CINDA-A
(1935–1976)

VOL. 2

CINDA-A

(1935-1976)

VOL. 2
Z ⩾ 51

AN INDEX TO THE LITERATURE ON
MICROSCOPIC NEUTRON DATA

PUBLISHED ON BEHALF OF
USA NATIONAL NUCLEAR DATA CENTER
USSR NUCLEAR DATA CENTRE
NEA DATA BANK
IAEA NUCLEAR DATA SECTION

BY THE
INTERNATIONAL ATOMIC ENERGY AGENCY, VIENNA, 1979

Printed by the IAEA in Austria
May 1979
ISBN 92—0—039179—6

LEGAL NOTICE

Neither the organizations which have contributed to this report and which are listed on the cover, nor any person acting on behalf of any of them or otherwise in the development, compilation, publication or distribution of the information in this report:

1. make any warranty or representation, expressed or implied, that the information in it is accurate, complete or useful, or that the use of any information, apparatus, method, or process disclosed may not infringe privately-owned rights; or

2. assume any liabilities with respect to the use of, or for damages resulting from the use of, any information, apparatus, method, or process disclosed.

AVIS

Les organisations qui ont contribué à l'établissement du présent rapport et dont les noms figurent sur la couverture, ou toute personne collaborant en leur nom ou d'autre manière à la collecte, compilation, publication ou distribution des renseignements contenus dans le présent rapport:

1. Ne garantissent d'aucune manière ni n'attestent, expressément ou implicitement, que lesdits renseignements sont exacts, complets ou utiles, ni que l'utilisation des renseignements, dispositifs, méthodes ou procédés divulgués ne risque pas de porter atteinte aux droits de personnes physiques ou morales privées;

2. N'assument aucune responsabilité civile afférente à l'usage, ou au dommage résultant de l'usage des renseignements, dispositifs, méthodes ou procédés divulgués.

ЮРИДИЧЕСКИЕ ПРИМЕЧАНИЯ

Ни одна из организаций, которые внесли свой вклад в данный сборник и которые перечислены на обложке, а также ни одно из лиц, действующих от имени какой-либо из этих организаций или каким-либо другим образом принимающих участие в разработке, сборе, публикации или распространении информации, которая содержится в данном сборнике, не имеют права:

1. Давать какие-либо гарантии или делать какие-либо представления, в выраженной или подразумеваемой форме, в отношении точности, полноты или полезности содержащейся в докладе информации или в отношении того, что использование какой-либо информации, аппаратуры, метода или описанного процесса не может не нарушить чьих-либо частных прав; или

2. Брать на себя какую-либо ответственность в отношении использования какой-либо информации, аппаратуры, метода или описанного процесса или за ущерб, причиненный в результате их использования.

ADVERTENCIA

Las organizaciones que han contribuido a elaborar el presente volumen, cuyos nombres figuran en la portada, y toda persona que haya actuado en nombre de cualquiera de ellas o participado de otra manera en la obtención, compilación, publicación o difusión de la información contenida en este volumen:

1. No garantizan ni afirman, explícita o implícitamente, la exactitud, integridad o utilidad de dicha información, ni que la utilización de cualquier información, aparato, método o proceso dado a conocer no infrinja derechos de propiedad privada;

2. No asumen responsabilidad alguna respecto de la utilización de cualquier información, aparato, método o proceso dado a conocer, ni por los daños que de tal utilización pudieran derivarse.

TABLE OF CONTENTS

VOL. 1

Foreword	VII
Computer retrievals available from the CINDA file	XI
A brief introduction to CINDA	XII
Computer libraries of cross-section data	XIII
Quick reference list of the 'quantities'	XVI
Elements or isotopes $Z \leqslant 50$	1
REF-codes (reference abbreviations)	Table 3
LAB-codes (laboratories and institutions)	Table 4
Some abbreviations used in 'Comments'	Table 5

VOL. 2

Entries (continued)

Elements or isotopes $Z \geqslant 51$	967
Collective entries 'Many'	1862
Collective entries 'FProd'	1893
Molecules and mixtures	1895

Annex

A detailed explanation of the CINDA listing	A.1
Acknowledgements	A.7
Abbreviations for molecules and mixtures	Table 1
Quantity definitions	Table 2
REF-codes (reference abbreviations)	Table 3
LAB-codes (laboratories and institutions)	Table 4
Some abbreviations used in 'Comments'	Table 5

FOREWORD

CINDA, the Computer Index of Neutron Data, contains bibliographical references to measurements, calculations, reviews and evaluations of neutron cross-sections and other microscopic neutron data; it includes also index references to computer libraries of numerical neutron data exchanged between four regional neutron data centres.

The present issue in two volumes, CINDA-A, is an index to all works on neutron nuclear data from the time of the discovery of the neutron until the end of 1976. Works completed after 1976 are indexed in the further CINDA-issues and their supplements, which will continue to be published in six months' intervals.

As compared to earlier cumulative CINDA publications, the information in this issue has been thoroughly revised with a special view to the correction of mistakes, the removal of superseded progress reports and occasional duplicates, to appropriate blocking of references to the same work and to adding index lines to the EXFOR data library (see p. XIII).

The compilation and publication of CINDA are the result of world-wide co-operation involving the following four data centres. Each centre is responsible for compiling the CINDA entries from the literature published in a defined geographical area given in brackets below:

* The USA National Nuclear Data Center at Brookhaven National Laboratory, USA (United States and Canada).

* The USSR Nuclear Data Centre at the Fiziko-Energeticheskij Institut, Obninsk, Soviet Union (USSR).

* The NEA Data Bank at Saclay, France (OECD member countries in Western Europe and Japan).

* The IAEA Nuclear Data Section at Vienna, Austria (all other countries in Eastern Europe, Asia, Australia, Africa, Central and South America; also IAEA publications and translation journals).

Besides the published CINDA books, up-to-date computer retrievals for specified CINDA information are currently available on request. For CINDA computer retrievals, as well as for suggestions and corrections, scientists are invited to contact their responsible Centre:

For USA and Canada:

Dr. Sol Pearlstein
National Nuclear Data Center
Brookhaven National Laboratory
Upton, N.Y. 11973
USA

For other OECD countries:

Dr. N. Tubbs
Banque de Données de l'AEN
NEA Data Bank
B.P. 9
F-91190 Gif-sur-Yvette
France

For USSR:

Д-ру В. Н. Манохину
Центр по ядерным данным
Физико-энергетический
    Институт
Обнинск, Калужской Обл.
СССР

For all other countries:

Dr. J.J. Schmidt
IAEA Nuclear Data Section
Kärntner Ring 11
A-1010 Vienna
Austria

AVANT-PROPOS

CINDA – Computer Index of Neutron Data (Index automatique de données neutroniques) – contient des références aux mesures, calculs et évaluations des sections efficaces et autres données neutroniques microscopiques; il comprend également des références aux index de bibliothèques automatiques de données neutroniques numériques échangées entre quatre centres régionaux de données neutroniques.

La présente édition CINDA-A en deux volumes sert d'index à tous les travaux sur les constantes neutroniques nucléaires, depuis la découverte du neutron jusqu'à la fin de 1976. Les travaux achevés après 1976 sont répertoriés dans les éditions ultérieures et dans leurs suppléments qui paraissent tous les six mois.

Par rapport aux publications précédentes, les renseignements contenus dans cette édition ont fait l'objet d'une révision minutieuse qui a permis notamment de corriger des erreurs, de supprimer les rapports intérimaires périmés et d'éventuelles entrées faisant double emploi, de regrouper les références portant sur les mêmes travaux et d'ajouter des rubriques à la bibliothèque de constantes EXFOR (voir p. XIII).

La compilation et la publication de CINDA sont le fruit de la collaboration sur le plan mondial des quatre centres de documentation ci-après. Chacun de ces centres est responsable de la compilation des entrées CINDA extraites des revues et ouvrages publiés dans la région géographique indiquée entre parenthèses ci-dessous:

* USA National Nuclear Data Center, Brookhaven National Laboratory, E.U. (E.U. d'Amérique et Canada).

* Centre des constantes nucléaires de l'URSS, Institut de physique énergétique d'Obninsk, Union soviétique (URSS).

* Banque de données de l'AEN, Saclay, France (Pays de l'Europe occidentale membres de l'OCDE et Japon).

* Section des constantes nucléaires de l'AIEA, Vienne, Autriche (tous autres pays de l'Europe orientale, d'Asie, d'Australie, d'Afrique, de l'Amérique centrale et de l'Amérique du Sud; également les publications et périodiques de l'AIEA).

Outre les volumes publiés de CINDA, on peut se procurer sur demande des restitutions automatiques d'une partie spécifique de CINDA mise à jour depuis la parution de ce volume. Pour ce service spécialisé, ainsi que pour les suggestions et les rectifications, les intéressés sont priés de se mettre en rapport avec leur centre responsable. (Les adresses sont indiquées à la page précédente.)

ПРЕДИСЛОВИЕ

СИНДА — компьютерный указатель нейтронных данных, содержащий библиографические ссылки на измерения, расчеты, обзоры и оценки нейтронных сечений и на другие микроскопические нейтронные данные. Он включает также ссылки на компьютерные библиотеки цифровых нейтронных данных, которыми обмениваются между собой четыре региональных нейтронных центра.

Настоящий двухтомный выпуск, СИНДА-А, представляет собой указатель всех работ по нейтронным ядерным данным с момента открытия нейтрона до конца 1976 года. Работы, завершенные после 1976 года, будут включены в последующие выпуски СИНДА и в дополнения к ним, которые будут по-прежнему публиковаться с интервалами в шесть месяцев.

В сравнении с прежними сводными публикациями СИНДА, информация в данном выпуске тщательно переработана, причем особое внимание обращено на исправление ошибок, на изъятие устаревших сообщений о достижениях и случайных дубликатов, на устранение ссылок на одну и ту же работу и на добавление индексных строк в библиотеку данных EXFOR (см. стр. XIII).

Сбор данных и публикация СИНДА являются результатом широкого международного сотрудничества с участием указанных ниже четырех центров. Каждый центр несет ответственность за сбор входных данных СИНДА из литературы, опубликованной в определенном географическом районе, указанном в скобках.

* Национальный центр по ядерным данным при Брукхейвенской национальной лаборатории, США (Соединенные Штаты Америки и Канада).

* Центр по ядерным данным СССР при Физико-энергетическом институте, Обнинск, СССР (Союз Советских Социалистических Республик).

* Банк данных АЯЭ в Сакле, Франция (страны Западной Европы — члены ОЭСР и Япония).

* Секция по ядерным данным МАГАТЭ в Вене, Австрия (все страны Восточной Европы, Азия, Австралия, Африка, Центральная и Южная Америка; также публикации МАГАТЭ и переводные журналы).

Помимо опубликованных сборников СИНДА, в настоящее время имеется возможность получать по запросу распечатки с ЭВМ по специфической информации, содержащейся в СИНДА. По вопросам получения этих распечаток, а также с различными предложениями и поправками ученым предлагается обращаться в свои соответствующие центры (см. адреса на странице VII).

PREFACIO

CINDA, Computer Index of Neutron Data, contiene referencias bibliográficas sobre medidas, cálculos, revisiones y evaluaciones de secciones eficaces neutrónicas y sobre otros datos neutrónicos microscópicos; incluye también referencias sobre colecciones de programas sobre datos numéricos nucleares intercambiados entre cuatro centros regionales de datos nucleares.

El presente volumen, CINDA-A, que está dividido en dos tomos, constituye un índice de todos los trabajos sobre datos neutrónicos desde que se descubrió la existencia del neutrón hasta el final de 1976. Los trabajos ultimados posteriormente se recogen en los volúmenes subsiguientes del CINDA y en sus suplementos, que se seguirán publicando a intervalos de seis meses.

La información contenida en el presente volumen, comparada con la incluida en anteriores publicaciones CINDA, ha sido examinada a fondo con miras, en particular, a corregir errores, a eliminar reseñas de informes sobre la marcha de trabajos que han quedado anulados por informes posteriores y corregir algunos casos de duplicación de la información, a agrupar debidamente las referencias a un mismo trabajo y a añadir nuevas líneas al índice para la biblioteca de datos EXFOR (véase la página XIII).

La compilación y publicación de CINDA es fruto de una colaboración a escala mundial, en la que participan los cuatro centros de datos enumerados a continuación. Cada uno de estos centros se encarga de compilar las reseñas correspondientes a la literatura publicada en la región geográfica que se indica entre paréntesis:

* El Centro Nacional de Datos Nucleares de los Estados Unidos, Laboratorio Nacional de Brookhaven, E.U. (Estados Unidos y Canadá).

* El Centro de Datos Nucleares de la Unión Soviética, Instituto de Físico-energética de Obninsk, Unión Soviética (URSS).

* El Banco de Datos de la AEN, Saclay, Francia (Países de Europa occidental miembros de la OCDE y el Japón).

* La sección de Datos Nucleares del OIEA en Viena, Austria (todos los restantes países de Europa oriental, Asia, Australia, Africa, América Central y América del Sur; también las publicaciones del OIEA y las revistas de traducciones).

Además de los volúmenes CINDA publicados, se pueden facilitar, previa petición, todas las reseñas almacenadas hasta la fecha en la computadora, correspondientes a informaciones específicas de CINDA. Para obtener esta información, así como para cualquier sugerencia o corrección, se invita a los científicos a dirigirse al Centro que les corresponda (véanse las direcciones en la página VII).

COMPUTER RETRIEVALS AVAILABLE FROM THE CINDA FILE

Requests for computer retrievals (which are free of charge!) should be addressed to one of the Centres given on page VII.
Special reasons which may decide you to ask for a retrieval are:
1. If you particularly need the most recent information available (i.e. information which is not yet contained in the last CINDA publication)
2. If you wish to check a part of the file which cannot easily be selected from the CINDA book
3. If you are requesting numeric experimental or evaluated data and wish at the same time to know of other data which may not yet be in the centres' numerical data files.

Specification of retrievals:
Possible search parameters are:
Element or Range of Z ⎫
Mass number A or range of A ⎭ or list of isotopes (ZA)
Quantity (for existing quantities see p. XIV), or list of reactions (ZA Quantity)
Energy range or alphabetic abbreviation (e.g. fission-spectrum average data)
Data type (experimental, evaluated, theoretical, etc.)
Laboratory
Country
Reference(s)
Publication date
Date of entry into the CINDA file
(a few more retrieval parameters exist that are mostly for usage of CINDA indexers).
The search parameters may be specified singly or in any reasonable combination. In order to avoid unwanted references on the output listing please specify your requirements as exactly as you can!

Examples:
1. Please send me a listing of all references on the Pu-239 neutron capture and absorption cross-sections.
2. Please send me all information entered in the CINDA file since the last CINDA book; but I am interested only in experimental data.
3. What has been published on capture cross-sections of fissile elements since 1970? (The search will specify quantity, Z-range and publication date.) I am interested only in point data $\sigma(E)$ and not in data averaged over a neutron spectrum.
4. Please send me all entries for (n,2n) reactions between 14 and 15 MeV and $A \leq 100$.

Output:
The requestor will receive a listing in either of three sorts:
"lab-sort":   this sort is firstly by the 3-character laboratory code in alphabetic order, then by nuclide and quantity.
"ZAQ-sort":   entries are sorted by element Z and mass-number A, then by Quantity (sorted as on page XIV).
"Quantity-sort": entries are sorted by Quantity (as on page XIV), then by nuclide ZA.
The requestor should specify which sort(s) he prefers. The usual format of computer listings is close to that of the book. (CINDA indexers may obtain retrievals in an "internal" format, which is needed for making corrections and grouping associated CINDA entries.)

A BRIEF INTRODUCTION TO CINDA

The CINDA bibliography allows its users to find the references to specific types of cross-section information or other microscopic data from neutron-induced reactions, for any given target nucleus.

CINDA entries are ordered in this publication first by element and mass number, then by cross-section or other quantity. Within these isotopes and quantity groups, the entries are ordered by date of publication.

References relating to the same work are listed in block form. The first line of a block refers usually to one of the main publications; in the following lines belonging to the same block, the codes for quantity and laboratory are omitted, and also the name of the first author if it is identical to the one in the line above. When a preliminary publication (e.g. progress report, abstract) becomes superseded by a more recent or final paper, it is often eliminated from the CINDA book. These entries are, however, kept in the CINDA master file, and will be included in retrievals from the file (as described on p. XI).

The Centres would appreciate notice of any errors of omission or commission users may find, so that the entries concerned can be corrected before the next cumulation.

To obtain the maximum amount of information from CINDA, it is suggested users read the detailed description given in the annex. However, the format of CINDA is rather simple and most of the conventions can easily be guessed. For the majority of uses to which CINDA can be put, the brief description on pages XIV and XV is all one needs.

COMPUTER LIBRARIES OF CROSS-SECTION DATA

This issue of CINDA indexes, for a given work, not only its bibliographic references but also its numerical data stored in computer libraries, which are available from the four regional neutron data centres. Since July 1970 the exchange of experimental neutron data between the U.S. National Nuclear Data Center, the NEA Data Bank, the USSR Centr po Jadernym Dannym and the IAEA Nuclear Data Section has been structured in the EXFOR exchange system, so that data entered at one centre are made available to the other three. Similarly, evaluated neutron data libraries or parts of them are generally available from the same four centres.

Whereas in earlier issues of CINDA the availability of data sets from the data centres was publicized by a simple tag (+) at the right-hand margin under the heading "Data", it was decided to include more information about these data by adding a "data-index line" below the bibliographic reference(s) of a given work. Users of CINDA-A will find such data-index lines for the experimental neutron data exchanged under the EXFOR agreement, as well as index lines referring to evaluated neutron data Libraries which are generally available.

More information about data-index lines and the availability of data can be found in Section 8 of the Annex.

24 Chromium

Quantity	Energy (eV) Min	Max	Lab	Type		Documentation Ref	Vol	Page	Date
(n, γ)	3.0+4	6.5+4	ORL	Expt	Jour	PR	129	2695	Mar 63
					Rept	BNL-653			Feb 62
					Conf	61 Vienna		§ 73	Aug 61
(n, γ)	1.0−4	5.0−2	WIN	Eval	Rept	AEEW-R 351			Feb 64
(n, γ)	3.0+1	5.0+4	CCP	Expt	Jour	AE	16	256	Mar 64
(n, γ)	8.5+3	9.4+4	SCT	Expt	Jour	NP/A 121		655	Dec 68
	8.1+3	9.4+4		Expt	Data	EXFOR 30114.			Mar 71
Spect (n, γ)	Maxwl		ISP	Expt	Conf	67 Juelich 64			Apr 67

Type of reference. The categories used are JOURnal, REPorT, CONFerence, PREPrint, PROGress report, ABSTract, BOOK, DISSertation, PRIVate communication, DATA in computer library.

Type of work. EXPT experimental, EXTH experiment with substantial theory, THEOretical, COMPilation, EVALuation, REVieW. See section 5 of the Annex.

Laboratory. The laboratory given in the paper for the first author.
The laboratories for these entries are:
ORL Oak Ridge National Laboratory
WIN AEE Winfrith
CCP Soviet Union, Laboratory unspecified
SCT Cape Town, South Africa
ISP Euratom, Ispra
Table 4 explains all the abbreviations used.

Energy range of incident neutrons in floating decimal point notation, explained more fully in section 3 of the Annex. The energy ranges covered by the references on this page are:
From 30 keV to 65 keV
From 0.1 meV to 50 meV
From 30 eV to 50 keV
From 8.5 keV to 94 keV
From 8.1 keV to 94 keV
Thermal Maxwellian energy spectrum

Cross-section or class of data. The list on page XXV shows the order in which quantities are listed, while full definitions are given in Table 2 at the end of this issue.

24 Chromium → Element and mass number

Author, Comments	Data
Macklin + LIQ SCINT, 10+ −3, 3.5+ −1MB SUPERSEDED* SUPERSEDED*	
LOW E PART UK DATA FILE. REFS HIGH E	
Kapchigashev + CURVE PB SLOWING DOWN ENGLISH SJA 16 306 FRANCAIS EAF 16 3 104	+
Spitz + VDG, M-R, TOF, REL TO IN, GRAPHS SIGMA AT 35 ES, THICK + THIN TARGET	+
Forte + CIRCULAR POLRZ (POLRZD NS). NDG	

Element and mass number
see the explanation on page A.1 at the end of this issue

24 Chromium
   means natural Cr
24 Chromium 052
   means Cr^{52}

Many
   refers to a whole range of nuclides

Fprod
   covers a mixture of fission products

1 Hydrogen CXX
   and similar codes refer to organic compounds and other molecules and mixtures; the abbreviations used are explained in Table 1 at the end of this issue

Numerical Data

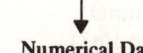

A cross under the heading "Data" indicates that the numerical data corresponding to this reference have been entered in the data files of one or more of the co-operating regional or national data centres. More information on the availability of numerical neutron data is given in section 8 of the Annex.

Reference Citations

The notation is explained fully in section 6 of the Annex, while abbreviations are expanded in Table 3; The examples are:

Physical Review 129, page 2695, March 1963. This article supersedes report BNL-653 and paper 73 of the IAEA conference on the Physics of Fast and Intermediate Reactors, Vienna, August 1961.

Report AEEW-R351, issued February 1964.

Atomnaja Energija 16, page 256, March 1964. Translations into English and French can be found in Soviet Atomic Energy and in Energie Atomique.

Nuclear Physics, Part A, vol.121, page 655, December 1968. A computer retrieval of the numerical data is available under the accession-number EXFOR 30114.

Symposium "Neutronenphysik an Forschungsreaktoren", Juelich, April 1967, page 64.

Comments

No fixed form, but the type of information given is discussed on page A.4, while common abbreviations are explained in Table 5.

Reading down these six entries we have:

Authors Macklin et al., experimental method liquid scintillator, two experimental values and a list of two previous publications on the same subject.

A section of the UK Nuclear Data File.

Authors Kapchigashev et al., a curve shows results from a neutron slowing down time experiment in lead.

Authors Spitz et al., an experiment using a Van-de-Graaff accelerator, Moxon-Rae detector, time-of-flight method; data relative to indium are given as graphs.

Authors Forte et al., circular polarization of gamma rays following capture of polarized neutrons. No data are given (NDG) in this paper.

XVII

QUICK REFERENCE LIST OF THE QUANTITIES

Evaluation	(n,γ)	Fission
Total	Res Int Capt	Res Int Fiss
Elastic	Spect (n,γ)	Alpha
Diff Elastic	Inelastic γ	Eta
Polarization	Nonelastic γ	Nu
Potntal Scat	$(n, 2n)$	Delayd Neuts
Tot Inelastc	(n,xn) $x > 2$	Frag Neuts
Diff Inelast	n Emission	Spect Fiss n
Thermal Scat	(n,p)	Spect Fiss γ
Scattering	(n,np)	Fiss Prod γ
Nonelastic	(n,d)	Fiss Prod β
Absorption	(n,nd)	Fiss Yield
Res Int Abs	(n,t)	Frag Spectra
	(n,nt)	Frag Charge
	$(n,He3)$	Reson Params
	(n,α)	Strnth Fnctn
	$(n,n\dot{\alpha})$	Lvl Density
		(γ,n)
		Photo-Fissn

The "Quantities" and their definitions are described at some length in table 2. In searching CINDA it should be kept in mind that information on a given cross-section sometimes appears under different quantities. Thus references on the cross-section for the thermal (n,γ) reaction should most likely be sought under '(n,γ)', but some might be listed under 'Absorption'. Similarly, information on 'Res Int Capt' should also be sought under 'Res Int Abs'. For most quantities information can also be found under 'Evaluation'.

The following specific conventions should also be noted:

Evaluation = Consistent evaluation of many quantities

Total = Elastic + Nonelastic = Scattering + Absorption

Scattering = Elastic + Inelastic = $\sigma_{n,n} + \sigma_{n,n'}$

Nonelastic = Inelastic + Absorption

= $\sigma_{n,n'} + \sigma_{n,2n} + \sigma_{n,3n} + \sigma_{n,f} + \sigma_{n,\gamma} + \sigma_{n,p} + \sigma_{n,d} + \ldots\ldots$

n Emission = $\sigma_{n,n'} + 2\sigma_{n,2n} + 3\sigma_{n,3n} + \bar{\nu}\sigma_{n,f} + \sigma_{n,np} + \ldots\ldots$

(n, xn) $x > 2$ = $(n,3n)$ and/or $(n,4n)$ and/or $\ldots\ldots$

51 Antimony

Quantity	Energy (ev) Min	Max	Lab	Type	Documentation Ref Vol Page	Date	Author, Comments	Data
Evaluation	5.0+5	1.5+7	LRL	Eval	Rept UCRL-5351	Nov 58	Howerton. CURVES	
Total	Maxwl		COL	Expt	Jour PR 48 265	Aug 35	Dunning+ IONCH,TRANS,RA-BE/PARAFIN N	
Total	1.0+5	1.8+5	ITY	Expt	Jour PR 56 881	Nov 39	Amaldi+ TRANSM.C-D NS. AVERAGE ES.	
Total	1.5-2	6.8-1	COL	Expt	Jour PR 71 65	Jan 47	Rainwater+ TOF	+
	1.5-2	6.8-1			Data EXFOR11685.004	Jun 76	. 28 PTS.	
Total	2.4+4	8.3+5	ANL	Expt	Jour PR 71 508	Apr 47	Fields+ GN SOURCES 6ES.	+
	2.4+4	8.3+5			Data EXFOR11057.018	Jun 76	. 6 PTS.	
Total	2.0+4	1.4+6	WIS	Expt	Jour PR 76 277	Jul 49	Bockelman+AVG.CS.CFD STATIST THEO	+
	2.0+4	1.4+6			Data EXFOR11881.005	Jun 76	. 31 PTS.	
Total	1.0+5	1.5+6	MIT	Theo	Jour PR 76 1550	Dec 49	Feshbach+ AVERAGE OVER RESON,CF EXPT	
Total	5.0+4	3.2+6	WIS	Expt	Jour PR 88 83	Oct 52	Miller+ 20 KEV SPREAD TRNSM.	+
	1.0+6	3.2+6			Data EXFOR11712.014	Jun 76	. 17 PTS.	
Total	1.4+7		ANL	Expt	Jour PR 88 686	Nov 52	Goodman+ T-D NEUTS 4.6+ -0.3B	
	1.4+7				Data EXFOR11057.018	Jun 76	. 1 PT.	
Total	1.4+7		LAS	Expt	Jour PR 88 562	Nov 52	Coon+	+
	1.4+7				Data EXFOR11056.041	Jun 76	. 1 PT.	
Total	3.5+7	1.9+8	BRK	Expt	Rept UCRL-2337	Aug 53	Ragent. TOF. SIG VARIATION WITH E.	+
	3.5+7	1.9+8			Data EXFOR11338.004	Jun 76	. 30 PTS.	
Total	2.8+6	1.3+7	LAS	Expt	Jour PR 94 1678	Jun 54	Nereson+ 10PC RSLN	+
	2.8+6	1.3+7			Data EXFOR11308.018	Jun 76	. 30 PTS.	
Total	5.5+0	3.1+1	BNL	Expt	Priv CARTER	Apr 55	Carter.	+
	5.5+0	3.1+1			Data EXFOR11878.003	Jun 76	. 62 PTS.	
Total	2.1+0	9.1+3	ANL	Expt	Jour PR 102 228	Apr 56	Palmer+ TRANSMISSION. RES. PARA.	+
	2.2+0	9.1+3			Data EXFOR11804.012	Jun 76	. 257 PTS.	
Total	7.7+8		BIR	Expt	Jour PPS 71 293	Mar 58	Booth+ 2149+ -74MB AT 765+ -30MEV	
Total	7.2+6	1.4+7	LRL	Expt	Jour PR 110 927	May 58	Bratenahl+ SC TRANS, 5ES	+
	7.1+6	1.4+7			Conf 58Geneva 14 109	Sep 58	- + TBL, CURV, CFD OPTMDL	
	7.0+6	1.4+7			Data EXFOR11155.025	Jun 76	. 5 PTS.	
Total	4.1+6		TNC	Expt	Rept WADD-TR-60-217	Apr 60	Vincent.TOF 4.4+ -0.1B	+
	4.1+6				Data EXFOR11621.016	Jun 76	. 1 PT.	
Total	1.8+7	2.9+7	LRL	Expt	Jour PR 120 521	Oct 60	Peterson+ T(D,N).MON.ENERGY. 1-2 PER	+
					Conf 58Geneva 14 109	Sep 58	Bratenahl+.P1881,TBL,CURV,CFD OPTMDL	
	1.8+7	2.9+7			Data EXFOR11108.032	Jun 76	. 4 PTS.	
Total	1.0+6		ANL	Theo	Jour PR 124 826	Nov 61	Sokoloff.HARMONIC OSCILLAT POT CURVE	
Total	3.7+6		BAR	Expt	Jour PR 125 331	Jan 62	Kent+ 400KEV SPREAD SEE PR114 1563	
	3.7+6				Data EXFOR11617.033	Jun 76	. 1 PT.	
Total	2.7-3	9.5-3	BUC	Expt	Jour AE 12 514	Jun 62	Bally+ CRYST SPEC, GRAPH, CFD TH	+
					Jour RSI 32 297	Mar 61	. DESCR OF MONOCHROMATOR	
					Jour RSI 31 640	Jun 60	. DESCR OF CRYST SPECTROM	
					Jour EAF 12 6 80	Oct 63	.FRENCH OF AE 12 514	
					Jour SJA 12 546	Jan 63	. ENGL OF AE 12 514	
	2.7-3	9.5-3			Data EXFOR30205.003	Nov 72	23 DATA POINTS, DATA FROM PRIV COM	
Total	2.4+4		LRC	Theo	Conf 66Paris 1 503	Oct 66	Bogart. VAL GVN, BETHE ANALYSIS	
Total	1.4+7		CCP	ExTh	Jour IZV 31 217	Feb 67	Dukarevich+.TBL,CURVES,CFD OPTMDL TH	
					Jour BAS 31 197	Feb 67	TRANSLATN.*	
Total	1.4+7		FTI	Expt	Jour NP/A 92 433	Feb 67	Dukarevich+ 4.67+ -0.02B	
Total	4.5+6	7.5+6	WIS	Expt	Jour PR 158 1142	Jun 67	Carlson+ VDG,CURV,50KEV RESOL,CFD TH	+
					Abst DA/B 28 1084	Sep 67	.THESIS ABST	
					Conf 66Gatlinbg § 2-1	Sep 66	Carlson+	
					Conf 65Antwerp 101	Jul 65	- +	
	4.5+6	7.6+6			Data EXFOR11497.022	Jun 76	. 61 PTS.	
Total	1.0+5	6.5+5	ANL	Expt	Prog WASH-1079 4	Oct 67	Whalen+ TO BE DONE	
Total	5.0-2	3.1+0	BUC	Expt	Jour RRP 12 10 907	Oct 67	Mateiciuc+,TRANSM,TOF,CURVE,FRENCH	+
	5.0-2	3.1+0			Data EXFOR30020.002	Oct 70	SIGMA TOTAL, PRIV COM MATEICIUÇ	
Total	6.0+0	5.0+3	COL	Expt	Jour PR 166 1234	Feb 68	Wynchank+ TOF 0.5NSEC/M RESOL CURVES	+
					Conf 65Antwerp 95	Jul 65	.SUPERSEDED	
	6.5+0	5.0+3			Data EXFOR11913.010	Jun 76	. 9316 PTS.	
Total	3.0+4	6.5+5	DKE	Expt	Jour AP 46 401	Feb 68	Tabony+ TRANS. CURV DERIVES S0,S1,S2	+
					Abst DA/B 27 2085	Dec 66	- .THESIS ABST	
	3.0+4	6.5+5			Data EXFOR11953.005	Jun 76	. 102 PTS.	
Total	1.4+7		OHO	Theo	Jour NC/B 53 2 363	Feb 68	Cassola+ OPTMDL CALC CFD EXPT	
Total	2.0-3	4.0-1	CAI	Expt	Jour JNE 22 389	Jun 68	ABU EL-ELA+,TOF SPECT,SIG(E) GRAPH	+
	2.5-3	2.3-1			Data EXFOR30217.003	Nov 72	113DATA POINTS, SIGMA VS E	
Total	2.0+7	3.0+7	AMS	Expt	Prog EANDC(E)127U	Apr 70	Rethmeier+,AVF CYCLOTRON,TOF	
Total	2.5+6	1.5+7	BNW	Expt	Jour PR/C 3 576	Feb 71	Foster+ TRANS, CURVS, CFD OTHERS+TH	+
					Jour NIM 36 1	Sep 65	.EXPT DETAILS	
	2.3+6	1.5+7			Data EXFOR10047.056	Aug 73	. 242 PTS.	

51 Antimony

Quantity	Energy (ev) Min	Max	Lab	Type	Documentation Ref Vol Page	Author, Comments Date	Data
Total	None		SAC	Expt Prog	EANDC(E)140U	Aug 71 Cauvin+	
Total	8.0+6		AE	Theo	AE - 430	Sep 71 Holmqvist+ CALC FROM OPTMOD PARAMS	
	8.1+6			Conf	70Helsinki 2 341	Jun 70 - + OPTMOD ANALYSIS. 8 MEV	
Total	5.0-2	1.5+2	BUC	Expt Jour	SCF 24 165	Feb 72 Mateiciuc.POWDER,TRANS,CFD LIT,GRPHS	
	3.0+1	1.5+2		Jour	RRP 15 339	Mar 70 - + SIG(NEUT-E) GRPH,TOF	
Total	2.7+3		MUN	Expt Prog	EANDC(E)150U	Oct 72 Dilg+ AVERAGE TOT XSECT+S0	+
				Conf	71Albany 327	Aug 71 - +TRNS.AVG CS GVN.31 ELEMENT GRP	
	2.7+3			Data	EXFOR20583.008	May 76 1PNT.	
Total	1.3+7	1.5+7	DEB	Eval Rept	IAEA - 153 173	73 Boedy+ MOST PROBABLE VAL OF SIG,TBL	
				Jour	AHP 30 115	Oct 71 Angeli+ AVG SIG,CFD CALC.TBLS.GRAPH	
Total	1.0+3	6.0+5	NBS	Expt Jour	PR/C 9 28	Jan 74 Camarda.LINAC.TOF.GRPH.TRANS.MEAS.S1	
Total	2.5+5	1.5+7	JAE	Theo Conf	JAERI-M - 5984	Feb 75 Tanaka.OPTMDL/COUPLD CH.GRPH CFD EXP	
Total	1.8-3	5.0+5	CAI	Expt Jour	AJN 9 155	Feb 76 Adib+ TRANS.B-W ANALYS,GRAPH TOTSIG	
Elastic	Maxwl		BNL	Expt Jour	PR 83 379	50 Weiss. COH SCAT. CS. PHASE.	+
	Maxwl			Data	EXFOR11580.007	Jun 76 .1 PT, COH	
Elastic	5.0-1		ANL	Expt Jour	PR 79 11	Jul 50 Harris+ EPI-CD,RES INT SCAT,B-W TH	
Elastic	2.5-2	7.3-2	ORL	Expt Jour	PR 81 527	Feb 51 Mc-Crary+ ACT NDG	+
	2.5-2	7.3-2		Data	EXFOR11043.	Jun 76 , 3 PTS, BAS, COH, COH AMP	
Elastic	1.0+6		WIS	Expt Jour	PR 93 1062	Mar 54 Walt+ 30 DEG.-150 DEG.	+
	1.0+6			Data	EXFOR11637.047	Jun 76 . 1 PT.	
Elastic	4.1+6		TNC	Expt Rept	WADD-TR-60-217	Apr 60 Vincent.TOF INT20-135DEG 2.1+-0.3B	+
	4.1+6			Data	EXFOR11621.014	Jun 76 . 1 PT.	
Elastic	Maxwl		LAS	Expt Jour	PR 131 2098	Sep 63 Arnold+	+
	Maxwl			Data	EXFOR11809.005	Jun 76 . 1 PT, COH AMP	
Elastic	1.0+6	1.4+7	AGN	Eval Rept	TID-21629	Dec 64 Perkins+ CALC FROM BNL325,UCRL5573	
Elastic	2.0+6		FEI	Expt Rept	EANDC-50 200	Jul 65 Kazakova+ EXPT,TABLE CFD OPTMODEL	+
				Prog	YFI-3 6	Sep 66 .TABLE	
				Prog	INDC-E-140 6	Sep 66 .ENGLISH TRANSL OF YFI-3 6 9/66	
Elastic	3.0+5	8.0+5	IFU	ExTh Jour	AE 20 8	Jan 66 Korzh+ SUMMARY OF SEVERAL YRS WORK	+
				Jour	UFZ 9 929	64 .	
				Jour	SJA 20 8	Jul 66 .ENGLISH TRANSL OF AE 20 8 1/66	
				Rept	INDSWG-101 112	65 .=UFZ9.ENGL NO GRPHS.RUSS LARGER GPH	
Elastic	3.0+5	1.5+6	ANL	Expt Jour	NP/A 93 609	Mar 67 Smith+ INTEG ANG DIST	+
	3.3+5	1.5+6		Rept	ANL-7274	Nov 66 - +TBLS OF DATA PTS.	
	3.0+5	1.5+6		Rept	EANDC(US)-62	Jun 64 - .TOF,TBL.50KEV STEPS,20KEV RSLN	
	3.3+5	1.5+6		Data	EXFOR10418.006	Aug 76 51PTS.37KEV LVL INEL CS INCLUDED	
Elastic	1.5+6		IFU	Expt Prog	YFI-5 42	Oct 67 Korzh+ TBL OPTMDL PARAMS + TOTELAST	
				Rept	INDC-232E	67 . ENGL OF YFI-5 42	
Elastic	1.5+6		IFU	Comp Jour	YF 7 277	Feb 68 Korzh+ OPTMOD PARS-FIT TO EXPTL-SIG	
				Jour	SNP 7 2 190	Aug 68 TRANSLATN.*	
Elastic	1.4+7		OHO	Theo Jour	NC/B 53 2 363	Feb 68 Cassola+ OPTMDL CALC CFD EXPT	
Elastic	1.5-3		MUN	Expt Jour	ZN/A 26 391	Mar 71 Koester+ SMALL ANGLE SCT.COH AMPLTDE	+
	2.5-2			Data	EXFOR20758.006	Jun 78 1PNT.COH.SC.AMP.	
Elastic	8.0+6		AE	Expt	AE - 430	Sep 71 Holmqvist+ INTEGRATED ANGDIST VALUES	+
				Conf	70Helsinki 2 341	Jun 70 - + OPTMOD ANALYSIS. 8 MEV	
	8.1+6			Data	EXFOR20162.017	May 74 1PNT	
Elastic	1.5+7		IJI	Expt Prog	YFI-12 84	72 Korzh+ ABST,INTEGRATED 20-145DEG,TBL	
				Prog	INDC(CCP)-30	Sep 72 .PAGE 74,ENGLISH OF YFI-12 84	
Elastic	8.7+5		ANL	Expt Jour	ANL-7935	Jun 72 COX+ 4 PI B(O)	+
	8.7+5			Data	EXFOR10332.106	Jun 74 . 1 PT.	
Elastic	7.0+6		AE	Expt Rept	AE - 482	Dec 73 Etemad. INTEGRATED.	+
	7.0+6			Data	EXFOR20346.011	Sep 74 1PNT.	
Diff Elastic	1.0+6		WIS	Expt Jour	PR 93 1062	Mar 54 Walt+ HE COUNTER 30-150DEG LAB CURVE	+
	1.0+6			Data	EXFOR11637.049	Jun 76 . 9 PTS, DSIG	
Diff Elastic	6.0+5	1.6+6	WIS	Expt Jour	PR 100 1315	Dec 55 Darden+ ALSO1MEV100KEVRSLN CF OPTMDL	+
	6.0+5	1.6+6		Data	EXFOR11638.007	Jun 76 . 8 PTS, DSIG	
Diff Elastic	1.4+7		GRN	Expt Diss	NAUTA	Jun 57 Nauta. C-W. D-T NS.	+
	1.4+7			Data	EXFOR20199.004	May 74 13PTS.D/DA.	
Diff Elastic	7.0+6		LRL	Theo Rept	UCRL-4927	Jul 57 Bjorklund+ OPTMDL CALC 6-PARAM FIT	
Diff Elastic	1.4+7		LRL	Theo Rept	UCRL-4926	Jul 57 Bjorklund+ OPTMDL CALC 6-PARAM FIT	
Diff Elastic	2.8+6		IFU	Expt Conf	58Geneva 15 18	Sep 58 Pasechnik+.PPR2030,CURV,N-ANGL-DISTR	+
Diff Elastic	2.8+6		IFU	ExTh Conf	59Tashkent 1 103	Sep 59 Pasechnik. XPT AND OPTMDL-TH,GRAPH	
				Rept	AEC-TR-6398	64 .VOL 1,P120.ENGL OF 59TASHKE 1 103	
Diff Elastic	2.9+6		CCP	Expt Jour	AE 7 477	Nov 59 Gofman+ P-RECOIL ION DETECT AT 90DEG	
				Jour	JNAB 14 140	May 61 TRANSLATN.*	
				Jour	SJA 7 946	Mar 61 TRANSLATN.*	
				Jour	KE 3 593	Jun 60 .TRANSLATN	

51 Antimony

Quantity	Energy (ev) Min	Max	Lab	Type	Documentation Ref Vol Page	Date	Author, Comments	Data
Diff Elastic	1.4+7		ANL	Expt	Jour PR 116 1571	Dec 59	Rayburn.MONTE CARLO CORRECT,CFD TH	+
	1.4+7				Data EXFOR11806.004	Jun 76	. 28 PTS, DSIG	
Diff Elastic	4.1+6		TNC	Expt	Rept WADD-TR-60-217	Apr 60	Vincent.TOF 20-135DEG.CURVE+TABLE	+
	4.1+6				Data EXFOR11621.017	Jun 76	. 15 PTS, DSIG	
Diff Elastic	1.0+6		ANL	Theo	Jour PR 124 826	Nov 61	Sokoloff.HARM OSC POT CFD EXPT CURVE	
Diff Elastic	4.0+6	7.0+6	LAS	Expt	Jour PR 129 1649	Feb 63	Thomson. SIG AT 90DEG	+
	4.0+6	7.0+6			Data EXFOR11495.034	Jun 76	. 2 PTS.	
Diff Elastic	1.0+6	1.4+7	AGN	Eval	Rept TID-21629	Dec 64	Perkins+ LEG COEF CALC FROM OTHERS	
Diff Elastic	8.0+5		IFU	Theo	Jour UFZ 10 6 586	Jun 65	Korzh.OPTMDL GRAPH SIG,CFD XPT	
					Jour IZV 29 862	May 65	.	
Diff Elastic	1.4+7		ORL	ExTh	Jour NP 68 97	Jun 65	Stelson+ XPT CFD DIST OPTMDL CALC	+
	1.4+7			Expt	Data EXFOR11527.022	Jun 76	. 9 PTS, DSIG	
Diff Elastic	2.0+6		FEI	Expt	Rept EANDC-50 200	Jul 65	Kazakova+ EXPT,CURVE CFD OPTMODEL	+
					Prog ICD-2 112	Jul 65	.CURVE	
					Prog INDSWG-101E	65	.ENGLISH TRANSL OF ICD-2 112 7/65	
Diff Elastic	8.0+5		IFU	Theo	Conf 65Antwerp § 193	Jul 65	Pasechnic+. OPT.MOD.PARAMETERS	
Diff Elastic	1.0+6		LAS	Theo	Prog WASH-1064 84	Oct 65	Rosen+ OPTMDL+ CPD ELST CFD WIS XPT	
Diff Elastic	3.0+5	8.0+5	IFU	ExTh	Jour AE 20 8	Jan 66	Korzh+ SUMMARY OF SEVERAL YRS WORK	+
					Jour UFZ 9 929	May 64	.GRPH SIG(COS),TBL DERIVED VALUES	
					Jour SJA 20 8	Jul 66	.ENGLISH TRANSL OF AE 20 8 1/66	
					Rept INDSWG-101 112	65	.=UFZ9.ENGL NO GRPHS.RUSS LARGER GPH	
Diff Elastic	5.0+6		DKE	Expt	Jour ZP 196 103	Sep 66	Buccino+ 20-140DEG,CFD OPTMOD. TABLE	+
					Abst DA 24 4248	Apr 64	- .CFD OPTMOD CALCS.	
	5.0+6				Data EXFOR11877.005	Jun 76	.13 PTS, DSIG	
Diff Elastic	3.2+6		BCM	Expt	Jour NP 89 154	Dec 66	Becker+ 12 ANGLES GRAPH CFD OPTMDL	+
	3.2+6				Data EXFOR11511.026	Jun 76	.13 PTS, DSIG	
Diff Elastic	3.0+5	1.5+6	ANL	Expt	Jour NP/A 93 609	Mar 67	Smith+ TOF, CFD OPTMDL	+
	3.3+5	1.5+6			Rept ANL-7274	Nov 66	+TBLS OF DATA PTS.	
	3.0+5	1.5+6			Rept EANDC(US)-62	Jun 64	- .TOF,TBL LEGEND COEF LAB SYSTEM	
	3.3+5	1.5+6			Data EXFOR10418.008	Aug 76	255PTS.37KEV LVL INEL INCLUDED	
Diff Elastic	1.0+6	1.4+7	AI	Eval	Rept NAA-SR-11980	Apr 67	Campbell+ LEG COEFS TBL+CURVS C-MSYS	
Diff Elastic	2.8+6		IFU	Theo	Jour UFZ 13 152	Jan 68	Strizhak+ GRPH SIG(ANG),OPTMOD CALC	
					Jour UPJ 13 106	Jul 68	TRANSLATN.*	
Diff Elastic	1.5+6		IFU	Comp	Jour YF 7 277	Feb 68	Korzh+ GRPH SIG(ANG),OPTMOD PARS-FIT	
					Jour SNP 7 2 190	Aug 68	TRANSLATN.*	
Diff Elastic	8.0+5	1.0+6	ANL	Expt	Abst BAP 13 681	Apr 68	COX+ CFD OPTMDL	
Diff Elastic	2.0+6	5.0+6	SCU	Theo	Rept ICD-6 236	69	Averyanov+CALC ANGDIST CFD EXPT,GRPH	
Diff Elastic	1.0+3	4.0+4	DUB	Expt	Jour YF 11 1152	Jun 70	Samosvat.LEGENDRECOEF(E) GRPH,OPTMOD	+
					Rept JINR-P3-4724	Oct 69	- . ASSYMMETRY,0+180DEG ANG	
					Jour SNP 11 639	Dec 70	- . ENGL OF YF 11 1152.	
	1.6+3	3.9+4			Data EXFOR40285.007	Apr 75	.LEGEND-COEF FOR 10 ES GVN	
Diff Elastic	8.0+6		AE	Expt	Rept AE-430	Sep 71	Holmqvist+ TBLS + GEN OPTMOD FITS	+
					Jour NP/A 188 24	Jun 72	- + OPTMOD ANAL OF 8MEV DATA	
	8.1+6				Rept AE-452	May 72	Salama.VDG TOF CURVES TABLES	
	8.0+6				Conf 70Helsinki 2 341	Jun 70	Holmqvist+ OPTMOD ANALYSIS. 8 MEV	
	8.1+6				Data EXFOR20162.	May 74	31PTS.D/DA,LEG.FIT.	
Diff Elastic	2.0+6		ANL	Expt	Prog NCSAC-42 10	Nov 71	Cox. NO DATA GIVEN.	
Diff Elastic	1.5+7		IJI	Expt	Prog YFI-12 84	72	Korzh+ ABST,20-145DEG,TBL LEG COEF	
					Prog INDC(CCP)-30	Sep 72	.PAGE 74,ENGLISH OF YFI-12 84	
Diff Elastic	8.7+5		ANL	Expt	Rept ANL-7935	Jun 72	COX+ CFD OPTMOD.HAUSER-FESHBACH	+
	8.7+5				Data EXFOR10332.020	Jun 74	. 8 PTS.	
Diff Elastic	2.0+6		SCU	Comp	Rept YK-15 153	Aug 73	Averyanov+ H-F,OPTMOD,DIFFSIG,GRAPH	
Diff Elastic	7.0+6		AE	Expt	Rept AE-482	Dec 73	Etemad. VDG. TOF.	+
	7.0+6				Data EXFOR20346.	Sep 74	31PTS.D/DA,LEG.FIT.	
Diff Elastic	3.2+6		AMS	Theo	Jour NP/A 222 93	Apr 74	Zijp+ LEG.COEFF COMPOUND ELASTIC.H-F	
Diff Elastic	8.0+6		JAE	Theo	Conf JAERI-M-5984	Feb 75	Tanaka.OPTMDL/COUPLD CH CFD EXPTS.	
Diff Elastic	1.4+7	1.5+7	JAE	Theo	Conf JAERI-M-5984	Feb 75	Tanaka.OPTMDL/COUPLD CH.GRPH CFD EXP	
Polarization	3.8+5	9.8+5	WIS	ExTh	Jour NP 6 177	Mar 58	Clement+ POLARIZATION, CFD OPT MDL	
				Expt	Rept AECU-3628	57	- + LI7(P,N) SOURCE. 3ANGLES.	
Polarization	3.3+6		FEI	Expt	Prog YFI-3 5	Sep 66	Kazakova+POLAR SCAT-NEUTS GVN,OPTMOD	
					Rept INDC-140E	66	. ENGL OF YFI-3 5	
Polarization	4.4+6	5.5+6	WIS	ExTh	Jour NP/A 95 193	Mar 67	Mahajan. OPTMDL ANALYSIS	
					Abst DA/B 28 1093	Sep 67	.SEE ALSO	
Polarization	2.0+6		ANL	Expt	Prog NCSAC-42 10	Nov 71	Cox. NO DATA GIVEN	
Polarization	1.5+7		IJI	Expt	Prog YFI-12 84	72	Korzh+ ABST,TBL P2 20-145 DEG	
					Prog INDC(CCP)-30	Sep 72	.PAGE 74,ENGLISH OF YFI-12 84	

51 Antimony

Quantity	Energy (ev) Min	Max	Lab	Type	Documentation Ref Vol Page	Date	Author, Comments	Data
Polarization	8.7+5		ANL	Expt	Rept ANL-7935	Jun 72	COX+ CFD OPTMOD.HAUSER-FESHBACH	+
	8.7+5				Data EXFOR10332.054	Jun 74	. 8 PTS.	
Polarization	3.2+6		AMS	Expt	Jour NP/A 222 93	Apr 74	Zijp+ TABLES,GRAPHS. CFD NON-SPH POT	+
					Conf 75Zurich 189	Aug 75	- + GRPH OF DATA IN REVIEW.	
					Conf 72Budapest 170	Aug 72	- + POLARIZTN,EXPT CFD OPTMOD,GRP	
	3.2+6				Data EXFOR20777.015	Apr 78	4PTS.	
Potntal Scat	1.2+2	3.0+2	ANL	Expt	Jour PR 76 100	Jul 49	Hibdon+TRNS.10PC RSLN.CO,MN SCT DET.	+
	1.2+2	3.0+2			Data EXFOR11261.027	Jun 76	. 2 PTS, SIG	
Potntal Scat		6.5+5	DKE	ExTh	Jour PL 13 70	Nov 64	Seth+0,1PHASE FRM SIG TOT AV 3-650KV	
Potntal Scat	2.4+4		LRC	Theo	Conf 66Paris 1 503	Oct 66	Bogart. VAL GVN, BETHE ANALYSIS	
Potntal Scat	1.0+0	3.0+0	BUC	Expt	Jour SCF 24 165	Feb 72	Mateiciuc.REGION OF CONSTANT TOTSIG	
Potntal Scat	1.8-3	5.0+0	CAI	Expt	Jour AJN 9 155	Feb 76	Adib+ FROM TOTSIG - RES SIG.TBL+GRPH	
Tot Inelastc	2.9+5	1.0+6	CCP	Expt	Jour ZET 30 1017	Jun 56	Poze.SIG AT 3ES GIVEN,AV E OF SCT NS	
	7.7+5	1.0+6			Jour ADP 20 3	Jul 57	Pose+,0.4+ - 0.2 B,0.7+ - 0.3 B	
	2.9+5	1.0+6			Jour JET 3 745	Dec 56	TRANSLATN.*	
Tot Inelastc	2.5+6		IFU	Expt	Jour JET 4 769	Jun 57	.ENGLISH OF ZET 31 907	
					Jour ZET 31 907	Nov 56	Strizhak. SPHERE METHOD,TABLE	
Tot Inelastc	1.4+7		LRL	Expt	Conf 58Paris § NS609	Jul 58	Mcgregor.FROM SNE 9AND14MEV CUTOFF	+
	1.4+7				Data EXFOR11205.019	Jun 76	. 1 PT.	
Tot Inelastc	2.5+6	1.4+7	IFU	Expt	Conf 58Geneva 15 18	Sep 58	Pasechnik+.PPR2030,NDG,EXPT DESCRIBD	
					Conf 55Geneva 2 3	Aug 55	- . INTEGR SIGMA,4ES,TABLE	
Tot Inelastc	4.0+5	1.2+6	FEI	Expt	Jour AE 15 416	Nov 63	Glazkov+	
					Jour JNE 18 654	64	. ENGL OF AE 15 416	
					Jour EAF 15 5	Nov 63	.FRENCH OF AE 15 416	
					Jour SJA 15 1173	Nov 63	. ENGL OF AE 15 416	
Tot Inelastc	8.0+5	4.0+6	IFU	Expt	Prog INDSWG-126 22	66	Pasechnik. AT 5 ES, TBP IN AE	
Tot Inelastc	1.5+7		TUD	Expt	Prog ZFK-262 28	Sep 73	Hermsdorf+ DEDUCED FROM N-EMIS,TABLE	
Diff Inelast	1.4+7		CCP	Expt	Jour AE 3 540	Dec 57	Zamyatnin+.P RECOIL, T=0.6+ - 0.06 MEV	
					Jour JNE 9 41	Jun 59	TRANSLATN.*	
					Jour SJA 3 1427	57	TRANSLATN.*	
Diff Inelast	2.9+6		CCP	Expt	Jour AE 7 477	Nov 59	Gofman+ SIGS TO 3 LEVELS,AT 90DEG	
					Jour JNAB 14 140	May 61	TRANSLATN.*	
					Jour SJA 7 946	Mar 61	TRANSLATN.*	
					Jour KE 3 593	Jun 60	.TRANSLATN	
Diff Inelast	4.1+6		TNC	Expt	Rept WADD-TR-60-217	Apr 60	Vincent.TOF ISOTROPIC 20-135DEG	+
	4.1+6				Data EXFOR11621.	Jun 76	. 22 PTS, DSIG	
	4.1+6				Data EXFOR11621.019	Jun 76	. 1 PT, SIG	
Diff Inelast	4.0+6	7.0+6	LAS	Expt	Jour PR 129 1649	Feb 63	Thomson+ 90DEG TEMP FOR NS TO 3MEV	+
	4.0+6	7.0+6			Data EXFOR11495.033	Jun 76	. 2 PTS, DSIG	
Diff Inelast	1.4+7		BAS	Expt	Jour PL 5 202	Jul 63	Huber+ GRPH OF INELASTIC N SPECT.	
					Jour HPA 36 1059	Dec 59	- +.T=0.89MEV	
Diff Inelast	4.0+6	6.5+6	DKE	Expt	Abst DA 24 4248	Apr 64	Buccino.ANG DIST.TOF.NUCL T.LVL DEN.	
Diff Inelast	1.4+7		ORL	ExTh	Jour NP 68 97	Jun 65	Stelson+TOF.GRPHS.CFD DWBA MDL CALCS	+
	1.4+7			Expt	Data EXFOR11527.023	Jun 76	. 17 PTS, DSIG	
Diff Inelast	3.0+5	8.0+5	IFU	Expt	Prog INDSWG-126 22	66	Pasechnik. AT 3 ES, TBP IN AE	
Diff Inelast	9.6+5		TUD	Expt	Jour KE 9 95	Mar 66	Oehler+ SIG TO 160, 500-600 KEV LVLS	+
	9.6+5				Data EXFOR30213.010	Nov 72	VALUE TO 160 KEV AND 300-600 KEV LEV	
Diff Inelast	1.4+7		FEI	Expt	Jour YF 4 1154	Dec 66	Sal'Nikov+ SPEC OF SECNDARY NS,CURVE	+
					Rept FEI-39	Jan 66	- +TOF SPECT,RING GEOM,E-SPEC	
					Jour SNP 4 831	Jun 67	.ENGLISH TRANSL OF YF 4 1154 12/66	
	1.4+7				Data EXFOR40134.011	Feb 73	N-SPECTRUM AT 92 DEG, 5EN'	
Diff Inelast	4.0+5	1.4+7	FEI	Comp	Rept ICD-4 57	67	Sluchevskaja.SELECTIV COMPIL ,TABLE	
Diff Inelast	1.5+7		TNC	Expt	Jour PR 186 1038	Oct 69	Mathur+TOF,DIST INEL SCT NEUTS	+
					Rept NDL-TR-86	Jan 67	- +TBLS.ANG=90DEG.EXPT DETAILS	
	1.5+7				Data EXFOR10043.	Jun 72	. 14 PTS.	
Diff Inelast	3.0+5	1.5+6	ANL	Expt	Jour NP/A 93 609	Mar 67	Smith+ TOF, CFD OPTMDL + H-F	+
	5.0+5	1.5+6			Rept ANL-7274	Nov 66	- +TBLS OF DATA PTS.	
	3.0+5	1.5+6			Data EXFOR10418.	Aug 76	306PTS.37KEV LVL INCLUDED IN DEL,SEL	
	5.0+5	1.5+6			Data EXFOR10418.009	Aug 76	33PTS.DIN CS FOR .16,.54MEV EXCIT.	
Diff Inelast	3.5+6	8.5+6	JAE	Expt	Prog EANDC(J)8L25	Jan 68	Maruyama+.TOF.CONTIN SPECT AT 90DEG.	
	3.6+6	8.5+6		ExTh	Jour NP/A 131 145	Jun 69	- . E DEPENDENCE,PARAM,TH FIT	
	3.5+6	8.5+6		Expt	Conf 67Tokyo 373	Sep 67	- + PPR8.127. ABST.	
Diff Inelast	1.4+7		TUD	Expt	Prog ZFK-223 24	Sep 71	Giera+ TOF,DOUBLE-DIFFSIG EXPT,NDG	
Diff Inelast	1.4+7		KFI	Theo	Rept KFKI-72-17	Feb 72	Kluge+ CALC N-SPEC INEL+N2N,TBL,GRPH	
Diff Inelast	1.4+7		TUD	Theo	Conf 73Kiev 1 258	May 73	Hermsdorf+ DESCRIPN OF N-SPEC	
Diff Inelast	1.4+7		FEI	Expt	Rept YK-23 6	76	Sal'Nikov+ TOF,NEUT-SPEC,TBLS	+
	1.4+7				Data EXFOR40324.	Dec 77	D2SIG/DA,DE. 3*51 PNTS	

51 Antimony

Quantity	Energy (ev) Min	Energy (ev) Max	Lab	Type	Documentation Ref Vol Page	Date	Author, Comments	Data
Thermal Scat	3.0−2		IBJ	Expt Rept	INR−1263/II/PS	Feb 71	Sosnowski+ PHONON DISPERSION CFD TH	
Thermal Scat	−		TOH	Expt Jour	PL/A 35 315	Jun 71	Waseda+ LIQUID SB STRUCTURE FACTORS	
Thermal Scat	1.8−3	5.0+0	CAI	Expt Jour	AJN 9 155	Feb 76	Adib+ COH SCAT AMP,BY TOTSIG.VAL GVN	
Thermal Scat	1.0−4	1.0+3	MUN	Revw Jour	EEN 80 1	77	Koester. SCAT LENGTH,FREE+INCOH SIG	
Scattering	Maxwl		CAV	Expt Jour	PRSA 162 127	Sep 37	Goldhaber+. 6.5B REL 4.83B FOR C	
Scattering	2.4+6	2.4+6	OSA	Expt Jour	SCP 34 865	Aug 38	Kikuchi+.D+D,G−M.SIG=3.1B.	
Scattering	Maxwl		JAP	Expt Jour	SCP 36 153	Jul 39	Kimura.SIG=3.0 PM 1.0B	
Scattering	2.0−2	2.0+0	IFU	Expt Prog	INDSWG−120 27	65	Vertebnyj.GRAPH,TOF,SIG(0.025)=4.1	
Scattering	Fast		FEI	Expt Jour	AE 18 409	Apr 65	Guseinov+ ANG DIST,TH(N,F)DETECTOR	
				Jour	JNE 20 700	Aug 66	. ENGL OF AE 18 409	
				Jour	SJA 18 526	Apr 65	. ENGL OF AE 18 409	
				Jour	EAF 18 526	Apr 65	.FRENCH OF AE 18 409	
Scattering	2.4+4		LRC	Theo Conf	66Paris 1 503	Oct 66	Bogart. VAL GVN, BETHE ANALYSIS	
Scattering	5.0−2	4.0−1	CAI	Expt Jour	JNE 22 389	Jun 68	El−Ela+ TOF SIG 4.20+−0.18B	
Nonelastic	+7		BRK	Expt Jour	PR 53 795	May 38	Grahame+ RA−BE,TRANS,BY FE56+AL(N,P)	
Nonelastic	1.0+6		WIS	Expt Jour	PR 93 1062	Mar 54	Walt+ 30DEG−150 DEG.	+
	1.0+6			Data	EXFOR11637.048	Jun 76	. 1 PT	
Nonelastic	2.5+6	4.1+6	IFU	Expt Conf	55Geneva 2 3	Aug 55	PASECHNIK SPH MEAS SPEC OF SCT N	+
				Jour	UFZ 3 185	58	.	
				Conf	56Kiev 102	56	.	
Nonelastic	1.4+7		CCP	Expt Jour	AE 1 4 155	Sep 56	Flerov+.SPHERE TRANSM, 2060+−40MB	+
				Jour	JNE 4 529	Apr 57	TRANSLATN.*	
				Jour	SJA 1 4 617	56	TRANSLATN.*	
Nonelastic	1.4+7		IFU	Expt Jour	AE 2 68	Jan 57	Strizhak.SPHERE TRANSMISS 1.87+−.08B	+
				Jour	JNE 5 253	Nov 57	TRANSLATN.*	
				Jour	SJA 2 72	57	TRANSLATN.*	
Nonelastic	1.4+7		LRL	Expt Jour	PR 108 726	Nov 57	Macgregor+,SPH TRNS CFD OPTMDL+XPTS	+
				Conf	58Geneva 14 109	Sep 58	Ball+ PPR1881,SPHERE TRANSM−METHOD	
	1.4+7			Data	EXFOR11226.019	Jun 76	. 1 PT.	
Nonelastic	1.4+7		CCP	Expt Jour	AE 5 522	Nov 58	Lebedev+ SPH GEOM,TR DET, 1.85+−.13B	+
				Jour	JNEA 11 39	59	TRANSLATN.*	
				Jour	SJA 5 1431	58	TRANSLATN.*	
Nonelastic	4.1+6		TNC	Expt Rept	WADD−TR−60−217	Apr 60	Vincent+	+
	4.1+6			Data	EXFOR11621.015	Jun 76	. 1 PT.	
Nonelastic	8.0+5	4.1+6	IFU	ExTh Jour	AE 20 8	Jan 66	Korzh+ SUMMARY OF SEVERAL YRS WORK	+
				Jour	UFZ 9 929	May 64	.	
				Jour	SJA 20 8	Jul 66	.ENGLISH TRANSL OF AE 20 8 1/66	
				Rept	INDSWG−101 112	65	.=UFZ9.ENGL NO GRPHS.RUSS LARGER GPH	
Nonelastic	1.5+7		BOS	Expt Conf	66Bombay 69	Feb 66	Chatterjee+.VAL GVN,PLASTIC SCINT	
Nonelastic	9.6+5		TUD	Expt Jour	KE 9 95	Mar 66	Oehler+ SIG GIVEN,NA−BE N−SOURCE	+
	9.6+5			Data	EXFOR30213.008	Nov 72	SINGLE VALUE	
Nonelastic	1.4+7		GHT	Expt Jour	ACA 64 187	73	Vandecasteele+ FLUX−ATTENUAT,SIG GVN	
Nonelastic	1.4+7		TUD	Theo Jour	KE 16 252	Aug 73	Hermsdorf+ INTEG FITTED DIFFSIG,TBL	
Absorption	Slow		OSA	Expt Jour	JPJO 18 188	36	Kikuchi+.SIG AND G−ENERGY DETERMIN	
Absorption	+7		BRK	Expt Jour	PR 53 795	May 38	Grahame+ RA−BE,TRANS,PB(NNGAMMA) DET	
Absorption	Pile		HAR	Expt Jour	PPSA 63 1175	Oct 50	Colmer+LITTLER.PILE OSC REL HAR B	+
				Rept	AERE−N/R−527	Jun 50	− + PILE OSC.	
Absorption	2.5+4	8.3+5	FEI	Expt Jour	ZET 34 574	Mar 58	Belanova.VALUES GIVEN AT 3 ES	
				Jour	JET 7 397	Sep 58	TRANSLATN.*	
Absorption	Fiss		KUR	Expt Conf	58Geneva 15 50	Sep 58	Leipunskij+.PPR2219,VAL GVN,SB−BE	
Absorption	2.4+4		FEI	Expt Jour	AE 19 3	Jul 65	Belanova+ 2 METHODS,ABSOL EXPT,TABLE	+
				Jour	JNE 20 411	66	.ENGLISH TRANSL OF AE 19 3 7/65	
				Jour	SJA 19 858	65	.ENGLISH TRANSL OF AE 19 3 7/65	
				Jour	EAF 19 1 11	65	. FRENCH TRANSL OF AE 19 3 7/65	
	2.4+4			Data	EXFOR40072.012	Jul 71	SIGMA AT 24 KEV AS PUBLISHED	
Absorption	9.6+5		TUD	Expt Jour	KE 9 95	Mar 66	Oehler+ SIG GIVEN,NA−BE N−SOURCE	+
	9.6+5			Data	EXFOR30213.009	Nov 72	SINGLE VALUE	
Absorption	5.0−2	4.0−1	CAI	Expt Jour	JNE 22 389	Jun 68	El−Ela+ TOF SIG 4.04+−.25B AT .025EV	
Absorption	8.1+6		AE	Theo Conf	70Helsinki 2 341	Jun 70	Holmqvist+55. OPTMODEL CALC SIGMA	
Res Int Abs	5.0−1	1.0+6	CCP	Expt Conf	55Geneva 5 91	Aug 55	Spivak+.VAL GVN CFD REF,PPR659	
Res Int Abs	−		CCP	Expt Jour	AE 3 507	Dec 57	Klimentov+.EPI CD REACTIVITY REL LI	+
				Jour	JNE 9 20	Jun 59	TRANSLATN.*	
				Jour	SJA 3 1387	57	TRANSLATN.*	
Res Int Abs	5.5−1		MUN	Comp Jour	JRC 29 175	Jan 76	Gryntakis+, 2 VALUES+STANDARDS GIVEN	
(n,γ)	Maxwl		UI	Expt Jour	PR 69 411	May 46	Coltman+ POWDERED SAMPLE+C. REL TO B	+
	Maxwl			Data	EXFOR12616.018	Jun 76	. 1 PT, SIGMA.	

51 Antimony

Quantity	Energy (ev) Min	Max	Lab	Type	Documentation Ref Vol Page	Date	Author, Comments	Data
(n,γ)	Pile		ANL	Expt	Jour PR 80 342	Nov 50	Harris+.PILE OSC.REL TO BORON.	+
	Pile				Data EXFOR11528.030	Jun 76	. 1 PT.	
(n,γ)	Maxwl		ORL	Expt	Jour PR 83 643	Aug 51	Pomerance.LOCAL OSC REL AU ABS 95	+
	Maxwl				Data EXFOR11047.061	Jun 76	. 1 PT.	
(n,γ)	2.0+5		KUR	Expt	Conf 58Geneva 15 50	Sep 58	Leipunskij+.PPR2219,VAL GVN,ACTIVATN	
(n,γ)	1.8+5	1.0+6	LAS	Expt	Jour PR 120 556	Oct 60	Diven.SC−T.	+
					Conf 58Geneva 15 60	Sep 58	.SUPERSEDED	
	1.8+5	1.0+6			Data EXFOR11616.002	Jun 76	. 7 PTS.	
(n,γ)	2.4+4		ORL	Expt	Jour NP 20 202	Oct 60	Schmitt.SHELL TRANSMISSION 565+ −45MB	+
					Prog EANDC−33 41	63	− + CORRECTION TO NP 20 202	
	2.4+4				Data EXFOR11778.010	Jun 76	. 1 PT.	
(n,γ)	7.0+3	1.8+5	ORL	Expt	Jour PR 122 182	Apr 61	Gibbons+ CURVE, CFD THEORY	+
	3.0+4	6.5+4			Jour PR 129 2695	Mar 63	Macklin+. LIQ SCINT,436 AND 245MB	
					Conf 61Vienna 1 95	Aug 61	Neiler.	
	7.5+3	1.8+5			Data EXFOR11329.	Jun 76	. 55 PTS.	
(n,γ)	2.0+2	8.0+3	ORL	Expt	Conf 61Saclay 203	Sep 61	Block+.LIQUID SCINTILLATOR	+
	2.1+2	8.0+3			Conf 61Vienna 1 95	Aug 61	Neiler.	
	2.1+2	8.4+3			Data EXFOR11935.008	Jun 76	. 36 PTS.	
(n,γ)	1.0+0	4.0+4	LEB	Expt	Jour ZET 42 988	Apr 62	Popov.PB−SLO−DOWN,GRPH SG(E)CFD OTHR	+
					Jour JET 15 683	Oct 62	TRANSLATN.*	
(n,γ)	1.0+3	1.0+5	DUB	Expt	Jour ZET 43 2000	Dec 62	Exp.COMP.WITH THEORY	
					Jour JET 16 1409	Jun 63	TRANSLATN.*	
(n,γ)	2.0+3	1.0+5	KUR	Theo	Jour NP 45 156	Jul 63	Nemirovsky+ OPTIC.THEOR.COMP.WITH EXP	
(n,γ)	2.4+4		CCP	Comp	Rept INDSWG−64 72	64	Belanova. SIG=692+ −60 MB	
(n,γ)	5.0+3	9.0+4	ORL	Theo	Jour RMP 37 166	Jan 65	Macklin+.CALC FOR KT=5TO90KEV	
(n,γ)	1.0+3	1.0+6	KFK	Eval	Conf 66Paris 1 277	Oct 66	Poenitz.TBL EVAL+RENORM TO AU	
(n,γ)	2.4+4		LRC	Eval	Conf 66Paris 1 503	Oct 66	Bogart. VAL GVN, BETHE ANALYSIS	
(n,γ)	5.0+0	1.0+5	HAR	Expt	Prog AERE−PR/NP13	Feb 68	Moxon+ LINAC TOF TO BE ANALYSED	
(n,γ)	3.0+5	2.7+6	FEI	ExTh	Jour AE 24 6 576	Jun 68	Tolstikov+ CURVE	+
					Jour EAF 24 6 111	Jun 68	.TRANSLATION	
	2.0+5	2.7+6		Expt	Data EXFOR40005.006	Jul 70	.SIGMA AT 18 ENERGIES GIVEN	
(n,γ)	1.1+4	7.3+4	PEL	Expt	Jour NP/A 121 655	Dec 68	Spitz+ TOF,SIG REL IN,GRAPHS	+
	1.1+4	7.3+4			Data EXFOR30114.008	Mar 71	VDG, 12 DATA LINES,PRIV COMM	
(n,γ)	1.0+3	1.0+7	BOL	Eval	Rept CEC(70)−2	Apr 70	Benzi.GRAPH=SUM OF SIG(ISOTOPES)	
(n,γ)	None		TOR	Expt	Abst DA/B 31 2200	Oct 70	ING.TOF.PARTL LVLS FOR SB122,SB124.	
(n,γ)	3.0+4		AUA	Theo	Rept AAEC/E−211	Nov 70	Musgrove. SIGMA GIVEN AND CFD OTHER	
(n,γ)	4.0+5		WWA	Expt	Jour APPB 2 489	71	Brzosko+ PARTIAL,TOTAL SIG CFD THEO	+
					Rept INR−1318 28	Apr 71	*SHORT REPORT,DATA GIV	
					Jour CJP 47 2849	Dec 69	*TH.CALCULATIONS OF SIG	
	4.0+5				Data EXFOR30159.	Apr 72	PARTIAL,TOTAL SIGMAS GIVEN	
(n,γ)	1.4+7		COL	Expt	Jour NSE 51 113	Jun 73	Stamatelatos+.E(GAM) ABOVE 14 MEV	
					Conf 71Knoxvill 267	Mar 71	.SUPERSEDED	
(n,γ)	1.0+3	1.0+7	FEI	Eval	Rept YK−8/2 97	Sep 72	Abagjan+ AVG SIG(ENERGY−GROUPS),TABL	
					Rept INDC(CCP)−39	Jul 74	.P102. ENGLISH OF YK−8/2 97	
Spect (n,γ)	Maxwl		CRC	Expt	Jour CJP 31 1025	Nov 53	Bartholomew+ PAIR SP,140KV LINEWIDTH	
Spect (n,γ)	Maxwl		GEA	Eval	Rept DC−58−1−30	Jan 58	Deloume. BY APPROXIMATION CURV+TABLE	
Spect (n,γ)	Maxwl		KUR	Expt	Jour AE 6 281	Mar 59	Groshev+ GRAPH+TABLE OF GAMMALINES	
					Jour SJA 6 170	Nov 60	. ENGL OF AE 6 281	
					Jour JNEA 12 47	May 60	. ENGL OF AE 6 281	
Spect (n,γ)	Maxwl		TAM	Expt	Abst BAP 4 97	Mar 59	Edens+	
Spect (n,γ)	Maxwl		YAL	Expt	Jour PR 114 268	Apr 59	Draper.SC SPECTR,GAM E 0 TO 600 KEV	
Spect (n,γ)	Maxwl		ARF	Expt	Prog ARF−1193−17	Dec 62	Greenwood+ NAI(TL) SPEC, 12 GAMMAS	
Spect (n,γ)	2.5−2		MIT	Comp	Rept MITNE−85	Jan 69	Rasmussen+TBL G INT.	
Spect (n,γ)	6.2+0	1.4+2	SAC	Expt	Conf 69Studsvik 657	Aug 69	Paya+ SPEC GRPH+TBL OF ISOTOPS,LINAC	
Spect (n,γ)	4.0+5		WWA	Expt	Jour APPB 2 489	Aug 71	Brzosko+ GAMMA−EN = 3 TO 7 MEV,GRAPH	
Spect (n,γ)	1.4+7		COL	Expt	Jour NSE 51 113	Jun 73	Stamatelatos+ PAIR SPECTR. CURVES	
					Conf 71Knoxvill 267	Mar 71	.SUPERSEDED	
Spect (n,γ)	1.4+7		NJS	Expt	Priv CVELBAR	Oct 73	.INTEGRAL EXPT,SCINT PAIR SPECTRMTR	+
	1.4+7				Data EXFOR30185.015	Oct 73	PROMPT GAMMA−RAY SPECT,25 DATA LINES	
Spect (n,γ)	4.6+5		AUA	Expt	Prog AAEC/PR−39P 44	Jan 74	Allen+ NA−I,GAMMA YIELD.FIGURE ONLY	
Inelastic γ	3.7+6		BAR	Expt	Jour PR 100 83	Oct 55	Rothman+1.00MEV G SIG=75MB AT 90DEG	+
	3.7+6				Data EXFOR11478.005	Jun 76	. 1 PT, DSIG	
Inelastic γ	2.8+6		CCP	Expt	Jour AE 4 132	Feb 58	Barchuk+ GAM ES+REL INTENS AT 100DEG	
					Jour JNE 9 120	Jun 59	TRANSLATN.*	
					Jour SJA 4 175	58	TRANSLATN.*	
Inelastic γ	2.8+6		IFU	Expt	Conf 58Geneva 15 18	Sep 58	Pasechnik+.PPR2030,CURVE	

51 Antimony

Quantity	Energy (ev) Min	Max	Lab	Type	Documentation Ref Vol Page	Date	Author, Comments	Data
Inelastic γ	3.0+6		FEI	Expt	Jour AE 9 403	Nov 60	Androsenko+ TABLE OF GAMMA-ENERGIES	
					Jour SJA 9 945	Sep 61	. ENGL OF AE 9 403	
					Jour KE 4 510	Jun 61	.GERMAN OF AE 9 403	
Inelastic γ	2.3+5	1.2+6	FEI	Expt	Jour IZV 25 309	Feb 61	Broder+ PRODUCTION CS FOR 1 GAM-E	+
	2.3+5	1.2+6			Data EXFOR40334.002	Jan 76	SIG AT 27 ES FOR PROD OF 1MEV-GAM	
Inelastic γ	1.1+6	2.5+6	CCP	Expt	Rept ANL-TR-177	64	Broder+,TBL+GRPH,1GAM+27N ES	
Inelastic γ	None		FEI	Expt	Prog YFI-7 4	Apr 69	Broder+ PRODUCTION SIG FOR 1 GAMMA-E	+
					Rept INDC(CCP)-7U5	Feb 70	TRANSLATN.*	
	2.2+5	1.2+6			Data EXFOR40036.009	Aug 70	SIGMA AT 27EN FOR PROD OF 153KEV GAM	
Inelastic γ	1.0+6	3.5+6	TNC	Expt	Rept ORO-2791-32	Feb 71	Buchanan+ ANG DIST+SIGS FOR 3NEUT ES	+
	1.0+6	1.5+6			Prog ORO-2791-26	Aug 67	Morgan+ NAI(TL) DET 2ES SPEC+ANGDIST	
	1.0+6				Data EXFOR11662.006	Jun 76	. 4 PTS, DSIG	
Inelastic γ	3.3+6		SBL	Expt	Jour NIM 134 545	76	Habbani+ 90 DEG TBL	+
	3.3+6				Data EXFOR20667.020	Oct 76	3PTS.D/DA.	
Nonelastic γ	2.4+6		OSA	Expt	Jour JMJ 21 75	39	Kikuchi+.D-D P LI-D N,SIG GIVN	
	2.1+6	2.8+6			Jour JMJ 21 232	39	Aoki.SIG GIVN	
		2.4+6			Jour JMJ 19 369	37	- .D+D NEUTRON.RELATIV SIG GIVN	
	Slow				Jour JPJO 18 115	36	Kikuchi+.REL SIG GIVN FOR G-EMISSION	
(n,2n)	Thrsh	Up	BRK	Expt	Jour PR 53 492	Mar 38	Sagane.LIMITS FOR N2N THRESHOLD E(N)	
(n,2n)	1.4+7		BRK	Expt	Conf 58Geneva 15 3	Sep 58	Ashby+ VALUE GIVEN, TOF	+
	1.4+7				Data EXFOR11632.018	Jun 76	. 1 PT.	
(n,2n)	1.4+7		CCP	Expt	Jour AE 5 522	Nov 58	Lebedev+ N2N+2(N3N)-REM=1.52+-0.2B	
					Jour JNEA 11 39	59	TRANSLATN.*	
					Jour SJA 5 1431	58	TRANSLATN.*	
(n,2n)	1.4+7		KFI	Theo	Rept KFKI-72-17	Feb 72	Kluge+ CALC N-SPEC INEL+N2N,TBL,GRPH	
(n,2n)	1.5+7		DEB	Eval	Jour REA 11 1 153	Mar 73	Boedy+ RECOMM.VALUE FROM N-Z SYSTEM.	
n Emission	1.4+7		CCP	Expt	Jour AE 5 522	Nov 58	Lebedev+ SPH GEOM,N COUNT,ETA GIVEN	
					Jour JNEA 11 39	59	.TRANSLATION	
					Jour SJA 5 1431	58	.ENGL OF AE 5 522 NOV58	
n Emission	1.5+7		TNC	Expt	Jour PR 186 1038	69	Mathur+TOF.90DEG.MULTISCT CORRC.	+
					Rept NDL-TR-86	Jan 67	- +EXPT+MULTISCAT CORRC DETAILS.	
	1.5+7				Data EXFOR10090.019	May 73	. 2PTS. NEM CS=136.77,131.64 MB/SR.	
n Emission	1.4+7		FEI	Expt	Rept YK- 23 10	76	Sal'Nikov+ INEL+(N,2N)+(N,PN)SIG GVN	+
	1.4+7				Data EXFOR40324.003	Dec 77	N-EMIS FROM IN+(N2N)+(NPN). 1 PNT	
n Emission	1.5+7		TUD	Expt	Jour KE 19 241	Aug 76	Hermsdorf+ ABSOL DOUBDIF,FIG.TOT,TBL	+
					Rept ZFK-277(U)	Aug 75	- + DIFFSIG AT 5ANGS,TBL+GRPH	
	1.5+7				Data EXFOR30397.025	May 77	49 PTS. ANGLE INT.N-EMISS.SPECT.	
	1.5+7				Data EXFOR30275.	Apr 74	DOUBLDIF(5ANG,555PTS)+PARTIAL ANGDIS	
(n,p)	1.4+7		BRN	Expt	Jour NP 10 418	Apr 59	Eubank+ 0 DEG SPEC. GRAPH. 5-15 MEV	
(n,p)	1.4+7		HAR	Expt	Jour NP 24 274	Apr 61	Allan.AT120DEG.EMULSION. CFD STATMOD	
	1.4+7				Data EXFOR20004.109	Nov 70	1PNT.CMPD.NUC.	
(n,p)	1.4+7		BRN	Expt	Jour PR 123 1738	Sep 61	Peck.YIELD SPECT.A DISTR OF GROUPS	+
					Jour NC 14 397	Oct 59	- +E AND ANG DISTRIB.OF PROTONS	
	1.4+7				Data EXFOR11913.012	Jun 76	. 5 PTS.	
(n,np)	1.4+7		BRN	Expt	Jour PR 123 1738	Sep 61	Peck.PROTON YLD SPECT,A DISTR OF GPS	+
	1.4+7				Data EXFOR11934.011	Jun 76	. 5 PTS, DSIG	
(n,d)	1.4+7		BRN	Expt	Jour PR 123 1738	Sep 61	Peck.YLD SPECT. A DISTR OF GROUPS	+
	1.4+7				Data EXFOR11934.010	Jun 76	. 5 PTS, DSIG	
(n,t)	2.3+7		JUL	Expt	Jour JIN 36 3639	Dec 74	Qaim+ (NT)+(NNT), 4.3+-1.3 MB	+
	2.3+7				Data EXFOR20524.010	Apr 76	1PNT.+NNT	
(n,nt)	2.3+7		JUL	Expt	Jour JIN 36 3639	Dec 74	Qaim+ (NT)+(NNT), 4.3+-1.3 MB	+
	2.3+7				Data EXFOR20524.010	Apr 76	1PNT.+NT.	
Reson Params	6.3+0	1.9+1	COL	Expt	Jour PR 70 159	Aug 46	Havens+ 2 RES, E0, WN	+
Reson Params	6.3+0	1.9+1			Data EXFOR11139.008	Jun 76	. 2 RES, E0,WT**2/PCS	
Reson Params	5.8+0	2.1+1	COL	Expt	Jour PR 71 65	Jan 47	Rainwater+ 3 RES OBSERVED	+
	5.8+0	2.1+1			Data EXFOR11685.010	Jun 76	. 3 RES, E0	
Reson Params	9.6+5		TUD	Expt	Jour KE 9 95	Mar 66	Oehler+.LEVELS+SPINS,CURVE,NA-BE NS	
Reson Params	2.4+4		LRC	Theo	Conf 66Paris 1 503	Oct 66	Bogart. VAL GVN, BETHE ANALYSIS	
Reson Params	1.5+1	3.0+3	COL	Expt	Jour PR 166 1234	Feb 68	Wynchank+ TOF G*WN FOR MANY ES AVG D	+
					Conf 65Antwerp 95	Jul 65	Rainwater+	
	1.5+1	3.0+3			Data EXFOR11913.012	Jun 76	. 295 RES, E0,WN0	
	1.5+1	3.0+3			Data EXFOR11913.011	Jun 76	. 15 RES, WT,WG	
Reson Params	6.2+0	2.5+2	JAE	Expt	Conf 68Wash. 789	Mar 68	Asami+ TRANS 34ES 2G*WN WT ISOT ASSG	+
Reson Params	2.2+2	3.0+2	CJD	Eval	Rept YK- 7	71	Zakharova+ SURVEY+SYSTEMATICS,GW,TBL	
					Rept INDC(CCP)-27	Nov 72	.ENGLISH TRANSLATION OF YK-7 /71	
Reson Params	6.2+0	1.5+2	BUC	Expt	Jour SCF 24 165	Feb 72	Mateiciuc.G-WID,N-WID 17RES,TBLS	
Reson Params	None		SAC	Expt	Conf 72Budapest 238	Aug 72	Jain+ CORREL N-,PARTIAL G-WIDTH,TBL	

51 Antimony

Quantity	Energy (ev) Min	Max	Lab	Type	Documentation Ref Vol Page	Date	Author, Comments	Data
Strnth Fnctn	1.0+4	2.0+5	ORL	Expt Jour	PR 122 182	Apr 61	Gibbons+	+
	1.0+4	2.0+5		Data	EXFOR11329.	Jun 76	. 3 PTS, STF, D, AVE WG	
Strnth Fnctn	1.0+3	1.5+4	DUB	Expt Rept	JINR-P-1010	62	Popov+. P-WAVE STF CFD OTHERS+OPTMDL	
Strnth Fnctn	2.4+4		LRC	Theo Conf	66Paris 1 503	Oct 66	Bogart. VAL GVN, BETHE ANALYSIS	
		2.5+6	COL	Expt Jour	PR 166 1234	Feb 68	Wynchank+ S.= .34+-.05	+
				Conf	65Antwerp 95	Jul 65	Rainwater+ S-WAVE STF=.35(X10-4)	
		2.5+6		Data	EXFOR11934.	Jun 76	. 3 PTS, STF, 2 PTS, D	
Strnth Fnctn	3.0+4	6.5+5	DKE	Expt Jour	AP 46 401	Feb 68	Tabony+ TRANS DERIVES S0, S1, S2	+
				Abst	DA/B 27 2085	Dec 66	- .THESIS ABST	
		3.3+5		ExTh Jour	PL 13 70	Nov 64	Seth+ S,P,D	
	5.0+4	1.5+5		Expt Conf	64Paris 2 916	Jul 64	- +S0,S1,S2 R PRIME/R DUKE U.	
	3.0+4	6.2+5			Data	EXFOR11953.004	Jun 76	. 3 PTS.	
Strnth Fnctn	8.0+3	3.0+4	PEL	Expt Jour	NP/A 121 655	Dec 68	Spitz+ FROM SIG(N,G)	+
	8.0+3	3.0+4		Data	EXFOR30114.011	Mar 71	P-WAVE STRENGTH FUNCTION.	
Strnth Fnctn	2.7+3		MUN	Expt Conf	71Albany 327	Aug 71	Dilg+TRNS.S0 STF GVN.31 ELEMENT GRPH	
Strnth Fnctn	None		SAC	Expt Prog	EANDC(E)140U	Aug 71	Cauvin+	
Strnth Fnctn	1.0+3	6.0+5	NBS	Expt Jour	PR/C 9 28	Jan 74	Camarda.LINAC.TRANS. S1 MEASURED.	+
	1.0+3	7.0+5		Prog	USNDC-7 147	Jun 73	- . LINAC. S1 MEASD. NO DATA	
	1.0+3	6.0+5		Data	EXFOR10765.008	Nov 78	. 1PT.S1=(2.1+-.5)-4	
Lvl Density	1.4+7		BAS	Expt Jour	PL 5 202	Jul 63	Huber+TBL OF NUC TEMP AND LVL DENSTY	
				Jour	HPA 36 1059	Dec 63	Plattner+TOF TBL12ELEM.CFD TH	
Lvl Density	None		ANL	Theo Jour	NP 60 70	Nov 64	Vonach+NUCL TEMP CFD ANGDIST INEL N	
Lvl Density	1.4+7		FEI	Expt Rept	FEI-30	Dec 65	Anufrienko+.PARAMS FROM NONELASTIC	+
Lvl Density	3.6+6	8.5+6	JAE	Expt Jour	NP/A 131 145	Jun 69	Maruyama. E DEPENDANCE,PARAM,TH FIT.	+
				Conf	67Tokyo 373	Sep 67	- + PPR8.127. ABST.	
Lvl Density	1.5+7		TNC	Expt Jour	PR 186 1038	Oct 69	Mathur+,FERMI GAS LVL DENSITY COEF	+
				Rept	NDL-TR-86	Jan 67	- +EXPT+MULTISCAT CORRC DETAILS.	
	1.5+7			Data	EXFOR10090.035	May 73	.2PTS. NUCLEAR T=.84,.33 MEV	
Lvl Density	1.4+7		TUD	Expt Prog	ZFK-223 25	Sep 71	Giera+ TOF,ELAS,LVL-DENSITY PAR,TBL	
(γ,n)	8.0+6	3.0+7	SAC	Expt Jour	NP/A 219 39	Jan 74	Lepretre+GDR,LORENTZ PARAM,GRPHS,TBL	

51 Antimony 113

Quantity	Energy (ev) Min	Max	Lab	Type	Documentation Ref Vol Page	Date	Author, Comments	Data
Reson Params	-		AUA	Theo Rept	AAEC/E-211	Nov 70	Musgrove. CALCULTD D+GAM WIDTH GIVEN	
Strnth Fnctn	-		AUA	Theo Rept	AAEC/E-211	Nov 70	Musgrove. SMOOTHED S0,S1 AND S2 GIVN	

51 Antimony 114

Quantity	Energy (ev) Min	Max	Lab	Type	Documentation Ref Vol Page	Date	Author, Comments	Data
Reson Params	-		AUA	Theo Rept	AAEC/E-211	Nov 70	Musgrove. CALCULTD D+GAM WIDTH GIVEN	
Strnth Fnctn	-		AUA	Theo Rept	AAEC/E-211	Nov 70	Musgrove. SMOOTHED S0,S1 AND S2 GIVN	

51 Antimony 115

Quantity	Energy (ev) Min	Max	Lab	Type	Documentation Ref Vol Page	Date	Author, Comments	Data
Reson Params	-		AUA	Theo Rept	AAEC/E-211	Nov 70	Musgrove. CALCULTD D+GAM WIDTH GIVEN	
Strnth Fnctn	-		AUA	Theo Rept	AAEC/E-211	Nov 70	Musgrove. SMOOTHED S0,S1 AND S2 GIVN	

51 Antimony 116

Quantity	Energy (ev) Min	Max	Lab	Type	Documentation Ref Vol Page	Date	Author, Comments	Data
Reson Params	-		AUA	Theo Rept	AAEC/E-211	Nov 70	Musgrove. CALCULTD D+GAM WIDTH GIVEN	
Strnth Fnctn	-		AUA	Theo Rept	AAEC/E-211	Nov 70	Musgrove. SMOOTHED S0,S1 AND S2 GIVN	
Lvl Density	+6	+7	WIS	ExTh Jour	NP 71 529	Sep 65	Wood+ DEDUCED FROM(P,N) ON SN 116	

51 Antimony 117

Quantity	Energy (ev) Min	Max	Lab	Type	Documentation Ref Vol Page	Date	Author, Comments	Data
(n,p)	6.0+6	1.4+7	WIS	Expt Abst	DA 25 6709	May 65	Wood.INVERSE REACTION	
(n,p)	1.9+6		ORL	Expt Jour	NP/A 176 449	Dec 71	Kernell+ INV REACT ANGDISTRIB.	
Reson Params	-		AUA	Theo Rept	AAEC/E-211	Nov 70	Musgrove. CALCULTD D+GAM WIDTH GIVEN	

51 Antimony 117

Quantity	Energy (ev) Min	Max	Lab	Type	Documentation Ref Vol Page	Date	Author, Comments	Data
Strnth Fnctn	–		AUA	Theo Rept	AAEC/E – 211	Nov 70	Musgrove. SMOOTHED S0,S1 AND S2 GIVN	
Lvl Density	+6	+7	WIS	ExTh Jour	NP 71 529	Sep 65	Wood+ DEDUCED FROM(P,N) ON SN 117	

51 Antimony 118

Quantity	Energy (ev) Min	Max	Lab	Type	Documentation Ref Vol Page	Date	Author, Comments	Data
(n,α)	–		BUC	Expt Jour	NP/A 140 23	Jan 70	Magda+ INVERSE,LVL DENS PAR,GRAPH	
				Rept	INDC(SEC) – 18	Aug 71	*P158.LVL DENS PAR,TBL	
Reson Params	–		AUA	Theo Rept	AAEC/E – 211	Nov 70	Musgrove. CALCULTD D+GAM WIDTH GIVEN	
Strnth Fnctn	–		AUA	Theo Rept	AAEC/E – 211	Nov 70	Musgrove. SMOOTHED S0,S1 AND S2 GIVN	
Lvl Density	+6	+7	WIS	ExTh Jour	NP 71 529	Sep 65	Wood+ DEDUCED FROM(P,N) ON SN 118	
Lvl Density	–		BUC	Expt Jour	NP/A 140 23	Jan 70	Magda+ (ALF,N),LVL DENSITY PAR,GRAPH	
				Rept	INDC(SEC) – 18	Aug 71	*P158.LVL DENS PAR,TBL	

51 Antimony 119

Quantity	Energy (ev) Min	Max	Lab	Type	Documentation Ref Vol Page	Date	Author, Comments	Data
(n,p)	6.0+6	1.4+7	WIS	Expt Abst	DA 25 6709	May 65	Wood.INVERSE REACTION	
Reson Params	–		AUA	Theo Rept	AAEC/E – 211	Nov 70	Musgrove. CALCULTD D+GAM WIDTH GIVEN	
Strnth Fnctn	–		AUA	Theo Rept	AAEC/E – 211	Nov 70	Musgrove. SMOOTHED S0,S1 AND S2 GIVN	

51 Antimony 120

Quantity	Energy (ev) Min	Max	Lab	Type	Documentation Ref Vol Page	Date	Author, Comments	Data
Spect (n,γ)		1.7+2	SAC	Expt Prog	EANDC(E)127U	Apr 70	Lottin+,GE(LI) DET	
(n,p)	Maxwl		IFU	Eval Rept	ICD – 4 20	67	Dadakina+ PENETR COEFF CALC,TABLE	
Reson Params	–		AUA	Theo Rept	AAEC/E – 211	Nov 70	Musgrove. CALCULTD D+GAM WIDTH GIVEN	
Strnth Fnctn	–		AUA	Theo Rept	AAEC/E – 211	Nov 70	Musgrove. SMOOTHED S0,S1 AND S2 GIVN	
Lvl Density	+6	+7	WIS	ExTh Jour	NP 71 529	Sep 65	Wood+ DEDUCED FROM(P,N) ON SN 120	
Lvl Density	9.0+6	1.7+7	ANL	Eval Rept	ANL – 75 – 34	Jun 75	Davey+N2NEVAL.CONSTANT T,LVL DEN FIT	

51 Antimony 121

Quantity	Energy (ev) Min	Max	Lab	Type	Documentation Ref Vol Page	Date	Author, Comments	Data
Evaluation	1.0–3	1.5+7	AUA	Eval Rept	AAEC/TM – 549	Jun 70	Cook.TOT,EL,INEL,NONEL,CAPT SIGS,NDG	+
				Rept	AAEC/E – 214	Jun 71	Bertram+GROUP SIGMAS SAME QUANTS.NDG	
				Rept	AAEC/TM – 587	Mar 71	*DESCRIPTION OF LIBRARY	
	1.0–3	1.5+7		Data	AUSTR – DFN 90.	Nov 71	POINT(223) AND GROUP(127) SIGMAS	
Total	1.4+7		FEI	Expt Prog	INDSWG – 126 33	66	Dukarevich.SIG=4.66+ – 0.02B	
Total	1.4+7		CCP	ExTh Jour	IZV 31 217	Feb 67	Dukarevich+.TBL,CURVES,CFD OPTMDL TH	
				Jour	BAS 31 197	Feb 67	TRANSLATN.*	
Total	1.4+7		FTI	Expt Jour	NP/A 92 433	Feb 67	Dukarevich+ CFD OPTMDL 4.66+ – 0.03B	+
Total	2.3+2	6.0+3	KUR	Expt Jour	YF 8 852	Nov 68	Muradyan+ TRANSMISS CV,TOTAL – POTNTAL	
				Jour	SNP 8 495	May 69	TRANSLATN.*	
Total	1.0–3	1.5+7	AUA	Eval Data	AUSTR – DFN 90.	Nov 71	COOK+POINT(223)+GROUP(127)SIG.CF EVL	+
Total	1.3+7	1.5+7	DEB	Eval Rept	IAEA – 153 173	73	Boedy+ MOST PROBABLE VAL OF SIG,TBL	
				Jour	AHP 30 115	Oct 71	Angeli+ AVG SIG,CFD CALC.TBLS.GRAPH	
Elastic	1.0–3	1.5+7	AUA	Eval Data	AUSTR – DFN 90.	Nov 71	COOK+POINT(223)+GROUP(127)SIG.CF EVL	+
Potntal Scat	2.3+2	6.0+3	KUR	Expt Jour	YF 8 852	Nov 68	Muradyan+ TRANSMISS CV,TOTAL – POTNTAL	
				Jour	SNP 8 495	May 69	. ENGL OF YF 8 852	
Tot Inelastc	+5	+6	HAR	Conf	67Kanpur § N108	Feb 67	Nath.VDG – NS LIFETIMES XCIT STATES	
Tot Inelastc	5.0+5	1.5+7	AUA	Eval Data	AUSTR – DFN 90.	Nov 71	COOK+POINT(11)+GROUP(127)SIG.CF EVL	+
Diff Inelast	4.0+5	1.2+6	FEI	Expt Jour	AE 15 416	Nov 63	Glazkov+ SPHER GEOM, 5 ENERGIES	
				Jour	JNE 18 654	64	. ENGL OF AE 15 416	
				Jour	EAF 15 5	Nov 63	.FRENCH OF AE 15 416	
				Jour	SJA 15 1173	Nov 63	. ENGL OF AE 15 416	
Diff Inelast	8.0+5	2.0+6	BHU	Expt Conf	67Tokyo § 4.109	Sep 67	Nath+ TOF(HAR VDG),6 LVLS+DECAY GAMS	
Nonelastic	1.0–3	1.5+7	AUA	Eval Data	AUSTR – DFN 90.	Nov 71	COOK+POINT(223)+GROUP(127)SIG.CF EVL	+
Nonelastic	1.4+7		TUD	Theo Conf	ZFK – 271 63	Nov 73	Seeliger+ N – SPEC,NDG.INTEG – SIG SHOWN	
Nonelastic	1.4+7	1.7+7	ANL	Eval Rept	ANL – 75 – 34	Jun 75	Davey+CORRC APPLIED TO N2N CS.TBLS.	
Absorption	Maxwl		PAV	Expt Jour	EN 14 541	Sep 67	Orvini+SIG 6.1+ – 0.25B	
Absorption	1.0–3	1.0+7	JUL	Eval Rept	JUEL – 678 – RG	Jul 70	Liu. EVALUATION+CALC,GRPH,FN OF E	
Res Int Abs	5.0–1		ANL	Expt Jour	PR 79 11	Jul 50	Harris+ EPI – CD,REL THERMAL ACT. B – W	+
	5.0–1			Data	EXFOR11343.021	Jun 76	. 1 PT.	

51 Antimony 121

Quantity	Energy (ev) Min	Max	Lab	Type	Documentation Ref Vol Page	Date	Author, Comments	Data
Res Int Abs	None		ORL Revw	Conf	55Geneva 5 96	Aug 55	Macklin+ TABLE,EXPT CFD THEORY.P833	
Res Int Abs	None		CRC Eval	Rept	AECL-1054	Mar 60	Walker.(CRP-913) REDUCED RES.INT.	
Res Int Abs	+3	+5	BOL Theo	Conf	61Vienna 1 179	Aug 61	Benzi+.PPR11,VAL GVN,L=0,L=1 .CAPT.	
Res Int Abs	5.0-1		BOL Eval	Conf	61Vienna 1 179	Aug 61	Benzi+ TBL TOTAL CAPT RES INTS.	
Res Int Abs	5.0-1		BOL Eval	Rept	RT/FI-4	Jan 67	Palmucci. CALC FROM (N,G) RES PARAMS	
Res Int Abs	5.0-1		BGK Expt	Rept	THAI-AEC-10	Oct 67	. ACTIV(NA-I),CD-RATIO,REL AU. TABLE	+
	5.0-1			Data	EXFOR30368.017	Jan 77	REL AU, PRELM.	
Res Int Abs	5.5-1		ISP Expt	Jour	JIN 30 1353	Jul 68	Orvini+ACT 200+ -17 B REL.TO AU197	+
	5.5-1			Data	EXFOR20633.005	Jun 76	1PNT.CAPTURE.	
Res Int Abs	5.0-1		CNE Expt	Conf	70Helsinki 2 589	Jun 70	Ricabarra+ RATIO TO THR-ACT SIGMA	+
	5.0-1			Data	EXFOR30190.003	Dec 72	RES INT AND RATIO TO THR-CAPT SIGMA	
Res Int Abs	5.0-1		NPL Expt	Jour	JNE 24 35	Feb 70	Ryves.REL AU.REDUCED INTGRL.ACTIV.	+
				Conf	71Canterby 139	Sep 71	- .REDUCED CAPT RES INTEGRAL,TBL	
	5.0-1			Data	EXFOR20789.084	Dec 78	1PNT.REDUCED INTEGRAL.CAPTURE	
Res Int Abs	5.5-1		CRC Eval	Rept	AECL-3037 1	Jan 72	Walker.REDUCED RES INT,DETAILED TBL	
Res Int Abs	5.0-1		AUA Eval	Rept	AAEC/TM-619	Sep 72	Clayton.CALC FROM SIG LIBRARY,TABLE	
Res Int Abs	5.0-1		KJL Expt	Jour	JIN 34 2699	Sep 72	Steinnes. ACT. AU MONITOR	+
	5.0-1			Data	EXFOR20188.012	May 74	1PNT.CAPTURE.	
Res Int Abs	5.0-1		SGA Eval	Conf	73Paris 1 233	Mar 73	Eder+ REDUCED RES INTEG CAPTURE,TBL	
				Rept	SGAE-PH-141	Feb 73	.SAME AS 73PARIS,EVAL OF EXPTL DATA	
Res Int Abs	5.0-1		GHT Expt	Jour	JRC 11 133	Jun 72	Van Der Linden+ BY(N,G).CFD OTHS,TBL	+
				Jour	JRC 23 113	74	- + (N,G).CD-RATIO,TABLE	
	5.5-1			Conf	73Paris 2 241	Mar 73	- + ACT,REL THR+GOLD,TBL	
	5.5-1			Data	EXFOR20643.060	Jul 76	1PNT.CAPTURE.	
Res Int Abs	5.5-1	+6	SAC Revw	Conf	IAEA-169 1 235	74	Ribon.CAPTURE,STATUS CFD REQUEST,TBL	
Res Int Abs	+0	+5	WIN Revw	Conf	IAEA-169 3 163	74	Pope+ DATA FILE CALC CFD XPTAL VALUE	
Res Int Abs	5.5-1		OAU Expt	Jour	RRL 23 317	Dec 75	Gleason. CD-RATIO,REL AU+MN,RI TABLE	+
	5.5-1			Data	EXFOR10644.034	Jul 77	. 1 PT. RIA=230.+ -10B	
Res Int Abs	5.0-1		MUN Comp	Jour	JRC 29 175	Jan 76	Gryntakis+ TO G+M. 9VALUES+STANDS GVN	
(n,γ)	2.2+5		PCF Expt	Jour	NAT 142 392	Aug 38	Halban+ ACT CS GIVEN	
(n,γ)	2.0+4	7.0+5	OXF Expt	Jour	PRSA 170 513	Apr 39	Griffiths.RA-BE PHOTONEUT ACTIVATION	
(n,γ)	Maxwl		LUQ Expt	Jour	PR 58 869	Nov 40	Rasseti. REL MG55(N,G), BETA ACT	
(n,γ)	Maxwl		JAP Expt	Jour	SCP 38 167	Jan 41	Sinma+.LI+D.RELATIVE SIG MEASUREMENT	
(n,γ)	Maxwl		UI Expt	Jour	PR 59 102	Jan 41	O-Neal+ ACT REL MN	
(n,γ)	Pile		ANL Expt	Jour	PR 72 888	Nov 47	Seren+ ACT METHOD.PILE IRRAD,METAL.	+
	Pile			Data	EXFOR11447.082	Jun 76	. 1 PT.	
(n,γ)	2.2+5	9.0+5	OXF Expt	Jour	NAT 161 727	May 48	Allen+ ACTIVATION RATIO	
(n,γ)	Fiss		ANL Expt	Jour	PR 75 1781	Jun 49	Hughes+ REL SIG(THERMAL),FOIL ACTIVN	+
	Fiss			Data	EXFOR11450.032	Jun 76	. 1 PT.	
(n,γ)	2.4+4		ANL Expt	Jour	PR 82 67	Apr 51	Hummel+ SB-BE PHOTONEUTS. ACTIVATION	+
	2.4+4			Data	EXFOR11010.013	Aug 76	. 1 PT. = 1.6B	
(n,γ)	Maxwl		ORL Expt	Jour	PR 88 412	Oct 52	Pomerance.PILE OSC.	+
	Maxwl			Data	EXFOR11507.058	Jun 76	. 1 PT.	
(n,γ)	Fiss		BNL Expt	Jour	PR 91 1423	Sep 53	Hughes+ ALSO LVL SPACINGS AT EXCIT E	
(n,γ)	Fast		HAR Expt	Rept	AERE-R/R-2151	57	Absalom+ ZEPHYR+TH ENVELOPE.	
(n,γ)	2.4+4		ORL Expt	Jour	PR 107 504	Jul 57	Macklin+ SB-BE NS,0.950B,ACT,REL I	+
	2.4+4			Data	EXFOR11399.031	Jun 76	. 1 PT.	
(n,γ)	2.5+4		LRL Expt	Jour	PR 112 226	Oct 58	Booth+ SB-BE REL I+THR,ACT 2.8D HL	+
				Abst	BAP 2 268	Oct 58	.ABST L6	
	2.5+4			Data	EXFOR11429.019	Jun 76	. 1 PT.	
(n,γ)	1.9+5		ORL Expt	Jour	PR 114 1619	Jun 59	Lyon+ ABS GAMMA COUNT 400+ -40MB ACT	+
	1.9+5			Data	EXFOR11407.021	Jun 76	. 1 PT.	
(n,γ)	Maxwl		MUA Expt	Jour	NP 12 261	Jul 59	Sehgal+0.19+ -0.03B METASTABLE	+
	Maxwl			Data	EXFOR31244.009	Jun 78	SIG TO ISOMER	
	Maxwl			Data	EXFOR31244.	Feb 70	SIG FOR 2.8D HALF-LIFE	
(n,γ)			CRC Eval	Rept	AECL-1054	Mar 60	Walker. (CRRP-913)	
(n,γ)	Maxwl Pile		ORL Expt	Jour	NSE 8 378	Nov 60	Lyon. ACTIVATION, 2 SIGMA VALUES GVN	+
	Maxwl			Data	EXFOR11625.	Jun 76	. 2 PTS, SIG TO GND + META	
(n,γ)	Fast		LAS Expt	Jour	NSE 8 608	Dec 60	Byers. GODIVA JEZEBEL ACT CS GIVEN	
(n,γ)	Maxwl		BNL Expt	Jour	PR 125 1615	Mar 62	DER MATEOSIAN.SIGS 2.8D,3.5M ACTIVTS	+
	Maxwl			Data	EXFOR11993.	Jun 76	. 2 PTS, SIG FOR GND + META	
(n,γ)	Maxwl		MTR Expt	Jour	PR 129 769	Jan 63	Keisch.RATIO ISOMER ACT TO GND ACT.	+
	Maxwl			Data	EXFOR11748.016	Jun 76	. 1 PT, ISOMER RATIO	
(n,γ)	Maxwl		ANL Comp	Jour	NP 60 241	Nov 64	Bishop+EXP AND TH ISOMER RATIOS CFD	
(n,γ)	7.8+3	6.4+4	KFK Expt	Prog	EANDC(E)-66	Feb 66	Poenitz. TO SB122G	
(n,γ)	Maxwl		KFI Expt	Jour	KFI 14 85	Apr 66	Kardon. IN HUN,ISOMERIC RATIO GIVEN	+
				Conf	64Paris 2 703	Jul 64	Gulyas+ISOMER RATIO,SEE ALSO LDL.	
	Maxwl			Data	EXFOR30341.004	Sep 76	ISOMERIC RATIO, 1 PNT	

51 Antimony 121

Quantity	Energy (ev) Min	Max	Lab	Type	Documentation Ref Vol Page	Date	Author, Comments	Data
(n,γ)	2.5-2		BOL	Eval	Rept RT/FI-4	Jan 67	Palmucci. CALC FROM RES PARAMETERS	
(n,γ)	3.0+6		DEB	Expt	Jour JNE 21 797	Oct 67	Peto+ACTIV,SIGMA REL TO AU(N,G)	+
	3.0+6				Data EXFOR30031.015	Aug 70	SINGLE VALUE	
(n,γ)	1.1+4	4.0+5	FEI	Expt	Prog YFI-6 11	68	Dovbenko+. TABLE. TO BE PUBL IN AE	+
	1.0+4	4.0+5			Jour EAF 27 41	Nov 69	.FRENCH TRANSL. OF AE 27 406	
					Jour SJA 27 1185	Nov 69	.ENGL. TRANSL. OF AE 27 406	
					Jour AE 27 406	Nov 69	Dovbenko+ SIG(E)GRPH,CFD OTHR+OPTMOD	
	1.1+4	4.0+5			Prog INDC(CCP)-3U	Mar 69	.ENGLISH TRANSL OF YFI-6 11 /68	
	1.1+4	3.9+5			Data EXFOR40331.014	Jan 76	SIG(E) AT 9 ES	
(n,γ)	+4	+6	FEI	Expt	Prog YFI-6 5	68	Kolesov+. NO DATA GIVEN	
					Conf 68Dubna § 5	Jun 68	.SEE ALSO	
					Prog INDC(CCP)-3U	Mar 69	.ENGLISH TRANSL OF YFI-6 5 /68	
(n,γ)	3.0+5	2.7+6	FEI	ExTh	Jour AE 24 6 576	Jun 68	Tolstikov+ EXPT+STATMOD CURVES	+
				Expt	Conf 68Riga	Jan 68	Dovbenko+ ABST,STATMOD CFD	
				ExTh	Jour EAF 24 6 111	Jun 68	.TRANSLATION	
	3.0+5	3.1+6		Expt	Data EXFOR40327.004	Nov 76	SIG(E), 23 PNTS	
	1.1+4	3.1+6			Data EXFOR40005.004	Jul 70	.SIGMA AT 28 ENERGIES GIVEN	
(n,γ)	-		IEA	Comp	Rept IEA-INF-10	Aug 68	Atalla. TABLES OF HL,SIG AND GAMM-E	
	2.4+4		MUA	Expt	Jour NC/B 58 402	Dec 68	Hasan+,SB-BE,ACT BETA-DET REL I-127.	+
	2.4+4				Data EXFOR30077.013	Dec 70	SIGMA FOR 2.8 D HALF-LIFE GIVEN	
	2.0+3		MTR	Expt	Prog WASH-1127 72	Apr 69	Schuman+ FILTERED BEAM,RELATVE CURVS	
(n,γ)	5.0+3	1.0+5	AUA	ExTh	Rept AAEC/E-198	May 69	Musgrove.S+P+D WAVE SIGMAS CALC,TBL	+
(n,γ)	+3		COL	Expt	Prog WASH-1136 22	Sep 69	Arbo+ TO BE DONE	
(n,γ)	1.0+3	1.0+7	BOL	Eval	Rept CCDN-NW/10	Dec 69	Benzi+H-F MOD,AXEL G(G)EST,ALL DATA	
					Rept CEC(70)-2	Apr 70	- +. GRAPH	
					Conf 66Paris 1 537	Oct 66	- + STATMOD.TBL AV VALS.SUPERSEDD	
					Jour NC 38 216	Jul 65	- + THEORY FOR CAPTURE EVALUATION	
					Conf 61Vienna 1 179	Aug 61	- + TBL AV VALS. SUPERSEDED.	
(n,γ)	Maxwl		MTR	Expt	Prog IN-1317 53	Jan 70	Hogg+ ACT, VALUE GIVEN	+
	Maxwl				Data EXFOR12602.004	Jun 76	. 1 PT, SIGMA.	
(n,γ)	3.0+4		AUA	Theo	Rept AAEC/E-211	Nov 70	Musgrove. SIGMA GIVEN AND CFD OTHER	
(n,γ)	2.5+4		AUW	Expt	Conf 70Madurai 2 19	Dec 70	Lakshmana Rao+. HIGH+LOW SPIN SIGMAS	+
	2.5+4				Data EXFOR30246.	Jun 73	.SIG TO GROUND AND META.ISOM RATIO	
(n,γ)	2.5-2		NPL	Expt	Jour JNE 24 35	Feb 70	Ryves.REL.AU,STANDARD NPL TH.FLUX.	
					Conf 71Canterby 139	71	- . VDG,GRAPHITE MODERATOR.ACTIVN	
	2.5-2				Data EXFOR20789.027	Dec 78	1PNT.SIGMA.	
(n,γ)	Maxwl		KFI	Comp	Jour JRC 7 365	Jun 71	Nagy+ SIGMA,GAMMA-E, HALF-LIFE GIVEN	
(n,γ)	Maxwl		GA	Eval	Rept GA-12071	Sep 71	Mathews+. RECOMMENDED VALUES	
(n,γ)	1.0-3	1.5+7	AUA	Eval	Data AUSTR-DFN 90.	Nov 71	COOK+POINT(223)+GROUP(127)SIG.CF EVL	
(n,γ)	Maxwl		CRC	Eval	Rept AECL-3037 1	Jan 72	Walker.RECOMMENDED SIG,DETAILED TBL	
(n,γ)	2.4+4		MUA	Theo	Jour IJP 46 114	Mar 72	Chaubey+ P-WAVE STRENGTH FUNC,TABLE	
(n,γ)	2.5+4		AUW	Theo	Jour PR/C 6 572	Aug 72	Rao+. ISOMER RATIOS CALCTD.CFD EXPT	+
	2.5+4			Expt	Data EXFOR30234.	Jun 73	.SIG TO GROUND AND META.ISOM RATIO	
(n,γ)	2.5-2		AUA	Eval	Rept AAEC/TM-619	Sep 72	Clayton.CALC FROM SIG LIBRARY,TABLE	
(n,γ)	Fast		MTR	Expt	Rept 72Kiamesha 2 614	Sep 72	Harker+ CFRMF INTEGRAL MEAS.	
(n,γ)	Maxwl		GHT	Comp	Jour JRC 16 39	73	Maenhaut+ACT TO SB122M+GS.GELI.SIG	
(n,γ)	Maxwl		SGA	Eval	Conf 73Paris 1 233	Mar 73	Eder+ RECOMMENDED SIG,TBL,NO DETAILS	
					Rept SGAE-PH-141	Feb 73	.SAME AS 73PARIS,EVAL OF EXPTL DATA	
(n,γ)	2.5-2	3.0+4	SAC	Revw	Conf IAEA-169 1 235	74	Ribon.STATUS SIG CFD REQUESTS,TABLE	
	Maxwl	Fiss	WIN	Revw	Conf IAEA-169 3 163	74	Pope+ MAXW+FIS-SPEC AVG DATA CFD XPT	
	Fiss				Conf IAEA-169 3 137	74	Dean. POINT DATA AVG OVER STAND-SPC	
(n,γ)	1.0+3	1.0+7	FEI	Eval	Rept YK-8/2 97	Sep 72	Abagjan+ AVG SIG(ENERGY-GROUPS),TABL	
					Rept INDC(CCP)-39	Jul 74	.P102. ENGLISH OF YK-8/2 97	
(n,γ)	Maxwl		OAU	Expt	Jour RRL 23 317	Dec 75	Gleason. CF-SOURC-ACT,REL AU+MN,TABL	+
	Maxwl				Data EXFOR10644.033	Jul 77	1PT.THR CS=6.90+-.3B	
(n,γ)	2.5-2		MUN	Comp	Jour JRC 29 175	Jan 76	Gryntakis+,TO M,G,M+G 4 VALUES GIVEN	
Spect (n,γ)	Pile		FAR	Expt	Jour CR 239 1130	Nov 54	Moreau. SINGLES SPEC+BETA-G COINC.	
Spect (n,γ)	2.5+4		ORL	Expt	Conf 58Geneva 15 68	Sep 58	Macklin.PPR671,SIGMA+G-ENERGY GVN	
Spect (n,γ)	5.0+0	2.0+2	ANL	Expt	Jour PR 124 1142	Nov 61	Jackson+ FC, LOW E GAMMAS	
Spect (n,γ)	Maxwl		KFI	Expt	Conf 64Paris 2 703	Jul 64	Gulyas+ALSO METASTABLE LEVEL	
Spect (n,γ)	6.3+0	1.6+1	JAE	Expt	Jour JAERI-1073	Mar 65	Kawarasaki. RES CAPT.LINAC.TOF.E,INT	+
					Rept INDSWG-90 6	Jul 65	- . TABLE E,INTS GIVEN.	
	6.3+0	1.6+1			Data EXFOR20277.007	Jun 74	11PTS.	
Spect (n,γ)	Maxwl		KFI	Expt	Jour YF 10 907	Nov 69	Kecskemeti+ AVG GAM-MULTIPLICITY,TBL	
					Jour SNP 10 524	May 70	TRANSLATN.*	
Spect (n,γ)		3.0+1	TOR	Expt	Jour NP/A 137 561	Nov 69	ING+ 2-DIM DATA COLL,4RES+CONTINUUM	
Spect (n,γ)	2.5-2	1.3+2	BNL	Expt	Jour PR/C 2 1115	Sep 70	Bhat+ GE(LI) DET,THERMAL+3RESON	
Spect (n,γ)	Maxwl		LAS	Expt	Abst BAP 15 1371	Nov 70	Shera.GE(LI) DET,NO DATA GIVEN	

51 Antimony 121

Quantity	Energy (ev) Min	Max	Lab	Type	Documentation Ref Vol Page	Date	Author, Comments	Data
Spect (n,γ)	Maxwl		KFI Comp	Jour	JRC 7 365	Jun 71	Nagy+ SIGMA,GAMMA−E, HALF−LIFE GIVEN	
Spect (n,γ)	Pile		KFK Expt	Rept	KFK−1401	Jun 71	Djadali.AVG POLRZ G EXPT,CFD T,SPIN	
	Maxwl			Jour	NP/A 147 150	May 70	Eichler+ POL NS.CIRC POL GS+ASSYMTRY	
Spect (n,γ)	1.0+7		WWATheo	Jour	NP/A 189 545	Jul 72	Brzosko+ CMPD NUCL DECAY.PARTIAL WG	
Spect (n,γ)	1.0+0	6.0+2	SAC Expt	Jour	NP/A 223 509	May 74	Jain+ GRAPHS,HIGH/LOW EG,WIDTH CORR	
	5.0+0	5.0+2		Jour	JPR 32 849	Dec 71	Lottin+CORRELATION (WGI,WN)	
	6.2+0	1.4+2		Conf	69Studsvik 657	Aug 69	Paya+ SPEC GRPH+TBL GVN,RESON,LINAC	
Spect (n,γ)	Maxwl		LIN Expt	Jour	NIM 138 299	76	Akhnazarov+ CONV.E SPECTROGR.NDG	
Inelastic γ	1.0+6	3.5+6	TNC Expt	Prog	ORO−2791−26	Aug 67	Morgan+ NAI(TL) 2ES CFD TH	+
	1.0+6	3.5+6		Data	EXFOR11662.007	Jun 76	. 2 PTS, DSIG	
Inelastic γ	8.0+5	2.0+6	BHU Expt	Conf	67Tokyo § 4.109	Sep 67	Nath+ TOF,PROMPT GATED,6LVLS+DECAY	
Inelastic γ	6.0+5	1.9+6	PEL Expt	Jour	NP/A 172 215	Aug 71	Barnard+ SPEC MEAS.ONLY LVLS SHOWN.	
				Jour	NP/A 167 511	Jun 71	− + METHOD DESCRIBED	
				Jour	NP/A 157 130	Nov 70	− + METHOD DESCRIBED	
Inelastic γ	8.0+6	8.8+6	BRC Expt	Prog	EANDC(E)150U	May 72	Lachkar+	
Inelastic γ	None		ALA Expt	Abst	PC 33 3	77	Hooper+ANG DISTR,PI.NDG.CFD MDL CALC	
(n,2n)	Fast		CAR Expt	Jour	PR 81 184	Jan 51	Cohen.AVR SIG,N SPEC.BETA ACT.	+
	Fast			Data	EXFOR11189.042	Jun 76	. 1 PT.	
(n,2n)	1.5+7		CRC Expt	Jour	CJP 31 267	Feb 53	Paul+ BETA ACT, CFD TH, HL=15M	+
	1.5+7			Data	EXFOR11274.079	Jun 76	. 1 PT.	
(n,2n)	1.4+7		CCP Expt	Jour	ZET 33 527	Aug 57	Vasil'Ev.SINGLE VALUE AT 14.3MEV	
(n,2n)	1.4+7		MUAExpt	Jour	NP 13 88	Oct 59	Khurana+C−W ABS BETA COUNT 453+−43MB	+
(n,2n)	Fiss		CRC Eval	Rept	CRC−1003	Dec 60	ROY+ ESTIMATED AVG SIG=0.9MB	
(n,2n)	1.2+7	2.0+7	LAS Expt	Jour	PR 121 1438	Mar 61	Prestwood. RADIO CHEM.	+
				Rept	LA−2493	Dec 60	.EXCITATION CURVE	
	1.2+7	2.0+7		Data	EXFOR11645.022	Jun 76	. 15 PTS.	
(n,2n)	1.4+7		ANL Expt	Jour	PR 122 168	Apr 61	Rayburn. 1056 MB	+
				Abst	BAP 3 337	61	.ABST R5	
	1.4+7			Data	EXFOR11328.027	Jun 76	. 1 PT.	
(n,2n)	1.5+7		MUAExpt	Jour	NP 28 560	Dec 61	Khurana+ ACTIV,CFD STATMOD	+
(n,2n)	1.2+7	1.8+7	RED Expt	Rept	NP−11667	Apr 62	Alford+	+
	1.2+7	1.8+7		Data	EXFOR11785.005	Jun 76	. 8 PTS.	
(n,2n)	1.2+7	2.0+7	ANL Expt	Jour	PR 130 731	Apr 63	Rayburn.TABLE+CURVE SIG REL CU63 N2N	+
	1.2+7	1.9+7		Data	EXFOR11784.005	Jun 76	. 13 PTS.	
(n,2n)	1.4+7		BOR Expt	Jour	CR 257 659	Jul 63	Carles.ACTIVATION.SIGMA REL CU63	+
(n,2n)	1.4+7		HAMCompJour		NP 65 257	Mar 65	Bormann. 6EXPT VALS.CFD SHELL EFFECT	
(n,2n)	1.3+7	1.5+7	BNL Theo	Jour	NSE 23 238	Nov 65	Pearlstein.3ES.STAT MDL CALC.TBL CS.	
(n,2n)	Fiss		BNL Theo	Jour	NSE 23 238	Nov 65	Pearlstein.STATMDL CALC.SPEC AVG.TBL	
(n,2n)	1.3+7	1.5+7	TIT Expt	Jour	JPJ 24 17	Jan 68	Kanda.C−W.ISOM RATIO P S GIVN	+
				Rept	JAERI−1102 43	Mar 66	− .C−W ISOM.S NORM.TO CU(N,2N).	
	1.3+7	1.5+7		Data	EXFOR20294.	Jun 74	28PTS.SIGMA.	
(n,2n)	1.3+7	1.9+7	HAMExpt	Jour	NP/A 115 309	Jul 68	Bormann+VDG.TO G,M.CFD STAT+OPTMDL	+
(n,2n)	1.5+7		TUR Expt	Jour	ZP 217 83	Oct 68	Minetti+GND + ISOM 1244B + 597B	
(n,2n)	9.0+6	2.0+7	AUA Expt	Rept	AAEC/TM−522	Nov 69	Bertram. CALC SIG(E)GRAPHS CFD EXPTS	
(n,2n)	1.5+7		DEB Comp	Jour	REA 7 4 93	Dec 69	Csikai+ SIG+HL COMPILTN,N−ACTIV−ANAL	
(n,2n)	1.5+7		BOS Expt	Prog	BARC−474 50	70	Chatterjee+ ABSOLUTE SIG EXPT	
(n,2n)	1.4+7		GIT Expt	Jour	PR/C 1 350	Jan 70	Fink+ACTIVATION,GRPHS,TBL.CFD OTH.	+
	1.4+7			Data	EXFOR10497.	Apr 76	2 PTS.M.GSTATE.427+−20.1188+−60MB.	
(n,2n)	1.4+7	1.5+7	JYV Eval	Rept	JU−RR−3/1970	Jun 70	Leppaemaeki+ TABLE OF EVAL AVG SIG	
(n,2n)	+7		KFI Comp	Rept	KFKI−71−8	Feb 71	Jeki. CALCULATED CFD EXPTL SIG VALUE	
(n,2n)	1.4+7	1.5+7	IRK ExTh	Jour	APA 33 285	Jul 71	Winiwarter+ ISOMERIC RATIO	
(n,2n)	1.4+7		GIT Theo	Jour	PR/C 4 1173	Oct 71	Fink+.STAT−MODEL CALCULATION,CFD EXP	
(n,2n)	1.5+7		DEB Eval	Jour	REA 11 1 153	Mar 73	Boedy. COMPILATION+RECOMM.VALUE,TBL	
				Rept	IAEA−153 173	73	− . RECOMM. VALUE ONLY	
(n,2n)	1.4+7		LOU Expt	Jour	INR−1464 12	May 73	Araminowicz+BRIEF,ACTIV,TABLE,GRAPH	+
	1.4+7			Data	EXFOR30264.035	Nov 73	SIGMA AT 14.6 MEV	
(n,2n)	9.0+6	2.0+7	IFL Eval	Rept	YK−15 63	Aug 73	Bondars+ SHORT. GRAPH OF EVAL DATA	
(n,2n)	Fiss		KOS Eval	Prog	INDC(HUN)−12	Jun 74	Boedy+ PG20.CALC+EXPTL SIG CFD,TABLE	
(n,2n)	1.5+7		TAT Theo	Jour	JP/A 7 1458	Aug 74	Kondaiah. CALC ON STAT MODEL	
(n,2n)	Fiss		KOS Eval	Conf	75Karlsrhe 29	Apr 75	Csikai. CF252,MAXW−SPC.AVG FOR 2TEMP	
(n,2n)	1.4+7		VLD Expt	Jour	ARS 71 123	Apr 75	Casanova+,SIG TO GRND+METAST STATES	+
				Prog	NEANDC(OR)140L	Dec 74	− + ACTIVATION.	
	1.4+7			Data	EXFOR20776.002	Dec 77	1PNT.SIGMA.	
(n,2n)	9.0+6	1.7+7	ANL Eval	Rept	ANL−75−34	Jun 75	Davey+CONSTANT T MDL,LVL DEN MDL FIT	
(n,2n)	1.3+7	1.5+7	TNC Expt	Abst	BAP 5 246	Apr 60	Mc−Crary+ ACT NDG	+
	1.3+7	1.5+7		Data	EXFOR11268.006	Jun 76	. 8 PTS.	
(n,xn) x>2	Fiss		BNL Theo	Jour	NSE 23 238	Nov 65	Pearlstein.SPEC AVG STATMDL CALC N3N	
n Emission	1.4+7		TUD Theo	Prog	ZFK−262 25	Sep 73	Hermsdorf+ CALC N−SPEC CFD EXPT,NDG	

51 Antimony 121

Quantity	Energy (ev) Min	Max	Lab	Type	Documentation Ref Vol Page	Date	Author, Comments	Data
(n,p)	+6	1.1+7	IBJ	Expt Jour	BPP 5 401	Apr 57	Wilhelmi. CYCLOTRON CFD BE+D SOURCE	
(n,p)	Fiss		CRC	Eval Rept	CRC-1003	Dec 60	ROY+ ESTIMATED AVG SIG=0.33MB	
(n,p)	+6	+7	BRN	Theo Jour	NP 27 596	Oct 61	Peck.GROSS STRUCT.FINITE CORE DEFORM	
(n,p)	1.4+7		SAH	Comp Jour	NUC 23 8 112	Aug 65	Chatterjee. TABLE WITH REFS.	
				Jour	NP 60 273	Nov 64	- .MEAN OF EXPT CFD SHELLMOD	
(n,p)	Maxwl		IFU	Theo Rept	ICD-4 20	67	Dadakina+ PENETR COEFF CALC,TABLE	
(n,p)	1.5+7		DEB	Comp Jour	REA 7 4 93	Dec 69	Csikai+ SIG+HL COMPILTN,N-ACTIV-ANAL	
(n,p)	1.5+7		KAZ	Expt Jour	YF 13 923	May 71	Levkovsky+ ACT,METHOD,TBL,CFD THEORY	
				Jour	SNP 13 529	Nov 71	. ENGL OF YF 10 923	
(n,p)	1.4+7		TUD	Theo Conf	ZFK-271 63	Nov 73	Seeliger+ P-EMISSION SPEC, NDG	
(n,p)	1.5+7		ARK	Expt Jour	JIN 36 5 953	May 74	Mavaddat+ ACTIV MEAS	
(n,α)	Fiss		CRC	Eval Rept	CRC-1003	Dec 60	ROY+ ESTIMATED AVG SIG=0.0005MB	
(n,α)	None		KFI	Comp Jour	JRC 7 365	Jun 71	Nagy+ GAMMA+BETA ES, HALF-LIFE GIVEN	
(n,α)	1.4+7		TUD	Theo Conf	ZFK-271 63	Nov 73	Seeliger+ A-EMISSION SPEC, NDG	
Reson Params	1.4+1		LUQ	Expt Jour	PR 61 469	Apr 42	Feeny+ G(TOT) BY ACTIVN+SELFSCREENNG	
Reson Params	6.3+0	9.0+1	ANL	Expt Jour	PR 102 228	Apr 56	Palmer+ TRNS.WT WN OTHER PARS 7 RES	+
	6.3+0	9.0+1		Data	EXFOR11804.	Jun 76	. 7 RES, E0,WT,WN,WN0,WG,PCS	
Reson Params	6.2+0	3.0+1	BNL	Expt Jour	PR 108 353	Oct 57	Stolovy+ FC, TRANS, 3 RES	+
	6.2+0	3.0+1		Data	EXFOR11866.005	Jun 76	. 3 RES, E0,WT,WN,WG	
Reson Params	6.2+0	1.7+2	ANL	Expt Jour	PR 124 1142	Nov 61	Jackson+ FAST CHOPPER	+
	6.2+0	1.7+2		Data	EXFOR11992.002	Jun 76	. 14 RES, E0	
Reson Params	6.2+0	3.0+1	BNL	Expt Jour	NP 42 676	Apr 63	Bolotin+ WG=80MEV,WN ALSO GIVEN	+
	6.2+0	3.0+1		Data	EXFOR11922.006	Jun 76	. 3 RES, E0,WN,PCS	
Reson Params	6.2+0	1.6+1	NRL	Expt Jour	PR 155 1330	Mar 67	Stolovy.2RES J=3.2 BY TRNS POLARZ NS	+
	6.2+0	1.6+1		Data	EXFOR11995.002	Jun 76	. 3 RES, E0,J	
Reson Params		1.0+6	AUA	Theo Jour	AUJ 20 477	Oct 67	Cook+ TBL OF AVG LVL SPACING D,L=0,1	
Reson Params	6.0+0	3.0+1	BUC	Expt Jour	RRP 12 10 907	Oct 67	Mateiciuc+, TOT+NEUT+GAMMA WIDTHS	+
	6.2+0	3.0+1		Data	EXFOR30020.	Oct 70	VALUES OF WN,WG AND WT AT 3 RESONANS	
Reson Params	1.5+1	1.7+2	COL	Expt Jour	PR 166 1234	Feb 68	Wynchank.	+
	1.5+1	1.7+2		Data	EXFOR11913.	Jun 76	. 15 PTS.	
Reson Params	6.2+0	1.7+2	KFK	Eval Rept	KFK-718	Apr 68	Schmidt+ RESOLVED+AVG RES PARAM(S,P)	
Reson Params	6.2+0	2.5+3	KUR	Expt Jour	YF 8 852	Nov 68	Muradyan+ 133RESON,TABLE WN,TOF	+
				Conf	68Dubna § 16	Jun 68	Muradjan+ SEE ALSO YFI-6 64	
	6.1+0	2.5+3		Prog	YFI-6 64	68	- + 135 RES,TABLE. TBP YF	
	6.2+0	2.5+3		Jour	SNP 8 495	May 69	. ENGL OF YF 8 852	
				Rept	INDC-260E	69	. ENGL OF YFI-6 64	
	6.2+0	2.5+3		Data	EXFOR40208.	Apr 74	.2G*NEUTRON WIDTH+2G*REDUCED N-WIDTH	
Reson Params	2.4+4		MUA	ExTh Jour	NC/B 58 402	Dec 68	Hasan+ AVERAGE LEVEL SPACING D GIVEN	+
	2.4+4			Expt Data	EXFOR30091.010	Dec 70	ESTIMATED AVERAGE LEVEL SPACING D	
Reson Params	5.4+1	1.5+2	BUC	Expt Jour	RRP 15 339	Mar 70	Mateiciuc+ RESON ES+D,WN CFD OTHER	+
	5.4+1	1.5+2		Data	EXFOR30372.002	Feb 77	N-WID, 9 PTS.	
Reson Params	6.2+0	2.5+3	KFK	Comp Rept	KFK-1233	Jul 70	Mueller. ES,WN,WG,G OF 127 RESON	
Reson Params	6.2+0	1.3+2	BNL	Expt Jour	PR/C 2 1115	Sep 70	Bhat+ J+PARTIAL WG FROM CAPT SPECTRA	+
	6.2+0	1.3+2		Data	EXFOR10065.002	Jan 70	. 8 PTS. E0, J.	
Reson Params	6.2+0		BUC	Expt Jour	JNE 24 245	Sep 70	Mateiciuc+ TOT,GAM,SCAT-WIDS	+
	6.2+0			Data	EXFOR30373.002	Feb 77	TOT,N-,G-WIDTHS	
Reson Params	-		AUA	Theo Rept	AAEC/E-211	Nov 70	Musgrove. CALCULTD D+GAM WIDTH GIVEN	
Reson Params	6.2+0	1.7+2	CJD	Eval Rept	YK-7	71	Zakharova+ SURVEY+SYSTEMATICS,GW,TBL	
				Rept	INDC(CCP)-27	Nov 72	.ENGLISH TRANSLATION OF YK-7 /71	
Reson Params	None		DUB	Theo Jour	YF 13 240	Feb 71	Malecki+ G-WID,THEO CFD EXPT.TBL,GRPH	
				Jour	SNP 13 133	Aug 71	- + ENGL OF YF 13 240.	
Reson Params	6.2+0	1.3+3	KUR	Expt Prog	YFI-12 27	72	Adamchuk+ TABLE OF RESPARS,ABST	+
				Rept	IAE-2108	71	- + S+P-WVE.114RES,N-WIDS,TBL	
				Prog	INDC(CCP)-30	Dec 72	.PG23,ENGLISH OF YFI-12 27	
	6.2+0	1.3+3		Data	EXFOR40164.002	Jun 73	.2G*REDUCED NEUTRON WIDTH	
Reson Params	6.0+0	4.2+3	SAC	Expt Prog	CEA-N-1522	72	.ANNUAL PROGR.REP,SPINS ASSIGNATION	+
	6.2+0	4.2+2		Prog	EANDC(E)140U	Sep 71	Paya+,SPIN ASSIGNMENTS	
	1.0+1	2.0+2		Prog	EANDC(E)127U	Apr 70	Cauvin+SPIN ASSIGN	
	6.2+0	4.2+2		Data	EXFOR20126.002	Sep 72	18PTS.J.	
Reson Params	6.2+0	1.5+2	BUC	Expt Jour	SCF 24 165	Feb 72	Mateiciuc+ THESIS.SEE REF'RRP 12,15'	
Reson Params	6.2+0	4.3+2	JAE	Expt Jour	JPJ 33 1185	Nov 72	Ohkubo+.LINAC.TOF.WN+WT,SO DERIVED	+
	1.5+2	1.5+2		Conf	68Wash. 789	Mar 68	Asami+ 2G*WN,WT. TRANS.NAT TGT	
Reson Params	+0	+2	BOL	Eval Conf	IAEA-169 3 123	74	Benzi+ AVG G-WID CFD OTHERS+XPT,TABL	
Reson Params	+0	+3	FEI	Eval Rept	YK-8/2 97	Sep 72	Abagyan+ AVG G-WID+D AT BINDNG-E,TBL	+
				Rept	INDC(CCP)-39	Jul 74	.PAGE 102.ENGLISH OF YK-8/2 97	
Reson Params	None		DUB	Expt Jour	YF 17 30	Aug 74	Karzhavina+ SPIN OF NEUT-RES	
Reson Params	None		SAC	Expt Conf	74Petten 165	Sep 74	Jain+ WIDTH CORRELATIONS OBSERVED	
Reson Params		1.0+5	ALA	Expt Abst	PC 33 3	77	Hooper+DNG DATA.E LVLS,I,PI.CFD CALC	

51 Antimony 121

Quantity	Energy (ev) Min	Max	Lab	Type	Documentation Ref Vol Page	Date	Author, Comments	Data
Strnth Fnctn	6.2+0	9.0+1	ANL	Expt	Jour PR 102 228	Apr 56	Palmer+ TRNS.AVG 7 RES ASSUMED WG	
Strnth Fnctn	+3		BNL	Expt	Jour PRL 1 461	Dec 58	Hughes+ FC 0.45+ −0.12	
Strnth Fnctn	+3	+5	BOL	Theo	Conf 61Vienna 1 179	Aug 61	Benzi+.PPR11,TABLE CFD EXPERIMENT	
Strnth Fnctn	None		ANL	Expt	Jour PR 124 1142	Nov 61	Jackson+ FAST CHOPPR	
Strnth Fnctn		7.0+2	KUR	Expt	Jour YF 8 852	Nov 68	Muradyan+ S0,S1,AVG D VALUES GVN	+
		+3			Conf 68Dubna § 16	Jun 68	Muradjan+ SEE ALSO YFI−6 64	
	6.1+0	7.0+2			Prog YFI−6 64	68	− + S0,S1 GIVEN. TBP YF	
		7.0+2			Jour SNP 8 495	May 69	. ENGL OF YF 8 852	
		+3			Rept INDC−260E	69	. ENGL OF YFI−6 64	
	6.2+0	7.0+2			Data EXFOR40208.006	Apr 74	.DATA FOR S−WAVE AND P−WAVE GVN	
Strnth Fnctn	−		AUA	Theo	Rept AAEC/E−211	Nov 70	Musgrove. SMOOTHED S0,S1 AND S2 GIVN	
Strnth Fnctn	6.2+0	1.3+3	KUR	Expt	Prog YFI−12 27	72	Adamchuk+ S0+S1 VALUES GIVEN,ABST	+
	None				Conf 71Kiev	May 71	− + S0 AND S1 VALUES GIVEN	
	6.2+0	1.3+3			Rept IAE−2108	71	− + S0+S1 GIVEN,GRAPH LVL−SPAC	
					Prog INDC(CCP)−30	Dec 72	.PG 23,ENGLISH OF YFI−12 27	
	6.2+0	1.3+3			Data EXFOR40164.004	Jun 73	.3 DATA LINES	
Strnth Fnctn		1.5+2	BUC	Expt	Jour SCF 24 165	Feb 72	Mateiciuc.S−WAVE CALC FROM RES PARS	+
					Jour RRP 15 339	Mar 70	+ VAL+ −ERROR GVN,TOF EXPT	
	6.0+1	1.5+2			Data EXFOR30372.004	Feb 77	1 PNT.	
Strnth Fnctn	2.4+4		MUA	Theo	Jour IJP 46 114	Mar 72	Chaubey+ P−WAVE.FOR A−SYSTEMTIC,GRPH	
Strnth Fnctn	None		AUA	Eval	Rept AAEC/E−277	Mar 73	Musgrove.TBLS EXPTL DATA+BEST VALUES	
Strnth Fnctn	2.5+4		AUW	Expt	Jour NP/A 213 35	Oct 73	Murty+ SB−BE.+ −5KEV.S,P−WAVE CONTRIB	
	1.8+4	2.8+4			Jour NP/A 213 35	Oct 73	− + P−WAVE.FIT TO P N−G AT 25KEV	
Strnth Fnctn	None		KUR	Theo	Prog IAE−2560	75	Adamchuk+ .S0−VALUE,TBL	
Lvl Density	Maxwl		KFI	Expt	Conf 64Paris 2 703	Jul 64	Gulyas+DISPERS PAR=3TO8 FROM ISOMRAT	
Lvl Density	−		FEI	Eval	Rept FEI−36	66	Kapchigashev+.TBL OF RELATD QUANTTYS	+
		5.0+4			Jour YF 4 686	Sep 66	.TABLE.SHORT VERSION OF FEI−36	
	−				Prog YFI−3 3	66	.ABSTRACT.TABLE LDL+NUCL EXCIT.E	
		5.0+4			Jour SNP 4 486	67	.ENGLISH OF YF 4.FROM(N,GAMMA).TABLE	
					Prog INDC−E−140 3	66	.ENGLISH TRANSL OF YFI−3	
Lvl Density	2.5+4		AUW	Expt	Conf 70Madurai 2 19	Dec 70	Lakshmana.EXPTL SPIN−CUT−OFF CFD TH	+
	2.5+4				Data EXFOR30246.030	Jun 73	SPIN CUT−OFF FACTOR FROM NG REACTION	
Lvl Density	None		AUW	Eval	Conf 70Madurai 2 267	Dec 70	Ramamurty+ A−PARAMETER GVN,LANG'S−TH	
Lvl Density	None		BOL	Eval	Rept IAEA−169 3 123	74	Benzi+ LVL DENS PARAM BY XPT,GRPH+TB	
Lvl Density	+0	+3	FEI	Eval	Rept YK−8/2 97	Sep 72	Abagyan+ LVL DENSITY PARAMETER,TBL	
					Rept INDC(CCP)−39	Jul 74	.PAGE 102.ENGLISH OF YK−8/2 97	
(γ,n)		+7	BSP	Revw	Conf 55Geneva 2 169	Aug 55	Souza−Santos+.P897,THRESHOLD VAL GVN	

51 Antimony 122

Quantity	Energy (ev) Min	Max	Lab	Type	Documentation Ref Vol Page	Date	Author, Comments	Data
Evaluation	1.0−3	1.5+7	AUA	Eval	Rept AAEC/TM−549	Jun 70	Cook.TOT,EL,INEL,NONEL,CAPT SIGS,NDG	+
					Rept AAEC/E−214	Jun 71	Bertram+GROUP SIGMAS SAME QUANTS.NDG	
					Rept AAEC/TM−587	Mar 71	*DESCRIPTION OF LIBRARY	
	1.0−3	1.5+7			Data AUSTR−DFN 91.	Nov 71	POINT(223) AND GROUP(127) SIGMAS	
Total	1.0−3	1.5+7	AUA	Eval	Data AUSTR−DFN 91.	Nov 71	COOK+POINT(223)+GROUP(127)SIG.CF EVL	+
Elastic	1.0−3	1.5+7	AUA	Eval	Data AUSTR−DFN 91.	Nov 71	COOK+POINT(223)+GROUP(127)SIG.CF EVL	+
Diff Elastic	1.0+6		LAS	Eval	Rept LA−2016	Jun 56	Longley.TBL ANG DIST 3−DEG STEPS	
Tot Inelastc	5.0+5	1.5+7	AUA	Eval	Data AUSTR−DFN 91.	Nov 71	COOK+POINT(11)+GROUP(127)SIG.CF EVL	+
Nonelastic	1.0−3	1.5+7	AUA	Eval	Data AUSTR−DFN 91.	Nov 71	COOK+POINT(223)+GROUP(127)SIG.CF EVL	+
Res Int Abs	5.0−1		AUA	Eval	Rept AAEC/TM−619	Sep 72	Clayton.CALC FROM SIG LIBRARY,TABLE	
Res Int Abs	+0	+5	WIN	Revw	Conf IAEA−169 3 163	74	Pope+ 1 VALUE WITH AUSTRAL DATA FILE	
(n,γ)	1.0−3	1.5+7	AUA	Eval	Data AUSTR−DFN 91.	Nov 71	COOK+POINT(223)+GROUP(127)SIG.CF EVL	+
(n,γ)	Pile		CRC	Eval	Rept AECL−3037 1	Jan 72	Walker.SIG ESTIMATED ACCORDING Z,A	
(n,γ)	2.5−2		AUA	Eval	Rept AAEC/TM−619	Sep 72	Clayton.CALC FROM SIG LIBRARY,TABLE	
(n,γ)	2.5−2		SGA	Eval	Conf 73Paris 1 233	Mar 73	Eder+ INTERPOLATED FROM CALC SIG,TBL	
					Rept SGAE−PH−141	Feb 73	.SAME AS 73PARIS,POINT SIG FROM COOK	
(n,γ)	Maxwl	Fiss	WIN	Revw	Conf IAEA−169 3 163	74	Pope+ MAXW+FIS−SPEC AVG EVAL DATA	
	Fiss				Conf IAEA−169 3 137	74	Dean. POINT DATA AVG OVER STAND−SPC	
(n,γ)	1.0+6	1.0+7	CRC	Revw	Conf 74Petten 119	Sep 74	Bartholomew+ PHOTON STRF GRPH	
(n,p)	Maxwl		IFU	Theo	Rept ICD−4 20	67	Dadakina+ PENETR COEFF CALC,TABLE	
Reson Params	None		MOL	Expt	Jour JPR 23 951	Nov 62	Vanhorenbeeck. = 1 DATA INDEX LINES	+
Reson Params	−		AUA	Theo	Rept AAEC/E−211	Nov 70	Musgrove. CALCULTD D+GAM WIDTH GIVEN	
Strnth Fnctn			AUA	Theo	Rept AAEC/E−211	Nov 70	Musgrove. SMOOTHED S0,S1 AND S2 GIVN	
Lvl Density	4.0+6	7.0+6	ISL	Theo	Conf 64Geneva § 511	May 64	Szwarcbaum+.T FROM 3 FORMLS CFD EXPS	
Lvl Density	+6		MIL	Theo	Jour EN 15 1 54	Jan 68	Facchini+ LDL PARS FROM LOW EN RES	
Lvl Density	None		MUN	Theo	Jour NP/A 217 269	Dec 73	Dilg+ A,DELTA. BACK SHIFTED FERMIGAS	

51 Antimony 122

Quantity	Energy (ev) Min	Max	Lab	Type	Documentation Ref Vol Page	Date	Author, Comments	Data
Lvl Density	None		COP	Theo Jour	NP/A 222 493	Apr 74	Dossing+COLL ROTAT.SPAC. ACCUR ESTIM	
Lvl Density	9.0+6	1.6+7	ANL	Eval Rept	ANL-75-34	Jun 75	Davey+N2NEVAL.CONSTANT T,LVL DEN FIT	

51 Antimony 123

Quantity	Energy (ev) Min	Max	Lab	Type	Documentation Ref Vol Page	Date	Author, Comments	Data
Evaluation	1.0-3	1.5+7	AUA	Eval Rept	AAEC/TM-549	Jun 70	Cook.TOT,EL,INEL,NONEL,CAPT SIGS,NDG	+
				Rept	AAEC/E-214	Jun 71	Bertram+GROUP SIGMAS SAME QUANTS.NDG	
				Rept	AAEC/TM-587	Mar 71	*DESCRIPTION OF LIBRARY	
	1.0-3	1.5+7		Data	AUSTR-DFN 92.	Nov 71	POINT(223) AND GROUP(127) SIGMAS	
Total	1.4+7		FEI	Expt Prog	INDSWG-126 33	66	Dukarevich.SIG=4.68+ - 0.03B	
Total	1.4+7		CCP	ExTh Jour	IZV 31 217	Feb 67	Dukarevich+.TBL,CURVES,CFD OPTMDL TH	
				Jour	BAS 31 197	Feb 67	TRANSLATN.*	
Total	1.4+7		FTI	Expt Jour	NP/A 92 433	Feb 67	Dukarevich+ CFD OPTMDL 4.68+ - 0.03B	+
Total	2.3+2	6.0+3	KUR	Expt Jour	YF 8 852	Nov 68	Muradyan+ TRANSMISS CV,TOTAL-POTNTAL	
				Jour	SNP 8 495	May 69	. ENGL OF YF 8 852	
Total	1.0-3	1.5+7	AUA	Eval Data	AUSTR-DFN 92.	Nov 71	COOK+POINT(223)+GROUP(127)SIG.CF EVL	+
Total	1.3+7	1.5+7	DEB	Eval Rept	IAEA-153 173	73	Boedy+ MOST PROBABLE VAL OF SIG,TBL	
				Jour	AHP 30 115	Oct 71	Angeli+ AVG SIG,CFD CALC.TBLS.GRAPH	
Elastic	1.0-3	1.5+7	AUA	Eval Data	AUSTR-DFN 92.	Nov 71	COOK+POINT(223)+GROUP(127)SIG.CF EVL	+
Polarization	8.5+5		ANL	Expt Prog	ANL-7410 3	Jan 69	Cox+,OPTMDL FIT TO DATA,CURVE+PARAMS	
Potntl Scat	2.3+2	6.0+3	KUR	Expt Jour	YF 8 852	Nov 68	Muradyan+ TRANSMISS CV,TOTAL-POTNTAL	
				Jour	SNP 8 495	May 69	. ENGL OF YF 8 852	
Tot Inelastc	5.0+5	1.5+7	AUA	Eval Data	AUSTR-DFN 92.	Nov 71	COOK+POINT(11)+GROUP(127)SIG.CF EVL	+
Diff Inelast	4.0+5	1.2+6	FEI	Expt Jour	AE 15 416	Nov 63	Glazkov+ SPHER GEOM, 5 ENERGIES	
				Jour	JNE 18 654	64	. ENGL OF AE 15 416	
				Jour	EAF 15 5	Nov 63	.FRENCH OF AE 15 416	
				Jour	SJA 15 1173	Nov 63	. ENGL OF AE 15 416	
Diff Inelast	8.0+5	2.0+6	BHU	Expt Conf	67Tokyo § 4.109	Sep 67	Nath+ TOF(HAR VDG),4 LVLS+DECAY GAMS	
Diff Inelast	2.2+5	1.2+6	FEI	Expt Rept	FEI-155	69	Broder+ EXCIT 1 LVL,TBL	
Nonelastic	1.0-3	1.5+7	AUA	Eval Data	AUSTR-DFN 92.	Nov 71	COOK+POINT(223)+GROUP(127)SIG.CF EVL	+
Nonelastic	1.4+7		TUD	Theo Conf	ZFK-271 63	Nov 73	Seeliger+ N-SPEC,NDG.INTEG - SIG SHOWN	
Nonelastic	1.4+7	1.6+7	ANL	Eval Rept	ANL-75-34	Jun 75	Davey+CORRC APPLIED TO N2N CS.TBLS.	
Absorption	Maxwl		PAV	Expt Rept	EN 14 541	Sep 67	Orvini+SIG 4.03+ - 0.16B	
Absorption	1.0-3	1.0+7	JUL	Eval Rept	JUEL-678-RG	Jul 70	Liu. EVALUATION+CALC,GRPH,FN OF E	
Res Int Abs	5.0-1		ANL	Expt Jour	PR 79 11	Jul 50	Harris+ EPI-CD,REL THERMAL ACT. B-W	+
	5.0-1			Data	EXFOR11343.022	Jun 76	. 1 PT.	
Res Int Abs	None		ORL	Revw Conf	55Geneva 5 96	Aug 55	Macklin+ TABLE.EXPT CFD THEORY,P833	
Res Int Abs	None		CRC	Eval Rept	AECL-1054	Mar 60	Walker.(CRP-913) REDUCED RES.INT.	
Res Int Abs	+3	+5	BOL	Theo Conf	61Vienna 1 179	Aug 61	Benzi+.PPR11,VAL GVN,L=0,L=1 .CAPT.	
Res Int Abs	5.0-1		BOL	Eval Conf	61Vienna 1 179	Aug 61	Benzi+ TBL TOTAL CAPT RES INTS.	
Res Int Abs	5.0-1		BOL	Eval Rept	RT/FI-4	Jan 67	Palmucci. CALC FROM (N,G) RES PARAMS	
Res Int Abs	5.0-1		BGK	Expt Rept	THAI-AEC-10	Oct 67	. ACTIV(NA-I),CD-RATIO,REL AU. TABLE	+
	5.0-1			Data	EXFOR30368.018	Jan 77	REL AU, PRELM.	
Res Int Abs	5.0-1		CPO	Expt Jour	JIN 30 349	Feb 68	Sims+ 142.6+ -4.0 REL TO CO59=69.9 B	+
	5.0-1			Data	EXFOR11658.	Jun 76	. 2 PTS, RI TO GND + META	
Res Int Abs	5.5-1		ISP	Expt Jour	JIN 30 1353	Jul 68	Orvini+ACT 116+ - 10 B REL.TO AU197	+
	5.5-1			Data	EXFOR20633.006	Jun 76	1PNT.CAPTURE.	
Res Int Abs	5.0-1		CNE	Expt Jour	CJP 47 2031	Oct 69	Ricabarra+ RATIO TO ACTIVAT SIG,TBL	+
				Conf	70Helsinki 2 589	Jun 70	. *SAME+MORE DATA TABLES	
				Rept	CNEA-282	70	*	
	6.0-1			Data	EXFOR30128.008	Dec 72	RES INTEG AND RATIO TO THR-ABS SIGM.	
Res Int Abs	None		GA	Eval Rept	GA-12071	Sep 71	Mathews+ RECOMMENDED VALUES	
Res Int Abs	5.0-1		NPL	Expt Jour	JNE 24 35	Feb 70	Ryves.REL AU.REDUCED INTGRL.ACTIV.	+
				Conf	71Canterby 139	Sep 71	- .REDUCED CAPT RES INTEGRAL,TBL	
	5.0-1			Data	EXFOR20789.304	Dec 78	1PNT.REDUCED INTEGRAL.CAPTURE	
Res Int Abs	5.5-1		CRC	Eval Rept	AECL-3037 1	Jan 72	Walker.REDUCED RES INT,DETAILED TBL	
Res Int Abs	5.0-1		AUA	Eval Rept	AAEC/TM-619	Sep 72	Clayton.CALC FROM SIG LIBRARY,TABLE	
Res Int Abs	5.0-1		MUN	Expt Jour	JRC 15 535	73	Alian+CAPT CD-R, 136.0B INCL 1/V	+
	5.0-1			Data	EXFOR20644.007	Jun 76	1PNT.CAPTURE.	
Res Int Abs	5.0-1		SGA	Eval Conf	73Paris 1 233	Mar 73	Eder+ REDUCED RES INTEG CAPTURE,TBL	
				Rept	SGAE-PH-141	Feb 73	.SAME AS 73PARIS,EVAL OF EXPTL DATA	
Res Int Abs	5.0-1		GHT	Expt Jour	JRC 11 133	Jun 72	Van Der Linden+ BY(N,G).CFD OTHS,TBL	+
				Jour	JRC 23 113	74	- + (N,G).CD-RATIO,TABLE	
	5.5-1			Conf	73Paris 2 241	Mar 73	- + ACT,REL THR+GOLD,TBL	
	5.5-1			Data	EXFOR20643.061	Jul 76	1PNT.CAPTURE.	
Res Int Abs	5.5-1	+6	SAC	Revw Conf	IAEA-169 1 235	74	Ribon.CAPTURE,STATUS CFD REQUEST,TBL	

51 Antimony 123

Quantity	Energy (ev) Min	Max	Lab	Type	Documentation Ref Vol Page	Date	Author, Comments	Data
Res Int Abs	+0	+5	WIN Revw	Conf	IAEA-169 3 163	74	Pope+ DATA FILE CALC CFD XPTAL VALUE	
Res Int Abs	5.5-1		MUNComp	Jour	JRC 29 175	Jan 76	Gryntakis+ TO G+M1+M2.10 VALUES GIVN	
(n,γ)	Maxwl		JAP Expt	Jour	SCP 38 167	Jan 41	Sinma+.LI+D.RELATIVE SIG MEASUREMENT	
(n,γ)	Maxwl		UI Expt	Jour	PR 59 102	Jan 41	O-Neal+ ACT REL MN	
(n,γ)	Pile		ANL Expt	Jour	PR 72 888	Nov 47	Seren+ ACT METHOD.PILE IRRAD, METAL.	+
	Pile			Data	EXFOR11447.083	Jun 76	. 1 PT.	
(n,γ)	Pile		ANL Expt	Jour	PR 72 1271	Dec 47	Der-Mateosian+MULT. NUCL. ISOMERISM.	+
	Pile			Data	EXFOR11997.002	Jun 76	. 1 PT.	
(n,γ)	Maxwl		ORL Expt	Jour	PR 88 412	Oct 52	Pomerance.PILE OSC.	+
	Maxwl			Data	EXFOR11507.059	Jun 76	. 1 PT.	
(n,γ)	2.4+4		ORL Expt	Jour	PR 107 504	Jul 57	Macklin+ SB-BE NS,456+ -46MB,.603MEV	+
	2.4+4			Data	EXFOR11399.032	Jun 76	. 1 PT.	
(n,γ)	2.5+4		LRL Expt	Jour	PR 112 226	Oct 58	Booth+ SB-BE REL I+THR,ACT 60D HL	+
				Abst	BAP 2 268	58	.ABST L6	
	2.5+4			Data	EXFOR11429.020	Jun 76	. 1 PT.	
(n,γ)	2.0+5		ORL Expt	Jour	PR 114 1619	Jun 59	Lyon+ ABS GAMMA COUNT 280+ -30MB ACT	+
	2.0+5			Data	EXFOR11407.022	Jun 76	. 1 PT.	
(n,γ)	Maxwl		CRC Eval	Rept	AECL-1054	Mar 60	Walker. (CRRP-913)	
(n,γ)	2.5-2	2.5-2	MOLExpt	Jour	NP 37 90	62	Vanhorenbeck. ACTIVATION.	+
	Pile			Data	EXFOR20207.	May 74	2PTS.SIGMA.	
(n,γ)	7.8+3	6.4+4	KFK Expt	Prog	EANDC(E)-66	Feb 66	Poenitz. TO SB124G	+
				Rept	ARB.BER-19	Nov 65	- . ACTIVATION OF SB-124 GS.	
(n,γ)	2.5-2		BOL Eval	Rept	RT/FI-4	Jan 67	Palmucci. CALC FROM RES PARAMETERS	
(n,γ)	Pile		ANL Expt	Abst	ANS 10 226	Jun 67	Plumlee. CP-5 REACTOR, 3.1+ -0.6B	+
	Pile			Data	EXFOR11987.002	Jun 76	. 1 PT.	
(n,γ)	Maxwl		CPO Expt	Jour	JIN 30 349	Feb 68	Sims+ 4.44+ -0.09 REL TO CO59=37.5 B	+
	Maxwl			Data	EXFOR11658.	Jun 76	. 2 PTS, SIG TO GND + META	
(n,γ)	1.5+7		DEB Expt	Jour	MFF 16 123	Feb 68	.THESIS CSIKAI IN HUNG,DATA+THEORY	
				Jour	NP/A 95 229	Mar 67	Csikai+ SIG REL CU63(N,2N) GIVEN	
	1.5+7			Data	EXFOR30067.013	Nov 70	SIGMA AT 14.7 MEV	
(n,γ)	3.0+5	2.7+6	FEI ExTh	Jour	AE 24 6 576	Jun 68	Tolstikov+ EXPT+STATMOD CURVES	+
				Expt Conf	68Riga	Jan 68	Dovbenko+ ABST,STATMOD CFD	
				ExTh Jour	EAF 24 6 111	Jun 68	.TRANSLATION	
	2.0+5	2.7+6		Expt Data	EXFOR40327.005	Nov 76	SIG(E), 18 PNTS	
	2.0+5	2.7+6		Data	EXFOR40005.005	Jul 70	.SIGMA AT 18 ENERGIES GIVEN	
(n,γ)	-		IEA Comp	Rept	IEA-INF-10	Aug 68	Atalla. TABLES OF HL,SIG AND GAMM-E	
(n,γ)	2.4+4		MUAExpt	Jour	NC/B 58 402	Dec 68	Hasan+,SB-BE,ACT BETA-DET REL I-127.	+
	2.4+4			Data	EXFOR30077.	Dec 70	SIGMAS FOR 2METASTABLE+ GROUND STATE	
(n,γ)	2.0+3		MTR Expt	Prog	WASH-1127 72	Apr 69	Schuman+ FILTERED BEAM,RELATVE CURVS	
(n,γ)	5.0+3	1.0+5	AUA ExTh	Jour	AAEC/E-198	May 69	Musgrove.S+P+D WAVE SIGMAS CALC,TBL	
(n,γ)	+3		COL Expt	Prog	WASH-1136 22	Sep 69	Arbo+ TO BE DONE	
(n,γ)	1.0+3	1.0+7	BOL Eval	Rept	CCDN-NW/10	Dec 69	Benzi+H-F MOD,AXEL G(G)EST,ALL DATA	
				Rept	CEC(70)-2	Apr 70	- +. GRAPH	
				Conf	66Paris 1 537	Oct 66	- + STATMOD.TBL AV VALS.SUPERSEDD	
				Jour	NC 38 216	Jul 65	- + THEORY FOR CAPTURE EVALUATION	
				Conf	61Vienna 1 179	Aug 61	- + TBL AV VALS. SUPERSEDED.	
(n,γ)	Pile		TRM Expt	Rept	BARC/I-84	70	Sankaranarayanan+ EFFECT SIG GIVEN	
(n,γ)	Maxwl		MTR Expt	Prog	IN-1317 53	Jan 70	Hogg+ ACT, VALUE GIVEN	+
	Maxwl			Data	EXFOR12602.005	Jun 76	. 1 PT, SIGMA.	
(n,γ)	3.0+4		AUA Theo	Rept	AAEC/E-211	Nov 70	Musgrove. SIGMA GIVEN AND CFD OTHER	
(n,γ)	2.5-2		NPL Expt	Jour	JNE 24 35	Feb 70	Ryves.REL.AU,STANDARD NPL TH.FLUX.	+
				Conf	71Canterby 139	71	- . VDG,GRAPHITE MODERATOR.ACTIVN	
	2.5-2			Data	EXFOR20789.029	Dec 78	1PNT.SIGMA.	
(n,γ)	1.4+7		COL Expt	Prog	NCSAC-38 73	May 71	Stamatelatos+. VALUE GIVEN	
(n,γ)	Maxwl		GA Eval	Rept	GA-12071	Sep 71	Mathews+ RECOMMENDED VALUES	
(n,γ)	1.0-3	1.5+7	AUA Eval	Data	AUSTR-DFN 92.	Nov 71	COOK+POINT(223)+GROUP(127)SIG.CF EVL	+
(n,γ)	Maxwl		CRC Eval	Rept	AECL-3037 1	Jan 72	Walker.RECOMMENDED SIG,DETAILED TBL	
(n,γ)	2.4+4		MUATheo	Jour	IJP 46 114	Mar 72	Chaubey+ P-WAVE STRENGTH FUNC,TABLE	
(n,γ)	2.5-2		AUA Eval	Rept	AAEC/TM-619	Sep 72	Clayton.CALC FROM SIG LIBRARY,TABLE	
(n,γ)	Fast		MTR Expt	Rept	72Kiamesha 2 614	Sep 72	Harker+ CFRMF INTEGRAL MEAS.	
(n,γ)	Maxwl		GHT Comp	Jour	JRC 16 39	73	Maenhaut+ACT TO SB124 .GELI.SIG GIVN	
(n,γ)	Maxwl		SGA Eval	Conf	73Paris 1 233	Mar 73	Eder+ RECOMMENDED SIG,TBL,NO DETAILS	
				Rept	SGAE-PH-141	Feb 73	.SAME AS 73PARIS,EVAL OF EXPTL DATA	
(n,γ)	2.5-2		SAC Revw	Conf	IAEA-169 1 235	74	Ribon.STATUS SIG CFD REQUESTS,TABLE	
(n,γ)	Maxwl Fiss		WIN Revw	Conf	IAEA-169 3 163	74	Pope+ MAXW+FIS-SPEC AVG DATA CFD XPT	
	Fiss			Conf	IAEA-169 3 137	74	Dean. POINT DATA AVG OVER STAND-SPC	

51 Antimony 123

Quantity	Energy (ev) Min	Energy (ev) Max	Lab	Type	Documentation Ref Vol Page	Author, Comments Date	Data
(n,γ)	1.0+3	1.0+7	FEI	Eval	Rept YK- 8/2 97	Sep 72 Abagjan+ AVG SIG(ENERGY-GROUPS),TBL	
				Expt	Rept YK- 8/2 97	Sep 72 Abagyan+ AVG SIG(ENERGY-GROUPS),TABL	
					Rept INDC(CCP)-39	Jul 74 .P102. ENGL OF YK-8/2 97	
(n,γ)	2.5-2		MUN	Comp Jour	JRC 29 175	Jan 76 Gryntakis+,TO M,G,M+G 8 VALUES GIVEN	
(n,γ)	1.5+7		IRK	Expt Priv	WAGNER	77 Wagner+	+
	1.4+7			Rept	INDC(SEC)-51	Oct 75 - + ABST PAGE 3	
	1.5+7			Data	EXFOR20718.009	Jan 76 1PNT.SIGMA.	
Spect (n,γ)	Pile		LND	Expt Jour	AF 5 427	Oct 52 Johansson+.NAI.COINC. TE124 GAMMAS	
Spect (n,γ)	Pile		FAR	Expt Jour	CR 239 800	Oct 54 Moreau. SINGLES SPEC+BETA-G COINC.	
Spect (n,γ)	None		RI	Expt Jour	NP 2 408	Dec 56 Dzhelepov+.600-2090 KEV GAMMAS.TABLE	
Spect (n,γ)	5.0+0	2.0+2	ANL	Expt Jour	PR 124 1142	Nov 61 Jackson+ FC, LOW ENERGY GAMMAS	
Spect (n,γ)	2.2+1		JAE	Expt Rept	JAERI-1073	Mar 65 Kawarasaki. RES CAPT.LINAC.TOF.E,INT	+
				Rept	INDSWG-90 6	Jul 65 - . TABLE E,INTS GIVEN.	
	2.2+1			Data	EXFOR20277.008	Jun 74 6PTS.	
Spect (n,γ)	2.2+1		TOR	Expt Jour	NP/A 137 561	Nov 69 ING+ 2-DIM DATA COLL. 500-700 KEV	
Spect (n,γ)	Pile		KFK	Expt Jour	ZP 233 458	Apr 70 Behrens+ BETA-G CIRCULAR POLRZ MEAS.	
Spect (n,γ)	Maxwl	+2	BNL	Expt Jour	PR/C 2 1115	Sep 70 Bhat+ GE(LI) DET.THERMAL+RESON CAPT	
Spect (n,γ)	Pile		KFK	Expt Rept	KFK-1401	Jun 71 Djadali.AVG POLRZ G EXPT,CFD T,SPIN	
	Maxwl			Jour	NP/A 147 150	May 70 Eichler+ POL NS.CIRC POL GS+ASSYMTRY	
Spect (n,γ)	-2	+2	SAC	Expt Rept	CEA-N-1522	Oct 72 Cauvin+ GAMMA SPECTR ANAL	
	1.0+1	3.0+2		Jour	JPR 32 849	Dec 71 Lottin+ CORRELATION (WGI,WN)	
	2.2+1	1.1+2		Conf	69Studsvik 657	Aug 69 Paya+ SPEC GRPH+TBL GVN,RESON,LINAC	
Inelastic γ	2.5+4		ORL	Expt Conf	58Geneva 15 68	Sep 58 Macklin.PPR671,SIGMA+G-ENERGY GVN	
Inelastic γ	1.0+6	1.5+6	TNC	Expt Rept	ORO-2791-26	Aug 67 Morgan+ NAI(TL) 2ES CFD TH	+
	1.0+6	3.5+6		Data	EXFOR11662.008	Jun 76 . 2 PTS, DSIG	
Inelastic γ	8.0+5	2.0+6	BHU	Expt Conf	67Tokyo § 4.109	Sep 67 Nath+ TOF,PROMPT GATED,4LVLS+DECAY	
Inelastic γ	2.2+5	1.2+6	FEI	Expt Rept	FEI-155	69 Broder+ 1 LVL, 27 ES, TABLE,GRAPH	
Inelastic γ	6.0+5	1.9+6	PEL	Expt Jour	NP/A 172 215	Aug 71 Barnard+ SPEC MEAS.ONLY LVLS SHOWN.	
				Jour	NP/A 167 511	Jun 71 - + METHOD DESCRIBED	
				Jour	NP/A 157 130	Nov 70 - + METHOD DESCRIBED	
Inelastic γ	8.0+6	8.8+6	BRC	Expt Prog	EANDC(E)150U	May 72 Lachkar+	
Inelastic γ	None	1.1+5	ALA	Expt Abst	PC 33 3	77 Hooper+DNG DATA.E LVLS,I,PI.CFD CALC	
(n,2n)	1.5+7		CRC	Expt Jour	CJP 31 267	Feb 72 Paul+ BETA ACT.CFD TH.HL=2.80	+
	1.5+7			Data	EXFOR11274.080	Jun 76 . 1 PT.	
(n,2n)	Fiss		CRC	Eval Rept	CRC-1003	Dec 60 ROY+ ESTIMATED AVG SIG=1.4MB	
(n,2n)	1.2+7	2.0+7	LAS	Expt Jour	PR 121 1438	Mar 61 Prestwood+ RADIO CHEM	+
				Rept	LA-2493	Dec 60 Bayhurst+,ACT EXCITATION CURVE	
	1.2+7	2.0+7		Data	EXFOR11645.023	Jun 76 . 15 PTS.	
(n,2n)	Thrsh	Up	LAS	Theo Jour	PR 123 859	Aug 61 Barr+ THEO FIT SIG(E,EP) DATA	
(n,2n)	1.5+7		MUA	Expt Jour	NP 28 560	Dec 61 Khurana+ ACTIV, CFD STATMOD	+
	1.4+7			Jour	NP 13 88	Oct 59 - +.C-W ABS BETA COUNT 1706MB	
(n,2n)	1.4+7		MUA	Expt Conf	64Chandgrh 99	Feb 64 Mangall+.NDG,ISOMERIC SIGMA RATIOS	+
	1.5+7			Jour	NP 49 510	Dec 63 Mangal+.SIG=1013+ - 12MB AT14.8MEV ACT	
	1.5+7			Data	EXFOR30060.	Apr 71 SIG AT 14.8 MEV AND ISOMERIC RATIO	
(n,2n)	1.4+7		HAM	Comp Jour	NP 65 257	Mar 65 Bormann. 3EXPT VALS.CFD SHELL EFFECT	
(n,2n)	1.3+7	1.5+7	BNL	Theo Jour	NSE 23 238	Nov 65 Pearlstein.3ES.STAT MDL CALC.TBL CS.	
(n,2n)	Fiss		BNL	Theo Jour	NSE 23 238	Nov 65 Pearlstein.STATMDL CALC.SPEC AVG.TBL	
(n,2n)	1.4+7		DEB	Revw Jour	MFF 16 123	Feb 68 Csikai. VAL GVN,RELATIVE MEASUREMENT	
(n,2n)	1.3+7	1.9+7	HAM	Expt Jour	NP/A 115 309	Jul 68 Bormann+ VDG.ACT.CFD STATMDL+OPTMDL	+
(n,2n)	1.5+7		TUR	Expt Jour	ZP 217 83	Oct 68 Minetti+,GND + ISOM 1594B + 686B	
(n,2n)	1.5+7		DEB	Comp Jour	REA 7 4 93	Dec 69 Csikai+ SIG+HL COMPILTN,N-ACTIV-ANAL	
(n,2n)	+7		KFI	Comp Jour	AHP 26 335	Dec 69 Adam+ GRPH+TBL,XPTL SIG CFD SHELL-TH	
				Jour	KFI 16 331	Oct 68 - + IN HUNGARIAN,SEE AHP 26 335	
(n,2n)	1.5+7		IBJ	Expt Jour	APPB 1 415	70 Rurarz+ ACTIV,NAI,SIG(M)+ISORATIO	+
	1.5+7			Data	EXFOR30154.	Feb 72 PARTIAL SIG,ISOM RATIO AT 14.5 MEV	
(n,2n)	1.4+7		GIT	Expt Jour	PR/C 1 350	Jan 70 Fink+ACTIVATION,GRPHS,TBL.CFD OTH.	+
	1.4+7			Data	EXFOR10497.026	Apr 76 1PT.CS=1542+ - 80MB.	
(n,2n)	1.4+7	1.5+7	JYV	Eval Rept	JU-RR-3/1970	Jun 70 Leppaemaeki+ TABLE OF EVAL AVG SIG	
(n,2n)	+7		KFI	Comp Jour	KFKI-71-8	Feb 71 Jeki. CALCULATED CFD EXPTL SIG VALUE	
(n,2n)	1.4+7	1.5+7	IRK	ExTh Jour	APA 33 285	Jul 71 Winiwarter+ ISOMERIC RATIO	
(n,2n)	1.4+7		GIT	Theo Jour	PR/C 4 1173	Oct 71 Fink+ STAT-MODEL CALCULATION.CFD EXP	
(n,2n)	1.5+7		DEB	Eval Jour	REA 11 1 153	Mar 73 Boedy. COMPILATION+RECOMM.VALUE,TBL	
				Rept	IAEA-153 173	73 - . RECOMM. VALUE ONLY	
(n,2n)	1.4+7		LOU	Expt Prog	INR-1464 12	May 73 Araminowicz+BRIEF,ACTIV,TABLE,GRAPH	+
	1.4+7			Data	EXFOR30264.036	Nov 73 SIGMA AT 14.6 MEV	
(n,2n)	Fiss		KOS	Eval Jour	AK 16 351	74 Boedy. U238,MAXW-SPC.AVG CFD XPT,TBL	
(n,2n)	1.5+7		TAT	Theo Jour	JP/A 7 1458	Aug 74 Kondaiah. CALC ON STAT MODEL	
(n,2n)	Fiss		KOS	Eval Conf	75Karlsrhe 29	Apr 75 Csikai. CF252,MAXW-SPC.AVG FOR 2TEMP	

51 Antimony 123

Quantity	Energy (ev) Min	Max	Lab	Type	Documentation Ref Vol Page	Date	Author, Comments	Data
(n,2n)	1.4+7		VLD	Expt Jour	ARS 71 123	Apr 75	Casanova+,SIG TO GRND+METAST STATES	+
				Prog	NEANDC(OR)140L	Dec 74	– + ACTIVATION.	
	1.4+7			Data	EXFOR20776.003	Dec 77	1PNT.SIGMA.	
(n,2n)	9.0+6	1.6+7	ANL	Eval Rept	ANL–75–34	Jun 75	Davey+CONSTANT T MDL,LVL DEN MDL FIT	
(n,xn) x>2	Fiss		BNL	Theo Jour	NSE 23 238	Nov 65	Pearlstein.SPEC AVG STATMDL CALC N3N	
n Emission	1.4+7		TUD	Theo Prog	ZFK–262 25	Sep 73	Hermsdorf+ CALC N–SPEC CFD EXPT,NDG	
(n,p)	Fiss		CRC	Eval Rept	CRC–1003	Dec 60	ROY+ ESTIMATED AVG SIG=0.08MB	
(n,p)	1.5+7		KAZ	Expt Jour	YF 13 923	May 71	Levkovsky+ ACT,SIG+ISOMER RATIO,TBL	
				Jour	SNP 13 529	Nov 71	. ENGL OF YF 10 923	
(n,p)	1.4+7	1.5+7	KAZ	Theo Jour	YF 18 705	Oct 73	Levkovsky.AVERAGED SIG,CALC,TBL	
				Jour	SNP 18 361	Apr 74	. ENGLISH OF YF 18,705	
(n,p)	1.4+7		TUD	Theo Conf	ZFK–271 63	Nov 73	Seeliger+ P–EMISSION SPEC, NDG	
(n,p)	1.5+7		ARK	Expt Jour	JIN 36 5 953	May 74	Mavaddat+ ACTIV MEAS	
(n,α)	Fiss		CRC	Eval Rept	CRC–1003	Dec 60	ROY+ ESTIMATED AVG SIG=BELO 0.0001MB	
(n,α)	1.4+7		KFI	Comp Jour	JRC 7 365	Jun 71	Nagy+ SIGMA,GAM+BETA ES,HALF–L GIVEN	
(n,α)	1.4+7		TUD	Theo Conf	ZFK–271 63	Nov 73	Seeliger+ A–EMISSION SPEC, NDG	
Reson Params	2.2+1	1.1+2	ANL	Expt Jour	PR 102 228	Apr 56	Palmer+ TRNS.WT WN OTHER PARS 4 RES	+
	2.2+1	1.1+2		Data	EXFOR11804.	Jun 76	. 4 RES, E0,WT,WN,WN0,PCS	
Reson Params	2.2+1		BNL	Expt Jour	PR 108 353	Oct 57	Stolovy+ FC, TRANS	+
	2.2+1			Data	EXFOR11866.006	Jun 76	. 1 RES, E0,WT,WN,WG	
Reson Params	2.2+1	1.9+2	ANL	Expt Jour	PR 124 1142	Nov 61	Jackson+ FAST CHOPPER	+
	2.2+1	1.9+2		Data	EXFOR11992.003	Jun 76	. 6 RES, E0	
Reson Params	2.2+1		BNL	Expt Jour	NP 42 676	Apr 63	Bolotin+ WG=58MEV,WN ALSO GIVEN	+
	2.2+1			Data	EXFOR11922.007	Jun 76	. 1 RES, E0,WN,WG	
Reson Params		1.0+6	AUA	Theo Jour	AUJ 20 477	Oct 67	Cook+ TBL OF AVG LVL SPACING D,L=0,1	
Reson Params	2.2+1		BUC	Expt Jour	RRP 12 10 907	Oct 67	Mateiciuc+, TOT+NEUT+GAMMA WIDTHS	+
	2.2+1			Data	EXFOR30020.	Oct 70	VALUES OF WN,WG AND WT AT 21.6 EV	
Reson Params	2.4+4		MUA	ExTh Jour	NC/B 58 402	Dec 68	Hasan+ AVERAGE LEVEL SPACING D GIVEN	+
	2.4+4			Expt	EXFOR30091.011	Dec 70	ESTIMATED AVERAGE LEVEL SPACING D	
Reson Params		1.2+3	CCP	Revw Jour	AE 28 38	Jan 70	Sukhoruchkin. EXPTL D–DISTRIB.CFD.TH	
				Jour	EAF 28 1 49	Jan 70	. FRENCH OF AE 28 38	
Reson Params	4.7+1	1.1+2	BUC	Expt Jour	RRP 15 339	Mar 70	Mateiciuc+ TBL–RESON E+WN,CFD OTHER	+
	4.7+1	1.1+2		Data	EXFOR30372.003	Feb 77	N–WID, 4 PTS.	
Reson Params	2.1+1	1.1+2	BNL	Expt Jour	PR/C 2 1115	Sep 70	Bhat+ J+PARTIAL WG FROM CAPT SPECTRA	+
	2.1+1	1.1+2		Data	EXFOR10065.003	Jan 70	4PTS.EO,J.	
Reson Params	–		AUA	Theo Rept	AAEC/E–211	Nov 70	Musgrove. CALCULTD D+GAM WIDTH GIVEN	
Reson Params	None		KUR	Expt Jour	AE 29 395	Nov 70	Muradjan+ ABST FRANC–SOV SEM DUBNA	+
	2.1+1	4.2+3		Jour	YF 8 852	Nov 68	Muradyan+ 110RESON,TABLE WN,TOF	
	2.1+0	4.2+3		Conf	68Dubna § 16	Jun 68	Muradjan+ SEE ALSO YFI–6 64	
	2.0+0	4.2+3		Prog	YFI–6 64	68	– + 112 RES,TABLE. TBP YF	
	None			Jour	SJA 29 1156	Nov 70	. ENGL OF AE 29 395	
	2.1+1	4.2+3		Jour	SNP 8 495	May 69	. ENGL OF YF 8 852	
	2.1+0	4.2+3		Rept	INDC–260E	69	. ENGL OF YFI–6 64	
	2.1+1	4.2+3		Data	EXFOR40208.	Apr 74	.2G*NEUTRON WIDTH+2G*REDUCED N–WIDTH	
Reson Params	2.1+1	1.9+2	CJD	Eval Rept	YK–7	71	Zakharova+ SURVEY+SYSTEMATICS,GW,TBL	
				Rept	INDC(CCP)–27	Nov 72	.ENGLISH TRANSLATION OF YK–7 /71	
Reson Params	None		DUB	Theo Jour	YF 13 240	Feb 71	Malecki+G–WID,THEO CFD EXPT.TBL,GRPH	
				Jour	SNP 13 133	Aug 71	– + ENGL OF YF 13 240.	
Reson Params	2.1+1	1.4+3	KUR	Expt Prog	YFI–12 27	72	Adamchuk+ TABLE OF RESPARS,ABST	+
				Rept	IAE–2108	71	– + S+P–WVE.65 RES,N–WIDS,TBL	
				Prog	INDC(CCP)–30	Dec 72	.PG23,ENGLISH OF YFI–12 27	
	2.1+1	1.4+3		Data	EXFOR40164.003	Jun 73	.2G*REDUCED NEUTRON WIDTH	
Reson Params	2.2+1	1.1+2	BUC	Expt Jour	SCF 24 165	Feb 72	Mateiciuc+ THESIS.SEE REF'RRP 12,15'	
Reson Params	2.1+1	3.0+2	SAC	Expt Conf	71Knoxvill 785	Mar 71	Cauvin+. J ASSIGNMENTS 7 RESON	+
				Conf	72Budapest 34	Aug 72	Lottin+SPIN ASSIGNM OF LEVELS,GRPH	
	2.1+1	3.0+2		Data	EXFOR20126.003	Sep 72	7PTS.J.	
Reson Params	2.1+1	3.5+2	JAE	Expt Jour	JPJ 33 1185	Nov 72	Ohkubo+.LINAC.TOF.WN+WT,SO DERIVED	+
	1.5+2	1.5+2		Conf	68Wash. 789	Mar 68	Asami+ 2G*WN,WT. TRANS.NAT TGT	
Reson Params	+0	+2	BOL	Eval Conf	IAEA–169 3 123	74	Benzi+ AVG G–WID CFD OTHERS+XPT,TABL	
Reson Params	+1	+3	FEI	Eval Rept	YK–8/2 97	Sep 72	Abagyan+ AVG G–WID+D AT BINDNG–E,TBL	
				Rept	INDC(CCP)–39	Jul 74	.PAGE 102.ENGLISH OF YK–8/2 97	
Reson Params	None		DUB	Expt Rept	YFI–17 30	Aug 74	Karzhavina+ SPIN OF NEUT–RES	
Reson Params		1.0+5	ALA	Expt Abst	PC 33 3	77	Hooper+DNG DATA.E LVLS,I,PI.CFD CALC	
Strnth Fnctn	2.2+1	1.0+2	ANL	Expt Jour	PR 102 228	Apr 56	Palmer+ TRNS.AVG 4RES ASSUMED WG	
Strnth Fnctn	+3		BNL	Expt Jour	PRL 1 461	Dec 58	Hughes.FC 0.60+–0.20	
Strnth Fnctn	+3	+5	BOL	Theo Conf	61Vienna 1 179	Aug 61	Benzi+.PPR11,TABLE CFD EXPERIMENT	

51 Antimony 123

Quantity	Energy (ev) Min	Max	Lab	Type	Documentation Ref Vol Page	Date	Author, Comments	Data
Strnth Fnctn		1.1+3	KUR	Expt Jour	YF 8 852	Nov 68	Muradyan+ S0,S1,AVG D VALUES GVN	+
		+3		Conf	68Dubna § 16	Jun 68	Muradjan+ SEE ALSO YFI-6 64	
	2.1+1	1.2+3		Prog	YFI-6 64	68	- + S0,S1 GIVEN. TBP YF	
		1.1+3		Jour	SNP 8 495	May 69	. ENGL OF YF 8 852	
		+3		Rept	INDC-260E	69	. ENGL OF YFI-6 64	
	2.1+1	1.2+3		Data	EXFOR40208.007	Apr 74	.DATA FOR S-WAVE AND P-WAVE GVN	
Strnth Fnctn	-		AUA	Theo Rept	AAEC/E-211	Nov 70	Musgrove. SMOOTHED S0,S1 AND S2 GVN	
Strnth Fnctn	2.1+1	1.4+3	KUR	Expt Prog	YFI-12 27	72	Adamchuk+ S0+S1 VALUES GIVEN,ABST	+
				Rept	IAE-2108	71	- + S0+S1 GIVEN,GRAPH LVL-SPAC	
				Prog	INDC(CCP)-30	Dec 72	.PG 23,ENGLISH OF YFI-12 27	
	2.1+1	1.4+3		Data	EXFOR40164.005	Jun 73	.3 DATA LINES	
Strnth Fnctn	2.4+4		MUA	Theo Jour	IJP 46 114	Mar 72	Chaubey+ P-WAVE.FOR A-SYSTEMIC,GRPH	
Strnth Fnctn	None		AUA	Eval Rept	AAEC/E-277	Mar 73	Musgrove.TBLS EXPTL DATA+BEST VALUES	
Strnth Fnctn	1.8+4	2.8+4	AUW	Expt Jour	NP/A 213 35	Oct 73	Murty+ P-WAVE.FIT TO P N-G AT 25KEV	
	2.5+4			Jour	NP/A 213 35	Oct 73	- + SB-BE.+-5KEV,S,P-WAVE CONTRIB	
Strnth Fnctn	None		KUR	Theo Prog	IAE-2560	75	Adamchuk+.S0-VALUE,TBL	
Lvl Density	-		FEI	Eval Rept	FEI-36	66	Kapchigashev+.TBL OF RELATD QUANTTYS	+
		5.0+4		Jour	YF 4 686	Sep 66	.TABLE.SHORT VERSION OF FEI-36	
	-			Prog	YFI-3 3	66	.ABSTRACT.TABLE LDL+NUCL EXCIT.E	
		5.0+4		Jour	SNP 4 486	67	.ENGLISH OF YF 4.FROM(N,GAMMA).TABLE	
				Prog	INDC-E-140 3	66	.ENGLISH TRANSL OF YFI-3	
Lvl Density	None		AUW	Theo Conf	70Madurai 2 267	Dec 70	Ramamurty+ A-PARAMETER GVN,LANG'S-TH	
Lvl Density	None		BOL	Eval Conf	IAEA-169 3 123	74	Benzi+.LVL DENS PARAM BY XPT,GRPH+TB	
Lvl Density	+1	+3	FEI	Eval Rept	YK-8/2 97	Sep 72	Abagyan+ LVL DENSITY PARAMETER,TBL	
				Rept	INDC(CCP)-39	Jul 74	.PAGE 102.ENGLISH OF YK-8/2 97	
Lvl Density	+0	7.5+2	JAE	ExTh Jour	JPJ 37 581	Sep 74	Ideno.LVL SPACING CORRELATIONS.TBL.	
	1.0+0	7.5+2		Rept	JAERI-M-5490	Nov 73	- .LEVEL SPACING CORRELATIONS.TBL	
	+0	7.5+2		Jour	JPJ 30 620	Mar 71	- + RES SPACING CORRELATION ANAL	

51 Antimony 124

Quantity	Energy (ev) Min	Max	Lab	Type	Documentation Ref Vol Page	Date	Author, Comments	Data
Evaluation	1.0-3	1.5+7	AUA	Eval Rept	AAEC/TM-549	Jun 70	Cook.TOT,EL,INEL,NONEL,CAPT SIGS,NDG	+
				Rept	AAEC/E-214	Jun 71	Bertram+GROUP SIGMAS SAME QUANTS.NDG	
				Rept	AAEC/TM-587	Mar 71	*DESCRIPTION OF LIBRARY	
	1.0-3	1.5+7		Data	AUSTR-DFN 93.	Nov 71	POINT(223) AND GROUP(127) SIGMAS	
Total	1.0-3	1.5+7	AUA	Eval Data	AUSTR-DFN 93.	Nov 71	COOK+POINT(223)+GROUP(127)SIG.CF EVL	+
Elastic	1.0-3	1.5+7	AUA	Eval Data	AUSTR-DFN 93.	Nov 71	COOK+POINT(223)+GROUP(127)SIG.CF EVL	+
Tot Inelastc	5.0+5	1.5+7	AUA	Eval Data	AUSTR-DFN 93.	Nov 71	COOK+POINT(11)+GROUP(127)SIG.CF EVL	+
Nonelastic	1.0-3	1.5+7	AUA	Eval Data	AUSTR-DFN 93.	Nov 71	COOK+POINT(223)+GROUP(127)SIG.CF EVL	+
Res Int Abs	5.0-1		BLN	Expt Abst	DA/B 32 3245	Dec 71	Elgart+PILE ACT.VAL GVN.	
				Diss	ELGART	71	- .SEE FOR DETAILS	
	5.0-1			Data	EXFOR10728.005	May 78	. 1PT.RIA=10,200B.	
Res Int Abs	5.0-1		AUA	Eval Rept	AAEC/TM-619	Sep 72	Clayton.CALC FROM SIG LIBRARY,TABLE	
Res Int Abs	+0	+5	WIN	Revw Conf	IAEA-169 3 163	74	Pope+ DATA FILE CALC CFD XPTAL VALUE	
(n,γ)	Pile		CCP	Expt Jour	AE 2 553	Jun 57	Murin+ ORDER OF 2000 BARNS	
				Jour	JNE 7 265	Sep 58	.TRANSLATION	
				Jour	SJA 2 677	57	.TRANSLATION	
(n,γ)	Maxwl		CRC	Expt Prog	PR-CM-36 7	63	Eastwood.	+
(n,γ)	Pile		CRC	Expt Jour	CJP 44 2956	Nov 66	Courtemanche. 6.5+-1.5B	+
	Pile			Data	EXFOR11990.002	Jun 76	. 1 PT.	
(n,γ)	1.0-3	1.5+7	AUA	Eval Data	AUSTR-DFN 93.	Nov 71	COOK+POINT(223)+GROUP(127)SIG.CF EVL	+
(n,γ)	Maxwl		BLN	Expt Abst	DA/B 32 3245	Dec 71	Elgart+PILE ACT.VAL GVN.	+
				Diss	ELGART	71	- .SEE FOR DETAILS	
	Maxwl			Data	EXFOR10728.004	May 78	. 1PT.SIG=2990B.	
(n,γ)	Pile		CRC	Eval Rept	AECL-3037 1	Jan 72	Walker.RECOMMENDED SIG,DETAILED TBL	
(n,γ)	2.5-2		AUA	Eval Rept	AAEC/TM-619	Sep 72	Clayton.CALC FROM SIG LIBRARY,TABLE	
(n,γ)	Fiss		WIN	Revw Conf	IAEA-169 3 137	74	Dean. POINT DATA AVG OVER STAND-SPC	
	Maxwl	Fiss		Conf	IAEA-169 3 163	74	Pope+ MAXW+FIS-SPEC AVG DATA CFD XPT	
Spect (n,γ)	Maxwl		LAS	Expt Abst	BAP 18 98	Jan 73	Shera+ GE(CI) DET. NO DATA GIVEN.	
(n,p)	Maxwl		IFU	Theo Rept	ICD-4 20	67	Dadakina+ PENETR COEFF CALC,TABLE	
Reson Params	-		AUA	Theo Rept	AAEC/E-211	Nov 70	Musgrove. CALCULTD D+GAM WIDTH GIVEN	
Strnth Fnctn	-		AUA	Theo Rept	AAEC/E-211	Nov 70	Musgrove. SMOOTHED S0,S1 AND S2 GIVN	
Lvl Density	1.4+7		HAM	Expt Jour	NP/A 186 65	May 72	Bormann+ A-PARAM,S CUTOFF. CS,I(N,A)	
Lvl Density	None		MUN	Theo Jour	NP/A 217 269	Dec 73	Dilg+ A,DELTA. BACK SHIFTED FERMIGAS	
Lvl Density	None		COP	Theo Jour	NP/A 222 493	Apr 74	Dossing+COLL ROTAT.SPAC. ACCUR ESTIM	

51 Antimony 125

Quantity	Energy (ev) Min	Max	Lab	Type	Documentation Ref Vol Page	Date	Author, Comments	Data
Evaluation	1.0−3	1.5+7	AUA	Eval	Rept AAEC/TM−549	Jun 70	Cook.TOT,EL,INEL,NONEL,CAPT SIGS,NDG	+
					Rept AAEC/E−214	Jun 71	Bertram+GROUP SIGMAS SAME QUANTS.NDG	
					Rept AAEC/TM−587	Mar 71	*DESCRIPTION OF LIBRARY	
	1.0−3	1.5+7		Data	AUSTR−DFN 94.	Nov 71	POINT(223) AND GROUP(127) SIGMAS	
Total	1.0−3	1.5+7	AUA Eval	Data	AUSTR−DFN 94.	Nov 71	COOK+POINT(223)+GROUP(127)SIG.CF EVL	+
Elastic	1.0−3	1.5+7	AUA Eval	Data	AUSTR−DFN 94.	Nov 71	COOK+POINT(223)+GROUP(127)SIG.CF EVL	+
Tot Inelastc	5.0+5	1.5+7	AUA Eval	Data	AUSTR−DFN 94.	Nov 71	COOK+POINT(11)+GROUP(127)SIG.CF EVL	+
Nonelastic	1.0−3	1.5+7	AUA Eval	Data	AUSTR−DFN 94.	Nov 71	COOK+POINT(223)+GROUP(127)SIG.CF EVL	+
Absorption	1.0−4	1.0+7	JUL Eval	Rept	JUEL−678−RG	Jul 70	Liu. EVALUATION+CALC,GRPH,FN OF E	
Res Int Abs	5.0−1		AUA Eval	Rept	AAEC/TM−619	Sep 72	Clayton.CALC FROM SIG LIBRARY,TABLE	
Res Int Abs	5.5−1	+6	SAC Revw	Conf	IAEA−169 1 235	74	Ribon.CAPTURE,STATUS CFD REQUEST,TBL	
Res Int Abs	+0	+5	WIN Revw	Conf	IAEA−169 3 163	74	Pope+ 1 VALUE WITH AUSTRAL DATA FILE	
(n,γ)	1.0+3	1.0+7	BOL Eval	Conf	66Paris 1 537	Oct 66	Benzi.STATIST MODEL+XPTAL MEAN D,WG	
(n,γ)	1.0−3	1.5+7	AUA Eval	Data	AUSTR−DFN 94.	Nov 71	COOK+POINT(223)+GROUP(127)SIG.CF EVL	+
(n,γ)	Pile		CRC Eval	Rept	AECL−3037 1	Jan 72	Walker.SIG ESTIMATED ACCORDING Z,A	
(n,γ)	2.5−2		AUA Eval	Rept	AAEC/TM−619	Sep 72	Clayton.CALC FROM SIG LIBRARY,TABLE	
(n,γ)	2.5−2	3.0+4	SAC Revw	Conf	IAEA−169 1 235	74	Ribon.STATUS SIG CFD REQUESTS,TBL	
(n,γ)	Fiss		WIN Revw	Conf	IAEA−169 3 137	74	Dean. POINT DATA AVG OVER STAND −SPC	
	Maxwl	Fiss		Conf	IAEA−169 3 163	74	Pope+ MAXW+FIS−SPEC AVG EVAL DATA	
Reson Params		1.0+6	AUA Theo	Jour	AUJ 20 477	Oct 67	Cook. TBL OF AVG LVL SPACING D,L=0,1	
Reson Params	−		AUA Theo	Rept	AAEC/E−211	Nov 70	Musgrove. CALCULTD D+GAM WIDTH GIVEN	
Strnth Fnctn	−		AUA Theo	Rept	AAEC/E−211	Nov 70	Musgrove. SMOOTHED S0,S1 AND S2 GIVN	

51 Antimony 126

Quantity	Energy (ev) Min	Max	Lab	Type	Documentation Ref Vol Page	Date	Author, Comments	Data
Evaluation	1.0−3	1.5+7	AUA	Eval	Rept AAEC/TM−549	Jun 70	Cook.TOT,EL,INEL,NONEL,CAPT SIGS,NDG	+
					Rept AAEC/E−214	Jun 71	Bertram+GROUP SIGMAS SAME QUANTS.NDG	
					Rept AAEC/TM−587	Mar 71	*DESCRIPTION OF LIBRARY	
	1.0−3	1.5+7		Data	AUSTR−DFN 95.	Nov 71	POINT(223) AND GROUP(127) SIGMAS	
Total	1.0−3	1.5+7	AUA Eval	Data	AUSTR−DFN 95.	Nov 71	COOK+POINT(223)+GROUP(127)SIG.CF EVL	+
Elastic	1.0−3	1.5+7	AUA Eval	Data	AUSTR−DFN 95.	Nov 71	COOK+POINT(223)+GROUP(127)SIG.CF EVL	+
Tot Inelastc	5.0+5	1.5+7	AUA Eval	Data	AUSTR−DFN 95.	Nov 71	COOK+POINT(11)+GROUP(127)SIG.CF EVL	+
Nonelastic	1.0−3	1.5+7	AUA Eval	Data	AUSTR−DFN 95.	Nov 71	COOK+POINT(223)+GROUP(127)SIG.CF EVL	+
Res Int Abs	5.0−1		AUA Eval	Rept	AAEC/TM−619	Sep 72	Clayton.CALC FROM SIG LIBRARY,TABLE	
Res Int Abs	+0	+5	WIN Revw	Conf	IAEA−169 3 163	74	Pope+ 1 VALUE WITH AUSTRAL DATA FILE	
(n,γ)	1.0−3	1.5+7	AUA Eval	Data	AUSTR−DFN 95.	Nov 71	COOK+POINT(223)+GROUP(127)SIG.CF EVL	+
(n,γ)	Pile		CRC Eval	Rept	AECL−3037 1	Jan 72	Walker.SIG ESTIMATED ACCORDING Z,A	
(n,γ)	2.5−2		AUA Eval	Rept	AAEC/TM−619	Sep 72	Clayton.CALC FROM SIG LIBRARY,TABLE	
(n,γ)	2.5−2		SGA Eval	Conf	73Paris 1 233	Mar 73	Eder+ INTERPOLATED FROM CALC SIG,TBL	
					Rept SGAE−PH−141	Feb 73	.SAME AS 73PARIS,POINT SIG FROM COOK	
(n,γ)	Maxwl	Fiss	WIN Revw	Conf	IAEA−169 3 163	74	Pope+ MAXW+FIS−SPEC AVG EVAL DATA	
	Fiss			Conf	IAEA−169 3 137	74	Dean. POINT DATA AVG OVER STAND −SPC	
Reson Params	−		AUA Theo	Rept	AAEC/E−211	Nov 70	Musgrove. CALCULTD D+GAM WIDTH GIVEN	
Strnth Fnctn	−		AUA Theo	Rept	AAEC/E−211	Nov 70	Musgrove. SMOOTHED S0,S1 AND S2 GIVN	

51 Antimony 127

Quantity	Energy (ev) Min	Max	Lab	Type	Documentation Ref Vol Page	Date	Author, Comments	Data
Evaluation	1.0−3	1.5+7	AUA	Eval	Rept AAEC/TM−549	Jun 70	Cook.TOT,EL,INEL,NONEL,CAPT SIGS,NDG	+
					Rept AAEC/E−214	Jun 71	Bertram+GROUP SIGMAS SAME QUANTS.NDG	
					Rept AAEC/TM−587	Mar 71	*DESCRIPTION OF LIBRARY	
	1.0−3	1.5+7		Data	AUSTR−DFN 96.	Nov 71	POINT(223) AND GROUP(127) SIGMAS	
Total	1.0−3	1.5+7	AUA Eval	Data	AUSTR−DFN 96.	Nov 71	COOK+POINT(223)+GROUP(127)SIG.CF EVL	+
Elastic	1.0−3	1.5+7	AUA Eval	Data	AUSTR−DFN 96.	Nov 71	COOK+POINT(223)+GROUP(127)SIG.CF EVL	+
Tot Inelastc	5.0+5	1.5+7	AUA Eval	Data	AUSTR−DFN 96.	Nov 71	COOK+POINT(11)+GROUP(127)SIG.CF EVL	+
Nonelastic	1.0−3	1.5+7	AUA Eval	Data	AUSTR−DFN 96.	Nov 71	COOK+POINT(223)+GROUP(127)SIG.CF EVL	+
Res Int Abs	5.0−1		AUA Eval	Rept	AAEC/TM−619	Sep 72	Clayton.CALC FROM SIG LIBRARY,TABLE	
Res Int Abs	+0	+5	WIN Revw	Conf	IAEA−169 3 163	74	Pope+ 1 VALUE WITH AUSTRAL DATA FILE	
(n,γ)	1.0−3	1.5+7	AUA Eval	Data	AUSTR−DFN 96.	Nov 71	COOK+POINT(223)+GROUP(127)SIG.CF EVL	+
(n,γ)	Pile		CRC Eval	Rept	AECL−3037 1	Jan 72	Walker.SIG ESTIMATED ACCORDING Z,A	
(n,γ)	2.5−2		AUA Eval	Rept	AAEC/TM−619	Sep 72	Clayton.CALC FROM SIG LIBRARY,TABLE	
(n,γ)	2.5−2		SGA Eval	Conf	73Paris 1 233	Mar 73	Eder+ INTERPOLATED FROM CALC SIG,TBL	
					Rept SGAE−PH−141	Feb 73	.SAME AS 73PARIS,POINT SIG FROM COOK	

51 Antimony 127

Quantity	Energy (ev) Min	Max	Lab	Type	Documentation Ref Vol Page	Author, Comments Date	Data
(n,γ)	Fiss		WIN Revw	Conf	IAEA – 169 3 137	74 Dean. POINT DATA AVG OVER STAND – SPC	
	Maxwl	Fiss		Conf	IAEA – 169 3 163	74 Pope+ MAXW+FIS – SPEC AVG EVAL DATA	
Reson Params	–		AUA Theo	Rept	AAEC/E – 211	Nov 70 Musgrove. CALCULTD D+GAM WIDTH GIVEN	
Strnth Fnctn	–		AUA Theo	Rept	AAEC/E – 211	Nov 70 Musgrove. SMOOTHED S0,S1 AND S2 GIVN	

51 Antimony 128

Quantity	Energy (ev) Min	Max	Lab	Type	Documentation Ref Vol Page	Author, Comments Date	Data
Evaluation	1.0 – 3	1.5+7	AUA Eval	Rept	AAEC/TM – 549	Jun 70 Cook.TOT,EL,INEL,NONEL,CAPT SIGS,NDG	+
				Rept	AAEC/E – 214	Jun 71 Bertram+GROUP SIGMAS SAME QUANTS.NDG	
				Rept	AAEC/TM – 587	Mar 71 *DESCRIPTION OF LIBRARY	
	1.0 – 3	1.5+7		Data	AUSTR – DFN 97.	Nov 71 POINT(223) AND GROUP(127) SIGMAS	
Total	1.0 – 3	1.5+7	AUA Eval	Data	AUSTR – DFN 97.	Nov 71 COOK+POINT(223)+GROUP(127)SIG.CF EVL	+
Elastic	1.0 – 3	1.5+7	AUA Eval	Data	AUSTR – DFN 97.	Nov 71 COOK+POINT(223)+GROUP(127)SIG.CF EVL	+
Tot Inelastc	5.0+5	1.5+7	AUA Eval	Data	AUSTR – DFN 97.	Nov 71 COOK+POINT(11)+GROUP(127)SIG.CF EVL	+
Nonelastic	1.0 – 3	1.5+7	AUA Eval	Data	AUSTR – DFN 97.	Nov 71 COOK+POINT(223)+GROUP(127)SIG.CF EVL	+
Res Int Abs	5.0 – 1		AUA Eval	Rept	AAEC/TM – 619	Sep 72 Clayton.CALC FROM SIG LIBRARY,TABLE	
Res Int Abs	+0	+5	WIN Revw	Conf	IAEA – 169 3 163	74 Pope+ 1 VALUE WITH AUSTRAL DATA FILE	
(n,γ)	1.0 – 3	1.5+7	AUA Eval	Data	AUSTR – DFN 97.	Nov 71 COOK+POINT(223)+GROUP(127)SIG.CF EVL	+
(n,γ)	2.5 – 2		AUA Eval	Rept	AAEC/TM – 619	Sep 72 Clayton.CALC FROM SIG LIBRARY,TABLE	
(n,γ)	Fiss		WIN Revw	Conf	IAEA – 169 3 137	74 Dean. POINT DATA AVG OVER STAND – SPC	
	Maxwl	Fiss		Conf	IAEA – 169 3 163	74 Pope+ MAXW+FIS – SPEC AVG EVAL DATA	
Reson Params	–		AUA Theo	Rept	AAEC/E – 211	Nov 70 Musgrove. CALCULTD D+GAM WIDTH GIVEN	
Strnth Fnctn	–		AUA Theo	Rept	AAEC/E – 211	Nov 70 Musgrove. SMOOTHED S0,S1 AND S2 GIVN	

51 Antimony 129

Quantity	Energy (ev) Min	Max	Lab	Type	Documentation Ref Vol Page	Author, Comments Date	Data
Reson Params	–		AUA Theo	Rept	AAEC/E – 211	Nov 70 Musgrove. CALCULTD D+GAM WIDTH GIVEN	
Strnth Fnctn	–		AUA Theo	Rept	AAEC/E – 211	Nov 70 Musgrove. SMOOTHED S0,S1 AND S2 GIVN	

52 Tellurium

Quantity	Energy (ev) Min	Max	Lab	Type	Documentation Ref Vol Page	Author, Comments Date	Data
Evaluation	5.0+5	1.5+7	LRL	Eval	Rept UCRL-5351	Nov 58 Howerton+ CURVES	
Total	Maxwl		COL	Expt	Jour PR 48 265	Aug 35 Dunning+ IONCH,TRANS,RA-BE/PARAFIN N	
Total	6.0-2	2.0+3	COL	Expt	Jour PR 83 660	Aug 51 Heindl+ THIN FILM TRANSM.5 CLEAR RES	+
	8.3-2	1.8+4			Data EXFOR11991.002	Jun 76 . 72 PTS.	
Total	1.4+7		LAS	Expt	Jour PR 88 562	Nov 52 Coon+	+
	1.4+7				Data EXFOR11056.042	Jun 76 . 1 PT.	
Total	9.0+4	3.0+6	WIS	Expt	Jour PR 89 1271	Mar 53 Walt+. GRAPH. ZR-T AND LI TARGETS	+
	9.0+4	3.0+6			Data EXFOR11746.006	Jun 76 . 20 PTS.	
Total	2.8+6	1.3+7	LAS	Expt	Jour PR 94 1678	Jun 54 Nereson+ RSLN 10PC	+
	2.8+6	1.3+7			Data EXFOR11308.019	Jun 76 . 30 PTS.	
Total	1.1+1	4.0+2	MTR	Expt	Priv SIMPSON	Jul 56 Simpson.	+
	1.1+1	4.0+2			Data EXFOR11996.002	Jun 76 . 191 PTS.	
Total	6.0+4	1.8+7	LAS	Theo	Rept LA-2099	Dec 56 Beyster+,OPTMDL CALC CFD EXPT,CURVE	
Total	1.0+3	3.2+4	HAR	Expt	Jour PPSA 70 51	Jan 57 Gayther+ FC THICK SAMPLE,AVSIG CF TH	
Total	7.0-1	+2	COL	Expt	Rept CU-192	Jun 59 Heindl. THESIS, TOF, 5 RES	
Total	3.7+6		BAR	Expt	Jour PR 125 331	Jan 62 Kent+400KEV SPREAD CONT PR114 1563.	+
	3.7+6				Data EXFOR11617.034	Jun 76 . 1 PT.	
Total	2.7-3	9.5-3	BUC	Expt	Jour AE 12 514	Jun 62 Bally+ CRYST SPEC, GRAPH, CFD TH	+
					Rept IFA-FN-23	Oct 62 . IN RUSSIAN	
					Jour RSI 32 297	Mar 61 . DESCR OF MONOCHROMATOR	
					Jour RSI 31 640	Jun 60 . DESCR OF CRYST SPECTROM	
					Jour EAF 12 6 80	Oct 63 .FRNCH OF AE 12 514	
					Jour SJA 12 546	Jan 63 . ENGL OF AE 12 514	
	2.7-3	9.5-3			Data EXFOR30205.005	Nov 72 19 DATA POINTS, DATA FROM PRIV COM	
Total		5.0+3	ANL	Expt	Prog WASH-1053 11	Oct 64 Cote.FC,NDG. TO FIND RES PAR 5 ISOTP	
Total	1.4+7		CCP	ExTh	Jour IZV 31 217	Feb 67 Dukarevich+.TBL,CURVES,CFD OPTMDL TH	
					Jour BAS 31 197	Feb 67 TRANSLATN.*	
Total	1.4+7		FTI	Expt	Jour NP/A 92 433	Feb 67 Dukarevich+ FROM ISOTOPES+DIRECT	
Total	6.0+0	5.0+3	COL	Expt	Jour PR 166 1234	Feb 67 Wynchank+ TOF 0.5NSEC/M RESOL CURVES	+
	6.1+0	5.2+3			Data EXFOR11913.015	Jun 76 . 9421 PTS.	
Total	1.4+7		OHO	Theo	Jour NC/B 53 2 363	Feb 68 Cassola+. OPTMOD CALC CFD EXPT.	
Total	1.4+7		DEB	Expt	Jour AHP 28 87	Mar 70 Angeli+ TRANSM,SHORT DESC,THEORY,TBL	+
	1.4+7				Data EXFOR30113.017	Feb 71 VALUE AT 14.5 MEV	
Total	2.5+6	1.5+7	BNW	Expt	Jour PR/C 3 576	Feb 71 Foster+,TRANS,CURVS,CFD OTHERS+TH	+
					Jour NIM 36 1	Sep 65 .EXPT DETAILS	
	2.3+6	1.5+7			Data EXFOR10047.057	Aug 73 . 248PTS.	
Total	2.1+2	6.2+3	SAC	Expt	Priv TELLIER	Sep 71 Tellier+.	+
	2.1+2	6.2+3			Data EXFOR20122.002	Sep 72 13105PTS.	
Total	2.7+3		MUN	Expt	Prog EANDC(E)150U	Oct 72 Dilg+ AVERAGE TOT XSECT+S0	+
					Conf 71Albany 327	Aug 71 - +TRNS.AVG CS GVN.31 ELEMENT GRP	
	2.7+3				Data EXFOR20583.009	Jun 76 1PNT.	
Total	1.3+7	1.5+7	DEB	Eval	Rept IAEA-153 173	73 Boedy+ MOST PROBABLE VAL OF SIG,TBL	
					Jour AHP 30 115	Oct 71 Angeli+ AVG SIG,CFD CALC.TBLS.GRAPH	
Total	1.0+6	2.0+6	RAM	Expt	Prog INDC(SEC)-50	Jan 76 Hussain+ P8,VERY BRIEF. CFD OTH,NDG	
Total	4.0-1	1.0+1	BNL	Expt	Abst PR 94 790	May 54 Foote. ABST WA3	+
	4.0-1	1.0+1			Data EXFOR12000.003	Jun 76 . 68 PTS.	
Elastic	1.0+6		WIS	Expt	Jour PR 93 1062	Mar 54 Walt+	+
	1.0+6				Data EXFOR11637.050	Jun 76 . 1 PT.	
Elastic	2.5-2		COL	Expt	Jour RSI 27 620	Aug 56 Heindl+	+
	2.5-2				Data EXFOR11786.003	Jun 76 . 1 PT.	
Elastic	1.0+6	1.4+7	AGN	Eval	Rept TID-21629	Dec 64 Perkins+ CALC FROM BNL325,UCRL5573	
Elastic	3.0+5	8.0+5	IFU	ExTh	Jour AE 20 8	Jan 66 Korzh+ SUMMARY OF SEVERAL YRS WORK	+
					Jour AE 16 260	64 .	
					Jour UFZ 8 389	63 .650KEV SEE P1323.300KEV SEE P1389	
					Jour SJA 20 8	Jul 66 .ENGLISH TRANSL OF AE 20 8 1/66	
Elastic	3.0+5	1.5+6	ANL	Expt	Jour NP/A 93 609	Mar 67 Smith+ INTEG ANG DIST	+
	3.3+5	1.5+6			Rept ANL-7274	Nov 66 - +TBLS OF DATA PTS.	
	3.3+5	1.5+6			Data EXFOR10418.010	Aug 76 . 53 PTS. CS DATA.	
Elastic	1.4+7		OHO	Theo	Jour NC/B 53 2 363	Feb 68 Cassola+. OPTMOD CALC CFD EXPT.	
Elastic	1.5-3		MUN	expt	Jour ZN/A 26 391	Mar 71 Koester+ SMALL ANGLE SCT.COH AMPLTDE	
	2.5-2				Data EXFOR20758.007	Jun 78 1PNT.COH.SC.AMP.	
Elastic	7.8-2		RIS	Expt	Jour ACS 27 85	Jan 73 Lindqvist+ COH.SC.LENGTH=5.80+-.05F	
Elastic	1.1+0	3.4+0	BNL	Expt	Abst PR 94 790	May 54 Foote. ABST WA3	+
	1.1+0	3.4+0			Data EXFOR12000.004	Jun 76 . 24 PTS.	
Diff Elastic	1.0+6		WIS	Expt	Jour PR 93 1062	Mar 54 Walt+ HE COUNTER 30-150DEG LAB CURVE	+
	1.0+6				Data EXFOR11637.052	Jun 76 . 5 PTS.	
Diff Elastic	1.0+5	1.8+7	LAS	Theo	Rept LA-2099	Dec 56 Beyster+,21ES,OPTMDL CALC CFD EXPT	

52 Tellurium

Quantity	Energy (ev) Min	Max	Lab	Type	Documentation Ref Vol Page	Author, Comments Date	Data
Diff Elastic	2.9+6		IFU Expt	Jour	UFZ 5 704	Oct 60 Strizhak+ IONIZ-CHAMBR,GRAPH SIG(ANG	+
Diff Elastic	1.4+7		IFU Expt	Jour	ZET 41 313	Aug 61 Strizhak+ SCINT-COUNTER,GRPH SIG(ANG	+
					Jour JET 14 225	Feb 62 TRANSLATN.*	
Diff Elastic	1.0+6	1.4+7	AGN Eval	Rept	TID-21629	Dec 64 Perkins+ LEG COEF CALC FROM OTHERS	
Diff Elastic	8.0+5		IFU Theo	Jour	UFZ 10 6 586	Jun 65 Korzh.OPTMDL GRAPH SIG,CFD XPT	
					Jour IZV 29 862	May 65 .	
Diff Elastic	8.0+5		IFU Theo	Conf	65Antwerp § 193	Jul 65 Pasechnic+. OPT.MOD.PARAMETERS	
Diff Elastic	1.0+6		LAS Theo	Prog	WASH-1064 84	Oct 65 Rosen+, OPTMDL+ CPD ELST CFD WIS XPT	
Diff Elastic	5.0+5	8.0+5	IFU Expt	Jour	AE 20 8	Jan 66 Korzh+ SUMMARY OF SEVERAL YEARS WORK	
					Jour AE 16 260	Mar 64 - + SPH GEOM,30-140 DEGREES	
					Jour UFZ 8 389	63 - +	
					Jour UFZ 8 1323	63 - + AT 650 KEV	
					Jour SJA 16 312	Mar 64 . ENGL OF AE 16 260	
Diff Elastic	3.2+6		BCM Expt	Jour	NP 89 154	Dec 66 Becker+ 12 ANGLES GRAPH CFD OPTMDL	+
	3.2+6			Data	EXFOR11511.027	Jun 76 . 13 PTS.	
Diff Elastic	3.0+5	1.5+6	ANL Expt	Jour	NP/A 93 609	Mar 67 Smith+ TOF, CFD OPTMDL	+
	3.3+5	1.5+6		Rept	ANL-7274	Nov 66 - +TBLS OF DATA PTS.	
	3.3+5	1.5+6		Data	EXFOR10418.011	Aug 76 265PTS.LEG COEFS.	
Diff Elastic	1.0+6	1.4+7	AI Eval	Rept	NAA-SR-11980	Apr 67 Campbell+ LEG COEFS TBL+CURVS C-MSYS	
Diff Elastic	2.8+6		IFU Theo	Jour	UFZ 13 152	Jan 68 Strizhak+ GRPH SIG(ANG),OPTMOD CALC	
					Jour UPJ 13 106	Jul 68 TRANSLATN.*	
Diff Elastic	3.0+5		IFU Expt	Rept	BNL-TR-232	Sep 68 Korzh+ ANGDIS(30-140DEG),GRPH+TBL	
	6.5+5			Rept	BNL-TR-242	Sep 68 - + ANGDIST(30-140DEG),GRAPH+TABL	
Diff Elastic	3.2+6		SCU Theo	Rept	ICD-6 236	69 Averyanov+CALC ANGDIST CFD EXPT,GRPH	
Diff Elastic	1.0+3	4.0+4	DUB Expt	Jour	YF 11 1152	Jun 70 Samosvat.LEGENDRECOEF(E) GRPH,OPTMOD	+
				Rept	JINR-P3-4724	Oct 69 - . ASSYMMETRY,0+180DEG ANG	
				Jour	SNP 11 639	Dec 70 - . ENGL OF YF 11 1152.	
	1.6+3	3.9+4		Data	EXFOR40285.008	Apr 75 .LEGEND-COEF FOR 10 ES GVN	
Diff Elastic	1.5+6		IJI Expt	Conf	72Kiev 2 4	Jan 72 Korzh+ ABST,NDG.OPTMOD,20-145DEG	
Diff Elastic	3.2+6		AMS Theo	Jour	NP/A 222 93	Apr 74 Zijp+ LEG.COEFF COMPOUND ELASTIC.H-F	
Diff Elastic	6.7+5	1.1+6	ANL Expt	Priv	COX	Apr 66 COX.	+
	6.7+5	1.1+6		Data	EXFOR11519.012	Jun 76 . 424 PTS.	
Polarization	3.8+5	9.8+5	WIS ExTh	Jour	NP 6 177	Mar 58 Clement+. POLARIZATION. CFD OPT MDL	+
			Expt	Rept	AECU-3628	57 - +.LI7(P,N) SOURCE. 3ANGLES.	
Polarization	1.5+6		DKE Expt	Rept	TID-19051	62 Olness+ TOF 51.5DEG POLARIZ MEASD	
Polarization	1.5+6		IJI Expt	Conf	72Kiev 2 4	Jan 72 Korzh+ ABST,NDG.OPTMOD	
Polarization	3.2+6		AMS Expt	Jour	NP/A 222 93	Apr 74 Zijp+ TABLES,GRAPHS. CFD NON-SPH POT	+
				Conf	75Zurich 189	Aug 75 - + GRPH OF DATA IN REVIEW.	
				Conf	72Budapest 170	Aug 72 - + POLARIZTN,EXPT CFD OPTMOD,GRP	
	3.2+6			Data	EXFOR20777.016	Apr 78 4PTS.	
Potntal Scat	1.2+2	3.0+2	ANL Expt	Jour	PR 76 100	Jul 49 Hibdon+1/10 ERSLN TRNSM MN CO SCATT	+
	1.2+2	3.0+2		Data	EXFOR11261.028	Jun 76 . 2 PTS.	
Potntal Scat	+4		HAR Expt	Jour	PPSA 70 51	Jan 57 Gayther+ FROM AVG SIGTOT. FC TRANSM	
Potntal Scat	+0	+2	BNL Expt	Rept	ORNL-2309	Jun 57 Seth+ 4.9+-.3B	
Potntal Scat	3.0-2	5.0+0	COL Expt	Rept	CU-192	Jun 59 Heindl. 4.5+-.1B FROM CURVE	
Tot Inelastc	2.5+6		IFU Expt	Jour	JET 4 769	Jun 57 .ENGLISH OF ZET 31 907	
				Jour	ZET 31 907	Nov 56 Strizhak. SPHERE METHOD,TABLE	
Tot Inelastc	8.0+5	4.0+6	IFU Expt	Prog	INDSWG-126 22	66 Pasechnik. AT 5 ES, TBP IN AE	
	2.5+6	1.4+7		Conf	55Geneva 2 3	Aug 55 - . INTEGR SIGMA,2ES,TABLE	
Tot Inelastc	1.1+6	1.6+6	FEI Comp	Rept	ICD-4 57	67 Sluchevskaja.SELECTIV COMPIL ,TABLE	
Diff Inelast	2.5+6		LAS Expt	Jour	PR 103 343	Jul 56 Cranberg+,TOF 90DEG 55MB .72MEV LVL	+
	2.5+6			Data	EXFOR11396.023	Jun 76 . 1 PT.	
Diff Inelast	6.0+6		DKE Expt	Rept	AD-299005	62 Seth+,NUCL TEMP+FERMI LVL DENS COEFF	
Diff Inelast	1.4+7		BAS Expt	Rept	PL 5 202	Jul 63 Huber+ GRPH OF INELASTIC N SPECT.	
				Jour	HPA 36 1059	Dec 59 - +.T=0.96MEV	
Diff Inelast	4.0+6	6.5+6	DKE Expt	Abst	DA 24 4248	Apr 64 Buccino.ANGDIST.TOF.NUCL T.LVL DEN.	
Diff Inelast	1.4+7		FEI Expt	Rept	FEI-4	65 Anufrienko+ SPEC OF SECONDARY NEUTNS	+
	1.4+7			Data	EXFOR40133.021	Feb 73 N-SPECTRUM AT 92 DEG	
Diff Inelast	3.0+5	8.0+5	IFU Expt	Prog	INDSWG-126 22	66 Pasechnik. AT 3 ES, TBP IN AE	
Diff Inelast	1.4+7		FEI Expt	Rept	FEI-39	Jan 66 Sal'Nikov+TOF SPECT,RING GEOM,E-SPEC	
Diff Inelast	3.0+5	1.5+6	ANL Expt	Jour	NP/A 93 609	Mar 67 Smith+ TOF, CFD OPTMDL + H-F	+
	1.1+6	1.5+6		Rept	ANL-7274	Nov 66 - +TBLS OF DATA PTS.	
	1.1+6	1.5+6		Data	EXFOR10418.012	Aug 76 13PTS.UNRESOLVED LVLS WITH 3 Q VALS	
Diff Inelast	1.4+7		CCP Theo	Jour	UFZ 14 342	Feb 69 Strizhak+ ANGDIST,OPTMOD FIT,GRAPH	
Thermal Scat	Maxwl		COL Expt	Jour	PR 83 660	51 Heindl.	+
	Maxwl			Data	EXFOR11991.004	Jun 76 . 1 PT. INCOHERENT SCAT.	

52 Tellurium

Quantity	Energy (ev) Min	Max	Lab	Type	Documentation Ref Vol Page	Date	Author, Comments	Data
Thermal Scat	5.0−2		JUL	Expt Jour	PSS 19 721	Feb 67	Axmann+ TOF. SCAT FROM POLYCRYSTAL	
				Rept	JUEL−479−NP	67	− + REPRINT OF PSS 19 721	
Thermal Scat	Cold		SAC	Expt Jour	PL/A 54 209	Sep 75	Tourand.DIFFRACTION BY LIQUID TE.	
Thermal Scat	1.0−4	1.0+3	MUN	Revw Jour	EEN 80 1	77	Koester. SCAT LENGTH,FREE+INCOH SIG	
Scattering	Maxwl		CAV	Expt Jour	PRSA 162 127	Sep 37	Goldhaber+. 5.3B REL 4.83B FOR C	
Scattering	6.0+4	1.8+6	ANL	Expt Jour	PR 107 1077	Aug 57	Langsdorf+,LEGENDRE COEFS CURVES	+
				Rept	ANL−5567	Oct 61	.REVISED DATA	
	6.0+4	1.8+6		Data	EXFOR11224.053	Jun 76	. 110 PTS, DSIG	
	6.0+4	1.8+6		Data	EXFOR11224.052	Jun 76	. 22 PTS, SIG	
Nonelastic	1.0+6		WIS	Expt Jour	PR 93 1062	Mar 54	Walt +	+
	1.0+6			Data	EXFOR11637.051	Jun 76	. 1 PT.	
Nonelastic	2.5+6	1.4+7	IFU	Expt Conf	55Geneva 2 3	Aug 55	PASECHNIK SPH MEAS SPEC OF SCT N	+
				Jour	UFZ 3 185	58	.	
				Conf	56Kiev 102	56	.	
Nonelastic	6.0+4	1.8+7	LAS	Theo Rept	LA−2099	Dec 56	Beyster+,OPTMDL CALC CFD EXPT,CURVE	
Nonelastic	1.4+7		IFU	Expt Jour	AE 2 68	Jan 57	Strizhak.SPHERE TRANSMISS 2.00+ − 10B	+
				Jour	JNE 5 253	Nov 57	TRANSLATN.*	
				Jour	SJA 2 72	57	TRANSLATN.*	
Nonelastic	8.0+5	3.6+6	IFU	Expt Jour	AE 20 8	Jan 66	Korzh+ SUMMARY OF SEVERAL YRS WORK	+
				ExTh Jour	UFZ 9 929	May 64	.	
				Expt Jour	AE 16 207	64	.	
				ExTh Jour	SJA 20 8	Jul 66	.ENGLISH TRANSL OF AE 20 8 1/66	
				Rept	INDSWG−101 112	65	.=UFZ9.ENGL NO GRPHS.RUSS LARGER GPH	
Absorption	Maxwl		HAR	Rept	AERE−R/R−2516	Mar 58	Jowitt+ PILE OSC.REL BORON.293DEGK.	
Absorption	2.5−2		HAR	Expt Jour	JNEA 12 32	May 60	Tattersall+ PILE OSCILLATOR.	+
	2.5−2			Data	EXFOR20638.036	Jul 76	1PNT.SIGMA.	
Absorption	2.4+4		FEI	Expt Jour	AE 8 549	Jun 60	Belanova.VAL FOR 3ES,SPHERE TRNSMISS	
				Jour	SJA 8 462	Jul 61	TRANSLATN.*GERMAN KE4 147 2/61	
Absorption	Maxwl		TOK	Expt Priv	OHNISHI+	Jul 68	TE(129G)/TE(131G) =0.68 PM 0.10	
Res Int Abs	None		ORL	Revw Conf	55Geneva 5 96	Aug 55	Macklin+.TABLE,EXPT CFD THEORY,P833	
Res Int Abs	−		CCP	Expt Jour	AE 3 507	Dec 57	Klimentov+.EPI CD REACTIVITY REL LI	+
				Jour	JNE 9 20	Jun 59	TRANSLATN.*	
				Jour	SJA 3 1387	57	TRANSLATN.*	
Res Int Abs	5.0−1		HAR	Expt Jour	JNE 12 32	May 60	Tattersall+ ABOVE 1/V,PILE OSC,ONE	+
				Rept	AERE−R−2887	Aug 59	−. PILE OSC.REL BORON	
	6.7−1			Data	EXFOR20638.037	Jul 76	1PNT.	
Res Int Abs	5.5−1		MUN	Comp Jour	JRC 29 175	Jan 76	Gryntakis+, 3 VALUES+STANDARDS GIVEN	
(n,γ)	2.2+5		PCF	Expt Jour	NAT 142 392	Aug 38	Halban+ ACT CS GIVEN	
(n,γ)	Pile		ANL	Expt Jour	PR 80 342	Nov 50	Harris+.PILE OSC.REL TO BORON.	
	Pile			Data	EXFOR11528.031	Jun 76	. 1 PT.	
(n,γ)	2.5−2		COL	Expt Jour	PR 83 660	Aug 51	Heindl+ FROM EXTRAPOL TRANSM CURVE	+
	2.5−2			Data	EXFOR11991.003	Jun 76	. 1 PT.	
(n,γ)	Maxwl		ORL	Expt Jour	PR 83 643	Aug 51	Pomerance. OSC REL AU ABS	+
	Maxwl			Data	EXFOR11047.043	Jun 76	. 1 PT.	
(n,γ)	2.5+6	4.0+6	IFU	Expt Conf	58Geneva 15 18	Sep 58	Pasechnik+.PPR2030,SIGMA AT 3ES	
(n,γ)	Pile		CRC	Eval Rept	CRRP−960	Jan 62	Westcott. EFF SIG, TABLE	
(n,γ)	3.0+4	6.5+4	ORL	Expt Jour	PR 129 2695	Mar 63	Macklin+ LIQ SCINT,97 AND 35MB	+
	3.0+4	6.5+4		Data	EXFOR11331.022	Jun 76	. 2 PTS.	
(n,γ)	2.4+4	8.3+5	CCP	Comp Jour	INDSWG−64 72	64	Belanova. TBL SIG AT 3 ES	
(n,γ)	Maxwl		TOK	Expt Priv	OHNISHI+	Jul 68	SIG(129G.S.)/SIG(131G.S.)=0.68PM0.10	
(n,γ)	1.0+3	1.0+7	BOL	Eval Rept	CEC(70)−2	Apr 70	Benzi.GRAPH=SUM OF SIG(ISOTOPES)	+
	1.0+3	1.0+7		Data	BENZI−DFN 676A	May 72	. 45 PNTS	
(n,γ)	3.0+4		AUA	Theo Rept	AAEC/E−211	Nov 70	Musgrove. SIGMA GIVEN AND CFD OTHER	
(n,γ)	5.0−1	7.0+3	LRL	Expt Jour	PR/C 8 2405	Dec 73	Browne+. 0.4PC RESOL. CURVES. LINAC.	+
				Prog	USNDC−7 107	Jun 73	− +. CURVES.	
	2.3+0	7.4+3		Data	EXFOR10340.008	Jun 76	7244PTS.CS DATA.	
(n,γ)	1.0+3	1.0+7	FEI	Eval Rept	YK−8/2 97	Sep 72	Abagjan+ AVG SIG(ENERGY−GROUPS),TABL	
				Rept	INDC(CCP)−39	Jul 74	.P102. ENGLISH OF YK−8/2 97	
Spect (n,γ)	Maxwl		ANL	Expt Jour	PR 88 916	Nov 52	Hamermesh. NAI(TL) SCINT	
Spect (n,γ)	None		CRC	Expt Prog	PR−P−41 44	Apr 59	Bartholomew+ WEAK 9.4 MEV GAMMA	
Spect (n,γ)	Maxwl		YAL	Expt Jour	PR 114 268	Apr 59	Draper.SC SPECTR,GAM E 0 TO 600 KEV	
Spect (n,γ)	Maxwl		UJV	Expt Jour	CZJ 10 119	60	Kopecky+ CRYSTSPEC,20−1000KEV G−SPEC	
Spect (n,γ)	Maxwl		ARF	Expt Prog	ARF−1193−17	Dec 62	Greenwood+ NAI(TL) SPEC, 8 GAMMAS	
Spect (n,γ)	Maxwl		KUR	Expt Jour	YF 4 238	Aug 66	Groshev+ SPEC,GRAPH.ES+INTS,TABLE	
				Rept	IAE−699	65	− + MAGNET COMPT−SPEC.TBL+GRAPH	
				Jour	SNP 4 172	Feb 67	. ENGL OF YF 4 238	
				Rept	ANL−TRANS−334	65	. ENGL OF IAE−699.	

52 Tellurium

Quantity	Energy (ev) Min	Max	Lab	Type	Documentation Ref Vol Page	Date	Author, Comments	Data
Spect (n,γ)	2.5-2		MIT	Comp Rept	MITNE-85	Jan 69	Rasmussen+TBL G INT.=AFCRL-69-0071	
Spect (n,γ)	Pile		ANL	Expt Prog	WASH-1127 10	Apr 69	Bollinger+ LVL STRUCTRE ONLY,NDG,TBC	
Spect (n,γ)	None		BNL	Expt Prog	WASH-1127 21	Apr 69	Chrien+ ANAL TO BE COMPLETED,NO DATA	
Spect (n,γ)	Maxwl		KFI	Expt Jour	YF 10 907	Nov 69	Kecskemeti+ AVG GAM-MULTIPLICITY,TBL	
				Jour	SNP 10 524	May 70	TRANSLATN.*	
Spect (n,γ)	+3	+4	AUA	Expt Prog	AAEC/PR-33P 7	70	Pattenden+ ANALYSIS TB CONT'D, NDG	
Spect (n,γ)	+3	+5	AUA	Expt Prog	AAEC/PR-34P	Apr 71	Bird+ SOME ISOTOPES.GAM-INT DRVD.NDG	
Spect (n,γ)		+3	BNL	Expt Prog	USNDC-1 30	May 72	Mughabghab+. P-WAVE RESON CAPT. CURV	
Spect (n,γ)	2.5+5		AUA	Expt Rept	INDC-17 7	Oct 74	Kenny+ NA-I GAM-SPEC,GRAPH	
Inelastic γ	3.3+6		SBL	Expt Jour	NIM 134 545	76	Habbani+ 90 DEG TBL	+
	3.3+6			Data	EXFOR20667.021	Oct 76	2PTS.D/DA.	
Nonelastic γ	3.2+6		NRL	Expt Jour	PR 96 386	Oct 54	Scherrer+ C-W+CRYST SPEC 4 PEAKS	
(n,2n)	1.5+7		DEB	Eval Jour	REA 11 1 153	Mar 73	Boedy+ RECOMM.VALUE FROM N-Z SYSTEM.	
(n,p)	1.4+7		BRN	Expt Jour	NP 10 418	Apr 59	Eubank+. 0 DEG XSECT.UPPER LIMIT.	
(n,p)	1.4+7		HAR	Expt Jour	NP 24 274	Apr 61	Allan.120DEG.PHOTOPLATE UPPER LIMIT	+
	1.4+7			Data	EXFOR20004.110	Nov 70	1PNT.CMPD.NUC.	
(n,p)	1.4+7		BRN	Expt Jour	PR 123 1738	Sep 61	Peck. YIELD SPECT, ADIST OF GROUPS	
(n,p)	1.4+7		WWA	Expt Jour	NSA 17 3464	Aug 63	Brzosko+ NDG,EFF CS , PAN-400/I	
(n,d)	1.4+7		BRN	Expt Jour	PR 123 1738	Sep 61	Peck. YIELD SPECT, ADIST OF GROUPS	
Reson Params	1.7+1	4.9+3	COL	Expt Jour	PR 166 1234	Feb 68	Wynchank+ TOF G*WN FOR MANY ES AVG D	+
				Conf	65Antwerp § 95	Jul 65	.SUPERSEDED	
	2.4+1	4.9+3		Data	EXFOR11913.016	Jun 76	. 169 RES, E0,WN0	
Reson Params	3.2+2	2.7+3	SAC	Expt Jour	CEA-N-1268	Feb 70	Tellier+.	+
	3.2+2	2.7+3		Data	EXFOR20120.	Sep 72	55PTS.AVG WG,2A*G*WN,2A*G*WN0.	
Strnth Fnctn	+4		HAR	Expt Jour	PPSA 70 51	Jan 57	Gayther+ FROM AVG SIGTOT. FC TRANSM	
Strnth Fnctn	None		BNL	Expt Prog	WASH-1028 12	Apr 60	Bolotin+ 0.6+-0.2	
Strnth Fnctn		5.0+3	COL	Expt Jour	PR 166 1234	Feb 68	Wynchank.S0=(.15+-.03)-4	+
	0.0+0	5.0+3		Data	EXFOR11913.	Jun 76	. 2 PTS, S0,D	
Strnth Fnctn	0.0+0	3.0+4	SAC	Expt Jour	CEA-N-1268	Feb 70	Tellier+.	+
	0.0+0	3.0+4		Data	EXFOR20120.	Sep 72	2PTS.L=0.	
Strnth Fnctn	2.7+3		MUN	Expt Conf	71Albany 327	Aug 76	Dilg+TRNS.S0 STF GVN.31 ELEMENT GRPH	
Lvl Density	6.0+6		DKE	Expt Rept	AD-299005	62	Seth+,NUCL TEMP+FERMI LVL DENS COEFF	
Lvl Density	1.4+7		BAS	Expt Jour	PL 5 202	Jul 63	Huber+TBL OF NUC TEMP AND LVL DENSTY	
				Jour	HPA 36 1059	Dec 63	Plattner+TOF TBL12ELEM.CFD TH	
Lvl Density	1.4+7		FEI	Expt Jour	YF 2 826	Nov 65	Anufrienko+.PARAMS FROM NONELASTIC	+
				Rept	FEI-30	Dec 65	.	
				Rept	EANDC-50 197	Jul 65	.FULL PAPER FROM 65ANTWERP	
				Rept	FEI-4	65	.	
				Jour	SNP 2 589	May 66	.ENGLISH TRANSL OF YF 2 826 11/65	
(γ,n)	8.0+6	3.0+7	SAC	Expt Jour	NP/A 219 39	Jan 74	Lepretre+GDR,LORENTZ PARAM,GRPHS,TBL	

52 Tellurium 116

Quantity	Energy (ev) Min	Max	Lab	Type	Documentation Ref Vol Page	Date	Author, Comments	Data
Reson Params	-		AUA	Theo Rept	AAEC/E-211	Nov 70	Musgrove. CALCULTD D+GAM WIDTH GIVEN	
Strnth Fnctn	-		AUA	Theo Rept	AAEC/E-211	Nov 70	Musgrove. SMOOTHED S0,S1 AND S2 GIVN	
Strnth Fnctn	-2	+3	SAC	Expt Rept	CEA-N-1522	Oct 72	Cauvin+ S0,S1 CALC	

52 Tellurium 117

Quantity	Energy (ev) Min	Max	Lab	Type	Documentation Ref Vol Page	Date	Author, Comments	Data
Reson Params	-		AUA	Theo Rept	AAEC/E-211	Nov 70	Musgrove. CALCULTD D+GAM WIDTH GIVEN	
Strnth Fnctn	-		AUA	Theo Rept	AAEC/E-211	Nov 70	Musgrove. SMOOTHED S0,S1 AND S2 GIVN	
Strnth Fnctn	-2	+3	SAC	Expt Rept	CEA-N-1522	Oct 72	Cauvin+ S0,S1 CALC	

52 Tellurium 118

Quantity	Energy (ev) Min	Max	Lab	Type	Documentation Ref Vol Page	Date	Author, Comments	Data
(n,p)	Maxwl		IFU	Theo Rept	ICD-4 20	67	Dadakina+ PENETR COEFF CALC,TABLE	
Reson Params	-		AUA	Theo Rept	AAEC/E-211	Nov 70	Musgrove. CALCULTD D+GAM WIDTH GIVEN	
Strnth Fnctn	-		AUA	Theo Rept	AAEC/E-211	Nov 70	Musgrove. SMOOTHED S0,S1 AND S2 GIVN	
Strnth Fnctn	-2	+3	SAC	Expt Rept	CEA-N-1522	Oct 72	Cauvin+ S0,S1 CALC	
Lvl Density	-3	+0	IFU	Theo Jour	UFZ 13 700	Apr 68	Pisanko+ LEVEL SPACING CALC,TBL	
				Jour	UPJ 13 498	Oct 68	TRANSLATN.*	

Quantity	Energy (ev) Min	Max	Lab	Type	Documentation Ref Vol Page	Date	Author, Comments	Data
					52 Tellurium 119			
(n,2n)	1.4+7		FIR	ExTh Jour	NCL 1 2 95	Jan 69	Guidetti+ CALC ISOM RATIO CFD EXP	
(n,p)	Maxwl		IFU	Theo Rept	ICD-4 20	67	Dadakina+ PENETR COEFF CALC,TABLE	
Reson Params	-		AUA	Theo Rept	AAEC/E-211	Nov 70	Musgrove. CALCULTD D+GAM WIDTH GIVEN	
Strnth Fnctn	-		AUA	Theo Rept	AAEC/E-211	Nov 70	Musgrove. SMOOTHED S0,S1 AND S2 GIVN	
Strnth Fnctn	-2	+3	SAC	Expt Rept	CEA-N-1522	Oct 72	Cauvin+ S0,S1 CALC	
					52 Tellurium 120			
Elastic	Maxwl		COL	Expt Prog	WASH-1053 11	Aug 56	Heindl+	+
	Maxwl			Data	EXFOR11786.004	Jun 76	. 1 PT, COH	+
(n,γ)	Maxwl		ORL	Expt Jour	PR 88 412	Oct 52	Pomerance.PILE OSC.ESTIM.ERROR 100PC	+
	Maxwl			Data	EXFOR11507.060	Jun 76	. 1 PT.	
(n,γ)	Maxwl		BNL	Expt Jour	PR 128 761	Oct 62	Sehgal.SIG FOR 154DAY,17DAY REL 110D	+
	Maxwl			Data	EXFOR11994.	Jun 76	. 3 PTS, SIG FOR GND,META,ISOMER RAT	
(n,γ)	Maxwl		ANL	Comp Jour	NP 60 241	Nov 64	Bishop+EXP AND TH ISOMER RATIOS CFD	
(n,γ)	-		IEA	Comp Rept	IEA-INF-10	Aug 68	Atalla. TABLES OF HL,SIG AND GAMM-E	
(n,γ)	1.0+3	1.0+7	BOL	Eval Rept	CCDN-NW/10	Dec 69	Benzi+H-F MOD,AXEL G(G)EST,ALL DATA	+
				Rept	CEC(70)-2	Apr 70	- +. GRAPH	
	1.0+3	1.0+7		Data	BENZI-DFN 640A	May 72	45 PNTS	
(n,γ)	3.0+4		AUA	Theo Rept	AAEC/E-211	Nov 70	Musgrove. SIGMA GIVEN AND CFD OTHER	
(n,γ)	Maxwl	Fiss	WIN	Revw Conf	IAEA-169 3 163	74	Pope+ FIS-SPEC AVG DATA CFD MAXW-XPT	
(n,γ)	1.0+3	1.0+7	FEI	Eval Rept	YK-8/2 97	Sep 72	Abagjan+ AVG SIG(ENERGY-GROUPS),TABL	
				Rept	INDC(CCP)-39	Jul 74	.P102. ENGLISH OF YK-8/2 97	
(n,γ)	2.5-2		BRK	Theo Jour	NP/A 237 3 419	Jan 75	Nardi+ ISOM RATIO,MTE-CARLO,CFD XPT	
(n,γ)	Maxwl		CNM	Expt Jour	RRL 25 327	May 76	Jimenez+ RADIOCHEM.ISOM RATIO GIVEN	+
	Pile			Data	EXFOR30351.002	Sep 76	ISOMERIC RATIO.	
(n,γ)	Maxwl		KAP	Expt Abst	BAP 6 70	Feb 61	Esch+.2.4+-1.0B TO 17-DAY TE121,ACT	
	Maxwl			Data	EXFOR11989.	Jun 76	. 2 PTS, SIG FOR GND + META	
Spect (n,γ)	Maxwl		KUR	Expt Jour	YF 4 238	Aug 66	Groshev+ ES+INTS FROM NAT TE.TBL+FIG	
				Rept	IAE-699	65	- + MAGNET COMPT SPEC.TBL+GRPH	
				Jour	SNP 4 172	Feb 67	. ENGL OF YF 4 238	
				Rept	ANL-TRANS-334	65	. ENGL OF IAE-699.	
(n,2n)	Fiss		CRC	Eval Rept	CRC-1003	Dec 60	Roy+,ESTIMATED AVG SIG=0.33MB	
(n,2n)	1.5+7		ARK	Expt Jour	NP/A 114 663	Jul 68	Husain+.TO GRND,METAST.T-D NS.	+
				Abst	DA/B 29 1626	Nov 68	- .TO TE119G SIG=685+-100MB	
	1.5+7			Data	EXFOR11999.	Jun 76	. 4 PTS,SIG TOT,GND,META,ISOM RAT	
(n,2n)	1.5+7		DEB	Comp Jour	REA 7 4 93	Dec 69	Csikai+ SIG+HL COMPILTN,N-ACTIV-ANAL	
(n,2n)	1.4+7	1.5+7	JYV	Eval Rept	JU-RR-3/1970	Jun 70	Leppaemaeki+ TABLE OF EVAL AVG SIG	
(n,2n)	1.4+7	1.5+7	IRK	ExTh Jour	APA 33 285	Jul 71	Winiwarter+ ISOMERIC RATIO	
(n,2n)	1.5+7		DEB	Eval Jour	REA 11 1 153	Mar 73	Boedy. COMPILATION+RECOMM.VALUE,TBL	
				Rept	IAEA-153 173	73	- . RECOMM. VALUE ONLY	
(n,2n)	1.5+7		IBJ	Theo Jour	ASL 27 186	77	Rurarz+ ISO RATIO,4MODLS,CFD XPT.TBL	
	1.4+7			Rept	INR-1464 10	May 73	- + ISOMERIC RATIO CFD EXPT,GRAF	
(n,p)	Fiss		CRC	Eval Rept	CRC-1003	Dec 60	Roy+,ESTIMATED AVG SIG=1.8MB	
(n,p)	Maxwl		IFU	Theo Rept	ICD-4 20	67	Dadakina+ PENETR COEFF CALC,TABLE	
(n,p)	1.5+7		RBZ	Expt Jour	FIZS 4 61	Dec 72	Lulic+ ISOMERIC SIG RATIO,CFD TH,TBL	
(n,α)	Fiss		CRC	Eval Rept	CRC-1003	Dec 60	Roy+,ESTIMATED AVG SIG=0.3MB	
(n,α)	Maxwl		ISL	Expt Prog	IA-822 42	63	Cheifetz.SIG CFD TH,TBL,ALF-SPCTR	
Reson Params	-		AUA	Theo Rept	AAEC/E-211	Nov 70	Musgrove. CALCULTD D+GAM WIDTH GIVEN	
Reson Params	+2	+3	FEI	Eval Rept	YK-8/2 97	Sep 72	Abagyan+ AVG G-WID+D AT BINDNG-E,TBL	
				Rept	INDC(CCP)-39	Jul 74	.PAGE 102.ENGLISH OF YK-8/2 97	
Strnth Fnctn	-		AUA	Theo Rept	AAEC/E-211	Nov 70	Musgrove. SMOOTHED S0,S1 AND S2 GIVN	
Strnth Fnctn	-2	+3	SAC	Expt Rept	CEA-N-1522	Oct 72	Cauvin+ S0,S1 CALC	
Lvl Density	+2	+3	FEI	Eval Rept	YK-8/2 97	Sep 72	Abagyan+ LVL DENSITY PARAMETER,TBL	
				Rept	INDC(CCP)-39	Jul 74	.PAGE 102.ENGLISH OF YK-8/2 97	
					52 Tellurium 121			
(n,2n)	1.4+7		FIR	ExTh Jour	NCL 1 2 95	Jan 69	Guidetti+ CALC ISOM RATIO CFD EXP	
(n,p)	Maxwl		IFU	Theo Rept	ICD-4 20	67	Dadakina+ PENETR COEFF CALC,TABLE	
Reson Params	-		AUA	Theo Rept	AAEC/E-211	Nov 70	Musgrove. CALCULTD D+GAM WIDTH GIVEN	
Strnth Fnctn	-		AUA	Theo Rept	AAEC/E-211	Nov 70	Musgrove. SMOOTHED S0,S1 AND S2 GIVN	
Strnth Fnctn	-2	+3	SAC	Expt Rept	CEA-N-1522	Oct 72	Cauvin+ S0,S1 CALC	

52 Tellurium 122

Quantity	Energy (ev) Min	Energy (ev) Max	Lab	Type	Documentation Ref Vol Page	Date	Author, Comments	Data
Evaluation	1.0−3	1.5+7	AUA	Eval	Rept AAEC/TM−549	Jun 70	Cook.TOT,EL,INEL,NONEL,CAPT SIGS,NDG	+
					Rept AAEC/E−214	Jun 71	Bertram+GROUP SIGMAS SAME QUANTS.NDG	
					Rept AAEC/TM−587	Mar 71	*DESCRIPTION OF LIBRARY	
	1.0−3	1.5+7			Data AUSTR−DFN 98.	Nov 71	POINT(223) AND GROUP(127) SIGMAS	
Total	1.4+7		FEI	Expt	Prog INDSWG−126 33	66	Dukarevich.SIG=4.65+−0.04B	
Total	1.4+7		CCP	ExTh	Jour IZV 31 217	Feb 67	Dukarevich+.TBL,CURVES,CFD OPTMDL TH	
					Jour BAS 31 197	Feb 67	TRANSLATN.*	
Total	1.4+7		FTI	Expt	Jour NP/A 92 433	Feb 67	Dukarevich+ CFD OPTMDL 4.65+−0.04B	+
Total		3.0+4	SAC	Expt	Priv TELLIER	Sep 71	Tellier+ NO DATA. RESONANCE ASSGNMNT	+
		3.0+4			Data EXFOR20122.003	Sep 72	0PTS.	
Total	1.0−3	1.5+7	AUA	Eval	Data AUSTR−DFN 98.	Nov 71	COOK+POINT(223)+GROUP(127)SIG.CF EVL	+
Total	1.3+7	1.5+7	DEB	Eval	Rept IAEA−153 173	73	Boedy+ MOST PROBABLE VAL OF SIG,TBL	
					Jour AHP 30 115	Oct 71	Angeli+ AVG SIG,CFD CALC.TBLS.GRAPH	
Elastic	1.0−3	1.5+7	AUA	Eval	Data AUSTR−DFN 98.	Nov 71	COOK+POINT(223)+GROUP(127)SIG.CF EVL	+
Tot Inelastc	1.0+6	1.5+7	AUA	Eval	Data AUSTR−DFN 98.	Nov 71	COOK+POINT(10)+GROUP(127)SIG.CF EVL	+
Nonelastic	1.0−3	1.5+7	AUA	Eval	Data AUSTR−DFN 98.	Nov 71	COOK+POINT(223)+GROUP(127)SIG.CF EVL	+
Absorption	1.0−3	1.0+7	JUL	Eval	Rept JUEL−678−RG	Jul 70	Liu. EVALUATION+CALC,GRPH,FN OF E	
Res Int Abs	None		CRC	Eval	Rept AECL−1054	Mar 60	Walker.(CRP−913) REDUCED RES.INT.	
Res Int Abs	5.0−1		BOL	Eval	Rept RT/FI−4	Jan 67	Palmucci. CALC FROM (N,G) RES PARAMS	
Res Int Abs	5.5−1		CRC	Eval	Rept AECL−3037 1	Jan 72	Walker.REDUCED RES INT FROM RES PARS	
Res Int Abs	5.0−1		AUA	Eval	Rept AAEC/TM−619	Sep 72	Clayton.CALC FROM SIG LIBRARY,TABLE	
Res Int Abs	+0	+5	WIN	Revw	Conf IAEA−169 3 163	74	Pope+ DATA FILE CALC CFD XPTAL VALUE	
Res Int Abs	5.5−1		MUN	Comp	Jour JRC 29 175	Jan 76	Gryntakis+, 2 VALUES ARE GIVEN	
(n,γ)	Pile		UI	Expt	Jour PR 76 333	Aug 49	Hill.	+
	Pile				Data EXFOR11998.003	Jun 76	. 1 PT.	
(n,γ)	Maxwl		ORL	Expt	Jour PR 88 412	Oct 52	Pomerance.PILE OSC.	+
	Maxwl				Data EXFOR11507.061	Jun 76	. 1 PT.	
(n,γ)	Maxwl		CRC	Eval	Rept AECL−1054	Mar 60	Walker. (CRRP−913)	
(n,γ)	2.0+1	1.5+3	CCP	Expt	Conf AEC−TR−5734 11	Dec 61	REL TOFRSLN.05MICROSEC/M	
(n,γ)	2.5−2		BOL	Eval	Rept RT/FI−4	Jan 67	Palmucci. CALC FROM RES PARAMETERS	
(n,γ)	3.0+4	2.2+5	ORL	Expt	Jour PR 159 1007	Jul 67	Macklin+. TOF. VDG. SCINT. 6 ES.ABSL	+
	3.0+4	1.3+5			Data EXFOR11679.011	Jun 76	. 7 PTS.	
(n,γ)	−		IEA	Comp	Rept IEA−INF− 10	Aug 68	Atalla. TABLES OF HL,SIG AND GAMM−E	
(n,γ)	5.0+3	1.0+5	AUA	ExTh	Rept AAEC/E−198	May 69	Musgrove.S+P+D WAVE SIGMAS CALC,TBL	
(n,γ)	1.0+3	1.0+7	BOL	Eval	Rept CCDN−NW/10	Dec 69	Benzi+H−F MOD,AXEL G(G)EST,ALL DATA	+
					Rept CEC(70)−2	Apr 70	−+. GRAPH	
	1.0+3	1.0+7			Data BENZI−DFN 641A	May 72	45 PNTS	
(n,γ)	3.0+4		AUA	Theo	Rept AAEC/E−211	Nov 70	Musgrove. SIGMA GIVEN AND CFD OTHER	
(n,γ)	1.0−3	1.5+7	AUA	Eval	Data AUSTR−DFN 98.	Nov 71	COOK+POINT(223)+GROUP(127)SIG.CF EVL	+
(n,γ)	3.0+3	5.0+5	ORL	Expt	Prog NCSAC−42 185	Nov 71	Macklin+. ORELA. ANAL TBC. NO DATA	
(n,γ)	Maxwl		CRC	Eval	Rept AECL−3037 1	Jan 72	Walker.RECOMMENDED SIG,DETAILED TBL	
(n,γ)	2.5+4		AUW	Expt	Jour JP/A 5 877	Jun 72	Siddappa+ ACT.	+
				ExTh	Conf 70Madurai 2 29	Dec 70	Sriramachandra Murty+.S+P WAVE SIGMA	
	2.5+4			Expt	Data EXFOR30248.005	Jun 73	SIGMA CAPTURE TO THE MS STATE	
(n,γ)	2.5−2		AUA	Eval	Rept AAEC/TM−619	Sep 72	Clayton.CALC FROM SIG LIBRARY,TABLE	
(n,γ)	7.5+6		BGN	Expt	Rept BUP−46	Oct 72	Vaagen+ DP DIFFSIG AND PROTON ANGDIS	
(n,γ)	Maxwl	Fiss	WIN	Revw	Conf IAEA−169 3 163	74	Pope+ MAXW+FIS−SPEC AVG DATA CFD XPT	
	Fiss				Conf IAEA−169 3 137	74	Dean. POINT DATA AVG OVER STAND−SPC	
(n,γ)	1.0+3	1.0+7	FEI	Eval	Jour YK−8/2 97	Sep 72	Bergman+ AVG SIG(ENERGY−GROUPS),TABL	
					Rept INDC(CCP)−39	Jul 74	.P102. ENGLISH OF YK−8/2 97	
(n,γ)	1.0+2	6.0+4	DUB	Expt	Jour YF 20 252	Aug 74	Bergman+ SDS.SIG(E),CFD OTHERS,GRAPH	
					Jour SNP 20 133	Feb 75	. ENGL OF YF 20 252	
(n,γ)	1.0+2	6.0+4	LEB	Expt	Jour YF 20 252	Aug 74	Bergman+ SIG(NEUT−E),GRAPH	+
	1.1+1	1.0+5			Jour SNP 20 133	Feb 75	. ENGLISH OF YF 20 252	
	5.0+1	6.4+4			Data EXFOR40292.002	Mar 75	.SIGMA FOR 54 ES GVN	
Spect (n,γ)	Pile		DLH	Expt	Conf 65Calcutta 174	Feb 65	Gupta+ GAM−GAM CORRELATN,104 DAYS HL	
Spect (n,γ)	Maxwl		KUR	Expt	Jour YF 4 238	Aug 66	Groshev+ ES+INTS FROM NAT TE.TBL+FIG	
					Rept IAE−699	65	−+ MAGNET COMPT SPEC.TBL+GRPH	
					Jour SNP 4 172	Feb 67	. ENGL OF YF 4 238	
					Rept ANL−TRANS−334	65	. ENGL OF IAE−699.	
Spect (n,γ)	Pile		CCP	Expt	Jour IZV 32 207	Feb 68	Kalinauskas+ TE123M,CONVERSN+G SPECS	
					Jour BAS 32 187	69	TRANSLATN.*NO 2	
Spect (n,γ)	Maxwl		BNL	Expt	Prog WASH−1127 18	Apr 69	Chrien+GROUND−STATE GAMMA E GIVEN	
(n,2n)	Fiss		CRC	Eval	Rept CRC−1003	Dec 60	Roy+,ESTIMATED AVG SIG=0.47MB	
(n,2n)	1.5+7		ARK	Expt	Rept NP/A 114 663	Jul 68	Husain+ .TO GRND,METAST.T−D NS.	+
					Abst DA/B 29 1626	Nov 68	− .TO TE121G SIG=750+−100MB	
	1.5+7				Data EXFOR11999.	Jun 76	. 4 PTS, SIG TOT,GND,META,ISM RATIO	

52 Tellurium 122

Quantity	Energy (ev) Min	Max	Lab	Type	Documentation Ref Vol Page	Date	Author, Comments	Data
(n,2n)	1.5+7		DEB	Comp Jour	REA 7 4 93	Dec 69	Csikai+ SIG+HL COMPILTN,N-ACTIV-ANAL	
(n,2n)	1.4+7		GIT	Expt Jour	PR/C 1 350	Jan 70	Fink+ACTIVATION,GRPHS,TBL.CFD OTH.	+
	1.4+7			Data	EXFOR10497.	Apr 76	2PTS.M,GSTATE.890+ -100,725+ -40 MB.	
(n,2n)	1.4+7	1.5+7	JYV	Eval Rept	JU-RR-3/1970	Jun 70	Leppaemaeki+ TABLE OF EVAL AVG SIG	
(n,2n)	+7		KFI	Theo Rept	KFKI-71-8	Feb 71	Jeki. CALCULATED CFD EXPTL SIG VALUE	
(n,2n)	1.4+7	1.5+7	IRK	ExTh Jour	APA 33 285	Jul 71	Winiwarter+ ISOMERIC RATIO	
(n,2n)	1.4+7		GIT	Expt Jour	PR/C 4 1173	Oct 71	Fink+.STAT-MODEL CALCULATION,CFD EXP	
(n,2n)	1.5+7		DEB	Eval Jour	REA 11 1 153	Mar 73	Boedy. COMPILATION+RECOMM.VALUE,TBL	
				Rept	IAEA-153 173	73	-. RECOMM. VALUE ONLY	
(n,2n)	1.5+7		TAT	Theo Jour	JP/A 7 1458	Aug 74	Kondaiah. CALC ON STAT MODEL	
(n,2n)	1.5+7		IBJ	Theo Jour	ASL 27 186	77	Rurarz+ ISO RATIO,4MODLS,CFD XPT.TBL	
	1.4+7				INR-1464 19	May 73	- + ISOMERIC RATIO CFD EXPT,GRAF	
(n,p)	Fiss		CRC	Eval Rept	CRC-1003	Dec 60	Roy+,ESTIMATED AVG SIG=0.23MB	
(n,p)	1.4+7		SAH	Comp Jour	NUC 23 8 112	Aug 65	Chatterjee. TABLE WITH REFS.	
(n,p)	1.4+7		IBJ	Expt Conf	JINR-3699 120	Feb 68	Turkiewicz+ P-SPEC GIVEN	
				Jour	PR 127 570	Jul 62	- + ANG+E DISTRIBUTION,GRAPH	
(n,p)	1.5+7		DEB	Comp Jour	REA 7 4 93	Dec 69	Csikai+ SIG+HL COMPILTN,N-ACTIV-ANAL	
(n,p)	1.5+7		KAZ	Expt Jour	YF 13 923	May 71	Levkovsky+ ACT,METHOD,TBL,CFD THEORY	
				Jour	SNP 13 529	Nov 71	. ENGL OF YF 10 923	
(n,p)	1.5+7		RBZ	Expt Jour	FIZS 4 61	Dec 72	Lulic+ ISOMERIC SIG RATIO,CFD TH,TBL	
(n,p)	1.4+7	1.5+7	KAZ	Theo Jour	YF 18 705	Oct 73	Levkovsky.AVERAGED SIG,CALC,TBL	
				Jour	SNP 18 361	Apr 74	. ENGLISH OF YF 18,705	
(n,p)	1.4+7		IRK	Expt Jour	NP/A 222 605	Apr 74	Struwe+ GELI. REL AL(N,A).	+
	1.5+7			Data	EXFOR20540.016	Apr 76	1PNT.SIGMA.	
(n,α)	Fiss		CRC	Eval Rept	CRC-1003	Dec 60	Roy+,ESTIMATED AVG SIG=0.02MB	
(n,α)	1.4+7		IBJ	Expt Jour	NP/A 110 11	Mar 68	Jaskola+ ALFA SPCTR CFD TH,FULL PAPR	+
				Rept	INR-1268	Apr 71	SEE ALSO * FULL INFORMATION	
				Jour	APPB 2 521	71	.SAME AS INR-1268	
				Rept	INR-1197 3	May 70	SEE ALSO *THEO,ALFA CLUSTRNG	
				Rept	INR-970	Feb 69	SEE ALSO * REVIEW	
	1.4+7			Data	EXFOR30158.002	Mar 71	NUM DATA NOT AVAILBL,SEE GRAF IN REF	
Reson Params	2.0+1	1.5+3	CCP	Expt Conf	AEC-TR-5734 11	Dec 61	AVERAGE D=140EV	
Reson Params	+0	1.5+3	KUR	Expt	AE 14 264	Mar 63	Daneljan. E0, D=140 EV	
				Jour	SJA 14 258	Mar 63	. ENGL OF AE 14 264	
Reson Params		3.0+4	ORL	Expt Prog	ORNL-4513 68	Jun 70	Dabbs+,LINAC,42 RESON,ONLY D GIVEN	
Reson Params	-		AUA	Theo Rept	AAEC/E-211	Nov 70	Musgrove. CALCULTD D+GAM WIDTH GIVEN	
Reson Params	7.2+1	1.1+4	SAC	Expt Priv	TELLIER	Sep 71	Tellier+ PARAMETERS FROM TRANS.	+
		1.1+4		Conf	71Knoxvill 680	Mar 71	- +.TRANS,AVG D=132.4EV 42RESON	
	7.2+1	1.1+4		Data	EXFOR20120.	Sep 72	116PTS.E0,WG,WT,2G*WN,2G*WN0.	
Reson Params	1.5+2	6.5+2	SAC	ExTh Diss	FRNC-TH-450	Oct 72	Delaroche.OPTICAL MODEL PARAMETERS	
Reson Params	None		DUB	Theo Rept	JINR-P4-7499	Oct 73	Soloviev+ CALC D CFD EXPTS,TABLE	
Reson Params	+1	+4	FEI	Eval Rept	YK-8/2 97	Sep 72	Abagyan+ AVG G-WID+D AT BINDNG-E,TBL	
				Rept	INDC(CCP)-39	Jul 74	.PAGE 102.ENGLISH OF YK-8/2 97	
			ANL	Expt Prog	WASH-1053 1	64	Cote.	+
Reson Params	7.3+1					Jun 76	. 1 RES, E0	
	7.3+1			Data	EXFOR12002.002			
Reson Params	7.3+1		BNL	Expt Abst	BAP 5 18	Jan 60	Bolotin+. 2G*(REDUCED WN) GIVEN	+
	7.3+1			Data	EXFOR11988.002	Jun 76	. 1 RES, E0,WN,WN0	
Strnth Fnctn		3.0+4	ORL	Expt Prog	ORNL-4513 68	Jun 70	Dabbs+,LINAC,S0 VALUE GIVEN	
Strnth Fnctn	-		AUA	Theo Rept	AAEC/E-211	Nov 70	Musgrove. SMOOTHED S0,S1 AND S2 GIVN	
Strnth Fnctn	0.0+0	1.1+4	SAC	Expt Priv	TELLIER	Sep 71	Tellier+ FROM RESONANCE ANALYSIS.	+
		1.1+4		Conf	71Knoxvill 680	Mar 71	- +. SO=0.79+ -0.20	
	0.0+0	1.1+4		Jour	CR 269 266	Aug 69	- +TOF ALSO D + A (STATPAR)	
		1.1+4		Data	EXFOR20120.012	Sep 72	.1PNT. L=0	
Strnth Fnctn	None		DUB	Theo Rept	JINR-P4-6947	73	Nikolenko. S0,ISOTOPIC DEPENDNC,GRPH	
				Rept	BNL-TR-556	Dec 73	. ENGLISH OF JINR-P4-6947	
Strnth Fnctn	None		AUA	Eval Rept	AAEC/E-277	Mar 73	Musgrove.TBLS EXPTL DATA+BEST VALUES	
Strnth Fnctn	None		KUR	Theo Prog	IAE-2560	75	Adamchuk+.S0-VALUE,TBL	
Strnth Fnctn	None		OSA	Theo Conf	JAERI-M-5984	Feb 75	Kitazoe+OPT MDLS.GRPH VS A.TBL PARS.	
Lvl Density	1.4+7		IBJ	Expt Jour	NP/A 110 11	Mar 68	Jaskola+ ALFA SPCTR CFD TH,FULL PAPR	+
				Rept	INR-1268	Apr 71	SEE ALSO * FULL INFORMATION	
				Jour	APPB 2 521	71	.SAME AS INR-1268	
	1.4+7			Data	EXFOR30158.003	Mar 71	LEVEL DENSITY PARAMETER OF SN119 GIV	
Lvl Density	0.0+0	1.1+4	SAC	Expt Rept	CEA-N-1268	Feb 70	Tellier+.	+
		1.1+4		Data	EXFOR20120.013	Sep 72	1PNT.SP.CUT(0).	
Lvl Density		3.0+4	ORL	Expt Prog	ORNL-4513 68	Jun 70	Dabbs+,LINAC,PARAMETER A GIVEN	
Lvl Density	+1	+4	FEI	Eval Rept	YK-8/2 97	Sep 72	Abagyan+ LVL DENSITY PARAMETER,TBL	
				Rept	INDC(CCP)-39	Jul 74	.PAGE 102.ENGLISH OF YK-8/2 97	

52 Tellurium 122

Quantity	Energy (ev) Min	Max	Lab	Type	Documentation Ref Vol Page	Author, Comments Date	Data
Lvl Density	+0		DUB	Theo Conf	75Kiev 3 23	May 75 Voronov. LVL SPACING OF TE123.TABLE	

52 Tellurium 123

Quantity	Energy (ev) Min	Max	Lab	Type	Documentation Ref Vol Page	Author, Comments Date	Data
Evaluation	1.0−3	1.5+7	AUA	Eval	Rept AAEC/TM−549	Jun 70 Cook.TOT,EL,INEL,NONEL,CAPT,G+M,NDG	+
					Rept AAEC/E−214	Jun 71 Bertram+GROUP SIGMAS SAME QUANTS.NDG	
					Rept AAEC/TM−587	Mar 71 *DESCRIPTION OF LIBRARY	
	1.0−3	1.5+7			Data AUSTR−DFN 99.	Nov 71 POINT(223) AND GROUP(127) SIGMAS	
	1.0−3	1.5+7			Data AUSTR−DFN 187.	Nov 71 TE−123M POINT+GROUP SIGS,SAME QUANTS	
Total	7.6−1	3.0+0	COL	Expt	Jour PR 83 660	51 Heindl.	+
	7.6−1	3.0+0			Data EXFOR11991.005	Jun 76 . 32 PTS.	
Total	None		MTR	Expt	Prog WASH−191	Jun 56 . FC, TBC, NDG	
Total		3.0+4	SAC	Expt	Priv TELLIER	Sep 71 Tellier+ NO DATA. RESONANCE ASSGNMNT	+
		3.0+4			Data EXFOR20122.004	Sep 72 0PTS.	
Total	1.0−3	1.5+7	AUA	Eval	Data AUSTR−DFN 99.	Nov 71 COOK+POINT(223)+GROUP(127)SIG.CF EVL	+
	1.0−3	1.5+7			Data AUSTR−DFN 187.	Nov 71 .TE−123M.POINT+GROUP SIGS.SEE EVAL	
Elastic	2.5−2		COL	Expt	Jour RSI 27 620	Aug 56 Heindl+	+
	2.5−2				Data EXFOR11786.005	Jun 76 . 1 PT, COH	
Elastic	2.0+2	1.0+3	SAC	Expt	Prog EANDC(E)115U	Mar 69 Trochon. LINAC TOF	
Elastic	1.0−3	1.5+7	AUA	Eval	Data AUSTR−DFN 187.	Nov 71 TE−123M.POINT+GROUP SIGS.SEE EVAL	+
	1.0−3	1.5+7			Data AUSTR−DFN 99.	Nov 71 COOK+POINT(223)+GROUP(127)SIG.CF EVL	
Tot Inelastc	1.4+7		GIT	Expt	Jour PR/C 1 350	Jan 70 Fink+ACTIVATION,GRPHS.TBL.CFD OTH.	+
	1.4+7				Data EXFOR10497.029	Apr 76 1PT.TE124 N2N+TE123 SIN=980+−100 MB	
Tot Inelastc	5.0+5	1.5+7	AUA	Eval	Data AUSTR−DFN 187.	Nov 71 .TE−123M.POINT+GROUP SIGS.SEE EVAL	+
	5.0+5	1.5+7			Data AUSTR−DFN 99.	Nov 71 COOK+POINT(11)+GROUP(127)SIG.CF EVL	
Diff Inelast	Fast		RIC	Expt	Jour NP 20 395	Nov 60 Bramblett+LVL DENS.PARAM13/MEV BY PN	
Diff Inelast	Maxwl		CLS	Expt	Jour PR/C 10 2397	Dec 74 Hamermesh. UPSCATTERING,ISOMER TARG.	+
	Maxwl				Data EXFOR10465.002	Jan 75 1PT,SIGMA	
Nonelastic	1.0−3	1.5+7	AUA	Eval	Data AUSTR−DFN 187.	Nov 71 .TE−123M.POINT+GROUP SIGS.SEE EVAL	+
	1.0−3	1.5+7			Data AUSTR−DFN 99.	Nov 71 COOK+POINT(223)+GROUP(127)SIG.CF EVL	
Absorption	1.0−3	1.0+7	JUL	Eval	Rept JUEL−678−RG	Jul 70 Liu. EVALUATION+CALC,GRPH,FN OF E	
Res Int Abs	None		CRC	Eval	Rept AECL−1054	Mar 60 Walker.(CRP−913) REDUCED RES.INT.	
Res Int Abs	+3	+5	BOL	Theo Conf	61Vienna 1 179	Aug 61 Benzi+.PPR11,VAL GVN,L=0,L=1 .CAPT.	
Res Int Abs	5.5−1		CRC	Eval	Rept AECL−3037 1	Jan 72 Walker.REDUCED RES INT FROM RES PARS	
Res Int Abs	5.0−1		AUA	Eval	Rept AAEC/TM−619	Sep 72 Clayton.CALC FROM SIG LIBRARY,TABLE	
Res Int Abs	+0	+5	WIN	Revw Conf	IAEA−169 3 163	74 Pope+ GND+META.DATA FILE CALC CFD XP	
Res Int Abs	5.5−1		MUN	Comp Jour	JRC 29 175	Jan 76 Gryntakis+, 2 VALUES ARE GIVEN	
(n,γ)	Maxwl		ORL	Expt	Jour PR 88 412	Oct 52 Pomerance.PILE OSC.	+
	Maxwl				Data EXFOR11507.062	Jun 76 . 1 PT.	
(n,γ)	Maxwl		CRC	Eval	Rept AECL−1054	Mar 60 Walker. (CRRP−913)	
(n,γ)	2.0+1	1.5+3	CCP	Expt	Conf AEC−TR−5734 11	Dec 61 REL TOFRSLN.05MICROSEC/M IMPURITIES	
(n,γ)	3.0+4	2.2+5	ORL	Expt	Jour PR 159 1007	Jul 67 Macklin+. TOF. VDG. SCINT. 5 ES.ABSL	+
	3.0+4	1.3+5			Data EXFOR11679.012	Jun 76 . 6 PTS.	
(n,γ)	5.0+3	1.0+5	AUA	ExTh	Rept AAEC/E−198	May 69 Musgrove.S+P+D WAVE SIGMAS CALC,TBL	
(n,γ)	1.0+3	1.0+7	BOL	Eval	Rept CCDN−NW/10	Dec 69 Benzi+H−F MOD,AXEL G(G)EST,ALL DATA	+
					Rept CEC(70)−2	Apr 70 −+. GRAPH	
					Conf 61Vienna 1 179	Aug 61 −+ TBL AV VALUES.SUPERSEDED	
	1.0+3	1.0+7			Data BENZI−DFN 642A	May 72 45 PNTS	
(n,γ)	3.0+4		AUA	Theo	Rept AAEC/E−211	Nov 70 Musgrove. SIGMA GIVEN AND CFD OTHER	
(n,γ)	1.0−3	1.5+7	AUA	Eval	Data AUSTR−DFN 187.	Nov 71 .TE−123M.POINT+GROUP SIGS.SEE EVAL	+
	1.0−3	1.5+7			Data AUSTR−DFN 99.	Nov 71 COOK+POINT(223)+GROUP(127)SIG.CF EVL	
(n,γ)	3.0+3	5.0+5	ORL	Expt	Prog NCSAC−42 185	Nov 71 Macklin+. ORELA. ANAL TBC. NO DATA	
(n,γ)	Maxwl		CRC	Eval	Rept AECL−3037 1	Jan 72 Walker.RECOMMENDED SIG,DETAILED TBL	
(n,γ)	2.5−2		AUA	Eval	Rept AAEC/TM−619	Sep 72 Clayton.CALC FROM SIG LIBRARY,TABLE	
(n,γ)	Maxwl	Fiss	WIN	Revw Conf	IAEA−169 3 163	74 Pope+ GND+META,DATA AVG OVER SPC,XPT	
	Fiss				Conf IAEA−169 3 137	74 Dean. GND+META,DATA AVG OVER FIS−SPC	
(n,γ)	1.0+3	1.0+7	FEI	Eval	Rept YK−8/2 97	Sep 72 Abagjan+ AVG SIG(ENERGY−GROUPS),TABL	
					Rept INDC(CCP)−39	Jul 74 .P102. ENGLISH OF YK−8/2 97	
(n,γ)	1.0+2	6.0+4	DUB	Expt	Jour YF 20 252	Aug 74 Bergman+ SDS.SIG(E),CFD OTHERS,GRAPH	
					Jour SNP 20 133	Feb 75 . ENGL OF YF 20 252	
(n,γ)	1.0+2	6.0+4	LEB	Expt	Jour YF 20 252	Aug 74 Bergman+ SIG(NEUT−E),GRAPH	+
	1.1+1	1.0+5			Jour SNP 20 133	Feb 75 . ENGLISH OF YF 20 252	
	1.6+1	6.4+4			Data EXFOR40292.003	Mar 75 .SIGMA FOR 65 ES GVN	
Spect (n,γ)	2.3+0		YAL	Expt	Jour PR 107 1650	Sep 57 Schultz+,625KEV G,TOF SPEC	

52 Tellurium 123

Quantity	Energy (ev) Min	Max	Lab	Type	Documentation Ref Vol Page	Date	Author, Comments	Data
Spect (n,γ)	Maxwl		CCP Expt	Jour	ZET 35 592	Sep 58	CRYST SC,SOFT LINES INTENSITIES	
				Jour	JET 8 410	Mar 59	TRANSLATN.*	
Spect (n,γ)	Maxwl		BNL Expt	Prog	WASH-1039 7	May 62	Febiger+ COINCIDENCES,NDG	
Spect (n,γ)	2.3+0		NRL Expt	Jour	NP 82 441	Jul 66	Vogt+ AT RESONANCE, NAT TARGET	
Spect (n,γ)	Maxwl		KUR Expt	Jour	YF 4 238	Aug 66	Groshev+ ES+INTS FROM NAT TE.TBL+FIG	
				Rept	IAE-699	65	- + MAGNET COMPT SPEC.TBL+GRAPH	
				Jour	SNP 4 172	Feb 67	. ENGL OF YF 4 238	
				Rept	ANL-TR-334	65	. ENGL OF IAE-699	
Spect (n,γ)	Maxwl		UEN Expt	Rept	BMWF-FBK67-20	Mar 67	Zehender.SUM COINC REL INTENS CASCAD	
Spect (n,γ)	Pile		ANL Expt	Jour	PR 179 1113	Mar 69	Bushnell+ CRYST SPEC+GE(LI),MANY GAM	
Spect (n,γ)	Maxwl		BNL Expt	Prog	WASH-1127 18	Apr 69	Chrien+GROUND-STATE GAMMA E GIVEN	
Spect (n,γ)	2.5-2		CLS Expt	Jour	PR/C 11 827	Mar 75	Hamermesh+ LEVEL CS FOR ISOM TARGET	+
	2.5-2			Data	EXFOR10478.002	Apr 75	4PTS,SIGMA	
Inelastic γ	Maxwl		CLS Expt	Jour	PR/C 11 827	Mar 75	Hamermesh+ TE-123M CAPT.CS FOR LVLS	
(n,2n)	Fiss		CRC Eval	Rept	CRC-1003	Dec 60	Roy+,ESTIMATED AVG SIG=14.5MB	
(n,2n)	1.5+7		DEB Eval	Jour	REA 11 1 153	Mar 73	Boedy+ RECOMM.VALUE FROM N-Z SYSTEM.	
(n,2n)	1.5+7		KFI Theo	Rept	KFKI-73-68	Dec 73	Jeki.NEW FIT,CALC SIG CFD OTHERS,TBL	
(n,p)	Fast		RIC Expt	Jour	NP 20 395	Nov 60	Bramblett+5.3MEV P ON SB123/INV REAC	
(n,p)	Fiss		CRC Eval	Rept	CRC-1003	Dec 60	Roy+,ESTIMATED AVG SIG=0.53MB	
(n,p)	Maxwl		IFU Theo	Rept	ICD-4 20	67	Dadakina+ PENETR COEFF CALC,TABLE	
(n,α)	Fiss		CRC Eval	Rept	CRC-1003	Dec 60	Roy+,ESTIMATED AVG SIG=1.2MB	
(n,α)	Maxwl		ISL Expt	Prog	IA-822 42	63	Cheifetz.SIG CFD TH,TBL,ALF-SPCTR	
(n,α)	Maxwl		ISL Expt	Jour	NP/A 91 238	Jan 67	Cheifetz+ 15+-10MUB TO GS LT FOR 1XS	
(n,α)	2.3+0	2.8+2	DUB Expt	Prog	YFI-7 52	Apr 69	Popov+ RES-E,SPIN,ALFA WIDTH AT 6 ES	
	2.0+0	1.0+3		Jour	YF 9 1163	Jun 69	- + ALF-INT+WIDTH,GRPH+TBL,6RES	
	2.3+0	2.8+2		Rept	INDC(CCP)-7U55	Feb 70	- + TRANSLATION.	
	2.0+0	1.0+3		Jour	SNP 9 680	Dec 69	. ENGLISH OF YF 9 1163	
(n,α)	Maxwl		LYO Expt	Jour	ZP/A 275 157	Nov 75	Emsallem+ SIG+LVL-WIDTH	+
	2.5-2			Data	EXFOR20612.003	Aug 76	2PTS.SIGMA.	
Reson Params	2.2+0		COL Expt	Jour	PR 83 660	Aug 51	Heindl+ AREA FROM B-W FIT.	+
	2.2+0			Data	EXFOR11991.006	Jun 76	. 1 RES, E0,WT**2/PCS	
Reson Params	2.3+0		COL Expt	Rept	CU-192	Jun 59	Heindl..01EV RSLN, B-W FIT, J WG WN	
Reson Params	2.0+1	1.5+3	CCP Expt	Conf	AEC-TR-5734 11	Dec 61	AVERAGE D=23EV	
Reson Params	+0	1.5+3	KUR Expt	Jour	AE 14 264	Mar 63	Daneljan. E0,WN,WG,J DETERMINED	
				Jour	SJA 14 258	Mar 63	. ENGL OF AE 14 264	
Reson Params	2.4+1	3.6+1	MTR Expt	Priv	SIMPSON	Jan 65	Simpson.	+
	2.4+1	3.6+1		Data	EXFOR11996.003	Jun 76	. 2 RES, E0,WN	
Reson Params		1.0+6	AUA Theo	Jour	AUJ 20 477	Oct 67	Cook. TBL OF AVG LVL SPACING D,L=0,1	+
Reson Params	2.3+0	2.8+2	DUB Expt	Prog	YFI-7 52	Apr 69	Popov+ RES-E,SPIN,ALFA WIDTH AT 6 ES	
	None			Rept	JINR-E3-5483	Dec 70	- . TABLE OF ALPHA+NEUTRON WIDTHS	
				Conf	70Helsinki 1 669	Jun 70	- +125. AVERAGE ALFA-WIDTH	
	2.3+0	2.8+2		Jour	YF 9 1163	Jun 69	- + TBL=EXPTL+STATMOD ALPHA WIDTH	
	None			Rept	UCRL-TR-10541	May 71	- + ENGL TRANSLATION.	
	2.3+0	2.8+2		Rept	INDC(CCP)-7U55	Feb 70	- + TRANSLATION.	
				Jour	SNP 9 6 680	Dec 69	- + TRANSLATION.	
	2.3+0	2.8+2		Data	EXFOR40304.004	Nov 75	.ALPHA-WIDTH FOR 6 EN GVN	
Reson Params		3.0+4	ORL Expt	Prog	ORNL-4513 68	Jun 70	Dabbs+,LINAC,26 RESON,ONLY D GIVEN	
Reson Params	-		AUA Theo	Rept	AAEC/E-211	Nov 70	Musgrove. CALCULTD D+GAM WIDTH GIVEN	
Reson Params	2.3+0	1.6+2	CJD Eval	Prog	YK-7	71	Zakharova+ SURVEY+SYSTEMATICS,GW,TBL	
				Rept	INDC(CCP)-27	Nov 72	.ENGLISH TRANSLATION OF YK-7 /71	
Reson Params	None		DUB Theo	Jour	YF 13 240	Feb 71	Malecki+G-WID,THEO CFD EXPT.TBL,GRPH	
				Jour	SNP 13 133	Aug 71	- + ENGL OF YF 13 240.	
Reson Params	2.4+1	6.6+2	SAC Expt	Conf	71Knoxvill 785	Mar 71	Cauvin+ J ASSIGNMENTS.19RESONANCES	+
	2.4+1	6.6+2		Data	EXFOR20126.004	Sep 72	19PTS.J.	
Reson Params	-		DUB Theo	Rept	JINR-E4-5711	Apr 71	Soloviev.RESONANCE STRUCTURE STUDY	
Reson Params	2.4+1	2.0+3	SAC Expt	Priv	TELLIER	Sep 71	Tellier+ PARAMETERS FROM TRANS.	+
				Conf	71Knoxvill 680	Mar 71	- +.TRANS,AVG D=26.3EV 26RESON	
	2.4+1	2.0+3		Data	EXFOR20120.	Sep 72	125PTS.WG,WT,2G*WN,2G*WN0.	
Reson Params	1.5+2	6.5+2	SAC ExTh	Diss	FRNC-TH-450	Oct 72	Delaroche.OPTICAL MODEL PARAMETERS	
Reson Params	None		DUB Theo	Rept	JINR-P4-7499	Oct 73	Soloviev+ CALC D CFD EXPTS,TABLE	
Reson Params	+0	+2	BOL Eval	Conf	IAEA-169 3 123	74	Benzi+ AVG G-WID CFD OTHERS+XPT,TABL	
Reson Params	+0	+3	FEI Eval	Rept	YK-8/2 97	Sep 72	Abagyan+ AVG G-WID+D AT BINDNG-E,TBL	
				Rept	INDC(CCP)-39	Jul 74	.PAGE 102.ENGLISH OF YK-8/2 97	
Reson Params	2.2+0		DUB Expt	Rept	JINR-P3-8140	Sep 74	Popov. PRELIM GAM-ALF WID(1+) GIVEN	
				Conf	74Petten 379	Sep 74	- +WIDTH FOR (N,G,A) PROCESS	
Reson Params	2.3+0	1.6+2	ANL Expt	Prog	WASH-1053 11	Oct 64	Cote.FC. OKS USSR XCEPT 2RES,P NEW	+
	2.3+0	3.7+2		Data	EXFOR12002.003	Jun 76	. 8 RES, E0,J	

52 Tellurium 123

Quantity	Energy (ev) Min	Max	Lab	Type	Documentation Ref Vol Page	Author, Comments Date	Data
Reson Params	2.4+1	1.6+2	BNL	Expt Abst	BAP 5 18	Jan 60 Bolotin+. 2G*(REDUCED WN) GIVEN	+
	2.4+1	1.6+2		Data	EXFOR11988.003	Jun 76 . 4 RES, E0,WN,WN0	
Reson Params	2.3+0	3.6+1	BNL	Expt Abst	BAP 13 1390	Nov 68 Mughabghab+ GE(LI) J=1 FROM N,G 3RES	+
	2.3+0	3.6+1		Data	EXFOR12637.002	Jun 76 . 3 RES, J	
Reson Params	2.3+0		BNL	Expt Abst	PR 94 790	54 Foote. ABST WA3	+
	2.3+0			Data	EXFOR12000.002	Jun 76 . 1 RES, E0,J,WT,WN,PCS	
Strnth Fnctn	2.3+0	3.6+2	CCP	Expt Jour	AE 14 264	Mar 63 .00016+ – .00007 DANELIAN+.SJA14 258	+
Strnth Fnctn	2.3+0	2.8+2	DUB	Expt Prog	YFI – 7 52	Apr 69 Popov+ (N,ALFA) TOF EXPT CFD STATMOD	
				Rept	INDC(CCP)–7U55	Feb 70 – + TRANSLATION.	
Strnth Fnctn		3.0+4	ORL	Expt Prog	ORNL–4513 68	Jun 70 Dabbs+,LINAC,S0 VALUE GIVEN	
Strnth Fnctn	–		AUA	Theo Rept	AAEC/E–211	Nov 70 Musgrove. SMOOTHED S0,S1 AND S2 GIVN	
Strnth Fnctn	0.0+0	6.6+2	SAC	Expt Priv	TELLIER	Sep 71 Tellier+ FROM RESONANCE ANALYSIS.	+
		6.6+2		Conf	71Knoxvill 680	Mar 71 – +. SO=0.98+ – 0.20	
	0.0+0	6.6+2		Jour	CR 269 266	Aug 69 – + TOF ALSO D + A (STATPAR)	
		6.6+2		Data	EXFOR20120.	Sep 72 . 3PTS.L=0.	
Strnth Fnctn	None		AUA	Eval Rept	AAEC/E–277	Mar 73 Musgrove.TBLS EXPTL DATA+BEST VALUES	
Strnth Fnctn	None		KUR	Theo Prog	IAE–2560	75 Adamchuk+.S0–VALUE,TBL	
Lvl Density	+6		MIL	Theo Jour	EN 15 1 54	Jan 68 Facchini+ LDL PARS FROM LOW EN RES	
Lvl Density	6.6+2	1.1+4	SAC	Expt Jour	CEA–N–1268	Feb 70 Tellier+.	+
	6.6+2	1.1+4		Data	EXFOR20120.	Sep 72 2PTS.A PARAM,SP.CUT(0).	
Lvl Density		3.0+4	ORL	Expt Prog	ORNL–4513 68	Jun 70 Dabbs+,LINAC,PARAMETER A GIVEN	
Lvl Density	None		DUB	Theo Rept	JINR–P4–7499	Oct 73 Soloviev+ CALC LVL–DENS–PARAM,GRAPH	
Lvl Density	None		MUN	Theo Jour	NP/A 217 269	Dec 73 Dilg+ A,DELTA. BACK SHIFTED FERMIGAS	
Lvl Density	None		BOL	Eval Conf	IAEA–169 3 123	74 Benzi+ LVL DENS PARAM BY XPT,GRPH+TB	
Lvl Density	None		COP	Theo Jour	NP/A 222 493	Apr 74 Dossing+COLL ROTAT.SPAC. ACCUR ESTIM	
Lvl Density	None		DUB	Theo Jour	NP/A 224 411	May 74 Soloviev+ 1/2 MICROSC MDL. SPH NUCL.	
Lvl Density	+0	+3	FEI	Eval Rept	YK– 8/2 97	Sep 72 Abagyan+ LVL DENSITY PARAMETER,TBL	
				Rept	INDC(CCP)–39	Jul 74 .PAGE 102.ENGLISH OF YK–8/2 97	

52 Tellurium 124

Quantity	Energy (ev) Min	Max	Lab	Type	Documentation Ref Vol Page	Author, Comments Date	Data
Evaluation	1.0–3	1.5+7	AUA	Eval Rept	AAEC/TM–549	Jun 70 Cook.TOT,EL,INEL,NONEL,CAPT SIGS,NDG	+
				Rept	AAEC/E–214	Jun 71 Bertram+GROUP SIGMAS SAME QUANTS.NDG	
				Rept	AAEC/TM–587	Mar 71 *DESCRIPTION OF LIBRARY	
	1.0–3	1.5+7		Data	AUSTR–DFN 100.	Nov 71 POINT(223) AND GROUP(127) SIGMAS	
Total	1.4+7		FEI	Expt Prog	INDSWG–126 33	66 Dukarevich.SIG=4.50+ – 0.05B	
Total	1.4+7		CCP	ExTh Jour	IZV 31 217	Feb 67 Dukarevich+.TBL,CURVES,CFD OPTMDL TH	
				Jour	BAS 31 197	Feb 67 TRANSLATN.*	
Total	1.4+7		FTI	Expt Jour	NP/A 92 433	Feb 67 Dukarevich+ CFD OPTMDL 4.60+ – 0.05B	+
Total		3.0+4	SAC	Expt Priv	TELLIER	Sep 71 Tellier+ NO DATA. RESONANCE ASSGNMNT	+
		3.0+4		Data	EXFOR20122.005	Sep 72 0PTS.	
Total	1.0–3	1.5+7	AUA	Eval Data	AUSTR–DFN 100.	Nov 71 COOK+POINT(223)+GROUP(127)SIG.CF EVL	
Total	1.3+7	1.5+7	DEB	Eval Rept	IAEA–153 173	73 Boedy+ MOST PROBABLE VAL OF SIG,TBL	
				Jour	AHP 30 115	Oct 71 Angeli+ AVG SIG,CFD CALC.TBLS.GRAPH	
Elastic	Maxwl		ORL	Expt Jour	ARN 11 303	61 Wilkinson.	+
	Maxwl			Data	EXFOR11005.006	Jun 76 . 1 PT, COH AMP	
Elastic	1.0–3	1.5+7	AUA	Eval Data	AUSTR–DFN 100.	Nov 71 COOK+POINT(223)+GROUP(127)SIG.CF EVL	
Tot Inelastc	1.0+6	1.5+7	AUA	Eval Data	AUSTR–DFN 100.	Nov 71 COOK+POINT(10)+GROUP(127)SIG.CF EVL	
Diff Inelast	6.0+5	7.5+5	LEB	Expt Jour	KSF 1976 6 20	76 Konobeevskij+ SIG(E) TO 2+ LVL,GRAPH	
				Jour	SPL 1976 6 16	76 . ENGL OF KSF 1976 6 20	
Nonelastic	1.0–3	1.5+7	AUA	Eval Data	AUSTR–DFN 100.	Nov 71 COOK+POINT(223)+GROUP(127)SIG.CF EVL	
Absorption	1.0–3	1.0+7	JUL	Eval Rept	JUEL–678–RG	Jul 70 Liu. EVALUATION+CALC,GRPH,FN OF E	
Res Int Abs	None		CRC	Eval Rept	AECL–1054	Mar 60 Walker.(CRP–913) REDUCED RES.INT.	
Res Int Abs	5.0–1		BOL	Eval Rept	RT/FI–4	Jan 67 Palmucci. CALC FROM (N,G) RES PARAMS	
Res Int Abs	5.0–1		AUA	Eval Rept	AAEC/TM–619	Sep 72 Clayton.CALC FROM SIG LIBRARY,TABLE	
Res Int Abs	+0	+5	WIN	Revw Conf	IAEA–169 3 163	74 Pope+ DATA FILE CALC CFD XPTAL VALUE	
Res Int Abs	5.5–1		MUN	Comp Jour	JRC 29 175	Jan 76 Gryntakis+, 2 VALUES ARE GIVEN	
(n,γ)	Pile		UI	Expt Jour	PR 76 333	Aug 49 Hill.	+
	Pile			Data	EXFOR11998.002	Jun 76 . 1 PT.	
(n,γ)	Maxwl		ORL	Expt Jour	PR 88 412	Oct 52 Pomerance.PILE OSC.	+
	Maxwl			Data	EXFOR11507.063	Jun 76 . 1 PT.	
(n,γ)	Maxwl		FTI	Expt Jour	JET 9 439	Aug 59 Gvozdev+ TRANSLATION	
				Jour	ZET 36 632	Feb 59 – + SIGMA (N,G)M GVN	
(n,γ)	Maxwl		CRC	Eval Jour	AECL–1054	Mar 60 Walker. (CRRP–913)	
(n,γ)	2.0+1	1.5+3	CCP	Expt Conf	AEC–TR–5734 11	Dec 61 REL TOFRSLN.05MICROSEC/M	
(n,γ)	2.0+1	1.5+3	CCP	Expt Jour	AE 14 264	Mar 63 COUNTS/TOF SHOWN DANELIAN+.SJA14 258	

52 Tellurium 124

Quantity	Energy (ev) Min	Energy (ev) Max	Lab	Type	Documentation Ref Vol Page	Date	Author, Comments	Data
(n,γ)	1.0+3	6.0+4	LEB	Expt Conf	65Antwerp § 182	Jul 65	Bergman.LEBEDEV. DO OBTAINED	+
(n,γ)	2.5-2		BOL	Eval Rept	RT/FI-4	Jan 67	Palmucci. CALC FROM RES PARAMETERS	
(n,γ)	2.5+4		FEI	ExTh Prog	YFI-4 22	May 67	Shorin+.,TBLS GIVEN,TBP YF	
				Rept	INDC-187E	67	. ENGL OF YFI-4 22	
(n,γ)	3.0+4	2.2+5	ORL	Expt Jour	PR 159 1007	Jul 67	Macklin+. TOF. VDG. SCINT. 5 ES.ABSL	+
	3.0+4	1.3+5		Data	EXFOR11679.013	Jun 76	. 6 PTS.	
(n,γ)	-		IEA	Comp Rept	IEA-INF- 10	Aug 68	Atalla. TABLES OF HL,SIG AND GAMM-E	
(n,γ)	1.0+3	1.0+7	BOL	Eval Rept	CCDN-NW/10	Dec 69	Benzi+H-F MOD,AXEL G(G)EST,ALL DATA	+
				Rept	CEC(70)-2	Apr 70	- +. GRAPH	
	1.0+3	1.0+7		Data	BENZI-DFN 643A	May 72	45 PNTS	
(n,γ)	3.0+4		AUA	Theo Rept	AAEC/E-211	Nov 70	Musgrove. SIGMA GIVEN AND CFD OTHER	
(n,γ)	1.0-3	1.5+7	AUA	Eval Data	AUSTR-DFN 100.	Nov 71	COOK+POINT(223)+GROUP(127)SIG.CF EVL	+
(n,γ)	3.0+5	5.0+5	ORL	Expt Prog	NCSAC-42 185	Nov 71	Macklin+ ORELA, ANALYSIS TBC, NDG	
(n,γ)	Maxwl		CRC	Eval Rept	AECL-3037 1	Jan 72	Walker.RECOMMEND SIG TO GND+META,TBL	
(n,γ)	2.5-2		AUA	Eval Rept	AAEC/TM-619	Sep 72	Clayton.CALC FROM SIG LIBRARY,TABLE	
(n,γ)	Maxwl	Fiss	WIN	Revw Conf	IAEA-169 3 163	74	Pope+ MAXW+FIS-SPEC AVG DATA CFD XPT	
	Fiss			Conf	IAEA-169 3 137	74	Dean. POINT DATA AVG OVER STAND SPEC	
(n,γ)	1.0+3	1.0+7	FEI	Eval Rept	YK- 8/2 97	Sep 72	Abagjan+ AVG SIG(ENERGY-GROUPS),TABL	
				Rept	INDC(CCP)-39	Jul 74	.P102. ENGLISH OF YK-8/2 97	
(n,γ)	1.0+2	6.0+4	DUB	Expt Jour	YF 20 252	Aug 74	Bergman+ SDS.SIG(E),CFD OTHERS,GRAPH	
				Jour	SNP 20 133	Feb 75	. ENGL OF YF 20 252	
(n,γ)	1.0+2	6.0+4	LEB	Expt Jour	YF 20 252	Aug 74	Bergman+ SIG(NEUT-E),GRAPH	
	1.1+1	1.0+5		Jour	SNP 20 133	Feb 75	. ENGLISH OF YF 20 252	
	3.6+1	6.4+4		Data	EXFOR40292.004	Mar 75	.SIGMA FOR 35 ES GVN	
Spect (n,γ)	Maxwl		KUR	Expt Jour	YF 4 238	Aug 66	Groshev+ ES+INTS FROM NAT TE.TBL+FIG	
				Rept	IAE-699	65	- + MAGNET COMPT SPEC.TBL+GRPH	
				Jour	SNP 4 172	Feb 67	. ENGL OF YF 4 238	
				Rept	ANL-TRANS-334	65	. ENGL OF IAE-699.	
Spect (n,γ)	Maxwl		BNL	Expt Prog	WASH-1127 18	Apr 69	Chrien+ GROUND-STATE GAMMA E GIVEN	
Spect (n,γ)	None		ORL	Theo Jour	NSE 36 220	May 69	Yost+ CALCUL BY GAMMA CASCADE MODEL	
Spect (n,γ)	Pile		KUR	Expt Conf	71Moscow	Feb 71	Groshev+.ABST,GE-LI,TBL,ES+INTENS	
Spect (n,γ)	Pile		KUR	Expt Jour	YF 13 681	Apr 71	Groshev+ GE-LI,TBD	
				Jour	SNP 13 387	Oct 71	. ENGL OF YF 13 681	
Inelastic γ	6.0+5	7.5+5	LEB	Expt Jour	KSF 1976 6 20	76	Konobeevskij+ SIG(E) TO 2+ LVL,GRAPH	
				Jour	SPL 1976 6 16	76	. ENGL OF KSF 1976 6 20	
(n,2n)	Fiss		CRC	Eval Rept	CRC-1003	Dec 60	Roy+,ESTIMATED AVG SIG=0.9MB	
(n,2n)	1.4+7		GIT	Expt Jour	PR/C 1 350	Jan 70	Fink+ACTIVATION,GRPHS.TBL.CFD OTH.	+
	1.4+7			Data	EXFOR10497.029	Apr 76	1PT.TE124 N2N+TE123 SIN=980+- 100 MB	
(n,2n)	1.5+7		DEB	Expt Jour	REA 11 1 153	Mar 73	Boedy+ RECOMM.VALUE FROM N-Z SYSTEM.	
(n,2n)	1.5+7		KFI	Theo Rept	KFKI-73-68	Dec 73	Jeki.NEW FIT,CALC SIG CFD OTHERS,TBL	
(n,2n)	1.5+7		IBJ	Theo Jour	ASL 27 186	77	Rurarz+ ISO RATIO,4MODLS,CFD XPT.TBL	
	1.4+7			Rept	INR-1464 19	May 73	- + ISOMERIC RATIO CFD EXPT,GRAF	
(n,p)	Fiss		CRC	Eval Rept	CRC-1003	Dec 60	Roy+,ESTIMATED AVG SIG=0.07MB	
(n,p)	1.4+7		SAH	Comp Jour	NUC 23 8 112	Aug 65	Chatterjee. TABLE WITH REFS.	
(n,p)	1.4+7		WWA	Expt Jour	NP 74 438	Dec 65	Brzosko+ ISOMERIC RATIOS,CFD THEORY	+
				Jour	NP 45 579	Aug 63	- + PARTIAL SIGMAS	
	1.4+7			Data	EXFOR30136.	Oct 71	PARTIALS AND TOTAL SIGMAS	
(n,p)	1.5+7		DEB	Comp Jour	REA 7 4 93	Dec 69	Csikai+ SIG+HL COMPILTN,N-ACTIV-ANAL	
(n,p)	1.4+7	1.5+7	JYV	Eval Rept	JU-RR-3/1970	Jun 70	Leppaemaeki+ TABLE OF EVAL AVG SIG	
(n,p)	1.5+7		KAZ	Expt Jour	YF 13 923	May 71	Levkovsky+ ACT,SIG+ISOMER RATIO,TBL	
				Jour	SNP 13 529	Nov 71	. ENGL OF YF 10 923	
(n,p)	1.5+7		RBZ	Expt Jour	FIZS 4 61	Dec 72	Lulic+ ISOMERIC SIG RATIO,CFD TH,TBL	
(n,p)	1.4+7	1.5+7	KAZ	Theo Jour	YF 18 705	Oct 73	Levkovsky.AVERAGED SIG,CALC,TBL	
				Jour	SNP 18 361	Apr 74	. ENGLISH OF YF 18,705	
(n,p)	1.4+7		IRK	Expt Jour	NP/A 222 605	Apr 74	Struwe+ GELI. REL AL(N,A).	+
	1.5+7			Data	EXFOR20540.017	Apr 76	1PNT.SIGMA.	
(n,α)	Fiss		CRC	Eval Rept	CRC-1003	Dec 60	Roy+,ESTIMATED AVG SIG=0.005MB	
(n,α)	1.5+7		SAH	Theo Jour	NP 89 329	Dec 66	Majumdar. STAT THEO CFD EXPTS	+
	1.5+7			Expt Jour	NP 41 192	Mar 63	Najumdar+ACTIVATION REL AL27(NP)	
				Data	EXFOR31117.002	Sep 72	.SIG GVN	
(n,α)	1.4+7		RBZ	Expt Priv	KULLISIC	Aug 68	Jurcevic.DIFSIG+ALFA SPEC AT 0 DEG.	+
	1.4+7			Data	EXFOR30203.	Nov 72	DIFF SIG AT 0 DEG	
(n,α)	1.4+7		RBZ	Expt Conf	69Bochum 210	Jul 69	Chatterjee+ ALFA-SPEC EXPT, NO DATA	
(n,α)	1.5+7		DEB	Comp Jour	REA 7 4 93	Dec 69	Csikai+ SIG+HL COMPILTN,N-ACTIV-ANAL	
(n,α)	1.4+7		RBZ	ExTh Conf	69Roorke 2 21	Dec 69	Chatterjee+ CFD P-ALFA REACTION, NDG	
(n,α)	1.4+7	1.5+7	JYV	Eval Rept	JU-RR-3/1970	Jun 70	Leppaemaeki+ TABLE OF EVAL AVG SIG	
(n,α)	1.5+7		KAZ	Expt Jour	YF 13 923	May 71	Levkovsky+ ACT,METHOD,TBL,CFD OTHERS	
				Jour	SNP 13 529	Nov 71	. ENGL OF YF 10 923	

52 Tellurium 124

Quantity	Energy (ev) Min	Max	Lab	Type	Documentation Ref Vol Page	Date	Author, Comments	Data
(n,α)	1.4+7		RBZ	Theo Conf	72Budapest 168	Aug 72	Caplar+ ANALYSIS OF SPECTRA,GRAPH	
Reson Params	2.0+1	1.5+3	CCP	Expt Conf	AEC-TR-5734 11	Dec 61	AVERAGE D=220EV	
Reson Params	+0	1.5+3	KUR	Expt Jour	AE 14 264	Mar 63	Daneljan. E0, D=220 EV	
				Jour	SJA 14 258	Mar 63	. ENGL OF AE 14 264	
Reson Params		1.0+6	AUA	Theo Jour	AUJ 20 477	Oct 67	Cook. TBL OF AVG LVL SPACING D,L=0,1	
Reson Params		3.0+4	ORL	Expt Prog	ORNL-4513 68	Jun 70	Dabbs+,LINAC,84 RESON,ONLY D GIVEN	
Reson Params	–		AUA	Theo Rept	AAEC/E-211	Nov 70	Musgrove. CALCULTD D+GAM WIDTH GIVEN	
Reson Params	3.5+2	2.8+4	SAC	Expt Priv	TELLIER	Sep 71	Tellier+ PARAMETERS FROM TRANS.	+
		2.8+4		Conf	71Knoxvill 680	Mar 71	– +.TRANS,AVG D=146.8EV 84RESON	
	3.5+2	2.8+4		Data	EXFOR20120.	Sep 72	214PTS.WG,WT,2G*WN,2G*WN0.	
Reson Params	1.5+2	6.5+2	SAC	ExTh Diss	FRNC-TH-450	Oct 72	Delaroche.OPTICAL MODEL PARAMETERS	
Reson Params	+2	+4	FEI	Eval Rept	YK-8/2 97	Sep 72	Abagyan+ AVG G-WID+D AT BINDNG-E,TBL	
				Rept	INDC(CCP)-39	Jul 74	.PAGE 102.ENGLISH OF YK-8/2 97	
Reson Params	2.0+2	2.0+2	ANL	Prog	WASH-1053 11	64	Cote+	+
	2.0+2	2.0+2		Data	EXFOR12002.004	Jun 76	. 1 RES, E0	
Reson Params	4.3+2		BNL	Expt Abst	BAP 5 18	Jan 60	Bolotin+. 2G*(REDUCED WN) GIVEN	+
	4.3+2			Data	EXFOR11988.004	Jun 76	. 1 RES, E0,WN,WN0	
Strnth Fnctn		3.0+4	ORL	Expt Prog	ORNL-4513 68	Jun 70	Dabbs+,LINAC,S0 VALUE GIVEN	
Strnth Fnctn	–		AUA	Theo Rept	AAEC/E-211	Nov 70	Musgrove. SMOOTHED S0,S1 AND S2 GIVN	
Strnth Fnctn	0.0+0	2.8+4	SAC	Expt Priv	TELLIER	Sep 71	Tellier+ FROM RESONANCE ANALYSIS.	+
		2.8+4		Conf	71Knoxvill 680	Mar 71	– +. S0=0.68+-0.20	
	0.0+0	2.8+4		Jour	CR 269 266	Aug 69	– + TOF ALSO D+A (STSTPAR)	
		2.8+4		Data	EXFOR20120.026	Sep 72	. 1PNT. L=0	
Strnth Fnctn	None		DUB	Theo Jour	JINR-P4-6947	73	Nikolenko. S0,ISOTOPIC DEPENDNC,GRPH	
				Rept	BNL-TR-556	Dec 73	. ENGLISH OF JINR-P4-6947	
Strnth Fnctn	None		AUA	Eval Rept	AAEC/E-277	Mar 73	Musgrove.TBLS EXPTL DATA+BEST VALUES	
Strnth Fnctn	None		KUR	Theo Prog	IAE-2560	75	Adamchuk+.S0-VALUE,TBL	
Strnth Fnctn	None		OSA	Theo Conf	JAERI-M-5984	Feb 75	Kitazoe+OPT MDLS.GRPH VS A.TBL PARS.	
Strnth Fnctn	+0	+6	DUB	Theo Jour	JINR-P4-9052	Oct 75	Soloviev+ S0,S1,SEMIMICROSC MODL,TBL	
Lvl Density	–		FEI	ExTh Prog	YFI-6 18	68	Ignatjuk+ TABLE VARIOUS PARAMETERS	
				Rept	INDC-260E	69	. ENGL OF YFI-6 18	
Lvl Density	+6		MIL	Theo Jour	EN 15 1 54	Jan 68	Facchini+ LDL PARS FROM LOW EN RES	
Lvl Density	–		FEI	Theo Jour	YF 8 1135	Dec 68	Ignatjuk+ TBL,A+ENTROPY+TEMP,CFD XPT	
				Jour	SNP 8 660	Jun 69	TRANSLATN.*	
Lvl Density	6.6+2	2.8+4	SAC	Expt Rept	CEA-N-1268	Feb 70	Tellier+.	+
	6.6+2	2.8+4		Data	EXFOR20120.	Sep 72	2PTS.A PARAM,SP.CUT(0).	
Lvl Density		3.0+4	ORL	Expt Prog	ORNL-4513 68	Jun 70	Dabbs+,LINAC,PARAMETER A GIVEN	
Lvl Density	None		DUB	Theo Rept	JINR-P4-7499	Oct 73	Soloviev+ CALC LVL-DENS-PARAM,GRAPH	
Lvl Density	None		MUN	Theo Jour	NP/A 217 269	Dec 73	Dilg+ A,DELTA. BACK SHIFTED FERMIGAS	
Lvl Density	None		COP	Theo Jour	NP/A 222 493	Apr 74	Dossing+COLL ROTAT.SPAC. ACCUR ESTIM	
Lvl Density	+2	+4	FEI	Eval Rept	YK-8/2 97	Sep 72	Abagyan+ LVL DENSITY PARAMETER,TBL	
				Rept	INDC(CCP)-39	Jul 74	.PAGE 102.ENGLISH OF YK-8/2 97	
(γ,n)	8.0+6	2.6+7	SAC	Expt Jour	NP/A 258 350	Feb 76	Lepretre+GDR,LORENTZ PARAM,GRPHS,TBL	

52 Tellurium 125

Quantity	Energy (ev) Min	Max	Lab	Type	Documentation Ref Vol Page	Date	Author, Comments	Data
Evaluation	1.0-3	1.5+7	AUA	Eval Rept	AAEC/TM-549	Jun 70	Cook.TOT,EL,INEL,NONEL,CAPT,G+M,NDG	+
				Rept	AAEC/E-214	Jun 71	Bertram+GROUP SIGMAS SAME QUANTS.NDG	
				Rept	AAEC/TM-587	Mar 71	*DESCRIPTION OF LIBRARY	
	1.0-3	1.5+7		Data	AUSTR-DFN 188.	Nov 71	TE-125M POINT+GROUP SIGS,SAME QUANTS	
	1.0-3	1.5+7		Data	AUSTR-DFN 101.	Nov 71	POINT(223) AND GROUP(127) SIGMAS	
Total	1.4+7		FEI	Expt Prog	INDSWG-126 33	66	Dukarevich.SIG=4.69+-0.04B	
Total	1.4+7		CCP	ExTh Jour	IZV 31 217	Feb 67	Dukarevich+.TBL,CURVES,CFD OPTMDL TH	
				Jour	BAS 31 197	Feb 67	TRANSLATN.*	
Total	1.4+7		FTI	Expt Jour	NP/A 92 433	Feb 67	Dukarevich+ CFD OPTMDL 4.69+-0.04B	+
Total		3.0+4	SAC	Expt Priv	TELLIER	Sep 71	Tellier+ NO DATA. RESONANCE ASSGNMNT	+
		3.0+4		Data	EXFOR20122.006	Sep 72	0PTS.	
Total	1.0-3	1.5+7	AUA	Eval Data	AUSTR-DFN 101.	Nov 71	COOK+POINT(223)+GROUP(127)SIG.CF EVL	+
	1.0-3	1.5+7		Data	AUSTR-DFN 188.	Nov 71	.TE-125M.POINT+GROUP SIGS.SEE EVAL	
Total	1.3+7	1.5+7	DEB	Eval Rept	IAEA-153 173	73	Boedy+ MOST PROBABLE VAL OF SIG,TBL	
				Jour	AHP 30 115	Oct 71	Angeli+ AVG SIG,CFD CALC.TBLS.GRAPH	
Elastic	Maxwl		ORL	Expt Jour	ARN 11 303	61	Wilkinson.	+
	Maxwl			Data	EXFOR11005.007	Jun 76	. 1 PT. COH.AMP.	
Elastic	2.0+2	4.0+3	SAC	Expt Prog	EANDC(E)115U	Mar 69	Trochon. LINAC TOF	
Elastic	1.0-3	1.5+7	AUA	Eval Data	AUSTR-DFN 101.	Nov 71	COOK+POINT(223)+GROUP(127)SIG.CF EVL	+
	1.0-3	1.5+7		Data	AUSTR-DFN 188.	Nov 71	.TE-125M.POINT+GROUP SIGS.SEE EVAL	

52 Tellurium 125

Quantity	Energy (ev) Min	Max	Lab	Type	Documentation Ref Vol Page	Date	Author, Comments	Data
Tot Inelastc	5.0+5	1.5+7	AUA Eval	Data	AUSTR – DFN 188.	Nov 71	.TE – 125M.POINT+GROUP SIGS.SEE EVAL	+
	5.0+5	1.5+7		Data	AUSTR – DFN 101.	Nov 71	COOK+POINT(11)+GROUP(127)SIG.CF EVL	
Nonelastic	1.0−3	1.5+7	AUA Eval	Data	AUSTR – DFN 101.	Nov 71	COOK+POINT(223)+GROUP(127)SIG.CF EVL	+
	1.0−3	1.5+7		Data	AUSTR – DFN 188.	Nov 71	.TE – 125M.POINT+GROUP SIGS.SEE EVAL	
Absorption	1.0−3	1.0+7	JUL Eval	Rept	JUEL – 678 – RG	Jul 70	Liu. EVALUATION+CALC,GRPH,FN OF E	
Res Int Abs	None		CRC Eval	Rept	AECL – 1054	Mar 60	Walker.(CRP – 913) REDUCED RES.INT.	
Res Int Abs	+3	+5	BOL Theo	Conf	61Vienna 1 179	Aug 61	Benzi+.PPR11,VAL GVN,L=0,L=1 .CAPT.	
Res Int Abs	5.0−1		BOL Eval	Rept	RT/FI – 4	Jan 67	Palmucci. CALC FROM (N,G) RES PARAMS	
Res Int Abs	None		GA Eval	Rept	GA – 12071	Sep 71	Mathews+. RECOMMENDED VALUES	
Res Int Abs	5.5−1		CRC Eval	Rept	AECL – 3037 1	Jan 72	Walker.REDUCED RES INT FROM RES PARS	
Res Int Abs	5.0−1		AUA Eval	Rept	AAEC/TM – 619	Sep 72	Clayton.CALC FROM SIG LIBRARY,TABLE	
Res Int Abs	+0	+5	WIN Revw	Conf	IAEA – 169 3 163	74	Pope+ META.DATA FILE CALC CFD XP	
Res Int Abs	5.5−1		MUNComp	Jour	JRC 29 175	Jan 76	Gryntakis+, 2 VALUES ARE GIVEN	
(n,γ)	Maxwl		ORL Expt	Jour	PR 88 412	Oct 52	Pomerance.PILE OSC.	+
	Maxwl			Data	EXFOR11507.064	Jun 76	. 1 PT.	
(n,γ)	Maxwl		CRC Eval	Rept	AECL – 1054	Mar 60	Walker. (CRRP – 913)	
(n,γ)	2.0+1	1.5+3	CCP Expt	Conf	AEC – TR – 5734 11	Dec 61	REL TOFRSLN.05MICROSEC/M IMPURITIES	
(n,γ)	2.0+1	1.5+3	CCP Expt	Jour	AE 14 264	Mar 63	COUNTS/TOF SHOWN DANELIAN+.SJA14 258	
(n,γ)	1.0+3	6.0+4	LEB Expt	Conf	65Antwerp § 182	Jul 65	Bergman.LEBEDEV. DO OBTAINED	
(n,γ)	2.5−2		BOL Eval	Rept	RT/FI – 4	Jan 67	Palmucci. CALC FROM RES PARAMETERS	
(n,γ)	3.0+4	2.2+5	ORL Expt	Jour	PR 159 1007	Jul 67	Macklin+. TOF. VDG. SCINT. 5 ES.ABSL	+
	3.0+4	1.3+5		Data	EXFOR11679.014	Jun 76	. 6 PTS.	
(n,γ)	1.0+3	1.0+7	BOL Eval	Rept	CCDN – NW/10	Dec 69	Benzi+H – F MOD,AXEL G(G)EST,ALL DATA	+
				Rept	CEC(70) – 2	Apr 70	– +. GRAPH	
				Conf	61Vienna 1 179	Aug 61	– + TBL AV VALUES.SUPERSEDED	
	1.0+3	1.0+7		Data	BENZI – DFN 644A	May 72	45 POINTS.	
(n,γ)	3.0+4		AUA Theo	Rept	AAEC/E – 211	Nov 70	Musgrove. SIGMA GIVEN AND CFD OTHER	
(n,γ)	Maxwl		GA Eval	Rept	GA – 12071	Sep 71	Mathews+. RECOMMENDED VALUES	
(n,γ)	1.0−3	1.5+7	AUA Eval	Conf	AUSTR – DFN 101.	Nov 71	COOK+POINT(223)+GROUP(127)SIG.CF EVL	+
	1.0−3	1.5+7		Data	AUSTR – DFN 188.	Nov 71	.TE – 125M.POINT+GROUP SIGS.SEE EVAL	
(n,γ)	3.0+3	5.0+5	ORL Expt	Prog	NCSAC – 42 185	Nov 71	Macklin+. ORELA. ANAL TBC. NO DATA	
(n,γ)	Maxwl		CRC Eval	Rept	AECL – 3037 1	Jan 72	Walker.RECOMMENDED SIG,DETAILED TBL	
(n,γ)	2.5−2		AUA Eval	Rept	AAEC/TM – 619	Sep 72	Clayton.CALC FROM SIG LIBRARY,TABLE	
(n,γ)	Pile	2.5−2	SGA Eval	Conf	73Paris 1 233	Mar 73	Eder+ 58 D ISOMER,SIG ESTIMATED,TBL	
				Rept	SGAE – PH – 141	Feb 73	.SAME AS 73PARIS,POINT SIG FROM COOK	
(n,γ)	Fiss		WIN Revw	Conf	IAEA – 169 3 137	74	Dean. GND+META,DATA AVG OVER FIS – SPC	
	Maxwl Fiss			Conf	IAEA – 169 3 163	74	Pope+ GND+META,DATA AVG OVER SPC,XPT	
(n,γ)	1.0+3	1.0+7	FEI Eval	Rept	YK – 8/2 97	Sep 72	Abagjan+ AVG SIG(ENERGY – GROUPS),TABL	
				Rept	INDC(CCP) – 39	Jul 74	.P102. ENGLISH OF YK – 8/2 97	
(n,γ)	1.0+2	6.0+4	DUB Expt	Jour	YF 20 252	Aug 74	Bergman+ SDS.SIG(E),CFD OTHERS,GRAPH	
				Jour	SNP 20 133	Feb 75	. ENGL OF YF 20 252	
(n,γ)	1.0+2	6.0+4	LEB Expt	Jour	YF 20 252	Aug 74	Bergman+ SIG(NEUT – E),GRAPH	+
	1.1+1	1.0+5		Jour	SNP 20 133	Feb 75	. ENGLISH OF YF 20 252	
	1.6+1	6.4+4		Data	EXFOR40292.005	Mar 75	.SIGMA FOR 65 ES GVN	
(n,γ)	2.0+3	2.4+4	BNL Expt	Conf	76Lowell 1297	Jul 76	Greenwood+2ES.LVL STRUC,PI TE126.NDG	
Spect (n,γ)	Maxwl		KUR Expt	Jour	YF 4 238	Aug 66	Groshev+ ES+INTS FROM NAT TE.TBL+FIG	
				Rept	IAE – 699	65	– + MAGNET COMPT SPEC.TBL+GRPH	
				Jour	SNP 4 172	Feb 67	. ENGL OF YF 4 238	
				Rept	ANL – TRANS – 334	65	. ENGL OF IAE – 699.	
Spect (n,γ)	Maxwl		BNL Expt	Prog	WASH – 1127 18	Apr 69	Chrien+ GROUND – STATE GAMMA E GIVEN	
Spect (n,γ)	Pile		ANL Expt	Conf	69Studsvik 601	Aug 69	Smither+ NO DATA GVN,OKS STATMOD	
Spect (n,γ)	2.0+3	2.4+4	BNL Expt	Conf	76Lowell 1297	Jul 76	Greenwood+2ES.LVL STRUC,PI TE126.NDG	
(n,2n)	Fiss		CRC Eval	Rept	CRC – 1003	Dec 60	Roy+,ESTIMATED AVG SIG=19.0MB	
(n,2n)	1.5+7		DEB Eval	Jour	REA 11 1 153	Mar 73	Boedy+ RECOMM.VALUE FROM N – Z SYSTEM.	
(n,2n)	1.5+7		KFI Theo	Rept	KFKI – 73 – 68	Dec 73	Jeki.NEW FIT,CALC SIG CFD OTHERS,TBL	
(n,p)	Fiss		CRC Eval	Rept	CRC – 1003	Dec 60	Roy+,ESTIMATED AVG SIG=0.17MB	
(n,p)	Maxwl		IFU Theo	Rept	ICD – 4 20	67	Dadakina+ PENETR COEFF CALC,TABLE	
(n,α)	Fiss		CRC Eval	Rept	CRC – 1003	Dec 60	Roy+,ESTIMATED AVG SIG=0.2MB	
(n,α)	1.4+7		RBZ Expt	Priv	KULLISIC	Aug 68	Jurcevic.DIFSIG+ALFA SPEC AT 0 DEG.	+
	1.4+7			Data	EXFOR30203.	Nov 72	DIFF SIG AT 0 DEG	
(n,α)	1.4+7		RBZ Expt	Conf	69Bochum 210	Jul 69	Chatterjee+ ALFA – SPEC EXPT, NO DATA	
(n,α)	1.4+7		RBZ ExTh	Conf	69Roorke 2 21	Dec 69	Chatterjee+ CFD P – ALFA REACTION, NDG	
(n,α)	1.4+7		RBZ Theo	Conf	72Budapest 168	Aug 72	Caplar+ ANALYSIS OF SPECTRA,GRAPH	
Reson Params	2.0+1	1.5+3	CCP Expt	Conf	AEC – TR – 5734 11	Dec 61	AVERAGE D=50EV	
Reson Params	+0	1.5+3	KUR Expt	Jour	AE 14 264	Mar 63	Daneljan. E0,WN,WG,J DETERMINED	
				Jour	SJA 14 258	Mar 63	. ENGL OF AE 14 264	
Reson Params		1.0+6	AUA Theo	Jour	AUJ 20 477	Oct 67	Cook. TBL OF AVG LVL SPACING D,L=0,1	
Reson Params	+3	+5	AUA ExTh	Rept	AAEC/E – 198	May 69	Musgrove.RES PARS +STF FROM (NG)FIT	+

52 Tellurium 125

Quantity	Energy (ev) Min	Max	Lab	Type	Documentation Ref Vol Page	Date	Author, Comments	Data
Reson Params		3.0+4	ORL	Expt Prog	ORNL-4513 68	Jun 70	Dabbs+,LINAC,114RESON,ONLY D GIVEN	
Reson Params	-		AUA	Theo Rept	AAEC/E-211	Nov 70	Musgrove. CALCULTD D+GAM WIDTH GIVEN	
Reson Params	2.6+1	2.9+2	CJD	Eval Rept	YK- 7	71	Zakharova+ SURVEY+SYSTEMATICS,GW,TBL	
				Rept	INDC(CCP)-27	Nov 72	.ENGLISH TRANSLATION OF YK-7 /71	
Reson Params	None		DUB	Theo Jour	YF 13 240	Feb 71	Malecki+G-WID,THEO CFD EXPT.TBL,GRPH	
				Jour	SNP 13 133	Aug 71	- + ENGL OF YF 13 240.	
Reson Params	1.4+2	3.4+3	SAC	Expt Conf	71Knoxvill 785	Mar 71	Cauvin+ J ASSIGNMENTS.38 RESONANCES	+
	1.4+2	3.4+3		Data	EXFOR20126.005	Sep 72	38PTS.J.	
Reson Params	9.0+1	7.8+3	SAC	Expt Priv	TELLIER	Sep 71	Tellier+ PARAMETERS FROM TRANS.	+
		7.8+3		Conf	71Knoxvill 680	Mar 71	- +.TRANS,AVG D=37.8EV 114RES	
	9.0+1	7.7+3		Data	EXFOR20120.	Sep 72	340PTS.WG,WT,2G*WN,2G*WN0.	
Reson Params	1.5+2	6.5+2	SAC	ExTh Diss	FRNC-TH-450	Oct 72	Delaroche.OPTICAL MODEL PARAMETERS	
Reson Params	None		DUB	Theo Rept	JINR-P4-7499	Oct 73	Soloviev+ CALC D CFD EXPTS,TABLE	
Reson Params	+0	+2	BOL	Eval Conf	IAEA-169 3 123	74	Benzi+ AVG G-WID CFD OTHERS+XPT,TABL	
Reson Params	+1	+3	FEI	Eval Rept	YK- 8/2 97	Sep 72	Abagyan+ AVG G-WID+D AT BINDNG-E,TBL	
				Rept	INDC(CCP)-39	Jul 74	.PAGE 102.ENGLISH OF YK-8/2 97	
Reson Params	2.6+1	4.3+2	ANL	Expt Prog	WASH-1053 11	Oct 64	Cote.FC. CORRECTS USSR,SOME NEW RES	+
	2.6+1	4.3+2		Data	EXFOR12002.005	Jun 76	. 10 RES, E0,J	
Reson Params	2.6+1	2.6+2	BNL	Expt Abst	BAP 13 1390	Nov 68	Mughabghab+ GE(LI) J=1 FROM N,G 3RES	+
	2.6+1	2.6+2		Data	EXFOR12637.003	Jun 76	. 3 RES, J	
Reson Params	2.6+1	2.9+2	BNL	Expt Abst	BAP 5 18	60	Bolotin.	+
	2.6+1	2.9+2		Data	EXFOR11988.005	Jun 76	. 5 RES, E0,WN,WN0	
Reson Params	2.0+3	2.4+4	BNL	Expt Conf	76Lowell 1297	Jul 76	Greenwood+2ES.LVL STRUC,PI TE126.NDG	
Reson Params	Maxwl		KUK	Theo Conf	76Ahmedabd 2 1	Dec 76	Sharma+AVG S-WAVE REDUCED N-WID ANAL	
Strnth Fnctn	+3	+5	BOL	Theo Conf	61Vienna 1 179	Aug 61	Benzi+.PPR11,TABLE CFD EXPERIMENT	
Strnth Fnctn	2.6+1	7.7+2	CCP	Expt Jour	AE 14 264	Mar 63	.000055+-.00004 DANELIAN+.SJA14 258	+
Strnth Fnctn	1.0+3	6.0+4	LEB	Expt Conf	65Antwerp § 182	Jul 65	Bergman.LEBEDEV.S1=5.1+-1.5.ALSO DO	
Strnth Fnctn	+3	+5	AUA	ExTh Rept	AAEC/E-198	May 69	Musgrove.S+P+D STF FROM (NG)FIT,TBL	
Strnth Fnctn		3.0+4	ORL	Expt Prog	ORNL-4513 68	Jun 70	Dabbs+,LINAC,S0 VALUE GIVEN	
Strnth Fnctn	-		AUA	Theo Rept	AAEC/E-211	Nov 70	Musgrove. SMOOTHED S0,S1 AND S2 GIVN	
Strnth Fnctn	0.0+0	7.8+3	SAC	Expt Priv	TELLIER	Sep 71	Tellier+ FROM RESONANCE ANALYSIS.	+
		7.8+3		Conf	71Knoxvill 680	Mar 71	- +. S0=0.49+-0.10	
	0.0+0	3.4+2		Jour	CR 269 266	Aug 69	- + TOF ALSO D + A (STATPAR)	
		7.8+3		Data	EXFOR20120.	Sep 72	. 3PTS.L=0.	
Strnth Fnctn	None		AUA	Eval Rept	AAEC/E-277	Mar 73	Musgrove.TBLS EXPTL DATA+BEST VALUES	
Strnth Fnctn	None		KUR	Theo Prog	IAE-2560	75	Adamchuk+.S0-VALUE,TBL	
Lvl Density	+6		MIL	Theo Jour	EN 15 1 54	Jan 68	Facchini+ LDL PARS FROM LOW EN RES	
Lvl Density	7.8+3	2.8+4	SAC	Expt Rept	CEA-N-1268	Feb 70	Tellier+.	+
	7.8+3	2.8+4		Data	EXFOR20120.	Sep 72	2PTS.A PARAM,SP.CUT(0).	
Lvl Density		3.0+4	ORL	Expt Prog	ORNL-4513 68	Jun 70	Dabbs+,LINAC,PARAMETER A GIVEN	
Lvl Density	None		MUN	Theo Jour	NP/A 217 269	Dec 73	Dilg+ A,DELTA. BACK SHIFTED FERMIGAS	
Lvl Density	None		BOL	Eval Conf	IAEA-169 3 123	74	Benzi+ LVL DENS PARAM BY XPT,GRPH+TB	
Lvl Density	None		COP	Theo Jour	NP/A 222 493	Apr 74	Dossing+COLL ROTAT.SPAC. ACCUR ESTIM	
Lvl Density	+1	+3	FEI	Eval Rept	YK- 8/2 97	Sep 72	Abagyan+ LVL DENSITY PARAMETER,TBL	
				Rept	INDC(CCP)-39	Jul 74	.PAGE 102.ENGLISH OF YK-8/2 97	

52 Tellurium 126

Quantity	Energy (ev) Min	Max	Lab	Type	Documentation Ref Vol Page	Date	Author, Comments	Data
Evaluation	1.0-3	1.5+7	AUA	Eval Rept	AAEC/TM-549	Jun 70	Cook.TOT,EL,INEL,NONEL,CAPT SIGS,NDG	+
				Rept	AAEC/E-214	Jun 71	Bertram+GROUP SIGMAS SAME QUANTS.NDG	
				Rept	AAEC/TM-587	Mar 71	*DESCRIPTION OF LIBRARY	
	1.0-3	1.5+7		Data	AUSTR-DFN 102.	Nov 71	POINT(223) AND GROUP(127) SIGMAS	
Total	1.4+7		FEI	Expt Prog	INDSWG-126 33	66	Dukarevich.SIG=4.73+-0.02B	
Total	1.4+7		CCP	ExTh Jour	IZV 31 217	Feb 67	Dukarevich+.TBL,CURVES,CFD OPTMDL TH	
				Jour	BAS 31 197	Feb 67	TRANSLATN.*	
Total	1.4+7		FTI	Expt Jour	NP/A 92 433	Feb 67	Dukarevich+ CFD OPTMDL 4.73+-0.02B	+
Total		3.0+4	SAC	Expt Priv	TELLIER	Sep 71	Tellier+ NO DATA. RESONANCE ASSGNMNT	+
		3.0+4		Data	EXFOR20122.007	Sep 72	0PTS.	
Total	1.0-3	1.5+7	AUA	Eval Data	AUSTR-DFN 102.	Nov 71	COOK+POINT(223)+GROUP(127)SIG.CF EVL	+
Total	1.3+7	1.5+7	DEB	Eval Rept	IAEA-153 173	73	Boedy+ MOST PROBABLE VAL OF SIG,TBL	
				Jour	AHP 30 115	Oct 71	Angeli+ AVG SIG,CFD CALC.TBLS.GRAPH	
Elastic	1.0-3	1.5+7	AUA	Eval Data	AUSTR-DFN 102.	Nov 71	COOK+POINT(223)+GROUP(127)SIG.CF EVL	+
Tot Inelastc	1.0+6	1.5+7	AUA	Eval Data	AUSTR-DFN 102.	Nov 71	COOK+POINT(10)+GROUP(127)SIG.CF EVL	+
Diff Inelast	6.8+5	1.3+6	LEB	Expt Jour	IZV 37 1900	Sep 73	Konobeevsky+ SIG OF EXCIT 1-ST LVL	+
				Jour	BAS 37 9 84	Sep 73	. ENGL OF IZV 37 1900	
	6.8+5	1.3+6		Data	EXFOR40214.010	May 74	.DIN=DNG,1 E-LVL,61 DATA LINES	

52 Tellurium 126

Quantity	Energy (ev) Min	Max	Lab	Type	Documentation Ref Vol Page	Date	Author, Comments	Data
Diff Inelast	6.8+5	8.3+5	LEB	Expt	Jour KSF 1976 6 20	76	Konobeevskij+ SIG(E) TO 2+ LVL,GRAPH	
					Jour SPL 1976 6 16	76	. ENGL OF KSF 1976 6 20	
Nonelastic	1.0−3	1.5+7	AUA	Eval	Data AUSTR−DFN 102.	Nov 71	COOK+POINT(223)+GROUP(127)SIG.CF EVL	+
Absorption	4.1−1	1.0+7	GA	Eval	Rept GA− 2451	Aug 61	Joanou+.68GROUP DATA FOR GAM−I	
Absorption	1.0−3	1.0+7	JUL	Eval	Rept JUEL−678−RG	Jul 70	Liu. EVALUATION+CALC,GRPH,FN OF E	
Res Int Abs	None		CRC	Eval	Rept AECL−1054	Mar 60	Walker.(CRP−913) REDUCED RES.INT.	
Res Int Abs	5.0−1		BOL	Eval	Rept RT/FI−4	Jan 67	Palmucci. CALC FROM (N,G) RES PARAMS	
Res Int Abs	None		GA	Eval	Rept GA− 12071	Sep 71	Mathews+. RECOMMENDED VALUES	
Res Int Abs	5.5−1		CRC	Eval	Rept AECL−3037 1	Jan 72	Walker.REDUCED RES INT TO GND+META	
Res Int Abs	5.0−1		AUA	Eval	Rept AAEC/TM−619	Sep 72	Clayton.CALC FROM SIG LIBRARY,TABLE	
Res Int Abs	4.6−1	1.0+6	RCN	Theo	Rept RCN−191	Jul 73	Lautenbach.CAPT INT FROM GROUP SIGMA	
Res Int Abs	5.0−1		GHT	Expt	Jour JRC 20 695	74	Van Der Linden+ BY(N,G).CFD OTHS,TBL	+
	5.5−1				Conf 73Paris 2 241	Mar 73	− + ACT,REL THR+GOLD,TBL	
	5.5−1				Data EXFOR20645.004	Jul 76	1PNT.CAPTURE.	
Res Int Abs	5.5−1	+6	SAC	Revw	Conf IAEA−169 1 235	74	Ribon.CAPTURE,STATUS CFD REQUEST,TBL	
Res Int Abs	+0	+5	WIN	Revw	Conf IAEA−169 3 163	74	Pope+ DATA FILE CALC CFD XPTAL VALUE	
Res Int Abs	5.5−1		MUN	Comp	Jour JRC 29 175	Jan 76	Gryntakis+, 4 VALUES TO META + GND	
(n,γ)	Pile		ANL	Expt	Jour PR 72 888	Nov 47	Seren+.ACT METHOD.TO9.3HR,90D ISOMER	+
	Pile				Data EXFOR11447.	Jun 76	. 2 PTS, SIG TO GND + ISOMER	
(n,γ)	Maxwl		ORL	Expt	Jour PR 88 412	Oct 52	Pomerance.PILE OSC.	+
	Maxwl				Data EXFOR11507.065	Jun 76	. 1 PT.	
(n,γ)	Maxwl		CRC	Eval	Rept AECL−1054	Mar 60	Walker. (CRRP−913)	
(n,γ)	None		ANL	Theo	Jour PR 120 1305	Nov 60	Huizenga+ ISOMER RATIO,TH CFD EXPT	
(n,γ)	Maxwl		MUA	Expt	Jour NP 36 542	Aug 62	Mangal+ SCINT SPECT,REL TO AU197,TBL	+
					Conf 62Madras 95	Feb 62	− +	
	Maxwl				Data EXFOR31248.009	Apr 73	.SIG TO GND−STATE GVN	
(n,γ)	Maxwl		MTR	Expt	Jour PR 129 769	Jan 63	Keisch.RATIO ISOMER ACT TO GND ACT.	+
	Maxwl				Data EXFOR11748.017	Jun 76	. 1 PT, ISOMER RATIO	
(n,γ)	2.0+1	1.5+3	CCP	Expt	Jour AE 14 264	Mar 63	ONLY 1RES AT 198EV FOUND SJA14 258	
(n,γ)	Maxwl		ANL	Comp	Jour NP 60 241	Nov 64	Bishop+EXP AND TH ISOMER RATIOS CFD	
(n,γ)	1.0+3	6.0+4	LEB	Expt	Conf 65Antwerp § 182	Jul 65	Bergman.LEBEDEV. DO OBTAINED	
(n,γ)	2.5−2		BOL	Eval	Rept RT/FI−4	Jan 67	Palmucci. CALC FROM RES PARAMETERS	
(n,γ)	1.3+5	3.0+5	ORL	Expt	Jour PR 159 1007	Jul 67	Macklin+. TOF. VDG. SCINT. 5 ES.ABSL	+
	3.0+4	1.3+5			Data EXFOR11679.015	Jun 76	. 6 PTS.	
(n,γ)	−		IEA	Comp	Rept IEA−INF− 10	Aug 68	Atalla. TABLES OF HL,SIG AND GAMM−E	
(n,γ)	2.4+4		MUA	Theo	Jour IJP 42 567	Sep 68	Chaubey+ METHD OF BOOTH,VAL CFD XPT	+
				Expt	Jour NP 66 267	May 65	− +,SB−BE,ACT BETA−DET REL I127	
	2.4+4				Data EXFOR30063.007	Dec 70	SIGMA FOR 9.3 H HALF−LIFE	
(n,γ)	1.0+3	1.0+7	BOL	Eval	Rept CCDN−NW/10	Dec 69	Benzi+H−F MOD,AXEL G(G)EST,ALL DATA	+
					Rept CEC(70)−2	Apr 70	− +. GRAPH	
					Conf 66Paris 1 537	Oct 66	− + STATMOD.TBL AV VALS.SUPERSEDD	
	1.0+3	1.0+7			Data BENZI−DFN 537D	May 72	45 PNTS	
(n,γ)	3.0+4		AUA	Theo	Rept AAEC/E−211	Nov 70	Musgrove. SIGMA GIVEN AND CFD OTHER	
(n,γ)	Maxwl		GA	Eval	Rept GA− 12071	Sep 71	Mathews+. RECOMMENDED VALUES	
(n,γ)	1.0−3	1.5+7	AUA	Eval	Data AUSTR−DFN 102.	Nov 71	COOK+POINT(223)+GROUP(127)SIG.CF EVL	+
(n,γ)	3.0+3	5.0+5	ORL	Expt	Prog NCSAC−42 185	Nov 71	Macklin+. ORELA. ANAL TBC. NO DATA	
(n,γ)	Maxwl		CRC	Eval	Rept AECL−3037 1	Jan 72	Walker.RECOMMEND SIG TO GND+META,TBL	
(n,γ)	2.4+4		MUA	Theo	Jour IJP 46 114	Mar 72	Chaubey+,P−WAVE STRENGTH FUNC,TABLE	
(n,γ)	2.5−2		AUA	Eval	Rept AAEC/TM−619	Sep 72	Clayton.CALC FROM SIG LIBRARY,TABLE	
(n,γ)		1.1+7	RCN	Theo	Rept RCN−191	Jun 73	Lautenbach. GROUP CONSTANTS TBL	
(n,γ)	2.5−2		SAC	Revw	Conf IAEA−169 1 235	74	Ribon.STATUS SIG CFD REQUESTS,TABLE	
(n,γ)	Maxwl	Fiss	WIN	Revw	Conf IAEA−169 3 163	74	Pope+ MAXW+FIS−SPEC AVG DATA CFD XPT	
	Fiss				Conf IAEA−169 3 137	74	Dean. POINT DATA AVG OVER STAND SPEC	
(n,γ)	1.0+3	1.0+7	FEI	Eval	Rept YK− 8/2 97	Sep 72	Abagjan+ AVG SIG(ENERGY−GROUPS),TABL	
					Rept INDC(CCP)−39	Jul 74	.P102. ENGLISH OF YK−8/2 97	
(n,γ)	1.0+2	6.0+4	DUB	Expt	Jour YF 20 252	Aug 74	Bergman+ SDS.SIG(E),CFD OTHERS,GRAPH	
					Jour SNP 20 133	Feb 75	. ENGL OF YF 20 252	
(n,γ)	1.0+2	6.0+4	LEB	Expt	Jour YF 20 252	Aug 74	Bergman+ SIG(NEUT−E),GRAPH	+
	1.1+1	1.0+5			Jour SNP 20 133	Feb 75	ENGLISH OF YF 20 252	
	1.4+2	6.4+4			Data EXFOR40292.006	Mar 75	.SIGMA FOR 40 ES GVN	
(n,γ)	2.5−2		BRK	Theo	Jour NP/A 237 3 419	Jan 75	Nardi+ ISOM RATIO,MTE−CARLO,CFD XPT	
Spect (n,γ)	+6		CNE	Expt	Conf 58Geneva 14 203	Sep 58	Bosch+.PPR2463,CURVE,EXPT DESCRIBED	
Spect (n,γ)	Maxwl		KUR	Expt	Jour YF 4 238	Aug 66	Groshev+ ES+INTS FROM NAT TE.TBL+FIG	
					Rept IAE−699	65	− + MAGNET COMPT SPEC.TBL+GRPH	
					Jour SNP 4 172	Feb 67	. ENGL OF YF 4 238	
					Rept ANL−TRANS−334	65	. ENGL OF IAE−699.	
Spect (n,γ)	Pile		CCP	Expt	Jour IZV 32 207	Feb 68	Kalinauskas+ TE127 META,CONVERS−SPEC	
					Jour BAS 32 187	69	TRANSLATN.*NO 2	

52 Tellurium 126

Quantity	Energy (ev) Min	Max	Lab	Type	Documentation Ref Vol Page	Date	Author, Comments	Data
Spect (n,γ)	Maxwl		BNL Expt	Prog	WASH – 1127 18	Apr 69	Chrien+ GROUND – STATE GAMMA E GIVEN	
Spect (n,γ)	Pile		KUR Expt	Jour	YF 13 681	Apr 71	Groshev+ GE – LI,TBD	
				Jour	SNP 13 387	Oct 71	. ENGL OF YF 13 681	
Inelastic γ	4.4+6		WES Expt	Jour	PR 102 461	Apr 56	Sinclair. 1.38MEV GAMMAS SEEN	+
				Rept	AECU – 3387	55	– .	
	4.4+6			Data	EXFOR11770.005	Jun 76	. 2 PTS.	
Inelastic γ	6.8+5	8.3+5	LEB Expt	Jour	KSF 1976 6 20	76	Konobeevskij+ SIG(E) TO 2+ LVL,GRAPH	
				Jour	SPL 1976 6 16	76	. ENGL OF KSF 1976 6 20	
(n,2n)	Fiss		CRC Eval	Rept	CRC – 1003	Dec 60	Roy+,ESTIMATED AVG SIG=1.5MB	
(n,2n)	1.5+7		DEB Eval	Jour	REA 11 1 153	Mar 73	Boedy+ RECOMM.VALUE FROM N – Z SYSTEM.	
(n,2n)	1.5+7		KFI Theo	Rept	KFKI – 73 – 68	Dec 73	Jeki.NEW FIT,CALC SIG CFD OTHERS,TBL	
(n,p)	Fiss		CRC Eval	Rept	CRC – 1003	Dec 60	Roy+,ESTIMATED AVG SIG=0.02MB	
(n,p)	1.5+7		ARK Expt	Jour	NP/A 114 663	Jul 68	Husain+.TO METASTABLE. T – D NS.	+
				Abst	DA/B 29 1626	Nov 68	– .1 P TO SB126M SIG=1.5+ – .2MB	
	1.5+7			Data	EXFOR11999.011	Jun 76	. 1 PT.	
(n,p)	1.5+7		DEB Comp	Jour	REA 7 4 93	Dec 69	Csikai+ SIG+HL COMPILTN,N – ACTIV – ANAL	
(n,p)	1.4+7	1.5+7	JYV Eval	Rept	JU – RR – 3/1970	Jun 70	Leppaemaeki+ TABLE OF EVAL AVG SIG	
(n,p)	1.5+7		KAZ Expt	Jour	YF 13 923	May 71	Levkovsky+ ACT,SIG+ISOMER RATIO,TBL	
				Jour	SNP 13 529	Nov 71	. ENGL OF YF 10 923	
(n,p)	1.5+7		RBZ Expt	Jour	FIZS 4 61	Dec 72	Lulic+ ISOMERIC SIG RATIO,CFD TH,TBL	
(n,p)	1.4+7	1.5+7	KAZ Theo	Jour	YF 18 705	Oct 73	Levkovsky.AVERAGED SIG,CALC,TBL	
				Jour	SNP 18 361	Apr 74	. ENGLISH OF YF 18,705	
(n,p)	1.4+7		IRK Expt	Jour	NP/A 222 605	Apr 74	Struwe+ GELI. REL AL(N,A).	+
	1.5+7			Data	EXFOR20540.	Apr 76	3PTS.SIGMA.	
(n,p)	1.5+7		SLO Expt	Jour	ASL 26 64	76	Hlavac+ ACTIV(GELI).TO META,CFD,TABL	+
	1.5+7			Data	EXFOR30286.008	Apr 75	1 DATA POINT	
(n,α)	Fiss		CRC Eval	Rept	CRC – 1003	Dec 60	Roy+,ESTIMATED AVG SIG=0.0016MB	
(n,α)	1.5+7		SAH Expt	Jour	NP 89 329	Dec 66	Majumdar. STAT THEO CFD EXPTS	+
			Expt	Jour	NP 41 192	Mar 63	Najumdar+ACTIVATION REL AL27(NP)	
	1.5+7			Data	EXFOR31117.003	Sep 72	.SIG GVN	
(n,α)	1.4+7		RBZ Expt	Priv	KULLISIC	Aug 68	Jurcevic.DIFSIG+ALFA SPEC AT 0 DEG.	+
	1.4+7			Data	EXFOR30203.	Nov 72	DIFF SIG AT 0 DEG	
(n,α)	1.5+7		ARK Expt	Jour	NP/A 114 663	Jul 68	Husain+.TO METASTABLE. T – D NS.	+
				Abst	DA/B 29 1626	Nov 68	– .1 A TO SN123G SIG=0.8+ – .1MB	
	1.5+7			Data	EXFOR11999.012	Jun 76	. 1 PT.	
(n,α)	1.4+7		RBZ Expt	Conf	69Bochum 210	Jul 69	Chatterjee+ ALFA – SPEC EXPT, NO DATA	
(n,α)	1.5+7		DEB Comp	Jour	REA 7 4 93	Dec 69	Csikai+ SIG+HL COMPILTN,N – ACTIV – ANAL	
(n,α)	1.4+7		RBZ ExTh	Conf	69Roorke 2 21	Dec 69	Chatterjee+ CFD P – ALFA REACTION, NDG	
(n,α)	1.4+7	1.5+7	JYV Eval	Rept	JU – RR – 3/1970	Jun 70	Leppaemaeki+ TABLE OF EVAL AVG SIG	
(n,α)	1.5+7		KAZ Expt	Jour	YF 13 923	May 71	Levkovsky+ ACT,SIG+ISOMER RATIO,TBL	
				Jour	SNP 13 529	Nov 71	. ENGL OF YF 10 923	
(n,α)	1.4+7		RBZ Theo	Conf	72Budapest 168	Aug 72	Caplar+ ANALYSIS OF SPECTRA,GRAPH	
(n,α)	1.4+7	1.5+7	KAZ Theo	Jour	YF 18 705	Oct 73	Levkovsky.AVERAGED SIG,CALC,TBL	
				Jour	SNP 18 361	Apr 74	. ENGLISH OF YF 18,705	
Reson Params	2.0+2		KUR Expt	Jour	AE 14 264	Mar 63	Daneljan. RESONANCE AT 198 EV	
				Jour	SJA 14 258	Mar 63	. ENGL OF AE 14 264	
Reson Params		1.0+6	AUA Theo	Jour	AUJ 20 477	Oct 67	Cook. TBL OF AVG LVL SPACING D,L=0,1	
Reson Params		3.0+4	ORL Expt	Prog	ORNL – 4513 68	Jun 70	Dabbs+,LINAC,65 RESON,D 2G*WN GIVEN	
Reson Params	–		AUA Theo	Rept	AAEC/E – 211	Nov 70	Musgrove. CALCULTD D+GAM WIDTH GIVEN	
Reson Params	2.0+2	1.8+4	SAC Expt	Priv	TELLIER	Sep 71	Tellier+ PARAMETERS FROM TRANS.	+
	1.8+4			Conf	71Knoxvill 680	Mar 71	– +.TRANS,AVG D=206.9EV 65RESON	
	2.0+2	1.8+4		Data	EXFOR20120.	Sep 72	141PTS.E0,WG,WT,2G*WN,2G*WN0.	
Reson Params		+3	BNL Expt	Prog	USNDC – 1 30	May 72	Mughabghab+. P – WAVE RESON FROM CAPT	
Reson Params	1.5+2	6.5+2	SAC ExTh	Diss	FRNC – TH – 450	Oct 72	Delaroche.OPTICAL MODEL PARAMETERS	
Reson Params	+2	+4	FEI Eval	Jour	YK – 8/2 97	Sep 72	Abagyan+ AVG G – WID+D AT BINDNG – E,TBL	
				Rept	INDC(CCP) – 39	Jul 74	.PAGE 102.ENGLISH OF YK – 8/2 97	
Reson Params	2.0+2		ANL Expt	Prog	WASH – 1053 1	64	Cote.	+
	2.0+2			Data	EXFOR12002.006	Jun 76	. 1 RES, E0	
Reson Params	2.0+2		ANL Expt	Prog	WASH – 1044 20	Aug 63	Singh+	+
	2.0+2			Data	EXFOR12001.003	Jun 76	. 1 RES, E0	
Reson Params	2.0+2		BNL Expt	Abst	BAP 5 18	60	Bolotin.	+
	2.0+2			Data	EXFOR11988.006	Jun 76	. 1 RES, E0,WN,WN0	
Strnth Fnctn		3.0+4	ORL Expt	Prog	ORNL – 4513 68	Jun 70	Dabbs+,LINAC,S0 VALUE GIVEN	
Strnth Fnctn	–		AUA Theo	Rept	AAEC/E – 211	Nov 70	Musgrove. SMOOTHED S0,S1 AND S2 GIVN	
Strnth Fnctn	0.0+0	1.8+4	SAC Expt	Priv	TELLIER	Sep 71	Tellier+ FROM RESONANCE ANALYSIS.	
		1.8+4		Conf	71Knoxvill 680	Mar 71	– +. SO=0.30+ – 0.10	
	0.0+0	1.8+4		Jour	CR 269 266	Aug 69	– + TOF ALSO D + A (STATPAR)	
				Data	EXFOR20120.042	Sep 72	1PNT.L=0.	

52 Tellurium 126

Quantity	Energy (ev) Min	Max	Lab	Type	Documentation Ref Vol Page	Date	Author, Comments	Data
Strnth Fnctn	2.4+4		MUA	Theo Jour	IJP 46 114	Mar 72	Chaubey+ P – WAVE.FOR A – SYSTEMTIC,GRPH	
Strnth Fnctn	None		DUB	Theo Rept	JINR – P4 – 6947	73	Nikolenko. S0,ISOTOPIC DEPENDNC,GRPH	
				Rept	BNL – TR – 556	Dec 73	. ENGLISH OF JINR – P4 – 6947	
Strnth Fnctn	None		AUA	Eval Rept	AAEC/E – 277	Mar 73	Musgrove.TBLS EXPTL DATA+BEST VALUES	
Strnth Fnctn	None		KUR	Theo Prog	IAE – 2560	75	Adamchuk+.S0 – VALUE,TBL	
Strnth Fnctn	None		OSA	Theo Conf	JAERI – M – 5984	Feb 75	Kitazoe+OPT MDLS.GRPH VS A.TBL PARS.	
Strnth Fnctn	+0	+6	DUB	Theo Rept	JINR – P4 – 9052	Oct 75	Soloviev+ S0,S1,SEMIMICROSC MODL,TBL	
Lvl Density	–		FEI	ExTh Prog	YFI – 6 18	68	Ignatjuk+ TABLE VARIOUS PARAMETERS	
				Rept	INDC – 260E	69	. ENGL OF YFI – 6 18	
Lvl Density	+6		MIL	Theo Jour	EN 15 1 54	Jan 68	Facchini+ LDL PARS FROM LOW EN RES	
Lvl Density	–		FEI	Theo Jour	YF 8 1135	Dec 68	Ignatjuk+ TBL,A+ENTROPY+TEMP,CFD XPT	
				Jour	SNP 8 660	Jun 69	TRANSLATN.*	
Lvl Density	7.8+3	1.8+4	SAC	Expt Rept	CEA – N – 1268	Feb 70	Tellier+.	+
	7.8+3	1.8+4		Data	EXFOR20120.	Sep 72	2PTS.A PARAM,SP.CUT(0).	
Lvl Density	–		FEI	Theo Conf	70Helsinki 2 885	Jun 70	Ignatjuk+76. SUPERFLUID CFD FERMI – TH	
Lvl Density		3.0+4	ORL	Expt Prog	ORNL – 4513 68	Jun 70	Dabbs+,LINAC,PARAMETER A GIVEN	
Lvl Density	None		AUW	Theo Conf	70Madurai 2 267	Dec 70	Ramamurty+ A – PARAMETER GVN,LANG'S TH	
Lvl Density	None		MUN	Theo Jour	NP/A 217 269	Dec 73	Dilg+ A,DELTA. BACK SHIFTED FERMIGAS	
Lvl Density	None		COP	Theo Jour	NP/A 222 493	Apr 74	Dossing+COLL ROTAT.SPAC. ACCUR ESTIM	
Lvl Density	+2	+4	FEI	Eval Rept	YK – 8/2 97	Sep 72	Abagyan+ LVL DENSITY PARAMETER,TBL	
				Rept	INDC(CCP) – 39	Jul 74	.PAGE 102.ENGLISH OF YK – 8/2 97	
(γ,n)	8.0+6	2.6+7	SAC	Expt Jour	NP/A 258 350	Feb 76	Lepretre+GDR,LORENTZ PARAM,GRPHS,TBL	

52 Tellurium 127

Quantity	Energy (ev) Min	Max	Lab	Type	Documentation Ref Vol Page	Date	Author, Comments	Data
Evaluation	1.0 – 3	1.5+7	AUA	Eval Rept	AAEC/TM – 549	Jun 70	Cook.TOT,EL,INEL,NONEL,CAPT,G+M,NDG	+
				Rept	AAEC/E – 214	Jun 71	Bertram+GROUP SIGMAS SAME QUANTS.NDG	
				Rept	AAEC/TM – 587	Mar 71	*DESCRIPTION OF LIBRARY	
	1.0 – 3	1.5+7		Data	AUSTR – DFN 189.	Nov 71	TE – 127M POINT+GROUP SIGS,SAME QUANTS	
	1.0 – 3	1.5+7		Data	AUSTR – DFN 103.	Nov 71	POINT(223) AND GROUP(127) SIGMAS	
Total	1.0 – 3	1.5+7	AUA	Eval Data	AUSTR – DFN 103.	Nov 71	COOK+POINT(223)+GROUP(127)SIG.CF EVL	+
	1.0 – 3	1.5+7		Data	AUSTR – DFN 189.	Nov 71	.TE – 127M.POINT+GROUP SIGS.SEE EVAL	
Elastic	1.0 – 3	1.5+7	AUA	Eval Data	AUSTR – DFN 103.	Nov 71	COOK+POINT(223)+GROUP(127)SIG.CF EVL	+
	1.0 – 3	1.5+7		Data	AUSTR – DFN 189.	Nov 71	.TE – 127M.POINT+GROUP SIGS.SEE EVAL	
Tot Inelastc	5.0+5	1.5+7	AUA	Eval Data	AUSTR – DFN 103.	Nov 71	COOK+POINT(11)+GROUP(127)SIG.CF EVL	+
	5.0+5	1.5+7		Data	AUSTR – DFN 189.	Nov 71	.TE – 127M.POINT+GROUP SIGS.SEE EVAL	
Nonelastic	1.0 – 3	1.5+7	AUA	Eval Data	AUSTR – DFN 189.	Nov 71	.TE – 127M.POINT+GROUP SIGS.SEE EVAL	
	1.0 – 3	1.5+7		Data	AUSTR – DFN 103.	Nov 71	COOK+POINT(223)+GROUP(127)SIG.CF EVL	
Res Int Abs	5.0 – 1		AUA	Eval Rept	AAEC/TM – 619	Sep 72	Clayton.CALC FROM SIG LIBRARY,TABLE	
Res Int Abs	+0	+5	WIN	Revw Conf	IAEA – 169 3 163	74	Pope+ GND+META.AUSTRL DATA FILE CALC	
(n,γ)	1.0 – 3	1.5+7	AUA	Eval Data	AUSTR – DFN 103.	Nov 71	COOK+POINT(223)+GROUP(127)SIG.CF EVL	+
(n,γ)	1.0 – 3	1.5+7		Data	AUSTR – DFN 189.	Nov 71	.TE – 127M.POINT+GROUP SIGS.SEE EVAL	
(n,γ)	Pile		CRC	Eval Rept	AECL – 3037 1	Jan 72	Walker.ESTIMATED SIG OF TE – 127M+GND	
(n,γ)	2.5 – 2		AUA	Eval Rept	AAEC/TM – 619	Sep 72	Clayton.CALC FROM SIG LIBRARY,TABLE	
(n,γ)	Pile	2.5 – 2	SGA	Eval Conf	73Paris 1 233	Mar 73	Eder+ 109 D ISOMER,SIG ESTIMATED,TBL	
				Rept	SGAE – PH – 141	Feb 73	.SAME AS 73PARIS,POINT SIG FROM COOK	
(n,γ)	Fiss		WIN	Revw Conf	IAEA – 169 3 137	74	Dean. GND+META,DATA AVG OVER FIS – SPC	
	Maxwl	Fiss		Conf	IAEA – 169 3 163	74	Pope+ GND+META,MAXW+FIS – SPC AVG DATA	
(n,2n)	1.4+7		FIR	ExTh Jour	NCL 1 2 95	Jan 69	Guidetti+ CALC ISOM RATIO CFD EXP	
Reson Params	–		AUA	Theo Rept	AAEC/E – 211	Nov 70	Musgrove. CALCULTD D+GAM WIDTH GIVEN	
Strnth Fnctn	–		AUA	Theo Rept	AAEC/E – 211	Nov 70	Musgrove. SMOOTHED S0,S1 AND S2 GIVN	
Strnth Fnctn	– 2	+3	SAC	Expt Rept	CEA – N – 1522	Oct 72	Cauvin+ S0,S1 CALC	
Lvl Density	None		MUN	Theo Jour	NP/A 217 269	Dec 73	Dilg+ A,DELTA. BACK SHIFTED FERMIGAS	
Lvl Density	None		COP	Theo Jour	NP/A 222 493	Apr 74	Dossing+COLL ROTAT.SPAC. ACCUR ESTIM	
Lvl Density	9.0+6	1.5+7	ANL	Eval Rept	ANL – 75 – 34	Jun 75	Davey+N2NEVAL.CONSTANT T,LVL DEN FIT	

52 Tellurium 128

Quantity	Energy (ev) Min	Max	Lab	Type	Documentation Ref Vol Page	Date	Author, Comments	Data
Evaluation	1.0 – 3	1.5+7	AUA	Eval Rept	AAEC/TM – 549	Jun 70	Cook.TOT,EL,INEL,NONEL,CAPT SIGS,NDG	+
				Rept	AAEC/E – 214	Jun 71	Bertram+GROUP SIGMAS SAME QUANTS.NDG	
				Rept	AAEC/TM – 587	Mar 71	*DESCRIPTION OF LIBRARY	
	1.0 – 3	1.5+7		Data	AUSTR – DFN 104.	Nov 71	POINT(223) AND GROUP(127) SIGMAS	
Total	1.4+7		FEI	Expt Prog	INDSWG – 126 33	66	Dukarevich.SIG=4.76+ – 0.03B	

52 Tellurium 128

Quantity	Energy (ev) Min	Max	Lab	Type	Documentation Ref Vol Page	Date	Author, Comments	Data
Total	1.4+7		CCP	ExTh	Jour IZV 31 217	Feb 67	Dukarevich+.TBL,CURVES,CFD OPTMDL TH	
					Jour BAS 31 197	Feb 67	TRANSLATN.*	
Total	1.4+7		FTI	Expt	Jour NP/A 92 433	Feb 67	Dukarevich+ CFD OPTMDL 4.76+ −0.03B	+
Total		3.0+4	SAC	Expt	Priv TELLIER	Sep 71	Tellier+ NO DATA. RESONANCE ASSGNMNT	+
		3.0+4			Data EXFOR20122.008	Sep 72	0PTS.	
Total	1.0−3	1.5+7	AUA	Eval	Data AUSTR−DFN 104.	Nov 71	COOK+POINT(223)+GROUP(127)SIG.CF EVL	+
Total	1.3+7	1.5+7	DEB	Eval	Rept IAEA−153 173	73	Boedy+ MOST PROBABLE VAL OF SIG,TBL	
					Jour AHP 30 115	Oct 71	Angeli+ AVG SIG,CFD CALC.TBLS.GRAPH	
Elastic	1.0−3	1.5+7	AUA	Eval	Data AUSTR−DFN 104.	Nov 71	COOK+POINT(223)+GROUP(127)SIG.CF EVL	+
Diff Elastic	1.0+6		LAS	Eval	Rept LA−2016	Jun 56	Longley.TBL ANG DIST 3−DEG STEPS	
Tot Inelastc	1.0+6	1.5+7	AUA	Eval	Data AUSTR−DFN 104.	Nov 71	COOK+POINT(10)+GROUP(127)SIG.CF EVL	+
Tot Inelastc	1.5+7		NIL	Expt	Prog INDC(SEC)−50	Jan 76	. ABST. NDG	
Diff Inelast	7.5+5	1.2+6	LEB	Expt	Jour IZV 37 1900	Sep 73	Konobeevsky+ SIG OF EXCIT 1−ST LVL	+
					Jour BAS 37 9 84	Sep 73	. ENGL OF IZV 37 1900	
	7.5+5	1.2+6			Data EXFOR40214.011	May 74	.DIN=DNG,1 E−LVL,56 DATA LINES	
Diff Inelast	7.4+5	8.9+5	LEB	Expt	Jour KSF 1976 6 20	76	Konobeevskij+ SIG(E) TO 2+ LVL,GRAPH	
					Jour SPL 1976 6 20	76	. ENGL OF KSF 1976 6 20	
Nonelastic	1.0−3	1.5+7	AUA	Eval	Data AUSTR−DFN 104.	Nov 71	COOK+POINT(223)+GROUP(127)SIG.CF EVL	+
Nonelastic	1.4+7	1.5+7	ANL	Eval	Rept ANL−75−34	Jun 75	Davey+CORRC APPLIED TO N2N CS.TBLS.	
Absorption	4.1−1	1.0+7	GA	Eval	Rept GA−2451	Aug 61	Joanou+.68GROUP DATA FOR GAM−I	
Absorption	1.0−4	1.0+7	JUL	Eval	Rept JUEL−678−RG	Jul 70	Liu. EVALUATION+CALC,GRPH,FN OF E	
Res Int Abs	None		CRC	Eval	Rept AECL−1054	Mar 60	Walker.(CRP−913) REDUCED RES.INT.	
Res Int Abs	5.0−1		BOL	Eval	Rept RT/FI−4	Jan 67	Palmucci. CALC FROM (N,G) RES PARAMS	
Res Int Abs	Maxwl		PAV	Expt	Jour NSE 35 88	Jan 69	Maxia+ ACT RI FOR GR,META FORMATION	
Res Int Abs	None		GA	Eval	Rept GA−12071	Sep 71	Mathews+. RECOMMENDED VALUES	
Res Int Abs	5.5−1		CRC	Eval	Rept AECL−3037 1	Jan 72	Walker.REDUCED RES INT TO GND+META	
Res Int Abs	5.0−1		AUA	Eval	Rept AAEC/TM−619	Sep 72	Clayton.CALC FROM SIG LIBRARY,TABLE	
Res Int Abs	5.0−1		SGA	Eval	Conf 73Paris 1 233	Mar 73	Eder+ SIG TO TE129M,REDUCED,CAPT,TBL	
					Rept SGAE−PH−141	Feb 73	.SAME AS 73PARIS,EVAL OF EXPTL DATA	
Res Int Abs	4.6−1	1.0+6	RCN	Theo	Rept RCN−191	Jul 73	Lautenbach.CAPT INT FROM GROUP SIGMA	
Res Int Abs	4.0−1		LRL	Expt	Jour PR/C 8 2405	Dec 73	Browne+DRVD FROM MEAS	+
	4.0−1				Data EXFOR10340.004	Jun 76	1PT RIA=1098+−105MB	
Res Int Abs	5.0−1		GHT	Expt	Jour JRC 20 695		74 Van Der Linden+ BY(N,G).CFD OTHS,TBL	+
	5.5−1				Conf 73Paris 2 241	Mar 73	− + ACT,REL THR+GOLD,TBL	
	5.5−1				Data EXFOR20645.005	Jul 76	1PNT.CAPTURE.	
Res Int Abs	5.5−1	+6	SAC	Revw	Conf IAEA−169 1 235		74 Ribon.CAPTURE,STATUS CFD REQUEST,TBL	
Res Int Abs	+0	+5	WIN	Revw	Conf IAEA−169 3 163		74 Pope+ DATA FILE CALC CFD XPTAL VALUE	
Res Int Abs	5.5−1		MUN	Comp	Jour JRC 29 175	Jan 76	Gryntakis+, 6 VALUES TO META + GND	
(n,γ)	Pile		ANL	Expt	Jour PR 72 888	Nov 47	Seren+.ACT METHOD.TO72MIN,32D ISOMER	+
	Pile				Data EXFOR11447.	Jun 76	. 2 PTS, SIG TO GND + META	
(n,γ)	Maxwl		ORL	Expt	Jour PR 88 412	Oct 52	Pomerance.PILE OSC.ESTIM.ERROR 100PC	+
	Maxwl				Data EXFOR11507.066	Jun 76	. 1 PT.	
(n,γ)	Maxwl		CRC	Eval	Rept AECL−1054	Mar 60	Walker. (CRRP−913)	
(n,γ)	None		ANL	Theo	Rept PR 120 1305	Nov 60	Huizenga+ ISOMER RATIO,TH CFD EXPT	
(n,γ)	Maxwl		MUA	Expt	Jour NP 36 542	Aug 62	Mangal+ SCINT SPECT,REL TO AU197,TBL	+
					Conf 62Madras 95	Feb 62	− +	
	Maxwl				Data EXFOR31248.010	Apr 73	.SIG TO GND−STATE GVN	
(n,γ)	Maxwl		ANL	Expt	Jour NP 60 241	Nov 64	Bishop+EXP AND TH ISOMER RATIOS CFD	+
	Maxwl					Jun 76	. 1 PT, ISOMER RATIO	
(n,γ)	1.0+3	6.0+4	LEB	Expt	Conf 65Antwerp § 182	Jul 65	Bergman.LEBEDEV. DO OBTAINED	
(n,γ)	2.4+4		MUA	Expt	Jour PR 152 1055	Dec 66	Chaubey+ SIG TO GND REL I−127,TABLE	+
	2.4+4				Data EXFOR30079.026	Dec 70	SIGMA FOR 72. MIN HALF−LIFE	
(n,γ)	2.5−2		BOL	Eval	Rept RT/FI−4	Jan 67	Palmucci. CALC FROM RES PARAMETERS	
(n,γ)	1.3+5	3.0+5	ORL	Expt	Jour PR 159 1007	Jul 67	Macklin+. TOF. VDG. SCINT. 5 ES.ABSL	+
	3.0+5	1.3+5			Data EXFOR11679.016	Jun 76	. 6 PTS.	
(n,γ)	1.1+4	3.4+5	FEI	Expt	Prog YFI−6 11	68	Dovbenko+. TABLE. TO BE PUBL IN AE	+
	1.0+4	4.0+5			Jour SJA 27 1185	Nov 69	.ENGL. TRANSL. OF AE 27 406	
					Jour EAF 27 41	Nov 69	.FRENCH TRANSL. OF AE 27 406	
					Jour AE 27 406	Nov 69	Dovbenko+ SIG(E)GRPH,CFD OTHR+OPTMOD	
	2.0+5	3.0+6			Jour AE 25 529	Dec 68	− +GRPH SIG(NEUT−E),CFD OPTMOD	
	1.1+4	3.4+5			Prog INDC(CCP)−3U	Mar 69	.ENGLISH TRANSL OF YFI−6 11 /68	
	2.0+5	3.0+6			Jour SJA 25 1367	Dec 68	.ENGLISH TRANSL OF AE 25 529 1268	
					Jour EAF 25 120	Dec 68	.FRENCH TRANSL OF AE 25 529 1268	
	1.1+4	3.9+5			Data EXFOR40331.012	Jan 76	SIG−GND AT10 ES	
	1.1+4	3.1+6			Data EXFOR40006.002	Jul 70	.SIGMA AT 25 ENERGIES GIVEN	
(n,γ)	−		IEA	Comp	Rept IEA−INF−10	Aug 68	Atalla. TABLES OF HL,SIG AND GAMM−E	
(n,γ)	Maxwl		PAV	Expt	Jour NSE 35 88	Jan 69	Maxia+ ACT SIGS FOR GR,META FORMATN	

52 Tellurium 128

Quantity	Energy (ev) Min	Energy (ev) Max	Lab	Type	Documentation Ref Vol Page	Date	Author, Comments	Data
(n,γ)	1.0+3	1.0+7	BOL	Eval	Rept CCDN-NW/10	Dec 69	Benzi+ H-F MOD,AXEL G(G)EST,ALL DATA	+
					Rept CEC(70)-2	Apr 70	- +. GRAPH	
					Conf 66Paris 1 537	Oct 66	- + STATMOD.TBL AV VALS.SUPERSEDD	
	1.0+3	1.0+7			Data BENZI-DFN 539D	May 72	45 PNTS	
(n,γ)	3.0+4		AUA	Theo	Rept AAEC/E-211	Nov 70	Musgrove. SIGMA GIVEN AND CFD OTHER	
(n,γ)	Maxwl		GA	Eval	Rept GA-12071	Sep 71	Mathews+. RECOMMENDED VALUES	
(n,γ)	1.0-3	1.5+7	AUA	Eval	Data AUSTR-DFN 104.	Nov 71	COOK+POINT(223)+GROUP(127)SIG.CF EVL	+
(n,γ)	None		BGN	Expt	Jour PNV 6 210	72	Vaagen. ABST DP CFD PD SPCTSCP INFO	
(n,γ)	Maxwl		CRC	Eval	Rept AECL-3037 1	Jan 72	Walker.RECOMMEND SIG TO GND+META,TBL	
(n,γ)	2.5-2		AUA	Eval	Rept AAEC/TM-619	Sep 72	Clayton.CALC FROM SIG LIBRARY,TABLE	
(n,γ)	Maxwl		SGA	Eval	Conf 73Paris 1 233	Mar 73	Eder+ SIG TO TE129M,TBL,NO DETAILS	
					Rept SGAE-PH-141	Feb 73	.SAME AS 73PARIS,EVAL OF EXPTL DATA	
(n,γ)		1.1+7	RCN	Theo	Rept RCN-191	Jun 73	Lautenbach. GROUP CONSTANTS TBL	
(n,γ)	2.0+2	7.4+3	LRL	Expt	Jour PR/C 8 2405	Dec 73	Browne+. 0.4PC RESOL. CURVES. LINAC.	+
	2.0+2	7.4+3			Data EXFOR10340.006	Jun 76	3469PTS.CS DATA	
(n,γ)	2.5-2		SAC	Revw	Conf IAEA-169 1 235	74	Ribon.STATUS SIG CFD REQUESTS,TABLE	
	Maxwl	Fiss	WIN	Revw	Conf IAEA-169 3 163	74	Pope+ MAXW+FIS-SPEC AVG DATA CFD XPT	
	Fiss				Conf IAEA-169 3 137	74	Dean. POINT DATA AVG OVER STAND SPEC	
(n,γ)	1.0+3	1.0+7	FEI	Eval	Rept YK-8/2 97	Sep 72	Abagjan+ AVG SIG(ENERGY-GROUPS),TABL	
					Rept INDC(CCP)-39	Jul 74	.P102. ENGLISH OF YK-8/2 97	
(n,γ)	1.0+2	6.0+4	DUB	Expt	Jour YF 20 252	Aug 74	Bergman+ SDS.SIG(E),CFD OTHERS,GRAPH	
					Jour SNP 20 133	Feb 75	. ENGL OF YF 20 252	
(n,γ)	1.0+2	6.0+4	LEB	Expt	Jour YF 20 252	Aug 74	Bergman+ SIG(NEUT-E),GRAPH	+
	1.1+1	1.0+5			Jour SNP 20 133	Feb 75	. ENGLISH OF YF 20 252	
	1.6+2	6.4+4			Data EXFOR40292.007	Mar 75	.SIGMA FOR 42 ES GVN	
(n,γ)	2.5+4		TAT	Expt	Conf 74Bombay 2 101	Dec 74	Kondaiah+ SIG TO GRND,REL I127 GIVEN	+
	2.5+4				Data EXFOR30390.011	Mar 77	1PNT. PARTIAL SIG TO GROUND.	
(n,γ)	2.5-2		BRK	Theo	Jour NP/A 237 3 419	Jan 75	Nardi+ ISOM RATIO,MTE-CARLO,CFD XPT	
(n,γ)	Fast		RCN	Expt	Rept ECN-10	Oct 76	Veenema+ STEK REACTIVITY WORTHS TBL.	
Spect (n,γ)	Maxwl		KUR	Expt	Jour YF 4 238	Aug 66	Groshev+ ES+INTS FROM NAT TE.TBL+FIG	
					Rept IAE-699	65	- + MAGNET COMPT SPEC.TBL+GRPH	
					Jour SNP 4 172	Feb 67	. ENGL OF YF 4 238	
					Rept ANL-TRANS-334	65	. ENGL OF IAE-699.	
Spect (n,γ)	Pile		KUR	Expt	Jour YF 13 681	Apr 71	Groshev+ GE-LI,TBD	
					Jour SNP 13 387	Oct 71	. ENGL OF YF 13 681	
Inelastic γ	4.4+6		WES	Expt	Jour PR 102 461	Apr 56	Sinclair. 0.76MEV GAMMAS SEEN	+
					Rept AECU-3387	55	- .	
	4.4+6				Data EXFOR11770.006	Jun 76	. 1 PT.	
Inelastic γ	7.4+5	8.9+5	LEB	Expt	Jour KSF 1976 6 20	76	Konobeevskij+ SIG(E) TO 2+ LVL,GRAPH	
					Jour SPL 1976 6 16	76	. ENGL OF KSF 1976 6 20	
(n,2n)	1.5+7		CRC	Expt	Jour CJP 31 267	Feb 53	Paul+ BETA ACT, CFD TH, HL=9.3H	+
	1.5+7				Data EXFOR11274.081	Jun 76	. 1 PT.	
(n,2n)	Fiss		CRC	Eval	Rept CRC-1003	Dec 60	Roy+,ESTIMATED AVG SIG=4.0MB	
(n,2n)	1.5+7		SAH	Expt	Jour NP 41 192	Mar 63	Najumdar+ACTIVATION REL AL27(NP)	
	1.5+7				Data EXFOR31117.005	Sep 72	.SIG GVN	
(n,2n)	1.5+7		TUR	Expt	Jour NP 51 337	Feb 64	Bonazzola+.BETA ACT.GS XSECT ONLY	+
(n,2n)	1.4+7		HAM	Comp	Jour NP 65 257	Mar 65	Bormann. 3EXPT VALS.CFD SHELL EFFECT	
(n,2n)	1.5+7		ARK	Expt	Jour NP/A 114 663	Jul 68	Husain+.TO GRNDSTATE. T-D NS.	+
					Abst DA/B 29 1626	Nov 68	- .TO TE127G SIG=760+-100MB	
	1.5+7				Data EXFOR11999.	Jun 76	. 3 PTS, SIG FOR TOT,GND,META	
(n,2n)	1.5+7		DEB	Comp	Jour REA 7 4 93	Dec 69	Csikai+ SIG+HL COMPILTN,N-ACTIV-ANAL	
(n,2n)	1.4+7		GIT	Expt	Jour PR/C 1 350	Jan 70	Fink+ACTIVATION,GRPHS,TBL.CFD OTH.	+
	1.4+7				Data EXFOR10497.	Apr 76	2PTS.M,GSTATE.949+-150,712+-60MB.	
(n,2n)	1.2+7	1.8+7	HAM	Expt	Jour NP/A 157 481	Nov 70	Bormann+ ACT. CFD STATIST TH.+ISOM R	
(n,2n)	+7		KFI	Theo	Rept KFKI-71-8	Feb 71	Jeki. CALCULATED CFD EXPTL SIG VALUE	
(n,2n)	1.4+7	1.5+7	IRK	ExTh	Jour APA 33 285	Jul 71	Winiwarter+ ISOMERIC RATIO	
(n,2n)	1.4+7		GIT	Theo	Jour PR/C 4 1173	Oct 71	Fink+.STAT-MODEL CALCULATION,CFD EXP	
(n,2n)	1.5+7		MUA	Expt	Jour NP/A 181 101	Feb 72	Hasan+ ACT. ENRICHED ISOTOPE. GND.	+
	1.5+7				Data EXFOR30041.008	Feb 73	SIG TO TE-127 GND-LVL (9.3 H)	
(n,2n)	1.5+7		DEB	Eval	Jour REA 11 1 153	Mar 73	Boedy. COMPILATION+RECOMM.VALUE,TBL	
					Rept IAEA-153 173	73	- . RECOMM. VALUE ONLY	
(n,2n)	1.5+7		TAT	Theo	Jour JP/A 7 1458	Aug 74	Kondaiah. CALC ON STAT MODEL	
(n,2n)	9.0+6	1.5+7	ANL	Eval	Rept ANL-75-34	Jun 75	Davey+CONSTANT T MDL,LVL DEN MDL FIT	
(n,2n)	1.5+7		IBJ	Theo	Rept ASL 27 186	77	Rurarz+ ISO RATIO,4MODLS,CFD XPT.TBL	
	1.4+7				Rept INR-1464 19	May 73	- . ISOMERIC RATIO CFD EXPT,GRAF	
(n,p)	Fiss		CRC	Eval	Rept CRC-1003	Dec 60	Roy+,ESTIMATED AVG SIG=0.006MB	
(n,p)	1.4+7		SAH	Comp	Jour NUC 23 8 112	Aug 65	Chatterjee. TABLE WITH REFS.	

52 Tellurium 128

Quantity	Energy (ev) Min	Max	Lab	Type	Documentation Ref Vol Page	Date	Author, Comments	Data
(n,p)	1.4+7		WWA	Expt	Jour NP 74 438	Dec 65	Brzosko+ ISOMERIC RATIOS,CFD THEORY	+
					Jour NP 45 579	Aug 63	− + PARTIAL SIGMAS	
	1.4+7				Data EXFOR30136.	Oct 71	PARTIALS AND TOTAL SIGMAS	
(n,p)	1.5+7		ARK	Expt	Jour NP/A 114 663	Jul 68	Husain+.TO GRND,METAST.T − D NS.	+
					Abst DA/B 29 1626	Nov 68	− .1 P TO SB128M SIG=1.0+ − .1MB	
	1.5+7				Data EXFOR11999.	Jun 76	. 4 PTS, SIG TOT,GND,META,ISOMER RAT	
(n,p)	1.5+7		DEB	Comp	Jour REA 7 4 93	Dec 69	Csikai+ SIG+HL COMPILTN,N − ACTIV − ANAL	
(n,p)	1.4+7	1.5+7	JYV	Eval	Rept JU − RR − 3/1970	Jun 70	Leppaemaeki+ TABLE OF EVAL AVG SIG	
(n,p)	1.5+7		KAZ	Expt	Jour YF 13 923	May 71	Levkovsky+ ACT,SIG+ISOMER RATIO,TBL	
					Jour SNP 13 529	Nov 71	. ENGL OF YF 10 923	
(n,p)	1.5+7		MUA	Expt	Jour NP/A 181 101	Feb 72	Hasan+ ACT. ENRICHED ISOTOPE. METAST	+
	1.5+7				Data EXFOR30041.013	Feb 73	SIG TO SB − 128 METASTABLE LVL (10 MIN	
(n,p)	1.5+7		RBZ	Expt	Jour FIZS 4 61	Dec 72	Lulic+ ISOMERIC SIG RATIO,CFD TH,TBL	
(n,p)	1.4+7		SAH	Expt	Conf 72Chandigr 2 115	Dec 72	Tikku+GAMMA ACT11M HL SIG18.7+ − 2.4MB	+
	1.5+7				Data EXFOR30394.014	Mar 77	1 PNT.	
(n,p)	1.4+7	1.5+7	KAZ	Theo	Jour YF 18 705	Oct 73	Levkovsky.AVERAGED SIG,CALC,TBL	
					Jour SNP 18 361	Apr 74	. ENGLISH OF YF 18,705	
(n,p)	1.4+7		IRK	Expt	Jour NP/A 222 605	Apr 74	Struwe+ GELI. REL AL(N,A).	+
	1.5+7				Data EXFOR20540.	Apr 76	3PTS.SIGMA.	
(n,p)	1.5+7		SLO	Expt	Jour ASL 26 64	76	Hlavac+ ACTIV(GELI).TO META,CFD TABL	+
	1.5+7				Data EXFOR30286.009	Apr 75	1 DATA POINT	
(n,np)	1.5+7		ALD	Expt	Jour PPS 74 632	Nov 59	Barry+ACTIV.0.33MB CFD DIRECT TH	+
(n,np)	1.5+7		KAZ	Expt	Jour YF 13 923	May 71	Levkovsky+ ACT,METHOD,TBL,CFD OTHERS	
					Jour SNP 13 529	Nov 71	. ENGL OF YF 10 923	
(n,d)	1.5+7		SAH	Comp	Jour NUC 23 8 112	Aug 65	Chatterjee. TABLE WITH REFS.	
(n,α)	Fiss		CRC	Eval	Rept CRC − 1003	Dec 60	Roy+,ESTIMATED AVG SIG=0.001MB	
(n,α)	1.5+7		SAH	Theo	Jour NP 89 329	Dec 66	Majumdar. STAT THEO CFD EXPTS	+
				Expt	Jour NP 41 192	Mar 63	Najumdar+ACTIVATION REL AL27(NP)	
	1.5+7				Data EXFOR31117.004	Sep 72	.SIG GVN	
(n,α)	1.4+7		RBZ	Expt	Priv KULLISIC	Aug 68	Jurcevic.DIFSIG+ALFA SPEC AT 0 DEG.	+
	1.4+7				Data EXFOR30203.	Nov 72	DIFF SIG AT 0 DEG	
(n,α)	1.5+7		ARK	Expt	Jour NP/A 114 663	Jul 68	Husain+.TO METASTABLE. T − D NS.	+
					Abst DA/B 29 1626	Nov 68	− .1 A TO SN125M SIG=0.5+ − .1MB	
	1.5+7				Data EXFOR11999.010	Jun 76	. 1 PT.	
(n,α)	1.4+7		RBZ	Expt	Conf 69Bochum 210	Jul 69	Chatterjee+ ALFA − SPEC GRAPH CFD(D,P)	
(n,α)	1.5+7		DEB	Comp	Jour REA 7 4 93	Dec 69	Csikai+ SIG+HL COMPILTN,N − ACTIV − ANAL	
(n,α)	1.4+7		RBZ	ExTh	Conf 69Roorke 2 21	Dec 69	Chatterjee+ CFD P − ALFA REACTION, NDG	
(n,α)	1.5+7		KAZ	Expt	Jour YF 13 923	May 71	Levkovsky+ ACT,METHOD,TBL,CFD OTHERS	
					Jour SNP 13 529	Nov 71	. ENGL OF YF 10 923	
(n,α)	1.4+7	1.5+7	CIS	Theo	Jour NP/A 210 297	Aug 73	Milazzo − Colli+ ALPHA E − DISTN CFD XPT	
	1.4+7				Jour PL/B 38 155	Feb 72	Colli − Milazzo+ A − SPECT CALC CFD EXPT	
(n,α)	1.4+7	1.5+7	KAZ	Theo	Jour YF 18 705	Oct 73	Levkovsky.AVERAGED SIG,CALC,TBL	
					Jour SNP 18 361	Apr 74	. ENGLISH OF YF 18,705	
Reson Params	2.0+2		BNL	Expt	Abst BAP 5 18	Jan 60	Bolotin+. 2G*(REDUCED WN) GIVEN	
Reson Params		1.0+6	AUA	Theo	Jour AUJ 20 477	Oct 67	Cook. TBL OF AVG LVL SPACING D,L=0,1	
Reson Params		3.0+4	ORL	Expt	Prog ORNL − 4513 68	Jun 70	Dabbs+,LINAC,38 RESON,ONLY D GIVEN	
Reson Params	−		AUA	Theo	Rept AAEC/E − 211	Nov 70	Musgrove. CALCULTD D+GAM WIDTH GIVEN	
Reson Params	3.5+2	2.2+4	SAC	Expt	Priv TELLIER	Sep 71	Tellier+ PARAMETERS FROM TRANS.	+
	2.2+4				Conf 71Knoxvill 680	Mar 71	− +.TRANS,AVG D=262.5EV 38RESON	
	3.5+2	2.2+4			Data EXFOR20120.	Sep 72	100PTS.WG,WT,2G*WN,2G*WN0.	
Reson Params		+3	BNL	Expt	Prog USNDC − 1 30	May 72	Mughabghab+. P − WAVE RESON FROM CAPT	
Reson Params	1.5+2	6.5+2	SAC	ExTh	Diss FRNC − TH − 450	Oct 72	Delaroche.OPTICAL MODEL PARAMETERS	
Reson Params	None		DUB	Theo	Rept JINR − P4 − 7499	Oct 73	Soloviev+ CALC D CFD EXPTS,TABLE	
Reson Params	3.5+2	7.1+3	LRL	Expt	Jour PR/C 8 2405	Dec 73	Browne+. G*WN*WG/WT,G*WG FOR 16RESON	+
	3.5+2	7.1+3			Data EXFOR10340.002	Jun 76	16RES ES.(WN*WG)/WT.	
Reson Params	+2	+4	FEI	Eval	Rept YK − 8/2 97	Sep 72	Abagyan+ AVG G − WID+D AT BINDNG − E,TBL	
					Rept INDC(CCP) − 39	Jul 74	.PAGE 102.ENGLISH OF YK − 8/2 97	
Reson Params	4.4+2		ANL	Expt	Prog WASH − 1053 1	64	Cote.	+
	4.4+2				Data EXFOR12002.007	Jun 76	. 1 RES, E0	
Reson Params	4.3+2	1.1+4	ANL	Expt	Prog WASH − 1044 20	Aug 63	Singh.	+
	4.3+2	1.1+4			Data EXFOR12001.002	Jun 76	. 7 RES, E0	
Strnth Fnctn		3.0+4	ORL	Expt	Prog ORNL − 4513 68	Jun 70	Dabbs+,LINAC,S0 VALUE GIVEN	
Strnth Fnctn	−		AUA	Theo	Rept AAEC/E − 211	Nov 70	Musgrove. SMOOTHED S0,S1 AND S2 GIVN	
Strnth Fnctn	0.0+0	2.2+4	SAC	Expt	Priv TELLIER	Sep 71	Tellier+ FROM RESONANCE ANALYSIS.	+
	2.2+4				Conf 71Knoxvill 680	Mar 71	− +. SO=0.25+ − 0.10	
	0.0+0	2.2+4			Jour CR 269 266	Aug 69	+ TOF ALSO D + A (STATPAR)	
	2.2+4				Data EXFOR20120.050	Sep 72	. 1PNT. L=0.	
Strnth Fnctn	−2	+3	SAC	Expt	Rept CEA − N − 1522	Oct 72	Cauvin+ S0,S1 CALC	

52 Tellurium 128

Quantity	Energy (ev) Min	Max	Lab	Type	Documentation Ref Vol Page	Date	Author, Comments	Data
Strnth Fnctn	None		DUB	Theo	Rept JINR – P4 – 6947	73	Nikolenko. S0,ISOTOPIC DEPENDNC,GRPH	
					Rept BNL – TR – 556	Dec 73	. ENGLISH OF JINR – P4 – 6947	
Strnth Fnctn	None		AUA	Eval	Rept AAEC/E – 277	Mar 73	Musgrove.TBLS EXPTL DATA+BEST VALUES	
Strnth Fnctn	None		KUR	Theo	Prog IAE – 2560	75	Adamchuk+ .S0 – VALUE,TBL	
Strnth Fnctn	None		OSA	Theo	Conf JAERI – M – 5984	Feb 75	Kitazoe+OPT MDLS.GRPH VS A.TBL PARS.	
Strnth Fnctn	+0	+6	DUB	Theo	Rept JINR – P4 – 9052	Oct 75	Soloviev+ S0,S1,SEMIMICROSC MODL,TBL	
Lvl Density	1.4+7		RBZ	Expt	Conf 69Bochum 210	Jul 69	Chatterjee+ TE128(N,A)SN125,LVL DENS	
Lvl Density	0.0+0	2.2+4	SAC	Expt	Rept CEA – N – 1268	Feb 70	Tellier+.	+
		2.2+4			Data EXFOR20120.051	Sep 72	1PNT.SP.CUT(0).	
Lvl Density		3.0+4	ORL	Expt	Prog ORNL – 4513 68	Jun 70	Dabbs+,LINAC,PARAMETER A GIVEN	
Lvl Density	+2	+4	FEI	Eval	Rept YK – 8/2 97	Sep 72	Abagyan+ LVL DENSITY PARAMETER,TBL	
					Rept INDC(CCP) – 39	Jul 74	.PAGE 102.ENGLISH OF YK – 8/2 97	
(γ,n)	8.0+6	2.6+7	SAC	Expt	Jour NP/A 258 350	Feb 76	Lepretre+GDR,LORENTZ PARAM,GRPHS,TBL	

52 Tellurium 129

Quantity	Energy (ev) Min	Max	Lab	Type	Documentation Ref Vol Page	Date	Author, Comments	Data
Evaluation	1.0-3	1.5+7	AUA	Eval	Rept AAEC/TM – 549	Jun 70	Cook.TOT,EL,INEL,NONEL,CAPT,G+M,NDG	+
					Rept AAEC/E – 214	Jun 71	Bertram+GROUP SIGMAS SAME QUANTS.NDG	
					Rept AAEC/TM – 587	Mar 71	*DESCRIPTION OF LIBRARY	
	1.0-3	1.5+7			Data AUSTR – DFN 105.	Nov 71	POINT(223) AND GROUP(127) SIGMAS	
	1.0-3	1.5+7			Data AUSTR – DFN 190.	Nov 71	TE – 129M POINT+GROUP SIGS,SAME QUANTS	
Total	1.0-3	1.5+7	AUA	Eval	Data AUSTR – DFN 105.	Nov 71	COOK+POINT(223)+GROUP(127)SIG.CF EVL	+
	1.0-3	1.5+7			Data AUSTR – DFN 190.	Nov 71	.TE – 129M.POINT+GROUP SIGS.SEE EVAL	
Elastic	1.0-3	1.5+7	AUA	Eval	Data AUSTR – DFN 190.	Nov 71	.TE – 129M.POINT+GROUP SIGS.SEE EVAL	+
	1.0-3	1.5+7			Data AUSTR – DFN 105.	Nov 71	COOK+POINT(223)+GROUP(127)SIG.CF EVL	
Tot Inelastc	5.0+5	1.5+7	AUA	Eval	Data AUSTR – DFN 105.	Nov 71	COOK+POINT(11)+GROUP(127)SIG.CF EVL	+
	5.0+5	1.5+7			Data AUSTR – DFN 190.	Nov 71	.TE – 129M.POINT+GROUP SIGS.SEE EVAL	
Nonelastic	1.0-3	1.5+7	AUA	Eval	Data AUSTR – DFN 190.	Nov 71	.TE – 129M.POINT+GROUP SIGS.SEE EVAL	+
	1.0-3	1.5+7			Data AUSTR – DFN 105.	Nov 71	COOK+POINT(223)+GROUP(127)SIG.CF EVL	
Res Int Abs	5.0-1		AUA	Eval	Rept AAEC/TM – 619	Sep 72	Clayton.CALC FROM SIG LIBRARY,TABLE	
Res Int Abs	+0	+5	WIN	Revw	Conf IAEA – 169 3 163	74	Pope+ GND+META.AUSTRL DATA FILE CALC	
(n,γ)	1.0-3	1.5+7	AUA	Eval	Data AUSTR – DFN 105.	Nov 71	COOK+POINT(223)+GROUP(127)SIG.CF EVL	+
	1.0-3	1.5+7			Data AUSTR – DFN 190.	Nov 71	.TE – 129M.POINT+GROUP SIGS.SEE EVAL	
(n,γ)	Pile		CRC	Eval	Rept AECL – 3037 1	Jan 72	Walker.ESTIMATED SIG OF TE – 129M	
(n,γ)	2.5-2		AUA	Eval	Rept AAEC/TM – 619	Sep 72	Clayton.CALC FROM SIG LIBRARY,TABLE	
(n,γ)	Pile	2.5-2	SGA	Eval	Conf 73Paris 1 233	Mar 73	Eder+ 34 D ISOMER,SIG ESTIMATED,TBL	
					Rept SGAE – PH – 141	Feb 73	.SAME AS 73PARIS,POINT SIG FROM COOK	
(n,γ)	Fiss		WIN	Revw	Conf IAEA – 169 3 137	74	Dean. GND+META,DATA AVG OVER FIS – SPC	
	Maxwl	Fiss			Conf IAEA – 169 3 163	74	Pope+ GND+META,MAXW+FIS – SPC AVG DATA	
(n,2n)	1.4+7		FIR	ExTh	Jour NCL 1 2 95	Jan 69	Guidetti+ CALC ISOM RATIO CFD EXP	
Reson Params	–		AUA	Theo	Rept AAEC/E – 211	Nov 70	Musgrove. CALCULTD D+GAM WIDTH GIVEN	
Reson Params	+2		BNL	Expt	Abst BAP 17 557	Apr 72	Mughabghab+. SEARCH FOR P – WAVE RESON	
Strnth Fnctn	–		AUA	Theo	Rept AAEC/E – 211	Nov 70	Musgrove. SMOOTHED S0,S1 AND S2 GIVN	
Strnth Fnctn	-2	+3	SAC	Expt	Rept CEA – N – 1522	Oct 72	Cauvin+ S0,S1 CALC	
Lvl Density	+6		MIL	Theo	Jour EN 15 1 54	Jan 68	Facchini+ LDL PARS FROM LOW EN RES	
Lvl Density	None		MUN	Theo	Jour NP/A 217 269	Dec 73	Dilg+ A,DELTA. BACK SHIFTED FERMIGAS	
Lvl Density	None		DUB	Theo	Jour NP/A 224 411	May 74	Soloviev+ 1/2 MICROSC MDL. SPH NUCL.	
Lvl Density	8.5+6	1.5+7	ANL	Eval	Rept ANL – 75 – 34	Jun 75	Davey+.N2NEVAL.CONSTANT T,LVL DEN FIT	

52 Tellurium 130

Quantity	Energy (ev) Min	Max	Lab	Type	Documentation Ref Vol Page	Date	Author, Comments	Data
Evaluation	1.0-3	1.5+7	AUA	Eval	Rept AAEC/TM – 549	Jun 70	Cook.TOT,EL,INEL,NONEL,CAPT SIGS,NDG	+
					Rept AAEC/E – 214	Jun 71	Bertram+GROUP SIGMAS SAME QUANTS.NDG	
					Rept AAEC/TM – 587	Mar 71	*DESCRIPTION OF LIBRARY	
	1.0-3	1.5+7			Data AUSTR – DFN 106.	Nov 71	POINT(223) AND GROUP(127) SIGMAS	
Total	1.0+3	1.2+5	DKE	Expt	Jour AP 14 387	Jul 61	Bilpuch+. 160 DEG SPECTROMETER	
Total	1.4+7		FEI	Expt	Prog INDSWG – 126 33	66	Dukarevich.SIG=4.81+ – 0.02B	
Total	1.4+7		CCP	ExTh	Jour IZV 31 217	Feb 67	Dukarevich+.TBL,CURVES,CFD OPTMDL TH	
					Jour BAS 31 197	Feb 67	TRANSLATN.*	
Total	1.4+7		FTI	Expt	Jour NP/A 92 433	Feb 67	Dukarevich+ CFD OPTMDL 4.81+ – 0.02B	+
Total	7.0+6	1.4+7	CJD	Theo	Rept ICD – 5 20	68	Vibrajanov+ VIBRATION MDL,AT 4ES,TBL	
Total		3.0+4	SAC	Expt	Priv TELLIER	Sep 71	Tellier+ NO DATA. RESONANCE ASSGNMNT	+
		3.0+4			Data EXFOR20122.009	Sep 72	0PTS.	
Total	1.0-3	1.5+7	AUA	Eval	Data AUSTR – DFN 106.	Nov 71	COOK+POINT(223)+GROUP(127)SIG.CF EVL	+

52 Tellurium 130

Quantity	Energy (ev) Min	Max	Lab	Type	Documentation Ref Vol Page	Date	Author, Comments	Data
Total	1.3+7	1.5+7	DEB Eval	Rept	IAEA – 153 173	73	Boedy+ MOST PROBABLE VAL OF SIG,TBL	
				Jour	AHP 30 115	Oct 71	Angeli+ AVG SIG,CFD CALC.TBLS.GRAPH	
Elastic	Maxwl		COL Expt	Jour	RSI 27 620	Aug 56	Heindl+	+
	Maxwl			Data	EXFOR11786.006	Jun 76	. 1 PT, COH	
Elastic	7.0+6	1.4+7	CJD Theo	Rept	ICD – 5 20	68	Averjanov+ VIBRATION MDL,AT 4ES,TBL	
Elastic	1.0–3	1.5+7	AUA Eval	Data	AUSTR – DFN 106.	Nov 71	COOK+POINT(223)+GROUP(127)SIG.CF EVL	+
Tot Inelastc	7.0+6	1.4+7	CJD Theo	Rept	ICD – 5 20	68	Averjanov+ VIBRATION MDL,AT 4ES,TBL	
Tot Inelastc	1.0+6	1.5+7	AUA Eval	Data	AUSTR – DFN 106.	Nov 71	COOK+POINT(10)+GROUP(127)SIG.CF EVL	+
Tot Inelastc	1.5+7		NIL Expt	Prog	INDC(SEC) – 50	Jan 76	. ABST. NDG	
Diff Inelast	1.4+7		LRL Theo	Rept	UCRL – 50181	Feb 67	Lutz+.CALC ANG DIST FOR FIRST 2+ LVL	
Diff Inelast	7.0+6	1.4+7	CJD Theo	Rept	ICD – 5 20	68	Averjanov+ TO 1ST LVL,ANGDIST,GRAPH	
Diff Inelast	8.4+5	1.3+6	LEB Expt	Jour	IZV 37 1900	Sep 73	Konobeevsky+ SIG OF EXCIT 1 – ST LVL	+
				Jour	BAS 37 9 84	Sep 73	. ENGL OF IZV 37 1900	
	8.4+5	1.3+6		Data	EXFOR40214.012	May 74	.DIN=DNG,1 E–LVL,48 DATA LINES	
Diff Inelast	8.4+5	9.9+5	LEB Expt	Jour	KSF 1976 6 20	76	Konobeevskij+ SIG(E) TO 2+ LVL,GRAPH	
				Jour	SPL 1976 6 16	76	. ENGL OF KSF 1976 6 20	
Nonelastic	1.0–3	1.5+7	AUA Eval	Data	AUSTR – DFN 106.	Nov 71	COOK+POINT(223)+GROUP(127)SIG.CF EVL	+
Nonelastic	1.4+7	1.5+7	ANL Eval	Rept	ANL – 75 – 34	Jun 75	Davey+CORRC APPLIED TO N2N CS.TBLS.	
Absorption	4.1–1	1.0+7	GA Eval	Rept	GA – 2451	Aug 61	Joanou+.68GROUP DATA FOR GAM – I	
Absorption	1.0–3	1.0+7	JUL Eval	Rept	JUEL – 678 – RG	Jul 70	Liu. EVALUATION+CALC,GRPH,FN OF E	
Res Int Abs	5.0–1		CNE Expt	Jour	CJP 46 2473	Nov 68	Ricabarra+,RATIO TO THR – ACT SIGMA	+
				Rept	CNEA – 274	70	– + SAME,IN SPANISH	
	5.0–1			Data	EXFOR30129.007	Oct 72	RESON INT AND RATIO TO THR ABS SIGM.	
Res Int Abs	None		GA Eval	Rept	GA – 12071	Sep 71	Mathews+. RECOMMENDED VALUES	
Res Int Abs	5.5–1		CRC Eval	Rept	AECL – 3037 1	Jan 72	Walker.REDUCED RES INT TO GND+META	
Res Int Abs	5.0–1		AUA Eval	Rept	AAEC/TM – 619	Sep 72	Clayton.CALC FROM SIG LIBRARY,TABLE	
Res Int Abs	4.6–1	1.0+6	RCN Theo	Rept	RCN – 191	Jul 73	Lautenbach.CAPT INT FROM GROUP SIGMA	
Res Int Abs	4.0–1		LRL Expt	Jour	PR/C 8 2405	Dec 73	Browne+DRVD FROM MEAS	+
	4.0–1			Data	EXFOR10340.005	Jun 76	1PT RIA=258+–32 MB	
Res Int Abs	5.0–1		GHT Expt	Jour	JRC 20 695	74	Van Der Linden+ BY(N,G).CFD OTHS,TBL	
	5.5–1			Conf	73Paris 2 241	Mar 73	– + ACT,REL THR+GOLD,TBL	
	5.5–1			Data	EXFOR20645.006	Jul 76	1PNT.CAPTURE.	
Res Int Abs	5.5–1	+6	SAC Revw	Conf	IAEA – 169 1 235	74	Ribon.CAPTURE,STATUS CFD REQUEST,TBL	
Res Int Abs	+0	+5	WIN Revw	Conf	IAEA – 169 3 163	74	Pope+ DATA FILE CALC CFD XPTAL VALUE	
Res Int Abs	5.5–1		MUNComp	Jour	JRC 29 175	Jan 76	Gryntakis+, 4 VALUES TO META + GND	
(n,γ)	Pile		ANL Expt	Jour	PR 72 888	Nov 47	Seren+.THR IRRAD. TO25MIN,30HR ISOM.	+
	Pile			Data	EXFOR11447.	Jun 76	. 2 PTS, SIG FOR GND + META	
(n,γ)	2.2+5	9.0+5	OXF Expt	Jour	NAT 161 727	May 48	Allen+ ACTIVATION RATIO	
(n,γ)	Maxwl		ORL Expt	Jour	PR 88 412	Oct 52	Pomerance.PILE OSC.	+
	Maxwl			Data	EXFOR11507.067	Jun 76	. 1 PT.	
(n,γ)	Maxwl		CRC Eval	Rept	AECL – 1054	Mar 60	Walker. (CRRP – 913)	
(n,γ)	Maxwl		MUA Expt	Jour	NP 36 542	Aug 62	Mangal+ SCINT SPECT,REL TO AU197,TBL	+
				Conf	62Madras 95	Feb 62	– +	
	Maxwl			Data	EXFOR31248.011	Apr 73	.SIG TO GND – STATE GVN	
(n,γ)	Maxwl		BNL Expt	Jour	PR 128 761	Oct 62	Sehgal.SIG FOR 25MIN,30HR REL AU197	+
	Maxwl			Data	EXFOR11994.	Jun 76	. 3 PTS, SIG FOR GND,META,ISOMER RAT	
(n,γ)	Maxwl		ANL Comp	Jour	NP 60 241	Nov 64	Bishop+EXP AND TH ISOMER RATIOS CFD	
(n,γ)	1.0+3	6.0+4	LEB Expt	Conf	65Antwerp § 182	Jul 65	Bergman.LEBEDEV. DO OBTAINED	
(n,γ)	Maxwl		KUR Expt	Jour	YF 4 238	Aug 66	Groshev+,TBL GIVEN ALSO IAE – 966 /65	
					–		ENGL ANL – TR – 334 /65	
(n,γ)	None		TRM Expt	Prog	AEET – 267 7	Aug 66	Namboodiri+ ISOMERIC SIG RATIO GIVEN	+
	Maxwl			Jour	JIN 28 1	Jan 66	– + ISOM RATIO GVN,CFD OTHRS	
	Maxwl			Data	EXFOR31078.003	Sep 72	.RATIO MS/GND+MS GVN	
(n,γ)	1.3+5	3.0+5	ORL Expt	Jour	PR 159 1007	Jul 67	Macklin+. TOF. VDG. SCINT. 4 ES.ABSL	+
	3.0+5	1.3+5		Data	EXFOR11679.017	Jun 76	. 5 PTS.	
(n,γ)	1.1+4	3.4+5	FEI Expt	Prog	YFI – 6 11	68	Dovbenko+. TABLE. TO BE PUBL IN AE	
	1.0+4	4.0+5		Jour	SJA 27 1185	Nov 69	.ENGL. TRANSL. OF AE 27 406	
				Jour	EAF 27 41	Nov 69	.FRENCH TRANSL. OF AE 27 406	
				Jour	AE 27 406	Nov 69	Dovbenko+ SIG(E)GRPH,CFD OTHR+OPTMOD	
	2.0+5	3.0+6		Jour	AE 25 529	Dec 68	– +GRPH SIG(NEUT – E),CFD OPTMOD	
	1.1+4	3.4+5		Prog	INDC(CCP) – 3U	Mar 69	.ENGLISH TRANSL OF YFI – 6 11 /68	
	2.0+5	3.0+6		Jour	EAF 25 120	Dec 68	.FRENCH TRANSL OF AE 25 529 1268	
				Jour	SJA 25 1367	Dec 68	.ENGLISH TRANSL OF AE 25 529 1268	
	1.1+4	3.9+5		Data	EXFOR40331.013	Jan 76	SIG – GND AT10 ES	
	1.1+4	3.1+6		Data	EXFOR40006.003	Jul 70	.SIGMA AT 26 ENERGIES GIVEN	
(n,γ)	–		IEA Comp	Rept	IEA – INF – 10	Aug 68	Atalla. TABLES OF HL,SIG AND GAMM – E	
(n,γ)	2.4+4		MUA Expt	Jour	NP/A 117 545	Sep 68	Chaubey+,SB – BE,ACT BETA – DET REL I127	+
	2.4+4			Data	EXFOR30086.	Dec 70	SIGMAS FOR 2 HALF – LIVES	

52 Tellurium 130

Quantity	Energy (ev) Min	Max	Lab	Type	Documentation Ref Vol Page	Date	Author, Comments	Data
(n,γ)	5.0+3	1.0+5	AUA	ExTh Rept	AAEC/E – 198	May 69	Musgrove.S+P+D WAVE SIGMAS CALC,TBL	+
(n,γ)	1.0+3	1.0+7	BOL	Eval Rept	CCDN – NW/10	Dec 69	Benzi+H – F MOD,AXEL G(G)EST,ALL DATA	+
				Rept	CEC(70) – 2	Apr 70	– +. GRAPH	
				Conf	66Paris 1 537	Oct 66	– + STATMOD.TBL AV VALS.SUPERSEDD	
	1.0+3	1.0+7		Data	BENZI – DFN 541D	May 72	45 PNTS	
(n,γ)	3.0+6		DEB	Expt Jour	AHP 28 257	Jan 70	Diksic+ SIG+ – ERROR,REL AU197(N,G)	+
	3.0+6			Data	EXFOR30023.009	Jun 70	SIGMA CAPT TO GND STATE	
(n,γ)	3.0+4		AUA	Theo Rept	AAEC/E – 211	Nov 70	Musgrove. SIGMA GIVEN AND CFD OTHER	
(n,γ)	Maxwl		GA	Eval Rept	GA – 12071	Sep 71	Mathews+. RECOMMENDED VALUES	
(n,γ)	1.0 – 3	1.5+7	AUA	Eval Data	AUSTR – DFN 106.	Nov 71	COOK+POINT(223)+GROUP(127)SIG.CF EVL	+
(n,γ)	3.0+3	5.0+5	ORL	Expt Prog	NCSAC – 42 185	Nov 71	Macklin+. ORELA. ANAL TBC. NO DATA	
(n,γ)	Maxwl		CRC	Eval Rept	AECL – 3037 1	Jan 72	Walker.RECOMMEND SIG TO GND+META,TBL	
(n,γ)	2.5+4		AUW	Expt Jour	JP/A 5 468	Mar 72	Thirumala+ ACT METHOD, RELATIVE TO I	
				Conf	68Madras 1 296	Feb 68	TIRUMALA RAO+ REL THR,NAI,SIG GIVEN	
(n,γ)	2.5 – 2		AUA	Eval Rept	AAEC/TM – 619	Sep 72	Clayton.CALC FROM SIG LIBRARY,TABLE	
(n,γ)		1.1+7	RCN	Theo Rept	RCN – 191	Jun 73	Lautenbach. GROUP CONSTANTS TBL	
(n,γ)	5.0+2	7.4+3	LRL	Expt Jour	PR/C 8 2405	Dec 73	Browne+. 0.4PC RESOL. CURVES. LINAC.	+
	5.0+2	7.4+3		Data	EXFOR10340.007	Jun 76	2162PTS.CS DATA	
(n,γ)	2.5 – 2		SAC	Revw Conf	IAEA – 169 1 235	74	Ribon.STATUS SIG CFD REQUESTS,TABLE	
(n,γ)	Fiss		WIN	Revw Conf	IAEA – 169 3 137	74	Dean. POINT DATA AVG OVER STAND SPEC	
	Maxwl	Fiss		Conf	IAEA – 169 3 163	74	Pope+ MAXW+FIS – SPEC AVG DATA CFD XPT	
(n,γ)	1.0+3	1.0+7	FEI	Eval Rept	YK – 8/2 97	Sep 72	Abagjan+ AVG SIG(ENERGY – GROUPS),TABL	
				Rept	INDC(CCP) – 39	Jul 74	.P102. ENGLISH OF YK – 8/2 97	
(n,γ)	1.0+2	6.0+4	DUB	Expt Jour	YF 20 252	Aug 74	Bergman+ SDS.SIG(E),CFD OTHERS,GRAPH	
				Jour	SNP 20 133	Feb 75	. ENGL OF YF 20 252	
(n,γ)	1.0+2	6.0+4	LEB	Expt Jour	YF 20 252	Aug 74	Bergman+ SIG(NEUT – E),GRAPH	+
	1.1+1	1.0+5		Jour	SNP 20 133	Feb 75	. ENGLISH OF YF 20 252	
	1.4+2	6.4+4		Data	EXFOR40292.008	Mar 75	.SIGMA FOR 43 ES GVN	
(n,γ)	2.5+4		TAT	Expt Conf	74Bombay 2 101	Dec 74	Kondaiah+ SIG TO 25MIN – ISOMER GIVEN	+
	2.5+4			Data	EXFOR30390.012	Mar 77	1PNT. PARTIAL SIG TO GROUND.	
(n,γ)	2.5 – 2		BRK	Theo Jour	NP/A 237 3 419	Jan 75	Nardi+ ISOM RATIO,MTE – CARLO,CFD XPT	
(n,γ)	1.4+7		IRK	Expt Jour	NP/A 264 105	Jun 76	Schwerer+ GE – LI.SIG(GS)=0.58+ – 0.12MB	+
	1.5+7			Data	EXFOR20670.010	Oct 76	1PNT.SIGMA.	
(n,γ)	Fast		RCN	Expt Rept	ECN – 10	Oct 76	Veenema+ STEK REACTIVITY WORTHS TBL.	
Spect (n,γ)	Maxwl		KUR	Expt Jour	YF 4 238	Aug 66	Groshev+ ES+INTS FROM NAT TE.TBL+FIG	
				Rept	IAE – 699	65	– + MAGNET COMPT SPEC.TBL+GRPH	
				Jour	SNP 4 172	Feb 67	. ENGL OF YF 4 238	
				Rept	ANL – TRANS – 334	65	. ENGL OF IAE – 699.	
Spect (n,γ)	Maxwl		BNL	Expt Prog	WASH – 1127 18	Apr 69	Chrien+ GROUND – STATE GAMMA E GIVEN	
Spect (n,γ)	Pile		KUR	Expt Jour	YF 13 681	Apr 71	Groshev+ GE – LI,TBD	
				Jour	SNP 13 387	Oct 71	. ENGL OF YF 13 681	
Inelastic γ	4.4+6		WES	Expt Jour	PR 102 461	Apr 56	Sinclair. 0.83MEV GAMMAS SEEN	+
				Rept	AECU – 3387	55	– .	
	4.4+6			Data	EXFOR11770.	Jun 76	. 3 PTS.	
Inelastic γ	8.4+5	9.9+5	LEB	Expt Jour	KSF 1976 6 20	76	Konobeevskij+ SIG(E) TO 2+ LVL,GRAPH	
				Jour	SPL 1976 6 16	76	. ENGL OF KSF 1976 6 20	
(n,2n)	1.5+7		CRC	Expt Jour	CJP 31 267	Feb 53	Paul+.BETA ACT.CFD TH. HL= 70M+32D	+
	1.5+7			Data	EXFOR11274.082	Jun 76	. 1 PT.	
(n,2n)	Fiss		CRC	Eval Rept	CRC – 1003	Dec 60	Roy+,ESTIMATED AVG SIG=3.4MB	
(n,2n)	1.5+7		SAH	Expt Jour	NP 41 192	Mar 63	Najumdar+ACTIVATION REL AL27(NP)	
	1.5+7			Data	EXFOR31117.	Sep 72	.SIG GVN	
(n,2n)	1.5+7		TUR	Expt Jour	NP 51 337	Feb 64	Bonazzola+ACT.BETA COUNT 580+ – 27MB	+
(n,2n)	1.4+7		HAM	Comp Jour	NP 65 257	Mar 65	Bormann. 2EXPT VALS.CFD SHELL EFFECT	
(n,2n)	1.4+7		IBJ	ExTh Jour	NP 74 438	Dec 65	Brzosko+ ACTIVATION,PARTIAL SIGMAS	+
	1.4+7			Expt Data	EXFOR30135.	Oct 71	PARTIAL AND TOTAL SIGMAS	
(n,2n)	1.4+7		KAZ	Expt Conf	67Kharkov	Feb 67	Shilin+. TBP IN IZV	
(n,2n)	1.5+7		ARK	Expt Jour	NP/A 114 663	Jul 68	Husain+.TO GRND,METAST.T – D NS.	+
				Abst	DA/B 29 1626	Nov 68	– .TO TE129G SIG=435+ – 50MB	
	1.5+7			Data	EXFOR11999.	Jun 76	. 4 PTS, SIG TOT,GND,META,ISOMER RAT	
(n,2n)	1.5+7		DEB	Comp Jour	REA 7 4 93	Dec 69	Csikai+ SIG+HL COMPILTN,N – ACTIV – ANAL	
(n,2n)	1.4+7		GIT	Expt Jour	PR/C 4 1173	Jan 70	Fink+ACTIVATION,GRPHS,TBL.CFD OTH.	+
	1.4+7			Data	EXFOR10497.	Apr 76	2PTS.M,GSTATE.885+ – 45,570+ – 30 MB.	
(n,2n)	1.4+7	1.5+7	JYV	Eval Rept	JU – RR – 3/1970	Jun 70	Leppaemaeki+ TABLE OF EVAL AVG SIG	
(n,2n)	1.2+7	1.8+7	HAM	Expt Jour	NP/A 157 481	Nov 70	Bormann+ ACT. CFD STATIST TH.+ISOM R	
(n,2n)	1.4+7	1.5+7	IRK	ExTh Jour	APA 33 285	Jul 71	Winiwarter+ ISOMERIC RATIO	
(n,2n)	1.4+7		GIT	Theo Jour	PR/C 4 1173	Oct 71	Fink+ .STAT – MODEL CALCULATION,CFD EXP	
(n,2n)	1.5+7		MUA	Expt Jour	NP/A 181 101	Feb 72	Hasan+ ACT. ENRICHED ISOTOPE. GND.	+
	1.5+7			Data	EXFOR30041.009	Feb 73	SIG TO TE – 129 GND – LVL (67MIN)	

52 Tellurium 130

Quantity	Energy (ev) Min	Max	Lab	Type	Documentation Ref Vol Page	Author, Comments Date	Data
(n,2n)	1.5+7		DEB	Eval Jour	REA 11 1 153	Mar 73 Boedy+ RECOMM.VALUE FROM N-Z SYSTEM.	
				Rept	IAEA-153 173	73 - . RECOMM. VALUE ONLY	
(n,2n)	1.4+7		LOU	Expt Prog	INR-1464 12	May 73 Araminowicz+BRIEF,ACTIV,TABLE,GRAPH	+
	1.4+7			Data	EXFOR30264.037	Nov 73 SIGMA AT 14.6 MEV	
(n,2n)	1.5+7		KFI	Theo Rept	KFKI-73-68	Dec 73 Jeki.NEW FIT,CALC SIG CFD OTHERS,TBL	
	+7			Rept	KFKI-71-8	Feb 71 - . CALCULATED CFD EXPTL SIG VALU	
(n,2n)	1.5+7		TAT	Theo Jour	JP/A 7 1458	Aug 74 Kondaiah. CALC ON STAT MODEL	
(n,2n)	8.5+6	1.5+7	ANL	Eval Jour	ANL-75-34	Jun 75 Davey+CONSTANT T MDL,LVL DEN MDL FIT	
(n,2n)	1.5+7		SLO	Expt Jour	ASL 26 64	76 Hlavac+ ACTIV(GELI).TO GRND,CFD,TABL	+
	1.5+7			Data	EXFOR30286.007	Apr 75 1 DATA POINT	
(n,2n)	1.5+7		IBJ	Theo Jour	ASL 27 186	77 Rurarz+ ISO RATIO,4MODLS,CFD XPT.TBL	
	1.4+7			Rept	INR-1464 19	May 73 - + ISOMERIC RATIO CFD EXPT,GRAF	
(n,p)	Fiss		CRC	Eval Rept	CRC-1003	Dec 60 Roy+,ESTIMATED AVG SIG=0.0015MB	
(n,p)	1.4+7		SAH	Comp Jour	NUC 23 8 112	Aug 65 Chatterjee. TABLE WITH REFS.	
				Jour	NP 60 273	Nov 64 - .MEAN OF EXPT CFD SHELLMOD	
(n,p)	1.4+7		WWA	Expt Jour	NP 74 438	Dec 65 Brzosko+ ISOMERIC RATIOS,CFD THEORY	+
				Jour	NP 45 579	Aug 63 - + PARTIAL SIGMAS	
	1.4+7			Data	EXFOR30136.	Oct 71 PARTIALS AND TOTAL SIGMAS	
(n,p)	1.5+7		DEB	Comp Jour	REA 7 4 93	Dec 69 Csikai+ SIG+HL COMPILTN,N-ACTIV-ANAL	
(n,p)	1.4+7	1.5+7	JYV	Eval Rept	JU-RR-3/1970	Jun 70 Leppaemaeki+ TABLE OF EVAL AVG SIG	
(n,p)	1.5+7		KAZ	Expt Jour	YF 13 923	May 71 Levkovsky+ ACT,SIG+ISOMER RATIO,TBL	
				Jour	SNP 13 529	Nov 71 . ENGL OF YF 10 923	
(n,p)	1.5+7		MUA	Expt Jour	NP/A 181 101	Feb 72 Hasan+ ACT. ENRICHED ISOTOPE. METAST	+
	1.5+7			Data	EXFOR30041.014	Feb 73 SIG TO SB-130 METASTABLE LVL (7 MIN	
(n,p)	1.5+7		RBZ	Expt Jour	FIZS 4 61	Dec 72 Lulic+ ISOMERIC SIG RATIO;CFD TH,TBL	
(n,p)	1.4+7		SAH	Expt Conf	72Chandigr 2 115	Dec 72 Tikku+GAMMA ACT7M HL SIG=20+-5 MB	+
	1.5+7			Data	EXFOR30394.015	Mar 77 1 PNT.	
(n,p)	1.4+7	1.5+7	KAZ	Theo Jour	YF 18 705	Oct 73 Levkovsky.AVERAGED SIG,CALC,TBL	
				Jour	SNP 18 361	Apr 74 . ENGLISH OF YF 18,705	
(n,p)	1.4+7		IRK	Expt Jour	NP/A 222 605	Apr 74 Struwe+ GELI. REL AL(N,A).	+
	1.5+7			Data	EXFOR20540.	Apr 76 3PTS.SIGMA.	
(n,np)	1.5+7		ALD	Expt Jour	PPS 74 632	Nov 59 Barry+ACTIV.0.17MB CFD DIRECT TH	+
(n,np)	1.5+7		KAZ	Expt Jour	YF 13 923	May 71 Levkovsky+ ACT,METHOD,TBL,CFD OTHERS	
				Jour	SNP 13 529	Nov 71 . ENGL OF YF 10 923	
(n,d)	1.5+7		SAH	Comp Jour	NUC 23 8 112	Aug 65 Chatterjee. TABLE WITH REFS.	
(n,He3)	1.5+7		RBZ	Expt Jour	JIN 36 477	74 Diksic+ ACTIV,GE(LI),TABLES	+
	1.4+7			Data	EXFOR30152.014	Apr 72 1 DATA LINE	
(n,α)	1.4+7		ALD	Expt Jour	PPS 73 215	Feb 59 Coleman+. ACTIVATION	+
(n,α)	Fiss		CRC	Eval Rept	CRC-1003	Dec 60 Roy+,ESTIMATED AVG SIG=BELO 0.0001MB	
(n,α)			CIS	Theo Jour	NP 51 460	Feb 64 Facchini+STATMOD SIG XPT/CALC200-260	
(n,α)	1.5+7		SAH	Theo Jour	NP 89 329	Dec 66 Majumdar. STAT THEO CFD EXPTS	+
				Expt Jour	NP 41 192	Mar 63 Najumdar+ACTIVATION REL AL27(NP)	
	1.5+7			Data	EXFOR31117.006	Sep 72 .SIG GVN	
(n,α)	1.4+7	1.5+7	NAP	Comp Rept	INFN/BE-67-11	Sep 67 Cuzzocrea+ AVERAGED CHOSEN DATA.	
(n,α)	1.5+7		DEB	Comp Jour	REA 7 4 93	Dec 69 Csikai+ SIG+HL COMPILTN,N-ACTIV-ANAL	
(n,α)	1.4+7	1.5+7	JYV	Eval Rept	JU-RR-3/1970	Jun 70 Leppaemaeki+ TABLE OF EVAL AVG SIG	
(n,α)	1.5+7		KAZ	Expt Jour	YF 13 923	May 71 Levkovsky+ ACT,METHOD,TBL,CFD OTHERS	
				Jour	SNP 13 529	Nov 71 . ENGL OF YF 10 923	
Reson Params	1.5+3	1.2+5	DKE	Expt Jour	AP 14 387	Jul 61 Bilpuch+. WN WN0 STF(S) AREA ANALYS	+
Reson Params	1.5+3	1.2+5		Data	EXFOR11599.	Jun 76 . 21 RES, WN,WN0	
Reson Params		1.0+6	AUA	Theo Jour	AUJ 20 477	Oct 67 Cook. TBL OF AVG LVL SPACING D,L=0,1	
Reson Params		3.0+4	ORL	Expt Prog	ORNL-4513 68	Jun 70 Dabbs+,LINAC,22 RESON,ONLY D GIVEN	
Reson Params	-		AUA	Theo Rept	AAEC/E-211	Nov 70 Musgrove. CALCULTD D+GAM WIDTH GIVEN	
Reson Params	1.1+3	3.0+4	SAC	Expt Priv	TELLIER	Sep 71 Tellier+ PARAMETERS FROM TRANS.	+
		3.0+4		Conf	71Knoxvill 680	Mar 71 - +.TRANS,AVG D=872EV 22RESON	
	1.1+3	3.0+4		Data	EXFOR20120.	Sep 72 56PTS.WG,WT,2G*WN,2G*WN0	
Reson Params		+3	BNL	Expt Prog	USNDC-1 30	May 72 Mughabghab+. P-WAVE RESON FROM CAPT	
Reson Params	1.5+2	6.5+2	SAC	ExTh Diss	FRNC-TH-450	Oct 72 Delaroche.OPTICAL MODEL PARAMETERS	
Reson Params	None		DUB	Theo Rept	JINR-P4-7499	Oct 73 Soloviev+ CALC D CFD EXPTS,TABLE	
Reson Params	1.1+3	7.0+3	LRL	Expt Jour	PR/C 8 2405	Dec 73 Browne+. G*WN*WG/WT,G*WG FOR 6 RESON	+
	1.1+3	4.4+3		Prog	USNDC-7 107	Jun 73 - +. TABLE G*WN AND G*WG.3 RESON	
	1.1+3	7.0+3		Data	EXFOR10340.003	Jun 76 6 RES ES.(WN*WG)/WT.	
Reson Params	+3	+4	FEI	Eval Rept	YK-8/2 97	Sep 72 Abagyan+ AVG G-WID+D AT BINDNG-E,TBL	
	+3			Rept	INDC(CCP)-39	Jul 74 .PAGE 102.ENGLISH OF YK-8/2 97	
Strnth Fnctn	0.0+0	1.2+5	DKE	Expt Jour	AP 14 346	61 Newson+	+
	0.0+0	1.2+5		Data	EXFOR11888.008	Jun 76 . 1 PT. D	
Strnth Fnctn	2.0+3	1.2+5	DKE	Expt Jour	AP 14 387	Jul 61 Bilpuch+. S WAVE	+
	2.0+3	1.2+5		Data	EXFOR11599.036	Jun 76 . 1 PT.	

52 Tellurium 130

Quantity	Energy (ev) Min	Max	Lab	Type	Documentation Ref Vol Page	Author, Comments Date	Data
Strnth Fnctn		3.0+4	ORL Expt	Prog	ORNL – 4513 68	Jun 70 Dabbs+,LINAC,S0 VALUE GIVEN	
Strnth Fnctn	–		AUA Theo	Rept	AAEC/E – 211	Nov 70 Musgrove. SMOOTHED S0,S1 AND S2 GIVN	
Strnth Fnctn	0.0+0	3.0+4	SAC Expt	Priv	TELLIER	Sep 71 Tellier+ FROM RESONANCE ANALYSIS.	+
		3.0+4		Conf	71Knoxvill 680	Mar 71 – +. S0=0.15+ –0.05	
	0.0+0	3.0+4		Jour	CR 269 266	Aug 69 – +TOF ALSO D + A (STATPAR)	
		3.0+4		Data	EXFOR20120.057	Sep 72 . 1PNT.L=0.	
Strnth Fnctn	None		DUB Theo	Rept	JINR – P4 – 6947	73 Nikolenko. S0,ISOTOPIC DEPENDNC,GRPH	
				Rept	BNL – TR – 556	Dec 73 . ENGLISH OF JINR – P4 – 6947	
Strnth Fnctn	None		AUA Eval	Rept	AAEC/E – 277	Mar 73 Musgrove.TBLS EXPTL DATA+BEST VALUES	
Strnth Fnctn	None		KUR Theo	Prog	IAE – 2560	75 Adamchuk+ .S0 – VALUE,TBL	
Strnth Fnctn	None		OSA Theo	Conf	JAERI – M – 5984	Feb 75 Kitazoe+OPT MDLS.GRPH VS A.TBL PARS.	
Strnth Fnctn	+0	+6	DUB Theo	Rept	JINR – P4 – 9052	Oct 75 Soloviev+ S0,S1,SEMIMICROSC MODL,TBL	
Lvl Density	2.4+4		MUA ExTh	Jour	NP/A 117 545	Sep 68 Chaubey+ SPIN – CUT – OFF – PARAMETER,TBL	+
	2.4+4			Expt	EXFOR30087.009	Dec 70 SPIN – CUT – OFF PARAM FROM CAPTURE EXPT	
Lvl Density	0.0+0	3.0+4	SAC Expt	Rept	CEA – N – 1268	Feb 70 Tellier+.	+
		3.0+4		Data	EXFOR20120.059	Sep 72 1PNT.A PARAM.FOR TE131 COMP NUCL	
Lvl Density		3.0+4	ORL Expt	Prog	ORNL – 4513 68	Jun 70 Dabbs+,LINAC,PARAMETER A GIVEN	
Lvl Density	None		AUW Theo	Conf	70Madurai 2 267	Dec 70 Ramamurty+ A – PARAMETER GVN,LANG'S – TH	
Lvl Density	+3	+4	FEI Eval	Rept	YK – 8/2 97	Sep 72 Abagyan+ LVL DENSITY PARAMETER,TBL	
				Rept	INDC(CCP) – 39	Jul 74 .PAGE 102.ENGLISH OF YK – 8/2 97	
(γ,n)	8.0+6	2.6+7	SAC Expt	Jour	NP/A 258 350	Feb 76 Lepretre+GDR,LORENTZ PARAM,GRPHS,TBL	

52 Tellurium 131

Quantity	Energy (ev) Min	Max	Lab	Type	Documentation Ref Vol Page	Author, Comments Date	Data
Evaluation	1.0–3	1.5+7	AUA Eval	Rept	AAEC/TM – 549	Jun 70 Cook.TOT,EL,INEL,NONEL,CAPT,G+M,NDG	+
				Rept	AAEC/E – 214	Jun 71 Bertram+GROUP SIGMAS SAME QUANTS.NDG	
				Rept	AAEC/TM – 587	Mar 71 *DESCRIPTION OF LIBRARY	
	1.0–3	1.5+7		Data	AUSTR – DFN 191.	Nov 71 TE – 131M POINT+GROUP SIGS,SAME QUANTS	
	1.0–3	1.5+7		Data	AUSTR – DFN 107.	Nov 71 POINT(223) AND GROUP(127) SIGMAS	
Total	1.0–3	1.5+7	AUA Eval	Data	AUSTR – DFN 191.	Nov 71 .TE – 131M.POINT+GROUP SIGS.SEE EVAL	+
	1.0–3	1.5+7		Data	AUSTR – DFN 107.	Nov 71 COOK+POINT(223)+GROUP(127)SIG.CF EVL	
Elastic	1.0–3	1.5+7	AUA Eval	Data	AUSTR – DFN 107.	Nov 71 COOK+POINT(223)+GROUP(127)SIG.CF EVL	+
	1.0–3	1.5+7		Data	AUSTR – DFN 191.	Nov 71 – TE – 131M.POINT+GROUP SIGS.SEE EVAL	
Tot Inelastc	5.0+5	1.5+7	AUA Eval	Data	AUSTR – DFN 107.	Nov 71 COOK+POINT(11)+GROUP(127)SIG.CF EVL	+
	5.0+5	1.5+7		Data	AUSTR – DFN 191.	Nov 71 .TE – 131M.POINT+GROUP SIGS.SEE EVAL	
Nonelastic	1.0–3	1.5+7	AUA Eval	Data	AUSTR – DFN 191.	Nov 71 .TE – 131M.POINT+GROUP SIGS.SEE EVAL	+
	1.0–3	1.5+7		Data	AUSTR – DFN 107.	Nov 71 COOK+POINT(223)+GROUP(127)SIG.CF EVL	
Res Int Abs	5.0–1		AUA Eval	Rept	AAEC/TM – 619	Sep 72 Clayton.CALC FROM SIG LIBRARY,TABLE	
Res Int Abs	+0	+5	WIN Revw	Conf	IAEA – 169 3 163	74 Pope+ GND+META.AUSTRL DATA FILE CALC	
(n,γ)	1.0–3	1.5+7	AUA Eval	Data	AUSTR – DFN 107.	Nov 71 COOK+POINT(223)+GROUP(127)SIG.CF EVL	+
	1.0–3	1.5+7		Data	AUSTR – DFN 191.	Nov 71 .TE – 131M.POINT+GROUP SIGS.SEE EVAL	
(n,γ)	Pile		CRC Eval	Rept	AECL – 3037 1	Jan 72 Walker.ESTIMATED SIG OF TE – 131M	
(n,γ)	2.5–2		AUA Eval	Rept	AAEC/TM – 619	Sep 72 Clayton.CALC FROM SIG LIBRARY,TABLE	
(n,γ)	Pile	2.5–2	SGA Eval	Conf	73Paris 1 233	Mar 73 Eder+ 30 H ISOMER,SIG ESTIMATED,TBL	
				Rept	SGAE – PH – 141	Feb 73 .SAME AS 73PARIS,POINT SIG FROM COOK	
(n,γ)	Fiss		WIN Revw	Conf	IAEA – 169 3 137	74 Dean. GND+META,DATA AVG OVER FIS – SPC	
	Maxwl	Fiss		Conf	IAEA – 169 3 163	74 Pope+ GND+META,MAXW+FIS – SPC AVG DATA	
(n,γ)	1.5+7		IRK Expt	Jour	NP/A 264 105	Jun 76 Schwerer+ GE – LI. SIG IN TBL	+
	1.5+7			Data	EXFOR20670.011	Oct 76 1PNT.SIGMA.	
Reson Params	–		AUA Theo	Rept	AAEC/E – 211	Nov 70 Musgrove. CALCULTD D+GAM WIDTH GIVEN	
Strnth Fnctn	–		AUA Theo	Rept	AAEC/E – 211	Nov 70 Musgrove. SMOOTHED S0,S1 AND S2 GIVN	
Strnth Fnctn	–2	+3	SAC Expt	Rept	CEA – N – 1522	Oct 72 Cauvin+ S0,S1 CALC	
Lvl Density	+6		MIL Theo	Jour	EN 15 1 54	Jan 68 Facchini+ LDL PARS FROM LOW EN RES	
Lvl Density	None		MUN Theo	Jour	NP/A 217 269	Dec 73 Dilg+ A,DELTA. BACK SHIFTED FERMIGAS	
Lvl Density	None		COP Theo	Jour	NP/A 222 493	Apr 74 Dossing+COLL ROTAT.SPAC. ACCUR ESTIM	
Lvl Density	None		DUB Theo	Jour	NP/A 224 411	May 74 Soloviev+ 1/2 MICROSC MDL. SPH NUCL.	

52 Tellurium 132

Quantity	Energy (ev) Min	Max	Lab	Type	Documentation Ref Vol Page	Author, Comments Date	Data
Evaluation	1.0–3	1.5+7	AUA Eval	Rept	AAEC/TM – 549	Jun 70 Cook.TOT,EL,INEL,NONEL,CAPT SIGS,NDG	+
				Rept	AAEC/E – 214	Jun 71 Bertram+GROUP SIGMAS SAME QUANTS.NDG	
				Rept	AAEC/TM – 587	Mar 71 *DESCRIPTION OF LIBRARY	
	1.0–3	1.5+7		Data	AUSTR – DFN 108.	Nov 71 POINT(223) AND GROUP(127) SIGMAS	
Total	1.0–3	1.5+7	AUA Eval	Data	AUSTR – DFN 108.	Nov 71 COOK+POINT(223)+GROUP(127)SIG.CF EVL	+

52 Tellurium 132

Quantity	Energy (ev) Min	Max	Lab	Type	Documentation Ref Vol Page	Date	Author, Comments	Data
Elastic	1.0−3	1.5+7	AUA	Eval Data	AUSTR−DFN 108.	Nov 71	COOK+POINT(223)+GROUP(127)SIG.CF EVL	+
Tot Inelastc	1.0+6	1.5+7	AUA	Eval Data	AUSTR−DFN 108.	Nov 71	COOK+POINT(10)+GROUP(127)SIG.CF EVL	+
Nonelastic	1.0−3	1.5+7	AUA	Eval Data	AUSTR−DFN 108.	Nov 71	COOK+POINT(223)+GROUP(127)SIG.CF EVL	+
Res Int Abs	5.0−1		AUA	Eval Rept	AAEC/TM−619	Sep 72	Clayton.CALC FROM SIG LIBRARY,TABLE	
Res Int Abs	+0	+5	WIN	Revw Conf	IAEA−169 3 163	74	Pope+ AUSTRL DATA FILE CALC	
(n,γ)	1.0−3	1.5+7	AUA	Eval Data	AUSTR−DFN 108.	Nov 71	COOK+POINT(223)+GROUP(127)SIG.CF EVL	+
(n,γ)	Pile		CRC	Eval Rept	AECL−3037 1	Jan 72	Walker.SIG ESTIMATED ACCORDING Z,A	
(n,γ)	2.5−2		AUA	Eval Rept	AAEC/TM−619	Sep 72	Clayton.CALC FROM SIG LIBRARY,TABLE	
(n,γ)	2.5−2		SGA	Eval Conf	73Paris 1 233	Mar 73	Eder+ INTERPOLATED FROM CALC SIG,TBL	
				Rept	SGAE−PH−141	Feb 73	.SAME AS 73PARIS,POINT SIG FROM COOK	
(n,γ)	Maxwl Fiss		WIN	Revw Conf	IAEA−169 3 163	74	Pope+ MAXW+FIS−SPEC AVG EVAL DATA	
	Fiss			Conf	IAEA−169 3 137	74	Dean. POINT DATA AVG OVER STAND SPEC	
Reson Params	−		AUA	Theo Rept	AAEC/E−211	Nov 70	Musgrove. CALCULTD D+GAM WIDTH GIVEN	
Strnth Fnctn	−		AUA	Theo Rept	AAEC/E−211	Nov 70	Musgrove. SMOOTHED S0,S1 AND S2 GIVN	
Strnth Fnctn	−2	+3	SAC	Expt Rept	CEA−N−1522	Oct 72	Cauvin+ S0,S1 CALC	

52 Tellurium 133

Quantity	Energy (ev) Min	Max	Lab	Type	Documentation Ref Vol Page	Date	Author, Comments	Data
Reson Params	−		AUA	Theo Rept	AAEC/E−211	Nov 70	Musgrove. CALCULTD D+GAM WIDTH GIVEN	
Strnth Fnctn	−		AUA	Theo Rept	AAEC/E−211	Nov 70	Musgrove. SMOOTHED S0,S1 AND S2 GIVN	
Strnth Fnctn	−2	+3	SAC	Expt Rept	CEA−N−1522	Oct 72	Cauvin+ S0,S1 CALC	

52 Tellurium 134

Quantity	Energy (ev) Min	Max	Lab	Type	Documentation Ref Vol Page	Date	Author, Comments	Data
Reson Params	−		AUA	Theo Rept	AAEC/E−211	Nov 70	Musgrove. CALCULTD D+GAM WIDTH GIVEN	
Strnth Fnctn	−		AUA	Theo Rept	AAEC/E−211	Nov 70	Musgrove. SMOOTHED S0,S1 AND S2 GIVN	
Strnth Fnctn	−2	+3	SAC	Expt Rept	CEA−N−1522	Oct 72	Cauvin+ S0,S1 CALC	

53 Iodine 119

Quantity	Energy (ev) Min Max	Lab	Type	Documentation Ref Vol Page	Author, Comments Date	Data
Reson Params	–	AUA	Theo Rept	AAEC/E-211	Nov 70 Musgrove. CALCULTD D+GAM WIDTH GIVEN	
Strnth Fnctn	–	AUA	Theo Rept	AAEC/E-211	Nov 70 Musgrove. SMOOTHED S0,S1 AND S2 GIVN	

53 Iodine 120

Quantity	Energy (ev) Min Max	Lab	Type	Documentation Ref Vol Page	Author, Comments Date	Data
Reson Params	–	AUA	Theo Rept	AAEC/E-211	Nov 70 Musgrove. CALCULTD D+GAM WIDTH GIVEN	
Strnth Fnctn	–	AUA	Theo Rept	AAEC/E-211	Nov 70 Musgrove. SMOOTHED S0,S1 AND S2 GIVN	

53 Iodine 121

Quantity	Energy (ev) Min Max	Lab	Type	Documentation Ref Vol Page	Author, Comments Date	Data
Reson Params	–	AUA	Theo Rept	AAEC/E-211	Nov 70 Musgrove. CALCULTD D+GAM WIDTH GIVEN	
Strnth Fnctn	–	AUA	Theo Rept	AAEC/E-211	Nov 70 Musgrove. SMOOTHED S0,S1 AND S2 GIVN	

53 Iodine 122

Quantity	Energy (ev) Min Max	Lab	Type	Documentation Ref Vol Page	Author, Comments Date	Data
Reson Params	–	AUA	Theo Rept	AAEC/E-211	Nov 70 Musgrove. CALCULTD D+GAM WIDTH GIVEN	
Strnth Fnctn	–	AUA	Theo Rept	AAEC/E-211	Nov 70 Musgrove. SMOOTHED S0,S1 AND S2 GIVN	

53 Iodine 123

Quantity	Energy (ev) Min Max	Lab	Type	Documentation Ref Vol Page	Author, Comments Date	Data
Reson Params	–	AUA	Theo Rept	AAEC/E-211	Nov 70 Musgrove. CALCULTD D+GAM WIDTH GIVEN	
Strnth Fnctn	–	AUA	Theo Rept	AAEC/E-211	Nov 70 Musgrove. SMOOTHED S0,S1 AND S2 GIVN	

53 Iodine 124

Quantity	Energy (ev) Min Max	Lab	Type	Documentation Ref Vol Page	Author, Comments Date	Data
(n,p)	Maxwl	IFU	Theo Rept	ICD-4 20	67 Dadakina+ PENETR COEFF CALC,TABLE	
Reson Params	–	AUA	Theo Rept	AAEC/E-211	Nov 70 Musgrove. CALCULTD D+GAM WIDTH GIVEN	
Strnth Fnctn	–	AUA	Theo Rept	AAEC/E-211	Nov 70 Musgrove. SMOOTHED S0,S1 AND S2 GIVN	

53 Iodine 125

Quantity	Energy (ev) Min Max	Lab	Type	Documentation Ref Vol Page	Author, Comments Date	Data
Res Int Abs	5.0-1	ISP	Expt Jour	JIN 26 1625	Oct 64 Bresesti+REFLECTOR POSITION 13730B	+
	5.0-1		Data	EXFOR20629.003	Oct 76 1PNT.CAPTURE.	
(n,γ)	Pile	ANL	Expt Rept	ACRH-15 92	61 Harper.	
(n,γ)	2.5-2	ISP	Expt Jour	JIN 26 1625	Oct 64 Bresesti+ACT CO60 FLUX DETECTOR	+
	2.5-2		Data	EXFOR20629.002	Oct 76 1PNT.SIGMA.	
(n,γ)	Maxwl	USA	Expt Jour	JIN 27 1727	65 Narang.	+
(n,p)	Maxwl	IFU	Theo Rept	ICD-4 20	67 Dadakina+ PENETR COEFF CALC,TABLE	
Reson Params	–	AUA	Theo Rept	AAEC/E-211	Nov 70 Musgrove. CALCULTD D+GAM WIDTH GIVEN	
Strnth Fnctn	–	AUA	Theo Rept	AAEC/E-211	Nov 70 Musgrove. SMOOTHED S0,S1 AND S2 GIVN	

53 Iodine 126

Quantity	Energy (ev) Min Max	Lab	Type	Documentation Ref Vol Page	Author, Comments Date	Data
Absorption	Maxwl	BLN	Expt Jour	NSE 58 291	Nov 75 Elgart+HFBR.WESTCOTT PROCEDURE.	+
	Maxwl		Data	EXFOR10546.004	Feb 76 1PT.ABS CS=(9.0+ -5.0)KB.	
Res Int Abs	5.0-1	BLN	Expt Abst	DA/B 32 3245	Dec 71 Elgart+PILE ACT.VAL GVN.	+
			Diss	ELGART	71 - .SEE FOR DETAILS	
	5.0-1		Data	EXFOR10728.003	May 78 . 1PT.RIA=40,600B	
(n,γ)	Maxwl	BLN	Expt Abst	DA/B 32 3245	Dec 71 Elgart+PILE ACT.VAL GVN.	+
			Diss	ELGART	71 - .SEE FOR DETAILS	
	Maxwl		Data	EXFOR10728.002	May 78 . 1PT.SIG=5960B.	
(n,p)	Maxwl	IFU	Theo Rept	ICD-4 20	67 Dadakina+ PENETR COEFF CALC,TABLE	
Reson Params	–	AUA	Theo Rept	AAEC/E-211	Nov 70 Musgrove. CALCULTD D+GAM WIDTH GIVEN	

53 Iodine 126

Quantity	Energy (ev) Min	Max	Lab	Type	Documentation Ref Vol Page	Author, Comments Date	Data
Strnth Fnctn	–		AUA	Theo Rept	AAEC/E – 211	Nov 70 Musgrove. SMOOTHED S0,S1 AND S2 GIVN	
Lvl Density	9.0+6	1.7+7	ANL	Eval Rept	ANL – 75 – 34	Jun 75 Davey+N2NEVAL.CONSTANT T,LVL DEN FIT	

53 Iodine 127

Quantity	Energy (ev) Min	Max	Lab	Type	Documentation Ref Vol Page	Author, Comments Date	Data
Evaluation	5.0+5	1.5+7	LRL	Eval Rept	UCRL – 5351	Nov 58 Howerton. CURVES	
Evaluation	1.0–3	1.5+7	AUA	Eval Rept	AAEC/TM – 549	Jun 70 Cook.TOT,EL,INEL,NONEL,CAPT SIGS,NDG	+
				Rept	AAEC/E – 214	Jun 71 Bertram+GROUP SIGMAS SAME QUANTS.NDG	
				Rept	AAEC/TM – 587	Mar 71 *DESCRIPTION OF LIBRARY	
	1.0–3	1.5+7		Data	AUSTR – DFN 109.	Nov 71 POINT(223) AND GROUP(127) SIGMAS	
Evaluation	1.0+3	1.0+7	BOL	Eval Rept	CEC(71) – 2	71 Benzi+ STAT+EVAP MDS.INEL,N2N,NG.TBL	+
	1.0+3	1.0+7		Data	BENZI – DFN 538D	Mar 71 4 QUANTITIES. UK FORMAT	
Total	Maxwl		COL	Expt Jour	PR 48 265	Aug 35 Dunning+ IONCH,TRANS,SIG SLOW+FAST N	
Total	1.0+5	1.8+5	ITY	Expt Jour	PR 56 881	Nov 39 Amaldi+ TRANSM.C–D NS. AVERAGE ES.	
Total	1.0–2	+4	COL	Expt Jour	PR 71 174	Feb 47 WU+ SLOW N SOURCE.TOF.TRANSM.	+
	8.2+3	1.7+1		Data	EXFOR11751.006	Jun 76 . 58 PTS.	
Total	2.4+4	8.3+5	ANL	Expt Jour	PR 71 508	Apr 47 Fields+GN SOURCES 6ES	
	2.4+4	8.3+5		Data	EXFOR11260.024	Jun 76 . 6 PTS.	
Total	2.6–3	1.0+3	COR	Expt Jour	PR 72 362	Sep 47 Jones.TRANSMISSION,TOF.	
Total	2.0+4	1.4+6	WIS	Expt Jour	PR 76 277	Jul 49 Bockelman+ CFD STATIST THEO	+
	2.4+4	1.4+6		Data	EXFOR11881.006	Jun 76 . 31 PTS.	
Total	1.0+5	1.5+6	MIT	Theo Jour	PR 76 1550	Dec 49 Feshbach+ AVERAGE OVER RESON,CF EXPT	
Total	4.2+7		BRK	Expt Jour	PR 80 842	Dec 50 Hildebrand+ BE–D NS.TRANSM. C DETECT	+
	4.2+7			Data	EXFOR11039.026	Jun 76 . 1 PT.	
Total	5.0+4	3.2+6	WIS	Expt Jour	PR 88 83	Oct 52 Miller+20KEV SPREAD TRNSM	+
	1.0+6	3.2+6		Data	EXFOR11712.015	Jun 76 . 14 PTS.	
Total	2.0+0	7.0+3	HAR	Expt Jour	PRSA 215 278	Nov 52 Merrison+.TOF TRANSMISSION	
Total	1.4+7		LAS	Expt Jour	PR 88 562	Nov 52 Coon+	+
	1.4+7			Data	EXFOR11056.043	Jun 76 . 1 PT.	
Total	1.5+1	2.0+2	BNL	Expt Jour	PR 95 476	Jul 54 Seidl+TRANSM INSTR RSLN UNCORCTD	+
	1.6+1	4.8+3		Data	EXFOR11671.009	Jun 76 . 122 PTS.	
Total	1.5+1	1.0+4	CCP	Expt Conf	55Geneva 4 22	Aug 55 Vladimirski+.CURVE,CHOPPER,TOF,P641	
Total	1.0+3	1.5+4	DKE	Expt Jour	PR 105 198	Jan 57 Newson+,TRNS 8.3B AVGD 2–4.5KEV	
Total	2.8+7		LVN	Expt Jour	JPR 22 652	Oct 61 Deconninck+TRANSMISS.3.80B AT 28.4MV	+
	2.8+7			Data	EXFOR20195.015	May 74 1PNT.	
Total	1.2+2	4.0+3	COL	Expt Jour	PR/B 137 547	Feb 65 Garg.TOF,CURVS,RSLN 5EV AT 5KEV	+
	2.9+2	1.9+3		Data	EXFOR11905.008	Jun 76 . 4034 PTS.	
Total	3.2+6	5.2+6	JNE	Expt Jour	NP 65 419	Mar 65 Manero.TRAMSMISS RES 30KEV BROAD RES	+
				ExTh Jour	NP/A 119 356	Oct 68 – +.FLUCT ANAL OF NP65 419	
	3.4+6	5.2+6		Expt Data	EXFOR20209.004	May 74 36PTS.	
Total		4.0+5	SAC	Expt Prog	EANDC(E)66U	Feb 66 Michaudon+ TBC.NDG	
Total	4.5+5	4.5+6	RPI	Expt Prog	WASH – 1068 185	Mar 66 Yergin+,TOF,NDG,TBC	
Total	4.0+6		LAS	Theo Rept	LA – 3538	Sep 66 Agee+ OPTMDL CALC	
Total	2.4+4		LRC	Theo Conf	66Paris 1 503	Oct 66 Bogart. VAL GVN, BETHE ANALYSIS	
Total	4.0+6		KUR	ExTh Jour	YF 6 910	Nov 67 Gorlov+ INCOM N POLARZD.CFD OPTMOD	
Total	4.0+6		IFU	Theo Jour	UFZ 13 51	Jan 68 Kashuba+ TBL,SIG – VAL,EXPT CFD OPTMOD	
				Jour	UPJ 13 33	Jul 68 TRANSLATN.*	
Total	3.0+4	6.5+5	DKE	Expt Jour	AP 46 401	Feb 68 Tabony+ TRANS CURV DERIVES S0,S1,S2	+
	3.0+4	6.5+5		Data	EXFOR11953.007	Jun 76 . 102 PTS.	
Total	6.0+5	2.0+6	RAM	Expt Prog	INDC(PAK) – 1 1	May 69 . EXPT TO BE DONE, NDG	
Total	1.4+7		DEB	Expt Jour	AHP 28 87	Mar 70 Angeli+ TRANSM,SHORT DESC,THEORY,TBL	+
	1.4+7			Data	EXFOR30113.018	Feb 71 VALUE AT 14.5 MEV	
Total	1.3+7		DAC	Expt Jour	JNE 24 385	Nov 70 Hussain+ XPT.AT 2 ES,AT BACKWARD ANG	+
	1.3+7			Data	EXFOR30245.003	Jun 73 SIGMA – TOTAL AT 13.36 AND 13.48 MEV	
Total	1.4+7		RAM	Expt Rept	AECD/EP – 21	Jan 71 Ullah+ OPTMOD FIT TO EXPTL DATA,GRPH	
Total	2.5+6	1.5+7	BNW	Expt Jour	PR/C 3 576	Feb 71 Foster+,TRANS,CURVS,CFD OTHERS+TH	+
				Jour	NIM 36 1	Sep 65 .SUPERSEDED	
	2.3+6	1.5+7		Data	EXFOR10047.058	Aug 73 . 243 PTS.	
Total	1.4+7		KOS	Expt Jour	AHP 30 115	Oct 71 Angeli+EXPT,DATA TABLE,LITER. SURVEY	+
	1.4+7			Data	EXFOR30141.012	Jan 72 SIGMA AT 14.7 MEV GIVEN	
Total	1.0–3	1.5+7	AUA	Eval Data	AUSTR – DFN 109.	Nov 71 COOK+POINT(223)+GROUP(127)SIG.CF EVL	+
Total	2.7+3		MUN	Expt Prog	EANDC(E)150U	Oct 72 Dilg+ AVERAGE TOT XSECT+S0	+
				Conf	71Albany 327	Aug 71 – +TRNS.AVG CS GVN.31 ELEMENT GRP	
	2.7+3			Data	EXFOR20583.010	May 76 1PNT.	
Total	1.3+7	1.5+7	DEB	Eval Rept	IAEA – 153 173	73 Boedy+ MOST PROBABLE VAL OF SIG,TBL	
Total	1.0+3	6.0+5	NBS	Expt Jour	PR/C 9 28	Jan 74 Camarda.LINAC.TOF.GRPH.TRANS.MEAS.S1	

53 Iodine 127

Quantity	Energy (ev) Min	Max	Lab	Type	Documentation Ref Vol Page	Author, Comments Date	Data
Total	1.8+1	5.0+2	ORL	Expt Prog	ORNL – 2501 26	Mar 58 Slaughter+FAST CHOPPER.CURV MANY RES	+
	1.7+1	6.8+2		Data	EXFOR11446.002	Jun 76 . 241 PTS.	
Elastic	3.6–2		ANL	Expt Jour	PR 71 666	May 47 Fermi+ SCATT LENGTH+SIGN FROM EXP+TH	+
	3.6–2			Data	EXFOR12593.011	Jun 76 . 1 PT, SIGMA.	
Elastic	5.0–1		ANL	Expt Jour	PR 79 11	Jul 50 Harris+ EPI – CD,RES INT SCAT,B – W TH	
Elastic	2.5–2		ORL	Expt Jour	PR 81 527	Feb 51 Shull+	+
	2.5–2			Data	EXFOR11043.	Jun 76 . 3 PTS, BAS, COH, COH AMP	
Elastic	3.0+5	1.5+6	ANL	Expt Rept	EANDC(US) – 62	Jun 64 Smith.TOF,TBL.50KEV STEPS,20KEV RSLN	+
	3.0+5	1.5+6		Data	EXFOR12039.003	Jun 76 . 23 PTS.	
Elastic	2.0+6		FEI	Expt Rept	EANDC – 50 200	Jul 65 Kazakova+ EXPT,TABLE CFD OPTMODEL	+
				Prog	YFI – 3 6	Sep 66 .TABLE	
				Prog	INDC – E – 140 6	Sep 66 .ENGLISH TRANSL OF YFI – 3 6 9/66	
Elastic	4.0+6		LAS	Theo Rept	LA – 3538	Sep 66 Agee+ OPTMDL + H – F FOR COMP	
Elastic	1.5+6		IFU	Expt Prog	YFI – 5 42	Oct 67 Korzh+ TBL OPTMDL PARAMS + TOTELAST	
				Rept	INDC – 232E	67 . ENGL OF YFI – 5 42	
Elastic	4.0+6		KUR	ExTh Jour	YF 6 910	Nov 67 Gorlov+ INCOM N POLARZD.CFD OPTMOD	+
				Expt Jour	DOK 158 574	Sep 64 – +	
	4.0+6			Data	EXFOR40221.030	May 74 .1 DATA LINE	
Elastic	1.5+6		IFU	Comp Jour	YF 7 277	Feb 68 Korzh+ OPTMOD PARS – FIT TO EXPTL – SIG	
				Jour	SNP 7 2 190	Aug 68 TRANSLATN.*	
Elastic	1.0–3	1.5+7	AUA	Eval Data	AUSTR – DFN 109.	Nov 71 COOK+POINT(223)+GROUP(127)SIG.CF EVL	+
Elastic	8.9+5		ANL	Expt Rept	ANL – 7935	Jun 72 COX+ 4 PI B(O)	+
	8.9+5			Data	EXFOR10332.108	Jun 74 . 1 PT	
Elastic	7.2–2		ANL	Expt Jour	ACR 28 663	Nov 72 Atoji. COH.SCAT.LENGTH = .525 + – .004	+
	7.2–2			Data	EXFOR10345.003	Feb 74 . 1 PT.	
Diff Elastic	7.0+6		LRL	Theo Rept	UCRL – 4927	Jul 57 Bjorklund+ OPTMDL CALC 6 – PARAM FIT	
Diff Elastic	4.0+6	7.0+6	LAS	Expt Jour	PR 129 1649	Feb 63 Thomson. SIG AT 90DEG	+
	4.0+6	7.0+6		Data	EXFOR11495.036	Jun 76 . 2 PTS., DIFFL. AMP.	
Diff Elastic	3.0+5	1.5+6	ANL	Expt Rept	EANDC(US) – 62	Jun 64 Smith.TOF,TBL.50KEV STEPS,20KEV RSLN	+
	3.0+5	1.5+6		Data	EXFOR12039.002	Jun 76 . 115 PTS., LEG.	
Diff Elastic	4.0+6		KUR	Expt Jour	DOK 158 574	Sep 64 Gorlov+,POLRZ NS,TBL SIG VS COS	+
				ExTh Jour	YF 6 910	Nov 67 – + INCOM N POLARZD.CFD OPTMOD	
				Expt Jour	PL/B 25 197	Aug 67 – +,CFD OPTMOD ANGLES 10 – 170DEGS	
				ExTh Conf	67Kharkov 175	Feb 67 – .POLRSD NS,ANGLES = 10 – 170 DEGRS	
				Expt Rept	INDSWG – 101 112	65 . LARGE GRPH.ALSO AVAILABLE IN ENGL	
				Jour	SPD 9 806	Mar 65 . ENGL OF DOK 158 574	
	4.0+6			Data	EXFOR40221.029	May 74 .SIGMA IN MB/SR AT 17 ANGLES GIVEN	
Diff Elastic	2.0+6		FEI	Expt Rept	EANDC – 50 200	Jul 65 Kazakova+ EXPT,CURVE CFD OPTMODEL	+
				Prog	ICD – 2 112	Jul 65 .CURVE	
				Prog	INDSWG – 101E	65 .ENGLISH TRANSL OF ICD – 2 112 7/65	
Diff Elastic	4.0+6		LAS	Theo Rept	LA – 3538	Sep 66 Agee+ OPTMDL + H – F FOR COMP	
Diff Elastic	4.0+6		LAS	Theo Rept	LA – 3788	67 Beery+.OPTMOD CALC POLARIZ ANG DISTR	
Diff Elastic	4.0+6		IFU	Theo Jour	UFZ 13 51	Jan 68 Kashuba+ GRPH,EXPT CFD OPTMOD – CALC	
				Jour	UPJ 13 33	Jul 68 TRANSLATN.*	
Diff Elastic	1.5+6		IFU	Comp Jour	YF 7 277	Feb 68 Korzh+ GRPH SIG(ANG),OPTMOD PARS – FIT	
				Jour	SNP 7 2 190	Aug 68 TRANSLATN.*	
Diff Elastic	2.0+6	4.0+6	SCU	Theo Rept	ICD – 6 236	69 Averyanov+CALC ANGDIST CFD EXPT,GRPH	
Diff Elastic	1.0+3	4.0+4	DUB	Expt Jour	YF 11 1152	Jun 70 Samosvat.LEGENDRECOEF(E) GRPH,OPTMOD	+
				Rept	JINR – P3 – 4724	Oct 69 – . ASSYMMETRY,0+180DEG ANG	
				Jour	SNP 11 639	Dec 70 – . ENGL OF YF 11 1152.	
	1.6+3	3.9+4		Data	EXFOR40285.009	Apr 75 .LEGEND – COEF FOR 10 ES GVN	
Diff Elastic	8.9+5		ANL	Expt Rept	ANL – 7935	Jun 72 Cox+. CFD OPTMOD,HAUSER – FESHBACH	
Diff Elastic	2.0+6		SCU	Comp Rept	YK – 15 153	Aug 73 Averjanov+ H – F,OPTMOD,DIFFSIG,GRAPH	
Diff Elastic	6.4+6		PAR	Expt Jour	JPR 37 6 651	Jun 76 Ramstein+ ANGDIST.5,130DEG.OPTMDL.	
				Diss	FRNC – TH – 418	Mar 73 – . ORSAY.VDG.	
Diff Elastic	1.0+6	6.0+6	BRC	Theo Conf	76Lowell 1446	Jul 76 Duchemin+CS,ANG DISTR CALC.CFD NDG	
Polarization	4.0+6		LAS	Theo Rept	LA – 3788	67 Beery+.OPTMOD CALC COS(THETA) DISTR	
Polarization	4.0+6		KUR	ExTh Jour	YF 6 910	Nov 67 Gorlov+ INCOM N POLARZD.CFD OPTMOD	+
				Expt Jour	DOK 158 574	Sep 64 – +	
	4.0+6			Data	EXFOR40221.031	May 74 .DIFF POLARZ OF EL SCAT,DATA AT16ANG	
Polarization	4.0+6		IJI	Theo Jour	YF 13 1026	May 71 Pasechnik+ POLRZ(ANG) CFD EXPT,GRAPH	
				Jour	SNP 13 589	Nov 71 . ENGL OF YF 13 1026	
Polarization	8.9+5		ANL	Expt Rept	ANL – 7935	Jun 72 COX+ CFD OPTMOD,HAUSER – FESHBACH	+
	8.9+5			Data	EXFOR10332.055	Jun 74 . 8 PTS.	
Potntal Scat	1.2+2	3.0+2	ANL	Expt Jour	PR 76 100	Jul 49 Hibdon.TRNSM MN CO SCATT DETCTRS	+
	1.2+2	3.0+2		Data	EXFOR11261.038	Jun 76 . 2 PTS.	
Potntal Scat	2.5–2		ORL	Expt Jour	PR 81 527	Feb 51 Shull+	+
	2.5–2			Data	EXFOR11043.154	Jun 76 . 1 PT.	

53 Iodine 127

Quantity	Energy (ev) Min	Max	Lab	Type	Documentation Ref Vol Page	Date	Author, Comments	Data
Potntal Scat		6.5+5	DKE	ExTh	Jour PL 13 70	Nov 64	Seth+0,1PHASE FRM SIG TOT AV 3-650KV	
Potntal Scat	2.4+4		LRC	Theo	Conf 66Paris 1 503	Oct 66	Bogart. VAL GVN, BETHE ANALYSIS	
Tot Inelastc	2.5+6		IFU	Expt	Jour JET 4 769	Jun 57	.ENGLISH OF ZET 31 907	
					Jour ZET 31 907	Nov 56	Strizhak. SPHERE METHOD,TABLE	
Tot Inelastc	2.5+6	1.4+7	IFU	Expt	Conf 58Geneva 15 18	Sep 58	Pasechnik+.PPR2030,NDG,EXPT DESCRIBD	
					Conf 55Geneva 2 3	Aug 55	- . INTEGR SIGMA,2ES,TABLE	
Tot Inelastc	4.0+5	1.2+6	FEI	Expt	Jour AE 15 416	Nov 63	Glazkov+	
					Jour JNE 18 654	64	. ENGL OF AE 15 416	
					Jour EAF 15 5	Nov 63	.FRENCH OF AE 15 416	
					Jour SJA 15 1173	Nov 63	. ENGL OF AE 15 416	
Tot Inelastc	8.0+5	4.0+6	IFU	Expt	Prog INDSWG-126 22	66	Pasechnik. AT 5 ES, TBP IN AE	
Tot Inelastc	2.0+5	9.0+5	BHU	Theo	Jour NP/A 106 241	Dec 67	Sharma+.H-F CALC.LVLS 203TO649KEV.	
Tot Inelastc	5.9+4	1.0+7	BOL	Eval	Rept CEC(71)-2	71	Benzi+ STAT MODEL. TBL GIVEN.	+
	5.9+4	1.0+7			Data BENZI-DFN 538D	Mar 71	65 PNTS	
Tot Inelastc	5.0+5	1.5+7	AUA	Eval	Data AUSTR-DFN 109.	Nov 71	COOK+POINT(11)+GROUP(127)SIG.CF EVL	+
Tot Inelastc	5.0+4	1.0+6	SAC	Theo	Conf 73Kiev 1 291	May 73	Krebs+ OPT+STATMDL,PRELIM CFD XP.GRF	
Tot Inelastc	1.4+7		TUD	Expt	Prog ZFK-262 39	Sep 73	Goebel+ INTEGRATED DIFFSIG,TB DONE	
Tot Inelastc	1.0-3	1.5+7	RCN	Eval	Prog RCN-239 11	Nov 75	Gruppelaar. EXP.+MODEL CALC. NDG	
Diff Inelast	2.0+5	1.2+6	WIS	Expt	Jour PR 101 103	Jan 56	Lind+,ANG DISTR ASSUMED ISOTR CURVE	
Diff Inelast	1.2+6		FR	Expt	Jour PA 60 9393	Nov 57	NO ASYMETRY OBS.(COMPTES RENDUS)	
Diff Inelast	1.3+7	1.7+7	PCF	Expt	Jour NC 9 664	Aug 58	Remy+NN N2N TOF SPECTRA RELATIV.ONLY	
Diff Inelast	1.4+7		VBT	Expt	Abst BAP 5 104	Mar 60	Arnold+.OKS TEMP.5-4MEV,T=8.1MEV	
Diff Inelast	3.2+6		SAC	Expt	Jour JPR 21 384	May 60	Naggiar+ ABST.SCAT BY 1ST EXCIT LVL	
	1.1+6	3.6+6			Jour JPR 19 54	Jan 58	Szteinsznaider+ ASYMMETRIC ANGDIST	
	1.1+6				Jour CR 245 668	Aug 57	Naggiar+ VDG. NAI + G-SPECT.	
Diff Inelast	4.0+6	7.0+6	LAS	Expt	Jour PR 129 1649	Feb 63	Thomson. TOF, 90DEG	+
	4.0+6	7.0+6			Data EXFOR11495.035	Jun 76	. 2 PTS, DSIG	
Diff Inelast	1.4+7		BAS	Expt	Jour PL 5 202	Jul 63	Huber+ GRPH OF INELASTIC N SPECT.	
					Jour HPA 36 1059	Dec 59	- +.T=0.89MEV	
Diff Inelast	1.2+7	2.2+7	HAM	Expt	Jour ZN/A 18 914	Sep 63	Langkau.CSI(TL) TARGET AND DETECTOR	
Diff Inelast	4.0+5	1.2+6	FEI	Expt	Jour AE 15 416	Nov 63	Glazkov+ SPHER GEOM, 5 ENERGIES	
					Jour JNE 18 654	64	. ENGL OF AE 15 416	
					Jour SJA 15 1173	Nov 63	. ENGL OF AE 15 416	
					Jour EAF 15 5	Nov 63	.FRENCH OF AE 15 416	
Diff Inelast	8.0+5		SAC	Expt	Jour JPR 24 1008	Nov 63	Cabe+ISOTROPIC FOR LVL AT 59+203KEV	
Diff Inelast	1.4+7		FEI	Expt	Jour YF 4 1154	Dec 66	Sal'Nikov+ SPEC OF SECNDARY NS,CURVE	+
					Rept FEI-39	Jan 66	- +TOF SPECT,RING GEOM,E-SPEC	
					Jour SNP 4 831	Jun 67	.ENGLISH TRANSL OF YF 4 1154 12/66	
					Data EXFOR40134.012	Feb 73	N-SPECTRUM AT 92 DEG, 50EN'	
Diff Inelast	3.5+6	8.5+6	JAE	Expt	Prog EANDC(J)8L25	Jan 68	Maruyama+.TOF.CONTIN SPECT AT 90DEG	
	3.6+6	8.5+6			Jour NP/A 131 145	Jun 69	- . E DEPENDENCE,PARAM,TH FIT	
Diff Inelast	5.9+4	1.0+7	BOL	Eval	Rept CEC(71)-2	71	Benzi+ DISCRETE INELASTIC.13 LVLS.	+
	5.9+4	1.0+6			Data BENZI-DFN 538D	Mar 71	1ST-13TH LVL +ANGDIST+E DIST	
	1.0+6	1.0+7			Data BENZI-DFN 538D	Mar 71	TO CONTINUUM, 30PNTS+ANGDIST+E DIST	
Diff Inelast	1.0+5	8.0+5	BHU	Theo	Rept PTP 45 1335	Apr 71	Sharma+ H-F,MOLDAUER TO 1ST,2ND LVLS	
	6.0+4	9.0+5			Jour NP/A 106 241	Dec 67	- +.H-F CALC TO 7 LVLS CFD EXPT.	
Diff Inelast	1.4+7		KFI	Theo	Rept KFKI-72-17	Feb 72	Kluge+ CALC N-SPEC INEL+N2N,TBL,GRPH	
Diff Inelast	1.4+7		TUD	Expt	Prog ZFK-262 39	Sep 73	Goebel+ DOUBLEDIFFSIG,IN PROGRESS	
Diff Inelast	1.5+7		TUD	Expt	Prog ZFK-283 89	Aug 74	Reif+ PREEQUIL N-SPEC CFD XPT,GRAPH	
Diff Inelast	1.4+7		FEI	Expt	Rept YK-23 6	76	Sal'Nikov+ TOF,NEUT-SPEC,TBLS	+
	1.4+7				Data EXFOR40324.	Dec 77	D2SIG/DA,DE. 4*51 PNTS	
Diff Inelast	1.0+6	6.0+6	BRC	Theo	Conf 76Lowell 1446	Jul 76	Duchemin+CS,ANG DISTR CALC.CFD NDG	
Thermal Scat	Cold		MUN	Expt	Prog EANDC(E)150U	Oct 72	Koester+ COH SCATT AMPL	+
	4.5-4				Data EXFOR20581.006	Jun 76	1PNT.COH.SC.AMP.	
Thermal Scat	1.0-4	1.0+3	MUN	Revw	Jour EEN 80 1	77	Koester. SCAT LENGTH,FREE+INCOH SIG	
Scattering	Maxwl		JAP	Expt	Jour SCP 36 153	Jul 39	Kimura.SIG=4.8B(UPPER LIMIT)	
Scattering	Slow		JAP	Expt	Jour JPJO 22 391	May 40	Kimura.RN+BE.SIG=2.5 TO 2.7B	
Scattering	Slow		JAP	Expt	Jour JPJO 25 481	Jul 43	Kimura.SIG + CURVE GIVN	
Scattering	1.5+6		FEI	Expt	Prog INDSWG-74	Jul 65	GUSEYNOV ETAL.SUBM.TO ATOMNAJA ENER.	
	Fast				Jour AE 18 409	Apr 65	Gusejnov+ ANG DIST,TH(N,F) DETECTOR	
					Jour SJA 18 526	Apr 65	. ENGL OF AE 18 409	
Scattering	2.4+4		LRC	Theo	Conf 66Paris 1 503	Oct 66	Bogart. VAL GVN, BETHE ANALYSIS	
Nonelastic	1.4+7		CCP	Expt	Jour AE 1 4 155	Sep 56	Flerov+.SPHERE TRANSM, 2110+-60MB	+
					Jour JNE 4 529	Apr 57	TRANSLATN.*	
					Jour SJA 1 4 617		56 TRANSLATN.*	
Nonelastic	1.4+7		IFU	Expt	Jour AE 2 68	Jan 57	Strizhak.SPHERE TRANSMISS 1.88+- 16B	+
					Jour JNE 5 253	Nov 57	TRANSLATN.*	
					Jour SJA 2 72		57 TRANSLATN.*	

53 Iodine 127

Quantity	Energy (ev) Min	Energy (ev) Max	Lab	Type	Documentation Ref Vol Page	Date	Author, Comments	Data
Nonelastic	2.5+6	3.6+6	IFU	Expt	Jour UFZ 3 185	Mar 58	Batalin+SPH TR DET EXPT DETAIL	+
					Conf 56Kiev 102	56	.	
					Conf 55Geneva 2 3	55	.	
Nonelastic	1.0−3	1.5+7	AUA	Eval	Data AUSTR−DFN 109.	Nov 71	COOK+POINT(223)+GROUP(127)SIG.CF EVL	+
Nonelastic	1.4+7		TUD	Theo	Conf ZFK−271 63	Nov 73	Seeliger+ N−SPEC,NDG.INTEG−SIG SHOWN	
Nonelastic	1.4+7	1.7+7	ANL	Eval	Rept ANL−75−34	Jun 75	Davey+CORRC APPLIED TO N2N CS.TBLS.	
Absorption	Slow		OSA	Expt	Jour JPJO 18 188	36	Kikuchi+.SIG AND G−ENERGY DETERMIN	
Absorption	+7		BRK	Expt	Jour PR 53 795	May 38	Grahame+ RA−BE,TRANS,PB(NNGAMMA) DET	
Absorption	Slow		JAP	Expt	Jour JPJO 25 481	Jul 43	Kimura.SIG + CURVE GIVN	
Absorption	Pile		HAR	Expt	Jour PPSA 63 1175	Oct 50	Colmer+LITTLER.PILE OSC REL HAR B	+
					Rept AERE−N/R−527	Jun 50	− + PILE OSC.	
Absorption	1.0+4	6.0+5	KAP	Theo	Rept NSE 2 334	May 57	Storm+,CALC 1.1 .28B CFD BNL325 NG	
Absorption	2.5+4	8.3+5	FEI	Expt	Jour ZET 34 574	Mar 58	Belanova.VALUES GIVEN AT 3 ES	
					Jour JET 7 397	Sep 58	TRANSLATN.*	
Absorption	2.5+4		KUR	Expt	Conf 58Geneva 15 50	Sep 58	Leipunskij+.PPR2219,VAL GVN,ACTIVATN	
Absorption	2.5−2		HAR	Expt	Jour JNEA 12 32	May 60	Tattersall+. PILE OSCILLATOR	+
					Rept AERE−R−2887	Aug 59	− . PILE OSC.REL BORON	
	2.5−2				Data EXFOR20638.038	Jul 76	1PNT.SIGMA.	
Absorption	2.4+4		FEI	Expt	Jour AE 8 549	Jun 60	Belanova.VAL FOR 3ES,SPHERE TRNSMISS	
					Jour SJA 8 462	Jul 61	TRANSLATN.*GERMAN KE4 147 2/61	
Absorption	Maxwl		GA	Eval	Rept GA−12071	Aug 61	Joanou+.68GROUP DATA FOR GAM−I	
Absorption	1.4+7	1.5+7	GLS	Expt	Jour NP 49 306	Nov 63	Robertson.SIG=26+−3MB	
Absorption	1.0−4	1.0+7	JUL	Eval	Rept JUEL−678−RG	Jul 70	Liu. EVALUATION+CALC,GRPH,FN OF E	
Absorption	3.0+6	1.6+8	VIP	Expt	Abst DA/B 31 331	Jul 70	Campbell. REL TO I127 AT 24 KEV	
Absorption	Fast		RCN	Revw	Conf IAEA−169 2 53	74	Bustraan.INTEG CFD SIG(N−E)FILES,TBL	
Res Int Abs	5.0−1		ANL	Expt	Jour PR 79 11	Jul 50	Harris+ EPI−CD,REL THERMAL ACT. B−W	+
	5.0−1				Data EXFOR11343.023	Jun 76	. 1 PT.	
Res Int Abs	5.0−1	1.0+6	CCP	Expt	Conf 55Geneva 5 91	Aug 55	Spivak+.VAL GVN CFD REF,PPR659	
Res Int Abs	None		ORL	Revw	Conf 55Geneva 5 96	Aug 55	Macklin+.TABLE,EXPT CFD THEORY,P833	
Res Int Abs	−		CCP	Expt	Jour AE 3 507	Dec 57	Klimentov+.EPI CD REACTIVITY REL LI	+
					Jour JNE 9 20	Jun 59	TRANSLATN.*	
					Jour SJA 3 1387	57	TRANSLATN.*	
Res Int Abs	None		ORL	Eval	Rept ORNL−2869	Mar 60	Nephew.1/V UP +TO100EV.ALSO 7 ES− UP	
Res Int Abs	5.0−1		HAR	Expt	Jour JNE 12 32	May 60	Tattersall+. ABOVE 1/V. OSC. CF CALC	+
					Rept AERE−R−2887	Aug 59	− . PILE OSC.REL BORON	
	6.7−1				Data EXFOR20638.039	Jul 76	1PNT.	
Res Int Abs	+3	+5	BOL	Theo	Conf 61Vienna 1 179	Aug 61	Benzi+.PPR11,VAL GVN,L=0,L=1 .CAPT.	
Res Int Abs	5.0−1		BOL	Expt	Conf 61Vienna 1 179	Aug 61	Benzi+ TBL TOTAL CAPT RES INTS.	
Res Int Abs	5.5−1		GA	Eval	Jour NSE 12 115	Jan 62	Garrison+,RI= 154+−40 B,FROM RES.PAR	
Res Int Abs	None		DKE	Expt	Abst DA 23 4719	Jun 63	Furr.RES INTEG REL TO I127.NDG	
Res Int Abs	5.0−1		ORL	Expt	Jour NSE 17 371	Nov 63	Pattenden.140+−20B	
Res Int Abs	−		FEI	Comp	Rept INDSWG−64 75	64	Prokhorov. 110+−20 B	
Res Int Abs	None		CRC	Eval	Rept AECL−2111	Nov 64	Walker. REDUCED RESONANCE INTEGRAL	
Res Int Abs	5.0−1		BOL	Eval	Rept RT/FI−4	Jan 67	Palmucci. CALC FROM (N,G) RES PARAMS	
Res Int Abs	5.0−1		BGK	Expt	Rept THAI−AEC−10	Oct 67	. ACTIV(NA−I),CD−RATIO,REL AU. TABLE	+
	5.0−1				Data EXFOR30368.019	Jan 77	REL AU, PRELM.	
Res Int Abs	5.0−1		CNE	Expt	Jour CJP 46 2473	Nov 68	Ricabarra+,RATIO TO THR−ACT SIGMA	+
					Rept CNEA−274	70	− + SAME,IN SPANISH	
	5.0−1				Data EXFOR30129.006	Oct 72	RESON INT AND RATIO TO THR ABS SIGM.	
Res Int Abs	5.0−1		GFK	Expt	Jour AKE 15 83	70	Breitenhuber+. CONTROL EXPT.ACTIV.	+
	5.0−1	1.0+6			Data EXFOR20029.004	Sep 71	1PNT.ACTIVATION.	
Res Int Abs	None		GA	Eval	Rept GA−12071	Sep 71	Mathews+. RECOMMENDED VALUES	
Res Int Abs	5.0−1		NPL	Expt	Jour JNE 24 35	Feb 70	Ryves.REL AU.REDUCED INTGRL.ACTIV.	+
					Conf 71Canterby 139	Sep 71	.REDUCED CAPT RES INTEGRAL,TBL	
	5.0−1				Data EXFOR20789.324	Dec 78	1PNT.REDUCED INTEGRAL.CAPTURE	
Res Int Abs	5.5−1		CRC	Eval	Rept AECL−3037 1	Jan 72	Walker.REDUCED RES INT,DETAILED TBL	
Res Int Abs	5.0−1		AUA	Eval	Rept AAEC/TM−619	Sep 72	Clayton.CALC FROM SIG LIBRARY,TABLE	
Res Int Abs	4.6−1	1.0+6	RCN	Theo	Rept RCN−191	Jul 73	Lautenbach.CAPT INT FROM GROUP SIGMA	
Res Int Abs	5.0−1		GHT	Expt	Jour JRC 20 695	74	Van Der Linden+ BY(N,G).CFD OTHS,TBL	+
	5.5−1				Conf 73Paris 2 241	Mar 73	− + ACT,REL THR+GOLD,TBL	
	5.5−1				Data EXFOR20645.007	Jul 76	1PNT.CAPTURE.	
Res Int Abs	5.5−1	+6	SAC	Revw	Conf IAEA−169 1 235	74	Ribon.CAPTURE,STATUS CFD REQUEST,TBL	
Res Int Abs	+0	+5	WIN	Revw	Conf IAEA−169 3 163	74	Pope+ DATA FILE CALC CFD XPTAL VALUE	
(n,γ)	Maxwl		COL	Expt	Jour PR 50 738	Oct 36	Fink. RATE OF ABSORPTION+SIGMA	
(n,γ)	2.2+5		PCF	Expt	Jour NAT 142 392	Aug 38	Halban+ ACT CS GIVEN	
(n,γ)	2.0+4	7.0+5	OXF	Expt	Jour PRSA 170 513	Apr 39	Griffiths.RA−BE PHOTONEUT ACTIVATION	
(n,γ)	Maxwl		LUQ	Expt	Jour PR 58 554	Sep 40	Lapointe+ ABS IN WATERBATH,REL BORON	
(n,γ)	Maxwl		LUQ	Expt	Jour PR 58 869	Nov 40	Rasetti. BETA ACT.REL MN55N,G	

53 Iodine 127

Quantity	Energy (ev) Min	Max	Lab	Type	Documentation Ref Vol Page	Author, Comments Date	Data
(n,γ)	Maxwl		JAP Expt	Jour	SCP 38 167	Jan 41 Sinma+.LI+D.RELATIVE SIG MEASUREMENT	
(n,γ)	Pile		MON Expt	Rept	MC- 70	44 Grummott.	+
	Pile			Data	EXFOR12040.002	Jun 76 . 1 PT.	
(n,γ)	3.0+3	5.9+6	LAS Expt	Rept	LA- 467	Jul 46 Linenberger+TBL.GRPH.REL TO H001	+
	3.0+3	5.9+6		Data	EXFOR11945.008	Jun 76 . 8 PTS.	
(n,γ)	Maxwl		LAS Expt	Rept	LA- 467	Jul 46 Linenberger+	+
	Maxwl			Data	EXFOR11945.008	Jun 76 . 1 PT, SIG	
(n,γ)	Pile		ANL Expt	Jour	PR 72 888	Nov 47 Seren+.THR IRRAD. THR IRRAD.PBI2.	+
	Pile			Data	EXFOR11447.090	Jun 76 . 1 PT.	
(n,γ)	2.2+5	9.0+5	OXF Expt	Jour	NAT 161 727	May 48 Allen+ ACTIVATION RATIO	
(n,γ)	Fiss		ANL Expt	Jour	PR 75 1781	Jun 49 Hughes+ REL SIG(THERMAL),FOIL ACTIVN	+
	Fiss			Data	EXFOR11450.033	Jun 76 . 1 PT.	
(n,γ)	Pile		ANL Expt	Jour	PR 80 342	Nov 50 Harris+.PILE OSC.REL TO BORON.	+
	Pile			Data	EXFOR11528.032	Jun 76 . 1 PT.	
(n,γ)	2.4+4		ANL Expt	Jour	PR 82 67	Apr 51 Hummel+ SB-BE PHOTONEUTS. ACTIVATION	+
	2.4+4			Data	EXFOR11010.014	Aug 76 . 1 PT. SIG=2.2B	
(n,γ)	Maxwl		ORL Expt	Jour	PR 83 641	Aug 51 Pomerance.LOCAL OSC REL AU ABS 95 B	+
	Maxwl			Data	EXFOR11047.044	Jun 76 . 1 PT.	
(n,γ)	2.5-2		KJL Expt	Jour	PR 86 937	Jun 52 Grimeland. = 2 DATA INDEX LINES	+
	Maxwl			Data	EXFOR20098.	Sep 71 2PTS.SIG.	
(n,γ)	2.7+5	1.6+6	LAS Expt	Jour	PR 89 1302	Mar 53 Martin+ NAI(TL) SCINT,EXCITATN CURVE	+
	2.7+5	1.6+6		Data	EXFOR12028.003	Jun 76 . 13 PTS.	
(n,γ)	Fiss		BNL Expt	Jour	PR 91 1423	Sep 53 Hughes+.ALSO LVL SPACINGS AT EXCIT E	
(n,γ)	Fast		HAR Expt	Jour	JNE 5 4	Jul 57 Rose. ACT CS GVN,ZEPHYR,TH DISCUSS	
				Rept	AERE-R/R-2151	57 Absalom+ ZEPHYR+TH ENVELOPE.	
				Revw Conf	55Geneva 5 331	Aug 55 Holmes+P404,SAME DATA AS JNE,5,4,57	
(n,γ)	1.0+4	6.0+5	ANL Theo	Abst	BAP 3 18	Jan 58 Moldauer. B-W AVERAGE NDG	
(n,γ)	2.4+4		ORL Expt	Jour	PR 107 504	Jul 57 Macklin+.SB-BE NS,820+-60MB,.455MEVG	+
				Conf	58Geneva 15 68	Sep 58 - .PPR671,VAL GVN,EXPT DESCRIBD	
	2.4+4			Data	EXFOR11399.033	Jun 76 . 1 PT.	
(n,γ)	1.4+7		ALD Expt	Jour	PPS 72 505	Oct 58 Perkin+ACT ANAL 2.5MB+-20PC, B-W TH	+
(n,γ)	2.0+4	1.0+6	LAS Expt	Jour	PR 113 256	Jan 59 Bame+,ACT 1B TO 0.08B CURVE	+
				Conf	58Geneva 15 60	Sep 58 .SUPERSEDED	
	1.9+4	6.6+5		Data	EXFOR11405.003	Jun 76 . 31 PTS.	
(n,γ)	2.5+4	6.0+5	RIC Expt	Jour	PR 114 201	Apr 59 Gabbard+,MONOTON DECREASING .7-.12B	+
				Jour	PRL 2 235	Mar 59 .SUPERSEDED	
	2.5+4	5.1+5		Data	EXFOR11098.010	Jun 76 . 9 PTS.	
(n,γ)	2.0+5		ORL Expt	Jour	PR 114 1619	Jun 59 Lyon+.ABS GAMMA COUNT 175+-15MB ACT	+
	2.0+5			Data	EXFOR11407.023	Jun 76 . 1 PT.	
(n,γ)	Maxwl		ETH Expt	Jour	ZP 156 293	Oct 59 Knoepfel+ PAIR SP,SUM INTENS 9GAMMAS	
(n,γ)	1.5+5	6.2+6	WIS Expt	Jour	PR 116 927	Nov 59 Johnsrud+ SC CFD OTHERS SIG VS E	+
	1.5+5	5.5+6		Data	EXFOR11675.015	Jun 76 . 28 PTS.	
(n,γ)	Maxwl		CRC Eval	Rept	AECL-1054	Mar 60 Walker. (CRRP-913)	
(n,γ)	1.0+3	4.0+5	DKE Expt	Jour	AP 10 477	Aug 60 Weston+ TH FIT TO DATA INCL S+P WAVE	+
	5.0+3	1.5+5		Data	EXFOR11818.010	Jun 76 . 14 PTS.	
(n,γ)	4.0+5	1.0+6	LAS Expt	Jour	PR 120 556	Oct 60 Diven.SC-T.	+
	4.0+5			Data	EXFOR11616.021	Jun 76 . 1 PT.	
(n,γ)	2.4+4		ORL Expt	Jour	NP 20 202	Oct 60 Schmitt.SHELL TRANSMISSION 885+-90MB	+
				Prog	EANDC-33 41	Sep 63 - + CORRECTION TO NP 20 202	
	2.4+4			Data	EXFOR11778.012	Jun 76 . 1 PT.	
(n,γ)	Fast		LAS Expt	Jour	NSE 8 608	Dec 60 Byers. GODIVA ACTIVATION CS GIVEN	
(n,γ)	2.5-2		ANL Expt	Jour	NSE 9 132	Feb 61 Meadows+,PULSED NEUTS,6.22+-0.15B	+
	2.5-2			Data	EXFOR11028.017	Sep 76 1PT.CS=6.22B	
(n,γ)	2.0+2	8.0+3	ORL Expt	Conf	61Saclay 203	Sep 61 Block+.LIQUID SCINTILLATOR	+
				Conf	61Vienna 1 95	Aug 61 Neiler.	
	2.0+2	8.0+3		Data	EXFOR11935.009	Jun 76 . 39 PTS.	
(n,γ)	2.5+4		DKE Expt	Rept	TID-16059	62 Furr.ACT 0.635+-0.180B ABSOLUTE	
(n,γ)	1.0+1	6.0+4	LEB Expt	Jour	ZET 42 988	Apr 62 Popov.PB-SLO-DOWN,GRPH SG(E)CFD OTHR	+
				Jour	JET 15 683	Oct 62 TRANSLATN.*	
(n,γ)	1.9+4	2.5+6	CCP Expt	Jour	JNAB 16 326	Jun 62 Stavisskii+ TRANSLATION	
				Jour	AE 10 158	Feb 61 - + REL U235 NF + THR VALUES	
(n,γ)	1.0+3	1.0+5	DUB Expt	Jour	ZET 43 2000	Dec 62 Exp.COMP.WITH THEORY	
				Jour	JET 16 1409	Jun 63 TRANSLATN.*	
(n,γ)	5.0+3	3.0+5	FOA Theo	Jour	NP 39 529	Dec 62 Bergqvist+. STATISTICAL MODEL	
(n,γ)	1.0+3	7.0+5	ORL Expt	Jour	PR 122 182	Apr 61 Gibbons+CURVE CFD THEORY REP BNL653	+
	3.0+4	6.5+4		Jour	PR 129 2695	Mar 63 Macklin+ LIQ SCINT,733 AND 440MB	
				Conf	61Vienna 1 95	Aug 61 Neiler.	
	9.5+3	1.7+5		Data	EXFOR11329.	Jun 76 . 49 PTS, SIG	

53 Iodine 127

Quantity	Energy (ev) Min	Max	Lab	Type	Documentation Ref Vol Page	Author, Comments Date	Data
(n,γ)		2.0+5	DKE	Theo Abst	DA/B 23 4719	Jun 63 Furr.CS PREDICTED FROM RES PARS.NDG	
(n,γ)	Maxwl		IBJ	Expt Jour	NKA 8 437	Jul 63 Jozefowicz. ACT CS GVN	+
				Rept	INR-407	Mar 63 - .BETA COUNT.5.8+ - 0.2B	
	Maxwl			Data	EXFOR31099.006	May 78 1 PNT	
(n,γ)	2.6+6		KFI	Expt Rept	KFKI-1467	Sep 63 Borbely+ ACTIVATION. TOTAL SIGMA	+
	2.6+6			Data	EXFOR30175.	May 72 TOTAL SIGMA	
(n,γ)	2.4+4		CCP	Comp Rept	INDSWG-64 43	64 Graph. BELANOVA AND OTHER XPTS	
(n,γ)	1.3+5	1.8+6	ANL	Expt Jour	PR/B 133 378	Jan 64 COX.CURV NORM TO THR AND AU ACTIVATN	+
	1.8+5	1.7+6		Data	EXFOR11835.009	Jun 76 . 30 PTS.	
(n,γ)	5.0+3	9.0+4	ORL	Theo Jour	RMP 37 166	Jan 65 Macklin+.CALC FOR KT=5TO90KEV	
(n,γ)	1.0+3	1.4+7	FEI	Theo Conf	65Antwerp	Jul 65 Zakharova.OBNINSK.FERMI GAS MODEL	
(n,γ)	Maxwl	+2	FEI	Expt Jour	AE 19 292	Sep 65 Stavisskij+ REL TO PU-239(N,F)	
				Jour	SJA 19 1210	Sep 65 . ENGL OF AE 19 292	
(n,γ)	Maxwl	2.4+4	NPL	Expt Jour	NP 71 417	Sep 65 Robertson.2ES,GLEEP+SB - BE,CFD OTHERS	+
				Conf	65Antwerp 552	Jul 65 - . SB-BE SOURE,ENERGY 22.8KV	
(n,γ)	1.0+5	1.4+7	UAR	Theo Jour	JNAB 20 373	May 66 Naguib+.HF,STATISTIC THEORY FIT DATA	
	Fiss			Jour	JNAB 20 373	May 66 - +. 65.6B BY THEOR FIT TO DATA	
(n,γ)	1.0+3	1.0+6	KFK	Eval Conf	66Paris 1 277	Oct 66 Poenitz.TBL EVAL+RENORM TO AU	
(n,γ)	2.4+4		LRC	Theo Conf	66Paris 1 503	Oct 66 Bogart. VAL GVN, BETHE ANALYSIS	
(n,γ)	2.5-2		BOL	Eval Rept	RT/FI-4	Jan 67 Palmucci. CALC FROM RES PARAMETERS	
(n,γ)	2.0+6	1.5+7	LOK	Theo Jour	JNE 21 577	Jul 67 Grench.COMPNUC METHODS IN MEV RANGE	
(n,γ)	1.3+5	1.8+5	ORL	Expt Jour	PR 159 1007	Jul 67 Macklin+ TOF,VDG, SCINT,3ES ABSL	+
	1.3+5	1.8+5		Data	EXFOR11679.018	Jun 76 . 3 PTS.	
(n,γ)	3.0+6		DEB	Expt Jour	JNE 21 797	Oct 67 Peto+ACTIV,SIGMA REL TO P-31(N,P)	
	3.0+6			Data	EXFOR30031.016	Aug 70 SINGLE VALUE	
(n,γ)	Pile		FEI	Expt Jour	AE 23 396	Nov 67 Lejpunskij.RATIO REL U235(N,F),PILE	
				Jour	EAF 23 5 21	Nov 67 . FRENCH TRANSL OF AE 23 396 11/67	
				Jour	SJA 23 1150	Nov 67 .ENGLISH TRANSL OF AE 23 396 11/67	
(n,γ)	Maxwl		AUA	Theo Jour	NSE 31 234	Feb 68 Cook+ STATISTICAL CALC CFD EXPT	
(n,γ)	1.4+7		UEN	Expt Jour	NP/A 111 360	Apr 68 Dinter. DERIVED FROM G SPECT. CFD TH	+
(n,γ)	2.9+6		IRK	Expt Jour	OAWA 105 236	Jun 68 Colditz+ ACTIVATION.	+
	2.9+6			Data	EXFOR20092.011	Sep 71 1PNT.SIG.	
(n,γ)	-		IEA	Comp Rept	IEA-INF- 10	Aug 68 Atalla. TABLES OF HL,SIG AND GAMM-E	
(n,γ)	1.4+7		NJS	Expt Rept	NIJS-R-545	Oct 68 Cvelbar+ SCINT TELESC SPECTR,SIG GIV	+
				Jour	FIZ 5 37	73 .FULL PAPER,INTG SIG CFD ACT SIG,TBL	
				Jour	FIZS 4 53	Dec 72 .SIG VS MASS NUMBER,GRAPH	
				Conf	72Budapest § D-21	Aug 72 .SIG VS MASS NUMBER,GRAPH	
				Jour	NP/A 158 251	Dec 70 .SIG VS MASS NUMBER,GRAPH	
	1.4+7			Data	EXFOR30184.012	Oct 72 1 DATA LINE	
(n,γ)	1.5+7		PAK	Expt Jour	JIN 30 2577	Oct 68 Qaim+,ACTIV	
	1.5+7			Data	EXFOR31080.005	Sep 72 .SIG GVN	
(n,γ)	1.0+6	1.0+7	WWA	Theo Rept	INR-967	Dec 68 Brzosko+ WG-MEAN LVL DIST,PIGMY RES	
(n,γ)	1.0+3	1.0+5	VIP	Expt Jour	NSE 35 364	Mar 69 Furr+ ACT FROM AVG RESON PARAMS	
(n,γ)	None		RPI	Theo Jour	PR 184 1201	Aug 69 Sperber.STATISTICAL CALC OF EXC FNCT	
(n,γ)	1.0+3	1.0+7	BOL	Eval Jour	CCDN-NW/10	Dec 69 Benzi+H-F MOD,AXEL G.DATA ENDF FORM.	
				Rept	CEC(70)-2	Apr 70 - +. GRAPH	
				Conf	66Paris 1 537	Oct 66 - + STATMOD.TBL AV VALS.SUPERSEDD	
				Jour	NC 38 216	Jul 65 - + THEORY FOR CAPTURE EVALUATION	
				Conf	61Vienna 1 179	Aug 61 - + TBL AV VALS. SUPERSEDED.	
(n,γ)	2.0+5		MUA	Theo Conf	69Roorke 2 129	Dec 69 Chaubey+ SIG VALUE GIVEN, STATIST-TH	
(n,γ)	1.0+2	6.0+3	WWA	Theo Jour	CJP 47 2849	Dec 69 Brzosko+,COMPOUND NUCL CALC CFD EXPT	
(n,γ)	Fiss		CAI	Expt Prog	IAEA-124 152	Feb 70 NO AUTHOR,BETA-ACT,REL THR SIG,NDG	
(n,γ)	2.0+6	1.4+7	BOL	Revw Conf	70Helsinki 2 379	Jun 70 Benzi.115. REVIEW, SIG(E) GRAPH	
(n,γ)	1.4+7	1.5+7	JYV	Eval Rept	JU-RR-3/1970	Jun 70 Leppaemaeki+ TABLE OF EVAL AVG SIG	
(n,γ)	1.0+3	1.0+6	GA	Revw Rept	70ANL 285	Oct 70 Carlson. STATUS AS STANDARD SIG,CURV	
(n,γ)	3.0+4		AUA	Theo Rept	AAEC/E-211	Nov 70 Musgrove. SIGMA GIVEN AND CFD OTHER	
(n,γ)	2.4+4		BHU	Expt Conf	70Madurai 2 615	Dec 70 Chaturvedi+ EXPTL+CALCULATED SIGMAS	
(n,γ)	1.0+3	1.0+7	BOL	Eval Rept	CEC(71)-2	71 Benzi+ OPTMOD EVAL.TBL GIVEN.	+
	1.0+3	1.0+7		Data	BENZI-DFN 538D	Mar 71 79 PNTS	
(n,γ)	2.5-2		NPL	Expt Jour	JNE 24 35	Feb 70 Ryves.REL.AU,STANDARD NPL TH.FLUX.	+
				Conf	71Canterby 139	71 - . VDG,GRAPHITE MODERATOR.ACTIVN	
	2.5-2			Data	EXFOR20789.031	Dec 78 1PNT.SIGMA.	
(n,γ)	4.0+5		WWA	Expt Jour	APPB 2 489	71 Brzosko+ PARTIAL,TOTAL SIG CFD THEO	+
				Rept	INR-1318 28	Apr 71 *SHORT REPORT,DATA GIV	
				Jour	CJP 47 2849	Dec 69 *TH.CALCULATIONS OF SIG	
	4.0+5			Data	EXFOR30159.	Apr 72 PARTIAL,TOTAL SIGMAS GIVEN	
(n,γ)	1.0+3	1.0+6	HED	Theo Rept	HEDL-TME-71106	Aug 71 Schmittroth. H-F CALCULATION	

53 Iodine 127

Quantity	Energy (ev) Min	Max	Lab	Type	Documentation Ref Vol Page	Date	Author, Comments	Data
(n,γ)	1.5+7		MUA	Expt Prog	BARC-553 19	Aug 71	Hasan+ SIG EXPT,CFD TH,ABST ONLY,NDG	
				Conf	70Madurai 2 36	Dec 70	. SAME ABSTRACT ONLY	
(n,γ)	Maxwl		GA	Eval Rept	GA- 12071	Sep 71	Mathews+. RECOMMENDED VALUES	
(n,γ)	1.0-3	1.5+7	AUA	Eval Data	AUSTR-DFN 109.	Nov 71	COOK+POINT(223)+GROUP(127)SIG.CF EVL	+
(n,γ)	Maxwl		CRC	Eval Rept	AECL-3037 1	Jan 72	Walker.RECOMMENDED SIG,DETAILED TBL	
(n,γ)	2.4+4		MUA	Theo Jour	IJP 46 114	Mar 72	Chaubey+ P-WAVE STRENGTH FUNCT,TABLE	
(n,γ)	1.0+2	1.0+7	HED	Theo Rept	HEDL-TME-71154	Aug 72	Mackellar+ REALISIC OPTMOD	
(n,γ)	2.5-2		AUA	Eval Rept	AAEC/TM-619	Sep 72	Clayton.CALC FROM SIG LIBRARY,TABLE	
(n,γ)	Fast		MTR	Expt Conf	72Kiamesha 2 614	Sep 72	Harker+ CFRMF INTEGRAL MEAS.	
(n,γ)	+6		KOS	Expt Jour	AHP 33 363	73	Peto+ AVERAGE SIG FOR ALF-BE N,TABLE	+
	+6			Data	EXFOR30265.014	Feb 74	1 DATA LINE	
(n,γ)	8.3+5		II	Expt Conf	73Kiev 4 312	May 73	Lakosi+ FOTO-N,REL AU197(N,G	
	+6			Data	EXFOR30268.009	Jul 74	1 POINT	
(n,γ)	1.0+3	1.0+6	SAC	Theo Conf	73Kiev 1 291	May 73	Krebs+ OPT+STATMDL,PRELIM CFD XP,GRF	
(n,γ)		1.1+7	RCN	Theo Rept	RCN-191	Jun 73	Lautenbach. GROUP CONSTANTS TBL	
(n,γ)	1.0+3	2.0+7	TUD	Theo Prog	ZFK-262 133	Sep 73	Hoehn+ CALC SIG CFD EXPT,GRAPH	
(n,γ)	2.5-2	3.0+4	SAC	Revw Conf	IAEA-169 1 235	74	Ribon.STATUS SIG CFD REQUESTS,TABLE	
	Maxwl	Fiss	WIN	Revw Conf	IAEA-169 3 163	74	Pope+ MAXW+FIS-SPEC AVG DATA CFD XPT	
	Fiss			Conf	IAEA-169 3 137	74	Dean. POINT DATA AVG OVER STAND SPEC	
(n,γ)	1.4+7		RBZ	Expt Jour	NCL 10 1	May 74	Vuletin+ ACT,GELI.CFD OTHRS+THEO,TBL	+
				Jour	FIZS 4 59	Dec 72	Holub+ ACTIV SIG,SUPSEDD BY NCL 10 1	
	1.4+7			Data	EXFOR30314.007	Dec 75	SIGMA AT 14.4 MEV	
	1.4+7			Data	EXFOR30145.010	Aug 73	.SUPERSEDED BY EXFOR30314.007	
(n,γ)	1.0+3	1.0+7	FEI	Eval Rept	YK- 8/2 97	Sep 72	Abagjan+ AVG SIG(ENERGY-GROUPS),TABL	
				Rept	INDC(CCP)-39	Jul 74	.P102. ENGLISH OF YK-8/2 97	
(n,γ)	1.5+7		BOR	Expt Jour	NSE 55 17	Sep 74	Rigaud+ MDL TH. CALC.TBLS.GRPHS.	+
				Conf	74Petten 233	Sep 74	- + IMPROVED ACT. METHOD	
	1.4+7			Diss	IN-2P3 1092	73	Destbuilliers.MEASURED BY 2 METHODS	
	1.5+7			Data	EXFOR20543.007	Apr 76	1PNT.SIGMA.	
(n,γ)	1.5+7		BOS	Expt Conf	74Calcutta 57	Nov 74	Majumdar+ CFD STATMOD.SIGMA GIVEN	+
				Jour	IJP 44 204	Mar 70	Majumder. BY BETA SATURATION ACT,TBL	
	1.5+7			Data	EXFOR30296.004	Jun 75	1 POINT	
(n,γ)	1.0+3	1.0+6	BOL	Theo Conf	JAERI-M-5984	Feb 75	Benzi+P.83.OPT/STATMOD.CURVES CFD	
(n,γ)	5.0+3	8.0+4	FEI	Expt Rept	YK- 19 57	May 75	Shorin+ TOF,SIG(NEUT-E),TBL,GRAPH	
(n,γ)	2.4+4		BNL	Expt Conf	75Wash. 920	Mar 75	Rimawi+ CS=722+-47MB.CFD OTHER EXPT	+
				Conf	AERE-R-8082	Jul 75	- +ABSTR,IRON FILTER TECHN,NDG	
	2.4+4			Data	EXFOR10434.005	Mar 75	1PT,SIGMA	
(n,γ)	1.0+3	1.0+6	SAC	Eval Rept	CEA-N-1832	Dec 75	Ribon+ EXP+TH ANAL,STAT MOL,CURVE	
(n,γ)	1.4+7		JYV	Expt Jour	PL/B 39 625	May 72	Kantele+ CAPT SIG MEASURED	+
	1.5+7			Rept	JU-RR-1/1976	Mar 76	Valkonen.(THESIS).ACTIV.TBL. 14.5MEV	
				Jour	NIM 103 549	Sep 72	- + ACTIV. GEOMETRY EFFS,TBL.	
	1.5+7			Data	EXFOR20673.027	Nov 76	1PNT.SIGMA.	
	1.5+7			Data	EXFOR20544.005	Apr 76	1PNT.SIGMA.	
(n,γ)	1.5+7		JYV	Comp Rept	JU-RR-1/1976	Mar 76	Valkonen.(THESIS).EXPTS CFD DSD MODL	
(n,γ)	1.4+7		IRK	Expt Jour	NP/A 264 105	Jun 76	Schwerer+ GE-LI.ACT SIG=1.12+-0.25MB	+
	1.5+7			Data	EXFOR20670.012	Oct 76	1PNT.SIGMA.	
(n,γ)	Maxwl		PSU	Expt Abst	DA/B 27 919	Sep 66	Kappe. ACT CS REL NA-23 GIVEN	+
	Maxwl			Data	EXFOR11277.008	Jun 76	. 1 PT.	
(n,γ)		1.0+3	KUK	Eval Conf	76Lowell 1280	Jul 76	Malik+VARIOUS CAPT DATA CFD AND ANAL	
(n,γ)	Fast		RCN	Expt Rept	ECN-10	Oct 76	Veenema+ STEK REACTIVITY WORTHS TBL.	
Spect (n,γ)	Maxwl		ANL	Expt Jour	PR 76 531	Aug 49	Kubitscheck+ MAX E.G.-M COINC+ABSORBR	
Spect (n,γ)	2.5+6		ANL	Expt Abst	PR 98 224	Apr 55	Hibdon+ MANY LINES IN CASCADE	
Spect (n,γ)	Maxwl		BNL	Expt Jour	PR 100 1302	Dec 55	Reier+,XTL SPEC .085AND.255MEVGAMMAS	
Spect (n,γ)	-		TAT	Expt Jour	NP 1 2	Jan 56	Gupta+JHA. NAI(TL)WELL. 3 NEW LINES	
Spect (n,γ)	2.0+5	1.9+6	RIC	Expt Prog	WASH-191 53	Jun 56	Zabel.SHAPE DOESNT CHANGE WITH E	
Spect (n,γ)	Maxwl		CCP	Expt Jour	ZET 31 886	Nov 56	Estulin.E-GAM 20-600KEV ,GRAPH	
				Jour	JET 4 752	Jun 57	TRANSLATN.*	
Spect (n,γ)	Maxwl		MOS	Expt Jour	ZET 32 979	May 57	Estulin+ SCINT SPEC 50-500KEV GAMMAS	
				Jour	JET 5 801	Dec 57	TRANSLATN.*	
Spect (n,γ)	Maxwl		MOS	Expt Jour	NP 4 91	Aug 57	Estulin+. INTESITY OF 1 SOFT GAMMA	
Spect (n,γ)	2.5+4		ORL	Expt Conf	58Geneva 15 68	Sep 58	Macklin. SIGMA+G-ENERGY GVN	
Spect (n,γ)	Maxwl		YAL	Expt Jour	PR 114 268	Apr 59	Draper.SC SPECTR,GAM E 0 TO 600 KEV	
Spect (n,γ)	Maxwl		ETH	Expt Jour	ZP 156 293	Oct 59	Knoeppel+ 3.9 TO 6.7MEV GAMMAS	
				Jour	NC 11 609	Jan 59	Balzer+ LINE ENS ONLY.CRYSTALSPEC.	
Spect (n,γ)	Maxwl		UJV	Expt Jour	CZJ 10 119	60	Kopecky+ CRYSTSPEC,20-1000KEV G-SPEC	
Spect (n,γ)	Maxwl	2.0+1	ANL	Expt Jour	PR 123 629	Jul 61	Du-Toit+ DELAYED GAMMAS	
Spect (n,γ)	2.0+4	3.0+5	FOA	ExTh Jour	NP 39 529	Dec 62	Bergqvist.+125KEV.GRAPH.CFD STATMDL	

53 Iodine 127

Quantity	Energy (ev) Min	Max	Lab	Type	Documentation Ref Vol Page	Date	Author, Comments	Data
Spect (n,γ)	7.5+6		AE	Expt Conf	65Antwerp 550	Jul 65	Bergqvist+ NAI. ABST.NDG.SHAPE ONLY.	
				Prog	EANDC(OR)36L14	Apr 65	- +VDG DISAGR.C COMPD.NUCL.TH	
Spect (n,γ)	Maxwl		BUC	Expt Jour	RRP 10 673	Aug 65	Cristu+ GSPEC INTENS,TBL+CRVS,LVLSCH	+
				Jour	SCF 20 577	Jun 68	- . THESIS, IN ROMANIAN	
	Maxwl			Data	EXFOR30211.002	Nov 72	INTENSITIES OF 13 SPECTRUM LINES	
Spect (n,γ)	Maxwl		MCM	Expt Jour	NP 83 241	Aug 66	Archer+ 184 GAMMAS OBSERVED	
Spect (n,γ)	1.4+7		UEN	Expt Jour	NP/A 111 360	Apr 68	Dinter. SIGMA, DSIGMA/DE CALC.CFD TH	
Spect (n,γ)	2.5-2		MIT	Comp Rept	MITNE-85	Jan 69	Rasmussen+TBL G INT.=AFCRL-69-0071	
Spect (n,γ)	+2		DUB	Expt Prog	YFI-7 59	Apr 69	Bechvarzh+ GAMMA-SPEC FOR 10 RESON	
				Rept	INDC(CCP)-7U63	Feb 70	TRANSLATN.*	
Spect (n,γ)	Maxwl		SFU	Expt Jour	NP/A 138 392	Nov 69	Korteling+.GE(LI).LOW E GAMMAS.	
Spect (n,γ)	Maxwl	1.0+3	CRC	Expt Prog	AECL-3666 62	Dec 69	Lone+,TOF,NO DATA GIVEN	
Spect (n,γ)	1.0+2	6.0+3	WWA	Theo Jour	CJP 47 2849	Dec 69	Brzosko+,COMPOUND NUCL CALC CFD EXPT	
Spect (n,γ)	Maxwl		FRS	Expt Jour	NP/A 165 415	Apr 71	Schaller+ .025-1.4,4.5-6.8MVGS,323ES	+
				Jour	HPA 42 917	Dec 69	Michaud+ PAIR+ANTICOMPTON-SPEC,GRPH	
	Maxwl			Data	EXFOR20531.	Apr 76	325PTS.	
Spect (n,γ)	Pile		KFK	Expt Rept	KFK-1401	Jun 71	Djadali.AVG POLRZ G EXPT,CFD T,SPIN	
	Maxwl			Jour	NP/A 147 150	May 70	Eichler+ POL NS.CIRC POL GS+ASSYMTRY	
Spect (n,γ)	4.0+5		WWA	Expt Jour	APPB 2 489	Aug 71	Brzosko+ GAMMA-EN = 3 TO 7 MEV,GRAPH	
Spect (n,γ)	1.0+7		WWA	Theo Jour	NP/A 189 545	Jul 72	Brzosko+ CMPD NUCL DECAY.PARTIAL WG	
Spect (n,γ)	1.4+7		NJS	Expt Jour	FIZ 5 37	73	Cvelbar+ SIGMA VS G-ENERGY,GRAPH	+
				Jour	NIM 44 292	Oct 66	.SCINT SPECTR DESCRIBED	
	1.4+7			Data	EXFOR30184.013	Oct 72	25 DATA LINES	
Spect (n,γ)	1.5+7		CCP	Expt Conf	73Tbilisi 159	Feb 73	Kravtsov+ ABST,GE-LI,G-SPEC AT 90DEG	
Spect (n,γ)	4.6+5		AUA	Expt Prog	AAEC/PR-39P 44	Jan 74	Allen+ NA-I,GAMMA YIELD,FIGURE ONLY	
Spect·(n,γ)	1.0+0	6.0+2	SAC	Expt Jour	NP/A 223 509	May 74	Jain+ GRAPHS,HIGH/LOW EG,WIDTH CORR	
	-2	+2		Rept	CEA-N-1522	Oct 72	Cauvin+ GAMMA SPECTR ANAL	
Inelastic γ	Thrsh	1.8+6	ANL	Expt Abst	PR 98 224	Apr 55	Hibdon+ MANY GAMMAS TBD	
Inelastic γ	2.0+5	1.2+6	LAS	Revw Conf	55Geneva 2 9	Aug 55	Day.P581, EXCITATN OF 5 LVLS,RINGGEO	
Inelastic γ	2.5+6		OXF	Expt Jour	PM 1 102	Jan 56	Wolf.NOT ABS.0.2 0.41 0.64 1.01MEV G	
Inelastic γ	2.0+5	1.2+6	WIS	Expt Jour	PR 101 103	Jan 56	Van-Loeff+ 4LINES ABSOLUTE CURVES	+
	1.4+5	1.2+6		Data	EXFOR11673.	Jun 76	. 85 PTS.,DIFFL. AMP.	
Inelastic γ	1.0+5	1.2+6	MIT	Expt Jour	PR 101 1516	Mar 56	Guernsey+,CS 60-KEV LEVEL CFD TH	+
	1.2+5	1.2+6		Data	EXFOR11691.003	Jun 76	. 27 PTS.	
Inelastic γ	8.0+5		TEX	Expt Jour	PR 103 1031	Aug 56	Morgan.5G ES	
Inelastic γ	Fast		HAM	Expt Jour	ZN/A 11 919	Nov 56	Heymann+NA(I)TL CRYSTAL	
Inelastic γ	5.0+5	1.5+6	WES	Expt Jour	PR 107 1306	Sep 57	Sinclair.XTL SPEC 62 145KEV GS	
Inelastic γ	3.0+6		FEI	Expt Jour	AE 7 268	Sep 59	Androsenko+ GRAPH+TABLE OF GAM-ENERG	
				Jour	SJA 7 763	Mar 61	. ENGL OF AE 7 268	
				Jour	JNEA 12 136	Jun 60	. ENGL OF AE 7 268	
				Jour	KE 3 565	Jun 60	.GERMAN OF AE 7 268	
Inelastic γ	2.0+5	3.5+6	CLU	Expt Jour	AP 12 485	Mar 61	Lind+SIG(94DEG) FOR 11 GAMMAS	+
	3.2+5	1.6+6		Data	EXFOR11188.012	Jun 76	. 148 PTS, DSIG	
Inelastic γ	3.1+6	4.3+6	CSR	Expt Jour	CZJ 11 229	Apr 61	Lehar. SC, TABLE OF GS CFD OTHR XPTS	
Inelastic γ	3.0+6		CCP	Expt Jour	IZV 25 1280	Oct 61	Graudynya+,SCINT,3 NEW GAMMA LINES	
Inelastic γ	5.8+6	7.5+6	FOA	Expt Jour	NP 80 198	May 66	Bergqvist+CFD SPEC IN CAPT.AT 0.1MEV	
Inelastic γ	5.7+5		CCP	Expt Jour	IZV 31 252	Feb 67	Musaelyan+.CURVE OF GAMMA SPECTR GVN	
				Jour	BAS 31 235	Feb 67	TRANSLATN.*	
Inelastic γ	5.0+5	1.0+6	PUC	Theo Jour	IPA 5 182	May 67	Vasudev+ H-F CALC,CFD XPT,LVL-SPINS	
Inelastic γ	5.0+4	5.0+5	SCT	Expt Jour	NP/A 125 312	Feb 69	Bain+ VDG,NAI(TL) 20-140 KEV GAMMAS	+
	4.6+4	5.1+5		Data	EXFOR30124.002	Mar 71	DATA FROM PRIVCOM	
Inelastic γ	4.6+4	5.1+5	SUN	Expt Jour	NP/A 125 312	Feb 69	Bain+ TO 59KEV LEVEL ,SIG(E),GRAPH	+
Inelastic γ	None		RAM	Expt Prog	INDC(PAK)-1 1	May 69	. VDG,GE-LI. NDG,CONTINUED	
Inelastic γ	1.0+3	1.8+6	PEL	Expt Jour	ZP 243 121	Apr 71	Barnard+ 17 LEVELS DETERMINED,TBL	
Inelastic γ	5.0+6	1.6+6	KQU	Expt Jour	NP/A 188 115	Jun 72	Sinclair+.GELI+NAITL. 34EG REL 418KV	
Nonelastic γ	2.4+6		OSA	Expt Jour	JMJ 21 75	39	Kikuchi+.D-D P LI-D N,SIG GIVN	
	2.1+6	2.8+6		Jour	JMJ 21 232	39	Aoki.SIG GIVN	
		2.4+6		Jour	JMJ 19 369	37	- .D+D NEUTRON.RELATIV SIG GIVN	
	Slow			Jour	JPJO 18 115	36	Kikuchi+.REL SIG GIVN FOR G-EMISSION	
Nonelastic γ	3.2+6		NRL	Expt Jour	PR 96 386	Oct 54	Scherrer+ C-W+CRYST SPEC 5 PEAKS	
(n,2n)	Fast		CAR	Expt Jour	PR 81 184	Jan 51	Cohen.AVR SIG,N SPEC.BETA ACT.	+
	Fast			Data	EXFOR11189.043	Jun 76	. 1 PT.	
(n,2n)	1.5+7		CRC	Expt Jour	CJP 31 267	Feb 53	Paul+.BETA ACT.CFD TH. HL= 70M+13D	+
	1.5+7			Data	EXFOR11274.085	Jun 76	. 1 PT.	
(n,2n)	9.5+6	1.8+7	LAS	Expt Jour	PR 89 1302	Mar 53	Martin+ NAI(TL) SCINT,EXCITATN CURVE	+
	9.5+6	1.8+7		Data	EXFOR12028.002	Jun 76	. 7 PTS.	
(n,2n)	1.2+7	1.8+7	LAS	Expt Jour	RMP 28 103	Apr 56	Brolley+ AVERAGED DATA	

53 Iodine 127

Quantity	Energy (ev) Min	Max	Lab	Type	Documentation Ref Vol Page	Date	Author, Comments	Data
(n,2n)	1.3+7	1.7+7	PCF Expt	Jour	NC 9 664	Aug 58	Remy+ NN AND N2N.TOF.N SPECTRA.	
	1.4+7			Jour	CR 246 1410	Mar 58	- +TOF+NSPECT+RESD GROUPS 1+1.3ME	
(n,2n)	Pile		CRC Expt	Rept	CRC-852	Jul 59	Roy+ ACTIVATION IN NRX FLUX	
(n,2n)	Fiss		BAT Expt	Rept	BMI-1486	Dec 60	Jung+ ACTIV.EFF SIG ABOV THRESH GIVN	
(n,2n)	Fiss		CRC Eval	Rept	CRC-1003	Dec 60	Roy+,ESTIMATED AVG SIG=0.9MB	
(n,2n)	1.2+7	2.0+7	HAMExpt	Jour	ZP 166 477	Feb 62	Bormann+ CURVE VS E. ALSO GAM SPECT.	+
(n,2n)	Pile		MUNExpt	Jour	ADP 12 57	63	Hertlein. ACTIV+REAC-SIG,AVG+EFF,TBL	
(n,2n)	Fiss		TRM Theo	Conf	63Bombay 232	Feb 63	Singh.VAL COMPUTD BY SEMIEMP FORMULA	
(n,2n)	Fast		AMS Expt	Jour	PHY 30 1762	Sep 64	Heertje+COMPARE WITH OTHER EXPTS	
(n,2n)	2.0+7		MIT Expt	Jour	JIN 27 1727	65	Narang.	+
	2.0+7			Data	EXFOR12020.	Jun 76	. 2 PTS, SIG FOR GND + META	
(n,2n)	1.4+7		HAMCompJour		NP 65 257	Mar 65	Bormann. 3EXPT VALS.CFD SHELL EFFECT	
(n,2n)	Fiss		IIT Comp	Conf	65IAEA 251	Mar 65	Barrall+CALC AVG SIGS OF 3FISS-SPECS	
(n,2n)	1.3+7	1.5+7	BNL Theo	Jour	NSE 23 238	Nov 65	Pearlstein.3ES.STAT MDL CALC.TBL CS.	
(n,2n)	Fiss		BNL Theo	Jour	NSE 23 238	Nov 65	Pearlstein.STATMDL CALC.SPEC AVG.TBL	
(n,2n)	Maxwl		GHT Expt	Jour	RCA 9 57	68	De Regge+0.647MICROBARN	
(n,2n)	Fiss		CCP Expt	Jour	DOK 180 836	Jun 68	Nasyrov.(AVG+EFFECTIV)THRESH-SIG-TBL	
				Jour	SPD 13 6 559	Dec 68	TRANSLATN.*	
				Jour	EAF 25 5 125	Nov 68	.TRANSLATN.*	
				Jour	AE 25 437	Nov 68	Nasyrov.(AVG+EFFECTIV)THRESH-SIG-TBL	
				Jour	SJA 25 1251	Nov 68	. ENGL OF AE 25 437	
(n,2n)	1.5+7		PAK Expt	Jour	JIN 30 2577	Oct 68	Qaim+,ACTIV	+
	1.5+7			Data	EXFOR31080.004	Sep 72	.SIG GVN	
(n,2n)	1.5+7		STF Expt	Rept	AFWL-TR-68-134	Mar 69	Barrall.	+
	1.5+7			Data	EXFOR10022.019	Nov 72	. 1 PT. SIGMA	
(n,2n)	1.4+7		KGUExpt	Jour	YF 10 699	Oct 69	Prokopets+ NEUT DOUBLE ANGDIST,GRPH	
				Jour	SNP 10 403	Apr 70	TRANSLATN.*	
				Jour	UFZ 14 687	Apr 69	Prokopec+ ANG CORREL BETWEEN NEUTS	
(n,2n)	9.0+6	1.9+7	AUA Theo	Rept	AAEC/TM-522	Nov 69	Bertram. CALC SIG(E)GRAPHS CFD EXPTS	
(n,2n)	1.5+7		STF Expt	Jour	NP/A 138 387	Nov 69	Barrall+. D-T NS. GAMMA ACTIVATION.	+
	1.5+7			Data	EXFOR10031.012	Jun 71	. 1 PT. SIGMA.	
(n,2n)	1.5+7		DEB Comp	Jour	REA 7 4 93	Dec 69	Csikai+ SIG+HL COMPILTN,N-ACTIV-ANAL	
(n,2n)	+7		KFI Comp	Jour	AHP 26 335	Dec 69	Adam+ GRPH+TBL,XPTL SIG CFD SHELL-TH	
				Jour	KFI 16 331	Oct 68	- + IN HUNGARIAN,SEE AHP 26 335	
(n,2n)	1.4+7		GIT Expt	Jour	PR/C 1 350	Jan 70	Fink+ACTIVATION,GRPHS,TBL.CFD OTH.	+
	1.4+7			Data	EXFOR10497.034	Apr 76	1PT.CS=1649+-80 MB.	
(n,2n)	1.0-4	1.8+7	BNWEval	Rept	BNWL-1312	May 70	Simons+.	
(n,2n)	1.4+7	1.5+7	JYV Eval	Rept	JU-RR-3/1970	Jun 70	Leppaemaeki+ TABLE OF EVAL AVG SIG	
(n,2n)	Fiss		KJL Expt	Jour	RCA 13 169	Jun 70	Steinnes.AVERAGE FISS NEUT CROSS-SEC	+
	Fiss			Data	EXFOR20109.007	Sep 71	1PNT.SIG.	
(n,2n)	9.2+6	1.0+7	BOL Eval	Rept	CEC(71)-2	71	Benzi+ STAT+EVAP MODELS.TBL GIVEN.	+
	9.2+6	1.0+7		Data	BENZI-DFN 538D	Mar 71	3 PNTS +ANGDIST+E DIST	
(n,2n)	+7		KFI Theo	Rept	KFKI-71-8	Feb 71	Jeki. CALCULATED CFD EXPTL SIG VALUE	
(n,2n)	Pile		ORL Expt	Abst	ANS 14 381	Jun 71	Jenkins+. EFFECTIVE SIG=0.837MB	
(n,2n)	1.5+7		IRK Expt	Jour	APA 34 209	Sep 71	Havlik. ACT. CC-W.	+
				Jour	OAWA 107 119	Apr 70	- . ACTIVATION METHOD.	
	1.5+7			Data	EXFOR20509.002	Apr 76	1PNT.SIGMA.	
(n,2n)	1.4+7		GIT Theo	Jour	PR/C 4 1173	Oct 71	Fink+.STAT-MODEL CALCULATION,CFD EXP	
(n,2n)	1.5+7	1.5+7	CCP Expt	Rept	YK-9 50	72	Maslov+ REL STAND,NA-I,SIG GIVEN	+
	1.4+7			Rept	INDC(CCP)-42	Aug 74	.P10. ENGLISH OF YK-9	
	1.4+7			Data	EXFOR40136.017	Feb 73	.1 DATA LINE	
(n,2n)	1.4+7		KFI Theo	Rept	KFKI-72-17	Feb 72	Kluge+ CALC N-SPEC INEL+N2N,TBL,GRPH	
(n,2n)	Fiss		MOLEval	Rept	BLG-465	May 72	Fabry.1.09+-0.0	
(n,2n)	1.3+7	1.8+7	HAMExpt	Prog	EANDC(E)150U	Oct 72	Bormann+ ACTIV MEAS	+
(n,2n)	1.5+7		DEB Eval	Rept	REA 11 1 153	Mar 73	Boedy. COMPILATION+RECOMM.VALUE,TBL	
				Rept	IAEA-153 173	73	- . RECOMM. VALUE ONLY	
(n,2n)	+7		KFK Expt	Rept	KFK-1783 87	Apr 73	Muenzel+DETECTION LIMITS,2 ES,CFD TH	
				Jour	JIN 34 2989	Sep 72	Krivan+ SYSTEMATICS OF EXCITATION	
(n,2n)	1.4+7		LOU Expt	Prog	INR-1464 12	May 73	Araminowicz+,BRIEF,ACTIV,TABLE,GRAPH	+
	1.4+7			Data	EXFOR30264.038	Nov 73	SIGMA AT 14.6 MEV	
(n,2n)	Thrsh	2.0+7	RCN Comp	Rept	RCN-196	Oct 73	Zijp+COMPIL.EVAL.CS.FAST N.METROLGY	
	Fiss			Revw Rept	INDC(NDS)-56	Sep 73	- .PG103, USE FOR DOSIMETRY,NDG	
				Conf	73Paris 2 271	Mar 73	- .RECOMM INTEG CFD DIFF CALC,TBL	
(n,2n)	Fiss		KOS Eval	Jour	AK 16 351	74	Boedy. U238,MAXW-SPC.AVG CFD XPT,TBL	
(n,2n)	1.5+7		TAT Theo	Jour	JP/A 7 1458	Aug 74	Kondaiah. CALC ON STAT MODEL	
(n,2n)	Fiss		KOS Eval	Conf	75Karlsrhe 29	Apr 75	Csikai. CF252,MAXW-SPC.AVG FOR 2TEMP	
(n,2n)	1.5+7		WPI Expt	Abst	BAP 20 560	Apr 75	Goloskie+TOF	
(n,2n)	1.4+7		TUD Theo	Conf	75Kiev 4 149	May 75	Seidel+ PREEQ-EFF ON CALC SIG.TABLE	

53 Iodine 127

Quantity	Energy (ev) Min	Max	Lab	Type	Documentation Ref Vol Page	Date	Author, Comments	Data
(n,2n)	9.0+6	1.7+7	ANL Eval	Rept	ANL-75-34	Jun 75	Davey+CONSTANT T MDL,LVL DEN MDL FIT	
(n,2n)	9.3+6	2.0+7	CRC Expt	Prog	INDC(CAN)-13 2	Oct 73	Santry+ BRIEF,GRPH,SIG FISS-SPEC GIV	+
	9.3+6	2.0+7		Data	EXFOR10424.002	Nov 76	9PTS.CS DATA.	
(n,xn) x>2	Fiss		BNL Theo	Jour	NSE 23 238	Nov 65	Pearlstein.SPEC AVG STATMDL CALC N3N	
(n,xn) x>2	2.0+7		GEL ExTh	Jour	NP/A 118 379	Oct 68	Liskien.ACT VDG REL CU65(N2N)CFD TH	+
	2.0+7			Expt Data	EXFOR20380.006	Oct 74	. 1PNT.SIGMA.	
(n,xn) x>2	1.5+7		PAK Expt	Jour	JIN 30 2577	Oct 68	Qaim+ (N,3N).ACTIV	+
	1.5+7			Data	EXFOR31080.006	Sep 72	.SIG FOR(N,3N)GVN	
n Emission	1.5+7	2.0+7	CCP Comp	Rept	ICD-6 215	70	Sluchevskaja.N,3N.2ES,2REFS CFD,TBL	
n Emission	1.4+7		TUD Theo	Prog	ZFK-262 25	Sep 73	Hermsdorf+ CALC N-SPEC CFD EXPT,NDG	
n Emission	1.4+7		FEI Expt	Rept	YK-23 10	76	Sal'Nikov+ INEL+(N,2N)+(N,PN)SIG GVN	+
	1.4+7			Data	EXFOR40324.002	Dec 77	N-EMIS FROM IN+(N2N)+(NPN). 1 PNT	
n Emission	1.5+7		TUD Expt	Jour	KE 19 241	Aug 76	Hermsdorf+ ABSOL DOUBDIF,FIG.TOT,TBL	+
				Rept	ZFK-277(U)	Aug 75	- + DIFFSIG AT 5ANGS,TBL+GRPH	
				Conf	ZFK-271 94	Nov 73	Goebel+ N-EMISSION SPEC,TOF.SUMMARY	
	1.5+7			Data	EXFOR30397.026	May 77	49 PTS. ANGLE INT.N-EMISS.SPECT.	
	1.5+7			Data	EXFOR30275.	Apr 74	DOUBLDIF(5ANG,482PTS)+PARTIAL ANGDIS	
(n,p)	1.5+7		CRC Expt	Jour	CJP 31 267	Feb 53	Paul+ BETA ACT, CFD TH, HL=9.3H	+
	1.5+7			Data	EXFOR11274.084	Jun 76	. 1 PT.	
(n,p)	1.5+7		GLS Theo	Jour	PM 2 473	Apr 57	Brown+ COMPNUCL 1 MB, DIRECT 16MB	
(n,p)	1.4+7		ALD Expt	Jour	PPS 73 215	Feb 59	Coleman+. ACT. CFD DIRECT INTERACTN	+
(n,p)	1.4+7		HAM Expt	Jour	ZN/A 15 200	Mar 60	Bormann+REL TO SIG I127(N,2N)=1.2B	+
(n,p)	Fiss		CRC Eval	Rept	CRC-1003	Dec 60	Roy+,ESTIMATED AVG SIG=0.13MB	
(n,p)	1.4+7		HAR Expt	Jour	NP 24 274	Apr 61	Allan.120DEG.PHOTOPLATE UPPER LIMIT	+
	1.4+7			Data	EXFOR20004.111	Nov 70	1PNT.CMPD.NUC.	
(n,p)	1.4+7		CIS Expt	Jour	NC 20 903	Jun 61	Marcazzan. = 1 DATA INDEX LINE	+
(n,p)	1.4+7		FRK Theo	Jour	ZP 171 379	Dec 62	Lindner.STATMOD,CF CJP 31 267,TH+XPT	
(n,p)	1.3+7	2.1+7	HAM Comp	Rept	EUR-122E	63	Neuert+.*P BORMANN+.HAMBOURG U.1961	
(n,p)	1.4+7		OTC Expt	Jour	NP 42 27	Apr 63	Dixon.MEAN8+-1MB WITH CS(I) CRYSTAL	
(n,p)	1.2+7	2.2+7	HAM Expt	Jour	ZN/A 18 914	Sep 63	Langkau.CSI(TL) TARGET AND DETECTOR	
(n,p)	2.6+6		KFI Expt	Rept	KFKI-1467	Sep 63	Borbely+ ACTIVATION. SIG TO GND STAT	+
	2.6+6			Data	EXFOR30175.	May 72	SIGMA TO GROUND STATE	
(n,p)	1.4+7	2.2+7	FRK Expt	Rept	EANDC(E)57U1	Feb 65	Bass+	+
(n,p)	1.4+7	1.5+7	SAH Comp	Jour	NUC 23 8 112	Aug 65	Chatterjee. TABLE WITH REFS.	
	1.4+7			Jour	NP 60 273	Nov 64	- .MEAN OF EXPT CFD SHELLMOD	
(n,p)	Maxwl		IFU Theo	Rept	ICD-4 20	67	Dadakina+ PENETR COEFF CALC,TABLE	
(n,p)	1.4+7	1.5+7	NAP Comp	Rept	INFN/BE-67-10	Jul 67	Cuzzocrea+ AVERAGED CHOSEN DATA.	
(n,p)	Maxwl		GHT Expt	Jour	RCA 9 57	68	De Regge+11.1MICROBARN FOR 127MTE	
(n,p)	1.5+7		PAK Expt	Jour	JIN 30 2577	Oct 68	Qaim+,ACTIV	+
	1.5+7			Data	EXFOR31080.	Sep 72	.SIG GVN	
(n,p)	1.5+7		KAZ Expt	Jour	YF 10 44	Jul 69	Levkovskij+ ABSOLUTE SIG+HL,ACTIVATN	+
				Jour	SNP 10 25	Jan 70	. ENGL OF YF 10 44	
	1.5+7			Data	EXFOR40226.	Dec 74	.2SIG GIVEN, GROUND+METASTABLE STATE	
(n,p)	1.5+7		DEB Comp	Jour	REA 7 4 93	Dec 69	Csikai+ SIG+HL COMPILTN,N-ACTIV-ANAL	
(n,p)	1.4+7	1.5+7	JYV Eval	Rept	JU-RR-3/1970	Jun 70	Leppaemaeki+ TABLE OF EVAL AVG SIG	
(n,p)	1.4+7	1.5+7	KAZ Theo	Jour	YF 18 705	Oct 73	Levkovsky.AVERAGED SIG,CALC,TBL	
				Jour	SNP 18 361	Apr 74	. ENGLISH OF YF 18,705	
(n,p)	1.4+7		TUD Theo	Conf	ZFK-271 63	Nov 73	Seeliger+ P-EMISSION SPEC, NDG	
(n,p)	1.5+7		ARK Expt	Jour	JIN 36 5 953	May 74	Mavaddat+ ACTIV MEAS	
(n,p)	2.2+7		SUN Expt	Prog	INDC(SEC)-42	Dec 74	Bharuth-Ram+ PRELIM ANGDIST,NDG	
(n,p)		7.5+8	IOW Expt	Jour	PR/C 12 1978	Dec 75	Hill+ ES TO 750 MEV.(N,2P) REACTION	
(n,np)	1.5+7		GLS Theo	Jour	PM 2 473	Apr 57	Brown+ N,PN* COMPNUCL 1MB,DIRECT NIL	
(n,np)	1.3+7	2.1+7	HAM Comp	Rept	EUR-I22E	63	Neuert+.*P BORMANN+.HAMBOURG U.1961	
(n,np)	1.2+7	2.2+7	HAM Expt	Jour	ZN/A 18 914	Sep 63	Langkau.CSI(TL) TARGET AND DETECTOR	
(n,np)	1.4+7	1.5+7	GLS Expt	Jour	NP 49 306	Nov 63	Robertson.SIG=3.5+-0.5MB	
(n,np)	1.4+7		TUD Theo	Conf	75Kiev 4 149	May 75	Seidel+ (NNP),(NPN).PREEQ-EFF.TABLE	
(n,np)		7.5+8	IOW Expt	Jour	PR/C 12 1978	Dec 75	Hill+ ES TO 750 MEV.(N,2PN) REACTION	
(n,d)	1.4+7		OTC Expt	Jour	NP 42 27	Apr 63	Dixon.MEAN1.2+-0.2MB FOR CSI CRYSTAL	
(n,d)	1.4+7	2.2+7	FRK Expt	Rept	EANDC(E)57U1	Feb 65	Bass+	+
(n,d)	1.4+7		SAH Comp	Jour	NUC 23 8 112	Aug 65	Chatterjee. TABLE WITH REFS.	
(n,α)	1.5+7		CRC Expt	Jour	CJP 31 267	Feb 53	Paul+ BETA ACT, CFD TH, HL=20M	+
	1.5+7			Data	EXFOR11274.083	Jun 76	. 1 PT.	
(n,α)	Fiss		CRC Eval	Rept	CRC-1003	Dec 60	Roy+,ESTIMATED AVG SIG=0.0026MB	
(n,α)	1.4+7		CIS Expt	Jour	NC 20 903	Jun 61	Marcazzan. = 2 DATA INDEX LINES	+
(n,α)	1.3+7	2.2+7	HAM Expt	Jour	ZN/A 17 479	Jun 62	Bormann.CSI,KI XTL. A SPECTR	+
(n,α)	1.4+7		FIR Expt	Jour	NP 36 38	Jul 62	Bizzeti+ SIG=1.39+-0.17MB	
(n,α)	1.4+7		FRK Theo	Jour	ZP 171 379	Dec 62	Lindner.STATMOD,CF CJP 31 267,TH+XPT	
(n,α)	1.4+7		OTC Expt	Jour	NP 42 27	Apr 63	Dixon.MEAN1.8+-0.2MB FOR CSI CRYSTAL	

53 Iodine 127

Quantity	Energy (ev) Min	Max	Lab	Type	Documentation Ref Vol Page	Date	Author, Comments	Data
(n,α)	1.4+7		ROM Comp	Jour	NCS 301	Sep 63	Amaldi.1.39+ −0.17MB AT E=14.1MEV	
(n,α)	1.4+7		CIS Theo	Jour	NP 51 460	Feb 64	Facchini+STATMOD SIG XPT/CALC=3−3.9	
(n,α)	1.4+7	2.2+7	FRK Expt	Rept	EANDC(E)57U1	Feb 65	Bass+	+
(n,α)	1.5+7		PAK Expt	Jour	JIN 30 2577	Oct 68	Qaim+,ACTIV OF METAST STATE 124SB	+
	1.5+7			Data	EXFOR31080.	Sep 72	.SIG GVN	
(n,α)	1.5+7		KAZ Expt	Jour	YF 10 44	Jul 69	Levkovskij+ ABSOLUTE SIG+HL,ACTIVATN	+
				Jour	SNP 10 25	Jan 70	. ENGL OF YF 10 44	
	1.5+7			Data	EXFOR40226.035	Dec 74	.SIGMA AT 14.8 MEV GIVEN	
(n,α)	1.5+7		DEB Comp	Jour	REA 7 4 93	Dec 69	Csikai+ SIG+HL COMPILTN,N−ACTIV−ANAL	
(n,α)	1.4+7	1.5+7	JYV Eval	Rept	JU−RR−3/1970	Jun 70	Leppaemaeki+ TABLE OF EVAL AVG SIG	
(n,α)	1.5+7		IRK Expt	Jour	APA 34 209	Sep 71	Havlik. ACT. CC−W.	+
				Jour	OAWA 107 119	Apr 70	− . ACTIVATION METHOD	
	1.5+7			Data	EXFOR20509.003	Apr 76	1PNT.SIGMA.	
(n,α)	1.4+7		HAM Expt	Jour	NP/A 186 65	May 72	Bormann+ SIG,A,E DISTR COMP+DIR.	
(n,α)	1.4+7	1.5+7	KAZ Theo	Jour	YF 18 705	Oct 73	Levkovsky.AVERAGED SIG,CALC,TBL	
				Jour	SNP 18 361	Apr 74	. ENGLISH OF YF 18,705	
(n,α)	1.4+7		TUD Expt	Conf	ZFK−271 63	Nov 73	Seeliger+ A−EMISSION SPEC, NDG	
(n,α)		7.5+8	IOW Expt	Jour	PR/C 12 1978	Dec 75	Hill+ ES TO 750 MEV.	
(n,nα)	1.3+7	2.2+7	HAM Expt	Jour	ZN/A 17 479	Jun 62	Bormann.CSI,KI XTL. A SPECTR	+
				Jour	ZP 166 477	Feb 62	− + CURVE.EXCIT FUNCTION.	
Reson Params	None		NYU Expt	Jour	PR 55 108	Jan 39	Hornbostel+ MULTI−RESON,C+FE+PB ABS	
Reson Params	2.1+1	4.2+1	COL Expt	Jour	PR 71 174	Feb 47	WU+ 3E0. APPROX STRENGTH GIVEN.	+
	2.1+1	4.2+1		Data	EXFOR11751.010	Jun 76	. 3 RES, E0,WT**2/PCS	
Reson Params	2.0+1		COR Expt	Jour	PR 72 362	Sep 47	Jones.WT BREIT−WIGNER FIT(.8EV UPPL)	
Reson Params	1.9+1	4.3+1	HAR Expt	Jour	PRSA 215 278	Nov 52	Merrison+.3 RES E. W.WN FOR 19EV RES	
Reson Params	2.0+1	9.1+1	BNL Expt	Jour	PR 95 476	Jul 54	Seidl+ RSLN.3TO3EV ASSUMED WG	+
	2.0+1	9.1+1		Data	EXFOR11671.010	Jun 76	. 7 RES, E0,WN	
Reson Params	2.1+1	9.2+1	CCP Expt	Jour	AE 1 5 55	Nov 56	Radkevich+. 7 RES, WN, WN.WT	+
	2.1+1	9.3+1		Jour	JNE 5 92	Jul 57	TRANSLATN.*	
	2.1+1	9.2+1		Jour	SJA 1 5 727	56	TRANSLATN.*	
Reson Params	2.1+1	2.0+2	ORL Expt	Prog	ORNL−2501 26	Jun 58	Slaughter+FASTCHOPPER. 10RESON	+
	2.1+1	2.0+2		Data	EXFOR11446.	Jun 76	. 11 RES, E0,WN,WN0	
Reson Params	1.1+1		ANL Expt	Jour	PR 123 629	Jul 61	Du−Toit+ RES.EN	
	1.1+1			Data	EXFOR12034.002	Jun 76	. 1 RES.EN	
Reson Params	2.0+1	1.7+2	ORL Expt	Jour	NSE 17 371	Nov 63	Pattenden.	+
	2.1+1	1.7+2		Data	EXFOR12025.002	Jun 76	. 9 RES, E0,WN0	
Reson Params	1.5+2	4.0+3	COL Expt	Jour	PR/B 137 547	Feb 65	Garg+.GWN 250LVLS,EXTENDS 1960 DATA	+
	1.5+2	4.0+3				Jun 76	. 280 RES, E0,WN0	
Reson Params	2.4+4		LRC Theo	Conf	66Paris 1 503	Oct 66	Bogart. VAL GVN, BETHE ANALYSIS	
Reson Params		1.0+6	AUA Theo	Jour	AUJ 20 477	Oct 67	Cook. TBL OF AVG LVL SPACING D,L=0,1	
Reson Params	3.2+6	5.2+6	JNE ExTh	Jour	NP/A 119 356	Oct 68	Manero+.AVERAGE WT FROM FLUCT ANAL.	
Reson Params	1.0+3	1.0+5	VIP Expt	Jour	NSE 35 364	Mar 69	Furr+ ACT AVG WG/WN S AND PWAVE NEUT	+
	1.0+3	1.0+5		Data	EXFOR10568.005	Apr 76	3PTS.WG/WN AVG.	
Reson Params	+3	+5	AUA ExTh	Rept	AAEC/E−198	May 69	Musgrove.RES PARS +STF FROM (NG)FIT	
Reson Params	2.0+5		MUA Theo	Conf	69Roorke 2 129	Dec 69	Chaubey+ D/GAM−WIDTH RATIO, STATMOD	
Reson Params	−		AUA Theo	Rept	AAEC/E−211	Nov 70	Musgrove. CALCULTD D+GAM WIDTH GIVEN	
Reson Params	2.0+1	2.4+2	SAC Expt	Conf	71Knoxvill 785	Mar 71	Cauvin+. J ASSIGNMENTS 13 RESON	+
	2.1+1	2.4+2		Data	EXFOR20126.006	Sep 72	13PTS.J.	
Reson Params	+1	+3	FEI Eval	Rept	YK− 8/2 97	Sep 72	Abagyan+ AVG G−WID+D AT BINDNG−E,TBL	
				Rept	INDC(CCP)−39	Jul 74	.PAGE 102.ENGLISH OF YK−8/2 97	
Reson Params	+1	+3	SAC Expt	Conf	74Petten 165	Sep 74	Jain+ NO WIDTH CORRELATIONS OBSERVED	
				Conf	72Budapest 238	Aug 72	− + N−,PARTIAL G−WIDTH CORREL.TBL	
Reson Params	0.0+0	1.5+7	BOL Theo	Conf	JAERI−M−5984	Feb 75	Benzi+P.83.OPT/STATMOD.CURV WG,WN.	
Reson Params	1.0+3	1.0+6	SAC Expt	Rept	CEA−N−1832	Dec 75	Ribon+ EXP+TH ANAL,RES PAR,TBL	
Strnth Fnctn	2.0+1	9.2+1	CCP Expt	Jour	AE 1 5 55	Nov 56	Radkevich+. S0=1.92+−0.6	
				Jour	JNE 5 92	Jul 57	TRANSLATN.*	
	2.0+1	9.3+1		Jour	SJA 1 5 727	56	TRANSLATN.*	
Strnth Fnctn	2.5+4	6.0+5	ANL Eval	Abst	BAP 3 18	Jan 58	Moldauer. STF CALC FROM NG	
Strnth Fnctn	0.0+0	2.0+3	ORL Expt	Prog	ORNL−2501 26	Mar 58	Slaughter+	+
	0.0+0	2.0+3		Data	EXFOR11446.005	Jun 76	. 1 PT.	
Strnth Fnctn		3.0+2	BNL Expt	Prog	WASH−1006	Oct 58	Harvey. TOF. CRYST SPEC. 1.3+−0.3	
Strnth Fnctn	+3		BNL Expt	Jour	PRL 1 461	Dec 58	Hughes+ FC, 1.2+−0.40	
Strnth Fnctn	+3	+5	ORL Expt	Prog	WASH−1029 55	Sep 60	Miller+ S(L=1)=+1−1.5	
						61	Gibbons+	+
Strnth Fnctn	1.0+4	2.0+5	ORL Expt	Jour	PR 122 182	Jun 76	. 3 PTS, STF, D, AVE WG	
	1.0+4	2.0+5		Data	EXFOR11329.			
Strnth Fnctn	+3	+5	BOL Theo	Conf	61Vienna 1 179	Aug 61	Benzi+.PPR11,TABLE CFD EXPERIMENT	
Strnth Fnctn	None		DKE Expt	Rept	TID−16059	62	Furr.ACT S,P FNCTS FOR N,G AVG	
				Abst	DA 23 4719	Jun 63	− .S,P WAVE.G,N STF CALC.NDG	

53 Iodine 127

Quantity	Energy (ev) Min	Max	Lab	Type	Documentation Ref Vol Page	Author, Comments Date	Data
Strnth Fnctn	1.0+3	1.5+4	DUB Expt	Rept	JINR – P – 1010	62 Popov+. P – WAVE STF CFD OTHERS+OPTMDL	
Strnth Fnctn		1.7+2	ORL Expt	Jour	NSE 17 371	Nov 63 Pattenden.0.7+ – 0.3	+
		1.7+2		Data	EXFOR12025.003	Jun 76 . 1 PT.	
Strnth Fnctn		1.0+4	COL Expt	Jour	PR/B 137 547	Feb 65 Garg+.GWN 250LVLS=1 DATA INDEX LINE	+
		4.0+3		Data	EXFOR11905.009	Jun 76 . 2 PTS, STF,D	
Strnth Fnctn	2.4+4		LRC Theo	Conf	66Paris 1 503	Oct 66 Bogart. VAL GVN, BETHE ANALYSIS	
Strnth Fnctn	3.0+4	6.5+5	DKE Expt	Jour	AP 46 401	Feb 68 Tabony+ TRANS DERIVES S0, S1, S2	+
				Jour	PL 13 70	Nov 64 .SUPERSEDED	
	5.0+4	1.5+5		Conf	64Paris 2 916	Jul 64 Seth+S0,S1,S2 R PRIME/R DUKE U.	
	3.0+4	6.5+5		Data	EXFOR11953.006	Jun 76 . 3 PTS.	
Strnth Fnctn	1.0+3	1.0+5	VIP Expt	Jour	NSE 35 364	Mar 69 Furr+ ACT S0=0.42,S1=0.83+ – 0.20	+
	1.0+3	1.0+5		Data	EXFOR10568.003	Apr 76 . 3 PTS. S, P WAVE STF.	
Strnth Fnctn	+3	+5	AUA ExTh	Rept	AAEC/E – 198	May 69 Musgrove.S+P+D STF FROM (NG)FIT,TBL	+
Strnth Fnctn	3.0+6	1.6+8	VIP Expt	Abst	DA/B 31 331	Jul 70 Campbell. G – RAY, SAME AS S,P WAVE NT	
Strnth Fnctn	–		AUA Theo	Rept	AAEC/E – 211	Nov 70 Musgrove. SMOOTHED S0,S1 AND S2 GIVN	
Strnth Fnctn	2.7+3		MUNExpt	Conf	71Albany 327	Aug 71 Dilg+TRNS.S0 STF GVN.31 ELEMENT GRPH	
Strnth Fnctn	2.4+4		MUATheo	Jour	IJP 46 114	Mar 72 Chaubey+ P – WAVE.FOR A – SYSTEMTIC,GRPH	
Strnth Fnctn	None		AUA Eval	Rept	AAEC/E – 277	Mar 73 Musgrove.TBLS EXPTL DATA+BEST VALUES	
Strnth Fnctn	1.0+3	6.0+5	NBS Expt	Jour	PR/C 9 28	Jan 74 Camarda.LINAC.TRANS. S1 MEASURED.	+
	1.0+3	7.0+5		Prog	USNDC – 7 147	Jun 73 – . LINAC. S1 MEASD. NO DATA	
	1.0+3	6.0+5		Data	EXFOR10765.009	Nov 78 . 1PT.S1=(1.55+ – .5) – 4	
Strnth Fnctn	None		KUR Theo	Prog	IAE – 2560	75 Adamchuk+.S0 – VALUE,TBL	
Strnth Fnctn	5.0+3	8.0+4	FEI Expt	Rept	YK – 19 57	May 75 Shorin+ RADIAT+P – NEUT STRENGTH FUNCT	
Lvl Density	–		HAMExpt	Rept	ZN/A 15 200	Mar 60 Bormann+NUCL TEMP FOR (N,P),(N,NP)	
Lvl Density	1.4+7		BAS Expt	Jour	PL 5 202	Jul 63 Huber+TBL OF NUC TEMP AND LVL DENSTY	
				Jour	HPA 36 1059	Dec 63 Plattner+TOF TBL12ELEM.CFD TH	
Lvl Density	4.0+6	7.0+6	ISL Theo	Conf	64Geneva § 511	May 64 Szwarcbaum+.T FROM 3 FORMLS CFD EXPS	
Lvl Density	1.0+3	1.4+7	FEI Theo	Conf	65Antwerp § 20	Jul 65 Zakharova.OBNINSK.FERMI GAS MODEL	
Lvl Density	1.4+7		FEI Expt	Rept	FEI – 30	Dec 65 Anufrienko+.PARAMS FROM NONELASTIC	+
Lvl Density	–		FEI Eval	Rept	FEI – 36	66 Kapchigashev+.TBL OF RELATD QUANTTYS	+
		5.0+4		Jour	YF 4 686	Sep 66 .TABLE.SHORT VERSION OF FEI – 36	
	–			Prog	YFI – 3 3	66 .ABSTRACT.TABLE LDL+NUCL EXCIT.E	
		5.0+4		Jour	SNP 4 486	67 .ENGLISH OF YF 4.FROM(N,GAMMA).TABLE	
				Prog	INDC – E – 140 3	66 .ENGLISH TRANSL OF YFI – 3	
Lvl Density	3.6+6	8.5+6	JAE Expt	Jour	NP/A 131 145	Jun 69 Maruyama. E DEPENDANCE,PARAM,TH FIT.	
	3.5+6	8.5+6		Prog	EANDC(J)3L10	Mar 66 Tsukada.TOF.SPEC CFD C THEORIES	
Lvl Density	+6	+7	AUA Theo	Rept	AAEC/TM – 522	Nov 69 Bertram. FORMULAE+PARS IN(N,2N) – ANAL	
Lvl Density	None		AUWTheo	Conf	70Madurai 2 267	Dec 70 Ramamurty+ A – PARAMETER GVN,LANG'S – TH	
Lvl Density	+1	+3	FEI Eval	Jour	YK – 8/2 97	Sep 72 Abagyan+ LVL DENSITY PARAMETER,TBL	
				Rept	INDC(CCP) – 39	Jul 74 .PAGE 102.ENGLISH OF YK – 8/2 97	
Lvl Density	2.0+3	3.5+3	JAE ExTh	Jour	JPJ 37 581	Sep 74 Ideno.LVL SPACING CORRELATIONS	
				Rept	JAERI – M – 5490	Nov 73 – .LEVEL SPACING CORRELATIONS.TBL	
(γ,n)	+7		BSP Revw	Conf	55Geneva 2 169	Aug 55 Souza – Santos+.P897,THRESHOLD VAL GVN	
(γ,n)	5.0+4	3.5+7	SAC Expt	Jour	NP/A 133 417	Aug 69 Bergere+LORENTZ LINE PARAM,GRPHS,TBL	

53 Iodine 128

Quantity	Energy (ev) Min	Max	Lab	Type	Documentation Ref Vol Page	Author, Comments Date	Data
Reson Params	–		AUA Theo	Rept	AAEC/E – 211	Nov 70 Musgrove. CALCULTD D+GAM WIDTH GIVEN	
Strnth Fnctn	–		AUA Theo	Rept	AAEC/E – 211	Nov 70 Musgrove. SMOOTHED S0,S1 AND S2 GIVN	
Lvl Density	+6		MIL Theo	Jour	EN 15 1 54	Jan 68 Facchini+ LDL PARS FROM LOW EN RES	
Lvl Density		+6	HAMExpt	Jour	NP/A 186 65	May 70 Bormann+ FROM CS OXD(N,A) 14MEV.	+
		+6		Data	EXFOR20471.	Jan 76 2PTS.A – PARAM,SPIN CUT – OFF.	
Lvl Density	None		MUNTheo	Jour	NP/A 217 269	Dec 73 Dilg+ A,DELTA. BACK SHIFTED FERMIGAS	
Lvl Density	None		COP Theo	Jour	NP/A 222 493	Apr 74 Dossing+COLL ROTAT.SPAC. ACCUR ESTIM	
Lvl Density	None		ROC Theo	Jour	NP/A 223 577	May 74 Huizenga+ EXP CFD MICROSC TH SPH NUC	

53 Iodine 129

Quantity	Energy (ev) Min	Max	Lab	Type	Documentation Ref Vol Page	Author, Comments Date	Data
Evaluation	1.0 – 3	1.5+7	AUA Eval	Rept	AAEC/TM – 549	Jun 70 Cook.TOT,EL,INEL,NONEL,CAPT SIGS,NDG	+
				Rept	AAEC/E – 214	Jun 71 Bertram+GROUP SIGMAS SAME QUANTS.NDG	
				Rept	AAEC/E – 587	Mar 71 *DESCRIPTION OF LIBRARY	
	1.0 – 3	1.5+7		Data	AUSTR – DFN 110.	Nov 71 POINT(223) AND GROUP(127) SIGMAS	
Evaluation	1.0+3	1.0+7	BOL Eval	Rept	CEC(71) – 2	71 Benzi+ STAT+EVAP MDS.INEL,N2N,NG.TBL	+
	1.0+3	1.0+7		Data	BENZI – DFN 540A	Mar 71 4 QUANTITIES. UK FORMAT	

53 Iodine 129

Quantity	Energy (ev) Min	Max	Lab	Type	Documentation Ref Vol Page	Date	Author, Comments	Data
Evaluation	1.0+2	1.5+7	JAE Eval	Rept	JAERI-M-5752	Jul 74	Igarasi+ JNDC FPND WG.TOT,EL,N',CAP	
Total	2.0-2	4.5-2	ORL Expt	Jour	NSE 8 112	Aug 60	Block+,FC SIG(.0253EV)=35+-4B TABLE	+
	-2	1.0+2		Conf	58Geneva 16 150	Sep 58	Harvey+.PPR673,TRANSMISSION CURV GVN	
	2.0-2	4.5-2		Data	EXFOR12024.003	Jun 76	. 24 PTS.	
Total	1.0-3	1.5+7	AUA Eval	Data	AUSTR-DFN 110.	Nov 71	COOK+POINT(223)+GROUP(127)SIG.CF EVL	+
Elastic	1.0-3	1.5+7	AUA Eval	Data	AUSTR-DFN 110.	Nov 71	COOK+POINT(223)+GROUP(127)SIG.CF EVL	+
Tot Inelastc	2.8+4	1.0+7	BOL Eval	Rept	CEC(71)-2	71	Benzi+ STAT MODEL. TBL GIVEN.	+
	2.8+4	1.0+7		Data	BENZI-DFN 540A	Mar 71	51 PNTS	
Tot Inelastc	5.0+5	1.5+7	AUA Eval	Data	AUSTR-DFN 110.	Nov 71	COOK+POINT(11)+GROUP(127)SIG.CF EVL	+
Diff Inelast	2.8+4	1.0+7	BOL Eval	Rept	CEC(71)-2	71	Benzi+ DISCRETE INELASTIC. 1 LVL	+
	2.8+4	2.0+5		Data	BENZI-DFN 540A	Mar 71	1ST LVL +ANGDIST+E DIST	
	2.0+5	1.0+7		Data	BENZI-DFN 540A	Mar 71	TO CONTINUUM, 39PNTS+ANGDIST+E DIST	
Nonelastic	1.0-3	1.5+7	AUA Eval	Data	AUSTR-DFN 110.	Nov 71	COOK+POINT(223)+GROUP(127)SIG.CF EVL	+
Absorption	Maxwl		ORL Expt	Jour	NSE 8 112	Aug 60	Block+,FC 31+-4B SIG(TOT)-SIG(SCT)	+
	Maxwl			Data	EXFOR12024.002	Jun 76	. 1 PT	
Absorption	4.1-1	1.0+7	GA Eval	Rept	GA-2451	Aug 61	Joanou+.68GROUP DATA FOR GAM-I	
Absorption	1.0-3	1.0+7	JUL Eval	Rept	JUEL-678-RG	Jul 70	Liu. EVALUATION+CALC,GRPH,FN OF E	
Res Int Abs	5.0-1		CRC Expt	Jour	CJC 36 1424	Oct 58	Roy+ ACT NRX CD RATIO,=36+-4B	+
				Conf	58Geneva 16 54	Sep 58	.SUPERSEDED	
	5.0-1			Data	EXFOR12005.004	Jun 76	. 1 PT.	
Res Int Abs	None		ORL Eval	Rept	ORNL-2869	Mar 60	Nephew.1/V UP +TO100EV.ALSO 3 ES- UP	
Res Int Abs	+3	+5	BOL Theo	Conf	61Vienna 1 179	Aug 61	Benzi+.PPR11,VAL GVN,L=0,L=1 .CAPT.	
Res Int Abs	5.0-1		BOL Eval	Conf	61Vienna 1 179	Aug 61	Benzi+ TBL TOTAL CAPT RES INTS.	
Res Int Abs	5.5-1		GA Eval	Jour	NSE 12 115	Jan 62	Garrison+,RI= 39+-10 B,FROM RES.PAR	
Res Int Abs	Maxwl	+2	ORL Expt	Jour	NSE 17 371	Nov 63	Pattenden.22+-7B	
Res Int Abs	None		CRC Eval	Rept	AECL-2111	Nov 64	Walker.REDUCED RESONANCE INTEGRAL	
Res Int Abs	5.0-1		BOL Eval	Rept	RT/FI-4	Jan 67	Palmucci. CALC FROM (N,G) RES PARAMS	
Res Int Abs	None		GA Eval	Rept	GA-12071	Sep 71	Mathews+. RECOMMENDED VALUES	
Res Int Abs	5.5-1		CRC Eval	Rept	AECL-3037 1	Jan 72	Walker.REDUCED RES INT,DETAILED TBL	
Res Int Abs	5.0-1		AUA Eval	Rept	AAEC/TM-619	Sep 72	Clayton.CALC FROM SIG LIBRARY,TABLE	
Res Int Abs	4.6-1	1.0+6	RCN Theo	Rept	RCN-191	Jul 73	Lautenbach.CAPT INT FROM GROUP SIGMA	
Res Int Abs	5.5-1	+6	SAC Revw	Conf	IAEA-169 1 235	74	Ribon.CAPTURE,STATUS CFD REQUEST,TBL	
Res Int Abs	+0	+5	WIN Revw	Conf	IAEA-169 3 163	74	Pope+ DATA FILE CALC CFD XPTAL VALUE	
(n,γ)	Pile		LAS Expt	Jour	PR 71 826	Jun 47	Katcoff.FROM U FISS,AND I131 ACT.	
(n,γ)	Pile		DUR Expt	Jour	CJC 34 293	Mar 56	Purkayastha+ NRX 35B	+
(n,γ)	Pile	2.5-2	CRC Expt	Jour	CJC 36 1424	Oct 58	Roy+ ACT 26.7 AND 27.7B EFFECTIVE	+
				Conf	58Geneva 16 54	Sep 58	.SUPERSEDED	
	Pile			Data	EXFOR12005.003	Jun 76	. 1 PT.	
(n,γ)	+3	+5	BOL Theo	Conf	61Vienna 1 179	Aug 61	Benzi+.PPR11,TABLE FOR 3ES	
(n,γ)	Maxwl		ORL Expt	Jour	NSE 17 371	Nov 63	Pattenden.28.0+-2B	+
	Maxwl			Data	EXFOR12025.006	Jun 76	. 1 PT.	
(n,γ)	Maxwl		CRC Eval	Rept	AECL-2111	Nov 64	Walker.	
(n,γ)	Maxwl		WIS Expt	Jour	JCP 44 970	Feb 66	Wilkey+	+
	Maxwl			Data	EXFOR12014.	Jun 76	. 3 PTS, SIG TO GND,META, ISM RAT	
(n,γ)	2.5-2		BOL Eval	Rept	RT/FI-4	Jan 67	Palmucci. CALC FROM RES PARAMETERS	
(n,γ)	Maxwl		AUA Theo	Jour	NSE 31 234	Feb 68	Cook+ STATISTICAL CALC CFD EXPT	
(n,γ)	5.0+3	1.0+5	AUA ExTh	Rept	AAEC/E-198	May 69	Musgrove.S+P+D WAVE SIGMAS CALC,TBL	+
(n,γ)	1.0+3	1.0+7	BOL Eval	Rept	CEC(71)-2	71	Benzi+ OPTMOD EVAL.TBL GIVEN.	+
				Conf	66Paris 1 537	Oct 66	- +,PPR.115,STATIST MOD +XPT D,WG	
				Jour	NC 38 216	Jul 65	- + THEORY FOR CAPTURE EVALUATION	
	1.0+3	1.0+7		Data	BENZI-DFN 540A	Mar 71	62 PNTS	
(n,γ)	Maxwl		GA Eval	Rept	GA-12071	Sep 71	Mathews+. RECOMMENDED VALUES	
(n,γ)	1.0-3	1.5+7	AUA Eval	Data	AUSTR-DFN 110.	Nov 71	COOK+POINT(223)+GROUP(127)SIG.CF EVL	+
(n,γ)	Maxwl		CRC Eval	Rept	AECL-3037 1	Jan 72	Walker.RECOMMENDED SIG,DETAILED TBL	
(n,γ)	2.5-2		AUA Eval	Rept	AAEC/TM-619	Sep 72	Clayton.CALC FROM SIG LIBRARY,TABLE	
(n,γ)		1.1+7	RCN Theo	Rept	RCN-191	Jun 73	Lautenbach. GROUP CONSTANTS TBL	
(n,γ)	Fast		MTR Expt	Prog	USNDC-9 6	Dec 73	Harker+.ACT. CFRMF. NO DATA GIVEN.	
(n,γ)	2.5-2	3.0+4	SAC Revw	Conf	IAEA-169 1 235	74	Ribon.STATUS SIG CFD REQUESTS,TABLE	
(n,γ)	Fiss		WIN Revw	Conf	IAEA-169 3 137	74	Dean. POINT DATA AVG OVER STAND SPEC	
	Maxwl Fiss			Conf	IAEA-169 3 163	74	Pope+ MAXW+FIS-SPEC AVG DATA CFD XPT	
(n,γ)	1.0+3	1.0+6	SAC Expt	Rept	CEA-N-1832	Dec 75	Ribon+ EXP+TH ANAL,STAT MOL,CURVE	
(n,γ)	Fast		RCN Expt	Rept	ECN-10	Oct 76	Veenema+ STEK REACTIVITY WORTHS TBL.	
(n,2n)	Fiss		CRC Eval	Rept	CRC-1003	Dec 60	Roy+,ESTIMATED AVG SIG=1.0MB	
(n,2n)	8.9+6	1.0+7	BOL Eval	Rept	CEC(71)-2	71	Benzi+ STAT+EVAP MODELS.TBL GIVEN.	+
	8.9+6	1.0+7		Data	BENZI-DFN 540A	Mar 71	4 PNTS +ANGDIST+E DIST	
(n,2n)	1.5+7		STR Expt	Jour	RRL 15 29	Sep 73	Kuhry+ D-T NS. REL CU63(N2N).	
	1.5+7			Data	EXFOR20365.002	Sep 74	1PNT.SIGMA.	
(n,p)	Fiss		CRC Eval	Rept	CRC-1003	Dec 60	Roy+,ESTIMATED AVG SIG=0.05MB	

53 Iodine 129

Quantity	Energy (ev) Min	Max	Lab	Type	Documentation Ref Vol Page	Author, Comments Date	Data
Reson Params	6.6+1	1.5+2	ORL Expt	Conf	58Geneva 16 150	Sep 58 Harvey+.PPR673,PARAMS FOR 6 RESONNCS	+
	6.6+1	1.5+2		Data	EXFOR12012.004	Jun 76 . 6 RES, E0,WN0	
Reson Params	2.0+1	1.7+2	ORL Expt	Jour	NSE 17 371	Nov 63 Pattenden.	+
	7.2+1	1.5+2		Data	EXFOR12025.004	Jun 76 . 5 RES, E0,WN0	
Reson Params	–		GRN Expt	Jour	NP 66 323	May 65 Pancholi. = 1 DATA INDEX LINE	+
Reson Params		1.0+6	AUA Theo	Jour	AUJ 20 477	Oct 67 Cook. TBL OF AVG LVL SPACING D,L=0,1	
Reson Params	–		AUA Theo	Rept	AAEC/E – 211	Nov 70 Musgrove. CALCULTD D+GAM WIDTH GIVEN	
Reson Params	1.0+3	1.0+6	SAC Eval	Rept	CEA – N – 1832	Dec 75 Ribon+ EXP+TH ANAL,RES PAR,TBL	
Strnth Fnctn	+3	+5	BOL Theo	Conf	61Vienna 1 179	Aug 61 Benzi+.PPR11,TABLE CFD EXPERIMENT	
Strnth Fnctn		1.5+2	ORL Expt	Jour	NSE 17 371	Nov 63 Pattenden.0.2+ – 0.1	+
		1.5+2		Data	EXFOR12025.005	Jun 76 . 1 PT.	
Strnth Fnctn	–		AUA Theo	Rept	AAEC/E – 211	Nov 70 Musgrove. SMOOTHED S0,S1 AND S2 GIVN	
Strnth Fnctn	None		KUR Theo	Prog	IAE – 2560	75 Adamchuk+.S0 – VALUE,TBL	

53 Iodine 130

Quantity	Energy (ev) Min	Max	Lab	Type	Documentation Ref Vol Page	Author, Comments Date	Data
Evaluation	1.0–3	1.5+7	AUA Eval	Rept	AAEC/TM – 549	Jun 70 Cook.TOT,EL,INEL,NONEL,CAPT SIGS,NDG	+
				Rept	AAEC/E – 214	Jun 71 Bertram+GROUP SIGMAS SAME QUANTS.NDG	
				Rept	AAEC/TM – 587	Mar 71 *DESCRIPTION OF LIBRARY	
	1.0–3	1.5+7		Data	AUSTR – DFN 111.	Nov 71 POINT(223) AND GROUP(127) SIGMAS	
Total	1.0–3	1.5+7	AUA Eval	Data	AUSTR – DFN 111.	Nov 71 COOK+POINT(223)+GROUP(127)SIG.CF EVL	+
Elastic	1.0–3	1.5+7	AUA Eval	Data	AUSTR – DFN 111.	Nov 71 COOK+POINT(223)+GROUP(127)SIG.CF EVL	+
Tot Inelastc	5.0+5	1.5+7	AUA Eval	Data	AUSTR – DFN 111.	Nov 71 COOK+POINT(11)+GROUP(127)SIG.CF EVL	+
Nonelastic	1.0–3	1.5+7	AUA Eval	Data	AUSTR – DFN 111.	Nov 71 COOK+POINT(223)+GROUP(127)SIG.CF EVL	+
Res Int Abs	5.0–1		AUA Eval	Rept	AAEC/E – 619	Sep 72 Clayton.CALC FROM SIG LIBRARY,TABLE	
Res Int Abs	+0	+5	WIN Revw	Conf	IAEA – 169 3 163	74 Pope+ CALC FROM AUSTRAL DATA FILE	
(n,γ)	Pile		CRC Expt	Jour	CJC 36 1424	Oct 58 Roy+ NRX BETA COUNT 18+ – 3B	+
	Pile			Data	EXFOR12005.002	Jun 76 . 1 PT.	
(n,γ)	1.0–3	1.5+7	AUA Eval	Data	AUSTR – DFN 111.	Nov 71 COOK+POINT(223)+GROUP(127)SIG.CF EVL	+
(n,γ)	Pile		CRC Eval	Rept	AECL – 3037 1	Jan 72 Walker.RECOMMENDED SIG,DETAILED TBL	
(n,γ)	2.5–2		AUA Eval	Rept	AAEC/E – 619	Sep 72 Clayton.CALC FROM SIG LIBRARY,TABLE	
(n,γ)	Maxwl	Fiss	WIN Revw	Conf	IAEA – 169 3 163	74 Pope+ MAXW+FIS – SPEC AVG DATA CFD XPT	
	Fiss			Conf	IAEA – 169 3 137	74 Dean. POINT DATA AVG OVER STAND SPEC	
Spect (n,γ)	Pile		LND Expt	Jour	AF 5 427	Oct 52 Johansson+.NAI.COINC. XE131 GAMMAS	
Spect (n,γ)	None		CAN Expt	Jour	NP 40 566	Feb 63 Hargrove+. TABLE 80 – 723KEV GAMMA INT	
Reson Params	–		AUA Theo	Rept	AAEC/E – 211	Nov 70 Musgrove. CALCULTD D+GAM WIDTH GIVEN	
Strnth Fnctn	–		AUA Theo	Rept	AAEC/E – 211	Nov 70 Musgrove. SMOOTHED S0,S1 AND S2 GIVN	
Lvl Density	+6		MIL Theo	Jour	EN 15 1 54	Jan 68 Facchini+ LDL PARS FROM LOW EN RES	
Lvl Density	None		COP Theo	Jour	NP/A 222 493	Apr 74 Dossing+COLL ROTAT.SPAC. ACCUR ESTIM	
Lvl Density	None		ROC Theo	Jour	NP/A 223 577	May 74 Huizenga+ EXP CFD MICROSC TH SPH NUC	

53 Iodine 131

Quantity	Energy (ev) Min	Max	Lab	Type	Documentation Ref Vol Page	Author, Comments Date	Data
Evaluation	1.0–3	1.5+7	AUA Eval	Rept	AAEC/TM – 549	Jun 70 Cook.TOT,EL,INEL,NONEL,CAPT SIGS,NDG	+
				Rept	AAEC/E – 214	Jun 71 Bertram+GROUP SIGMAS SAME QUANTS.NDG	
				Rept	AAEC/TM – 587	Mar 71 *DESCRIPTION OF LIBRARY	
	1.0–3	1.5+7		Data	AUSTR – DFN 112.	Nov 71 POINT(223) AND GROUP(127) SIGMAS	
Evaluation	1.0–5	1.5+7	HED Eval	Prog	HEDL – TME – 71143	Oct 71 Schenter+. EVALUATION FOR ENDF/B	
Total	3.0+4	6.5+5	DKE Expt	Abst	DA/B 27 2085	Dec 66 Tabony.TRNSM. DERIVES S,P,D STR FNS	
Total	1.0–3	1.5+7	AUA Eval	Data	AUSTR – DFN 112.	Nov 71 COOK+POINT(223)+GROUP(127)SIG.CF EVL	+
Elastic	1.0–3	1.5+7	AUA Eval	Data	AUSTR – DFN 112.	Nov 71 COOK+POINT(223)+GROUP(127)SIG.CF EVL	+
Tot Inelastc	5.0+5	1.5+7	AUA Eval	Data	AUSTR – DFN 112.	Nov 71 COOK+POINT(11)+GROUP(127)SIG.CF EVL	+
Nonelastic	1.0–3	1.5+7	AUA Eval	Data	AUSTR – DFN 112.	Nov 71 COOK+POINT(223)+GROUP(127)SIG.CF EVL	+
Absorption	1.0–4	1.0+7	JUL Eval	Rept	JUEL – 678 – RG	Jul 70 Liu. EVALUATION+CALC,GRPH,FN OF E	
Res Int Abs	5.0–1		ORL Expt	Prog	ORNL – 3488 15	Oct 63 Halperin+ PRELIM RESULT GVN	
	5.0–1			Data	EXFOR12026.003	Jun 76 . 1 PT.	
Res Int Abs	5.5–1		CRC Eval	Rept	AECL – 3037 1	Jan 72 Walker.REDUCED RES INT,DETAILED TBL	
Res Int Abs	5.0–1		AUA Eval	Rept	AAEC/TM – 619	Sep 72 Clayton.CALC FROM SIG LIBRARY,TABLE	
Res Int Abs	5.5–1	+6	SAC Revw	Conf	IAEA – 169 1 235	74 Ribon.CAPTURE,STATUS CFD REQUEST,TBL	
Res Int Abs	+0	+5	WIN Revw	Conf	IAEA – 169 3 163	74 Pope+ DATA FILE CALC CFD XPTAL VALUE	
(n,γ)	Pile		CRC Expt	Rept	BNL – C – 9 70	49 Yaffe.	
	Pile			Data	EXFOR12045.002	Jun 76 . 1 PT.	
(n,γ)	Maxwl		MCM Expt	Jour	JIN 5 253	Oct 58 Kennett+MASS SPECTROMETER	+
	Maxwl			Data	EXFOR12016.002	Jun 76 . 1 PT.	

53 Iodine 131

Quantity	Energy (ev) Min	Max	Lab	Type	Documentation Ref Vol Page	Author, Comments Date	Data
(n,γ)	Maxwl		CRC	Eval	Rept AECL – 1054	Mar 60 Walker. (CRRP – 913)	
(n,γ)	Maxwl		ORL	Expt	Prog ORNL – 3488 1	63 Halperin.	+
	Maxwl				Data EXFOR12026.002	Jun 76 . 1 PT.	
(n,γ)	1.0 – 3	1.5 + 7	AUA	Eval	Data AUSTR – DFN 112.	Nov 71 COOK + POINT(223) + GROUP(127)SIG.CF EVL	+
(n,γ)	Maxwl		CRC	Eval	Rept AECL – 3037 1	Jan 72 Walker.RECOMMENDED SIG,DETAILED TBL	
(n,γ)	2.5 – 2		AUA	Eval	Rept AAEC/TM – 619	Sep 72 Clayton.CALC FROM SIG LIBRARY,TABLE	
(n,γ)	2.5 – 2		SGA	Eval	Conf 73Paris 1 233	Mar 73 Eder+ INTERPOLATED FROM CALC SIG,TBL	
					Rept SGAE – PH – 141	Feb 73 .SAME AS 73PARIS,POINT SIG FROM COOK	
(n,γ)	Fiss		SAC	Revw	Conf IAEA – 169 1 235	74 Ribon.STATUS SIG CFD REQUESTS,TABLE	
	2.5 – 2				Conf IAEA – 169 1 235	74 – .STATUS SIG CFD REQUESTS,TABLE	
(n,γ)	Maxwl	Fiss	WIN	Revw	Conf IAEA – 169 3 163	74 Pope+ MAXW + FIS – SPEC AVG DATA CFD XPT	
	Fiss				Conf IAEA – 169 3 137	74 Dean. POINT DATA AVG OVER STAND SPEC	
Fiss Prod γ	Pile		SGA	Theo	Jour APA 28 94	Apr 69 Higats+.COMP.PROGR.BUILDUP FISS.PROD.	
Reson Params		1.0 + 6	AUA	Theo	Jour AUJ 20 477	Oct 67 Cook. TBL OF AVG LVL SPACING D,L=0,1	
Reson Params	–		AUA	Theo	Rept AAEC/E – 211	Nov 70 Musgrove. CALCULTD D + GAM WIDTH GIVEN	
Strnth Fnctn	3.0 + 4	6.5 + 5	DKE	Expt	Abst DA/B 27 2085	Dec 66 Tabony.S,P,D STF FROM TRANSMISS DATA	
Strnth Fnctn	–		AUA	Theo	Rept AAEC/E – 211	Nov 70 Musgrove. SMOOTHED S0,S1 AND S2 GIVN	

53 Iodine 132

Quantity	Energy (ev) Min	Max	Lab	Type	Documentation Ref Vol Page	Author, Comments Date	Data
Reson Params	–		AUA	Theo	Rept AAEC/E – 211	Nov 70 Musgrove. CALCULTD D + GAM WIDTH GIVEN	
Strnth Fnctn	–		AUA	Theo	Rept AAEC/E – 211	Nov 70 Musgrove. SMOOTHED S0,S1 AND S2 GIVN	

53 Iodine 133

Quantity	Energy (ev) Min	Max	Lab	Type	Documentation Ref Vol Page	Author, Comments Date	Data
Evaluation	1.0 – 3	1.5 + 7	AUA	Eval	Rept AAEC/TM – 549	Jun 70 Cook.TOT,EL,INEL,NONEL,CAPT SIGS,NDG	+
					Rept AAEC/E – 214	Jun 71 Bertram + GROUP SIGMAS SAME QUANTS.NDG	
					Rept AAEC/TM – 587	Mar 71 *DESCRIPTION OF LIBRARY	
	1.0 – 3	1.5 + 7			Data AUSTR – DFN 113.	Nov 71 POINT(223) AND GROUP(127) SIGMAS	
Total	1.0 – 3	1.5 + 7	AUA	Eval	Data AUSTR – DFN 113.	Nov 71 COOK + POINT(223) + GROUP(127)SIG.CF EVL	+
Elastic	1.0 – 3	1.5 + 7	AUA	Eval	Data AUSTR – DFN 113.	Nov 71 COOK + POINT(223) + GROUP(127)SIG.CF EVL	+
Tot Inelastc	5.0 + 5	1.5 + 7	AUA	Eval	Data AUSTR – DFN 113.	Nov 71 COOK + POINT(11) + GROUP(127)SIG.CF EVL	+
Nonelastic	1.0 – 3	1.5 + 7	AUA	Eval	Data AUSTR – DFN 113.	Nov 71 COOK + POINT(223) + GROUP(127)SIG.CF EVL	+
Res Int Abs	5.0 – 1		AUA	Eval	Rept AAEC/TM – 619	Sep 72 Clayton.CALC FROM SIG LIBRARY,TABLE	
Res Int Abs	+0	+5	WIN	Revw	Conf IAEA – 169 3 163	74 Pope+ CALC FROM AUSTRAL DATA FILE	
(n,γ)	1.0 – 3	1.5 + 7	AUA	Eval	Data AUSTR – DFN 113.	Nov 71 COOK + POINT(223) + GROUP(127)SIG.CF EVL	+
(n,γ)	Pile		CRC	Eval	Rept AECL – 3037 1	Jan 72 Walker.SIG ESTIMATED ACCORDING Z,A	
(n,γ)	2.5 – 2		AUA	Eval	Rept AAEC/TM – 619	Sep 72 Clayton.CALC FROM SIG LIBRARY,TABLE	
(n,γ)	2.5 – 2		SGA	Eval	Conf 73Paris 1 233	Mar 73 Eder+ INTERPOLATED FROM CALC SIG,TBL	
					Rept SGAE – PH – 141	Feb 73 .SAME AS 73PARIS,POINT SIG FROM COOK	
(n,γ)	2.5 – 2		SAC	Revw	Conf IAEA – 169 1 235	74 Ribon.STATUS SIG CFD REQUESTS,TABLE	
(n,γ)	Maxwl	Fiss	WIN	Revw	Conf IAEA – 169 3 163	74 Pope+ MAXW + FIS – SPEC AVG EVAL DATA	
	Fiss				Conf IAEA – 169 3 137	74 Dean. POINT DATA AVG OVER STAND SPEC	
Reson Params	–		AUA	Theo	Rept AAEC/E – 211	Nov 70 Musgrove. CALCULTD D + GAM WIDTH GIVEN	
Strnth Fnctn	–		AUA	Theo	Rept AAEC/E – 211	Nov 70 Musgrove. SMOOTHED S0,S1 AND S2 GIVN	

53 Iodine 134

Quantity	Energy (ev) Min	Max	Lab	Type	Documentation Ref Vol Page	Author, Comments Date	Data
Reson Params	–		AUA	Theo	Rept AAEC/E – 211	Nov 70 Musgrove. CALCULTD D + GAM WIDTH GIVEN	
Strnth Fnctn	–		AUA	Theo	Rept AAEC/E – 211	Nov 70 Musgrove. SMOOTHED S0,S1 AND S2 GIVN	

53 Iodine 135

Quantity	Energy (ev) Min	Max	Lab	Type	Documentation Ref Vol Page	Author, Comments Date	Data
Evaluation	1.0 – 3	1.5 + 7	AUA	Eval	Rept AAEC/TM – 549	Jun 70 Cook.TOT,EL,INEL,NONEL,CAPT SIGS,NDG	+
					Rept AAEC/E – 214	Jun 71 Bertram + GROUP SIGMAS SAME QUANTS.NDG	
					Rept AAEC/TM – 587	Mar 71 *DESCRIPTION OF LIBRARY	
	1.0 – 3	1.5 + 7			Data AUSTR – DFN 114.	Nov 71 POINT(223) AND GROUP(127) SIGMAS	
Evaluation	1.0 – 5	1.5 + 7	HED	Eval	Prog HEDL – TME – 71143	Oct 71 Schenter+. EVALUATION FOR ENDF/B	
Total	1.0 – 3	1.5 + 7	AUA	Eval	Data AUSTR – DFN 114.	Nov 71 COOK + POINT(223) + GROUP(127)SIG.CF EVL	+
Elastic	1.0 – 3	1.5 + 7	AUA	Eval	Data AUSTR – DFN 114.	Nov 71 COOK + POINT(223) + GROUP(127)SIG.CF EVL	+

53 Iodine 135

Quantity	Energy (ev) Min	Max	Lab	Type	Documentation Ref Vol Page	Author, Comments Date	Data
Tot Inelastc	5.0+5	1.5+7	AUA Eval	Data	AUSTR – DFN 114.	Nov 71 COOK+POINT(11)+GROUP(127)SIG.CF EVL	+
Nonelastic	1.0−3	1.5+7	AUA Eval	Data	AUSTR – DFN 114.	Nov 71 COOK+POINT(223)+GROUP(127)SIG.CF EVL	+
Absorption	1.0−4	1.0+7	JUL Eval	Rept	JUEL – 678 – RG	Jul 70 Liu. EVALUATION+CALC,GRPH,FN OF E	
Res Int Abs	5.0−1		AUA Eval	Rept	AAEC/TM – 619	Sep 72 Clayton.CALC FROM SIG LIBRARY,TABLE	
Res Int Abs	5.5−1	+6	SAC Revw	Conf	IAEA – 169 1 235	74 Ribon.CAPTURE,STATUS CFD REQUEST,TBL	
Res Int Abs	+0	+5	WIN Revw	Conf	IAEA – 169 3 163	74 Pope+ DATA FILE CALCS COMPARED	
(n,γ)	1.0−3	1.5+7	AUA Eval	Data	AUSTR – DFN 114.	Nov 71 COOK+POINT(223)+GROUP(127)SIG.CF EVL	+
(n,γ)	Pile		CRC Eval	Rept	AECL – 3037 1	Jan 72 Walker.SIG ESTIMATED ACCORDING Z,A	
(n,γ)	2.5−2		AUA Eval	Rept	AAEC/TM – 619	Sep 72 Clayton.CALC FROM SIG LIBRARY,TABLE	
(n,γ)	2.5−2		SGA Eval	Conf	73Paris 1 233	Mar 73 Eder+ INTERPOLATED FROM CALC SIG,TBL	
				Rept	SGAE – PH – 141	Feb 73 .SAME AS 73PARIS,POINT SIG FROM COOK	
(n,γ)	2.5−2		SAC Revw	Conf	IAEA – 169 1 235	74 Ribon.STATUS SIG CFD REQUESTS,TABLE	
(n,γ)	Maxwl	Fiss	WIN Revw	Conf	IAEA – 169 3 163	74 Pope+ MAXW+FIS – SPEC AVG DATA CFD XPT	
	Fiss			Conf	IAEA – 169 3 137	74 Dean. POINT DATA AVG OVER STAND SPEC	
Reson Params		1.0+6	AUA Theo	Jour	AUJ 20 477	Oct 67 Cook. TBL OF AVG LVL SPACING D,L=0,1	
Reson Params	–		AUA Theo	Rept	AAEC/E – 211	Nov 70 Musgrove. CALCULTD D+GAM WIDTH GIVEN	
Strnth Fnctn	–		AUA Theo	Rept	AAEC/E – 211	Nov 70 Musgrove. SMOOTHED S0,S1 AND S2 GIVN	

53 Iodine 136

Quantity	Energy (ev) Min	Max	Lab	Type	Documentation Ref Vol Page	Author, Comments Date	Data
Reson Params	–		AUA Theo	Rept	AAEC/E – 211	Nov 70 Musgrove. CALCULTD D+GAM WIDTH GIVEN	
Strnth Fnctn	–		AUA Theo	Rept	AAEC/E – 211	Nov 70 Musgrove. SMOOTHED S0,S1 AND S2 GIVN	

54 Xenon

Quantity	Energy (ev) Min	Max	Lab	Type	Documentation Ref Vol Page	Date	Author, Comments	Data
Evaluation	5.0+5	1.5+7	LRL	Eval	Rept UCRL-5351	Nov 58	Howerton. CURVS	
Total	6.3+0	2.3+5	ANL	Expt	Jour PR 89 904	Feb 53	Harris+ .2 EV RSLN	+
	6.3+0	9.3+3			Data EXFOR12027.002	Jun 76	. 55 PTS. SIGMA.	
Total	1.0+0	1.5+2	BNL	Expt	Jour PR 116 1516	Dec 59	Mann+ TRNS+FC, PEAK IDENTIFIED	+
	5.2-1	1.4+2			Data EXFOR11868.013	Jun 76	. 121 PTS, SIG	
Total	1.2+5	2.0+7	LOK	Expt	Jour PR 118 683	May 60	Vaughn+ TRANS	+
	1.2+5	2.0+7			Data EXFOR11106.007	Jun 76	. 152 PTS. SIGMA.	
Total	3.0-3	2.5-2	SAC	Expt	Jour JPR 24 21	Jan 63	Genin+CS COMPARED WITH EARLIER DATA	+
					Prog EANDC(E)23L	Feb 62	- .DEDUCED THR SCAT+ABS XSECT	
Total	2.1+0	4.1+3	SAC	Expt	Priv RIBON	Jan 70	Ribon. DATA FOR COMPILATION.	+
					Rept CEA-N-1149	Jan 69	- .TOF,TRANSMISSION.+SCATTERING	
					Conf 66Paris 1 119	Oct 66	- +NDG,TOF,LINAC,HIGH RESOLUTION	
	2.1+0	4.1+3			Data EXFOR20149.	May 73	25582PTS.	
Total	1.3+7	1.5+7	DEB	Eval	Rept IAEA-153 173	73	Boedy+ MOST PROBABLE VAL OF SIG,TBL	
					Jour AHP 30 115	Oct 71	Angeli+ AVG SIG,CFD CALC.TBLS.GRAPH	
Elastic	Maxwl		ANL	Expt	Jour PR 80 20	Oct 50	Harris. AVERAGE SCATTERING	+
	Maxwl				Data EXFOR11181.006	Jun 76	. 1 PT. SIGMA.	
Elastic	Maxwl		ANL	Expt	Jour PR 102 1321	Jun 56	Crouch+ COHERENT 3.27+-0.34B	+
	Maxwl				Data EXFOR11863.003	Jun 76	. 1 PT. COH AMP.	
Elastic	Maxwl		ORL	Expt	Book NB.GS.COMP 211	63	Burns+	
Elastic	2.5-2		ANL	Expt	Jour PR 148 1303	Aug 66	Krohn+ FREE ATOM S + COH SCAT LENGTH	+
	2.5-2				Data EXFOR11417.010	Jun 76	. 1 PT. FAS.	
Elastic	1.0+2	2.3+3	SAC	Expt	Rept CEA-N-1149	Jan 69	Ribon. 2EXPTS, 2 TOF PATHS	+
	1.0+0	4.0+2			Conf 66Paris 1 119	Oct 66	- +LINAC TOF OPTIM RESOL 45NS/M	
	1.0+0	2.3+3			Data EXFOR20149.002	May 73	0PTS. SEE RESONANCE PARAMETERS.	
Potntl Scat	0.0+0	6.5+2	SAC	Expt	Rept CEA-N-1149	Jan 69	Ribon.	+
		6.5+2			Data EXFOR20149.011	May 73	1PNT.RADIUS.	
Thermal Scat	-3	+0	IND	Theo	Conf 69Roorke 3 149	Dec 69	Dave+ SOLID, MORSE POTENTIAL PARAMS	
Thermal Scat	1.0-4	1.0+3	MUN	Revw	Jour EEN 80 1	77	Koester. SCAT LENGTH	
Absorption	2.0-2	2.4-1	CUW	Theo	Rept CWR-400-1	Sep 57	Roberts.MAXWELL-BOLTZMANN AVGD SIGS.	
Absorption	3.0-3	2.5-2	SAC	Expt	Jour JPR 24 21	Jan 63	Genin+ COMPARED WITH PREVIOUS DATA	+
Absorption	2.5-2		ANL	Expt	Jour PR 148 1303	Aug 66	Krohn+ 25.1+-1.0B DEDUCED FROM TRANS	+
	2.5-2				Data EXFOR11417.011	Jun 76	. 1 PT, SIG	
(n,γ)	Pile		MCM	Expt	Jour PR 80 296	Oct 50	Macnamara+ MASS SPEC. ABUNDANCE VAR.	+
	Pile				Data EXFOR11858.004	Jun 76	. 1 PT. SIGMA.	
(n,γ)	1.0+3	1.0+7	BOL	Eval	Rept CEC(70)-2	Apr 70	Benzi.GRAPH=SUM OF SIG(ISOTOPES)	
(n,γ)	3.0+4		AUA	Theo	Rept AAEC/E-211	Nov 70	Musgrove. SIGMA GIVEN AND CFD OTHER	
(n,γ)	1.0+3	1.0+7	FEI	Eval	Rept YK-8/2 97	Sep 72	Abagjan+ AVG SIG(ENERGY-GROUPS),TABL	
					Rept INDC(CCP)-39	Jul 74	.P102. ENGLISH OF YK-8/2 97	
Spect (n,γ)	None		CRC	Expt	Abst BAP 7 470	Aug 62	Bartholomew+ G PAIR SPEC	
Spect (n,γ)	Maxwl		BNL	Expt	Abst BAP 9 176	Feb 64	Monaro+ 10GS 5.74-9.30 MEV	
Spect (n,γ)	Maxwl		KFI	Expt	Jour YF 10 907	Nov 69	Kecskemeti+ AVG GAM-MULTIPLICITY,TBL	
					Jour SNP 10 524	May 70	TRANSLATN.*	
Spect (n,γ)	Maxwl		KFI	Expt	Rept KFKI-71-46	Aug 71	Kardon+ REL INTENS VS GAM ES,TABLE	+
	Maxwl				Data EXFOR30170.	May 72	145 DATA LINES	
(n,2n)	1.5+7		DEB	Eval	Jour REA 11 1 153	Mar 73	Boedy+ RECOMM.VALUE FROM N-Z SYSTEM.	
(n,p)	1.4+7		SAH	Comp	Jour NP 60 273	Nov 64	Chatterjee.MEAN OF EXPT CFD SHELLMOD	
(n,α)	1.3+7	1.8+7	TUE	Expt	Jour ZP 207 359	Oct 67	Mack+,AT 6 ENERGY POINTS	
(n,α)	1.3+7	1.8+7	CIS	Expt	Jour NP/A 210 297	Aug 73	Milazzo-Colli+ CALC EXCIT FN CFD XPT	
					Jour PL/B 38 155	Feb 72	Colli-Milazzo+ A-SPECT+EXCIT FN CALC	
(n,α)	1.3+7	1.8+7	BRC	Theo	Conf 76Lowell 347	Jul 76	Cindro.N-INDUCED REAC.MED.-HVY.NUCL.	
Reson Params	9.3+0	1.4+1	ANL	Expt	Jour PR 89 904	Feb 53	Harris+ STRENGTH FROM AREA METHOD	+
	9.3+0	1.4+1			Data EXFOR12027.003	Jun 76	. 2 RES, E0,WT**2/PCS	
Reson Params	4.6+1	3.4+2	ITE	Expt	Prog INDSWG-120 19	65	Ignat'Ev.TOF,TABLE OF 9 RES ES	
Reson Params	9.9+0	4.0+3	SAC	Expt	Priv RIBON	Jan 70	Ribon. DATA FOR COMPILATION.	+
	5.2+0	4.1+4			Rept CEA-N-1149	Jan 69	- .7EXPTS;3 TOF PATHS,3 SAMPLES	
	9.2+1	5.1+2			Conf 66Paris 1 119	Oct 66	- +WT,WN,WN0,WG FROM SHAPE ANAL	
	9.9+0	4.0+3			Data EXFOR20149.	May 73	97PTS.E0,WG,WT,J,A*G*WN.	
Strnth Fnctn		1.3+2	BNL	Expt	Jour PR 116 1516	Dec 59	Mann.	+
		1.3+2			Data EXFOR11868.008	Jun 76	. 1 PT, S0	
Lvl Density	None		FEI	Theo	Jour YF 11 1213	Jun 70	Ignatyuk+ SPIN DEPENDENCE OF DENSITY	
					Jour SNP 11 674	Dec 70	. ENGL OF YF 11 1213	

54 Xenon 121

Quantity	Energy (ev) Min	Max	Lab	Type	Documentation Ref Vol Page	Author, Comments Date	Data
(n,2n)	Fiss		CRC	Eval Rept	CRC - 1003	Dec 60 ROY+ ESTIMATED AVG SIG=20.0MB	
Reson Params	–		AUA	Theo Rept	AAEC/E - 211	Nov 70 Musgrove. CALCULTD D+GAM WIDTH GIVEN	
Strnth Fnctn	–		AUA	Theo Rept	AAEC/E - 211	Nov 70 Musgrove. SMOOTHED S0,S1 AND S2 GIVN	

54 Xenon 122

Quantity	Energy (ev) Min	Max	Lab	Type	Documentation Ref Vol Page	Author, Comments Date	Data
Reson Params	–		AUA	Theo Rept	AAEC/E - 211	Nov 70 Musgrove. CALCULTD D+GAM WIDTH GIVEN	
Strnth Fnctn	–		AUA	Theo Rept	AAEC/E - 211	Nov 70 Musgrove. SMOOTHED S0,S1 AND S2 GIVN	

54 Xenon 123

Quantity	Energy (ev) Min	Max	Lab	Type	Documentation Ref Vol Page	Author, Comments Date	Data
Reson Params	–		AUA	Theo Rept	AAEC/E - 211	Nov 70 Musgrove. CALCULTD D+GAM WIDTH GIVEN	
Strnth Fnctn	–		AUA	Theo Rept	AAEC/E - 211	Nov 70 Musgrove. SMOOTHED S0,S1 AND S2 GIVN	

54 Xenon 124

Quantity	Energy (ev) Min	Max	Lab	Type	Documentation Ref Vol Page	Author, Comments Date	Data
Evaluation	1.0 - 5	2.0+7	BNL	Eval Rept	BNL - 50374	Feb 73 Bhat+ TABLE RESON PARAMS+SIG CURVES	
Res Int Abs	5.0 - 1		CRC	Expt Prog	EANDC(CAN) - 16	Jan 63 Eastwood+P6 NRX SPECT 2690B INC 1/V	+
	5.0 - 1			Data	EXFOR11849.004	Jun 76 . 1 PT. SIGMA.	
Res Int Abs	5.0 - 1	+6	ISP	Expt Jour	JIN 26 9	Jan 64 Bresesti+ACT INT=3600+ - 500B	+
	5.0 - 1			Data	EXFOR20628.003	Oct 76 1PNT.CAPTURE.	
Res Int Abs	+0	+5	WIN	Revw Conf	IAEA - 169 3 163	74 Pope+ EVALUATED VALUE GIVEN	
(n,γ)	Pile		HAN	Expt Jour	JAP 29 1373	58 Tobin+	+
	Pile			Data	EXFOR12013.002	Jun 76 . 1 PT. SIGMA.	
(n,γ)	Pile		CRC	Expt Prog	EANDC(CAN) - 16	Jan 63 Eastwood+P6 NRX SPECT 2690B INC 1/V	+
	Pile			Data	EXFOR11849.005	Jun 76 . 1 PT. SIGMA.	
(n,γ)	2.5 - 2		ISP	Expt Jour	JIN 26 9	Jan 64 Bresesti+SIGMA=111+ - 11B	+
	2.5 - 2			Data	EXFOR20628.002	Oct 76 1PNT.SIGMA.	
(n,γ)	Maxwl		COR	Expt Rept	NYO - 3664 - 6	Jun 68 Winn.PILE ACT 18+ - 4B TO XE125M	
(n,γ)	–		IEA	Comp Rept	IEA - INF - 10	Aug 68 Atalla. TABLES OF HL,SIG AND GAMM - E	
(n,γ)	Maxwl		GIT	Expt Jour	NP/A 120 329	Nov 68 Kondaiah+ PILE,EPI CD CORR.META,GRND	+
				Prog	BARC - 401	69 .SUPERSEDED	
	Maxwl			Data	EXFOR11883.	Jun 76 . 2 PTS. SIGMA FOR GND + ISM.	
(n,γ)	Maxwl		KFI	Expt Jour	YF 10 27	Jul 69 Kardon+ ISOM SIG RATIO, META/GROUND	+
				Jour	SNP 10 15	Jan 70 . ENGL OF YF 10 27	
	2.5 - 2			Data	EXFOR30323.002	Feb 76 1 PNT	
(n,γ)	1.0+3	1.0+7	BOL	Eval Rept	CCDN - NW/10	Dec 69 Benzi+H - F MOD,AXEL G(G)EST,ALL DATA	
				Rept	CEC(70) - 2	Apr 70 - +. GRAPH	
(n,γ)	1.0+3	1.0+7	SAC	Eval Prog	EANDC(E)127U	Apr 70 Ribon+	
(n,γ)	3.0+4		AUA	Theo Rept	AAEC/E - 211	Nov 70 Musgrove. SIGMA GIVEN AND CFD OTHER	
(n,γ)	Maxwl		KFI	Comp Jour	JRC 7 365	Jun 71 Nagy+ SIGMA,GAM+XRAY ES,HALF-L GIVEN	
(n,γ)	Maxwl	Fiss	WIN	Revw Conf	IAEA - 169 3 163	74 Pope+ FIS - SPEC AVG DATA CFD MAXW - XPT	
(n,γ)	1.0+3	1.0+7	FEI	Eval Rept	YK - 8/2 97	Sep 72 Abagjan+ AVG SIG(ENERGY - GROUPS),TABL	
				Rept	INDC(CCP) - 39	Jul 74 .P102. ENGLISH OF YK - 8/2 97	
(n,γ)	2.5 - 2	3.0+1	BNL	Expt Prog	ERDA - NDC - 3 48	May 76 Kane+CS ESTABLISHED THR TO 50EV.NDG	
Spect (n,γ)	Maxwl		KFI	Comp Jour	JRC 7 365	Jun 71 Nagy+ SIGMA,GAM+XRAY ES,HALF-L GIVEN	
Spect (n,γ)	Pile		UPP	Expt Jour	ZP 265 65	Oct 73 Karlsson+,INT CONVERSION,DECAY SCH	
(n,2n)	Fiss		CRC	Eval Rept	CRC - 1003	Dec 60 Roy+,ESTIMATED AVG SIG=0.2MB	
(n,2n)	1.4+7		GIT	Expt Jour	NP/A 120 337	Nov 68 Kondaiah+ACT.CS,HL.TBL.CFD.TH,EXPT	+
				Prog	BARC - 401	69 .SUPERSEDED	
	1.4+7			Data	EXFOR11884.011	Jun 76 . 1 PT. SIGMA.	
(n,2n)	1.5+7		DEB	Comp Jour	REA 7 4 93	Dec 69 Csikai+ SIG+HL COMPILTN,N - ACTIV - ANAL	
(n,2n)	1.4+7	1.5+7	JYV	Eval Rept	JU - RR - 3/1970	Jun 70 Leppaemaeki+ TABLE OF EVAL AVG SIG	
(n,2n)	+7		KFI	Theo Rept	KFKI - 71 - 8	Feb 71 Jeki. CALCULATED CFD EXPTL SIG VALUE	
(n,2n)	1.5+7		DEB	Eval Jour	REA 11 1 153	Mar 73 Boedy. COMPILATION+RECOMM.VALUE,TBL	
				Rept	IAEA - 153 173	73 - . RECOMM. VALUE ONLY	
(n,2n)	1.5+7		TAT	Theo Jour	JP/A 7 1458	Aug 74 Kondaiah. CALC ON STAT MODEL	

54 Xenon 124

Quantity	Energy (ev) Min	Max	Lab	Type	Documentation Ref Vol Page	Author, Comments Date	Data
(n,2n)	1.5+7		ARK	Expt Jour	NSE 60 235	Jul 76 Sigg+ACT.TBL OF HL,CS.CFD WITH OTH.	+
				Abst	DA/B 37 2237	Nov 76 - .ACT TECH.CFD OTH EXPT AND PRED	
				Diss	SIGG	76 - .ACT.TBLS,GRPHS.CFD OTH.	
	1.5+7			Data	EXFOR10775.002	Jan 79 . 1 PT.CS=997+ - 80 MB.HL GVN.	
	1.5+7			Data	EXFOR10775.003	Jan 79 . 1 PT.META CS,META+ GND CS.HL GVN.	
(n,2n)	8.0+6	1.7+7	LRC	Theo Jour	MED 3 358	Oct 76 Blue+EFFECTIVE CS CALC=.36MB.	
(n,p)	Fiss		CRC	Eval Rept	CRC - 1003	Dec 60 Roy+,ESTIMATED AVG SIG=2.2MB	
(n,p)	Maxwl		IFU	Theo Rept	ICD - 4 20	67 Dadakina+ PENETR COEFF CALC,TABLE	
(n,α)	Fiss		CRC	Eval Rept	CRC - 1003	Dec 60 ROY+ ESTIMATED AVG SIG=0.36MB	
Reson Params	5.2+0		BNL	Expt Jour	PR 116 1516	Dec 59 Mann.	+
	5.2+0			Data	EXFOR11868.009	Jun 76 . 1 RES, EO, WN, WNO	
Reson Params	5.2+0	2.5+2	SAC	Expt Rept	CEA - N - 1149	Jan 69 Ribon. TOF.TRANSM + SCT.TBL.	+
				Priv	RIBON	Jan 70 - . DATA FOR COMPILATION.	
	5.2+0	2.5+2		Data	EXFOR20149.	May 73 4PTS.J,A*G*WN.	
Reson Params	-		AUA	Theo Rept	AAEC/E - 211	Nov 70 Musgrove. CALCULTD D+GAM WIDTH GIVEN	
Reson Params	5.2+0		CJD	Eval Rept	YK - 7	71 Zakharova+ SURVEY+SYSTEMATICS,GW,TBL	
				Rept	INDC(CCP) - 27	Nov 72 .ENGLISH TRANSLATION OF YK - 7 /71	
Reson Params	5.2+0	2.5+2	FEI	Theo Rept	YK - 8/2 97	Sep 72 Abagyan+ AVG G - WID+D AT BINDNG - E,TBL	
				Rept	INDC(CCP) - 39	Jul 74 .PAGE 102.ENGLISH OF YK - 8/2 97	
Reson Params	5.2+0	9.9+0	BNL	Expt Prog	ERDA - NDC - 3 48	May 76 Kane+5.16,9.88EV RES PARS TBD.	
Strnth Fnctn	-		AUA	Theo Rept	AAEC/E - 211	Nov 70 Musgrove. SMOOTHED S0,S1 AND S2 GIVN	
Lvl Density	None		GIT	Expt Jour	NP/A 120 329	Nov 68 Kondaiah+ SPIN CUTOFF FROM ISOMRATIO	
Lvl Density	5.2+0	2.5+2	FEI	Expt Rept	YK - 8/2 97	Sep 72 Abagyan+ LVL DENSITY PARAMETER,TBL	
				Rept	INDC(CCP) - 39	Jul 74 .PAGE 102.ENGLISH OF YK - 8/2 97	

54 Xenon 125

Quantity	Energy (ev) Min	Max	Lab	Type	Documentation Ref Vol Page	Author, Comments Date	Data
(n,γ)	Pile		CRC	Expt Prog	PR - CM - 32 13	63 Brown.	+
				Prog	EANDC(CAN) - 16	Jan 63 Eastwood+P6 NRX SPECT 2690B INC 1/V	
	Pile			Data	EXFOR12035.002	Jun 76 . 1 PT. SIGMA.	
Reson Params	-		AUA	Theo Rept	AAEC/E - 211	Nov 70 Musgrove. CALCULTD D+GAM WIDTH GIVEN	
Strnth Fnctn	-		AUA	Theo Rept	AAEC/E - 211	Nov 70 Musgrove. SMOOTHED S0,S1 AND S2 GIVN	
Lvl Density	None		COP	Theo Jour	NP/A 222 493	Apr 74 Dossing+COLL ROTAT.SPAC. ACCUR ESTIM	

54 Xenon 126

Quantity	Energy (ev) Min	Max	Lab	Type	Documentation Ref Vol Page	Author, Comments Date	Data
Res Int Abs	5.0-1	+6	ISP	Expt Jour	JIN 27 1175	Jun 65 Bresesti+RES CAPT INTEGRAL 38+ - 3.8B	+
	5.0-1			Data	EXFOR20630.004	Oct 76 1PNT.CAPTURE.	
Res Int Abs	+0	+5	WIN	Revw Conf	IAEA - 169 3 163	74 Pope+ EVALUATED VALUE GIVEN	
(n,γ)	Pile		CRC	Expt Prog	EANDC(CAN) - 16	Jan 63 Eastwood+P6 NRX SPECT 2690B INC 1/V	+
	Pile			Data	EXFOR11849.006	Jun 76 . 1 PT. SIGMA.	
(n,γ)	2.5-2		ISP	Expt Jour	JIN 27 1175	Jun 65 Bresesti+2.2+ - .22B	
	2.5-2			Data	EXFOR20630.002	Oct 76 1PNT.SIGMA.	
(n,γ)	Pile		ROS	Expt Jour	NP 73 91	Nov 65 Winter+ .7+ - .4B NATURAL TARGET	
(n,γ)	Maxwl		COR	Expt Rept	NYO - 3664 - 6	Jun 68 Winn.PILE ACT 0.23+ - 0.07B TO XE127M	
(n,γ)	-		IEA	Comp Rept	IEA - INF - 10	Aug 68 Atalla. TABLES OF HL,SIG AND GAMM - E	
(n,γ)	Maxwl		GIT	Expt Jour	NP/A 120 329	Nov 68 Kondaiah+ PILE,EPI CD CORR.META,GRND	+
				Prog	BARC - 401	69 .SUPERSEDED	
	Maxwl			Data	EXFOR11883.	Jun 76 . 2 PTS. SIGMA FOR GND + META.	
(n,γ)	Maxwl		KFI	Expt Jour	YF 10 27	Jul 69 Kardon+ ISOM SIG RATIO, META/GROUND	+
				Jour	SNP 10 15	Jan 70 . ENGL OF YF 10 27	
	2.5-2			Data	EXFOR30323.003	Feb 76 1 PNT	
(n,γ)	1.0+3	1.0+7	BOL	Eval Rept	CCDN - NW/10	Dec 69 Benzi+H - F MOD,AXEL G(G)EST,ALL DATA	
				Rept	CEC(70) - 2	Apr 70 - +. GRAPH	
(n,γ)	1.0+3	1.0+7	SAC	Eval Rept	EANDC(E)127U	Apr 70 Ribon+	
(n,γ)	3.0+4		AUA	Theo Rept	AAEC/E - 211	Nov 70 Musgrove. SIGMA GIVEN AND CFD OTHER	
(n,γ)	Maxwl	Fiss	WIN	Revw Conf	IAEA - 169 3 163	74 Pope+ FIS - SPEC AVG DATA CFD MAXW - XPT	
(n,γ)	1.0+3	1.0+7	FEI	Eval Rept	YK - 8/2 97	Sep 72 Abagjan+ AVG SIG(ENERGY - GROUPS),TABL	
				Rept	INDC(CCP) - 39	Jul 74 .P102. ENGLISH OF YK - 8/2 97	
Spect (n,γ)	Pile		IPS	Expt Jour	AF 5 191	Aug 52 Bergstroem.XE127,I127 GAMMAS.LEVELS	
Spect (n,γ)	-		ISP	Expt Jour	NP 58 491	64 Bresesti+.GRPH COUNTS/CHANNEL. L/K	
(n,2n)	Fiss		CRC	Eval Rept	CRC - 1003	Dec 60 ROY+ ESTIMATED AVG SIG=0.4MB	

54 Xenon 126

Quantity	Energy (ev) Min	Max	Lab	Type	Documentation Ref Vol Page	Author, Comments Date	Data
(n,2n)	1.4+7		GIT	Expt Jour	NP/A 120 337	Nov 68 Kondaiah+ACT.CS,HL.TBL.CFD.TH,EXPT	+
				Prog	BARC-401	69 .SUPERSEDED	
	1.4+7			Data	EXFOR11884.	Jun 76 . 2 PTS. SIGMA FOR GND + META.	
(n,2n)	1.5+7		DEB	Comp Jour	REA 7 4 93	Dec 69 Csikai+ SIG+HL COMPILTN,N–ACTIV–ANAL	
(n,2n)	1.4+7	1.5+7	JYV	Eval Rept	JU–RR–3/1970	Jun 70 Leppaemaeki+ TABLE OF EVAL AVG SIG	
(n,2n)	+7		KFI	Theo Rept	KFKI–71–8	Feb 71 Jeki. CALCULATED CFD EXPTL SIG VALUE	
(n,2n)	Maxwl		KFI	Comp Jour	JRC 7 365	Jun 71 Nagy+ SIGMA,GAM+XRAY ES,HALF–L GIVEN	
(n,2n)	1.4+7	1.5+7	IRK	ExTh Jour	APA 33 285	Jul 71 Winiwarter+ ISOMERIC RATIO	
(n,2n)	1.5+7		DEB	Eval Jour	REA 11 1 153	Mar 73 Boedy. COMPILATION+RECOMM.VALUE,TBL	
				Rept	IAEA–153 173	73 – . RECOMM. VALUE ONLY	
(n,2n)	1.5+7		TAT	Theo Jour	JP/A 7 1458	Aug 74 Kondaiah. CALC ON STAT MODEL	
(n,2n)	1.5+7		ARK	Expt Jour	NSE 60 235	Jul 76 Sigg+ACT.TBL OF HL,CS.CFD WITH OTH.	
				Abst	DA/B 37 2237	Nov 76 – .ACT TECH.CFD OTH EXPT AND PRED	
				Diss	SIGG	76 – .TBLS,GRPHS.CFD OTH.2META.	
(n,p)	Fiss		CRC	Eval Rept	CRC–1003	Dec 60 ROY+ ESTIMATED AVG SIG=0.5MB	
(n,α)	Fiss		CRC	Eval Rept	CRC–1003	Dec 60 ROY+ ESTIMATED AVG SIG=0.024MB	
Reson Params	4.6+2	2.3+3	SAC	Expt Rept	CEA–N–1149	Jan 69 Ribon. TOF.TRANSM + SCT.TBL.	+
				Priv	RIBON	Jan 70 – . DATA FOR COMPILATION.	
	4.6+2	2.3+3		Data	EXFOR20149.	May 73 4PTS.J,A*G*WN.	
Reson Params	–		AUA	Theo Rept	AAEC/E–211	Nov 70 Musgrove. CALCULTD D+GAM WIDTH GIVEN	
Reson Params	4.6+2		BNL	Eval Rept	BNL–50374	Feb 73 Bhat+.J WT WN WG. ENDF/B–3 DATA.	
Reson Params	4.6+2		FEI	Eval Rept	YK– 8/2 97	Sep 72 Abagyan+ AVG G–WID+D AT BINDNG–E,TBL	
				Rept	INDC(CCP)–39	Jul 74 .PAGE 102.ENGLISH OF YK–8/2 97	
Strnth Fnctn	–		AUA	Theo Rept	AAEC/E–211	Nov 70 Musgrove. SMOOTHED S0,S1 AND S2 GIVN	
Lvl Density	None		GIT	Expt Jour	NP/A 120 329	Nov 68 Kondaiah+ SPIN CUTOFF FROM ISOMRATIO	
Lvl Density	4.6+2		FEI	Eval Rept	YK– 8/2 97	Sep 72 Abagyan+ LVL DENSITY PARAMETER,TBL	
				Rept	INDC(CCP)–39	Jul 74 .PAGE 102.ENGLISH OF YK–8/2 97	

54 Xenon 127

Quantity	Energy (ev) Min	Max	Lab	Type	Documentation Ref Vol Page	Author, Comments Date	Data
(n,p)	Maxwl		IFU	Theo Rept	ICD–4 20	67 Dadakina+ PENETR COEFF CALC,TABLE	
(n,α)	Maxwl		ILL	Expt Conf	76Corsica 39	May 76 Hagberg+ NOT SEEN. UPPER LIMIT GIVEN	
Reson Params	–		AUA	Theo Rept	AAEC/E–211	Nov 70 Musgrove. CALCULTD D+GAM WIDTH GIVEN	
Strnth Fnctn	–		AUA	Theo Rept	AAEC/E–211	Nov 70 Musgrove. SMOOTHED S0,S1 AND S2 GIVN	

54 Xenon 128

Quantity	Energy (ev) Min	Max	Lab	Type	Documentation Ref Vol Page	Author, Comments Date	Data
Evaluation	1.0–3	1.5+7	AUA	Eval Rept	AAEC/TM–549	Jun 70 Cook.TOT,EL,INEL,NONEL,CAPT SIGS,NDG	+
				Rept	AAEC/E–214	Jun 71 Bertram+GROUP SIGMAS SAME QUANTS.NDG	
				Rept	AAEC/TM–587	Mar 71 *DESCRIPTION OF LIBRARY	
	1.0–3	1.5+7		Data	AUSTR–DFN 115.	Nov 71 POINT(223) AND GROUP(127) SIGMAS	
Total	1.0–3	1.5+7	AUA	Eval Data	AUSTR–DFN 115.	Nov 71 COOK+POINT(223)+GROUP(127)SIG.CF EVL	+
Elastic	1.0–3	1.5+7	AUA	Eval Data	AUSTR–DFN 115.	Nov 71 COOK+POINT(223)+GROUP(127)SIG.CF EVL	+
Tot Inelastc	5.0+5	1.5+7	AUA	Eval Data	AUSTR–DFN 115.	Nov 71 COOK+POINT(11)+GROUP(127)SIG.CF EVL	+
Nonelastic	1.0–3	1.5+7	AUA	Eval Data	AUSTR–DFN 115.	Nov 71 COOK+POINT(223)+GROUP(127)SIG.CF EVL	+
Absorption	Maxwl		KAP	Expt Jour	NUC 13 30	Dec 55 Robb+0TO5B TBL OF Q S RCTR POIS	
Absorption	4.1–1	1.0+7	GA	Eval Prog	GA–2451	Aug 61 Joanou+ 68 GROUP DATA FOR GAM–I	
Res Int Abs	5.5–1		CRC	Eval Rept	AECL–3037 1	Jan 72 Walker.REDUCED RES INT TO GND+META	
Res Int Abs	5.0–1		AUA	Eval Rept	AAEC/TM–619	Sep 72 Clayton.CALC FROM SIG LIBRARY,TABLE	
Res Int Abs	+0	+5	WIN	Revw Conf	IAEA–169 3 163	74 Pope+ DATA FILE CALC CFD XPTAL VALUE	
(n,γ)	Pile		MCM	Expt Jour	PR 80 296	50 Macnamara+ MASS SPEC.	+
	Pile			Data	EXFOR11858.005	Jun 76 . 1 PT. SIGMA.	
(n,γ)	Maxwl		CRC	Eval Prog	AECL–1054	Mar 60 Walker. (CRRP–913)	
(n,γ)	Pile		CRC	Expt Prog	EANDC(CAN)–16	Jan 63 Eastwood+P6 NRX SPECT 2690B INC 1/V	+
	Pile			Data	EXFOR11849.007	Jun 76 . 1 PT. SIGMA.	
(n,γ)	2.5+4		FEI	ExTh Prog	YFI–4 22	May 67 Shorin+.,TBLS GIVEN,TBP YF	
				Theo Jour	YF 6 769	Oct 67 – + STATMOD. SIGMA GIVEN	
				ExTh Rept	INDC–187E	67 . ENGL OF YFI–4 22	
(n,γ)	Maxwl		UCS	Expt Jour	NSE 31 545	Mar 68 Tilbury+ ACTIV 0.43+–0.10B TO ISOM	+
	Maxwl			Data	EXFOR11927.007	Jun 76 . 1 PT. SIGMA.	
(n,γ)	–		IEA	Comp Rept	IEA–INF– 10	Aug 68 Atalla. TABLES OF HL,SIG AND GAMM–E	
(n,γ)	Maxwl		GIT	Expt Jour	NP/A 120 329	Nov 68 Kondaiah+ PILE,EPI CD CORR.TO METAST	+
				Prog	BARC–401	69 .SUPERSEDED	
	Maxwl			Data	EXFOR11883.011	Jun 76 . 1 PT. SIGMA TO META.	

54 Xenon 128

Quantity	Energy (ev) Min	Max	Lab	Type	Documentation Ref Vol Page	Author, Comments Date	Data
(n,γ)	1.0+3	1.0+7	BOL	Eval	Rept CCDN – NW/10	Dec 69 Benzi+H – F MOD,AXEL G(G)EST,ALL DATA	
					Rept CEC(70) – 2	Apr 70 – +. GRAPH	
(n,γ)	1.0+3	1.0+7	SAC	Eval	Prog EANDC(E)127U	Apr 70 Ribon+	
(n,γ)	3.0+4		AUA	Theo	Rept AAEC/E – 211	Nov 70 Musgrove. SIGMA GIVEN AND CFD OTHER	
(n,γ)	1.0–3	1.5+7	AUA	Eval	Data AUSTR – DFN 115.	Nov 71 COOK+POINT(223)+GROUP(127)SIG.CF EVL	+
(n,γ)	Maxwl		CRC	Eval	Rept AECL – 3037 1	Jan 72 Walker.RECOMMEND SIG TO GND+META,TBL	
(n,γ)	2.5–2		AUA	Eval	Rept AAEC/TM – 619	Sep 72 Clayton.CALC FROM SIG LIBRARY,TABLE	
(n,γ)	Fiss		WIN	Revw	Conf IAEA – 169 3 137	74 Dean. POINT DATA AVG OVER STAND SPEC	
	Maxwl	Fiss			Conf IAEA – 169 3 163	74 Pope+ MAXW+FIS – SPEC AVG DATA CFD XPT	
(n,γ)	1.0+3	1.0+7	FEI	Eval	Rept YK – 8/2 97	Sep 72 Abagjan+ AVG SIG(ENERGY – GROUPS),TABL	
					Rept INDC(CCP) – 39	Jul 74 .P102. ENGLISH OF YK – 8/2 97	
Spect (n,γ)	Pile		IPS	Expt	Jour AF 7 239	Mar 54 Bergstroem+.XE129M DEC. NAI.CONVCOEF	
					Jour AF 5 191	Aug 52 – .ISOMER XE129M DISCOVERED	
Spect (n,γ)	Pile		IPS	Expt	Jour AF 14 373	Oct 58 Alvaeger+. DECAY OF XE129M. M2 HL	
(n,2n)	Fiss		CRC	Eval	Rept CRC – 1003	Dec 60 ROY+ ESTIMATED AVG SIG=0.7MB	
(n,2n)	1.4+7		GIT	Expt	Jour NP/A 120 337	Nov 68 Kondaiah+ACT.CS,HL.TBL.CFD.TH,EXPT	+
					Prog BARC – 401	69 .SUPERSEDED	
	1.4+7				Data EXFOR11884.	Jun 76 . 2 PTS. SIGMA FOR GND + META.	
(n,2n)	1.5+7		DEB	Comp	Jour REA 7 4 93	Dec 69 Csikai+ SIG+HL COMPILTN,N – ACTIV – ANAL	
(n,2n)	1.4+7	1.5+7	JYV	Eval	Rept JU – RR – 3/1970	Jun 70 Leppaemaeki+ TABLE OF EVAL AVG SIG	
(n,2n)	+7		KFI	Theo	Rept KFKI – 71 – 8	Feb 71 Jeki. CALCULATED CFD EXPTL SIG VALUE	
(n,2n)	1.4+7	1.5+7	IRK	ExTh	Jour APA 33 285	Jul 71 Winiwarter+ ISOMERIC RATIO	
(n,2n)	1.5+7		DEB	Eval	Rept REA 11 1 153	Mar 73 Boedy. COMPILATION+RECOMM.VALUE,TBL	
					Rept IAEA – 153 173	73 – . RECOMM. VALUE ONLY	
(n,2n)	1.5+7		TAT	Theo	Jour JP/A 7 1458	Aug 74 Kondaiah. CALC ON STAT MODEL	
(n,2n)	1.5+7		ARK	Expt	Jour NSE 60 235	Jul 76 Sigg+ACT.TBL OF HL,CS.CFD WITH OTH.	+
					Abst DA/B 37 2237	Nov 76 – .ACT TECH.CFD OTH EXPT AND PRED	
					Diss SIGG	76 – .TBLS,GRPHS.CFD OTH.2META.	
	1.5+7				Data EXFOR10775.004	Jan 79 . 1PT.META,GND,META+GND CS.HL GVN.	
(n,p)	Fiss		CRC	Eval	Rept CRC – 1003	Dec 60 ROY+ ESTIMATED AVG SIG=0.2MB	
(n,p)	1.5+7		ARK	Expt	Jour NSE 60 235	Jul 76 Sigg+ACT.TBL OF HL,CS.CFD WITH OTH	+
					Abst DA/B 37 2237	Nov 76 – .ACT TECH.CFD OTH EXPT AND PRED	
					Diss SIGG	76 – .ACT.TBLS,GRPHS.CFD OTH.	
	1.5+7				Data EXFOR10775.009	Jan 79 . 1PT.CS=27+ – 4MB.HL.GVN.	
(n,α)	Fiss		CRC	Eval	Rept CRC – 1003	Dec 60 ROY+ ESTIMATED AVG SIG=0.007MB	
Reson Params	2.5+4		FEI	ExTh	Prog YFI – 4 22	May 67 Shorin+.,TBLS GIVEN,TBP YF	
					Rept INDC – 187E	67 . ENGL OF YFI – 4 22	
Reson Params	2.4+2	3.4+3	SAC	Expt	Rept CEA – N – 1149	Jan 69 Ribon. TOF.TRANSM + SCT.TBL.	+
					Priv RIBON	Jan 70 – . DATA FOR COMPILATION.	
	2.4+2	3.4+3			Data EXFOR20149.	May 73 23PTS.WG,WT,J,A*G*WN.	
Reson Params	–		AUA	Theo	Rept AAEC/E – 211	Nov 70 Musgrove. CALCULTD D+GAM WIDTH GIVEN	
Reson Params	1.5+2	6.5+2	SAC	ExTh	Diss FRNC – TH – 450	Oct 72 Delaroche.OPTICAL MODEL PARAMETERS	
Reson Params	2.4+2	3.4+3	BNL	Eval	Rept BNL – 50374	Feb 73 Bhat+ J WT WN WG. ENDF/B – 3 DATA	
Reson Params	+2	+3	FEI	Eval	Rept YK – 8/2 97	Sep 72 Abagyan+ AVG G – WID+D AT BINDNG – E,TBL	
					Rept INDC(CCP) – 39	Jul 74 .PAGE 102.ENGLISH OF YK – 8/2 97	
Strnth Fnctn	0.0+0	3.4+3	SAC	Expt	Rept CEA – N – 1149	Jan 69 Ribon. FROM RESONANCE ANALYSIS.	+
		3.4+3			Priv RIBON	Jan 70 – . DATA FOR COMPILATION.	
		3.4+3			Data EXFOR20149.020	May 73 1PNT.L=0.	
Strnth Fnctn	–		AUA	Theo	Rept AAEC/E – 211	Nov 70 Musgrove. SMOOTHED S0,S1 AND S2 GIVN	
Strnth Fnctn	None		KUR	Theo	Rept IAE – 2560	75 Adamchuk+.S0 – VALUE,TBL	
Strnth Fnctn	None		OSA	Theo	Conf JAERI – M – 5984	Feb 75 Kitazoe+OPT MDLS.GRPH VS A.TBL PARS	
Lvl Density	0.0+0	3.4+3	SAC	Expt	Rept CEA – N – 1149	Jan 69 Ribon. FROM RESONANCE ANALYSIS.	+
		3.4+3			Priv RIBON	Jan 70 – . DATA FOR COMPILATION.	
		3.4+3			Data EXFOR20149.021	May 73 1PNT.SP.CUT(0).	
Lvl Density	+2	+3	FEI	Eval	Rept YK – 8/2 97	Sep 72 Abagyan+ LVL DENSITY PARAMETER,TBL	
					Rept INDC(CCP) – 39	Jul 74 .PAGE 102.ENGLISH OF YK – 8/2 97	

54 Xenon 129

Quantity	Energy (ev) Min	Max	Lab	Type	Documentation Ref Vol Page	Author, Comments Date	Data
Total	0.0+0	4.2+3	SAC	Expt	Rept CEA – N – 1149	Jan 69 Ribon. ENRICHED TO 50PC.RES ASSGNMNT	+
		4.2+3			Priv RIBON	Jan 70 – . NO DATA. ISOTOPIC RES ASSGN.	
		4.2+3			Data EXFOR20149.022	May 73 0PTS.	
Absorption	1.0–3	1.0+7	JUL	Eval	Rept JUEL – 678 – RG	Jul 70 Liu. EVALUATION+CALC,GRPH,FN OF E	
Res Int Abs	None		CRC	Eval	Prog AECL – 1054	Mar 60 Walker. (CRP – 913) REDUCED RES. INT.	
Res Int Abs	5.0–1		BOL	Eval	Rept RT/FI – 4	Jan 67 Palmucci. CALC FROM (N,G) RES PARAMS	
Res Int Abs	5.5–1		CRC	Eval	Rept AECL – 3037 1	Jan 72 Walker.REDUCED RES INT FROM RES PARS	

54 Xenon 129

Quantity	Energy (ev) Min	Max	Lab	Type	Documentation Ref Vol Page	Date	Author, Comments	Data
Res Int Abs	+0	+5	WIN Revw	Conf	IAEA – 169 3 163	74	Pope+ DATA FILE CALC CFD XPTAL VALUE	
(n,γ)	Pile		MCM Expt	Jour	PR 80 296	Oct 50	Macnamara+ MASS SPEC. ABUNDANCE VAR.	+
	Pile			Data	EXFOR11858.006	Jun 76	. 1 PT. SIGMA.	
(n,γ)	Maxwl		CRC Eval	Prog	AECL – 1054	Mar 60	Walker. (CRRP – 913)	
(n,γ)	Pile		CRC Expt	Prog	EANDC(CAN) – 16	Jan 63	Eastwood+P6 NRX SPECT 2690B INC 1/V	+
	Pile			Data	EXFOR11849.008	Jun 76	. 1 PT. SIGMA.	
(n,γ)	2.5 – 2		BOL Eval	Rept	RT/FI – 4	Jan 67	Palmucci. CALC FROM RES PARAMETERS	
(n,γ)	1.0+3	1.0+7	BOL Eval	Rept	CCDN – NW/10	Dec 69	Benzi+H – F MOD,AXEL G(G)EST,ALL DATA	
				Rept	CEC(70) – 2	Apr 70	– +. GRAPH	
(n,γ)	1.0+3	1.0+7	SAC Eval	Prog	EANDC(E)127U	Apr 70	Ribon+	
(n,γ)	3.0+4		AUA Theo	Rept	AAEC/E – 211	Nov 70	Musgrove. SIGMA GIVEN AND CFD OTHER	
(n,γ)	Maxwl		CRC Eval	Rept	AECL – 3037 1	Jan 72	Walker.RECOMMENDED SIG,DETAILED TBL	
(n,γ)	Maxwl	Fiss	WIN Revw	Conf	IAEA – 169 3 163	74	Pope+ FIS – SPEC AVG DATA CFD MAXW – XPT	
(n,γ)	1.0+3	1.0+7	FEI Eval	Rept	YK – 8/2 97	Sep 72	Abagjan+ AVG SIG(ENERGY – GROUPS),TABL	
				Rept	INDC(CCP) – 39	Jul 74	.P102. ENGLISH OF YK – 8/2 97	
Spect (n,γ)	9.4+0		ITE Expt	Jour	ZET 45 875	Oct 63	Ignat'Ev.GRAPH G – SPEC FROM 9.4EV – RES	
				Jour	JET 18 602	Mar 64	TRANSLATN.*	
Spect (n,γ)	9.5+0		ITE Expt	Jour	JINR – 1845 1400	Jun 64	Beljaev+ TOF,TBL,E – GAMM=4.7 MEV	
Spect (n,γ)	Maxwl		KUR Expt	Jour	YF 13 1129	Jun 71	Groshev+ GE – LI,G – E+INT+LVLS IN GRAPH	+
				Jour	SNP 13 647	Dec 71	. ENGL OF YF 13 1129	
	2.5 – 2			Data	EXFOR40182.002	Nov 73	.GAM/100N FOR 38 E GVN	
Spect (n,γ)	Pile		KUR Expt	Jour	YF 13 1129	Jun 71	Groshev+ GE – LI,ES+INTENS,G – TRANSITN	
Spect (n,γ)	Maxwl		KFI Expt	Rept	KFKI – 71 – 46	Aug 71	Kardon+ REL INTENS,TBL,LVL SCHEME,Q	+
	Maxwl			Data	EXFOR30170.	May 72	11 DATA LINES	
Spect (n,γ)	5.2+0	1.4+1	BNL Expt	Jour	PR/C 9 2363	Jun 74	Gelletly+ GE(LI) DET	
(n,2n)	Fiss		CRC Eval	Rept	CRC – 1003	Dec 60	ROY+ ESTIMATED AVG SIG=7.3MB	
(n,2n)	1.5+7		DEB Eval	Jour	REA 11 1 153	Mar 73	Boedy+ RECOMM.VALUE FROM N – Z SYSTEM.	
(n,2n)	1.5+7		KFI Theo	Rept	KFKI – 73 – 68	Dec 73	Jeki.NEW FIT,CALC SIG CFD OTHERS,TBL	
(n,p)	Fiss		CRC Eval	Rept	CRC – 1003	Dec 60	ROY+ ESTIMATED AVG SIG=0.26MB	
(n,p)	Maxwl		IFU Theo	Rept	ICD – 4 20	67	Dadakina+ PENETR COEFF CALC,TABLE	
(n,α)	Fiss		CRC Eval	Rept	CRC – 1003	Dec 60	ROY+ ESTIMATED AVG SIG=0.08MB	
(n,α)	9.4+0	1.3+2	DUB Expt	Prog	YFI – 7 52	Apr 69	Popov+ RES – E,SPIN,ALFA WIDTH AT 3 ES	
				Jour	YF 9 1163	Jun 69	– + ALF – INT+WIDTH,GRPH+TBL,3RES	
				Rept	INDC(CCP) – 7U55	Feb 70	– + TRANSLATION.	
				Jour	SNP 9 680	Dec 69	. ENGLISH OF YF 9 1163	
Reson Params	9.5+0	1.3+2	BNL Expt	Jour	PR 116 1516	Dec 59	Mann+	+
	9.5+0	1.3+2		Data	EXFOR11868.010	Jun 76	. 3 RES. EO, WN, WNO	
Reson Params	9.4+0		CCP Comp	Rept	INDSWG – 64 19	64	Ignat'Ev. 1 RES, SUPERSEDS ZET45 875	
Reson Params		1.0+6	AUA Theo	Jour	AUJ 20 477	Oct 67	Cook. TBL OF AVG LVL SPACING D,L=0,1	
Reson Params	9.4+0	1.3+2	DUB Expt	Prog	YFI – 7 52	Apr 69	Popov+ RES – E,SPIN,ALFA WIDTH AT 3 ES	+
				Jour	YF 9 1163	Jun 69	– + TBL=EXPTL+STATMOD ALPHA WIDTH	
				Rept	INDC(CCP) – 7U55	Feb 70	– + TRANSLATION.	
				Jour	SNP 9 6 680	Dec 69	– + TRANSLATION.	
	9.4+0	1.3+2		Data	EXFOR40304.006	Nov 75	.ALPHA – WIDTH FOR 3 EN GVN	
Reson Params	9.6+0	4.1+3	SAC Expt	Rept	CEA – N – 1149	Jan 69	Ribon. TOF.TRANSM + SCT.TBL.	
	1.0+1	2.0+2		Prog	EANDC(E)127U	Apr 70	Cauvin+SPIN ASSIGN	
	9.6+0	4.1+3		Priv	RIBON	Jan 70	Ribon. DATA FOR COMPILATION.	
	9.7+0	1.9+2		Conf	66Paris 1 119	Oct 66	– +WT,WN,WN0,WG FROM SHAPE ANAL	
	9.6+0	4.1+3		Data	EXFOR20149.	May 73	219PTS.WG,AVG WG,WT,J,A*G*WN.	
Reson Params	–		AUA Theo	Rept	AAEC/E – 211	Nov 70	Musgrove. CALCULTD D+GAM WIDTH GIVEN	
Reson Params	9.7+0	3.7+2	CJD Eval	Rept	YK – 7	71	Zakharova+ SURVEY+SYSTEMATICS,GW,TBL	
				Rept	INDC(CCP) – 27	Nov 72	.ENGLISH TRANSLATION OF YK – 7 /71	
Reson Params	1.5+2	6.5+2	SAC ExTh	Diss	FRNC – TH – 450	Oct 72	Delaroche.OPTICAL MODEL PARAMETERS	
Reson Params	9.4+0	4.1+3	BNL Eval	Rept	BNL – 50374	Feb 73	Bhat+ J WT WN WG. MOD. ENDF/B – 3 DATA.	
Reson Params	+0	+2	BOL Eval	Conf	IAEA – 169 3 123	74	Benzi+ AVG G – WID CFD OTHERS+XPT,TABL	
Reson Params	+0	+3	FEI Eval	Rept	YK – 8/2 97	Sep 72	Abagjan+ AVG G – WID+D AT BINDNG – E,TBL	
				Rept	INDC(CCP) – 39	Jul 74	.PAGE 102.ENGLISH OF YK – 8/2 97	
Strnth Fnctn	9.4+0	1.3+2	DUB Expt	Prog	YFI – 7 52	Apr 69	Popov+ (N,ALFA) TOF EXPT CFD STATMOD	
				Rept	INDC(CCP) – 7U55	Feb 70	– + TRANSLATION.	
Strnth Fnctn	–		DUB Revw	Jour	YF 11 111	Jan 71	Malecki+ VALUES FOR TWO SPIN STATES	
				Jour	SNP 11 61	Jul 70	– + ENGL OF YF 11 61.	
Strnth Fnctn	0.0+0	4.1+3	SAC Expt	Rept	CEA – N – 1149	Jan 69	Ribon. FROM RESONANCE ANALYSIS.	+
		4.1+3		Priv	RIBON	Jan 70	– . DATA FOR COMPILATION.	
		4.0+3		Prog	EANDC(E)89U185	Feb 68	Michaudon+ L=0,NO VARIATN WITH SPIN.	
		4.1+3		Data	EXFOR20149.028	May 73	1PNT.L=0.	
Strnth Fnctn	–		AUA Theo	Rept	AAEC/E – 211	Nov 70	Musgrove. SMOOTHED S0,S1 AND S2 GIVN	
Strnth Fnctn	None		AUA Eval	Rept	AAEC/E – 277	Mar 73	Musgrove.TBLS EXPTL DATA+BEST VALUES	
Strnth Fnctn	None		KUR Theo	Prog	IAE – 2560	75	Adamchuk+ .S0 – VALUE,TBL	

54 Xenon 129

Quantity	Energy (ev) Min	Max	Lab	Type	Documentation Ref Vol Page	Author, Comments Date	Data
Lvl Density	0.0+0	4.1+3	SAC	Expt Rept	CEA-N-1149	Jan 69 Ribon. FROM RESONANCE ANALYSIS.	+
		4.1+3		Priv	RIBON	Jan 70 - . DATA FOR COMPILATION.	
		4.1+3		Data	EXFOR20149.029	May 73 1PNT.SP.CUT(0).	
Lvl Density	None		AUW	Theo Conf	70Madurai 2 267	Dec 70 Ramamurty+ A-PARAMETER GVN,LANG'S-TH	
Lvl Density	None		BOL	Eval Conf	IAEA-169 3 123	74 Benzi+ LVL DENS PARAM BY XPT,GRPH+TB	
Lvl Density	+0	+3	FEI	Eval Rept	YK-8/2 97	Sep 72 Abagyan+ LVL DENSITY PARAMETER,TBL	
				Rept	INDC(CCP)-39	Jul 74 .PAGE 102.ENGLISH OF YK-8/2 97	

54 Xenon 130

Quantity	Energy (ev) Min	Max	Lab	Type	Documentation Ref Vol Page	Author, Comments Date	Data
Evaluation	1.0-3	1.5+7	AUA	Eval Rept	AAEC/TM-549	Jun 70 Cook.TOT,EL,INEL,NONEL,CAPT SIGS,NDG	+
				Rept	AAEC/E-214	Jun 71 Bertram+GROUP SIGMAS SAME QUANTS.NDG	
				Rept	AAEC/TM-587	Mar 71 *DESCRIPTION OF LIBRARY	
	1.0-3	1.5+7		Data	AUSTR-DFN 116.	Nov 71 POINT(223) and GROUP(127) SIGMAS	
Total	1.0-3	1.5+7	AUA	Eval Data	AUSTR-DFN 116.	Nov 71 COOK+POINT(223)+GROUP(127)SIG.CF EVL	+
Elastic	1.0-3	1.5+7	AUA	Eval Data	AUSTR-DFN 116.	Nov 71 COOK+POINT(223)+GROUP(127)SIG.CF EVL	+
Tot Inelastc	1.0+6	1.5+7	AUA	Eval Data	AUSTR-DFN 116.	Nov 71 COOK+POINT(10)+GROUP(127)SIG.CF EVL	+
Nonelastic	1.0-3	1.5+7	AUA	Eval Data	AUSTR-DFN 116.	Nov 71 COOK+POINT(223)+GROUP(127)SIG.CF EVL	+
Absorption	Maxwl		KAP	Expt Jour	NUC 13 30	Dec 55 Robb+0TO5B TBL OF Q S RCTR POIS	
Absorption	4.1-1	1.0+7	GA	Eval Prog	GA-2451	Aug 61 Joanou+ 68 GROUP DATA FOR GAM-I	
Res Int Abs	5.5-1		CRC	Eval Prog	AECL-3037 1	Jan 72 Walker.REDUCED RES INT TO GND+META	
Res Int Abs	5.0-1		AUA	Eval Rept	AAEC/TM-619	Sep 72 Clayton.CALC FROM SIG LIBRARY,TABLE	
Res Int Abs	+0	+5	WIN	Revw Conf	IAEA-169 3 163	74 Pope+ DATA FILE CALC CFD XPTAL VALUE	
(n,γ)	Pile		MCM	Expt Jour	PR 80 296	50 Macnamara+ MASS SPEC.	+
	Pile			Data	EXFOR11858.007	Jun 76 . 1 PT. SIGMA.	
(n,γ)	Maxwl		CRC	Eval Prog	AECL-1054	Mar 60 Walker. (CRRP-913)	
	Pile		CRC	Expt Prog	EANDC(CAN)-16	Jan 63 Eastwood+P6 NRX REACTOR SPECT	+
	Pile			Data	EXFOR11849.009	Jun 76 . 1 PT. SIGMA.	
(n,γ)	2.5+4		FEI	ExTh Prog	YFI-4 22	May 67 Shorin+.,TBLS GIVEN,TBP YF	
				Theo Jour	YF 6 769	Oct 67 - + STATMOD. SIGMA GIVEN	
				ExTh Rept	INDC-187E	67 . ENGL OF YFI-4 22	
(n,γ)	Maxwl		UCS	Expt Jour	NSE 31 545	Mar 68 Tilbury+ ACTIV 0.34+-0.08B TO ISOM	+
	Pile			Data	EXFOR11927.008	Jun 76 . 1 PT. SIGMA.	
(n,γ)	-		IEA	Comp Rept	IEA-INF-10	Aug 68 Atalla. TABLES OF HL,SIG AND GAMM-E	
(n,γ)	Maxwl		GIT	Expt Jour	NP/A 120 329	Nov 68 Kondaiah+ PILE,EPI CD CORR.TO METAST	+
				Prog	BARC-401	69 .SUPERSEDED	
	Maxwl			Data	EXFOR11883.012	Jun 76 . 1 PT. SIGMA.	
(n,γ)	1.0-3	1.0+7	BOL	Eval Rept	CCDN-NW/10	Dec 69 Benzi+H-F MOD,AXEL G(G)EST,ALL DATA	
				Rept	CEC(70)-2	Apr 70 - +. GRAPH	
(n,γ)	3.0+4		AUA	Theo Rept	AAEC/E-211	Nov 70 Musgrove. SIGMA GIVEN AND CFD OTHER	
(n,γ)	1.0-3	1.5+7	AUA	Eval Data	AUSTR-DFN 116.	Nov 71 COOK+POINT(223)+GROUP(127)SIG.CF EVL	+
(n,γ)	Maxwl		CRC	Eval Prog	AECL-3037 1	Jan 72 Walker.RECOMMEND SIG TO GND+META,TBL	
(n,γ)	2.5-2		AUA	Eval Rept	AAEC/TM-619	Sep 72 Clayton.CALC FROM SIG LIBRARY,TABLE	
(n,γ)	Maxwl	Fiss	WIN	Revw Conf	IAEA-169 3 163	74 Pope+ MAXW+FIS-SPEC AVG DATA CFD XPT	
	Fiss			Conf	IAEA-169 3 137	74 Dean. POINT DATA AVG OVER STAND SPEC	
(n,γ)	1.0-3	1.0+7	FEI	Eval Rept	YK-8/2 97	Sep 72 Abagyan+ AVG SIG(ENERGY-GROUPS),TABL	
				Rept	INDC(CCP)-39	Jul 74 .P102. ENGLISH OF YK-8/2 97	
Spect (n,γ)	Pile		IPS	Expt Jour	AF 7 239	Mar 54 Bergstroem+.XE131 DECAY.NAI.CONVCOEF	
				Jour	AF 5 191	Aug 52 - .XE131,131M DECAY.LEVELS	
(n,2n)	Fiss		CRC	Eval Rept	CRC-1003	Dec 60 ROY+ ESTIMATED AVG SIG=1.0MB	
(n,2n)	1.4+7		GIT	Expt Jour	NP/A 120 337	Nov 68 Kondaiah+ACT.CS,HL.TBL.CFD.TH,EXPT	+
				Prog	BARC-401	69 .SUPERSEDED	
	1.4+7			Data	EXFOR11884.020	Jun 76 . 1 PT. SIGMA.	
(n,2n)	1.5+7		DEB	Comp Jour	REA 7 4 93	Dec 69 Csikai+ SIG+HL COMPILTN,N-ACTIV-ANAL	
(n,2n)	1.4+7	1.5+7	JYV	Eval Rept	JU-RR-3/1970	Jun 70 Leppaemaeki+ TABLE OF EVAL AVG SIG	
(n,2n)	1.5+7		DEB	Eval Jour	REA 11 1 153	Mar 73 Boedy+ RECOMM.VALUE FROM N-Z SYSTEM.	
(n,2n)	1.5+7		ARK	Expt Jour	NSE 60 235	Jul 76 Sigg+ACT.TBL OF HL,CS.CFD WITH OTH.	+
				Abst	DA/B 37 2237	Nov 76 - .ACT TECH.CFD OTH EXPT AND PRED	
				Diss	SIGG	76 - .TBLS,GRPHS.CFD OTH.	
	1.5+7			Data	EXFOR10775.005	Jan 79 . 1PT.CS=2031+-165 MB.HL GVN.	
(n,2n)	1.5+7		IBJ	Theo Jour	ASL 27 186	77 Rurarz+ ISO RATIO,4MODLS,CFD XPT.TBL	
	1.4+7			Rept	INR-1464 19	May 73 - + ISOMERIC RATIO CFD EXPT,GRAF	
(n,p)	Fiss		CRC	Eval Rept	CRC-1003	Dec 60 ROY+ ESTIMATED AVG SIG=0.5MB	
(n,p)	1.4+7		GIT	Expt Jour	NP/A 120 337	Nov 68 Kondaiah+ACT.CS,HL.TBL.CFD.TH,EXPT	+
				Prog	BARC-401	69 .SUPERSEDED	
	1.4+7			Data	EXFOR11884.016	Jun 76 .1 PT. SIGMA.	

54 Xenon 130

Quantity	Energy (ev) Min	Max	Lab	Type	Documentation Ref Vol Page	Author, Comments Date	Data
(n,p)	1.5+7		DEB Comp	Jour	REA 7 4 93	Dec 69 Csikai+ SIG+HL COMPILTN,N-ACTIV-ANAL	
(n,p)	1.4+7	1.5+7	JYV Eval	Rept	JU-RR-3/1970	Jun 70 Leppaemaeki+ TABLE OF EVAL AVG SIG	
(n,p)	1.4+7	1.5+7	KAZ Theo	Jour	YF 18 705	Oct 73 Levkovsky.AVERAGED SIG,CALC,TBL	
				Jour	SNP 18 361	Apr 74 . ENGLISH OF YF 18,705	
(n,p)	1.5+7		ARK Expt	Jour	NSE 60 235	Jul 76 Sigg+ACT.TBL OF HL,CS.CFD WITH OTH	+
				Abst	DA/B 37 2237	Nov 76 - .ACT TECH.CFD OTH EXPT AND PRED	
				Diss	SIGG	76 - .ACT.TBLS,GRPHS.CFD OTH.	
	1.5+7			Data	EXFOR10775.010	Jan 79 . 1PT.CS=11.1+-1.2 MB.HL GVN.	
(n,α)	Fiss		CRC Eval	Rept	CRC-1003	Dec 60 ROY+ ESTIMATED AVG SIG=0.0007 MB	
Reson Params	1.3+2		BNL Expt	Jour	PR 116 1516	Dec 59 Mann.	+
	1.3+2			Data	EXFOR11868.011	Jun 76 . 1 RES. EO,WN,WNO	
Reson Params	2.5+4		FEI ExTh	Prog	YFI-4 22	May 67 Shorin+.,TBLS GIVEN,TBP YF	
				Rept	INDC-187E	67 . ENGL OF YFI-4 22	
Reson Params	-		DUB Expt	Conf	68DUBSY 283	Jul 68 Shapiro.AVERAGE ALFA WIDTH,LVL SPAC.	
Reson Params	4.3+2	3.6+3	SAC Expt	Rept	CEA-N-1149	Jan 69 Ribon. TOF.TRANSM + SCT.TBL.	+
				Priv	RIBON	Jan 73 - . DATA FOR COMPILATION.	
	4.3+2	3.6+3		Data	EXFOR20149.	May 73 47PTS.WG,WT,J,A*G*WN.	
Reson Params	-		AUA Theo	Rept	AAEC/E-211	Nov 70 Musgrove. CALCULTD D+GAM WIDTH GIVEN	
Reson Params	2.4+2		CJD Eval	Rept	YK-7	71 Zakharova+ SURVEY+SYSTEMATICS,GW,TBL	
				Rept	INDC(CCP)-27	Nov 72 .ENGLISH TRANSLATION OF YK-7 /71	
Reson Params	1.5+2	6.5+2	SAC ExTh	Diss	FRNC-TH-450	Oct 72 Delaroche.OPTICAL MODEL PARAMETERS	
Reson Params	1.5+3	3.6+3	BNL Eval	Rept	BNL-50374	Feb 73 Bhat+ J WT WN WG. ENDF/B-3 DATA.	
Reson Params	+2	+3	FEI Eval	Rept	YK-8/2 97	Sep 72 Abagyan+ AVG G-WID+D AT BINDNG-E,TBL	
				Rept	INDC(CCP)-39	Jul 74 .PAGE 102.ENGLISH OF YK-8/2 97	
Strnth Fnctn	0.0+0	3.6+3	SAC Expt	Rept	CEA-N-1149	Jan 69 Ribon. FROM RESONANCE ANALYSIS.	+
		3.6+2		Priv	RIBON	Jan 70 - . DATA FOR COMPILATION.	
		3.6+3		Data	EXFOR20149.034	May 73 1PNT.L=0.	
Strnth Fnctn	-		AUA Theo	Rept	AAEC/E-211	Nov 70 Musgrove. SMOOTHED S0,S1 AND S2 GIVN	
Strnth Fnctn	None		KUR Theo	Prog	IAE-2560	75 Adamchuk+.S0-VALUE,TBL	
Strnth Fnctn	None		OSA Theo	Conf	JAERI-M-5984	Feb 75 Kitazoe+OPT MDLS.GRPH VS A.TBL PARS	
Lvl Density	0.0+0	3.6+3	SAC Expt	Rept	CEA-N-1149	Jan 69 Ribon. FROM RESONANCE ANALYSIS.	+
		3.6+2		Priv	RIBON	Jan 70 - . DATA FOR COMPILATION.	
		3.6+3		Data	EXFOR20149.035	May 73 1PNT.SP.CUT(0).	
Lvl Density	-		FEI Theo	Conf	70Helsinki 2 885	Jun 70 Ignatjuk+76. SUPERFLUID CFD FERMI-TH	
Lvl Density	None		MUN Theo	Jour	NP/A 217 269	Dec 73 Dilg+ A,DELTA. BACK SHIFTED FERMIGAS	
Lvl Density	None		COP Theo	Jour	NP/A 222 493	Apr 74 Dossing+COLL ROTAT.SPAC. ACCUR ESTIM	
Lvl Density	None		ROC Theo	Jour	NP/A 223 577	May 74 Huizenga+ EXP CFD MICROSC TH SPH NUC	
Lvl Density	+2	+3	FEI Eval	Rept	YK-8/2 97	Sep 72 Abagyan+ LVL DENSITY PARAMETER,TBL	
				Rept	INDC(CCP)-39	Jul 74 .PAGE 102.ENGLISH OF YK-8/2 97	

54 Xenon 131

Quantity	Energy (ev) Min	Max	Lab	Type	Documentation Ref Vol Page	Author, Comments Date	Data
Evaluation	1.0-3	1.5+7	AUA Eval	Rept	AAEC/TM-549	Jun 70 Cook.TOT,EL,INEL,NONEL,CAPT SIGS,NDG	+
				Rept	AAEC/E-214	Jun 71 Bertram+GROUP SIGMAS SAME QUANTS.NDG	
				Rept	AAEC/TM-587	Mar 71 *DESCRIPTION OF LIBRARY	
	1.0-3	1.5+7		Data	AUSTR-DFN 117.	Nov 71 POINT(223) AND GROUP(127) SIGMAS	
Evaluation	1.0+3	1.0+7	BOL Eval	Rept	CEC(71)-2	71 Benzi+ STAT+EVAP INEL,N2N,NG.TBL	+
	1.0+3	1.0+7		Data	BENZI-DFN 542D	Mar 71 4 QUANTITIES. UK FORMAT	
Evaluation	1.0-5	1.5+7	HED Eval	Prog	HEDL-TME-71143	Oct 71 Schenter+ EVALUATION FOR ENDF/B	
Evaluation	1.0+2	1.5+7	JAE Eval	Rept	JAERI-M-5752	Jul 74 Igarasi+ JNDC FPND WG.TOT,EL,N',CAP	
Total	1.0-3	1.5+7	AUA Eval	Data	AUSTR-DFN 117.	Nov 71 COOK+POINT(223)+GROUP(127)SIG.CF EVL	+
Elastic	1.0-3	1.5+7	AUA Eval	Data	AUSTR-DFN 117.	Nov 71 COOK+POINT(223)+GROUP(127)SIG.CF EVL	+
Tot Inelastc	8.1+4	1.0+7	BOL Eval	Rept	CEC(71)-2	71 Benzi+ STAT MODEL. TBL GIVEN.	+
	8.1+4	1.0+7		Data	BENZI-DFN 542D	Mar 71 51 PNTS	
Tot Inelastc	5.0+5	1.5+7	AUA Eval	Data	AUSTR-DFN 117.	Nov 71 COOK+POINT(11)+GROUP(127)SIG.CF EVL	+
Diff Inelast	8.1+4	1.0+7	BOL Eval	Rept	CEC(71)-2	71 Benzi+ DISCRETE INELASTIC. 6 LVLS	+
	8.0+5	1.0+7		Data	BENZI-DFN 542D	Mar 71 TO CONTINUUM, 29PNTS+ANGDIST+E DIST	
	8.1+4	8.0+5		Data	BENZI-DFN 542D	Mar 71 1ST- 6TH LVL+ANGDIST+E DIST	
Nonelastic	1.0-3	1.5+7	AUA Eval	Data	AUSTR-DFN 117.	Nov 71 COOK+POINT(223)+GROUP(127)SIG.CF EVL	+
Absorption	4.1-1	1.0+7	GA Eval	Prog	GA-2451	Aug 61 Joanou+ 68 GROUP DATA FOR GAM-I	
Absorption	1.0-3	1.0+7	JUL Eval	Rept	JUEL-678-RG	Jul 70 Liu. EVALUATION+CALC,GRPH,FN OF E	
Absorption	Pile		CRC Eval	Conf	73Paris 1 459	Mar 73 Walker.FISS PRODUCT ABS,TBL PILE SIG	
Res Int Abs	None		CRC Eval	Rept	AECL-1054	Mar 60 Walker. (CRP-913) REDUCED RES. INT.	
Res Int Abs	None		ORL Eval	Rept	ORNL-2869	Mar 60 Nephew.1/V UP +TO100EV.ALSO 14 EV-UP	
Res Int Abs	5.0-1		BOL Eval	Rept	RT/FI-4	Jan 67 Palmucci. CALC FROM (N,G) RES PARAMS	
Res Int Abs	None		GA Eval	Prog	GA-12071	Sep 71 Mathews+ RECOMMENDED VALUES	

54 Xenon 131

Quantity	Energy (ev) Min	Max	Lab	Type	Documentation Ref Vol Page	Date	Author, Comments	Data
Res Int Abs	5.5−1		CRC	Eval Rept	AECL−3037 1	Jan 72	Walker.REDUCED RES INT FROM RES PARS	
Res Int Abs	5.0−1		AUA	Eval Rept	AAEC/TM−619	Sep 72	Clayton.CALC FROM SIG LIBRARY,TABLE	
Res Int Abs	4.6−1	1.0+6	RCN	Theo Rept	RCN−191	Jul 73	Lautenbach.CAPT INT FROM GROUP SIGMA	
Res Int Abs	5.5−1	+6	SAC	Revw Conf	IAEA−169 1 235	74	Ribon.CAPTURE,STATUS CFD REQUEST,TBL	
Res Int Abs	+0	+5	WIN	Revw Conf	IAEA−169 3 163	74	Pope+ DATA FILE CALC CFD XPTAL VALUE	
(n,γ)	Pile		MCM	Expt Jour	PR 80 296	Oct 50	Macnamara+ MASS SPEC. ABUNDANCE VAR.	+
	Pile			Data	EXFOR11858.008	Jun 76	. 1 PT. SIGMA.	
(n,γ)	Maxwl		CRC	Eval Prog	AECL−1054	Mar 60	Walker. (CRRP−913)	
(n,γ)	5.0−3	2.5+0	GA	Eval Rept	GA−2113	Jun 61	Wikner+ TABLE + CURVE, 100 E POINTS	
(n,γ)	2.8−3	1.0+6	GA	Eval Jour	NSE 12 115	Jan 62	Garrison+ EVAL FROM XPT+AVERAGE RES	
(n,γ)	Pile		CRC	Expt Prog	EANDC(CAN)−16	Jan 63	Eastwood+P6 NRX SPECT 2690B INC 1/V	+
	Pile			Data	EXFOR11849.010	Jun 76	. 1 PT. SIGMA.	
(n,γ)	2.5−2		BOL	Eval Jour	RT/FI−4	Jan 67	Palmucci. CALC FROM RES PARAMETERS	
(n,γ)	Maxwl		AUA	Theo Jour	NSE 31 234	Feb 68	Cook+ STATISTICAL CALC CFD EXPT	
(n,γ)	5.0+3	1.0+5	AUA	ExTh Rept	AAEC/E−198	May 69	Musgrove.S+P+D WAVE SIGMAS CALC,TBL	+
(n,γ)	3.0+4		AUA	Theo Rept	AAEC/E−211	Nov 70	Musgrove. SIGMA GIVEN AND CFD OTHER	
(n,γ)	1.0+3	1.0+7	BOL	Eval Rept	CEC(71)−2	71	Benzi+ OPTMOD EVAL.TBL GIVEN.	+
				Rept	CEC(70)−2	Apr 70	− +. GRAPH	
				Rept	CCDN−NW/10	Dec 69	− +H−F MOD,AXEL G(G)EST,ALL DATA	
				Conf	66Paris 1 537	Oct 66	− + STATMOD.TBL AV VALS.SUPERSEDD	
	1.0+3	1.0+7		Data	BENZI−DFN 542D	Mar 71	68 PNTS	
(n,γ)	Maxwl		GA	Eval Prog	GA−12071	Sep 71	Mathews+ RECOMMENDED VALUES	
(n,γ)	1.0−3	1.5+7	AUA	Eval Data	AUSTR−DFN 117.	Nov 71	COOK+POINT(223)+GROUP(127)SIG.CF EVL	+
(n,γ)	Maxwl		CRC	Eval Rept	AECL−3037 1	Jan 72	Walker.RECOMMENDED SIG,DETAILED TBL	
(n,γ)	Maxwl		IAE	Revw Rept	IAEA−143 897	Apr 72	Lemmel.RECENT EVALUATIONS,TABLE	
	2.5−2			Rept	IAEA−143 897	Apr 72	− .RECENT EVALUATIONS,TABLE+GRPH	
(n,γ)	2.5−2		AUA	Eval Rept	AAEC/TM−619	Sep 72	Clayton.CALC FROM SIG LIBRARY,TABLE	
(n,γ)		1.1+7	RCN	Theo Rept	RCN−191	Jun 73	Lautenbach. GROUP CONSTANTS TBL	
(n,γ)	Fiss		SAC	Revw Conf	IAEA−169 1 235	74	Ribon.STATUS SIG CFD REQUESTS,TABLE	
	2.5−2	3.0+4		Conf	IAEA−169 1 235	74	− .STATUS SIG CFD REQUESTS,TABLE	
(n,γ)	Fiss		WIN	Revw Conf	IAEA−169 3 137	74	Dean. POINT DATA AVG OVER STAND SPEC	
	Maxwl	Fiss		Conf	IAEA−169 3 163	74	Pope+ MAXW+FIS−SPEC AVG DATA CFD XPT	
(n,γ)	1.0+3	1.0+7	FEI	Eval Rept	YK−8/2 97	Sep 72	Abagjan+ AVG SIG(ENERGY−GROUPS),TABL	
				Rept	INDC(CCP)−39	Jul 74	.P102. ENGLISH OF YK−8/2 97	
(n,γ)	Fast		RCN	Expt Rept	ECN−10	Oct 76	Veenema+ STEK REACTIVITY WORTHS TBL.	
(n,γ)	1.0−3	1.0+7	RCN	Revw Rept	ECN−12	Nov 76	Gruppelaar+ INTERCOMP. RECENT WORKS	
Spect (n,γ)	+1		ITE	Expt Jour	ZET 45 875	Oct 63	Ignat'Ev.GRAPH G−SPEC FROM 1RES	
				Jour	JET 18 602	Mar 64	TRANSLATN.*	
Spect (n,γ)	1.4+1		ITE	Expt Conf	JINR−1845 1400	Jun 64	Beljaev+ TOF,TBL,E−GAMM=4.5 TO6.4MEV	
Spect (n,γ)	1.4+1		BNL	Expt Jour	PR/C 3 1678	Apr 71	Gelletly+ GE(LI) DET.CURVS+TABLES	
Spect (n,γ)	Maxwl		KUR	Expt Jour	YF 13 1129	Jun 71	Groshev+ GE−LI,G−E+INT+LVLS IN GRAPH	+
				Jour	SNP 13 647	Dec 71	. ENGL OF YF 13 1129	
	2.5−2			Data	EXFOR40182.003	Nov 73	.GAM/100N FOR 33 E GVN	
Spect (n,γ)	Pile		KUR	Expt Jour	YF 13 1129	Jun 71	Groshev+ GE−LI,ES+INTENS,G−TRANSITN	
Spect (n,γ)	Maxwl		KFI	Expt Jour	KFKI−71−46	Aug 71	Kardon+ REL INTENS,TBL,LVL SCHEME,Q	+
	Maxwl			Data	EXFOR30170.	May 72	85 DATA LINES	
(n,2n)	6.7+6	1.0+7	BOL	Eval Rept	CEC(71)−2	71	Benzi+ STAT+EVAP MODELS.TBL GIVEN.	+
	6.7+6	1.0+7		Data	BENZI−DFN 542D	Mar 71	8 PNTS +ANGDIST+E DIST	
(n,2n)	1.5+7		DEB	Eval Jour	REA 11 1 153	Mar 73	Boedy+ RECOMM.VALUE FROM N−Z SYSTEM.	
(n,2n)	1.5+7		KFI	Theo Rept	KFKI−73−68	Dec 73	Jeki.NEW FIT,CALC SIG CFD OTHERS,TBL	
(n,p)	Fiss		CRC	Eval Rept	CRC−1003	Dec 60	ROY+ ESTIMATED AVG SIG=0.09MB	
(n,p)	1.4+7		GIT	Expt Jour	NP/A 120 337	Nov 68	Kondaiah+ACT.CS,HL.TBL.CFD.TH,EXPT	+
				Prog	BARC−401	69	.SUPERSEDED	
	1.4+7			Data	EXFOR11884.017	Jun 76	. 1 PT. SIGMA.	
(n,p)	1.5+7		DEB	Comp Jour	REA 7 4 93	Dec 69	Csikai+ SIG+HL COMPILTN,N−ACTIV−ANAL	
(n,p)	1.4+7	1.5+7	JYV	Eval Jour	JU−RR−3/1970	Jun 70	Leppaemaeki+ TABLE OF EVAL AVG SIG	
(n,p)	1.4+7	1.5+7	KAZ	Theo Jour	YF 18 705	Oct 73	Levkovsky.AVERAGED SIG,CALC,TBL	
				Jour	SNP 18 361	Apr 74	. ENGLISH OF YF 18,705	
(n,p)	1.5+7		ARK	Expt Jour	NSE 60 235	Jul 76	Sigg+ACT.TBL OF HL,CS.CFD WITH OTH	+
				Abst	DA/B 37 2237	Nov 76	− .ACT TECH.CFD OTH EXPT AND PRED	
				Diss	SIGG	76	− .ACT.TBLS,GRPHS.CFD OTH.	
	1.5+7			Data	EXFOR10775.011	Jan 79	. 1PT.CS=7.0+−.8 MB.HL GVN	
(n,α)	Fiss		CRC	Eval Rept	CRC−1003	Dec 60	Roy+,ESTIMATED AVG SIG=0.0093MB	
Reson Params	1.4+1	7.6+1	BNL	Expt Jour	PR 116 1516	Dec 59	Mann+	+
	1.4+1	7.6+1		Data	EXFOR11868.012	Jun 76	. 3 RES. EO, WN, WNO	
Reson Params		1.0+6	AUA	Theo Jour	AUJ 20 477	Oct 67	Cook. TBL OF AVG LVL SPACING D,L=0,1	

54 Xenon 131

Quantity	Energy (ev) Min	Max	Lab	Type	Documentation Ref Vol Page	Author, Comments Date	Data
Reson Params	1.4+1	3.9+3	SAC	Expt Rept	CEA – N – 1149	Jan 69 Ribon. TOF.TRANSM + SCT.TBL.	+
	1.0+1	2.0+2		Prog	EANDC(E)127U	Apr 70 Cauvin+SPIN ASSIGN	
	1.4+1	3.9+3		Priv	RIBON	Jan 70 Ribon. DATA FOR COMPILATION.	
	1.4+1	2.8+2		Conf	66Paris 1 119	Oct 66 – +WT,WN WN0,WG FROM SHAPE ANAL	
	1.4+1	3.9+3		Data	EXFOR20149.	May 73 122PTS.WG,AVG WG,WT,J,A*G*WN.	
Reson Params	–		AUA	Theo Rept	AAEC/E – 211	Nov 70 Musgrove. CALCULTD D+GAM WIDTH GIVEN	
Reson Params	1.4+1	2.8+2	CJD	Eval Rept	YK – 7	71 Zakharova+ SURVEY+SYSTEMATICS,GW,TBL	
				Rept	INDC(CCP) – 27	Nov 72 .ENGLISH TRANSLATION OF YK – 7 /71	
Reson Params	–		DUB	Theo Rept	JINR – E4 – 5711	Apr 71 Soloviev.RESONANCE STRUCTURE STUDY	
Reson Params	1.5+2	6.5+2	SAC	ExTh Diss	FRNC – TH – 450	Oct 72 Delaroche.OPTICAL MODEL PARAMETERS	
Reson Params	1.4+1	3.9+3	BNL	Eval Rept	BNL – 50374	Feb 73 Bhat+ J WT WN WG. ENDF/B – 3 DATA.	
Reson Params	None		DUB	Theo Rept	JINR – P4 – 7499	Oct 73 Soloviev+ CALC D CFD EXPTS,TABLE	
Reson Params	+0	+2	BOL	Eval Conf	IAEA – 169 3 123	74 Benzi+ AVG G – WID CFD OTHERS+XPT,TABL	
Reson Params	+1	+3	FEI	Eval Rept	YK – 8/2 97	Sep 72 Abagyan+ AVG G – WID+D AT BINDNG – E,TBL	
				Rept	INDC(CCP) – 39	Jul 74 .PAGE 102.ENGLISH OF YK – 8/2 97	
Strnth Fnctn	–		DUB	Revw Jour	YF 11 111	Jan 70 Malecki+ VALUES FOR TWO SPIN STATES	
				Jour	SNP 11 61	Jul 70 – + ENGL OF YF 11 61.	
Strnth Fnctn	0.0+0	4.0+3	SAC	Expt Rept	CEA – N – 1149	Jan 69 Ribon. FROM RESONANCE ANALYSIS.	+
		4.0+3		Priv	RIBON	Jan 70 – . DATA FOR COMPILATION.	
				Prog	EANDC(E)89U185	Feb 68 Michaudon+L=0,NO VARIATN WITH SPIN.	
		4.0+3		Data	EXFOR20149.041	May 73 1PNT.L=0.	
Strnth Fnctn	–		AUA	Theo Rept	AAEC/E – 211	Nov 70 Musgrove. SMOOTHED S0,S1 AND S2 GIVN	
Strnth Fnctn	None		AUA	Eval Rept	AAEC/E – 277	Mar 73 Musgrove.TBLS EXPTL DATA+BEST VALUES	
Strnth Fnctn	None		KUR	Theo Prog	IAE – 2560	75 Adamchuk+.S0 – VALUE,TBL	
Lvl Density	0.0+0	4.0+3	SAC	Expt Rept	CEA – N – 1149	Jan 69 Ribon. FROM RESONANCE ANALYSIS.	+
		4.0+3		Priv	RIBON	Jan 70 – . DATA FOR COMPILATION.	
		4.0+3		Data	EXFOR20149.042	May 73 1PNT.SP.CUT(0).	
Lvl Density	None		AUW	Theo Conf	70Madurai 2 267	Dec 70 Ramamurty+ A – PARAMETER GVN,LANG'S – TH	
Lvl Density	None		BOL	Eval Conf	IAEA – 169 3 123	74 Benzi+ LVL DENS PARAM BY XPT,GRPH+TB	
Lvl Density	+1	+3	FEI	Eval Rept	YK – 8/2 97	Sep 72 Abagyan+ LVL DENSITY PARAMETER,TBL	
				Rept	INDC(CCP) – 39	Jul 74 .PAGE 102.ENGLISH OF YK – 8/2 97	

54 Xenon 132

Quantity	Energy (ev) Min	Max	Lab	Type	Documentation Ref Vol Page	Author, Comments Date	Data
Evaluation	1.0 – 3	1.5+7	AUA	Eval Rept	AAEC/TM – 549	Jun 70 Cook.TOT,EL,INEL,NONEL,CAPT SIGS,NDG	+
				Rept	AAEC/E – 214	Jun 71 Bertram+GROUP SIGMAS SAME QUANTS.NDG	
				Rept	AAEC/TM – 587	Mar 71 *DESCRIPTION OF LIBRARY	
	1.0 – 3	1.5+7		Data	AUSTR – DFN 118.	Nov 71 POINT(223) AND GROUP(127) SIGMAS	
Evaluation	1.0+3	1.0+7	BOL	Eval Rept	CEC(71) – 2	71 Benzi+ STAT+EVAP MDS.INEL,N2N,NG.TBL	+
	1.0+3	1.0+7		Data	BENZI – DFN 543D	Mar 71 4 QUANTITIES. UK FORMAT	
Total	7.0+6	1.4+7	CJD	Theo Rept	ICD – 5 20	68 Averjanov+ VIBRATION MDL,AT 4ES,TBL	
Total	0.0+0	4.2+3	SAC	Expt Rept	CEA – N – 1149	Jan 69 Ribon. ENRICHED TO 27PC.RES ASSGNMNT	+
	4.2+3			Priv	RIBON	Jan 70 – . NO DATA. ISOTOPIC RES ASSGN.	
	4.2+3			Data	EXFOR20149.043	May 73 0PTS.	
Total	1.0 – 3	1.5+7	AUA	Eval Data	AUSTR – DFN 118.	Nov 71 COOK+POINT(223)+GROUP(127)SIG.CF EVL	+
Elastic	7.0+6	1.4+7	CJD	Theo Rept	ICD – 5 20	68 Averjanov+ VIBRATION MDL,AT 4ES,TBL	
Elastic	1.0 – 3	1.5+7	AUA	Eval Data	AUSTR – DFN 118.	Nov 71 COOK+POINT(223)+GROUP(127)SIG.CF EVL	
Tot Inelastc	7.0+6	1.4+7	CJD	Theo Rept	ICD – 5 20	68 Averjanov+ VIBRATION MDL,AT 4ES,TBL	
Tot Inelastc	6.7+5	1.0+7	BOL	Eval Rept	CEC(71) – 2	71 Benzi+ STAT MODEL. TBL GIVEN.	+
	6.7+5	1.0+7		Data	BENZI – DFN 543D	Mar 71 49 PNTS	
Tot Inelastc	1.0+6	1.5+7	AUA	Eval Data	AUSTR – DFN 118.	Nov 71 COOK+POINT(10)+GROUP(127)SIG.CF EVL	+
Diff Inelast	1.4+7		LRL	Theo Rept	UCRL – 50181	Feb 67 Lutz+ CALC ANG DIST FOR FIRST 2+ LVL	
Diff Inelast	7.0+6	1.4+7	CJD	Theo Rept	ICD – 5 20	68 Averjanov+ TO 1ST LVL,ANGDIST,GRAPH	
Diff Inelast	6.7+5	1.0+7	BOL	Eval Rept	CEC(71) – 2	71 Benzi+ DISCRETE INELASTIC. 6 LVLS	+
	6.7+5	2.0+6		Data	BENZI – DFN 543D	Mar 71 1ST – 6TH LVL +ANGDIST+E DIST	
	2.0+6	1.0+7		Data	BENZI – DFN 543D	Mar 71 TO CONTINUUM, 24PNTS+ANGDIST+E DIST	
Nonelastic	1.0 – 3	1.5+7	AUA	Eval Data	AUSTR – DFN 118.	Nov 71 COOK+POINT(223)+GROUP(127)SIG.CF EVL	+
Absorption	Maxwl		KAP	Expt Jour	NUC 13 30	Dec 55 Halperin+0TO5D2B TBL OF Q S RCTR POIS	
Absorption	4.1 – 1	1.0+7	GA	Eval Prog	GA – 2451	Aug 61 Joanou+ 68 GROUP DATA FOR GAM – I	
Absorption	1.0 – 4	1.0+7	JUL	Eval Rept	JUEL – 678 – RG	Jul 70 Liu. EVALUATION+CALC,GRPH,FN OF E	
Res Int Abs	5.0 – 1		CAN	Expt Prog	EANDC(CAN) – 16	Jan 63 Eastwood+ P6 NRX SPECT .106B INC 1/V	+
	5.0 – 1			Data	EXFOR11849.	Jun 76 . 2 PTS. RI FOR GND + META.	
Res Int Abs	None		GA	Eval Prog	GA – 12071	Sep 71 Mathews+ RECOMMENDED VALUES	
Res Int Abs	5.5 – 1		CRC	Eval Rept	AECL – 3037 1	Jan 72 Walker.REDUCED RES INT TO GND+META	
Res Int Abs	5.0 – 1		AUA	Eval Rept	AAEC/TM – 619	Sep 72 Clayton.CALC FROM SIG LIBRARY,TABLE	
Res Int Abs	4.6 – 1	1.0+6	RCN	Theo Rept	RCN – 191	Jul 73 Lautenbach.CAPT INT FROM GROUP SIGMA	

54 Xenon 132

Quantity	Energy (ev) Min	Max	Lab	Type	Documentation Ref Vol Page	Date	Author, Comments	Data
Res Int Abs	5.5−1	+6	SAC	Revw Conf	IAEA−169 1 235	74	Ribon.CAPTURE,STATUS CFD REQUEST,TBL	
Res Int Abs	+0	+5	WIN	Revw Conf	IAEA−169 3 163	74	Pope+ DATA FILE CALC CFD XPTAL VALUE	
(n,γ)	Maxwl		CRC	Eval Prog	AECL−1054	Mar 60	Walker. (CRRP−913)	
(n,γ)	Pile		CRC	Expt Prog	EANDC(CAN)−16	Jan 63	Eastwood+P6 NRX REACTOR SPECT ISOMER	+
	Pile			Data	EXFOR11849.	Jun 76	. 2 PTS. SIGMA FOR GND + META.	
(n,γ)	Maxwl		UCS	Expt Jour	NSE 31 545	Mar 68	Tilbury+ ACTIV TO GND AND ISOM	+
	Maxwl			Data	EXFOR11927.	Jun 76	. 2 PTS. SIGMA FOR GND + META.	
	−		IEA	Comp Rept	IEA−INF− 10	Aug 68	Atalla. TABLES OF HL,SIG AND GAMM−E	
(n,γ)	Maxwl		GIT	Expt Jour	NP/A 120 329	Nov 68	Kondaiah+ PILE,EPI CD CORR.META,GRND	+
				Prog	BARC−401	69	.SUPERSEDED	
	Maxwl			Data	EXFOR11883.	Jun 76	. 2 PTS. SIGMA FOR GND + META.	
(n,γ)	Maxwl		KFI	Expt Jour	YF 10 27	Jul 69	Kardon+ ISOM SIG RATIO, META/GROUND	+
				Jour	SNP 10 15	Jan 70	. ENGL OF YF 10 27	
	2.5−2			Data	EXFOR30323.004	Feb 76	1 PNT	
(n,γ)	3.0+4		AUA	Theo Rept	AAEC/E−211	Nov 70	Musgrove. SIGMA GIVEN AND CFD OTHER	
(n,γ)	1.0+3	1.0+7	BOL	Eval Rept	CEC(71)−2	71	Benzi+ OPTMOD EVAL.TBL GIVEN.	+
				Rept	CEC(70)−2	Apr 70	− +. GRAPH	
				Rept	CCDN−NW/10	Dec 69	− +H−F MOD,AXEL G(G)EST,ALL DATA	
				Conf	66Paris 1 537	Oct 66	− + STATMOD.TBL AV VALS.SUPERSEDD	
	1.0+3	1.0+7		Data	BENZI−DFN 543D	Mar 71	73 PNTS	
(n,γ)	Maxwl		GA	Eval Prog	GA− 12071	Sep 71	Mathews+ RECOMMENDED VALUES	
(n,γ)	1.0−3	1.5+7	AUA	Eval Data	AUSTR−DFN 118.	Nov 71	COOK+POINT(223)+GROUP(127)SIG.CF EVL	+
(n,γ)	Maxwl		CRC	Eval Rept	AECL−3037 1	Jan 72	Walker.RECOMMEND SIG TO GND+META,TBL	
(n,γ)	2.5−2		AUA	Eval Rept	AAEC/TM−619	Sep 72	Clayton.CALC FROM SIG LIBRARY,TABLE	
(n,γ)	Fast		INL	Expt Prog	USNDC−7 1	Jun 73	Harker+ CFRMF INTEGRAL MEAS.	
(n,γ)		1.1+7	RCN	Theo Rept	RCN−191	Jun 73	Lautenbach. GROUP CONSTANTS TBL	
(n,γ)	2.5−2	3.0+4	SAC	Revw Conf	IAEA−169 1 235	74	Ribon.STATUS SIG CFD REQUESTS,TABLE	
(n,γ)	Fiss		WIN	Revw Conf	IAEA−169 3 137	74	Dean. POINT DATA AVG OVER STAND SPEC	
	Maxwl Fiss			Conf	IAEA−169 3 163	74	Pope+ MAXW+FIS−SPEC AVG DATA CFD XPT	
(n,γ)	1.0+3	1.0+7	FEI	Eval Rept	INDC(CCP)−39	Jul 74	.P102. ENGLISH OF YK−8/2 97	
				Rept	YK− 8/2 97	Sep 72	Abagjan+ AVG SIG(ENERGY−GROUPS),TABL	
Spect (n,γ)	Pile		IPS	Expt Jour	AF 7 239	Mar 54	Bergstroem+.XE133,133M DEC. CONVCOEF	
				Jour	AF 5 191	Aug 52	− .XE133,133M DECAY.LEVELS	
(n,2n)	Fiss		CRC	Eval Rept	CRC−1003	Dec 60	ROY+ ESTIMATED AVG SIG=1.5MB	
(n,2n)	1.4+7		GIT	Expt Jour	NP/A 120 337	Nov 68	Kondaiah+ACT.CS,HL.TBL.CFD.TH,EXPT	+
				Prog	BARC−401	69	.SUPERSEDED	
	1.4+7			Data	EXFOR11884.021	Jun 76	. 1 PT. SIGMA.	
(n,2n)	1.5+7		DEB	Comp Jour	REA 7 4 93	Dec 69	Csikai+ SIG+HL COMPILTN,N−ACTIV−ANAL	
(n,2n)	1.4+7	1.5+7	JYV	Eval Rept	JU−RR−3/1970	Jun 70	Leppaemaeki+ TABLE OF EVAL AVG SIG	
(n,2n)	9.0+6	1.0+7	BOL	Eval Rept	CEC(71)−2	71	Benzi+ STAT+EVAP MODELS.TBL GIVEN.	+
	9.0+6	1.0+7		Data	BENZI−DFN 543D	Mar 71	3 PNTS+ANGDIST+E DIST , 1RANGE	
(n,2n)	1.5+7		DEB	Eval Jour	REA 11 1 153	Mar 73	Boedy+ RECOMM.VALUE FROM N−Z SYSTEM.	
(n,2n)	1.5+7		KFI	Theo Rept	KFKI−73−68	Dec 73	Jeki.NEW FIT,CALC SIG CFD OTHERS,TBL	
(n,2n)	1.5+7		ARK	Expt Jour	NSE 60 235	Jul 76	Sigg+ACT.TBL OF HL,CS.CFD WITH OTH.	+
				Abst	DA/B 37 2237	Nov 76	− .ACT TECH.CFD OTH EXPT AND PRED	
				Diss	SIGG	76	− .TBLS,GRPHS.CFD OTH.	
	1.5+7			Data	EXFOR10775.006	Jan 79	. 1PT.CS =1000+−80 MB.HL GVN.	
(n,2n)	1.5+7		IBJ	Theo Jour	ASL 27 186	77	Rurarz+ ISO RATIO,4MODLS,CFD XPT.TBL	
	1.4+7			Rept	INR−1464 19	May 73	− + ISOMERIC RATIO CFD EXPT,GRAF	
(n,p)	Fiss		CRC	Eval Rept	CRC−1003	Dec 60	ROY+ ESTIMATED AVG SIG=0.02MB	
(n,p)	1.4+7		SAH	Comp Jour	NP 60 273	Nov 64	Chatterjee.MEAN OF EXPT CFD SHELLMOD	
(n,p)	1.4+7		GIT	Expt Jour	NP/A 120 337	Nov 68	Kondaiah+ACT.CS,HL.TBL.CFD.TH,EXPT	+
				Rept	BARC−401	69	.SEE ALSO	
	1.4+7			Data	EXFOR11884.018	Jun 76	. 1 PT. SIGMA.	
(n,p)	1.5+7		DEB	Comp Jour	REA 7 4 93	Dec 69	Csikai+ SIG+HL COMPILTN,N−ACTIV−ANAL	
(n,p)	1.4+7	1.5+7	JYV	Eval Rept	JU−RR−3/1970	Jun 70	Leppaemaeki+ TABLE OF EVAL AVG SIG	
(n,p)	1.5+7		ARK	Expt Jour	NSE 60 235	Jul 76	Sigg+ACT.TBL OF HL,CS.CFD WITH OTH	+
				Abst	DA/B 37 2237	Nov 76	− .ACT TECH.CFD OTH EXPT AND PRED	
				Diss	SIGG	76	− .ACT.TBLS,GRPHS.CFD OTH.	
	1.5+7			Data	EXFOR10775.012	Jan 79	. 1PT.CS =3.7+−.4 MB.	
(n,α)	Fiss		CRC	Eval Rept	CRC−1003	Dec 60	ROY+ ESTIMATED AVG SIG=0.0003MB	
Reson Params		1.0+6	AUA	Theo Jour	AUJ 20 477	Oct 67	Cook. TBL OF AVG LVL SPACING D,L=0,1	
Reson Params	6.4+2	3.9+3	SAC	Expt Rept	CEA−N−1149	Jan 69	Ribon. TOF.TRANSM + SCT.TBL.	+
				Priv	RIBON	Jan 70	− . DATA FOR COMPILATION.	
	6.4+2	3.9+3		Data	EXFOR20149.	May 73	20PTS.WG,WT,J,A*G*WN.	
Reson Params	1.4+1	+1	BNL	Expt Prog	NCSAC−31 28	May 70	Kane+ PROBABLE J GIVEN	
Reson Params	−		AUA	Theo Rept	AAEC/E−211	Nov 70	Musgrove. CALCULTD D+GAM WIDTH GIVEN	

54 Xenon 132

Quantity	Energy (ev) Min	Max	Lab	Type	Documentation Ref Vol Page	Date	Author, Comments	Data
Reson Params	5.1+2		CJD	Eval	Rept YK- 7	71	Zakharova+ SURVEY+SYSTEMATICS,GW,TBL	
					Rept INDC(CCP)- 27	Nov 72	.ENGLISH TRANSLATION OF YK-7 /71	
Reson Params	1.5+2	6.5+2	SAC	ExTh Diss	FRNC- TH- 450	Oct 72	Delaroche.OPTICAL MODEL PARAMETERS	
Reson Params	6.4+2	3.9+3	BNL	Eval	Rept BNL- 50374	Feb 73	Bhat+ J WT WN WG ENDF/B-3 DATA.	
Reson Params	+2	+3	FEI	Eval	Rept YK- 8/2 97	Sep 72	Abagyan+ AVG G-WID+D AT BINDNG-E,TBL	
					Rept INDC(CCP)-39	Jul 74	.PAGE 102.ENGLISH OF YK-8/2 97	
Strnth Fnctn	0.0+0	4.0+3	SAC	Expt	Rept CEA-N-1149	Jan 69	Ribon. FROM RESONANCE ANALYSIS.	+
		4.0+3		Priv	RIBON	Jan 70	- . DATA FOR COMPILATION.	
		4.0+3		Data	EXFOR20149.048	May 73	1PNT.L=0.	
Strnth Fnctn	-		AUA	Theo	Rept AAEC/E-211	Nov 70	Musgrove. SMOOTHED S0,S1 AND S2 GIVN	
Strnth Fnctn	None		OSA	Theo	Conf JAERI-M-5984	Feb 75	Kitazoe+OPT MDLS.GRPH VS A.TBL PARS	
Lvl Density	None		GIT	Expt	Jour NP/A 120 329	Nov 68	Kondaiah+ SPIN CUTOFF FROM ISOMRATIO	
Lvl Density	0.0+0	4.0+3	SAC	Expt	Rept CEA-N-1149	Jan 69	Ribon. FROM RESONANCE ANALYSIS.	+
		4.0+3		Priv	RIBON	Jan 70	- . DATA FOR COMPILATION.	
		4.0+3		Data	EXFOR20149.049	May 73	1PNT.SP.CUT(0).	
Lvl Density	-		FEI	Theo	Conf 70Helsinki 2 885	Jun 70	Ignatjuk+76. SUPERFLUID CFD FERMI-TH	
Lvl Density	None		AUW	Theo	Conf 70Madurai 2 267	Dec 70	Ramamurty+ A-PARAMETER GVN,LANG'S-TH	
Lvl Density	None		MUN	Theo	Jour NP/A 217 269	Dec 73	Dilg+ A,DELTA. BACK SHIFTED FERMIGAS	
Lvl Density	None		COP	Theo	Jour NP/A 222 493	Apr 74	Dossing+COLL ROTAT.SPAC. ACCUR ESTIM	
Lvl Density	None		ROC	Theo	Jour NP/A 223 577	May 74	Huizenga+ EXP CFD MICROSC TH SPH NUC	
Lvl Density	+2	+3	FEI	Eval	Rept YK- 8/2 97	Sep 72	Abagyan+ LVL DENSITY PARAMETER,TBL	
					Rept INDC(CCP)-39	Jul 74	.PAGE 102.ENGLISH OF YK-8/2 97	

54 Xenon 133

Quantity	Energy (ev) Min	Max	Lab	Type	Documentation Ref Vol Page	Date	Author, Comments	Data
Evaluation	1.0-3	1.5+7	AUA	Eval	Rept AAEC/TM-549	Jun 70	Cook.TOT,EL,INEL,NONEL,CAPT SIGS,NDG	+
					Rept AAEC/E-214	Jun 71	Bertram+GROUP SIGMAS SAME QUANTS.NDG	
					Rept AAEC/TM-587	Mar 71	*DESCRIPTION OF LIBRARY	
	1.0-3	1.5+7			Data AUSTR-DFN 119.	Nov 71	POINT(223) AND GROUP(127) SIGMAS	
Evaluation	1.0-5	1.5+7	HED	Eval	Prog HEDL-TME-71143	Oct 71	Schenter+ EVALUATION FOR ENDF/B	
Total	1.0-3	1.5+7	AUA	Eval	Data AUSTR-DFN 119.	Nov 71	COOK+POINT(223)+GROUP(127)SIG.CF EVL	+
Elastic	1.0-3	1.5+7	AUA	Eval	Data AUSTR-DFN 119.	Nov 71	COOK+POINT(223)+GROUP(127)SIG.CF EVL	+
Tot Inelastc	1.0+6	1.5+7	AUA	Eval	Data AUSTR-DFN 119.	Nov 71	COOK+POINT(10)+GROUP(127)SIG.CF EVL	+
Nonelastic	1.0-3	1.5+7	AUA	Eval	Data AUSTR-DFN 119.	Nov 71	COOK+POINT(223)+GROUP(127)SIG.CF EVL	+
Absorption	1.0-4	1.0+7	JUL	Eval	Rept JUEL-678-RG	Jul 70	Liu. EVALUATION+CALC,GRPH,FN OF E	
Res Int Abs	5.0-1		AUA	Eval	Rept AAEC/TM-619	Sep 72	Clayton.CALC FROM SIG LIBRARY,TABLE	
Res Int Abs	5.5-1	+6	SAC	Revw	Conf IAEA-169 1 235	74	Ribon.CAPTURE,STATUS CFD REQUEST,TBL	
Res Int Abs	+0	+5	WIN	Revw	Conf IAEA-169 3 163	74	Pope+ DATA FILE CALCS COMPARED	
(n,γ)	Maxwl		MCM	Expt	Jour JIN 5 253	Feb 58	Kennett+NRX MS 188PM89B THR IFVMI	+
	Maxwl			Data	EXFOR12016.004	Jun 76	. 1 PT. SIGMA.	
(n,γ)	Maxwl		CRC	Eval	Prog AECL-1054	Mar 60	Walker. (CRRP-913)	
(n,γ)	1.0-3	1.5+7	AUA	Eval	Data AUSTR-DFN 119.	Nov 71	COOK+POINT(223)+GROUP(127)SIG.CF EVL	+
(n,γ)	Pile		CRC	Eval	Prog AECL-3037 1	Jan 72	Walker.RECOMMENDED SIG,DETAILED TBL	
(n,γ)	2.5-2		AUA	Eval	Rept AAEC/TM-619	Sep 72	Clayton.CALC FROM SIG LIBRARY,TABLE	
(n,γ)	2.5-2		SAC	Revw	Conf IAEA-169 1 235	74	Ribon.STATUS SIG CFD REQUESTS,TABLE	
	Fiss			Conf	IAEA-169 1 235	74	- .STATUS SIG CFD REQUESTS,TABLE	
(n,γ)	Maxwl	Fiss	WIN	Revw	Conf IAEA-169 3 163	74	Pope+ MAXW+FIS-SPEC AVG DATA CFD XPT	
	Fiss			Conf	IAEA-169 3 137	74	Dean. POINT DATA AVG OVER STAND SPEC	
Reson Params		1.0+6	AUA	Theo	Jour AUJ 20 477	Oct 67	Cook. TBL OF AVG LVL SPACING D,L=0,1	
Reson Params	-		AUA	Theo	Rept AAEC/E-211	Nov 70	Musgrove. CALCULTD D+GAM WIDTH GIVEN	
Strnth Fnctn	-		AUA	Theo	Rept AAEC/E-211	Nov 70	Musgrove. SMOOTHED S0,S1 AND S2 GIVN	

54 Xenon 134

Quantity	Energy (ev) Min	Max	Lab	Type	Documentation Ref Vol Page	Date	Author, Comments	Data
Evaluation	1.0-3	1.5+7	AUA	Eval	Rept AAEC/TM-549	Jun 70	Cook.TOT,EL,INEL,NONEL,CAPT SIGS,NDG	+
					Rept AAEC/E-214	Jun 71	Bertram+GROUP SIGMAS SAME QUANTS.NDG	
					Rept AAEC/TM-587	Mar 71	*DESCRIPTION OF LIBRARY	
	1.0-3	1.5+7			Data AUSTR-DFN 120.	Nov 71	POINT(223) AND GROUP(127) SIGMAS	
Evaluation	1.0+3	1.0+7	BOL	Eval	Rept CEC(71)-2	71	Benzi+ STAT+EVAP MDS.INEL,N2N,NG.TBL	+
	1.0+3	1.0+7			Data BENZI-DFN 545D	Mar 71	4 QUANTITIES. UK FORMAT	
Total	1.0-3	1.5+7	AUA	Eval	Data AUSTR-DFN 120.	Nov 71	COOK+POINT(223)+GROUP(127)SIG.CF EVL	+
Elastic	1.0-3	1.5+7	AUA	Eval	Data AUSTR-DFN 120.	Nov 71	COOK+POINT(223)+GROUP(127)SIG.CF EVL	+
Tot Inelastc	8.5+5	1.0+7	BOL	Eval	Rept CEC(71)-2	71	Benzi+ STAT MODEL. TBL GIVEN.	+
	8.5+5	1.0+7			Data BENZI-DFN 545D	Mar 71	42 PNTS	

54 Xenon 134

Quantity	Energy (ev) Min	Max	Lab	Type	Documentation Ref Vol Page	Date	Author, Comments	Data
Tot Inelastc	1.0+6	1.5+7	AUA	Eval	Data AUSTR-DFN 120.	Nov 71	COOK+POINT(10)+GROUP(127)SIG.CF EVL	+
Diff Inelast	8.5+5	1.0+7	BOL	Eval	Rept CEC(71)-2	71	Benzi+ DISCRETE INELASTIC. 4 LVLS	
	8.5+5	2.0+6			Data BENZI-DFN 545D	Mar 71	1ST- 4TH LVL+ANGDIST+E DIST	
	2.0+6	1.0+7			Data BENZI-DFN 545D	Mar 71	TO CONTINUUM, 23PNTS+ANGDIST+E DIST	
Nonelastic	1.0-3	1.5+7	AUA	Eval	Data AUSTR-DFN 120.	Nov 71	COOK+POINT(223)+GROUP(127)SIG.CF EVL	+
Absorption	Maxwl		KAP	Expt	Jour NUC 13 30	Dec 55	Robb+0TO5D2B TBL OF Q S RCTR POIS	
Absorption	4.1-1	1.0+7	GA	Eval	Prog GA-2451	Aug 61	Joanou+ 68 GROUP DATA FOR GAM-I	
Absorption	1.0-4	1.0+7	JUL	Eval	Rept JUEL-678-RG	Jul 70	Liu. EVALUATION+CALC,GRPH,FN OF E	
Res Int Abs	5.0-1		CRC	Expt	Prog EANDC(CAN)-16	Jan 63	Eastwood+P6 NRX SPECT .302B INC 1/V	+
	5.0-1				Data EXFOR11849.017	Jun 76	. 1 PT. RI	
Res Int Abs	None		GA	Eval	Prog GA- 12071	Sep 71	Mathews+ RECOMMENDED VALUES	
Res Int Abs	5.5-1		CRC	Eval	Rept AECL-3037 1	Jan 72	Walker.REDUCED RES INT TO GND+META	
Res Int Abs	5.0-1		AUA	Eval	Rept AAEC/TM-619	Sep 72	Clayton.CALC FROM SIG LIBRARY,TABLE	
Res Int Abs	4.6-1	1.0+6	RCN	Theo	Rept RCN-191	Jul 73	Lautenbach.CAPT INT FROM GROUP SIGMA	
Res Int Abs	5.5-1	+6	SAC	Revw	Conf IAEA-169 1 235	74	Ribon.CAPTURE,STATUS CFD REQUEST,TBL	
Res Int Abs	+0	+5	WIN	Revw	Conf IAEA-169 3 163	74	Pope+ DATA FILE CALC CFD XPTAL VALUE	
(n,γ)	Pile		MCM	Expt	Jour PR 80 296	50	Macnamara+ MASS SPEC	+
	Pile				Data EXFOR11858.019	Jun 76	. 1 PT, SIG	
(n,γ)	Maxwl		CRC	Eval	Prog AECL-1054	Mar 60	Walker. (CRRP-913)	
(n,γ)	Pile		CRC	Expt	Prog EANDC(CAN)-16	Jan 63	Eastwood+P6 NRX SPECT .302B INC 1/V	+
	Pile				Data EXFOR11849.013	Jun 76	. 1 PT. SIGMA.	
(n,γ)	-		IEA	Comp	Rept IEA-INF- 10	Aug 68	Atalla. TABLES OF HL,SIG AND GAMM-E	
(n,γ)	Maxwl		GIT	Expt	Jour NP/A 120 329	Nov 68	Kondaiah+ PILE,EPI CD CORR.META,GRND	+
					Prog BARC-401	69	.SUPERSEDED	
	Maxwl				Data EXFOR11883.	Jun 76	. 2 PTS. SIGMA FOR GND + META.	
(n,γ)	Maxwl		KFI	Expt	Jour YF 10 27	Jul 69	Kardon+ ISOM SIG RATIO, META/GROUND	+
					Jour SNP 10 15	Jan 70	. ENGL OF YF 10 27	
	2.5-2				Data EXFOR30323.005	Feb 76	1 PNT	
(n,γ)	3.0+4		AUA	Theo	Rept AAEC/E-211	Nov 70	Musgrove. SIGMA GIVEN AND CFD OTHER	
(n,γ)	1.0+3	1.0+7	BOL	Eval	Rept CEC(71)-2	71	Benzi+ OPTMOD EVAL.TBL GIVEN.	+
					Rept CEC(70)-2	Apr 70	- +. GRAPH	
					Rept CCDN-NW/10	Dec 69	- +H-F MOD,AXEL G(G)EST,ALL DATA	
					Conf 66Paris 1 537	Oct 66	- + STATMOD.TBL AV VALS.SUPERSEDD	
	1.0+3	1.0+7			Data BENZI-DFN 545D	Mar 71	68 PNTS	
(n,γ)	Maxwl		GA	Eval	Prog GA- 12071	Sep 71	Mathews+ RECOMMENDED VALUES	
(n,γ)	1.0-3	1.5+7	AUA	Eval	Data AUSTR-DFN 120.	Nov 71	COOK+POINT(223)+GROUP(127)SIG.CF EVL	
(n,γ)	Maxwl		CRC	Eval	Rept AECL-3037 1	Jan 72	Walker.RECOMMEND SIG TO GND+META,TBL	
(n,γ)	2.5-2		AUA	Eval	Rept AAEC/TM-619	Sep 72	Clayton.CALC FROM SIG LIBRARY,TABLE	
(n,γ)	Fast		INL	Eval	Rept USNDC-7 1	Jun 73	Harker+ CFRMF INTEGRAL MEAS.	
(n,γ)		1.1+7	RCN	Theo	Rept RCN-191	Jun 73	Lautenbach. GROUP CONSTANTS TBL	
(n,γ)	2.5-2	3.0+4	SAC	Revw	Conf IAEA-169 1 235	74	Ribon.STATUS SIG CFD REQUESTS,TABLE	
(n,γ)	Fiss		WIN	Revw	Conf IAEA-169 3 137	74	Dean. POINT DATA AVG OVER STAND SPEC	
	Maxwl	Fiss			Conf IAEA-169 3 163	74	Pope+ MAXW+FIS-SPEC AVG DATA CFD XPT	
(n,γ)	1.0+3	1.0+7	FEI	Eval	Rept YK- 8/2 97	Sep 72	Abagjan+ AVG SIG(ENERGY-GROUPS),TABL	
					Rept INDC(CCP)-39	Jul 74	.P102. ENGLISH OF YK-8/2 97	
Spect (n,γ)	Pile		IPS	Expt	Jour AF 5 191	Aug 52	Bergstroem.DECAY GAMMAS	
(n,2n)	Fiss		CRC	Eval	Rept CRC-1003	Dec 60	Roy+,ESTIMATED AVG SIG=2.2MB	
(n,2n)	1.4+7		GIT	Expt	Jour NP/A 120 337	Nov 68	Kondaiah+ACT.CS,HL.TBL.CFD.TH,EXPT	+
					Rept BARC-401	69	.SEE ALSO	
	1.4+7				Data EXFOR11884.	Jun 76	. 2 PTS. SIGMA FOR GND + META.	
(n,2n)	1.5+7		DEB	Comp	Jour REA 7 4 93	Dec 69	Csikai+ SIG+HL COMPILTN,N-ACTIV-ANAL	
(n,2n)	1.4+7	1.5+7	JYV	Eval	Rept JU-RR-3/1970	Jun 70	Leppaemaeki+ TABLE OF EVAL AVG SIG	
(n,2n)	8.5+6	1.0+7	BOL	Eval	Rept CEC(71)-2	71	Benzi+ STAT+EVAP MODELS.TBL GIVEN.	+
	8.5+6	1.0+7			Data BENZI-DFN 545D	Mar 71	4 PNTS, ANGDIST+E DIST, 1 RANGE	
(n,2n)	+7		KFI	Theo	Rept KFKI-71-8	Feb 71	Jeki. CALCULATED CFD EXPTL SIG VALUE	
(n,2n)	1.4+7	1.5+7	IRK	ExTh	Jour APA 33 285	Jul 71	Winiwarter+ ISOMERIC RATIO	
(n,2n)	1.5+7		DEB	Expt	Jour REA 11 1 153	Mar 73	Boedy. COMPILATION+RECOMM.VALUE,TBL	
					Rept IAEA-153 173	73	- . RECOMM. VALUE ONLY	
(n,2n)	1.5+7		TAT	Theo	Jour JP/A 7 1458	Aug 74	Kondaiah. CALC ON STAT MODEL	
(n,2n)	1.5+7		ARK	Expt	Rept NSE 60 235	Jul 76	Sigg+ACT.TBL OF HL,CS.CFD WITH OTH.	
					Abst DA/B 37 2237	Nov 76	- .ACT TECH.CFD OTH EXPT AND PRED	
					Diss SIGG	76	- .TBLS,GRPHS.CFD OTH.2META.	
	1.5+7				Data EXFOR10775.007	Jan 79	. 1PT.META,GND,META+GND CS GVN.	
(n,2n)	1.5+7		IBJ	Theo	Jour ASL 27 186	77	Rurarz+ ISO RATIO,4MODLS,CFD XPT.TBL	
	1.4+7				Rept INR-1464 19	May 73	- + ISOMERIC RATIO CFD EXPT,GRAF	
(n,p)	Fiss		CRC	Eval	Rept CRC-1003	Dec 60	Roy+,ESTIMATED AVG SIG=0.03MB	

54 Xenon 134

Quantity	Energy (ev) Min	Max	Lab	Type	Documentation Ref Vol Page	Date	Author, Comments	Data
(n,p)	1.4+7		GIT	Expt Jour	NP/A 120 337	Nov 68	Kondaiah+ACT.CS,HL.TBL.CFD.TH,EXPT	+
				Rept	BARC-401	69	.SEE ALSO	
	1.4+7			Data	EXFOR11884.019	Jun 76	. 1 PT. SIGMA.	
(n,p)	1.5+7		DEB	Comp Jour	REA 7 4 93	Dec 69	Csikai+ SIG+HL COMPILTN,N-ACTIV-ANAL	
(n,p)	1.4+7	1.5+7	JYV	Eval Rept	JU-RR-3/1970	Jun 70	Leppaemaeki+ TABLE OF EVAL AVG SIG	
(n,p)	1.4+7	1.5+7	KAZ	Theo Jour	YF 18 705	Oct 73	Levkovsky.AVERAGED SIG,CALC,TBL	
				Jour	SNP 18 361	Apr 74	. ENGLISH OF YF.18,705	
(n,p)	1.5+7		ARK	Expt Jour	NSE 60 235	Jul 76	Sigg+ACT.TBL OF HL,CS.CFD WITH OTH	+
				Abst	DA/B 37 2237	Nov 76	- .ACT TECH.CFD OTH EXPT AND PRED	
				Diss	SIGG	76	- .ACT.TBLS,GRPHS.CFD OTH.	
	1.5+7			Data	EXFOR10775.013	Jan 79	. 1PT.CS=1.8+-.3 MB.	
(n,α)	Fiss		CRC	Eval Rept	CRC-1003	Dec 60	Roy+,ESTIMATED AVG SIG=BELO 0.0001MB	
Reson Params		1.0+6	AUA	Theo Jour	AUJ 20 477	Oct 67	Cook. TBL OF AVG LVL SPACING D,L=0,1	
Reson Params	1.0+3		SAC	Expt Rept	CEA-N-1149	Jan 69	Ribon. TOF.TRANSM + SCT.TBL.	+
				Priv	RIBON	Jan 70	- . DATA FOR COMPILATION.	
	4.5+2			Conf	66Paris 1 119	Oct 66	- +WT,WN,WG FROM SHAPE ANALYSIS	
	1.0+3			Data	EXFOR20149.	May 73	2PTS.J,A*G*WN.	
Reson Params	-		AUA	Theo Rept	AAEC/E-211	Nov 70	Musgrove. CALCULTD D+GAM WIDTH GIVEN	
Reson Params	4.5+2		CJD	Eval Rept	YK-7	71	Zakharova+ SURVEY+SYSTEMATICS,GW,TBL	
				Rept	INDC(CCP)-27	Nov 72	.ENGLISH TRANSLATION OF YK-7 /71	
Reson Params	1.5+2	6.5+2	SAC	ExTh Diss	FRNC-TH-450	Oct 72	Delaroche.OPTICAL MODEL PARAMETERS	
Reson Params	1.0+3		BNL	Eval Rept	BNL-50374	Feb 73	Bhat+. J WT WN WG. ENDF/B-3 DATA.	
Reson Params	1.0+3		FEI	Eval Rept	YK-8/2 97	Sep 72	Abagyan+ AVG G-WID+D AT BINDNG-E,TBL	
				Rept	INDC(CCP)-39	Jul 74	.PAGE 102.ENGLISH OF YK-8/2 97	
Strnth Fnctn	-		AUA	Theo Rept	AAEC/E-211	Nov 70	Musgrove. SMOOTHED S0,S1 AND S2 GIVN	
Strnth Fnctn	None		OSA	Theo Conf	JAERI-M-5984	Feb 75	Kitazoe+OPT MDLS.GRPH VS A.TBL PARS	
Lvl Density	None		GIT	Expt Jour	NP/A 120 329	Nov 68	Kondaiah+ SPIN CUTOFF FROM ISOMRATIO	
Lvl Density	None		AUW	Theo Conf	70Madurai 2 267	Dec 70	Ramamurty+ A-PARAMETER GVN,LANG'S-TH	
Lvl Density	1.0+3		FEI	Eval Rept	YK-8/2 97	Sep 72	Abagyan+ LVL DENSITY PARAMETER,TBL	
				Rept	INDC(CCP)-39	Jul 74	.PAGE 102.ENGLISH OF YK-8/2 97	

54 Xenon 135

Quantity	Energy (ev) Min	Max	Lab	Type	Documentation Ref Vol Page	Date	Author, Comments	Data
Evaluation	4.1-1	1.0+7	GA	Eval Prog	GA-2451	Aug 61	Joanou+.68GRP TRANSFER(EL,INEL),ABS	
Evaluation	2.5-2	1.0+7	GEN	Eval Rept	APEX-704	Nov 61	Cooper+. CONTENT OF C-FINE TAPES	
Evaluation	1.0-2	1.0+3	UK	Eval Rept	AEEW-R-116	Jun 62	Sumner.SUPERSEDED.	
Evaluation	1.0-2	1.0+3	UK	Eval Rept	AEEW-R-351	Feb 64	Barrington+(WIN).FROM AEEW-116.	
Evaluation	1.0-3	1.5+7	AUA	Eval Rept	AAEC/TM-549	Jun 70	Cook.TOT,EL,INEL,NONEL,CAPT SIGS,NDG	+
				Rept	AAEC/E-214	Jun 71	Bertram+GROUP SIGMAS SAME QUANTS.NDG	
				Rept	AAEC/TM-587	Mar 71	*DESCRIPTION OF LIBRARY	
	1.0-3	1.5+7		Data	AUSTR-DFN 121.	Nov 71	POINT(223) AND GROUP(127) SIGMAS	
Total	1.5-2	2.0-1	ORL	Expt Jour	PR 102 823	May 56	Bernstein+ CS EXC FN 2.2MEGAB .025EV	
	1.0-2	5.0-1		Conf	55Geneva 4 153	Aug 55	- +.P591,GRAPH,CH+CRYST-SPECT	
Total	1.0-2	+3	ORL	Expt Jour	PR 115 1693	Sep 59	Smith+ TOF, CURVES, .084EV RES	+
	1.0-2	3.2-1		Data	EXFOR12032.002	Jun 76	. 77 PTS, SIGMA.	
Total	1.0-2	1.0+3	UK	Eval Rept	AEEW-R-116	Jun 62	Sumner.TABLE+CURVE.BR-WIGN+DOPPLCORR	+
	1.0-4	1.0+3		Data	UKNDL-DFN 4F	Mar 73	54 PNTS	
Total	1.0-2	1.0+3	UK	Eval Rept	AEEW-R-351	Feb 64	Barrington+(WIN).UKNDL FILE.	
Total	1.0-3	1.5+7	AUA	Eval Data	AUSTR-DFN 121.	Nov 71	COOK+POINT(223)+GROUP(127)SIG.CF EVL	+
Total	-3	1.9+0	THS	Theo Rept	IKE-6 89 65	Jun 75	Keinert. DATA LIBRARY	
Elastic	1.0-2	1.0+3	UK	Eval Rept	AEEW-R-116	Jun 62	Sumner.SUPERSEDED.	+
	1.0-4	1.0+3		Data	UKNDL-DFN 4F	Mar 73	54 PNTS	
Elastic	1.0-2	1.0+3	UK	Eval Rept	AEEW-R-351	Feb 64	Barrington+(WIN).UKNDL FILE.	
Elastic	1.0-3	1.5+7	AUA	Eval Data	AUSTR-DFN 121.	Nov 71	COOK+POINT(223)+GROUP(127)SIG.CF EVL	
Diff Elastic	1.0-2	1.0+3	UK	Eval Rept	AEEW-R-351	Feb 64	Barrington+(WIN).UKNDL FILE.	
Diff Elastic	1.0-4	1.0+3	UK	Eval Data	UKNDL-DFN 4F	Mar 73	1 RNGS,C.M.	
Tot Inelastc	1.0+6	1.5+7	AUA	Eval Data	AUSTR-DFN 121.	Nov 71	COOK+POINT(10)+GROUP(127)SIG.CF EVL	+
Scattering	1.0-3	2.0+0	JUL	Theo Rept	JUEL-746-RG 50	Apr 71	Bonka.KUGEL-THERMOS-LIBR,T=300K,CURV	
Nonelastic	1.0-3	1.5+7	AUA	Eval Data	AUSTR-DFN 121.	Nov 71	COOK+POINT(223)+GROUP(127)SIG.CF EVL	+
Absorption	2.9-2		KAP	Expt Jour	PR 104 555	Oct 56	Deutsch+ 2.45+-0.1MEGABARNS IF MAXWL	
Absorption	1.0-3	1.0+7	JUL	Eval Rept	JUEL-678-RG	Jul 70	Liu. EVALUATION+CALC,GRPH,FN OF E	
Absorption	1.0-3	2.0+0	JUL	Theo Rept	JUEL-746-RG 49	Apr 71	Bonka.KUGEL-THERMOS-LIBR,T=300K,CURV	
Absorption	Pile		CRC	Calc Conf	73Paris 1 459	Mar 73	Walker.FISS PRODUCT ABS,TBL PILE SIG	
Res Int Abs	5.0-1		BOL	Eval Rept	RT/FI-4	Jan 67	Palmucci. CALC FROM (N,G) RES PARAMS	
Res Int Abs	5.0-1		AUA	Eval Rept	AAEC/TM-619	Sep 72	Clayton.CALC FROM SIG LIBRARY,TABLE	
Res Int Abs	5.5-1	+6	SAC	Revw Conf	IAEA-169 1 235	74	Ribon.CAPTURE,STATUS CFD REQUEST,TBL	

54 Xenon 135

Quantity	Energy (ev) Min	Max	Lab	Type	Documentation Ref Vol Page	Date	Author, Comments	Data
Res Int Abs	+0	+5	WIN Revw	Conf	IAEA - 169 3 163	74	Pope+ DATA FILE CALC CFD XPTAL VALUE	
(n,γ)	Maxwl		MCM Expt	Jour	CJP 33 640	Nov 55	Petruska+CHANGE IN CS135 YLD,REL B10	+
	Maxwl			Data	EXFOR12007.002	Jun 76	. 1 PT. ISM RATIO	
(n,γ)	Pile		ANL Expt	Jour	JIN 2 271	Jul 56	Freedman+NEGAT.ACT.METHOD,3EXPERIMT	+
	Pile			Data	EXFOR12015.002	Jun 76	. 1 PT. SIGMA.	
(n,γ)	Maxwl		CCP Expt	Jour	AE 3 546	Dec 57	Ivanov+. 3.2+ −1 MEGABARN FROM F YLD	
				Jour	JNE 9 46	Jun 59	TRANSLATN.*	
				Jour	SJA 3 1436	57	TRANSLATN.*	
(n,γ)	Maxwl		MCM Expt	Jour	CJP 37 531	May 59	Fickel+ NEUT TEMPS 120,137 DEGC	+
	Maxwl			Data	EXFOR12009.002	Jun 76	. 1 PT. SIGMA.	
(n,γ)	Maxwl		CRC Eval	Prog	AECL - 1054	Mar 60	Walker. (CRRP-913)	
(n,γ)	5.0-3	2.5+0	GA Eval	Rept	GA- 2113	Jun 61	Wikner+.TABLE + CURVE.100 E POINTS	
(n,γ)	Pile		CRC Eval	Rept	CRRP - 960	Jan 62	Westcott. EFF SIG TABLE 27 - 827 DEG C	
(n,γ)	2.8-3	1.0+6	GA Eval	Jour	NSE 12 115	Jan 62	Garrison+.EVAL FROM XPT+AVERAGE RES	
(n,γ)	1.0-2	1.0+3	UK Eval	Rept	AEEW-R - 116	Jun 62	Sumner.SUPERSEDED.	+
	1.0-4	1.0+3		Data	UKNDL - DFN 4F	Mar 73	54 PNTS	
(n,γ)	1.0-2	1.0+3	UK Eval	Rept	AEEW-R - 351	Feb 64	Barrington+(WIN).UKNDL FILE.	
(n,γ)	2.5-2		BOL Eval	Rept	RT/FI-4	Jan 67	Palmucci. CALC FROM RES PARAMETERS	
(n,γ)	Maxwl		AUA Theo	Jour	NSE 31 234	Feb 68	Cook+ STATISTICAL CALC CFD EXPT	
(n,γ)	1.0-3	1.5+7	AUA Eval	Data	AUSTR - DFN 121.	Nov 71	COOK+POINT(223)+GROUP(127)SIG.CF EVL	+
(n,γ)	Maxwl		CRC Eval	Rept	AECL - 3037 1	Jan 72	Walker.RECOMMENDED SIG,DETAILED TBL	
(n,γ)	Maxwl		IAE Revw	Rept	IAEA - 143 897	Apr 72	Lemmel.RECENT EVALUATIONS,TABLE	
	2.5-2			Rept	IAEA - 143 897	Apr 72	- .RECENT EVALUATIONS,TABLE+GRPH	
(n,γ)	2.5-2		AUA Eval	Rept	AAEC/TM - 619	Sep 72	Clayton.CALC FROM SIG LIBRARY,TABLE	
(n,γ)	Maxwl	2.5-2	SGA Eval	Conf	73Paris 1 233	Mar 73	Eder+ EVAL G - FACTOR,CALC THR SIG,TBL	
				Rept	SGAE - PH - 141	Feb 73	.SAME AS 73PARIS,EVAL OF EXPTL DATA	
(n,γ)	Maxwl		CRC Expt	Jour	JNE 27 409	Jun 73	Santry+ NTN TEMP 318K,REL CO059 NG	+
	Maxwl			Data	EXFOR10261.002	Apr 78	. 1PT.CS=3.09+ - .07B.	
(n,γ)	2.5-2		SAC Revw	Conf	IAEA - 169 1 235	74	Ribon.STATUS SIG CFD REQUESTS,TABLE	
(n,γ)	Maxwl Fiss		WIN Revw	Conf	IAEA - 169 3 163	74	Pope+ MAXW+FIS - SPEC AVG DATA CFD XPT	
	Fiss			Conf	IAEA - 169 3 137	74	Dean. POINT DATA AVG OVER STAND SPEC	
(n,α)	1.0-2	1.0+3	UK Eval	Rept	AEEW-R - 351	Feb 64	Barrington+(WIN).UKNDL FILE.	
Reson Params	8.5-2		ORL Expt	Jour	PR 102 823	May 56	Bernstein+,CS 2POSSIBLE VALUES WN WG	
				Conf	55Geneva 4 153	Aug 55	- +TOTAL WIDTH,G - FACTOR,P591	
	8.5-2			Data	EXFOR12031.002	Jun 76	1 RES, EO, WNO, WG	
Reson Params	8.5-2		ORL Expt	Jour	PR 115 1693	Sep 59	Smith+ TOF, G WN WG CALCTD	+
	8.5-2			Data	EXFOR12032.003	Jun 76	. 1 RES. EO, WN, WG	
Reson Params	8.4-2		UK Eval	Rept	AEEW-R - 116	Jun 62	Sumner.RECOMMENDED WN(0),WG,G	
Reson Params		1.0+6	AUA Eval	Jour	AUJ 20 477	Oct 67	Cook. TBL OF AVG LVL SPACING D,L=0,1	
Reson Params	-		AUA Theo	Rept	AAEC/E - 211	Nov 70	Musgrove. CALCULTD D+GAM WIDTH GIVEN	
Reson Params	8.5-2		CJD Eval	Rept	YK- 7	71	Zakharova+ SURVEY+SYSTEMATICS,GW,TBL	
				Rept	INDC(CCP) - 27	Nov 72	.ENGLISH TRANSLATION OF YK-7 /71	
Reson Params	None		DUB Theo	Rept	JINR - P4 - 7499	Oct 73	Soloviev+ CALC D CFD EXPTS,TABLE	
Strnth Fnctn	-		AUA Theo	Rept	AAEC/E - 211	Nov 70	Musgrove. SMOOTHED S0,S1 AND S2 GIVN	

54 Xenon 136

Quantity	Energy (ev) Min	Max	Lab	Type	Documentation Ref Vol Page	Date	Author, Comments	Data
Evaluation	1.0-3	1.5+7	AUA Eval	Rept	AAEC/TM - 549	Jun 70	Cook.TOT,EL,INEL,NONEL,CAPT SIGS,NDG	+
				Rept	AAEC/E - 214	Jun 71	Bertram+GROUP SIGMAS SAME QUANTS.NDG	
				Rept	AAEC/TM - 587	Mar 71	*DESCRIPTION OF LIBRARY	
	1.0-3	1.5+7		Data	AUSTR - DFN 122.	Nov 71	POINT(223) AND GROUP(127) SIGMAS	
Evaluation	1.0+3	1.0+7	BOL Eval	Rept	CEC(71) - 2	71	Benzi+ STAT+EVAP MDS.INEL,N2N,NG.TBL	+
	1.0-3	1.0+7		Data	BENZI - DFN 547D	Mar 71	4 QUANTITIES. UK FORMAT	
Total	1.0-3	1.5+7	AUA Eval	Data	AUSTR - DFN 122.	Nov 71	COOK+POINT(223)+GROUP(127)SIG.CF EVL	+
Elastic	1.0-3	1.5+7	AUA Eval	Data	AUSTR - DFN 122.	Nov 71	COOK+POINT(223)+GROUP(127)SIG.CF EVL	+
Tot Inelastc	1.3+6	1.0+7	BOL Eval	Rept	CEC(71) - 2	71	Benzi+ STAT MODEL. TBL GIVEN.	+
	1.3+6	1.0+7		Data	BENZI - DFN 547D	Mar 71	37 PNTS	
Tot Inelastc	2.0-6	1.5+7	AUA Eval	Data	AUSTR - DFN 122.	Nov 71	COOK+POINT(9)+GROUP(127)SIG.CF EVL	+
Diff Inelast	1.3+6	1.0+7	BOL Eval	Rept	CEC(71) - 2	71	Benzi+ DISCRETE INELASTIC. 3 LVLS	+
	3.0+6	1.0+7		Data	BENZI - DFN 547D	Mar 71	TO CONTINUUM, 19PNTS+ANGDIST+E DIST	
	1.3+6	3.0+6		Data	BENZI - DFN 547D	Mar 71	1ST - 3RD LVL+ANGDIST+E DIST	
Nonelastic	1.0-3	1.5+7	AUA Eval	Data	AUSTR - DFN 122.	Nov 71	COOK+POINT(223)+GROUP(127)SIG.CF EVL	
Absorption	4.1-1	1.0+7	GA Eval	Prog	GA- 2451	Aug 61	Joanou+ 68 GROUP DATA FOR GAM - I	
Absorption	1.0-4	1.0+7	JUL Eval	Rept	JUEL - 678 - RG	Jul 70	Liu. EVALUATION+CALC,GRPH,FN OF E	
Res Int Abs	None		GA Eval	Prog	GA- 12071	Sep 71	Mathews+ RECOMMENDED VALUES	
Res Int Abs	5.5-1		CRC Eval	Rept	AECL - 3037 1	Jan 72	Walker.REDUCED RES INT,DETAILED TBL	

54 Xenon 136

Quantity	Energy (ev) Min	Max	Lab	Type	Documentation Ref Vol Page	Author, Comments Date	Data
Res Int Abs	5.0 $-$ 1		AUA	Eval Rept	AAEC/TM $-$ 619	Sep 72 Clayton.CALC FROM SIG LIBRARY,TABLE	
Res Int Abs	4.6 $-$ 1	1.0 $+$ 6	RCN	Theo Rept	RCN $-$ 191	Jul 73 Lautenbach.CAPT INT FROM GROUP SIGMA	
Res Int Abs	5.5 $-$ 1	$+$ 6	SAC	Revw Conf	IAEA $-$ 169 1 235	74 Ribon.CAPTURE,STATUS CFD REQUEST,TBL	
Res Int Abs	$+$ 0	$+$ 5	WIN	Revw Conf	IAEA $-$ 169 3 163	74 Pope$+$ DATA FILE CALCS COMPARED	
(n,γ)	2.5 $-$ 2		ORL	Expt Rept	AECD $-$ 2274	48 Goldhaber.	+
(n,γ)	Pile		MCM	Expt Jour	PR 80 296	50 Macnamara$+$ MASS SPEC.	+
	Pile			Data	EXFOR11858.010	Jun 76 . 1 PT. SIGMA.	
(n,γ)	Fiss		ANL	Expt Jour	PR 78 632	Jun 50 Hughes$+$ REL SIG(THERMAL).	+
	Fiss			Data	EXFOR11596.010	Jun 76 . 1 PT. SIGMA.	
(n,γ)	Fiss		BNL	Expt Jour	PR 91 1423	Sep 53 Hughes$+$.ALSO LVL SPACINGS AT EXCIT E	
(n,γ)	Maxwl		CRC	Eval Prog	AECL $-$ 1054	Mar 60 Walker. (CRRP $-$ 913)	
(n,γ)	Pile		CRC	Eval Prog	EANDC(CAN) $-$ 16	Jan 63 Eastwood$+$P6 NRX SPECT .302B INC 1/V	
(n,γ)	Maxwl		ISP	Expt Jour	JIN 27 1175	Jun 65 BRESESTI .281$+-$.028B	+
	2.5 $-$ 2			Data	EXFOR20630.003	Oct 76 1PNT.SIGMA.	
(n,γ)	$-$		IEA	Comp Rept	IEA $-$ INF $-$ 10	Aug 68 Atalla. TABLES OF HL,SIG AND GAMM $-$ E	
(n,γ)	Maxwl		GIT	Expt Jour	NP/A 120 329	Nov 68 Kondaiah$+$ PILE,EPI CD CORR.HL 3.9MIN	+
				Prog	BARC $-$ 401	69 .SUPERSEDED	
	Maxwl			Data	EXFOR11883.007	Jun 76 . 1 PT. SIGMA	
(n,γ)	1.0 $+$ 3	1.0 $+$ 7	BOL	Eval Rept	CCDN $-$ NW/10	Dec 69 Benzi$+$H $-$ F MOD,AXEL G(G)EST,ALL DATA	+
				Rept	CEC(71) $-$ 2	71 $-$ $+$ OPTMOD EVAL.TBL GIVEN.	
				Rept	CEC(70) $-$ 2	Apr 70 $-$ $+$. GRAPH	
				Conf	66Paris 1 537	Oct 66 $-$ $+$ STATMOD.TBL AV VALS.SUPERSEDD	
	1.0 $+$ 3	1.0 $+$ 7		Data	BENZI $-$ DFN 547D	Mar 71 65 PNTS	
(n,γ)	3.0 $+$ 4		AUA	Theo Rept	AAEC/E $-$ 211	Nov 70 Musgrove. SIGMA GIVEN AND CFD OTHER	
(n,γ)	1.0 $-$ 3	1.5 $+$ 7	AUA	Eval Data	AUSTR $-$ DFN 122.	Nov 71 COOK$+$POINT(223)$+$GROUP(127)SIG.CF EVL	+
(n,γ)	Maxwl		CRC	Eval Rept	AECL $-$ 3037 1	Jan 72 Walker.RECOMMENDED SIG,DETAILED TBL	
(n,γ)	2.5 $-$ 2		AUA	Eval Rept	AAEC/TM $-$ 619	Sep 72 Clayton.CALC FROM SIG LIBRARY,TABLE	
(n,γ)		1.1 $+$ 7	RCN	Theo Rept	RCN $-$ 191	Jun 73 Lautenbach. GROUP CONSTANTS TBL	
(n,γ)	2.5 $-$ 2	3.0 $+$ 4	SAC	Revw Conf	IAEA $-$ 169 1 235	74 Ribon.STATUS SIG CFD REQUESTS,TABLE	
(n,γ)	Fiss		WIN	Revw Conf	IAEA $-$ 169 3 137	74 Dean. POINT DATA AVG OVER STAND SPEC	
	Maxwl Fiss			Conf	IAEA $-$ 169 3 163	74 Pope$+$ MAXW$+$FIS $-$ SPEC AVG DATA CFD XPT	
(n,γ)	1.0 $+$ 3	1.0 $+$ 7	FEI	Eval Rept	YK $-$ 8/2 97	Sep 72 Abagjan$+$ AVG SIG(ENERGY $-$ GROUPS),TABL	
				Rept	INDC(CCP) $-$ 39	Jul 74 .P102. ENGLISH OF YK $-$ 8/2 97	
(n,2n)	Fiss		CRC	Eval Rept	CRC $-$ 1003	Dec 60 Roy$+$,ESTIMATED AVG SIG=4.8MB	
(n,2n)	1.4 $+$ 7		GIT	Expt Jour	NP/A 120 337	Nov 68 Kondaiah$+$ACT.CS,HL.TBL.CFD.TH,EXPT	+
				Prog	BARC $-$ 401	69 .SUPERSEDED	
	1.4 $+$ 7			Data	EXFOR11884.	Jun 76 . 2 PTS. SIGMA TO GND $+$ ISM.	
(n,2n)	1.5 $+$ 7		DEB	Comp Jour	REA 7 4 93	Dec 69 Csikai$+$ SIG$+$HL COMPILTN,N $-$ ACTIV $-$ ANAL	
(n,2n)	1.4 $+$ 7	1.5 $+$ 7	JYV	Eval Jour	JU $-$ RR $-$ 3/1970	Jun 70 Leppaemaeki$+$ TABLE OF EVAL AVG SIG	
(n,2n)	7.9 $+$ 6	1.0 $+$ 7	BOL	Eval Rept	CEC(71) $-$ 2	71 Benzi$+$ STAT$+$EVAP MODELS.TBL GIVEN.	+
	7.9 $+$ 6	1.0 $+$ 7		Data	BENZI $-$ DFN 547D	Mar 71 6 PNTS$+$ANGDIST$+$E DIST, 1 RANGE	
(n,2n)	$+$ 7		KFI	Theo Rept	KFKI $-$ 71 $-$ 8	Feb 71 Jeki. CALCULATED CFD EXPTL SIG VALUE	
(n,2n)	1.4 $+$ 7	1.5 $+$ 7	IRK	ExTh Jour	APA 33 285	Jul 71 Winiwarter$+$ ISOMERIC RATIO	
(n,2n)	1.5 $+$ 7		DEB	Eval Jour	REA 11 1 153	Mar 73 Boedy. COMPILATION$+$RECOMM.VALUE,TBL	
				Rept	IAEA $-$ 153 173	73 $-$. RECOMM. VALUE ONLY	
(n,2n)	1.5 $+$ 7		TAT	Theo Jour	JP/A 7 1458	Aug 74 Kondaiah. CALC ON STAT MODEL	
(n,2n)	1.5 $+$ 7		ARK	Expt Jour	NSE 60 235	Jul 76 Sigg$+$ACT.TBL OF HL,CS.CFD WITH OTH	+
				Abst	DA/B 37 2237	Nov 76 $-$ .ACT TECH.CFD OTH EXPT AND PRED	
				Diss	SIGG	76 $-$ .TBLS,GRPHS.CFD OTH.2META.	
	1.5 $+$ 7			Data	EXFOR10775.008	Jan 79 . 1PT.META,GND,META$+$GND CS GVN.	
(n,2n)	1.5 $+$ 7		IBJ	Theo Jour	ASL 27 186	77 Rurarz$+$ ISO RATIO,4MODLS,CFD XPT.TBL	
	1.4 $+$ 7			Rept	INR $-$ 1464 19	May 73 $-$ $+$ ISOMERIC RATIO CFD EXPT,GRAF	
(n,p)	Fiss		CRC	Eval Rept	CRC $-$ 1003	Dec 60 Roy$+$,ESTIMATED AVG SIG=0.0005MB	
(n,α)	Fiss		CRC	Eval Rept	CRC $-$ 1003	Dec 60 Roy$+$,ESTIMATED AVG SIG=BELO 0.0001MB	
Reson Params		1.0 $+$ 6	AUA	Theo Jour	AUJ 20 477	Oct 67 Cook. TBL OF AVG LVL SPACING D,L=0,1	
Reson Params	$-$		AUA	Theo Rept	AAEC/E $-$ 211	Nov 70 Musgrove. CALCULTD D$+$GAM WIDTH GIVEN	
Reson Params	$+$ 2	$+$ 3	FEI	Eval Rept	YK $-$ 8/2 97	Sep 72 Abagjan$+$ AVG G $-$ WID$+$D AT BINDNG $-$ E,TBL	
				Rept	INDC(CCP) $-$ 39	Jul 74 .PAGE 102.ENGLISH OF YK $-$ 8/2 97	
Strnth Fnctn	$-$		AUA	Theo Rept	AAEC/E $-$ 211	Nov 70 Musgrove. SMOOTHED S0,S1 AND S2 GIVN	
Lvl Density	None		ROC	Theo Jour	NP/A 223 577	May 74 Huizenga$+$ EXP CFD MICROSC TH SPH NUC	
Lvl Density	$+$ 2	$+$ 3	FEI	Eval Rept	YK $-$ 8/2 97	Sep 72 Abagjan$+$ LVL DENSITY PARAMETER,TBL	
				Rept	INDC(CCP) $-$ 39	Jul 74 .PAGE 102.ENGLISH OF YK $-$ 8/2 97	

54 Xenon 137

Quantity	Energy (ev) Min	Max	Lab	Type	Documentation Ref Vol Page	Author, Comments Date	Data
Reson Params	$-$		AUA	Theo Rept	AAEC/E $-$ 211	Nov 70 Musgrove. CALCULTD D$+$GAM WIDTH GIVEN	

54 Xenon 137

Quantity	Energy (ev) Min	Max	Lab	Type	Documentation Ref Vol Page	Author, Comments Date	Data
Strnth Fnctn	–		AUA	Theo Rept	AAEC/E – 211	Nov 70 Musgrove. SMOOTHED S0,S1 AND S2 GIVN	

54 Xenon 138

Quantity	Energy (ev) Min	Max	Lab	Type	Documentation Ref Vol Page	Author, Comments Date	Data
Reson Params	–		AUA	Theo Rept	AAEC/E – 211	Nov 70 Musgrove. CALCULTD D+GAM WIDTH GIVEN	
Strnth Fnctn	–		AUA	Theo Rept	AAEC/E – 211	Nov 70 Musgrove. SMOOTHED S0,S1 AND S2 GIVN	

55 Cesium 125

Quantity	Energy (ev) Min	Max	Lab	Type	Documentation Ref Vol Page	Date	Author, Comments	Data
Reson Params	–		AUA	Theo Rept	AAEC/E – 211	Nov 70	Musgrove. CALCULTD D+GAM WIDTH GIVEN	
Strnth Fnctn	–		AUA	Theo Rept	AAEC/E – 211	Nov 70	Musgrove. SMOOTHED S0,S1 AND S2 GIVN	

55 Cesium 126

Quantity	Energy (ev) Min	Max	Lab	Type	Documentation Ref Vol Page	Date	Author, Comments	Data
Reson Params	–		AUA	Theo Rept	AAEC/E – 211	Nov 70	Musgrove. CALCULTD D+GAM WIDTH GIVEN	
Strnth Fnctn	–		AUA	Theo Rept	AAEC/E – 211	Nov 70	Musgrove. SMOOTHED S0,S1 AND S2 GIVN	

55 Cesium 127

Quantity	Energy (ev) Min	Max	Lab	Type	Documentation Ref Vol Page	Date	Author, Comments	Data
Reson Params	–		AUA	Theo Rept	AAEC/E – 211	Nov 70	Musgrove. CALCULTD D+GAM WIDTH GIVEN	
Strnth Fnctn	–		AUA	Theo Rept	AAEC/E – 211	Nov 70	Musgrove. SMOOTHED S0,S1 AND S2 GIVN	
Lvl Density	–		HAM	Expt Jour	ZN/A 15 200	Mar 60	Bormann+NUCL TEMP FOR (N,P),(N,NP)	

55 Cesium 128

Quantity	Energy (ev) Min	Max	Lab	Type	Documentation Ref Vol Page	Date	Author, Comments	Data
Reson Params	–		AUA	Theo Rept	AAEC/E – 211	Nov 70	Musgrove. CALCULTD D+GAM WIDTH GIVEN	
Strnth Fnctn	–		AUA	Theo Rept	AAEC/E – 211	Nov 70	Musgrove. SMOOTHED S0,S1 AND S2 GIVN	

55 Cesium 129

Quantity	Energy (ev) Min	Max	Lab	Type	Documentation Ref Vol Page	Date	Author, Comments	Data
(n,p)	Maxwl		IFU	Theo Rept	ICD – 4 20	67	Dadakina+ PENETR COEFF CALC,TABLE	
Reson Params	–		AUA	Theo Rept	AAEC/E – 211	Nov 70	Musgrove. CALCULTD D+GAM WIDTH GIVEN	
Strnth Fnctn	–		AUA	Theo Rept	AAEC/E – 211	Nov 70	Musgrove. SMOOTHED S0,S1 AND S2 GIVN	

55 Cesium 130

Quantity	Energy (ev) Min	Max	Lab	Type	Documentation Ref Vol Page	Date	Author, Comments	Data
Reson Params	–		AUA	Theo Rept	AAEC/E – 211	Nov 70	Musgrove. CALCULTD D+GAM WIDTH GIVEN	
Strnth Fnctn	–		AUA	Theo Rept	AAEC/E – 211	Nov 70	Musgrove. SMOOTHED S0,S1 AND S2 GIVN	

55 Cesium 131

Quantity	Energy (ev) Min	Max	Lab	Type	Documentation Ref Vol Page	Date	Author, Comments	Data
(n,p)	Maxwl		IFU	Theo Rept	ICD – 4 20	67	Dadakina+ PENETR COEFF CALC,TABLE	
Reson Params	–		AUA	Theo Rept	AAEC/E – 211	Nov 70	Musgrove. CALCULTD D+GAM WIDTH GIVEN	
Strnth Fnctn	–		AUA	Theo Rept	AAEC/E – 211	Nov 70	Musgrove. SMOOTHED S0,S1 AND S2 GIVN	

55 Cesium 132

Quantity	Energy (ev) Min	Max	Lab	Type	Documentation Ref Vol Page	Date	Author, Comments	Data
(n,p)	Maxwl		IFU	Theo Rept	ICD – 4 20	67	Dadakina+ PENETR COEFF CALC,TABLE	
(n,α)	Maxwl		ILL	Expt Conf	76Corsica 39	May 76	Hagberg+ NOT SEEN. UPPER LIMIT GIVEN	
Reson Params	–		AUA	Theo Rept	AAEC/E – 211	Nov 70	Musgrove. CALCULTD D+GAM WIDTH GIVEN	
Strnth Fnctn	–		AUA	Theo Rept	AAEC/E – 211	Nov 70	Musgrove. SMOOTHED S0,S1 AND S2 GIVN	
Lvl Density	9.0+6	1.6+7	ANL	Eval Rept	ANL – 75 – 34	Jun 75	Davey+N2NEVAL.CONSTANT T,LVL DEN FIT	

55 Cesium 133

Quantity	Energy (ev) Min	Max	Lab	Type	Documentation Ref Vol Page	Date	Author, Comments	Data
Evaluation	5.0+5	1.5+7	LRL	Eval Rept	UCRL – 5351	Nov 58	Howerton. CURVES	
Evaluation	1.0–3	1.5+7	AUA	Eval Rept	AAEC/TM – 549	Jun 70	Cook.TOT,EL,INEL,NONEL,CAPT SIGS,NDG	+
				Rept	AAEC/E – 214	Jun 71	Bertram+GROUP SIGMAS SAME QUANTS.NDG	
				Rept	AAEC/TM – 587	Mar 71	*DESCRIPTION OF LIBRARY	
	1.0–3	1.5+7		Data	AUSTR – DFN 123.	Nov 71	POINT(223) AND GROUP(127) SIGMAS	

55 Cesium 133

Quantity	Energy (ev) Min	Max	Lab	Type	Documentation Ref Vol Page	Date	Author, Comments	Data
Evaluation	1.0+3	1.0+7	BOL	Eval	Rept CEC(71)-2	71	Benzi+ STAT+EVAP MDS.INEL,N2N,NG.TBL	+
	1.0+3	1.0+7			Data BENZI-DFN 544D	Mar 71	4 QUANTITIES. UK FORMAT	
Evaluation	+0	+6	BNL	Eval	Rept BNL-50383	Apr 73	Bhat+	
Evaluation	1.0+2	1.5+7	JAE	Eval	Rept JAERI-M-5752	Jul 74	Igarasi+ JNDC FPND WG.TOT,EL,N',CAP	
Total	8.0-1	9.0+1	BNL	Expt	Jour PR 93 1030	Mar 54	Landon+ BE CRYSTLSPECTR CSF SAMPLE	+
	8.0-1	9.0+1			Data EXFOR12029.004	Jun 76	. 48 PTS. SIGMA.	
Total	1.1-1	5.7+2	BNL	Expt	Jour PR 99 10	Jul 55	Harvey+	+
	1.1-1	5.7+2			Data EXFOR11917.034	Jun 76	. 188 PTS. SIGMA.	
Total	1.0+3	4.5+3	DKE	Expt	Jour PR 105 198	Jan 57	Newson+ TRNS 10.2B AVGD 2-4.5KEV	
Total	1.0+2	3.5+3	COL	Expt	Jour PR/B 137 547	Feb 65	Garg+ NEVIS, TOF, CURVES	+
	1.0+2	4.0+3			Data EXFOR11905.012	Jun 76	. 7551 PTS. SIGMA.	
Total	1.4+7		DEB	Expt	Jour AHP 20 193	Jan 66	Angeli.SIG=4.96+-0.21B, R=7.67FERMI	+
					Jour AK 7 95	Jun 65	- . ORGANIC SCIN,TOT=4.96+-.21B	
	1.4+7				Data EXFOR30174.002	Jul 72	SIGMA AT 14.1 MEV	
Total	2.8-2	3.0-1	KAP	Expt	Priv HICKMAN	Jun 66	Brazos.	+
	2.8-2	3.0-1			Data EXFOR12087.002	Jun 76	. 7 PTS, SIG	
Total	1.7+0	1.1+3	KIL	Expt	Jour AKE 14 271	Aug 69	Jung+ TOF. PARTIAL WIDTHS ONLY.	
					Conf 70Helsinki 1 679	Jun 70	- + PRELIMINARY RESULTS	
	1.7+0	1.1+3			Data EXFOR20553.	Apr 76	0PTS. SEE RESONANCE PARAMETERS.	
Total	2.5+6	1.5+7	BNW	Expt	Jour PR/C 3 576	Feb 71	Foster+ TRANS,CURVS,CFD OTHERS+TH	+
					Jour NIM 36 1	Sep 65	.EXPT DETAILS	
	2.3+6	1.5+7			Data EXFOR10047.059	Aug 73	. 243 PTS.	
Total	1.4+7		KOS	Expt	Jour AHP 30 115	Oct 71	Angeli+EXPT,DATA TABLE,LITER. SURVEY	
	1.4+7				Data EXFOR30141.013	Jan 72	SIGMA AT 14.7 MEV GIVEN	
Total	1.0-3	1.5+7	AUA	Eval	Data AUSTR-DFN 123.	Nov 71	COOK+ POINT(223)+GROUP(127)SIG.CF EVL	+
Total	2.7+3		MUN	Expt	Prog EANDC(E)150U	Oct 72	Dilg+ AVERAGE TOT XSECT+S0	+
					Conf 71Albany 327	Aug 71	- +TRNS.AVG CS GVN.31 ELEMENT GRP	
	2.7+3				Data EXFOR20583.011	May 76	1PNT.	
Total	1.2+5	1.9+6	PEL	Expt	Jour ZP 271 1	Nov 74	Barnard+.GRPH,CFD WITH OPTMOD CALC.	
	2.5+5	1.2+6			Rept PEL-191	Oct 69	Coetzee.TRANS,SIG AT 482 ES,TBL,GRPH	
	2.5+5	1.2+6			Data EXFOR30178.003	Feb 72	.SIG AT 482 ES. TRANSMISSION	
Total	1.0-2	1.0+1	KAP	Expt	Rept CONF-758-2	Jan 65	Hickman. TOF+SLOW CHOPPER.	+
	1.6-2	4.4+0			Data EXFOR12004.002	Jun 76	. 61 PTS. SIGMA.	
Total		4.0+2	ITE	Expt	Conf 76Lowell 1251	Jul 76	Kalebin+TRNS.RES PARS DRVD.NDG	
Elastic	2.5-2		ORL	Expt	Jour PR 81 527	Feb 51	Shull+	+
	2.5-2				Data EXFOR11043.	Jun 76	. 3 PTS, BAS, COH, COH AMP	
Elastic	1.2+5	1.1+6	PEL	Expt	Rept PEL-191	Oct 69	Coetzee.LEG FIT TO ANGDIST, TBL,GRPH	
	1.2+5	1.1+6			Data EXFOR30179.010	Feb 72	.FROM LEG FIT OF DIFFSIG. AT 19 ES.	
Elastic	7.7-2		ANL	Expt	Jour ACRA 27 494	Sep 71	COX+ COH SCAT AMP	
Elastic	1.0-3	1.5+7	AUA	Eval	Data AUSTR-DFN 123.	Nov 71	COOK+ POINT(223)+GROUP(127)SIG.CF EVL	+
Elastic	8.8+5		ANL	Expt	Rept ANL-7935	Jun 72	COX+ 4 PI B(O)	+
	8.8+5				Data EXFOR10332.110	Jun 74	. 1 PT.	
Diff Elastic	8.8+5		ANL	Expt	Rept ANL-7935	Jun 72	COX+ CFD OPTMOD, HAUSER-FESHBACH	+
	8.8+5				Data EXFOR10332.022	Jun 74	. 8 PTS.	
Diff Elastic	1.2+5	1.1+6	PEL	Expt	Jour ZP 271 1	Nov 74	Barnard+.GRPH,4 LEG COEF GIVEN	
					Rept PEL-191	Oct 69	Coetzee.DIFFSIG AT 18 ES,10 ANGS,TBL	
	1.2+5	1.1+6			Data EXFOR30179.	Feb 72	.4-TERM LEG FIT +DIFFSIG. AT 19 ES.	
Polarization	8.8+5		ANL	Expt	Rept ANL-7935	Jun 72	COX+ CFD OPTMOD, HAUSER-FESHBACH	+
	8.8+5				Data EXFOR10332.056	Jun 74	. 8 PTS.	
Potntal Scat	2.5-2		ORL	Expt	Jour PR 81 527	Feb 51	Shull+	+
	2.5-2				Data EXFOR11043.	Jun 76	. 1 PT. SIGMA.	
Tot Inelastc	8.2+4	1.0+7	BOL	Eval	Rept CEC(71)-2	71	Benzi+ STAT MODEL. TBL GIVEN.	+
	8.2+4	1.0+7			Data BENZI-DFN 544D	Mar 71	50 PNTS	
Tot Inelastc	5.5+5	9.7+5	JAE	Expt	Jour NP/A 171 480	Aug 71	Kikuchi. P-T NS. EXCIT FUNCTIONS	
	5.5+5	9.7+5			Data EXFOR20306.	Jun 74	205PTS.SIGMA.	
Tot Inelastc	5.0+5	1.5+7	AUA	Eval	Data AUSTR-DFN 123.	Nov 71	COOK+ POINT(11)+GROUP(127)SIG.CF EVL	
Tot Inelastc	8.0+4	1.0+6	SAC	Theo	Conf 73Kiev 1 291	May 73	Krebs+ OPT+STATMDL,PRELIM,GRAPH	
Tot Inelastc	1.0-3	1.5+7	RCN	Eval	Prog RCN-239 11	Nov 75	Gruppelaar. EXP.+MODEL CALC. NDG	
Diff Inelast	1.2+7	2.2+7	HAM	Expt	Jour ZN/A 18 914	Sep 63	Langkau.CSI(TL) TARGET AND DETECTOR	
Diff Inelast	1.4+7		FEI	Expt	Rept FEI-39	Jan 66	Sal'Nikov+TOF SPECT,RING GEOM,E-SPEC	+
Diff Inelast	1.4+7		FEI	Expt	Jour YF 4 1154	Dec 66	Sal'Nikow+ SPEC OF SECNDARY NS,CURVE	+
					Jour SNP 4 831	Jun 67	.ENGLISH TRANSL OF YF 4 1154 12/66	
	1.4+7				Data EXFOR40134.013	Feb 73	N-SPECTRUM AT 92 DEG, 51EN'	
Diff Inelast	3.5+6	8.5+6	JAE	Expt	Prog EANDC(J)8L25	Jan 68	Maruyama+.TOF.CONTIN SPECT AT 90DEG.	
	3.6+6	8.5+6			Jour NP/A 131 145	Jun 69	- . E DEPENDENCE,PARAM,TH FIT	
	3.5+6	8.5+6			Conf 67Tokyo 373	Sep 67	- + PPR8.127. ABST.	

55 Cesium 133

Quantity	Energy (ev) Min	Max	Lab	Type	Documentation Ref Vol Page	Author, Comments Date	Data
Diff Inelast	8.2+4	1.0+7	BOL Eval	Rept	CEC(71)-2	71 Benzi+ DISCRETE INELASTIC. 4 LVLS	+
	8.2+4	5.0+5		Data	BENZI-DFN 544D	Mar 71 1ST- 4TH LVL, +ANGDIST+E DIST	
	5.0+5	1.0+7		Data	BENZI-DFN 544D	Mar 71 TO CONTINUUM,31PNTS+ANGDIST+E DIST	
Diff Inelast	1.4+7		KFI Theo	Rept	KFKI-72-17	Feb 72 Kluge+ CALC N-SPEC INEL+N2N,TBL,GRPH	
Diff Inelast	1.2+5	1.9+6	PEL Expt	Jour	ZP 271 1	Nov 74 Barnard+ GRPH,AT 90 DEG,H-F CALC	+
	2.4+5	1.3+6		Rept	PEL-191	Oct 69 Coetzee.SIG TO LVLS+ANGDIST,TBL,GRPH	
	2.4+5	1.3+6		Data	EXFOR30179.	Feb 72 .90-DEG DIFFSIG,8 LVLS,56 ES,ANGDIST	
Thermal Scat	Cold		MUN Expt	Prog	EANDC(E)150U	Oct 72 Koester+ COH SCATT AMPL	+
	4.5-4			Data	EXFOR20581.007	Jun 76 1PNT.COH.SC.AMP.	
Thermal Scat	1.0-4	1.0+3	MUN Revw	Jour	EEN 80 1	77 Koester. SCAT LENGTH,FREE+INCOH SIG	
Scattering	1.5+6		FEI Expt	Prog	INDSWG-74	Jul 65 GUSEYNOV ETAL.SUBM.TO ATOMNAJA ENER.	
	Fast			Jour	AE 18 409	Apr 65 Gusejnov+ ANG DIST,TH(N,F) DETECTOR	
				Jour	SJA 18 526	Apr 65 . ENGL OF AE 18 409	
Nonelastic	1.0-3	1.5+7	AUA Eval	Data	AUSTR-DFN 123.	Nov 71 COOK+POINT(223)+GROUP(127)SIG.CF EVL	+
Nonelastic	1.4+7	1.6+7	ANL Eval	Rept	ANL-75-34	Jun 75 Davey+CORRC APPLIED TO N2N CS.TBLS.	
Absorption	Pile		ANL Expt	Jour	PR 80 342	Nov 50 Harris+ PILE OSC. REL TO BORON.	+
	Pile			Data	EXFOR11528.033	Jun 76 . 1 PT. SIGMA.	
Absorption	2.5-2		HAR Expt	Rept	AERE-R/R-2333	57 Cummins+ PILE OSC.	+
Absorption	Maxwl		HAR Expt	Rept	AERE-R/R-2516	Mar 58 Jowitt+ PILE OSC.REL BORON.293DEGK.	
Absorption	2.5-2		HAR Expt	Jour	JNEA 12 32	May 60 Tattersall+ PILE OSCILLATOR.	+
	2.5-2			Data	EXFOR20638.040	Jul 76 1PNT.SIGMA.	
Absorption	Maxwl		KAP Expt	Prog	KAPL-2000-12	Dec 60 Fehr. PAGE 33	
	Maxwl			Data	EXFOR12023.002	Jun 76 . 1 PT. SIGMA.	
Absorption	4.1-1	1.0+7	GA Eval	Prog	GA-2451	Aug 61 Joanou+ 68 GROUP DATA FOR GAM-I	
Absorption	1.4+7	1.5+7	GLS Expt	Jour	NP 49 306	Nov 63 Robertson.SIG=26+-3MB AT14.1MEV,CSI	
Absorption	2.5-2		FAR Expt	Conf	66Paris 1 479	Oct 66 Carre+ OSCILLATOR MEHTOD.	+
	2.5-2			Data	EXFOR20658.022	Jul 76 1PNT.SIGMA.	
Absorption	Fast		AE Expt	Conf	70Helsinki 2 603	Jun 70 Andersson.PILE OSC. 3 SPECS.CFD CALC	
Absorption	1.0-3	1.0+7	JUL Eval	Rept	JUEL-678-RG	Jul 70 Liu. EVALUATION+CALC,GRPH,FN OF E	
Absorption	Pile		CRC Eval	Conf	73Paris 1 459	Mar 73 Walker.FISS PRODUCT ABS,TBL PILE SIG	
Absorption	Fast		RCN Revw	Conf	IAEA-169 2 53	74 Bustraan.INTEG CFD SIG(N-E)FILES,TBL	
Res Int Abs	-		CCP Expt	Jour	AE 3 507	Dec 57 Klimentov+.EPI CD REACTIVITY REL LI	+
				Jour	JNE 9 20	Jun 59 TRANSLATN.*	
				Jour	SJA 3 1387	57 TRANSLATN.*	
Res Int Abs	5.0-1		MCM Expt	Conf	58Geneva 15 459	Sep 58 Bidinosti+ P.201.MASS SPEC REL CO	+
	5.0-1			Data	EXFOR12022.002	Jun 76 . 1 PT.	
Res Int Abs	None		CRC Eval	Prog	AECL-1054	Mar 60 Walker.(CRP-913) REDUCED RES.INT.	
Res Int Abs	None		ORL Eval	Prog	ORNL-2869	Mar 60 Nephew.1/V UP +TO100EV.ALSO 6 ES- UP	
Res Int Abs	5.0-1		HAR Expt	Jour	JNE 12 32	May 60 Tattersall+ ABOVE 1/V,OSCIL,REL B+AU	+
				Rept	AERE-R-2887	Aug 59 - . PILE OSC.REL BORON	
				Conf	58Geneva 16 34	Sep 58 Rose+ SUPERSEDED	
	6.7-1			Data	EXFOR20638.041	Jul 76 1PNT.	
Res Int Abs	5.0-1		CRC Expt	Jour	CJC 38 2528	Dec 60 Baerg+ 34.4 TO META,461B TO GROUND	+
	5.0-1			Data	EXFOR12006.003	Jun 76 . 1 PT, RI	
Res Int Abs	5.0-1		KAP Expt	Prog	KAPL-2000-12	Dec 60 Fehr. PAGE 33	+
	5.0-1			Data	EXFOR12023.002	Jun 76 . 1 PT, RI	
Res Int Abs	5.0-1		CRC Expt	Jour	JNEA 13 141	Jan 61 Brown+ 370+-50B.CD RATIO REL CO59	+
	5.0-1			Data	EXFOR12022.003	Jun 76 . 1 PT.	
Res Int Abs	5.0-1		BOL Eval	Conf	61Vienna 1 179	Aug 61 Benzi+ TBL TOTAL CAPT RES INTS.	
Res Int Abs	5.0-1		FAR Expt	Conf	66Paris 1 479	Oct 66 Carre+ OSCILLATOR METHOD.	+
				Conf	66Paris 2 371	Oct 66 Vidal+.PPR73,RES INT,E ABOVE 1EV	
				Rept	CEA-R-2486	Jul 64 - + PILE OSC REL B AND AU	
	5.5-1			Data	EXFOR20658.023	Jul 76 1PNT.	
Res Int Abs	5.0-1		BOL Eval	Rept	RT/FI-4	Jan 67 Palmucci. CALC FROM (N,G) RES PARAMS	
Res Int Abs	5.0-1		BGK Expt	Rept	THAI-AEC-10	Oct 67 . CD-RATIO REL AU.TO GRND,META.TABLE	+
	5.0-1			Data	EXFOR30368.	Jan 77 REL AU, PRELM. TO CS-134M AND -134G	
Res Int Abs	5.0-1		CPO Expt	Jour	JIN 30 349	Feb 68 Sims+ 495+-17 REL TO CO59=69.9 B	+
	5.0-1			Data	EXFOR11658.	Jun 76 . 2 PTS, RI TO GND + META	
Res Int Abs	5.0-1		NPL Expt	Jour	JNE 24 35	Feb 70 Ryves.REL.AU.REDUCD INT.PROD CS134M	
	5.0-1			Data	EXFOR20789.334	Dec 78 1PNT.REDUCED INTEGRAL.CAPTURE	
Res Int Abs	None		GA Eval	Prog	GA-12071	Sep 71 Mathews+ RECOMMENDED VALUES	
Res Int Abs	5.5-1		CRC Eval	Rept	AECL-3037 1	Jan 72 Walker.REDUCED RES INT,DETAILED TBL	
Res Int Abs	5.0-1		AUA Eval	Rept	AAEC/TM-619	Sep 72 Clayton.CALC FROM SIG LIBRARY,TABLE	
Res Int Abs	5.0-1		KJL Expt	Jour	JIN 34 2699	Sep 72 Steinnes. ACT. AU MONITOR	+
	5.0-1			Data	EXFOR20188.013	May 74 1PNT.CAPTURE.	
Res Int Abs	5.0-1		MUN Expt	Jour	JRC 15 535	73 Alian+CAPT CD-R, 386 B INCL 1/V	
	5.0-1			Data	EXFOR20644.008	Jun 76 1PNT.CAPTURE.	
Res Int Abs	4.6-1	1.0+6	RCN Theo	Rept	RCN-191	Jul 73 Lautenbach.CAPT INT FROM GROUP SIGMA	

55 Cesium 133

Quantity	Energy (ev) Min	Max	Lab	Type	Documentation Ref Vol Page	Author, Comments Date	Data
Res Int Abs	5.0-1		GHT	Expt	Jour JRC 20 695	74 Van Der Linden+ BY(N,G).CFD OTHS,TBL	+
	5.5-1			Conf	73Paris 2 241	Mar 73 - + ACT,REL THR+GOLD,TBL	
	5.5-1			Data	EXFOR20645.	Jul 76 2PTS.CAPTURE.	
Res Int Abs	5.5-1	+6	SAC	Revw Conf	IAEA-169 1 235	74 Ribon.CAPTURE,STATUS CFD REQUEST,TBL	
Res Int Abs	+0	+5	WIN	Revw Conf	IAEA-169 3 163	74 Pope+ DATA FILE CALC CFD XPTAL VALUE	
Res Int Abs		4.0+2	ITE	Expt Conf	76Lowell 1251	Jul 76 Kalebin+TRNS.RES PARS,INTEG.NDG	
(n,γ)	Pile		ANL	Expt	Jour PR 72 888	Nov 47 Seren+ ACT METHOD.TO3HR,1.7YR ISOMER	+
	Pile			Data	EXFOR11447.	Jun 76 . 2 PTS,SIG TO GND + META	
(n,γ)	Maxwl		ORL	Expt	Jour PR 83 643	Aug 51 Pomerance. LOCAL OSC REL AU ABS 95B	+
	Maxwl			Data	EXFOR11047.045	Jun 76 . 1 PT. SIGMA.	
(n,γ)	Maxwl		CRC	Expt	Jour JIN 5 259	Feb 58 Bayly+ PILE, (N,G)CS GVN	
	Maxwl			Data	EXFOR12017.002	Jun 76 . 1 PT. SIGMA.	
(n,γ)	Pile		MCM	Expt	Conf 58Geneva 15 459	Sep 58 Bidinosti+ PAPER 201, REL CO	+
	Pile			Data	EXFOR12010.003	Jun 76 . 1 PT.	
(n,γ)	2.5+4		LRL	Expt	Jour PR 112 226	Oct 58 Booth+ SB-BE REL I+THR,ACT 3.1H,2.3Y	+
	2.5+4			Data	EXFOR11429.	Jun 76 . 2 PTS, SIG TO GND + META	
(n,γ)	Maxwl		ETH	Expt	Jour ZP 156 293	Oct 59 Knoepfel+ PAIR SP,SUM INTENS 12GAMS	
(n,γ)	2.5-2		CRC	Eval	Prog AECL-1054	Mar 60 Walker. (CRRP-913)	
(n,γ)	None		ANL	Theo	Jour PR 120 1305	Nov 60 Huizenga+ ISOMER RATIO,TH CFD EXPT	
(n,γ)	Pile		ORL	Expt	Jour NSE 8 378	Nov 60 Lyon. ACTIVATION,SIGMA GIVEN	+
	Pile			Data	EXFOR11625.021	Jun 76 . 1 PT. SIGMA.	
(n,γ)	2.5-2		CRC	Expt	Jour CJC 38 2528	Dec 60 Baerg+ 2.82B TO META,30.4B TO GROUND	+
	2.5-2			Data	EXFOR12006.002	Jun 76 . 1 PT. SIGMA.	
(n,γ)	Pile		MTR	Expt	Jour JIN 17 180	61 Keisch. SIG TO ISO-STATE	
	Pile			Data	EXFOR12018.002	Jun 76 . 1 PT. SIGMA.	
(n,γ)	Maxwl		CRC	Expt	Jour JNEA 13 141	Jan 61 Brown+ 33.4+-2.6B,CD DIFF REL CO59	+
	Maxwl			Data	EXFOR12022.002	Jun 76 . 1 PT, SIG	
(n,γ)	5.0-3	2.5+0	GA	Eval	Rept GA-2113	Jun 61 Wikner+.TABLE + CURVE.100 E POINTS	
(n,γ)	Pile		KSU	Expt	Rept TID-22165	62 Simons.ISOMERIC SIG RATIOS CFD TH	
	Pile			Data	EXFOR12631.	Jun 76 . 2 PTS , SIG FOR GND + META	
(n,γ)	2.8-3	1.0+6	GA	Eval	Jour NSE 12 115	Jan 62 Garrison+ 55 GROUPS	
(n,γ)	1.0+0	4.0+4	LEB	Expt	Jour ZET 42 988	Apr 62 Popov.PB-SLO-DOWN,GRPH SG(E)CFD OTHR	+
					Jour JET 15 683	Oct 62 TRANSLATN.*	
(n,γ)	1.0+3	1.0+5	DUB	Expt	Jour ZET 43 2000	Dec 62 Exp.COMP.WITH THEORY	
					Jour JET 16 1409	Jun 63 TRANSLATN.*	
(n,γ)	5.0+3	3.0+5	FOA	Theo	Jour NP 39 529	Dec 62 Bergqvist+. GRAPH. STATISTICAL MODEL	
(n,γ)	Maxwl	+0	MTR	Expt	Jour PR 129 769	Jan 63 Keisch.RATIO ISOMER ACT TO GND ACT.	+
	Maxwl			Data	EXFOR11748.018	Jun 76 . 2 PTS, SIG TO GND + META	
(n,γ)	2.0+5	1.0+5	KUR	Theo	Jour NP 45 156	Jul 63 Nemirovsky+OPTIC.THEOR.COMP.WITH EXP	
(n,γ)	2.6+6		KFI	Expt	Rept KFKI-1467	Sep 63 Borbely+ ACTIVATION. SIG TO ISO STAT	+
	2.6+6			Data	EXFOR30175.	May 72 SIGMA TO ISOMERIC STATE	
(n,γ)	Pile		KFI	Expt	Rept KFKI-63-18	Sep 63 Gulyas+ ISOMERIC RATIO	+
	Pile			Data	EXFOR30176.	May 72 ISOMERIC RATIO	
(n,γ)	Maxwl	Pile	ANL	Expt	Jour NP 60 241	Nov 64 Bishop+ISOMER YIELD RATIO,THR+EPICD	+
	Maxwl			Data	EXFOR11831.006	Jun 76 . 2 PTS, SIG TO GND + META	
(n,γ)	Maxwl		ORL	Theo	Jour RMP 37 166	Jan 65 Macklin+ CALC FOR KT=5TO90KEV	
(n,γ)	2.5-2		BOL	Eval	Rept RT/FI-4	Jan 67 Palmucci. CALC FROM RES PARAMETERS	
(n,γ)	1.4+5	1.3+6	FEI	Expt	Prog YFI-5 13	Oct 67 Tolstikov+ TABLE SIGMA AT 8 ES	
	1.5+5	1.0+6			Jour AE 23 566	Jun 67 - + REL THERML SIG,CFD OTHERS	
					Rept BNL-TR-240	Oct 68 . ENGLISH OF AE 23 576	
					Jour SJA 23 1347	Jun 67 . ENGL OF AE 23 566	
	1.4+5	1.3+6			Rept INDC-232E	67 . ENGL OF YFI-5 13	
(n,γ)	Maxwl		FEI	Theo	Jour YF 6 1174	Dec 67 Malyshev.STATMOD ISOM SIG,HIGH+LOW L	
					Jour SNP 6 853	Jun 68 .TRANSLATION	
(n,γ)	Maxwl		AUA	Theo	Jour NSE 31 234	Feb 68 Cook+ STATISTICAL CALC CFD EXPT	
(n,γ)	Maxwl		CPO	Expt	Jour JIN 30 349	Feb 68 Sims+ 29.2+-2.3 REL TO CO59=37.5 B	+
	Maxwl			Data	EXFOR11658.	Jun 76 . 2 PTS, SIG TO GND + META	
(n,γ)	+3	+6	WWA	Theo	Conf JINR-D3893 131	May 68 Brzosko+ ABSTRACT,SIG CALCULATED,NDG	
(n,γ)	-		IEA	Comp	Rept IEA-INF-10	Aug 68 Atalla. TABLES OF HL,SIG AND GAMM-E	
(n,γ)	2.0+3				Rept WASH-1127 72	Apr 69 Schuman+ FILTERED BEAM,TO GND+ISOMER	
(n,γ)	5.0+3	1.0+5	AUA	ExTh	Rept AAEC/E-198	May 69 Musgrove.S+P+D WAVE SIGMAS CALC,TBL	+
(n,γ)	1.0+4	1.5+5	KFK	Expt	Jour NP/A 133 513	Aug 69 Kompe. RENORMAL OF 66PARIS,GRAPH	+
					Rept EANDC(E)89U3	Feb 68 - + DATA RENORMALISED.	
					Rept KFK-635	Oct 67 Ponitz+ SUPERSEEDED BY NP/A 133	
					Rept EANDC(E)76U7	Jan 67 Kompe. ABSTRACT,GRAPH	
					Conf 66Paris 1 513	Oct 66 - . SUPERSEEDED BY NP/A 133	
	1.3+4	1.7+5			Data EXFOR20358.020	Sep 74 72PTS.SIGMA.	
(n,γ)	None		COL	Expt	Prog NCSAC-31 50	May 70 Arbo+,NEVIS,MOXON-RAE DET,TO BE DONE	

55 Cesium 133

Quantity	Energy (ev) Min	Energy (ev) Max	Lab	Type	Documentation Ref Vol Page	Author, Comments Date	Data
(n,γ)	1.5+7		MNZ	Expt Jour	JIN 32 1799	Jun 70 Qaim+ ACTIV MEAS.+ISOM RATIO	+
	1.5+7			Data	EXFOR20519.	Apr 76 4PTS.SIGMA.	
(n,γ)	–		CCP	Revw Jour	AE 29 187	Sep 70 Sukhoruchkin. (D,P GAM) CFD (N,GAM)	
				Jour	SJA 29 896	Sep 70 TRANSLATN.*	
(n,γ)	3.0+4		AUA	Theo Rept	AAEC/E – 211	Nov 70 Musgrove. SIGMA GIVEN AND CFD OTHER	
(n,γ)	1.0+3	1.0+7	BOL	Eval Rept	CEC(71) – 2	71 Benzi+ OPTMOD EVAL.TBL GIVEN.	+
				Rept	CEC(70) – 2	Apr 70 – +. GRAPH	
				Rept	CCDN – NW/10	Dec 69 – +H – F MOD,AXEL G(G)EST,ALL DATA	
				Conf	66Paris 1 537	Oct 66 – + STATMOD.TBL AV VALS.SUPERSEDD	
				Conf	61Vienna 1 179	Aug 61 – + TBL AV VALS. SUPERSEDED.	
	1.0+3	1.0+7		Data	BENZI – DFN 544D	Mar 71 67 PNTS	
(n,γ)	4.0+5		WWA	Expt Jour	APPB 2 489	71 Brzosko+ PARTIAL,TOTAL SIG CFD THEO	+
				Rept	INR – 1318 28	Apr 71 *SHORT REPORT,DATA GIV	
				Jour	CJP 47 2849	Dec 69 *TH.CALCULATIONS OF SIG	
	4.0+5			Data	EXFOR30159.	Apr 72 PARTIAL,TOTAL SIGMAS GIVEN	
(n,γ)	Maxwl		GA	Eval Rept	GA – 12071	Sep 71 Mathews+. RECOMMENDED VALUES	
(n,γ)	1.0 – 3	1.5+7	AUA	Eval Data	AUSTR – DFN 123.	Nov 71 COOK+POINT(223)+GROUP(127)SIG.CF EVL	+
(n,γ)	2.5 – 2		CRC	Eval Rept	AECL – 3037 1	Jan 72 Walker.RECOMMENDED SIG,DETAILED TBL	
(n,γ)	2.4+4		MUA	Theo Jour	IJP 46 114	Mar 72 Chaubey+ P – WAVE STRENGTH FUNCT,TABLE	
(n,γ)	Maxwl		IAE	Revw Rept	IAEA – 143 897	Apr 72 Lemmel.RECENT EVALUATIONS,TABLE	
	2.5 – 2			Rept	IAEA – 143 897	Apr 72 – .RECENT EVALUATIONS,TABLE+GRPH	
(n,γ)	Pile		RIS	Expt Rept	RISO – M – 1516	Jun 72 Olsen. ACT. REL NI58(N,P)	+
	Pile			Data	EXFOR20231.006	May 74 1PNT.SIGMA.	
(n,γ)	1.4+7		BOR	Expt Jour	NP/A 176 545	Dec 71 Rigaud+ INTEGRATED FROM NG SPECTRUM	+
				Conf	72Budapest 220	Aug 72 – +INTEGRATD SIG FROM SPEC,GRPH	
				Jour	JPRS 32 10 231	Oct 71 Irigaray+COLL.5B,MEAS.G.SPC.WITH INA	
	1.4+7			Data	EXFOR20533.002	Apr 76 1PNT.SIGMA.	
(n,γ)	2.5 – 2		AUA	Eval Rept	AAEC/TM – 619	Sep 72 Clayton.CALC FROM SIG LIBRARY,TABLE	
(n,γ)	Fast		MTR	Expt Conf	72Kiamesha 2 614	Sep 72 Harker+ CFRMF INTEGRAL MEAS.	+
				Conf	71Knoxvill 241	Mar 71 – .INTEGRAL MEAST,0.096B RELAU	
	Fast			Data	EXFOR10218.006	Oct 72 . 1 PT. SIGMA.	
(n,γ)	Fast		DUB	Expt Rept	JINR – P12 – 6810	Nov 72 Ngo Quoc Buu+ ACT ANALYS, CD – RATIOS	
(n,γ)		1.1+7	RCN	Theo Rept	RCN – 191	Jun 73 Lautenbach. GROUP CONSTANTS TBL	
(n,γ)	2.4+4		AUW	Expt Jour	JPJ 35 8	Jul 73 Murty+.ACTIV – METHOD.SIG=56+ – 7MB	
(n,γ)	Fiss		SAC	Revw Conf	IAEA – 169 1 235	74 Ribon.STATUS SIG CFD REQUESTS,TABLE	
	2.5 – 2	3.0+4		Conf	IAEA – 169 1 235	74 – .STATUS SIG CFD REQUESTS,TABLE	
(n,γ)	1.0+3	2.0+6	SAC	Eval Rept	CEA – CONF – 2407	74 Krebs. IDENTICAL TO KIEV MAY – JUNE73	
	1.0+3	1.0+6		Theo Conf	73Kiev 1 291	May 73 – + OPT+STATMDL,PRELIM CFD XP.GRF	
	Maxwl	Fiss	WIN	Revw Conf	IAEA – 169 3 163	74 Pope+ MAXW+FIS – SPEC AVG DATA CFD XPT	
	Fiss			Conf	IAEA – 169 3 137	74 Dean. POINT DATA AVG OVER STAND SPEC	
(n,γ)	Pile		NSU	Expt Jour	KNS 6 89	Jun 74 BAK. ACTIV,ISOM RATIO GVN,CFD THEORY	+
				Prog	INDC(SEC) – 35	Sep 73 BAK+ P154. ISOM RATIO,SHORT NOTE,TBL	
	Pile			Data	EXFOR30388.006	Mar 77 ISOM.RATIO.	
(n,γ)	Fast		NSU	Expt Jour	KNS 6 89	Jun 74 BAK. EPI – CD.ACTIV,ISOM RATIO GVN,TBL	+
	Fast			Data	EXFOR30388.006	Mar 77 ISOM.RATIO, FOR EPI – CD NEUTRON.	
(n,γ)	1.0+3	1.0+7	FEI	Eval Rept	YK – 8/2 97	Sep 72 Abagjan+ AVG SIG(ENERGY – GROUPS),TABL	
				Rept	INDC(CCP) – 39	Jul 74 .P102. ENGLISH OF YK – 8/2 97	
(n,γ)	1.3 – 2	4.7+1	WUR	Expt Rept	EIR – 217	Apr 75 Widder. POWDER SAMPLE	+
				Conf	74Petten 757	Sep 74 – . M – R DET,ABS.EXP.,NDG	
				Priv	SWISS PH S	Oct 71 – . TOF+MOXON – RAE.CURVS CFD SIGT	
	1.3 – 2	4.7+1		Data	EXFOR20437.004	Nov 75 270PTS.SIGMA.	
(n,γ)	1.5+7		JYV	Comp Rept	JU – RR – 1/1976	Mar 76 Valkonen.(THESIS).EXPTS CFD DSD MODL	
(n,γ)	2.4+4	2.4+4	KTO	Expt Prog	NEANDC(J)44L	Aug 76 Yamamuro+.LINAC,FE – FILTER.SIG=580MB	+
	2.4+4			Data	EXFOR20697.003	Nov 76 1PNT.SIGMA.	
(n,γ)	Fast		RCN	Expt Rept	ECN – 10	Oct 76 Veenema+ STEK REACTIVITY WORTHS TBL.	
(n,γ)	1.0 – 3	1.0+7	RCN	Revw Rept	ECN – 12	Nov 76 Gruppelaar+ INTERCOMP. RECENT WORKS	
(n,γ)	1.5+7		IRK	Expt Priv	WAGNER	77 Wagner+	+
	1.4+7			Rept	INDC(SEC) – 51	Oct 75 – + ABST PAGE 3	
	1.5+7			Data	EXFOR20718.	Jan 76 2PTS.SIGMA.	
Spect (n,γ)	Maxwl		CCP	Expt Jour	ZET 35 592	Sep 58 CRYST SC,SOFT LINES INTENSITIES	
				Jour	JET 8 410	Mar 59 TRANSLATN.*	
Spect (n,γ)	Maxwl		ETH	Expt Jour	ZP 156 293	Oct 59 Knoeppel+ 4.5 TO 6.7MEV GAMMAS	
				Jour	NC 11 609	Jan 59 Balzer+ LINE ENS ONLY.CRYSTALSPEC.	
Spect (n,γ)	Pile		MOS	Expt Jour	NP 16 168	Apr 60 Estulin+ NAI(TL),10 – 350KEV GS.SCHEME	
Spect (n,γ)	Maxwl		BUC	Expt Conf	60Vienna 177	Oct 60 Dragomirescu+.NDG,REFS GVN,EXPT DSCR	
Spect (n,γ)	2.0+4	3.0+5	FOA	ExTh Jour	NP 39 529	Dec 62 Bergqvist+.+125KEV.GRAPH.CFD STATMDL	
	Maxwl			Theo Jour	NP 53 397	Apr 64 Starfelt.STATMOD CALC LARGE DISCREP.	
	2.0+4			Rept	FOA4 – A4355 411	Feb 64 Bergqvist+.M1 GIANT RES (=ANL – 6797)	

55 Cesium 133

Quantity	Energy (ev) Min	Max	Lab	Type	Documentation Ref Vol Page	Author, Comments Date	Data
Spect (n,γ)	None		FTI	Expt	Jour ZET 45 892	Oct 63 Berestovoj.GRPHS PROMPT+DELAYED G-SP	
					Jour JET 18 613	Mar 64 TRANSLATN.*	
Spect (n,γ)	Maxwl		IFU	Expt	Jour IZV 30 359	Feb 66 Berestovoj+ CURVES,GE-DETECTOR	
	None			Prog	INDSWG-120 33	65 - .TABLE OF 10G-ES AND INTNS	
	Maxwl				Jour BAS 30 364	Feb 66 . ENGL OF IZV 30 359	
Spect (n,γ)	Maxwl		MCM	Expt	Jour NP 83 241	Aug 66 Archer+ 86 GAMMAS OBSERVED	
Spect (n,γ)	-		FTI	Expt	Prog YFI-5 32	Oct 67 Berestovoj+ EXCITED STATE OF CS-134	
					Rept INDC-232E	67 . ENGL OF YFI-5 32	
Spect (n,γ)	Maxwl		MOS	Expt	Jour IZV 32 81	Jan 68 Rozantsev+ GAMMA,TIME DISTRIBUTION	
					Jour BAS 32 80	Jan 68 TRANSLATN.*NO 1	
Spect (n,γ)	Maxwl		FTI	Expt	Jour IZV 32 296	Feb 68 Berestovoi+ GAM E+TIME SPECS,GRAPHS	
					Jour BAS 32 269	69 TRANSLATN.*NO 2	
Spect (n,γ)	None		FTI	Expt	Jour IZV 32 713	Apr 68 Kadashevich+ GAM+T SPEC,ON LINE COMP	
					Jour BAS 32 659	69 TRANSLATN.*NO 4	
Spect (n,γ)	+0	+3	DUB	Expt	Conf 68DUBSY 283	Jul 68 Shapiro.GE-LI DET. RESOL=80NS/M,CURV	
Spect (n,γ)	2.5-2		MIT	Comp	Rept MITNE-85	Jan 69 Rasmussen+TBL G INT.=AFCRL-69-0071	
Spect (n,γ)	5.6+0	4.8+1	DUB	Expt	Conf CZJB 19 248	Feb 69 Becvar.F+GAM INTENSITY+ENERGY AT 3ES	
					Rept JINR-P3-3697	Feb 68 - + GE-LI,GRPH G-SPEC+LVL SCHEME	
	5.9+0	4.8+1			Conf 67Tokyo § 4.117	Sep 67 - + TOF,GE-LI.CAPT AT 3RES,GRAPH	
				Theo	Rept BNL-TR-284	69 . ENGLISH OF CZJB 19 248	
Spect (n,γ)	Pile		ANL	Expt	Conf 69Studsvik 601	Aug 69 Smither+ NO DATA GVN,TB CFD STATMOD	
Spect (n,γ)	Maxwl		KFI	Expt	Jour YF 10 907	Nov 69 Kecskemeti+ AVG GAM-MULTIPLICITY,TBL	
					Jour SNP 10 524	May 70 TRANSLATN.*	
Spect (n,γ)	Maxwl		SFU	Expt	Jour NP/A 138 392	Nov 69 Korteling+ GE(LI). LOW E GAMMAS.	
Spect (n,γ)	Maxwl	4.8+1	CRC	Expt	Prog AECL-3666 62	Dec 69 Lone+ ANAL TBC,TBL HIGH-E GAMS GIVEN	
Spect (n,γ)	Pile		THD	Expt	Jour ZP 230 37	Dec 69 Hofmann+,DECAY-SCH OF CS134 CF	
Spect (n,γ)	2.0+5	2.2+6	TUL	Expt	Jour NP/A 142 619	Mar 70 Dave+ VDG,GE(LI). INELASTIC G SEPAR.	
Spect (n,γ)	5.9+0	1.3+2	BNL	Expt	Prog NCSAC-31 17	May 70 Chrien+ CAPT IN 6 RES, CURVS FOR 2	
Spect (n,γ)	Maxwl		CCP	Expt	Jour IZV 35 112	Jan 71 Rozantsev. 52 NSEC STATE,INTENS.,TBL	
					Jour BAS 35 102	Jan 73 . ENGLISH OF IZV 35 112 1/71	
Spect (n,γ)	Pile		KFK	Expt	Rept KFK-1401	Jun 71 Djadali.AVG POLRZ G EXPT,CFD T,SPIN	
	Maxwl				Jour NP/A 147 150	May 70 Eichler+ POL NS.CIRC POL GS+ASSYMTRY	
Spect (n,γ)	4.0+5		WWA	Expt	Jour APPB 2 489	Aug 71 Brzosko+ GAMMA-EN = 3 TO 7 MEV,GRAPH	
Spect (n,γ)		3.6+2	HAR	Expt	Rept AERE-PR/NP18	Mar 72 Thomas+.LINAC TOF LOW EN GS TO GET J	
Spect (n,γ)	1.0+7		WWA	Theo	Jour NP/A 189 545	Jul 72 Brzosko+ CMPD NUCL DECAY.PARTIAL WG	
Spect (n,γ)	1.4+7		BOR	Expt	Conf 72Budapest 220	Aug 72 Rigaud+ TOF,NDG	
					Jour NP/A 176 545	Dec 71 - + TOF. E(GAMMA)=14 TO 22 MEV.	
Spect (n,γ)	7.0+0	9.0+2	USP	Expt	Prog INDC(SEC)-35	Sep 73 Barros+ P47.TOF,SPIN ASSIGNMENT,NDG	
Spect (n,γ)	Maxwl		MUN	Expt	Conf 74Petten 552	Sep 74 Rabenstein+BRANCH RATIOS LVL CS-134	
Spect (n,γ)	5.0+0	9.0+2	GEL	Expt	Prog NEANDC(E)162 3	Feb 75 Coceva+LINAC TOF	
Spect (n,γ)	Maxwl		LIN	Expt	Jour NP/A 248 249	Aug 75 Alexeev+E+INT OF GAM+CONV ELECT,TBL	+
	2.5-2				Rept LIJAF-121	Oct 74 Alekseev+ DATA ARE GIVEN	
	Maxwl				Conf 72Kiev 1 95	Jan 72 - + ABST.GAM-ES+REL INTS,TABLE	
	2.5-2				Data EXFOR40299.002	May 75 .DATA IN GAM/100N FOR 165 ES GVN	
Spect (n,γ)	Maxwl		LIN	Expt	Jour NIM 138 299	76 Akhnazarov+ CONV.E SPECTROGR.GRPH	
Inelastic γ	2.5+6		NTS	Expt	Abst BAP 4 103	Mar 59 Lamb+ GAMMA ENERGY	
Inelastic γ	1.4+7		NTS	Expt	Abst BAP 11 741	Jul 66 Foster+ NDG	
Inelastic γ	1.0+6	2.2+6	TUL	Expt	Jour NP/A 142 619	Mar 70 Dave+GAMMA PROD SIG.95DEG.REL FE.	+
	1.0+6	2.2+6			Data EXFOR10038.	May 71 . 78 PTS AT 95 DEG.	
Inelastic γ	5.0+5	1.2+6	JAE	Expt	Jour NP/A 171 480	Aug 71 Kikuchi.PROD C.S. 9LVLS+EXCIT FUNCTS	+
	5.0+5	1.0+6			Jour JPJ 28 1089	Apr 70 - +.VDG GE(LI).LVLS	
	5.5+5	1.2+6			Data EXFOR20306.	Jun 74 501PTS.D/DA,G-SPEC.	
Inelastic γ	1.2+5	1.1+6	PEL	Expt	Jour ZP 271 1	Nov 74 Barnard+.DECAY-SCH OF CS-133 GIVEN	
(n,2n)	1.4+7		IRK	Expt	Jour OAWA 96 120	Mar 59 Vonach. ACTIVATION.	+
	1.4+7				Data EXFOR20087.007	Sep 71 1PNT.SIG.	
(n,2n)	Fiss		CRC	Eval	Rept CRC-1003	Dec 60 ROY+ ESTIMATED AVG SIG=1.3MB	
(n,2n)	1.4+7		HAM	Expt	Jour ZN/A 16 227	Mar 61 Pollehn+SIG=704MB	+
(n,2n)	1.2+7	2.0+7	HAM	Expt	Jour ZP 166 477	Feb 62 Bormann+ CURVE VS E. ALSO GAM SPECT.	+
	1.4+7		HAM	Comp	Jour NP 66 257	Mar 65 Bormann. 2EXPT VALS.CFD SHELL EFFECT	
(n,2n)	1.4+7	1.5+7	AMS	Expt	Jour PHY 31 1091	Jul 65 Nagel+.REL FE56(NP)+CU65(N2N)	
					Diss NAGEL	Dec 66 - .D-T NS.ACT.FINAL	
	1.4+7	1.5+7			Data EXFOR20198.	May 74 4PTS.SIGMA.	
(n,2n)	1.3+7	1.5+7	BNL	Theo	Jour NSE 23 238	Nov 65 Pearlstein.3ES.STAT MDL CALC.TBL CS.	
(n,2n)	Fiss		BNL	Theo	Jour NSE 23 238	Nov 65 Pearlstein.STATMDL CALC.SPEC AVG.TBL	
(n,2n)	9.0+6	2.0+7	AUA	Theo	Rept AAEC/TM-522	Nov 69 Bertram. CALC SIG(E)GRAPHS CFD EXPTS	
(n,2n)	1.5+7		DEB	Comp	Jour REA 7 4 93	Dec 69 Csikai+ SIG+HL COMPILTN,N-ACTIV-ANAL	
(n,2n)	1.4+7		GIT	Expt	Jour PR/C 1 350	Jan 70 Fink+ ACTIVATION, SIG=1542+-75MB	+
	1.4+7				Data EXFOR10497.035	Apr 76 . 1 PT. CS=1542+-75 MB	

55 Cesium 133

Quantity	Energy (ev) Min	Max	Lab	Type	Documentation Ref Vol Page	Date	Author, Comments	Data
(n,2n)	1.4+7	1.5+7	JYV	Eval Rept	JU-RR-3/1970	Jun 70	Leppaemaeki+ TABLE OF EVAL AVG SIG	
(n,2n)	1.5+7		MNZ	Expt Jour	JIN 32 1799	Jun 70	Qaim+ ACTIV MEAS.	+
	1.5+7			Data	EXFOR20519.006	Apr 76	1PNT.SIGMA.	
(n,2n)	9.1+6	1.0+7	BOL	Eval Rept	CEC(71)-2	71	Benzi+ STAT+EVAP MODELS.TBL GIVEN.	+
	9.1+6	1.0+7		Data	BENZI-DFN 544D	Mar 71	3 PNTS+ANGDIST+E DIST. 1 RANGE	
(n,2n)	+7		KFI	Theo Rept	KFKI-71-8	Feb 71	Jeki. CALCULATED CFD EXPTL SIG VALUE	
(n,2n)	1.5+7		IRK	Expt Jour	APA 34 209	Sep 71	Havlik. ACT. CC-W.	+
				Jour	OAWA 107 119	Apr 70	- . ACTIVATION METHOD	
	1.5+7			Data	EXFOR20509.004	Apr 76	1PNT.SIGMA.	
(n,2n)	1.4+7		GIT	Theo Jour	PR/C 4 1173	Oct 71	Fink+ STAT-MODEL CALCULATION,CFD EXP	
(n,2n)	1.4+7		CCP	Expt Rept	YK- 9 50	72	Maslov+ REL CU65(N,2N),NA-I,SIG GIVN	+
				Rept	INDC(CCP)-42	Aug 74	.P10.ENGLISH OF YK-9	
	1.4+7			Data	EXFOR40136.018	Sep 74	.1 DATA LINE	
(n,2n)	1.4+7		KFI	Theo Rept	KFKI-72-17	Feb 72	Kluge+ CALC N-SPEC INEL+N2N,TBL,GRPH	
(n,2n)	+7		KFK	Expt Jour	JIN 34 2989	Sep 72	Krivan+ SYSTEMATICS OF EXCITATION	
(n,2n)	1.3+7	1.8+7	HAM	Expt Prog	EANDC(E)150U	Oct 72	Bormann+ ACTIV MEAS	+
	1.3+7	1.8+7		Data	EXFOR20797.007	Dec 78	7PTS.SIGMA.	
(n,2n)	1.5+7		DEB	Eval Jour	REA 11 1 153	Mar 73	Boedy. COMPILATION+RECOMM.VALUE,TBL	
				Rept	IAEA-153 173	73	- . RECOMM. VALUE ONLY	
(n,2n)	1.4+7		LOU	Expt Prog	INR-1464 12	May 73	Araminowicz+ BRIEF,ACTIV,TABLE,GRAPH	+
	1.4+7			Data	EXFOR30264.039	Nov 73	SIGMA AT 14.6 MEV	
(n,2n)	1.5+7		TAT	Theo Jour	JP/A 7 1458	Aug 74	Kondaiah. CALC ON STAT MODEL	
(n,2n)	9.0+6	1.6+7	ANL	Eval Rept	ANL-75-34	Jun 75	Davey+CONSTANT T MDL,LVL DEN MDL FIT	
(n,xn) x>2	Fiss		BNL	Theo Jour	NSE 23 238	Nov 65	Pearlstein.SPEC AVG STATMDL CALC N3N	
(n,xn) x>2	2.0+7		GEL	ExTh Jour	NP/A 118 379	Oct 68	Liskien.ACT VDG REL CU65(N2N)CFD TH	+
	2.0+7			Expt Data	EXFOR20380.007	Oct 74	. 1PNT.N3N SIGMA.	
(n,p)	Fiss		CRC	Eval Rept	CRC-1003	Dec 60	ROY+ ESTIMATED AVG SIG=0.2MB	
(n,p)	1.4+7		CIS	Expt Jour	NC 20 903	Jun 61	Marcazzan. = 1 DATA INDEX LINE	
(n,p)	1.3+7	2.1+7	HAM	Comp Rept	EUR-122E	63	Neuert+.*P BORMANN+.HAMBOURG U.1961	
(n,p)	1.4+7		OTC	Expt Jour	NP 42 27	Apr 63	Dixon.AVERAGE=8+-1MB FOR CSI CRYSTAL	
(n,p)	1.5+7		ARK	Expt Jour	PR 131 2649	Sep 63	Bramlitt+ LESS THAN 0.005MB N2P	+
				Rept	TID-16949	62	.THESIS	
	1.5+7			Data	EXFOR11590.069	Jun 76	. 1 PT, SIG N,2P	
(n,p)	1.2+7	2.2+7	HAM	Expt Jour	ZN/A 18 914	Sep 63	Langkau.CSI(TL) TARGET AND DETECTOR	
(n,p)	2.6+6		KFI	Expt Rept	KFKI-1467	Sep 63	Borbely+ ACTIVATION. PARTIAL SIGMAS	+
	2.6+6			Data	EXFOR30175.	May 72	SIGMA TO GROUND AND ISOMERIC STATES	
(n,p)	1.4+7	2.2+7	FRK	Expt Rept	EANDC(E)57U1	Feb 65	Bass+	+
(n,p)	1.4+7		SAH	Comp Jour	NUC 23 8 112	Aug 65	Chatterjee. TABLE WITH REFS.	
				Jour	NP 60 273	Nov 64	- .MEAN OF EXPT CFD SHELLMOD	
(n,p)	1.5+7		RBZ	Expt Jour	JIN 27 2471	Dec 65	Kolar+ ISOMERIC SIG RATIO,CFD THEORY	+
	1.5+7			Data	EXFOR31077.004	Sep 72	.RATIO MS/GND GVN	
(n,p)	Maxwl		IFU	Theo Rept	ICD-4 20	67	Dadakina+ PENETR COEFF CALC,TABLE	
(n,p)	1.5+7		DEB	Expt Jour	REA 7 4 93	Dec 69	Csikai+ SIG+HL COMPILTN,N-ACTIV-ANAL	
(n,p)	1.4+7	1.5+7	JYV	Eval Rept	JU-RR-3/1970	Jun 70	Leppaemaeki+ (N,2P) UPPER LIMIT,TBL	
(n,p)	1.5+7		MNZ	Expt Jour	JIN 32 1799	Jun 70	Qaim+ ACTIV MEAS.+ISOM RATIO+(N,2P)	+
	1.5+7			Data	EXFOR20519.	Apr 76	5PTS.SIGMA,N2P.	
(n,p)	1.5+7		RBZ	Expt Jour	NP/A 154 273	Oct 70	Lulic+ SIG(N,2P) MEASURED BY ACTIV	+
	1.5+7			Data	EXFOR30106.011	Apr 72	SIG(N,2P) AT 14.6 MEV	
(n,p)		7.5+8	IOW	Expt Jour	PR/C 12 1978	Dec 75	Hill+ ES TO 750 MEV.(N,P) REACTION	
(n,np)	1.3+7	2.1+7	HAM	Comp Rept	EUR-122E	63	Neuert+.*P BORMANN+.HAMBOURG U.1961	
(n,np)	1.2+7	2.2+7	HAM	Expt Jour	ZN/A 18 914	Sep 63	Langkau.CSI(TL) TARGET AND DETECTOR	
(n,np)	1.4+7	1.5+7	GLS	Expt Jour	NP 49 306	Nov 63	Robertson.SIG=3.5+-0.5MB	
(n,np)		7.5+8	IOW	Expt Jour	PR/C 12 1978	Dec 75	Hill+ ES TO 750 MEV.(N,2PN) REACTION	
(n,d)	1.4+7		OTC	Expt Jour	NP 42 27	Apr 63	Dixon.SIG=1.2+-0.2MB FOR CSI CRYSTAL	
(n,d)	1.4+7	2.2+7	FRK	Expt Rept	EANDC(E)57U1	Feb 65	Bass+	+
(n,d)	1.4+7		SAH	Comp Jour	NUC 23 8 112	Aug 65	Chatterjee. TABLE WITH REFS.	
(n,t)	1.5+7		SAH	Comp Jour	NUC 23 8 112	Aug 65	Chatterjee. TABLE WITH REFS.	
(n,He3)	1.5+7		ARK	Expt Jour	PR 125 297	Jan 62	Bramlitt.ACTIVATN SIG M 0.15MB,8 DAY	+
	1.5+7			Data	EXFOR11491.019	Jun 76	. 1 PT. SIGMA.	
(n,He3)	1.5+7		DEB	Expt Jour	NP 68 546	Jul 65	Csikai+.RATIO N,HE3/N,ALFA. VAL GIVN	+
	1.5+7			Data	EXFOR30214.	Nov 72	RATIO N,HE3/N,ALFA = .005+-.003	
(n,He3)	1.4+7	1.5+7	JYV	Eval Rept	JU-RR-3/1970	Jun 70	Leppaemaeki+ TABLE OF EVAL AVG SIG	
(n,He3)	1.5+7		MNZ	Expt Jour	JIN 32 1799	Jun 70	Qaim+ ACTIV MEAS.	+
				Jour	JRC 21 395	74	- +(JUL) CHEM SEP,SIG VS Z SYSTEM	
				Conf	72Budapest 50	Aug 72	- +(JUL) ACTIVATION. GRPH	
	1.5+7			Data	EXFOR20519.012	Apr 76	1PNT.SIGMA.	
(n,α)	+5	+7	KJL	Expt Conf	57Paris 1 48	Sep 57	Samsahl.SAELAN. EXPTL VALUE OF 1954	

55 Cesium 133

Quantity	Energy (ev) Min	Max	Lab	Type	Documentation Ref Vol Page	Date	Author, Comments	Data
(n,α)	1.4+7		ORL Expt	Jour	PR 110 531	Apr 58	Blosser+ ACT,REL FE56(N,P),1.0+ −.3MB	+
	1.4+7			Data	EXFOR11747.006	Jun 76	. 1 PT. SIGMA.	
(n,α)	Fiss		HAR Expt	Rept	AERE − I/R − 2630	Jul 58	Mellish+FAST REACTOR,ACTIV	
				Conf	57Paris 1 35	Sep 57	− + UNESCO CONF.	
(n,α)	Fiss		GES Revw	Jour	NUC 17 1 54	Jan 59	Rochlin.47 ISOTOPES.ACT.RVS.TBL	
(n,α)	1.4+7		ALD Expt	Jour	PPS 73 215	Feb 59	Coleman+. ACTIVATION	+
(n,α)	Fiss		CRC Eval	Rept	CRC − 1003	Dec 60	ROY+ ESTIMATED AVG SIG=0.0008MB	
(n,α)	1.4+7		CIS Expt	Jour	NC 20 903	Jun 61	Marcazzan. = 2 DATA INDEX LINES	
(n,α)	1.3+7	2.2+7	HAM Expt	Jour	ZN/A 17 479	Jun 62	Bormann.CSI XTL.A SPECTR.CFD STAT TH	+
(n,α)	1.4+7		OTC Expt	Jour	NP 42 27	Apr 63	Dixon. SIG=1.8+ −0.2MBFOR CSI CRYSTAL	
(n,α)	1.5+7		ARK Expt	Jour	PR 131 2649	Sep 63	Bramlitt+ 1.0+ −0.9MB TO 12.6H I130	+
				Rept	TID − 16949	62	.THESIS	
	1.5+7			Data	EXFOR11590.070	Jun 76	. 1 PT. SIGMA.	
(n,α)	1.4+7		CIS Theo	Jour	NP 51 460	Feb 64	Facchini+STATMOD SIG XPT/CALC2.8 − 5.2	
(n,α)	1.4+7	2.2+7	FRK Expt	Rept	EANDC(E)57U1	Feb 65	Bass+	+
(n,α)	1.4+7	1.5+7	NAP Comp	Rept	INFN/BE − 67 − 11	Sep 67	Cuzzocrea+ AVERAGED CHOSEN DATA.	+
(n,α)	Fast		KJL Expt	Rept	KR − 123	Dec 67	Steinnes.ACT.REL TO AL(NA).	
	Fast			Data	EXFOR20053.005	Sep 71	1PNT.SIG.	
(n,α)	1.5+7		KAZ Expt	Jour	YF 8 7	Jul 68	Levkovskij+ SIG VAL + − ERROR GVN,TBL	+
				Jour	SNP 8 4	Jan 69	TRANSLATN.*	
	1.5+7			Data	EXFOR40223.021	May 74	.SIGMA GIVEN,1 DATA LINE	
(n,α)	1.5+7		DEB Comp	Jour	REA 7 4 93	Dec 69	Csikai+ SIG+HL COMPILTN,N − ACTIV − ANAL	
(n,α)	1.4+7		GIT Expt	Jour	PR/C 1 358	Jan 70	Fink+ SIG=1.96+ −0.15MB	+
	1.4+7			Data	EXFOR10145.031	Apr 75	. 1 PT. SIGMA.	
(n,α)	1.4+7	1.5+7	JYV Eval	Rept	JU − RR − 3/1970	Jun 70	Leppaemaeki+ TABLE OF EVAL AVG SIG	
(n,α)	1.5+7		MNZ Expt	Jour	JIN 32 1799	Jun 70	Qaim+ ACTIV MEAS.+ISOM RATIO	+
	1.5+7			Data	EXFOR20519.	Apr 76	5PTS.SIGMA.	
(n,α)	1.5+7		IRK Expt	Jour	APA 34 209	Sep 71	Havlik. ACT. CC − W.	+
				Jour	OAWA 107 119	Apr 70	− . ACTIVATION METHOD	
	1.5+7			Data	EXFOR20509.005	Apr 76	1PNT.SIGMA.	
(n,α)	1.4+7		GIT Theo	Jour	PR/C 4 1173	Oct 71	Fink+.STAT − MODEL CALCULATION,CFD EXP	
(n,α)	1.4+7		HAM Expt	Jour	NP/A 186 65	May 72	Bormann+ SIG,A,E DISTR COMP+DIR.	
(n,α)	+7		KFK Expt	Rept	KFK−1783 87	Apr 73	Muenzel+ DETECTION LIMITS,2 ES,CFD TH	
				Jour	JIN 34 2093	Jul 72	Krivan+ ACTIVITY CFD SYSTEMATICS	
(n,α)	1.4+7	1.5+7	KAZ Theo	Jour	YF 18 705	Oct 73	Levkovsky.AVERAGED SIG,CALC,TBL	
				Jour	SNP 18 361	Apr 74	. ENGLISH OF YF 18,705	
(n,α)		7.5+8	IOW Expt	Jour	PR/C 12 1978	Dec 75	Hill+ ES TO 750 MEV.	
(n,nα)	1.3+7	2.2+7	HAM Expt	Jour	ZN/A 17 479	Jun 62	Bormann.CSI,XTL.A SPECTR.CFD STAT TH	+
				Jour	ZP 166 477	Feb 62	− + CURVE. EXCIT FUNCTION	
Reson Params	5.9+0		BNL Expt	Jour	PR 93 1030	Mar 54	Landon+ SIG.WT WN BREIT − WGNER ANAL	+
	5.9+0			Data	EXFOR12029.003	Jun 76	. 1 RES, E0,WT,WN0,PCS	
Reson Params	2.3+1	5.3+2	BNL Expt	Jour	PR 99 10	Jul 55	Harvey+ FC TRANSM. 16 RES. AREA ANL	+
	2.3+1	5.3+2		Data	EXFOR11912.032	Jun 76	. 16 RES, E0,WN,WN0,WG	
Reson Params	1.3+2	3.5+3	COL Expt	Jour	PR/B 137 547	Feb 65	Garg+G*WN,145 RES.TBL.D VAL GVN.	+
	1.3+2	3.5+3		Data	EXFOR11905.014	Jun 76	. 160 RES, E0,WN0	
Reson Params	1.0+4	1.0+6	FEI Expt	Jour	AE 23 566	Jun 67	Tolstikov+ MEAN WG,OPTMOD OKS EXPT	
				Jour	SJA 23 1347	Jun 67	. ENGL OF AE 23 566	
Reson Params		1.0+6	AUA Theo	Jour	AUJ 20 477	Oct 67	Cook. TBL OF AVG LVL SPACING D,L=0,1	
Reson Params	5.9+0	3.5+3	KFK Eval	Rept	KFK − 718	Apr 68	Schmidt+ RESOLVED+AVG RES PARAM(S,P)	
Reson Params	None		BNL Theo	Conf	69Studsvik 627	Aug 69	Chrien+ WG − DISTR CFD PORTER − THOM,TBL	
Reson Params	1.7+0	1.1+3	KIL Expt	Jour	AKE 14 271	Aug 69	Jung+ PARTIAL WIDTHS.	+
				Conf	70Helsinki 1 679	Jun 70	− + PRELIMINARY RESULTS	
	1.7+0	5.9+2		Data	EXFOR20553.	Apr 76	53PTS.WG,WN,WT,MEAN LVLSP,AVG.WN0	
Reson Params	5.9+0	3.5+3	KFK Comp	Rept	KFK − 1233	Jul 70	Mueller. ES,WN,WG,G OF 165 RESON	
Reson Params	−		AUA Eval	Rept	AAEC/E − 211	Nov 70	Musgrove. CALCULTD D+GAM WIDTH GIVEN	
Reson Params	5.9+0	1.3+2	CJD Eval	Rept	YK − 7	71	Zakharova+ SURVEY+SYSTEMATICS,GW,TBL	
				Rept	INDC(CCP) − 27	Nov 72	.ENGLISH TRANSLATION OF YK − 7 /71	
Reson Params	None		DUB Theo	Jour	YF 13 240	Feb 71	Malecki+G − WID,THEO CFD EXPT.TBL,GRPH	
				Jour	SNP 13 133	Aug 71	− + ENGL OF YF 13 240.	
Reson Params	None		SAC Expt	Conf	72Budapest 238	Aug 72	Jain+ CORREL N−,PARTIAL G − WIDTH,TBL	
Reson Params	+0	+2	BOL Eval	Conf	IAEA − 169 3 123	74	Benzi+ AVG G − WID CFD OTHERS+XPT,TABL	
Reson Params	+0	+3	FEI Eval	Rept	YK − 8/2 97	Sep 72	Abagyan+ AVG G − WID+D AT BINDNG − E,TBL	
				Rept	INDC(CCP) − 39	Jul 74	.PAGE 102.ENGLISH OF YK − 8/2 97	
Reson Params	2.0+4	8.0+5	HAR Expt	Conf	74Petten 300	Sep 74	Riehs+ SPINS INT.RATIOS OF G	+
	1.5+2	9.0+2		Prog	EANDC(UK) 151	Aug 73	− . LOW EN GS TO GET J TBC	
	5.9+0	3.6+2		Prog	AERE − PR/NP18	Mar 74	Thomas+ J ASSIGNED FROM CAPT GS TBL	
	5.9+0	3.6+2		Data	EXFOR20451.002	Jan 76	12PTS.J.	
Reson Params	1.0+3	1.0+6	SAC Eval	Rept	CEA − N − 1832	Dec 75	Ribon+ EXP+TH ANAL,RES PAR,TBL	

55 Cesium 133

Quantity	Energy (ev) Min	Max	Lab	Type	Documentation Ref Vol Page	Author, Comments Date	Data
Reson Params		4.0+2	ITE	Expt Conf	76Lowell 1251	Jul 76 Kalebin+SHAPE AND AREA ANAL.NDG	
Strnth Fnctn		5.3+2	BNL	Expt Jour	PR 99 10	Jul 55 Harvey+	+
		5.3+2		Data	EXFOR11912.	Jun 76 . 2 PTS, S0,D	
Strnth Fnctn	+3		BNL	Expt Jour	PRL 1 461	Dec 58 Hughes+ FC 1.0+ −0.20	
Strnth Fnctn	+3	+5	BOL	Theo Conf	61Vienna 1 179	Aug 61 Benzi+.PPR11,TABLE CFD EXPERIMENT	
Strnth Fnctn	1.0+3	1.5+4	DUB	Expt Rept	JINR−P−1010	62 Popov+. P−WAVE STF CFD OTHERS+OPTMDL	
Strnth Fnctn	3.5+3		COL	Expt Jour	PR/B 137 547	Feb 65 Garg+ =0.68+ −0.09 CORRECTED FOR L=1	+
	3.5+3			Data	EXFOR11905.	Jun 76 . 2 PTS, S0,D	
Strnth Fnctn	1.0+4	1.5+5	KFK	Expt Jour	NP/A 133 513	Aug 69 Kompe. S1,S2,S(GAMMA)LEAST SQ NG FIT	+
				Rept	KFK−1071	Aug 69 − . REPRINT OF NP/A 133 513	
	1.0+4	1.5+5		Data	EXFOR20358.	Sep 74 3PTS.GAMMA STF.	
Strnth Fnctn	1.7+0	1.1+3	KIL	Expt Jour	70Helsinki 1 679	Jun 70 Jung+ PRELIMINARY RESULTS	+
	1.7+0	2.5+2		Data	EXFOR20553.006	Apr 76 1PNT.	
Strnth Fnctn	−		AUA	Theo Rept	AAEC/E−211	Nov 70 Musgrove. SMOOTHED S0,S1 AND S2 GIVN	
Strnth Fnctn	2.7+3		MUN	Expt Conf	71Albany 327	Aug 71 Dilg+TRNS.S0 STF GVN.31 ELEMENT GRPH	
Strnth Fnctn	2.4+4		MUA	Theo Jour	IJP 46 114	Mar 72 Chaubey+ P−WAVE.FOR A−SYSTEMTIC,GRPH	
Strnth Fnctn	None		AUA	Eval Rept	AAEC/E−277	Mar 73 Musgrove.TBLS EXPTL DATA+BEST VALUES	
Strnth Fnctn	2.5+4		AUW	Expt Jour	NP/A 213 35	Oct 73 Murty+ SB−BE.+ −5KEV.S,P−WAVE CONTRIB	
	1.8+4	2.8+4		Jour	NP/A 213 35	Oct 73 − + P−WAVE.FIT TO P N−G AT 25KEV	
Strnth Fnctn	None		KUR	Theo Prog	IAE−2560	75 Adamchuk+.S0−VALUE,TBL	
Strnth Fnctn	2.0+1	1.0+5	RPI	Expt Abst	BAP 21 537	Apr 76 Hockenbury+S0,S1 DRVD.NDG	
Lvl Density	1.4+7		FEI	Expt Rept	FEI−30	Dec 66 Anufrienko+.PARAMS FROM NONELASTIC	+
Lvl Density	−		FEI	Eval Rept	FEI−36	66 Kapchigashev+.TBL OF RELATD QUANTTYS	+
		5.0+4		Jour	YF 4 686	Sep 66 .TABLE.SHORT VERSION OF FEI−36	
	−			Prog	YFI−3 3	66 .ABSTRACT.TABLE LDL+NUCL EXCIT.E	
		5.0+4		Jour	SNP 4 486	67 .ENGLISH OF YF 4.FROM(N,GAMMA).TABLE	
				Prog	INDC−E−140 3	66 .ENGLISH TRANSL OF YFI−3	
Lvl Density	3.6+6	8.5+6	JAE	Expt Jour	NP/A 131 145	Jun 69 Maruyama. E DEPENDANCE,PARAM,TH FIT.	
	3.5+6	8.5+6		Prog	EANDC(J)8L25	Jan 68 − +.TOF.SPEC NO FIT C THEORIES	
				Conf	67Tokyo 373	Sep 67 − + PPR8.127. ABST.	
Lvl Density	None		AUW	Theo Conf	70Madurai 2 267	Dec 70 Ramamurty+ A−PARAMETER GVN,LANG'S−TH	
Lvl Density	None		BOL	Eval Conf	IAEA−169 3 123	74 Benzi+ LVL DENS PARAM BY XPT,GRPH+TB	
Lvl Density	+0	+3	FEI	Eval Rept	YK−8/2 97	Sep 72 Abagyan+ LVL DENSITY PARAMETER,TBL	
				Rept	INDC(CCP)−39	Jul 74 .PAGE 102.ENGLISH OF YK−8/2 97	
Lvl Density	2.0+3	3.5+3	JAE	ExTh Jour	JPJ 37 581	Sep 74 Ideno.LVL SPACING CORRELATIONS.	
				Rept	JAERI−M−5490	Nov 73 − .LEVEL SPACING CORRELATIONS.TBL	
(γ,n)	8.0+6	3.0+7	SAC	Expt Jour	NP/A 219 39	Jan 74 Lepretre+GDR,LORENTZ PARAM,GRPHS,TBL	

55 Cesium 134

Quantity	Energy (ev) Min	Max	Lab	Type	Documentation Ref Vol Page	Author, Comments Date	Data
Evaluation	1.0−3	1.5+7	AUA	Eval Rept	AAEC/TM−549	Jun 70 Cook.TOT,EL,INEL,NONEL,CAPT SIGS,NDG	+
				Rept	AAEC/E−214	Jun 71 Bertram+GROUP SIGMAS SAME QUANTS.NDG	
				Rept	AAEC/TM−587	Mar 71 *DESCRIPTION OF LIBRARY	
	1.0−3	1.5+7		Data	AUSTR−DFN 124.	Nov 71 POINT(223) AND GROUP(127) SIGMAS	
Total	1.0−3	1.5+7	AUA	Eval Data	AUSTR−DFN 124.	Nov 71 COOK+POINT(223)+GROUP(127)SIG.CF EVL	+
Total		4.0+2	ITE	Expt Conf	76Lowell 1251	Jul 76 Kalebin+TRNS.RES PARS DRVD.NDG	
Elastic	1.0−3	1.5+7	AUA	Eval Data	AUSTR−DFN 124.	Nov 71 COOK+POINT(223)+GROUP(127)SIG.CF EVL	+
Tot Inelastc	5.0+5	1.5+7	AUA	Eval Data	AUSTR−DFN 124.	Nov 71 COOK+POINT(11)+GROUP(127)SIG.CF EVL	+
Nonelastic	1.0−3	1.5+7	AUA	Eval Data	AUSTR−DFN 124.	Nov 71 COOK+POINT(223)+GROUP(127)SIG.CF EVL	+
Absorption	Pile		ROS	Expt Rept	ZFK−201	Apr 70 Adam.THR+EFFECTIV SIG,PRODUCTION SIG	
Absorption	1.0−4	1.0+7	JUL	Eval Rept	JUEL−678−RG	Jul 70 Liu. EVALUATION+CALC,GRPH,FN OF E	
Res Int Abs	5.0−1		AUA	Eval Rept	AAEC/TM−619	Sep 72 Clayton.CALC FROM SIG LIBRARY,TABLE	
Res Int Abs	5.5−1	+6	SAC	Revw Conf	IAEA−169 1 235	74 Ribon.CAPTURE,STATUS CFD REQUEST,TBL	
Res Int Abs	+0	+5	WIN	Revw Conf	IAEA−169 3 163	74 Pope+ DATA FILE CALCS COMPARED	
Res Int Abs		4.0+2	ITE	Expt Conf	76Lowell 1251	Jul 76 Kalebin+TRNS.RES PARS,INTEG.NDG	
(n,γ)	Maxwl		CRC	Expt Jour	JIN 5 259	Feb 58 Bayly+PILE MS 134PM12B THR IFVMI	+
(n,γ)	Maxwl			Data	EXFOR12017.003	Jun 76 . 1 PT. SIGMA.	
(n,γ)	Maxwl		CRC	Expt Prog	AECL−1054	Mar 60 Walker. (CRRP−913)	
(n,γ)	1.0−3	1.5+7	AUA	Eval Data	AUSTR−DFN 124.	Nov 71 COOK+POINT(223)+GROUP(127)SIG.CF EVL	
(n,γ)	Pile		CRC	Eval Rept	AECL−3037 1	Jan 72 Walker.RECOMMENDED SIG,DETAILED TBL	
(n,γ)	2.5−2		AUA	Eval Rept	AAEC/TM−619	Sep 72 Clayton.CALC FROM SIG LIBRARY,TABLE	
(n,γ)	2.5−2		SGA	Eval Conf	73Paris 1 233	Mar 73 Eder+ INTERPOLATED FROM CALC SIG,TBL	
				Rept	SGAE−PH−141	Feb 73 .SAME AS 73PARIS,POINT SIG FROM COOK	
(n,γ)	2.5−2		SAC	Revw Conf	IAEA−169 1 235	74 Ribon.STATUS SIG CFD REQUESTS,TABLE	
(n,γ)	Fiss		WIN	Revw Conf	IAEA−169 3 137	74 Dean. POINT DATA AVG OVER STAND SPEC	
	Maxwl	Fiss		Conf	IAEA−169 3 163	74 Pope+ MAXW+FIS−SPEC AVG DATA CFD XPT	

55 Cesium 134

Quantity	Energy (ev) Min	Max	Lab	Type	Documentation Ref Vol Page	Date	Author, Comments	Data
Spect (n,γ)	Maxwl		LIN	Expt	Jour NP/A 248 249	Aug 75	Alexeev+COMPLEMENT FROM CS133 STUDY	
(n,p)	Maxwl		IFU	Theo	Rept ICD-4 20	67	Dadakina+ PENETR COEFF CALC,TABLE	
Fiss Prod γ	Pile		SGA	Theo	Jour APA 28 94	Apr 69	Higats+COMP.PROGR.BUILDUP FISS.PROD.	
Reson Params		1.0+6	AUA	Theo	Jour AUJ 20 477	Oct 67	Cook. TBL OF AVG LVL SPACING D,L=0,1	
Reson Params	−		AUA	Theo	Rept AAEC/E-211	Nov 70	Musgrove. CALCULTD D+GAM WIDTH GIVEN	
Reson Params		4.0+2	ITE	Expt	Conf 76Lowell 1251	Jul 76	Kalebin+SHAPE AND AREA ANAL.NDG	
Strnth Fnctn	−		AUA	Theo	Rept AAEC/E-211	Nov 70	Musgrove. SMOOTHED S0,S1 AND S2 GIVN	
Lvl Density	+6		MIL	Theo	Jour EN 15 1 54	Jan 68	Facchini+ LDL PARS FROM LOW EN RES	
Lvl Density	None		MUN	Theo	Jour NP/A 217 269	Dec 73	Dilg+ A,DELTA. BACK SHIFTED FERMIGAS	
Lvl Density	None		COP	Theo	Jour NP/A 222 493	Apr 74	Dossing+COLL ROTAT.SPAC. ACCUR ESTIM	
Lvl Density	None		ROC	Theo	Jour NP/A 223 577	May 74	Huizenga+ EXP CFD MICROSC TH SPH NUC	

55 Cesium 135

Quantity	Energy (ev) Min	Max	Lab	Type	Documentation Ref Vol Page	Date	Author, Comments	Data
Evaluation	1.0−3	1.5+7	AUA	Eval	Rept AAEC/TM-549	Jun 70	Cook.TOT,EL,INEL,NONEL,CAPT SIGS,NDG	+
					Rept AAEC/E-214	Jun 71	Bertram+GROUP SIGMAS SAME QUANTS.NDG	
					Rept AAEC/TM-587	Mar 71	*DESCRIPTION OF LIBRARY	
	1.0−3	1.5+7			Data AUSTR-DFN 125.	Nov 71	POINT(223) AND GROUP(127) SIGMAS	
Evaluation	1.0+3	1.0+7	BOL	Eval	Rept CEC(71)-2	71	Benzi+ STAT+EVAP MDS.INEL,N2N,NG.TBL	+
	1.0+3	1.0+7			Data BENZI-DFN 546A	Mar 71	4 QUANTITIES. UK FORMAT	
Evaluation	1.0−5	1.5+7	HED	Eval	Prog HEDL-TME-71143	Oct 71	Schenter+ EVALUATION FOR ENDF/B	
Evaluation	1.0+2	1.5+7	JAE	Eval	Rept JAERI-M-5752	Jul 74	Igarasi+ JNDC FPND WG.TOT,EL,N',CAP	
Total	1.7+0	1.1+3	KIL	Expt	Conf 70Helsinki 1 679	Jun 70	Jung+ PRELIMINARY RESULTS	+
	1.7+0	1.1+3			Data EXFOR20553.	Apr 76	0PTS. SEE RESONANCE PARAMETERS.	
Total	1.0−3	1.5+7	AUA	Eval	Data AUSTR-DFN 125.	Nov 71	COOK+POINT(223)+GROUP(127)SIG.CF EVL	+
Elastic	1.0−3	1.5+7	AUA	Eval	Data AUSTR-DFN 125.	Nov 71	COOK+POINT(223)+GROUP(127)SIG.CF EVL	+
Elastic	+1	+6	GEL	Expt	Prog INDC(SEC)-26	May 72	Theobald+ HE3-SCINT,EXPLOSN,PROPOSED	
Tot Inelastc	2.5+5	1.0+7	BOL	Eval	Rept CEC(71)-2	71	Benzi+ STAT MODEL. TBL GIVEN.	+
	2.5+5	1.0+7			Data BENZI-DFN 546A	Mar 71	41 PNTS	
Tot Inelastc	5.0+5	1.5+7	AUA	Eval	Data AUSTR-DFN 125.	Nov 71	COOK+POINT(11)+GROUP(127)SIG.CF EVL	+
Diff Inelast	2.5+5	1.0+7	BOL	Eval	Rept CEC(71)-2	71	Benzi+ DISCRETE INELASTIC. 3 LVLS	+
	8.0+5	1.0+7			Data BENZI-DFN 546A	Mar 71	TO CONTINUUM,26PNTS+ANGDIST+E DIST	
	2.5+5	8.0+5			Data BENZI-DFN 546A	Mar 71	1ST-3RD LVL+ANGDIST+E DIST	
Nonelastic	1.0−3	1.5+7	AUA	Eval	Data AUSTR-DFN 125.	Nov 71	COOK+POINT(223)+GROUP(127)SIG.CF EVL	+
Absorption	4.1−1	1.0+7	GA	Eval	Prog GA-2451	Aug 61	Joanou+.68GROUP DATA FOR GAM-I	
Absorption	1.0−4	1.0+7	JUL	Eval	Rept JUEL-678-RG	Jul 70	Liu. EVALUATION+CALC,GRPH,FN OF E	
Res Int Abs	5.0−1		CRC	Expt	Jour CJP 36 863	Jul 58	Baerg+ ACT,61.7+−2.3B	+
	5.0−1				Data EXFOR12008.003	Jun 76	. 1 PT, RI	
Res Int Abs	None		CRC	Eval	Prog AECL-1054	Mar 60	Walker.(CRP-913) REDUCED RES.INT.	
Res Int Abs	None		GA	Eval	Rept GA-12071	Sep 71	Mathews+. RECOMMENDED VALUES	
Res Int Abs	5.5−1		CRC	Eval	Rept AECL-3037 1	Jan 72	Walker.REDUCED RES INT,DETAILED TBL	
Res Int Abs	5.0−1				Rept AAEC/TM-619	Sep 72	Clayton.CALC FROM SIG LIBRARY,TABLE	
Res Int Abs	4.6−1	1.0+6	RCN	Theo	Rept RCN-191	Jul 73	Lautenbach.CAPT INT FROM GROUP SIGMA	
Res Int Abs	5.5−1	+6	SAC	Revw	Conf IAEA-169 1 235	74	Ribon.CAPTURE,STATUS CFD REQUEST,TBL	
Res Int Abs	+0	+5	WIN	Revw	Conf IAEA-169 3 163	74	Pope+ DATA FILE CALC CFD XPTAL VALUE	
(n,γ)	Pile		LAS	Expt	Jour PR 75 1473	May 49	Sugarman.	+
	Pile				Data EXFOR12038.002	Jun 76	. 1 PT.	
(n,γ)	Pile		CRC	Expt	Jour CJP 36 863	Jul 58	Baerg+ SIG=10.4+−0.5B EFFECTIVE,ACT	+
	Pile				Data EXFOR12008.002	Jun 76	. 1 PT. SIGMA.	
(n,γ)	Maxwl		CRC	Eval	Prog AECL-1054	Mar 60	Walker. (CRRP-913)	
(n,γ)	5.0−3	2.5+0	GA	Eval	Rept GA-2113	Jun 61	Wikner+ TABLE + CURVE. 100 E PTS.	
(n,γ)	1.0+3	1.0+7	BOL	Eval	Rept CEC(71)-2	71	Benzi+ OPTMOD EVAL.TBL GIVEN.	+
					Conf 66Paris 1 537	Oct 66	− .STATIST MODEL+XPTAL MEAN D,WG	
	1.0+3	1.0+7			Data BENZI-DFN 546A	Mar 71	61 PNTS	
(n,γ)	1.0−3	1.5+7	AUA	Eval	Data AUSTR-DFN 125.	Nov 71	COOK+POINT(223)+GROUP(127)SIG.CF EVL	+
(n,γ)	Maxwl		CRC	Eval	Rept AECL-3037 1	Jan 72	Walker.RECOMMENDED SIG,DETAILED TBL	
(n,γ)	+1	+6	GEL	Expt	Prog INDC(SEC)-26	May 72	Theobald+ M-R+CERENCOV,BOMB,PROPOSED	
(n,γ)	2.5−2		AUA	Eval	Rept AAEC/TM-619	Sep 72	Clayton.CALC FROM SIG LIBRARY,TABLE	
(n,γ)		1.1+7	RCN	Theo	Rept RCN-191	Jun 73	Lautenbach. GROUP CONSTANTS TBL	
(n,γ)	Fiss		SAC	Revw	Conf IAEA-169 1 235	74	Ribon.STATUS SIG CFD REQUESTS,TABLE	
	2.5−2	3.0+4			Conf IAEA-169 1 235	74	− .STATUS SIG CFD REQUESTS,TABLE	
(n,γ)	Maxwl	Fiss	WIN	Revw	Conf IAEA-169 3 163	74	Pope+ MAXW+FIS-SPEC AVG DATA CFD XPT	
	Fiss				Conf IAEA-169 3 137	74	Dean. POINT DATA AVG OVER STAND SPEC	
(n,γ)	1.0−3	1.0+7	RCN	Revw	Rept ECN-12	Nov 76	Gruppelaar+ INTERCOMP. RECENT WORKS	
(n,2n)	Fiss		CRC	Eval	Rept CRC-1003	Dec 60	ROY+ ESTIMATED AVG SIG=1.2MB	

55 Cesium 135

Quantity	Energy (ev) Min	Max	Lab	Type	Documentation Ref Vol Page	Date	Author, Comments	Data
(n,2n)	9.1+6	1.0+7	BOL	Eval	Rept CEC(71) – 2	71	Benzi+ STAT+EVAP MODELS.TBL GIVEN.	+
	9.1+6	1.0+7			Data BENZI – DFN 546A	Mar 71	3 PNTS+ANGDIST+E DIST. 1 RANGE	
(n,p)	Fiss		CRC	Eval	Rept CRC – 1003	Dec 60	ROY+ ESTIMATED AVG SIG=0.06MB	
(n,p)	Maxwl		IFU	Theo	Rept ICD – 4 20	67	Dadakina+ PENETR COEFF CALC,TABLE	
(n,α)	Fiss		CRC	Eval	Rept CRC – 1003	Dec 60	ROY+ ESTIMATED AVG SIG=0.0003MB	
Reson Params		1.0+6	AUA	Theo	Jour AUJ 20 477	Oct 67	Cook. TBL OF AVG LVL SPACING D,L=0,1	
Reson Params	4.2+1	8.8+2	KIL	Expt	Conf 70Helsinki 1 679	Jun 70	Jung+ PRELIMINARY RESULTS	+
	4.2+1	8.8+2			Data EXFOR20553.008	Apr 76	2PTS.WN.	
Reson Params	–		AUA	Theo	Rept AAEC/E – 211	Nov 70	Musgrove. CALCULTD D+GAM WIDTH GIVEN	
Reson Params	+1	+6	GEL	Expt	Prog INDC(SEC) – 26	May 72	Theobald+ FROM CAPT+EL SIG,PROPOSED	
Reson Params	1.0+3	1.0+6	SAC	Eval	Rept CEA – N – 1832	Dec 75	Ribon+ EXP+TH ANAL,RES PAR,TBL	
Strnth Fnctn	–		AUA	Theo	Rept AAEC/E – 211	Nov 70	Musgrove. SMOOTHED S0,S1 AND S2 GIVN	

55 Cesium 136

Quantity	Energy (ev) Min	Max	Lab	Type	Documentation Ref Vol Page	Date	Author, Comments	Data
Evaluation	1.0–3	1.5+7	AUA	Eval	Rept AAEC/TM – 549	Jun 70	Cook.TOT,EL,INEL,NONEL,CAPT SIGS,NDG	+
					Rept AAEC/E – 214	Jun 71	Bertram+GROUP SIGMAS SAME QUANTS.NDG	
					Rept AAEC/TM – 587	Mar 71	*DESCRIPTION OF LIBRARY	
	1.0–3	1.5+7			Data AUSTR – DFN 126.	Nov 71	POINT(223) AND GROUP(127) SIGMAS	
Total	1.0–3	1.5+7	AUA	Eval	Data AUSTR – DFN 126.	Nov 71	COOK+POINT(223)+GROUP(127)SIG.CF EVL	+
Elastic	1.0–3	1.5+7	AUA	Eval	Data AUSTR – DFN 126.	Nov 71	COOK+POINT(223)+GROUP(127)SIG.CF EVL	+
Tot Inelastc	5.0+5	1.5+7	AUA	Eval	Data AUSTR – DFN 126.	Nov 71	COOK+POINT(11)+GROUP(127)SIG.CF EVL	+
Nonelastic	1.0–3	1.5+7	AUA	Eval	Data AUSTR – DFN 126.	Nov 71	COOK+POINT(223)+GROUP(127)SIG.CF EVL	+
Res Int Abs	5.0–1		AUA	Eval	Rept AAEC/TM – 619	Sep 72	Clayton.CALC FROM SIG LIBRARY,TABLE	
Res Int Abs	+0	+5	WIN	Revw	Conf IAEA – 169 3 163	74	Pope+ CALC FROM AUSTRAL DATA FILE	
(n,γ)	1.0–3	1.5+7	AUA	Eval	Data AUSTR – DFN 126.	Nov 71	COOK+POINT(223)+GROUP(127)SIG.CF EVL	+
(n,γ)	Pile		CRC	Eval	Rept AECL – 3037 1	Jan 72	Walker.SIG ESTIMATED ACCORDING Z,A	
(n,γ)	2.5–2		AUA	Eval	Rept AAEC/TM – 619	Sep 72	Clayton.CALC FROM SIG LIBRARY,TABLE	
(n,γ)	2.5–2		SGA	Eval	Conf 73Paris 1 233	Mar 73	Eder+ INTERPOLATED FROM CALC SIG,TBL	
					Rept SGAE – PH – 141	Feb 73	.SAME AS 73PARIS,POINT SIG FROM COOK	
(n,γ)	Fiss		WIN	Revw	Conf IAEA – 169 3 137	74	Dean. POINT DATA AVG OVER STAND SPEC	
	Maxwl	Fiss			Conf IAEA – 169 3 163	74	Pope+ MAXW+FIS – SPEC AVG EVAL DATA	
Reson Params	–		AUA	Theo	Rept AAEC/E – 211	Nov 70	Musgrove. CALCULTD D+GAM WIDTH GIVEN	
Strnth Fnctn	–		AUA	Theo	Rept AAEC/E – 211	Nov 70	Musgrove. SMOOTHED S0,S1 AND S2 GIVN	

55 Cesium 137

Quantity	Energy (ev) Min	Max	Lab	Type	Documentation Ref Vol Page	Date	Author, Comments	Data
Evaluation	1.0–3	1.5+7	AUA	Eval	Rept AAEC/TM – 549	Jun 70	Cook.TOT,EL,INEL,NONEL,CAPT SIGS,NDG	+
					Rept AAEC/E – 214	Jun 71	Bertram+GROUP SIGMAS SAME QUANTS.NDG	
					Rept AAEC/TM – 587	Mar 71	*DESCRIPTION OF LIBRARY	
	1.0–3	1.5+7			Data AUSTR – DFN 127.	Nov 71	POINT(223) AND GROUP(127) SIGMAS	
Evaluation	1.0+3	1.0+7	BOL	Eval	Rept CEC(71) – 2	71	Benzi+ STAT+EVAP MDS.INEL,N2N,NG.TBL	+
	1.0+3	1.0+7			Data BENZI – DFN 548A	Mar 71	4 QUANTITIES. UK FORMAT	
Evaluation	1.0–5	1.5+7	HED	Eval	Prog HEDL – TME – 71143	Oct 71	Schenter+ EVALUATION FOR ENDF/B	
Evaluation	1.0+2	1.5+7	JAE	Eval	Rept JAERI – M – 5752	Jul 74	Igarasi+ JNDC FPND WG.TOT,EL,N',CAP	
Total	1.7+0	1.1+3	KIL	Expt	Conf 70Helsinki 1 679	Jun 70	Jung+ PRELIMINARY RESULTS	+
	1.7+0	1.1+3			Data EXFOR20553.	Apr 76	0PTS. SEE RESONANCE PARAMETERS.	
Total	1.0–3	1.5+7	AUA	Eval	Data AUSTR – DFN 127.	Nov 71	COOK+POINT(223)+GROUP(127)SIG.CF EVL	+
Elastic	1.0–3	1.5+7	AUA	Eval	Data AUSTR – DFN 127.	Nov 71	COOK+POINT(223)+GROUP(127)SIG.CF EVL	+
Tot Inelastc	4.6+5	1.0+7	BOL	Eval	Rept CEC(71) – 2	71	Benzi+ STAT MODEL. TBL GIVEN.	+
	4.6+5	1.0+7			Data BENZI – DFN 548A	Mar 71	40 PNTS	
Tot Inelastc	5.0+5	1.5+7	AUA	Eval	Data AUSTR – DFN 127.	Nov 71	COOK+POINT(11)+GROUP(127)SIG.CF EVL	+
Diff Inelast	4.6+5	1.0+7	BOL	Eval	Rept CEC(71) – 2	71	Benzi+ DISCRETE INELASTIC. 1 LVL	+
	7.0+5	1.0+7			Data BENZI – DFN 548A	Mar 71	TO CONTINUUM, 35PNTS+ANGDIST+E DIST	
	4.6+5	7.0+5			Data BENZI – DFN 548A	Mar 71	1ST LVL+ANGDIST+E DIST	
Nonelastic	1.0–3	1.5+7	AUA	Eval	Data AUSTR – DFN 127.	Nov 71	COOK+POINT(223)+GROUP(127)SIG.CF EVL	+
Absorption	Pile		ANL	Expt	Prog BNL – C – 9 89	49	Engelkemeir.	
	Pile				Data EXFOR12044.002	Jun 76	. 1 PT.	
Absorption	Maxwl		KAP	Expt	Jour NUC 14 89	Sep 56	Deutsch.FISS PROD S EST BY STEHN	
Absorption	4.1–1	1.0+7	GA	Eval	Prog GA – 2451	Aug 61	Joanou+ 68 GROUP DATA FOR GAM – I	
Absorption	1.0–4	1.0+7	JUL	Eval	Rept JUEL – 678 – RG	Jul 70	Liu. EVALUATION+CALC,GRPH,FN OF E	
Res Int Abs	None		GA	Eval	Rept GA – 12071	Sep 71	Mathews+. RECOMMENDED VALUES	
Res Int Abs	5.0–1		AUA	Eval	Rept AAEC/TM – 619	Sep 72	Clayton.CALC FROM SIG LIBRARY,TABLE	
Res Int Abs	4.6–1	1.0+6	RCN	Theo	Rept RCN – 191	Jul 73	Lautenbach.CAPT INT FROM GROUP SIGMA	

55   Cesium   137

Quantity	Energy (ev) Min	Max	Lab	Type	Documentation Ref Vol Page	Date	Author, Comments	Data
Res Int Abs	5.5−1	+6	SAC	Revw Conf	IAEA − 169 1 235	74	Ribon.CAPTURE,STATUS CFD REQUEST,TBL	
Res Int Abs	+0	+5	WIN	Revw Conf	IAEA − 169 3 163	74	Pope+ DATA FILE CALCS COMPARED	
(n,γ)	Maxwl		ANL	Expt Jour	JNEA 12 16	May 60	Stupegia. SIGMA GVN	+
	Maxwl			Data	EXFOR12021.002	Jun 76	. 1 PT. SIGMA.	
(n,γ)	Maxwl		CRC	Eval Rept	AECL − 2111	Nov 64	Walker.	
(n,γ)	1.0+3	1.0+7	BOL	Eval Rept	CEC(71) − 2	71	Benzi+ OPTMOD EVAL.TBL GIVEN.	+
				Conf	66Paris 1 537	Oct 66	− .STATIST MODEL+XPTAL MEAN D,WG	
	1.0+3	1.0+7		Data	BENZI − DFN 548A	Mar 71	62 PNTS	
(n,γ)	Maxwl		GA	Eval Rept	GA − 12071	Sep 71	Mathews+. RECOMMENDED VALUES	
(n,γ)	1.0−3	1.5+7	AUA	Eval Data	AUSTR − DFN 127.	Nov 71	COOK+ POINT(223)+GROUP(127)SIG.CF EVL	+
(n,γ)	Pile		CRC	Eval Rept	AECL − 3037 1	Jan 72	Walker.RECOMMENDED SIG,DETAILED TBL	
(n,γ)	2.5−2		AUA	Eval Rept	AAEC/TM − 619	Sep 72	Clayton.CALC FROM SIG LIBRARY,TABLE	
(n,γ)		1.1+7	RCN	Theo Rept	RCN − 191	Jun 73	Lautenbach. GROUP CONSTANTS TBL	
(n,γ)	2.5−2	3.0+4	SAC	Revw Conf	IAEA − 169 1 235	74	Ribon.STATIS SIG CFD REQUESTS,TABLE	
	Fiss			Conf	IAEA − 169 1 235	74	− .STATIS SIG CFD REQUESTS,TABLE	
(n,γ)	Maxwl	Fiss	WIN	Revw Conf	IAEA − 169 3 163	74	Pope+ MAXW+FIS − SPEC AVG DATA CFD XPT	
	Fiss			Conf	IAEA − 169 3 137	74	Dean. POINT DATA AVG OVER STAND SPEC	
Spect (n,γ)	−		CCP	Expt Rept	AEC − TR − 6449	63	Gritchenko. GAM SPEC,FISS PRODUCT	
(n,2n)	Fiss		CRC	Eval Rept	CRC − 1003	Dec 60	ROY+ ESTIMATED AVG SIG=5.3MB	
(n,2n)	8.7+6	1.0+7	BOL	Eval Rept	CEC(71) − 2	71	Benzi+ STAT+EVAP MODELS.TBL GIVEN.	+
	8.7+6	1.0+7		Data	BENZI − DFN 548A	Mar 71	4 PNTS+ANGDIST+E DIST. 1 RANGE	
(n,α)	Fiss		CRC	Eval Prog	GA − B − 12271	Sep 71	Roy+,ESTIMATED AVG SIG=0.0003MB	
Fiss Prod γ	Pile		SGA	Theo Jour	APA 28 94	Apr 69	Higats+COMP.PROGR.BUILDUP FISS.PROD.	
Reson Params		1.0+6	AUA	Theo Jour	AUJ 20 477	Oct 67	Cook. TBL OF AVG LVL SPACING D,L=0,1	
Reson Params	4.2+1	8.8+2	KIL	Expt Conf	70Helsinki 1 679	Jun 70	Jung+ PRELIMINARY RESULTS	+
	4.2+1	8.8+2		Data	EXFOR20553.009	Apr 76	2PTS.WN.	
Reson Params	−		AUA	Theo Rept	AAEC/E − 211	Nov 70	Musgrove. CALCULTD D+GAM WIDTH GIVEN	
Strnth Fnctn	−		AUA	Theo Rept	AAEC/E − 211	Nov 70	Musgrove. SMOOTHED S0,S1 AND S2 GIVN	

55   Cesium   138

Quantity	Energy (ev) Min	Max	Lab	Type	Documentation Ref Vol Page	Date	Author, Comments	Data
Reson Params	−		AUA	Theo Rept	AAEC/E − 211	Nov 70	Musgrove. CALCULTD D+GAM WIDTH GIVEN	
Strnth Fnctn	−		AUA	Theo Rept	AAEC/E − 211	Nov 70	Musgrove. SMOOTHED S0,S1 AND S2 GIVN	

55   Cesium   139

Quantity	Energy (ev) Min	Max	Lab	Type	Documentation Ref Vol Page	Date	Author, Comments	Data
Reson Params	−		AUA	Theo Rept	AAEC/E − 211	Nov 70	Musgrove. CALCULTD D+GAM WIDTH GIVEN	
Strnth Fnctn	−		AUA	Theo Rept	AAEC/E − 211	Nov 70	Musgrove. SMOOTHED S0,S1 AND S2 GIVN	

56 Barium

Quantity	Energy (ev) Min	Max	Lab	Type	Documentation Ref Vol Page	Author, Comments Date	Data
Evaluation	2.5−2	1.4+7	PCT	Eval	Rept NP− 8216	Oct 58 Lamarsh+ ALL DATA	
Evaluation	5.0+5	1.5+7	LRL	Eval	Rept UCRL−5351	Nov 58 Howerton. CURVS TOT SEL SNE STN N2N	
Total	Maxwl		COL	Expt	Jour PR 48 265	Aug 35 Dunning+ IONCH,TRANS,RA−BE/PARAFIN N	
Total	4.2+7		BRK	Expt	Jour PR 80 842	Dec 50 Hildebrand+ BE−D NS.TRANSM. C DETECT	+
	4.2+7			Data	EXFOR11039.027	Jun 76 . 1 PT, SIGMA.	
Total	1.6+8		HAR	Expt	Jour PM 42 751	Jul 51 Taylor+. 2476+−88MB AT 156+−3MEV	
Total	2.4−2	9.6−1	COL	Expt	Priv HAVENS	52 Havens.	+
	2.4−2	9.6−1		Data	EXFOR11361.007	Jun 76 . 33 PTS, SIGMA.	
Total	5.0+4	3.2+6	WIS	Expt	Jour PR 88 83	Oct 52 Miller+ 20KEV SPREAD TRNSM	+
	5.0+4	3.2+6		Data	EXFOR11712.016	Jun 76 . 71 PTS, SIGMA.	
Total	1.4+7		LAS	Expt	Jour PR 88 562	Nov 52 Coon+ SIMPLE TRANS, GOOD GEOMETRY.	+
	1.4+7			Data	EXFOR11056.044	Jun 76 . 1 PT, SIGMA.	
Total	1.6+4	1.0+5	DKE	Expt	Jour PR 102 1580	Jun 56 Newson+ ABS CURV ISOTOPIC ASSIGNMENT	+
	1.6+4	1.0+5		Data	EXFOR11834.007	Jun 76 . 57 PTS, SIGMA.	
Total	5.0+4	1.8+7	LAS	Theo	Rept LA− 2099	Dec 56 Beyster+ OPTMDL CALC CFD EXPT,CURVE	
Total	1.3+7	1.6+7	LAS	Expt	Jour PR 109 1268	Feb 58 Conner.TRNS SC 3ES 5.01 5.02 4.97B	+
					Conf 58Geneva 15 11	Sep 58 Coon+ PPR666,SIGMA AT 3ES GVN,TOF	
	1.3+7	1.6+7		Data	EXFOR11320.005	Jun 76 . 3 PTS, SIGMA.	
Total	1.1+2	2.4+2	BNL	Expt	Jour PR 110 692	May 58 Seth+ TRANSMISSION EXPERIMENT.	+
	1.1+2	2.4+2		Data	EXFOR11788.032	Jun 76 . 10 PTS, SIGMA.	
Total	4.1+6		TNC	Expt	Rept WADD−TR−60−217	Apr 60 Vincent.TOF 4.3+−0.1B	+
	4.1+6			Data	EXFOR11621.022	Jun 76 . 1 PT, SIGMA.	
Total	+0	2.0+5	DKE	Expt	Jour AP 14 387	Jul 61 Bilpuch+. 160 DEG SPECTROMETER	
	1.5+4	1.2+5			Jour NIM 7 67	Apr 60 Newson+ HIGH RESOLUTION N SPECTROSCOP	
	1.7+4	2.0+5		Data	EXFOR11599.044	Jun 76 . 140 PTS, SIGMA.	
Total	2.8+7		LVN	Expt	Jour JPR 22 652	Oct 61 Deconninck+TRANSMISS.4.09B AT 28.4MV	+
	2.8+7			Data	EXFOR20195.016	May 74 1PNT.	
Total	1.2+6	1.8+6	STF	Expt	Jour PR 131 1644	Aug 63 Wells+ CURVE GIVEN	+
	1.2+6	1.8+6		Data	EXFOR11121.015	Jun 76 . 24 PTS, SIGMA.	
Total	1.0+6	1.6+7	HAR	Theo	Jour NP 55 673	Jul 64 Wilmore+ OPTMOD USING LOCAL EQUIV P−B	
					Rept AERE−R−4649	Jun 64 − + OPTICAL MDL	
Total	3.0+0	1.0+3	IFU	Expt	Prog YFI−6 112	68 Vertebnyj+. TRANSMISSION,TIME−OF−FL	
					Rept INDC−260E	69 . ENGL OF YFI−6 112	
Total	5.0+5	1.5+7	AUA	Theo	Rept AAEC/TM−536	Apr 70 Bertram. OPTMOD SIG(E)GRAPH CFD EXPT	
Total	2.5+6	1.5+7	BNW	Expt	Jour PR/C 3 576	Feb 71 Foster+,TRANS,CURVS,CFD OTHERS+TH	
					Jour NIM 36 1	Sep 65 − + EXPERIMENTAL DETAILS.	
Total	5.0+4	8.8+5	DKE	Expt	Prog NCSAC−38 182	May 71 Newson+. NO SIG GIVEN	
Total	1.3+7	1.5+7	DEB	Eval	Rept IAEA−153 173	73 Boedy+ MOST PROBABLE VAL OF SIG,TBL	
					Jour AHP 30 115	Oct 71 Angeli+ AVG SIG,CFD CALC.TBLS.GRAPH	
Total	5.7+6	9.6+6	THS	Expt	Jour ZP/A 275 17	Nov 75 Heuer+ TRANSMISSION EXPT.	+
					Diss HEUER	Apr 74 − . TRANSMISSION	
	5.7+6	9.6+6		Data	EXFOR20560.004	Mar 76 41PTS.	
Total	1.8+1	1.2+3	ANL	Expt	Prog WASH−1013	Nov 58 Bollinger+ FC NDG EXPECTS TO GIVE IA	+
	1.8+1	1.2+3		Data	EXFOR11643.002	Jun 76 . 723 PTS, SIGMA.	
Total	2.3+6	2.7+6	TEX	Expt	Abst BAP 2 232	Apr 57 Bennett. ABST X1, FAST COINCIDENCE	+
	2.3+6	2.7+6		Data	EXFOR11265.007	Jun 76 . 14 PTS, SIGMA.	
Elastic	3.6−2		ANL	Expt	Jour PR 71 666	May 47 Fermi+ SCATT LENGTH+SIGN FROM INTERF	+
	3.6−2			Data	EXFOR12593.002	Jun 76 . 1 PT, SIGMA.	
Elastic	1.0+6		WIS	Expt	Jour PR 93 1062	Mar 54 Walt+ SEE TABLE I.	+
	1.0+6			Data	EXFOR11637.053	Jun 76 . 1 PT, SIGMA.	
Elastic	4.1+6		TNC	Expt	Rept WADD−TR−60−217	Apr 60 Vincent.TOF INT20−135DEG 2.5+−0.3B	+
	4.1+6			Data	EXFOR11621.020	Jun 76 . 1 PT, SIGMA.	
Elastic	6.5+5		IFU	Expt	Jour UFZ 8 1323	Dec 63 Korzh.INTEGRATD FROM ANGDSTRB 5.94	
Elastic	1.0+6	1.6+7	HAR	Theo	Jour NP 55 673	Jul 64 Wilmore+ OPTMOD SHAPE ELASTIC ONLY	
Elastic	1.0+6	5.0+6	AGN	Eval	Rept TID−21629	Dec 64 Perkins. 3 ES, CALC FROM BNL 400.	
Elastic	2.0+6		FEI	Expt	Rept EANDC−50 200	Jul 65 Kazakova+ EXPT,TABLE CFD OPTMODEL	+
					Prog YFI−3 6	Sep 66 .TABLE	
					Conf 65Antwerp 576	Jul 65 .ABSTRACT ONLY OF EANDC−50	
					Prog INDC−E−140 6	Sep 66 .ENGLISH TRANSL OF YFI−3 6 9/66	
Elastic	5.0+5	8.0+5	IFU	ExTh	Jour AE 20 8	Jan 66 Korzh+ SUMMARY OF SEVERAL YRS WORK	
					Jour UFZ 8 1323	63 .	
					Jour SJA 20 8	Jul 66 .ENGLISH TRANSL OF AE 20 8 1/66	
Elastic	5.0+5	1.5+7	AUA	Theo	Rept AAEC/TM−536	Apr 70 Bertram. OPTMOD SIG(E)GRAPH CFD EXPT	
Elastic	8.8+5		ANL	Expt	Rept ANL−7935	Jun 72 COX+ 4 PI B(O)	+
	8.8+5			Data	EXFOR10332.112	Jun 74 . 1 PT, SIGMA.	
Elastic	Cold		MUN	Expt	Prog EANDC(E)157U	Mar 73 Koester+COH SCT AMP.BAF2,W3,(N03)2	

56 Barium

Quantity	Energy (ev) Min	Max	Lab	Type	Documentation Ref Vol Page	Author, Comments Date	Data
Diff Elastic	1.0+6		WIS	Expt	Jour PR 93 1062	Mar 54 Walt+ HE COUNTER 30-150DEG LAB CURVE	+
	1.0+6				Data EXFOR11637.055	Jun 76 . 9 PTS, DSIGMA.	
Diff Elastic	1.0+5	1.8+7	LAS	Theo	Rept LA-2099	Dec 56 Beyster+,21ES,OPTMDL CALC CFD EXPT	
Diff Elastic	7.0+6		LRL	Theo	Rept UCRL-4927	Jul 57 Bjorklund+ OPTMDL CALC 6-PARAM FIT	
Diff Elastic	1.4+7		LRL	Theo	Rept UCRL-4926	Jul 57 Bjorklund+ OPTMDL CALC 6-PARAM FIT	
Diff Elastic	5.0+6		WES	Expt	Jour PR 109 2105	Mar 58 Hill. 30-150 DEG CFD OPTMDL CALCS.	+
	5.0+6				Data EXFOR11321.009	Jun 76 . 10 PTS, DSIGMA.	
Diff Elastic	4.1+6		TNC	Expt	Rept WADD-TR-60-217	Apr 60 Vincent.TOF 20-135DEG CURVE+TABLE	+
	4.1+6				Data EXFOR11621.023	Jun 76 . 15 PTS, DSIGMA.	
Diff Elastic	1.2+6	1.7+6	STF	Expt	Jour PR 131 1644	Aug 63 Wells+ THRS EFFECTS CURVES AT 2ANGLS	+
	1.2+6	1.7+6			Data EXFOR11121.	Jun 76 . 45PTS, DSIGMA AT 90DEG AND 125DEG.	
Diff Elastic	6.5+5		IFU	Expt	Jour UFZ 8 1323	Dec 63 Korzh.GRAPH SIG(COS),TBL DERIVD VLUS	+
Diff Elastic	5.0+5	8.0+5	FEI	Expt	Jour AE 16 207	Mar 64 Pasechnik+	
					Jour JNE 19 278	65 . ENGL OF AE 16 207	
					Jour SJA 16 246	Mar 64 . ENGL OF AE 16 207	
					Jour EAF 16 3 2	64 .FRENCH OF AE 16 207	
Diff Elastic	4.0+6	5.0+6	HAR	Theo	Jour NP 55 673	Jul 64 Wilmore+OPTMOD SHAPE +COMP.ELASTIC	
					Rept AERE-R-4649	Jun 64 - + OPTICAL MDL	
Diff Elastic	1.0+6	5.0+6	AGN	Eval	Rept TID-21629	Dec 64 Perkins. 3ES CALC LEGNDR COEF.	
Diff Elastic	8.0+5		IFU	Theo	Jour UFZ 10 6 586	Jun 65 Korzh.OPTMDL GRAPH SIG,CFD XPT	
					Jour IZV 29 862	May 65 .	
Diff Elastic	2.0+6		FEI	Expt	Rept EANDC-50 200	Jul 65 Kazakova+ EXPT,CURVE CFD OPTMODEL	+
					Prog ICD-2 112	Jul 65 .CURVE	
					Conf 65Antwerp 576	Jul 65 .ABSTRACT ONLY OF EANDC-50	
					Prog INDSWG-101E	65 .ENGLISH TRANSL OF ICD-2 112 7/65	
Diff Elastic	8.0+5		IFU	Theo	Conf 65Antwerp § 193	Jul 65 Pasechnic+. OPT.MOD.PARAMETERS	
Diff Elastic	1.0+6		LAS	Theo	Prog WASH-1064 84	Oct 65 Rosen+ OPTMDL+ CPD ELST CFD WIS XPT.	
Diff Elastic	5.0+5	8.0+5	IFU	ExTh	Jour AE 20 8	Jan 66 Korzh+ SUMMARY OF SEVERAL YRS WORK	+
				Theo	Jour AE 16 207	Mar 64 Pasechnik+ SPH 30-140 DEGREES	
				ExTh	Jour UFZ 8 1323	63 .	
	6.5+5			Expt	Rept BNL-TR-242	Sep 68 Korzh+ ANGDIST(30-140DEG),GRAPH+TABL	
	5.0+5	8.0+5		ExTh	Jour SJA 20 8	Jul 66 .ENGLISH TRANSL OF AE 20 8 1/66	
				Theo	Jour JNE 19 278	Apr 65 . ENGL OF AE 16 207	
					Jour SJA 16 246	Mar 64 . ENGL OF AE 16 207	
Diff Elastic	3.2+6		BCM	Expt	Jour NP 89 154	Dec 66 Becker+ 12 ANGLES GRAPH CFD OPTMODL	+
	3.2+6				Data EXFOR11511.028	Jun 76 . 13 PTS, DSIGMA.	
Diff Elastic	1.0+6	5.0+6	AI	Eval	Rept NAA-SR-11980	Apr 67 Campbell+ LEG COEFS TBL+CURVS C-MSYS	
Diff Elastic	2.0+6	3.2+6	SCU	Theo	Rept ICD-6 236	69 Averyanov+CALC ANGDIST CFD EXPT,GRPH	
Diff Elastic	8.8+5		ANL	Expt	Rept ANL-7935	Jun 72 COX+ CFD OPTMOD,HAUSER-FESHBACH.	+
	8.8+5				Data EXFOR10332.023	Jun 74 . 8 PTS, DSIGMA	
Diff Elastic	8.0+5		SCU	Comp	Rept YK-15 153	Aug 73 Aver'Janov+ H-F,OPTMOD,DIFFSIG,GRAPH	
Diff Elastic	3.2+6		AMS	Theo	Jour NP/A 222 93	Apr 74 Zijp+ LEG.COEFF COMPOUND ELASTIC.H-F	
Polarization	3.3+6		FEI	Expt	Prog YFI-3 5	Sep 66 Kazakova+POLAR SCAT-NEUTS GVN,OPTMOD	
					Rept INDC-140E	66 . ENGL OF YFI-3 5	
Polarization	8.8+5		ANL	Expt	Rept ANL-7935	Jun 72 COX+ CFD OPTMOD,HAUSER-FESHBACH	+
	8.8+5				Data EXFOR10332.057	Jun 74 . 8 PTS	
Polarization	3.2+6		AMS	Expt	Jour NP/A 222 93	Apr 74 Zijp+ TABLES,GRAPHS. CFD NON-SPH POT	+
					Conf 75Zurich 189	Aug 75 - + GRPH OF DATA IN REVIEW.	
					Conf 72Budapest 170	Aug 72 - + POLARIZTN,EXPT CFD OPTMOD,GRP	
	3.2+6				Data EXFOR20777.017	Apr 78 9PTS.	
Potntal Scat	1.2+2	3.4+2	ANL	Expt	Jour PR 79 747	Sep 50 Hibdon. REL MN+CO RESON SCAT. BAF2	
Potntal Scat	+0	+3	BNL	Expt	Jour PR 110 692	May 58 Seth+ 4.3+ -1.0B CALCTD FROM TOT SIG	+
	1.8+2				Data EXFOR11788.014	Jun 76 . 1 PT, SIGMA.	
Potntal Scat	1.0+6	1.4+7	HAR	Theo	Rept AERE-R-4649	Jun 64 Wilmore.OPTMDL TH.TBLS,CURVES	
Tot Inelastc	2.5+6		IFU	Expt	Jour JET 4 769	Jun 57 .ENGLISH OF ZET 31 907	
					Jour ZET 31 907	Nov 56 Strizhak. SPHERE METHOD,TABLE	
Tot Inelastc	Fiss		KUR	Revw	Conf 60Vienna 159	Oct 60 Bondarenko+.TABLE,EXPT DESCRIBED	
Tot Inelastc	2.5+6		FEI	Expt	Book NEJTRONFIZ 294	61 Lovchikova. NP237 AND U238 TR-DETECT	
					Book SPN 216	61 . ENGL OF NEJTRONFIZ 294	
Tot Inelastc	Fiss		CCP		Jour AE 11 442	Nov 61 FISCH 1.36PM.10B FOR N BELO1.4MEV	
					Jour SJA 11 1087	May 62 TRANSLATN.*	
Tot Inelastc	4.0+5	1.2+6	FEI	Expt	Jour AE 15 416	Nov 63 Glazkov+	
					Jour JNE 18 654	64 . ENGL OF AE 15 416	
					Jour SJA 15 1173	Nov 63 . ENGL OF AE 15 416	
					Jour EAF 15 5	Nov 63 .FRENCH OF AE 15 416	
Tot Inelastc	8.0+5	4.0+6	IFU	Expt	Prog INDSWG-126 22	66 Pasechnik. AT 5 ES, TBP IN AE	
	2.5+6	4.1+6			Conf 55Geneva 2 3	Aug 55 - . INTEGR SIGMA,3ES,TABLE	

56 Barium

Quantity	Energy (ev) Min	Max	Lab	Type	Documentation Ref Vol Page	Date	Author, Comments	Data
Diff Inelast	4.1+6		TNC	Expt Rept	WADD-TR-60-217	Apr 60	Vincent.TOF ISOTROPIC 90-135DEG	+
	4.1+6			Data	EXFOR11621.024	Jun 76	. 17 PTS, DSIGMA.	
Diff Inelast	1.4+7		BAS	Expt Jour	PL 5 202	Jul 63	Huber+ GRPH OF INELASTIC N SPECT.	
				Jour	HPA 36 1059	Dec 59	- +.T=1.01MEV	
Diff Inelast	3.0+5	8.0+5	IFU	Expt Prog	INDSWG-126 22	66	Pasechnik. AT 3 ES, TBP IN AE	
Diff Inelast	3.5+6	8.5+6	JAE	Expt Prog	EANDC(J)8L25	Jan 68	Maruyama+.TOF.CONTIN SPECT AT 90DEG.	
	3.6+6	8.5+6		Jour	NP/A 131 145	Jun 69	- . E DEPENDENCE,PARAM,TH FIT	
	3.5+6	8.5+6		Conf	67Tokyo 373	Sep 67	- + PPR8.127. ABST.	
Thermal Scat	1.0-4	1.0+3	MUN	Revw Jour	EEN 80 1	77	Koester. SCAT LENGTH,FREE SIG	
Scattering	Maxwl		CAV	Expt Jour	PRSA 162 127	Sep 37	Goldhaber+. 8.2B REL 4.83B FOR C	
Scattering	1.5+6		FEI	Expt Prog	INDSWG-74	Jul 65	GUSEYNOV ETAL.SUBM.TO ATOMNAJA ENER.	
Nonelastic	1.0+6		WIS	Expt Jour	PR 93 1062	Mar 54	Walt+	+
	1.0+6			Data	EXFOR11637.054	Jun 76	. 1 PT, SIGMA.	
Nonelastic	3.3+6	4.1+6	IFU	Expt Conf	55Geneva 2 3	Aug 55	Pasechnik.SPH MEAS SPEC OF SCT N	+
Nonelastic	5.0+4	1.8+7	LAS	Theo Rept	LA-2099	Dec 56	Beyster+ OPTMDL CALC CFD EXPT,CURVE	
Nonelastic	1.4+7		IFU	Expt Jour	AE 2 68	Jan 57	Strizhak.SPHERE TRANSMISS 1.90+-.17B	+
				Jour	JNE 5 253	Nov 57	TRANSLATN.*	
				Jour	SJA 2 72	57	TRANSLATN.*	
Nonelastic	4.1+6		TNC	Expt Rept	WADD-TR-60-217	Apr 60	Vincent.	+
	4.1+6			Data	EXFOR11621.021	Jun 76	. 1 PT, SIGMA.	
Nonelastic	1.0+6	1.6+7	HAR	Theo Jour	NP 55 673	Jul 64	Wilmore+OPTMOD INCLUDES COMP.ELASTIC	
Nonelastic	3.3+6	4.1+6	IFU	ExTh Jour	AE 20 8	Jan 66	Korzh+ SUMMARY OF SEVERAL YRS WORK	+
				Jour	AE 16 207	64	.	
	3.0+6	4.1+6		Jour	SJA 20 8	Jul 66	.ENGLISH TRANSL OF AE 20 8 1/66	
Nonelastic	5.0+5	1.5+7	AUA	Theo Rept	AAEC/TM-536	Apr 70	Bertram. OPTMOD SIG(E)GRAPH CFD EXPT	
Absorption	Pile		HAR	Expt Jour	PPSA 63 1175	Oct 50	Colmer+LITTLER.PILE OSC REL HAR B	+
				Rept	AERE-N/R-527	Jun 50	- + PILE OSC.	
Absorption	Pile		ANL	Expt Jour	PR 80 342	Nov 50	Harris+ PILE OSC.REL TO BORON.	
	Pile			Data	EXFOR11528.034	Jun 76	. 1 PT, SIGMA.	
Absorption	2.5+4	8.3+5	FEI	Expt Jour	ZET 34 574	Mar 58	Belanova. LIMITS GIVEN AT 3ES	+
				Jour	JET 7 397	Sep 58	TRANSLATN.*	
Absorption	2.5+4		KUR	Expt Conf	58Geneva 15 50	Sep 58	Leipunskij+.PPR2219,VAL GVN,ACTIVATN	
Absorption	1.0+6	1.4+7	HAR	Theo Rept	AERE-R-4649	Jun 64	WILMORE OPTMOD.TBLS,CURVES, +-10PC	
Absorption	2.4+4		FEI	Expt Prog	INDSWG-74	Jul 65	BELANOVA ET AL.TBP ATOMNAJA ENERGIJA	
Res Int Abs	None		ORL	Revw Conf	55Geneva 5 96	Aug 55	Macklin+ TABLE,EXPT CFD THEORY,P833	
Res Int Abs	-		CCP	Expt Jour	AE 3 507	Dec 57	Klimentov+.EPI CD REACTIVITY REL LI	+
				Jour	JNE 9 20	Jun 59	TRANSLATN.*	
				Jour	SJA 3 1387	57	TRANSLATN.*	
Res Int Abs	-		FEI	Comp Rept	INDSWG-64 75	64	Prokhorov. 9.0+-2 B	
(n,γ)	Slow	9.9+6	JAP	Expt Jour	JPJO 22 551	Jul 40	Nonaka-D+D.EXCIT CURVE GIVN	
(n,γ)	Maxwl		LUQ	Expt Jour	PR 58 554	Sep 40	Lapointe+ ABS IN WATERBATH,UPPER LIM	
(n,γ)	Maxwl		UI	Expt Jour	PR 69 411	May 46	Coltman+ POWDERED SAMPLE+C. REL TO B	+
	Maxwl			Data	EXFOR12616.019	Jun 76	. 1 PT, SIGMA.	
(n,γ)	Maxwl		ORL	Expt Jour	PR 83 643	Aug 51	Pomerance. LOCAL OSC REL AU ABS 95 B	+
	Maxwl			Data	EXFOR11047.062	Jun 76	. 1PT, SIGMA.	
(n,γ)	2.0+5		KUR	Expt Conf	58Geneva 15 50	Sep 58	Leipunskij+.PPR2219,VAL GVN,ACTIVATN	+
(n,γ)	3.0+4	6.5+4	ORL	Expt Jour	PR 129 2695	Mar 63	Macklin+ SIGMA=61 AND 33MB,SCINT	+
	3.0+4	6.5+4		Data	EXFOR11331.023	Jun 76	. 2 PTS, SIGMA.	
(n,γ)	5.0+3	9.0+4	ORL	Theo Jour	RMP 37 166	Jan 65	Macklin+ CALC FOR KT=5TO90KEV	
(n,γ)	1.0+3	1.0+7	BOL	Eval Rept	CEC(70)-2	Apr 70	Benzi.GRAPH=SUM OF SIG(ISOTOPES)	
(n,γ)	3.0+4		AUA	Theo Rept	AAEC/E-211	Nov 70	Musgrove. SIGMA GIVEN AND CFD OTHER	
(n,γ)	1.4+7		NJS	Expt Jour	FIZS 4 53	Dec 72	.SIG VS MASS NUMBER,GRAPH	+
				Jour	NP/A 158 251	Dec 70	Cvelbar+MEAS INTEGRATES G-SPEC.CFDTH	
	1.4+7			Data	EXFOR30185.006	Dec 72	1 DATA LINE	
(n,γ)	1.0+3	1.0+7	FEI	Eval Rept	YK-8/2 97	Sep 72	Abagjan+ AVG SIG(ENERGY-GROUPS),TABL	
				Rept	INDC(CCP)-39	Jul 74	.P102. ENGLISH OF YK-8/2 97	
(n,γ)	5.0+0	7.0+7	FEI	Theo Rept	YFI-17 16	Aug 74	Dovbenko+ SIG(NEUT-E)	
Spect (n,γ)	Maxwl		CRC	Expt Jour	CJP 31 1051	Nov 53	Kinsey+ PAIR SPECT,LINE WIDTH=140KEV	
Spect (n,γ)	Maxwl		GEA	Eval Rept	DC-58-1-30	Jan 58	Deloume. BY APPROXIMATION CURV+TABLE	
Spect (n,γ)	None		DUB	Expt Conf	67Tokyo § 4.117	Sep 67	Becvar+ RES CAPT.46+57EV TO 131/132	
Spect (n,γ)	2.5-2		MIT	Comp Rept	MITNE-85	Jan 69	Rasmussen+TBL G INT.=AFCRL-69-0071	
Spect (n,γ)	Maxwl		KUR	Expt Jour	YF 10 681	Oct 69	Groshev+ TABLE GAM-SPECTRA,TRANSITNS	+
				Jour	SNP 10 392	Apr 70	TRANSLATN.*	
	2.5-2			Data	EXFOR40237.005	Nov 74	.GAM/100N FOR 10 ES GVN	
Spect (n,γ)	Maxwl		KFI	Expt Jour	YF 10 907	Nov 69	Kecskemeti+ AVG GAM-MULTIPLICITY,TBL	
				Jour	SNP 10 524	May 70	TRANSLATN.*	

56 Barium

Quantity	Energy (ev) Min	Energy (ev) Max	Lab	Type	Documentation Ref Vol Page	Date	Author, Comments	Data
Spect (n,γ)	Pile		KUR	Expt	Jour IZV 34 768	Apr 70	Groshev+ MAGNET SPEC,TBL GAM ES+INTS	+
					Jour BAS 34 680	Apr 71	* ENGL OF IZV 34 768	
	2.5−2				Data EXFOR40181.002	Jan 74	.72 GAMMA ES AND GAM/100N GIVEN	
Spect (n,γ)	5.0+3	8.1+4	AUA	Expt	Conf 72Budapest 92	Aug 72	Bird+ REL INTENSITIES OF GAMMAS,TBL	
Spect (n,γ)	1.4+7		NJS	Expt	Priv CVELBAR	Oct 72	.PROMPT GAMMA−RAY SPECTRUM	+
	1.4+7				Data EXFOR30185.007	Oct 72	25 DATA LINES	
Spect (n,γ)	4.6+5		AUA	Expt	Prog AAEC/PR−39P 44	Jan 74	Allen+ NA−I,GAMMA YIELD,FIGURE ONLY	
Inelastic γ	3.0+6		FEI	Expt	Jour AE 7 268	Sep 59	Androsenko+ GRAPH+TABLE OF GAM−ENERG	
					Jour SJA 7 763	Mar 61	. ENGL OF AE 7 268	
					Jour JNEA 12 136	Jun 60	. ENGL OF AE 7 268	
					Jour KE 3 565	Jun 60	.GERMAN OF AE 7 268	
Inelastic γ	4.0+6	1.5+7	TNC	Expt	Abst BAP 7 120	Feb 62	Nellis+ TOF+ CRYST SPECTROMETER NDG	
Inelastic γ	1.0+6	1.4+7	ORL	Expt	Jour NSE 42 335	Dec 70	Maerker+ NAI(TL) DET,GAM SPEC+SIGS	
Nonelastic γ	2.1+6	2.8+6	OSA	Expt	Jour JMJ 21 232	39	Aoki.SIG GIVN	
	2.4+6				Jour JMJ 21 75	39	Kikuchi+.D−D P LI−D N,SIG GIVN	
		2.4+6			Jour JMJ 19 369	37	Aoki.D+D NEUTRON.RELATIV SIG GIVN	
	Slow				Jour JMJ 18 188	36	Kikuchi+.SIG GIVN BY D+D NEUTRON	
					Jour JPJO 18 115	36	− +.REL SIG GIVN FOR G−EMISSION	
Nonelastic γ	3.2+6		NRL	Expt	Jour PR 96 386	Oct 54	Scherrer+ C−W+CRYST SPEC 8 PEAKS	
Nonelastic γ	3.5+6	8.5+6	ALD	Expt	Jour NP 60 561	Dec 64	Perkin.TABLE OF G PROD SIG GIVEN.	+
(n,2n)	1.5+7		DEB	Eval	Jour REA 11 1 153	Mar 73	Boedy+ RECOMM.VALUE FROM N−Z SYSTEM.	
Reson Params	5.4+4	1.3+5	DKE	Expt	Jour AP 14 387	Jul 61	Bilpuch+ AREA ANALYSIS.	+
	5.4+4	1.3+5			Data EXFOR11599.039	Jun 76	.5 RESONANCES E0 AND WN.	
Reson Params	3.0+0	1.0+3	IFU	Expt	Conf 69Erevan	Feb 69	Vertebnij+.ABST,LVL DENS ISOT DEPEND	
Reson Params	2.6+1	8.0+1	IFU	Expt	Jour UFZ 14 227	Feb 69	Vertebnis+.TOF,TRANSPARENSY CURVE	
Reson Params	4.6+1	2.1+3	SAC	Expt	Jour NP/A 134 118	Sep 69	Alves+ LINAC TOF.WN,WN0,25E0.	+
					Rept CEA−R−3128	Jun 66	Chevillon−Pitollat. LINAC.SUPERSEDED	
	4.6+1	2.1+3			Data EXFOR20688.008	Jun 77	26PTS.E0,J,A*G*WN	
Lvl Density	1.4+7		BAS	Expt	Jour PL 5 202	Jul 63	Huber+TBL OF NUC TEMP AND LVL DENSTY	
					Jour HPA 36 1059	Dec 63	Plattner+TOF TBL12ELEM.CFD TH	
Lvl Density	3.6+6	8.5+6	JAE	Expt	Jour NP/A 131 145	Jun 69	Maruyama. E DEPENDANCE,PARAM,TH FIT.	
	3.5+6	8.5+6			Prog EANDC(J)8L25	Jan 68	− +.TOF.SPEC FIT TO EXP(E/T)	
					Conf 67Tokyo 373	Sep 67	− + PPR8.127. ABST.	
Lvl Density	5.0+0	7.0+7	FEI	Theo	Rept YFI−17 16	Aug 74	Dovbenko+ CALCULATION	
(γ,n)	9.0+6	2.4+7	SAC	Expt	Jour NP/A 172 426	Sep 71	Beil+LORENTZ LINE PARAM,GRAPHS,TBLS	

56 Barium 126

Quantity	Energy (ev) Min	Max	Lab	Type	Documentation Ref Vol Page	Date	Author, Comments	Data
Reson Params	−		AUA	Theo	Rept AAEC/E−211	Nov 70	Musgrove. CALCULTD D+GAM WIDTH GIVEN	
Strnth Fnctn	−		AUA	Theo	Rept AAEC/E−211	Nov 70	Musgrove. SMOOTHED S0,S1 AND S2 GIVN	

56 Barium 127

Quantity	Energy (ev) Min	Max	Lab	Type	Documentation Ref Vol Page	Date	Author, Comments	Data
Reson Params	−		AUA	Theo	Rept AAEC/E−211	Nov 70	Musgrove. CALCULTD D+GAM WIDTH GIVEN	
Strnth Fnctn	−		AUA	Theo	Rept AAEC/E−211	Nov 70	Musgrove. SMOOTHED S0,S1 AND S2 GIVN	

56 Barium 128

Quantity	Energy (ev) Min	Max	Lab	Type	Documentation Ref Vol Page	Date	Author, Comments	Data
(n,p)	Maxwl		IFU	Theo	Rept ICD−4 20	67	Dadakina+ PENETR COEFF CALC,TABLE	
Reson Params	−		AUA	Theo	Rept AAEC/E−211	Nov 70	Musgrove. CALCULTD D+GAM WIDTH GIVEN	
Strnth Fnctn	−		AUA	Theo	Rept AAEC/E−211	Nov 70	Musgrove. SMOOTHED S0,S1 AND S2 GIVN	
Lvl Density	−3	+0	IFU	Theo	Jour UFZ 13 700	Apr 68	Pisanko+ LEVEL SPACING CALC,TBL	
					Jour UPJ 13 498	Oct 68	TRANSLATN.*	

56 Barium 129

Quantity	Energy (ev) Min	Max	Lab	Type	Documentation Ref Vol Page	Date	Author, Comments	Data
Reson Params	−		AUA	Theo	Rept AAEC/E−211	Nov 70	Musgrove. CALCULTD D+GAM WIDTH GIVEN	
Strnth Fnctn	−		AUA	Theo	Rept AAEC/E−211	Nov 70	Musgrove. SMOOTHED S0,S1 AND S2 GIVN	

56 Barium 130

Quantity	Energy (ev) Min	Max	Lab	Type	Documentation Ref Vol Page	Author, Comments Date	Data
Total	3.0+0	1.0+3	IFU	Expt	Prog YFI-6 112	68 Vertebnyj+. TRANSMISSION,TIME-OF-FL	
					Rept INDC-260E	69 . ENGL OF YFI-6 112	
Res Int Abs	5.0-1		LRL	Expt	Prog USNDC-1 95	May 72 Browne+. LINAC. VALUE GIVEN	
Res Int Abs	5.0-1		KJL	Expt	Jour JIN 34 2699	Sep 72 Steinnes. ACT. AU MONITOR	+
	5.0-1				Data EXFOR20188.014	May 74 1PNT.CAPTURE.	
Res Int Abs	5.0-1		MUN	Expt	Jour JRC 15 535	73 Alian+CAPT CD-R, 205 B INCL 1/V	+
	5.0-1				Data EXFOR20644.009	Jun 76 1PNT.CAPTURE.	
Res Int Abs	5.0-1		GHT	Expt	Jour JRC 20 695	74 Van Der Linden+ BY(N,G).CFD OTHS,TBL	+
	5.5-1				Conf 73Paris 2 241	Mar 73 - + ACT,REL THR+GOLD,TBL	
	5.5-1				Data EXFOR20645.010	Jul 76 1PNT.CAPTURE.	
Res Int Abs	+0	+5	WIN	Revw	Conf IAEA-169 3 163	74 Pope+ EVALUATED VALUE GIVEN	
(n,γ)	Pile		ARK	Expt	Jour PR 101 149	56 Beggs+ GAMMA DECAY OF BA-131	
	Pile				Data EXFOR12030.002	Jun 76 . 1 PT, CS RATIO BA130 TO BA132 (MS)	
(n,γ)	Pile		ORL	Expt	Jour NSE 8 378	Nov 60 Lyon. ACTIVATION,SIGMA GIVEN	+
	Pile				Data EXFOR11625.022	Jun 76 . 1 PT, SIGMA.	
(n,γ)	Pile		ORL	Expt	Jour JIN 25 1079	Nov 63 Lyon. CS RATIO BA130 TO BA132 GVN.	+
	Pile				Data EXFOR12019.002	Jun 76 . 1 PT. CS RATIO BA130 TO BA132.	
(n,γ)	Maxwl		UCB	Expt	Rept NYO-10175	Dec 64 Arino+ACT.TBLS.GRAPHS.PRODUCT HL.	+
	Maxwl				Data EXFOR11817.	Jun 76 . 1 PT. GND + MS SIGMA	
(n,γ)	Maxwl		UCS	Expt	Jour NSE 31 545	Mar 68 Tilbury+ ACTIV 2.5+ -0.3 TO ISOM	+
	Maxwl				Data EXFOR11927.011	Jun 76 . 1 PT, SIGMA.	
(n,γ)	-		IEA	Comp	Rept IEA-INF- 10	Aug 68 Atalla. TABLES OF HL,SIG AND GAMM-E	
(n,γ)	1.0+3	1.0+7	BOL	Eval	Rept CCDN-NW/10	Dec 69 Benzi+H-F MOD,AXEL G(G)EST,ALL DATA	
					Rept CEC(70)-2	Apr 70 - +. GRAPH	
(n,γ)	3.0+4		AUA	Theo	Rept AAEC/E-211	Nov 70 Musgrove. SIGMA GIVEN AND CFD OTHER	
(n,γ)	2.0+1	5.0+3	LRL	Expt	Jour PR/C 7 2522	Jun 73 Berman+.LINAC. 0.4PC RESOL. CURVES.	+
	2.0+1	1.2+3			Data EXFOR10313.002	Aug 75 . 5865 PTS, SIGMA	
(n,γ)	Maxwl	Fiss	WIN	Revw	Conf IAEA-169 3 163	74 Pope+ FIS-SPEC AVG DATA CFD MAXW-XPT	
(n,γ)	1.0+3	1.0+7	FEI	Eval	Rept INDC(CCP)-39	Jul 74 .P102. ENGLISH OF YK-8/2 97	
					Rept YK-8/2 97	Sep 72 Abagjan+ AVG SIG(ENERGY-GROUPS),TABL	
Spect (n,γ)	Pile		IPS	Expt	Jour AF 2 295	Dec 50 Kondaiah. E+INT FOR CS131 GS.	
Spect (n,γ)	Maxwl		DUB	Expt	Jour IZV 31 1672	Oct 67 Batist+ GAM E+INTENS,216-1048KEV,TBL	
					Jour BAS 31 1712	Oct 67 . ENGL OF IZV 31 1672	
Spect (n,γ)	-		MBG	Expt	Jour ZP 252 312	Jun 72 Sturm+, GS-GS CORR IN BA131+CS131	
(n,2n)	Fiss		CRC	Eval	Rept CRC-1003	Dec 60 ROY+ ESTIMATED AVG SIG=0.3MB	
(n,2n)	1.4+7		GIT	Expt	Jour PR/C 1 350	Jan 70 Fink+ACTIVATION,GRPHS,TBL CFD OTH.	+
	1.4+7				Data EXFOR10497.036	Apr 76 . 1PT BA130 N2N+BA130 NNP=1371+70MB.	
(n,2n)	1.4+7		GIT	Theo	Jour PR/C 4 1173	Oct 71 Fink+ STAT-MODEL CALCULATION,CFD EXP	
(n,2n)	1.5+7		DEB	Eval	Rept REA 11 1 153	Mar 73 Boedy. COMPILATION+RECOMM.VALUE,TBL	
					Rept IAEA-153 173	73 - . RECOMM. VALUE ONLY	
(n,p)	Fiss		CRC	Eval	Rept CRC-1003	Dec 60 ROY+ ESTIMATED AVG SIG=1.1MB	
(n,p)	Maxwl		IFU	Theo	Rept ICD-4 20	67 Dadakina+ PENETR COEFF CALC,TABLE	
(n,np)	1.4+7		GIT	Expt	Jour PR/C 1 350	Jan 70 Fink+ACTIVATION,GRPHS,TBL CFD OTH.	+
	1.4+7				Data EXFOR10497.036	Apr 76 . 1PT BA130 N2N+BA 130 NNP=137+-70MB	
(n,α)	Fiss		CRC	Eval	Rept CRC-1003	Dec 60 ROY+ ESTIMATED AVG SIG=0.014MB	
Reson Params	3.0+0	1.0+3	IFU	Expt	Conf 69Erevan	Feb 69 Vertebnij+.ABST,LVL DENS ISOT DEPEND	
Reson Params	4.7+1	9.0+2	IFU	Expt	Jour UFZ 14 227	Feb 69 Vertebnis+.WN,8 RES,TBL,CURVE	
Reson Params	2.0+1	9.4+2	SAC	Expt	Jour NP/A 134 118	Sep 69 Alves+ DATA TBL. IN FRENCH. NAT TGT	+
					Rept CEA-R-3128	Jan 66 Chevillon+ (THESIS).NAT TGT.	
	2.0+1	9.4+2			Data EXFOR20688.009	Jun 77 6PTS.E0,WN,J,G*WN.	
Reson Params	-		AUA	Theo	Rept AAEC/E-211	Nov 70 Musgrove. CALCULTD D+GAM WIDTH GIVEN	
Reson Params	3.8+2	9.1+2	CJD	Eval	Rept YK-7	71 Zakharova+ SURVEY+SYSTEMATICS,GW,TBL	
					Rept INDC(CCP)-27	Nov 72 .ENGLISH TRANSLATION OF YK-7 /71	
Reson Params	-		DUB	Theo	Rept JINR-E4-5711	Apr 71 Soloviev. AVG LVL SPACING, EXPTS TBD	
Reson Params	4.9+1	5.8+1	HAR	Expt	Jour NP/A 177 393	Dec 71 Van De Vyver+	+
	4.9+1	5.8+1			Data EXFOR20469.002	Jan 76 2PTS.G*WN.	
Reson Params	4.6+1	1.2+3	LRL	Expt	Jour PR/C 7 2522	Jun 73 Berman+ CAPT MEAST.G*WN*WG/WT,WN,WG	+
	4.6+1	2.8+3			Data EXFOR10313.003	Aug 75 . 41 PTS G(WG)(WN)/WT,EN	
Reson Params	None		DUB	Theo	Rept JINR-P4-7499	Oct 73 Soloviev+ CALC D CFD EXPTS,TABLE	
Reson Params	+1	+3	FEI	Eval	Rept YK-8/2 97	Sep 72 Abagjan+ AVG G-WID+D AT BINDNG-E,TBL	
					Rept INDC(CCP)-39	Jul 74 .PAGE 102.ENGLISH OF YK-8/2 97	
Strnth Fnctn	-		AUA	Theo	Rept AAEC/E-211	Nov 70 Musgrove. SMOOTHED S0,S1 AND S2 GIVN	
Lvl Density	+1	+3	FEI	Eval	Rept YK-8/2 97	Sep 72 Abagjan+ LVL DENSITY PARAMETER,TBL	
					Rept INDC(CCP)-39	Jul 74 .PAGE 102.ENGLISH OF YK-8/2 97	

56 Barium 131

Quantity	Energy (ev) Min	Max	Lab	Type	Documentation Ref Vol Page	Date	Author, Comments	Data
(n,p)	Maxwl		IFU Theo	Rept	ICD-4 20	67	Dadakina+ PENETR COEFF CALC,TABLE	
Reson Params	-		AUA Theo	Rept	AAEC/E-211	Nov 70	Musgrove. CALCULTD D+GAM WIDTH GIVEN	
Strnth Fnctn	-		AUA Theo	Rept	AAEC/E-211	Nov 70	Musgrove. SMOOTHED S0,S1 AND S2 GIVN	
Lvl Density	+6		MIL Theo	Jour	EN 15 1 54	Jan 68	Facchini+ LDL PARS FROM LOW EN RES	
Lvl Density	None		DUB Theo	Jour	NP/A 224 411	May 74	Soloviev+ 1/2 MICROSC MDL. SPH NUCL.	
Lvl Density	None		ROC Theo	Jour	NP/A 223 577	May 74	Huizenga+ EXP CFD MICROSC TH SPH NUC	

56 Barium 132

Quantity	Energy (ev) Min	Max	Lab	Type	Documentation Ref Vol Page	Date	Author, Comments	Data
Total	3.0+0	1.0+3	IFU Expt	Prog	YFI-6 112	68	Vertebnyj+. TRANSMISSION,TIME-OF-FL	
				Rept	INDC-260E	69	. ENGL OF YFI-6 112	
Res Int Abs	5.0-1		GHT Expt	Jour	JRC 20 695	74	Van Der Linden+ BY(N,G).CFD OTHS,TBL	+
	5.5-1			Conf	73Paris 2 241	Mar 73	- + ACT,REL THR+GOLD,TBL	
	5.5-1			Data	EXFOR20645.011	Jul 76	1PNT.CAPTURE.	
(n,γ)	Pile		ANL Expt	Jour	PR 72 1160	Dec 47	Katcoff.	+
	Pile			Data	EXFOR12037.002	Jun 76	. 1 PT, SIGMA.	
(n,γ)	Pile		ARK Expt	Jour	PR 101 149	56	Beggs+ GAMMA DECAY OF BA-131	+
	Pile			Data	EXFOR12030.002	Jun 76	. 1 PT CS RATIO BA130 TO BA132 (MS).	
(n,γ)	Maxwl		MUAExpt	Jour	NP 20 183	Oct 60	Hans+ CS OF BA132(NG)BA133M GIVEN	+
	Maxwl			Data	EXFOR31246.008	Sep 72	.SIG TO MS-STATE GVN	
(n,γ)	Maxwl		MUAExTh	Jour	NP 41 372	Mar 63	Mangal+ (N,G)M SIGMA GVN,TH CFD EXPT	+
	Maxwl			Expt Data	EXFOR31249.004	Sep 72	.SIG TO MS-STATE GVN	
(n,γ)	Pile		ORL Expt	Jour	JIN 25 1079	Nov 63	Lyon. CS RATIO BA130 TO BA132 GVN	+
	Pile			Data	EXFOR12019.	Jun 76	. 1 PT NG+ CS RATIO BA130 TO BA132.	
(n,γ)	Maxwl		ANL Comp	Jour	NP 60 241	Nov 64	Bishop+EXP AND TH ISOMER RATIOS CFD	
(n,γ)	-		IEA Comp	Rept	IEA-INF- 10	Aug 68	Atalla. TABLES OF HL,SIG AND GAMM-E	
(n,γ)	Maxwl		JAP Expt	Priv	ISHII	Nov 69	Ishii.SIG 288KV ISOMER=0.98+-0.15 B	
(n,γ)	1.0+3	1.0+7	BOL Eval	Rept	CCDN-NW/10	Dec 69	Benzi+H-F MOD,AXEL G(G)EST,ALL DATA	
				Rept	CEC(70)-2	Apr 70	- +. GRAPH	
(n,γ)	3.0+4		AUA Theo	Rept	AAEC/E-211	Nov 70	Musgrove. SIGMA GIVEN AND CFD OTHER	
(n,γ)	Maxwl	Fiss	WIN Revw	Conf	IAEA-169 3 163	74	Pope+ FIS-SPEC AVG DATA CFD MAXW-XPT	
(n,γ)	1.0+3	1.0+7	FEI Eval	Jour	YK- 8/2 97	Sep 72	Abagjan+ AVG SIG(ENERGY-GROUPS),TABL	
				Rept	INDC(CCP)-39	Jul 74	.P102. ENGLISH OF YK-8/2 97	
(n,γ)	2.5-2		BRK Theo	Jour	NP/A 237 3 419	Jan 75	Nardi+ ISOM RATIO,MTE-CARLO,CFD XPT	
Spect (n,γ)	Maxwl		DUB Expt	Jour	IZV 31 1672	Oct 67	Batist+ GAM E+INTENS,ISOMERIC STATE	
				Jour	BAS 31 1712	Oct 67	. ENGL OF IZV 31 1672	
(n,2n)	Fiss		CRC Eval	Rept	CRC-1003	Dec 60	ROY+ ESTIMATED AVG SIG=0.55MB	
(n,2n)	1.4+7		GIT Expt	Jour	PR/C 1 350	Jan 70	Fink+ ACTIVATION,SIG=1574+- 100	+
	1.4+7			Data	EXFOR10497.037	Apr 76	. 1PT CS=1574+- 100 MB.	
(n,2n)	1.4+7		GIT Theo	Jour	PR/C 4 1173	Oct 71	Fink+ STAT-MODEL CALCULATION,CFD EXP	
(n,2n)	1.5+7		IBJ Expt	Jour	APPB 3 637	72	Rurarz+ SIG TO METASTABLE STATE	+
				Prog	INR-1401 4	May 72	- + ACTIV,SIG TO ISOMERIC LEVEL	
	1.5+7			Data	EXFOR30183.002	Aug 72	1 DATA LINE	
(n,2n)	1.5+7		DEB Eval	Jour	REA 11 1 153	Mar 73	Boedy. COMPILATION+RECOMM.VALUE,TBL	
				Rept	IAEA-153 173	73	- . RECOMM. VALUE ONLY	
(n,2n)	1.5+7		TAT Theo	Jour	JP/A 7 1458	Aug 74	Kondaiah. CALC ON STAT MODEL	
(n,2n)	1.5+7		IBJ Theo	Jour	ASL 27 186	77	Rurarz+ ISO RATIO,4MODLS,CFD XPT.TBL	
	1.4+7			Rept	INR-1464 19	May 73	- + ISOMERIC RATIO CFD EXPT,GRAF	
(n,p)	Pile		ARK Expt	Abst	BAP 1 40	Jan 56	Robinson+ 0.7+-0.2MB Q=0MEV	
(n,p)	Fiss		GES Revw	Jour	NUC 17 1 54	Jan 59	Rochlin.47 ISOTOPES.ACT.RVW.TBL.	
(n,p)	Fiss		CRC Eval	Rept	CRC-1003	Dec 60	ROY+ ESTIMATED AVG SIG=1.0MB	
(n,α)	Fiss		CRC Eval	Rept	CRC-1003	Dec 60	ROY+ ESTIMATED AVG SIG=0.041MB	
Reson Params	3.0+0	1.0+3	IFU Expt	Conf	69Erevan	Feb 69	Vertebnij+.ABST,LVL DENS ISOT DEPEND	
Reson Params	5.7+1		SAC Expt	Jour	NP/A 134 118	Sep 69	Alves+ LINAC TOF.WN,WN0,WG,WT,J	+
				Conf	68Wash. 867	Mar 68	Morgenstern.WG.VS. A. AVG WG GIVEN	
	5.7+1			Data	EXFOR20688.010	Jun 77	1PNT.E0,WT,J,G*WN.	
Reson Params	-		AUA Theo	Rept	AAEC/E-211	Nov 70	Musgrove. CALCULTD D+GAM WIDTH GIVEN	
Reson Params	5.7+1		CJD Eval	Rept	YK- 7	71	Zakharova+ SURVEY+SYSTEMATICS,GW,TBL	
				Rept	INDC(CCP)-27	Nov 72	.ENGLISH TRANSLATION OF YK-7 /71	
Reson Params	4.9+1	5.8+1	HAR Expt	Jour	NP/A 177 393	Dec 71	Van De Vyver+	+
	4.9+1	5.8+1		Data	EXFOR20469.003	Jan 76	2PTS.G*WN.	
Reson Params	1.0+2	1.1+3	LRL Expt	Jour	PR/C 7 2522	Jun 73	Berman+ CAPT MEAST,ES ONLY 10 RESON.	+
	1.0+2	2.1+3		Data	EXFOR10313.004	Jun 75	. 17 PTS EN	
Reson Params	+1	+3	FEI Eval	Rept	YK- 8/2 97	Sep 72	Abagyan+ AVG G-WID+D AT BINDNG-E,TBL	
				Rept	INDC(CCP)-39	Jul 74	.PAGE 102.ENGLISH OF YK-8/2 97	

56 Barium 132

Quantity	Energy (ev) Min	Max	Lab	Type	Documentation Ref Vol Page	Author, Comments Date	Data
Strnth Fnctn	–		AUA	Theo Rept	AAEC/E – 211	Nov 70 Musgrove. SMOOTHED S0,S1 AND S2 GIVN	
Lvl Density	+1	+3	FEI	Eval Rept	YK – 8/2 97	Sep 72 Abagyan+ LVL DENSITY PARAMETER,TBL	
				Rept	INDC(CCP) – 39	Jul 74 .PAGE 102.ENGLISH OF YK – 8/2 97	

56 Barium 133

Quantity	Energy (ev) Min	Max	Lab	Type	Documentation Ref Vol Page	Author, Comments Date	Data
(n,p)	Maxwl		IFU	Theo Rept	ICD – 4 20	67 Dadakina+ PENETR COEFF CALC,TABLE	
Reson Params	–		AUA	Theo Rept	AAEC/E – 211	Nov 70 Musgrove. CALCULTD D+GAM WIDTH GIVEN	
Strnth Fnctn	–		AUA	Theo Rept	AAEC/E – 211	Nov 70 Musgrove. SMOOTHED S0,S1 AND S2 GIVN	
Lvl Density	+7		MIL	Theo Jour	NC/A 51 4 1074	Oct 67 Gadioli+THEOR EVAL EVAPORATION SPECT	

56 Barium 134

Quantity	Energy (ev) Min	Max	Lab	Type	Documentation Ref Vol Page	Author, Comments Date	Data
Evaluation	1.0 – 3	1.5+7	AUA	Eval Rept	AAEC/TM – 549	Jun 70 Cook.TOT,EL,INEL,NONEL,CAPT SIGS,NDG	+
				Rept	AAEC/E – 214	Jun 71 Bertram+GROUP SIGMAS SAME QUANTS.NDG	
				Rept	AAEC/TM – 587	Mar 71 *DESCRIPTION OF LIBRARY	
	1.0 – 3	1.5+7		Data	AUSTR – DFN 128.	Nov 71 POINT(223) AND GROUP(127) SIGMAS	
Total	1.0 – 3	1.5+7	AUA	Eval Data	AUSTR – DFN 128.	Nov 71 COOK+ POINT(223)+GROUP(127) SIGMAS	+
Total	4.0+0	2.0+3	HAR	Expt Jour	NP/A 177 393	Dec 71 VAN DE VIJVER+ TRANSM.ENRICHED SAMPL	+
	4.0+0	2.0+3		Data	EXFOR20469.	Jan 76 0PTS. SEE RESONANCE PARAMETERS.	
Elastic	1.0 – 3	1.5+7	AUA	Eval Data	AUSTR – DFN 128.	Nov 71 COOK+ POINT(223)+GROUP(127) SIGMAS	+
Tot Inelastc	1.0 – 3	1.5+7	AUA	Eval Data	AUSTR – DFN 128.	Nov 71 COOK+ POINT(223)+GROUP(127) SIGMAS	+
Nonelastic	1.0 – 3	1.5+7	AUA	Eval Data	AUSTR – DFN 128.	Nov 71 COOK+ POINT(223)+GROUP(127) SIGMAS	+
Absorption	4.1 – 1	1.0+7	GA	Eval Rept	GA – 2451	Aug 61 Joanou+ 68GROUP DATA FOR GAM – I ABS	
Absorption	1.0 – 3	1.0+7	JUL	Eval Rept	JUEL – 678 – RG	Jul 70 Liu. EVALUATION+CALC,GRPH,FN OF E	
Res Int Abs	5.5 – 1		CRC	Eval Rept	AECL – 3037 1	Jan 72 Walker.REDUCED RES INT FROM RES PARS	
Res Int Abs	5.0 – 1		AUA	Eval Rept	AAEC/TM – 619	Sep 72 Clayton.CALC FROM SIG LIBRARY,TABLE	
Res Int Abs	5.0 – 1		GHT	Expt Jour	JRC 20 695	74 Van Der Linden+ BY(N,G).CFD OTHS,TBL	+
	5.5 – 1			Conf	73Paris 2 241	Mar 73 – + ACT,REL THR+GOLD,TBL	
	5.5 – 1			Data	EXFOR20645.012	Jul 76 1PNT.CAPTURE.	
Res Int Abs	+0	+5	WIN	Revw Conf	IAEA – 169 3 163	74 Pope+ DATA FILE CALC CFD XPTAL VALUE	
(n,γ)	Maxwl		ORL	Expt Jour	PR 88 412	Oct 52 Pomerance.PILE OSC.ESTIM.ERROR 100PC	+
	Maxwl			Data	EXFOR11507.068	Jun 76 . 1 PT, SIGMA.	
(n,γ)	Maxwl		CRC	Eval Rept	AECL – 1054	Mar 60 Walker. (CRRP – 913)	
(n,γ)	Maxwl		MUA	Expt Jour	NP 20 183	Oct 60 Hans+ CS OF BA134(NG)BA135M GIVEN	+
	Maxwl			Data	EXFOR31246.009	Sep 72 .SIG TO MS – STATE GVN	
(n,γ)	Maxwl		MUA	ExTh Jour	NP 41 372	Mar 63 Mangal+ (N,G)M SIGMA GVN,TH CFD EXPT	+
	Maxwl			Expt Data	EXFOR31249.005	Sep 72 .SIG TO MS – STATE GVN	
(n,γ)	–		IEA	Comp Rept	IEA – INF – 10	Aug 68 Atalla. TABLES OF HL,SIG AND GAMM – E	
(n,γ)	Maxwl		JAP	Priv	ISHII	Nov 69 Ishii.SIG 268KV ISOMER=0.33+ – 0.06 B	
(n,γ)	1.0+3	1.0+7	BOL	Eval Rept	CCDN – NW/10	Dec 69 Benzi+H – F MOD,AXEL G(G)EST,ALL DATA	
				Rept	CEC(70) – 2	Apr 70 – +. GRAPH	
(n,γ)	1.0 – 3	1.5+7	AUA	Eval Data	AUSTR – DFN 128.	Nov 71 COOK+ POINT(223)+GROUP(127) SIGMAS	+
(n,γ)	Maxwl		CRC	Eval Rept	AECL – 3037 1	Jan 72 Walker.RECOMMENDED SIG,DETAILED TBL	
(n,γ)	2.5 – 2		AUA	Eval Rept	AAEC/TM – 619	Sep 72 Clayton.CALC FROM SIG LIBRARY,TABLE	
(n,γ)	+6		KOS	Expt Jour	AHP 33 363	73 Peto+ BA – 135(INL)+BA – 134(N,G)BA – 135M	+
	+6			Data	EXFOR30265.015	Feb 74 AVERAGE SIG FOR PU – BE NEUTRONS	
(n,γ)	Fiss		WIN	Revw Conf	IAEA – 169 3 137	74 Dean. POINT DATA AVG OVER STAND SPEC	
	Maxwl	Fiss		Conf	IAEA – 169 3 163	74 Pope+ MAXW+FIS – SPEC AVG DATA CFD XPT	
(n,γ)	1.0+3	1.0+7	FEI	Eval Rept	YK – 8/2 97	Sep 72 Abagyan+ AVG SIG(ENERGY – GROUPS),TABL	
				Rept	INDC(CCP) – 39	Jul 74 .P102. ENGLISH OF YK – 8/2 97	
(n,γ)	3.0+4		AUA	Expt Jour	NP/A 256 173	Jan 75 Musgrove+AVG SIG=225+ – 35MB AT 30 KEV	+
				Theo Rept	AAEC/E – 211	Nov 70 – . SIGMA GIVEN AND CFD OTHER	
	Maxwl			Expt Data	EXFOR30328.	Mar 76 AVERAGE SIG,KT=30KEV. 1 PNT	
(n,γ)	Fiss		KOS	Expt Conf	75Karlsrhe 29	Apr 75 Csikai. CF252.+135(N,N')META.SIG GVN	
	1.4+6			Data	EXFOR30400.050	Oct 78 1 PNT. BA134(N,G)+BA135(N,N')BA135M	
Spect (n,γ)	Maxwl		DUB	Expt Jour	IZV 31 1672	Oct 67 Batist+ BA 135 M – G – TRANSITN=268.7KEV	
				Jour	BAS 31 1712	Oct 67 . ENGL OF IZV 31 1672	
Spect (n,γ)	Maxwl		KUR	Expt Jour	YF 10 681	Oct 69 Groshev+ TABLE GAM – SPECTRA,TRANSITNS	+
				Rept	IAE – 1780	Jan 69 – + TBL OF GAMMA YLD+E,GE(LI)	
				Jour	SNP 10 392	Apr 70 . ENGL OF YF 10 681	
				Rept	LA – TR – 69 – 29	Oct 69 . ENGLISH OF IAE – 1780	
	2.5 – 2			Data	EXFOR40237.002	Nov 74 .GAM/100N FOR 11 ES GVN	

56 Barium 134

Quantity	Energy (ev) Min	Max	Lab	Type	Documentation Ref Vol Page	Date	Author, Comments	Data
(n,2n)	1.5+7		ARK	Expt Jour	PR 118 242	Apr 60	Wille. MEAS ACT SIG=940+ - 80 MB	+
	1.5+7			Data	EXFOR12033.002	Jun 76	. 1 PT, SIGMA.	
(n,2n)	Fiss		CRC	Eval Rept	CRC - 1003	Dec 60	ROY+ ESTIMATED AVG SIG=0.7MB	
(n,2n)	1.4+7		HAM	Comp Jour	NP 65 257	Mar 65	Bormann. 1EXPT VALS.CFD SHELL EFFECT	
(n,2n)	1.5+7		TUR	Theo Jour	NC 56 18 201	Jul 68	Minetti+THEOR ISOM RATIO SPIN CO PAR	
(n,2n)	1.5+7		DEB	Comp Jour	REA 7 4 93	Dec 69	Csikai+ SIG+HL COMPILTN,N - ACTIV - ANAL	
(n,2n)	1.4+7		GIT	Expt Jour	PR/C 1 350	Jan 70	Fink+ACTIVATION,GRPHS,TBL CFD OTH.	+
	1.4+7			Data	EXFOR10497.038	Apr 76	. 1PT CS=783+ - 56MB.	
(n,2n)	1.4+7	1.5+7	JYV	Eval Rept	JU - RR - 3/1970	Jun 70	Leppaemaeki+ TABLE OF EVAL AVG SIG	
(n,2n)	1.4+7	1.5+7	IRK	ExTh Jour	APA 33 285	Jul 71	Winiwarter+ ISOMERIC RATIO	
(n,2n)	1.5+7		IBJ	Expt Jour	APPB 3 637	72	Rurarz+ SIG TO METASTABLE STATE	+
				Prog	INR - 1401 4	May 72	- + ACTIV,SIG TO ISOMERIC LEVEL	
	1.5+7			Data	EXFOR30183.003	Aug 72	1 DATA LINE	
(n,2n)	1.5+7		DEB	Eval Jour	REA 11 1 153	Mar 73	Boedy+ RECOMM.VALUE FROM N - Z SYSTEM.	
(n,2n)	1.5+7		KFI	Theo Rept	KFKI - 73 - 68	Dec 73	Jeki.NEW FIT,CALC SIG CFD OTHERS,TBL	
(n,2n)	1.5+7		RBZ	Expt Jour	JP/G 2 405	Jun 76	Holub+ STUDY OF SYSTEMATICS,SIG GIVN	+
				ExTh Prog	INDC(SEC) - 50	Jan 76	- + GELI,ACTIV.CFD OTH+THEO,TABLE	
				Jour	ASL 25 180	75	- . TBL SIG,TO META,GND.CFD OTHRS	
	1.4+7			Expt Data	EXFOR30348.	Sep 76	SIGMA ISOM+GND+TOTAL.	
(n,2n)	1.5+7		IBJ	Theo Jour	ASL 27 186	77	Rurarz+ ISO RATIO,4MODLS,CFD XPT.TBL	
	1.4+7			Rept	INR - 1464 19	May 73	- + ISOMERIC RATIO CFD EXPT,GRAF	
(n,p)	Fiss		CRC	Eval Rept	CRC - 1003	Dec 60	ROY+ ESTIMATED AVG SIG=0.15MB	
(n,α)	Fiss		CRC	Eval Rept	CRC - 1003	Dec 60	ROY+ ESTIMATED AVG SIG=0.0021MB	
Reson Params	1.0+2	5.0+2	SAC	Expt Jour	NP/A 134 118	Sep 69	Alves+ LINAC TOF.WN,WN0,WG,WT,J,2E0	+
				Conf	68Wash. 867	Mar 68	Morgenstern.WG VS. A. AVG WG GIVEN	
				Rept	CEA - R - 3128	Jun 66	Chevillon+ TRANS+CAPT. SUPERSEDED.	
	2.0+1	9.4+2		Data	EXFOR20688.011	Jun 77	2PTS.E0,WN,WT,J,G*WN.	
Reson Params	-		AUA	Theo Rept	AAEC/E - 211	Nov 70	Musgrove. CALCULTD D+GAM WIDTH GIVEN	
Reson Params	1.0+2		CJD	Eval Rept	YK - 7	71	Zakharova+ SURVEY+SYSTEMATICS,GW,TBL	
				Rept	INDC(CCP) - 27	Nov 72	.ENGLISH TRANSLATION OF YK - 7 /71	
Reson Params	-		DUB	Theo Rept	JINR - E4 - 5711	Apr 71	Soloviev. AVG LVL SPACING, EXPTS TBD	
Reson Params	1.0+2	1.9+3	HAR	Expt Jour	NP/A 177 393	Dec 71	VAN DE VYVER+ S - WAVE AREA ANAL. 8E0.	+
	1.0+2	4.6+3		Data	EXFOR20469.	Jan 76	17PTS.E0,G*WN.	
Reson Params	1.0+2	1.1+3	LRL	Expt Jour	PR/C 7 2522	Jun 73	Berman+ CAPT MEAST.ES ONLY 6 RESON.	+
	1.0+2	2.0+3		Data	EXFOR10313.005	Jun 75	. 11 PTS EN	
Reson Params	None		DUB	Theo Rept	JINR - P4 - 7499	Oct 73	Soloviev+ CALC D CFD EXPTS,TABLE	
Reson Params	+2	+3	FEI	Eval Rept	YK - 8/2 97	Sep 72	Abagyan+ AVG G - WID+D AT BINDNG - E,TBL	
				Rept	INDC(CCP) - 39	Jul 74	.PAGE 102.ENGLISH OF YK - 8/2 97	
Strnth Fnctn	-		AUA	Theo Rept	AAEC/E - 211	Nov 70	Musgrove. SMOOTHED S0,S1 AND S2 GIVN	
Strnth Fnctn	1.0+2	1.9+3	HAR	Expt Jour	NP/A 177 393	Dec 71	VAN DE VYVER+ S - WAVE.	+
	4.0+0	2.0+3		Data	EXFOR20469.006	Jan 76	1PNT.L=0.	
Strnth Fnctn	None		AUA	Eval Rept	AAEC/E - 277	Mar 73	Musgrove.TBLS EXPTL DATA+BEST VALUES	
Strnth Fnctn	None		KUR	Theo Prog	IAE - 2560	75	Adamchuk+.S0 - VALUE,TBL	
Strnth Fnctn	None		OSA	Theo Conf	JAERI - M - 5984	Feb 75	Kitazoe+OPT MDLS.GRPH VS A.TBL PARS	
Lvl Density	+2	+3	FEI	Eval Rept	YK - 8/2 97	Sep 72	Abagyan+ LVL DENSITY PARAMETER,TBL	
				Rept	INDC(CCP) - 39	Jul 74	.PAGE 102.ENGLISH OF YK - 8/2 97	

56 Barium 135

Quantity	Energy (ev) Min	Max	Lab	Type	Documentation Ref Vol Page	Date	Author, Comments	Data
Total	4.0+0	2.0+3	HAR	Expt Jour	NP/A 177 393	Dec 71	VAN DE VIJVER+ TRANSM.ENRICHED SAMPL	+
	4.0+0	2.0+3		Data	EXFOR20469.	Jan 76	0PTS. SEE RESONANCE PARAMETERS.	
Potntal Scat		1.3+3	SAC	Expt Jour	NP/A 123 561	Jan 69	Morgenstern+ RADIUS FROM RES ANAL	+
				Rept	CEA - R - 3609	Sep 68	- + (THESIS) RADIUS.	
	0.0+0	1.3+3		Data	EXFOR20688.014	Jun 77	1PNT.RADIUS.	
Diff Inelast	4.0+5	1.2+6	FEI	Expt Jour	AE 15 416	Nov 63	Glazkov+ SPHER GEOM, 5 ENERGIES	
				Jour	JNE 18 654	64	. ENGL OF AE 15 416	
				Jour	EAF 15 5	Nov 63	.FRENCH OF AE 15 416	
				Jour	SJA 15 1173	Nov 63	. ENGL OF AE 15 416	
Diff Inelast	2.8+6		DEB	Expt Jour	AK 10 112	Jul 68	Bornemisza+ TBL HL+SIGMA FOR BA135M	+
	2.8+6			Data	EXFOR30338.005	Aug 76	TO ISOM. 1 PNT	
Diff Inelast	1.5+7		IBJ	Expt Prog	INR - 1401 4	May 72	Rurarz+ ACTIV,PAR SIG TO ISOM LVL	+
	1.5+7			Data	EXFOR30183.004	Aug 72	1 DATA LINE	
Diff Inelast	1.4+7		ITJ	Expt Jour	JRC 14 201	73	Janczyszyn+ ISO - PROD BY NAT - BA ACTIV	+
	1.4+7			Data	EXFOR30322.013	Feb 76	MEAN OF BA135(N,N')+BA136(N,2N)	

56 Barium 135

Quantity	Energy (ev) Min	Max	Lab	Type	Documentation Ref Vol Page	Date	Author, Comments	Data
Diff Inelast	+6		KOS Expt	Jour	AHP 33 363	73	Peto+ BA−135(INL)+BA−134(N,G)BA−135M	+
	−			Prog	INDC(HUN)−1G	Apr 70	.PROG REPORT. ISOM−SIG XPT TB CONTIN	
		+6		Data	EXFOR30265.015	Feb 74	AVG SIG FOR PU−BE NEUTRONS	
Diff Inelast	Fiss		KOS Expt	Conf	75Karlsrhe 29	Apr 75	Csikai. CF252.+134(N,G)META. SIG GVN	+
	1.4+6			Data	EXFOR30400.050	Oct 78	1 PNT. BA134(N,G)+BA135(N,N')BA135M	
Diff Inelast	Thrsh	Up	CAI Theo	Jour	AKE 28 3 201	76	Abboud. EXCITATION−FN,STATMOD	
Absorption	1.0−3	1.0+7	JUL Eval	Rept	JUEL−678−RG	Jul 70	Liu. EVALUATION+CALC,GRPH,FN OF E	
Res Int Abs	5.5−1		CRC Eval	Rept	AECL−3037 1	Jan 72	Walker.REDUCED RES INT FROM RES PARS	
Res Int Abs	+0	+5	WIN Revw	Conf	IAEA−169 3 163	74	Pope+ EVALUATED VALUE GIVEN	
(n,γ)	Maxwl		ORL Expt	Jour	PR 88 412	Oct 52	Pomerance.PILE OSC.	+
	Maxwl			Data	EXFOR11507.069	Jun 76	. 1 PT, SIGMA.	
(n,γ)	Maxwl		COR Expt	Rept	NYO−3664−6	Jun 68	Winn.PILE ACT 13.9+−0.7MB TO BA136M	
(n,γ)	5.0+3	1.0+5	AUA ExTh	Jour	AAEC/E−198	May 69	Musgrove.S+P+D WAVE SIGMAS CALC,TBL	+
(n,γ)	1.0+3	1.0+7	BOL Eval	Rept	CCDN−NW/10	Dec 69	Benzi+H−F MOD,AXEL G(G)EST,ALL DATA	
				Rept	CEC(70)−2	Apr 70	− +. GRAPH	
(n,γ)	3.0+4		AUA Theo	Rept	AAEC/E−211	Nov 70	Musgrove. SIGMA GIVEN AND CFD OTHER	
(n,γ)	Maxwl		KFI Comp	Jour	JRC 7 365	Jun 71	Nagy+ SIGMA,GAM+XRAY+ELECTR ES GIVEN	
(n,γ)	Maxwl			Rept	AECL−3037 1	Jan 72	Walker.RECOMMENDED SIG,DETAILED TBL	
(n,γ)	Maxwl	Fiss	WIN Revw	Conf	IAEA−169 3 163	74	Pope+ FIS−SPEC AVG DATA CFD MAXW XPT	
(n,γ)	1.0+3	1.0+7	FEI Eval	Rept	YK−8/2 97	Sep 72	Abagjan+ AVG SIG(ENERGY−GROUPS),TABL	
				Rept	INDC(CCP)−39	Jul 74	.P102. ENGLISH OF YK−8/2 97	
(n,γ)	3.0+3	1.0+5	ORL Expt	Prog	ERDA−NDC−3 176	May 76	Musgrove+CS MEAS.NDG.	+
	3.0+3	5.0+4		Data	EXFOR10538.007	Feb 76	. 15PTS, AVG NG CS.	
Spect (n,γ)	1.8+1	1.5+3	DUB Expt	Jour	ZET 49 80	Jul 65	Urbanec+ 0.4−10MEV GS, RESON CAPTURE	
				Conf	67Tokyo § 4.117	Sep 67	− + NEW LEVEL.	
				Conf	65Antwerp § 188	Jul 65	− .DUBNA.5 N RES.J GIVEN	
	1.8+1	1.5+3		Jour	JET 22 57	Jan 66	− + ENGL OF ZET 49 80	
Spect (n,γ)	Maxwl		BNL Expt	Rept	PR 181 1682	May 69	Gelletly+ GE(LI),GAM ES+INTENS GIVEN	
Spect (n,γ)	−2	5.0+3	DUB Expt	Jour	CZJB 19 899	Jul 69	Becvar+ G−SPECS,24.5EV RESON ANAL	
	+0	+3		Conf	68DUBSY 283	Jul 68	Shapiro.GE−LI DET. RESOL=80NS/M,NDG	
	2.4+1			Rept	JINR−P3−3696	Feb 68	Becvar+ GE−LI.490−850KEV G−SPEC,GRPH	
Spect (n,γ)	Pile		ANL Expt	Conf	69Studsvik 601	Aug 69	Smither+ NO DATA GVN,TB CFD STATMOD	
Spect (n,γ)	Pile		KUR Expt	Jour	IZV 34 768	Apr 70	Groshev+ GE−LI,TBL G ES+INTS,LVL SCH	+
				Jour	BAS 34 680	Apr 71	* ENGL OF IZV 34 768	
	2.5−2			Data	EXFOR40181.003	Jan 74	.19 GAMMA ES AND GAM/100N GIVEN	
Spect (n,γ)	Maxwl		KFI Comp	Jour	JRC 7 365	Jun 71	Nagy+ SIGMA,GAM+XRAY+ELECTR ES GIVEN	
Spect (n,γ)	2.4+4		BNL Expt	Prog	USNDC−9 52	Dec 73	Rimawi+ GAM SPEC+INTENSITY GIVEN.	
Spect (n,γ)	2.4+1	4.6+2	BNL Expt	Jour	PR/C 9 1622	Apr 74	Chrien+ RESON CAPT SPECT 10 RESON.	
Inelastic γ	1.4+7		GIT Expt	Jour	PR/C 1 350	Jan 70	LU+ ACTIVATION.	+
	1.4+7			Data	EXFOR10497.039	Apr 76	. 1PT BA136 N2N+BA135 SIN=1149+−80MB	
Inelastic γ	1.5+7		IBJ Expt	Jour	APPB 3 637	72	Rurarz+ 268 KEV GAMMA, SIG GIVEN	
(n,2n)	Fiss		CRC Eval	Rept	CRC−1003	Dec 60	ROY+ ESTIMATED AVG SIG=6.4MB	
(n,2n)	−		KOS Expt	Prog	INDC(HUN)−1G	Apr 70	.PROG REPORT. EXPT TO BE DONE	
(n,2n)	1.5+7		DEB Expt	Jour	REA 11 1 153	Mar 73	Boedy+ RECOMM.VALUE FROM N−Z SYSTEM.	
(n,2n)	1.5+7		KFI Theo	Rept	KFKI−73−68	Dec 73	Jeki.NEW FIT,CALC SIG CFD OTHERS,TBL	
(n,p)	Fiss		CRC Eval	Rept	CRC−1003	Dec 60	ROY+ ESTIMATED AVG SIG=0.35MB	
(n,p)	Maxwl		IFU Theo	Rept	ICD−4 20	67	Dadakina+ PENETR COEFF CALC,TABLE	
(n,p)	−		KOS Expt	Prog	INDC(HUN)−1G	Apr 70	.PROG REPORT. EXPT TO BE DONE	
(n,α)	Fiss		CRC Eval	Rept	CRC−1003	Dec 60	ROY+ ESTIMATED AVG SIG=0.035MB	
(n,α)	−		KOS Expt	Prog	INDC(HUN)−1G	Apr 70	.PROG REPORT. EXPT TO BE DONE	
Reson Params	8.2+1	5.2+2	BNL Expt	Priv	PILCHER	Apr 55	Pilcher.	+
	8.2+1	5.2+2		Data	EXFOR12041.	Jun 76	. 10 RES, WN,WN0, 1 RES, WG	
Reson Params	2.5+1	1.1+2	BNL Expt	Jour	PR 108 353	Oct 57	Stolovy+ FC,TRANS,WT WG WN.	
	2.5+1	1.1+2		Data	EXFOR11866.007	Jun 76	. 4 RESONANCES, E0, WG, WN, AND WT.	
Reson Params	2.5+1	3.2+2	ANL Expt	Conf	64Paris 2 673	Jul 64	Bollinger+SPIN OF FEW LVLS	
	2.5+1	3.2+2		Data	EXFOR12043.002	Jun 76	. 7 RESONANCES, J GIVEN.	
Reson Params	2.4+1	3.2+2	DUB Expt	Rept	JINR−P−1972	Jul 65	Urbanec+,7 RESONS,TBL WG,WN,*XTLSPEC	
	2.4+1	5.2+2		Jour	ZET 49 80	Jul 65	− + CS,E,WG FOR 11RES.CFD OTHER	
				Jour	JET 22 57	Jan 66	− + ENGL OF ZET 49 80	
	2.4+1	3.2+2		Rept	ANL−TRANS−202		65 . ENGL OF JINR−P−1972	
Reson Params	2.4+1	2.9+2	DUB Expt	Conf	65Antwerp § 188	Jul 65	Kim Hi San.DUBNA.5 RES.WT,WG,J	+
Reson Params		1.0+6	AUA Theo	Jour	AUJ 20 477	Oct 67	Cook. TBL OF AVG LVL SPACING D,L=0,1	
Reson Params	2.4+1	1.3+3	SAC Expt	Jour	NP/A 134 118	Sep 69	Alves+LINAC TOF.WN,WN0,J 20E;10WGWT	+
				Conf	68Wash. 867	Mar 68	Morgenstern. WG VS. A. AVG WG GIVEN	
				Conf	66Paris 1 559	Oct 66	Huynh+ ABST.NDG. SEE INDC−156	
				Rept	CEA−R−3128	Jun 66	Chevillon+ TRANS+CAPT. SUPERSEDED.	
				Conf	65Antwerp 525	Jul 65	De Barros+ PPR73.ABST.NDG	
	0.0+0	1.3+3		Data	EXFOR20688.	Jun 77	21PTS.E0,AVG WG,WN,WT,J,G*WN.	

56 Barium 135

Quantity	Energy (ev) Min	Max	Lab	Type	Documentation Ref Vol Page	Date	Author, Comments	Data
Reson Params	2.5+1	2.9+2	DUB	Expt	Jour CZJB 19 899	Jul 69	Becvar+ LOW LVL DECAY-SCH OF 136-BA	
Reson Params	2.4+1	8.8+1	ANL	Expt	Jour PR/C 1 1501	Apr 70	Wetzel+J FROM CAPT MEAS.TBL GVN.	+
	2.4+1	8.8+1			Data EXFOR10080.003	Feb 76	. 3 PTS J,E0.	
Reson Params	–		AUA	Theo	Rept AAEC/E-211	Nov 70	Musgrove. CALCULTD D+GAM WIDTH GIVEN	
Reson Params	2.4+1	4.3+2	CJD	Eval	Rept YK-7	71	Zakharova+ SURVEY+SYSTEMATICS,GW,TBL	
					Rept INDC(CCP)-27	Nov 72	.ENGLISH TRANSLATION OF YK-7 /71	
Reson Params	None		DUB	Theo	Jour YF 13 240	Feb 71	Malecki+G-WID,THEO CFD EXPT.TBL,GRPH	
					Jour SNP 13 133	Aug 71	– + ENGL OF YF 13 240.	
Reson Params	2.4+1	1.4+3	HAR	Expt	Jour NP/A 177 393	Dec 71	VAN DE VYVER+ S-WAVE AREA ANAL.25E0.	+
	2.4+1	2.0+3			Data EXFOR20469.	Jan 76	56PTS.E0,WG,G*WN.	
Reson Params	2.4+1	1.0+3	LRL	Expt	Jour PR/C 7 2522	Jun 73	Berman+ CAPT MEAST.ES ONLY 13 RESON.	+
	2.4+1	2.3+3			Data EXFOR10313.006	Jun 75	. 20 PTS EN	
Reson Params	None		DUB	Theo	Rept JINR-P4-7499	Oct 73	Soloviev+ CALC D CFD EXPTS,TABLE	
Reson Params	+0	+2	BOL	Eval	Conf IAEA-169 3 123	74	Benzi+ AVG G-WID CFD OTHERS+XPT,TABL	
Reson Params	2.4+1	4.6+2	BNL	Expt	Jour PR/C 9 1622	Apr 74	Chrien+ TABLE PARTIAL WG. 10 RESON.	+
	2.4+1	4.6+2			Data EXFOR10643.002	Aug 78	. 10 RES.J GVN.	
Reson Params	+1	+3	FEI	Eval	Rept YK-8/2 97	Sep 72	Abagyan+ AVG G-WID+D AT BINDNG-E,TBL	
					Rept INDC(CCP)-39	Jul 74	.PAGE 102.ENGLISH OF YK-8/2 97	
Reson Params	3.0+3	6.0+3	ORL	Expt	Prog ERDA-NDC-3 176	May 76	Musgrove+AVG WG.	+
	3.1+3	6.0+3			Data EXFOR10538.	Feb 76	. 186PTS WN,WG,WT,LVL SPACING.	
Strnth Fnctn	+3		BNL	Expt	Jour PRL 1 461	Dec 58	Hughes. FC 1.1+ – 0.30	
Strnth Fnctn		1.4+3	SAC	Expt	Jour NP/A 123 569	Jan 69	Morgenstern+ TBL. FROM RES ANALYSIS	
					Rept CEA-R-3609	Sep 68	– . (THESIS) S-WAVE. RADIUS	
					Conf 68Wash. 867	Mar 68	– +	
					Conf 66Paris 1 183	Oct 66	– + PPR65.ABST.NDG.INDC-156	
					Conf 66Paris 1 205	Oct 66	Julien+ PPR64.ABST.NDG. SEE INDC-156	
					Rept CEA-R-3128	Jun 66	Chevillon+ TRANS+CAPT. SUPERSEDED.	
	0.0+0	1.3+3			Data EXFOR20688.015	Jun 77	1PNT.L=0.	
Strnth Fnctn	–		DUB	Revw	Jour YF 11 111	Jan 70	Malecki+ VALUES FOR TWO SPIN STATES	
					Jour SNP 11 61	Jul 70	– + ENGL OF YF 11 61.	
Strnth Fnctn	–		AUA	Theo	Rept AAEC/E-211	Nov 70	Musgrove. SMOOTHED S0,S1 AND S2 GIVN	
Strnth Fnctn	2.4+1	1.4+3	HAR	Expt	Jour NP/A 177 393	Dec 71	VAN DE VYVER+ S-WAVE.	+
	4.0+1	2.0+3			Data EXFOR20469.010	Jan 76	1PNT.L=0.	
Strnth Fnctn	None		AUA	Eval	Rept AAEC/E-277	Mar 73	Musgrove.TBLS EXPTL DATA+BEST VALUES	
Strnth Fnctn	None		KUR	Theo	Prog IAE-2560	75	Adamchuk+.S0-VALUE,TBL	
Strnth Fnctn		+5	KFK	Theo	Conf JAERI-M-5984	Feb 75	Newstead.P230.TBL S0,S1 CFD EXP.	
Strnth Fnctn	3.0+3	6.0+3	ORL	Expt	Prog ERDA-NDC-3 176	May 76	Musgrove+P WAVE. VAL GVN	+
	3.1+3	5.8+3			Data EXFOR10538.006	Feb 76	. 1PT P WAVE STF=(.8+ – .2)–4.	
Lvl Density	+6		MIL	Theo	Jour EN 15 1 54	Jan 68	Facchini+ LDL PARS FROM LOW EN RES	
Lvl Density	None		MUN	Theo	Jour NP/A 217 269	Dec 73	Dilg+ A,DELTA. BACK SHIFTED FERMIGAS	
Lvl Density	None		BOL	Eval	Conf IAEA-169 3 123	74	Benzi+ LVL DENS PARAM BY XPT,GRPH+TB	
Lvl Density	None		DUB	Theo	Jour NP/A 224 411	May 74	Soloviev+ 1/2 MICROSC MDL. SPH NUCL.	
Lvl Density	None		ROC	Theo	Jour NP/A 223 577	May 74	Huizenga+ EXP CFD MICROSC TH SPH NUC	
Lvl Density	+1	+3	FEI	Eval	Rept YK-8/2 97	Sep 72	Abagyan+ LVL DENSITY PARAMETER,TBL	
					Rept INDC(CCP)-39	Jul 74	.PAGE 102.ENGLISH OF YK-8/2 97	

56 Barium 136

Quantity	Energy (ev) Min	Max	Lab	Type	Documentation Ref Vol Page	Date	Author, Comments	Data
Evaluation	1.0–3	1.5+7	AUA	Eval	Rept AAEC/TM-549	Jun 70	Cook.TOT,EL,INEL,NONEL,CAPT SIGS,NDG	+
					Rept AAEC/E-214	Jun 71	Bertram+GROUP SIGMAS SAME QUANTS.NDG	
					Rept AAEC/TM-587	Mar 71	*DESCRIPTION OF LIBRARY	
	1.0–3	1.5+7			Data AUSTR-DFN 129.	Nov 71	POINT(223) AND GROUP(127) SIGMAS	
Total	2.7+3	2.2+4	DKE	Expt	Jour AP 14 387	Jul 61	Bilpuch+	+
	2.7+3	2.2+4			Data EXFOR11599.045	Jun 76	. 44 PTS, SIGMA.	
Total	1.0–3	1.5+7	AUA	Eval	Data AUSTR-DFN 129.	Nov 71	COOK+ POINT(223)+GROUP(127) SIGMAS	
Total	4.0+0	2.0+3	HAR	Expt	Jour NP/A 177 393	Dec 71	VAN DE VIJVER+ TRANSM.ENRICHED SAMPL	+
	4.0+0	2.0+3			Data EXFOR20469.	Jan 76	0PTS. SEE RESONANCE PARAMETERS.	
Elastic	1.0–3	1.5+7	AUA	Eval	Data AUSTR-DFN 129.	Nov 71	COOK+ POINT(223)+GROUP(127) SIGMAS	
Tot Inelastc	1.0–3	1.5+7	AUA	Eval	Data AUSTR-DFN 129.	Nov 71	COOK+ POINT(223)+GROUP(127) SIGMAS	
Diff Inelast	4.0+5	1.2+6	FEI	Expt	Jour AE 15 416	Nov 63	Glazkov+ SPHER GEOM, 5 ENERGIES	
					Jour JNE 18 654	64	. ENGL OF AE 15 416	
					Jour SJA 11 173	Nov 63	. ENGL OF AE 15 416	
					Jour EAF 15 5	Nov 63	.FRENCH OF AE 15 416	
Diff Inelast	Thrsh	1.7+6	LEB	Expt	Conf 72Kiev 2 4	Jan 72	Konobeevskij+ ABST,NDG.SIG TO 2-LVL	
Nonelastic	1.0–3	1.5+7	AUA	Eval	Data AUSTR-DFN 129.	Nov 71	COOK+ POINT(223)+GROUP(127) SIGMAS	+
Absorption	4.1–1	1.0+7	GA	Eval	Rept GA-2451	Aug 61	Joanou+ 68GROUP DATA FOR GAM-I ABS	

56 Barium 136

Quantity	Energy (ev) Min	Max	Lab	Type	Documentation Ref Vol Page	Date	Author, Comments	Data
Absorption	1.0−3	1.0+7	JUL Eval	Rept	JUEL−678−RG	Jul 70	Liu. EVALUATION+CALC,GRPH,FN OF E	
Res Int Abs	None		CRC Eval	Rept	AECL−1054	Mar 60	Walker.(CRP−913) REDUCED RES.INT.	
Res Int Abs	5.0−1		BOL Eval	Rept	RT/FI−4	Jan 67	Palmucci. CALC FROM (N,G) RES PARAMS	
Res Int Abs	5.5−1		CRC Eval	Rept	AECL−3037 1	Jan 72	Walker.REDUCED RES INT FROM RES PARS	
Res Int Abs	5.0−1		AUA Eval	Rept	AAEC/TM−619	Sep 72	Clayton.CALC FROM SIG LIBRARY,TABLE	
Res Int Abs	5.0−1		GHT Expt	Jour	JRC 20 695	74	Van Der Linden+ BY(N,G).CFD OTHS,TBL	+
	5.5−1			Conf	73Paris 2 241	Mar 73	− + ACT,REL THR+GOLD,TBL	
	5.5−1			Data	EXFOR20645.013	Jul 76	1PNT.CAPTURE.	
Res Int Abs	5.5−1	+6	SAC Revw	Conf	IAEA−169 1 235	74	Ribon.CAPTURE,STATUS CFD REQUEST,TBL	
Res Int Abs	+0	+5	WIN Revw	Conf	IAEA−169 3 163	74	Pope+ DATA FILE CALC CFD XPTAL VALUE	
(n,γ)	Maxwl		ORL Expt	Jour	PR 88 412	Oct 52	Pomerance.PILE OSC.ESTIM.ERROR 100PC	+
	Maxwl			Data	EXFOR11507.070	Jun 76	. 1 PT, SIGMA.	
(n,γ)	Maxwl		CRC Eval	Rept	AECL−1054	Mar 60	Walker.(CRP−913)	
(n,γ)	Maxwl		MUA Expt	Jour	NP 20 183	Oct 60	Hans+ CS OF BA136(NG)BA137M GIVEN	+
	Maxwl			Data	EXFOR31246.010	Sep 72	.SIG TO MS−STATE GVN	
(n,γ)	Maxwl		UCS Expt	Jour	NSE 22 373	Jul 65	Kramer+ ACTIVATION.	+
	Maxwl			Data	EXFOR11832.007	Jun 76	. 1 PT, SIGMA.	
(n,γ)	2.5−2		BOL Eval	Rept	RT/FI−4	Jan 67	Palmucci. CALC FROM RES PARAMETERS	
(n,γ)	Maxwl		MIL Expt	Jour	EN 14 4 228	Apr 67	FOGLIO PARA+.SIG GS+ISOM CFD THEORY.	
(n,γ)	−		IEA Comp	Rept	IEA−INF−10	Aug 68	Atalla. TABLES OF HL,SIG AND GAMM−E	
(n,γ)	1.0+3	1.0+7	BOL Eval	Rept	CCDN−NW/10	Dec 69	Benzi+H−F MOD,AXEL G(G)EST,ALL DATA	
				Rept	CEC(70)−2	Apr 70	− +. GRAPH	
(n,γ)	3.0+4		AUA Theo	Rept	AAEC/E−211	Nov 70	Musgrove. SIGMA GIVEN AND CFD OTHER	
(n,γ)	1.0−3	1.5+7	AUA Eval	Data	AUSTR−DFN 129.	Nov 71	COOK+ POINT(223)+GROUP(127) SIGMAS	+
(n,γ)	Maxwl		CRC Eval	Rept	AECL−3037 1	Jan 72	Walker.RECOMMENDED SIG,DETAILED TBL	
(n,γ)	2.5−2		AUA Eval	Rept	AAEC/TM−619	Sep 72	Clayton.CALC FROM SIG LIBRARY,TABLE	
(n,γ)	+6		KOS Expt	Jour	AHP 33 363	73	Peto+ BA−137(INL)+BA−136(N,G)BA−137M	+
	+6			Data	EXFOR30265.016	Feb 74	AVERAGE SIG FOR PU−BE NEUTRONS	
(n,γ)	2.5−2		SAC Revw	Conf	IAEA−169 1 235	74	Ribon.STATUS SIG CFD REQUESTS,TABLE	
(n,γ)	Maxwl	Fiss	WIN Revw	Conf	IAEA−169 3 163	74	Pope+ MAXW+FIS−SPEC AVG DATA CFD XPT	
	Fiss			Conf	IAEA−169 3 137	74	Dean. POINT DATA AVG OVER STAND SPEC	
(n,γ)	1.0+3	1.0+7	FEI Eval	Rept	YK−8/2 97	Sep 72	Abagjan+ AVG SIG(ENERGY−GROUPS),TABL	
				Rept	INDC(CCP)−39	Jul 74	.P102. ENGLISH OF YK−8/2 97	
(n,γ)	3.0+4		AUA Expt	Jour	NP/A 256 173	Jan 75	Musgrove+AVG SIG=61+−10MB AT 30 KEV	+
	Maxwl			Data	EXFOR30328.	Mar 76	AVERAGE SIG,KT=30KEV. 1 PNT	
(n,γ)	Fiss		KOS Expt	Conf	75Karlsrhe 29	Apr 75	Csikai. CF252.+137(N,N')META.SIG GVN	
	1.4+6			Data	EXFOR30400.051	Oct 78	1 PNT. BA136(N,G)+BA137(N,N')BA137M	
Spect (n,γ)	Maxwl		KUR Expt	Jour	YF 10 681	Oct 69	Groshev+ TABLE GAM−SPECTRA,TRANSITNS	+
				Rept	IAE−1780	Jan 69	− + TBL OF GAMMA YLD+E,GE(LI)	
				Jour	SNP 10 392	Apr 70	. ENGL OF YF 10 681	
				Rept	LA−TR−69−29	Oct 69	. ENGLISH OF IAE−1780	
	2.5−2			Data	EXFOR40237.003	Nov 74	.GAM/100N FOR 4 ES GVN	
(n,2n)	1.5+7		ARK Expt	Jour	PR 118 242	Apr 60	Wille. MEAS ACT SIG=700+−80 MB	+
	1.5+7			Data	EXFOR12033.003	Jun 76	. 1 PT, SIGMA.	
(n,2n)	Fiss		CRC Eval	Rept	CRC−1003	Dec 60	ROY+ ESTIMATED AVG SIG=0.76MB	
(n,2n)	1.4+7		HAM Comp	Jour	NP 65 257	Mar 65	Bormann. 1EXPT VALS.CFD SHELL EFFECT	
(n,2n)	1.5+7		TUR Theo	Jour	NC 56 18 201	Jul 68	Minetti+THEOR ISOM RATIO SPIN CO PAR	
(n,2n)	1.5+7		DEB Comp	Jour	REA 7 4 93	Dec 69	Csikai+ SIG+HL COMPILTN,N−ACTIV−ANAL	
(n,2n)	1.4+7		GIT Expt	Jour	PR/C 1 350	Jan 70	Fink+ACTIVATION,GRPHS,TBL CFD OTH.	+
	1.4+7			Data	EXFOR10497.039	Apr 76	. 1PT BA136 N2N+BA135 SIN=1149+−80MB	
(n,2n)	1.5+7		IBJ Expt	Jour	APPB 3 637	72	Rurarz+ SIG TO METASTABLE STATE	+
				Prog	INR−1401 4	May 72	− + ACTIV,PAR SIG TO ISOM LVL	
	1.5+7			Data	EXFOR30183.004	Aug 72	1 DATA LINE	
(n,2n)	1.4+7		ITJ Expt	Jour	JRC 14 201	73	Janczyszyn+ ISO−PROD BY NAT−BA ACTIV	
	1.4+7			Data	EXFOR30322.013	Feb 76	MEAN OF BA135(N,N')+BA136(N,2N)	
(n,2n)	1.5+7		DEB Eval	Jour	REA 11 1 153	Mar 73	Boedy+ RECOMM.VALUE FROM N−Z SYSTEM.	
(n,2n)	1.5+7		KFI Theo	Rept	KFKI−73−68	Dec 73	Jeki.NEW FIT,CALC SIG CFD OTHERS,TBL	
(n,2n)	1.5+7		RBZ Expt	Jour	JP/G 2 405	Jun 76	Holub+ STUDY OF SYSTEMATICS,SIG GIVN	+
				ExTh	INDC(SEC)−50	Jan 76	− + ACTIV.CFD OTH+THEO,TABLE	
				Jour	ASL 25 180	75	− . TBL SIG,TO META,GND.CFD OTHRS	
	1.4+7			Expt Data	EXFOR30348.	Sep 76	SIGMA ISOM+GND+TOTAL.	
(n,2n)	1.4+7		AUW Expt	Conf	76Ahmedabd 2 18	Dec 76	Lakshmana Das+ ABST. REL AL−27,TABLE	+
				Data	EXFOR30433.003	Mar 78	SIG TO BA−135M.	
(n,2n)	1.5+7		IBJ Theo	Jour	ASL 27 186	77	Rurarz+ ISO RATIO,4MODLS,CFD XPT.TBL	
	1.4+7			Rept	INR−1464 19	May 73	− + ISOMERIC RATIO CFD EXPT,GRAF	
(n,p)	Pile		ARK Expt	Abst	BAP 1 40	Jan 56	Robinson+ 0.2+−0.05MUB Q=0.92MEV	
(n,p)	Fiss		GES Revw	Jour	NUC 17 1 54	Jan 59	Rochlin.47 ISOTOPES.ACT.RVS.TBL	
(n,p)	1.4+7		ALD Expt	Jour	PPS 73 215	Feb 59	Coleman+. ACT. CFD DIRECT INTERACTN	+

56 Barium 136

Quantity	Energy (ev) Min	Max	Lab	Type	Documentation Ref Vol Page	Date	Author, Comments	Data
(n,p)	1.5+7		ARK Expt	Jour	PR 118 242	Apr 60	Wille. MEAS ACT SIG = 49 +- 10 MB	+
	1.5+7			Data	EXFOR12033.004	Jun 76	. 1 PT, SIGMA.	
(n,p)	Fiss		CRC Eval	Rept	CRC - 1003	Dec 60	ROY+ ESTIMATED AVG SIG=0.1MB	
(n,p)	1.5+7		SAH Comp	Jour	NUC 23 8 112	Aug 65	Chatterjee. TABLE WITH REFS.	
(n,p)	1.4+7	1.5+7	NAP Comp	Rept	INFN/BE - 67 - 10	Jul 67	Cuzzocrea+ AVERAGED CHOSEN DATA.	
(n,p)	1.5+7		KAZ Expt	Jour	YF 8 7	Jul 68	Levkovskij+ SIG VAL +- ERROR GVN,TBL	+
				Jour	SNP 8 4	Jan 69	TRANSLATN.*	
	1.5+7			Data	EXFOR40223.023	May 74	.SIGMA GIVEN,1 DATA LINE	
(n,p)	1.5+7		DEB Comp	Jour	REA 7 4 93	Dec 69	Csikai+ SIG+HL COMPILTN,N - ACTIV - ANAL	
(n,p)	1.4+7	1.5+7	KAZ Theo	Jour	YF 18 705	Oct 73	Levkovsky.AVERAGED SIG,CALC,TBL	
				Jour	SNP 18 361	Apr 74	. ENGLISH OF YF 18,705	
(n,α)	Fiss		CRC Eval	Rept	CRC - 1003	Dec 60	ROY+ ESTIMATED AVG SIG = 0.0004MB	
Reson Params	1.0+2		BNL Expt	Priv	PILCHER	Apr 55	Pilcher.	+
	1.0+2			Data	EXFOR12041.005	Jun 76	. 1 RESONANCE, WN.	
Reson Params	1.0+2		BNL Expt	Jour	PR 108 353	Oct 57	Stolovy+ FC, TRANS	+
Reson Params	8.0+3		DKE Expt	Jour	AP 14 387	Jul 61	Bilpuch+ REDUCED NEUTRON WIDTHS.	+
	8.0+3			Data	EXFOR11599.040	Jun 76	. 1 RESONANCE, WN AND E0.	
Reson Params		1.0+6	AUA Theo	Jour	AUJ 20 477	Oct 67	Cook. TBL OF AVG LVL SPACING D,L=0,1	
Reson Params	5.1+2		SAC Expt	Jour	NP/A 134 118	Sep 69	Alves+ LINAC TOF.WN,WN0,J.	+
	1.0+2	5.1+2		Conf	66Paris 1 559	Oct 66	Huynh+ ABST.NDG. SEE INDC - 156	
				Rept	CEA - R - 3128	Jun 66	Chevillon - P.WN,WN0,WT,WG,J.TRNS+CAPT	
	5.1+2			Data	EXFOR20688.016	Jun 77	1PNT.E0,WN,J,G*WN.	
Reson Params	-		AUA Theo	Rept	AAEC/E - 211	Nov 70	Musgrove. CALCULTD D+GAM WIDTH GIVEN	
Reson Params	1.0+2		CJD Eval	Rept	YK - 7	71	Zakharova+ SURVEY+SYSTEMATICS,GW,TBL	
				Rept	INDC(CCP) - 27	Nov 72	.ENGLISH TRANSLATION OF YK - 7 /71	
Reson Params	4.5+2	5.1+2	HAR Expt	Jour	NP/A 177 393	Dec 71	VAN DE VYVER+ S - WAVE AREA ANAL. 2E0.	+
	4.5+2	7.3+3		Data	EXFOR20469.	Jan 76	11PTS.E0,G*WN.	
Reson Params	4.2+2	6.5+2	LRL Expt	Jour	PR/C 7 2522	Jun 73	Berman+ CAPT MEAST.ES ONLY 3 RESON.	+
	4.2+2	2.0+3		Data	EXFOR10313.007	Jun 75	. 4 PTS EN	
Reson Params	None		DUB Theo	Rept	JINR - P4 - 7499	Oct 73	Soloviev+ CALC D CFD EXPTS,TABLE	
	-			Rept	JINR - E4 - 5711	Apr 71	- . AVG LVL SPACING, EXPTS TBD	
Reson Params	+2	+3	FEI Eval	Rept	YK - 8/2 97	Sep 72	Abagyan+ AVG G - WID+D AT BINDNG - E,TBL	
				Rept	INDC(CCP) - 39	Jul 74	.PAGE 102.ENGLISH OF YK - 8/2 97	
Strnth Fnctn		1.0+4	DKE Expt	Jour	AP 14 346	Jul 61	Newson+ TRANSMISSION.	+
		1.0+4		Data	EXFOR11888.009	Jun 76	. 1 PT, LEVEL SPACING.	
Strnth Fnctn	-		AUA Theo	Rept	AAEC/E - 211	Nov 70	Musgrove. SMOOTHED S0,S1 AND S2 GIVN	
Strnth Fnctn	4.5+2	5.1+2	HAR Expt	Jour	NP/A 177 393	Dec 71	VAN DE VYVER+ S - WAVE.	+
	4.0+0	2.0+3		Data	EXFOR20469.013	Jan 76	1PNT.L=0.	
Strnth Fnctn	None		AUA Theo	Rept	AAEC/E - 277	Mar 73	Musgrove.TBLS EXPTL DATA+BEST VALUES	
Strnth Fnctn	None		KUR Theo	Prog	IAE - 2560	75	Adamchuk+.S0 - VALUE,TBL	
Strnth Fnctn	None		OSA Theo	Conf	JAERI - M - 5984	Feb 75	Kitazoe+OPT MDLS.GRPH VS A.TBL PARS	
Lvl Density	+6		MIL Theo	Jour	EN 15 1 54	Jan 68	Facchini+ LDL PARS FROM LOW EN RES	
Lvl Density	-		FEI Theo	Conf	70Helsinki 2 885	Jun 70	Ignatjuk+76. SUPERFLUID CFD FERMI - TH	
Lvl Density	None		MUN Theo	Jour	NP/A 217 269	Dec 73	Dilg+ A,DELTA. BACK SHIFTED FERMIGAS	
Lvl Density	None		COP Theo	Jour	NP/A 222 493	Apr 74	Dossing+COLL ROTAT.SPAC. ACCUR ESTIM	
Lvl Density	None		ROC Theo	Jour	NP/A 223 577	May 74	Huizenga+ EXP CFD MICROSC TH SPH NUC	
Lvl Density	+2	+3	FEI Eval	Rept	YK - 8/2 97	Sep 72	Abagyan+ LVL DENSITY PARAMETER,TBL	
				Rept	INDC(CCP) - 39	Jul 74	.PAGE 102.ENGLISH OF YK - 8/2 97	

56 Barium 137

Quantity	Energy (ev) Min	Max	Lab	Type	Documentation Ref Vol Page	Date	Author, Comments	Data
Evaluation	1.0-3	1.5+7	AUA Eval	Rept	AAEC/TM - 549	Jun 70	Cook.TOT,EL,INEL,NONEL,CAPT SIGS,NDG	+
				Rept	AAEC/E - 214	Jun 71	Bertram+GROUP SIGMAS SAME QUANTS.NDG	
				Rept	AAEC/TM - 587	Mar 71	*DESCRIPTION OF LIBRARY	
	1.0-3	1.5+7		Data	AUSTR - DFN 130.	Nov 71	POINT(223) AND GROUP(127) SIGMAS	
Total	1.0-3	1.5+7	AUA Eval	Data	AUSTR - DFN 130.	Nov 71	COOK+ POINT(223)+GROUP(127) SIGMAS	+
Total	4.0+0	2.0+3	HAR Expt	Jour	NP/A 177 393	Dec 71	VAN DE VIJVER+ TRANSM.ENRICHED SAMPL	+
	4.0+0	2.0+3		Data	EXFOR20469.	Jan 76	0PTS. SEE RESONANCE PARAMETERS.	
Elastic	1.0-3	1.5+7	AUA Eval	Data	AUSTR - DFN 130.	Nov 71	COOK+ POINT(223)+GROUP(127) SIGMAS	+
Diff Elastic	4.0+5	3.0+6	BAR Expt	Jour	PR 100 1329	Dec 55	Swann+ EXC CURV FOR 661KEV METAST	
Diff Elastic	1.0+6		LAS Eval	Rept	LA - 2016	Jun 56	Longley+ TBL ANG DIST 3 - DEG STEPS.	
Potntal Scat		1.3+3	SAC Expt	Jour	NP/A 123 561	Jan 69	Morgenstern+ RADIUS FROM RES ANAL	+
				Rept	CEA - R - 3609	Sep 68	- + (THESIS) RADIUS.	
	0.0+0	1.3+3		Data	EXFOR20688.018	Jun 77	1PNT.RADIUS.	
Tot Inelastc	6.7+5	1.0+6	KUR Theo	Jour	NP 45 156	Jul 63	Nemirovsky+ EXCITATION OF 661KEV LVL	
Tot Inelastc	Fiss		IIT Comp	Conf	65IAEA 251	Mar 65	Barrall+CALC AVG SIGS OF 3FISS - SPECS	

56 Barium 137

Quantity	Energy (ev) Min	Max	Lab	Type	Documentation Ref Vol Page	Date	Author, Comments	Data
Tot Inelastc	Pile		FEI	Comp Rept	ICD-4 57	67	Sluchevskaja.SELECTIV COMPIL ,TABLE	
Tot Inelastc	Fast		MUN	Expt Jour	NUK 10 181	Oct 67	Koehler+H2O MODER REACT. .1MEVCUTOFF	
				Rept	FRM-81	Aug 66	- + SUPERSEDED.	
Tot Inelastc	1.0-3	1.5+7	AUA	Eval Data	AUSTR-DFN 130.	Nov 71	COOK+ POINT(223)+GROUP(127) SIGMAS	+
Diff Inelast	4.0+5	1.2+6	FEI	Expt Jour	AE 15 416	Nov 63	Glazkov+ SPHER GEOM, 5 ENERGIES	
				Jour	JNE 18 654	64	. ENGL OF AE 15 416	
				Jour	SJA 15 1173	Nov 63	. ENGL OF AE 15 416	
				Jour	EAF 15 5	Nov 63	.FRENCH OF AE 15 416	
Diff Inelast	Fiss		UCB	Expt Rept	NYO-10175	Dec 64	Arino+ACT.TBLS.GRAPHS.PRODUCT HL.	+
	Fiss			Data	EXFOR11817.029	Jun 76	. 1 PT, DSIGMA.	
Diff Inelast	Fiss		UCS	Expt Jour	NSE 22 373	Jul 65	Kramer+ ACTIVATION.	+
	Fiss			Data	EXFOR11832.016	Jun 76	. 1 PT, SIGMA.	
Diff Inelast	2.8+6		DEB	Expt Jour	AK 10 112	Jul 68	Bornemisza+ TBL HL+SIGMA FOR BA137M	+
	2.8+6			Data	EXFOR30338.006	Aug 76	TO ISOM. 1 PNT	
Diff Inelast	1.5+7		IBJ	Expt Jour	APPB 1 415	70	Rurarz+ ACTIV,NAI,SIG(M)+ISORATIO	+
	1.5+7			Data	EXFOR30154.	Feb 72	PARTIAL SIG	
Diff Inelast	+7		FEI	Theo Conf	72Kiev 2 19	Jan 72	Tertychnyj+ ABST,NDG.H-F,DOUBLEDIFF	
Diff Inelast	+6		KOS	Expt Jour	AHP 33 363	73	Peto+ BA-137(INL)+BA-136(N,G)BA-137M	+
	+6			Data	EXFOR30265.016	Feb 74	AVG SIG FOR PU-BE NEUTRONS	
Diff Inelast	Fiss		KOS	Expt Conf	75Karlsrhe 29	Apr 75	Csikai. CF252.+136(N,G)META. SIG GVN	+
	1.4+6			Data	EXFOR30400.051	Oct 78	1 PNT. BA136(N,G)+BA137(N,N')BA137M	
Diff Inelast	Thrsh	Up	CAI	Theo Jour	AKE 28 3 201	76	Abboud. EXCITATION-FN,STATMOD	
Nonelastic	1.0-3	1.5+7	AUA	Eval Data	AUSTR-DFN 130.	Nov 71	COOK+ POINT(223)+GROUP(127) SIGMAS	+
Absorption	4.1-1	1.0+7	GA	Eval Rept	GA-2451	Aug 61	Joanou+ 68GROUP DATA FOR GAM-I ABS	
Absorption	1.0-3	1.0+7	JUL	Eval Rept	JUEL-678-RG	Jul 70	Liu. EVALUATION+CALC,GRPH,FN OF E	
Res Int Abs	5.0-1		BOL	Eval Rept	RT/FI-4	Jan 67	Palmucci. CALC FROM (N,G) RES PARAMS	
Res Int Abs	5.5-1		CRC	Eval Rept	AECL-3037 1	Jan 72	Walker.REDUCED RES INT FROM RES PARS	
Res Int Abs	5.0-1		AUA	Eval Rept	AAEC/TM-619	Sep 72	Clayton.CALC FROM SIG LIBRARY,TABLE	
Res Int Abs	5.5-1	+6	SAC	Revw Conf	IAEA-169 1 235	74	Ribon.CAPTURE,STATUS CFD REQUEST,TBL	
Res Int Abs	+0	+5	WIN	Revw Conf	IAEA-169 3 163	74	Pope+ DATA FILE CALC CFD XPTAL VALUE	
(n,γ)	Maxwl		ORL	Expt Jour	PR 88 412	Oct 52	Pomerance.PILE OSC.	+
	Maxwl			Data	EXFOR11507.071	Jun 76	. 1 PT, SIGMA.	
(n,γ)	2.5-2		BOL	Eval Rept	RT/FI-4	Jan 67	Palmucci. CALC FROM RES PARAMETERS	
(n,γ)	1.0+3	1.0+7	BOL	Eval Rept	CCDN-NW/10	Dec 69	Benzi+H-F MOD,AXEL G(G)EST,ALL DATA	
				Rept	CEC(70)-2	Apr 70	- +. GRAPH	
(n,γ)	3.0+4		AUA	Theo Rept	AAEC/E-211	Nov 70	Musgrove. SIGMA GIVEN AND CFD OTHER	
(n,γ)	1.0-3	1.5+7	AUA	Eval Data	AUSTR-DFN 130.	Nov 71	COOK+ POINT(223)+GROUP(127) SIGMAS	+
(n,γ)	Maxwl		CRC	Eval Rept	AECL-3037 1	Jan 72	Walker.RECOMMENDED SIG,DETAILED TBL	
(n,γ)	2.5-2		AUA	Eval Rept	AAEC/TM-619	Sep 72	Clayton.CALC FROM SIG LIBRARY,TABLE	
(n,γ)	2.5-2		SAC	Revw Conf	IAEA-169 1 235	74	Ribon.STATUS SIG CFD REQUESTS,TABLE	
(n,γ)	Fiss		WIN	Revw Conf	IAEA-169 3 137	74	Dean. POINT DATA AVG OVER STAND SPEC	
(n,γ)	Maxwl	Fiss		Conf	IAEA-169 3 163	74	Pope+ MAXW+FIS-SPEC AVG DATA CFD XPT	
(n,γ)	1.0+3	1.0+7	FEI	Eval Rept	YK-8/2 97	Sep 72	Abagjan+ AVG SIG(ENERGY-GROUPS),TABL	
				Rept	INDC(CCP)-39	Jul 74	.P102. ENGLISH OF YK-8/2 97	
Spect (n,γ)	Maxwl		BNL	Expt Jour	PR 174 1485	Oct 68	Kane+ GE(LI)+NAI 91GAMS BA138 LVLS	
Spect (n,γ)	Pile		ANL	Expt Conf	69Studsvik 601	Aug 69	Smither+ NO DATA GVN,TB CFD STATMOD	
Spect (n,γ)	Pile		KUR	Expt Jour	IZV 34 768	Apr 70	Groshev+ GE-LI,TBL G ES+INTS,LVL SCH	+
				Jour	BAS 34 680	Apr 71	* ENGL OF IZV 34 768	
	2.5-2			Data	EXFOR40181.004	Jan 74	.25 GAMMA ES AND GAM/100N GIVEN	
Inelastic γ	5.0+5	3.0+6	BAR	Expt Jour	PR 100 1329	Dec 55	Swan+661KEV METASTABLE LVL OF BA-137	+
	5.0+5	3.0+6		Data	EXFOR11862.003	Jun 76	. 36 PTS.	
Inelastic γ	2.8+6		REN	Expt Jour	ARI 18 279	May 67	Broadhead+ ACTIV 2.6MIN ISOMER 465MB	+
	2.8+6			Data	EXFOR11850.007	Jun 76	. 1 PT.	
Inelastic γ	None		KFI	Comp Jour	JRC 7 365	Jun 71	Nagy+ GAMMA-E AND HALF-LIFE GIVEN	
(n,2n)	Fiss		CRC	Eval Rept	CRC-1003	Dec 60	ROY+ ESTIMATED AVG SIG=7.4MB	
(n,2n)	1.5+7		DEB	Eval Jour	REA 11 1 153	Mar 73	Boedy+ RECOMM.VALUE FROM N-Z SYSTEM.	
(n,2n)	1.5+7		KFI	Theo Rept	KFKI-73-68	Dec 73	Jeki.NEW FIT,CALC SIG CFD OTHERS,TBL	
(n,p)	Fiss		CRC	Eval Rept	CRC-1003	Dec 60	ROY+ ESTIMATED AVG SIG=0.06MB	
(n,α)	Fiss		CRC	Eval Rept	CRC-1003	Dec 60	ROY+ ESTIMATED AVG SIG=0.035MB	
Reson Params	4.2+2	5.9+2	BNL	Expt Priv	PILCHER	Apr 55	Pilcher.	+
	4.2+2	5.9+2		Data	EXFOR12041.006	Jun 76	. 2 RESONANCES, WN.	
Reson Params		1.0+6	AUA	Theo Jour	AUJ 20 477	Oct 67	Cook. TBL OF AVG LVL SPACING D,L=0,1	
Reson Params	4.2+2	1.3+3	SAC	Expt Jour	NP/A 134 118	Sep 69	Alves+ LINAC TOF.WN,WN0,J 3E0;2WG,WT	+
				Rept	CEA-R-3128	Jun 66	Chevillon-P.WN,WN0,WT,WG,J TRNS+CAPT	
	4.2+2	1.3+3		Data	EXFOR20688.017	Jun 77	3PTS.E0,WN,WT,J,G*WN.	
Reson Params	-		AUA	Theo Rept	AAEC/E-211	Nov 70	Musgrove. CALCULTD D+GAM WIDTH GIVEN	
Reson Params	4.5+2	5.8+2	CJD	Eval Rept	YK-7	71	Zakharova+ SURVEY+SYSTEMATICS,GW,TBL	
				Rept	INDC(CCP)-27	Nov 72	.ENGLISH TRANSLATION OF YK-7 /71	

56 Barium 137

Quantity	Energy (ev) Min	Max	Lab	Type	Documentation Ref Vol Page	Author, Comments Date	Data
Reson Params	1.3+2	1.7+3	HAR	Expt Jour	NP/A 177 393	Dec 71 VAN DE VYVER+ S-WAVE AREA ANAL. 8E0.	+
	1.3+2	5.0+3		Data	EXFOR20469.	Jan 76 18PTS.E0,G*WN.	
Reson Params	4.2+2	1.0+3	LRL	Expt Jour	PR/C 7 2522	Jun 73 Berman+ CAPT MEAST.ES ONLY 3 RESON	+
	4.2+2	2.0+3		Data	EXFOR10313.008	Jun 75 . 5 PTS EN	
Reson Params	None		DUB	Theo Rept	JINR-P4-7499	Oct 73 Soloviev+ CALC D CFD EXPTS,TABLE	
Reson Params	+0	+2	BOL	Eval Conf	IAEA-169 3 123	74 Benzi+ AVG G-WID CFD OTHERS+XPT,TABL	
Reson Params	+2	+3	FEI	Eval Rept	YK- 8/2 97	Sep 72 Abagyan+ AVG G-WID+D AT BINDNG-E,TBL	
				Rept	INDC(CCP)-39	Jul 74 .PAGE 102.ENGLISH OF YK-8/2 97	
Strnth Fnctn	None		BNL	Expt Prog	WASH-1021 10	Jun 59 Hughes+ NDG	
Strnth Fnctn		1.4+3	SAC	Expt Jour	NP/A 123 569	Jan 69 Morgenstern+ TBL. FROM RES ANALYSIS	+
				Rept	CEA-R-3609	Sep 68 - . (THESIS) S-WAVE. RADIUS	
				Conf	68Wash. 867	Mar 68 - +	
				Conf	66Paris 1 183	Oct 66 - + PPR65.ABST.NDG.INDC-156	
				Rept	CEA-R-3128	Jun 66 Chevillon+ FROM TRANS+CAPT RES ANAL	
	0.0+0	1.3+3		Data	EXFOR20688.019	Jun 77 1PNT.L=0.	
Strnth Fnctn	-		AUA	Theo Rept	AAEC/E-211	Nov 70 Musgrove. SMOOTHED S0,S1 AND S2 GIVN	
Strnth Fnctn	1.3+2	1.7+3	HAR	Expt Jour	NP/A 177 393	Dec 71 VAN DE VYVER+ S-WAVE.	+
	4.0+0	2.0+3		Data	EXFOR20469.016	Jan 76 1PNT.L=0.	
Strnth Fnctn	None		AUA	Eval Rept	AAEC/E-277	Mar 73 Musgrove.TBLS EXPTL DATA+BEST VALUES	
Strnth Fnctn	None		KUR	Theo Prog	IAE-2560	75 Adamchuk+.S0-VALUE,TBL	
Strnth Fnctn		+5	KFK	Theo Conf	JAERI-M-5984	Feb 75 Newstead.P230.TBL S0,S1 CFD EXP.	
Lvl Density	+6		MIL	Theo Jour	EN 15 1 54	Jan 68 Facchini+ LDL PARS FROM LOW EN RES	
Lvl Density	None		AUW	Theo Conf	70Madurai 2 267	Dec 70 Ramamurty+ A-PARAMETER GVN,LANG'S-TH	
Lvl Density	None		MUN	Theo Jour	NP/A 217 269	Dec 73 Dilg+ A,DELTA. BACK SHIFTED FERMIGAS	
Lvl Density	None		BOL	Eval Conf	IAEA-169 3 123	74 Benzi+ LVL DENS PARAM BY XPT,GRPH+TB	
Lvl Density	None		COP	Theo Jour	NP/A 222 493	Apr 74 Dossing+COLL ROTAT.SPAC. ACCUR ESTIM	
Lvl Density	None		DUB	Theo Jour	NP/A 224 411	May 74 Soloviev+ 1/2 MICROSC MDL. SPH NUCL.	
Lvl Density	None		ROC	Theo Jour	NP/A 223 577	May 74 Huizenga+ EXP CFD MICROSC TH SPH NUC	
Lvl Density	+2	+3	FEI	Eval Rept	YK- 8/2 97	Sep 72 Abagyan+ LVL DENSITY PARAMETER,TBL	
				Rept	INDC(CCP)-39	Jul 74 .PAGE 102.ENGLISH OF YK-8/2 97	

56 Barium 138

Quantity	Energy (ev) Min	Max	Lab	Type	Documentation Ref Vol Page	Author, Comments Date	Data
Evaluation	1.0-3	1.5+7	AUA	Eval Rept	AAEC/TM-549	Jun 70 Cook.TOT,EL,INEL,NONEL,CAPT SIGS,NDG	+
				Rept	AAEC/E-214	Jun 71 Bertram+GROUP SIGMAS SAME QUANTS.NDG	
				Rept	AAEC/TM-587	Mar 71 *DESCRIPTION OF LIBRARY	
	1.0-3	1.5+7		Data	AUSTR-DFN 131.	Nov 71 POINT(223) AND GROUP(127) SIGMAS	
Total	7.0+6	1.4+7	CJD	Theo Rept	ICD-5 20	68 Averjanov+ VIBRATION MDL,AT 4ES,TBL	
Total	1.0-3	1.5+7	AUA	Eval Data	AUSTR-DFN 131.	Nov 71 COOK+ POINT(223)+GROUP(127) SIGMAS	+
Elastic	7.0+6	1.4+7	CJD	Theo Rept	ICD-5 20	68 Averjanov+ VIBRATION MDL,AT 4ES,TBL	
Elastic	1.0-3	1.5+7	AUA	Eval Data	AUSTR-DFN 131.	Nov 71 COOK+ POINT(223)+GROUP(127) SIGMAS	
Tot Inelastc	7.0+6	1.4+7	CJD	Theo Rept	ICD-5 20	68 Averjanov+ VIBRATION MDL,AT 4ES,TBL	
Tot Inelastc	1.0-3	1.5+7	AUA	Eval Data	AUSTR-DFN 131.	Nov 71 COOK+ POINT(223)+GROUP(127) SIGMAS	+
Diff Inelast	1.4+6	2.1+6	STF	Expt Abst	DA/B 26 6800	May 66 Tucker.SIG FIRST 2 LVLS PROD.CFD H-F	+
	Thrsh			Conf	64Paris 2 671	Jul 64 - +10KEVRSLN XPT+OPTMDLFIT.NDG	
	1.4+6	2.1+6		Data	EXFOR11720.	Jun 76 . 54 PTS, SIGMA.	
Diff Inelast	1.4+7		LRL	Theo Rept	UCRL-50181	Feb 67 Lutz+ CALC ANG DIST FOR FIRST 2+ LVL	
Diff Inelast	7.0+6	1.4+7	CJD	Theo Rept	ICD-5 20	68 Averjanov+ TO 1ST LVL,ANGDIST,GRAPH	
Diff Inelast	Thrsh	1.7+6	LEB	Expt Conf	72Kiev 2 4	Jan 72 Konobeevskij+ ABST,NDG.SIG TO 2+LVL	
Nonelastic	1.0-3	1.5+7	AUA	Eval Data	AUSTR-DFN 131.	Nov 71 COOK+ POINT(223)+GROUP(127) SIGMAS	+
Absorption	2.5+4		ORL	Expt Conf	58Geneva 15 68	Sep 58 Macklin.PPR671,VAL GVN,EXPT DESCRIBD	
Absorption	4.1-1	1.0+7	GA	Expt Rept	GA-2451	Aug 61 Joanou+ 68GROUP DATA FOR GAM-I ABS	
Absorption	1.0-3	1.0+7	JUL	Eval Rept	JUEL-678-RG	Jul 70 Liu. EVALUATION+CALC,GRPH,FN OF E	
Res Int Abs	5.0-1		CNE	Expt Jour	CJP 46 2473	Nov 68 Ricabarra+,RATIO TO THR-ACT SIGMA	+
				Rept	CNEA-274	70 - + SAME,IN SPANISH	
	5.0-1			Data	EXFOR30129.008	Oct 72 RESON INT AND RATIO TO THR ABS SIGM.	
Res Int Abs	None		GA	Eval Rept	GA-12071	Sep 71 Mathews+ RECOMMENDED VALUES	
Res Int Abs	5.5-1		CRC	Eval Rept	AECL-3037 1	Jan 72 Walker.REDUCED RES INT,DETAILED TBL	
Res Int Abs	5.0-1		AUA	Eval Rept	AAEC/TM-619	Sep 72 Clayton.CALC FROM SIG LIBRARY,TABLE	
Res Int Abs	4.6-1	1.0+6	RCN	Theo Rept	RCN-191	Jul 73 Lautenbach.CAPT INT FROM GROUP SIGMA	
Res Int Abs	5.0-1		GHT	Expt Jour	JRC 20 695	74 Van Der Linden+ BY(N,G).CFD OTHS,TBL	+
	5.5-1			Conf	73Paris 2 241	Mar 73 - + ACT,REL THR+GOLD,TBL	
	5.5-1			Data	EXFOR20645.014	Jul 76 1PNT.CAPTURE.	
Res Int Abs	5.5-1	+6	SAC	Revw Conf	IAEA-169 1 235	74 Ribon.CAPTURE,STATUS CFD REQUEST,TBL	
Res Int Abs	+0	+5	WIN	Revw Conf	IAEA-169 3 163	74 Pope+ DATA FILE CALC CFD XPTAL VALUE	
(n,γ)	2.2+5		PCF	Expt Jour	NAT 142 392	Aug 38 Halban+ ACT CS GIVEN	

56 Barium 138

Quantity	Energy (ev) Min	Max	Lab	Type	Documentation Ref Vol Page	Date	Author, Comments	Data
(n,γ)	Maxwl		JAP	Expt Jour	SCP 38 167	Jan 41	Sinma+.LI+D.RELATIVE SIG MEASUREMENT	
(n,γ)	Pile		ANL	Expt Jour	PR 72 888	Nov 47	Seren+ THR IRRAD. THR IRRAD.BAO2.	+
	Pile			Data	EXFOR11447.093	Jun 76	. 1 PT, SIGMA.	
(n,γ)	2.2+5	9.0+5	OXF	Expt Jour	NAT 161 727	May 48	Allen+ ACTIVATION RATIO	
(n,γ)	Fiss		ANL	Expt Jour	PR 75 1781	Jun 49	Hughes+ REL SIG(THERMAL),FOIL ACTIVN	+
	Fiss			Data	EXFOR11450.034	Jun 76	. 1 PT, SIGMA.	
(n,γ)	Maxwl		ORL	Expt Jour	PR 88 412	Oct 52	Pomerance.PILE OSC.	+
	Maxwl			Data	EXFOR11507.072	Jun 76	. 1 PT, SIGMA.	
(n,γ)	2.5+4		ANL	Expt Rept	AECU−2394	Jan 53	Kimball+ ACT SB−BE PHOTONEUTS 53MB	
				Jour	PR 89 1306	Mar 53	− + SEE AECU−2394	
(n,γ)	Fiss		BNL	Expt Jour	PR 91 1423	Sep 53	Hughes+ ALSO LVL SPACINGS AT EXCIT E	
(n,γ)	2.4+4		ORL	Expt Jour	PR 107 504	Jul 57	Macklin+ SB−BE NEUTS.11.4+ −1.1 MB	+
	2.4+4			Data	EXFOR11399.034	Jun 76	. 1 PT, SIGMA.	
(n,γ)	2.5+6	4.0+6	IFU	Expt Conf	58Geneva 15 18	Sep 58	Pasechnik+.PPR2030,SIGMA AT 3ES	+
(n,γ)	2.5+4	4.0+6	KUR	Expt Conf	58Geneva 15 50	Sep 58	Leipunskij+.PPR2219,TBL AT 4ES	+
(n,γ)	1.4+7		ALD	Expt Jour	PPS 72 505	Oct 58	Perkin+ACT ANAL 1.3MB+ −30PC, B−W TH	+
(n,γ)	2.5+4		FEI	Expt Jour	AE 5 564	Nov 58	Kononov+ ACT CS REL TO I127(N,G) GVN	+
				Jour	JNEA 11 46	59	.TRANSLATION	
				Jour	SJA 5 1483	58	.TRANSLATION	
(n,γ)	2.0+5		ORL	Expt Jour	PR 114 1619	Jun 59	Lyon+ ABS GAMMA COUNT 3.2+ −0.3MB ACT	+
	2.0+5			Data	EXFOR11407.024	Jun 76	. 1 PT, SIGMA.	
(n,γ)	1.5+5	3.0+6	WIS	Expt Jour	PR 116 927	Nov 59	Johnsrud+ SC CFD OTHERS SIG VS E	+
	1.5+5	2.2+6		Data	EXFOR11675.016	Jun 76	17PTS, SIG	
(n,γ)	Maxwl		CRC	Eval Rept	AECL−1054	Mar 60	Walker. (CRRP−913)	
(n,γ)	Pile		ORL	Expt Jour	NSE 8 378	Nov 60	Lyon. ACTIVATION,SIGMA GIVEN	+
	Pile			Data	EXFOR11625.023	Jun 76	. 1 PT, SIGMA.	
(n,γ)	2.4+4	2.0+6	CCP	Expt Jour	AE 10 508	May 61	Stavisskii+ GRAPH,ACT REL I127 + THR	+
				Jour	JNE 17 579	Dec 63	TRANSLATN.*	
				Jour	SJA 10 498	Mar 62	TRANSLATN.*	
(n,γ)	Maxwl		UCB	Expt Rept	NYO−10175	Dec 64	Arino+ACT.TBLS.GRAPHS.PRODUCT HL.	+
	Maxwl			Data	EXFOR11817.030	Jun 76	. 1 PT, SIGMA.	
(n,γ)	Maxwl		UCS	Expt Jour	NSE 22 373	Jul 65	Kramer+ ACTIVATION	+
	Maxwl			Data	EXFOR11832.008	Jun 76	. 1 PT, SIGMA.	
(n,γ)	2.4+4		MUA	Expt Jour	PR 152 1055	Dec 66	Chaubey+ BETA−DET,SIG REL I−127,TBL	+
				Theo Jour	IJP 42 567	Sep 68	− + METHD OF BOOTH,VAL CFD XPT	
	2.4+4			Expt Data	EXFOR30079.027	Dec 70	SIGMA FOR 84. MIN HALF−LIFE	
(n,γ)	3.0+6		DEB	Expt Jour	JNE 21 797	Oct 67	Peto+ACTIV,SIGMA REL TO P−31(N,P)	+
	3.0+6			Data	EXFOR30031.017	Aug 70	SINGLE VALUE	
(n,γ)	1.4+7		LYO	Comp Rept	LYCEN/6780	Nov 67	Crouzet+COMPILATN FOR ACTIVTN ANALYS	
(n,γ)	1.4+7		NAP	Expt Jour	NC/B 52 2 476	Dec 67	Cuzzocrea+. ACT ANAL.SIG=1+ −.2 MB	
(n,γ)	Maxwl		AUA	Theo Jour	NSE 31 234	Feb 68	Cook+ STATISTICAL CALC CFD EXPT	
(n,γ)	2.9+6		IRK	Expt Jour	OAWA 105 236	Jun 68	Colditz+ ACTIVATION.	+
	2.9+6			Data	EXFOR20092.012	Sep 71	1PNT.SIG.	
(n,γ)	−		IEA	Comp Rept	IEA−INF− 10	Aug 68	Atalla. TABLES OF HL,SIG AND GAMM−E	
(n,γ)	Maxwl		BNL	Expt Jour	PR 180 1105	Apr 69	Moragues+ EVIDENCE FOR DIRECT CAPT	
(n,γ)	5.0+3	1.0+5	AUA	ExTh Rept	AAEC/E−198	May 69	Musgrove.S+P+D WAVE SIGMAS CALC,TBL	+
(n,γ)	1.0+3	1.0+7	BOL	Eval Rept	CCDN−NW/10	Dec 69	Benzi+H−F MOD,AXEL G(G)EST,ALL DATA	
				Rept	CEC(70)−2	Apr 70	− +. GRAPH	
				Conf	66Paris 1 537	Oct 66	− + STATMOD.TBL AV VALS.SUPERSEDD	
				Jour	NC 38 216	Jul 65	− + THEORY FOR CAPTURE EVALUATION	
(n,γ)	2.0+5		MUA	Theo Conf	69Roorke 2 129	Dec 69	Chaubey+ SIG VALUE GIVEN, STATIST−TH	
(n,γ)	Maxwl		GA	Eval Rept	GA−12071	Sep 71	Mathews+ RECOMMENDED VALUES	
(n,γ)	1.0−3	1.5+7	AUA	Eval Data	AUSTR−DFN 131.	Nov 71	COOK+ POINT(223)+GROUP(127) SIGMAS	+
(n,γ)	Maxwl		CRC	Eval Rept	AECL−3037 1	Jan 72	Walker.RECOMMENDED VAL,DETAILED TBL	
(n,γ)	2.4+4		MUA	Theo Jour	IJP 46 114	Mar 72	Chaubey+ P−WAVE STRENGTH FUNCT,TABLE	
(n,γ)	2.5−2		AUA	Eval Rept	AAEC/TM−619	Sep 72	Clayton.CALC FROM SIG LIBRARY,TABLE	
(n,γ)	0.0+0	1.0+7	CCP	Theo Conf	73Kiev 2 3	May 73	Dovbenko+ STATMOD,SIG(NEUT−E),GRAPH	
(n,γ)		1.1+7	RCN	Theo Rept	RCN−191	Jun 73	Lautenbach. GROUP CONSTANTS TBL	
(n,γ)	1.4+7		NJS	Expt Jour	NP/A 213 525	Oct 73	Potokar+ INTEGRATED FROM SPECTRUM	
(n,γ)	2.5+4		AUW	Expt Jour	NC/A 18 48	Nov 73	Sidappa+ ACTIV SIG,CFD.TABLE	
(n,γ)	2.5−2		SAC	Revw Conf	IAEA−169 1 235	74	Ribon.STATUS SIG CFD REQUESTS,TABLE	
(n,γ)	Fiss		WIN	Revw Conf	IAEA−169 3 137	74	Dean. POINT DATA AVG OVER STAND SPEC	
	Maxwl	Fiss		Conf	IAEA−169 3 163	74	Pope+ MAXW+FIS−SPEC AVG DATA CFD XPT	
(n,γ)	1.4+7		RBZ	Expt Jour	NCL 10 1	May 74	Vuletin+ ACT,GELI.CFD OTHRS+THEO,TBL	+
	1.4+7			Data	EXFOR30314.008	Dec 75	SIGMA AT 14.4 MEV	
	1.4+7			Data	EXFOR30145.011	Aug 73	.SUPERSEDED BY EXFOR30314.008	
(n,γ)	1.0+3	1.0+7	FEI	Eval Rept	YK− 8/2 97	Sep 72	Abagjan+ AVG SIG(ENERGY−GROUPS),TABL	
				Rept	INDC(CCP)−39	Jul 74	.P102. ENGLISH OF YK−8/2 97	

56 Barium 138

Quantity	Energy (ev) Min	Max	Lab	Type	Documentation Ref Vol Page	Author, Comments Date	Data
(n,γ)	1.5+7		BOS Expt	Conf	74Calcutta 57	Nov 74 Majumdar+ CFD STATMOD.SIGMA GIVEN	+
				Jour	IJP 44 204	Mar 70 Majumder. BY BETA SATURATION ACT,TBL	
	1.5+7			Data	EXFOR30296.005	Jun 75 1 POINT	
(n,γ)	Fiss		KOS Expt	Conf	75Karlsrhe 29	Apr 75 Csikai. CF252.ACTIV(1GAMMA).SIG GIVN	+
	1.4+6			Data	EXFOR30400.049	Oct 78 1 PNT.	
(n,γ)	3.0+4		AUA Expt	Jour	NP/A 252 301	Nov 75 Musgrove+MAXWELLIAN AVGD SIG=5.7MB	+
				Theo Rept	AAEC/E-211	Nov 70 - . SIGMA GIVEN AND CFD OTHER	
	3.0+4			Expt Data	EXFOR30328.	Mar 76 AVERAGE SIG. 1PNT.	
(n,γ)	1.5+7		JYV Comp	Rept	JU-RR-1/1976	Mar 76 Valkonen.(THESIS).EXPTS CFD DSD MODL	
(n,γ)		1.0+5	ORL Expt	Prog	ORNL-TM-5450	May 76 Perey+IDENTICAL TO ERDA-NDC-3 MAY 76	
(n,γ)	1.4+7		IRK Expt	Jour	NP/A 264 105	Jun 76 Schwerer+ GE-LI.ACT SIG=1.10+-0.11MB	+
	1.5+7			Data	EXFOR20670.013	Oct 76 1PNT.SIGMA.	
Spect (n,γ)	2.5+4		ORL Expt	Conf	58Geneva 15 68	Sep 58 Macklin.PPR671,SIGMA+G-ENERGY GVN	
Spect (n,γ)	Pile		MSU Expt	Jour	NP 19 79	Sep 60 Kelly+ UNCORRECTED GRAPHS.BRANCH RT	
Spect (n,γ)	Maxwl		DUB Expt	Jour	IZV 31 1672	Oct 67 Batist+ GAMMA ENERGY+INTENS,TBL+GRPH	
				Conf	68Riga	Jan 68 - + ABST,G ES,INT,GE-LI SPECTROM	
				Jour	BAS 31 1712	Oct 67 . ENGL OF IZV 31 1672	
Spect (n,γ)	Maxwl		BNL Expt	Jour	PR 180 1105	Apr 69 Moragues+ GE(LI)+NAI DET,BA139 LVLS	
Spect (n,γ)	Maxwl		KUR Expt	Jour	YF 10 681	Oct 69 Groshev+ TABLE GAM-SPECTRA,TRANSITNS	+
				Rept	IAE-1780	Jan 69 - + TBL OF GAMMA YLD+E,GE(LI)	
				Jour	SNP 10 392	Apr 70 . ENGL OF YF 10 681	
				Rept	LA-TR-69-29	Oct 69 . ENGLISH OF IAE-1780	
	2.5-2			Data	EXFOR40237.004	Nov 74 .GAM/100N FOR 3 ES GVN	
Spect (n,γ)	Maxwl		SAC Expt	Prog	EANDC(E)127U	Apr 70 Audias+,GE(LI) DET	
				Conf	69Studsvik 337	Aug 69 Irigaray+ G-SPEC TBL,20LINES,GE(LI)	
Spect (n,γ)	1.4+7		NJS Expt	Jour	NP/A 213 525	Oct 73 Potokar+ D-T NS. PAIR SPECTROMETER.	
				Theo Conf	72Budapest 250	Aug 72 - + CALC SPECTRA CFD EXPTS,NDG	
Spect (n,γ)	2.5-2		IFB Theo	Conf	76Lowell 1283	Jul 76 Martsynkevich+DOORWAY STATE ROLE.	
	Maxwl			Jour	NP/A 262 261	May 76 - +LVL SPEC.COL E1 DECAYS	
	None			Jour	YF 15 1132	Jun 72 Knat'Ko+ CALC E1 INTS CFD EXPT,GRAPH	
				Jour	SNP 15 626	Dec 72 - + ENGLISH OF YF 15 1132	
Inelastic γ	1.4+6	2.1+6	STF Expt	Jour	PR/B 137 1181	Mar 65 Tucker+ 90 DEG SIG FOR 2 GAMMAS	
(n,2n)	1.5+7		ARK Expt	Jour	PR 118 242	Apr 60 Wille. MEAS ACT SIG=1250+-100MB	+
	1.5+7			Data	EXFOR12033.005	Jun 76 . 1 PT, SIGMA.	
(n,2n)	Fiss		CRC Eval	Rept	CRC-1003	Dec 60 ROY+ ESTIMATED AVG SIG=1.1MB	
(n,2n)	1.4+7		HAMComp	Jour	NP 65 257	Mar 65 Bormann. 1EXPT VALS.CFD SHELL EFFECT	
(n,2n)	Fiss		UCS Expt	Jour	NSE 22 373	Jul 65 Kramer+ ACTIVATION	+
	Fiss			Data	EXFOR11832.017	Jun 76 . 1 PT, SIGMA.	
(n,2n)	1.4+7		NAP Expt	Jour	NC/B 52 2 476	Dec 67 Cuzzocrea+. 1020+-70 MB METAST STATE	
(n,2n)	1.5+7		TUR Theo	Jour	NC 56 18 201	Jul 68 Minetti+THEOR ISOM RATIO SPIN CO PAR	
(n,2n)	1.5+7		IBJ Expt	Jour	APPB 1 415	70 Rurarz+ ACTIV,NAI,SIG(M)+ISORATIO	+
				Jour	NKA 14 933	Oct 69 - + ACTIV,NAI(TL),SIG TO ISOMER	
	1.5+7			Data	EXFOR30154.011	May 72 ISOMERIC RATIO	
	1.5+7			Data	EXFOR30098.002	Mar 71 SIGMA TO MS AT 14.5MEV FROM INR-1197	
(n,2n)	1.5+7		DEB Comp	Jour	REA 7 4 93	Dec 69 Csikai+ SIG+HL COMPILTN,N-ACTIV-ANAL	
(n,2n)	1.4+7	1.5+7	JYV Eval	Rept	JU-RR-3/1970	Jun 70 Leppaemaeki+ TABLE OF EVAL AVG SIG	
(n,2n)	1.4+7		DEB Eval	Jour	REA 11 1 153	Mar 73 Boedy+ RECOMM.VALUE FROM N-Z SYSTEM.	
(n,2n)	1.5+7		KFI Theo	Rept	KFKI-73-68	Dec 73 Jeki.NEW FIT,CALC SIG CFD OTHERS,TBL	
(n,2n)	1.5+7		WKU Expt	Jour	BAP 20 700	May 75 KAO+ ACT CS TO ISOMER	+
	1.5+7			Data	EXFOR10486.004	May 75 . 1 PT, SIGMA.	
(n,2n)	1.5+7		RBZ Expt	Prog	INDC(SEC)-50	Jan 76 Holub+ GELI,ACTIV.CFD OTH+THEO,TABLE	
(n,2n)			IBJ Theo	Jour	ASL 27 186	77 Rurarz+ ISO RATIO,4MODLS,CFD XPT.TBL	
	1.4+7			Rept	INR-1464 19	May 73 - + ISOMERIC RATIO CFD EXPT,GRAF	
(n,p)	Fast		CAR Expt	Jour	PR 81 184	Jan 51 Cohen.AVR SIG,N SPEC.BETA ACT.UPPLIM	+
	Fast			Data	EXFOR11189.024	Jun 76 . 1 PT, SIGMA.	
(n,p)	1.5+7		CRC Expt	Jour	CJP 31 267	Feb 53 Paul+ BETA ACT.CFD TH HL=33M	+
	1.5+7			Data	EXFOR11274.086	Jun 76 . 1 PT, SIGMA.	
(n,p)			GLS Theo	Jour	PM 2 473	Apr 57 Brown+ COMPNUCL NIL, DIRECT 3MB	
(n,p)	1.4+7		ALD Expt	Jour	PPS 73 215	Feb 59 Coleman+. ACT. CFD DIRECT INTERACTN	
(n,p)	1.5+7		ARK Expt	Jour	PR 118 242	Apr 60 Wille. MEAS ACT SIG=2.5+-1.0MB	+
	1.5+7			Data	EXFOR12033.006	Jun 76 . 1 PT, SIGMA.	
(n,p)	Fiss		CRC Eval	Rept	CRC-1003	Dec 60 ROY+ ESTIMATED AVG SIG=0.003MB	
(n,p)	1.4+7		CCP Expt	Jour	ZET 45 305	Aug 63 Levkovskij.ACTIVATION METHOD	+
				Jour	JET 18 213	Jan 64 TRANSLATN.*	
(n,p)	1.5+7		SAH Comp	Jour	NUC 23 8 112	Aug 65 Chatterjee. TABLE WITH REFS.	
	1.4+7			Jour	NP 60 273	Nov 64 - .MEAN OF EXPT CFD SHELLMOD	
(n,p)	1.4+7	1.5+7	NAP Comp	Rept	INFN/BE-67-10	Jul 67 Cuzzocrea+ AVERAGED CHOSEN DATA.	
(n,p)	1.4+7		NAP Expt	Jour	NC/B 52 2 476	Dec 67 Cuzzocrea+. 3.13+-.24 MB.TH OKS EXPT	

56 Barium 138

Quantity	Energy (ev) Min	Max	Lab	Type	Documentation Ref Vol Page	Date	Author, Comments	Data
(n,p)	1.5+7		KAZ	Expt Jour	YF 8 7	Jul 68	Levkovskij+ SIG VAL +- ERROR GVN,TBL	+
				Jour	SNP 8 4	Jan 69	TRANSLATN.*	
	1.5+7			Data	EXFOR40223.022	May 74	.SIGMA GIVEN,1 DATA LINE	
(n,p)	1.5+7		DEB	Comp Jour	REA 7 4 93	Dec 69	Csikai+ SIG+HL COMPILTN,N-ACTIV-ANAL	
(n,p)	1.4+7		GIT	Expt Jour	PR/C 1 358	Jan 70	Fink+ ACT,SIG=3.8+-0.6MB	+
	1.4+7			Data	EXFOR10145.020	Sep 75	. 1PNT.SIGMA	
(n,p)	1.4+7	1.5+7	JYV	Eval Rept	JU-RR-3/1970	Jun 70	Leppaemaeki+ TABLE OF EVAL AVG SIG	
(n,p)	1.4+7		GIT	Theo Jour	PR/C 4 1173	Oct 71	Fink+ STAT-MODEL CALCULATION,CFD EXP	
(n,p)	1.4+7	1.5+7	KAZ	Theo Jour	YF 18 705	Oct 73	Levkovsky.AVERAGED SIG,CALC,TBL	
				Jour	SNP 18 361	Apr 74	. ENGLISH OF YF 18,705	
(n,p)	1.4+7		IRK	Expt Jour	OAWA 113 9 153	Jun 76	Schwerer+SIG.CORR.BY SELF-ABS.ETC.	+
	1.4+7			Data	EXFOR20811.012	Oct 78	1PNT.SIGMA.	
(n,np)	1.5+7		GLS	Theo Jour	PM 2 473	Apr 57	Brown+ N,PN* COMPNUCL NIL,DIRECT NIL	
(n,np)		7.5+8	IOW	Expt Jour	PR/C 12 1978	Dec 75	Hill+ ES TO 750 MEV.(N,3PN)REACTION	
(n,α)	Fiss		CRC	Eval Rept	CRC-1003	Dec 60	ROY+ ESTIMATED AVG SIG=0.0004MB	
(n,α)	1.4+7		HYO	Expt Jour	JPJ 16 2371	Dec 61	Fukuzawa.TO XE135+XE135M CFD STATMOD	+
	1.4+7			Data	EXFOR20289.	Jun 74	2PTS.SIGMA.	
(n,α)	Fiss	1.5+7	BER	Expt Jour	ZN/A 20 1583	Dec 65	Lagerwall. AVG VAL CFD 15MEV SIG.	
	Fiss			Data	EXFOR20741.004	Apr 77	1PNT.SIGMA.	
(n,α)	1.5+7		TUE	Expt Jour	ZP 201 105	Apr 67	STAUDT ALPHA E+ANGDIST,SIGTOT.SC DET	
(n,α)	1.4+7		NAP	Expt Jour	NC/B 52 2 476	Dec 67	Cuzzocrea+. 3.6+-0.5 MB CFD THEORY	
(n,α)	1.5+7		DEB	Comp Jour	REA 7 4 93	Dec 69	Csikai+ SIG+HL COMPILTN,N-ACTIV-ANAL	
(n,α)	1.4+7	1.5+7	JYV	Eval Rept	JU-RR-3/1970	Jun 70	Leppaemaeki+ TABLE OF EVAL AVG SIG	
(n,α)	1.4+7		GIT	Expt Jour	PR/C 1 358	Jan 70	Fink+ GND STATE + 15.6M ISM	+
				Abst	DA/B 31 6488	May 71	LU.MIXD POWDR.SHELL CLOSURE EFFECT.	
	1.4+7			Data	EXFOR10145.	Apr 75	. 2 PTS, SIG FOR GND + META	
(n,α)	1.4+7		GIT	Theo Jour	PR/C 4 1173	Oct 71	Fink+ STAT-MODEL CALCULATION,CFD EXP	
(n,α)	1.4+7		IRK	Expt Jour	OAWA 113 9 153	Jun 76	Schwerer+SIG XE135M,135G	+
	1.4+7			Data	EXFOR20811.	Oct 78	2PTS.SIGMA.	
Reson Params	3.2+4	1.9+5	DKE	Expt Jour	AP 14 387	Jul 61	Bilpuch+ WN WN0 STF(S) ISOT UNCERTN	+
	3.2+4	1.9+5		Data	EXFOR11599.	Jun 76	. 35 RES E0 AND WN, 23 RES WN0.	
Reson Params		1.0+6	AUA	Theo Jour	AUJ 20 477	Oct 67	Cook. TBL OF AVG LVL SPACING D,L=0,1	
Reson Params	+3	+5	AUA	ExTh Rept	AAEC/E-198	May 69	Musgrove.RES PARS +STF FROM (NG)FIT	
Reson Params	2.0+5		MUA	Conf	69Roorke 2 129	Dec 69	Chaubey+ D/GAM-WIDTH RATIO, STATMOD	
Reson Params	-		AUA	Theo Rept	AAEC/E-211	Nov 70	Musgrove. CALCULTD D+GAM WIDTH GIVEN	
Reson Params	None		DUB	Theo Rept	JINR-P4-7499	Oct 73	Soloviev+ CALC D CFD EXPTS,TABLE	
	-			Rept	JINR-E4-5711	Apr 71	- . AVG LVL SPACING, EXPTS TBD	
Reson Params	+1	+2	FEI	Eval Rept	YK-8/2 97	Sep 72	Abagyan+ AVG G-WID+D AT BINDNG-E,TBL	
				Rept	INDC(CCP)-39	Jul 74	.PAGE 102.ENGLISH OF YK-8/2 97	
Reson Params		1.0+5	ORL	Expt Prog	ORNL-TM-5450	May 76	Perey+IDENTICAL TO ERDA-NDC-3 MAY 76	
Strnth Fnctn	3.0+4	1.9+5	DKE	Expt Jour	AP 14 387	Jul 61	Bilpuch+ S WAVE STF	+
	3.0+4	1.9+5		Data	EXFOR11599.046	Jun 76	. 1 PT, STF ALL LEVELS.	
	3.0+4	1.9+5		Data	EXFOR11599.043	Jun 76	. 1 PT, STF ASSIGNED LEVELS.	
Strnth Fnctn		2.2+5	DKE	Expt Jour	AP 14 346	Jul 61	Newson+ TRANSMISSION.	
		2.2+5		Data	EXFOR11888.010	Jun 76	. 1 PT, LEVEL SPACING.	
Strnth Fnctn	+3	+5	AUA	ExTh Rept	AAEC/E-198	May 69	Musgrove.S+P+D STF FROM (NG)FIT,TBL	+
Strnth Fnctn	-		AUA	Theo Rept	AAEC/E-211	Nov 70	Musgrove. SMOOTHED S0,S1 AND S2 GIVN	
Strnth Fnctn	2.4+4		MUA	Theo Jour	IJP 46 114	Mar 72	Chaubey+ P-WAVE.FOR A-SYSTEMTIC,GRPH	
Strnth Fnctn	None		AUA	Eval Rept	AAEC/E-277	Mar 73	Musgrove.TBLS EXPTL DATA+BEST VALUES	
Strnth Fnctn	1.8+4	2.8+4	AUW	Expt Jour	NP/A 213 35	Oct 73	Murty+ P-WAVE.FIT TO P N-G AT 25KEV	
	2.5+4			Jour	NP/A 213 35	Oct 73	- + SB-BE.+-5KEV.S,P-WAVE CONTRIB	
Strnth Fnctn	None		KUR	Theo Prog	IAE-2560	75	Adamchuk+.S0-VALUE,TBL	
Strnth Fnctn	None		OSA	Theo Conf	JAERI-M-5984	Feb 75	Kitazoe+OPT MDLS.GRPH VS A.TBL PARS	
Strnth Fnctn		1.0+5	ORL	Expt Prog	ERDA-NDC-2 132	May 75	Musgrove+S0=(0.9+-0.4)E-04S1=0.5E-04	
Lvl Density	+6		MIL	Theo Jour	EN 15 1 54	Jan 68	Facchini+ LDL PARS FROM LOW EN RES	
Lvl Density	+6		FEI	Theo Prog	YFI-7 7	Apr 69	Ignatyuk+ TEMP+DENS+A VS EXCIT-E,CRV	
	+6	+7		Jour	YF 11 1012	May 70	- + DENSITY+A+TEMP VS EXCIT-E	
	+6			Rept	INDC(CCP)-7U5	Feb 70	TRANSLATN.*	
	+6	+7		Jour	SNP 11 563	Nov 70	. ENGL OF YF 11 1012	
Lvl Density	-		FEI	Theo Conf	70Helsinki 2 885	Jun 70	Ignatjuk+76. SUPERFLUID CFD FERMI-TH	
Lvl Density	+6	+7	FEI	Theo Jour	YF 12 960	Nov 70	Stavinskij. (N,N')-ANAL,A-PARAM GRPH	
Lvl Density	None		AUW	Theo Conf	70Madurai 2 267	Dec 70	Ramamurty+ A-PARAMETER GVN,LANG'S-TH	
Lvl Density	0.0+0	1.0+7	CCP	Theo Conf	73Kiev 2 3	May 73	Dovbenko+ SEPERFLUID+FERMIGAS MODLS	
Lvl Density	None		MUN	Theo Jour	NP/A 217 269	Dec 73	Dilg+ A,DELTA. BACK SHIFTED FERMIGAS	
Lvl Density	None		COP	Theo Jour	NP/A 222 493	Apr 74	Dossing+COLL ROTAT.SPAC. ACCUR ESTIM	
Lvl Density	None		ROC	Theo Jour	NP/A 223 577	May 74	Huizenga+ EXP CFD MICROSC TH SPH NUC	
Lvl Density	+1	+2	FEI	Eval Rept	YK-8/2 97	Sep 72	Abagyan+ LVL DENSITY PARAMETER,TBL	
				Rept	INDC(CCP)-39	Jul 74	.PAGE 102.ENGLISH OF YK-8/2 97	

56 Barium 139

Quantity	Energy (ev) Min	Max	Lab	Type	Documentation Ref Vol Page	Author, Comments Date	Data
Absorption	Pile		LAS Expt	Rept	CC – 2908	Jul 45 Katcoff.	+
	Pile			Data	EXFOR12603.002	Jun 76 . 1 PT, SIGMA.	
(n,γ)	Maxwl		CRC Expt	Jour	PR 76 617	Sep 49 Yaffe+ BY LA140 BETAS,REL BA138 SIG	
Reson Params	–		AUA Theo	Rept	AAEC/E – 211	Nov 70 Musgrove. CALCULTD D+GAM WIDTH GIVEN	
Strnth Fnctn	–		AUA Theo	Rept	AAEC/E – 211	Nov 70 Musgrove. SMOOTHED S0,S1 AND S2 GIVN	
Lvl Density	+6	+7	FEI Theo	Jour	YF 12 960	Nov 70 Stavinsky. LVL DENSITY(EXCIT – E) GRPH	
Lvl Density	0.0+0	1.0+7	CCP Theo	Conf	73Kiev 2 3	May 73 Dovbenko+ SEPERFLUID+FERMIGAS MODLS	
Lvl Density	None		MUN Theo	Jour	NP/A 217 269	Dec 73 Dilg+ A,DELTA. BACK SHIFTED FERMIGAS	
Lvl Density	None		COP Theo	Jour	NP/A 222 493	Apr 74 Dossing+COLL ROTAT.SPAC. ACCUR ESTIM	
Lvl Density	None		DUB Theo	Jour	NP/A 224 411	May 74 Soloviev+ 1/2 MICROSC MDL. SPH NUCL.	
Lvl Density	None		ROC Theo	Jour	NP/A 223 577	May 74 Huizenga+ EXP CFD MICROSC TH SPH NUC	

56 Barium 140

Quantity	Energy (ev) Min	Max	Lab	Type	Documentation Ref Vol Page	Author, Comments Date	Data
Evaluation	1.0 – 3	1.5+7	AUA Eval	Rept	AAEC/TM – 549	Jun 70 Cook.TOT,EL,INEL,NONEL,CAPT SIGS,NDG	+
				Rept	AAEC/E – 214	Jun 71 Bertram+GROUP SIGMAS SAME QUANTS.NDG	
				Rept	AAEC/TM – 587	Mar 71 *DESCRIPTION OF LIBRARY	
	1.0 – 3	1.5+7		Data	AUSTR – DFN 132.	Nov 71 POINT(223) AND GROUP(127) SIGMAS	
Total	1.0 – 3	1.5+7	AUA Eval	Data	AUSTR – DFN 132.	Nov 71 COOK+ POINT(223)+GROUP(127) SIGMAS	+
Elastic	1.0 – 3	1.5+7	AUA Eval	Data	AUSTR – DFN 132.	Nov 71 COOK+ POINT(223)+GROUP(127) SIGMAS	+
Tot Inelastc	1.0 – 3	1.5+7	AUA Eval	Data	AUSTR – DFN 132.	Nov 71 COOK+ POINT(223)+GROUP(127) SIGMAS	+
Nonelastic	1.0 – 3	1.5+7	AUA Eval	Data	AUSTR – DFN .	Nov 71 COOK+ POINT(223)+GROUP(127) SIGMAS	+
Res Int Abs	5.0 – 1		ORL Expt	Prog	ORNL – 4164 1	Sep 67 Halperin+ VALUE GIVEN	+
	5.0 – 1			Data	EXFOR10348.003	Jun 74 . 1 PT	
Res Int Abs	5.5 – 1		CRC Eval	Rept	AECL – 3037 1	Jan 72 Walker.REDUCED RES INT,DETAILED TBL	
Res Int Abs	5.0 – 1		AUA Eval	Rept	AAEC/TM – 619	Sep 72 Clayton.CALC FROM SIG LIBRARY,TABLE	
Res Int Abs	5.5 – 1	+6	SAC Revw	Conf	IAEA – 169 1 235	74 Ribon.CAPTURE,STATUS CFD REQUEST,TBL	
Res Int Abs	+0	+5	WIN Revw	Conf	IAEA – 169 3 163	74 Pope+ DATA FILE CALC CFD XPTAL VALUE	
(n,γ)	Pile		CRC Expt	Conf	58Geneva 16 54	Sep 58 Eastwood+ ABOUT 12B	+
	Pile			Data	EXFOR12011.002	Jun 76 . 1 PT, SIGMA.	
(n,γ)	Maxwl		CRC Eval	Rept	AECL – 1054	Mar 60 Walker. (CRRP – 913)	
(n,γ)	2.5 – 2		ORL Expt	Prog	ORNL – 4164 1	Sep 67 Halperin+ VALUE GIVEN	+
	2.5 – 2			Data	EXFOR10348.002	Jun 74 . 1 PT, SIGMA	
(n,γ)	1.0 – 3	1.5+7	AUA Eval	Data	AUSTR – DFN .	Nov 71 COOK+ POINT(223)+GROUP(127) SIGMAS	+
(n,γ)	Maxwl		CRC Eval	Rept	AECL – 3037 1	Jan 72 Walker.RECOMMENDED SIG,DETAILED TBL	
(n,γ)	2.5 – 2		AUA Eval	Rept	AAEC/TM – 619	Sep 72 Clayton.CALC FROM SIG LIBRARY,TABLE	
(n,γ)	2.5 – 2		SAC Revw	Conf	IAEA – 169 1 235	74 Ribon.STATUS SIG CFD REQUESTS,TABLE	
(n,γ)	Maxwl Fiss		WIN Revw	Conf	IAEA – 169 3 163	74 Pope+ MAXW+FIS – SPEC AVG DATA CFD XPT	
	Fiss			Conf	IAEA – 169 3 137	74 Dean. POINT DATA AVG OVER STAND SPEC	
Spect (n,γ)	–		CCP Expt	Rept	AEC – TR – 6449	63 Gritchenko. GAM SPEC,FISS PRODUCT	
Fiss Prod γ	Pile		SGA Theo	Jour	APA 28 94	Apr 69 Higats+COMP.PROGR.BUILDUP FISS.PROD.	
Reson Params	–		AUA Theo	Rept	AAEC/E – 211	Nov 70 Musgrove. CALCULTD D+GAM WIDTH GIVEN	
Strnth Fnctn	–		AUA Theo	Rept	AAEC/E – 211	Nov 70 Musgrove. SMOOTHED S0,S1 AND S2 GIVN	
Lvl Density	– 3	+0	IFU Theo	Jour	UFZ 13 700	Apr 68 Pisanko+ LEVEL SPACING CALC,TBL	
				Jour	UPJ 13 498	Oct 68 TRANSLATN.*	

56 Barium 141

Quantity	Energy (ev) Min	Max	Lab	Type	Documentation Ref Vol Page	Author, Comments Date	Data
Reson Params	–		AUA Theo	Rept	AAEC/E – 211	Nov 70 Musgrove. CALCULTD D+GAM WIDTH GIVEN	
Strnth Fnctn	–		AUA Theo	Rept	AAEC/E – 211	Nov 70 Musgrove. SMOOTHED S0,S1 AND S2 GIVN	

57 Lanthanum 129

Quantity	Energy (ev) Min	Max	Lab	Type	Documentation Ref Vol Page	Author, Comments Date	Data
Reson Params	–		AUA	Theo Rept	AAEC/E-211	Nov 70 Musgrove. CALCULTD D+GAM WIDTH GIVEN	
Strnth Fnctn	–		AUA	Theo Rept	AAEC/E-211	Nov 70 Musgrove. SMOOTHED S0,S1 AND S2 GIVN	

57 Lanthanum 130

Quantity	Energy (ev) Min	Max	Lab	Type	Documentation Ref Vol Page	Author, Comments Date	Data
Reson Params	–		AUA	Theo Rept	AAEC/E-211	Nov 70 Musgrove. CALCULTD D+GAM WIDTH GIVEN	
Strnth Fnctn	–		AUA	Theo Rept	AAEC/E-211	Nov 70 Musgrove. SMOOTHED S0,S1 AND S2 GIVN	

57 Lanthanum 131

Quantity	Energy (ev) Min	Max	Lab	Type	Documentation Ref Vol Page	Author, Comments Date	Data
Reson Params	–		AUA	Theo Rept	AAEC/E-211	Nov 70 Musgrove. CALCULTD D+GAM WIDTH GIVEN	
Strnth Fnctn	–		AUA	Theo Rept	AAEC/E-211	Nov 70 Musgrove. SMOOTHED S0,S1 AND S2 GIVN	

57 Lanthanum 132

Quantity	Energy (ev) Min	Max	Lab	Type	Documentation Ref Vol Page	Author, Comments Date	Data
Reson Params	–		AUA	Theo Rept	AAEC/E-211	Nov 70 Musgrove. CALCULTD D+GAM WIDTH GIVEN	
Strnth Fnctn	–		AUA	Theo Rept	AAEC/E-211	Nov 70 Musgrove. SMOOTHED S0,S1 AND S2 GIVN	

57 Lanthanum 134

Quantity	Energy (ev) Min	Max	Lab	Type	Documentation Ref Vol Page	Author, Comments Date	Data
Spect (n,γ)	Maxwl		UJV	Expt Rept	UJV-363	Oct 59 Urbanec. SCINT SPECTRMTR,SPEC GS	
Reson Params	–		AUA	Theo Rept	AAEC/E-211	Nov 70 Musgrove. CALCULTD D+GAM WIDTH GIVEN	
Strnth Fnctn	–		AUA	Theo Rept	AAEC/E-211	Nov 70 Musgrove. SMOOTHED S0,S1 AND S2 GIVN	

57 Lanthanum 135

Quantity	Energy (ev) Min	Max	Lab	Type	Documentation Ref Vol Page	Author, Comments Date	Data
Reson Params	–		AUA	Theo Rept	AAEC/E-211	Nov 70 Musgrove. CALCULTD D+GAM WIDTH GIVEN	
Strnth Fnctn	–		AUA	Theo Rept	AAEC/E-211	Nov 70 Musgrove. SMOOTHED S0,S1 AND S2 GIVN	

57 Lanthanum 136

Quantity	Energy (ev) Min	Max	Lab	Type	Documentation Ref Vol Page	Author, Comments Date	Data
Reson Params	–		AUA	Theo Rept	AAEC/E-211	Nov 70 Musgrove. CALCULTD D+GAM WIDTH GIVEN	
Strnth Fnctn	–		AUA	Theo Rept	AAEC/E-211	Nov 70 Musgrove. SMOOTHED S0,S1 AND S2 GIVN	

57 Lanthanum 137

Quantity	Energy (ev) Min	Max	Lab	Type	Documentation Ref Vol Page	Author, Comments Date	Data
(n,p)	–		BUC	Expt Rept	IFA-CRD-26	Mar 63 Magda+,INV,EVAP SPECT,TBL,CURV,TH	
(n,p)	Maxwl		IFU	Theo Rept	ICD-4 20	67 Dadakina+ PENETR COEFF CALC,TABLE	
Reson Params	–		AUA	Theo Rept	AAEC/E-211	Nov 70 Musgrove. CALCULTD D+GAM WIDTH GIVEN	
Strnth Fnctn	–		AUA	Theo Rept	AAEC/E-211	Nov 70 Musgrove. SMOOTHED S0,S1 AND S2 GIVN	

57 Lanthanum 138

Quantity	Energy (ev) Min	Max	Lab	Type	Documentation Ref Vol Page	Author, Comments Date	Data
Total	2.0+1	4.0+2	RPI	Expt Prog	WASH-1048 71	Jun 64 Block+ 9 RESES TBL.TRNS,TOF,RPI LINC	
Res Int Abs	5.0-1		IJI	Eval Rept	KIYAI-76-6	76 Fedorova+ CALC FROM BNL-325 RESPARS	
				Conf	75Kiev 1 169	May 75 – + CALC FROM RESPARS, TABLE	
Res Int Abs	Pile		JUL	Expt Jour	ARI 27 533	Oct 76 Michael+ MASS SPEC. 384B EXCL 1/V	+
				Prog	NEANDC(E)172 5	Jul 76 – +P.43.(NG)RI= 384+ -90 B	
	2.5-2			Data	EXFOR20666.003	Nov 76 1PNT.CAPTURE.	
(n,γ)	5.0+3	1.0+5	AUA	ExTh Rept	AAEC/E-198	May 69 Musgrove.S+P+D WAVE SIGMAS CALC,TBL	+

57 Lanthanum 138

Quantity	Energy (ev) Min	Max	Lab	Type	Documentation Ref Vol Page	Date	Author, Comments	Data
(n,γ)	1.0+3	1.0+7	BOL	Eval	Rept CCDN-NW/10	Dec 69	Benzi+H-F MOD,AXEL G(G)EST,ALL DATA	
					Rept CEC(70)-2	Apr 70	- +. GRAPH	
(n,γ)	3.0+4		AUA	Theo	Rept AAEC/E-211	Nov 70	Musgrove. SIGMA GIVEN AND CFD OTHER	
(n,γ)	Fiss		WIN	Revw	Conf IAEA-169 3 163	74	Pope+ BENZI EVAL DATA AVG OVER SPEC	
(n,γ)	1.0+3	1.0+7	FEI	Eval	Rept YK- 8/2 97	Sep 72	Abagjan+ AVG SIG(ENERGY-GROUPS),TABL	
					Rept INDC(CCP)-39	Jul 74	.P102. ENGLISH OF YK-8/2 97	
(n,γ)	Pile		JUL	Expt	Jour ARI 27 533	Oct 76	Michael+ ENRICH SAMPL,MASS-SP, 57.2B	+
					Prog NEANDC(E)172 5	Jul 76	- +.P.43. 57.2+-5.7 B	
	2.5-2				Data EXFOR20666.002	Nov 76	1PNT.SIGMA.	
(n,2n)	Fiss		CRC	Eval	Rept CRC-1003	Dec 60	Roy+,ESTIMATED AVG SIG=4.8MB	
(n,p)	Fiss		CRC	Eval	Rept CRC-1003	Dec 60	Roy+,ESTIMATED AVG SIG=10.0MB	
(n,p)	-		BUC	Expt	Rept IFA-CRD-26	Mar 63	Magda+,INV,EVAP SPECT,TBL,CURV,TH	
(n,p)	-		BUC	Expt	Prog INDC(SEC)-18	Aug 71	Alevra+P158.INVERSE,LVL DENS PAR,TBL	
					Jour NP/A 140 23	Jan 70	* EXPERIMENTAL SET-UP	
(n,α)	Fiss		CRC	Eval	Rept CRC-1003	Dec 60	Roy+,ESTIMATED AVG SIG=0.013MB	
Reson Params	3.1+0	3.1+2	ORL	Expt	Conf 65Antwerp § 77	Jul 65	Harvey+. AREA ANAL. 10 RES.2GGAMN0	+
					Prog ORNL-1354 28	65	.EQUIVALENT.	
	3.1+0	3.1+2			Data EXFOR12071.002	Jun 76	. 10 RES. E0,WN0,WG.	
Reson Params	3.0+0	2.0+1	ANL	Expt	Jour PR 159 1050	Jul 67	Shwe+ TRANS.WT,WG,WN. 2 RESONANCES.	+
	3.0+0	2.0+1			Data EXFOR12065.005	Jun 76	. 2 RES. E0,WT,WN,WG,PCS.	
Reson Params		1.0+6	AUA	Theo	Jour AUJ 20 477	Oct 67	Cook. TBL OF AVG LVL SPACING D,L=0,1	
Reson Params	-1	+2	BNL	Expt	Prog WASH-1127 15	Apr 69	Chrien+ J,PI FOUND FROM N,G	
Reson Params	-		AUA	Theo	Rept AAEC/E-211	Nov 70	Musgrove. CALCULTD D+GAM WIDTH GIVEN	
Reson Params	3.1+0	2.0+1	CJD	Eval	Rept YK-7	71	Zakharova+ SURVEY+SYSTEMATICS,GW,TBL	
					Rept INDC(CCP)-27	Nov 72	.ENGLISH TRANSLATION OF YK-7 /71	
Reson Params	+0	+2	FEI	Eval	Rept YK- 8/2 97	Sep 72	Abagyan+ AVG G-WID+D AT BINDNG-E,TBL	
					Rept INDC(CCP)-39	Jul 74	.PAGE 102.ENGLISH OF YK-8/2 97	
Reson Params	3.1+0		ORL	Expt	Abst BAP 4 385	Aug 59	Harvey+ WG,WN.	+
	3.1+0				Data EXFOR12050.004	Jun 76	. 1 RES. E0,WN.	
Reson Params	2.1+1	3.6+2	RPI	Expt	Prog WASH-1048 71	Jun 64	Block+ 9 RES ES TBL.TOF,RSLN 6NS/M.	+
	2.1+1	3.6+2			Data EXFOR12074.003	Jun 76	. 9 RES. E0.	
Strnth Fnctn	3.1+0	2.8+2	ORL	Expt	Conf 65Antwerp § 77	Jul 65	Harvey+. BASED ON 8 RES S WAVE	
					Prog ORNL-1354 28	65	.EQUIVALENT.	
Strnth Fnctn	-		AUA	Theo	Rept AAEC/E-211	Nov 70	Musgrove. SMOOTHED S0,S1 AND S2 GIVN	
Strnth Fnctn	None		AUA	Eval	Rept AAEC/E-277	Mar 73	Musgrove.TBLS EXPTL DATA+BEST VALUES	
Strnth Fnctn	None		KUR	Theo	Prog IAE-2560	75	Adamchuk+.S0-VALUE,TBL	
Lvl Density	-		BUC	Expt	Prog INDC(SEC)-18	Aug 71	Alevra+P158.(ALF,N),LVL DENS PAR,TBL	
					Jour NP/A 140 23	Jan 70	* EXPERIMENTAL SET-UP	
Lvl Density	1.0+0	3.7+2	JAE	ExTh	Rept JAERI-M-5490	Nov 73	Ideno.LEVEL SPACING CORRELATIONS.TBL	
	+0	3.7+2			Jour JPJ 30 620	Mar 71	- + RES SPACING CORRELATION ANAL	
Lvl Density	+0	+2	FEI	Eval	Rept YK- 8/2 97	Sep 72	Abagyan+ LVL DENSITY PARAMETER,TBL	
					Rept INDC(CCP)-39	Jul 74	.PAGE 102.ENGLISH OF YK-8/2 97	

57 Lanthanum 139

Quantity	Energy (ev) Min	Max	Lab	Type	Documentation Ref Vol Page	Date	Author, Comments	Data
Evaluation	5.0+5	1.5+7	LRL	Eval	Rept UCRL-5351	Nov 58	Howerton. CURVS,TOT,SEL,SNE,STN,N2N.	
Evaluation	1.0-3	1.5+7	AUA	Eval	Rept AAEC/E-549	Jun 70	Cook.TOT,EL,INEL,NONEL,CAPT SIGS,NDG	+
					Rept AAEC/E-214	Jun 71	Bertram+GROUP SIGMAS SAME QUANTS.NDG	
					Rept AAEC/TM-587	Mar 71	*DESCRIPTION OF LIBRARY	
	1.0-3	1.5+7			Data AUSTR-DFN 133.	Nov 71	POINT(223) AND GROUP(127) SIGMAS	
Evaluation	1.0+3	1.0+7	BOL	Eval	Rept CEC(71)-2	71	Benzi+ STAT+EVAP MDS.INEL,N2N,NG,TBL	+
	1.0+3	1.0+7			Data BENZI-DFN 550E	Mar 71	4 QUANTITIES. UK FORMAT	
Evaluation	1.0-5	1.5+7	HED	Eval	Rept HEDL-TME-71143	Oct 71	Schenter+. EVALUATION FOR ENDF/B	
Evaluation	1.0-5	1.5+7	BOL	Eval	Prog NEANDC(E)182 7	Dec 76	Fabri+ COMPLETE EVAL IN ENDF/B DONE	+
	1.0-5	1.5+7			Data CNEN-CEA 5	Jan 78	PRELIM.ALL QUANTITIES.ENDF FORMAT	
Total	Maxwl		COL	Expt	Jour PR 48 265	Aug 35	Dunning+ IONCH,TRANS,RA-BE/PARAFIN N	
Total	1.3-2	2.3+3	COL	Expt	Priv HAVENS	52	Havens.	+
	1.3-2	2.3+3			Data EXFOR11361.008	Jun 76	. 42 PTS. SIGMA.	
Total	5.0+4	3.2+6	WIS	Expt	Jour PR 88 83	Oct 52	Miller+ 20KEV SPREAD, TRNSM.	+
	1.0+4	3.2+6			Data EXFOR11712.017	Jun 76	. 85 PTS. SIGMA.	
Total	1.4+7		LAS	Expt	Jour PR 88 562	Nov 52	Coon+	+
	1.4+7				Data EXFOR11056.045	Jun 76	. 1 PT. SIGMA.	
Total	2.7+6	1.3+7	LAS	Expt	Jour PR 94 1678	Jun 54	Nereson+ RSLN 10 PERCENT.	+
	2.7+6	1.3+7			Data EXFOR11308.020	Jun 76	. 30 PTS. SIGMA.	
Total	1.0+3	1.0+4	DKE	Expt	Jour PR 105 198	Jan 57	Newson+,TRNS CURV ABS PKS Q STATISTC	+
	1.0+3	1.0+4			Data EXFOR11569.011	Jun 76	. 55 PTS. SIGMA.	

57 Lanthanum 139

Quantity	Energy (ev) Min	Energy (ev) Max	Lab	Type	Documentation Ref Vol Page	Date	Author, Comments	Data
Total	6.4+1	8.3+1	BNL Expt	Jour	PR 108 353	Oct 57	Stolovy+ FC,TRANS.	+
	6.4+1	8.3+1		Data	EXFOR11866.009	Jun 76	. 21 PTS. SIGMA.	
Total	1.3+7	1.6+7	LAS Expt	Jour	PR 109 1268	Feb 58	Conner.TRNS SC 6ES 4.81BMAX 4.69BMIN	+
				Conf	58Geneva 15 11	Sep 58	Coon+.PPR666,SIGMA AT 6ES GVN,TOF	
	1.3+7	1.6+7		Data	EXFOR11320.006	Jun 76	. 6 PTS. SIGMA.	
Total	2.0-2	1.0+1	WUR Expt	Jour	HPA 37 224	May 64	Verdan.NDG TRANSMIS.MEAS	
Total	1.0+0	2.0+4	ORL Expt	Prog	WASH-1048 71	Jun 64	Block.NDG,TRNS,TOF,RSLN 6 NS/M	
Total	9.8+5		SHE Theo	Jour	NP 54 417	Jun 64	Maddison.OPTMOD FIT TO TOWLE GILBOY	
Total	3.0+4	6.5+5	DKE Expt	Abst	DA/B 27 2085	Dec 66	Tabony.TRNSM. DERIVES S,P,D STR FNS	+
	3.0+4	6.5+5		Data	EXFOR11936.003	Jun 76	. 100 PTS. SIGMA.	
Total	1.0-1	1.0+3	ANL Expt	Jour	PR 159 1050	Jul 67	Shwe+ TRANS. 46 RES. ISOTOPIC ASSGN.	+
	1.0-1	1.5+3		Data	EXFOR12065.004	Jun 76	. 58 PTS. SIGMA.	
Total	3.3+6	5.2+6	JNE Expt	Jour	ARS 64 63	Feb 68	Manero. VDG. TRANSMISSION	+
	3.3+6	5.2+6		Data	EXFOR20170.003	May 74	65PTS.	
Total		4.0+5	DKE Expt	Abst	DA/B 28 3834	Mar 68	Divadeenam.TRNS.AV SIG CFD OPTMDL.	+
	1.2+5	6.4+5		Data	EXFOR10523.011	Jan 76	. 28 PTS. SIGMA.	
Total	5.0+1	3.0+4	SAC Expt	Jour	NP/A 123 561	Jan 69	Morgenstern+LINAC 1.5-.34NS/M NDG	
				Jour	JPR 24 997	Nov 63	Bianchi+ TOF 2.5NS/M SUPERSEDED.	
	5.0+1	3.0+4		Data	EXFOR20684.	Jul 77	0PTS. SEE RESONANCE PARAMETERS.	
Total	2.5+6	1.5+7	BNW Expt	Jour	PR/C 3 576	Feb 71	Foster+,TRANS,CURVS,CFD OTHERS+TH	+
				Jour	NIM 36 1	Sep 65	.EXPT DETAILS	
	2.3+6	1.5+7		Data	EXFOR10047.061	Aug 73	. 254 PTS. SIGMA.	
Total	1.0-3	1.5+7	AUA Eval	Data	AUSTR-DFN 133.	Nov 71	COOK+POINT(223)+GROUP(127)SIG.CF EVL	+
Total	2.7+3		MUN Expt	Prog	EANDC(E)150U	Oct 72	Dilg+ AVERAGE TOT XSECT+S0	+
				Conf	71Albany 327	Aug 71	- +TRNS.AVG CS GVN.31 ELEMENT GRP	
	2.7+3			Data	EXFOR20583.012	Jun 76	1PNT.	
Total	1.3+7	1.5+7	DEB Eval	Rept	IAEA-153 173	73	Boedy+ MOST PROBABLE VAL OF SIG,TBL	
				Rept	AHP 30 115	Oct 71	Angeli+ AVG SIG,CFD CALC.TBLS.GRAPH	
Total	1.0+6	2.0+6	DAC Eval	Jour	NSPB 6 59	Oct 73	Enayetullah+ SIG(E),LSQ-FIT,TBL+GRPH	
			Expt	Jour	NP/A 209 189	Jul 73	Islam+ VDG,TRANS,CFD OPTICAL MODEL	
			Theo	Jour	NP/A 209 202	Jul 73	- + FLUCTUATION ANALYSIS,OWN DATA	
			Comp	Rept	AECD/EP-18	Dec 70	Ameen+ EXPTL DATA FROM DAC,TABLES	
	1.0+6	2.0+6		Expt Data	EXFOR30134.004	Nov 71	SIGMA-TOT AT 100 ES,PRIVATE COMM.	
Total	1.0+3	6.0+5	NBS Expt	Jour	PR/C 9 28	Jan 74	Camarda.LINAC.TOF.GRPH.TRANS.MEAS.S1	
Total	7.0+5	9.0+6	GLS Expt	Jour	JP/A 7 1758	Sep 74	Kellie+ SIG IN CURVE,STAT ERROR 2 PC	+
	7.0+5	9.0+6		Data	EXFOR20418.002	Sep 75	642PTS.	
Total	2.5+5	1.5+7	JAE Theo	Conf	JAERI-M-5984	Feb 75	Tanaka.OPTMDL/COUPLD CH.GRPH CFD EXP	
Total	-3	1.9+0	THS Theo	Rept	IKE-6 89 65	Jun 75	Keinert. DATA LIBRARY	
Total	3.0+0	7.6+4	COL Expt	Jour	PR/C 13 1884	May 76	Hacken+TOF.TRNS.CURVS.RES PARS DRVD.	+
	3.0+1	7.6+4		Data	EXFOR10579.006	Aug 76	. DATA UNOBTAINABLE FROM AUTHORS.	
Total	3.9+0	4.2+1	ORL Expt	Abst	BAP 4 385	Aug 59	Harvey+ WG,WN.	+
	3.9+0	4.2+1		Data	EXFOR12050.002	Jun 76	. 335 PTS. SIGMA.	
Elastic	2.5-2		ORL Expt	Jour	PR 91 597	Aug 53	Koehler+	+
	2.5-2			Data	EXFOR12060.	Jun 76	. 2 PTS. COH, COH AMP.	
Elastic	7.3-2		ANL Expt	Jour	JCP 35 1950	Dec 61	Atoji+.	+
	7.3-2			Data	EXFOR11606.004	Jun 76	. 1 PT. COH AMP.	
Elastic	1.0+6		ALD Expt	Jour	NP 42 86	Apr 63	Gilboy+.SIG=7.20B+-3PC	+
Elastic	9.8+5		AGN Eval	Rept	TID-21629	Dec 64	Perkins+ CALC FROM OTHER DATA.	
Elastic	8.0+6		VIR Expt	Conf	68Wash. 2 755	Mar 68	Bernard+ TOF, INT ANG DIST.	+
	8.0+6			Data	EXFOR12054.004	Jun 76	. 1 PT. SIGMA.	
Elastic	2.3+5	1.6+6	SUN Expt	Jour	NP/A 124 111	Feb 69	Malan.JG+,VDG,TOF,LEG FIT,TABLE	+
	2.3+5	1.6+6		Data	EXFOR30125.	Dec 72	SIGMA AT 8 ENERGIES	
Elastic	1.0-3	1.5+7	AUA Eval	Data	AUSTR-DFN 133.	Nov 71	COOK+POINT(223)+GROUP(127)SIG.CF EVL	+
Elastic	2.5-2		IJI Eval	Rept	KIYAI-76-6	76	Fedorova+ COMP+EVAL,REFS GIVEN.TABLE	
				Conf	75Kiev 1 169	May 75	- + EVAL SIG GIVEN,TABLE	
Diff Elastic	4.0+6	7.0+6	LAS Expt	Jour	PR 129 1649	Feb 63	Thomson. SIG AT 90DEG	+
	4.0+6	7.0+6		Data	EXFOR11495.038	Jun 76	. 3 PTS. DSIGMA.	
Diff Elastic	1.0+6		ALD Expt	Jour	NP 42 86	Apr 63	Gilboy+30TO137DEG.COMP.WITH OPTICMOD	+
Diff Elastic	9.8+5		SHE Theo	Jour	NP 54 417	Jun 64	Maddison.OPTMOD FIT TO TOWLE GILBOY	
Diff Elastic	9.8+5		AGN Eval	Rept	TID-21629	Dec 64	Perkins+ LEGENDRE COEF CALC.	
Diff Elastic	3.2+6		BCM Expt	Jour	NP 89 154	Dec 66	Becker+ 12 ANGLES GRAPH CFD OPTMDL	+
	3.2+6			Data	EXFOR11511.029	Jun 76	. 12 PTS. DSIGMA.	
Diff Elastic	8.0+6		VIR Expt	Conf	68Wash. 2 755	Mar 68	Bernard+ TOF 25-160DEG REL N-P SIG	+
	8.0+6			Data	EXFOR11054.	Jun 76	. 18 PTS,DSIGMA. 11 PTS, LEG COEF.	
Diff Elastic	3.2+6		SCU Theo	Rept	ICD-6 236	69	Averyanov+CALC ANGDIST CFD EXPT,GRPH	

57 Lanthanum 139

Quantity	Energy (ev) Min	Max	Lab	Type	Documentation Ref Vol Page	Date	Author, Comments	Data
Diff Elastic	2.3+5	1.6+6	SUN	Expt	Jour NP/A 124 111	Feb 69	Malan+ ANG DISTR GRPH,LEGENDRE COEFF	+
				Diss	MALAN	70	- . (UNIV OF STELLENBOSCH)	
	2.3+5	1.6+6		Data	EXFOR31263.	Mar 73	.LEGENDRE-COEF. GVN	
	2.3+5	1.6+6		Data	EXFOR30125.	Dec 72	DATA FROM PRIVCOM MALAN,DBLE DIFF CS	
Diff Elastic	2.3+5	1.6+6	CCP	Comp Rept	ICD-6 50	70	Bazazjanc+ ANGDIST,LEG COEF,8 ES,TBL	
Diff Elastic	8.0+6		CCP	Comp Rept	ICD-6 50	70	Bazazjanc+ ANGDIST EXPTS,GRPH	
Diff Elastic	1.0+3	4.0+4	DUB	Expt	Jour YF 11 1152	Jun 70	Samosvat.LEGENDRECOEF(E) GRPH,OPTMOD	
					Rept JINR-P3-4724	Oct 69	- . ASSYMMETRY,0+180DEG ANG	
					Jour SNP 11 639	Dec 70	- . ENGL OF YF 11 1152.	
Diff Elastic	1.5+6	3.6+6	JAE	Expt Priv	TANAKA	Aug 71	Tanaka. TOF.REL H(N,N),+LEGENDRE FIT	+
					Jour NP/A 179 513	Jan 72	- . ANG DIST CFD OPTMDL, C-CHNL	
Diff Elastic	1.0+0	2.6+5	DUB	Expt	Conf 73Kiev 2 330	May 73	Mirzaakhmedov+ ANOMAL ANGDIST CFD TH	
					Conf 72Budapest 188	Aug 72	- + ANGDIST ANOMALY,GRAPH	
Potntl Scat	1.2+2	3.4+2	ANL	Expt	Jour PR 79 747	Sep 50	Hibdon. REL MN+CO RESON SCAT. METAL	
Potntl Scat		6.5+5	DKE	ExTh	Jour PL 13 70	Nov 64	Seth+0,1PHASE FRM SIG TOT AV 3-650KV	
Potntl Scat	None		DKE	Expt	Abst DA/B 28 3834	Mar 68	Divadeenam.TRNS.EFFECTIVE RADIUS	
Potntl Scat		+5	SAC	Expt	Jour NP/A 123 561	Jan 69	Morgenstern+ RADIUS.RES SHAPE ANAL.	+
		+6			Rept CEA-R-3609	Sep 68	- .(THESIS).DATA GIVEN	
					Conf 68Wash. 867	Mar 68	- + PPR E27	
	0.0+0	1.0+4			Data EXFOR20684.021	Jul 77	1PNT.RADIUS.	
Tot Inelastc	1.2+6	1.8+6	LEB	Expt	Jour YF 1 443	Mar 65	Bukarev+	+
	1.2+6	1.8+6			Data EXFOR40040.	Aug 70	EXCIT FCTN AT 6ES FOR 4 LEVELS	
Tot Inelastc	5.0+5	7.0+6	ALD	Expt	Jour NP/A 112 337	May 68	Owens+.3ES.FROM N SPECT 90DEG.	+
Tot Inelastc	3.6+5	1.4+6	SUN	Expt	Jour NP/A 124 111	Feb 69	Malan+ INTEGRATED DIFF INEL SIGMAS	+
Tot Inelastc	1.7+5	1.0+7	BOL	Eval	Rept CEC(71)-2	71	Benzi+ STAT MODEL. TBL GIVEN.	+
	1.7+5	1.0+7			Data BENZI-DFN 550E	Mar 71	43 PNTS	
Tot Inelastc	5.0+5	1.5+7	AUA	Eval	Data AUSTR-DFN 133.	Nov 71	COOK+POINT(11)+GROUP(127)SIG.CF EVL	+
Tot Inelastc	1.2+5	1.2+6	SAC	Theo	Conf 73Kiev 1 291	May 73	Krebs+ OPT+STATMDL,PRELIM CFD XP.GRF	
Tot Inelastc	1.0-3	1.5+7	RCN	Eval	Prog RCN-239 11	Nov 75	Gruppelaar. EXP.+MODEL CALC. NDG	
Diff Inelast	4.0+6	7.0+6	LAS	Expt	Jour PR 129 1649	Feb 63	Thomson+ 90DEG TEMP FOR NS TO 5MEV	+
	4.0+6	7.0+6			Data EXFOR11495.037	Jun 76	. 4 PTS. DSIGMA.	
	5.0+6				Data EXFOR11495.041	Jun 76	. 1 PT. SIGMA.	
Diff Inelast	4.0+6	6.5+6	DKE	Expt	Abst DA 24 4248	Apr 64	Buccino.ANG DIST.TOF.NUCL T.LVL DEN.	
Diff Inelast	3.5+6	8.5+6	JAE	Expt	Prog EANDC(J)8L25	Jan 68	Maruyama+.TOF.CONTIN SPECT AT 90DEG	+
					Conf 67Tokyo 373	Sep 67	- + PPR8.127. ABST.	
Diff Inelast	5.0+6	7.0+6	ALD	Expt	Jour NP/A 112 337	May 68	Owens+.3ES.FROM N SPECT 90DEG NDG.	+
					Conf 65Antwerp 547	Jul 65	- + PPR122.ABST.SPECT N' AT 90DEG	
Diff Inelast	1.7+5	2.1+6	SUN	Expt	Jour NP/A 124 111	Feb 69	Malan+ ANG DISTR,EXC FUNCTION,GRAPH	+
				Diss	MALAN	70	- . (UNIV OF STELLENBOSCH)	
	3.5+5	2.1+6			Data EXFOR30125.	Dec 72	DBLE DIFF SIG AT 90DEG,14 LVLS,22 ES	
	1.7+5	1.4+6			Data EXFOR30125.	Dec 72	DBLE DIFF SIG 7 ANGS, 4 LVLS, 3 ES	
Diff Inelast	6.1+5	7.5+5	CCP	Comp	Rept ICD-6 106	70	Sluchevskaja.SIG(ANG) TO LVLS,GRAPHS	
Diff Inelast	1.7+5	1.0+7	BOL	Eval	Rept CEC(71)-2	71	Benzi+ DISCRETE INELASTIC. 5 LVLS	+
	1.6+6	1.0+7			Data BENZI-DFN 550E	Mar 71	TO CONTINUUM, 19PNTS+ANGDIST+E DIST	
	1.7+5	1.6+6			Data BENZI-DFN 550E	Mar 71	1ST- 5TH LVL+ANGDIST+E DIST	
Diff Inelast	1.5+6	3.5+6	JAE	Expt	Jour NP/A 179 513	Jan 72	Tanaka+. ANGDIST CFD OPTMDL,C-CHANNL	+
	1.5+6	3.6+6			Priv TANAKA	Aug 71	- . TOF.REL H(N,N),+LEGENDRE FIT	
	1.5+6	3.6+6			Data EXFOR20337.	Jul 74	175PTS.D/DA,LEG.FIT.	
Diff Inelast	1.0+3	1.0+6	SAC	Eval	Conf CEA-N-1832	Dec 75	Ribon+ EXP+OPT MDL ANAL,CURVES	
Thermal Scat	1.0-4	1.0+3	MUN	Revw	Jour EEN 80 1	77	Koester. SCAT LENGTH,FREE+INCOH SIG	
Scattering	2.5-2		ORL	Expt	Jour PR 91 597	Aug 53	Koehler+ TRANS 9.3+-0.7B	+
	2.5-2				Data EXFOR12060.004	Jun 76	. 1 PT, SIG	
Scattering	None		SAC	Expt	Jour PRL 33 102	Jul 74	Roubeau+ SLOW N SPIN-DEP SCT LENGTH	
Nonelastic	1.0-3	1.5+7	AUA	Eval	Data AUSTR-DFN 133.	Nov 71	COOK+POINT(223)+GROUP(127)SIG.CF EVL	+
Absorption	Maxwl		FAR	Expt	Jour JPR 12 584	May 51	Benoist+. PILE OSC. CD-DIFFERENCE.	
Absorption	2.5-2		HAR	Expt	Rept AERE-R/R-2333	57	Cummins+ PILE OSCILLATOR.	+
Absorption	4.1-1	1.0+7	GA	Eval	Rept GA-2451	Aug 61	Joanou+.68GROUP DATA FOR GAM-I	
Absorption	1.0-3	1.0+7	JUL	Eval	Rept JUEL-678-RG	Jul 70	Liu. EVALUATION+CALC,GRPH,FN OF E	
Absorption	2.5-2		IJI	Eval	Rept KIYAI-K-6	76	Fedorova+ COMP+EVAL,MANY REFS.TABLE	
					Conf 75Kiev 1 169	May 75	- + EVAL SIG GIVEN,TABLE	
Res Int Abs	5.0-1		ANL	Expt	Rept ANL-4277 46	Apr 49	Thomas. CD-RATIO MEAS = 29.3	
Res Int Abs	5.0-1	1.0+6	CCP	Expt	Conf 55Geneva 5 91	Aug 55	Spivak+.VAL GVN CFD REF,PPR659	
Res Int Abs	None		ORL	Revw	Conf 55Geneva 5 96	Aug 55	Macklin+.TABLE,EXPT CFD THEORY,P833	
Res Int Abs	None		CRC	Eval	Rept AECL-1054	Mar 60	Walker.(CRP-913) REDUCED RES.INT.	
Res Int Abs	None		ORL	Eval	Rept ORNL-2869	Mar 60	Nephew.1/V UP +TO100EV.ALSO73.5EV-UP	
Res Int Abs	5.5-1		GA	Eval	Jour NSE 12 115	Jan 62	Garrison+,RI= 10+-2.5B,FROM RES.PAR	
Res Int Abs		1.0+5	LEB	Expt	Jour ZET 46 80	Jan 64	Konks.TBL 3E- RANGES.ENGL JET 19 59	
Res Int Abs	5.0-1		BOL	Eval	Rept RT/FI-4	Jan 67	Palmucci. CALC FROM (N,G) RES PARAMS	

57 Lanthanum 139

Quantity	Energy (ev) Min	Max	Lab	Type	Documentation Ref Vol Page	Author, Comments Date	Data
Res Int Abs	5.4−1		ORL	Expt	Jour JIN 29 584	May 67 Obrien+CD FILTER.CFD OTHERS.	+
					Jour NUC 25 2 41	Feb 67 − +NEW WAY TO MAKE PURE CE141.	
	5.4−1				Data EXFOR10085.004	Apr 74 1PT.RIA=11.2+−.6B.	
Res Int Abs	5.0−1		ANL	Expt	Jour PR 159 1050	Jul 67 Cote+ 12.1+−1.0B INCLUDING 1/V	
Res Int Abs	Pile		GFK	Expt	Rept EANDC(OR)68L	Jan 68 Breitenhuber+. CONTROL EXPT.ACTIV.	
Res Int Abs	5.0−1		MTR	Expt	Rept IN− 1195	May 68 Scoville+	+
	5.0−1				Data EXFOR11820.006	Jun 76 . 1 PT. RI.	
Res Int Abs	5.5−1		ISP	Expt	Jour JIN 30 1353	Jul 68 Orvini+ACT 10.8+−1.1 B REL.TO AU197	+
	5.5−1				Data EXFOR20633.007	Jun 76 1PNT.CAPTURE.	
Res Int Abs	5.5−1		GHT	Expt	Jour JRC 9 9	71 De Corte+CAPT CD−R,11.0B INCL 1/V	+
	5.0−1				Data EXFOR20646.009	Sep 76 1PNT.CAPTURE.	
Res Int Abs	None		GA	Eval	Rept GA− 12071	Sep 71 Mathews+. RECOMMENDED VALUES	
Res Int Abs	5.0−1		NPL	Expt	Jour JNE 25 129	Mar 71 Ryves+REL AU.LESS 1/V PART.ACT EXPT.	
					Conf 71Canterby 139	Sep 71 − .REDUCED CAPT RES INTEGRAL,TBL	
	5.0−1				Data EXFOR20791.015	Dec 78 1PNT.REDUCED CAPT INTGRL.	
Res Int Abs	5.5−1		CRC	Eval	Rept AECL−3037 1	Jan 72 Walker.REDUCED RES INT,DETAILED TBL	
Res Int Abs	5.0−1		AUA	Eval	Rept AAEC/TM−619	Sep 72 Clayton.CALC FROM SIG LIBRARY,TABLE	
Res Int Abs	5.0−1		MUN	Expt	Jour JRC 15 535	73 Alian+CAPT CD−R,117.1B INCL 1/V	+
	5.0−1				Data EXFOR20644.010	Jun 76 1PNT.CAPTURE.	
Res Int Abs	5.5−1		RCN	Revw	Conf 73Paris 2 271	Mar 73 Zijp.ACT,RECOMM FROM LITERATURE,TBL	
Res Int Abs	4.6−1	1.0+6	RCN	Theo	Rept RCN−191	Jul 73 Lautenbach.CAPT INT FROM GROUP SIGMA	
Res Int Abs	5.0−1		GHT	Expt	Jour JRC 20 695	74 Van Der Linden+ BY(N,G).CFD OTHS,TBL	+
	5.5−1				Conf 73Paris 2 241	Mar 73 − + ACT,REL THR+GOLD,TBL	
	5.5−1				Data EXFOR20645.015	Jul 76 1PNT.CAPTURE.	
Res Int Abs	5.5−1	+6	SAC	Revw	Conf IAEA−169 1 235	74 Ribon.CAPTURE,STATUS CFD REQUEST,TBL	
Res Int Abs	+0	+5	WIN	Revw	Conf IAEA−169 3 163	74 Pope+ DATA FILE CALC CFD XPTAL VALUE	
Res Int Abs	5.0−1		KJL	Expt	Jour JIN 37 1591	Aug 75 Steinnes. CD−RAT+ACTIV INTEG,CFD,TBL	+
					Jour JIN 34 2699	Sep 72 − . ACT. AU MONITOR	
	5.0−1				Data EXFOR20635.002	Aug 76 1PNT.CAPTURE.	
	5.0−1				Data EXFOR20188.015	May 74 1PNT.CAPTURE.	
Res Int Abs	5.5−1		OAU	Expt	Jour RRL 23 317	Dec 75 Gleason. CD−RATIO,REL AU+MN,RI TABLE	+
	5.5−1				Data EXFOR10644.036	Jul 77 1PT.RIA=12.5+−.4B	
Res Int Abs	5.0−1		IJI	Eval	Rept KIYAI−76−6	76 Fedorova+ EVAL CFD CALC.TBL RI,REFS	
					Conf 75Kiev 1 169	May 75 − + EVAL+CALC RI GIVEN,TABLE	
(n,γ)	2.0+4	7.0+5	OXF	Expt	Jour PRSA 170 513	Apr 39 Griffiths.RA−BE PHOTONEUT ACTIVATION	
(n,γ)	Maxwl		JAP	Expt	Jour SCP 38 167	Jan 41 Sinma+.LI+D.RELATIVE SIG MEASUREMENT	
(n,γ)	Pile		ANL	Expt	Jour PR 72 888	Nov 47 Seren+.ACT METHOD.PILE IRRAD.	+
	Pile				Data EXFOR11447.094	Jun 76 . 1 PT. SIGMA.	
(n,γ)	Fiss		ANL	Expt	Jour PR 78 632	Jun 50 Hughes+ REL SIG(THERMAL).	+
	Fiss				Data EXFOR11596.011	Jun 76 . 1 PT. SIGMA.	
(n,γ)	Pile		ANL	Expt	Jour PR 80 342	Nov 50 Harris+.PILE OSC.REL TO BORON.	+
	Pile				Data EXFOR11528.035	Jun 76 . 1 PT. SIGMA.	
(n,γ)	Maxwl		ORL	Expt	Jour PR 83 643	Aug 51 Pomerance. LOCAL OSC REL AU ABS=95B.	+
	Maxwl				Data EXFOR11047.063	Jun 76 . 1 PT. SIGMA.	
(n,γ)	Fiss		BNL	Expt	Jour PR 91 1423	Sep 53 Hughes+.ALSO LVL SPACINGS AT EXCIT E	
(n,γ)	2.4+4		ORL	Expt	Jour PR 107 504	Jul 57 Macklin+.SB−BE NEUTS 50+−7MB,1.6MEVG	+
					Conf 58Geneva 15 68	Sep 58 .SUPERSEDED.	
	2.4+4				Data EXFOR11399.035	Jun 76 . 1 PT. SIGMA.	
(n,γ)	Pile		KUR	Expt	Conf 58Geneva 15 50	Sep 58 Leipunskij+.PPR2219,VAL GVN	
(n,γ)	1.4+7		ALD	Expt	Jour PPS 72 505	Oct 58 Perkin+ACT ANAL 1.48MB+−10PC,B−W TH	+
(n,γ)	2.5+4		LRL	Expt	Jour PR 112 226	Oct 58 Booth+ SB−BE REL I+THR,ACT 40.2H HL	+
	2.5+4				Data EXFOR11429.023	Jun 76 . 1 PT. SIGMA.	
(n,γ)	2.0+5		ORL	Expt	Jour PR 114 1619	Jun 59 Lyon+.ABS GAMMA COUNT 10+−2MB ACT	+
	2.0+5				Data EXFOR11625.024	Jun 76 . 1 PT. SIGMA.	
(n,γ)	1.5+5	3.0+6	WIS	Expt	Jour PR 116 927	Nov 59 Johnsrud+ SC CFD OTHERS,SIG VS E.	+
	1.7+5	2.0+6			Data EXFOR11675.017	Jun 76 . 4 PTS. SIGMA.	
(n,γ)	Maxwl		CRC	Eval	Rept AECL−1054	Mar 60 Walker. (CRRP−913).	
(n,γ)	1.5+7		ARK	Expt	Jour PR 118 242	Apr 60 Wille+ MEAS ACT SIG=1.1+−0.2 MB.	+
	1.5+7				Data EXFOR12033.008	Jun 76 . 1 PT. SIGMA.	
(n,γ)	Pile		ORL	Expt	Jour NSE 8 378	Nov 60 Lyon. ACTIVATION,SIGMA GIVEN	+
	Pile				Data EXFOR11625.024	Jun 76 . 1 PT. SIGMA.	
(n,γ)	Fast		LAS	Expt	Jour NSE 8 608	Dec 60 Byers. GODIVA JEZEBEL ACT CS GIVEN	
(n,γ)	3.0+4	6.5+4	ORL	Expt	Jour PR 122 182	Apr 61 Gibbons+	+
					Jour PR 129 2695	Mar 63 Macklin+ LIQ SCINT,55+−10,18+−3MB	
					Conf 61Vienna 1 95	Aug 61 Neiler.	
	3.0+4	6.5+4			Data EXFOR11329.038	Jun 76 . 2 PTS. SIGMA.	
(n,γ)	4.0+1	4.0+4	LEB	Expt	Jour ZET 46 80	Jan 64 Konks.PB−SLOW−DOWN,GRAPH SIG(E)	+
					Jour JET 19 59	Jul 64 TRANSLATN.*	

57 Lanthanum 139

Quantity	Energy (ev) Min	Energy (ev) Max	Lab	Type	Documentation Ref Vol Page	Documentation Date	Author, Comments	Data
(n,γ)	1.0+0	2.0+4	ORL	Expt Prog	WASH-1048 71	Jun 64	Block. NDG,TOF, RSLN 6 NS/M	
(n,γ)	5.0+3	9.0+4	ORL	Theo Jour	RMP 37 166	Jan 65	Macklin+.CALC FOR KT=5TO90KEV	
(n,γ)	2.5−2		BOL	Eval Rept	RT/FI-4	Jan 67	Palmucci. CALC FROM RES PARAMETERS	
(n,γ)	1.5+7		DEB	Expt Jour	NP/A 95 229	Mar 67	Csikai+,ACTIV,THEORY SIG=F(N),TABLE	+
				Jour	MFF 16 123	Feb 68	- .THESIS,IN HUNGARIAN,EXPT,GRPH	
	1.5+7			Data	EXFOR30067.014	Nov 70	VALUE AT 14.7 MEV, (= NP A95 TBL 1)	
(n,γ)	Maxwl		ORL	Expt Jour	JIN 29 584	May 67	Obrien+ORNL REACTOR.CFD OTHERS.	+
				Jour	NUC 25 2 41	Feb 67	- +NEW WAY TO MAKE PURE CE141.	
	Maxwl			Data	EXFOR10085.	Apr 74	. 2 PTS. MEAS EFFECTIVE CS,THRML VAL	
(n,γ)	Maxwl		ANL	Theo Jour	PR 159 1050	Jul 67	Cote+ CALCTD FROM MEASD RESON ES	
(n,γ)	3.0+6		DEB	Expt Jour	JNE 21 797	Oct 67	Peto+ACTIV,SIGMA REL TO AU(N,G)	+
	3.0+6			Data	EXFOR30031.018	Aug 70	SINGLE VALUE	
(n,γ)	1.4+7		LYO	Comp Rept	LYCEN/6780	Nov 67	Crouzet+COMPILATN FOR ACTIVTN ANALYS	
(n,γ)	1.4+7		NAP	Expt Jour	NC/B 52 2 476	Dec 67	Cuzzocrea+. ACT ANAL.SIG=1.9+-.4 MB	
(n,γ)	Maxwl		AUA	Theo Jour	NSE 31 234	Feb 68	Cook+ STATISTICAL CALC CFD EXPT	
(n,γ)	1.1+4	2.0+6	ANL	Expt Jour	JNE 22 267	May 68	Stupegia+ ACT 19ES REL U235 NF,TABLE	+
	1.1+4	2.0+6		Data	EXFOR11624.007	Jun 76	. 19 PTS. SIGMA.	
(n,γ)	-		IEA	Comp Rept	IEA-INF-10	Aug 68	Atalla. TABLES OF HL,SIG AND GAMM-E	
(n,γ)	2.4+4		MUA	Theo Jour	IJP 42 567	Sep 68	Chaubey+ METHD OF BOOTH,VAL CFD XPT	+
				Expt Jour	PR 152 1055	Dec 66	- + BETA-DET,SIG REL I-127,TBL	
	2.4+4			Data	EXFOR30079.028	Dec 70	SIGMA FOR 40. H HALF-LIFE	
(n,γ)	2.0+3		MTR	Expt Prog	WASH-1127 72	Apr 69	Schuman+ FILTERED BEAM,RELATVE CURVS	
(n,γ)	2.0+5		MUA	Theo Conf	69Roorke 2 129	Dec 69	Chaubey+ SIG VALUE GIVEN, STATIST-TH	
(n,γ)	1.0+6	1.0+6	GA	Theo Conf	70Helsinki 2 281	Jun 70	Fricke+44. SIG(E) GRAPH,STATMOD CALC	
(n,γ)	3.0+4		AUA	Theo Rept	AAEC/E-211	Nov 70	Musgrove. SIGMA GIVEN AND CFD OTHER	
(n,γ)	3.0+4		AUA	Theo Rept	AAEC/E-211	Nov 70	Musgrove. SIGMA GIVEN AND CFD OTHER	
(n,γ)	Pile		MTR	Expt Abst	ANS 13 755	Nov 70	Scoville+.CFRMF MEAST.VALUE GIVEN.	
(n,γ)	2.4+4		BHU	Expt Conf	70Madurai 2 615	Dec 70	Chaturvedi+ EXPTL+CALCULATED SIGMAS	
(n,γ)	1.0+3	1.0+7	BOL	Eval Conf	CEC(71)-2	71	Benzi+ OPTMOD EVAL.TBL GIVEN.	+
				Rept	CEC(70)-2	Apr 70	- +. GRAPH	
				Rept	CEC(70)-2	Apr 70	- .GRAPH=SUM OF SIG(ISOTOPES)	
				Rept	CCDN-NW/10	Dec 69	- +H-F MOD,AXEL G(G)EST,ALL DATA	
				Conf	66Paris 1 537	Oct 66	- + STATMOD.TBL AV VALS.SUPERSEDD	
				Jour	NC 38 216	Jul 65	- + THEORY FOR CAPTURE EVALUATION	
	1.0+3	1.0+7		Data	BENZI-DFN 550E	Mar 71	62 PNTS	
(n,γ)	2.5−2		NPL	Expt Jour	JNE 25 129	Mar 71	Ryves Rel Au.SIG=9.03+-.33B.ACT EXPT	+
				Conf	71Canterby 139	71	Ryves. VDG,GRAPHITE MODERATOR.ACTIVN	
	2.5−2			Data	EXFOR20791.014	Dec 78	1PNT.SIGMA.	
(n,γ)	2.0+5	5.9+6	IFU	Expt Jour	UFZ 16 1205	Jul 71	Zaikin+ ACT METH,SIG(NEUT-E),GRPHS	+
				Prog	YFI-10 47	May 71	- + TBL SIG VS N-E,+-ERRORS	
				Rept	INDC(CCP)-15	Dec 71	.P52. ENGLISH OF YFI-10 47	
	2.0+5	5.9+6		Data	EXFOR40255.004	Dec 75	.SIGMA FOR 21 EN GVN	
(n,γ)	Maxwl		GA	Eval Rept	GA-12071	Sep 71	Mathews+. RECOMMENDED VALUES	
	1.0−3	1.5+7	AUA	Eval Data	AUSTR-DFN 133.	Nov 71	COOK+POINT(223)+GROUP(127)SIG.CF EVL	
(n,γ)	1.4+7		BOR	Expt Jour	NP/A 176 545	Dec 71	Rigaud+ INTEGRATED FROM NG SPECTRUM	+
				Conf	72Budapest 220	Aug 72	- + INTEGRATD SIG FROM SPEC,GRPH	
				Jour	JPRS 32 10 231	Oct 71	Irigaray+COLL.5B,MEAS.G.SPC.WITH INA	
	1.4+7			Data	EXFOR20533.003	Apr 76	1PNT.SIGMA.	
(n,γ)	1.4+7		RBZ	Expt Data	LNS-4-72	72	Holub+ACTIVATION SIGMA,TBL,GRAPH	+
	1.4+7			Data	EXFOR30145.012	Aug 73		
(n,γ)	Maxwl		CRC	Eval Rept	AECL-3037 1	Jan 72	Walker.RECOMMENDED SIG,DETAILED TBL	
(n,γ)	2.4+4		MUA	Theo Jour	IJP 46 114	Mar 72	Chaubey+ P-WAVE STRENGTH FUNCT,TABLE	
(n,γ)	2.5−2		IAE	Revw Rept	IAEA-143 897	Apr 72	Lemmel.RECENT EVALUATIONS,TABLE+GRPH	
	Maxwl			Rept	IAEA-143 897	Apr 72	- .RECENT EVALUATIONS,TABLE	
(n,γ)	None		CAS	Expt Rept	NCL 4 430	Jul 72	Fubini.CORR BETWEEN NG AND DP REACT	
(n,γ)	1.0+2	1.0+7	HED	Theo Rept	HEDL-TME-71154	Aug 72	Mackellar+ REALISIC OPTMOD	
(n,γ)	2.5−2		AUA	Eval Rept	AAEC/TM-619	Sep 72	Clayton.CALC FROM SIG LIBRARY,TABLE	
(n,γ)	Fast		MTR	Expt Conf	72Kiamesha 2 614	Sep 72	Harker+ CFRMF INTEGRAL MEAS.	
(n,γ)	Fast		DUB	Expt Rept	JINR-P12-6810	Nov 72	Ngo Quoc Buu+ ACT ANALYS, CD-RATIOS	
(n,γ)	2.5−2		RCN	Revw Conf	73Paris 2 271	Mar 73	Zijp.RECOMMENDED FROM LITERATURE,TBL	
(n,γ)		1.1+6	RCN	Theo Rept	RCN-191	Jun 73	Lautenbach. GROUP CONSTANTS TBL	
(n,γ)	2.5−2	3.0+4	SAC	Revw Conf	IAEA-169 1 235	74	Ribon.STATUS SIG CFD REQUESTS,TABLE	
	Fiss			Conf	IAEA-169 1 235	74	- .STATUS SIG CFD REQUESTS,TABLE	
(n,γ)	1.0+3	2.0+6	SAC	Eval Rept	CEA-CONF-2407	74	Krebs. IDENTICAL TO KIEV MAY-JUNE73	
	1.0+3	1.0+6		Theo Conf	73Kiev 1 291	May 73	- + OPT+STATMDL,PRELIM CFD XP.GRF	
(n,γ)	Maxwl	Fiss	WIN	Revw Conf	IAEA-169 3 163	74	Pope+ MAXW+FIS-SPEC AVG DATA CFD XPT	
	Fiss			Conf	IAEA-169 3 137	74	Dean. POINT DATA AVG OVER STAND SPEC	

57 Lanthanum 139

Quantity	Energy (ev) Min	Energy (ev) Max	Lab	Type	Documentation Ref Vol Page	Date	Author, Comments	Data
(n,γ)	1.0+3	1.0+7	FEI	Eval	Rept YK- 8/2 97	Sep 72	Abagjan+ AVG SIG(ENERGY-GROUPS),TABL	
					Rept INDC(CCP)-39	Jul 74	.P102. ENGLISH OF YK-8/2 97	
(n,γ)	1.5+7		BOR	Expt	Jour NSE 55 17	Sep 74	Rigaud+ MDL TH.CALCS.TBLS.GRAPHS.	+
					Conf 74Petten 233	Sep 74	- + IMPROVED ACTIVATION METHOD	
					Diss IN- 2P3 1092	73	Desthilliers+ 2 METHODS.	
	1.5+7				Data EXFOR20543.008	Apr 76	1PNT.SIGMA.	
(n,γ)	Maxwl		MUN	Expt	Jour ZP/A 272 273	Mar 75	Mannhart+8.933 +- 0.036 B	+
					Diss MANNHART	Jul 74	- . 8.933+-0.036 B	
	2.5-2				Data EXFOR20610.004	May 76	1PNT.SIGMA.	
(n,γ)	Maxwl		OAU	Expt	Jour RRL 23 317	Dec 75	Gleason. CF-SOURC-ACT,REL AU+MN,TABL	+
	Maxwl				Data EXFOR10644.035	Jul 77	. 1 PT THR CS=9.15+-0.25B.	
(n,γ)	1.0+3	1.0+6	SAC	Eval	Rept CEA-N-1832	Dec 75	Ribon+ EXP+TH ANAL,STAT MOL,CURVE	
(n,γ)	1.5+7		JYV	Comp	Rept JU-RR-1/1976	Mar 76	Valkonen.(THESIS).EXPTS CFD DSD MODL	
(n,γ)	3.1+0	3.2+3	COL	Expt	Jour PR/C 13 1884	May 76	Hacken+CAPT MEAS.RES OBS.	
(n,γ)	1.4+7		IRK	Expt	Jour NP/A 264 105	Jun 76	Schwerer+ GE-LI.ACT SIG=1.01+-0.10MB	+
	1.5+7				Data EXFOR20670.014	Oct 76	1PNT.SIGMA.	
(n,γ)	Fast		RCN	Expt	Rept ECN-10	Oct 76	Veenema+ STEK REACTIVITY WORTHS TBL.	
Res Int Capt	None		ROS	Revw	Jour KE 8 88	Jan 65	Schumann+ VAL GVN,EXPT DESCRIBED	
					Rept ZFK-RN-23	Sep 64	- + VAL GVN,NO DETAILS	
Spect (n,γ)	Maxwl		ANL	Expt	Jour PR 80 415	Nov 50	Hamermesh+ FOTOPLATE, GAM ABV 3 MEV	
Spect (n,γ)	2.5+4		ORL	Expt	Conf 58Geneva 15 68	Sep 58	Macklin.PPR671,SIGMA+G-ENERGY GVN	
Spect (n,γ)	-		UJV	Expt	Jour CZJ 10 275	60	Urbanec+. SCINT SPEC.20-1000KEV GAMS	
Spect (n,γ)	-		CCP	Expt	Jour ZET 38 282	Jan 60	Dzhelepov.GRAPH G-SPC 2.6-3.9 MEV	
					Jour JET 11 205	Jul 60	TRANSLATN.*	
Spect (n,γ)	Maxwl		CCP	Expt	Book NEJTRONFIZ 335	61	Groshev.TBL+GRAPH.ENGL TRNSL=SPN 248	
Spect (n,γ)	Maxwl		ARF	Expt	Prog ARF-1193-12	Jul 62	Greenwood+,CRYST SPEC,LOW-E GAMMAS	
Spect (n,γ)	Maxwl		CAS	Expt	Jour NC 29 977	Aug 63	Giannini+ NAI, E+INTENSITY,TO 277KEV	+
Spect (n,γ)	7.2+1		ANL	Expt	Prog WASH-1071 12	Nov 66	Sheve+2.CAPTURE BY J=3 72.3EV RES	
Spect (n,γ)	Maxwl		MCM	Expt	Jour NP 89 241	Dec 66	Hughes+ GE(LI) SPECTROMETER	
Spect (n,γ)	2.5-2		MIT	Comp	Jour MITNE-85	Jan 69	Rasmussen+TBL G INT.=AFCRL-69-0071	
Spect (n,γ)	Maxwl		RIS	Expt	Prog EANDC(OR)85L	Mar 69	Baader+ BENT CRYST SPECT.	
Spect (n,γ)	1.0-1	1.5+2	BNL	Expt	Prog WASH-1127 21	Apr 69	Chrien+ 13 HIGH-E GAMMAS MEASURED	
Spect (n,γ)	Maxwl		BKB	Expt	Jour FIZS 1 56	Aug 69	Simic+ GRPH LOW-E G-SPEC.LVL SCH,NDG	
					Conf 69Studsvik 349	Aug 69	- + ABSTR,0-5200KEV GAM-E,TB PUBL	
Spect (n,γ)	5.5-1	7.4-1	BNL	Expt	Conf 69Studsvik 105	Aug 69	Kane+ GRPH GAM-SPEC,NEUT-MONOCHROMTR	
Spect (n,γ)	Maxwl		KFI	Revw	Jour YF 10 907	Nov 69	Kecskemeti+ AVG GAM-MULTIPLICITY,TBL	
					Jour SNP 10 524	May 70	TRANSLATN.*	
Spect (n,γ)	Maxwl		BOR	Expt	Prog EANDC(E)127U	Apr 70	Audias+,GE(LI) DET	
					Conf 69Studsvik 337	Aug 69	Irigaray+ G-SPEC TBL,45LINES,GE(LI)	
Spect (n,γ)	Maxwl		LAS	Expt	Jour PR/C 2 2323	Dec 70	Jurney+,GE(LI)+SI(LI) DET,MANY GAMS	
Spect (n,γ)	Pile		KFK	Expt	Rept KFK-1401	Jun 71	Djadali.AVG POLRZ G EXPT,CFD T,SPIN	
					Jour NP/A 165 560	Apr 71	- + POL N, CIRC POL GS.	
					Rept KFK-1296	Sep 70	- +POLRZ GAMS,LA-140 LVLS+SPINS	
Spect (n,γ)	1.4+7		BOR	Expt	Jour NP/A 176 545	Dec 71	Rigaud+ TOF. E(GAMMA)=14 TO 22 MEV.	
Spect (n,γ)	1.0+7		WWA	Theo	Jour NP/A 189 545	Jul 72	Brzosko+ CMPD NUCL DECAY.PARTIAL WG	
Spect (n,γ)	5.0+5	2.0+6	CAS	Expt	Conf 72Budapest 228	Aug 72	Fubini+ CORRELATION (N,G)-(D,P),NDG	+
	Maxwl				Data EXFOR20444.002	Nov 75	54PTS.	
Spect (n,γ)	1.4+7		FR	Expt	Conf 72Budapest 220	Aug 72	Rigaud+ TOF,NDG	
Spect (n,γ)	Pile		MUN	Expt	Jour ZP 258 315	Mar 73	Henkelmann. E + INT OF GS GIVEN	+
	2.5-2				Data EXFOR20606.007	Jun 76	7PTS.	
Spect (n,γ)	4.6+5		AUA	Expt	Prog AAEC/PR-39P 44	Jan 74	Allen+ NA-I,GAMMA YIELD,FIGURE ONLY	
Inelastic γ	3.0+6		FEI	Expt	Jour AE 9 403	Nov 60	Androsenko+ TABLE OF GAMMA-ENERGIES	
Inelastic γ	3.0+6		CCP	Expt	Jour IZV 25 1280	Oct 61	Graudynya+,SCINT,0.64-2.08MEV GAMS	
Inelastic γ	1.0+6	2.0+6	LEB	Expt	Jour YF 1 443	Mar 65	Bukarev.GRAPH G-SPEC,TBL SIG PER LVL	+
					Jour SNP 1 316	Sep 65	TRANSLATN.*	
Inelastic γ	4.0+5	1.7+6	LAS	Expt	Prog WASH-1068 115	Mar 66	DAY+,TBC,NDG	
Inelastic γ	5.0+6	7.0+6	ALD	Expt	Jour NP/A 112 337	May 68	Owens+.3ES.TOF SPECT 90 DEG. NDG.	+
Inelastic γ	2.9+6		TOR	Expt	Jour CJP 46 1849	Sep 68	Daniels+ GE(LI)+NAI 18 GAMMA PEAKS	
					Abst DA/B 29 3436	Mar 69	Felsteiner. ES REL INT.COINCS.	
Inelastic γ	5.0+5	2.3+6	SUN	Expt	Jour NP/A 124 433	Feb 69	VAN DER MERWE+TOF GATED GE-LI.LEVELS	
Inelastic γ	2.8+6		KGU	Expt	Jour YF 9 1129	Jun 69	Romanenko+ GRPH,E+INT TBL,LVL-SCHEME	+
					Jour SNP 9 660	Dec 69	*	
					Conf 67Kharkov 49	Feb 67	* ABST ONLY	
Inelastic γ	2.8+6				Data EXFOR40414.004	Dec 77	E+ABS INT OF 10 GAMMAS	
	None		ITK	Expt	Prog INDC(SEC)-35	Sep 73	Singh+ P119.LEVEL SCHEME,GE-LI,TBL	
(n,2n)	Fiss		CRC	Eval	Rept CRC-1003	Dec 60	Roy+,ESTIMATED AVG SIG=1.6MB	
(n,2n)	8.9+6	1.0+7	BOL	Eval	Rept CEC(71)-2	71	Benzi+ STAT+EVAP MODELS.TBL GIVEN.	+
	8.9+6	1.0+7			Data BENZI-DFN 550E	Mar 71	4 PNTS+ANGDIST+E DIST. 1 RANGE	

57 Lanthanum 139

Quantity	Energy (ev) Min	Max	Lab	Type	Documentation Ref Vol Page	Date	Author, Comments	Data
(n,2n)	1.5+7		DEB	Eval Jour	REA 11 1 153	Mar 73	Boedy+ RECOMM.VALUE FROM N-Z SYSTEM.	
(n,2n)	1.5+7		KFI	Theo Rept	KFKI-73-68	Dec 73	Jeki.NEW FIT,CALC SIG CFD OTHERS,TBL	
(n,p)	Fast		CAR	Expt Jour	PR 81 184	Jan 51	Cohen.AVR SIG,N SPEC.BETA ACT.UPPLIM	+
	Fast			Data	EXFOR11189.025	Jun 76	. 1 PT. SIGMA	
(n,p)	1.5+7		CRC	Expt Jour	CJP 31 267	Feb 53	Paul+ BETA ACT. CFD TH. HL=85M.	+
	1.5+7			Data	EXFOR11274.087	Jun 76	. 1 PT. SIGMA.	
(n,p)	1.5+7		GLS	Theo Jour	PM 2 473	Apr 57	Brown+ COMPNUCL NIL, DIRECT 9MB	
(n,p)	1.4+7		ALD	Expt Jour	PPS 73 215	Feb 59	Coleman+. ACT. CFD DIRECT INTERACTN	+
(n,p)	1.5+7		ARK	Expt Jour	PR 118 242	Apr 60	Wille+ MEAS ACT SIG=5+ -1MB.	+
	1.5+7			Data	EXFOR12033.009	Jun 76	. 1 PT. SIGMA.	
(n,p)	Fiss		CRC	Eval Rept	CRC-1003	Dec 60	Roy+,ESTIMATED AVG SIG=0.001MB	
(n,p)	1.5+7		ARK	Expt Jour	PR 131 2649	Sep 63	Bramlitt+ LESS THAN 0.046MB N2P	+
				Rept	TID-16949	62	.THESIS	
	1.5+7			Data	EXFOR11590.071	Jun 76	. 1 PT. SIGMA, N,2P.	
(n,p)	1.5+7		SAH	Comp Jour	NUC 23 8 112	Aug 65	Chatterjee. TABLE WITH REFS.	
	1.4+7			Jour	NP 60 273	Nov 64	- .MEAN OF EXPT CFD SHELLMOD	
(n,p)	1.4+7		DEB	Expt Jour	NP/A 91 222	Jan 67	Csikai+ ACTIV, VALUE AT 14.7MEV,TBL	+
				Jour	MFF 16 123	Feb 68	SEE ALSO *THESIS HUNG	
	1.5+7			Data	EXFOR30115.009	Jan 71	SIGMA AT 14.7 MEV FROM NP A91 222	
(n,p)	1.4+7	1.5+7	NAP	Comp Rept	INFN/BE-67-10	Jul 67	Cuzzocrea+ AVERAGED CHOSEN DATA.	
(n,p)	1.4+7		LYO	Comp Rept	LYCEN/6780	Nov 67	Crouzet+COMPILATN FOR ACTIVTN ANALYS	
(n,p)	1.4+7		NAP	Comp Rept	NC/B 52 2 476	Dec 67	Cuzzocrea+. 4.47+ -.32 MB.TH OKS EXPT	
(n,p)	1.5+7		KAZ	Expt Jour	YF 8 7	Jul 68	Levkovskij+ SIG VAL + -ERROR GVN,TBL	+
				Jour	SNP 8 4	Jan 69	TRANSLATN.*	
	1.5+7			Data	EXFOR40223.024	May 74	.SIGMA GIVEN,1 DATA LINE	
(n,p)	1.5+7		DEB	Comp Jour	REA 7 4 93	Dec 69	Csikai+ SIG+HL COMPILTN,N-ACTIV-ANAL	
(n,p)	1.4+7	1.5+7	JYV	Eval Rept	JU-RR-3/1970	Jun 70	Leppaemaeki+ (N,2P) UPPER LIMIT,TBL	
(n,p)	1.4+7	1.5+7	JYV	Eval Rept	JU-RR-3/1970	Jun 70	Leppaemaeki+ TABLE OF EVAL AVG SIG	
(n,p)	1.5+7		RBZ	Expt Jour	NP/A 154 273	Oct 70	Lulic+ SIG(N,2P) MEASURED BY ACTIV	
	1.5+7			Data	EXFOR30106.012	Apr 72	SIG(N,2P) AT 14.6 MEV	
(n,p)	1.5+7		IRK	Expt Jour	APA 34 209	Sep 71	Havlik. ACT. CC-W.	+
				Jour	OAWA 107 119	Apr 70	- . ACTIVATION METHOD	
	1.5+7			Data	EXFOR20509.006	Apr 76	1PNT.SIGMA.	
(n,p)	1.5+7		ARK	Expt Abst	DA/B 32 5091	Mar 72	Bari. GE(LI) DET. ACT. SIG GIVEN	
	1.5+7			Data	EXFOR10431.011	Aug 75	1PT,SIGMA	
(n,p)	1.4+7	1.5+7	KAZ	Theo Jour	YF 18 705	Oct 73	Levkovsky.AVERAGED SIG,CALC,TBL	
				Jour	SNP 18 361	Apr 74	. ENGLISH OF YF 18,705	
(n,p)		7.5+8	IOW	Expt Jour	PR/C 12 1978	Dec 75	Hill+ ES TO 750 MEV.(N,2P) REACTION	
(n,np)	1.5+7		GLS	Theo Jour	PM 2 473	Apr 57	Brown+ N,PN* COMPNUCL NIL,DIRECT NIL	
(n,d)	1.5+7		SAH	Comp Jour	NUC 23 8 112	Aug 65	Chatterjee. TABLE WITH REFS.	
(n,t)	1.5+7		JUL	Expt Jour	JRC 21 395	74	Qaim+ DIRECT GAMS,SIG VS Z SYSTEMATC	+
	1.4+7			Jour	JIN 35 1 19	Jan 73	- +ACTIVATION	
	1.5+7			Conf	72Budapest 50	Aug 72	- . ACTIVATION ,GRP	
				Conf	71Canterby 121	Sep 71	.PRELIMINARY, 00624269	
	1.5+7			Data	EXFOR20522.012	Apr 76	1PNT.SIGMA.	
(n,α)	1.4+7		ALD	Expt Jour	PPS 73 215	Feb 59	Coleman+. ACTIVATION	+
(n,α)	1.5+7		ARK	Expt Jour	PR 118 242	Apr 60	Wille+ MEAS ACT SIG=1.3 MB.	+
	1.5+7			Data	EXFOR12033.007	Jun 76	. 1 PT. SIGMA.	
(n,α)	Fiss		CRC	Eval Rept	CRC-1003	Dec 60	Roy+,ESTIMATED AVG SIG=0.0014MB	
(n,α)	1.4+7		CIS	Theo Jour	NP 51 460	Feb 64	Facchini+STATMOD SIG XPT/CALC=0.7	
(n,α)	1.4+7		IBJ	Expt Jour	NP 53 270	Apr 64	Jaskola+ EXPT DESCRBD,ALFA SPCTR GIV	+
				Rept	INR-1268	Jan 71	SEE ALSO * FULL INFORMATION	
				Jour	APPB 2 521	71	.SAME AS INR-1268	
				Jour	NP 66 361	May 65	SEE ALSO * THEO,ALFA CLUSTRNG	
	1.4+7			Data	EXFOR30158.004	Mar 71	NUM DATA NOT AVAILBL,SEE GRAF IN REF	
(n,α)	1.5+7		MUA	Expt Jour	NP 69 153	Jul 65	Khurana+ FE-STANDARD	
(n,α)	1.5+7		RBZ	Expt Jour	NP 73 548	Nov 65	Kulisic.E+ANGDIST+SIGTOT.CFD TH.CURV	+
				Rept	EANDC-50S148	Jul 65	. FULL PAPER PRESENTD AT 65ANTWERP	
				Conf	64Paris 2 769	Jul 64	.	
	1.5+7			Data	EXFOR30127.	Mar 71	SIGMA, ANG-DISTR, ALFA-SPECTR(0DEG)	
(n,α)	1.4+7	1.5+7	NAP	Comp Rept	INFN/BE-67-11	Sep 67	Cuzzocrea+ AVERAGED CHOSEN DATA.	
(n,α)	1.4+7		LYO	Comp Rept	LYCEN/6780	Nov 67	Crouzet+COMPILATN FOR ACTIVTN ANALYS	
(n,α)	1.6+7		TUE	Expt Jour	ZP 214 127	Jul 68	Brendle.ASYMMETRY-MEASUREMENT	
(n,α)	1.5+7		DEB	Expt Jour	REA 7 4 93	Dec 69	Csikai+ SIG+HL COMPILTN,N-ACTIV-ANAL	
(n,α)	1.4+7	1.5+7	JYV	Eval Rept	JU-RR-3/1970	Jun 70	Leppaemaeki+ TABLE OF EVAL AVG SIG	
(n,α)	1.5+7		IRK	Expt Jour	APA 34 209	Sep 71	Havlik. ACT. CC-W.	+
				Jour	OAWA 107 119	Apr 70	- . ACTIVATION METHOD	
	1.5+7			Data	EXFOR20509.007	Apr 76	1PNT.SIGMA.	

57 Lanthanum 139

Quantity	Energy (ev) Min	Max	Lab	Type	Documentation Ref Vol Page	Author, Comments Date	Data
(n,α)	1.5+7		ARK	Expt	Abst DA/B 32 5091	Mar 72 Bari. GE(LI) DET. ACT. SIG GIVEN	+
	1.5+7				Data EXFOR10431.021	Aug 75 . 1 PT. SIGMA.	
(n,α)	1.4+7		RBZ	Theo	Conf 72Budapest 168	Aug 72 Caplar+ ANALYSIS OF SPECTRA,GRAPH	
(n,α)	1.4+7	1.5+7	KAZ	Theo	Jour YF 18 705	Oct 73 Levkovsky.AVERAGED SIG,CALC,TBL	
					Jour SNP 18 361	Apr 74 . ENGLISH OF YF 18,705	
(n,α)		7.5+8	IOW	Expt	Jour PR/C 12 1978	Dec 75 Hill+ ES TO 750 MEV.	
Reson Params	7.4+1		BNL	Expt	Jour PR 108 353	Oct 57 Stolovy+ FC,TRNS. WT,WN,WG.	+
	7.4+1				Data EXFOR11866.008	Jun 76 . 1 RES. E0,WT,WN,WG.	
Reson Params	−.4+3	1.0+4	ANL	Expt	Jour PR 159 1050	Jul 67 Shwe+ 46 RES + NEG E RES. ISOT ASSGN	+
	2.1+2	4.0+3			Data EXFOR12065.002	Jun 76 . 6 RES. E0 FOR LA.	
	7.3−1	1.2+3			Data EXFOR12065.008	Jun 76 . 4 RES, E0,WT,WN,WG,PCS FOR LA139	
	2.4+2	1.7+6			Data EXFOR12065.	Jun 76 . 38 RES, E0 FOR LA139	
Reson Params		1.0+6	AUA	Theo	Jour AUJ 20 477	Oct 67 Cook. TBL OF AVG LVL SPACING D,L=0,1	
Reson Params	7.2+1		KFK	Eval	Rept KFK−718	Apr 68 Schmidt+ RESOLVED+AVG RES PARAM(S,P)	
Reson Params	7.2+1	3.1+4	SAC	Expt	Jour NP/A 123 561	Jan 69 Morgenstern+ WN,WN0 TO10KEV.MULTILVL	+
					Rept CEA−R−3609	Sep 68 − .(THESIS).DATA GIVEN	
					Conf 68Wash. 867	Mar 68 − +AVERAGE WG GIVEN	
					Conf 66Paris 1 559	Oct 66 Huynh+ ABST.NDG. SEE INDC−156	
					Conf 65Antwerp 525	Jul 65 De Barros+ PPR73.ABST.NDG	
					Jour JPR 24 997	Nov 63 Bianchi+ TOF 2.5NS/M. SUPERSEDED	
	7.2+1	3.1+4			Data EXFOR20684.020	Jul 77 166PTS.E0,J,L,G*WN.	
Reson Params	−1	+2	BNL	Expt	Prog WASH−1127 15	Apr 69 Chrien+ J,PI FOUND FROM N,G	
Reson Params	+3	+5	AUA	ExTh	Rept AAEC/E−198	May 69 Musgrove.RES PARS +STF FROM (NG)FIT	+
Reson Params	None		BNL	Comp	Conf 69Studsvik 627	Aug 69 Chrien. WG/WN, NG/DP − CORRELTN TBL	
Reson Params	2.0+5		MUA	Theo	Conf 69Roorke 2 129	Dec 69 Chaubey+ D/GAM−WIDTH RATIO, STATMOD	
Reson Params	7.2+1	1.0+4	KFK	Comp	Rept KFK−1233	Jul 70 Mueller. ES,WN,WG,G OF 31 RESON	
Reson Params	−		AUA	Theo	Rept AAEC/E−211	Nov 70 Musgrove. CALCULTD D+GAM WIDTH GIVEN	
Reson Params	7.6−1	7.3+1	CJD	Eval	Rept YK−7	71 Zakharova+ SURVEY+SYSTEMATICS,GW,TBL	
					Rept INDC(CCP)−27	Nov 72 .ENGLISH TRANSLATION OF YK−7 /71	
Reson Params	−1	+3	FEI	Eval	Rept YK−8/2 97	Sep 72 Abagyan+ AVG G−WID+D AT BINDNG−E,TBL	
					Rept INDC(CCP)−39	Jul 74 .PAGE 102.ENGLISH OF YK−8/2 97	
Reson Params	1.0+3	1.0+6	SAC	Eval	Rept CEA−N−1832	Dec 75 Ribon+ EXP+TH ANAL,RES PAR,TBL	
Reson Params	7.2+1	2.6+4	COL	Expt	Prog PR/C 13 1884	May 76 Hacken+TOF.TRNS,CAPT.RESPARS DRVD.	+
	7.2+1	2.6+4			Data EXFOR10579.	Aug 76 150RES ES.G*WN RED.D VAL GVN.	
Reson Params	7.2+1	3.7+4	COL	Expt	Prog WASH−1068 35	Mar 66 Garg+,TRNS,NDG,TBP	+
	7.2+1	3.7+4			Data EXFOR12068.002	Jun 76 . 102 RES. E0.	
Reson Params	7.5−1	2.1+1	ORL	Expt	Abst BAP 4 385	Aug 59 Harvey+ WG,WN.	+
	2.1+1				Data EXFOR12050.003	Jun 76 . 1 RES. E0 FOR LA.	
	7.5−1				Data EXFOR12050.005	Jun 76 . 1 RES. E0,WN,WG FOR LA139.	
Strnth Fnctn		4.0+4	LEB	Expt	Jour ZET 46 80	Jan 64 Konks.PB−SLOW−DOWN,VALUE GIVEN	
					Jour JET 19 59	Jul 64 TRANSLATN.*	
Strnth Fnctn	3.0+3	6.5+5	DKE	Expt	Abst DA/B 27 2085	Dec 66 Tabony.S,P,D STF FROM TRANSMISS DATA	+
		6.5+5		ExTh	Jour PL 13 70	Nov 64 Seth+S,P,D STF FRM SIG TOT 3−650KEV	
	5.0+3	1.5+5		Expt	Conf 64Paris 2 916	Jul 64 − +S0,S1,S2 R PRIME/R DUKE U.	
	3.0+3	6.5+5			Data EXFOR11665.021	Jun 76 . 3 PTS. STF.	
Strnth Fnctn	1.1+4		ANL	Expt	Jour PR 159 1050	Jul 67 Shwe+ S0=0.7+1.0−0.3.	+
	1.1+4				Data EXFOR12065.003	Jun 76 . 1 PT. S0.	
Strnth Fnctn	None		DKE	Expt	Abst DA/B 28 3834	Mar 68 Divadeenam.S,P,D WAVES.CFD POTMDLS.	
Strnth Fnctn	+3	+4	DUB	Expt	Jour YF 7 493	Mar 68 Konks+ UPPER LIMIT OF S2 ESTIMATED	
					Jour SNP 7 310	Sep 68 − + ENGL OF YF 7 493.	
Strnth Fnctn		1.0+4	SAC	Expt	Jour NP/A 123 561	Jan 69 Morgenstern+ S,WAVE,P WAVE UPPRLIMIT	+
					Rept CEA−R−3609	Sep 68 − .(THESIS).DATA GIVEN	
					Conf 68Wash. 867	Mar 68 − +	
	0.0+0	1.0+4			Data EXFOR20684.022	Jul 77 2PTS.	
Strnth Fnctn	+3	+5	AUA	ExTh	Rept AAEC/E−198	May 69 Musgrove.S+P+D STF FROM (NG)FIT,TBL	+
Strnth Fnctn	−		AUA	Theo	Rept AAEC/E−211	Nov 70 Musgrove. SMOOTHED S0,S1 AND S2 GIVN	
Strnth Fnctn	2.4+4		MUA	Theo	Jour IJP 46 114	Mar 72 Chaubey+ P−WAVE.FOR A−SYSTEMTIC,GRPH	
Strnth Fnctn	1.5+2	6.5+2	SAC	ExTh	Diss FRNC−TH−450	Oct 72 Delaroche.OPTICAL MODEL PARAMETERS	
Strnth Fnctn	None		AUA	Eval	Rept AAEC/E−277	Mar 73 Musgrove.TBLS EXPTL DATA+BEST VALUES	
Strnth Fnctn	1.0+3	6.0+5	NBS	Expt	Jour PR/C 9 28	Jan 74 Camarda.LINAC.TRANS. S1 MEASURED.	+
	1.0+3	6.0+5			Data EXFOR10765.010	Nov 78 . 1PT.S1=(0.5+−.4)−4	
Strnth Fnctn	None		KUR	Theo	Prog IAE−2560	75 Adamchuk+ .S0−VALUE,TBL	
Strnth Fnctn		+5	KFK	Theo	Conf JAERI−M−5984	Feb 75 Newstead.P230.TBL S0,S1 CFD EXP.	
Strnth Fnctn	6.0+3	2.6+4	COL	Expt	Jour PR/C 13 1884	May 76 Hacken+P−T DATA FIT.S0,S1 GVN.CURV.	
	6.0+3	2.6+4			Data EXFOR10579.005	Aug 76 2PTS.S0=.76+−.13 S1=.6+.3−.2	
Strnth Fnctn	2.7+3		MUN	Expt	Conf 71Albany 327	Aug 76 Dilg+TRNS.S0 STF GVN.31 ELEMENT GRPH	
Lvl Density	4.0+6	7.0+6	ISL	Theo	Conf 64Geneva § 511	May 64 Szwarcbaum+.T FROM 3 FORMLS CFD EXPS	

57 Lanthanum 139

Quantity	Energy (ev) Min	Energy (ev) Max	Lab	Type	Documentation Ref Vol Page	Date	Author, Comments	Data
Lvl Density	–		FEI	Eval	Rept FEI – 36	66	Kapchigashev+.TBL OF RELATD QUANTTYS	+
		5.0+4			Jour YF 4 686	Sep 66	.TABLE.SHORT VERSION OF FEI – 36	
	–				Prog YFI – 3 3	66	.ABSTRACT.TABLE LDL+NUCL.EXCIT.E	
		5.0+4			Jour SNP 4 486	67	.ENGLISH OF YF 4.FROM(N,GAMMA).TABLE	
					Prog INDC – E – 140 3	66	.ENGLISH TRANSL OF YFI – 3	
Lvl Density	+6		MIL	Theo	Jour EN 15 1 54	Jan 68	Facchini+ LDL PARS FROM LOW EN RES	
Lvl Density	5.0+6	7.0+6	ALD	Expt	Jour NP/A 112 337	May 68	Owens+.LVL DENS VERSUS EXCIT.MEAN T	+
					Conf 65Antwerp 547	Jul 65	– + PPR122. TBL FERMI GAS CONST.	
Lvl Density	–		CCP	Theo	Jour YF 7 1193	Jun 68	Shubin.CALC OKS EXPT,ROSENZWEIG – EFCT	
					Jour SNP 7 712	Dec 68	TRANSLATN.*	
Lvl Density	3.6+6	8.5+6	JAE	Expt	Jour NP/A 131 145	Jun 69	Maruyama. E DEPENDANCE,PARAM,TH FIT.	
Lvl Density	None		AUW	Theo	Conf 70Madurai 2 267	Dec 70	Ramamurty+ A – PARAMETER GVN,LANG'S – TH	
Lvl Density	1.4+7		IBJ	Expt	Rept INR – 1268	Jan 71	Jaskola+ ALFA SPCTR CFD TH,FULL PAPR	+
					Jour APPB 2 521	71	.SAME AS INR – 1268	
	1.4+7				Data EXFOR30158.005	Mar 71	LEVEL DENSITY PARAMETER OF CS136 GIV	
Lvl Density	None		MUN	Theo	Jour NP/A 217 269	Dec 73	Dilg+ A,DELTA. BACK SHIFTED FERMIGAS	
Lvl Density	None		COP	Theo	Jour NP/A 222 493	Apr 74	Dossing+COLL ROTAT.SPAC. ACCUR ESTIM	
Lvl Density	None		ROC	Theo	Jour NP/A 223 577	May 74	Huizenga+ EXP CFD MICROSC TH SPH NUC	
Lvl Density	–1	+3	FEI	Eval	Rept YK – 8/2 97	Sep 72	Abagyan+ LVL DENSITY PARAMETER,TBL	
					Rept INDC(CCP) – 39	Jul 74	.PAGE 102.ENGLISH OF YK – 8/2 97	
(γ,n)	+7		BSP	Revw	Conf 55Geneva 2 169	Aug 55	Souza – Santos+.P897,THRESHOLD VAL GVN	
(γ,n)	8.0+6	3.0+7	SAC	Expt	Jour NP/A 121 463	Dec 68	Bergere+LORENTZ LINE PARAM,GRPHS,TBL	
(γ,n)	9.0+6	2.4+7	SAC	Expt	Jour NP/A 172 426	Sep 71	Beil+LORENTZ LINE PARAM,GRAPHS,TBLS	

57 Lanthanum 140

Quantity	Energy (ev) Min	Energy (ev) Max	Lab	Type	Documentation Ref Vol Page	Date	Author, Comments	Data
Evaluation	1.0 – 3	1.5+7	AUA	Eval	Rept AAEC/TM – 549	Jun 70	Cook.TOT,EL,INEL,NONEL,CAPT SIGS,NDG	+
					Rept AAEC/E – 214	Jun 71	Bertram+GROUP SIGMAS SAME QUANTS.NDG	
					Rept AAEC/TM – 587	Mar 71	*DESCRIPTION OF LIBRARY	
	1.0 – 3	1.5+7			Data AUSTR – DFN 134.	Nov 71	POINT(223) AND GROUP(127) SIGMAS	
Total	1.0 – 3	1.5+7	AUA	Eval	Data AUSTR – DFN 134.	Nov 71	COOK+POINT(223)+GROUP(127)SIG.CF EVL	+
Elastic	1.0 – 3	1.5+7	AUA	Eval	Data AUSTR – DFN 134.	Nov 71	COOK+POINT(223)+GROUP(127)SIG.CF EVL	+
Tot Inelastc	5.0+5	1.5+7	AUA	Eval	Data AUSTR – DFN 134.	Nov 71	COOK+POINT(11)+GROUP(127)SIG.CF EVL	+
Nonelastic	1.0 – 3	1.5+7	AUA	Eval	Data AUSTR – DFN 134.	Nov 71	COOK+POINT(223)+GROUP(127)SIG.CF EVL	+
Absorption	2.5 – 2		IJI	Eval	Rept KIYAI – 76 – 6	76	Fedorova+ COMP(REFS,SIGS),EVAL.TABLE	
					Conf 75Kiev 1 169	May 75	– + EVAL SIG GIVEN,TABLE	
Res Int Abs	5.4 – 1		ORL	Expt	Jour JIN 29 584	May 67	Obrien+CD FILTER CFD OTHERS.	
					Jour NUC 25 2 41	Feb 67	+MAKING PURE CE141.	
	5.4 – 1				Data EXFOR10085.006	Apr 74	. 1 PT. RIA=69+ – 0.4B.	
Res Int Abs	5.5 – 1		CRC	Eval	Rept AECL – 3037 1	Jan 72	Walker.REDUCED RES INT,DETAILED TBL	
Res Int Abs	5.0 – 1		AUA	Eval	Rept AAEC/TM – 619	Sep 72	Clayton.CALC FROM SIG LIBRARY,TABLE	
Res Int Abs	5.5 – 1	+6	SAC	Revw	Conf IAEA – 169 1 235	74	Ribon.CAPTURE,STATUS CFD REQUEST,TBL	
Res Int Abs	+0	+5	WIN	Revw	Conf IAEA – 169 3 163	74	Pope+ DATA FILE CALC CFD XPTAL VALUE	
Res Int Abs	5.0 – 1		IJI	Eval	Rept KIYAI – 76 – 6	76	Fedorova+ EVAL CFD CALC.TBL RI,REFS	
					Conf 75Kiev 1 169	May 75	– + CALC+EVAL RI GIVEN,TABLE	
(n,γ)	2.5 – 2		LAS	Expt	Jour JCP 17 421	Apr 49	Katcoff+	+
(n,γ)	Maxwl		CRC	Eval	Rept AECL – 1054	Mar 60	Walker. (CRRP – 913).	
(n,γ)	Maxwl		ORL	Expt	Jour JIN 29 584	May 67	Obrien+ORNL REACTOR. CFD OTHERS.	
(n,γ)	Maxwl				Data EXFOR10085.	Apr 74	. 2 PTS. MEAS EFF.CS. THERMAL VALUE.	
(n,γ)	1.0 – 3	1.5+7	AUA	Eval	Data AUSTR – DFN 134.	Nov 71	COOK+POINT(223)+GROUP(127)SIG.CF EVL	+
(n,γ)	Maxwl		CRC	Eval	Rept AECL – 3037 1	Jan 72	Walker.RECOMMENDED SIG,DETAILED TBL	
(n,γ)	2.5 – 2		AUA	Eval	Rept AAEC/TM – 619	Sep 72	Clayton.CALC FROM SIG LIBRARY,TABLE	
(n,γ)	2.5 – 2		SAC	Revw	Conf IAEA – 169 1 235	74	Ribon.STATUS SIG CFD REQUESTS,TABLE	
(n,γ)	Maxwl Fiss		WIN	Revw	Conf IAEA – 169 3 163	74	Pope+ MAXW+FIS – SPEC AVG DATA CFD XPT	
	Fiss				Conf IAEA – 169 3 137	74	Dean. POINT DATA AVG OVER STAND SPEC	
Spect (n,γ)	–		CCP	Expt	Rept AEC – TR – 6449	63	Gritchenko. GAM SPEC,FISS PRODUCT	
Spect (n,γ)	Maxwl		LAS	Expt	Prog WASH – 1074 82	Apr 67	Jurney+ GE(LI) NAI SPECT. NDG.	
Reson Params	–		AUA	Theo	Rept AAEC/E – 211	Nov 70	Musgrove. CALCULTD D+GAM WIDTH GIVEN	
Strnth Fnctn	–		AUA	Theo	Rept AAEC/E – 211	Nov 70	Musgrove. SMOOTHED S0,S1 AND S2 GIVN	
Lvl Density	+6		MIL	Theo	Jour EN 15 1 54	Jan 68	Facchini+ LDL PARS FROM LOW EN RES	
Lvl Density	None		MUN	Theo	Jour NP/A 217 269	Dec 73	Dilg+ A,DELTA. BACK SHIFTED FERMIGAS	
Lvl Density	None		COP	Theo	Jour NP/A 222 493	Apr 74	Dossing+COLL ROTAT.SPAC. ACCUR ESTIM	
Lvl Density	None		ROC	Theo	Jour NP/A 223 577	May 74	Huizenga+ EXP CFD MICROSC TH SPH NUC	

57 Lanthanum 141

Quantity	Energy (ev) Min Max	Lab	Type	Documentation Ref Vol Page	Author, Comments Date	Data
Reson Params	–	AUA	Theo Rept	AAEC/E-211	Nov 70 Musgrove. CALCULTD D+GAM WIDTH GIVEN	
Strnth Fnctn	–	AUA	Theo Rept	AAEC/E-211	Nov 70 Musgrove. SMOOTHED S0,S1 AND S2 GIVN	

57 Lanthanum 142

Quantity	Energy (ev) Min Max	Lab	Type	Documentation Ref Vol Page	Author, Comments Date	Data
Reson Params	–	AUA	Theo Rept	AAEC/E-211	Nov 70 Musgrove. CALCULTD D+GAM WIDTH GIVEN	
Strnth Fnctn	–	AUA	Theo Rept	AAEC/E-211	Nov 70 Musgrove. SMOOTHED S0,S1 AND S2 GIVN	

57 Lanthanum 143

Quantity	Energy (ev) Min Max	Lab	Type	Documentation Ref Vol Page	Author, Comments Date	Data
Reson Params	–	AUA	Theo Rept	AAEC/E-211	Nov 70 Musgrove. CALCULTD D+GAM WIDTH GIVEN	
Strnth Fnctn	–	AUA	Theo Rept	AAEC/E-211	Nov 70 Musgrove. SMOOTHED S0,S1 AND S2 GIVN	

57 Lanthanum 144

Quantity	Energy (ev) Min Max	Lab	Type	Documentation Ref Vol Page	Author, Comments Date	Data
Spect (n,γ)	Spont Spont	GRE	Expt Rept Data	CEA-R-4563 EXFOR20511.002	Apr 74 Monnand+ GE(LI) Apr 76 10PTS.	+

58 Cerium

Quantity	Energy (ev) Min	Max	Lab	Type	Documentation Ref Vol Page	Author, Comments Date	Data
Evaluation	5.0+5	1.5+7	LRL Eval	Rept	UCRL-5351	Nov 58 Howerton.CURVES	
Total	Maxwl		COL Expt	Jour	PR 48 265	Aug 35 Dunning+ IONCH,TRANS,RA-BE/PARAFIN	N
Total	1.2+2	3.0+2	ANL Expt	Jour	PR 76 100	Jul 49 Hibdon+1/10 ERSLN TRN MN CO SCAT DET	+
	1.2+2	3.0+2		Data	EXFOR11261.029	Jun 76 . 2 PTS. SIG	
Total	5.0+3	3.2+6	WIS Expt	Jour	PR 88 83	Oct 52 Miller+20KEVSPREAD TRNSM	+
	5.0+3	3.2+6		Data	EXFOR11712.018	Jun 76 . 90 PTS. SIGMA	
Total	1.4+7		LAS Expt	Jour	PR 88 562	Nov 52 Coon+ SIGMA=5.08+-0.10 B.	+
	1.4+7			Data	EXFOR11056.046	Jun 76 . 1 PT. SIGMA	
Total	4.6+0	1.9+2	BNL Expt	Priv	CARTER	Mar 55 Carter.	+
	4.6+0	1.9+2		Data	EXFOR11897.003	Jun 76 . 38 PTS. SIG	
Total	2.9+0	3.4+1	HAR Expt	Priv	EGELSTAFF4	Jun 55 Egelstaff. CHOPPER.	+
Total	5.0+3	5.5+4	DKE Expt	Jour	PR 102 1580	Jun 56 Newson+ ABS CURV ISOTOPIC ASSIGNMENT	+
	5.0+3	1.2+5		Abst	PR 98 1162	May 55 - .ABSTRACT HA10 RES ES GIVEN	
	5.0+3	5.5+4		Data	EXFOR11834.008	Jun 76 . 86 PTS. SIGMA	
Total	1.0+3	3.2+4	HAR Expt	Jour	PPSA 70 51	Jan 57 Gayther+ FC THICK SAMPLE,AVSIG CF TH	
Total	1.3+7	1.6+7	LAS Expt	Jour	PR 109 1268	Feb 58 Conner.TRNS SC 3ES 4.99 5.01 5.00B	+
				Conf	58Geneva 15 11	Sep 58 Coon+ PPR666,SIGMA AT 3ES GVN,TOF	
	1.3+7	1.6+7		Data	EXFOR11320.007	Jun 76 . 3 PTS. SIGMA	
Total	1.8+7	2.8+7	LRL Expt	Jour	PR 120 521	Oct 60 Peterson+ TRANS 4ES CURV CFD OPTMDL	+
	1.8+7	2.8+7		Data	EXFOR11108.033	Jun 76 . 4 PTS. SIGMA	
Total	1.0+6		ANL Theo	Jour	PR 124 826	Nov 61 Sokoloff.HARMONIC OSCILLAT POT CURVE	
Total	1.2+6	1.8+6	STF Expt	Jour	PR 131 1644	Aug 63 Wells+ CURVE GIVEN	+
	1.2+6	1.8+6		Data	EXFOR11121.018	Jun 76 . 24 PTS. SIGMA	
Total	3.2+6	5.2+6	JNE Expt	Jour	ARS 64 63	Feb 68 Manero.30KEV RESOL,2.4PC,OXIDE TGT	+
	3.3+6	5.2+6		Data	EXFOR20170.004	May 74 67PTS.	
Total	2.5+6	1.5+7	BNW Expt	Jour	PR/C 3 576	Feb 71 Foster+ TRANS,CURVS,CFD OTHERS+TH	+
				Jour	NIM 36 1	Sep 65 .EXPT DETAILS	
	2.3+6	1.5+7		Data	EXFOR10047.062	Aug 73 . 254PTS.	
Total	1.4+7		KOS Expt	Jour	AHP 30 115	Oct 71 Angeli+EXPT,DATA TABLE,LITER. SURVEY	+
	1.4+7			Data	EXFOR30141.014	Jan 72 SIGMA AT 14.7 MEV GIVEN	
Total	2.7+3		MUN Expt	Prog	EANDC(E)150U	Oct 72 Dilg+ AVERAGE TOT XSECT+S0	+
				Conf	71Albany 327	Aug 71 - +TRNS.AVG CS GVN.31 ELEMENT GRP	
	2.7+3			Data	EXFOR20583.013	Jun 76 1PNT.	
Total	1.3+7	1.5+7	DEB Eval	Rept	IAEA-153 173	73 Boedy+ MOST PROBABLE VAL OF SIG,TBL	
Total	1.0+6	2.0+6	DAC Eval	Jour	NSPB 6 59	Oct 73 Enayetullah+ SIG(E),LSQ-FIT,TBL+GRPH	+
			Theo	Jour	NP/A 209 202	Jul 73 Islam+ FLUCTUATION ANALYSIS,OWN DATA	
			Expt	Jour	NP/A 209 189	Jul 73 - + VDG,TRANS,CFD OPTICAL MODEL	
			Comp	Rept	AECD/EP-18	Dec 70 Ameen+ EXPTL DATA FROM DAC,TABLES	
	1.0+6	2.0+6		Expt	EXFOR30134.005	Nov 71 SIGMA-TOT AT 100 ES,PRIVATE COMM.	
Total	1.4+5	6.3+5	DKE Expt	Jour	AP 84 165	May 74 Pineo+TRNS.AVG CS.TBL GRPHS.OPTMDL	+
	1.0+5	6.5+5		Abst	DA/B 31 6821	May 71 - .2E RANGES.CFD OPTMDL.	
	1.5+4	6.0+5		Diss	PINEO	70 .AVG CS.GRPHS.CFD.STF CALC.TBL.CFD.	
	1.5+4	6.0+5		Data	EXFOR10542.013	Jan 79 . DATA UNOBTAINABLE FROM AUTHORS.	
Total	7.0+5	9.0+6	GLS Expt	Jour	JP/A 7 1758	Sep 74 Kellie+TOF.LINAC.CFD OPTMDL.GRPH.	+
	7.0+5	9.0+6		Data	EXFOR20418.003	Sep 75 642PTS.	
Total	1.0+6	1.9+7	RAM Expt	Jour	NSPB 9 73	Oct 76 Molla+ VDG. SIG(E)FIG,CFD OTH+OPTMOD	
Elastic	2.5-2		ORL Expt	Jour	PR 91 597	Aug 53 Koehler+ COH.SCAT.=2.7+-0.2 BARNS	+
	2.5-2			Data	EXFOR12060.	Jun 76 . 2 PTS. COH, COH AMP	
Elastic	1.0+6		WIS Expt	Jour	PR 93 1062	Mar 54 Walt. FROM ANG. DIST.	
	1.0+6			Data	EXFOR11637.056	Jun 76 . 1 PT. SIGMA	
Elastic	7.3-2		ANL Expt	Jour	JCP 35 1950	Dec 61 Atoji. FROM NEUTRON DIFF. STUDIES	+
	7.3-2			Data	EXFOR11606.005	Jun 76 . 1 PT. COH. AMP.	
Elastic	1.0+6		ALD Expt	Jour	NP 42 86	Apr 63 Gilboy+ .SIG=6.85B+-3PC	
Elastic	6.8+5	1.1+6	ANL Expt	Prog	ANL-7210 3	Dec 66 Cox.CURVE 50-KEV STEPS	
Elastic	8.8+5		ANL Expt	Rept	ANL-7935	Jun 72 COX+ 4 PI B(O)	+
	8.8+5			Data	EXFOR10332.114	Jun 74 . 1 PT.	
Diff Elastic	1.0+6		WIS Expt	Jour	PR 93 1062	Mar 54 Walt+ HE COUNTER 30-150DEG LAB CURVE	+
	1.0+6			Data	EXFOR11637.058	Jun 76 . 9 PTS. DSIGMA	
Diff Elastic	5.0+5	1.6+6	WIS Expt	Jour	PR 100 1315	Dec 55 Darden+ ALSO1MEV100KEVRSLN CF OPTMDL	+
	5.0+5	1.6+6		Data	EXFOR11638.008	Jun 76 . 8 PTS. DSIGMA	
Diff Elastic	1.0+6		ANL Theo	Jour	PR 124 826	Nov 61 Sokoloff.HARM OSC POT CFD EXPT CURVE	
Diff Elastic	5.0+6	7.0+6	LAS Expt	Jour	PR 129 1649	Feb 63 Thomson. SIG AT 90DEG	+
	5.0+6	7.0+6		Data	EXFOR11495.040	Jun 76 . 2 PTS. DSIGMA	
Diff Elastic	1.0+6		ALD Expt	Jour	NP 42 86	Apr 63 Gilboy+30TO137DEG.COMP.WITH OPTICMOD	
Diff Elastic	1.2+6	2.0+6	STF Expt	Jour	PR 131 1644	Aug 63 Wells+ THRS EFFECTS CURVES AT10ANGLS	+
	1.2+6	2.0+6		Data	EXFOR11121.019	Jun 76 . 226 PTS. DSIGMA AT 226ES	
	1.2+6	2.0+6		Data	EXFOR11121.020	Jun 76 . 305 PTS. DSIGMA AT 34ES	

58 Cerium

Quantity	Energy (ev) Min	Max	Lab	Type	Documentation Ref Vol Page	Date	Author, Comments	Data
Diff Elastic	1.0+6		LAS	Theo Prog	WASH-1064 84	Oct 65	Rosen+ OPTMDL CPD ELST CFD WIS XPT	
Diff Elastic	5.0+6		DKE	Expt Jour	ZP 196 103	Sep 66	Buccino+ 20-140DEG,CFD OPTMOD. TABLE	+
				Abst	DA 24 4248	Apr 64	- .CFD OPTMDL CALCS	
	5.0+6			Data	EXFOR11877.006	Jun 76	. 13 PTS. DSIGMA	
Diff Elastic	6.8+5	1.1+6	ANL	Expt Prog	ANL-7210 3	Dec 66	Cox.50KEV AVG,LEG COEF VS N-E,GRAPH	+
	6.8+5	1.1+6		Data	EXFOR11519.013	Jun 76	. 408 PTS. DSIGMA	
Diff Elastic	3.2+6		BCM	Expt Jour	NP 89 154	Dec 66	Becker+ 12 ANGLES GRAPH CFD OPTMDL	
	3.2+6			Data	EXFOR11511.030	Jun 76	. 12 PTS. DSIGMA	
Diff Elastic	4.4+6	5.5+6	WIS	ExTh Jour	NP/A 95 193	Mar 67	Mahajan.POLARIZATION OPTMDL ANALYSIS	
				Abst	DA/B 28 1093	Sep 67	.SEE ALSO	
Diff Elastic	3.2+6	5.0+6	SCU	Theo Rept	ICD-6 236	69	Averyanov+CALC ANGDIST CFD EXPT,GRPH	
Diff Elastic	8.8+5		ANL	Expt Rept	ANL-7935	Jun 72	COX+ CFD OPTMOD,HAUSER-FESHBACH	+
	8.8+5			Data	EXFOR10332.024	Jun 74	. 8 PTS.	
Polarization	3.8+5	9.8+5	WIS	ExTh Jour	NP 6 177	Mar 58	Clement+ POLARIZATION. CFD OPT MDL	
				Expt Rept	AECU-3628	57	- + LI7(P,N) SOURCE. 3ANGLES.	
Polarization	8.7+5		ANL	Expt Rept	ANL-7935	Jun 72	COX+ CFD OPTMOD,HAUSER-FESHBACH	+
	8.7+5			Data	EXFOR10332.058	Jun 74	.8 PTS.	
Potntal Scat	+4		HAR	Expt Jour	PPSA 70 51	Jan 57	Gayther+ FROM AVG SIGTOT. FC TRANSM	
Potntal Scat	3.0+3	6.5+5	DKE	Expt Jour	AP 84 165	May 74	Pineo+TRNS.S WAVE SCT LENGTH.TBL.CFD	
				Abst	DA/B 31 6821	May 71	.THESIS ABST.	
				Diss	PINEO	70	.TBL.GRPHS.CFD TO 3 COLLECTIVE MDLS.	
Tot Inelastc	5.0+6	7.0+6	ALD	Expt Jour	NP/A 112 337	May 68	Owens+.3ES.FROM N SPECT 90DEG.	+
Diff Inelast	5.0+6	7.0+6	LAS	Expt Jour	PR 129 1649	Feb 63	Thomson+ 90DEG TEMP FOR NS TO 5MEV	+
	5.0+6	7.0+6		Data	EXFOR11495.042	Jun 76	. 2 PTS. SIGMA	
	5.0+6	7.0+6		Data	EXFOR11495.039	Jun 76	. 4 PTS. DSIGMA	
Diff Inelast	1.4+7		BAS	Expt Jour	PL 5 202	Jul 63	Huber+ GRAPH OF INELASTIC N SPECTRUM	
				Jour	HPA 36 1059	Dec 59	- +.T=0.90MEV	
Diff Inelast	1.4+7		FEI	Expt Jour	YF 4 1154	Dec 66	Sal'Nikow+ SPEC OF SECNDARY NS,CURVE	+
				Rept	FEI-39	Jan 66	Sal'Nikov+TOF SPECT,RING GEOM,E-SPEC	
				Prog	YFI-2 11	66	.ABSTRACT	
				Rept	FEI-30	Dec 65	.SAME CURVE,SIMILAR TEXT AS YF 4	
				Jour	SNP 4 831	Jun 67	.ENGLISH TRANSL OF YF 4 1154 12/66	
				Prog	INDSWG-126E 10	66	.ABSTRACT.ENGLISH TRANSL OF YFI-2	
	1.4+7			Data	EXFOR40134.014	Feb 73	N-SPECTRUM AT 92 DEG, 50EN'	
Diff Inelast	3.5+6	8.5+6	JAE	Expt Prog	EANDC(J)8L25	Jan 68	Maruyama+.TOF.CONTIN SPECT AT 90DEG	+
	3.6+6	8.5+6		Jour	NP/A 131 145	Jun 69	- . E DEPENDENCE,PARAM,TH FIT	
	3.5+6	8.5+6		Conf	67Tokyo 373	Sep 67	- + PPR8.127. ABST.	
Diff Inelast	5.0+6	7.0+6	ALD	Expt Jour	NP/A 112 337	May 68	Owens+.3ES.FROM N SPECT 90DEG NDG.	+
				Conf	65Antwerp 547	Jul 65	- + PPR122.ABST.SPECT N' AT 90DEG	
Diff Inelast	1.5+7		TNC	Expt Jour	PR 186 1038	Oct 69	Mathur+TOF,DIST INEL SCT NEUTS	
				Rept	NDL-TR-86	Jan 67	- +TBLS.ANG=90DEG.EXPT DETAILS	
	1.5+7			Data	EXFOR10043.	Jun 72	11PTS.D/DA	
Diff Inelast	1.4+7		KFI	Theo Rept	KFKI-72-17	Feb 72	Kluge+ CALC N-SPEC INEL+N2N,TBL,GRPH	
Thermal Scat	Cold		ORL	Revw Jour	JAP 36 1078	Mar 65	Koehler.MAG. PROPS FROM N DIFFR XPTS	
Thermal Scat	7.7-2		BKB	Expt Jour	ACR 20 315	Feb 66	N DIFFRACTION SAM=.75+-.02CM-12	
Thermal Scat	2.0-4	1.5-1	BSP	ExTh Jour	JCP 48 520	Jan 68	Mattos.TRIVALENT ION PARAMAG SIG	+
Thermal Scat	1.0-4	1.0+3	MUN	Revw Jour	EEN 80 1	77	Koester. SCAT LENGTH	
Scattering	2.5-2		ORL	Expt Jour	PR 91 597	Aug 53	Koehler+ TRANS 2.7+-0.2B	+
	2.5-2			Data	EXFOR12060.007	Jun 76	. 1 PT. SIGMA	
Scattering	2.5-2		IFU	Expt Conf	70Helsinki 1 651	Jun 70	Vertebnij+ 2200M/SEC SIGMA GIVEN,TBL	
				Rept	BNL-TR-495	Jul 72	. ENGLISH OF 70HELSIN 1 651	
Nonelastic	1.0+6		WIS	Expt Jour	PR 93 1062	Mar 54	Walt.	+
	1.0+6			Data	EXFOR11637.057	Jun 76	. 1 PT. SIGMA	
Nonelastic	1.5+7		BOS	Expt Jour	PR 161 1181	Sep 67	Chatterjee+ SPHERE .2.03+-.08B	+
	1.5+7			Data	EXFOR30337.008	Jun 76	1 PNT	
Absorption	Pile		HAR	Expt Jour	PPSA 63 1175	Oct 50	Colmer+LITTLER.PILE OSC REL HAR B	
				Rept	AERE-N/R-527	Jun 50	- + PILE OSC.	
Res Int Abs	-		CCP	Expt Jour	AE 3 507	Dec 57	Klimentov+.EPI CD REACTIVITY REL LI	+
				Jour	JNE 9 20	Jun 59	TRANSLATN.*	
				Jour	SJA 3 1387	57	TRANSLATN.*	
Res Int Abs	-		SAC	Revw Conf	64Geneva § 102	May 64	Carre+CF CALC VAL+EXP BY TATTERSAL	
(n,γ)	Pile		ANL	Expt Jour	PR 80 342	Nov 50	Harris+ PILE OSC.REL TO BORON.APPROX	+
	Pile			Data	EXFOR11528.036	Jun 76	. 1 PT. SIGMA	
(n,γ)	Maxwl		ORL	Expt Jour	PR 83 641	Aug 51	Pomerance.LOCAL OSC REL AU ABS 95 B	+
	Maxwl			Data	EXFOR11047.064	Jun 76	. 1 PT. SIGMA	
(n,γ)	4.0+5		LAS	Expt Jour	PR 120 556	Oct 60	Diven.SC-T.	+
	4.0+5			Data	EXFOR11616.023	Jun 76	. 1 PT. SIGMA	

58 Cerium

Quantity	Energy (ev) Min	Max	Lab	Type	Documentation Ref Vol Page	Date	Author, Comments	Data
(n,γ)	3.0+4	6.5+4	ORL Expt	Jour	PR 122 182	Apr 61	Gibbons+	+
				Jour	PR 129 2695	Mar 63	Macklin+ LIQ SCINT,35+ − 5,8+ − 2MB	
				Conf	61Vienna 1 95	Aug 61	Neiler.	
	3.0+4	6.5+4		Data	EXFOR11329.039	Jun 76	. 2 PTS. SIGMA	
(n,γ)	1.0+4	2.0+5	KFK Expt	Jour	NP/A 141 602	Jan 70	Kompe+ VDG.REL TO AU.ALSO MAXWELL AV	
				Rept	KFK − 1165	Feb 70	− + EQU TO NP/A 141 602	
(n,γ)	3.0+4		AUA Theo	Rept	AAEC/E − 211	Nov 70	Musgrove. SIGMA GIVEN AND CFD OTHER	
(n,γ)	1.5+6		LND Expt		EANDC(OR)115L	Jul 72	Bergqvist+	
(n,γ)	1.4+7		BOR Expt	Conf	72Budapest 220	Aug 72	Rigaud+INTEGRATD SIG FROM SPEC,GRPH	+
				Jour	NP/A 176 545	Dec 71	− + INTEGRATED FROM NG SPECTRUM	
				Jour	JPRS 32 10 231	Oct 71	Irigaray+COLL.5B,MEAS.G.SPC.WITH INA	
	1.4+7			Data	EXFOR20533.004	Apr 76	1PNT.SIGMA.	
(n,γ)	1.0+3	1.0+7	FEI Eval	Rept	YK − 8/2 97	Sep 72	Abagjan+ AVG SIG(ENERGY − GROUPS),TABL	
				Rept	INDC(CCP) − 39	Jul 74	.P102. ENGLISH OF YK − 8/2 97	
Spect (n,γ)	None		BNL Expt	Prog	WASH − 1124 14	Nov 68	Chrien+ NDG TO BE COMPLETED	
Spect (n,γ)	Maxwl		AUW Expt	Prog	BARC − 401 28	69	Chintalapudi+,E − GAMMA BELOW 900 KEV.	
Spect (n,γ)	2.5−2		MIT Comp	Rept	MITNE − 85	Jan 69	Rasmussen+TBL G INT.=AFCRL − 69 − 0071	
Spect (n,γ)	1.4+7		BOR Expt	Conf	72Budapest 220	Aug 72	Rigaud+ TOF,NDG	
				Jour	NP/A 176 545	Dec 71	− + TOF. E(GAMMA)=14 TO 22 MEV.	
Inelastic γ	3.0+6	4.5+6	FEI Comp	Rept	ICD − 4 57	67	Sluchevskaja.SELECTIV COMPIL ,TABLE	
Inelastic γ	5.0+6	7.0+6	ALD Expt	Jour	NP/A 112 337	May 68	Owens+.3ES.TOF SPECT 90 DEG. NDG.	+
Inelastic γ	2.8+6		NRD Expt	Prog	WASH − 1127 158	Apr 69	Engesser+ TO BE COMPLETED,NO DATA	
Inelastic γ	3.0+6	4.5+6	TNC Expt	Rept	ORO − 2791 − 32	Feb 71	Buchanan+ 90 − DEG SIGS FOR 4NEUT ES	
	4.0+6	1.5+6		Prog	ORO − 2791 − 19 66	Aug 66	Morgan+ 2ES. GAMMA SPECT.55DEG.CRVS	
Nonelastic γ	3.2+6		NRL Expt	Jour	PR 96 386	Oct 54	Scherrer+ C − W+CRYST SPEC 4 PEAKS	
Nonelastic γ	1.4+7		LRL Expt	Rept	UCRL − 7440	Jul 63	Chazan+ TOT G PROD.CURVES ROUGH,P2ME	
(n,2n)	1.4+7		KFI Theo	Rept	KFKI − 72 − 17	Feb 72	Kluge+ CALC N − SPEC INEL+N2N,TBL,GRPH	
(n,2n)	1.5+7		DEB Eval	Jour	REA 11 1 153	Mar 73	Boedy+ RECOMM.VALUE FROM N − Z SYSTEM.	
n Emission	1.5+7		TNC Expt	Jour	PR 186 1038	69	Mathur+TOF.90DEG.MULTISCT CORRC.	+
				Rept	NDL − TR − 86	Jan 67	− +EXPT+MULTISCAT CORRC DETAILS.	
	1.5+7			Data	EXFOR10090.020	May 73	2PTS.NEM CS=154.10,173.14 MB/SR.	
(n,p)	4.5+6	1.5+7	UPP Expt	Prog	KDK − 12 32	Apr 76	Lindholm+.	
Reson Params	3.0+0	1.0+3	IFU Expt	Conf	69Erevan	Feb 69	Vertebnij+.ABST,LVL DENS ISOT DEPEND	
Strnth Fnctn	8.0+0	2.3+5	WIS Expt	Jour	PR 99 748	Aug 55	Darden. TRANSM STRENGTH FN DATA	
Strnth Fnctn	3.0+3	6.5+5	DKE Expt	Abst	DA/B 31 6821	May 71	Pineo.S,P,D WAVE.THESIS ABST	
Strnth Fnctn	2.7+3		MUN Expt	Conf	71Albany 327	Aug 76	Dilg+TRNS.S0 STF GVN.31 ELEMENT GRPH	
Lvl Density	1.4+7		BAS Expt	Jour	PL 5 202	Jul 63	Huber+TBL OF NUC TEMP AND LVL DENSTY	
				Jour	HPA 36 1059	Dec 63	Plattner+TOF TBL12ELEM.CFD TH	
Lvl Density	4.0+6	6.5+6	DKE Expt	Abst	DA 24 4248	Apr 64	Buccino.ANG DIST.TOF.NUCL T.LVL DEN	
Lvl Density	1.4+7		FEI Expt	Rept	FEI − 30	Dec 65	Anufrienko+.PARAMS FROM NONELASTIC	+
Lvl Density	5.0+6	7.0+6	ALD Expt	Jour	NP/A 112 337	May 68	Owens+.LVL DENS VERSUS EXCIT.MEAN T	+
				Conf	65Antwerp 547	Jul 65	− + PPR122. TBL FERMI GAS CONST.	
Lvl Density	3.6+6	8.5+6	JAE Expt	Jour	NP/A 131 145	Jun 69	Maruyama. E DEPENDANCE,PARAM,TH FIT.	+
				Conf	67Tokyo 373	Sep 67	− + PPR8.127. ABST.	
Lvl Density	1.5+7		TNC Expt	Jour	PR 186 1038	Oct 69	Mathur+ FERMI GAS LVL DENSITY COEF	+
				Rept	NDL − TR − 86	Jan 67	− +EXPT+MULTISCAT CORRC DETAILS.	
	1.5+7			Data	EXFOR10090.036	May 73	2PTS.NUCLEAR T=.85,.35 MEV.	
Lvl Density	None		FEI Theo	Jour	YF 11 1213	Jun 70	Ignatyuk+ SPIN DEPENDENCE OF DENSITY	
				Jour	SNP 11 674	Dec 70	. ENGL OF YF 11 1213	
Lvl Density	1.4+7		BAS Expt	Jour	HPA 44 487	Jul 71	Schacher+ LVL DENS NUCL TEMP TOF	
				Diss	SCHACHER	Dec 70	− . LVL DENSITY FROM N2N+N,N'	
(γ,n)	5.0+6	3.5+7	SAC Expt	Jour	NP/A 133 417	Aug 69	Bergere+LORENTZ LINE PARAM,GRPHS,TBL	
(γ,n)	9.0+6	2.4+7	SAC Expt	Jour	NP/A 172 426	Sep 71	Beil+LORENTZ LINE PARAM,GRAPHS,TBLS	

58 Cerium 131

Quantity	Energy (ev) Min	Max	Lab	Type	Documentation Ref Vol Page	Date	Author, Comments	Data
Reson Params	−		AUA Theo	Rept	AAEC/E − 211	Nov 70	Musgrove. CALCULTD D+GAM WIDTH GIVEN	
Strnth Fnctn	−		AUA Theo	Rept	AAEC/E − 211	Nov 70	Musgrove. SMOOTHED S0,S1 AND S2 GIVN	

58 Cerium 132

Quantity	Energy (ev) Min	Max	Lab	Type	Documentation Ref Vol Page	Date	Author, Comments	Data
Reson Params	−		AUA Theo	Rept	AAEC/E − 211	Nov 70	Musgrove. CALCULTD D+GAM WIDTH GIVEN	
Strnth Fnctn	−		AUA Theo	Rept	AAEC/E − 211	Nov 70	Musgrove. SMOOTHED S0,S1 AND S2 GIVN	

58 Cerium 134

Quantity	Energy (ev) Min	Energy (ev) Max	Lab	Type	Documentation Ref Vol Page	Author, Comments Date	Data
(n,p)	Maxwl		IFU	Theo Rept	ICD-4 20	67 Dadakina+ PENETR COEFF CALC,TABLE	
Reson Params	-		AUA	Theo Rept	AAEC/E-211	Nov 70 Musgrove. CALCULTD D+GAM WIDTH GIVEN	
Strnth Fnctn	-		AUA	Theo Rept	AAEC/E-211	Nov 70 Musgrove. SMOOTHED S0,S1 AND S2 GIVN	
Lvl Density	-3	+0	IFU	Theo Jour	UFZ 13 700	Apr 68 Pisanko+ LEVEL SPACING CALC,TBL	
				Jour	UPJ 13 498	Oct 68 TRANSLATN.*	

58 Cerium 135

Quantity	Energy (ev) Min	Energy (ev) Max	Lab	Type	Documentation Ref Vol Page	Author, Comments Date	Data
Reson Params	-		AUA	Theo Rept	AAEC/E-211	Nov 70 Musgrove. CALCULTD D+GAM WIDTH GIVEN	
Strnth Fnctn	-		AUA	Theo Rept	AAEC/E-211	Nov 70 Musgrove. SMOOTHED S0,S1 AND S2 GIVN	

58 Cerium 136

Quantity	Energy (ev) Min	Energy (ev) Max	Lab	Type	Documentation Ref Vol Page	Author, Comments Date	Data
Absorption	2.5-2		IJI	Eval Rept	KIYAI-76-6	76 Fedorova+ COMP(REFS,SIGS),EVAL.TABLE	
				Conf	75Kiev 1 169	May 75 - + EVAL SIGS OF 3ISOMERS,TABL	
Res Int Abs	5.0-1		IJI	Eval Rept	KIYAI-76-6	76 Fedorova+ CALC FROM BNL-325 RESPARS	
				Conf	75Kiev 1 169	May 75 - + RI CALC FROM RESPARS,TABLE	
(n,γ)	Maxwl		ORL	Expt Jour	PR 88 412	Oct 52 Pomerance.PILE OSC.ESTIM.ERROR 100PC	+
	Maxwl			Data	EXFOR11507.073	Jun 76 . 1 PT. SIGMA	
(n,γ)	Pile		ORL	Expt Jour	PR 103 917	Aug 56 Brosi+ (N,G),(N,G)M SIGMAS GVN	+
	Pile			Data	EXFOR12062.	Jun 76 . 2 PT. SIGMA FOR GND + META	
(n,γ)	None		ANL	Theo Jour	PR 120 1305	Nov 60 Huizenga+ ISOMER RATIO,TH CFD EXPT	
(n,γ)	Maxwl		MTR	Expt Jour	PR 129 769	Jan 63 Keish. RATIO ISOMER ACT TO GND ACT.	+
	Maxwl			Data	EXFOR11748.019	Jun 76 . 1 PT. ISOMER RATIO	
(n,γ)	Maxwl		ANL	Comp Jour	NP 60 241	Nov 64 Bishop+EXP AND TH ISOMER RATIOS CFD	
(n,γ)	-		IEA	Comp Rept	IEA-INF- 10	Aug 68 Atalla. TABLES OF HL,SIG AND GAMM-E	
(n,γ)	1.0+3	1.0+7	BOL	Eval Rept	CCDN-NW/10	Dec 69 Benzi+H-F MOD,AXEL G(G)EST,ALL DATA	
				Rept	CEC(70)-2	Apr 70 - +. GRAPH	
(n,γ)	3.0+4		AUA	Theo Rept	AAEC/E-211	Nov 70 Musgrove. SIGMA GIVEN AND CFD OTHER	
(n,γ)	Maxwl	Fiss	WIN	Revw Conf	IAEA-169 3 163	74 Pope+ FIS-SPEC AVG DATA CFD MAXW-XPT	
(n,γ)	1.0+3	1.0+7	FEI	Eval Rept	YK- 8/2 97	Sep 72 Abagjan+ AVG SIG(ENERGY-GROUPS),TABL	
				Rept	INDC(CCP)-39	Jul 74 .P102. ENGLISH OF YK-8/2 97	
(n,γ)	2.5-2		BRK	Theo Jour	NP/A 237 3 419	Jan 75 Nardi+ ISOM RATIO,MTE-CARLO,CFD XPT	
Spect (n,γ)	Pile		KUR	Expt Conf	69Erevan	Feb 69 Groshev+ ABSTR,GE-DETECTOR	
(n,2n)	Fiss		CRC	Eval Rept	CRC-1003	Dec 60 ROY+ ESTIMATED AVG SIG=0.3MB	
(n,2n)	1.4+7		LYO	Comp Rept	LYCEN/6780	Nov 67 Crouzet+COMPILATN FOR ACTIVTN ANALYS	
(n,2n)	1.4+7		GIT	Expt Jour	PR/C 1 350	Jan 70 Fink+ ACTIVATION,SIG=1318+- 90MB	+
	1.4+7			Data	EXFOR10497.040	Apr 76 1PT.CS=1318+- 90MB.	
(n,2n)	1.4+7	1.5+7	JYV	Eval Rept	JU-RR-3/1970	Jun 70 Leppaemaeki+ TABLE OF EVAL AVG SIG	
(n,2n)	+7		KFI	Expt Rept	KFKI-71-8	Feb 71 Jeki. CALCULATED CFD EXPTL SIG VALUE	
(n,2n)	1.4+7		GIT	Theo Jour	PR/C 4 1173	Oct 71 Fink+ STAT -MODEL CALCULATION,CFD EX	
(n,2n)	1.5+7		ARK	Expt Abst	DA/B 32 5091	Mar 72 Bari. GE(LI) DET. ACT. SIG GIVEN	+
	1.5+7			Data	EXFOR10431.041	Aug 75 1PT,SIGMA	
(n,2n)	1.5+7		DEB	Eval Jour	REA 11 1 153	Mar 73 Boedy. COMPILATION+RECOMM.VALUE,TBL	
				Rept	IAEA-153 173	73 - . RECOMM. VALUE ONLY	
(n,2n)	1.5+7		TAT	Theo Jour	JP/A 7 1458	Aug 74 Kondaiah. CALC ON STAT MODEL	
(n,2n)	1.5+7		JUL	Expt Jour	NP/A 224 319	May 74 Qaim. ACT.GE(LI)	+
				Jour	RRL 25 335	May 76 - + SIG IN GRPH. SYST VS (N-Z)/A	
	1.5+7			Data	EXFOR20541.002	Apr 76 1PNT.SIGMA.	
(n,p)	Fiss		CRC	Eval Rept	CRC-1003	Dec 60 ROY+ ESTIMATED AVG SIG=2.6MB	
(n,p)	Maxwl		IFU	Theo Rept	ICD-4 20	67 Dadakina+ PENETR COEFF CALC,TABLE	
(n,p)	1.4+7		LYO	Comp Rept	LYCEN/6780	Nov 67 Crouzet+COMPILATN FOR ACTIVTN ANALYS	
(n,α)	Fiss		CRC	Eval Rept	CRC-1003	Dec 60 ROY+ ESTIMATED AVG SIG=0.032MB	
(n,α)	1.4+7		LYO	Comp Rept	LYCEN/6780	Nov 67 Crouzet+COMPILATN FOR ACTIVTN ANALYS	
Reson Params	-		AUA	Theo Rept	AAEC/E-211	Nov 70 Musgrove. CALCULTD D+GAM WIDTH GIVEN	
Reson Params	6.6+1	8.8+2	IFU	Expt Prog	YFI-10 44	May 71 Vertebnyj+ TRANS,N-WID,D,E-LVL,TABLE	
				Jour	UFZ 15 2050	Dec 70 Verteboy+.WN,9RES,D,TBLS	
				Rept	INDC(CCP)-15	Dec 71 . ENGL OF YFI-10 44	
Reson Params	None		DUB	Theo Rept	JINR-P4-7499	Oct 73 Soloviev+ CALC D CFD EXPTS,TABLE	
Reson Params	+1	+2	FEI	Eval Rept	YK- 8/2 97	Sep 72 Abagjan+ AVG G-WID+D AT BINDNG-E,TBL	
				Rept	INDC(CCP)-39	Jul 74 .PAGE 102.ENGLISH OF YK-8/2 97	
Strnth Fnctn	-		AUA	Theo Rept	AAEC/E-211	Nov 70 Musgrove. SMOOTHED S0,S1 AND S2 GIVN	

58 Cerium 136

Quantity	Energy (ev) Min	Max	Lab	Type	Documentation Ref Vol Page	Date	Author, Comments	Data
Lvl Density	+1	+2	FEI	Eval	Rept YK - 8/2 97	Sep 72	Abagyan+ LVL DENSITY PARAMETER,TBL	
					Rept INDC(CCP) - 39	Jul 74	.PAGE 102.ENGLISH OF YK - 8/2 97	

58 Cerium 137

Quantity	Energy (ev) Min	Max	Lab	Type	Documentation Ref Vol Page	Date	Author, Comments	Data
(n,α)	None		PUR	Expt	Jour NP/A 144 344	Apr 70	Swanson+INV SIG VS E(ALPHA) 15 - 28MEV	
(n,α)	None		PUR	Expt	Jour NP/A 144 355	Apr 70	Swanson+INV RECOIL DISTR 19 - 24 MEV	
Reson Params	–		AUA	Theo	Rept AAEC/E - 211	Nov 70	Musgrove. CALCULTD D+GAM WIDTH GIVEN	
Strnth Fnctn	–		AUA	Theo	Rept AAEC/E - 211	Nov 70	Musgrove. SMOOTHED S0,S1 AND S2 GIVN	
Lvl Density	None		MUN	Theo	Jour NP/A 217 269	Dec 73	Dilg+ A,DELTA. BACK SHIFTED FERMIGAS	
Lvl Density	None		DUB	Theo	Jour NP/A 224 411	May 74	Soloviev+ 1/2 MICROSC MDL. SPH NUCL.	
Lvl Density	None		ROC	Theo	Jour NP/A 223 577	May 74	Huizenga+ EXP CFD MICROSC TH SPH NUC	

58 Cerium 138

Quantity	Energy (ev) Min	Max	Lab	Type	Documentation Ref Vol Page	Date	Author, Comments	Data
Absorption	2.5 - 2		IJI	Eval	Rept KIYAI - 76 - 6	76	Fedorova+ COMP(REFS,SIGS),EVAL.TABLE	
					Conf 75Kiev 1 169	May 75	- + EVAL SIGS OF 2ISOMERS,TABL	
Res Int Abs	5.0 - 1		GHT	Expt	Jour JRC 23 113	74	Van Der Linden+ (N,G).CD - RATIO,TABLE	
(n,γ)	Maxwl		ISU	Expt	Jour PR 79 467	Aug 50	Moses+ RATIO CA.1.4 TO SIG(CE140)	+
	Maxwl				Data EXFOR12058.002	Jun 76	. 1 PT. SIGMA	
(n,γ)	Maxwl		ORL	Expt	Jour PR 88 412	Oct 52	Pomerance.PILE OSC.	+
	Maxwl				Data EXFOR11507.074	Jun 76	. 1 PT. SIGMA	
(n,γ)	Maxwl		ORL	Expt	Jour PR 103 190	Jul 56	Ketelle+	+
	Maxwl				Data EXFOR12063.	Jun 76	. 2 PTS. SIG TO GND + META	
(n,γ)	None		ANL	Theo	Jour PR 120 1305	Nov 60	Huizenga+ ISOMER RATIO,TH CFD EXPT	
(n,γ)	Pile		BNL	Expt	Jour PR 128 761	Oct 62	Sehgal.0.65+ - .22B REL CE140.140D ACT	+
	Pile				Data EXFOR11994.	Jun 76	. 2 PTS. SIGMA TO GND + META	
(n,γ)	Maxwl		ANL	Comp	Jour NP 60 241	Nov 64	Bishop+EXP AND TH ISOMER RATIOS CFD	
(n,γ)	–		IEA	Comp	Rept IEA - INF - 10	Aug 68	Atalla. TABLES OF HL,SIG AND GAMM - E	
(n,γ)	1.0+3	1.0+7	BOL	Eval	Rept CCDN - NW/10	Dec 69	Benzi+H - F MOD,AXEL G(G)EST,ALL DATA	
					Rept CEC(70) - 2	Apr 70	- +. GRAPH	
(n,γ)	3.0+4		AUA	Theo	Rept AAEC/E - 211	Nov 70	Musgrove. SIGMA GIVEN AND CFD OTHER	
(n,γ)	Maxwl		KFI	Comp	Jour JRC 7 365	Jun 71	Nagy+ SIGMA,GAM+XRAY+ELECTR ES GIVEN	
(n,γ)	Maxwl	Fiss	WIN	Revw	Conf IAEA - 169 3 163	74	Pope+ FIS - SPEC AVG DATA CFD MAXW - XPT	
(n,γ)	1.0+3	1.0+7	FEI	Eval	Rept YK - 8/2 97	Sep 72	Abagjan+ AVG SIG(ENERGY - GROUPS),TABL	
					Rept INDC(CCP) - 39	Jul 74	.P102. ENGLISH OF YK - 8/2 97	
Spect (n,γ)	Maxwl		KUR	Expt	Jour YF 10 681	Oct 69	Groshev+ TABLE GAM - SPECTRA,TRANSITNS	+
					Rept IAE - 1780	Jan 69	- + TBL OF GAMMA YLD+E,GE(LI)	
					Jour SNP 10 392	Apr 70	. ENGL OF YF 10 681	
					Rept LA - TR - 69 - 29	Oct 69	. ENGLISH OF IAE - 1780	
	2.5 - 2				Data EXFOR40237.006	Nov 74	.GAM/100N FOR 3 ES GVN	
Spect (n,γ)	Maxwl		KFI	Comp	Jour JRC 7 365	Jun 71	Nagy+ SIGMA,GAM+XRAY+ELECTR ES GIVEN	
(n,2n)	Fiss		CRC	Eval	Rept CRC - 1003	Dec 60	ROY+ ESTIMATED AVG SIG=0.7MB	
(n,2n)	1.4+7		LYO	Comp	Rept LYCEN/6780	Nov 67	Crouzet+COMPILATN FOR ACTIVTN ANALYS	
(n,2n)	1.4+7		GIT	Expt	Jour PR/C 1 350	Jan 70	Fink+ACTIVATION,GRPHS,TBL CFD OTH.	+
	1.4+7				Data EXFOR10497.041	Apr 76	1PT.CS=958+ - 100 MB.	
(n,2n)	1.5+7		ARK	Expt	Abst DA/B 32 5091	Mar 72	Bari. GE(LI) DET. ACT. SIG GIVEN	+
	1.5+7				Data EXFOR10431.042	Aug 75	1PT,SIGMA	
(n,2n)	1.5+7		DEB	Eval	Jour REA 11 1 153	Mar 73	Boedy+ RECOMM.VALUE FROM N - Z SYSTEM.	
(n,2n)	1.5+7		KFI	Theo	Rept KFKI - 73 - 68	Dec 73	Jeki.NEW FIT,CALC SIG CFD OTHERS,TBL	
(n,2n)	1.5+7		JUL	Expt	Jour NP/A 224 319	May 74	Qaim. ACT.GE(LI).TO GRND, METAST	
					Jour RRL 25 335	May 76	- + SIG IN GRPH. SYST VS (N - Z)/A	
	1.5+7				Data EXFOR20541.	Apr 76	4PTS.SIGMA.	
(n,2n)	1.5+7		IBJ	Theo	Jour ASL 27 186	77	Rurarz+ ISO RATIO,4MODLS,CFD XPT.TBL	
	1.4+7				Rept INR - 1464 19	May 73	- + ISOMERIC RATIO CFD EXPT,GRAF	
(n,p)	Fiss		CRC	Eval	Rept CRC - 1003	Dec 60	ROY+ ESTIMATED AVG SIG=0.9MB	
(n,α)	Fiss		CRC	Eval	Rept CRC - 1003	Dec 60	ROY+ ESTIMATED AVG SIG=0.0032MB	
Reson Params	–		AUA	Theo	Rept AAEC/E - 211	Nov 70	Musgrove. CALCULTD D+GAM WIDTH GIVEN	
Reson Params	1.0-2	5.0+3	IFU	Expt	Prog YFI - 10 44	May 71	Vertebnyj+ NO LVLS DETECTD IN E - RANG	
					Rept INDC(CCP) - 15	Dec 71	. ENGL OF YFI - 10 44	
Reson Params	None		DUB	Theo	Rept JINR - P4 - 7499	Oct 73	Soloviev+ CALC D CFD EXPTS,TABLE	
Reson Params	+1	+4	FEI	Eval	Rept YK - 8/2 97	Sep 72	Abagyan+ AVG G - WID+D AT BINDNG - E,TBL	
					Rept INDC(CCP) - 39	Jul 74	.PAGE 102.ENGLISH OF YK - 8/2 97	
Strnth Fnctn	–		AUA	Theo	Rept AAEC/E - 211	Nov 70	Musgrove. SMOOTHED S0,S1 AND S2 GIVN	

58 Cerium 138

Quantity	Energy (ev) Min	Max	Lab	Type	Documentation Ref Vol Page	Date	Author, Comments	Data
Lvl Density	None		AUW	Theo Conf	70Madurai 2 267	Dec 70	Ramamurty+ A – PARAMETER GVN,LANG'S – TH	
Lvl Density	+1	+4	FEI	Eval Rept	YK – 8/2 97	Sep 72	Abagyan+ LVL DENSITY PARAMETER,TBL	
				Rept	INDC(CCP) – 39	Jul 74	.PAGE 102.ENGLISH OF YK – 8/2 97	

58 Cerium 139

Quantity	Energy (ev) Min	Max	Lab	Type	Documentation Ref Vol Page	Date	Author, Comments	Data
(n,γ)	Pile		BNL	Expt Jour	PR 128 761	Oct 62	Sehgal.ACT,18+ – 5MB TO 55SEC ISOMER	
(n,p)	6.0+6	1.4+7	WIS	Expt Abst	DA 25 6709	May 65	Wood.INVERSE REACTION	
(n,p)	Maxwl		IFU	Theo Rept	ICD – 4 20	67	Dadakina+ PENETR COEFF CALC,TABLE	
Reson Params	–		AUA	Theo Rept	AAEC/E – 211	Nov 70	Musgrove. CALCULTD D+GAM WIDTH GIVEN	
Strnth Fnctn	–		AUA	Theo Rept	AAEC/E – 211	Nov 70	Musgrove. SMOOTHED S0,S1 AND S2 GIVN	
Strnth Fnctn	1.0+3	2.1+4	COL	Expt Prog	USNDC – 3 50	Oct 72	Hacken+ S0 GIVEN	
Lvl Density	None		DUB	Theo Jour	NP/A 224 411	May 74	Soloviev+ 1/2 MICROSC MDL. SPH NUCL.	
Lvl Density	9.0+6	1.7+7	ANL	Eval Rept	ANL – 75 – 34	Jun 75	Davey+N2NEVAL.CONSTANT T,LVL DEN FIT	

58 Cerium 140

Quantity	Energy (ev) Min	Max	Lab	Type	Documentation Ref Vol Page	Date	Author, Comments	Data
Evaluation	1.0–3	1.5+7	AUA	Eval Rept	AAEC/TM – 549	Jun 70	Cook.TOT,EL,INEL,NONEL,CAPT SIGS,NDG	+
				Rept	AAEC/E – 214	Jun 71	Bertram+GROUP SIGMAS SAME QUANTS.NDG	
				Rept	AAEC/TM – 587	Mar 71	*DESCRIPTION OF LIBRARY	
	1.0–3	1.5+7		Data	AUSTR – DFN 135.	Nov 71	POINT(223) AND GROUP(127) SIGMAS	
Evaluation	1.0–5	1.5+7	BOL	Eval Prog	NEANDC(E)182 7	Dec 76	Fabri+ COMPLETE EVAL IN ENDF/B DONE	+
	1.0–5	1.5+7		Data	CNEN – CEA 3	Jan 78	PRELIM.ALL QUANTITIES.ENDF FORMAT	
Total	1.0+3	6.0+4	DKE	Expt Jour	AP 8 211	Oct 59	Newson+ THIN – SAMPLE TRANSMISSN DATA	+
	1.0+3	6.0+4		Data	EXFOR11452.014	Jun 76	. 101 PTS. SIGMA	
Total	9.8+5		SHE	Theo Jour	NP 54 417	Jun 64	Maddison.OPTMOD FIT TO TOWLE GILBOY	
Total	7.0+6	1.4+7	CJD	Theo Rept	ICD – 5 20	68	Averjanov+ VIBRATION MDL,AT 4ES,TBL	
Total	1.0+3	1.5+3	IFU	Expt Prog	YFI – 7 37	Apr 69	Vertebny+NO RESONANCES FOUND,NO DATA	
				Rept	INDC(CCP) – 7U40	Feb 71	TRANSLATN.*	
Total	1.0–3	1.5+7	AUA	Eval Data	AUSTR – DFN 135.	Nov 71	COOK+ POINT(223)+GROUP(127) SIGMAS	+
Total	+3		DKE	Expt Jour	AP 84 165	May 74	Pineo+ N STRENGTH FUNC, TBLS, GRPHS.	
Total		6.3+4	COL	Expt Prog	USNDC – 11 68	Jun 74	Hacken+TRNS+SELF IND ANAL FOR CS.NDG	+
	1.0+0	6.8+1		Data	EXFOR10411.002	Apr 76	UNCORRECTED CS DATA AVAILABLE.	
Elastic	2.5–2		ORL	Expt Jour	PR 91 597	Aug 53	Koehler+ COM.SCAT.=2.8+ – 0.1 BARNS	+
	2.5–2			Data	EXFOR12060.	Jun 76	. 2 PTS. COH. SIGMA, COH AMP	
Elastic	7.0+6	1.4+7	CJD	Expt Rept	ICD – 5 20	68	Averjanov+ VIBRATION MDL,AT 4ES,TBL	
Elastic	1.0–3	1.5+7	AUA	Eval Data	AUSTR – DFN 135.	Nov 71	COOK+ POINT(223)+GROUP(127) SIGMAS	+
Elastic	2.5–2		IJI	Eval Rept	KIYAI – 76 – 6	76	Fedorova+ RECOMM SIG GIVEN,TABLE	
				Conf	75Kiev 1 169	May 75	– + EVAL 2200M/S SIG,TABLE	
Diff Elastic	1.0+6		LAS	Expt Jour	LA – 2016	Jun 56	Longley+ TBL ANG DIST 3 – DEG STEPS	
Diff Elastic	9.8+5		SHE	Theo Jour	NP 54 417	Jun 64	Maddison.OPTMOD FIT TO TOWLE GILBOY	
Diff Elastic	1.5+6	7.0+6	IJI	Theo Conf	71Moscow	Feb 71	Kashuba+ ABST.CALC OPTMOD,TABLE GIVN	
Potntal Scat	2.5–2		ORL	Expt Jour	PR 91 597	Aug 53	Koehler+ SIGMA=7.94 BARNS	+
Tot Inelastc	7.0+6	1.4+7	CJD	Theo Rept	ICD – 5 20	68	Averjanov+ VIBRATION MDL,AT 4ES,TBL	
Tot Inelastc	1.0–3	1.5+7	AUA	Eval Data	AUSTR – DFN 135.	Nov 71	COOK+ POINT(223)+GROUP(127) SIGMAS	+
Diff Inelast	2.5+6		LAS	Expt Jour	PRL 11 341	Oct 63	Cranberg. ANG DISTR FOR 3 LEVELS	
Diff Inelast	2.2+6		TNC	Theo Prog	WASH – 1068 197	Mar 66	Mathur+SIG+ANG DISTR CALCS.TBC	
Diff Inelast	1.6+6	2.2+6	STF	Expt Abst	DA/B 26 6800	May 66	Tucker.SIG FIRST 3 LVLS PROD.CFD H – F	+
	1.6+6	1.8+6		Conf	64Paris 2 671	Jul 64	– + GRPH SIG VS E 1 LVL.CFD H – F	
	1.6+6	2.2+6		Data	EXFOR11720.	Jun 76	. 44 PTS. SIG	
Diff Inelast	1.4+7		LRL	Expt Jour	UCRL – 50181	Feb 67	Lutz+ CALC ANG DIST FOR FIRST 2+ LVL	
Diff Inelast	7.0+6	1.4+7	CJD	Theo Rept	ICD – 5 20	68	Averjanov+ TO 1ST LVL,ANGDIST,GRAPH	
Scattering	2.5–2		ORL	Expt Jour	PR 91 597	Aug 53	Koehler+ TRANS 2.8+ – 0.1B	+
	2.5–2			Data	EXFOR12060.012	Jun 76	. 1 PT. SIGMA	
Scattering	2.5–2		IFU	Expt Conf	70Helsinki 1 651	Jun 70	Vertebnij+ 2200M/SEC SIGMA GIVEN,TBL	
				Rept	BNL – TR – 495	Jul 72	. ENGLISH OF 70HELSIN 1 651	
Nonelastic	1.0–3	1.5+7	AUA	Eval Data	AUSTR – DFN 135.	Nov 71	COOK+ POINT(223)+GROUP(127) SIGMAS	+
Nonelastic	1.4+7	1.7+7	ANL	Eval Rept	ANL – 75 – 34	Jun 75	Davey+CORRC APPLIED TO N2N CS.TBLS.	
Absorption	4.1–1	1.0+7	GA	Eval Rept	GA – 2451	Aug 61	Joanou+ 68GROUP DATA FOR GAM – I ABS	
Absorption	1.0–4	1.0+7	JUL	Eval Rept	JUEL – 678 – RG	Jul 70	Liu. EVALUATION+CALC,GRPH,FN OF E	
Absorption	2.5–2		IJI	Eval Rept	KIYAI – 76 – 6	76	Fedorova+ COMP(REFS,SIGS),EVAL.TABLE	
				Conf	75Kiev 1 169	May 75	– + EVAL SIG GIVEN,TABLE	
Res Int Abs	None		CRC	Eval Rept	AECL – 2111	Nov 64	Walker.REDUCED RESONANCE INTEGRAL	

58 Cerium 140

Quantity	Energy (ev) Min	Max	Lab	Type	Documentation Ref Vol Page	Author, Comments Date	Data
Res Int Abs	5.0-1		ORL Expt	Jour	NSE 20 302	Nov 64 Lantz+ RES INTGRL=0.48+-0.05B MTR	+
	5.0-1			Data	EXFOR12056.003	Jun 76 . 1 PT. RI	
Res Int Abs	5.0-1		CNE Expt	Jour	CJP 46 2473	Nov 68 Ricabarra+,RATIO TO THR-ACT SIGMA	+
				Rept	CNEA-274	70 - + SAME,IN SPANISH	
	5.0-1			Data	EXFOR30129.009	Oct 72 RESON INT AND RATIO TO THR ABS SIGM.	
Res Int Abs	None		GA Eval	Rept	GA- 12071	Sep 71 Mathews+ RECOMMENDED VALUES	
Res Int Abs	5.5-1		CRC Eval	Rept	AECL-3037 1	Jan 72 Walker.REDUCED RES INT,DETAILED TBL	
Res Int Abs		1.0+6	OSL Expt	Prog	INDC(NOR)-1 1	May 72 Alstad+ RES CAPT INT REL AU.TBL.ABST	+
	0.0+0	1.0+6		Jour	JIN 29 2155	Sep 67 - + ACTIV REL AU,AND CD RATIO	
		1.0+6		Data	EXFOR20044.003	Sep 71 1PNT.CAPTURE.	
Res Int Abs	5.0-1		AUA Eval	Rept	AAEC/TM-619	Sep 72 Clayton.CALC FROM SIG LIBRARY,TABLE	
Res Int Abs	5.0-1		KJL Expt	Jour	JIN 34 2699	Sep 72 Steinnes. ACT. AU MONITOR	
	5.0-1			Data	EXFOR20188.016	May 74 1PNT.CAPTURE.	
Res Int Abs	5.0-1		MUN Expt	Jour	JRC 15 535	73 Alian+CAPT CD-R, 0.66B INCL 1/V	+
	5.0-1			Data	EXFOR20644.012	Jun 76 1PNT.CAPTURE.	
Res Int Abs	4.6-1	1.0+6	RCN Theo	Rept	RCN-191	Jul 73 Lautenbach.CAPT INT FROM GROUP SIGMA	
Res Int Abs	5.0-1		GHT Expt	Jour	JRC 20 695	74 Van Der Linden+ BY(N,G).CFD OTHS,TBL	+
	5.5-1			Conf	73Paris 2 241	Mar 73 - + ACT,REL THR+GOLD,TBL	
	5.5-1			Data	EXFOR20645.016	Jul 76 1PNT.CAPTURE.	
Res Int Abs	5.5-1	+6	SAC Revw	Conf	IAEA-169 1 235	74 Ribon.CAPTURE,STATUS CFD REQUEST,TBL	
Res Int Abs	+0	+5	WIN Revw	Conf	IAEA-169 3 163	74 Pope+ DATA FILE CALC CFD XPTAL VALUE	
Res Int Abs	5.0-1		IJI Eval	Rept	KIYAI-76-6	76 Fedorova+ COMP(REFS,RI),EVAL.TABLE	
				Conf	75Kiev 1 169	May 75 - + EVAL OF RI-EXPTS.TABLE	
(n,γ)	Pile		LAS Expt	Jour	JCP 17 421	Apr 49 Katcoff+ SIGMA=.27+-.06B/ATOM CE	+
	Pile			Data	EXFOR12053.002	Jun 76 . 1 PT. SIGMA	
(n,γ)	Fiss		ANL Expt	Jour	PR 78 632	Jun 50 Hughes+ REL SIG(THERMAL).	+
	Fiss			Data	EXFOR11596.012	Jun 76 . 1 PT. SIGMA	
(n,γ)	Maxwl		ANL Expt	Jour	PR 78 632	Jun 50 Hughes+	+
	Maxwl			Data	EXFOR11596.015	Jun 76 . 1 PT. SIGMA	
(n,γ)	Maxwl		ISU Expt	Jour	PR 79 467	Aug 50 Moses+	+
	Maxwl			Data	EXFOR12058.002	Jun 76 . 1 PT. SIG	
(n,γ)	Maxwl		ORL Expt	Jour	PR 88 412	Oct 52 Pomerance.PILE OSC.	+
	Maxwl			Data	EXFOR11507.075	Jun 76 . 1 PT. SIGMA	
(n,γ)	Fiss		BNL Expt	Jour	PR 91 1423	Sep 53 Hughes+ ALSO LVL SPACINGS AT EXCIT E	
(n,γ)	2.4+4		ORL Expt	Jour	PR 107 504	Jul 57 Macklin+.SB-BE NS,31+-4MB,.145MEV G	+
				Conf	58Geneva 15 68	Sep 58 - .PPR671,VAL GVN,EXPT DESCRIBD	
	2.4+4			Data	EXFOR11399.036	Jun 76 . 1 PT. SIGMA	
(n,γ)	Maxwl		CRC Eval	Rept	AECL-2111	Nov 64 Walker.	
(n,γ)	Maxwl		ORL Expt	Jour	NSE 20 302	Nov 64 Lantz+.59PM.06B.ACT.MTR.OKS POMRNC	
				Conf	60Vienna 239	Oct 60 Stoughton+ NDG,EXPT DESCRIBED	
	Maxwl			Data	EXFOR12056.002	Jun 76 . 1 PT. SIGMA	
(n,γ)	Maxwl		OSL Expt	Jour	JIN 27 2155	Sep 67 Alstad+ ACTIVATION REL AU,+CD RATIO	+
	Maxwl			Data	EXFOR20044.002	Sep 71 1PNT.SIG.	
(n,γ)	-		IEA Comp	Rept	IEA-INF- 10	Aug 68 Atalla. TABLES OF HL,SIG AND GAMM-E	
(n,γ)	Maxwl		BNL Expt	Prog	WASH-1127 23	Apr 69 Moragues+ SEARCH FOR DIRECT CAPT,NDG	
(n,γ)	5.0+3	1.0+5	AUA ExTh	Rept	AAEC/E-198	May 69 Musgrove.S+P+D WAVE SIGMAS CALC,TBL	+
(n,γ)	1.0+3	1.0+7	BOL Eval	Rept	CCDN-NW/10	Dec 69 Benzi+H-F MOD,AXEL G(G)EST,ALL DATA	
				Rept	CEC(70)-2	Apr 70 - +. GRAPH	
				Conf	66Paris 1 537	Oct 66 - + STATMOD.TBL AV VALS.SUPERSEDD	
(n,γ)	3.0+4		AUA Theo	Rept	AAEC/E-211	Nov 70 Musgrove. SIGMA GIVEN AND CFD OTHER	
(n,γ)	Fast		MTR Expt	Abst	ANS 13 755	Nov 70 Scoville+CFRMF MRAST.VALUE GIVEN.	
(n,γ)	Maxwl		GA Eval	Rept	GA- 12071	Sep 71 Mathews+ RECOMMENDED VALUES	
(n,γ)	1.0-3	1.5+7	AUA Eval	Data	AUSTR-DFN 135.	Nov 71 COOK+ POINT(223)+GROUP(127) SIGMAS	+
(n,γ)	Maxwl		CRC Eval	Rept	AECL-3037 1	Jan 72 Walker.RECOMMENDED SIG,DETAILED TBL	
(n,γ)	2.5-2		AUA Eval	Rept	AAEC/TM-619	Sep 72 Clayton.CALC FROM SIG LIBRARY,TABLE	
(n,γ)	Fast		MTR Expt	Conf	72Kiamesha 2 614	Sep 72 Harker+ CFRMF INTEGRAL MEAS.	
(n,γ)	Maxwl		MUN Expt	Jour	JRC 15 535	73 Alian+ ACT, 0.68B REL TO CO-59	+
	2.5-2			Data	EXFOR20644.011	Jun 76 1PNT.SIGMA.	
(n,γ)		1.1+7	RCN Theo	Rept	RCN-191	Jun 73 Lautenbach. GROUP CONSTANTS TBL	
(n,γ)	2.5+4		AUW Expt	Jour	NC/A 18 48	Nov 73 Sidappa+ ACTIV SIG,CFD.TABLE	
(n,γ)	2.5-2	3.0+4	SAC Revw	Conf	IAEA-169 1 235	74 Ribon.STATUS SIG CFD REQUESTS,TABLE	
(n,γ)	Maxwl	Fiss	WIN Revw	Conf	IAEA-169 3 163	74 Pope+ MAXW+FIS-SPEC AVG DATA CFD XPT	
	Fiss			Conf	IAEA-169 3 137	74 Dean. POINT DATA AVG OVER STAND SPEC	
(n,γ)	1.0+3	1.0+7	FEI Eval	Rept	YK- 8/2 97	Sep 72 Abagjan+ AVG SIG(ENERGY-GROUPS),TABL	
				Rept	INDC(CCP)-39	Jul 74 .P102. ENGLISH OF YK- 8/2 97	
(n,γ)	2.5+4		TAT Expt	Conf	74Bombay 2 101	Dec 74 Kondaiah+ SIGMA GIVEN	+
	2.5+4			Data	EXFOR30390.013	Mar 77 1PNT.	
(n,γ)	5.0+6	2.0+7	TIT Theo	Conf	JAERI-M-5984	Feb 75 Kitazawa+PART-VIB COUPLING. CURVES	

58 Cerium 140

Quantity	Energy (ev) Min	Max	Lab	Type	Documentation Ref Vol Page	Date	Author, Comments	Data
(n,γ)	1.5+7		JYV Comp	Rept	JU – RR – 1/1976	Mar 76	Valkonen.(THESIS).EXPTS CFD DSD MODL	
(n,γ)	8.0+6	2.0+7	UBO Theo	Jour	NSE 61 40	Sep 76	Longo+HIGH E G.CS CALC,CFD EXPT.GRPH	
(n,γ)	Fast		RCN Expt	Rept	ECN – 10	Oct 76	Veenema+ STEK REACTIVITY WORTHS TBL.	
Spect (n,γ)	Pile		IPS Expt	Jour	AF 4 81	Aug 52	Kondaiah. B – G SPECTROSCOPY	
Spect (n,γ)	Pile		LND Expt	Jour	AF 3 533	Aug 52	Johansson. NAI(TL). E. K – CONV COEFF.	
Spect (n,γ)	2.5+4		ORL Expt	Conf	58Geneva 15 68	Sep 58	Macklin.PPR671,SIGMA+G – ENERGY GVN	
Spect (n,γ)	Maxwl		ORL Expt	Prog	ORNL – 4230 45	May 68	Slaughter+ GE(LI),TO VLS IN CE141	
Spect (n,γ)	Maxwl		AUW Expt	Jour	IPA 7 8 542	Aug 69	Surya.E OF G,RELATIVE INT GIVEN	
Spect (n,γ)	Maxwl		KUR Expt	Jour	YF 10 681	Oct 69	Groshev+ TABLE GAM – SPECTRA,TRANSITNS	+
				Rept	IAE – 1780	Jan 69	– + TBL OF GAMMA YLD+E,GE(LI)	
				Jour	SNP 10 392	Apr 70	. ENGL OF YF 10 681	
				Rept	LA – TR – 69 – 29	Oct 69	. ENGLISH OF IAE – 1780	
	2.5 – 2			Data	EXFOR40237.007	Nov 74	.GAM/100N FOR 2 ES GVN	
Spect (n,γ)	Maxwl		BNL Expt	Jour	PR/C 1 1052	Mar 70	Gelletly+ GE(LI) DET.CE141 LVLS GIVN	
Spect (n,γ)	Maxwl		BOR Expt	Prog	EANDC(E)127U	Apr 70	Audias+ GE(LI) DET	
				Conf	69Studsvik 337	Aug 69	Irigaray+ G – SPEC TBL,37LINES,GE(LI)	
Spect (n,γ)	Pile		KFK Expt	Rept	KFK – 1401	Jun 71	Djadali.POLRZ G EXPT,CE – 141LVL+SPIN	
				Jour	NP/A 165 560	Apr 71	– + POL N, CIRC POL GS.	
				Rept	KFK – 1296	Sep 70	– +POLRZ GAMS,CE – 141 LVLS+SPINS	
Spect (n,γ)	1.4+7		BOR Expt	Conf	73Pacif.Gr 2 953	Mar 73	Rigaud+ HIGH – E G – SPEC CFD THEO,GRAPH	
Spect (n,γ)	6.2+6	1.1+7	UPP Expt	Rept	INDC – 17 27	Oct 74	Lindholm+ NAI SPECS CFD SEMI – DIR MDL	
				Conf	74Petten 239	Sep 74	– + TOF SEMI DIRECT MODEL GRPH	
	8.2+6	1.4+7		Conf	74Petten 199	Sep 74	Bergqvist+(LND) FAST CAPT EXP+CALC	
	6.2+6	1.1+7		Conf	73Munich 1 655	Aug 73	Lindholm+ SEMIDIRECT MDL OKS XPT,NDG	
Spect (n,γ)	1.4+7		TIT Theo	Conf	JAERI – M – 5984	Feb 75	Kitazawa+PART – VIB CALC CFD EXP.CURVS	
Spect (n,γ)	9.9+6	1.1+7	BOL Theo	Conf	75Wash. 346	Mar 75	Longo+2 EN.G SPECT 9 – 19MEV CFD EXP	
Spect (n,γ)	2.5 – 2		IFB Theo	Conf	76Lowell 1283	Jul 76	Martsynkevich+DOORWAY STATE ROLE.	
	Maxwl			Jour	NP/A 262 261	May 76	– +LVL SPEC.COL E1 DECAYS	
	None			Jour	YF 15 1132	Jun 72	Knat'Ko+ CALC E1 INTS CFD EXPT,GRAPH	
				Jour	SNP 15 626	Dec 72	– + ENGLISH OF YF 15 1132	
Spect (n,γ)	8.0+6	2.0+7	UBO Theo	Jour	NSE 61 40	Sep 76	Longo+HIGH E G.SPEC CALC,CFD EX.GRPH	
Inelastic γ	1.9+6	2.1+6	STF Expt	Jour	PR/B 137 1181	Mar 65	Tucker+CS 90DEG COINC 0.3,1.6MEVGS	+
	1.9+6	2.1+6		Data	EXFOR11720.009	Jun 76	. 9 PTS. SIG	
Inelastic γ	1.6+6	1.9+6	STF Expt	Jour	NP/A 111 513	Apr 68	Torop. ANG DIST OF GS. 1ST EXCTSTATE	
				Abst	DA/B 28 4715	May 68	– .GAM ANGDIST AT 5ES CFD THEORY	
Inelastic γ	2.8+6		KGU Expt	Jour	YF 9 1129	Jun 69	Romanenko+ GRPH,E+INT TBL,LVL – SCHEME	+
				Jour	SNP 9 660	Dec 69	*	
				Conf	67Kharkov 49	Feb 67	* ABST ONLY	
	2.8+6			Data	EXFOR40414.005	Dec 77	E+ABS INT OF 8 GAMMAS	
Inelastic γ	1.6+6	1.9+6	CCP Comp	Rept	ICD – 6 106	70	Sluchevskaja.SIG(ANG) FOR GS,GRAPHS	
Inelastic γ	1.8+6	2.1+6	TNC Expt	Rept	ORO – 2791 – 32	Feb 71	Buchanan+ 2NEUT ES,1.596MEV GAMMA	+
	1.8+6	2.1+6		Data	EXFOR11662.009	Jun 76	. 2 PTS. DSIG	
Inelastic γ	None		ITK Expt	Prog	INDC(SEC) – 35	Sep 73	Singh+ P119.LEVEL SCHEME,GE – LI,TBL	
(n,2n)	1.5+7		ARK Expt	Jour	PR 118 242	Apr 60	Wille+ MEAS ACT SIG=1200+ – 400MB	
	1.5+7			Data	EXFOR12033.010	Jun 76	. 1 PT. SIGMA	
(n,2n)	Fiss		CRC Eval	Rept	CRC – 1003	Dec 60	ROY+ ESTIMATED AVG SIG=1.3MB	
(n,2n)	1.4+7		HAM Expt	Jour	ZN/A 16 227	Mar 61	Pollehn+SIG=1440MB	+
(n,2n)	1.4+7		HAM Comp	Jour	NP 65 257	Mar 65	Bormann. 2EXPT VALS.CFD SHELL EFFECT	
(n,2n)	1.5+7		MUA Expt	Jour	NP 88 349	Nov 66	Prasad+,T – D NEUT ACT REL TO FE56(NP)	+
	1.5+7			Data	EXFOR30015.003	May 70	PARTIAL SIGMA(METASTABLE)	
(n,2n)	1.5+7		TAM Expt	Jour	PR 156 1340	Apr 67	Menon+ ACT TO CE139M, REL CU63(N,2N)	+
	1.5+7			Data	EXFOR12066.	Jun 76	. 2 PTS. SIGMA TO GND + META	
(n,2n)	1.4+7		LYO Comp	Rept	LYCEN/6780	Nov 67	Crouzet+COMPILATN FOR ACTIVTN ANALYS	
(n,2n)	1.4+7		NAP Expt	Jour	NC/B 52 2 476	Dec 67	Cuzzocrea+. SIG TO GROUND AND METAST	
(n,2n)	1.4+7		IRK Expt	Diss	WINKLER	68	Winkler.(THESIS)	
(n,2n)	1.5+7		DEB Expt	Jour	AHP 24 233	Feb 68	Csikai+ ACTIV,ABS VALUE,THEORY CFD	+
				Jour	MFF 16 123	Feb 68	SEE ALSO *THESIS IN HUNG	
	1.5+7			Data	EXFOR30040.004	Nov 70	SIGMA AT 14.8 MEV RESP TO PR – 141(NP)	
(n,2n)	1.3+7	1.9+7	HAM Expt	Jour	NP/A 115 309	Jul 68	Bormann+ VDG.ACT.CFD STATMDL+OPTMDL	+
(n,2n)	1.5+7		TUR Theo	Jour	NC 56 18 201	Jul 68	Minetti+THEOR ISOM RATIO SPIN CO PAR	
(n,2n)	1.5+7		MUN Expt	Jour	NP/A 118 9	Sep 68	Dilg+ ACTIV.REL AL(N,A)	
				Jour	OAWS 177 323	69	Winkler+(IRK) ACTIVATION.	
	1.5+7			Data	EXFOR20802.002	Dec 78	1PNT.SIGMA.	
(n,2n)	1.4+7	1.5+7	IRK Comp	Jour	OAWS 177 469	69	Hille.	
(n,2n)	1.5+7		IBJ Expt	Jour	APPB 1 415	70	Rurarz+ ACTIV,NAI,ISORATIO VS THEORY	
				Jour	NKA 14 933	Oct 69	– + ACTIV,NAI(TL),SIG TO ISOMER	
	1.5+7			Data	EXFOR30154.012	May 72	ISOMERIC RATIO	
	1.5+7			Data	EXFOR30098.003	Mar 71	VALUE TO METASTABLE STATE AT 14.5MEV	

58 Cerium 140

Quantity	Energy (ev) Min	Max	Lab	Type	Documentation Ref Vol Page	Date	Author, Comments	Data
(n,2n)	1.5+7		DEB Comp	Jour	REA 7 4 93	Dec 69	Csikai+ SIG+HL COMPILTN,N-ACTIV-ANAL	
(n,2n)	1.5+7		CCP Comp	Rept	ICD-6 215	70	Sluchevskaja.SIG FROM 2 REFERENC,TBL	
(n,2n)	1.4+7		GIT Expt	Jour	PR/C 1 350	Jan 70	Fink+ ACTIVATION,SIG=1593+ -130	+
	1.4+7			Data	EXFOR10497.	Apr 76	2PTS.M STATE CS, M+G STATE CS	
(n,2n)	1.4+7	1.5+7	JYV Eval	Rept	JU-RR-3/1970	Jun 70	Leppaemaeki+ TABLE OF EVAL AVG SIG	
(n,2n)	+7		KFI Theo	Rept	KFKI-71-8	Feb 71	Jeki. CALCULATED CFD EXPTL SIG VALUE	
(n,2n)	Maxwl	1.4+7	KFI Comp	Jour	JRC 7 365	Jun 71	Nagy+ SIGMAS,GAM+XRAY+ELECTR ES GIVN	
(n,2n)	1.4+7	1.5+7	IRK ExTh	Jour	APA 33 285	Jul 71	Winiwarter+ ISOMERIC RATIO	
(n,2n)	1.4+7		GIT Theo	Jour	PR/C 4 1173	Oct 71	Fink+ STAT-MODEL CALCULATION,CFD EXP	
(n,2n)	1.5+7		ARK Expt	Abst	DA/B 32 5091	Mar 72	Bari. GE(LI) DET. ACT. SIG GIVEN	+
	1.5+7			Data	EXFOR10431.	Aug 75	2PTS,SIGMA,META AND GND+META	
(n,2n)	1.4+7		ITJ Expt	Jour	JRC 14 201	73	Janczyszyn+ TO ISO,ACTIV.CFD OTH,TBL	+
	1.4+7			Data	EXFOR30322.014	Feb 76	1 PNT.	
(n,2n)	1.5+7		DEB Eval	Jour	REA 11 1 153	Mar 73	Boedy. COMPILATION+RECOMM.VALUE,TBL	
				Rept	IAEA-153 173	73	-. RECOMM. VALUE ONLY	
(n,2n)	Fiss		KOS Eval	Jour	AK 16 351	74	Boedy. U238,MAXW-SPC.AVG CFD XPT,TBL	
(n,2n)	1.5+7		TAT Theo	Jour	JP/A 7 1458	Aug 74	Kondaiah. CALC ON STAT MODEL	
(n,2n)	Fiss		KOS Eval	Conf	75Karlsrhe 29	Apr 75	Csikai. CF252,MAXW-SPC.AVG FOR 2TEMP	
(n,2n)	1.5+7		SMU Expt	Jour	JIN 37 1121	May 75	Eapen+ TO GND,META.RATIO CFD TH,TBLS	+
				Conf	74Columbia 95	Jul 74	Salita+ ACT,SIG TO GND+META,TABLE	
	1.5+7			Data	EXFOR10493.	May 75	3 PTS. ISOM,GND ST PROD CS + RATIO	
(n,2n)	9.0+6	1.7+7	ANL Eval	Rept	ANL-75-34	Jun 75	Davey+CONSTANT T MDL,LVL DEN MDL FIT	
(n,2n)	1.5+7		JUL Expt	Jour	NP/A 224 319	May 74	Qaim. ACT.GE(LI).TO GRND, METAST	
				Jour	RRL 25 335	May 76	- + SIG IN GRPH. SYST VS (N-Z)/A	
	1.5+7			Data	EXFOR20541.	Apr 76	4PTS.SIGMA.	
(n,2n)			IBJ Theo	Jour	ASL 27 186	77	Rurarz+ ISO RATIO,4MODLS,CFD XPT.TBL	
	1.4+7			Rept	INR-1464 19	May 73	- + ISOMERIC RATIO CFD EXPT,GRAF	
(n,p)	1.4+7		CCP Expt	Jour	ZET 33 1520	Dec 57	Act+RDCHEM,REL TO CE142 1/.60	
				Jour	JET 6 1174	Jun 58	TRANSLATN.*	
(n,p)	1.4+7		ALD Expt	Jour	PPS 73 215	Feb 59	Coleman+. ACT. CFD DIRECT INTERACTN	+
(n,p)	1.5+7		ARK Expt	Jour	PR 118 242	Apr 60	Wille+ MEAS ACT SIG=10+ -2MB	+
	1.5+7			Data	EXFOR12033.012	Jun 76	1 PT. SIGMA	
(n,p)	Fiss		CRC Eval	Jour	CRC-1003	Dec 60	ROY+ ESTIMATED AVG SIG=0.01MB	
(n,p)	1.4+7		FRK Theo	Jour	ZP 171 379	Dec 62	Lindner.STATMOD,CF CJP 31 267(EXPT)	
(n,p)	1.5+7		SAH Comp	Jour	NUC 23 8 112	Aug 65	Chatterjee. TABLE WITH REFS.	
	1.4+7			Jour	NP 60 273	Nov 64	- .MEAN OF EXPT CFD SHELLMOD	
(n,p)	1.4+7	1.5+7	ARK Theo	Prog	ORO-3235-29	Jan 67	Koch+ STAT MODEL CALC CFD EXPTS	
(n,p)	1.4+7	1.5+7	NAP Comp	Rept	INFN/BE-67-10	Jul 67	Cuzzocrea+ AVERAGED CHOSEN DATA.	
(n,p)			LYO Comp	Rept	LYCEN/6780	Nov 67	Crouzet+COMPILATN FOR ACTIVTN ANALYS	
(n,p)	1.4+7		NAP Expt	Jour	NC/B 52 2 476	Dec 67	Cuzzocrea+. 7.71+ -.85 MB.TH OKS EXPT	
(n,p)	Pile		GHT Expt	Jour	RCA 10 11	68	Deschuyter+MEAN REACT SIG+CHEMISTRY	+
	1.5+6			Data	EXFOR20738.002	Apr 77	10PTS.SIGMA.	
(n,p)	1.5+7		DEB Comp	Jour	REA 7 4 93	Dec 69	Csikai+ SIG+HL COMPILTN,N-ACTIV-ANAL	
(n,p)	1.4+7		GIT Expt	Jour	PR/C 1 358	Jan 70	Fink+ ACT.SIG=6.3+ -0.5MB	+
	1.4+7			Data	EXFOR10145.021	Sep 75	1PNT.SIGMA.	
(n,p)	1.4+7	1.5+7	JYV Eval	Rept	JU-RR-3/1970	Jun 70	Leppaemaeki+ TABLE OF EVAL AVG SIG	
(n,p)	1.5+7		IRK Expt	Jour	APA 34 209	Sep 71	Havlik. ACT. CC-W.	+
				Jour	OAWA 107 119	Apr 70	- . ACTIVATION METHOD	
	1.5+7			Data	EXFOR20509.008	Apr 76	1PNT.SIGMA.	
(n,p)	1.4+7		GIT Theo	Jour	PR/C 4 1173	Oct 71	Fink+ STAT-MODEL CALCULATION,CFD EXP	
(n,p)	1.5+7		ARK Expt	Abst	DA/B 32 5091	Mar 72	Bari. GE(LI) DET. ACT. SIG GIVEN	+
	1.5+7			Data	EXFOR10431.012	Aug 75	1PT,SIGMA	
(n,p)	1.4+7	1.5+7	KAZ Theo	Jour	YF 18 705	Oct 73	Levkovsky.AVERAGED SIG,CALC,TBL	
				Jour	SNP 18 361	Apr 74	. ENGLISH OF YF 18,705	
(n,p)	1.5+7		JUL Expt	Jour	RRL 25 335	May 76	Qaim+ ACTIV,GELI.CFD OTHERS,TBL+GRPH	+
	1.5+7			Data	EXFOR20716.002	Jun 77	1PNT.SIGMA.	
(n,α)	1.5+7		CRC Expt	Jour	CJP 31 267	Feb 53	Paul+ BETA ACT.CFD TH.HL=2.6M	+
	1.5+7			Data	EXFOR11274.088	Jun 76	1 PT. SIGMA	
(n,α)	1.5+7		ARK Expt	Jour	PR 118 242	Apr 60	Wille+ MEAS ACT SIG=9.+ -2.MB	+
	1.5+7			Data	EXFOR12033.011	Jun 76	1 PT. SIGMA	
(n,α)	Fiss		CRC Eval	Rept	CRC-1003	Dec 60	ROY+ ESTIMATED AVG SIG=0.0002MB	
(n,α)	1.4+7		FRK Theo	Jour	ZP 171 379	Dec 62	Lindner.STATMOD,CF CJP 31 267,TH+XPT	
(n,α)	1.4+7		CIS Theo	Jour	NP 51 460	Feb 64	Facchini+STATMOD SIG XPT/CALC0.9-1.4	
(n,α)	1.3+7	1.7+7	HAM Expt	Prog	EANDC(E)66U	Feb 66	Bormann+. TBP.TABLE.TO BA137M	+
(n,α)	1.5+7		TUE Expt	Jour	ZP 201 105	Apr 67	STAUDT ALPHA E+ANGDIST,SIGTOT.SC DET	+
(n,α)			LYO Comp	Rept	LYCEN/6780	Nov 67	Crouzet+COMPILATN FOR ACTIVTN ANALYS	
(n,α)	1.5+7		DEB Comp	Jour	REA 7 4 93	Dec 69	Csikai+ SIG+HL COMPILTN,N-ACTIV-ANAL	
(n,α)	1.4+7	1.5+7	JYV Eval	Rept	JU-RR-3/1970	Jun 70	Leppaemaeki+ TABLE OF EVAL AVG SIG	

58 Cerium 140

Quantity	Energy (ev) Min	Max	Lab	Type	Documentation Ref Vol Page	Date	Author, Comments	Data
(n,α)	1.5+7		IRK Expt	Jour	APA 34 209	Sep 71	Havlik. ACT. CC – W.	+
				Jour	OAWA 107 119	Apr 70	– . ACTIVATION METHOD	
	1.5+7			Data	EXFOR20509.009	Apr 76	1PNT.SIGMA.	
Reson Params	5.0+2	1.2+5	DKE Expt	Abst	PR 98 1162	May 55	Newson.ABSTRACT HA10 RES ES GIVEN	
Reson Params		1.0+6	AUA Theo	Jour	AUJ 20 477	Oct 67	Cook. TBL OF AVG LVL SPACING D,L=0,1	
Reson Params	3.0+0	1.0+3	IFU Expt	Conf	69Erevan	Feb 69	Vertebnij + .ABST,LVL DENS ISOT DEPEND	
Reson Params	–		AUA Theo	Rept	AAEC/E – 211	Nov 70	Musgrove. CALCULTD D+GAM WIDTH GIVEN	
Reson Params	None		DUB Theo	Rept	JINR – P4 – 7499	Oct 73	Soloviev+ CALC D CFD EXPTS,TABLE	
Reson Params	2.5+3	6.3+4	COL Expt	Prog	USNDC – 11 68	Jun 74	Hacken+WN 23 LVLS.TBL.D GVN.	+
	2.5+3	6.3+4		Data	EXFOR10411.002	Apr 76	24PTS.WN,23 RES ES.D VAL.	
Reson Params	+4		FEI Eval	Rept	YK – 8/2 97	Sep 72	Abagyan+ AVG G – WID+D AT BINDNG – E,TBL	
				Rept	INDC(CCP) – 39	Jul 74	.PAGE 102.ENGLISH OF YK – 8/2 97	
Strnth Fnctn		2.0+5	DKE Expt	Rept	AP 8 211	Oct 59	Newson+ FROM RESON PARAMS 1.0+ – 0.4	+
		2.0+5		Data	EXFOR11888.011	Jun 76	. 1 PT. D	
Strnth Fnctn	–		AUA Theo	Rept	AAEC/E – 211	Nov 70	Musgrove. SMOOTHED S0,S1 AND S2 GIVN	
Strnth Fnctn	None		AUA Eval	Rept	AAEC/E – 277	Mar 73	Musgrove.TBLS EXPTL DATA+BEST VALUES	
Strnth Fnctn	1.8+4	2.8+4	AUW Expt	Jour	NP/A 213 35	Oct 73	Murty+ P – WAVE.FIT TO P N – G AT 25KEV	
	2.5+4			Jour	NP/A 213 35	Oct 73	– + SB – BE. + – 5KEV.S,P – WAVE CONTRIB	
Strnth Fnctn	2.5+3	6.3+4	COL Expt	Prog	USNDC – 11 68	Jun 74	Hacken+S WAVE STF VAL GVN.	+
	2.5+3	6.3+4		Data	EXFOR10411.004	Apr 76	1PT S0=1.4+ – .4	
Strnth Fnctn	None		KUR Theo	Prog	IAE – 2560	75	Adamchuk+.S0 – VALUE,TBL	
Lvl Density	5.0+6	7.0+6	ISL Theo	Conf	64Geneva § 511	May 64	Szwarcbaum+.T FROM 3 FORMLS CFD EXPS	
Lvl Density	+6		FEI Theo	Prog	YFI – 7 7	Apr 69	Ignatyuk+ TEMP+DENS+A VS EXCIT – E,CRV	
	+6	+7		Jour	YF 11 1012	May 70	– + DENSITY+A+TEMP VS EXCIT – E	
	+6			Rept	INDC(CCP) – 7U5	Feb 70	TRANSLATN.*	
	+6	+7		Jour	SNP 11 563	Nov 70	. ENGL OF YF 11 1012	
Lvl Density	None		SAC Expt	Jour	NP/A 133 417	Aug 69	Bergere+NUCL TEMP,A PARAM,FROM NG	
Lvl Density	+6	+7	FEI Theo	Jour	YF 12 960	Nov 70	Stavinskij. (N,N') – ANAL,A – PARAM GRPH	
Lvl Density	None		AUW Theo	Conf	70Madurai 2 267	Dec 70	Ramamurty+ A – PARAMETER GVN,LANG'S – TH	
Lvl Density	+4		FEI Eval	Rept	YK – 8/2 97	Sep 72	Abagyan+ LVL DENSITY PARAMETER,TBL	
				Rept	INDC(CCP) – 39	Jul 74	.PAGE 102.ENGLISH OF YK – 8/2 97	
(γ,n)	8.0+6	2.6+7	SAC Expt	Jour	NP/A 258 350	Feb 76	Lepretre+GDR,LORENTZ PARAM,GRPHS,TBL	

58 Cerium 141

Quantity	Energy (ev) Min	Max	Lab	Type	Documentation Ref Vol Page	Date	Author, Comments	Data
Evaluation	1.0 – 3	1.5+7	AUA Eval	Rept	AAEC/TM – 549	Jun 70	Cook.TOT,EL,INEL,NONEL,CAPT SIGS,NDG	+
				Rept	AAEC/E – 214	Jun 71	Bertram+GROUP SIGMAS SAME QUANTS.NDG	
				Rept	AAEC/TM – 587	Mar 71	*DESCRIPTION OF LIBRARY	
Evaluation	1.0 – 5	1.5+7	BOL Eval	Prog	NEANDC(E)182 7	Dec 76	Fabri+ COMPLETE EVAL IN ENDF/B DONE	+
	1.0 – 5	1.5+7		Data	CNEN – CEA 3	Jan 78	PRELIM.ALL QUANTITIES.ENDF FORMAT	
Total	1.0 – 3	1.5+7	AUA Eval	Data	AUSTR – DFN 136.	Nov 71	COOK+POINT(223)+GROUP(127)SIG.CF EVL	+
Elastic	1.0 – 3	1.5+7	AUA Eval	Data	AUSTR – DFN 136.	Nov 71	COOK+POINT(223)+GROUP(127)SIG.CF EVL	+
Elastic	2.5 – 2		IJI Eval	Rept	KIYAI – 76 – 6	76	Fedorova+ RECOMM SIG GIVEN,TABLE	
Nonelastic	1.0 – 3	1.5+7	AUA Eval	Data	AUSTR – DFN 136.	Nov 71	COOK+POINT(223)+GROUP(127)SIG.CF EVL	+
Absorption	2.5 – 2		IJI Eval	Rept	KIYAI – 76 – 6	76	Fedorova+ ONLY 1LIT – VALUE=RECOMM.TBL	
				Conf	75Kiev 1 169	May 75	– + EVAL SIG GIVEN,TABLE	
Res Int Abs	5.0 – 1		AUA Eval	Rept	AAEC/TM – 619	Sep 72	Clayton.CALC FROM SIG LIBRARY,TABLE	
Res Int Abs	5.5 – 1	+6	SAC Revw	Conf	IAEA – 169 1 235	74	Ribon.CAPTURE,STATUS CFD REQUEST,TBL	
Res Int Abs	+0	+5	WIN Revw	Conf	IAEA – 169 3 163	74	Pope+ DATA FILE CALC CFD XPTAL VALUE	
(n,γ)	Pile		ORL Expt	Jour	NSE 20 302	Nov 64	Lantz+ 29 PM3B.MAS SPECT MET.EFF B	+
	Pile			Data	EXFOR12056.004	Jun 76	. 1 PT. SIGMA	
(n,γ)	Pile		CRC Eval	Rept	AECL – 3037 1	Jan 72	Walker.RECOMMENDED SIG,DETAILED TBL	
(n,γ)	2.5 – 2		AUA Eval	Rept	AAEC/TM – 619	Sep 72	Clayton.CALC FROM SIG LIBRARY,TABLE	
(n,γ)	2.5 – 2		SAC Revw	Conf	IAEA – 169 1 235	74	Ribon.STATUS SIG CFD REQUESTS,TABLE	
(n,γ)	Maxwl	Fiss	WIN Revw	Conf	IAEA – 169 3 163	74	Pope+ MAXW+FIS – SPEC AVG DATA CFD XPT	
	Fiss			Conf	IAEA – 169 3 137	74	Dean. POINT DATA AVG OVER STAND SPEC	
Spect (n,γ)	Maxwl		LAS Expt	Prog	WASH – 1074 82	Apr 67	Jurney.GE(LI) NAI SPECTROMETER NDG	
Reson Params	–		AUA Theo	Rept	AAEC/E – 211	Nov 70	Musgrove. CALCULTD D+GAM WIDTH GIVEN	
Strnth Fnctn	–		AUA Theo	Rept	AAEC/E – 211	Nov 70	Musgrove. SMOOTHED S0,S1 AND S2 GIVN	
Lvl Density	None		MUN Theo	Jour	NP/A 217 269	Dec 73	Dilg+ A,DELTA. BACK SHIFTED FERMIGAS	
Lvl Density	None		DUB Theo	Jour	NP/A 224 411	May 74	Soloviev+ 1/2 MICROSC MDL. SPH NUCL.	
Lvl Density	None		ROC Theo	Jour	NP/A 223 577	May 74	Huizenga+ EXP CFD MICROSC TH SPH NUC	

58 Cerium 142

Quantity	Energy (ev) Min	Max	Lab	Type	Documentation Ref Vol Page	Date	Author, Comments	Data
Evaluation	1.0-3	1.5+7	AUA	Eval	Rept AAEC/TM - 549	Jun 70	Cook.TOT,EL,INEL,NONEL,CAPT SIGS,NDG	+
					Rept AAEC/E - 214	Jun 71	Bertram+GROUP SIGMAS SAME QUANTS.NDG	
					Rept AAEC/TM - 587	Mar 71	*DESCRIPTION OF LIBRARY	
	1.0-3	1.5+7			Data AUSTR - DFN 137.	Nov 71	POINT(223) AND GROUP(127) SIGMAS	
Evaluation	1.0-5	1.5+7	BOL	Eval	Prog NEANDC(E)182 7	Dec 76	Fabri+ COMPLETE EVAL IN ENDF/B DONE	+
	1.0-5	1.5+7			Data CNEN - CEA 3	Jan 78	PRELIM.ALL QUANTITIES.ENDF FORMAT	
Total	3.0+3	3.0+5	DKE	Expt	Jour AP 8 211	Oct 59	Newson+ THIN - SAMPLE TRANSMISSN DATA	+
	2.0+2	6.0+4			Data EXFOR11452.015	Jun 76	. 118 PTS. SIGMA	
Total	1.0-3	1.5+7	AUA	Data	AUSTR - DFN 137.	Nov 71	COOK+POINT(223)+GROUP(127)SIG.CF EVL	+
Elastic	2.5-2		ORL	Expt	Jour PR 91 597	Aug 53	Koehler+ COH.SCAT.=2.6+ - 0.2 BARNS	+
	2.5-2				Data EXFOR12060.010	Jun 76	. 2 PTS, COH. SCAT, COH AMP	
Elastic	1.0-3	1.5+7	AUA	Eval	Data AUSTR - DFN 137.	Nov 71	COOK+POINT(223)+GROUP(127)SIG.CF EVL	+
Elastic	2.5-2		IJI	Eval	Conf 75Kiev 1 169	May 75	Fedorova+ EVAL 2200M/S SIG,TABLE	
Potntal Scat	2.5-2		ORL	Expt	Jour PR 91 597	Aug 53	Koehler+ SIGMA= 8.00 BARNS	+
Tot Inelastc	1.0+6	1.5+7	AUA	Eval	Data AUSTR - DFN 137.	Nov 71	COOK+POINT(10)+GROUP(127)SIG.CF EVL	+
Diff Inelast	Thrsh	1.7+6	LEB	Expt	Conf 72Kiev 2 4	Jan 72	Konobeevskij+ ABST,NDG.SIG TO 2+LVL	
Scattering	2.5-2		ORL	Expt	Jour PR 91 597	Aug 53	Koehler+ TRANS 2.6+ - 0.2B	+
	2.5-2				Data EXFOR12060.013	Jun 76	. 1 PT. SIGMA	
Scattering	2.5-2		IFU	Expt	Conf 70Helsinki 1 651	Jun 70	Vertebnij+ 2200M/SEC SIGMA GIVEN,TBL	
					Rept BNL - TR - 495	Jul 72	. ENGLISH OF 70HELSIN 1 651	
Nonelastic	1.0-3	1.5+7	AUA	Eval	Data AUSTR - DFN 137.	Nov 71	COOK+POINT(223)+GROUP(127)SIG.CF EVL	+
Absorption	4.1-1	1.0+7	GA	Eval	Rept GA - 2451	Aug 61	Joanou+ 68GROUP DATA FOR GAM - I ABS	
Absorption	1.0-4	1.0+7	JUL	Eval	Rept JUEL - 670 - RG	Jul 70	Liu. EVALUATION+CALC,GRPH,FN OF E	
Absorption	2.5-2		IJI	Eval	Rept KIYAI - 76 - 6	76	Fedorova+ COMP(REFS,SIGS),EVAL.TABLE	
					Conf 75Kiev 1 169	May 75	- + EVAL SIG GIVEN,TABLE	
Res Int Abs	5.0-1		CNE	Expt	Jour CJP 46 2473	Nov 68	Ricabarra+,RATIO TO THR - ACT SIGMA	+
					Rept CNEA - 274	70	- + SAME,IN SPANISH	
	5.0-1				Data EXFOR30129.010	Oct 72	RESON INT AND RATIO TO THR ABS SIGM.	
Res Int Abs	None		GA	Eval	Rept GA - 12071	Sep 71	Mathews+ RECOMMENDED VALUES	
Res Int Abs	5.5-1		CRC	Eval	Rept AECL - 3037 1	Jan 72	Walker.REDUCED RES INT,DETAILED TBL	
Res Int Abs		1.0+6	OSL	Expt	Prog INDC(NOR) - 1 1	May 72	Alstad+ RES CAPT INT REL AU.TBL.ABST	+
	0.0+0	1.0+6			Jour JIN 29 2155	Sep 67	- + ACTIV REL AU,AND CD RATIO	
		1.0+6			Data EXFOR20044.005	Sep 71	1PNT.CAPTURE.	
Res Int Abs	5.0-1		AUA	Eval	Rept AAEC/TM - 619	Sep 72	Clayton.CALC FROM SIG LIBRARY,TABLE	
Res Int Abs	4.6-1	1.0+6	RCN	Theo	Rept RCN - 191	Jul 73	Lautenbach.CAPT INT FROM GROUP SIGMA	
Res Int Abs	5.0-1		GHT	Expt	Jour JRC 20 695	74	Van Der Linden+ BY(N,G).CFD OTHS,TBL	+
	5.5-1				Conf 73Paris 2 241	Mar 73	- + ACT,REL THR+GOLD,TBL	
	5.5-1				Data EXFOR20645.017	Jul 76	1PNT.CAPTURE.	
Res Int Abs	5.5-1	+6	SAC	Revw	Conf IAEA - 169 1 235	74	Ribon.CAPTURE,STATUS CFD REQUEST,TBL	
Res Int Abs	+0	+5	WIN	Revw	Conf IAEA - 169 3 163	74	Pope+ DATA FILE CALC CFD XPTAL VALUE	
Res Int Abs	5.0-1		IJI	Eval	Rept KIYAI - 76 - 6	76	Fedorova+ COMP(REFS,RI),EVAL.TABLE	
					Conf 75Kiev 1 169	May 75	- + EVAL OF RI - EXPTS.TABLE	
(n,γ)	Maxwl		LAS	Expt	Jour JCP 17 421	Apr 49	Katcoff+SIGMA=.105+ - 02B/ATOM CE	+
	Maxwl				Data EXFOR12053.003	Jun 76	. 1 PT. SI8GMA	
(n,γ)	Fiss		ANL	Expt	Jour PR 78 632	Jun 50	Hughes+ REL SIG(THERMAL).	+
	Fiss				Data EXFOR11596.014	Jun 76	. 1 PT. SIGMA	
(n,γ)	Maxwl		ANL	Expt	Jour PR 78 632	Jun 50	Hughes+	+
	Maxwl				Data EXFOR11596.016	Jun 76	. 1 PT. SIGMA	
(n,γ)	Maxwl		ORL	Expt	Jour PR 88 412	Oct 52	Pomerance.PILE OSC.	+
	Maxwl				Data EXFOR11507.076	Jun 76	. 1 PT. SIGMA	
(n,γ)	Fiss		BNL	Expt	Jour PR 91 1423	Sep 53	Hughes+ ALSO LVL SPACINGS AT EXCIT E	
(n,γ)	Maxwl		MCG	Expt	Jour CJC 34 1023	Aug 56	Roy+ ACT 0.95+ - 0.05B REL CO59 36.3B	+
	Maxwl				Data EXFOR12051.002	Jun 76	. 1 PT. SIGMA	
(n,γ)	2.4+4		ORL	Expt	Jour PR 107 504	Jul 57	Macklin+ SB - BE NS,425+ - 43MB,.29MEV G	+
					Conf 58Geneva 15 68	Sep 58	- .PPR671,VAL GVN,EXPT DESCRIBD	
	2.4+4				Data EXFOR11399.037	Jun 76	. 1 PT. SIGMA	
(n,γ)	1.4+7		ALD	Expt	Jour PPS 72 505	Oct 58	Perkin+ACT ANAL BELOW 7.5MB, B - W TH	+
(n,γ)	2.0+5		ORL	Expt	Jour PR 114 1619	Jun 59	Lyon+ ABS GAMMA COUNT 22+ - 5MB ACT	+
	2.0+5				Data EXFOR11407.026	Jun 76	. 1 PT. SIGMA	
(n,γ)	Maxwl		CRC	Eval	Rept AECL - 1054	Mar 60	Walker.(CRRP - 913)	
(n,γ)	Pile		ORL	Expt	Jour NSE 8 378	Nov 60	Lyon. ACTIVATION,SIGMA GIVEN	+
					Conf 60Vienna 239	Oct 60	Stoughton+ NDG, EXPT DESCRIBED	
	Pile				Data EXFOR11625.025	Jun 76	. 1 PT. SIGMA	
(n,γ)	2.4+4		MUA	Expt	Jour PR 152 1055	Dec 66	Chaubey+ BETA - DET,SIG REL I - 127,TBL	+
	2.4+4				Data EXFOR30079.029	Dec 70	SIGMA FOR 33. H HALF - LIFE	
(n,γ)	Maxwl		OSL	Expt	Jour JIN 27 2155	Sep 67	Alstad+ ACTIVATION REL AU, +CD RATIO	+
	Maxwl				Data EXFOR20044.004	Sep 71	1PNT.SIG.	

58 Cerium 142

Quantity	Energy (ev) Min	Max	Lab	Type	Documentation Ref Vol Page	Date	Author, Comments	Data
(n,γ)	3.0+6		DEB	Expt Jour	JNE 21 797	Oct 67	Peto+ACTIV,SIGMA REL TO S-32(N,P)	+
	3.0+6			Data	EXFOR30031.020	Aug 70	SINGLE VALUE	
(n,γ)	1.4+7		LYO	Comp Rept	LYCEN/6780	Nov 67	Crouzet+COMPILATN FOR ACTIVTN ANALYS	
(n,γ)	−		IEA	Comp Rept	IEA−INF− 10	Aug 68	Atalla. TABLES OF HL,SIG AND GAMM−E	
(n,γ)	5.0+3	1.0+5	AUA	ExTh Rept	AAEC/E−198	May 69	Musgrove.S+P+D WAVE SIGMAS CALC,TBL	+
(n,γ)	1.0+3	1.0+7	BOL	Eval Rept	CCDN−NW/10	Dec 69	Benzi+H−F MOD,AXEL G(G)EST,ALL DATA	
				Rept	CEC(70)−2	Apr 70	− +. GRAPH	
				Conf	66Paris 1 537	Oct 66	− + STATMOD.TBL AV VALS.SUPERSEDD	
(n,γ)	3.0+4		AUA	Theo Rept	AAEC/E−211	Nov 70	Musgrove. SIGMA GIVEN AND CFD OTHER	
(n,γ)	Fast		MTR	Expt Abst	ANS 13 755	Nov 70	Scoville+ CFRMF MEAST.VALUE GIVEN.	
				Prog	IN− 1407 29	Jun 70	− + ACT.FAST SPECT.VALUE GIVEN	
(n,γ)	Maxwl		GA	Eval Rept	GA− 12071	Sep 71	Mathews+ RECOMMENDED VALUES	
(n,γ)	1.0−3	1.5+7	AUA	Eval Data	AUSTR−DFN 137.	Nov 71	COOK+POINT(223)+GROUP(127)SIG.CF EVL	+
(n,γ)	Maxwl		CRC	Eval Rept	AECL−3037 1	Jan 72	Walker.RECOMMENDED SIG,DETAILED TBL	
(n,γ)	2.5−2		AUA	Eval Rept	AAEC/TM−619	Sep 72	Clayton.CALC FROM SIG LIBRARY,TABLE	
(n,γ)	Fast		MTR	Expt Conf	72Kiamesha 2 614	Sep 72	Harker+ CFRMF INTEGRAL MEAS.	
(n,γ)		1.1+7	RCN	Theo Rept	RCN−191	Jun 73	Lautenbach. GROUP CONSTANTS TBL	
(n,γ)	2.5−2	3.0+4	SAC	Revw Conf	IAEA−169 1 235	74	Ribon.STATUS SIG CFD REQUESTS,TABLE	
(n,γ)	Fiss		WIN	Revw Conf	IAEA−169 3 137	74	Dean. POINT DATA AVG OVER STAND SPEC	
	Maxwl	Fiss		Conf	IAEA−169 3 163	74	Pope+ MAXW+FIS−SPEC AVG DATA CFD XPT	
(n,γ)	1.0+3	1.0+7	FEI	Eval Rept	YK− 8/2 97	Sep 72	Abagjan+ AVG SIG(ENERGY−GROUPS),TABL	
				Rept	INDC(CCP)−39	Jul 74	.P102. ENGLISH OF YK−8/2 97	
(n,γ)	2.5+4		TAT	Expt Conf	74Bombay 2 101	Dec 74	Kondaiah+ SIGMA GIVEN	+
	2.5+4			Data	EXFOR30390.014	Mar 77	1PNT.	
(n,γ)	1.4+7		IRK	Expt Jour	NP/A 264 105	Jun 76	Schwerer+ GE−LI.ACT SIG=1.11+−0.17MB	+
	1.5+7			Data	EXFOR20670.015	Oct 76	1PNT.SIGMA.	
(n,γ)	Fast		RCN	Expt Rept	ECN−10	Oct 76	Veenema+ STEK REACTIVITY WORTHS TBL.	
Spect (n,γ)	Pile		IPS	Expt Jour	AF 4 81	Aug 52	Kondaiah. DECAY SCHEME. GRAPHS	
Spect (n,γ)	2.5+4		ORL	Expt Jour	58Geneva 15 68	Sep 58	Macklin.PPR671,SIGMA+G−ENERGY GVN	
Spect (n,γ)	Maxwl		CCP	Expt Jour	IZV 30 1253	Aug 66	Arutjunjan+.TABLE+GRAPH OF GAM−SPECT	
				Jour	BAS 30 1310	66	. ENGL OF IZV 30 1253	
Spect (n,γ)	Maxwl		KUR	Expt Jour	YF 10 681	Oct 69	Groshev+ TABLE GAM−SPECTRA,TRANSITNS	+
				Rept	IAE−1780	Jan 69	− + TBL OF GAMMA YLD+E,GE(LI)	
				Jour	SNP 10 392	Apr 70	. ENGL OF YF 10 681	
				Rept	LA−TR−69−29	Oct 69	. ENGLISH OF IAE−1780	
	2.5−2			Data	EXFOR40237.008	Nov 74	.GAM/100N FOR 4 ES GVN	
Spect (n,γ)	2.5−2		MAN	Expt Jour	PR/C 13 1434	Apr 76	Gelletly+G SPEC 100KEV−6MEV.TBL,GRPH	
	Maxwl			Rept	BNL−19168	Jan 75	− +TBL.LVL.SCHEME	
				Conf	74Petten 526	Sep 74	− + DECAY SCHEME CE−143, TBL	
Inelastic γ	1.5+6		TNC	Theo Prog	WASH−1071 192	Nov 66	Mathur+ .645−MEV GAMMA DISTR,NDG,TBC	
Inelastic γ	8.0+5	1.8+6	TNC	Expt Rept	ORO−2791−32	Feb 71	Buchanan+ 4NEUT ES,0.645MEV GAMMA	+
	8.0+5	1.8+6		Data	EXFOR11662.010	Jun 76	. 13 PTS. DSIG	
(n,2n)	1.5+7		ARK	Expt Jour	PR 118 242	Apr 60	Wille+ MEAS ACT SIG=1600+−300MB	+
	1.5+7			Data	EXFOR12033.015	Jun 76	. 1 PT. SIGMA	
(n,2n)	Fiss		CRC	Eval Rept	CRC−1003	Dec 60	ROY+ ESTIMATED AVG SIG=10.0MB	
(n,2n)	1.4+7		HAM	Comp Jour	NP 65 257	Mar 65	Bormann. 1EXPT VALS.CFD SHELL EFFECT	
(n,2n)	1.4+7		NAP	Expt Priv	CUZZOCREA+	Nov 66	Cuzzocrea+ PRELIM.ABST TO SIF 66	+
(n,2n)	1.4+7		LYO	Comp Rept	LYCEN/6780	Nov 67	Crouzet+COMPILATN FOR ACTIVTN ANALYS	
(n,2n)	1.5+7		DEB	Expt Jour	AHP 24 233	Feb 68	Csikai+ ACTIV,ABS VALUE,THEORY CFD	+
				Jour	MFF 16 123	Feb 68	SEE ALSO *THESIS IN HUNG	
	1.5+7			Data	EXFOR30040.005	Nov 70	SIGMA AT 14.8 MEV RESP TO PR−141(NP)	
(n,2n)	1.3+7	1.9+7	HAM	Expt Jour	NP/A 115 309	Jul 68	Bormann+ VDG.ACT.CFD STATMDL+OPTMDL	+
(n,2n)	1.5+7		MUN	Expt Jour	NP/A 118 9	Sep 68	Dilg+ ACTIV.REL AL(N,A)	+
	1.5+7	1.5+7		Jour	OAWS 177 323	69	Winkler+(IRK) ACTIVATION.	
	1.5+7			Data	EXFOR20802.003	Dec 78	1PNT.SIGMA.	
(n,2n)	1.5+7		DEB	Comp Jour	REA 7 4 93	Dec 69	Csikai+ SIG+HL COMPILTN,N−ACTIV−ANAL	
(n,2n)	1.5+7		CCP	Comp Rept	ICD−6 215	70	Sluchevskaja.SIG FROM 2 REFERENC,TBL	
(n,2n)	1.4+7		GIT	Expt Jour	PR/C 1 350	Jan 70	Fink+ACTIVATION,GRPHS,TBL CFD OTH.	+
	1.4+7			Data	EXFOR10497.044	Apr 76	1PT. CS=1730+−170MB.	
(n,2n)	1.4+7	1.5+7	JYV	Eval Rept	JU−RR−3/1970	Jun 70	Leppaemaeki+ TABLE OF EVAL AVG SIG	
(n,2n)	+7		KFI	Theo Rept	KFKI−71−8	Feb 71	Jeki. CALCULATED CFD EXPTL SIG VALUE	
(n,2n)	1.4+7		GIT	Theo Jour	PR/C 4 1173	Oct 71	Fink+ STAT−MODEL CALCULATION,CFD EXP	
(n,2n)	1.5+7		ARK	Expt Abst	DA/B 32 5091	Mar 72	Bari. GE(LI) DET. ACT. SIG GIVEN	+
	1.5+7			Data	EXFOR10431.045	Aug 75	1PT,SIGMA	
(n,2n)	1.5+7		DEB	Eval Jour	REA 11 1 153	Mar 73	Boedy. COMPILATION+RECOMM.VALUE,TBL	
				Rept	IAEA−153 173	73	− . RECOMM. VALUE ONLY	
(n,2n)	1.5+7		TAT	Theo Jour	JP/A 7 1458	Aug 74	Kondaiah. CALC ON STAT MODEL	

58 Cerium 142

Quantity	Energy (ev) Min	Max	Lab	Type	Documentation Ref Vol Page	Author, Comments Date	Data
(n,2n)	1.5+7		JUL	Expt Jour	NP/A 224 319	May 74 Qaim. ACT.GE(LI)	+
				Jour	RRL 25 335	May 76 − + SIG IN GRPH. SYST VS (N−Z)/A	
	1.5+7			Data	EXFOR20541.011	Apr 76 1PNT.SIGMA.	
(n,2n)	1.4+7		IRK	Expt Jour	OAWA 113 9 153	Jun 76 Schwerer+SIG.CORR.BY SELF−ABS.ETC.	+
	1.5+7			Prog	EANDC(OR)117L	Aug 72 Rohatsch. TBL ABST	
	1.4+7			Data	EXFOR20811.015	Oct 78 1PNT.SIGMA.	
(n,p)	1.4+7		CCP	Expt Jour	ZET 33 1520	Dec 57 Act+RDCHEM,REL TO CE140 .60/1	
				Jour	JET 6 1174	Jun 58 TRANSLATN.*	
(n,p)	1.4+7		ALD	Expt Jour	PPS 73 215	Feb 59 Coleman+. ACT. CFD DIRECT INTERACTN	+
(n,p)	1.5+7		ARK	Expt Jour	PR 118 242	Apr 60 Wille+ MEAS ACT SIG=5.+−2MB	+
	1.5+7			Data	EXFOR12033.014	Jun 76 . 1 PT. SIGMA	
(n,p)	Fiss		CRC	Eval Rept	CRC−1003	Dec 60 ROY+ ESTIMATED AVG SIG=0.002MB	
(n,p)	1.4+7	1.5+7	SAH	Comp Jour	NUC 23 8 112	Aug 65 Chatterjee. TABLE WITH REFS.	
(n,p)	1.4+7		NAP	Expt Priv	CUZZOCREA+	Nov 66 Cuzzocrea+ PRELIM.ABST TO SIF 66	+
(n,p)	1.4+7	1.5+7	ARK	Theo Prog	ORO−3235−29	Jan 67 Koch+ STAT MODEL CALC CFD EXPTS	
(n,p)	1.4+7	1.5+7	NAP	Comp Rept	INFN/BE−67−10	Jul 67 Cuzzocrea+ AVERAGED CHOSEN DATA.	
(n,p)	1.4+7		LYO	Comp Rept	LYCEN/6780	Nov 67 Crouzet+COMPILATN FOR ACTIVTN ANALYS	
(n,p)	1.5+7		DEB	Comp Jour	REA 7 4 93	Dec 69 Csikai+ SIG+HL COMPILTN,N−ACTIV−ANAL	
(n,p)	1.4+7	1.5+7	JYV	Eval Rept	JU−RR−3/1970	Jun 70 Leppaemaeki+ TABLE OF EVAL AVG SIG	
(n,p)	1.5+7		MUA	Expt Jour	NC/A 3 3 467	Jun 71 Prasad+ ACTIVATION CFD STATMOD	+
				Conf	69Roorke 2 112	Dec 69 − + SIG VALUE FOR 1.35 H HALF−L	
	1.5+7			Data	EXFOR30336.037	76 1 PNT	
(n,p)	1.4+7	1.5+7	KAZ	Theo Jour	YF 18 705	Oct 73 Levkovsky.AVERAGED SIG,CALC,TBL	
				Jour	SNP 18 361	Apr 74 . ENGLISH OF YF 18,705	
(n,p)	1.5+7		JUL	Expt Jour	RRL 25 335	May 76 Qaim+ ACTIV,GELI.CFD OTHERS,TBL+GRPH	+
	1.5+7			Data	EXFOR20716.003	Jun 77 1PNT.SIGMA.	
(n,p)	1.4+7		IRK	Expt Jour	OAWA 113 9 153	Jun 76 Schwerer+SIG.CORR.BY SELF−ABS.ET3§	+
	1.4+7			Data	EXFOR20811.016	Oct 78 1PNT.SIGMA.	
(n,np)	1.5+7		LON	Expt Jour	NP 1 278	Mar 56 Cohen+. ACT METHOD. UPPER LIMIT	
(n,np)	1.5+7		ALD	Expt Jour	PPS 74 632	Nov 59 Barry+ACTIV.1.0+−0.2MB CFD DIRECT TH	+
(n,np)	1.4+7		OSM	Theo Jour	PHY 27 1113	Dec 61 Hyder. DIRECT INTERACT,NUMER VALUES	
(n,np)	1.4+7	1.5+7	JYV	Eval Rept	JU−RR−3/1970	Jun 70 Leppaemaeki+ TABLE OF EVAL AVG SIG	
(n,np)		7.5+8	IOW	Expt Jour	PR/C 12 1978	Dec 75 Hill+ ES TO 750 MEV.(N,2PN) REACTION	
(n,d)	1.4+7	1.5+7	SAH	Comp Jour	NUC 23 8 112	Aug 65 Chatterjee. TABLE WITH REFS.	
(n,d)			JUL	Expt Rept	EUR−5182E 939	Sep 74 Qaim+ ACT METHOD,SUM OF ND+NNP SIG	+
	1.5+7			Data	EXFOR20513.036	Apr 76 1PNT.+NNP.	
(n,He3)			JUL	Expt Prog	NEANDC(E)161U	Aug 74 Qaim+ VACUUM SEPERATION	
(n,α)	1.4+7		ALD	Expt Jour	PPS 73 215	Feb 59 Coleman+. ACTIVATION	+
(n,α)	1.5+7		ARK	Expt Jour	PR 118 242	Apr 60 Wille+ MEAS ACT SIG=8.+−2.MB	+
	1.5+7			Data	EXFOR12033.013	Jun 76 . 1 PT. SIGMA	
(n,α)	Fiss		CRC	Eval Rept	CRC−1003	Dec 60 ROY+ ESTIMATED AVG SIG=0.0033MB	
(n,α)			CIS	Theo Jour	NP 51 460	Feb 64 Facchini+STATMOD XPT/CALC=2−3.3	
(n,α)	1.4+7		NAP	Expt Priv	CUZZOCREA+	Nov 66 Cuzzocrea+ PRELIM.ABST TO SIF 66	+
(n,α)	1.4+7	1.5+7	NAP	Comp Rept	INFN/BE−67−11	Sep 67 Cuzzocrea+ AVERAGED CHOSEN DATA.	
(n,α)	1.4+7		LYO	Comp Rept	LYCEN/6780	Nov 67 Crouzet+COMPILATN FOR ACTIVTN ANALYS	
(n,α)	1.5+7		KAZ	Expt Jour	YF 8 7	Jul 68 Levkovskij+ SIG VAL +−ERROR GVN,TBL	+
				Jour	SNP 8 4	Jan 69 TRANSLATN.*	
	1.5+7			Data	EXFOR40223.025	May 74 .SIGMA GIVEN,1 DATA LINE	
(n,α)	1.5+7		DEB	Comp Jour	REA 7 4 93	Dec 69 Csikai+ SIG+HL COMPILTN,N−ACTIV−ANAL	
(n,α)	1.4+7		GIT	Expt Jour	PR/C 1 358	Jan 70 Fink+ SIG=6.0+−1.0MB	+
	1.4+7			Data	EXFOR10145.034	Apr 75 1PT,SIGMA	
(n,α)	1.4+7	1.5+7	JYV	Eval Rept	JU−RR−3/1970	Jun 70 Leppaemaeki+ TABLE OF EVAL AVG SIG	
(n,α)	1.4+7		GIT	Theo Jour	PR/C 4 1173	Oct 71 Fink+ STAT−MODEL CALCULATION,CFD EXP	
(n,α)	1.5+7		ARK	Expt Abst	DA/B 32 5091	Mar 72 Bari. GE(LI) DET. ACT. SIG GIVEN	
	1.5+7			Data	EXFOR10431.022	Aug 75 1PT,SIGMA	
Reson Params		1.0+6	AUA	Theo Jour	AUJ 20 477	Oct 67 Cook. TBL OF AVG LVL SPACING D,L=0,1	
Reson Params	3.0+0	1.0+3	IFU	Expt Conf	69Erevan	Feb 69 Vertebnij+.ABST,LVL DENS ISOT DEPEND	
Reson Params	−		AUA	Theo Rept	AAEC/E−211	Nov 70 Musgrove. CALCULTD D+GAM WIDTH GIVEN	
Reson Params	1.3+3	4.4+3	IJI	Expt Jour	UFZ 15 2050	Dec 70 Vertebny+ N−WIDTH,4 RES,D,TBLS	+
				Prog	YFI−7 37	Apr 69 − + 4 RES−ES, D AND NEUT−WIDTH	
				Rept	INDC(CCP)−7U40	Feb 70 .TRANSLATION OF YFI−7 37	
	1.3+3	4.4+3		Data	EXFOR40052.	Jul 73 .4 RES−ES,N−WIDTH AND D GIVEN	
Reson Params	None		DUB	Theo Jour	ZEP 14 194	Aug 71 Solovev.LARGE N−WID G−WID CORREL.NDG	
				Rept	JINR−E4−5880	71 Soloviev.N−GAM−WIDS CORR.SHORT NOTE	
				Jour	JEL 14 129	Aug 71 − . ENGL OF ZEP 14 194.	
Reson Params	None		DUB	Theo Rept	JINR−P4−7499	Oct 73 Soloviev+ CALC D CFD EXPTS,TABLE	

58 Cerium 142

Quantity	Energy (ev) Min	Max	Lab	Type	Documentation Ref Vol Page	Author, Comments Date	Data
Reson Params	+3		FEI	Eval	Rept YK – 8/2 97	Sep 72 Abagyan+ AVG G – WID+D AT BINDNG – E,TBL	
					Rept INDC(CCP) – 39	Jul 74 .PAGE 102.ENGLISH OF YK – 8/2 97	
Strnth Fnctn		2.0+5	DKE	Expt	Jour AP 8 211	Oct 59 Newson+ FROM RESON PARAMS 1.2+ – 0.5	+
		2.0+5		Data	EXFOR11888.012	Jun 76 . 1 PT, D	
Strnth Fnctn	–		AUA	Theo	Rept AAEC/E – 211	Nov 70 Musgrove. SMOOTHED S0,S1 AND S2 GIVN	
Strnth Fnctn	None		AUA	Eval	Rept AAEC/E – 277	Mar 73 Musgrove.TBLS EXPTL DATA+BEST VALUES	
Strnth Fnctn	None		KUR	Theo	Prog IAE – 2560	75 Adamchuk+.S0 – VALUE,TBL	
Lvl Density	None		SAC	Expt	Jour NP/A 133 417	Aug 69 Bergere+NUCL TEMP,A PARAM,FROM NG	
Lvl Density	None		AUW	Theo	Conf 70Madurai 2 267	Dec 70 Ramamurty+ A – PARAMETER GVN,LANG'S – TH	
Lvl Density	+3		FEI	Eval	Rept YK – 8/2 97	Sep 72 Abagyan+ LVL DENSITY PARAMETER,TBL	
					Rept INDC(CCP) – 39	Jul 74 .PAGE 102.ENGLISH OF YK – 8/2 97	
(γ,n)	8.0+6	2.6+7	SAC	Expt	Jour NP/A 258 350	Feb 76 Lepretre+GDR,LORENTZ PARAM,GRPHS,TBL	

58 Cerium 143

Quantity	Energy (ev) Min	Max	Lab	Type	Documentation Ref Vol Page	Author, Comments Date	Data
Evaluation	1.0 – 3	1.5+7	AUA	Eval	Rept AAEC/TM – 549	Jun 70 Cook.TOT,EL,INEL,NONEL,CAPT SIGS,NDG	+
					Rept AAEC/E – 214	Jun 71 Bertram+GROUP SIGMAS SAME QUANTS.NDG	
					Rept AAEC/TM – 587	Mar 71 *DESCRIPTION OF LIBRARY	
	1.0 – 3	1.5+7		Data	AUSTR – DFN 138.	Nov 71 POINT(223) AND GROUP(127) SIGMAS	
Total	1.0 – 3	1.5+7	AUA	Eval	Data AUSTR – DFN 138.	Nov 71 COOK+POINT(223)+GROUP(127)SIG.CF EVL	+
Elastic	1.0 – 3	1.5+7	AUA	Eval	Data AUSTR – DFN 138.	Nov 71 COOK+POINT(223)+GROUP(127)SIG.CF EVL	+
Tot Inelastc	1.0+6	1.5+7	AUA	Eval	Data AUSTR – DFN 138.	Nov 71 COOK+POINT(10)+GROUP(127)SIG.CF EVL	+
Nonelastic	1.0 – 3	1.5+7	AUA	Eval	Data AUSTR – DFN 138.	Nov 71 COOK+POINT(223)+GROUP(127)SIG.CF EVL	+
Absorption	2.5 – 2		IJI	Eval	Rept KIYAI – 76 – 6	76 Fedorova+ ONLY 1LIT – VALUE=RECOMM.TBL	
					Conf 75Kiev 1 169	May 75 – + EVAL SIG GIVEN,TABLE	
Res Int Abs	5.0 – 1		AUA	Eval	Rept AAEC/TM – 619	Sep 72 Clayton.CALC FROM SIG LIBRARY,TABLE	
Res Int Abs	5.5 – 1	+6	SAC	Revw	Conf IAEA – 169 1 235	74 Ribon.CAPTURE,STATUS CFD REQUEST,TBL	
Res Int Abs	+0	+5	WIN	Revw	Conf IAEA – 169 3 163	74 Pope+ CALC FROM AUSTRAL DATA FILE	
(n,γ)	Pile		MCG	Expt	Jour CJC 34 238	Mar 56 Roy+ 6.0+ – 0.7B BY PR144DECAY ABSCRVS	+
(n,γ)	1.0 – 3	1.5+7	AUA	Eval	Data AUSTR – DFN 138.	Nov 71 COOK+POINT(223)+GROUP(127)SIG.CF EVL	+
(n,γ)	Pile		CRC	Eval	Rept AECL – 3037 1	Jan 72 Walker.RECOMMENDED SIG,DETAILED TBL	
(n,γ)	2.5 – 2		AUA	Eval	Rept AAEC/TM – 619	Sep 72 Clayton.CALC FROM SIG LIBRARY,TABLE	
(n,γ)	2.5 – 2		SAC	Revw	Conf IAEA – 169 1 235	74 Ribon.STATUS SIG CFD REQUESTS,TABLE	
(n,γ)	Maxwl	Fiss	WIN	Revw	Conf IAEA – 169 3 163	74 Pope+ MAXW+FIS – SPEC AVG DATA CFD XPT	
	Fiss				Conf IAEA – 169 3 137	74 Dean. POINT DATA AVG OVER STAND SPEC	
Spect (n,γ)	Maxwl		LAS	Expt	Prog WASH – 1074 82	Apr 67 Jurney.GE(LI) NAI SPECTROMETER NDG	
Reson Params	–		AUA	Theo	Rept AAEC/E – 211	Nov 70 Musgrove. CALCULTD D+GAM WIDTH GIVEN	
Strnth Fnctn	–		AUA	Theo	Rept AAEC/E – 211	Nov 70 Musgrove. SMOOTHED S0,S1 AND S2 GIVN	
Lvl Density	None		MUN	Theo	Jour NP/A 217 269	Dec 73 Dilg+ A,DELTA. BACK SHIFTED FERMIGAS	
Lvl Density	None		COP	Theo	Jour NP/A 222 493	Apr 74 Dossing+COLL ROTAT.SPAC. ACCUR ESTIM	
Lvl Density	None		DUB	Theo	Jour NP/A 224 411	May 74 Soloviev+ 1/2 MICROSC MDL. SPH NUCL.	
Lvl Density	None		ROC	Theo	Jour NP/A 223 577	May 74 Huizenga+ EXP CFD MICROSC TH SPH NUC	

58 Cerium 144

Quantity	Energy (ev) Min	Max	Lab	Type	Documentation Ref Vol Page	Author, Comments Date	Data
Evaluation	1.0 – 3	1.5+7	AUA	Eval	Rept AAEC/TM – 549	Jun 70 Cook.TOT,EL,INEL,NONEL,CAPT SIGS,NDG	+
					Rept AAEC/E – 214	Jun 71 Bertram+GROUP SIGMAS SAME QUANTS.NDG	
					Rept AAEC/TM – 587	Mar 71 *DESCRIPTION OF LIBRARY	
	1.0 – 3	1.5+7		Data	AUSTR – DFN 139.	Nov 71 POINT(223) AND GROUP(127) SIGMAS	
Evaluation	1.0+2	1.5+7	JAE	Eval	Rept JAERI – M – 5752	Jul 74 Igarasi+ JNDC FPND WG.TOT,EL,N',CAP	
Evaluation	1.0 – 5	1.5+7	BOL	Eval	Prog NEANDC(E)182 7	Dec 76 Fabri+ COMPLETE EVAL IN ENDF/B DONE	+
	1.0 – 5	1.5+7		Data	CNEN – CEA 3	Jan 78 PRELIM.ALL QUANTITIES.ENDF FORMAT	
Total	1.0 – 3	1.5+7	AUA	Eval	Data AUSTR – DFN 139.	Nov 71 COOK+POINT(223)+GROUP(127)SIG.CF EVL	+
Elastic	1.0 – 3	1.5+7	AUA	Eval	Data AUSTR – DFN 139.	Nov 71 COOK+POINT(223)+GROUP(127)SIG.CF EVL	+
Tot Inelastc	5.0+5	1.5+7	AUA	Eval	Data AUSTR – DFN 139.	Nov 71 COOK+POINT(11)+GROUP(127)SIG.CF EVL	+
Nonelastic	1.0 – 3	1.5+7	AUA	Eval	Data AUSTR – DFN 139.	Nov 71 COOK+POINT(223)+GROUP(127)SIG.CF EVL	+
Absorption	2.5 – 2		IJI	Eval	Rept KIYAI – 76 – 6	76 Fedorova+ ONLY 1LIT – VALUE=RECOMM.TBL	
					Conf 75Kiev 1 169	May 75 – + EVAL SIG GIVEN,TABLE	
Res Int Abs	5.0 – 1		ORL	Expt	Jour NSE 13 289	Jul 62 Lantz.ACTIVATION RI=2.60+ – 0.26B	+
					Conf 60Vienna 239	Oct 60 Stoughton+ VAL GVN,EXPT DESCRIBED	
	5.0 – 1			Data	EXFOR12055.003	Jun 76 . 1 PT, RI	
Res Int Abs	None		CRC	Eval	Rept AECL – 2111	Nov 64 Walker.REDUCED RESONANCE INTEGRAL	
Res Int Abs	5.5 – 1		CRC	Eval	Rept AECL – 3037 1	Jan 72 Walker.REDUCED RES INT,DETAILED TBL	

58 Cerium 144

Quantity	Energy (ev) Min	Max	Lab	Type	Documentation Ref Vol Page	Date	Author, Comments	Data
Res Int Abs	5.0 – 1		AUA	Eval Rept	AAEC/TM – 619	Sep 72	Clayton.CALC FROM SIG LIBRARY,TABLE	
Res Int Abs	5.5 – 1	+6	SAC	Revw Conf	IAEA – 169 1 235	74	Ribon.CAPTURE,STATUS CFD REQUEST,TBL	
Res Int Abs	+0	+5	WIN	Revw Conf	IAEA – 169 3 163	74	Pope+ DATA FILE CALC CFD XPTAL VALUE	
Res Int Abs	5.0 – 1		IJI	Eval Rept	KIYAI – 76 – 6	76	Fedorova+ COMP(REFS,RI),EVAL.TABLE	
				Conf	75Kiev 1 169	May 75	– + EVAL OF RI – EXPTS.TABLE	
(n,γ)	Maxwl		ORL	Expt Jour	NSE 13 289	Jul 62	Lantz.ACTIVATION SIG = 1.00 + – 0.10B	+
				Conf	60Vienna 239	Oct 60	Stoughton+ VAL GVN,EXPT DESCRIBED	
	Maxwl			Data	EXFOR12055.002	Jun 76	. 1 PT. SIG	
(n,γ)	Maxwl		CRC	Eval Rept	AECL – 3037 1	Dec 69	Walker.RECOMMENDED SIG,DETAILED TBL	
(n,γ)	1.0 – 3	1.5+7	AUA	Eval Data	AUSTR – DFN 139.	Nov 71	COOK+ POINT(223)+ GROUP(127)SIG.CF EVL	+
(n,γ)	Maxwl		CRC	Eval Rept	AECL – 2111	Jan 72	Walker.REDUCED RESONANCE INTEGRAL	
(n,γ)	2.5 – 2		AUA	Eval Rept	AAEC/TM – 619	Sep 72	Clayton.CALC FROM SIG LIBRARY,TABLE	
(n,γ)	2.5 – 2	3.0+4	SAC	Revw Conf	IAEA – 169 1 235	74	Ribon.STATUS SIG CFD REQUESTS,TABLE	
	Fiss			Conf	IAEA – 169 1 235	74	– .STATUS SIG CFD REQUESTS,TABLE	
(n,γ)	Maxwl Fiss		WIN	Revw Conf	IAEA – 169 3 163	74	Pope+ MAXW+ FIS – SPEC AVG DATA CFD XPT	
	Fiss			Conf	IAEA – 169 3 137	74	Dean. POINT DATA AVG OVER STAND SPEC	
Fiss Prod γ	Pile		SGA	Theo Jour	APA 28 94	Apr 69	Higats+ COMP.PROGR.BUILDUP FISS.PROD.	
Reson Params	–		AUA	Theo Rept	AAEC/E – 211	Nov 70	Musgrove. CALCULTD D+GAM WIDTH GIVEN	
Reson Params	None		DUB	Theo Jour	ZEP 14 194	Aug 71	Solovev.LARGE N – WID G – WID CORREL.NDG	
				Rept	JINR – E4 – 5880	71	Soloviev.N – GAM – WIDS CORR.SHORT NOTE	
				Jour	JEL 14 129	Aug 71	– . ENGL OF ZEP 14 194.	
Strnth Fnctn	–		AUA	Theo Rept	AAEC/E – 211	Nov 70	Musgrove. SMOOTHED S0,S1 AND S2 GIVEN	
Lvl Density	– 3	+0	IFU	Theo Jour	UFZ 13 700	Apr 68	Pisanko+ LEVEL SPACING CALC,TBL	
				Jour	UPJ 13 498	Oct 68	TRANSLATN.*	

58 Cerium 145

Quantity	Energy (ev) Min	Max	Lab	Type	Documentation Ref Vol Page	Date	Author, Comments	Data
Reson Params	–		AUA	Theo Rept	AAEC/E – 211	Nov 70	Musgrove. CALCULTD D+GAM WIDTH GIVEN	
Strnth Fnctn	–		AUA	Theo Rept	AAEC/E – 211	Nov 70	Musgrove. SMOOTHED S0,S1 AND S2 GIVN	

59 Praseodymium 137

Quantity	Energy (ev) Min	Max	Lab	Type	Documentation Ref Vol Page	Author, Comments Date	Data
Reson Params	–		AUA	Theo Rept	AAEC/E – 211	Nov 70 Musgrove. CALCULTD D+GAM WIDTH GIVEN	
Strnth Fnctn	–		AUA	Theo Rept	AAEC/E – 211	Nov 70 Musgrove. SMOOTHED S0,S1 AND S2 GIVN	

59 Praseodymium 138

Quantity	Energy (ev) Min	Max	Lab	Type	Documentation Ref Vol Page	Author, Comments Date	Data
Reson Params	–		AUA	Theo Rept	AAEC/E – 211	Nov 70 Musgrove. CALCULTD D+GAM WIDTH GIVEN	
Strnth Fnctn	–		AUA	Theo Rept	AAEC/E – 211	Nov 70 Musgrove. SMOOTHED S0,S1 AND S2 GIVN	

59 Praseodymium 139

Quantity	Energy (ev) Min	Max	Lab	Type	Documentation Ref Vol Page	Author, Comments Date	Data
Reson Params	–		AUA	Theo Rept	AAEC/E – 211	Nov 70 Musgrove. CALCULTD D+GAM WIDTH GIVEN	
Strnth Fnctn	–		AUA	Theo Rept	AAEC/E – 211	Nov 70 Musgrove. SMOOTHED S0,S1 AND S2 GIVN	

59 Praseodymium 140

Quantity	Energy (ev) Min	Max	Lab	Type	Documentation Ref Vol Page	Author, Comments Date	Data
Reson Params	–		AUA	Theo Rept	AAEC/E – 211	Nov 70 Musgrove. CALCULTD D+GAM WIDTH GIVEN	
Strnth Fnctn	–		AUA	Theo Rept	AAEC/E – 211	Nov 70 Musgrove. SMOOTHED S0,S1 AND S2 GIVN	
Lvl Density	9.5+6	1.8+7	ANL	Eval Rept	ANL – 75 – 34	Jun 75 Davey+N2NEVAL.CONSTANT T,LVL DEN FIT	

59 Praseodymium 141

Quantity	Energy (ev) Min	Max	Lab	Type	Documentation Ref Vol Page	Author, Comments Date	Data
Evaluation	5.0+5	1.5+7	LRL	Eval Rept	UCRL – 5351	Nov 58 Howerton. CURVS TOT SEL SNE STN N2N	
Evaluation	1.0 – 3	1.5+7	AUA	Eval Rept	AAEC/TM – 549	Jun 70 Cook.TOT,EL,INEL,NONEL,CAPT SIGS,NDG	+
				Rept	AAEC/E – 214	Jun 71 Bertram+GROUP SIGMAS SAME QUANTS.NDG	
				Rept	AAEC/TM – 587	Mar 71 *DESCRIPTION OF LIBRARY	
	1.0 – 3	1.5+7		Data	AUSTR – DFN 140.	Nov 71 POINT(226) AND GROUP(127) SIGMAS	
Evaluation	1.0+3	1.0+7	BOL	Eval Rept	CEC(71) – 2	71 Benzi+ STAT+EVAP MDS.INEL,N2N,NG.TBL	+
	1.0+3	1.0+7		Data	BENZI – DFN 552E	Mar 71 4 QUANTITIES. UK FORMAT	
Total	Maxwl		COL	Expt Jour	PR 48 265	Aug 35 Dunning+ IONCH,TRANS,RA – BE/PARAFIN N	
Total	5.0+4	3.2+6	WIS	Expt Jour	PR 88 83	Oct 52 Miller+ 20KEV SPREAD TRNSM	+
	5.0+4	3.2+6		Data	EXFOR11712.019	Jun 76 . 79 PTS.	
Total	1.4+7		LAS	Expt Jour	PR 88 562	Nov 52 Coon+	
	1.4+7			Data	EXFOR11056.047	Jun 76 . 1 PT.	
Total	1.0+0	5.0+0	BNL	Expt Priv	SAILOR	Mar 55 Sailor.	+
	1.0+0	5.0+0		Data	EXFOR12075.002	Jun 76 . 2 PTS.	
Total	1.1+1	2.1+3	BNL	Expt Priv	CARTER	Mar 55 Carter.	+
	1.1+1	2.1+3		Data	EXFOR11879.004	Jun 76 . 143 PTS.	
Total	4.5+0	1.0+4	CCP	Expt Conf	55Geneva 4 22	Aug 55 Vladimirski+.P641,CURVE,CHOPPER,TOF	+
Total	4.0+2	2.0+3	HAR	Theo Jour	PPS 71 910	Jun 58 Egelstaff.FLUCTUATIONS CFD THEORY	+
	1.0+3	3.2+4		Expt Jour	PPSA 70 51	Jan 57 Gayther+ FC THICK SAMPLE,AVSIG CF TH	
	8.0+0	2.4+4		Priv	EGELSTAFF5	Jun 56 Egelstaff.	
Total	1.4+7		CHF	Expt Jour	CHP 1 39	Oct 63 Hsu+.VAL GVN,VDG,PLASTIC SCINT	
Total	2.0 – 2	1.0+1	WUR	Expt Jour	HPA 37 224	May 64 Verdan.NDG TRANSMIS.MEAS	
Total	1.0+0	2.0+3	RPI	Expt Prog	WASH – 1048 71	Jun 64 Block.26 RES ES TBL,TRNS,TOF,6NS/M	
Total	9.8+5		SHE	Theo Jour	NP 54 417	Jun 64 Maddison.OPTMOD FIT TO TOWLE GILBOY	
Total	1.0 – 2	1.0+1	KAP	Expt Rept	CONF – 758 – 2	Jan 65 Hickman. TOF+SLOW CHOPPER.	+
	1.7 – 2	7.6+0		Data	EXFOR12004.003	Jun 76 . 61 PTS.	
Total	2.9 – 2	1.6 – 1	KAP	Expt Priv	HICKMAN	Jun 66 Brazos.	+
	2.9 – 2	1.6 – 1		Data	EXFOR12087.003	Jun 76 . 6 PTS.	
Total	1.7 – 2	8.3+0	KAP	Expt Priv	HICKMAN	Jun 66 Eiland.	+
	1.7 – 2	8.3+0		Data	EXFOR12070.002	Jun 76 . 89 PTS.	
Total	2.6 – 3	9.7 – 1	BSP	Expt Conf	66Paris 1 53	Oct 66 Zimmerman+,P.129, SIG(E) GRAPH	+
				Jour	NP/A 95 683	Apr 67 SEE ALSO *	
	2.6 – 3	9.7 – 1		Data	EXFOR30224.	Dec 72 SIG AT 32ES, SIG AT 0.025 EV,PRIVCOM	
Total	4.5+6	7.5+6	WIS	Expt Jour	PR 158 1142	Jun 67 Carlson+ VDG,CURV,50KEV RESOL,CFD TH	+
				Abst	DA/B 28 1084	Sep 67 .THESIS, ABST.	
				Conf	66Gatlinbg § 2.1	Sep 66 .SUPERSEDED	
	4.5+6	7.5+6		Data	EXFOR11497.025	Jun 76 . 60 PTS, SIG	

59 Praseodymium 141

Quantity	Energy (ev) Min	Max	Lab	Type	Documentation Ref Vol Page	Date	Author, Comments	Data
Total	6.0+0	2.5+5	COL	Expt	Jour PR 166 1234	Feb 68	Wynchank+ TOF 0.5NSEC/M RESOL CURVES	+
	5.5+1	3.0+5			Data EXFOR11913.023	Jun 76	. 9657 PTS.	
Total	3.2+6	5.2+6	JNE	Expt	Jour ARS 64 63	Feb 68	Manero.30KEV RESOL,3PC,OXIDE TARGET	+
	3.3+6	6.0+6			Data EXFOR20170.005	May 74	68PTS.	
Total	5.0+2	6.0+3	SAC	Expt	Jour NP/A 123 561	Jan 69	Morgenstern+LINAC 1 - 0.6NS/M NDG	+
	5.0+2	6.0+3			Data EXFOR20684.	Jul 77	0PTS. SEE RESONANCE PARAMETERS.	
Total	1.2+5	1.0+6	RAM	Expt	Prog INDC(PAK)-1 1	May 69	. VDG,EXPT TO BE DONE. NDG	
Total	1.3+7		DAC	Expt	Jour JNE 24 385	Nov 70	Hussain+ XPT.AT 2 ES,AT BACKWARD ANG	
	1.3+7				Data EXFOR30245.004	Jun 73	SIGMA - TOTAL AT 13.36 AND 13.48 MEV	
Total	1.4+7		RAM	Expt	Rept AECD/EP - 21	Jan 71	Ullah+ OPTMOD FIT TO EXPTL DATA,GRPH	
Total	2.5+6	1.5+7	BNW	Expt	Jour PR/C 3 576	Feb 71	Foster+,TRANS,CURVS,CFD OTHERS+TH	+
					Jour NIM 36 1	Sep 65	.EXPT DETAILS	
	2.3+6	1.5+7			Data EXFOR10047.063	Aug 73	. 246 PTS.	
Total	1.0+6	1.8+7	RAM	Expt	Rept AECD/EP - 24	Jul 71	Enayetullah+ CFD OPTMOD,GRPH,TBP NSE	
	1.6+7	1.8+7			Rept AECD/EP - 18	Dec 70	Husain.VDG,TRANS,SIG AT 6 ES,TABLE	
	1.0+6	2.0+6			Rept AECD/EP - 18	Dec 70	- .VDG,TRANS,SIG AT 101ES,TABLE	
	3.8+6	5.6+6			Rept AECD/EP - 18	Dec 70	- .VDG,TRANS,SIG AT 14 ES,TABLE	
Total	1.0-3	1.5+7	AUA	Eval	Data AUSTR - DFN 140.	Nov 71	COOK+POINT(226)+GROUP(127)SIG.CF EVL	+
Total	2.7+3		MUN	Expt	Prog EANDC(E)150U	Oct 72	Dilg+ AVERAGE TOT XSECT+S0	+
					Conf 71Albany 327	Aug 71	- +TRNS.AVG CS GVN.31 ELEMENT GRP	
	2.7+3				Data EXFOR20583.014	May 76	1PNT.	
Total	1.3+7	1.5+7	DEB	Eval	Rept IAEA - 153 173	73	Boedy+ MOST PROBABLE VAL OF SIG,TBL	
					Jour AHP 30 115	Oct 71	Angeli+ AVG SIG,CFD CALC.TBLS.GRAPH	
Total	1.0+6	1.8+7	DAC	Expt	Rept NSE 46 148	Oct 71	Enayetullah+ TRANS,CFD OPTMOD,GRPH	+
				ExTh	Jour JNE 27 123	Feb 73	.DEDUCE PARAMETERS OF OPTICAL MODEL	
				Comp	Rept AECD/EP - 18	Dec 70	Ameen+ COMPILATION OF EXP VALUES	
	1.0+6	1.8+7		Expt	Data EXFOR30243.002	Jun 73	SIG - TOT FROM 3 TO 18 MEV AT 20 ES	
Total	1.0+6	2.0+6	DAC	Expt	Jour NSPB 6 59	Oct 73	Enayetullah+ SIG(E),LSQ - FIT,TBL+GRPH	+
				Expt	Jour NP/A 209 189	Jul 73	Islam+ VDG,TRANS,CFD OPTICAL MODEL	
				Theo	Jour NP/A 209 202	Jul 73	- + FLUCTUATION ANALYSIS,OWN DATA	
				Comp	Rept AECD/EP - 18	Dec 70	Ameen+ EXPTL DATA FROM DAC,TABLES	
	1.0+6	2.0+6		Expt	Data EXFOR30134.006	Nov 71	SIGMA - TOT AT 100 ES,PRIVATE COMM.	
Total	7.0+5	9.0+6	GLS	Expt	Jour JP/A 7 1758	Sep 74	Kellie+ SIG IN CURVE,STAT ERROR 2 PC	+
	7.0+5	9.0+6			Data EXFOR20418.004	Sep 75	646PTS.	
Total	5.0+5	2.4+6	ITK	Expt	Prog BARC - 831 45	75	Singh+ TRANSMISSN,CFD OPTMOD, NDG	
Total	2.5+5	1.5+7	JAE	Theo	Conf JAERI - M - 5984	Feb 75	Tanaka.OPTMDL/COUPLD CH.GRPH CFD EXP	
Total	2.5-2		IJI	Comp	Rept KIYAI - 76 - 6	76	Fedorova+ TO GET RECOM ABS - SIG.TABLE	
Total	5.0+5	2.4+6	GEL	Expt	Prog NEANDC(E)172 3	Feb 76	Singh+VDG TOF	
					Prog NEANDC(E)162 3	Feb 75	- +VDG TOF	
					Jour ZP/A 272 47	Jan 75	Knitter+ MEAS + CFD WITH OPTMOD - CALC	
Elastic	5.0-1		ANL	Expt	Jour PR 79 11	Jul 50	Harris+ EPI - CD,RES INT SCAT,B - W TH	
Elastic	Maxwl		ORL	Expt	Jour PR 91 597	Aug 53	Koehler+	+
	Maxwl				Data EXFOR12060.	Jun 76	. 2 PTS, COH, COH AMP	
Elastic	1.0+6		ALD	Expt	Jour NP 42 86	Apr 63	Gilboy+.SIG=6.83B + - 3PC	
Elastic	9.8+5		AGN	Eval	Rept TID - 21629	Dec 64	Perkins+ BNL325,UCRL5573 DATA	
Elastic	8.0+6		VIR	Expt	Conf 68Wash. § E10	Mar 68	Bernard+ INTEG ANG DIST	
	8.0+6				Data EXFOR12054.007	Jun 76	. 1 PT, SIG	
Elastic	2.3+5	1.6+6	SUN	Expt	Jour NP/A 124 111	Feb 69	Malan.JG+,VDG,TOF,LEG FIT,TABLE	+
	2.3+5	1.6+6			Data EXFOR30125.	Dec 72	SIGMA AT 8 ENERGIES	
Elastic	1.0-3	1.5+7	AUA	Eval	Data AUSTR - DFN 140.	Nov 71	COOK+POINT(226)+GROUP(127)SIG.CF EVL	+
Elastic	8.8+5		ANL	Expt	Rept ANL - 7935	Jun 72	COX+ 4 PI B(O)	+
	8.8+5				Data EXFOR10332.116	Jun 74	. 1 PT.	
Elastic	2.5-2		IJI	Eval	Rept KIYAI - 76 - 6	76	Fedorova+ COMP(REFS,SIGS),EVAL.TABLE	
					Conf 75Kiev 1 169	May 75	- + EVAL 2200M/S SIG,TABLE	
Elastic	2.5-2	1.0+0	DUB	Expt	Conf 76Lowell 1243	Jul 76	Akopian+THR SCT AMP,1EV TOT SCT CS.	
	5.0-1	1.0+2			Rept JINR - P3 - 7800	Apr 74	- + COHERENT+TOT SCAT SIG GIVEN	
Diff Elastic	1.0+6		ALD	Expt	Jour NP 42 86	Apr 63	Gilboy+30TO137DEG.COMP.WITH OPTICMOD	+
Diff Elastic	9.8+5		SHE	Theo	Jour NP 54 417	Jun 64	Maddison.OPTMOD FIT TO TOWLE GILBOY	
Diff Elastic	9.8+5		AGN	Eval	Rept TID - 21629	Dec 64	Perkins+ LEG COEFS CALCULATED	
Diff Elastic	5.0+6		DKE	Expt	Jour ZP 196 103	Sep 66	Buccino+ 20 - 140DEG,CFD OPTMOD. TABLE	+
					Abst DA 24 4248	Apr 64	- .CFD OPTMOD CALCS.	
	5.0+6				Data EXFOR11877.007	Jun 76	. 13 PTS.	
Diff Elastic	3.2+6		BCM	Expt	Jour NP 89 154	Dec 66	Becker+ 12 ANGLES GRAPH CFD OPTMDL	+
	3.2+6				Data EXFOR11511.031	Jun 76	. 12 PTS.	
Diff Elastic	8.0+6		VIR	Expt	Conf 68Wash. § E10	Mar 68	Bernard+ TOF 25 - 160DEG REL N - P SIG	+
	8.0+6				Data EXFOR12054.006	Jun 76	. 10 LEG COEFS	
	8.0+6				Data EXFOR12054.005	Jun 76	. 19 PTS, DSIG	
Diff Elastic	3.2+6	5.0+6	SCU	Theo	Rept ICD - 6 236	69	Averyanov+CALC ANGDIST CFD EXPT,GRPH	

59 Praseodymium 141

Quantity	Energy (ev) Min	Max	Lab	Type	Documentation Ref Vol Page	Date	Author, Comments	Data
Diff Elastic	2.3+5	1.6+6	SUN	Expt	Jour NP/A 124 111	Feb 69	Malan+ ANG DISTR GRPH,LEGENDRE COEFF	+
					Diss MALAN	70	- . (UNIV OF STELLENBOSCH)	
	2.3+5	1.6+6			Data EXFOR31263.	Mar 73	.LEGENDRE-COEF. GVN	
	2.3+5	1.6+6			Data EXFOR30125.	Dec 72	DBLE DIFF SIG, DATA FROM PRIV COM.	
Diff Elastic	2.3+5	1.6+6	CCP	Comp	Rept ICD-6 50	70	Bazajanc+ ANGDIST,LEG COEF,8 ES,TBL	
Diff Elastic	8.0+6		CCP	Comp	Rept ICD-6 50	70	Bazajanc+ ANGDIST EXPTS,GRPH	
Diff Elastic	1.5+6	3.6+6	JAE	Expt	Jour NP/A 179 513	Jan 72	Tanaka+ ANGDIST CFD OPTMDL,C-CHANNEL	+
					Priv TANAKA	Aug 71	- . TOF.REL H(N,N),+LEGENDRE FIT	
	1.5+6	3.6+6			Data EXFOR20337.	Jul 74	101PTS.D/DA,LEG.FIT.	
Diff Elastic	8.8+5		ANL	Expt	Rept ANL-7935	Jun 72	Cox+. CFD OPTMOD,HAUSER-FESHBACH	+
	8.8+5				Data EXFOR10332.025	Jun 74	. 8 PTS.	
Diff Elastic	1.0+0	2.6+5	DUB	Expt	Conf 73Kiev 2 330	May 73	Mirzaakhmedov+ ANOMAL ANGDIST CFD TH	
					Conf 72Budapest 188	Aug 72	- + ANGDIST ANOMALY,GRAPH	
Diff Elastic	1.2+6	1.9+6	ITK	Expt	Prog BARC-831 45	75	Singh+ 20-150DEG,TOF.CFD OPTMOD,NDG	
Diff Elastic	1.2+6	1.9+6	GEL	Expt	Prog NEANDC(E)172 3	Feb 76	Singh+VDG TOF	
					Prog NEANDC(E)162 3	Feb 75	- +VDG TOF	
					Jour ZP/A 272 47	Jan 75	Knitter+ ANGDIST AT 3 N-ES,GRPHS	
Polarization	4.4+6	5.5+6	WIS	ExTh	Jour NP/A 95 193	Mar 67	Mahajan. POLRZ OPTMDL ANALYSIS	
					Abst DA/B 28 1093	Sep 67	.SEE ALSO	
Polarization	8.8+5		ANL	Expt	Rept ANL-7935	Jun 72	Cox+. CFD OPTMOD,HAUSER-FESHBACH	+
	8.8+5				Data EXFOR10332.059	Jun 74	. 8 PTS.	
Potntal Scat	+4		HAR	Expt	Jour PPSA 70 51	Jan 57	Gayther+ FROM AVG SIGTOT. FC TRANSM	
Potntal Scat		+5	SAC	Expt	Jour NP/A 123 561	Jan 69	Morgenstern+ RADIUS.RES SHAPE ANAL.	+
		+6			Rept CEA-R-3609	Sep 68	- .(THESIS).DATA GIVEN	
					Conf 68Wash. 867	Mar 68	- + PPR E27	
		+5			Jour JPR 24 997	Nov 63	Bianchi+5.5+-2B DEDUCD FRM RES1120EV	
	0.0+0	6.0+3			Data EXFOR20684.026	Jul 77	1PNT.RADIUS.	
Tot Inelastc	1.2+6	1.8+6	LEB	Expt	Jour YF 1 443	Mar 65	Bukarev+	+
	1.3+6	1.9+6			Data EXFOR40040.	Aug 70	EXCIT FCTN AT 6ES FOR 2 LEVELS	
Tot Inelastc	5.0+6	7.0+6	ALD	Expt	Jour NP/A 112 337	May 68	Owens+.3ES.FROM N SPECT 90DEG.	
Tot Inelastc	2.6+5	1.3+6	SUN	Expt	Jour NP/A 124 111	Feb 69	Malan+ INTEGRATED DIFF INEL SIGMAS	+
Tot Inelastc	1.5+5	1.0+7	BOL	Eval	Rept CEC(71)-2	71	Benzi+ STAT MODEL. TBL GIVEN.	+
	1.5+5	1.0+7			Data BENZI-DFN 552E	Mar 71	49 PNTS	
Tot Inelastc	5.0+6	1.5+7	AUA	Eval	Data AUSTR-DFN 140.	Nov 71	COOK+POINT(11)+GROUP(127)SIG.CF EVL	
Tot Inelastc	3.0+6	9.0+6	BOL	Theo	Rept RT/FI-72 7	Mar 72	Reffo+ COMPNUC+EVAPOR,FORTRN,TBL SIG	
Tot Inelastc	1.0-3	1.5+7	RCN	Eval	Prog RCN-239 11	Nov 75	Gruppelaar. EXP.+MODEL CALC. NDG	
Diff Inelast	4.0+6	6.5+6	DKE	Expt	Abst DA 24 4248	Apr 64	Buccino.ANG DIST.TOF.NUCL T.LVL DEN	
Diff Inelast	3.5+6	8.5+6	JAE	Expt	Prog EANDC(J)8L25	Jan 68	Maruyama+.TOF.CONTIN SPECT AT 90DEG	+
	8.0+6				Jour NP/A 131 145	Jun 69	- .ANGDIST OF NS 0.5-2MEV,GRPH	
	3.5+6	8.5+6			Conf 67Tokyo 373	Sep 67	- + PPR8.127. ABST.	
Diff Inelast	5.0+6	7.0+6	ALD	Expt	Jour NP/A 112 337	May 68	Owens+.3ES.FROM N SPECT 90DEG NDG.	+
					Conf 65Antwerp 547	Jul 65	- + PPR122.ABST.SPECT N' AT 90DEG	
Diff Inelast	1.5+5	2.2+6	SUN	Expt	Jour NP/A 124 111	Feb 69	Malan+ ANG DISTR,EXC FUNCTION,GRAPH	+
					Diss MALAN	70	- . (UNIV OF STELLENBOSCH)	
	2.6+5	2.2+6			Data EXFOR30125.	Dec 72	DBLE DIFF SIG AT 90DEG,12 LVLS,26 ES	
	1.5+5	1.3+6			Data EXFOR30125.	Dec 72	DBLE DIFF SIG AT 7 ANG, 3 LVLS, 3 ES	
Diff Inelast	6.1+6	1.6+6	CCP	Comp	Rept ICD-6 106	70	Sluchevskaja.SIG(ANG) TO LVLS,GRAPHS	
Diff Inelast	1.5+5	1.0+7	BOL	Eval	Rept CEC(71)-2	71	Benzi+ DISCRETE INELASTIC. 7 LVLS	+
	1.5+5	1.9+6			Data BENZI-DFN 552E	Mar 71	1ST- 7TH LVL+ANGDIST+E DIST	
	1.9+6	1.0+7			Data BENZI-DFN 552E	Mar 71	TO CONTINUUM, 19PNTS+ANGDIST+E DIST	
Diff Inelast	1.5+6	3.5+6	JAE	Expt	Jour NP/A 179 513	Jan 72	Tanaka+. ANGDIST CFD OPTMDL,C-CHANNL	+
	1.5+6	3.6+6			Priv TANAKA	Aug 71	- . TOF.REL H(N,N),+LEGENDRE FIT	
	1.5+6	3.6+6			Data EXFOR20337.	Jul 74	231PTS.D/DA,LEG.FIT.	
Diff Inelast	1.7+6	1.9+6	ITK	Expt	Prog BARC-831 45	75	Singh+ TO 2LVLS,ANGDIS.CFD CALC,NDG	
Diff Inelast	+7		CCP	Expt	Rept YK- 23 4	76	Brodskaja+ ACTIV,AVG SIG,TBL	
Diff Inelast	1.7+6	1.9+6	GEL	Expt	Prog NEANDC(E)172 3	Feb 76	Singh+VDG TOF	
					Prog NEANDC(E)162 3	Feb 75	- +VDG TOF	
					Jour ZP/A 272 47	Jan 75	Knitter+ ANGDIST AT 2 N-ES,GRPHS	
Thermal Scat	Maxwl		ORL	Expt	Jour PR 92 1380	Dec 65	Koehler+TRIVALENT ION PARAMAG SCAT	
Thermal Scat	Cold		ORL	Revw	Jour JAP 36 1078	Mar 65	Koehler+ MAGNETIC PROPS	
Thermal Scat	Cold		GRE	Expt	Jour JAP 37 1038	Mar 66	MAGNETIC PROPS FROM N DIFFR XPTS	
Thermal Scat	2.0-4	1.5-1	BSP	ExTh	Jour JCP 48 520	Jan 68	Mattos.,TRIVALENT ION PARAMAG SIG	+
					Jour NP/A 95 683	Apr 67	SEE ALSO * SAME CURVE.	
Thermal Scat	1.0-4	1.0+3	MUN	Revw	Jour EEN 80 1	77	Koester. SCAT LENGTH	
Scattering	Maxwl		ORL	Expt	Jour PR 91 597	Aug 53	Koehler+ TRANS 4.0+-1.0B	
	Maxwl				Data EXFOR12060.016	Jun 76	. 1 PT.	

59 Praseodymium 141

Quantity	Energy (ev) Min	Energy (ev) Max	Lab	Type	Documentation Ref Vol Page	Author, Comments Date	Data
Scattering	2.5 – 2		BSP	Expt Conf	66Paris 1 53	Oct 66 Zimmerman+,P.129,DEDUCED SIG(.025EV)	+
				Jour	NP/A 95 683	Apr 67 SEE ALSO *	
	2.5 – 2			Data	EXFOR30224.024	Dec 72 DEDUCED SIGMA	
Nonelastic	1.0 – 3	1.5+7	AUA	Eval Data	AUSTR – DFN 140.	Nov 71 COOK+POINT(226)+GROUP(127)SIG.CF EVL	+
Nonelastic	1.4+7	1.8+7	ANL	Eval Rept	ANL – 75 – 34	Jun 75 Davey+CORRC APPLIED TO N2N CS.TBLS.	
Absorption	2.5 – 2		HAR	Expt Rept	AERE – R/R – 2333	57 Cummins+. PILE OSCILLATOR.	
Absorption	4.1 – 1	1.0+7	GA	Eval Prog	GA – 2451	Aug 61 Joanou+.68GROUP DATA FOR GAM – I	
Absorption	1.0 – 3	1.0+7	JUL	Eval Rept	JUEL – 678 – RG	Jul 70 Liu. EVALUATION+CALC,GRPH,FN OF E	
Absorption	2.5 – 2		IJI	Eval Rept	KIYAI – 76 – 6	76 Fedorova+ COMP(REFS,SIGS),EVAL.TABLE	
				Conf	75Kiev 1 169	May 75 – + EVAL SIGS OF 3ISOMERS,TABL	
Res Int Abs	5.0 – 1		ANL	Expt Jour	PR 79 11	Jul 50 Harris+ EPI – CD,REL THERMAL ACT. B – W	+
	5.0 – 1			Data	EXFOR11343.024	Jun 76 . 1 PT.	
Res Int Abs	5.0 – 1	1.0+6	CCP	Expt Conf	55Geneva 5 91	Aug 55 Spivak+.VAL GVN CFD REF,PPR659	
Res Int Abs	None		ORL	Revw Conf	55Geneva 5 96	Aug 55 Macklin+.TABLE,EXPT CFD THEORY,P833	
Res Int Abs	5.0 – 1		KAP	Expt Rept	KAPL – 2000 – 12	60 Fehr+ PAGE 33	
Res Int Abs	None		CRC	Eval Rept	AECL – 1054	Mar 60 Walker.(CRP – 913) REDUCED RES.INT.	
Res Int Abs	None		ORL	Eval Rept	ORNL – 2869	Mar 60 Nephew.1/V UP +TO100EV.ALSO85.5EV – UP	
Res Int Abs	+3	+5	BOL	Theo Conf	61Vienna 1 179	Aug 61 Benzi+.PPR11,VAL GVN,L=0,L=1 .CAPT.	
Res Int Abs	5.0 – 1		BOL	Expt Conf	61Vienna 1 179	Aug 61 Benzi+ TBL TOTAL CAPT RES INTS.	
Res Int Abs	5.5 – 1		GA	Eval Jour	NSE 12 115	Jan 62 Garrison+,RI=23.5+ – 9 B,FROM RES.PAR	
Res Int Abs		1.0+5	LEB	Expt Jour	ZET 46 80	Jan 64 Konks.TBL 3E – RANGES.ENGL JET 19 59	
Res Int Abs	5.0 – 1		BOL	Expt Rept	RT/FI – 4	Jan 67 Palmucci. CALC FROM (N,G) RES PARAMS	
Res Int Abs	None		GA	Eval Rept	GA – 12071	Sep 71 Mathews+. RECOMMENDED VALUES	
Res Int Abs	5.5 – 1		CRC	Eval Rept	AECL – 3037 1	Jan 72 Walker.REDUCED INTEG FROM RESPAR,TBL	
Res Int Abs	5.0 – 1		AUA	Eval Rept	AAEC/TM – 619	Sep 72 Clayton.CALC FROM SIG LIBRARY,TABLE	
Res Int Abs	5.0 – 1		KJL	Expt Jour	JIN 34 2699	Sep 72 Steinnes. ACT. AU MONITOR	+
	5.0 – 1			Data	EXFOR20188.017	May 74 1PNT.CAPTURE.	
Res Int Abs	4.6 – 1	1.0+6	RCN	Theo Rept	RCN – 191	Jul 73 Lautenbach.CAPT INT FROM GROUP SIGMA	
Res Int Abs	5.0 – 1		GHT	Expt Jour	JRC 20 695	74 Van Der Linden+ BY(N,G).CFD OTHS,TBL	
	5.5 – 1			Conf	73Paris 2 241	Mar 73 – + ACT,REL THR+GOLD,TBL	
	5.5 – 1			Data	EXFOR20645.018	Jul 76 1PNT.CAPTURE.	
Res Int Abs	5.5 – 1	+6	SAC	Revw Conf	IAEA – 169 1 235	74 Ribon.CAPTURE,STATUS CFD REQUEST,TBL	
Res Int Abs	+0	+5	WIN	Revw Conf	IAEA – 169 3 163	74 Pope+ DATA FILE CALC CFD XPTAL VALUE	
Res Int Abs	5.0 – 1		IJI	Eval Rept	KIYAI – 76 – 6	76 Fedorova+ EVAL CFD CALC.TBL RI,REFS	
				Conf	75Kiev 1 169	May 75 – + EVAL+CALC RI GIVEN,TABLE	
(n,γ)	2.0+4	7.0+5	OXF	Expt Jour	PRSA 170 513	Apr 39 Griffiths.RA – BE PHOTONEUT ACTIVATION	
(n,γ)	Pile		ANL	Expt Jour	PR 72 888	Nov 47 Seren+.THR IRRAD. THR IRRAD.PR4O7.	+
	Pile			Data	EXFOR11447.095	Jun 76 . 1 PT.	
(n,γ)	Fiss		ANL	Expt Jour	PR 78 632	Jun 50 Hughes+ REL SIG(THERMAL).	
	Fiss			Data	EXFOR11596.013	Jun 76 . 1 PT.	
(n,γ)	Maxwl		ORL	Expt Jour	PR 83 643	Aug 51 Pomerance. LOCAL OSC REL AU ABS 95 B	+
	Maxwl			Data	EXFOR11047.046	Jun 76 . 1 PT.	
(n,γ)	Fiss		BNL	Expt Jour	PR 91 1423	Sep 53 Hughes+.ALSO LVL SPACINGS AT EXCIT E	
(n,γ)	1.0+4	6.0+5	KAP	Theo Jour	NSE 2 334	May 57 Storm+,CALC AVG RATIO TO U235 CFDXPT	
(n,γ)	2.4+4		ORL	Expt Jour	PR 107 504	Jul 57 Macklin+.SB – BE NS,547+ – 55MB,1.59MEVG	+
				Jour	PR 114 1619	Jun 59 . REVISED VALUE GIVEN	
				Conf	58Geneva 15 68	Sep 58 Macklin.PPR671,VAL GVN,EXPT DESCRIBD	
	2.4+4			Data	EXFOR11399.038	Jun 76 . 1 PT, SIG FROM PR 114 1619	
(n,γ)	2.5+6	4.0+6	IFU	Expt Conf	58Geneva 15 18	Sep 58 Pasechnik+.PPR2030,SIGMA AT 3ES	
(n,γ)	Pile		KUR	Expt Conf	58Geneva 15 50	Sep 58 Leipunskij+.PPR2219,VAL GVN	
(n,γ)	1.4+7		ALD	Expt Jour	PPS 72 505	Oct 58 Perkin+ACT ANAL 3.33MB+ – 10PC,B – W TH	
(n,γ)	2.5+4		LRL	Expt Jour	PR 112 226	Oct 58 Booth+ SB – BE REL I+THR,ACT 19.1H HL	+
	2.5+4			Data	EXFOR11429.024	Jun 76 . 1 PT.	
(n,γ)	2.0+5		ORL	Expt Jour	PR 114 1619	Jun 59 Lyon+.ABS GAMMA COUNT 155,38MB 2ES	
	2.0+5			Data	EXFOR11407.027	Jun 76 . 1 PT.	
(n,γ)	1.5+5	2.0+6	WIS	Expt Jour	PR 116 927	Nov 59 Johnsrud+ CFD OTHERS	+
	1.7+5	2.0+6		Data	EXFOR11675.018	Jun 76 . 4 PTS.	
(n,γ)	Maxwl		KAP	Expt Rept	KAPL – 2000 – 12	60 Fehr+ PAGE 33	
(n,γ)	Maxwl		CRC	Eval Prog	AECL – 1054	Mar 60 Walker.(CRP – 913)	
(n,γ)	1.5+7		ARK	Expt Jour	PR 118 242	Apr 60 Willie. MEAS ACT SIG – 2.1+ – 1.0 MB	+
	1.5+7			Data	EXFOR12033.016	Jun 76 . 1 PT.	
(n,γ)	Maxwl		ORL	Expt Conf	60Vienna 239	Oct 60 Stoughton+.NDG,EXPT DESCRIBED	
(n,γ)	Pile		ORL	Expt Jour	NSE 8 378	Nov 60 Lyon. ACTIVATION,SIGMA GIVEN	
	Pile			Data	EXFOR11625.026	Jun 76 . 1 PT.	
(n,γ)	5.0+3	3.0+5	ORL	Expt Jour	PR 122 182	Apr 61 Gibbons.CRV CFD THEORY REP BNL653	+
	3.0+4	6.5+4		Jour	PR 129 2695	Mar 63 Macklin+ LIQ SCINT,115 AND 59MB	
				Conf	61Vienna 1 95	Aug 61 Neiler.	
	1.2+4	1.6+5		Data	EXFOR11329.	Jun 76 . 51 PTS.	

59 Praseodymium 141

Quantity	Energy (ev) Min	Max	Lab	Type	Documentation Ref Vol Page	Date	Author, Comments	Data
(n,γ)	+0	+3	CCP		Jour NSA 17 2952	Jul 63	ABSTR 22557 JINR-P-1223 USSR	
(n,γ)	1.5+7		ARK	Expt	Jour PR 131 2649	Sep 63	Bramlitt+ 2.3+ -1.1MB	+
					Rept TID-16949	62	.THESIS	
	1.5+7				Data EXFOR11590.074	Jun 76	. 1 PT.	
(n,γ)	2.0+1	4.0+4	LEB	Expt	Jour ZET 46 80	Jan 64	Konks.PB-SLOW-DOWN,GRAPH SIG(E)	+
					Jour JET 19 59	Jul 64	TRANSLATN.*	
(n,γ)	1.0+0	2.0+3	RPI	Expt	Prog WASH-1048 71	Jun 64	Block. 26 RES ES TBL, TOF,RSLN 6NS/M	
(n,γ)	5.0+3	9.0+4	ORL	Theo	Jour RMP 37 166	Jan 65	Macklin+.CALC FOR KT=5TO90KEV	
(n,γ)	2.5-2		BSP	Expt	Conf 66Paris 1 53	Oct 66	Zimmerman+,P.129,DEDUCED SIG(.025EV)	+
					Jour NP/A 95 683	Apr 67	SEE ALSO *	
	2.5-2				Data EXFOR30224.025	Dec 72	DEDUCED SIGMA	
(n,γ)	2.4+4		MUA	Expt	Jour PR 152 1055	Dec 66	Chaubey+ REL I-127,ISOM UNKNOWN,TBL	
				Theo	Jour IJP 42 567	Sep 68	- + METHD OF BOOTH,VAL CFD XPT	
	2.4+4			Expt	Data EXFOR30079.030	Dec 70	SIGMA FOR 19. H HALF-LIFE	
(n,γ)	2.5-2		BOL	Eval	Rept RT/FI-4	Jan 67	Palmucci. CALC FROM RES PARAMETERS	
(n,γ)	Maxwl		FRS	Expt	Jour PL/B 24 400	Apr 67	Kern+3.7+ -0.5B TO 14.6M ISOMER	+
(n,γ)	3.0+6		DEB	Expt	Jour JNE 21 797	Oct 67	Peto+ ACTIV,SIGMA REL TO P-31(N,P)	
	3.0+6				Data EXFOR30031.019	Aug 70	SINGLE VALUE	
(n,γ)	1.4+7		LYO	Comp	Rept LYCEN/6780	Nov 67	Crouzet+COMPILATN FOR ACTIVTN ANALYS	
(n,γ)	1.4+7		NAP	Expt	Jour NC/B 52 2 476	Dec 67	Cuzzocrea+. ACT ANAL.SIG=2.6+ -.5 MB	
(n,γ)	Maxwl		AUA	Theo	Jour NSE 31 234	Feb 68	Cook+ STATISTICAL CALC CFD EXPT	
(n,γ)	1.3+7	1.5+7	DEB	Expt	Jour MFF 16 123	Feb 68	Csikai+,ACTIV,SIG(E)/SIG(14.7),GRAPH	+
					Jour NP/A 95 229	Mar 67	.EQUIVALENT*	
	1.5+7				Data EXFOR30067.015	Nov 70	VALUE AT 14.7 MEV, (= NP A95 TBL 1)	
	1.3+7	1.5+7			Data EXFOR30074.005	Nov 70	SIGMA AT 8ES REL VALUE AT 14.7 MEV	
(n,γ)	1.4+5	2.5+6	ANL	Expt	Jour JNE 22 267	May 68	Stupegia+ ACT 24ES REL U235 NF,TABLE	+
					Rept INDC-156	67	.FULL TEXT OF PAPERS51	
					Conf 66Paris 1 520	Oct 66	.SUPERSEDED	
	1.9+5	2.5+6			Data EXFOR11624.008	Jun 76	. 24 PTS	
(n,γ)	-		IEA	Comp	Rept IEA-INF-10	Aug 68	Atalla. TABLES OF HL,SIG AND GAMM-E	
(n,γ)	2.5+5	3.1+5	IRK	Expt	Jour OAWA 106 153	Jun 69	Colditz+	
(n,γ)	Maxwl		UJV	Expt	Jour CZJB 19 1307	Oct 69	Urbanec+ 85.1+515 EV LVL,SIG-CONTRIB	
(n,γ)	2.0+5		MUA	Theo	Jour 69Roorke 2 129	Dec 69	Chaubey+ SIG VALUE GIVEN, STATIST-TH	
(n,γ)	3.0+6		DEB	Expt	Jour AHP 28 257	Jan 70	Diksic+ SIG+ISOMRATIO,REL P31(N,P)	+
	3.0+6				Data EXFOR30023.	Jun 70	CAPT-SIG TO G,M.ISOM RATIO	
(n,γ)	1.4+7	1.5+7	JYV	Eval	Rept JU-RR-3/1970	Jun 70	Leppaemaeki+ TABLE OF EVAL AVG SIG	
(n,γ)	3.0+4		AUA	Theo	Rept AAEC/E-211	Nov 70	Musgrove. SIGMA GIVEN AND CFD OTHER	
(n,γ)	2.4+4		BHU	Expt	Conf 70Madurai 2 615	Dec 70	Chaturvedi+ EXPTL+CALCULATED SIGMAS	
(n,γ)	1.0+3	1.0+7	BOL	Eval	Rept CEC(71)-2	71	Benzi+ OPTMOD EVAL.TBL GIVEN.	+
					Rept CEC(70)-2	Apr 70	- +. GRAPH	
					Rept CCDN-NW/10	Dec 69	- +H-F MOD,AXEL G(G)EST,ALL DATA	
					Conf 66Paris 1 537	Oct 66	- + STATMOD.TBL AV VALS.SUPERSEDD	
					Jour NC 38 216	Jul 65	- + THEORY FOR CAPTURE EVALUATION	
					Conf 61Vienna 1 179	Aug 61	- + TBL AV VALS. SUPERSEDED.	
	1.0+3	1.0+7			Data BENZI-DFN 552E	Mar 71	68 PNTS	
(n,γ)	2.0+5	5.9+6	IFU	Expt	Jour UFZ 16 1205	Jul 71	Zaikin+ ACT METH,SIG(NEUT-E),GRPHS	+
					Prog YFI-10 47	May 71	- + TBL SIG VS N-E,+ - ERRORS	
					Rept INDC(CCP)-15	Dec 71	.P52. ENGLISH OF YFI-10 47	
	8.4+4	5.9+6			Data EXFOR40255.005	Dec 75	.SIGMA FOR 30 EN GVN	
(n,γ)	Maxwl		GA	Eval	Rept GA-12071	Sep 71	Mathews+ RECOMMENDED VALUES	
(n,γ)	1.0-3	1.5+7	AUA	Eval	Data AUSTR-DFN 140.	Nov 71	COOK+POINT(226)+GROUP(127)SIG.CF EVL	+
(n,γ)	Maxwl		CRC	Eval	Rept AECL-3037 1	Jan 72	Walker.RECOMMENDED SIG,DETAILED TBL	
(n,γ)	2.4+4		MUA	Theo	Jour IJP 46 114	Mar 72	Chaubey+ P-WAVE STRENGTH FUNCT,TABLE	
(n,γ)	2.5-2		IAE	Revw	Rept IAEA-143 897	Apr 72	Lemmel.RECENT EVALUATIONS,TABLE+GRPH	
	Maxwl				Rept IAEA-143 897	Apr 72	- .RECENT EVALUATIONS,TABLE	
(n,γ)	2.5-2		AUA	Eval	Rept AAEC/TM-619	Sep 72	Clayton.CALC FROM SIG LIBRARY,TABLE	
(n,γ)	Fast		MTR	Expt	Conf 72Kiamesha 2 614	Sep 72	Harker+ CFRMF INTEGRAL MEAS.	+
					Conf 71Knoxvill 113	Mar 71	- .INTEGRAL MEAST,0.19B REL AU	
	Fast				Data EXFOR10218.007	Oct 72	. 1 PT. SIGMA	
(n,γ)		1.1+7	RCN	Theo	Rept RCN-191	Jun 73	Lautenbach. GROUP CONSTANTS TBL	
(n,γ)	+3	+7	TUD	Theo	Prog ZFK-262 133	Sep 73	Hoehn+ CALC SIG CFD EXP,GRPH AT 1MEV	
(n,γ)	2.5-2	3.0+4	SAC	Revw	Conf IAEA-169 1 235	74	Ribon.STATUS SIG CFD REQUESTS,TABLE	
(n,γ)	Maxwl	Fiss	WIN	Revw	Conf IAEA-169 3 163	74	Pope+ MAXW+FIS-SPEC AVG DATA CFD XPT	
	Fiss				Conf IAEA-169 3 137	74	Dean. POINT DATA AVG OVER STAND SPEC	
(n,γ)	1.4+7		RBZ	Expt	Jour NCL 10 1	May 74	Vuletin+ ACT,GELI.CFD OTHRS+THEO,TBL	
	1.4+7				Data EXFOR30314.009	Dec 75	SIGMA AT 14.4 MEV	
	1.4+7				Data EXFOR30145.013	Aug 73	.SUPERSEDED BY EXFOR30314.009	

59 Praseodymium 141

Quantity	Energy (ev) Min	Max	Lab	Type	Ref	Vol	Page	Date	Author, Comments	Data
(n,γ)	1.0+3	1.0+7	FEI	Eval	Rept	YK-	8/2	97	Sep 72 Abagjan+ AVG SIG(ENERGY-GROUPS),TABL	
					Rept	INDC(CCP)-		39	Jul 74 .P102. ENGLISH OF YK-8/2 97	
(n,γ)	1.5+7		BOS	Expt	Conf	74Calcutta		57	Nov 74 Majumdar+ CFD STATMOD.SIGMA GIVEN	+
					Jour	IJP	44	204	Mar 70 Majumder. BY BETA SATURATION ACT,TBL	
	1.5+7				Data	EXFOR30296.006			Jun 75 1 POINT	
(n,γ)	Fast		RCN	Expt	Rept	ECN-		10	Oct 76 Veenema+ STEK REACTIVITY WORTHS TBL.	
(n,γ)	1.0-3	1.0+7	RCN	Revw	Rept	ECN-		12	Nov 76 Gruppelaar+ INTERCOMP. RECENT WORKS	
(n,γ)	1.5+7		IRK	Expt	Priv	WAGNER			77 Wagner+	+
	1.4+7				Rept	INDC(SEC)-		51	Oct 75 - + ABST PAGE 3	
	1.5+7				Data	EXFOR20718.012			Jan 76 1PNT.SIGMA.	
Spect (n,γ)	Maxwl		CRC	Expt	Jour	CJP	31	1025	Nov 53 Bartholomew+ PAIR SP,140KV LINEWIDTH	
Spect (n,γ)	Maxwl		GEA	Eval	Rept	DC-	58-1-	30	Jan 58 Deloume. BY APPROXIMATION CURV+TABLE	
Spect (n,γ)	8.8+5		ARF	Expt	Prog	ARF-	1193-	12	Jul 62 Greenwood+,CRYST SPEC,LOW-E GAMMAS	
Spect (n,γ)	Maxwl		CAS	Expt	Jour	NC	29	977	Aug 63 Giannini+ NAI, E+INTENSITY,TO 177KEV	+
Spect (n,γ)	8.5+1	5.2+2	DUB	Expt	Jour	ZET	45	93	Aug 63 Urbanec.TOF,NAI,G-SPEC 3-7.5MEV,6RES	
					Rept	JINR-P-		1223	Mar 63 - + CALC DETAILS.	
					Jour	JET	18	68	Jan 64 - + ENGL OF ZET 45 93	
Spect (n,γ)	Pile		RIS	Expt	Prog	EANDC(OR)32L			Jun 64 Maier+ (MUN) 30 LINES OBSERVED.P12.	
Spect (n,γ)	Maxwl		MIL	Expt	Jour	EN	11	612	Nov 64 Para+ GAMMAS TO 170 KEV	
Spect (n,γ)	Maxwl		MCM	Expt	Jour	NP	89	241	Dec 66 Hughes+ GE(LI) SPECTROMETER	
Spect (n,γ)	+3		AUA	Revw	Jour	NSP	3 2	64	Oct 67 Allen.NDG,PUBLSHD IN PRIV COMMUNICTN	
Spect (n,γ)	+0	+3	DUB	Expt	Conf	68DUBSY		283	Jul 68 Shapiro.GE-LI DET. RESOL=80NS/M,NDG	
Spect (n,γ)	Maxwl		FSU	Expt	Jour	PR	173	1133	Sep 68 Kern+ GE(LI)+CRYST SPEC .032-5.8MEV	
Spect (n,γ)	+0	+4	COL	Expt	Prog	WASH-	1124	31	Nov 68 Camarda+ MOXON-RAE DET TBC NO DATA	
Spect (n,γ)	2.5-2		MIT	Comp	Rept	MITNE-		85	Jan 69 Rasmussen+TBL G INT.=AFCRL-69-0071	
Spect (n,γ)	+1	+2	BNL	Expt	Prog	WASH-	1127	21	Apr 69 Chrien+SPIN ASSIGNMENTS FOR 11RESON	
Spect (n,γ)	8.5+1	6.4+2	DUB	Expt	Conf	69Studsvik		651	Aug 69 Becvar+ SPEC GRPH AT 84.8EV N-RESON	
					Conf	72Budapest		230	Aug 72 - + PULSED REACTOR,GE-LI,GRPH	
					Jour	CZJB	19	899	Jul 69 - + G-SPECS,85.1EV RESON ANAL	
Spect (n,γ)	8.5+1	1.5+3	UJV	Expt	Jour	CZJB	19	1307	Oct 69 Urbanec+ THIS+OTHER XPT,NEW DEDUCTNS	
Spect (n,γ)	Maxwl		LEI	Expt	Jour	NP/A	157	577	70 Mellema+LEVEL SPIN+NUCL ORIENTATION	
Spect (n,γ)	1.2+6	2.2+6	TUL	Expt	Jour	NP/A	142	619	Mar 70 Dave+ VDG,GE(LI). INELASTIC G SEPAR.	
Spect (n,γ)	Pile		KFK	Expt	Rept	KFK-		1401	Jun 71 Djadali.AVG POLRZ G EXPT,CFD T,SPIN	
	Maxwl				Jour	NP/A	147	150	May 70 Eichler+. POL NS.CIRC POL GS+ASSYMTRY	
Spect (n,γ)	None		RCN	Expt	Prog	EANDC(E)140U			Aug 71 Mellema+,SPIN ASSIGNM.,ORIENT.NUCL	
Spect (n,γ)	Maxwl		MUN	Expt	Jour	ZP	258	315	Mar 73 Henkelmann. E + INT OF GS GIVEN	+
	2.5-2				Data	EXFOR20606.008			Jun 76 7PTS.	
Spect (n,γ)	4.6+5		AUA	Expt	Prog	AAEC/PR-		39P 44	Jan 74 Allen+ NA-I,GAMMA YIELD,FIGURE ONLY	
Spect (n,γ)	Pile		AUW	Expt	Jour	CS	43	739	Dec 74 Sriramamurthi+ NA-I SPEC,TBL ES+INTS	+
	Pile				Data	EXFOR30291.001			Apr 75 10PTS.	
Spect (n,γ)	1.4+7		NJS	Expt	Rept	INDC(YUG)-		5	Dec 76 Budnar+ SCINT PAIRSPEC.TBL SIG(EGAM)	+
	1.4+7				Data	EXFOR30364.006			Dec 76 DIFFSIG(GAM-E:11 TO 22MEV).25 PNTS	
Inelastic γ	1.0+6	2.0+6	LEB	Expt	Jour	YF	1	443	Mar 65 Bukarev.GRAPH G-SPEC,TBL SIG PER LVL	+
					Jour	SNP	1	316	Sep 65 TRANSLATN.*	
Inelastic γ	5.0+6	7.0+6	ALD	Expt	Jour	NP/A	112	337	May 68 Owens+.3ES.TOF SPECT 90 DEG. NDG.	
Inelastic γ	2.9+6		TOR	Expt	Jour	CJP	46	1849	Sep 68 Daniels+ GE(LI)+NAI 12 GAMMA PEAKS	
					Abst	DA/B	29	3436	Mar 69 Felsteiner. ES, REL INT. COINCS.	
Inelastic γ	5.0+5	2.3+6	SUN	Expt	Jour	NP/A	124	433	Feb 69 VAN DER MERWE+TOF GATED GE-LI.LEVELS	
Inelastic γ	2.8+6		NRD	Expt	Prog	WASH-	1127	158	Apr 69 Engesser+ TO BE COMPLETED,NO DATA	
Inelastic γ	1.3+6	2.2+6	TUL	Expt	Jour	NP/A	142	619	Mar 70 Dave+GAMMA PROD SIG.95DEG.REL FE	+
	1.3+6	2.2+6			Data	EXFOR10038.			May 71 . 74 PTS. D/DA AT 95 DEG.	
Inelastic γ	2.7+6		KGU	Expt	Conf	71Moscow			Feb 71 .ABST ONLY,GAM ES+REL INTENS,SPEC	
Inelastic γ	2.7+6		KGU	Expt	Jour	YF	15	856	May 72 Andreev+ GAM ES GIVEN,GRPH ANGDIST	
					Jour	SNP	15	479	Nov 72 .ENGLISH TRANSLATION OF YF 15 856	
Inelastic γ	None		ITK	Expt	Rept	INDC(SEC)-		35	Sep 73 Singh+ P119.LEVEL SCHEME,GE-LI,TBL	
Inelastic γ	1.1+6	2.2+6	GEL	Expt	Jour	ZP	270	97	Oct 74 Knitter+.G-RAY-SPEC AT 8 N-ES MEAS.	
					Prog	NEANDC(E)-		161U	Aug 74 - +	
(n,2n)	2.0+7		OHO	Expt	Jour	PR	53	437	Mar 38 Pool+ LI+D NS,BETA ACT,RATIO TO (NG)	
(n,2n)	Fast		CAR	Expt	Jour	PR	81	184	Jan 51 Cohen.AVR SIG,N SPEC.BETA ACT.	+
	Fast				Data	EXFOR11189.044			Jun 76 . 1 PNT.	
(n,2n)	1.5+7		CRC	Expt	Jour	CJP	31	267	Feb 53 Paul+.BETA ACT.CFD TH. HL= 70M+3.4M	
	1.5+7				Data	EXFOR11274.089			Jun 76 . 1 PT.	
(n,2n)	1.5+7		ARK	Expt	Jour	PR	118	242	Apr 60 Wille. MEAS ACT SIG=2100+ -300MB.	+
	1.5+7				Data	EXFOR12033.018			Jun 76 . 1 PT.	
(n,2n)	1.2+7	1.8+7	NRD	Expt	Jour	PR	118	228	Apr 60 Ferguson. MEAS ACT SIG=1231-1737 MB.	
	1.2+7	1.8+7			Data	EXFOR11356.005			Jun 76 . 6 PTS.	
(n,2n)	Fiss		CRC	Eval	Rept	CRC-		1003	Dec 60 Roy+,ESTIMATED AVG SIG=0.76MB	

59 Praseodymium 141

Quantity	Energy (ev) Min	Max	Lab	Type	Documentation Ref Vol Page	Date	Author, Comments	Data
(n,2n)	1.4+7		ANL	Expt Jour	PR 122 168	Apr 61	Rayburn. 1801 MB	+
				Abst	BAP 3 337	Aug 58	. ABST R5	
	1.4+7			Data	EXFOR11328.028	Jun 76	. 1 PT.	
(n,2n)	1.5+7		MUA	Expt Jour	NP 28 560	Dec 61	Khurana+HANS.ACTIVATION,CFD STATMOD.	+
	1.5+7			Data	EXFOR31247.015	Mar 73	.SIG GVN	
(n,2n)	1.2+7	1.8+7	RED	Expt Rept	NP– 11667	Apr 62	Alford+.XCIT FNC NORM TO 1591MB14MEV	+
	1.2+7	1.8+7		Data	EXFOR11785.006	Jun 76	. 8 PTS.	
(n,2n)	1.4+7		BOL	Expt Jour	NC 26 1328	Dec 62	Cevolani+RESULTS CFD OTHER DATA+THEO	+
(n,2n)	Pile		MUN	Expt Jour	ADP 12 57	63	Hertlein. ACTIV+REAC–SIG,AVG+EFF,TBL	
(n,2n)	1.4+7		ROM	Comp Jour	NCS 301	Sep 63	Amaldi.1240+ – 74MB AT E=14.1MEV	
(n,2n)	1.4+7		HAM	Comp Jour	NP 65 257	Mar 65	Bormann. 7EXPT VALS.CFD SHELL EFFECT	
(n,2n)	1.5+7		TAM	Expt Jour	PR 156 1340	Apr 67	Menon+ ACT 1082MB,	+
	1.5+7			Data	EXFOR12066.004	Jun 76	. 1 PT.	
(n,2n)	1.4+7		LYO	Comp Rept	LYCEN/6780	Nov 67	Crouzet+COMPILATN FOR ACTIVTN ANALYS	
(n,2n)	1.4+7		NAP	Expt Jour	NC/B 52 2 476	Dec 67	Cuzzocrea+. 2002+ – 225 MB.TH OKS EXPT	
(n,2n)	1.5+7		DEB	Expt Jour	AHP 24 93	Apr 68	Peto+,SIG(15MEV) REL CU–63(N,2N)	+
	1.5+7			Data	EXFOR30100.006	Feb 71	SIGMA TOTAL	
(n,2n)	1.3+7	1.9+7	HAM	Expt Jour	NP/A 115 309	Jul 68	Bormann+ VDG.ACT.CFD STATMDL+OPTMDL	+
(n,2n)	1.5+7		DEB	Comp Jour	REA 7 4 93	Dec 69	Csikai+ SIG+HL COMPILTN,N–ACTIV–ANAL	
(n,2n)	1.5+7		BOS	Expt Prog	BARC–474 50	70	Chatterjee+ ABSOLUTE SIG EXPT	
(n,2n)	1.4+7	1.5+7	JYV	Eval Rept	JU–RR–3/1970	Jun 70	Leppaemaeki+ (N,3N) UPPER LIMIT,TBL	
(n,2n)	1.4+7	1.5+7	JYV	Eval Rept	JU–RR–3/1970	Jun 70	Leppaemaeki+ TABLE OF EVAL AVG SIG	
(n,2n)	9.5+6	1.0+7	BOL	Eval Rept	CEC(71)–2	71	Benzi+ STAT+EVAP MODELS.TBL GIVEN.	+
	9.5+6	1.0+7			BENZI–DFN 552E	Mar 71	3 PNTS+ANGDIST+E DIST. 1 RANGE	
(n,2n)	+7		KFI	Theo Rept	KFKI–71–8	Feb 71	Jeki. CALCULATED CFD EXPTL SIG VALUE	
(n,2n)	1.5+7		ARK	Expt Abst	DA/B 32 5091	Mar 72	Bari. GE(LI) DET. ACT. SIG GIVEN	+
	1.5+7			Data	EXFOR10431.046	Aug 75	. 1 PT. SIGMA.	
(n,2n)	1.5+7		DEB	Eval Jour	REA 11 1 153	Mar 73	Boedy. COMPILATION+RECOMM.VALUE,TBL	
				Rept	IAEA–153 173	73	– . RECOMM. VALUE ONLY	
(n,2n)	1.4+7		LOU	Expt Prog	INR–1464 12	May 73	Araminowicz+ BRIEF,ACTIV,TABLE,GRAPH	+
	1.4+7			Data	EXFOR30264.040	Nov 73	SIGMA AT 14.6 MEV	
(n,2n)	Fiss		KOS	Eval Jour	AK 16 351	74	Boedy. U238,MAXW–SPC.AVG CFD XPT,TBL	
(n,2n)	1.5+7		TAT	Theo Jour	JP/A 7 1458	Aug 74	Kondaiah. CALC ON STAT MODEL.	
(n,2n)	Fiss		KOS	Eval Conf	75Karlsrhe 29	Apr 75	Csikai. CF252,MAXW–SPC.AVG FOR 2TEMP	
(n,2n)	9.5+6	1.8+7	ANL	Eval Rept	ANL–75–34	Jun 75	Davey+CONSTANT T MDL,LVL DEN MDL FIT	
(n,2n)	+7		CCP	Expt Rept	YK– 23 4	76	Brodskaja+ ACTIV,AVG SIG,TBL	
(n,2n)	1.5+7		JYV	Expt Rept	JU–RR–1/1976	Mar 76	Valkonen.(THESIS).ACTIV.TBL.14.7MEV	+
	1.5+7			Data	EXFOR20673.028	Nov 76	1PNT.SIGMA.	
(n,2n)	1.2+7	1.8+7	GEO	Expt Abst	BAP 8 60	Jan 63	Rayburn+ ABST R7	
	1.2+7	1.8+7		Data	EXFOR11954.003	Jun 76	. 20 PTS.	
(n,2n)	1.5+7		ARK	Expt Jour	JIN 37 631	Mar 75	Sigg+ TO GROUND,FOR SYSTEMATICS,TBL	+
				Abst	DA/B 37 2237	Nov 76	– .ACT TECH.CFD OTH EXPT AND PRED	
	1.5+7			Data	EXFOR10477.013	May 75	. 1 PT. SIGMA.	
(n,xn) x>2	1.5+7		ARK	Expt Jour	PR 131 2649	Sep 63	Bramlitt+N3N.LESS THAN 10 MB.HL GVN	+
				Rept	TID–16949	62	.THESIS	
	1.5+7			Data	EXFOR11590.073	Jun 76	. 1 PT, (N,3N)	
(n,xn) x>2	1.8+7	2.0+7	GEL	ExTh Jour	NP/A 118 379	Oct 68	Liskien.ACT VDG REL CU65(N2N)CFD TH	+
	1.8+7	2.0+7		Expt Data	EXFOR20380.008	Oct 74	. 6PTS.N3N SIGMA.	
(n,p)	1.5+7		ARK	Expt Jour	PR 118 242	Apr 60	Wille. MEAS ACT SIG=4.5+ – 1.0 MB	+
	1.5+7			Data	EXFOR12033.017	Jun 76	. 1 PT.	
(n,p)	Fiss		CRC	Eval Rept	CRC–1003	Dec 60	Roy+,ESTIMATED AVG SIG=0.09MB	
(n,p)	1.5+7		ARK	Expt Jour	PR 131 2649	Sep 63	Bramlitt+ LESS THAN 0.84MB N2P	+
				Rept	TID–16949	62	.THESIS	
	1.5+7			Data	EXFOR11590.053	Jun 76	. 1 PT, SIG (N,2P)	
(n,p)	1.5+7		SAH	Comp Jour	NUC 23 8 112	Aug 65	Chatterjee. TABLE WITH REFS.	
	1.4+7			Jour	NP 60 273	Nov 64	– .MEAN OF EXPT CFD SHELLMOD	
(n,p)	Maxwl		IFU	Theo Rept	ICD–4 20	67	Dadakina+ PENETR COEFF CALC,TABLE	
(n,p)	Fiss		ORL	Expt Jour	NUC 25 2 41	Feb 67	O–Brien. SIG=.12MB, IRRAD IN ORR	
(n,p)	1.4+7	1.5+7	NAP	Comp Rept	INFN/BE–67–10	Jul 67	Cuzzocrea+ AVERAGED CHOSEN DATA.	
(n,p)	1.4+7		LYO	Comp Rept	LYCEN/6780	Nov 67	Crouzet+COMPILATN FOR ACTIVTN ANALYS	
(n,p)	1.4+7		NAP	Expt Jour	NC/B 52 2 476	Dec 67	Cuzzocrea+. 11.5+ – 1.1 MB.TH OKS EXPT	
(n,p)	1.5+7		DEB	Expt Jour	AHP 24 233	Feb 68	Csikai+ ACTIV,ABS VALUE,THEORY CFD	+
				Jour	MFF 16 123	Feb 68	SEE ALSO *THESIS IN HUNG	
	1.5+7			Data	EXFOR30040.002	Nov 70	SIGMA AT 14.8 MEV RESP TO PR–141(NP)	
(n,p)	1.5+7		DEB	Comp Jour	REA 7 4 93	Dec 69	Csikai+ SIG+HL COMPILTN,N–ACTIV–ANAL	
(n,p)	1.4+7	1.5+7	JYV	Eval Rept	JU–RR–3/1970	Jun 70	Leppaemaeki+ TABLE OF EVAL AVG SIG	
(n,p)	1.4+7	1.5+7	JYV	Eval Rept	JU–RR–3/1970	Jun 70	Leppaemaeki+ (N,2P) UPPER LIMIT,TBL	

59 Praseodymium 141

Quantity	Energy (ev) Min	Energy (ev) Max	Lab	Type	Documentation Ref Vol Page	Author, Comments Date	Data
(n,p)	1.5+7		IRK	Expt	Jour APA 34 209	Sep 71 Havlik. ACT. CC−W.	+
					Jour OAWA 107 119	Apr 70 − . ACTIVATION METHOD	
	1.5+7				Data EXFOR20509.010	Apr 76 1PNT.SIGMA.	
(n,p)	1.5+7		ARK	Expt	Abst DA/B 32 5091	Mar 72 Bari. GE(LI) DET. ACT. SIG GIVEN	+
	1.5+7				Data EXFOR10431.013	Aug 75 . 1 PT. SIGMA.	
(n,p)	1.4+7	1.5+7	KAZ	Theo	Jour YF 18 705	Oct 73 Levkovsky.AVERAGED SIG,CALC,TBL	
					Jour SNP 18 361	Apr 74 . ENGLISH OF YF 18,705	
(n,p)	+7		CCP	Expt	Rept YK− 23 4	76 Brodskaja+ ACTIV,AVG SIG,TBL	
(n,p)	1.5+7		JUL	Expt	Jour RRL 25 335	May 76 Qaim+ ACTIV,GELI.CFD OTHERS,TBL+GRPH	+
	1.5+7				Data EXFOR20716.004	Jun 77 1PNT.SIGMA.	
(n,d)	1.5+7		SAH	Comp	Jour NUC 23 8 112	Aug 65 Chatterjee. TABLE WITH REFS.	
(n,d)	1.4+7		WWA	Expt	Prog INDC(POL)−2 3	Apr 69 Dabrowska+ TO GND−ST,ANGDIST.GRAPH	
(n,t)	1.5+7		DEB	Expt	Jour AHP 24 233	Feb 68 Csikai+ ACTIV,UPPER LIMIT OF SIGMA	+
	1.5+7				Data EXFOR30040.003	Nov 70 SIGMA AT 14.8 MEV MAX LIMIT ONLY	
(n,t)	1.5+7		JUL	Expt	Jour NP/A 257 233	Feb 76 Qaim+ACT,TBL,GRPH,CFD OTHER ISOTOPE	+
					Jour JRC 21 395	74 − + CHEM SEPAR,SIG VS Z SYSTEMATI	
	1.5+7				Data EXFOR20669.009	Oct 76 1PNT.SIGMA.	
(n,α)	Fiss		CRC	Eval	Rept CRC−1003	Dec 60 Roy+,ESTIMATED AVG SIG=0.0024MB	
(n,α)	1.5+7		RBZ	Expt	Jour NP 54 17	May 64 Kulisic.E+ANGDIST+SIGTOT.CFD TH.CURV	+
					Jour NP 73 548	Nov 65 − . CONTINUATION OF NP 54 17	
					Rept EANDC−50S148	Jul 65 . FULL PAPER PRESENTD AT 65ANTWERP	
					Conf 64Paris 2 769	Jul 64 .	
	1.5+7				Data EXFOR30130.	Mar 71 SIGMA, ANG−DISTR, ALFA−SPEC(3ANGLES)	
(n,α)	1.4+7	1.5+7	JYV	Eval	Rept JU−RR−3/1970	Jun 70 Leppaemaeki+ TABLE OF EVAL AVG SIG	
(n,α)	1.4+7		TIT	Expt	Jour NP/A 149 513	Jul 70 Kitazawa. S SPEC 0 DEG+SIGMA+ANDISTR	+
	1.5+7				Data EXFOR20336.	Jul 74 18PTS.D/DA,D/DA.DE.	
(n,α)	1.4+7		RBZ	Theo	Jour FIZ 6 41	May 74 Caplar+ DOUBLE−DIFFSIG,CFD EXPT,GRPH	
	None				Prog INDC(SEC)−35	Sep 73 − + PRE−EQUILIBRIUM STATMDL,GRPH	
	1.4+7				Conf 73Munich 1 517	Aug 73 − + DIFFSIG FORMULA GIVN,NO DATA	
					Conf 72Budapest 168	Aug 72 − + ANALYSIS OF SPECTRA,GRAPH	
(n,α)	+7		CCP	Expt	Rept YK− 23 4	76 Brodskaja+ ACTIV,AVG SIG,TBL	
Reson Params	8.6+1	1.8+3	BNL	Expt	Priv PILCHER	Apr 55 Pilcher.	+
	8.6+1	1.8+3			Data EXFOR12041.007	Jun 76 . 10 RES, WN0	
Reson Params	8.5+1	5.2+2	DUB	Expt	Jour ZET 45 93	Aug 63 Urbanec.TOF,NAI,PARTL G−WID,TBL,6RES	
					Rept JINR−P−1223	Mar 63 − + CALC DETAILS.	
					Jour JET 18 68	Jan 64 − + ENGL OF ZET 45 93	
Reson Params	5.1+1	9.4+2	CCP	Comp	Rept INDSWG−64 19	64 TBL OF 14 RES FROM IGNAT'EV+URBANEC	
Reson Params	5.0+1	9.4+2	DUB	Expt	Jour ZET 47 43	Jul 64 .TRNS+TOF,E+J+WG+GWN FOR 14 RES	+
					Jour JET 20 30	Jan 65 .TRANSLATN.	
Reson Params		1.0+6	AUA	Theo	Jour AUJ 20 477	Oct 67 Cook. TBL OF AVG LVL SPACING D,L=0,1	
Reson Params	8.5+1	1.0+4	COL	Expt	Jour PR 166 1234	Feb 68 Wynchank+ TOF G*WN FOR MANY ES AVG D	+
					Conf 65Antwerp § 95	Jul 65 .SUPERSEDED.	
	8.5+1	1.0+4			Data EXFOR11913.019	Jun 76 . 1 RES, E0,J,WN0	
Reson Params	8.5+1	5.7+3	SAC	Expt	Jour NP/A 123 561	Jan 69 Morgenstern+ J,WN,WN0,80E0.MULTILEVL	+
					Rept CEA−R−3609	Sep 68 − +. (THESIS).	
					Conf 68Wash. 867	Mar 68 − + AVERAGE WG GIVEN	
					Conf 66Paris 1 559	Oct 66 Huynh+ ABST.NDG. SEE INDC−156	
					Conf 65Antwerp 525	Jul 65 De Barros+ PPR73.ABST.NDG	
					Jour JPR 24 999	Nov 63 Bianchi+ SUPERSEDED	
	8.5+1	2.3+2			Jour JPR 22 724	Oct 61 Corge+ TOF.3 RES G−SPECS.RES SPINS.	
	8.5+1	9.3+2			Jour JPR 22 719	Oct 61 − + DATA GIVEN.SUPERSEDED	
	8.5+1	5.7+3			Conf 61Saclay 581	Sep 61 − + ES+MULTILVL ANAL.SOME J ASSGN	
	9.8+2	2.9+3			Jour CR 253 859	Jun 61 − + DATA. SUPERSEDED	
	2.1+2	2.3+2			Jour CR 252 3233	May 61 Julien+ SPIN 3 FOR 2 LEVELS	
	0.0+0	6.0+3			Data EXFOR20684.	Jul 77 99PTS.E0,WG,AVG WG,WN,J,L,G*WN.	
Reson Params	+3	+5	AUA	ExTh	Rept AAEC/E−198	May 69 Musgrove.RES PARS + STF FROM (NG)FIT	+
Reson Params	None		BNL	Expt	Conf 69Studsvik 627	Aug 69 Chrien. WG−DISTR CFD PORTER−THOM,TBL	
Reson Params	8.5+1	6.4+2	DUB	ExTh	Conf 69Studsvik 651	Aug 69 Becvar+5 N−RESON SPIN VAL,WG CFD P−T	
				Expt	Rept JINR−P−5309	Mar 70 − + P67.J DIST,WG.	
	2.5+1	1.1+2			Jour CZJB 19 899	Jul 69 − + LOW LVL DECAY−SCH OF 142−PR	
Reson Params	8.5+1	7.2+4	UJV	Expt	Jour CZJB 19 1307	Oct 69 Urbanec+ NEW LVL ANAL,SPIN,WN−DISTR	
	8.5+1	6.4+2			Rept UJV−2228	69 Becvar+ DISTRIBUT.OF WG,ANAL,TBL+CVS	
Reson Params	2.0+5		MUA	Theo	Conf 69Roorke 2 129	Dec 69 Chaubey+ D/GAM−WIDTH RATIO, STATMOD	
Reson Params	−		AUA	Theo	Rept AAEC/E−211	Nov 70 Musgrove. CALCULTD D+GAM WIDTH GIVEN	
Reson Params	8.6+1	1.5+3	CJD	Eval	Rept YK− 7	71 Zakharova+ .SURVEY+SYSTEMATICS,GW,TBL	
					Rept INDC(CCP)−27	Nov 72 .ENGLISH TRANSLATION OF YK−7 /71	
Reson Params	None		DUB	Theo	Jour YF 13 240	Feb 71 Malecki+G−WID,THEO CFD EXPT.TBL,GRPH	
					Jour SNP 13 133	Aug 71 − + ENGL OF YF 13 240.	

59 Praseodymium 141

Quantity	Energy (ev) Min	Max	Lab	Type	Documentation Ref Vol Page	Author, Comments Date	Data
Reson Params	+0	+2	BOL	Eval	Conf IAEA – 169 3 123	74 Benzi+ AVG G – WID CFD OTHERS+XPT,TABL	
Reson Params	+1	+4	FEI	Eval	Rept YK – 8/2 97	Sep 72 Abagyan+ AVG G – WID+D AT BINDNG – E,TBL	
					Rept INDC(CCP) – 39	Jul 74 .PAGE 102.ENGLISH OF YK – 8/2 97	
Reson Params	1.0+3	1.0+6	SAC	Rept	CEA – N – 1832	Dec 75 Ribon+ EXP+TH ANAL,RES PAR,TBL	
Reson Params	8.5+1	9.6+2	BNL	Expt	Prog WASH – 1127 15	Apr 69 Chrien+SPIN ASSIGNMENTS FOR 11RESON	+
	8.5+1	9.6+2			Data EXFOR12638.002	Jun 76 . 13 RES, E0,J	
Reson Params	8.5+1	1.4+3	RPI	Expt	Prog WASH – 1048 71	Jun 64 Block+	+
	8.5+1	1.9+3			Data EXFOR12074.002	Jun 76 . 26 RES, E0	
Strnth Fnctn	+4		HAR	Expt	Jour PPSA 70 51	Jan 57 Gayther+ FROM AVG SIGTOT. FC TRANSM	
Strnth Fnctn	+3		BNL	Expt	Jour PRL 1 461	Dec 58 Hughes. FC 2.5+ – 0.7	
Strnth Fnctn	1.0+4	2.0+5	ORL	Expt	Jour PR 122 182	61 Gibbons. AVG WG+D FROM FIT TO NGAMMA	+
	1.0+4	2.0+5			Data EXFOR11329.	Jun 76 . 3 PTS, S0,D,AVE WG	
Strnth Fnctn	+3	+5	BOL	Theo	Conf 61Vienna 1 179	Aug 61 Benzi+.PPR11,TABLE CFD EXPERIMENT	
Strnth Fnctn		4.0+4	LEB	Expt	Jour ZET 46 80	Jan 64 Konks.PB – SLOW – DOWN,VALUE GIVEN	
					Jour JET 19 59	Jul 64 TRANSLATN.*	
Strnth Fnctn		1.0+4	COL	Expt	Jour PR 166 1234	Feb 68 Wynchank+	+
	None				Conf 65Antwerp § 95	Jul 65 Rainwater+. S – WAVE STF=2.48(X10 – 4)	
		1.0+4			Data EXFOR11913.023	Jun 76 . 6 PTS, S, AND 1 PT, D	
Strnth Fnctn	+3	+4	DUB	Expt	Jour YF 7 493	Mar 68 Konks+ UPPER LIMIT OF S2 ESTIMATED	
					Jour SNP 7 310	Sep 68 – + ENGL OF YF 7 493.	
Strnth Fnctn		5.7+3	SAC	Expt	Jour NP/A 123 561	Jan 69 Morgenstern+ S,WAVE	+
					Rept CEA – R – 3609	Sep 68 – .(THESIS).DATA GIVEN	
					Conf 68Wash. 867	Mar 68 – +	
					Conf 66Paris 1 205	Oct 66 Julien+ PPR64.ABST.NDG. SEE INDC – 156	
	0.0+0	6.0+3			Data EXFOR20684.027	Jul 77 1PNT.L=0.	
Strnth Fnctn	+3	+5	AUA	ExTh	Rept AAEC/E – 198	May 69 Musgrove.S+P+D STF FROM (NG)FIT,TBL	+
Strnth Fnctn	–		DUB	Revw	Jour YF 11 111	Jan 70 Malecki+ VALUES FOR TWO SPIN STATES	
					Jour SNP 11 61	Jul 70 – + ENGL OF YF 11 61.	
Strnth Fnctn	–		AUA	Theo	Rept AAEC/E – 211	Nov 70 Musgrove. SMOOTHED S0,S1 AND S2 GIVN	
Strnth Fnctn	2.7+3		MUN	Expt	Conf 71Albany 327	Aug 71 Dilg+TRNS.S0 STF GVN.31 ELEMENT GRPH	
Strnth Fnctn	2.4+4		MUA	Theo	Jour IJP 46 114	Mar 72 Chaubey+ P – WAVE.FOR A – SYSTEMTIC,GRPH	
Strnth Fnctn	None		AUA	Eval	Rept AAEC/E – 277	Mar 73 Musgrove.TBLS EXPTL DATA+BEST VALUES	
Strnth Fnctn		+5	KFK	Theo	Conf JAERI – M – 5984	Feb 75 Newstead.P230.TBL S0,S1 OFD EXP.	
Lvl Density			FEI	Eval	Rept FEI – 36	66 Kapchigashev+.TBL OF RELATD QUANTTYS	+
		5.0+4			Jour YF 4 686	Sep 66 .TABLE.SHORT VERSION OF FEI – 36	
	–				Prog YFI – 3 3	66 .ABSTRACT.TABLE LDL+NUCL.EXCIT.E	
		5.0+4			Jour SNP 4 486	67 .ENGLISH OF YF 4.FROM(N,GAMMA).TABLE	
					Prog INDC – E – 140 3	66 .ENGLISH TRANSL OF YFI – 3	
Lvl Density	5.0+6	7.0+6	ALD	Expt	Jour NP/A 112 337	May 68 Owens+.LVL DENS VERSUS EXCIT.MEAN T	+
					Conf 65Antwerp 547	Jul 65 – + PPR122. TBL FERMI GAS CONST.	
Lvl Density	3.6+6	8.5+6	JAE	Expt	Jour NP/A 131 145	Jun 69 Maruyama. E DEPENDANCE,PARAM,TH FIT.	
	3.5+6	8.5+6			Conf 67Tokyo 373	Sep 67 – + PPR8.127. ABST.	
Lvl Density	None		AUW	Theo	Conf 70Madurai 2 267	Dec 70 Ramamurty+ A – PARAMETER GVN,LANG'S – TH	
Lvl Density	None		ITE	Theo	Conf 72Budapest 270	Aug 72 Sukhoruchkin. STATIST DIST OF LVLS	
Lvl Density	None		BOL	Eval	Conf IAEA – 169 3 123	74 Benzi+ LVL DENS PARAM BY XPT,GRPH+TB	
Lvl Density	+1	+4	FEI	Eval	Rept YK – 8/2 97	Sep 72 Abagyan+ LVL DENSITY PARAMETER,TBL	
					Rept INDC(CCP) – 39	Jul 74 .PAGE 102.ENGLISH OF YK – 8/2 97	
(γ,n)	9.0+6	2.4+7	SAC	Expt	Jour NP/A 172 426	Sep 71 Beil+LORENTZ LINE PARAM,GRAPHS,TBLS	

59 Praseodymium 142

Quantity	Energy (ev) Min	Max	Lab	Type	Documentation Ref Vol Page	Author, Comments Date	Data
Evaluation	1.0 – 3	1.5+7	AUA	Eval	Rept AAEC/TM – 549	Jun 70 Cook.TOT,EL,INEL,NONEL,CAPT SIGS,NDG	+
					Rept AAEC/E – 214	Jun 71 Bertram+GROUP SIGMAS SAME QUANTS.NDG	
					Rept AAEC/TM – 587	Mar 71 *DESCRIPTION OF LIBRARY	
	1.0 – 3	1.5+7			Data AUSTR – DFN 141.	Nov 71 POINT(223) AND GROUP(127) SIGMAS	
Total	1.0 – 3	1.5+7	AUA	Eval	Data AUSTR – DFN 141.	Nov 71 COOK+POINT(223)+GROUP(127)SIG.CF EVL	+
Elastic	1.0 – 3	1.5+7	AUA	Eval	Data AUSTR – DFN 141.	Nov 71 COOK+POINT(223)+GROUP(127)SIG.CF EVL	+
Tot Inelastc	5.0+5	1.5+7	AUA	Eval	Data AUSTR – DFN 141.	Nov 71 COOK+POINT(11)+GROUP(127)SIG.CF EVL	+
Nonelastic	1.0 – 3	1.5+7	AUA	Eval	Data AUSTR – DFN 141.	Nov 71 COOK+POINT(223)+GROUP(127)SIG.CF EVL	+
Absorption	2.5 – 2		IJI	Eval	Rept KIYAI – 76 – 6	76 Fedorova+ ONLY 1LIT – VALUE,RENORM.TBL	
					Conf 75Kiev 1 169	May 75 – + EVAL SIG GIVEN,TABLE	
Res Int Abs	5.0 – 1		AUA	Eval	Rept AAEC/TM – 619	Sep 72 Clayton.CALC FROM SIG LIBRARY,TABLE	
Res Int Abs	+0	+5	WIN	Revw	Conf IAEA – 169 3 163	74 Pope+ CALC FROM AUSTRAL DATA FILE	
(n,γ)	Maxwl		MTR	Expt	Jour JCP 23 2108	Nov 55 Smith+	+
	Maxwl				Data EXFOR11851.003	Jun 76 . 1 PT.	
(n,γ)	1.0 – 3	1.5+7	AUA	Eval	Data AUSTR – DFN 141.	Nov 71 COOK+POINT(223)+GROUP(127)SIG.CF EVL	+

59 Praseodymium 142

Quantity	Energy (ev) Min	Max	Lab	Type	Documentation Ref Vol Page	Date	Author, Comments	Data
(n,γ)	Pile		CRC	Eval Rept	AECL - 3037 1	Jan 72	Walker.RECOMMENDED SIG,DETAILED TBL	
(n,γ)	2.5 - 2		AUA	Eval Rept	AAEC/TM - 619	Sep 72	Clayton.CALC FROM SIG LIBRARY,TABLE	
(n,γ)	Maxwl Fiss		WIN	Revw Conf	IAEA - 169 3 163	74	Pope+ MAXW+FIS - SPEC AVG DATA CFD XPT	
	Fiss			Conf	IAEA - 169 3 137	74	Dean. POINT DATA AVG OVER STAND SPEC	
Spect (n,γ)	1.6+6		ORL	Expt Conf	61Saclay 203	Sep 61	Block+.DIFF PULSE - HEIGHT.LIQUIDSCINT	
Spect (n,γ)	Maxwl		LAS	Expt Prog	WASH - 1074 82	Apr 67	Jurney. GE(LI) NAI SPECTROMETER NDG.	
Spect (n,γ)	Maxwl		BNL	Expt Prog	WASH - 1127 18	Apr 69	Chrien+ GROUND - STATE GAMMA E GIVEN	
Reson Params	-		AUA	Theo Rept	AAEC/E - 211	Nov 70	Musgrove. CALCULTD D+GAM WIDTH GIVEN	
Strnth Fnctn	-		AUA	Theo Rept	AAEC/E - 211	Nov 70	Musgrove. SMOOTHED S0,S1 AND S2 GIVN	
Lvl Density	+6		MIL	Theo Jour	EN 15 1 54	Jan 68	Facchini+ LDL PARS FROM LOW EN RES	
Lvl Density	-		BUC	Expt Jour	NP/A 140 23	Jan 70	Magda+ PARAM A FROM (ALPHA,N) SPECTR	
Lvl Density	None		MUN	Theo Jour	NP/A 217 269	Dec 73	Dilg+ A,DELTA. BACK SHIFTED FERMIGAS	
Lvl Density	None		COP	Theo Jour	NP/A 222 493	Apr 74	Dossing+COLL ROTAT.SPAC. ACCUR ESTIM	
Lvl Density	None		ROC	Theo Jour	NP/A 223 577	May 74	Huizenga+ EXP CFD MICROSC TH SPH NUC	

59 Praseodymium 143

Quantity	Energy (ev) Min	Max	Lab	Type	Documentation Ref Vol Page	Date	Author, Comments	Data
Evaluation	1.0 - 3	1.5+7	AUA	Eval Rept	AAEC/TM - 549	Jun 70	Cook.TOT,EL,INEL,NONEL,CAPT SIGS,NDG	+
				Rept	AAEC/E - 214	Jun 71	Bertram+GROUP SIGMAS SAME QUANTS.NDG	
				Rept	AAEC/TM - 587	Mar 71	*DESCRIPTION OF LIBRARY	
	1.0 - 3	1.5+7		Data	AUSTR - DFN 142.	Nov 71	POINT(223) AND GROUP(127) SIGMAS	
Evaluation	1.0 - 5	1.5+7	BOL	Eval Prog	NEANDC(E)182 7	Dec 76	Fabri+ COMPLETE EVAL IN ENDF/B DONE	+
	1.0 - 5	1.5+7		Data	CNEN - CEA 3	Jan 78	PRELIM.ALL QUANTITIES.ENDF FORMAT	
Total	1.0 - 3	1.5+7	AUA	Eval Data	AUSTR - DFN 142.	Nov 71	COOK+POINT(223)+GROUP(127)SIG.CF EVL	+
Elastic	1.0 - 3	1.5+7	AUA	Eval Data	AUSTR - DFN 142.	Nov 71	COOK+POINT(223)+GROUP(127)SIG.CF EVL	+
Tot Inelastc	5.0+5	1.5+7	AUA	Eval Data	AUSTR - DFN 142.	Nov 71	COOK+POINT(11)+GROUP(127)SIG.CF EVL	+
Nonelastic	1.0 - 3	1.5+7	AUA	Eval Data	AUSTR - DFN 142.	Nov 71	COOK+POINT(223)+GROUP(127)SIG.CF EVL	+
Absorption	2.5 - 2		IJI	Eval Rept	KIYAI - 76 - 6	76	Fedorova+ ONLY 1LIT - VALUE,RENORM.TBL	
				Conf	75Kiev 1 169	May 75	- + EVAL SIG GIVEN,TABLE	
Res Int Abs	5.0 - 1		CRC	Expt Jour	CJP 37 907	Aug 59	ROY. NRX ACT 190+ - 25B	+
	5.0 - 1			Data	EXFOR12052.003	Jun 76	. 1 PT.	
Res Int Abs	None		CRC	Eval Prog	AECL - 1054	Mar 60	Walker.(CRP - 913) REDUCED RES.INT.	
Res Int Abs	5.5 - 1		CRC	Eval Rept	AECL - 3037 1	Jan 72	Walker.REDUCED RES INT,DETAILED TBL	
Res Int Abs	5.0 - 1		AUA	Eval Rept	AAEC/TM - 619	Sep 72	Clayton.CALC FROM SIG LIBRARY,TABLE	
Res Int Abs	5.5 - 1	+6	SAC	Revw Conf	IAEA - 169 1 235	74	Ribon.CAPTURE,STATUS CFD REQUEST,TBL	
Res Int Abs	+0	+5	WIN	Revw Conf	IAEA - 169 3 163	74	Pope+ DATA FILE CALC CFD XPTAL VALUE	
Res Int Abs	5.0 - 1		IJI	Eval Rept	KIYAI - 76 - 6	76	Fedorova+ ONLY 1LIT - VALUE=RECOMM.TBL	
				Conf	75Kiev 1 169	May 75	- + EVAL OF RI - EXPTS.TABLE	
(n,γ)	Pile		CRC	Expt Jour	CJP 37 907	Aug 59	ROY. NRX ACT EFFECTIVE+2200M.SEC SIG	+
	Pile			Data	EXFOR12052.002	Jun 76	. 1 PT.	
(n,γ)	Maxwl		CRC	Eval Prog	AECL - 1054	Mar 60	Walker. (CRP - 913)	
(n,γ)	Maxwl		ORL	Expt Conf	60Vienna 239	Oct 60	Stoughton+.NDG,EXPT DESCRIBED	
(n,γ)	1.0 - 3	1.5+7	AUA	Eval Data	AUSTR - DFN 142.	Nov 71	COOK+POINT(223)+GROUP(127)SIG.CF EVL	+
(n,γ)	Maxwl		CRC	Eval Rept	AECL - 3037 1	Jan 72	Walker.RECOMMENDED SIG,DETAILED TBL	
(n,γ)	2.5 - 2		AUA	Eval Rept	AAEC/TM - 619	Sep 72	Clayton.CALC FROM SIG LIBRARY,TABLE	
(n,γ)	Fiss		SAC	Revw Conf	IAEA - 169 1 235	74	Ribon.STATUS SIG CFD REQUESTS,TABLE	
	2.5 - 2			Conf	IAEA - 169 1 235	74	- .STATUS SIG CFD REQUESTS,TABLE	
(n,γ)	Maxwl Fiss		WIN	Revw Conf	IAEA - 169 3 163	74	Pope+ MAXW+FIS - SPEC AVG DATA CFD XPT	
	Fiss			Conf	IAEA - 169 3 137	74	Dean. POINT DATA AVG OVER STAND SPEC	
Reson Params	-		AUA	Theo Rept	AAEC/E - 211	Nov 70	Musgrove. CALCULTD D+GAM WIDTH GIVEN	
Strnth Fnctn	-		AUA	Theo Rept	AAEC/E - 211	Nov 70	Musgrove. SMOOTHED S0,S1 AND S2 GIVN	

59 Praseodymium 144

Quantity	Energy (ev) Min	Max	Lab	Type	Documentation Ref Vol Page	Date	Author, Comments	Data
Reson Params	-		AUA	Theo Rept	AAEC/E - 211	Nov 70	Musgrove. CALCULTD D+GAM WIDTH GIVEN	
Strnth Fnctn	-		AUA	Theo Rept	AAEC/E - 211	Nov 70	Musgrove. SMOOTHED S0,S1 AND S2 GIVN	

59 Praseodymium 145

Quantity	Energy (ev) Min	Max	Lab	Type	Documentation Ref Vol Page	Date	Author, Comments	Data
Evaluation	1.0 – 3	1.5+7	AUA	Eval	Rept AAEC/TM – 549	Jun 70	Cook.TOT,EL,INEL,NONEL,CAPT SIGS,NDG	+
					Rept AAEC/E – 214	Jun 71	Bertram+GROUP SIGMAS SAME QUANTS.NDG	
					Rept AAEC/TM – 587	Mar 71	*DESCRIPTION OF LIBRARY	
	1.0 – 3	1.5+7		Data	AUSTR – DFN 143.	Nov 71	POINT(223) AND GROUP(127) SIGMAS	
Total	1.0 – 3	1.5+7	AUA Eval	Data	AUSTR – DFN 143.	Nov 71	COOK+POINT(223)+GROUP(127)SIG.CF EVL	+
Elastic	1.0 – 3	1.5+7	AUA Eval	Data	AUSTR – DFN 143.	Nov 71	COOK+POINT(223)+GROUP(127)SIG.CF EVL	+
Tot Inelastc	5.0+5	1.5+7	AUA Eval	Data	AUSTR – DFN 143.	Nov 71	COOK+POINT(11)+GROUP(127)SIG.CF EVL	+
Nonelastic	1.0 – 3	1.5+7	AUA Eval	Data	AUSTR – DFN 143.	Nov 71	COOK+POINT(223)+GROUP(127)SIG.CF EVL	+
Res Int Abs	5.0 – 1		AUA Eval	Rept	AAEC/TM – 619	Sep 72	Clayton.CALC FROM SIG LIBRARY,TABLE	
Res Int Abs	+0	+5	WIN Revw	Conf	IAEA – 169 3 163	74	Pope+ CALC FROM AUSTRAL DATA FILE	
(n,γ)	1.0 – 3	1.5+7	AUA Eval	Data	AUSTR – DFN 143.	Nov 71	COOK+POINT(223)+GROUP(127)SIG.CF EVL	+
(n,γ)	Pile		CRC Eval	Rept	AECL – 3037 1	Jan 72	Walker.SIG ESTIMATED ACCORDING Z,A	
(n,γ)	2.5 – 2		AUA Eval	Rept	AAEC/TM – 619	Sep 72	Clayton.CALC FROM SIG LIBRARY,TABLE	
(n,γ)	Maxwl	Fiss	WIN Revw	Conf	IAEA – 169 3 163	74	Pope+ MAXW+FIS – SPEC AVG EVAL DATA	
	Fiss			Conf	IAEA – 169 3 137	74	Dean. POINT DATA AVG OVER STAND SPEC	
Reson Params	–		AUA Theo	Rept	AAEC/E – 211	Nov 70	Musgrove. CALCULTD D+GAM WIDTH GIVEN	
Strnth Fnctn	–		AUA Theo	Rept	AAEC/E – 211	Nov 70	Musgrove. SMOOTHED S0,S1 AND S2 GIVN	

59 Praseodymium 146

Quantity	Energy (ev) Min	Max	Lab	Type	Documentation Ref Vol Page	Date	Author, Comments	Data
Reson Params	–		AUA Theo	Rept	AAEC/E – 211	Nov 70	Musgrove. CALCULTD D+GAM WIDTH GIVEN	
Strnth Fnctn	–		AUA Theo	Rept	AAEC/E – 211	Nov 70	Musgrove. SMOOTHED S0,S1 AND S2 GIVN	

59 Praseodymium 147

Quantity	Energy (ev) Min	Max	Lab	Type	Documentation Ref Vol Page	Date	Author, Comments	Data
Reson Params	–		AUA Theo	Rept	AAEC/E – 211	Nov 70	Musgrove. CALCULTD D+GAM WIDTH GIVEN	
Strnth Fnctn	–		AUA Theo	Rept	AAEC/E – 211	Nov 70	Musgrove. SMOOTHED S0,S1 AND S2 GIVN	

60 Neodymium

Quantity	Energy (ev) Min	Max	Lab	Type	Documentation Ref Vol Page	Author, Comments Date	Data
Evaluation	5.0+5	1.5+7	LRL Eval	Rept	UCRL-5351	Nov 58 Howerton+ CURVES	
Total	Maxwl		COL Expt	Jour	PR 48 265	Aug 35 Dunning+ IONCH,TRANS,RA-BE/PARAFIN N	
Total	6.0-2	5.0+0	ANL Expt	Jour	PR 71 556	Apr 47 Sturm+ CURV. USE OF LIF(111) CRYSTAL	
Total	Maxwl		ANL Expt	Jour	PR 76 300	Jul 49 Hess+ 53B QUOTED.ISOTP SIG BY MASSSP	
Total	6.0+4	3.0+6	WIS Expt	Jour	PR 93 461	Feb 54 Okazaki+ TRANS AVG OVER RESON OKS TH	+
	5.0+4	2.9+6		Data	EXFOR12061.002	Jun 76 . 23 PTS.	
Total	4.5+0	1.0+4	CCP Expt	Conf	55Geneva 4 22	Aug 55 Vladimirski+.P641,CURVE,CHOPPER,TOF	+
Total	4.1+1	4.5+1	BNL Expt	Priv	PILCHER	Sep 55 Pilcher.	+
	4.1+1	4.5+1		Data	EXFOR12225.002	Jun 76 . 10 PTS.	
Total	1.3+7	1.6+7	LAS Expt	Jour	PR 109 1268	Feb 58 Conner.TRNS SC 3ES 4.92 5.09 5.06B	+
				Conf	58Geneva 15 11	Sep 58 Coon+ SIGMA AT 3ES GVN. TOF	
	1.3+7	1.6+7		Data	EXFOR11320.008	Jun 76 . 3 PTS.	
Total	9.6-1	1.3+4	MTR Expt	Priv	SIMPSON	Mar 58 Simpson.	+
	9.6-1	1.3+4		Data	EXFOR12072.002	Jun 76 . 448 PTS.	
Total	5.0-1	6.8+1	BNL Expt	Jour	PR 110 692	May 58 Seth+ FC ABS CURV.	+
	5.0-1	9.0+1		Data	EXFOR11788.033	Jun 76 . 40 PTS.	
Total	3.2+6	5.2+6	JNE Expt	Jour	ARS 59 179	Sep 63 Manero.ND OXIDE TGT.GOOD GEOM. +-5PC	
Total	3.0+3	6.5+5	DKE ExTh	Jour	PL 16 306	Jun 65 Seth.AV CS 8-10KEV RSN INT RES OBSV	+
				Jour	PL 13 70	64 - + ANALLYZED TRANS FOR STF	
	2.0+3	6.4+5		Expt Data	EXFOR11781.014	Jun 76 . 103 PTS.	
Total	1.4+7		ANL Expt	Abst	DA/B 28 3835	Mar 68 Haugsnes. SIG=5.06+-0.03B, CFD OPTMD	+
				Rept	ANL-5609	Nov 56 .SUPERSEDED.	
				Rept	ANL-5554	Aug 56 .SUPERSEDED.	
	1.4+7			Data	EXFOR11733.007	Jun 76 . 1 PT.	
Total	3.3-2	2.7-1	BNL Expt	Jour	NIM 86 83	Sep 70 Malik+ TBL. NO CORR. FOR CONTAMINANT	+
	3.3-2	2.7-1		Data	EXFOR10501.021	May 75 . 4 PTS. SIGMA	
Total		6.2+5	CCP Revw	Jour	AE 29 187	Sep 70 Sukhoruchkin. AVERAGED SIG(E) GRAPH	
				Jour	SJA 29 896	Sep 70 TRANSLATN.*	
Total	2.5+6	1.5+7	BNW Expt	Jour	PR/C 3 576	Feb 71 Foster+ TRANS, CURVS, CFD OTHERS+ TH	+
				Jour	NIM 36 1	Sep 65 .EXPT DETAILS	
	2.4+6	1.5+7		Data	EXFOR10047.064	Aug 73 . 244 PTS.	
Total	2.7+3		MUN Expt	Prog	EANDC(E)150U	Oct 72 Dilg+ AVERAGE TOT XSECT+S0	+
				Conf	71Albany 327	Aug 71 - +TRNS.AVG CS GVN.31 ELEMENT GRP	
	2.7+3			Data	EXFOR20583.015	Jun 76 1PNT.	
Total	1.3+7	1.5+7	DEB Eval	Rept	IAEA-153 173	73 Boedy+ MOST PROBABLE VAL OF SIG,TBL	
				Jour	AHP 30 115	Oct 71 Angeli+ AVG SIG,CFD CALC.TBLS.GRAPH	
Total	1.4+7		CCP Expt	Conf	73Kiev 3 108	May 73 Djumin+ OPTMOD CALC,SIG(A),GRAPH	
				Conf	73Tbilisi 147	Feb 73 - + ABST,SIG,PARAM OF DEFORM,NDG	
Total	1.0+5	6.5+5	DKE Expt	Jour	AP 84 165	May 74 Pineo+ CURV. AVE. SIGMA	
				Abst	DA/B 31 6821	May 71 - .2 E RANGE AVGS.CFD OPTMDL	
	1.5+4	6.0+5		Diss	PINEO	70 .AVG CS.GRPHS.CFD.STF CALC.TBL.CFD.	
	1.5+4	6.0+5		Data	EXFOR10542.017	Jan 79 . DATA UNOBTAINABLE FROM AUTHORS.	
Total	7.0+5	9.0+6	GLS Expt	Jour	JP/A 7 1758	Sep 74 Kellie+ SIG IN CURVE,STAT ERROR 2 PC	+
	7.0+5	9.0+6		Data	EXFOR20418.005	Sep 75 646PTS.	
Elastic	Maxwl		ORL Expt	Jour	PR 91 597	Aug 53 Koehler+	+
	Maxwl			Data	EXFOR12060.	Jun 76 . 2 PTS, COH, COH AMP	
Elastic	1.0+6		ALD Expt	Jour	NP 42 86	Apr 63 Gilboy+.SIG=6.088B+-3PC	+
Elastic	9.8+5		AGN Eval	Rept	TID-21629	Dec 64 Perkins+ FROM BNL325 AND OTHERS	
Elastic	Cold		GRE Expt	Jour	ACRB 31 2745	Nov 75 Boucherle+ SC.LENGTH=0.769+-0.005	+
	2.5-2			Data	EXFOR20746.002	Jun 78 3PTS.COH.SC.AMP.	
Diff Elastic	1.4+7		LRL Theo	Rept	UCRL-4926	Jul 57 Bjorklund+ OPTMDL CALC 6-PARAM FIT	
	7.0+6			Rept	UCRL-4927	Jul 57 - + OPTMDL CALC 6-PARAM FIT	
Diff Elastic	+5	+6	ANL Expt	Prog	WASH-1006	Oct 58 Lane+	
Diff Elastic	1.0+6		ALD Expt	Jour	NP 42 86	Apr 63 Gilboy+30TO137DEG.COMP.WITH OPTICMOD	
Diff Elastic	9.8+5		AGN Eval	Rept	TID-21629	Dec 64 Perkins+ LEG COEF DERIVED	
Polarization	3.8+5		WIS ExTh	Jour	NP 6 177	Mar 58 Walker. REDUCED RESONANCE INTEGRAL	
				Expt Rept	AECU-3628	57 Clement+ LI7(P,N) SOURCE. 2ANGLES.	
Polarization	+5	+6	ANL Expt	Prog	WASH-1006 1	Oct 58 Lane+	
Potntal Scat	3.8+5	+3	BNL Expt	Jour	PR 110 692	May 58 Seth+ 5.0+-0.6B CALCTD FROM TOT SIG	+
	4.5+1			Data	EXFOR11788.015	Jun 76 . 1 PT.	
Potntal Scat		6.5+5	DKE ExTh	Jour	PL 13 70	Nov 64 Seth+0,1PHASE FRM SIG TOT AV 3-650KV	
Potntal Scat	1.0+5	6.5+5	DKE Expt	Jour	AP 84 165	May 74 Pineo+TRNS.S WAVE SCT LENGTH.TBL.CFD	
	3.0+3	6.5+5		Diss	PINEO	70 .TBL.GRPHS.CFD TO 3 COLLECTIVE MDLS.	
Tot Inelastc	5.0+6	7.0+6	ALD Expt	Jour	NP/A 112 337	May 68 Owens+.3ES.FROM N SPECT 90DEG.	+
Diff Inelast	5.0+6	7.0+6	ALD Expt	Jour	NP/A 112 337	May 68 Owens+.3ES.FROM N SPECT 90DEG NDG.	
				Conf	65Antwerp' 547	Jul 65 - + PPR122.ABST.SPECT N' AT 90DEG	
Thermal Scat	Maxwl		ORL Expt	Jour	PR 92 1380	Dec 53 Koehler+TRIVALENT ION PARAMAG SCAT	

60 Neodymium

Quantity	Energy (ev) Min	Max	Lab	Type	Documentation Ref Vol Page	Date	Author, Comments	Data
Thermal Scat	Maxwl		ORL	Theo Jour	PR 92 1387	Dec 53	Trammel.TRIVAL.ION MAG.SCAT.CFD XPT	
Thermal Scat	2.0−4	1.5−1	BSP	ExTh Jour	JCP 48 520	Jan 68	Mattos.,TRIVALENT ION PARAMAG SIG	+
Thermal Scat	1.0−4	1.0+3	MUN	revw Jour	EEN 80 1	77	Koester. SCAT LENGTH,INCOH SIG	
Scattering	Maxwl		ORL	Expt Jour	PR 91 597	Aug 53	Koehler+ TRANS 16+−3B	+
	Maxwl			Data	EXFOR12060.019	Jun 76	. 1 PT, SIG	
Scattering		6.0+2	GEL	Expt Jour	JNE 23 369	Jul 69	Migneco+ TOF.RES.PARAMS.LISTED	
Scattering	2.0−2	1.0+1	IJI	Expt Conf	73Kiev 2 104	May 73	Vertebny+ TOF,SIG(NEUT−E),GRAPH	
Scattering	−3		JUL	Expt Conf	75Wash. 823	Mar 75	Schmatz+ INCOH.CS REV VANADIUM	
Nonelastic	Maxwl		ANL	Expt Jour	PR 76 300	Jul 49	Hess+ 45B = (TOT−EL)	
Absorption	Maxwl		FAR	Expt Rept	CEA−137	Mar 52	Ailloud.43.2+−1BARN PILE OSCILLATOR	+
	Pile			Jour	JPR 13 171	Mar 52	− +. PILE OSC. CFD OTHER EXPTS	
Res Int Abs	5.0−1	1.0+6	CCP	Expt Conf	55Geneva 5 91	Aug 55	Spivak+.VAL GVN CFD REF,PPR659	
Res Int Abs	5.0−1		MTR	Expt Jour	IN− 1195	May 68	Scoville+	+
				Jour	ANS 8 290	Jun 65	.SUPERSEDED	
	5.0−1			Data	EXFOR11820.007	Jun 76	. 1 PT.	
(n,γ)	Pile		ANL	Expt Jour	PR 80 342	Nov 50	Harris+ PILE OSC. REL TO BORON.	+
	Pile			Data	EXFOR11528.007	Jun 76	. 1 PT.	
(n,γ)	Maxwl		ORL	Expt Jour	PR 83 641	Aug 51	Pomerance. LOCAL OSC REL AU ABS 95 B	+
	Maxwl			Data	EXFOR11047.047	Jun 76	. 1 PT.	
(n,γ)	2.5−2		ANL	Expt Jour	NSE 9 132	Feb 61	Meadows+ PULSED NEUTS.49.9+0.3−2.2B	+
	2.5−2			Data	EXFOR11028.018	Sep 76	. 1 PT. CS=49.9B	
(n,γ)	1.2+2	6.0+2	GEL	Expt Prog	EANDC(E)115U	Mar 69	Weigmann+,LINAC TOF	
(n,γ)		6.0+2	GEL	Expt Jour	JNE 23 369	Jul 69	Migneco+ TOF.ABS.NORM USING AG RES.	
(n,γ)	1.0+3	1.0+7	BOL	Eval Rept	CEC(70)−2	Apr 70	Benzi.GRAPH=SUM OF SIG(ISOTOPES)	
(n,γ)	3.3−2	8.3−1	BNL	Expt Jour	NIM 86 83	Sep 70	Malik+MOXON RAE DET RELATIVE TO AU	+
	3.3−2	2.7−1		Data	EXFOR10501.020	May 75	. 4 PTS. SIGMA	
(n,γ)	3.0+4		AUA	Theo Rept	AAEC/E−211	Nov 70	Musgrove. SIGMA GIVEN AND CFD OTHER	
(n,γ)	1.0+3	1.0+7	FEI	Eval Rept	YK− 8/2 97	Sep 72	Abagjan+ AVG SIG(ENERGY−GROUPS),TABL	
				Rept	INDC(CCP)−39	Jul 74	.P102. ENGLISH OF YK−8/2 97	
(n,γ)	Fast		RCN	Expt Rept	ECN−10	Oct 76	Veenema+ STEK REACTIVITY WORTHS TBL.	
Spect (n,γ)	Maxwl		CRC	Expt Prog	PR−P−41 44	Apr 59	Bartholomew+LOW E GAMMAS−HIGH GAMMAS	
Spect (n,γ)	Maxwl	4.4+0	YAL	Expt Jour	NP 19 436	Nov 60	Draper+ TABLE, GRAPH 400−900KEV GAMS	
Spect (n,γ)	Maxwl		CCP	Expt Book	NEJTRONFIZ 335	61	Groshev.TBL+GRAPH.ENGL TRNSL=SPN 248	
Spect (n,γ)	Maxwl		ARF	Expt Prog	ARF−1193−12	Jul 62	Greenwood+ CRYST SPEC. LOW−E GAMMAS	
Spect (n,γ)	Maxwl		CAS	Expt Jour	NC 29 977	Aug 63	Giannini+ NAI, E+INTENSITY,TO 262KEV	+
Spect (n,γ)	+0	+4	COL	Expt Prog	WASH−1124 31	Nov 68	Camarda+ MOXON−RAE DET TBC NO DATA	
Spect (n,γ)	Maxwl		KUR	Expt Jour	YF 8 1067	Dec 68	Groshev+ GAMMA−COMPT−SPEC,GRPH+TBL	+
				Jour	SNP 8 619	Jun 69	TRANSLATN.*	
	2.5−2			Data	EXFOR40236.006	Oct 74	.GAM/100N FOR MANY ES BY 2METHODS GVN	
Spect (n,γ)	2.5−2		MIT	Comp Rept	MITNE−85	Jan 69	Rasmussen+TBL G INT.=AFCRL−69−0071	
Spect (n,γ)	Pile		CNE	Expt Prog	INDC(SEC)−18	Aug 71	Mariscotti+ PG2.NAI+GE−LI,NDG,TBP	
Spect (n,γ)	+0	+2	NRL	Expt Jour	PR/C 5 2030	Jun 72	Stolovy+ NAI(TL) DET.RESON ASSIGN, J	
Spect (n,γ)	Maxwl		MUN	Expt Jour	ZP 258 315	Mar 73	Henkelmann. E + INT OF GS GIVEN	+
	2.5−2			Data	EXFOR20606.009	Jun 76	2PTS.	
Spect (n,γ)	Maxwl		NIL	Expt Prog	INDC(SEC)−50	Jan 76	. ABST. ANALYS COMPLETD,NDG	
Inelastic γ	4.4+6		WES	Expt Jour	PR 107 1306	Sep 57	Sinclair.XTL SPEC .46 1.60MEV GS IA	
Inelastic γ	5.0+6	7.0+6	ALD	Expt Jour	NP/A 112 337	May 68	Owens+.3ES.TOF SPECT 90 DEG. NDG.	+
(n,2n)	1.5+7		DEB	Eval Jour	REA 11 1 153	Mar 73	Boedy+ RECOMM.VALUE FROM N−Z SYSTEM.	
(n,α)	5.0+1	1.0+3	DUB	Expt Jour	JINR−P3−3104	Jan 67	Kvitek+,ALPHA EMISS VS E(N),GRAPH	
	6.0+0	4.1+2		Rept	YFI−3 26	Sep 66	− + ALFA−WIDTH,EXPT CFD THEORY	
				Rept	INDC−140E 28	67	. ENGL TRANSL OF YFI−3 26	
Reson Params	3.0+2	5.0+2	GEL	ExTh Jour	JNE 23 369	Jul 69	Migneco+ TOF.WG,WN.AREA ANAL.	
Reson Params	5.8+2	1.1+3	SAC	Expt Jour	NP/A 134 118	Sep 69	Alves+LINAC TOF.35E0,8WN.	+
	5.2+2	1.1+3		Data	EXFOR20688.020	Jun 77	36PTS.E0,WT,A*G*WN.	
Reson Params	0.0+0	2.0+3	SAC	Expt Rept	CEA−N−1459	Aug 71	Tellier. AVERAGE G−WIDTH.	+
		2.0+3		Data	EXFOR20121.002	Sep 72	1PNT.AVG WG.	
Strnth Fnctn		6.5+5	DKE	ExTh Jour	PL 13 70	Nov 64	Seth+S,P,D STF FRM SIG TOT AV 3−650K	+
	5.0+4	1.5+5		Expt Conf	64Paris 2 916	Jul 64	− + S0, S1, S2 R PRIME/R	
	3.0+5	6.5+5		Data	EXFOR11665.022	Jun 75	. 1 PT. EACH. S, P, D	
Strnth Fnctn	6.0+0	+6	COL	Expt Abst	BAP 13 722	Apr 68	Hacken+ PRELIMINARY LVL SPACINGS	
Strnth Fnctn	0.0+0	4.7+3	SAC	Expt Rept	CEA−N−1459	Aug 71	Tellier. FROM SEPERATED ISOTOPE EXPT	+
		4.7+3		Data	EXFOR20121.003	Sep 72	1PNT.L=0.	
Strnth Fnctn	3.0+3	6.5+5	DKE	Expt Jour	AP 84 165	May 74	Pineo+ S, P, D WAVE.	
	None			Abst	DA/B 31 6821	May 71	.S,P,D WAVE.	
Strnth Fnctn	2.7+3		MUN	Expt Conf	71Albany 327	Aug 76	Dilg+TRNS.S0 STF GVN.31 ELEMENT GRPH	
Lvl Density	5.0+6	7.0+6	ALD	Expt Jour	NP/A 112 337	May 68	Owens+.LVL DENS VERSUS EXCIT.MEAN T	
				Conf	65Antwerp 547	Jul 65	− + PPR122. TBL FERMI GAS CONST.	

60 Neodymium

Quantity	Energy (ev) Min	Max	Lab	Type	Documentation Ref Vol Page	Author, Comments Date	Data
Lvl Density	0.0+0	3.0+2	SAC	Theo Conf	72Budapest 180	Aug 72 Jain+ HIGHER ORDER SPACING DIST,GRPH	
(γ,n)	9.0+6	2.4+7	SAC	Expt Jour	NP/A 172 426	Sep 71 Beil+LORENTZ LINE PARAM,GRAPHS,TBLS	

60 Neodymium 139

Quantity	Energy (ev) Min	Max	Lab	Type	Documentation Ref Vol Page	Author, Comments Date	Data
Reson Params	–		AUA	Theo Rept	AAEC/E – 211	Nov 70 Musgrove. CALCULTD D+GAM WIDTH GIVEN	
Strnth Fnctn	–		AUA	Theo Rept	AAEC/E – 211	Nov 70 Musgrove. SMOOTHED S0,S1 AND S2 GIVN	
Strnth Fnctn	–2	+3	SAC	Expt Rept	CEA – N – 1522	Oct 72 Cauvin+ S0,S1 CALC	

60 Neodymium 140

Quantity	Energy (ev) Min	Max	Lab	Type	Documentation Ref Vol Page	Author, Comments Date	Data
(n,p)	Maxwl		IFU	Theo Rept	ICD – 4 20	67 Dadakina+ PENETR COEFF CALC,TABLE	
Reson Params	–		AUA	Theo Rept	AAEC/E – 211	Nov 70 Musgrove. CALCULTD D+GAM WIDTH GIVEN	
Strnth Fnctn	–		AUA	Theo Rept	AAEC/E – 211	Nov 70 Musgrove. SMOOTHED S0,S1 AND S2 GIVN	
Strnth Fnctn	–2	+3	SAC	Expt Rept	CEA – N – 1522	Oct 72 Cauvin+ S0,S1 CALC	
Lvl Density	–3	+0	IFU	Theo Jour	UFZ 13 700	Apr 68 Pisanko+ LEVEL SPACING CALC,TBL	
				Jour	UPJ 13 498	Oct 68 TRANSLATN.*	

60 Neodymium 141

Quantity	Energy (ev) Min	Max	Lab	Type	Documentation Ref Vol Page	Author, Comments Date	Data
Reson Params	–		AUA	Theo Rept	AAEC/E – 211	Nov 70 Musgrove. CALCULTD D+GAM WIDTH GIVEN	
Strnth Fnctn	–		AUA	Theo Rept	AAEC/E – 211	Nov 70 Musgrove. SMOOTHED S0,S1 AND S2 GIVN	
Strnth Fnctn	–2	+3	SAC	Expt Rept	CEA – N – 1522	Oct 72 Cauvin+ S0,S1 CALC	
Lvl Density	1.0+7	1.8+7	ANL	Eval Rept	ANL – 75 – 34	Jun 75 Davey+N2NEVAL.CONSTANT T,LVL DEN FIT	

60 Neodymium 142

Quantity	Energy (ev) Min	Max	Lab	Type	Documentation Ref Vol Page	Author, Comments Date	Data
Evaluation	1.0–3	1.5+7	AUA	Eval Rept	AAEC/TM – 549	Jun 70 Cook.TOT,EL,INEL,NONEL,CAPT SIGS,NDG	+
				Rept	AAEC/E – 214	Jun 71 Bertram+GROUP SIGMAS SAME QUANTS.NDG	
				Rept	AAEC/TM – 587	Mar 71 *DESCRIPTION OF LIBRARY	
	1.0–3	1.5+7		Data	AUSTR – DFN 144.	Nov 71 POINT(223) AND GROUP(127) SIGMAS	
Total	1.0+2	3.2+4	SAC	Expt Rept	CEA – N – 1459	Aug 71 Tellier. ENRICHED TO 95PC.EXPT DETS.	+
				Priv	TELLIER	Oct 71 – . DATA FOR COMPILATION.	
				Jour	CR 272 695	Mar 71 – . LINAC.TOF.PRELIM ANALYSIS.	
	1.0+2	3.2+4		Data	EXFOR20118.002	Sep 72 .10461PTS	
Total	1.0–3	1.5+7	AUA	Eval Data	AUSTR – DFN 144.	Nov 71 COOK+POINT(223)+GROUP(127)SIG.CF EVL	+
Total	2.0–2	1.0+1	IJI	Expt Conf	73Kiev 2 104	May 73 Vertebny+ TOF,SIG(NEUT – E)	
Total	1.4+7		LIN	Expt Jour	IZV 37 1019	May 73 Djumin+ SIG(A),OPTMODEL CALC,GRAPH	+
				Conf	73Kiev 3 108	May 73 – + OPTMOD CALC,SIG	
				Jour	BAS 37 5 91	May 73 .ENGLISH OF IZV 37 1019	
	1.4+7			Data	EXFOR40302.002	Feb 76 1 PNT	
Total	7.5+5	1.4+7	BRC	Expt Abst	BAP 20 1196	Sep 75 Shamu+ MEAS TOT CS DIFF WITH 144ND	
Elastic	Maxwl		ORL	Expt Jour	PR 91 597	Aug 53 Koehler+	+
	Maxwl			Data	EXFOR12060.	Jun 76 . 2 PTS, COH, COH AMP	
Elastic	1.0–3	1.5+7	AUA	Eval Data	AUSTR – DFN 144.	Nov 71 COOK+POINT(223)+GROUP(127)SIG.CF EVL	+
Elastic	2.5–2		IJI	Eval Rept	KIYAI – 76 – 6	76 Fedorova+ COMP(REFS,SIGS),EVAL.TABLE	
				Conf	75Kiev 1 169	May 75 – + EVAL 2200M/S SIG,TABLE	
Tot Inelastc	2.0+6	1.5+7	AUA	Eval Data	AUSTR – DFN 144.	Nov 71 COOK+POINT(9)+GROUP(127)SIG.CF EVL	+
Diff Inelast	1.4+7		LRL	Theo Rept	UCRL – 50181	Feb 67 Lutz+ CALC ANG DIST FOR FIRST 2+ LVL	
Diff Inelast	2.5+6		KTY	Expt Prog	U/KTY – 77 70	77 Coope+STRUCT STUDY USING DIN,DNG.NDG	
Scattering	Maxwl		ORL	Expt Jour	PR 91 597	Aug 53 Koehler+ TRANS 7.5+ – 0.6B	+
	Maxwl			Data	EXFOR12060.022	Jun 76 . 1 PT, SIG	
Scattering	2.0–2	1.0+1	IJI	Expt Conf	73Kiev 2 104	May 73 Vertebny+ TOF,SIG(NEUT – E),GRAPH	
Nonelastic	1.0–3	1.5+7	AUA	Eval Data	AUSTR – DFN 144.	Nov 71 COOK+POINT(223)+GROUP(127)SIG.CF EVL	+
Nonelastic	1.4+7	1.8+7	ANL	Eval Rept	ANL – 75 – 34	Jun 75 Davey+CORRC APPLIED TO N2N CS.TBLS.	
Absorption	4.1–1	1.0+7	GA	Eval Rept	GA – 2451	Aug 61 Joanou+ 68GROUP DATA FOR GAM – I	
Absorption	2.5–2		IJI	Eval Rept	KIYAI – 76 – 6	76 Fedorova+ COMP(REFS,SIGS),EVAL.TABLE	
				Conf	75Kiev 1 169	May 75 – + EVAL SIG GIVEN,TABLE	
Res Int Abs	5.5–1		CRC	Eval Rept	AECL – 3037 1	Jan 72 Walker. RED RIA RES PARS(JINR – 3 – 3564	

60 Neodymium 142

Quantity	Energy (ev) Min	Max	Lab	Type	Documentation Ref Vol Page	Date	Author, Comments	Data
Res Int Abs	5.0−1		AUA	Eval	Rept AAEC/TM−619	Sep 72	Clayton.CALC FROM SIG LIBRARY,TABLE	
Res Int Abs	+0	+5	WIN	Revw	Conf IAEA−169 3 163	74	Pope+ DATA FILE CALC CFD XPTAL VALUE	
Res Int Abs	5.0−1		IJI	Eval	Rept KIYAI−76−6	76	Fedorova+ CALC FROM BNL−325 RESPARS	
					Conf 75Kiev 1 169	May 75	− + RI CALC FROM RESPARS,TABLE	
(n,γ)	Maxwl		ANL	Expt	Jour PR 76 300	Jul 49	Hess+ NAT ND TGT,MASS−SPEC.UPPER LIM	+
	Maxwl			Data	EXFOR12067.004	Jun 76	. 1 PT.	
(n,γ)	Maxwl		ORL	Expt	Jour PR 88 412	Oct 52	Pomerance.PILE OSC.	+
	Maxwl			Data	EXFOR11507.077	Jun 76	. 1 PT.	
(n,γ)	Pile		MCM	Expt	Jour PR 90 447	May 53	Walker+NRX,MASS SP. 13+−5B REL ND148	+
	Pile			Data	EXFOR12059.005	Jun 76	. 1 PT.	
(n,γ)	+0	1.5+3	HAR	Expt	Jour NP 3 553	Jun 57	Bowey. TOF. CAPT GAM YLD CURVE	
(n,γ)	Maxwl		CRC	Eval	Rept AECL−1054	Mar 60	Walker. SAME AS CRRP−913	
(n,γ)	2.5+4		FEI	ExTh	Prog YFI−4 22	May 67	Shorin+.,TBLS GIVEN,TBP YF	
				Theo	Jour YF 6 769	Oct 67	− + VAL GIVN,STAT THEORY	
					Jour SNP 6 558	Apr 68	. ENGL OF YF 6 769	
				ExTh	Rept INDC−187E	67	. ENGL OF YFI−4 22	
(n,γ)	Maxwl	3.0+0	BNL	Expt	Prog WASH−1127 23	Apr 69	Moragues+ SEARCH FOR DIRECT CAPT,NDG	
(n,γ)	1.0+3	1.0+7	BOL	Eval	Rept CCDN−NW/10	Dec 69	Benzi+H−F MOD,AXEL G(G)EST,ALL DATA	
					Rept CEC(70)−2	Apr 70	− +. GRAPH	
(n,γ)	Maxwl		HAR	Expt	Rept AERE−R−6384	May 70	Cabell+ TBL.SIG=18.76+−0.73B. T=82C	
	Pile				Jour JIN 30 897	May 68	− + IRR PLUTO MASS ANAL	
	Maxwl				Rept AERE−R−5520	Jul 67	− +.MASS SPECTR METHD.82+−13DEGC	
(n,γ)	3.0+4		AUA	Theo	Rept AAEC/E−211	Nov 70	Musgrove. SIGMA GIVEN AND CFD OTHER	
(n,γ)	1.0−3	1.5+7	AUA	Eval	Data AUSTR−DFN 144.	Nov 71	COOK+POINT(223)+GROUP(127)SIG.CF EVL	+
(n,γ)	Maxwl		CRC	Eval	Rept AECL−3037 1	Jan 72	Walker.RECOMMENDED SIG,DETAILED TBL	
(n,γ)	2.5−2		AUA	Eval	Rept AAEC/TM−619	Sep 72	Clayton.CALC FROM SIG LIBRARY,TABLE	
(n,γ)	Maxwl	Fiss	WIN	Revw	Conf IAEA−169 3 163	74	Pope+ MAXW+FIS−SPEC AVG EVAL DATA	
	Fiss				Conf IAEA−169 3 137	74	Dean. POINT DATA AVG OVER STAND SPEC	
(n,γ)	1.0+3	1.0+7	FEI	Eval	Rept YK−8/2 97	Sep 72	Abagjan+ AVG SIG(ENERGY−GROUPS),TABL	
					Rept INDC(CCP)−39	Jul 74	.P102. ENGLISH OF YK−8/2 97	
(n,γ)	Fast		RCN	Expt	Rept ECN−10	Oct 76	Veenema+ STEK REACTIVITY WORTHS TBL.	
Res Int Capt	5.0−1		HAR	Expt	Rept AERE−R−6384	May 70	Cabell+ REDUCED VAL=−34+−11.4B TBL	
Spect (n,γ)	+0	+4	COL	Expt	Prog WASH−1124 31	Nov 68	Camarda+ MOXON−RAE DET TBC NO DATA	
Spect (n,γ)	Maxwl		KUR	Expt	Jour YF 8 1067	Dec 68	Groshev+ GE−LI,GAM−SPEC,GRPH+TBL	
					Jour SNP 8 619	Jun 69	TRANSLATN.*	
Spect (n,γ)	2.5−2		IFB	Theo	Conf 76Lowell 1283	Jul 76	Martsynkevich+DOORWAY STATE ROLE.	
	Maxwl				Jour NP/A 262 261	May 76	− +LVL SPEC.COL E1 DECAYS	
	None				Jour YF 15 1132	Jun 72	Knat'Ko+ CALC E1 INTS CFD EXPT,GRAPH	
					Jour SNP 15 626	Dec 72	− + ENGLISH OF YF 15 1132	
Spect (n,γ)	Maxwl		NIL	Expt	Jour NP/A 272 133	Nov 76	Mirza+ GELI−NAI.ES+INTS,LVL SCHEME	+
					Conf 74Petten 557	Sep 74	− + DECAY SCHEME ND−143	
	Maxwl				Data EXFOR30366.002	Jan 77	343 G−LINES.	
$(n,2n)$	1.5+7		ARK	Expt	Jour PR 118 242	Apr 60	Wille+ MEAS ACT SIG=2060+−200MB	+
	1.5+7				Data EXFOR12033.021	Jun 76	. 1 PT.	
$(n,2n)$	Fiss		CRC	Eval	Rept CRC−1003	Dec 60	ROY+ ESTIMATED AVG SIG=0.63MB	
$(n,2n)$	1.4+7		ANL	Expt	Jour PR 122 168	Apr 61	Rayburn. 2411 MB+−8.3 PERCENT	+
					Rept ANL−5955	Jan 59	.SUPERSEDED	
	1.4+7				Data EXFOR11328.029	Jun 76	. 1 PT.	
$(n,2n)$	Pile		MUN	Expt	Jour ADP 12 57		63 Hertlein. ACTIV+REAC−SIG,AVG+EFF,TBL	
$(n,2n)$	1.4+7		HAM	Comp	Jour NP 65 257	Mar 65	Bormann. 4EXPT VALS.CFD SHELL EFFECT	
$(n,2n)$	1.5+7		REN	Expt	Jour PR/B 139 1525	Sep 65	Broadhead+ C−W ACT	+
	1.5+7				Data EXFOR11874.003	Jun 76	. 1 PT.	
$(n,2n)$	1.5+7		RED	Expt	Jour PR 142 725	Feb 66	Grissom+ ACT,ISOMERIC YIELD	+
	1.5+7				Data EXFOR12064.	Jun 76	. 1 PT. EACH,GND,META,AND RATIO	
$(n,2n)$	1.5+7		TAM	Expt	Jour PR 156 1340	Apr 67	Menon+ ACT TO ND141M,	+
	1.5+7				Data EXFOR12066.006	Jun 76	. 1 PT.	
$(n,2n)$	1.4+7		LYO	Comp	Rept LYCEN/6780	Nov 67	Crouzet+COMPILATN FOR ACTIVTN ANALYS	
$(n,2n)$	1.4+7		NAP	Expt	Jour NC/B 52 2 476	Dec 67	Cuzzocrea+. SIG TO GROUND AND METAST	
$(n,2n)$	1.5+7		TUR	Theo	Jour NC 56 18 201	Jul 68	Minetti+THEOR ISOM RATIO SPIN CO PAR	
$(n,2n)$	1.5+7		MUN	Expt	Jour NP/A 118 9	Sep 68	Dilg+ ACTIV.REL AL(N,A)	+
	1.5+7				Data EXFOR20802.004	Dec 78	1PNT.SIGMA.	
$(n,2n)$	1.5+7		DEB	ExTh	Jour NP/A 122 234	Dec 68	Karolyi.ISOMERIC RATIO,HUIZ−VANDENB.	+
	1.5+7			Expt	Data EXFOR30101.012	Feb 71	ISOMERIC RATIO	
$(n,2n)$	1.4+7		AUW	Expt	Jour NP/A 125 57	Feb 69	RAMA PRASAD+,ACTIVATION,CFD OTHERS	+
				ExTh	Jour IPA 12 640	Sep 74	Rama Prasad+ CFD STATMDL COMPND VALU	
	1.4+7			Expt	Data EXFOR30051.	Dec 70	SIGMA N2N,ALSO N2N+NA+NP FOR OTHERS.	

60 Neodymium 142

Quantity	Energy (ev) Min	Max	Lab	Type	Documentation Ref Vol Page	Date	Author, Comments	Data
(n,2n)	1.5+7		IBJ	Expt Jour	APPB 1 415	70	Rurarz+ ACTIV,NAI,ISORATIO VS THEORY	+
				Jour	NKA 14 933	Oct 69	− + ACTIV,NAI(TL),SIG TO ISOMER	
	1.5+7			Data	EXFOR30154.013	May 72	ISOMERIC RATIO	
	1.5+7			Data	EXFOR30098.004	Mar 71	VALUE TO METASTABLE STATE AT 14.5MEV	
(n,2n)	1.5+7		DEB	Comp Jour	REA 7 4 93	Dec 69	Csikai+ SIG+HL COMPILTN,N−ACTIV−ANAL	
(n,2n)	1.4+7	1.5+7	CCP	Comp Rept	ICD−6 215	70	Sluchevskaja.SIGS GND+ISOM,RATIO,TBL	
(n,2n)	1.4+7	1.5+7	JYV	Eval Rept	JU−RR−3/1970	Jun 70	Leppaemaeki+ TABLE OF EVAL AVG SIG	
(n,2n)	1.2+7	1.8+7	HAM	Expt Jour	NP/A 157 481	Nov 70	Bormann+ ACT. CFD STATIST TH.	
(n,2n)	+7		KFI	Theo Rept	KFKI−71−8	Feb 71	Jeki. CALCULATED CFD EXPTL SIG VALUE	
(n,2n)	1.4+7	1.5+7	IRK	ExTh Jour	APA 33 285	Jul 71	Winiwarter+ ISOMERIC RATIO	
(n,2n)	1.5+7		ARK	Expt Abst	DA/B 32 5091	Mar 72	Bari. GE(LI) DET. ACT. SIG GIVEN	+
	1.5+7			Data	EXFOR10431.	Aug 75	. 2 PTS. SIGMA, META AND GND+META	
(n,2n)	1.5+7		DEB	Eval Jour	REA 11 1 153	Mar 73	Boedy. COMPILATION+RECOMM.VALUE,TBL	
				Rept	IAEA−153 173	73	− . RECOMM. VALUE ONLY	
(n,2n)	1.5+7		TAT	Theo Jour	JP/A 7 1457	Aug 74	Kondaiah. CALC ON STAT MODEL	
(n,2n)	1.4+7		AUW	Expt Conf	74Bombay 2 105	Dec 74	Lakshmandas+ ACTIV,GELI.SIGMA GIVEN	+
	1.4+7			Data	EXFOR30389.002	Mar 77	1 PNT, PART'L SIG TO ND−141G.	
(n,2n)	1.0+7	1.8+7	ANL	Eval Rept	ANL−75−34	Jun 75	Davey+CONSTANT T MDL,LVL DEN MDL FIT	
(n,2n)	1.5+7		JUL	Expt Jour	NP/A 224 319	May 74	Qaim. ACT.GE(LI).TO GRND, METAST	+
				Jour	RRL 25 335	May 76	− + SIG IN GRPH. SYST VS (N−Z)/A	
	1.5+7			Data	EXFOR20541.	Apr 76	4PTS.SIGMA.	
(n,2n)	1.5+7		IBJ	Theo Jour	ASL 27 186	77	Rurarz+ ISO RATIO,4MODLS,CFD XPT.TBL	
	1.4+7			Rept	INR−1464 19	May 73	− + ISOMERIC RATIO CFD EXPT,GRAF	
(n,xn) x>2	1.4+7		BRC	ExTh Prog	CEA−N−1875 60	Apr 76	Frehaut+N3N.SYSTEMATIC LAWS SEARCH	
(n,p)	Fast		OHO	Expt Jour	PR 53 437	Mar 38	Pool+ BETAS,CLOUDCH,RATIO ND150(N2N)	
(n,p)	1.4+7		ALD	Expt Jour	PPS 73 215	Feb 59	Coleman+. ACT. CFD DIRECT INTERACTN	+
(n,p)	Fiss		CRC	Eval Rept	CRC−1003	Dec 60	ROY+ ESTIMATED AVG SIG=0.07MB	
(n,p)	1.5+7		SAH	Comp Jour	NUC 23 8 112	Aug 65	Chatterjee. TABLE WITH REFS.	
	1.4+7			Jour	NP 60 273	Nov 64	− .MEAN OF EXPT CFD SHELLMOD	
(n,p)	1.4+7	1.5+7	NAP	Comp Rept	INFN/BE−67−10	Jul 67	Cuzzocrea+ AVERAGED CHOSEN DATA.	
(n,p)			LYO	Comp Rept	LYCEN/6780	Nov 67	Crouzet+COMPILATN FOR ACTIVTN ANALYS	
(n,p)	1.4+7		NAP	Expt Jour	NC/B 52 2 476	Dec 67	Cuzzocrea+. 11.9+−.9 MB. TH OKS EXPT	
(n,p)	1.5+7		DEB	Comp Jour	REA 7 4 93	Dec 69	Csikai+ SIG+HL COMPILTN,N−ACTIV−ANAL	
(n,p)	1.4+7	1.5+7	JYV	Eval Rept	JU−RR−3/1970	Jun 70	Leppaemaeki+ TABLE OF EVAL AVG SIG	
(n,p)	1.4+7	1.5+7	KAZ	Theo Jour	YF 18 705	Oct 73	Levkovsky.AVERAGED SIG,CALC,TBL	
				Jour	SNP 18 361	Apr 74	. ENGLISH OF YF 18,705	
(n,α)	1.5+7		ARK	Expt Jour	PR 118 242	Apr 60	Wille+ MEAS ACT PROD. 2 ISOMERS	+
	1.5+7			Data	EXFOR12033.	Jun 76	. 1 PT. EACH FOR 2 ISO.	
(n,α)	Fiss		CRC	Eval Rept	CRC−1003	Dec 60	ROY+ ESTIMATED AVG SIG=0.005MB	
(n,α)	1.4+7		CIS	Theo Jour	NP 51 460	Feb 64	Facchini+STATMOD SIG XPT/CALC0.6−1.0	
(n,α)	1.5+7		RED	Expt Jour	PR 142 725	Feb 66	Grissom+ ACT	+
	1.5+7			Data	EXFOR12064.002	Jun 76	. 1 PT.	
(n,α)	1.5+7		TUE	Expt Jour	ZP 201 105	Apr 67	STAUDT ALPHA E+ANGDIST,SIGTOT.SC DET	+
(n,α)	1.4+7	1.5+7	NAP	Comp Rept	INFN/BE−67−11	Sep 67	Cuzzocrea+ AVERAGED CHOSEN DATA.	
(n,α)			LYO	Comp Rept	LYCEN/6780	Nov 67	Crouzet+COMPILATN FOR ACTIVTN ANALYS	
(n,α)	1.5+7		DEB	Comp Jour	REA 7 4 93	Dec 69	Csikai+ SIG+HL COMPILTN,N−ACTIV−ANAL	
(n,α)	1.4+7	1.5+7	JYV	Eval Rept	JU−RR−3/1970	Jun 70	Leppaemaeki+ TABLE OF EVAL AVG SIG	
(n,α)	1.4+7		KFI	Comp Jour	JRC 7 365	Jun 71	Nagy+ SIGMA,GAM+XRAY+ELECTR ES GIVEN	
(n,α)	1.5+7		ARK	Expt Abst	DA/B 32 5091	Mar 72	Bari. GE(LI) DET. ACT. SIG GIVEN	+
	1.5+7			Data	EXFOR10431.023	Aug 75	. 1 PT. SIGMA	
Reson Params	4.0+0	+3	COL	Expt Abst	BAP 10 575	Jun 65	Ceulemans+TRNS+SELF INDICATION.TBD	
Reson Params	2.5+4		FEI	ExTh Prog	YFI−4 22	May 67	Shorin+.,TBLS GIVEN,TBP YF	
				Rept	INDC−187E	67	. ENGL OF YFI−4 22	
Reson Params		1.0+4	DUB	Expt Conf	68DUBSY 349	Jul 68	Pikelner.LVL SPAC,AVERG. WG ,S0 VS A	
Reson Params	1.6+3	1.0+4	DUB	Expt	YF 8 639	Oct 68	Karzhavina+TRANS+G−YLD EXPT,WN 7RES	+
				Rept	YFI−6 124	68	− + TABLE.	
				Rept	JINR−P3−3564	Nov 67	− + FULL PAPER.	
				Jour	SNP 8 371	Apr 69	− + TRANSLATION.	
				Rept	INDC−260E	69	− + ENGL OF YFI−6 124.	
	1.7+3	1.0+4		Data	EXFOR40113.	Sep 72	N−WIDTH AT 7 RES, D	
Reson Params	7.4+5	6.1+6	KUR	Expt Jour	YF 8 1067	Dec 68	Groshev+ LVL SCHEME DISCUSSED	
				Jour	SNP 8 619	Jun 69	TRANSLATN.*	
Reson Params	−		AUA	Theo Rept	AAEC/E−211	Nov 70	Musgrove. CALCULTD D+GAM WIDTH GIVEN	
Reson Params	2.2+2	3.1+4	SAC	Expt Rept	CEA−N−1459	Aug 71	Tellier. SHAPE−ANALYSIS 37 LEVELS	+
				Priv	TELLIER	Oct 71	− . VALUES FOR COMPILATION.	
				Conf	71Knoxvill 680	Mar 71	− +.TRANS,AVG D=415EV 37RESON	
	2.2+2	3.1+4		Data	EXFOR20121.	Sep 72	74PTS.2G*WN,2G*WN0.	
Reson Params	None		DUB	Theo Rept	JINR−P4−7499	Oct 73	Soloviev+ CALC D CFD EXPTS,TABLE	

PAGE 1119

60 Neodymium 142

Quantity	Energy (ev) Min	Max	Lab	Type	Documentation Ref Vol Page	Date	Author, Comments	Data
Reson Params	+2	+4	FEI	Eval	Rept YK- 8/2 97	Sep 72	Abagyan+ AVG G-WID+D AT BINDNG-E,TBL	
					Rept INDC(CCP)-39	Jul 74	.PAGE 102.ENGLISH OF YK-8/2 97	
Strnth Fnctn		1.0+4	DUB	Expt	Conf 68DUBSY 349	Jul 68	Pikelner.LVL SPAC,AVERG. WG,S0 VS A	
Strnth Fnctn	1.7+3	1.0+4	DUB	Expt	Jour YF 8 639	Oct 68	Karzhavina+TRANS+G-YLD EXPT,S-RES	+
					Rept YFI-6 124	68	- + TABLE.	
					Rept JINR-P3-3564	Nov 67	- + FULL PAPER.	
					Jour SNP 8 371	Apr 69	- + TRANSLATION.	
					Rept INDC-260E	69	- + ENGL OF YFI-6 124.	
	0.0+0	6.3+3			Data EXFOR40113.006	Sep 72	(60-ND-142,STF) STRENGTH-	
Strnth Fnctn	-		AUA	Theo	Rept AAEC/E-211	Nov 70	Musgrove. SMOOTHED S0,S1 AND S2 GIVN	
Strnth Fnctn	2.0+2	3.1+4	SAC	Expt	Rept CEA-N-1459	Aug 71	Tellier. VERSUS ENERGY	+
	-2	+3			Rept CEA-N-1522	Oct 72	Cauvin+ S0,S1 CALC	
	2.0+2	3.1+4			Jour CR 272 695	Mar 71	Tellier. LINAC,TOF. 37 LEVELS,+D,+A	
					Conf 71Knoxvill 680	Mar 71	- +.S0=1.4+-0.35	
	2.0+2	3.1+4			Data EXFOR20121.006	Sep 72	. 1PNT.L=0.	
Strnth Fnctn	None		AUA	Eval	Rept AAEC/E-277	Mar 73	Musgrove.TBLS EXPTL DATA+BEST VALUES	
Lvl Density	-		DUB	Expt	Jour YF 8 639	Oct 68	Karzhavina+ VAL+PARS GVN,TBL+GRPH	+
					Jour SNP 8 371	Apr 69	- + TRANSLATION.	
	None				Data EXFOR40113.053	Sep 72	LEVEL-DENSITY PARAMETER	
Lvl Density	+7		DEB	ExTh	Jour NP/A 122 234	Dec 68	Karolyi+ SPIN CUTOFF,M OF INERT,N2N	+
	+7			Expt	Data EXFOR30101.029	Feb 71	CUT-OFF PARAMETER	
Lvl Density	0.0+0	3.1+4	SAC	Expt	Rept CEA-N-1459	Aug 71	Tellier. FROM STAT RES ANALYSIS.	+
		3.1+4			Jour CR 272 695	Mar 71	- .	
		3.1+4			Data EXFOR20121.007	Sep 72	1PNT.SP.CUT(0).	
Lvl Density	+2	+4	FEI	Eval	Rept YK- 8/2 97	Sep 72	Abagyan+ LVL DENSITY PARAMETER,TBL	
					Rept INDC(CCP)-39	Jul 74	.PAGE 102.ENGLISH OF YK-8/2 97	
(γ,n)	9.0+6	2.0+7	SAC	Expt	Jour NP/A 172 437	Sep 71	Carlos+LORENTZ LINE PARAM,GRPHS,TBL	

60 Neodymium 143

Quantity	Energy (ev) Min	Max	Lab	Type	Documentation Ref Vol Page	Date	Author, Comments	Data
Evaluation	1.0-3	1.5+7	AUA	Eval	Rept AAEC/TM-549	Jun 70	Cook.TOT,EL,INEL,NONEL,CAPT SIGS,NDG	+
					Rept AAEC/E-214	Jun 71	Bertram+GROUP SIGMAS SAME QUANTS.NDG	
					Rept AAEC/TM-587	Mar 71	*DESCRIPTION OF LIBRARY	
	1.0-3	1.5+7			Data AUSTR-DFN 145.	Nov 71	POINT(223) AND GROUP(127) SIGMAS	
Evaluation	1.0+2	1.5+7	JAE	Eval	Rept JAERI-M-5752	Jul 74	Igarasi+ JNDC FPND WG.TOT,EL,N',CAP	
Total	None		MTR	Expt	Prog WASH-191	Jun 56	. FC, TBC, NDG	
Total	-2	+1	HAR	Expt	Conf 58Geneva 16 44	Sep 58	Pattenden.PPR11,CURVE,CRYSTALSPECTRM	
Total	1.0-2	1.0+1	HAR	Expt	Jour JNE 7 199	Sep 58	Hay.CS TRANS.GRAPHS,410+-20B AT THR	
Total	6.5+1	3.0+4	SAC	Expt	Rept CEA-N-1459	Aug 71	Tellier. ENRICHED TO 83PC.EXPT DETS.	+
					Priv TELLIER	Oct 71	- . DATA FOR COMPILATION.	
					Jour CR 272 695	Mar 71	- . LINAC.TOF.PRELIM ANALYSIS.	
	6.5+1	3.0+4			Data EXFOR20118.003	Sep 72	11200PTS.	
Total	1.0-3	1.5+7	AUA	Eval	Data AUSTR-DFN 145.	Nov 71	COOK+POINT(223)+GROUP(127)SIG.CF EVL	+
Total	2.0-2	1.0+1	IJI	Expt	Conf 73Kiev 2 104	May 73	Vertebny+ TOF,SIG(NEUT-E),GRAPH	
Total	1.4+7		LIN	Expt	Jour IZV 37 1019	May 73	Djumin+ SIG(A),OPTMODEL CALC,GRAPH	+
					Conf 73Kiev 3 108	May 73	- + OPTMOD CALC,SIG	
					Jour BAS 37 5 91	May 73	.ENGLISH OF IZV 37 1019	
	1.4+7				Data EXFOR40302.003	Feb 76	1 PNT	
Total	5.0+1	2.0+2	MOL	Expt	Rept RCN-203 219	Dec 73	Ceulemans+ RESONANCE PARAM ANALYSIS	
Total	2.5-2		IJI	Comp	Rept KIYAI-76-6	76	Fedorova+ TO GET RECOM ABS-SIG.TABLE	
Elastic	Maxwl		HAR	Expt	Jour JNE 7 199	Sep 58	Hay. 75+-7B FROM B-W FIT TO SIGTOT	+
Elastic	1.0-3	1.5+7	AUA	Eval	Data AUSTR-DFN 145.	Nov 71	COOK+POINT(223)+GROUP(127)SIG.CF EVL	
Elastic	2.5-2		IJI	Eval	Rept KIYAI-76-6	76	Fedorova+ ONLY 1LIT-VALUE=RECOMM.TBL	
					Conf 75Kiev 1 169	May 75	- + EVAL 2200M/S SIG,TABLE	
Potntl Scat		7.4+2	SAC	Expt	Jour NP/A 123 561	Jan 69	Morgenstern+ RADIUS IN TBL.	+
	0.0+0	7.4+2			Data EXFOR20688.023	Jun 77	1PNT.RADIUS.	
Tot Inelastc	1.0+6	1.5+7	AUA	Eval	Data AUSTR-DFN 145.	Nov 71	COOK+POINT(10)+GROUP(127)SIG.CF EVL	
Scattering	2.0-2	1.0+1	IJI	Expt	Conf 73Kiev 2 104	May 73	Vertebny+ TOF,SIG(NEUT-E),GRAPH	
Nonelastic	1.0-3	1.5+7	AUA	Eval	Data AUSTR-DFN 145.	Nov 71	COOK+POINT(223)+GROUP(127)SIG.CF EVL	
Absorption	Maxwl		HAR	Expt	Rept NRDC-113	Mar 59	HAY+ 343+-20B SUPERSEDES TNCCUK24+36	+
					Jour JNE 7 199	Sep 58	Hay. 335+-20B FROM B-W FIT TO SIGTOT	
Absorption	2.5-2		HAR	Expt	Jour JNEA 12 32	May 60	Tattersall+. PILE OSCILLATOR	+
					Rept AERE-R-2887	Aug 59	- . PILE OSC.REL BORON	
	Maxwl				Rept AERE-R/R-2516	Mar 58	Jowitt+ PILE OSC.REL BORON.293DEGK.	
	2.5-2				Data EXFOR20638.042	Jul 76	1PNT.SIGMA.	
Absorption	4.1-1	1.0+7	GA	Eval	Rept GA-2451	Aug 61	Joanou+ 68GROUP DATA FOR GAM-I	

60 Neodymium 143

Quantity	Energy (ev) Min	Max	Lab	Type	Documentation Ref Vol Page	Date	Author, Comments	Data
Absorption	1.0-3	1.0+7	JUL Eval	Rept	JUEL-678-RG	Jul 70	Liu. EVALUATION+CALC,GRPH,FN OF E	
Absorption	Pile		CRC Eval	Conf	73Paris 1 459	Mar 73	Walker.FISS PRODUCT ABS,TBL PILE SIG	
Absorption	2.5-2		IJI Eval	Rept	KIYAI-76-6	76	Fedorova+ COMP(REFS,SIGS),EVAL.TABLE	
				Conf	75Kiev 1 169	May 75	- + EVAL SIG GIVEN,TABLE	
Res Int Abs	None		CRC Eval	Rept	AECL-1054	Mar 60	Walker. SAME AS CRRP-913.	
Res Int Abs	None		ORL Eval	Rept	ORNL-2869	Mar 60	Nephew.1/V UP +TO100EV.ALSO 56 EV-UP	
Res Int Abs	5.0-1		HAR Expt	Jour	JNE 12 32	May 60	Tattersall+. ABOVE 1/V. UPPER LIMIT	+
				Rept	AERE-R-2887	Aug 59	- . PILE OSC.REL BORON	
	6.7-1			Data	EXFOR20638.043	Jul 76	1PNT.	
Res Int Abs	5.5-1		GA Eval	Jour	NSE 12 115	Jan 62	Garrison+ =130+-60 B. FROM RES. PAR	
Res Int Abs	None		CRC Eval	Rept	AECL-2111	Nov 64	Walker. RED RESONANCE INTEGRAL	
Res Int Abs	5.0-1		BOL Eval	Rept	RT/FI-4	Jan 67	Palmucci. CALC FROM (N,G) RES PARAMS	
Res Int Abs	None		GA Eval	Rept	GA-12071	Sep 71	Mathews+ RECOMMENDED VALUES	
Res Int Abs	5.5-1		CRC Eval	Rept	AECL-3037 1	Jan 72	Walker.REDUCED RES INT FROM RES PARS	
Res Int Abs	5.0-1		AUA Eval	Rept	AAEC/TM-619	Sep 72	Clayton.CALC FROM SIG LIBRARY,TABLE	
Res Int Abs	4.6-1	1.0+6	RCN Theo	Rept	RCN-191	Jul 73	Lautenbach.CAPT INT FROM GROUP SIGMA	
Res Int Abs	5.5-1	+6	SAC Revw	Conf	IAEA-169 1 235	74	Ribon.CAPTURE,STATUS CFD REQUEST,TBL	
Res Int Abs	+0	+5	WIN Revw	Conf	IAEA-169 3 163	74	Pope+ DATA FILE CALC CFD XPTAL VALUE	
Res Int Abs	5.0-1		IJI Eval	Rept	KIYAI-76-6	76	Fedorova+ EVAL CFD CALC.TBL RI,REFS	
				Conf	75Kiev 1 169	May 75	- + EVAL+CALC RI GIVEN,TABLE	
(n,γ)	Maxwl		ANL Expt	Jour	PR 76 300	Jul 49	Hess+ NAT ND TGT,MASS-SPECT. 240BARN	+
	Maxwl			Data	EXFOR12067.002	Jun 76	. 1 PT.	
(n,γ)	Maxwl		ORL Expt	Jour	PR 88 412	Oct 52	Pomerance.PILE OSC.	+
	Maxwl			Data	EXFOR11507.078	Jun 76	. 1 PT.	
(n,γ)	Pile		MCMExpt	Jour	PR 90 447	May 53	Walker+NRX,MASS SP.334+ -12B REL ND48	+
	Pile			Data	EXFOR12059.002	Jun 76	. 1 PT.	
(n,γ)	+0	1.5+3	HAR Expt	Jour	NP 3 553	Jun 57	Bowey. TOF. CAPT GAM YLD CURVE	
(n,γ)	Maxwl		CRC Eval	Rept	AECL-1054	Mar 60	Walker. SAME AS CRRP-913	
(n,γ)	None		CRC Expt	Conf	60Kingston 933	Aug 60	Campion+ NDG.STUDY ON 3+ STATE	
(n,γ)	5.0-3	2.5+0	GA Eval	Rept	GA-2113	Jun 61	Wikner+ TABLE + CURVE.100 E POINTS	
(n,γ)	2.8-3	1.0+6	GA Eval	Jour	NSE 12 115	Jan 62	Garrison+ EVAL FROM XPT+AVERAGE RES	
(n,γ)	2.5-2		BOL Eval	Rept	RT/FI-4	Jan 67	Palmucci. CALC FROM RES PARAMETERS	
(n,γ)	Maxwl		AUA Theo	Jour	NSE 31 234	Feb 68	Cook+ STATISTICAL CALC CFD EXPT	
(n,γ)	Maxwl		MCMExpt	Jour	PL/B 26 11 662	Apr 68	Oakey+ SIG=0.3MB FOR (N,NA)	+
	Maxwl			Data	EXFOR12057.002	Jun 76	. 1 PT. (N,NA)	
(n,γ)	-2	+0	BNL Expt	Prog	WASH-1124 17	Nov 68	Sailor+ PROPOSED EXPT MOXON-RAE DET	
(n,γ)	5.0+3	1.0+5	AUA ExTh	Rept	AAEC/E-198	May 69	Musgrove.S+P+D WAVE SIGMAS CALC,TBL	+
(n,γ)	1.0+3	1.0+7	BOL Eval	Rept	CCDN-NW/10	Dec 69	Benzi+H-F MOD,AXEL G(G)EST,ALL DATA	
				Rept	CEC(70)-2	Apr 70	- +. GRAPH	
				Conf	66Paris 1 537	Oct 66	- + STATMOD.TBL AV VALS.SUPERSEDD	
(n,γ)	Maxwl		HAR Expt	Rept	AERE-R-6384	May 70	Cabell+ TBL.SIG=316.1+ -13.5B. T=82C	
				Jour	JIN 30 897	May 68	- + IRR PLUTO MASS ANAL	
	Pile			Rept	AERE-R-5520	Jul 67	- +.MASS SPECTR METHD.PLUTO CORE	
(n,γ)	4.0-2	9.0+2	DUB Expt	Jour	NP/A 154 177	Sep 70	Kvitek+ TOF. M-R DET. CURVE GIVEN	
(n,γ)	3.0+4		AUA Theo	Rept	AAEC/E-211	Nov 70	Musgrove. SIGMA GIVEN AND CFD OTHER	
(n,γ)	Maxwl		GA Eval	Rept	GA-12071	Sep 71	Mathews+ RECOMMENDED VALUES	
(n,γ)	1.0-3	1.5+7	AUA Eval	Data	AUSTR-DFN 145.	Nov 71	COOK+POINT(223)+GROUP(127)SIG.CF EVL	+
(n,γ)	Maxwl		CRC Eval	Rept	AECL-3037 1	Jan 72	Walker.RECOMMENDED SIG,DETAILED TBL	
(n,γ)	2.5-2		IAE Revw	Rept	IAEA-143 897	Apr 72	Lemmel.RECENT EVALUATIONS,TABLE+GRPH	
	Maxwl				IAEA-143 897	Apr 72	- .RECENT EVALUATIONS,TABLE	
(n,γ)	2.5-2		AUA Eval	Rept	AAEC/TM-619	Sep 72	Clayton.CALC FROM SIG LIBRARY,TABLE	
(n,γ)	5.5+0		DUB ExTh	Jour	PL/B 44 5	May 73	Furman+ RESONANCE STUDY	+
(n,γ)	2.0-2	1.0+1	IJI Expt	Conf	73Kiev 2 104	May 73	Vertebny+ TOF,SIG(NEUT-E),GRAPH	
		1.1+7	RCN Theo	Rept	RCN-191	Jun 73	Lautenbach. GROUP CONSTANTS TBL	
(n,γ)	2.5-2	3.0+4	SAC Revw	Conf	IAEA-169 1 235	74	Ribon.STATUS SIG CFD REQUESTS,TABLE	
	Fiss			Conf	IAEA-169 1 235	74	- .STATUS SIG CFD REQUESTS,TABLE	
(n,γ)	Maxwl Fiss		WIN Revw	Conf	IAEA-169 3 163	74	Pope+ MAXW+FIS-SPEC AVG EVAL DATA	
	Fiss			Conf	IAEA-169 3 137	74	Dean. POINT DATA AVG OVER STAND SPEC	
(n,γ)	None		INL Expt	Prog	USNDC-11 11	Jun 74	Harker+ INTEG CS, HL	
(n,γ)	1.0+3	1.0+7	FEI Eval	Jour	YK-8/2 97	Sep 72	Abagjan+ AVG SIG(ENERGY-GROUPS),TABL	
				Rept	INDC(CCP)-39	Jul 74	.P102. ENGLISH OF YK-8/2 97	
(n,γ)	Fast		RCN Expt	Rept	ECN-10	Oct 76	Veeneema+ STEK REACTIVITY WORTHS TBL.	
Spect (n,γ)	Maxwl		KUR Expt	Jour	NP 16 645	Jun 60	Groshev+ 0.5 TO 8MEV GAMS,CFD THEORY	
Spect (n,γ)	Maxwl		CRC Expt	Conf	AEC-TR-6465	Jul 60	Bartholomew+ MOSCOW CONF NUC REACTNS	
Spect (n,γ)	Maxwl		YAL Expt	Jour	NP 19 436	Nov 60	Draper+ TABLE. GRAPH 400-900KEV GAMS	
Spect (n,γ)	Maxwl		UEN Expt	Jour	ZP 188 93	Oct 65	Zehender+Z-STEP-CASCADES,ND144-LE	
Spect (n,γ)	4.8-2		RCN Expt	Jour	PHY 38 48	Mar 68	Reddingius+POSTMA.ALIGNED NUCLEI,ANG	+
	4.8-2			Data	EXFOR20235.002	May 74	16PTS.	

60 Neodymium 143

Quantity	Energy (ev) Min	Max	Lab	Type	Documentation Ref Vol Page	Date	Author, Comments	Data
Spect (n,γ)	Maxwl		CRC	Expt	Prog AECL – 3166 57	Sep 68	Earle+ GE(LI). PRELIM GAMMA ES GIVN	
Spect (n,γ)	Pile		KUR	Expt	Jour YF 8 1067	Dec 68	Groshev+.GE – LI,LVL SCH,TBL,GRPH	+
	Maxwl				Jour SNP 8 619	Jun 69	. ENGL OF YF 8 1067	
	2.5 – 2				Data EXFOR40236.002	Oct 74	.GAM/100N FOR 3 ES GVN	
Spect (n,γ)	None		ORL	Theo	Jour NSE 36 220	May 69	Yost+ CALCUL BY GAMMA CASCADE MODEL	
Spect (n,γ)	Pile		CCP	Expt	Jour IZV 34 449	Feb 70	Berzin+ TBL GS+CONV – EL ES+INTS,LVLS	
					Jour BAS 34 389	Feb 71	* ENGL OF IZV 34 449	
Spect (n,γ)	Pile		KUR	Expt	Jour IZV 35 786	Apr 71	Groshev+ INTERNAL CONV,INTENS.TABLE	
					Jour BAS 35 723	Apr 72	. ENGL OF IZV 35 786	
Spect (n,γ)	Pile		KFK	Expt	Rept KFK – 1401	Jun 71	Djadali.POLRZ G EXPT,ND – 144 LVL+SPIN	
					Jour NP/A 165 560	Apr 71	– + POL N, CIRC POL GS.	
					Rept KFK – 1296	Sep 70	+POLRZ GAMS,ND – 144 LVLS+SPINS	
Spect (n,γ)	Maxwl		GEL	Expt	Conf 72Budapest 54	Aug 72	Weigmann+ INTENSITIES OF TRANSIT,TBL	
	5.5+1	4.5+2			Jour NP/A 185 229	Apr 72	– + LINAC TOF. SPECTRA AT RES.	
Spect (n,γ)	Maxwl		IFL	Expt	Book PROKOFJEV	73	. TBL GAM,CONV ELECTR ES+INT,LVL SCH	
					Conf 67Kharkov	Feb 67	Lure+. TBP IN IZV	
Spect (n,γ)	Pile		CCP	Expt	Conf 73Tbilisi 76	Feb 73	Berzin+ ABST,GE – LI,ES+INTENSITIES	
Spect (n,γ)	Maxwl	4.0+2	ORL	Expt	Conf 74Petten 562	Sep 74	Raman+ LVL SCHEME ND – 144, TBL.PREL.	
	Maxwl				Prog USNDC – 3 121	Oct 72	Jurney+ SOME DATA.TBP APS MEETING	
Spect (n,γ)	Fast		MUN	Expt	Jour IZV 40 68	Jan 75	Rabenstein+ G – ES+INTS,TBL.LVL SCHEME	
	Maxwl				Conf 74Petten 565	Sep 74	– +SPINS,PARITIES LVL ND – 144	
	Fast				Jour BAS 40 1 55	Jan 76	. ENGL OF IZV 40 68	
Spect (n,γ)	+0	1.2+3	GEL	Expt	Rept NEANDC(E)162 3	Feb 75	Rohr+LINAC TOF	
Spect (n,γ)	Maxwl		ANL	Expt	Jour PR/C 14 75	Jul 76	Bushnell+INT,ES.LVL SCHEME ND144.NDG	
(n,2n)	Fiss		CRC	Eval	Rept CRC – 1003	Dec 60	ROY+ ESTIMATED AVG SIG=36.0MB	
(n,2n)	1.5+7		DEB	Eval	Jour REA 11 1 153	Mar 73	Boedy+ RECOMM.VALUE FROM N – Z SYSTEM.	
(n,2n)	1.5+7		KFI	Theo	Rept KFKI – 73 – 68	Dec 73	Jeki.NEW FIT,CALC SIG CFD OTHERS,TBL	
(n,p)	1.4+7		ALD	Expt	Rept PPS 73 215	Feb 59	Coleman+. ACT. CFD DIRECT INTERACTN	+
(n,p)	Fiss		CRC	Eval	Rept CRC – 1003	Dec 60	ROY+ ESTIMATED AVG SIG=0.05MB	
(n,p)	1.5+7		SAH	Comp	Jour NUC 23 8 112	Aug 65	Chatterjee. TABLE WITH REFS.	
(n,p)	1.4+7	1.5+7	ARK	Theo	Prog ORO – 3235 – 29	Jan 67	Koch+ STAT MODEL CALC CFD EXPTS	
(n,p)	1.4+7		LYO	Comp	Rept LYCEN/6780	Nov 67	Crouzet+COMPILATN FOR ACTIVTN ANALYS	
(n,p)	1.5+7		DEB	Comp	Rept REA 7 4 93	Dec 69	Csikai+ SIG+HL COMPILTN,N – ACTIV – ANAL	
(n,p)	1.4+7	1.5+7	JYV	Eval	Rept JU – RR – 3/1970	Jun 70	Leppaemaeki+ TABLE OF EVAL AVG SIG	
(n,p)	1.4+7	1.5+7	KAZ	Theo	Jour YF 18 705	Oct 73	Levkovsky.AVERAGED SIG,CALC,TBL	
					Jour SNP 18 361	Apr 74	. ENGLISH OF YF 18,705	
(n,α)	Fiss		CRC	Eval	Rept CRC – 1003	Dec 60	ROY+ ESTIMATED AVG SIG=0.88MB	
(n,α)	Maxwl		ISL	Expt	Jour PL 1 289	Jul 62	Cheifetz. TBL Q – VALU,SIG,BRANCHRATIO	+
	Maxwl				Data EXFOR31151.002	Mar 73	.SIG GVN	
(n,α)	Maxwl		CCP	Expt	Jour YF 1 252	Feb 65	Andreev.IONIZ – CHAMBER,SIG=23MB GND	+
					Jour SNP 1 177	Aug 65	TRANSLATN.*	
(n,α)	Maxwl		LEB	Expt	Conf 65Antwerp § 176	Jul 65	Andreev+CFD TH 23+ – 5 MB	
(n,α)	1.0+0	1.0+3	DUB	Expt	Conf 66Dubna 147	Jul 66	Frank+,REVIEW,BRIEF DISCUSSION	
(n,α)	1.0+0	1.0+4	DUB	Expt	Conf 68DUBSY 283	Jul 68	Shapiro.RESONANCES,TOF,100 NS/M,WA	
(n,α)	Pile	2.5 – 2	JAE	Expt	Jour NP/A 141 193	Jan 70	Okamoto. BI FILTER.A SPECT.EFF SIG.	+
	2.5 – 2				Data EXFOR20335.002	Jul 74	3PTS.SIGMA.	
(n,α)	4.0 – 2	9.0+2	DUB	Expt	Jour NP/A 154 177	Sep 70	Kvitek+ TOF. SCINT DET CURVE GIVEN	
	Maxwl				Rept JINR – P3 – 4982	Apr 70	– + ALFA SPEC GRAPHS,ALFA WIDTH	
	5.0+1	1.0+3			Rept JINR – E3 – 3029	Nov 66	– +,ALPHA EMISS VS E(N),GRAPH	
	6.0+0	4.1+2			Rept YFI – 3 26	Sep 66	+ ALPHA – WIDTH,EXPT CFD THEORY	
					Rept INDC – 140E 28	67	. ENGL TRANSL OF YFI – 3 26	
(n,α)	Maxwl		LYO	Expt	Abst 75Harwell 38	Mar 75	Asghar+ (ILL).(N,GAM ALPHA) SIG.TBC	
					Conf 74Petten 395	Sep 74	Emsallem+ ALSO PARTIAL CR. SECT.	
(n,α)	2.5 – 2		IJI	Eval	Rept KIYAI – 76 – 6	76	Fedorova+ COMP(REFS,SIGS),EVAL.TABLE	
Reson Params	5.6+1	1.8+2	HAR	Expt	Jour NP 3 553	Jun 57	Bowey.TOF.4ES FROM CAPT GAMMA YIELDS	
Reson Params	5.6+1	1.3+2	BNL	Expt	Jour PR 108 353	Oct 57	Stolovy+ FC. TRANS	+
	5.6+1	1.3+2			Data EXFOR11866.010	Jun 76	. 2 RES, E0,WN,WN0,WG	
Reson Params	– .6+1		HAR	Expt	Jour JNE 7 199	Sep 58	Hay.ER= – 6+ – 1EV,WNO=68 WG=86 + – 15MV	+
Reson Params	5.6+1	1.9+2	ANL	Expt	Prog ANL – 6589	Aug 62	Carpenter.	+
	5.6+1	1.9+2			Data EXFOR12048.002	Jun 76	. 5 RES, E0,J	
Reson Params	+0	+3	COL	Expt	Prog NYO – GEN72 – 132	Jan 67	Garg+ P,1, NDG. NEW RUN SINCE BAP10	
Reson Params		1.0+6	AUA	Theo	Jour AUJ 20 477	Oct 67	Cook. TBL OF AVG LVL SPACING D,L=0,1	

60 Neodymium 143

Quantity	Energy (ev) Min	Max	Lab	Type	Documentation Ref Vol Page	Date	Author, Comments	Data
Reson Params	5.5+1	6.6+2	SAC	Expt	Jour NP/A 134 118	Sep 69	Alves+LINAC TOF.WN,WN0 11E0,7WT4J3WG	+
					Conf 68Wash. 867	Mar 68	Morgenstern. WG VS. A. AVG WG GIVEN	
					Conf 66Paris 1 559	Oct 66	Huynh+ ABST.NDG. SEE INDC-156	
					Conf 65Antwerp 525	Jul 65	De Barros+ PPR73.ABST.NDG	
	5.5+1	1.3+2			Jour JPR 24 997	Nov 63	Bianchi. DATA. SUPERSEDED	
	8.0+1				Jour CR 254 4162	Jun 62	Julien+ RES CAPT G - SPEC.ISOT ASSGN.	
	0.0+0	7.4+2			Data EXFOR20688.	Jun 77	12PTS.E0,AVG WG,WN,WT,G*WN.	
Reson Params		4.0+2	DUB	Expt	Conf 68DUBSY 283	Jul 68	Shapiro.ALFA WIDTH,TOF, 100NS/M	
	-.6+2	4.1+2			Jour ZEP 5 365	May 67	Kvitek+. N,ALFA REACTION,IMP REACTOR	
		4.0+2		ExTh	Conf 67Kharkov 201	Feb 67	- .EMITT ALFA PARTICLES,CFD H-F	
		4.1+2		Expt	Rept JINR-P3-3104	Jan 67	- +,TABLE OF WIDTHS AT FEW E(N)	
Reson Params		1.0+3	DUB	Expt	Conf 68DUBSY 349	Jul 68	Pikelner.LVL SPAC,AVERG. WG	
Reson Params	5.5+1	1.4+3	DUB	Expt	Jour YF 8 639	Oct 68	Karzhavina+23RES,WT,WN,WG,LVL D,TBL	+
					Rept YFI-6 124	68	- + TABLE.	
					Rept JINR-P3-3564	Nov 67	- + FULL PAPER.	
					Jour SNP 8 371	Apr 69	- + TRANSLATION.	
					Rept INDC-260E	69	- + ENGL OF YFI-6 124.	
	5.5+1	1.3+3			Data EXFOR40113.	Sep 72	N-WIDTH AT 23RES, TOT-WID,CAPT-WID,D	
Reson Params	7.0+5	7.8+6	KUR	Expt	Jour YF 8 1067	Dec 68	Groshev+ LVL SCHEME DISCUSSED	
					Jour SNP 8 619	Jun 69	TRANSLATN.*	
Reson Params	5.5+1	5.5+2	GEL	Expt	Jour JNE 23 369	Jul 69	Migneco+ TOF.WG,WN.AREA ANAL.	
Reson Params	-.6+1	7.2+2	DUB	Expt	Conf 70Helsinki 1 669	Jun 70	Popov+125. TABLE ALPHA WIDTH + SPIN	+
					Rept JINR-E3-5483	Dec 70	- . TABLE OF ALPHA+NEUTRON WIDTHS	
	-.6+1	7.0+2			Jour NP/A 154 177	Sep 70	Kvitek+ J,PI,ALPHA,GAMMA WIDTHS	
	Maxwl				Rept JINR-P3-4982	Apr 70	- + ALFA WIDTH GIVEN,N-RESONANCS	
	-.6+1	7.2+2			Rept UCRL-TR-105 41	May 71	.ENGLISH	
	-.6+1	7.1+2			Data EXFOR40225.002	Jul 75	.ALPHA WIDTH AT 9 ES GIVEN	
Reson Params	-		AUA	Theo	Rept AAEC/E-211	Nov 70	Musgrove. CALCULTD D+GAM WIDTH GIVEN	
Reson Params	-.6+1	7.8+2	CJD	Eval	Rept YK-7	71	Zakharova+ SURVEY+SYSTEMATICS,GW,TBL	
					Rept INDC(CCP)-27	Nov 72	.ENGLISH TRANSLATION OF YK-7 /71	
Reson Params	None		DUB	Theo	Jour YF 13 240	Feb 71	Malecki+G-WID,THEO CFD EXPT.TBL,GRPH	
					Jour SNP 13 133	Aug 71	- + ENGL OF YF 13 240.	
Reson Params	-.6-2	6.6+2	SAC	Expt	Conf 71Knoxvill 785	Mar 71	Cauvin+.J ASSIGNMENTS 19RESON	+
	6.0-2	6.6+2			Rept CEA-N-1522	Oct 72	- + RESONANCES SPINS ANAL	
	-.6-1	6.6+2			Data EXFOR20126.007	Sep 72	. 19PTS.J.	
Reson Params	5.5+1	5.5+3	SAC	Expt	Rept CEA-N-1459	Aug 71	Tellier. SHAPE-ANALYSIS 109 LEVELS	+
					Priv TELLIER	Oct 71	- . VALUES FOR COMPILATION.	
					Conf 71Knoxvill 680	Mar 71	- +.TRANS,AVG D=32EV 109RES	
	5.5+1	5.5+3			Data EXFOR20121.	Sep 72	245PTS.AVG WG,WT,2G*WN,2G*WN0.	
Reson Params	5.5+1	8.5+2	NRL	Expt	Jour PR/C 5 2030	Jun 72	Stolovy+ J FOR 23 RESONANCES	+
	5.5+1	8.5+2			Data EXFOR10256.002	Oct 72	. 23 RES. J	
Reson Params	None		DUB	Theo	Rept JINR-P4-7499	Oct 73	Soloviev+ CALC D CFD EXPTS,TABLE	
Reson Params	5.5+1	2.1+3	MOL	Expt	Rept RCN-203 219	Dec 73	Ceulemans+2G * WN WT	
Reson Params	+0	+2	BOL	Eval	Conf IAEA-169 3 123	74	Benzi+ AVG G-WID CFD OTHERS+XPT,TABL	
Reson Params	+1	+3	FEI	Eval	Rept YK-8/2 97	Sep 72	Abagyan+ AVG G-WID+D AT BINDNG-E,TBL	
					Rept INDC(CCP)-39	Jul 74	.PAGE 102.ENGLISH OF YK-8/2 97	
Reson Params	5.5+1	1.2+5	GEL	Expt	Conf 74Petten 306	Sep 74	Rohr+ SPINS INT.RATIOS OF G	+
	5.5+1	2.0+3			Conf 71Knoxvill 743	Mar 71	- +.LINAC,PARAMS FROM CAPT MEASTS	
	5.5+1	2.0+3			Data EXFOR20397.	Oct 74	92PTS.AVG WG,J,G*WN,AVG.G*WG,G*WG	
Reson Params	-.6+1	5.5+1	DUB	Expt	Jour ASL 25 211	75	Niedzwiedzuk+ (N,GA).TBL SIG,GAM-WID	
	-.6+0				Rept JINR-P3-8140	Sep 74	Popov. PRELIM GAM-ALF WID(3-) GIVEN	
	-.6+1	5.5+1			Conf 74Petten 379	Sep 74	- +WIDTH FOR (N,G,A) PROCESS	
	5.5+1				Rept RCN-203 89	Dec 73	Furman+(N,GA) REACTION	
	-.6+1	5.5+1		ExTh	Jour APPB 4 275	73	Popov+ ALFA WIDTH DISTRIBUTION,GRPH	
	5.5+1	7.1+2		Expt	Rept JINR-P3-6754	Oct 72	Winiwarter+ TOTAL ALPHA-WIDTHS,TBL	
Reson Params	1.0+3	1.0+6	SAC	Eval	Rept CEA-N-1832	Dec 75	Ribon+ EXP+TH ANAL,RES PAR,TBL	
Strnth Fnctn	+3		BNL	Expt	Jour PRL 1 461	Dec 58	Hughes+ FC 3.7+-0.6	
		1.0+3	DUB	Expt	Conf 68DUBSY 349	Jul 68	Pikelner.LVL SPAC,AVERG. WG,S0 VS A	
Strnth Fnctn	5.5+1	1.4+3	DUB	Expt	Jour YF 8 639	Oct 68	Karzhavina+TRANS+G-YLD EXPT,S-RES	+
					Rept YFI-6 124	68	- + TABLE.	
					Rept JINR-P3-3564	Nov 67	- + FULL PAPER.	
					Conf 67Tokyo § 8.133	Sep 67	- + ABST.NDG.	
					Jour SNP 8 371	Apr 69	- + TRANSLATION.	
					Rept INDC-260E	69	- + ENGL OF YFI-6 124.	
	0.0+0	8.4+2			Data EXFOR40113.014	Sep 72	STRENGTH-FUNCTION	

60 Neodymium 143

Quantity	Energy (ev) Min	Max	Lab	Type	Documentation Ref Vol Page	Date	Author, Comments	Data
Strnth Fnctn		7.4+2	SAC Expt	Jour	NP/A 123 561	Jan 69	Morgenstern+ TBL.FROM RES ANALYSIS	+
				Jour	NP/A 134 118	Sep 69	Alves+LINAC TOF. S0=4.5 +1.5 −1.1	
				Rept	CEA−R−3609	Sep 68	Morgenstern. (THESIS)	
				Conf	68Wash. 867	Mar 68	− +	
	0.0+0	7.4+2		Data	EXFOR20688.024	Jun 77	1PNT.L=0.	
Strnth Fnctn	−		AUA Theo	Rept	AAEC/E−211	Nov 70	Musgrove. SMOOTHED S0,S1 AND S2 GIVN	
Strnth Fnctn	5.6+2	5.5+3	SAC Expt	Rept	CEA−N−1459	Aug 71	Tellier. VERSUS ENERGY	+
				Priv	TELLIER	Oct 71	− . VALUES FOR COMPILATION.	
				Jour	CR 272 695	Mar 71	− .LINAC,TOF.109 LEVELS,+D,+A	
				Conf	71Knoxvill 680	Mar 71	− + S0=3.1+ −0.5	
	5.6+2	5.5+3		Data	EXFOR20121.	Sep 72	5PTS.L=0.	
Strnth Fnctn	0.0+0	8.4+2	NRL Expt	Jour	PR/C 5 2030	Jun 72	Stolovy+ S0 FOR J=3, J=4 RESON	+
		8.5+2		Data	EXFOR10256.004	Oct 72	. 2 PTS. S0, S1	
Strnth Fnctn	1.5+2	6.5+2	SAC ExTh	Diss	FRNC−TH−450	Oct 72	Delaroche.OPTICAL MODEL PARAMETERS	
Strnth Fnctn	−2	+3	SAC Expt	Rept	CEA−N−1522	Oct 72	Cauvin+ S0,S1 CALC	
	None			Prog	EANDC(E)140U	Sep 71	− +, J=3,4 S−WAVE	
Strnth Fnctn	None		AUA Eval	Rept	AAEC/E−277	Mar 73	Musgrove.TBLS EXPTL DATA+BEST VALUES	
Strnth Fnctn		2.0+3	MOLEXP	Prog	INDC(SEC)−43	Dec 72	Ceulemans. 0.5(S0(3−)+S0(4−)) GIVEN	
Strnth Fnctn	2.0+1	1.0+5	RPI Expt	Abst	BAP 21 537	Apr 76	Hockenbury+S0,S1 DRVD.NDG	
Strnth Fnctn	0.0+0	1.2+3	GEL Expt	Conf	76Lowell 1258	Jul 76	Rohr.STF E DEP OVER 2 E RANGES.	
	5.5+1	1.2+5		Conf	74Petten 306	Sep 74	− + S−NEUTRON STF FOR J=3,4	
Lvl Density	−		DUB Expt	Jour	YF 8 639	Oct 68	Karzhavina+ VAL+PARS GVN,TBL+GRPH	+
				Jour	SNP 8 371	Apr 69	− + TRANSLATION.	
	None			Data	EXFOR40113.054	Sep 72	LEVEL−DENSITY PARAMETER	
Lvl Density	None		AUWTheo	Conf	70Madurai 2 267	Dec 70	Ramamurty+ A−PARAMETER GVN,LANG'S−TH	
Lvl Density	0.0+0	5.5+3	SAC Expt	Rept	CEA−N−1459	Aug 71	Tellier. FROM STAT RES ANALYSIS.	+
		5.5+3		Jour	CR 272 695	Mar 71	− . LINAC,TOF. D AND A,109 LVLS	
		5.5+3		Data	EXFOR20121.014	Sep 72	1PNT.SP.CUT(0).	
Lvl Density	None		MUNTheo	Jour	NP/A 217 269	Dec 73	Dilg+ A,DELTA. BACK SHIFTED FERMIGAS	
Lvl Density	None		BOL Eval	Conf	IAEA−169 3 123	74	Benzi+ LVL DENS PARAM BY XPT,GRPH+TB	
Lvl Density	None		DUB Theo	Jour	NP/A 224 411	May 74	Soloviev+ 1/2 MICROSC MDL. SPH NUCL.	
Lvl Density	None		ROC Theo	Jour	NP/A 223 577	May 74	Huizenga+ EXP CFD MICROSC TH SPH NUC	
Lvl Density	+1	+3	FEI Eval	Rept	YK−8/2 97	Sep 72	Abagyan+ LVL DENSITY PARAMETER,TBL	
					INDC(CCP)−39	Jul 74	.PAGE 102.ENGLISH OF YK−8/2 97	
Lvl Density	+0	1.2+3	JAE ExTh	Jour	JPJ 37 581	Sep 74	Ideno.LVL SPACING CORRELATIONS.TBL	
	1.0+0	1.2+3		Rept	JAERI−M−5490	Nov 73	− .LEVEL SPACING CORRELATIONS.TBL	
(γ,n)	9.0+6	2.0+7	SAC Expt	Jour	NP/A 172 437	Sep 71	Carlos+LORENTZ LINE PARAM,GRPHS,TBL	

60 Neodymium 144

Quantity	Energy (ev) Min	Max	Lab	Type	Documentation Ref Vol Page	Date	Author, Comments	Data
Evaluation	1.0−3	1.5+7	AUA Eval	Rept	AAEC/TM−549	Jun 70	Cook.TOT,EL,INEL,NONEL,CAPT SIGS,NDG	+
				Rept	AAEC/E−214	Jun 71	Bertram+GROUP SIGMAS SAME QUANTS.NDG	
				Rept	AAEC/TM−587	Mar 71	*DESCRIPTION OF LIBRARY	
	1.0−3	1.5+7		Data	AUSTR−DFN 146.	Nov 71	POINT(223) AND GROUP(127) SIGMAS	
Evaluation	1.0+2	1.5+7	JAE Eval	Rept	JAERI−M−5752	Jul 74	Igarasi+ JNDC FPND WG.TOT,EL,N',CAP	
Evaluation	1.0−5	1.5+7	BOL Eval	Prog	NEANDC(E)182 7	Dec 76	Fabri+ COMPLETE EVAL IN ENDF/B DONE	+
	1.0−5	1.5+7		Data	CNEN−CEA 5	Jan 77	PRELIM.ALL QUANTITIES.ENDF FORMAT	
Total	9.8+5		SHE Theo	Jour	NP 54 417	Jun 64	Maddison.OPTMOD FIT TO TOWLE GILBOY	
Total	7.0+6	1.4+7	CJD Theo	Rept	ICD−5 20	68	Averjanov+ VIBRATION MDL,AT 4ES,TBL	
Total	9.0+1	2.9+4	SAC Expt	Rept	CEA−N−1459	Aug 71	Tellier. ENRICHED TO 91PC.EXPT DETS.	+
				Priv	TELLIER	Oct 71	− . DATA FOR COMPILATION.	
				Jour	CR 272 695	Mar 71	− . LINAC.TOF.PRELIM ANALYSIS.	
	9.0+1	2.9+4		Data	EXFOR20118.004	Sep 72	9498PTS.	
Total	1.0−3	1.5+7	AUA Eval	Data	AUSTR−DFN 146.	Nov 71	COOK+POINT(223)+GROUP(127)SIG.CF EVL	+
Total	1.4+7		LIN Expt	Conf	73Kiev 3 108	May 73	Djumin+ OPTMOD CALC,SIG	+
				Jour	IZV 37 1019	May 73	− + SIG(A),OPTMODEL CALC,GRAPH	
				Jour	BAS 37 5 91	May 73	.ENGLISH OF IZV 37 1019	
	1.4+7			Data	EXFOR40302.004	Feb 76	1 PNT	
Total	1.0+5	6.5+5	DKE Expt	Jour	AP 84 165	May 74	Pineo+TRNS.AVG CS.TBL GRPHS.OPTMDL	
				Abst	DA/B 31 6821	May 71	− .2E RANGE AVGS.CFD OPTMDL.	
	1.5+4	6.0+5		Diss	PINEO	70	.AVG CS.GRPHS.CFD.STF CALC.TBL.CFD.	
	1.5+4	6.0+5		Data	EXFOR10542.014	Jan 79	. DATA UNOBTAINABLE FROM AUTHORS.	
Total	7.5+5	1.4+7	BRC Expt	Abst	BAP 20 1196	Sep 75	Shamu+ALSO MEAS DIFF OTHER EVEN A ND	
Elastic	Maxwl		ORL Expt	Jour	PR 91 597	Aug 53	Koehler+.	
	Maxwl			Data	EXFOR12060.	Jun 76	. 2 PTS, COH, COH AMP	
Elastic	7.0+6	1.4+7	CJD Theo	Rept	ICD−5 20	68	Averjanov+ VIBRATION MDL,AT 4ES,TBL	

60 Neodymium 144

Quantity	Energy (ev) Min	Max	Lab	Type	Documentation Ref Vol Page	Date	Author, Comments	Data
Elastic	1.0−3	1.5+7	AUA	Eval	Data AUSTR−DFN 146.	Nov 71	COOK+POINT(223)+GROUP(127)SIG.CF EVL	+
Elastic	2.5−2		IJI	Eval	Rept KIYAI−76−6	76	Fedorova+ ONLY 1LIT−VALUE=RECOMM.TBL	
					Conf 75Kiev 1 169	May 75	− + EVAL 2200M/S SIG,TABLE	
Diff Elastic	9.8+5		SHE	Theo	Jour NP 54 417	Jun 64	Maddison.OPTMOD FIT TO TOWLE GILBOY	
Potntal Scat	3.0+3	6.5+5	DKE	Expt	Jour AP 84 165	May 74	Pineo+TRNS.S WAVE SCT LENGTH.TBL.CFD	
					Abst DA/B 31 6821	May 71	.THESIS ABST.	
					Diss PINEO	70	.TBL.GRPHS.CFD TO 3 COLLECTIVE MDLS.	
Tot Inelastc	7.0+6	1.4+7	CJD	Theo	Rept ICD−5 20	68	Averjanov+ VIBRATION MDL,AT 4ES,TBL	
Tot Inelastc	1.0+6	1.5+7	AUA	Eval	Data AUSTR−DFN 146.	Nov 71	COOK+POINT(10)+GROUP(127)SIG.CF EVL	+
Diff Inelast	7.0+6	1.4+7	CJD	Theo	Rept ICD−5 20	68	Averjanov+ TO 1ST LVL,ANGDIST,GRAPH	
Scattering	Maxwl		ORL	Expt	Jour PR 91 597	Aug 53	Koehler+ TRANS 1.0+ − 0.2B	+
	Maxwl				Data EXFOR12060.025	Jun 76	. 1 PT, SIG	
Scattering	2.0−2	1.0+1	IJI	Expt	Conf 73Kiev 2 104	May 73	Vertebny+ TOF,SIG(NEUT−E),GRAPH	
Nonelastic	1.0−3	1.5+7	AUA	Eval	Data AUSTR−DFN 146.	Nov 71	COOK+POINT(223)+GROUP(127)SIG.CF EVL	+
Absorption	4.1−1	1.0+7	GA	Eval	Rept GA−2451	Aug 61	Joanou+ 68GROUP DATA FOR GAM−I	
Absorption	1.0−4	1.0+7	JUL	Eval	Rept JUEL−678−RG	Jul 70	Liu. EVALUATION+CALC,GRPH,FN OF E	
Absorption	2.5−2		IJI	Eval	Rept 75Kiev 1 169	May 75	Fedorova+ EVAL SIG GIVEN,TABLE	
Res Int Abs	None		CRC	Eval	Rept AECL−1054	Mar 60	Walker. SAME AS CRRP−913	
Res Int Abs	None		GA	Eval	Rept GA−12071	Sep 71	Mathews+ RECOMMENDED VALUES	
Res Int Abs	5.5−1		CRC	Eval	Rept AECL−3037 1	Jan 72	Walker. RED RIA RES PARS(JINR−3−3564	
Res Int Abs	5.0−1		AUA	Eval	Rept AAEC/TM−619	Sep 72	Clayton.CALC FROM SIG LIBRARY,TABLE	
Res Int Abs	4.6−1	1.0+6	RCN	Theo	Rept RCN−191	Jul 73	Lautenbach.CAPT INT FROM GROUP SIGMA	
Res Int Abs	5.5−1	+6	SAC	Revw	Conf IAEA−169 1 235	74	Ribon.CAPTURE,STATUS CFD REQUEST,TBL	
Res Int Abs	+0	+5	WIN	Revw	Conf IAEA−169 3 163	74	Pope+ DATA FILE CALC CFD XPTAL VALUE	
Res Int Abs	5.0−1		IJI	Eval	Rept KIYAI−76−6	76	Fedorova+ EVAL CFD CALC.TBL RI,REFS	
					Conf 75Kiev 1 169	May 75	− + EVAL+CALC RI GIVEN,TABLE	
(n,γ)	Maxwl		ANL	Expt	Jour PR 76 300	Jul 49	Hess+ NAT ND TGT,MASS−SPEC.UPPER LIM	+
	Maxwl				Data EXFOR12067.005	Jun 76	. 1 PT.	
(n,γ)	Maxwl		ORL	Expt	Jour PR 88 412	Oct 52	Pomerance.PILE OSC.	+
	Maxwl				Data EXFOR11507.079	Jun 76	. 1 PT.	
(n,γ)	Pile		MCM	Expt	Jour PR 90 447	May 53	Walker+ NRX,MASS SP.0+−6B REL ND 48B	+
	Pile				Data EXFOR12059.006	Jun 76	. 1 PT.	
(n,γ)	+0	1.5+3	HAR	Expt	Jour NP 3 553	Jun 57	Bowey. TOF. CAPT GAM YLD CURVE	
(n,γ)	Maxwl		CRC	Eval	Rept AECL−1054	Mar 60	Walker. SAME AS CRRP−913	
(n,γ)	1.0+3	1.0+7	BOL	Eval	Rept CCDN−NW/10	Dec 69	Benzi+H−F MOD,AXEL G(G)EST,ALL DATA	
					Rept CEC(70)−2	Apr 70	− +. GRAPH	
					Conf 66Paris 1 537	Oct 66	− + STATMOD.TBL AV VALS.SUPERSEDD	
(n,γ)	Maxwl		HAR	Expt	Rept AERE−R−6384	May 70	Cabell+ TBL.SIG=3.58+−0.31B. T=82C	+
	Pile				Jour JIN 30 897	May 68	− + IRR PLUTO MASS ANAL	
					Rept AERE−R−5520	Jul 67	− +.MASS SPECTR METHD.PLUTO CORE	
(n,γ)	3.0+4		AUA	Theo	Rept AAEC/E−211	Nov 70	Musgrove. SIGMA GIVEN AND CFD OTHER	
(n,γ)	Maxwl		GA	Eval	Rept GA−12071	Sep 71	Mathews+ RECOMMENDED VALUES	
(n,γ)	1.0−3	1.5+7	AUA	Eval	Data AUSTR−DFN 146.	Nov 71	COOK+POINT(223)+GROUP(127)SIG.CF EVL	+
(n,γ)	Maxwl		CRC	Eval	Rept AECL−3037 1	Jan 72	Walker.RECOMMENDED SIG,DETAILED TBL	
(n,γ)	2.5−2		AUA	Eval	Rept AAEC/TM−619	Sep 72	Clayton.CALC FROM SIG LIBRARY,TABLE	
(n,γ)		1.1+7	RCN	Theo	Rept RCN−191	Jun 73	Lautenbach. GROUP CONSTANTS TBL	
(n,γ)	2.5−2	3.0+4	SAC	Revw	Conf IAEA−169 1 235	74	Ribon.STATUS SIG CFD REQUESTS,TABLE	
(n,γ)	Maxwl	Fiss	WIN	Revw	Conf IAEA−169 3 163	74	Pope+ MAXW+FIS−SPEC AVG EVAL DATA	
	Fiss				Conf IAEA−169 3 137	74	Dean. POINT DATA AVG OVER STAND SPEC	
(n,γ)	None		INL	Expt	Prog USNDC−11 11	Jun 74	Harker+ INTEG CS, HL	
(n,γ)	1.0+3	1.0+7	FEI	Eval	Rept YK−8/2 97	Sep 72	Abagjan+ AVG SIG(ENERGY−GROUPS),TABL	
					Rept INDC(CCP)−39	Jul 74	.P102. ENGLISH OF YK−8/2 97	
(n,γ)	2.5−2		IJI	Eval	Rept KIYAI−76−6	76	Fedorova+ COMP(REFS,SIGS),EVAL.TABLE	
(n,γ)	Fast		RCN	Expt	Rept ECN−10	Oct 76	Veenema+ STEK REACTIVITY WORTHS TBL.	
Spect (n,γ)	Maxwl		CCP	Expt	Jour ZET 39 584	Sep 60	4 TWO−CASCADE GS STUDIED	
					Jour JET 12 411	Mar 61	TRANSLATN.*	
Spect (n,γ)	+0	+4	COL	Expt	Prog WASH−1124 31	Nov 68	Camarda+ MOXON−RAE DET TBC NO DATA	
Spect (n,γ)	Maxwl		KUR	Expt	Jour YF 8 1067	Dec 68	Groshev+ 2 GAM LINES,ENRICHED SAMPLE	+
					Jour SNP 8 619	Jun 69	TRANSLATN.*	
	2.5−2				Data EXFOR40236.003	Oct 74	. GAM/100N FOR 25 ES GIVEN	
Spect (n,γ)	Maxwl		NIL	Expt	Conf 74Petten 566	Sep 74	Najam+ DECAY SC.ND−145, Q−VALUE	
Spect (n,γ)	Maxwl		ORL	Expt	Jour PR/C 12 260	Jul 75	Hillis+ LEVEL STRUCT INFO.TBL,GRPH	
					Jour NIM 121 573	74	Kendrick+ ONLY FIGURE GIVEN	
					Prog ORNL−4844 82	Apr 73	Mc−Clure+ SUPERSEDED	
					Conf 72Budapest 128	Aug 72	+ LVEL SCHEME OF ND145, GRPH	
Inelastic γ	+6		CCP	Conf	Conf 75Leningrd 348	Jan 75	Andreev+ ABST,GE−LI	
Inelastic γ	2.7+6		KGU	Expt	Jour YF 23 12	Jan 76	Andreev+ SPEC,SIG TO 6 LVLS,GRPH+TBL	
					Jour SNP 23 6	Jan 76	. ENGL OF YF 23 12	

60 Neodymium 144

Quantity	Energy (ev) Min	Energy (ev) Max	Lab	Type	Documentation Ref Vol Page	Date	Author, Comments	Data
(n,2n)	Fiss		CRC	Eval	Rept CRC-1003	Dec 60	ROY+ ESTIMATED AVG SIG=7.3MB	
(n,2n)	1.5+7		DEB	Eval	Jour REA 11 1 153	Mar 73	Boedy+ RECOMM.VALUE FROM N-Z SYSTEM.	
(n,2n)	1.5+7		KFI	Theo	Rept KFKI-73-68	Dec 73	Jeki.NEW FIT,CALC SIG CFD OTHERS,TBL	
(n,xn) x>2	1.4+7		BRC	ExTh	Prog CEA-N-1875 60	Apr 76	Frehaut+N3N.SYSTEMATIC LAWS SEARCH	
(n,p)	Fiss		CRC	Eval	Rept CRC-1003	Dec 60	ROY+ ESTIMATED AVG SIG=0.02MB	
(n,p)	1.4+7		LYO	Comp	Rept LYCEN/6780	Nov 67	Crouzet+COMPILATN FOR ACTIVTN ANALYS	
(n,p)	1.4+7	1.5+7	KAZ	Theo	Jour YF 18 705	Oct 73	Levkovsky.AVERAGED SIG,CALC,TBL	
					Jour SNP 18 361	Apr 74	. ENGLISH OF YF 18,705	
(n,α)	Fiss		CRC	Eval	Rept CRC-1003	Dec 60	ROY+ ESTIMATED AVG SIG=0.055MB	
(n,α)	1.4+7		LYO	Comp	Rept LYCEN/6780	Nov 67	Crouzet+COMPILATN FOR ACTIVTN ANALYS	
(n,α)	1.4+7		AUW	Expt	Jour NP/A 125 57	Feb 69	RAMA PRASAD+,ACTIVATION,CFD OTHERS	+
				ExTh	Jour IPA 12 640	Sep 74	Rama Prasad+ CFD STATMDL COMPND VALU	
	1.4+7			Expt	Data EXFOR30051.	Dec 70	SIGMA NA,ALSO N2N+NA+NP FOR OTHERS.	
(n,α)	1.5+7		DEB	Comp	Jour REA 7 4 93	Dec 69	Csikai+ SIG+HL COMPILTN,N-ACTIV-ANAL	
(n,α)	1.4+7	1.5+7	JYV	Eval	Rept JU-RR-3/1970	Jun 70	Leppaemaeki+ TABLE OF EVAL AVG SIG	
(n,α)	1.5+7		IRK	Expt	Jour APA 34 209	Sep 71	Havlik. ACT. CC-W.	+
					Jour OAWA 107 119	Apr 70	- . ACTIVATION METHOD	
	1.5+7				Data EXFOR20509.011	Apr 76	1PNT.SIGMA.	
Reson Params	+0	+3	COL	Expt	Prog NYO-GEN72-132	Jan 67	Garg+ P, 1,MORE THAN BAP10 575.NDG	
Reson Params		1.0+6	AUA	Theo	Jour AUJ 20 477	Oct 67	Cook. TBL OF AVG LVL SPACING D,L=0,1	
Reson Params	-		DUB	Expt	Conf 68DUBSY 283	Jul 68	Shapiro.AVERAGE ALFA WIDTH,LVL SPAC.	
Reson Params		1.4+4	DUB	Expt	Conf 68DUBSY 349	Jul 68	Pikelner.LVL SPAC,AVERG. WG	
Reson Params	3.7+2	1.4+4	DUB	Expt	Jour YF 8 639	Oct 68	Karzhavina+20RES,WN,WG,TABLES	+
					Rept YFI-6 124	68	- + TABLE.	
					Rept JINR-P3-3564	Nov 67	- + FULL PAPER.	
					Jour SNP 8 371	Apr 69	- + TRANSLATION.	
					Rept INDC-260E	69	- + ENGL OF YFI-6 124.	
	7.8-2				Data EXFOR40113.	Sep 72	N-WIDTH AT 20RES, CAPT-WIDTH, D	
Reson Params	6.7+4	5.8+6	KUR	Expt	Jour YF 8 1067	Dec 68	Groshev+ LVL SCHEME DISCUSSED	
					Jour SNP 8 619	Jun 69	TRANSLATN.*	
Reson Params	7.3+2		SAC	Expt	Jour NP/A 134 118	Sep 69	Alves+LINAC TOF.WN,WN0,J,WT.	+
	7.3+2				Data EXFOR20688.025	Jun 77	1PNT.E0,WN,WT,G*WN.	
Reson Params	-		AUA	Theo	Rept AAEC/E-211	Nov 70	Musgrove. CALCULTD D+GAM WIDTH GIVEN	
Reson Params	7.5+2	1.6+3	CJD	Eval	Rept YK-7	71	Zakharova+ SURVEY+SYSTEMATICS,GW,TBL	
					Rept INDC(CCP)-27	Nov 72	.ENGLISH TRANSLATION OF YK-7 /71	
Reson Params	None		DUB	Theo	Jour YF 13 240	Feb 71	Malecki+G-WID,THEO CFD EXPT.TBL,GRPH	
					Jour SNP 13 133	Aug 71	- + ENGL OF YF 13 240.	
Reson Params	3.7+2	1.9+4	SAC	Expt	Rept CEA-N-1459	Aug 71	Tellier. SHAPE-ANALYSIS 35 LEVELS	+
					Priv TELLIER	Oct 71	- . VALUES FOR COMPILATION.	
					Conf 71Knoxvill 680	Mar 71	- +.TRANS,AVG D=537EV 35RESON	
	3.7+2	1.9+4			Data EXFOR20121.	Sep 72	76PTS.WG,WT,2G*WN,2G*WN0.	
Reson Params	None		DUB	Theo	Rept JINR-P4-7499	Oct 73	Soloviev+ CALC D CFD EXPTS,TABLE	
Reson Params	+0	+2	BOL	Eval	Conf IAEA-169 3 123	74	Benzi+ AVG G-WID CFD OTHERS+XPT,TABL	
Reson Params	+2	+4	FEI	Eval	Rept YK-8/2 97	Sep 72	Abagyan+ AVG G-WID+D AT BINDNG-E,TBL	
					Rept INDC(CCP)-39	Jul 74	.PAGE 102.ENGLISH OF YK-8/2 97	
Strnth Fnctn		1.4+4	DUB	Expt	Conf 68DUBSY 349	Jul 68	Pikelner.LVL SPAC,AVERG. WG,S0 VS A	
Strnth Fnctn	3.7+2	1.4+4	DUB	Expt	Jour YF 8 639	Oct 68	Karzhavina+TRANS+G-YLD EXPT,S-RES	+
					Rept YFI-6 124	68	- + TABLE.	
					Rept JINR-P3-3564	Nov 67	- + FULL PAPER.	
					Conf 67Tokyo § 8.133	Sep 67	- + ABST.NDG.	
					Jour SNP 8 371	Apr 69	- + TRANSLATION.	
					Rept INDC-260E	69	- + ENGL OF YFI-6 124.	
	0.0+0	7.6+3			Data EXFOR40113.021	Sep 72	STRENGTH-FUNCTION	
Strnth Fnctn	-		AUA	Theo	Rept AAEC/E-211	Nov 70	Musgrove. SMOOTHED S0,S1 AND S2 GIVN	
Strnth Fnctn	3.0+2	1.9+4	SAC	Expt	Rept CEA-N-1459	Aug 71	Tellier. VERSUS ENERGY	+
					Priv TELLIER	Oct 71	- . VALUE FOR COMPILATION.	
					Conf 71Knoxvill 680	Mar 71	- + SO=4.0+-1.2	
					Jour CR 272 695	Mar 71	- .LINAC,TOF. 35LEVELS,+D,+A	
	3.0+2	1.9+4			Data EXFOR20121.019	Sep 72	1PNT.L=0.	
Strnth Fnctn	-2	+3	SAC	Expt	Rept CEA-N-1522	Oct 72	Cauvin+ S0,S1 CALC	
Strnth Fnctn	None		AUA	Eval	Rept AAEC/E-277	Mar 73	Musgrove.TBLS EXPTL DATA+BEST VALUES	
Strnth Fnctn	3.0+3	6.5+5	DKE	Expt	Jour AP 84 165	May 74	Pineo+ S, P, D WAVE.	
					Abst DA/B 31 6821	May 71	- .S,P,D WAVE.THESIS ABST	
					Diss PINEO	70	.S0,S1.TBL.GRPHS.CFD CALC,OTH EXPTS.	
Lvl Density	-		FEI	ExTh	Prog YFI-6 18	68	Ignatjuk+ TABLE VARIOUS PARAMETERS	
	None			Theo	Jour SNP 8 660	Jun 69	.TRANSLATN.*	
					Jour YF 8 1135	Dec 68	Ignatjuk+ TBL,A+ENTROPY+TEMP,CFD XPT	
	-			ExTh	Rept INDC-260E	69	. ENGL OF YFI-6 18	

60 Neodymium 144

Quantity	Energy (ev) Min	Max	Lab	Type	Documentation Ref Vol Page	Author, Comments Date	Data
Lvl Density	+6		MIL	Theo Jour	EN 15 1 54	Jan 68 Facchini+ LDL PARS FROM LOW EN RES	
Lvl Density	-		DUB	Expt Jour	YF 8 639	Oct 68 Karzhavina+ VAL+PARS GVN,TBL+GRPH	+
				Jour	SNP 8 371	Apr 69 - + TRANSLATION.	
	None			Data	EXFOR40113.055	Sep 72 LEVEL-DENSITY PARAMETER	
Lvl Density	None		CCP	Theo Jour	YF 11 1028	May 70 Rubchenya. DENSITY+A+TEMP GIVEN,GRPH	
				Jour	SNP 11 571	Nov 70 . ENGL OF YF 11 571.	
Lvl Density	-		FEI	Theo Conf	70Helsinki 2 885	Jun 70 Ignatjuk+76. SUPERFLUID CFD FERMI-TH	
Lvl Density	None		AUW	Theo Conf	70Madurai 2 267	Dec 70 Ramamurty+ A-PARAMETER GVN,LANG'S-TH	
Lvl Density	0.0+0	1.9+4	SAC	Expt Rept	CEA-N-1459	Aug 71 Tellier. FROM STAT RES ANALYSIS.	+
		1.9+4		Jour	CR 272 695	Mar 71 - .LINAC,TOF.D AND A,35 LVLS	
		1.9+4		Data	EXFOR20121.020	Sep 72 1PNT.SP.CUT(0).	
Lvl Density	None		MUN	Theo Jour	NP/A 217 269	Dec 73 Dilg+ A,DELTA. BACK SHIFTED FERMIGAS	
Lvl Density	None		BOL	Eval Conf	IAEA-169 3 123	74 Benzi+ LVL DENS PARAM BY XPT,GRPH+TB	
Lvl Density	None		COP	Theo Jour	NP/A 222 493	Apr 74 Dossing+COLL ROTAT.SPAC. ACCUR ESTIM	
Lvl Density	None		ROC	Theo Jour	NP/A 223 577	May 74 Huizenga+ EXP CFD MICROSC TH SPH NUC	
Lvl Density	+2	+4	FEI	Eval Rept	YK- 8/2 97	Sep 72 Abagyan+ LVL DENSITY PARAMETER,TBL	
				Rept	INDC(CCP)-39	Jul 74 .PAGE 102.ENGLISH OF YK-8/2 97	
Lvl Density	+0	2.0+4	JAE	ExTh Jour	JPJ 37 581	Sep 74 Ideno.LVL SPACING CORRELATIONS.TBL.	
	1.0+0	2.0+4		Rept	JAERI-M-5490	Nov 73 - .LEVEL SPACING CORRELATIONS.TBL	
(γ,n)	9.0+6	2.0+7	SAC	Expt Jour	NP/A 172 437	Sep 71 Carlos+LORENTZ LINE PARAM,GRPHS,TBL	

60 Neodymium 145

Quantity	Energy (ev) Min	Max	Lab	Type	Documentation Ref Vol Page	Author, Comments Date	Data
Evaluation	1.0-3	1.5+7	AUA	Eval Rept	AAEC/TM-549	Jun 70 Cook.TOT,EL,INEL,NONEL,CAPT SIGS,NDG	+
				Rept	AAEC/E-214	Jun 71 Bertram+GROUP SIGMAS SAME QUANTS.NDG	
				Rept	AAEC/TM-587	Mar 71 *DESCRIPTION OF LIBRARY	
	1.0-3	1.5+7		Data	AUSTR-DFN 147.	Nov 71 POINT(223) AND GROUP(127) SIGMAS	
Evaluation	1.0+2	1.5+7	JAE	Eval Rept	JAERI-M-5752	Jul 74 Igarasi+ JNDC FPND WG.TOT,EL,N',CAP	
Total	-2	+1	HAR	Expt Conf	58Geneva 16 44	Sep 58 Pattenden.PPR11,CURVE,CRYSTALSPECTRM	
Total	3.1+1	2.5+4	SAC	Expt Rept	CEA-N-1459	Aug 71 Tellier. ENRICHED TO 71PC.EXPT DETS.	+
				Priv	TELLIER	Oct 71 - . DATA FOR COMPILATION.	
				Jour	CR 272 695	Mar 71 - . LINAC.TOF.PRELIM ANALYSIS.	
	3.1+1	2.5+4		Data	EXFOR20118.005	Sep 72 13815PTS.	
Total	1.0-3	1.5+7	AUA	Eval Data	AUSTR-DFN 147.	Nov 71 COOK+POINT(223)+GROUP(127)SIG.CF EVL	+
Total	2.0-2	1.0+1	IJI	Expt Conf	73Kiev 2 104	May 73 Vertebny+ TOF,SIG(NEUT-E),GRAPH	+
Total	1.4+7		LIN	Expt Jour	IZV 37 1019	May 73 Djumin+ SIG(A),OPTMODEL CALC,GRAPH	+
				Conf	73Kiev 3 108	May 73 - + OPTMOD CALC,SIG	
				Jour	BAS 37 5 91	May 73 .ENGLISH OF IZV 37 1019	
	1.4+7			Data	EXFOR40302.005	Feb 76 1 PNT	
Total	2.5-2		IJI	Comp Rept	KIYAI-76-6	76 Fedorova+ TO GET RECOM ABS-SIG.TABLE	
Total	2.0+1	2.0+5	RPI	Expt Prog	ERDA-NDC-3 255	May 76 Hockenbury+TRNS MEAS.NDG	
Elastic	1.0-3	1.5+7	AUA	Eval Data	AUSTR-DFN 147.	Nov 71 COOK+POINT(223)+GROUP(127)SIG.CF EVL	+
Elastic	2.5-2		IJI	Eval Rept	KIYAI-76-6	76 Fedorova+ COMP(REFS,SIGS),EVAL.TABLE	
				Conf	75Kiev 1 169	May 75 - + EVAL 2200M/S SIG,TABLE	
Potntal Scat		7.4+2	SAC	Expt Jour	NP/A 123 561	Jan 69 Morgenstern+ RADIUS IN TBL.	+
	0.0+0	7.4+2		Data	EXFOR20688.028	Jun 77 1PNT.RADIUS.	
Tot Inelastc	5.0+5	1.5+7	AUA	Eval Data	AUSTR-DFN 147.	Nov 71 COOK+POINT(11)+GROUP(127)SIG.CF EVL	+
Scattering	2.0-2	1.0+1	IJI	Expt Conf	73Kiev 2 104	May 73 Vertebny+ TOF,SIG(NEUT-E),GRAPH	
Nonelastic	1.0-3	1.5+7	AUA	Eval Data	AUSTR-DFN 147.	Nov 71 COOK+POINT(223)+GROUP(127)SIG.CF EVL	+
Absorption	2.5-2		HAR	Expt Jour	JNEA 12 32	May 60 Tattersall+. PILE OSCILLATOR	+
				Rept	AERE-R-2887	Aug 59 - . PILE OSC.REL BORON	
	2.5-2			Data	EXFOR20638.044	Jul 76 1PNT.SIGMA.	
Absorption	4.1-1	1.0+7	GA	Eval Rept	GA-2451	Aug 61 Joanou+ 68GROUP DATA FOR GAM-I	
Absorption	1.0-3	1.0+7	JUL	Eval Rept	JUEL-678-RG	Jul 70 Liu. EVALUATION+CALC,GRPH,FN OF E	
Absorption	Pile		CRC	Eval Conf	73Paris 1 459	Mar 73 Walker.FISS PRODUCT ABS,TBL PILE SIG	
Absorption	2.5-2		IJI	Eval Rept	KIYAI-76-6	76 Fedorova+ COMP(REFS,SIGS),EVAL.TABLE	
				Conf	75Kiev 1 169	May 75 - + EVAL SIG GIVEN,TABLE	
Res Int Abs	None		CRC	Eval Rept	AECL-1054	Mar 60 Walker. SAME AS CRRP-913	
Res Int Abs	None		ORL	Eval Rept	ORNL-2869	Mar 60 Nephew.1/V UP +TO100EV.ALSO 43 EV-UP	
Res Int Abs	5.0-1		HAR	Expt Jour	JNE 12 32	May 60 Tattersall+. ABOVE 1/V. OSC.CF CALC	+
				Rept	AERE-R-2887	Aug 59 - . PILE OSC.REL BORON	
	6.7-1			Data	EXFOR20638.045	Jul 76 1PNT.	
Res Int Abs	5.5-1		GA	Expt Rept	NSE 12 115	Jan 62 Garrison+ RI= 316+-170B,FROM RES.PAR	
Res Int Abs	None		CRC	Eval Rept	AECL-2111	Nov 64 Walker. REDUCED RESONANCE INTEGRAL	
Res Int Abs	5.0-1		BOL	Eval Rept	RT/FI-4	Jan 67 Palmucci. CALC FROM (N,G) RES PARAMS	
Res Int Abs	None		GA	Eval Rept	GA-12071	Sep 71 Mathews+ RECOMMENDED VALUES	

60 Neodymium 145

Quantity	Energy (ev) Min	Max	Lab	Type	Documentation Ref Vol Page	Date	Author, Comments	Data
Res Int Abs	5.5 – 1		CRC	Eval	Rept AECL – 3037 1	Jan 72	Walker.REDUCED RES INT,DETAILED TBL	
Res Int Abs	5.0 – 1		AUA	Eval	Rept AAEC/TM – 619	Sep 72	Clayton.CALC FROM SIG LIBRARY,TABLE	
Res Int Abs	4.6 – 1	1.0+6	RCN	Theo	Rept RCN – 191	Jul 73	Lautenbach.CAPT INT FROM GROUP SIGMA	
Res Int Abs	5.5 – 1	+6	SAC	Revw	Conf IAEA – 169 1 235	74	Ribon.CAPTURE,STATUS CFD REQUEST,TBL	
Res Int Abs	+0	+5	WIN	Revw	Conf IAEA – 169 3 163	74	Pope+ DATA FILE CALC CFD XPTAL VALUE	
Res Int Abs	5.0 – 1		IJI	Eval	Rept KIYAI – 76 – 6	76	Fedorova+ EVAL CFD CALC.TBL RI,REFS	
					Conf 75Kiev 1 169	May 75	– + EVAL+CALC RI GIVEN,TABLE	
(n,γ)	Maxwl		ANL	Expt	Jour PR 76 300	Jul 49	Hess+ NAT ND TGT,MASS – SPEC.UPPER LIM	+
	Maxwl				Data EXFOR12067.003	Jun 76	. 1 PT.	
(n,γ)	Maxwl		ORL	Expt	Jour PR 88 412	Oct 52	Pomerance.PILE OSC.	+
	Maxwl				Data EXFOR11507.080	Jun 76	. 1 PT.	
(n,γ)	Pile		MCM	Expt	Jour PR 90 447	May 53	Walker+NRX,MASS SP,37+ – 6B REL ND 48B	+
	Pile				Data EXFOR12059.003	Jun 76	. 1 PT.	
(n,γ)	+0	1.5+3	HAR	Expt	Jour NP 3 553	Jun 57	Bowey. TOF. CAPT GAM YLD CURVE	
(n,γ)	Maxwl		CRC	Eval	Rept AECL – 1054	Mar 60	Walker. SAME AS CRRP – 913	
(n,γ)	5.0 – 3	2.5+0	GA	Eval	Rept GA – 2113	Jun 61	Wikner+TABLE + CURVE.100 E POINTS	
(n,γ)	2.8 – 3	1.0+6	GA	Eval	Rept NSE 12 115	Jan 62	Garrison+ EVAL FROM XPT+AVERAGE RES	
(n,γ)	2.5 – 2		BOL	Eval	Rept RT/FI – 4	Jan 67	Palmucci. CALC FROM RES PARAMETERS	
(n,γ)	Maxwl		AUA	Theo	Jour NSE 31 234	Feb 68	Cook+ STATISTICAL CALC CFD EXPT	
(n,γ)	5.0+3	1.0+5	AUA	ExTh	Rept AAEC/E – 198	May 69	Musgrove.S+P+D WAVE SIGMAS CALC,TBL	+
(n,γ)	1.0+3	1.0+7	BOL	Eval	Rept CCDN – NW/10	Dec 69	Benzi+H – F MOD,AXEL G(G)EST,ALL DATA	
					Rept CEC(70) – 2	Apr 70	– +. GRAPH	
					Conf 66Paris 1 537	Oct 66	– + STATMOD.TBL AV VALS.SUPERSEDD	
(n,γ)	Maxwl		HAR	Expt	Rept AERE – R – 6384	May 70	Cabell+ TBL.SIG=42.9+ – 2.2B. T=82C	
					Jour JIN 30 897	May 68	– + IRR PLUTO MASS ANAL	
	Pile				Rept AERE – R – 5520	Jul 67	– +.MASS SPECTR METHD.PLUTO CORE	
(n,γ)	3.0+4		AUA	Theo	Rept AAEC/E – 211	Nov 70	Musgrove. SIGMA GIVEN AND CFD OTHER	
(n,γ)	Maxwl		GA	Eval	Rept GA – 12071	Sep 71	Mathews+ RECOMMENDED VALUES	
(n,γ)	1.0 – 3	1.5+7	AUA	Eval	Data AUSTR – DFN 147.	Nov 71	COOK+POINT(223)+GROUP(127)SIG.CF EVL	+
(n,γ)	Maxwl		CRC	Eval	Rept AECL – 3037 1	Jan 72	Walker.RECOMMENDED SIG,DETAILED TBL	
(n,γ)	2.5 – 2		IAE	Revw	Rept IAEA – 143 897	Apr 72	Lemmel.RECENT EVALUATIONS,TABLE+GRPH	
	Maxwl				Rept IAEA – 143 897	Apr 72	– .RECENT EVALUATIONS,TABLE	
(n,γ)	2.5 – 2		AUA	Eval	Rept AAEC/TM – 619	Sep 72	Clayton.CALC FROM SIG LIBRARY,TABLE	
(n,γ)	2.0 – 2	1.0+1	IJI	Expt	Conf 73Kiev 2 104	May 73	Vertebny+ TOF,SIG(NEUT – E),GRAPH	
(n,γ)		1.1+7	RCN	Theo	Rept RCN – 191	Jun 73	Lautenbach. GROUP CONSTANTS TBL	
(n,γ)	Fiss		SAC	Revw	Conf IAEA – 169 1 235	74	Ribon.STATUS SIG CFD REQUESTS,TABLE	
	2.5 – 2	3.0+4			Conf IAEA – 169 1 235	74	– .STATUS SIG CFD REQUESTS,TABLE	
(n,γ)	Maxwl	Fiss	WIN	Revw	Conf IAEA – 169 3 163	74	Pope+ MAXW+FIS – SPEC AVG EVAL DATA	
	Fiss				Conf IAEA – 169 3 137	74	Dean. POINT DATA AVG OVER STAND SPEC	
(n,γ)	None		INL	Expt	Prog USNDC – 11 11	Jun 74	Harker+ INTEG CS, HL	
(n,γ)	1.0+3	1.0+7	FEI	Eval	Rept YK – 8/2 97	Sep 72	Abagjan+ AVG SIG(ENERGY – GROUPS),TABL	
					Rept INDC(CCP) – 39	Jul 74	.P102. ENGLISH OF YK – 8/2 97	
(n,γ)	2.0+1	1.5+5	RPI	Expt	Abst BAP 20 560	Apr 75	Hockenbury+ LINAC.	+
	6.6+3	7.1+4			Data EXFOR10552.005	Nov 78	. 434 PTS.CAPT CS.	
(n,γ)	Fast		RCN	Expt	Rept ECN – 10	Oct 76	Veenema+ STEK REACTIVITY WORTHS TBL.	
Res Int Capt	5.0 – 1		HAR	Expt	Rept AERE – R – 6384	May 70	Cabell+ REDUCED VAL=245+ – 32B TBL	
Spect (n,γ)	4.4+0		YAL	Expt	Jour NP 19 436	Nov 60	Draper+TABLE, GRAPH 400 – 900KEV GAMS	
Spect (n,γ)	4.8 – 2		RCN	Expt	Jour PHY 38 48	Mar 68	Reddingius+ TBL.GS.	+
	4.8 – 2				Data EXFOR20235.003	May 74	16PTS.	
Spect (n,γ)	Maxwl		KUR	Expt	Jour IZV 32 1629	Oct 68	Groshev+ GAM – SPEC – GRAPH,GE(LI) – DET	+
					Jour BAS 32 1514	69	TRANSLATN.*NO 10	
	Pile				Jour YF 8 1067	Dec 68	Groshev+.GE – LI,LVL SCH,TABLE	
	Maxwl				Conf 68Riga	Jan 68	ABSTRACT *	
					Jour SNP 8 619	Jun 69	. ENGL OF YF 8 1067	
	2.5 – 2				Data EXFOR40236.004	Oct 74	.GAM/100N FOR 2 ES GVN	
Spect (n,γ)	None		ORL	Theo	Jour NSE 36 220	May 69	Yost+ CALCUL BY GAMMA CASCADE MODEL	
Spect (n,γ)	Pile		CCP	Expt	Jour IZV 34 824	Apr 70	Berzin+ TBL CONV – EL+G ES,LVL SCHEME	
					Jour BAS 34 733	Apr 71	* ENGL OF IZV 34 824	
Spect (n,γ)	Maxwl		CCP	Expt	Conf 72Kiev 1 104	Jan 72	Berzin'+ ABSTR.GAM – ES+ABS INTS,TABLE	
Spect (n,γ)	Maxwl		IFL	Expt	Book PROKOFJEV	73	. TBL GAM,CONV ELECTR ES+INT,LVL SCH	
Spect (n,γ)	None		ORL	Expt	Abst BAP 21 657	Apr 76	Wells+10 N RES BELOW 300EV.SEP E.GVN	
Spect (n,γ)	Maxwl		ANL	Expt	Jour PR/C 14 75	Jul 76	Bushnell+INT,ES.GRPH,TBLS.LVL SCHEME	
(n,2n)	Fiss		CRC	Eval	Rept CRC – 1003	Dec 60	ROY+ESTIMATED AVG SIG=44.0MB	
(n,2n)	1.5+7		DEB	Eval	Jour REA 11 1 153	Mar 73	Boedy+ RECOMM.VALUE FROM N – Z SYSTEM.	
(n,2n)	1.5+7		KFI	Eval	Rept KFKI – 73 – 68	Dec 73	Jeki.NEW FIT,CALC SIG CFD OTHERS,TBL	
(n,p)	Fiss		CRC	Eval	Rept CRC – 1003	Dec 60	ROY+ ESTIMATED AVG SIG=0.006MB	
(n,p)	1.4+7		LYO	Comp	Rept LYCEN/6780	Nov 67	Crouzet+COMPILATN FOR ACTIVTN ANALYS	

60 Neodymium 145

Quantity	Energy (ev) Min	Max	Lab	Type	Documentation Ref Vol Page	Date	Author, Comments	Data
(n,p)	1.4+7	1.5+7	KAZ	Theo	Jour YF 18 705	Oct 73	Levkovsky.AVERAGED SIG,CALC,TBL	
					Jour SNP 18 361	Apr 74	. ENGLISH OF YF 18,705	
(n,α)	Fiss		CRC	Eval	Rept CRC-1003	Dec 60	ROY+ ESTIMATED AVG SIG=0.24MB	
(n,α)	Maxwl		ISL	Expt	Jour PL 1 289	Jul 62	Cheifetz. TBL Q-VALU,SIG,BRANCHRATIO	+
	Maxwl				Data EXFOR31151.003	Mar 73	.SIG GVN	
(n,α)	Maxwl		CCP	Expt	Jour YF 1 252	Feb 65	Andreev.IONIZ-CHAMBER,	
					Jour SNP 1 177	Aug 65	TRANSLATN.*	
(n,α)	1.0+0	1.0+3	DUB	Expt	Conf 66Dubna 147	Jul 66	Frank+,REVIEW,BRIEF DISCUSSION	
(n,α)		4.1+2	DUB	Expt	Rept JINR-E3-3029	Nov 66	Kvitek+,AVERAGE ALPHA WIDTH,THEORCLC	+
(n,α)	Pile	2.5-2	JAE	Expt	Jour NP/A 141 193	Jan 70	Okamoto. BI FILTER.A SPECT.EFF SIG.	+
	2.5-2				Data EXFOR20335.003	Jul 74	2PTS.SIGMA.	
(n,α)	4.4+0	1.0+2	DUB	Expt	Conf 70Helsinki 1 669	Jun 70	Popov+125. SPECTRUM OF ALFAS, CURVE	
					Rept JINR-P3-5073	May 70	- .Y.P.+ ALFA SPEC GRAPHS,W-ALFA	
					Prog YFI-11 45	70	- + ABST,SAME TBL AS JINR-5073	
					Prog INDC(CCP)-31	Dec 72	.PAGE 44,ENGLISH OF YFI-11 45	
(n,α)	4.4+0	1.7+3	RPI	Expt	Conf 75Wash. 93	Mar 75	Block+ GRPH COUNTS VS CHANNEL	
(n,α)	Maxwl		LYO	Expt	Jour ZP 275 157	Nov 75	Emsallem+ SIG+LVL-WIDTH	+
	2.5-2				Data EXFOR20612.004	Aug 76	2PTS.SIGMA.	
(n,α)	2.5-2		IJI	Eval	Rept KIYAI-76-6	76	Fedorova+ RECOMMENDED SIG GIVEN	
Reson Params	4.4+1	2.4+2	HAR	Expt	Jour NP 3 553	Jun 57	Bowey.TOF.4ES FROM CAPT GAMMA YIELDS	
Reson Params	4.4+0		BNL	Expt	Jour PR 108 353	Oct 57	Stolovy+ FC, TRNS WT WN WG	+
	4.4+0				Data EXFOR11866.	Jun 76	. 1 RES, E0,WT,WN,WG	
Reson Params	4.4+0	1.0+2	ANL	Expt	Prog ANL-6589	Aug 62	Carpenter.	+
	4.4+0	1.0+2			Data EXFOR12048.003	Jun 76	. 5 RES, E0,J	
Reson Params	+0	+3	COL	Expt	Prog NYO-GEN72-132	Jan 67	Garg+ P.1,BAP10 575 +NEW RUN,BUT NDG	
Reson Params		1.0+6	AUA	Theo	Jour AUJ 20 477	Oct 67	Cook. TBL OF AVG LVL SPACING D,L=0,1	
Reson Params	4.3+0	6.5+2	SAC	Expt	Jour NP/A 134 118	Sep 69	Alves+LINAC TOF.22WN,WN0;SOME J,WGWT	+
	4.0+0	6.5+2			Conf 68Wash. 867	Mar 68	Morgenstern. WG VS. A. AVG WG GIVEN	
					Conf 66Paris 1 559	Oct 66	Huynh+ ABST.NDG. SEE INDC-156	
					Conf 65Antwerp 525	Jul 65	De Barros+ PPR73.ABST.NDG	
	4.3+0	1.0+2			Jour JPR 24 997	Nov 63	Bianchi+ DATA. SUPERSEDED	
	1.5+2				Jour CR 254 4162	Jun 62	Julien+ TOF.G-SPEC,ISOT ASSIGNMENT.	
	0.0+0	7.4+2			Data EXFOR20688.	Jun 77	23PTS.E0,AVG WG,WN,WT,G*WN.	
Reson Params	4.2+1	1.1+3	DUB	Expt	Jour YF 8 639	Oct 68	Karzhavina+49RES,WT,WN,WG,TABLES	+
					Rept YFI-6 124	68	- + TABLE.	
					Rept JINR-P3-3564	Nov 67	- + FULL PAPER.	
					Jour SNP 8 371	Apr 69	- + TRANSLATION.	
					Rept INDC-260E	69	- + ENGL OF YFI-6 124.	
	4.3+1	1.0+3			Data EXFOR40113.	Sep 72	N-WIDTH AT 49RES, CAPT-WID,TOT-WID,D	
Reson Params	4.5+5	7.6+6	KUR	Expt	Jour YF 8 1067	Dec 68	Groshev+ LVL SCHEME DISCUSSED	
					Jour SNP 8 619	Jun 69	TRANSLATN.*	
Reson Params	4.2+1	5.7+2	GEL	Expt	Jour JNE 23 369	Jul 69	Migneco+ TOF.WG,WN.AREA ANAL.	
Reson Params	7.5+2	1.7+3	MOL	Expt	Prog EANDC(E)127U	Apr 70	Ceulemans+ FROM TOTAL SIG ANALYSIS.	
Reson Params	-		AUA	Theo	Jour AAEC/E-211	Nov 70	Musgrove. CALCULTD D+GAM WIDTH GIVEN	
Reson Params	None		DUB	Expt	Jour AE 29 395	Nov 70	Pikel'Ner+ ABST FRANC-SOV SEM DUBNA	
		1.0+3			Conf 68DUBSY 349	Jul 68	Pikelner.LVL SPAC,AVERG. WG	
	None				Jour SJA 29 1156	Nov 70	- + ENGL OF AE 29 395	
Reson Params	4.4+0	1.0+2	DUB	Expt	Rept JINR-E3-5483	Dec 70	Popov. TABLE OF ALPHA+NEUTRON WIDTHS	
					Jour NP/A 154 177	Sep 70	Kvitek+ J,PI,ALPHA,GAMMA WIDTHS	
					Conf 70Helsinki 1 669	Jun 70	Popov+125. AVERAGE ALFA-WIDTH	
					Rept JINR-P3-5073	May 70	- .Y.P.+ ALFA WIDTH GVN,N-RESON	
					Jour ZEP 5 365	May 67	Kvitek+. N,ALFA REACTION,IMP REACTOR	
	1.0+0	4.0+2		ExTh	Conf 67Kharkov 201	Feb 67	- .EMITT ALFA PARTICLES,CFD H-F	
	4.0+0	1.0+2		Expt	Rept JINR-P3-3104	Jan 67	- +,TABLE OF WIDTHS AT FEW E(N)	
	4.4+0	1.0+2			Rept UCRL-TR-105	May 71	. ENGL OF 70HELSIN.FULL RPT-N0=10541	
Reson Params	4.4+1	6.4+2	CJD	Eval	Rept YK-7	71	Zakharova+ SURVEY+SYSTEMATICS,GW,TBL	
					Rept INDC(CCP)-27	Nov 72	.ENGLISH TRANSLATION OF YK-7 /71	
Reson Params	None		DUB	Theo	Jour YF 13 240	Feb 71	Malecki+G-WID,THEO CFD EXPT.TBL,GRPH	
					Jour SNP 13 133	Aug 71	+ ENGL OF YF 13 240.	
Reson Params	4.3+1	1.5+3	GEL	Expt	Conf 71Knoxvill 743	Mar 71	Rohr+.LINAC,PARAMS FROM CAPT MEASTS	+
	4.3+1	3.1+4			Data EXFOR20397.	Oct 74	129PTS.AVG WG,J,G*WN,AVG*G*WG,G*WG	
Reson Params	4.3+0	4.1+2	SAC	Expt	Conf 71Knoxvill 785	Mar 71	Cauvin+.J ASSIGNMENTS 23RESON	+
	4.3+0	4.1+2			Data EXFOR20126.008	Sep 72	. 23PTS.J.	
Reson Params	4.3+1	4.6+3	SAC	Expt	Rept CEA-N-1459	Aug 71	Tellier. SHAPE-ANALYSIS 178 LEVELS	+
					Priv TELLIER	Oct 71	- . VALUES FOR COMPILATION.	
					Conf 71Knoxvill 680	Mar 71	- +.TRANS,AVG D=18.9EV 179RES	
	4.3+1	4.6+3			Data EXFOR20121.	Sep 72	421PTS.AVG WG,WT,2G*WN,2G*WN0.	

60 Neodymium 145

Quantity	Energy (ev) Min	Energy (ev) Max	Lab	Type	Documentation Ref Vol Page	Author, Comments Date	Data
Reson Params	4.3+0	6.6+2	NRL Expt	Jour	PR/C 5 2030	Jun 72 Stolovy+ J FOR 36 RESONANCES	+
	4.3+0	6.6+2		Data	EXFOR10256.003	Oct 72 . 36 RES. J	
Reson Params	None		DUB Theo	Rept	JINR – P4 – 7499	Oct 73 Soloviev+ CALC D CFD EXPTS,TABLE	
Reson Params	+0	+2	BOL Eval	Conf	IAEA – 169 3 123	74 Benzi+ AVG G – WID CFD OTHERS+XPT,TABL	
Reson Params	+0	+3	FEI Eval	Rept	YK – 8/2 97	Sep 72 Abagyan+ AVG G – WID+D AT BINDNG – E,TBL	
				Rept	INDC(CCP) – 39	Jul 74 .PAGE 102.ENGLISH OF YK – 8/2 97	
Reson Params	2.0+1	1.5+5	RPI Expt	Abst	BAP 20 560	Apr 75 Hockenbury+D=14.4+ – 2.0EV.RESPARS TBP	+
	8.6+1			Data	EXFOR10552.010	Nov 78 . 1PT.WN=(10.2+ – .4) – 3 EV AT 85.6 EV.	
Reson Params	1.0+3	1.0+6	SAC Eval	Rept	CEA – N – 1832	Dec 75 Ribon+ EXP+TH ANAL,RES PAR,TBL	
Reson Params	2.5 – 2	+3	ANL Expt	Jour	PR/C 14 75	Jul 76 Bushnell+SNG MEAS.I,PI ASSIGNED	
Strnth Fnctn	+3		BNL Expt	Jour	PRL 1 461	Dec 58 Hughes+ FC, 3.3+ – 1.5	
Strnth Fnctn		1.0+3	DUB Expt	Conf	68DUBSY 349	Jul 68 Pikelner.LVL SPAC,AVERG. WG,S0 VS A	
Strnth Fnctn	4.2+1	1.0+3	DUB Expt	Rept	YF 8 639	Oct 68 Karzhavina+TRANS+G – YLD EXPT,S – RES	+
				Rept	YFI – 6 124.	68 – + TABLE.	
				Rept	JINR – P3 – 3564	Nov 67 – + FULL PAPER.	
				Conf	67Tokyo § 8.133	Sep 67 – + ABST.NDG.	
				Jour	SNP 8 371	Apr 69 – + TRANSLATION.	
				Rept	INDC – 260E	69 – + ENGL OF YFI – 6 124.	
	0.0+0	1.0+3		Data	EXFOR40113.028	Sep 72 STRENGTH – FUNCTION	
Strnth Fnctn		7.4+2	SAC Expt	Jour	NP/A 123 561	Jan 69 Morgenstern+ TBL.FROM RES ANALYSIS	+
				Jour	NP/A 134 118	Sep 69 Alves+LINAC TOF. S0=2.8 +0.9 – 0.6	
				Rept	CEA – R – 3609	Sep 68 Morgenstern. (THESIS)	
				Conf	68Wash. 867	Mar 68 – +	
	0.0+0	7.4+2		Data	EXFOR20688.029	Jun 77 1PNT.L=0.	
Strnth Fnctn	–		AUA Theo	Rept	AAEC/E – 211	Nov 70 Musgrove. SMOOTHED S0,S1 AND S2 GIVN	
Strnth Fnctn	4.0+2	4.7+3	SAC Expt	Rept	CEA – N – 1459	Aug 71 Tellier. VERSUS ENERGY	+
				Priv	TELLIER	Oct 71 – . VALUES FOR COMPILATION.	
				Jour	CR 272 695	Mar 71 – .LINAC,TOF.179 LEVELS,+D,+A	
				Conf	71Knoxvill 680	Mar 71 – + SO=4.2+ – 0.5	
	4.0+2	4.7+3		Data	EXFOR20121.	Sep 72 6PTS.L=0.	
Strnth Fnctn	0.0+0	6.6+2	NRL Expt	Jour	PR/C 5 2030	Jun 72 Stolovy+ S0 FOR J 3 AND 4 RESON	+
		6.6+2		Data	EXFOR10256.005	Oct 72 . 2 PTS. S0, S1	
Strnth Fnctn	1.5+2	6.5+2	SAC ExTh	Diss	FRNC – TH – 450	Oct 72 Delaroche.OPTICAL MODEL PARAMETERS	
Strnth Fnctn		+3	SAC ExTh	Rept	CEA – N – 1522	Oct 72 Cauvin+ S0,S1 VALUES.	
Strnth Fnctn	None		AUA Eval	Rept	AAEC/E – 277	Mar 73 Musgrove.TBLS EXPTL DATA+BEST VALUES	
Strnth Fnctn	6.5+3	7.1+4	RPI Expt	Abst	BAP 20 560	Apr 75 Hockenbury+RESPARS.TBP.	+
	6.5+3	7.1+4		Data	EXFOR10552.019	Nov 78 . 4PTS.S0,S1,S2,AVG WG GVN.	
Lvl Density	–		DUB Expt	Jour	YF 8 639	Oct 68 Karzhavina+ VAL+PARS GVN,TBL+GRPH	+
				Jour	SNP 8 371	Apr 69 – + TRANSLATION.	
	None			Data	EXFOR40113.056	Sep 72 LEVEL – DENSITY PARAMETER	
Lvl Density	0.0+0	4.7+3	SAC Expt	Rept	CEA – N – 1459	Aug 71 Tellier. FROM STAT RES ANALYSIS.	+
		4.7+3		Jour	CR 272 695	Mar 71 – .LINAC,TOF. D AND A,179 LVLS	
		4.7+3		Data	EXFOR20121.027	Sep 72 1PNT.SP.CUT(0).	
Lvl Density	None		MUN Theo	Jour	NP/A 217 269	Dec 73 Dilg+ A,DELTA. BACK SHIFTED FERMIGAS	
Lvl Density	None		BOL Eval	Conf	IAEA – 169 3 123	74 Benzi+ LVL DENS PARAM BY XPT,GRPH+TB	
Lvl Density	None		DUB Theo	Jour	NP/A 224 411	May 74 Soloviev+ 1/2 MICROSC MDL. SPH NUCL.	
Lvl Density	None		ROC Theo	Jour	NP/A 223 577	May 74 Huizenga+ EXP CFD MICROSC TH SPH NUC	
Lvl Density	+0	+3	FEI Eval	Rept	YK – 8/2 97	Sep 72 Abagyan+ LVL DENSITY PARAMETER,TBL	
				Rept	INDC(CCP) – 39	Jul 74 .PAGE 102.ENGLISH OF YK – 8/2 97	
Lvl Density	+0	1.0+4	JAE ExTh	Jour	JPJ 37 581	Sep 74 Ideno.LVL SPACING CORRELATIONS	
	1.0+0	1.4+3		Rept	JAERI – M – 5490	Nov 73 – .LEVEL SPACING CORRELATIONS.TBL	
Lvl Density	+0		DUB Theo	Conf	75Kiev 3 23	May 75 Voronov. LVL SPACING OF ND146.TABLE	
(γ,n)	9.0+6	2.0+7	SAC Expt	Jour	NP/A 172 437	Sep 71 Carlos+LORENTZ LINE PARAM,GRPHS,TBL	

60 Neodymium 146

Quantity	Energy (ev) Min	Energy (ev) Max	Lab	Type	Documentation Ref Vol Page	Author, Comments Date	Data
Evaluation	1.0 – 3	1.5+7	AUA Eval	Rept	AAEC/TM – 549	Jun 70 Cook.TOT,EL,INEL,NONEL,CAPT SIGS,NDG	+
				Rept	AAEC/E – 214	Jun 71 Bertram+GROUP SIGMAS SAME QUANTS.NDG	
				Rept	AAEC/TM – 587	Mar 71 *DESCRIPTION OF LIBRARY	
	1.0 – 3	1.5+7		Data	AUSTR – DFN 148.	Nov 71 POINT(223) AND GROUP(127) SIGMAS	
Evaluation	1.0 – 5	1.5+7	BOL Eval	Prog	NEANDC(E)182 7	Dec 76 Fabri+ COMPLETE EVAL IN ENDF/B DONE	+
	1.0 – 5	1.5+7		Data	CNEN – CEA 5	Jan 78 PRELIM.ALL QUANTITIES.ENDF FORMAT	
Total	3.0+1	5.0+3	SAC Expt	Rept	CEA – N – 1459	Aug 71 Tellier. ENRICHED TO 95PC.EXPT DETS.	+
				Priv	TELLIER	Oct 71 – . DATA FOR COMPILATION.	
				Jour	CR 272 695	Mar 71 – . LINAC.TOF.PRELIM ANALYSIS.	
	3.0+1	5.0+3		Data	EXFOR20118.006	Sep 72 10994PTS.	

60   Neodymium   146

Quantity	Energy (ev) Min	Max	Lab	Type	Documentation Ref Vol Page	Date	Author, Comments	Data
Total	1.0−3	1.5+7	AUA Eval	Data	AUSTR−DFN 148.	Nov 71	COOK+POINT(223)+GROUP(127)SIG.CF EVL	+
Total	1.4+7		LIN Expt	Conf	73Kiev 3 108	May 73	Djumin+ OPTMOD CALC,SIG	+
				Jour	IZV 37 1019	May 73	− + SIG(A),OPTMODEL CALC,GRAPH	
				Jour	BAS 37 5 91	May 73	.ENGLISH OF IZV 37 1019	
	1.4+7				Data	EXFOR40302.006	Feb 76	1 PNT
Total	1.0+5	6.5+5	DKE Expt	Jour	AP 84 165	May 74	Pineo+TRNS.AVG CS.TBL GRPHS.OPTMDL	+
	1.5+4	6.0+5		Diss	PINEO	70	.AVG CS.GRPHS.CFD.STF CALC.TBL.CFD.	
	1.5+4	6.0+5		Data	EXFOR10542.015	Jan 79	. DATA UNOBTAINABLE FROM AUTHORS.	
Total	7.5+5	1.4+7	BRC Expt	Abst	BAP 20 1196	Sep 75	Shamu+ MEAS TOT CS DIFF WITH 144ND	
Elastic	Maxwl		ORL Expt	Jour	PR 91 597	Aug 53	Koehler+	+
	Maxwl			Data	EXFOR12060.	Jun 76	. 2 PTS, COH, COH AMP	
Elastic	1.0−3	1.5+7	AUA Eval	Data	AUSTR−DFN 148.	Nov 71	COOK+POINT(223)+GROUP(127)SIG.CF EVL	+
Elastic	2.5−2		IJI Eval	Rept	KIYAI−76−6	76	Fedorova+ COMP(REFS,SIGS),EVAL.TABLE	
				Conf	75Kiev 1 169	May 75	− + EVAL 2200M/S SIG,TABLE	
Potntal Scat	3.0+3	6.5+5	DKE Expt	Jour	AP 84 165	May 74	Pineo+TRNS.S WAVE SCT LENGTH.TBL.CFD	
				Abst	DA/B 31 6821	May 71	.THESIS ABST.	
				Diss	PINEO	70	.TBL.GRPHS.CFD TO 3 COLLECTIVE MDLS.	
Tot Inelastc	5.0+5	1.5+7	AUA Eval	Data	AUSTR−DFN 148.	Nov 71	COOK+POINT(11)+GROUP(127)SIG.CF EVL	+
Diff Inelast	Thrsh	1.7+6	LEB Expt	Conf	72Kiev 2 4	Jan 72	Konobeevskij+ ABST,NDG.SIG TO 2+LVL	
Diff Inelast	5.0+5	2.5+6	KTY Expt	Prog	U/KTY−77 14	77	Mcellistrem+ INEL CS CFD WHF.GRPH.	
Scattering	Maxwl		ORL Expt	Jour	PR 91 597	Aug 53	Koehler+ TRANS 9.5+ −0.4B	+
	Maxwl			Data	EXFOR12060.028	Jun 76	. 1 PT, SIG	
Scattering	2.0−2	1.0+1	IJI Expt	Conf	73Kiev 2 104	May 73	Vertebny+ TOF,SIG(NEUT−E),GRAPH	
Nonelastic	1.0−3	1.5+7	AUA Eval	Data	AUSTR−DFN 148.	Nov 71	COOK+POINT(223)+GROUP(127)SIG.CF EVL	+
Absorption	4.1−1	1.0+7	GA Eval	Rept	GA− 2451	Aug 61	Joanou+ 68GROUP DATA FOR GAM−I	
Absorption	1.0−4	1.0+7	JUL Eval	Rept	JUEL−678−RG	Jul 70	Liu. EVALUATION+CALC,GRPH,FN OF E	
Absorption	2.5−2		IJI Eval	Rept	KIYAI−76−6	76	Fedorova+ COMP(REFS,SIGS),EVAL.TABLE	
				Conf	75Kiev 1 169	May 75	− + EVAL SIG GIVEN,TABLE	
Res Int Abs	None		GA Eval	Rept	GA− 12071	Sep 71	Mathews+ RECOMMENDED VALUES	
Res Int Abs	5.5−1		CRC Eval	Rept	AECL−3037 1	Jan 72	Walker.REDUCED RES INT,DETAILED TBL	
Res Int Abs		1.0+6	OSL Expt	Prog	INDC(NOR)−1 1	May 72	Alstad+ RES CAPT INT REL AU.TBL.ABST	+
	0.0+0	1.0+6		Jour	JIN 29 2155	Sep 67	− + ACTIV REL AU,AND CD RATIO	
		1.0+6		Data	EXFOR20044.007	Sep 71	1PNT.CAPTURE.	
Res Int Abs	5.0−1		AUA Eval	Rept	AAEC/TM−619	Sep 72	Clayton.CALC FROM SIG LIBRARY,TABLE	
Res Int Abs	5.0−1		KJL Expt	Jour	JIN 34 2699	Sep 72	Steinnes. ACT. AU MONITOR	+
	5.0−1			Data	EXFOR20188.018	May 74	1PNT.CAPTURE.	
Res Int Abs	5.5−1		CNE Expt	Jour	CJP 51 1454	Jul 73	Ricabarra+ ACTIV,REL THR+GOLD,TABLES	+
	6.0−1			Data	EXFOR30239.	May 73	RES INTEGS + RATIO TO THR−ABS SIGMA	
Res Int Abs	4.6−1	1.0+6	RCN Theo	Rept	RCN−191	Jul 73	Lautenbach.CAPT INT FROM GROUP SIGMA	
Res Int Abs	5.0−1		GHT Expt	Jour	JRC 20 695	74	Van Der Linden+ BY(N,G).CFD OTHS,TBL	
	5.5−1			Conf	73Paris 2 241	Mar 73	− + ACT,REL THR+GOLD,TBL	
	5.5−1			Data	EXFOR20645.019	Jul 76	1PNT.CAPTURE.	
Res Int Abs	5.5−1	+6	SAC Revw	Conf	IAEA−169 1 235	74	Ribon.CAPTURE,STATUS CFD REQUEST,TBL	
Res Int Abs	+0	+5	WIN Revw	Conf	IAEA−169 3 163	74	Pope+ DATA FILE CALC CFD XPTAL VALUE	
Res Int Abs	5.0−1		IJI Eval	Rept	KIYAI−76−6	76	Fedorova+ EVAL CFD CALC.TBL RI,REFS	
				Conf	75Kiev 1 169	May 75	− + EVAL+CALC RI GIVEN,TABLE	
Res Int Abs	5.5−1		MUNExpt	Diss	GRYNTAKIS	Mar 76	Gryntakis.ACT 2.57+ − 0.14 B, INCL 1/V	+
				Jour	RCA 17 191	Mar 72	KIM+ACTIV.EQUIVALENT TO THESIS	
	5.5−1			Data	EXFOR20625.019	Aug 76	1PNT.CAPTURE.	
(n,γ)	Maxwl		OHO Expt	Jour	PR 53 437	Mar 38	Pool+ BETAS,CLOUD CH,RATIO ND148(NG)	
(n,γ)	Maxwl		ANL Expt	Jour	PR 76 300	Jul 49	Hess+ NAT ND TGT,MASS−SPEC.UPPER LIM	+
	Maxwl			Data	EXFOR12067.006	Jun 76	. 1 PT.	
(n,γ)	Maxwl		ORL Expt	Jour	PR 88 412	Oct 52	Pomerance.PILE OSC.	+
	Maxwl			Data	EXFOR11507.081	Jun 76	. 1 PT.	
(n,γ)	Pile		MCMExpt	Jour	PR 90 447	May 53	Walker+NRX,MASS SP,3.7+ − 5B REL ND 48	+
	Pile			Data	EXFOR12059.007	Jun 76	. 1 PT.	
(n,γ)	Fiss		BNL Expt	Jour	PR 91 1423	Sep 53	Hughes+ ALSO LVL SPACINGS AT EXCIT E	+
	Fiss			Data	EXFOR11562.013	Jun 76	. 1 PT.	
(n,γ)	+0	1.5+3	HAR Expt	Jour	NP 3 553	Jun 57	Bowey. TOF. CAPT GAM YLD CURVE	
(n,γ)	Maxwl		CRC Eval	Rept	AECL−1054	Mar 60	Walker. SAME AS CRRP−913.	
(n,γ)	Maxwl		OSL Expt	Jour	JIN 27 2155	Sep 67	Alstad+ ACTIVATION REL AU,+CD RATIO	+
	Maxwl			Data	EXFOR20044.006	Sep 71	1PNT.SIG.	
(n,γ)	Pile		CRC Expt	Prog	EANDC(CAN)−34	Jan 68	Mowatt+ RELATIVE TO ND148	
(n,γ)	−		IEA Comp	Rept	IEA−INF− 10	Aug 68	Atalla. TABLES OF HL,SIG AND GAMM−E	
(n,γ)	1.0+3	1.0+7	BOL Eval	Rept	CCDN−NW/10	Dec 69	Benzi+H−F MOD,AXEL G(G)EST,ALL DATA	
				Rept	CEC(70)−2	Apr 70	− . GRAPH	
				Conf	66Paris 1 537	Oct 66	− + STATMOD.TBL AV VALS.SUPERSEDD	
(n,γ)	3.0+4		AUA Theo	Rept	AAEC/E−211	Nov 70	Musgrove. SIGMA GIVEN AND CFD OTHER	

60 Neodymium 146

Quantity	Energy (ev) Min	Energy (ev) Max	Lab	Type	Documentation Ref Vol Page	Documentation Date	Author, Comments	Data
(n,γ)	Maxwl		GA	Eval Rept	GA - 12071	Sep 71	Mathews+ RECOMMENDED VALUES	
(n,γ)	1.0-3	1.5+7	AUA	Eval Data	AUSTR - DFN 148.	Nov 71	COOK+POINT(223)+GROUP(127)SIG.CF EVL	+
(n,γ)	Maxwl		CRC	Eval Rept	AECL - 3037 1	Jan 72	Walker.RECOMMENDED SIG,DETAILED TBL	
(n,γ)	2.5+4		AUW	Expt Jour	JP/A 5 468	Mar 72	Thirumala+ ACT METHOD, RELATIVE TO I	+
				ExTh Conf	70Madurai 2 25	Dec 70	Thirumala Rao+ SIGMAS FOR S+P WAVES	
	2.5+4			Expt Data	EXFOR30247.002	Jun 73	CAPTURE CROSS SECTION	
(n,γ)	2.5-2		AUA	Eval Rept	AAEC/TM - 619	Sep 72	Clayton.CALC FROM SIG LIBRARY,TABLE	
(n,γ)		1.1+7	RCN	Theo Rept	RCN - 191	Jun 73	Lautenbach. GROUP CONSTANTS TBL	
(n,γ)	2.5+4		AUW	Expt Jour	NC/A 18 48	Nov 73	Sidappa+ ACTIV SIG,CFD.TABLE	
(n,γ)	2.5-2	3.0+4	SAC	Revw Conf	IAEA - 169 1 235	74	Ribon.STATUS SIG CFD REQUESTS,TABLE	
(n,γ)	Maxwl	Fiss	WIN	Revw Conf	IAEA - 169 3 163	74	Pope+ MAXW+FIS - SPEC AVG EVAL DATA	
	Fiss			Conf	IAEA - 169 3 137	74	Dean. POINT DATA AVG OVER STAND SPEC	
(n,γ)	None		INL	Expt Prog	USNDC - 11 11	Jun 74	Harker+ INTEG CS, HL	
(n,γ)	1.0+3	1.0+7	FEI	Eval Rept	YK - 8/2 97	Sep 72	Abagjan+ AVG SIG(ENERGY - GROUPS),TABL	
				Rept	INDC(CCP) - 39	Jul 74	.P102. ENGLISH OF YK - 8/2 97	
(n,γ)	Maxwl		MUN	Expt Diss	GRYNTAKIS	Mar 76	Gryntakis.,ACT.,1.31+ - 0.06 B,REL. AU	+
				Jour	RCA 17 191	Mar 72	KIM+,EQUIVALENT TO THESIS	
	2.5-2			Data	EXFOR20625.018	Aug 76	1PNT.SIGMA	
(n,γ)	Fast		RCN	Expt Rept	ECN - 10	Oct 76	Veenema+ STEK REACTIVITY WORTHS TBL.	
Spect (n,γ)	Pile		IPS	Expt Jour	AF 4 81	Aug 52	Kondaiah. DECAY SCHEME.E+INT BETA - GA	
				Jour	PR 81 1056	51	- + SUPERSEDED.	
Spect (n,γ)	Maxwl		CCP	Expt Jour	IZV 30 1260	Aug 66	Arutjunjan+.TABLE+GRAPH OF GAM - SPECT	
				Jour	BAS 30 1310	66	. ENGL OF IZV 30 1253	
Spect (n,γ)	Pile		LND	Expt Jour	ZP 207 105	Oct 67	Dougan+,GAMMA - SPEC,13GAMMA - E GIVEN	
Spect (n,γ)	Pile		SWR	Expt Jour	AF 34 531	Dec 67	Baecklin+. HL FOR 1ST LVL.DELD COINC	
				Rept	AE - 265	Feb 67	- + DECAY PROPERTIES ND - 147	
Spect (n,γ)	+0	+4	COL	Expt Prog	WASH - 1124 31	Nov 68	Camarda+ MOXON - RAE DET TBC NO DATA	
Spect (n,γ)	Pile		KUR	Expt Jour	YF 8 1067	Dec 68	Groshev+.GE - LI,LVL SCH,GRPH	
	Maxwl			ExTh Conf	68Riga	Jan 68	- + ABST,G ES,INT,GE DETECTOR	
				Expt Jour	SNP 8 619	Jun 69	. ENGL OF YF 8 1067	
	2.5-2			Data	EXFOR40236.005	Oct 74	.GAM/100N FOR 11 ES GVN	
Spect (n,γ)	Pile		JUL	Expt Jour	ZP 257 177	Dec 72	Fellmann+,LVL - SCHEME OF PM - 147 GIVEN	
Spect (n,γ)	Maxwl		NIL	Expt Prog	INDC(SEC) - 42	Dec 74	. GELI - NAI,TBD.	
Spect (n,γ)	2.5-2		ILL	Expt Conf	76Lowell 1300	Jul 76	Pinston+LVL SCHEMES DEDUCED.NDG	
	Maxwl			Jour	NP/A 246 380	Jul 75	Roussille+ CURV,TBL,E,INT,LVL SHEME	
				Abst	75Harwell 39	Mar 75	Borner+CURVD CRYST. NDG. TBC.	
	2.5-2			Data	EXFOR20586.002	Aug 76	231PTS.	
(n,2n)	Fiss		CRC	Eval Rept	CRC - 1003	Dec 60	ROY+ ESTIMATED AVG SIG = 13.3MB	
(n,2n)	1.5+7		DEB	Eval Rept	REA 11 1 153	Mar 73	Boedy+ RECOMM.VALUE FROM N - Z SYSTEM.	
(n,2n)	1.5+7		KFI	Theo Rept	KFKI - 73 - 68	Dec 73	Jeki.NEW FIT,CALC SIG CFD OTHERS,TBL	
(n,2n)	1.4+7		AUW	Expt Prog	BARC - 831 34	75	Lakshamana Das+ ACTIV(GELI),CFD,NDG	
(n,xn) x>2	1.4+7		BRC	ExTh Prog	CEA - N - 1875 60	Apr 76	Frehaut+N3N.SYSTEMATIC LAWS SEARCH	+
	1.5+7			Expt Conf	75Gothenbg	Jun 75	- +	
	1.5+7				Data	EXFOR20571.011	Mar 76	1PNT.N3N.	
(n,p)	Fiss		CRC	Eval Rept	CRC - 1003	Dec 60	ROY+ ESTIMATED AVG SIG = 0.005MB	
(n,p)	1.4+7	1.5+7	ARK	Theo Prog	ORO - 3235 - 29	Jan 67	Koch+ STAT MODEL CALC CFD EXPTS	
(n,p)	1.4+7		LYO	Comp Rept	LYCEN/6780	Nov 67	Crouzet+COMPILATN FOR ACTIVTN ANALYS	
(n,p)	1.5+7		ARK	Expt Abst	DA/B 32 5091	Mar 72	Bari. GE(LI) DET. ACT. SIG GIVEN	+
	1.5+7			Data	EXFOR10431.014	Aug 75	. 1 PT. SIGMA	
(n,p)	1.4+7	1.5+7	KAZ	Theo Jour	YF 18 705	Oct 73	Levkovsky.AVERAGED SIG,CALC,TBL	
(n,p)	1.5+7		JUL	Expt Jour	RRL 25 335	May 76	Qaim+ ACTIV,GELI.CFD OTHERS,TBL+GRPH	+
	1.5+7			Data	EXFOR20716.005	Jun 77	1PNT.SIGMA.	
(n,α)	1.4+7		ALD	Expt Jour	PPS 73 215	Feb 59	Coleman+. ACTIVATION	
(n,α)	1.5+7		ARK	Expt Jour	PR 118 242	Apr 60	Wille+ MEAS ACT SIG = 8.3+ - 2.0 MB	+
	1.5+7			Data	EXFOR12033.022	Jun 76	. 1 PT.	
(n,α)	Fiss		CRC	Eval Rept	CRC - 1003	Dec 60	ROY+ ESTIMATED AVG SIG = 0.0078MB	
(n,α)	1.4+7	1.5+7	NAP	Comp Rept	INFN/BE - 67 - 11	Sep 67	Cuzzocrea+ AVERAGED CHOSEN DATA.	
(n,α)	1.4+7		LYO	Comp Rept	LYCEN/6780	Nov 67	Crouzet+COMPILATN FOR ACTIVTN ANALYS	
(n,α)	1.5+7		DEB	Comp Jour	REA 7 4 93	Dec 69	Csikai+ SIG+HL COMPILTN,N - ACTIV - ANAL	
(n,α)	1.4+7	1.5+7	JYV	Eval Rept	JU - RR - 3/1970	Jun 70	Leppaemaeki+ TABLE OF EVAL AVG SIG	
(n,α)	1.5+7		KYU	Expt Jour	NST 12 681	Nov 75	Sato+.ACTIVATION SIG = 4.42+ - 0.47 MB	+
	1.5+7			Data	EXFOR20595.002	Aug 76	1PNT.SIGMA.	
Reson Params	+0	+3	COL	Expt Rept	NYO - GEN72 - 132	Jan 67	Garg+ P.1,BAP10 575 +NEW RUN,BUT NDG	
Reson Params		1.0+6	AUA	Theo Jour	AUJ 20 477	Oct 67	Cook. TBL OF AVG LVL SPACING D,L=0,1	
Reson Params	-		DUB	Expt Conf	68DUBSY 283	Jul 68	Shapiro.AVERAGE ALFA WIDTH,LVL SPAC.	
Reson Params		7.0+3	DUB	Expt Conf	68DUBSY 349	Jul 68	Pikelner.LVL SPAC,AVERG. WG	

60 Neodymium 146

Quantity	Energy (ev) Min	Energy (ev) Max	Lab	Type	Documentation Ref Vol Page	Date	Author, Comments	Data
Reson Params	3.6+2	6.8+3	DUB	Expt	Jour YF 8 639	Oct 68	Karzhavina+18RES,WT,WN,WG,TABLES	+
					Rept YFI-6 124	68	- + TABLE.	
					Rept JINR-P3-3564	Nov 67	- + FULL PAPER.	
					Jour SNP 8 371	Apr 69	- + TRANSLATION.	
					Rept INDC-260E	69	- + ENGL OF YFI-6 124.	
	3.6+2	6.7+3			Data EXFOR40113.	Sep 72	N-WIDTH AT 18 RES,TOT-WID,CAPT-WID,D	
Reson Params	7.8+4	5.2+6	KUR	Expt	Jour YF 8 1067	Dec 68	Groshev+ LVL SCHEME DISCUSSED	
					Jour SNP 8 619	Jun 69	TRANSLATN.*	
Reson Params	-		AUA	Theo	Rept AAEC/E-211	Nov 70	Musgrove. CALCULTD D+GAM WIDTH GIVEN	
Reson Params	3.6+2	8.2+2	CJD	Eval	Rept YK-7	71	Zakharova+ SURVEY+SYSTEMATICS,GW,TBL	
					Rept INDC(CCP)-27	Nov 72	.ENGLISH TRANSLATION OF YK-7 /71	
Reson Params	None		DUB	Theo	Jour YF 13 240	Feb 71	Malecki+G-WID,THEO CFD EXPT.TBL,GRPH	
					Jour SNP 13 133	Aug 71	- + ENGL OF YF 13 240.	
Reson Params	3.6+2	3.1+4	SAC	Expt	Rept CEA-N-1459	Aug 71	Tellier.SHAPE-ANALYSIS 69LEVELS	+
					Priv TELLIER	Oct 71	- . VALUES FOR COMPILATION.	
		1.8+4			Conf 71Knoxvill 680	Mar 71	- +.TRANS,AVG D=211EV 44RESON	
	3.6+2	3.1+4			Data EXFOR20121.	Sep 72	117PTS.E0,WG,WT,2G*WN,2G*WN0.	
Reson Params	None		CNE	Expt	Prog INDC(ARG)-3	72	Ricabarra+ G-WID FROM ACT-INTEG,NDG	
Reson Params	None		DUB	Theo	Rept JINR-P4-7499	Oct 73	Soloviev+ CALC D CFD EXPTS,TABLE	
Reson Params	+0	+2	BOL	Eval	Conf IAEA-169 3 123	74	Benzi+ AVG G-WID CFD OTHERS+XPT,TABL	
Reson Params	+2	+4	FEI	Eval	Rept YK-8/2 97	Sep 72	Abagyan+ AVG G-WID+D AT BINDNG-E,TBL	
					Rept INDC(CCP)-39	Jul 74	.PAGE 102.ENGLISH OF YK-8/2 97	
Strnth Fnctn		7.0+3	DUB	Expt	Conf 68DUBSY 349	Jul 68	Pikelner.LVL SPAC,AVERG. WG,S0 VS A	
Strnth Fnctn	3.6+2	6.8+3	DUB	Expt	Jour YF 8 639	Oct 68	Karzhavina+,TRANS+G-YLD EXPT,S-RES	+
					Rept YFI-6 124	68	- + TABLE.	
					Rept JINR-P3-3564	Nov 67	- + FULL PAPER.	
					Jour SNP 8 371	Apr 69	- + TRANSLATION.	
					Rept INDC-260E	69	- + ENGL OF YFI-6 124.	
	0.0+0	4.0+3			Data EXFOR40113.036	Sep 72	STRENGTH-FUNCTION	
Strnth Fnctn	-		AUA	Theo	Rept AAEC/E-211	Nov 70	Musgrove. SMOOTHED S0,S1 AND S2 GIVN	
Strnth Fnctn	2.5+4		AUW	ExTh	Conf 70Madurai 2 25	Dec 70	Thirumala Rao+ S1 GIVEN,CAPTURE-EXPT	+
	2.5+4			Expt	Data EXFOR30247.006	Jun 73	S1-VALUE	
Strnth Fnctn	3.0+2	1.8+4	SAC	Expt	Priv TELLIER	Oct 71	Tellier. VALUES FOR COMPILATION.	+
					Rept CEA-N-1459	Aug 71	- . VERSUS ENERGY	
					Jour CR 272 695	Mar 71	- .LINAC,TOF.44 LEVELS,+D,+A	
					Conf 71Knoxvill 680	Mar 71	- +. S0=2.3+-0.6	
	3.0+2	1.8+4			Data EXFOR20121.033	Sep 72	1PNT.L=0.	
Strnth Fnctn	-2	+3	SAC	Expt	Rept CEA-N-1522	Oct 72	Cauvin+ S0,S1 CALC	
Strnth Fnctn	None		AUA	Eval	Rept AAEC/E-277	Mar 73	Musgrove.TBLS EXPTL DATA+BEST VALUES	
Strnth Fnctn	3.0+3	6.5+5	DKE	Expt	Jour AP 84 165	May 74	Pineo+ S, P, D WAVE	
					Abst DA/B 31 6821	May 71	- .S,P,D WAVE.THESIS ABST	
					Diss PINEO	70	.S0,S1.TBL.GRPHS.CFD CALC,OTH EXPTS.	
Lvl Density	-		FEI	ExTh	Prog YFI-6 18	68	Ignatjuk+ TABLE VARIOUS PARAMETERS	
	None			Theo	Jour SNP 8 660	Jun 69	.TRANSLATN.*	
					Jour YF 8 1135	Dec 68	Ignatjuk+ TBL,A+ENTROPY+TEMP,CFD XPT	
	-			ExTh	Rept INDC-260E	69	. ENGL OF YFI-6 18	
Lvl Density	+6		MIL	Theo	Jour EN 15 1 54	Jan 68	Facchini+ LDL PARS FROM LOW EN RES	
Lvl Density	-		DUB	Expt	Jour YF 8 639	Oct 68	Karzhavina+ VAL+PARS GVN,TBL+GRPH	+
					Jour SNP 8 371	Apr 69	- + TRANSLATION.	
	None				Data EXFOR40113.057	Sep 72	LEVEL-DENSITY PARAMETER	
Lvl Density	None		CCP	Theo	Jour YF 11 1028	May 70	Rubchenya. DENSITY+A+TEMP GIVEN	
					Jour SNP 11 571	Nov 70	. ENGL OF YF 11 571.	
Lvl Density	-		FEI	Theo	Conf 70Helsinki 2 885	Jun 70	Ignatjuk+76. SUPERFLUID CFD FERMI-TH	
Lvl Density	None		AUW	Theo	Conf 70Madurai 2 267	Dec 70	Ramamurty+ A-PARAMETER GVN,LANG'S-TH	
Lvl Density	0.0+0	1.8+4	SAC	Expt	Rept CEA-N-1459	Aug 71	Tellier. FROM STAT RES ANALYSIS.	+
		1.8+4			Jour CR 272 695	Mar 71	- .LINA,TOF D AND A, 44'LVLS	
		1.8+4			Data EXFOR20121.034	Sep 72	1PNT.SP.CUT(0).	
Lvl Density	None		MUN	Theo	Jour NP/A 217 269	Dec 73	Dilg+ A,DELTA. BACK SHIFTED FERMIGAS	
Lvl Density	None		BOL	Eval	Conf IAEA-169 3 123	74	Benzi+ LVL DENS PARAM BY XPT,GRPH+TB	
Lvl Density	None		COP	Theo	Jour NP/A 222 493	Apr 74	Dossing+COLL ROTAT.SPAC. ACCUR ESTIM	
Lvl Density	None		ROC	Theo	Jour NP/A 223 577	May 74	Huizenga+ EXP CFD MICROSC TH SPH NUC	
Lvl Density	+2	+4	FEI	Eval	Rept YK-8/2 97	Sep 72	Abagyan+ LVL DENSITY PARAMETER,TBL	
					Rept INDC(CCP)-39	Jul 74	.PAGE 102.ENGLISH OF YK-8/2 97	
Lvl Density	+0	1.8+4	JAE	ExTh	Jour JPJ 37 581	Sep 74	Ideno.LVL SPACING CORRELATIONS.TBL.	
	1.0+0	1.8+4			Rept JAERI-M-5490	Nov 73	.LEVEL SPACING CORRELATIONS.TBL	
	+0	6.8+3			Jour JPJ 30 620	Mar 71	- + RES SPACING CORRELATION ANAL	
Lvl Density	+0		DUB	Theo	Conf 75Kiev 3 23	May 75	Voronov. LVL SPACING OF ND147.TABLE	
(γ,n)	9.0+6	2.0+7	SAC	Expt	Jour NP/A 172 437	Sep 71	Carlos+LORENTZ LINE PARAM,GRPHS,TBL	

60   Neodymium   147

Quantity	Energy (ev) Min	Max	Lab	Type	Documentation Ref Vol Page	Date	Author, Comments	Data
Evaluation	1.0-3	1.5+7	AUA	Eval	Rept AAEC/TM-549	Jun 70	Cook.TOT,EL,INEL,NONEL,CAPT SIGS,NDG	+
					Rept AAEC/E-214	Jun 71	Bertram+GROUP SIGMAS SAME QUANTS.NDG	
					Rept AAEC/TM-587	Mar 71	*DESCRIPTION OF LIBRARY	
	1.0-3	1.5+7			Data AUSTR-DFN 149.	Nov 71	POINT(223) AND GROUP(127) SIGMAS	
Evaluation	1.0-5	1.5+7	BOL	Eval	Prog NEANDC(E)182 7	Dec 76	Fabri+ COMPLETE EVAL IN ENDF/B DONE	+
	1.0-5	1.5+7			Data CNEN-CEA 3	Jan 78	PRELIM.ALL QUANTITIES.ENDF FORMAT	
Total	1.0-3	1.5+7	AUA	Eval	Data AUSTR-DFN 149.	Nov 71	COOK+POINT(223)+GROUP(127)SIG.CF EVL	+
Elastic	1.0-3	1.5+7	AUA	Eval	Data AUSTR-DFN 149.	Nov 71	COOK+POINT(223)+GROUP(127)SIG.CF EVL	+
Elastic	+1	+6	GEL	Expt	Prog INDC(SEC)-26	May 72	Theobald+ HE3-SCINT,EXPLOSN,PROPOSED	
Tot Inelastc	5.0+5	1.5+7	AUA	Eval	Data AUSTR-DFN 149.	Nov 71	COOK+POINT(11)+GROUP(127)SIG.CF EVL	+
Nonelastic	1.0-3	1.5+7	AUA	Eval	Data AUSTR-DFN 149.	Nov 71	COOK+POINT(223)+GROUP(127)SIG.CF EVL	+
Res Int Abs	None		GA	Eval	Rept GA-12071	Sep 71	Mathews+ RECOMMENDED VALUES	
Res Int Abs	5.0-1		AUA	Eval	Rept AAEC/TM-619	Sep 72	Clayton.CALC FROM SIG LIBRARY,TABLE	
Res Int Abs	5.5-1	+6	SAC	Revw	Conf IAEA-169 1 235	74	Ribon.CAPTURE,STATUS CFD REQUEST,TBL	
Res Int Abs	+0	+5	WIN	Revw	Conf IAEA-169 3 163	74	Pope+ DATA FILE CALCS COMPARED	
(n,γ)	Maxwl		GA	Eval	Rept GA-12071	Sep 71	Mathews+ RECOMMENDED VALUES	
(n,γ)	1.0-3	1.5+7	AUA	Eval	Data AUSTR-DFN 149.	Nov 71	COOK+POINT(223)+GROUP(127)SIG.CF EVL	+
(n,γ)	Pile		CRC	Eval	Rept AECL-3037 1	Jan 72	Walker.SIG ESTIMATED ACCORDING Z,A	
(n,γ)	+1	+6	GEL	Expt	Prog INDC(SEC)-26	May 72	Theobald+ M-R+CERENCOV,BOMB,PROPOSED	
(n,γ)	2.5-2		AUA	Eval	Rept AAEC/TM-619	Sep 72	Clayton.CALC FROM SIG LIBRARY,TABLE	
(n,γ)	Pile	2.5-2	SGA	Eval	Conf 73Paris 1 233	Mar 73	Eder+ ESTIMATED FROM POINT SIG,TABLE	
					Rept SGAE-PH-141	Feb 73	.SAME AS 73PARIS,POINT SIG FROM COOK	
(n,γ)	Pile		GRE	Expt	Jour AKE 24 141	74	Heck+ CAPT GAM EXPT, 440+-150B	+
	2.5-2				Data EXFOR20556.002	Mar 76	1PNT.SIGMA.	
(n,γ)	Fiss		SAC	Revw	Conf IAEA-169 1 235	74	Ribon.STATUS SIG CFD REQUESTS,TABLE	
	2.5-2				Conf IAEA-169 1 235	74	-.STATUS SIG CFD REQUESTS,TABLE	
(n,γ)	Maxwl	Fiss	WIN	Revw	Conf IAEA-169 3 163	74	Pope+ MAXW+FIS-SPEC AVG EVAL DATA	
	Fiss				Conf IAEA-169 3 137	74	Dean. POINT DATA AVG OVER STAND SPEC	
Reson Params	-		AUA	Theo	Rept AAEC/E-211	Nov 70	Musgrove. CALCULTD D+GAM WIDTH GIVEN	
Reson Params	+1	+6	GEL	Expt	Prog INDC(SEC)-26	May 72	Theobald+ FROM CAPT+EL SIG,PROPOSED	
Reson Params	+0	+2	BOL	Eval	Conf IAEA-169 3 123	74	Benzi+ AVG G-WID CFD OTHERS+XPT,TABL	
Strnth Fnctn	-		AUA	Theo	Rept AAEC/E-211	Nov 70	Musgrove. SMOOTHED S0,S1 AND S2 GIVN	
Strnth Fnctn	-2	+3	SAC	Expt	Rept CEA-N-1522	Oct 72	Cauvin+ S0,S1 CALC	
Lvl Density	None		MUN	Theo	Jour NP/A 217 269	Dec 73	Dilg+ A,DELTA. BACK SHIFTED FERMIGAS	
Lvl Density	None		BOL	Eval	Conf IAEA-169 3 123	74	Benzi+ LVL DENS PARAM BY XPT,GRPH+TB	
Lvl Density	None		DUB	Theo	Jour NP/A 224 411	May 74	Soloviev+ 1/2 MICROSC MDL. SPH NUCL.	

60   Neodymium   148

Quantity	Energy (ev) Min	Max	Lab	Type	Documentation Ref Vol Page	Date	Author, Comments	Data
Evaluation	1.0-3	1.5+7	AUA	Eval	Rept AAEC/TM-549	Jun 70	Cook.TOT,EL,INEL,NONEL,CAPT SIGS,NDG	+
					Rept AAEC/E-214	Jun 71	Bertram+GROUP SIGMAS SAME QUANTS.NDG	
					Rept AAEC/TM-587	Mar 71	*DESCRIPTION OF LIBRARY	
	1.0-3	1.5+7			Data AUSTR-DFN 150.	Nov 71	POINT(223) AND GROUP(127) SIGMAS	
Evaluation	1.0-5	1.5+7	BOL	Eval	Prog NEANDC(E)182 7	Dec 76	Fabri+ COMPLETE EVAL IN ENDF/B DONE	+
	1.0-5	1.5+7			Data CNEN-CEA 5	Jan 78	PRELIM.ALL QUANTITIES.ENDF FORMAT	
Total	4.0+1	1.1+4	SAC	Expt	Rept CEA-N-1459	Aug 71	Tellier. ENRICHED TO 89PC.EXPT DETS.	+
					Priv TELLIER	Oct 71	- . DATA FOR COMPILATION.	
					Jour CR 272 695	Mar 71	- . LINAC.TOF.PRELIM ANALYSIS.	
	4.0+1	1.1+4			Data EXFOR20118.007	Sep 72	12077PTS.	
Total	1.0-3	1.5+7	AUA	Eval	Data AUSTR-DFN 150.	Nov 71	COOK+POINT(223)+GROUP(127)SIG.CF EVL	+
Total	1.4+7		LIN	Expt	Conf 73Kiev 3 108	May 73	Djumin+ OPTMOD CALC,SIG	+
					Jour IZV 37 1019	May 73	- + SIG(A),OPTMODEL CALC,GRAPH	
					Jour BAS 37 5 91	May 73	.ENGLISH OF IZV 37 1019	
	1.4+7				Data EXFOR40302.007	Feb 76	1 PNT	
Total	1.0+5	6.5+5	DKE	Expt	Jour AP 84 165	May 74	Pineo+TRNS.AVG CS.TBL GRPHS.OPTMDL	+
					Abst DA/B 31 6821	May 71	- .2E RANGE AVGS.CFD OPTMDL.	
	1.5+4	6.0+5			Diss PINEO	70	.AVG CS.GRPHS.CFD.STF CALC.TBL.CFD.	
	1.5+4	6.0+5			Data EXFOR10542.016	Jan 79	. DATA UNOBTAINABLE FROM AUTHORS.	
Total	7.5+5	1.4+7	BRC	Expt	Abst BAP 20 1196	Sep 75	Shamu+ MEAS TOT CS DIFF WITH 144ND	
Elastic	1.0-3	1.5+7	AUA	Eval	Data AUSTR-DFN 150.	Nov 71	COOK+POINT(223)+GROUP(127)SIG.CF EVL	+
Elastic	2.5-2		IJI	Eval	Rept KIYAI-76-6	76	Fedorova+ ONLY 1LIT-VALUE=RECOMM.TBL	
					Conf 75Kiev 1 169	May 75	- + EVAL 2200M/S SIG,TABLE	
Potntal Scat	3.0+3	6.5+5	DKE	Expt	Jour AP 84 165	May 74	Pineo+TRNS.S WAVE SCT LENGTH.TBL.CFD	
					Abst DA/B 31 6821	May 71	.THESIS ABST.	
					Diss PINEO	70	.TBL.GRPHS.CFD TO 3 COLLECTIVE MDLS.	

60 Neodymium 148

Quantity	Energy (ev) Min	Max	Lab	Type	Documentation Ref Vol Page	Date	Author, Comments	Data
Tot Inelastc	5.0+5	1.5+7	AUA Eval	Data	AUSTR – DFN 150.	Nov 71	COOK+POINT(11)+GROUP(127)SIG.CF EVL	+
Diff Inelast	2.5+6		KTY Expt	Prog	U/KTY – 77 70	77	Coope+STRUCT STUDY USING DIN,DNG.	
Scattering	2.0-2	1.0+1	IJI Expt	Conf	73Kiev 2 104	May 73	Vertebny+ TOF,SIG(NEUT – E),GRAPH	
Nonelastic	1.0-3	1.5+7	AUA Eval	Data	AUSTR – DFN 150.	Nov 71	COOK+POINT(223)+GROUP(127)SIG.CF EVL	+
Absorption	4.1-1	1.0+7	GA Eval	Rept	GA – 2451	Aug 61	Joanou+ 68GROUP DATA FOR GAM – I	
Absorption	1.0-4	1.0+7	JUL Eval	Rept	JUEL – 678 – RG	Jul 70	Liu. EVALUATION+CALC,GRPH,FN OF E	
Absorption	2.5-2		IJI Eval	Rept	KIYAI – 76 – 6	76	Fedorova+ COMP(REFS,SIGS),EVAL.TABLE	
				Conf	75Kiev 1 169	May 75	– + EVAL SIG GIVEN,TABLE	
Res Int Abs	None		GA Eval	Rept	GA – 12071	Sep 71	Mathews+ RECOMMENDED VALUES	
Res Int Abs	5.5-1		CRC Eval	Rept	AECL – 3037 1	Jan 72	Walker.REDUCED RES INT,DETAILED TBL	
Res Int Abs		1.0+6	OSL Expt	Prog	INDC(NOR) – 1 1	May 72	Alstad+ RES CAPT INT REL AU.TBL.ABST	+
	0.0+0	1.0+6		Jour	JIN 29 2155	Sep 67	– + ACTIV REL AU,AND CD RATIO	
		1.0+6		Data	EXFOR20044.009	Sep 71	1PNT.CAPTURE.	
Res Int Abs	5.0-1		AUA Eval	Rept	AAEC/TM – 619	Sep 72	Clayton.CALC FROM SIG LIBRARY,TABLE	
Res Int Abs	5.5-1		CNE Expt	Jour	CJP 51 1454	Jul 73	Ricabarra+ ACTIV,REL THR+GOLD,TABLES	+
	6.0-1			Data	EXFOR30239.	May 73	RES INTEGS + RATIO TO THR – ABS SIGMA	
Res Int Abs	4.6-1	1.0+6	RCN Theo	Rept	RCN – 191	Jul 73	Lautenbach.CAPT INT FROM GROUP SIGMA	
Res Int Abs	5.0-1		GHT Expt	Jour	JRC 20 695	74	Van Der Linden+ BY(N,G).CFD OTHS,TBL	
	5.5-1			Conf	73Paris 2 241	Mar 73	– + ACT,REL THR+GOLD,TBL	
	5.5-1			Data	EXFOR20645.020	Jul 76	1PNT.CAPTURE.	
Res Int Abs	5.5-1	+6	SAC Revw	Conf	IAEA – 169 1 235	74	Ribon.CAPTURE,STATUS CFD REQUEST,TBL	
Res Int Abs	+0	+5	WIN Revw	Conf	IAEA – 169 3 163	74	Pope+ DATA FILE CALC CFD XPTAL VALUE	
Res Int Abs	5.0-1		KJL Expt	Jour	JIN 37 1591	Aug 75	Steinnes. CD – RAT+ACTIV INTEG,CFD,TBL	+
	5.0-1			Data	EXFOR20635.003	Aug 76	1PNT.CAPTURE.	
Res Int Abs	5.0-1		IJI Eval	Rept	KIYAI – 76 – 6	76	Fedorova+ EVAL CFD CALC.TBL RI,REFS	
				Conf	75Kiev 1 169	May 75	– + EVAL+CALC RI GIVEN,TABLE	
Res Int Abs	5.5-1		MUN Expt	Diss	GRYNTAKIS	Mar 72	Gryntakis.ACT 13.77+ – 1.00B, INCL 1/V	
				Jour	RCA 17 191	Mar 72	KIM+ACTIV.EQUIVALENT TO THESIS	
	5.5-1			Data	EXFOR20625.021	Aug 76	1PNT.CAPTURE.	
Res Int Abs	5.0-1		GEV Expt	Abst	ANS 7 270	Nov 64	Ruiz.	+
	5.0-1			Data	EXFOR12049.002	Jun 76	. 1 PT. RIG.	
(n,γ)	Maxwl		OHO Expt	Jour	PR 53 437	Mar 38	Pool+ BETAS CLOUD CH RATIO ND148(NDG	
(n,γ)	Maxwl		ANL Expt	Jour	PR 76 300	Jul 49	Hess+ NAT ND TGT,MASS – SPEC.UPPER LIM	
	Maxwl			Data	EXFOR12067.007	Jun 76	. 1 PT.	
(n,γ)	Maxwl		ORL Expt	Jour	PR 88 412	Oct 52	Pomerance.PILE OSC.	+
	Maxwl			Data	EXFOR11507.082	Jun 76	. 1 PT.	
(n,γ)	Pile		MCM Expt	Jour	PR 90 447	May 53	Walker+NRX,MASS SP,3.7+ – 9B REL ND 48	+
	Pile			Data	EXFOR12059.004	Jun 76	. 1 PT.	
(n,γ)	Fiss		BNL Expt	Jour	PR 91 1423	Sep 53	Hughes+ ALSO LVL SPACINGS AT EXCIT	+
	Fiss			Data	EXFOR11562.014	Jun 76	. 1 PT.	
(n,γ)	+0	1.5+3	HAR Expt	Jour	NP 3 553	Jun 57	Bowey. TOF. CAPT GAM YLD CURVE	
(n,γ)	1.5+5	3.0+6	WIS Expt	Jour	PR 116 927	Nov 59	Johnsrud+ SC CPD OTHERS SIG VS E	+
	1.8+5	2.5+6		Data	EXFOR11675.019	Jun 76	. 14 PTS.	
(n,γ)	Maxwl		CRC Eval	Rept	AECL – 1054	Mar 60	Walker. SAME AS CRRP – 913	
(n,γ)	Maxwl		OSL Expt	Jour	JIN 27 2155	Sep 67	Alstad+ ACTIVATION REL AU,+CD RATIO	+
	Maxwl			Data	EXFOR20044.008	Sep 71	1PNT.SIG.	
(n,γ)	Maxwl		AUA Theo	Jour	NSE 31 234	Feb 68	Cook+ STATISTICAL CALC CFD EXPT	
(n,γ)	–		IEA Comp	Rept	IEA – INF – 10	Aug 68	Atalla. TABLES OF HL,SIG AND GAMM – E	
(n,γ)	2.4+4		MUA Expt	Jour	NC/B 58 402	Dec 68	Hasan+,SB – BE,ACT BETA – DET REL I – 127.	+
	2.4+4			Data	EXFOR30077.017	Dec 70	SIGMA FOR 1.9 H HALF LIFE GIVEN	
(n,γ)	1.0+3	1.0+7	BOL Eval	Rept	CCDN – NW/10	Dec 69	Benzi+H – F MOD,AXEL G(G)EST,ALL DATA	
				Rept	CEC(70) – 2	Apr 70	– +. GRAPH	
				Conf	66Paris 1 537	Oct 66	– + STATMOD.TBL AV VALS.SUPERSEDD	
				Jour	NC 38 216	Jul 65	– + THEORY FOR CAPTURE EVALUATION	
(n,γ)	3.0+4		AUA Theo	Rept	AAEC/E – 211	Nov 70	Musgrove. SIGMA GIVEN AND CFD OTHER	
(n,γ)	Maxwl		GA Eval	Rept	GA – 12071	Sep 71	Mathews+ RECOMMENDED VALUES	
(n,γ)	1.0-3	1.5+7	AUA Eval	Data	AUSTR – DFN 150.	Nov 71	COOK+POINT(223)+GROUP(127)SIG.CF EVL	
(n,γ)	Maxwl		CRC Eval	Rept	AECL – 3037 1	Jan 72	Walker.RECOMMENDED SIG,DETAILED TBL	
(n,γ)	2.5+4		AUW Expt	Jour	JP/A 5 468	Mar 72	Thirumala+ ACT METHOD, RELATIVE TO I	+
				ExTh	70Madurai 2 25	Dec 70	Thirumala Rao+ SIGMAS FOR S+P WAVES	
	2.5+4			Expt Data	EXFOR30247.003	Jun 73	CAPTURE CROSS SECTION	
(n,γ)	2.5-2		AUA Eval	Rept	AAEC/TM – 619	Sep 72	Clayton.CALC FROM SIG LIBRARY,TABLE	
(n,γ)	Fast		INL Expt	Conf	72Kiamesha 2 614	Sep 72	Harker+ CFRMF INTEGRAL MEAS.	
(n,γ)		1.1+7	RCN Theo	Rept	RCN – 191	Jun 73	Lautenbach. GROUP CONSTANTS TBL	
(n,γ)	2.5+4		AUW Expt	Jour	NC/A 18 48	Nov 73	Sidappa+ ACTIV SIG,CFD.TABLE	
(n,γ)	2.5-2		SAC Revw	Conf	IAEA – 169 1 235	74	Ribon.STATUS SIG CFD REQUESTS,TABLE	
(n,γ)	Maxwl Fiss		WIN Revw	Conf	IAEA – 169 3 163	74	Pope+ MAXW+FIS – SPEC AVG EVAL DATA	
	Fiss			Conf	IAEA – 169 3 137	74	Dean. POINT DATA AVG OVER STAND SPEC	

60 Neodymium 148

Quantity	Energy (ev) Min	Max	Lab	Type	Documentation Ref Vol Page	Date	Author, Comments	Data
(n,γ)	1.0+3	1.0+7	FEI	Eval	Rept YK- 8/2 97	Sep 72	Abagjan+ AVG SIG(ENERGY-GROUPS),TABL	
					Rept INDC(CCP)-39	Jul 74	.P102. ENGLISH OF YK-8/2 97	
(n,γ)	Maxwl		MUN	Expt	Diss GRYNTAKIS	Mar 76	Gryntakis.,ACT.,2.45+ -0.14 B,REL. AU	+
					Jour RCA 17 191	Mar 72	KIM+,EQUIVALENT TO THESIS	
	2.5-2				Data EXFOR20625.020	Aug 76	1PNT.SIGMA.	
(n,γ)	Maxwl		GEV	Expt	Abst ANS 7 270	Nov 64	Ruiz.	+
	Maxwl				Data EXFOR12049.002	Jun 76	. 1 PT.	
(n,γ)	Fast		RCN	Expt	Rept ECN-10	Oct 76	Veenema+ STEK REACTIVITY WORTHS TBL.	
Spect (n,γ)	Maxwl		ILL	Expt	Jour NP/A 264 1	Jun 76	Pinston+ GELI.G E+INTS.G-G,SPIN+PIS	+
	2.5-2				Conf 76Lowell 1300	Jul 76	- +LVL SCHEMES DEDUCED.NDG	
	Maxwl				Conf 74Petten 691	Sep 74	Borner+ BENT XTL+GELI,GRAPH ONLY	
	Maxwl				Data EXFOR20590.002	Aug 76	308PTS. GAMMA ENERGIES,INTENSITIES	
(n,2n)	Fast		OHO	Expt	Jour PR 53 437	Mar 38	Pool+ BETAS,CLOUDCH,RATIO ND150(N2N)	
(n,2n)	1.5+7		ARK	Expt	Jour PR 118 242	Apr 60	Wille+ MEAS ACT SIG=2160+ -200MB	+
	1.5+7				Data EXFOR12033.025	Jun 76	. 1 PT.	
(n,2n)	Fiss		CRC	Eval	Rept CRC-1003	Dec 60	ROY+ ESTIMATED AVG SIG=35.0MB	
(n,2n)	1.4+7		HAM	Comp	Jour NP 65 257	Mar 65	Bormann. 1EXPT VALS.CFD SHELL EFFECT	
(n,2n)	1.4+7		LYO	Comp	Rept LYCEN/6780	Nov 67	Crouzet+COMPILATN FOR ACTIVTN ANALYS	
(n,2n)	1.4+7		AUW	Expt	Jour NP/A 125 57	Feb 69	RAMA PRASAD+,ACTIVATION,CFD OTHERS	+
				ExTh	Jour IPA 12 640	Sep 74	Rama Prasad+ CFD STATMDL COMPND VALU	
	1.4+7			Expt	Data EXFOR30051.	Dec 70	SIGMA N2N,ALSO N2N+NA+NP FOR OTHERS.	
(n,2n)	1.5+7		DEB	Comp	Jour REA 7 4 93	Dec 69	Csikai+ SIG+HL COMPILTN,N-ACTIV-ANAL	
(n,2n)	1.4+7	1.5+7	JYV	Eval	Rept JU-RR-3/1970	Jun 70	Leppaemaeki+ TABLE OF EVAL AVG SIG	
(n,2n)	+7		KFI	Theo	Rept KFKI-71-8	Feb 71	Jeki. CALCULATED CFD EXPTL SIG VALUE	
(n,2n)	1.5+7		ARK	Expt	Abst DA/B 32 5091	Mar 72	Bari. GE(LI) DET. ACT. SIG GIVEN	+
	1.5+7				Data EXFOR10431.049	Aug 75	. 1 PT. SIGMA	
(n,2n)	1.5+7		DEB	Eval	Jour REA 11 1 153	Mar 73	Boedy. COMPILATION+RECOMM.VALUE,TBL	
					Rept IAEA-153 173	73	- . RECOMM. VALUE ONLY	
(n,2n)	1.5+7		TAT	Theo	Jour JP/A 7 1457	Aug 74	Kondaiah. CALC ON STAT MODEL	
(n,2n)	1.5+7		JUL	Expt	Jour NP/A 224 319	May 74	Qaim. ACT.GE(LI)	+
					Jour RRL 25 335	May 76	- + SIG IN GRPH. SYST VS (N-Z)/A	
	1.5+7				Data EXFOR20541.016	Apr 76	1PNT.SIGMA.	
(n,xn) x>2	1.4+7		BRC	ExTh	Prog CEA-N-1875 60	Apr 76	Frehaut+N3N.SYSTEMATIC LAWS SEARCH	
	1.4+7	1.5+7		Expt	Conf 75Gothenbg	Jun 75	- +	
	1.4+7	1.5+7			Data EXFOR20571.013	Mar 76	3PTS.N3N.	
(n,xn) x>2	1.5+7		ARK	Expt	Prog A-ARK-61 7	Feb 61	Poularikas+ N3N	+
	1.5+7				Data EXFOR11790.003	Jun 76	. 1 PT. N3N	
(n,p)	1.5+7		ARK	Expt	Jour PR 118 242	Apr 60	Wille+ MEAS ACT SIG= 3.5+ - .8 MB	+
	1.5+7				Data EXFOR12033.024	Jun 76	. 1 PT.	
(n,p)	Fiss		CRC	Eval	Rept CRC-1003	Dec 60	ROY+ ESTIMATED AVG SIG=0.002MB	
(n,p)	1.5+7		SAH	Comp	Jour NUC 23 8 112	Aug 65	Chatterjee. TABLE WITH REFS.	
(n,p)	1.4+7		LYO	Comp	Rept LYCEN/6780	Nov 67	Crouzet+COMPILATN FOR ACTIVTN ANALYS	
(n,p)	1.5+7		DEB	Comp	Jour REA 7 4 93	Dec 69	Csikai+ SIG+HL COMPILTN,N-ACTIV-ANAL	
(n,p)	1.4+7	1.5+7	JYV	Eval	Rept JU-RR-3/1970	Jun 70	Leppaemaeki+ TABLE OF EVAL AVG SIG	
(n,p)	1.4+7	1.5+7	KAZ	Theo	Jour YF 18 705	Oct 73	Levkovsky.AVERAGED SIG,CALC,TBL	
					Jour SNP 18 361	Apr 74	. ENGLISH OF YF 18,705	
(n,α)	1.5+7		ARK	Expt	Jour PR 118 242	Apr 60	Wille+ MEAS ACT SIG= 5. +-1. MB	+
	1.5+7				Data EXFOR12033.023	Jun 76	. 1 PT.	
(n,α)	Fiss		CRC	Eval	Rept CRC-1003	Dec 60	ROY+ ESTIMATED AVG SIG=0.001MB	
(n,α)	1.4+7		CIS	Theo	Jour NP 51 460	Feb 64	Facchini+STATMOD SIG XPT/CALC=4-6	
(n,α)	1.4+7		LYO	Comp	Rept LYCEN/6780	Nov 67	Crouzet+COMPILATN FOR ACTIVTN ANALYS	
(n,α)	1.5+7		DEB	Comp	Jour REA 7 4 93	Dec 69	Csikai+ SIG+HL COMPILTN,N-ACTIV-ANAL	
(n,α)	1.4+7	1.5+7	JYV	Eval	Rept JU-RR-3/1970	Jun 70	Leppaemaeki+ TABLE OF EVAL AVG SIG	
Reson Params	1.6+2	2.9+2	HAR	Expt	Jour NP 3 553	Jun 57	Bowey.TOF.2ES FROM CAPT GAMMA YIELDS	
Reson Params	+0	+3	COL	Expt	Rept NYO-GEN72-132	Jan 67	Garg P.1,BAP10 575 +NEW RUN,BUT NDG	
Reson Params		1.0+6	AUA	Theo	Jour AUJ 20 477	Oct 67	Cook. TBL OF AVG LVL SPACING D,L=0,1	
Reson Params	9.0+3		DUB	Expt	Conf 68DUBSY 349	Jul 68	Pikelner.LVL SPAC,AVERG. WG	
Reson Params	1.5+2	8.8+3	DUB	Expt	Jour YF 8 639	Oct 68	Karzhavina+,29RES,WN,WG,TABLES	+
					Rept YFI-6 124	68	- + TABLE.	
					Rept JINR-P3-3564	Nov 67	- + FULL PAPER.	
					Jour SNP 8 371	Apr 69	- + TRANSLATION.	
					Rept INDC-260E	69	- + ENGL OF YFI-6 124.	
	1.6+2	8.8+3			Data EXFOR40113.	Sep 72	N-WIDTH AT 29RES, CAPT-WIDTH, D	
Reson Params	2.4+4		MUA	ExTh	Jour NC/B 58 402	Dec 68	Hasan+ AVERAGE LEVEL SPACING D GIVEN	+
	2.4+4			Expt	Data EXFOR30091.012	Dec 70	ESTIMATED AVERAGE LEVEL SPACING D	
Reson Params	1.5+2	2.8+2	GEL	Expt	Jour JNE 23 369	Jul 69	Migneco+ TOF.WG,WN.AREA ANAL.	
Reson Params	1.6+2	7.1+2	SAC	Expt	Jour NP/A 134 118	Sep 69	Alves+LINAC TOF.WN,WN0,J 3E0,2WT.	+
	1.6+2	7.1+2			Data EXFOR20688.030	Jun 77	3PTS.E0,WN,WT,G*WN.	

60 Neodymium 148

Quantity	Energy (ev) Min	Max	Lab	Type	Documentation Ref Vol Page	Date	Author, Comments	Data
Reson Params	–		AUA	Theo	Rept AAEC/E-211	Nov 70	Musgrove. CALCULTD D+GAM WIDTH GIVEN	
Reson Params	1.5+2	1.2+3	CJD	Eval	Rept YK-7	71	Zakharova+ SURVEY+SYSTEMATICS,GW,TBL	
					Rept INDC(CCP)-27	Nov 72	.ENGLISH TRANSLATION OF YK-7 /71	
Reson Params	None		DUB	Theo	Jour YF 13 240	Feb 71	Malecki+G-WID,THEO CFD EXPT.TBL,GRPH	
					Jour SNP 13 133	Aug 71	- + ENGL OF YF 13 240.	
Reson Params	9.0+1	3.0+4	SAC	Expt	Rept CEA-N-1459	Aug 71	Tellier.SHAPE ANALYSIS 102LEVELS	+
	9.5+1	2.3+4			Conf 71Knoxvill 680	Mar 71	- +TRANS,AVG D=72EV 67RESON	
					Priv TELLIER	Oct 71	- . VALUES FOR COMPILATION.	
	9.5+1	2.3+4			Data EXFOR20121.	Sep 72	181PTS.E0,WG,WT,2G*WN,2G*WN0.	
Reson Params	None		CNE	Expt	Prog INDC(ARG)-3	72	Ricabarra+ G-WID FROM ACT-INTEG,NDG	
Reson Params	None		DUB	Expt	Rept JINR-P4-7499	Oct 73	Soloviev+ CALC D CFD EXPTS,TABLE	
Reson Params	+0	+2	BOL	Eval	Conf IAEA-169 3 123	74	Benzi+ AVG G-WID CFD OTHERS+XPT,TABL	
Reson Params	+1	+4	FEI	Eval	Rept YK-8/2 97	Sep 72	Abagyan+ AVG G-WID+D AT BINDNG-E,TBL	
					Rept INDC(CCP)-39	Jul 74	.PAGE 102.ENGLISH OF YK-8/2 97	
Strnth Fnctn		9.0+3	DUB	Expt	Conf 68DUBSY 349	Jul 68	Pikelner.LVL SPAC,AVERG. WG,S0 VS A	
Strnth Fnctn	1.5+2	8.8+3	DUB	Expt	Jour YF 8 639	Oct 68	Karzhavina+,TRANS+G-YLD EXPT,S-RES	+
					Jour SNP 8 371	Apr 69	SEE ALSO *	
					Rept YFI-6 124	68	Karzhavina+ TABLE.	
					Jour SNP 8 371	Apr 69	- + TRANSLATION.	
					Rept INDC-260E	69	- + ENGL OF YFI-6 124.	
	0.0+0	4.5+3			Data EXFOR40113.043	Sep 72	STRENGTH-FUNCTION	
Strnth Fnctn			AUA	Theo	Rept AAEC/E-211	Nov 70	Musgrove. SMOOTHED S0,S1 AND S2 GIVN	
	2.5+4		AUW	ExTh	Conf 70Madurai 2 25	Dec 70	Thirumala Rao+ S1 GIVEN,CAPTURE-EXPT	+
	2.5+4			Expt	Data EXFOR30247.007	Jun 73	S1-VALUE	
Strnth Fnctn	-2	+3	SAC	Expt	Rept CEA-N-1522	Oct 72	Cauvin+ S0,S1 CALC	+
	9.0+1	1.2+4			Priv TELLIER	Oct 71	Tellier. VALUES FOR COMPILATION.	
	9.0+1	3.0+4			Rept CEA-N-1459	Aug 71	- . VERSUS ENERGY	
	9.0+1	1.2+4			Jour CR 272 695	Mar 71	- .LINAC,TOF 67LEVELS,+D,+A	
					Conf 71Knoxvill 680	Mar 71	- +.S0=3.0+ - 0.6	
	9.0+1	1.2+4			Data EXFOR20121.040	Sep 72	1PNT.L=0.	
Strnth Fnctn	None		AUA	Eval	Rept AAEC/E-277	Mar 73	Musgrove.TBLS EXPTL DATA+BEST VALUES	
Strnth Fnctn	3.0+3	6.5+5	DKE	Expt	Jour AP 84 165	May 74	Pineo+ S, P, D WAVE	
					Abst DA/B 31 6821	May 71	- .S,P,D WAVE.THESIS ABST	
Lvl Density	–		DUB	Theo	Jour YF 8 639	Oct 68	Karzhavina+ VAL+PARS GVN,TBL+GRPH	+
					Jour SNP 8 371	Apr 69	- + TRANSLATION.	
	None				Data EXFOR40113.058	Sep 72	LEVEL-DENSITY PARAMETER	
Lvl Density	0.0+0	1.2+4	SAC	Expt	Rept CEA-N-1459	Aug 71	Tellier. FROM STAT RES ANALYSIS.	+
		1.2+4			Jour CR 272 695	Mar 71	- .LINAC,TOF.D AND A, 67 LVLS	
		1.2+4			Data EXFOR20121.041	Sep 72	1PNT.SP.CUT(0).	
Lvl Density	0.0+0	1.0+4	ITE	Theo	Conf 72Budapest 268	Aug 72	Belyaev+ GROUPINGS OF LVL SPACNG,TBL	
Lvl Density	1.0+0	1.0+4	JAE	ExTh	Rept JAERI-M-5490	Nov 73	Ideno.LEVEL SPACING CORRELATIONS.TBL	
Lvl Density	None		BOL	Eval	Conf IAEA-169 3 123	74	Benzi+ LVL DENS PARAM BY XPT,GRPH+TB	
Lvl Density	+1	+4	FEI	Eval	Rept YK-8/2 97	Sep 72	Abagyan+ LVL DENSITY PARAMETER,TBL	
					Rept INDC(CCP)-39	Jul 74	.PAGE 102.ENGLISH OF YK-8/2 97	
(γ,n)	8.0+6	2.2+7	CCP	Expt	Jour YF 10 460	Sep 69	Vasil'Ev+ SIG(GAM-E) GRAPH GIVEN	
					Jour SNP 10 263	Mar 70	. ENGL TRANSL OF YF 10 460	
(γ,n)	9.0+6	2.0+7	SAC	Expt	Jour NP/A 172 437	Sep 71	Carlos+LORENTZ LINE PARAM,GRPHS,TBL	

60 Neodymium 149

Quantity	Energy (ev) Min	Max	Lab	Type	Documentation Ref Vol Page	Date	Author, Comments	Data
Reson Params	–		AUA	Theo	Rept AAEC/E-211	Nov 70	Musgrove. CALCULTD D+GAM WIDTH GIVEN	
Strnth Fnctn	–		AUA	Theo	Rept AAEC/E-211	Nov 70	Musgrove. SMOOTHED S0,S1 AND S2 GIVN	
Strnth Fnctn	-2	+3	SAC	Expt	Rept CEA-N-1522	Oct 72	Cauvin+ S0,S1 CALC	
Lvl Density	None		DUB	Theo	Jour NP/A 224 411	May 74	Soloviev+ 1/2 MICROSC MDL. SPH NUCL.	

60 Neodymium 150

Quantity	Energy (ev) Min	Max	Lab	Type	Documentation Ref Vol Page	Date	Author, Comments	Data
Evaluation	1.0-3	1.5+7	AUA	Eval	Rept AAEC/TM-549	Jun 70	Cook.TOT,EL,INEL,NONEL,CAPT SIGS,NDG	+
					Rept AAEC/E-214	Jun 71	Bertram+GROUP SIGMAS SAME QUANTS.NDG	
					Rept AAEC/TM-587	Mar 71	*DESCRIPTION OF LIBRARY	
	1.0-3	1.5+7			Data AUSTR-DFN 151.	Nov 71	POINT(223) AND GROUP(127) SIGMAS	
Evaluation	1.0-5	1.5+7	BOL	Eval	Prog NEANDC(E)182 7	Dec 76	Fabri+ COMPLETE EVAL IN ENDF/B DONE	+
	1.0-5	1.5+7			Data CNEN-CEA 5	Jan 78	PRELIM.ALL QUANTITIES.ENDF FORMAT	

60 Neodymium 150

Quantity	Energy (ev) Min	Max	Lab	Type	Documentation Ref Vol Page	Date	Author, Comments	Data
Total	1.8+1	1.4+4	SAC Expt	Rept	CEA – N – 1459	Aug 71	Tellier. ENRICHED TO 88PC.EXPT DETS.	+
				Priv	TELLIER	Oct 71	– . DATA FOR COMPILATION.	
				Jour	CR 272 695	Mar 71	– . LINAC.TOF.PRELIM ANALYSIS.	
	1.8+1	1.4+4		Data	EXFOR20118.008	Sep 72	15109PTS.	
Total	1.0 – 3	1.5+7	AUA Eval	Data	AUSTR – DFN 151.	Nov 71	COOK+POINT(223)+GROUP(127)SIG.CF EVL	+
Total	1.4+7		LIN Expt	Conf	73Kiev 3 108	May 73	Djumin+ OPTMOD CALC,SIG	+
				Jour	IZV 37 1019	May 73	– + SIG(A),OPTMODEL CALC,GRAPH	
				Jour	BAS 37 5 91	May 73	.ENGLISH OF IZV 37 1019	
	1.4+7			Data	EXFOR40302.008	Feb 76	1 PNT	
Total	7.5+5	1.4+7	BRC Expt	Abst	BAP 20 1196	Sep 75	Shamu+ MEAS TOT CS DIFF WITH 144ND	
Elastic	1.0 – 3	1.5+7	AUA Eval	Data	AUSTR – DFN 151.	Nov 71	COOK+POINT(223)+GROUP(127)SIG.CF EVL	+
Elastic	2.5 – 2		IJI Eval	Rept	KIYAI – 76 – 6	76	Fedorova+ ONLY 1LIT – VALUE = RECOMM.TBL	
				Conf	75Kiev 1 169	May 75	– + EVAL 2200M/S SIG,TABLE	
Tot Inelastc	5.0+5	1.5+7	AUA Eval	Data	AUSTR – DFN 151.	Nov 71	COOK+POINT(11)+GROUP(127)SIG.CF EVL	+
Diff Inelast	2.5+6		KTY Expt	Prog	U/KTY – 77 70	77	Coope+STRUCT STUDY USING DIN,DNG	
Scattering	2.0 – 2	1.0+1	IJI Expt	Conf	73Kiev 2 104	May 73	Vertebny+ TOF,SIG(NEUT – E),GRAPH	
Nonelastic	1.0 – 3	1.5+7	AUA Eval	Data	AUSTR – DFN 151.	Nov 71	COOK+POINT(223)+GROUP(127)SIG.CF EVL	+
Absorption	4.1 – 1	1.0+7	GA Eval	Rept	GA – 2451	Aug 61	Joanou+ 68GROUP DATA FOR GAM – I	
Absorption	1.0 – 4	1.0+7	JUL Eval	Rept	JUEL – 678 – RG	Jul 70	Liu. EVALUATION+CALC,GRPH,FN OF E	
Absorption	2.5 – 2		IJI Eval	Rept	KIYAI – 76 – 6	76	Fedorova+ COMP(REFS,SIGS),EVAL.TABLE	
				Conf	75Kiev 1 169	May 75	– + EVAL SIG GIVEN,TABLE	
Res Int Abs	0.0+0	1.0+6	OSL Expt	Jour	JIN 29 2155	Sep 67	Alstad+ ACTIV REL AU,AND CD RATIO	+
		1.0+6		Data	EXFOR20044.011	Sep 71	1PNT.CAPTURE.	
Res Int Abs	None		GA Eval	Rept	GA – 12071	Sep 71	Mathews+ RECOMMENDED VALUES	
Res Int Abs	5.5 – 1		CRC Eval	Rept	AECL – 3037 1	Jan 72	Walker.REDUCED RES INT,DETAILED TBL	
Res Int Abs	5.0 – 1		AUA Eval	Rept	AAEC/TM – 619	Sep 72	Clayton.CALC FROM SIG LIBRARY,TABLE	
Res Int Abs	5.5 – 1		CNE Expt	Jour	CJP 51 1454	Jul 73	Ricabarra+ ACTIV,REL THR+GOLD,TABLES	+
	6.0 – 1			Data	EXFOR30239.	May 73	RES INTEGS + RATIO TO THR – ABS SIGMA	
Res Int Abs	4.6 – 1	1.0+6	RCN Theo	Rept	RCN – 191	Jul 73	Lautenbach.CAPT INT FROM GROUP SIGMA	
Res Int Abs	5.0 – 1		GHT Expt	Jour	JRC 20 695	74	Van Der Linden+ BY(N,G).CFD OTHS,TBL	+
	5.5 – 1			Conf	73Paris 2 241	Mar 73	– + ACT,REL THR+GOLD,TBL	
	5.5 – 1			Data	EXFOR20645.021	Jul 76	1PNT.CAPTURE.	
Res Int Abs	5.5 – 1	+6	SAC Revw	Conf	IAEA – 169 1 235	74	Ribon.CAPTURE,STATUS CFD REQUEST,TBL	
Res Int Abs	+0	+5	WIN Revw	Conf	IAEA – 169 3 163	74	Pope+ DATA FILE CALC CFD XPTAL VALUE	
Res Int Abs	5.0 – 1		KJL Expt	Jour	JIN 37 1591	Aug 75	Steinnes. CD – RAT+ACTIV INTEG,CFD,TBL	+
	5.0 – 1			Data	EXFOR20635.004	Aug 76	1PNT.CAPTURE.	
Res Int Abs	5.0 – 1		IJI Eval	Rept	KIYAI – 76 – 6	76	Fedorova+ COMP(REFS,RI),EVAL.TABLE	
				Conf	75Kiev 1 169	May 75	– + EVAL+CALC RI GIVEN,TABLE	
Res Int Abs	5.5 – 1		MUNExpt	Diss	GRYNTAKIS	Mar 76	Gryntakis.ACT 16.48+ – 0.67B, INCL 1/V	
				Jour	RCA 17 191	Mar 72	KIM+ACTIV.EQUIVALENT TO THESIS	
	5.5 – 1			Data	EXFOR20625.023	Aug 76	2PTS.CAPTURE.	
(n,γ)	Maxwl		OHOExpt	Jour	PR 53 437	Mar 38	Pool+ BETAS,CLOUD CH,RATIO ND148(NG)	
(n,γ)	Maxwl		ANL Expt	Jour	PR 76 300	Jul 49	Hess+ NAT ND TGT,MASS – SPEC.UPPER LIM	+
	Maxwl			Data	EXFOR12067.008	Jun 76	. 1 PT.	
(n,γ)	Maxwl		ORL Expt	Jour	PR 88 412	Oct 52	Pomerance.PILE OSC.	
	Maxwl			Data	EXFOR11507.083	Jun 76	. 1 PT.	
(n,γ)	Pile		MCMExpt	Jour	PR 90 447	May 53	Walker+NRX,MASS SP,0+12B REL ND 48B	+
	Pile			Data	EXFOR12059.008	Jun 76	. 1 PT.	
(n,γ)	+0	1.5+3	HAR Expt	Jour	NP 3 553	Jun 57	Bowey. TOF. CAPT GAM YLD CURVE	
(n,γ)	Maxwl		MUAExpt	Jour	NP 12 261	Jul 59	Sehgal+1.5+ – 0.2B	+
	Maxwl			Data	EXFOR31244.010	Jun 78	1 PNT	
	Maxwl			Data	EXFOR31244.010	Dec 70	SIG FOR 12MIN HALF – LIFE	
(n,γ)	1.5+5	3.0+6	WIS Expt	Jour	PR 116 927	Nov 59	Johnsrud+ SC CFD OTHERS SIG VS E	+
	1.8+5	2.5+6		Data	EXFOR11675.020	Jun 76	. 1 PT.	
(n,γ)	Maxwl		CRC Eval	Rept	AECL – 1054	Mar 60	Walker. SAME AS CRRP – 913	
(n,γ)	Maxwl		OSL Expt	Jour	JIN 27 2155	Sep 67	Alstad+ ACTIVATION REL AU,+CD RATIO	+
	Maxwl			Data	EXFOR20044.010	Sep 71	1PNT.SIG.	
(n,γ)	1.4+7		LYO Comp	Rept	LYCEN/6780	Nov 67	Crouzet+COMPILATN FOR ACTIVTN ANALYS	
(n,γ)	Maxwl		AUA Theo	Jour	NSE 31 234	Feb 68	Cook+ STATISTICAL CALC CFD EXPT	
(n,γ)	–		IEA Comp	Rept	IEA – INF – 10	Aug 68	Atalla. TABLES OF HL,SIG AND GAMM – E	
(n,γ)	2.4+4		MUAExpt	Jour	NC/B 58 402	Dec 68	Hasan+,SB – BE,ACT BETA – DET REL I – 127.	+
	2.4+4			Data	EXFOR30077.018	Dec 70	SIGMA FOR 12MIN HALF – LIFE GIVEN	
(n,γ)	1.0+3	1.0+7	BOL Eval	Rept	CCDN – NW/10	Dec 69	Benzi+H – F MOD,AXEL G(G)EST,ALL DATA	
				Rept	CEC(70) – 2	Apr 70	– +. GRAPH	
				Conf	66Paris 1 537	Oct 66	– + STATMOD.TBL AV VALS.SUPERSEDD	
(n,γ)	3.0+4		AUA Theo	Rept	AAEC/E – 211	Nov 70	Musgrove. SIGMA GIVEN AND CFD OTHER	
(n,γ)	Maxwl		GA Eval	Rept	GA – 12071	Sep 71	Mathews+ RECOMMENDED VALUES	
(n,γ)	1.0 – 3	1.5+7	AUA Eval	Data	AUSTR – DFN 151.	Nov 71	COOK+POINT(223)+GROUP(127)SIG.CF EVL	+

60 Neodymium 150

Quantity	Energy (ev) Min	Max	Lab	Type	Documentation Ref Vol Page	Date	Author, Comments	Data
(n,γ)	Maxwl		CRC	Eval	Rept AECL-3037 1	Jan 72	Walker.RECOMMENDED SIG,DETAILED TBL	
(n,γ)	2.5+4		AUW	Expt	Jour JP/A 5 468	Mar 72	Thirumala+ ACT METHOD, RELATIVE TO I	+
				ExTh	Conf 70Madurai 2 25	Dec 70	Thirumala Rao+ SIGMAS FOR S+P WAVES	
	2.5+4			Expt	Data EXFOR30247.004	Jun 73	CAPTURE CROSS SECTION	
(n,γ)	2.5-2		AUA	Eval	Rept AAEC/TM-619	Sep 72	Clayton.CALC FROM SIG LIBRARY,TABLE	
(n,γ)	Fast		INL	Expt	Conf 72Kiamesha 2 614	Sep 72	Harker+ CFRMF INTEGRAL MEAS.	
(n,γ)		1.1+7	RCN	Theo	Rept RCN-191	Jun 73	Lautenbach. GROUP CONSTANTS TBL	
(n,γ)	2.5-2		SAC	Revw	Conf IAEA-169 1 235	74	Ribon.STATUS SIG CFD REQUESTS,TABLE	
(n,γ)	Maxwl	Fiss	WIN	Revw	Conf IAEA-169 3 163	74	Pope+ MAXW+FIS-SPEC AVG EVAL DATA	
	Fiss				Conf IAEA-169 3 137	74	Dean. POINT DATA AVG OVER STAND SPEC	
(n,γ)	1.0+3	1.0+7	FEI	Eval	Rept YK-8/2 97	Sep 72	Abagjan+ AVG SIG(ENERGY-GROUPS),TABL	
					Rept INDC(CCP)-39	Jul 74	.P102. ENGLISH OF YK-8/2 97	
(n,γ)	Maxwl		MUN	Expt	Diss GRYNTAKIS	Mar 76	Gryntakis.,ACT.,1.17+-0.07 B,REL. AU	+
					Jour RCA 17 191	Mar 72	KIM+,EQUIVALENT TO THESIS	
	2.5-2				Data EXFOR20625.022	Aug 76	2PTS.SIGMA.	
(n,γ)	Fast		RCN	Expt	Rept ECN-10	Oct 76	Veenema+ STEK REACTIVITY WORTHS TBL.	
Spect (n,γ)	Pile		AE	Expt	Jour AF 35 237	Mar 68	Malmskog+. DECAY SPECTRUM OF PM-151	
Spect (n,γ)	Maxwl		FTI	Expt	Conf 68Debrecen 3 458	Jul 68	Voinova+ GAM-SPEC,151PM INT-CONVERSN	
Spect (n,γ)	Maxwl		FTI	Expt	Jour IZV 33 626	Apr 69	Voinova+ ND151,G+CONV EL,GRAPHS+TBL	
					Jour BAS 33 576	70	TRANSLATN.*NO 4	
Spect (n,γ)	Maxwl		LAS	Expt	Prog USNDC-3 121	Oct 72	Smith+ ND151 LEVELS GIVEN	
Spect (n,γ)	Maxwl		ILL	Expt	Jour NP/A 270 61	Oct 76	Pinston+GELI+BETA DET.LVLS IN ND-151	
	2.5-2				Conf 76Lowell 1300	Jul 76	- +LVL SCHEMES DEDUCED.NDG	
(n,2n)	Fast		OHO	Expt	Jour PR 53 437	Mar 38	Pool+ BETAS CLOUD CH RATIO ND148(NDG	
(n,2n)	1.5+7		ARK	Expt	Jour PR 118 242	Apr 60	Wille+ MEAS ACT SIG=2200+-300MB	+
	1.5+7				Data EXFOR12033.026	Jun 76	. 1 PT.	
(n,2n)	Fiss		CRC	Eval	Rept CRC-1003	Dec 60	ROY+ ESTIMATED AVG SIG=10.0MB	
(n,2n)	1.4+7		HAM	Comp	Jour NP 65 257	Mar 65	Bormann. 1EXPT VALS.CFD SHELL EFFECT	
(n,2n)	1.5+7		TAM	Expt	Jour PR 156 1340	Apr 67	Menon+ ACT = 1728MB,	+
	1.5+7				Data EXFOR12066.007	Jun 76	. 1 PT.	
(n,2n)	1.4+7		LYO	Comp	Rept LYCEN/6780	Nov 67	Crouzet+COMPILATN FOR ACTIVTN ANALYS	
(n,2n)	1.5+7		DEB	Comp	Jour REA 7 4 93	Dec 69	Csikai+ SIG+HL COMPILTN,N-ACTIV-ANAL	
(n,2n)	1.4+7	1.5+7	JYV	Expt	Jour JU-RR-3/1970	Jun 70	Leppaemaeki+ TABLE OF EVAL AVG SIG	
(n,2n)	+7		KFI	Theo	Rept KFKI-71-8	Feb 71	Jeki. CALCULATED CFD EXPTL SIG VALUE	
(n,2n)	1.5+7		ARK	Expt	Abst DA/B 32 5091	Mar 72	Bari. GE(LI) DET. ACT. SIG GIVEN	+
	1.5+7				Data EXFOR10431.050	Aug 75	. 1 PT. SIGMA	
(n,2n)	1.5+7		DEB	Eval	Jour REA 11 1 153	Mar 73	Boedy. COMPILATION+RECOMM.VALUE,TBL	
					Rept IAEA-153 173	73	- . RECOMM. VALUE ONLY	
(n,2n)	1.5+7		TAT	Theo	Jour JP/A 7 1457	Aug 74	Kondaiah. CALC ON STAT MODEL	
(n,2n)	1.5+7		JUL	Expt	Jour NP/A 224 319	May 74	Qaim. ACT.GE(LI)	+
					Jour RRL 25 335	May 76	- + SIG IN GRPH. SYST VS (N-Z)/A	
	1.5+7				Data EXFOR20541.017	Apr 76	1PNT.SIGMA.	
(n,xn) x>2	1.4+7		BRC	ExTh	Prog CEA-N-1875 60	Apr 76	Frehaut+N3N.SYSTEMATIC LAWS SEARCH	+
	1.3+7	1.5+7		Expt	Conf 75Gothenbg	Jun 75	- +	
	1.3+7	1.5+7			Data EXFOR20571.015	Mar 76	3PTS.N3N.	
(n,p)	Fiss		CRC	Eval	Rept CRC-1003	Dec 60	ROY+ ESTIMATED AVG SIG=0.0004MB	
(n,p)	1.4+7		LYO	Comp	Rept LYCEN/6780	Nov 67	Crouzet+COMPILATN FOR ACTIVTN ANALYS	
(n,α)	Fiss		CRC	Eval	Rept CRC-1003	Dec 60	ROY+ ESTIMATED AVG SIG=0.0001MB	
(n,α)	1.4+7		LYO	Comp	Rept LYCEN/6780	Nov 67	Crouzet+COMPILATN FOR ACTIVTN ANALYS	
Reson Params	2.4+2	3.8+2	HAR	Expt	Jour NP 3 553	Jun 57	Bowey.TOF.2ES FROM CAPT GAMMA YIELDS	
Reson Params		1.0+6	AUA	Theo	Jour AUJ 20 477	Oct 67	Cook. TBL OF AVG LVL SPACING D,L=0,1	
Reson Params	4.0+3		DUB	Expt	Conf 68DUBSY 349	Jul 68	Pikelner.LVL SPAC,AVERG. WG	
Reson Params	7.9+1	3.9+3	DUB	Expt	Jour YF 8 639	Oct 68	Karzhavina+,16RES,WT,WN,WG,TABLES	+
					Rept YFI-6 124	68	- + TABLE.	
					Rept JINR-P3-3564	Nov 67	- + FULL PAPER.	
					Jour SNP 8 371	Apr 69	- + TRANSLATION.	
					Rept INDC-260E	69	- + ENGL OF YFI-6 124.	
	7.9+1	3.8+3			Data EXFOR40113.	Sep 72	N-WIDTH AT 16RES,CAPT-WID,TOT-WID, D	
Reson Params	2.4+4		MUA	ExTh	Jour NC/B 58 402	Dec 68	Hasan+ AVERAGE LEVEL SPACING D GIVEN	+
	2.4+4			Expt	Data EXFOR30091.013	Dec 70	ESTIMATED AVERAGE LEVEL SPACING D	
Reson Params	7.8+1		GEL	Expt	Jour JNE 23 369	Jul 69	Migneco+ TOF.WG,WN.AREA ANAL.	
Reson Params	7.9+1	4.9+2	SAC	Expt	Jour NP/A 134 118	Sep 69	Alves+LINAC TOF.WN,WN0 2E0;1WT	+
	7.9+1	4.9+2			Data EXFOR20688.031	Jun 77	2PTS.E0,WT,G*WN.	
Reson Params	–		AUA	Theo	Rept AAEC/E-211	Nov 70	Musgrove. CALCULTD D+GAM WIDTH GIVEN	
Reson Params	8.0+1	1.0+3	CJD	Eval	Rept YK-7	71	Zakharova+ SURVEY+SYSTEMATICS,GW,TBL	
					Rept INDC(CCP)-27	Nov 72	.ENGLISH TRANSLATION OF YK-7 /71	
Reson Params	None		DUB	Theo	Jour YF 13 240	Feb 71	Malecki+G-WID,THEO CFD EXPT.TBL,GRPH	
					Jour SNP 13 133	Aug 71	- + ENGL OF YF 13 240.	

60 Neodymium 150

Quantity	Energy (ev) Min	Max	Lab	Type	Documentation Ref Vol Page	Author, Comments Date	Data
Reson Params	7.9+1	2.5+4	SAC	Expt	Conf 71Knoxvill 680	Mar 71 Tellier+TRANS,AVG D=121EV 79RESON	+
					Priv TELLIER	Oct 71 − . VALUES FOR COMPILATION.	
	7.0+1	3.0+4			Rept CEA−N−1459	Aug 71 − . SHAPE−ANALYSIS 91 LEVELS	
	7.9+1	2.5+4			Data EXFOR20121.	Sep 72 187PTS.E0,WG,WT,2G*WN,2G*WN0.	
Reson Params	None		CNE	Expt	Prog INDC(ARG)−3	72 Ricabarra+ G−WID FROM ACT−INTEG,NDG	
Reson Params	+0	+2	BOL	Eval	Conf IAEA−169 3 123	74 Benzi+ AVG G−WID CFD OTHERS+XPT,TABL	
Reson Params	+1	+4	FEI	Eval	Rept YK−8/2 97	Sep 72 Abagyan+ AVG G−WID+D AT BINDNG−E,TBL	
					Rept INDC(CCP)−39	Jul 74 .PAGE 102.ENGLISH OF YK−8/2 97	
Strnth Fnctn		4.0+3	DUB	Expt	Conf 68DUBSY 349	Jul 68 Pikelner.LVL SPAC,AVERG. WG,S0 VS A	
Strnth Fnctn	7.9+1	3.9+3	DUB	Expt	Jour YF 8 639	Oct 68 Karzhavina+,TRANS+G−YLD EXPT,S−RES	+
					Rept YFI−6 124	68 − + TABLE.	
					Rept JINR−P3−3564	Nov 67 − + FULL PAPER.	
					Jour SNP 8 371	Apr 69 − + TRANSLATION.	
					Rept INDC−260E	69 − + ENGL OF YFI−6 124.	
	0.0+0	3.8+4			Data EXFOR40113.051	Sep 72 STRENGTH−FUNCTION	
Strnth Fnctn	−		AUA	Theo	Rept AAEC/E−211	Nov 70 Musgrove. SMOOTHED S0,S1 AND S2 GIVN	
Strnth Fnctn	2.5+4		AUW	ExTh	Conf 70Madurai 2 25	Dec 70 Thirumala Rao+ S1 GIVEN,CAPTURE−EXPT	+
	2.5+4			Expt	Data EXFOR30247.008	Jun 73 S1−VALUE	
Strnth Fnctn	7.0+1	1.4+4	SAC	Expt	Rept CEA−N−1459	Aug 71 Tellier. VERSUS ENERGY	+
	−2	+3			Rept CEA−N−1522	Oct 72 Cauvin+ S0,S1 CALC	
	7.0+1	1.4+4			Priv TELLIER	Oct 71 Tellier. VALUES FOR COMPILATION.	
					Jour CR 272 695	Mar 71 − .LINAC,TOF.79LEVELS,+D,+A	
					Conf 71Knoxvill 680	Mar 71 − +.S0=3.2+−0.6	
	7.0+1	1.4+4			Data EXFOR20121.047	Sep 72 1PNT.L=0.	
Strnth Fnctn	None		AUA	Eval	Rept AAEC/E−277	Mar 73 Musgrove.TBLS EXPTL DATA+BEST VALUES	
Lvl Density	−		DUB	Expt	Jour YF 8 639	Oct 68 Karzhavina+ VAL+PARS GVN,TBL+GRPH	+
					Jour SNP 8 371	Apr 69 − + TRANSLATION.	
	None				Data EXFOR40113.059	Sep 72 LEVEL−DENSITY PARAMETER	
Lvl Density	0.0+0	1.4+4	SAC	Expt	Rept CEA−N−1459	Aug 71 Tellier. FROM STAT RES ANALYSIS.	+
		1.4+4			Jour CR 272 695	Mar 71 − .LINAC,TOF.D AND A,79 LVLS	
		1.4+4			Data EXFOR20121.048	Sep 72 1PNT.SP.CUT(0).	
Lvl Density	None		BOL	Eval	Conf IAEA−169 3 123	74 Benzi+ LVL DENS PARAM BY XPT,GRPH+TB	
Lvl Density	+1	+4	FEI	Eval	Rept YK−8/2 97	Sep 72 Abagyan+ LVL DENSITY PARAMETER,TBL	
					Rept INDC(CCP)−39	Jul 74 .PAGE 102.ENGLISH OF YK−8/2 97	
Lvl Density	+0	1.0+4	JAE	ExTh	Jour JPJ 37 581	Sep 74 Ideno.LVL SPACING CORRELATIONS.TBL.	
	1.0+0	1.0+4			Rept JAERI−M−5490	Nov 73 − .LEVEL SPACING CORRELATIONS.TBL	
	+0	4.0+3			Jour JPJ 30 620	Mar 71 − + RES SPACING CORRELATION ANAL	
(γ,n)	8.0+6	2.2+7	CCP	Expt	Jour YF 10 460	Sep 69 Vasil'Ev+ SIG(GAM−E) GRAPH GIVEN	
					Jour SNP 10 263	Mar 70 . ENGL TRANSL OF YF 10 460	
(γ,n)	9.0+6	2.0+7	SAC	Expt	Jour NP/A 172 437	Sep 71 Carlos+LORENTZ LINE PARAM,GRPHS,TBL	

60 Neodymium 151

Quantity	Energy (ev) Min	Max	Lab	Type	Documentation Ref Vol Page	Author, Comments Date	Data
Strnth Fnctn	−2	+3	SAC	Expt	Rept CEA−N−1522	Oct 72 Cauvin+ S0,S1 CALC	
Lvl Density	None		MUN	Theo	Jour NP/A 217 269	Dec 73 Dilg+ A,DELTA. BACK SHIFTED FERMIGAS	

61 Promethium 141

Quantity	Energy (ev) Min	Max	Lab	Type	Documentation Ref Vol Page	Author, Comments Date	Data
Reson Params	–		AUA	Theo Rept	AAEC/E-211	Nov 70 Musgrove. CALCULTD D+GAM WIDTH GIVEN	
Strnth Fnctn	–		AUA	Theo Rept	AAEC/E-211	Nov 70 Musgrove. SMOOTHED S0,S1 AND S2 GIVN	

61 Promethium 142

Quantity	Energy (ev) Min	Max	Lab	Type	Documentation Ref Vol Page	Author, Comments Date	Data
Reson Params	–		AUA	Theo Rept	AAEC/E-211	Nov 70 Musgrove. CALCULTD D+GAM WIDTH GIVEN	
Strnth Fnctn	–		AUA	Theo Rept	AAEC/E-211	Nov 70 Musgrove. SMOOTHED S0,S1 AND S2 GIVN	

61 Promethium 143

Quantity	Energy (ev) Min	Max	Lab	Type	Documentation Ref Vol Page	Author, Comments Date	Data
(n,p)	Maxwl		IFU	Theo Rept	ICD-4 20	67 Dadakina+ PENETR COEFF CALC,TABLE	
Reson Params	–		AUA	Theo Rept	AAEC/E-211	Nov 70 Musgrove. CALCULTD D+GAM WIDTH GIVEN	
Strnth Fnctn	–		AUA	Theo Rept	AAEC/E-211	Nov 70 Musgrove. SMOOTHED S0,S1 AND S2 GIVN	

61 Promethium 144

Quantity	Energy (ev) Min	Max	Lab	Type	Documentation Ref Vol Page	Author, Comments Date	Data
(n,p)	Maxwl		IFU	Theo Rept	ICD-4 20	67 Dadakina+ PENETR COEFF CALC,TABLE	
Reson Params	–		AUA	Theo Rept	AAEC/E-211	Nov 70 Musgrove. CALCULTD D+GAM WIDTH GIVEN	
Strnth Fnctn	–		AUA	Theo Rept	AAEC/E-211	Nov 70 Musgrove. SMOOTHED S0,S1 AND S2 GIVN	

61 Promethium 145

Quantity	Energy (ev) Min	Max	Lab	Type	Documentation Ref Vol Page	Author, Comments Date	Data
(n,p)	Maxwl		IFU	Theo Rept	ICD-4 20	67 Dadakina+ PENETR COEFF CALC,TABLE	
Reson Params	–		AUA	Theo Rept	AAEC/E-211	Nov 70 Musgrove. CALCULTD D+GAM WIDTH GIVEN	
Strnth Fnctn	–		AUA	Theo Rept	AAEC/E-211	Nov 70 Musgrove. SMOOTHED S0,S1 AND S2 GIVN	

61 Promethium 146

Quantity	Energy (ev) Min	Max	Lab	Type	Documentation Ref Vol Page	Author, Comments Date	Data
Absorption	$2.5-2$		IJI	Eval Rept	KIYAI-76-6	76 Fedorova+ ONLY 1LIT-VALUE=RECOMM.TBL	
				Conf	75Kiev 1 169	May 75 – + EVAL SIG GIVEN,TABLE	
(n,γ)	Pile		ORL	Expt Jour	JIN 29 2117	Sep 67 Pinajian+HYDR. TUBE FACIL	+
				Rept	ORNL-P-2926	65 – + 8400B TBP JIN	
	Pile			Data	EXFOR12089.002	Jun 76 . 1 PT.	
(n,p)	Maxwl		IFU	Theo Rept	ICD-4 20	67 Dadakina+ PENETR COEFF CALC,TABLE	
Reson Params	–		AUA	Theo Rept	AAEC/E-211	Nov 70 Musgrove. CALCULTD D+GAM WIDTH GIVEN	
Strnth Fnctn	–		AUA	Theo Rept	AAEC/E-211	Nov 70 Musgrove. SMOOTHED S0,S1 AND S2 GIVN	

61 Promethium 147

Quantity	Energy (ev) Min	Max	Lab	Type	Documentation Ref Vol Page	Author, Comments Date	Data
Evaluation	$1.0-3$	$1.5+7$	AUA	Eval Rept	AAEC/TM-549	Jun 70 Cook.TOT,EL,INEL,NONEL,CAPT SIGS,NDG	+
				Rept	AAEC/E-214	Jun 71 Bertram+GROUP SIGMAS SAME QUANTS.NDG	
				Rept	AAEC/E-587	Mar 71 *DESCRIPTION OF LIBRARY	
	$1.0-3$	$1.5+7$		Data	AUSTR-DFN 152.	Nov 71 POINT(223) AND GROUP(127) SIGMAS	
Evaluation	$1.0+3$	$1.0+7$	BOL	Eval Rept	CEC(71)-2	71 Benzi+ STAT+EVAP MDS.INEL,N2N,NG.TBL	+
	$1.0+3$	$1.0+7$		Data	BENZI-DFN 558A	Mar 71 4 QUANTITIES. UK FORMAT	
Evaluation	$1.0+2$	$1.5+7$	JAE	Eval Rept	JAERI-M-5752	Jul 74 Igarasi+ JNDC FPND WG.TOT,EL,N',CAP	
Total	$4.0-2$	$1.0+2$	ORL	Expt Conf	58Geneva 16 150	Sep 58 Harvey+ PPR673,CURVE,CRYSTALSPECTRUM	+
	$4.0-2$	$1.0+2$		Data	EXFOR12012.005	Jun 76 .DATA UNOBTAINABLE	
Total	$1.0-2$	$1.0+3$	MTR	Expt Jour	NSE 43 58	Jan 71 Codding+FAST CHOPR.GRPHS,2200M/S VAL	+
	$2.5-2$			Data	EXFOR10114.010	Mar 76 . 1 PT. CS=200+5-7B.	
Total	$2.5+6$	$1.5+7$	BNW	Expt Jour	PR/C 3 576	Feb 71 Foster+ TRANS,CURVS,CFD OTHERS+TH	+
				Jour	NIM 36 1	Sep 65 .EXPT DETAILS	
	$2.5+6$	$1.5+7$		Data	EXFOR10047.065	Aug 73 . 229PTS. SIGMA	
Total	$1.0-3$	$1.5+7$	AUA	Eval Data	AUSTR-DFN 152.	Nov 71 COOK+POINT(223)+GROUP(127)SIG.CF EVL	+

61 Promethium 147

Quantity	Energy (ev) Min	Max	Lab	Type	Documentation Ref Vol Page	Author, Comments Date	Data
Total	$7.0-2$		ORL Expt	Rept	CONF-721114-4	Oct 72 Koehler+	+
	$7.0-2$			Data	EXFOR10453.002	Nov 74 . 1 PT. SIGMA	
Total	$1.0-2$	$4.0+2$	KAP Expt	Jour	NSE 52 310	Nov 73 Kirouac+ TRANS, THERMAL VALUE	+
				Rept	KAPL-3974	Nov 71 - .SEE ALSO	
	$2.5-2$			Data	EXFOR10258.002	Nov 78 . 1PT.CS=198+ - 8B.	
Total	$5.4+0$	$2.0+2$	CCP Expt	Conf	75Kiev	May 75 Kalebin+ TOT SIG	
Total	-3	$1.9+0$	THS Theo	Rept	IKE-6 89 65	Jun 75 Keinert. DATA LIBRARY	
Total	$2.5-2$		IJI Comp	Rept	KIYAI-76-6	76 Fedorova+ TO GET RECOM ABS-SIG.TABLE	
Total	$1.0-2$	$4.0+2$	NIR Expt	Conf	76Lowell 1252	Jul 76 Anufriev+TRNS.TOT CS.RES PARS.NDG	
Elastic	$1.0-3$	$1.5+7$	AUA Eval	Data	AUSTR-DFN 152.	Nov 71 COOK+POINT(223)+GROUP(127)SIG.CF EVL	+
Elastic	$+1$	$+6$	GEL Expt	Prog	INDC(SEC)-26	May 72 Theobald+ HE3-SCINT,EXPLOSN,PROPOSED	
Potntl Scat	$2.0+0$	$1.3+1$	MTR Expt	Jour	NSE 43 58	Jan 71 Codding+FROM SHAPE FIT ANAL	+
	$2.0+0$	$1.3+1$		Data	EXFOR10114.009	Mar 76 . 1PT=13B. FROM SHAPE FIT.	
Tot Inelastc	$9.2+4$	$1.0+7$	BOL Eval	Rept	CEC(71)-2	71 Benzi+ STAT MODEL. TBL GIVEN.	+
	$9.2+4$	$1.0+7$		Data	BENZI-DFN 558A	Mar 71 60 PNTS	
Tot Inelastc	$5.0+5$	$1.5+7$	AUA Eval	Data	AUSTR-DFN 152.	Nov 71 COOK+POINT(11)+GROUP(127)SIG.CF EVL	
Diff Inelast	$9.2+4$	$1.0+7$	BOL Eval	Rept	CEC(71)-2	71 Benzi+ DISCRETE INELASTIC. 6 LVLS	+
	$9.2+4$	$8.0+5$		Data	BENZI-DFN 558A	Mar 71 1ST- 6TH LVL+ANGDIST+E DIST	
	$8.0+5$	$1.0+7$		Data	BENZI-DFN 558A	Mar 71 TO CONTINUUM, 31PNTS+ANGDIST+E DIST	
Nonelastic	$1.0-3$	$1.5+7$	AUA Eval	Data	AUSTR-DFN 152.	Nov 71 COOK+POINT(223)+GROUP(127)SIG.CF EVL	+
Absorption	Pile		CCP Expt	Jour	AE 3 11	Jul 57 Gorshkov+.M/S ANAL U235 FPS, 90+ - 20B	+
Absorption	Maxwl		ORL Expt	Prog	WASH-745	Nov 57 Harvey+ 50B FROM RESPARS	
Absorption	Maxwl		CCP Expt	Conf	58Geneva 15 446	Sep 58 Anikina+.PPR2040,VAL GVN	
Absorption	$4.1-1$	$1.0+7$	GA Eval	Rept	GA-2451	Aug 61 Joanou+ 68GROUP DATA FOR GAM-I	
Absorption	Fast		AE Expt	Conf	70Helsinki 2 603	Jun 70 Andersson.PILE OSC. 3 SPECS.CFD CALC	
Absorption	$1.0-4$	$1.0+7$	JUL Eval	Rept	JUEL-678-RG	Jul 70 Liu. EVALUATION+CALC,GRPH,FN OF E	
Absorption	$2.5-2$		MTR Expt	Jour	NSE 43 58	Jan 71 Codding+CALC VAL FROM TRNS.DATA.CFD.	+
	$2.5-2$			Data	EXFOR10114.011	Mar 76 1PT.CALC VAL=192B.	
Absorption	Pile		CRC Eval	Conf	73Paris 1 459	Mar 73 Walker.FISS PRODUCT ABS,TBL PILE SIG	
Absorption	Fast		RCN Revw	Conf	IAEA-169 2 53	74 Bustraan.INTEG CFD SIG(N-E)FILES,TBL	
Absorption	$2.5-2$		IJI Eval	Rept	KIYAI-76-6	76 Fedorova+ COMP(REFS,SIGS),EVAL.TABLE	
				Conf	75Kiev 1 169	May 75 - + EVAL SIGS OF 3ISOMERS,TABL	
Res Int Abs	None		ORL Expt	Conf	60Vienna 239	Oct 60 Stoughton+.VAL GVN,EXPT DESCRIBED	+
	None			Data	EXFOR12126.	Jun 76 . 2 PTS, RI FOR 2 ISOMERS	
Res Int Abs	$5.0-1$		BOL Eval	Conf	61Vienna 1 179	Aug 61 Benzi+ TBL TOTAL CAPT RES INTS.	
Res Int Abs	$5.5-1$		GA Eval	Jour	NSE 12 115	Jan 62 Garrison+,RI=2270+ - 700B,FROM RES.PAR	
Res Int Abs	Pile		MTR Expt	Jour	NSE 12 519	Apr 62 Schuman+ TO BOTH PM148 ISOMERS	+
	Pile			Data	EXFOR12100.	Jun 76 . 2 PTS, RI FOR 2 ISOMERS	
Res Int Abs	None		CRC Eval	Rept	AECL-2111	Nov 64 Walker. REDUCED RESONANCE INTEGRAL	
Res Int Abs	$5.0-1$		BOL Eval	Rept	RT/FI-4	Jan 67 Palmucci. CALC FROM (N,G) RES PARAMS	
Res Int Abs	$5.5-1$		MCME Expt	Prog	EANDC(CAN)-32	Jan 67 Tomlinson+ NDG	
Res Int Abs	$5.0-1$		ALD Expt	Jour	JIN 29 2147	Sep 67 Fenner+,TO MS AND GRD, REL.TO CO	+
	$2.0-1$			Data	EXFOR20631.	Sep 76 2PTS.CAPTURE.	
Res Int Abs	Pile		HAR Expt	Jour	JIN 32 3433	Nov 70 Cabell.	+
	$5.0-1$			Rept	AERE-R-6384	May 70 - + REDUCED VAL=1274+ -66B TBL	
	Pile			Data	EXFOR20458.003	Jan 76 1PNT.CAPTURE.	
Res Int Abs	$5.0-1$		MTR Expt	Jour	NSE 43 58	Jan 71 Codding+CALC FROM RES.PARS.	
Res Int Abs	$5.5-1$		CRC Eval	Rept	AECL-3037 1	Jan 72 Walker.REDUCED RES INT TO GND+META	
Res Int Abs	$5.0-1$		AUA Eval	Rept	AAEC/TM-619	Sep 72 Clayton.CALC FROM SIG LIBRARY,TABLE	
Res Int Abs	$5.0-1$		SGA Eval	Conf	73Paris 1 233	Mar 73 Eder+ SIG TO PM148M,G,CAPTURE,TABLE	
				Rept	SGAE-PH-141	Feb 73 .SAME AS 73PARIS,EVAL OF EXPTL DATA	
Res Int Abs	$4.6-1$	$1.0+6$	RCN Theo	Rept	RCN-191	Jul 73 Lautenbach.CAPT INT FROM GROUP SIGMA	
Res Int Abs	$5.0-1$		KAP Expt	Jour	NSE 52 310	Nov 73 Kirouac+ RI=2280+ -200B	+
				Rept	KAPL-3974	Nov 71 - .SEE ALSO	
	$5.0-1$			Data	EXFOR10258.012	Nov 78 . 1PT.CALC RIA=2280+ -200B.	
Res Int Abs	$5.5-1$	$+6$	SAC Revw	Conf	IAEA-169 1 235	74 Ribon.CAPTURE,STATUS CFD REQUEST,TBL	
Res Int Abs	$+0$	$+5$	WIN Revw	Conf	IAEA-169 3 163	74 Pope+ DATA FILE CALC CFD XPTAL VALUE	
Res Int Abs	$5.0-1$		IJI Eval	Rept	KIYAI-76-6	76 Fedorova+ COMP(REFS,RI),EVAL.TABLE	
				Rept	KIYAI-76-6	76 - + EVAL CFD CALC.TBL RI,REFS	
				Conf	75Kiev 1 169	May 75 - + EVAL+CALC RI GIVEN,TABLE	
(n,γ)	Pile		ANL Expt	Jour	PR 72 85	Jan 47 Parker+ SIGMA	+
	Pile			Data	EXFOR12149.002	Jun 76 . 1 PT.	
(n,γ)	Pile		MCME Expt	Conf	58Geneva 15 459	Sep 58 Bidinosti+ PPR201,MASS SPEC REL CO	+
	Pile			Data	EXFOR12010.004	Jun 76 . 1 PT.	
(n,γ)	Maxwl		ORL Expt	Conf	60Vienna 239	Oct 60 Stoughton+.VAL GVN,PRELIM RESULTS	+
	Maxwl			Data	EXFOR12126.	Jun 76 . 2 PTS, SIG FOR 2 ISOMERS	
(n,γ)	$5.0-3$	$2.5+0$	GA Eval	Rept	GA-2113	Jun 61 Wikner+ TABLE+CURVE. 100 E POINTS	
(n,γ)	$2.8-3$	$1.0+6$	GA Eval	Jour	NSE 12 115	Jan 62 Garrison+.EVAL FROM XPT+AVERAGE RES	

61 Promethium 147

Quantity	Energy (ev) Min	Energy (ev) Max	Lab	Type	Documentation Ref Vol Page	Date	Author, Comments	Data
(n,γ)	Pile		MTR	Expt	Jour NSE 12 519	Apr 62	Schuman+ PILE+THR CS TO BOTH(NG)PROD	+
	Pile			Data	EXFOR12100.	Jun 76	. 2 PTS, SIG FOR 2 ISOMERS	
(n,γ)	Maxwl		CRC	Eval	Rept AECL-2111	Nov 64	Walker.	
(n,γ)	+1	+5	LAS	Expt	Prog WASH-1064 94	Oct 65	Glass+BOMB TBD1966,FOR41D PM148	
(n,γ)	1.0+3	1.0+4	LAS	Theo	Rept LA-3463	Jan 66	Bell. TH CAPTURE OF RARE EARTHS	
(n,γ)	Pile		CRC	Revw	Conf 66Paris 1 521	Oct 66	Walker. REVIEW OF SIGMA MEASTS	
(n,γ)	2.5-2		BOL	Eval	Rept RT/FI-4	Jan 67	Palmucci. CALC FROM RES PARAMETERS	
(n,γ)	Maxwl		MCM	Expt	Prog EANDC(CAN)-32	Jan 67	Tomlinson+ NDG	
(n,γ)	Maxwl		ALD	Expt	Jour JIN 29 2147	Sep 67	Fenner+ SIG TO GND+ISO-STATE.REL CO	+
	2.5-2			Data	EXFOR20631.	Sep 76	2PTS.SIGMA.	
(n,γ)	Maxwl		AUA	Theo	Jour NSE 31 234	Feb 68	Cook+ STATISTICAL CALC CFD EXPT	
(n,γ)	2.0+1	1.0+4	LAS	Expt	Abst BAP 13 1391	Nov 68	Beery+ TOF BOMB SOURCE MOXON-RAE DET	
(n,γ)	5.0+3	1.0+5	AUA	ExTh	Rept AAEC/E-198	May 69	Musgrove.S+P+D WAVE SIGMAS CALC,TBL	+
(n,γ)	+3	+7	CCP	Revw	Conf 70Helsinki 2 245	Jun 70	Abramov.114. REVIEW OF DATA STATUS	
(n,γ)	Pile		HAR	Expt	Jour JIN 32 3433	Dec 70	Cabell.CD CUT-OFF.	+
	Maxwl				Rept AERE-R-6384	May 70	- + TBL.SIG=96.0+-1.8B TO GS.	
	Pile				Data EXFOR20458.002	Jan 76	1PNT.SIGMA.	
(n,γ)	1.0+3	1.0+7	BOL	Eval	Rept CEC(71)-2	71	Benzi+ OPTMOD EVAL.TBL GIVEN.	+
					Conf 66Paris 1 537	Oct 66	- +,PPR.115,STATIST MOD +XPT D,WG	
					Jour NC 38 216	Jul 65	- + THEORY FOR CAPTURE EVALUATION	
					Conf 61Vienna 1 179	Aug 61	- + TBL AV VALS. SUPERSEDED.	
	1.0+3	1.0+7			Data BENZI-DFN 558A	Mar 71	78 PNTS	
(n,γ)	Maxwl		CRC	Eval	Jour CJP 49 108	Jan 71	Mowatt+ ACT.84B TO GND.72.4B TO MET	+
	Maxwl				Data EXFOR10151.	Aug 75	2PTS.SIGMA.	
(n,γ)	1.0-3	1.5+7	AUA	Eval	Data AUSTR-DFN 152.	Nov 71	COOK+POINT(223)+GROUP(127)SIG.CF EVL	+
(n,γ)	Maxwl		CRC	Eval	Rept AECL-3037 1	Jan 72	Walker.RECOMMEND SIG TO GND+META,TBL	
(n,γ)	Maxwl		IAE	Revw	Rept IAEA-143 897	Apr 72	Lemmel.RECENT EVALUATIONS,TABLE	
	2.5-2				Rept IAEA-143 897	Apr 72	- .RECENT EVALUATIONS,TABLE+GRPH	
(n,γ)	+1	+6	GEL	Expt	Prog INDC(SEC)-26	May 72	Theobald+ M-R+CERENCOV,BOMB,PROPOSED	
(n,γ)	2.5-2		AUA	Eval	Rept AAEC/TM-619	Sep 72	Clayton.CALC FROM SIG LIBRARY,TABLE	
(n,γ)	Fast		MTR	Expt	Conf 72Kiamesha 2 614	Sep 72	Harker+ CFRMF INTEGRAL MEAS.	
(n,γ)	Maxwl		SGA	Eval	Conf 73Paris 1 233	Mar 73	Eder+ SIG TO PM148 META,GND,TABLE	
					Rept SGAE-PH-141	Feb 73	.SAME AS 73PARIS,EVAL OF EXPTL DATA	
(n,γ)		1.1+7	RCN	Theo	Rept RCN-191	Jun 73	Lautenbach. GROUP CONSTANTS TBL	
(n,γ)	2.5-2	3.0+4	SAC	Revw	Conf IAEA-169 1 235	74	Ribon.STATUS SIG CFD REQUESTS,TABLE	
	Fiss				Conf IAEA-169 1 235	74	- .STATUS SIG CFD REQUESTS,TABLE	
(n,γ)	Maxwl	Fiss	WIN	Revw	Conf IAEA-169 3 163	74	Pope+ MAXW+FIS-SPEC AVG EVAL DATA	
	Fiss				Conf IAEA-169 3 137	74	Dean. POINT DATA AVG OVER STAND SPEC	
(n,γ)	Fast		RCN	Expt	Conf ECN-10	Oct 76	Veenema+ STEK REACTIVITY WORTHS TBL.	
Spect (n,γ)	Maxwl		OKL	Expt	Jour ZP 233 391	Apr 70	Fischbeck+ BETA-G DIRECTIONAL CORR	
(n,2n)	7.7+6	1.0+7	BOL	Eval	Rept CEC(71)-2	71	Benzi+ STAT+EVAP MODELS.TBL GIVEN.	+
	7.7+6	1.0+7			Data BENZI-DFN 558A	Mar 71	6 PNTS+ANGDIST+E DIST. 1 RANGE	
Reson Params	1.1+0	5.0+1	ORL	Expt	Conf 58Geneva 16 150	Sep 58	Harvey+ PPR673,PARAMS FOR 12ES	+
	1.0+0	5.0+1			Data EXFOR12012.006	Jun 76	. 12 RES, E0,WN,WN0	
Reson Params		1.0+6	AUA	Theo	Jour AUJ 20 477	Oct 67	Cook. TBL OF AVG LVL SPACING D,L=0,1	
Reson Params	2.0+1	1.0+4	LAS	Expt	Abst BAP 13 1391	Nov 68	Beery+ MOXON-RAE,BOMB 70RESON SEEN	
Reson Params	-		AUA	Theo	Rept AAEC/E-211	Nov 70	Musgrove. CALCULTD D+GAM WIDTH GIVEN	
Reson Params	-.1+1	6.9+0	CJD	Eval	Rept YK-7	71	Zakharova+ SURVEY+SYSTEMATICS,GW,TBL	
					Rept INDC(CCP)-27	Nov 72	.ENGLISH TRANSLATION OF YK-7 /71	
Reson Params	-.2+1	2.4+2	MTR	Expt	Jour NSE 43 58	Jan 71	Codding+SHAPE AND PEAK FITS.	+
	-.2+1	2.4+2			Data EXFOR10114.	Mar 76	. 79 PTS.2G*WN AND WG.	
Reson Params	+1	+6	GEL	Expt	Prog INDC(SEC)-26	May 72	Theobald+ FROM CAPT+EL SIG,PROPOSED	
Reson Params	-.4+1	3.2+2	KAP	Expt	Jour NSE 52 310	Nov 73	Kirouac+ WT WG FOR 3.2G*WN D FOR 39	+
	-.4-3	3.2+2			Rept KAPL-3974	Nov 71	- .SEE ALSO	
	-.2+1	3.2+2			Data EXFOR10258.	Nov 78	. 36 RES WN0*2G.3RES WT,WG,WN0*G.	
Reson Params	+0	+2	BOL	Eval	Conf IAEA-169 3 123	74	Benzi+ AVG G-WID CFD OTHERS+XPT,TABL	
Reson Params	-.2+1	1.7+2	NIR	Expt	Conf 75Kiev 3 205	May 75	Belanova+ BY TOTSIG.N,TOT WIDS,TABLE	
Reson Params	1.0+3	1.0+6	SAC	Eval	Rept CEA-N-1832	Dec 75	Ribon+ EXP+TH ANAL,RES PAR,TBL	
Reson Params	1.0-2	4.0+2	NIR	Expt	Rept 76Lowell 1252	Jul 76	Anufriev+SHAPE AND AREA ANAL.NDG	
Strnth Fnctn	2.0-1	2.0+1	ORL	Expt	Abst BAP 3 177	May 58	Harvey+ TRANS TOF STF=3.0+-1.1	
Strnth Fnctn	1.0+0	5.0+1	BNL	Expt	Prog WASH-1006	Oct 58	Harvey. STF=4.2+-1.2	
Strnth Fnctn	+3	+5	BOL	Theo	Conf 61Vienna 1 179	Aug 61	Benzi+.PPR11,TABLE CFD EXPERIMENT	
Strnth Fnctn	-		AUA	Theo	Rept AAEC/E-211	Nov 70	Musgrove. SMOOTHED S0,S1 AND S2 GIVN	
Strnth Fnctn	0.0+0	2.0+2	MTR	Expt	Jour NSE 43 58	Jan 71	Codding+S0 TAKEN FROM SLOPE.	+
	0.0+0	2.0+2			Data EXFOR10114.	Mar 76	. 1 PT, S0, 1 PT, D	
Strnth Fnctn	None		AUA	Eval	Rept AAEC/E-277	Mar 73	Musgrove.TBLS EXPTL DATA+BEST VALUES	

61 Promethium 147

Quantity	Energy (ev) Min	Max	Lab	Type	Documentation Ref Vol Page	Date	Author, Comments	Data
Strnth Fnctn	0.0+0	1.0+2	KAP	Expt	Jour NSE 52 310	Nov 73	Kirouac+TRNS.S0 FROM 18 RES.	+
					Rept KAPL-3974	Nov 71	- .SEE ALSO	
	0.0+0	1.0+2			Data EXFOR10258.004	Nov 78	. 1PT.S0=(2.8+ -.6)-4.	
Strnth Fnctn	1.0-2	4.0+2	NIR	Expt	Conf 76Lowell 1252	Jul 76	Anufriev+TRNS.RES PARS DRVD.STF TBD	
Lvl Density	None		BOL	Eval	Conf IAEA-169 3 123	74	Benzi+ LVL DENS PARAM BY XPT,GRPH+TB	

61 Promethium 148

Quantity	Energy (ev) Min	Max	Lab	Type	Documentation Ref Vol Page	Date	Author, Comments	Data
Evaluation	1.0-3	1.5+7	AUA	Eval	Rept AAEC/TM-549	Jun 70	Cook.TOT,EL,INEL,NONEL,CAPT,G+M,NDG	+
					Rept AAEC/E-214	Jun 71	Bertram+GROUP SIGMAS SAME QUANTS.NDG	
					Rept AAEC/TM-587	Mar 71	*DESCRIPTION OF LIBRARY	
	1.0-3	1.5+7			Data AUSTR-DFN 153.	Nov 71	POINT(223) AND GROUP(127) SIGMAS	
	1.0-3	1.5+7			Data AUSTR-DFN 192.	Nov 71	PM-148M POINT+GROUP SIGS,SAME QUANTS	
Total	1.0-3	1.5+7	AUA	Eval	Data AUSTR-DFN 153.	Nov 71	COOK+POINT(223)+GROUP(127)SIG.CF EVL	+
	1.0-3	1.5+7			Data AUSTR-DFN 192.	Nov 71	.PM-148M.POINT+GROUP SIGS.SEE EVAL	
Total	1.3+7	1.5+7	DEB	Eval	Rept IAEA-153 173	73	Boedy+ MOST PROBABLE VAL OF SIG,TBL	
					Jour AHP 30 115	Oct 71	Angeli+ AVG SIG,CFD CALC.TBLS.GRAPH	
Total	1.0-2	4.0+2	KAP	Expt	Jour NSE 52 310	Nov 73	Kirouac+ TRANS,THERM VALUE	
					Rept KAPL-3974	Nov 71	-	+
Elastic	1.0-3	1.5+7	AUA	Eval	Data AUSTR-DFN 153.	Nov 71	COOK+POINT(223)+GROUP(127)SIG.CF EVL	
	1.0-3	1.5+7			Data AUSTR-DFN 192.	Nov 71	.PM-148M.POINT+GROUP SIGS.SEE EVAL	
Tot Inelastc	Maxwl		TOK	Expt	Jour JPJ 26 576	Feb 69	Miyano+,CS OF TRANS FROM META TO GS	+
	Pile				Data EXFOR20295.003	Jun 74	1PNT.SIGMA.	
Tot Inelastc	5.0+5	1.5+7	AUA	Eval	Data AUSTR-DFN 192.	Nov 71	.PM-148M.POINT+GROUP SIGS.SEE EVAL	
	5.0+5	1.5+7			Data AUSTR-DFN 153.	Nov 71	COOK+POINT(11)+GROUP(127)SIG.CF EVL	
Nonelastic	1.0-3	1.5+7	AUA	Eval	Data AUSTR-DFN 192.	Nov 71	.PM-148M.POINT+GROUP SIGS.SEE EVAL	
	1.0-3	1.5+7			Data AUSTR-DFN 153.	Nov 71	COOK+POINT(223)+GROUP(127)SIG.CF EVL	
Absorption	1.0-4	1.0+7	JUL	Eval	Rept JUEL-678-RG	Jul 70	Liu. EVALUATION+CALC,GRPH,FN OF E	
Absorption	Pile		CRC	Eval	Conf 73Paris 1 459	Mar 73	Walker.FISS PRODUCT ABS,TBL PILE SIG	
Absorption	2.5-2		IJI	Eval	Rept KIYAI-76-6	76	Fedorova+ PM148G AND M.COMP+EVAL.TBL	
					Conf 75Kiev 1 169	May 75	- + EVAL SIG GIVEN,TABLE	
Res Int Abs	5.0-1		MTR	Expt	Jour NSE 12 519	Apr 62	Schuman+ RI FOR PM148 AND PM148M	+
	5.0-1				Data EXFOR12100.	Jun 76	. 2 PTS, RI FOR PM148 AND PM148M	
Res Int Abs	5.5-1		MCM	Expt	Prog EANDC(CAN)-32	Jan 67	Tomlinson+ NDG	
Res Int Abs	5.0-1		ALD	Expt	Jour JIN 29 2147	Sep 67	Fenner+,FOR THE PM148M(N,G) REACTION	+
	2.0-1				Data EXFOR20631.007	Sep 76	1PNT.CAPTURE.	
Res Int Abs	5.0-1		AUA	Eval	Rept AAEC/TM-619	Sep 72	Clayton.CALC FROM SIG LIBRARY,TABLE	
Res Int Abs	5.0-1		KAP	Expt	Jour NSE 52 310	Nov 73	Kirouac+UPPER LIMIT=6000B.	+
					Rept KAPL-3974	Nov 71	- .SEE ALSO	
	5.0-1				Data EXFOR10258.013	Nov 78	. 1PT.CALC RIA=3600B+ -2400B.	
Res Int Abs	5.5-1	+6	SAC	Revw	Conf IAEA-169 1 235	74	Ribon.CAPTURE,STATUS CFD REQUEST,TBL	
Res Int Abs	+0	+5	WIN	Revw	Conf IAEA-169 3 163	74	Pope+ GND+META.DATA FILE CALC CFD XP	
Res Int Abs	5.0-1		IJI	Eval	Rept KIYAI-76-6	76	Fedorova+ PM148G AND M.COMP+EVAL.TBL	
					Conf 75Kiev 1 169	May 75	- + EVAL OF RI-EXPTS.TABLE	
(n,γ)	Pile		MTR	Expt	Jour NSE 12 519	Apr 62	Schuman+,SIG FOR PM148 AND PM148M	+
	Pile				Data EXFOR12100.	Jun 76	. 2 PTS, SIG FOR PM148 AND PM148M	
(n,γ)	Pile		MCM	Expt	Jour PR-CM-35 102	63	Mathews+	+
	Pile				Data EXFOR12143.	Jun 76	. 2 PTS, SIG FOR PM148 AND PM148M	
(n,γ)	2.0+1	3.0+2	LAS	Expt	Rept LA-DC-7864	Aug 66	Brown. TBD DIVEN SEEGER BOMB N(S)	
(n,γ)	Pile		CRC	Revw	Conf 66Paris 1 521	Oct 66	Walker. REVIEW OF SIGMA MEASTS	
(n,γ)	Maxwl		MCM	Expt	Prog EANDC(CAN)-32	Jan 67	Tomlinson+ NDG	
(n,γ)	2.5-2		ALD	Expt	Jour JIN 29 2147	Sep 67	Fenner+ SIG GIVEN REL TO CO	+
	2.5-2				Data EXFOR20631.006	Sep 76	1PNT.SIGMA.	
(n,γ)	Pile		TOK	Expt	Jour JPJ 26 576	Feb 69	Miyano+ PM148M DE-EXCITATION C.S.	+
	Pile				Data EXFOR20295.002	Jun 74	1PNT.SIGMA.	
(n,γ)	1.0-3	1.5+7	AUA	Eval	Data AUSTR-DFN 153.	Nov 71	COOK+POINT(223)+GROUP(127)SIG.CF EVL	+
	1.0-3	1.5+7			Data AUSTR-DFN 192.	Nov 71	.PM-148M.POINT+GROUP SIGS.SEE EVAL	
(n,γ)	Pile		CRC	Eval	Rept AECL-3037 1	Jan 72	Walker.RECOMMENDED SIG OF PM-148M+G	
(n,γ)	Maxwl		IAE	Revw	Rept IAEA-143 897	Apr 72	Lemmel.RECENT EVALUATIONS,TABLE	
	2.5-2				Rept IAEA-143 897	Apr 72	- .RECENT EVALUATIONS,TABLE+GRPH	
(n,γ)	2.5-2		AUA	Eval	Rept AAEC/TM-619	Sep 72	Clayton.CALC FROM SIG LIBRARY,TABLE	
(n,γ)	Pile		SGA	Eval	Conf 73Paris 1 233	Mar 73	Eder+ 41 D ISOMER,RECOMMENDD SIG,TBL	
					Rept SGAE-PH-141	Feb 73	.SAME AS 73PARIS,EVAL OF EXPTL DATA	
(n,γ)	2.5-2		SAC	Revw	Conf IAEA-169 1 235	74	Ribon.STATUS SIG CFD REQUESTS,TABLE	
	Fiss				Conf IAEA-169 1 235	74	- .STATUS SIG CFD REQUESTS,TABLE	

61 Promethium 148

Quantity	Energy (ev) Min	Max	Lab	Type	Documentation Ref Vol Page	Date	Author, Comments	Data
(n,γ)	Maxwl	Fiss	WIN	Revw Conf	IAEA-169 3 163	74	Pope+ MAXW+FIS-SPEC AVG EVAL DATA	
	Fiss			Conf	IAEA-169 3 137	74	Dean. GND+META,DATA AVG OVER FIS-SPC	
(n,p)	Maxwl		IFU	Theo Rept	ICD-4 20	67	Dadakina+ PENETR COEFF CALC,TABLE	
Reson Params		1.0+6	AUA	Theo Jour	AUJ 20 477	Oct 67	Cook. TBL OF AVG LVL SPACING D,L=0,1	
Reson Params	–		AUA	Theo Rept	AAEC/E-211	Nov 70	Musgrove. CALCULTD D+GAM WIDTH GIVEN	
Reson Params	1.7-1		KAP	Expt Jour	NSE 52 310	Nov 73	Kirouac+ WT WG 2G*WN.TRANS. META.	+
				Rept	KAPL-3974	Nov 71	– .SEE ALSO	
	1.7-1			Data	EXFOR10258.008	Nov 78	. 1 RES.WT,WG,WN0*G FOR .169 EV RES.	
Strnth Fnctn	–		AUA	Theo Rept	AAEC/E-211	Nov 70	Musgrove. SMOOTHED S0,S1 AND S2 GIVN	
Lvl Density	None		COP	Theo Jour	NP/A 222 493	Apr 74	Dossing+COLL ROTAT.SPAC. ACCUR ESTIM	
Lvl Density	None		ROC	Theo Jour	NP/A 223 577	May 74	Huizenga+ EXP CFD MICROSC TH SPH NUC	

61 Promethium 149

Quantity	Energy (ev) Min	Max	Lab	Type	Documentation Ref Vol Page	Date	Author, Comments	Data
Evaluation	1.0-3	1.5+7	AUA	Eval Rept	AAEC/TM-549	Jun 70	Cook.TOT,EL,INEL,NONEL,CAPT SIGS,NDG	+
				Rept	AAEC/E-214	Jun 71	Bertram+GROUP SIGMAS SAME QUANTS.NDG	
				Rept	AAEC/TM-587	Mar 71	*DESCRIPTION OF LIBRARY	
	1.0-3	1.5+7		Data	AUSTR-DFN 154.	Nov 71	POINT(223) AND GROUP(127) SIGMAS	
Total	1.0-3	1.5+7	AUA	Eval Data	AUSTR-DFN 154.	Nov 71	COOK+POINT(223)+GROUP(127)SIG.CF EVL	+
Elastic	1.0-3	1.5+7	AUA	Eval Data	AUSTR-DFN 154.	Nov 71	COOK+POINT(223)+GROUP(127)SIG.CF EVL	+
Tot Inelastc	5.0+5	1.5+7	AUA	Eval Data	AUSTR-DFN 154.	Nov 71	COOK+POINT(11)+GROUP(127)SIG.CF EVL	+
Nonelastic	1.0-3	1.5+7	AUA	Eval Data	AUSTR-DFN 154.	Nov 71	COOK+POINT(223)+GROUP(127)SIG.CF EVL	+
Absorption	2.5-2		IJI	Eval Rept	KIYAI-76-6	76	Fedorova+ COMP(REFS,SIGS),EVAL.TABLE	
				Conf	75Kiev 1 169	May 75	– + EVAL SIG GIVEN,TABLE	
Res Int Abs	5.0-1		AUA	Eval Rept	AAEC/E-619	Sep 72	Clayton.CALC FROM SIG LIBRARY,TABLE	
Res Int Abs	5.5-1	+6	SAC	Revw Conf	IAEA-169 1 235	74	Ribon.CAPTURE,STATUS CFD REQUEST,TBL	
Res Int Abs	+0	+5	WIN	Revw Conf	IAEA-169 3 163	74	Pope+ DATA FILE CALCS COMPARED	
(n,γ)	Maxwl		FTI	Expt Jour	AE 19 188	Aug 65	Kondurov+ 1700+ -30MB	
				Jour	JNE 20 814	Sep 66	. ENGL OF AE 19 188	
				Jour	SJA 19 1086	Aug 65	. ENGL OF AE 19 188	
				Jour	EAF 19 2 125	Aug 65	. FRENCH OF AE 19 188	
(n,γ)	Pile		CRC	Expt Conf	68Wash. 1291	Mar 68	Mowatt+ DEPLETION METHOD 1000+ -400B	+
	Pile			Data	EXFOR12141.002	Jun 76	. 1 PT.	
(n,γ)	1.0-3	1.5+7	AUA	Eval Data	AUSTR-DFN 154.	Nov 71	COOK+POINT(223)+GROUP(127)SIG.CF EVL	+
(n,γ)	Pile		CRC	Eval Rept	AECL-3037 1	Jan 72	Walker.RECOMMENDED SIG,DETAILED TBL	
(n,γ)	2.5-2		AUA	Eval Rept	AAEC/E-619	Sep 72	Clayton.CALC FROM SIG LIBRARY,TABLE	
(n,γ)	2.5-2		SAC	Revw Conf	IAEA-169 1 235	74	Ribon.STATUS SIG CFD REQUESTS,TABLE	
	Fiss			Conf	IAEA-169 1 235	74	– .STATUS SIG CFD REQUESTS,TABLE	
(n,γ)	Maxwl	Fiss	WIN	Revw Conf	IAEA-169 3 163	74	Pope+ MAXW+FIS-SPEC AVG EVAL DATA	
	Fiss			Conf	IAEA-169 3 137	74	Dean. POINT DATA AVG OVER STAND SPEC	
Reson Params	–		AUA	Theo Rept	AAEC/E-211	Nov 70	Musgrove. CALCULTD D+GAM WIDTH GIVEN	
Strnth Fnctn	–		AUA	Theo Rept	AAEC/E-211	Nov 70	Musgrove. SMOOTHED S0,S1 AND S2 GIVN	

61 Promethium 150

Quantity	Energy (ev) Min	Max	Lab	Type	Documentation Ref Vol Page	Date	Author, Comments	Data
Reson Params	–		AUA	Theo Rept	AAEC/E-211	Nov 70	Musgrove. CALCULTD D+GAM WIDTH GIVEN	
Strnth Fnctn	–		AUA	Theo Rept	AAEC/E-211	Nov 70	Musgrove. SMOOTHED S0,S1 AND S2 GIVN	

61 Promethium 151

Quantity	Energy (ev) Min	Max	Lab	Type	Documentation Ref Vol Page	Date	Author, Comments	Data
Evaluation	1.0-3	1.5+7	AUA	Eval Rept	AAEC/TM-549	Jun 70	Cook.TOT,EL,INEL,NONEL,CAPT SIGS,NDG	+
				Rept	AAEC/E-214	Jun 71	Bertram+GROUP SIGMAS SAME QUANTS.NDG	
				Rept	AAEC/TM-587	Mar 71	*DESCRIPTION OF LIBRARY	
	1.0-3	1.5+7		Data	AUSTR-DFN 155.	Nov 71	POINT(223) AND GROUP(127) SIGMAS	
Total	1.0-3	1.5+7	AUA	Eval Data	AUSTR-DFN 155.	Nov 71	COOK+POINT(223)+GROUP(127)SIG.CF EVL	+
Elastic	1.0-3	1.5+7	AUA	Eval Data	AUSTR-DFN 155.	Nov 71	COOK+POINT(223)+GROUP(127)SIG.CF EVL	+
Tot Inelastc	5.0+5	1.5+7	AUA	Eval Data	AUSTR-DFN 155.	Nov 71	COOK+POINT(11)+GROUP(127)SIG.CF EVL	+
Nonelastic	1.0-3	1.5+7	AUA	Eval Data	AUSTR-DFN 155.	Nov 71	COOK+POINT(223)+GROUP(127)SIG.CF EVL	+
Absorption	2.5-2		IJI	Eval Rept	KIYAI-76-6	76	Fedorova+ ONLY 1LIT-VALUE=RECOMM.TBL	
				Conf	75Kiev 1 169	May 75	– + EVAL SIG GIVEN,TABLE	
Res Int Abs	5.0-1		AUA	Eval Rept	AAEC/TM-619	Sep 72	Clayton.CALC FROM SIG LIBRARY,TABLE	
Res Int Abs	5.5-1	+6	SAC	Revw Conf	IAEA-169 1 235	74	Ribon.CAPTURE,STATUS CFD REQUEST,TBL	

61   Promethium   151

Quantity	Energy (ev) Min	Max	Lab	Type	Documentation Ref Vol Page	Author, Comments Date	Data
Res Int Abs	+0	+5	WIN Revw	Conf	IAEA – 169 3 163	74 Pope+ DATA FILE CALCS COMPARED	
(n,γ)	Pile		CRC Expt	Conf	68Wash. 1291	Mar 68 Mowatt+ DEPLETION METH.LESS THAN 700	+
	Pile			Data	EXFOR12141.003	Jun 76 . 1 PT.	
(n,γ)	1.0 – 3	1.5 + 7	AUA Eval	Data	AUSTR – DFN 155.	Nov 71 COOK+POINT(223)+GROUP(127)SIG.CF EVL	+
(n,γ)	Pile		CRC Eval	Rept	AECL – 3037 1	Jan 72 Walker.RECOMMENDED SIG,DETAILED TBL	
(n,γ)	2.5 – 2		AUA Eval	Rept	AAEC/TM – 619	Sep 72 Clayton.CALC FROM SIG LIBRARY,TABLE	
(n,γ)	2.5 – 2		SAC Revw	Conf	IAEA – 169 1 235	74 Ribon.STATUS SIG CFD REQUESTS,TABLE	
	Fiss			Conf	IAEA – 169 1 235	74 – .STATUS SIG CFD REQUESTS,TABLE	
(n,γ)	Maxwl	Fiss	WIN Revw	Conf	IAEA – 169 3 163	74 Pope+ MAXW+FIS – SPEC AVG EVAL DATA	
	Fiss			Conf	IAEA – 169 3 137	74 Dean. POINT DATA AVG OVER STAND SPEC	
Reson Params	–		AUA Theo	Rept	AAEC/E – 211	Nov 70 Musgrove. CALCULTD D+GAM WIDTH GIVEN	
Strnth Fnctn	–		AUA Theo	Rept	AAEC/E – 211	Nov 70 Musgrove. SMOOTHED S0,S1 AND S2 GIVN	

61   Promethium   152

Quantity	Energy (ev) Min	Max	Lab	Type	Documentation Ref Vol Page	Author, Comments Date	Data
Reson Params	–		AUA Theo	Rept	AAEC/E – 211	Nov 70 Musgrove. CALCULTD D+GAM WIDTH GIVEN	
Strnth Fnctn	–		AUA Theo	Rept	AAEC/E – 211	Nov 70 Musgrove. SMOOTHED S0,S1 AND S2 GIVN	

62 Samarium

Quantity	Energy (ev) Min	Max	Lab	Type	Documentation Ref Vol Page	Date	Author, Comments	Data
Evaluation	5.0+5	1.5+7	LRL Eval	Rept	UCRL-5351	Nov 58	Howerton+ CURVES	
Evaluation	2.5-2	1.0+7	GEN Eval	Rept	APEX-704	Nov 61	Cooper+ CONTENT OF C-FINE TAPES	
Evaluation	2.5-2	1.0+7	KFK Eval	Rept	KFK-352	Aug 65	Schmidt+.TOT SEL DEL(MUXI)SNE SIN NG	
Total	Maxwl		COL Expt	Jour	PR 48 265	Aug 35	Dunning+ IONCH,TRANS,RA-BE/PARAFIN N	
Total	Maxwl		COL Expt	Jour	PR 49 453	Mar 36	Mitchell. TRANS. CD STOPPED.CFD METH	
Total	4.0-2	6.5+1	ANL Expt	Jour	PR 71 757	Jun 47	Sturm. CRYSPC.TRNS 3 RES APPAR. CRV	+
	4.0-2	7.4-1		Data	EXFOR12136.008	Jun 76	. 34 PTS.	
Total	5.0-3	1.8-1	KJL Expt	Jour	PR 93 195	Jan 54	Mcreynolds+ PB CRYST SPEC B-W FIT	+
	5.0-3	9.6-1		Data	EXFOR20101.002	Sep 71	40PTS.	
Total	6.0+4	3.0+6	WIS Expt	Jour	PR 93 461	Feb 54	Okazaki+ TRANS AVG OVER RESON OKS TH	+
	7.0+4	3.0+6		Data	EXFOR12061.003	Jun 76	. 46 PTS.	
Total	4.0-2	1.0+0	BNL Expt	Jour	PR 96 1014	Nov 54	Sailor+	+
	4.0-2	1.0+0		Data	EXFOR12110.002	Jun 76	. 58 PTS.	
Total	1.4+2	2.9+5	HAR Expt	Priv	EGELSTAFF4	Jun 55	Egelstaff. TOF.CHOPPER.	+
Total	2.5+0	1.0+4	CCP Expt	Conf	55Geneva 4 22	Aug 55	Vladimirski+.P641,CURVE,CHOPPER,TOF	
Total	6.0+4	1.8+7	LAS Theo	Rept	LA-2099	Dec 56	Schrandt+OPTMDL CALC CFD EXPT,CURVE	
Total	1.0+3	3.2+4	HAR Expt	Jour	PPSA 70 51	Jan 57	Gayther+ FC THICK SAMPLE,AVSIG CF TH	
Total	1.2+0	4.4+3	BNL Expt	Priv	ZIMMERMAN	Apr 57	Zimmerman.	+
	1.2+0	4.4+3		Data	EXFOR12145.002	Jun 76	. 207 PTS.	
Total	1.2+1	7.4+2	MTR Expt	Prog	IDO-16373 39	Jul 57	Simpson+RES PARS FROM TOT CS DATA	+
	1.1+1	7.4+2		Data	EXFOR11983.002	Jun 76	. 616 PTS.	
Total	1.3+7	1.6+7	LAS Expt	Jour	PR 109 1268	Feb 58	Conner.TRNS SC 3ES 5.10 5.14 5.24B	+
				Conf	58Geneva 15 11	Sep 58	Coon+ SIGMA AT 3ES VN. TOF.	
	1.3+7	1.6+7		Data	EXFOR11320.009	Jun 76	. 3 PTS.	
Total	6.0-1	1.8+1	MTR Expt	Priv	SIMPSON	Mar 58	Simpson.	+
	6.0-1	1.8+1		Data	EXFOR12072.003	Jun 76	. 373 PTS.	
Total	4.0+2	2.0+3	HAR Theo	Jour	PPS 71 910	Jun 58	Egelstaff.FLUCTUATIONS CFD THEORY	
Total	4.0-2	3.0+1	ORL Expt	Conf	58Geneva 16 150	Sep 58	Harvey+ PPR673,CURVE,CRYSTALSPECTROM	
	6.0-1	2.5+1		Conf	57Col.Univ 105	Sep 57	- + CURV.	
Total	Maxwl		CRC Expt	Jour	NUC 16 10 108	Oct 58	Westcott. NRX ABSOL CURVE 20-76DEGC	
Total	1.5-4	3.0-3	MUN Expt	Jour	ADP 7 50	Jan 61	Hoehne. TOF RSLN FUNCT GIVEN	+
Total	4.0-1	5.0-1	FEI Expt	Prog	INDSWG-120 17	65	Doil'Nicyn.TOF,RESONANC STRUCTR, NDG	
Total	8.5-4	2.8-1	JAE Expt	Prog	INDSWG-90 2	Jul 65	Ohno.ENRICHED SAMPL FOR LO-E-RES,NDG	+
	8.5-4	2.8-1		Data	EXFOR20327.002	Jul 74	67PTS.	
Total	1.0+4	1.0+7	KFK Eval	Rept	KFK-352	Aug 65	Schmidt.GRAPHS+TABULATED DATA(NO.12)	
Total	1.4+7		ANL Expt	Abst	DA/B 28 3835	Mar 68	Haugsnes. SIG=5.01=-0.04B CFD OPTMDS	+
				Rept	ANL-5609	Nov 56	.SUPERSEDED.	
	1.4+7			Data	EXFOR11733.008	Jun 76	. 1 PT.	
Total	6.2-2	9.5-1	CNA Expt	Rept	CNAEM-52	Jun 68	Akyuz+ CRYST SPEC,GAP .32-.78EV,2RES	+
	6.2-2	9.5-1		Data	EXFOR20173.	May 74	47PTS.A*TOT(RES).	
Total	3.0+5	1.5+6	ANL Expt	Jour	NSE 39 67	Jan 70	Sherwood+ TOF, CFD ENDF/B DATA	+
				Prog	ANL-7610 14	Jan 70	Whalen+ CURVE	
				Rept	ANL-7567	May 69	Sherwood+DATA PTS. IN APPENDIX	
	3.0+5	1.5+6		Data	EXFOR10007.015	May 75	. 347 PTS.	
Total	5.0+5	1.5+7	AUA Theo	Rept	AAEC/TM-536	Apr 70	Bertram. OPTMOD SIG(E)GRAPH CFD EXPT	
Total	2.5+6	1.5+7	BNW Expt	Jour	PR/C 3 576	Feb 71	Foster+ TRANS,CURVS,CFD OTHERS + TH	+
				Jour	NIM 36 1	Sep 65	.EXPT DETAILS	
	2.2+6	1.5+7		Data	EXFOR10047.066	Aug 73	. 254 PTS.	
Total	2.7+3		MUN Expt	Prog	EANDC(E)150U	Oct 72	Dilg+ AVERAGE TOT XSECT+S0	+
				Conf	71Albany 327	Aug 71	- +TRNS.AVG CS GVN.31 ELEMENT GRP	
	2.7+3			Data	EXFOR20583.016	May 76	1PNT.	
Total	1.3+7	1.5+7	DEB Eval	Rept	IAEA-153 173	73	Boedy+ MOST PROBABLE VAL OF SIG,TBL	
Total	1.4+7		LIN Expt	Conf	73Kiev 3 108	May 73	Djumin+ OPTMOD CALC,SIG(A),GRAPH	
Total	1.4+5	6.3+5	DKE Expt	Jour	AP 84 165	May 74	Pineo+ TRNS.AVG CS.TBL GRPHS.OPTMDL	+
	1.0+5	6.5+5		Jour	AP 84 1 165	May 74	- + CURV. TBL. CFD OPT. MOD.	
	1.5+4	6.0+5		Diss	PINEO	70	.AVG CS.GRPHS.CFD.STF CALC.TBL.CFD.	
	1.5+4	6.0+5		Data	EXFOR10542.020	Jan 79	. DATA UNOBTAINABLE FROM AUTHORS.	
Total	7.0+5	9.0+6	GLS Expt	Jour	JP/A 7 1758	Sep 74	Kellie+ SIG IN CURVE,STAT ERROR 2 PC	+
	7.0+5	9.0+6		Data	EXFOR20418.006	Sep 75	646PTS.	
Total	None		SAC Theo	Jour	JPR 35 4	Sep 74	Lagrange+OPTMDL FOR EVEN ISO.DEFORMT	
Elastic	2.0-2	1.5-1	CRC Expt	Jour	PR 83 841	Aug 51	Brockhouse+ RATIO SCATT/ABS REL V.	+
	2.5-2	1.6-1		Data	EXFOR11653.005	Jun 76	. 15 PTS. RATIO.	
Elastic	1.0+6		ALD Expt	Jour	NP 42 86	Apr 63	Gilboy+.SIG=6.54B+-3PC	+
Elastic	1.0+4	1.0+7	KFK Eval	Rept	KFK-352	Aug 65	Schmidt.GRAPHS+TABULATED DATA(NO.12)	
Elastic	1.5+6		IFU Expt	Prog	YFI-5 42	Oct 67	Korzh+ TBL OPTMDL PARAMS + TOTELAST	
				Rept	INDC-232E	67	. ENGL OF YFI-5 42	

62 Samarium

Quantity	Energy (ev) Min	Energy (ev) Max	Lab	Type	Documentation Ref Vol Page	Date	Author, Comments	Data
Elastic	1.5+6		IFU	Comp	Jour YF 7 277	Feb 68	Korzh+ OPTMOD PARS-FIT TO EXPTL-SIG	
					Jour SNP 7 2 190	Aug 68	TRANSLATN.*	
Elastic	3.0+5	1.5+6	ANL	Expt	Jour NSE 39 67	Jan 70	Sherwood+ INTEGRATED SIG. CURVE	+
					Abst DA 30 3211	Jan 70	- +	
					Rept ANL-7567	May 69	- +CALC CS AND LEG COEFS GVN.	
					Prog EANDC(US)-62	Mar 65	Smith.TOF,TBL.50KEV STEPS,20KEV RSLN	
	3.0+5	1.5+6			Data EXFOR10007.012	May 75	. 55 PTS. INTEGRATED CS.	
Elastic	5.0+5	1.5+7	AUA	Theo	Rept AAEC/TM-536	Apr 70	Bertram. OPTMOD SIG(E)GRAPH CFD EXPT	
Diff Elastic	1.0+5	1.8+7	LAS	Theo	Rept LA-2099	Dec 56	Beyster+ 21ES. OPTMDl CALC cFD ExPT*	
Diff Elastic	1.0+6		ALD	Expt	Jour NP 42 86	Apr 63	Gilboy+30TO137DEG.COMP.WITH OPTICMOD	+
Diff Elastic	1.5+6		IFU	Comp	Jour YF 7 277	Feb 68	Korzh+ GRPH SIG(ANG),OPTMOD PARS-FIT	
					Jour SNP 7 2 190	Aug 68	TRANSLATN.*	
Diff Elastic	3.0+5	1.5+6	ANL	Expt	Jour NSE 39 67	Jan 70	Sherwood+ TOF,CFD OPTMDL,20KEV RESOL	
					Abst DA/B 30 3211	Jan 70	- .	
					Rept ANL-7567	May 69	- +GRPH DEL VS ANG AT .98 MEV.	
					Prog EANDC(US)-62	Mar 65	Smith+TOF.TBL.50KEV STEPS,20KEV RSLN	
Polarization	3.8+5		WIS	ExTh	Jour NP 6 177	Mar 58	Clement+ POLARIZATION. CFD OPT MDL	
				Expt	Rept AECU-3628	57	- + LI7 (P,N)SOURCE. 2 ANGLES.	
Potntal Scat		+5	ANL	Expt	Jour PR 79 11	Jul 50	Harris+ FROM RES INT SCATTERING.	
Potntal Scat	9.6-2		CRC	Expt	Jour CJP 31 432	Mar 53	Brockhouse.FROM ASSUMD ABS AND WIDTH	
Potntal Scat	+4		HAR	Expt	Jour PPSA 70 51	Jan 57	Gayther+ FROM AVG SIGTOT. FC TRANSM	
Potntal Scat	1.0+0		CNA	Expt	Rept CNAEM-52	Jun 68	Akyuz+. CALCULATED WITH R(EFF).	+
Potntal Scat	3.0+3	6.5+5	DKE	Expt	Jour AP 84 165	May 74	Pineo+TRNS.S WAVE SCT LENGTH.TBL.CFD	
	3.0+5	6.5+5			Jour AP 84 1 165	May 74	- + S-WAVE SCATTERING LENGTH.	
	3.0+3	6.5+5			Diss PINEO	70	.TBL.GRPHS.CFD TO 3 COLLECTIVE MDLS.	
Tot Inelastc	1.0+4	1.0+7	KFK	Eval	Rept KFK-352	Aug 65	Schmidt.GRAPHS+TABULATED DATA(NO.12)	
Tot Inelastc	5.0+6	7.0+6	ALD	Expt	Jour NP/A 112 337	May 68	Owens+.3ES.FROM N SPECT 90DEG.	+
Diff Inelast	5.0+6	7.0+6	ALD	Expt	Jour NP/A 112 337	May 68	Owens+.3ES.FROM N SPECT 90DEG NDG.	+
					Conf 65Antwerp 547	Jul 65	- + PPR122.ABST.SPECT N' AT 90DEG	
Diff Inelast	5.2+5	1.5+6	ANL	Expt	Jour NSE 39 67	Jan 70	Sherwood+ TOF, CFD OPTICAL MODEL	+
					Abst DA/B 30 3211	Jan 70	- .	
					Rept ANL-7567	May 69	- +DIN VS ANG .98 MEV.	
	5.2+5	1.5+6			Data EXFOR10007.014	May 75	. 112 PTS. CALC CS.	
Scattering	2.5-2	1.0+7	GEA	Eval	Rept TID-11824	Jan 61	Zwick. GROUP AVGD+MAXWELL AVGD 18GRP	
Nonelastic	6.0+4	1.8+7	LAS	Theo	Rept LA-2099	Dec 56	Beyster+ OPTMDL CALC CFD EXPT, CURVE	
Nonelastic	1.0+4	1.0+7	KFK	Eval	Rept KFK-352	Aug 65	Schmidt.GRAPHS+TABULATED DATA(NO.12)	
Nonelastic	5.0+5	1.5+7	AUA	Theo	Rept AAEC/TM-536	Apr 70	Bertram. OPTMOD SIG(E)GRAPH CFD EXPT	
Absorption	Pile		ANL	Expt	Jour PR 74 505	Aug 48	Dempster.EVIDENCE FOR ABS IN SM149	
					Jour PR 71 745	Jun 47	Lapp+ LARGE ABS. DUE TO SM149	
Absorption	2.0-2	1.5-1	CRC	Expt	Jour PR 83 841	Aug 51	Brockhouse+ RATIO SCATT/ABS REL V.	+
	2.5-2	1.6-1			Data EXFOR11653.005	Jun 76	. 15 PTS. RATIO.	
Absorption	Maxwl		HAR	Expt	Rept AERE-R/M-100	Dec 56	Cummins+.PILE OSC THR WELL REL HAR E	
Absorption	Pile		HAR	Expt	Jour JNE 4 33	Jan 57	Aitken+ 10380+-160B,PILE OSCIL REL B	+
Absorption	2.0-2	2.4-1	CUW	Theo	Rept CWR-400-1	Sep 57	Roberts.MAXWELL-BOLTZMANN AVGD SIGS.	
Absorption	Maxwl	Pile	HAR	Expt	Jour JNEA 12 32	May 60	Tattersall+. EFF SIG IN THREE SPECTR	
					Rept AERE-R-2887	Aug 59	- . PILE OSC.REL BORON	
	Maxwl				Rept AERE-R/R-2516	Mar 58	Jowitt+ PILE OSC.REL BORON.293DEGK.	
Absorption	2.5-2	1.0+7	GEA	Eval	Rept TID-11824	Jan 61	Zwick. GROUP AVGD+MAXWELL AVGD 18GRP	
Absorption	2.5-2		ROS	Expt	Jour KE 10 25	Jan 67	Albert.VAL 2200M/SEC GVN,LOCAL OSCIL	
Absorption	Maxwl		ROS	Expt	Rept ZFK-132 19	Dec 67	Faehrmann. CFD WITH OTHER AUTHORS	
Res Int Abs		+5	ANL	Expt	Jour PR 79 11	Jul 50	Harris+ EPI-CD, B-W TH	
Res Int Abs	Pile		FAR	Expt	Jour CR 234 2448	Jun 52	Netter+. PILE OSC. REL B.LOWER LIMIT	
Res Int Abs	-		CCP	Expt	Jour AE 3 507	Dec 57	Klimentov+.EPI CD REACTIVITY REL LI	+
					Jour JNE 9 20	Jun 59	TRANSLATN.*	
					Jour SJA 3 1387	57	TRANSLATN.*	
(n,γ)	Maxwl		COL	Expt	Jour PR 50 738	Oct 36	Fink. RATE OF ABS+SIGMA AS FCT OF T	
(n,γ)	Pile		ANL	Expt	Jour PR 72 888	Nov 47	Seren+ ACT METHOD.21MIN.60D OBSERVED	+
	Pile				Data EXFOR11447.097	Jun 76	. 1 PT.	
(n,γ)	Pile		ANL	Expt	Jour PR 80 342	Nov 50	Harris+ PILE OSC.REL TO BORON,APPROX	
	Pile				Data EXFOR11528.038	Jun 76	. 1 PT.	
(n,γ)	Maxwl		ORL	Expt	Jour PR 83 643	Aug 51	Pomerance. LOCAL OSC REL AU ABS 95 B	+
	Maxwl				Data EXFOR11047.048	Jun 76	. 1 PT.	
(n,γ)	Pile		CRC	Eval	Rept CRRP-960	Nov 60	Westcott.G,S FACTORS EFFECTIVE CAPT.	
					Rept CRRP-862	Aug 59	.SUPERSEDED.	
					Rept CRRP-787	Aug 58	.SUPERSEDED.	
					Rept CRRP-680	Jan 57	.SUPERSEDED.	

62 Samarium

Quantity	Energy (ev) Min	Max	Lab	Type	Documentation Ref Vol Page	Date	Author, Comments	Data
(n,γ)	2.5−2		ANL Expt	Jour	NSE 9 132	Feb 61	Meadows+ PULSED NEUTS. 5828+ −30B	+
	2.5−2			Data	EXFOR11028.019	Sep 76	. 1 PT. CS=5828 B	
(n,γ)	3.0+4	1.7+5	ORL Expt	Jour	PR 122 182	Apr 61	Gibbons+ 875, 450MB AND 330MB.	+
	3.0+4	6.5+4		Jour	PR 129 2695	Mar 63	Macklin+ LIQ SCINT,875 AND 450MB	
	3.0+4	1.7+5		Conf	61Vienna 1 95	Aug 61	Neiler.	
	9.5+3	1.7+5		Data	EXFOR11329.	Jun 76	. 3 PTS(30−170KEV).52 PTS(9.5−170KEV	
(n,γ)	2.0+2	8.0+3	ORL Expt	Conf	61Saclay 203	Sep 61	Block+ LARGE LIQUID SCINTILLATOR	+
				Conf	61Vienna 1 95	Aug 61	Neiler. TABLE FOR 3ES GVN, GRAPH	
	2.1+2	7.8+3		Data	EXFOR11935.011	Jun 76	. 43 PTS.	
(n,γ)	5.0+3	9.0+4	ORL Theo	Jour	RMP 37 166	Jan 65	Macklin+ CALC ASSUM.MAX. SHAPE	
(n,γ)	1.0+3	1.0+5	FEI Theo	Jour	AE 18 114	Feb 65	Dovbenko+ H−F THEORY CFD DATA	
				Jour	JNE 20 675	66	. ENGL OF AE 18 114	
				Jour	SJA 18 140	Feb 65	. ENGL OF AE 18 114	
(n,γ)	1.0+4	1.0+7	KFK Eval	Rept	KFK−352	Aug 65	Schmidt.GRAPHS+TABULATED DATA(NO.12)	
(n,γ)	2.5−2	2.5−2	AE Expt	Jour	NUK 6 245	Sep 68	Sokolowski+.PILE OSC. FAST CHOPPER.	+
	Pile			Data	EXFOR20077.	Sep 71	3PTS.SIG.	
(n,γ)	1.0+0	1.0+7	BOL Eval	Rept	CEC(70)−2	Apr 70	Benzi.GRAPH=SUM OF SIG(ISOTOPES)	
(n,γ)	3.0+4		AUA Theo	Rept	AAEC/E−211	Nov 70	Musgrove. SIGMA GIVEN AND CFD OTHER	
(n,γ)	3.0+4	1.6+5	USP Expt	Jour	NP/A 196 83	Nov 72	Lepine+ LI7−P NS.TOF.M−R. REL TO IN	+
	3.0+4	1.6+5		Data	EXFOR30233.002	Mar 73	NDS,RELATIVE TO IN,ABSOLUTE ERROR	
(n,γ)	1.1+0	3.1+4	KFK Expt	Jour	JNE 27 811	Nov 73	Chou+ ABSOL EXPT.SDT SPECTROM.	+
				Rept	KFK−EXT−4 28	Nov 70	− . ABS EXPT	
	1.1+0	3.1+4		Data	EXFOR20352.	Sep 74	314 PTS.SIGMA.	
(n,γ)	1.0+3	1.0+7	FEI Eval	Rept	YK−8/2 97	Sep 72	Abagjan+ AVG SIG(ENERGY−GROUPS),TABL	
				Rept	INDC(CCP)−39	Jul 74	.P102. ENGLISH OF YK−8/2 97	
(n,γ)	1.0+6	1.0+7	CRC Revw	Conf	74Petten 119	Sep 74	Bartholomew+ PHOTON STRF GRPH	
(n,γ)	1.0+3	3.7+5	FEI ExTh	Conf	75Kiev 3 190	May 75	Jurlov+ REL B10(N,A).SIG(E),GRAPH	
(n,γ)	None		MUNTheo	Diss	GRYNTAKIS	Mar 76	Gryntakis.,CALC.OF WESTCOTTS G−FUNCT	
				Jour	RCA 22 128	Mar 75	− +,EQUIVALENT TO THESIS	
Spect (n,γ)	Maxwl		ANL Expt	Jour	PR 76 531	Aug 49	Kubitscheck+ MAX E.G−M COINC+ABSORBR	
Spect (n,γ)	Maxwl		CRC Expt	Jour	CJP 31 1051	Nov 53	Kinsey+ PAIR SPECT,LINE WIDTH=100KEV	
Spect (n,γ)	Maxwl		CCP Expt	Conf	55Moscow 270	Jul 55	Adjasevich+. CURVES AND DISCUSSION	
				Rept	AEC−TR−2435	55	.PAGE 195,ENGL OF 55MOSCOW 270	
Spect (n,γ)	Maxwl		CCP		Rept AEC−TR−2435PT1	56	.USSR PAGE 196	
Spect (n,γ)	Maxwl		GEA Eval	Rept	DC−58−1−30	Jan 58	Deloume. BY APPROXIMATION.TABLE+CURV	
Spect (n,γ)	Maxwl		YAL Expt	Jour	PR 114 268	Apr 59	Draper.SC SPECTR,GAM E 0 TO 600 KEV	
Spect (n,γ)	Maxwl		ARF Expt	Prog	ARF−1193−12	Jul 62	Greenwood+ CRYST SPEC., LOW−E GAMMAS	
Spect (n,γ)	Pile		MUNExpt	Conf	63ANL 148	Oct 63	Bieber+ CONVERSION ELECTRON SPECTRUM	
Spect (n,γ)		8.6−1	FEI Expt	Jour	JINR−1845 137	Jun 64	Alnikov+,CHOPPER,.096+.86EV*RES,GRPH	
				Conf	64Paris 2 820	Jul 64	.	
				Rept	ANL−TRANS−178	64	.	
Spect (n,γ)	2.5−2		MIT Comp	Rept	MITNE−85	Jan 69	Rasmussen+TBL G INT.=AFCRL−69−0071	
Spect (n,γ)	Pile		ANL Expt	Prog	WASH−1127 10	Apr 69	Bollinger+. AVE RES LVL ONLY, NDG.TBC	
Spect (n,γ)	Maxwl		MUNExpt	Jour	ZP 258 315	Mar 73	Henkelmann. E + INT OF GS GIVEN	+
	2.5−2			Data	EXFOR20606.010	Jun 76	2PTS.	
Inelastic γ	4.4+6		WES Expt	Jour	PR 107 1306	Sep 57	Sinclair.XTL SPEC NONE OBSERVED	
Inelastic γ	5.0+6	7.0+6	ALD Expt	Jour	NP/A 112 337	May 68	Owens+.3ES.TOF SPECT 90 DEG. NDG.	+
(n,2n)	1.5+7		DEB Eval	Jour	REA 11 1 153	Mar 73	Boedy+ RECOMM.VALUE FROM N−Z SYSTEM.	
(n,p)	1.4+7		MNZExpt	Jour	RCA 22 11	75	Weigel+SUM OF (N,P)+(N,NP)+(N,D)SIG	
(n,np)	1.4+7		MNZExpt	Jour	RCA 22 11	75	Weigel+ TOT SIG, ACT METHOD	
(n,α)	2.0+0	4.0+2	DUB Expt	Rept	JINR−E3−3029	Nov 66	Kvitek+,ALPHA EMISS VS E(N),GRAPH	
	6.0+0	4.1+2		Rept	YFI−3 26	Sep 66	− + ALFA−WIDTH,EXPT CFD THEORY	
	1.1+0	1.4+2		Jour	IZV 30 1371	Jul 66	− + GRAPH SIG(E),TBL OF PARAMS	
	6.0+0	4.1+2		Rept	INDC−140E 28	67	. ENGL TRANSL OF YFI−3 26	
	1.1+0	1.4+2		Jour	BAS 30 1432	66	. ENGL OF IZV 30 1371	
Reson Params	9.6−2	3.3+1	ANL Expt	Jour	PR 71 757	Jun 47	Sturm+ CRYSTSPEC TRANS SIG.WT=.074EV	+
	9.6−2	3.3+1		Data	EXFOR12136.005	Jun 76	. 3 RES, E0,WT,PCS.	
Reson Params	1.2+1		BNL Expt	Jour	PR 96 1014	Nov 54	Sailor+	+
	1.2+1			Data	EXFOR12110.010	Jun 76	. 1 RES, E0.	
Reson Params	3.4+0	5.2+1	BNL Expt	Priv	PILCHER	Apr 55	Pilcher.	+
	3.4+0	5.2+1		Data	EXFOR12041.008	Jun 76	. 24 RES, E0,WN.	
Reson Params	1.2+1	9.9+1	MTR Expt	Prog	IDO−16373 39	Jul 57	Simpson.G*WN,WG,RED WN.TBL	+
	4.8+1	9.3+1		Data	EXFOR11983.004	Jun 76	. 4 RES, E0.	
Reson Params	−.6−1		MUNExpt	Jour	ADP 7 50	Jan 61	SIG=48B.EV1/2 WT=.1EV G.REDUCED WN	
Reson Params	9.7−2		AE Expt	Jour	NUK 6 245	Sep 68	Sokolowski+ E0,WG BREIT−WIGNER FIT.	+
	9.7−2			Data	EXFOR20077.009	Sep 71	1PNT.WG.	
Reson Params	1.8+2		DUB Expt	Jour	PL 22 186	Aug 66	Kvitek+POPOV ALPHA WIDTHS 1RES	

62 Samarium

Quantity	Energy (ev) Min	Max	Lab	Type	Documentation Ref Vol Page	Author, Comments Date	Data
Reson Params	9.7−2	8.7−1	CNA Expt	Rept	CNAEM−52	Jun 68 Akyuz+ B−W SINGLE LVL ANALYSIS	+
	9.7−2	8.7−1		Data	EXFOR20173.	May 74 12PTS.A*WG,A*WN,A*S0*WT,A*WT,−−	
Strnth Fnctn	+4		HAR Expt	Jour	PPSA 70 51	Jan 57 Gayther+ FROM AVG SIGTOT. FC TRANSM	
Strnth Fnctn	2.7+3		MUN Expt	Conf	71Albany 327	Aug 71 Dilg+TRNS.S0 STF GVN.31 ELEMENT GRPH	
Strnth Fnctn	1.1+0	3.1+4	KFK Expt	Jour	JNE 27 811	Nov 73 Chou+ P−WAVE,WG/D.FROM ABSOL NG−EXPT	+
				Rept	KFK−EXT−4 28	Nov 70 −. SI=0.61	
	1.0+0	5.0+4		Data	EXFOR20352.	Sep 74 2PTS.GAMMA STRNGTH FUNC,L=1.	
Strnth Fnctn	3.0+3	6.5+5	DKE Expt	Jour	AP 84 1 165	May 74 Pineo+ S−WAVE SCATTERING LENGTH.	
Lvl Density	5.0+6	7.0+6	ALD Expt	Jour	NP/A 112 337	May 68 Owens+.LVL DENS VERSUS EXCIT.MEAN T	+
				Conf	65Antwerp 547	Jul 65 − + PPR122. TBL FERMI GAS CONST.	
Lvl Density	None		SAC Expt	Jour	NP/A 133 417	Aug 69 Bergere+NUCL TEMP,A PARAM,FROM NG	
Lvl Density	None		FEI Theo	Jour	YF 11 1213	Jun 70 Ignatyuk+ SPIN DEPENDENCE OF DENSITY	
				Jour	SNP 11 674	Dec 70 − ENGL OF YF 11 1213	
(γ,n)	5.0+6	3.5+7	SAC Expt	Jour	NP/A 133 417	Aug 69 Bergere+LORENTZ LINE PARAM,GRPHS,TBL	

62 Samarium 142

Quantity	Energy (ev) Min	Max	Lab	Type	Documentation Ref Vol Page	Author, Comments Date	Data
Reson Params	−		AUA Theo	Rept	AAEC/E−211	Nov 70 Musgrove. CALCULTD D+GAM WIDTH GIVEN	
Strnth Fnctn	−		AUA Theo	Rept	AAEC/E−211	Nov 70 Musgrove. SMOOTHED S0,S1 AND S2 GIVN	

62 Samarium 143

Quantity	Energy (ev) Min	Max	Lab	Type	Documentation Ref Vol Page	Author, Comments Date	Data
(n,2n)	1.5+7		FIR Expt	Jour	NC/B 54 2 319	Apr 68 Curzio+ ISOM RATIO SPIN CUTOFF EVAL	
(n,2n)	1.4+7		AUW Expt	Prog	BARC−474 39	70 RAMA PRASAD+ ISOM SIG RATIO,NAI(TL)	
Reson Params	−		AUA Theo	Rept	AAEC/E−211	Nov 70 Musgrove. CALCULTD D+GAM WIDTH GIVEN	
Strnth Fnctn	−		AUA Theo	Rept	AAEC/E−211	Nov 70 Musgrove. SMOOTHED S0,S1 AND S2 GIVN	
Lvl Density	1.1+7	1.9+7	ANL Eval	Rept	ANL−75−34	Jun 75 Davey+N2NEVAL.CONSTANT T,LVL DEN FIT	

62 Samarium 144

Quantity	Energy (ev) Min	Max	Lab	Type	Documentation Ref Vol Page	Author, Comments Date	Data
Total	1.4+7		LIN Expt	Jour	IZV 37 1019	May 73 Djumin+ SIG(A),OPTMODEL CALC,GRAPH	+
				Conf	73Kiev 3 108	May 73 − + OPTMOD CALC,SIG	
				Jour	BAS 37 5 91	May 73 .ENGLISH OF IZV 37 1019	
	1.4+7			Data	EXFOR40302.009	Feb 76 1 PNT	
Nonelastic	1.4+7	1.9+7	ANL Eval	Rept	ANL−75−34	Jun 75 Davey+CORRC APPLIED TO N2N CS.TBLS.	
Absorption	Pile		MTR Expt	Abst	BAP 3 63	Jan 58 Carey+ SIG=APPROX. 0.03B.	
Absorption	2.5−2		IJI Eval	Conf	75Kiev 1 169	May 75 Fedorova+ EVAL SIG GIVEN,TABLE	
(n,γ)	Pile		MCM Expt	Diss	WALKER	May 56 Walker.	+
	Pile			Data	EXFOR12127.002	Jun 76 . 1 PT.	
(n,γ)	Pile		HLS Expt	Jour	PR 127 943	Aug 62 Kauranen+.ESTIMATE S=.7B.	+
	Pile			Data	EXFOR20104.002	Sep 71 1PNT.SIG.	
(n,γ)	3.0+4		ORL Expt	Jour	NAT 197 370	Jan 63 Macklin. 119+−55 MB.	+
	3.0+4			Data	EXFOR12095.002	Jun 76 . 1 PT.	
(n,γ)	5.0+3	9.0+4	ORL Theo	Jour	RMP 37 166	Jan 65 Macklin+ CALC ASSUMING MAX. SHAPE.	
(n,γ)	1.0+3	1.0+5	CCP Theo	Jour	AE 18 114	Feb 65 Dovbenko+ STATIST MOD CURVE CFD DATA	
				Jour	JNE 20 675	Aug 66 TRANSLATN.*	
				Jour	EAF 18 2 44	Feb 65 TRANSLATN.*	
				Jour	SJA 18 140	Feb 65 TRANSLATN.*	
(n,γ)	−		IEA Comp	Rept	IEA−INF−10	Aug 68 Atalla. TABLES OF HL,SIG AND GAMM−E	
(n,γ)	1.0+3	1.0+7	BOL Eval	Rept	CCDN−NW/10	Dec 69 Benzi+H−F MOD,AXEL G(G)EST,ALL DATA	
				Rept	CEC(70)−2	Apr 70 − +. GRAPH	
(n,γ)	3.0+4		AUA Theo	Rept	AAEC/E−211	Nov 70 Musgrove. SIGMA GIVEN AND CFD OTHER	
(n,γ)	Maxwl	Fiss	WIN Revw	Conf	IAEA−169 3 163	74 Pope+ FIS−SPEC AVG DATA CFD MAXW−XPT	
(n,γ)	1.0+3	1.0+7	FEI Eval	Conf	YK−8/2 97	Sep 72 Abagjan+ AVG SIG(ENERGY−GROUPS),TABL	
				Rept	INDC(CCP)−39	Jul 74 .P102. ENGLISH OF YK−8/2 97	
(n,γ)	2.5−2		IJI Eval	Rept	KIYAI−76−6	76 Fedorova+ ONLY 1LIT−VALUE=RECOMM.TBL	
Spect (n,γ)	Pile		SWR Expt	Jour	AF 34 531	Dec 67 Baecklin+. HL FOR 1ST LVL.DELD COINC	
Spect (n,γ)	None		ANL Expt	Conf	74Petten 358	Sep 74 Smither+AVG NEUTR.CAPT. (PROGR.)	
(n,2n)	1.5+7		ARK Expt	Jour	PR 118 242	Apr 60 Wille+ MEAS ACT SIG=1200+−300MB.	+
				Jour	PR 112 1950	Dec 58 − + 1200+−300MB. CFD TH	
	1.5+7			Data	EXFOR12033.027	Jun 76 . 1 PT.	

62 Samarium 144

Quantity	Energy (ev) Min	Energy (ev) Max	Lab	Type	Documentation Ref Vol Page	Author, Comments Date	Data
(n,2n)	Fiss		CRC	Eval Rept	CRC - 1003	Dec 60 ROY+ ESTIMATED AVG SIG=0.4MB.	
(n,2n)	1.4+7		ANL	Expt Jour	PR 122 168	Apr 61 Rayburn. 1484 MB+ -8 PERCENT.	+
	1.4+7			Data	EXFOR11328.030	Jun 76 . 1 PT.	
(n,2n)	1.5+7		RED	Expt Jour	PR 129 703	Jan 63 Alford+ XSECT,ISOM YLD REL CU63(N2N)	+
	1.5+7			Data	EXFOR12116.	Jun 76 . 2 PTS. SIG+ISM RATIO.	
(n,2n)	1.4+7		HAM	Comp Jour	NP 65 257	Mar 65 Bormann. 3EXPT VALS.CFD SHELL EFFECT	
(n,2n)	1.5+7		REN	Expt Jour	PR/B 139 1525	Sep 65 Broadhead+ C-W ACT	+
	1.5+7			Data	EXFOR11874.004	Jun 76 . 1 PT.	
(n,2n)	1.5+7		TAM	Expt Jour	PR 156 1340	Apr 67 Menon+ ACT GND, ISOM,	+
	1.5+7			Data	EXFOR12066.	Jun 76 . 1 PT EACH. GND, ISOM, + RATIO.	
(n,2n)	1.3+7		DEB	Expt Jour	AHP 23 87	May 67 Csikai+ ACTIV,SIG AT THR+3MEV, TABLE	+
				Jour	MFF 16 123	Feb 68 SEE ALSO *THEORY+TABLES	
	1.4+7			ExTh Jour	PL 20 52	Jan 66 Csikai+ CFD CURVE VS (N-Z)	
	1.3+7			Expt Data	EXFOR30033.017	Sep 70 SINGLE VALUE	
(n,2n)	1.4+7		LYO	Comp Rept	LYCEN/6780	Nov 67 Crouzet+COMPILATN FOR ACTIVTN ANALYS	
(n,2n)	1.4+7		NAP	Expt Jour	NC/B 52 2 476	Dec 67 Cuzzocrea+. SIG TO GROUND AND METAST	
(n,2n)	1.5+7		FIR	Expt Jour	NC/B 55 319	Apr 68 Curzio+ ISOM RATIO SPIN CUTOFF EVAL	
(n,2n)	1.3+7	1.9+7	HAM	Expt Jour	NP/A 115 309	Jul 68 Bormann++ VDG.ACT.CFD STATMDL+OPTMDL	+
(n,2n)	1.5+7		DEB	Expt Jour	NP/A 122 234	Dec 68 Karolyi+,ACT,D-T NS,ISOM RAT,CFD TH	+
	1.5+7			Data	EXFOR30101.013	Feb 71 ISOMERIC RATIO	
(n,2n)	1.4+7		AUW	Expt Jour	NP/A 125 57	Feb 69 RAMA PRASAD+,ACTIVATION,CFD OTHERS	+
				ExTh Jour	IPA 12 640	Sep 74 Rama Prasad+ CFD STATMDL COMPND VALU	
	1.4+7			Expt Data	EXFOR30051.	Dec 70 SIGMA N2N,ALSO N2N+NA+NP FOR OTHERS.	
(n,2n)	1.5+7		IBJ	Expt Jour	APPB 1 415	70 Rurarz+ ACTIV,NAI,ISORATIO VS THEORY	+
				Jour	NKA 14 933	Oct 69 - + ACTIV,NAI(TL),SIG TO ISOMER	
	1.5+7			Data	EXFOR30154.014	May 72 ISOMERIC RATIO	
	1.5+7			Data	EXFOR30098.005	Mar 71 VALUE TO METASTABLE STATE AT 14.5MEV	
(n,2n)	1.5+7		DEB	Comp Jour	REA 7 4 93	Dec 69 Csikai+ SIG+HL COMPILTN,N-ACTIV-ANAL	
(n,2n)	1.4+7	1.5+7	CCP	Comp Jour	ICD-6 215	70 Sluchevskaja.SIGS GND+ISOM,RATIO,TBL	
(n,2n)	1.4+7	1.5+7	JYV	Eval Rept	JU-RR-3/1970	Jun 70 Leppaemaeki+ TABLE OF EVAL AVG SIG	
(n,2n)	+7		KFI	Theo Rept	KFKI-71-8	Feb 71 Jeki. CALCULATED CFD EXPTL SIG VALUE	
(n,2n)	None		KFI	Comp Jour	JRC 7 365	Jun 71 Nagy+ GAMMA-E AND HALF-LIFE GIVEN	
(n,2n)	1.4+7	1.5+7	IRK	ExTh Jour	APA 33 285	Jul 71 Winiwarter+ ISOMERIC RATIO	
(n,2n)	1.5+7		RPI	Expt Jour	JIN 34 1105	Apr 72 Dewanjee+ ACT,GND AND META	+
	1.5+7			Data	EXFOR10288.	Sep 73 . 2 PTS. SIGMA.	
(n,2n)	1.4+7		CCP	Expt Jour	YF 15 1099	Jun 72 Victorov+ ACTIV,TBL CFD OTHERS+THEO	+
				Jour	SNP 15 608	Dec 72 - + ENGLISH OF YF 15 1099	
	1.4+7			Data	EXFOR40107.005	Dec 72 1 VALUE	
(n,2n)	1.5+7		DEB	Eval Jour	REA 11 1 153	Mar 73 Boedy. COMPILATION+RECOMM.VALUE,TBL	
				Rept	IAEA-153 173	73 - . RECOMM. VALUE ONLY	
(n,2n)	Fiss		KOS	Eval Jour	AK 16 351	74 Boedy. U238,MAXW-SPC.AVG CFD XPT,TBL	
(n,2n)	1.5+7	1.7+7	AUB	Expt Jour	NP/A 223 118	Apr 74 Ghori+	+
	1.5+7	1.7+7		Data	EXFOR10359.005	Jan 75 . 4 PTS. SIGMA.	
(n,2n)	1.5+7		TAT	Theo Jour	JP/A 7 1457	Aug 74 Kondaiah. CALC ON STAT MODEL	
(n,2n)	1.4+7		MNZ	Expt Jour	RCA 22 11	75 Weigel+SUM OF (N,2N)+(N,NP)+(N,D)SIG	
(n,2n)	Fiss		KOS	Eval Conf	75Karlsrhe 29	Apr 75 Csikai. CF252,MAXW-SPC.AVG FOR 2TEMP	
(n,2n)	1.1+7	1.9+7	ANL	Eval Rept	ANL-75-34	Jun 75 Davey+CONSTANT T MDL,LVL DEN MDL FIT	
(n,2n)	1.5+7		ARK	Expt Abst	DA/B 32 5091	Mar 72 Bari. GE(LI) DET. ACT. SIG GIVEN	+
	1.5+7			Data	EXFOR10431.	Aug 75 . 3 PTS. GND,META,META+GND.	
(n,2n)	1.4+7		AUW	Expt Conf	75Calcutta 2 31	Dec 75 Lakshmandas+ 981+ -90 MB ACTIVATION	
(n,2n)	1.5+7		JYV	Expt Rept	JU-RR-1/1976	Mar 76 Valkonen.(THESIS).ACTIV.TBL.14.7MEV	+
	1.5+7			Data	EXFOR20673.029	Nov 76 1PNT.SIGMA.	
(n,2n)	1.5+7		JUL	Expt Jour	NP/A 224 319	May 74 Qaim. ACT.GE(LI).TO GRND, METAST	+
				Jour	RRL 25 335	May 76 - + SIG IN GRPH. SYST VS (N-Z)/A	
	1.5+7			Data	EXFOR20541.	Apr 76 4PTS.SIGMA.	
(n,2n)	1.2+7	1.8+7	GEO	Expt Abst	BAP 8 121	Feb 63 Rayburn+900TO2300MB.CFD COMP NUCL MD	+
	1.3+7	1.8+7		Data	EXFOR11955.003	Jun 76 . 13 PTS.	
(n,2n)	1.5+7		ARK	Expt Jour	JIN 37 631	Mar 75 Sigg+ TO GND,META.FOR SYSTEMTICS,TBL	+
				Abst	DA/B 37 2237	Nov 76 - .ACT TECH.CFD OTH EXPT AND PRED	
				Diss	SIGG	76 - .TBLS,GRPHS.CFD OTH.2META.	
	1.5+7			Data	EXFOR10477.	May 75 . 3 PTS, SIGMA,GND,META,GND AND META	
(n,2n)	1.5+7		IBJ	Theo Jour	ASL 27 186	77 Rurarz+ ISO RATIO,4MODLS,CFD XPT.TBL	
	1.4+7			Rept	INR-1464 19	May 73 - + ISOMERIC RATIO CFD EXPT,GRAF	
(n,p)	Fiss		CRC	Eval Rept	CRC-1003	Dec 60 ROY+ ESTIMATED AVG SIG=1.1MB	
(n,p)	Maxwl		IFU	Theo Rept	ICD-4 20	67 Dadakina+ PENETR COEFF CALC,TABLE	
(n,p)	1.4+7		LYO	Comp Rept	LYCEN/6780	Nov 67 Crouzet+COMPILATN FOR ACTIVTN ANALYS	
(n,p)	1.4+7		MNZ	Expt Jour	RCA 22 11	75 Weigel+ TOT SIG, ACT METHOD	

62 Samarium 144

Quantity	Energy (ev) Min	Max	Lab	Type	Documentation Ref Vol Page	Date	Author, Comments	Data
(n,p)	$1.5+7$		JUL	Expt Jour	RRL 25 335	May 76	Qaim+ ACTIV,GELI.CFD OTHERS,TBL+GRPH	+
	$1.5+7$			Data	EXFOR20716.006	Jun 77	1PNT.SIGMA.	
(n,np)	$1.4+7$		MNZ	Expt Jour	RCA 22 11	75	Weigel+SUM OF (N,2N)+(N,NP)+(N,D)SIG	
(n,α)	Fiss		CRC	Eval Rept	CRC-1003	Dec 60	ROY+ ESTIMATED AVG SIG=0.014MB	
(n,α)	$1.4+7$		RED	Expt Abst	BAP 10 260	Feb 65	Alford+ ACT REL N2N	
(n,α)	$1.4+7$		LYO	Comp Rept	LYCEN/6780	Nov 67	Crouzet+COMPILATN FOR ACTIVTN ANALYS	
(n,α)	–		IBJ	Expt Jour	INR-1109/FIAPL	Sep 69	Kownacki+ INV AT ALPHA 31 MEV 2N OUT	
(n,α)	$1.5+7$		DEB	Comp Jour	REA 7 4 93	Dec 69	Csikai+ SIG+HL COMPILTN,N-ACTIV-ANAL	
Reson Params	$1.0+3$	$1.0+5$	CCP	Theo Jour	AE 18 114	Feb 65	Dovbenko+ WG, AVERAGE RES SPACING	
				Jour	JNE 20 675	Aug 66	TRANSLATN.*	
				Jour	SJA 18 140	Feb 65	TRANSLATN.*	
				Jour	EAF 18 2 44	Feb 65	TRANSLATN.*	
Reson Params	$+3$	$+5$	AUA	ExTh Rept	AAEC/E-198	May 69	Musgrove.RES PARS +STF FROM (NG)FIT	+
Reson Params	–		AUA	Theo Rept	AAEC/E-211	Nov 70	Musgrove. CALCULTD D+GAM WIDTH GIVEN	
Reson Params	None		DUB	Theo Rept	JINR-P4-7499	Oct 73	Soloviev+ CALC D CFD EXPTS,TABLE	
Reson Params	$+0$	$+3$	FEI	Eval Rept	YK-8/2 97	Sep 72	Abagyan+ AVG G-WID+D AT BINDNG-E,TBL	
				Rept	INDC(CCP)-39	Jul 74	.PAGE 102.ENGLISH OF YK-8/2 97	
Strnth Fnctn	$+3$	$+5$	AUA	ExTh Rept	AAEC/E-198	May 69	Musgrove.S+P+D STF FROM (NG)FIT,TBL	
Strnth Fnctn	–		AUA	Theo Rept	AAEC/E-211	Nov 70	Musgrove. SMOOTHED S0,S1 AND S2 GIVN	
Strnth Fnctn	None		AUA	Eval Rept	AAEC/E-277	Mar 73	Musgrove.TBLS EXPTL DATA+BEST VALUES	
Lvl Density	$+7$		DEB	ExTh Jour	NP/A 122 234	Dec 68	Karolyi+ SPIN CUTOFF,M OF INERT,N2N	+
	$+7$			Expt Data	EXFOR30101.030	Feb 71	CUT-OFF PARAMETER	
Lvl Density	$+0$	$+3$	FEI	Eval Rept	YK-8/2 97	Sep 72	Abagyan+ LVL DENSITY PARAMETER,TBL	
				Rept	INDC(CCP)-39	Jul 74	.PAGE 102.ENGLISH OF YK-8/2 97	
(γ,n)	$2.4+7$		BSP	Expt Conf	55Geneva 2 169	Aug 55	Souza-Santos+.P897,THRESHOLD+CURVE	
(γ,n)	$7.0+6$	$3.0+7$	SAC	Expt Jour	NP/A 225 171	Jun 74	Carlos+GDR,LORENTZ PARAM,GRAPHS,TBLS	

62 Samarium 145

Quantity	Energy (ev) Min	Max	Lab	Type	Documentation Ref Vol Page	Date	Author, Comments	Data
Absorption	$2.5-2$		IJI	Eval Conf	75Kiev 1 169	May 75	Fedorova+ EVAL SIG GIVEN,TABLE	
(n,γ)	Pile		HLS	Expt Jour	PR 127 943	Aug 62	Kauranen+.ESTIMATE S=110B.	+
	Pile			Data	EXFOR20104.003	Sep 71	1PNT.SIG.	
(n,γ)	$2.5-2$		IJI	Eval Rept	KIYAI-76-6	76	Fedorova+ ONLY 1LIT-VALUE=RECOMM.TBL	
(n,p)	Maxwl		IFU	Theo Rept	ICD-4 20	67	Dadakina+ PENETR COEFF CALC,TABLE	
Reson Params	–		AUA	Theo Rept	AAEC/E-211	Nov 70	Musgrove. CALCULTD D+GAM WIDTH GIVEN	
Strnth Fnctn	–		AUA	Theo Rept	AAEC/E-211	Nov 70	Musgrove. SMOOTHED S0,S1 AND S2 GIVN	
Lvl Density	None		DUB	Theo Jour	NP/A 224 411	May 74	Soloviev+ 1/2 MICROSC MDL. SPH NUCL.	

62 Samarium 146

Quantity	Energy (ev) Min	Max	Lab	Type	Documentation Ref Vol Page	Date	Author, Comments	Data
Spect (n,γ)	None		ANL	Expt Conf	74Petten 358	Sep 74	Smither+AVG NEUTR.CAPT. (PROGR.)	
Reson Params	–		AUA	Theo Rept	AAEC/E-211	Nov 70	Musgrove. CALCULTD D+GAM WIDTH GIVEN	
Strnth Fnctn	–		AUA	Theo Rept	AAEC/E-211	Nov 70	Musgrove. SMOOTHED S0,S1 AND S2 GIVN	
Lvl Density	-3	$+0$	IFU	Theo Jour	UFZ 13 700	Apr 68	Pisanko+ LEVEL SPACING CALC,TBL	
				Jour	UPJ 13 498	Oct 68	TRANSLATN.*	

62 Samarium 147

Quantity	Energy (ev) Min	Max	Lab	Type	Documentation Ref Vol Page	Date	Author, Comments	Data
Evaluation	$2.5-2$	$1.0+7$	KFK	Eval Rept	KFK-352	Aug 65	Schmidt+.RES	
Evaluation	$1.0-3$	$1.5+7$	AUA	Eval Rept	AAEC/TM-549	Jun 70	Cook.TOT,EL,INEL,NONEL,CAPT SIGS,NDG	+
				Rept	AAEC/E-214	Jun 71	Bertram+GROUP SIGMAS SAME QUANTS.NDG	
				Rept	AAEC/TM-587	Mar 71	*DESCRIPTION OF LIBRARY	
	$1.0-3$	$1.5+7$		Data	AUSTR-DFN 156.	Nov 71	POINT(223) AND GROUP(127) SIGMAS	
Evaluation	$1.0+2$	$1.5+7$	JAE	Eval Rept	JAERI-M-5752	Jul 74	Igarasi+ JNDC FPND WG.TOT,EL,N',CAP	
Total	$1.0-3$	$1.5+7$	AUA	Eval Data	AUSTR-DFN 156.	Nov 71	COOK+POINT(223)+GROUP(127)SIG.CF EVL	+
Total	$1.0-1$	$1.2+3$	KAP	Expt Jour	NSE 54 286	Jul 74	Eiland+TRNS.CURVS.THR VAL.RES ANAL.	
Total	$2.5-2$		KAP	Expt Jour	NSE 54 28	Jul 74	Eiland+77+-6B FRM 10-1TO12+3 EV DATA	+
				Conf	71Knoxvill 673	Mar 71	-+LINAC, TRANS, SIG=75+-6B	
	$2.5-2$			Data	EXFOR10147.008	Jan 78	.1PT.CS=77+-6B.	
Total	-3	$1.9+0$	THS	Theo Rept	IKE-6 89 65	Jun 75	Keinert. DATA LIBRARY	
Elastic	$1.0-3$	$1.5+7$	AUA	Eval Data	AUSTR-DFN 156.	Nov 71	COOK+POINT(223)+GROUP(127)SIG.CF EVL	+
Tot Inelastc	$5.0+5$	$1.5+7$	AUA	Eval Data	AUSTR-DFN 156.	Nov 71	COOK+POINT(11)+GROUP(127)SIG.CF EVL	+

62 Samarium 147

Quantity	Energy (ev) Min	Energy (ev) Max	Lab	Type	Documentation Ref Vol Page	Date	Author, Comments	Data
Nonelastic	1.0−3	1.5+7	AUA	Eval Data	AUSTR−DFN 156.	Nov 71	COOK+POINT(223)+GROUP(127)SIG.CF EVL	+
Absorption	Maxwl		KAP	Expt Jour	NUC 14 89	Sep 56	Deutsch.FISS PROD S EST BY STEHN	
Absorption	Pile		CCP	Expt Jour	AE 3 11	Jul 57	Gorshkov+.U235 FP YLD,M/S, 1000+ −50B	+
				Jour	JNE 8 69	Nov 58	TRANSLATN.*	
				Jour	SJA 3 729	57	TRANSLATN.*	
Absorption	Maxwl		HAR	Expt Rept	AERE−R/R−2516	Mar 58	Jowitt+ PILE OSC.REL BORON.293DEGK.	
Absorption	2.5−2		HAR	Expt Jour	JNEA 12 32	May 60	Tattersall+ PILE OSCILLATOR.	+
	2.5−2			Data	EXFOR20638.046	Jul 76	1PNT.SIGMA.	
Absorption	4.1−1	1.0+7	GA	Eval Prog	GA−2451	Aug 61	Joanou+ 68GROUP DATA FOR GAM−I	
Absorption	1.0−3	1.0+7	JUL	Eval Rept	JUEL−678−RG	Jul 70	Liu. EVALUATION+CALC,GRPH,FN OF E	
Absorption	Maxwl	Pile	SGA	Expt Jour	JMS 6 435	71	Dobrozemsky+ CHANGE OF ABUND.TBL SIG	+
				Rept	SGAE−PH−104	71	− + MASS−SPECT METHOD	
				Rept	AEC−TR−7574	74	− + ENGLISH OF JMS 6 435	
	2.5−2			Data	EXFOR20637.002	Sep 76	1PNT.SIGMA.	
Absorption	2.5−2		IJI	Eval Rept	KIYAI−76−6	76	Fedorova+ COMP(REFS,SIGS),EVAL.TABLE	
				Conf	75Kiev 1 169	May 75	− + EVAL SIG GIVEN,TABLE	
Res Int Abs	None		CRC	Eval Rept	AECL−1054	Mar 60	Walker. SAME AS CRRP−913	
Res Int Abs	5.0−1		HAR	Expt Jour	JNE 12 32	May 60	Tattersall+. ABOVE 1/V. UPPER LIMIT	+
				Rept	AERE−R−2887	Aug 59	− . PILE OSC.REL BORON	
	6.7−1			Data	EXFOR20638.047	Jul 76	1PNT.	
Res Int Abs	+3	+5	BOL	Theo Conf	61Vienna 1 179	Aug 61	Benzi+.PPR11,VAL GVN,L=0,L=1 .CAPT.	
Res Int Abs	5.5−1		GA	Eval Jour	NSE 12 115	Jan 62	Garrison+ RIG=690+ −150B.FROM RES.PAR	
Res Int Abs	5.0−1		ALD	Expt Jour	JIN 29 2147	Sep 67	Fenner+,RI=640+ −200 B, REL.TO CO	
	2.0−1			Data	EXFOR20631.009	Sep 76	1PNT.CAPTURE.	
Res Int Abs	5.5−1		SGA	Expt Jour	JMS 6 435	71	Dobrozemsky+ EFF ABS RES INT GIVEN.	+
				Prog	SGAE−PH−104	71	− +MASS−SPECTROMETRIC	
				Rept	AEC−TR−7574	74	. ENGLISH OF JMS 6 415	
	5.5−1			Data	EXFOR20637.003	Sep 76	1PNT.	
Res Int Abs	5.5−1		CRC	Eval Rept	AECL−3037 1	Jan 72	Walker.REDUCED RES INT,DETAILED TBL	
Res Int Abs	5.0−1		AUA	Eval Rept	AAEC/TM−619	Sep 72	Clayton.CALC FROM SIG LIBRARY,TABLE	
Res Int Abs	5.0−1		SGA	Eval Conf	73Paris 1 233	Mar 73	Eder+ REDUCED RES INTEG CAPTURE,TBL	
				Rept	SGAE−PH−141	Feb 73	.SAME AS 73PARIS,EVAL OF EXPTL DATA	
Res Int Abs	4.6−1	1.0+6	RCN	Theo Rept	RCN−191	Jul 73	Lautenbach.CAPT INT FROM GROUP SIGMA	
Res Int Abs	5.5−1	+6	SAC	Revw Conf	IAEA−169 1 235	74	Ribon.CAPTURE,STATUS CFD REQUEST,TBL	
Res Int Abs	+0	+5	WIN	Revw Conf	IAEA−169 3 163	74	Pope+ DATA FILE CALC CFD XPTAL VALUE	
Res Int Abs	5.0−1		KAP	Expt Jour	NSE 54 286	Jul 74	Eiland+ CAPT INTEG CALC,714+ −50B.	+
				Conf	71Knoxvill 673	Mar 71	− +CAPT INTEG DRVD.	
	5.0−1			Data	EXFOR10147.015	Jan 78	. RIG=714+ −50B.	
Res Int Abs	5.0−1		IJI	Eval Rept	KIYAI−76−6	76	Fedorova+ EVAL CFD CALC.TBL RI,REFS	
				Conf	75Kiev 1 169	May 75	− + EVAL+CALC RI GIVEN,TABLE	
(n,γ)	Pile		MCM	Expt Diss	WALKER	May 56	Walker.	+
	Pile			Data	EXFOR12127.003	Jun 76	. 1 PT.	
(n,γ)	2.5−2		CRC	Eval Rept	AECL−1054	Mar 60	Walker. SAME AS CRRP−913	
(n,γ)	2.5−2		GA	Eval Jour	NSE 12 115	Jan 62	Garrison+ 87+ −60B.	
(n,γ)	3.0+4		ORL	Expt Jour	NAT 197 370	Jan 63	Macklin.1.17+ −.19B	+
	3.0+4			Data	EXFOR12095.003	Jun 76	. 1 PT.	
(n,γ)	5.0+3	9.0+4	ORL	Theo Jour	RMP 37 166	Jan 65	Macklin+ CALC ASSUM. MAX. SHAPE.	
(n,γ)	1.0+3	1.0+5	CCP	Theo Jour	AE 18 114	Feb 65	Dovbenko+ STATIST MOD CURVE CFD DATA	
				Jour	JNE 20 675	Aug 66	TRANSLATN.*	
				Jour	EAF 18 2 44	Feb 65	TRANSLATN.*	
				Jour	SJA 18 140	Feb 65	TRANSLATN.*	
(n,γ)	1.0+3	1.0+4	LAS	Theo Rept	LA−3463	Jan 66	Bell. TH CAPTURE OF RARE EARTHS	
(n,γ)	Maxwl		RPI	Expt Jour	NSE 28 139	Apr 67	Forman+ 75+ −11B IRRAD+MASS SPEC	+
				Abst	DA/B 27 3635	Apr 67	− .	
	Maxwl			Data	EXFOR12103.002	Jun 76	. 1 PT.	
(n,γ)	2.5−2		ALD	Expt Jour	JIN 29 2147	Sep 67	Fenner+ SIG GIVEN REL TO CO	+
	2.5−2			Data	EXFOR20631.008	Sep 76	1PNT.SIGMA.	
(n,γ)	Maxwl		AUA	Theo Jour	NSE 31 234	Feb 68	Cook+ STATISTICAL CALC CFD EXPT	
(n,γ)	1.0+3	1.0+7	BOL	Eval Rept	CCDN−NW/10	Dec 69	Benzi+H−F MOD,AXEL G(G)EST,ALL DATA	
				Rept	CEC(70)−2	Apr 70	− +. GRAPH	
				Conf	61Vienna 1 179	Aug 61	− + TBL AV VALUES. SUPERSEDED	
(n,γ)	3.0+4		AUA	Theo Rept	AAEC/E−211	Nov 70	Musgrove. SIGMA GIVEN AND CFD OTHER	
(n,γ)	1.0−3	1.5+7	AUA	Eval Data	AUSTR−DFN 156.	Nov 71	COOK+POINT(223)+GROUP(127)SIG.CF EVL	+
(n,γ)	Maxwl		CRC	Eval Rept	AECL−3037 1	Jan 72	Walker.RECOMMENDED SIG,DETAILED TBL	
(n,γ)	2.5−2		AUA	Eval Rept	AAEC/TM−619	Sep 72	Clayton.CALC FROM SIG LIBRARY,TABLE	
(n,γ)	Maxwl		SGA	Eval Conf	73Paris 1 233	Mar 73	Eder+ RECOMMENDED SIG,TBL,NO DETAILS	
				Rept	SGAE−PH−141	Feb 73	.SAME AS 73PARIS,EVAL OF EXPTL DATA	
(n,γ)		1.1+7	RCN	Theo Rept	RCN−191	Jun 73	Lautenbach. GROUP CONSTANTS TBL	

62 Samarium 147

Quantity	Energy (ev) Min	Max	Lab	Type	Documentation Ref Vol Page	Date	Author, Comments	Data
(n,γ)	2.5-2	3.0+4	SAC	Revw	Conf IAEA-169 1 235	74	Ribon.STATUS SIG CFD REQUESTS,TABLE	
	Fiss				Conf IAEA-169 1 235	74	- .STATUS SIG CFD REQUESTS,TABLE	
(n,γ)	Fiss		WIN	Revw	Conf IAEA-169 3 137	74	Dean. POINT DATA AVG OVER STAND SPEC	
	Maxwl Fiss				Conf IAEA-169 3 163	74	Pope+ MAXW+FIS-SPEC AVG DATA CFD XPT	
(n,γ)	1.0+3	1.0+7	FEI	Eval	Rept YK- 8/2 97	Sep 72	Abagjan+ AVG SIG(ENERGY-GROUPS),TABL	
					Rept INDC(CCP)-39	Jul 74	.P102. ENGLISH OF YK-8/2 97	
(n,γ)	2.5-2		KAP	Expt	Jour NSE 54 286	Jul 74	Eiland+ ABS=TOT-POT SCT-RES SCT.	+
					Conf 71Knoxvill 673	Mar 71	- +ABS=TOT-POT SCT-RES SCT.	
	2.5-2				Data EXFOR10147.012	Jan 78	. 1PT.SIG=56+-7B.	
(n,γ)	1.0+3	3.7+5	FEI	ExTh	Conf 75Kiev 3 190	May 75	Jurlov+ REL B10(N,A).SIG(E),GRAPH	
(n,γ)	Fast		RCN	Expt	Rept ECN-10	Oct 76	Veeneema+ STEK REACTIVITY WORTHS TBL.	
Spect (n,γ)	3.4+0		YAL	Expt	Jour PR 107 1650	Sep 57	Fenstermacher+ 565KEV G,P-H SPECT.	
Spect (n,γ)	3.4+0		JAE	Expt	Jour JAERI-1073	Mar 65	Kawarasaki. RES CAPT.LINAC.TOF.E,INT	+
					Rept INDSWG-90 6	Jul 65	- . TABLE E,INTS GIVEN.	
	3.4+0				Data EXFOR20277.009	Jun 74	6PTS.	
Spect (n,γ)	None		MTR	Expt	Prog IN- 1218 123	Dec 68	Spencer+ GE-LI DET	
Spect (n,γ)	Pile		LEI	Expt	Jour PHY 40 567	Jan 69	Reddingius+ GE-LI TABLE INT GRAPHS	
Spect (n,γ)	Pile		RCN	Expt	Jour PHY 40 567	Jan 69	Reddingius+ N FILTER 77DEG K	+
	Pile				Data EXFOR20236.002	May 74	8PTS.	
Spect (n,γ)	1.0+2	+5	ANL	Expt	Jour PR/C 2 1513	Oct 70	Buss+ GE(LI) DET. 33 GAMMAS.	
					Conf 69Studsvik 601	Aug 69	.SUPERSEDED	
Spect (n,γ)	Pile		KUR	Expt	Jour YF 14 473	Sep 71	Groshev+ GE-LI,TBL G ES+INTS,LVL-SCH	
					Jour SNP 14 265	Mar 72	* ENGL OF YF 14 473	
					Jour SNP 13 387	Oct 71	* ENGL OF YF 13 681	
					Jour YF 13 681	Apr 71	*DESCRIPTION OF EXPT	
Spect (n,γ)	3.4+0		BNL	Expt	Prog USNDC-1 36	May 72	Gelletly+ SM148 LEVELS.	
Spect (n,γ)	3.4+0	2.1+2	DUB	Expt	Conf 73Kiev 2 295	May 73	Aldea+ TOF,SPIN-DEP OF G-INT RATIOS	
Spect (n,γ)	None		ANL	Expt	Prog USNDC-9 24	Dec 73	Smither+ AVG RESON CAPT SPEC. NDG.	
Spect (n,γ)	1.0+7		CCP	Expt	Conf 74Kharkov 100	Feb 74	Nejburg+ ABST,GE-LI,ES+INTENS,TBL	
(n,2n)	Fiss		CRC	Eval	Rept CRC-1003	Dec 60	ROY+ ESTIMATED AVG SIG=24.0MB	
(n,2n)	1.4+7		LYO	Comp	Rept LYCEN/6780	Nov 67	Crouzet+COMPILATN FOR ACTIVTN ANALYS	
(n,2n)	1.5+7		DEB	Eval	Jour REA 11 1 153	Mar 73	Boedy+ RECOMM.VALUE FROM N-Z SYSTEM.	
(n,2n)	1.5+7		KFI	Theo	Rept KFKI-73-68	Dec 73	Jeki.NEW FIT,CALC SIG CFD OTHERS,TBL	
(n,p)	Fiss		CRC	Eval	Rept CRC-1003	Dec 60	ROY+ ESTIMATED AVG SIG=0.11MB	
(n,p)	Maxwl		IFU	Theo	Rept ICD-4 20	67	Dadakina+ PENETR COEFF CALC,TABLE	
(n,p)	1.4+7		LYO	Comp	Rept LYCEN/6780	Nov 67	Crouzet+COMPILATN FOR ACTIVTN ANALYS	
(n,α)	Fiss		CRC	Eval	Rept CRC-1003	Dec 60	ROY+ ESTIMATED AVG SIG=0.67MB	
(n,α)	Maxwl		ISL	Expt	Jour PL 1 289	Jul 62	Cheifetz. TBL Q-VALU,SIG,BRANCHRATIO	+
	Maxwl				Data EXFOR31151.	Mar 73	.SIG GVN	
(n,α)	Maxwl		CCP	Expt	Jour YF 1 252	Feb 65	Andreev.IONIZ-CHAMBER,	
					Jour SNP 1 177	Aug 65	TRANSLATN.*	
(n,α)	1.1+0	1.4+2	CCP	Expt	Jour IZV 30 1371	Jul 66	Kvitek+. GRAPH SIG(E), TBL OF PARAMS	
					-		ENGL TRANSL SEE BAS 30 1432 (66)	
(n,α)	1.1+0	1.4+2	DUB	Expt	Jour IZV 30 1371	Jul 66	Kvitek+ GRAPH SIG(E),TBL OF PARAMS	
(n,α)	Maxwl	2.0+2	DUB	Expt	Jour PL 22 186	Aug 66	Kvitek+POPOV LIFETIMES OF XCIT STATE	
	1.0+0	4.0+2			Rept JINR-P-2625	Mar 66	- +(N,A)+(N,G)REACTNS,HALF-LIFES	
	1.1+0	1.4+2			Jour BAS 30 1432	66	. ENGL OF IZV 30 1371	
(n,α)		4.0+2	DUB	Expt	Rept JINR-E3-3029	Nov 66	Kvitek+,AVER ALPHA WIDTH,THEOR CALC	+
(n,α)	3.4+0	1.8+1	DUB	Expt	Jour IZV 32 1994	Dec 68	Popov+ ALFA SPEC GRAPHS,WIDTH TABLE	
	3.4+0	3.0+2			Rept JINR-E3-5483	Dec 70	- . ALFA SPECS VS NEUT-E,CRVS	
	2.5-2	9.0+2			Rept JINR-P3-4982	Apr 70	Kvitek+ ALFA SPEC,GRAPHS	
	3.4+0	1.8+1			Rept JINR-P6-3605	Dec 67	.SEE ALSO *	
					Jour BAS 32 12 1836	69	. ENGLISH OF IZV 32 1994 D/68	
(n,α)	Pile	2.5-2	JAE	Expt	Jour NP/A 141 193	Jan 70	Okamoto. BI FILTER.A SPECT.EFF SIG.	+
	2.5-2				Data EXFOR20335.004	Jul 74	2PTS.SIGMA.	
(n,α)	3.4+0	1.8+2	DUB	Expt	Jour IZV 35 8 1542	Aug 71	Wilhelm+ ALFA SPECS, 11 RES, GRPHS	
	3.0+0	3.0+2			Rept JINR-P3-5553	Feb 71	- + ALFA SPECTRA, GRAPHS+ TABLE	
	3.4+0	1.8+2			Jour BAS 35 8 1406	Aug 72	. ENGLISH OF IZV 35 1542 8/71	
(n,α)	Maxwl		LYO	Expt	Jour NP/A 231 437	Oct 74	Emsallem+ILL HF REACTOR,SIG+GRPH+TBL	+
					Abst 75Harwell 38	Mar 75	Asghar+ (ILL).(N,GAM ALPHA) SIG.TBC	
					Conf 74Petten 395	Sep 74	Emsallem+ ALSO PARTIAL CR. SECT.	
	2.5-2				Data EXFOR20564.002	Sep 75	4PTS.SIGMA.	
(n,α)	2.5-2		IJI	Eval	Rept KIYAI-76-6		76 Fedorova+ COMP(REFS,SIGS),EVAL.TABLE	
(n,α)	0.0+0	2.0+2	DUB	Theo	Conf JINR-D-9920	Jun 76	Popov. P 126.A-WIDS,SEMIMIC THEO,FIG	

62 Samarium 147

Quantity	Energy (ev) Min	Max	Lab	Type	Documentation Ref Vol Page	Date	Author, Comments	Data
(n,α)	None		DUB	Expt	Conf 76Lowell 1250	Jul 76	Antonov+TOT ALPHA WIDS OF N-RES.GRPH	
	2.0+0	4.0+2			Jour NP/A 261 35	Apr 76	Balabanov+RES ALPHA WT. TOF SPECTS.	
	1.5+1	5.0+2			Rept JINR-P3-9099	Aug 75	- + ALFAS VS EN,GRPH. RES,TBL	
	+2	1.0+3			Conf 73Kiev 2 148	May 73	- + TOT ALF-WID,CFD OPTMDL	
	2.0+0	+3			Rept JINR-P13-6602	Aug 72	- + TOF SPEC WITH E-SCALE	
(n,α)	1.8+7		IBJ	Expt	Conf 76Lowell 1352	Jul 76	Glowacka+ E-SPEC.CFD HF,PRE-EQ,KNOCK	+
					Jour ASL 25 203	75	- + A-SPEC CFD TH,GRPH	
				ExTh	Conf ZFK-271 109	Nov 73	- + A-SPEC CFD 2 MODELS,NDG.	
				Expt	Prog INR-1464 1	May 73	- +BRIEF,ALPHA SPECTRUM,TABLES	
	1.8+7				Data EXFOR30261.	Nov 73	ALFA-SPEC(49 PTS)+SIGMA AT 35 DEGREE	
(n,α)	1.4+7		IBJ	Expt	Conf 76Lowell 1352	Jul 76	Glowacka+ E-SPEC.CFD HF,PRE-EQ,KNOCK	+
					Jour ASL 25 203	75	- + A-SPEC CFD TH,GRPH	
					Prog INDC(SEC)-42	Dec 74	- + TBL DIFFSIG,GRPH E+ANG-DIS	
	1.4+7				Data EXFOR30298.	Jul 75	DOUBLE DIFFSIG(44 PTS)+ANGDIST(1 PT)	
Reson Params	3.4+0	1.9+1	BNL	Expt	Jour PR 96 1014	Nov 54	Sailor.	+
	3.4+0	1.9+1			Data EXFOR12110.006	Jun 76	. 2 RES. E0.	
Reson Params	1.8+1	9.9+2	MTR	Expt	Prog IDO-16373 39	Jul 57	Simpson.WG,G*WN,WN0.TBL.11RES ES.	
	1.0+1	1.0+2			Abst BAP 2 42	Feb 57	- +WG GVN.RES PARS.NDG	
	1.8+1	9.9+1			Data EXFOR11983.005	Jun 76	. 12 RES. E0,WN,WN0,WG.	
Reson Params	3.4+0	1.6+2	HAR	Expt	Jour NP 5 294	Jan 58	Bowey+. 15 RESONANCE ES GVN. LINAC	+
Reson Params	None		GA	Eval	Jour NSE 12 115	Jan 62	Garrison+	
Reson Params	3.4+0	3.2+1	ANL	Expt	Prog ANL-6589	Aug 62	Carpenter+	+
	3.4+0	3.2+1			Data EXFOR12048.004	Jun 76	. 5 RES. E0,J.	
Reson Params	3.4+0		ORL	Expt	Jour NSE 17 37	63	Pattenden.	+
	3.4+0				Data EXFOR12025.008	Jun 76	. 1 RES. E0,WN0.	
Reson Params	1.0+3	1.0+5	CCP	Theo	Jour AE 18 114	Feb 65	Dovbenko+ WG, AVERAGE RES SPACING	
					Jour JNE 20 675	Aug 66	TRANSLATN.*	
					Jour SJA 18 140	Feb 65	TRANSLATN.*	
					Jour EAF 18 2 44	Feb 65	TRANSLATN.*	
Reson Params	-		KFK	Eval	Rept KFK-352	Aug 65	Schmidt.AVERAGE S-WAWE RES PAR(TAB19	
Reson Params	3.4+0	1.8+1	MOL	Expt	Jour NP/A 97 657	May 67	Poortmans+.FROM RES SCATTERING EXPT.	+
	3.4+0	1.8+1			Data EXFOR20213.	May 74	4PTS.J, WN/WT.	
Reson Params		1.0+6	AUA	Theo	Jour AUJ 20 477	Oct 67	Cook. TBL OF AVG LVL SPACING D,L=0,1	
Reson Params	+3	+5	AUA	ExTh	Rept AAEC/E-198	May 69	Musgrove.RES PARS +STF FROM (NG)FIT	
Reson Params			AUA	Theo	Rept AAEC/E-211	Nov 70	Musgrove. CALCULTD D+GAM WIDTH GIVEN	
Reson Params	-		DUB	Revw	Rept JINR-E4-5469	Nov 70	Soloviev. REDUCED ALFA-WIDTH, TABLE	
Reson Params	3.4+0	3.2+1	CJD	Eval	Rept YK-7	71	Zakharova+ SURVEY+SYSTEMATICS,GW,TBL	
					Rept INDC(CCP)-27	Nov 72	.ENGLISH TRANSLATION OF YK-7 /71	
Reson Params	3.4+0	5.8+1	MTR	Expt	Jour NSE 43 58	Jan 71	Codding+ 2G*WN AND WG 8 RESON	+
	6.0-1	2.5+2			Data EXFOR10114.	Mar 76	. 36 PTS. WN, WG.	
Reson Params	None		DUB	Theo	Jour YF 13 240	Feb 71	Malecki+G-WID,THEO CFD EXPT.TBL,GRPH	
					Jour SNP 13 133	Aug 71	- + ENGL OF YF 13 240.	
Reson Params	1.8+1	1.9+2	SAC	Expt	Conf 71Knoxvill 785	Mar 71	Cauvin+.J ASSIGNMENTS 27RESON	+
	1.8+1	1.9+2			Data EXFOR20126.009	Sep 72	27PTS.J.	
Reson Params	3.4+0	1.8+2	DUB	Expt	Jour IZV 35 1542	Aug 71	Wilhelm+ TOT+PARTIAL ALFA-WIDTHS,TBL	
					Rept JINR-P3-5553	Feb 71	- + TABLE OF ALFA WIDTH + SPINS	
					Jour BAS 35 1406	Aug 72	. ENGLISH OF IZV 35 1542 8/71	
					Rept UCRL-TR-10541	May 71	Popov+ ENGL TRANSLATION.	
Reson Params	3.4+0	4.1+2	DUB	Expt	Rept JINR-P3-6237	Jan 72	Karzhavina+ SPINS OF RESONANCES,TBL	+
					Rept RCN-203 254	Dec 73	- + G-MULTIPL METH.J,D,S0	
					Conf 73Kiev 2 337	May 73	- + SPIN IDENT,G-MULTIP METH	
	3.4+0	2.8+2			Conf 72Budapest 20	Aug 72	- + SPINS OF RESONANCES,TBL	
	3.4+0	1.2+2			Rept JINR-P3-6092	Nov 71	- .GS MULTIPLICITY,SPINS,TBL	
	3.4+0	4.1+2			Data EXFOR40098.002	May 72	SPINS OF 58 RES.	
Reson Params	1.8+1	4.2+2	DUB	Expt	Jour YF 15 401	Mar 72	Karzhavina+ AREA ANALYS,GRPHS,D GIVN	+
					Prog YFI-12 49	72	- + ABST,TBL TOT-,N-,G-WIDS	
					Rept JINR-P3-5655	Mar 71	- + TABLE,WN,WG.	
					Jour SNP 15 225	Sep 72	- + ENGL OF YF 15 401.	
					Prog INDC(CCP)-30	Sep 72	.PAGE 42,ENGLISH OF YFI-12 49	
	1.8+1	4.2+2			Data EXFOR40071.	Jul 71	N-WID 60RESON,TOT+G-WIDS 7RESON,D	
Reson Params	3.4+0		BNL	Expt	Prog USNDC-1 36	May 72	Gelletly+ J PI GIVEN FROM CAPT	

62 Samarium 147

Quantity	Energy (ev) Min	Energy (ev) Max	Lab	Type	Documentation Ref Vol Page	Date	Author, Comments	Data
Reson Params	3.4+0	1.8+2	DUB	Expt Jour	NP/A 154 177	Sep 70	Kvitek+ J,PI,ALPHA,GAMMA WIDTHS	+
	3.4+0	9.9+2		ExTh Jour	APPB 4 275	73	Popov+ ALFA WIDTH DISTRIBUTION,GRAPH	
	3.4+0	1.9+2		Expt Jour	IZV 35 1542	Aug 71	.SIMILAR	
	3.4+0	9.9+2		Rept	JINR-E3-5483	Dec 70	Popov. ALFA WIDTH ANAL, TABLE+GRAPHS	
				Rept	JINR-E3-5469	Dec 70	- . ALFA WIDTH ANAL, TABLE+GRAPHS	
	3.4+0	9.9+2		Conf	70Helsinki 1 669	Jun 70	- +P125. TBL ALFA-WIDTH, SPIN	
	3.4+0	9.0+2		Rept	JINR-P3-4982	Apr 70	Kvitek+ TOT ALFA WIDTHS	
	3.4+0	1.8+1		Jour	IZV 32 1994	Dec 68	Popov+ ALPHA WIDTHS AT 2 RES.,TBL	
				Rept	JINR-P6-3605	Dec 67	. SEE ALSO,IN RUSSIAN	
	3.4+0	4.0+2		Conf	67Kharkov 201	Feb 67	Kvitek. EMITT ALFA PARTICLES,CFD H-F	
	3.4+0	8.4+1		Jour	PL 22 186	Aug 66	- + ALFA WIDTHS, 4 RES	
				Rept	JINR-P-2625	Mar 66	- + (N,A)+(N,G) REACTNS	
	3.4+0	1.9+2		Rept	UCRL-TR-10541	May 71	Popov+ ENGL TRANSLATION	
	3.4+0	1.8+1		Jour	BAS 32 1836	69	. ENGLISH OF IZV 32 1994 D/68	
	3.4+0	1.8+2		Data	EXFOR40225.003	Jul 75	.ALPHA WIDTH AT 12 ES GIVEN	
Reson Params	None		CCP	Expt Jour	IZV 37 1129	May 73	Danelyan.I=3,CORREL G-INT A-WID,TBL	
				Jour	BAS 37 5 190	May 73	.ENGLISH OF IZV 37 1129	
Reson Params	+0	+3	KUR	Theo Conf	73Kiev 2 301	May 73	Daneljan. CORREL N+G-WID+PARTL G-WID	
Reson Params	None		DUB	Theo Rept	JINR-P4-7499	Oct 73	Soloviev+ CALC D CFD EXPTS,TABLE	
Reson Params	+0	+2	BOL	Eval Conf	IAEA-169 3 123	74	Benzi+ AVG G-WID CFD OTHERS+XPT,TABL	
Reson Params	3.4+0	2.1+2	DUB	Expt Rept	JINR-P3-7885	May 74	Aldea+ BY(N,G).SPIN,GG.CFD CALC,TBLS	
				Conf	73Kiev 2 289	May 73	- + TOF,HARD GS.EXC-E+FINAL SPINS	
Reson Params	+0	+3	FEI	Eval Rept	YK-8/2 97	Sep 72	Abagyan+ AVG G-WID+D AT BINDNG-E,TBL	
				Rept	INDC(CCP)-39	Jul 74	.PAGE 102.ENGLISH OF YK-8/2 97	
Reson Params	-.2+1	1.2+3	KAP	Expt Jour	NSE 54 286	Jul 74	Eiland+TRNS.AREA ANAL.WN,WG.TBL.	+
	1.0-2	1.2+3		Conf	71Knoxvill 673	Mar 71	- + LINAC,TRANS,AVG D, AVG G*WN	
	-.2+1	1.2+3		Data	EXFOR10147.	Jan 78	. 128 E0S.WN*G,WG,D GVN.	
Reson Params	2.0+0	4.0+2	DUB	Expt Jour	NP/A 261 35	Apr 76	Balabanov+TBLS OF ALPHA RES PARS	
	+2	1.0+3		Conf	73Kiev 2 148	May 73	- + TOT ALF-WIDTH,CFD OPTMOD	
	None			Conf	72Budapest 140	Aug 72	- + ALPHA-WIDTHS ,TBL	
	+2	1.0+3		Rept	YFI-17	Aug 74	. ABSTR OF 73KIEV,2,148	
Reson Params	3.4+0		DUB	Expt Jour	YF 23 1165	Jun 76	Vtjurin+ A-WID,A-YLD REL LI(N,T).TBL	
				Jour	BAS 23 619	Jun 76	.ENGL OF YF 23 619	
Strnth Fnctn	1.0+1	1.0+2	MTR	Expt Abst	BAP 2 42	Feb 57	Simpson+AVG STF= (6.0+-1.5)-4	
Strnth Fnctn	+3		BNL	Expt Jour	PRL 1 461	Dec 58	Hughes+ FC 4.3+-1.3	
Strnth Fnctn	+3	+5	BOL	Theo Conf	61Vienna 1 179	Aug 61	Benzi+.PPR11,TABLE CFD EXPERIMENT	
Strnth Fnctn	None		GA	Eval Jour	NSE 12 115	Jan 62	Garrison+ STF+ D.	
Strnth Fnctn	+3	+5	AUA	Expt Rept	AAEC/E-198	May 69	Musgrove.S+P+D STF FROM (NG)FIT,TBL	+
Strnth Fnctn	-		AUA	Theo Rept	AAEC/E-211	Nov 70	Musgrove. SMOOTHED S0,S1 AND S2 GIVN	
Strnth Fnctn	3.4+0	4.1+2	DUB	Expt Rept	JINR-P3-6237	Feb 72	Karzhavina+ TOF	+
	3.4+0	4.1+2		Data	EXFOR40098.	May 72	STRENGTH-FUNCTION, 2 EN. INTERVALS	
Strnth Fnctn	1.8+1	4.2+2	DUB	Expt Jour	YF 15 401	Mar 72	Karzhavina+ S0 FOR DIFFERENT E-RANGE	+
				Prog	YFI-12 49	72	- + ABST,S0 GIVEN	
				Conf	71Kiev	May 71	- + S0 AND S1 VALUES GIVEN	
				Rept	JINR-P3-5655	Mar 71	- + TABLE,WN,WG.	
				Jour	SNP 15 225	Sep 72	- + ENGL OF YF 15 401.	
				Prog	INDC(CCP)-30	Sep 72	.PAGE 42,ENGLISH OF YFI-12 49	
	1.8+1	4.2+2		Data	EXFOR40071.007	Jul 71	STRENGTH FUNCTION	
Strnth Fnctn	1.5+2	6.5+2	SAC	ExTh Diss	FRNC-TH-450	Oct 72	Delaroche.OPTICAL MODEL PARAMETERS	
Strnth Fnctn	None		AUA	Eval Rept	AAEC/E-277	Mar 73	Musgrove.TBLS EXPTL DATA+BEST VALUES	
Strnth Fnctn	1.0-2	1.2+3	KAP	Expt Jour	NSE 54 286	Jul 74	Eiland+TRNS.S WAVE CALC.	+
				Conf	71Knoxvill 673	Mar 71	- + LINAC,TRANS. SO=4.6+-0.4	
	1.0-2	1.2+3		Data	EXFOR10147.010	Jan 78	. 1PT.S0=(4.3+-1.3)-4	
Lvl Density	-		FEI	Eval Rept	FEI-36	66	Kapchigashev+.TBL OF RELATD QUANTTYS	+
		5.0+4		Jour	YF 4 686	Sep 66	.TABLE.SHORT VERSION OF FEI-36	
	-			Prog	YFI-3 3	66	.ABSTRACT.TABLE LDL+NUCL.EXCIT.E	
		5.0+4		Jour	SNP 4 486	67	.ENGLISH OF YF 4.FROM(N,GAMMA).TABLE	
				Prog	INDC-E-140 3	66	.ENGLISH TRANSL OF YFI-3	
Lvl Density	None		AUW	Theo Conf	70Madurai 2 267	Dec 70	Ramamurty+ A-PARAMETER GVN,LANG'S-TH	
Lvl Density	3.4+0	4.1+2	DUB	Expt Rept	JINR-P3-6237	Feb 72	Karzhavina+ TOF	+
	3.4+0	4.1+2		Data	EXFOR40098.004	May 72	AVERAGE LEVEL SPACING	
Lvl Density	None		BOL	Eval Conf	IAEA-169 3 123	74	Benzi+ LVL DENS PARAM BY XPT,GRPH+TB	
Lvl Density	+0	+3	FEI	Eval Rept	YK-8/2 97	Sep 72	Abagyan+ LVL DENSITY PARAMETER,TBL	
				Rept	INDC(CCP)-39	Jul 74	.PAGE 102.ENGLISH OF YK-8/2 97	

62 Samarium 148

Quantity	Energy (ev) Min	Max	Lab	Type	Documentation Ref Vol Page	Date	Author, Comments	Data
Evaluation	1.0−3	1.5+7	AUA	Eval	Rept AAEC/TM−549	Jun 70	Cook.TOT,EL,INEL,NONEL,CAPT SIGS,NDG	+
					Rept AAEC/E−214	Jun 71	Bertram+GROUP SIGMAS SAME QUANTS.NDG	
					Rept AAEC/TM−587	Mar 71	*DESCRIPTION OF LIBRARY	
	1.0−3	1.5+7			Data AUSTR−DFN 157.	Nov 71	POINT(223) AND GROUP(127) SIGMAS	
Total	1.0−3	1.5+7	AUA	Eval	Data AUSTR−DFN 157.	Nov 71	COOK+POINT(223)+GROUP(127)SIG.CF EVL	+
Total	1.4+7		LIN	Expt	Conf 73Kiev 3 108	May 73	Djumin+ OPTMOD CALC,SIG	+
					Jour IZV 37 1019	May 73	− + SIG(A),OPTMODEL CALC,GRAPH	
					Jour BAS 37 5 91	May 73	.ENGLISH OF IZV 37 1019	
	1.4+7				Data EXFOR40302.010	Feb 76	1 PNT	
Total	1.0+6	2.0+7	BRC	Theo	Conf JAERI−M−5984	Feb 75	Lagrange.EFF OF DEFORMATION.GRPHS	
	2.0+6	2.0+7			Jour JPRL 33 111	Sep 74	− .DEFORMAT EFFECT ON STG TOT	
Total	7.5+5	1.5+7	WMU	Expt	Jour PL/B 61 29	Mar 76	Shamu+QUAD DEFORM PARS FROM TOT CS.	+
	7.5+5	1.4+7			Data EXFOR10615.002	Nov 76	. 27 PTS. TOT CS DATA	
Total	1.0+6	1.6+7	KTY	Revw	Conf 76Lowell 171	Jul 76	Mcellistrem.COUP−CHAN CALC.	
Elastic	1.0−3	1.5+7	AUA	Eval	Data AUSTR−DFN 157.	Nov 71	COOK+POINT(223)+GROUP(127)SIG.CF EVL	+
Diff Elastic	6.3+6		KTY	Expt	Jour PL/B 58 293	Sep 75	Lagrange+TOF.NUC DEFORMATION EFFECT	+
	6.3+6				Data EXFOR10528.	Mar 76	. 32 PTS. DIFF CS AND LEG COEFS.	
Diff Elastic	6.2+6		BRC	ExTh	Conf IAEA−190 251		76 Delaroche+ ANGDIS,COUPL−CHANNEL,GRPH	
				Expt	Jour PL/B 58 293	Sep 75	Lagrange+VDG,TOF.QUAD DEFORM EFFECTS	
Tot Inelastc	1.0+6	1.5+7	AUA	Eval	Data AUSTR−DFN 157.	Nov 71	COOK+POINT(10)+GROUP(127)SIG.CF EVL	+
Diff Inelast	6.2+6		BRC	Expt	Jour PL/B 58 293	Sep 75	Lagrange+VDG,TOF.QUAD DEFORM EFFECTS	
Diff Inelast	6.3+6		KTY	Expt	Jour PL/B 58 293	Sep 75	Lagrange+ TOF,NUC DEFORMATION EFFECT	
Diff Inelast	2.5+6	1.4+7	KTY	Revw	Conf 76Lowell 171	Jul 76	Mcellistrem.SCAT TO 2+ LVL.	
Nonelastic	1.0−3	1.5+7	AUA	Eval	Data AUSTR−DFN 157.	Nov 71	COOK+POINT(223)+GROUP(127)SIG.CF EVL	+
Absorption	Maxwl		KAP	Expt	Jour NUC 14 89	Sep 56	Deutsch.FISS PROD S EST BY STEHN	
Absorption	4.1−1	1.0+7	GA	Eval	Prog GA−2451	Aug 61	Joanou+ 68GROUP DATA FOR GAM−I	
Absorption	1.0−3	1.0+7	JUL	Eval	Rept JUEL−678−RG	Jul 70	Liu. EVALUATION+CALC,GRPH,FN OF E	
Absorption	Maxwl	Pile	SGA	Expt	Jour JMS 6 435		71 Dobrozemsky+ CHANGE OF ABUND.TBL SIG	+
					Rept SGAE−PH−104		71 − + MASS−SPEC METHOD	
					Rept AEC−TR−7574		74 − + ENGLISH OF JMS 6 435	
	2.5−2				Data EXFOR20637.004	Sep 76	1PNT.SIGMA.	
Absorption	2.5−2		IJI	Eval	Rept KIYAI−76−6		76 Fedorova+ ONLY 1LIT−VALUE=RECOMM.TBL	
					Conf 75Kiev 1 169	May 75	− + EVAL SIG GIVEN,TABLE	
Res Int Abs	4.0−1		GA	Eval	Jour NSE 12 115	Jan 62	Garrison+ EST. RIG=50+−50B	
Res Int Abs	5.5−1		SGA	Expt	Jour JMS 6 435		71 Dobrozemsky+ EFF ABS RES INT GIVEN.	+
					Prog SGAE−PH−104		71 − +MASS−SPECTROMETRIC	
					Rept AEC−TR−7574		74 . ENGLISH OF JMS 6 415	
	5.5−1				Data EXFOR20637.005	Sep 76	1PNT.	
Res Int Abs	5.5−1		CRC	Eval	Rept AECL−3037 1	Jan 72	Walker.REDUCED RES INT FROM RES PARS	
Res Int Abs	5.0−1		AUA	Eval	Rept AAEC/TM−619	Sep 72	Clayton.CALC FROM SIG LIBRARY,TABLE	
Res Int Abs	5.0−1		SGA	Eval	Conf 73Paris 1 233	Mar 73	Eder+ REDUCED RES INTEG CAPTURE,TBL	
					Rept SGAE−PH−141	Feb 73	.SAME AS 73PARIS,EVAL OF EXPTL DATA	
Res Int Abs	4.6−1	1.0+6	RCN	Theo	Rept RCN−191	Jul 73	Lautenbach.CAPT INT FROM GROUP SIGMA	
Res Int Abs	5.5−1	+6	SAC	Revw	Conf IAEA−169 1 235		74 Ribon.CAPTURE,STATUS CFD REQUEST,TBL	
Res Int Abs	+0	+5	WIN	Revw	Conf IAEA−169 3 163		74 Pope+ DATA FILE CALC CFD XPTAL VALUE	
Res Int Abs	5.0−1		IJI	Eval	Rept KIYAI−76−6		76 Fedorova+ ONLY 1LIT−VALUE=RECOMM.TBL	
					Conf 75Kiev 1 169	May 75	− + EVAL OF RI−EXPTS.TABLE	
(n,γ)	Pile		MCM	Expt	Diss WALKER	May 56	Walker.	+
	Pile				Data EXFOR12127.004	Jun 76	. 1 PT.	
(n,γ)	2.5−2		CRC	Eval	Rept AECL−1054	Mar 60	Walker. SAME AS CRRP−913	
(n,γ)	2.5−2		GA	Eval	Jour NSE 12 115	Jan 62	Garrison+ RANGE OF POSSIBLE VALUES.	
(n,γ)	3.0+4		ORL	Expt	Jour NAT 197 370	Jan 63	Macklin. 258+−48 MB.	+
	3.0+4				Data EXFOR12095.004	Jun 76	. 1 PT.	
(n,γ)	5.0+3	9.0+4	ORL	Theo	Jour RMP 37 166	Jan 65	Macklin+ CALC ASSUM. MAX. SHAPE.	
(n,γ)	1.0+3	1.0+5	CCP	Theo	Jour AE 18 114	Feb 65	Dovbenko+ STATIST MOD CURVE CFD DATA	
					Jour JNE 20 675	Aug 66	TRANSLATN.*	
					Jour EAF 18 2 44	Feb 65	TRANSLATN.*	
					Jour SJA 18 140	Feb 65	TRANSLATN.*	
(n,γ)	2.5+4		FEI	ExTh	Prog YFI−4 22	May 67	Shorin+.,TBLS GIVEN,TBP YF	
					Rept INDC−187E		67 . ENGL OF YFI−4 22	
(n,γ)	Maxwl		AUA	Theo	Jour NSE 31 234	Feb 68	Cook+ STATISTICAL CALC CFD EXPT	
(n,γ)	Pile	2.5−2	AUA	Expt	Rept AAEC/TM−443	Mar 68	Whittem.MASS−SPEC.SIG(EFF),SIG(.025)	+
	Pile	2.5−2			Data EXFOR30059.	Nov 71	EFFECTIVE AND 0.0253EV CROSS SECTION	
(n,γ)	1.0+3	1.0+7	BOL	Eval	Rept CCDN−NW/10	Dec 69	Benzi+H−F MOD,AXEL G(G)EST,ALL DATA	
					Rept CEC(70)−2	Apr 70	− +. GRAPH	
(n,γ)	3.0+4		AUA	Theo	Rept AAEC/E−211	Nov 70	Musgrove. SIGMA GIVEN AND CFD OTHER	
(n,γ)	1.0−3	1.5+7	AUA	Eval	Data AUSTR−DFN 157.	Nov 71	COOK+POINT(223)+GROUP(127)SIG.CF EVL	+

62 Samarium 148

Quantity	Energy (ev) Min	Max	Lab	Type	Documentation Ref Vol Page	Date	Author, Comments	Data
(n,γ)	Maxwl		CRC	Eval	Rept AECL – 3037 1	Jan 72	Walker.RECOMMENDED SIG,DETAILED TBL	
(n,γ)	2.5 – 2		AUA	Eval	Rept AAEC/TM – 619	Sep 72	Clayton.CALC FROM SIG LIBRARY,TABLE	
(n,γ)	Maxwl		SGA	Eval	Conf 73Paris 1 233	Mar 73	Eder+ RECOMMENDED SIG,TBL,NO DETAILS	
					Rept SGAE – PH – 141	Feb 73	.SAME AS 73PARIS,EVAL OF EXPTL DATA	
(n,γ)		1.1+7	RCN	Theo	Rept RCN – 191	Jun 73	Lautenbach. GROUP CONSTANTS TBL	
(n,γ)	Fiss		SAC	Revw	Conf IAEA – 169 1 235	74	Ribon.STATUS SIG CFD REQUESTS,TABLE	
	2.5 – 2				Conf IAEA – 169 1 235	74	– .STATUS SIG CFD REQUESTS,TABLE	
(n,γ)	Fiss		WIN	Revw	Conf IAEA – 169 3 137	74	Dean. POINT DATA AVG OVER STAND SPEC	
	Maxwl	Fiss			Conf IAEA – 169 3 163	74	Pope+ MAXW+FIS – SPEC AVG DATA CFD XPT	
(n,γ)	1.0+3	1.0+7	FEI	Eval	Rept YK – 8/2 97	Sep 72	Abagjan+ AVG SIG(ENERGY – GROUPS),TABL	
					Rept INDC(CCP) – 39	Jul 74	.P102. ENGLISH OF YK – 8/2 97	
(n,γ)	Fast		RCN	Expt	Rept ECN – 10	Oct 76	Veenema+ STEK REACTIVITY WORTHS TBL.	
Spect (n,γ)	None		ANL	Expt	Conf 74Petten 358	Sep 74	Smither+AVG NEUTR.CAPT. (PROGR.)	
Inelastic γ	8.0+6		BRC	Expt	Rept CEA – N – 1798 34	Jun 75	Sigaud+ VDG TOF	
(n,2n)	Fiss		CRC	Eval	Rept CRC – 1003	Dec 60	ROY+ ESTIMATED AVG SIG=7.8MB.	
(n,2n)	1.5+7		DEB	Eval	Jour REA 11 1 153	Mar 73	Boedy+ RECOMM.VALUE FROM N – Z SYSTEM.	
(n,2n)	1.5+7		KFI	Theo	Rept KFKI – 73 – 68	Dec 73	Jeki.NEW FIT,CALC SIG CFD OTHERS,TBL	
(n,xn) x>2	1.4+7		BRC	ExTh	Prog CEA – N – 1875 60	Apr 76	Frehaut+N3N.SYSTEMATIC LAWS SEARCH	
(n,p)	Fiss		CRC	Eval	Rept CRC – 1003	Dec 60	ROY+ ESTIMATED AVG SIG=0.03MB.	
(n,p)	1.4+7		LYO	Comp	Rept LYCEN/6780	Nov 67	Crouzet+COMPILATN FOR ACTIVTN ANALYS	
(n,p)	1.4+7		AUW	Expt	Jour NP/A 125 57	Feb 69	RAMA PRASAD+,ACTIVATION,CFD OTHERS	+
				ExTh	Jour IPA 12 640	Sep 74	Rama Prasad+ CFD STATMDL COMPND VALU	
	1.4+7			Expt	Data EXFOR30051.	Dec 70	SIGMA NP,ALSO N2N+NA+NP FOR OTHERS.	
(n,p)	1.5+7		DEB	Comp	Jour REA 7 4 93	Dec 69	Csikai+ SIG+HL COMPILTN,N – ACTIV – ANAL	
(n,p)	1.4+7	1.5+7	JYV	Eval	Rept JU – RR – 3/1970	Jun 70	Leppaemaeki+ TABLE OF EVAL AVG SIG	
(n,p)	1.5+7		JUL	Expt	Jour RRL 25 335	May 76	Qaim+ ACTIV,GELI.TO GND,META.TBL+FIG	+
	1.5+7				Data EXFOR20716.	Jun 77	2PTS.SIGMA.	
(n,α)	Fiss		CRC	Eval	Rept CRC – 1003	Dec 60	ROY+ ESTIMATED AVG SIG=0.045MB.	
(n,α)	2.5 – 2		IJI	Eval	Rept KIYAI – 76 – 6	76	Fedorova+ RECOMMENDED SIG GIVEN	
Reson Params	9.4+1		HAR	Expt	Jour NP 5 294	Jan 58	Bowey+. 1 RESONANCE E GVN. LINAC	
Reson Params	None		GA	Eval	Jour NSE 12 115	Jan 62	Garrison+	
Reson Params	1.0+3	1.0+5	CCP	Theo	Jour AE 18 114	Feb 65	Dovbenko+ WG, AVERAGE RES SPACING	
					Jour JNE 20 675	Aug 66	TRANSLATN.*	
					Jour SJA 18 140	Feb 65	TRANSLATN.*	
					Jour EAF 18 2 44	Feb 65	TRANSLATN.*	
Reson Params		1.0+6	AUA	Theo	Jour AUJ 20 477	Oct 67	Cook. TBL OF AVG LVL SPACING D,L=0,1	
Reson Params	–		DUB	Expt	Conf 68DUBSY 283	Jul 68	Shapiro.AVERAGE ALFA WIDTH,LVL SPAC.	
Reson Params	+3	+5	AUA	ExTh	Rept AAEC/E – 198	May 69	Musgrove.RES PARS +STF FROM (NG)FIT	+
Reson Params	–		AUA	Theo	Rept AAEC/E – 211	Nov 70	Musgrove. CALCULTD D+GAM WIDTH GIVEN	
Reson Params	None		DUB	Theo	Rept JINR – P4 – 7499	Oct 73	Soloviev+ CALC D CFD EXPTS,TABLE	
Reson Params	+0	+3	FEI	Eval	Rept YK – 8/2 97	Sep 72	Abagyan+ AVG G – WID+D AT BINDNG – E,TBL	
					Rept INDC(CCP) – 39	Jul 74	.PAGE 102.ENGLISH OF YK – 8/2 97	
Strnth Fnctn	None		GA	Eval	Jour NSE 12 115	Jan 62	Garrison+ STF + D.	
Strnth Fnctn	+3	+5	AUA	ExTh	Rept AAEC/E – 198	May 69	Musgrove.S+P+D STF FROM (NG)FIT,TBL	+
Strnth Fnctn	–		AUA	Theo	Rept AAEC/E – 211	Nov 70	Musgrove. SMOOTHED S0,S1 AND S2 GIVN	
Strnth Fnctn	None		AUA	Eval	Rept AAEC/E – 277	Mar 73	Musgrove.TBLS EXPTL DATA+BEST VALUES	
Strnth Fnctn	3.0+3	6.5+5	DKE	Expt	Jour AP 84 165	May 74	Pineo+ S0, S1, S2	
Lvl Density	–		FEI	ExTh	Prog YFI – 6 18	68	Ignatjuk+ TABLE VARIOUS PARAMETERS	
	None			Theo	Jour SNP 8 660	Jun 69	.TRANSLATN.*	
					Jour YF 8 1135	Dec 68	Ignatjuk+ TBL,A+ENTROPY+TEMP,CFD XPT	
	–			ExTh	Rept INDC – 260E	69	. ENGL OF YFI – 6 18	
Lvl Density	+6		MIL	Theo	Jour EN 15 1 54	Jan 68	Facchini+ LDL PARS FROM LOW EN RES	
Lvl Density	None		CCP	Theo	Jour YF 11 1028	May 70	Rubchenya. DENSITY+A+TEMP GIVEN	
					Jour SNP 11 571	Nov 70	. TRANSLATN OF YF 11 571.	
Lvl Density	–		FEI	Theo	Conf 70Helsinki 2 885	Jun 70	Ignatjuk+76. SUPERFLUID CFD FERMI – TH	
Lvl Density	None		AUW	Theo	Conf 70Madurai 2 267	Dec 70	Ramamurty+ A – PARAMETER GVN,LANG'S – TH	
Lvl Density	None		MUN	Theo	Jour NP/A 217 269	Dec 73	Dilg+ A,DELTA. BACK SHIFTED FERMIGAS	
Lvl Density	None		COP	Theo	Jour NP/A 222 493	Apr 74	Dossing+COLL ROTAT.SPAC. ACCUR ESTIM	
Lvl Density	None		ROC	Theo	Jour NP/A 223 577	May 74	Huizenga+ EXP CFD MICROSC TH SPH NUC	
Lvl Density	+0	+3	FEI	Eval	Rept YK – 8/2 97	Sep 72	Abagyan+ LVL DENSITY PARAMETER,TBL	
					Rept INDC(CCP) – 39	Jul 74	.PAGE 102.ENGLISH OF YK – 8/2 97	
(γ,n)	7.0+6	3.0+7	SAC	Expt	Jour NP/A 225 171	Jun 74	Carlos+GDR,LORENTZ PARAM,GRAPHS,TBLS	

62 Samarium 149

Quantity	Energy (ev) Min	Max	Lab	Type	Documentation Ref Vol Page	Date	Author, Comments	Data
Evaluation	4.1-1	1.0+7	GA Eval	Prog	GA- 2451	Aug 61	Joanou+ 68GROUP CS MATRIX FOR GAM-I	
Evaluation	2.5-2	1.0+7	GEN Eval	Rept	APEX-704	Nov 61	Cooper+ CONTENT OF C-FINE TAPES	
Evaluation	2.5-2	1.0+7	KFK Eval	Rept	KFK-352	Aug 65	Schmidt+.RES	
Evaluation	1.0-3	1.5+7	AUA Eval	Rept	AAEC/TM-549	Jun 70	Cook.TOT,EL,INEL,NONEL,CAPT SIGS,NDG	+
				Rept	AAEC/E-214	Jun 71	Bertram+GROUP SIGMAS SAME QUANTS.NDG	
				Rept	AAEC/TM-587	Mar 71	*DESCRIPTION OF LIBRARY	
	1.0-3	1.5+7		Data	AUSTR-DFN 158.	Nov 71	POINT(223) AND GROUP(127) SIGMAS	
Evaluation	1.0+2	1.5+7	JAE Eval	Rept	JAERI-M-5752	Jul 74	Igarasi+ JNDC FPND WG.TOT,EL,N',CAP	
Evaluation	-2	+3	WIN Eval	Prog	UKNDC(75)P71	Jul 75	Pope+ THERMAL + RESON PARAM	
Total	6.0-2	2.0+1	BNL Expt	Jour	PR 109 1219	Feb 58	Marshak+ TOF CS RES ABS CURVES	
Total	-2	+1	HAR Expt	Conf	58Geneva 16 44	Sep 58	Pattenden.PPR11,CURVE,CRYSTALSPECTRM	
Total	4.0-1	8.0+0	CCP Expt	Jour	AE 16 523	Jun 64	Begzhanov+TRANS.2.5MICROS/M RSLN	
				Jour	SJA 16 647	Jun 64	. ENGL OF AE 16 523	
Total	6.5-4	2.8-1	JAE Expt	Rept	INDSWG-90 2	Jul 65	Ohno+ ENRICHED.LOW EN RES STUDIED.	+
	6.5-4	2.8-1		Data	EXFOR20327.003	Jul 74	80PTS.	
Total	2.5-2		JAE Expt	Rept	EANDC(J)8 1	Jan 68	Okamoto. BI FILTER.	+
Total	6.0-4	1.0+0	JAE Expt	Jour	JPJ 26 225	Feb 69	Asami.V-SELECT P CRYST-SPECT,CURVE	+
				Rept	EANDC(J)10L1	Nov 68	- .	
	2.5-2			Data	EXFOR20328.002	Jul 74	1PNT.	
	2.5-2			Data	EXFOR20331.002	Jul 74	1PNT.	
Total	1.0-3	1.5+7	AUA Eval	Data	AUSTR-DFN 158.	Nov 71	COOK+POINT(223)+GROUP(127)SIG.CF EVL	+
Total	1.4+7		LIN Expt	Jour	IZV 37 1019	May 73	Djumin+ SIG(A),OPTMODEL CALC,GRAPH	+
				Conf	73Kiev 3 108	May 73	- + OPTMOD CALC,SIG	
				Jour	BAS 37 5 91	May 73	.ENGLISH OF IZV 37 1019	
	1.4+7			Data	EXFOR40302.011	Feb 76	1 PNT	
Total	1.4+5	6.3+5	DKE Expt	Jour	AP 84 165	May 74	Pineo+TRNS.AVG CS.TBL GRPHS.OPTMDL	+
	1.0+5	6.5+5		Jour	AP 84 165	May 74	- + N STRENGTH FUNC, TBLS, GRPHS.	
				Abst	DA/B 31 6821	May 71	- .2E RANGE AVGS.CFD OPTMDL.	
	1.5+4	6.0+5		Diss	PINEO	70	.AVG CS.GRPHS.CFD.STF CALC.TBL.CFD.	
	1.5+4	6.0+5		Data	EXFOR10542.018	Jan 79	. DATA UNOBTAINABLE FROM AUTHORS.	
Total	-3	1.9+0	THS Theo	Rept	IKE-6 89 65	Jun 75	Keinert. DATA LIBRARY	
Total	2.5-2		IJI Comp	Rept	KIYAI-76-6		76 Fedorova+ TO GET RECOM ABS-SIG.TABLE	
Total	2.0+1	2.0+5	RPI Expt	Prog	ERDA-NDC-3 255	May 76	Hockenbury+TRNS MEAS.NDG	
Total	1.0-2	4.0+2	NIR Expt	Conf	76Lowell 1252	Jul 76	Anufriev+TRNS.TOT CS.RES PARS.NDG	
Elastic	1.0-3	1.5+7	AUA Eval	Data	AUSTR-DFN 158.	Nov 71	COOK+POINT(223)+GROUP(127)SIG.CF EVL	+
Potntal Scat	3.0+3	6.5+5	DKE Expt	Jour	AP 84 165	May 74	Pineo+TRNS.S WAVE SCT LENGTH.TBL.CFD	
	3.0+5	6.5+5		Jour	AP 84 165	May 74	- + S-WAVE SCATT LENGTH.	
	3.0+3	6.5+5		Diss	PINEO	70	.TBL.GRPHS.CFD TO 3 COLLECTIVE MDLS.	
Tot Inelastc	5.0+5	1.5+7	AUA Eval	Data	AUSTR-DFN 158.	Nov 71	COOK+POINT(11)+GROUP(127)SIG.CF EVL	+
Scattering	2.5-2	1.0+7	GEA Eval	Rept	TID-11824	Jan 61	Zwick. GROUP AVGD+MAXWELL AVGD 18GRP	
Nonelastic	1.0-3	1.5+7	AUA Eval	Data	AUSTR-DFN 158.	Nov 71	COOK+POINT(223)+GROUP(127)SIG.CF EVL	+
Absorption	Pile		HAR Expt	Rept	AERE-R/R-2333	57	Cummins.NOT CORR FOR 1/V.TENTATIVE.	
Absorption	Pile		HAR Expt	Jour	JNE 4 33	Jan 57	Aitken+ SM149 MAIN ABS.IN NAT SM,M/S	+
Absorption	Pile		CCP Expt	Jour	AE 3 11	Jul 57	Gorshkov+.ABOVE 58000+-9000B,MASS SP	+
				Jour	JNE 8 69	Nov 58	. ENGL OF AE 3 729	
				Jour	SJA 3 729	57	. ENGL OF AE 3 729	
Absorption	Maxwl		CCP Expt	Conf	58Geneva 15 446	Sep 58	Anikina+.PPR2040,VAL GVN	
Absorption	Pile		MCME Expt	Conf	58Geneva 15 459	Sep 58	Bidinosti+ MASS SPEC REL CO	+
	Pile			Data	EXFOR12010.005	Jun 76	. 1 PT.	
Absorption	Maxwl	Pile	HAR Expt	Jour	JNEA 12 32	May 60	Tattersall+. EFF SIG IN THREE SPECTR	
				Rept	AERE-R-2887	Aug 59	- . PILE OSC.REL BORON	
	Maxwl			Rept	AERE-R/R-2516	Mar 58	Jowitt+ PILE OSC.REL BORON.293DEGK.	
Absorption	2.5-2	1.0+7	GEA Eval	Rept	TID-11824	Jan 61	Zwick.GROUP AVGD+MAXWELL AVGD 18GRPS	
Absorption	Fast		AE Expt	Conf	70Helsinki 2 603	Jun 70	Andersson.PILE OSC. 3 SPECS.CFD CALC	
Absorption	1.0-3	1.0+7	JUL Eval	Rept	JUEL-678-RG	Jul 70	Liu. EVALUATION+CALC,GRPH,FN OF E	
Absorption	1.0-3	2.0+0	JUL Theo	Rept	JUEL-746-RG 49	Apr 71	Bonka.KUGEL-THERMOS-LIBR,T=300K,CURV	
Absorption	Pile		CRC Eval	Conf	73Paris 1 459	Mar 73	Walker.FISS PRODUCT ABS,TBL PILE SIG	
Absorption	Fast		RCN Revw	Conf	IAEA-169 2 53		74 Bustraan.INTEG CFD SIG(N-E)FILES,TBL	
Absorption	2.5-2		IJI Eval	Conf	KIYAI-76-6		76 Fedorova+ COMP(REFS,SIGS),EVAL.TABLE	
				Conf	75Kiev 1 169	May 75	- + EVAL SIG GIVEN,TABLE	
Res Int Abs	5.5-1		GA Eval	Jour	NSE 12 115	Jan 62	Garrison+ RIG=3400+-300B.	
Res Int Abs	5.0-1		BOL Eval	Rept	RT/FI-4	Jan 67	Palmucci. CALC FROM (N,G) RES PARAMS	
Res Int Abs	None		GA Revw	Rept	GA-12071	Sep 71	Mathews+ RECOMMENDED VALUES.	
Res Int Abs	5.0-1		AUA Eval	Rept	AAEC/TM-619	Sep 72	Clayton.CALC FROM SIG LIBRARY,TABLE	
Res Int Abs	4.6-1	1.0+6	RCN Theo	Rept	RCN-191	Jul 73	Lautenbach.CAPT INT FROM GROUP SIGMA	
Res Int Abs	5.5-1	+6	SAC Revw	Rept	IAEA-169 1 235		74 Ribon.CAPTURE,STATUS CFD REQUEST,TBL	
Res Int Abs	+0	+5	WIN Revw	Conf	IAEA-169 3 163		74 Pope+ DATA FILE CALCS COMPARED	

62 Samarium 149

Quantity	Energy (ev) Min	Energy (ev) Max	Lab	Type	Documentation Ref Vol Page	Author, Comments Date	Data
(n,γ)	Pile		ANL Expt	Jour	PR 79 271	Jul 50 Inghram+	+
	Pile			Data	EXFOR12106.002	Jun 76 . 1 PT.	
(n,γ)	Maxwl		MCM Expt	Jour	CJC 33 830	May 55 Melaika+ 66200+ − 2500B REL NAT B 755B	+
	Maxwl			Data	EXFOR12086.002	Jun 76 . 1 PT.	
(n,γ)	Pile		MCM Expt	Priv	WALKER	May 56 Walker.	+
	Pile			Data	EXFOR12127.005	Jun 76 . 1 PT.	
(n,γ)	Maxwl		CCP Expt	Jour	AE 3 546	Dec 57 Ivanov+. 49000+ − 8000B FROM FISS YLD	
				Jour	JNE 9 46	Jun 59 TRANSLATN.*	
				Jour	SJA 3 1436	57 TRANSLATN.*	
(n,γ)	2.5−2		CRC Eval	Rept	AECL − 1054	Mar 60 Walker. SAME AS CRRP−913	
(n,γ)	Pile		HAR Expt	Jour	JIN 17 6	61 Aitken+ WELL−CHARACTERISED SPECTRUM	
(n,γ)	5.0−3	2.5+0	GA Eval	Rept	GA− 2113	Jun 61 Wikner+ TABLE + CURVE.100 E POINTS.	
(n,γ)	Pile		CRC Eval	Rept	CRRP−960	Jan 62 Westcott.EFF SIG TABLE 20−1300DEG C	
(n,γ)	2.5−2		GA Eval	Jour	NSE 12 115	Jan 62 Garrison+ EVAL FROM XPT+AVERAGE RES	
(n,γ)	3.0+4		ORL Expt	Jour	NAT 197 370	Jan 63 Macklin. 1.62+ −.28 B.	+
	3.0+4			Data	EXFOR12095.005	Jun 76 . 1 PT.	
(n,γ)	5.0+3	9.0+4	ORL Theo	Jour	RMP 37 166	Jan 65 Macklin+ CALC ASSUM. MAX. SHAPE.	
(n,γ)	1.0+3	1.0+5	CCP Theo	Jour	AE 18 114	Feb 65 Dovbenko+ STATIST MOD CURVE CFD DATA	
				Jour	JNE 20 675	Aug 66 TRANSLATN.*	
				Jour	SJA 18 140	Feb 65 TRANSLATN.*	
				Jour	EAF 18 2 44	Feb 65 TRANSLATN.*	
(n,γ)	1.0−1	1.1+0	ITE Expt	Jour	ITE−450	Apr 66 Kirpichnikov.GAMMA YLD VS NE.CURVES	+
				Rept	YFI−3 14	Sep 66 − . INTERFERENCE EFFECTS	
	9.9−2	1.0+0		Rept	INDC−140E 15	66 . ENGL OF YFI−3 14	
(n,γ)	3.5−1	1.1+1	CCP Expt	Rept	YFI−3 14	Sep 66 Kirpichnikov.INTERFERENCE EFFECTS	
				−		ENGL TRANSL SEE INDC−140E 15	
(n,γ)	2.5−2		BOL Eval	Rept	RT/FI−4	Jan 67 Palmucci. CALC FROM RES PARAMETERS	
(n,γ)	Maxwl		AUA Theo	Jour	NSE 31 234	Feb 68 Cook+ STATISTICAL CALC CFD EXPT	
(n,γ)	Pile		AUA Expt	Rept	AAEC/TM−443	Mar 68 Whittem.MASS−SPEC,SIG(EFF) R=0.0004	+
	Pile			Data	EXFOR30059.005	Nov 71 SIGMA(EFF) IN PILE SPEC WITH R=.0004	
(n,γ)	Pile		MUN Revw	Conf	69Studsvik 127	Aug 69 Egidy.PART'L SIGS OF CONV LINES,GRPH	
(n,γ)	1.0+3	1.0+7	BOL Eval	Rept	CCDN−NW/10	Dec 69 Benzi+H−F MOD,AXEL G(G)EST,ALL DATA	
				Rept	CEC(70)−2	Apr 70 − +. GRAPH	
				Conf	66Paris 1 537	Oct 66 − + STATMOD.TBL AV VALS.SUPERSEDD	
(n,γ)	4.0−2	9.0+2	DUB Expt	Jour	NP/A 154 177	Sep 70 Kvitek+ TOF. M−R DET. CURVE GIVEN	
(n,γ)	3.0+4		AUA Theo	Rept	AAEC/E−211	Nov 70 Musgrove. SIGMA GIVEN AND CFD OTHER	
(n,γ)	Maxwl		GA Eval	Rept	GA− 12071	Sep 71 Mathews+ RECOMMENDED VALUES.	
(n,γ)	1.0−3	1.5+7	AUA Eval	Data	AUSTR−DFN 158.	Nov 71 COOK+POINT(223)+GROUP(127)SIG.CF EVL	+
(n,γ)	2.5−2		CRC Eval	Rept	AECL−3037 1	Jan 72 Walker.RECOMMENDED SIG,DETAILED TBL	
(n,γ)	2.5−2		IAE Revw	Rept	IAEA−143 897	Apr 72 Lemmel.RECENT EVALUATIONS,TABLE+GRPH	
	Maxwl			Rept	IAEA−143 897	Apr 72 − .RECENT EVALUATIONS,TABLE	
(n,γ)	2.5−2		AUA Eval	Rept	AAEC/TM−619	Sep 72 Clayton.CALC FROM SIG LIBRARY,TABLE	
(n,γ)	2.5−2		SGA Eval	Conf	73Paris 1 233	Mar 73 Eder+ RECOMMENDED SIG,TBL,NO DETAILS	
				Rept	SGAE−PH−141	Feb 73 .SAME AS 73PARIS,EVAL OF EXPTL DATA	
(n,γ)		1.1+7	RCN Theo	Rept	RCN−191	Jun 73 Lautenbach. GROUP CONSTANTS TBL	
(n,γ)	2.5−2	3.0+4	SAC Revw	Conf	IAEA−169 1 235	74 Ribon.STATUS SIG CFD REQUESTS,TABLE	
	Fiss			Conf	IAEA−169 1 235	74 − .STATUS SIG CFD REQUESTS,TABLE	
	Fiss		WIN Revw	Conf	IAEA−169 3 137	74 Dean. POINT DATA AVG OVER STAND SPEC	
	Maxwl	Fiss		Conf	IAEA−169 3 163	74 Pope+ MAXW+FIS−SPEC AVG DATA CFD XPT	
(n,γ)	Pile		ANL Expt	Abst	BAP 19 525	Apr 74 Smither+ EFFECTIVE SIG=64670+ − 1000B	
(n,γ)	1.0+3	1.0+7	FEI Eval	Rept	YK− 8/2 97	Sep 72 Abagjan+ AVG SIG(ENERGY−GROUPS),TABL	
				Rept	INDC(CCP)−39	Jul 74 .P102. ENGLISH OF YK−8/2 97	
(n,γ)	2.0+1	1.5+5	RPI Expt	Abst	BAP 20 560	Apr 75 Hockenbury+ LINAC	+
	6.6+3	7.1+4		Data	EXFOR10552.006	Nov 76 . 434 PTS.CAPT CS.	
	6.6+3	7.1+4		Data	EXFOR10552.006	Nov 76 . 43 PTS. CAPT CS.	
(n,γ)	1.0+3	3.7+5	FEI ExTh	Conf	75Kiev 3 190	May 75 Jurlov+ REL B10(N,A).SIG(E),GRAPH	
(n,γ)	None		MUN Theo	Diss	GRYNTAKIS	Mar 76 Gryntakis.,CALC.OF WESTCOTTS G−FUNCT	
				Jour	RCA 22 128	Mar 75 − +,EQUIVALENT TO THESIS	
(n,γ)	Fast		RCN Expt	Rept	ECN−10	Oct 76 Veenema+ STEK REACTIVITY WORTHS TBL.	
Spect (n,γ)	Pile		ANL Expt	Jour	PR 88 943	Nov 52 Hibdon+ INTERNAL CONVERSION,GAMMA ES	
Spect (n,γ)	Maxwl		MOS Expt	Jour	ZET 32 979	May 57 Estulin+ SCINT SPEC 50−500KEV GAMMAS	
				Jour	JET 5 801	Dec 57 TRANSLATN.*	
Spect (n,γ)	9.6−2	4.9+0	YAL Expt	Jour	PR 107 1650	Sep 57 Fenstermacher+ 3 ES 340 440 KEV GS	
Spect (n,γ)	Maxwl		CCP Expt	Conf	58Geneva 15 138	Sep 58 Groshev+.PPR2029,CURVE,COMPTON−SPECT	
Spect (n,γ)	9.7−2	8.6−1	YAL Expt	Abst	BAP 4 35	Jan 59 Springer+ NAI(TL),GAMMA MULTIPLICITY	
Spect (n,γ)	Slow		CCP	Jour	NSA 14 1134	May 60 BLG−39 VERVIER,BRUSSELS	
Spect (n,γ)	Maxwl		CCP ExTh	Jour	NP 16 645	Jun 60 Groshev+COMPTON SPEC, +THEOR DISCUSS	

62 Samarium 149

Quantity	Energy (ev) Min	Max	Lab	Type	Documentation Ref Vol Page	Date	Author, Comments	Data
Spect (n,γ)	–		MUN Expt	Jour	ZN/A 16 927	Sep 61	Schult.LVLS IN SM150 XTAL SPECTROMET	
Spect (n,γ)	Maxwl		AUW Expt	Conf	63Bombay 160	Feb 63	Sastry+.TBL,GAMMA – E +INTENSITY	
Spect (n,γ)	Maxwl		KUR Expt	Jour	NP 43 669	Jun 63	Groshev+.DECAY SCHEME SM150 GIVEN	
Spect (n,γ)	Pile		RIS Expt	Prog	EANDC(OR)32L	Jun 64	Maier+ (MUN) 200 LOW EN LINES.NDG	
Spect (n,γ)	Maxwl		UEN Expt	Jour	ZP 183 217	Feb 65	Zehender+CASCADES THR 330+770KEV	
Spect (n,γ)	9.6–2	8.9–1	JAE Expt	Rept	JAERI–1073	Mar 65	Kawarasaki. RES CAPT.LINAC.TOF.E,INT	+
				Rept	INDSWG–90 6	Jul 65	– . TABLE E,INTS GIVEN.	
	9.6–2	8.9–1		Data	EXFOR20277.	Jun 74	9PTS.	
Spect (n,γ)	9.6–2	8.7–1	FEI Expt	Prog	INDSWG–74	Jul 65	BRODER ET AL.2 ES.	+
Spect (n,γ)	9.0–2	2.0+0	ISP Expt	Prog	EANDC(E)66U	Feb 66	.TBC.YIELD OF 7.21MEV TRNSIT.WG.NDG	
Spect (n,γ)	1.0+0	4.0+2	DUB Expt	Rept	JINR–P–2625	Mar 66	Kvitek+(N,A)+(N,G)REACTNS,HALF–LIFES	
Spect (n,γ)	Maxwl		BUC Expt	Jour	RRP 11 283	Apr 66	Cojocaru.ANG CORREL OF GS,GRPHS,TBLS	
Spect (n,γ)	Maxwl		MUN Expt	Jour	ZP 194 280	Jul 66	Elze.INTCONVERSION.392LINES3KEV–8MEV	
				Conf	67Juelich 56	Apr 67	– .	
				Jour	ZP 184 229	Apr 65	– .	
Spect (n,γ)	Pile		MUN Expt	Jour	ZN/A 21 1328	Sep 66	Neumann. CRYST SPEC EXPT OF GAM INT	
				Rept	ANL–TRANS–941	73	. ENGLISH OF ZN/A 1328	
Spect (n,γ)	Maxwl		ANL Expt	Jour	PR 150 964	Oct 66	Smither.BENT–XTL GS 70–2331KEV,LEVEL	+
Spect (n,γ)	Pile		MUN Expt	Jour	ZN/A 21 1729	Oct 66	Lang. LVL SCH OF SM 150	
Spect (n,γ)	Maxwl		FEI Expt	Conf	68Riga	Jan 68	Broder+ ABST,G ES,INT,GE–LI SPECTROM	
Spect (n,γ)	None		IFL Expt	Jour	IZV 32 74	Jan 68	Lure+ GAM+CONVERSION TBLS,LVL SCHEME	
	Maxwl			Book	PROKOFJEV	73	. TBL GAM,CONV ELECTR ES+INT,LVL SCH	
	None			Jour	BAS 32 74	Jan 69	. ENGL OF IZV 32 74	
Spect (n,γ)	1.0+0	4.0+1	FEI Expt	Rept	FEI–116	Feb 68	Broder+ GAMMA SPEC,TBL OF GAM YLD+E	
Spect (n,γ)		+3	DUB Expt	Conf	68DUBSY 283	Jul 68	Shapiro.RESONANCES,TOF,100 NS/M	
Spect (n,γ)	Maxwl		KUR Expt	Jour	IZV 32 1719	Oct 68	Govor+ GAM+K X RAY COINCIDENCE SPECS	
				Jour	BAS 32 1584	Oct 69	. ENGL OF IZV 32 1719	
Spect (n,γ)	Pile		KFK Expt	Jour	ZP 219 114	Jan 69	Eichler.POLZN. PARITY TEST.	
Spect (n,γ)	Pile		LEI Expt	Jour	NP/A 137 389	Nov 69	Reddingius+ GELI.LVL–SCHEME.	
				Jour	PHY 40 567	Jan 69	– + GE–LI TABLE INT GRAPHS	
Spect (n,γ)	1.2–1	1.5+0	CCP Expt	Conf	69Erevan	Feb 69	Kirpichnikov+.ABST,INTERFER OF RES	
Spect (n,γ)	None		CCP Theo	Jour	YF 9 740	Apr 69	Trusov. TABLE OF CALC INT–CONV–COEF	
				Jour	SNP 9 429	Oct 69	TRANSLATN.*NO4	
Spect (n,γ)	None		ORL Theo	Jour	NSE 36 220	May 69	Yost+ CALCULAT BY GAMMA CASCADE MDL	
Spect (n,γ)	Maxwl		IFL Expt	Conf	69Kinshasa 481	Jul 69	Lindsay. AEC GHANA,CONV EL SPEC GRPH	
Spect (n,γ)	Maxwl		KFI Revw	Jour	YF 10 907	Nov 69	Kecskemeti+ AVG GAM–MULTIPLICITY,TBL	
				Jour	SNP 10 524	May 70	TRANSLATN.*	
Spect (n,γ)	4.7–2	1.2–1	RCN Expt	Jour	NP/A 137 389	Nov 69	Reddingius+SPEC+ANISOTR+LVLS.ALIGNED	+
	Pile			Jour	PHY 40 567	Jan 69	– + N FILTER 77DEG K	
	Pile			Data	EXFOR20236.003	May 74	23PTS.	
Spect (n,γ)	Pile		KUR Expt	Jour	IZV 34 804	Apr 70	Panin+ CONVERSN–EL SPECS,ES+INTS,TBL	
				Jour	BAS 34 714	Apr 71	* ENGL OF IZV 34 804	
				Jour	BAS 33 617	Apr 70	* ENGL OF IZV 33 670	
				Jour	IZV 33 670	Apr 69	*METHOD DESCRIBED,SPECS	
Spect (n,γ)	Pile		ANL Expt	Jour	PR/C 2 1513	Oct 70	Buss+ GE(LI) DET,46 GAMMAS	
				Conf	69Studsvik 601	Aug 69	.SUPERSEDED	
				Conf	JINR–D–3893	May 68	Burson. ABSTRACT,GAM+CONV E XPT,NDG	
Spect (n,γ)		2.5+2	DUB Expt	Rept	JINR–P3–5655	Mar 71	Karzhavina+ TABLE,WN,WG.	
Spect (n,γ)	Maxwl		KUR Expt	Jour	IZV 35 1593	Aug 71	Panin+ MULTIPOLE ORDER OF TRANS,TBL	
				Jour	BAS 35 1453	Aug 72	. ENGL OF IZV 35 1593	
Spect (n,γ)	Maxwl		CCP Theo	Jour	ZET 65 12	Jul 73	Nosov+ THERMODYN CALC CFD EXPT,GRAPH	
				Jour	JET 38 6	Jan 74	. ENGLISH OF ZET 65 6	
Spect (n,γ)	Pile		ANL Expt	Abst	BAP 19 525	Apr 74	Smither+ NDG.	
Spect (n,γ)	Maxwl		BNL Revw	Conf	74Petten 247	Sep 74	Chrien+LEVEL–LEVEL INTERFERENCE GRPH	
Spect (n,γ)	4.0–2	3.4+1	BNL Expt	Jour	NP/A 236 198	Dec 74	Becvar+ G–LINE INTS(NEUT–E),CURVES	
				Jour	NP/A 236 173	Dec 74	– + GRPH SPEC.ES+INTS(RES–E),TBL	
Spect (n,γ)	Maxwl	Pile	SGA ExTh	Jour	APA 41 4 338	75	Korn+ SPEC SHAPE	
				Rept	SGAE–PH–174	Nov 74	– + SPEC SHAPE	
Spect (n,γ)	Maxwl		ATI ExTh	Rept	INDC(SEC)–51	Oct 75	Korn+ ABST ON PAGE 2 SHAPE G–SPECT	
Spect (n,γ)	9.7–2		CNA Expt	Prog	INDC(SEC)–51	Dec 75	Cansoy+P141,ABST.109–1806KEV ANALYSD	
(n,2n)	Fiss		CRC Eval	Rept	CRC–1003	Dec 60	ROY+ ESTIMATED AVG SIG=25.0MB.	
(n,2n)	1.5+7		DEB Eval	Jour	REA 11 1 153	Mar 73	Boedy+ RECOMM.VALUE FROM N–Z SYSTEM.	
(n,2n)	1.5+7		KFI Theo	Rept	KFKI–73–68	Dec 73	Jeki.NEW FIT,CALC SIG CFD OTHERS,TBL	
(n,p)	Fiss		CRC Eval	Rept	CRC–1003	Dec 60	ROY+ ESTIMATED AVG SIG=0.024MB.	
(n,p)	1.4+7		LYO Comp	Rept	LYCEN/6780	Nov 67	Crouzet+COMPILATN FOR ACTIVTN ANALYS	
(n,α)	Fiss		CRC Eval	Rept	CRC–1003	Dec 60	ROY+ ESTIMATED AVG SIG=0.038MB.	

62 Samarium 149

Quantity	Energy (ev) Min	Energy (ev) Max	Lab	Type	Documentation Ref Vol Page	Date	Author, Comments	Data
(n,α)	Maxwl		ISL	Expt	Jour PL 1 289	Jul 62	Cheifetz. TBL Q − VALU,SIG,BRANCHRATIO	+
	Maxwl				Data EXFOR31151.	Mar 73	.SIG GVN	
(n,α)	Maxwl		PR	Expt	Jour PR 127 1665	Sep 62	Macfarlane+SIG 2ALPHA ES. NEG E RES	+
	Maxwl				Data EXFOR12132.002	Jun 76	. 2 ALPHA ENERGIES.	
(n,α)	Maxwl		CCP	Expt	Jour YF 1 252	Feb 65	Andreev.IONIZ − CHAMBER,SIG= 7MB GND	+
					Jour SNP 1 177	Aug 65	TRANSLATN.*	
(n,α)	Maxwl		LEB		Conf 65Antwerp § 176	Jul 65	Andreev+CFD TH 48+ − 10MB	
(n,α)	1.1+0	1.4+2	CCP	Expt	Jour IZV 30 1371	Jul 66	Kvitek+. GRAPH SIG(E), TBL OF PARAMS	
					−		ENGL TRANSL SEE BAS 30 1432 (66)	
(n,α)	1.1+0	1.4+2	DUB	Expt	Jour IZV 30 1371	Jul 66	Kvitek+ GRAPH SIG(E),TBL OF PARAMS	
(n,α)	1.0+0	1.0+3	DUB	Expt	Conf 66Dubna 147	Jul 66	Frank+,REVIEW, GRAPH GIVEN	
(n,α)	4.0−3	1.0−1	MOL	Expt	Jour NP 82 331	Jul 66	Poortmans+ FIRST XCIT/GROUND STATE	
					Conf 64Paris 2 554	Jul 64	− + ISOMERIC RATIO.	
(n,α)	Maxwl	2.0+2	DUB	Expt	Jour PL 22 186	Aug 66	Kvitek+POPOV LIFETIMES OF XCIT STATE	
	1.0+0	4.0+2			Rept JINR − P − 2625	Mar 66	− +(N,A)+(N,G)REACTNS,HALF − LIFES	
	1.1+0	1.4+2			Jour BAS 30 1432	66	. ENGL OF IZV 30 1371	
(n,α)		4.0+2	DUB	Expt	Jour JINR − E3 − 3029	Nov 66	Kvitek+,AVER ALPHA WIDTH,TEOR CALC	+
(n,α)	Maxwl		MCM	Expt	Jour PL/B 24 142	Feb 67	Oakey+ SIG TO 10 ND146 LEVELS	+
					Jour NIM 49 220	Apr 67	.SEE ALSO	
	Maxwl				Data EXFOR12084.002	Jun 76	. 1 PT.	
(n,α)	2.5−2		IBJ	Expt	Jour NP/A 97 187	Apr 67	.SEE ALSO *	+
					Rept INR − 755/IA/PL	Sep 66	Dakowski+ GRAPHS,SPIN ASSIGNMENT	
	2.5−2				Data EXFOR30402.002	Jul 77	2 PTS, PART.SIG TO ND − 146 GND+1ST.	
(n,α)	Maxwl		NBS	Expt	Prog WASH − 1074 83	Apr 67	Schroder+ ALFA PARTICLE SPEC TBC NDG	
(n,α)	Pile	2.5−2	JAE	Expt	Jour NP/A 141 193	Jan 70	Okamoto. BI FILTER.A SPECT.EFF SIG.	+
	2.5−2				Data EXFOR20335.005	Jul 74	10PTS.SIGMA.	
(n,α)	Maxwl	9.0+2	DUB	Expt	Rept JINR − P3 − 4982	Apr 70	Kvitek+ ALFA SPEC GRAPHS,ALFA WIDTH	
	4.0−2	9.0+2	DUB	Expt	Jour NP/A 154 177	Sep 70	Kvitek+ TOF. SCINT DET CURVE GIVEN	
		+3			Conf 68DUBSY 283	Jul 68	Shapiro.RESONANCES,TOF,100 NS/M,WA	
(n,α)	Maxwl		TAM	Expt	Jour PL/B 36 74	Aug 71	Mueller+ RATIO ALPHA INT AS FN TEMP	
(n,α)	2.5−2	4.0+1	DUB	Expt	Jour YF 20 3	Jul 74	Winiwarter+ GRPH SIG(E),TBL ALF − WIDS	
					Rept JINR − P3 − 7245	Aug 73	− + RESPARS,TBL,SIG+ALF − SPEC	
	2.5−2	1.0+0			Conf 73Kiev 2 154	May 73	− + TOF,SIG(NEUT − E),GRAPH	
	2.5−2	4.0+1			Jour SNP 20 1	Jan 75	. ENGLISH OF YF 20 3	
(n,α)	1.8+7		IBJ	ExTh	Conf ZFK − 271 109	Nov 73	Glowacka+ A − SPEC CFD 2 MODELS,NDG.	+
				Expt	Prog INR − 1464 1	May 73	− +BRIEF,ALPHA SPECTRUM,TABLES	
	1.8+7				Data EXFOR30261.	Nov 73	ALFA − SPEC(48 PTS)+SIGMA AT 35 DEGREE	
(n,α)	Maxwl		LYO	Expt	Abst 75Harwell 38	Mar 75	Asghar+ (ILL).(N,GAM ALPHA) SIG.TBC	
					Conf 74Petten 395	Sep 74	Emsallem+ ALSO PARTIAL CR. SECT.	
(n,α)	1.4+7		IBJ	Expt	Prog INR − 1502 4	May 75	Glowacka+ ALPHA SPECTRUM, TABLE	+
	1.4+7				Data EXFOR30298.	May 75	DOUBLE DIFFSIG(42 PTS)+ANGDIST(1 PT)	
(n,α)	2.5−2		IJI	Eval	Rept KIYAI − 76 − 6	76	Fedorova+ COMP(REFS,SIGS),EVAL.TABLE	
(n,α)	0.0+0	2.0+2	DUB	Theo	Conf JINR − D − 9920	Jun 76	Popov. P 126.A − WIDS,SEMIMIC THEO,FIG	
(n,α)	None		DUB	Expt	Conf 76Lowell 1250	Jul 76	Antonov+TOT ALPHA WIDS OF N − RES.GRPH	
	2.0+0	4.0+2			Jour NP/A 261 35	Apr 76	Balabanov+RES ALPHA WT. TOF SPECTS.	
	3.5+0	2.0+2			Rept JINR − P3 − 9099	Aug 75	− + ALFAS VS EN,GRPH. RES,TBL	
	Fast				Conf 75Kiev 4 60	May 75	− + FOR ALF − WID.SIG NOT GIVEN	
	+0	2.0+2			Rept JINR − P3 − 8653	Mar 75	− + CORREL N − ,A − WIDS,CFD THEO	
Reson Params	9.6−2		ORL	Expt	Jour PR 70 557	Oct 46	Borst+ N DIFF METHOD SIG − WT − RESCURVE	+
	9.6−2				Data EXFOR11756.004	Jun 76	. 1 RES. E0,WT,PCS.	
Reson Params	9.6−2		CRC	Expt	Jour CJP 31 432	May 53	Brockhouse.	+
	9.6−2				Data EXFOR11653.010	Jun 76	. 1 RES. J.	
Reson Params	9.6−2		KJL	Expt	Jour PR 93 195	Jan 54	Mcreynolds+ PB CRYST SPEC.E0,WT,SIG0	+
	9.6−2				Data EXFOR20101.	Sep 71	2PTS.WT,TOT(RES).	
Reson Params	9.4−2		ORL	Expt	Jour PR 95 105	Jul 54	Roberts.	+
	9.4−2				Data EXFOR12148.001	Jun 76	. 1 RES. J.	
Reson Params	9.8−2	1.7+1	BNL	Expt	Jour PR 96 1014	Nov 54	Sailor+	+
	9.8−2	1.7+1			Data EXFOR12110.007	Jun 76	. 7 RES. E0,WT**2/PCS.	
Reson Params	1.2+1	9.9+2	MTR	Prog	IDO − 16373 39	Jul 57	Simpson.WG,G*WN,WN0.TBL.23RES ES	
	1.0+1	1.0+2			Abst BAP 2 42	Feb 57	− +BREIT − WIGNER PAR.NDG	
	3.2+1	9.9+2			Data EXFOR11983.006	Jun 76	. 23 RES. E0,WN,WN0.	
Reson Params	9.8−2	9.8−2	HAR	Expt	Conf 58Geneva 16 4	58	Pattenden. PPR11. FROM TRANSMISSION	+
Reson Params	5.0+0	1.8+2	HAR	Expt	Jour NP 5 294	Jan 58	Bowey+. 22 RESONANCE ES GVN. LINAC	+
Reson Params	1.2+1	1.7+1	BNL	Expt	Jour PR 109 1219	Feb 58	Marshak+	+
	9.8−2	1.7+1			Data EXFOR11766.002	Jun 76	. 8 RES. E0,WT,WN0,WG,PCS.	
Reson Params	None		GA	Eval	Jour NSE 12 115	Jan 62	Garrison+	

62 Samarium 149

Quantity	Energy (ev) Min	Max	Lab	Type	Documentation Ref Vol Page	Author, Comments Date	Data
Reson Params	2.5+1	4.2+1	ANL	Expt Prog	ANL-6589	Aug 62 Carpenter.	+
	2.5+1	4.2+1		Data	EXFOR12048.005	Jun 76 . 2 RES. E0,J.	
Reson Params	-.3-1		PR	Expt Jour	PR 127 1665	Sep 62 Macfarlane+	+
	-.3-1			Data	EXFOR12132.003	Jun 76 . 1 RES. J.	
Reson Params	9.8-2	8.9+0	BNL	Expt Jour	PR 128 1287	Nov 62 Marshak+ 4 RESONANCES ALL J=4	+
	9.6-2	8.9+0		Data	EXFOR12147.002	Jun 76 . 4 RES. J.	
Reson Params	8.7-1		ORL	Expt Jour	NSE 17 371	63 Pattenden.	+
	8.7-1			Data	EXFOR12025.009	Jun 76 . 1 RES. E0,WN0.	
Reson Params	4.0-1	8.0+0	CCP	Expt Jour	AE 16 523	Jun 64 Begzhanov+3RES.E0,SIGZERO,TOT WIDTH	+
				Jour	SJA 16 647	Jun 64 . ENGL OF AE 16 523	
Reson Params	1.0+3	1.0+5	CCP	Theo Jour	AE 18 114	Feb 65 Dovbenko+ WG, AVERAGE RES SPACING	
				Jour	JNE 20 675	Aug 66 TRANSLATN.*	
				Jour	EAF 18 2 44	Feb 65 TRANSLATN.*	
				Jour	SJA 18 140	Feb 65 TRANSLATN.*	
Reson Params	1.0+0	4.0+2	DUB	ExTh Conf	67Kharkov 201	Feb 67 Kvitek.EMITT ALFA PARTICLES,CFD H-F	
Reson Params	9.8-2	8.7-1	MOL	Expt Jour	NP/A 97 657	May 67 Poortmans+.FROM RES SCATTERING EXPT.	+
	9.8-2	8.7-1		Data	EXFOR20213.	May 74 4PTS.J,WN/WT.	
Reson Params		1.0+6	AUA	Theo Jour	AUJ 20 477	Oct 67 Cook. TBL OF AVG LVL SPACING D,L=0,1	
Reson Params	9.7-2	8.7-1	CNA	Expt Rept	CNAEM-52	Jun 68 Akyuz+ CRYST SPEC 2RESON WN WT WG	+
	9.7-2	8.7-1		Data	EXFOR20173.	May 74 8PTS.WG,WN,WN0,TOT(RES).	
Reson Params		+3	DUB	Expt Conf	68DUBSY 283	Jul 68 Shapiro.ALFA WIDTH,TOF, 100NS/M	
Reson Params	9.9-2		JAE	Expt Jour	JPJ 26 225	Feb 69 Asami.CRYST-SPECT,WT WN GIVN	+
	9.9-2			Data	EXFOR20331.	Jul 74 3PTS.WN0,WT,TOT(RES).	
Reson Params	+3	+5	AUA	ExTh Rept	AAEC/E-198	May 69 Musgrove.RES PARS +STF FROM (NG)FIT	+
Reson Params	9.8-2	5.2+1	DUB	Expt Conf	70Helsinki 1 669	Jun 70 Popov+125. TABLE ALPHA WIDTH + SPIN	+
	None			Rept	JINR-E3-5483	Dec 70 - . TABLE OF ALPHA+NEUTRON WIDTHS	
	9.8-2	1.0+2		Jour	NP/A 154 177	Sep 70 Kvitek+ J,PI,ALPHA,GAMMA WIDTHS	
	Maxwl			Rept	JINR-P3-4982	Apr 70 - + ALFA WIDTH GIVEN,N-RESONANCS	
	9.8-2	1.7+1		Jour	PL 22 186	Aug 66 - +POPOV ALPHA WIDTHS 8RES	
				Rept	JINR-P-2625	Mar 66 - +(N,A)+(N,G)REACTNS,HALF-LIFES	
	9.8-2	5.2+1		Rept	UCRL-TR-105	May 71 . ENGL OF 70HELSIN.FULL RPT-N0=10541	
	9.8-2	5.2+1		Data	EXFOR40225.004	Jul 75 .ALPHA WIDTH AT 16 ES GIVEN	
Reson Params	-		AUA	Theo Rept	AAEC/E-211	Nov 70 Musgrove. CALCULTD D+GAM WIDTH GIVEN	
Reson Params	9.8-2	9.1+0	CJD	Eval Rept	YK-7	71 Zakharova+ SURVEY+SYSTEMATICS,GW,TBL	
				Rept	INDC(CCP)-27	Nov 72 .ENGLISH TRANSLATION OF YK-7 /71	
Reson Params	None		DUB	Theo Jour	YF 13 240	Feb 71 Malecki+G-WID,THEO CFD EXPT.TBL,GRPH	
				Jour	SNP 13 133	Aug 71 - + ENGL OF YF 13 240.	
Reson Params	5.0+0	1.9+2	SAC	Expt Conf	71Knoxvill 785	Mar 71 Cauvin+.J ASSIGNMENTS 41RESON	
	5.0+0	1.9+2		Data	EXFOR20126.010	Sep 72 41PTS.J.	
Reson Params	6.5+0		BNL	Expt Prog	NCSAC-38 30	May 71 Brunhart+ J TO BE MEASD, POLAR EXPT	
Reson Params	1.6+1	2.5+2	DUB	Expt Jour	YF 15 401	Mar 72 Karzhavina+ AREA ANALYS,GRPHS,D GIVN	+
				Prog	YFI-12 49	72 - + ABST,TBL E-RES,N-WIDTHS	
				Rept	JINR-P3-5655	Mar 71 - + TABLE,WN,WG.	
				Jour	SNP 15 225	Sep 72 - + ENGL OF YF 15 401.	
				Prog	INDC(CCP)-30	Sep 72 .PAGE 42,ENGLISH OF YFI-12 49	
	1.6+1	2.5+2		Data	EXFOR40071.	Jul 71 ELAS-WIDTH+REDUCED,82 RESONANCES,D	
Reson Params	+1	+6	GEL	Expt Prog	INDC(SEC)-26	May 72 Theobald+ FROM CAPT+EL SIG,PROPOSED	
Reson Params	5.0-1	2.6+2	DUB	Expt Rept	RCN-203 254	Dec 73 Karzhavina+ G-MULT METH.J,D,S0 GIVEN	+
	+0	+3		Conf	73Kiev 2 337	May 73 - + SPIN IDENT,G-MULTIP MTHD	
	5.0+0	2.0+2		Conf	72Budapest 20	Aug 72 - + SPINS OF RESONANCES,TBL	
	5.0+0	2.6+2		Rept	JINR-P3-6237	Jan 72 - + SPINS OF RESONANCES,TBL	
	4.9+0	6.5+2		Rept	JINR-P3-6092	Nov 71 - .GS MULTIPLICITY,SPINS,TBL	
	5.0+0	2.6+2		Data	EXFOR40098.003	May 72 SPINS OF 84 RES.	
Reson Params	+0	+2	BOL	Eval Conf	IAEA-169 3 123	74 Benzi+ AVG G-WID CFD OTHERS+XPT,TABL	
Reson Params	-.5+0	1.7+1	DUB	Expt Jour	YF 20 3	Jul 74 Winiwarter+ TOT+PART ALF-WIDTHS,TBL	
				Rept	JINR-P3-7245	Aug 73 - + RES-ES,A-WID,SPIN,TABLE	
				Jour	SNP 20 1	Jan 75 . ENGLISH OF YF 20 3	
Reson Params	+0	+2	FEI	Eval Rept	YK-8/2 97	Sep 72 Abagyan+ AVG G-WID+D AT BINDNG-E,TBL	
				Rept	INDC(CCP)-39	Jul 74 .PAGE 102.ENGLISH OF YK-8/2 97	
Reson Params	-.5-3	9.0+0	BNL	Expt Rept	NP/A 236 198	Dec 74 Becvar+ G-WID-AMPLIT(RES-E,LVL),TBL	+
	9.8-2	3.4+1		Jour	NP/A 236 173	Dec 74 - + SPIN+PARITY OF 41G-LINES,TBL	
	9.8-2	3.4+1		Data	EXFOR10464.002	Feb 75 . 16 RES., J, PI	
Reson Params	+3		RPI	Expt Prog	ERDA-NDC-3 255	May 76 Hockenbury+RES PARS DRVD.NDG	+
	2.0+1	1.5+5		Abst	BAP 20 560	Apr 75 - +D=2.7+-.3EV RES PARS TBP.	
	3.4+1			Data	EXFOR10552.011	Nov 78 . 1PT.WN=(6.62+-.2)-3EV AT 33.9 EV.	
Reson Params	1.0+3	1.0+6	SAC	Eval Rept	CEA-N-1832	Dec 75 Ribon+ EXP+TH ANAL,RES PAR,TBL	

62 Samarium 149

Quantity	Energy (ev) Min	Max	Lab	Type	Documentation Ref Vol Page	Date	Author, Comments	Data
Reson Params	2.0+0	4.0+2	DUB	Expt	Jour NP/A 261 35	Apr 76	Balabanov+TBLS OF ALPHA RES PARS	
	Fast				Conf 75Kiev 4 60	May 75	- + AVG ALF-WIDTHS.TABLE	
	+0	2.0+2			Rept JINR-P3-8653	Mar 75	- + CORREL N-,A-WIDS,CFD THEO	
Reson Params	1.0-2	4.0+2	NIR	Expt	Conf 76Lowell 1252	Jul 76	Anufriev+SHAPE AND AREA ANAL.NDG	
Reson Params	Maxwl		KUK	Theo	Conf 76Ahmedabd 2 1	Dec 76	Sharma+AVG S-WAVE REDUCED N-WID ANAL	
Strnth Fnctn	2.0+1	1.0+3	MTR	Expt	Abst BAP 3 176	May 58	Simpson+ FAST CHOPPER STF=3.11+-0.28	
Strnth Fnctn	+3		BNL	Expt	Jour PRL 1 461	Dec 58	Hughes+ FC 3.2+-0.1	
Strnth Fnctn	6.0-2	2.0+1			Jour PR 109 1219	Feb 58	Marshak+ TOF CS 2.0 8 LEVELS.	
Strnth Fnctn	None		GA	Eval	Jour NSE 12 115	Jan 62	Garrison+ STF + D.	
Strnth Fnctn	+3	+5	AUA	ExTh	Rept AAEC/E-198	May 69	Musgrove.S+P+D STF FROM (NG)FIT,TBL	+
Strnth Fnctn	-		AUA	Theo	Rept AAEC/E-211	Nov 70	Musgrove. SMOOTHED S0,S1 AND S2 GIVN	
Strnth Fnctn	1.6+1	2.5+2	DUB	Expt	Jour YF 15 401	Mar 72	Karzhavina+ S0 FOR DIFFERENT E-RANGE	+
					Prog YFI-12 49	72	- + ABST,S0 GIVEN	
					Conf 71Kiev	May 71	- + S0 AND S1 VALUES GIVEN	
					Rept JINR-P3-5655	Mar 71	- + TABLE,WN,WG.	
					Jour SNP 15 225	Sep 72	- + ENGL OF YF 15 401.	
					Prog INDC(CCP)-30	Sep 72	.PAGE 42,ENGLISH OF YFI-12 49	
	1.6+1	2.5+2			Data EXFOR40071.	Jul 71	FOR 16-134 EV AND FOR 16-250 EV GIVN	
Strnth Fnctn	1.5+2	6.5+2	SAC	ExTh	Diss FRNC-TH-450	Oct 72	Delaroche.OPTICAL MODEL PARAMETERS	
Strnth Fnctn	None		AUA	Eval	Rept AAEC/E-277	Mar 73	Musgrove.TBLS EXPTL DATA+BEST VALUES	
Strnth Fnctn	3.0+3	6.5+5	DKE	Expt	Jour AP 84 1 165	May 74	Pineo+ S-WAVE SCATTERING LENGTH.	
					Diss PINEO	70	.S0,S1.TBL.GRPHS.CFD CALC,OTH EXPTS.	
Strnth Fnctn	6.5+3	7.1+4	RPI	Expt	Abst BAP 20 560	Apr 75	Hockenbury+RESPARS.TBP.	+
	6.5+3	7.1+4			Data EXFOR10552.	Nov 78	. 4PTS.S0,S1,S2,AVG WG GVN.	
Strnth Fnctn	1.0-2	4.0+2	NIR	Expt	Conf 76Lowell 1252	Jul 76	Anufriev+TRNS.RES PARS DRVD.STF TBD	
Lvl Density	-		FEI	Eval	Rept FEI-36	66	Kapchigashev+.TBL OF RELATD QUANTTYS	+
		5.0+4			Jour YF 4 686	Sep 66	.TABLE.SHORT VERSION OF FEI-36	
	-				Prog YFI-3 3	66	.ABSTRACT.TABLE LDL+NUCL.EXCIT.E	
		5.0+4			Jour SNP 4 486	67	.ENGLISH OF YF 4.FROM(N,GAMMA).TABLE	
					Prog INDC-E-140 3	66	.ENGLISH TRANSL OF YFI-3	
Lvl Density	None		AUW	Theo	Conf 70Madurai 2 267	Dec 70	Ramamurty+ A-PARAMETER GVN,LANG'S-TH	
Lvl Density	5.0+0	1.6+2	DUB	Expt	Rept JINR-P3-6237	Feb 72	Karzhavina+ TOF	+
	5.0+0	1.6+2			Data EXFOR40098.005	May 72	AVERAGE LEVEL SPACING	
Lvl Density	None		BOL	Eval	Conf IAEA-169 3 123	74	Benzi+ LVL DENS PARAM BY XPT,GRPH+TB	
Lvl Density	None		DUB	Theo	Jour NP/A 224 411	May 74	Soloviev+ 1/2 MICROSC MDL. SPH NUCL.	
Lvl Density	+0	+2	FEI	Eval	Rept YK-8/2 97	Sep 72	Abagyan+ LVL DENSITY PARAMETER,TBL	
					Rept INDC(CCP)-39	Jul 74	.PAGE 102.ENGLISH OF YK-8/2 97	

62 Samarium 150

Quantity	Energy (ev) Min	Max	Lab	Type	Documentation Ref Vol Page	Date	Author, Comments	Data
Evaluation	1.0-3	1.5+7	AUA	Eval	Rept AAEC/TM-549	Jun 70	Cook.TOT,EL,INEL,NONEL,CAPT SIGS,NDG	+
					Rept AAEC/E-214	Jun 71	Bertram+GROUP SIGMAS SAME QUANTS.NDG	
					Rept AAEC/TM-587	Mar 71	*DESCRIPTION OF LIBRARY	
	1.0-3	1.5+7			Data AUSTR-DFN 159.	Nov 71	POINT(223) AND GROUP(127) SIGMAS	
Total	9.8+5		SHE	Theo	Jour NP 54 417	Jun 64	Maddison.OPTMOD FIT TO TOWLE GILBOY	
Total	1.3+7	1.5+7	DEB	Eval	Jour AHP 30 115	Oct 71	Angeli+ AVG SIG,CFD CALC.TBLS.GRAPH	
Total	1.0-3	1.5+7	AUA	Eval	Data AUSTR-DFN 159.	Nov 71	COOK+POINT(223)+GROUP(127)SIG.CF EVL	+
Total	1.4+7		LIN	Expt	Conf 73Kiev 3 108	May 73	Djumin+ OPTMOD CALC,SIG	+
					Jour IZV 37 1019	May 73	- + SIG(A),OPTMODEL CALC,GRAPH	
					Jour BAS 37 5 91	May 73	.ENGLISH OF IZV 37 1019	
	1.4+7				Data EXFOR40302.012	Feb 76	1 PNT	
Total	8.0+5	1.5+7	WMU	Expt	Jour PL/B 45 241	Jul 73	Shamu+TRANSMISSION METHOD	+
	7.5+5	1.4+7			Data EXFOR10615.003	Nov 76	. 27PTS.(SM150TOT-SM148TOT)/SM148TOT	
Total	-1	1.2+3	KAP	Expt	Jour NSE 54 286	Jul 74	Eiland+TRNS.CURV.THR VAL.RES ANAL.	
Total	2.5-2		KAP	Expt	Jour NSE 54 286	Jul 74	Eiland+	+
					Conf 71Knoxvill 673	Mar 71	- + LINAC, TRANS, SIG=133+-8 B	
	2.5-2				Data EXFOR10147.009	Jul 72	1PT.SIG=135+-8B.	
Total	1.0+6	1.5+7	BRC	Theo	Conf JAERI-M-5984	Feb 75	Lagrange.EFF OF DEFORMATION.GRPHS	
	2.0+6	2.0+7			Jour JPRL 33 111	Sep 74	- .DEFORMAT EFFECT ON STG TOT	
Total	-3	1.9+0	THS	Theo	Rept IKE-6 89 65	Jun 75	Keinert. DATA LIBRARY	
Total	1.0+6	1.6+7	KTY	Revw	Conf 76Lowell 171	Jul 76	Mcellistrem.COUP-CHAN CALC.	
Elastic	1.0-3	1.5+7	AUA	Eval	Data AUSTR-DFN 159.	Nov 71	COOK+POINT(223)+GROUP(127)SIG.CF EVL	+
Diff Elastic	9.8+5		SHE	Theo	Jour NP 54 417	Jun 64	Maddison.OPTMOD FIT TO TOWLE GILBOY	
Tot Inelastc	5.0-2	1.5+7	AUA	Eval	Data AUSTR-DFN 159.	Nov 71	COOK+POINT(11)+GROUP(127)SIG.CF EVL	+
Diff Inelast	2.5+6	1.4+7	KTY	Revw	Conf 76Lowell 171	Jul 76	Mcellistrem.SCAT TO 2+ LVL.	

62 Samarium 150

Quantity	Energy (ev) Min	Energy (ev) Max	Lab	Type	Documentation Ref Vol Page	Date	Author, Comments	Data
Nonelastic	1.0−3	1.5+7	AUA	Eval Data	AUSTR−DFN 159.	Nov 71	COOK+POINT(223)+GROUP(127)SIG.CF EVL	+
Absorption	Maxwl		KAP	Expt Jour	NUC 14 89	Sep 56	Deutsch.FISS PROD S EST BY STEHN	
Absorption	4.1−1	1.0+7	GA	Eval Prog	GA− 2451	Aug 61	Joanou+ 68GROUP DATA FOR GAM−I	
Absorption	1.0−3	1.0+7	JUL	Eval Rept	JUEL−678−RG	Jul 70	Liu. EVALUATION+CALC,GRPH,FN OF E	
Absorption	Pile		CRC	Eval Conf	73Paris 1 459	Mar 73	Walker.FISS PRODUCT ABS,TBL PILE SIG	
Absorption	2.5−2		IJI	Eval Conf	75Kiev 1 169	May 75	Fedorova+ EVAL SIG GIVEN,TABLE	
Res Int Abs	5.5−1		GA	Eval Jour	NSE 12 115	Jan 62	Garrison+ RIG=400+−130B.	
Res Int Abs	5.5−1		ORL	Expt Prog	WASH−1039 30	May 62	Halperin+ SIGMA GVN	
Res Int Abs	None		CRC	Eval Rept	AECL−2111	Nov 64	Walker. REDUCED RESONANCE INTEGRAL	
Res Int Abs	5.0−1		BOL	Eval Rept	RT/FI−4	Jan 67	Palmucci. CALC FROM (N,G) RES PARAMS	
Res Int Abs	5.5−1		CRC	Eval Rept	AECL−3037 1	Jan 72	Walker.REDUCED RES INT,DETAILED TBL	
Res Int Abs	5.0−1		AUA	Eval Rept	AAEC/TM−619	Sep 72	Clayton.CALC FROM SIG LIBRARY,TABLE	
Res Int Abs	4.6−1	1.0+6	RCN	Theo Rept	RCN−191	Jul 73	Lautenbach.CAPT INT FROM GROUP SIGMA	
Res Int Abs	5.5−1	+6	SAC	Revw Conf	IAEA−169 1 235	74	Ribon.CAPTURE,STATUS CFD REQUEST,TBL	
Res Int Abs	+0	+5	WIN	Revw Conf	IAEA−169 3 163	74	Pope+ DATA FILE CALC CFD XPTAL VALUE	
Res Int Abs	5.0−1		KAP	Expt Jour	NSE 54 286	Jul 74	Eiland+CAPT INTEG CALC.VAL GVN	+
				Conf	71Knoxville 673	Mar 71	− +CAPT INTEG DRVD.	
	5.0−1			Data	EXFOR10147.016	Jan 78	. RIA=310+−15B	
Res Int Abs	5.0−1		IJI	Eval Rept	KIYAI−76−6	76	Fedorova+ EVAL CFD CALC.TBL RI,REFS	
				Conf	75Kiev 1 169	May 75	− + EVAL+CALC RI GIVEN,TABLE	
(n,γ)	Fast		OHO	Expt Jour	PR 53 437	Mar 38	Pool+ BETAS,CLOUD CH,RAT SM152.	
	Maxwl			Jour	PR 53 437	Mar 38	− + BETAS,CLOUD CH, RATIO SM152.	
(n,γ)	Pile		MCM	Expt Diss	WALKER	May 56	Walker.	+
	Pile			Data	EXFOR12127.006	Jun 76	. 1 PT.	
(n,γ)	Pile		HAR	Expt Jour	JIN 17 6	61	Aitken+ WELL−CHARACTERISED SPECTRUM	
(n,γ)	Maxwl		GA	Eval Jour	NSE 12 115	Jan 62	Garrison+ 85+−25B.	
(n,γ)	Maxwl		ORL	Expt Prog	WASH−1039 30	May 62	Halperin+ SIGMA GVN	
(n,γ)	3.0+4		ORL	Expt Jour	NAT 197 370	Jan 63	Macklin. 370+−72 MB	+
	3.0+4			Data	EXFOR12095.006	Jun 76	. 1 PT.	
(n,γ)	Maxwl		CRC	Eval Rept	AECL−2111	Nov 64	Walker.	
(n,γ)	5.0+3	9.0+4	ORL	Theo Jour	RMP 37 166	Jan 65	Macklin+ CALC ASSUM. MAX. SHAPE.	
(n,γ)	1.0+3	1.0+5	CCP	Theo Jour	AE 18 114	Feb 65	Dovbenko+ STATIST MOD CURVE CFD DATA	
				Jour	JNE 20 675	Aug 66	TRANSLATN.*	
				Jour	EAF 18 2 44	Feb 65	TRANSLATN.*	
				Jour	SJA 18 140	Feb 65	TRANSLATN.*	
(n,γ)	2.5−2		BOL	Eval Rept	RT/FI−4	Jan 67	Palmucci. CALC FROM RES PARAMETERS	
(n,γ)	2.5+4		FEI	ExTh Prog	YFI−4 22	May 67	Shorin+.,TBLS GIVEN,TBP YF	
				Rept	INDC−187E	67	. ENGL OF YFI−4 22	
(n,γ)	Maxwl		AUA	Theo Jour	NSE 31 234	Feb 68	Cook+ STATISTICAL CALC CFD EXPT	
(n,γ)	−		IEA	Comp Rept	IEA−INF−10	Aug 68	Atalla. TABLES OF HL,SIG AND GAMM−E	
(n,γ)	1.0+3	1.0+7	BOL	Eval Rept	CCDN−NW/10	Dec 69	Benzi+H−F MOD,AXEL G(G)EST,ALL DATA	
				Rept	CEC(70)−2	Apr 70	− +. GRAPH	
(n,γ)	3.0+4		AUA	Theo Rept	AAEC/E−211	Nov 70	Musgrove. SIGMA GIVEN AND CFD OTHER	
(n,γ)	2.5−2		KAP	Expt Conf	71Knoxvill 673	Mar 71	Eiland+ABS=TOT−POT SCT−RES SCT.	+
	2.5−2			Data	EXFOR10147.013	Jan 78	. 1 PT. SIG=107+−9 B.	
(n,γ)	1.0−3	1.5+7	AUA	Eval Data	AUSTR−DFN 159.	Nov 71	COOK+POINT(223)+GROUP(127)SIG.CF EVL	+
(n,γ)	Maxwl		CRC	Eval Rept	AECL−3037 1	Jan 72	Walker.RECOMMENDED SIG,DETAILED TBL	
(n,γ)	Maxwl		IAE	Revw Rept	IAEA−143 897	Apr 72	Lemmel.RECENT EVALUATIONS,TABLE	
	2.5−2			Rept	IAEA−143 897	Apr 72	− .RECENT EVALUATIONS,TABLE+GRPH	
(n,γ)	2.5−2		AUA	Eval Rept	AAEC/TM−619	Sep 72	Clayton.CALC FROM SIG LIBRARY,TABLE	
(n,γ)		1.1+7	RCN	Theo Rept	RCN−191	Jun 73	Lautenbach. GROUP CONSTANTS TBL	
(n,γ)	2.5−2		SAC	Revw Conf	IAEA−169 1 235	74	Ribon.STATUS SIG CFD REQUESTS,TABLE	
	Fiss			Conf	IAEA−169 1 235	74	− .STATUS SIG CFD REQUESTS,TABLE	
(n,γ)	Maxwl Fiss		WIN	Revw Conf	IAEA−169 3 163	74	Pope+ MAXW+FIS−SPEC AVG DATA CFD XPT	
	Fiss			Conf	IAEA−169 3 137	74	Dean. POINT DATA AVG OVER STAND SPEC	
(n,γ)	1.0+3	1.0+7	FEI	Eval Rept	YK−8/2 97	Sep 72	Abagjan+ AVG SIG(ENERGY−GROUPS),TABL	
				Rept	INDC(CCP)−39	Jul 74	.P102. ENGLISH OF YK−8/2 97	
(n,γ)	2.5−2		IJI	Eval Rept	KIYAI−76−6	76	Fedorova+ COMP(REFS,SIGS),EVAL.TABLE	
(n,γ)	Fast		RCN	Expt Rept	ECN−10	Oct 76	Veenema+ STEK REACTIVITY WORTHS TBL.	
Spect (n,γ)	Pile		MUN	Expt Jour	ZP 170 465	Nov 62	Bieber+CRYSTSPEC .059−1.7MEV,LVL SCH	
Spect (n,γ)	−		CCP	Expt Jour	IZV 31 277	Feb 67	Govor+.CURVE OF GAMMAS,LVL DIAGRAM	
				Jour	BAS 31 261	Feb 67	TRANSLATN.*	
Spect (n,γ)	Maxwl		KUR	Expt Rept	IAE−1832	69	Panin+ CONVERS−EL SPEC,TBL ES+INTS	
				Rept	BNL−TR−306	Nov 69	. ENGLISH OF IAE−1832	
Spect (n,γ)	None		LEI	Expt Conf	69Montreal 690	Aug 69	Postma+SPIN ASSIGNMENTS.ANISOT.NDG.	

62 Samarium 150

Quantity	Energy (ev) Min	Max	Lab	Type	Documentation Ref Vol Page	Date	Author, Comments	Data
Spect (n,γ)	Pile		KUR	Expt	Jour YF 13 681	Apr 71	Groshev+ GE-LI,GAM-ES+INT.TBL,GRAPHS	+
					Conf 71Moscow	Feb 71	- + ABST.GE-LI,TBL ES+INTENS	
					Jour SNP 13 387	Oct 71	. ENGL OF YF 13 681	
	2.5-2				Data EXFOR40146.003	Apr 73	.32 GAMMA ES AND GAM/100N GIVEN	
Spect (n,γ)	Maxwl		RIS	Expt	Prog EANDC(E)140U	Aug 71	Van Assche+ (MUN) CRYST SPEC.NDG.	
Spect (n,γ)		2.0+5	MUN	Expt	Rept PTUM-E-18	May 73	Schreckenbach. THESIS. CONV-EL,LVLS	
Spect (n,γ)	None		ANL	Expt	Conf 74Petten 358	Sep 74	Smither+AVG NEUTR.CAPT. (PROGR.)	
Spect (n,γ)	2.5-2		LVN	Expt	Conf 76Lowell 1438	Jul 76	Vandenput+EXPT LVL SCHEME CFD MDL.	
Inelastic γ	2.5+6		KTY	Expt	Conf 76Lowell 1326	Jul 76	Coope+CS MEAS.STAT MDL,CC CALCS.NDG	
(n,2n)	Fiss		CRC	Eval	Rept CRC-1003	Dec 60	ROY+ESTIMATED AVG SIG=2.8MB.	
(n,2n)	1.5+7		DEB	Eval	Jour REA 11 1 153	Mar 73	Boedy+ RECOMM.VALUE FROM N-Z SYSTEM.	
(n,2n)	1.5+7		KFI	Theo	Rept KFKI-73-68	Dec 73	Jeki.NEW FIT,CALC SIG CFD OTHERS,TBL	
(n,xn) x>2	1.4+7		BRC	ExTh	Prog CEA-N-1875 60	Apr 76	Frehaut+N3N.SYSTEMATIC LAWS SEARCH	
(n,p)	Fiss		CRC	Eval	Rept CRC-1003	Dec 60	ROY+ ESTIMATED AVG SIG=0.0008MB.	
(n,p)	1.4+7	1.5+7	ARK	Theo	Prog ORO-3235-29	Jan 67	Koch+ STAT MODEL CALC CFD EXPTS.	
(n,p)	1.4+7		LYO	Comp	Rept LYCEN/6780	Nov 67	Crouzet+COMPILATN FOR ACTIVTN ANALYS	
(n,p)	1.5+7		ARK	Expt	Abst DA/B 32 5091	Mar 72	Bari. GE(LI) DET. ACT. SIG GIVEN	+
	1.5+7				Data EXFOR10431.015	Aug 75	. 1 PT. SIGMA.	
(n,p)	1.5+7		KYU	Expt	Jour NST 12 681	Nov 75	Sato+.ACTIVATION SIG=7.19+-1.01 MB	+
	1.5+7				Data EXFOR20595.003	Aug 76	1PNT.SIGMA.	
(n,p)	1.5+7		JUL	Expt	Jour RRL 25 335	May 76	Qaim+ ACTIV,GELI.CFD OTHERS,TBL+GRPH	
(n,α)	Fiss		CRC	Eval	Rept CRC-1003	Dec 60	ROY+ ESTIMATED AVG SIG=0.0025MB.	
(n,α)	1.4+7		LYO	Comp	Rept LYCEN/6780	Nov 67	Crouzet+COMPILATN FOR ACTIVTN ANALYS	
(n,α)	1.4+7		MNZ	Expt	Jour RCA 22 11	75	Weigel+ TOT SIG, ACT METHOD	
(n,α)	1.5+7		ARK	Expt	Abst DA/B 32 5091	Mar 72	Bari. GE(LI) DET. ACT. SIG GIVEN	+
	1.5+7				Data EXFOR10431.024	Aug 75	. 1 PT. SIGMA.	
(n,α)	2.5-2		IJI	Eval	Rept KIYAI-76-6	76	Fedorova+ RECOMMENDED SIG GIVEN	
Reson Params	2.1+1		BNL	Expt	Jour PR 96 1014	Nov 56	Sailor+	+
	2.1+1				Data EXFOR12110.008	Jun 76	. 1 RES. E0.	
Reson Params	2.1+1	4.4+1	MTR	Expt	Prog IDO-16373 39	Jul 57	Simpson.WG,G*WN,WN0.TBL 2 RES ES.	+
	2.1+1				Data EXFOR11983.007	Jun 76	. 1 RES. E0.	
Reson Params	2.1+1	4.8+1	HAR	Expt	Jour NP 5 294	Jan 58	Bowey+. 2 RESONANCE ES GVN. LINAC	+
Reson Params	None		GA	Eval	Jour NSE 12 115	Jan 62	Garrison+	
Reson Params	1.0+3	1.0+5	CCP	Theo	Jour AE 18 114	Feb 65	Dovbenko+ WG, AVERAGE RES SPACING	
					Jour JNE 20 675	Aug 66	TRANSLATN.*	
					Jour EAF 18 2 44	Feb 65	TRANSLATN.*	
					Jour SJA 18 140	Feb 65	TRANSLATN.*	
Reson Params	9.7-2		WWA	Expt	Jour NP/A 97 187	Apr 67	Dakowski+.SPIN=4- WITH 3- BOUND ST	
Reson Params		1.0+6	AUA	Theo	Jour AUJ 20 477	Oct 67	Cook. TBL OF AVG LVL SPACING D,L=0,1	
Reson Params	-		DUB	Expt	Conf 68DUBSY 283	Jul 68	Shapiro.AVERAGE ALFA WIDTH,LVL SPAC.	
Reson Params	+3	+5	AUA	ExTh	Rept AAEC/E-198	May 69	Musgrove.RES PARS +STF FROM (NG)FIT	+
Reson Params	-		AUA	Theo	Rept AAEC/E-211	Nov 70	Musgrove. CALCULTD D+GAM WIDTH GIVEN	
Reson Params	+1	+3	FEI	Eval	Rept YK-8/2 97	Sep 72	Abagyan+ AVG G-WID+D AT BINDNG-E,TBL	
					Rept INDC(CCP)-39	Jul 74	.PAGE 102.ENGLISH OF YK-8/2 97	
Reson Params	-.3+1	1.6+3	KAP	Expt	Jour NSE 54 286	Jul 74	Eiland+TRNS.RESPARS DRVD.	+
	1.0-2	1.6+3			Conf 71Knoxvill 673	Mar 71	- + LINAC,TRANS.AVG D,AVG G*WN	
	-.3+1	1.6+3			Data EXFOR10147.	Jan 78	. 23 RES. E0,WN,WG,D.	
Strnth Fnctn	None		GA	Eval	Jour NSE 12 115	Jan 62	Garrison+ STF + D.	
Strnth Fnctn	+3	+5	AUA	ExTh	Rept AAEC/E-198	May 69	Musgrove.S+P+D STF FROM (NG)FIT,TBL	+
Strnth Fnctn	-		AUA	Theo	Rept AAEC/E-211	Nov 70	Musgrove. SMOOTHED S0,S1 AND S2 GIVN	
Strnth Fnctn	1.0-2	1.6+3	KAP	Expt	Jour NSE 54 286	Jul 74	Eiland+ TRNS. S WAVE CALC.	+
					Conf 71Knoxvill 673	Mar 71	- + LINAC, TRANS, S0=3.6+-0.3	
	1.0-2	1.6+3			Data EXFOR10147.011	Jan 78	. 1PT.S0=(3.3+-1.1)-4	
Lvl Density	-		FEI	ExTh	Prog YFI-6 18	68	Ignatjuk+ TABLE VARIOUS PARAMETERS	
	None			Theo	Jour SNP 8 660	Jun 69	.TRANSLATN.*	
					Jour YF 8 1135	Dec 68	Ignatjuk+ TBL,A+ENTROPY+TEMP,CFD XPT	
	-			ExTh	Rept INDC-260E	69	. ENGL OF YFI-6 18	
Lvl Density	+6		MIL	Theo	Jour EN 15 1 54	Jan 68	Facchini+ LDL PARS FROM LOW EN RES	
Lvl Density	-		CCP	Theo	Jour YF 7 1193	Jun 68	Shubin.CALC OKS EXPT,ROSENZWEIG-EFCT	
					Jour SNP 7 712	Dec 68	TRANSLATN.*	
Lvl Density	None		CCP	Theo	Jour YF 11 1028	May 70	Rubchenya. DENSITY+A+TEMP GIVEN	
					Jour SNP 11 571	Nov 70	. ENGL OF YF 11 571.	
Lvl Density	None		MUN	Theo	Jour NP/A 217 269	Dec 73	Dilg+ A,DELTA. BACK SHIFTED FERMIGAS	
Lvl Density	None		COP	Theo	Jour NP/A 222 493	Apr 74	Dossing+COLL ROTAT.SPAC. ACCUR ESTIM	
Lvl Density	+1	+3	FEI	Eval	Rept YK-8/2 97	Sep 72	Abagyan+ LVL DENSITY PARAMETER,TBL	
					Rept INDC(CCP)-39	Jul 74	.PAGE 102.ENGLISH OF YK-8/2 97	
(γ,n)	8.0+6	2.2+7	CCP	Expt	Jour YF 10 460	Sep 69	Vasil'Ev+ SIG(GAM-E) GRAPH GIVEN	
					Jour SNP 10 263	Mar 70	. ENGL TRANSL OF YF 10 460	

62 Samarium 150

Quantity	Energy (ev) Min	Max	Lab	Type	Documentation Ref Vol Page	Date	Author, Comments	Data
(γ,n)	7.0+6	3.0+7	SAC	Expt	Jour NP/A 225 171	Jun 74	Carlos+GDR,LORENTZ PARAM,GRAPHS,TBLS	

62 Samarium 151

Quantity	Energy (ev) Min	Max	Lab	Type	Documentation Ref Vol Page	Date	Author, Comments	Data
Evaluation	1.0−3	1.5+7	AUA	Eval	Rept AAEC/TM−549	Jun 70	Cook.TOT,EL,INEL,NONEL,CAPT SIGS,NDG	+
					Rept AAEC/E−214	Jun 71	Bertram+GROUP SIGMAS SAME QUANTS.NDG	
					Rept AAEC/TM−587	Mar 71	*DESCRIPTION OF LIBRARY	
	1.0−3	1.5+7			Data AUSTR−DFN 160.	Nov 71	POINT(223) AND GROUP(127) SIGMAS	
Evaluation	1.0+3	1.0+7	BOL	Eval	Rept CEC(71)−2	71	Benzi+ STAT+EVAP MDS.INEL,N2N,NG.TBL	+
	1.0+3	1.0+7			Data BENZI−DFN 562A	Mar 71	4 QUANTITIES. UK FORMAT	
Evaluation	1.0+2	1.5+7	JAE	Eval	Rept JAERI−M−5752	Jul 74	Igarasi+ JNDC FPND WG.TOT,EL,N',CAP	
Total	Maxwl		ORL	Expt	Jour NSE 17 371	Nov 63	Pattenden.15000+−1800B	+
					Conf 60Vienna 535	Oct 60	Block+ VAL(2200M/SEC) GVN,EXPT DESCR	
	Maxwl				Data EXFOR12025.007	Jun 76	. 1 PT. SIGMA.	
Total	1.0−3	1.5+7	AUA	Eval	Data AUSTR−DFN 160.	Nov 71	COOK+POINT(223)+GROUP(127)SIG.CF EVL	+
Total	1.0−2	2.5+3	KAP	Expt	Jour PR/C 11 895	Mar 75	Kirouac+ LINAC.93PCT ENRICHED.GRPHS	+
	1.0−2	2.4+0			Data EXFOR10503.008	May 75	. 139 PTS. SIGMA.	
Total	−3	1.9+0	THS	Theo	Rept IKE−6 89 65	Jun 75	Keinert. DATA LIBRARY	
Elastic	1.0−3	1.5+7	AUA	Eval	Data AUSTR−DFN 160.	Nov 72	COOK+POINT(223)+GROUP(127)SIG.CF EVL	+
Elastic	+1	+6	GEL	Expt	Prog INDC(SEC)−26	May 72	Theobald+ HE3−SCINT,EXPLOSN,PROPOSED	
Tot Inelastc	4.8+3	1.0+7	BOL	Eval	Rept CEC(71)−2	71	Benzi+ STAT MODEL. TBL GIVEN.	+
	4.8+3	1.0+7			Data BENZI−DFN 562A	Mar 71	59 PNTS	
Tot Inelastc	5.0+5	1.5+7	AUA	Eval	Data AUSTR−DFN 160.	Nov 71	COOK+POINT(11)+GROUP(127)SIG.CF EVL	+
Diff Inelast	4.8+3	1.0+7	BOL	Eval	Rept CEC(71)−2	71	Benzi+ DISCRETE INELASTIC. 1 LVL	+
	9.0+3	1.0+7			Data BENZI−DFN 562A	Mar 71	TO CONTINUUM, 53PNTS+ANGDIST+E DIST	
	4.8+3	9.0+3			Data BENZI−DFN 562A	Mar 71	1ST LVL+ANGDIST+E DIST	
Nonelastic	1.0−3	1.5+7	AUA	Eval	Data AUSTR−DFN 160.	Nov 71	COOK+POINT(223)+GROUP(127)SIG.CF EVL	+
Absorption	Maxwl		CCP	Expt	Conf 58Geneva 15 446	Sep 58	Anikina+.PPR2040,VAL GVN	
Absorption	Pile		MCM	Expt	Conf 58Geneva 15 459	Sep 58	Bidinosti+ PPR201,MASS SPEC REL CO	+
	Pile				Data EXFOR12010.006	Jun 76	. 1 PT.	
Absorption	4.1−1	1.0+7	GA	Eval	Prog GA−2451	Aug 61	Joanou+ 68GROUP DATA FOR GAM−I	
Absorption	1.0−3	1.0+7	JUL	Eval	Rept JUEL−678−RG	Jul 70	Liu. EVALUATION+CALC,GRPH,FN OF E	
Absorption	Pile		CRC	Eval	Conf 73Paris 1 459	Mar 73	Walker.FISS PRODUCT ABS,TBL PILE SIG	
Absorption	2.5−2		IJI	Eval	Rept KIYAI−76−6	76	Fedorova+ COMP(REFS,SIGS),EVAL.TABLE	
					Conf 75Kiev 1 169	May 75	− + EVAL SIG GIVEN,TABLE	
Res Int Abs	5.5−1		GA	Eval	Jour NSE 12 115	Jan 62	Garrison+ RIG=2500+−480B.	
Res Int Abs	Maxwl	+2	ORL	Expt	Jour NSE 17 371	Nov 63	Pattenden.3300+−700B	
Res Int Abs	None		CRC	Eval	Rept AECL−2111	Nov 64	Walker. REDUCED RESONANCE INTEGRAL.	
Res Int Abs	5.0−1		BOL	Eval	Rept RT/FI−4	Jan 67	Palmucci. CALC FROM (N,G) RES PARAMS	
Res Int Abs	5.5−1		CRC	Eval	Rept AECL−3037 1	Jan 72	Walker.REDUCED RES INT,DETAILED TBL	
Res Int Abs	5.0−1		AUA	Eval	Rept AAEC/TM−619	Sep 72	Clayton.CALC FROM SIG LIBRARY,TABLE	
Res Int Abs	4.6−1	1.0+6	RCN	Theo	Rept RCN−191	Jul 73	Lautenbach.CAPT INT FROM GROUP SIGMA	
Res Int Abs	5.5−1	+6	SAC	Revw	Conf IAEA−169 1 235	74	Ribon.CAPTURE,STATUS CFD REQUEST,TBL	
Res Int Abs	+0	+5	WIN	Revw	Conf IAEA−169 3 163	74	Pope+ DATA FILE CALC CFD XPTAL VALUE	
Res Int Abs	5.0−1		KAP	Expt	Jour PR/C 11 895	Mar 75	Kirouac+UNRESOLV GT 300EV +RES PAR	+
	5.0−1				Data EXFOR10503.005	May 75	. 1 PT.	
Res Int Abs	5.0−1		IJI	Eval	Rept KIYAI−76−6	76	Fedorova+ EVAL CFD CALC.TBL RI,REFS	
					Conf 75Kiev 1 169	May 75	− + EVAL+CALC RI GIVEN,TABLE	
(n,γ)	Pile		ANL	Expt	Jour PR 79 271	Jul 50	Inghram+	+
	Pile				Data EXFOR12106.005	Jun 76	. 1 PT.	
(n,γ)	Maxwl		MCM	Expt	Jour CJC 33 830	May 55	Melaika+ 12000B REL NAT B 755B	+
	Maxwl				Data EXFOR12086.003	Jun 76	. 1 PT.	
(n,γ)	Pile		MCM	Expt	Diss WALKER	May 56	Walker.	+
	Pile				Data EXFOR12127.007	Jun 76	. 1 PT.	
(n,γ)	5.0−3	2.5+0	GA	Eval	Rept GA−2113	Jun 61	Wikner+ TABLE+CURVE. 100 E POINTS.	
(n,γ)	Pile		CRC	Eval	Rept CRRP−960	Jan 62	Westcott.EFF SIG TABLE 20−1300DEG C	
(n,γ)	2.5−2		GA	Eval	Jour NSE 12 115	Jan 62	Garrison+ EVAL FROM XPT+AVERAGE RES	
(n,γ)	Maxwl		CRC	Eval	Rept AECL−2111	Nov 64	Walker.	
(n,γ)	2.5−2		BOL	Eval	Rept RT/FI−4	Jan 67	Palmucci. CALC FROM RES PARAMETERS	
(n,γ)	Maxwl		AUA	Theo	Jour NSE 31 234	Feb 68	Cook+ STATISTICAL CALC CFD EXPT	
(n,γ)	1.0+3	1.0+7	BOL	Eval	Rept CEC(71)−2	71	Benzi+ OPTMOD EVAL.TBL GIVEN.	+
					Conf 66Paris 1 537	Oct 66	− .STATIST MODEL+XPTAL MEAN D,WG	
	1.0+3	1.0+7			Data BENZI−DFN 562A	Mar 71	63 PNTS	
(n,γ)	1.0−3	1.5+7	AUA	Eval	Data AUSTR−DFN 160.	Nov 71	COOK+POINT(223)+GROUP(127)SIG.CF EVL	+
(n,γ)	Maxwl		CRC	Eval	Rept AECL−3037 1	Jan 72	Walker.RECOMMENDED SIG,DETAILED TBL	

62 Samarium 151

Quantity	Energy (ev) Min	Max	Lab	Type	Documentation Ref Vol Page	Author, Comments Date	Data
(n,γ)	2.5−2		IAE Revw	Rept	IAEA−143 897	Apr 72 Lemmel.RECENT EVALUATIONS,TABLE+GRPH	
	Maxwl			Rept	IAEA−143 897	Apr 72 − .RECENT EVALUATIONS,TABLE	
(n,γ)	+1	+6	GEL Expt	Prog	INDC(SEC)−26	May 72 Theobald+ M−R+CERENCOV,BOMB,PROPOSED	
(n,γ)	2.5−2		AUA Eval	Rept	AAEC/TM−619	Sep 72 Clayton.CALC FROM SIG LIBRARY,TABLE	
(n,γ)		1.1+7	RCN Theo	Rept	RCN−191	Jun 73 Lautenbach. GROUP CONSTANTS TBL	
(n,γ)	Fiss		SAC Revw	Conf	IAEA−169 1 235	74 Ribon.STATUS SIG CFD REQUESTS,TABLE	
	2.5−2	3.0+4		Conf	IAEA−169 1 235	74 − .STATUS SIG CFD REQUESTS,TABLE	
(n,γ)	Fiss		WIN Revw	Conf	IAEA−169 3 137	74 Dean. POINT DATA AVG OVER STAND SPEC	
	Maxwl	Fiss		Conf	IAEA−169 3 163	74 Pope+ MAXW+FIS−SPEC AVG DATA CFD XPT	
(n,γ)	2.5−2		KAP Expt	Jour	PR/C 11 895	Mar 75 Kirouac+CS=15200B.NON 1/V.	
(n,γ)	Fast		RCN Expt	Jour	ECN−10	Oct 76 Veenema+ STEK REACTIVITY WORTHS TBL.	
Spect (n,γ)	Pile		KUR Expt	Jour	YF 13 681	Apr 71 Groshev+ GE−LI,GAM−ES+INT.TBL,GRAPHS	+
				Conf	71Moscow	Feb 71 − + ABST.GE−LI,TBL ES+INTENS	
				Jour	SNP 13 387	Oct 71 . ENGL OF YF 13 681	
	2.5−2			Data	EXFOR40146.002	Apr 73 .20 GAMMA ES AND GAM/100N GIVEN	
(n,2n)	5.6+6	1.0+7	BOL Eval	Rept	CEC(71)−2	71 Benzi+ STAT+EVAP MODELS.TBL GIVEN.	+
	5.6+6	1.0+7		Data	BENZI−DFN 562A	Mar 71 10 PNTS+ANGDIST. (1 RANGE, LAB)	
Reson Params	1.0+0	6.3+0	ORL Expt	Conf	58Geneva 16 150	Sep 58 Harvey+ NDG. TOF.	
	1.1+0	6.3+0		Data	EXFOR12012.007	Jun 76 . 5 RES. E0,WN.	
Reson Params	None		GA Eval	Jour	NSE 12 115	Jan 62 Garrison+	
Reson Params	−.2−4	1.3+1	ORL Expt	Jour	NSE 17 371	Nov 63 Pattenden.	+
	−.2−4	1.3+1		Data	EXFOR12025.	Jun 76 . 10RES(1.1−13)4RES(−0.015−2.)WN,WN0	
Reson Params		1.0+6	AUA Theo	Jour	AUJ 20 477	Oct 67 Cook. TBL OF AVG LVL SPACING D,L=0,1	
Reson Params			AUA Theo	Rept	AAEC/E−211	Nov 70 Musgrove. CALCULTD D+GAM WIDTH GIVEN	
Reson Params	−.1−1	2.0+0	CJD Eval	Rept	YK−7	71 Zakharova+ SURVEY+SYSTEMATICS,GW,TBL	
				Rept	INDC(CCP)−27	Nov 72 .ENGLISH TRANSLATION OF YK−7 /71	
Reson Params	4.6−1	3.0+2	KAP Expt	Jour	PR/C 11 895	Mar 75 Kirouac+ TBL E0,WG,GWN0,WT	+
	−.1−3	3.0+2		Data	EXFOR10503.	May 75 . 121 RES. RED WN, 14 WT, WG	
Reson Params	1.0+3	1.0+6	SAC Eval	Rept	CEA−N−1832	Dec 75 Ribon+ EXP+TH ANAL,RES PAR,TBL	
Strnth Fnctn	None		GA Eval	Jour	NSE 12 115	Jan 62 Garrison+ STF + D.	
Strnth Fnctn	None		ORL Expt	Jour	NSE 17 371	Nov 63 Pattenden.4.0+−1.8	
	+0	1.1+1		Conf	60Vienna 535	Oct 60 Block+ VAL GVN, EXPT DESCRIBED.	
Strnth Fnctn			AUA Theo	Rept	AAEC/E−211	Nov 70 Musgrove. SMOOTHED S0,S1 AND S2 GIVN	
Strnth Fnctn	None		AUA Eval	Rept	AAEC/E−277	Mar 73 Musgrove.TBLS EXPTL DATA+BEST VALUES	
Strnth Fnctn	+0	2.3+3	KAP Expt	Jour	PR/C 11 895	Mar 75 Kirouac+ D=1.72+−0.07 EV.	+
		2.3+3		Data	EXFOR10503.006	May 75 . 4 PTS. DIFF ENERGY RANGES.	
Lvl Density	None		MUN Theo	Jour	NP/A 217 269	Dec 73 Dilg+ A,DELTA. BACK SHIFTED FERMIGAS	
Lvl Density	None		COP Theo	Jour	NP/A 222 493	Apr 74 Dossing+COLL ROTAT.SPAC. ACCUR ESTIM	
Lvl Density	None		ROC Theo	Jour	NP/A 223 589	May 74 Huizenga+ EXP CFD MICROSC TH AX SYMM	

62 Samarium 152

Quantity	Energy (ev) Min	Max	Lab	Type	Documentation Ref Vol Page	Author, Comments Date	Data
Evaluation	1.0−3	1.5+7	AUA Eval	Rept	AAEC/TM−549	Jun 70 Cook.TOT,EL,INEL,NONEL,CAPT SIGS,NDG	+
				Rept	AAEC/E−214	Jun 71 Bertram+GROUP SIGMAS SAME QUANTS.NDG	
				Rept	AAEC/TM−587	Mar 71 *DESCRIPTION OF LIBRARY	
	1.0−3	1.5+7		Data	AUSTR−DFN 161.	Nov 71 POINT(223) AND GROUP(127) SIGMAS	
Total	−2	+1	HAR Expt	Conf	58Geneva 16 44	Sep 58 Pattenden.PPR11,CURVE,CRYSTALSPECTRM	+
Total	6.8+0	9.2+0	BNL Expt	Jour	NSE 12 63	Jan 62 Bernabei+	+
	7.5+0	8.5+0		Data	EXFOR12099.003	Jun 76 . 24 PTS.	
Total	1.0−3	1.5+7	AUA Eval	Data	AUSTR−DFN 161.	Nov 71 COOK+POINT(223)+GROUP(127)SIG.CF EVL	+
Total	9.8−1	5.2+3	COL Expt	Jour	PR/C 6 251	Jul 72 Rahn+TRNS,SELF INDIC.RES PAR ANAL.	
	4.6+1	5.1+3		Rept	NYO−72−281	Oct 70 − .SEE FOR DETAILS	
Total	1.4+7		LIN Expt	Jour	IZV 37 1019	May 73 Djumin+ SIG(A),OPTMODEL CALC,GRAPH	+
				Conf	73Kiev 3 108	May 73 − + OPTMOD CALC,SIG	
				Jour	BAS 37 5 91	May 73 .ENGLISH OF IZV 37 1019	
	1.4+7			Data	EXFOR40302.013	Feb 76 1 PNT	
Total	1.0+5	6.5+5	DKE Expt	Jour	AP 84 165	May 74 Pineo+ N STRENGTH FUNC, TBLS, GRPHS.	+
	1.4+5	6.3+5		Jour	AP 84 165	May 74 − +TRNS.AVG CS.TBL GRPHS.OPTMDL	
	1.5+4	6.0+5		Diss	PINEO	70 .AVG CS.GRPHS.CFD.STF CALC.TBL.CFD.	
	1.5+4	6.0+5		Data	EXFOR10542.019	Jan 79 . DATA UNOBTAINABLE FROM AUTHORS.	
Total	1.0+6	1.5+7	BRC Theo	Conf	JAERI−M−5984	Feb 75 Lagrange.EFF OF DEFORMATION.GRPHS	
	2.0+5	2.0+7		Jour	JPRL 33 111	Sep 74 − .DEFORMAT EFFECT ON STG TOT	
Total	2.5−2		IJI Comp	Rept	KIYAI−76−6	76 Fedorova+ TO GET RECOM ABS−SIG.TABLE	
Total	7.5+5	1.4+7	WMU ExTh	Jour	PL/B 61 29	Mar 76 Shamu+QUAD DEFORM PARS FROM TOT CS.	+
	8.0+5	1.5+7		Expt	PL/B 45 241	Jul 73 − +TRANSMISSION METHOD	
	7.5+5	1.4+7		Data	EXFOR10615.004	Nov 76 27PTS.(SM152TOT−SM148TOT)/SM148TOT.	

62 Samarium 152

Quantity	Energy (ev) Min	Max	Lab	Type	Documentation Ref Vol Page	Author, Comments Date	Data
Total	1.0+6	1.6+7	KTY Revw	Conf	76Lowell 171	Jul 76 Mcellistrem.COUP–CHAN CALC.	
Elastic	2.5–2		ORL Expt	Jour	PR 91 597	Aug 53 Koehler+	+
	2.5–2			Data	EXFOR12060.	Jun 76 . 2 PTS. COH, COH AMP.	
Elastic	1.0–3	1.5+7	AUA Eval	Data	AUSTR–DFN 161.	Nov 71 COOK+POINT(223)+GROUP(127)SIG.CF EVL	+
Diff Elastic	7.0+6	1.6+7	KTY Revw	Conf	76Lowell 171	Jul 76 Mcellistrem.COUP–CHAN CALC.	
Potntal Scat	3.0+3	6.5+5	DKE Expt	Jour	AP 84 165	May 74 Pineo+TRNS.S WAVE SCT LENGTH.TBL.CFD	
				Diss	PINEO	70 .TBL.GRPHS.CFD TO 3 COLLECTIVE MDLS.	
Tot Inelastc	5.0+5	1.5+7	AUA Eval	Data	AUSTR–DFN 161.	Nov 71 COOK+POINT(11)+GROUP(127)SIG.CF EVL	
Diff Inelast	1.4+7		LRL Theo	Rept	UCRL–50181	Feb 67 Lutz+ CALC ANG DIST FOR FIRST 2+ LVL	
Diff Inelast	2.5+6	1.6+7	KTY Revw	Conf	76Lowell 171	Jul 76 Mcellistrem.COUP–CHAN CALC.	
Nonelastic	1.0–3	1.5+7	AUA Eval	Data	AUSTR–DFN 161.	Nov 71 COOK+POINT(223)+GROUP(127)SIG.CF EVL	+
Absorption	Maxwl		HAR Expt	Rept	AERE–R/R–2516	Mar 58 Jowitt+ PILE OSC.REL BORON.293DEGK.	
Absorption	2.5–2		HAR Expt	Jour	JNEA 12 32	May 60 Tattersall+ PILE OSCILLATOR.	+
	2.5–2			Data	EXFOR20638.048	Jul 76 1PNT.SIGMA.	
Absorption	4.1–1	1.0+7	GA Eval	Prog	GA–2451	Aug 61 Joanou+ 68GROUP DATA FOR GAM–I.	
Absorption	1.0–3	1.0+7	JUL Eval	Rept	JUEL–678–RG	Jul 70 Liu. EVALUATION+CALC,GRPH,FN OF E	
Absorption	Pile		CRC Eval	Rept	73Paris 1 459	Mar 73 Walker.FISS PRODUCT ABS,TBL PILE SIG	
Absorption	2.5–2		IJI Eval	Rept	KIYAI–76–6	76 Fedorova+ COMP(REFS,SIGS),EVAL.TABLE	
				Conf	75Kiev 1 169	May 75 – + EVAL SIG GIVEN,TABLE	
Res Int Abs	5.0–1		ANL Expt	Jour	PR 79 11	Jul 50 Harris+ EPI–CD,REL THERMAL ACT. B–W	+
	5.0–1			Data	EXFOR11343.025	Jun 76 . 1 PT.	
Res Int Abs	None		ORL Revw	Conf	55Geneva 5 96	Aug 55 Macklin+ TABLE,EXPT CFD THEORY,P 833	
Res Int Abs	5.0–1		KAP Expt	Rept	KAPL–2000–12	60 Fehr+ VOL.I, P. 33.	+
	5.0–1			Data	EXFOR12023.007	Jun 76 . 1 PT. RI.	
Res Int Abs	5.0–1		HAR Expt	Jour	JNE 12 32	May 60 Tattersall+ ABOVE 1/V,OSCIL,REL B+AU	+
				Rept	AERE–R–2887	Aug 59 – . PILE OSC.REL BORON	
				Conf	58Geneva 16 34	Sep 58 Rose+ SUPERSEDED	
	6.7–1			Data	EXFOR20638.049	Jul 76 1PNT.	
Res Int Abs	5.5–1		BNL Expt	Jour	CJP 39 1193	Aug 61 Chrien. RIG=3090+ –220B,FROM RES,PAR.	
Res Int Abs	5.0–1	+6	CRC Expt	Jour	CJP 39 1184	Aug 61 Walker+ ZEEP CD RATIO,3100+ –200B	
Res Int Abs	5.5–1		GA Eval	Jour	NSE 12 115	Jan 62 Garrison+ RI=2230+ –1200B,FROM RE,PAR	
Res Int Abs	5.0–1		HAR Expt	Jour	JIN 24 749	Dec 62 Cabell.ACTIVATION.ABOVE 1/V RANGE	+
	5.0–1			Data	EXFOR20627.003	Oct 76 1PNT.CAPTURE.	
Res Int Abs	None		CRC Eval	Rept	AECL–2111	Nov 64 Walker. REDUCED RESONANCE INTEGRAL.	
Res Int Abs	5.0–1		BOL Eval	Rept	RT/FI–4	Jan 67 Palmucci. CALC FROM (N,G) RES PARAMS	
Res Int Abs	5.0–1		BGK Expt	Rept	THAI–AEC–10	Oct 67 . ACTIV(NA–I),CD–RATIO,REL AU. TABLE	+
	5.0–1			Data	EXFOR30368.023	Jan 77 REL AU, PRELM.	
Res Int Abs	None		GA Eval	Prog	GA–12071	Sep 71 Mathews+ RECOMMENDED VALUES.	
Res Int Abs	5.5–1		CRC Eval	Rept	AECL–3037 1	Jan 72 Walker.REDUCED RES INT,DETAILED TBL	
Res Int Abs	5.0–1	+6	COL Expt	Jour	NSE 48 219	Jun 72 Rahn+. RI=2644+ –604B	
	4.1–1	+6		Prog	COO–2176–1 1	Jun 72 Rainwater+ VALUE GIVEN	
Res Int Abs	5.0–1		AUA Eval	Rept	AAEC/TM–619	Sep 72 Clayton.CALC FROM SIG LIBRARY,TABLE	
Res Int Abs	5.0–1		KJL Expt	Jour	JIN 34 2699	Sep 72 Steinnes. ACT. AU MONITOR	+
	5.0–1			Data	EXFOR20188.019	May 74 1PNT.CAPTURE.	
Res Int Abs	4.6–1	1.0+6	RCN Theo	Rept	RCN–191	Jul 73 Lautenbach.CAPT INT FROM GROUP SIGMA	
Res Int Abs	5.0–1		GHT Expt	Jour	JRC 20 695	74 Van Der Linden+ BY(N,G).CFD OTHS,TBL	+
	5.5–1			Conf	73Paris 2 241	Mar 73 – + ACT,REL THR+GOLD,TBL	
	5.5–1			Data	EXFOR20645.022	Jul 76 1PNT.CAPTURE.	
Res Int Abs	5.5–1	+6	SAC Revw	Conf	IAEA–169 1 235	74 Ribon.CAPTURE,STATUS CFD REQUEST,TBL	
Res Int Abs	+0	+5	WIN Revw	Conf	IAEA–169 3 163	74 Pope+ DATA FILE CALC CFD XPTAL VALUE	
Res Int Abs	5.0–1		IJI Eval	Rept	KIYAI–76–6	76 Fedorova+ EVAL CFD CALC.TBL RI,REFS	
				Conf	75Kiev 1 169	May 75 – + EVAL+CALC RI GIVEN,TABLE	
(n,γ)	Maxwl		OHO Expt	Jour	PR 53 437	Mar 38 Pool+ BETAS,CLOUD CH,RATIO SM150(NG)	
	Fast			Jour	PR 53 437	Mar 38 – + BETAS,CLOUD CH,RATIO SM150(NG	
(n,γ)	Pile		ANL Expt	Jour	PR 72 888	Nov 47 Seren+ THR IRRAD, THR IRRAD. SM153.	+
	Pile			Data	EXFOR11447.096	Jun 76 . 1 PT.	
(n,γ)	Pile		MCM Expt	Diss	WALKER	May 56 Walker.	+
	Pile			Data	EXFOR12127.008	Jun 76 . 1 PT.	
(n,γ)	2.4+4		ORL Expt	Jour	PR 107 504	Jul 57 Macklin+ SB–BE NS,668+ –100MB,105MEVG	+
				Conf	58Geneva 15 68	Sep 58 – . VAL GVN, EXPT DESCRIBED	
	2.4+4			Data	EXFOR11399.040	Jun 76 . 1 PT.	
(n,γ)	2.0+5		ORL Expt	Jour	PR 114 1619	Jun 59 Lyon+ ABS GAMMA COUNT 150+ –20MB ACT.	+
	2.0+5			Data	EXFOR11407.028	Jun 76 . 1 PT.	
(n,γ)	Maxwl		KAP Expt	Rept	KAPL–2000–12	60 Fehr+ VOL. I,P. 33.	
	Maxwl			Data	EXFOR12023.006	Jun 76 . 1 PT.	
(n,γ)	5.0–3	2.5+0	GA Eval	Rept	GA–2113	Jun 61 Wikner+ TABLE + CURVE. 100 E POINTS.	
(n,γ)	2.5–2		GA Eval	Jour	NSE 12 115	Jan 62 Garrison+ EVAL FROM XPT+AVERAGE RES.	

62 Samarium 152

Quantity	Energy (ev) Min	Max	Lab	Type	Documentation Ref Vol Page	Date	Author, Comments	Data
(n,γ)	Maxwl		HAR	Expt Jour	JIN 24 749	Dec 62	Cabell.ACTIVATION.209+ −9B	+
	2.5−2			Data	EXFOR20627.002	Oct 76	1PNT.SIGMA.	
(n,γ)	3.0+4		ORL	Expt Jour	NAT 197 370	Jan 63	Macklin. 411+ −71 MB.	+
	3.0+4			Data	EXFOR12095.007	Jun 76	. 1 PT.	
(n,γ)	Maxwl		CRC	Eval Rept	AECL−2111	Nov 64	Walker.	
(n,γ)	5.0+3	9.0+4	ORL	Theo Jour	RMP 37 166	Jan 65	Macklin+ CALC ASSUM. MAX.SHAPE.	
(n,γ)	1.0+3	1.0+5	CCP	Theo Jour	AE 18 114	Feb 65	Dovbenko+ STATIST MOD CURVE CFD DATA	
				Jour	JNE 20 675	Aug 66	TRANSLATN.*	
				Jour	SJA 18 140	Feb 65	TRANSLATN.*	
				Jour	EAF 18 2 44	Feb 65	TRANSLATN.*	
(n,γ)	2.4+4		MUA	Expt Jour	PR 152 1055	Dec 66	Chaubey+ BETA−DET,SIG REL I−127,TBL	+
	2.4+4			Data	EXFOR30079.031	Dec 70	SIGMA FOR 47. H HALF−LIFE	
(n,γ)	2.5−2		BOL	Eval Rept	RT/FI−4	Jan 67	Palmucci. CALC FROM RES PARAMETERS	
(n,γ)	3.0+6		DEB	Expt Jour	JNE 21 797	Oct 67	Peto+ACTIV,SIGMA REL TO AU(N,G)	+
	3.0+6			Data	EXFOR30031.021	Aug 70	SINGLE VALUE	
(n,γ)	Maxwl		AUA	Theo Jour	NSE 31 234	Feb 68	Cook+ STATISTICAL CALC CFD EXPT	
(n,γ)	−		IEA	Comp Rept	IEA−INF− 10	Aug 68	Atalla. TABLES OF HL,SIG AND GAMM−E	
(n,γ)	1.0+3	1.0+7	BOL	Eval Rept	CCDN−NW/10	Dec 69	Benzi+H−F MOD,AXEL G(G)EST,ALL DATA	
				Rept	CEC(70)−2	Apr 70	− +. GRAPH	
				Conf	66Paris 1 537	Oct 66	− + STATMOD.TBL AV VALS.SUPERSEDD	
(n,γ)	2.0+5		MUA	Theo Conf	69Roorke 2 129	Dec 69	Chaubey+ SIG VALUE GIVEN, STATIST−TH	
(n,γ)	3.0+4		AUA	Theo Rept	AAEC/E−211	Nov 70	Musgrove. SIGMA GIVEN AND CFD OTHER	
(n,γ)	2.4+4	9.7+5	ATI	Expt Prog	EANDC(OR)105L	Aug 71	Bensch+,PHOTO− NEUTRON SOURCES	
(n,γ)	Maxwl		GA	Eval Prog	GA− 12071	Sep 71	Mathews+ RECOMMENDED VALUES.	
(n,γ)	1.0−3	1.5+7	AUA	Eval Data	AUSTR−DFN 161.	Nov 71	COOK+POINT(223)+GROUP(127)SIG.CF EVL	+
(n,γ)	Maxwl		CRC	Eval Rept	AECL−3037 1	Jan 72	Walker.RECOMMENDED SIG,DETAILED TBL	
(n,γ)	2.5−2		IAE	Revw Rept	IAEA−143 897	Apr 72	Lemmel.RECENT EVALUATIONS,TABLE+GRPH	
	Maxwl			Rept	IAEA−143 897	Apr 72	− .RECENT EVALUATIONS,TABLE	
(n,γ)	2.5−2		AUA	Eval Rept	AAEC/TM−619	Sep 72	Clayton.CALC FROM SIG LIBRARY,TABLE	
(n,γ)	Fast		MTR	Expt Conf	72Kiamesha 2 614	Sep 72	Harker+ CFRMF INTEGRAL MEAS.	
(n,γ)	Fast		DUB	Expt Rept	JINR−P12−6810	Nov 72	Ngo Quoc Buu+ ACT ANALYS, CD−RATIOS	
(n,γ)	8.3+5		II	Expt Conf	73Kiev 4 312	May 73	Lakosi+ FOTO−N,REL AU197(N,G	+
	+6			Data	EXFOR30268.010	Jul 74	1 POINT	
(n,γ)		1.1+7	RCN	Theo Rept	RCN−191	Jun 73	Lautenbach. GROUP CONSTANTS TBL	
(n,γ)	Fiss		SAC	Revw Conf	IAEA−169 1 235	74	Ribon.STATUS SIG CFD REQUESTS,TABLE	
	2.5−2			Conf	IAEA−169 1 235	74	− .STATUS SIG CFD REQUESTS,TABLE	
(n,γ)	Maxwl	Fiss	WIN	Revw Conf	IAEA−169 3 163	74	Pope+ MAXW+FIS−SPEC AVG DATA CFD XPT	
	Fiss			Conf	IAEA−169 3 137	74	Dean. POINT DATA AVG OVER STAND SPEC	
(n,γ)	1.0+3	1.0+7	FEI	Eval Rept	YK− 8/2 97	Sep 72	Abagjan+ AVG SIG(ENERGY−GROUPS),TABL	
				Rept	INDC(CCP)−39	Jul 74	.P102. ENGLISH OF YK−8/2 97	
(n,γ)	Maxwl		BNL	Expt Prog	ERDA−NDC−2 31	May 75	Chrien+TABLE	
				Conf	74Petten 271	Sep 74	Cole+ DIRECT CAPT.COMP. TBL	
(n,γ)	Fast		RCN	Expt Rept	ECN−10	Oct 76	Veenema+ STEK REACTIVITY WORTHS TBL.	
Res Int Capt	None		ROS	Revw Rept	ZFK−RN−23	Sep 64	Schumann+ VAL GVN,NO DETAILS	
Spect (n,γ)	8.2+0		YAL	Expt Jour	PR 107 1650	Sep 57	Fenstermacher+ PULSE−HEIGHT SPECTRUM	
Spect (n,γ)	Pile		CAV	Expt Jour	NP 5 187	Jan 58	Mccutchen. GRPH,TBL OF 5 REL INTENST	
Spect (n,γ)	2.5+4		ORL	Expt Conf	58Geneva 15 68	Sep 58	Macklin. SIGMA+G−ENERGY GVN	
Spect (n,γ)	8.0+0		YAL	Expt Abst	BAP 4 35	Jan 59	Springer+,NAI(TL),GAMMA MULTIPLICITY	
Spect (n,γ)	−		MUN	Expt Jour	ZN/A 16 927	Sep 61	Schult.LVLS IN SM153 XTAL SPECTROMET	
Spect (n,γ)	Pile		CTH	Expt Jour	NP 39 286	Dec 62	Hardell+. PRECISION E DETERMINATION	
Spect (n,γ)	8.2+0		JAE	Expt Rept	JAERI−1073	Mar 65	Kawarasaki. RES CAPT.LINAC.TOF.E,INT	+
				Rept	INDSWG−90 6	Jul 65	− . TABLE E,INTS GIVEN.	
	8.2+0			Data	EXFOR20277.012	Jun 74	7PTS.	
Spect (n,γ)	Pile		ROS	Expt Rept	ZFK−PHA−18	Dec 65	Funke+ G SPEC SM 153, 25 TO 700 KEV	
Spect (n,γ)	Pile		MUN	Expt Jour	ZN/A 21 1328	Sep 66	Neumann. CRYST SPEC EXPT OF GAM INT	
				Rept	ANL−TRANS−941	73	. ENGLISH OF ZN/A 1328	
Spect (n,γ)	Maxwl		MUN	Expt Conf	67Juelich 56	Apr 67	Egidy+ CONV ELECTRONS.10LVL DECAYSCH	
Spect (n,γ)	+0	+4	COL	Expt Prog	WASH−1124 31	Nov 68	Camarda+ MOXON−RAE DET TBC NO DATA	
Spect (n,γ)	Pile		LEI	Expt Jour	PHY 40 567	Jan 69	Reddingius+ GE−LI TABLE INT GRAPHS	
Spect (n,γ)	Pile		RCN	Expt Jour	PHY 40 567	Jan 69	Reddingius+ N FILTER 77DEG K	+
	Pile			Data	EXFOR20236.004	May 74	30PTS.	
Spect (n,γ)	None		ORL	Theo Jour	NSE 36 220	May 69	Yost+ CALCULAT BY GAMMA CASCADE MDL	
Spect (n,γ)	Pile		ANL	Expt Jour	PR 187 1632	Nov 69	Smither+ CRYST SPECT+GE(LI),251LINES	
				Conf	69Studsvik	Aug 69	.SUPERSEDED	
Spect (n,γ)	Pile		LAS	Expt Jour	NP/A 171 113	Aug 71	Bennett+GE(LI)+NA RING.SPEC+SIG104EG	+
	Pile			Data	EXFOR10240.	Jul 74	. 104 PTS. DSIGMA.	
Spect (n,γ)	−1		BNL	Expt Prog	USNDC−9 39	Dec 73	Cole+. DIRECT CAPTURE SPECTRA SHOWN	
Spect (n,γ)	None		ANL	Expt Conf	74Petten 358	Sep 74	Smither+AVG NEUTR.CAPT. (PROGR.)	

62 Samarium 152

Quantity	Energy (ev) Min	Max	Lab	Type	Documentation Ref Vol Page	Date	Author, Comments	Data
Inelastic γ	8.0+6		BRC	Expt Rept	CEA-N-1798 34	Jun 75	Sigaud+ VDG TOF	
Inelastic γ	2.8+6		CCP	Expt Conf	76Lowell 1334	Jul 76	Andreev+G SPEC.EXCIT CS CFD H-F.TBL	
Inelastic γ	2.5+6		KTY	Revw Conf	76Lowell 171	Jul 76	Mcellistrem.4+TO2+,6+TO4+ TRANSITION	
Inelastic γ	2.0+6	3.0+6	KGU	Theo Conf	77Kiev	77	Zajchenko+ OPTMODL,CALCULATION	
(n,2n)	Fiss		CRC	Eval Rept	CRC-1003	Dec 60	Roy+,ESTIMATED AVG SIG=5.8MB	
(n,2n)	1.4+7		LYO	Comp Rept	LYCEN/6780	Nov 67	Crouzet+COMPILATN FOR ACTIVTN ANALYS	
(n,2n)	1.5+7		DEB	Eval Jour	REA 11 1 153	Mar 73	Boedy+ RECOMM.VALUE FROM N-Z SYSTEM.	
(n,2n)	1.5+7		KFI	Theo Rept	KFKI-73-68	Dec 73	Jeki.NEW FIT,CALC SIG CFD OTHERS,TBL	
(n,xn) x>2	1.4+7		BRC	ExTh Prog	CEA-N-1875 60	Apr 76	Frehaut+N3N.SYSTEMATIC LAWS SEARCH	+
	1.5+7			Expt Conf	75Gothenbg	Jun 75	- +	
	1.5+7			Data	EXFOR20571.019	Mar 76	1PNT.N3N.	
(n,p)	1.5+7		ARK	Expt Jour	PR 118 242	Apr 60	Wille+ MEAS ACT SIG=3.7+-.2 MB.	+
				Jour	PR 112 1950	Dec 58	- + 3.7+-0.2 MB, CFD TH	
	1.5+7			Data	EXFOR12033.029	Jun 76	. 1 PT.	
(n,p)	Fiss		CRC	Eval Rept	CRC-1003	Dec 60	Roy+,ESTIMATED AVG SIG=0.004MB	
(n,p)	1.4+7		FRK	Theo Jour	ZP 171 379	Dec 62	Lindner.STATMOD,CF CJP 31 267(EXPT)	
(n,p)	1.5+7		SAH	Comp Jour	NUC 23 8 112	Aug 65	Chatterjee. TABLE WITH REFS.	
	1.4+7				NP 60 273	Nov 64	- .MEAN OF EXPT CFD SHELLMO4	
(n,p)	1.4+7	1.5+7	ARK	Theo Prog	ORO-3235-29	Jan 67	Koch+,STAT MODEL CALC CFD EXPTS	
(n,p)	1.4+7		LYO	Comp Rept	LYCEN/6780	Nov 67	Crouzet+COMPILATN FOR ACTIVTN ANALYS	
(n,p)	1.5+7		DEB	Comp Jour	REA 7 4 93	Dec 69	Csikai+ SIG+HL COMPILTN,N-ACTIV-ANAL	
(n,p)	None		SAH	Expt Prog	BARC-474 29	70	Murty+ GAM+BETA DECAY OF PM-152	
	-			Conf	69Roorke 2 175	Dec 69	- + DECAY OF 6 MIN PM-152 TABLES	
(n,p)	1.4+7	1.5+7	JYV	Eval Rept	JU-RR-3/1970	Jun 70	Leppaemaeki+ TABLE OF EVAL AVG SIG	
(n,p)	1.4+7	1.5+7	KAZ	Theo Jour	YF 18 705	Oct 73	Levkovsky.AVERAGED SIG,CALC,TBL	
				Jour	SNP 18 361	Apr 74	. ENGLISH OF YF 18,705	
(n,p)	1.4+6		MNZ	Expt Jour	ZP/A 272 291	Mar 75	Herrmann+ DECAY OF(4.2 MIN)-PM-152	
(n,α)	1.5+7		CRC	Expt Jour	CJP 31 267	Feb 53	Paul+ BETA ACT. CFD TH. HL=1.7H.	+
	1.5+7			Data	EXFOR11274.090	Jun 76	. 1 PT.	
(n,α)	1.5+7		ARK	Expt Jour	PR 118 242	Apr 60	Wille+ MEAS ACT SIG=10+-2. MB.	+
				Jour	PR 112 1950	Dec 58	- + 10+-2MB, CFD TH	
	1.5+7			Data	EXFOR12033.028	Jun 76	. 1 PT.	
(n,α)	Fiss		CRC	Eval Rept	CRC-1003	Dec 60	Roy+,ESTIMATED AVG SIG=0.0004MB	
(n,α)	1.4+7		FRK	Theo Jour	ZP 171 379	Dec 62	Lindner.STATMOD,CF CJP 31 267,TH+XPT	
(n,α)	1.4+7		CIS	Theo Jour	NP 51 460	Feb 64	Facchini+STATMOD SIG XPT/CALC230-350	
(n,α)	1.4+7	1.5+7	NAP	Comp Rept	INFN/BE-67-11	Sep 67	Cuzzocrea+ AVERAGED CHOSEN DATA.	
(n,α)	1.4+7		LYO	Comp Rept	LYCEN/6780	Nov 67	Crouzet+COMPILATN FOR ACTIVTN ANALYS	
(n,α)	1.5+7		DEB	Comp Jour	REA 7 4 93	Dec 69	Csikai+ SIG+HL COMPILTN,N-ACTIV-ANAL	
(n,α)	1.4+7	1.5+7	JYV	Eval Rept	JU-RR-3/1970	Jun 70	Leppaemaeki+ TABLE OF EVAL AVG SIG	
(n,α)	1.5+7		ARK	Expt Abst	DA/B 32 5091	Mar 72	Bari. GE(LI) DET. ACT. SIG GIVEN	+
	1.5+7			Data	EXFOR10431.025	Aug 75	. 1 PT. SIGMA.	
(n,α)	1.5+7		KYU	Expt Jour	NST 12 681	Nov 75	Sato+.ACTIVATION SIG=2.81+-0.42 MB	+
	1.5+7			Data	EXFOR20595.004	Aug 76	1PNT.SIGMA.	
Reson Params	8.2+0		BNL	Expt Jour	PR 96 1014	Nov 54	Sailor+	+
	8.2+0			Data	EXFOR12110.009	Jun 76	. 1 RES. E0.	
Reson Params	8.0+0	1.7+2	HAR	Expt Jour	NP 5 294	Jan 58	Bowey+. 4 RESONANCE ES GVN. LINAC	+
Reson Params	8.0+0		BNL	Expt Jour	CJP 39 1193	Aug 61	Chrien. NRU FAST CHOPPER WN,WT,SIGO.	
Reson Params	8.0+0		CRC	Expt Jour	CJP 39 1184	Aug 61	Walker.	
Reson Params	8.0+0		BNL	Expt Jour	NSE 12 63	Jan 62	Bernabei+CSWT=.201EV,WG=.07EV,WN=.13	+
	8.0+0			Data	EXFOR12099.004	Jun 76	. 1 RES. E0,WT,WN,WG,PCS.	
Reson Params	None		GA	Eval Jour	NSE 12 115	Jan 62	Garrison+	
Reson Params	8.1+0		ORL	Expt Jour	NSE 17 371	63	Pattenden.	+
	8.1+0			Data	EXFOR12025.012	Jun 76	. 1 RES. E0,WN0.	
Reson Params	1.0+3	1.0+5	CCP	Theo Jour	AE 18 114	Feb 65	Dovbenko+ WG, AVERAGE RES SPACING	
				Jour	JNE 20 675	Aug 66	TRANSLATN.*	
				Jour	EAF 18 2 44	Feb 65	TRANSLATN.*	
				Jour	SJA 18 140	Feb 65	TRANSLATN.*	
Reson Params		1.0+6	AUA	Theo Jour	AUJ 20 477	Oct 67	Cook. TBL OF AVG LVL SPACING D,L=0,1	
Reson Params	8.0+0	1.3+3	DUB	Expt Rept	JINR-P3-3882	Oct 68	Karzhavina+	+
	8.0+0	1.4+3		Prog	YFI-6 135	68	- +.RES-E ONLY.ALSO DUB-3882	
				Rept	INDC-260E	69	- + ENGL OF YFI-6 124.	
	8.0+0	1.3+3		Data	EXFOR40165.	Jul 73	.27 RES-E,D	
Reson Params	8.0+0		KFK	Eval Rept	KFK-718	Apr 68	Schmidt+ RESOLVED+AVG RES PARAM(S,P)	
Reson Params	+3	+5	AUA	ExTh Rept	AAEC/E-198	May 69	Musgrove.RES PARS +STF FROM (NG)FIT	+
Reson Params	2.0+5		MUA	Theo Conf	69Roorke 2 129	Dec 69	Chaubey+ D/GAM-WIDTH RATIO, STATMOD	
Reson Params	8.0+0		KFK	Comp Rept	KFK-1233	Jul 70	Mueller. ES,WN,WG,G OF 1 RESON	
Reson Params	-		AUA	Theo Rept	AAEC/E-211	Nov 70	Musgrove. CALCULTD D+GAM WIDTH GIVEN	

PAGE 1171

62 Samarium 152

Quantity	Energy (ev) Min	Max	Lab	Type	Documentation Ref Vol Page	Author, Comments Date	Data
Reson Params	8.1+0		CJD	Eval	Rept YK - 7	71 Zakharova+ SURVEY+SYSTEMATICS,GW,TBL	
					Rept INDC(CCP) - 27	Nov 72 .ENGLISH TRANSLATION OF YK - 7 /71	
Reson Params	None		DUB	Theo	Rept YF 13 240	Feb 71 Malecki+G - WID,THEO CFD EXPT.TBL,GRPH	
					Jour SNP 13 133	Aug 71 - + ENGL OF YF 13 240.	
Reson Params	8.1+0	5.1+3	COL	Expt	Jour PR/C 6 251	Jul 72 Rahn+. WN FOR 91 RESON.SOME WG,AVG D	+
	None				Conf 75Wash. 780	Mar 75 Hacken+ TBL AVG WG,STF,NUMBER GWN,WG	
					Jour NSE 48 219	Jun 72 Rahn+. AVG WG=65MEV OVER 9 RESON	
	8.1+0	5.1+3			Conf 71Albany 205	Aug 71 Camarda+ WG GVN, TBP PR.	
					Rept NYO - 72 - 281	Oct 70 Rahn.SEE FOR DETAILS.	
	8.6+0	5.1+3			Data EXFOR10046.	Jan 78 . 92 RES ES.WN RED,WG.D GVN.	
Reson Params	8.0+0	2.4+2	BNL	Expt	Prog USNDC - 9 39	Dec 73 Cole+. WN+WG FOR 6 RESON FROM CAPTUR	
Reson Params	+0	+2	BOL	Eval	Conf IAEA - 169 3 123	74 Benzi+ AVG G - WID CFD OTHERS+XPT,TABL	
Reson Params	+0	+3	FEI	Eval	Rept YK - 8/2 97	Sep 72 Abagyan+ AVG G - WID+D AT BINDNG - E,TBL	
					Rept INDC(CCP) - 39	Jul 74 .PAGE 102.ENGLISH OF YK - 8/2 97	
Reson Params	2.5 - 2		COL	Theo	Conf 75Wash. 335	Mar 75 Felvinci+MOD ERICSON CALC CFD EXPT.	
Strnth Fnctn	None		GA	Eval	Jour NSE 12 115	Jan 62 Garrison+ STF + D.	
Strnth Fnctn		+3	DUB	Expt	Prog YFI - 6 135	68 Karzhavina+.TABLE. FULL PPR DUB - 3882	
	8.0+0	1.4+3			Rept JINR - P3 - 3882	Oct 68 - + FULL PAPER.	
		+3			Rept INDC - 260E	69 - + ENGL OF YFI - 6 124.	
Strnth Fnctn	+3	+5	AUA	ExTh	Rept AAEC/E - 198	May 69 Musgrove.S+P+D STF FROM (NG)FIT,TBL	+
Strnth Fnctn	3.0+3	6.5+5	DKE	Expt	Diss PINEO	70 .S0,S1.TBL.GRPHS.CFD CALC,OTH EXPTS.	
Strnth Fnctn	-		AUA	Theo	Rept AAEC/E - 211	Nov 70 Musgrove. SMOOTHED S0,S1 AND S2 GIVN	
Strnth Fnctn	8.1+0	5.1+3	COL	Expt	Jour PR/C 6 251	Jul 72 Rahn+. S0=2.2+ - 0.4	+
	None				Conf 75Wash. 780	Mar 75 Hacken+ NEVIS TOF S - WAVE STF	
	8.1+0	5.1+3			Conf 71Albany 205	Aug 71 Camarda+ S0 GVN.	
	8.1+0	1.5+3			Rept NYO - 72 - 281	Oct 70 Rahn.EXPT DETAILS	
	0.0+0	3.7+3			Data EXFOR10046.025	Jan 78 . 1PT.S0=(2.2+ - .4) - 4	
Strnth Fnctn	None		AUA	Eval	Rept AAEC/E - 277	Mar 73 Musgrove.TBLS EXPTL DATA+BEST VALUES	
Lvl Density	+6		MIL	Theo	Jour EN 15 1 54	Jan 68 Facchini+ LDL PARS FROM LOW EN RES	
Lvl Density	-		CCP	Theo	Jour YF 7 1193	Jun 68 Shubin.CALC OKS EXPT,ROSENZWEIG - EFCT	
					Jour SNP 7 712	Dec 68 TRANSLATN.*	
Lvl Density	-		FEI	Theo	Jour YF 8 1135	Dec 68 Ignatjuk+ A+TEMP+ENTROPY,GRPH+TBL	
					Jour SNP 8 660	Jun 69 TRANSLATN.*	
Lvl Density	None		CCP	Theo	Jour YF 11 1028	May 70 Rubchenya. DENSITY+A+TEMP GIVEN,GRPH	
					Jour SNP 11 571	Nov 70 . ENGL OF YF 11 571.	
Lvl Density	None		AUWTheo		Conf 70Madurai 2 267	Dec 70 Ramamurty+ A - PARAMETER GVN,LANG'S - TH	
Lvl Density	0.0+0	5.2+3	ITE	Theo	Conf 72Budapest 268	Aug 72 Belyaev+ GROUPINGS OF LVL SPACNG,TBL	
Lvl Density	None		MUNTheo		Jour NP/A 217 269	Dec 73 Dilg+ A,DELTA. BACK SHIFTED FERMIGAS	
Lvl Density	None		BOL	Eval	Conf IAEA - 169 3 123	74 Benzi+ LVL DENS PARAM BY XPT,GRPH+TB	
Lvl Density	None		COP	Theo	Jour NP/A 222 493	Apr 74 Dossing+COLL ROTAT.SPAC. ACCUR ESTIM	
Lvl Density	None		ROC	Theo	Jour NP/A 223 589	May 74 Huizenga+ EXP CFD MICROSC TH AX SYMM	
Lvl Density	+0	+3	FEI	Eval	Rept YK - 8/2 97	Sep 72 Abagyan+ LVL DENSITY PARAMETER,TBL	
					Rept INDC(CCP) - 39	Jul 74 .PAGE 102.ENGLISH OF YK - 8/2 97	
Lvl Density	+0	5.2+3	JAE	ExTh	Jour JPJ 37 581	Sep 74 Ideno.LVL SPACING CORRELATIONS.TBL.	
	1.0+0	5.2+3			Rept JAERI - M - 5490	Nov 73 - .LEVEL SPACING CORRELATIONS.TBL	
(γ,n)	8.0+6	2.2+7	CCP	Expt	Jour YF 10 460	Sep 69 Vasil'Ev+ SIG(GAM - E) GRAPH GIVEN	
					Jour SNP 10 263	Mar 70 . ENGL TRANSL OF YF 10 460	
(γ,n)	7.0+6	3.0+7	SAC	Expt	Jour NP/A 225 171	Jun 74 Carlos+GDR,LORENTZ PARAM,GRAPHS,TBLS	

62 Samarium 153

Quantity	Energy (ev) Min	Max	Lab	Type	Documentation Ref Vol Page	Author, Comments Date	Data
Evaluation	1.0 - 3	1.5+7	AUA	Eval	Rept AAEC/TM - 549	Jun 70 Cook.TOT,EL,INEL,NONEL,CAPT SIGS,NDG	+
					Rept AAEC/E - 214	Jun 71 Bertram+GROUP SIGMAS SAME QUANTS.NDG	
					Rept AAEC/TM - 587	Mar 71 *DESCRIPTION OF LIBRARY	
	1.0 - 3	1.5+7			Data AUSTR - DFN 162.	Nov 71 POINT(223) AND GROUP(127) SIGMAS	
Total	1.0 - 3	1.5+7	AUA	Eval	Data AUSTR - DFN 162.	Nov 71 COOK+POINT(223)+GROUP(127)SIG.CF EVL	+
Elastic	1.0 - 3	1.5+7	AUA	Eval	Data AUSTR - DFN 162.	Nov 71 COOK+POINT(223)+GROUP(127)SIG.CF EVL	+
Tot Inelastc	5.0+5	1.5+7	AUA	Eval	Data AUSTR - DFN 162.	Nov 71 COOK+POINT(11)+GROUP(127)SIG.CF EVL	+
Nonelastic	1.0 - 3.	1.5+7	AUA	Eval	Data AUSTR - DFN 162.	Nov 71 COOK+POINT(223)+GROUP(127)SIG.CF EVL	+
Res Int Abs	5.0 - 1		AUA	Eval	Rept AAEC/TM - 619	Sep 72 Clayton.CALC FROM SIG LIBRARY,TABLE	
Res Int Abs	5.5 - 1	+6	SAC	Revw	Conf IAEA - 169 1 235	74 Ribon.CAPTURE,STATUS CFD REQUEST,TBL	
Res Int Abs	+0	+5	WIN	Revw	Conf IAEA - 169 3 163	74 Pope+ DATA FILE CALCS COMPARED	
(n,γ)	Pile		MCM	Expt	Diss WALKER	May 56 Walker.	
	Pile				Data EXFOR12127.009	Jun 76 . 1 PT.	
(n,γ)	1.0 - 3	1.5+7	AUA	Eval	Data AUSTR - DFN 162.	Nov 71 COOK+POINT(223)+GROUP(127)SIG.CF EVL	+
(n,γ)	Pile		CRC	Eval	Rept AECL - 3037 1	Jan 72 Walker.SIG ESTIMATED ACCORDING Z,A	

62 Samarium 153

Quantity	Energy (ev) Min	Max	Lab	Type	Documentation Ref Vol Page	Date	Author, Comments	Data
(n,γ)	2.5−2		AUA	Eval Rept	AAEC/TM−619	Sep 72	Clayton.CALC FROM SIG LIBRARY,TABLE	
(n,γ)	Pile	2.5−2	SGA	Eval Conf	73Paris 1 233	Mar 73	Eder+ ESTIMATED FROM POINT SIG,TABLE	
				Rept	SGAE−PH−141	Feb 73	.SAME AS 73PARIS,POINT SIG FROM COOK	
(n,γ)	Fiss		SAC	Revw Conf	IAEA−169 1 235	74	Ribon.STATUS SIG CFD REQUESTS,TABLE	
	2.5−2			Conf	IAEA−169 1 235	74	− .STATUS SIG CFD REQUESTS,TABLE	
(n,γ)	Maxwl	Fiss	WIN	Revw Conf	IAEA−169 3 163	74	Pope+ MAXW+FIS−SPEC AVG EVAL DATA	
	Fiss			Conf	IAEA−169 3 137	74	Dean. POINT DATA AVG OVER STAND SPEC	
Reson Params	−		AUA	Theo Rept	AAEC/E−211	Nov 70	Musgrove. CALCULTD D+GAM WIDTH GIVEN	
Strnth Fnctn	−		AUA	Theo Rept	AAEC/E−211	Nov 70	Musgrove. SMOOTHED S0,S1 AND S2 GIVN	
Lvl Density	−		CCP	Theo Jour	YF 7 1193	Jun 68	Shubin.CALC OKS EXPT,ROSENZWEIG−EFCT	
				Jour	SNP 7 712	Dec 68	TRANSLATN.*	
Lvl Density	8.0+0	7.0+2	DUB	Expt Rept	JINR−P3−3882	Oct 68	Karzhavina+	+
				Prog	YFI−6 135	68	.KARZHAVINA+	
	8.0+0	7.0+2		Data	EXFOR40165.006	Jul 73	.1 DATA LINE	
Lvl Density	None		MUN	Theo Jour	NP/A 217 269	Dec 73	Dilg+ A,DELTA. BACK SHIFTED FERMIGAS	
Lvl Density	None		COP	Theo Jour	NP/A 222 493	Apr 74	Dossing+COLL ROTAT.SPAC. ACCUR ESTIM	
Lvl Density	None		DUB	Theo Jour	NP/A 224 396	May 74	Malov+ 1/2 MICROSC.MODEL. DEFORM NUC	
Lvl Density	None		ROC	Theo Jour	NP/A 223 589	May 74	Huizenga+ EXP CFD MICROSC TH AX SYMM	

62 Samarium 154

Quantity	Energy (ev) Min	Max	Lab	Type	Documentation Ref Vol Page	Date	Author, Comments	Data
Evaluation	1.0−3	1.5+7	AUA	Eval Rept	AAEC/TM−549	Jun 70	Cook.TOT,EL,INEL,NONEL,CAPT SIGS,NDG	+
				Rept	AAEC/E−214	Jun 71	Bertram+GROUP SIGMAS SAME QUANTS.NDG	
				Rept	AAEC/TM−587	Mar 71	*DESCRIPTION OF LIBRARY	
	1.0−3	1.5+7		Data	AUSTR−DFN 163.	Nov 71	POINT(223) AND GROUP(127) SIGMAS	
Total	1.0−3	1.5+7	AUA	Eval Data	AUSTR−DFN 163.	Nov 71	COOK+POINT(223)+GROUP(127)SIG.CF EVL	+
Total	9.8−1	5.2+3	COL	Expt Jour	PR/C 6 251	Jul 72	Rahn+TRNS,SELF INDIC.RES PAR ANAL.	
	4.6+1	2.5+3		Rept	NYO−72−281	Oct 70	− .SEE FOR DETAILS	
Total	1.4+7		LIN	Expt Conf	73Kiev 3 108	May 73	Djumin+ OPTMOD CALC,SIG	+
				Jour	IZV 37 1019	May 73	− + SIG(A),OPTMODEL CALC,GRAPH	
				Jour	BAS 37 5 91	May 73	.ENGLISH OF IZV 37 1019	
	1.4+7			Data	EXFOR40302.014	Feb 76	1 PNT	
Total	1.0+6	1.5+7	BRC	Theo Conf	JAERI−M−5984	Feb 75	Lagrange.EFF OF DEFORMATION.GRPHS	
	2.0+6	2.0+7		Jour	JPRL 33 111	Sep 74	− .DEFORMAT EFFECT ON STG TOT	
Total	7.5+5	1.5+7	WMU	Expt Jour	PL/B 61 29	Mar 76	Shamu+QUAD DEFORM PARS FROM TOT CS.	+
	8.0+5	1.5+7		Jour	PL/B 45 241	Jul 73	+TRANSMISSION METHOD	
	7.5+5	1.4+7		Data	EXFOR10615.005	Nov 76	. 27 PTS.(SM154TOT−SM148TOT)/SM148TO	
Elastic	2.5−2		ORL	Expt Jour	PR 91 597	Aug 53	Koehler.	+
	2.5−2			Data	EXFOR12060.	Jun 76	. 2 PTS. COH, COH AMP.	
Elastic	1.0−3	1.5+7	AUA	Eval Data	AUSTR−DFN 163.	Nov 71	COOK+POINT(223)+GROUP(127)SIG.CF EVL	
Diff Elastic	6.3+6		KTY	Expt Jour	PL/B 58 293	Sep 75	Lagrange+TOF.NUC DEFORMATION EFFECT	+
	6.3+6			Data	EXFOR10528.	Mar 76	. 21PTS.SM154DEL+SM154DIN. LEG COEFF	
Diff Elastic	6.2+6		BRC	ExTh Conf	IAEA−190 251	76	Delaroche+ ANGDIS,COUPL−CHANNEL,GRPH	
				Expt Jour	PL/B 58 293	Sep 75	Lagrange+VDG,TOF.QUAD DEFORM EFFECTS	
Tot Inelastc	5.0+5	1.5+7	AUA	Eval Data	AUSTR−DFN 163.	Nov 71	COOK+POINT(11)+GROUP(127)SIG.CF EVL	
Diff Inelast	1.1+6	2.3+6	ALA	Expt Jour	NP/A 211 493	Sep 73	Elbakr+ FROM DNG	
Diff Inelast	6.3+6		KTY	Expt Jour	PL/B 58 293	Sep 75	Lagrange+TOF.NUC DEFORMATION EFFECT	
	6.3+6			Data	EXFOR10528.	Mar 76	. 11PTS.SM154DEL+SM154DIN. LEG COEFF	
Diff Inelast	6.2+6		BRC	ExTh Conf	IAEA−190 251	76	Delaroche+ ANGDIS(1ST EXC STATE)GRPH	
				Expt Jour	PL/B 58 293	Sep 75	Lagrange+VDG,TOF.QUAD DEFORM EFFECTS	
Nonelastic	1.0−3	1.5+7	AUA	Eval Data	AUSTR−DFN 163.	Nov 71	COOK+POINT(223)+GROUP(127)SIG.CF EVL	+
Absorption	4.1−1	1.0+7	GA	Eval Rept	GA−2451	Aug 61	Joanou+ 68GROUP DATA FOR GAM−I	
Absorption	1.0−4	1.0+7	JUL	Eval Rept	JUEL−678−RG	Jul 70	Liu. EVALUATION+CALC,GRPH,FN OF E	
Absorption	2.5−2		IJI	Eval Rept	KIYAI−76−6	76	Fedorova+ ONLY 1LIT−VALUE,RENORM.TBL	
				Conf	75Kiev 1 169	May 75	− + EVAL SIG GIVEN,TABLE	
Res Int Abs	5.5−1		GA	Eval Jour	NSE 12 115	Jan 62	Garrison+ EST. RIG=25+−23B.	
Res Int Abs	None		GA	Eval Rept	GA−12071	Sep 71	Mathews+ RECOMMENDED VALUES.	
Res Int Abs	5.5−1		CRC	Eval Rept	AECL−3037 1	Jan 72	Walker.REDUCED RES INT FROM RES PARS	
Res Int Abs	5.0−1		COL	Eval Jour	NSE 48 219	Jun 72	Rahn+. RI=31+−6B	
Res Int Abs	5.0−1		AUA	Eval Rept	AAEC/TM−619	Sep 72	Clayton.CALC FROM SIG LIBRARY,TABLE	
Res Int Abs	4.6−1	1.0+6	RCN	Theo Rept	RCN−191	Jul 73	Lautenbach.CAPT INT FROM GROUP SIGMA	
Res Int Abs	5.0−1		GHT	Expt Jour	JRC 20 695	74	Van Der Linden+ BY(N,G).CFD OTHS,TBL	+
	5.5−1			Conf	73Paris 2 241	Mar 73	− + ACT,REL THR+GOLD,TBL	
	5.5−1			Data	EXFOR20645.023	Jul 76	1PNT.CAPTURE.	
Res Int Abs	5.5−1	+6	SAC	Revw Conf	IAEA−169 1 235	74	Ribon.CAPTURE,STATUS CFD REQUEST,TBL	
Res Int Abs	+0	+5	WIN	Revw Conf	IAEA−169 3 163	74	Pope+ DATA FILE CALC CFD XPTAL VALUE	

62 Samarium 154

Quantity	Energy (ev) Min	Max	Lab	Type	Documentation Ref Vol Page	Date	Author, Comments	Data
Res Int Abs	5.0−1		IJI	Eval	Rept KIYAI−76−6	76	Fedorova+ CALC FROM BNL−325 RESPARS	
					Conf 75Kiev 1 169	May 75	− + RI CALC FROM RESPARS,TABLE	
(n,γ)	Pile		ANL	Expt	Jour PR 72 888	Nov 47	Seren+	+
	Pile				Data EXFOR11447.132	Jun 76	. 1 PT.	
(n,γ)	2.4+4		ORL	Expt	Jour PR 107 504	Jul 57	Macklin+.SB−BE NS,527+ −70MB,0.25MEVG	+
					Conf 58Geneva 15 68	Sep 58	− . VAL GVN, EXPT DESCRIBED	
	2.4+4				Data EXFOR11399.041	Jun 76	. 1 PT.	
(n,γ)	1.5+5	6.2+6	WIS	Expt	Jour PR 116 927	Nov 59	Johnsrud+ SC CFD OTHERS SIG VS E	+
	1.5+5	6.2+6			Data EXFOR11675.021	Jun 76	. 23 PTS. SIGMA.	
(n,γ)	Maxwl		CRC	Eval	Rept AECL−1054	Mar 60	Walker. SAME AS CRRP−913	
(n,γ)	2.5−2		GA	Eval	Jour NSE 12 115	Jan 62	Garrison+ 5.5+ −3.1B.	
(n,γ)	3.0+4		ORL	Expt	Jour NAT 197 369	Jan 63	Macklin. 325+ −61MB	+
	3.0+4				Data EXFOR12095.008	Jun 76	. 1 PT.	
(n,γ)	5.0+3	9.0+4	ORL	Theo	Jour RMP 37 166	Jan 65	Macklin+ CALC ASSUM MAX. SHAPE.	
(n,γ)	1.0+3	1.0+5	CCP	Theo	Jour AE 18 114	Feb 65	Dovbenko+ STATIST MOD CURVE CFD DATA	
					Jour JNE 20 675	Aug 66	TRANSLATN.*	
					Jour EAF 18 2 44	Feb 65	TRANSLATN.*	
					Jour SJA 18 140	Feb 65	TRANSLATN.*	
(n,γ)	2.4+4		MUA	Expt	Jour PR 152 1055	Dec 66	Chaubey+ BETA−DET,SIG REL I−127,TBL	+
	2.4+4				Data EXFOR30079.032	Dec 70	SIGMA FOR 22. MIN HALF−LIFE	
(n,γ)	3.0+6		DEB	Expt	Jour JNE 21 797	Oct 67	Peto+ACTIV,SIGMA REL TO P−31(N,P)	+
	3.0+6				Data EXFOR30031.022	Aug 70	SINGLE VALUE	
(n,γ)	1.4+7		LYO	Comp	Rept LYCEN/6780	Nov 67	Crouzet+COMPILATN FOR ACTIVTN ANALYS	
(n,γ)	Maxwl		AUA	Theo	Jour NSE 31 234	Feb 68	Cook+ STATISTICAL CALC CFD EXPT	
(n,γ)	−		IEA	Comp	Rept IEA−INF− 10	Aug 68	Atalla. TABLES OF HL,SIG AND GAMM−E	
(n,γ)	1.0+3	1.0+7	BOL	Eval	Rept CCDN−NW/10	Dec 69	Benzi+H−F MOD,AXEL G(G)EST,ALL DATA	
					Rept CEC(70)−2	Apr 70	− +. GRAPH	
					Conf 66Paris 1 537	Oct 66	− + STATMOD.TBL AV VALS.SUPERSEDD	
(n,γ)	3.0+4		AUA	Theo	Rept AAEC/E−211	Nov 70	Musgrove. SIGMA GIVEN AND CFD OTHER	
(n,γ)	Maxwl		GA	Eval	Rept GA−12071	Sep 71	Mathews+. RECOMMENDED VALUES	
(n,γ)	1.0−3	1.5+7	AUA	Eval	Data AUSTR−DFN 163.	Nov 71	COOK+POINT(223)+GROUP(127)SIG.CF EVL	+
(n,γ)	Maxwl		CRC	Eval	Rept AECL−3037 1	Jan 72	Walker.RECOMMENDED SIG,DETAILED TBL	
(n,γ)	2.5−2		AUA	Eval	Rept AAEC/TM−619	Sep 72	Clayton.CALC FROM SIG LIBRARY,TABLE	
(n,γ)	Fast		MTR	Expt	Conf 72Kiamesha 2 614	Sep 72	Harker+ CFRMF INTEGRAL MEAS.	
(n,γ)	5.0+3	1.6+5	VIP	Expt	Jour NSE 49 317	Nov 72	Fawcett+. ACTIVATION. CURVE.	+
					Abst DA/B 32 2929	Nov 71	− .	
	5.0+3	1.6+5			Data EXFOR10298.005	Oct 73	. 16 PTS. SIGMA.	
(n,γ)	8.3+5		II	Expt	Conf 73Kiev 4 312	May 73	Lakosi+ FOTO−N,REL AU197(N,G	+
	+6				Data EXFOR30268.011	Jul 74	1 POINT	
(n,γ)		1.1+7	RCN	Theo	Rept RCN−191	Jun 73	Lautenbach.GROUP CONSTANTS TBL	
(n,γ)	2.5−2		SAC	Revw	Conf IAEA−169 1 235	74	Ribon.STATUS SIG CFD REQUESTS,TABLE	
(n,γ)	Fiss		WIN	Revw	Conf IAEA−169 3 137	74	Dean. POINT DATA AVG OVER STAND SPEC	
	Maxwl	Fiss			Conf IAEA−169 3 163	74	Pope+ MAXW+FIS−SPEC AVG DATA CFD XPT	
(n,γ)	1.0+3	1.0+7	FEI	Eval	Rept YK−8/2 97	Sep 72	Abagjan+ AVG SIG(ENERGY−GROUPS),TABL	
					Rept INDC(CCP)−39	Jul 74	.P102. ENGLISH OF YK−8/2 97	
(n,γ)	1.5+7		JYV	Expt	Jour PL/B 39 625	May 72	Kantele+ CAPT SIG MEASURED	+
					Rept JU−RR−1/1976	Mar 76	Valkonen.(THESIS).ACTIV.TBL. 14.5MEV	
	1.5+7				Data EXFOR20673.030	Nov 76	1PNT.SIGMA.	
	1.5+7				Data EXFOR20544.006	Apr 76	1PNT.SIGMA.	
(n,γ)	Fast		RCN	Expt	Rept ECN−10	Oct 76	Veenema+ STEK REACTIVITY WORTHS TBL.	
Spect (n,γ)	Pile		MIL	Expt	Jour NP 6 252	Mar 58	Bisi+. GRAPH. EU155 DECAY. TABLE	
Spect (n,γ)	2.5+4		ORL	Expt	Conf 58Geneva 15 68	Sep 58	Macklin. SIGMA+G−ENERGY GVN.	
Spect (n,γ)	Pile		CTH	Expt	Jour NP 39 286	Dec 62	Hardell+. PRECISION E DETERMINATION	
Spect (n,γ)	Pile		ROS	Expt	Rept ZFK−138	Jan 68	Kemnitz. CURVES,LVL SCH EU 155	
Spect (n,γ)	+0	+4	COL	Expt	Prog WASH−1124 31	Nov 68	Camarda+ MOXON−RAE DET TBC NO DATA	
Spect (n,γ)	Pile		KUR	Expt	Jour YF 13 681	Apr 71	Groshev+ GE−LI,TBD	
	Maxwl				Jour IZV 35 1644	Aug 71	− + GAMMA TRANSITIONS,GRAPH	
	Pile				Conf 71Moscow	Feb 71	− + ABSTR,GE−LI,TABLE OF ES	
	Maxwl				Jour BAS 35 1497	Aug 72	. ENGL OF IZV 35 1644	
	Pile				Jour SNP 13 387	Oct 71	. ENGL OF YF 13 681	
Spect (n,γ)	None		ANL	Expt	Conf 74Petten 358	Sep 74	Smither+AVG NEUTR.CAPT. (PROGR.)	
Inelastic γ	1.5+6		SUN	Expt	Prog SUNI−14	Dec 70	Elbakr+. GAMMA SPECTRA SHOWN	
Inelastic γ	1.1+6	2.3+6	ALA	Expt	Jour NP/A 211 493	Sep 73	Elbakr+ GAMMA YLDS, LVL SCH TO 1.7MV	+
		1.9+5			Jour NIM 97 283	Dec 71	− +EXPT DETAILS FOR NPA.211 P493	
	1.1+6	2.3+6			Data EXFOR10362.	Apr 76	DATA UNOBTAINABLE FROM AUTHORS.	
Inelastic γ	8.0+6		BRC	Expt	Rept CEA−N−1798 34	Jun 75	Sigaud+ VDG TOF	
(n,2n)	2.0+7		OHO	Expt	Jour PR 53 437	Mar 38	Pool+ BETAS,CLOUDCH,RATIO SM152(N2N)	

62 Samarium 154

Quantity	Energy (ev) Min	Max	Lab	Type	Documentation Ref Vol Page	Author, Comments Date	Data
(n,2n)	1.5+7		CRC	Expt Jour	CJP 31 267	Feb 53 Paul+.BETA ACT.CFD TH. HL= 70M+47H	+
	1.5+7			Data	EXFOR11274.091	Jun 76 . 1 PT.	
(n,2n)	1.5+7		ARK	Expt Jour	PR 118 242	Apr 60 Wille+ MEAS ACT SIG=1500+ −300MB.	+
				Jour	PR 112 1950	Dec 58 − + 1.5+ −0.3B, CFD TH	
	1.5+7			Data	EXFOR12033.032	Jun 76 . 1 PT.	
(n,2n)	Fiss		CRC	Eval Rept	CRC−1003	Dec 60 Roy+,ESTIMATED AVG SIG=6.9MB	
(n,2n)	1.4+7		HAM	Comp Jour	NP 65 257	Mar 65 Bormann. 2EXPT VALS.CFD SHELL EFFECT	
(n,2n)	1.4+7		LYO	Comp Rept	LYCEN/6780	Nov 67 Crouzet+COMPILATN FOR ACTIVTN ANALYS	
(n,2n)	1.5+7		DEB	Comp Jour	REA 7 4 93	Dec 69 Csikai+ SIG+HL COMPILTN,N−ACTIV−ANAL	
(n,2n)	1.4+7	1.5+7	JYV	Eval Rept	JU−RR−3/1970	Jun 70 Leppaemaeki+ TABLE OF EVAL AVG SIG	
(n,2n)	+7		KFI	Theo Rept	KFKI−71−8	Feb 71 Jeki. CALCULATED CFD EXPTL SIG VALUE	
(n,2n)	1.4+7		CCP	Expt Jour	YF 15 1099	Jun 72 Victorov+ ACTIV,TBL CFD OTHERS+THEO	+
				Jour	SNP 15 608	Dec 72 − + ENGLISH OF YF 15 1099	
	1.4+7			Data	EXFOR40107.006	Dec 72 1 VALUE	
(n,2n)	1.5+7		DEB	Eval Jour	REA 11 1 153	Mar 73 Boedy. COMPILATION+RECOMM.VALUE,TBL	
				Rept	IAEA−153 173	73 − . RECOMM. VALUE ONLY	
(n,2n)	1.5+7		TAT	Theo Jour	JP/A 7 1457	Aug 74 Kondaiah. CALC ON STAT MODEL	
(n,2n)	1.4+7		MNZ	Expt Jour	RCA 22 11	75 Weigel+ TOT SIG, ACT METHOD	
(n,2n)	1.5+7		ARK	Expt Abst	DA/B 32 5091	Mar 72 Bari. GE(LI) DET. ACT. SIG GIVEN	+
	1.5+7			Data	EXFOR10431.054	Aug 75 . 1 PT. SIGMA.	
(n,2n)	1.5+7		JUL	Expt Jour	NP/A 224 319	May 74 Qaim. ACT.GE(LI)	+
				Jour	RRL 25 335	May 76 − + SIG IN GRPH. SYST VS (N−Z)/A	
	1.5+7			Data	EXFOR20541.022	Apr 76 1PNT.SIGMA.	
(n,xn) x>2	1.4+7		BRC	ExTh Prog	CEA−N−1875 60	Apr 76 Frehaut+N3N.SYSTEMATIC LAWS SEARCH	+
	1.5+7			Expt Conf	75Gothenbg	Jun 75 − +	
	1.5+7			Data	EXFOR20571.021	Mar 76 1PNT.N3N.	
(n,p)	1.5+7		ARK	Expt Jour	PR 118 242	Apr 60 Wille+ MEAS ACT SIG=3.5+ −.2MB.	+
				Jour	PR 112 1950	Dec 58 − + 3.5+ −0.2MB, CFD TH	
	1.5+7			Data	EXFOR12033.031	Jun 76 . 1 PT.	
(n,p)	Fiss		CRC	Eval Rept	CRC−1003	Dec 60 Roy+,ESTIMATED AVG SIG=0.001MB	
(n,p)	1.5+7		SAH	Comp Jour	NUC 23 8 112	Aug 65 Chatterjee. TABLE WITH REFS.	
(n,p)	1.4+7	1.5+7	ARK	Theo Prog	ORO−3235−29	Jan 67 Koch+,STAT MODEL CALC CFD EXPTS	
(n,p)	1.4+7		LYO	Comp Rept	LYCEN/6780	Nov 67 Crouzet+COMPILATN FOR ACTIVTN ANALYS	
(n,p)	1.5+7		DEB	Comp Jour	REA 7 4 93	Dec 69 Csikai+ SIG+HL COMPILTN,N−ACTIV−ANAL	
(n,p)	1.4+7	1.5+7	JYV	Eval Rept	JU−RR−3/1970	Jun 70 Leppaemaeki+ TABLE OF EVAL AVG SIG	
(n,p)	1.4+7	1.5+7	KAZ	Theo Jour	YF 18 705	Oct 73 Levkovsky.AVERAGED SIG,CALC,TBL	
				Jour	SNP 18 361	Apr 74 . ENGLISH OF YF 18,705	
(n,α)	1.5+7		ARK	Expt Jour	PR 118 242	Apr 60 Wille+ MEAS ACT SIG=9.+ −3.MB.	+
				Jour	PR 112 1950	Dec 58 − + 9+ −3MB, CFD TH	
	1.5+7			Data	EXFOR12033.030	Jun 76 . 1 PT.	
(n,α)	Fiss		CRC	Eval Rept	CRC−1003	Dec 60 Roy+,ESTIMATED AVG SIG=BELO 0.0001MB	
(n,α)	1.4+7		CIS	Theo Jour	NP 51 460	Feb 64 Facchini+STATMOD SIG XPT/CALC=20K	
(n,α)	1.4+7		LYO	Comp Rept	LYCEN/6780	Nov 67 Crouzet+COMPILATN FOR ACTIVTN ANALYS	
(n,α)	1.5+7		DEB	Comp Jour	REA 7 4 93	Dec 69 Csikai+ SIG+HL COMPILTN,N−ACTIV−ANAL	
(n,α)	1.4+7	1.5+7	JYV	Eval Rept	JU−RR−3/1970	Jun 70 Leppaemaeki+ TABLE OF EVAL AVG SIG	
(n,α)	1.5+7		ARK	Expt Abst	DA/B 32 5091	Mar 72 Bari. GE(LI) DET. ACT. SIG GIVEN	+
	1.5+7			Data	EXFOR10431.026	Aug 75 . 1 PT, SIGMA.	
Reson Params	9.0+1		HAR	Expt Jour	NP 5 294	Jan 58 Bowey+. 1 RESONANCE E GVN. LINAC	
Reson Params	None		GA	Eval Jour	NSE 12 115	Jan 62 Garrison+	
Reson Params	1.0+3	1.0+5	CCP	Theo Jour	AE 18 114	Feb 65 Dovbenko+ WG, AVERAGE RES SPACING	
				Jour	JNE 20 675	Aug 66 TRANSLATN.*	
				Jour	SJA 18 140	Feb 65 TRANSLATN.*	
				Jour	EAF 18 2 44	Feb 65 TRANSLATN.*	
Reson Params		1.0+6	AUA	Theo Jour	AUJ 20 477	Oct 67 Cook. TBL OF AVG LVL SPACING D,L=0,1	
Reson Params	9.3+1	1.8+3	DUB	Expt Rept	JINR−P3−3882	Oct 68 Karzhavina+	+
	9.3+1	1.9+3		Prog	YFI−6 135	68 − +.RES−E ONLY.ALSO DUB−3882	
				Rept	INDC−260E	69 − + ENGL OF YFI−6 124.	
	9.3+1	1.8+3		Data	EXFOR40165.	Jul 73 .21 RES−E,D	
Reson Params	+3	+5	AUA	ExTh Rept	AAEC/E−198	May 69 Musgrove.RES PARS +STF FROM (NG)FIT	+
Reson Params	−		AUA	Theo Rept	AAEC/E−211	Nov 70 Musgrove. CALCULTD D+GAM WIDTH GIVEN	
Reson Params	None		DUB	Theo Jour	ZEP 14 194	Aug 71 Solovev.LARGE N−WID G−WID CORREL.NDG	
				Rept	JINR−E4−5880	71 Soloviev.N−GAM−WIDS CORR.SHORT NOTE	
				Jour	JEL 14 129	Aug 71 − . ENGL OF ZEP 14 194.	

62 Samarium 154

Quantity	Energy (ev) Min	Max	Lab	Type	Documentation Ref Vol Page	Author, Comments Date	Data
Reson Params	9.3+1	5.1+3	COL	Expt	Jour PR/C 6 251	Jul 72 Rahn+. WN FOR 35 RESON.SOME WG,AVG D	+
	None				Conf 75Wash. 780	Mar 75 Hacken+ TBL AVG WG,STF,NUMBER GWN,WG	
					Jour NSE 48 219	Jun 72 Rahn+. AVG WG=79MEV OVER 3 RESON	
	9.3+1	5.1+3			Conf 71Albany 205	Aug 71 Camarda+ WG GVN, TBP PR.	
	9.3+1	1.5+3			Rept NYO-72-281	Oct 70 Rahn.SEE FOR DETAILS.	
	9.3+1	5.1+3			Data EXFOR10046.	Jan 78 . 35 RES ES.WN RED,WG.D GVN.	
Reson Params	+0	+2	BOL	Eval	Conf IAEA-169 3 123	74 Benzi+ AVG G-WID CFD OTHERS+XPT,TABL	
Reson Params	None		ANL	Expt	Prog USNDC-11 42	Jun 74 Cole+ 4S GIANT RES, NDG.	
Reson Params	+1	+3	FEI	Eval	Rept YK-8/2 97	Sep 72 Abagyan+ AVG G-WID+D AT BINDNG-E,TBL	
					Rept INDC(CCP)-39	Jul 74 .PAGE 102.ENGLISH OF YK-8/2 97	
Strnth Fnctn	None		GA	Expt	Jour NSE 12 115	Jan 62 Garrison+ STF + D.	
Strnth Fnctn		+3	DUB	Expt	Prog YFI-6 135	68 Karzhavina+.TABLE. FULL PPR DUB-3882	
	9.3+1	1.9+3			Rept JINR-P3-3882	Oct 68 - + FULL PAPER.	
		+3			Rept INDC-260E	69 - + ENGL OF YFI-6 124.	
Strnth Fnctn	+3	+5	AUA	ExTh	Rept AAEC/E-198	May 69 Musgrove.S+P+D STF FROM (NG)FIT,TBL	+
Strnth Fnctn	-		AUA	Theo	Rept AAEC/E-211	Nov 70 Musgrove. SMOOTHED S0,S1 AND S2 GIVEN	
	9.3+1	5.1+3	COL	Expt	Jour PR/C 6 251	Jul 72 Rahn+. S0=1.8+-0.5	+
	None			Revw	Conf 75Wash. 780	Mar 75 Hacken+ NEVIS TOF S-WAVE STF	
	9.3+1	5.1+3		Expt	Conf 71Albany 205	Aug 71 Camarda+ S0 GVN.	
	9.3+1	2.5+3			Rept NYO-72-281	Oct 70 Rahn.EXPT DETAILS	
	0.0+0	3.1+3			Data EXFOR10046.028	Jan 78 . 1PT.S0=(1.8+-.5)-4	
Strnth Fnctn	5.0+3	1.6+5	VIP	Expt	Jour NSE 49 317	Nov 72 Fawcett+. GAMMA,S0,AND S1 GIVEN	
					Abst DA/B 32 2929	Nov 71 .SUPERSEDED	
Strnth Fnctn	None		AUA	Eval	Rept AAEC/E-277	Mar 73 Musgrove.TBLS EXPTL DATA+BEST VALUES	
Lvl Density	None		BOL	Eval	Conf IAEA-169 3 123	74 Benzi+ LVL DENS PARAM BY XPT,GRPH+TB	
Lvl Density	+1	+3	FEI	Eval	Rept YK-8/2 97	Sep 72 Abagyan+ LVL DENSITY PARAMETER,TBL	
					Rept INDC(CCP)-39	Jul 74 .PAGE 102.ENGLISH OF YK-8/2 97	
Lvl Density	+0	5.2+3	JAE	ExTh	Jour JPJ 37 581	Sep 74 Ideno.LVL SPACING CORRELATIONS.TBL.	
	1.0+0	5.2+3			Rept JAERI-M-5490	Nov 73 - .LEVEL SPACING CORRELATIONS.TBL	
(γ,n)	8.0+6	2.2+7	CCP	Expt	Jour YF 10 460	Sep 69 Vasil'Ev+ SIG(GAM-E) GRAPH GIVEN	
					Jour SNP 10 263	Mar 70 . ENGL TRANSL OF YF 10 460	
(γ,n)	7.0+6	3.0+7	SAC	Expt	Jour NP/A 225 171	Jun 74 Carlos+GDR,LORENTZ PARAM,GRAPHS,TBLS	

62 Samarium 155

Quantity	Energy (ev) Min	Max	Lab	Type	Documentation Ref Vol Page	Author, Comments Date	Data
Reson Params	-		AUA	Theo	Rept AAEC/E-211	Nov 70 Musgrove. CALCULTD D+GAM WIDTH GIVEN	
Strnth Fnctn	-		AUA	Theo	Rept AAEC/E-211	Nov 70 Musgrove. SMOOTHED S0,S1 AND S2 GIVN	
Lvl Density	9.3+1	1.8+3	DUB	Expt	Rept JINR-P3-3882	Oct 68 Karzhavina+	+
					Prog YFI-6 135	68 .KARZHAVINA+	
	9.3+1	1.8+3			Data EXFOR40165.007	Jul 73 .1 DATA LINE	
Lvl Density	None		MUN	Theo	Jour NP/A 217 269	Dec 73 Dilg+ A,DELTA. BACK SHIFTED FERMIGAS	
Lvl Density	None		ROC	Theo	Jour NP/A 223 589	May 74 Huizenga+ EXP CFD MICROSC TH AX SYMM	

62 Samarium 156

Quantity	Energy (ev) Min	Max	Lab	Type	Documentation Ref Vol Page	Author, Comments Date	Data
Evaluation	1.0-3	1.5+7	AUA	Eval	Rept AAEC/TM-549	Jun 70 Cook.TOT,EL,INEL,NONEL,CAPT SIGS,NDG	+
					Rept AAEC/E-214	Jun 71 Bertram+GROUP SIGMAS SAME QUANTS.NDG	
					Rept AAEC/TM-587	Mar 71 *DESCRIPTION OF LIBRARY	
	1.0-3	1.5+7			Data AUSTR-DFN 164.	Nov 71 POINT(223) AND GROUP(127) SIGMAS	
Total	1.0-3	1.5+7	AUA	Eval	Data AUSTR-DFN 164.	Nov 71 COOK+POINT(223)+GROUP(127)SIG.CF EVL	+
Elastic	1.0-3	1.5+7	AUA	Eval	Data AUSTR-DFN 164.	Nov 71 COOK+POINT(223)+GROUP(127)SIG.CF EVL	+
Tot Inelastc	5.0+5	1.5+7	AUA	Eval	Data AUSTR-DFN 164.	Nov 71 COOK+POINT(11)+GROUP(127)SIG.CF EVL	+
Nonelastic	1.0-3	1.5+7	AUA	Eval	Data AUSTR-DFN 164.	Nov 71 COOK+POINT(223)+GROUP(127)SIG.CF EVL	+
Res Int Abs	5.0-1		AUA	Eval	Rept AAEC/TM-619	Sep 72 Clayton.CALC FROM SIG LIBRARY,TABLE	
Res Int Abs	+0	+5	WIN	Revw	Conf IAEA-169 3 163	74 Pope+ CALC FROM AUSTRAL DATA FILE	
(n,γ)	1.0-3	1.5+7	AUA	Eval	Data AUSTR-DFN 164.	Nov 71 COOK+POINT(223)+GROUP(127)SIG.CF EVL	+
(n,γ)	Pile		CRC	Eval	Rept AECL-3037 1	Jan 72 Walker.SIG ESTIMATED ACCORDING Z,A	
(n,γ)	2.5-2		AUA	Eval	Rept AAEC/TM-619	Sep 72 Clayton.CALC FROM SIG LIBRARY,TABLE	
(n,γ)	Maxwl	Fiss	WIN	Revw	Conf IAEA-169 3 163	74 Pope+ MAXW+FIS-SPEC AVG EVAL DATA	
	Fiss				Conf IAEA-169 3 137	74 Dean. POINT DATA AVG OVER STAND SPEC	
Reson Params	-		AUA	Theo	Rept AAEC/E-211	Nov 70 Musgrove. CALCULTD D+GAM WIDTH GIVEN	
Strnth Fnctn	-		AUA	Theo	Rept AAEC/E-211	Nov 70 Musgrove. SMOOTHED S0,S1 AND S2 GIVN	

63 Europium

Quantity	Energy (ev) Min	Max	Lab	Type	Documentation Ref Vol Page	Date	Author, Comments	Data
Evaluation	5.0+5	1.5+7	LRL Eval	Rept	UCRL-5351	Nov 58	Howerton. CURVS.	
Evaluation	Pile		CRC Eval	Rept	CRRP-960	Nov 60	Westcott.G,S FACTORS EFFECTIVE CAPT.	
Evaluation	2.5-2	1.0+7	GEN Eval	Rept	APEX-704	Nov 61	Cooper+ CONTENT OF C-FINE TAPES	
Evaluation	2.5-2	1.0+7	KFK Eval	Rept	KFK-352	Aug 65	Schmidt+.TOT SEL DEL SNE SIN NG	
Total	Maxwl		COL Expt	Jour	PR 48 265	Aug 35	Dunning+ IONCH,TRANS,RA-BE/PARAFIN N	
Total	7.0-3	6.5+1	ANL Expt	Jour	PR 71 757	Jun 47	Sturm. SPECT TRNSM 4RES APPARENT	+
	7.0-3	8.3-1		Data	EXFOR12136.009	Jun 76	. 44 PTS. SIGMA.	
Total	7.8-2	6.0+1	BNL Expt	Jour	PR 93 1292	Mar 54	Sailor+ TOT CURVE CRYSTLSPECT.	+
	7.8-2	7.9-1		Data	EXFOR12109.002	Jun 76	. 52 PTS. SIGMA.	
Total	8.0-2	1.0+1	BNL Expt	Jour	PR 95 453	Jul 54	Wood. TRANS CURV 12 RESON ASSIGNED	
Total	1.0-3	1.0+2	KJL Expt	Abst	PR 98 1162	May 55	Holt.ABSTRACT HA11 RES VALUES GIVEN	+
	1.1-3	8.5-3		Data	EXFOR20103.002	Sep 71	12PTS.	
Total	2.0-1	1.3+0	BNL Expt	Jour	PR 98 1267	Jun 55	Landon+ .327 .461 1.056EV RES	+
	8.2-1	4.4+0		Data	EXFOR11966.004	Jun 76	. 119 PTS. SIGMA.	
Total	4.0+0	8.4+1	BNL Expt	Jour	PR 99 10	Jul 55	Harvey+ BNL FAST CHOPPER.	+
	4.0+0	8.4+1		Data	EXFOR11912.035	Jun 76	. 330 PTS. SIGMA.	
Total	8.0+2	2.4+4	HAR Expt	Priv	EGELSTAFF5	Jun 56	Egelstaff. TRANSMISSION.	+
Total	1.0+3	3.2+4	HAR Expt	Jour	PPSA 70 51	Jan 57	Gayther+ FC THICK SAMPLE,AVSIG CF TH	
Total	4.0+2	2.0+3	HAR Theo	Jour	PPS 71 910	Jun 58	Egelstaff.FLUCTUATIONS CFD THEORY	
Total	1.8-2	1.0+0	BNL Expt	Prog	WASH-1028 11	Apr 60	Hellsten+ TRANS,NDG	
Total	Cold		KJL Revw	Conf	60Vienna 169	Oct 60	Riste.NDG,TBP	
Total	1.5-4	3.0-3	MUN Expt	Jour	ADP 7 50	Jan 61	Hoehne. TOF RSLN FUNCT GIVEN	+
Total	5.0-4	5.0-2	JAE Expt	Jour	INDSWG-90 2	Jul 65	Ohno.TRNS,CRYST.+MECH.MONOCHR.,GRPHS	
Total	1.0+4	1.0+7	KFK Eval	Rept	KFK-352	Aug 65	Schmidt.GRAPHS+TABULATED DATA(NO.12)	
Total	2.5+1	1.5+3	LAS Expt	Conf	68Wash. 837	Mar 68	Harlow+ TOF BOMB CURVE 50/50 151+153	
Total	2.5+6	1.5+7	BNW Expt	Jour	PR/C 3 576	Feb 71	Foster+ TRANS,CURVS,CFD OTHERS+TH	+
				Jour	NIM 36 1	Sep 65	.EXPT DETAILS	
	2.3+6	1.5+7		Data	EXFOR10047.067	Aug 73	. 241 PTS, SIGMA.	
Total	1.0-2	3.0-1	IFU Expt	Prog	YFI-12 74	Jun 71	Vertebny+	+
	1.0-2	3.0-1		Data	EXFOR40109.004	Dec 72	SIGMA AT 30 ES	
Total	2.3-2	7.5-1	MOL Expt	Jour	NP/A 172 489	Sep 71	Poortmans+ CRYST SPEC.EU-151 RES ANL	+
	1.0-1	6.5-1		Conf	68Wash. 2 883	Mar 68	- + 3 ENERGIES. SUPERSEDED.	
	2.3-2	7.5-1		Data	EXFOR20221.	May 74	127PTS.	
Total	1.0-2	3.0-1	IJI Expt	Prog	YFI-12 74	72	Vertebny+ ABSTRACT,TBL SIG(N-E)	
				Prog	INDC(CCP)-30	Sep 72	.PAGE 64,ENGLISH OF YFI-12 74	
Total	2.7+3		MUN Expt	Prog	EANDC(E)150U	Oct 72	Dilg+ AVERAGE TOT XSECT+S0	+
				Conf	71Albany 327	Aug 71	- +TRNS.AVG CS GVN.31 ELEMENT GRP	
	2.7+3			Data	EXFOR20583.017	May 76	1PNT.	
Total	1.3+7	1.5+7	DEB Eval	Rept	IAEA-153 173	73	Boedy+ MOST PROBABLE VAL OF SIG,TBL	
				Jour	AHP 30 115	Oct 71	Angeli+ AVG SIG,CFD CALC.TBLS.GRAPH	
Elastic	5.0-1		ANL Expt	Jour	PR 79 11	Jul 50	Harris+ EPI-CD,RES INT SCAT,B-W TH	
Elastic	2.0-2	1.6-1	CRC Expt	Jour	CJP 31 432	Mar 53	Brockhouse. CRYST SPEC EU203 SCT/ABS	+
	2.0-2	1.6-1		Data	EXFOR11653.006	Jun 76	. 9 PTS. RADIO SIGEL/SIG ABS.	
Elastic	4.0-4		LAS Expt	Jour	PR 124 1848	Dec 61	Arnold. COH,INCOH SEE PR126 2262 ERR	
Elastic	4.2-2		LAS Expt	Jour	PR 127 2101	Sep 62	Nereson+ DIFFRACTION GIVE SCAT LNGTH	+
	4.2-2			Data	EXFOR12150.002	Jun 76	. 1 PT. COH AMP.	
Elastic	1.0+4	1.0+7	KFK Eval	Rept	KFK-352	Aug 65	Schmidt.GRAPHS+TABULATED DATA(NO.12)	
Potntal Scat	+4		HAR Expt	Jour	PPSA 70 51	Jan 57	Gayther+ FROM AVG SIGTOT. FC TRANSM	
Tot Inelastc	1.0+4	1.0+7	KFK Eval	Rept	KFK-352	Aug 65	Schmidt.GRAPHS+TABULATED DATA(NO.12)	
Thermal Scat	Cold		ORL Revw	Jour	JAP 36 1078	Mar 65	Koehler. MAGN PROPS FROM N DIFFR XPT	
Nonelastic	1.0+4	1.0+7	KFK Eval	Rept	KFK-352	Aug 65	Schmidt.GRAPHS+TABULATED DATA(NO.12)	
Absorption	Maxwl		HAR Expt	Rept	AERE-R/M-100	Dec 56	Cummins+.PILE OSC THR WELL REL HAR E	
Absorption	2.5-2		ROS Expt	Jour	KE 10 25	Jan 67	Albert.VAL 2200M/SEC GVN,LOCAL OSCIL	
Absorption	Maxwl		ROS Expt	Jour	ZFK-132 19	Dec 67	Faehrmann. CFD WITH OTHER AUTHORS	
Absorption	1.0-2		CAS Eval	Prog	EANDC(E)127U	Apr 70	Gibello+	
Res Int Abs	5.0-1		MTR Expt	Rept	IN- 1195	May 68	Scoville+	+
	5.0-1			Data	EXFOR11820.008	Jun 76	.RI ABS	
Res Int Abs	2.0-1	1.0+4	LRL Expt	Rept	UCRL-50804	Feb 70	Czirr+ CALC FROM DIFF DATA	+
	2.0-1	1.0+4		Data	EXFOR10169.004	Jul 72	. 1 PT.	
Res Int Abs	5.5-1		MUN Expt	Diss	GRYNTAKIS	Mar 76	Gryntakis.,SUM OF ISOT.RES.INTEGRALS	+
				Jour	RCA 22 20	75	KIM+,EQUIVALENT TO THESIS	
	2.0-1	5.5-1		Data	EXFOR20657.003	Aug 76	2PTS.CAPTURE.	
(n,γ)	Pile		ANL Expt	Jour	PR 72 888	Nov 47	Seren+ THR IRRAD. TO EU152,154,	+
	Pile			Data	EXFOR11447.099	Jun 76	. 1 PT. SIGMA	
(n,γ)	Maxwl		ORL Expt	Jour	PR 83 641	Aug 51	Pomerance.LOCAL OSC REL AU ABS 95 B	+
	Maxwl			Data	EXFOR11047.049	Jun 76	. 1 PT. SIGMA	

63 Europium

Quantity	Energy (ev) Min	Energy (ev) Max	Lab	Type	Documentation Ref Vol Page	Author, Comments Date	Data
(n,γ)	2.0−2	1.6−1	CRC	Expt	Jour CJP 31 432	Mar 53 Brockhouse.CRYST SPEC EU203 SCT/ABS	+
	2.0−2	1.6−1		Data	EXFOR11653.006	Jun 76 . 9 PTS. RATIO SIG EL/SIG ABS.	
(n,γ)	2.5−2		ANL	Expt	Jour NSE 9 132	Feb 61 Meadows+ PULSED NEUTS,4406+ −30B	+
	2.5−2			Data	EXFOR11028.020	Sep 76 . 1 PT CS=4406B.	
(n,γ)	2.1+2	9.5+3	ORL	Expt	Conf 61Saclay 203	Sep 61 Block+ LIQUID SCINTILLATOR	+
	2.0+2	8.0+3			Conf 61Vienna 1 95	Aug 61 Neiler.PPR73,GRAPH,FAST CHOPPER	
	2.1+2	9.5+3			Data EXFOR11935.012	Jun 76 . 49 PTS. SIGMA	
(n,γ)	3.0+4	6.5+4	ORL	Expt	Jour PR 129 2695	Mar 63 Macklin+ LIQ SCINT,2.56 AND 1.58B	+
	3.0+4	6.5+4			Data EXFOR11331.024	Jun 76 . 2 PTS. SIGMA	
(n,γ)	8.0−1	5.0+4	LEB	Expt	Conf JINR−1845 100	Jun 64 Konks.PB−SLOWDOWN, GRAPH SIG(E)	+
					Rept ICD−1 43	64 . BETTER GRAPH.(ENGL=INDSWG−64E)	
					Rept KFK−352	65 . DISCUSS OF RESULTS	
(n,γ)	5.0+3	9.0+4	ORL	Theo	Jour RMP 37 166	Jan 65 Macklin+ CALC FOR KT=5TO90 KEV	
(n,γ)	1.0+4	1.0+7	KFK	Eval	Rept KFK−352	Aug 65 Schmidt.GRAPHS+TABULATED DATA(NO.12)	
(n,γ)	2.5+1	3.0+4	KFK	Eval	Rept KFK−352	Aug 65 Schmidt+.GRAPHS+TABLE(NO.7)	
(n,γ)	3.0+4	2.0+5	ORL	Expt	Jour PR 159 1007	Jul 67 Macklin+ TOF,TOTAL−E DET, 7ES,ABSL	+
	3.0+4	2.0+5			Data EXFOR11679.019	Jun 76 . 7 PTS. SIGMA	
(n,γ)	1.0+0	5.0+4	DUB	Expt	Jour YF 7 493	Mar 68 Konks+ SIG(NEUT−E) GRPH,PB−SLOW−DOWN	
					Jour SNP 7 310	Sep 68 − + ENGL OF YF 7 493.	
(n,γ)	2.0+2	1.2+4	LRL	Expt	Rept UCRL−50804	Feb 70 Czirr.TOF+LINAC.PULSED NEUTS.CURVE	+
	2.0+2	1.3+4			Data EXFOR10169.007	Jul 72 . 98PTS, SIG.	
(n,γ)	1.0+3	1.0+7	BOL	Eval	Rept CEC(70)−2	Apr 70 Benzi.GRAPH=SUM OF SIG(ISOTOPES)	
(n,γ)	+3	+7	FEI	Revw	Conf 70Helsinki 2 245	Jun 70 Abramov. PPR114.REVW OF DATA STATUS	
(n,γ)	3.0+4		AUA	Theo	Rept AAEC/E−211	Nov 70 Musgrove. SIGMA GIVEN AND CFD OTHER	
(n,γ)	3.0+4	3.0+5	USP	Expt	Jour NP/A 196 83	Nov 72 Lepine+ LI7−P NS.TOF.M−R. REL TO IN	+
	3.0+4	3.0+5			Data EXFOR30233.003	Mar 73 NDS,RELATIVE TO IN,ABSOLUTE ERROR	
(n,γ)	1.1+0	3.1+4	KFK	Expt	Jour JNE 27 811	Nov 73 Chou+ ABSOL EXPT.SDT SPECTROM.	+
	1.0+0	3.0+4			Rept KFK−EXT−4 28	Nov 70 − . ABS EXPT	
	7.7−1	5.0+4			Data EXFOR20352.	Sep 74 . 352 PTS.SIGMA.	
(n,γ)	1.0+3	1.0+7	FEI	Eval	Rept YK−8/2 97	Sep 72 Abagjan+ AVG SIG(ENERGY−GROUPS),TABL	
					Rept INDC(CCP)−39	Jul 74 .P102. ENGLISH OF YK−8/2 97	
(n,γ)	1.0+6	1.0+7	CRC	Revw	Conf 74Petten 119	Sep 74 Bartholomew+ PHOTON STRF GRPH	
(n,γ)	1.0+3	3.7+5	FEI	ExTh	Conf 75Kiev 3 190	May 75 Jurlov+ REL B10(N,A).SIG(E),GRAPH	
(n,γ)	Maxwl		MUN	ExTh	Diss GRYNTAKIS	Mar 76 Gryntakis.,ACT.MEAS.,CALC OF G−FUNCT	+
					Jour RCA 22 128	Mar 75 − +,CALC WESTCOTTS G−FUNCTION	
					Jour RCA 22 20	Jan 75 KIM+,EQUIVALENT TO THESIS	
	2.5−2			Expt	EXFOR20657.002	Aug 76 2PTS.SIGMA.	
(n,γ)	1.0−2	1.0+1	WUR	Expt	Jour NSE 60 53	May 76 Widder.TOF.CS VS.E GRPHS.2200M/S CS	+
	1.1−2	1.0+1			Rept EIR−217	Apr 75 − . POWDER SAMPLE	
					Conf 74Petten 757	Sep 74 − . M−R DET,ABS.EXP.,NDG	
	1.1−2	1.0+1			Data EXFOR20437.005	Nov 75 . 379PTS.SIGMA.	
(n,γ)	Fast		RCN	Expt	Rept ECN−10	Oct 76 Veenema+ STEK REACTIVITY WORTHS TBL.	
(n,γ)	1.0−2	1.0+5	HAR	Expt	Jour ANE 3 399	Nov 76 Moxon+LINAC.M−R.TBL.GRPHS. +.025EV	+
	1.0+2	1.0+5			Rept EANDC(UK)−158	Feb 74 − + AVERAGED. CALC FROM EU151,153	
	1.0+2	1.0+5			Data EXFOR20489.002	Mar 76 27PTS.SIGMA.	
Spect (n,γ)	Maxwl		TAT	Expt	Jour NP 4 44	Aug 57 Bhattacherjee+.TBL+GRPH.LONGLVD ACTV	
Spect (n,γ)	Pile		HEB	ExTh	Jour NP 4 477	Sep 57 Ofer. SINGLES SPECTRUM GIVEN	
Spect (n,γ)	Maxwl		YAL	Expt	Jour PR 114 268	Apr 59 Draper.SC SPECTR,GAM E 0 TO 600 KEV	
Spect (n,γ)	Maxwl		ARF	Expt	Prog ARF−1193−12	Jul 62 Greenwood+ CRYST SPEC,LOW−E GAMMAS	
Spect (n,γ)	Maxwl		FTI	Expt	Conf 64Paris 2 811	Jul 64 Kaminker.LIFE TIME OF EXCITED STATE	
Spect (n,γ)	2.5−2		MIT	Comp	Rept MITNE−85	Jan 69 Rasmussen+TBL G INT.=AFCRL−69−0071	
Spect (n,γ)	Pile		CAI	Expt	Jour ZN/A 27 1229	Sep 72 El−Aasser+ G+INT CONVERSION SM−152	
Spect (n,γ)	Pile		MUN	Expt	Jour ZP 258 315	Mar 73 Henkelmann. E+INT OF GS GIVEN	+
	2.5−2				Data EXFOR20606.011	Jun 76 5PTS.	
(n,2n)	1.5+7		DEB	Eval	Jour REA 11 1 153	Mar 73 Boedy+ RECOMM.VALUE FROM N−Z SYSTEM.	
Reson Params	−.1−3	2.2+1	ANL	Expt	Jour PR 71 757	Jun 47 Sturm.CRYSTLSPECT TRNSM SIG WT	+
	−.1−3	2.2+1			Data EXFOR12136.006	Jun 76 . 5 RES. E0, WT, AND TOT PCS.	
Reson Params	3.3−1	1.5+1	BNL	Expt	Jour PR 93 1292	Mar 54 Sailor+RSLN.001TO.2EV 15RES CRYSTLSP	
	3.3−1	1.5+1			Data EXFOR12109.003	Jun 76 . 10 RES, E0,WN,WT**2/PCS	
Reson Params	2.0−1	1.3+0	BNL	Expt	Jour PR 98 1267	Jun 55 Landon+	+
	3.3−1	2.5+0			Jour PR 96 1014	Nov 54 Sailor+ RSLN .001EV STRGTH 4RES	
	3.3−1	1.1+0			Data EXFOR11966.005	Jun 76 . 3 RES, E0,WT,WG,PCS	
Reson Params	4.8+0	4.7+1	BNL	Expt	Jour PR 99 10	Jul 55 Harvey+ BNL FAST CHOPPER.	+
	4.8+0	4.7+1			Data EXFOR11912.051	Jun 76 . 33 RES E0, WN, AND WNO.	
Reson Params	1.8−2	1.0+0	BNL	Expt	Prog WASH−1028 11	Apr 60 Hellsten+ NDG	
Reson Params	None		BNL	Expt	Prog WASH−1048 13	Jun 64 Sailor. OKS STOLOVYS SPIN VALUES	
Strnth Fnctn	2.0+2	6.0+3	BNL	Expt	Jour PHY 22 994	Nov 56 Hughes.3.3+−0.5TRANSMISS.V.TOF CURVE	

63 Europium

Quantity	Energy (ev) Min	Max	Lab	Type	Documentation Ref Vol Page	Date	Author, Comments	Data
Strnth Fnctn	+4		HAR	Expt Jour	PPSA 70 51	Jan 57	Gayther+ FROM AVG SIGTOT. FC TRANSM	
Strnth Fnctn	+3	+5	BNL	Expt Conf	ORNL-2309	Jun 57	Block+ PRELIM 3D3PMD6	
Strnth Fnctn	8.0-1	5.0+4	LEB	Expt Conf	JINR-1845 100	Jun 64	Konks+ PB-SLOWDOWN-TIME, TABLE	
Strnth Fnctn		5.0+4	RI	Expt Prog	YFI-5 59	Oct 67	Konks+ TABLE	
				Rept	INDC-232E	Jan 69	. ENGL OF YFI-5 59	
Strnth Fnctn	2.7+3		MUN	Expt Conf	71Albany 327	Aug 71	Dilg+TRNS.S0 STF GVN.31 ELEMENT GRPH	
Strnth Fnctn	1.1+0	3.1+4	KFK	Expt Jour	JNE 27 811	Nov 73	Chou+ P-WAVE,WG/D.FROM ABSOL NG-EXPT+	
	1.0+0	5.0+4		Data	EXFOR20352.	Sep 74	2PTS.GAMMA STRNGTH FUNC,L=1.	

63 Europium 145

Quantity	Energy (ev) Min	Max	Lab	Type	Documentation Ref Vol Page	Date	Author, Comments	Data
(n,p)	Maxwl		IFU	Theo Rept	ICD-4 20	67	Dadakina+ PENETR COEFF CALC,TABLE	
Reson Params	-		AUA	Theo Rept	AAEC/E-211	Nov 70	Musgrove. CALCULTD D+GAM WIDTH GIVEN	
Strnth Fnctn	-		AUA	Theo Rept	AAEC/E-211	Nov 70	Musgrove. SMOOTHED S0,S1 AND S2 GIVN	

63 Europium 146

Quantity	Energy (ev) Min	Max	Lab	Type	Documentation Ref Vol Page	Date	Author, Comments	Data
(n,p)	Maxwl		IFU	Theo Rept	ICD-4 20	67	Dadakina+ PENETR COEFF CALC,TABLE	
Reson Params	-		AUA	Theo Rept	AAEC/E-211	Nov 70	Musgrove. CALCULTD D+GAM WIDTH GIVEN	
Strnth Fnctn	-		AUA	Theo Rept	AAEC/E-211	Nov 70	Musgrove. SMOOTHED S0,S1 AND S2 GIVN	

63 Europium 147

Quantity	Energy (ev) Min	Max	Lab	Type	Documentation Ref Vol Page	Date	Author, Comments	Data
(n,p)	Maxwl		IFU	Theo Rept	ICD-4 20	67	Dadakina+ PENETR COEFF CALC,TABLE	
Reson Params	-		AUA	Theo Rept	AAEC/E-211	Nov 70	Musgrove. CALCULTD D+GAM WIDTH GIVEN	
Strnth Fnctn	-		AUA	Theo Rept	AAEC/E-211	Nov 70	Musgrove. SMOOTHED S0,S1 AND S2 GIVN	

63 Europium 148

Quantity	Energy (ev) Min	Max	Lab	Type	Documentation Ref Vol Page	Date	Author, Comments	Data
(n,p)	Maxwl		IFU	Theo Rept	ICD-4 20	67	Dadakina+ PENETR COEFF CALC,TABLE	
Reson Params	-		AUA	Theo Rept	AAEC/E-211	Nov 70	Musgrove. CALCULTD D+GAM WIDTH GIVEN	
Strnth Fnctn	-		AUA	Theo Rept	AAEC/E-211	Nov 70	Musgrove. SMOOTHED S0,S1 AND S2 GIVN	

63 Europium 149

Quantity	Energy (ev) Min	Max	Lab	Type	Documentation Ref Vol Page	Date	Author, Comments	Data
(n,p)	Maxwl		IFU	Theo Rept	ICD-4 20	67	Dadakina+ PENETR COEFF CALC,TABLE	
Reson Params	-		AUA	Theo Rept	AAEC/E-211	Nov 70	Musgrove. CALCULTD D+GAM WIDTH GIVEN	
Strnth Fnctn	-		AUA	Theo Rept	AAEC/E-211	Nov 70	Musgrove. SMOOTHED S0,S1 AND S2 GIVN	

63 Europium 150

Quantity	Energy (ev) Min	Max	Lab	Type	Documentation Ref Vol Page	Date	Author, Comments	Data
Reson Params	-		AUA	Theo Rept	AAEC/E-211	Nov 70	Musgrove. CALCULTD D+GAM WIDTH GIVEN	
Strnth Fnctn	-		AUA	Theo Rept	AAEC/E-211	Nov 70	Musgrove. SMOOTHED S0,S1 AND S2 GIVN	

63 Europium 151

Quantity	Energy (ev) Min	Max	Lab	Type	Documentation Ref Vol Page	Date	Author, Comments	Data
Evaluation	2.5-2	1.0+7	KFK	Eval Rept	KFK-352	Aug 65	Schmidt+.RES NG	
Evaluation	None		SAC	Eval Prog	EANDC(E)-157U2	May 73	Ribon.	
Evaluation	1.0-5	2.0+7	BNL	Eval Rept	BNL-19455	Nov 74	Takahashi.GRPH.	
Evaluation		9.0+3	WIN	Eval Prog	UKNDC(75)P71	Jul 75	Smith.GENEX DATA PREPARED	
Total	-2	+1	HAR	Expt Conf	58Geneva 16 44	Sep 58	Pattenden.PPR11,CURVE,CRYSTALSPECTRM	
Total	1.0+0	1.0+1	BNL	Expt Jour	PR 114 1577	Jun 59	Patronis+ CS CURVES GIVEN	

63 Europium 151

Quantity	Energy (ev) Min	Max	Lab	Type	Documentation Ref Vol Page	Date	Author, Comments	Data
Total	1.0 − 1	1.0 + 0	BNL	Expt	Jour NSE 10 169	Jun 61	Tassan+ CURVE,RES PARAMS .321 .460EV	+
	2.0 − 1	6.7 − 1			Data EXFOR12151.002	Jun 76	. 80 PTS. SIGMA	
Total	2.5 − 2		JAE	Expt	Prog EANDC(J)10L1	Nov 68	Ohno+ .CRYST − SPECT + V − SELECT	+
	5.0 − 4	5.0 − 2			Prog INDSWG − 90 2	Jul 65	− .TRNS,CRYST.+MECH.MONOCHR.,GRPH	
	2.5 − 2				Data EXFOR20328.003	Jul 74	1PNT.	
Total	1.0 − 2	3.0 − 1	IFU	Expt	Prog YFI − 12 74	Jun 71	Vertebny+	+
	1.0 − 2	3.0 − 1			Data EXFOR40109.003	Dec 72	SIGMA AT 30 ES	
Total	1.0 − 2	3.0 − 1	IJI	Expt	Prog YFI − 12 74	72	Vertebny+ ABSTRACT,TBL SIG(N − E)	
					Prog INDC(CCP) − 30	Sep 72	.PAGE 64,ENGLISH OF YFI − 12 74	
Total	8.1 − 1	5.2 + 3	COL	Expt	Jour PR/C 6 251	Jul 72	Rahn+TRNS.SELF INDIC.RES PAR ANAL.	+
	4.6 + 1	3.0 + 3			Rept NYO − 72 − 281	Oct 70	− .SEE FOR DETAILS	
	2.6 + 2	3.0 + 3			Data EXFOR10046.032	Jan 78	. 4419 PTS.CS DATA.	
Total	2.0 + 3		IJI	Expt	Conf 76Lowell 1244	Jul 76	Vertebnyi+ TRANSM VS THICKNESS,NDG	
					Conf 75Kiev 3 151	May 75	Vertebnyj+ RES − NEUT FILTRAT.SIG GIVN	
Total	6.5 − 3	1.7 − 1	IJI	Expt	Rept YFI − 22 19	Dec 76	Razbudey+ TOF,SIG(NEUT − E),TBL	
	1.0 − 2	3.0 − 1			Conf 75Kiev 3 161	May 75	Razbudej+ TRANS.SIG(E,N − DOSE),GRAPH	
					Rept KIYAI − 75 − 17	75	− + TOF,CAPILL SAMPLES.SIG GVN	
Elastic		3.0 + 0	BET	Eval	Rept WAPD − T − 1630	Oct 63	Harris.MULTILEVEL EFFECTS	
Elastic	2.5 − 2		IJI	Eval	Conf 75Kiev 1 169	May 75	Fedorova+ EVAL 2200M/S SIG,TABLE	
Potntal Scat	2.0 + 3		IJI	Expt	Conf 76Lowell 1244	Jul 76	Vertebnyi+ SCT − LNGTH GVN,FRM TOT + SCT	
Scattering	6.0 + 0	9.0 + 0	IJI	Expt	Conf 73Kiev 2 85	May 73	Vertebny+ SIG(NEUT − E),GRAPH,TOF	
Scattering	+7		IJI	Expt	Conf 77Kiev	77	Trofimova+ SIG	
	2.0 + 3				Conf 76Lowell 1244	Jul 76	Vertebnyi+ SCT − SIG VS THICKNESS,NDG	
					Conf 75Kiev 3 151	May 75	Vertebnyj+ RES − NEUT FILTRAT.SIG GIVN	
Nonelastic	2.0 + 3		IJI	Expt	Conf 75Kiev 3 151	May 75	Vertebnyj+ RES − NEUT FILTRAT.SIG GIVN	
Absorption	2.0 − 2	2.4 − 1	CUW	Theo	Rept CWR − 400 − 1	Sep 57	Roberts.MAXWELL − BOLTZMANN AVGD SIGS.	
Absorption	2.5 − 2		HAR	Expt	Jour JNEA 12 32	May 60	Tattersall+ . PILE OSCILLATOR	+
					Rept AERE − R − 2887	Aug 59	− . PILE OSC.REL BORON	
	2.5 − 2				Data EXFOR20638.050	Jul 76	1PNT.SIGMA.	
Absorption	4.1 − 1	1.0 + 7	GA	Eval	Rept GA − 2451	Aug 61	Joanou+ 68GROUP DATA FOR GAM − I ABS	
Absorption	2.5 − 2		ROS	Expt	Jour KE 10 25	Jan 67	Albert.VAL 2200M/SEC GVN,LOCAL OSCIL	
Absorption	Maxwl		ROS	Expt	Rept ZFK − 132 19	Dec 67	Faehrmann. CFD WITH OTHER AUTHORS	
Absorption	1.0 − 3	1.0 + 7	JUL	Eval	Rept JUEL − 678 − RG	Jul 70	Liu. EVALUATION+CALC,GRPH,FN OF E	
Absorption	1.0 − 3	2.0 + 0	JUL	Theo	Rept JUEL − 746 − RG144	Apr 71	Bonka.KUGEL − THERMOS − LIBR,CURVE	
Absorption	2.5 − 2		IJI	Eval	Conf 75Kiev 1 169	May 75	Fedorova+ EVAL SIG OF 3ISOMERS,TABLE	
Absorption	Maxwl		IJI	Expt	Rept YFI − 22 21	Dec 76	Razbudey+ ACT,SIG = 8900+ − 1100 BARN	
Res Int Abs	5.0 − 1		ANL	Expt	Jour PR 79 11	Jul 50	Harris+ EPI − CD,REL THERMAL ACT. B − W	+
	5.0 − 1				Data EXFOR11343.026	Jun 76	. RI GIVEN	
Res Int Abs	2.5 − 2		HAR	Expt	Jour JNE 12 32	May 60	Tattersall+ PILE OSCILLATOR.	+
	6.7 − 1				Data EXFOR20638.051	Jul 76	1PNT.	
Res Int Abs	5.5 − 1		MOL	Theo	Rept BLG − 421	Sep 67	Damle+,EVAL ACT R.I. = 665+ − 100B,TO MS	
Res Int Abs	5.5 − 1		MOL	Eval	Rept BLG − 421	Sep 67	Damle+,EVAL ACT R.I. = 665+ − 100B,TO MS	
Res Int Abs	5.0 − 1		BGK	Expt	Rept THAI − AEC − 10	Oct 67	. ACTIV(NA − I),CD − RATIO,REL AU. TABLE	+
	5.0 − 1				Data EXFOR30368.022	Jan 77	REL AU, PRELM.	
Res Int Abs	5.0 − 1		CPO	Expt	Jour JIN 29 2671	Nov 67	Sims+ ACTIVATION.RI FOR CAPTURE	+
	5.0 − 1				Data EXFOR12090.	Jun 76	. RI FOR MS AND GND STATE.	
Res Int Abs	5.0 − 1		MTR	Expt	Rept IN − 1195	May 68	Scoville+	+
	5.0 − 1				Data EXFOR11820.009	Jun 76	. RI ABS.	
Res Int Abs	6.3 − 1		CAS	Eval	Jour NSE 40 51	70	Gibello+, 1230 B, TO 9.2 H ISOMER	
					Jour NSE 37 478	69	Orestano+,SAME RESULTS	
Res Int Abs	2.0 − 1	1.0 + 4	LRL	Expt	Rept UCRL − 50804	Feb 70	Czirr+ CALC FROM DIFF DATA	+
	2.0 − 1	1.0 + 4			Data EXFOR10169.003	Jul 72	. 1 PT.	
Res Int Abs	5.5 − 1		GHT	Expt	Jour JRC 9 9	71	De Corte+CAPT CD − R,2014B TO EU − 152M	+
	5.0 − 1				Data EXFOR20646.010	Sep 76	1PNT.CAPTURE.	
Res Int Abs	None		GA	Eval	Rept GA − 12071	Sep 71	Mathews+ RECOMMENDED VALUES	
Res Int Abs	5.5 − 1		CRC	Comp	Rept AECL − 3037 1	Jan 72	Walker.TBL OF CORRECTED EXPTL VALUES	
Res Int Abs	5.0 − 1		COL	Expt	Jour NSE 48 219	Jun 72	Rahn+ RI = 3265+ − 310B.	
Res Int Abs	5.0 − 1		MUN	Expt	Jour JRC 15 535	73	Alian+CAPT CD − R, 2928B INCL 1/V	+
	5.0 − 1				Data EXFOR20644.014	Jun 76	1PNT.CAPTURE.	
Res Int Abs	5.5 − 1		RCN	Revw	Conf 73Paris 2 271	Mar 73	Zijp.ACT,RECOMM FROM LITERATURE,TBL	
Res Int Abs	5.0 − 1		GHT	Expt	Jour JRC 20 695	74	Van Der Linden+ BY(N,G).CFD OTHS,TBL	+
	5.5 − 1				Conf 73Paris 2 241	Mar 73	− + ACT,REL THR+GOLD,TBL	
	5.5 − 1				Data EXFOR20645.	Jul 76	2PTS.CAPTURE.	
Res Int Abs	5.5 − 1	+6	SAC	Revw	Conf IAEA − 169 1 235	74	Ribon.CAPTURE,STATUS CFD REQUEST,TBL	
Res Int Abs	+0	+5	WIN	Revw	Conf IAEA − 169 3 163	74	Pope+ DATA FILE CALC CFD XPTAL VALUE	
Res Int Abs	5.0 − 1		IJI	Eval	Conf 75Kiev 1 169	May 75	Fedorova+ EVAL RI OF 3ISOMERS,TABLE	
Res Int Abs	5.0 − 1		KJL	Expt	Jour JIN 37 1591	Aug 75	Steinnes. CD − RAT+ACTIV INTEG,CFD,TBL	+
	5.0 − 1				Data EXFOR20635.	Aug 76	2PTS.CAPTURE.	

63 Europium 151

Quantity	Energy (ev) Min	Energy (ev) Max	Lab	Type	Documentation Ref Vol Page	Date	Author, Comments	Data
Res Int Abs	5.5−1		MUN	Expt Diss	GRYNTAKIS	Mar 76	Gryntakis.ACT MS AND GRD,WITHOUT CD	+
				Jour	RCA 22 20	75	KIM+ACTIV.EQUIVALENT TO THESIS	
	2.0−1	5.5−1		Data	EXFOR20657.	Aug 76	6PTS.CAPTURE.	
(n,γ)	2.0+4	7.0+5	OXF Expt	Jour	PRSA 170 513	Apr 39	Griffiths.RA − BE PHOTONEUT ACTIVATION	
(n,γ)	Maxwl		JAP Expt	Jour	SCP 38 167	Jan 41	Sinma+.LI+D.RELATIVE SIG MEASUREMENT	
(n,γ)	Pile		ANL Expt	Jour	PR 72 888	Nov 47	Seren+ THR IRRAD. THR IRRAD.OXALATE.	+
	Pile			Data	EXFOR11447.098	Jun 76	. 1 PT. SIGMA	
(n,γ)	Maxwl		ANL Expt	Jour	PR 75 1500	May 49	Hayden+ ISOTOPIC DILUTION,TO +−15PC	+
	Maxwl			Data	EXFOR12138.002	Jun 76	. 1 PT. SIGMA	
(n,γ)	1.5+5	3.0+6	WIS Expt	Jour	PR 116 927	Nov 59	Johnsrud+ SC CFD OTHERS SIG VS E	+
	1.7+5	2.5+6		Data	EXFOR11675.022	Jun 76	. 14 PTS, SIG	
(n,γ)	Maxwl		KAP Expt	Prog	KAPL−2000−8	Dec 59	Moore+	+
	Maxwl			Data	EXFOR12093.002	Jun 76	. RATIO SIG(GND)/SIG(MS).	
(n,γ)	Maxwl		MUA Expt	Jour	NP 20 183	Oct 60	Hans+ SIGMA GIVEN	+
	Maxwl			Data	EXFOR31246.011	Sep 72	.SIG TO MS−STATE GVN	
(n,γ)	None		ANL Theo	Jour	PR 120 1305	Nov 60	Huizenga+ ISOMER RATIO,TH CFD EXPT	
(n,γ)	Maxwl	+0	MTR Expt	Jour	PR 129 769	Jan 63	Keisch.RATIO ISOMER ACT TO GND ACT.	+
	Maxwl			Data	EXFOR11748.020	Jun 76	.SIGMA RATIO MS/GND.	
(n,γ)		3.0+0	BET Eval	Rept	WAPD−T−1630	Oct 63	Harris. MULTILEVEL EFFECTS	
(n,γ)	8.0−1	5.0+4	LEB Expt	Conf	JINR−1845 100	Jun 64	Konks. PB − SLOWDOWN, GRAPH SIG(E)	+
				Rept	ICD−1 43	64	. BETTER GRAPH.(ENGL=INDSWG−64E)	
				Rept	KFK−352	65	. DISCUSS OF RESULTS	
(n,γ)	Maxwl		ANL Comp	Jour	NP 60 241	Nov 64	Bishop+EXP AND TH ISOMER RATIOS CFD	
(n,γ)	Maxwl		BNL Expt	Jour	PR/B 137 763	Feb 65	Takahashi.	+
	Maxwl			Data	EXFOR12117.	Jun 76	. 1 PT. MS AND MS/M2 RATIO(SPA)	
(n,γ)	2.5+1	3.0+4	KFK Eval	Rept	KFK−352	Aug 65	Schmidt+.GRAPHS+TABLE(NO.7)	
(n,γ)	1.0−2	3.0+1	MOL Eval	Rept	BLG−421	66	Damle+. CURVE RECOMMENDED SIGS	
(n,γ)	1.0+3	1.0+4	LAS Theo	Rept	LA−3463	Jan 66	Bell. TH CAPTURE OF RARE EARTHS	
(n,γ)	+3		LAS Eval	Jour	LA−3643	Dec 66	Barr+ ESTIMATED SIGS CFD EXPTS	
(n,γ)	Pile		CPO Expt	Jour	JIN 29 2671	Nov 67	Sims+ ACTIVATION.	+
	Pile			Data	EXFOR12090.	Jun 76	. 1 PT. SIGMA MS AND GND STATE.	
(n,γ)	Maxwl		FEI Theo	Jour	YF 6 1174	Dec 67	Malyshev.STATMOD ISOM SIG,HIGH+LOW L	
				Jour	SNP 6 853	Jun 68	.TRANSLATION	
(n,γ)	Maxwl Pile		MOL Eval	Rept	BLG−421	68	Damle+ TBP THRSIG RESINTG GIVEN	
(n,γ)	Maxwl Pile		MOL Eval	Rept	BLG−421	68	Damle+ TBP THRSIG RESINTG GIVEN	
(n,γ)	Maxwl		AUA Theo	Jour	NSE 31 234	Feb 68	Cook+ STATISTICAL CALC CFD EXPT	
(n,γ)	1.0+0	5.0+4	DUB Expt	Jour	YF 7 493	Mar 68	Konks+ SIG(NEUT−E) GRPH,PB−SLOW−DOWN	
				Jour	SNP 7 310	Sep 68	− + ENGL OF YF 7 493.	
(n,γ)	2.5+1	1.0+4	LAS Expt	Conf	68Wash. 837	Mar 68	Harlow+ TOF BOMB SOURCE CURVE	+
	None			Data	EXFOR10324.	Dec 73	. 0 PTS. DATA WITHDRAWN	
(n,γ)	−		IEA Comp	Rept	IEA−INF−10	Aug 68	Atalla. TABLES OF HL,SIG AND GAMM−E	
(n,γ)	1.0+3	1.0+7	BOL Eval	Rept	CCDN−NW/10	Dec 69	Benzi+H−F MOD,AXEL G(G)EST,ALL DATA	
				Rept	CEC(70)−2	Apr 70	− +. GRAPH	
				Jour	NC 38 216	Jul 65	− + THEORY FOR CAPTURE EVALUATION	
(n,γ)	2.0+2	1.2+4	LRL Expt	Jour	UCRL−50804	Feb 70	Czirr.TOF+LINAC.PULSED NEUTS.TABLE	+
	2.0+2	1.3+4		Data	EXFOR10169.006	Jul 72	. 98 PTS, SIGMA.	
(n,γ)	3.0+4		AUA Theo	Rept	AAEC/E−211	Nov 70	Musgrove. SIGMA GIVEN AND CFD OTHER	
(n,γ)	2.5−2		NPL Expt	Jour	JNE 25 129	Mar 71	Ryves+PROD EU152M.REL AU.ACT.EXPT.	+
				Conf	71Canterby 139	71	− . VDG,GRAPHITE MODERATOR.ACTIVN	
	2.5−2			Data	EXFOR20791.016	Dec 78	1PNT.SIGMA.	
(n,γ)	Maxwl		GA Eval	Rept	GA−12071	Sep 71	Mathews+ RECOMMENDED VALUES	
(n,γ)	−.3−3	4.6−1	MOL Expt	Jour	NP/A 172 489	Sep 71	Poortmans+ CRYST SPEC+ACT CS(.025EV)	+
	2.5−2	4.6−1		Conf	68Wash. 2 883	Mar 68	− + 3 ENERGIES. SUPERSEDED.	
	−.3−2	4.6−1		Data	EXFOR20221.	May 74	14PTS.SIGMA.	
(n,γ)	Maxwl		CRC Comp	Rept	AECL−3037 1	Jan 72	Walker.TBL OF CORRECTED EXPTAL SIGS	
(n,γ)	2.5+4		AUW Expt	Jour	JP/A 5 1262	Aug 72	Lakshimana+ ACT. ISOMER RATIO	+
				Conf	70Madurai 2 19	Dec 70	Lakshmana Rao+. HIGH+LOW SPIN SIGMAS	
	2.5+4			Data	EXFOR30246.	Jun 73	.SIG TO MS(J=8) AND MS(J=0).ISORATIO	
(n,γ)	2.5+4		AUW Theo	Jour	PR/C 6 572	Aug 72	Rao+. ISOMER RATIOS CALCTD.CFD EXPT	
	2.5+4			Expt	EXFOR30234.	Jun 73	.SIG TO GROUND AND META.ISOM RATIO	
(n,γ)	Fast		DUB Expt	Rept	JINR−P12−6810	Nov 72	Ngo Quoc Buu+ ACT ANALYS, CD−RATIOS	
(n,γ)	Maxwl		MUN Expt	Jour	JRC 15 535	73	Alian+ ACT, 4056B REL TO CO−59	+
	2.5−2			Data	EXFOR20644.013	Jun 76	1PNT.SIGMA.	
(n,γ)	Pile		BKB Expt	Prog	INDC(SEC)−35	Sep 73	Koicki+ GE−LI,COINC,SHORT NOTE,NDG	
(n,γ)	Maxwl		RCN Revw	Prog	INDC(NDS)−56	Sep 73	Zijp.PG103,FOR DOSIMETRY,SIG GIVEN	
	2.5−2			Conf	73Paris 2 271	Mar 73	− .RECOMMENDED FROM LITERATURE,TB	
(n,γ)	Fiss		SAC Revw	Conf	IAEA−169 1 235	74	Ribon.STATUS SIG CFD REQUESTS,TABLE	
	2.5−2			Conf	IAEA−169 1 235	74	− .STATUS SIG CFD REQUESTS,TABLE	

63 Europium 151

Quantity	Energy (ev) Min	Energy (ev) Max	Lab	Type	Documentation Ref Vol Page	Date	Author, Comments	Data
(n,γ)	Maxwl	Fiss	WIN	Revw Conf	IAEA – 169 3 163	74	Pope+ MAXW+FIS – SPEC AVG DATA CFD XPT	
(n,γ)	1.0+3	1.0+7	FEI	Eval Rept	YK – 8/2 97	Sep 72	Abagjan+ AVG SIG(ENERGY – GROUPS),TABL	
				Rept	INDC(CCP) – 39	Jul 74	.P102. ENGLISH OF YK – 8/2 97	
(n,γ)	1.0+2	1.0+7	BNL	Theo Conf	JAERI – M – 5984	Feb 75	Takahashi.P257.CALC CFD EVAL AND EXP	
(n,γ)	Fast		INL	Expt Abst	BAP 20 173	Feb 75	Anderl+SIG FOR GD ST,M1,M2 75WASH	
(n,γ)	2.0+1	2.0+5	RPI	Expt Conf	75Wash. 905	Mar 75	Hockenbury+GRPH CFD CALC	+
	6.3+3	3.0+5		Data	EXFOR10435.002	Oct 74	. 566 PTS, SIGMA	
(n,γ)	1.0+3	3.7+5	FEI	ExTh Conf	75Kiev 3 190	May 75	Jurlov+ REL B10(N,A).SIG(E),GRAPH	
(n,γ)	Maxwl		MUN	ExTh Diss	GRYNTAKIS	Mar 76	Gryntakis.,ACT.MEAS.,CALC OF G – FUNCT	+
				Jour	RCA 22 128	Mar 75	– +,CALC WESTCOTTS G – FUNCTION	
				Jour	RCA 22 20	Jan 75	KIM+,EQUIVALENT TO THESIS	
	2.5 – 2			Expt Data	EXFOR20657.	Aug 76	6PTS.SIGMA.	
(n,γ)	1.0 – 2	1.5+0	WUR	Expt Jour	NSE 60 53	May 76	Widder.TOF.CS VS.E GRPHS.2200M/S CS	+
				Rept	EIR – 217	Apr 75	– . EU NAT – 153.	
				Conf	74Petten 757	Sep 74	– . M – R DET,ABS.EXP.,NDG	
	1.0 – 2	1.6+0		Data	EXFOR20437.006	Nov 75	271PTS.SIGMA.	
(n,γ)	None		RCN	Revw Jour	ECN – 2	Sep 76	Zijp+ INTERCOMP. INTEGRAL SIG SAND – 2	
(n,γ)	1.0 – 2	1.0+5	HAR	Expt Jour	ANE 3 399	Nov 76	Moxon+LINAC.M – R.TBL.GRPHS. +.025EV	+
	1.0+2	1.0+5		Rept	EANDC(UK) – 158	Feb 74	– + AVERAGED. TOF. REL B10(N,A)	
	1.0+2	1.0+5		Data	EXFOR20489.003	Mar 76	27PTS.SIGMA.	
Spect (n,γ)	Maxwl		TAT	Expt Jour	NP 4 44	Aug 57	Bhattacherjee+. DECAY SCHEME DERIVED	
Spect (n,γ)	Maxwl		CCP	Expt Jour	AE 4 22	Jan 59	Sklyarevskii+.EGS+INTENS BELOW .3MEV	
				Jour	JNE 9 69	Jun 59	TRANSLATN.*	
				Jour	SJA 4 19	58	TRANSLATN.*	
Spect (n,γ)	Maxwl		KUR	Expt Conf	58Geneva 15 138	Sep 58	Groshev+ PPR2029.CURV,COMPTON – SPEC	
Spect (n,γ)	+0	+5	BNL	Expt Prog	WASH – 1006 6	Oct 58	Marshak+	
Spect (n,γ)	Pile		IPS	Expt Jour	NP 10 118	Feb 59	Nathan+.TBL OF 10 GAM INT.INT CONV.	
Spect (n,γ)	Pile		SAH	Expt Conf	59Calcutta 44	Feb 59	Mukherjee. INT – CONV,9H+13V HLS 152EV	
Spect (n,γ)	3.3 – 1	2.5+0	YAL	Expt Jour	NP 13 53	Oct 59	Draper+RESONANT CAPT,INT.OF 95KEV G.	
Spect (n,γ)	Maxwl		MUN	Revw Conf	60Vienna 63	Oct 60	Maierleibnitz.CURVE DISCUSS OF RESLT	
Spect (n,γ)	–		MUN	Expt Jour	ZN/A 16 927	Sep 61	Schult.LVLS IN EU152 XTAL SPECTROMET	
Spect (n,γ)	Pile		UPP	Expt Jour	NP 40 329	Jan 63	Marklund+.E DETERM. NO INTENS MEAS.	
Spect (n,γ)	None		FTI	Expt Jour	ZET 45 892	Oct 63	Berestovoj.GRPHS PROMPT+DELAYED G – SP	
				Jour	JET 18 613	Mar 64	TRANSLATN.*	
Spect (n,γ)	4.6 – 1		JAE	Expt Rept	JAERI – 1073	Mar 65	Kawarasaki. RES CAPT.LINAC.TOF.E,INT	+
				Rept	INDSWG – 90 6	Jul 65	– . TABLE E,INTS GIVEN.	
Spect (n,γ)	Pile		FTI	Expt Jour	YF 3 3	Jan 66	Voinova.NEW GAMMA LINES,GRAPH,TABLE	
				Jour	SNP 3 1	Jul 66	TRANSLATN.*	
Spect (n,γ)	Pile		MUN	Expt Jour	ZN/A 21 1328	Sep 66	Neumann. CRYST SPEC EXPT OF GAM INT	
				Rept	ANL – TRANS – 941	73	. ENGLISH OF ZN/A 1328	
Spect (n,γ)	Maxwl		LAS	Expt Prog	WASH – 1071 137	Nov 66	Shera. NDG	
Spect (n,γ)	Maxwl		IFL	Expt Jour	YF 5 929	May 67	Bondarenko+ CONV ELECS,E+REL INT.TBL	
				Jour	SNP 5 662	Nov 67	. ENGL OF YF 5 929	
Spect (n,γ)	Maxwl		FTI	Expt Jour	YF 7 1161	Jun 68	Borovikof+ GAM – SPEC – GRPH,DECAY – SCHEM	
				Jour	SNP 7 694	Dec 68	TRANSLATN.*	
Spect (n,γ)	+0	+4	COL	Expt Prog	WASH – 1124 31	Nov 68	Camarda+ MOXON – RAE DET TBC NO DATA	
Spect (n,γ)	Maxwl		KFI	Revw Jour	YF 10 907	Nov 69	Kecskemeti+ AVG GAM – MULTIPLICITY,TBL	
				Jour	SNP 10 524	May 70	TRANSLATN.*	
Spect (n,γ)	Maxwl		KFK	Expt Jour	NP/A 155 21	Oct 70	Michaelis.GE(LI) 273LINES 150 – 877KEV	+
	Maxwl			Data	EXFOR20153.002	Oct 73	272PTS.	
Spect (n,γ)	4.0 – 3	4.6 – 1	BNL	Expt Prog	USNDC – 1 37	May 72	Kane+ HIGH – E GAMMAS. NO DATA GIVEN	
Spect (n,γ)	None		VBT	Expt Jour	ZP 256 387	Dec 72	Baker+ LVL – SCHEMES OF GD – 152 +SM – 152	
Spect (n,γ)	Maxwl		IFL	Expt Book	PROKOFJEV	73	. TBL CONV ELECTR ES+INT(20 – 225KEV)	
Spect (n,γ)	3.2 – 1	3.4+0	BNL	Expt Abst	BAP 18 36	Jan 73	Breitig+ GE((I) DET. SPEC OF 5RESON	
Spect (n,γ)	Maxwl		CCP	Theo Jour	ZET 65 12	Jul 73	Nosov+ THERMODYN CALC CFD EXPT,GRAPH	
				Jour	JET 38 6	Jan 74	. ENGLISH OF ZET 65 6	
Spect (n,γ)	Pile		GER	Expt Jour	ZP/A 273 239	Jul 75	Hauser+ INT CONVERSION OF EU – 152ISOM	
Spect (n,γ)	Pile		WUR	Expt Rept	EIR – 285	Jul 75	Pruys+ LVL SCH EU152 ISOM	
(n,2n)	1.5+7		ARK	Expt Jour	PR 118 242	Apr 60	Wille+ MEAS ACT SIG= 500+ – 200 MB	+
	1.5+7			Data	EXFOR12033.033	Jun 76	. 1 PT. SIGMA	
(n,2n)	Fiss		CRC	Eval Rept	CRC – 1003	Dec 60	Roy+,ESTIMATED AVG SIG=4.8MB	
(n,2n)	1.5+7		MUA	Expt Jour	NP 28 560	Dec 61	Khurana+ ACTIV,CFD STATMOD	+
	1.5+7			Data	EXFOR31247.016	Mar 73	.SIG GVN	
(n,2n)	1.5+7		IRK	Expt Jour	NP 51 329	Feb 64	Spenke.ACTIVATION,ABS BETA COUNT	+
				Jour	OAWA 100 197	Jun 63	– . SUPERSEDED	
	1.5+7			Data	EXFOR20058.002	Sep 71	1PNT.SIG.	
(n,2n)	1.4+7		HAM	Comp Jour	NP 65 257	Mar 65	Bormann. 3EXPT VALS.CFD SHELL EFFECT	
(n,2n)	1.3+7	1.5+7	BNL	Theo Jour	NSE 23 238	Nov 65	Pearlstein.3ES.STAT MDL CALC.TBL CS.	

63 Europium 151

Quantity	Energy (ev) Min	Max	Lab	Type	Documentation Ref Vol Page	Date	Author, Comments	Data
(n,2n)	Fiss		BNL Theo	Jour	NSE 23 238	Nov 65	Pearlstein.STATMDL CALC.SPEC AVG.TBL	
(n,2n)	1.4+7		LYO Comp	Rept	LYCEN/6780	Nov 67	Crouzet+COMPILATN FOR ACTIVTN ANALYS	
(n,2n)	1.5+7		DEB Comp	Jour	REA 7 4 93	Dec 69	Csikai+ SIG+HL COMPILTN,N−ACTIV−ANAL	
(n,2n)	1.4+7	1.5+7	JYV Eval	Rept	JU−RR−3/1970	Jun 70	Leppaemaeki+ TABLE OF EVAL AVG SIG	
(n,2n)	1.4+7	1.5+7	IRK ExTh	Jour	APA 33 285	Jul 71	Winiwarter+ ISOMERIC RATIO	
(n,2n)	1.5+7		ARK Expt	Abst	DA/B 32 5091	Mar 72	Bari. GE(LI) DET. ACT. SIG GIVEN	+
	1.5+7			Data	EXFOR10431.003	Aug 75	. 1PT, SIGMA.	
(n,2n)	1.5+7		LRL Expt	Jour	NP/A 190 635	Aug 72	Nethaway. D−T NS. 1180+−150 MB	+
	1.5+7			Data	EXFOR10312.006	May 75	. 1PNT, SIGMA.	
(n,2n)	1.5+7		DEB Eval	Jour	REA 11 1 153	Mar 73	Boedy+ RECOMM.VALUE FROM N−Z SYSTEM.	
(n,2n)	1.5+7		KFI Theo	Rept	KFKI−73−68	Dec 73	Jeki.NEW FIT,CALC SIG CFD OTHERS,TBL	
(n,2n)	1.5+7		TAT Theo	Jour	JP/A 7 1457	Aug 74	Kondaiah. CALC ON STAT MODEL	
(n,2n)	1.5+7		JUL Expt	Jour	NP/A 224 319	May 74	Qaim. ACT.GE(LI).TO GRND, METAST	+
				Jour	RRL 25 335	May 76	− + SIG IN GRPH. SYST VS (N−Z)/A	
	1.5+7			Data	EXFOR20541.	Apr 76	4PTS.SIGMA.	
(n,xn) x>2	Fiss		BNL Theo	Jour	NSE 23 238	Nov 65	Pearlstein.SPEC AVG STATMDL CALC N3N	
(n,xn) x>2	1.5+7	2.8+7	LAS Expt	Jour	PR/C 12 451	Aug 75	Bayhurst+N3N,N4N.TBL,GRPH.CFD CALC.	+
	1.5+7	2.8+7		Data	EXFOR10536.	Apr 76	. 9PTS. N3N, 2PTS N4N.	
(n,p)	Fiss		CRC Eval	Rept	CRC−1003	Dec 60	Roy+,ESTIMATED AVG SIG=0.1MB	
(n,p)	Maxwl		IFU Theo	Rept	ICD−4 20	67	Dadakina+ PENETR COEFF CALC,TABLE	
(n,p)	1.4+7	1.5+7	ARK Theo	Prog	ORO−3235−29	Jan 67	Koch+,STAT MODEL CALC CFD EXPTS	
(n,p)	1.4+7		LYO Comp	Rept	LYCEN/6780	Nov 67	Crouzet+COMPILATN FOR ACTIVTN ANALYS	
(n,α)	Fiss		CRC Eval	Rept	CRC−1003	Dec 60	Roy+,ESTIMATED AVG SIG=0.0068MB	
(n,α)	Maxwl		CCP Expt	Jour	YF 1 252	Feb 65	Andreev.IONIZ−CHAMBER,SIG=.009MB	+
				Jour	SNP 1 177	Aug 65	TRANSLATN.*	
(n,α)	Maxwl		LEB Expt	Conf	65Antwerp § 176	Jul 65	Andreev+CFD TH 9+−2MICROB	
(n,α)	1.4+7		LYO Comp	Rept	LYCEN/6780	Nov 67	Crouzet+COMPILATN FOR ACTIVTN ANALYS	
(n,α)	1.4+7		AUW Expt	Jour	NP/A 125 57	Feb 69	RAMA PRASAD+,ACTIVATION,CFD OTHERS	+
	1.4+7			Data	EXFOR30051.	Dec 70	SIGMA NA,ALSO N2N+NA+NP FOR OTHERS.	
(n,α)	1.5+7		DEB Comp	Jour	REA 7 4 93	Dec 69	Csikai+ SIG+HL COMPILTN,N−ACTIV−ANAL	
(n,α)	Maxwl	9.0+2	DUB Expt	Rept	JINR−P3−4982	Apr 70	Kvitek+ ALFA SPEC GRAPHS,ALFA WIDTH	
(n,α)	1.4+7	1.5+7	JYV Eval	Rept	JU−RR−3/1970	Jun 70	Leppaemaeki+ TABLE OF EVAL AVG SIG	
(n,α)	3.2−1	3.7+0	DUB Expt	Rept	JINR−P3−7376	Sep 73	Balabanov+ RES−E,ALF−WID,SPIN,TABLE	
	+2	1.0+3		Conf	73Kiev 2 148	May 73	− + TOT ALF−WID,CFD OPTMDL	
(n,α)	Maxwl		LYO Expt	Jour	NP/A 231 437	Oct 74	Emsallem+ILL HF REACTOR,SIG+GRPH+TBL	+
	2.5−2			Data	EXFOR20564.003	Sep 75	1PNT.SIGMA.	
(n,α)	1.4+7		IBJ Expt	Prog	INDC(SEC)−42	Dec 74	Glowacka+ TBL DIFFSIG,GRPH E+ANG−DIS	+
	1.4+7			Data	EXFOR30298.	Jul 75	DOUBLE DIFFSIG(36 PTS)+ANGDIST(1 PT)	
(n,α)	1.8+7		IBJ Expt	Jour	NP/A 244 117	Jun 75	Glowacka+ ALF E−SPEC CFD MODLS,GRAPH	+
	1.4+7	1.8+7		Jour	ASL 25 203	75	− + A−SPEC AT 2ES,CFD THEO,FIG	
	1.8+7			Prog	INR−1464 1	May 73	− +BRIEF,ALPHA SPECTRUM,TABLES	
	1.8+7			Data	EXFOR30261.	Nov 73	ALFA−SPEC(38 PTS)+SIGMA AT 35 DEGREE	
(n,α)	1.9+7		BRC Theo	Conf	76Lowell 347	Jul 76	Cindro.N−INDUCED REAC.MED.−HVY.NUCL.	
Reson Params	3.0+4		ORL Expt	Jour	PR 70 557	Nov 46	Borst.	
Reson Params	3.3−1	7.4+0	BNL Expt	Jour	PR 93 1292	Mar 54	Sailor+	+
	3.3−1	7.4+0		Data	EXFOR12109.	Jun 76	. 6 RES, E0,WT,WN,PCS,WT**2/PCS	
Reson Params	−.1−1	7.4+0	BNL Expt	Jour	PR 95 453	Jul 54	Wood. ACT 7RESON ES ONLY	+
	−.1−3	7.4+0		Data	EXFOR11613.002	Jun 76	. 7 RES, E0.	
Reson Params	6.0−4	6.0−4	KJL Expt	Abst	PR 98 1162	May 55	Holt.ABSTRACT HA11. TOT(RES)=8.4E+4B	+
	−.6−3			Data	EXFOR20103.	Sep 71	2PTS.WG,TOT(RES).	
Reson Params	4.0+0	1.8+1	BNL Expt	Conf	ORNL−2309	Jun 57	Block+ PRELIM 20ES AV D D9PMD2EV	+
	4.0+0	1.0+1		Prog	WASH−192 13	Mar 57	Zimmerman+ NDG	
	4.8+0	2.7+1		Data	EXFOR12224.	Jun 76	. 20 RES. E0 AND WN0.	
Reson Params	1.0+0	1.0+1	ORL Expt	Conf	ORNL−2309	Jun 57	Block+ FC 14ES AV D D65EV	+
	1.1+0	9.0+0		Prog	ORNL−2204 33	Feb 57	Harvey+	
	1.1+0	9.0+0		Data	EXFOR11613.002	Jun 76	. 11 RES, E0,WN,WT**2	
Reson Params	1.1+0	3.7+0	BNL Expt	Jour	PR 114 1577	Jun 59	Domanic+ WG AND WN FOR 4 RESONANCES.	+
				Jour	PRL 2 488	Jun 59	.SUPERSEDED	
	1.1+0	9.1+0		Data	EXFOR11688.002	Jun 76	12 RES E0, WG, WN0, WT, TOT PCS.	
Reson Params	3.2−1	4.6−1	BNL Expt	Jour	NSE 10 169	Jun 61	Tassan+ LOW ENERGY RESONANCES	+
	3.2−1	4.6−1		Data	EXFOR12151.003	Jun 76	. 2 RES E0,WG,WN0,WT,TOT PCS.	
Reson Params	3.2−1	3.4+0	NRL Expt	Jour	PR/B 134 68	Apr 64	Stolovy. SPIN STATES ASSIGNED	+
	3.2−1	3.4+0		Data	EXFOR11436.002	Jun 76	. 4 RES. E0 AND J.	
Reson Params	3.3−1	1.1+0	BNL Expt	Prog	WASH−1056 14	Mar 65	Passell.3RES,ALL J=I+1/2	
Reson Params	−		KFK Eval	Rept	KFK−352	Aug 65	Schmidt.AVERAGE S−WAWE RES PAR(TAB.6	
Reson Params	−.6−2	2.7+1	MOL Eval	Rept	BLG−421	66	Damle+. RECOMMENDED PARAMS 28RESON	
Reson Params	+3		LAS Eval	Rept	LA−3643	Dec 66	Barr+ ESTIMATED RES PARS CFD EXPTS	
Reson Params		1.0+6	AUA Theo	Jour	AUJ 20 477	Oct 67	Cook. TBL OF AVG LVL SPACING D,L=0,1	

63 Europium 151

Quantity	Energy (ev) Min	Max	Lab	Type	Documentation Ref Vol Page	Date	Author, Comments	Data
Reson Params	+3	+5	AUA	ExTh Rept	AAEC/E – 198	May 69	Musgrove.RES PARS +STF FROM (NG)FIT	+
Reson Params	Maxwl	9.0+2	DUB	Expt Rept	JINR – P3 – 4982	Apr 70	Kvitek+ ALFA WIDTH GIVEN,N – RESONANCS	
Reson Params	–		AUA	Theo Rept	AAEC/E – 211	Nov 70	Musgrove. CALCULTD D+GAM WIDTH GIVEN	
Reson Params	3.0 – 1	3.7+0	CJD	Eval Rept	YK – 7	71	Zakharova+ SURVEY+SYSTEMATICS,GW,TBL	
				Rept	INDC(CCP) – 27	Nov 72	.ENGLISH TRANSLATION OF YK – 7 /71	
Reson Params	None		DUB	Theo Jour	YF 13 240	Feb 71	Malecki+G – WID,THEO CFD EXPT.TBL,GRPH	
				Jour	SNP 13 133	Aug 71	+ ENGL OF YF 13 240.	
Reson Params	3.2 – 1	1.1+2	IFU	Expt Prog	YFI – 10 44	May 71	Vertebny+ ABST,TBL OF RESONANCE – ES	
				Rept	INDC(CCP) – 15	Dec 71	*P50,ENG OF YFI – 10	
Reson Params	–.4 – 2		MOL	Expt Jour	NP/A 172 489	Sep 71	Poortmans+ 1 LVL FIT TO TOT C.S.	+
	–.3 – 2			Data	EXFOR20221.	May 74	. 2PTS.WT,S0*E1/2.	
Reson Params	None		COL	Expt Jour	NSE 48 219	Jun 72	Rahn+. AVG WG=90MEV OVER 70RESON	
Reson Params	3.2 – 1	9.9+1	COL	Expt Jour	PR/C 6 251	Jul 72	Rahn+. G*WN FOR 105RES.SOME WG,AVG D	+
	None			Conf	75Wash. 780	Mar 75	Hacken+ TBL AVG WG,STF,NUMBER GWN,WG	
	1.1+0	9.9+1		Rept	NYO – 72 – 281	Oct 70	Rahn.SEE FOR DETAILS.	
	1.1+0	9.9+2		Data	EXFOR10046.032	Jan 78	. 103 RES ES.WN RED*G,WG.D GVN.	
Reson Params	3.2 – 1	3.4+0	BNL	Expt Abst	BAP 18 36	Jan 73	Breitig+ 5 RESONANCES.	
Reson Params	3.2 – 1	3.7+0	DUB	Expt Rept	JINR – P3 – 7376	Sep 73	Balabanov+ RES – E,ALF – WID,SPIN,TABLE	
	+2	1.0+3		Conf	73Kiev 2 148	May 73	– + TOT ALF – WID,CFD OPTMDL	
Reson Params	+0	+2	BOL	Eval Conf	IAEA – 169 3 123	74	Benzi+ AVG G – WID CFD OTHERS+XPT,TABL	
Reson Params	– 1	+2	FEI	Eval Rept	YK – 8/2 97	Sep 72	Abagyan+ AVG G – WID+D AT BINDNG – E,TBL	
				Rept	INDC(CCP) – 39	Jul 74	.PAGE 102.ENGLISH OF YK – 8/2 97	
Reson Params	None		RPI	Expt Conf	75Wash. 905	Mar 75	Hockenbury+ AVG WG,D	
Reson Params	–.2 – 1	1.8+0	HAR	Expt Jour	ANE 3 399	Nov 76	Moxon+LINAC.M – R.TBL ADJ LOW E ERSPAR	
Strnth Fnctn	1.0+0	1.0+1	ORL	Expt Conf	ORNL – 2309	Jun 57	Block+ FC 3D1PMD8.	
Strnth Fnctn		+3	BNL	Expt Jour	PRL 1 461	Dec 58	Hughes. FC 2.7+ – 0.5	
	6.0+3			Conf	ORNL – 2309	Jun 57	Block+ PRELIM 2D7PMD5 20RES AVG2WAYS	
Strnth Fnctn	8.0 – 1	5.0+4	LEB	Expt Conf	JINR – 1845 100	Jun 64	Konks+ PB – SLOWDOWN – TIME, TABLE	
Strnth Fnctn	+0	+2	MOL	Eval Rept	BLG – 421	66	Damle+. RECOMMENDED S0=3.35+ – 0.5META	
Strnth Fnctn		5.0+4	RI	Expt Prog	YFI – 5 59	Oct 67	Konks+ TABLE	
				Rept	INDC – 232E	Jan 69	. ENGL OF YFI – 5 59	
Strnth Fnctn	1.0+0	5.0+4	DUB	Expt Jour	YF 7 493	Mar 68	Konks+ TABLE OF S0+S1 VALS,CFD OTHER	
				Jour	SNP 7 310	Sep 68	– + ENGL OF YF 7 493.	
Strnth Fnctn	+3	+5	AUA	ExTh Rept	AAEC/E – 198	May 69	Musgrove.S+P+D STF FROM (NG)FIT,TBL	+
Strnth Fnctn	–		AUA	Theo Rept	AAEC/E – 211	Nov 70	Musgrove. SMOOTHED S0,S1 AND S2 GIVN	
Strnth Fnctn	None		KFK	Expt Rept	KFK – EXT – 4 28	Nov 70	Chou. S1=0.37	
Strnth Fnctn	3.2 – 1	9.9+1	COL	Expt Jour	PR/C 6 251	Jul 72	Rahn+. S0=3.2+ – 0.5	+
	None			Conf	75Wash. 780	Mar 75	Hacken+ NEVIS TOF S – WAVE STF	
	1.1+0	9.9+1		Rept	NYO – 72 – 281	Oct 70	Rahn.EXPT DETAILS	
	0.0+0	1.0+2		Data	EXFOR10046.019	Jan 78	. 1PT, S0=(3.25+ – .51) – 4	
Strnth Fnctn	None		AUA	Eval Rept	AAEC/E – 277	Mar 73	Musgrove.TBLS EXPTL DATA+BEST VALUES	
Strnth Fnctn	None		RPI	Expt Conf	75Wash. 905	Mar 75	Hockenbury+ AVG S0,S1	
Lvl Density	–		COP	Theo Jour	NP 6 62	Mar 58	Ericson. LVL DENSITY FORM CFD EXP	
Lvl Density	–		FEI	Eval Rept	FEI – 36	66	Kapchigashev+.TBL OF RELATD QUANTTYS	
		5.0+4		Jour	YF 4 686	Sep 66	.TABLE.SHORT VERSION OF FEI – 36	
	–			Prog	YFI – 3 3	66	.ABSTRACT.TABLE LDL+NUCL.EXCIT.E	
		5.0+4		Jour	SNP 4 486	67	.ENGLISH OF YF 4.FROM(N,GAMMA).TABLE	
				Prog	INDC – E – 140 3	66	.INGLSH TRANSL OF YFI – 3	
Lvl Density	2.5+4		AUW	Expt Conf	70Madurai 2 19	Dec 70	Lakshmana.EXPTL SPIN – CUT – OFF CFD TH	+
	2.5+4			Data	EXFOR30246.032	Jun 73	SPIN CUT – OFF FACTOR FROM NG REACTION	
Lvl Density	None		AUW	Theo Conf	70Madurai 2 267	Dec 70	Ramamurty+ A – PARAMETER GVN,LANG'S – TH	
Lvl Density	None		BOL	Eval Conf	IAEA – 169 3 123	74	Benzi+ LVL DENS PARAM BY XPT,GRPH+TB	
Lvl Density	– 1	+2	FEI	Eval Rept	YK – 8/2 97	Sep 72	Abagyan+ LVL DENSITY PARAMETER,TBL	
				Rept	INDC(CCP) – 39	Jul 74	.PAGE 102.ENGLISH OF YK – 8/2 97	
(γ,n)	8.0+6	2.2+7	CCP	Expt Jour	ZEP 11 520	Jun 70	Vasil'Ev+ EXPTL SIG(GAMMA – E) GRAPH	

63 Europium 152

Quantity	Energy (ev) Min	Max	Lab	Type	Documentation Ref Vol Page	Date	Author, Comments	Data
Evaluation	1.0 – 2	2.0+7	BNL	Eval Rept	BNL – 19456	Nov 74	Takahashi.GRPH.	
Total	2.0 – 2	2.0 – 1	IJI	Expt Conf	75Kiev 3 145	May 75	Vertebnyj+ 12.4YRS.SIG(E) GRAPH	
Diff Inelast	Maxwl		LIN	Expt Jour	AE 36 77	Jan 74	Kondurov+ MS TO GND,SIG FOR N – ACCEL	
				Jour	SJA 36 92	Jul 74	. ENGL OF AE 36 77	
Absorption	2.5 – 2		IJI	Eval Conf	75Kiev 1 169	May 75	Fedorova+ EVAL 2200M/S SIG,TABLE	
(n,γ)	Maxwl		ANL	Expt Jour	PR 75 1500	May 49	Hayden+ ISOTOPIC DILUTION,TO + – 15PC	+
	Maxwl			Data	EXFOR12138.004	Jun 76	. 1 PT. SIGMA (SPA).	
(n,γ)	+3		LAS	Eval Rept	LA – 3643	Dec 66	Barr+ ESTIMATED SIGS CFD EXPTS	

63 Europium 152

Quantity	Energy (ev) Min	Max	Lab	Type	Documentation Ref Vol Page	Date	Author, Comments	Data
(n,γ)	1.0+3	6.0+3	LAS	Expt Prog	WASH – 1127 123	Apr 69	Harlow+ POMMARD EVENT,RATIO TO EU151	
(n,γ)	2.5–2	3.4+0	JAE	Expt Prog	EANDC(J)19L1	Aug 70	Asami+.GE(LI),ISOM RATIO	
(n,γ)	Maxwl		CRC	Comp Rept	AECL – 3037 1	Jan 72	Walker.TBL OF CORRECTED EXPTAL SIGS	
Spect (n,γ)	Pile		HEB	ExTh Jour	NP 4 477	Sep 57	Ofer. ANGULAR CORR. DECAY SCHEME.	
Spect (n,γ)	Maxwl		BNL	Expt Jour	PR 115 1287	Sep 59	Patronis+,SC SPECT,81 AND 92 KEV GS	
Spect (n,γ)	Pile		MUN	Expt Jour	ZN/A 21 1328	Sep 66	Neumann. CRYST SPEC EXPT OF GAM INT	
				Rept	ANL – TRANS – 941	73	. ENGLISH OF ZN/A 1328	
Spect (n,γ)	Maxwl		MUN	Expt Jour	ZP 230 18	Dec 69	Muehlbauer. LVL – SCH OF EU153	+
				Conf	69Studsvik 65	Aug 69	Koch+ ANALYSIS TBC. NDG.	
	2.5–2			Data	EXFOR20604.	Jul 76	87PTS.	
(n,p)	Maxwl		IFU	Theo Rept	ICD – 4 20	67	Dadakina+ PENETR COEFF CALC,TABLE	
Reson Params	1.8+0	9.0+0	BNL	Expt Jour	PR 95 453	Jul 54	Wood. ACT 5RESON ES ONLY	
Reson Params	+3		LAS	Eval Rept	LA – 3643	Dec 66	Barr+ ESTIMATED RES PARS CFD EXPTS	
Reson Params	–		AUA	Theo Rept	AAEC/E – 211	Nov 70	Musgrove. CALCULTD D+GAM WIDTH GIVEN	
Reson Params	1.4+1		IJI	Expt Conf	76Lowell 1254	Jul 76	Vertebnyi+ AVG WG,D GVN.WG,G*WN TABL	
Strnth Fnctn	–		AUA	Theo Rept	AAEC/E – 211	Nov 70	Musgrove. SMOOTHED S0,S1 AND S2 GIVN	
Lvl Density	+6		MIL	Theo Jour	EN 15 1 54	Jan 68	Facchini+ LDL PARS FROM LOW EN RES	
Lvl Density	None		MUN	Theo Jour	NP/A 217 269	Dec 73	Dilg+ A,DELTA. BACK SHIFTED FERMIGAS	
Lvl Density	None		COP	Theo Jour	NP/A 222 493	Apr 74	Dossing+COLL ROTAT.SPAC. ACCUR ESTIM	
Lvl Density	None		ROC	Theo Jour	NP/A 223 589	May 74	Huizenga+ EXP CFD MICROSC TH AX SYMM	

63 Europium 153

Quantity	Energy (ev) Min	Max	Lab	Type	Documentation Ref Vol Page	Date	Author, Comments	Data
Evaluation	2.5–2	1.0+7	KFK	Eval Rept	KFK – 352	Aug 65	Schmidt+.RES NG	
Evaluation	1.0–3	1.5+7	AUA	Eval Rept	AAEC/TM – 549	Jun 70	Cook.TOT,EL,INEL,NONEL,CAPT SIGS,NDG	+
				Rept	AAEC/E – 214	Jun 71	Bertram+GROUP SIGMAS SAME QUANTS.NDG	
				Rept	AAEC/TM – 587	Mar 71	*DESCRIPTION OF LIBRARY	
	1.0–3	1.5+7		Data	AUSTR – DFN 165.	Nov 71	POINT(223) AND GROUP(127) SIGMAS	
Evaluation	None		SAC	Eval Prog	EANDC(E) – 157U2	May 73	Ribon.	
Evaluation	1.0–5	2.0+7	BNL	Eval Rept	BNL – 19455	Nov 74	Takahashi.GRPH.	
Evaluation		9.0+3	WIN	Eval Rept	UKNDC(75)P71	Jul 75	Smith.GENEX DATA PREPARED	
Total	–2	+1	HAR	Expt Conf	58Geneva 16 44	Sep 58	Pattenden.PPR11,CURVE,CRYSTALSPECTRM	
Total	1.0+0	1.0+1	BNL	Expt Jour	PR 114 1577	Jun 59	Domanic+ CS CURVES GIVEN.	
Total	1.0–2	3.0–1	IFU	Expt Prog	YFI – 12 74	Jun 71	Verteby+	+
	1.0–2	3.0–1		Data	EXFOR40109.002	Dec 72	SIGMA AT 30 ES	
Total	1.0–3	1.5+7	AUA	Eval Data	AUSTR – DFN 165.	Nov 71	COOK+POINT(223)+GROUP(127)SIG.CF EVL	+
Total	1.0–2	3.0–1	IJI	Expt Prog	YFI – 12 74	72	Vertebny+ ABSTRACT,TBL SIG(N – E)	
				Prog	INDC(CCP) – 30	Sep 72	.PAGE 64,ENGLISH OF YFI – 12 74	
Total	8.1–1	5.2+3	COL	Expt Jour	PR/C 6 251	Jul 72	Rahn+TRNS.CURVS.RES PAR ANAL	
	9.8–1	5.2+3		Jour	PR/C 6 251	Jul 72	– +TRNS,SELF INDIC.RES PAR ANAL.	
	4.6+1	3.0+3		Rept	NYO – 72 – 281	Oct 70	– .SEE FOR DETAILS	
Total	–3	1.9+0	THS	Theo Rept	IKE – 6 89 65	Jun 75	Keinert. DATA LIBRARY	
Total	2.0+3		IJI	Expt Conf	76Lowell 1244	Jul 76	Vertebnyi+ TRANSM VS THICKNESS,NDG	
				Conf	75Kiev 3 151	May 75	Vertebnyj+ RES – NEUT FILTRAT.SIG GIVN	
Elastic	1.4–2		ORL	Expt Jour	PRL 27 741	Sep 71	Nielsen+ COH SCAT AMP	+
	1.4–2			Data	EXFOR10185.002	Jul 72	. 1 PT.	
Elastic	1.0–3	1.5+7	AUA	Eval Data	AUSTR – DFN 165.	Nov 71	COOK+POINT(223)+GROUP(127)SIG.CF EVL	+
Elastic	2.5–2		IJI	Eval Conf	75Kiev 1 169	May 75	Fedorova+ EVAL 2200M/S SIG,TABLE	
Potntal Scat	2.0+3		IJI	Expt Conf	76Lowell 1244	Jul 76	Vertebnyi+ SCT – LNGTH GVN,FRM TOT+SCT	
Tot Inelastc	5.0+5	1.5+7	AUA	Eval Data	AUSTR – DFN 165.	Nov 71	COOK+POINT(11)+GROUP(127)SIG.CF EVL	+
Scattering	2.0–2	3.0–2	IFU	Expt Conf	70Helsinki 1 651	Jun 70	Vertebnij+ 2200M/SEC SIGMA GIVEN,TBL	
				Rept	BNL – TR – 495	Jul 72	. ENGLISH OF 70HELSIN 1 651	
Scattering	+7		IJI	Expt Conf	77Kiev	77	Trofimova+ SIG	
	2.0+3			Conf	76Lowell 1244	Jul 76	Vertebnyi+ SCT – SIG VS THICKNESS,NDG	
				Conf	75Kiev 3 151	May 75	Vertebnyj+ RES – NEUT FILTRAT.SIG GIVN	
Nonelastic	1.0–3	1.5+7	AUA	Eval Data	AUSTR – DFN 165.	Nov 71	COOK+POINT(223)+GROUP(127)SIG.CF EVL	+
Nonelastic	2.0+3		IJI	Expt Conf	75Kiev 3 151	May 75	Vertebnyj+ RES – NEUT FILTRAT.SIG GIVN	
Absorption	2.5–2		HAR	Expt Jour	JNEA 12 32	May 60	Tattersall+. PILE OSCILLATOR	+
				Rept	AERE – R – 2887	Aug 59	– . PILE OSC.REL BORON	
	2.5–2			Data	EXFOR20638.052	Jul 76	1PNT.SIGMA.	
Absorption	4.1–1	1.0+7	GA	Eval Rept	GA – 2451	Aug 61	Joanou+.68GROUP DATA FOR GAM – I ABS	
Absorption	1.0–3	1.0+7	JUL	Eval Rept	JUEL – 678 – RG	Jul 70	Liu. EVALUATION+CALC,GRPH,FN OF E	
Absorption	1.0–3	2.0+0	JUL	Eval Rept	JUEL – 746 – RG144	Apr 71	Bonka.KUGEL – THERMOS.LIBR,CURVE	
Absorption	Pile		CRC	Eval Conf	73Paris 1 459	Mar 73	Walker.FISS PRODUCT ABS,TBL PILE SIG	
Absorption	2.5–2		IJI	Eval Conf	75Kiev 1 169	May 75	Fedorova+ EVAL 2200M/S SIG,TABLE	
Res Int Abs	None		ORL	Revw Conf	55Geneva 5 96	Aug 55	Macklin+.TABLE,EXPT CFD THEORY,P833	

63 Europium 153

Quantity	Energy (ev) Min	Max	Lab	Type	Documentation Ref Vol Page	Author, Comments Date	Data
Res Int Abs	None		CRC	Eval	Rept AECL-1054	Mar 60 Walker.(CRP-913) REDUCED RES.INT.	
Res Int Abs	None		ORL	Eval	Rept ORNL-2869	Mar 60 Nephew.1/V UP +TO100EV.ALSO 5 ES- UP	
Res Int Abs	5.0-1		HAR	Expt	Jour JNE 12 32	May 60 Tattersall+. ABOVE 1/V. OSC. CF CALC	+
					Rept AERE-R-2887	Aug 59 - . PILE OSC.REL BORON	
	6.7-1				Data EXFOR20638.053	Jul 76 1PNT.	
Res Int Abs	+3	+5	BOL	Theo	Conf 61Vienna 1 179	Aug 61 Benzi+.PPR11,VAL GVN,L=0,L=1 .CAPT.	
Res Int Abs	5.0-1		BOL	Eval	Conf 61Vienna 1 179	Aug 61 Benzi+ TBL TOTAL CAPT RES INTS.	
Res Int Abs	5.5-1		GA	Eval	Jour NSE 12 115	Jan 62 Garrison+,RI=1380+-200B,FROM RES.PAR	
Res Int Abs	5.0-1		BOL	Eval	Rept RT/FI-4	Jan 67 Palmucci. CALC FROM (N,G) RES PARAMS	
Res Int Abs	Pile		CPO	Expt	Jour JIN 29 2671	Nov 67 Sims+ ACTIVATION.RI FOR CAPTURE	+
	Pile				Data EXFOR12090.006	Jun 76 . RI ABS.	
Res Int Abs	5.0-1		MTR	Expt	Jour IN-1195	May 68 Scoville+	+
	5.0-1				Data EXFOR11820.010	Jun 76 . RI ABS.	
Res Int Abs	None		GA	Eval	Rept GA-12071	Sep 71 Mathews+. RECOMMENDED VALUES	
Res Int Abs	5.5-1		CRC	Eval	Rept AECL-3037 1	Jan 72 Walker.REDUCED RES INT,DETAILED TBL	
Res Int Abs	5.0-1		COL	Eval	Jour NSE 48 219	Jun 72 Rahn+. RI=1632+-195B	
Res Int Abs	5.0-1		AUA	Eval	Rept AAEC/TM-619	Sep 72 Clayton.CALC FROM SIG LIBRARY,TABLE	
Res Int Abs	4.6-1	1.0+6	RCN	Theo	Rept RCN-191	Jul 73 Lautenbach.CAPT INT FROM GROUP SIGMA	
Res Int Abs	5.0-1		GHT	Expt	Jour JRC 20 695	74 Van Der Linden+ BY(N,G).CFD OTHS,TBL	+
	5.5-1				Conf 73Paris 2 241	Mar 73 - + ACT,REL THR+GOLD,TBL	
	5.5-1				Data EXFOR20645.026	Jul 76 1PNT.CAPTURE.	
Res Int Abs	5.5-1	+6	SAC	Revw	Conf IAEA-169 1 235	74 Ribon.CAPTURE,STATUS CFD REQUEST,TBL	
Res Int Abs	+0	+5	WIN	Revw	Conf IAEA-169 3 163	74 Pope+ DATA FILE CALC CFD XPTAL VALUE	
Res Int Abs	5.0-1		IJI	Eval	Conf 75Kiev 1 169	May 75 Fedorova+ EVAL+CALC RI GIVEN,TABLE	
Res Int Abs	5.5-1		MUN	Expt	Diss GRYNTAKIS	Mar 76 Gryntakis.ACT 3414+-197 B, INCL 1/V	+
					Jour RCA 22 20	75 KIM+ACTIV.EQUIVALENT TO THESIS	
	5.5-1				Data EXFOR20657.011	Aug 76 1PNT.CAPTURE.	
(n,γ)	Maxwl		ANL	Expt	Rept PR 75 1500	May 49 Hayden+ ISOTOPIC DILUTION,TO +-15PC	+
(n,γ)	Maxwl				Data EXFOR12138.003	Jun 76 . 1 PT. SIGMA	
(n,γ)	Maxwl		CRC	Eval	Rept AECL-1054	Mar 60 Walker. (CRRP-913)	
(n,γ)	5.0-3	2.5+0	GA	Eval	Rept GA-2113	Jun 61 Wikner+.TABLE + CURVE.100 E POINTS	
(n,γ)	2.8-3	1.0+6	GA	Eval	Jour NSE 12 115	Jan 62 Garrison+.EVAL FROM XPT+AVERAGE RES	
(n,γ)	8.0-1	5.0+4	LEB	Expt	Conf JINR-1845 100	Jun 64 Konks. PB-SLOWDOWN, GRAPH SIG(E)	+
					Rept ICD-1 43	64 . BETTER GRAPH.(ENGL=INDSWG-64E)	
(n,γ)	2.5+1	3.0+4	KFK	Eval	Rept KFK-352	Aug 65 Schmidt+.GRAPHS+TABLE(NO.7)	
(n,γ)	1.0+3	1.0+4	LAS	Theo	Rept LA-3463	Jan 66 Bell. TH CAPTURE OF RARE EARTHS	
(n,γ)	+3		LAS	Eval	Rept LA-3643	Dec 66 Barr+ ESTIMATED SIGS CFD EXPTS	
(n,γ)	2.5-2		BOL	Eval	Rept RT/FI-4	Jan 67 Palmucci. CALC FROM RES PARAMETERS	
(n,γ)	Pile		CPO	Expt	Jour JIN 29 2671	Nov 67 Sims+ ACTIVATION.	+
	Pile				Data EXFOR12090.007	Jun 76 . 1 PT. SIGMA.	
(n,γ)	1.4+7		LYO	Comp	Rept LYCEN/6780	Nov 67 Crouzet+COMPILATN FOR ACTIVTN ANALYS	
(n,γ)	Maxwl		AUA	Theo	Jour NSE 31 234	Feb 68 Cook+ STATISTICAL CALC CFD EXPT	
(n,γ)	1.0+0	5.0+4	DUB	Expt	Jour YF 7 493	Mar 68 Konks+ SIG(NEUT-E) GRPH,PB-SLOW-DOWN	
					Jour SNP 7 310	Sep 68 - + ENGL OF YF 7 493.	
(n,γ)	2.5+1	1.0+4	LAS	Expt	Conf 68Wash. 837	Mar 68 Harlow+ TOF BOMB SOURCE CURVE	+
	None				Data EXFOR10324.	Dec 73 . 0 PTS. DATA WITHDRAWN.	
(n,γ)	-		IEA	Comp	Rept IEA-INF-10	Aug 68 Atalla. TABLES OF HL,SIG AND GAMM-E	
(n,γ)	1.0+3	1.0+7	BOL	Eval	Rept CCDN-NW/10	Dec 69 Benzi+H-F MOD,AXEL G(G)EST,ALL DATA	
					Rept CEC(70)-2	Apr 70 - +. GRAPH	
					Conf 66Paris 1 537	Oct 66 - + STATMOD.TBL AV VALS.SUPERSEDD	
					Jour NC 38 216	Jul 65 - + THEORY FOR CAPTURE EVALUATION	
					Conf 61Vienna 1 179	Aug 61 - + TBL AV VALS. SUPERSEDED.	
(n,γ)	3.0+4		AUA	Theo	Rept AAEC/E-211	Nov 70 Musgrove. SIGMA GIVEN AND CFD OTHER	
(n,γ)	Maxwl		GA	Eval	Rept GA-12071	Sep 71 Mathews+. RECOMMENDED VALUES	
(n,γ)	1.0-3	1.5+7	AUA	Eval	Data AUSTR-DFN 165.	Nov 71 COOK+POINT(223)+GROUP(127)SIG.CF EVL	+
(n,γ)	Maxwl		CRC	Eval	Rept AECL-3037 1	Jan 72 Walker.RECOMMENDED SIG,DETAILED TBL	
(n,γ)	2.5-2		IAE	Revw	Rept IAEA-143 897	Apr 72 Lemmel.RECENT EVALUATIONS,TABLE+GRPH	
(n,γ)	Maxwl				Rept IAEA-143 897	Apr 72 - .RECENT EVALUATIONS,TABLE	
(n,γ)	2.5-2		AUA	Eval	Rept AAEC/TM-619	Sep 72 Clayton.CALC FROM SIG LIBRARY,TABLE	
(n,γ)		1.1+7	RCN	Theo	Rept RCN-191	Jun 73 Lautenbach.GROUP CONSTANTS TBL	
(n,γ)	2.5-2	3.0+4	SAC	Revw	Conf IAEA-169 1 235	74 Ribon.STATUS SIG CFD REQUESTS,TABLE	
	Fiss				Conf IAEA-169 1 235	74 - .STATUS SIG CFD REQUESTS,TABLE	
(n,γ)	Fiss		WIN	Revw	Conf IAEA-169 3 137	74 Dean. POINT DATA AVG OVER STAND SPEC	
	Maxwl	Fiss			Conf IAEA-169 3 163	74 Pope+ MAXW+FIS-SPEC AVG DATA CFD XPT	
(n,γ)	1.0+3	1.0+7	FEI	Eval	Jour YK- 8/2 97	Sep 72 Abagjan+ AVG SIG(ENERGY-GROUPS),TABL	
					Rept INDC(CCP)-39	Jul 74 .P102. ENGLISH OF YK-8/2 97	
(n,γ)	1.0+2	1.0+7	BNL	Theo	Conf JAERI-M-5984	Feb 75 Takahashi.P257.CALC CFD EVAL AND EXP	
(n,γ)	Fast		INL	Expt	Abst BAP 20 173	Feb 75 Anderl+ SPECTRUM AVG SIG 75WASH	

63 Europium 153

Quantity	Energy (ev) Min	Max	Lab	Type	Documentation Ref Vol Page	Author, Comments Date	Data
(n,γ)	2.0+1	2.0+5	RPI Expt	Conf	75Wash. 905	Mar 75 Hockenbury+GRPH CFD CALC	+
	6.3+3	3.0+5		Data	EXFOR10435.003	Oct 74 . 566PTS, SIGMA.	
(n,γ)	1.0+3	3.7+5	FEI ExTh	Conf	75Kiev 3 190	May 75 Jurlov+ REL B10(N,A).SIG(E),GRAPH	
(n,γ)	Maxwl		MUNExTh	Diss	GRYNTAKIS	Mar 76 Gryntakis.,ACT.MEAS.,CALC OF G – FUNCT	+
	None		Theo	Jour	RCA 22 128	Mar 75 – +,CALC WESTCOTTS G – FUNCTION	
	Maxwl		ExTh	Jour	RCA 22 20	Jan 75 KIM+,EQUIVALENT TO THESIS	
	2.5 – 2		Expt	Data	EXFOR20657.010	Aug 76 1PNT.SIGMA.	
(n,γ)	1.0 – 2	1.0+1	WURExpt	Jour	NSE 60 53	May 76 Widder.TOF.CS VS.E GRPHS.2200M/S CS	+
	1.0 – 2	9.8+0		Rept	EIR – 217	Apr 75 – . POWDER SAMPLE	
				Conf	74Petten 757	Sep 74 – . M – R DET,ABS.EXP.,NDG	
	1.0 – 2	9.8+0		Data	EXFOR20437.007	Nov 75 286PTS.SIGMA.	
(n,γ)	Fast		RCN Expt	Rept	ECN – 10	Oct 76 Veeenema+ STEK REACTIVITY WORTHS TBL.	
(n,γ)	1.0 – 2	1.0+5	HAR Expt	Jour	ANE 3 399	Nov 76 Moxon+LINAC.M – R.TBL.GRPHS. +.025EV	+
	1.0+2	1.0+5		Rept	EANDC(UK) – 158	Feb 74 – + AVERAGED. TOF. REL B10(N,A)	
	1.0+2	1.0+5		Data	EXFOR20489.004	Mar 76 27PTS.SIGMA.	
Spect (n,γ)	Maxwl		TAT Expt	Jour	NP 4 44	Aug 57 Bhattacherjee+. DECAY SCHEME DERIVED	
Spect (n,γ)	+0	+5	BNL Expt	Prog	WASH – 1006 6	Oct 58 Marshak+	
Spect (n,γ)	3.3 – 1	2.5+0	YAL Expt	Jour	NP 13 53	Oct 59 Draper+,RESONANT CAPT,INT.OF 74+94KEV	
Spect (n,γ)	Maxwl		MUNExpt	Jour	ZN/A 18 576	May 63 Orecher+ROENTGEN SPECTROMETRY	
Spect (n,γ)	Maxwl		CCP Expt	Jour	IZV 30 394	66 Dzhelepov+.TBL+GRAPHS,ELOTRON	
				Jour	IZV 30 1265	Aug 66 – +.TABLE+GRAPH OF GAM – SPECTR	
				Jour	BAS 30 401	66 . ENGL OF IZV 30 394	
				Jour	BAS 30 1322	66 .ENGLISH TRANSLATION	
Spect (n,γ)	Pile		MUNExpt	Jour	ZN/A 21 1328	Sep 66 Neumann. CRYST SPEC EXPT OF GAM INT	
				Rept	ANL – TRANS – 941	73 . ENGLISH OF ZN/A 1328	
Spect (n,γ)	Maxwl		LAS Expt	Prog	WASH – 1071 137	Nov 66 Shera. NDG	
Spect (n,γ)	Maxwl		IFL Expt	Jour	YF 5 929	May 67 Bondarenko+ CONV ELECS,E+REL INT.TBL	
				Jour	SNP 5 662	Nov 67 . ENGL OF YF 5 929	
Spect (n,γ)	+0	+4	COL Expt	Jour	WASH – 1124 31	Nov 68 Camarda+ MOXON – RAE DET TBC NO DATA	
Spect (n,γ)	Maxwl		JUL Expt	Jour	ZP 255 450	Nov 72 Delang+,ANG – CORR MEASURM. OF GD – 154	
(n,2n)	1.5+7		ARK Expt	Jour	PR 118 242	Apr 60 Wille+ MEAS ACT SIG= 750+ – 200 MB	+
	1.5+7			Data	EXFOR12033.034	Jun 76 . 1 PT. SIGMA	
(n,2n)	Fiss		CRC Eval	Rept	CRC – 1003	Dec 60 ROY+ ESTIMATED AVG SIG=4.4MB	
(n,2n)	1.5+7		MUAExpt	Jour	NP 28 560	Dec 61 Khurana+ ACTIV,CFD STATMOD	
	1.5+7			Data	EXFOR31247.017	Mar 73 .SIG GVN	
(n,2n)	1.4+7		HAMCompJour		NP 65 257	Mar 65 Bormann. 2EXPT VALS.CFD SHELL EFFECT	
(n,2n)	1.3+7	1.5+7	BNL Theo	Jour	NSE 23 238	Nov 65 Pearlstein.3ES.STAT MDL CALC.TBL CS.	
(n,2n)	Fiss		BNL Theo	Jour	NSE 23 238	Nov 65 Pearlstein.STATMDL CALC.SPEC AVG.TBL	
(n,2n)	1.4+7		LYO Comp	Rept	LYCEN/6780	Nov 67 Crouzet+COMPILATN FOR ACTIVTN ANALYS	
(n,2n)	1.5+7		TUR Theo	Jour	NC 56 18 201	Jul 68 Minetti+THEOR ISOM RATIO SPIN CO PAR	
(n,2n)	1.4+7		AUWExpt	Jour	NP/A 125 57	Feb 69 RAMA PRASAD+,ACTIVATION,CFD OTHERS	+
	1.4+7			Data	EXFOR30051.	Dec 70 SIGMA N2N,ALSO N2N+NA+NP FOR OTHERS.	
(n,2n)	1.5+7		DEB Comp	Jour	REA 7 4 93	Dec 69 Csikai+ SIG+HL COMPILTN,N – ACTIV – ANAL	
(n,2n)	1.4+7	1.5+7	JYV Eval	Rept	JU – RR – 3/1970	Jun 70 Leppaemaeki+ TABLE OF EVAL AVG SIG	
(n,2n)	1.5+7		ARK Expt	Abst	DA/B 32 5091	Mar 72 Bari. GE(LI) DET. ACT. SIG GIVEN	
	1.5+7			Data	EXFOR10431	Aug 75 . 2PTS, SIGMA, PROD 2 META STATES	
(n,2n)	1.5+7		DEB Eval	Jour	REA 11 1 153	Mar 73 Boedy+ RECOMM.VALUE FROM N – Z SYSTEM.	
(n,2n)	1.5+7		KFI Theo	Rept	KFKI – 73 – 68	Dec 73 Jeki.NEW FIT,CALC SIG CFD OTHERS,TBL	
(n,2n)	1.5+7		SMU Expt	Conf	74Columbia 95	Jul 74 Salaita+ ACTIV.SIG TO GRND+META.TABL	
(n,2n)	1.4+7		WURExpt	Jour	JIN 37 1587	Aug 75 Pruys+ GE – LI.SIG TO 2ISO GVN,CFD OTH	
				Rept	EIR – 285	Jul 75 – + DECAY OF M1 AND M2 IN EU – 152	
(n,2n)	1.5+7		JUL Expt	Jour	NP/A 224 319	May 74 Qaim. ACT.GE(LI).TO GRND, METAST1+2	+
				Jour	RRL 25 335	May 76 – + SIG IN GRPH. SYST VS (N – Z)/A	
	1.5+7			Data	EXFOR20541.	Apr 76 6PTS.SIGMA.	
(n,xn) x>2	Fiss		BNL Theo	Jour	NSE 23 238	Nov 65 Pearlstein.SPEC AVG STATMDL CALC N3N	
(n,p)	1.4+7		ALD Expt	Jour	PPS 73 215	Feb 59 Coleman+. ACT. CFD DIRECT INTERACTN	+
(n,p)	Fiss		CRC Eval	Rept	CRC – 1003	Dec 60 Roy+,ESTIMATED AVG SIG=0.03MB	
(n,p)	1.5+7		SAH Comp	Jour	NUC 23 8 112	Aug 65 Chatterjee. TABLE WITH REFS.	
	1.4+7			Jour	NP 60 273	Nov 64 – .MEAN OF EXPT CFD SHELLMOD	
(n,p)	1.4+7	1.5+7	ARK Theo	Prog	ORO – 3235 – 29	Jan 67 Koch+,STAT MODEL CALC CFD EXPTS	
(n,p)	1.4+7		LYO Comp	Rept	LYCEN/6780	Nov 67 Crouzet+COMPILATN FOR ACTIVTN ANALYS	
(n,p)	1.5+7		DEB Comp	Jour	REA 7 4 93	Dec 69 Csikai+ SIG+HL COMPILTN,N – ACTIV – ANAL	
(n,p)	1.4+7	1.5+7	JYV Eval	Rept	JU – RR – 3/1970	Jun 70 Leppaemaeki+ TABLE OF EVAL AVG SIG	
(n,p)	1.5+7		ARK Expt	Abst	DA/B 32 5091	Mar 72 Bari. GE(LI) DET. ACT. SIG GIVEN	+
	1.5+7			Data	EXFOR10431.002	Aug 75 . 1 PT, SIGMA	
(n,p)	1.4+7	1.5+7	KAZ Theo	Jour	YF 18 705	Oct 73 Levkovsky.AVERAGED SIG,CALC,TBL	
				Jour	SNP 18 361	Apr 74 . ENGLISH OF YF 18,705	

63 Europium 153

Quantity	Energy (ev) Min	Energy (ev) Max	Lab	Type	Documentation Ref Vol Page	Date	Author, Comments	Data
(n,p)	1.4+7		WUR	Expt	Jour JIN 37 1587	Aug 75	Pruys+ GE−LI.SIG GIVEN,CFD OTHER	
				Rept	EIR−285	Jul 75	− +	
	1.5+7			Prog	EANDC(OR)−133L	Jun 73	− + REL.TO EU(N,2N) 9.3H =650 MB	
(n,p)	1.5+7		JUL	Expt	Jour RRL 25 335	May 76	Qaim+ ACTIV,GELI.CFD OTHERS,TBL+GRPH	
(n,α)	1.4+7		MUA	Expt	Conf 60Waltair 297	Feb 60	Khurana+.VAL GVN REL FE056(N,P),C−W	+
	1.4+7			Data	EXFOR30403.024	Jul 77	1 PNT. REL TO FE56(N,P)= 110 MB	
(n,α)	Fiss		CRC	Eval	Rept CRC−1003	Dec 60	Roy+,ESTIMATED AVG SIG=0.0006MB	
(n,α)	1.5+7		MUA	Expt	Jour NP 69 153	Jul 65	Khurana+ FE−STANDARD	+
	1.5+7			Data	EXFOR31316.017	Feb 71	.SIG GVN	
(n,α)	1.5+7		DEB	Comp	Jour REA 7 4 93	Dec 69	Csikai+ SIG+HL COMPILTN,N−ACTIV−ANAL	
(n,α)	1.4+7	1.5+7	JYV	Eval	Rept JU−RR−3/1970	Jun 70	Leppaemaeki+ TABLE OF EVAL AVG SIG	
(n,α)	1.4+7		IBJ	Expt	Rept INR−1318 16	Apr 71	Jaskola+ ALFA SPCTR CFD TH,SMALL RPT	+
					Prog INDC(SEC)−42	Dec 74	Glowacka+ TBL DIFFSIG,GRPH E+ANG−DIS	
				Theo	Jour CJP 51 1765	Aug 73	− + KNOCKON EFF.CFD EXPT,GRAPH	
				Expt	Rept INDC(SEC)−18	Aug 71	SEE ALSO *P107, =INR−1318	
	1.4+7			Data	EXFOR30298.	Jul 75	DOUBLE DIFFSIG(25 PTS)+ANGDIST(1 PT)	
(n,α)	1.4+7		WWA	Theo	Rept INDC(SEC)−28	Sep 72	Kozlowski+ ENERGY SPECT CALC. ,GRPH	
(n,α)	1.4+7	1.8+7	IBJ	ExTh	Conf ZFK−271 109	Nov 73	Glowacka+ A−SPEC AT 2ES,GRPH	
				Conf	73Munich 1 519	Aug 73	− + A−SPEC CFD TH,GRPH	
(n,α)	Maxwl		LYO	Expt	Jour NP/A 231 437	Oct 74	Emsallem+ILL HF REACTOR,SIG+GRPH+TBL	+
	2.5−2			Data	EXFOR20564.004	Sep 75	1PNT.SIGMA.	
(n,α)	1.8+7		IBJ	Expt	Jour NP/A 244 117	Jun 75	Glowacka+ ALF E−SPEC CFD MODLS,GRAPH	+
				Prog	INDC(SEC)−42	Dec 74	− + TBL DIFFSIG,GRPH E+ANG−DIS	
	1.8+7			Data	EXFOR30299.	Jul 75	DOUBLE DIFFSIG(31 PTS)+ANGDIST(1 PT)	
(n,α)	1.4+7		WUR	Expt	Jour JIN 37 1587	Aug 75	Pruys+ GE−LI.SIG GIVEN,CFD OTHER	
				Rept	EIR−285	Jul 75	− +	
	1.5+7			Prog	EANDC(OR)−133L	Jun 73	− + REL.TO EU(N,2N) 9.3H =650 MB	
Reson Params	5.4−1		ORL	Expt	Jour PR 70 557	Nov 46	Borst.	+
	5.4−1			Data	EXFOR11756.005	Jun 76	. 1 RES. E0,WT,AND TOT PCS.	
Reson Params	1.8+0	9.0+0	BNL	Expt	Jour PR 93 1292	Mar 54	Sailor+ CRYSTL SPECTR	+
Reson Params	1.8+0	9.0+0	BNL	Expt	Jour PR 95 453	Jul 54	Wood. ACTIVATION.	+
	1.8+0	9.0+0		Data	EXFOR11424.003	Jun 76	. 5 RES E0	
Reson Params	4.0+0	2.4+1	BNL	Expt	Conf ORNL−2309	Jun 57	Block+ PRELIM 16ES AV D 1D5PMD3EV	+
	4.0+0	2.0+1		Prog	WASH−192 13	Mar 57	Zimmerman+ NDG	
	4.7+0	2.4+1		Data	EXFOR12224.003	Jun 76	. 13 RES. E0 AND WN0.	
Reson Params	1.0+0	1.0+1	ORL	Expt	Conf ORNL−2309	Jun 57	Block+ FC 8ES AV D 1D15EV.	+
	1.8+0	8.9+0		Prog	ORNL−2204 33	Feb 57	Harvey+	
	1.8+0	8.9+0		Data	EXFOR11613.003	Jun 76	. 8 RES, E0,WN,WT**2	
Reson Params	4.6−1		HAR	Expt	Conf 58Geneva 16 44	Sep 58	Pattenden+.PPR11,PARAMS GVN,WN	
Reson Params	1.7+0	8.9+0	BNL	Expt	Jour PR 114 1577	Jun 59	Domanic+ WG AND WN FOR 6 RESONANCES.	+
	1.7+0	8.9+0		Data	EXFOR11688.003	Jun 76	. 6 RES.E0,WT,WN0,WG,TOT PCS.	
Reson Params	2.5+0		NRL	Expt	Jour PR/B 134 68	Apr 64	Stolovy. POLARZD NUC,NS.J=3	+
	2.5+0			Data	EXFOR11436.003	Jun 76	. 1 RES. E0 AND J.	
Reson Params	−		KFK	Eval	Rept KFK−352	Aug 65	Schmidt.AVERAGE S−WAWE RES PAR(TAB.6	
Reson Params	+3		LAS	Eval	Rept LA−3643	Dec 66	Barr+ ESTIMATED RES PARS CFD EXPTS	
Reson Params		1.0+6	AUA	Theo	Jour AUJ 20 477	Oct 67	Cook. TBL OF AVG LVL SPACING D,L=0,1	
Reson Params	+3	+5	AUA	ExTh	Rept AAEC/E−198	May 69	Musgrove.RES PARS +STF FROM (NG)FIT	+
Reson Params	−		AUA	Theo	Rept AAEC/E−211	Nov 70	Musgrove. CALCULTD D+GAM WIDTH GIVEN	
						71	Zakharova+ SURVEY+SYSTEMATICS,GW,TBL	
Reson Params	1.7+0	9.0+0	CJD	Eval	Jour YK−7			
					Rept INDC(CCP)−27	Nov 72	.ENGLISH TRANSLATION OF YK−7 /71	
Reson Params	None		DUB	Theo	Jour YF 13 240	Feb 71	Malecki+G−WID,THEO CFD EXPT.TBL,GRPH	
					Jour SNP 13 533	Aug 71	− + ENGL OF YF 13 240.	
Reson Params	4.6−1	6.6+2	IFU	Expt	Prog YFI−10 44	May 71	Vertebny+ ABST,TBL OF RESONANCE−ES	
					Rept INDC(CCP)−15	Dec 71	*P50,ENG OF YFI−10	
Reson Params	None		COL	Expt	Jour NSE 48 219	Jun 72	Rahn+. AVG WG=94.8MEV OVER 44RESON	
Reson Params	4.6−1	9.8+1	COL	Expt	Jour PR/C 6 251	Jul 72	Rahn+. G*WN FOR 77 RES.SOME WG,AVG D	+
	None			Conf	75Wash. 780	Mar 75	Hacken+ TBL AVG WG,STF,NUMBER GWN,WG	
	1.7+0	9.8+1		Rept	NYO−72−281	Oct 70	Rahn.SEE FOR DETAILS.	
	1.7+0	9.8+1		Data	EXFOR10046.	Jan 78	. 76 RES ES.WN RED*G,WG.D GVN.	
Reson Params	+0	+2	BOL	Eval	Conf IAEA−169 3 123	74	Benzi+ AVG G−WID CFD OTHERS+XPT,TABL	
Reson Params	+0	+2	FEI	Eval	Rept YK−8/2 97	Sep 72	Abagyan+ AVG G−WID+D AT BINDNG−E,TBL	
					Rept INDC(CCP)−39	Jul 74	.PAGE 102.ENGLISH OF YK−8/2 97	
Reson Params	None		RPI	Expt	Conf 75Wash. 905	Mar 75	Hockenbury+ AVG WG,D	
Strnth Fnctn	1.0+0	1.0+1	ORL	Expt	Conf ORNL−2309	Jun 57	Block+ FC, 8 RES	
Strnth Fnctn		+3	BNL	Expt	Conf PRL 1 461	Dec 58	Hughes. FC 2.7−+ −0.6	
		2.4+1			Conf ORNL−2309	Jun 57	Block+ PRELIM 2D7PMD6 16 AVG2WAYS.	
Strnth Fnctn	+3	+5	BOL	Theo	Conf 61Vienna 1 179	Aug 61	Benzi+.PPR11,TABLE CFD EXPERIMENT	
Strnth Fnctn	8.0−1	5.0+4	LEB	Expt	Conf JINR−1845 100	Jun 64	Konks+ PB−SLOWDOWN−TIME, TABLE	

63 Europium 153

Quantity	Energy (ev) Min	Max	Lab	Type	Documentation Ref Vol Page	Date	Author, Comments	Data
Strnth Fnctn		5.0+4	RI	Expt Prog	YFI-5 59	Oct 67	Konks+ TABLE	
				Rept	INDC-232E	Jan 69	. ENGL OF YFI-5 59	
Strnth Fnctn	1.0+0	5.0+4	DUB	Expt Jour	YF 7 493	Mar 68	Konks+ TABLE OF S0+S1 VALS,CFD OTHER	
				Jour	SNP 7 310	Sep 68	- + ENGL OF YF 7 493.	
Strnth Fnctn	+3	+5	AUA	ExTh Rept	AAEC/E-198	May 69	Musgrove.S+P+D STF FROM (NG)FIT,TBL	+
Strnth Fnctn	-		AUA	Theo Rept	AAEC/E-211	Nov 70	Musgrove. SMOOTHED S0,S1 AND S2 GIVN	
Strnth Fnctn	4.6-1	9.8+1	COL	Expt Jour	PR/C 6 251	Jul 72	Rahn+. S0=2.3+-0.4	+
	None			Revw Conf	75Wash. 780	Mar 75	Hacken+ NEVIS TOF S-WAVE STF	
	1.7+0	9.8+1		Expt Rept	NYO-72-281	Oct 70	Rahn.EXPT DETAILS	
	0.0+0	1.0+2		Data	EXFOR10046.022	Jan 78	. 1PT.S0=(2.3+-.4)-4	
Strnth Fnctn	None		AUA	Eval Rept	AAEC/E-277	Mar 73	Musgrove.TBLS EXPTL DATA+BEST VALUES	
Strnth Fnctn	None		RPI	Eval Rept	75Wash. 905	Mar 75	Hockenbury+ AVG S0,S1	
Lvl Density	-		COP	Theo Jour	NP 6 62	Mar 58	Ericson. LVL DENSITY FORM CFD EXP	
Lvl Density	-		FEI	Eval Rept	FEI-36	66	Kapchigashev+.TBL OF RELATD QUANTTYS	+
		5.0+4		Jour	YF 4 686	Sep 66	.TABLE.SHORT VERSION OF FEI-36	
	-			Prog	YFI-3 3	66	.ABSTRACT.TABLE LDL+NUCL.EXCIT.E	
		5.0+4		Jour	SNP 4 486	67	.ENGLISH OF YF 4.FROM(N,GAMMA).TABLE	
				Prog	INDC-E-140 3	66	.ENGLISH TRANSL OF YFI-3	
Lvl Density	None		AUW	Theo Conf	70Madurai 2 267	Dec 70	Ramamurty+ A-PARAMETER GVN,LANG'S-TH	
Lvl Density	1.4+7		IBJ	Expt Prog	INR-1318 16	Apr 71	Jaskola+ ALFA SPCTR CFD TH,SMALL RPT	+
	1.4+7			Data	EXFOR30158.007	Mar 71	LEVEL DENSITY PARAMETER OF PM150 GIV	
Lvl Density	None		BOL	Eval Conf	IAEA-169 3 123	74	Benzi+ LVL DENS PARAM BY XPT,GRPH+TB	
Lvl Density	None		DUB	Theo Jour	JINR-P4-8102	Jul 74	Malov+ SEMI-MICROSC CALC OKS XPT,TBL	
				Rept	UCRL-TR-10845	Apr 75	. ENGL OF JINR-P4-8102	
Lvl Density	+0	+2	FEI	Eval Rept	YK-8/2 97	Sep 72	Abagyan+ LVL DENSITY PARAMETER,TBL	
				Rept	INDC(CCP)-39	Jul 74	.PAGE 102.ENGLISH OF YK-8/2 97	
(γ,n)	8.0+6	2.2+7	CCP	Expt Jour	ZEP 11 520	Jun 70	Vasil'Ev+ EXPTL SIG(GAMMA-E) GRAPH	

63 Europium 154

Quantity	Energy (ev) Min	Max	Lab	Type	Documentation Ref Vol Page	Date	Author, Comments	Data
Evaluation	1.0-3	1.5+7	AUA	Eval Rept	AAEC/TM-549	Jun 70	Cook.TOT,EL,INEL,NONEL,CAPT SIGS,NDG	+
				Rept	AAEC/E-214	Jun 71	Bertram+GROUP SIGMAS SAME QUANTS.NDG	
				Rept	AAEC/TM-587	Mar 71	*DESCRIPTION OF LIBRARY	
	1.0-3	1.5+7		Data	AUSTR-DFN 166.	Nov 71	POINT(223) AND GROUP(127) SIGMAS	
Evaluation	1.0-2	2.0+7	BNL	Eval Rept	BNL-19456	Nov 74	Takahashi.GRPH.	
Evaluation	1.0-5	1.5+7	BOL	Eval Prog	NEANDC(E)182 7	Dec 76	Fabri+ COMPLETE EVAL IN ENDF/B DONE	+
	1.0-5	1.5+7		Data	CNEN-CEA 3	Jan 78	PRELIM.ALL QUANTITIES.ENDF FORMAT	
Total	1.0-3	1.5+7	AUA	Eval Data	AUSTR-DFN 166.	Nov 71	COOK+POINT(223)+GROUP(127)SIG.CF EVL	+
Elastic	1.0-3	1.5+7	AUA	Eval Data	AUSTR-DFN 166.	Nov 71	COOK+POINT(223)+GROUP(127)SIG.CF EVL	+
Tot Inelastc	5.0+5	1.5+7	AUA	Eval Data	AUSTR-DFN 166.	Nov 71	COOK+POINT(11)+GROUP(127)SIG.CF EVL	
Nonelastic	1.0-3	1.5+7	AUA	Eval Data	AUSTR-DFN 166.	Nov 71	COOK+POINT(223)+GROUP(127)SIG.CF EVL	+
Absorption	4.1-1	1.0+7	GA	Eval Rept	GA-2451	Aug 61	Joanou+.68GROUP DATA FOR GAM-I ABS	
Absorption	Pile		ROS	Expt Rept	ZFK-201	Apr 70	Adam.THR+EFFECTIV SIG,PRODUCTION SIG	
Absorption	1.0-4	1.0+7	JUL	Eval Rept	JUEL-678-RG	Jul 70	Liu. EVALUATION+CALC,GRPH,FN OF E	
Absorption	Pile		CRC	Eval Conf	73Paris 1 459	Mar 73	Walker.FISS PRODUCT ABS,TBL PILE SIG	
Absorption	2.5-2		IJI	Eval Conf	75Kiev 1 169	May 75	Fedorova+ EVAL 2200M/S SIG,TABLE	
Res Int Abs			AUA	Eval Rept	AAEC/TM-619	Sep 72	Clayton.CALC FROM SIG LIBRARY,TABLE	
Res Int Abs	4.6-1	1.0+6	RCN	Theo Rept	RCN-191	Jul 73	Lautenbach.CAPT INT FROM GROUP SIGMA	
Res Int Abs	5.5-1	+6	SAC	Revw Conf	IAEA-169 1 235	74	Ribon.CAPTURE,STATUS CFD REQUEST,TBL	
Res Int Abs	+0	+5	WIN	Revw Conf	IAEA-169 3 163	74	Pope+ DATA FILE CALCS COMPARED	
(n,γ)	Maxwl		ANL	Expt Jour	PR 75 1500	May 49	Hayden+ ISOTOPIC DILUTION,TO +-15PC	+
	Maxwl			Data	EXFOR12138.005	Jun 76	. 1 PT. SIGMA (SPA)	
(n,γ)	Maxwl		CRC	Eval Rept	AECL-1054	Mar 60	Walker. (CRRP-913)	
(n,γ)	+3		LAS	Eval Rept	LA-3643	Dec 66	Barr+ ESTIMATED SIGS CFD EXPTS	
(n,γ)	1.0-3	1.5+7	AUA	Eval Data	AUSTR-DFN 166.	Nov 71	COOK+POINT(223)+GROUP(127)SIG.CF EVL	+
(n,γ)	Maxwl		CRC	Eval Rept	AECL-3037 1	Jan 72	Walker.RECOMMENDED SIG,DETAILED TBL	
(n,γ)	2.5-2		IAE	Revw Rept	IAEA-143 897	Apr 72	Lemmel.RECENT EVALUATIONS,TABLE+GRPH	
	Maxwl			Rept	IAEA-143 897	Apr 72	- .RECENT EVALUATIONS,TABLE	
(n,γ)	2.5-2		AUA	Eval Rept	AAEC/TM-619	Sep 72	Clayton.CALC FROM SIG LIBRARY,TABLE	
(n,γ)		1.1+7	RCN	Theo Rept	RCN-191	Jun 73	Lautenbach.GROUP CONSTANTS TBL	
(n,γ)	2.5-2		SAC	Revw Conf	IAEA-169 1 235	74	Ribon.STATUS SIG CFD REQUESTS,TABLE	
	Fiss			Conf	IAEA-169 1 235	74	- .STATUS SIG CFD REQUESTS,TABLE	
(n,γ)	Maxwl	Fiss	WIN	Revw Conf	IAEA-169 3 163	74	Pope+ MAXW+FIS-SPEC AVG DATA CFD XPT	
	Fiss			Conf	IAEA-169 3 137	74	Dean. POINT DATA AVG OVER STAND SPEC	
Spect (n,γ)	Maxwl		BNL	Expt Jour	PR 115 1287	Sep 59	Patronis+,SC SPECT,75 AND 91 KEV GS	
Spect (n,γ)	Pile		AE	Expt Rept	AE-179	Feb 65	Malmskog.HL,E1 PROB,GINT 104,246KEVL	

63 Europium 154

Quantity	Energy (ev) Min	Max	Lab	Type	Documentation Ref Vol Page	Date	Author, Comments	Data
(n,p)	Maxwl		IFU	Theo Rept	ICD – 4 20	67	Dadakina+ PENETR COEFF CALC,TABLE	
Reson Params	+3		LAS	Eval Rept	LA – 3643	Dec 66	Barr+ ESTIMATED RES PARS CFD EXPTS	
Reson Params		1.0+6	AUA	Theo Jour	AUJ 20 477	Oct 67	Cook. TBL OF AVG LVL SPACING D,L=0,1	
Reson Params	–		AUA	Theo Rept	AAEC/E – 211	Nov 70	Musgrove. CALCULTD D+GAM WIDTH GIVEN	
Strnth Fnctn	–		AUA	Theo Rept	AAEC/E – 211	Nov 70	Musgrove. SMOOTHED S0,S1 AND S2 GIVN	
Lvl Density	+6		MIL	Theo Jour	EN 15 1 54	Jan 68	Facchini+ LDL PARS FROM LOW EN RES	
Lvl Density	None		MUN	Theo Jour	NP/A 217 269	Dec 73	Dilg+ A,DELTA. BACK SHIFTED FERMIGAS	
Lvl Density	None		COP	Theo Jour	NP/A 222 493	Apr 74	Dossing+COLL ROTAT.SPAC. ACCUR ESTIM	
Lvl Density	None		ROC	Theo Jour	NP/A 223 589	May 74	Huizenga+ EXP CFD MICROSC TH AX SYMM	

63 Europium 155

Quantity	Energy (ev) Min	Max	Lab	Type	Documentation Ref Vol Page	Date	Author, Comments	Data
Evaluation	1.0 – 3	1.5+7	AUA	Eval Rept	AAEC/TM – 549	Jun 70	Cook.TOT,EL,INEL,NONEL,CAPT SIGS,NDG	+
				Rept	AAEC/E – 214	Jun 71	Bertram+GROUP SIGMAS SAME QUANTS.NDG	
				Rept	AAEC/TM – 587	Mar 71	*DESCRIPTION OF LIBRARY	
	1.0 – 3	1.5+7		Data	AUSTR – DFN 167.	Nov 71	POINT(223) AND GROUP(127) SIGMAS	
Evaluation	1.0 – 5	1.5+7	BOL	Eval Prog	NEANDC(E)182 7	Dec 76	Fabri+ COMPLETE EVAL IN ENDF/B DONE	+
	1.0 – 5	1.5+7		Data	CNEN – CEA 3	Jan 78	PRELIM.ALL QUANTITIES.ENDF FORMAT	
Total	1.0 – 3	1.5+7	AUA	Eval Data	AUSTR – DFN 167.	Nov 71	COOK+POINT(223)+GROUP(127)SIG.CF EVL	+
Elastic	1.0 – 3	1.5+7	AUA	Eval Data	AUSTR – DFN 167.	Nov 71	COOK+POINT(223)+GROUP(127)SIG.CF EVL	+
Tot Inelastc	5.0+5	1.5+7	AUA	Eval Data	AUSTR – DFN 167.	Nov 71	COOK+POINT(11)+GROUP(127)SIG.CF EVL	+
Nonelastic	1.0 – 3	1.5+7	AUA	Eval Data	AUSTR – DFN 167.	Nov 71	COOK+POINT(223)+GROUP(127)SIG.CF EVL	+
Absorption	4.1 – 1	1.0+7	GA	Eval Rept	GA – 2451	Aug 61	Joanou+.68GROUP DATA FOR GAM – I ABS	
Absorption	Pile		CRC	Expt Prog	INDC(CAN) – 7 2	Jun 70	Walker+ SHORT NOTE,VALUE GIVEN	
Absorption	1.0 – 4	1.0+7	JUL	Eval Rept	JUEL – 678 – RG	Jul 70	Liu. EVALUATION+CALC,GRPH,FN OF E	
Absorption	Pile		CRC	Eval Conf	73Paris 1 459	Mar 73	Walker.FISS PRODUCT ABS,TBL PILE SIG	
Absorption	2.5 – 2		IJI	Eval Conf	75Kiev 1 169	May 75	Fedorova+ EVAL 2200M/S SIG,TABLE	
Res Int Abs	5.0 – 1		AUA	Eval Rept	AAEC/TM – 619	Sep 72	Clayton.CALC FROM SIG LIBRARY,TABLE	
Res Int Abs	5.5 – 1	+6	SAC	Revw Conf	IAEA – 169 1 235	74	Ribon.CAPTURE,STATUS CFD REQUEST,TBL	
Res Int Abs	+0	+5	WIN	Revw Conf	IAEA – 169 3 163	74	Pope+ DATA FILE CALCS COMPARED	
(n,γ)	Maxwl		ANL	Expt Jour	PR 75 1500	May 49	Hayden+ ISOTOPIC DILUTION,TO + – 15PC	+
	Maxwl			Data	EXFOR12138.006	Jun 76	. 1 PT. SIGMA (SPA)	
(n,γ)	Maxwl		CRC	Eval Rept	AECL – 1054	Mar 60	Walker. (CRRP – 913)	
(n,γ)	1.0+3	1.0+7	BOL	Eval Conf	66Paris 1 537	Oct 66	Benzi.STATIST MODEL+XPTAL MEAN D,WG	
(n,γ)	+3		LAS	Eval Rept	LA – 3643	Dec 66	Barr+ ESTIMATED SIGS CFD EXPTS	
(n,γ)	Maxwl		AUA	Theo Jour	NSE 31 234	Feb 68	Cook+ STATISTICAL CALC CFD EXPT	
(n,γ)	Maxwl		CRC	Expt Jour	CJP 48 1933	Aug 70	Mowatt.GE(LI) DET.SIG=4040+ – 125B	+
	Maxwl			Data	EXFOR10154.002	Jun 72	. 1PNT, SIGMA.	
(n,γ)	1.0 – 3	1.5+7	AUA	Eval Data	AUSTR – DFN 167.	Nov 71	COOK+POINT(223)+GROUP(127)SIG.CF EVL	+
(n,γ)	Maxwl		CRC	Eval Rept	AECL – 3037 1	Jan 72	Walker.RECOMMENDED SIG,DETAILED TBL	
(n,γ)	Maxwl		IAE	Revw Rept	IAEA – 143 897	Apr 72	Lemmel.RECENT EVALUATIONS,TABLE	
	2.5 – 2			Rept	IAEA – 143 897	Apr 72	– .RECENT EVALUATIONS,TABLE+GRPH	
(n,γ)	2.5 – 2		AUA	Eval Rept	AAEC/TM – 619	Sep 72	Clayton.CALC FROM SIG LIBRARY,TABLE	
(n,γ)	Pile		SGA	Eval Conf	73Paris 1 233	Mar 73	Eder+ RECOMMENDED SIG,TBL,NO DETAILS	
	Maxwl			Rept	SGAE – PH – 141	Feb 73	.SAME AS 73PARIS,EVAL OF EXPTL DATA	
(n,γ)		1.1+7	RCN	Theo Rept	RCN – 191	Jun 73	Lautenbach.GROUP CONSTANTS TBL	
(n,γ)	2.5 – 2	3.0+4	SAC	Revw Conf	IAEA – 169 1 235	74	Ribon.STATUS SIG CFD REQUESTS,TABLE	
	Fiss			Conf	IAEA – 169 1 235	74	– .STATUS SIG CFD REQUESTS,TABLE	
(n,γ)	Maxwl	Fiss	WIN	Revw Conf	IAEA – 169 3 163	74	Pope+ MAXW+FIS – SPEC AVG DATA CFD XPT	
	Fiss			Conf	IAEA – 169 3 137	74	Dean. POINT DATA AVG OVER STAND SPEC	
Reson Params		1.0+6	AUA	Theo Jour	AUJ 20 477	Oct 67	Cook. TBL OF AVG LVL SPACING D,L=0,1	
Reson Params	–		AUA	Theo Rept	AAEC/E – 211	Nov 70	Musgrove. CALCULTD D+GAM WIDTH GIVEN	
Strnth Fnctn	–		AUA	Theo Rept	AAEC/E – 211	Nov 70	Musgrove. SMOOTHED S0,S1 AND S2 GIVN	

63 Europium 156

Quantity	Energy (ev) Min	Max	Lab	Type	Documentation Ref Vol Page	Date	Author, Comments	Data
Evaluation	1.0 – 3	1.5+7	AUA	Eval Rept	AAEC/TM – 549	Jun 70	Cook.TOT,EL,INEL,NONEL,CAPT SIGS,NDG	+
				Rept	AAEC/E – 214	Jun 71	Bertram+GROUP SIGMAS SAME QUANTS.NDG	
				Rept	AAEC/TM – 587	Mar 71	*DESCRIPTION OF LIBRARY	
	1.0 – 3	1.5+7		Data	AUSTR – DFN 168.	Nov 71	POINT(223) AND GROUP(127) SIGMAS	
Total	1.0 – 3	1.5+7	AUA	Eval Data	AUSTR – DFN 168.	Nov 71	COOK+POINT(223)+GROUP(127)SIG.CF EVL	+
Elastic	1.0 – 3	1.5+7	AUA	Eval Data	AUSTR – DFN 168.	Nov 71	COOK+POINT(223)+GROUP(127)SIG.CF EVL	+
Tot Inelastc	5.0+5	1.5+7	AUA	Eval Data	AUSTR – DFN 168.	Nov 71	COOK+POINT(11)+GROUP(127)SIG.CF EVL	+
Nonelastic	1.0 – 3	1.5+7	AUA	Eval Data	AUSTR – DFN 168.	Nov 71	COOK+POINT(223)+GROUP(127)SIG.CF EVL	+

63 Europium 156

Quantity	Energy (ev) Min	Max	Lab	Type	Documentation Ref Vol Page	Date	Author, Comments	Data
Res Int Abs	5.0 – 1		AUA	Eval Rept	AAEC/TM – 619	Sep 72	Clayton.CALC FROM SIG LIBRARY,TABLE	
Res Int Abs	5.5 – 1	+6	SAC	Revw Conf	IAEA – 169 1 235	74	Ribon.CAPTURE,STATUS CFD REQUEST,TBL	
Res Int Abs	+0	+5	WIN	Revw Conf	IAEA – 169 3 163	74	Pope+ DATA FILE CALCS COMPARED	
(n,γ)	1.0 – 3	1.5 + 7	AUA	Eval Data	AUSTR – DFN 168.	Nov 71	COOK+POINT(223)+GROUP(127)SIG.CF EVL	+
(n,γ)	Maxwl		CRC	Eval Rept	AECL – 3037 1	Jan 72	Walker.SIG ESTIMATED ACCORDING Z,A	
(n,γ)	2.5 – 2		AUA	Eval Rept	AAEC/TM – 619	Sep 72	Clayton.CALC FROM SIG LIBRARY,TABLE	
(n,γ)	Pile	2.5 – 2	SGA	Eval Conf	73Paris 1 233	Mar 73	Eder+ ESTIMATED FROM POINT SIG,TABLE	
				Rept	SGAE – PH – 141	Feb 73	.SAME AS 73PARIS,POINT SIG FROM COOK	
(n,γ)	Fiss		SAC	Revw Conf	IAEA – 169 1 235	74	Ribon.STATUS SIG CFD REQUESTS,TABLE	
	2.5 – 2			Conf	IAEA – 169 1 235	74	– .STATUS SIG CFD REQUESTS,TABLE	
(n,γ)	Maxwl	Fiss	WIN	Revw Conf	IAEA – 169 3 163	74	Pope+ MAXW+FIS – SPEC AVG EVAL DATA	
	Fiss			Conf	IAEA – 169 3 137	74	Dean. POINT DATA AVG OVER STAND SPEC	
(n,p)	Maxwl		IFU	Theo Rept	ICD – 4 20	67	Dadakina+ PENETR COEFF CALC,TABLE	
Reson Params	–		AUA	Theo Rept	AAEC/E – 211	Nov 70	Musgrove. CALCULTD D+GAM WIDTH GIVEN	
Strnth Fnctn	–		AUA	Theo Rept	AAEC/E – 211	Nov 70	Musgrove. SMOOTHED S0,S1 AND S2 GIVN	

63 Europium 157

Quantity	Energy (ev) Min	Max	Lab	Type	Documentation Ref Vol Page	Date	Author, Comments	Data
Evaluation	1.0 – 3	1.5 + 7	AUA	Eval Rept	AAEC/TM – 549	Jun 70	Cook.TOT,EL,INEL,NONEL,CAPT SIGS,NDG	+
				Rept	AAEC/E – 214	Jun 71	Bertram+GROUP SIGMAS SAME QUANTS.NDG	
				Rept	AAEC/TM – 587	Mar 71	*DESCRIPTION OF LIBRARY	
	1.0 – 3	1.5 + 7		Data	AUSTR – DFN 169.	Nov 71	POINT(223) AND GROUP(127) SIGMAS	
Total	1.0 – 3	1.5 + 7	AUA	Eval Data	AUSTR – DFN 169.	Nov 71	COOK+POINT(223)+GROUP(127)SIG.CF EVL	+
Elastic	1.0 – 3	1.5 + 7	AUA	Eval Data	AUSTR – DFN 169.	Nov 71	COOK+POINT(223)+GROUP(127)SIG.CF EVL	+
Tot Inelastc	5.0 + 5	1.5 + 7	AUA	Eval Data	AUSTR – DFN 169.	Nov 71	COOK+POINT(11)+GROUP(127)SIG.CF EVL	+
Nonelastic	1.0 – 3	1.5 + 7	AUA	Eval Data	AUSTR – DFN 169.	Nov 71	COOK+POINT(223)+GROUP(127)SIG.CF EVL	+
Res Int Abs	5.0 – 1		AUA	Eval Rept	AAEC/TM – 619	Sep 72	Clayton.CALC FROM SIG LIBRARY,TABLE	
Res Int Abs	+0	+5	WIN	Revw Conf	IAEA – 169 3 163	74	Pope+ DATA FILE CALCS COMPARED	
(n,γ)	1.0 – 3	1.5 + 7	AUA	Eval Data	AUSTR – DFN 169.	Nov 71	COOK+POINT(223)+GROUP(127)SIG.CF EVL	+
(n,γ)	Maxwl		CRC	Eval Rept	AECL – 3037 1	Jan 72	Walker.SIG ESTIMATED ACCORDING Z,A	
(n,γ)	2.5 – 2		AUA	Eval Rept	AAEC/TM – 619	Sep 72	Clayton.CALC FROM SIG LIBRARY,TABLE	
(n,γ)	Pile	2.5 – 2	SGA	Eval Conf	73Paris 1 233	Mar 73	Eder+ ESTIMATED FROM POINT SIG,TABLE	
				Rept	SGAE – PH – 141	Feb 73	.SAME AS 73PARIS,POINT SIG FROM COOK	
(n,γ)	Maxwl	Fiss	WIN	Revw Conf	IAEA – 169 3 163	74	Pope+ MAXW+FIS – SPEC AVG EVAL DATA	
	Fiss			Conf	IAEA – 169 3 137	74	Dean. POINT DATA AVG OVER STAND SPEC	
Reson Params	–		AUA	Theo Rept	AAEC/E – 211	Nov 70	Musgrove. CALCULTD D+GAM WIDTH GIVEN	
Strnth Fnctn	–		AUA	Theo Rept	AAEC/E – 211	Nov 70	Musgrove. SMOOTHED S0,S1 AND S2 GIVN	

63 Europium 158

Quantity	Energy (ev) Min	Max	Lab	Type	Documentation Ref Vol Page	Date	Author, Comments	Data
(n,p)	1.4 + 7	1.5 + 7	SGA	ExTh Rept	SGAE – PH – 172	Oct 74	Blinouska+ LVL SCH GD 158	

63 Europium 159

Quantity	Energy (ev) Min	Max	Lab	Type	Documentation Ref Vol Page	Date	Author, Comments	Data
Reson Params	–		AUA	Theo Rept	AAEC/E – 211	Nov 70	Musgrove. CALCULTD D+GAM WIDTH GIVEN	
Strnth Fnctn	–		AUA	Theo Rept	AAEC/E – 211	Nov 70	Musgrove. SMOOTHED S0,S1 AND S2 GIVN	

64 Gadolinium

Quantity	Energy (ev) Min	Max	Lab	Type	Documentation Ref Vol Page	Date	Author, Comments	Data
Evaluation	2.5−2	1.0+7	UNC	Eval Rept	NDA−57−27	Sep 56	Monroe+.TOT,ABS,SCT.TABLE+CURVE	
Evaluation	5.0+5	1.5+7	LRL	Eval Rept	UCRL−5351	Nov 58	Howerton. CURVS SAME AS CE +NG,N3N.	
Evaluation	2.5−2	1.0+7	GEN	Eval Rept	APEX−704	Nov 61	Cooper+. CONTENT OF C−FINE TAPES	
Evaluation	2.5−2	1.0+7	KFK	Eval Rept	KFK−352	Aug 65	Schmidt+.TOT SEL DEL(MUXI)SNE SIN NG	
Evaluation	1.0−3	1.8+7	ANL	Eval Rept	ANL−7387	Mar 68	Pennington+ COMPILATION ENDF/B DATA	
Total	Maxwl		COL	Expt Jour	PR 48 265	Aug 35	Dunning+ IONCH,TRANS,RA−BE/PARAFIN N	
Total	2.0−2	2.0−1	ANL	Expt Jour	PR 71 757	Jun 47	Sturm. TRNSM APPROX RES PARAMS.	
Total	2.0−3	2.0−1	ANL	Expt Jour	PR 72 585	Oct 47	Brill+.ROTATING SHUTTER. TRANSM.	+
	2.0−3	2.0−1		Data	EXFOR12137.002	Jun 76	. 64 PTS.	
Total	6.6−1	2.7+3	ANL	Expt Priv	PALMER.	Mar 53	Palmer.	+
	6.6−1	2.7+3		Data	EXFOR12129.	Jun 76	. 291 PTS. SIGMA.	
Total	8.0+2	2.4+4	HAR	Expt Priv	EGELSTAFF5	Jun 56	Egelstaff. TRANSMISSION.	+
Total	8.9+0	8.0+2	MTR	Expt Prog	IDO−16297 77	Aug 56	Simpson.FAST CHOPPER.GRPHS.	+
	8.9+0	8.0+2		Data	EXFOR11983.003	Jun 76	. 725 PTS.	
Total	1.0+3	3.2+4	HAR	Expt Jour	PPSA 70 51	Jan 57	Gayther+ FC THICK SAMPLE,AVSIG CF TH	
Total	1.3+7	1.6+7	LAS	Expt Jour	PR 109 1268	Feb 58	Conner.TRNS SC 3ES 5.33 5.14 5.40B	+
				Conf	58Geneva 15 11	Sep 58	Coon+.PPR666,SIGMA AT 3ES GVN,TOF	
	1.3+7	1.6+7		Data	EXFOR11320.010	Jun 76	. 3 PTS.	
Total	1.2+0	1.0+1	MTR	Expt Priv	SIMPSON	Mar 58	Simpson. FAST CHOPPER	+
	1.2+0	1.0+1		Data	EXFOR12072.004	Jun 76	. 203 PTS.	
Total	4.0+2	2.0+3	HAR	Theo Jour	PPS 71 910	Jun 58	Egelstaff.FLUCTUATIONS CFD THEORY	
Total	Maxwl		CRC	Expt Jour	NUC 16 10 108	Oct 58	Westcott.NRX ABSOL CURVE 20−760DEGC	
Total	2.0−2	2.8−1	BNL	Expt Jour	NSE 8 183	60	Moller. CRYS. SPECT.	+
	2.0−2	2.8−1		Data	EXFOR12097.002	Jun 76	. 50 PTS.	
Total	1.5−4	3.0−3	MUN	Expt Jour	ADP 7 50	Jan 61	Hoehne. TOF RSLN FUNCT GIVEN	
Total	1.0+6		ALD	Expt Jour	NP 42 86	Apr 63	Gilboy+ INTEGRATING EL,INELAS.SPECTRA	+
Total	1.5+0	3.0+0	BNL	ExTh Jour	PR/B 138 1361	Jun 65	Shore+, CF RESPAR	
Total	4.0+3	6.4+5	DKE	ExTh Jour	PL 16 306	Jun 65	Seth. AV CS 8−10KEV RSN INT RES OBSV	+
	4.0+3	6.4+5		Expt Data	EXFOR11781.015	Jun 76	. 95 PTS.	
Total	9.0−3	2.3−1	COL	Expt Jour	RSI 36 887	Jul 65	Rustad+ CS, 50400+−500B TH C/S.	+
	9.0−3	2.3−1		Data	EXFOR11586.	Jun 76	. 15 PTS. SIGMA.	
Total	None		JAE	Expt Prog	INDSWG−90 2	Jul 65	Ohno.ENRICHED SAMPL FOR LO−E−RES,NDG	
Total	1.0+4	1.0+7	KFK	Eval Rept	KFK−352	Aug 65	Schmidt.GRAPHS+TABULATED DATA(NO.12)	
Total	2.4+6	1.6+7	NDL	Expt Jour	NSE 25 291	Jul 66	Wickstrom+SIG 5 TO 6 B MPL SCAT CORR	+
	2.4+6	1.6+7		Data	EXFOR12102.002	Jun 76	. 7 PTS.	
Total	1.2+3	2.0+6	ANL	Expt Priv	STUPEGIA.	Jul 67	Stupegia.	+
	1.2+3	2.0+6		Data	EXFOR12125.002	Jun 76	. 99 PTS.	
Total	3.0+0	1.0+3	IFU	Expt Prog	YFI−6 113	68	Vertebnyj+. TRANSMISSION, TIME−OF−FL	
				Rept	INDC−260E	69	. ENGL OF YFI−6 113	
Total	1.5+0	2.7+2	SAC	Expt Rept	CEA−N−1149	Jan 69	Ribon. TOF, TRANSMISSION. +SCATTERNG	+
	1.5+0	2.7+2		Data	EXFOR20148.007	May 73	0PTS.	
Total	3.9+6	1.9+7	RAM	Expt Jour	JNE 23 113	Mar 69	Hussain+ TRANSM,VDG,TBL 16−19MEV	+
	1.6+7	1.9+7		Rept	AECD/EP−18	Dec 70	Husain.VDG,TRANS,SIG AT 12 ES,TABLE	
	1.6+7	1.9+7		Data	EXFOR31086.002	Sep 72	.SIG AT 12 ES GVN	
	3.9+6	5.6+6		Data	EXFOR30016.003	Dec 71	SIG AT 33 ES FROM PRIV COMM.	
	1.6+7	1.9+7		Data	EXFOR30016.002	May 70	SIG AT 12 ES FROM JNE 23 113 TABLE 1	
Total	1.0+5	1.5+6	ANL	Expt Jour	NSE 39 67	Jan 70	Sherwood+,TOF,CFD OPTMDL+ENDF/B	+
				Rept	ANL−7567	May 69	− .	
	1.0+5	1.5+6		Data	EXFOR10007.	May 75	. 709 PTS.	
Total	3.0+0	2.0+1	GA	Expt Jour	NP/A 146 337	May 70	Friesenhahn+ TRANSMISSION. NDG.	
Total		6.2+5	CCP	Revw Jour	AE 29 187	Sep 70	Sukhoruchkin. AVERAGED SIG(E) GRAPH	
				Jour	SJA 29 896	Sep 70	TRANSLATN.*	
Total	2.5+6	1.5+7	BNW	Expt Jour	PR/C 3 576	Feb 71	Foster+,TRANS,CURVS,CFD OTHERS+TH	+
				Jour	NIM 36 1	Sep 65	.EXPT DETAILS	
	2.3+6	1.5+7		Data	EXFOR10047.068	Aug 73	. 256 PTS.	
Total	2.7+3		MUN	Expt Prog	EANDC(E)150U	Oct 72	Dilg+ AVERAGE TOT XSECT+S0	+
				Conf	71Albany 327	Aug 71	− +TRNS.AVG CS GVN.31 ELEMENT GRP	
	2.7+3			Data	EXFOR20583.018	May 76	1PNT.	
Total	1.3+7	1.5+7	DEB	Eval Rept	IAEA−153 173		73 Boedy+ MOST PROBABLE VAL OF SIG,TBL	
				Jour	AHP 30 115	Oct 71	Angeli+ AVG SIG,CFD CALC.TBLS.GRAPH	
Total	1.4+7		LIN	Expt Conf	73Kiev 3 108	May 73	Djumin+ OPTMOD CALC,SIG(A),GRAPH	

64 Gadolinium

Quantity	Energy (ev) Min	Max	Lab	Type	Documentation Ref Vol Page	Author, Comments Date	Data
Total	1.0+6	2.0+6	DAC	Eval Jour	NSPB 6 59	Oct 73 Enayetullah+ SIG(E),LSQ – FIT,TBL+GRPH	+
				Theo Jour	NP/A 209 202	Jul 73 Islam+ FLUCTUATION ANALYSIS,OWN DATA	
				Expt Jour	NP/A 209 189	Jul 73 – + VDG,TRANS,CFD OPTICAL MODEL	
				Comp Rept	AECD/EP – 18	Dec 70 Ameen+ EXPTL DATA FROM DAC,TABLES	
				Expt Jour	NSPB 4 3	Oct 68 Hussain+ TRANSM,VDG,TBL 20KEV RESOL	
	1.0+6	2.0+6		Data	EXFOR30134.007	Nov 71 SIGMA – TOT AT 100 ES,PRIVATE COMM.	
	1.0+6	2.0+6		Data	EXFOR30054.002	Dec 70 SIG TOT AT 34 ES	
Total	1.4+5	6.3+5	DKE	Expt Jour	AP 84 165	May 74 Pineo+TRNS.AVG CS.TBL GRPHS.OPTMDL	+
	+3	+5		Jour	AP 84 165	May 74 – +TRNS.AVG CS TBL,GRPHS.OPTMDL.	
	1.0+5	6.5+5		Abst	DA/B 31 6821	May 71 – .2E RANGE AVGS.CFD OPTMDL.	
	1.5+4	6.0+5		Diss	PINEO	70 .AVG CS.GRPHS.CFD.STF CALC.TBL.CFD.	
	1.5+4	6.0+5		Data	EXFOR10542.021	Jan 79 . DATA UNOBTAINABLE FROM AUTHORS.	
Total	7.0+5	9.0+6	GLS	Expt Jour	JP/A 7 1758	Sep 74 Kellie+ SIG IN CURVE,STAT ERROR 2 PC	+
	7.0+5	9.0+6		Data	EXFOR20418.007	Sep 75 646PTS.	
Total	2.5+5	1.5+7	JAE	Theo Conf	JAERI – M – 5984	Feb 75 Tanaka.OPTMDL/COUPLD CH.GRPH CFD EXP	
	1.5+6	3.6+6		Conf	INDC(SEC) – 31	Jan 73 – .P51.CALC SIG CFD EXPT,TBL	
Total	– 3	1.9+0	THS	Theo Jour	IKE – 6 89 65	Jun 75 Keinert. DATA LIBRARY	
Elastic	2.0 – 2	1.6 – 1	CRC	Expt Jour	CJP 31 432	53 Brockhouse. RATIO SCT/ABS REL V.	+
	2.0 – 2	1.5 – 1		Data	EXFOR11653.007	Jun 76 . 16 PTS.	
Elastic	1.0+6		ALD	Expt Jour	NP 42 86	Apr 63 Gilboy+.SIG=6.55B+ – 3PC	
Elastic	9.8+5		AGN	Eval Rept	TID – 21629	Dec 64 Perkins. CALC FROM BNL400,UCRL5573 D	
Elastic	1.0+4	1.0+7	KFK	Eval Rept	KFK – 352	Aug 65 Schmidt.GRAPHS+TABULATED DATA(NO.12)	
Elastic	1.5+0	2.5+2	SAC	Expt Rept	CEA – N – 1149	Jan 69 Ribon.2EXPTS,2TOF PATHS	+
	1.5+0	2.5+2		Data	EXFOR20148.006	May 73 . OPTS.SIG.	
Elastic	3.0+5	1.5+6	ANL	Expt Jour	NSE 39 67	Jan 70 Sherwood+. INTEGRATED SIG,CURVE	+
				Abst	DA 30 3211	Jan 70 – .	
				Rept	ANL – 7567	May 69 – +CALC CS AND LEG COEFS GVN.	
				Rept	EANDC(US) – 62	Jun 64 Smith.TOF,TBL.50KEV STEPS,20KEV RSLN	
	3.0+5	1.5+6		Data	EXFOR10007.007	May 75 . 65 PTS. CALC CS.	
Diff Elastic	1.4+7		LRL	Theo Rept	UCRL – 4926	Jul 57 Bjorklund+ OPTMDL CALC 6 – PARAM FIT	
Diff Elastic	None		ANL	Expt Prog	WASH – 1006	Oct 58 Langsdorf. LLT10 – 20KV+POLXPTSTBD	
Diff Elastic	1.0+6		ALD	Expt Jour	NP 42 86	Apr 63 Gilboy+30TO137DEG.COMP.WITH OPTICMOD	+
Diff Elastic	9.8+5		AGN	Eval Rept	TID – 21629	Dec 64 Perkins.LEG.COEF CALC FRM OTHER DATA	
Diff Elastic	4.4+6	5.5+6	WIS	ExTh Jour	NP/A 95 193	Mar 67 Mahajan.POLARIZATION OPTMDL ANALYSIS	
				Jour	DA/B 28 1093	Sep 67 – .	
Diff Elastic	3.0+5	1.5+6	ANL	Expt Jour	NSE 39 67	Jan 70 Sherwood+,TOF,CFD OPTMDL+ENDF/B	+
				Abst	DA 30 3211	Jan 70 – .	
				Rept	ANL – 7567	May 69 – +DEL VS ANG AT .5,.98 MEV.	
				Rept	EANDC(US) – 62	Jun 64 Smith+TOF.TBL.50KEV STEPS,20KEV RSLN	
	3.0+5	1.5+6		Data	EXFOR10007.008	May 75 . 260 PTS.LEG COEFS GVN.	
Diff Elastic	1.5+6	3.6+6	JAE	Theo Conf	INDC(SEC) – 31	Jan 73 Tanaka.P51.CALC ANGDIST CFD EXP,GRPH	+
	1.5+6	3.5+6		Expt Prog	EANDC(J)26L6	Aug 72 – +.TOF.500KEV STEP FIGS GIVEN	
				Conf	72Budapest 148	Aug 72 – + ANGULAR DISTRIBUTIONS ,GRPH	
				Prog	EANDC(J)22L10	Aug 71 – +.VDG. .5MEV,10D STEPS 25 – 145D	
	1.5+6	3.6+6		Data	EXFOR20326.004	Jun 74 65PTS.D/DA	
Polarization	1.5+6		JAE	Expt Prog	EANDC(J)30L 5	Sep 73 Tomita.VDG,TOF.FIG GIVEN	
Potntal Scat	+4		HAR	Expt Jour	PPSA 70 51	Jan 57 Gayther+ FROM AVG SIGTOT. FC TRANSM	
Potntal Scat		6.5+5	DKE	ExTh Jour	PL 13 70	Nov 64 Seth+0,1PHASE FRM SIG TOT AV 3 – 650KV	
Potntal Scat	3.0+3	6.5+5	DKE	Expt Jour	AP 84 165	May 74 Pineo+TRNS.S WAVE SCT LENGTH.TBL.CFD	
				Abst	DA/B 31 6821	May 71 .THESIS ABST.	
				Diss	PINEO	70 .TBL.GRPHS.CFD TO 3 COLLECTIVE MDLS.	
Tot Inelastc	1.0+4	1.0+7	KFK	Eval Rept	KFK – 352	Aug 65 Schmidt.GRAPHS+TABULATED DATA(NO.12)	
Tot Inelastc	5.0+6	7.0+6	ALD	Expt Jour	NP/A 112 337	May 68 Owens+.3ES.FROM N SPECT 90DEG.	+
Diff Inelast	4.0+6	6.5+6	DKE	Expt Abst	DA 24 4248	Apr 64 Buccino.ANGDIST.TOF.NUCL T.LVL DEN.	
Diff Inelast	5.0+6	7.0+6	ALD	Expt Jour	NP/A 112 337	May 68 Owens+.3ES.FROM N SPECT 90DEG NDG.	
				Conf	65Antwerp 547	Jul 65 – + PPR122.ABST.SPECT N' AT 90DEG	
Diff Inelast	3.2+5	1.5+6	ANL	Expt Jour	NSE 39 67	Jan 70 Sherwood+,TOF,CFD OPTMDL+ENDF/B	+
				Abst	DA 30 3211	Jan 70 – .	
				Rept	ANL – 7567	May 69 – +DIN VS ANG AT 2 ES.	
	3.2+5	1.5+6		Data	EXFOR10007.009	May 75 . 91 PTS. CALC CS.	
Diff Inelast	1.5+6	3.6+6	JAE	Theo Conf	INDC(SEC) – 31	Jan 73 Tanaka.P51.CALC ANGDIST TO LVLS,GRPH	
				Expt Conf	72Budapest 148	Aug 72 – + TOF. REL H(N,N)	
	1.5+6	3.5+6		Prog	EANDC(J)26L6	Aug 72 – +.TOF.500KEV STEP FIGS GIVEN	
	1.5+6	3.6+6		Data	EXFOR20326.005	Jun 74 107PTS.D/DA.	
Thermal Scat	Cold		ORL	Revw Jour	JAP 36 1078	Mar 65 Kohler. MAG PROPS FROM N DIFFR XPTS	
Thermal Scat	2.0 – 4	1.5 – 1	BSP	ExTh Jour	JCP 48 520	Jan 68 Mattos.,TRIVALENT ION PARAMAG SIG	+
Nonelastic	1.0+4	1.0+7	KFK	Eval Rept	KFK – 352	Aug 65 Schmidt.GRAPHS+TABULATED DATA(NO.12)	

64 Gadolinium

Quantity	Energy (ev) Min	Max	Lab	Type	Documentation Ref Vol Page	Date	Author, Comments	Data
Absorption	Pile		HAR	Expt	Jour PPSA 63 1175	Oct 50	Colmer+LITTLER.PILE OSC REL HAR B	+
					Rept AERE−N/R−527	Jun 50	− + PILE OSC.	
Absorption	2.0−2	1.6−1	CRC	Expt	Jour CJP 31 342	53	Brockhouse. RATIO SCT/ABS REL V.	+
	2.0−2	1.5−1			Data EXFOR11653.007	Jun 76	. 16 PTS.	
Absorption	2.0−2	2.4−1	CUW	Theo	Rept CWR−400−1	Sep 57	Roberts.MAXWELL−BOLTZMANN AVGD SIGS.	
Absorption	Maxwl		HAR	Expt	Rept AERE−R/R−2516	Mar 58	Jowitt+ PILE OSC.REL BORON.293DEGK.	
					Rept AERE−R/M−100	Dec 56	Cummins+.PILE OSC THR WELL REL HAR E	
Absorption	2.5−2		ROS	Expt	Jour KE 10 25	Jan 67	Albert.VAL 2200M/SEC GVN,LOCAL OSCIL	
Absorption	Pile		CCP	Expt	Jour AE 22 133	Feb 67	Grishanin+.VAL GVN,DISCUSSN OF RESLT	
					Jour SJA 22 144	Feb 67	TRANSLATN.*	
Absorption	Maxwl		ROS	Expt	Rept ZFK−132 19	Dec 67	Faehrmann. CFD WITH OTHER AUTHORS	
Res Int Abs	−		CCP	Expt	Jour AE 3 507	Dec 57	Klimentov+.EPI CD REACTIVITY REL LI	+
					Jour JNE 9 20	Jun 59	TRANSLATN.*	
					Jour SJA 3 1387	57	TRANSLATN.*	
Res Int Abs	5.0−1		BNL	Expt	Rept BNL−13074	68	Mughabghab. FAST CHOPPER	
Res Int Abs	5.0−1	1.0+5	GA	Expt	Prog NCSAC−31 63	May 70	Friesenhahn+,VALUE GIVEN,TBP IN NP	
(n,γ)	Maxwl		COL	Expt	Jour PR 50 738	Oct 36	Fink. RATE OF ABSORPTION+SIGMA	
(n,γ)	Pile		ANL	Expt	Jour PR 72 888	Nov 47	Seren+.ACT METHOD.APPROX.4DECAYS OBS	+
	Pile				Data EXFOR11447.	Jun 76	. 3 PTS, 3 ISOMERS.	
(n,γ)	Pile		ANL	Expt	Jour PR 80 342	Nov 50	Harris+.PILE OSC.REL TO BORON.	+
	Pile				Data EXFOR11528.039	Jun 76	. 1 PT.	
(n,γ)	Maxwl		ORL	Expt	Jour PR 83 643	Aug 51	Pomerance.LOCAL OSC REL AU ABS 95 B	+
	Maxwl				Data EXFOR11047.050	Jun 76	. 1 PT.	
(n,γ)	2.5−2		ANL	Expt	Jour NSE 9 132	Feb 61	Meadows+.PULSED NEUTS,46617+ − 100B	+
	2.5−2				Data EXFOR11028.021	Sep 76	. 1 PT. CS=46,617B.	
(n,γ)	3.0+4	1.7+5	ORL	Expt	Jour PR 122 182	Apr 61	Gibbons.1175,310MB AND 670MB AT 65KV	+
	3.0+4	6.5+4			Jour PR 129 2695	Mar 63	Macklin+ LIQ SCINT,1.175 AND .670B	
	3.0+4	1.7+5			Conf 61Vienna 1 95	Aug 61	Neiler.	
	7.5+3	1.7+5			Data EXFOR11329.	Jun 76	. 57 PTS.	
(n,γ)	2.0+2	7.3+3	ORL	Expt	Conf 61Saclay 203	Sep 61	Block+.LIQUID SCINTILLATOR	+
	2.0+2	8.0+3			Conf 61Vienna 1 95	Aug 61	Neiler.	
	2.0+2	7.3+3			Data EXFOR11935.013	Jun 76	. 41 PTS.	
(n,γ)	Pile		CRC	Eval	Rept CRRP−960	Jan 62	Westcott. EFF SIG TABLE 20−1300DEG C	
(n,γ)	5.0+3	9.0+4	ORL	Theo	Jour RMP 37 166	Jan 65	Macklin+.CALC FOR KT=5TO90KEV	
(n,γ)	1.0+4	1.0+7	KFK	Eval	Rept KFK−352	Aug 65	Schmidt.GRAPHS+TABULATED DATA(NO.12)	
(n,γ)	2.5−2	2.5−2	AE	Expt	Jour NUK 6 245	Sep 68	Sokolowski+.PILE OSC. FAST CHOPPER.	+
	Pile				Data EXFOR20077.	Sep 71	2PTS.SIG.	
(n,γ)	1.0+3	1.0+7	BOL	Eval	Rept CEC(70)−2	Apr 70	Benzi.GRAPH=SUM OF SIG(ISOTOPES)	
(n,γ)	3.0+4		AUA	Theo	Rept AAEC/E−211	Nov 70	Musgrove. SIGMA GIVEN AND CFD OTHER	
(n,γ)	1.0+3	1.0+6	GA	Expt	Conf 71Knoxvill 252	Mar 71	Fricke+,ABSOL AVG SIG,NO DATA GIVEN	+
			ExTh		Conf 70Helsinki 2 265	Jun 70	− + TOF	
	3.0+0	2.0+4		Expt	Jour NP/A 146 337	May 70	Friesenhahn+ AVERAGE NG 200EV UP.NDG	
	1.0+3	7.5+5			Data EXFOR10049.003	Jul 71	. 89 PTS, SIGMA.	
(n,γ)	1.4+7		LAS	Expt	Jour PL/B 36 557	Oct 71	Drake+ SPECTRUM SUMMED CFD PB208 NG	+
					Conf 71Knoxvill 266	Mar 71	Bergqvist+,NO DATA,ABSTRACT ONLY	
	1.4+7				Data EXFOR10193.002	Jun 72	. 1 PT, SIGMA.	
(n,γ)	3.0+4	3.0+5	USP	Expt	Jour NP/A 196 83	Nov 72	Lepine+ LI7−P NS.TOF.M−R. REL TO IN	+
	3.0+4	3.0+5			Data EXFOR30233.004	Mar 73	NDS,RELATIVE TO IN,ABSOLUTE ERROR	
(n,γ)	5.0+3	7.0+4	CCP	Expt	Jour 73Kiev 2 206	May 73	Kononov+ TOF,SIG(NEUT−E),GRAPH	
(n,γ)	1.0+3	1.0+7	FEI	Eval	Rept YK−8/2 97	Sep 72	Abagjan+ AVG SIG(ENERGY−GROUPS),TABL	
					Rept INDC(CCP)−39	Jul 74	.P102. ENGLISH OF YK−8/2 97	
(n,γ)	None		MUN	Theo	Diss GRYNTAKIS	Mar 76	Gryntakis.,CALC.OF WESTCOTTS G−FUNCT	
					Jour RCA 22 128	Mar 75	− +,EQUIVALENT TO THESIS	
Spect (n,γ)	Maxwl		ANL	Expt	Jour PR 76 531	Aug 49	Kubitscheck+ MAX E.G−M COINC+ABSORBR	
Spect (n,γ)	Pile		ANL	Expt	Jour PR 88 943	Nov 52	Hibdon+ INTERNAL CONVERSION,GAMMA ES	
Spect (n,γ)	Maxwl		CRC	Expt	Jour CJP 31 1051	Nov 53	Kinsey+ PAIR SPECT,LINE WIDTH=140KEV	
Spect (n,γ)	+0		YAL	Expt	Abst BAP 2 218	Apr 57	Springer+,LVLS TRNSITS INTS	
Spect (n,γ)	Maxwl		GEA	Eval	Rept DC−58−1−30	Jan 58	Deloume.BY APPROXIMATION CURV+TABLE	
Spect (n,γ)	Maxwl		KUR	Expt	Jour AE 4 5	Jan 58	Groshev+ SPECTRUM+LINES 0.3−7.33MEV	
					Jour JNE 9 50	Jun 59	. ENGL OF AE 4 5	
					Jour SJA 4 1	58	. ENGL OF AE 4 5	
Spect (n,γ)	Maxwl		YAL	Expt	Jour PR 114 268	Apr 59	Draper.SC SPECTR,GAM E 0 TO 600 KEV	
Spect (n,γ)	Maxwl		ARF	Expt	Prog ARF−1193−12	Jul 62	Greenwood+,CRYST SPEC,LOW−E GAMMAS	
					Prog ARF−1193−9	Apr 62	− +,CRYST SPEC,LOW−E GAMMAS	
Spect (n,γ)	3.7+4	9.0+4	MUN	Expt	Jour ZAP 17 452	Aug 64	Noekenberg. CONVERSION ELECTRON−SPEC	
Spect (n,γ)	2.5−2		MIT	Comp	Rept MITNE−85	Jan 69	Rasmussen+TBL G INT.=AFCRL−69−0071	

64 Gadolinium

Quantity	Energy (ev) Min	Max	Lab	Type	Documentation Ref Vol Page	Author, Comments Date	Data
Spect (n,γ)	Maxwl		KFI	Revw Jour	YF 10 907	Nov 69 Kecskemeti+ AVG GAM - MULTIPLICITY,TBL	
				Jour	SNP 10 524	May 70 TRANSLATN.*	
Spect (n,γ)	Pile		KFK	Expt Jour	NP/A 150 151	Jul 70 Michaelis+ GD - 156,158 LVL SCHEMES.	
				Rept	KFK - 1267	Jul 70 - + GD156,158 LVLS DEDUCED	
Spect (n,γ)	Maxwl		WAL	Eval Rept	WANL - TME - 2713	Jul 70 Fody.GAM YLDS FOR WANL POINT LIBRARY	
Spect (n,γ)	Pile		ANL	Expt Jour	PR/C 2 1951	Nov 70 Bollinger+,B10 COVER,GE(LI) DET	
Spect (n,γ)	1.4+7		LAS	Expt Conf	71Knoxvill 266	Mar 71 Bergqvist+,NO DATA,ABSTRACT ONLY	
Spect (n,γ)	Pile		MUN	Expt Jour	ZP 258 315	Mar 73 Henkelmann. E + INT OF GS GIVEN	+
	2.5 - 2			Data	EXFOR20606.012	Jun 76 5PTS.	
Spect (n,γ)	2.4+4		BNL	Expt Prog	USNDC - 7 36	Jun 73 Wasson+. GE(LI) DET. NO DATA GIVEN	
Inelastic γ	4.4+6		WES	Expt Jour	PR 107 1306	Sep 57 Sinclair.XTL SPEC NONE OBSERVED	
Inelastic γ	5.0+6	7.0+6	ALD	Expt Jour	NP/A 112 337	May 68 Owens+.3ES.TOF SPECT 90 DEG. NDG.	+
(n,2n)	1.5+7		DEB	Eval Jour	REA 11 1 153	Mar 73 Boedy+ RECOMM.VALUE FROM N - Z SYSTEM.	
(n,p)	1.4+7		MNZ	Expt Jour	RCA 22 11	75 Weigel+SUM OF (N,P)+(N,NP)+(N,D)SIG	
(n,np)	1.4+7		MNZ	Expt Jour	RCA 22 11	75 Weigel+ TOT SIG, ACT METHOD	
Reson Params	3.1 - 2		ANL	Expt Jour	PR 71 757	Jun 47 Strum+CRYS SPEC E WT PCS.	+
	3.1+2			Data	EXFOR12136.004	Jun 76 . 1 RES, E0,WT,PCS.	
Reson Params	2.8 - 2		ANL	Expt Jour	PR 72 585	Oct 47 Brill+ E,PCS,WT.	+
	2.8 - 2			Data	EXFOR12137.003	Jun 76 . 1 RES, E0,WT,PCS.	
Reson Params	2.0+0	3.4+1	BNL	Expt Jour	PR 96 1014	Nov 54 Sailor+	+
	2.0+0	3.4+1		Data	EXFOR12110.011	Jun 76 . 11 RES, E0.	
Reson Params	1.0+0	5.0+1	MTR	Expt Abst	BAP 2 42	Feb 57 Simpson+ BREIT WIGNER ANAL.	+
	1.8+1	3.4+1		Data	EXFOR11983.008	Jun 76 . 5 RES, E0.	
Reson Params	3.3 - 2		MUN	Expt Jour	ADP 7 50	Jan 61 Hoehne. SIG=4400.0B WT=0.120EV.	
Reson Params	3.1 - 2	2.8+0	BNL	Expt Abst	BAP 9 21	Jan 64 Shore+ J=2,1,2,2 AT .03,2,2,6,2.8EV	
Reson Params	None		BNL	Expt Abst	BAP 11 29	Jan 66 Chrien+ R,=8.5F FROM SIGTOT	
Reson Params	7.0 - 1	1.0+3	IFU	Expt Conf	68Riga	Jan 68 Vertebnyj+ ABST,LVLS,TOF 50 NS/M	
Reson Params	3.8+0	2.0+2	SAC	Expt Rept	CEA - N - 1149	Jan 69 Ribon. FROM TOTAL+SCT MEASUREMENTS.	+
	3.8+0	2.0+2		Data	EXFOR20148.008	May 73 12PTS.E0.	
Reson Params	3.0+0	5.0+2	IFU	Expt Jour	UFZ 14 520	Mar 69 Vertebnis+.TOF,TRANSPARENSY CURVE	
Strnth Fnctn	+4		HAR	Expt Jour	PPSA 70 51	Jan 57 Gayther+ FROM AVG SIGTOT. FC TRANSM	
Strnth Fnctn	+0	+3	BNL	Expt Prog	WASH - 1046 21	Jan 64 Palevsky.FC,NDG.TO BE ANALYSED,L=0.	
Strnth Fnctn	3.0+3	6.5+5	DKE	ExTh Jour	PL 13 70	Nov 64 Seth+S,P,D STF FRM SIG TOT 3 - 650KEV	+
	5.0+4	3.4+5		Expt Conf	64Paris 2 916	Jul 64 - +S0,S1,S2 R PRIME/R DUKE U.	
	3.0+3	6.5+5		Data	EXFOR11665.023	Jun 76 . 3 PTS.	
Strnth Fnctn	3.0+3	6.5+5	DKE	Expt Abst	DA/B 31 6821	May 71 Pineo.S,P,D WAVE.THESIS ABST	
				Diss	PINEO	70 .S0,S1.TBL.GRPHS.CFD CALC,OTH EXPTS.	
Strnth Fnctn	2.7+3		MUN	Expt Conf	71Albany 327	Aug 71 Dilg+TRNS.S0 STF GVN.31 ELEMENT GRPH	
Lvl Density	5.0+6	7.0+6	ALD	Expt Jour	NP/A 112 337	May 68 Owens+.LVL DENS VERSUS EXCIT.MEAN T	+
				Conf	65Antwerp 547	Jul 65 - + PPR122. TBL FERMI GAS CONST.	

64 Gadolinium 146

Quantity	Energy (ev) Min	Max	Lab	Type	Documentation Ref Vol Page	Author, Comments Date	Data
Reson Params	-		AUA	Theo Rept	AAEC/E - 211	Nov 70 Musgrove. CALCULTD D+GAM WIDTH GIVEN	
Strnth Fnctn	-		AUA	Theo Rept	AAEC/E - 211	Nov 70 Musgrove. SMOOTHED S0,S1 AND S2 GIVN	

64 Gadolinium 147

Quantity	Energy (ev) Min	Max	Lab	Type	Documentation Ref Vol Page	Author, Comments Date	Data
Spect (n,γ)	+6		DUB	Expt Conf	75Leningrd 105	Jan 75 Vylov+ ABST,GE - LI,ES + INTENSIT,TBL	
(n,p)	Maxwl		IFU	Theo Rept	ICD - 4 20	67 Dadakina+ PENETR COEFF CALC,TABLE	
Reson Params	-		AUA	Theo Rept	AAEC/E - 211	Nov 70 Musgrove. CALCULTD D+GAM WIDTH GIVEN	
Strnth Fnctn	-		AUA	Theo Rept	AAEC/E - 211	Nov 70 Musgrove. SMOOTHED S0,S1 AND S2 GIVN	

64 Gadolinium 148

Quantity	Energy (ev) Min	Max	Lab	Type	Documentation Ref Vol Page	Author, Comments Date	Data
(n,p)	Maxwl		IFU	Theo Rept	ICD - 4 20	67 Dadakina+ PENETR COEFF CALC,TABLE	
Strnth Fnctn	-		AUA	Theo Rept	AAEC/E - 211	Nov 70 Musgrove. SMOOTHED S0,S1 AND S2 GIVN	
Lvl Density	- 3	+0	IFU	Theo Jour	UFZ 13 700	Apr 68 Pisanko+ LEVEL SPACING CALC,TBL	
				Jour	UPJ 13 498	Oct 68 TRANSLATN.*	

64 Gadolinium 149

Quantity	Energy (ev) Min	Max	Lab	Type	Documentation Ref Vol Page	Author, Comments Date	Data
(n,p)	Maxwl		IFU	Theo Rept	ICD-4 20	67 Dadakina+ PENETR COEFF CALC,TABLE	
Reson Params	−		AUA	Theo Rept	AAEC/E-211	Nov 70 Musgrove. CALCULTD D+GAM WIDTH GIVEN	
Strnth Fnctn	−		AUA	Theo Rept	AAEC/E-211	Nov 70 Musgrove. SMOOTHED S0,S1 AND S2 GIVN	

64 Gadolinium 150

Quantity	Energy (ev) Min	Max	Lab	Type	Documentation Ref Vol Page	Author, Comments Date	Data
Reson Params	−		AUA	Theo Rept	AAEC/E-211	Nov 70 Musgrove. CALCULTD D+GAM WIDTH GIVEN	
Strnth Fnctn	−		AUA	Theo Rept	AAEC/E-211	Nov 70 Musgrove. SMOOTHED S0,S1 AND S2 GIVN	
Lvl Density	−3	+0	IFU	Theo Jour	UFZ 13 700	Apr 68 Pisanko+ LEVEL SPACING CALC,TBL	
				Jour	UPJ 13 498	Oct 68 TRANSLATN.*	

64 Gadolinium 151

Quantity	Energy (ev) Min	Max	Lab	Type	Documentation Ref Vol Page	Author, Comments Date	Data
(n,p)	Maxwl		IFU	Theo Rept	ICD-4 20	67 Dadakina+ PENETR COEFF CALC,TABLE	
Reson Params	−		AUA	Theo Rept	AAEC/E-211	Nov 70 Musgrove. CALCULTD D+GAM WIDTH GIVEN	
Strnth Fnctn	−		AUA	Theo Rept	AAEC/E-211	Nov 70 Musgrove. SMOOTHED S0,S1 AND S2 GIVN	

64 Gadolinium 152

Quantity	Energy (ev) Min	Max	Lab	Type	Documentation Ref Vol Page	Author, Comments Date	Data
Evaluation	1.0+6		BOL	Eval Prog	EANDC(E)157U 2	May 73 Menapace+ TO BE CONTINUED ABOVE 1MEV	
Total	3.0+0	1.0+3	IFU	Expt Prog	YFI-6 113	68 Vertebnyj+. TRANSMISSION, TIME-OF-FL	
				Rept	INDC-260E	69 . ENGL OF YFI-6 113	
Absorption	2.5−2		IJI	Eval Conf	75Kiev 1 169	May 75 Fedorova+ EVAL 2200M/S SIG,TABLE	
Res Int Abs	5.0−1		KJL	Expt Jour	JIN 34 2699	Sep 72 Steinnes. ACT. AU MONITOR	+
	5.0−1			Data	EXFOR20188.021	May 74 1PNT.CAPTURE.	
Res Int Abs	+0	+5	WIN	Revw Conf	IAEA-169 3 163	74 Pope+ EVALUATED VALUE GIVEN	
Res Int Abs	5.0−1		IJI	Eval Conf	75Kiev 1 169	May 75 Fedorova+ EVAL OF RI-EXPTS.TABLE	
(n,γ)	−		IEA	Comp Rept	IEA-INF-10	Aug 68 Atalla. TABLES OF HL,SIG AND GAMM-E	
(n,γ)	1.0+3	1.0+7	BOL	Eval Rept	CCDN-NW/10	Dec 69 Benzi+H-F MOD,AXEL G(G)EST,ALL DATA	
				Rept	CEC(70)-2	Apr 70 − +. GRAPH	
(n,γ)	3.0+4		AUA	Theo Rept	AAEC/E-211	Nov 70 Musgrove. SIGMA GIVEN AND CFD OTHER	
(n,γ)	Maxwl		KJL	Expt Jour	JIN 34 2699	72 Steinnes. 97KEV,103KEV ACTIVITY.	+
	2.5−2			Data	EXFOR20188.020	May 74 1PNT.SIGMA.	
(n,γ)	Maxwl	Fiss	WIN	Revw Conf	IAEA-169 3 163	74 Pope+ FIS-SPEC AVG DATA CFD MAXW-XPT	
(n,γ)	1.0+3	1.0+7	FEI	Eval Rept	YK-8/2 97	Sep 72 Abagjan+ AVG SIG(ENERGY-GROUPS),TABL	
				Rept	INDC(CCP)-39	Jul 74 .P102. ENGLISH OF YK-8/2 97	
Spect (n,γ)	Pile		CAV	Expt Jour	NP 5 187	Jan 58 Mccutchen. GRPH,TBL OF 3 REL INTENST	
(n,2n)	Fiss		CRC	Eval Rept	CRC-1003	Dec 60 Roy+,ESTIMATED AVG SIG=3.3MB	
(n,2n)	1.4+7		LYO	Comp Rept	LYCEN/6780	Nov 67 Crouzet+COMPILATN FOR ACTIVTN ANALYS	
(n,2n)	1.5+7		DEB	Eval Jour	REA 11 1 153	Mar 73 Boedy+ RECOMM.VALUE FROM N-Z SYSTEM.	
(n,2n)	1.5+7		KFI	Theo Rept	KFKI-73-68	Dec 73 Jeki.NEW FIT,CALC SIG CFD OTHERS,TBL	
(n,2n)	1.5+7		JUL	Expt Jour	NP/A 224 319	May 74 Qaim. ACT.GE(LI)	+
				Jour	RRL 25 335	May 76 − + SIG IN GRPH. SYST VS (N−Z)/A	
	1.5+7			Data	EXFOR20541.033	Apr 76 1PNT.SIGMA.	
(n,p)	Fiss		CRC	Eval Rept	CRC-1003	Dec 60 Roy+,ESTIMATED AVG SIG=0.14MB	
(n,p)	1.4+7		LYO	Comp Rept	LYCEN/6780	Nov 67 Crouzet+COMPILATN FOR ACTIVTN ANALYS	
(n,α)	Fiss		CRC	Eval Rept	CRC-1003	Dec 60 Roy+,ESTIMATED AVG SIG=0.019MB	
(n,α)	Maxwl		CCP	Expt Jour	YF 1 252	Feb 65 Andreev.IONIZ-CHAMBER,SIG=M7MB	+
				Jour	SNP 1 177	Aug 65 TRANSLATN.*	
Reson Params	3.3+0	9.4+1	IFU	Expt Prog	YFI-6 113	68 Vertebnyj+. TABLE 10 RES	
				Rept	INDC-260E	69 . ENGL OF YFI-6 113	
Reson Params		2.3+2	DUB	Expt Conf	68DUBSY 349	Jul 68 Pikelner.LVL SPAC,AVERG. WG	
Reson Params	3.3+0	9.4+1	IFU	Expt Rept	UFZ 13 2085	Dec 68 Vertebnyj+10RESON,WN,EXPT-D CFD TH-D	+
				Jour	UPJ 13 1492	Jun 69 TRANSLATN.*	
Reson Params	3.3+0	9.4+1	IFU	Expt Jour	UFZ 14 520	Mar 69 Vertebnis+.TOF,WN,10 RES,TBL,GRAPH	

64 Gadolinium 152

Quantity	Energy (ev) Min	Max	Lab	Type	Documentation Ref Vol Page	Date	Author, Comments	Data
Reson Params	8.0+0	2.9+2	DUB	Expt	Jour YF 9 897	May 69	Karzhavina+,TRANS+AREA ANAL,TBL+GRPH	+
					Prog YFI-6 135	Oct 68	- + SHORTER TEXT, TABLE	
					Rept JINR-P3-3882	Jun 68	- + FULL PAPER.	
	2.2+2	2.7+3			Rept BNL-TR-322	Jan 70	- + ENGL OF YF 9 897.	
	8.0+0	2.9+2			Jour SNP 9 523	Nov 69	- + ENGL OF YF 9 897.	
	8.0+0	3.0+2			Rept INDC-E-260	69	.ENGL TRANSL OF YFI-6 135	
	8.0+0	2.9+2			Data EXFOR40162.	Jul 73	.EN-RES,WID,GAMMA-WID,D,AVER G-WID	
Reson Params	-		AUA	Theo	Rept AAEC/E-211	Nov 70	Musgrove. CALCULTD D+GAM WIDTH GIVEN	
Reson Params	3.7+1	1.8+2	CJD	Eval	Rept YK-7	71	Zakharova+ SURVEY+SYSTEMATICS,GW,TBL	
					Rept INDC(CCP)-27	Nov 72	.ENGLISH TRANSLATION OF YK-7 /71	
Reson Params	None		DUB	Theo	Jour YF 13 240	Feb 71	Malecki+G-WID,THEO CFD EXPT.TBL,GRPH	
					Jour SNP 13 133	Aug 71	- + ENGL OF YF 13 240.	
Reson Params	+0	+2	BOL	Eval	Conf IAEA-169 3 123	74	Benzi+ AVG G-WID CFD OTHERS+XPT,TABL	
Reson Params	+0	+2	FEI	Eval	Rept YK-8/2 97	Sep 72	Abagyan+ AVG G-WID+D AT BINDNG-E,TBL	
					Rept INDC(CCP)-39	Jul 74	.PAGE 102.ENGLISH OF YK-8/2 97	
Strnth Fnctn		2.3+2	DUB	Expt	Conf 68DUBSY 349	Jul 68	Pikelner.LVL SPAC,AVERG. WG,S0 VS A	
Strnth Fnctn	3.3+0	9.4+1	IFU	Expt	Jour UFZ 13 2085	Dec 69	Vertebnyj+ VAL GVN,S-RESONANCE	
					Jour UPJ 13 1492	Jun 69	TRANSLATN.*	
Strnth Fnctn		2.3+2	DUB	Expt	Jour YF 9 897	May 69	Karzhavina+,TRANSMISSION,RES-PARAMS	+
					Prog YFI-6 135	Oct 68	- + SHORTER TEXT, TABLE	
					Rept JINR-P3-3882	Jun 68	- + FULL PAPER.	
					Rept BNL-TR-322	Jan 70	- + ENGL OF YF 9 897.	
					Jour SNP 9 523	Nov 69	- + ENGL OF YF 9 897.	
		3.0+2			Rept INDC-E-260	69	.ENGL TRANSL OF YFI-6 135	
	8.0+0	2.3+2			Data EXFOR40162.038	Jul 73	.2 DATA LINES	
Strnth Fnctn	-		AUA	Theo	Rept AAEC/E-211	Nov 70	Musgrove. SMOOTHED S0,S1 AND S2 GIVN	
Strnth Fnctn	None		AUA	Eval	Rept AAEC/E-277	Mar 73	Musgrove.TBLS EXPTL DATA+BEST VALUES	
Lvl Density	None		BOL	Eval	Conf IAEA-169 3 123	74	Benzi+ LVL DENS PARAM BY XPT,GRPH+TB	
Lvl Density	+0	+2	FEI	Eval	Rept YK-8/2 97	Sep 72	Abagyan+ LVL DENSITY PARAMETER,TBL	
					Rept INDC(CCP)-39	Jul 74	.PAGE 102.ENGLISH OF YK-8/2 97	
(γ,n)	8.0+6	2.2+7	CCP	Expt	Jour ZEP 11 520	Jun 70	Vasil'Ev+ EXPTL SIG(GAMMA-E) GRAPH	

64 Gadolinium 153

Quantity	Energy (ev) Min	Max	Lab	Type	Documentation Ref Vol Page	Date	Author, Comments	Data
(n,p)	Maxwl		IFU	Theo	Rept ICD-4 20	67	Dadakina+ PENETR COEFF CALC,TABLE	
Reson Params	-		AUA	Theo	Rept AAEC/E-211	Nov 70	Musgrove. CALCULTD D+GAM WIDTH GIVEN	
Strnth Fnctn	-		AUA	Theo	Rept AAEC/E-211	Nov 70	Musgrove. SMOOTHED S0,S1 AND S2 GIVN	
Lvl Density	8.0+0	2.3+2	DUB	Expt	Rept JINR-P3-3882	Oct 68	Karzhavina+	+
					Rept YFI-6 135	Nov 68	- +	
	8.0+0	2.3+2			Data EXFOR40162.039	Jul 73	.1 DATA LINE	
Lvl Density	None		MUN	Theo	Jour NP/A 217 269	Dec 73	Dilg+ A,DELTA. BACK SHIFTED FERMIGAS	
Lvl Density	None		ROC	Theo	Jour NP/A 223 589	May 74	Huizenga+ EXP CFD MICROSC TH AX SYMM	

64 Gadolinium 154

Quantity	Energy (ev) Min	Max	Lab	Type	Documentation Ref Vol Page	Date	Author, Comments	Data
Evaluation	1.0+6		BOL	Eval	Prog EANDC(E)157U 2	May 73	Menapace+ TO BE CONTINUED ABOVE 1MEV	
Total	3.0+0	1.0+3	IFU	Expt	Prog YFI-6 113	68	Vertebnyj+. TRANSMISSION, TIME-OF-FL	
					Rept INDC-260E	69	. ENGL OF YFI-6 113	
Total	1.4+7		LIN	Expt	Conf 73Kiev 3 108	May 73	Djumin+ OPTMOD CALC,SIG	+
					Jour IZV 37 1019	May 73	- + SIG(A),OPTMODEL CALC,GRAPH	
					Jour BAS 37 5 91	May 73	.ENGLISH OF IZV 37 1019	
	1.4+7				Data EXFOR40302.015	Feb 76	1 PNT	
Total	0.0+0	1.0+4	COL	Expt	Jour PR/C 10 1904	Nov 74	Rahn+ANAL.FOR.RES,STF,AVG. D.TBLES.	
Absorption	4.1-1	1.0+7	GA	Eval	Rept GA-2451	Aug 61	Joanou+.68GROUP DATA FOR GAM-I	
Absorption	Pile		FEI	Expt	Prog INDSWG-126 8	66	Grishanin. SIG=100+ -20 B	
Absorption	Maxwl	Pile	SGA	Expt	Jour JMS 6 435	71	Dobrozemsky+ CHANGE OF ABUND.TBL SIG	+
					Rept SGAE-PH-104	71	- + MASS-SPEC METHOD	
	Pile				Conf 66Paris 1 495	Oct 66	- + PPR82. MASS-SPEC. TBL.	
					Rept SGAE-PH-47	Oct 66	- + PRELIM VALUE.	
	Maxwl	Pile			Rept AEC-TR-7574	74	- + ENGLISH OF JMS 6 435	
	2.5-2				Data EXFOR20637.006	Sep 76	1PNT.SIGMA.	
Absorption	2.5-2		IJI	Eval	Conf 75Kiev 1 169	May 75	Fedorova+ EVAL 2200M/S SIG,TABLE	
Res Int Abs	5.0-1		ORL	Expt	Prog ORNL-3832 7	Sep 65	Lantz. VALUE GIVEN.	+
	5.0-1				Data EXFOR11938.003	Jun 76	. 1 PT, RI.	

64 Gadolinium 154

Quantity	Energy (ev) Min	Max	Lab	Type	Documentation Ref Vol Page	Date	Author, Comments	Data
Res Int Abs	5.5−1		SGA	Expt	Jour JMS 6 435	71	Dobrozemsky+ EFF ABS RES INT GIVEN.	+
					Prog SGAE−PH−104	71	− +MASS−SPECTROMETRIC	
					Rept AEC−TR−7574	74	. ENGLISH OF JMS 6 415	
	5.5−1				Data EXFOR20637.007	Sep 76	1PNT.	
Res Int Abs	5.5−1		CRC	Eval	Rept AECL−3037 1	Jan 72	Walker.REDUCED RES INT,DETAILED TBL	
Res Int Abs	5.0−1		COL	Expt	Jour NSE 48 219	Jun 72	Rahn+ RI=177+ −17B	
Res Int Abs	+0	+5	WIN	Revw	Conf IAEA−169 3 163	74	Pope+ EVALUATED VALUE GIVEN	
Res Int Abs	5.0−1		IJI	Eval	Conf 75Kiev 1 169	May 75	Fedorova+ EVAL+CALC RI GIVEN,TABLE	
(n,γ)	Maxwl		MCM	Expt	Priv WALKER	May 56	Walker.	+
	Maxwl				Data EXFOR12127.010	Jun 76	. 1 PT.	
(n,γ)	Maxwl		ORL	Expt	Prog ORNL−3832 7	Sep 65	Lantz. VALUE GIVEN.	+
	Maxwl				Data EXFOR11938.002	Jun 76	. 1 PT.	
(n,γ)	2.5+4		FEI	ExTh	Prog YFI−4 22	May 67	Shorin+.,TBLS GIVEN,TBP YF	
				Theo	Jour YF 6 769	Oct 67	− + STATMOD. SIGMA GIVEN	
				ExTh	Rept INDC−187E	67	. ENGL OF YFI−4 22	
(n,γ)	1.0+3	1.0+7	BOL	Eval	Rept CCDN−NW/10	Dec 69	Benzi+H−F MOD,AXEL G(G)EST,ALL DATA	
					Rept CEC(70)−2	Apr 70	− +. GRAPH	
(n,γ)	3.0+4		AUA	Theo	Rept AAEC/E−211	Nov 70	Musgrove. SIGMA GIVEN AND CFD OTHER	
(n,γ)	Maxwl		CRC	Eval	Rept AECL−3037 1	Jan 72	Walker.RECOMMENDED SIG,DETAILED TBL	
(n,γ)	5.0+3	7.0+4	CCP	Expt	Conf 73Kiev 2 206	May 73	Kononov+ TOF,SIG(NEUT−E),GRAPH	
(n,γ)	Maxwl	Fiss	WIN	Revw	Conf IAEA−169 3 163	74	Pope+ FIS−SPEC AVG DATA CFD MAXW−XPT	
(n,γ)	1.0+3	1.0+7	FEI	Eval	Rept YK−8/2 97	Sep 72	Abagjan+ AVG SIG(ENERGY−GROUPS),TABL	
					Rept INDC(CCP)−39	Jul 74	.P102. ENGLISH OF YK−8/2 97	
(n,γ)	5.0+3	7.0+4	FEI	Expt	Rept YFI−17 9	Aug 74	Shorin+ TOF,SIG(NEUT−E),TBL	+
					Jour YF 19 5	Jan 74	− + TOF,SIG(NEUT−E),GRAPHS	
	5.3+3	6.8+4			Rept INDC(CCP)−48	Feb 75	. ENGLISH OF YFI−17 9	
	5.0+3	7.0+4			Jour SNP 19 2	Jul 74	. ENGLISH OF YF 19 5	
	5.3+3	6.8+4			Data EXFOR40222.004	Mar 74	.SIGMA FOR 32 EN−RANGES GVN	
(n,γ)	0.0+0	1.0+4	COL	Expt	Jour PR/C 10 1904	Nov 74	Rahn+ANAL.FOR AVG.WG=88MIL−EV,25LVLS	
Spect (n,γ)	+0	+4	COL	Expt	Prog WASH−1124 31	Nov 68	Camarda+ MOXON−RAE DET TBC NO DATA	
Spect (n,γ)	2.4+4		INL	Expt	Conf 75Wash. 912	Mar 75	Greenwood+ GRPH COUNTS VS CHANNEL	
					Rept ANCR−1177 58	Jan 75	− + SUPERSEDED	
					Conf 74Petten 353	Sep 74	− + FILTERED BEAM,GRPH	
(n,2n)	Fiss		CRC	Eval	Rept CRC−1003	Dec 60	Roy+,ESTIMATED AVG SIG=3.0MB	
(n,2n)	1.3+7	1.5+7	BNL	Theo	Jour NSE 23 238	Nov 65	Pearlstein.3ES.STAT MDL CALC.TBL CS.	
(n,2n)	Fiss		BNL	Theo	Jour NSE 23 238	Nov 65	Pearlstein.STATMDL CALC.SPEC AVG.T	
(n,2n)	1.4+7		LYO	Comp	Rept LYCEN/6780	Nov 67	Crouzet+COMPILATN FOR ACTIVTN ANALYS	
(n,2n)	1.5+7		MUN	Expt	Jour NP/A 118 9	Sep 68	Dilg+ ACTIV.REL AL(N,A)	+
	1.5+7				Data EXFOR20802.005	Dec 78	1PNT.SIGMA.	
(n,2n)	1.5+7		DEB	Comp	Jour REA 7 4 93	Dec 69	Csikai+ SIG+HL COMPILTN,N−ACTIV−ANAL	
(n,2n)	1.4+7	1.5+7	JYV	Eval	Rept JU−RR−3/1970	Jun 70	Leppaemaeki+ TABLE OF EVAL AVG SIG	
(n,2n)	+7		KFI	Theo	Rept KFKI−71−8	Feb 71	Jeki. CALCULATED CFD EXPTL SIG VALUE	
(n,2n)	1.5+7		DEB	Eval	Jour REA 11 1 153	Mar 73	Boedy. COMPILATION+RECOMM.VALUE,TBL	
					Rept IAEA−153 173	73	− . RECOMM. VALUE ONLY	
(n,2n)	1.5+7		TAT	Theo	Jour JP/A 7 1457	Aug 74	Kondaiah. CALC ON STAT MODEL	
(n,2n)	1.4+7		MNZ	Expt	Jour RCA 22 11	75	Weigel+ TOT SIG, ACT METHOD	
(n,2n)	1.5+7		JUL	Expt	Jour NP/A 224 319	May 74	Qaim. ACT.GE(LI)	+
					Jour RRL 25 335	May 76	− + SIG IN GRPH. SYST VS (N−Z)/A	
	1.5+7				Data EXFOR20541.034	Apr 76	1PNT.SIGMA.	
(n,xn) x>2	Fiss		BNL	Theo	Jour NSE 23 238	Nov 65	Pearlstein.SPEC AVG STATMDL CALC N3N	
(n,p)	Fiss		CRC	Eval	Rept CRC−1003	Dec 60	Roy+,ESTIMATED AVG SIG=0.02MB	
(n,p)	1.4+7	1.5+7	ARK	Theo	Prog ORO−3235−29	Jan 67	Koch+,STAT MODEL CALC CFD EXPTS	
(n,p)	1.4+7		LYO	Comp	Rept LYCEN/6780	Nov 67	Crouzet+COMPILATN FOR ACTIVTN ANALYS	
(n,He3)	None		OSU	Expt	Abst DA 24 4748	May 64	Kelley. INVERSE REACT.	
(n,α)	Fiss		CRC	Eval	Rept CRC−1003	Dec 60	Roy+,ESTIMATED AVG SIG=0.0018MB	
(n,α)	Maxwl		CCP	Expt	Jour YF 1 252	Feb 65	Andreev.IONIZ−CHAMBER,SIG=M.6MB	+
					Jour SNP 1 177	Aug 65	TRANSLATN.*	
Reson Params	2.2+1	6.4+1	HAR	Expt	Jour NP 5 294	Jan 58	Bowey+. 2 RESONANCE ES GVN. LINAC	
Reson Params	2.5+4		FEI	ExTh	Prog YFI−4 22	May 67	Shorin+.,TBLS GIVEN,TBP YF	
					Rept INDC−187E	67	. ENGL OF YFI−4 22	
Reson Params	9.4+0	1.5+2	IFU	Expt	Prog YFI−6 113	68	Vertebnyj+. TABLE 14 RES	
					Rept INDC−260E	69	. ENGL OF YFI−6 113	
Reson Params	7.0−1	1.0+3	IFU	Expt	Conf 68Riga	Jan 68	Vertebnyj+ ABST,LVLS,TOF 50 NS/M	
Reson Params		2.3+2	DUB	Expt	Conf 68DUBSY 349	Jul 68	Pikelner.LVL SPAC,AVERG. WG	
Reson Params	9.4+0	1.5+2	IFU	Expt	Jour UFZ 13 2085	Dec 69	Vertebnyj+14RESON,WN,EXPT−D CFD TH−D	+
					Jour UPJ 13 1492	Jun 69	TRANSLATN.*	
Reson Params	2.2+1	2.2+1	SAC	Expt	Rept CEA−N−1149	Jan 69	Ribon. FROM TOTAL+SCT MEASUREMENTS.	+
	2.2+1				Data EXFOR20148.009	May 73	1PNT.2A*G*WN.	

64 Gadolinium 154

Quantity	Energy (ev) Min	Max	Lab	Type	Documentation Ref Vol Page	Date	Author, Comments	Data
Reson Params	9.4+0	1.5+2	IFU	Expt	Jour UFZ 14 520	Mar 69	Vertebnis+.TOF,WN,14 RES,TBL,GRAPH	
Reson Params	2.2+1		BNL	Expt	Jour PR 180 1131	Apr 69	Mughabghab. E, WN, WN0.	
					Rept BNL-13074	68	- . E, WN, WN0.	
Reson Params	1.1+1	2.2+2	DUB	Expt	Jour YF 9 897	May 69	Karzhavina+,TRANS+AREA ANAL,TBL+GRPH	+
					Prog YFI-6 135	Oct 68	- + SHORTER TEXT, TABLE	
					Rept JINR-P3-3882	Jun 68	- + FULL PAPER.	
	2.2+2	2.7+3			Rept BNL-TR-322	Jan 70	- + ENGL OF YF 9 897.	
	1.1+1	2.2+2			Jour SNP 9 523	Nov 69	- + ENGL OF YF 9 897.	
	1.1+1	2.5+2			Rept INDC-E-260	69	.ENGL TRANSL OF YFI-6 135	
	1.1+1	2.2+2			Data EXFOR40162.	Jul 73	.EN-RES,WID,GAMMA WID,D,AVER G-WID	
Reson Params	-		AUA	Theo	Rept AAEC/E-211	Nov 70	Musgrove. CALCULTD D+GAM WIDTH GIVEN	
Reson Params	6.5+1	1.6+2	CJD	Eval	Rept YK-7	71	Zakharova+ SURVEY+SYSTEMATICS,GW,TBL	
					Rept INDC(CCP)-27	Nov 72	.ENGLISH TRANSLATION OF YK-7 /71	
Reson Params	None		DUB	Theo	Jour YF 13 240	Feb 71	Malecki+G-WID,THEO CFD EXPT.TBL,GRPH	
					Jour SNP 13 133	Aug 71	- + ENGL OF YF 13 240.	
Reson Params	None		DUB	Theo	Jour ZEP 14 194	Aug 71	Solovev.LARGE N-WID G-WID COR95L.ND7	
					Rept JINR-E4-5880	71	Soloviev.N-GAM-WIDS CORR.SHORT NOTE	
					Jour JEL 14 129	Aug 71	- . ENGL OF ZEP 14 194.	
Reson Params	+0	+2	BOL	Eval	Conf IAEA-169 3 123	74	Benzi+ AVG G-WID CFD OTHERS+XPT,TABL	
Reson Params	+0	+3	FEI	Eval	Rept YK-8/2 97	Sep 72	Abagyan+ AVG G-WID+D AT BINDNG-E,TBL	
					Rept INDC(CCP)-39	Jul 74	.PAGE 102.ENGLISH OF YK-8/2 97	
Reson Params	1.2+1	9.9+2	COL	Expt	Jour PR/C 10 1904	Nov 74	Rahn+ 47 RES. WG= 0.088 EV	+
	0.0+0	1.0+4			Jour NSE 48 219	Jun 72	- +AVG WG=1008MEV OVER 24 RESON.	
	1.2+1	9.9+2			Data EXFOR10458.	Jan 75	.47 WN0,25 WG GIVEN.	
Reson Params	None		COL	Theo	Conf 75Wash. 335	Mar 75	Felvinci+MOD ERICSON CALC CFD EXPT.	
Strnth Fnctn		2.3+2	DUB	Expt	Conf 68DUBSY 349	Jul 68	Pikelner.LVL SPAC,AVERG. WG,S0 VS A	
Strnth Fnctn	9.4+0	1.5+2	IFU	Expt	Jour UFZ 13 2085	Dec 68	Vertebnyj+ VAL GVN,S-RESONANCE	
					Jour UPJ 13 1492	Jun 69	TRANSLATN.*	
Strnth Fnctn		2.3+2	DUB	Expt	Jour YF 9 897	May 69	Karzhavina+,TRANSMISSION,RES-PARAMS	+
					Prog YFI-6 135	Oct 68	- + SHORTER TEXT, TABLE	
					Rept JINR-P3-3882	Jun 68	- + FULL PAPER.	
					Rept BNL-TR-322	Jan 70	- + ENGL OF YF 9 897.	
					Jour SNP 9 523	Nov 69	- + ENGL OF YF 9 897.	
		2.5+2			Rept INDC-E-260	69	.ENGL TRANSL OF YFI-6 135	
	1.1+1	2.3+2			Data EXFOR40162.040	Jul 73	.2 DATA LINES	
Strnth Fnctn	-		AUA	Theo	Rept AAEC/E-211	Nov 70	Musgrove. SMOOTHED S0,S1 AND S2 GIVN	
Strnth Fnctn	None		AUA	Eval	Rept AAEC/E-277	Mar 73	Musgrove.TBLS EXPTL DATA+BEST VALUES	
Strnth Fnctn	1.2+1	9.9+2	COL	Expt	Jour PR/C 10 1904	Nov 74	Rahn+ SO=(2.0+-0.3)-4.47RES	
Lvl Density	None		CCP	Theo	Jour YF 13 43	Jan 71	Bravin+.DEFORM PAR CALC,TBL,CFD EXPT	
Lvl Density	None		BOL	Eval	Conf IAEA-169 3 123	74	Benzi+ LVL DENS PARAM BY XPT,GRPH+TB	
Lvl Density	+0	+3	FEI	Eval	Rept YK-8/2 97	Sep 72	Abagyan+ LVL DENSITY PARAMETER,TBL	
					Rept INDC(CCP)-39	Jul 74	.PAGE 102.ENGLISH OF YK-8/2 97	
(γ,n)	8.0+6	2.2+7	CCP	Expt	Jour ZEP 11 520	Jun 70	Vasil'Ev+ EXPTL SIG(GAMMA-E) GRAPH	

64 Gadolinium 155

Quantity	Energy (ev) Min	Max	Lab	Type	Documentation Ref Vol Page	Date	Author, Comments	Data
Evaluation	2.5-2	1.0+7	KFK	Eval	Rept KFK-352	Aug 65	Schmidt+.RES	
Evaluation	1.0-3	1.5+7	AUA	Eval	Rept AAEC/TM-549	Jun 70	Cook.TOT,EL,INEL,NONEL,CAPT SIGS,NDG	+
					Rept AAEC/E-214	Jun 71	Bertram+GROUP SIGMAS SAME QUANTS.NDG	
					Rept AAEC/TM-587	Mar 71	*DESCRIPTION OF LIBRARY	
	1.0-3	1.5+7			Data AUSTR-DFN 170.	Nov 71	POINT(223) AND GROUP(127) SIGMAS	
Evaluation	1.0+6		BOL	Eval	Prog EANDC(E)157U 2	May 73	Menapace+ TO BE CONTINUED ABOVE 1MEV	
Evaluation	-2	+3	WIN	Eval	Prog UKNDC(75)P71	Jul 75	Pope+ THERMAL + RESON PARAM	
Total	None		MTR	Expt	Abst BAP 2 42	Feb 57	Simpson+MEAS FOR RES PARS.NDG	
Total	-2	+1	HAR	Expt	Conf 58Geneva 16 44	Sep 58	Pattenden.PPR11,CURVE,CRYSTALSPECTRM	
Total	2.0-2	2.8-1	BNL	Expt	Jour NSE 8 183	Sep 60	Moller+,CURVE RES PARS GIVEN.	+
	2.0-2	2.8-1			Data EXFOR12097.	Jun 76	. 51 PTS. SIGMA.	
Total	7.8-2		BNL	ExTh	Jour PR/B 138 1361	Jun 65	Shore+ POLRZ EFFECT USED FOR R.P.	
Total	2.5-2		JAE	Expt	Prog EANDC(J)10L1	Nov 68	Ohno+.CRYST-SPECT+V-SELECT	+
	2.5-2				Data EXFOR20328.004	Jul 74	1PNT.	
Total	5.0+1	2.7+2	SAC	Expt	Rept CEA-N-1149	Jan 69	Ribon. RESONANCE PARAMETERS.	+
					Conf 66Paris 1 119	Oct 66	- + PPR72,CURVES OF TRANSMISSION	
		2.7+2			Data EXFOR20148.011	May 73	. OPTS.	
Total	1.0-3	1.5+7	AUA	Eval	Data AUSTR-DFN 170.	Nov 71	COOK+POINT(223)+GROUP(127)SIG.CF EVL	+

64 Gadolinium 155

Quantity	Energy (ev) Min	Max	Lab	Type	Documentation Ref Vol Page	Date	Author, Comments	Data
Total	1.4+7		LIN	Expt	Conf 73Kiev 3 108	May 73	Djumin+ OPTMOD CALC,SIG	+
					Jour IZV 37 1019	May 73	- + SIG(A),OPTMODEL CALC,GRAPH	
					Jour BAS 37 5 91	May 73	.ENGLISH OF IZV 37 1019	
	1.4+7				Data EXFOR40302.016	Feb 76	1 PNT	
Elastic	1.0-3	1.5+7	AUA	Eval	Data AUSTR-DFN 170.	Nov 71	COOK+POINT(223)+GROUP(127)SIG.CF EVL	+
Potntal Scat	None		BNL	Expt	Jour PL/B 24 573	May 67	Chrien+ FROM ANALYSIS OF RESONANCES	
Tot Inelastc	5.0+5	1.5+7	AUA	Eval	Data AUSTR-DFN 170.	Nov 71	COOK+POINT(11)+GROUP(127)SIG.CF EVL	+
Scattering	0.0+0	2.5+2	SAC	Expt	Rept CEA-N-1149	Jan 69	Ribon. RESONANCE PARAMETER ANALYSIS.	+
		2.5+2			Data EXFOR20148.010	May 73	0PTS.SIG.	
Nonelastic	1.0-3	1.5+7	AUA	Eval	Data AUSTR-DFN 170.	Nov 71	COOK+POINT(223)+GROUP(127)SIG.CF EVL	+
Absorption	Maxwl		HEB	Expt	Rept PR 115 424	Jul 59	Low+,AERE PILE,PAR RES SPECT,88700B	
Absorption	Maxwl	Pile	HAR	Expt	Jour JNEA 12 32	May 60	Tattersall+. EFF SIG IN THREE SPECTR	
					Rept AERE-R-2887	Aug 59	- . PILE OSC.REL BORON	
	Maxwl				Rept AERE-R/R-2516	Mar 58	Jowitt+ PILE OSC.REL BORON.293DEGK.	
Absorption	4.1-1	1.0+7	GA	Eval	Rept GA-2451	Aug 61	Joanou+.68GROUP DATA FOR GAM-I	
Absorption	1.0-3	1.0+7	JUL	Eval	Rept JUEL-678-RG	Jul 70	Liu. EVALUATION+CALC,GRPH,FN OF E	
Absorption	2.5-2		IJI	Eval	Conf 75Kiev 1 169	May 75	Fedorova+ EVAL 2200M/S SIG,TABLE	
Res Int Abs	5.0-1		BNL	Expt	Rept BNL-13074	68	Mughabghab. FAST CHOPPER	
Res Int Abs	5.0-1		GA	Expt	Prog NCSAC-31 63	May 70	Friesenhahn+,VALUE GIVEN,TBP IN NP	
Res Int Abs	None		GA	Eval	Rept GA-12071	Sep 71	Mathews+. RECOMMENDED VALUES	
Res Int Abs	5.0-1		AUA	Eval	Rept AAEC/TM-619	Sep 72	Clayton.CALC FROM SIG LIBRARY,TABLE	
Res Int Abs	4.6-1	1.0+6	RCN	Theo	Rept RCN-191	Jul 73	Lautenbach.CAPT INT FROM GROUP SIGMA	
Res Int Abs	+0	+5	WIN	Revw	Conf IAEA-169 3 163	74	Pope+ DATA FILE CALCS COMPARED	
(n,γ)	Pile		ANL	Expt	Jour PR 71 745	Jun 47	Lapp+	+
	Pile				Data EXFOR12135.002	Jun 76	1 PT.	
(n,γ)	Pile		ANL	Expt	Jour PR 79 271	Jul 50	Ingraham+	+
	Pile				Data EXFOR12106.003	Jun 76	1 PT.	
(n,γ)	Maxwl		HEB	Expt	Jour NCS 11 468	Mar 59	LOW+ ABST. RATIO GD157/GD155,=2.82	
(n,γ)	Maxwl		CRC	Eval	Rept AECL-1054	Mar 60	Walker. (CRRP-913)	
(n,γ)	5.0-3	2.5+0	GA	Eval	Rept GA-2113	Jun 61	Wikner+.TABLE + CURVE.100 E POINTS	
(n,γ)	2.8-3	1.0+6	GA	Eval	Jour NSE 12 115	Jan 62	Garrison+.EVAL FROM XPT+AVERAGE RES	
(n,γ)	1.0+3	1.0+4	LAS	Theo	Rept LA-3463	Jan 66	Bell. TH CAPTURE OF RARE EARTHS	
(n,γ)	2.6-2	6.2+1	KUR	Expt	Prog YFI-6 76	68	Daneljan+ ONLY RES PARS GIVEN	
					Rept INDC-260E	69	. ENGL OF YFI-6 76	
(n,γ)	Maxwl		AUA	Theo	Jour NSE 31 234	Feb 68	Cook+ STATISTICAL CALC CFD EXPT	
(n,γ)	1.2+1	4.3+1	CCP	Expt	Jour ZET 54 401	Feb 68	Danelyan+ SIG IN REL UNITS VS NEUT-E	
					Jour JET 24 216	Aug 68	TRANSLATN.*	
(n,γ)	5.0+3	1.0+5	AUA	ExTh	Rept AAEC/E-198	May 69	Musgrove.S+P+D WAVE SIGMAS CALC,TBL	+
(n,γ)	1.0+3	1.0+7	BOL	Eval	Rept CCDN-NW/10	Dec 69	Benzi+H-F MOD,AXEL G(G)EST,ALL DATA	
					Rept CEC(70)-2	Apr 70	- +. GRAPH	
(n,γ)	3.0+0	2.0+4	GA	Expt	Prog NCSAC-31 63	May 70	Friesenhahn+,NO DATA,TBP IN NP	
(n,γ)	3.0+4		AUA	Theo	Rept AAEC/E-211	Nov 70	Musgrove. SIGMA GIVEN AND CFD OTHER	
(n,γ)	Maxwl		GA	Eval	Rept GA-12071	Sep 71	Mathews+. RECOMMENDED VALUES	
(n,γ)	1.0-3	1.5+7	AUA	Eval	Data AUSTR-DFN 170.	Nov 71	COOK+POINT(223)+GROUP(127)SIG.CF EVL	
(n,γ)	Maxwl		CRC	Eval	Rept AECL-3037 1	Jan 72	Walker.RECOMMENDED SIG,DETAILED TBL	
(n,γ)	2.5-2		AUA	Eval	Rept AAEC/TM-619	Sep 72	Clayton.CALC FROM SIG LIBRARY,TABLE	
(n,γ)	5.0+3	7.0+4	CCP	Expt	Conf 73Kiev 2 206	May 73	Kononov+ TOF,SIG(NEUT-E),GRAPH	
(n,γ)		1.1+7	RCN	Theo	Rept RCN-191	Jun 73	Lautenbach.GROUP CONSTANTS TBL	
(n,γ)	Maxwl	Fiss	WIN	Revw	Conf IAEA-169 3 163	74	Pope+ MAXW+FIS-SPEC AVG DATA CFD XPT	
	Fiss				Conf IAEA-169 3 137	74	Dean. POINT DATA AVG OVER STAND SPEC	
(n,γ)	1.0+3	1.0+7	FEI	Eval	Rept YK-8/2 97	Sep 72	Abagjan+ AVG SIG(ENERGY-GROUPS),TABL	
					Rept INDC(CCP)-39	Jul 74	.P102. ENGLISH OF YK-8/2 97	
(n,γ)	5.0+3	7.0+4	FEI	Expt	Rept YFI-17 9	Aug 74	Shorin+ TOF,SIG(NEUT-E),TBL	+
					Jour YF 19 5	Jan 74	+ TOF,SIG(NEUT-E),GRAPHS	
	5.3+3	6.8+4			Rept INDC(CCP)-48	Feb 75	. ENGLISH OF YFI-17 9	
	5.0+3	7.0+4			Jour SNP 19 2	Jul 74	. ENGLISH OF YF 19 5	
	5.3+3	6.8+4			Data EXFOR40222.005	Mar 74	.SIGMA FOR 32 EN-RANGES GVN	
(n,γ)	2.4+4		INL	Expt	Prog ERDA-NDC-2 35	May 75	Greenwood+LVL.STRUCT.GRPH.TBL.	
	None				Prog USNDC-11 4	Jun 74	+ E-LVL STUDY	
(n,γ)	None		MUN	Theo	Diss GRYNTAKIS	Mar 76	Gryntakis.,CALC.OF WESTCOTTS G-FUNCT	
					Jour RCA 22 128	Mar 75	- +,EQUIVALENT TO THESIS	
(n,γ)	Maxwl		MCM	Expt	Priv WALKER	May 56	Walker.	+
	Maxwl				Data EXFOR12127.011	Jun 76	1 PT.	
Spect (n,γ)	Maxwl		CCP	Expt	Jour AE 4 22	Jan 58	Sklyarevskii+.EGS+INTENS BELOW .3MEV	
					Jour JNE 9 69	Jun 59	TRANSLATN.*	
					Jour SJA 4 19	58	TRANSLATN.*	

64 Gadolinium 155

Quantity	Energy (ev) Min	Max	Lab	Type	Documentation Ref Vol Page	Date	Author, Comments	Data
Spect (n,γ)	Maxwl		KUR Expt	Jour	AE 4 5	Jan 58	Groshev+ SPECTRUM+LINES 0.3 – 7.33MEV	
				Jour	JNE 9 50	Jun 59	. ENGL OF AE 4 5	
				Jour	SJA 4 1	58	. ENGL OF AE 4 5	
Spect (n,γ)	2.6+0		YAL Expt	Abst	BAP 4 35	Jan 59	Springer+,NAI(TL),GAMMA MULTIPLICITY	
Spect (n,γ)	Maxwl		CRC Expt	Conf	AEC – TR – 6465	Jul 60	Bartholomew+ MOSCOW CONF NUC REACTNS	
Spect (n,γ)	Maxwl		UNC Theo	Jour	PR 122 212	Apr 61	Troubetzkoy. STAT TH CFD DATA.	
Spect (n,γ)	–		MUN Expt	Jour	ZN/A 16 927	Sep 61	Schult.LVLS IN GD156 XTAL SPECTROMET	
Spect (n,γ)	2.0+0	8.0+1	CCP Expt	Jour	ZET 45 1858	Dec 63	20RES.3 GAMMA E INTERVLS.P – T 8.44MEV	
				Jour	JET 18 1274	64	TRANSLATN.*DANELYAN	
Spect (n,γ)	Maxwl		CCP Theo	Jour	YF 2 4 657	Oct 65	Kosorukov.GRPH SPCTR,CFD EXP	
				Jour	SNP 2 470	Apr 66	TRANSLATN.*	
Spect (n,γ)	Pile		MUN Expt	Jour	ZN/A 21 1328	Sep 66	Neumann. CRYST SPEC EXPT OF GAM INT	
				Rept	ANL – TRANS – 941	73	. ENGLISH OF ZN/A 1328	
Spect (n,γ)	None		KUR Expt	Priv	DANELYAN	Jun 68	Danelyan+.8.44+8.52 MEV TRANS INTENS	
Spect (n,γ)	Maxwl		KUR Expt	Jour	IZV 32 1719	Oct 68	Govor+ GAM+K X RAY COINCIDENCE SPECS	
				Jour	BAS 32 1584	Oct 69	. ENGL OF IZV 32 1719	
Spect (n,γ)	None		MTR Expt	Jour	IN – 1218 123	Dec 68	Spencer+ GE – LI DET	
Spect (n,γ)	Maxwl		RIS Expt	Conf	69Montreal 701	Aug 69	Koch+CRYS DIFFRACT.MEASMT RVW.NDG	
Spect (n,γ)	Maxwl		KFI Revw	Jour	YF 10 907	Nov 69	Kecskemeti+ AVG GAM – MULTIPLICITY,TBL	
				Jour	SNP 10 524	May 70	TRANSLATN.*	
Spect (n,γ)	Maxwl	6.3+1	KUR Expt	Prog	YFI – 8 13	Dec 69	Daneljan+ GAMMA INTENS IN RES REGN	
				Rept	INDC(CCP) – 8U18	Dec 70	TRANSLATN.*	
	2.6 – 2	6.3+1		Jour	ZET 58 456	Feb 70	Daneljan+ GAM – INT OR ROTAT+VIBRAT	
				Jour	ZET 54 401	Feb 68	– + GAM – SPECS AT 10 RESONANCES	
				Jour	JET 31 242	Aug 70	. ENGL OF ZET 58 456	
				Jour	JET 24 216	Aug 68	. ENGL OF ZET 54 401	
Spect (n,γ)	Maxwl		UPP Expt	Prog	EANDC(OR)99 19	Aug 70	Baecklin+. ELECTR+GAM SPEC 500 LINES	
	Pile			Conf	69Studsvik 147	Aug 69	– +LABS=UPP+MTR+MUN,G+EL SPECS	
Spect (n,γ)	Pile		ANL Expt	Jour	PR/C 2 1951	Nov 70	Bollinger+,B10 COVER,GE(LI) DET	
				Conf	69Studsvik 601	Aug 69	Smither+ NO DATA GVN,OKS STATMOD	
Spect (n,γ)	Pile		KFK Expt	Rept	KFK – 1401	Jun 71	Djadali.AVG POLRZ G EXPT,CFD T,SPIN	
	Maxwl			Jour	NP/A 147 150	May 70	Eichler+ POL NS.CIRC POL GS+ASSYMTRY	
Spect (n,γ)	Maxwl		MUN Expt	Prog	EANDC(E)140U	Aug 71	Egidy+ INT.CONVERSION.	
				Conf	67Juelich 56	Apr 67	– + CONVERSION ELECTRONS162 – 6.NDG	
Spect (n,γ)	2.0+3		MTR Expt	Prog	ANCR – 1088 63	72	Greenwood+. 5045 – 8537KEV GAMMAS	
Spect (n,γ)	6.3+6	8.7+6	KUR Expt	Jour	ZET 62 1228	Apr 72	Danelya+ INTENS. OF G – TRANSIT., NDG	
				Jour	JET 35 649	Oct 72	. ENGLISH OF ZET 62 1228	
Spect (n,γ)	None		KUR Expt	Prog	INDC(SEC) – 28	Sep 72	Danelyan+ PAGE62,GE – LI,G – INTENS,NDG	
Spect (n,γ)	Maxwl		IFL Expt	Book	PROKOFJEV	73	. TBL GAM,CONV ELECTR ES+INT,LVL SCH	
Spect (n,γ)	Maxwl		KFI Expt	Prog	KFKI – YB – 72 31	May 73	Kardon+ VERY BRIEF,G – SPECT,G – WID,NDG	
Spect (n,γ)	Maxwl		CCP Theo	Jour	ZET 65 12	Jul 73	Nosov+ THERMODYN CALC CFD EXPT,GRAPH	
				Jour	JET 38 6	Jan 74	. ENGLISH OF ZET 65 6	
Spect (n,γ)	8.9+4	4.5+6	MUN Expt	Jour	ZN/A 29 17	Jan 74	Schreckenbach. INT CONVERSION,TBL	
	8.0+4	1.0+7		Rept	PTUM – E – 18	May 73	– . THESIS. CONV – EL,LVLS	
Spect (n,γ)	Maxwl		KUR Expt	Jour	YF 19 712	Apr 74	Efimov+ TBL G – ES+INTS+SPIN(FINAL ST)	
				Jour	SNP 19 361	Oct 74	. ENGLISH OF YF 19 712	
Spect (n,γ)	2.0+3		BNL Expt	Jour	NIM 138 125	76	Greenwood+ FILTERED BEAM GRPH	
(n,2n)	Fiss		CRC Eval	Rept	CRC – 1003	Dec 60	Roy+,ESTIMATED AVG SIG=10.0MB	
(n,2n)	1.3+7	1.5+7	BNL Theo	Jour	NSE 23 238	Nov 65	Pearlstein.3ES.STAT MDL CALC.TBL CS.	
(n,2n)	Fiss		BNL Theo	Jour	NSE 23 238	Nov 65	Pearlstein.STATMDL CALC.SPEC AVG.TBL	
(n,2n)	1.5+7		DEB Eval	Jour	REA 11 1 153	Mar 73	Boedy+ RECOMM.VALUE FROM N – Z SYSTEM.	
(n,2n)	1.5+7		KFI Theo	Rept	KFKI – 73 – 68	Dec 73	Jeki.NEW FIT,CALC SIG CFD OTHERS,TBL	
(n,xn) x>2	Fiss		BNL Theo	Jour	NSE 23 238	Nov 65	Pearlstein.SPEC AVG STATMDL CALC N3N	
(n,p)	Fiss		CRC Eval	Rept	CRC – 1003	Dec 60	Roy+,ESTIMATED AVG SIG=0.08MB	
(n,p)	Maxwl		IFU Theo	Rept	ICD – 4 20	67	Dadakina+ PENETR COEFF CALC,TABLE	
(n,p)	1.4+7	1.5+7	ARK Theo	Prog	ORO – 3235 – 29	Jan 67	Koch+,STAT MODEL CALC CFD EXPTS	
(n,α)	Fiss		CRC Eval	Rept	CRC – 1003	Dec 60	Roy+,ESTIMATED AVG SIG=0.016MB	
(n,α)	Maxwl		ISL Expt	Jour	PL 1 289	Jul 62	Cheifetz. TBL Q – VALU,SIG,BRANCHRATIO	+
	Maxwl			Data	EXFOR31151.	Mar 73	.SIG GVN	
(n,α)	Maxwl		CCP Expt	Jour	YF 1 252	Feb 65	Andreev.IONIZ – CHAMBER,SIG=M.09MB	+
				Jour	SNP 1 177	Aug 65	TRANSLATN.*	
(n,α)	Maxwl		MCM Expt	Jour	NP/A 129 571	May 69	Beg+ ALPHA SPEC GD155+ND143(STANDRD)	+
	Maxwl			Data	EXFOR12139.002	Jun 76	. 1 PT.	
(n,α)	2.0+0	2.1+1	DUB Expt	Rept	JINR – P3 – 7376	Sep 73	Balabanov+ RES – PARS+TOF SPEC,TBL,GRF	
(n,α)	Fiss		LYO Expt	Jour	LYCEN/75 – 01 27	74	Emsallem+ABST,NDG	
Reson Params	2.1+0	4.7+1	MTR Expt	Prog	IDO – 16373 39	Jul 57	Simpson.WG,G*WN,WN0.TBL.23 RES ES.	+
	2.1+0	4.7+1		Data	EXFOR11983.009	Jun 76	. 23 RES, E0,WN,WN0,WG.	
Reson Params	6.4+0	7.8+1	HAR Expt	Jour	NP 5 294	Jan 58	Bowey+. 18 RESONANCE ES GVN. LINAC	+

64 Gadolinium 155

Quantity	Energy (ev) Min	Max	Lab	Type	Documentation Ref Vol Page	Author, Comments Date	Data
Reson Params	2.7−2		CRC Expt	Conf	60Kingston 573	Aug 60 Bartholomew. E,J GIVEN.	+
	2.7−2			Data	EXFOR11444.002	Jun 76 . 1 RES, J.	
Reson Params	2.7−2	2.4+1	BNL Expt	Jour	NSE 8 183	Sep 60 Moller+,WT WG 2GWN OTHER PARAMETERS	+
	2.7−2	2.4+1		Data	EXFOR12097.009	Jun 76 . 11 RES, E0,WT,WG,PCS.	
Reson Params	2.0+0	4.4+1	ANL Expt	Prog	ANL−6589	Aug 62 Carpenter. E,J GIVEN.	+
	2.0+0	4.4+1		Data	EXFOR12048.006	Jun 76 . 12 RES, E0,J.	
Reson Params	2.7−2	6.3+0	NRL Expt	Jour	PR/B 134 68	Apr 64 Stolovy. J=1 2EV RES,3RES J=2	+
	2.7−2	6.3+0		Data	EXFOR11436.004	Jun 76 . 4 RES, E0,J.	
Reson Params	2.7−2	2.6+0	BNL ExTh	Jour	PR/B 138 1361	Jun 65 Shore+ J=2,3RD AT2.0EV J=1.	+
	2.7−2	2.6+0		Expt Data	EXFOR11440.002	Jun 76 . 3 RES, E0,J.	
Reson Params	−		KFK Eval	Rept	KFK−352	Aug 65 Schmidt+AVERAGE S−WAWE RES PAR(TAB19	
Reson Params		1.0+6	AUA Theo	Jour	AUJ 20 477	Oct 67 Cook. TBL OF AVG LVL SPACING D,L=0,1	
Reson Params	2.6−2	6.2+1	KUR Expt	Prog	YFI−6 76	68 Daneljan+ TABLE 23 RES	
				Rept	INDC−260E	69 . ENGL OF YFI−6 76	
Reson Params	1.2+1	4.3+1	CCP Expt	Jour	ZET 54 401	Feb 68 Danelyan+ SPINS OF 5 (N,G) RESONANCS	
				Jour	JET 24 216	Aug 68 TRANSLATN.*	
Reson Params	6.3+0	3.3+1	SAC Expt	Jour	NP/A 132 129	Jul 69 Julien+ TBL RESONANCE PARAMS.	+
				Diss	CEA−R−3602	Jul 69 Alves.THESIS,WN,WG,WT,7E0,3J GIVEN	
				Conf	68Wash. 867	Mar 68 Morgenstern. WG VS. A. AVG WG GIVEN	
				Conf	66Paris 1 559	Oct 66 Huynh+ ABST.NDG. SEE INDC−156	
	0.0+0	8.0+0		Data	EXFOR20687.	Aug 77 3PTS.E0,WG,AVG WG,WT,J,G*WN.	
Reson Params		1.8+2	DUB Expt	Conf	68DUBSY 349	Jul 68 Pikelner.LVL SPAC,AVERG. WG	
Reson Params	−		IFU Expt	Jour	UFZ 13 2085	Dec 68 Vertebnyj+ OTHER EXPTL+TH D VAL GVN	
				Jour	UPJ 13 1492	Jun 69 TRANSLATN.*	
Reson Params	3.6+0	8.5+1	SAC Expt	Rept	CEA−N−1149	Jan 69 Ribon.TOF TRANSMISSION. +SCATTERING	+
	3.6+0	8.5+1		Data	EXFOR20148.	May 73 126PTS.WG,AVG WG,WT,2G*WN.	
Reson Params	2.0+0	7.0+1	BNL Expt	Jour	PR 180 1131	Apr 69 Mughabghab+ TRANS,2G*WN AVG D 32RESN	+
				Rept	BNL−13074	68 − .	
	2.0+0	7.0+1		Data	EXFOR10051.	May 73 . 93 PTS.E0,2G*WN,2G*WN0.	
Reson Params	6.2+0	1.8+2	DUB Expt	Jour	YF 9 897	May 69 Karzhavina+,TRANS+AREA ANAL,TBL+GRPH	+
				Prog	YFI−6 135	Oct 68 − + SHORTER TEXT, TABLE	
				Rept	JINR−P3−3882	Jun 68 − + FULL PAPER.	
	2.2+2	2.7+3		Rept	BNL−TR−322	Jan 70 − + ENGL OF YF 9 897.	
	6.2+0	1.8+2		Jour	SNP 9 523	Nov 69 − + ENGL OF YF 9 897.	
	6.2+0	1.9+2		Rept	INDC−E−260	69 .ENGL TRANSL OF YFI−6 135	
	6.3+0	1.8+2		Data	EXFOR40162.	Jul 73 .EN−RES,TOT WID,GAMMA WID,D,AVER G−W	
Reson Params	7.8+0	6.3+1	CCP Expt	Jour	ZET 58 456	Feb 70 Danelyan+ SPINS OF 13(N,G) RESONANCS	
				Jour	JET 31 242	Aug 70 TRANSLATN.*	
Reson Params	2.0+0	9.3+1	SAC Expt	Jour	NP/A 145 549	Apr 70 Asghar+ WN,WNO,WT,J. 28E0+J FOR 93EV	+
	2.0+0	9.3+1		Data	EXFOR20147.002	May 73 29PTS.J.	
Reson Params	3.6+0	1.8+2	GA Expt	Jour	NP/A 146 337	May 70 Friesenhahn+WN,WG,90E0,AREA,SHAPE AN	+
	3.6+0	1.7+2		Data	EXFOR10049.	May 73 . 90 RES,N−WID, 28RES,G−WID.	
Reson Params	−		AUA Theo	Rept	AAEC/E−211	Nov 70 Musgrove. CALCULTD D+GAM WIDTH GIVEN	
Reson Params	None		KUR Expt	Jour	AE 29 395	Nov 70 Muradjan+ ABST FRANC−SOV SEM DUBNA	
				Jour	SJA 29 1156	Nov 70 TRANSLATN.*	
Reson Params	−		DUB Expt	Rept	JINR−E3−5483	Dec 70 Popov. TABLE OF ALPHA+NEUTRON WIDTHS	
Reson Params	2.7−2	5.2+1	CJD Eval	Rept	YK−7	71 Zakharova+ SURVEY+SYSTEMATICS,GW,TBL	
				Rept	INDC(CCP)−27	Nov 72 .ENGLISH TRANSLATION OF YK−7 /71	
Reson Params	None		DUB Theo	Jour	YF 13 240	Feb 71 Malecki+G−WID,THEO CFD EXPT.TBL,GRPH	
				Jour	SNP 13 133	Aug 71 − + ENGL OF YF 13 240.	
Reson Params	6.3+6	8.7+6	KUR Expt	Jour	ZET 62 1228	Apr 72 Danelya+ REDUCED G−WIDTHS,23RES.,NDG	
				Jour	JET 35 649	Oct 72 . ENGLISH OF ZET 62 1228	
Reson Params	+2	1.0+3	CCP Expt	Conf	73Kiev 2 148	May 73 Balabanov+ TOT ALF−WID,CFD OPTMDL	
Reson Params	+0	+3	KUR Theo	Conf	73Kiev 2 301	May 73 Daneljan. CORREL N+G−WID+PARTL G−WID	
Reson Params	2.0+0	2.1+1	DUB Expt	Rept	JINR−P3−7376	Sep 73 Balabanov+ RES−E,ALF−WID,SPIN,TABLE	
				Conf	72Budapest 140	Aug 72 − + ALPHA−WIDTHS ,TBL	
Reson Params	+0	+2	BOL Eval	Conf	IAEA−169 3 123	74 Benzi+ AVG G−WID CFD OTHERS+XPT,TABL	
Reson Params	Maxwl		KUR Expt	Jour	YF 19 712	Apr 74 Efimov+ CORREL RED N−WID,G−WID STUDY	
				Jour	SNP 19 361	Oct 74 . ENGLISH OF YF 19 712	
Reson Params	+0	+2	FEI Eval	Rept	YK−8/2 97	Sep 72 Abagyan+ AVG G−WID+D AT BINDNG−E,TBL	
				Rept	INDC(CCP)−39	Jul 74 .PAGE 102.ENGLISH OF YK−8/2 97	
Reson Params	8.5+6		DUB Theo	Conf	74Petten 175	Sep 74 Malov+ DOBS,SEMI−MICROSCOPIC CALC.	
Reson Params	+0		DUB Theo	Jour	YF 21 40	Jan 75 Voronov+ MEAN D,WITH ROTAT.CFD EXPT	
				Jour	SNP 21 20	Jul 75 . ENGLISH OF YF 21,40	
Reson Params	Maxwl		KUK Theo	Conf	76Ahmedabd 2 1	Dec 76 Sharma+AVG S−WAVE REDUCED N−WID ANAL	
Strnth Fnctn	1.0+1	5.0+1	MTR Expt	Abst	BAP 2 42	Feb 57 Simpson+AVG STF=(2.0+−.2)−4	
Strnth Fnctn	+3		BNL Expt	Jour	PRL 1 461	Dec 58 Hughes. FC 1.8+−0.7	
Strnth Fnctn		1.8+2	DUB Expt	Conf	68DUBSY 349	Jul 68 Pikelner.LVL SPAC,AVERG. WG,S0 VS A	

64 Gadolinium 155

Quantity	Energy (ev) Min	Max	Lab	Type	Documentation Ref Vol Page	Date	Author, Comments	Data
Strnth Fnctn	0.0+0	8.5+1	SAC	Expt	Rept CEA-N-1149	Jan 69	Ribon. RES PARAM ANALYSIS.TBL	+
		8.5+1		Jour	JPRC 29 1 203	Jan 68	- + S-WAVE.NO VARIATION WITH SPIN	
		8.5+1		Data	EXFOR20148.016	May 73	. 1PNT.L=0	
Strnth Fnctn	2.7-2	1.5+4	BNL	Expt	Jour PR 180 1131	Apr 69	Mughabghab+ TRANS,2.4+ -0.3FROM RESON	+
		+4		Jour	PL/B 24 573	May 67	Chrien+ FROM RES+UNRESOLVED REGIONS	
		5.0+3		Conf	65Antwerp 69	Jul 65	- +TOT SIG SLOPE SWAVE STF 2.35+	
	2.7-2	1.5+4		Data	EXFOR10051.	May 73	. 4 PTS. L=0.	
Strnth Fnctn		1.8+2	DUB	Expt	Jour YF 9 897	May 69	Karzhavina+,TRANSMISSION,RES-PARAMS	+
				Prog	YFI-6 135	Oct 68	- + SHORTER TEXT, TABLE	
				Rept	JINR-P3-3882	Jun 68	- + FULL PAPER.	
		2.3+2		Rept	BNL-TR-322	Jan 70	- + ENGL OF YF 9 897.	
		1.8+2		Jour	SNP 9 523	Nov 69	- + ENGL OF YF 9 897.	
		1.9+2		Rept	INDC-E-260	69	.ENGL TRANSL OF YFI-6 135	
	6.0+0	1.8+2		Data	EXFOR40162.051	Jul 73	.STRNTH FNCTN GVN	
Strnth Fnctn	-		DUB	Revw	Jour YF 11 111	Jan 70	Malecki+ VALUES FOR TWO SPIN STATES	
				Jour	SNP 11 61	Jul 70	- + ENGL OF YF 11 61.	
Strnth Fnctn	0.0+0	9.3+1	SAC	Expt	Jour NP/A 145 549	Apr 70	Asghar+.S-WAVE J=1,2.NO SPIN DEPEND	+
	0.0+0	9.3+1		Data	EXFOR20147.003	May 73	2PTS.L=0.	
Strnth Fnctn	2.7-2	2.4+2	BNL	Expt	Jour PR/C 1 1850	May 70	Mughabghab+,STF FROM SIGMA+RESON	
Strnth Fnctn	3.6+0	1.8+4	GA	Expt	Jour NP/A 146 337	May 70	Friesenhahn+L=0 FROM RES,L=1 FROM NG	+
	3.0+0	2.0+4		Data	EXFOR10049.	May 73	. 3 PTS.	
Strnth Fnctn	-		AUA	Theo	Rept AAEC/E-211	Nov 70	Musgrove. SMOOTHED S0,S1 AND S2 GIVN	
Strnth Fnctn	1.5+2	6.5+2	SAC	ExTh	Diss FRNC-TH-450	Oct 72	Delaroche.OPTICAL MODEL PARAMETERS	
Strnth Fnctn	None		AUA	Eval	Rept AAEC/E-277	Mar 73	Musgrove.TBLS EXPTL DATA+BEST VALUES	
Lvl Density	1.1+1	2.3+2	DUB	Expt	Rept JINR-P3-3882	Oct 68	Karzhavina+	+
				Rept	YFI-6 135	Nov 68	- +	
	1.1+1	2.3+2		Data	EXFOR40162.045	Jul 73	.1 DATA LINES	
Lvl Density	0.0+0	8.5+1	SAC	Expt	Rept CEA-N-1149	Jan 69	Ribon. RESONANCE PARAMETER ANALYSIS.	
		8.5+1		Data	EXFOR20148.017	May 73	1PNT.SP.CUT(0).	
Lvl Density	None		AUW	Theo	Conf 70Madurai 2 267	Dec 70	Ramamurty+ A-PARAMETER GVN,LANG'S-TH	
Lvl Density	None		MUN	Theo	Jour NP/A 217 269	Dec 73	Dilg+ A,DELTA. BACK SHIFTED FERMIGAS	
Lvl Density	None		BOL	Eval	Conf IAEA-169 3 123	74	Benzi+ LVL DENS PARAM BY XPT,GRPH+TB	
Lvl Density	None		ROC	Theo	Jour NP/A 223 589	May 74	Huizenga+ EXP CFD MICROSC TH AX SYMM	
Lvl Density	+0	+2	FEI	Eval	Rept YK- 8/2 97	Sep 72	Abagyan+ LVL DENSITY PARAMETER,TBL	
				Rept	INDC(CCP)-39	Jul 74	.PAGE 102.ENGLISH OF YK-8/2 97	
Lvl Density	+0		DUB	Theo	Conf 75Kiev 3 23	May 75	Voronov. LVL SPACING OF GD156.TABLE	

64 Gadolinium 156

Quantity	Energy (ev) Min	Max	Lab	Type	Documentation Ref Vol Page	Date	Author, Comments	Data
Evaluation	1.0-3	1.5+7	AUA	Eval	Rept AAEC/TM-549	Jun 70	Cook.TOT,EL,INEL,NONEL,CAPT SIGS,NDG	+
					Rept AAEC/E-214	Jun 71	Bertram+GROUP SIGMAS SAME QUANTS.NDG	
					Rept AAEC/TM-587	Mar 71	*DESCRIPTION OF LIBRARY	
	1.0-3	1.5+7			Data AUSTR-DFN 171.	Nov 71	POINT(223) AND GROUP(127) SIGMAS	
Evaluation	1.0-5	1.5+7	BOL	Eval	Prog NEANDC(E)182 7	Dec 76	Fabri+ COMPLETE EVAL IN ENDF/B DONE	+
	1.0-5	1.5+7			Data CNEN-CEA 5	Jan 78	PRELIM.ALL QUANTITIES.ENDF FORMAT	
Total	1.0+6	1.0+7	BOL	Revw	Conf 70Helsinki 2 379	Jun 70	Benzi.115. REVIEW, SIG(E) GRAPH	
Total	1.0-3	1.5+7	AUA	Eval	Data AUSTR-DFN 171.	Nov 71	COOK+POINT(223)+GROUP(127)SIG.CF EVL	+
Total	1.4+7		LIN	Expt	Jour IZV 37 1019	May 73	Djumin+ SIG(A),OPTMODEL CALC,GRAPH	+
					Conf 73Kiev 3 108	May 73	- + OPTMOD CALC,SIG	
					Jour BAS 37 5 91	May 73	.ENGLISH OF IZV 37 1019	
	1.4+7				Data EXFOR40302.017	Feb 76	1 PNT	
Total	0.0+0	1.0+7	BOL	Theo	Conf JAERI-M-5984	Feb 75	Benzi+P.83.OPT/STATMOD.CURVES CFD.	
Elastic	1.0-3	1.5+7	AUA	Eval	Data AUSTR-DFN 171.	Nov 71	COOK+POINT(223)+GROUP(127)SIG.CF EVL	+
Diff Elastic	4.0+6		BOL	Revw	Conf 70Helsinki 2 379	Jun 70	Benzi.115. REVIEW, SIG(E) GRAPH	
Diff Elastic	4.0+6		BOL	Theo	Conf JAERI-M-5984	Feb 75	Benzi+P.83.OPT/STATMOD.ANG CURVS CFD	
Potntal Scat	None		BNL	Expt	Jour PL/B 24 573	May 67	Chrien+ FROM ANALYSIS OF RESONANCES	
Tot Inelastc	1.4+7	1.5+7	JYV	Expt	Rept JU-RR-3/1970	Jun 70	Leppaemaeki+ TABLE OF EVAL AVG SIG	
Tot Inelastc	5.0+5	1.5+7	AUA	Eval	Data AUSTR-DFN 171.	Nov 71	COOK+POINT(11)+GROUP(127)SIG.CF EVL	+
Diff Inelast	1.0+6		BOL	Revw	Conf 70Helsinki 2 379	Jun 70	Benzi.115. REVIEW, SIG(ANG) GRAPHS	
Diff Inelast	1.0+6		BOL	Theo	Conf JAERI-M-5984	Feb 75	Benzi+P.83.OPT/STATMOD.ANG CURVS CFD	
Nonelastic	1.0-3	1.5+7	AUA	Eval	Data AUSTR-DFN 171.	Nov 71	COOK+POINT(223)+GROUP(127)SIG.CF EVL	+
Absorption	Maxwl		KAP	Expt	Jour NUC 14 89	Sep 56	Deutsch.FISS PROD S EST BY STEHN	
Absorption	4.1-1	1.0+7	GA	Eval	Rept GA- 2451	Aug 61	Joanou+.68GROUP DATA FOR GAM-I	

64 Gadolinium 156

Quantity	Energy (ev) Min	Energy (ev) Max	Lab	Type	Documentation Ref Vol Page	Date	Author, Comments	Data
Absorption	Pile		FEI	Expt	Prog INDSWG – 126 8	66	Grishanin. SIG=11.5+ – 7.2 B	
					Jour AE 19 459	Nov 65	– + SIG=9.8 + – 2.58 B	
					Jour JNE 21 203	66	. ENGL OF AE 19 459	
					Jour SJA 19 1432	Nov 65	. ENGL OF AE 19 459	
Absorption	1.0 – 3	1.0 + 7	JUL	Eval	Rept JUEL – 678 – RG	Jul 70	Liu. EVALUATION+CALC,GRPH,FN OF E	
Absorption	Maxwl	Pile	SGA	Expt	Jour JMS 6 435	71	Dobrozemsky+ CHANGE OF ABUND.TBL SIG	+
					Rept SGAE – PH – 104	71	– + MASS – SPEC METHOD.	
	Pile				Conf 66Paris 1 495	Oct 66	– + PPR82.MASS SPEC,VAL GVN	
	Maxwl	Pile			Jour APA 23 64	May 66	Lugmair+ REL CO – 59 BY MASS – SPEC	
	Pile				Rept SGAE – PH – 47	66	Dobrozemsky+ SUPERSEDED.	
					Rept SGAE – PH – 35	65	– + SUPERSEDED.	
	Maxwl	Pile			Rept AEC – TR – 7574	74	– + ENGLISH OF JMS 6 435	
	2.5 – 2				Data EXFOR20637.008	Sep 76	1PNT.SIGMA.	
Absorption	2.5 – 2		IJI	Eval	Conf 75Kiev 1 169	May 75	Fedorova+ EVAL 2200M/S SIG,TABLE	
Res Int Abs	5.0 – 1		ORL	Expt	Prog ORNL – 3832 7	Sep 65	Lantz. VALUE GIVEN.	+
	5.0 – 1				Data EXFOR11938.005	Jun 76	. 1 PT.	
Res Int Abs	5.0 – 1		BNL	Expt	Rept BNL – 13074	68	Mughabghab.	
Res Int Abs	5.5 – 1		SGA	Expt	Jour JMS 6 435	71	Dobrozemsky+ EFF ABS RES INT GIVEN.	+
					Prog SGAE – PH – 104	71	– +MASS – SPECTROMETRIC	
					Rept AEC – TR – 7574	74	. ENGLISH OF JMS 6 415	
	5.5 – 1				Data EXFOR20637.009	Sep 76	1PNT.	
Res Int Abs	None		GA	Eval	Rept GA – 12071	Sep 71	Mathews+. RECOMMENDED VALUES	
Res Int Abs	5.5 – 1		CRC	Eval	Rept AECL – 3037 1	Jan 72	Walker.REDUCED RES INT,DETAILED TBL	
Res Int Abs	5.0 – 1		AUA	Eval	Rept AAEC/TM – 619	Sep 72	Clayton.CALC FROM SIG LIBRARY,TABLE	
Res Int Abs	5.5 – 1	+6	SAC	Revw	Conf IAEA – 169 1 235	74	Ribon.CAPTURE,STATUS CFD REQUEST,TBL	
Res Int Abs	+0	+5	WIN	Revw	Conf IAEA – 169 3 163	74	Pope+ DATA FILE CALC CFD XPTAL VALUE	
Res Int Abs	5.0 – 1		IJI	Eval	Conf 75Kiev 1 169	May 75	Fedorova+ EVAL+CALC RI GIVEN,TABLE	
(n,γ)	Maxwl		MCM	Expt	Priv WALKER	May 56	Walker.	+
	Maxwl				Data EXFOR12127.012	Jun 76	. 1 PT.	
(n,γ)	Maxwl		CRC	Eval	Rept AECL – 1054	Mar 60	Walker. (CRRP – 913)	
(n,γ)	Maxwl		ORL	Expt	Prog ORNL – 3832 7	Sep 65	Lantz. VALUE GIVEN.	+
	Maxwl				Data EXFOR11938.004	Jun 76	. 1 PT.	
(n,γ)	5.0 + 3	1.0 + 5	AUA	ExHt	Rept AAEC/E – 198	May 69	Musgrove.S+P+D WAVE SIGMAS CALC,TBL	+
(n,γ)	1.0 + 3	1.0 + 7	BOL	Eval	Rept CCDN – NW/10	Dec 69	Benzi+H – F MOD,AXEL G(G)EST,ALL DATA	
					Rept CEC(70) – 2	Apr 70	– +. GRAPH	
					Conf 66Paris 1 537	Oct 66	– + STATMOD.TBL AV VALS.SUPERSEDD	
(n,γ)	1.4 + 7	1.5 + 7	JYV	Eval	Rept JU – RR – 3/1970	Jun 70	Leppaemaeki+ TABLE OF EVAL AVG SIG	
(n,γ)	3.0 + 4		AUA	Theo	Rept AAEC/E – 211	Nov 70	Musgrove. SIGMA GIVEN AND CFD OTHER	
(n,γ)	Maxwl		GA	Eval	Rept GA – 12071	Sep 71	Mathews+. RECOMMENDED VALUES	
(n,γ)	1.0 – 3	1.5 + 7	AUA	Eval	Data AUSTR – DFN 171.	Nov 71	COOK+POINT(223)+GROUP(127)SIG.CF EVL	+
(n,γ)	Maxwl		CRC	Eval	Rept AECL – 3037 1	Jan 72	Walker.RECOMMENDED SIG,DETAILED TBL	
(n,γ)	2.5 – 2		AUA	Eval	Rept AAEC/TM – 619	Sep 72	Clayton.CALC FROM SIG LIBRARY,TABLE	
(n,γ)	5.0 + 3	7.0 + 4	CCP	Expt	Conf 73Kiev 2 206	May 73	Kononov+ TOF,SIG(NEUT – E),GRAPH	
(n,γ)		1.1 + 7	RCN	Theo	Rept RCN – 191	Jun 73	Lautenbach.GROUP CONSTANTS TBL	
(n,γ)	2.5 – 2		SAC	Revw	Conf IAEA – 169 1 235	74	Ribon.STATUS SIG CFD REQUESTS,TABLE	
(n,γ)	Maxwl	Fiss	WIN	Revw	Conf IAEA – 169 3 163	74	Pope+ MAXW+FIS – SPEC AVG DATA CFD XPT	
	Fiss				Conf IAEA – 169 3 137	74	Dean. POINT DATA AVG OVER STAND SPEC	
(n,γ)	1.0 + 3	1.0 + 7	FEI	Eval	Rept YK – 8/2 97	Sep 72	Abagjan+ AVG SIG(ENERGY – GROUPS),TABL	
					Rept INDC(CCP) – 39	Jul 74	.P102. ENGLISH OF YK – 8/2 97	
(n,γ)	5.0 + 3	7.0 + 4	FEI	Expt	Rept YFI – 17 9	Aug 74	Shorin+ TOF,SIG(NEUT – E),TBL	+
					Jour YF 19 5	Jan 74	– + TOF,SIG(NEUT – E),GRAPHS	
	5.3 + 3	6.8 + 4			Rept INDC(CCP) – 48	Feb 75	. ENGLISH OF YFI – 17 9	
	5.0 + 3	7.0 + 4			Jour SNP 19 2	Jul 74	. ENGLISH OF YF 19 5	
	5.3 + 3	6.8 + 4			Data EXFOR40222.006	Feb 74	.SIGMA FOR 32 EN – RANGES GVN	
(n,γ)	Maxwl		BNL	Expt	Prog ERDA – NDC – 2 31	May 75	Chrien+TABLE	
					Conf 74Petten 271	Sep 74	Cole+ DIRECT CAPT.COMP. TBL	
(n,γ)	Fast		RCN	Expt	Rept ECN – 10	Oct 76	Veenema+ STEK REACTIVITY WORTHS TBL.	
(n,γ)		3.0 + 3	GEL	Expt	Prog NEANDC(E)182 7	Dec 76	Coceva+ LINAC(GEEL).TBC	
Spect (n,γ)	Maxwl		AUW	Expt	Conf 63Bombay 160	Feb 63	Sastry+.TBL,GAMMA – E +INTENSITY	
Spect (n,γ)	Pile		KUR	Expt	Jour YF 13 681	Apr 71	Groshev+ GE – LI,TBD	
	Maxwl				Jour IZV 35 1644	May 73	– + GAMMA TRANSITIONS,GRAPH	
					Jour BAS 35 1497	Aug 72	. ENGL OF IZV 35 1644	
	Pile				Jour SNP 13 387	Oct 71	. ENGL OF YF 13 681	
Spect (n,γ)	1.0 + 3	2.4 + 4	INL	Expt	Conf 75Wash. 912	Mar 75	Greenwood+ GRPH COUNTS VS CHANNEL	
					Rept ANCR – 1177 58	Jan 75	– + SUPERSEDED	
					Conf 74Petten 353	Sep 74	– + FILTERED BEAM,GRPH	
Inelastic γ	8.5 + 6		UNC	Theo	Jour PR 122 212	Apr 61	Troubetzkoy. STAT TH CFD DATA.	
(n,2n)	Fiss		CRC	Eval	Rept CRC – 1003	Dec 60	Roy+,ESTIMATED AVG SIG = 5.6MB	

64 Gadolinium 156

Quantity	Energy (ev) Min	Max	Lab	Type	Documentation Ref Vol Page	Date	Author, Comments	Data
(n,2n)	1.3+7	1.5+7	BNL Theo	Jour	NSE 23 238	Nov 65	Pearlstein.3ES.STAT MDL CALC.TBL CS.	
(n,2n)	Fiss		BNL Theo	Jour	NSE 23 238	Nov 65	Pearlstein.STATMDL CALC.SPEC AVG.TBL	
(n,2n)	1.4+7	1.5+7	HLS Expt	Jour	AAF 6 325	Nov 69	Liukkonen+ ANALYS OF 31MS ISOM STATE	
(n,2n)	1.4+7	1.5+7	JYV Eval	Rept	JU−RR−3/1970	Jun 70	Leppaemaeki+ TABLE OF EVAL AVG SIG	
(n,2n)	1.5+7		DEB Eval	Jour	REA 11 1 153	Mar 73	Boedy+ RECOMM.VALUE FROM N−Z SYSTEM.	
(n,2n)	1.5+7		KFI Theo	Rept	KFKI−73−68	Dec 73	Jeki.NEW FIT,CALC SIG CFD OTHERS,TBL	
(n,xn) x>2	Fiss		BNL Theo	Jour	NSE 23 238	Nov 65	Pearlstein.SPEC AVG STATMDL CALC N3N	
(n,p)	Fiss		CRC Eval	Rept	CRC−1003	Dec 60	Roy+,ESTIMATED AVG SIG=0.04MB	
(n,p)	1.4+7	1.5+7	ARK Theo	Prog	ORO−3235−29	Jan 67	Koch+,STAT MODEL CALC CFD EXPTS	
(n,p)	1.4+7		LYO Comp	Rept	LYCEN/6780	Nov 67	Crouzet+COMPILATN FOR ACTIVTN ANALYS	
(n,p)	1.5+7		IRK Expt	Jour	APA 34 245	Sep 71	Havlik. ACT. CC−W.	+
				Jour	OAWA 107 119	Apr 70	−. ACTIVATION METHOD	
	1.5+7			Data	EXFOR20509.012	Apr 76	1PNT.SIGMA.	
(n,α)	1.4+7		ALD Expt	Jour	PPS 73 215	Feb 59	Coleman+. ACTIVATION	+
(n,α)	Fiss		CRC Eval	Rept	CRC−1003	Dec 60	Roy+,ESTIMATED AVG SIG=0.0002MB	
(n,α)	1.4+7		CIS Theo	Jour	NP 51 460	Feb 64	Facchini+STATMOD SIG XPT/CALC127−163	
(n,α)	1.4+7		LYO Comp	Rept	LYCEN/6780	Nov 67	Crouzet+COMPILATN FOR ACTIVTN ANALYS	
(n,α)	1.4+7		AUW Expt	Jour	NP/A 125 57	Feb 69	RAMA PRASAD+,ACTIVATION,CFD OTHERS	+
			ExTh	Jour	IPA 12 640	Sep 74	Rama Prasad+ CFD STATMDL COMPND VALU	
	1.4+7			Expt Data	EXFOR30051.	Dec 70	SIGMA NA,ALSO N2N+NA+NP FOR OTHERS.	
(n,α)	1.5+7		DEB Comp	Jour	REA 7 4 93	Dec 69	Csikai+ SIG+HL COMPILTN,N−ACTIV−ANAL	
(n,α)	1.4+7	1.5+7	JYV Eval	Rept	JU−RR−3/1970	Jun 70	Leppaemaeki+ TABLE OF EVAL AVG SIG	
Reson Params	3.2+1	8.0+1	HAR Expt	Jour	NP 5 294	Jan 58	Bowey+. 2 RESONANCE ES GVN. LINAC	+
Reson Params		1.0+6	AUA Theo	Jour	AUJ 20 477	Oct 67	Cook. TBL OF AVG LVL SPACING D,L=0,1	
Reson Params		1.2+2	DUB Expt	Conf	68DUBSY 349	Jul 68	Pikelner.LVL SPAC,AVERG. WG	
Reson Params	−		IFU Expt	Jour	UFZ 13 2085	Dec 68	Vertebnyj+ OTHER EXPTL+TH D VAL GVN	
				Jour	UPJ 13 1492	Jun 69	TRANSLATN.*	
Reson Params	3.3+1	2.0+2	SAC Expt	Rept	CEA−N−1149	Jan 69	Ribon. RESONANCE PARAMETER ANALYSIS.	+
	3.3+1	2.0+2		Data	EXFOR20148.	May 73	10PTS.WG,WT,2A*G*WN.	
Reson Params	3.3+1	8.5+2	BNL Expt	Jour	PR 180 1131	Apr 69	Mughabghab+ TRANS,WN AVG D 11RESON	+
				Jour	PR/C 1 1850	May 70	− +, AVG WG=105+−10	
	3.3+1	8.5+2		Data	EXFOR10051.	May 73	34 PTS. E0,WG,WN,WN0.	
Reson Params	3.3+1	1.6+3	DUB Expt	Jour	YF 9 897	May 69	Karzhavina+,TRANS+AREA ANAL,TBL+GRPH	+
				Prog	YFI−6 135	Oct 68	− + SHORTER TEXT, TABLE	
				Rept	JINR−P3−3882	Jun 68	− + FULL PAPER.	
	2.2+2	2.7+3		Rept	BNL−TR−322	Jan 70	− + ENGL OF YF 9 897.	
	3.3+1	1.6+3		Jour	SNP 9 523	Nov 69	− + ENGL OF YF 9 897.	
				Rept	INDC−E−260	69	.ENGL TRANSL OF YFI−6 135	
	3.3+1	1.6+3		Data	EXFOR40162.	Jul 73	.EN−RES,N−WID,TOT−W,GAMMA−W,D	
Reson Params	−		AUA Theo	Rept	AAEC/E−211	Nov 70	Musgrove. CALCULTD D+GAM WIDTH GIVEN	
Reson Params	3.3+1	9.1+2	CJD Eval	Rept	YK−7	71	Zakharova+ SURVEY+SYSTEMATICS,GW,TBL	
				Rept	INDC(CCP)−27	Nov 72	.ENGLISH TRANSLATION OF YK−7 /71	
Reson Params	None		DUB Theo	Rept	YF 13 240	Feb 71	Malecki+G−WID,THEO CFD EXPT.TBL,GRPH	
				Jour	SNP 13 133	Aug 71	− + ENGL OF YF 13 240.	
Reson Params	None		DUB Theo	Conf	73Munich 1 246	Aug 73	Malov+ SUPERFLUID MDL,TBL D VS EXC−E	
				Jour	ZEP 14 194	Aug 71	Solovev.LARGE N−WID G−WID CORREL.NDG	
				Rept	JINR−E4−5880	71	Soloviev.N−GAM−WIDS CORR.SHORT NOTE	
				Jour	JEL 14 129	Aug 71	−. ENGL OF ZEP 14 194.	
Reson Params	+0	+2	BOL Eval	Conf	IAEA−169 3 123	74	Benzi+ AVG G−WID CFD OTHERS+XPT,TABL	
Reson Params	None		ANL Expt	Prog	USNDC−11 42	Jun 74	Cole+ 4S GIANT RES, TO BE DONE	
Reson Params	+1	+3	FEI Eval	Rept	YK−8/2 97	Sep 72	Abagyan+ AVG G−WID+D AT BINDNG−E,TBL	
				Rept	INDC(CCP)−39	Jul 74	.PAGE 102.ENGLISH OF YK−8/2 97	
Strnth Fnctn		1.2+2	DUB Expt	Conf	68DUBSY 349	Jul 68	Pikelner.LVL SPAC,AVERG. WG,S0 VS A	
Strnth Fnctn	3.3+1	1.5+4	BNL Expt	Jour	PR 180 1131	Apr 69	Mughabghab+ TRANS,2.4+−0.3FROM RESON	+
		+4		Jour	PL/B 24 573	May 67	Chrien+ FROM RES+UNRESOLVED REGIONS	
		5.0+3		Conf	65Antwerp 69	Jul 65	− +.TOT SIG SLOPE SWAVE STF 1.9+	
	3.3+1	1.5+4		Data	EXFOR10051.	May 73	. 4 PTS. L=0.	
Strnth Fnctn		1.2+3	DUB Expt	Jour	YF 9 897	May 69	Karzhavina+,TRANSMISSION,RES−PARAMS	+
				Prog	YFI−6 135	Oct 68	− + SHORTER TEXT, TABLE	
				Rept	JINR−P3−3882	Jun 68	− + FULL PAPER.	
		2.3+2		Rept	BNL−TR−322	Jan 70	− + ENGL OF YF 9 897.	
		1.2+3		Jour	SNP 9 523	Nov 69	− + ENGL OF YF 9 897.	
		1.6+3		Rept	INDC−E−260	69	.ENGL TRANSL OF YFI−6 135	
	3.3+1	1.2+3		Data	EXFOR40162.041	Jul 73	.2 DATA LINES	
Strnth Fnctn	3.3+1	8.5+2	BNL Expt	Jour	PR/C 1 1850	May 70	Mughabghab+,STF FROM SIGMA+RESON	+
Strnth Fnctn	−		AUA Theo	Rept	AAEC/E−211	Nov 70	Musgrove. SMOOTHED S0,S1 AND S2 GIVN	
Strnth Fnctn	None		AUA Eval	Rept	AAEC/E−277	Mar 73	Musgrove.TBLS EXPTL DATA+BEST VALUES	
Lvl Density	+6		MIL Theo	Jour	EN 15 1 54	Jan 68	Facchini+ LDL PARS FROM LOW EN RES	

64 Gadolinium 156

Quantity	Energy (ev) Min	Max	Lab	Type	Documentation Ref Vol Page	Date	Author, Comments	Data
Lvl Density	6.0+0	1.8+2	DUB	Expt	Rept JINR – P3 – 3882	Oct 68	Karzhavina +	+
					Rept YFI – 6 135	Nov 68	– +	
	6.0+0	1.8+2			Data EXFOR40162.046	Jul 73	.1 DATA LINE	
Lvl Density	None		CCP	Theo	Jour YF 11 1028	May 70	Rubchenya. DENSITY + A + TEMP GIVEN,GRPH	
					Jour SNP 11 571	Nov 70	. ENGL OF YF 11 571.	
Lvl Density	None		AUW	Theo	Conf 70Madurai 2 267	Dec 70	Ramamurty + A – PARAMETER GVN,LANG'S – TH	
Lvl Density	None		CCP	Theo	Jour YF 13 43	Jan 71	Bravin +.DEFORM PAR CALC,TBL,CFD EXPT	
Lvl Density	7.6+6		BUC	Expt	Prog INDC(SEC) – 35	Sep 73	Trutia + P170.FROM (N,P) REACTION,TBL	
Lvl Density	None		MUN	Theo	Jour NP/A 217 269	Dec 73	Dilg + A,DELTA. BACK SHIFTED FERMIGAS	
Lvl Density	None		BOL	Eval	Conf IAEA – 169 3 123	74	Benzi + LVL DENS PARAM BY XPT,GRPH + TB	
Lvl Density	None		COP	Theo	Jour NP/A 222 493	Apr 74	Dossing +COLL ROTAT.SPAC. ACCUR ESTIM	
Lvl Density	None		ROC	Theo	Jour NP/A 223 589	May 74	Huizenga + EXP CFD MICROSC TH AX SYMM	
Lvl Density	+1	+3	FEI	Eval	Rept YK – 8/2 97	Sep 72	Abagyan + LVL DENSITY PARAMETER,TBL	
					Rept INDC(CCP) – 39	Jul 74	.PAGE 102.ENGLISH OF YK – 8/2 97	
Lvl Density	None		DUB	Theo	Jour YF 21 40	Jan 75	Voronov + LVL DENS(EXC – E,SPIN),GRAPHS	
					Jour NP/A 224 396	May 74	Malov + 1/2 MICROSC.MODEL. DEFORM NUC	
					Jour SNP 21 20	Jul 75	. ENGLISH OF YF 21,40	
(γ,n)	8.0+6	2.2+7	CCP	Expt	Jour ZEP 11 520	Jun 70	Vasil'Ev + EXPTL SIG(GAMMA – E) GRAPH	

64 Gadolinium 157

Quantity	Energy (ev) Min	Max	Lab	Type	Documentation Ref Vol Page	Date	Author, Comments	Data
Evaluation	1.0 – 3	1.5+7	AUA	Eval	Rept AAEC/TM – 549	Jun 70	Cook.TOT,EL,INEL,NONEL,CAPT SIGS,NDG	+
					Rept AAEC/E – 214	Jun 71	Bertram +GROUP SIGMAS SAME QUANTS.NDG	
					Rept AAEC/TM – 587	Mar 71	*DESCRIPTION OF LIBRARY	
	1.0 – 3	1.5+7			Data AUSTR – DFN 172.	Nov 71	POINT(223) AND GROUP(127) SIGMAS	
Evaluation	–2	+3	WIN	Eval	Prog UKNDC(75)P71	Jul 75	Pope + THERMAL + RESON PARAM	
Evaluation	1.0 – 5	1.5+7	BOL	Eval	Prog NEANDC(E)182 7	Dec 76	Fabri + COMPLETE EVAL IN ENDF/B DONE	+
	1.0 – 5	1.5+7			Data CNEN – CEA 5	Jan 78	PRELIM.ALL QUANTITIES.ENDF FORMAT	
Total	–2	+1	HAR	Expt	Conf 58Geneva 16 44	Sep 58	Pattenden.PPR11,CURVE,CRYSTALSPECTRM	
Total	None		MTR	Expt	Prog IDO – 16373 39	Jul 59	Simpson.RES PARS NO CS DATA	
Total	2.0 – 2	2.8 – 1	BNL	Expt	Jour NSE 8 183	Sep 60	Moller +.CURVE RES PARS GIVEN.	+
	2.0 – 2	2.8 – 1			Data EXFOR12097.	Jun 76	. 51 PTS. SIGMA.	
Total	9.8+5		SHE	Theo	Jour NP 54 417	Jun 64	Maddison.OPTMOD FIT TO TOWLE GILBOY	
Total	7.8 – 2		BNL	ExTh	Jour PR/B 138 1361	Jun 65	Shore + POLRZ EFFECT USED FOR R.P.	
Total	2.5 – 2		JAE	Expt	Prog EANDC(J)10L1	Nov 68	Ohno +.CRYST – SPECT + V – SELECT	+
	2.5 – 2				Data EXFOR20328.005	Jul 74	1PNT.	
Total	0.0+0	2.7+2	SAC	Expt	Rept CEA – N – 1149	Jan 69	Ribon. RESONANCE PARAMETER ANALYSIS.	+
		2.7+2			Conf 66Paris 1 119	Oct 66	– + PPR72,CURVES OF TRANSMISSION	
		2.7+2			Data EXFOR20148.022	May 73	. OPTS.	
Total	1.0 – 3	1.5+7	AUA	Eval	Data AUSTR – DFN 172.	Nov 71	COOK + POINT(223) + GROUP(127)SIG.CF EVL	+
Total	1.4+7		LIN	Expt	Conf 73Kiev 3 108	May 73	Djumin + OPTMOD CALC,SIG	+
					Jour IZV 37 1019	May 73	– + SIG(A),OPTMODEL CALC,GRAPH	
					Jour BAS 37 5 91	May 73	.ENGLISH OF IZV 37 1019	
	1.4+7				Data EXFOR40302.018	Feb 76	1 PNT	
Elastic	1.0 – 3	1.5+7	AUA	Eval	Data AUSTR – DFN 172.	Nov 71	COOK + POINT(223) + GROUP(127)SIG.CF EVL	+
Diff Elastic	9.8+5		SHE	Theo	Jour NP 54 417	Jun 64	Maddison.OPTMOD FIT TO TOWLE GILBOY	
Potntal Scat	None		BNL	Expt	Jour PL/B 24 573	May 67	Chrien + FROM ANALYSIS OF RESONANCES	
Tot Inelastc	5.0+5	1.5+7	AUA	Eval	Data AUSTR – DFN 172.	Nov 71	COOK + POINT(11) + GROUP(127)SIG.CF EVL	
Scattering	0.0+0	2.6+2	SAC	Expt	Rept CEA – N – 1149	Jan 69	Ribon. RESONANCE PARAMETER ANALYSIS	+
		2.6+2			Data EXFOR20148.021	May 73	0PTS.SIG.	
Nonelastic	1.0 – 3	1.5+7	AUA	Eval	Data AUSTR – DFN 172.	Nov 71	COOK + POINT(223) + GROUP(127)SIG.CF EVL	+
Absorption	Maxwl		HEB	Expt	Jour PR 115 424	Jul 59	Low +,AERE RILE,PAR RES SPECT,210000B	
Absorption	Maxwl	Pile	HAR	Expt	Jour JNEA 12 32	May 60	Tattersall +. EFF SIG IN THREE SPECTR	
					Rept AERE – R – 2887	Aug 59	– . PILE OSC.REL BORON	
	Maxwl				Rept AERE – R/R – 2516	Mar 58	Jowitt + PILE OSC.REL BORON.293DEGK.	
Absorption	4.1 – 1	1.0+7	GA	Eval	Rept GA – 2451	Aug 61	Joanou +.68GROUP DATA FOR GAM – I	
Absorption	1.0 – 3	1.0+7	JUL	Eval	Rept JUEL – 678 – RG	Jul 70	Liu. EVALUATION +CALC,GRPH,FN OF E	
Absorption	2.5 – 2		IJI	Eval	Conf 75Kiev 1 169	May 75	Fedorova + EVAL 2200M/S SIG,TABLE	
Res Int Abs	5.0 – 1		BOL	Eval	Rept RT/FI – 4	Jan 67	Palmucci. CALC FROM (N,G) RES PARAMS	
Res Int Abs	5.0 – 1		BNL	Expt	Rept BNL – 13074	68	Mughabghab.	
Res Int Abs	5.0 – 1		GA	Expt	Prog NCSAC – 31 63	May 70	Friesenhahn +,VALUE GIVEN,TBP IN NP	
Res Int Abs	None		GA	Eval	Rept GA – 12071	Sep 71	Mathews +. RECOMMENDED VALUES	
Res Int Abs	5.0 – 1		AUA	Eval	Rept AAEC/TM – 619	Sep 72	Clayton. CALC FROM SIG LIBRARY,TABLE	
Res Int Abs	4.6 – 1	1.0+6	RCN	Theo	Rept RCN – 191	Jul 73	Lautenbach.CAPT INT FROM GROUP SIGMA	
Res Int Abs	5.5 – 1	+6	SAC	Revw	Conf IAEA – 169 1 235	74	Ribon.CAPTURE,STATUS CFD REQUEST,TBL	
Res Int Abs	+0	+5	WIN	Revw	Conf IAEA – 169 3 163	74	Pope + DATA FILE CALCS COMPARED	

64 Gadolinium 157

Quantity	Energy (ev) Min	Max	Lab	Type	Documentation Ref Vol Page	Date	Author, Comments	Data
(n,γ)	Pile		ANL	Expt	Jour PR 71 745	Jun 47	Lapp+	+
	Pile			Data	EXFOR12135.002	Jun 76	. 1 PT.	
(n,γ)	Pile		ANL	Expt	Jour PR 79 271	Jul 50	Ingraham.	+
	Pile			Data	EXFOR12106.004	Jun 76	. 1 PT.	
(n,γ)	Maxwl		MCM	Expt	Priv WALKER	May 56	Walker.	+
	Maxwl			Data	EXFOR12127.013	Jun 76	. 1 PT.	
(n,γ)	Maxwl		HEB	Expt	Jour NCS 11 468	Mar 59	LOW+ ABST. RATIO GD157/GD155, =2.82	
(n,γ)	Maxwl		CRC	Eval	Rept AECL-1054	Mar 60	Walker. (CRRP-913)	
(n,γ)	5.0-3	2.5+0	GA	Eval	Rept GA-2113	Jun 61	Wikner+.TABLE + CURVE.100 E POINTS	
(n,γ)	2.8-3	1.0+6	GA	Eval	Jour NSE 12 115	Jan 62	Garrison+.EVAL FROM XPT+AVERAGE RES	
(n,γ)	1.0+3	1.0+4	LAS	Theo	Rept LA-3463	Jan 66	Bell. TH CAPTURE OF RARE EARTHS	
(n,γ)	2.5-2		BOL	Eval	Rept RT/FI-4	Jan 67	Palmucci. CALC FROM RES PARAMETERS	
(n,γ)	Maxwl		AUA	Theo	Jour NSE 31 234	Feb 68	Cook+ STATISTICAL CALC CFD EXPT	
(n,γ)	5.0+3	1.0+5	AUA	ExTh	Rept AAEC/E-198	May 69	Musgrove.S+P+D WAVE SIGMAS CALC,TBL	+
(n,γ)	1.0+3	1.0+7	BOL	Eval	Rept CCDN-NW/10	Dec 69	Benzi+H-F MOD,AXEL G(G)EST,ALL DATA	
					Rept CEC(70)-2	Apr 70	- +. GRAPH	
					Conf 66Paris 1 537	Oct 66	- + STATMOD.TBL AV VALS.SUPERSEDD	
(n,γ)	2.8+0	1.5+2	CCP	Expt	Jour ZET 58 456	Feb 70	Danelyan+ SIG IN REL UNITS VS NEUT-E	
					Jour JET 31 242	Aug 70	TRANSLATN.*	
(n,γ)	3.0+0	2.0+4	GA	Expt	Prog NCSAC-31 63	May 70	Friesenhahn+,NO DATA,TBP IN NP	
(n,γ)	3.0+4		AUA	Theo	Rept AAEC/E-211	Nov 70	Musgrove. SIGMA GIVEN AND CFD OTHER	
(n,γ)	Maxwl		GA	Eval	Rept GA-12071	Sep 71	Mathews+. RECOMMENDED VALUES	
(n,γ)	1.0-3	1.5+4	AUA	Eval	Data AUSTR-DFN 172.	Nov 71	COOK+POINT(223)+GROUP(127)SIG.CF EVL	+
(n,γ)	Maxwl		CRC	Eval	Rept AECL-3037 1	Jan 72	Walker.RECOMMENDED SIG,DETAILED TBL	
(n,γ)	2.5-2		AUA	Eval	Rept AAEC/TM-619	Sep 72	Clayton.CALC FROM SIG LIBRARY,TABLE	
(n,γ)	5.0+3	7.0+4	CCP	Expt	Conf 73Kiev 2 206	May 73	Kononov+ TOF,SIG(NEUT-E),GRAPH	
(n,γ)		1.1+7	RCN	Theo	Rept RCN-191	Jun 73	Lautenbach.GROUP CONSTANTS TBL	
(n,γ)	2.5-2		SAC	Revw	Conf IAEA-169 1 235	74	Ribon.STATUS SIG CFD REQUESTS,TABLE	
	Fiss				Conf IAEA-169 1 235	74	- .STATUS SIG CFD REQUESTS,TABLE	
(n,γ)	Fiss		WIN	Revw	Conf IAEA-169 3 137	74	Dean. POINT DATA AVG OVER STAND SPEC	
	Maxwl	Fiss			Conf IAEA-169 3 163	74	Pope+ MAXW+FIS-SPEC AVG DATA CFD XPT	
(n,γ)	1.0+3	1.0+7	FEI	Eval	Rept YK-8/2 97	Sep 72	Abagjan+ AVG SIG(ENERGY-GROUPS),TABL	
					Rept INDC(CCP)-39	Jul 74	.P102. ENGLISH OF YK-8/2 97	
(n,γ)	5.0+3	7.0+4	FEI	Expt	Rept YFI-17 9	Aug 74	Shorin+ TOF,SIG(NEUT-E),TBL	+
					Jour YF 19 5	Jan 74	- + TOF,SIG(NEUT-E),GRAPHS	
	5.3+3	6.8+4			Rept INDC(CCP)-48	Feb 75	. ENGLISH OF YFI-17 9	
	5.0+3	7.0+4			Jour SNP 19 2	Jul 74	. ENGLISH OF YF 19 5	
	5.3+3	6.8+4			Data EXFOR40222.007	Mar 74	.SIGMA FOR 32 EN-RANGES GVN	
(n,γ)	2.4+4		INL	Expt	Prog ERDA-NDC-2 35	May 75	Greenwood+LVL.STRUCT.GRPH.TBL.	
	None				Prog USNDC-11 4	Jun 74	- + E-LVL STUDY	
(n,γ)	None		MUN	Theo	Diss GRYNTAKIS	Mar 76	Gryntakis.,CALC.OF WESTCOTTS G-FUNCT	
					Jour RCA 22 128	Mar 75	- +,EQUIVALENT TO THESIS	
(n,γ)	Fast		RCN	Expt	Rept ECN-10	Oct 76	Veenema+ STEK REACTIVITY WORTHS TBL.	
Spect (n,γ)	Maxwl		CCP	Expt	Jour AE 4 22	Jan 58	Sklyarevskii+.EGS+INTENS BELOW .3MEV	
					Jour JNE 9 69	Jun 59	TRANSLATN.*	
					Jour SJA 4 19	58	TRANSLATN.*	
Spect (n,γ)	3.0-2		YAL	Expt	Abst BAP 4 35	Jan 59	Springer+,NAI(TL),GAMMA MULTIPLICITY	
Spect (n,γ)	Maxwl		KUR	ExTh	Jour NP 16 645	Jun 60	Groshev+ COMPT SPEC. THEOR DISCUSSN	
				Expt	Jour AE 4 5	Jan 58	- + SPECTRUM+LINES 0.3-6.74MEV	
					Jour JNE 9 50	Jun 59	. ENGL OF AE 4 5	
					Jour SJA 4 1	58	. ENGL OF AE 4 5	
Spect (n,γ)	Maxwl		UNC	Theo	Jour PR 122 212	Apr 61	Troubetzkoy. STAT TH CFD DATA.	
Spect (n,γ)	-		MUN	Expt	Jour ZN/A 16 927	Sep 61	Schult.LVLS IN GD158 XTAL SPECTROMET	
Spect (n,γ)	Maxwl		CRC	Expt	Jour ARN 11 259	Oct 61	Bartholomew.	
					Conf AEC-TR-6465	Jul 60	- + MOSCOW CONF NUC REACTNS	
	None				Prog PR-P-41 43	Apr 59	- + 80,277,359 KEV GAMMAS.	
Spect (n,γ)	Pile		MUN	Expt	Jour ZN/A 21 1328	Sep 66	Neumann. CRYST SPEC EXPT OF GAM INT	
					Rept ANL-TRANS-941	73	. ENGLISH OF ZN/A 21 1328	
Spect (n,γ)	Maxwl		RIS	Expt	Conf 69Montreal 701	Aug 69	Koch+CRYS DIFFRACT.MEASMT RVW.NDG.	
Spect (n,γ)	Maxwl		KFI	Revw	Jour YF 10 907	Nov 69	Kecskemeti+ AVG GAM-MULTIPLICITY,TBL	
					Jour SNP 10 524	May 70	TRANSLATN.*	
Spect (n,γ)	Maxwl	6.3+1	KUR	Expt	Prog YFI-8 13	Dec 69	Daneljan+ GAMMA INTENS IN RES REGN	
					Rept INDC(CCP)-8U18	Dec 70	TRANSLATN.*	
	3.0-2	1.5+2			Jour ZET 58 456	Feb 70	Daneljan+ GAM-INT OR ROTAT+VIBRAT	
					Jour JET 31 242	Aug 70	. ENGL OF ZET 58 456	
Spect (n,γ)	Pile		KUR	Expt	Jour IZV 34 804	Apr 70	Panin+ CONVERSN-EL SPECS,ES+INTS,TBL	
					Jour BAS 34 714	Apr 71	* ENGL OF IZV 34 804	
Spect (n,γ)	Maxwl		UPP	Expt	Prog EANDC(OR)99 19	Aug 70	Baecklin+. ELECTR+GAM SPEC 500 LINES	

64 Gadolinium 157

Quantity	Energy (ev) Min	Max	Lab	Type	Documentation Ref Vol Page	Date	Author, Comments	Data
Spect (n,γ)	Pile		ANL	Expt	Jour PR/C 2 1951	Nov 70	Bollinger+,B10 COVER,GE(LI) DET	
					Conf 69Studsvik 601	Aug 69	Smither+ NO DATA GVN,OKS STATMOD	
Spect (n,γ)	Pile		KFK	Expt	Rept KFK-1401	Jun 71	Djadali.AVG POLRZ G EXPT,CFD T,SPIN	
	Maxwl				Jour NP/A 147 150	May 70	Eichler+ POL NS.CIRC POL GS+ASSYMTRY	
Spect (n,γ)	Maxwl		KUR	Expt	Jour IZV 35 1593	Aug 71	Panin+ MULTIPOLE ORDER OF TRANS,TBL	
					Jour BAS 35 1453	Aug 72	. ENGL OF IZV 35 1593	
Spect (n,γ)	Maxwl		MUN	Eval	Prog EANDC(E)140U	Aug 71	Baader+, LEVEL SCHEME GD-158	
				Revw	Conf 69Studsvik 127	Aug 69	Egidy. CONV-ELECTRON-SPEC GRPHS CFD	
				Expt	Conf 67Juelich 56	Apr 67	- + CONVERSION ELECTRONS162-6.NDG	
Spect (n,γ)	Maxwl		IFL	Expt	Book PROKOFJEV	73	. TBL GAM,CONV ELECTR ES+INT,LVL SCH	
Spect (n,γ)	Maxwl		CCP	Theo	Jour ZET 65 12	Jul 73	Nosov+ THERMODYN CALC CFD EXPT,GRAPH	
					Jour JET 38 6	Jan 74	. ENGLISH OF ZET 65 6	
Spect (n,γ)	Pile		LRL	Expt	Jour NP/A 217 410	Dec 73	White+ GE(LI)+NAI(TL). 74 EG VALUES.	
Spect (n,γ)	Maxwl Pile		SGA	ExTh	Jour APA 41 4 338	75	Korn+ SPEC SHAPE	
				Rept	SGAE-PH-174	Nov 74	- + SPEC SHAPE	
Spect (n,γ)	Maxwl		ATI	ExTh	Rept INDC(SEC)-51	Oct 75	Korn+ ABST ON PAGE 2 SHAPE G-SPECT	
Spect (n,γ)	2.0+3		BNL	Expt	Jour NIM 138 125	76	Greenwood+ FILTERED BEAM GRPH	
(n,2n)	Fiss		CRC	Eval	Rept CRC-1003	Dec 60	Roy+,ESTIMATED AVG SIG=2.2MB	
(n,2n)	1.3+7	1.5+7	BNL	Theo	Jour NSE 23 238	Nov 65	Pearlstein.3ES.STAT MDL CALC.TBL CS.	
(n,2n)	Fiss		BNL	Theo	Jour NSE 23 238	Nov 65	Pearlstein.STATMDL CALC.SPEC AVG.TBL	
(n,2n)	1.5+7		DEB	Eval	Jour REA 11 1 153	Mar 73	Boedy+ RECOMM.VALUE FROM N-Z SYSTEM.	
(n,2n)			KFI	Expt	Rept KFKI-73-68	Dec 73	Jeki.NEW FIT,CALC SIG CFD OTHERS,TBL	
(n,xn) x>2	Fiss		BNL	Theo	Jour NSE 23 238	Nov 65	Pearlstein.SPEC AVG STATMDL CALC N3N	
(n,p)	1.4+7		ALD	Expt	Jour PPS 73 215	Feb 59	Coleman+. ACT. CFD DIRECT INTERACTN	+
(n,p)	Fiss		CRC	Eval	Rept CRC-1003	Dec 60	Roy+,ESTIMATED AVG SIG=0.013MB	
(n,p)	1.5+7		SAH	Comp	Jour NUC 23 8 112	Aug 65	Chatterjee. TABLE WITH REFS.	
(n,p)	1.4+7	1.5+7	ARK	Theo	Prog ORO-3235-29	Jan 67	Koch+,STAT MODEL CALC CFD EXPTS	
(n,p)	1.4+7		LYO	Comp	Rept LYCEN/6780	Nov 67	Crouzet+COMPILATN FOR ACTIVTN ANALYS	
(n,p)	1.5+7		DEB	Comp	Jour REA 7 4 93	Dec 69	Csikai+ SIG+HL COMPILTN,N-ACTIV-ANAL	
(n,p)	1.4+7	1.5+7	JYV	Eval	Rept JU-RR-3/1970	Jun 70	Leppaemaeki+ TABLE OF EVAL AVG SIG	
(n,p)	1.5+7		JUL	Expt	Jour RRL 25 335	May 76	Qaim+ ACTIV,GELI.CFD OTHERS,TBL+GRPH	+
	1.5+7				Data EXFOR20716.009	Jun 77	1PNT.SIGMA.	
(n,α)	Fiss		CRC	Eval	Rept CRC-1003	Dec 60	Roy+,ESTIMATED AVG SIG=0.0002MB	
(n,α)	Maxwl		ISL	Expt	Jour PL 1 289	Jul 62	Cheifetz. TBL Q-VALU,SIG,BRANCHRATIO	+
	Maxwl				Data EXFOR31151.	Mar 73	.SIG GVN	
(n,α)	Maxwl		CCP	Expt	Jour YF 1 252	Feb 65	Andreev.IONIZ-CHAMBER,SIG=M.08MB	+
					Jour SNP 1 177	Aug 65	TRANSLATN.*	
(n,α)	Fast		DUB	Expt	Conf 75Kiev 4 60	May 75	Balabanov+ FOR ALF-WID.SIG NOT GIVEN	
Reson Params	4.4-2		ORL	Expt	Jour PR 70 557	Oct 46	Borst+ E, PCS, WT GIVEN.	+
	4.4-2				Data EXFOR11756.006	Jun 76	. 1 RES, E0,WT,PCS.	
Reson Params	3.1-2		ANL	Expt	Jour PR 71 757	Jun 47	Brill+,WT FROM BREIT-WIGNER FIT.	
Reson Params	2.7+0	4.9+1	MTR	Expt	Prog IDO-16373 39	Jul 57	Simpson.WG,G*WN,WN0.TBL.4 RES ES	+
	3.0+0	4.9+1			Data EXFOR11983.010	Jun 76	. 4 RES, E0,WN,WN0,WG.	
Reson Params	1.7+1	8.1+1	HAR	Expt	Jour NP 5 294	Jan 58	Bowey+. 7 RESONANCE ES GVN. LINAC	+
Reson Params	3.1-2		CRC	Expt	Conf 60Kingston 573	Aug 60	Bartholomew. E, J, GIVEN.	
	3.1-2				Data EXFOR11444.003	Jun 76	. 1 RES, J.	
Reson Params	3.1-2	2.4+1	BNL	Expt	Jour NSE 8 183	Sep 60	Moller+WT WG 2GWN OTHER PARAMETERS.	+
	3.1-2	2.4+1			Data EXFOR12097.010	Jun 76	. 5 RES, E0,WT,WN,WG,PCS.	
Reson Params	2.9+0	4.4+1	ANL	Expt	Prog ANL-6589	Aug 62	Carpenter.	+
Reson Params	3.1-2		MOL	Expt	Conf 63ANL 363	Oct 63	Poortmans+ WN/W,G,J MEASD CRYST SPCT	+
				Rept	AERE-R-4131	Sep 62	- + PRELIMINARY	
	3.1-2				Data EXFOR20166.	May 74	2PTS.J,WN/WT.	
Reson Params	3.1-2		NRL	Expt	Jour PR/B 134 68	Apr 64	Stolovy. POLRZD NUC,NS.J=2.	+
	3.1-2				Data EXFOR11436.005	Jun 76	. 1 RES, E0,J.	
Reson Params	3.1-2	2.8+0	BNL	ExTh	Jour PR/B 138 1361	Jun 65	Shore+BOTH RES J=2,FROM POLRZ EFFECT	+
	3.1-2	2.8+0		Expt	Data EXFOR11440.003	Jun 76	. 2 RES, E0,J.	
Reson Params	1.7+1		MOL	Expt	Jour NP/A 97 657	May 67	Poortmans+ FROM SCATTERING EXPT	+
	1.7+1				Data EXFOR20213.	May 74	1PTS.J,WN/WT.	
Reson Params		1.0+6	AUA	Theo	Jour AUJ 20 477	Oct 67	Cook. TBL OF AVG LVL SPACING D,L=0,1	
Reson Params	1.7+1	4.9+1	SAC	Expt	Jour NP/A 132 129	Jul 69	Julien+ WN WG WT 2E0 J=2 FOR 16.8EV	
					Conf 68Wash. 867	Mar 68	Morgenstern. WG VS. A. AVG WG GIVEN	
					Diss CEA-R-3602	Jul 69	Alves.	
					Conf 66Paris 1 559	Oct 66	Huynh+ ABST.NDG. SEE INDC-156	
	1.7+1	4.9+1			Data EXFOR20687.036	Aug 77	2PTS.E0,WG,WT,J,G*WN.	
Reson Params		3.0+2	DUB	Expt	Conf 68DUBSY 349	Jul 68	Pikelner.LVL SPAC,AVERG. WG	
Reson Params	-		IFU	Expt	Jour UFZ 13 2085	Dec 68	Vertebnyj+ OTHER EXPTL+TH D VAL GVN	
					Jour UPJ 13 1492	Jun 69	TRANSLATN.*	

64 Gadolinium 157

Quantity	Energy (ev) Min	Energy (ev) Max	Lab	Type	Documentation Ref Vol Page	Date	Author, Comments	Data
Reson Params	1.6+1	2.5+2	SAC	Expt	Rept CEA-N-1149	Jan 69	Ribon. TOF, TRANSMISSION. +SCATTERNG	+
	1.6+1	2.5+2			Data EXFOR20148.	May 73	130PTS.WG,AVG WG,WT,2G*WN	
Reson Params	3.1-2	1.8+2	BNL	Expt	Jour PR 180 1131	Apr 69	Mughabghab+ TRANS,2G*WN AVG D 29RESN	+
	2.8+0	1.8+2			Data EXFOR10051.	May 73	. 87 PTS,E0,WG,2G*WN,2G*WN0.	
Reson Params	1.6+1	3.1+2	DUB	Expt	Jour YF 9 897	May 69	Karzhavina+,TRANS+AREA ANAL,TBL+GRPH	+
					Prog YFI-6 135	Oct 68	- + SHORTER TEXT, TABLE	
					Rept JINR-P3-3882	Jun 68	- + FULL PAPER.	
	2.2+2	2.7+3			Rept BNL-TR-322	Jan 70	- + ENGL OF YF 9 897.	
	1.6+1	3.1+2			Jour SNP 9 523	Nov 69	- + ENGL OF YF 9 897.	
					Rept INDC-E-260	69	.ENGL TRANSL OF YFI-6 135	
	1.6+1	3.1+2			Data EXFOR40162.	Jul 73	.EN-RES,N-WID,TOT-W,GAMMA-W,D	
Reson Params	1.7+1	2.4+2	SAC	Expt	Jour NP/A 145 549	Apr 70	Asghar+ WN,WN0,WT,J.25 E0+J AT 93EV	+
	1.7+1	2.4+2			Data EXFOR20147.004	May 73	24PTS.J.	
Reson Params	3.1-2	6.0+2	BNL	Expt	Jour PR/C 1 1850	May 70	Mughabghab+, AVG WG=107+-8	+
Reson Params	1.6+1	1.8+2	GA	Expt	Jour NP/A 146 337	May 70	Friesenhahn+WN,WG,32E0,AREA,SHAPE AN	+
	3.0+0	2.0+2			Data EXFOR10049.	May 73	. 32 RES,N-WID, 19RES,G-WID.	
Reson Params	-		AUA	Theo	Rept AAEC/E-211	Nov 70	Musgrove. CALCULTD D+GAM WIDTH GIVEN	
Reson Params	None		KUR	Expt	Jour AE 29 395	Nov 70	Muradjan+ ABST FRANC-SOV SEM DUBNA	
					Jour SJA 29 1156	Nov 70	TRANSLATN.*	
Reson Params	3.1-2	1.1+2	CJD	Eval	Rept YK-7	71	Zakharova+ SURVEY+SYSTEMATICS,GW,TBL	
					Rept INDC(CCP)-27	Nov 72	.ENGLISH TRANSLATION OF YK-7 /71	
Reson Params	None		DUB	Theo	Jour YF 13 240	Feb 71	Malecki+G-WID,THEO CFD EXPT.TBL,GRPH	
					Jour SNP 13 133	Aug 71	- + ENGL OF YF 13 240.	
Reson Params		1.8+2	CCP	Expt	Jour IZV 37 1129	May 73	Daneljan.I=1,GAMS FROM 9 LEVELS,NDG	
					Jour BAS 37 5 190	May 73	.ENGLISH OF IZV 37 1129	
Reson Params	+0	+3	KUR	Theo	Conf 73Kiev 2 301	May 73	Daneljan. CORREL N+G-WID+PARTL G-WID	
Reson Params	1.6+1	3.4+2	DUB	Expt	Jour RCN-203 242	Dec 73	Karzhavina+ G MULTIPL.METH,J,SO,D	
	3.1-2	3.0+2			Conf 73Kiev 2 337	May 73	- + SPIN-IDENT,G-MULTIP MTHD	
	1.6+1	3.4+2			Rept JINR-P3-6948	Feb 73	- + SPINS OF RESONANCES, TBL	
Reson Params	+0	+2	BOL	Eval	Conf IAEA-169 3 123	74	Benzi+ AVG G-WID CFD OTHERS+XPT,TABL	
Reson Params	+0	+2	FEI	Eval	Rept YK-8/2 97	Sep 72	Abagyan+ AVG G-WID+D AT BINDNG-E,TBL	
					Rept INDC(CCP)-39	Jul 74	.PAGE 102.ENGLISH OF YK-8/2 97	
Reson Params	+0		DUB	Theo	Jour YF 21 40	Jan 75	Voronov+ MEAN D,WITH ROTAT.CFD EXPT	
	7.9+6				Conf 74Petten 175	Sep 74	Malov+ DOBS,SEMI-MICROSCOPIC CALC.	
	None				Conf 73Munich 1 246	Aug 73	- + SUPERFLUID MDL,TBL D VS STATE	
	+0				Jour SNP 21 20	Jul 75	. ENGLISH OF YF 21,40	
Reson Params	Fast		DUB	Expt	Conf 75Kiev 4 60	May 75	Balabanov+ AVG ALF-WIDTHS.TABLE	
Strnth Fnctn	1.0+1	5.0+1	MTR	Expt	Abst BAP 2 42	Feb 57	Simpson+NDG.ANAL TBD	
Strnth Fnctn	+3		BNL	Expt	Jour PRL 1 461	Dec 58	Hughes. FC 1.5+-0.3	
Strnth Fnctn		2.4+2	SAC	Expt	Jour NP/A 145 549	Apr 70	Asghar+S-WAVE J=1,2.NO SPIN DEPEND	+
					Jour JPRC 29 1 203	Jan 68	Michaudon+ L=0.NO SPIN VARTN	
	0.0+0	2.4+2			Data EXFOR20147.005	May 73	. 2PTS.L=0.	
Strnth Fnctn		3.0+2	DUB	Expt	Conf 68DUBSY 349	Jul 68	Pikelner.LVL SPAC,AVERG. WG,S0 VS A	
Strnth Fnctn		2.5+2	SAC	Expt	Jour CEA-N-1149	Jan 69	Ribon. VALUE FROM RESONANCE ANALYSIS	+
		2.5+2			Data EXFOR20148.027	May 73	1PNT.L=0.	
Strnth Fnctn	3.1-2	1.8+4	BNL	Expt	Jour PR 180 1131	Apr 69	Mughabghab+ TRANS,1.8+-0.8FROM RESON	+
		+4			Jour PL/B 24 573	May 67	Chrien+ FROM RES+UNRESOLVED REGIONS	
		5.0+3			Conf 65Antwerp 69	Jul 65	- +TOT SIG SLOPE SWAVE STF 2.16+	
	3.1-2	1.5+4			Data EXFOR10051.	May 73	. 4 PTS. L=0.	
Strnth Fnctn		3.0+2	DUB	Expt	Jour YF 9 897	May 69	Karzhavina+,TRANSMISSION,RES-PARAMS	+
					Prog YFI-6 135	Oct 68	- + SHORTER TEXT, TABLE	
					Rept JINR-P3-3882	Jun 68	- + FULL PAPER.	
		2.3+2			Rept BNL-TR-322	Jan 70	- + ENGL OF YF 9 897.	
		3.0+2			Jour SNP 9 523	Nov 69	- + ENGL OF YF 9 897.	
		3.1+2			Rept INDC-E-260	69	.ENGL TRANSL OF YFI-6 135	
	1.6+1	3.0+2			Data EXFOR40162.042	Jul 73	.1 DATA LINE	
Strnth Fnctn	-		DUB	Revw	Jour YF 11 111	Jan 70	Malecki+ VALUES FOR TWO SPIN STATES	
					Jour SNP 11 61	Jul 70	- + ENGL OF YF 11 61.	
Strnth Fnctn	3.1-2	6.0+2	BNL	Expt	Jour PR/C 1 1850	May 70	Mughabghab+,STF FROM SIGMA+RESON	+
Strnth Fnctn	1.6+1	1.8+4	GA	Expt	Jour NP/A 146 337	May 70	Friesenhahn+L=0 FROM RES,L=1 FROM NG	+
	3.0+0	2.0+4			Data EXFOR10049.	May 73	. 3 PTS.	
Strnth Fnctn	-		AUA	Theo	Rept AAEC/E-211	Nov 70	Musgrove. SMOOTHED S0,S1 AND S2 GIVN	
Strnth Fnctn	1.5+2	6.5+2	SAC	ExTh	Diss FRNC-TH-450	Oct 72	Delaroche.OPTICAL MODEL PARAMETERS	
Strnth Fnctn	None		AUA	Eval	Rept AAEC/E-277	Mar 73	Musgrove.TBLS EXPTL DATA+BEST VALUES	
Strnth Fnctn	3.1-2	3.0+2	DUB	Expt	Conf 73Kiev 2 337	May 73	Karzhavina+ S0 FOR I=1,2 GIVEN	
	1.6+1	3.4+2			Rept JINR-P3-6948	Feb 73	- + FOR J=1 AND J=2	
Lvl Density	+6		MIL	Theo	Jour EN 15 1 54	Jan 68	Facchini+ LDL PARS FROM LOW EN RES	

64 Gadolinium 157

Quantity	Energy (ev) Min	Max	Lab	Type	Documentation Ref Vol Page	Date	Author, Comments	Data
Lvl Density	3.3+1	1.2+3	DUB	Expt	Rept YFI-6 135	Nov 68	.KARZHAVINA+	+
					Rept JINR-P3-3882	Jun 68	.KARZHAVINA+	
	3.3+1	1.2+3			Data EXFOR40162.047	Jul 73	.1 DATA LINE	
Lvl Density	0.0+0	2.5+2	SAC	Expt	Rept CEA-N-1149	Jan 69	Ribon. RESONANCE PARAMETER ANALYSIS	+
		2.5+2			Data EXFOR20148.028	May 73	1PNT.SP.CUT(0).	
Lvl Density	None		AUW	Theo	Conf 70Madurai 2 267	Dec 70	Ramamurty+ A−PARAMETER GVN,LANG'S−TH	
Lvl Density	1.6+1	3.4+2	DUB	Expt	Rept JINR-P3-6948	Feb 73	Karzhavina+ D AND SPIN CUTOFF FACTOR	
Lvl Density	7.6+6		BUC	Expt	Prog INDC(SEC)-35	Sep 73	Trutia+ P170.FROM (N,P) REACTION,TBL	
Lvl Density	None		MUN	Theo	Jour NP/A 217 269	Dec 73	Dilg+ A,DELTA. BACK SHIFTED FERMIGAS	
Lvl Density	None		BOL	Eval	Conf IAEA-169 3 123	74	Benzi+ LVL DENS PARAM BY XPT,GRPH+TB	
Lvl Density	None		ROC	Theo	Jour NP/A 223 589	May 74	Huizenga+ EXP CFD MICROSC TH AX SYMM	
Lvl Density	+0	+2	FEI	Theo	Rept YK-8/2 97	Sep 72	Abagyan+ LVL DENSITY PARAMETER,TBL	
					Rept INDC(CCP)-39	Jul 74	.PAGE 102.ENGLISH OF YK-8/2 97	
Lvl Density	None		DUB	Theo	Jour YF 21 40	Jan 75	Voronov+ LVL DENS(EXC-E,SPIN),GRAPHS	
					Jour NP/A 224 396	May 74	Malov+ 1/2 MICROSC.MODEL. DEFORM NUC	
					Jour SNP 21 20	Jul 75	. ENGLISH OF YF 21,40	

64 Gadolinium 158

Quantity	Energy (ev) Min	Max	Lab	Type	Documentation Ref Vol Page	Date	Author, Comments	Data
Evaluation	1.0-3	1.5+7	AUA	Eval	Rept AAEC/TM-549	Jun 70	Cook.TOT,EL,INEL,NONEL,CAPT SIGS,NDG	+
					Rept AAEC/E-214	Jun 71	Bertram+GROUP SIGMAS SAME QUANTS.NDG	
					Rept AAEC/TM-587	Mar 71	*DESCRIPTION OF LIBRARY	
	1.0-3	1.5+7			Data AUSTR-DFN 173.	Nov 71	POINT(223) AND GROUP(127) SIGMAS	
Evaluation	1.0+6		BOL	Eval	Prog EANDC(E)157U 2	May 73	Menapace+ TO BE CONTINUED ABOVE 1MEV	
Total	1.0-3	1.5+7	AUA	Eval	Data AUSTR-DFN 173.	Nov 71	COOK+POINT(223)+GROUP(127)SIG.CF EVL	+
Total	0.0+0	1.0+4	COL	Expt	Jour PR/C 10 1904	Nov 74	Rahn+ANAL.FOR RES.PAR,STF,AVG D	
Elastic	1.0-3	1.5+7	AUA	Eval	Data AUSTR-DFN 173.	Nov 71	COOK+POINT(223)+GROUP(127)SIG.CF EVL	+
Potntl Scat	None		BNL	Expt	Jour PL/B 24 573	May 67	Chrien+ FROM ANALYSIS OF RESONANCES	
Tot Inelastc	5.0+5	1.5+7	AUA	Eval	Data AUSTR-DFN 173.	Nov 71	COOK+POINT(11)+GROUP(127)SIG.CF EVL	+
Diff Inelast	1.4+7		LRL	Theo	Rept UCRL-50181	Feb 67	Lutz+.CALC ANG DIST FOR FIRST 2+ LVL	
Nonelastic	1.0-3	1.5+7	AUA	Eval	Data AUSTR-DFN 173.	Nov 71	COOK+POINT(223)+GROUP(127)SIG.CF EVL	
Absorption	4.1-1	1.0+7	GA	Eval	Rept GA-2451	Aug 61	Joanou+.68GROUP DATA FOR GAM-I	
Absorption	1.0-3	1.0+7	JUL	Eval	Rept JUEL-678-RG	Jul 70	Liu. EVALUATION+CALC,GRPH,FN OF E	
Absorption	2.5-2		IJI	Eval	Conf 75Kiev 1 169	May 75	Fedorova+ EVAL 2200M/S SIG,TABLE	
Res Int Abs	5.0-1		BNL	Expt	Rept BNL-13074	68	Mughabghab.	
Res Int Abs	None		GA	Eval	Rept GA-12071	Sep 71	Mathews+. RECOMMENDED VALUES	
Res Int Abs	5.5-1		CRC	Eval	Rept AECL-3037 1	Jan 72	Walker.REDUCED RES INT FROM RES PARS	
Res Int Abs	5.0-1		COL	Expt	Jour NSE 48 219	Jun 72	Rahn+. RI=60.5+-6.0B	
Res Int Abs	5.0-1		AUA	Eval	Rept AAEC/TM-619	Sep 72	Clayton.CALC FROM SIG LIBRARY,TABLE	
Res Int Abs	4.6-1	1.0+6	RCN	Theo	Rept RCN-191	Jul 73	Lautenbach.CAPT INT FROM GROUP SIGMA	
Res Int Abs	5.0-1		GHT	Expt	Jour JRC 20 695	74	Van Der Linden+ BY(N,G).CFD OTHS,TBL	
	5.5-1				Conf 73Paris 2 241	Mar 73	- + ACT,REL THR+GOLD,TBL	
	5.5-1				Data EXFOR20645.027	Jul 76	1PNT.CAPTURE.	
Res Int Abs	5.5-1	+6	SAC	Revw	Conf IAEA-169 1 235	74	Ribon.CAPTURE,STATUS CFD REQUEST,TBL	
Res Int Abs	+0	+5	WIN	Revw	Conf IAEA-169 3 163	74	Pope+ DATA FILE CALC CFD XPTAL VALUE	
Res Int Abs	5.0-1		IJI	Eval	Conf 75Kiev 1 169	May 75	Fedorova+ EVAL+CALC RI GIVEN,TABLE	
Res Int Abs	5.0-1		KJL	Expt	Jour JIN 37 1591	Aug 75	Steinnes. CD-RAT+ACTIV INTEG,CFD,TBL	
					Jour JIN 34 2699	Sep 72	- . ACT. AU MONITOR	
	5.0-1				Data EXFOR20635.007	Aug 76	1PNT.CAPTURE.	
	5.0-1				Data EXFOR20188.022	May 74	1PNT.CAPTURE.	
(n,γ)	Maxwl		OHO	Expt	Jour PR 53 437	Mar 38	Pool+ BETAS,CLOUDCH,RATIO GD160(NG)	
(n,γ)	Pile		ANL	Expt	Jour PR 72 888	Nov 47	Seren+	+
	Pile				Data EXFOR11447.101	Jun 76	. 1 PT.	
(n,γ)	2.4+4		ORL	Expt	Jour PR 107 504	Jul 57	Macklin+.SB-BE NS,710+-71MB,.364MEVG	+
					Conf 58Geneva 671	Sep 58	.SUPERSEDED	
	2.4+4				Data EXFOR11399.042	Jun 76	. 1 PT.	
(n,γ)	2.0+5		ORL	Expt	Jour PR 114 1619	Jun 59	Lyon+. ABS GAMMA COUNT 111+-15MB ACT	+
	2.0+5				Data EXFOR11407.029	Jun 76	. 1 PT.	
(n,γ)	Maxwl		CRC	Eval	Rept AECL-1054	Mar 60	Walker. (CRRP-913)	
(n,γ)	Maxwl		ORL	Expt	Jour NSE 8 378	Nov 60	Lyon. ACTIVATION, SIGMA GIVEN	+
	Maxwl				Data EXFOR11625.027	Jun 76	. 1 PT.	
	1.5+7		ARK	Expt	Prog A-ARK-61 2	61	Bramlitt+	
	1.5+7				Data EXFOR11880.009	Jun 76	. 1 PT.	
(n,γ)	Maxwl		MUA	ExTh	Jour NP 41 372	Mar 63	Mangal+ (N,G) SIGMA GVN,TH CFD EXPT	+
	Maxwl			Expt	Data EXFOR31249.006	Sep 72	.SIG GVN	

64 Gadolinium 158

Quantity	Energy (ev) Min	Max	Lab	Type	Documentation Ref Vol Page	Date	Author, Comments	Data
(n,γ)	2.4+4		MUA	Expt Jour	PR 152 1055	Dec 66	Chaubey+ BETA-DET,SIG REL I-127,TBL	+
	2.4+4			Data	EXFOR30079.033	Dec 70	SIGMA FOR 18. H HALF-LIFE	
(n,γ)	3.0+6		DEB	Expt Jour	JNE 21 797	Oct 67	Peto+ACTIV,SIGMA REL TO P-31(N,P)	+
	3.0+6			Data	EXFOR30031.023	Aug 70	SINGLE VALUE	
(n,γ)	Maxwl		AUA	Theo Jour	NSE 31 234	Feb 68	Cook+ STATISTICAL CALC CFD EXPT	
(n,γ)	4.9+3	2.1+6	ANL	Expt Jour	JNE 22 267	May 68	Stupegia+ ACT 21ES REL U235 NF,TABLE	+
	4.9+3	2.1+6		Data	EXFOR11624.010	Jun 76	. 21 PTS.	
(n,γ)	–		IEA	Comp Rept	IEA-INF- 10	Aug 68	Atalla. TABLES OF HL,SIG AND GAMM-E	
(n,γ)	1.0+3	1.0+7	BOL	Eval Rept	CCDN-NW/10	Dec 69	Benzi+H-F MOD,AXEL G(G)EST,ALL DATA	
				Rept	CEC(70)-2	Apr 70	- +. GRAPH	
				Conf	66Paris 1 537	Oct 66	- + STATMOD.TBL AV VALS.SUPERSEDD	
(n,γ)	1.0+3	1.0+6	GA	Theo Conf	70Helsinki 2 281	Jun 70	Fricke+44. SIG(E) GRAPH,STATMOD CALC	
(n,γ)	3.0+4		AUA	Theo Rept	AAEC/E-211	Nov 70	Musgrove. SIGMA GIVEN AND CFD OTHER	
(n,γ)	Fast		MTR	Expt Prog	NCSAC-33 90	Dec 70	Scoville+.ACT.FAST SPECT.VALUE GIVEN	
(n,γ)	Maxwl		GA	Eval Rept	GA- 12071	Sep 71	Mathews+. RECOMMENDED VALUES	
(n,γ)	1.0-3	1.5+7	AUA	Eval Data	AUSTR-DFN 173.	Nov 71	Cook+POINT(223)+GROUP(127)SIG.CF EVL	+
(n,γ)	Maxwl		CRC	Eval Rept	AECL-3037 1	Jan 72	Walker.RECOMMENDED SIG,DETAILED TBL	
(n,γ)	2.5+4		AUW	Expt Jour	JP/A 5 468	Mar 72	Thirumala+ ACT METHOD, RELATIVE TO I	+
				ExTh Conf	70Madurai 2 25	Dec 70	Thirumala Rao+ SIGMAS FOR S+P WAVES	
	2.5+4			Expt Data	EXFOR30247.005	Jun 73	CAPTURE CROSS SECTION	
(n,γ)	2.5-2		AUA	Eval Rept	AAEC/TM-619	Sep 72	Clayton.CALC FROM SIG LIBRARY,TABLE	
(n,γ)	Fast		MTR	Expt Conf	72Kiamesha 2 614	Sep 72	Harker+ CFRMF INTEGRAL MEAS.	
(n,γ)	5.0+3	7.0+4	CCP	Expt Conf	73Kiev 2 206	May 73	Kononov+ TOF,SIG(NEUT-E),GRAPH	
(n,γ)		1.1+7	RCN	Theo Rept	RCN-191	Jun 73	Lautenbach.GROUP CONSTANTS TBL	
(n,γ)	2.5-2		SAC	Revw Conf	IAEA-169 1 235	74	Ribon.STATUS SIG CFD REQUESTS,TABLE	
(n,γ)	Maxwl	Fiss	WIN	Revw Conf	IAEA-169 3 163	74	Pope+ MAXW+FIS-SPEC AVG DATA CFD XPT	
	Fiss			Conf	IAEA-169 3 137	74	Dean. POINT DATA AVG OVER STAND SPEC	
(n,γ)	1.0+3	1.0+7	FEI	Eval Rept	YK- 8/2 97	Sep 72	Abagjan+ AVG SIG(ENERGY-GROUPS),TABL	
				Rept	INDC(CCP)-39	Jul 74	.P102. ENGLISH OF YK-8/2 97	
(n,γ)	5.0+3	7.0+4	FEI	Expt Rept	YFI-17 9	Aug 74	Shorin+ TOF,SIG(NEUT-E),TBL	+
				Jour	YF 19 5	Jan 74	- + TOF,SIG(NEUT-E),GRAPHS	
	5.3+3	6.8+4		Rept	INDC(CCP)-48	Feb 75	. ENGLISH OF YFI-17 9	
	5.0+3	7.0+4		Jour	SNP 19 2	Jul 74	. ENGLISH OF YF 19 5	
	5.3+3	6.8+4		Data	EXFOR40222.008	Mar 74	.SIGMA FOR 32 EN-RANGES GVN	
(n,γ)	2.5-2		BNL	Expt Prog	ERDA-NDC-2 31	May 75	Chrien+NDG.TBC.	
(n,γ)	None		COL	Expt Prog	ERDA-NDC-2 55	May 75	Hacken+ NG/WID CALC.	
(n,γ)	Maxwl		MCM	Expt Priv	WALKER	May 56	Walker.	+
	Maxwl			Data	EXFOR12127.014	Jun 76	. 1 PT.	
(n,γ)	+7		FEI	Theo Rept	YK- 21 3	Oct 76	Blokhin+ SIG(NEUT-E),GRAPH	
Spect (n,γ)	Pile		FAR	Expt Jour	CR 241 389	Jul 55	Barloutaud+. COINCIDENCE. GRPH.	
Spect (n,γ)	2.5+4		ORL	Expt Conf	58Geneva 15 68	Sep 58	Macklin.PPR671,SIGMA+G-ENERGY GVN	
Spect (n,γ)	Pile		TAT	Expt Conf	62Madras 126	Feb 62	SUBBA RAO.GRAPH,TBL OF GS-INTENSITY	
Spect (n,γ)	Maxwl		AUW	Expt Conf	63Bombay 160	Feb 63	Sastry+.TBL,GAMMA-E+INTENSITY	
Spect (n,γ)	Pile		AE	ExTh Jour	NP/A 103 481	Nov 67	Malmskog+. DED HL FOR 363 KEV LEVEL	
Spect (n,γ)	+0	+4	COL	Expt Prog	WASH-1124 31	Nov 68	Camarda+ MOXON-RAE DET TBC NO DATA	
Spect (n,γ)	Maxwl		KUR	Expt Rept	IAE-1832	69	Panin+ CONVERS-EL SPEC,TBL ES+INTS	
				Rept	BNL-TR-306	Nov 69	. ENGLISH OF IAE-1832	
Spect (n,γ)	Pile		KUR	Expt Jour	YF 13 681	Apr 71	Groshev+ GE-LI,TBD	
	Maxwl			Jour	IZV 35 1644	May 73	- + GAMMA TRANSITIONS,GRAPH	
	Pile			Conf	71Moscow	Feb 71	- + ABST.GE-LI,TBL OF ES	
	Maxwl			Jour	BAS 35 1497	Aug 72	. ENGL OF IZV 35 1644	
	Pile			Jour	SNP 13 387	Oct 71	. ENGL OF YF 13 681	
(n,2n)	Fiss		CRC	Eval Rept	CRC-1003	Dec 60	Roy+,ESTIMATED AVG SIG=29.0MB	
(n,2n)	1.3+7	1.5+7	BNL	Theo Jour	NSE 23 238	Nov 65	Pearlstein.3ES.STAT MDL CALC.TBL CS.	
(n,2n)	Fiss		BNL	Theo Jour	NSE 23 238	Nov 65	Pearlstein.STATMDL CALC.SPEC AVG.TBL	
(n,2n)	1.5+7		DEB	Eval Jour	REA 11 1 153	Mar 73	Boedy+ RECOMM.VALUE FROM N-Z SYSTEM.	
(n,2n)	1.5+7		KFI	Theo Rept	KFKI-73-68	Dec 73	Jeki.NEW FIT,CALC SIG CFD OTHERS,TBL	
(n,xn) x>2	Fiss		BNL	Theo Jour	NSE 23 238	Nov 65	Pearlstein.SPEC AVG STATMDL CALC N3N	
(n,p)	Fiss		CRC	Eval Rept	CRC-1003	Dec 60	Roy+,ESTIMATED AVG SIG=0.003MB	
(n,p)	1.4+7		SAH	Comp Jour	NP 60 273	Nov 64	Chatterjee.MEAN OF EXPT CFD SHELLMOD	
(n,p)	1.4+7	1.5+7	ARK	Theo Prog	ORO-3235-29	Jan 67	Koch+,STAT MODEL CALC CFD EXPTS	
(n,p)	1.4+7		LYO	Comp Rept	LYCEN/6780	Nov 67	Crouzet+COMPILATN FOR ACTIVTN ANALYS	
(n,p)	1.5+7		IRK	Expt Jour	APA 34 209	Sep 71	Havlik. ACT. CC-W.	+
				Jour	OAWA 107 119	Apr 70	- . ACTIVATION METHOD	
	1.5+7			Data	EXFOR20509.013	Apr 76	1PNT.SIGMA.	
(n,α)	Fiss		CRC	Eval Rept	CRC-1003	Dec 60	Roy+,ESTIMATED AVG SIG=BELO 0.0001MB	
(n,α)	1.4+7		LYO	Comp Rept	LYCEN/6780	Nov 67	Crouzet+COMPILATN FOR ACTIVTN ANALYS	

64 Gadolinium 158

Quantity	Energy (ev) Min	Max	Lab	Type	Documentation Ref Vol Page	Date	Author, Comments	Data
(n,α)	1.4+7		AUW	Expt Jour	NP/A 125 57	Feb 69	RAMA PRASAD+,ACTIVATION,CFD OTHERS	+
				ExTh Jour	IPA 12 640	Sep 74	Rama Prasad+ CFD STATMDL COMPND VALU	
	1.4+7			Expt Data	EXFOR30051.	Dec 70	SIGMA NA,ALSO N2N+NA+NP FOR OTHERS.	
(n,α)	1.5+7		DEB	Comp Jour	REA 7 4 93	Dec 69	Csikai+ SIG+HL COMPILTN,N−ACTIV−ANAL	
(n,α)	1.4+7	1.5+7	JYV	Eval Rept	JU−RR−3/1970	Jun 70	Leppaemaeki+ TABLE OF EVAL AVG SIG	
(n,α)	1.5+7		IRK	Expt Jour	APA 34 209	Sep 71	Havlik. ACT. CC−W.	+
				Jour	OAWA 107 119	Apr 70	−. ACTIVATION METHOD	
	1.5+7			Data	EXFOR20509.014	Apr 76	1PNT.SIGMA.	
Reson Params	2.2+1		HAR	Expt Jour	NP 5 294	Jan 58	Bowey+. 1 RESONANCE E GVN. LINAC	
Reson Params	2.2+1		BNL	Expt Jour	NSE 8 183	Sep 60	Moller+	+
	2.2+1			Data	EXFOR12097.011	Jun 76	. 1 RES, E0.	
Reson Params		2.0+3	DUB	Expt Conf	68DUBSY 349	Jul 68	Pikelner.LVL SPAC,AVERG. WG	
Reson Params	−		IFU	Expt Jour	UFZ 13 2085	Dec 68	Vertebnyj+ OTHER TH D VAL GVN	
				Jour	UPJ 13 1492	Jun 69	TRANSLATN.*	
Reson Params	2.2+1	2.2+1	SAC	Expt Rept	CEA−N−1149	Jan 69	Ribon. RESONANCE PARAMETER ANALYSIS	+
	2.2+1			Data	EXFOR20148.029	May 73	1PNT.2A*G*WN.	
Reson Params	2.2+1	9.2+2	BNL	Expt Jour	PR 180 1131	Apr 69	Mughabghab+ TRANS,WN AVG D 10RESON	+
	2.2+1	9.2+2		Data	EXFOR10051.	May 73	. 42 PTS,E0,WG,WN,WN0.	
Reson Params	2.2+1	2.3+3	DUB	Expt Jour	YF 9 897	May 69	Karzhavina+,TRANS+AREA ANAL,TBL+GRPH	+
				Prog	YFI−6 135	Oct 68	−+ SHORTER TEXT, TABLE	
				Rept	JINR−P3−3882	Jun 68	−+ FULL PAPER.	
	2.2+2	2.7+3		Rept	BNL−TR−322	Jan 70	−+ ENGL OF YF 9 897.	
	2.2+1	2.3+3		Jour	SNP 9 523	Nov 69	−+ ENGL OF YF 9 897.	
	2.2+1	2.4+3		Rept	INDC−E−260	69	.ENGL TRANSL OF YFI−6 135	
	2.2+1	2.3+3		Data	EXFOR40162.	Jul 73	.EN−RES,N−WID,TOT−W,GAMMA−W,D	
Reson Params	2.2+1	9.2+2	BNL	Expt Jour	PR/C 1 1850	May 70	Mughabghab+, AVG WG=108+−20	+
Reson Params	−		AUA	Theo Rept	AAEC/E−211	Nov 70	Musgrove. CALCULTD D+GAM WIDTH GIVEN	
Reson Params	2.2+1	1.4+3	CJD	Eval Jour	YK−7	71	Zakharova+ SURVEY+SYSTEMATICS,GW,TBL	
				Rept	INDC(CCP)−27	Nov 72	.ENGLISH TRANSLATION OF YK−7 /71	
Reson Params	None		DUB	Theo Jour	YF 13 240	Feb 71	Malecki+G−WID,THEO CFD EXPT.TBL,GRPH	
				Jour	SNP 13 133	Aug 71	−+ ENGL OF YF 13 240.	
Reson Params	None		DUB	Theo Jour	ZEP 14 194	Aug 71	Soloviev.LARGE N−WID G−WID CORREL.NDG	
				Rept	JINR−E4−5880	71	Soloviev.N−GAM−WIDS CORR.SHORT NOTE	
				Jour	JEL 14 129	Aug 71	−. ENGL OF ZEP 14 194.	
Reson Params	+0	+2	BOL	Eval Conf	IAEA−169 3 123	74	Benzi+ AVG G−WID CFD OTHERS+XPT,TABL	
Reson Params	+1	+4	FEI	Eval Rept	YK−8/2 97	Sep 72	Abagyan+ AVG G−WID+D AT BINDNG−E,TBL	
				Rept	INDC(CCP)−39	Jul 74	.PAGE 102.ENGLISH OF YK−8/2 97	
Reson Params	2.2+1	1.0+4	COL	Expt Jour	PR/C 10 1904	Nov 74	Rahn+95 RES.WG=0.105 EV	+
	0.0+0	1.0+4		Jour	NSE 48 219	Jun 72	−+AVG WG=1068MEV.OVER 27 RESON.	
	2.2+1	1.0+3		Data	EXFOR10458.	Jan 75	.93 WN0,27 WG, 2 G*WN0.GIVEN.	
Reson Params	+7		FEI	Theo Rept	YK−21 3	Oct 76	Blokhin+ D,WG,WG/D,TBL	
Strnth Fnctn		2.0+3	DUB	Expt Conf	68DUBSY 349	Jul 68	Pikelner.LVL SPAC,AVERG. WG,S0 VS A	
Strnth Fnctn	2.2+1	9.2+2	BNL	Expt Jour	PR 180 1131	Apr 69	Mughabghab+ TRANS,1.6+−0.6FROM RESON	
		+4		Jour	PL/B 24 573	May 67	Chrien+ FROM RES+UNRESOLVED REGIONS	
	2.2+1	9.2+2		Data	EXFOR10051.027	May 73	. 2 PTS. L=0.	
Strnth Fnctn		2.0+3	DUB	Expt Jour	YF 9 897	May 69	Karzhavina+,TRANSMISSION,RES−PARAMS	+
				Prog	YFI−6 135	Oct 68	−+ SHORTER TEXT, TABLE	
				Rept	JINR−P3−3882	Jun 68	−+ FULL PAPER.	
		2.3+2		Rept	BNL−TR−322	Jan 70	−+ ENGL OF YF 9 897.	
		2.0+3		Jour	SNP 9 523	Nov 69	−+ ENGL OF YF 9 897.	
		2.4+3		Rept	INDC−E−260	69	.ENGL TRANSL OF YFI−6 135	
	2.2+1	2.0+3		Data	EXFOR40162.043	Jul 73	.2 DATA LINES	
Strnth Fnctn	2.2+1	9.2+2	BNL	Expt Jour	PR/C 1 1850	May 70	Mughabghab+,STF FROM RESON=1.6+−0.6	+
Strnth Fnctn	−		AUA	Theo Rept	AAEC/E−211	Nov 70	Musgrove. SMOOTHED S0,S1 AND S2 GIVN	
Strnth Fnctn	2.5+4		AUW	ExTh Conf	70Madurai 2 25	Dec 70	Thirumala Rao+ S1 GIVEN,CAPTURE−EXPT	
	2.5+4			Expt Data	EXFOR30247.009	Jun 73	S1−VALUE	
Strnth Fnctn	None		AUA	Eval Rept	AAEC/E−277	Mar 73	Musgrove.TBLS EXPTL DATA+BEST VALUES	
Strnth Fnctn	2.2+1	1.0+4	COL	Expt Jour	PR/C 10 1904	Nov 74	Rahn+ SO=(1.5+−0.2)−4.95RES	
Lvl Density	+6		MIL	Theo Jour	EN 15 1 54	Jan 68	Facchini+ LDL PARS FROM LOW EN RES	
Lvl Density	1.6+1	3.0+2	DUB	Expt Rept	JINR−P3−3882	Jun 68	Karzhavina+	+
				Rept	YFI−6 135	Nov 68	−+	
	1.6+1	3.0+2		Data	EXFOR40162.048	Jul 73	.1 DATA LINE	
Lvl Density	None		CCP	Theo Jour	YF 11 1028	May 70	Rubchenya. DENSITY+A+TEMP GIVEN	
				Jour	SNP 11 571	Nov 70	. ENGL OF YF 11 571.	
Lvl Density	None		AUW	Conf	70Madurai 2 267	Dec 70	Ramamurty+ A−PARAMETER GVN,LANG'S−TH	
Lvl Density	None		CCP	Theo Jour	YF 13 43	Jan 71	Bravin+.DEFORM PAR CALC,TBL,CFD EXPT	
Lvl Density	None		MUN	Theo Jour	NP/A 217 269	Dec 73	Dilg+ A,DELTA. BACK SHIFTED FERMIGAS	
Lvl Density	None		BOL	Eval Conf	IAEA−169 3 123	74	Benzi+ LVL DENS PARAM BY XPT,GRPH+TB	

64 Gadolinium 158

Quantity	Energy (ev) Min	Max	Lab	Type	Documentation Ref Vol Page	Date	Author, Comments	Data
Lvl Density	None		COP	Theo	Jour NP/A 222 493	Apr 74	Dossing+COLL ROTAT.SPAC. ACCUR ESTIM	
Lvl Density	None		DUB	Theo	Jour NP/A 224 396	May 74	Malov+ 1/2 MICROSC.MODEL. DEFORM NUC	
Lvl Density	None		ROC	Theo	Jour NP/A 223 589	May 74	Huizenga+ EXP CFD MICROSC TH AX SYMM	
Lvl Density	+1	+4	FEI	Eval	Rept YK– 8/2 97	Sep 72	Abagyan+ LVL DENSITY PARAMETER,TBL	
					Rept INDC(CCP)–39	Jul 74	.PAGE 102.ENGLISH OF YK–8/2 97	
Lvl Density	+0	1.0+4	JAE	ExTh	Jour JPJ 37 581	Sep 74	Ideno.LVL SPACING CORRELATIONS.TBL.	
	1.0+0	1.0+4			Rept JAERI–M–5490	Nov 73	– .LEVEL SPACING CORRELATIONS.TBL	
(γ,n)	8.0+6	2.2+7	CCP	Expt	Jour ZEP 11 520	Jun 70	Vasil'Ev+ EXPTL SIG(GAMMA–E) GRAPH	

64 Gadolinium 159

Quantity	Energy (ev) Min	Max	Lab	Type	Documentation Ref Vol Page	Date	Author, Comments	Data
Evaluation	1.0–3	1.5+7	AUA	Eval	Rept AAEC/TM–549	Jun 70	Cook.TOT,EL,INEL,NONEL,CAPT SIGS,NDG	+
					Rept AAEC/E–214	Jun 71	Bertram+GROUP SIGMAS SAME QUANTS.NDG	
					Rept AAEC/TM–587	Mar 71	*DESCRIPTION OF LIBRARY	
	1.0–3	1.5+7			Data AUSTR–DFN 174.	Nov 71	POINT(223) AND GROUP(127) SIGMAS	
Total	1.0–3	1.5+7	AUA	Eval	Data AUSTR–DFN 174.	Nov 71	COOK+POINT(223)+GROUP(127)SIG.CF EVL	+
Elastic	1.0–3	1.5+7	AUA	Eval	Data AUSTR–DFN 174.	Nov 71	COOK+POINT(223)+GROUP(127)SIG.CF EVL	+
Tot Inelastc	5.0+5	1.5+7	AUA	Eval	Data AUSTR–DFN 174.	Nov 71	COOK+POINT(11)+GROUP(127)SIG.CF EVL	+
Nonelastic	1.0–3	1.5+7	AUA	Eval	Data AUSTR–DFN 174.	Nov 71	COOK+POINT(223)+GROUP(127)SIG.CF EVL	+
Res Int Abs	5.0–1		AUA	Eval	Rept AAEC/TM–619	Sep 72	Clayton.CALC FROM SIG LIBRARY,TABLE	
Res Int Abs	+0	+5	WIN	Revw	Conf IAEA–169 3 163	74	Pope+ CALC FROM AUSTRAL DATA FILE	
(n,γ)	1.0–3	1.5+7	AUA	Eval	Data AUSTR–DFN 174.	Nov 71	COOK+POINT(223)+GROUP(127)SIG.CF EVL	+
(n,γ)	Pile		CRC	Eval	Rept AECL–3037 1	Jan 72	Walker.SIG ESTIMATED ACCORDING Z,A	
(n,γ)	2.5–2		AUA	Eval	Rept AAEC/TM–619	Sep 72	Clayton.CALC FROM SIG LIBRARY,TABLE	
(n,γ)	Fiss		WIN	Revw	Conf IAEA–169 3 137	74	Dean. POINT DATA AVG OVER STAND SPEC	
	Maxwl	Fiss			Conf IAEA–169 3 163	74	Pope+ MAXW+FIS–SPEC AVG EVAL DATA	
Reson Params	–		AUA	Theo	Rept AAEC/E–211	Nov 70	Musgrove. CALCULTD D+GAM WIDTH GIVEN	
Reson Params	None		COL	Theo	Conf 75Wash. 335	Mar 75	Felvinci+ MOD ERICSON CALC CFD EXPT.	
Strnth Fnctn	–		AUA	Theo	Rept AAEC/E–211	Nov 70	Musgrove. SMOOTHED S0,S1 AND S2 GIVN	
Lvl Density	+6		MIL	Theo	Jour EN 15 1 54	Jan 68	Facchini+ LDL PARS FROM LOW EN RES	
Lvl Density	2.2+1	2.0+3	DUB	Expt	Jour JINR–P3–3882	Jun 68	Karzhavina+	+
					Rept YFI–6 135	Nov 68	– +	
	2.2+1	2.0+3			Data EXFOR40162.049	Jul 73	.1 DATA LINE	
Lvl Density	None		MUN	Theo	Jour NP/A 217 269	Dec 73	Dilg+ A,DELTA. BACK SHIFTED FERMIGAS	
Lvl Density	None		DUB	Theo	Jour NP/A 224 396	May 74	Malov+ 1/2 MICROSC.MODEL. DEFORM NUC	
Lvl Density	None		ROC	Theo	Jour NP/A 223 589	May 74	Huizenga+ EXP CFD MICROSC TH AX SYMM	

64 Gadolinium 160

Quantity	Energy (ev) Min	Max	Lab	Type	Documentation Ref Vol Page	Date	Author, Comments	Data
Evaluation	1.0–3	1.5+7	AUA	Eval	Rept AAEC/TM–549	Jun 70	Cook.TOT,EL,INEL,NONEL,CAPT SIGS,NDG	+
					Rept AAEC/E–214	Jun 71	Bertram+GROUP SIGMAS SAME QUANTS.NDG	
					Rept AAEC/TM–587	Mar 71	*DESCRIPTION OF LIBRARY	
	1.0–3	1.5+7			Data AUSTR–DFN 175.	Nov 71	POINT(223) AND GROUP(127) SIGMAS	
Evaluation	1.0+6		BOL	Eval	Prog EANDC(E)157U 2	May 73	Menapace+ TO BE CONTINUED ABOVE 1MEV	
Total	1.0–3	1.5+7	AUA	Eval	Data AUSTR–DFN 175.	Nov 71	COOK+POINT(223)+GROUP(127)SIG.CF EVL	+
Total	1.4+7		LIN	Expt	Jour IZV 37 1019	May 73	Djumin+ SIG(A),OPTMODEL CALC,GRAPH	+
					Conf 73Kiev 3 108	May 73	– + OPTMOD CALC,SIG	
					Jour BAS 37 5 91	May 73	.ENGLISH OF IZV 37 1019	
	1.4+7				Data EXFOR40302.019	Feb 76	1 PNT	
Total	0.0+0	1.0+4	COL	Expt	Jour PR/C 10 1904	Nov 74	Rahn+ANAL.FOR RES,STF,AVG D.TBLS.	
Elastic	1.0–3	1.5+7	AUA	Eval	Data AUSTR–DFN 175.	Nov 71	COOK+POINT(223)+GROUP(127)SIG.CF EVL	+
Tot Inelastc	5.0+5	1.5+7	AUA	Eval	Data AUSTR–DFN 175.	Nov 71	COOK+POINT(11)+GROUP(127)SIG.CF EVL	+
Diff Inelast	1.0+6	3.0+6	ALA	Expt	Jour PR/C 10 1864	Nov 74	Elbakr+ 14 LEVELS	+
	1.1+6	2.9+6			Rept ALBERTA–67	May 74	Gill+ TABLE,INTEGRAL SIGMA,14 LEVELS	
	1.0+6	3.0+6			Data EXFOR10456.002	Jan 75	. 80 PTS, DSIGMA, 14 LEVELS.	
Thermal Scat	6.5–2		CCP	Expt	Jour ZET 55 1241	Oct 68	Kuchin+ MAGNETIC+CRYSTAL STRUCTURE	
					Jour JET 28 649	Apr 69	TRANSLATN.*	
Nonelastic	1.0–3	1.5+7	AUA	Eval	Data AUSTR–DFN 175.	Nov 71	COOK+POINT(223)+GROUP(127)SIG.CF EVL	+
Res Int Abs	5.0–1		BNL	Expt	Rept BNL–13074	68	Mughabghab. FAST CHOPPER	+
Res Int Abs	5.5–1		CRC	Eval	Rept AECL–3037 1	Jan 72	Walker.REDUCED RES INT FROM RES PARS	
Res Int Abs	5.0–1		COL	Expt	Jour NSE 48 219	Jun 72	Rahn+ 6.9+–1.0B	
Res Int Abs	5.0–1		AUA	Eval	Rept AAEC/TM–619	Sep 72	Clayton.CALC FROM SIG LIBRARY,TABLE	
Res Int Abs	5.0–1		GHT	Expt	Jour JRC 23 113	74	Van Der Linden+ (N,G).CD–RATIO,TABLE	
Res Int Abs	+0	+5	WIN	Revw	Conf IAEA–169 3 163	74	Pope+ DATA FILE CALC CFD XPTAL VALUE	

64 Gadolinium 160

Quantity	Energy (ev) Min	Max	Lab	Type	Documentation Ref Vol Page	Date	Author, Comments	Data
Res Int Abs	5.0-1		IJI Eval	Conf	75Kiev 1 169	May 75	Fedorova+ EVAL+CALC RI GIVEN,TABLE	
(n,γ)	Maxwl		MCMExpt	Priv	WALKER	May 56	Walker.	+
	Maxwl			Data	EXFOR12127.015	Jun 76	. 1 PT.	
(n,γ)	1.4+7		ALD Expt	Jour	PPS 72 505	Oct 58	Perkin+ACT ANAL 18.5MB+ -30PC,B-W TH	+
(n,γ)	1.5+7		ARK Expt	Jour	PR 118 242	Apr 60	Wille. MEAS ACT SIG= 3.0+ -1.0 MB.	+
	1.5+7			Data	EXFOR12033.036	Jun 76	. 1 PT.	
(n,γ)	Maxwl		MUAExTh	Jour	NP 41 372	Mar 63	Mangal+ (N,G) SIGMA GVN,TH CFD EXPT	
	Maxwl			Expt Data	EXFOR31249.007	Sep 72	.SIG GVN	
(n,γ)	2.4+4		MUAExpt	Jour	PR 152 1055	Dec 66	Chaubey+ BETA-DET,SIG REL I-127,TBL	+
	2.4+4			Data	EXFOR30079.034	Dec 70	SIGMA FOR 3.7 MIN HALF-LIFE	
(n,γ)	2.8+6		REN Expt	Jour	ARI 18 279	May 67	Broadhead+ ACTIV 3.7MIN GD161, 17MB	+
	2.8+6			Data	EXFOR11850.008	Jun 76	. 1 PT.	
(n,γ)	1.4+7		LYO Comp	Rept	LYCEN/6780	Nov 67	Crouzet+COMPILATN FOR ACTIVTN ANALYS	
(n,γ)	-		IEA Comp	Rept	IEA-INF- 10	Aug 68	Atalla. TABLES OF HL,SIG AND GAMM-E	
(n,γ)	1.0+3	1.0+7	BOL Eval	Rept	CCDN-NW/10	Dec 69	Benzi+H-F MOD,AXEL G(G)EST,ALL DATA	
				Rept	CEC(70)-2	Apr 70	- +. GRAPH	
(n,γ)	3.0+4		AUA Theo	Rept	AAEC/E-211	Nov 70	Musgrove. SIGMA GIVEN AND CFD OTHER	
(n,γ)	Fast		MTR Expt	Prog	NCSAC-33 90	Dec 70	Scoville+.ACT.FAST SPEC.VALUE GIVEN.	
(n,γ)	1.0-3	1.5+7	AUA Eval	Data	AUSTR-DFN 175.	Nov 71	COOK+POINT(223)+GROUP(127)SIG.CF EVL	+
(n,γ)	Maxwl		CRC Eval	Rept	AECL-3037 1	Jan 72	Walker.RECOMMENDED SIG,DETAILED TBL	
(n,γ)	2.5+4		AUWExpt	Jour	JP/A 5 468	Mar 72	Thirumala+ ACT METHOD, RELATIVE TO I	
(n,γ)	1.4+7		GRE Theo	Jour	NP/A 189 334	Jul 72	Boisson+.DIR,COLLECT.CURV. DEFORMNUC	
(n,γ)	2.5-2		AUA Eval	Rept	AAEC/TM-619	Sep 72	Clayton.CALC FROM SIG LIBRARY,TABLE	
(n,γ)	Fast		MTR Expt	Conf	72Kiamesha 2 614	Sep 72	Harker+ CFRMF INTEGRAL MEAS.	
(n,γ)	5.0+3	1.6+5	VIP Expt	Jour	NSE 49 317	Nov 72	Fawcett+. ACTIVATION. CURVE.	+
				Abst	DA/B 32 2929	Nov 71	- .	
	5.0+3	1.6+5		Data	EXFOR10298.004	Oct 73	. 16 PTS. SIGMA.	
(n,γ)	5.0+3	7.0+4	CCP Expt	Conf	73Kiev 2 206	May 73	Kononov+ TOF,SIG(NEUT-E),GRAPH	
(n,γ)	2.5+4		AUWExpt	Jour	NC/A 18 48	Nov 73	Sidappa+ ACTIV SIG,CFD.TABLE	
(n,γ)	Fiss		WIN Revw	Conf	IAEA-169 3 137	74	Dean. POINT DATA AVG OVER STAND SPEC	
	Maxwl	Fiss		Conf	IAEA-169 3 163	74	Pope+ MAXW+FIS-SPEC AVG DATA CFD XPT	
(n,γ)	1.0+3	1.0+7	FEI Eval	Rept	YK- 8/2 97	Sep 72	Abagjan+ AVG SIG(ENERGY-GROUPS),TABL	
				Rept	INDC(CCP)-39	Jul 74	.P102. ENGLISH OF YK- 8/2 97	
(n,γ)	5.0+3	7.0+4	FEI Expt	Rept	YFI-17 9	Aug 74	Shorin+ TOF,SIG(NEUT-E),TBL	+
				Jour	YF 19 5	Jan 74	- + TOF,SIG(NEUT-E),GRAPHS	
	5.3+3	6.8+4		Rept	INDC(CCP)-48	Feb 75	. ENGLISH OF YFI-17 9	
	5.0+3	7.0+4		Jour	SNP 19 2	Jul 74	. ENGLISH OF YF 19 5	
	5.3+3	6.8+4		Data	EXFOR40222.009	Mar 74	.SIGMA FOR 32 EN-RANGES GVN	
(n,γ)	2.5-2		BNL Expt	Prog	ERDA-NDC-2 31	May 75	Chrien+NDG.TBC.	
(n,γ)	None		COL Expt	Prog	ERDA-NDC-2 55	May 75	Hacken+ NG/WID CALC.	
(n,γ)	1.5+7		JYV Expt	Jour	PL/B 39 625	May 72	Kantele+ CAPT SIG MEASURED	+
				Rept	JU-RR-1/1976	Mar 76	Valkonen.(THESIS).ACTIV.TBL. 14.5MEV	
	1.5+7			Data	EXFOR20673.031	Nov 76	1PNT.SIGMA.	
	1.5+7			Data	EXFOR20544.007	Apr 76	1PNT.SIGMA.	
Spect (n,γ)	Pile		COP Expt	Jour	NP 6 630	May 58	GREGERS HANSEN+.GRPH+TBL. LVLS DY161	
Spect (n,γ)	Pile		KUR Expt	Jour	YF 13 681	Apr 71	Groshev+ GE-LI,TBD	
	Maxwl			Jour	IZV 35 1644	May 73	- + GAMMA TRANSITIONS,GRAPH	
				Jour	BAS 35 1497	Aug 72	. ENGL OF IZV 35 1644	
	Pile			Jour	SNP 13 387	Oct 71	. ENGL OF YF 13 681	
Inelastic γ	1.1+6	3.2+6	ALA Expt	Jour	PR/C 10 1864	Nov 74	Elbakr+ 14.LVLS.UP.TO.1599KEV	
(n,2n)	1.5+7		CRC Expt	Jour	CJP 31 267	Feb 53	Paul+.BETA ACT.CFD TH. HL= 70M+18H	+
	1.5+7			Data	EXFOR11274.092	Jun 76	. 1 PT.	
(n,2n)	1.5+7		ARK Expt	Jour	PR 118 242	Apr 60	Wille. MEAS ACT SIG=1450+ -300 MB	+
	1.5+7			Data	EXFOR12033.037	Jun 76	. 1 PT.	
(n,2n)	Fiss		CRC Eval	Rept	CRC-1003	Dec 60	Roy+,ESTIMATED AVG SIG=19.0MB	
(n,2n)	1.5+7		MUAExpt	Jour	NP 28 560	Dec 61	Khurana+HANS.ACTIVATION,CFD STATMOD.	+
	1.5+7			Data	EXFOR31247.018	Mar 73	.SIG GVN	
(n,2n)	1.4+7		HAMCompJour		NP 65 257	Mar 65	Bormann. 3EXPT VALS.CFD SHELL EFFECT	
(n,2n)	1.3+7	1.5+7	BNL Theo	Jour	NSE 23 238	Nov 65	Pearlstein.3ES.STAT MDL CALC.TBL CS.	
(n,2n)	Fiss		BNL Theo	Jour	NSE 23 238	Nov 65	Pearlstein.STATMDL CALC.SPEC AVG.TBL	
(n,2n)	1.4+7		LYO Comp	Rept	LYCEN/6780	Nov 67	Crouzet+COMPILATN FOR ACTIVTN ANALYS	
(n,2n)	1.4+7		AUWExpt	Jour	NP/A 125 57	Feb 69	RAMA PRASAD+,ACTIVATION,CFD OTHERS	+
				ExTh Jour	IPA 12 640	Sep 74	Rama Prasad+ CFD STATMDL COMPND VALU	
	1.4+7			Expt Data	EXFOR30051.	Dec 70	SIGMA N2N,ALSO N2N+NA+NP FOR OTHERS.	
(n,2n)	1.5+7		DEB Comp	Jour	REA 7 4 93	Dec 69	Csikai+ SIG+HL COMPILTN,N-ACTIV-ANAL	
(n,2n)	1.4+7	1.5+7	JYV Eval	Rept	JU-RR-3/1970	Jun 70	Leppaemaeki+ TABLE OF EVAL AVG SIG	
(n,2n)	+7		KFI Theo	Rept	KFKI-71-8	Feb 71	Jeki. CALCULATED CFD EXPTL SIG VALUE	

64 Gadolinium 160

Quantity	Energy (ev) Min	Max	Lab	Type	Documentation Ref Vol Page	Date	Author, Comments	Data
(n,2n)	1.5+7		IRK Expt	Jour	APA 34 209	Sep 71	Havlik. ACT. CC−W.	+
				Jour	OAWA 107 119	Apr 70	− . ACTIVATION METHOD	
	1.5+7			Data	EXFOR20509.015	Apr 76	1PNT.SIGMA.	
(n,2n)	1.5+7		ARK Expt	Abst	DA/B 32 5091	Mar 72	Bari. GE(LI) DET. ACT. SIG GIVEN	+
	1.5+7			Data	EXFOR10431.055	Aug 75	. 1 PT, SIGMA.	
(n,2n)	1.4+7		CCP Expt	Jour	YF 15 1099	Jun 72	Victorov+ ACTIV,TBL CFD OTHERS+THEO	+
	1.4+7			Data	EXFOR40107.007	Dec 72	1 VALUE	
(n,2n)	1.5+7		DEB Eval	Jour	REA 11 1 153	Mar 73	Boedy. COMPILATION+RECOMM.VALUE,TBL	
				Rept	IAEA−153 173	73	− . RECOMM. VALUE ONLY	
(n,2n)	1.5+7		NPL Expt	Jour	JNE 27 531	Aug 73	Robertson+ SIG=1456MB.REL FE056 NP	+
	1.5+7			Data	EXFOR20799.017	Oct 78	1PNT.SIGMA.	
(n,2n)	1.5+7		TAT Theo	Jour	JP/A 7 1457	Aug 74	Kondaiah. CALC ON STAT MODEL	
(n,2n)	1.4+7		AUW Expt	Conf	74Bombay 2 105	Dec 74	Lakshmandas+ ACTIV,GELI.SIGMA GIVEN	+
	1.4+7			Data	EXFOR30389.004	Mar 77	1 PNT.	
(n,2n)	1.5+7		JUL Expt	Jour	NP/A 224 319	May 74	Qaim. ACT.GE(LI)	+
				Jour	RRL 25 335	May 76	− + SIG IN GRPH. SYST VS (N−Z)/A	
	1.5+7			Data	EXFOR20541.035	Apr 76	1PNT.SIGMA.	
(n,xn) x>2	Fiss		BNL Theo	Jour	NSE 23 238	Nov 65	Pearlstein.SPEC AVG STATMDL CALC N3N	
(n,p)	Fiss		CRC Eval	Rept	CRC−1003	Dec 60	Roy+,ESTIMATED AVG SIG=0.0006MB	
(n,p)	1.4+7	1.5+7	ARK Theo	Prog	ORO−3235−29	Jan 67	Koch+,STAT MODEL CALC CFD EXPTS	
(n,p)	1.4+7		LYO Comp	Rept	LYCEN/6780	Nov 67	Crouzet+COMPILATN FOR ACTIVTN ANALYS	
(n,α)	1.5+7		ARK Expt	Jour	PR 180 242	Apr 60	Wille. MEAS ACT SIG=2.+−1. MB.	+
	1.5+7			Data	EXFOR12033.035	Jun 76	. 1 PT.	
(n,α)	Fiss		CRC Eval	Rept	CRC−1003	Dec 60	Roy+,ESTIMATED AVG SIG=BELO 0.0001MB	
(n,α)	1.4+7		CIS Theo	Jour	NP 51 460	Feb 64	Facchini+STATMOD SIG XPT/CALC120−370	
(n,α)	1.4+7		LYO Comp	Rept	LYCEN/6780	Nov 67	Crouzet+COMPILATN FOR ACTIVTN ANALYS	
(n,α)	1.5+7		DEB Comp	Jour	REA 7 4 93	Dec 69	Csikai+ SIG+HL COMPILTN,N−ACTIV−ANAL	
(n,α)	1.4+7	1.5+7	JYV Eval	Rept	JU−RR−3/1970	Jun 70	Leppaemaeki+ TABLE OF EVAL AVG SIG	
(n,α)	1.4+7		KFI Comp	Jour	JRC 7 365	Jun 71	Nagy+ SIGMA,GAMMA−E AND HALF−L GIVEN	
Reson Params		2.5+3	DUB Expt	Conf	68DUBSY 349	Jul 68	Pikelner.LVL SPAC,AVERG. WG	
Reson Params	−		IFU Expt	Jour	UFZ 13 2085	Dec 68	Vertebnyj+ OTHER TH D VAL GVN	
				Jour	UPJ 13 1492	Jun 69	TRANSLATN.*	
Reson Params	2.2+2	2.7+3	BNL Expt	Jour	PR 180 1131	Apr 69	Mughabghab+ TRANS,WN AVG D 8 RESON	+
	2.2+2	2.7+3		Data	EXFOR10051.	Aug 72	. 16 PTS. E0,WN,WN0.	
Reson Params	2.2+2	2.7+3	DUB Expt	Jour	YF 9 897	May 69	Karzhavina+,TRANS+AREA ANAL,TBL+GRPH	+
				Prog	YFI−6 135	Oct 68	− + SHORTER TEXT, TABLE	
				Rept	JINR−P3−3882	Jun 68	− + FULL PAPER.	
				Rept	BNL−TR−322	Jan 70	− + ENGL OF YF 9 897.	
				Jour	SNP 9 523	Nov 69	− + ENGL OF YF 9 897.	
	2.2+1	2.7+3		Rept	INDC−E−260	69	.ENGL TRANSL OF YFI−6 135	
	2.2+2	2.7+3		Data	EXFOR40162.	Jul 73	.EN−RES,N−WID,TOT−W,GAMMA−W,D	
Reson Params	−		AUA Theo	Rept	AAEC/E−211	Nov 70	Musgrove. CALCULTD D+GAM WIDTH GIVEN	
Reson Params	None		DUB Theo	Jour	YF 13 240	Feb 71	Malecki+G−WID,THEO CFD EXPT.TBL,GRPH	
				Jour	SNP 13 133	Aug 71	− + ENGL OF YF 13 240.	
Reson Params	+0	+2	BOL Eval	Conf	IAEA−169 3 123	74	Benzi+ AVG G−WID CFD OTHERS+XPT,TABL	
Reson Params	+2	+4	FEI Eval	Rept	YK−8/2 97	Sep 72	Abagyan+ AVG G−WID+D AT BINDNG−E,TBL	
				Rept	INDC(CCP)−39	Jul 74	.PAGE 102.ENGLISH OF YK−8/2 97	
Reson Params	2.2+2	9.7+3	COL Expt	Jour	PR/C 10 1904	Nov 74	Rahn+ 58 RES.WG=0.111 EV	+
	0.0+0	1.0+4		Jour	NSE 48 219	Jun 72	−+AVG WG=1298MEV OVER 5 RESON.	
	2.2+2	9.7+3		Data	EXFOR10458.	Jan 75	.43 WN0,4 WG, 13 G*WN0 GIVEN.	
Strnth Fnctn		2.5+3	DUB Expt	Conf	68DUBSY 349	Jul 68	Pikelner.LVL SPAC,AVERG. WG,S0 VS A	
Strnth Fnctn	2.2+2	2.7+3	BNL Expt	Jour	PR 180 1131	Apr 69	Mughabghab+ TRANS,2.5+−1.3FROM RESON	+
	2.2+2	2.7+3		Data	EXFOR10051.030	May 73	. 2 PTS, L=0.	
Strnth Fnctn		2.5+3	DUB Expt	Jour	YF 9 897	May 69	Karzhavina+,TRANSMISSION,RES−PARAMS	+
				Prog	YFI−6 135	Oct 68	− + SHORTER TEXT, TABLE	
				Rept	JINR−P3−3882	Jun 68	− + FULL PAPER.	
		2.3+2		Rept	BNL−TR−322	Jan 70	− + ENGL OF YF 9 897.	
		2.5+3		Jour	SNP 9 523	Nov 69	− + ENGL OF YF 9 897.	
		2.7+3		Rept	INDC−E−260	69	− + ENGL TRANSL OF YFI−6 135	
	2.2+2	2.5+3		Data	EXFOR40162.044	Jul 73	.2 DATA LINES	
Strnth Fnctn	2.2+2	2.7+3	BNL Expt	Jour	PR/C 1 1850	May 70	Mughabghab+,STF FROM RESON=2.5+−1.3	+
Strnth Fnctn	−		AUA Theo	Rept	AAEC/E−211	Nov 70	Musgrove. SMOOTHED S0,S1 AND S2 GIVN	
Strnth Fnctn		1.0+5	VIP Expt	Abst	DA/B 32 2932	Nov 71	Lindsay. GAMMA, S,P WAVE, GOLD STD.	
Strnth Fnctn	5.0+3	1.6+5	VIP Expt	Jour	NSE 49 317	Nov 72	Fawcett+. GAMMA,S0,AND S1 GIVEN	
				Abst	DA/B 32 2929	Nov 71	.SUPERSEDED	
Strnth Fnctn	None		AUA Eval	Rept	AAEC/E−277	Mar 73	Musgrove.TBLS EXPTL DATA+BEST VALUES	
Strnth Fnctn	2.2+2	9.7+3	COL Expt	Jour	PR/C 10 1904	Nov 74	Rahn+ SO=(1.8+−0.4)−4.51=(1.7+−.3)−4	
	None			Conf	75Wash. 780	Mar 75	Hacken+ NEVIS TOF S−WAVE STF	

64 Gadolinium 160

Quantity	Energy (ev) Min	Max	Lab	Type	Documentation Ref Vol Page	Date	Author, Comments	Data
Lvl Density	None		AUW	Theo Conf	70Madurai 2 267	Dec 70	Ramamurty+ A – PARAMETER GVN,LANG'S – TH	
Lvl Density	None		BOL	Eval Conf	IAEA – 169 3 123	74	Benzi+ LVL DENS PARAM BY XPT,GRPH+TB	
Lvl Density	+2	+4	FEI	Eval Rept	YK – 8/2 97	Sep 72	Abagyan+ LVL DENSITY PARAMETER,TBL	
				Rept	INDC(CCP) – 39	Jul 74	.PAGE 102.ENGLISH OF YK – 8/2 97	
Lvl Density	+0	1.0+4	JAE	ExTh Jour	JPJ 37 581	Sep 74	Ideno.LVL SPACING CORRELATIONS.TBL.	
	1.0+0	1.0+4		Rept	JAERI – M – 5490	Nov 73	– .LEVEL SPACING CORRELATIONS.TBL	

64 Gadolinium 161

Quantity	Energy (ev) Min	Max	Lab	Type	Documentation Ref Vol Page	Date	Author, Comments	Data
(n,γ)	Maxwl		ANL	Expt Jour	PR 153 1310	Jan 67	Wahlgren+,FROM 162ACT,96+ – 50KILOBARN	
Reson Params	–		AUA	Theo Rept	AAEC/E – 211	Nov 70	Musgrove. CALCULTD D+GAM WIDTH GIVEN	
Strnth Fnctn	–		AUA	Theo Rept	AAEC/E – 211	Nov 70	Musgrove. SMOOTHED S0,S1 AND S2 GIVN	
Lvl Density	2.2+2	2.5+3	DUB	Expt Rept	JINR – P3 – 3882	Jun 68	Karzhavina+	+
				Rept	YFI – 6 135	Nov 68	– +	
	2.2+2	2.5+3		Data	EXFOR40162.050	Jul 73	.1 DATA LINE	
Lvl Density	None		MUN	Theo Jour	NP/A 217 269	Dec 73	Dilg+ A,DELTA. BACK SHIFTED FERMIGAS	
Lvl Density	None		ROC	Theo Jour	NP/A 223 589	May 74	Huizenga+ EXP CFD MICROSC TH AX SYMM	

65 Terbium 148

Quantity	Energy (ev) Min Max	Lab	Type	Documentation Ref Vol Page	Author, Comments Date	Data
Reson Params	–	AUA	Theo Rept	AAEC/E-211	Nov 70 Musgrove. CALCULTD D+GAM WIDTH GIVEN	
Strnth Fnctn	–	AUA	Theo Rept	AAEC/E-211	Nov 70 Musgrove. SMOOTHED S0,S1 AND S2 GIVN	

65 Terbium 150

Quantity	Energy (ev) Min Max	Lab	Type	Documentation Ref Vol Page	Author, Comments Date	Data
Reson Params	–	AUA	Theo Rept	AAEC/E-211	Nov 70 Musgrove. CALCULTD D+GAM WIDTH GIVEN	
Strnth Fnctn	–	AUA	Theo Rept	AAEC/E-211	Nov 70 Musgrove. SMOOTHED S0,S1 AND S2 GIVN	

65 Terbium 151

Quantity	Energy (ev) Min Max	Lab	Type	Documentation Ref Vol Page	Author, Comments Date	Data
Reson Params	–	AUA	Theo Rept	AAEC/E-211	Nov 70 Musgrove. CALCULTD D+GAM WIDTH GIVEN	
Strnth Fnctn	–	AUA	Theo Rept	AAEC/E-211	Nov 70 Musgrove. SMOOTHED S0,S1 AND S2 GIVN	

65 Terbium 152

Quantity	Energy (ev) Min Max	Lab	Type	Documentation Ref Vol Page	Author, Comments Date	Data
Reson Params	–	AUA	Theo Rept	AAEC/E-211	Nov 70 Musgrove. CALCULTD D+GAM WIDTH GIVEN	
Strnth Fnctn	–	AUA	Theo Rept	AAEC/E-211	Nov 70 Musgrove. SMOOTHED S0,S1 AND S2 GIVN	

65 Terbium 153

Quantity	Energy (ev) Min Max	Lab	Type	Documentation Ref Vol Page	Author, Comments Date	Data
(n,p)	Maxwl	IFU	Theo Rept	ICD-4 20	67 Dadakina+ PENETR COEFF CALC,TABLE	
Reson Params	–	AUA	Theo Rept	AAEC/E-211	Nov 70 Musgrove. CALCULTD D+GAM WIDTH GIVEN	
Strnth Fnctn	–	AUA	Theo Rept	AAEC/E-211	Nov 70 Musgrove. SMOOTHED S0,S1 AND S2 GIVN	

65 Terbium 154

Quantity	Energy (ev) Min Max	Lab	Type	Documentation Ref Vol Page	Author, Comments Date	Data
Reson Params	–	AUA	Theo Rept	AAEC/E-211	Nov 70 Musgrove. CALCULTD D+GAM WIDTH GIVEN	
Strnth Fnctn	–	AUA	Theo Rept	AAEC/E-211	Nov 70 Musgrove. SMOOTHED S0,S1 AND S2 GIVN	

65 Terbium 155

Quantity	Energy (ev) Min Max	Lab	Type	Documentation Ref Vol Page	Author, Comments Date	Data
(n,p)	Maxwl	IFU	Theo Rept	ICD-4 20	67 Dadakina+ PENETR COEFF CALC,TABLE	
Reson Params	–	AUA	Theo Rept	AAEC/E-211	Nov 70 Musgrove. CALCULTD D+GAM WIDTH GIVEN	
Strnth Fnctn	–	AUA	Theo Rept	AAEC/E-211	Nov 70 Musgrove. SMOOTHED S0,S1 AND S2 GIVN	

65 Terbium 156

Quantity	Energy (ev) Min Max	Lab	Type	Documentation Ref Vol Page	Author, Comments Date	Data
(n,p)	Maxwl	IFU	Theo Rept	ICD-4 20	67 Dadakina+ PENETR COEFF CALC,TABLE	
Reson Params	–	AUA	Theo Rept	AAEC/E-211	Nov 70 Musgrove. CALCULTD D+GAM WIDTH GIVEN	
Strnth Fnctn	–	AUA	Theo Rept	AAEC/E-211	Nov 70 Musgrove. SMOOTHED S0,S1 AND S2 GIVN	

65 Terbium 157

Quantity	Energy (ev) Min Max	Lab	Type	Documentation Ref Vol Page	Author, Comments Date	Data
Reson Params	–	AUA	Theo Rept	AAEC/E-211	Nov 70 Musgrove. CALCULTD D+GAM WIDTH GIVEN	
Strnth Fnctn	–	AUA	Theo Rept	AAEC/E-211	Nov 70 Musgrove. SMOOTHED S0,S1 AND S2 GIVN	

65 Terbium 158

Quantity	Energy (ev) Min Max	Lab	Type	Documentation Ref Vol Page	Author, Comments Date	Data
Reson Params	–	AUA	Theo Rept	AAEC/E-211	Nov 70 Musgrove. CALCULTD D+GAM WIDTH GIVEN	

65 Terbium 158

Quantity	Energy (ev) Min	Max	Lab	Type	Documentation Ref Vol Page	Author, Comments Date	Data
Strnth Fnctn	–		AUA	Theo Rept	AAEC/E – 211	Nov 70 Musgrove. SMOOTHED S0,S1 AND S2 GIVN	

65 Terbium 159

Quantity	Energy (ev) Min	Max	Lab	Type	Documentation Ref Vol Page	Author, Comments Date	Data
Evaluation	1.0 – 3	1.5+7	AUA	Eval Rept	AAEC/TM – 549	Jun 70 Cook.TOT,EL,INEL,NONEL,CAPT SIGS,NDG	+
				Rept	AAEC/E – 214	Jun 71 Bertram+GROUP SIGMAS SAME QUANTS.NDG	
				Rept	AAEC/TM – 587	Mar 71 *DESCRIPTION OF LIBRARY	
	1.0 – 3	1.5+7		Data	AUSTR – DFN 176.	Nov 71 POINT(223) AND GROUP(127) SIGMAS	
Evaluation	1.0 – 5	1.5+7	BOL	Eval Prog	NEANDC(E)182 7	Dec 76 Fabri+ COMPLETE EVAL IN ENDF/B DONE	+
	1.0 – 5	1.5+7		Data	CNEN – CEA 5	Jan 78 PRELIM.ALL QUANTITIES.ENDF FORMAT	
Total	Maxwl		COL	Expt Jour	PR 48 265	Aug 35 Dunning+ IONCH,TRANS,RA – BE/PARAFIN N	
Total	2.5+0	1.7+2	BNL	Expt Jour	PR 99 10	Jul 55 Harvey.+ CHOPF.TRNS.RES PAR ANAL.	+
	2.5+0	1.7+2		Data	EXFOR11912.036	Jun 76 . 206 PTS. CS DATA.	
Total	+0	3.0+3	BNL	Expt Jour	PRL 1 461	Dec 58 Hughes+ TRNS. NDG. STF ANAL. TBL.	
Total	7.3 – 2		ISU	Expt Jour	PR 121 610	Jan 61 Atoji. TRNS. CS=29.8+ – 1.0B.	
Total	1.0 – 4	3.0 – 3	MUN	Expt Jour	AKE 16 49	70 Knorr+ TRANS EXPT, TBL	
Total	3.0+6	1.5+7	KFK	Revw Conf	70Helsinki 2 219	Jun 70 Cierjacks.113. SIG(E) GRPH CFD OPTMD	
Total	3.3 – 2	2.7 – 1	BNL	Expt Jour	NIM 86 83	Sep 70 Malik+ TRNS. 4ES. TBL. CFD.	+
	3.3 – 2	2.7 – 1		Data	EXFOR10501.024	May 75 . 4 PTS, SIGMA.	
Total	3.5 – 1	3.7+0	CNA	Expt Prog	EANDC(OR)100	Jan 71 Cansoy.CRYST SPEC,NDG,TBP CNAEM – 76	+
	3.5 – 1	3.1+0		Data	EXFOR20174.002	May 74 29PTS.	
Total	2.5+6	1.5+7	BNW	Expt Jour	PR/C 3 576	Feb 71 Foster+,TRANS,CURVS,CFD OTHERS+TH	+
	3.0+6	1.5+7		Jour	PRL 22 139	Jan 69 Glasgow+ TOF.CURV.CFD P – B TBP SOON.	
	2.5+6	1.5+7		Jour	NIM 36 1	Sep 65 .EXPT DETAILS	
	2.3+6	1.5+7		Data	EXFOR10047.069	Aug 73 . 252 PTS.	
Total	1.0 – 3	1.5+7	AUA	Eval Data	AUSTR – DFN 176.	Nov 71 COOK+POINT(223)+GROUP(127)SIG.CF EVL	+
Total	2.7+3		MUN	Expt Prog	EANDC(E)150U	Oct 72 Dilg+ AVERAGE TOT XSECT+S0	+
				Conf	71Albany 327	Aug 71 – +TRNS.AVG CS GVN.31 ELEMENT GRP	
	2.7+3			Data	EXFOR20583.019	May 76 1PNT.	
Total	1.3+7	1.5+7	DEB	Eval Rept	IAEA – 153 173	73 Boedy+ MOST PROBABLE VAL OF SIG,TBL	
				Jour	AHP 30 115	Oct 71 Angeli+ AVG SIG,CFD CALC.TBLS.GRAPH	
Total	3.5 – 3	1.8+0	RHI	Expt Jour	PR/B 8 2595	Sep 73 Malik+ CFD CALC, TBLS, GRPH	+
	3.5 – 3	1.8+0		Data	EXFOR10383.002	Jun 74 . 67 PTS.	
Total	3.0+3	6.5+5	DKE	Expt Jour	AP 84 165	May 74 Pineo+ AVG CS CURV, TBLS, GRPHS.	+
	1.0+5	6.5+5		Abst	DA/B 31 6821	May 71 – .2E RANGE AVGS.CFD OPTMDL.	
	1.5+4	6.0+5		Diss	PINEO	70 .AVG CS.GRPHS.CFD.STF CALC.TBL.CFD.	
	1.5+4	6.0+5		Data	EXFOR10542.022	Jan 79 . DATA UNOBTAINABLE FROM AUTHORS.	
Total	2.0+1	9.0+2	SAC	Expt Prog	NEANDC(E)166L	Feb 76 Derrien+ TOF,TRANS,RES PARAM DEDUCED	+
	2.0+1	9.0+2		Data	EXFOR20577.	Feb 76 0PTS. SEE RESONANCE PARAMETERS.	
Elastic	7.3 – 2		ISU	Expt Jour	PR 121 610	Jan 61 Atoji. N DIFFRACTION COH SCT, SC CS.	+
	7.3 – 2			Data	EXFOR12113.	Jun 76 . 2 PTS, COH, COH AMP	
Elastic	7.5 – 2		ANL	Expt Jour	JCP 35 1950	Dec 61 Atoji+ N DIFFRACTION. AMPL GVN.	+
	7.5 – 2			Data	EXFOR11606.006	Jun 76 . 1 PT. COH AMP=(7.62+ – .3) – 13.	
Elastic	1.0 – 3	1.5+7	AUA	Eval Data	AUSTR – DFN 176.	Nov 71 COOK+POINT(223)+GROUP(127)SIG.CF EVL	+
Elastic	1.0 – 3		RHI	Theo Jour	PR/B 8 2595	Sep 73 Malik+ PARAMAGN.SCAT,COH,INCOH SCAT	
Elastic	2.5 – 2		IJI	Eval Conf	75Kiev 1 169	May 75 Fedorova+ EVAL 2200M/S SIG,TABLE	
Elastic	1.0+0		DUB	Expt Conf	76Lowell 1243	Jul 76 Akopian+TOF.SCT CS=COH+INCOH.TBL	
	Cold			Rept	JINR – P3 – 8458	Mar 75 – + SPIN – INCOHERENT SIGMA GIVEN	
Diff Elastic	7.0+6		LRL	Theo Rept	UCRL – 4927	Jul 57 Bjorklund+ OPTMDL CALC 6 – PARAM FIT	
Diff Elastic	3.0+5	1.5+6	ANL	Expt Prog	WASH – 1068 1	Mar 66 Elwyn+,POL+SIG,ANALYSIS TBC.NDG.	
Polarization	3.0+5	1.5+6	ANL	Expt Prog	WASH – 1068 1	Mar 66 Elwyn+,POL+SIG,ANALYSIS TBC.NDG.	
Polarization	Maxwl		DUB	Expt Jour	ZET 69 777	Sep 75 Akopjan+ ANTIFERROM,.05DEGK.(A+) – (A –	
				Jour	JET 42 397	Sep 75 . ENGLISH OF ZET 69 777	
Polarization	2.0+0	3.1+2	DUB	Expt Rept	JINR – P3 – 9852	Jul 76 Alfimenkov+ TRANSMIS – EFF VS N – E,GRP	
	2.0+1	1.0+5		Conf	76Lowell 1361	Jul 76 – +TRNS EFFECT.TBL,GRPH	
Potntal Scat	3.0+3	6.5+5	DKE	Expt Abst	DA/B 31 6821	May 71 .THESIS ABST.	
				Diss	PINEO	70 .TBL.GRPHS.CFD TO 3 COLLECTIVE MDLS.	
Potntal Scat	3.5 – 1	3.1+0	CNA	Expt Prog	INDC(TUR) – 3	May 72 Cansoy. B – W SINGLE LEVEL FIT	+
	3.5 – 1	3.1+0		Data	EXFOR20174.004	May 74 1PNT.	
Potntal Scat	1.0 – 3		RHI	Theo Jour	PR/B 8 2595	Sep 73 Malik+ SIG = 7.5+ – .5B.	
Potntal Scat	6.2 – 2	1.0+0	CNA	Expt Prog	INDC(SEC) – 51	Dec 75 Cansoy+P139,ABST.FROM (N,G),SIG GIVN	
Tot Inelastc	1.0 – 3	3.0 – 3	MUN	Theo Jour	AKE 16 49	70 Knorr+ PARAMAGNETIC SCAT SIG CALC	
Tot Inelastc	5.0+5	1.5+7	AUA	Eval Data	AUSTR – DFN 176.	Nov 71 COOK+POINT(11)+GROUP(127)SIG.CF EVL	+
Diff Inelast	1.0 – 3	3.0 – 3	MUN	Expt Jour	AKE 16 49	70 Knorr+PARAMAGNETIC SCAT,2 ANG,CFD TH	
Thermal Scat	Cold		ORL	Revw Jour	JAP 36 1078	Mar 65 Koehler+ MAGN PROP FROM N DIFFRAC.	
Thermal Scat	Cold		GRE	Expt Jour	JAP 37 1038	Mar 66 MAGNETIC PROPS FROM N DIFFR XPTS	

65 Terbium 159

Quantity	Energy (ev) Min	Energy (ev) Max	Lab	Type	Documentation Ref Vol Page	Date	Author, Comments	Data
Thermal Scat	2.0−4	1.5−1	BSP	ExTh Jour	JCP 48 520	Jan 68	Mattos.,TRIVALENT ION PARAMAG SIG	+
Thermal Scat	None		RIS	Expt Prog	EANDC(OR)85L	Mar 69	Dietrich+	
Thermal Scat	1.0−4	1.0+3	MUN	Revw Jour	EEN 80 1	77	Koester. SCAT LENGTH	
Nonelastic	1.0−3	1.5+7	AUA	Eval Data	AUSTR−DFN 176.	Nov 71	COOK+POINT(223)+GROUP(127)SIG.CF EVL	+
Absorption	1.0−4	3.0−3	MUN	Theo Jour	AKE 16 49	70	Knorr+ FROM TOT SIG EXPT CALC, TBL	
Absorption	1.0−3	1.0+7	JUL	Eval Rept	JUEL−678−RG	Jul 70	Liu. EVALUATION+CALC,GRPH,FN OF E	
Absorption	2.5−2		IJI	Eval Conf	75Kiev 1 169	May 75	Fedorova+ EVAL 2200M/S SIG,TABLE	
Res Int Abs	None		CRC	Eval Rept	AECL−1054	Mar 60	Walker+ RED RES INT = 370B	
Res Int Abs	+3	+5	BOL	Theo Conf	61Vienna 1 179	Aug 61	Benzi+.PPR11,VAL GVN,L=0,L=1 .CAPT.	
Res Int Abs	5.0−1		BOL	Eval Conf	61Vienna 1 179	Aug 61	Benzi+ TBL TOTAL CAPT RES INTS.	
Res Int Abs	5.0−1		BOL	Eval Rept	RT/FI−4	Jan 67	Palmucci. CALC FROM (N,G) RES PARAMS	
Res Int Abs	0.0+0	1.0+6	OSL	Expt Rept	JIN 29 2155	Sep 67	Alstad+ ACTIV REL AU,AND CD RATIO	+
		1.0+6		Data	EXFOR20044.013	Sep 71	1PNT.CAPTURE.	
Res Int Abs	5.0−1		BGK	Expt Rept	THAI−AEC−10	Oct 67	. ACTIV(NA−I),CD−RATIO,REL AU. TABLE	+
	5.0−1			Data	EXFOR30368.024	Jan 77	REL AU, PRELM.	
Res Int Abs	5.0−1		MTR	Expt Rept	IN−1195	May 68	Scoville+.REACTIVITY MEAS. TBL. CFD.	+
				Jour	ANS 8 290	Jun 65	− + REACTIV. 6 ELS. CFD CALC.	
	5.0−1			Data	EXFOR11820.011	Jun 76	. 1 PT. RIA= 630+−25B.	
Res Int Abs	5.0−1		CNE	Expt Conf	70Helsinki 2 589	Jun 70	Ricabarra+ RATIO TO THR−ACT SIGMA	+
	5.0−1			Data	EXFOR30190.004	Dec 72	RES INT AND RATIO TO THR−CAPT SIGMA	
Res Int Abs	None		GA	Eval Rept	GA−12071	Sep 71	Mathews+. RECOMMENDED VALUES	
Res Int Abs	5.5−1		CRC	Eval Rept	AECL−3037 1	Jan 72	Walker.REDUCED RES INT,DETAILED TBL	
Res Int Abs	5.0−1		AUA	Eval Rept	AAEC/TM−619	Sep 72	Clayton.CALC FROM SIG LIBRARY,TABLE	
Res Int Abs	5.0−1		KJL	Expt Jour	JIN 34 2699	Sep 72	Steinnes. ACT. AU MONITOR	+
	5.0−1			Data	EXFOR20188.023	May 74	1PNT.CAPTURE.	
Res Int Abs	5.0−1		MUN	Expt Jour	JRC 15 535	73	Alian+CAPT CD−R, 313 B INCL 1/V	+
	5.0−1			Data	EXFOR20644.015	Jun 76	1PNT.CAPTURE.	
Res Int Abs	4.6−1	1.0+6	RCN	Theo Rept	RCN−191	Jul 73	Lautenbach.CAPT INT FROM GROUP SIGMA	
Res Int Abs	5.0−1		GHT	Expt Rept	JRC 20 695	74	Van Der Linden+ BY(N,G).CFD OTHS,TBL	
	5.5−1			Conf	73Paris 2 241	Mar 73	− + ACT,REL THR+GOLD,TBL	
	5.5−1			Data	EXFOR20645.028	Jul 76	1PNT.CAPTURE.	
Res Int Abs	+0	+5	WIN	Revw Conf	IAEA−169 3 163	74	Pope+ DATA FILE CALC CFD XPTAL VALUE	
Res Int Abs	1.0−1		NPL	Expt Jour	JP/A 7 2318	Dec 74	Ryves+ REL TO MN AU,REDUCED INTEGRAL	+
	1.0−1	1.4+7		Data	EXFOR20561.009	Oct 75	1PNT.	
Res Int Abs	5.0−1		IJI	Eval Conf	75Kiev 1 169	May 75	Fedorova+ EVAL+CALC RI GIVEN,TABLE	
(n,γ)	2.0+4	7.0+5	OXF	Expt Jour	PRSA 170 513	Apr 39	Griffiths.RA−BE PHOTONEUT ACTIVATION	
(n,γ)	Pile		ANL	Expt Jour	PR 72 888	Nov 47	Seren+.ACT 65 ELEMENTS. TBL.	+
	Pile			Data	EXFOR11447.104	Jun 76	. 1 PT. CS =10.7B+−20PCT.	
(n,γ)	Maxwl		ORL	Expt Jour	PR 83 643	Aug 51	Pomerance. LOCAL OSC REL AU ABS.	+
	Maxwl			Data	EXFOR11047.065	Jun 76	. 1 PT. CS= 44B+−10PCT.	
(n,γ)	Maxwl		CRC	Eval Rept	AECL−1054	Mar 60	Walker+ 2200M/SEC CS= 46B.	
(n,γ)	2.0+2	8.0+3	ORL	Expt Conf	61Saclay 203	Sep 61	Block+. CHOPF. LIQ SCINT. CFD OTH.	+
				Conf	61Vienna 1 95	Aug 61	Neiler.PPR73,TABLE FOR 3ES GVN,GRAPH	
	2.0+2	9.4+3		Data	EXFOR11935.014	Jun 76	. 52 PTS.	
(n,γ)	3.0+3	4.0+5	ORL	Expt Conf	PR 122 182	Apr 61	Gibbons+ TOF. CURV. CFD CALC.	+
	3.0+4	6.5+4		Jour	PR 129 2695	Mar 63	Macklin+ LIQ SCINT,1.85 AND 1.07B	
	3.0+4	1.7+5		Conf	61Vienna 1 95	Aug 61	Neiler.	
	1.1+4	1.7+5		Data	EXFOR11329.	Jun 76	. 48 PTS.	
(n,γ)	5.0+3	9.0+4	ORL	Theo Prog	ARF−1193−12	Jan 65	Macklin+.CALC FOR KT=5TO90KEV	
(n,γ)	1.0−3	1.0+4	LAS	Theo Rept	LA−3463	Jan 66	Bell. TH CAPTURE OF RARE EARTHS	
(n,γ)	2.5−2		BOL	Eval Rept	RT/FI−4	Jan 67	Palmucci. CALC FROM RES PARAMETERS	
(n,γ)	3.4+0		TRM	Expt Conf	67Kanpur 409	Feb 67	Chandramoleswar. WG= 40+−4 MICRO S	
(n,γ)	Maxwl		OSL	Expt Jour	JIN 27 2155	Sep 67	Alstad+ ACTIVATION REL AU,+CD RATIO	+
	Pile			Data	EXFOR20044.012	Sep 71	1PNT.SIG.	
(n,γ)	3.0+6		DEB	Expt Jour	JNE 21 797	Oct 67	Peto+ACTIV,SIGMA REL TO S−32(N,P)	
	3.0+6			Data	EXFOR30031.024	Aug 70	SINGLE VALUE	
(n,γ)	1.4+7		LYO	Comp Rept	LYCEN/6780	Nov 67	Crouzet+COMPILATN FOR ACTIVTN ANALYS	
(n,γ)	−		IEA	Comp Rept	IEA−INF−10	Aug 68	Atalla. TABLES OF HL,SIG AND GAMM−E	
(n,γ)	2.0+3		MTR	Expt Prog	WASH−1127 72	Apr 69	Schuman+ FILTERED BEAM,RELATVE CURVS	
(n,γ)	1.0+3	1.0+7	BOL	Eval Conf	CCDN−NW/10	Dec 69	Benzi+H−F MOD,AXEL G(G)EST,ALL DATA	
				Rept	CEC(70)−2	Apr 70	− +. GRAPH	
				Conf	66Paris 1 537	Oct 66	− + STATMOD.TBL AV VALS.SUPERSEDD	
				Jour	NC 38 216	Jul 65	− + THEORY FOR CAPTURE EVALUATION	
				Conf	61Vienna 1 179	Aug 61	− + TBL AV VALS. SUPERSEDED.	
(n,γ)	3.3−2	8.3−1	BNL	Expt Jour	NIM 86 83	Sep 70	Malik+MOXON RAE DET. REL AU .4ES TBL	+
	3.3−2	2.7−1		Data	EXFOR10501.023	May 75	. 4 PTS, SIGMA.	
(n,γ)	1.0+3	1.0+6	GA	Revw Conf	70ANL 285	Oct 70	Carlson. STATUS AS STANDARD SIG,CURV	
(n,γ)	3.0+4		AUA	Theo Rept	AAEC/E−211	Nov 70	Musgrove. SIGMA GIVEN AND CFD OTHER	

65 Terbium 159

Quantity	Energy (ev) Min	Energy (ev) Max	Lab	Type	Documentation Ref Vol Page	Date	Author, Comments	Data
(n,γ)	Pile		MTR	Expt Abst	ANS 13 755	Nov 70	Scoville+.CFRMF MEAST.VALUE GIVEN.	
(n,γ)	4.0+5		WWA	Expt Jour	APPB 2 489	71	Brzosko+ PARTIAL,TOTAL SIG CFD THEO	+
				Rept	INR–1318 28	Apr 71	*SHORT REPORT,DATA GIV	
				Jour	CJP 47 2849	Dec 69	*TH.CALCULATIONS OF SIG	
	4.0+5			Data	EXFOR30159.	Apr 72	PARTIAL,TOTAL SIGMAS GIVEN	
(n,γ)	Maxwl		GA	Eval Rept	GA– 12071	Sep 71	Mathews+. RECOMMENDED VALUES	
(n,γ)	1.0–3	1.5+7	AUA	Eval Data	AUSTR–DFN 176.	Nov 71	COOK+POINT(223)+GROUP(127)SIG.CF EVL	+
(n,γ)	Maxwl		CRC	Eval Rept	AECL–3037 1	Jan 72	Walker.RECOMMENDED SIG,DETAILED TBL	
(n,γ)	2.5+4		AUW	Expt Jour	JP/A 5 877	Jun 72	Siddappa+ ACT. S,P–WAVE CS GIVEN	+
				ExTh Conf	70Madurai 2 29	Dec 70	Sriramachandra Murty+.S+P WAVE SIGMA	
	2.5+4			Expt Data	EXFOR30248.006	Jun 73	SIGMA CAPTURE VALUE	
(n,γ)	1.4+7		GRE	Theo Jour	NP/A 189 334	Jul 72	Boisson+.DIR,COLLECT.CURV. DEFORMNUC	
(n,γ)	1.4+7		BOR	Expt Conf	72Budapest 220	Aug 72	Rigaud+INTEGRATD SIG FROM SPEC,GRPH	+
				Jour	NP/A 176 545	Dec 71	– + INTEGRATED FROM NG SPECTRUM	
				Jour	JPRS 32 10 231	Oct 71	Irigaray+COLL.5B,MEAS.G.SPC.WITH INA	
	1.4+7			Data	EXFOR20533.005	Apr 76	1PNT.SIGMA.	
(n,γ)	2.5–2		AUA	Eval Rept	AAEC/TM–619	Sep 72	Clayton.CALC FROM SIG LIBRARY,TABLE	
(n,γ)	Fast		MTR	Expt Conf	72Kiamesha 2 614	Sep 72	Harker+ CFRMF INTEGRAL MEAS.	
(n,γ)	3.0+4	3.0+5	USP	Expt Jour	NP/A 196 83	Nov 72	Lepine+ LI7–P NS.TOF.M–R. REL TO IN	+
	3.0+4	3.0+5		Data	EXFOR30233.005	Mar 73	NDS,RELATIVE TO IN,ABSOLUTE ERROR	
(n,γ)		1.1+7	RCN	Theo Rept	RCN–191	Jun 73	Lautenbach.GROUP CONSTANTS TBL	
(n,γ)	2.5–2		NPL	Expt Prog	EANDC(UK)–151	Aug 73	Ryves+ MEASURED REL AU MN,TBP	
(n,γ)	Fiss		WIN	Revw Conf	IAEA–169 3 137	74	Dean. POINT DATA AVG OVER STAND SPEC	
	Maxwl	Fiss		Conf	IAEA–169 3 163	74	Pope+ MAXW+FIS–SPEC AVG DATA CFD XPT	
(n,γ)	1.0+3	1.0+7	FEI	Eval Rept	YK–8/2 97	Sep 72	Abagjan+ AVG SIG(ENERGY–GROUPS),TABL	
				Rept	INDC(CCP)–39	Jul 74	.P102. ENGLISH OF YK–8/2 97	
(n,γ)	2.5–2		NPL	Expt Jour	JP/A 7 2318	Dec 74	Ryves+	+
	2.5–2			Data	EXFOR20561.008	Oct 75	1PNT.SIGMA.	
(n,γ)	6.2–2	1.0+0	CNA	Expt Prog	INDC(SEC)–51	Dec 75	Cansoy+P139.70N–ES,RES–PARS(1RES)GVN	
(n,γ)	1.0+3	1.0+6	SAC	Eval Rept	CEA–N–1832	Dec 75	Ribon+ EXP+TH ANAL,STAT MOL,CURVE	
(n,γ)	1.5+7		JYV	Comp Rept	JU–RR–1/1976	Mar 76	Valkonen.(THESIS).EXPTS CFD DSD MODL	
(n,γ)	2.1+3	1.0+4	DUB	Theo Conf	JINR–D–9920	Jun 76	Pikel'Ner. P285.POL NS,SPIN–DEP.TABL	
(n,γ)	Fast		RCN	Expt Prog	ECN–10	Oct 76	Veenema+ STEK REACTIVITY WORTHS TBL.	
Spect (n,γ)	Pile		COP	ExTh Jour	NP 4 125	Aug 57	Nathan.GRPHS+TBL.DECAY SCH.CFD UNFDM	
Spect (n,γ)	Pile		HEB	ExTh Jour	NP 5 331	Jan 58	Ofer. GRAPH+TABLE. DECAY SCHEME. NAI	
Spect (n,γ)	Maxwl		YAL	Expt Jour	PR 114 268	Apr 59	Draper.SC SPECTR,GAM E 0 TO 600 KEV	
Spect (n,γ)	Maxwl		ARF	Expt Prog	ARF–1193 12	Jul 62	Greenwood+,CRYST SPEC,LOW–E GAMMAS	
Spect (n,γ)	Maxwl		CAS	Expt Jour	NC 27 1032	Feb 63	Giannini+ NA–I,E+INTENSITY TO253 KEV	+
Spect (n,γ)	Maxwl		MIL	Expt Jour	EN 11 612	Nov 64	Para+ GAMMAS TO 260 KEV	
Spect (n,γ)	Maxwl		AUW	Expt Conf	67Kanpur § N75	Mar 67	Sriramamurthy+ G–G COINCS,SCINT SP	
Spect (n,γ)	Maxwl		MUN	Expt Conf	67Juelich 56	Apr 67	Egidy+ CONVERSION–ELECTRONS.NDG.	
				Jour	ZP 195 489	66	– + BETA–SPECTROMETER.CONV–ELS.	
Spect (n,γ)	Maxwl		MOS	Expt Jour	IZV 32 81	Jan 68	Rozantsev+ GAMMA,TIME DISTRIBUTION	
				Jour	BAS 32 80	Jan 68	TRANSLATN.*NO 1	
Spect (n,γ)	Maxwl		UPP	Expt Jour	NP/A 120 561	Nov 68	Nilsson+.INT CONVERSION. PURE E2 TR.	
Spect (n,γ)	2.5–2		MIT	Comp Rept	MITNE–85	Jan 69	Rasmussen+TBL G INT.=AFCRL–69–0071	
Spect (n,γ)	Pile		DUB	Expt Jour	CZJB 19 1017	Aug 69	Finger+ 160–TB DECAY–SCH GVN	
Spect (n,γ)	None		MOS	Expt Jour	IZV 33 1315	Aug 69	Rozantsev+ DELAYED–COINC,GRPHS+TABLE	
				Jour	BAS 33 1215	70	TRANSLATN.*NO 8	
Spect (n,γ)	2.0+3		MTR	Expt Prog	NCSAC–31 76	May 70	Greenwood+,ANAL TO BE COMPL,NO DATA	
Spect (n,γ)	Maxwl		MUN	Expt Jour	ZP 239 57	Oct 70	Bosh.G–RAY–SPECT + ANG.DISTR.	
Spect (n,γ)	4.3+1	7.0+1	CRC	Expt Prog	AECL–3912 61	Mar 71	Lone+.GE(LI) DET.TABLE GAMS 2RESON	
Spect (n,γ)	Pile		KFK	Expt Rept	KFK–1401	Jun 71	Djadali.AVG POLRZ G EXPT,CFD T,SPIN	
	Maxwl			Jour	NP/A 147 150	May 70	Eichler+ POL NS.CIRC POL GS+ASSYMTRY	
Spect (n,γ)	4.0+5		WWA	Expt Jour	APPB 2 489	Aug 71	Brzosko+ GAMMA–EN = 3 TO 7 MEV,GRAPH	
Spect (n,γ)	1.4+7		BOR	Expt Conf	72Budapest 220	Aug 72	Rigaud+ TOF,NDG	
				Jour	NP/A 176 545	Dec 71	– + TOF. E(GAMMA)=14 TO 22 MEV.	
Spect (n,γ)	Pile		MUN	Expt Jour	ZP 258 315	Mar 73	Henkelmann. E + INT OF GS GIVEN	+
	2.5–2			Data	EXFOR20606.013	Jun 76	7PTS.	
Spect (n,γ)	3.3+0	5.0+2	BNL	Expt Prog	USNDC–9 48	Dec 73	Ribon+. TABLE OF RESON J VALUES.	
Spect (n,γ)	Maxwl		FRS	Expt Jour	NP/A 221 333	Mar 74	Kern+PAIR+ANTI–C.HIGH+LOW GS. TBL.	
				Jour	HPA 46 60	73	– + PRELIMINARY RESULTS	
				Conf	72Budapest 102	Aug 72	– + PRELIM LVL SCHEME +SPINS TB16	
				Jour	HPA 45 93	Jun 72	Michaud+ E(G), I CALIBRAT PAIR SPECT	
				Jour	HPA 42 917	Dec 69	– + PAIR+ANTICOMPTON–SPEC,GRPH	
Spect (n,γ)	Maxwl		MUN	Expt Jour	NP/A 221 333	Mar 74	Schreckenbach+TBL,GRPH CONV ELS.	
				Rept	PTUM–E–18	May 73	– . THESIS. CONV–EL,LVLS	

65 Terbium 159

Quantity	Energy (ev) Min	Max	Lab	Type	Documentation Ref Vol Page	Date	Author, Comments	Data
Spect (n,γ)	Maxwl		RIS	Expt	Jour NP/A 221 333	Mar 74	Koch+ CURVD XTL.+GELI.LOW EN GS. TBL	
				Conf	69Studsvik 65	Aug 69	− +AUTMTD−CURVD−CRYST−SPEC,NDG+TB	
					Jour KT 5 17	63	Gruber+ BENT XTL.ABOVE 24KEV GS	
					Jour KT 5 19	63	Maier+ LOW EN GAMMAS.	
Spect (n,γ)	1.0+0	6.0+2	SAC	Expt	Jour NP/A 223 509	May 74	Jain+ GRAPHS,HIGH/LOW EG,WIDTH CORR	
Spect (n,γ)	Maxwl		LRL	Expt	Jour NP/A 221 333	Mar 74	Larson+LOW EN (N,GG) COINC.TBL.GRPHS	
				Conf	74Petten 578	Sep 74	Mann+ GG−COINC, ONLY GRPH GIVEN	
Inelastic γ	4.0+5	2.2+6	CCP	Expt	Jour UFZ 14 683	Apr 69	Romanenko+.SOME NEW LVLS,G−SPEC CURV	
Inelastic γ	3.7+6		HFA	Expt	Jour PR/C 8 1929	Nov 73	Felsteiner+. GE(LI) DET. CURVE+TABLE	+
	3.7+6			Data	EXFOR30387.002	Mar 77	29 G−LINES.	
(n,2n)	Fiss		CRC	Eval	Rept CRC−1003	Dec 60	Roy+,ESTIMATED AVG SIG=3.0MB	
(n,2n)	1.5+7		REN	Expt	Jour PR/B 139 1525	Sep 65	Broadhead+ C−W.ACT.HL=10.2SEC. CFD.	+
	1.5+7			Data	EXFOR11874.005	Jun 76	. 1 PT. CS = 160+ −19MB.	
(n,2n)	1.5+7		MUA	Expt	Jour NP 88 349	Nov 66	Prasad+,T−D NEUT ACT REL TO FE56(NP)	+
	1.5+7			Data	EXFOR30015.004	May 70	PARTIAL SIGMA(METASTABLE)	
(n,2n)	1.4+7		LYO	Comp	Rept LYCEN/6780	Nov 67	Crouzet+COMPILATN FOR ACTIVTN ANALYS	
(n,2n)	1.5+7		TUR	Theo	Jour NC/B 56 1 201	Jul 68	Minetti+THEOR ISOM RATIO SPIN CO PAR	
(n,2n)	1.4+7		AUW	Expt	Jour NP/A 125 57	Feb 69	RAMA PRASAD+,ACTIVATION,CFD OTHERS	+
	1.4+7			Data	EXFOR30051.	Dec 70	SIGMA N2N,ALSO N2N+NA+NP FOR OTHERS.	
(n,2n)	1.5+7		DEB	Comp	Jour REA 7 4 93	Dec 69	Csikai+ SIG+HL COMPILTN,N−ACTIV−ANAL	
(n,2n)	1.4+7	1.5+7	JYV	Eval	Rept JU−RR−3/1970	Jun 70	Leppaemaeki+ TABLE OF EVAL AVG SIG	
(n,2n)	None		KFI	Expt	Jour JRC 7 365	Jun 71	Nagy+ GAM+XRAY+ELECTR ES, HALF−L GVN	
(n,2n)	1.5+7		DEB	Eval	Jour REA 11 1 153	Mar 73	Boedy+ RECOMM.VALUE FROM N−Z SYSTEM.	
(n,2n)	1.5+7		KFI	Theo	Rept KFKI−73−68	Dec 73	Jeki.NEW FIT,CALC SIG CFD OTHERS,TBL	
(n,2n)	1.5+7		JUL	Expt	Jour NP/A 224 319	May 74	Qaim. ACT.GE(LI).TO GRND, METAST	+
					Jour RRL 25 335	May 76	− + SIG IN GRPH. SYST VS (N−Z)/A	
	1.5+7			Data	EXFOR20541.	Apr 76	4PTS.SIGMA.	
(n,p)	Fiss		CRC	Eval	Rept CRC−1003	Dec 60	Roy+,ESTIMATED AVG SIG=0.025MB	
(n,p)	1.5+7		ARK	Expt	Jour PR 131 2649	Sep 63	Bramlitt+ ACT.NP,N2P. TBL. CFD.	+
				Rept	TID−16949	62	.THESIS	
	1.5+7			Data	EXFOR11590.	Jun 76	. 2 PTS, NP AND N2P	
(n,p)	1.5+7		SAH	Comp	Jour NUC 23 8 112	Aug 65	Chatterjee. TABLE WITH REFS.	
	1.4+7				Jour NP 60 273	Nov 64	− .MEAN OF EXPT CFD SHELLMOD	
(n,p)	1.4+7	1.5+7	ARK	Theo	Prog ORO−3235−29	Jan 67	Koch+,STAT MODEL CALC CFD EXPTS	
(n,p)	1.4+7		LYO	Comp	Rept LYCEN/6780	Nov 67	Crouzet+COMPILATN FOR ACTIVTN ANALYS	
(n,p)	1.4+7		AUW	Expt	Jour NP/A 125 57	Feb 69	RAMA PRASAD+,ACTIVATION,CFD OTHERS	+
				ExTh	Jour IPA 12 640	Sep 74	Rama Prasad+ CFD STATMDL COMPND VALU	
	1.4+7			Expt Data	EXFOR30051.	Dec 70	SIGMA NP,ALSO N2N+NA+NP FOR OTHERS.	
(n,p)	1.5+7		DEB	Comp	Jour REA 7 4 93	Dec 69	Csikai+ SIG+HL COMPILTN,N−ACTIV−ANAL	
(n,p)	1.4+7	1.5+7	JYV	Eval	Rept JU−RR−3/1970	Jun 70	Leppaemaeki+ (N,2P) UPPER LIMIT,TBL	
(n,p)	1.4+7	1.5+7	JYV	Eval	Rept JU−RR−3/1970	Jun 70	Leppaemaeki+ TABLE OF EVAL AVG SIG	
(n,p)	1.5+7		IRK	Expt	Jour APA 34 209	Sep 71	Havlik. ACT. CC−W.	+
					Jour OAWA 107 119	Apr 70	− . ACTIVATION METHOD	
	1.5+7			Data	EXFOR20509.016	Apr 76	1PNT.SIGMA.	
(n,p)	1.5+7		ARK	Expt	Abst DA/B 32 5091	Mar 72	Bari. GE(LI) DET. ACT. SIG GIVEN	+
	1.5+7			Data	EXFOR10431.016	Aug 75	. 1 PT, SIGMA, GND+META.	
(n,p)	1.5+7		JUL	Expt	Jour RRL 25 335	May 76	Qaim+ ACTIV,GELI.CFD OTHERS,TBL+GRPH	+
	1.5+7			Data	EXFOR20716.010	Jun 77	1PNT.SIGMA.	
(n,d)	1.5+7		SAH	Comp	Jour NUC 23 8 112	Aug 65	Chatterjee. TABLE WITH REFS.	
(n,He3)	1.5+7		JUL	Expt	Jour JRC 21 395	74	Qaim+ CHEM SEPAR,SIG VS Z SYSTEMATIC	
(n,α)	Fiss		CRC	Eval	Rept CRC−1003	Dec 60	Roy+,ESTIMATED AVG SIG=0.0001MB	
(n,α)	1.5+7		RBZ	Expt	Jour NP 73 548	Nov 65	Kulisic.E+ANGDIST+SIGTOT.CFD TH.CURV	+
				Rept	EANDC−50S148	Jul 65	. FULL PAPER PRESENTD AT 65ANTWERP	
				Conf	64Paris 2 769	Jul 64	.	
	1.5+7			Data	EXFOR30127.	Mar 71	SIGMA, ANG−DISTR, ALFA−SPECTR(0DEG)	
(n,α)	1.4+7		LYO	Comp	Rept LYCEN/6780	Nov 67	Crouzet+COMPILATN FOR ACTIVTN ANALYS	
(n,α)	1.4+7		IBJ	Expt	Jour NP/A 110 11	Mar 68	Jaskola+ ALFA SPCTR CFD TH,FULL PAPR	+
				Theo	Jour CJP 51 1765	Aug 73	Glowacka+ KNOCKON EFF.CFD EXPT,GRAPH	
				Expt	Rept INR−1268	Jan 68	SEE ALSO * FULL INFORMATION	
					Jour APPB 2 521	71	.SAME AS INR−1268	
					Rept INR−1197 3	May 70	SEE ALSO *THEO,ALFA CLUSTRNG	
					Rept INR−970	Feb 69	SEE ALSO * REVIEW	
					Rept EANDC−50 11	Jul 65	SEE ALSO * SMALL REPORT	
					Conf 65Antwerp § 11	Jul 65	.PAGE 497. ABSTRACT ONLY	
					Rept INR−596	Jan 65	SEE ALSO * FULL INFORMATION	
	1.4+7			Data	EXFOR30158.008	Mar 71	NUM DATA NOT AVAILBL,SEE GRAF IN REF	
(n,α)	1.4+7		IBJ	Expt	Rept INR−918/DN 14	May 68	SEE ALSO *	
(n,α)	1.4+7		RBZ	Expt	Conf 69Bochum 210	Jul 69	Chatterjee+ ALFA−SPEC GRAPH,LVL DENS	

65 Terbium 159

Quantity	Energy (ev) Min	Max	Lab	Type	Documentation Ref Vol Page	Date	Author, Comments	Data
(n,α)	1.5+7		DEB	Comp Jour	REA 7 4 93	Dec 69	Csikai+ SIG+HL COMPILTN,N-ACTIV-ANAL	
(n,α)	1.5+7		IRK	Expt Jour	APA 34 209	Sep 71	Havlik. ACT. CC-W.	+
				Jour	OAWA 107 119	Apr 70	- . ACTIVATION METHOD	
	1.5+7			Data	EXFOR20509.017	Apr 76	1PNT.SIGMA.	
(n,α)	1.4+7	1.5+7	CIS	Theo Jour	NP/A 210 297	Aug 73	Milazzo-Colli+ ALPHA E-DISTN CFD XPT	
	1.4+7			Jour	PL/B 38 155	Feb 72	Colli-Milazzo+ A-SPECT CALC CFD EXPT	
(n,α)	1.8+7		IBJ	Expt Jour	NP/A 244 117	Jun 75	Glowacka+ ALF E-SPEC CFD MODLS,GRAPH	+
				Prog	INDC(SEC)-42	Dec 74	- + TBL DIFFSIG,GRPH E+ANG-DIS	
	1.8+7			Data	EXFOR30299.	Jul 75	DOUBLE DIFFSIG(33 PTS)+ANGDIST(1 PT)	
Reson Params	3.4+0	1.1+1	BNL	Expt Jour	PR 96 1014	Nov 54	Sailor.+CRYST SPEC. 4 ES. TBL.	+
	3.4+0	1.1+1		Data	EXFOR12110.012	Jun 76	. 4 RES, E0	
Reson Params	3.4+0	1.6+2	BNL	Expt Jour	PR 99 10	Jul 55	Harvey+ TRNS. CHOPF. AREA ANAL. TBL.	+
	3.3+0	1.6+2		Data	EXFOR11912.052	Jun 76	. 24 RES, E0,WN,WN0	
Reson Params	3.3+0	9.8+1	CCP	Comp Rept	INDSWG-64 19	64	VAN NAJ-JAN', TABLE OF 22 RES WN WG	
Reson Params	3.4+0	1.1+1	BNL	Expt Jour	PHY 30 713	Apr 64	Postma+EO=3.35,4.99,11.11 SPIN=2,1,2	+
Reson Params	3.3+0	9.8+1	DUB	Expt Jour	ZET 47 43	Jul 64	.TRNS+TOF,E+J+WG+GWN FOR 22 RES	+
				Jour	JET 20 30	Jan 65	.TRANSLATN.	
Reson Params	2.4+1	1.1+2	HAR	Expt Conf	65Antwerp 522	Jul 65	Asghar.GIVE WN WG J COMPAR WITH OTHR	+
Reson Params		1.0+6	AUA	Theo Jour	AUJ 20 477	Oct 67	Cook. TBL OF AVG LVL SPACING D,L=0,1	
Reson Params	+3	+5	AUA	ExTh Rept	AAEC/E-198	May 69	Musgrove.RES PARS +STF FROM (NG)FIT	+
Reson Params	0.0+0	7.6+2	SAC	Expt Jour	NP/A 132 129	Jul 69	Julien+ AVG G-WIDTH. SEE 68WASH.	+
				Conf	68Wash. 867	Mar 68	Morgenstern. WG VS. A. AVG WG GIVEN	
	0.0+0	7.6+2		Data	EXFOR20687.037	Aug 77	1PNT.AVG WG.	
Reson Params	-		AUA	Theo Rept	AAEC/E-211	Nov 70	Musgrove. CALCULTD D+GAM WIDTH GIVEN	
Reson Params	3.3+0	1.1+2	CJD	Eval Rept	YK-7	71	Zakharova+ SURVEY+SYSTEMATICS,GW,TBL	
				Rept	INDC(CCP)-27	Nov 72	.ENGLISH TRANSLATION OF YK-7 /71	
Reson Params	3.3+0		CNA	Expt Prog	EANDC(OR)100	Jan 71	Cansoy.NEW ANALYS,TBL,TBP CNAEM-76	+
	3.3+0			Data	EXFOR20174.003	May 74	1PNT.S0*(WT)2.	
Reson Params	None		DUB	Theo Jour	YF 13 240	Feb 71	Malecki+G-WID,THEO CFD EXPT.TBL,GRPH	
				Jour	SNP 13 133	Aug 71	- + ENGL OF YF 13 240.	
Reson Params	3.3+0	9.8+1	BNL	Expt Prog	USNDC-9 48	Dec 73	Ribon+. TABLE OF RESON J VALUES.	
Reson Params	+0	+2	BOL	Eval Conf	IAEA-169 3 123	74	Benzi+ AVG G-WID CFD OTHERS+XPT,TABL	
Reson Params	1.0+0	6.0+2	SAC	Expt Jour	NP/A 223 509	May 74	Jain+ G-SPECS FOR WIDTH CORRELATIONS	
	5.0+2			Conf	74Petten 165	Sep 74	- + WIDTH CORRELATIONS OBSERVED	
Reson Params	+0	+2	FEI	Eval Rept	YK-8/2 97	Sep 72	Abagyan+ AVG G-WID+D AT BINDNG-E,TBL	
				Rept	INDC(CCP)-39	Jul 74	.PAGE 102.ENGLISH OF YK-8/2 97	
Reson Params	6.2-2	1.0+0	CNA	Expt Prog	INDC(SEC)-51	Dec 75	Cansoy+P139,ABST.1RES,BY (N,G),J GVN	
Reson Params	1.0+3		SAC	Expt Rept	CEA-N-1832	Dec 75	Ribon+ EXP+TH ANAL,RES PAR,TBL	
Reson Params	0.0+0	7.5+2	SAC	Expt Rept	CEA-N-1867	Mar 75	Derrien+ SHAPE ANALYSIS	+
	2.1+1	7.6+2		Prog	NEANDC(E)166L	Feb 76	- + TABLE OF EN+N-WID+G-WID	
	0.0+0	7.5+2		Data	EXFOR20577.	Feb 76	171PTS.AVG WG,WT,MEANLVLSP0.	
Strnth Fnctn	+3		BNL	Expt Jour	PRL 1 461	Dec 58	Hughes+ FC. TRNS. STF=(1.5+-.2)-4.	
Strnth Fnctn	1.0+4	2.0+5	ORL	Expt Jour	PR 122 182	61	Gibbons+ TOF CAPT. S0, S1 GVN.	+
	1.0+4	2.0+5		Data	EXFOR11329.094	Jun 76	. 4 PTS, S0,S1,D,AVE WG	
Strnth Fnctn	+3	+5	BOL	Theo Conf	61Vienna 1 179	Aug 61	Benzi+.PPR11,TABLE CFD EXPERIMENT	
Strnth Fnctn		4.0+5	SAC	Expt Prog	EANDC(E)66U172	Feb 66	Julien+ TBP	
Strnth Fnctn	+3	+5	AUA	ExTh Rept	AAEC/E-198	May 69	Musgrove.S+P+D STF FROM (NG)FIT,TBL	+
Strnth Fnctn	-		DUB	Revw Jour	YF 11 111	Jan 70	Malecki+ VALUES FOR TWO SPIN STATES	
				Jour	SNP 11 61	Jul 70	- + ENGL OF YF 11 61.	
Strnth Fnctn	-		AUA	Theo Rept	AAEC/E-211	Nov 70	Musgrove. SMOOTHED S0,S1 AND S2 GIVN	
Strnth Fnctn	3.0+3	6.5+5	DKE	Expt Abst	DA/B 31 6821	May 71	Pineo.S,P,D WAVE.THESIS ABST	
				Diss	PINEO	70	.S0,S1.TBL.GRPHS.CFD CALC,OTH EXPTS.	
Strnth Fnctn	2.7+3		MUN	Expt Conf	71Albany 327	Aug 71	Dilg+TRNS.S0 STF GVN.31 ELEMENT GRPH	
Strnth Fnctn	None		AUA	Eval Rept	AAEC/E-277	Mar 73	Musgrove.TBLS EXPTL DATA+BEST VALUES	
Strnth Fnctn	2.0+1	9.0+2	SAC	Expt Rept	CEA-N-1867	Mar 75	Derrien. RES PAR ANALYSIS	+
	2.1+1	7.6+2		Rept	NEANDC(E)166L	Feb 76	- + S0=1.56 FROM RES PARAM	
	0.0+0	7.5+2		Data	EXFOR20577.004	Feb 76	1PNT.L=0.	
Lvl Density	-		COP	Theo Jour	NP 6 62	Mar 58	Ericson. LVL DENSITY FORM CFD EXP	
Lvl Density	-		FEI	Eval Rept	FEI-36	66	Kapchigashev+.TBL OF RELATD QUANTTYS	
		5.0+4		Jour	YF 4 686	Sep 66	.TABLE.SHORT VERSION OF FEI-36	
				Prog	YFI-3 3	66	.ABSTRACT.TABLE LDL+NUCL.EXCIT.E	
		5.0+4		Jour	SNP 4 486	67	.ENGLISH OF YF 4.FROM(N,GAMMA).TABLE	
				Prog	INDC-E-140 3	66	.ENGLISH TRANSL OF YFI-3	
Lvl Density	1.4+7		IBJ	Expt Jour	NP/A 110 11	Mar 68	Jaskola+ ALFA SPCTR CFD TH,FULL PAPR	+
	1.4+7			Data	EXFOR30158.009	Mar 71	LEVEL DENSITY PARAMETER OF EU156 GIV	
Lvl Density	1.4+7		RBZ	Expt Conf	69Bochum 210	Jul 69	Chatterjee+ TB159(N,A)EU156,LVL DENS	
Lvl Density	None		AUW	Theo Conf	70Madurai 2 267	Dec 70	Ramamurty+ A-PARAMETER GVN,LANG'S-TH	
Lvl Density	None		BOL	Eval Conf	IAEA-169 3 123	74	Benzi+ LVL DENS PARAM BY XPT,GRPH+TB	

65 Terbium 159

Quantity	Energy (ev) Min	Max	Lab	Type	Documentation Ref Vol Page	Author, Comments Date	Data
Lvl Density	None		DUB	Theo Rept	JINR – P4 – 8102	Jul 74 Malov+ SEMI – MICROSC CALC OKS XPT,TBL	
				Rept	UCRL – TR – 10845	Apr 75 . ENGL OF JINR – P4 – 8102	
Lvl Density	+0	+2	FEI	Eval Rept	YK – 8/2 97	Sep 72 Abagyan+ LVL DENSITY PARAMETER,TBL	
				Rept	INDC(CCP) – 39	Jul 74 .PAGE 102.ENGLISH OF YK – 8/2 97	
Lvl Density	2.0+1	9.0+2	SAC	ExTh Rept	CEA – N – 1867	Mar 75 Derrien. RES PAR ANALYSIS	
(γ,n)	8.0+6	3.0+7	SAC	Expt Jour	NP/A 121 463	Dec 68 Bergere+LORENTZ LINE PARAM,GRPHS,TBL	

65 Terbium 160

Quantity	Energy (ev) Min	Max	Lab	Type	Documentation Ref Vol Page	Author, Comments Date	Data
Evaluation	1.0–3	1.5+7	AUA	Eval Rept	AAEC/TM – 549	Jun 70 Cook.TOT,EL,INEL,NONEL,CAPT SIGS,NDG	+
				Rept	AAEC/E – 214	Jun 71 Bertram+GROUP SIGMAS SAME QUANTS.NDG	
				Rept	AAEC/TM – 587	Mar 71 *DESCRIPTION OF LIBRARY	
	1.0–3	1.5+7		Data	AUSTR – DFN 177.	Nov 71 POINT(223) AND GROUP(127) SIGMAS	
Total	1.0–3	1.5+7	AUA	Eval Data	AUSTR – DFN 177.	Nov 71 COOK+POINT(223)+GROUP(127)SIG.CF EVL	+
Elastic	1.0–3	1.5+7	AUA	Eval Data	AUSTR – DFN 177.	Nov 71 COOK+POINT(223)+GROUP(127)SIG.CF EVL	+
Tot Inelastc	5.0+5	1.5+7	AUA	Eval Data	AUSTR – DFN 177.	Nov 71 COOK+POINT(11)+GROUP(127)SIG.CF EVL	+
Nonelastic	1.0–3	1.5+7	AUA	Eval Data	AUSTR – DFN 177.	Nov 71 COOK+POINT(223)+GROUP(127)SIG.CF EVL	+
Absorption	2.5–2		IJI	Eval Conf	75Kiev 1 169	May 75 Fedorova+ EVAL 2200M/S SIG,TABLE	
Res Int Abs	5.0–1		AUA	Eval Rept	AAEC/TM – 619	Sep 72 Clayton.CALC FROM SIG LIBRARY,TABLE	
Res Int Abs	+0	+5	WIN	Revw Conf	IAEA – 169 3 163	74 Pope+ CALC FROM AUSTRAL DATA FILE	
(n,γ)	Pile		MTR	Expt Jour	JCP 25 502	Sep 56 Smith+.525+ – 100B FROM SUCCESSIV CAPT	
(n,γ)	1.0–3	1.5+7	AUA	Eval Data	AUSTR – DFN 177.	Nov 71 COOK+POINT(223)+GROUP(127)SIG.CF EVL	+
(n,γ)	Pile		CRC	Eval Rept	AECL – 3037 1	Jan 72 Walker.RECOMMENDED SIG,DETAILED TBL	
(n,γ)	2.5–2		AUA	Eval Rept	AAEC/TM – 619	Sep 72 Clayton.CALC FROM SIG LIBRARY,TABLE	
(n,γ)	Fiss		WIN	Revw Conf	IAEA – 169 3 137	74 Dean. POINT DATA AVG OVER STAND SPEC	
	Maxwl	Fiss		Conf	IAEA – 169 3 163	74 Pope+ MAXW+FIS – SPEC AVG DATA CFD XPT	
(n,γ)	Pile		KFK	Expt Prog	KFK – 2223 50	Dec 75 Heck+ GAM – TRANSITIONS OF TB – 161	
(n,p)	Maxwl		IFU	Theo Rept	ICD – 4 20	67 Dadakina+ PENETR COEFF CALC,TABLE	
Reson Params	–		AUA	Theo Rept	AAEC/E – 211	Nov 70 Musgrove. CALCULTD D+GAM WIDTH GIVEN	
Strnth Fnctn	–		AUA	Theo Rept	AAEC/E – 211	Nov 70 Musgrove. SMOOTHED S0,S1 AND S2 GIVN	
Lvl Density	+6		MIL	Theo Jour	EN 15 1 54	Jan 68 Facchini+ LDL PARS FROM LOW EN RES	
Lvl Density	None		MUN	Theo Jour	NP/A 217 269	Dec 73 Dilg+ A,DELTA. BACK SHIFTED FERMIGAS	
Lvl Density	None		COP	Theo Jour	NP/A 222 493	Apr 74 Dossing+COLL ROTAT.SPAC. ACCUR ESTIM	
Lvl Density	None		ROC	Theo Jour	NP/A 223 589	May 74 Huizenga+ EXP CFD MICROSC TH AX SYMM	

65 Terbium 161

Quantity	Energy (ev) Min	Max	Lab	Type	Documentation Ref Vol Page	Author, Comments Date	Data
Evaluation	1.0–3	1.5+7	AUA	Eval Rept	AAEC/TM – 549	Jun 70 Cook.TOT,EL,INEL,NONEL,CAPT SIGS,NDG	+
				Rept	AAEC/E – 214	Jun 71 Bertram+GROUP SIGMAS SAME QUANTS.NDG	
				Rept	AAEC/TM – 587	Mar 71 *DESCRIPTION OF LIBRARY	
	1.0–3	1.5+7		Data	AUSTR – DFN 178.	Nov 71 POINT(223) AND GROUP(127) SIGMAS	
Total	1.0–3	1.5+7	AUA	Eval Data	AUSTR – DFN 178.	Nov 71 COOK+POINT(223)+GROUP(127)SIG.CF EVL	+
Elastic	1.0–3	1.5+7	AUA	Eval Data	AUSTR – DFN 178.	Nov 71 COOK+POINT(223)+GROUP(127)SIG.CF EVL	+
Tot Inelastc	5.0+5	1.5+7	AUA	Eval Data	AUSTR – DFN 178.	Nov 71 COOK+POINT(11)+GROUP(127)SIG.CF EVL	+
Nonelastic	1.0–3	1.5+7	AUA	Eval Data	AUSTR – DFN 178.	Nov 71 COOK+POINT(223)+GROUP(127)SIG.CF EVL	+
Res Int Abs	5.0–1		AUA	Eval Rept	AAEC/TM – 619	Sep 72 Clayton.CALC FROM SIG LIBRARY,TABLE	
Res Int Abs	+0	+5	WIN	Revw Conf	IAEA – 169 3 163	74 Pope+ CALC FROM AUSTRAL DATA FILE	
(n,γ)	1.0–3	1.5+7	AUA	Eval Data	AUSTR – DFN 178.	Nov 71 COOK+POINT(223)+GROUP(127)SIG.CF EVL	+
(n,γ)	Pile		CRC	Eval Rept	AECL – 3037 1	Jan 72 Walker.SIG ESTIMATED ACCORDING Z,A	
(n,γ)	2.5–2		AUA	Eval Rept	AAEC/TM – 619	Sep 72 Clayton.CALC FROM SIG LIBRARY,TABLE	
(n,γ)	Fiss		WIN	Revw Conf	IAEA – 169 3 137	74 Dean. POINT DATA AVG OVER STAND SPEC	
	Maxwl	Fiss		Conf	IAEA – 169 3 163	74 Pope+ MAXW+FIS – SPEC AVG EVAL DATA	
Reson Params	–		AUA	Theo Rept	AAEC/E – 211	Nov 70 Musgrove. CALCULTD D+GAM WIDTH GIVEN	
Strnth Fnctn	–		AUA	Theo Rept	AAEC/E – 211	Nov 70 Musgrove. SMOOTHED S0,S1 AND S2 GIVN	

65 Terbium 162

Quantity	Energy (ev) Min	Max	Lab	Type	Documentation Ref Vol Page	Author, Comments Date	Data
Reson Params	–		AUA	Theo Rept	AAEC/E – 211	Nov 70 Musgrove. CALCULTD D+GAM WIDTH GIVEN	
Strnth Fnctn	–		AUA	Theo Rept	AAEC/E – 211	Nov 70 Musgrove. SMOOTHED S0,S1 AND S2 GIVN	

65 Terbium 163

Quantity	Energy (ev) Min Max	Lab	Type	Documentation Ref Vol Page	Date	Author, Comments	Data
Reson Params	–	AUA	Theo Rept	AAEC/E-211	Nov 70	Musgrove. CALCULTD D+GAM WIDTH GIVEN	
Strnth Fnctn	–	AUA	Theo Rept	AAEC/E-211	Nov 70	Musgrove. SMOOTHED S0,S1 AND S2 GIVN	

66 Dysprosium

Quantity	Energy (ev) Min	Max	Lab	Type	Documentation Ref Vol Page	Author, Comments Date	Data
Evaluation	Maxwl		GEN Eval	Rept	APEX – 467	Jun 58 Tralli+.68 – 3000DEG F SCT ABS	
Evaluation	3.2 – 2	1.0+7	GEN Eval	Rept	APEX – 467	Jun 58 Tralli+.18GROUPS AS IN AG + TOT SNE	
Total	Maxwl		COL Expt	Jour	PR 48 265	Aug 35 Dunning+ IONCH,TRANS,RA – BE/PARAFIN N	
Total	8.0 – 2	2.0+1	ANL Expt	Jour	PR 71 556	Apr 47 Sturm+ USE OF LIF(111) CRYSTALS	
Total	7.0 – 3	1.5 – 1	ANL Expt	Jour	PR 72 585	Oct 47 Brill+ ROTATING SHUTTER. TRANSM.	
Total	3.2 – 1	2.7+0	BNL Expt	Jour	PR 96 1014	Nov 54 Sailor.	+
	3.2 – 1	2.7+0		Data	EXFOR12110.003	Jun 76 . 40 PTS.	
Total	2.4+0	4.3+1	BNL Expt	Priv	CARTER	Mar 55 Carter.	+
	2.4+0	4.3+1		Data	EXFOR11897.005	Jun 76 . 256 PTS, SIG	
Total	1.4+2	3.6+4	HAR Expt	Priv	EGELSTAFF4	Jun 55 Egelstaff. TRANSMISSION.	+
Total	1.0+3	3.2+4	HAR Expt	Jour	PPSA 70 51	Jan 57 Gayther+ FC THICK SAMPLE,AVSIG CF TH	
Total	4.0+2	2.0+3	HAR Theo	Jour	PPS 71 910	Jun 58 Egelstaff.FLUCTUATIONS CFD THEORY	
Total	1.8 – 2	1.0+0	BNL Expt	Prog	WASH – 1028 11	Apr 60 Hellsten+ TRANS,NDG	
Total	1.3+4	2.1+5	ANL Expt	Prog	ANL – 6580 29	Jun 62 Hibdon+ – 1.5KEV RSLN	
Total	1.0+6		ALD Expt	Jour	NP 42 86	Apr 63 Gilboy+.SIG = 6.73B	+
Total	1.1+4	2.0+6	ANL Expt	Priv	STUPEGIA	Jun 65 Stupegia+100 E PTS. DELTA E	+
	1.1+4	2.0+6		Data	EXFOR12125.003	Jun 66 . 101 PTS.	
Total	5.0 – 4	5.0 – 2	JAE Expt	Prog	INDSWG – 90 2	Jul 65 Ohno.TRNS,CRYST. + MECH.MONOCHR.,GRPHS	+
	6.0 – 4	2.3 – 2		Rept	JAERI – 1069	Dec 64 Okamoto.VELOCITY – SELECTOR,ABS – CURVE.	
	6.3 – 4	2.2 – 2		Data	EXFOR20276.002	Jun 74 35PTS.	
Total	2.0 – 2	1.0+0	IFU Expt	Prog	YFI – 4 38	May67 Vertebnyj+.,TBL,CURVES,TBP UFZ	
				Rept	INDC – 187E	67 . ENGL OF YFI – 4 38	
Total	1.5 – 2	1.0+1	WUR Expt	Rept	EIR – 123	Jul 67 Brunner+.TOF TRANS CFD OTHER EXPTS	+
				Conf	66Paris 1 61	Oct 66 – + PPR 20. PRELIM DATA.	
Total	1.0 – 4	3.0 – 3	MUN Expt	Jour	AKE 16 49	70 Knorr+ TRANS EXPT, TBL	
Total	2.5+6	1.5+7	BNW Expt	Jour	PR/C 3 576	Feb 71 Foster+ TRANS.CURVES.CFD OTHERS+TH	+
				Jour	NIM 36 1	Sep 65 .EXPT DETAILS	
	2.3+6	1.5+7		Data	EXFOR10047.070	Aug 73 . 249PTS.	
Total	2.7+3		MUN Expt	Prog	EANDC(E)150U	Oct 72 Dilg+ AVERAGE TOT XSECT+S0	+
				Conf	71Albany 327	Aug 71 – +TRNS.AVG CS GVN.31 ELEMENT GRP	
	2.7+3			Data	EXFOR20583.020	May 76 1PNT.	
Total	2.0 – 3	7.0 – 1	CAI Expt	Jour	AKE 20 149	Nov 72 Abdel – Kawi+ TOF EXPT, CURVE	
	2.2 – 3	7.9 – 1		Data	EXFOR30467.006	Jan 79 126 PTS. AND SIG(0.025 EV)	
Total	1.3+7	1.5+7	DEB Eval	Rept	IAEA – 153 173	73 Boedy+ MOST PROBABLE VAL OF SIG,TBL	
				Jour	AHP 30 115	Oct 71 Angeli+ AVG SIG,CFD CALC.TBLS.GRAPH	
Total	1.4+5	6.3+5	DKE Expt	Jour	AP 84 165	May 74 Pineo+TRNS.AVG CS TBL,GRPHS.OPTMDL.	+
	1.5+4	6.0+5		Diss	PINEO	70 .AVG CS.GRPHS.CFD.STF CALC.TBL.CFD.	
	1.5+4	6.0+5		Data	EXFOR10542.023	Jan 79 . DATA UNOBTAINABLE FROM AUTHORS.	
Total	7.0+5	9.0+6	GLS Expt	Jour	JP/A 7 1758	Sep 74 Kellie+ SIG IN CURVE,STAT ERROR 2 PC	+
	7.0+5	9.0+6		Data	EXFOR20418.008	Sep 75 646PTS.	
Total	1.0 – 3	4.0 – 1	KAP Expt	Abst	BAP 6 70	Feb 61 Moore.TRANS,1/V .001 – 0.4EV RANGE	
	5.3 – 4	4.0 – 1		Data	EXFOR12083.002	Jun 76 . 75 PTS.	
Elastic	2.0 – 2	1.2 – 1	CRC Expt	Jour	CJP 31 432	Mar 53 Brockhouse. CRYST SPEC SCT/ABS DY2O0	
	2.0 – 2	1.2 – 1		Data	EXFOR11653.008	Jun 76 . 8 PTS, RATIO TO ABS	
Elastic	1.0+6		ALD Expt	Jour	NP 42 86	Apr 63 Gilboy+.SIG = 5.87B+ – 3PC	+
Elastic	9.8+5		AGN Eval	Rept	TID – 21629	Dec 64 Perkins+CALC FROM BNL400,UCRL5573 DA	
Elastic	2.0 – 2	1.0+0	IFU Expt	Jour	UFZ 13 605	Apr 68 Vertebnyi+.GRPH,EXPTL SIG = NUCL+MAGN	
				Jour	UPJ 13 425	Oct 68 TRANSLATN.*	
Elastic	Cold		MUN Expt	Prog	EANDC(E)157U	Mar 73 Koester+COH SCT AMP.FROM DY2(S04)3	
Diff Elastic	1.0+6		ALD Expt	Jour	NP 42 86	Apr 63 Gilboy+30TO137DEG.COMP.WITH OPTICMOD	+
Diff Elastic	9.8+5		AGN Eval	Rept	TID – 21629	Dec 64 Perkins+LEG COEF CALC FROM OTHER DAT	
Potntal Scat	+4		HAR Expt	Jour	PPSA 70 51	Jan 57 Gayther+ FROM AVG SIGTOT. FC TRANSM	
Potntal Scat	2.2 – 3	7.9 – 1	CAI Expt	Jour	AKE 20 149	Nov 72 Abdel – Kawi+ TOTSIG,1/V – RELATNSHIP	
	2.2 – 3	7.9 – 1		Data	EXFOR30467.008	Jan 79 1 PNT.	
Potntal Scat	3.0+3	6.5+5	DKE Expt	Jour	AP 84 165	May 74 Pineo+TRNS.S WAVE SCT LENGTH.TBL.CFD	
				Abst	DA/B 31 6821	May 71 .THESIS ABST.	
				Diss	PINEO	70 .TBL.GRPHS.CFD TO 3 COLLECTIVE MDLS.	
Tot Inelastc	5.0+6	7.0+6	ALD Expt	Jour	NP/A 112 337	May 68 Owens+.3ES.FROM N SPECT 90DEG.	
Tot Inelastc	1.0 – 3	3.0 – 3	MUN Theo	Jour	AKE 16 49	70 Knorr+ PARAMAGNETIC SCAT SIG CALC	
Diff Inelast	5.0+6	7.0+6	ALD Expt	Jour	NP/A 112 337	May 68 Owens+.3ES.FROM N SPECT 90DEG NDG.	+
				Conf	65Antwerp 547	Jul 65 – + PPR122.ABST.SPECT N' AT 90DEG	
Thermal Scat	Cold		ORL Expt	Jour	JAP 32 485	Mar 61 Koehler+ 1 – XLT DIFFRACTION	
Thermal Scat	Cold		ORL Revw	Jour	JAP 36 1078	Mar 65 Koehler+ MAGN PROPS FRM N DIFFR XPTS	
Thermal Scat	2.0 – 4	1.5 – 1	BSP ExTh	Jour	JCP 48 520	Jan 68 Mattos.,TRIVALENT ION PARAMAG SIG	
Thermal Scat	2.0 – 2	1.0+0	IFU Expt	Jour	UFZ 13 605	Apr 68 Vertebnyi+ GRPH SIG(E),MAGN CONTRIB	
				Jour	UPJ 13 425	Oct 68 TRANSLATN.*	

66 Dysprosium

Quantity	Energy (ev) Min	Max	Lab	Type	Documentation Ref Vol Page	Author, Comments Date	Data
Thermal Scat	2.0−2	1.4+0	IJI	Expt Prog	YFI−12 67	72 Vertebny+ ABST,TOT SCAT SIG 15ES,TBL	
				Prog	INDC(CCP)−30	Sep 72 .PAGE 58,ENGLISH OF YFI−12 67	
Thermal Scat	1.0−4	1.0+3	MUN	Revw Jour	EEN 80 1	77 Koester. SCAT LENGTH,FREE SIG	
Scattering	2.0−2	3.0+1	IFU	Expt Conf	68Riga	Jan 68 Gnidak+ ABST,TOF,4PI−GEOMETRY	
Scattering	2.0−2	3.0−2	IFU	Expt Conf	70Helsinki 1 651	Jun 70 Vertebnij+ 2200M/SEC SIGMA GIVEN,TBL	
				Rept	BNL−TR−495	Jul 72 . ENGLISH OF 70HELSIN 1 651	
Absorption	Maxwl		HAR	Expt Rept	AERE−R/M−100	Dec 56 Cummins+.PILE OSC THR WELL REL HAR E	
Absorption	1.0−4	3.0−3	MUN	Theo Jour	AKE 16 49	70 Knorr+ FROM TOT SIG EXPT CALC, TBL	
Res Int Abs	5.0−1		MTR	Expt Jour	NSE 25 12	May 66 Scoville. 1840+−180B	+
	5.0−1			Data	EXFOR12101.003	Jun 76 . 1 PT.	
Res Int Abs	5.0−1	+7	IFU	Revw Jour	ICD−4 7	67 Vertebnyj.ANAL + REVW OF RES PARAMS	
Res Int Abs	5.0−1		MTR	Expt Rept	IN−1195	May 68 Scoville.	
Res Int Abs	+1	+6	MRY	Expt Abst	DA/B 29 2465	Jan 69 Kopp. CFD REACT. WORTHS B AND DY	
Res Int Abs	Pile		ROS	Expt Jour	KE 14 73	Mar 71 Huettel.VALUES GIVEN VS ATOM DENSITY	+
	Pile			Data	EXFOR30137.004	Nov 71 INF DILUTE RES−INT	
Res Int Abs	5.0−1		MTR	Expt Abst	ANS 5 377	62 Scoville.	+
	5.0−1			Data	EXFOR12080.002	Jun 76 . 1 PT.	
(n,γ)	Maxwl		ORL	Expt Jour	PR 83 643	Aug 51 Pomerance.LOCAL OSC REL AU ABS 95 B	+
	Maxwl			Data	EXFOR11047.051	Jun 76 . 1 PT.	
(n,γ)	2.0−2	1.2−1	CRC	Expt Jour	CJP 31 432	Mar 53 Brockhouse.CRYST SPEC SCT/ABS DY2OO	+
	2.0−2	1.2−1		Data	EXFOR11653.008	Jun 76 . 18 PTS, RATIO TO SEL	
(n,γ)	2.5−2		ANL	Expt Jour	NSE 9 132	Feb 61 Meadows+ PULSED NEUTS,936+−20B	+
	2.5−2			Data	EXFOR11028.022	Sep 76 . 1PT.CS=936B	
(n,γ)	2.0+2	8.0+3	ORL	Expt Conf	61Saclay 203	Sep 61 Block+ LIQUID SCINTILLATOR	+
				Conf	61Vienna 1 95	Aug 61 Neiler.PPR73,TABLE FOR 2ES GVN,GRAPH	
	2.0+2	7.8+3		Data	EXFOR11935.015	Jun 76 . 43 PTS.	
(n,γ)	3.0+4	1.7+5	ORL	Expt Jour	PR 122 182	Apr 61 Gibbons.775,240MB REPL BNL653	+
	3.0+4	6.5+4		Jour	PR 129 2695	Mar 63 Macklin+ LIQ SCINT,775 AND 570MB	
	3.0+4	1.7+5		Conf	61Vienna 1 95	Aug 61 Neiler.	
	6.4+3	1.7+5		Data	EXFOR11329.	Jun 76 . 57 PTS, SIG FROM PR 122 182	
	6.5+4			Data	EXFOR11331.025	Jun 76 . 1 PT, SIG FROM PR 129 2695	
(n,γ)	5.0+3	9.0+4	ORL	Theo Jour	RMP 37 166	Jan 65 Macklin+ CALC FOT KT=5TO90KEV	
(n,γ)	Maxwl		MTR	Expt Jour	NSE 25 12	May 66 Scoville. 950+−50 B	+
	Maxwl			Data	EXFOR12101.002	Jun 76 . 1 PT.	
(n,γ)	1.0+3	1.0+7	BOL	Eval Rept	CEC(70)−2	Apr 70 Benzi.GRAPH=SUM OF SIG(ISOTOPES)	
(n,γ)	3.0+4		AUA	Theo Rept	AAEC/E−211	Nov 70 Musgrove. SIGMA GIVEN AND CFD OTHER	
(n,γ)	3.0+4	3.0+5	USP	Expt Jour	NP/A 196 83	Nov 72 Lepine+ LI7−P NS.TOF.M−R. REL TO IN	+
	3.0+4	3.0+5		Data	EXFOR30233.006	Mar 73 NDS,RELATIVE TO IN,ABSOLUTE ERROR	
(n,γ)	1.0+3	1.0+7	FEI	Eval Rept	YK−8/2 97	Sep 72 Abagjan+ AVG SIG(ENERGY−GROUPS),TABL	
				Rept	INDC(CCP)−39	Jul 74 .P102. ENGLISH OF YK−8/2 97	
(n,γ)	1.2−2	1.2+1	WUR	Expt Rept	EIR−217	Apr 75 Widder. POWDER SAMPLE	+
				Conf	74Petten 757	Sep 74 -. M−R DET,ABS.EXP.,NDG	
				Priv	SWISS PH S	Oct 71 -. TOF+MOXON−RAE.CURVS CFD SIGT	
	1.3−2	1.2+1		Data	EXFOR20437.008	Nov 75 367PTS.SIGMA.	
Spect (n,γ)	1.7+0	5.5+0	YAL	Expt Abst	BAP 2 218	Apr 57 Springer+ 4 GAMMA ES	
Spect (n,γ)	Maxwl		KUR	Expt Jour	AE 4 5	Jan 58 Groshev+ SPECTRUM+LINES 0.3−5.87MEV	
				Jour	JNE 9 50	Jun 59 . ENGL OF AE 4 5	
				Jour	SJA 4 1	58 . ENGL OF AE 4 5	
Spect (n,γ)	Maxwl		YAL	Expt Jour	PR 114 268	Apr 59 Draper.SC SPECTR,GAM E 0 TO 600 KEV	
Spect (n,γ)	Maxwl		CRC	Revw Jour	ARN 11 259	Oct 61 Bartholomew.	
Spect (n,γ)	Maxwl		ARF	Expt Prog	ARF−1193−17	Dec 62 Greenwood+ NAI(TL) SPEC, 9 GAMMAS	
				Prog	ARF−1193−9	Apr 62 - +,CRYST SPEC,LOW−E GAMMAS	
Spect (n,γ)	Maxwl		CTH	Expt Jour	NIM 24 185	Aug 63 Arnell+ NAI 3CRYST SPECT,INTERNL TGT	
Spect (n,γ)	Maxwl		LAS	Expt Conf	63ANL 133	Oct 63 Motz+ COMPTON SPEC TABLE+CURVE HI−E	
Spect (n,γ)	2.5−2	.	MIT	Comp Rept	MITNE−85	Jan 69 Rasmussen+TBL G INT.=AFCRL−69−0071	
Spect (n,γ)	Pile		ANL	Expt Prog	WASH−1127 10	Apr 69 Bollinger+ LVL STRUCTRE ONLY,TBC,NDG	
Spect (n,γ)	2.0+3		MTR	Expt Prog	NCSAC−31 76	May 70 Greenwood+ ANAL TO BE COMPPL,NO DATA	
Spect (n,γ)	None		PEL	Expt Prog	INIS−MF−310 31	71 .SHORT NOTE,LIFE−TIME VS GAM−E,NDG	
Spect (n,γ)	Pile		MUN	Expt Jour	ZP 258 315	Mar 73 Henkelmann. E + INT OF GS GIVEN	+
	2.5−2			Data	EXFOR20606.014	Jun 76 9PTS.	
Inelastic γ	5.0+6	7.0+6	ALD	Expt Jour	NP/A 112 337	May 68 Owens+.3ES.TOF SPECT 90 DEG. NDG.	+
(n,2n)	1.5+7		DEB	Eval Jour	REA 11 1 153	Mar 73 Boedy+ RECOMM.VALUE FROM N−Z SYSTEM.	
(n,p)	1.4+7		MNZ	Expt Jour	RCA 22 11	75 Weigel+SUM OF (N,P)+(N,NP)+(N,D)SIG	
(n,np)	1.4+7		MNZ	Expt Jour	RCA 22 11	75 Weigel+ TOT SIG, ACT METHOD	
Reson Params	−.1+0	1.0+1	ANL	Expt Jour	PR 71 757	Jun 47 Strum. CRYST TRN 0.031EV RESON.	+
	−.1+0	1.0+1		Data	EXFOR12136.007	Jun 76 . 1 RES, E0,WT,PCS	

66 Dysprosium

Quantity	Energy (ev) Min	Max	Lab	Type	Documentation Ref Vol Page	Date	Author, Comments	Data
Reson Params	1.7+0	7.4+1	BNL	Expt Jour	PR 96 1014	Nov 54	Sailor.	+
	1.7+0	7.4+1		Data	EXFOR12110.013	Jun 76	. 12 RES, E0	
Reson Params	2.7+0	3.8+1	BNL	Expt Priv	PILCHER	Aug 56	Pilcher.	+
	2.7+0	3.8+1		Data	EXFOR12041.009	Jun 76	. 21 RES, E0,WN	
Reson Params	1.8-2	1.0+0	BNL	Expt Prog	WASH-1028 11	Apr 60	Hellsten+ NDG	
Reson Params	None		IFU	Expt Jour	UFZ 14 1810	Nov 69	Vertebny+.TOF,3 RES, AVG D,CURVS,TBL	
Strnth Fnctn	+4		HAR	Expt Jour	PPSA 70 51	Jan 57	Gayther+ FROM AVG SIGTOT. FC TRANSM	
Strnth Fnctn	+3		BNL	Expt Jour	PRL 1 461	Dec 58	Hughes.FC 2.4+ -0.4	
Strnth Fnctn	+0	+3	BNL	Expt Prog	WASH-1046 21	Jan 64	Palevsky.FC,NDG.TO BE ANALYSED,L=0.	
Strnth Fnctn	2.7+3		MUN	Expt Conf	71Albany 327	Aug 71	Dilg+TRNS.S0 STF GVN.31 ELEMENT GRPH	
Strnth Fnctn	+3	+5	DKE	Expt Prog	USNDC-7 224	Jun 73	Pineo+ S0,S1,S2.NO DATA GIVEN.TBPAP	
Lvl Density	5.0+6	7.0+6	ALD	Expt Jour	NP/A 112 337	May 68	Owens+.LVL DENS VERSUS EXCIT.MEAN T	+
				Conf	65Antwerp 547	Jul 65	- + PPR122. TBL FERMI GAS CONST.	
Lvl Density	None		FEI	Theo Jour	YF 11 1213	Jun 70	Ignatyuk+ SPIN DEPENDENCE OF DENSITY	
				Jour	SNP 11 674	Dec 70	. ENGL OF YF 11 1213	

66 Dysprosium 150

Quantity	Energy (ev) Min	Max	Lab	Type	Documentation Ref Vol Page	Date	Author, Comments	Data
Reson Params	-		AUA	Theo Rept	AAEC/E-211	Nov 70	Musgrove. CALCULTD D+GAM WIDTH GIVEN	
Strnth Fnctn	-		AUA	Theo Rept	AAEC/E-211	Nov 70	Musgrove. SMOOTHED S0,S1 AND S2 GIVN	

66 Dysprosium 151

Quantity	Energy (ev) Min	Max	Lab	Type	Documentation Ref Vol Page	Date	Author, Comments	Data
Reson Params	-		AUA	Theo Rept	AAEC/E-211	Nov 70	Musgrove. CALCULTD D+GAM WIDTH GIVEN	
Strnth Fnctn	-		AUA	Theo Rept	AAEC/E-211	Nov 70	Musgrove. SMOOTHED S0,S1 AND S2 GIVN	

66 Dysprosium 152

Quantity	Energy (ev) Min	Max	Lab	Type	Documentation Ref Vol Page	Date	Author, Comments	Data
Reson Params	-		AUA	Theo Rept	AAEC/E-211	Nov 70	Musgrove. CALCULTD D+GAM WIDTH GIVEN	
Strnth Fnctn	-		AUA	Theo Rept	AAEC/E-211	Nov 70	Musgrove. SMOOTHED S0,S1 AND S2 GIVN	

66 Dysprosium 153

Quantity	Energy (ev) Min	Max	Lab	Type	Documentation Ref Vol Page	Date	Author, Comments	Data
Reson Params	-		AUA	Theo Rept	AAEC/E-211	Nov 70	Musgrove. CALCULTD D+GAM WIDTH GIVEN	
Strnth Fnctn	-		AUA	Theo Rept	AAEC/E-211	Nov 70	Musgrove. SMOOTHED S0,S1 AND S2 GIVN	

66 Dysprosium 154

Quantity	Energy (ev) Min	Max	Lab	Type	Documentation Ref Vol Page	Date	Author, Comments	Data
Reson Params	-		AUA	Theo Rept	AAEC/E-211	Nov 70	Musgrove. CALCULTD D+GAM WIDTH GIVEN	
Strnth Fnctn	-		AUA	Theo Rept	AAEC/E-211	Nov 70	Musgrove. SMOOTHED S0,S1 AND S2 GIVN	

66 Dysprosium 155

Quantity	Energy (ev) Min	Max	Lab	Type	Documentation Ref Vol Page	Date	Author, Comments	Data
Reson Params	-		AUA	Theo Rept	AAEC/E-211	Nov 70	Musgrove. CALCULTD D+GAM WIDTH GIVEN	
Strnth Fnctn	-		AUA	Theo Rept	AAEC/E-211	Nov 70	Musgrove. SMOOTHED S0,S1 AND S2 GIVN	

66 Dysprosium 156

Quantity	Energy (ev) Min	Max	Lab	Type	Documentation Ref Vol Page	Date	Author, Comments	Data
Elastic	2.5-2		IJI	Eval Conf	75Kiev 1 169	May 75	Fedorova+ EVAL 2200M/S SIG,TABLE	
Absorption	2.5-2		IJI	Eval Conf	75Kiev 1 169	May 75	Fedorova+ EVAL 2200M/S SIG,TABLE	
Res Int Abs	5.0-1		OSL	Expt Prog	INDC(NOR)-1 2	May 72	Alstad+ REL AU. TABLES	+
	5.0-1			Data	EXFOR20187.003	May 74	1PNT.CAPTURE.	
Res Int Abs	+0	+5	WIN	Revw Conf	IAEA-169 3 163	74	Pope+ EVALUATED VALUE GIVEN	

66 Dysprosium 156

Quantity	Energy (ev) Min	Max	Lab	Type	Documentation Ref Vol Page	Date	Author, Comments	Data
Res Int Abs	5.0-1		IJI	Eval	Conf 75Kiev 1 169	May 75	Fedorova+ RI CALC FROM RESPARS,TABLE	
(n,γ)	-		IEA	Comp	Rept IEA-INF- 10	Aug 68	Atalla. TABLES OF HL,SIG AND GAMM-E	
(n,γ)	1.0+3	1.0+7	BOL	Eval	Rept CCDN-NW/10	Dec 69	Benzi+H-F MOD,AXEL G(G)EST,ALL DATA	
					Rept CEC(70)-2	Apr 70	- +. GRAPH	
(n,γ)	3.0+4		AUA	Theo	Rept AAEC/E-211	Nov 70	Musgrove. SIGMA GIVEN AND CFD OTHER	
(n,γ)	Maxwl		OSL	Expt	Prog INDC(NOR)-1 2	May 72	Alstad+ ACTIVATION REL AU-197,TABLE	+
	2.5-2				Data EXFOR20187.002	May 74	1PNT.SIGMA.	
(n,γ)	Maxwl		WIN	Revw	Conf IAEA-169 3 163	74	Pope+ FIS-SPEC AVG DATA CFD MAXW-XPT	
	Fiss				Conf IAEA-169 3 163	74	- + FIS-SPEC AVG DATA CFD MAXW-XP	
(n,γ)	1.0+3	1.0+7	FEI	Eval	Rept YK- 8/2 97	Sep 72	Abagjan+ AVG SIG(ENERGY-GROUPS),TABL	
					Rept INDC(CCP)-39	Jul 74	.P102. ENGLISH OF YK-8/2 97	
(n,2n)	Fiss		CRC	Eval	Rept CRC-1003	Dec 60	ROY+ ESTIMATED AVG SIG=1.5MB	
(n,2n)	1.4+7		LYO	Comp	Rept LYCEN/6780	Nov 67	Crouzet+COMPILATN FOR ACTIVTN ANALYS	
(n,2n)	1.4+7	1.5+7	JYV	Eval	Rept JU-RR-3/1970	Jun 70	Leppaemaeki+ TABLE OF EVAL AVG SIG	
(n,2n)	1.5+7		ARK	Expt	Abst DA/B 32 5091	Mar 72	Bari. GE(LI) DET. ACT. SIG GIVEN	+
	1.5+7				Data EXFOR10431.056	Aug 75	. 1 PT,SIGMA	
(n,2n)	1.5+7		DEB	Eval	Jour REA 11 1 153	Mar 73	Boedy+ RECOMM.VALUE FROM N-Z SYSTEM.	
(n,2n)	1.5+7		KFI	Theo	Jour KFKI-73- 68	Dec 73	Jeki.NEW FIT,CALC SIG CFD OTHERS,TBL	
(n,2n)	1.5+7		TAT	Theo	Jour JP/A 7 1457	Aug 74	Kondaiah. CALC ON STAT MODEL	
(n,2n)	1.5+7		JUL	Expt	Jour NP/A 224 319	May 74	Qaim. ACT.GE(LI)	+
					Jour RRL 25 335	May 76	- + SIG IN GRPH. SYST VS (N-Z)/A	
	1.5+7				Data EXFOR20541.040	Apr 76	1PNT.SIGMA.	
(n,2n)	1.4+7		GIT	Expt	Abst BAP 13 1699	Dec 68	OMS+ ACT, REL FE56 NP	+
	1.4+7				Data EXFOR12131.002	Jun 76	. 1 PT, SIG	
(n,p)	Fiss		CRC	Eval	Rept CRC-1003	Dec 60	ROY+ ESTIMATED AVG SIG=0.5MB	
(n,α)	Fiss		CRC	Eval	Rept CRC-1003	Dec 60	ROY+ ESTIMATED AVG SIG=0.01MB	
(n,α)	Maxwl		CCP	Expt	Jour YF 1 252	Feb 65	Andreev.IONIZ-CHAMBER,SIG=M9MB	+
					Jour SNP 1 177	Aug 65	TRANSLATN.*	
Reson Params	2.1+0	1.2+2	IFU	Revw	Rept ICD-4 7	67	Vertebnyj.ANAL + REVW OF RES PARAMS	
Reson Params	1.0-2	1.0+3	IFU	Expt	Prog YFI-4 42	May 67	Vertebnyj+.,TBL GIVEN,TRNS	
					Rept INDC-187E	67	. ENGL OF YFI-4 42	
Reson Params	2.1+0	1.3+2	IFU	Expt	Prog YFI-5 44	Oct 67	Vertebnyj+ TABLE 20 RESONANCES	
					Conf 67Tokyo § 8.134	Sep 67	.SUPERSEDD.SOME E+GN	
					Rept INDC-232E	67	. ENGL OF YFI-5 44	
Reson Params	2.0-2	1.0+3	IFU	Expt	Conf 68Riga	Jan 68	Vertebnyj+ ABSTRACT,LVLS,PARAMETERS	
Reson Params	-		IFU	Expt	Jour UFZ 13 2085	Dec 68	Vertebnyj+TBL,EXPTL-D CFD OTHER TH-D	
					Jour UPJ 13 1492	Jun 69	TRANSLATN.*	
Reson Params	2.2+0	2.8+1	IFU	Expt	Jour UFZ 14 1810	Nov 69	Vertebny+.TOF,10 RES,AVG D,CURVS,TBL	+
	2.2+0	1.2+2			Data EXFOR40097.	May 72	E-RES,N-WIDTH,RED.N-WIDTH, 20 RES.	
Reson Params	-		AUA	Theo	Rept AAEC/E-211	Nov 70	Musgrove. CALCULTD D+GAM WIDTH GIVEN	
Reson Params	2.1+0	3.1+0	CJD	Eval	Rept YK- 7	71	Zakharova+ SURVEY+SYSTEMATICS,GW,TBL	
					Rept INDC(CCP)-27	Nov 72	.ENGLISH TRANSLATION OF YK-7 /71	
Reson Params	None		DUB	Theo	Rept ZEP 14 194	Aug 71	Solovev.LARGE N-WID G-WID CORREL.NDG	
					Rept JINR-E4-5880	71	Soloviev.N-GAM-WIDS CORR.SHORT NOTE	
					Jour JEL 14 129	Aug 71	- . ENGL OF ZEP 14 194.	
Reson Params	+0	+2	BOL	Eval	Conf IAEA-169 3 123	74	Benzi+ AVG G-WID CFD OTHERS+XPT,TABL	
Reson Params	+0	+1	FEI	Eval	Rept YK- 8/2 97	Sep 72	Abagyan+ AVG G-WID+D AT BINDNG-E,TBL	
					Rept INDC(CCP)-39	Jul 74	.PAGE 102.ENGLISH OF YK-8/2 97	
Strnth Fnctn	-		IFU	Expt	Jour UFZ 13 2085	Dec 68	Vertebnyj+ VAL GVN,S-RESONANCE	
					Jour UPJ 13 1492	Jun 69	TRANSLATN.*	
Strnth Fnctn	2.2+0	4.7+1	IFU	Expt	Jour UFZ 14 1810	Nov 69	Vertebny+	+
	2.2+0	4.7+1			Data EXFOR40097.011	May 72	STRENGTH-FUNCTION	
Strnth Fnctn	-		AUA	Theo	Rept AAEC/E-211	Nov 70	Musgrove. SMOOTHED S0,S1 AND S2 GIVN	
Lvl Density	None		BOL	Eval	Conf IAEA-169 3 123	74	Benzi+ LVL DENS PARAM BY XPT,GRPH+TB	
Lvl Density	+0	+1	FEI	Eval	Rept YK- 8/2 97	Sep 72	Abagyan+ LVL DENSITY PARAMETER,TBL	
					Rept INDC(CCP)-39	Jul 74	.PAGE 102.ENGLISH OF YK-8/2 97	

66 Dysprosium 157

Quantity	Energy (ev) Min	Max	Lab	Type	Documentation Ref Vol Page	Date	Author, Comments	Data
Reson Params	-		AUA	Theo	Rept AAEC/E-211	Nov 70	Musgrove. CALCULTD D+GAM WIDTH GIVEN	
Strnth Fnctn	-		AUA	Theo	Rept AAEC/E-211	Nov 70	Musgrove. SMOOTHED S0,S1 AND S2 GIVN	
Lvl Density	None		MUN	Theo	Jour NP/A 217 269	Dec 73	Dilg+ A,DELTA. BACK SHIFTED FERMIGAS	
Lvl Density	None		ROC	Theo	Jour NP/A 223 589	May 74	Huizenga+ EXP CFD MICROSC TH AX SYMM	

66 Dysprosium 158

Quantity	Energy (ev) Min	Max	Lab	Type	Documentation Ref Vol Page	Author, Comments Date	Data
Absorption	2.5−2		IJI	Eval Conf	75Kiev 1 169	May 75 Fedorova+ EVAL 2200M/S SIG,TABLE	
Res Int Abs	5.0−1		OSL	Expt Prog	INDC(NOR)−1 2	May 72 Alstad+ REL AU. TABLES	+
	5.0−1			Data	EXFOR20187.005	May 74 1PNT.CAPTURE.	
Res Int Abs	+0	+5	WIN	Revw Conf	IAEA−169 3 163	74 Pope+ EVALUATED VALUE GIVEN	
(n,γ)	Maxwl		MUA	Expt Jour	NP 12 261	Jul 59 Sehgal+96+−20B	+
	Maxwl			Data	EXFOR31244.004	Jun 78 1 PNT	
(n,γ)	−		IEA	Comp Rept	IEA−INF− 10	Aug 68 Atalla. TABLES OF HL,SIG AND GAMM−E	
(n,γ)	1.0+3	1.0+7	BOL	Eval Rept	CCDN−NW/10	Dec 69 Benzi+H−F MOD,AXEL G(G)EST,ALL DATA	
				Rept	CEC(70)−2	Apr 70 − +. GRAPH	
(n,γ)	3.0+4		AUA	Theo Rept	AAEC/E−211	Nov 70 Musgrove. SIGMA GIVEN AND CFD OTHER	
(n,γ)	Maxwl		OSL	Expt Prog	INDC(NOR)−1 2	May 72 Alstad+ ACTIVATION REL AU−197,TABLE	+
	2.5−2			Data	EXFOR20187.004	May 74 1PNT.SIGMA.	
(n,γ)	Maxwl		WIN	Revw Conf	IAEA−169 3 163	74 Pope+ FIS−SPEC AVG DATA CFD MAXW−XPT	
	Fiss			Conf	IAEA−169 3 163	74 − + FIS−SPEC AVG DATA CFD MAXW−XP	
(n,γ)	1.0+3	1.0+7	FEI	Eval Rept	YK− 8/2 97	Sep 72 Abagjan+ AVG SIG(ENERGY−GROUPS),TABL	
				Rept	INDC(CCP)−39	Jul 74 .P102. ENGLISH OF YK−8/2 97	
(n,2n)	Fiss		CRC	Eval Rept	CRC−1003	Dec 60 ROY+ ESTIMATED AVG SIG=1.6MB	
(n,2n)	1.4+7		LYO	Comp Rept	LYCEN/6780	Nov 67 Crouzet+COMPILATN FOR ACTIVTN ANALYS	
(n,2n)	1.4+7	1.5+7	JYV	Eval Rept	JU−RR−3/1970	Jun 70 Leppaemaeki+ TABLE OF EVAL AVG SIG	
(n,2n)	1.5+7		ARK	Expt Abst	DA/B 32 5091	Mar 72 Bari. GE(LI) DET. ACT. SIG GIVEN	+
	1.5+7			Data	EXFOR10431.057	Aug 75 1PT,SIGMA	
(n,2n)	1.5+7		DEB	Eval Jour	REA 11 1 153	Mar 73 Boedy+ RECOMM.VALUE FROM N−Z SYSTEM.	
(n,2n)	1.5+7		KFI	Theo Jour	KFKI−73−68	Dec 73 Jeki.NEW FIT,CALC SIG CFD OTHERS,TBL	
(n,2n)	1.5+7		TAT	Theo Jour	JP/A 7 1457	Aug 74 Kondaiah. CALC ON STAT MODEL	
(n,2n)	1.5+7		JUL	Expt Jour	NP/A 224 319	May 74 Qaim. ACT.GE(LI)	+
				Jour	RRL 25 335	May 76 − + SIG IN GRPH. SYST VS (N−Z)/A	
	1.5+7			Data	EXFOR20541.041	Apr 76 1PNT.SIGMA.	
(n,2n)	1.4+7		GIT	Expt Abst	BAP 13 1699	Dec 68 OMS+ ACT, REL FE56 NP	+
	1.4+7			Data	EXFOR12131.003	Jun 76 . 1 PT, SIG	
(n,p)	Fiss		CRC	Eval Rept	CRC−1003	Dec 60 ROY+ ESTIMATED AVG SIG=0.1MB	
(n,p)	Maxwl		IFU	Theo Rept	ICD−4 20	67 Dadakina+ PENETR COEFF CALC,TABLE	
(n,p)	1.4+7		LYO	Comp Rept	LYCEN/6780	Nov 67 Crouzet+COMPILATN FOR ACTIVTN ANALYS	
(n,p)	None		KFI	Comp Jour	JRC 7 365	Jun 71 Nagy+ GAM+XRAY+ELECTR ES, HALF−L GVN	
(n,α)	Fiss		CRC	Eval Rept	CRC−1003	Dec 60 ROY+ ESTIMATED AVG SIG=0.001MB	
(n,α)	Maxwl		CCP	Expt Jour	YF 1 252	Feb 65 Andreev.IONIZ−CHAMBER,SIG=M6MB	+
				Jour	SNP 1 177	Aug 65 TRANSLATN.*	
Reson Params	3.8+0	2.7+2	IFU	Revw Rept	ICD−4 7	67 Vertebnyj.ANAL + REVW OF RES PARAMS	
Reson Params	3.8+1	2.8+2	IFU	Expt Prog	YFI−5 44	Oct 67 Vertebnyj+ TABLE 6 RESONANCES	
				Rept	INDC−232E	67 . ENGL OF YFI−5 44	
Reson Params	2.0−2	1.0+3	IFU	Expt Conf	68Riga	Jan 68 Vertebnyj+ ABSTRACT,LVLS,PARAMETERS	
Reson Params	3.8+1	2.7+2	IFU	Expt Jour	UFZ 13 2085	Dec 68 Vertebnyj+ 6RESON,WN,EXPT−D CFD TH−D	+
				Jour	UPJ 13 1492	Jun 69 TRANSLATN.*	
Reson Params	3.8+1	6.0+1	IFU	Expt Jour	UFZ 14 1810	Nov 69 Vertebny+.TOF,3 RES, AVG D,CURVS,TBL	+
	3.8+1	2.7+2		Data	EXFOR40097.	May 72 E−RES,N−WIDTH,RED.N−WIDTH, 6 RES.	
Reson Params	−		AUA	Theo Rept	AAEC/E−211	Nov 70 Musgrove. CALCULTD D+GAM WIDTH GIVEN	
Reson Params	None		DUB	Theo Jour	ZEP 14 194	Aug 71 Solovev.LARGE N−WID G−WID CORREL.NDG	
				Rept	JINR−E4−5880	71 Soloviev.N−GAM−WIDS CORR.SHORT NOTE	
				Jour	JEL 14 129	Aug 71 − . ENGL OF ZEP 14 194.	
Reson Params	+1		FEI	Eval Rept	YK− 8/2 97	Sep 72 Abagyan+ AVG G−WID+D AT BINDNG−E,TBL	
				Rept	INDC(CCP)−39	Jul 74 .PAGE 102.ENGLISH OF YK−8/2 97	
Strnth Fnctn	−		AUA	Theo Rept	AAEC/E−211	Nov 70 Musgrove. SMOOTHED S0,S1 AND S2 GIVN	
Lvl Density	None		CCP	Theo Jour	YF 13 43	Jan 71 Bravin+.DEFORM PAR,CALC,TBL,CFD EXPT	
Lvl Density	+1		FEI	Eval Rept	YK− 8/2 97	Sep 72 Abagyan+ LVL DENSITY PARAMETER,TBL	
				Rept	INDC(CCP)−39	Jul 74 .PAGE 102.ENGLISH OF YK−8/2 97	

66 Dysprosium 159

Quantity	Energy (ev) Min	Max	Lab	Type	Documentation Ref Vol Page	Author, Comments Date	Data
(n,p)	Maxwl		IFU	Theo Rept	ICD−4 20	67 Dadakina+ PENETR COEFF CALC,TABLE	
Reson Params	−		AUA	Theo Rept	AAEC/E−211	Nov 70 Musgrove. CALCULTD D+GAM WIDTH GIVEN	
Strnth Fnctn	−		AUA	Theo Rept	AAEC/E−211	Nov 70 Musgrove. SMOOTHED S0,S1 AND S2 GIVN	
Lvl Density	None		MUN	Theo Jour	NP/A 217 269	Dec 73 Dilg+ A,DELTA. BACK SHIFTED FERMIGAS	
Lvl Density	None		ROC	Theo Jour	NP/A 223 589	May 74 Huizenga+ EXP CFD MICROSC TH AX SYMM	

66 Dysprosium 160

Quantity	Energy (ev) Min	Max	Lab	Type	Documentation Ref Vol Page	Date	Author, Comments	Data
Evaluation	1.0−3	1.5+7	AUA	Eval	Rept AAEC/TM−549	Jun 70	Cook.TOT,EL,INEL,NONEL,CAPT SIGS,NDG	+
					Rept AAEC/E−214	Jun 71	Bertram+GROUP SIGMAS SAME QUANTS.NDG	
					Rept AAEC/TM−587	Mar 71	*DESCRIPTION OF LIBRARY	
	1.0−3	1.5+7		Data	AUSTR−DFN 179.	Nov 71	POINT(223) AND GROUP(127) SIGMAS	
Total	2.5−2		KAP	Expt	Abst BAP 3 337	Aug 58	House+ABST.R6.PILE.	+
Total	1.0−1		ORL	Expt	Jour PR 174 1553	Oct 68	Child+ FROM NEUT DIFFRACT 36.4+−6B	
Total	1.0−3	1.5+7	AUA	Data	AUSTR−DFN 179.	Nov 71	COOK+POINT(223)+GROUP(127)SIG.CF EVL	
Total	1.0+0	2.0+3	COL	Expt	Jour PR/C 11 462	Feb 75	Liou+ANAL.FOR RES,STF,AVG D	
					Conf 75Wash. 780	Mar 75	Hacken+12ELEMENT RVW.RES PAR SUMMARY	
Total	1.4+7		LIN	Expt	Conf 75Kiev 4 140	May 75	Djumin+ SIG GIVEN.OPTMOD ANAL,RADIUS	
Elastic	1.0−1		ORL	Expt	Jour PR 174 1553	Oct 68	Child+ COHERENT SCAT AMPLITUDE	
Elastic	1.0−3	1.5+7	AUA	Data	AUSTR−DFN 179.	Nov 71	COOK+POINT(223)+GROUP(127)SIG.CF EVL	
Elastic	2.5−2		IJI	Eval	Conf 75Kiev 1 169	May 75	Fedorova+ EVAL 2200M/S SIG,TABLE	
Tot Inelastc	5.0+5	1.5+7	AUA	Data	AUSTR−DFN 179.	Nov 71	COOK+POINT(11)+GROUP(127)SIG.CF EVL	
Nonelastic	1.0−3	1.5+7	AUA	Data	AUSTR−DFN 179.	Nov 71	COOK+POINT(223)+GROUP(127)SIG.CF EVL	+
Absorption	Maxwl		MTR	Expt	Jour NSE 25 12	May 66	Scoville. 55+−9 B	+
	Maxwl			Data	EXFOR12101.004	Jun 76	. 1 PT.	
Absorption	Maxwl	Pile	SGA	Expt	Jour JMS 6 435	71	Dobrozemsky+ CHANGE OF ABUND.TBL SIG	+
					Rept SGAE−PH−104	71	−+ MASS−SPEC METHOD	
					Rept AEC−TR−7574	74	−+ ENGLISH OF JMS 6 435	
	2.5−2			Data	EXFOR20637.010	Sep 76	1PNT.SIGMA.	
Absorption	2.5−2		IJI	Eval	Conf 75Kiev 1 169	May 75	Fedorova+ EVAL 2200M/S SIG,TABLE	
Res Int Abs	5.0−1		MTR	Expt	Jour NSE 25 12	May 66	Scoville. 1160+−130B	+
	5.0−1			Data	EXFOR12101.005	Jun 76	. 1 PT.	
Res Int Abs	5.0−1		MTR	Expt	Rept IN−1195	May 68	Scoville.	+
Res Int Abs	5.5−1		SGA	Expt	Jour JMS 6 435	71	Dobrozemsky+ EFF ABS RES INT GIVEN.	+
					Prog SGAE−PH−104	71	−+MASS−SPECTROMETRIC	
					Rept AEC−TR−7574	74	. ENGLISH OF JMS 6 415	
	5.5−1			Data	EXFOR20637.011	Sep 76	1PNT.	
Res Int Abs	5.5−1		CRC	Eval	Rept AECL−3037 1	Jan 72	Walker.REDUCED RES INT,DETAILED TBL	
Res Int Abs	5.0−1		AUA	Eval	Rept AAEC/TM−619	Sep 72	Clayton.CALC FROM SIG LIBRARY,TABLE	
Res Int Abs	+0	+5	WIN	Revw	Conf IAEA−169 3 163	74	Pope+ DATA FILE CALC CFD XPTAL VALUE	
Res Int Abs	5.0−1		IJI	Eval	Conf 75Kiev 1 169	May 75	Fedorova+ EVAL+CALC RI GIVEN,TABLE	
(n,γ)	Maxwl		MCM	Expt	Priv WALKER	May 56	Walker.	+
	Maxwl			Data	EXFOR12127.016	Jun 76	. 1 PT.	
(n,γ)	Maxwl		CRC	Eval	Rept AECL−1054	Mar 60	Walker. (CRRP−913)	
(n,γ)	2.5+4		FEI	ExTh	Prog YFI−4 22	May 67	Shorin+.,TBLS GIVEN,TBP YF	
					Rept INDC−187E	67	. ENGL OF YFI−4 22	
(n,γ)	2.5+4		CCP	Theo	Jour YF 6 769	Oct 67	Shorin+ VAL GVN,STATISTICAL−THEORY	
					Jour SNP 6 558	Apr 68	TRANSLATN.*	
(n,γ)	1.0+3	1.0+7	BOL	Eval	Rept CCDN−NW/10	Dec 69	Benzi+H−F MOD,AXEL G(G)EST,ALL DATA	
					Rept CEC(70)−2	Apr 70	−+. GRAPH	
(n,γ)	3.0+4		AUA	Theo	Rept AAEC/E−211	Nov 70	Musgrove. SIGMA GIVEN AND CFD OTHER	
(n,γ)	1.0−3	1.5+7	AUA	Data	AUSTR−DFN 179.	Nov 71	COOK+POINT(223)+GROUP(127)SIG.CF EVL	+
(n,γ)	Maxwl		CRC	Eval	Rept AECL−3037 1	Jan 72	Walker.RECOMMENDED SIG,DETAILED TBL	
(n,γ)	2.5−2		AUA	Eval	Rept AAEC/TM−619	Sep 72	Clayton.CALC FROM SIG LIBRARY,TABLE	
(n,γ)	Maxwl		WIN	Revw	Conf IAEA−169 3 163	74	Pope+ MAXW+FIS−SPEC AVG DATA CFD XPT	
	Fiss				Conf IAEA−169 3 137	74	Dean. POINT DATA AVG OVER STAND SPEC	
(n,γ)	1.0+3	1.0+7	FEI	Eval	Rept YK−8/2 97	Sep 72	Abagjan+ AVG SIG(ENERGY−GROUPS),TABL	
					Rept INDC(CCP)−39	Jul 74	.P102. ENGLISH OF YK−8/2 97	
(n,γ)	Maxwl		KAP	Expt	Abst BAP 3 337	Aug 58	House+ PILE OSC.SIG=130+−130B	+
	Maxwl			Data	EXFOR12082.002	Jun 76	. 1 PT, SIG	
(n,2n)	Fiss		CRC	Eval	Rept CRC−1003	Dec 60	ROY+ ESTIMATED AVG SIG=2.0MB	
(n,2n)	1.3+7	1.5+7	BNL	Theo	Jour NSE 23 238	Nov 65	Pearlstein.3ES.STAT MDL CALC.TBL CS.	
(n,2n)	Fiss		BNL	Theo	Jour NSE 23 238	Nov 65	Pearlstein.STATMDL CALC.SPEC AVG.TBL	
(n,2n)	1.4+7		LYO	Comp	Rept LYCEN/6780	Nov 67	Crouzet+COMPILATN FOR ACTIVTN ANALYS	
(n,2n)	1.4+7		IRK	Expt	Diss WINKLER	68	Winkler.(THESIS)	
(n,2n)	1.5+7		MUN	Expt	Jour NP/A 118 9	Sep 68	Dilg+ ACTIV.REL AL(N,A)	+
					Jour OAWS 177 323	69	Winkler+(IRK) ACTIVATION.	
	1.5+7			Data	EXFOR20802.006	Dec 78	1PNT.SIGMA.	
(n,2n)	1.4+7	1.5+7	IRK	Comp	Jour OAWS 177 469	69	Hille.	
(n,2n)	1.5+7		DEB	Comp	Jour REA 7 4 93	Dec 69	Csikai+ SIG+HL COMPILTN,N−ACTIV−ANAL	
(n,2n)	1.4+7	1.5+7	JYV	Eval	Rept JU−RR−3/1970	Jun 70	Leppaemaeki+ TABLE OF EVAL AVG SIG	
(n,2n)	+7		KFI	Theo	Rept KFKI−71−8	Feb 71	Jeki. CALCULATED CFD EXPTL SIG VALUE	
(n,2n)	1.5+7		DEB	Eval	Jour REA 11 1 153	Mar 73	Boedy. COMPILATION+RECOMM.VALUE,TBL	
					Rept IAEA−153 173	73	−. RECOMM. VALUE ONLY	

PAGE 1230

66 Dysprosium 160

Quantity	Energy (ev) Min	Max	Lab	Type	Documentation Ref Vol Page	Author, Comments Date	Data
(n,2n)	1.5+7		JUL	Expt	Jour NP/A 224 319	May 74 Qaim. ACT.GE(LI)	+
					Jour RRL 25 335	May 76 - + SIG IN GRPH. SYST VS (N-Z)/A	
	1.5+7				Data EXFOR20541.042	Apr 76 1PNT.SIGMA.	
(n,xn) x>2	Fiss		BNL	Theo	Jour NSE 23 238	Nov 65 Pearlstein.SPEC AVG STATMDL CALC N3N	
(n,p)	Fiss		CRC	Eval	Rept CRC - 1003	Dec 60 ROY+ ESTIMATED AVG SIG=0.06MB	
(n,p)	1.4+7	1.5+7	ARK	Theo	Prog ORO - 3235 - 29	Jan 67 Koch+ STAT MODEL CALC CFD EXPTS	
(n,p)	1.4+7		LYO	Comp	Rept LYCEN/6780	Nov 67 Crouzet+COMPILATN FOR ACTIVTN ANALYS	
(n,p)	1.5+7		IRK	Expt	Jour APA 34 209	Sep 71 Havlik. ACT. CC-W.	+
					Jour OAWA 107 119	Apr 70 - . ACTIVATION METHOD	
	1.5+7				Data EXFOR20509.018	Apr 76 1PNT.SIGMA.	
(n,p)	1.5+7		JUL	Expt	Jour RRL 25 335	May 76 Qaim+ ACTIV,GELI.CFD OTHERS,TBL+GRPH	
(n,α)	Fiss		CRC	Eval	Rept CRC - 1003	Dec 60 ROY+ ESTIMATED AVG SIG=0.035MB	
(n,α)	Maxwl		CCP	Expt	Jour YF 1 252	Feb 65 Andreev.IONIZ-CHAMBER,SIG=M.3MB	+
					Jour SNP 1 177	Aug 65 TRANSLATN.*	
(n,α)	1.4+7		IBJ	Expt	Rept INR - 1268	Jan 71 Jaskola+ ALFA SPCTR CFD TH,FULL PAPR	+
					Rept INR - 1275	Jan 71 SEE ALSO * FULL INFORMATION	
					Jour APPB 2 521	71 .SAME AS INR - 1268	
	1.4+7				Data EXFOR30158.026	Jul 72 INTEGRATED CROSS SECTION,1 DATA LINE	
	1.4+7				Data EXFOR30158.010	Jul 72 28 DATA LINES (ALPHA SPECTRUM)	
(n,α)	1.8+7		IBJ	Expt	Prog INR - 1401 13	May 72 Glowacka+ E DISTRBT OF ALPHAS,TABLE	+
					Rept INR - 1468/I/PLA	73 - + ALFA E - SPEC,GRAPH.	
					Conf 72Budapest 16	Aug 72 . ALFA-SPEC KNOCK-ON TH,GRAPH	
					Rept INR - 1401 22	May 72 * ALPHA SPCTR AT 1 ANGL	
	1.8+7				Data EXFOR30172.	Aug 72 DISTRBT OF ALF(35 DATA)+SIG AT 1 ANG	
(n,α)	1.4+7		WWA	Theo	Conf 72Budapest 18	Aug 72 Glowacka+ KNOCK ON,SPEC CFD XPT,GRPH	
					Jour NP/A 187 177	May 72 Kozlowski+. 30DEG E-SPEC.KNOCK-ON OK	
(n,α)	1.4+7	1.8+7	IBJ	ExTh	Jour ZFK - 271 109	Nov 73 Glowacka+ A-SPEC AT 2ES,GRPH	
					Conf 73Munich 1 519	Aug 73 - + A-SPEC CFD TH,GRPH	
Reson Params	1.9+0	8.5+1	IFU	Revw	Rept ICD - 4 7	67 Vertebnyj.ANAL + REVW OF RES PARAMS	
Reson Params	2.5+4		FEI	ExTh	Prog YFI - 4 22	May 67 Shorin+.,TBLS GIVEN,TBP YF	
					Rept INDC - 187E	67 . ENGL OF YFI - 4 22	
Reson Params	1.8+0	8.5+1	IFU	Expt	Prog YFI - 5 44	Oct 67 Vertebnyj+ TABLE 6 RESONANCES	
					Rept INDC - 232E	67 . ENGL OF YFI - 5 44	
Reson Params	2.0-2	1.0+3	IFU	Expt	Conf 68Riga	Jan 68 Vertebnyj+ ABSTRACT,LVLS,PARAMETERS	
Reson Params	-		IFU	Expt	Jour UFZ 13 2085	Dec 68 Vertebnyj+ OTHER TH D VAL GVN	
					Jour UPJ 13 1492	Jun 69 TRANSLATN.*	
Reson Params	1.9+0	8.5+1	IFU	Expt	Jour UFZ 13 2085	Dec 68 Vertebnyj+ 6RESON,WN,EXPT-D CFD TH-D	+
					Jour UPJ 13 1492	Jun 69 TRANSLATN.*	
Reson Params	1.9+0	1.0+1	IFU	Expt	Jour UFZ 14 1810	Nov 69 Vertebny+.TOF,3 RES, AVG D,CURVS,TBL	+
	1.9+0	8.5+1			Data EXFOR40097.	May 72 E-RES,N-WIDTH,RED.N-WIDTH, 6 RES.	
Reson Params	-		AUA	Theo	Rept AAEC/E - 211	Nov 70 Musgrove. CALCULTD D+GAM WIDTH GIVEN	
Reson Params	1.9+0		CJD	Eval	Rept YK - 7	71 Zakharova+ SURVEY+SYSTEMATICS,GW,TBL	
					Rept INDC(CCP) - 27	Nov 72 .ENGLISH TRANSLATION OF YK-7 /71	
Reson Params	1.0+0	2.0+1	BNL	Expt	Jour ZN/A 26 334	Mar 71 Brunhart+ SPINS OF 9 RESON DY 161	
Reson Params	+0	+1	FEI	Eval	Rept YK - 8/2 97	Sep 72 Abagyan+ AVG G-WID+D AT BINDNG-E,TBL	
					Rept INDC(CCP) - 39	Jul 74 .PAGE 102.ENGLISH OF YK-8/2 97	
Reson Params	1.0+1	2.0+3	COL	Expt	Jour PR/C 11 462	Feb 75 Liou+TABLE E0, WN0. STF,AVG D,AVG WG	+
					Conf 75Wash. 780	Mar 75 Hacken+12 ELEMENT RES PAR RVW.TBL	
	1.0+1	7.3+3			Data EXFOR10525.	Mar 76 . 74PTS.WN RED,WG,D GVN.	
Strnth Fnctn	-		AUA	Theo	Rept AAEC/E - 211	Nov 70 Musgrove. SMOOTHED S0,S1 AND S2 GIVN	
Strnth Fnctn	1.0+1	2.0+3	COL	Expt	Jour PR/C 11 462	Feb 75 Liou+SWAVE.64LVLS.GRPH.TBL CFD.	+
					Conf 75Wash. 780	Mar 75 Hacken+12 ELEMENT RVW. TBL	
	1.1+1	2.0+3			Data EXFOR10525.007	Mar 76 . 1PT.S0=(2.7+ - .36)-4	
Lvl Density	None		CCP	Theo	Jour YF 13 43	Jan 71 Bravin+.DEFORM PAR,CALC,TBL,CFD EXPT	
Lvl Density	1.4+7		IBJ	Expt	Rept INR - 1268	Jan 71 Jaskola+ ALFA SPCTR CFD TH,FULL PAPR	+
					Rept INR - 1275	Jan 71 SEE ALSO * FULL INFORMATION	
					Jour APPB 2 521	71 .SAME AS INR - 1268	
	1.4+7				Data EXFOR30158.011	Mar 71 LEVEL DENSITY PARAMETER OF GD157 GIV	
Lvl Density	+0	+1	FEI	Eval	Rept YK - 8/2 97	Sep 72 Abagyan+ LVL DENSITY PARAMETER,TBL	
					Rept INDC(CCP) - 39	Jul 74 .PAGE 102.ENGLISH OF YK-8/2 97	

66 Dysprosium 161

Quantity	Energy (ev) Min	Max	Lab	Type	Documentation Ref Vol Page	Date	Author, Comments	Data
Evaluation	1.0-3	1.5+7	AUA	Eval	Rept AAEC/TM-549	Jun 70	Cook.TOT,EL,INEL,NONEL,CAPT SIGS,NDG	+
					Rept AAEC/E-214	Jun 71	Bertram+GROUP SIGMAS SAME QUANTS.NDG	
					Rept AAEC/TM-587	Mar 71	*DESCRIPTION OF LIBRARY	
	1.0-3	1.5+7			Data AUSTR-DFN 180.	Nov 71	POINT(223) AND GROUP(127) SIGMAS	
Total	2.5-2		KAP	Expt	Abst BAP 3 337	Aug 58	House+ ABST.R6. PILE.	+
Total	1.0-1		ORL	Expt	Jour PR 174 1553	Oct 68	Child+ FROM NEUT DIFFRACT 366+ -13B	
Total	2.5-2	1.5+0	IFU	Expt	Prog YFI-11 59	70	Vertebny+ ABST,OXIDE,TBL SIG AT 28ES	+
					Prog INDC(CCP)-31	Dec 72	.PAGE 58,ENGLISH OF YFI-11 59	
	2.5-2	1.5+0			Data EXFOR40090.002	Jan 72	SIG TOT AT 27 EN.	
Total	2.5-2	7.0-1	IFU	Expt	Conf 70Helsinki 1 651	Jun 70	Vertebnij+.87. SIG(E) GRAPH+2200M/SEC	
					Rept BNL-TR-495	Jul 72	. ENGLISH OF 70HELSIN 1 651	
Total	1.0-3	1.5+7	AUA	Eval	Data AUSTR-DFN 180.	Nov 71	COOK+POINT(223)+GROUP(127)SIG.CF EVL	+
Total	1.0+0	1.0+4	COL	Expt	Jour PR/C 11 462	Feb 75	Liou+ANAL.FOR RES,STF,AVG D.TABLES.	
					Conf 75Wash. 780	Mar 75	Hacken+12ELEMENT RVW.RES PAR SUMMARY	
Total	1.4+7		LIN	Expt	Conf 75Kiev 4 140	May 75	Djumin+ SIG GIVEN.OPTMOD ANAL,RADIUS	
Elastic	1.0-1		ORL	Expt	Jour PR 174 1553	Oct 68	Child+ COHERENT SCAT AMPLITUDE	
Elastic	1.0-3	1.5+7	AUA	Eval	Data AUSTR-DFN 180.	Nov 71	COOK+POINT(223)+GROUP(127)SIG.CF EVL	
Elastic	2.5-2		IJI	Eval	Conf 75Kiev 1 169	May 75	Fedorova+ EVAL 2200M/S SIG,TABLE	
Potntal Scat	None		BNL	Expt	Jour PR/C 1 1850	May 70	Chrien+ SCAT RADINS FROM ANAL OF RES	
					Jour PL/B 24 573	May 67	.SUPERSEDED	
Tot Inelastc	5.0+5	1.5+7	AUA	Eval	Data AUSTR-DFN 180.	Nov 71	COOK+POINT(11)+GROUP(127)SIG.CF EVL	+
Thermal Scat	2.5-2	1.5+0	IFU	Expt	Prog YFI-11 59	70	Vertebny+ OXIDE,TOTSCAT,TBL 2200M/S	
					Prog INDC(CCP)-31	Dec 72	.PAGE 58,ENGLISH OF YFI-11 59	
Scattering	2.5-2	1.2+0	IFU	Expt	Prog YFI-6 108	68	Vertebnyj+. TABLE SIG(E).TBP UFZ	
					Rept INDC-260E	69	. ENGL OF YFI-6 108	
Scattering	2.0-2	3.0-2	IFU	Expt	Conf 70Helsinki 1 651	Jun 70	Vertebnij+ 2200M/SEC SIGMA GIVEN,TBL	
					Rept BNL-TR-495	Jul 72	. ENGLISH OF 70HELSIN 1 651	
Scattering	2.5-2	1.1+0	IFU	Expt	Conf 70Helsinki 1 651	Jun 70	Vertebnij+.87. SIG(E) GRAPH+2200M/SEC	
					Rept BNL-TR-495	Jul 72	. ENGLISH OF 70HELSIN 1 651	
Scattering	Maxwl		IFU	Expt	Prog YFI-11 59	Dec 71	Vertebny+	+
	Maxwl				Data EXFOR40090.003	Jan 72	THERMAL SCATTERING CS.	
Nonelastic	1.0-3	1.5+7	AUA	Eval	Data AUSTR-DFN 180.	Nov 71	COOK+POINT(223)+GROUP(127)SIG.CF EVL	+
Absorption	1.0-3	1.0+7	JUL	Eval	Rept JUEL-678-RG	Jul 70	Liu. EVALUATION+CALC,GRPH,FN OF E	
Absorption	Maxwl	Pile	SGA	Expt	Jour JMS 6 435	71	Dobrozemsky+ CHANGE OF ABUND.TBL SIG	
					Rept SGAE-PH-104	71	- + MASS-SPEC METHOD	
					Rept AEC-TR-7574	74	- + ENGLISH OF JMS 6 435	
	2.5-2				Data EXFOR20637.012	Sep 76	1PNT.SIGMA.	
Absorption	Maxwl		IFU	Expt	Prog YFI-11 59	Dec 71	Vertebny+	+
	Maxwl				Data EXFOR40090.004	Jan 72	THERMAL ABSORPTION CS.	
Absorption	2.5-2		IJI	Eval	Conf 75Kiev 1 169	May 75	Fedorova+ EVAL 2200M/S SIG,TABLE	
Res Int Abs	None		CRC	Eval	Rept AECL-1054	Mar 60	Walker.(CRP-913) REDUCED RES.INT.	
Res Int Abs	+3	+5	BOL	Theo	Conf 61Vienna 1 179	Aug 61	Benzi+.PPR11,VAL GVN,L=0,L=1 .CAPT.	
Res Int Abs	5.0-1		BOL	Eval	Conf 61Vienna 1 179	Aug 61	Benzi+ TBL TOTAL CAPT RES INTS.	
Res Int Abs	5.0-1		MTR	Expt	Jour NSE 25 12	May 66	Scoville. 1670+ -167B	+
					Abst ANS 7 85	Jun 64	.SUPERSEDED	
	5.0-1				Data EXFOR12101.007	Jun 76	. 1 PT.	
Res Int Abs	5.0-1		BOL	Eval	Rept RT/FI-4	Jan 67	Palmucci. CALC FROM (N,G) RES PARAMS	
Res Int Abs	5.0-1	+6	MTR	Expt	Rept IN-1195	May 68	Scoville.	+
Res Int Abs	5.5-1		SGA	Expt	Jour JMS 6 435	71	Dobrozemsky+ EFF ABS RES INT GIVEN.	+
					Prog SGAE-PH-104	71	- +MASS-SPECTROMETRIC	
					Rept AEC-TR-7574	74	. ENGLISH OF JMS 6 415	
	5.5-1				Data EXFOR20637.013	Sep 76	1PNT.	
Res Int Abs	5.5-1		CRC	Eval	Rept AECL-3037 1	Jan 72	Walker.REDUCD INTEG FROM RESPARS,TBL	
Res Int Abs	5.0-1		AUA	Eval	Rept AAEC/TM-619	Sep 72	Clayton.CALC FROM SIG LIBRARY,TABLE	
Res Int Abs	+0	+5	WIN	Revw	Conf IAEA-169 3 163	74	Pope+ DATA FILE CALC CFD XPTAL VALUE	
Res Int Abs	5.0-1		IJI	Eval	Conf 75Kiev 1 169	May 75	Fedorova+ EVAL+CALC RI GIVEN,TABLE	
(n,γ)	Maxwl		MCM	Expt	Priv WALKER	May 56	Walker.	+
	Maxwl				Data EXFOR12127.017	Jun 76	. 1 PT.	
(n,γ)	Maxwl		CRC	Eval	Rept AECL-1054	Mar 60	Walker. (CRRP-913)	
(n,γ)	Maxwl	1.0+0	CCP	Expt	Jour AE 16 56	Jan 64	Danelian+.TOF CURVE GIVEN	+
					Jour EAF 16 1 81	Jan 64	- +. FRENCH	
					Jour SJA 16 58	64	- +. ENGLISH	
(n,γ)	Maxwl		CCP	Expt	Jour IZV 29 2168	Dec 65	Bondarenko+.SIG GIVN.ENGL BAS29 2004	
(n,γ)	1.0+3	1.0+4	LAS	Theo	Rept LA-3463	Jan 66	Bell. TH CAPTURE OF RARE EARTHS	
(n,γ)	Maxwl		MTR	Expt	Jour NSE 25 12	May 66	Scoville. 583+ -95 B	+
	Maxwl				Data EXFOR12101.006	Jun 76	. 1 PT.	

66 Dysprosium 161

Quantity	Energy (ev) Min	Max	Lab	Type	Documentation Ref Vol Page	Date	Author, Comments	Data
(n,γ)	2.9+4	1.7+5	FEI	Expt	Conf 66Paris 1 469	Oct 66	Kononov+ TOF,SCIN TANK,PLSD C-W,GRPH	+
					Conf 66Moscow	Feb 66	.SAME EXPT,GRAPHS	
					Prog ICD-3 108	66	.ABSTRACT.GRAPH,COMPARED OTHER DATA	
					Prog INDSWG-152 108	66	.ENGLISH TRANSL OF ICD-3	
	2.9+4	1.7+5			Data EXFOR40076.008	Jul 71	SIG AT 20 ENERGIES FROM PRIV COMMUN	
(n,γ)	2.5-2		BOL	Eval	Rept RT/FI-4	Jan 67	Palmucci. CALC FROM RES PARAMETERS	
(n,γ)	5.0+3	1.0+5	AUA	ExTh	Rept AAEC/E-198	May 69	Musgrove.S+P+D WAVE SIGMAS CALC,TBL	+
(n,γ)	1.0+3	1.0+7	BOL	Eval	Rept CCDN-NW/10	Dec 69	Benzi+H-F MOD,AXEL G(G)EST,ALL DATA	
					Rept CEC(70)-2	Apr 70	- +. GRAPH	
					Conf 66Paris 1 537	Oct 66	- + STATMOD.TBL AV VALS.SUPERSEDD	
					Jour NC 38 216	Jul 65	- + THEORY FOR CAPTURE EVALUATION	
					Conf 61Vienna 1 179	Aug 61	- + TBL AV VALS. SUPERSEDED.	
(n,γ)	2.5-2	1.5+0	IFU	Expt	Prog YFI-11 59	70	Vertebny+ ABST,TBL 2200M/S VALUES	
					Prog INDC(CCP)-31	Dec 72	.PAGE 58,ENGLISH OF YFI-11 59	
(n,γ)	2.5-2		IFU	Expt	Conf 70Helsinki 1 651	Jun 70	Vertebnij+87. SIGMA GIVEN	
					Rept BNL-TR-495	Jul 72	. ENGLISH OF 70HELSIN 1 651	
(n,γ)	3.0+4		AUA	Theo	Rept AAEC/E-211	Nov 70	Musgrove. SIGMA GIVEN AND CFD OTHER	
(n,γ)	1.0-3	1.5+7	AUA	Eval	Data AUSTR-DFN 180.	Nov 71	COOK+POINT(223)+GROUP(127)SIG.CF EVL	+
(n,γ)	Maxwl		CRC	Eval	Rept AECL-3037 1	Jan 72	Walker.RECOMMENDED SIG,DETAILED TBL	
(n,γ)	2.5-2		AUA	Eval	Rept AAEC/TM-619	Sep 72	Clayton.CALC FROM SIG LIBRARY,TABLE	
(n,γ)	Maxwl	Fiss	WIN	Revw	Conf IAEA-169 3 163	74	Pope+ MAXW+FIS-SPEC AVG DATA CFD XPT	
	Fiss				Conf IAEA-169 3 137	74	Dean. POINT DATA AVG OVER STAND SPEC	
(n,γ)	1.0+3	1.0+7	FEI	Eval	Rept YK-8/2 97	Sep 72	Abagjan+ AVG SIG(ENERGY-GROUPS),TABL	
					Rept INDC(CCP)-39	Jul 74	.P102. ENGLISH OF YK-8/2 97	
(n,γ)	Maxwl		KAP	Expt	Abst BAP 3 337	Aug 58	House+ PILE OSC.SIG=130+-130B	+
	Maxwl				Data EXFOR12082.003	Jun 76	. 1 PT.	
Spect (n,γ)	2.7+0	3.7+0	YAL	Expt	Conf 57Col.Univ § V4	Sep 57	Schultz+ TOF, EG = 190KEV	
Spect (n,γ)	None		MIT	Expt	Rept MITNE-37	Aug 63	Neill+ HARD GS AND LOW E GG COINCS	
Spect (n,γ)	Pile		MUN	Expt	Jour ZN/A 21 1328	Sep 66	Neumann. CRYST SPEC EXPT OF GAM INT	
					Rept ANL-TRANS-941	73	. ENGLISH OF ZN/A 1328	
Spect (n,γ)	Pile		RIS	Expt	Jour PR 160 1011	Aug 67	Schult+ BENT CRYST,INT GS .03-1.3MEV	
					Conf 65Antwerp 518	Jul 65	- + PPR56. ABST. LVL SPINS.	
Spect (n,γ)	Maxwl		FSU	Expt	Conf 68DUBSY 71	Jul 68	Sheline.ANAL.WAVE FUNCT. DEFORM.STAT	
					Jour PR 160 1001	67	-	
Spect (n,γ)	Maxwl		UPP	Expt	Jour AF 39 221	Jun 69	Baecklin+.GE(LI).TBL E+REL INTENSTS	
Spect (n,γ)	Pile		ANL	Expt	Conf 69Studsvik 601	Aug 69	Smither+ NO DATA GVN,TB CFD STATMOD	
(n,2n)	Fiss		CRC	Eval	Rept CRC-1003	Dec 60	ROY+ ESTIMATED AVG SIG=26.0MB	
(n,2n)	1.3+7	1.5+7	BNL	Theo	Jour NSE 23 238	Nov 65	Pearlstein.3ES.STAT MDL CALC.TBL CS.	
(n,2n)	Fiss		BNL	Theo	Jour NSE 23 238	Nov 65	Pearlstein.STATMDL CALC.SPEC AVG.TBL	
(n,2n)	1.5+7		DEB	Eval	Jour REA 11 1 153	Mar 73	Boedy+ RECOMM.VALUE FROM N-Z SYSTEM.	
(n,2n)	1.5+7		KFI	Theo	Rept KFKI-73-68	Dec 73	Jeki.NEW FIT,CALC SIG CFD OTHERS,TBL	
(n,xn) x>2	Fiss		BNL	Theo	Jour NSE 23 238	Nov 65	Pearlstein.SPEC AVG STATMDL CALC N3N	
(n,p)	Fiss		CRC	Eval	Rept CRC-1003	Dec 60	ROY+ ESTIMATED AVG SIG=0.03MB	
(n,p)	Maxwl		IFU	Theo	Rept ICD-4 20	67	Dadakina+ PENETR COEFF CALC,TABLE	
(n,p)	1.4+7	1.5+7	ARK	ExTh	Prog ORO-3235-29	Jan 67	Koch+STAT MODEL CALC CFD EXPTS	
(n,p)	1.4+7		LYO	Comp	Rept LYCEN/6780	Nov 67	Crouzet+COMPILATN FOR ACTIVTN ANALYS	
(n,p)	1.5+7		JUL	Expt	Jour RRL 25 335	May 76	Qaim+ ACTIV,GELI.CFD OTHERS,TBL+GRPH	
(n,α)	Fiss		CRC	Eval	Rept CRC-1003	Dec 60	ROY+ESTIMATED AVG SIG=0.003MB	
(n,α)	Maxwl		CCP	Expt	Jour YF 1 252	Feb 65	Andreev.IONIZ-CHAMBER,SIG=M.03MB	+
					Jour SNP 1 177	Aug 65	TRANSLATN.*	
(n,α)	1.4+7		IBJ	Expt	Rept INR-1268	Jan 71	Jaskola+ ALFA SPCTR CFD TH,FULL PAPR	+
					Prog INDC(SEC)-42	Dec 74	Glowacka+ TBL DIFFSIG,GRPH E+ANG-DIS	
					Rept INR-1275	Jan 71	SEE ALSO * FULL INFORMATION	
					Jour APPB 2 521	71	.SAME AS INR-1268	
	1.4+7				Data EXFOR30298.	Jul 75	DOUBLE DIFFSIG(38 PTS)+ANGDIST(1 PT)	
	1.4+7				Data EXFOR30158.012	Mar 71	NUM DATA NOT AVAILBL,SEE GRAF IN REF	
(n,α)	Maxwl		LYO	Expt	Prog LYCEN/75-01 27	74	Emsallem+ABST,NDG	
Reson Params	2.7+0	3.7+0	BNL	Expt	Abst BAP 7 305	Apr 62	Brunhart+ ABST.K16 WO RES. SPINS.	+
	2.7+0	3.7+0			Data EXFOR11470.002	Jun 76	. 2 RES, J	
Reson Params	-.2+1	1.0+0	CCP	Expt	Jour AE 16 56	Jan 64	Danelian+.PARITY FOR NEG E RES GIVEN	+
					Jour SJA 16 58	64	. ENGLISH	
					Jour EAF 16 1 81	64	. FRENCH	
Reson Params	-.2+1	3.7+0	IFU	Revw	Rept ICD-4 7	67	Vertebnyj.ANAL + REVW OF RES PARAMS	
Reson Params	-.2+1	3.7+0	IFU	Revw	Rept ICD-4 7	67	Vertebnyj.ANAL + REVW OF RES PARAMS	
Reson Params		1.0+6	AUA	Theo	Jour AUJ 20 477	Oct 67	Cook. TBL OF AVG LVL SPACING D,L=0,1	
Reson Params	-		IFU	Expt	Jour UFZ 13 2085	Dec 68	Vertebnyj+ OTHER EXPTL+TH D VAL GVN	
					Jour UPJ 13 1492	Jun 69	TRANSLATN.*	

66 Dysprosium 161

Quantity	Energy (ev) Min	Max	Lab	Type	Documentation Ref Vol Page	Author, Comments Date	Data
Reson Params	2.7+0	1.4+2	BNL	Expt	Jour PR/C 1 1850	May 70 Chrien+ TRANS,WN WG AVG D FOR 14RES	+
Reson Params	-		AUA	Theo	Rept AAEC/E - 211	Nov 70 Musgrove. CALCULTD D+GAM WIDTH GIVEN	
Reson Params	2.7+0	3.7+0	CJD	Eval	Rept YK- 7	71 Zakharova+ SURVEY+SYSTEMATICS,GW,TBL	
					Rept INDC(CCP) - 27	Nov 72 .ENGLISH TRANSLATION OF YK-7 /71	
Reson Params	1.3+1	1.7+1	BNL	Expt	Prog NCSAC - 38 30	May 71 Rorer+ TRANS,J FOR 2 RESON GIVEN	
Reson Params	+0	+2	BOL	Eval	Conf IAEA - 169 3 123	74 Benzi+ AVG G - WID CFD OTHERS+XPT,TABL	
Reson Params	+0	+2	FEI	Eval	Rept YK - 8/2 97	Sep 72 Abagyan+ AVG G - WID+D AT BINDNG - E,TBL	
					Rept INDC(CCP) - 39	Jul 74 .PAGE 102.ENGLISH OF YK - 8/2 97	
Reson Params	8.2+6		DUB	Theo	Conf 74Petten 175	Sep 74 Malov+ DOBS,SEMI - MICROSCOPIC CALC.	
					Conf 73Munich 1 246	Aug 73 - + SUPERFLUID MDL,TABLE D VS E.	
Reson Params	+0		DUB	Theo	Jour YF 21 40	Jan 75 Voronov+ MEAN D,WITH ROTAT.CFD EXPT	
					Jour SNP 21 20	Jul 75 . ENGLISH OF YF 21,40	
Reson Params	2.7+0	1.0+4	COL	Expt	Jour PR/C 11 462	Feb 75 Liou+TBL.E0,G*WN0,STF,AVG D,WG.	+
	2.7+0	1.0+3			Conf 75Wash. 780	Mar 75 Hacken+12 ELEMENT RES PAR RVW.TBL	
	2.7+0	1.0+3			Data EXFOR10525.	Mar 76 . 278PR-TS.WN RED,WG,D GVN.	
Reson Params	2.7+0	1.4+2	DUB	Expt	Jour YF 22 3	Jul 75 Karzhavina+ SPINS+N - WIDS,TABLE	
	4.0+0	1.5+2			Rept JINR - P3 - 7980	May 74 - + SPINS,NEUTR WIDTHS,TABLE	
	7.7+0	6.6+1			Rept RCN - 203 242	Dec 73 - + G MULTIPL.METH,J	
	7.7+0	6.6+2			Conf 73Kiev 2 337	May 73 - + SPIN - IDENT,G - MULTIP MTHD	
	7.7+0	6.6+1			Rept JINR - P3 - 6948	Feb 73 - + SPINS OF RESONANCES, TBL	
	2.7+0	1.4+2			Jour SNP 22 1	Jul 75 .ENGL OF YF 22 3	
Reson Params	2.7+0	1.4+2	BNL	Expt	Abst BAP 2 42	Jan 57 Zimmerman+ FC, WG WN GIVEN	+
	2.7+0	1.4+2			Data EXFOR11438.002	Jun 76 . 36 RES, E0,WN,WG	
Strnth Fnctn	+3		BNL	Expt	Jour PRL 1 461	Dec 58 Hughes. FC 1.75+ - 0.3	
Strnth Fnctn	+3	+5	BOL	Theo	Conf 61Vienna 1 179	Aug 61 Benzi+.PPR11,TABLE CFD EXPERIMENT	
Strnth Fnctn	+0	+2	BNL	Expt	Jour PR/C 1 1850	May 70 Chrien+ TRANS,S0 = 1.85+ - 0.15 FROM RES	+
					Jour PL/B 24 573	May 67 .SUPERSEDED	
					Conf 65Antwerp 69	Jul 65 .SUPERSEDED	
Strnth Fnctn	-		AUA	Theo	Rept AAEC/E - 211	Nov 70 Musgrove. SMOOTHED S0,S1 AND S2 GIVN	
Strnth Fnctn	None		AUA	Eval	Rept AAEC/E - 277	Mar 73 Musgrove.TBLS EXPTL DATA+BEST VALUES	
Strnth Fnctn	2.7+0	1.0+3	COL	Expt	Jour PR/C 11 462	Feb 75 Liou+SWAVE.251 LVLS.GRPH.TBL.CFD.	+
					Conf 75Wash. 780	Mar 75 Hacken+12 ELEMENT RVW. TBL	
	2.7+0	1.0+3			Data EXFOR10525.008	Mar 76 . 1 PT.S0 = (1.73+ - .17) - 4	
Strnth Fnctn	2.7+0	2.0+2	DUB	Expt	Jour YF 22 3	Jul 75 Karzhavina+ S0,S0(J = 2,J = 3) GIVEN	
	4.0+0	1.5+2			Rept JINR - P3 - 7980	May 74 - +S0 FOR J = 2,3,SPIN FACTOR	
Lvl Density	1.4+7		IBJ	Expt	Rept INR - 1268	Jan 71 Jaskola+ ALFA SPCTR CFD TH,FULL PAPR	+
					Rept INR - 1275	Jan 71 SEE ALSO * FULL INFORMATION	
					Jour APPB 2 521	71 .SAME AS INR - 1268	
	1.4+7				Data EXFOR30158.013	Mar 71 LEVEL DENSITY PARAMETER OF GD158 GIV	
Lvl Density	None		MUN	Theo	Rept NP/A 217 269	Dec 73 Dilg+ A,DELTA. BACK SHIFTED FERMIGAS	
Lvl Density	None		BOL	Eval	Conf IAEA - 169 3 123	74 Benzi+ LVL DENS PARAM BY XPT,GRPH+TB	
Lvl Density	None		ROC	Theo	Jour NP/A 223 589	May 74 Huizenga+ EXP CFD MICROSC TH AX SYMM	
Lvl Density	+0	+2	FEI	Eval	Rept YK - 8/2 97	Sep 72 Abagyan+ LVL DENSITY PARAMETER,TBL	
					Rept INDC(CCP) - 39	Jul 74 .PAGE 102.ENGLISH OF YK - 8/2 97	

66 Dysprosium 162

Quantity	Energy (ev) Min	Max	Lab	Type	Documentation Ref Vol Page	Author, Comments Date	Data
Evaluation	1.0-3	1.5+7	AUA	Eval	Rept AAEC/TM - 549	Jun 70 Cook.TOT,EL,INEL,NONEL,CAPT SIGS,NDG	+
					Rept AAEC/E - 214	Jun 71 Bertram+GROUP SIGMAS SAME QUANTS.NDG	
					Rept AAEC/TM - 587	Mar 71 *DESCRIPTION OF LIBRARY	
	1.0-3	1.5+7			Data AUSTR - DFN 181.	Nov 71 POINT(223) AND GROUP(127) SIGMAS	
Total	2.5-2		KAP	Expt	Abst BAP 3 337	Aug 58 House+. ABST. R6. PILE	+
Total	9.8+5		SHE	Theo	Jour NP 54 417	Jun 64 Maddison.OPTMOD FIT TO TOWLE GILBOY	
Total	1.0-1		ORL	Expt	Jour PR 174 1553	Oct 68 Child+ FROM NEUT DIFFRACT 111+ - 6B	
Total	2.5-2	1.5+0	IFU	Expt	Prog YFI - 11 59	70 Vertebny+ ABST,OXIDE,TBL SIG AT 28ES	+
					Prog INDC(CCP) - 31	Dec 72 .PAGE 58,ENGLISH OF YFI - 11 59	
	2.5-2	1.5+0			Data EXFOR40090.005	Jan 72 SIG TOT AT 27 EN.	
Total	2.5-2	7.0-1	IFU	Expt	Conf 70Helsinki 1 651	Jun 70 Vertebnij+87. SIG(E) GRAPH+2200M/SEC	
					Rept BNL - TR - 495	Jul 72 . ENGLISH OF 70HELSIN 1 651	
Total	1.0-3	1.5+7	AUA	Eval	Data AUSTR - DFN 181.	Nov 71 COOK+POINT(223)+GROUP(127)SIG.CF EVL	+
Total	1.0+0	1.6+4	COL	Expt	Jour PR/C 11 462	Feb 75 Liou+ANAL.FOR RES,STF,AVG D.TABLES.	
	1.0+0	1.0+4			Conf 75Wash. 780	Mar 75 Hacken+12ELEMENT RVW.RES PAR SUMMARY	
Total	1.4+7		LIN	Expt	Conf 75Kiev 4 140	May 75 Djumin+ SIG GIVEN.OPTMOD ANAL,RADIUS	
Elastic	1.0-1		ORL	Expt	Jour PR 174 1553	Oct 68 Child+ COHERENT SCAT AMPLITUDE	
Elastic	2.0-2	2.0+0	IFU	Expt	Rept IF - 69 5	69 Vertebny+ SIG(E) GRAPH,SCAT AMPLITUD	

66 Dysprosium 162

Quantity	Energy (ev) Min	Max	Lab	Type	Documentation Ref Vol Page	Date	Author, Comments	Data
Elastic	1.0-3	1.5+7	AUA Eval	Data	AUSTR-DFN 181.	Nov 71	COOK+POINT(223)+GROUP(127)SIG.CF EVL	+
Elastic	2.5-2		IJI Eval	Conf	75Kiev 1 169	May 75	Fedorova+ EVAL 2200M/S SIG,TABLE	
Diff Elastic	9.8+5		SHE Theo	Jour	NP 54 417	Jun 64	Maddison.OPTMOD FIT TO TOWLE GILBOY	
Potntal Scat	None		BNL Expt	Jour	PR/C 1 1850	May 70	Chrien+ SCAT RADINS FROM ANAL OF RES	
				Jour	PL/B 24 573	May 67	.SUPERSEDED	
Tot Inelastc	5.0+5	1.5+7	AUA Eval	Data	AUSTR-DFN 181.	Nov 71	COOK+POINT(11)+GROUP(127)SIG.CF EVL	+
Thermal Scat	2.5-2	1.5+0	IFU Expt	Prog	YFI-11 59	70	Vertebny+ OXIDE,TOTSCAT,TBL 2200M/S	
				Prog	INDC(CCP)-31	Dec 72	.PAGE 58,ENGLISH OF YFI-11 59	
Scattering	2.5-2	3.0+0	IFU Expt	Prog	YFI-6 108	68	Vertebnyj+. TABLE SIG(E).TBP UFZ	
				Rept	INDC-260E	69	. ENGL OF YFI-6 108	
Scattering	2.0-2	3.0-2	IFU Expt	Conf	70Helsinki 1 651	Jun 70	Vertebnij+ 2200M/SEC SIGMA GIVEN,TBL	
	2.0-2	3.0-1		Rept	BNL-TR-495	Jul 72	. ENGLISH OF 70HELSIN 1 651	
Scattering	2.5-2	1.5+0	IFU Expt	Conf	70Helsinki 1 651	Jun 70	Vertebnij+87. SIG(E) GRAPH+2200M/SEC	
				Rept	BNL-TR-495	Jul 72	. ENGLISH OF 70HELSIN 1 651	
Scattering	Maxwl		IFU Expt	Prog	YFI-11 59	Dec 71	Vertebny+	+
	Maxwl			Data	EXFOR40090.006	Jan 72	THERMAL SCATTERING CS.	
Nonelastic	1.0-3	1.5+7	AUA Eval	Data	AUSTR-DFN 181.	Nov 71	COOK+POINT(223)+GROUP(127)SIG.CF EVL	+
Absorption	Maxwl	Pile	SGA Expt	Jour	JMS 6 435	71	Dobrozemsky+ CHANGE OF ABUND.TBL SIG	+
				Rept	SGAE-PH-104	71	- + MASS-SPEC METHOD	
				Rept	AEC-TR-7574	74	- + ENGLISH OF JMS 6 435	
	2.5-2			Data	EXFOR20637.014	Sep 76	1PNT.SIGMA.	
Absorption	Maxwl		IFU Expt	Prog	YFI-11 59	Dec 71	Vertebny+	+
	Maxwl			Data	EXFOR40090.007	Jan 72	THERMAL ABSORPTION CS.	
Absorption	2.5-2		IJI Eval	Conf	75Kiev 1 169	May 75	Fedorova+ EVAL 2200M/S SIG,TABLE	
Res Int Abs	None		CRC Eval	Rept	AECL-1054	Mar 60	Walker.(CRP-913) REDUCED RES.INT.	
Res Int Abs	+3	+5	BOL Theo	Conf	61Vienna 1 179	Aug 61	Benzi+.PPR11,VAL GVN,L=0,L=1 .CAPT.	
Res Int Abs	5.0-1		MTR Expt	Jour	NSE 25 12	May 66	Scoville. 3324+ - 400B	+
				Jour	ANS 7 85	Jun 64	.SUPERSEDED	
	5.0-1			Data	EXFOR12101.009	Jun 76	. 1 PT.	
Res Int Abs	5.0-1		BOL Eval	Rept	RT/FI-4	Jan 67	Palmucci. CALC FROM (N,G) RES PARAMS	
Res Int Abs	5.0-1		MTR Expt	Rept	IN-1195	May 68	Scoville.	+
Res Int Abs	5.5-1		SGA Expt	Jour	JMS 6 435	71	Dobrozemsky+ EFF ABS RES INT GIVEN.	+
				Prog	SGAE-PH-104	71	- +MASS-SPECTROMETRIC	
				Rept	AEC-TR-7574	74	. ENGLISH OF JMS 6 415	
	5.5-1			Data	EXFOR20637.015	Sep 76	1PNT.	
Res Int Abs	5.5-1		CRC Eval	Rept	AECL-3037 1	Jan 72	Walker.REDUCD INTEG FROM RESPARS,TBL	
Res Int Abs	5.0-1		AUA Eval	Rept	AAEC/TM-619	Sep 72	Clayton.CALC FROM SIG LIBRARY,TABLE	
Res Int Abs	+0	+5	WIN Revw	Conf	IAEA-169 3 163	74	Pope+ DATA FILE CALC CFD XPTAL VALUE	
Res Int Abs	5.0-1		IJI Eval	Conf	75Kiev 1 169	May 75	Fedorova+ EVAL+CALC RI GIVEN,TABLE	
(n,γ)	Maxwl		MCM Expt	Priv	WALKER	May 56	Walker.	+
	Maxwl			Data	EXFOR12127.018	Jun 76	. 1 PT.	
(n,γ)	Maxwl		CRC Eval	Rept	AECL-1054	Mar 60	Walker. (CRRP-913)	
(n,γ)	Maxwl	1.0+0	CCP Expt	Jour	AE 16 56	Jan 64	Danelian+.TOF CURVE GIVEN	+
				Jour	EAF 16 1 81	Jan 64	- +. FRENCH.	
				Jour	SJA 16 58	64	- +. ENGLISH	
(n,γ)	Maxwl		CCP Expt	Jour	IZV 29 2168	Dec 65	Bondarenko+.SIG GIVN.ENGL BAS29 2004	
(n,γ)	1.0+3	1.0+4	LAS Theo	Rept	LA-3463	Jan 66	Bell. TH CAPTURE OF RARE EARTHS	
(n,γ)	Maxwl		MTR Expt	Jour	NSE 25 12	May 66	Scoville. 152+ - 27 B	+
	Maxwl			Data	EXFOR12101.008	Jun 76	. 1 PT.	
(n,γ)	2.9+4	1.6+5	FEI Expt	Conf	66Paris 1 469	Oct 66	Kononov+ TOF,SCIN TANK,PLSD C-W,GRPH	+
				Conf	66Moscow	Feb 66	.SAME EXPT,GRAPHS	
				Prog	ICD-3 108	66	.ABSTRACT.GRAPH,COMPARED OTHER DATA	
				Prog	INDSWG-152 108	66	.ENGLISH TRANSL OF ICD-3	
	2.9+4	1.7+5		Data	EXFOR40076.009	Jul 71	SIG AT 21 ENERGIES FROM PRIV COMMUN	
(n,γ)	2.5-2		BOL Eval	Rept	RT/FI-4	Jan 67	Palmucci. CALC FROM RES PARAMETERS	
(n,γ)	5.0+3	1.0+5	AUA ExTh	Rept	AAEC/E-198	May 69	Musgrove.S+P+D WAVE SIGMAS CALC,TBL	+
(n,γ)	1.0+3	1.0+7	BOL Eval	Rept	CCDN-NW/10	Dec 69	Benzi+H-F MOD,AXEL G(G)EST,ALL DATA	
				Rept	CEC(70)-2	Apr 70	- +. GRAPH	
				Conf	66Paris 1 537	Oct 66	- + STATMOD.TBL AV VALS.SUPERSEDD	
(n,γ)	2.5-2	1.5+0	IFU Expt	Prog	YFI-11 59	70	Vertebny+ ABST,TBL 2200M/S VALUES	
				Prog	INDC(CCP)-31	Dec 72	.PAGE 58,ENGLISH OF YFI-11 59	
(n,γ)	2.5-2		IFU Expt	Conf	70Helsinki 1 651	Jun 70	Vertebnij+87. SIGMA GIVEN	
				Rept	BNL-TR-495	Jul 72	. ENGLISH OF 70HELSIN 1 651	
(n,γ)	3.0+4		AUA Theo	Rept	AAEC/E-211	Nov 70	Musgrove. SIGMA GIVEN AND CFD OTHER	
(n,γ)	1.0-3	1.5+7	AUA Eval	Data	AUSTR-DFN 181.	Nov 71	COOK+POINT(223)+GROUP(127)SIG.CF EVL	+
(n,γ)	Maxwl		CRC Eval	Rept	AECL-3037 1	Jan 72	Walker.RECOMMENDED SIG,DETAILED TBL	
(n,γ)	2.5-2		AUA Eval	Rept	AAEC/TM-619	Sep 72	Clayton.CALC FROM SIG LIBRARY,TABLE	

66 Dysprosium 162

Quantity	Energy (ev) Min	Max	Lab	Type	Documentation Ref Vol Page	Author, Comments Date	Data
(n,γ)	Maxwl	Fiss	WIN	Revw Conf	IAEA – 169 3 163	74 Pope+ MAXW+FIS – SPEC AVG DATA CFD XPT	
	Fiss			Conf	IAEA – 169 3 137	74 Dean. POINT DATA AVG OVER STAND SPEC	
(n,γ)	1.0+3	1.0+7	FEI	Eval Rept	YK – 8/2 97	Sep 72 Abagjan+ AVG SIG(ENERGY – GROUPS),TABL	
				Rept	INDC(CCP) – 39	Jul 74 .P102. ENGLISH OF YK – 8/2 97	
(n,γ)	Maxwl	2.0+1	BNL	Revw Conf	74Petten 247	Sep 74 Chrien+DIRECT CAPTURE COMP. GRPH.	
(n,γ)	2.5 – 2		BNL	Expt Conf	74Petten 271	Sep 74 Cole+ DIRECT CAPT.COMP. GRPH+TBL	
	2.5 – 2	7.0+1		Conf	72Budapest 226	Aug 72 – + SEARCH.NONSTATIST.EFFECTS,NDG	
(n,γ)	Maxwl		KAP	Expt Abst	BAP 3 337	Aug 58 House+ PILE OSC,SIG = 240+ – 30B	+
	Maxwl			Data	EXFOR12082.004	Jun 76 . 1 PT.	
Spect (n,γ)	5.5+0		JAE	Expt Rept	JAERI – 1073	Mar 65 Kawarasaki. RES CAPT.LINAC.TOF.E,INT	+
				Rept	INDSWG – 90 6	Jul 65 – . TABLE E,INTS GIVEN.	
	5.5+0			Data	EXFOR20277.013	Jun 74 5PTS.	
Spect (n,γ)	Pile		MUN	Expt Jour	ZN/A 21 1328	Sep 66 Neumann. CRYST SPEC EXPT OF GAM INT	
				Rept	ANL – TRANS – 941	73 . ENGLISH OF ZN/A 1328	
Spect (n,γ)	Maxwl		RIS	Expt Jour	PR 154 1146	Feb 67 Schult+.CRV – XTL,GS 38KEV TO 1 MEV	+
				Conf	65Antwerp 518	Jul 65 – + PPR57. ABST. LVL SPINS.	
Spect (n,γ)	None		ORL	Theo Jour	NSE 36 220	May 69 Yost+ CALCULAT BY GAMMA CASCADE MDL	
Spect (n,γ)	Maxwl		IFL	Expt Book	PROKOFJEV	73 . TBL GAM,CONV ELECTR ES+INT,LVL SCH	
Spect (n,γ)	Maxwl	1.0+2	BNL	Revw Conf	74Petten 247	Sep 74 Chrien+DIRECT CAPTURE COMP. GRPH.	
Inelastic γ	+0	+7	CCP	Expt Conf	75Leningrd 121	Jan 75 Avchukhov+ ABST,ES + INTENSIT,TBL	+
	Fast			Data	EXFOR40316.002	Oct 75 .GAM/100N FOR 57 GAM – E AT 90 DEG GVN	
(n,2n)	Fiss		CRC	Eval Rept	CRC – 1003	Dec 60 ROY+ ESTIMATED AVG SIG = 3.0MB	
(n,2n)	1.3+7	1.5+7	BNL	Theo Jour	NSE 23 238	Nov 65 Pearlstein.3ES.STAT MDL CALC.TBL CS.	
(n,2n)	Fiss		BNL	Theo Jour	NSE 23 238	Nov 65 Pearlstein.STATMDL CALC.SPEC AVG.TBL	
(n,2n)	1.5+7		DEB	Eval Jour	REA 11 1 153	Mar 73 Boedy+ RECOMM.VALUE FROM N – Z SYSTEM.	
(n,2n)	1.5+7		KFI	Theo Rept	KFKI – 73 – 68	Dec 73 Jeki.NEW FIT,CALC SIG CFD OTHERS,TBL	
(n,xn) x>2	Fiss		BNL	Theo Jour	NSE 23 238	Nov 65 Pearlstein.SPEC AVG STATMDL CALC N3N	
(n,p)	Fiss		CRC	Eval Rept	CRC – 1003	Dec 60 ROY+ ESTIMATED AVG SIG = 0.006MB	
(n,p)	1.5+7		SAH	Expt Prog	AEET – 267 50	Aug 66 Gujrathi+DECAY TB – 162,LEVELS DY – 162	
(n,p)	1.4+7	1.5+7	ARK	ExTh Prog	ORO – 3235 – 29	Jan 67 Koch+ STAT MODEL CALC CFD EXPTS	
(n,p)	1.4+7		LYO	Comp Rept	LYCEN/6780	Nov 67 Crouzet+COMPILATN FOR ACTIVTN ANALYS	
(n,p)	1.4+7	1.5+7	JYV	Eval Rept	JU – RR – 3/1970	Jun 70 Leppaemaeki+ TABLE OF EVAL AVG SIG	
(n,p)	1.5+7		JUL	Expt Jour	RRL 25 335	May 76 Qaim+ ACTIV,GELI.CFD OTHERS,TBL+GRPH	+
	1.5+7			Data	EXFOR20716.011	Jun 77 1PNT.SIGMA.	
(n,p)	1.4+7		GIT	Expt Abst	BAP 13 1699	Dec 68 OMS+ ACT, REL FE56 NP	+
	1.4+7			Data	EXFOR12131.004	Jun 76 . 1 PT.	
(n,α)	1.4+7		ALD	Expt Jour	PPS 73 215	Feb 59 Coleman+. ACTIVATION	+
(n,α)	Fiss		CRC	Eval Rept	CRC – 1003	Dec 60 ROY+ ESTIMATED AVG SIG = BELO 0.0001MB	
(n,α)	1.4+7		CIS	Theo Jour	NP 51 460	Feb 64 Facchini+STATMOD SIG XPT/CALC210 – 265	
(n,α)	1.4+7		LYO	Comp Rept	LYCEN/6780	Nov 67 Crouzet+COMPILATN FOR ACTIVTN ANALYS	
(n,α)	1.5+7		DEB	Comp Jour	REA 7 4 93	Dec 69 Csikai+ SIG+HL COMPILTN,N – ACTIV – ANAL	
(n,α)	1.4+7	1.5+7	JYV	Eval Rept	JU – RR – 3/1970	Jun 70 Leppaemaeki+ TABLE OF EVAL AVG SIG	
(n,α)	1.4+7		IBJ	Expt Prog	INR – 1318 16	Apr 71 Jaskola+ ALFA SPCTR CFD TH,SMALL RPT	+
				Rept	INR – 1197 3	May 70 SEE ALSO *THEO,ALFA CLUSTRNG	
	1.4+7			Data	EXFOR30158.027	Jul 72 INTEGRATED CROSS SECTION,1 DATA LINE	
	1.4+7			Data	EXFOR30158.014	Jul 72 29 DATA LINES (ALPHA SPECTRUM)	
(n,α)	1.5+7		ARK	Expt Abst	DA/B 32 5091	Mar 72 Bari. GE(LI) DET. ACT. SIG GIVEN	+
	1.5+7			Data	EXFOR10431.027	Aug 75 1PT,SIGMA	
	1.8+7		IBJ	Expt Prog	INR – 1401 13	May 72 Glowacka+ E DISTRBT OF ALPHAS,TABLE	+
				Rept	INR – 1468/I/PLA	73 – + ALFA E – SPEC,GRAPH.	
				Conf	72Budapest 16	Aug 72 . ALFA – SPEC CFD KNOCK – ON TH,GRAPH	
				Rept	INR – 1401 22	May 72 * ALPHA SPCTR AT 1 ANGL	
	1.8+7			Data	EXFOR30172.	Aug 72 DISTRBT OF ALF(28 DATA)+SIG AT 1 ANG	
(n,α)	1.4+7		WWA	Theo Conf	72Budapest 18	Aug 72 Glowacka+ KNOCK ON,SPEC CFD XPT,GRPH	
				Jour	NP/A 187 177	May 72 Kozlowski+. 30DEG E – SPEC.KNOCK – ON OK	
Reson Params	1.0+4	2.0+6	FEI	ExTh Jour	YF 5 129	Jan 67 Kononov.Lσ2 N CAPTURE,TBL,CURVES GVN	+
				Jour	SNP 5 89	Jul 67 TRANSLATN.*	
Reson Params	+0	+3	IFU	Expt Conf	67Kharkov 171	Feb 67 Vertebny.TRANSMISSION EXPT	
Reson Params		1.0+6	AUA	Theo Jour	AUJ 20 477	Oct 67 Cook. TBL OF AVG LVL SPACING D,L=0,1	
Reson Params	None		IFU	Expt Jour	UFZ 13 679	Apr 68 Vertebnyi+ OTHER D VAL GVN	
				Jour	UPJ 13 477	Oct 68 TRANSLATN.*	
Reson Params	–		IFU	Expt Jour	UFZ 13 2085	Dec 68 Vertebnyj+ OTHER EXPTL+TH D VAL GVN	
				Jour	UPJ 13 1492	Jun 69 TRANSLATN.*	
Reson Params	5.4+0	8.6+2	BNL	Expt Jour	PR/C 1 1850	May 70 Chrien+,TRANS,WN WG AVG D FOR 14RES	+
Reson Params	–		AUA	Theo Rept	AAEC/E – 211	Nov 70 Musgrove. CALCULTD D+GAM WIDTH GIVEN	
Reson Params	5.4+0		CJD	Eval Rept	YK – 7	71 Zakharova+ SURVEY+SYSTEMATICS,GW,TBL	
				Rept	INDC(CCP) – 27	Nov 72 .ENGLISH TRANSLATION OF YK – 7 /71	
Reson Params	1.0+0	2.0+1	BNL	Expt Jour	ZN/A 26 334	Mar 71 Brunhart+ SPINS OF 2 RESON DY 163	

66 Dysprosium 162

Quantity	Energy (ev) Min	Max	Lab	Type	Documentation Ref Vol Page	Date	Author, Comments	Data
Reson Params	5.4+0	2.7+2	BNL	Expt	Prog USNDC-3 26	Oct 72	Cole+9WN AND WG FOR 3 RESON GIVEN	
Reson Params	+0	+2	BOL	Eval	Conf IAEA-169 3 123	74	Benzi+ AVG G-WID CFD OTHERS+XPT,TABL	
Reson Params	+0	+2	FEI	Eval	Rept YK-8/2 97	Sep 72	Abagyan+ AVG G-WID+D AT BINDNG-E,TBL	
					Rept INDC(CCP)-39	Jul 74	.PAGE 102.ENGLISH OF YK-8/2 97	
Reson Params	5.5+0	1.6+4	COL	Expt	Jour PR/C 11 462	Feb 75	Liou+TABLE E0,WN09STF,AVG D,WG.	+
					Conf 75Wash. 780	Mar 75	Hacken+12 ELEMENT RES PAR RVW.TBL	
					Data EXFOR10525.	Mar 76	. 159 PTS. WN RED,WG,D GVN.	
Reson Params	5.4+0	6.5+0	BNL	Expt	Abst BAP 2 42	Jan 57	Zimmerman.FC WG=174+-45 WN=21+-7MV	+
	5.4+0	6.5+0			Data EXFOR11438.003	Jun 76	. 4 RES, E0,WN,WG	
Strnth Fnctn	+3	+5	BOL	Theo	Conf 61Vienna 1 179	Aug 61	Benzi+.PPR11,TABLE CFD EXPERIMENT	
Strnth Fnctn	1.0+4	2.0+6	FEI	ExTh	Jour YF 5 129	Jan 67	Kononov.Lσ2 N CAPTURE,TBL,CURVES GVN	+
					Jour SNP 5 89	Jul 67	TRANSLATN.*	
	1.0+4	2.0+6		Expt	Data EXFOR40013.003	Mar 73	.VALUE GIVEN	
Strnth Fnctn	+0	+2	BNL	Expt	Jour PR/C 1 1850	May 70	Chrien+ TRANS,S0=2.3+-0.5 FROM RES	+
					Jour PL/B 24 573	May 67	.SUPERSEDED	
					Conf 65Antwerp 69	Jul 65	.SUPERSEDED	
Strnth Fnctn	–		AUA	Theo	Rept AAEC/E-211	Nov 70	Musgrove. SMOOTHED S0,S1 AND S2 GIVN	
Strnth Fnctn	None		AUA	Eval	Rept AAEC/E-277	Mar 73	Musgrove.TBLS EXPTL DATA+BEST VALUES	
Strnth Fnctn	5.5+0	1.6+4	COL	Expt	Jour PR/C 11 462	Feb 75	Liou+S0(135LVLS)S1(7LVLS).TBL CFD	+
					Conf 75Wash. 780	Mar 75	Hacken+12 ELEMENT RVW. TBL	
	5.5+0	1.6+4			Data EXFOR10525.	Mar 76	.2PTS.S0=(1.88+-.25)-4S1=(1.1+-.4)-4	
Lvl Density	+6		MIL	Theo	Jour EN 15 1 54	Jan 68	Facchini+ LDL PARS FROM LOW EN RES	
Lvl Density	None		CCP	Theo	Jour YF 11 1028	May 70	Rubchenya. DENSITY+A+TEMP GIVEN	
					Jour SNP 11 571	Nov 70	. ENGL OF YF 11 571.	
Lvl Density	None		AUW	Theo	Conf 70Madurai 2 267	Dec 70	Ramamurty+ A-PARAMETER GVN,LANG'S-TH	
Lvl Density	None		CCP	Theo	Jour YF 13 43	Jan 71	Bravin+.DEFORM PAR,CALC,TBL,CFD EXPT	
Lvl Density	1.4+7		IBJ	Expt	Prog INR-1318 16	Apr 71	Jaskola+ ALFA SPCTR CFD TH,SMALL RPT	+
	1.4+7				Data EXFOR30158.015	Mar 71	LEVEL DENSITY PARAMETER OF GD159 GIV	
Lvl Density	None		MUN	Theo	Jour NP/A 217 269	Dec 73	Dilg+ A,DELTA. BACK SHIFTED FERMIGAS	
Lvl Density	None		BOL	Eval	Conf IAEA-169 3 123	74	Benzi+ LVL DENS PARAM BY XPT,GRPH+TB	
Lvl Density	None		COP	Theo	Jour NP/A 222 493	Apr 74	Dossing+COLL ROTAT.SPAC. ACCUR ESTIM	
Lvl Density	None		ROC	Theo	Jour NP/A 223 589	May 74	Huizenga+ EXP CFD MICROSC TH AX SYMM	
Lvl Density	+0	+2	FEI	Eval	Rept YK-8/2 97	Sep 72	Abagyan+ LVL DENSITY PARAMETER,TBL	
					Rept INDC(CCP)-39	Jul 74	.PAGE 102.ENGLISH OF YK-8/2 97	
Lvl Density	+0		DUB	Theo	Conf 75Kiev 3 23	May 75	Voronov. LVL SPACING OF DY163.TABLE	
	None				Jour NP/A 224 396	May 74	Malov+ 1/2 MICROSC.MODEL. DEFORM NUC	
	8.2+6				Conf 73Munich 1 246	Aug 73	- + SUPERFLUID MDL,TABLE D VS E.	

66 Dysprosium 163

Quantity	Energy (ev) Min	Max	Lab	Type	Documentation Ref Vol Page	Date	Author, Comments	Data
Evaluation	1.0-3	1.5+7	AUA	Eval	Rept AAEC/TM-549	Jun 70	Cook.TOT,EL,INEL,NONEL,CAPT SIGS,NDG	+
					Rept AAEC/E-214	Jun 71	Bertram+GROUP SIGMAS SAME QUANTS.NDG	
					Rept AAEC/TM-587	Mar 71	*DESCRIPTION OF LIBRARY	
	1.0-3	1.5+7			Data AUSTR-DFN 182.	Nov 71	POINT(223) AND GROUP(127) SIGMAS	
Total	2.5-2		KAP	Expt	Abst BAP 3 337	Aug 58	Rayburn.	+
Total	1.0-1		ORL	Expt	Jour PR 174 1553	Oct 68	Child+ FROM NEUT DIFFRACT 85.9+-8B	
Total	2.5-2	1.5+0	IFU	Expt	Prog YFI-11 59	70	Vertebny+. ABST,OXIDE,TBL SIG AT 28ES	+
					Prog INDC(CCP)-31	Dec 72	.PAGE 58,ENGLISH OF YFI-11 59	
	2.5-2	1.5+0			Data EXFOR40090.008	Jan 72	SIG TOT AT 27 EN.	
Total	2.5-2	7.0-1	IFU	Expt	Conf 70Helsinki 1 651	Jun 70	Vertebnij+87. SIG(E) GRAPH+2200M/SEC	
					Rept BNL-TR-495	Jul 72	. ENGL OF 70HELSIN 1 651	
Total	1.0-3	1.5+7	AUA	Eval	Data AUSTR-DFN 182.	Nov 71	COOK+POINT(223)+GROUP(127)SIG.CF EVL	+
Total	1.0+0	1.0+4	COL	Expt	Jour PR/C 11 462	Feb 75	Liou+ANAL.FOR RES,STF,AVG D.TABLES.	
					Conf 75Wash. 780	Mar 75	Hacken+12ELEMENT RVW.RES PAR SUMMARY	
Total	1.4+7		LIN	Expt	Conf 75Kiev 4 140	May 75	Djumin+ SIG GIVEN.OPTMOD ANAL,RADIUS	
Elastic	1.0-1		ORL	Expt	Jour PR 174 1553	Oct 68	Child+ COHERENT SCAT AMPLITUDE	
Elastic	1.0-3	1.5+7	AUA	Eval	Data AUSTR-DFN 182.	Nov 71	COOK+POINT(223)+GROUP(127)SIG.CF EVL	+
Elastic	2.5-2		IJI	Eval	Conf 75Kiev 1 169	May 75	Fedorova+ EVAL 2200M/S SIG,TABLE	
Potntal Scat	None		BNL	Expt	Jour PR/C 1 1850	May 70	Chrien+ SCAT RADINS FROM ANAL OF RES	
					Jour PL/B 24 573	May 67	.SUPERSEDED	
Tot Inelastc	5.0+5	1.5+7	AUA	Eval	Data AUSTR-DFN 182.	Nov 71	COOK+POINT(11)+GROUP(127)SIG.CF EVL	+
Thermal Scat	2.5-2	1.5+0	IFU	Expt	Prog YFI-11 59	70	Vertebny+ OXIDE,TOTSCAT,TBL 2200M/S	
					Prog INDC(CCP)-31	Dec 72	.PAGE 58,ENGLISH OF YFI-11 59	
Scattering	2.5-2	1.2+0	IFU	Expt	Prog YFI-6 108	68	Vertebnyj+. TABLE SIG(E).TBP UFZ	
					Rept INDC-260E	69	. ENGL OF YFI-6 108	

Quantity	Energy (ev) Min	Energy (ev) Max	Lab	Type	Documentation Ref Vol Page	Author, Comments Date	Data
Scattering	2.0−2	3.0−2	IFU	Expt	Conf 70Helsinki 1 651	Jun 70 Vertebnij+ 2200M/SEC SIGMA GIVEN,TBL	
					Rept BNL−TR−495	Jul 72 . ENGLISH OF 70HELSIN 1 651	
Scattering	2.5−2	1.1+0	IFU	Expt	Conf 70Helsinki 1 651	Jun 70 Vertebnij+87. SIG(E) GRAPH+2200M/SEC	
					Rept BNL−TR−495	Jul 72 . ENGLISH OF 70HELSIN 1 651	
Scattering	Maxwl		IFU	Expt	Prog YFI−11 59	Dec 71 Vertebny+	+
	Maxwl				Data EXFOR40090.009	Jan 72 THERMAL SCATTERING CS.	
Nonelastic	1.0−3	1.5+7	AUA	Eval	Data AUSTR−DFN 182.	Nov 71 COOK+POINT(223)+GROUP(127)SIG.CF EVL	+
Absorption	Maxwl	Pile	SGA	Expt	Jour JMS 6 435	71 Dobrozemsky+ CHANGE OF ABUND.TBL SIG	+
					Rept SGAE−PH−104	71 − + MASS−SPEC METHOD	
					Rept AEC−TR−7574	74 − + ENGLISH OF JMS 6 435	
	2.5−2				Data EXFOR20637.016	Sep 76 1PNT.SIGMA.	
Absorption	Maxwl		IFU	Expt	Prog YFI−11 59	Dec 71 Vertebny+	+
	Maxwl				Data EXFOR40090.010	Jan 72 THERMAL ABSORPTION CS.	
Absorption	2.5−2		IJI	Eval	Conf 75Kiev 1 169	May 75 Fedorova+ EVAL 2200M/S SIG,TABLE	
Res Int Abs	None		CRC	Eval	Rept AECL−1054	Mar 60 Walker.(CRP−913) REDUCED RES.INT.	
Res Int Abs	+3	+5	BOL	Theo	Conf 61Vienna 1 179	Aug 61 Benzi+.PPR11,VAL GVN,L=0,L=1 .CAPT.	
Res Int Abs	5.0−1		MTR	Expt	Jour NSE 25 12	May 66 Scoville. 1962+ −176B	+
					Jour ANS 7 85	Jun 64 .SUPERSEDED	
	5.0−1				Data EXFOR12101.011	Jun 76 . 1 PT.	
Res Int Abs	5.0−1		BOL	Eval	Rept RT/FI−4	Jan 67 Palmucci. CALC FROM (N,G) RES PARAMS	
Res Int Abs	5.0−1		MTR	Expt	Rept IN− 1195	May 68 Scoville.	+
Res Int Abs	5.5−1		SGA	Expt	Jour JMS 6 435	71 Dobrozemsky+ EFF ABS RES INT GIVEN.	+
					Prog SGAE−PH−104	71 − +MASS−SPECTROMETRIC	
					Rept AEC−TR−7574	74 . ENGLISH OF JMS 6 415	
	5.5−1				Data EXFOR20637.017	Sep 76 1PNT.	
Res Int Abs	5.5−1		CRC	Eval	Rept AECL−3037 1	Jan 72 Walker.REDUCD INTEG FROM RESPARS,TBL	
Res Int Abs	5.0−1		AUA	Eval	Rept AAEC/TM−619	Sep 72 Clayton.CALC FROM SIG LIBRARY,TABLE	
Res Int Abs	+0	+5	WIN	Revw	Conf IAEA−169 3 163	74 Pope+ DATA FILE CALC CFD XPTAL VALUE	
Res Int Abs	5.0−1		IJI	Eval	Conf 75Kiev 1 169	May 75 Fedorova+ EVAL+CALC RI GIVEN,TABLE	
(n,γ)	Maxwl		MCM	Expt	Priv WALKER	May 56 Walker.	+
	Maxwl				Data EXFOR12127.019	Jun 76 . 1 PT.	
(n,γ)	Maxwl		CRC	Eval	Rept AECL−1054	Mar 60 Walker. (CRRP−913)	
(n,γ)	Maxwl		CCP	Eval	Jour IZV 29 2168	Dec 65 Bondarenko+.SIG GIVN.ENGL BAS29 2004	
(n,γ)	1.0+3	1.0+4	LAS	Theo	Rept LA− 3463	Jan 66 Bell. TH CAPTURE OF RARE EARTHS	
(n,γ)	Maxwl		MTR	Expt	Jour NSE 25 12	May 66 Scoville. 121+ −19 B	+
	Maxwl				Data EXFOR12101.010	Jun 76 . 1 PT.	
(n,γ)	2.9+4	1.5+5	FEI	Expt	Conf 66Paris 1 469	Oct 66 Kononov+ TOF,SCIN TANK,PLSD C−W,GRPH	+
					Conf 66Moscow	Feb 66 .SAME EXPT,GRAPHS	
					Prog ICD−3 108	66 .ABSTRACT.GRAPH,COMPARED OTHER DATA	
					Prog INDSWG−152 108	66 .ENGLISH TRANSL OF ICD−3	
	2.9+4	1.7+5			Data EXFOR40076.010	Jul 71 SIG AT 19 ENERGIES FROM PRIV COMMUN	
(n,γ)	2.5−2		BOL	Eval	Rept RT/FI−4	Jan 67 Palmucci. CALC FROM RES PARAMETERS	
(n,γ)	5.0+3	1.0+5	AUA	ExTh	Rept AAEC/E−198	May 69 Musgrove.S+P+D WAVE SIGMAS CALC,TBL	+
(n,γ)	1.0+3	1.0+7	BOL	Eval	Rept CCDN−NW/10	Dec 69 Benzi+H−F MOD,AXEL G(G)EST,ALL DATA	
					Rept CEC(70)−2	Apr 70 − +. GRAPH	
					Conf 61Vienna 1 179	Aug 61 − + TBL AV VALUES. SUPERSEDED.	
(n,γ)	2.5−2	1.5+0	IFU	Expt	Prog YFI−11 59	70 Vertebny+ ABST,TBL 2200M/S VALUES	
					Prog INDC(CCP)−31	Dec 72 .PAGE 58,ENGLISH OF YFI−11 59	
(n,γ)	2.5−2		IFU	Expt	Conf 70Helsinki 1 651	Jun 70 Vertebnij+87. SIGMA GIVEN	
					Rept BNL−TR−495	Jul 72 . ENGLISH OF 70HELSIN 1 651	
(n,γ)	3.0+4		AUA	Theo	Rept AAEC/E−211	Nov 70 Musgrove. SIGMA GIVEN AND CFD OTHER	
(n,γ)	1.0−3	1.5+7	AUA	Eval	Data AUSTR−DFN 182.	Nov 71 COOK+POINT(223)+GROUP(127)SIG.CF EVL	+
(n,γ)	Maxwl		CRC	Eval	Rept AECL−3037 1	Jan 72 Walker.RECOMMENDED SIG,DETAILED TBL	
(n,γ)	2.5−2		AUA	Eval	Rept AAEC/TM−619	Sep 72 Clayton.CALC FROM SIG LIBRARY,TABLE	
(n,γ)	Maxwl	Fiss	WIN	Revw	Conf IAEA−169 3 163	74 Pope+ MAXW+FIS−SPEC AVG DATA CFD XPT	
	Fiss				Conf IAEA−169 3 137	74 Dean. POINT DATA AVG OVER STAND SPEC	
(n,γ)	1.0+3	1.0+7	FEI	Eval	Rept YK−8/2 97	Sep 72 Abagjan+ AVG SIG(ENERGY−GROUPS),TABL	+
					Rept INDC(CCP)−39	Jul 74 .P102. ENGLISH OF YK−8/2 97	+
(n,γ)	Maxwl		KAP	Expt	Abst BAP 3 337	Aug 58 House+ PILE OSC,SIG=220+−50B	
	Maxwl				Data EXFOR12082.005	Jun 76 . 1 PT.	
Spect (n,γ)	1.7+0		YAL	Expt	Abst BAP 4 35	Jan 59 Springer+ NAI(TL),GAMMA MULTIPLICITY	
Spect (n,γ)	Maxwl		RIS	Expt	Jour ZP 180 298	Aug 64 Schult.BENT XTL,TBL OF GS,DY164−LVLS	
Spect (n,γ)	1.7+0		JAE	Expt	Rept JAERI−1073	Mar 65 Kawarasaki. RES CAPT.LINAC.TOF.E,INT	+
					Rept INDSWG−90 6	Jul 65 . TABLE E,INTS GIVEN.	
	1.7+0				Data EXFOR20277.014	Jun 74 10PTS.	
Spect (n,γ)	1.7+0		NRL	Expt	Jour NP 82 441	Jul 66 Vogt. AT RES, NAT TARGET	
Spect (n,γ)	Pile		MUN	Expt	Jour ZN/A 21 1328	Sep 66 Neumann. CRYST SPEC EXPT OF GAM INT	
					Rept ANL−TRANS−941	73 . ENGLISH OF ZN/A 1328	

66 Dysprosium 163

Quantity	Energy (ev) Min	Max	Lab	Type	Documentation Ref Vol Page	Date	Author, Comments	Data
Spect (n,γ)	Maxwl		LAS	Expt Jour	PR 152 1084	Dec 66	Hafemeister+ABSINT 15LINES5-7.6MEV	
Spect (n,γ)	None		MTR	Expt Prog	IN- 1218 123	Dec 68	Spencer+ GE-LI DET	
Spect (n,γ)	5.0+6	8.0+6	LAS	Expt Conf	69Erevan	Feb 69	Daneljan+ ABST,SPEC FOR PARTIC RES	
Spect (n,γ)	Pile		ANL	Expt Conf	69Studsvik 601	Aug 69	Smither+ NO DATA GVN,TB CFD STATMOD	
Spect (n,γ)	Maxwl	1.4+2	KUR	Expt Rept	ICD-6 47	Oct 69	Daneljan+ GAM-INTENS, 11RES,TABLE	
	8.0-2	1.5+2		Conf	69Studsvik 663	Aug 69	Danelyan+ THR+RES NEUTS,TBL G-INTENS	
Spect (n,γ)	1.6+1	2.0+2	KUR	Expt Jour	ZET 62 425	Feb 72	Daneljan+ 5GAMS, TBL INTENS AT 9 RES	
	1.7+0	2.0+2		Rept	IAE-2170	Dec 71	Daneljan+ GAM ES+INTENS AT 14RES,TBL	
	1.6+1	2.0+2		Jour	JET 35 227	Aug 72	Daneljan+ ENGLISH OF ZET 62 425	
				Rept	BNL-TR-490	72	.ENGLISH TRANS	
Spect (n,γ)	1.6+1	2.5+2	BNL	Expt Conf	72Budapest 214	Aug 72	Mughabghab+ G-RAY SPECTRA ,NDG	
	+1	+2		Prog	ORNL-TM-3808	Apr 72	Slaughter+ GE(LI) DET. NO DATA GIVN	
Spect (n,γ)	Maxwl		CTH	Expt Prog	EANDC(OR)115L	Jul 72	Larsson+, TO OBTAIN LEVEL STRUCTURE	
Spect (n,γ)	None		KUR	Expt Prog	INDC(SEC)-28	Sep 72	Danelyan+ NDG	
Spect (n,γ)	Maxwl		KFI	Expt Prog	KFKI-YB-72 31	May 73	Kardon+ VERY BRIEF,G-SPECT,G-WID,NDG	
Spect (n,γ)	None		LIE	Theo Jour	NP/A 222 525	Apr 74	Baudinet-Robinet.STAT CORR PART WID	
(n,2n)	Fiss		CRC	Eval Rept	CRC-1003	Dec 60	ROY+ ESTIMATED AVG SIG=40.0MB	
(n,2n)	1.3+7	1.5+7	BNL	Theo Jour	NSE 23 238	Nov 65	Pearlstein.3ES.STAT MDL CALC.TBL CS.	
(n,2n)	Fiss		BNL	Theo Jour	NSE 23 238	Nov 65	Pearlstein.STATMDL CALC.SPEC AVG.TBL	
(n,2n)	1.5+7		DEB	Eval Jour	REA 11 1 153	Mar 73	Boedy+ RECOMM.VALUE FROM N-Z SYSTEM.	
(n,2n)	1.5+7		KFI	Theo Rept	KFKI-73-68	Dec 73	Jeki.NEW FIT,CALC SIG CFD OTHERS,TBL	
(n,xn) x>2	Fiss		BNL	Theo Jour	NSE 23 238	Nov 65	Pearlstein.SPEC AVG STATMDL CALC N3N	
(n,p)	1.5+7		ARK	Expt Jour	PR 118 242	Apr 60	Wille. MEAS ACT SIG=3.0+ -1.0 MB	+
	1.5+7			Data	EXFOR12033.038	Jun 76	. 1 PT.	
(n,p)	Fiss		CRC	Eval Rept	CRC-1003	Dec 60	ROY+ ESTIMATED AVG SIG=0.007MB	
(n,p)	1.5+7		SAH	Comp Jour	NUC 23 8 112	Aug 65	Chatterjee. TABLE WITH REFS.	
	1.4+7			Jour	NP 60 273	Nov 64	- .MEAN OF EXPT CFD SHELLMOD	
(n,p)	1.4+7	1.5+7	ARK	Theo Prog	ORO-3235-29	Jan 67	Koch+ STAT MODEL CALC CFD EXPTS	
(n,p)			LYO	Comp Rept	LYCEN/6780	Nov 67	Crouzet+COMPILATN FOR ACTIVTN ANALYS	
(n,p)	1.5+7		DEB	Comp Jour	REA 7 4 93	Dec 69	Csikai+ SIG+HL COMPILTN,N-ACTIV-ANAL	
(n,p)	1.4+7	1.5+7	JYV	Eval Rept	JU-RR-3/1970	Jun 70	Leppaemaeki+ TABLE OF EVAL AVG SIG	
(n,p)	1.4+7	1.5+7	KAZ	Theo Jour	YF 18 705	Oct 73	Levkovsky.AVERAGED SIG,CALC,TBL	
				Jour	SNP 18 361	Apr 74	. ENGLISH OF YF 18,705	
(n,p)	1.5+7		JUL	Expt Jour	RRL 25 335	May 76	Qaim+ ACTIV,GELI.CFD OTHERS,TBL+GRPH	+
	1.5+7			Data	EXFOR20716.012	Jun 77	1PNT.SIGMA.	
(n,p)	1.4+7		GIT	Expt Abst	BAP 13 1699	Dec 68	OMS+ ACT, REL FE56 NP	+
	1.4+7			Data	EXFOR12131.005	Jun 76	. 1PT.	
(n,α)	Fiss		CRC	Eval Rept	CRC-1003	Dec 60	ROY+ ESTIMATED AVG SIG=0.0008MB	
(n,α)	Maxwl		CCP	Expt Jour	YF 1 252	Feb 65	Andreev.IONIZ-CHAMBER,SIG=M.02MB	+
				Jour	SNP 1 177	Aug 65	TRANSLATN.*	
(n,α)	1.4+7		IBJ	Expt Rept	INR-1268	Jan 71	Jaskola+ ALFA SPCTR CFD TH,FULL PAPR	+
				Rept	INR-1275	Jan 71	SEE ALSO * FULL INFORMATION	
				Jour	APPB 2 521	71	.SAME AS INR-1268	
	1.4+7			Data	EXFOR30158.016	Mar 71	NUM DATA NOT AVAILBL,SEE GRAF IN REF	
(n,α)	1.4+7	1.5+7	CIS	Theo Jour	NP/A 210 297	Aug 73	Milazzo-Colli+ ALPHA E-DISTN CFD XPT	
	1.4+7			Jour	PL/B 38 155	Feb 72	Colli-Milazzo+ A-SPECT CALC CFD EXPT	
(n,α)	1.8+7		IBJ	Expt Prog	INDC(SEC)-42	Dec 74	Glowacka+ TBL DIFFSIG,GRPH E+ANG-DIS	+
	1.8+7			Data	EXFOR30299.	Jul 75	DOUBLE DIFFSIG(35 PTS)+ANGDIST(1 PT)	
Reson Params	1.7+0		BNL	Expt Abst	BAP 7 305	Apr 62	Brunhart+ABST.K16. 1RES J=2	
	1.7+0			Data	EXFOR11470.003	Jun 76	. 1 RES, J	
Reson Params	-.5+0	1.0+0	CCP	Expt Jour	AE 16 56	Jan 64	Danelian+.PARITY FOR NEG E RES GIVEN	+
				Jour	EAF 16 1 81		64 . FRENCH	
				Jour	SJA 16 58		64 . ENGLISH	
Reson Params	1.7+0		MOL	Expt Jour	NP 62 641	Feb 65	Ceulemans+J=2 FROM GAMMA(N)/GAMMA	
	1.7+0			Data	EXFOR20208.	May 74	2PTS.J,WN/WT.	
Reson Params	-.5+0	1.7+0	IFU	Revw Rept	ICD-4 7	67	Vertebnyj.ANAL+REVW OF RES PARAMS	
Reson Params	1.7+0		WUR	Expt Rept	EIR-123	Jul 67	Brunner+.SHAPE ANAL CFD OTHER EXPTS	+
				Conf	66Paris 1 61	Oct 66	- + PPR 20. PRELIM DATA.	
Reson Params		1.0+6	AUA	Theo Jour	AUJ 20 477	Oct 67	Cook. TBL OF AVG LVL SPACING D,L=0,1	
Reson Params	-		IFU	Expt Jour	UFZ 13 2085	Dec 68	Vertebnyj+ OTHER EXPTL+TH D VAL GVN	
				Jour	UPJ 13 1492	Jun 69	TRANSLATN.*	
Reson Params	1.6+1	1.4+2	KUR	Expt Conf	69Studsvik 663	Aug 69	Danelyan+ TBL OF J VALUES,10NEUT-RES	
Reson Params	1.7+0	2.2+2	BNL	Expt Jour	PR/C 1 1850	May 70	Chrien+ TRANS, WN WGAVG D FOR 14RES	+
Reson Params	-		AUA	Theo Rept	AAEC/E-211	Nov 70	Musgrove. CALCULTD D+GAM WIDTH GIVEN	
Reson Params	1.7+0		CJD	Eval Rept	YK-7	71	Zakharova+ SURVEY+SYSTEMATICS,GW,TBL	
				Rept	INDC(CCP)-27	Nov 72	.ENGLISH TRANSLATION OF YK-7 /71	

66 Dysprosium 163

Quantity	Energy (ev) Min	Max	Lab	Type	Documentation Ref Vol Page	Author, Comments Date	Data
Reson Params	1.6+1	2.0+2	KUR	Expt	Jour ZET 62 425	Feb 72 Daneljan+ N-WIDS 9 RESON,REL THR,TBL	
	1.7+0	2.0+2			Rept IAE-2170	Dec 71 Danelyan+ PARTIAL G-WID,DISTR CORREL	
	1.6+1	2.0+2			Jour JET 35 227	Aug 72 Daneljan+ ENGLISH OF ZET 62 425	
Reson Params	1.6+1	2.5+2	BNL	Expt	Conf 72Budapest 214	Aug 72 Mughabghab+ SPINS OF RESONANCES	+
					Prog ORNL-TM-3808	Apr 72 Slaughter+ GE(LI) DET. J FOR 29RES	
	1.7+0	2.9+2			Data EXFOR10118.002	Jul 71 . 8 PTS. EO,J.	
Reson Params	None		KUR	Expt	Prog INDC(SEC)-28	Sep 72 Daneljan+ CORR OF G-AND N-WIDTH,NDG	
Reson Params	+0	+3	KUR	Theo	Conf 73Kiev 2 301	May 73 Daneljan. CORREL N+G-WID+PARTL G-WID	
Reson Params	+0	+2	BOL	Eval	Conf IAEA-169 3 123	74 Benzi+ AVG G-WID CFD OTHERS+XPT,TABL	
Reson Params	None		LIE	Theo	Jour NP/A 222 525	Apr 74 Baudinet-Robinet.STAT CORR PART WID	
Reson Params	+0	+3	FEI	Eval	Rept YK-8/2 97	Sep 72 Abagyan+ AVG G-WID+D AT BINDNG-E,TBL	
					Rept INDC(CCP)-39	Jul 74 .PAGE 102.ENGLISH OF YK-8/2 97	
Reson Params	7.7+6		DUB	Theo	Conf 74Petten 175	Sep 74 Malov+ DOBS,SEMI-MICROSCOPIC CALC.	
Reson Params	+0		DUB	Theo	Jour YF 21 40	Jan 75 Voronov+ MEAN D,WITH ROTAT.CFD EXPT	
					Jour SNP 21 20	Jul 75 . ENGLISH OF YF 21,40	
Reson Params	1.7+0	1.0+3	COL	Expt	Jour PR/C 11 462	Feb 75 Liou+NEVIS.TBL,E0,GWN0,AVG WG,D,S0	+
					Conf 75Wash. 780	Mar 75 Hacken+12 ELEMENT RES PAR RVW.TBL	
	1.7+0	1.0+3			Data EXFOR10525.	Mar 76 . 154PTS.WN RED,WG,D GVN.	
Reson Params	1.7+0	3.2+2	DUB	Expt	Jour YF 22 3	Jul 75 Karzhavina+ SPINS+N-WIDS,TABLE	
	1.6+1	3.0+2			Rept JINR-P3-7980	May 74 - +SPINS,NEUTR WIDTHS,TABLE	
	1.6+1	6.6+1			Rept RCN-203 242	Dec 73 - + G MULTIPL.METH,J	
	7.7+0	6.6+2			Conf 73Kiev 2 337	May 73 Karzhavina+ SPIN-IDENT,G-MULTIP MTHD	
	7.7+0	6.6+1			Rept JINR-P3-6948	Feb 75 Karzhavina+ SPINS OF RESONANCES, TBL	
	1.7+0	3.2+2			Jour SNP 22 1	Jul 75 .ENGL OF YF 22 3	
Reson Params	1.7+0	2.2+2	BNL	Expt	Abst BAP 2 42	Jan 57 Zimmerman+FC WG=103+-10 WN=1.48+-.12	+
	1.7+0	2.2+2			Data EXFOR11438.004	Jun 76 . 17 RES, E0,WN,WG	
Reson Params	Maxwl		KUK	Theo	Conf 76Ahmedabd 2 1	Dec 76 Sharma+AVG S-WAVE REDUCED N-WID ANAL	
Strnth Fnctn	+3		BNL	Expt	Jour PRL 1 461	Dec 58 Hughes. FC 1.45+-0.3	
	+3	+5	BOL	Theo	Conf 61Vienna 1 179	Aug 61 Benzi+.PPR11,TABLE CFD EXPERIMENT	
	+0	+2	BNL	Expt	Jour PR/C 1 1850	May 70 Chrien+,TRANS,SO=1.7+-0.2 FROM RES	+
	+0	+3			Jour PL/B 24 573	May 67 .SUPERSEDED	
	+0	+2			Conf 65Antwerp 69	Jul 65 .SUPERSEDED	
Strnth Fnctn	-		AUA	Theo	Rept AAEC/E-211	Nov 70 Musgrove. SMOOTHED S0,S1 AND S2 GIVN	
Strnth Fnctn	0.0+0	2.2+2	ANL	Expt	Jour NSE 48 219	Jun 72 Whalen. AVERAGE RESON SPACING	
Strnth Fnctn	1.5+2	6.5+2	SAC	ExTh	Diss FRNC-TH-450	Oct 72 Delaroche.OPTICAL MODEL PARAMETERS	
Strnth Fnctn	None		AUA	Eval	Rept AAEC/E-277	Mar 73 Musgrove.TBLS EXPTL DATA+BEST VALUES	
Strnth Fnctn	1.7+0	1.0+3	COL	Expt	Jour PR/C 11 462	Feb 75 Liou+SWAVE.114 LVLS.GRPH.TBL.CFD.	+
					Conf 75Wash. 780	Mar 75 Hacken+12 ELEMENT RVW. TBL	
	1.7+0	1.0+3			Data EXFOR10525.011	Mar 76 . 1 PT.S0=(2.02+-.3)-4	
Strnth Fnctn	2.7+0	4.5+2	DUB	Expt	Jour YF 22 3	Jul 75 Karzhavina+ S0,S0(J=2,J=3) GIVEN	
	1.6+1	3.0+2			Rept JINR-P3-7980	May 74 - +S0 FOR J=2,3,SPIN FACTOR	
Lvl Density	+6		MIL	Theo	Jour EN 15 1 54	Jan 68 Facchini+ LDL PARS FROM LOW EN RES	
Lvl Density	None		AUW	Theo	Conf 70Madurai 2 267	Dec 70 Ramamurty+ A-PARAMETER GVN,LANG'S-TH	
Lvl Density	1.4+7		IBJ	Expt	Rept INR'-1268	Jan 71 Jaskola+ ALFA SPCTR CFD TH,FULL PAPR	+
					Rept INR-1275	Jan 71 SEE ALSO * FULL INFORMATION	
					Jour APPB 2 521	71 .SAME AS INR-1268	
	1.4+7				Data EXFOR30158.017	Mar 71 LEVEL DENSITY PARAMETER OF GD160 GIV	
Lvl Density	None		MUN	Theo	Jour NP/A 217 269	Dec 73 Dilg+ A,DELTA. BACK SHIFTED FERMIGAS	
Lvl Density	None		BOL	Eval	Conf IAEA-169 3 123	74 Benzi+ LVL DENS PARAM BY XPT,GRPH+TB	
Lvl Density	None		COP	Theo	Jour NP/A 222 493	Apr 74 Dossing+COLL ROTAT.SPAC. ACCUR ESTIM	
Lvl Density	None		DUB	Theo	Jour NP/A 224 396	May 74 Malov+ 1/2 MICROSC.MODEL. DEFORM NUC	
Lvl Density	None		ROC	Theo	Jour NP/A 223 589	May 74 Huizenga+ EXP CFD MICROSC TH AX SYMM	
Lvl Density	+0	+3	FEI	Eval	Rept YK-8/2 97	Sep 72 Abagyan+ LVL DENSITY PARAMETER,TBL	
					Rept INDC(CCP)-39	Jul 74 .PAGE 102.ENGLISH OF YK-8/2 97	

66 Dysprosium 164

Quantity	Energy (ev) Min	Max	Lab	Type	Documentation Ref Vol Page	Author, Comments Date	Data
Evaluation	1.0-3	1.5+7	AUA	Eval	Rept AAEC/TM-549	Jun 70 Cook.TOT,EL,INEL,NONEL,CAPT SIGS,NDG	+
					Rept AAEC/E-214	Jun 71 Bertram+GROUP SIGMAS SAME QUANTS.NDG	
					Rept AAEC/TM-587	Mar 71 *DESCRIPTION OF LIBRARY	
	1.0-3	1.5+7			Data AUSTR-DFN 183.	Nov 71 POINT(223) AND GROUP(127) SIGMAS	
Total	2.5-2		KAP	Expt	Abst BAP 3 337	Aug 58 House+ ABST. PILE	+
Total	1.8-2	1.0+0	BNL	Expt	Prog WASH-1028 11	Apr 60 Hellsten+ NON 1/V	
Total	2.0-2	2.0+0	BNL	Expt	Jour NSE 11 369	Dec 61 Sher+ CS NOT 1/V ABOVE .1EV CFD B-W	+
					Jour ANS 3 464	Dec 60 .SUPERSEDED	
	2.0-2	1.6+0			Data EXFOR12098.003	Jun 76 . 32 PTS.	

66 Dysprosium 164

Quantity	Energy (ev) Min	Energy (ev) Max	Lab	Type	Documentation Ref Vol Page	Date	Author, Comments	Data
Total	1.0 – 1		ORL	Expt	Jour PR 174 1553	Oct 68	Child+ FROM NEUT DIFFRACT 1880+ – 30B	
Total	2.5 – 2		JAE	Expt	Prog EANDC(J)10L1	Nov 68	Ohno+ .CRYST – SPECT+V – SELECT	+
	2.5 – 2				Data EXFOR20328.006	Jul 74	1PNT.	
Total	1.0+0	3.2+2	IJI	Expt	Prog YFI – 7 37	Apr 69	Vertebny+ TABLE OF SIG AT 51 NEUT – ES	+
					Rept INDC(CCP) – 7U40	Feb 70	.TRANSLATION	
	1.0+0	3.2+2			Data EXFOR40052.002	Jul 73	.SIGMA AT 51 ENERGIES GIVEN	
Total	2.5 – 2	1.5+0	IFU	Expt	Prog YFI – 11 59	70	Vertebny+ ABST,OXIDE,TBL SIG AT 28ES	+
					Prog INDC(CCP) – 31	Dec 72	.PAGE 58,ENGLISH OF YFI – 11 59	
	2.5 – 2	1.5+0			Data EXFOR40090.011	Jan 72	SIG TOT AT 27 EN.	
Total	2.5 – 2	7.0 – 1	IFU	Expt	Conf 70Helsinki 1 651	Jun 70	Vertebnij+87. SIG(E) GRAPH+2200M/SEC	
					Rept BNL – TR – 495	Jul 72	. ENGLISH OF 70HELSIN 1 651	
Total	1.0 – 3	1.5+7	AUA	Eval	Data AUSTR – DFN 183.	Nov 71	COOK+POINT(223)+GROUP(127)SIG.CF EVL	+
Total	+3		DKE	Expt	Jour AP 84 165	May 74	Pineo+ N STRENGTH FUNC, TBLS, GRPHS.	
Total	1.0+0	2.1+4	COL	Expt	Jour PR/C 11 462	Feb 75	Liou+ANAL.FOR RES,STF,AVG D.TABLES.	
	1.0+0	1.0+4			Conf 75Wash. 780	Mar 75	Hacken+12ELEMENT RVW.RES PAR SUMMARY	
Total	1.4+7		LIN	Expt	Jour 75Kiev 4 140	May 75	Djumin+ SIG GIVEN.OPTMOD ANAL,RADIUS	
Total	6.0 – 4	1.0 – 1	KAP	Expt	Abst BAP 6 70	Feb 61	Moore.TRANS,1/V OVER FULL RANGE	+
	5.3 – 4	1.4 – 1			Data EXFOR12083.003	Jun 76	. 37 PTS.	
Elastic	1.0 – 1		ORL	Expt	Jour PR 174 1553	Oct 68	Child+ COHERENT SCAT AMPLITUDE	
Elastic	2.0 – 2	1.0+1	IFU	Expt	Rept IF – 69 5	69	Vertebny+ SIG(E) GRAPH,SCAT AMPLITUD	
Elastic	Maxwl	+5	IFU	Comp	Prog YFI – 7 43	Apr 69	Vertebny+ SCATTERING – LENGTH DERIVED	
					Rept INDC(CCP) – 7U46	Feb 70	TRANSLATN.*	
Elastic	1.0 – 3	1.5+7	AUA	Eval	Data AUSTR – DFN 183.	Nov 71	COOK+POINT(223)+GROUP(127)SIG.CF EVL	+
Elastic	2.5 – 2		IJI	Eval	Conf 75Kiev 1 169	May 75	Fedorova+ EVAL 2200M/S SIG,TABLE	
Potntl Scat	None		BNL	Expt	Jour PR/C 1 1850	May 70	Chrien+,SCAT RADINS FROM ANAL OF RES	
					Jour PL/B 24 573	May 67	.SUPERSEDED	
Tot Inelastc	5.0+5	1.5+7	AUA	Eval	Data AUSTR – DFN 183.	Nov 71	COOK+POINT(11)+GROUP(127)SIG.CF EVL	+
Diff Inelast	1.4+7		LRL	Theo	Rept UCRL – 50181	Feb 67	Lutz+ CALC ANG DIST FOR FIRST 2+ LVL	
Thermal Scat	2.5 – 2	1.5+0	IFU	Expt	Prog YFI – 11 59	70	Vertebny+ OXIDE,TOTSCAT,TBL 2200M/S	
					Prog INDC(CCP) – 31	Dec 72	.PAGE 58,ENGLISH OF YFI – 11 59	
Scattering	2.5 – 2	1.0+1	IFU	Expt	Prog YFI – 6 108	68	Vertebnyj+. TABLE SIG(E).TBP UFZ	
					Rept INDC – 260E	69	. ENGL OF YFI – 6 108	
Scattering	2.0 – 2	3.0 – 2	IFU	Expt	Conf 70Helsinki 1 651	Jun 70	Vertebnij+ 2200M/SEC SIGMA GIVEN,TBL	
					Rept BNL – TR – 495	Jul 72	. ENGLISH OF 70HELSIN 1 651	
Scattering	2.5 – 2	1.0+1	IFU	Expt	Conf 70Helsinki 1 651	Jun 70	Vertebnij+87. SIG(E) GRAPH+2200M/SEC	
					Rept BNL – TR – 495	Jul 72	. ENGLISH OF 70HELSIN 1 651	
Scattering	Maxwl		IFU	Expt	Prog YFI – 11 59	Dec 71	Vertebny+	+
	Maxwl				Data EXFOR40090.012	Jan 72	THERMAL SCATTERING CS.	
Nonelastic	1.0 – 3	1.5+7	AUA	Eval	Data AUSTR – DFN 183.	Nov 71	COOK+POINT(223)+GROUP(127)SIG.CF EVL	+
Absorption	Maxwl		IFU	Expt	Prog YFI – 11 59	Dec 71	Vertebny+	+
	Maxwl				Data EXFOR40090.013	Jan 72	THERMAL ABSORPTION CS.	
Absorption	2.5 – 2		IJI	Eval	Conf 75Kiev 1 169	May 75	Fedorova+ EVAL 2200M/S SIG,TABLE	
Res Int Abs	4.4 – 1		ANL	Theo	Abst ANS 6 39	Jun 63	Persiani+ RNEGCRESRCONTRIB.INFNITLDIL	
Res Int Abs	5.0 – 1		MTR	Expt	Jour NSE 25 12	May 66	Scoville. 377+ – 34B	+
					Jour ANS 7 85	Jun 64	.SUPERSEDED	
	5.0 – 1				Data EXFOR12101.013	Jun 76	. 1 PT.	
Res Int Abs	5.0 – 1		BOL	Eval	Rept RT/FI – 4	Jan 67	Palmucci. CALC FROM (N,G) RES PARAMS	
Res Int Abs	5.5 – 1		MOL	Theo	Rept BLG – 421	Sep 67	Damle+,EVAL ACT R.I.=332+ – 10B,TO GND	
Res Int Abs	5.5 – 1		MOL	Eval	Rept BLG – 421	Sep 67	Damle+,EVAL ACT R.I.=332+ – 10B,TO GND	
Res Int Abs	5.0 – 1		MTR	Expt	Rept IN – 1195	May 68	Scoville.	+
Res Int Abs	5.0 – 1		OSL	Expt	Prog INDC(NOR) – 1 2	May 72	Alstad+ REL AU. TABLES	+
	5.0 – 1				Data EXFOR20187.009	May 74	1PNT.CAPTURE.	
Res Int Abs	5.0 – 1		AUA	Eval	Rept AAEC/TM – 619	Sep 72	Clayton.CALC FROM SIG LIBRARY,TABLE	
Res Int Abs	5.5 – 1		RCN	Revw	Conf 73Paris 2 271	Mar 73	Zijp.ACT,RECOMM FROM LITERATURE,TBL	
Res Int Abs	5.0 – 1		GHT	Expt	Jour JRC 20 695	74	Van Der Linden+ BY(N,G).CFD OTHS,TBL	+
					Jour JRC 23 113	74	– + (N,G).CD – RATIO,TABLE	
	5.5 – 1				Conf 73Paris 2 241	Mar 73	– + ACT,REL THR+GOLD,TBL	
	5.5 – 1				Data EXFOR20645.029	Jul 76	1PNT.CAPTURE.	
Res Int Abs	+0	+5	WIN	Revw	Conf IAEA – 169 3 163	74	Pope+ DATA FILE CALC CFD XPTAL VALUE	
Res Int Abs	1.0 – 1		NPL	Expt	Jour JP/A 7 2318	Dec 74	Ryves+ REL TO MN AU,REDUCED INTEGRAL	+
	1.0 – 1	1.4+7			Data EXFOR20561.011	Oct 75	1PNT.	
Res Int Abs	5.0 – 1		IJI	Eval	Conf 75Kiev 1 169	May 75	Fedorova+ EVAL+CALC RI GIVEN,TABLE	
Res Int Abs	5.0 – 1		KJL	Expt	Jour JIN 37 1591	Aug 75	Steinnes. CD – RAT+ACTIV INTEG,CFD,TBL	+
	5.0 – 1				Data EXFOR20635.008	Aug 76	1PNT.CAPTURE.	
Res Int Act	–		ISL	Expt	Jour JNAB 16 291	Jun 62	Ben – David+.NEGLIGIBLE IN THR REACTOR	
(n,γ)	2.0+7		OHO	Expt	Jour PR 53 437	Mar 38	Pool+ BETAS,CLOUDCH,RATIO DY160(N2N)	
(n,γ)	2.2+5		PCF	Expt	Jour NAT 142 392	Aug 38	Halban+ ACT CS GIVEN	
(n,γ)	Maxwl		JAP	Expt	Jour SCP 38 167	Jan 41	Sinma+.LI+D.RELATIVE SIG MEASUREMENT	

66 Dysprosium 164

Quantity	Energy (ev) Min	Energy (ev) Max	Lab	Type	Documentation Ref Vol Page	Author, Comments Date	Data
(n,γ)	Pile		ANL	Expt Rept	ANL-4010 55	47 Goldhaber.	+
	Pile			Data	EXFOR12077.002	Jun 76 .1 PT.	
(n,γ)	Pile		ANL	Expt Jour	PR 72 888	Nov 47 Seren+ THR IRRAD. TO EU152, TTO140MI	+
				Rept	CP-2376	44 - .	
	Pile			Data	EXFOR11447.	Jun 76 . 2 PTS, SIG FOR 2 ISOMERS	
(n,γ)	2.2+5	9.0+5	OXF	Expt Jour	NAT 161 727	May 48 Allen+ ACTIVATION RATIO	
(n,γ)	Maxwl		MCM	Expt Priv	WALKER	May 56 Walker.	+
	Maxwl			Data	EXFOR12127.020	Jun 76 . 1 PT.	
(n,γ)	2.5+4		LRL	Expt Jour	PR 112 226	Oct 58 Booth+ SB-BE REL I+THR,ACT 2.32H HL	+
				Abst	BAP 2 268	Oct 58 .ABST. L6,WASH190 192 194	
	2.5+4			Data	EXFOR11429.025	Jun 76 . 1 PT.	
(n,γ)	Maxwl		MUA	Expt Jour	NP 12 261	Jul 59 Sehgal+2490+-300B METASTABLE	+
	Maxwl			Data	EXFOR31244.	Mar 73 .SIG TO GND AND MS-STATE GVN	
(n,γ)	1.5+5	6.0+6	WIS	Expt Jour	PR 116 927	Nov 59 Johnsrud+ SC CFD OTHERS	+
	1.5+5	6.0+6		Data	EXFOR11615.023	Jun 76 . 17 PTS, SIG	
(n,γ)	1.5+7		ARK	Expt Jour	PR 118 242	Apr 60 Wille. MEAS ACT PROD 2 ISOMERS	+
	1.5+7			Data	EXFOR12033.	Jun 76 . 2 PTS, SIG FOR 2 ISOMERS	
(n,γ)	6.0-2	2.0+0	BNL	Expt Jour	NSE 11 369	Dec 61 Sher+ (N,G)SIGMA AT 8 ES GVN	+
	6.0-2	2.0+0		Data	EXFOR12098.002	Jun 76 . 8 PTS, SIG	
(n,γ)	Maxwl		MUA	Expt Jour	NP 36 542	Aug 62 Mangal+ SCINT SPECT,REL TO AU197,TBL	+
	Maxwl			Data	EXFOR31248.012	Apr 73 .SIG TO GND-STATE GVN	
(n,γ)	Maxwl		ANL	Comp Jour	NP 60 241	Nov 64 Bishop+EXP AND TH ISOMER RATIOS CFD	
(n,γ)	2.4+4		MUA	Expt Jour	NP 66 267	May 65 Chaubey+ SB-BE,ACT,BETA-DET,REL I127	+
	2.4+4			Data	EXFOR30063.008	Dec 70 1966-EXPT.TOTAL SIGMA	
(n,γ)	Maxwl		CCP	Expt Jour	IZV 29 2168	Dec 65 Bondarenko+.SIG GIVN.ENGL BAS29 2004	
(n,γ)	1.0-1	1.5+2	MOL	Eval Rept	BLG-421	66 Damle+. CURVE RECOMMENDED SIGS	
(n,γ)	Maxwl		MTR	Expt Jour	NSE 25 12	May 66 Scoville. 2600+-410 B	+
	Maxwl			Data	EXFOR12101.012	Jun 76 . 1 PT.	
(n,γ)	2.5-2		BOL	Eval Rept	RT/FI-4	Jan 67 Palmucci. CALC FROM RES PARAMETERS	
(n,γ)	Maxwl		ROS	Expt Jour	KE 10 306	Oct 67 Albert+ ACT CS,VAL CFD REFS,IN GERMN	
(n,γ)	1.4+7		LYO	Comp Rept	LYCEN/6780	Nov 67 Crouzet+COMPILATN FOR ACTIVTN ANALYS	
(n,γ)	Maxwl Pile		MOL	Eval Rept	BLG-421	68 Damle+ TBP THRSIG RESINTG GIVEN	
(n,γ)	Maxwl Pile		MOL	Eval Rept	BLG-421	68 Damle+ TBP THRSIG RESINTG GIVEN	
(n,γ)	Fiss		MOL	Expt Conf	68Wash. 2 1263	Mar 68 Fabry+ ACT 23.3+-2.5MB TO DY165G	+
	Fiss			Data	EXFOR20264.004	May 74 1PNT.SIGMA.	
(n,γ)	-		IEA	Comp Rept	IEA-INF-10	Aug 68 Atalla. TABLES OF HL,SIG AND GAMM-E	
(n,γ)	2.4+4		MUA	Expt Jour	NP/A 117 545	Sep 68 Chaubey+,SB-BE,ACT BETA-DET REL I127	+
				Theo Jour	IJP 42 567	Sep 68 - + METHD OF BOOTH,VAL CFD XPT	
	2.4+4			Expt Data	EXFOR30086.	Dec 70 PARTL SIG TO META,GROUND	
(n,γ)	Pile		MUN	Revw Conf	69Studsvik 127	Aug 69 Egidy.PART'L SIGS OF CONV LINES,GRPH	
(n,γ)	1.0+3	1.0+7	BOL	Eval Rept	CCDN-NW/10	Dec 69 Benzi+H-F MOD,AXEL G(G)EST,ALL DATA	
				Rept	CEC(70)-2	Apr 70 - +. GRAPH	
(n,γ)	2.0+5		MUA	Theo Rept	Roorke 2 129	Dec 69 Chaubey+ SIG VALUE GIVEN, STATIST-TH	
(n,γ)	2.5-2	1.5+0	IFU	Expt Prog	YFI-11 59	70 Vertebny+ ABST,TBL 2200M/S VALUES	
				Prog	INDC(CCP)-31	Dec 72 .PAGE 58,ENGLISH OF YFI-11 59	
(n,γ)	Fiss		CAI	Expt Prog	IAEA-124 152	Feb 70 NO AUTHOR,BETA-ACT,REL THR SIG,NDG	
(n,γ)	2.5-2		IFU	Expt Conf	70Helsinki 1 651	Jun 70 Vertebnij+87. SIGMA GIVEN	
				Rept	BNL-TR-495	Jul 72 . ENGLISH OF 70HELSIN 1 651	
(n,γ)	3.0+4		AUA	Theo Rept	AAEC/E-211	Nov 70 Musgrove. SIGMA GIVEN AND CFD OTHER	
(n,γ)	Maxwl	1.4+7	KFI	Comp Jour	JRC 7 365	Jun 71 Nagy+ SIGMAS,GAMMA-E AND HALF-L GIVN	
(n,γ)	-		ATI	Expt Prog	EANDC(OR)105L	Aug 71 Bensch+,PHOTO-NEUTRON SOURCES	
(n,γ)	1.0-3	1.5+7	AUA	Eval Data	AUSTR-DFN 183.	Nov 71 COOK+POINT(223)+GROUP(127)SIG.CF EVL	+
(n,γ)	Maxwl		CRC	Eval Rept	AECL-3037 1	Jan 72 Walker.RECOMMENDED SIG,DETAILED TBL	
(n,γ)	2.4+4		MUA	Theo Jour	IJP 46 114	Mar 72 Chaubey+ P-WAVE STRENGTH FUNCT,TABLE	
(n,γ)	Maxwl		OSL	Expt Prog	INDC(NOR)-1 2	May 72 Alstad+ REL AU,TO ISOM,GND(+SUM),TBL	+
	2.5-2			Data	EXFOR20187.	May 74 3PTS.SIGMA.	
(n,γ)	2.5+4		AUW	Theo Jour	PR/C 6 572	Aug 72 Rao+. ISOMER RATIOS CALCTD.CFD EXPT	+
	2.5+4			Expt Data	EXFOR30234.	Jun 73 .SIG TO GROUND AND META.ISOM RATIO	
(n,γ)	2.5-2		AUA	Eval Rept	AAEC/TM-619	Sep 72 Clayton.CALC FROM SIG LIBRARY,TABLE	
(n,γ)	Pile		ROS	ExTh Prog	ZFK-243 93	Sep 72 Mohsen+ NG-SYSTEMAT. FOR RARE EARTHS	
(n,γ)	5.0+3	1.6+5	VIP	Expt Jour	NSE 49 317	Nov 72 Fawcett+ ACTIVATION. CURVE.	+
				Abst	DA/B 32 2929	Nov 71 - +	
	5.0+3	1.6+5		Data	EXFOR10298.003	Oct 73 16PTS.SIGMA.	
(n,γ)	Maxwl		RCN	Revw Rept	INDC(NDS)-56	Sep 73 Zijp.PG103,FOR DOSIMETRY,SIG GIVEN	
	2.5-2			Conf	73Paris 2 271	Mar 73 - .RECOMMENDED FROM LITERATURE,TB	
(n,γ)	1.0+5	2.5+6	CRC	Expt Jour	NP/A 213 349	Oct 73 Clarke+ ISOM RAT CFD G-CASCADE MODEL	
(n,γ)	Maxwl Fiss		WIN	Revw Conf	IAEA-169 3 163	74 Pope+ MAXW+FIS-SPEC AVG DATA CFD XPT	
	Fiss			Conf	IAEA-169 3 137	74 Dean. POINT DATA AVG OVER STAND SPEC	

66 Dysprosium 164

Quantity	Energy (ev) Min	Max	Lab	Type	Documentation Ref Vol Page	Author, Comments Date	Data
(n,γ)	1.0+3	1.0+7	FEI	Eval	Rept YK- 8/2 97	Sep 72 Abagjan+ AVG SIG(ENERGY - GROUPS),TABL	
					Rept INDC(CCP) - 39	Jul 74 .P102. ENGLISH OF YK-8/2 97	
(n,γ)	Maxwl	1.0+2	BNL	Revw	Conf 74Petten 247	Sep 74 Chrien+DIRECT CAPTURE COMP. GRPH.	
(n,γ)	Maxwl		BNL	Expt	Conf 74Petten 271	Sep 74 Cole+ DIRECT CAPT.COMP. GRPH+TBL	
(n,γ)	2.5-2		NPL	Expt	Jour JP/A 7 2318	Dec 74 Ryves+	+
	2.5-2			Data	EXFOR20561.010	Oct 75 1PNT.SIGMA.	
(n,γ)	Maxwl		KAP	Expt	Abst BAP 3 337	Aug 58 House+ PILE OSC.SIG=2780+ - 50B	+
	Maxwl			Data	EXFOR12082.006	Jun 76 . 1 PT.	
(n,γ)	None		RCN	Revw	Rept ECN-2	Sep 76 Zijp+ INTERCOMP. INTEGRAL SIG SAND-2	
Spect (n,γ)	Pile		ANL	Expt	Jour PR 88 943	Nov 52 Hibdon+ INTERNAL CONVERSION,GAMMA ES	
Spect (n,γ)	Maxwl		CCP	Expt	Jour AE 4 22	Jan 58 Sklyarevskii+.EGS+INTENS BELOW .3MEV	
					Jour JNE 9 69	Jun 59 TRANSLATN.*	
					Jour SJA 4 19	58 TRANSLATN.*	
Spect (n,γ)	Maxwl		YAL	Expt	Abst BAP 4 35	Jan 59 Springer+,NAI(TL),GAMMA MULTIPLICITY	
Spect (n,γ)	Pile		UPP	Expt	Jour NP 40 329	Jan 63 Marklund+.E DETERM. NO INTENS MEAS.	
Spect (n,γ)	None		MIT	Expt	Rept MITNE-37	Aug 63 Neill+ GG COINCS	
Spect (n,γ)	Pile		CTH	Expt	Jour AF 25 333	Jan 64 Hardell+.E+INT OF GS FROM DY165M DEC	
					Jour NP 39 286	Dec 62 - +. PRECISION E DET OF ISOM LV	
Spect (n,γ)	Maxwl		LAS	Expt	Jour PR/B 136 355	Oct 64 Motz.CURV,TBL MOSTLY ES,SOME INTNSTS	
Spect (n,γ)	Maxwl		MIL	Expt	Jour EN 11 612	Nov 64 Para+ GAMMAS TO 190 KEV	
Spect (n,γ)	Maxwl		RIS	Expt	Jour ZP 182 171	Dec 64 Schult.BENT XTL,TBL OF GS,DY165-LVLS	
Spect (n,γ)	Pile		MUN	Expt	Jour ZN/A 21 1328	Sep 66 Neumann. CRYST SPEC EXPT OF GAM INT	
					Rept ANL-TRANS-941	73 . ENGLISH OF ZN/A 1328	
Spect (n,γ)	2.5-2		LAS	Expt	Jour PR 152 1084	Dec 66 Hafemeister.	+
Spect (n,γ)	Maxwl		KFK	Expt	Jour ZP 206 84	Sep 67 Markus+ 5*GE-LI +ANTICOMPTN SP.E+INT	
					Conf 67Tokyo 4 107	Sep 67 - + GELI. NDG	
					Rept KFK-678	Sep 67 - + REPRINT OF ZP 206 84	
					Rept KFK-562	Mar 67 Michaelis+ LVL SCHEME DY-165	
					Conf 65Antwerp 516	Jul 65 Markus+ PPR52. ABST.NDG.	
Spect (n,γ)	Maxwl		MUN	Expt	Jour ZP 207 153	Oct 67 Dutta+.INTCONVERSN.225LINES0KEV-7MEV	
					Conf 67Juelich 56	Apr 67 - + SUPERSEDED.	
					Jour ADP 9 221	Jul 62 - + CONVERSION-EL SPECTRUM	
Spect (n,γ)	Maxwl		MUN	Theo	Jour 69Studsvik 541	Aug 69 Egidy. STATMOD CALC GRPHS CFD EXPT	
Spect (n,γ)	Maxwl		KFI	Revw	Jour YF 10 907	Nov 69 Kecskemeti+ AVG GAM-MULTIPLICITY,TBL	
					Jour SNP 10 524	May 70 TRANSLATN.*	
Spect (n,γ)	Maxwl	1.4+7	KFI	Comp	Jour JRC 7 365	Jun 71 Nagy+ SIGMAS,GAMMA-E AND HALF-L GIVN	
Spect (n,γ)	Maxwl		CTH	Expt	Prog EANDC(OR)115L	Jul 72 Larsson+, TO OBTAIN LEVEL STRUCTURE	
Spect (n,γ)	Maxwl		IFL	Expt	Book PROKOFJEV	73 . TBL GAM,CONV ELECTR ES+INT,LVL SCH	
Spect (n,γ)	Maxwl		CCP	Theo	Jour ZET 65 12	Jul 73 Nosov+ THERMODYN CALC CFD EXPT,GRAPH	
					Jour JET 38 6	Jan 74 . ENGLISH OF ZET 65 6	
Spect (n,γ)	Maxwl	1.0+2	BNL	Revw	Conf 74Petten 247	Sep 74 Chrien+DIRECT CAPTURE COMP. GRPH.	
Inelastic γ	+7		CCP	Expt	Conf 75Leningrd 347	Jan 75 Avchukhov+ ABST,ES+INTENSITIES,TBL	+
	Fast			Data	EXFOR40315.002	Nov 75 .GAM/100N FOR 53 GAM-E AT 90 DEG GVN	
(n,2n)	Fiss		CRC	Eval	Rept CRC-1003	Dec 60 ROY+ ESTIMATED AVG SIG=5.8MB.	
(n,2n)	1.3+7	1.5+7	BNL	Theo	Jour NSE 23 238	Nov 65 Pearlstein.3ES.STAT MDL CALC.TBL CS.	
(n,2n)	Fiss		BNL	Theo	Jour NSE 23 238	Nov 65 Pearlstein.STATMDL CALC.SPEC AVG.TBL	
(n,2n)	1.5+7		DEB	Eval	Jour REA 11 1 153	Mar 73 Boedy+ RECOMM.VALUE FROM N-Z SYSTEM.	
(n,2n)	1.5+7		KFI	Theo	Rept KFKI-73-68	Dec 73 Jeki.NEW FIT,CALC SIG CFD OTHERS,TBL	
(n,xn) x>2	Fiss		BNL	Theo	Jour NSE 23 238	Nov 65 Pearlstein.SPEC AVG STATMDL CALC N3N	
(n,p)	Fiss		CRC	Eval	Rept CRC-1003	Dec 60 ROY+ ESTIMATEDAVG SIG=0.001MB	
(n,p)	1.4+7	1.5+7	ARK	ExTh	Prog ORO-3235-29	Jan 67 Koch+ STAT MODEL CALC CFD EXPTS	
(n,p)	1.4+7		LYO	Comp	Rept LYCEN/6780	Nov 67 Crouzet+COMPILATN FOR ACTIVTN ANALYS	
(n,p)	1.5+7		JUL	Expt	Jour RRL 25 335	May 76 Qaim+ ACTIV,GELI.CFD OTHERS,TBL+GRPH	+
	1.5+7			Data	EXFOR20716.013	Jun 77 1PNT.SIGMA.	
(n,α)	1.4+7		MUA	Expt	Conf 60Waltair 297	Feb 60 Khurana+.VAL GVN REL FE056(N,P),C-W	+
	1.4+7			Data	EXFOR30403.025	Jul 77 1 PNT. REL TO FE056(N,P)= 110 MB	
(n,α)	1.5+7		ARK	Expt	Jour PR 118 242	Apr 60 Wille. MEAS ACT SIG = 4.5+- .8 MB	+
	1.5+7			Data	EXFOR12033.039	Jun 76 . 1 PT.	
(n,α)	Fiss		CRC	Eval	Rept CRC-1003	Dec 60 ROY+ ESTIMATED AVG SIG=BELO 0.0001MB	
(n,α)	1.4+7		CIS	Theo	Jour NP 51 460	Feb 64 Facchini+STATMOD SIG XPT/CALC=41000	
(n,α)	1.5+7		MUA	Expt	Jour NP 69 153	Jul 65 Khurana+ FE STANDARD	+
	1.5+7			Data	EXFOR31316.018	Feb 71 .SIG GVN	
(n,α)	1.4+7	1.5+7	NAP	Comp	Rept INFN/BE-67-11	Sep 67 Cuzzocrea+ AVERAGED CHOSEN DATA.	
(n,α)	1.4+7		LYO	Comp	Rept LYCEN/6780	Nov 67 Crouzet+COMPILATN FOR ACTIVTN ANALYS	
(n,α)	1.5+7		DEB	Comp	Jour REA 7 4 93	Dec 69 Csikai+ SIG+HL COMPILTN,N-ACTIV-ANAL	
(n,α)	1.4+7	1.5+7	JYV	Eval	Rept JU-RR-3/1970	Jun 70 Leppaemaeki+ TABLE OF EVAL AVG SIG	

66 Dysprosium 164

Quantity	Energy (ev) Min	Max	Lab	Type	Documentation Ref Vol Page	Author, Comments Date	Data
(n,α)	1.4+7		IBJ	Expt	Rept INR-1268	Jan 71 Jaskola+ ALFA SPCTR CFD TH,FULL PAPR	+
					Rept INR-1275	Jan 71 SEE ALSO * FULL INFORMATION	
					Jour APPB 2 521	71 .SAME AS INR-1268	
	1.4+7				Data EXFOR30158.018	Jul 72 24 DATA LINES (ALPHA SPECTRUM)	
	1.4+7				Data EXFOR30158.028	Jul 72 INTEGRATED CROSS SECTION,1 DATA LINE	
(n,α)	1.5+7		IRK	Expt	Jour APA 34 209	Sep 71 Havlik. ACT. CC-W.	+
					Jour OAWA 107 119	Apr 70 - . ACTIVATION METHOD	
	1.5+7				Data EXFOR20509.019	Apr 76 1PNT.SIGMA.	
(n,α)	1.8+7		IBJ	Expt	Prog INR-1401 13	May 72 Glowacka+ E DISTRBT OF ALPHAS,TABLE	+
					Rept INR-1468/I/PLA	73 - + ALFA E-SPEC,GRAPH.	
					Conf 72Budapest 16	Aug 72 . ALFA-SPEC CFD KNOCK-ON TH,GRAPH	
					Rept INR-1401 22	May 72 * ALPHA SPCTR AT 1 ANGL	
	1.8+7				Data EXFOR30172.	Aug 72 DISTRBT OF ALF(26 DATA)+SIG AT 1 ANG	
(n,α)	1.4+7		WWA	Theo	Conf 72Budapest 18	Aug 72 Glowacka+ KNOCK ON,SPEC CFD XPT,GRPH	
					Jour NP/A 187 177	May 72 Kozlowski+. 30DEG E-SPEC.KNOCK-ON OK	
(n,α)	1.4+7		DUB	Theo	Rept JINR-P4-6832	Dec 72 Kozlowski.DEFORMD NUC STRUCTURE,GRPH	
(n,α)	1.4+7		GIT	Expt	Abst BAP 13 1699	Dec 68 OMS+ ACT, REL FE56 NP	+
	1.4+7				Data EXFOR12131.006	Jun 76 . 1 PT.	
Reson Params	-.2+1		BNL	Expt	Jour NSE 11 369	Dec 61 Sher+	+
	-.2+1				Data EXFOR12098.004	Jun 76 . 1 RES, E0,WT,WN0	
Reson Params	-.2+0	1.5+2	MOL	Eval	Rept BLG-421	66 Damle+. RECOMMENDED PARAMS 2 RESON	
Reson Params		1.0+6	AUA	Theo	Jour AUJ 20 477	Oct 66 Cook. TBL OF AVG LVL SPACING D,L=0,1	
Reson Params	1.0+0	3.2+2	IJI	Expt	Prog YFI-7 37	Apr 69 Vertebny+ N+G WIDTH AT 146EV,NEG.RES	+
					Rept INDC(CCP)-7U40	Feb 70 .TRANSLATION	
	1.4+2				Data EXFOR40052.006	Jul 73 .ONE DATA-LINE	
Reson Params	2.0+5		MUA	Theo	Conf 69Roorke 2 129	Dec 69 Chaubey+ D/GAM-WIDTH RATIO, STATMOD	
Reson Params	-.2+1	1.3+3	BNL	Expt	Jour PR/C 1 1850	May 70 Chrien+ TRANS,WN WG AVG D FOR 14RES	+
Reson Params	-		AUA	Theo	Rept AAEC/E-211	Nov 70 Musgrove. CALCULTD D+GAM WIDTH GIVEN	
Reson Params	-.2+1	1.4+2	CJD	Eval	Jour YK-7	71 Zakharova+ SURVEY+SYSTEMATICS,GW,TBL	
					Rept INDC(CCP)-27	Nov 72 .ENGLISH TRANSLATION OF YK-7 /71	
Reson Params	+2	+3	FEI	Eval	Rept YK-8/2 97	Sep 72 Abagyan+ AVG G-WID+D AT BINDNG-E,TBL	
					Rept INDC(CCP)-39	Jul 74 .PAGE 102.ENGLISH OF YK-8/2 97	
Reson Params	1.5+2	2.1+4	COL	Expt	Jour PR/C 11 462	Feb 75 Liou+TBL.E0,WN0,AVG WG,D,S0.NEVIS.	+
					Conf 75Wash. 780	Mar 75 Hacken+12 ELEMENT RES PAR RVW.TBL	
	1.5+2	2.1+4			Data EXFOR10525.	Mar 76 . 122PTS. WN RED,WG,D GVN.	
Reson Params	1.5+2		BNL	Expt	Abst BAP 2 42	Feb 57 Zimmerman.	+
	1.5+2				Data EXFOR11438.005	Jun 76 . 1 RES, E0,WN,WG	
Strnth Fnctn	+0	+2	MOL	Eval	Rept BLG-421	66 Damle+. RECOMMENDED S0=2.0 GROUND	
Strnth Fnctn	+0	+3	BNL	Expt	Jour PR/C 1 1850	May 70 Chrien+,TRANS,SO=1.2+-0.5 FROM RES	+
					Jour PL/B 24 573	May 67 .SUPERSEDED	
Strnth Fnctn	-		AUA	Theo	Rept AAEC/E-211	Nov 70 Musgrove. SMOOTHED S0,S1 AND S2 GIVN	
Strnth Fnctn	2.4+4		MUA	Theo	Jour IJP 46 114	Mar 72 Chaubey+ P-WAVE.FOR A-SYSTEMTIC,GRPH	
Strnth Fnctn	5.0+3	1.6+5	VIP	Expt	Jour NSE 49 317	Nov 72 Fawcett+. GAMMA,S0,AND S1 GIVEN	
					Abst DA/B 32 2929	Nov 71 .SUPERSEDED	
Strnth Fnctn	None		AUA	Eval	Rept AAEC/E-277	Mar 73 Musgrove.TBLS EXPTL DATA+BEST VALUES	
Strnth Fnctn	+2	+3	FEI	Eval	Rept YK-8/2 97	Sep 72 Abagyan+ LVL DENSITY PARAMETER,TABLE	
					Rept INDC(CCP)-39	Jul 74 .PAGE 102.ENGLISH OF YK-8/2 97	
Strnth Fnctn	1.5+2	2.1+4	COL	Expt	Jour PR/C 11 462	Feb 75 Liou+S0(91LVLS)S1(25LVLS).TBL.CFD.	+
					Conf 75Wash. 780	Mar 75 Hacken+12 ELEMENT RES PAR RVW.TBL	
	1.5+2	2.1+4			Data EXFOR10525.012	Mar 76 .2PTS.S0=(1.70+-.25)-4S1=(1.3+-.3)-4	
Lvl Density	+6		MIL	Theo	Jour EN 15 1 54	Jan 68 Facchini+ LDL PARS FROM LOW EN RES	
Lvl Density	2.4+4		MUA	ExTh	Jour NP/A 117 545	Sep 68 Chaubey+ SPIN-CUT-OFF-PARAMETER,TBL	+
	2.4+4			Expt	Data EXFOR30087.010	Dec 70 SPIN-CUT-OFF PARAM FROM CAPTURE EXPT	
Lvl Density	None		CCP	Theo	Jour YF 11 1028	May 70 Rubchenya. DENSITY+A+TEMP GIVEN	
					Jour SNP 11 571	Nov 70 . ENGL OF YF 11 571.	
Lvl Density	None		AUW	Theo	Conf 70Madurai 2 267	Dec 70 Ramamurty+ A-PARAMETER GVN,LANG'S-TH	
Lvl Density	None		CCP	Theo	Jour YF 13 43	Jan 71 Bravin+.DEFORM PAR,CALC,TBL,CFD EXPT	
Lvl Density	1.4+7		IBJ	Expt	Rept INR-1268	Jan 71 Jaskola+ ALFA SPCTR CFD TH,FULL PAPR	+
					Rept INR-1275	Jan 71 SEE ALSO * FULL INFORMATION	
					Jour APPB 2 521	71 .SAME AS INR-1268	
	1.4+7				Data EXFOR30158.019	Mar 71 LEVEL DENSITY PARAMETER OF GD161 GIV	
Lvl Density	None		MUN	Theo	Jour NP/A 217 269	Dec 73 Dilg+ A,DELTA. BACK SHIFTED FERMIGAS	
Lvl Density	None		COP	Theo	Jour NP/A 222 493	Apr 74 Dossing+COLL ROTAT.SPAC. ACCUR ESTIM	
Lvl Density	None		DUB	Theo	Jour NP/A 224 396	May 74 Malov+ 1/2 MICROSC.MODEL. DEFORM NUC	
Lvl Density	None		ROC	Theo	Jour NP/A 223 589	May 74 Huizenga+ EXP CFD MICROSC TH AX SYMM	

66 Dysprosium 165

Quantity	Energy (ev) Min Max	Lab	Type	Documentation Ref Vol Page	Author, Comments Date	Data
Absorption	2.5 – 2	IJI	Eval Conf	75Kiev 1 169	May 75 Fedorova+ EVAL 2200M/S SIG,TABLE	
Res Int Abs	5.0 – 1	OSL	Expt Prog	INDC(NOR) – 1 2	May 72 Alstad+ REL AU. TABLES	+
	5.0 – 1		Data	EXFOR20187.011	May 74 1PNT.CAPTURE.	
(n,γ)	–	GOE	Expt Jour	ZP 159 101	Apr 60 Tornau. SIG=475+ –60B TO MS.GAM SPECT	
(n,γ)	Maxwl	OSL	Expt Prog	INDC(NOR) – 1 2	May 72 Alstad+ ACTIVATION REL AU – 197,TABLE	+
	2.5 – 2		Data	EXFOR20187.010	May 74 1PNT.SIGMA.	
(n,γ)	Pile	JAE	Expt Prog	NEANDC(J)44L	Aug 76 Sekine+ ACTIV.SIG TO MS AND GS.	+
	2.5 – 2		Data	EXFOR20695.002	Oct 76 1PNT.SIGMA.	
Reson Params	–	AUA	Theo Rept	AAEC/E – 211	Nov 70 Musgrove. CALCULTD D+GAM WIDTH GIVEN	
Strnth Fnctn	–	AUA	Theo Rept	AAEC/E – 211	Nov 70 Musgrove. SMOOTHED S0,S1 AND S2 GIVN	
Lvl Density	None	MUN	Theo Jour	NP/A 217 269	Dec 73 Dilg+ A,DELTA. BACK SHIFTED FERMIGAS	
Lvl Density	None	COP	Theo Jour	NP/A 222 493	Apr 74 Dossing+COLL ROTAT.SPAC. ACCUR ESTIM	
Lvl Density	None	DUB	Theo Jour	NP/A 224 396	May 74 Malov+ 1/2 MICROSC.MODEL. DEFORM NUC	
Lvl Density	None	ROC	Theo Jour	NP/A 223 589	May 74 Huizenga+ EXP CFD MICROSC TH AX SYMM	

66 Dysprosium 166

Quantity	Energy (ev) Min Max	Lab	Type	Documentation Ref Vol Page	Author, Comments Date	Data
Reson Params	–	AUA	Theo Rept	AAEC/E – 211	Nov 70 Musgrove. CALCULTD D+GAM WIDTH GIVEN	
Strnth Fnctn	–	AUA	Theo Rept	AAEC/E – 211	Nov 70 Musgrove. SMOOTHED S0,S1 AND S2 GIVN	

Quantity	Energy (ev) Min Max	Lab	Type	**67 Holmium 152** Documentation Ref Vol Page	Author, Comments Date	Data
Reson Params	–	AUA	Theo Rept	AAEC/E – 211	Nov 70 Musgrove. CALCULTD D+GAM WIDTH GIVEN	
Strnth Fnctn	–	AUA	Theo Rept	AAEC/E – 211	Nov 70 Musgrove. SMOOTHED S0,S1 AND S2 GIVN	

Quantity	Energy (ev) Min Max	Lab	Type	**67 Holmium 153** Documentation Ref Vol Page	Author, Comments Date	Data
Reson Params	–	AUA	Theo Rept	AAEC/E – 211	Nov 70 Musgrove. CALCULTD D+GAM WIDTH GIVEN	
Strnth Fnctn	–	AUA	Theo Rept	AAEC/E – 211	Nov 70 Musgrove. SMOOTHED S0,S1 AND S2 GIVN	

Quantity	Energy (ev) Min Max	Lab	Type	**67 Holmium 158** Documentation Ref Vol Page	Author, Comments Date	Data
Reson Params	–	AUA	Theo Rept	AAEC/E – 211	Nov 70 Musgrove. CALCULTD D+GAM WIDTH GIVEN	
Strnth Fnctn	–	AUA	Theo Rept	AAEC/E – 211	Nov 70 Musgrove. SMOOTHED S0,S1 AND S2 GIVN	

Quantity	Energy (ev) Min Max	Lab	Type	**67 Holmium 159** Documentation Ref Vol Page	Author, Comments Date	Data
Reson Params	–	AUA	Theo Rept	AAEC/E – 211	Nov 70 Musgrove. CALCULTD D+GAM WIDTH GIVEN	
Strnth Fnctn	–	AUA	Theo Rept	AAEC/E – 211	Nov 70 Musgrove. SMOOTHED S0,S1 AND S2 GIVN	

Quantity	Energy (ev) Min Max	Lab	Type	**67 Holmium 160** Documentation Ref Vol Page	Author, Comments Date	Data
Reson Params	–	AUA	Theo Rept	AAEC/E – 211	Nov 70 Musgrove. CALCULTD D+GAM WIDTH GIVEN	
Strnth Fnctn	–	AUA	Theo Rept	AAEC/E – 211	Nov 70 Musgrove. SMOOTHED S0,S1 AND S2 GIVN	

Quantity	Energy (ev) Min Max	Lab	Type	**67 Holmium 161** Documentation Ref Vol Page	Author, Comments Date	Data
Reson Params	–	AUA	Theo Rept	AAEC/E – 211	Nov 70 Musgrove. CALCULTD D+GAM WIDTH GIVEN	
Strnth Fnctn	–	AUA	Theo Rept	AAEC/E – 211	Nov 70 Musgrove. SMOOTHED S0,S1 AND S2 GIVN	

Quantity	Energy (ev) Min Max	Lab	Type	**67 Holmium 162** Documentation Ref Vol Page	Author, Comments Date	Data
Reson Params	–	AUA	Theo Rept	AAEC/E – 211	Nov 70 Musgrove. CALCULTD D+GAM WIDTH GIVEN	
Strnth Fnctn	–	AUA	Theo Rept	AAEC/E – 211	Nov 70 Musgrove. SMOOTHED S0,S1 AND S2 GIVN	

Quantity	Energy (ev) Min Max	Lab	Type	**67 Holmium 163** Documentation Ref Vol Page	Author, Comments Date	Data
Reson Params	–	AUA	Theo Rept	AAEC/E – 211	Nov 70 Musgrove. CALCULTD D+GAM WIDTH GIVEN	
Strnth Fnctn	–	AUA	Theo Rept	AAEC/E – 211	Nov 70 Musgrove. SMOOTHED S0,S1 AND S2 GIVN	

Quantity	Energy (ev) Min Max	Lab	Type	**67 Holmium 164** Documentation Ref Vol Page	Author, Comments Date	Data
Spect (n,γ)	Pile	MUN	Expt Jour Rept	ZN/A 21 1328 ANL – TRANS – 941	Sep 66 Neumann. CRYST SPEC EXPT OF GAM INT 73 . ENGLISH OF ZN/A 1328	
Reson Params	–	AUA	Theo Rept	AAEC/E – 211	Nov 70 Musgrove. CALCULTD D+GAM WIDTH GIVEN	
Strnth Fnctn	–	AUA	Theo Rept	AAEC/E – 211	Nov 70 Musgrove. SMOOTHED S0,S1 AND S2 GIVN	

Quantity	Energy (ev) Min Max	Lab	Type	**67 Holmium 165** Documentation Ref Vol Page	Author, Comments Date	Data
Evaluation	5.0+5 1.5+7	LRL	Eval Rept	UCRL – 5351	Nov 58 Howerton. CURVES	

67 Holmium 165

Quantity	Energy (ev) Min	Energy (ev) Max	Lab	Type	Documentation Ref Vol Page	Date	Author, Comments	Data
Evaluation	1.0−3	1.5+7	AUA	Eval	Rept AAEC/TM−549	Jun 70	Cook.TOT,EL,INEL,NONEL,CAPT SIGS,NDG	+
					Rept AAEC/E−214	Jun 71	Bertram+GROUP SIGMAS SAME QUANTS.NDG	
					Rept AAEC/TM−587	Mar 71	*DESCRIPTION OF LIBRARY	
	1.0−3	1.5+7			Data AUSTR−DFN 184.	Nov 71	POINT(223) AND GROUP(127) SIGMAS	
Total	Maxwl		COL	Expt	Jour PR 48 265	Aug 35	Dunning+ IONCH,TRANS,RA−BE/PARAFIN N	
Total	3.0−2	5.0−1	ORL	Expt	Jour PR 87 487	Aug 52	Bernstein+ TRANS+CRYST SPEC CURVE	+
	2.6−2	5.0−1			Rept ORNL−1068	Oct 51	Stephenson.TRANS CRYST SPECT,CURVES	
	2.6−2	5.0−1			Data EXFOR11745.008	Jun 76	. 20 PTS.	
Total	3.0−1	5.0+1	BNL	Expt	Jour PR 92 656	Nov 53	Foote+ CRYSTL SPECT.	+
	2.2−1	1.1+1			Data EXFOR12107.002	Jun 76	. 54 PTS.	
Total	5.0+4	2.9+6	WIS	Expt	Jour PR 93 461	Feb 54	Okazaki.	+
Total	3.0+0	3.4+2	BNL	Expt	Jour PR 99 10	Jul 55	Harvey+	+
	3.0+0	3.4+2			Data EXFOR11912.038	Jun 76	. 258 PTS.	
Total	1.0+6		ALD	Expt	Jour NP 42 86	Apr 63	Gilboy+.SIG=6.34B	+
Total	5.0−4	5.0−2	JAE	Expt	Abst BAP 9 179	Feb 64	Ohno+. DISAGREE WITH BNL325(2ED)	
Total	9.8+5		SHE	Theo	Jour NP 54 417	Jun 64	Maddison.OPTMOD FIT TO TOWLE GILBOY	
Total	3.0−2	5.0−1	BNL	Expt	Jour PR/B 136 1285	Dec 64	Schermer. CURV CORR PARAMAG SCATT	+
	1.7−2	1.3+0			Data EXFOR12123.002	Jun 76	. 63 PTS.	
Total	2.5+3	2.0+6	ANL	Expt	Priv STUPEGIA	Jun 65	Stupegia+ 100 E PTS. DELTA E 2−30KEV	+
	2.5+3	2.0+6			Data EXFOR12125.004	Jun 76	. 96 PTS.	
Total	3.0+5	4.0+5	ORL	ExTh	Jour PR/B 139 29	Jul 65	Wagner+ TRANS. CURVE.	+
					Conf 65Antwerp § 154	Jul 65	.SUPERSEDED	
	3.0+5	4.0+5		Expt	Data EXFOR12133.002	Jun 76	. 11 PTS.	
Total	2.9+5	4.2+5	ORL	Theo	Jour RMP 37 679	Oct 65	Tamura. CALCD SIG.	
Total	1.4+7		NBS	Expt	Jour PR 150 996	Oct 66	Marshak+ 5.29B, 3.5+−.75PC	+
					Jour PRL 16 194	Jan 66	.SUPERSEDED	
	1.4+7				Data EXFOR12142.002	Jun 76	. 1 PT.	
Total	1.0+6	1.5+7	YAL	Expt	Prog WASH−1071 196	Nov 66	Firk.TOF,NDG	
Total	8.3+5	1.1+6	ISS	Expt	Jour JPJ 22 368	Feb 67	Kobayashi+TOF.POL TGT+NS.FIG.P−B ANL	+
					Jour PTP 36 1071	Nov 66	− + SUPERSEDED.	
	8.3+5	1.1+6			Data EXFOR20293.002	Jun 74	6PTS.	
Total	1.0−3	9.4−1	IEA	Expt	Jour NP/A 95 683	Apr 67	. SEE ALSO *	+
					Conf 66Paris 1 53	Oct 66	Zimmerman+ P.129,SIG(E),SIG AT.025EV	
	1.0−3	9.4−1			Data EXFOR30224.	Dec 72	SIG AT 110ES,SIG AT 0.025EV,PRIVCOMM	
Total	2.0−2	1.0+0	IFU	Expt	Prog YFI−4 38	May 67	Vertebnyj+.,TBL,CURVES,TBP UFZ	
					Rept INDC−187E	67	. ENGL OF YFI−4 38	
Total	7.9+6	1.5+7	STF	ExTh	Jour PR 157 1149	May 67	Fisher+ 2ES,AT 8MEV POLRZ NS,TARGET	+
				Expt	Abst DA/B 27 4514	Jun 67	Shelley.POL+UNPOL DATA OK ROT−OPTMDL	
					Jour PRL 17 36	Jul 66	.SUPERSEDED	
	8.0+6	1.5+7			Jour PL 19 684	Jan 66	.SUPERSEDED	
	7.9+6	1.5+7			Data EXFOR12118.002	Jun 76	. 2 PTS.	
Total	3.3+5	5.6+6	STF	Expt	Jour PRL 20 502	Mar 68	Mccarthy+4. EFFECT OF ORIENTATION	+
	3.3+5	5.6+6			Data EXFOR12122.002	Jun 76	. 5 PTS.	
Total	2.0+6	1.4+8	HAR	Expt	Abst BAP 13 681	Apr 68	Marshak+3. EFFECT OF ORIENTATION	
Total	3.0+6	7.5+6	PAD	Expt	Jour NP/A 133 572	Aug 69	Fasoli+ ATTN METHOD. 4ENS. GRPH.	
Total	1.0−4	3.0−3	MUN	Expt	Jour AKE 16 49	70	Knorr+ TRANS EXPT, TBL	
Total	None		SAC	Expt	Prog EANDC(E)140U	Apr 70	Cauvin+	
Total	3.0+6	1.5+7	KFK	Revw	Conf 70Helsinki 2 219	Jun 70	Cierjacks.113. SIG(E) GRPH CFD OPTMD	
Total	1.0+6	1.4+8	NBS	Expt	Jour PR/C 2 1862	Nov 70	Marshak+,TOF,ALIGNED TARGET,CURVES	+
	2.0+6	1.4+8			Jour PRL 20 554	Mar 68	− +SUMMARY OF JPR/C 2.	
	1.1+6	1.4+8			Data EXFOR10076.002	May 71	103PTS.	
Total	2.5+6	1.5+7	BNW	Expt	Jour PR/C 3 576	Feb 71	Foster+.,TRANS,CURVS,CFD OTHERS+TH	+
					Jour PRL 22 139	Jan 69	.SUPERSEDED	
					Jour NIM 36 1	Sep 65	.SUPERSEDED	
	2.4+6	1.5+7			Data EXFOR10047.071	Aug 73	233PTS.	
Total	1.0+5	1.5+6	ANL	Expt	Jour ZP 243 171	Apr 71	Meadows+ 2.5KEV RESOLUTION	+
	1.0+5	1.5+6			Data EXFOR10034.	May 71	. 752 PTS.	
Total	1.5+7	1.9+7	RAM	Expt	Rept AECD/EP−23	Jul 71	Farooque+ TRANS,SIG AT 31ES,GRAPH	
					Rept AECD/EP−18	Dec 70	Husain.VDG,TRANS,SIG AT 31 ES,TABLE	
Total	2.0+5	1.9+7	RAM	Theo	Jour NSPB 6 7	Oct 73	Enayetullah+ OPTMDL−FIT,CURV CFD XPT	
	+5	1.9+7			Rept AECD/EP−23	Jul 71	Farooque+ OPTMOD CALC CFD EXPTS GRPH	
Total	1.0−3	1.5+7	AUA	Eval	Data AUSTR−DFN 184.	Nov 71	COOK+POINT(223)+GROUP(127)SIG.CF EVL	+
Total	1.0+1	5.0+2	BNL	Eval	Jour NSE 46 266	Nov 71	Stephenson+. PARAMETRIC FIT. CURVES	
	1.0−4	5.0+1			Conf 68Wash. § F14	Mar 68	− . B−W FIT TO DATA	

67 Holmium 165

Quantity	Energy (ev) Min	Max	Lab	Type	Documentation Ref Vol Page	Author, Comments Date	Data
Total	3.6+1	3.1+3	SAC	Expt Priv	TELLIER	Dec 71 Tellier. LINAC.TOF.DATA FOR COMPILTN	+
				Conf	72Budapest 38	Aug 72 − + NDG	
				Conf	71Knoxvill 680	Mar 71 − + TRANSMISSION. RES PARAMETRS	
				Rept	CEA − N − 1338	Nov 70 − . RESONANCE ANALYSIS.	
	3.6+1	3.1+3		Data	EXFOR20123.002	Sep 72 13787PTS.	
Total	2.7+3		MUN	Expt Prog	EANDC(E)150U	Oct 72 Dilg+ AVERAGE TOT XSECT+S0	+
				Conf	71Albany 327	Aug 71 − +TRNS.AVG CS GVN.31 ELEMENT GRP	
	2.7+3			Data	EXFOR20583.021	May 76 1PNT.	
Total		5.0+4	SAC	ExTh Diss	FRNC − TH − 450	Oct 72 Delaroche.TOF	
Total	1.3+7	1.5+7	DEB	Eval Rept	IAEA − 153 173	73 Boedy+ MOST PROBABLE VAL OF SIG,TBL	
				Jour	AHP 110 115	Oct 71 Angeli+ AVG SIG,CFD CALC.TBLS.GRAPH	
Total	1.4+7	1.9+7	DAC	Expt Jour	JNE 27 43	Jan 73 Farooque+ TRANS,CFD OPTMOD,GRAPH,NDG	+
				Comp Rept	AECD/EP − 18 17	Dec 70 Ameen+ COMPILATION OF EXP. DATA,TBLS	
	1.4+7	1.9+7		Expt Data	EXFOR30244.002	Jun 73 TOTAL SIGMA AT 31 ES,FROM AECD/EP/18	
Total	1.0+6	2.0+6	DAC	Eval Jour	NSPB 6 59	Oct 73 Enayetullah+ SIG(E),LSQ − FIT,TBL+GRPH	+
				Expt Jour	NP/A 209 189	Jul 73 Islam+ AVG,TRANS,CFD OPTICAL MODEL	
				Theo Jour	NP/A 209 202	Jul 73 − + FLUCTUATION ANALYSIS,OWN DATA	
				Comp Rept	AECD/EP − 18	Dec 70 Ameen+ EXPTL DATA FROM DAC,TABLES	
	1.0+6	2.0+6		Expt Data	EXFOR30134.008	Nov 71 SIGMA − TOT AT 100 ES,PRIVATE COMM.	
Total	1.0+3	6.0+5	NBS	Expt Jour	PR/C 9 28	Jan 74 Camarda.LINAC.TOF.GRPH.TRANS.MEAS.S1	
Total	1.5+4	6.0+5	DKE	Expt Jour	AP 84 165	May 74 Pineo+TRNS.AVG CS.TBLS,GRPHS.OPTMDL.	+
	1.0+6	6.5+5		Abst	DA/B 31 6821	May 71 − .2E RANGE AVGS.CFD OPTMDL.	
	1.5+4	6.0+5		Diss	PINEO	70 .AVG CS.GRPHS.CFD.STF CALC.TBL.CFD.	
	1.5+4	6.0+5		Data	EXFOR10542.024	Jan 79 . DATA UNOBTAINABLE FROM AUTHORS.	
Total	7.0+5	9.0+6	GLS	Expt Jour	JP/A 7 1758	Sep 74 Kellie+ SIG IN CURVE,STAT ERROR 2 PC	+
	8.0+5	9.0+6		Data	EXFOR20418.009	Sep 75 588PTS.	
Total	6.1+5	4.0+6	PAD	Expt Jour	NCL 6 485	Mar 73 Fasoli+ VDG	+
	2.0+6			Jour	NCL 11 169	Sep 74 − + THEORY COMPARED WITH EXPT	
	6.1+5	4.0+6		Data	EXFOR20497.002	Mar 76 12PTS.	
Total	+7		IJI	Expt Conf	77Kiev	77 Trofimova+ SIG	
	2.0+3			Conf	76Lowell 1244	Jul 76 Vertebnyi+ TRANSM VS THICKNESS,NDG	
Elastic	2.5−2		ORL	Expt Jour	PR 110 37	Apr 58 Koehler+ COHERENT SIG=9.1+−.5B.	+
	2.5−2			Data	EXFOR12112.	Jun 76 . 2 PTS, COH, COH AMP	
Elastic	1.0+6		ALD	Expt Jour	NP 42 86	Apr 63 Gilboy+.SIG=4.91B+−3PC	+
Elastic	3.0+5	1.4+7	ORL	Theo Jour	NP 53 1	Apr 64 Davies+ OPTMOD+SPIN−SPIN.INT,.3,14MV	
Elastic	9.8+5		AGN	Eval Rept	TID − 21629	Dec 64 Perkins+ CALC FROM BNL400,UCRL5573	
Elastic	7.9−1		BNL	Expt Jour	PR/B 136 1285	Dec 64 Schermer. POLRZ NS.	
Elastic	3.5+1	7.5+2	HAR	Expt Jour	NP/A 108 535	Feb 68 Asghar+.TOF.2SAMPLES.REL PB.CURVE	
Elastic	1.0−2	1.0+1	IFU	Expt Jour	UFZ 13 605	Apr 68 Vertebnyi+ GRPHS,EXPTL SIG=NUCL+MAGN	
				Jour	UPJ 13 425	Oct 68 TRANSLATN.*	
Elastic	3.0+5	1.5+6	ANL	Expt Jour	ZP 243 171	Apr 71 Meadows+INTGRTED CS + LEG COEF CURVS	+
	3.0+5	1.5+6		Data	EXFOR10034.002	Sep 75 62 PTS	
Elastic	1.0−3	1.5+7	AUA	Eval Data	AUSTR − DFN 184.	Nov 71 COOK+POINT(223)+GROUP(127)SIG.CF EVL	+
Elastic	2.5−2		IJI	Eval Conf	75Kiev 1 169	May 75 Fedorova+ EVAL 2200M/S SIG,TABLE	
Elastic	1.0+0		DUB	Expt Conf	76Lowell 1243	Jul 76 Akopian+TOF.SCT CS=COH+INCOH.TBL	
Elastic	Cold		NZA	Theo Jour	PL/B 65 309	Dec 76 Thompson.SPIN−SPIN SIG CALC.	
Diff Elastic	1.0+6		ALD	Expt Jour	NP 42 86	Apr 63 Gilboy+30TO137DEG.COMP.WITH.OPTICMOD	+
Diff Elastic	3.0+5	1.4+7	ORL	Theo Jour	NP 53 1	Apr 64 Davies+ OPTMOD+SPIN−SPIN.INT,.3,14MV	
Diff Elastic	9.8+5		SHE	Theo Jour	NP 54 417	Jun 64 Maddison.OPTMOD FIT TO TOWLE GILBOY	
Diff Elastic	9.8+5		AGN	Eval Rept	TID − 21629	Dec 64 Perkins+ LEG COEF CALC OTHERS,DATA	
Diff Elastic	1.0+6		ITY	Theo Priv	IANEVA	May 65 Cnen.OPTMDL+APPROX DEFORM. OKS NP51	
Diff Elastic	3.5+5		ORL	ExTh Jour	PR/B 139 29	Jul 65 Wagner+ NO SPIN−SPIN POT. POLRZ.	+
				Conf	65Antwerp § 154	Jul 65 .SUPERSEDED	
	3.5+5			Expt Data	EXFOR12133.003	Jun 76 . 12 PTS.	
Diff Elastic	3.5+5		ORL	Theo Jour	RMP 37 679	Oct 65 Tamura. CALCD SIG.	
Diff Elastic	9.2+5		ISS	Expt Jour	JPJ 22 368	Feb 67 Kobayashi+,TOF.REL SIG CFD OPTMDL	
Diff Elastic	8.0+6	1.5+7	STF	Expt Jour	PR 157 1149	May 67 Fisher+ 2ES,ABS CURV,ELAS+2EXCT LVLS	
				Abst	DA/B 27 4514	Jun 67 .ABST	
Diff Elastic	3.5+5	1.5+7	STF	Theo Jour	NP/A 130 609	Jun 69 Fisher+ OPTMDL FIT.	
Diff Elastic	3.0+6	7.5+6	PAD	Expt Jour	NP/A 133 572	Aug 69 Fasoli+ VDG TOF.4ES. CFD OPTMDL.	
Diff Elastic	3.0+5	1.5+6	ANL	Expt Jour	ZP 243 171	Apr 71 Meadows+,CFD DEFORMED POTENTIAL	+
	3.0+5	1.5+6		Data	EXFOR10034.003	Sep 75 310 PTS LIG.FIT.	
Diff Elastic	None		ANL	Expt Prog	USNDC − 11 25	Jun 74 Smith. NDG	
Polarization	3.5+5	1.5+7	STF	Expt Jour	NP/A 130 609	Jun 69 Fisher+ OPTMDL FIT+ASSYM FOR POLR NS	
Potntal Scat	0.0+0	1.2+3	SAC	Expt Rept	CEA − N − 1338	Nov 71 Tellier. 1PNT RADIUS	+
		1.2+3		Data	EXFOR20119.002	Sep 72 1PNT.RADIUS.	
Potntal Scat	3.0+3	6.5+5	DKE	Expt Jour	AP 84 165	May 74 Pineo+TRNS.S WAVE SCT LENGTH.TBL.CFD	
	None			Abst	DA/B 31 6821	May 71 − .S − WAVE SCATT LENGTH	

67 Holmium 165

Quantity	Energy (ev) Min	Max	Lab	Type	Documentation Ref Vol Page	Date	Author, Comments	Data
Potntal Scat	2.0+3		IJI	Expt Conf	76Lowell 1244	Jul 76	Vertebnyi+ SCT-LNGTH GVN,FRM TOT+SCT	
Tot Inelastc	5.0+6	7.0+6	ALD	Expt Jour	NP/A 112 337	May 68	Owens+.3ES.FROM N SPECT 90DEG.	+
Tot Inelastc	1.0-3	3.0-3	MUN	Theo Jour	AKE 16 49	70	Knorr+ PARAMAGNETIC SCAT SIG CALC	
Tot Inelastc	5.0+5	1.5+7	AUA	Eval Data	AUSTR-DFN 184.	Nov 71	COOK+POINT(11)+GROUP(127)SIG.CF EVL	+
Diff Inelast	1.0+6		OXF	Theo Jour	NP 51 27	Feb 64	Barrett.H-F.DIRECT SIG FOR 2+ROT LVL	
Diff Inelast	9.8+5		SHE	Theo Jour	NP 54 417	Jun 64	Maddison.H-F FOR COMP EL 5LVL DEFORM	
Diff Inelast	5.0+6	7.0+6	ALD	Expt Jour	NP/A 112 337	May 68	Owens+.3ES.FROM N SPECT 90DEG NDG.	+
Diff Inelast	1.0+6	1.4+8	ORL	Revw Conf	68DUBSY 213	Jul 68	Tamura.INEL SCT DEFORMED NUCLEI REVW	
Diff Inelast	3.6+6	8.5+6	JAE	Expt Jour	NP/A 131 145	Jun 69	Maruyama. ANGDIST OF NS.-SPECT N'	
				Priv	MARUYAMA	Jul 68	-. N(EN')/EN',EN'.55TO1.95MEV	
Diff Inelast	3.0+6	7.5+6	PAD	Expt Jour	NP/A 133 572	Aug 69	Fasoli+ VDG TOF.4ES.ANGDIST.N'GROUPS	
Diff Inelast	3.0+5	1.5+6	ANL	Expt Jour	ZP 243 171	Apr 71	Meadows+12LVLS.CFD.OPTMDL POTENTIAL	+
	4.2+5	1.5+6		Data	EXFOR10034.	May 71	173 PTS 9 STATES.	
Diff Inelast	4.0+5	1.4+6	PEL	Expt Jour	ZP 257 137	Dec 72	Barnard+,CURVES OF TOF-SPEC GIVEN	
Thermal Scat	Cold		ORL	Revw Jour	JAP 36 1078	Mar 65	Koehler. MAG PROPS, N DIFFR EXPTS	
Thermal Scat	Cold		BNL	Expt Jour	JAP 37 1032	Mar 66	Corliss. MAG PROPS, N DIFFR EXPTS	
Thermal Scat	Cold		GRE	Expt Jour	JAP 37 1038	Mar 66	MAGNETIC PROPS FROM N DIFFR XPTS	
Thermal Scat	Cold		CRC	Expt Jour	JAP 39 457	Feb 68	Holden+ TOF CRYST SPEC PARAMAGN SCAT	
Thermal Scat	1.0-2	1.0+1	IFU	Expt Jour	UFZ 13 605	Apr 68	Vertebnyi+ GRPH SIG(E),MAGN CONTRIB	
				Jour	UPJ 13 425	Oct 68	TRANSLATN.*	
Thermal Scat	2.0-2	1.4+0	IJI	Expt Prog	YFI-12 67	72	Verteby+ ABST,TOT SCAT SIG 15ES,TBL	
				Prog	INDC(CCP)-30	Sep 72	.PAGE 58,ENGLISH OF YFI-12 67	
Thermal Scat	1.0-4	1.0+3	MUN	Revw Jour	EEN 80 1	77	Koester. SCAT LENGTH,FREE SIG	
Scattering	2.5-2		IEA	Expt Jour	NP/A 95 683	Apr 67	. SEE ALSO *	+
				Conf	66Paris 1 53	Oct 66	Zimmerman+ P.129,SIG AT.025EV DEDUCD	
	2.5-2			Data	EXFOR30224.008	Dec 72	DEDUCED SIGMA	
Scattering	2.0-2	3.0+1	IFU	Expt Conf	68Riga	Jan 68	Gnidak+ ABST,TOF,4PI-GEOMETRY	
Scattering	2.0-2	3.0-2	IFU	Expt Conf	70Helsinki 1 651	Jun 70	Vertebnij+ 2200M/SEC SIGMA GIVEN,TBL	
				Rept	BNL-TR-495	Jul 72	. ENGLISH OF 70HELSIN 1 651	
Scattering	2.0+3		IJI	Expt Conf	76Lowell 1244	Jul 76	Vertebnyi+ SCT-SIG VS THICKNESS,NDG	
Nonelastic	1.0-3	1.5+7	AUA	Eval Data	AUSTR-DFN 184.	Nov 71	COOK+POINT(223)+GROUP(127)SIG.CF EVL	+
Absorption	1.0-4	3.0-3	MUN	Theo Jour	AKE 16 49	70	Knorr+ FROM TOT SIG EXPT CALC, TBL	
Absorption	2.5-2		IJI	Eval Conf	75Kiev 1 169	May 75	Fedorova+ EVAL SIGS OF 3ISOMERS,TABL	
Res Int Abs	1.3+2		DUB	Expt Conf	65Antwerp	Jul 65	Konks.DUBNA.64+-6 B ABOVE 130 EV	
Res Int Abs	5.0-1		STF	Expt Conf	66S.Diego 2 175	Feb 66	Lesage+	+
	5.0-1			Data	EXFOR11754.009	Jun 76	. 1 PT.	
Res Int Abs	5.0-1		BOL	Eval Rept	RT/FI-4	Jan 67	Palmucci. CALC FROM (N,G) RES PARAMS	
Res Int Abs	5.0-1		BGK	Expt Rept	THAI-AEC-10	Oct 67	. ACTIV(NA-I),CD-RATIO,REL AU. TABLE	+
	5.0-1			Data	EXFOR30368.025	Jan 77	REL AU, PRELM.	
Res Int Abs	5.0-1	5.0+2	BNL	Eval Conf	68Wash. § F14	Mar 68	Stephenson. 672B FROM EVALUATD SIGMS	
Res Int Abs	5.0-1		MTR	Expt Rept	IN-1195	May 68	Scoville.	+
	5.0-1			Data	EXFOR11820.012	Jun 76	. 1 PT.	
Res Int Abs	2.0-1	1.0+4	LRL	Expt Rept	UCRL-50804	Feb 70	Czirr+ CALC FROM DIFF DATA	+
	2.0-1	1.0+4			Data	EXFOR10169.002	Jul 72	1PT	
Res Int Abs	5.5-1		CRC	Eval Rept	AECL-3037 1	Jan 72	Walker.REDUCED RES INT FROM RES PARS	
Res Int Abs	5.0-1		AUA	Eval Rept	AAEC/TM-619	Sep 72	Clayton.CALC FROM SIG LIBRARY,TABLE	
Res Int Abs	5.0-1		GHT	Expt Jour	JRC 20 695	74	Van Der Linden+ BY(N,G).CFD OTHS,TBL	+
	5.5-1			Conf	73Paris 2 241	Mar 73	- + ACT,REL THR+GOLD,TBL	
	5.5-1			Data	EXFOR20645.030	Jul 76	1PNT.CAPTURE.	
Res Int Abs	+0	+5	WIN	Revw Conf	IAEA-169 3 163	74	Pope+ DATA FILE CALC CFD XPTAL VALUE	
Res Int Abs	1.0-1		NPL	Expt Jour	JP/A 7 2318	Dec 74	Ryves+ REL TO MN AU,REDUCED INTEGRAL	+
	1.0-1	1.4+7		Data	EXFOR20561.013	Oct 75	1PNT.	
Res Int Abs	5.0-1		IJI	Eval Conf	75Kiev 1 169	May 75	Fedorova+ EVAL+CALC RI GIVEN,TABLE	
Res Int Abs	5.0-1		KJL	Expt Jour	JIN 37 1591	Aug 75	Steinnes. CD-RAT+ACTIV INTEG,CFD,TBL	+
				Jour	JIN 34 2699	Sep 72	-. ACT. AU MONITOR	
	5.0-1			Data	EXFOR20635.009	Aug 76	1PNT.CAPTURE.	
	5.0-1			Data	EXFOR20188.024	May 74	1PNT.CAPTURE.	
(n,γ)	2.0+7		OHO	Expt Jour	PR 53 437	Mar 38	Pool+ BETAS,CLOUDCH,RATIO 27H HO/N2N	
(n,γ)	Pile		ANL	Expt Jour	PR 72 888	Nov 47	Seren+.THR IRRAD. TO EU152, HO2O4	+
	Pile			Data	EXFOR11447.107	Jun 76	. 1 PT.	
(n,γ)	Maxwl		ORL	Expt Jour	PR 83 643	Aug 51	Pomerance. LOCAL OSC REL AU ABS 95 B	
	Maxwl			Data	EXFOR11047.052	Jun 76	. 1 PT.	
(n,γ)	1.4+7		ALD	Expt Jour	PPS 72 505	Oct 58	Perkin+ACT ANAL ABOVE 9.45MB,B-W TH	+
(n,γ)	1.5+5	6.0+6	WIS	Expt Jour	PR 116 927	Nov 59	Johnsrud+ SC CFD OTHERS SIG VS E	+
	1.7+5	2.5+6		Data	EXFOR11675.024	Jun 76	. 15 PTS.	

67 Holmium 165

Quantity	Energy (ev) Min	Max	Lab	Type	Documentation Ref Vol Page	Date	Author, Comments	Data
(n,γ)	3.0+4	1.7+5	ORL Expt	Jour	PR 122 182	Apr 61	Gibbons+ 1720,515,1070 MB AT 65 KEV.	+
	3.0+4	6.5+4		Jour	PR 129 2695	Mar 63	Macklin+ LIQ SCINT,1.72 AND 1.07B	
	3.0+4	1.7+5		Conf	61Vienna 1 95	Aug 61	Neiler.	
				Prog	BNL–653	Feb 61	.SUPERSEDED	
	9.5+3	1.7+5		Data	EXFOR11329.	Jun 76	. 57 PTS.	
(n,γ)	2.0+2	8.0+3	ORL Expt	Conf	61Saclay 203	Sep 61	Block+.LIQUID SCINTILLATOR	+
				Conf	61Vienna 1 95	Aug 61	Neiler.PPR73,TABLE FOR SOME ES,GRAPH	
	2.1+2	9.4+3		Data	EXFOR11935.016	Jun 76	. 50 PTS.	
(n,γ)	Maxwl		ROS Expt	Rept	ZFK–RN–16	Sep 62	Brinckmann+VAL GVN,PRODCTN OF HO166M	
(n,γ)	Maxwl		MTR Expt	Prog	WASH–1041 36	Oct 62	Keisch+	+
	Maxwl			Data	EXFOR12094.002	Jun 76	. 1 PT.	
(n,γ)	2.0–1	3.0+4	LEB Comp	Rept	INDSWG–64 43	64	Konks.PB–SLOW–DOWN,GRAPH SIG(E)	
(n,γ)	3.0+4		LEB Expt	Conf	JINR–1845 100	Jun 64	Konks+ PB–SLOWDOWN–TIME, NDG	
(n,γ)	6.4–2	7.9–1	BNL Expt	Jour	PR/B 136 1285	Dec 64	Schermer. POLRZ NS.3ES.60PC.	
(n,γ)	5.0+3	9.0+4	ORL Theo	Jour	RMP 37 166	Jan 65	Macklin+.CALC FOR KT=5TO90KEV	
(n,γ)	Maxwl		RIS Expt	Jour	PR/B 140 816	Nov 65	185MICROS ISOMER .58+–.08 OF CAPTURE	
(n,γ)	1.0+3	1.0+4	LAS Theo	Rept	LA–3463	Jan 66	Bell. TH CAPTURE OF RARE EARTHS	
(n,γ)	2.5–2		IEA Expt	Conf	66Paris 1 53	Oct 66	Zimmerman+ P.129,SIG AT.025EV DEDUCD	+
	2.5–2			Data	EXFOR30224.009	Dec 72	DEDUCED SIGMA	
(n,γ)	2.5–2		BOL Eval	Rept	RT/FI–4	Jan 67	Palmucci. CALC FROM RES PARAMETERS	
(n,γ)	3.9+0		TRM Expt	Conf	67Kanpur 409	Feb 67	Chandramoleswar. WG= 43+–4 MICRO S	
				Prog	AEET–267 4	Aug 66	– + VALUE GIVEN,CFD BNL	
(n,γ)	1.3+7	1.5+7	DEB Expt	Conf	NP/A 95 229	Mar 67	Csikai+,SIG TO G–STATE AT 9ES	+
				Jour	MFF 16 123	Feb 68	SEE ALSO *IN HUNGARIAN	
	1.3+7	1.5+7		Data	EXFOR30074.006	Nov 70	SIG TO G–STATE AT 8ES REL TO 14.7MEV	
	1.5+7			Data	EXFOR30067.016	Nov 70	SIGMA TO GND–STATE AT 14.7 MEV	
(n,γ)	3.0+0	5.2+2	DUB Expt	Jour	YF 5 471	Mar 67	Karzhavina+.JRNSM–CURVE,PULSD REACTR	
				–			ENGL SNP5 329 (9/67)	
(n,γ)	Maxwl		LAS Expt	Jour	PR 155 1265	Mar 67	Motz+ SIG FOR 1200Y ISOMER =3.5+–.5B	
(n,γ)	3.0+6		DEB Expt	Jour	JNE 21 797	Oct 67	Peto+ACTIV,SIGMA REL TO P–31(N,P)	+
	3.0+6			Data	EXFOR30031.025	Aug 70	SINGLE VALUE	
(n,γ)	1.0+6	1.9+7	LOK Expt	Jour	PR 163 1299	Nov 67	Menlove+ ACT,17ES REL THR,U235 FISS	+
				Conf	66Wash. 746	Mar 66	.SUPERSEDED	
	9.7+5	1.9+7		Data	EXFOR11420.005	Jun 76	. 17 PTS.	
(n,γ)	1.4+7		LYO Comp	Rept	LYCEN/6780	Nov 67	Crouzet+COMPILATN FOR ACTIVTN ANALYS	
(n,γ)	Maxwl		LRL Expt	Jour	JIN 30 15	Jan 68	Nethaway+ TO ISOM ONLY.REL TO TM169	+
	Maxwl			Data	EXFOR12091.002	Jun 76	. 1 PT.	
(n,γ)	–1	5.0+4	DUB Expt	Jour	YF 7 493	Mar 68	Konks+ SIG(NEUT–E) GRPH,PB–SLOW–DOWN	
				Jour	SNP 7 310	Sep 68	– + ENGL OF YF 7 493.	
(n,γ)	1.0+3	1.0+5	HAR Expt	Rept	NP–17644	Jul 68	Moxon.THESIS.MOXON–RAE DET.AVG SIG	
	2.5+0	1.0+5		Jour	NP/A 108 535	Feb 68	Asghar+.TOF.3SAMPLES.CURVE AVERAG CS	
(n,γ)	–		IEA Comp	Rept	IEA–INF–10	Aug 68	Atalla. TABLES OF HL,SIG AND GAMM–E	
(n,γ)	2.4+4		MUA Theo	Jour	IJP 42 567	Sep 68	Chaubey+ METHD OF BOOTH,VAL CFD XPT	+
			Expt	Jour	NP 66 267	May 65	– +,SB–BE,ACT BETA–DET REL I127	
	2.4+4			Data	EXFOR30063.009	Dec 70	SIGMA FOR 2.73 H HALF–LIFE	
(n,γ)	2.0+5		MUA Theo	Conf	69Roorke 2 129	Dec 69	Chaubey+ SIG VALUE GIVEN, STATIST–TH	
(n,γ)	2.0+2	1.2+4	LRL Expt	Rept	UCRL–50804	Feb 70	Czirr.TOF+LINAC.PULSED NEUTS.CURVE	+
	2.0+2	1.3+4		Data	EXFOR10169.005	Jul 72	98PTS.SIGMA.	
(n,γ)	1.0+7	2.2+7	BOL Revw	Conf	70Helsinki 2 379	Jun 70	Benzi.115. REVIEW, SIG(E) GRAPH	
(n,γ)	1.0+3	1.0+6	GA Revw	Conf	70ANL 285	Oct 70	Carlson. STATUS AS STANDARD SIG,CURV	
(n,γ)	3.0+4		AUA Theo	Rept	AAEC/E–211	Nov 70	Musgrove. SIGMA GIVEN AND CFD OTHER	
(n,γ)	Fast		MTR Expt	Prog	NCSAC–33 90	Dec 70	Scoville+.ACT.FAST SPEC.VALUE GIVEN.	
(n,γ)	4.0+5		WWA Expt	Jour	APPB 2 489	71	Brzosko+ PARTIAL,TOTAL SIG CFD THEO	+
				Rept	INR–1318 28	Apr 71	*SHORT REPORT,DATA GIV	
				Jour	CJP 47 2849	Dec 69	*TH.CALCULATIONS OF SIG	
	4.0+5			Data	EXFOR30159.	Apr 72	PARTIAL,TOTAL SIGMAS GIVEN	
(n,γ)	Fast		MTR Expt	Conf	71Knoxvill 113	Mar 71	Harker.INTEGRAL MEAST,1.46B REL AU	+
	Fast			Data	EXFOR10218.008	Oct 72	1PNT.SIGMA.	
(n,γ)	Maxwl		KFI Comp	Jour	JRC 7 365	Jun 71	Nagy+ SIGMA,GAMMA–E AND HALF–LIFE	
(n,γ)		+5	ATI Expt	Prog	EANDC(OR)105L	Aug 71	Bensch+,PHOTO–NEUTRON SOURCES	
(n,γ)	1.4+7		LAS Expt	Jour	PL/B 36 557	Oct 71	Drake+ SPECTRUM SUMMED CFD PB208 NG	+
	1.4+7			Data	EXFOR10193.003	Jun 72	1PT,SIGMA	
(n,γ)	1.0–3	1.5+7	AUA Eval	Data	AUSTR–DFN 184.	Nov 71	COOK+POINT(223)+GROUP(127)SIG.CF EVL	+
(n,γ)	Maxwl		CRC Eval	Rept	AECL–3037 1	Jan 72	Walker.RECOMMENDED SIG,DETAILED TBL	
(n,γ)	2.4+4		MUA Theo	Jour	IJP 46 114	Mar 72	Chaubey+ P–WAVE STRENGTH FUNCT,TABLE	
(n,γ)	1.0+3	1.0+7	BOL Eval	Data	BENZI–DFN 690.	May 72	40 PNTS	
(n,γ)	2.5–2		AUA Eval	Rept	AAEC/TM–619	Sep 72	Clayton.CALC FROM SIG LIBRARY,TABLE	

67 Holmium 165

Quantity	Energy (ev) Min	Max	Lab	Type	Documentation Ref Vol Page	Date	Author, Comments	Data
(n,γ)	3.0+4	3.0+5	USP	Expt Jour	NP/A 196 83	Nov 72	Lepine+ LI7-P NS.TOF.M-R. REL TO IN	+
	3.0+4	3.0+5		Data	EXFOR30233.007	Mar 73	NDS,RELATIVE TO IN,ABSOLUTE ERROR	
(n,γ)	5.0+3	1.6+5	VIP	Expt Jour	NSE 49 317	Nov 72	Fawcett+. ACTIVATION. CURVE.	+
				Abst	DA/B 32 2929	Nov 71	- . ABST.	
	5.0+3	1.6+5		Data	EXFOR10298.002	Oct 73	16PTS.SIGMA.	
(n,γ)	7.2+6	1.4+7	ORE	Expt Conf	73Pacif.Gr 2 951	Mar 73	Mcdaniels+ TO GND,1ST ST,GRPH SIG(E)	
(n,γ)	2.5+4		AUW	Expt Jour	NC/A 18 48	Nov 73	Sidappa+ ACTIV SIG,CFD.TABLE	
(n,γ)	1.7+2	6.0+5	LRL	Expt Jour	NSE 52 299	Nov 73	Czirr+. ABSOL+RELATIVE MEASTS	+
	1.0+2	1.0+6		Prog	UCID-16037 1	May 72	- + REL U235(N,F),NDG	
	1.9+2	2.5+5		Data	EXFOR10305.002	Nov 75	29 PTS	
(n,γ)	Fiss		WIN	Revw Conf	IAEA-169 3 137	74	Dean. POINT DATA AVG OVER STAND SPEC	
	Maxwl	Fiss		Conf	IAEA-169 3 163	74	Pope+ MAXW+FIS-SPEC AVG DATA CFD XPT	
(n,γ)	1.4+7		LAS	Expt Prog	USNDC-11 151	Jun 74	Arthur+ ANG DISTR GAMMAS, NDG.	+
(n,γ)	+3	3.0+4	JAE	Expt Prog	NEANDC(J)36L 4	Sep 74	Mizumoto+.LINAC,TOF.LIQ-SCINT.NDG	
(n,γ)	2.5-2		NPL	Expt Jour	JP/A 7 2318	Dec 74	Ryves+	+
	2.5-2			Data	EXFOR20561.012	Oct 75	1PNT.SIGMA.	
(n,γ)	2.5+4		TAT	Expt Conf	74Bombay 2 101	Dec 74	Kondaiah+ SIG TO 27HRS-ISOMER GIVEN	+
	2.5+4			Data	EXFOR30390.015	Mar 77	1PNT. PARTIAL SIG TO GROUND	
(n,γ)	2.0+4	3.5+6	ANL	Expt Conf	AERE-R-8082	Jul 75	Poenitz. ABSTR LIQ SCINT. REL AU	
	3.0+5	3.0+6		Rept	ANL-NDM-15	Jun 75	- . TBL,GRPH CFD OPT MODEL CALC	
	4.0+5	3.0+6		Data	EXFOR10401.002	Feb 76	16PTS.	
(n,γ)	1.5+7		JYV	Expt Jour	PL/B 39 625	May 72	Kantele+ CAPT SIG MEASURED	+
				Rept	JU-RR-1/1976	Mar 76	Valkonen.(THESIS).ACTIV.TBL. 14.5MEV	
	1.5+7			Data	EXFOR20673.032	Nov 76	1PNT.SIGMA.	
	1.5+7			Data	EXFOR20544.008	Apr 76	1PNT.SIGMA.	
(n,γ)	1.5+7		JYV	Comp Rept	JU-RR-1/1976	Mar 76	Valkonen.(THESIS).EXPTS CFD DSD MODL	
(n,γ)	2.1+3	1.0+4	DUB	Theo Conf	JINR-D-9920	Jun 76	Pikel'Ner. P285.POL NS,SPIN-DEP.TABL	
(n,γ)	4.0+2	2.0+3	BOL	Expt Conf	76Lowell 1242	Jul 76	Coceva+CAPT YLDS.S0 STF.NDG	
(n,γ)		1.0+3	KUK	Eval Conf	76Lowell 1280	Jul 76	Malik+ VARIOUS CAPT DATA CFD AND ANAL	
Spect (n,γ)	Maxwl		YAL	Expt Jour	PR 114 268	Apr 59	Draper.SC SPECTR,GAM E 0 TO 600 KEV	
Spect (n,γ)	Maxwl		ARF	Expt Prog	ARF-1193-9	Apr 62	Greenwood+,CRYST SPEC,LOW-E GAMMAS	
Spect (n,γ)	Pile		CTH	Expt Jour	NP 39 286	Dec 62	Hardell+. PRECISION E DETERMINATION	
Spect (n,γ)	Maxwl		CAS	Expt Jour	NC 27 538	Jan 63	Giannini+ NAI(TL),E+INTENSTY,TO .4MV	+
Spect (n,γ)	Pile		UPP	Expt Jour	NP 40 329	Jan 63	Marklund+.E DETERM. NO INTENS MEAS.	
Spect (n,γ)	Maxwl		MUN	Expt Jour	ZN/A 18 576	May 63	Orecher+ROENTGEN SPECTROMETRY	
Spect (n,γ)	None		MIT	Expt Rept	MITNE-37	Aug 63	Neill+. HARD GS AND GG COINCS.	
Spect (n,γ)	Maxwl		IFL	Expt Jour	NP 66 325	May 65	Balodis+ INT CONV,HO166LVLS TO 240KV	+
				Jour	ZN/A 18 576	63	*(ORECHER)	
Spect (n,γ)			KUR	Expt Jour	IZV 29 782	May 65	Groshev+.TBL + GRAPH. ENGL BAS29 786	
				Conf	64Paris 2 585	Jul 64	SEE ALSO *	
				Book	NEJTRONFIZ 335	61	Groshev. TABLE+GRAPH	
				Jour	NP 16 645	Jun 60	- + 0.5 TO 6MEV GAMS,CFD THEORY	
				Book	SPN 248	61	. ENGL TRANSL OF NEJTRONFIZ 335	
Spect (n,γ)	Maxwl		CCP	Theo Jour	YF 2 4 657	Oct 65	Kosorukov.GRPH SPCTR,CFD EXP	
				Jour	SNP 2 470	Apr 66	TRANSLATN.*	
Spect (n,γ)	Pile		MUN	Expt Jour	ZN/A 21 1328	Sep 66	Neumann. CRYST SPEC EXPT OF GAM INT	
				Rept	ANL-TRANS-941	73	. ENGLISH OF ZN/A 1328	
Spect (n,γ)	Maxwl		LAS	Expt Jour	PR 155 1265	Mar 67	Motz+ GE-LI +MAGNT SPECT,4.9-6.1MEV	
				Jour	PR/B 140 816	Nov 65	.SUPERSEDED	
				Conf	65Antwerp § 53	Jul 65	.SUPERSEDED	
				Prog	EANDC(OR)-35	Apr 65	.SUPERSEDED	
Spect (n,γ)	Maxwl		MUN	Expt Conf	67Juelich 56	Apr 67	Egidy+ CONVERSION ELECTRONS162-6.NDG	
Spect (n,γ)	Pile		ANL	Expt Prog	WASH-1124 8	Nov 68	Jackson+ NAI NDG TO GND+1MEV REGION	
Spect (n,γ)	Maxwl		UPP	Expt Jour	NP/A 120 561	Nov 68	Nilsson+.INT CONVERSION. PURE E2 TR.	
				Jour	NP/A 120 569	Nov 68	Hoegberg+ M INT CONVERSION. PURE E2.	
Spect (n,γ)		1.0+3	HAR	Expt Prog	EANDC(OR)86L	Jan 69	Axmann+(IRK) LINAC.	
Spect (n,γ)	2.5-2		MIT	Comp Rept	MITNE-85	Jan 69	Rasmussen+TBL G INT.=AFCRL-69-0071	
Spect (n,γ)	+1		BNL	Expt Rept	IAEA-124 303	Feb 70	Chrien.G-SPEC EPITHERMAL AVG	
	1.3+1	1.8+1		Conf	69Studsvik 627	Aug 69	- . SPEC GRPHS FOR 2 NEUT-RESON	
Spect (n,γ)	1.8+1	8.6+1	ANL	Expt Jour	NP/A 155 569	Aug 70	Poenitz+GE(LI) LOW LVL OCCUP PROB	
Spect (n,γ)	Pile		ANL	Expt Jour	PR/C 2 1951	Nov 70	Bollinger+,B10 COVER,GE(LI) DET	
				Conf	69Studsvik 601	Aug 69	Smither+ NO DATA GVN,OKS STATMOD	
Spect (n,γ)	Pile		CCP	Expt Jour	IZV 35 770	Apr 71	Belyaev+ INTENSITIES OF GAMMAS,TBL	
				Jour	BAS 35 709	Apr 72	. ENGLISH OF IZV 35 770 4/71	
Spect (n,γ)	Maxwl		KFI	Comp Jour	JRC 7 365	Jun 71	Nagy+ SIGMA,GAMMA-E AND HALF-LIFE	
Spect (n,γ)	Pile		KFK	Expt Rept	KFK-1401	Jun 71	Djadali.AVG POLRZ G EXPT,CFD T,SPIN	
	Maxwl			Jour	NP/A 147 150	May 70	Eichler+ POL NS.CIRC POL GS+ASSYMTRY	
Spect (n,γ)	4.0+5		WWA	Expt Jour	APPB 2 489	Aug 71	Brzosko+ GAMMA-EN = 3 TO 7 MEV,GRAPH	

67 Holmium 165

Quantity	Energy (ev) Min	Max	Lab	Type	Documentation Ref Vol Page	Author, Comments Date	Data
Spect (n,γ)	1.4+7		LAS Expt	Jour	PL/B 36 557	Oct 71 Drake+ SPECTRUM CFD PB208 AND U238	
Spect (n,γ)	Maxwl		IFL Expt	Book	PROKOFJEV	73 . TBL GAM,CONV ELECTR ES+INT,LVL SCH	
Spect (n,γ)	Pile		MUNExpt	Jour	ZP 258 315	Mar 73 Henkelmann. E + INT OF GS GIVEN	+
	2.5-2			Data	EXFOR20606.015	Jun 76 8PTS.	
Spect (n,γ)	1.0+0	2.0+3	GEL Expt	Prog	NEANDC(E)162 3	Feb 75 Coceva+REL.CONTRIB.DIFF.SPINS T CAPT	
Spect (n,γ)	6.5-2		LEI Expt	Rept	INIS-MF-3169	Jun 76 Bosman. THESIS.POL NS+TARG.LVL SCHEM	
Spect (n,γ)	Maxwl		RCN Expt	Diss	INIS-MF-3169	Jun 76 Bosman. POL N,POL TARGET, SPINS HO66	
				Diss	BOSMAN-LEIDEN	76 - .POL N POL TGT DEC SCH SPINS	
				Conf	74Petten 638	Sep 74 - + NUCL.ORIENTATION,SPINS HO166	
Spect (n,γ)	1.4+7		NJS Expt	Rept	INDC(YUG)-5	Dec 76 Budnar+ SCINT PAIRSPEC.TBL SIG(EGAM)	+
	1.4+7			Data	EXFOR30364.008	Dec 76 DIFFSIG(GAM - E:11 TO 22MEV).25 PNTS	+
Inelastic γ	5.0+6	7.0+6	ALD Expt	Jour	NP/A 112 337	May 68 Owens+.3ES.TOF SPECT 90 DEG. NDG.	+
Inelastic γ	2.7+6		KGUExpt	Conf	71Moscow	Feb 71 .ABST ONLY,GAM ES+REL INTENS,SPEC	
Inelastic γ	+7		CCP Expt	Conf	72Kiev	Jan 72 Simonenko+ ABST,SPIN OF 8 STATES	
Inelastic γ	4.0+5	1.8+6	PEL Expt	Jour	ZP 257 137	Dec 72 Barnard+, TBL OF GS GIVEN	
Inelastic γ	2.7+6		KGUTheo	Jour	YF 18 473	Sep 73 Simonenko+ PAIRCORREL-MDL CFD XP,TBL	
			Expt	Jour	YF 15 856	May 72 Andreev+ GAM ES GIVEN,ANGDIST NDG	
			Theo	Jour	SNP 18 243	Apr 74 .ENGLISH OF YF 18 473	
			Expt	Jour	SNP 15 479	Nov 72 .ENGLISH TRANSLATION OF YF 15 856	
Inelastic γ	5.2+5	1.0+6	DAC Expt	Jour	NSPB 6 32	Oct 73 Siddiq+ NA-I G-SPEC(300-800KEV),CURV	
(n,2n)	Fiss		CRC Eval	Rept	CRC-1003	Dec 60 Roy+,ESTIMATED AVG SIG=4.5MB	
(n,2n)	1.5+7		MUAExpt	Jour	NP 28 560	Dec 61 Khurana+HANS.ACTIVATION,CFD STATMOD.	+
	1.5+7			Data	EXFOR31247.019	Mar 73 .SIG GVN	
(n,2n)	1.5+7		TUR Expt	Jour	NP 51 337	Feb 64 Bonazzola+ACT BETA COUNT 2760+-55MB	+
(n,2n)	1.4+7		HAMCompJour		NP 65 257	Mar 65 Bormann. 2EXPT VALS.CFD SHELL EFFECT	
(n,2n)	1.3+7	1.5+7	BNL Theo	Jour	NSE 23 238	Nov 65 Pearlstein.3ES.STAT MDL CALC.TBL CS.	
(n,2n)	Fiss		BNL Theo	Jour	NSE 23 238	Nov 65 Pearlstein.STATMDL CALC.SPEC AVG.TBL	
(n,2n)	1.4+7		SAH Expt	Jour	NP 85 227	Sep 66 Sethi+ GS+133KV ISOMER,DECAY OBSERVD	+
				Prog	AEET-267 51	Aug 66 - +SIGS GVN,METAST+GROUND STATE	
				Conf	66Bombay 224	Feb 66 - +.SIGMA FOR 2STATES GVN,ACTIVTN	
	1.4+7			Data	EXFOR31280.	Mar 73 .SIG POPULATING MS AND GND STATE GVN	
(n,2n)	1.3+7	1.9+7	LOK Expt	Jour	PR 163 1308	Nov 67 Menlove+ ACT,PROBABLY TO HO164M,TABL	+
				Abst	DA/B 27 3638	Apr 67 .ABSTRACT	
	1.3+7	1.9+7		Data	EXFOR11421.008	Jun 76 . 10 PTS.	
(n,2n)	1.4+7		LYO Comp	Rept	LYCEN/6780	Nov 67 Crouzet+COMPILATN FOR ACTIVTN ANALYS	
(n,2n)	1.3+7	1.9+7	HAMExpt	Jour	NP/A 115 309	Jul 68 Bormann+VDG.TO META.CFD STAT+OPTMDL	+
(n,2n)	1.5+7		MUNexpt	Jour	NP/A 118 9	Sep 68 Dilg+ ACTIV.REL AL(N,A) .TO G,METAST	+
	1.5+7			Data	EXFOR20802.	Dec 78 2PTS.SIGMA.	
(n,2n)	1.5+7		DEB ExTh	Jour	NP/A 122 234	Dec 69 Karolyi.ISOMERIC RATIO,HUIZ-VANDENB.	+
	1.5+7		Expt		EXFOR30101.014	Feb 71 ISOMERIC RATIO	
(n,2n)	1.5+7		DEB Comp	Jour	REA 7 4 93	Dec 69 Csikai+ SIG+HL COMPILTN,N-ACTIV-ANAL	
(n,2n)	1.5+7		CCP Comp	Rept	ICD-6 215	70 Sluchevskaja.SIGS GND+ISOM,RATIO,TBL	
(n,2n)	1.2+7	1.8+7	BAS Expt	Jour	HPA 43 17	Feb 70 Steiner+ ACT ANAL CFD STATMOD TBL	+
	1.3+7	1.9+7		Prog	EANDC(OR)90L	Jun 69 - +,ISOM XSECT RATIOS	
	1.3+7	1.9+7		Data	EXFOR20514.	Apr 76 11PTS.SIGMA.	
(n,2n)	1.4+7	1.5+7	JYV Eval	Rept	JU-RR-3/1970	Jun 70 Leppaemaeki+ TABLE OF EVAL AVG SIG	
(n,2n)	+7		KFI Theo	Rept	KFKI-71-8	Feb 71 Jeki. CALCULATED CFD EXPTL SIG VALUE	
(n,2n)	1.4+7	1.5+7	IRK ExTh	Jour	APA 33 285	Jul 71 Winiwarter+ ISOMERIC RATIO	
(n,2n)	1.5+7		DEB Eval	Rept	REA 11 1 153	Mar 73 Boedy. COMPILATION+RECOMM.VALUE,TBL	
				Rept	IAEA-153 173	73 - . RECOMM. VALUE ONLY	
(n,2n)	1.5+7		TAT Theo	Jour	JP/A 7 1457	Aug 74 Kondaiah. CALC ON STAT MODEL	
(n,2n)	1.5+7		JUL Expt	Jour	NP/A 224 319	May 74 Qaim. ACT.GE(LI).TO GRND, METAST	+
				Jour	RRL 25 335	May 76 - + SIG IN GRPH. SYST VS (N-Z)/A	
	1.5+7			Data	EXFOR20541.	Apr 76 4PTS.SIGMA.	
(n,xn) x>2	Fiss		BNL Theo	Rept	NSE 23 238	Nov 65 Pearlstein.SPEC AVG STATMDL CALC N3N	
(n,p)	Fiss		CRC Eval	Rept	CRC-1003	Dec 60 Roy+,ESTIMATED AVG SIG=0.013MB	
(n,p)	1.4+7		HYO Expt	Jour	JPJ 16 2371	Dec 61 Fukuzawa.TO DY165+DY165M CFD STATMOD	+
	1.4+7			Data	EXFOR20289.	Jun 74 2PTS.SIGMA.	
(n,p)	1.4+7		SAH Comp	Jour	NUC 23 8 112	Aug 65 Chatterjee. TABLE WITH REFS.	
					NP 60 273	Nov 64 - .MEAN OF EXPT CFD SHELLMOD	
(n,p)	1.4+7	1.5+7	ARK Theo	Prog	ORO-3235-29	Jan 67 Koch+,STAT MODEL CALC CFD EXPTS	
(n,p)	1.4+7	1.5+7	NAP Comp	Rept	INFN/BE-67-10	Jul 67 Cuzzocrea+ AVERAGED CHOSEN DATA.	
(n,p)	1.4+7		LYO Comp	Rept	LYCEN/6780	Nov 67 Crouzet+COMPILATN FOR ACTIVTN ANALYS	
(n,p)	1.5+7		DEB Comp	Jour	REA 7 4 93	Dec 69 Csikai+ SIG+HL COMPILTN,N-ACTIV-ANAL	
(n,p)	1.4+7	1.5+7	JYV Eval	Rept	JU-RR-3/1970	Jun 70 Leppaemaeki+ TABLE OF EVAL AVG SIG	
(n,p)	1.4+7		KFI Comp	Jour	JRC 7 365	Jun 71 Nagy+ SIG-LIMIT,GAM-ES AND HALF-LIFE	
(n,α)	Fiss		CRC Eval	Rept	CRC-1003	Dec 60 Roy+,ESTIMATED AVG SIG=BELO 0.0001MB	
(n,α)	1.5+7		CIS Expt	Jour	NP 46 51	Jul 63 Marcazzan+.DIFF.SIG-AT 30DEG MEASURE	+

67 Holmium 165

Quantity	Energy (ev) Min	Energy (ev) Max	Lab	Type	Documentation Ref Vol Page	Date	Author, Comments	Data
(n,α)	Maxwl		CCP	Expt	Jour YF 1 252	Feb 65	Andreev.SIG UPPER LIMIT,TBL(HO167?)	+
					Jour SNP 1 177	Aug 65	*	
(n,α)	1.5+7		SAH	Expt	Prog AEET-267 50	Aug 66	Gujrathi+ABSTRACT,DECAY OF TB-162	
(n,α)	1.4+7		LYO	Comp	Rept LYCEN/6780	Nov 67	Crouzet+COMPILATN FOR ACTIVTN ANALYS	
(n,α)	1.4+7		AUW	Expt	Jour NP/A 125 57	Feb 69	RAMA PRASAD+,ACTIVATION,CFD OTHERS	+
				ExTh	Jour IPA 12 640	Sep 74	Rama Prasad+ CFD STATMDL COMPND VALU	
	1.4+7			Expt	Data EXFOR30051.	Dec 70	SIGMA NA,ALSO N2N+NA+NP FOR OTHERS	
(n,α)	1.5+7		DEB	Comp	Jour REA 7 4 93	Dec 69	Csikai+ SIG+HL COMPILTN,N-ACTIV-ANAL	
(n,α)	1.4+7	1.5+7	JYV	Eval	Rept JU-RR-3/1970	Jun 70	Leppaemaeki+ TABLE OF EVAL AVG SIG	
(n,α)	1.4+7		TIT	Expt	Jour NP/A 149 513	Jul 70	Kitazawa. S SPEC 0 DEG+SIGMA+ANDISTR	+
	1.5+7				Data EXFOR20336.004	Jul 74	12PTS.D/DA.DE.	
(n,α)	+7		KFK	Expt	Jour JIN 34 2093	Jul 72	Krivan+ ACTIVITY CFD SYSTEMATICS	
(n,α)	1.4+7		RBZ	Theo	Jour FIZ 6 41	May 74	Caplar+ DOUBLE-DIFFSIG,CFD EXPT,GRPH	
	None				Prog INDC(SEC)-35	Sep 73	- + PRE-EQUILIBRIUM STATMDL,GRPH	
	1.4+7				Conf 73Munich 1 517	Aug 73	- + DIFFSIG FORMULA GIVN,NO DATA	
(n,α)	1.4+7	1.8+7	IBJ	Expt	Jour ASL 25 203	75	Glowacka+ A-SPEC,ANGDIS,CFD THEO,FIG	
(n,α)	1.8+7		IBJ	Expt	Jour NP/A 244 117	Jun 75	Glowacka+ ALF E-SPEC+ANGDIST.GRAPHS	+
				ExTh	Conf ZFK-271 109	Nov 73	- + A-SPEC CFD 2 MODELS,NDG	
				Expt	Prog INR-1464 1	May 73	- +BRIEF,ALPHA SPECTRUM,TABLES	
	1.8+7				Data EXFOR30261.	Nov 73	ALFA-SPEC(28 PTS)+SIGMA AT 35 DEGREE	
Reson Params	4.0+0	1.3+1	BNL	Expt	Jour PR 92 656	Nov 53	Foote+ CRYSTSPEC STRENGTH ESTIMATED	+
	4.0+0	3.9+1			Data EXFOR12107.	Jun 76	. 5 RES, E0,WT**2/PCS	
Reson Params	4.0+0		BNL	Expt	Jour PR 96 1014	Nov 54	Sailor+ CRYSTL SPECTR RSLN.03EV	+
Reson Params	3.9+0	1.3+2	BNL	Expt	Jour PR 99 10	Jul 55	Harvey+.FC TRANSM. 19 RES. AREA ANAL	+
	3.9+0	1.3+2			Data EXFOR11912.053	Jun 76	. 19 RES, E0,WN,WNO	
Reson Params	+0	+2	BNL	Expt	Prog WASH-745	Nov 57	Hughes. FC NDG	
Reson Params	3.9+0	1.3+1	BNL	Expt	Jour PR 126 979	May 62	Postma+TRNS OF POLARIZED HO,J=4.2RES	+
	3.9+0	1.3+1			Data EXFOR11160.002	Jun 76	. 2 RES., J	
Reson Params	3.9+0		BNL	Expt	Priv SCHERMER.	Feb 64	. Schermer.	
	3.9+0				Data EXFOR12123.003	Jun 76	. 1 RES, E0,WT,PCS	
Reson Params	1.8+1	2.1+1	BNL	Expt	Jour PR/B 137 1484	Mar 65	Brunhart.	+
	1.8+1	2.1+1			Data EXFOR11771.002	Jun 76	. 2 PTS., J	
Reson Params	3.9+0	5.4+1	DUB	Expt	Jour YF 3 55	Jan 66	Alfimenkov+,PLRZD NS AND TRGT TABLE	+
	3.9+0	2.4+2			Rept JINR-P3-3208	Apr 67	- +.TRANS POL N.SPINS.TBL	
	3.9+0	5.4+1			Jour SNP 3 39	Jul 66	TRANSLATN.*BNL-TR-36 N/65	
					Rept JINR-P-2209	Jun 65	.SEE ALSO	
		5.5+2			Rept JINR-P-2209	Jun 65	Alfimenkov+SPINS OF 11 EXTD STATES	
Reson Params	3.9+0		TRM	Expt	Prog AEET-267 4	Aug 66	Chandramoleswar+TABLE WN,WT, CFD BNL	+
	3.9+0				Data EXFOR30408.004	Aug 77	N-,TOT-WIDTHS, PEAK SIG.	
Reson Params	3.9+0	4.9+2	DUB	Expt	Jour YF 5 471	Mar 67	Karzhavina+ TBL+CURV,TOT+N-WIDTH,	+
	3.9+0	5.1+2			Rept JINR-P-2593	Mar 66	.TRANSM-XPT,WN+WG TABLE	
	3.9+0	4.9+2			Jour SNP 5 329	Sep 67	. ENGL OF YF 5 471	
	3.9+0	5.1+2			Data EXFOR40032.	Aug 70	.89 RES-EN,6 SUBENTRIES	
Reson Params		1.0+6	AUA	Theo	Jour AUJ 20 477	Oct 67	Cook. TBL OF AVG LVL SPACING D,L=0,1	
Reson Params	3.9+0	2.6+2	HAR	Expt	Jour NP/A 108 535	Feb 68	Asghar+.WN WG J SCATT+CAPT AREA METH	
	3.5+1	9.3+1		Revw	Conf 66Trieste 831	Dec 66	RAE.N-WID,G-WID,AREA ANALYSIS,GRAPH	
Reson Params	None		IFU	Expt	Jour UFZ 13 679	Apr 68	Vertebnyi+ OTHER D VAL GVN	
					Jour UPJ 13 477	Oct 68	TRANSLATN.*	
Reson Params		5.0+2	DUB	Expt	Rept 68DUBSY 349	Jul 68	Pikelner.LVL SPAC,AVERG. WG	
Reson Params	1.0+3	1.0+5	HAR	Expt	Rept NP-17644	Jul 68	Moxon.THESIS. AVG D,WG,AND WG/D	
Reson Params	+0	+2	ANL	Expt	Prog WASH-1124 8	Nov 68	Jackson+ WN+PARTIAL WG CORRELATN NDG	
Reson Params	+3	+5	AUA	ExTh	Rept AAEC/E-198	May 69	Musgrove.RES PARS +STF FROM (NG)FIT	+
Reson Params	1.3+1	1.8+1	BNL	ExTh	Conf 69Studsvik 627	Aug 69	Chrien.GRPH=RES-SPIN INFL ON GAM-INT	
Reson Params	1.3+1		HAR	Expt	Prog AERE-PR/NP16	Aug 69	Marshak+ LINAC POLRZ SAMPLE J TBD	
Reson Params	2.0+5		MUA	Theo	Conf 69Roorke 2 129	Dec 69	Chaubey+ D/GAM-WIDTH RATIO, STATMOD	
Reson Params	1.8+1	8.6+1	ANL	Expt	Jour NP/A 151 569	Aug 70	Poenitz+SPIN ASSIGN 14 N-G RESON.	
	1.8+1	8.6+1			Data EXFOR10167.002	Nov 72	14PTS.E0,J.	
Reson Params	-		AUA	Theo	Rept AAEC/E-211	Nov 70	Musgrove. CALCULTD D+GAM WIDTH GIVEN	
Reson Params	3.9+0	2.5+2	CJD	Eval	Rept YK-7	71	Zakharova+ SURVEY+SYSTEMATICS,GW,TBL	
					Rept INDC(CCP)-27	Nov 72	.ENGLISH TRANSLATION OF YK-7 /71	
Reson Params	None		DUB	Theo	Jour YF 13 240	Feb 71	Malecki+G-WID,THEO CFD EXPT.TBL,GRPH	
					Jour SNP 13 133	Aug 71	- + ENGL OF YF 13 240.	
Reson Params	None		GEL	Expt	Prog EANDC(E)150U	May 72	Coceva+,CAPTURE GAMMAS	
	1.5+2	5.4+2			Prog EANDC(E)115U	Mar 69	- +,ANAL OF MULT OF CAPT GAMMAS	

67 Holmium 165

Quantity	Energy (ev) Min	Energy (ev) Max	Lab	Type	Documentation Ref Vol Page	Date	Author, Comments	Data
Reson Params	8.2+0	1.7+3	SAC	Expt	Conf 72Budapest 38	Aug 72	Tellier+ NDG	+
				Priv	TELLIER	Dec 71	- . VALUES FOR COMPILATION.	
	8.2+0	1.3+3		Conf	71Knoxvill 680	Mar 71	- + TRANS,AVG D=2.65EV 278RES	
	8.2+0	1.7+3		Rept	CEA-N-1338	Nov 70	- . 350 RESONANCES WGN	
	8.2+0	1.7+3		Data	EXFOR20119.	Sep 72	840PTS.E0,WG,WT,2G*WN,2G*WN0.	
Reson Params	1.5+2	6.5+2	SAC	ExTh Diss	FRNC-TH-450	Oct 72	Delaroche. J	
Reson Params	+0	+3	DUB	Expt Conf	73Kiev 2 337	May 73	Karzhavina+ SPIN IDENT,G-MULTIP MTHD	
Reson Params	2.6+3	3.1+3	ORL	Expt Jour	NSE 59 231	Mar 76	Macklin+(G*WG WN/WT) TBL	+
	2.6+3	3.1+3		Data	EXFOR10531.006	Feb 78	. 50 RES ES.WN*G*WG/WT.	
Reson Params	4.0+0	1.3+1	BNL	Expt Prog	WASH-1033 5	61	Marshak+	+
	4.0+0	1.3+1		Data	EXFOR11984.003	Jun 76	. 2 RES., J	
Reson Params	Maxwl		KUK	Theo Conf	76Ahmedabd 2 1	Dec 58	Sharma+AVG S-WAVE REDUCED N-WID ANAL	
Strnth Fnctn	+3		BNL	Expt Conf	PRL 1 461	Dec 58	Hughes. FC, 2.5+-0.4	
Strnth Fnctn	1.0+4	2.0+5	ORL	Expt Jour	PR 122 182	61	Gibbons+	+
	1.0+4	2.0+5		Data	EXFOR11329.	Jun 76	. 4 PTS, S0,S1,D,AVE WG	
Strnth Fnctn	8.0-1	5.0+4	LEB	Expt Conf	JINR-1845 100	Jun 64	Konks+ PB-SLOWDOWN-TIME, TABLE	
Strnth Fnctn	3.9+0	5.1+2	DUB	Expt Jour	YF 5 471	Mar 67	Karzhavina+TOF, STRENGTH FN GIVEN	+
				Rept	JINR-P-2593	Mar 66	.S0 VAL GIVEN	
				Jour	SNP 5 329	Sep 67	. ENGL OF YF 5 471	
	3.9+0	5.0+2		Data	EXFOR40032.007	Aug 70	.1 DATA LINE	
Strnth Fnctn		5.0+4	RI	Expt Prog	YFI-5 59	Oct 67	Konks+ TABLE	
				Rept	INDC-232E	Jan 69	. ENGL OF YFI-5 59	
Strnth Fnctn	-1	5.0+4	DUB	Expt Jour	YF 7 493	Mar 68	Konks+ TABLE OF S0+S1 VALS,CFD OTHER	
	+3	+5		Conf	65Antwerp	Jul 65	- .DUBNA.S0,S1	
	-1	5.0+4		Jour	SNP 7 310	Sep 68	- + ENGL OF YF 7 493.	
Strnth Fnctn		5.0+2	DUB	Expt Conf	68DUBSY 349	Jul 68	Pikelner.LVL SPAC,AVERG. WG,S0 VS A	
Strnth Fnctn	1.0+3	1.0+5	HAR	Expt Rept	NP- 17644	Jul 68	Moxon.THESIS.MOXON-RAE DET.S+P+DWAVE	
Strnth Fnctn	+3	+5	AUA	ExTh Rept	AAEC/E-198	May 69	Musgrove.S+P+D STF FROM (NG)FIT,TBL	+
Strnth Fnctn	-		DUB	Revw Jour	YF 11 111	Jan 70	Malecki+ VALUES FOR TWO SPIN STATES	
				Jour	SNP 11 61	Jul 70	- + ENGL OF YF 11 61.	
Strnth Fnctn	-		AUA	Theo Rept	AAEC/E-211	Nov 70	Musgrove. SMOOTHED S0,S1 AND S2 GIVN	
Strnth Fnctn	3.0+3	6.5+5	DKE	Expt Abst	DA/B 31 6821	May 71	Pineo.S,P,D WAVE.THESIS ABST	
				Diss	PINEO	70	.S0,S1.TBL.GRPHS.CFD CALC,OTH EXPTS.	
Strnth Fnctn	2.4+4		MUA	Theo Jour	IJP 46 114	Mar 72	Chaubey+ P-WAVE.FOR A-SYSTEMTIC,GRPH	
Strnth Fnctn	1.0+4	1.0+6	SAC	Theo Prog	EANDC(E)150U	May 72	Cauvin+,CALC OF S0 AND S1	
Strnth Fnctn	5.0+0	2.0+3	SAC	Expt Rept	CEA-N-1338	Nov 70	Tellier. S0=1.77	+
	1.0+1	2.0+2		Conf	72Budapest 38	Aug 72	- + S-WAVE STRENGTHFUNCTION	
	1.2+3	2.0+5		Priv	TELLIER	Dec 71	- .VALUES FOR COMPILATION.	
	1.3+3			Conf	71Knoxvill 680	Mar 71	- +. S0=1.77+-0.15	
	1.2+3	2.0+5		Data	EXFOR20119.	Sep 72	2PTS.L=0.	
Strnth Fnctn	1.5+2	6.5+2	SAC	ExTh Diss	FRNC-TH-450	Oct 72	Delaroche.OPTICAL MODEL PARAMETERS	
Strnth Fnctn	5.0+3	1.6+5	VIP	Expt Jour	NSE 49 317	Nov 72	Fawcett+. GAMMA,S0,AND S1 GIVEN	
				Abst	DA/B 32 2929	Nov 71	.SUPERSEDED	
Strnth Fnctn	None		AUA	Eval Rept	AAEC/E-277	Mar 73	Musgrove.TBLS EXPTL DATA+BEST VALUES	
Strnth Fnctn	1.0+3	6.0+5	NBS	Expt Jour	PR/C 9 28	Jan 74	Camarda.LINAC.TRANS. S1 MEASURED.	+
	1.0+3	6.0+5		Data	EXFOR10765.011	Nov 78	. 1PT.S1=(0.7+-.4)-4	
Strnth Fnctn		+5	KFK	Theo Conf	JAERI-M-5984	Feb 75	Newstead.P230.TBL S0,S1 CFD EXP.	
Strnth Fnctn	2.6+3	3.1+3	ORL	Expt Jour	NSE 59 231	Mar 76	Macklin+S,P,D WAVE STF	
Strnth Fnctn	2.7+3		MUN	Expt Conf	71Albany 327	Aug 76	Dilg+TRNS.S0 STF GVN.31 ELEMENT GRPH	
Lvl Density			COP	Theo Jour	NP 6 62	Mar 58	Ericson. LVL DENSITY FORM CFD EXP	
Lvl Density	-		FEI	Eval Rept	FEI-36	66	Kapchigashev+.TBL OF RELATD QUANTTYS	+
		5.0+4		Jour	YF 4 686	Sep 66	.TABLE.SHORT VERSION OF FEI-36	
	-			Prog	YFI-3 3	66	.ABSTRACT.TABLE LDL+NUCL.EXCIT.E	
		5.0+4		Jour	SNP 4 486	67	.ENGLISH OF YF 4.FROM(N,GAMMA).TABLE	
				Prog	INDC-E-140 3	66	.ENGLISH TRANSL OF YFI-3	
Lvl Density		5.4+1	DUB	Expt Jour	YF 3 55	Jan 66	Alfimenkov+,PLRZD NS AND TRGT	
				Jour	SNP 3 39	Jul 66	TRANSLATN.*BNL-TR-36 N/65	
				Rept	JINR-P-2209	Jun 65	.SEE ALSO	
Lvl Density	5.0+6	7.0+6	ALD	Expt Jour	NP/A 112 337	May 68	Owens+.LVL DENS VERSUS EXCIT.MEAN T	+
Lvl Density	+7		DEB	ExTh Jour	NP/A 122 234	Dec 68	Karolyi+ SPIN CUTOFF,M OF INERT,N2N	+
	+7			Expt Data	EXFOR30101.031	Feb 71	CUT-OFF PARAMETER	
Lvl Density	3.6+6	8.5+6	JAE	Expt Jour	NP/A 131 145	Jun 69	Maruyama. E DEPENDANCE,PARAM,TH FIT.	
Lvl Density	1.4+7		BAS	Expt Jour	HPA 43 559	Nov 70	Sobottka+ LVL DENS,NUCL TEMP,TOF	
				Abst	HPA 42 563	Jul 69	- +.TOF LD PARAM ANAL NDG	
Lvl Density	None		AUW	Theo Conf	70Madurai 2 267	Dec 70	Ramamurty+ A-PARAMETER GVN,LANG'S-TH	
Lvl Density	0.0+0	1.2+3	SAC	Expt Rept	CEA-N-1338	Nov 71	Tellier.	+
	0.0+0	1.2+3		Data	EXFOR20119.010	Sep 72	1PNT.SP.CUT(0).	
Lvl Density	0.0+0	1.3+3	ITE	Theo Conf	72Budapest 268	Aug 72	Belyaev+ GROUPINGS OF LVL SPACNG,TBL	

67 Holmium 165

Quantity	Energy (ev) Min	Max	Lab	Type	Documentation Ref Vol Page	Author, Comments Date	Data
Lvl Density	None		DUB	Theo Rept	JINR - P4 - 8102	Jul 74 Malov+ SEMI - MICROSC CALC OKS XPT,TBL	
				Rept	UCRL - TR - 10845	Apr 75 . ENGL OF JINR - P4 - 8102	
(γ,n)	8.0+6	3.0+7	SAC	Expt Jour	NP/A 121 463	Dec 68 Bergere+LORENTZ LINE PARAM,GRPHS,TBL	

67 Holmium 166

Quantity	Energy (ev) Min	Max	Lab	Type	Documentation Ref Vol Page	Author, Comments Date	Data
(n,γ)	1.4+7		ROM	Expt Jour	NCS 370	Sep 63 Giannini+LVLS.EXCITED IN CAPTURE NDG	
(n,γ)	None		TUD	Expt Conf	64Paris	64 Kastner+ CHAIN OF 4 ISOMERIC TRANS	
Spect (n,γ)	3.9+0		YAL	Expt Abst	BAP 4 35	Jan 59 Springer+,NAI(TL),GAMMA MULTIPLICITY	
Spect (n,γ)		8.5+5	ANL	Expt Jour	PL/B 32 457	Aug 70 Bollinger+ AVG - RES - CAPT METHOD	
(n,p)	Maxwl		IFU	Theo Rept	ICD - 4 20	67 Dadakina+ PENETR COEFF CALC,TABLE	
Reson Params	–		AUA	Theo Rept	AAEC/E - 211	Nov 70 Musgrove. CALCULTD D+GAM WIDTH GIVEN	
Strnth Fnctn	–		AUA	Theo Rept	AAEC/E - 211	Nov 70 Musgrove. SMOOTHED S0,S1 AND S2 GIVN	
Lvl Density	+6		MIL	Theo Jour	EN 15 1 54	Jan 68 Facchini+ LDL PARS FROM LOW EN RES	
Lvl Density	None		MUN	Theo Jour	NP/A 217 269	Dec 73 Dilg+ A,DELTA. BACK SHIFTED FERMIGAS	
Lvl Density	None		COP	Theo Jour	NP/A 222 493	Apr 74 Dossing+COLL ROTAT.SPAC. ACCUR ESTIM	
Lvl Density	None		ROC	Theo Jour	NP/A 223 589	May 74 Huizenga+ EXP CFD MICROSC TH AX SYMM	

67 Holmium 167

Quantity	Energy (ev) Min	Max	Lab	Type	Documentation Ref Vol Page	Author, Comments Date	Data
Spect (n,γ)	Maxwl		CCP	Expt Jour	AE 4 22	Jan 58 Sklyarevskii+.EGS+INTENS BELOW .3MEV	
				Jour	JNE 9 69	Jun 59 TRANSLATN.*	
				Jour	SJA 4 19	58 TRANSLATN.*	
Reson Params	–		AUA	Theo Rept	AAEC/E - 211	Nov 70 Musgrove. CALCULTD D+GAM WIDTH GIVEN	
Strnth Fnctn	–		AUA	Theo Rept	AAEC/E - 211	Nov 70 Musgrove. SMOOTHED S0,S1 AND S2 GIVN	

67 Holmium 168

Quantity	Energy (ev) Min	Max	Lab	Type	Documentation Ref Vol Page	Author, Comments Date	Data
Reson Params	–		AUA	Theo Rept	AAEC/E - 211	Nov 70 Musgrove. CALCULTD D+GAM WIDTH GIVEN	
Strnth Fnctn	–		AUA	Theo Rept	AAEC/E - 211	Nov 70 Musgrove. SMOOTHED S0,S1 AND S2 GIVN	

67 Holmium 169

Quantity	Energy (ev) Min	Max	Lab	Type	Documentation Ref Vol Page	Author, Comments Date	Data
Reson Params	–		AUA	Theo Rept	AAEC/E - 211	Nov 70 Musgrove. CALCULTD D+GAM WIDTH GIVEN	
Strnth Fnctn	–		AUA	Theo Rept	AAEC/E - 211	Nov 70 Musgrove. SMOOTHED S0,S1 AND S2 GIVN	

68 Erbium

Quantity	Energy (ev) Min	Max	Lab	Type	Documentation Ref Vol Page	Date	Author, Comments	Data
Evaluation	5.0+5	1.5+7	LRL	Eval	Rept UCRL-5351	Nov 58	Howerton. CURVS TOT SEL SNE STN N2N	
Evaluation	Pile		CRC	Eval	Rept CRRP-960	Nov 60	Westcott.G,S FACTORS EFFECTIVE CAPT.	
Total	Maxwl		COL	Expt	Jour PR 48 265	Aug 35	Dunning+ IONCH,TRANS,RA-BE/PARAFIN N	
Total	3.0-2	7.0-1	ORL	Expt	Jour PR 87 487	Aug 52	Bernstein+ TRANS+CRYST SPEC CURVE	+
	3.0-2	2.3-1			Data EXFOR11745.012	Jun 76	. 20 PTS.	
Total	Maxwl		ORL	Expt	Jour PR 87 487	Aug 52	Bernstein+	+
	Maxwl				Data EXFOR11745.009	Jun 76	. 1 PT. SIG.	
Total	6.0+4	3.0+6	WIS	Expt	Jour PR 93 461	Feb 54	Okazaki+ TRANS AVG OVER RESON OKS TH	+
	5.0+4	3.0+6			Data EXFOR12061.004	Jun 76	. 27 PTS.	
Total	1.0+0	5.6+1	BNL	Expt	Jour PR 96 1014	Nov 54	Sailor.	+
	1.0+0	5.6+1			Data EXFOR12110.004	Jun 76	. 77 PTS.	
Total	6.0+4	1.8+7	LAS	Theo	Rept LA-2099	Dec 56	Beyster+,OPTMDL CALC CFD EXPT,CURVE	
Total	1.3+7	1.6+7	LAS	Expt	Jour PR 109 1268	Feb 58	Conner.TRNS SC 3ES 5.37 5.37 5.41B	+
					Conf 58Geneva 15 11	Sep 58	Coon+.PPR666,SIGMA FOR 3ES,TOF	
	1.3+7	1.6+7			Data EXFOR11320.011	Jun 76	. 3 PTS.	
Total	2.1-1	8.9-1	BNL	Expt	Jour NSE 8 183	60	Moller.	+
	2.1-1	8.9-1			Data EXFOR12097.007	Jun 76	. 86 PTS.	
Total	1.0-3	6.0-1	KAP	Expt	Abst ANS 3 462	Dec 60	Roesser+ SLOWCHOP ERSLN UNDER 1/10.	+
	1.0-3	6.0-1			Data EXFOR12079.002	Jun 76	. 126 PTS.	
Total	3.0+3	6.5+5	DKE	ExTh	Jour PL 16 306	Jun 65	Seth. AV CS 8-10KEV RSN INT RES OBSV	+
	5.0+3	6.4+5		Expt	Data EXFOR11781.	Jun 76	. 93 PTS.	
Total	5.0-4	5.0-2	JAE	Expt	Prog INDSWG-90 2	Jul 65	Ohno.TRNS,CRYST.+MECH.MONOCHR.,GRPHS	
Total	5.5-3	3.0-1	BSP	Expt	Conf 66Paris 1 53	Oct 66	Zimmerman+,P.129,SIG(E),SIG(.025EV)	+
					Jour NP/A 95 683	Apr 67	SEE ALSO * +IEA-86	
					Conf 64Geneva 7 82	May 64	SEE ALSO *P.118	
	5.5-3	3.0-1			Data EXFOR30224.	Dec 72	SIG AT 23ES, SIG AT 0.025 EV,PRIVCOM	
Total	7.0-3	3.3-1	UFT	Expt	Rept ICD-3 85	Oct 66	Vertebny+.GRAPH,NO CORRECTIONS	
Total	1.4+7		ANL	Expt	Abst DA/B 28 3835	Mar 68	Haugsnes.SIG=5.32+-.05B,CFD OPTMDL	+
	1.4+7				Data EXFOR11733.009	Jun 76	. 1 PT.	
Total	1.0-4	3.0-3	MUN	Expt	Jour AKE 16 49	70	Knorr+ TRANS EXPT, TBL	
Total	3.3-2	2.7-1	BNL	Expt	Jour NIM 86 83	Sep 70	Malik+ MOXON-RAE DET REL AU	+
	3.3-2	2.7-1			Data EXFOR10501.027	May 75	4PTS,SIGMA	
Total	2.5+6	1.5+7	BNW	Expt	Jour PR/C 3 576	Feb 71	Foster+,TRANS,CURVS,CFD OTHERS+TH	+
					Jour NIM 36 1	Sep 65	.SUPERSEDED	
	2.3+6	1.5+7			Data EXFOR10047.072	Aug 73	. 234 PTS.	
Total	2.7+3		MUN	Expt	Prog EANDC(E)150U	Oct 72	Dilg+ AVERAGE TOT XSECT+S0	+
					Conf 71Albany 327	Aug 71	- +TRNS.AVG CS GVN.31 ELEMENT GRP	
	2.7+3				Data EXFOR20583.022	Jun 76	1PNT.	
Total	1.3+7	1.5+7	DEB	Eval	Rept IAEA-153 173	73	Boedy+ MOST PROBABLE VAL OF SIG,TBL	
					Jour AHP 30 115	Oct 71	Angeli+ AVG SIG,CFD CALC.TBLS.GRAPH	
Total	6.0+0	1.6+5	COL	Expt	Jour PR/C 5 974	Mar 73	Liou+TOF.TRNS.RES PAR.ANAL.NDG.	+
					Rept NYO-72-190	68	- .TRNS+SELF INDICATION.NDG	
	None				Jour RSI 35 263	Mar 64	Rainwater+SEE FOR EXPT DETAILS.	
	6.8+2	1.0+4			Data EXFOR10591.002	Jan 78	. RAW DATA AVAILABLE FROM NNDC.	
Total	7.0+5	9.0+6	GLS	Expt	Jour JP/A 7 1758	Sep 74	Kellie+ SIG IN CURVE,STAT ERROR 2 PC	+
	8.0+5	9.0+6			Data EXFOR20418.010	Sep 75	588PTS.	
Total	2.5+5	1.5+7	JAE	Theo	Conf JAERI-M-5984	Feb 75	Tanaka.OPTMDL/COUPLD CH.GRPH CFD EXP	
Total	1.1+0	4.4+3	BNL	Expt	Prog WASH-745	Nov 57	Hughes+ FC, NDG.	+
	1.1+0	4.4+3			Data EXFOR11259.003	Jun 76	. 522 PTS.	
Elastic	Maxwl		ORL	Expt	Jour PR 91 597	Aug 53	Koehler+	+
	Maxwl				Data EXFOR12060.	Jun 76	. 1 PT COH, COH AMP	
Elastic	1.0+6		ALD	Expt	Jour NP 42 86	Apr 63	Gilboy+.SIG=6.25B+-3PC	+
Elastic	9.8+5		AGN	Eval	Rept TID-21629	Dec 64	Perkins+ CALC FRM BNL400,UCRL5973	
Elastic	7.0-3	1.0+0	IFU	Expt	Jour IZV 31 353	Feb 71	Vertebnyj+.CURVES,CHOPPER,TOF	+
	2.5-2				Data EXFOR40061.017	Mar 71	SIGMA FOR 2200 M/SEC	
Elastic	1.0-2	1.7-1	IFU	Expt	Jour UFZ 13 599	Apr 68	Kolotyi+ GRPH SIG(E),SCAT-AMPLITUDE	
					Jour UPJ 13 420	Oct 68	TRANSLATN.*	
Elastic	9.5+5		ANL	Expt	Rept ANL-7935	Jun 72	COX+ 4 PI B(O)	+
	9.5+5				Data EXFOR10332.118	Jun 74	. 1 PT.	
Diff Elastic	1.0+5	1.8+7	LAS	Theo	Rept LA-2099	Dec 56	Beyster+,21ES,OPTMDL CALC CFD EXPT	
Diff Elastic	1.0+6		ALD	Expt	Jour NP 42 86	Apr 63	Gilboy+30TO137DEG.COMP.WITH OPTICMOD	+
Diff Elastic	9.8+5		AGN	Eval	Rept TID-21629	Dec 64	Perkins+ LEGENDRE COEF.	
Diff Elastic	1.5+6	3.5+6	JAE	Expt	Jour NP/A 179 513	Jan 72	Tanaka+ ANGDIST CFD OPTMDL,C-CHANNEL	+
	1.4+6				Priv TANAKA	Aug 71	- . TOF, REL H(NN).+LEGENDRE FIT	
	1.5+6	3.6+6			Data EXFOR20337.	Jul 74	98PTS.D/DA,SOME N',LEG.FIT,-	
Diff Elastic	9.5+5		ANL	Expt	Rept ANL-7935	Jun 72	Cox+. CFD OPTMOD,HAUSER-FESHBACH	+
	9.5+5				Data EXFOR10332.026	Jun 74	. 8 PTS.	

68 Erbium

Quantity	Energy (ev) Min	Max	Lab	Type	Documentation Ref Vol Page	Author, Comments Date	Data
Polarization	3.8+5	9.8+5	WIS ExTh	Jour	NP 6 177	Mar 58 Clement+. POLARIZATION. CFD OPT MDL	
				Expt Rept	AECU-3628	57 - +.LI7(P,N) SOURCE. 3ANGLES.	
Polarization	9.4+5		ANL Expt	Rept	ANL-7935	Jun 72 Cox+. CFD OPTMOD,HAUSER-FESHBACH	+
	9.4+5			Data	EXFOR10332.060	Jun 74 . 8 PTS.	
Potntal Scat	0.0+0		BNL Expt	Prog	WASH-745	Nov 57 Hughes+ FC ZW RES NDG	
Potntal Scat		6.5+5	DKE ExTh	Jour	PL 13 70	Nov 64 Seth+.0,1PHASE FRM SIG TOT AV 3-650KV	
Tot Inelastc	5.0+6	7.0+6	ALD Expt	Jour	NP/A 112 337	May 68 Owens+.3ES.FROM N SPECT 90DEG.	+
Tot Inelastc	1.0-3	3.0-3	MUNTheo	Jour	AKE 16 49	70 Knorr+ PARAMAGNETIC SCAT SIG CALC	
Diff Inelast	1.0+6		DKE Expt	Prog	WASH-1028 21	Apr 60 Bevington+NDG.TOF.TBC	
Diff Inelast	4.0+6	6.5+6	DKE Expt	Jour	NP 60 17	Nov 64 Buccino+N SPEC MEASURED 4ES+NUC TEMP	
				Abst	DA 24 4248	Apr 64 - .ANGDIST,TOF, NUCL T,LVL DEN.	
Diff Inelast	5.0+6	7.0+6	ALD Expt	Jour	NP/A 112 337	May 68 Owens+.3ES.FROM N SPECT 90DEG NDG.	+
				Conf	65Antwerp 547	Jul 65 - + PPR122.ABST.SPECT N' AT 90DEG	
Thermal Scat	Maxwl		ORL Expt	Jour	PR 92 1380	Dec 53 Koehler+TRIVALENT ION PARAMAG SCAT	
Thermal Scat	Maxwl		ORL Theo	Jour	PR 92 1387	Dec 53 Trammel.TRIVAL.ION MAG.SCAT.CFD XPT	
Thermal Scat	Cold		ORL Expt	Jour	JAP 32 49	Mar 61 Cable+ P.49S 1-XTL DIFRACTION	
Thermal Scat	Cold		ORL Revw	Jour	JAP 36 1078	Mar 65 Koehler.MAGNETIC PROPS FRM N DIFFR X	
Thermal Scat	Cold		BNL Expt	Jour	JAP 37 1032	Mar 66 Corliss+ MAGNETIC PROPS FROM DIFFR	
Thermal Scat	Cold		GRE Expt	Jour	JAP 37 1038	Mar 66 MAGNETIC PROPS FROM N DIFFR XPTS	
Thermal Scat	2.0-4	1.5-1	BSP ExTh	Jour	JCP 48 520	Jan 68 Mattos.,TRIVALENT ION PARAMAG SIG	+
				Jour	NP/A 95 683	Apr 67 SEE ALSO * SAME CURVE.	
Thermal Scat	Cold		CRC Expt	Jour	JAP 39 457	Feb 68 Holden+ TOF CRYST SPEC PARAMAGN SCAT	
Thermal Scat	1.0-2	3.0-1	IFU Expt	Jour	UFZ 13 599	Apr 68 Kolotyi+ GRPH MAGN-SIG(NEUT-E),ER+++	+
				Jour	UPJ 13 420	Oct 68 TRANSLATN.*	
	2.0-2	4.0-1		Data	EXFOR40301.	Feb 76 .THERM AND BOUND-ATOM SCAT CS AT10ES	
Thermal Scat	2.0-2	1.4+0	IJI Expt	Prog	YFI-12 67	72 Vertebny+ ABST,TOT SCAT SIG 15ES,TBL	
				Prog	INDC(CCP)-30	Sep 72 .PAGE 58,ENGLISH OF YFI-12 67	
Thermal Scat	1.0-4	1.0+3	MUNRevw	Jour	EEN 80 1	77 Koester. SCAT LENGTH,FREE SIG	
Scattering	Maxwl		ORL Expt	Jour	PR 91 597	Aug 53 Koehler+ TRANS 15+-4B,COHER=7.8+-0.4	+
	Maxwl			Data	EXFOR12060.035	Jun 76 . 1 PT.	
Scattering	2.5-2		BSP Expt	Conf	66Paris 1 53	Oct 66 Zimmerman+,P.129,SIG(.025EV)DEDUCED	+
				Jour	NP/A 95 683	Apr 67 SEE ALSO * +IEA-86	
				Conf	64Geneva 7 82	May 64 SEE ALSO *P.118	
Scattering	6.0-2	1.7-1	IFU Expt	Jour	UFZ 13 599	Apr 68 Koloty+	+
	6.0-2	1.7-1		Data	EXFOR40039.008	Sep 70 AVERAGE SIGMA	
Scattering	2.0-2	3.0-2	IFU Expt	Conf	70Helsinki 1 651	Jun 70 Vertebnij+ 2200M/SEC SIGMA GIVEN,TBL	
				Rept	BNL-TR-495	Jul 72 . ENGLISH OF 70HELSIN 1 651	
Nonelastic	6.0+4	1.8+7	LAS Theo	Rept	LA-2099	Dec 56 Beyster+,OPTMDL CALC CFD EXPT,CURVE	
Absorption	2.0-2	2.4-1	CUWTheo	Rept	CWR-400-1	Sep 57 Roberts.MAXWELL-BOLTZMANN AVGD SIGS.	
Absorption	1.0-4	3.0-3	MUNTheo	Jour	AKE 16 49	70 Knorr+ FROM TOT SIG EXPT CALC, TBL	
Res Int Abs	5.0-1		MTR Expt	Rept	IN-1195	May 68 Scoville.	+
	5.0-1			Data	EXFOR11820.013	Jun 76 . 1 PT.	
(n,γ)	Maxwl		ORL Expt	Jour	PR 83 643	Aug 51 Pomerance. OSC REL AU ABS 95B	
	Maxwl			Data	EXFOR11047.053	Jun 76 . 1 PT.	
(n,γ)	3.0+4	1.7+5	ORL Expt	Conf	61Vienna 1 95	Aug 61 Neiler.	+
				Jour	PR 122 182	Apr 61 Gibbons+ 960 , 230 MB REPL BNL 653	
	3.0+4	1.7+5		Data	EXFOR11329.	Jun 76 . 51 PTS.	
(n,γ)	2.0+2	8.0+3	ORL Expt	Conf	61Saclay 203	Sep 61 Block+.LIQUID SCINTILLATOR	+
				Conf	61Vienna 1 95	Aug 61 Neiler.PPR73,TABLE FOR SOME ES,GRAPH	
	2.0+2	7.8+3		Data	EXFOR11935.010	Jun 76 . 45 PTS.	
(n,γ)	2.0-2	2.0+4	GA Expt	Rept	GA-3874	Mar 63 Haddad+LINAC TOF LIQ SC-T CURVE ONLY	+
	1.0-2	1.2+0		Data	EXFOR11944.	Jun 76 . 88 PTS.	
(n,γ)	3.0+4	6.5+4	ORL Expt	Jour	PR 129 2695	Mar 63 Macklin+ LIQ SCINT,960 AND 540MB	+
	6.5+4			Data	EXFOR11331.026	Jun 76 . 1 PT.	
(n,γ)	5.0+3	9.0+4	ORL Theo	Jour	RMP 37 166	Jan 65 Macklin+ CALC FOR KT=5TO90 KEV	
(n,γ)	2.5-2		BSP Expt	Conf	66Paris 1 53	Oct 66 Zimmerman+,P.129,SIG(.025EV)DEDUCED	+
				Jour	NP/A 95 683	Apr 67 SEE ALSO * +IEA-86	
				Conf	64Geneva 7 82	May 64 SEE ALSO *P.118	
	2.5-2			Data	EXFOR30224.012	Dec 72 DEDUCED SIGMA	
(n,γ)	3.3-1	8.3-1	BNL Expt	Jour	NIM 86 83	Sep 70 Malik+ MOXON-RAE DET REL AU	+
	3.3-1	2.7-1		Data	EXFOR10501.026	May 75 4PTS,SIGMA	
(n,γ)	3.0+4		AUA Theo	Rept	AAEC/E-211	Nov 70 Musgrove. SIGMA GIVEN AND CFD OTHER	
(n,γ)	3.0+4		AUA Expt	Prog	INDC(SEC)-28	Sep 72 Stroud+P285. VDG, SIG MEASURED,NDG	
(n,γ)	3.0+4	3.0+5	USP Expt	Jour	NP/A 196 83	Nov 72 Lepine+ LI7-P NS.TOF.M-R. REL TO IN	+
	3.0+4	3.0+5		Data	EXFOR30233.008	Mar 73 NDS,RELATIVE TO IN,ABSOLUTE ERROR	
(n,γ)	5.0+3	7.0+4	CCP Expt	Conf	73Kiev 2 206	May 73 Kononov+ TOF,SIG(NEUT-E),GRAPH	
(n,γ)	1.0+6	1.0+7	CRC Revw	Conf	74Petten 119	Sep 74 Bartholomew+ PHOTON STRF GRPH	

68 Erbium

Quantity	Energy (ev) Min	Max	Lab	Type	Documentation Ref Vol Page	Author, Comments Date	Data
Spect (n,γ)	Maxwl		KUR	Expt	Jour AE 4 5	Jan 58 Groshev+ SPECTRUM+LINES 0.3-6.68MEV	
					Jour JNE 9 50	Jun 59 . ENGL OF AE 4 5	
					Jour SJA 4 1	58 . ENGL OF AE 4 5	
Spect (n,γ)	Maxwl		YAL	Expt	Jour PR 114 268	Apr 59 Draper.SC SPECTR,GAM E 0 TO 600 KEV	
Spect (n,γ)	Maxwl	9.4+0	YAL	Expt	Jour NP 10 386	Apr 59 Fenstermacher+ GRAPH.5NES.ASSGN 167	
Spect (n,γ)	Maxwl		ARF	Expt	Prog ARF-1193-12	Jul 62 Greenwood+ CRYST SPEC. LOW-E GAMMAS	
Spect (n,γ)	Maxwl		CAS	Expt	Jour NC 27 1032	Feb 63 Giannini+ NA-I,E+INTENSITY TO280 KEV	+
Spect (n,γ)	4.6-1	5.8-1	JAE	Expt	Rept JAERI-1073	Mar 65 Kawarasaki. RES CAPT.LINAC.TOF.E,INT	+
					Rept INDSWG-90 6	Jul 65 - . TABLE E,INTS GIVEN.	
	4.6-1	5.8-1			Data EXFOR20277.015	Jun 74 8PTS.	
Spect (n,γ)	+0	+4	COL	Expt	Prog WASH-1124 31	Nov 68 Camarda+ MOXON-RAE DET TBC NO DATA	
Spect (n,γ)	2.5-2		MIT	Comp	Rept MITNE-85	Jan 69 Rasmussen+TBL G INT.=AFCRL-69-0071	
Spect (n,γ)	Pile		ANL	Expt	Prog WASH-1127 10	Apr 69 Bollinger+ LVL STRUCTRE ONLY,TBC,NDG	
Spect (n,γ)	Pile		MUN	Expt	Jour ZP 258 315	Mar 73 Henkelmann. E + INT OF GS GIVEN	+
	2.5-2				Data EXFOR20606.016	Jun 76 5PTS.	
Inelastic γ	5.0+6	7.0+6	ALD	Expt	Jour NP/A 112 337	May 68 Owens+.3ES.TOF SPECT 90 DEG, NDG.	+
(n,2n)	1.5+7		DEB	Eval	Jour REA 11 1 153	Mar 73 Boedy+ RECOMM.VALUE FROM N-Z SYSTEM.	
Reson Params	4.7-1	2.8+1	BNL	Expt	Jour PR 96 1014	Nov 54 Sailor+	+
	4.7-1	2.8+1			Data EXFOR12110.014	Jun 76 . 7 RES, E0.	
Reson Params	4.6-1	9.8+1	CCP	Expt	Jour AE 15 247	Sep 63 Vlasov+.TRANSMISSION,CFD ISOTOPE TGT	
					Jour SJA 15 952	Sep 63 . ENGL OF AE 15 247	
Reson Params	3.0+1	8.0+1	GA	Expt	Priv HADDAD	Feb 64 Haddad.	+
	3.0+1	8.0+1			Data EXFOR11944.005	Jun 76 . 3 RES, E0.	
Reson Params	4.6-1	5.8-1	BNL	Expt	Prog WASH-1048 13	Jun 64 Sailor+ SPIN OF 2 LOW RESONS	
Reson Params	None		BNL	Expt	Abst BAP 11 29	Jan 66 Chrien+ RADIUS PARAMETER, =9.	
Reson Params	3.0+0	5.0+2	DUB	Expt	Jour YF 7 225	Feb 68 Karzhavina+,TRANSMISSION+NG YIELD	
					Rept YFI-4 47	May 67 - + RES ANAL.	
					Rept JINR-P3-3097	Feb 67 - + TOT+NG,TBL.	
					Jour SNP 7 161	Aug 68 - + ENGL OF YF 7 225.	
					Rept INDC-187E	67 - + ENGL OF YFI-4 47.	
Reson Params	2.3+1	2.8+2	IFU	Expt	Rept ICD-5 5	Dec 71 Vertebny+	+
	2.3+1	2.8+2			Data EXFOR40061.010	Mar 71 14 RESONANCE-ENERGIES	
Reson Params	6.0+0	1.6+5	COL	Expt	Jour PR/C 5 974	Mar 73 Liou+ISOTOPE RES PARS.GVN.	
					Rept NYO-72-190	68 - .SEE ALSO	
Reson Params	+0	+2	BNL	Expt	Prog WASH-745	Nov 57 Hughes+ FC NDG.	+
	4.3+0	3.1+2			Data EXFOR11259.004	Jun 76 . 45 RES, EN,WN0	
Strnth Fnctn	+0	+5	BNL	Expt	Prog WASH-745	Nov 57 Hughes. FC ANAL P AVG NDG.	
Strnth Fnctn	3.0+3	6.5+5	DKE	ExTh	Jour PL 13 70	Nov 64 Seth+S,P,D STF FRM SIG TOT 3-650KEV	+
	5.0+4	1.5+5		Expt	Conf 64Paris 2 916	Jul 64 - +S0,S1,S2 R PRIME/R	
	3.0+3	6.5+5			Data EXFOR11665.024	Jun 76 . 3 PTS.	
Strnth Fnctn	2.7+3		MUN	Expt	Conf 71Albany 327	Aug 76 Dilg+TRNS.S0 STF GVN.31 ELEMENT GRPH	
Lvl Density	5.0+6	7.0+6	ALD	Expt	Jour NP/A 112 337	May 68 Owens+.LVL DENS VERSUS EXCIT.MEAN T	+
					Conf 65Antwerp 547	Jul 65 - + PPR122. TBL FERMI GAS CONST.	
Lvl Density	None		SAC	Expt	Jour NP/A 133 417	Aug 69 Bergere+NUCL TEMP,A PARAM,FROM NG	
(γ,n)	5.0+6	3.5+7	SAC	Expt	Jour NP/A 133 417	Aug 69 Bergere+LORENTZ LINE PARAM,GRPHS,TBL	

68 Erbium 160

Quantity	Energy (ev) Min	Max	Lab	Type	Documentation Ref Vol Page	Author, Comments Date	Data
Lvl Density	None		CCP	Theo	Jour YF 13 43	Jan 71 Bravin+.DEFORM PAR,CALC,TBL,CFD EXPT	

68 Erbium 161

Quantity	Energy (ev) Min	Max	Lab	Type	Documentation Ref Vol Page	Author, Comments Date	Data
Reson Params	-		AUA	Theo	Rept AAEC/E-211	Nov 70 Musgrove. CALCULTD D+GAM WIDTH GIVEN	
Strnth Fnctn	-		AUA	Theo	Rept AAEC/E-211	Nov 70 Musgrove. SMOOTHED S0,S1 AND S2 GIVN	

68 Erbium 162

Quantity	Energy (ev) Min	Max	Lab	Type	Documentation Ref Vol Page	Author, Comments Date	Data
Total	2.5-2		IFU	Expt	Conf 65Antwerp § 186	Jul 65 Vertebny.KIEV.FC XPT.LESS THAN 315B	
Total	5.0-3	1.0-1	CCP	Expt	Jour UFZ 11 240	Mar 66 TOF,CURVES GIVEN	
Total	7.0-3	3.3-1	UFT	Expt	Rept ICD-3 85	Oct 66 Vertebny+.GRAPH,NO CORRECTIONS	
					Rept INDC-152E 85	67 . ENGL OF ICD-3 85	

68 Erbium 162

Quantity	Energy (ev) Min	Max	Lab	Type	Documentation Ref Vol Page	Date	Author, Comments	Data
Total	None		BNL	Expt	Jour PL/B 24 573	May 67	Chrien+ FROM ANALYSIS OF RESONANCES	
Total	3.0+0	5.0+2	IFU	Expt	Prog YFI-5 35	Oct 67	Vertebnyj+ TRANSMISSION CURVE	
					Rept INDC-232E	67	. ENGL OF YFI-5 35	
Total	1.1-2	1.2-1	IFU	Expt	Rept ICD-5 5	Dec 71	Vertebny+	+
	1.1-2	1.2-1			Data EXFOR40061.002	Mar 71	SIGMA AT 121 ENERGIES	
Total	1.0-2	1.4+7	CCP	Eval	Data SOKRATOR-2006	77	SIG(E)	+
Elastic	7.0-3	1.0+0	IFU	Expt	Jour IZV 31 353	Feb 67	Vertebnyj+.CURVES,CHOPPER,TOF	
Elastic	1.0-2	1.7-1	IFU	Expt	Jour UFZ 13 599	Apr 68	Kolotyi+ GRPH SIG(E),SCAT-AMPLITUDE	+
					Jour UPJ 13 420	Oct 68	TRANSLATN.*	
	2.5-2				Data EXFOR40061.011	Mar 71	SIGMA FOR 2200 M/SEC	
Elastic	2.5-2		IJI	Eval	Conf 75Kiev 1 169	May 75	Fedorova+ EVAL 2200M/S SIG,TABLE	
Elastic	1.0-2	1.4+7	CCP	Eval	Data SOKRATOR-2006	77	SIG(E)	+
Diff Elastic	1.0-3	1.5+7	CCP	Eval	Data SOKRATOR-2006	77	ANGDIST(E)	+
Tot Inelastc	1.0-3	1.5+7	CCP	Eval	Data SOKRATOR-2006	77	SIG(E)	+
Diff Inelast	1.0-3	1.5+7	CCP	Eval	Data SOKRATOR-2006	77	SIG TO 8 LVLS	+
Thermal Scat	1.0-2	1.7-1	IFU	Expt	Jour UFZ 13 599	Apr 68	Kolotyi+ GRPHS,EXPTL SIG=NUCL+MAGN	+
					Jour UPJ 13 420	Oct 68	TRANSLATN.*	
	1.0-2	4.0-1			Data EXFOR40301.	Feb 76	.THERM AND BOUND-ATOM SCAT CS AT11ES	
Scattering	6.0-2	1.7-1	IFU	Expt	Jour UFZ 13 599	Apr 68	Koloty+	+
	6.0-2	1.7-1			Data EXFOR40039.002	Sep 70	AVERAGE SIGMA	
Scattering	2.0-2	3.0-2	IFU	Expt	Conf 70Helsinki 1 651	Jun 70	Vertebnij+ 2200M/SEC SIGMA GIVEN,TBL	
					Rept BNL-TR-495	Jul 72	. ENGLISH OF 70HELSIN 1 651	
Absorption	2.5-2		IJI	Eval	Conf 75Kiev 1 169	May 75	Fedorova+ EVAL 2200M/S SIG,TABLE	
Res Int Abs	5.0-1		OSL	Expt	Prog INDC(NOR)-1 3	May 72	Glomset+ REDUCD CAPTINTEG REL AU,TBL	+
					Priv PAPPAS	Nov 70	Pappas. ACT. POWD,LIQ SOLUT.TBP JIN	
	0.0+0	1.0+6			Data EXFOR20093.003	Sep 71	1PNT.CAPTURE.	
(n,γ)	-		IEA	Comp	Rept IEA-INF- 10	Aug 68	Atalla. TABLES OF HL,SIG AND GAMM-E	
(n,γ)	5.0+3	1.0+5	AUA	ExTh	Rept AAEC/E-198	May 69	Musgrove.S+P+D WAVE SIGMAS CALC,TBL	+
(n,γ)	3.0+4		AUA	Theo	Rept AAEC/E-211	Nov 70	Musgrove. SIGMA GIVEN AND CFD OTHER	
(n,γ)	2.5-2		IFU	Expt	Rept ICD-5 5	Dec 71	Vertebny+	+
	2.5-2				Data EXFOR40061.018	Mar 71	SIGMA FOR 2200 M/SEC	
(n,γ)	1.0+3	1.0+7	BOL	Eval	Data BENZI-DFN 691.	May 72	40 PNTS	+
(n,γ)	Maxwl		OSL	Expt	Prog INDC(NOR)-1 3	May 72	Glomset+ REL AU,ASSUMING 1/V,TABLE	+
					Priv PAPPAS	Nov 70	Pappas. ACT. POWD,LIQ SOLUT.TBP JIN	
	Maxwl				Data EXFOR20093.002	Sep 71	1PNT.SIG.	
(n,γ)	Maxwl	Fiss	WIN	Revw	Conf IAEA-169 3 163	74	Pope+ FIS-SPEC AVG DATA CFD MAXW-XPT	
(n,γ)	1.0-3	1.4+7	CCP	Eval	Data SOKRATOR-2006	77	SIG(E)	+
(n,2n)	Fiss		CRC	Eval	Rept	Dec 60	ROY+ ESTIMATED AVG SIG=1.2MB	
(n,2n)	1.4+7		AUW	Expt	Jour NP/A 125 57	Feb 69	RAMA PRASAD+,ACTIVATION,CFD OTHERS	+
				ExTh	Jour IPA 12 640	Sep 74	Rama Prasad+ CFD STATMDL COMPND VALU	
	1.4+7			Expt	Data EXFOR30051.	Dec 70	SIGMA N2N,ALSO N2N+NA+NP FOR OTHERS.	
(n,2n)	1.5+7		DEB	Comp	Jour REA 7 4 93	Dec 69	Csikai+ SIG+HL COMPILTN,N-ACTIV-ANAL	
(n,2n)	1.4+7	1.5+7	JYV	Eval	Rept JU-RR-3/1970	Jun 70	Leppaemaeki+ TABLE OF EVAL AVG SIG	
(n,2n)	1.5+7		IRK	Expt	Rept APA 34 209	Sep 71	Havlik. ACT. CC-W.	+
					Jour OAWA 107 119	Apr 70	- . ACTIVATION METHOD	
	1.5+7				Data EXFOR20509.020	Apr 76	1PNT.SIGMA.	
(n,2n)	1.5+7		ARK	Expt	Abst DA/B 32 5091	Mar 72	Bari. GE(LI) DET. ACT. SIG GIVEN	
(n,2n)	1.5+7		DEB	Eval	Jour REA 11 1 153	Mar 73	Boedy. COMPILATION+RECOMM.VALUE,TBL	
					Rept IAEA-153 173	73	- . RECOMM. VALUE ONLY	
(n,2n)	1.5+7		TAT	Theo	Jour JP/A 7 1457	Aug 74	Kondaiah. CALC ON STAT MODEL	
(n,2n)	1.4+7		AUW	Expt	Conf 74Bombay 2 105	Dec 74	Lakshmandas+ ACTIV,GELI.SIGMA GIVEN	+
	1.4+7				Data EXFOR30389.003	Mar 77	1 PNT.	
(n,2n)	1.5+7		JUL	Expt	Jour NP/A 224 319	May 74	Qaim. ACT.GE(LI)	+
					Jour RRL 25 335	May 76	- + SIG IN GRPH. SYST VS (N-Z)/A	
	1.5+7				Data EXFOR20541.047	Apr 76	1PNT.SIGMA.	
(n,p)	Fiss		CRC	Eval	Rept CRC-1003	Dec 60	ROY+ ESTIMATED AVG SIG=0.24MB	
(n,α)	Fiss		CRC	Eval	Rept CRC-1003	Dec 60	ROY+ ESTIMATED AVG SIG=0.0019MB	
(n,α)	Maxwl		CCP	Expt	Jour YF 1 252	Feb 65	Andreev.IONIZ-CHAMBER,SIG=M11MB	+
					Jour SNP 1 177	Aug 65	TRANSLATN.*	
Reson Params	7.0+0	2.1+1	IFU	Expt	Conf 65Antwerp § 186	Jul 65	Vertebny.KIEV.FC XPT.3 RES WNS	
Reson Params	-2	+0	IFU	Expt	Conf 67Kharkov	Feb 67	Vertebnyj+. TBP IN IZV	
Reson Params	+0	+3	IFU	Expt	Conf 67Kharkov 171	Feb 67	Vertebny.TRANSMISSION EXPT	
Reson Params	5.5+0	2.3+1	BNL	Expt	Jour PR 162 1130	Oct 67	Mughabghab+ TRANS WN FOR 17RESON ES	+
	5.5+0	2.3+2			Data EXFOR12120.004	Jun 76	. 17 RES. EN, WN.	
Reson Params	7.6+0	1.4+2	IFU	Expt	Prog YFI-5 35	Oct 67	Vertebnyj+ TABLE 10 RESONANCES	
					Rept INDC-232E	67	. ENGL OF YFI-5 35	
Reson Params	1.4+1	6.6+1	COL	Expt	Rept NYO-72-190	68	Liou+ TOF, WN FOR 6 RESONANCES	+

68 Erbium 162

Quantity	Energy (ev) Min	Max	Lab	Type	Documentation Ref Vol Page	Author, Comments Date	Data
Reson Params	7.6+0	1.3+2	IFU	Expt	Jour UFZ 13 679	Apr 68 Vertebnyi+ 10 RES,WN D VALS GVN,TBLS	
					Jour UPJ 13 477	Oct 68 TRANSLATN.*	
Reson Params	-		AUA	Theo	Rept AAEC/E-211	Nov 70 Musgrove. CALCULTD D+GAM WIDTH GIVEN	
Reson Params	7.6+0	1.4+2	IFU	Expt	Rept ICD-5 5	Dec 71 Vertebny+	+
	7.6+0	1.4+2			Data EXFOR40061.	Mar 71 N-WID AT 10 RES, D	
Strnth Fnctn		+4	BNL	Expt	Jour PL/B 24 573	May 67 Chrien+ FROM RES+UNRESOLVED REGIONS	
Strnth Fnctn	5.5+0	2.3+2	BNL	Expt	Jour PR 162 1130	Oct 67 Mughabghab+ TRANS 2.1+-0.7 FROM RES	+
Strnth Fnctn	-		IFU	Expt	Prog YFI-5 35	Oct 67 Vertebnyj+ VALUE GIVEN	
					Rept INDC-232E	67 . ENGL OF YFI-5 35	
Strnth Fnctn	+0	+2	IFU	Expt	Jour UFZ 13 679	Apr 68 Vertebnyi+ VAL +-ERROR GVN	
					Jour UPJ 13 477	Oct 68 TRANSLATN.*	
Strnth Fnctn	5.5+0	1.4+2	BNL	Expt	Jour PR/C 1 1850	May 70 Mughabghab+ STF FROM RESON+SIGMA	
Strnth Fnctn	-		AUA	Theo	Rept AAEC/E-211	Nov 70 Musgrove. SMOOTHED S0,S1 AND S2 GIVN	
Strnth Fnctn	None		AUA	Eval	Rept AAEC/E-277	Mar 73 Musgrove.TBLS EXPTL DATA+BEST VALUES	
Lvl Density	+0	+3	IFU	Expt	Conf 67Kharkov 171	Feb 67 Vertebny.TRANSMISSION EXPT	
Lvl Density	-		DUB	Expt	Jour YF 7 225	Feb 68 Karzhavina+OTHER VAL GVN,CFD ER-ISOT	
					Jour SNP 7 2 161	Aug 68 - + ENGL OF YF 7 225.	
Lvl Density	None		CCP	Theo	Jour YF 13 43	Jan 71 Bravin+.DEFORM PAR,CALC,TBL,CFD EXPT	

68 Erbium 163

Quantity	Energy (ev) Min	Max	Lab	Type	Documentation Ref Vol Page	Author, Comments Date	Data
Reson Params	-		AUA	Theo	Rept AAEC/E-211	Nov 70 Musgrove. CALCULTD D+GAM WIDTH GIVEN	
Strnth Fnctn	-		AUA	Theo	Rept AAEC/E-211	Nov 70 Musgrove. SMOOTHED S0,S1 AND S2 GIVN	
Lvl Density	+6		MIL	Theo	Jour EN 15 1 54	Jan 68 Facchini+ LDL PARS FROM LOW EN RES	
Lvl Density	None		MUN	Theo	Jour NP/A 217 269	Dec 73 Dilg+ A,DELTA. BACK SHIFTED FERMIGAS	
Lvl Density	None		ROC	Theo	Jour NP/A 223 589	May 74 Huizenga+ EXP CFD MICROSC TH AX SYMM	

68 Erbium 164

Quantity	Energy (ev) Min	Max	Lab	Type	Documentation Ref Vol Page	Author, Comments Date	Data
Total	2.5-2		IFU	Expt	Conf 65Antwerp § 186	Jul 65 Vertebny.KIEV.FC XPT.LESS THAN 50B	
Total	7.0-3	3.3-1	UFT	Expt	Rept ICD-3 85	Oct 66 Vertebny+.GRAPH,NO CORRECTIONS	
					Rept INDC-152E 85	67 . ENGL OF ICD-3 85	
Total	2.5-2		BNL	Expt	Jour PR 162 1130	Oct 67 Mughabghab.	+
	None				Jour PL/B 24 573	May 67 Chrien+ FROM ANALYSIS OF RESONANCES	
	2.5-2				Data EXFOR12120.002	Jun 76 . 1 PT.	
Total	4.5+0	2.5+2	IFU	Expt	Prog YFI-5 35	Oct 67 Vertebnyj+ TRANSMISSION CURVE	
					Rept INDC-232E	67 . ENGL OF YFI-5 35	
Total	5.6+1	1.6+5	COL	Expt	Jour PR/C 5 974	Mar 73 Liou+TOF.TRNS.RES PAR.ANAL.NDG.	
					Rept NYO-72-190	68 - . TOF, TRANS, CURVE	
	None				Jour RSI 35 263	Mar 64 Rainwater+SEE FOR EXPT DETAILS.	
Total	1.4+7		LIN	Expt	Conf 75Kiev 4 140	May 75 Djumin+ SIG GIVEN.OPTMOD ANAL,RADIUS	
Total	1.0-2	1.4+7	CCP	Eval	Data SOKRATOR-2007	77 SIG(E)	+
Elastic	7.0-3	1.0+0	IFU	Expt	Jour IZV 31 353	Feb 67 Vertebnyj+.CURVES,CHOPPER,TOF	+
	2.5-2				Data EXFOR40061.012	Mar 71 SIGMA FOR 2200 M/SEC	
Elastic	1.0-2	1.7-1	IFU	Expt	Jour UFZ 13 599	Apr 68 Kolotyi+ GRPH SIG(E),SCAT-AMPLITUDE	
					Jour UPJ 13 420	Oct 68 TRANSLATN.*	
Elastic	2.6-2		IFU	Expt	Rept IF-69 5	69 Vertebny+ SIG+SCATAMPL AT 2200 M/SEC	
Elastic	2.5-2		IJI	Eval	Conf 75Kiev 1 169	May 75 Fedorova+ EVAL 2200M/S SIG,TABLE	
Elastic	1.0-2	1.4+7	CCP	Eval	Data SOKRATOR-2007	77 SIG(E)	+
Diff Elastic	1.0-3	1.5+7	CCP	Eval	Data SOKRATOR-2007	77 ANGDIST(E)	+
Tot Inelastc	1.0-2	1.5+7	CCP	Eval	Data SOKRATOR-2007	77 SIG(E)	+
Diff Inelast	1.0-3	1.5+7	CCP	Eval	Data SOKRATOR-2007	77 SIG TO 10 LVLS	+
Thermal Scat	1.0-2	1.7-1	IFU	Expt	Jour UFZ 13 599	Apr 68 Kolotyi+ GRPHS,EXPTL SIG=NUCL+MAGN	+
					Jour UPJ 13 420	Oct 68 TRANSLATN.*	
	1.0-2	4.0-1			Data EXFOR40301.	Feb 76 .THERM AND BOUND-ATOM SCAT CS AT11ES	
Scattering	6.0-2	1.7-1	IFU	Expt	Jour UFZ 13 599	Apr 68 Koloty+	+
	6.0-2	1.7-1			Data EXFOR40039.003	Sep 70 AVERAGE SIGMA	
Scattering	2.0-2	3.0-2	IFU	Expt	Conf 70Helsinki 1 651	Jun 70 Vertebnij+ 2200M/SEC SIGMA GIVEN,TBL	
					Rept BNL-TR-495	Jul 72 . ENGLISH OF 70HELSIN 1 651	
Absorption	2.5-2		IJI	Eval	Conf 75Kiev 1 169	May 75 Fedorova+ EVAL 2200M/S SIG,TABLE	
Res Int Abs	5.0-1		OSL	Expt	Prog INDC(NOR)-1 3	May 72 Glomset+ REDUCD CAPTINTEG REL AU,TBL	+
					Priv PAPPAS	Nov 70 Pappas. ACT. POWD,LIQ SOLUT.TBP JIN	
	0.0+0	1.0+6			Data EXFOR20093.005	Sep 71 1PNT.CAPTURE.	
(n,γ)	Maxwl		GOE	Expt	Jour ZP 175 54	Jul 63 Schoeneberg. SIG (N,G) GVN,IN GERMAN	

68 Erbium 164

Quantity	Energy (ev) Min	Max	Lab	Type	Documentation Ref Vol Page	Author, Comments Date	Data
(n,γ)	–		IEA Comp	Rept	IEA – INF – 10	Aug 68 Atalla. TABLES OF HL,SIG AND GAMM – E	
(n,γ)	5.0+3	1.0+5	AUA ExTh	Rept	AAEC/E – 198	May 69 Musgrove.S+P+D WAVE SIGMAS CALC,TBL	+
(n,γ)		3.0+4	HAR Expt	Prog	EANDC(OR)94L	Jan 70 Axmann+ ABST.	
(n,γ)	3.0+4		AUA Theo	Rept	AAEC/E – 211	Nov 70 Musgrove. SIGMA GIVEN AND CFD OTHER	
(n,γ)	1.0+3	1.0+7	BOL Eval	Data	BENZI – DFN 692.	May 72 40 PNTS	+
(n,γ)	Maxwl		OSL Expt	Prog	INDC(NOR) – 1 3	May 72 Glomset+ REL AU,ASSUMING 1/V,TABLE	+
				Priv	PAPPAS	Nov 70 Pappas. ACT. POWD,LIQ SOLUT.TBP JIN	
	Maxwl			Data	EXFOR20093.004	Sep 71 1PNT.SIG.	
(n,γ)	Maxwl	Fiss	WIN Revw	Conf	IAEA – 169 3 163	74 Pope+ FIS – SPEC AVG DATA CFD MAXW – XPT	
(n,γ)	2.5 – 2		BNL Expt	Prog	ERDA – NDC – 2 31	May 75 Chrien+NDG.TBC.	
(n,γ)	1.0 – 3	1.4+7	CCP Eval	Data	SOKRATOR – 2007	77 SIG(E)	+
Spect (n,γ)		3.0+4	HAR Expt	Prog	EANDC(OR)94L	Jan 70 Axmann+ ABST. TBC	
Spect (n,γ)	Pile		ANL Expt	Jour	PR/C 2 1951	Nov 70 Bollinger+ B10 COVER, GE(LI) DET.	
(n,2n)	Fiss		CRC Eval	Rept	CRC – 1003	Dec 60 Roy+,ESTIMATED AVG SIG=1.7MB	
(n,2n)	1.5+7		DEB Eval	Jour	REA 11 1 153	Mar 73 Boedy+ RECOMM.VALUE FROM N – Z SYSTEM.	
(n,2n)	1.5+7		KFI Theo	Rept	KFKI – 73 – 68	Dec 73 Jeki.NEW FIT,CALC SIG CFD OTHERS,TBL	
(n,2n)	1.5+7		JUL Expt	Jour	NP/A 224 319	May 74 Qaim. ACT.GE(LI)	+
				Jour	RRL 25 335	May 76 – + SIG IN GRPH. SYST VS (N – Z)/A	
	1.5+7			Data	EXFOR20541.048	Apr 76 1PNT.SIGMA.	
(n,p)	Fiss		CRC Eval	Rept	CRC – 1003	Dec 60 ROY+ ESTIMATED AVG SIG=0.13MB	
(n,p)	1.4+7	1.5+7	ARK Theo	Prog	ORO – 3235 – 29	Jan 67 Koch+ STAT MODEL CALC CFD EXPTS.	
(n,α)	Fiss		CRC Eval	Rept	CRC – 1003	Dec 60 ROY+ ESTIMATED AVG SIG=0.0004MB	
(n,α)	Maxwl		CCP Expt	Jour	YF 1 252	Feb 65 Andreev.IONIZ – CHAMBER,SIG=M1.2MB	+
				Jour	SNP 1 177	Aug 65 TRANSLATN.*	
Reson Params	8.1+0		IFU Expt	Conf	65Antwerp § 186	Jul 65 Vertebny.KIEV.FC XPT.WN=.55+ – .1MEV	
Reson Params	– 2	+0	IFU Expt	Conf	67Kharkov	Feb 67 Vertebnyj+. TBP IN IZV	
Reson Params	+0	+3	IFU Expt	Conf	67Kharkov 171	Feb 67 Vertebny.TRANSMISSION EXPT	
Reson Params	7.9+0	2.3+2	BNL Expt	Jour	PR 162 1130	Oct 67 Mughabghab+ TRNS. WN FOR 12 RESON.	+
	7.9+0	2.3+2		Data	EXFOR12120.005	Jun 76 . 12 RES, EN, WN, WN0.	
Reson Params	7.8+0	1.3+2	IFU Expt	Prog	YFI – 5 35	Oct 67 Vertebnyj+ TABLE 5 RESONANCES	
				Rept	INDC – 232E	67 . ENGL OF YFI – 5 35	
Reson Params	7.8+0	6.1+2	DUB Expt	Jour	YF 7 225	Feb 68 Karzhavina+,TRANS+NG YLD,RES – PAR+STF	+
				Rept	YFI – 4 47	May 67 – + RES ANAL.	
				Rept	JINR – P3 – 3097	Feb 67 – + TOT+NG,TBL.	
				Jour	SNP 7 161	Aug 68 – + ENGL OF YF 7 225.	
				Rept	INDC – 187E	67 – + ENGL OF YFI – 4 47.	
	7.7+0	6.1+2		Data	EXFOR40147.	May 73 .N – WIDTH,AVERAGE LVL SPACING	
Reson Params	7.8+0	1.3+2	IFU Expt	Jour	UFZ 13 679	Apr 68 Vertebnyi+ 5 RES,WN D VALS GVN,TBLS	
				Jour	UPJ 13 477	Oct 68 TRANSLATN.*	
Reson Params		6.0+2	DUB Expt	Conf	68DUBSY 349	Jul 68 Pikelner.LVL SPAC,AVERG. WG,S0 VS A	
Reson Params	–		AUA Theo	Rept	AAEC/E – 211	Nov 70 Musgrove. CALCULTD D+GAM WIDTH GIVEN	
Reson Params	8.0+0		IFU Expt	Rept	ICD – 5 5	Dec 71 Vertebny+	
	8.0+0			Data	EXFOR40061.006	Mar 71 N – WID AT 1 RES	+
Reson Params	3.1+1	7.5+2	COL Expt	Jour	PR/C 5 974	Mar 72 Liou+.WN FOR 13 RESONANCES	+
	3.1+1	7.6+2		Rept	NYO – 72 – 190	68 . TOF, WN FOR 13 RESON ES.	
	3.1+1	7.5+2		Data	EXFOR10591.007	Jan 78 . 13 RES ES.RED WN GVN.	
Reson Params	None		COL Expt	Conf	75Wash. 335	Mar 75 Felvinci+MOD ERICSON CALC CFD EXPT.	
Reson Params	2.0+3	2.4+4	BNL Expt	Prog	ERDA – NDC – 3 51	May 76 Koene+PARTIAL WG REL AU197.PI. NDG	
Strnth Fnctn	3.1+1	2.3+2	COL Expt	Prog	NYO – GEN72 – 132	Jan 72 Garg+,P.1,NEVIS,TRNSM, L=0 VALUE,TBL	
Strnth Fnctn	7.9+0	2.3+2	BNL Expt	Jour	PR 162 1130	Oct 67 Mughabghab+ TRANS 9.2+ – 0.8 FROM RES	+
		+4		Jour	PL/B 24 573	May 67 Chrien+ FROM RES+UNRESOLVED REGIONS	
Strnth Fnctn	7.8+0	6.1+2	DUB Expt	Jour	YF 7 225	Feb 68 Karzhavina+,TRANS+NG YLD,RES – PAR+STF	+
				Rept	YFI – 4 47	May 67 – + RES ANAL.	
				Rept	JINR – P3 – 3097	Feb 67 – + TOT+NG,TBL.	
				Jour	SNP 7 161	Aug 68 – + ENGL OF YF 7 225.	
				Rept	INDC – 187E	67 – + ENGL OF YFI – 4 47.	
	7.7+0	6.1+2		Data	EXFOR40147.	May 73 .1 DATA LINE	
Strnth Fnctn		6.0+2	DUB Expt	Conf	68DUBSY 349	Jul 68 Pikelner.LVL SPAC,AVERG. WG,S0 VS A	
Strnth Fnctn	7.9+0	2.4+2	BNL Expt	Jour	PR/C 1 1850	May 70 Mughabghab+,STF FROM RESON+SIGMA	
Strnth Fnctn	–		AUA Theo	Rept	AAEC/E – 211	Nov 70 Musgrove. SMOOTHED S0,S1 AND S2 GIVN	
Strnth Fnctn	None		AUA Eval	Rept	AAEC/E – 277	Mar 73 Musgrove.TBLS EXPTL DATA+BEST VALUES	
Lvl Density	None		CCP Theo	Jour	YF 13 43	Jan 71 Bravin+.DEFORM PAR,CALC,TBL,CFD EXPT	

68 Erbium 165

Quantity	Energy (ev) Min	Max	Lab	Type	Documentation Ref Vol Page	Date	Author, Comments	Data
Spect (n,γ)	Pile		MUN	Expt	Jour ZN/A 21 1328	Sep 66	Neumann. CRYST SPEC EXPT OF GAM INT	
					Rept ANL-TRANS-941	73	. ENGLISH OF ZN/A 1328	
Reson Params	–		AUA	Theo	Rept AAEC/E-211	Nov 70	Musgrove. CALCULTD D+GAM WIDTH GIVEN	
Strnth Fnctn	–		AUA	Theo	Rept AAEC/E-211	Nov 70	Musgrove. SMOOTHED S0,S1 AND S2 GIVN	
Lvl Density	+6		MIL	Theo	Jour EN 15 1 54	Jan 68	Facchini+ LDL PARS FROM LOW EN RES	
Lvl Density	7.8+0	6.0+2	DUB	Expt	Jour YF 7 225	Feb 68	Karzhavina+LVL-DEN(EXCIT-E),GRPH,TBL	+
					Rept JINR-P3-3097	Feb 67	- + TOT+NG,TBL.	
					Jour SNP 7 2 161	Aug 68	- + ENGL OF YF 7 225.	
	7.8+0	6.0+2			Data EXFOR40147.	May 73	.1 DATA LINE	
Lvl Density	None		MUN	Theo	Jour NP/A 217 269	Dec 73	Dilg+ A,DELTA. BACK SHIFTED FERMIGAS	
Lvl Density	None		ROC	Theo	Jour NP/A 223 589	May 74	Huizenga+ EXP CFD MICROSC TH AX SYMM	

68 Erbium 166

Quantity	Energy (ev) Min	Max	Lab	Type	Documentation Ref Vol Page	Date	Author, Comments	Data
Total	2.5-2	2.0+2	IFU	Expt	Conf JINR-1845 50	Jun 64	Vertebnij+ TRANSMISSN-TOF, NDG	
Total	2.5-2		IFU	Expt	Conf 65Antwerp § 186	Jul 65	Vertebny.KIEV.FC XPT.SIG 94+ -5B	
Total	7.0-3	3.3-1	UFT	Expt	Rept ICD-3 85	Oct 66	Vertebny+.GRAPH,NO CORRECTIONS	
					Rept INDC-152E 85	67	. ENGL OF ICD-3 85	
Total	None		BNL	Expt	Jour PL/B 24 573	May 67	Chrien+ FROM ANALYSIS OF RESONANCES	
Total	1.1-2	1.2-1	IFU	Expt	Rept ICD-5 5	Dec 71	Vertebny+	+
	1.1-2	1.2-1			Data EXFOR40061.003	Mar 71	SIGMA AT 121 ENERGIES	
Total	4.0+0	1.0+4	HAR	Expt	Prog AERE-PR/NP18	Mar 72	Axmann+ LINAC TOF NDG	
Total	6.0+0	1.6+5	COL	Expt	Jour PR/C 5 974	Mar 73	Liou+TOF.TRNS.RES PAR.ANAL.NDG.	+
					Rept NYO-72-190	68	- .TRNS+SELF INDIC.CURV.	
	None				Jour RSI 35 263	Mar 64	Rainwater+SEE FOR EXPT DETAILS.	
	6.8+2	1.0+4			Data EXFOR10591.003	Jan 78	. RAW DATA AVAILABLE FROM NNDC.	
Total	1.4+7		LIN	Expt	Conf 75Kiev 4 140	May 75	Djumin+ SIG GIVEN.OPTMOD ANAL,RADIUS	
Total	1.0-2	1.4+7	CCP	Eval	Data SOKRATOR-2008	76	SIG(E)	+
Total	+7		IJI	Expt	Conf 77Kiev	77	Trofimova+ SIG	
	2.0+3				Conf 76Lowell 1244	Jul 76	Vertebnyi+ TRANSM VS THICKNESS,NDG	
Elastic	7.0-3	1.0+0	IFU	Expt	Jour IZV 31 353	Feb 67	Vertebnyj+.CURVES,CHOPPER,TOF	+
	2.5-2				Data EXFOR40061.013	Mar 71	SIGMA FOR 2200 M/SEC	
Elastic	1.0-2	1.7-1	IFU	Expt	Jour UFZ 13 599	Apr 68	Kolotyi+ GRPH SIG(E),SCAT-AMPLITUDE	
					Jour UPJ 13 420	Oct 68	TRANSLATN.*	
Elastic	2.6-2		IFU	Expt	Rept IF-69 5	69	Vertebny+ SIG+SCATAMPL AT 2200 M/SEC	
Elastic	Maxwl	+5	IFU	Comp	Prog YFI-7 43	Apr 69	Vertebny+ SCATTERING-LENGTH DERIVED	
					Rept INDC(CCP)-7U46	Feb 70	TRANSLATN.*	
Elastic	2.5-2		IJI	Eval	Conf 75Kiev 1 169	May 75	Fedorova+ EVAL 2200M/S SIG,TABLE	
Elastic	1.0-2	1.4+7	CCP	Eval	Data SOKRATOR-2008	76	SIG(E)	+
Diff Elastic	1.4+7		ORL	Theo	Jour NP 68 97	Jun 65	Stelson+ DIST OPTMDL CALC	
Diff Elastic	1.0-3	1.5+7	CCP	Eval	Data SOKRATOR-2008	76	ANGDIST(E)	+
Potntal Scat	2.0+3		IJI	Expt	Conf 76Lowell 1244	Jul 76	Vertebnyi+ SCT-LNGTH GVN,FRM TOT+SCT	
Tot Inelastc	1.0-3	1.5+7	CCP	Eval	Data SOKRATOR-2008	76	SIG(E)	+
Diff Inelast	1.4+7		ORL	Theo	Jour NP 68 97	Jun 65	Stelson+ DIST OPTMDL CALC AD TO 2+	
Diff Inelast	1.4+7		LRL	Theo	Rept UCRL-50181	Feb 67	Lutz+.CALC ANG DIST FOR FIRST 2+ LVL	
Diff Inelast	1.0-3	1.5+7	CCP	Eval	Data SOKRATOR-2008	76	SIG TO 7 LVLS	+
Thermal Scat	1.0-2	1.7-1	IFU	Expt	Jour UFZ 13 599	Apr 68	Kolotyi+ GRPHS,EXPTL SIG=NUCL+MAGN	+
					Jour UPJ 13 420	Oct 68	TRANSLATN.*	
	1.0-2	4.0-1			Data EXFOR40301.	Feb 76	.THERM AND BOUND-ATOM SCAT CS AT11ES	
Scattering	1.7-2	6.0-2	IFU	Expt	Jour UFZ 13 599	Apr 68	Koloty+	+
	1.7-2	6.0-2			Data EXFOR40039.004	Sep 70	AVERAGE SIGMA	
Scattering	2.0-2	3.0-2	IFU	Expt	Conf 70Helsinki 1 651	Jun 70	Vertebnij+ 2200M/SEC SIGMA GIVEN,TBL	
					Rept BNL-TR-495	Jul 72	. ENGLISH OF 70HELSIN 1 651	
Scattering	2.0+3		IJI	Expt	Conf 76Lowell 1244	Jul 76	Vertebnyi+ SCT-SIG VS THICKNESS,NDG	
Absorption	Maxwl	Pile	SGA	Expt	Jour JMS 6 435	71	Dobrozemsky+ CHANGE OF ABUND.TBL SIG	+
					Rept SGAE-PH-104	71	- + MASS-SPEC METHOD.	
	2.5-2				Data EXFOR20637.018	Sep 76	1PNT.SIGMA.	
Absorption	2.5-2		IJI	Eval	Conf 75Kiev 1 169	May 75	Fedorova+ EVAL 2200M/S SIG,TABLE	
Res Int Abs	5.5-1		SGA	Expt	Jour JMS 6 435	71	Dobrozemsky+ EFF ABS RES INT GIVEN.	+
	Maxwl	Pile			Rept SGAE-PH-104	71	- + MASS SPEC. ACTIVATION.	
	5.5-1				Data EXFOR20637.019	Sep 76	1PNT.	
Res Int Abs	5.0-1		COL	Expt	Jour NSE 48 219	Jun 72	Rahn+. RI=122+ -13B	
Res Int Abs	+0	+5	WIN	Revw	Conf IAEA-169 3 163	74	Pope+ EVALUATED VALUE GIVEN	
Res Int Abs	5.0-1		IJI	Eval	Conf 75Kiev 1 169	May 75	Fedorova+ EVAL+CALC RI GIVEN,TABLE	

68 Erbium 166

Quantity	Energy (ev) Min	Max	Lab	Type	Documentation Ref Vol Page	Author, Comments Date	Data
(n,γ)	Maxwl		ROS	Expt Jour	ADP 12 225	63 Alexander+ ACTIV,SIG TO ISOM GIVEN	
				Rept	ZFK-RN-16	Sep 62 Brinckmann+VAL GVN,PRODCTN OF ER167M	
				Rept	RFP-TRANS-78	71 . ENGLISH OF ADP 12 225	
(n,γ)	Maxwl		UCS	Expt Rept	NYO-10175	Dec 64 Arino+ACT.TBLS.GRAPHS.PRODUCT HL.	+
	Maxwl			Data	EXFOR11817.012	Jun 76 . 1 PT.	
(n,γ)	–		IEA	Comp Rept	IEA-INF- 10	Aug 68 Atalla. TABLES OF HL,SIG AND GAMM-E	
(n,γ)	5.0+3	1.0+5	AUA	ExTh Rept	AAEC/E-198	May 69 Musgrove.S+P+D WAVE SIGMAS CALC,TBL	+
(n,γ)		3.0+4	HAR	Expt Prog	EANDC(OR)94L	Jan 70 Axmann+ ABST.	
(n,γ)	3.0+4		AUA	Theo Rept	AAEC/E-211	Nov 70 Musgrove. SIGMA GIVEN AND CFD OTHER	
(n,γ)	Maxwl		KFI	Comp Jour	JRC 7 365	Jun 71 Nagy+ SIGMA,GAM+XRAY+ELECTR ES GIVEN	
(n,γ)	2.5-2		IFU	Expt Rept	ICD-5 5	Dec 71 Vertebny+	+
	2.5-2			Data	EXFOR40061.019	Mar 71 SIGMA FOR 2200 M/SEC	
(n,γ)	1.0+3	1.0+7	BOL	Eval Data	BENZI-DFN 693.	May 72 40 PNTS	+
(n,γ)	Pile		ROS	ExTh Prog	ZFK-243 93	Sep 72 Mohsen+ NG-SYSTEMAT. FOR RARE EARTHS	
(n,γ)	5.0+3	7.0+4	CCP	Expt Conf	73Kiev 2 206	May 73 Kononov+ TOF,SIG(NEUT-E),GRAPH	
(n,γ)	+6		II	Expt Conf	73Kiev 4 312	May 73 Lakosi+ ACTIV BY PHOTONEUTRONS,TABLE	+
	+6			Data	EXFOR30268.012	Jul 74 ER-167(INL)+ER-166(NG)TO ISOMER,1PT	
(n,γ)	Maxwl	Fiss	WIN	Revw Conf	IAEA-169 3 163	74 Pope+ FIS-SPEC AVG DATA CFD MAXW-XPT	
(n,γ)	5.0+3	7.0+4	FEI	Expt Jour	YFI-17 9	Aug 74 Shorin+ TOF,SIG(NEUT-E),TBL	+
				Jour	YF 19 5	Jan 74 - + TOF,SIG(NEUT-E),GRAPHS	
	5.3+3	6.8+4		Rept	INDC(CCP)-48	Feb 75 . ENGLISH OF YFI-17 9	
	5.0+3	7.0+4		Jour	SNP 19 2	Jul 74 . ENGLISH OF YF 19 5	
	5.3+3	6.8+4		Data	EXFOR40222.010	Mar 74 .SIGMA FOR 32 EN-RANGES GVN	
(n,γ)	2.5-2		BNL	Expt Prog	ERDA-NDC-2 31	May 75 Chrien+NDG.TBC.	
(n,γ)	1.0-3	1.4+7	CCP	Eval Data	SOKRATOR-2008	76 SIG(E)	+
(n,γ)	Maxwl		WES	Expt Abst	BAP 3 336	Aug 58 Hopkins. DANGER COEF METH 45B+-20PC	+
	Maxwl			Data	EXFOR12081.002	Jun 76 . 1 PT.	
Spect (n,γ)	Maxwl		RIS	Expt Jour	ZP 187 450	Sep 65 Koch.TBL OF GS TO 800KEV,ER167-LEVLS	
Spect (n,γ)	Maxwl		ANL	Expt Jour	PR 162 1112	Oct 67 Prestwich+ GE(LI) 25 HIGH-E GAM PKS	+
Spect (n,γ)	+0	+4	COL	Expt Prog	WASH-1124 31	Nov 68 Camarda+ MOXON-RAE DET TBC NO DATA	
Spect (n,γ)	Maxwl		KFK	Expt Jour	NP/A 143 225	Mar 70 Michaelis+ G-G COINC,LVLS ER-167	
				Rept	KFK-1194	Mar 70 - + EQU TO NP/A 143 225	
				Rept	KFK-1197	Feb 70 - + LVL SCHEME ER-167 +SPECT	
				Rept	KFK-1096	Aug 69 - + REPRINT OF 69STUDSVIK	
				Conf	69Studsvik 469	Aug 69 - + ER167LVL-SCH GVN+DISCUSSD	
				Conf	JINR-D3893 37	May 68 - + EXPT DONE,BUT NO DATA GVN	
				Rept	KFK-616	Sep 67 Fanger+ LVLS CFD DY165+YB169+THEORY	
				Conf	67Tokyo § 4.107	Sep 67 Markus+ DATA GIVEN. TBP ZP 206.	
				Jour	ZP 206 84	Sep 67 - + PRELIM LVLS ER-167.CFD DY,YB	
Spect (n,γ)	Maxwl		KFI	Comp Jour	JRC 7 365	Jun 71 Nagy+ SIGMA,GAM+XRAY+ELECTR ES GIVEN	
(n,2n)	1.5+7		ARK	Expt Jour	PR 118 242	Apr 60 Wille+ MEAS ACT SIG=1000+-400 MB	+
	1.5+7			Data	EXFOR12033.042	Jun 76 . 1 PT.	
(n,2n)	Fiss		CRC	Eval Rept	CRC-1003	Dec 60 Roy+,ESTIMATED AVG SIG=2.6MB	
(n,2n)	1.4+7		HAM	Comp Jour	NP 65 257	Mar 65 Bormann. 1EXPT VALS.CFD SHELL EFFECT	
(n,2n)	1.5+7		MUN	Expt Jour	NP/A 118 9	Sep 68 Dilg+ ACTIV.REL AL(N,A)	+
				Jour	OAWS 177 323	69 Winkler+(IRK) ACTIVATION.	
	1.5+7			Data	EXFOR20802.009	Dec 78 1PNT.SIGMA.	
(n,2n)	1.5+7		DEB	Comp Jour	REA 7 4 93	Dec 69 Csikai+ SIG+HL COMPILTN,N-ACTIV-ANAL	
(n,2n)	1.4+7	1.5+7	JYV	Eval Rept	JU-RR-3/1970	Jun 70 Leppaemaeki+ TABLE OF EVAL AVG SIG	
(n,2n)	+7		KFI	Theo Rept	KFKI-71-8	Feb 71 Jeki. CALCULATED CFD EXPTL SIG VALUE	
(n,2n)	1.5+7		DEB	Eval Jour	REA 11 1 153	Mar 73 Boedy. COMPILATION+RECOMM.VALUE,TBL	
				Rept	IAEA-153 173	73 - . RECOMM. VALUE ONLY	
(n,2n)	1.5+7		TAT	Theo Jour	JP/A 7 1457	Aug 74 Kondaiah. CALC ON STAT MODEL	
(n,2n)	1.5+7		JUL	Expt Jour	NP/A 224 319	May 74 Qaim. ACT.GE(LI)	+
				Jour	RRL 25 335	May 76 - + SIG IN GRPH. SYST VS (N-Z)/A	
	1.5+7			Data	EXFOR20541.049	Apr 74 1PNT.SIGMA.	
(n,p)	Fiss		CRC	Eval Rept	CRC-1003	Dec 60 Roy+,ESTIMATED AVG SIG=0.012MB	
(n,p)	1.4+7		SAH	Comp Jour	NP 60 273	Nov 64 Chatterjee.MEAN OF EXPT CFD SHELLMOD	
(n,p)	1.4+7	1.5+7	ARK	ExTh Prog	ORO-3235-29	Jan 67 Koch+,STAT MODEL CALC CFD EXPTS	
(n,p)	1.5+7		ARK	Expt Abst	DA/B 32 5091	Mar 72 Bari. GE(LI) DET. ACT. SIG GIVEN	+
	1.5+7			Data	EXFOR10431.017	Aug 75 . 1 PT. SIGMA.	
(n,p)	1.5+7		JUL	Expt Jour	RRL 25 335	May 76 Qaim+ ACTIV,GELI.CFD OTHERS,TBL+GRPH	
(n,α)	Fiss		CRC	Eval Rept	CRC-1003	Dec 60 Roy+,ESTIMATED AVG SIG=0.0001MB	
(n,α)	Maxwl		CCP	Expt Jour	YF 1 252	Feb 65 Andreev.IONIZ-CHAMBER,SIG=M.07MB	+
				Jour	SNP 1 177	Aug 65 TRANSLATN.*	

68 Erbium 166

Quantity	Energy (ev) Min	Max	Lab	Type	Documentation Ref Vol Page	Author, Comments Date	Data
(n,α)	1.4+7		IBJ	Expt	Rept INR−1268	Jan 71 Jaskola+ ALFA SPCTR CFD TH,FULL PAPR	+
					Jour APPB 2 521	71 .SAME AS INR−1268	
					Rept INR−1175	Mar 70 SEE ALSO * FULL INFORMATION	
	1.4+7				Data EXFOR30158.020	Mar 71 NUM DATA NOT AVAILBL,SEE GRAF IN REF	
(n,α)	1.4+7		WWA	Theo	Prog INDC(SEC)−28	Sep 72 Kozlowski+ ENERGY SPECT CALC. ,GRPH	
					Jour NP/A 187 177	May 72 − +.30DEG E−SPEC.KNOCK−ON OK	
(n,α)	1.4+7		DUB	Theo	Rept JINR−P4−6832	Dec 72 Kozlowski.DEFORMD NUC STRUCTURE,GRPH	
(n,α)	1.4+7		IBJ	ExTh	Conf ZFK−271 109	Nov 73 Glowacka+ A−SPEC CFD 2 MODELS,NDG	
				Theo	Conf 72Budapest 18	Aug 72 − + ENERGY SPECTRA, GRPH	
Reson Params	6.0+0	1.4+2	GA	Expt	Rept GA−3874	Mar 63 Haddad+LINAC TOF LIQ SC T ISO ASSNG	+
	1.6+1	8.2+1			Data EXFOR11944.006	Jun 76 . 3 RES. EN, WN, WNG.	
Reson Params	1.5+1		CCP	Expt	Rept AE 15 247	Sep 63 Vlasov+.TRANSMISSION, 3 RES	
					Jour SJA 15 952	Sep 63 . ENGL OF AE 15 247	
Reson Params	1.6+1		IFU	Expt	Conf 65Antwerp § 186	Jul 65 Vertebny.KIEV.FC XPT.WN=2.1+−.2MEV	
Reson Params	+0	+3	IFU	Expt	Conf 67Kharkov 171	Feb 67 Vertebny.TRANSMISSION EXPT	
Reson Params	1.6+1	6.0+2	BNL	Expt	Jour PR 162 1130	Oct 67 Mughabghab+ TRANS WN FOR 13RESON ES	+
	1.6+1	6.0+2			Data EXFOR12120.006	Jun 76 . 13 RES. EN, WN, WN0.	
Reson Params	1.5+1	1.8+2	IFU	Expt	Prog YFI−5 35	Oct 67 Vertebnyj+ TABLE 4 RESONANCES	
					Rept INDC−232E	67 . ENGL OF YFI−5 35	
Reson Params	1.5+1	1.4+3	DUB	Expt	Jour YF 7 225	Feb 68 Karzhavina+,TRANS+NG YLD,RES−PAR+STF	+
					Rept YFI−4 47	May 67 − + RES ANAL.	
					Rept JINR−P3−3097	Feb 67 − + TOT+NG,TBL.	
					Jour SNP 7 161	Aug 68 − + ENGL OF YF 7 225.	
					Rept INDC−187E	67 − + ENGL OF YFI−4 47.	
	1.5+1	1.4+3			Data EXFOR40147.	May 73 .NW,GW,TOT−WIDTH,D,AVER GW	
Reson Params	1.6+1	1.7+2	IFU	Expt	Jour UFZ 13 679	Apr 68 Vertebnyi+ 4 RES,WN D VALS GVN,TBLS	
					Jour UPJ 13 477	Oct 68 TRANSLATN.*	
Reson Params		1.4+3	DUB	Expt	Conf 68DUBSY 349	Jul 68 Pikelner.LVL SPAC,AVERG. WG,S0 VS A	
Reson Params	None		BNL	Eval	Conf 69Studsvik 627	Aug 69 Chrien. WG/WN−CORREL,WG CFD P−T,TBLS	
Reson Params	−		AUA	Theo	Rept AAEC/E−211	Nov 70 Musgrove. CALCULTD D+GAM WIDTH GIVEN	
Reson Params	1.5+1	3.0+2	CJD	Eval	Rept YK−7	71 Zakharova+ SURVEY+SYSTEMATICS,GW,TBL	
					Rept INDC(CCP)−27	Nov 72 .ENGLISH TRANSLATION OF YK−7 /71	
Reson Params	None		DUB	Theo	Jour YF 13 240	Feb 71 Malecki+G−WID,THEO CFD EXPT.TBL,GRPH	
					Jour SNP 13 133	Aug 71 − + ENGL OF YF 13 240.	
Reson Params	1.6+1		IFU	Expt	Rept ICD−5 5	Dec 71 Vertebny+	+
	1.6+1				Data EXFOR40061.007	Mar 71 N−WID AT 1 RES	
Reson Params	1.6+1	9.5+3	COL	Expt	Jour PR/C 5 974	Mar 72 Liou+.WN WG G*WN D. P−T+WIGNER DISTS	+
					Conf 71Albany 205	Aug 71 Camarda+ D, WG GVN. TBP PR.	
	1.6+1	3.0+3			Rept NYO−72−190	68 Liou.TOF.51 WN,3WG.AVG D.TBLS	
	1.6+1	9.5+3			Data EXFOR10591.	Jan 78 . 174 RES ES.WG,RED WN GVN.D GVN.	
Reson Params	None		DUB	Theo	Conf 73Munich 1 246	Aug 73 Malov+ SUPERFLUID MDL,TBL D VS EXC−E	
Reson Params	None		COL	Expt	Conf 75Wash. 780	Mar 75 Hacken+ TBL AV WG,STF,NUMBER GWN,WG	
					Jour NSE 48 219	Jun 72 Rahn+. AVG WG=92.4MEV OVER 10RESON	
Reson Params	None		COL	Expt	Conf 75Wash. 335	Mar 75 Felvinci+MOD ERICSON CALC CFD EXPT.	
Strnth Fnctn	1.6+1	6.0+2	BNL	Expt	Jour PR 162 1130	Oct 67 Mughabghab+ TRANS 7.7+−0.9 FROM RES	
		+4			Jour PL/B 24 573	May 67 Chrien+ FROM RES+UNRESOLVED REGIONS	
Strnth Fnctn	1.5+1	1.4+3	DUB	Expt	Jour YF 7 225	Feb 68 Karzhavina+,TRANS+NG YLD,RES−PAR+STF	+
					Rept YFI−4 47	May 67 − + RES ANAL.	
					Rept JINR−P3−3097	Feb 67 − + TOT+NG,TBL.	
					Jour SNP 7 161	Aug 68 − + ENGL OF YF 7 225.	
					Rept INDC−187E	67 − + ENGL OF YFI−4 47.	
	1.5+1	1.4+3			Data EXFOR40147.	May 73 .1 DATA LINE	
Strnth Fnctn		1.4+3	DUB	Expt	Conf 68DUBSY 349	Jul 68 Pikelner.LVL SPAC,AVERG. WG,S0 VS A	
Strnth Fnctn	1.6+1	6.0+2	BNL	Expt	Jour PR/C 1 1850	May 70 Mughabghab+,STF FROM RESON=1.9+−0.7	
Strnth Fnctn	−		AUA	Theo	Rept AAEC/E−211	Nov 70 Musgrove. SMOOTHED S0,S1 AND S2 GIVN	
Strnth Fnctn	1.6+1	9.5+3	COL	Expt	Jour PR/C 5 974	Mar 72 Liou+.S0 AND S1 GIVEN	+
					Conf 71Albany 205	Aug 71 Camarda+ S0, S1 GVN.	
	1.6+1	3.0+3			Rept NYO−72−190	68 Liou.S0=1.70+−.45.	
	0.0+0	4.2+3			Data EXFOR10591.014	Jan 78 . 2 PTS.S0=1.70+−.23.S1=.75+−.04.	
Strnth Fnctn	None		AUA	Eval	Rept AAEC/E−277	Mar 73 Musgrove.TBLS EXPTL DATA+BEST VALUES	
Strnth Fnctn	None		COL	Revw	Conf 75Wash. 780	Mar 75 Hacken+ NEVIS TOF S−WAVE STF	
Lvl Density	None		AUW	Theo	Conf 70Madurai 2 267	Dec 70 Ramamurty+ A−PARAMETER GVN,LANG'S−TH	
Lvl Density	None		CCP	Theo	Jour YF 13 43	Jan 71 Bravin+.DEFORM PAR,CALC,TBL,CFD EXPT	
Lvl Density	1.4+7		IBJ	Expt	Rept INR−1268	Jan 71 Jaskola+ ALFA SPCTR CFD TH,FULL PAPR	+
					Jour APPB 2 521	71 .SAME AS INR−1268	
	1.4+7				Data EXFOR30158.021	Mar 71 LEVEL DENSITY PARAMETER OF DY163 GIV	

68 Erbium 166

Quantity	Energy (ev) Min	Energy (ev) Max	Lab	Type	Documentation Ref Vol Page	Author, Comments Date	Data
Lvl Density	+0	2.0+3	JAE	ExTh Jour	JPJ 37 581	Sep 74 Ideno.LVL SPACING CORRELATIONS.TBL	
	1.0+0	2.0+3		Rept	JAERI – M – 5490	Nov 73 – .LEVEL SPACING CORRELATIONS.TBL	
	+0	6.5+2		Jour	JPJ 30 620	Mar 71 – + RES SPACING CORRELATION ANAL	

68 Erbium 167

Quantity	Energy (ev) Min	Energy (ev) Max	Lab	Type	Documentation Ref Vol Page	Author, Comments Date	Data
Total	2.0–2	9.0–1	BNL Expt	Jour	NSE 8 183	Sep 60 Moller+ CURVE RES PARS GIVEN.	+
	2.1–2	8.9–1		Data	EXFOR12097.008	Jun 76 . 86 PTS.	
Total	2.5–2	2.0+2	IFU Expt	Conf	JINR – 1845 50	Jun 64 Vertebnij+ TRANSMISSN – TOF, NDG	
Total	9.8+5		SHE Theo	Jour	NP 54 417	Jun 64 Maddison.OPTMOD FIT TO TOWLE GILBOY	
Total	2.5–2		IFU Expt	Conf	65Antwerp § 186	Jul 65 Vertebny.KIEV.FC XPT.SIG 670+ – 30B	
Total	7.0–3	3.3–1	UFT Expt	Rept	ICD – 3 85	Oct 66 Vertebny+.GRAPH,NO CORRECTIONS	
				Rept	INDC – 152E 85	67 . ENGL OF ICD – 3 85	
Total	None		BNL Expt	Jour	PL/B 24 573	May 67 Chrien+ FROM ANALYSIS OF RESONANCES	
Total	1.1–2	1.2–1	IFU Expt	Rept	ICD – 5 5	Dec 71 Vertebny+	+
	1.1–2	1.2–1		Data	EXFOR40061.004	Mar 71 SIGMA AT 121 ENERGIES	
Total	6.0+0	1.2+3	COL Expt	Jour	PR/C 5 974	Mar 73 Liou+TOF.TRNS.RES PAR.ANAL.NDG.	+
				Rept	NYO – 72 – 190	68 – + TOF, TRANS, CURVE.	
	None			Jour	RSI 35 263	Mar 64 Rainwater+SEE FOR EXPT DETAILS.	
	1.0+0	1.7+3		Data	EXFOR10591.004	Jan 78 . RAW DATA AVAILABLE FROM NNDC.	
Total	1.4+7		LIN Expt	Conf	75Kiev 4 140	May 75 Djumin+ SIG GIVEN.OPTMOD ANAL,RADIUS	
Total	1.0–2	1.4+7	CCP Eval	Data	SOKRATOR – 2009	76 SIG(E)	+
Total	5.0+0	1.3+2	HAR Expt	Conf	76Lowell 1257	Jul 76 Axmann.(IRK).TOF.RES PARS DERVD.NDG	
Total	+7		IJI Expt	Conf	77Kiev	77 Trofimova+ SIG	
	2.0+3			Conf	76Lowell 1244	Jul 76 Vertebnyi+ TRANSM VS THICKNESS,NDG	
Elastic	7.0–3	1.0+0	IFU Expt	Jour	IZV 31 353	Feb 67 Vertebnyj+.CURVES,CHOPPER,TOF	
	2.5–2			Data	EXFOR40061.014	Mar 71 SIGMA FOR 2200 M/SEC	
Elastic	1.0–2	1.7–1	IFU Expt	Jour	UFZ 13 599	Apr 68 Kolotyi+ GRPH SIG(E),SCAT – AMPLITUDE	
				Jour	UPJ 13 420	Oct 68 TRANSLATN.*	
Elastic	2.5–2		IJI Eval	Conf	75Kiev 1 169	May 75 Fedorova+ EVAL 2200M/S SIG,TABLE	
Elastic	1.0–2	1.4+7	CCP Eval	Data	SOKRATOR – 2009	76 SIG(E)	+
Elastic	5.0+0	1.3+2	HAR Expt	Conf	76Lowell 1257	Jul 76 Axmann.(IRK).TOF.RES PARS.SCT YIELD	
		1.0+3		Prog	EANDC(UK) 151	Aug 73 – .TOF LINAC TO GET BETTER WG	
Diff Elastic	9.8+5		SHE Theo	Jour	NP 54 417	Jun 64 Maddison.OPTMOD FIT TO TOWLE GILBOY	
Diff Elastic	1.0–3	1.5+7	CCP Eval	Data	SOKRATOR – 2009	76 ANGDIST(E)	+
Potntal Scat	2.0+3		IJI Expt	Conf	76Lowell 1244	Jul 76 Vertebnyi+ SCT – LNGTH GVN,FRM TOT+SCT	
Tot Inelastc	Fiss		UCS Expt	Jour	NYO – 10175	Dec 64 Arino+ACT.TBLS.GRAPHS.PRODUCT HL.	+
	Fiss			Data	EXFOR11817.013	Jun 76 . 1 PT.	
Tot Inelastc	1.0–3	1.5+7	CCP Eval	Data	SOKRATOR – 2009	76 SIG(E)	+
Diff Inelast	1.5+7		IBJ Expt	Jour	APPB 1 415	Dec 70 Rurarz+ NA – I,SIG TO ISOM GVN,G – SPEC	+
				Jour	APPB 1 415	70 – + ACTIV,NAI,SIG(M)+ISORATIO	
	1.5+7			Data	EXFOR30154.	Feb 72 PARTIAL SIG	
Diff Inelast	1.4+7		ITJ Expt	Jour	JRC 14 201	73 Janczyszyn+ ISO – PROD BY NAT – ER ACTIV	
	1.4+7			Data	EXFOR30322.015	Feb 76 MEAN OF ER167(N,N')+ER168(N,2N)	
Diff Inelast	8.3+5		II Expt	Conf	73Kiev 4 312	May 73 Lakosi+ TO MS,REL AU197(N,G)	
	+6			Data	EXFOR30268.	Jul 74 ER – 167(INL)+ER – 166(NG)TO ISOMER,2PTS	
Diff Inelast	Thrsh	Up	CAI Theo	Jour	AKE 28 3 201	76 Abboud. EXCITATION – FN,STATMOD	
Diff Inelast	1.0–3	1.5+7	CCP Eval	Data	SOKRATOR – 2009	76 SIG TO 7 LVLS	+
Thermal Scat	1.0–2	1.7–1	IFU Expt	Jour	UFZ 13 599	Apr 68 Kolotyi+ GRPHS,EXPTL SIG=NUCL+MAGN	+
				Jour	UPJ 13 420	Oct 68 TRANSLATN.*	
	2.0–2	1.5–1		Data	EXFOR40301.	Feb 76 .THERM AND BOUND – ATOM SCAT CS AT18ES	
Scattering	6.0–2	1.7–1	IFU Expt	Jour	UFZ 13 599	Apr 68 Koloty+	+
	6.0–2	1.7–1		Data	EXFOR40039.005	Sep 70 AVERAGE SIGMA	
Scattering	2.0–2	3.0–2	IFU Expt	Conf	70Helsinki 1 651	Jun 70 Vertebnij+ 2200M/SEC SIGMA GIVEN,TBL	
				Rept	BNL – TR – 495	Jul 72 . ENGLISH OF 70HELSIN 1 651	
Scattering	2.0+3		IJI Expt	Conf	76Lowell 1244	Jul 76 Vertebnyi+ SCT – SIG VS THICKNESS,NDG	
Absorption	1.0–3	2.0+0	JUL Theo	Rept	JUEL – 746 – RG144	Apr 71 Bonka.KUGEL – THERMOS – LIBR,CURVE	
Absorption	2.5–2		IJI Eval	Conf	75Kiev 1 169	May 75 Fedorova+ EVAL 2200M/S SIG,TABLE	
Res Int Abs	5.4–1		ORL Expt	Prog	ORNL – 4155 15	Aug 67 Gillette+	+
	5.4–1			Data	EXFOR10259.011	Jul 74 . 1 PT. SIGMA	
Res Int Abs	5.0–1		COL Expt	Jour	NSE 48 219	Jun 72 Rahn+. RI=3177+ – 325B	
Res Int Abs	+0	+5	WIN Revw	Conf	IAEA – 169 3 163	74 Pope+ EVALUATED VALUE GIVEN	
Res Int Abs	5.0–1		IJI Eval	Conf	75Kiev 1 169	May 75 Fedorova+ EVAL+CALC RI GIVEN,TABLE	
(n,γ)	Maxwl	5.0+2	GA Expt	Abst	BAP 9 31	Jan 64 Lopez+ SIG=160+ – 8B AT THERMAL	
(n,γ)	1.0+3	1.0+4	LAS Theo	Rept	LA – 3463	Jan 66 Bell. TH CAPTURE OF RARE EARTHS	

68 Erbium 167

Quantity	Energy (ev) Min	Energy (ev) Max	Lab	Type	Documentation Ref Vol Page	Date	Author, Comments	Data
(n,γ)	Maxwl		RPI	Expt	Jour IRE 14 1	Apr 67	SU+	+
				Abst	DA/B 28 720	Aug 67	SU.MASS-SP OF IRRAD SAMLES,699+ -20B	
				Prog	RPI-328-68 165	Jun 66	SU+ MASS SPECTROMET ANAL,VALUE GIVEN	
	Maxwl			Data	EXFOR12128.003	Jun 67	. 1 PT.	
(n,γ)	Maxwl		ORL	Expt	Prog ORNL-4155 15	Aug 67	Gillette+	+
	Maxwl			Data	EXFOR10259.005	Jul 74	. 1 PT. SIGMA	
(n,γ)	2.5-2		IFU	Expt	Rept ICD-5 5	Nov 68	Vertebny+	+
	2.5-2			Data	EXFOR40061.020	Mar 71	SIGMA FOR 2200 M/SEC	
(n,γ)	5.0+3	1.0+5	AUA	ExTh	Rept AAEC/E-198	May 69	Musgrove.S+P+D WAVE SIGMAS CALC,TBL	+
(n,γ)	3.0+4		AUA	Theo	Rept AAEC/E-211	Nov 70	Musgrove. SIGMA GIVEN AND CFD OTHER	
(n,γ)	1.0-2	1.0+2	HAR	Expt	Prog AERE-PR/NP17	Dec 70	Moxon+ TOF LINAC ANAL TBC	
(n,γ)	1.0+3	1.0+7	BOL	Expt	Jour BENZI-DFN 694.	May 72	40 PNTS	+
(n,γ)	5.0+3	7.0+4	CCP	Expt	Conf 73Kiev 2 206	May 73	Kononov+ TOF,SIG(NEUT-E),GRAPH	
(n,γ)	Maxwl	Fiss	WIN	Revw	Conf IAEA-169 3 163	74	Pope+ FIS-SPEC AVG DATA CFD MAXW-XPT	
(n,γ)	5.0+3	7.0+4	FEI	Expt	Rept YFI-17 9	Aug 74	Shorin+ TOF,SIG(NEUT-E),TBL	+
					Jour YF 19 5	Jan 74	- + TOF,SIG(NEUT-E),GRAPHS	
	5.3+3	6.8+4			Rept INDC(CCP)-48	Feb 75	. P 5.ENGLISH OF YFI-17 9	
	5.0+3	7.0+4			Jour SNP 19 2	Jul 74	. ENGLISH OF YF 19 5	
	6.0+3	6.8+4			Data	EXFOR40222.011	Mar 74 .SIGMA FOR 31 EN-RANGES GVN	
(n,γ)	1.0-3	1.4+7	CCP	Eval	Data SOKRATOR-2009	76	SIG(E)	+
(n,γ)	Maxwl		WES	Expt	Abst BAP 3 336	Aug 58	Hopkins. DANGER COEF METH 620B+ -20PC	+
	Maxwl			Data	EXFOR12081.003	Jun 76	. 1 PT.	
	5.0+0	1.3+2	HAR	Expt	Conf 76Lowell 1257	Jul 76	Axmann.(IRK).TOF.RES PARS.CAPT YLD	
Spect (n,γ)	Maxwl		CCP	Expt	Jour AE 4 22	Jan 58	Sklyarevskii+.EGS+INTENS BELOW .3MEV	
					Jour JNE 9 69	Jun 59	TRANSLATN.*	
					Jour SJA 4 19	58	TRANSLATN.*	
Spect (n,γ)	4.7-1	6.0+0	YAL	Expt	Abst BAP 4 35	Jan 59	Springer+,NAI(TL),GAMMA MULTIPLICITY	
Spect (n,γ)	Maxwl	9.4+0	YAL	Expt	Jour NP 10 386	Apr 59	Fenstermacher+.GRAPH.TBL. 5 NEUT ES.	
Spect (n,γ)	Maxwl		KUR	Expt	Jour IZV 29 772	May 65	Groshev+.TBL + GRAPH. ENGL BAS29 775	
Spect (n,γ)	Maxwl		MUN	Expt	Jour ZP 192 142	Mar 66	Koch+ ER168 LVL SCHEME,RISO CRYSTSPC	
					Conf 65Antwerp 516	Jul 65	- . ABST.NDG.PPR51.	
Spect (n,γ)	Maxwl		CTH	Expt	Jour NIM 50 29	Apr 67	Broman+ CRYSTSP LOWERS BKGRND IN DET	
					Conf 69Studsvik 351	Aug 67	Falkstroem+(LUND) GRPHS,GE-MONOCHRMR	
					Rept LFF-22	66	Broman+ REPORT.	
Spect (n,γ)	+0	+4	COL	Expt	Prog WASH-1124 31	Nov 68	Camarda+ MOXON-RAE DET TBC NO DATA	
Spect (n,γ)	3.0-1	3.0+1	IFU	Expt	Jour UFZ 13 2083	Dec 68	Pavlenko+GRPHS GAM-YLD(GAM-E,NEUT-E)	
					Jour UPJ 13 1490	Jun 69	TRANSLATN.*	
Spect (n,γ)	Maxwl		KFI	Revw	Jour YF 10 907	Nov 69	Kecskemeti+ AVG GAM-MULTIPLICITY,TBL	
					Jour SNP 10 524	May 70	TRANSLATN.*	
Spect (n,γ)	Pile		CCP	Expt	Jour IZV 34 719	Apr 70	Prokofev+ TBL CONV-EL ES+INTS,LVLSCH	
					Jour BAS 34 635	Apr 71	* ENGL OF IZV 34 719	
Spect (n,γ)	Maxwl		KFK	Expt	Jour NP/A 150 161	Jul 70	Michaelis+GE(LI)ANTICOMPT.TBL,LVL168	
					Rept KFK-1197	Feb 70	- + LVL SCHEME ER-168	
Spect (n,γ)	Maxwl		UPP	Expt	Prog EANDC(OR)99 19	Aug 70	Baecklin+. GAM SPEC. SEVERAL NEW LNS	
Spect (n,γ)	Pile		ANL	Expt	Jour PR/C 2 1951	Nov 70	Bollinger+,B10 COVER,GE(LI) DET	
					Conf 69Studsvik 601	Aug 69	Smither+ NO DATA GVN,OKS STATMOD	
					Conf JINR-D-3893	May 68	Bollinger+ GAM E VS INTENS PLOT,J+PI	
Spect (n,γ)	+0	+2	BNL	Expt	Prog NCSAC-42 43	Nov 71	Chrien+. GE(LI). TOF SPECTRUM SHOWN	
Spect (n,γ)	Maxwl		IFL	Expt	Book PROKOFJEV	73	. TBL GAM,CONV ELECTR ES+INT,LVL SCH	
Spect (n,γ)	5.0+0	1.3+2	HAR	Expt	Prog AERE-PR/NP20	Mar 73	Axmann.SPECRA TAKEN.TO BE ANALYSED.	
Spect (n,γ)	2.0+1	1.5+2			Prog AERE-PR/NP19	Sep 72	Thomas+ TO BE ANAL NON STAT EFFECTS	
		1.4+2			Prog AERE-PR/NP18	Mar 72	- + LINAC TOF LOW EN GS TO GET J	
Spect (n,γ)	Maxwl		BKB	Expt	Jour FIZS 6 21	Jun 73	Simic+ ABST.HIGH EXCIT STATS INVESTG	
Spect (n,γ)	Maxwl		CCP	Theo	Jour ZET 65 12	Jul 73	Nosov+ THERMODYN CALC CFD EXPT,GRAPH	
					Jour JET 38 6	Jan 74	. ENGLISH OF ZET 65 6	
Spect (n,γ)	None		MUU	Expt	Jour ZP 268 379	Jul 74	Olma+.,INT CONVERSION,LVL-SCH GIVEN	
Spect (n,γ)	1.5+1	5.5+2	DUB	Expt	Rept JINR-P3-8511	Jan 75	Kharzavina+ GAMMA-SPECTRUM,GRAPH	
Inelastic γ	2.8+6		REN	Expt	Jour ARI 18 279	May 67	Broadhead+ ACTIV 2.3SEC ISOMER 790MB	+
	2.8+6				Data EXFOR11850.009	Jun 76	. 1 PT, SIG	
Inelastic γ	Maxwl		KFI	Comp	Jour JRC 7 365	Jun 71	Nagy+ GAM+XRAY+ELECTR ES,HALF-L GIVN	
(n,2n)	Fiss		CRC	Eval	Rept CRC-1003	Dec 60	Roy+,ESTIMATED AVG SIG=33.0MB	
(n,2n)	1.5+7		DEB	Eval	Jour REA 11 1 153	Mar 73	Boedy+ RECOMM.VALUE FROM N-Z SYSTEM.	
(n,2n)	1.5+7		KFI	Theo	Rept KFKI-73-68	Dec 73	Jeki.NEW FIT,CALC SIG CFD OTHERS,TBL	
(n,p)	1.5+7		ARK	Expt	Jour PR 118 242	Apr 60	Wille+ MEAS ACT SIG= 3.0+ -1.0 MB	+
	1.5+7				Data EXFOR12033.043	Jun 76	. 1 PT.	
(n,p)	Fiss		CRC	Eval	Rept CRC-1003	Dec 60	Roy+,ESTIMATED AVG SIG=0.015MB	
(n,p)	1.5+7		SAH	Comp	Jour NUC 23 8 112	Aug 65	Chatterjee. TABLE WITH REFS.	
(n,p)	1.4+7	1.5+7	ARK	ExTh	Prog ORO-3235-29	Jan 67	Koch+,STAT MODEL CALC CFD EXPTS	

68 Erbium 167

Quantity	Energy (ev) Min	Energy (ev) Max	Lab	Type	Documentation Ref Vol Page	Date	Author, Comments	Data
(n,p)	1.5+7		DEB	Comp Jour	REA 7 4 93	Dec 69	Csikai+ SIG+HL COMPILTN,N−ACTIV−ANAL	
(n,p)	1.4+7	1.5+7	JYV	Eval Rept	JU−RR−3/1970	Jun 70	Leppaemaeki+ TABLE OF EVAL AVG SIG	
(n,p)	1.5+7		MUA	Expt Jour	NC/A 3 3 467	Jun 71	Prasad+ ACTIVATION CFD STATMOD	+
				Conf	69Roorke 2 112	Dec 69	− + SIG VALUE FOR 2.8 H HALF−L	
	1.5+7			Data	EXFOR30336.038	76	1 PNT	
(n,p)	1.4+7	1.5+7	KAZ	Theo Jour	YF 18 705	Oct 73	Levkovsky.AVERAGED SIG,CALC,TBL	
				Jour	SNP 18 361	Apr 74	. ENGLISH OF YF 18,705	
(n,α)	Fiss		CRC	Eval Rept	CRC−1003	Dec 60	Roy+,ESTIMATED AVG SIG=0.0024MB	
(n,α)	Maxwl		CCP	Expt Jour	YF 1 252	Feb 65	Andreev.IONIZ−CHAMBER,SIG=M.07MB	+
				Jour	SNP 1 177	Aug 65	TRANSLATN.*	
(n,α)	Maxwl		LYO	Expt Prog	LYCEN/75−01 27	74	Emsallem+ABST,NDG	
Reson Params	4.7−1	9.4+0	YAL	Expt Jour	NP 10 386	Apr 59	Fenstermacher+	+
	4.7−1	9.4+0		Data	EXFOR11171.002	Jun 76	. 4 RES. EN.	
Reson Params	4.6−1	5.8−1	BNL	Expt Jour	NSE 8 183	Sep 60	Sailor+,WT WG 2GWN OTHER PARAMETERS	+
Reson Params	6.0+0	1.4+2	GA	Expt Rept	GA−3874	Mar 63	Haddad. LINAC TOF LIQ SC−T	
	7.9+0			ExTh Jour	NP 71 129	Sep 65	Frohner+ PARS BY SH+AREA ANAL	
	6.0+0	1.1+2		Expt Data	EXFOR11944.007	Jun 76	. 23 RES. EN, WN, WNG	
Reson Params	4.6−1	2.8+1	CCP	Expt Jour	AE 15 247	Sep 63	Vlasov+.TRANSMISSION, 7 RES	
				Jour	SJA 15 952	Sep 63	. ENGL OF AE 15 247	
Reson Params	4.6−1	5.8−1	HAR	Expt Prog	AERE−PR/NP2 1	May 65	Moxon+ PARAMETERS FOR 2 RES GIVEN.	+
Reson Params	4.6−1	2.8+1	IFU	Expt Conf	65Antwerp § 186	Jul 65	Vertebny.KIEV.FC XPT.7 RES IA. 5 WNS	
Reson Params	−2	+0	IFU	Expt Conf	67Kharkov	Feb 67	Vertebnyj+. TBP IN IZV	
Reson Params	+0	+3	IFU	Expt Conf	67Kharkov 171	Feb 67	Vertebny.TRANSMISSION EXPT	
Reson Params		1.0+6	AUA	Theo Jour	AUJ 20 477	Oct 67	Cook. TBL OF AVG LVL SPACING D,L=0,1	
Reson Params	4.6−1	1.4+2	BNL	Expt Jour	PR 162 1130	Oct 67	Mughabghab+ TRANS WN FOR 28RESON ES	+
	4.6−1	1.4+2		Data	EXFOR12120.007	Jun 76	. 28 RES, EN, WN, WN0	
Reson Params	4.6−1	6.3+1	IFU	Expt Prog	YFI−5 35	Oct 67	Vertebnyj+ TABLE 17 RESONANCES	
				Rept	INDC−232E	67	. ENGL OF YFI−5 35	
Reson Params	5.9+1	3.2+2	DUB	Expt Jour	YF 7 225	Feb 68	Karzhavina+,TRANS+NG YLD,RES−PAR+STF	+
				Rept	YFI−4 47	May 67	− + RES ANAL.	
				Rept	JINR−P3−3097	Feb 67	− + TOT+NG,TBL.	
				Jour	SNP 7 161	Aug 68	− + ENGL OF YF 7 225.	
				Rept	INDC−187E	67	− + ENGL OF YFI−4 47.	
	5.9+1	3.2+2		Data	EXFOR40147.	May 73	.NW,GW,TOT−WIDTH,D,AVER GW	
Reson Params	4.6−1	6.2+1	IFU	Expt Jour	UFZ 13 679	Apr 68	Vertebnyi+ 17 RES,WN D VALS GVN,TBLS	
				Jour	UPJ 13 477	Oct 68	TRANSLATN.*	
Reson Params		3.2+2	DUB	Expt Conf	68DUBSY 349	Jul 68	Pikelner.LVL SPAC,AVERG. WG,S0 VS A	
Reson Params	4.6−1	2.7+1	ANL	Expt Jour	PR/C 1 1501	Apr 70	Wetzel+J FROM CAPT MEAS.TBL GVN.	+
	4.6−1	2.7+1		Data	EXFOR10080.005	Feb 76	. 8 PTS. J, E0.	
Reson Params	4.6−1	9.6+0	BNL	Expt Jour	PR/C 2 1137	Sep 70	Brunhart+,TRANS,J FOR 4RESON,ABSOL	+
	4.6−1	9.6+0		Data	EXFOR10066.002	Jan 70	. 4 PTS. E0,J	
Reson Params			AUA	Theo Rept	AAEC/E−211	Nov 70	Musgrove. CALCULTD D+GAM WIDTH GIVEN	
Reson Params	4.6−1	2.1+2	CJD	Eval Rept	YK−7	71	Zakharova+ SURVEY+SYSTEMATICS,GW,TBL	
				Rept	INDC(CCP)−27	Nov 72	.ENGLISH TRANSLATION OF YK−7 /71	
Reson Params	None		DUB	Theo Jour	YF 13 240	Feb 71	Malecki+G−WID,THEO CFD EXPT.TBL,GRPH	
				Jour	SNP 13 133	Aug 71	− + ENGL OF YF 13 240.	
Reson Params	6.0+0	+2	BNL	Expt Prog	NCSAC−42 43	Nov 71	Chrien+. FROM CAPT SPECT. NO DATA	
Reson Params	4.6−1	6.3+1	IFU	Expt Rept	ICD−5 5	Dec 71	Vertebny+	+
	4.6−1	6.3+1		Data	EXFOR40061.	Mar 71	N−WID AT 17 RES, D	
Reson Params	6.0+0	1.7+3	COL	Expt Jour	PR/C 5 974	Mar 72	Liou+.WN WG G*WN D J. P−T+WIGNER	+
				Conf	71Albany 205	Aug 71	Camarda+ DA+D,WG GVN. TBP PR.	
	8.0+0	6.5+2		Rept	NYO−72−190	68	Liou.TOF.G*WN.SOME WG,J,D.TBLS.	
	6.0+1	1.7+3		Data	EXFOR10591.	Jan 78	. 268 RES ES.J,WG,RED WN GVN.D GVN.	
Reson Params	2.0+1	1.4+2	HAR	Expt Prog	AERE−PR/NP18	Mar 72	Thomas+ J ASSIGNED FROM CAPT GS.TBL.	+
	2.0+1	1.4+2		Data	EXFOR20451.003	Jan 76	21PTS.J.	
Reson Params	None		COL	Expt Jour	NSE 48 219	Jun 72	Rahn+. AVG WG=91 MEV OVER 54RESON	
Reson Params	4.6−1	5.8−1	DUB	Expt Rept	JINR−P3−6611	Jul 72	Alfimenkov+ MAGNETIC MOMENTS OF RES.	
				Rept	BNL−TR−519	73	Karzhavina+ ENGL TRANSLATION.	
Reson Params	7.8+6		DUB	Theo Conf	74Petten 175	Sep 74	Malov+ DOBS,SEMI−MICROSCOPIC CALC.	
Reson Params	2.0+4	1.5+5	HAR	Expt Conf	74Petten 300	Sep 74	Riehs+. SPINS INT.RATIOS OF G	
Reson Params	+0		DUB	Theo Jour	YF 21 40	Jan 75	Voronov+ MEAN D,WITH ROTAT.CFD EXPT	
				Jour	SNP 21 20	Jul 75	. ENGLISH OF YF 21,40	
Reson Params	6.0+0	2.9+2	DUB	Expt Rept	JINR−P3−8511	Jan 75	Kharzavina+ GAM−ANALYS,RES−SPINS TBL	
Reson Params	None		COL	Revw Conf	75Wash. 780	Mar 75	Hacken+ TBL AV WG,STF,NUMBER GWN,WG	
Reson Params	4.6−1	9.6+0	BNL	Expt Prog	WASH−1039 6	May 62	Sailor. 4.2EV RESON NOT IN ER167	+
	4.6−1	9.6+0		Data	EXFOR11179.002	Jun 76	. 4 RES. J.	
Reson Params		2.8+2	HAR	Expt Conf	76Lowell 1257	Jul 76	Axmann.(IRK).TOF.D GVN.WN.WG.I NDG	
	5.0+0	1.3+2		Prog	EANDC(UK) 151	Aug 73	− .TOF LINAC J WN WG 30 RES	

68 Erbium 167

Quantity	Energy (ev) Min	Max	Lab	Type	Documentation Ref Vol Page	Author, Comments Date	Data
Strnth Fnctn	+3		BNL	Expt Jour	PRL 1 461	Dec 58 Hughes. FC 1.6+ – 0.4	
Strnth Fnctn	4.6 – 1	1.4+2 +4	BNL	Expt Jour Jour	PR 162 1130 PL/B 24 573	Oct 67 Mughabghab+ TRANS 9.9+ – 0.9 FROM RES May 67 Chrien+ FROM RES+UNRESOLVED REGIONS	+
Strnth Fnctn	–		IFU	Expt Prog Rept	YFI – 5 35 INDC – 232E	Oct 67 Vertebnyj+ VALUE GIVEN 67 . ENGL OF YFI – 5 35	
Strnth Fnctn	5.9+1	3.2+2	DUB	Expt Jour Rept Rept Jour Rept	YF 7 225 YFI – 4 47 JINR – P3 – 3097 SNP 7 161 INDC – 187E	Feb 68 Karzhavina+,TRANS+NG YLD,RES – PAR+STF May 67 – + RES ANAL. Feb 67 – + TOT+NG,TBL. Aug 68 – + ENGL OF YF 7 225. 67 – + ENGL OF YFI – 4 47.	+
	5.9+1	3.2+2		Data	EXFOR40147.	May 73 .1 DATA LINE	
Strnth Fnctn	+0	+2	IFU	Expt Jour Jour	UFZ 13 679 UPJ 13 477	Apr 68 Vertebnyi+ VAL + – ERROR GVN Oct 68 TRANSLATN.*	
Strnth Fnctn		3.2+2	DUB	Expt Conf	68DUBSY 349	Jul 68 Pikelner.LVL SPAC,AVERG. WG,S0 VS A	
Strnth Fnctn	–		DUB	Theo Rept	JINR – E4 – 4908	Feb 70 Gabrakov+ S0,S1 AND GAM – WIDTH GRPHS	
Strnth Fnctn	4.6 – 1	3.2+2	BNL	Expt Jour	PR/C 1 1850	May 70 Mughabghab+,STF FROM RESON+SIGMA	
Strnth Fnctn	–		AUA	Theo Rept	AAEC/E – 211	Nov 70 Musgrove. SMOOTHED S0,S1 AND S2 GIVN	
Strnth Fnctn	4.6 – 1	6.3+1	IFU	Expt Rept	ICD – 5 5	Dec 71 Vertebny+	+
	5.0+0	6.3+1		Data	EXFOR40061.023	Mar 71 STRENGTH FUNC FROM RESON PARAM	
Strnth Fnctn	6.0+0	1.7+3	COL	Expt Jour Conf Rept Data	PR/C 5 974 71Albany 205 NYO – 72 – 190 EXFOR10591.015	Mar 72 Liou+.S0 GIVEN Aug 71 Camarda+ S0 GIVEN. 68 Liou.TOF.S0=1.95+ – 0.32. Jan 78 . 1 PT. S0=1.89+ – .20	+
Strnth Fnctn	1.5+2	6.5+2	SAC	ExTh Diss	FRNC – TH – 450	Oct 72 Delaroche.OPTICAL MODEL PARAMETERS	
Strnth Fnctn	None		AUA	Eval Rept	AAEC/E – 277	Mar 73 Musgrove.TBLS EXPTL DATA+BEST VALUES	
Strnth Fnctn	6.0+0	2.9+2	DUB	Expt Rept	JINR – P3 – 8511	Jan 75 Kharzavina+ GAM – ANALYS,S0(I=+, – 1/2)	
Strnth Fnctn	None		COL	Revw Conf	75Wash. 780	Mar 75 Hacken+ NEVIS TOF S – WAVE STF	
Lvl Density	+0	+3	IFU	Expt Conf	67Kharkov 171	Feb 67 Vertebny.TRANSMISSION EXPT	
Lvl Density	+6		MIL	Theo Jour	EN 15 1 54	Jan 68 Facchini+ LDL PARS FROM LOW EN RES	
Lvl Density	1.5+1	1.4+3	DUB	Expt Jour Rept Jour	YF 7 225 JINR – P3 – 3097 SNP 7 2 161	Feb 68 Karzhavina+LVL – DEN(EXCIT – E),GRPH,TBL Feb 67 – + TOT+NG,TBL. Aug 68 – + ENGL OF YF 7 225.	+
	1.5+1	1.4+3		Data	EXFOR40147.	May 73 .1 DATA LINE	
Lvl Density	None		AUW	Theo Jour	NP/A 70Madurai 2 267	Dec 70 Ramamurty+ A – PARAMETER GVN,LANG'S – TH	
Lvl Density	None		MUN	Theo Jour	NP/A 217 269	Dec 73 Dilg+ A,DELTA. BACK SHIFTED FERMIGAS	
Lvl Density	None		DUB	Theo Jour	NP/A 224 396	May 74 Malov+ 1/2 MICROSC.MODEL. DEFORM NUC	
Lvl Density	None		ROC	Theo Jour	NP/A 223 589	May 74 Huizenga+ EXP CFD MICROSC TH AX SYMM	

68 Erbium 168

Quantity	Energy (ev) Min	Max	Lab	Type	Documentation Ref Vol Page	Author, Comments Date	Data
Total	2.5 – 2	2.0+2	IFU	Expt Conf	JINR – 1845 50	Jun 64 Vertebnij+ TRANSMISSN – TOF, NDG	
Total	2.5 – 2		IFU	Expt Conf	65Antwerp § 186	Jul 65 Vertebny.KIEV.FC XPT.SIG 35+ – 10B	
Total	7.0 – 3	3.3 – 1	UFT	Expt Jour Rept	ICD – 3 85 INDC – 152E 85	Oct 66 Vertebny+.GRAPH,NO CORRECTIONS 67 . ENGL OF ICD – 3 85	
Total	2.5 – 2		BNL	Expt Jour Jour Data	PR 162 1130 PL/B 24 573 EXFOR12120.003	Oct 67 Mughabghab. May 67 Chrien+ FROM ANALYSIS OF RESONANCES Jun 76 . 1 PT.	+
	None 2.5 – 2						
Total	5.6+1	1.6+5	COL	Expt Jour Rept	PR/C 5 974 NYO – 72 – 190	Mar 73 Liou+TOF.TRNS.RES PAR.ANAL.NDG. 68 – .TRNS+SELF INDIC.CURV.	+
	None			Jour	RSI 35 263	Mar 64 Rainwater+SEE FOR EXPT DETAILS.	
	1.0+0	1.5+4		Data	EXFOR10591.005	Jan 78 . RAW DATA AVAILABLE FROM NNDC.	
Total	1.4+7		LIN	Expt Conf	75Kiev 4 140	May 75 Djumin+ SIG GIVEN.OPTMOD ANAL,RADIUS	
Total	1.0 – 2	1.4+7	CCP	Eval Data	SOKRATOR – 2010	76 SIG(E)	+
Total	+7		IJI	Expt Data	77Kiev	77 Trofimova+ SIG	
	2.0+3			Conf	76Lowell 1244	Jul 76 Vertebnyi+ TRANSM VS THICKNESS,NDG	
Elastic	7.0 – 3	1.0+0	IFU	Expt Jour Data	IZV 31 353 EXFOR40061.015	Feb 67 Vertebnyj+.CURVES,CHOPPER,TOF Mar 71 SIGMA FOR 2200 M/SEC	+
Elastic	1.0 – 2	1.7 – 1	IFU	Expt Jour Jour	UFZ 13 599 UPJ 13 420	Apr 68 Kolotyi+ GRPH SIG(E),SCAT – AMPLITUDE Oct 68 TRANSLATN.*	
Elastic	2.6 – 2		IFU	Expt Rept	IF – 69 5	69 Vertebny+ SIG+SCATAMPL AT 2200 M/SEC	
Elastic	Maxwl	+5	IFU	Comp Prog Rept	YFI – 7 43 INDC(CCP) – 7U46	Apr 69 Vertebny+ SCATTERING – LENGTH DERIVED Feb 70 TRANSLATN.*	
Elastic	2.5 – 2		IJI	Eval Conf	75Kiev 1 169	May 75 Fedorova+ EVAL 2200M/S SIG,TABLE	
Elastic	1.0 – 2	1.4+7	CCP	Eval Data	SOKRATOR – 2010	76 SIG(E)	+
Diff Elastic	1.0 – 3	1.5+7	CCP	Eval Data	SOKRATOR – 2010	76 ANGDIST(E)	+
Potntl Scat	2.0+3		IJI	Expt Conf	76Lowell 1244	Jul 76 Vertebnyi+ SCT – LNGTH GVN,FRM TOT+SCT	

68 Erbium 168

Quantity	Energy (ev) Min	Max	Lab	Type	Documentation Ref Vol Page	Date	Author, Comments	Data
Tot Inelastc	1.0−3	1.5+7	CCP	Eval	Data SOKRATOR−2010	76	SIG(E)	+
Diff Inelast	1.0−3	1.5+7	CCP	Eval	Data SOKRATOR−2010	76	SIG TO 9 LVLS	+
Thermal Scat	1.0−2	1.7−1	IFU	Expt	Jour UFZ 13 599	Apr 68	Kolotyi+ GRPHS,EXPTL SIG=NUCL+MAGN	+
					Jour UPJ 13 420	Oct 68	TRANSLATN.*	
	1.0−2	4.0−1			Data EXFOR40301.	Feb 76	.THERM AND BOUND−ATOM SCAT CS AT11ES	
Scattering	6.0−2	1.7−1	IFU	Expt	Jour UFZ 13 599	Apr 68	Kolotyi+	+
	6.0−2	1.7−1			Data EXFOR40039.006	Sep 70	AVERAGE SIGMA	
Scattering	2.0−2	3.0−2	IFU	Expt	Conf 70Helsinki 1 651	Jun 70	Vertebnij+ 2200M/SEC SIGMA GIVEN,TBL	
					Rept BNL−TR−495	Jul 72	. ENGLISH OF 70HELSIN 1 651	
Scattering	2.0+3		IJI	Expt	Conf 76Lowell 1244	Jul 76	Vertebnyi+ SCT−SIG VS THICKNESS,NDG	
Absorption	2.5−2		IJI	Eval	Conf 75Kiev 1 169	May 75	Fedorova+ EVAL 2200M/S SIG,TABLE	
Res Int Abs	5.4−1		ORL	Expt	Prog ORNL−4155 15	Aug 67	Gillette+	+
	5.4−1				Data EXFOR10259.012	Jul 74	. 1 PT. SIGMA.	
Res Int Abs	5.0−1		OSL	Expt	Prog INDC(NOR)−1 3	May 72	Glomset+ REDUCD CAPTINTEG REL AU,TBL	+
					Priv PAPPAS	Nov 70	Pappas. ACT. POWD,LIQ SOLUT.TBP JIN	
	0.0+0	1.0+6			Data EXFOR20093.007	Sep 71	1PNT.CAPTURE.	
Res Int Abs	5.0−1		COL	Expt	Jour NSE 48 219	Jun 72	Rahn+. RI=35.5+−7.0B	
Res Int Abs	+0	+5	WIN	Revw	Conf IAEA−169 3 163	74	Pope+ EVALUATED VALUE GIVEN	
Res Int Abs	5.0−1		IJI	Eval	Conf 75Kiev 1 169	May 75	Fedorova+ EVAL+CALC RI GIVEN,TABLE	
(n,γ)	Maxwl		ANL	Expt	Rept ANL−5287	Jul 54	Barnes+ ACT SIG=2.03+−0.41B	+
	Maxwl				Data EXFOR12078.002	Jun 76	. 1 PT.	
(n,γ)	Maxwl		ORL	Expt	Prog ORNL−4155 15	Aug 67	Gillette+	+
	Maxwl				Data EXFOR10259.006	Jul 74	. 1 PT. SIGMA	
	−		IEA	Comp	Rept IEA−INF−10	Aug 68	Atalla. TABLES OF HL,SIG AND GAMM−E	
(n,γ)	2.5−2		IFU	Expt	Rept ICD−5 5	Nov 68	Vertebny+	+
	2.5−2				Data EXFOR40061.021	Mar 71	SIGMA FOR 2200 M/SEC	
(n,γ)	5.0+3	1.0+5	AUA	ExTh	Rept AAEC/E−198	May 69	Musgrove.S+P+D WAVE SIGMAS CALC,TBL	
(n,γ)	3.0+4		AUA	Theo	Rept AAEC/E−211	Nov 70	Musgrove. SIGMA GIVEN AND CFD OTHER	
(n,γ)	1.0+3	1.0+7	BOL	Eval	Data BENZI−DFN 695.	May 72	40 PNTS	+
(n,γ)	Maxwl		OSL	Expt	Prog INDC(NOR)−1 3	May 72	Glomset+ REL AU,ASSUMING 1/V,TABLE	+
					Priv PAPPAS	Nov 70	Pappas. ACT. POWD,LIQ SOLUT.TBP JIN	
	Maxwl				Data EXFOR20093.006	Sep 71	1PNT.SIG.	
(n,γ)	Pile		ROS	ExTh	Prog ZFK−243 93	Sep 72	Mohsen+ NG−SYSTEMAT. FOR RARE EARTHS	
(n,γ)	5.0+3	7.0+4	CCP	Expt	Conf 73Kiev 2 206	May 73	Kononov+ TOF,SIG(NEUT−E),GRAPH	
(n,γ)	Maxwl	Fiss	WIN	Revw	Conf IAEA−169 3 163	74	Pope+ FIS−SPEC AVG DATA CFD MAXW−XPT	
(n,γ)	5.0+3	7.0+4	FEI	Expt	Rept YFI−17 9	Aug 74	Shorin+ TOF,SIG(NEUT−E),TBL	+
					Jour YF 19 5	Jan 74	− + TOF,SIG(NEUT−E),GRAPHS	
	5.3+3	6.8+4			Rept INDC(CCP)−48	Feb 75	. P 5.ENGLISH OF YFI−17 9	
	5.0+3	7.0+4			Jour SNP 19 2	Jul 74	. ENGLISH OF YF 19 5	
	5.3+3	6.8+4			Data EXFOR40222.012	Mar 74	.SIGMA FOR 32 EN−RANGES GVN	
(n,γ)	2.5−2		BNL	Expt	Prog ERDA−NDC−2 31	May 75	Chrien+NDG.TBC.	
(n,γ)	1.0−3	1.4+7	CCP	Eval	Data SOKRATOR−2010	76	SIG(E)	+
Spect (n,γ)	Maxwl		LAS	Expt	Prog WASH−1079 105	Oct 67	Jurney++ 93GAMS 25KEV−2.5MEV NDG	
Spect (n,γ)	None		ANL	Expt	Abst BAP 13 721	Apr 68	Bollinger+.RATIO AV WG FOR M1,E1	
Spect (n,γ)	+0	+4	COL	Expt	Prog WASH−1124 31	Nov 68	Camarda+ MOXON−RAE DET TBC NO DATA	
Spect (n,γ)	Pile		KUR	Expt	Jour YF 13 681	Apr 71	Groshev+ GE−LI,TBD	
					Jour SNP 13 387	Oct 71	. ENGL OF YF 13 681	
Spect (n,γ)	2.5−2	1.0+3	BNL	Expt	Rept PR/C 13 1139	Mar 76	Garg+HFBR.RES CAPT.SPEC GRPHS	
(n,2n)	Fiss		CRC	Eval	Rept CRC−1003	Dec 60	Roy+,ESTIMATED AVG SIG=4.8MB	
	Fiss		UCS	Expt	Rept NYO−10175	Dec 64	Arino+ACT.TBLS.GRAPHS.PRODUCT HL.	+
	Fiss				Data EXFOR11817.014	Jun 76	. 1 PT.	
(n,2n)	1.5+7		REN	Expt	Jour PR/B 139 1525	Sep 65	Broadhead+ C−W ACT	+
	1.5+7				Data EXFOR11874.006	Jun 76	. 1 PT.	
(n,2n)	1.5+7		MUA	Expt	Jour NP 88 349	Nov 66	Prasad+,T−D NEUT ACT REL TO FE56(NP)	+
	1.5+7				Data EXFOR30015.005	May 70	PARTIAL SIGMA(METASTABLE)	
(n,2n)	1.5+7		TUR	Theo	Jour NC 56 18 201	Jul 68	Minetti+THEOR ISOM RATIO SPIN CO PAR	
(n,2n)	1.5+7		DEB	Comp	Jour REA 7 4 93	Dec 69	Csikai+ SIG+HL COMPILTN,N−ACTIV−ANAL	
(n,2n)	1.4+7	1.5+7	JYV	Eval	Rept JU−RR−3/1970	Jun 70	Leppaemaeki+ TABLE OF EVAL AVG SIG	
(n,2n)	1.5+7		IBJ	Expt	Rept APPB 1 415	Dec 70	Rurarz+ NA−I,SIG TO ISOM GVN,CFD OTH	+
					Jour APPB 1 415	70	− + ACTIV,NAI,SIG(M)+ISORATIO	
	1.5+7				Data EXFOR30154.	Feb 72	PAR SIG,ISOM RATIO,SPIN CUT−OFF FACT	
(n,2n)	1.4+7		KFI	Comp	Jour JRC 7 365	Jun 71	Nagy+ SIGMA,GAM+XRAY ES, HALF−L GIVN	
(n,2n)	1.4+7		ITJ	Expt	Jour JRC 14 201	73	Janczyszyn+ ISO−PROD BY NAT−ER ACTIV	+
	1.4+7				Data EXFOR30322.015	Feb 76	MEAN OF ER167(N,N')+ER168(N,2N)	
(n,2n)	1.5+7		DEB	Eval	Jour REA 11 1 153	Mar 73	Boedy+ RECOMM.VALUE FROM N−Z SYSTEM.	
(n,2n)	1.5+7		KFI	Theo	Rept KFKI−73−68	Dec 73	Jeki.NEW FIT,CALC SIG CFD OTHERS,TBL	
(n,p)	1.5+7		ARK	Expt	Jour PR 118 242	Apr 60	Wille+ MEAS ACT SIG=2.5+−1.0 MB	+
	1.5+7				Data EXFOR12033.046	Jun 76	. 1 PT.	

68 Erbium 168

Quantity	Energy (ev) Min	Max	Lab	Type	Documentation Ref Vol Page	Date	Author, Comments	Data
(n,p)	Fiss		CRC Eval	Rept	CRC – 1003	Dec 60	Roy+,ESTIMATED AVG SIG = 0.003MB	
(n,p)	1.5+7		SAH Comp	Jour	NUC 23 8 112	Aug 65	Chatterjee. TABLE WITH REFS.	
(n,p)	1.4+7	1.5+7	ARK ExTh	Prog	ORO – 3235 – 29	Jan 67	Koch+,STAT MODEL CALC CFD EXPTS	
(n,p)	1.5+7		DEB Comp	Jour	REA 7 4 93	Dec 69	Csikai+ SIG+HL COMPILTN,N – ACTIV – ANAL	
(n,p)	1.4+7	1.5+7	JYV Eval	Rept	JU – RR – 3/1970	Jun 70	Leppaemaeki+ TABLE OF EVAL AVG SIG	
(n,p)	1.4+7	1.5+7	KAZ Theo	Jour	YF 18 705	Oct 73	Levkovsky.AVERAGED SIG,CALC,TBL	
				Jour	SNP 18 361	Apr 74	. ENGLISH OF YF 18,705	
(n,p)	1.5+7		JUL Expt	Jour	RRL 25 335	May 76	Qaim+ ACTIV,GELI.CFD OTHERS,TBL+GRPH	+
	1.5+7			Data	EXFOR20716.014	Jun 77	1PNT.SIGMA.	
(n,α)	1.5+7		ARK Expt	Jour	PR 118 242	Apr 60	Wille+ MEAS ACT PROD. 2 ISOMERS	+
	1.5+7			Data	EXFOR12033.	Jun 76	. 2 PTS, SIG FOR 2 ISM.	
(n,α)	Fiss		CRC Eval	Rept	CRC – 1003	Dec 60	Roy+,ESTIMATED AVG SIG = BELO 0.0001MB	
(n,α)	1.4+7		CIS Theo	Jour	NP 51 460	Feb 64	Facchini+STATMOD SIG XPT/CALC 45 – 80	
(n,α)	Maxwl		CCP Expt	Jour	YF 1 252	Feb 65	Andreev.IONIZ – CHAMBER,SIG = M.09MB	+
				Jour	SNP 1 177	Aug 65	TRANSLATN.*	
(n,α)	1.5+7		DEB Comp	Jour	REA 7 4 93	Dec 69	Csikai+ SIG+HL COMPILTN,N – ACTIV – ANAL	
(n,α)	1.4+7	1.5+7	JYV Eval	Rept	JU – RR – 3/1970	Jun 70	Leppaemaeki+ TABLE OF EVAL AVG SIG	
(n,α)	1.4+7		IBJ Expt	Rept	INR – 1268	Jan 71	Jaskola+ ALFA SPCTR CFD TH,FULL PAPR	+
				Theo Conf	72Budapest 18	Aug 72	Glowacka+ ENERGY SPECTRA, GRPH	
				Expt Jour	APPB 2 521	71	.SAME AS INR – 1268	
				Rept	INR – 1197 3	May 70	SEE ALSO *THEO,ALFA CLUSTRNG	
				Rept	INR – 1175	Mar 70	SEE ALSO * FULL INFORMATION	
	1.4+7			Data	EXFOR30158.022	Mar 71	NUM DATA NOT AVAILBL,SEE GRAF IN REF	
(n,α)	1.4+7		KFI Comp	Jour	JRC 7 365	Jun 71	Nagy+ SIG LIMIT,GAMMA – ES,HALF – LIFE	
(n,α)	1.4+7		WWA Theo	Prog	INDC(SEC) – 28	Sep 72	Kozlowski+ ENERGY SPECT CALC. ,GRPH	
				Jour	NP/A 187 177	May 72	– +. 30DEG E – SPEC.KNOCK – ON OK	
(n,α)	1.4+7	1.5+7	CIS Theo	Jour	NP/A 210 297	Aug 73	Milazzo – Colli+ ALPHA E – DISTN CFD XPT	
	1.4+7			Jour	PL/B 38 155	Feb 72	Colli – Milazzo+ A – SPECT CALC CFD EXPT	
(n,α)	1.4+7	1.5+7	KAZ Theo	Jour	YF 18 705	Oct 73	Levkovsky.AVERAGED SIG,CALC,TBL	
				Jour	SNP 18 361	Apr 74	. ENGLISH OF YF 18,705	
Reson Params	3.0+1	1.7+2	IFU Expt	Conf	65Antwerp § 186	Jul 65	Vertebny.KIEV.FC XPT.14RES IA. 7 WNS	
Reson Params	8.0+1	1.4+3	BNL Expt	Jour	PR 162 1130	Oct 67	Mughabghab+ TRANS WN FOR 8 RESON ES	+
	8.0+1	1.4+3		Data	EXFOR12120.008	Jun 76	. 8 RES. EN, WN, WNO	
Reson Params	7.3+0	1.5+3	DUB Expt	Jour	YF 7 225	Feb 68	Karzhavina+,TRANS+NG YLD,RES – PAR+STF	+
				Rept	YFI – 4 47	May 67	– + RES ANAL.	
				Rept	JINR – P3 – 3097	Feb 67	– + TOT+NG,TBL.	
				Jour	SNP 7 161	Aug 68	– + ENGL OF YF 7 225.	
				Rept	INDC – 187E	67	– + ENGL OF YFI – 4 47.	
	7.2+0	1.5+3		Data	EXFOR40147.	May 73	.NW,GW,TOT – WIDTH,D,AVER GW	
Reson Params		1.5+3	DUB Expt	Conf	68DUBSY 349	Jul 68	Pikelner.LVL SPAC,AVERG. WG,S0 VS A	
Reson Params	–		AUA Theo	Rept	AAEC/E – 211	Nov 70	Musgrove. CALCULTD D+GAM WIDTH GIVEN	
Reson Params	8.1+1	5.3+2	CJD Eval	Rept	YK – 7	71	Zakharova+ SURVEY+SYSTEMATICS,GW,TBL	
				Rept	INDC(CCP) – 27	Nov 72	.ENGLISH TRANSLATION OF YK – 7 /71	
Reson Params	None		DUB Theo	Jour	YF 13 240	Feb 71	Malecki+G – WID,THEO CFD EXPT.TBL,GRPH	
				Jour	SNP 13 133	Aug 71	– + ENGL OF YF 13 240.	
Reson Params	8.0+1	1.5+4	COL Expt	Jour	PR/C 5 974	Mar 72	Liou+.WN WG G*WN D. P – T+WIGNER DIST	+
				Conf	71Albany 205	Aug 71	Camarda+ D,WG GVN. TBP PR.	
	8.0+1	4.4+3		Rept	NYO – 72 – 190	68	Liou.TOF.WN FOR 28 RES.AVG D.	
	8.0+1	1.5+4		Data	EXFOR10591.	Jan 78	. 128 RES ES.WG,WN RED,WN*G RED.D.	
Reson Params	None		COL Expt	Jour	NSE 48 219	Jun 72	Rahn+. AVG WG = 85 MEV OVER 2 RESON	
Reson Params	None		DUB Theo	Conf	73Munich 1 246	Aug 73	Malov+ SUPERFLUID MDL,TBL D VS EXC – E	
				Jour	ZEP 14 194	Aug 71	Soloviev.LARGE N – WID G – WID CORREL.NDG	
				Rept	JINR – E4 – 5880	Jul 71	Soloviev.N – GAM – WIDS CORR.SHORT NOTE	
				Jour	JEL 14 129	Aug 71	– . ENGL OF ZEP 14 194.	
Reson Params	None		COL Revw	Conf	75Wash. 780	Mar 75	Hacken+ TBL AV WG,STF,NUMBER GWN,WG	
Reson Params	2.5 – 2		COL Expt	Conf	75Wash. 335	Mar 75	Felvinci+MOD ERICSON CALC CFD EXPT.	
Reson Params	7.9+1	1.0+3	BNL Expt	Jour	PR/C 13 1139	Mar 76	Garg+PARTAL WIDS 7ES.TBL.PI,I,G STF.	+
	7.9+1	1.0+3		Data	EXFOR10622.002	Jul 77	202PTS.PARTIAL RAD WIDTHS FOR 7 RES.	
Strnth Fnctn	8.0+1	1.4+3	BNL Expt	Jour	PR 162 1130	Oct 67	Mughabghab+ TRANS 6.6 – 0.8 FROM RES	+
		+4		Jour	PL/B 24 573	May 67	Chrien+ FROM RES+UNRESOLVED REGIONS	
Strnth Fnctn	7.3+0	1.5+3	DUB Expt	Jour	YF 7 225	Feb 68	Karzhavina+,TRANS+NG YLD,RES – PAR+STF	+
				Rept	YFI – 4 47	May 67	– + RES ANAL.	
				Rept	JINR – P3 – 3097	Feb 67	– + TOT+NG,TBL.	
				Jour	SNP 7 161	Aug 68	– + ENGL OF YF 7 225.	
				Rept	INDC – 187E	67	– + ENGL OF YFI – 4 47.	
	7.2+0	1.5+3		Data	EXFOR40147.	May 73	.1 DATA LINE	
Strnth Fnctn		1.5+3	DUB Expt	Conf	68DUBSY 349	Jul 68	Pikelner.LVL SPAC,AVERG. WG,S0 VS A	
Strnth Fnctn	8.0+1	1.4+3	BNL Expt	Jour	PR/C 1 1850	May 70	Mughabghab+,STF FROM RESON = 1.4+ – 0.7	

68 Erbium 168

Quantity	Energy (ev) Min	Max	Lab	Type	Documentation Ref Vol Page	Author, Comments Date	Data
Strnth Fnctn	–		AUA	Theo Rept	AAEC/E – 211	Nov 70 Musgrove. SMOOTHED S0,S1 AND S2 GIVN	
Strnth Fnctn	8.0+1	1.5+4	COL	Expt Jour	PR/C 5 974	Mar 72 Liou+.S0 AND S1 GIVEN	+
				Conf	71Albany 205	Aug 71 Camarda+ S0, S1 GVN.	
	8.0+1	4.4+3		Rept	NYO – 72 – 190	68 Liou.TOF.S0 = 1.43 + – 0.40.	
	0.0+0	4.7+3		Data	EXFOR10591.016	Jan 78 . 2PTS. S0 =1.50+ – .21 S1 =.70+ – .20	
Strnth Fnctn	None		AUA	Eval Rept	AAEC/E – 277	Mar 73 Musgrove.TBLS EXPTL DATA+BEST VALUES	
Strnth Fnctn	None		COL	Revw Conf	75Wash. 780	Mar 75 Hacken+ NEVIS TOF S – WAVE STF	
Lvl Density	+6		MIL	Theo Jour	EN 15 1 54	Jan 68 Facchini+ LDL PARS FROM LOW EN RES	
Lvl Density	5.0+0	2.0+2	DUB	Expt Jour	YF 7 225	Feb 68 Karzhavina+LVL – DEN(EXCIT – E),GRPH,TBL	+
				Rept	JINR – P3 – 3097	Feb 67 – + TOT+NG,TBL.	
				Jour	SNP 7 2 161	Aug 68 – + ENGL OF YF 7 225.	
	5.0+0	2.0+2		Data	EXFOR40147.	May 73 .1 DATA LINE	
Lvl Density	None		CCP	Theo Jour	YF 11 1028	May 70 Rubchenya. DENSITY+A+TEMP GIVEN	
				Jour	SNP 11 571	Nov 70 . ENGL OF YF 11 571.	
Lvl Density	None		AUW	Theo Conf	70Madurai 2 267	Dec 70 Ramamurty+ A – PARAMETER GVN,LANG'S – TH	
Lvl Density	1.4+7		IBJ	Expt Rept	INR – 1268	Jan 71 Jaskola+ ALFA SPCTR CFD TH,FULL PAPR	+
				Jour	APPB 2 521	71 .SAME AS INR – 1268	
	1.4+7			Data	EXFOR30158.023	Mar 71 LEVEL DENSITY PARAMETER OF DY165 GIV	
Lvl Density	None		MUN	Theo Jour	NP/A 217 269	Dec 73 Dilg+ A,DELTA. BACK SHIFTED FERMIGAS	
Lvl Density	None		COP	Theo Jour	NP/A 222 493	Apr 74 Dossing+COLL ROTAT.SPAC. ACCUR ESTIM	
Lvl Density	None		DUB	Theo Jour	NP/A 224 396	May 74 Malov+ 1/2 MICROSC.MODEL. DEFORM NUC	
Lvl Density	None		ROC	Theo Jour	NP/A 223 589	May 74 Huizenga+ EXP CFD MICROSC TH AX SYMM	
Lvl Density	+0	1.0+4	JAE	ExTh Jour	JPJ 37 581	Sep 74 Ideno.LVL SPACING CORRELATIONS.TBL.	
	1.0+0	1.0+4		Rept	JAERI – M – 5490	Nov 73 – .LEVEL SPACING CORRELATIONS.TBL	

68 Erbium 169

Quantity	Energy (ev) Min	Max	Lab	Type	Documentation Ref Vol Page	Author, Comments Date	Data
Total	+7		IJI	Expt Conf	77Kiev	77 Trofimova+ SIG	
Spect (n,γ)	Maxwl		LAS	Expt Prog	NCSAC – 31 155	May 70 Bunker+,ABSTRACT ONLY,TBP IN PR	
Reson Params	–		AUA	Theo Rept	AAEC/E – 211	Nov 70 Musgrove. CALCULTD D+GAM WIDTH GIVEN	
Strnth Fnctn	–		AUA	Theo Rept	AAEC/E – 211	Nov 70 Musgrove. SMOOTHED S0,S1 AND S2 GIVEN	
Lvl Density	+6		MIL	Theo Jour	EN 15 1 54	Jan 68 Facchini+ LDL PARS FROM LOW EN RES	
Lvl Density	7.3+0	1.4+3	DUB	Expt Jour	YF 7 225	Feb 68 Karzhavina+LVL – DEN(EXCIT – E),GRPH,TBL	+
				Rept	JINR – P3 – 3097	Feb 67 – + TOT+NG,TBL.	
				Jour	SNP 7 2 161	Aug 68 – + ENGL OF YF 7 225.	
	7.3+0	1.4+3		Data	EXFOR40147.	May 73 .1 DATA LINE	
Lvl Density	None		MUN	Theo Jour	NP/A 217 269	Dec 73 Dilg+ A,DELTA. BACK SHIFTED FERMIGAS	
Lvl Density	None		DUB	Theo Jour	NP/A 224 396	May 74 Malov+ 1/2 MICROSC.MODEL. DEFORM NUC	
Lvl Density	None		ROC	Theo Jour	NP/A 223 589	May 74 Huizenga+ EXP CFD MICROSC TH AX SYMM	

68 Erbium 170

Quantity	Energy (ev) Min	Max	Lab	Type	Documentation Ref Vol Page	Author, Comments Date	Data
Total	2.5 – 2	2.0+2	IFU	Expt Conf	JINR – 1845 50	Jun 64 Vertebnij+ TRANSMISSN – TOF, NDG	
Total	2.5 – 2		IFU	Expt Conf	65Antwerp § 186	Jul 65 Verteb ny.KIEV.FC XPT.LESS THAN 45B	
Total	7.0 – 3	3.3 – 1	UFT	Expt Rept	ICD – 3 85	Oct 66 Vertebnyi+.GRAPH,NO CORRECTIONS	
				Rept	INDC – 152E 85	67 . ENGL OF ICD – 3 85	
Total	4.0+0	1.0+4	HAR	Expt Prog	AERE – PR/NP18	Mar 72 Axmann+ LINAC TOF NDG	
Total	5.6+1	1.6+5	COL	Expt Jour	PR/C 5 974	Mar 73 Liou+TOF.TRNS.RES PAR.ANAL.NDG.	+
				Rept	NYO – 72 – 190	68 – .TRNS+SELF INDIC.AREA ANAL.	
	None			Jour	RSI 35 263	Mar 64 Rainwater+SEE FOR EXPT DETAILS.	
	1.0+0	2.4+4		Data	EXFOR10591.006	Jan 78 . RAW DATA AVAILABLE FROM NNDC.	
Total	1.4+7		LIN	Expt Conf	75Kiev 4 140	May 75 Djumin+ SIG GIVEN.OPTMOD ANAL,RADIUS	
Total	1.0 – 2	1.4+7	CCP	Eval Data	SOKRATOR – 2011	76 SIG(E)	+
Total	+7		IJI	Expt Conf	77Kiev	77 Trofimova+ SIG	
	2.0+3			Conf	76Lowell 1244	Jul 76 Vertebnyi+ TRANSM VS THICKNESS,NDG	
Elastic	7.0 – 3	1.0+0	IFU	Expt Jour	IZV 31 353	Feb 67 Vertebnyj+.CURVES,CHOPPER,TOF	+
	2.5 – 2			Data	EXFOR40061.016	Mar 71 SIGMA FOR 2200 M/SEC	
Elastic	1.0 – 2	1.7 – 1	IFU	Expt Jour	UFZ 13 599	Apr 68 Kolotyi+ GRPH SIG(E),SCAT – AMPLITUDE	
				Jour	UPJ 13 420	Oct 68 TRANSLATN.*	
Elastic	2.6 – 2		IFU	Expt Rept	IF – 69 5	69 Vertebny+ SIG+SCATAMPL AT 2200 M/SEC	
Elastic	Maxwl	+5	IFU	Comp Prog	YFI – 7 43	Apr 69 Vertebny+ SCATTERING – LENGTH DERIVED	
				Rept	INDC(CCP) – 7U46	Feb 70 TRANSLATN.*	
Elastic	2.5 – 2		IJI	Eval Conf	75Kiev 1 169	May 75 Fedorova+ EVAL 2200M/S SIG,TABLE	
Elastic	1.0 – 2	1.4+7	CCP	Eval Data	SOKRATOR – 2011	76 SIG(E)	+

68 Erbium 170

Quantity	Energy (ev) Min	Max	Lab	Type	Documentation Ref Vol Page	Date	Author, Comments	Data
Diff Elastic	1.0−3	1.5+7	CCP	Eval	Data SOKRATOR−2011	76	ANGDIST(E)	+
Potntal Scat	2.0+3		IJI	Expt	Conf 76Lowell 1244	Jul 76	Vertebnyi+ SCT−LNGTH GVN,FRM TOT+SCT	
Tot Inelastc	1.0−3	1.5+7	CCP	Eval	Data SOKRATOR−2011	76	SIG(E)	+
Diff Inelast	1.0−3	1.5+7	CCP	Eval	Data SOKRATOR−2011	76	SIG TO 7 LVLS	+
Thermal Scat	1.0−2	1.7−1	IFU	Expt	Jour UFZ 13 599	Apr 68	Kolotyi+ GRPHS,EXPTL SIG=NUCL+MAGN	+
					Jour UPJ 13 420	Oct 68	TRANSLATN.*	
	1.0−2	4.0−1			Data EXFOR40301.	Feb 76	.THERM AND BOUND−ATOM SCAT CS AT11ES	
Scattering	6.0−2	1.7−1	IFU	Expt	Jour UFZ 13 599	Apr 68	Koloty+	+
	6.0−2	1.7−1			Data EXFOR40039.007	Sep 70	AVERAGE SIGMA	
Scattering	2.0−2	3.0−2	IFU	Expt	Conf 70Helsinki 1 651	Jun 70	Vertebnij+ 2200M/SEC SIGMA GIVEN,TBL	
					Rept BNL−TR−495	Jul 72	. ENGLISH OF 70HELSIN 1 651	
Scattering	2.0+3		IJI	Expt	Conf 76Lowell 1244	Jul 76	Vertebnyi+ SCT−SIG VS THICKNESS,NDG	
Absorption	2.5−2		IJI	Eval	Conf 75Kiev 1 169	May 75	Fedorova+ EVAL 2200M/S SIG,TABLE	
Res Int Abs	5.4−1		ORL	Expt	Prog ORNL−4155 15	Aug 67	Gillette+	+
	5.4−1				Data EXFOR10259.013	Jul 74	1PT,SIGMA	
Res Int Abs	5.0−1		BGK	Expt	Rept THAI−AEC−10	Oct 67	. ACTIV(NA−I),CD−RATIO,REL AU. TABLE	+
	5.0−1				Data EXFOR30368.026	Jan 77	REL AU, PRELM.	
Res Int Abs	5.0−1		OSL	Expt	Prog INDC(NOR)−1 3	May 72	Glomset+ REDUCD CAPTINTEG REL AU,TBL	+
					Priv PAPPAS	Nov 70	Pappas. ACT. POWD,LIQ SOLUT.TBP JIN	
	0.0+0	1.0+6			Data EXFOR20093.009	Sep 71	1PNT.CAPTURE.	
Res Int Abs	5.0−1		COL	Expt	Jour NSE 48 219	Jun 72	Rahn+. RI=44+−7B	
Res Int Abs	5.0−1		GHT	Expt	Jour JRC 20 695	74	Van Der Linden+ BY(N,G).CFD OTHS,TBL	+
	5.5−1				Conf 73Paris 2 241	Mar 73	− + ACT,REL THR+GOLD,TBL	
	5.5−1				Data EXFOR20645.031	Jul 76	1PNT.CAPTURE.	
Res Int Abs	+0	+5	WIN	Revw	Conf IAEA−169 3 163	74	Pope+ EVALUATED VALUE GIVEN	
Res Int Abs	5.0−1		IJI	Eval	Conf 75Kiev 1 169	May 75	Fedorova+ EVAL+CALC RI GIVEN,TABLE	
Res Int Abs	5.0−1		KJL	Expt	Jour JIN 37 1591	Aug 75	Steinnes. CD−RAT+ACTIV INTEG,CFD,TBL	+
	5.0−1				Data EXFOR20635.010	Aug 76	1PNT.CAPTURE.	
(n,γ)	Maxwl		OHO	Expt	Jour PR 53 437	Mar 38	Pool+ BETAS,CLOUDCH,RATIO ER168(NG)	
(n,γ)	Maxwl		ANL	Expt	Rept ANL−5287	Jul 54	Barnes+ ACT SIG=8.72+−1.78B	+
	Maxwl				Data EXFOR12078.003	Jun 76	. 1 PT.	
(n,γ)	2.4+4		ORL	Expt	Jour PR 107 504	Jul 57	Macklin+.SB−BE NS,298+−30MB	
					Conf 58Geneva 671	Sep 58	.SUPERSEDED	
	2.4+4				Data EXFOR11399.043	Jun 76	. 1 PT.	
(n,γ)	Maxwl		MUAExTh	Jour	NP 41 372	Mar 63	Mangal+ (N,G) SIGMA GVN,TH CFD EXPT	+
	Maxwl			Expt	Data EXFOR31249.008	Sep 72	.SIG GVN	
(n,γ)	Maxwl		ORL	Expt	Prog ORNL−4155 15	Aug 67	Gillette+	+
	Maxwl				Data EXFOR10259.007	Jul 74	1PT,SIGMA	
(n,γ)	3.0+6		DEB	Expt	Jour JNE 21 797	Oct 67	Peto+ACTIV,SIGMA REL TO P−31(N,P)	+
	3.0+6				Data EXFOR30031.026	Aug 70	SINGLE VALUE	
(n,γ)	4.9+3	2.6+6	ANL	Expt	Jour JNE 22 267	May 68	Stupegia+ ACT 20ES REL U235 NF,TABLE	+
	4.9+3	2.6+6			Data EXFOR11624.011	Jun 76	. 20 PTS.	
(n,γ)	−		IEA	Comp	Rept IEA−INF−10	Aug 68	Atalla. TABLES OF HL,SIG AND GAMM−E	
(n,γ)	2.5−2		IFU	Expt	Rept ICD−5 5	Nov 68	Vertebny+	+
	2.5−2				Data EXFOR40061.022	Mar 71	SIGMA FOR 2200 M/SEC	
(n,γ)	2.4+4		MUA	Expt	Jour NC/B 58 402	Dec 68	Hasan+,SB−BE,ACT BETA−DET REL I−127.	+
	2.4+4				Data EXFOR30077.019	Dec 70	SIGMA FOR 7.8 H HALF LIFE GIVEN	
(n,γ)		3.0+4	HAR	Expt	Prog EANDC(OR)94L	Jan 70	Axmann+ ABST.	
(n,γ)	1.0+3	1.0+6	GA	Theo	Conf 70Helsinki 2 281	Jun 70	Fricke+44. SIG(E) GRAPH,STATMAT CALC	
(n,γ)	3.0+4		AUA	Theo	Rept AAEC/E−211	Nov 70	Musgrove. SIGMA GIVEN AND CFD OTHER	
(n,γ)	2.4+4		MUA	Theo	Jour IJP 46 114	Mar 72	Chaubey+ P−WAVE STRENGTH FUNCT,TABLE	
(n,γ)	1.0+3	1.0+7	BOL	Eval	Data BENZI−DFN 696.	May 72	40 PNTS	+
(n,γ)	Maxwl		OSL	Expt	Prog INDC(NOR)−1 3	May 72	Glomset+ REL AU,ASSUMING 1/V,TABLE	+
					Priv PAPPAS	Nov 70	Pappas. ACT. POWD,LIQ SOLUT.TBP JIN	
	Maxwl				Data EXFOR20093.008	Sep 71	1PNT.SIG.	
(n,γ)	1.5+7		JYV	Expt	Jour NIM 103 549	Sep 72	Valkonen+ ACTIV.TARG GEOM EFFS.TBL.	
(n,γ)	Pile		ROS	ExTh	Prog ZFK−243 93	Sep 72	Mohsen+ NG−SYSTEMAT. FOR RARE EARTHS	
(n,γ)	5.0+3	7.0+4	CCP	Expt	Conf 73Kiev 2 206	May 73	Kononov+ TOF,SIG(NEUT−E),GRAPH	
(n,γ)	8.3+5		II	Expt	Conf 73Kiev 4 312	May 73	Lakosi+ FOTO−N,REL AU197(N,G	+
	+6				Data EXFOR30268.014	Jul 74	1 POINT	
(n,γ)	Maxwl	Fiss	WIN	Revw	Conf IAEA−169 3 163	74	Pope+ FIS−SPEC AVG DATA CFD MAXW−XPT	
(n,γ)	1.4+7		RBZ	Expt	Jour NCL 10 1	May 74	Vuletin+ ACT,GELI.CFD OTHRS+THEO,TBL	+
	1.4+7				Data EXFOR30314.010	Dec 75	SIGMA AT 14.4 MEV	
	1.4+7				Data EXFOR30145.014	Aug 73	.SUPERSEDED BY EXFOR30314.010	

68 Erbium 170

Quantity	Energy (ev) Min	Max	Lab	Type	Documentation Ref Vol Page	Author, Comments Date	Data
(n,γ)	5.0+3	7.0+4	FEI	Expt	Rept YFI-17 9	Aug 74 Shorin+ TOF,SIG(NEUT-E),TBL	+
					Jour YF 19 5	Jan 74 - + TOF,SIG(NEUT-E),GRAPHS	
	5.3+3	6.8+4			Rept INDC(CCP)-48	Feb 75 . P 5.ENGLISH OF YFI-17 9	
	5.0+3	7.0+4			Jour SNP 19 2	Jul 74 . ENGLISH OF YF 19 5	
	5.3+3	6.8+4			Data EXFOR40222.013	Mar 74 .SIGMA FOR 32 EN-RANGES GIVEN	
(n,γ)	1.0-3	1.4+7	CCP	Eval	Data SOKRATOR-2011	76 SIG(E)	+
(n,γ)	1.5+7		JYV	Expt	Jour PL/B 39 625	May 72 Kantele+ CAPT SIG MEASURED	+
					Rept JU-RR-1/1976	Mar 76 Valkonen.(THESIS).ACTIV.TBL. 14.5MEV	
	1.5+7				Data EXFOR20673.033	Nov 76 1PNT.SIGMA.	
	1.5+7				Data EXFOR20544.009	Apr 76 1PNT.SIGMA.	
(n,γ)	+7		FEI	Theo	Rept YK- 21 3	Oct 76 Blokhin+ SIG(NEUT-E),GRAPH	
Spect (n,γ)	2.5+4		ORL	Expt	Conf 58Geneva 15 68	Sep 58 Macklin.PPR671,SIGMA+G-ENERGY GVN	
Spect (n,γ)	+0	+4	COL	Expt	Prog WASH-1124 31	Nov 68 Camarda+ MOXON-RAE DET TBC NO DATA	
Spect (n,γ)	Pile		CTH	Expt	Jour NP/A 161 209	Jan 71 Alenius+ PAIR,ANTICO SPEC. 96 LINES.	
Spect (n,γ)	Pile		KUR	Expt	Jour YF 13 681	Apr 71 Groshev+ GE-LI,TBD	
					Jour SNP 13 387	Oct 71 . ENGL OF YF 13 681	
Spect (n,γ)	Maxwl		ROS	Expt	Prog ZFK-243 65	Sep 72 Mohsen+ HIGH-E GAMS,GE-LI,4 ES GIVEN	+
	Maxwl				Data EXFOR30276.	Oct 74 GAMMA SPECTRUM, 74 POINTS	
(n,2n)	1.5+7		ARK	Expt	Jour PR 118 242	Apr 60 Wille+ MEAS ACT SIG=1200+ -500 MB	+
	1.5+7				Data EXFOR12033.047	Jun 76 . 1 PT.	
(n,2n)	Fiss		CRC	Eval	Rept CRC-1003	Dec 60 Roy+,ESTIMATED AVG SIG=7.6MB	
(n,2n)	1.5+7		IRK	Expt	Jour NP 51 329	Feb 64 Spenke.ACTIVATION,ABS BETA COUNT	+
					Jour OAWA 100 197	Jun 63 - . SUPERSEDED	
	1.5+7				Data EXFOR20058.003	Sep 71 1PNT.SIG.	
(n,2n)	1.4+7		HAM	Comp Jour	NP 65 257	Mar 65 Bormann. 2EXPT VALS.CFD SHELL EFFECT	
(n,2n)	1.5+7		DEB	Comp Jour	REA 7 4 93	Dec 69 Csikai+ SIG+HL COMPILTN,N-ACTIV-ANAL	
(n,2n)	1.4+7	1.5+7	JYV	Eval	Rept JU-RR-3/1970	Jun 70 Leppaemaeki+ TABLE OF EVAL AVG SIG	
(n,2n)	+7		KFI	Theo	Rept KFKI-71-8	Feb 71 Jeki. CALCULATED CFD EXPTL SIG VALUE	
(n,2n)	1.5+7		DEB	Eval	Jour REA 11 1 153	Mar 73 Boedy. COMPILATION+RECOMM.VALUE,TBL	
					Rept IAEA-153 173	73 - . RECOMM. VALUE ONLY	
(n,2n)	1.5+7		TAT	Theo	Jour JP/A 7 1457	Aug 74 Kondaiah. CALC ON STAT MODEL	
(n,p)	1.5+7		ARK	Expt	Jour PR 118 242	Apr 60 Wille+ MEAS ACT SIG= 1.8+ - .5 MB	+
	1.5+7				Data EXFOR12033.048	Jun 76 . 1 PT.	
(n,p)	Fiss		CRC	Eval	Rept CRC-1003	Dec 60 Roy+,ESTIMATED AVG SIG=0.0008MB	
(n,p)	1.5+7		SAH	Comp Jour	NUC 23 8 112	Aug 65 Chatterjee. TABLE WITH REFS.	
(n,p)	1.4+7	1.5+7	ARK	ExTh	Prog ORO-3235-29	Jan 67 Koch+,STAT MODEL CALC CFD EXPTS	
(n,p)	1.5+7		DEB	Comp Jour	REA 7 4 93	Dec 69 Csikai+ SIG+HL COMPILTN,N-ACTIV-ANAL	
(n,p)	1.4+7	1.5+7	JYV	Eval	Rept JU-RR-3/1970	Jun 70 Leppaemaeki+ TABLE OF EVAL AVG SIG	
(n,p)	None		KFI	Comp Jour	JRC 7 365	Jun 71 Nagy+ GAM+BETA ES AND HALF-LIFE GIVN	
(n,p)	1.4+7	1.5+7	KAZ	Theo	Jour YF 18 705	Oct 73 Levkovsky.AVERAGED SIG,CALC,TBL	
					Jour SNP 18 361	Apr 74 . ENGLISH OF YF 18,705	
(n,α)	1.5+7		ARK	Expt	Jour PR 118 242	Apr 60 Wille+ MEAS ACT SIG= 1.0+ - .2 MB	+
	1.5+7				Data EXFOR12033.049	Jun 76 . 1 PT. SIG.	
(n,α)	Fiss		CRC	Eval	Rept CRC-1003	Dec 60 Roy+,ESTIMATED AVG SIG=BELO 0.0001MB	
(n,α)	1.4+7		CIS	Theo	Jour NP 51 460	Feb 64 Facchini+STATMOD SIG XPT/CALC260-400	
(n,α)	1.5+7		DEB	Comp Jour	REA 7 4 93	Dec 69 Csikai+ SIG+HL COMPILTN,N-ACTIV-ANAL	
(n,α)	1.4+7	1.5+7	JYV	Eval	Rept JU-RR-3/1970	Jun 70 Leppaemaeki+ TABLE OF EVAL AVG SIG	
(n,α)	1.4+7	1.5+7	KAZ	Theo	Jour YF 18 705	Oct 73 Levkovsky.AVERAGED SIG,CALC,TBL	
					Jour SNP 18 361	Apr 74 . ENGLISH OF YF 18,705	
Reson Params	9.6+1		IFU	Expt	Conf 65Antwerp § 186	Jul 65 Vertebny.KIEV.FC XPT.WN=716+ -30MEV	
Reson Params	9.5+1		BNL	Expt	Jour PR 162 1130	Oct 67 Mughabghab+ TRANS WN+REDUCED WN	+
	9.5+1				Data EXFOR12120.009	Jun 76 . 1 RES. EN, WN, WNO	
Reson Params	7.4+0	2.9+3	DUB	Expt	Jour YF 7 225	Feb 68 Karzhavina+,TRANS+NG YLD,RES-PAR+STF	+
					Rept YFI-4 47	May 67 - + RES ANAL.	
					Rept JINR-P3-3097	Feb 67 - + TOT+NG,TBL.	
					Jour SNP 7 161	Aug 68 - + ENGL OF YF 7 225.	
					Rept INDC-187E	67 - + ENGL OF YFI-4 47.	
	7.3+0	2.9+3			Data EXFOR40147.	May 73 .NW,TOT-WIDTH,D,RES-EN	
Reson Params		3.0+3	DUB	Expt	Conf 68DUBSY 349	Jul 68 Pikelner.LVL SPAC,AVERG. WG,S0 VS A	
Reson Params	9.5+1		IFU	Expt	Rept ICD-5 5	Nov 68 Vertebny+	+
	9.5+1				Data EXFOR40061.009	Mar 71 N-WID AT 1 RES	
Reson Params	2.4+4		MUA	ExTh Jour	NC/B 58 402	Dec 68 Hasan+ AVERAGE LEVEL SPACING D GIVEN	+
	2.4+4			Expt	Data EXFOR30091.014	Dec 70 ESTIMATED AVERAGE LEVEL SPACING D	
Reson Params	-		AUA	Theo	Rept AAEC/E-211	Nov 70 Musgrove. CALCULTD D+GAM WIDTH GIVEN	
Reson Params	9.6+1		CJD	Eval	Rept YK- 7	71 Zakharova+ SURVEY+SYSTEMATICS,GW,TBL	
					Rept INDC(CCP)-27	Nov 72 .ENGLISH TRANSLATION OF YK-7 /71	

68 Erbium 170

Quantity	Energy (ev) Min	Max	Lab	Type	Documentation Ref Vol Page	Author, Comments Date	Data
Reson Params	9.5+1	2.4+4	COL	Expt	Jour PR/C 5 974	Mar 72 Liou+.WN WG G*WN D. P−T+WIGNER DIST	+
					Conf 71Albany 205	Aug 71 Camarda+ D GVN. TBP PR.	
	9.5+1	8.4+3			Rept NYO−72−190	68 Liou+TOF.WN FOR 27 RES ES.AVG D GVN	
	9.5+1	2.4+4			Data EXFOR10591.	Jan 78 . 124 RES ES.WG,WN RED,WN*G RED.D.	
Reson Params	None		COL	Revw	Conf 75Wash. 780	Mar 75 Hacken+ TBL AV WG,STF,NUMBER GWN,WG	
Reson Params	+7		FEI	Theo	Rept YK− 21 3	Oct 76 Blokhin+ D,WG,WG/D,TBL	
Strnth Fnctn	7.4+0	2.9+3	DUB	Expt	Jour YF 7 225	Feb 68 Karzhavina+,TRANS+NG YLD,RES−PAR+STF	+
					Rept YFI−4 47	May 67 − + RES ANAL.	
					Rept JINR−P3−3097	Feb 67 − + TOT+NG,TBL.	
					Jour SNP 7 161	Aug 68 − + ENGL OF YF 7 225.	
					Rept INDC−187E	67 − + ENGL OF YFI−4 47.	
	7.3+0	2.9+3			Data EXFOR40147.	May 73 .1 DATA LINE	
Strnth Fnctn		3.0+3	DUB	Expt	Conf 68DUBSY 349	Jul 68 Pikelner.LVL SPAC,AVERG. WG,S0 VS A	
Strnth Fnctn	−		AUA	Theo	Rept AAEC/E−211	Nov 70 Musgrove. SMOOTHED S0,S1 AND S2 GIVN	
Strnth Fnctn	9.5+1	2.4+4	COL	Expt	Jour PR/C 5 974	Mar 72 Liou+.S0 AND S1 GIVEN	+
					Conf 71Albany 205	Aug 71 Camarda+ S0, S1 GVN.	
	9.5+1	8.4+3			Rept NYO−72−190	68 Liou+TOF.WN FOR 27 RES ES.AVG D GVN.	
	0.0+0	4.8+3			Data EXFOR10591.017	Jan 78 . 2PTS. S0=1.54+ −.22 S1=.80+ −.25	
Strnth Fnctn	2.4+4		MUA	Theo	Jour IJP 46 114	Mar 72 Chaubey+ P−WAVE.FOR A−SYSTEMTIC,GRPH	
Strnth Fnctn	None		AUA	Eval	Rept AAEC/E−277	Mar 73 Musgrove.TBLS EXPTL DATA+BEST VALUES	
Strnth Fnctn	None		COL	Revw	Conf 75Wash. 780	Mar 75 Hacken+ NEVIS TOF S−WAVE STF	
Lvl Density	None		AUW	Theo	Conf 70Madurai 2 267	Dec 70 Ramamurty+ A−PARAMETER GVN,LANG'S−TH	
Lvl Density	+0	1.0+4	JAE	ExTh	Jour JPJ 37 581	Sep 74 Ideno.LVL SPACING CORRELATIONS.TBL.	
	1.0+0	1.0+4			Rept JAERI−M−5490	Nov 73 − .LEVEL SPACING CORRELATIONS.TBL	

68 Erbium 171

Quantity	Energy (ev) Min	Max	Lab	Type	Documentation Ref Vol Page	Author, Comments Date	Data
Absorption	2.5−2		IJI	Eval	Conf 75Kiev 1 169	May 75 Fedorova+ EVAL 2200M/S SIG,TABLE	
Reson Params	−		AUA	Theo	Rept AAEC/E−211	Nov 70 Musgrove. CALCULTD D+GAM WIDTH GIVEN	
Strnth Fnctn	−		AUA	Theo	Rept AAEC/E−211	Nov 70 Musgrove. SMOOTHED S0,S1 AND S2 GIVN	
Lvl Density	7.4+0	2.8+3	DUB	Expt	Jour YF 7 225	Feb 68 Karzhavina+LVL−DEN(EXCIT−E),GRPH,TBL	+
					Rept JINR−P3−3097	Feb 67 − + TOT+NG,TBL.	
					Jour SNP 7 2 161	Aug 68 − + ENGL OF YF 7 225.	
	7.4+0	2.8+3			Data EXFOR40147.	May 73 .1 DATA LINE	
Lvl Density	None		MUN	Theo	Jour NP/A 217 269	Dec 73 Dilg+ A,DELTA. BACK SHIFTED FERMIGAS	
Lvl Density	None		ROC	Theo	Jour NP/A 223 589	May 74 Huizenga+ EXP CFD MICROSC TH AX SYMM	

68 Erbium 172

Quantity	Energy (ev) Min	Max	Lab	Type	Documentation Ref Vol Page	Author, Comments Date	Data
Reson Params	−		AUA	Theo	Rept AAEC/E−211	Nov 70 Musgrove. CALCULTD D+GAM WIDTH GIVEN	
Strnth Fnctn	−		AUA	Theo	Rept AAEC/E−211	Nov 70 Musgrove. SMOOTHED S0,S1 AND S2 GIVN	

69 Thulium 161

Quantity	Energy (ev) Min	Max	Lab	Type	Documentation Ref Vol Page	Author, Comments Date	Data
Reson Params	–		AUA	Theo Rept	AAEC/E-211	Nov 70 Musgrove. CALCULTD D+GAM WIDTH GIVEN	
Strnth Fnctn	–		AUA	Theo Rept	AAEC/E-211	Nov 70 Musgrove. SMOOTHED S0,S1 AND S2 GIVN	

69 Thulium 162

Quantity	Energy (ev) Min	Max	Lab	Type	Documentation Ref Vol Page	Author, Comments Date	Data
Reson Params	–		AUA	Theo Rept	AAEC/E-211	Nov 70 Musgrove. CALCULTD D+GAM WIDTH GIVEN	
Strnth Fnctn	–		AUA	Theo Rept	AAEC/E-211	Nov 70 Musgrove. SMOOTHED S0,S1 AND S2 GIVN	

69 Thulium 163

Quantity	Energy (ev) Min	Max	Lab	Type	Documentation Ref Vol Page	Author, Comments Date	Data
Reson Params	–		AUA	Theo Rept	AAEC/E-211	Nov 70 Musgrove. CALCULTD D+GAM WIDTH GIVEN	
Strnth Fnctn	–		AUA	Theo Rept	AAEC/E-211	Nov 70 Musgrove. SMOOTHED S0,S1 AND S2 GIVN	

69 Thulium 164

Quantity	Energy (ev) Min	Max	Lab	Type	Documentation Ref Vol Page	Author, Comments Date	Data
Reson Params	–		AUA	Theo Rept	AAEC/E-211	Nov 70 Musgrove. CALCULTD D+GAM WIDTH GIVEN	
Strnth Fnctn	–		AUA	Theo Rept	AAEC/E-211	Nov 70 Musgrove. SMOOTHED S0,S1 AND S2 GIVN	

69 Thulium 165

Quantity	Energy (ev) Min	Max	Lab	Type	Documentation Ref Vol Page	Author, Comments Date	Data
Reson Params	–		AUA	Theo Rept	AAEC/E-211	Nov 70 Musgrove. CALCULTD D+GAM WIDTH GIVEN	
Strnth Fnctn	–		AUA	Theo Rept	AAEC/E-211	Nov 70 Musgrove. SMOOTHED S0,S1 AND S2 GIVN	

69 Thulium 166

Quantity	Energy (ev) Min	Max	Lab	Type	Documentation Ref Vol Page	Author, Comments Date	Data
Reson Params	–		AUA	Theo Rept	AAEC/E-211	Nov 70 Musgrove. CALCULTD D+GAM WIDTH GIVEN	
Strnth Fnctn	–		AUA	Theo Rept	AAEC/E-211	Nov 70 Musgrove. SMOOTHED S0,S1 AND S2 GIVN	

69 Thulium 167

Quantity	Energy (ev) Min	Max	Lab	Type	Documentation Ref Vol Page	Author, Comments Date	Data
(n,p)	Maxwl		IFU	Theo Rept	ICD-4 20	67 Dadakina+ PENETR COEFF CALC,TABLE	
Reson Params	–		AUA	Theo Rept	AAEC/E-211	Nov 70 Musgrove. CALCULTD D+GAM WIDTH GIVEN	
Strnth Fnctn	–		AUA	Theo Rept	AAEC/E-211	Nov 70 Musgrove. SMOOTHED S0,S1 AND S2 GIVN	

69 Thulium 168

Quantity	Energy (ev) Min	Max	Lab	Type	Documentation Ref Vol Page	Author, Comments Date	Data
(n,p)	Maxwl		IFU	Theo Rept	ICD-4 20	67 Dadakina+ PENETR COEFF CALC,TABLE	
Reson Params	–		AUA	Theo Rept	AAEC/E-211	Nov 70 Musgrove. CALCULTD D+GAM WIDTH GIVEN	
Strnth Fnctn	–		AUA	Theo Rept	AAEC/E-211	Nov 70 Musgrove. SMOOTHED S0,S1 AND S2 GIVN	
Lvl Density	8.0+6	1.5+7	ANL	Eval Prog	ANL-75-34 31	Jun 75 Davey+N2NEVAL.CONSTANT T,LVL DEN FIT	

69 Thulium 169

Quantity	Energy (ev) Min	Max	Lab	Type	Documentation Ref Vol Page	Author, Comments Date	Data
Total	Maxwl		COL	Expt Jour	PR 48 265	Aug 35 Dunning+ IONCH,TRANS,RA-BE/PARAFIN N	
Total	1.0-1	5.0+1	BNL	Expt Jour	PR 92 656	Nov 53 Foote+ CRYSTLSPECT.	+
	1.1+0	5.8+0			Data EXFOR12107.003	Jun 76 . 56 PTS, SIG	
Total	3.0+0	2.0+2	BNL	Expt Jour	PR 99 10	Jul 55 Harvey+.FC TRANSM. 8+ -2B	+
	6.0+0	3.4+2			Data EXFOR11912.037	Jun 76 . 318 PTS, SIG	
Total	3.8-2	1.6+0	MTR	Expt Jour	PR 103 1326	Sep 56 Joki+,TRNS+CS,134+ -3B AT 0.0253EV	+
	3.7-2	1.6+0			Data EXFOR12111.	Jun 76 . 363 PTS, SIG	

69 Thulium 169

Quantity	Energy (ev) Min	Energy (ev) Max	Lab	Type	Documentation Ref Vol Page	Date	Author, Comments	Data
Total	9.5−4	9.5−1	BSP	Expt	Conf 66Paris 1 53	Oct 66	Zimmerman+,P.129,SIG(E),+SIG(.025EV)	+
					Jour NP/A 95 683	Apr 67	SEE ALSO *	
	9.5−4	9.5−1			Data EXFOR30224.	Dec 72	SIG AT 62ES, SIG AT 0.025 EV,PRIVCOM	
Total	3.4+0	4.6+0	BNL	Expt	Jour NP/A 91 644	Feb 67	Al−Kital+ XPT CFD CALCULATED CURVE	
Total	4.0+0	8.3+2	SAC	Expt	Jour NP/A 131 305	Jun 69	DE BARROS+ LINAC.TRANSM. NDG	+
	4.0+0	8.3+2			Data EXFOR20685.	Jul 77	0PTS. SEE RESONANCE PARAMETERS.	
Total	1.0−3	3.0−3	MUN	Expt	Jour AKE 16 49	70	Knorr+ TRANS EXPT, TBL	
Total	3.0+6	1.5+7	KFK	Revw	Conf 70Helsinki 2 219	Jun 70	Cierjacks.113. SIG(E) GRPH CFD OPTMD	
Total	3.5−1	3.2+0	CNA	Expt	Prog EANDC(OR)100	Jan 71	Cansoy.CRYST SPEC,NDG,TBP CNAEM−76	+
	3.5−1	3.2+0			Data EXFOR20174.005	May 74	30PTS.	
Total	2.5+6	1.5+7	BNW	Expt	Jour PR/C 3 576	Feb 71	Foster+,TRANS,CURVS,CFD OTHERS+TH	+
					Jour PRL 22 139	Jan 69	.SUPERSEDED	
					Jour NIM 36 1	Sep 65	.EXPT DETAILS	
	2.3+6	1.5+7			Data EXFOR10047.073	Aug 73	. 235 PTS. SIGMA	
Total	None		COL	Expt	Prog NCSAC−42 61	Nov 71	Hacken+. TRANS. ANAL TBC. NO DATA	
Total	4.0+0	1.0+4	HAR	Expt	Prog AERE−PR/NP18	Mar 72	Axmann+ LINAC TOF NDG	
Total	2.7+3		MUN	Expt	Prog EANDC(E)150U	Oct 72	Dilg+ AVERAGE TOT XSECT+S0	+
					Conf 71Albany 327	Aug 71	− +TRNS.AVG CS GVN.31 ELEMENT GRP	
	2.7+3				Data EXFOR20583.023	Jun 76	1PNT.	
Total	2.6+1	5.0+3	SAC	Expt	Rept CEA−N−1563	Oct 72	Tellier+ D,S0,WN,WG ANAL	+
					Conf 72Budapest 38	Aug 72	− + ABST.NDG.LINAC.	
					Priv TELLIER	May 72	− + DATA FOR COMPILATN.	
	2.6+1	5.0+3			Data EXFOR20125.002	Sep 72	. 12406PTS.	
Total	1.3+7	1.5+7	DEB	Eval	Rept IAEA−153 173	73	Boedy+ MOST PROBABLE VAL OF SIG,TBL	
					Jour AHP 30 115	Oct 71	Angeli+ AVG SIG,CFD CALC.TBLS.GRAPH	
Total	2.0+3		IJI	Expt	Conf 76Lowell 1244	Jul 76	Vertebnyi+ TRANSM VS THICKNESS,NDG	
Elastic	Cold		ORL	Revw	Jour JAP 36 1078	Mar 65	Koehler. N DIFFR XPTS.	
Elastic	1.0+1	4.3+2	HAR	Expt	Jour NIM 39 68	Jan 66	Asghar+LI−6 DET. FOR RES ANALYSIS	
					Rept AERE−NP/GEN40	Jun 65	− +MATEHED LI−6 DET.LINAC.GRPH	
Elastic	None		ANL	Expt	Prog USNDC−3 25	Oct 72	Lander+ COHERENT SCAT LENGTH GIVEN	
Elastic	2.5−2		IJI	Eval	Conf 75Kiev 1 169	May 75	Fedorova+ EVAL 2200M/S SIG,TABLE	
Elastic	1.0+0		DUB	Expt	Conf 76Lowell 1243	Jul 76	Akopian+TOF.SCT CS=COH+INCOH.TBL	
Diff Elastic	1.4+7		LRL	Theo	Rept UCRL−4926	Jul 57	Bjorklund+ OPTMDL CALC 6−PARAM FIT	
Potntal Scat		7.6+2	SAC	Expt	Jour NP/A 123 561	Jan 69	Morgenstern+ RADIUS FROM RES ANAL	+
					Rept CEA−R−3609	Sep 68	− + (THESIS) RADIUS.	
	0.0+0	7.6+2			Data EXFOR20685.011	Jul 77	1PNT.RADIUS.	
Potntal Scat	0.0+0	2.0+3	SAC	Expt	Priv TELLIER	Feb 72	Tellier+.	+
		2.0+3			Data EXFOR20124.002	Sep 72	1PNT.RADIUS.	
Potntal Scat	3.5−1	3.2+0	CNA	Expt	Prog INDC(TUR)−3	May 72	Cansoy. B−W SINGLE LEVEL FIT	+
	3.5−1	3.2+0			Data EXFOR20174.007	May 74	1PNT.	
Potntal Scat	2.0+3		IJI	Expt	Conf 76Lowell 1244	Jul 76	Vertebnyi+ SCT−LNGTH GVN,FRM TOT+SCT	
Tot Inelastc	1.0−3	3.0−3	MUN	Theo	Jour AKE 16 49	70	Knorr+ PARAMAGNETIC SCAT SIG CALC	
Tot Inelastc	8.0+6	2.0+7	LRL	Theo	Conf 75Wash. 651	Mar 75	Gardner.GRAPH CALC	
Diff Inelast	+7		CCP	Expt	Rept YK−23 4	76	Brodskaja+ ACTIV,AVG SIG,TBL	
Thermal Scat	Cold		GRE	Expt	Jour JAP 37 1038	Mar 66	MAGNETIC PROPS FROM N DIFFR XPTS	
Thermal Scat	2.0−4	1.5−1	BSP	ExTh	Jour JCP 48 520	Jan 68	Mattos.,TRIVALENT ION PARAMAG SIG	+
					Jour NP/A 95 683	Apr 67	SEE ALSO * SAME CURVE.	
Thermal Scat	2.0−2	1.4+0	IJI	Expt	Prog YFI−12 67	72	Vertebny+ ABST,TOT SCAT SIG 15ES,TBL	
					Prog INDC(CCP)−30	Sep 72	.PAGE 58,ENGLISH OF YFI−12 67	
Thermal Scat	1.0−4	1.0+3	MUN	Revw	Jour EEN 80 1	77	Koester. SCAT LENGTH,FREE SIG	
Scattering	2.5−2		BSP	Expt	Conf 66Paris 1 53	Oct 66	Zimmerman+,P.129,SIG(.025EV)DEDUCED	+
					Jour NP/A 95 683	Apr 67	SEE ALSO *	
	2.5−2				Data EXFOR30224.015	Dec 72	DEDUCED SIGMA	
Scattering	2.0+3		IJI	Expt	Conf 76Lowell 1244	Jul 76	Vertebnyi+ SCT−SIG VS THICKNESS,NDG	
Nonelastic	1.4+7	1.5+7	ANL	Eval	Prog ANL−75−34 182	Jun 75	Davey+CORRC APPLIED TO N2N CS.TBLS.	
Absorption	1.0−4	3.0−3	MUN	Theo	Jour AKE 16 49	70	Knorr+ FROM TOT SIG EXPT CALC, TBL	
Absorption	2.5−2		IJI	Eval	Conf 75Kiev 1 169	May 75	Fedorova+ EVAL 2200M/S SIG,TABLE	
Res Int Abs	5.0−1		BOL	Eval	Rept RT/FI−4	Jan 67	Palmucci. CALC FROM (N,G) RES PARAMS	
Res Int Abs	5.4−1		ORL	Expt	Rept ORNL−4155 15	Aug 67	Gillette+	+
	5.4−1				Data EXFOR10259.008	Jul 74	. 1 PT. SIGMA	
Res Int Abs	5.0−1		MTR	Expt	Rept IN−1195	May 68	Scoville.	+
	5.0−1				Data EXFOR11820.014	Jun 76	. 1 PT, RI	
Res Int Abs	5.5−1		CPO	Expt	Jour JIN 32 2839	Oct 70	Sims+ (N,G).CD CUT−OFF,VALUE GIVEN	+
	5.5−1				Data EXFOR10608.	Aug 76	. 2 PTS.MAXW SPEC MEAS AND 1/V RMVD.	
Res Int Abs	5.0−1		OSL	Expt	Prog INDC(NOR)−1 1	May 72	Alstad+ REDUCED CAPTINTEG REL AU,TBL	+
					Priv PAPPAS	Nov 70	Pappas. ACT. POWD,LIQ SOLUT.TBP JIN	
	0.0+0	1.0+6			Data EXFOR20094.003	Sep 71	1PNT.CAPTURE.	

69 Thulium 169

Quantity	Energy (ev) Min Max	Lab	Type	Documentation Ref Vol Page	Author, Comments Date	Data
Res Int Abs	5.0-1	KJL	Expt	Jour JIN 34 2699	Sep 72 Steinnes. ACT. AU MONITOR	+
	5.0-1			Data EXFOR20188.025	May 74 1PNT.CAPTURE.	
Res Int Abs	5.0-1	GHT	Expt	Jour JRC 20 695	74 Van Der Linden+ BY(N,G).CFD OTHS,TBL	+
	5.5-1			Conf 73Paris 2 241	Mar 73 - + ACT,REL THR+GOLD,TBL	
	5.5-1			Data EXFOR20645.032	Jul 76 1PNT.CAPTURE.	
Res Int Abs	5.0-1	IJI	Eval	Conf 75Kiev 1 169	May 75 Fedorova+ EVAL+CALC RI GIVEN,TABLE	
(n,γ)	None	PAR	Expt	Jour CR 203 787	Oct 36 Curie+ HALF-LIFE OF 170TM	
(n,γ)	Pile	ANL	Expt	Jour PR 72 888	Nov 47 Seren+.THR IRRAD. TO EU152, TM2O3.	+
	Pile			Data EXFOR11447.108	Jun 76 . 1 PT, SIG	
(n,γ)	Maxwl	ORL	Expt	Jour PR 83 643	Aug 51 Pomerance. LOCAL OSC REL AU ABS 95 B	+
	Maxwl			Data EXFOR11047.066	Jun 76 . 1 PT, SIG	
(n,γ)	3.0+4 1.7+5	ORL	Expt	Jour PR 122 182	Apr 61 Gibbons+	
	3.0+4 6.5+4			Jour PR 129 2695	Mar 63 Macklin+ LIQ SCINT,1.31 AND 0.70B	
	3.0+4 1.7+5			Conf 61Vienna 1 95	Aug 61 Neiler.	
	9.5+3 1.7+5			Data EXFOR11329.	Jun 76 . 60 PTS, SIG	
(n,γ)	2.0+2 8.0+3	ORL	Expt	Conf 61Saclay 203	Sep 61 Block+.LIQUID SCINTILLATOR	
				Conf 61Vienna 1 95	Aug 61 Neiler.PPR73,TABLE FOR SOME ES,GRAPH	
	2.0+2 7.8+3			Data EXFOR11935.017	Jun 76 . 46 PTS, SIG	
(n,γ)	5.0+3 9.0+4	ORL	Theo	Jour RMP 37 166	Jan 65 Macklin+.CALC FOR KT=5TO90KEV	
(n,γ)	1.0+3 1.0+4	LAS	Theo	Prog LA-3463 15	Jan 66 Bell. TH CAPTURE OF RARE EARTHS	
(n,γ)	2.5-2	BSP	Expt	Conf 66Paris 1 53	Oct 66 Zimmerman+,P.129,SIG(.025EV)DEDUCED	+
				Jour NP/A 95 683	Apr 67 SEE ALSO *	
	2.5-2			Data EXFOR30224.016	Dec 72 DEDUCED SIGMA	
(n,γ)	2.5-2	BOL	Eval	Rept RT/FI-4	Jan 67 Palmucci. CALC FROM RES PARAMETERS	
(n,γ)	Maxwl	ORL	Expt	Prog ORNL-4155 15	Aug 67 Gillette+	+
	Maxwl			Data EXFOR10259.002	Jul 74 . 1 PT. SIGMA	
(n,γ)	None	BNL	Expt	Abst BAP 12 1167	Dec 67 Chrien. DIRECT. LVL INTERFERENCE.	
(n,γ)	-	IEA	Comp	Rept IEA-INF- 10	Aug 68 Atalla. TABLES OF HL,SIG AND GAMM-E	
(n,γ)	3.9+0 1.7+2	RIO	Expt	Jour NDF 15 167	Aug 69 Barros+ TOTAL NEUT CAPT,TOF SPECTRUM	
(n,γ)	2.4+1	BNL	Revw	Rept IAEA-124 303	Feb 70 Chrien.REL PARTIAL SIG(6MEV-G)CFD TH	
(n,γ)	1.0+2 1.0+5	LRL	Expt	Prog NCSAC-31 108	May 70 Gardner+,OPTMDL CALCULATION,CURVE	
(n,γ)	Maxwl	CPO	Expt	Jour JIN 32 2839	Oct 70 Sims+ CD CUT-OFF,REL CO59,SIG GIVEN	+
	Maxwl			Data EXFOR10608.	Aug 76 . 2 PTS. EFF. AND MAXW SPEC CALC.	
(n,γ)	1.0+3 1.0+6	GA	Revw	Conf 70ANL 285	Oct 70 Carlson. STATUS AS STANDARD SIG,CURV	
(n,γ)	3.0+4	AUA	Theo	Rept AAEC/E-211	Nov 70 Musgrove. SIGMA GIVEN AND CFD OTHER	
(n,γ)	Fast	INL	Expt	Conf 71Knoxvill 113	Mar 71 Harker.INTEGRAL MEAST,0.70B REL AU	+
	Fast			Data EXFOR10218.009	Oct 72 . 1 PNT. SIGMA.	
(n,γ)	1.0+7	BOL	Eval	Data BENZI-DFN 697.	May 72 40 PNTS	+
(n,γ)	1.0+2 1.0+6	LRL	Expt	Prog USNDC-1 94	May 72 Czirr+. TO BE COMPLETED. NO DATA GVN	
(n,γ)	Maxwl	OSL	Expt	Prog INDC(NOR)-1 1	May 72 Alstad+ ACTIVATION REL AU-197,TABLE	+
				Priv PAPPAS	Nov 70 Pappas. ACT. POWD,LIQ SOLUT.TBP JIN	
	Maxwl			Data EXFOR20094.002	Sep 71 1PNT.SIG.	
(n,γ)	2.5+4	AUW	Expt	Jour JP/A 5 877	Jun 72 Siddappa+ ACT. S,P-WAVE CS GIVEN	+
			ExTh	Conf 70Madurai 2 29	Dec 70 Sriramachandra Murty+.S+P WAVE SIGMA	
	2.5+4		Expt	Data EXFOR30248.010	Jun 73 SIGMA CAPTURE VALUE	
(n,γ)	+2 2.0+3	COL	Expt	Abst ANS 19 394	Oct 74 Arbo+ ORELA+NEVIS.GRPH.REL.TO.AU	
	3.1+2 4.0+2			Prog COO-2176-20 8	Jun 73 - +.TOF.MOXON-RAE DETECTOR. CURVE	
(n,γ)	3.5+4 1.7+5	BRC	Eval	Prog CEA-N-1875 119	Apr 76 Bertrand - Lepage+RECOMMENDED VALUES	
Spect (n,γ)	Maxwl	CCP	Expt	Jour AE 4 22	Jan 58 Sklyarevskii+.EGS+INTENS BELOW .3MEV	
				Jour JNE 9 69	Jun 59 TRANSLATN.*	
				Jour SJA 4 19	58 TRANSLATN.*	
Spect (n,γ)	3.9+0	YAL	Expt	Abst BAP 4 35	Jan 59 Springer+,NAI(TL),GAMMA MULTIPLICITY	
Spect (n,γ)	Maxwl	YAL	Expt	Jour PR 114 268	Apr 59 Draper.SC SPECTR,GAM E 0 TO 600 KEV	
Spect (n,γ)	Maxwl	KUR	Expt	Book NEJTRONFIZ 335	61 Groshev. TABLE+GRAPH	
				Jour NP 16 645	Jun 60 - + 0.5 TO 6MEV GAMS,CFD THEORY	
				Book SPN 248	61 . ENGL TRANSL OF NEJTRONFIZ 335	
Spect (n,γ)	Maxwl	ARF	Expt	Prog ARF-1193-9	Apr 62 Greenwood+,CRYST SPEC,LOW-E GAMMAS	
Spect (n,γ)	Maxwl	CAS	Expt	Jour NC 27 538	Jan 63 Giannini+ NAI(TL),E+INTENSTY,TO .3MV	+
Spect (n,γ)	Pile	UPP	Expt	Jour NP 40 329	Jan 63 Marklund+.E DETERM. NO INTENS MEAS.	
Spect (n,γ)	3.9+0	JAE	Expt	Rept JAERI-1073	Mar 65 Kawarasaki. RES CAPT.LINAC.TOF.E,INT	+
				Rept INDSWG-90 6	Jul 65 - . TABLE E,INTS GIVEN.	
	3.9+0			Data EXFOR20277.016	Jun 74 4PTS.	
Spect (n,γ)	Maxwl	IFL	Expt	Jour YF 2 236	Aug 65 . ES+INTS OF CONVERSION ELECTRONS	
				Jour SNP 2 168	Feb 66 . ENGLISH OF YF 2 236	
Spect (n,γ)	Maxwl	LAS	Expt	Jour PR 143 857	Mar 66 Motz+,14 LINES ABOVE 5.7MEV,ABS INT	
Spect (n,γ)	Maxwl	RIS	Expt	Jour PR 143 857	Mar 66 Maier+,BENT XTL,LINES TO 870KEV,ABS	+
Spect (n,γ)	None	RPI	Expt	Prog WASH-1068 183	Mar 66 Rae+,SC+TOF,NDG	

69 Thulium 169

Quantity	Energy (ev) Min	Max	Lab	Type	Documentation Ref Vol Page	Author, Comments Date	Data
Spect (n,γ)	Maxwl		MUN	Expt Jour	PR 143 857	Mar 66 Egidy+ JOINT PUBLICATION.LVL SCHME.	
				Conf	67Juelich 56	Apr 67 - + CONVERSION ELECTRONS162-6.NDG	
Spect (n,γ)	Maxwl		MRY	Expt Abst	DA/B 28 1093	Sep 67 Mehta.SINGLE+COINC SPECT, NAI SCINT	
Spect (n,γ)	Maxwl	1.4+2	BNL	Expt Jour	PR 174 1512	Oct 68 Chrien+ GE(LI) RESON+NONRESON CAPT	
	Maxwl			Conf	69Studsvik 627	Aug 69 - .SPEC GRPHS GVN,THR+RESON NEUT	
	Maxwl	1.4+2		Jour	PRL 20 342	Feb 68 .SUPERSEDED	
				Jour	NIM 53 108	Jul 67 .SUPERSEDED	
				Jour	NIM 53 93	Jul 67 .SUPERSEDED	
Spect (n,γ)	Maxwl		UPP	Expt Jour	NP/A 120 569	Nov 68 Hoegberg+ M INT CONVERSION. PURE E2.	
				Jour	NP/A 120 561	Nov 68 Nilsson+.INT CONVERSION. PURE E2 TR.	
Spect (n,γ)	2.5-2		MIT	Comp Rept	MITNE-85	Jan 69 Rasmussen+TBL G INT.=AFCRL-69-0071	
Spect (n,γ)	Maxwl		ROS	Expt Rept	ZFK-166	Jan 69 Andreeff. DELAYED GAM EXPT	
				Jour	NP/A 102 241	Oct 67 Andreef+.NAT.TARGET. DEDUCED LEVELS.	
Spect (n,γ)	Pile		ANL	Expt Conf	69Studsvik 601	Aug 69 Smither+ NDG,DISAGREES STATMOD	
				Conf	68DUBSY 317	Jul 68 Bollinger.ANAL.RAD. TRANSITIONS.	
				Conf	JINR-D-3893	May 68 - + ABSTRACT,NO DATA GIVEN	
Spect (n,γ)	Maxwl		SAC	Expt Jour	NP/A 135 241	Oct 69 Alves+ LINAC GE(LI) 5130-6556KEV GAM	
				Rept	CEA-R-3602	Jul 69 - . (THESIS).SEE ALSO	
Spect (n,γ)	1.4+1	1.2+2	BNL	Expt Jour	PR/C 2 2030	Nov 70 Bhat+,CAPT IN 13RESON.P-H SPECTRA	
	1.5+2			Conf	68DUBSY 342	Jul 68 Chrien. GAM E+INTENSITY TABLE	
Spect (n,γ)	None		BNL	Expt Prog	NCSAC-42 33	Nov 71 Chrien+. ORELA. GAMMA SPECTRA SHOWN	
Spect (n,γ)		1.5+2	HAR	Expt Prog	AERE-PR/NP18	Mar 72 Thomas+ LOW EN GS TO GET J GRPH	
		1.6+2		Conf	71Albany 251	Aug 71 - .TBL G INT.	
Spect (n,γ)	Maxwl		IFL	Expt Book	PROKOFJEV	73 . TBL GAM,CONV ELECTR ES+INT,LVL SCH	
Spect (n,γ)	Pile		MUN	Expt Jour	ZP 258 315	Mar 73 Henkelmann. E + INT OF GS GIVEN	+
	2.5-2			Data	EXFOR20606.017	Jun 76 8PTS.	
Spect (n,γ)	None		LIE	Theo Jour	NP/A 222 525	Apr 74 Baudinet-Robinet.STAT CORR PART WID	
Inelastic γ	2.8+6		KGU	Expt Jour	YF 9 1129	Jun 69 Romanenko+ GRPH,E+INT TBL,LVL-SCHEME	+
				Jour	SNP 9 660	Dec 69 *	
				Conf	67Kharkov 49	Feb 67 * ABST ONLY	
	2.8+6			Data	EXFOR40414.006	Dec 77 E+ABS INT OF 7 GAMMAS	
(n,2n)	1.0+7	1.5+7	LRL	Expt Prog	UCRL-6028 6	Jun 60 Tewes.ACT 7ES .4 TO .9B + -40PC,TBC	+
	9.8+6	1.5+7		Data	EXFOR11504.014	Jun 76 . 7 PTS. SIGMA.	
(n,2n)	Fiss		CRC	Eval Prog	CRC-1003 30	Dec 60 ROY+ ESTIMATED AVG SIG=3.3MB.	
	Fiss		ORL	Expt Prog	ORNL-CF-66 6	66 Lewis. REF=ORNL-CF-66-12-9	+
	Fiss			Data	EXFOR10368.002	Apr 75 . 1 PT. SIGMA.	
(n,2n)	1.4+7		ALD	Expt Rept	AWRE-O-76/66	Dec 66 Vallis. ACTIV. AL27(N,ALPHA) STANDRD	+
	1.5+7			Data	EXFOR20347.007	Sep 74 1PNT.SIGMA.	
(n,2n)	+7		NDL	Expt Prog	WASH-1079 128	Oct 67 Temperley. ACT, GE-LI, TBD	
(n,2n)	1.5+7		MUN	Expt Jour	NP/A 118 9	Sep 68 Dilg+ ACTIV.REL AL(N,A)	+
				Jour	OAWS 177 323	69 Winkler+(IRK) ACTIVATION.	
	1.5+7			Data	EXFOR20802.010	Dec 78 1PNT.SIGMA.	
(n,2n)	1.5+7		DEB	Comp Jour	REA 7 4 93	Dec 69 Csikai+ SIG+HL COMPILTN,N-ACTIV-ANAL	
(n,2n)	1.4+7	1.5+7	JYV	Eval Rept	JU-RR-3/1970	Jun 70 Leppaemaeki+ TABLE OF EVAL AVG SIG	
(n,2n)	+7		KFI	Theo Rept	KFKI-71-8	Feb 71 Jeki. CALCULATED CFD EXPTL SIG VALUE	
(n,2n)	1.5+7		CCP	Expt Jour	YF 14 682	Oct 71 Druzhinin+ NAI,ABSOL,TBL CFD OTHERS	
				Jour	SNP 14 383	Apr 72 *ENGL OF YF 14 682	
(n,2n)	1.5+7		ARK	Expt Abst	DA/B 32 5091	Mar 72 Bari. GE(LI) DET. ACT. SIG GIVEN	+
	1.5+7			Data	EXFOR10431.059	Aug 75 . 1 PT. SIGMA.	
(n,2n)	1.4+7	1.5+7	LRL	Expt Jour	NP/A 190 635	Aug 72 Nethaway. D-T NS.TO METST.+-5PC ACCU	+
	1.4+7	1.5+7		Data	EXFOR10312.007	May 75 . 9 PTS. SIGMA.	
(n,2n)	1.2+7	1.4+7	ALD	Expt Rept	AWRE-O-72/72	Nov 72 Mather+ LARGE LIQ SCINTILLATOR.	+
	1.2+7	1.4+7		Data	EXFOR20795.007	Oct 78 2PTS.SIGMA.	
(n,2n)	1.5+7		DEB	Eval Jour	REA 11 1 153	Mar 73 Boedy. COMPILATION+RECOMM.VALUE,TBL	
				Rept	IAEA-153 173	73 - . RECOMM. VALUE ONLY	
(n,2n)	+7		KFK	Expt Rept	KFK-1783 87	Apr 73 Muenzel+DETECTION LIMITS,2 ES,CFD TH	
				Jour	JIN 34 2989	Sep 72 Krivan+ SYSTEMATICS OF EXCITATION	
(n,2n)	1.3+7	1.5+7	AUB	Expt Abst	BAP 18 775	May 73 Alford+. SIGS AT 3ES GIVEN.	
(n,2n)	Fiss		KOS	Expt Jour	AK 16 351	74 Boedy. U238,MAXW-SPC.AVG CFD XPT,TBL	
(n,2n)	1.5+7		TAT	Theo Jour	JP/A 7 1457	Aug 74 Kondaiah. CALC ON STAT MODEL	
(n,2n)	8.0+6	2.0+7	LRL	Theo Conf	75Wash. 651	Mar 75 Gardner.CFD LLL EXPT.GRPH.	
(n,2n)	Fiss		KOS	Eval Conf	75Karlsrhe 29	Apr 75 Csikai. CF252,MAXW-SPC.AVG FOR 2TEMP	
(n,2n)	8.0+6	1.5+7	ANL	Eval Prog	ANL-75-34 182	Jun 75 Davey+CONSTANT T MDL,LVL DEN MDL FIT	
(n,2n)	8.4+6	2.0+7	BRC	Eval Rept	CEA-R-4712	Dec 74 Philis+EXP+STAT MDL ANAL,TBL,CURVES	
				Rept	CEA-N-1798 100	Jun 75 - + CURVES	
(n,2n)	8.7+6	2.8+7	LAS	Expt Jour	PR/C 12 451	Aug 75 Bayhurst+TBL,GRPH	+
	8.7+6	2.8+7		Data	EXFOR10536.	Apr 76 . 15 PTS. SIGMA.	
(n,2n)	+7		CCP	Expt Rept	YK-23 4	76 Brodskaja+ ACTIV,AVG SIG,TBL	

69 Thulium 169

Quantity	Energy (ev) Min	Max	Lab	Type	Documentation Ref Vol Page	Date	Author, Comments	Data
(n,2n)	1.5+7		JUL	Expt	Jour RRL 25 335	May 76	Qaim+ SIG IN GRPH. SYST VS (N−Z)/A	+
					Jour NP/A 224 319	May 74	− . ACT.GE(LI)	
◆	1.5+7				Data EXFOR20541.050	Apr 76	1PNT.SIGMA.	
(n,2n)	8.4+6	1.5+7	BRC	Expt	Jour NIM 135 511	Jun 76	Frehaut.GD LOADED SCIN.EXPT DETAILS.	+
					Conf 75Kiev 4 303	May 75	− + LIQSCIN.SIG(E),CFD.GRPH+TBL	
					Conf 75Wash. 855	Mar 75	− + TBL.GRPH.REL 238U(N,F)	
					Rept CEA−R−4627	Nov 74	− + LARGE LIQ SCINT METH 9 VAL	
	8.4+6	1.5+7			Data EXFOR20416.014	Jul 75	14PTS.SIGMA.	
(n,2n)	8.5+6	2.8+7	BRC	Theo	Conf 76Lowell 365	Jul 76	Frehaut.SYST.NT.CASCADE REACTIONS.	
(n,2n)	Thrsh	1.5+7	BRC	Expt	Conf 76Lowell 1350	Jul 76	Cindro+EXCIT FN CALC.CFD EXPT.NDG.	
(n,xn) x>2	1.5+7	2.0+7	LRL	Theo	Conf 75Wash. 651	Mar 75	Gardner.N3N.GRPH.CALC CFD LRL EXPT	
(n,xn) x>2	1.7+7	2.8+7	LAS	Expt	Jour PR/C 12 451	Aug 75	Bayhurst+N3N,N4N TBL,GRPH.CFD CALC.	+
	1.7+7	2.8+7			Data EXFOR10536.	Apr 76	. 11 PTS. N3N,2 PTS. N4N.	
(n,xn) x>2	None		LAS	Theo	Prog LA−6472 9	Aug 76	Arthur+GNASH CODE CALC.NDG.TBC.	
(n,p)	Fiss		CRC	Eval	Prog CRC−1003 30	Dec 60	ROY+ ESTIMATED AVG SIG=0.015MB.	
(n,p)	1.4+7		SAH	Comp	Jour NP 60 273	Nov 64	Chatterjee.MEAN OF EXPT CFD SHELLMOD	
(n,p)	Maxwl		IFU	Theo	Rept ICD−4 20	67	Dadakina+ PENETR COEFF CALC,TABLE	
(n,p)	1.4+7	1.5+7	ARK	Theo	Jour ORO−3235 29	Jan 67	Koch+,STAT MODEL CALC CFD EXPTS	
(n,p)	+7		CCP	Expt	Rept YK−23 4	76	Brodskaja+ ACTIV,AVG SIG,TBL	
(n,α)	Fiss		CRC	Eval	Prog CRC−1003 30	Dec 60	ROY+ ESTIMATED AVG SIG=0.0001MB.	
(n,α)	Maxwl		CCP	Expt	Jour YF 1 252	Feb 65	Andreev.IONIZ−CHAMBER,SIG=M.01MB	+
					Jour SNP 1 177	Aug 65	TRANSLATN.*	
(n,α)	1.4+7		IBJ	Expt	Jour NP/A 110 11	Mar 68	Jaskola+ ALFA SPCTR CFD TH,FULL PAPR	+
				Theo	Jour CJP 51 1765	Aug 73	Glowacka+KNOCK−ON EFF.TH CF XPT,GRPH	
				Expt	Rept INR−1268	Jan 71	SEE ALSO * FULL INFORMATION	
					Jour APPB 2 521	71	.SAME AS INR−1268	
	1.4+7				Data EXFOR30158.024	Mar 71	NUM DATA NOT AVAILBL,SEE GRAF IN REF	
(n,α)	1.4+7		DUB	Theo	Rept JINR−P4−6832	Dec 72	Kozlowski.DEFORMD NUC STRUCTURE,GRPH	
(n,α)	1.4+7	1.5+7	CIS	Theo	Jour NP/A 210 297	Aug 73	Milazzo−Colli+ ALPHA E−DISTN CFD XPT	
	1.4+7				Jour PL/B 38 155	Feb 72	Colli−Milazzo+ A−SPECT CALC CFD EXPT	
(n,α)	1.8+7		IBJ	Expt	Jour NP/A 244 117	Jun 75	Glowacka+ ALF E−SPEC CFD MODLS,GRAPH	+
					Prog INDC(SEC)−42	Dec 74	− + TBL DIFFSIG,GRPH E+ANG−DIS	
	1.8+7				Data EXFOR30299.	Jul 75	DOUBLE DIFFSIG(38 PTS)+ANGDIST(1 PT)	
(n,α)	+7		CCP	Expt	Rept YK−23 4	76	Brodskaja+ ACTIV,AVG SIG,TBL	
(n,α)	1.9+7		BRC	Theo	Conf 76Lowell 347	Jul 76	Cindro.N−INDUCED REAC.MED.−HVY.NUCL.	
Reson Params	3.9+0	1.8+1	BNL	Expt	Jour PR 92 656	Nov 53	Foote+	+
	3.9+0	1.8+1			Data EXFOR12107.006	Jun 76	. 3 RES,WT**2./PCS	
Reson Params	3.9+0		BNL	Expt	Jour PR 96 1014	Nov 54	Sailor+ CRYST SPEC, RSLN .03 EV	+
Reson Params	3.9+0	1.6+2	BNL	Expt	Jour PR 99 10	Jul 55	Harvey+.FC TRANSM. 17 RES. AREA ANAL	+
	3.9+0	1.6+2			Data EXFOR11912.054	Jun 76	. 17 RES,E0,WN,WN0.	
Reson Params	+0	+2	BNL	Expt	Prog WASH−745	Nov 57	Hughes. FC NDG	
Reson Params	4.5+1	4.5+1	HAR	Expt	Prog AERE−PR/NP4 2	May 63	Corvi+ 45EV RESONANCE PARAMETERS.	+
		1.6+2			Prog AERE−PR/NP3 20	Sep 62	Pattenden+16LVLS CF BNL PR V99 P10	
		4.5+1		Revw	Prog AERE−PR/NP3 21	Sep 62	Corvi.7LVLS NDG	
Reson Params	3.9+0		MOL	Expt	Jour NP 62 481	Feb 65	Ceulemans+J=1 FROM GAMMA(N)/GAMMA	+
	3.9+0				Data EXFOR20208.	May 74	2PTS.J,WN/WT.	
Reson Params	1.7+1		HAR	Expt	Jour NIM 39 68	Jan 66	Asghar+ WN VERSUS WT J=0,1 FROM SCT	+
	1.4+1	3.0+2			Conf 65Antwerp 522	Jul 65	− + PPR65. TBL RES PARS.	
	1.0+1	4.3+2			Rept AERE−NP/GEN40	Jun 65	− +LI−6 DET. SCAT EXPT.FOR RES	
	1.0+1	3.0+2			Rept AERE−R−4131 25	Sep 62	Brooks. AERE TOF NDG	
Reson Params	3.9+0		BNL	Expt	Jour NP/A 91 644	Feb 67	Al−Kital+ J=1 POLARIZED N AND TARGET	
Reson Params		1.0+6	AUA	Theo	Jour AUJ 20 477	Oct 67	Cook. TBL OF AVG LVL SPACING D,L=0,1	
Reson Params	3.9+0	7.7+2	SAC	Expt	Jour IAN 131 305	Jun 69	De Barros+ LINAC.SAME DATA CEA−R3385	
	3.9+0	7.6+2			Conf 68Wash. 867	Mar 68	Morgenstern.WG VS.A.AVG WG GIVEN	
					Rept CEA−R−3385	Feb 68	Julien+ PARS,ANAL.WN.DIST.S VS J.	
					Rept CEA−R−3077	Dec 67	De Barros.TBL WN,WG,W,SPINS.	
	3.9+0	7.7+2			Conf 66Paris 1 193	Oct 66	− + LVL SPAC.SEE ALSO P559.	
	3.9+0	7.6+2			Conf 65Antwerp 525	Jul 65	− + PPR73.ABST.NDG	
					Jour JPR 24 994	Nov 63	Bianchi+LIST RES ENS.SUPERSEDED.	
	0.0+0	7.6+2			Data EXFOR20685.	Jul 77	96PTS.E0,WG,AVG WG,WN,WT,J,G*WN.	
Reson Params	3.9+0	8.3+1	BNL	Expt	Jour PR 174 1512	Oct 68	Chrien+ J+PARTIAL WG FROM N,G	
					Jour PRL 20 342	Feb 68	− +6. CORRELATION OF WN,WG	
Reson Params	+3	+5	AUA	ExTh	Rept AAEC/E−198	May 69	Musgrove.RES PARS +STF FROM (NG)FIT	+
Reson Params	None		BNL	Eval	Conf 69Studsvik 627	Aug 69	Chrien. WG/WN−CORREL,WG CFD P−T,TBLS	
Reson Params	2.0+0	7.6+2	RIO	Expt	Jour NDF 15 167	Aug 69	Barros+ 95RESON,WN+WG+SPIN+D,TBL+CRV	
Reson Params	−		AUA	Theo	Rept AAEC/E−211	Nov 70	Musgrove. CALCULTD D+GAM WIDTH GIVEN	
Reson Params	1.4+1	1.2+2	BNL	Expt	Jour PR/C 2 2030	Nov 70	Bhat+,J FOR 13RESON FROM CAPT SPECT	

69 Thulium 169

Quantity	Energy (ev) Min	Max	Lab	Type	Documentation Ref Vol Page	Author, Comments Date	Data
Reson Params	3.9+0	7.4+2	CJD	Eval	Rept YK-7	71 Zakharova+ SURVEY+SYSTEMATICS,GW,TBL	
					Rept INDC(CCP)-27	Nov 72 .ENGLISH TRANSLATION OF YK-7 /71	
Reson Params	3.9+0		CNA	Expt	Prog EANDC(OR)100	Jan 71 Cansoy.NEW ANALYS,TBL,TBP CNAEM-76	+
	3.9+0				Data EXFOR20174.006	May 74 1PNT.S0*(WT)2.	
Reson Params	None		DUB	Theo	Jour YF 13 240	Feb 71 Malecki+G - WID,THEO CFD EXPT.TBL,GRPH	
					Jour SNP 13 133	Aug 71 - + ENGL OF YF 13 240.	
Reson Params	3.9+0	1.9+3	SAC	Expt	Conf 71Knoxvill 680	Mar 71 Tellier+ TRANSM.LINAC.	+
					Rept CEA-N-1563	Oct 72 - + D,S0,WN,WG ANALYSIS.	
					Conf 72Budapest 38	Aug 72 - + ABST.NDG	
					Priv TELLIER	Feb 72 - +.	
	3.9+0	1.9+3			Data EXFOR20124.	Sep 72 775PTS.E0,WG,AVG WG,WT,J,2G*WN,- -	
Reson Params	3.9+0	7.2+2	BNL	Expt	Prog ORNL-4743 79	Dec 71 Chrien+ J VALUES FOR 68 RESON,ORELA	+
	3.9+0	7.2+2			Data EXFOR10483.002	Apr 75 .68 RES.J.	
Reson Params	1.4+1	1.5+2	HAR	Expt	Prog AERE-PR/NP18	Mar 72 Thomas+ J ASSIGNED FROM CAPT GS TBL	+
					Conf 71Albany 251	Aug 71 - .SPIN ASSIGN.INT CORR WITH WN.	
	1.4+1	1.5+2			Data EXFOR20451.004	Jan 76 13PTS.J.	
Reson Params	3.9+0	2.1+3	COL	Expt	Prog COO-2176-20 8	Jun 73 Arbo+.CAPT AREAS+DIST.TABLES+CURVES.	
Reson Params	None		LIE	Theo	Jour NP/A 222 525	Apr 74 Baudinet-Robinet.STAT CORR PART WID	
Reson Params	3.9+0	1.6+2	CRC	Expt	Abst BAP 8 334	Apr 63 Singh.	+
	3.9+0	1.6+2			Data EXFOR11942.003	Jun 76 . 20 RES, E0,J	
Reson Params	Maxwl		KUK	Theo	Conf 76Ahmedabd 2 1	Dec 76 Sharma+AVG S-WAVE REDUCED N-WID ANAL	
Strnth Fnctn	+3		BNL	Expt	Jour PRL 1 461	Dec 58 Hughes. FC 1.6+-0.3	
Strnth Fnctn	1.0+4	2.0+5	ORL	Expt	Jour PR 122 182	Apr 61 Gibbons+	+
	1.0+4	2.0+5			Data EXFOR11329.	Jun 76 . 3 PTS, STF,D,AVE WG	
Strnth Fnctn	3.9+0	7.7+2	SAC	Expt	Jour NP/A 131 305	Jun 69 De Barros+S0(S,P)SAME DATA CEA-R3385	+
	3.9+0	7.6+2			Rept CEA-R-3609	Sep 68 Morgenstern.S-WAVE,RADIUS	
					Conf 68Wash. 867	Mar 68 - + PPR E27. BRIEF REPORT	
					Rept CEA-R-3385	Feb 68 Julien. (THESIS).SEE ALSO.S0 VS J.	
					Rept CEA-R-3077	Dec 67 De Barros.S+P WV.S0=1.5+-0.4(10-4)	
	0.0+0	7.6+2			Data EXFOR20685.012	Jul 77 1PNT.L=0.	
Strnth Fnctn	+3	+5	AUA	ExTh	Rept AAEC/E-198	May 69 Musgrove.S+P+D STF FROM (NG)FIT,TBL	+
Strnth Fnctn	2.0+0	7.6+2	RIO	Expt	Jour NDF 15 167	Aug 69 Barros+ S0 VALUE +- ERROR GVN	
Strnth Fnctn	-		DUB	Revw	Jour YF 11 111	Jan 70 Malecki+ VALUES FOR TWO SPIN STATES	
					Jour SNP 11 61	Jul 70 - + ENGL OF YF 11 61.	
Strnth Fnctn	-		AUA	Theo	Rept AAEC/E-211	Nov 70 Musgrove. SMOOTHED S0,S1 AND S2 GIVN	
Strnth Fnctn	1.0+1	1.9+3	SAC	Expt	Conf 72Budapest 38	Aug 72 Tellier+S-WAVE STRENGTHFUNCTION	+
	1.2+3	8.0+4			Rept CEA-N-1563	Oct 72 - + D,S0,WN,WG ANALYSIS.	
					Priv TELLIER	Feb 72 - + VALUES FOR COMPILATION.	
	1.0+1	1.9+3			Conf 71Knoxvill 680	Mar 71 - +. S0=1.3+-0.4 PRELIMINARY	
	1.2+3	8.0+4			Data EXFOR20124.	Sep 72 4PTS.L=0.	
Strnth Fnctn	None		AUA	Eval	Rept AAEC/E-277	Mar 73 Musgrove.TBLS EXPTL DATA+BEST VALUES	
Strnth Fnctn	2.0+3		IJI	Expt	Conf 76Lowell 1244	Jul 76 Vertebnyi+ S0 GVN.FROM TOT,SCAT-DATA	
Strnth Fnctn	2.7+3		MUN	Expt	Conf 71Albany 327	Aug 76 Dilg+TRNS.S0 STF GVN.31 ELEMENT GRPH	
Lvl Density	-		COP	Theo	Jour NP 6 62	Mar 58 Ericson. LVL DENSITY FORM CFD EXP	
Lvl Density	1.4+7		IBJ	Expt	Jour NP/A 110 11	Mar 68 Jaskola+ ALFA SPCTR CFD TH,FULL PAPR	+
					Rept INR-1268	Jan 71 SEE ALSO * FULL INFORMATION	
					Jour APPB 2 521	71 .SAME AS INR-1268	
	1.4+7				Data EXFOR30158.025	Mar 71 LEVEL DENSITY PARAMETER OF HO166 GIV	
Lvl Density	None		AUW	Theo	Conf 70Madurai 2 267	Dec 70 Ramamurty+ A-PARAMETER GVN,LANG'S-TH	
Lvl Density	None		DUB	Theo	Rept JINR-P4-8102	Jul 74 Malov+ SEMI-MICROSC CALC OKS XPT,TBL	
					Rept UCRL-TR-10845	Apr 75 . ENGL OF JINR-P4-8102	

69 Thulium 170

Quantity	Energy (ev) Min	Max	Lab	Type	Documentation Ref Vol Page	Author, Comments Date	Data
Total	1.0+0	1.0+2	MTR	Expt	Prog WASH-1136 44	Sep 69 Stokes+,FAST CHOPPER,TRANS,CURVES	+
	5.0-2	1.0+2			Data EXFOR10405.002	Sep 74 . 394 PTS. SIGMA.	
Absorption	Pile		MTR	Expt	Prog WASH-192 36	Mar 57 Reeder+ 150+-20B.	
Absorption	2.5-2		IJI	Eval	Conf 75Kiev 1 169	May 75 Fedorova+ EVAL 2200M/S SIG,TABLE	
Res Int Abs	5.4-1		ORL	Expt	Prog ORNL-4155 15	Aug 67 Gillette+	+
	5.4-1				Data EXFOR10259.009	Jul 74 . 1 PT. SIGMA.	
Res Int Abs	1.0+0	1.0+2	MTR	Expt	Prog WASH-1136 44	Sep 69 Stokes+,VALUE GIVEN	
(n,γ)	Pile		GOE	Expt	Jour ZP 149 215	Oct 57 Houtermans.110+-10B CO 60 STD=36B	
(n,γ)	1.4+7		ROM	Expt	Jour NCS 370	Sep 63 Giannini+LVLS.EXCITED IN CAPTURE NDG	
(n,γ)	Maxwl		ORL	Expt	Prog ORNL-4155 15	Aug 67 Gillette+	+
	Maxwl				Data EXFOR10259.003	Jul 74 . 1 PT. SIGMA.	
(n,γ)	Pile		JAP	Expt	Jour JPJ 31 1304	Nov 71 Miyano.160B IN HIGH FLUX PILE	

69 Thulium 170

Quantity	Energy (ev) Min	Max	Lab	Type	Documentation Ref Vol Page	Author, Comments Date	Data
Spect (n,γ)	None		ANL	Expt Abst	BAP 13 721	Apr 68 Bollinger+.RATIO AV WG FOR M1,E1	
(n,p)	Maxwl		IFU	Theo Rept	ICD-4 20	67 Dadakina+ PENETR COEFF CALC,TABLE	
Reson Params	–		AUA	Theo Rept	AAEC/E-211	Nov 70 Musgrove. CALCULTD D+GAM WIDTH GIVEN	
Reson Params	2.8+0	9.0+1	MTR	Expt Prog	WASH-1136 44	Sep 69 Stokes+,WN+WG FOR 13RES FROM TOT SIG	+
	2.8+0	9.0+1		Data	EXFOR10405.	Sep 74 . 14 RES. 4 RES. WN,WG.	
Strnth Fnctn	2.8+0	9.0+1	MTR	Expt Prog	WASH-1136 44	Sep 69 Stokes+,VALUE GIVEN	
Strnth Fnctn	–		AUA	Theo Rept	AAEC/E-211	Nov 70 Musgrove. SMOOTHED S0,S1 AND S2 GIVN	
Strnth Fnctn	None		AUA	Eval Rept	AAEC/E-277	Mar 73 Musgrove.TBLS EXPTL DATA+BEST VALUES	
Lvl Density	+6		MIL	Theo Jour	EN 15 1 54	Jan 68 Facchini+ LDL PARS FROM LOW EN RES	
Lvl Density	None		MUN	Theo Jour	NP/A 217 269	Dec 73 Dilg+ A,DELTA. BACK SHIFTED FERMIGAS	
Lvl Density	None		COP	Theo Jour	NP/A 222 493	Apr 74 Dossing+COLL ROTAT.SPAC. ACCUR ESTIM	
Lvl Density	None		ROC	Theo Jour	NP/A 223 589	May 74 Huizenga+ EXP CFD MICROSC TH AX SYMM	

69 Thulium 171

Quantity	Energy (ev) Min	Max	Lab	Type	Documentation Ref Vol Page	Author, Comments Date	Data
Total	5.0-2	1.0+2	MTR	Expt Priv	STOKES	Apr 74 Stokes+ MTR CHOPPER	+
	5.0-2	1.0+2		Data	EXFOR10405.003	Sep 74 . 347 PTS. SIGMA.	
Absorption	2.5-2		IJI	Eval Conf	75Kiev 1 169	May 75 Fedorova+ EVAL 2200M/S SIG,TABLE	
Res Int Abs	5.4-1		ORL	Expt Prog	ORNL-4155 15	Aug 67 Gillette+	+
	5.4-1			Data	EXFOR10259.010	Jul 74 . 1 PT. SIGMA.	
(n,γ)	Maxwl		ORL	Expt Prog	ORNL-4155 15	Aug 67 Gillette+	+
	Maxwl			Data	EXFOR10259.004	Jul 74 . 1 PT. SIGMA.	
Reson Params	–		AUA	Theo Rept	AAEC/E-211	Nov 70 Musgrove. CALCULTD D+GAM WIDTH GIVEN	
Reson Params	4.9+0	6.4+1	MTR	Expt Priv	STOKES	Apr 74 Stokes+ MTR CHOPPER	+
	4.9+0	6.4+1		Data	EXFOR10405.	Sep 74 . 4 RES,WN,.1RES,WG.	
Strnth Fnctn	–		AUA	Theo Rept	AAEC/E-211	Nov 70 Musgrove. SMOOTHED S0,S1 AND S2 GIVN	

69 Thulium 172

Quantity	Energy (ev) Min	Max	Lab	Type	Documentation Ref Vol Page	Author, Comments Date	Data
Reson Params	–		AUA	Theo Rept	AAEC/E-211	Nov 70 Musgrove. CALCULTD D+GAM WIDTH GIVEN	
Strnth Fnctn	–		AUA	Theo Rept	AAEC/E-211	Nov 70 Musgrove. SMOOTHED S0,S1 AND S2 GIVN	

69 Thulium 173

Quantity	Energy (ev) Min	Max	Lab	Type	Documentation Ref Vol Page	Author, Comments Date	Data
Reson Params	–		AUA	Theo Rept	AAEC/E-211	Nov 70 Musgrove. CALCULTD D+GAM WIDTH GIVEN	
Strnth Fnctn	–		AUA	Theo Rept	AAEC/E-211	Nov 70 Musgrove. SMOOTHED S0,S1 AND S2 GIVN	

69 Thulium 174

Quantity	Energy (ev) Min	Max	Lab	Type	Documentation Ref Vol Page	Author, Comments Date	Data
Reson Params	–		AUA	Theo Rept	AAEC/E-211	Nov 70 Musgrove. CALCULTD D+GAM WIDTH GIVEN	
Strnth Fnctn	–		AUA	Theo Rept	AAEC/E-211	Nov 70 Musgrove. SMOOTHED S0,S1 AND S2 GIVN	

69 Thulium 175

Quantity	Energy (ev) Min	Max	Lab	Type	Documentation Ref Vol Page	Author, Comments Date	Data
Reson Params	–		AUA	Theo Rept	AAEC/E-211	Nov 70 Musgrove. CALCULTD D+GAM WIDTH GIVEN	
Strnth Fnctn	–		AUA	Theo Rept	AAEC/E-211	Nov 70 Musgrove. SMOOTHED S0,S1 AND S2 GIVN	

70 Ytterbium

Quantity	Energy (ev) Min	Max	Lab	Type	Documentation Ref Vol Page	Author, Comments Date	Data
Evaluation	5.0+5	1.5+7	LRL Eval	Rept	UCRL-5351	Nov 58 Howerton. CURVS.	
Total	Maxwl		COL Expt	Jour	PR 48 265	Aug 35 Dunning+ IONCH,TRANS,RA-BE/PARAFIN N	
Total	6.0+4	3.0+6	WIS Expt	Jour	PR 93 461	Feb 54 Okazaki+ TRANS AVG OVER RESON OKS TH	+
	5.0+4	2.9+6		Data	EXFOR12061.005	Jun 76 . 43 PTS. SIGMA	
Total	1.5-1	2.9+1	BNL Expt	Jour	PR 96 1014	Nov 54 Sailor+ CRYSTAL SPECTROMETER MEAS.	+
	1.5-1	2.9+1		Data	EXFOR12110.005	Jun 76 . 96 PTS. SIGMA	
Total	1.0+3	3.2+4	HAR Expt	Jour	PPSA 70 51	Jan 57 Gayther+ FC THICK SAMPLE,AVSIG CF TH	
Total	4.0+2	2.0+3	HAR Theo	Jour	PPS 71 910	Jun 58 Egelstaff.FLUCTUATIONS CFD THEORY	
Total	7.4-2		ISU Expt	Jour	PR 121 610	Jan 61 Atoji. TRANSMISSION 48.5+ -0.3 B	
Total	2.5-3	2.4-1	BSP Expt	Conf	66Paris 1 53	Oct 66 Zimmerman+,P.129,SIG(E)CURVE,THR SIG	+
				Jour	NP/A 95 683	Apr 67 SEE ALSO *	
	1.8-3	4.1-1		Data	EXFOR30224.	Dec 72 SIG AT 40ES, SIG AT 0.025 EV,PRIVCOM	
Total	2.5-2		BNL Expt	Jour	PR 174 1400	Oct 68 Mughabghab+ TRANS SIG=67.6+ -2.0B.	+
	2.5-2			Data	EXFOR12130.002	Jun 76 . 1 PT. SIGMA	
Total	2.5+6	1.5+7	BNW Expt	Jour	PR/C 3 576	Feb 71 Foster+,TRANS,CURVS,CFD OTHERS+TH	+
				Jour	NIM 36 1	Sep 65 .EXPT DETAILS	
	2.5+6	1.5+7		Data	EXFOR10047.074	Aug 73 . 231 PTS.	
Total	2.7+3		MUN Expt	Prog	EANDC(E)150U	Oct 72 Dilg+ AVERAGE TOT XSECT+S0	+
				Conf	71Albany 327	Aug 71 - +TRNS.AVG CS GVN.31 ELEMENT GRP	
	2.7+3			Data	EXFOR20583.024	Jun 76 1PNT.	
Total	1.3+7	1.5+7	DEB Eval	Rept	IAEA-153 173	73 Boedy+ MOST PROBABLE VAL OF SIG,TBL	
				Jour	AHP 30 115	Oct 72 Angeli+ AVG SIG,CFD CALC.TBLS.GRAPH	
Total	1.0+0	2.0+4	COL Expt	Jour	PR/C 7 823	Feb 73 Liou+TRNS.TOF.RES PAR ANAL.NO CS GVN	+
	6.0+0	3.7+2		Rept	NYO-72-190	68 - .TOF.TRNS.SELF INDIC.	
	None			Data	EXFOR10081.065	Jan 78 .RAW DATA GVN UPON REQUEST TO NNDC.	
Total	7.0+5	9.0+6	GLS Expt	Jour	JP/A 7 1758	Sep 74 Kellie+ SIG IN CURVE,STAT ERROR 2 PC	+
	7.0+5	9.0+6		Data	EXFOR20418.011	Sep 75 642PTS.	
Elastic	7.3-2		ISU Expt	Jour	PR 121 610	Jan 61 Atoji. 30 B SCHOL=20.0+ -0.4 B	+
	7.3-2			Data	EXFOR12113.	Jun 76 . 2 PTS. COH, COH AMP.	
Elastic	7.5-2		ANL Expt	Jour	JCP 35 1950	Dec 61 Atoji.SCAT.AMPL.=1.262X10-12CM+ -.012	+
	7.5-2			Data	EXFOR11606.007	Jun 76 . 1 PT, COH SCAT.	
Elastic	1.0+6		ALD Expt	Jour	NP 42 86	Apr 63 Gilboy+.SIG=6.54B+ -3PC	
Elastic	3.0+5	1.5+6	ANL Expt	Rept	EANDC(US)-62	Jun 64 Smith.TOF,TBL.50KEV STEPS,20KEV RSLN	+
	3.0+5	1.5+6		Data	EXFOR12039.005	Jun 76 . 24 PTS. SIGMA	
Elastic	9.8+5		AGN Eval	Rept	TID-21629	Dec 64 Perkins+ CALC FRM BNL400,UCRL5573	
Elastic	1.5+6		IFU Expt	Prog	YFI-5 42	Oct 67 Korzh+ TBL OPTMDL PARAMS + TOTELAST	
				Rept	INDC-232E	67 . ENGL OF YFI-5 42	
Elastic	1.5+6		IFU Comp	Jour	YF 7 277	Feb 68 Korzh+ OPTMOD PARS-FIT TO EXPTL-SIG	
				Jour	SNP 7 2 190	Aug 68 TRANSLATN.*	
Elastic	2.5-2	4.1+0	IFU Expt	Prog	YFI-7 41	Apr 69 Vertebny+ SIGMA AT 54 NEUT-ES,TABLE	
				Rept	INDC(CCP)-7U44	Feb 70 TRANSLATN.*	
Diff Elastic	1.0+6		ALD Expt	Jour	NP 42 86	Apr 63 Gilboy+30TO137DEG.COMP.WITH OPTICMOD	+
Diff Elastic	3.0+5	1.5+6	ANL Expt	Rept	EANDC(US)-62	Jun 64 Smith.TOF,TBL LEGEND COEF LAB SYSTEM	+
	3.0+5	1.5+6		Data	EXFOR12039.004	Jun 76 . 120 PTS. DSIGMA AT 24 ES.	
Diff Elastic	9.8+5		AGN Eval	Rept	TID-21629	Dec 64 Perkins+ LEG.COEF CALC OTHER DATA	
Diff Elastic	1.5+6		IFU Comp	Jour	YF 7 277	Feb 68 Korzh+ GRPH SIG(ANG),OPTMOD PARS-FIT	
				Jour	SNP 7 2 190	Aug 68 TRANSLATN.*	
Diff Elastic	3.0+5	1.5+6	ANL Expt	Prog	WASH-1093 1	Apr 68 Smith+ TOF TBC NDG NEAR COMPLETION	
Potntal Scat	Maxwl		MUU Theo	Jour	ZN/A 11 757	Sep 56 Kenschitzki+NO SPIN ORBIT COUPLIND	
Potntal Scat	+4		HAR Expt	Jour	PPSA 70 51	Jan 57 Gayther+ FROM AVG SIGTOT. FC TRANSM	
Potntal Scat	None		BNL Expt	Abst	BAP 11 29	Jan 66 Mughabghab+R.RADIUS PAR.=7.8F SIGTOT	
Tot Inelastc	5.0+6	7.0+6	ALD Expt	Jour	NP/A 112 337	May 68 Owens+.3ES.FROM N SPECT 90DEG.	+
Diff Inelast	3.0+5	1.5+6	ANL Expt	Prog	WASH-1093 1	Apr 68 Smith+ TOF TBC NDG NEAR COMPLETION	
Diff Inelast	5.0+6	7.0+6	ALD Expt	Jour	NP/A 112 337	May 68 Owens+.3ES.FROM N SPECT 90DEG NDG.	+
				Conf	65Antwerp 547	Jul 65 - + PPR122.ABST.SPECT N' AT 90DEG	
Thermal Scat	2.0-4	1.5-1	BSP ExTh	Jour	JCP 48 520	Jan 68 Mattos.,TRIVALENT ION PARAMAG SIG	+
				Jour	NP/A 95 683	Apr 67 SEE ALSO * SAME CURVE.	
Thermal Scat	2.5-2		BNL Expt	Jour	PR 174 1400	Oct 68 Mughabghab+ PARAMAGN SIG=5.2+ -0.9B.	
Thermal Scat	2.0-2	1.4+0	IJI Expt	Prog	YFI-12 67	72 Vertebny+ ABST,TOT SCAT SIG 15ES,TBL	
				Prog	INDC(CCP)-30	Sep 72 .PAGE 58,ENGLISH OF YFI-12 67	
Thermal Scat	1.0-4	1.0+3	MUN Revw	Jour	EEN 80 1	77 Koester. SCAT LENGTH,FREE SIG	
Scattering	7.3-2		ISU Expt	Jour	PR 121 610	Jan 61 Atoji.	+
	7.3-2			Data	EXFOR12113.006	Jun 76 . 1 PT, SIG.	
Scattering	2.5-2		BSP Expt	Conf	66Paris 1 53	Oct 66 Zimmerman+,P.129,DEDUCED SIG(.025EV)	
				Jour	NP/A 95 683	Apr 67 SEE ALSO *	
				Conf	64Geneva 7 82	May 64 SEE ALSO *P.118	
	2.5-2			Data	EXFOR30224.019	Dec 72 DEDUCED SIGMA	

70 Ytterbium

Quantity	Energy (ev) Min	Max	Lab	Type	Documentation Ref Vol Page	Author, Comments Date	Data
Scattering	2.5−2		BNL Expt	Jour	PR 174 1400	Oct 68 Mughabghab+ TRANS SIG=25.6+ −3.5B.	
Scattering	2.5−2	4.1+0	IFU Expt	Prog	YFI−7 41	Apr 69 Vertebny+	+
	2.5−2	4.1+0		Data	EXFOR40048.002	Aug 70 INTEGRAL SIGMA AT 54 ENERGIES	
Scattering	2.0−2	3.0−2	IFU Expt	Conf	70Helsinki 1 651	Jun 70 Vertebnij+ 2200M/SEC SIGMA GIVEN,TBL	
				Rept	BNL−TR−495	Jul 72 . ENGLISH OF 70HELSIN 1 651	
Absorption	2.5−2		BNL Expt	Jour	PR 174 1400	Oct 68 Mughabghab+ TRANS SIG=36.8+ −4.1B.	
Res Int Abs	5.0−1		MTR Expt	Rept	IN− 1195 14	May 68 Scoville. RI=195+ −10MEAS.129CALC.	+
				Jour	ANS 8 290	Jun 65 .SUPERSEDED	
	5.0−1			Data	EXFOR11820.015	Jun 76 . 1 PT. R.I.	
Res Int Abs	−1	+3	BNL Expt	Jour	PR 174 1400	Oct 68 Mughabghab+TRNS177+ −24B FRM SEP ISOT	
(n,γ)	Maxwl		ORL Expt	Jour	PR 83 641	Aug 51 Pomerance.LOCAL OSC REL AU ABS 95	+
	Maxwl			Data	EXFOR11047.054	Jun 76 . 1 PT. SIGMA	
(n,γ)	9.5+3	1.7+5	ORL Expt	Jour	PR 122 182	Apr 61 Gibbons+575,170MB AND 390MB AT 65KEV	+
	3.0+4	6.5+4		Jour	PR 129 2695	Mar 63 Macklin+ LIQ SCINT,575 AND 390MB	
	3.0+4	1.7+5		Conf	61Vienna 1 95	Aug 61 Neiler.	
				Prog	BNL−653	Feb 61 .SUPERSEDED	
	3.0+4	1.7+5		Data	EXFOR11329.	Jun 76 . 51 PTS. SIGMA	
(n,γ)	2.0+2	8.0+3	ORL Expt	Conf	61Saclay 203	Sep 61 Block+.LIQUID SCINTILLATOR	+
				Conf	61Vienna 1 95	Aug 61 Neiler.PPR73,TABLE FOR SOME ES,GRAPH	
	2.0+2	5.9+3		Data	EXFOR11935.018	Jun 76 . 41 PTS. SIGMA	
(n,γ)	5.0+3	9.0+4	ORL Theo	Jour	RMP 37 166	Jan 65 Macklin+.CALC FOR KT=5TO90KEV	
(n,γ)	2.5−2		BSP Expt	Conf	66Paris 1 53	Oct 66 Zimmerman+,P.129,DEDUCED SIG(.025EV)	+
				Jour	NP/A 95 683	Apr 67 SEE ALSO *	
				Conf	64Geneva 7 82	May 64 SEE ALSO *P.118	
	2.5−2			Data	EXFOR30224.020	Dec 72 DEDUCED SIGMA	
(n,γ)	3.0+4		AUA Theo	Rept	AAEC/E−211	Nov 70 Musgrove. SIGMA GIVEN AND CFD OTHER	
(n,γ)	8.1+0	2.0+2	NRL Expt	Jour	NP/A 173 477	Oct 71 Ritter+ LINAC TOF. TOF SPECTRUM.	
(n,γ)	3.0+4	1.6+5	USP Expt	Jour	NP/A 196 83	Nov 72 Lepine+ LI7−P NS.TOF.M−R. REL TO IN	+
	3.0+4	1.6+5		Data	EXFOR30233.009	Mar 73 NDS,RELATIVE TO IN,ABSOLUTE ERROR	
(n,γ)	5.0+3	8.0+4	FEI Expt	Jour	YF 20 1092	Dec 74 Shorin+ SIG(E) CFD H−F,OTHERS,GRAPH	
				Jour	SNP 20 572	Jun 75 . ENGLISH OF YF 20 1092	
Spect (n,γ)	Maxwl		ARF Expt	Prog	ARF−1193−9	Apr 62 Greenwood+,CRYST SPEC,LOW−E GAMMAS	
Spect (n,γ)	Maxwl		CAS Expt	Jour	NC 27 1032	Feb 63 Giannini+ NA−I,E+INTENSITY TO173 KEV	+
Spect (n,γ)	1.4+7	1.5+7	HLS Expt	Jour	ZP 204 456	Aug 67 Kantele+,YB−OXYD IRRADIATED	
Spect (n,γ)	+0	+4	COL Expt	Prog	WASH−1124 31	Nov 68 Camarda+ MOXON−RAE DET TBC NO DATA	
Spect (n,γ)	2.5−2		MIT Comp	Rept	MITNE−85	Jan 69 Rasmussen+TBL G INT.=AFCRL−69−0071	
Spect (n,γ)	Pile		ANL Expt	Prog	WASH−1127 10	Apr 69 Bollinger+ LVL STRUCTRE ONLY,TBC,NDG	
Spect (n,γ)	Maxwl		INL Expt	Jour	NP/A 252 260	Nov 75 Greenwood+.LVL STRUCTURE TO 171YB EXPT	
Inelastic γ	5.0+6	7.0+6	ALD Expt	Jour	NP/A 112 337	May 68 Owens+.3ES.TOF SPECT 90 DEG. PLOT.	+
(n,2n)	1.5+7		DEB Eval	Jour	REA 11 1 153	Mar 73 Boedy+ RECOMM.VALUE FROM N−Z SYSTEM.	
Reson Params	6.0−1	1.8+1	BNL Expt	Jour	PR 96 1014	Nov 54 Sailor+	+
	6.0−1	1.8+1		Data	EXFOR12110.015	Jun 76 . 5 RES, E0,WT**2/PCS.	
Reson Params	4.5+0	1.5+2	DUB Expt	Jour	YF 3 1 48	Jan 66 Wang Nai Yang+ TRANS.CHOP.TBL.	
				Rept	JINR−P−2158	Jun 65 Wang Nai−Yang+ 42RES,TBL	
				Jour	SNP 3 34	Jul 66 Wang Nai Yang+ ENGL OF YF 3 48.	
Reson Params	1.0+0	2.0+5	COL Expt	Jour	PR/C 7 823	Feb 73 Liou+TRNS.TOF.ISOTOPE RES PAR ANAL.	
Strnth Fnctn	+4		HAR Expt	Jour	PPSA 70 51	Jan 57 Gayther+ FROM AVG SIGTOT. FC TRANSM	
Strnth Fnctn	2.7+3		MUN Expt	Conf	71Albany 327	Aug 76 Dilg+TRNS.S0 STF GVN.31 ELEMENT GRPH	
Lvl Density	5.0+6	7.0+6	ALD Expt	Jour	NP/A 112 337	May 68 Owens+.LVL DENS VERSUS EXCIT.MEAN T	+
				Conf	65Antwerp 547	Jul 65 − + PPR122. TBL FERMI GAS CONST.	
Lvl Density	None		FEI Theo	Jour	YF 11 1213	Jun 70 Ignatyuk+ SPIN DEPENDENCE OF DENSITY	
				Jour	SNP 11 674	Dec 70 . ENGL OF YF 11 1213	

70 Ytterbium 165

Quantity	Energy (ev) Min	Max	Lab	Type	Documentation Ref Vol Page	Author, Comments Date	Data
Reson Params	−		AUA Theo	Rept	AAEC/E−211	Nov 70 Musgrove. CALCULTD D+GAM WIDTH GIVEN	
Strnth Fnctn	−		AUA Theo	Rept	AAEC/E−211	Nov 70 Musgrove. SMOOTHED S0,S1 AND S2 GIVN	

70 Ytterbium 166

Quantity	Energy (ev) Min	Max	Lab	Type	Documentation Ref Vol Page	Author, Comments Date	Data
(n,p)	Maxwl		IFU Theo	Rept	ICD−4 20	67 Dadakina+ PENETR COEFF CALC,TABLE	
Reson Params	−		AUA Theo	Rept	AAEC/E−211	Nov 70 Musgrove. CALCULTD D+GAM WIDTH GIVEN	
Strnth Fnctn	−		AUA Theo	Rept	AAEC/E−211	Nov 70 Musgrove. SMOOTHED S0,S1 AND S2 GIVN	

70 Ytterbium 166

Quantity	Energy (ev) Min	Max	Lab	Type	Documentation Ref Vol Page	Date	Author, Comments	Data
Lvl Density	−3	+0	IFU	Theo	Jour UFZ 13 700	Apr 68	Pisanko+ LEVEL SPACING CALC,TBL	
					Jour UPJ 13 498	Oct 68	TRANSLATN.*	
Lvl Density	None		CCP	Theo	Jour YF 13 43	Jan 71	Bravin+.DEFORM PAR,CALC,TBL,CFD EXPT	

70 Ytterbium 167

Quantity	Energy (ev) Min	Max	Lab	Type	Documentation Ref Vol Page	Date	Author, Comments	Data
Reson Params	−		AUA	Theo	Rept AAEC/E−211	Nov 70	Musgrove. CALCULTD D+GAM WIDTH GIVEN	
Strnth Fnctn	−		AUA	Theo	Rept AAEC/E−211	Nov 70	Musgrove. SMOOTHED S0,S1 AND S2 GIVN	

70 Ytterbium 168

Quantity	Energy (ev) Min	Max	Lab	Type	Documentation Ref Vol Page	Date	Author, Comments	Data
Absorption	2.5−2		IJI	Eval	Conf 75Kiev 1 169	May 75	Fedorova+ EVAL 2200M/S SIG,TABLE	
Res Int Abs	6.0−1	2.3+1	BNL	Expt	Jour PR 174 1400	Oct 68	Mughabghab+ TRANS, 30950B FRM RES	
					Conf 68Wash. § E28	Mar 68	.SUPERSEDED	
Res Int Abs	5.0−1		CNE	Expt	Conf 70Helsinki 2 589	Jun 70	Ricabarra+ RATIO TO THR−ACT SIGMA	+
	5.0−1				Data EXFOR30190.005	Dec 72	RES INT AND RATIO TO THR−CAPT SIGMA	
Res Int Abs	5.5−1		CPO	Expt	Jour JIN 32 2839	Oct 70	Sims+ (N,G).CD CUT−OFF,VALUE GIVEN	+
	5.5−1				Data EXFOR10608.	Aug 76	. 2PTS.MAXW SPEC MEAS AND 1/V REMOVE	
Res Int Abs	5.0−1		OSL	Expt	Prog INDC(NOR)−1 1	May 72	Alstad+ REDUCED CAPTINTEG REL AU,TBL	+
					Priv PAPPAS	Nov 70	Pappas. ACT. POWD,LIQ SOLUT.TBP JIN	
	0.0+0	1.0+6			Data EXFOR20094.005	Sep 71	1PNT.CAPTURE.	
Res Int Abs	5.0−1		COL	Expt	Jour NSE 48 219	Jun 72	Rahn+. RI=31900+−4500B	
Res Int Abs	5.0−1		KJL	Expt	Jour JIN 34 2699	Sep 72	Steinnes. ACT. AU MONITOR	+
	5.0−1				Data EXFOR20188.026	May 74	1PNT.CAPTURE.	
Res Int Abs	5.0−1		GHT	Expt	Jour JRC 20 695	74	Van Der Linden+ BY(N,G).CFD OTHS,TBL	+
	5.5−1				Conf 73Paris 2 241	Mar 73	− + ACT,REL THR+GOLD,TBL	
	5.5−1				Data EXFOR20645.033	Jul 76	1PNT.CAPTURE.	
Res Int Abs	5.0−1		IJI	Eval	Conf 75Kiev 1 169	May 75	Fedorova+ EVAL+CALC RI GIVEN,TABLE	
(n,γ)	Maxwl		LAS	Expt	Jour PR 170 1108	Jun 68	Shera+ GE(LI) + SI (LI)	+
	Maxwl				Data EXFOR12134.002	Jun 76	. 1 PT. SIGMA	
(n,γ)	−		IEA	Comp	Rept IEA−INF−10	Aug 68	Atalla. TABLES OF HL,SIG AND GAMM−E	
(n,γ)	Maxwl		CPO	Expt	Jour JIN 32 2839	Oct 70	Sims+ CD CUT−OFF,REL CO59,SIG GIVEN	+
	Maxwl				Data EXFOR10608.	Aug 76	2PTS.EFFECTIVE CS AND MAXW SPEC CALC	
(n,γ)	3.0+4		AUA	Theo	Rept AAEC/E−211	Nov 70	Musgrove. SIGMA GIVEN AND CFD OTHER	
(n,γ)	2.5+4		AUW	ExTh	Conf 70Madurai 2 29	Dec 70	Sriramachandra Murty+.S+P WAVE SIGMA	+
	2.5+4				Expt Data EXFOR30248.007	Jun 73	SIGMA CAPTURE VALUE	
(n,γ)	2.5−2		IJI	Expt	Prog YFI−12 66	72	Vertebny+ ABST,SIG GIVEN	
					Prog INDC(CCP)−30	Sep 72	.PAGE 57,ENGLISH OF YFI−12 66	
(n,γ)	1.0+3	1.0+7	BOL	Eval	Data BENZI−DFN 698.	May 72	40 PNTS	+
(n,γ)	Maxwl		OSL	Expt	Prog INDC(NOR)−1 1	May 72	Alstad+ ACTIVATION REL AU−197,TABLE	+
					Priv PAPPAS	Nov 70	Pappas. ACT. POWD,LIQ SOLUT.TBP JIN	
	Maxwl				Data EXFOR20094.004	Sep 71	1PNT.SIG.	
(n,γ)	Pile		ROS	ExTh	Prog ZFK−243 93	Sep 72	Mohsen+ NG−SYSTEMAT. FOR RARE EARTHS	
(n,γ)	Maxwl		TNC	Expt	Abst BAP 6 506	Dec 61	Hudson+.ACTIVATION. NO DATA GIVEN	+
	Maxwl				Data EXFOR11844.003	Jun 76	. 1 PT. SIGMA	
Spect (n,γ)	Pile		NRL	Expt	Abst BAP 13 722	Apr 68	Ritter+. PILE BEAM.6778KEV G ONLY	
Spect (n,γ)	Maxwl		LAS	Expt	Jour PR 170 1108	Jun 68	Shera+ GE(LI)+SI(LI) .06−6.8MEV GAMS	
Spect (n,γ)	Maxwl		KFK	Expt	Jour NP/A 119 609	Nov 68	Michaelis+GELI PAIR+ANTI−C. =KFK−919	
					Rept KFK−919	Nov 68	− + LVL SCH YB 169	
					Conf 69Studsvik 469	Aug 69	− + YB−169.TBL GS GIVN.+REVW.	
					Rept KFK−1096	Aug 69	− + REPRINT OF 69STUDSVIK	
					Conf JINR−D3893 37	May 68	− + TABLE OF 32GAM LVLS,I+PI	
					Jour NIM 56 181	Nov 67	− + METHOD.	
					Jour ZP 206 84	Sep 67	Markus+ PRELIM LVLS,CFD DY165+ER167	
					Rept KFK−562	Mar 67	Michaelis+ LVL SCHEME YB−169.ANTI−C.	
Spect (n,γ)	Maxwl		MUN	Expt	Conf 69Studsvik 65	Aug 69	Koch+ SPEC GRPH GVN. BENT CRYST.RISO	
Spect (n,γ)	None		RIS	Expt	Conf 69Montreal 701	Aug 69	Koch+CRYS DIFFRACT.MEASMT RVW.NDG.	
Spect (n,γ)	None		KFI	Comp	Jour JRC 7 365	Jun 71	Nagy+ GAM+XRAY+ELECTRON ES,HALF−LIFE	
Spect (n,γ)	Maxwl		IFL	Expt	Book PROKOFJEV	73	. TBL GAM,CONV ELECTR ES+INT,LVL SCH	
(n,2n)	Fiss		CRC	Eval	Rept CRC−1003	Dec 60	Roy+,ESTIMATED AVG SIG=1.8MB	
(n,2n)	1.5+7		ARK	Expt	Abst DA/B 32 5091	Mar 72	Bari. GE(LI) DET. ACT. SIG GIVEN	+
	1.5+7				Data EXFOR10431.060	Aug 75	. 1 PT. SIGMA	
(n,2n)	1.5+7		DEB	Eval	Jour REA 11 1 153	Mar 73	Boedy+ RECOMM.VALUE FROM N−Z SYSTEM.	
(n,2n)	1.5+7		KFI	Theo	Rept KFKI−73−68	Dec 73	Jeki.NEW FIT,CALC SIG CFD OTHERS,TBL	

70 Ytterbium 168

Quantity	Energy (ev) Min	Max	Lab	Type	Documentation Ref Vol Page	Date	Author, Comments	Data
(n,2n)	1.4+7		MNZ Expt	Jour	RCA 22 11	75	Weigel+ SUM OF (N,2N)+(N,NP)+(N,D)SIG	
(n,2n)	1.5+7		JUL Expt	Jour	RRL 25 335	May 76	Qaim+ SIG IN GRPH. SYST VS (N−Z)/A	+
				Jour	NP/A 224 319	May 74	− . ACT.GE(LI)	
	1.5+7			Data	EXFOR20541.051	Apr 76	1PNT.SIGMA.	
(n,p)	Fiss		CRC Eval	Rept	CRC−1003	Dec 60	Roy+,ESTIMATED AVG SIG=0.1MB	
(n,p)	Maxwl		IFU Theo	Rept	ICD−4 20	67	Dadakina+ PENETR COEFF CALC,TABLE	
(n,np)	1.4+7		MNZ Expt	Jour	RCA 22 11	75	Weigel+ SUM OF (N,2N)+(N,NP)+(N,D)SIG	
(n,α)	Fiss		CRC Eval	Rept	CRC−1003	Dec 60	Roy+,ESTIMATED AVG SIG=0.001MB	
(n,α)	Maxwl		CCP Expt	Jour	YF 1 252	Feb 65	Andreev.IONIZ−CHAMBER,SIG=M4MB	+
				Jour	SNP 1 177	Aug 65	TRANSLATN.*	
(n,α)	Maxwl		LYO Expt	Jour	NP/A 231 437	Oct 74	Emsallem+ ILL HF REACTOR,SIG+GRPH+TBL	+
	2.5−2			Data	EXFOR20564.005	Sep 75	1PNT.SIGMA.	
Reson Params		1.0+6	AUA Theo	Jour	AUJ 20 477	Oct 67	Cook. TBL OF AVG LVL SPACING D,L=0,1	
Reson Params	6.0−1		BNL Expt	Jour	PR 174 1400	Oct 68	Mughabghab+ RES. ENERGIES, WIDTHS.	+
	6.0−1			Data	EXFOR12130.	Jun 76	. 1 RES, E0	
Reson Params	−		AUA Theo	Rept	AAEC/E−211	Nov 70	Musgrove. CALCULTD D+GAM WIDTH GIVEN	
Reson Params	6.0−1		CJD Eval	Rept	YK−7	71	Zakharova+ SURVEY+SYSTEMATICS,GW,TBL	
				Rept	INDC(CCP)−27	Nov 72	.ENGLISH TRANSLATION OF YK−7 /71	
Reson Params	−		DUB Theo	Rept	JINR−E4−5711	Apr 71	Soloviev. AVG LVL SPACING, EXPTS TBD	
Reson Params	6.0+0	2.9+2	IJI Expt	Prog	YFI−12 70	72	Vertebny+ ABSTRACT,TBL E,N−,G−WIDS	
				Prog	INDC(CCP)−30	Sep 72	.PAGE 60,ENGLISH OF YFI−12 70	
Reson Params	6.0−1	2.9+2	IFU Expt	Jour	YFI−10 74	Jun 72	Vertebny+	+
	6.0−1	2.9+2		Data	EXFOR40127.	Jan 73	13RES, RED N−WIDTH, CAPT−WIDTH, D	
Reson Params	2.2+1	1.9+2	COL Expt	Jour	PR/C 7 823	Feb 73	Liou+.TOF.G*WN FOR 2 RESONANCES	+
	2.3+1	1.7+2		Rept	NYO−72−190	68	− .TOF.WN FOR 2 RES ES.	
	2.3+1	1.9+2		Data	EXFOR10081.	Jan 78	. 2RES ES.WN RED GVN.	
Strnth Fnctn	−		AUA Theo	Rept	AAEC/E−211	Nov 70	Musgrove. SMOOTHED S0,S1 AND S2 GIVN	
Lvl Density	None		CCP Theo	Jour	YF 13 43	Jan 71	Bravin+.DEFORM PAR,CALC,TBL,CFD EXPT	

70 Ytterbium 169

Quantity	Energy (ev) Min	Max	Lab	Type	Documentation Ref Vol Page	Date	Author, Comments	Data
(n,γ)	Pile		JUL Expt	Prog	NEANDC(E)−161U	Aug 74	Ihle+ USING MASS SPECTROMETRY	
(n,p)	Maxwl		IFU Theo	Rept	ICD−4 20	67	Dadakina+ PENETR COEFF CALC,TABLE	
Reson Params	−		AUA Theo	Rept	AAEC/E−211	Nov 70	Musgrove. CALCULTD D+GAM WIDTH GIVEN	
Strnth Fnctn	−		AUA Theo	Rept	AAEC/E−211	Nov 70	Musgrove. SMOOTHED S0,S1 AND S2 GIVN	
Lvl Density	None		ROC Theo	Jour	NP/A 223 589	May 74	Huizenga+ EXP CFD MICROSC TH AX SYMM	

70 Ytterbium 170

Quantity	Energy (ev) Min	Max	Lab	Type	Documentation Ref Vol Page	Date	Author, Comments	Data
Total	2.5−2		BNL Expt	Jour	PR 174 1400	Oct 68	Mughabghab+ TRANS SIG=17.0+−1.0B.	+
				Conf	68Wash. § E28	Mar 68	.SUPERSEDED	
	2.5−2			Data	EXFOR12130.003	Jun 76	. 1 PT. SIGMA	
Total	1.4+7		LIN Expt	Conf	75Kiev 4 140	May 75	Djumin+ SIG GIVEN.OPTMOD ANAL,RADIUS	
Elastic	2.5−2		IJI Eval	Conf	75Kiev 1 169	May 75	Fedorova+ EVAL 2200M/S SIG,TABLE	
Potntal Scat	None		BNL Expt	Jour	PL/B 24 573	May 67	Chrien+ FROM ANALYSIS OF RESONANCES	
Thermal Scat	2.5−2		BNL Expt	Jour	PR 174 1400	Oct 68	Mughabghab+ PARAMAGN SIG=5.0+−1.5B.	
Scattering	2.5−2		BNL Expt	Jour	PR 174 1400	Oct 68	Mughabghab+ TRANS SIG=2.6+−0.5B.	
Absorption	2.5−2		BNL Expt	Jour	PR 174 1400	Oct 68	Mughabghab+ TRANS SIG=9.4+−0.9B.	
Absorption	Maxwl	Pile	SGA Expt	Jour	JMS 6 435	71	Dobrozemsky+ CHANGE OF ABUND.TBL SIG	+
				Rept	SGAE−PH−104	71	− + MASS−SPEC METHOD	
	Pile			Conf	66Paris 1 495	Oct 66	− + PPR82.MASS−SPEC VAL GVN	
				Rept	SGAE−PH−47	Oct 66	− + SUPERSEDED	
	Maxwl	Pile		Rept	AEC−TR−7574	74	− + ENGLISH OF JMS 6 435	
	2.5−2			Data	EXFOR20637.020	Sep 76	1PNT.SIGMA.	
Absorption	2.5−2		IJI Eval	Conf	75Kiev 1 169	May 75	Fedorova+ EVAL 2200M/S SIG,TABLE	
Res Int Abs	8.1+0	1.3+3	BNL Expt	Jour	PR 174 1400	Oct 68	Mughabghab+ TRANS 326B FROM RES.	
				Conf	68Wash. § E28	Mar 68	.SUPERSEDED	
Res Int Abs	5.5−1		SGA Expt	Jour	JMS 6 435	71	Dobrozemsky+ EFF ABS RES INT GIVEN.	+
				Prog	SGAE−PH−104	71	− +MASS−SPECTROMETRIC	
				Rept	AEC−TR−7574	74	. ENGLISH OF JMS 6 415	
	5.5−1			Data	EXFOR20637.021	Sep 76	1PNT.	
Res Int Abs	5.0−1		COL Expt	Jour	NSE 48 219	Jun 72	Rahn+. RI=211+−20B	
Res Int Abs	5.0−1		IJI Eval	Conf	75Kiev 1 169	May 75	Fedorova+ EVAL+CALC RI GIVEN,TABLE	

70 Ytterbium 170

Quantity	Energy (ev) Min	Max	Lab	Type	Documentation Ref Vol Page	Author, Comments Date	Data
(n,γ)	Maxwl		MCM	Expt Priv	WALKER	May 56 Walker. SIGMA −24B.	+
	Maxwl			Data	EXFOR12127.021	Jun 76 . 1 PT. SIGMA	
(n,γ)	2.5+4		FEI	ExTh Prog	YFI−4 22	May 67 Shorin+.,TBLS GIVEN,TBP YF	
				Theo Jour	YF 6 769	Oct 67 − + VALUE GIVEN,STATIST THEORY	
				Jour	SNP 6 558	Apr 68 . ENGL OF YF 6 769	
				ExTh Prog	INDC−187E	67 . ENGL OF YFI−4 22	
(n,γ)	5.0+3	1.0+5	AUA	ExTh Rept	AAEC/E−198	May 69 Musgrove.S+P+D WAVE SIGMAS CALC,TBL	+
(n,γ)	3.0+4		AUA	Theo Rept	AAEC/E−211	Nov 70 Musgrove. SIGMA GIVEN AND CFD OTHER	
(n,γ)	8.1+0	2.0+2	NRL	Expt Jour	NP/A 173 477	Oct 71 Ritter+ LINAC TOF. TOF SPECTRUM.	
(n,γ)	1.0+3	1.0+7	BOL	Eval Data	BENZI−DFN 699.	May 72 40 PNTS	+
(n,γ)	Pile		ROS	ExTh Prog	ZFK−243 93	Sep 72 Mohsen+ NG−SYSTEMAT. FOR RARE EARTHS	
Spect (n,γ)	Maxwl		NRL	Expt Jour	PR 183 983	Jul 69 Namenson+,GE(LI) DET,+−3KEV ERROR	
				Conf	69Montreal 660	Aug 69 − +GELI DET.CFD OTHER NEAR Z/A	
Spect (n,γ)	8.1+0	7.3+1	NRL	Expt Jour	NP/A 173 477	Oct 71 Ritter+ LINAC TOF.4N RES. 9EG.	
Spect (n,γ)	Maxwl		CTH	Expt Jour	NP/A 188 129	Jun 72 Wallander+PAIR,ANTICOMP. 103 E(G).	+
	Pile			Data	EXFOR20225.	May 74 73PTS.	
Spect (n,γ)	Maxwl		BNL	Expt Conf	74Petten 271	Sep 74 Cole+ DIRECT CAPT.COMP. TBL	
(n,2n)	Fiss		CRC	Eval Rept	CRC−1003	Dec 60 Roy+,ESTIMATED AVG SIG=2.3MB	
(n,2n)	1.5+7		MUN	Expt Jour	NP/A 118 9	Sep 68 Dilg+ ACTIV.REL AL(N,A)	+
				Jour	OAWS 177 323	69 Winkler+(IRK) ACTIVATION.	
	1.5+7			Data	EXFOR20802.011	Dec 78 1PNT.SIGMA.	
(n,2n)	1.5+7		DEB	Comp Jour	REA 7 4 93	Dec 69 Csikai+ SIG+HL COMPILTN,N−ACTIV−ANAL	
(n,2n)	1.4+7	1.5+7	JYV	Eval Jour	JU−RR−3/1970	Jun 70 Leppaemaeki+ TABLE OF EVAL AVG SIG	
(n,2n)	+7		KFI	Theo Rept	KFKI−71−8	Feb 71 Jeki. CALCULATED CFD EXPTL SIG VALUE	
(n,2n)	None		KFI	Comp Jour	JRC 7 365	Jun 71 Nagy+ GAM+XRAY+ELECTR ES, HALF−LIFE	
(n,2n)	1.5+7		ARK	Expt Abst	DA/B 32 5091	Mar 72 Bari. GE(LI) DET. ACT. SIG GIVEN	+
	1.5+7			Data	EXFOR10431.061	Aug 75 . 1 PT. SIGMA	
(n,2n)	1.5+7		DEB	Eval Rept	REA 11 1 153	Mar 73 Boedy. COMPILATION+RECOMM.VALUE,TBL	
				Rept	IAEA−153 173	73 − . RECOMM. VALUE ONLY	
(n,2n)	1.5+7		TAT	Theo Jour	JP/A 7 1457	Aug 74 Kondaiah. CALC ON STAT MODEL	
(n,2n)	1.4+7		MNZ	Expt Jour	RCA 22 11	75 Weigel+ TOT SIG, ACT METHOD	
(n,2n)	1.5+7		JUL	Expt Jour	NP/A 224 319	May 74 Qaim. ACT.GE(LI)	+
				Jour	RRL 25 335	May 76 − + SIG IN GRPH. SYST VS (N−Z)/A	
	1.5+7			Data	EXFOR20541.052	Apr 76 1PNT.SIGMA.	
(n,p)	Fiss		CRC	Eval Rept	CRC−1003	Dec 60 Roy+,ESTIMATED AVG SIG=0.02MB	
(n,p)	1.4+7	1.5+7	ARK	Theo Prog	ORO−3235−29	Jan 67 Koch+,STAT MODEL CALC CFD EXPTS	
(n,α)	Fiss		CRC	Eval Rept	CRC−1003	Dec 60 Roy+,ESTIMATED AVG SIG=0.0003MB	
(n,α)	Maxwl		CCP	Expt Jour	YF 1 252	Feb 65 Andreev.IONIZ−CHAMBER,SIG=M.04MB	+
				Jour	SNP 1 177	Aug 65 TRANSLATN.*	
(n,α)	None		KFI	Comp Jour	JRC 7 365	Jun 71 Nagy+ GAM+XRAY+ELECTR ES, HALF−LIFE	
(n,α)	Maxwl		LYO	Expt Jour	NP/A 231 437	Oct 74 Emsallem+ILL HF REACTOR,SIG+GRPH+TBL	+
	2.5−2			Data	EXFOR20564.006	Sep 75 1PNT.SIGMA.	
Reson Params	4.0+1	7.3+1	DUB	Expt Jour	YF 3 48	Jan 66 Wang+ TOF, TRNS, TBL, 2 RES	+
				Rept	INDSWG−126	66 .	
				Conf	65Antwerp 187	Jul 65 .SEE ALSO	
				Rept	JINR−P−2158	Jun 65 Wang+ 16RES, TBL, GWN, AVG D	
				Jour	SNP 3 34	Jul 66 .ENGL TRANSL	
	4.0+1	7.3+1		Data	EXFOR40030.	Aug 70 N−WIDTH AT 2RES, TOT−WIDTH	
Reson Params	2.5+4		FEI	ExTh Prog	YFI−4 22	May 67 Shorin+.,TBLS GIVEN,TBP YF	
				Prog	INDC−187E	67 . ENGL OF YFI−4 22	
Reson Params	8.1+0	4.5+2	BNL	Expt Jour	PR 174 1400	Oct 68 Mughabghab+ TRANS 13ES WN+AVERAGE D	+
	8.1+0	4.5+2		Data	EXFOR12130.010	Jun 76 . 13 RES,E0,WN,WN0	
Reson Params	−		AUA	Theo Rept	AAEC/E−211	Nov 70 Musgrove. CALCULTD D+GAM WIDTH GIVEN	
Reson Params	4.0+1	7.4+1	CJD	Eval Rept	YK−7	71 Zakharova+ SURVEY+SYSTEMATICS,GW,TBL	
				Rept	INDC(CCP)−27	Nov 72 .ENGLISH TRANSLATION OF YK−7 /71	
Reson Params	None		DUB	Theo Rept	JINR−E4−5880	Jul 71 Soloviev.N−GAM−WIDS CORR.SHORT NOTE	
	−			Rept	JINR−E4−5711	Apr 71 − . AVG LVL SPACING, EXPTS TBD	
Reson Params	8.1+0	1.3+3	COL	Expt Jour	PR/C 7 823	Feb 73 Liou+. TOF. G*WN FOR 23 RESONANCES	+
	4.0+1	3.6+2		Rept	NYO−72−190	68 − .TOF.WN FOR 7 RES ES.	
	4.0+2	1.3+3		Data	EXFOR10081.	Jan 78 . 19 RES ES.WN RED GVN.D GVN.	
Strnth Fnctn	8.1+0	9.9+2	BNL	Expt Jour	PR 174 1400	Oct 68 Mughabghab+ STF=2.46+−0.6 FROM RES	
		+4		Jour	PL/B 24 573	May 67 Chrien+ FROM RES+UNRESOLVED REGIONS	
		5.0+3		Conf	65Antwerp 69	Jul 65 − +TOTSIG SLOPE SWAVE STF1.32+−.	
Strnth Fnctn	8.1+0	9.9+2	BNL	Expt Jour	PR/C 7 823	May 70 Mughabghab+,STF FROM RESON+SIGMA	
Strnth Fnctn	−		AUA	Theo Rept	AAEC/E−211	Nov 70 Musgrove. SMOOTHED S0,S1 AND S2 GIVN	
Strnth Fnctn	8.1+0	1.3+3	COL	Expt Jour	PR/C 7 823	Feb 73 Liou+.TOF.S0=2.25+−1.0	+
	4.0+2	1.3+3		Data	EXFOR10081.064	Jan 78 . 1PT.S0=(2.25+−1.0)−4	
Strnth Fnctn	None		AUA	Eval Rept	AAEC/E−277	Mar 73 Musgrove.TBLS EXPTL DATA+BEST VALUES	

70 Ytterbium 170

Quantity	Energy (ev) Min Max	Lab	Type	Documentation Ref Vol Page	Author, Comments Date	Data
Strnth Fnctn	None	COL	Revw Conf	75Wash. 780	Mar 75 Hacken+ NEVIS TOF S-WAVE STF	
Lvl Density	None	CCP	Theo Jour	YF 13 43	Jan 71 Bravin+.DEFORM PAR,CALC,TBL,CFD EXPT	

70 Ytterbium 171

Quantity	Energy (ev) Min Max	Lab	Type	Documentation Ref Vol Page	Author, Comments Date	Data
Total	2.5-2	BNL	Expt	Jour PR 174 1400	Oct 68 Mughabghab+ TRANS SIG=57+ -3B.	+
				Conf 68Wash. § E28	Mar 68 .SUPERSEDED	
	2.5-2			Data EXFOR12130.004	Jun 76 . 1 PT. SIGMA	
Total	1.0+0 2.0+4	COL	Expt	Jour PR/C 7 823	Feb 73 Liou+TRNS.TOF.RES PAR ANAL.NO CS GVN	+
	7.5+1 1.5+2			Rept NYO-72-190	68 - . TOF, TRANS, CURVE.	
	None			Data EXFOR10081.066	Jan 78 .RAW DATA GVN UPON REQUEST TO NNDC.	
Total	1.4+7	LIN	Expt	Conf 75Kiev 4 140	May 75 Djumin+ SIG GIVEN.OPTMOD ANAL,RADIUS	
Elastic	2.5-2	IJI	Eval	Conf 75Kiev 1 169	May 75 Fedorova+ EVAL 2200M/S SIG,TABLE	
Potntl Scat	None	BNL	Expt	Jour PL/B 24 573	May 67 Chrien+ FROM ANALYSIS OF RESONANCES	
Thermal Scat	2.5-2	BNL	Expt	Jour PR 174 1400	Oct 68 Mughabghab+ PARAMAGN SIG=5.2+ -0.9B.	
Scattering	2.5-2	BNL	Expt	Jour PR 174 1400	Oct 68 Mughabghab+ TRANS SIG=3.4+ -0.9B.	
Absorption	2.5-2	BNL	Expt	Jour PR 174 1400	Oct 68 Mughabghab+ TRANS SIG=48.4+ -3.3B.	
Absorption	Maxwl Pile	SGA	Expt	Jour JMS 6 435	71 Dobrozemsky+ CHANGE OF ABUND.TBL SIG	+
				Rept SGAE-PH-104	71 - + MASS-SPEC METHOD	
	Pile			Conf 66Paris 1 495	Oct 66 - +PPR82 MASS-SPEC VAL GIVN	
	Maxwl Pile			Rept AEC-TR-7574	74 - + ENGLISH OF JMS 6 435	
	2.5-2			Data EXFOR20637.022	Sep 76 1PNT.SIGMA.	
Absorption	2.5-2	IJI	Eval	Conf 75Kiev 1 169	May 75 Fedorova+ EVAL 2200M/S SIG,TABLE	
Res Int Abs	7.9+0 3.5+2	BNL	Expt	Jour PR 174 1400	Oct 68 Mughabghab+ TRANS 313B FROM RES.	
				Conf 68Wash. § E28	Mar 68 .SUPERSEDED	
Res Int Abs	5.5-1	SGA	Expt	Jour JMS 6 435	71 Dobrozemsky+ EFF ABS RES INT GIVEN.	+
				Prog SGAE-PH-104	71 - +MASS-SPECTROMETRIC	
				Rept AEC-TR-7574	74 . ENGLISH OF JMS 6 415	
	5.5-1			Data EXFOR20637.023	Sep 76 1PNT.	
Res Int Abs	5.0-1	COL	Expt	Jour NSE 48 219	Jun 72 Rahn+. RI=344+ -39B	
Res Int Abs	5.0-1	IJI	Eval	Conf 75Kiev 1 169	May 75 Fedorova+ RI CALC FROM RESPARS,TABLE	
(n,γ)	Maxwl	MCM	Expt	Diss WALKER	May 56 Walker.SIGMA=64+ -7B.	+
	Maxwl			Data EXFOR12127.022	Jun 76 . 1 PT. SIGMA	
(n,γ)	5.0+3 1.0+5	AUA	ExTh	Rept AAEC/E-198	May 69 Musgrove.S+P+D WAVE SIGMAS CALC,TBL	+
(n,γ)	3.0+4	AUA	Theo	Rept AAEC/E-211	Nov 70 Musgrove. SIGMA GIVEN AND CFD OTHER	
(n,γ)	1.0+3 1.0+7	BOL	Expt	Data BENZI-DFN 700.	May 72 40 PNTS	
(n,γ)	5.0+3 8.0+4	FEI	Expt	Jour YF 20 1092	Dec 74 Shorin+ SIG(E)GRPH CFD H-F.RES-PARS	+
	5.0+3 8.4+4			Data EXFOR40274.002	Mar 75 SIGMA AT 32 E-RANGES GIVEN	
Spect (n,γ)	+0 +4	COL	Expt	Prog WASH-1124 31	Nov 68 Camarda+ MOXON-RAE DET TBC NO DATA	
Spect (n,γ)	Maxwl	NRL	Expt	Jour PR 183 983	Jul 69 Namenson+,GE(LI) DET,+ -3KEV ERROR	
Spect (n,γ)	Pile	ANL	Expt	Conf 69Studsvik 601	Aug 69 Smither+ NO DATA GVN,TB CFD STATMOD	
Spect (n,γ)	Maxwl	MUN	Expt	Conf 69Studsvik 65	Aug 69 Koch+ AUT-CURVD-CRYST SPEC.NDG.TBP.	
Spect (n,γ)	Maxwl 2.0+3	MTR	Expt	Jour PL/B 33 213	Oct 70 Greenwood+ G ES 4BANDS BELOW 2MV GVN	
Spect (n,γ)	Pile	CTH	Expt	Jour PS 3 55	71 Alenius+ GE(LI) PAIR+ANTICOINC	+
	Pile			Data EXFOR20244.	May 74 76PTS.	
Spect (n,γ)	+0 +2	BNL	Expt	Prog NCSAC-38 23	May 71 Chrien+. RESONANCE CAPTURE,CURVES	
Spect (n,γ)	7.9+4 1.2+6	MUN	Expt	Jour ZN/A 28 226	Feb 73 Wimmer. TBL, LVL-SCH OF YB-172	
Spect (n,γ)	Maxwl	BNL	Expt	Jour PL/B 58 39	Aug 75 Macphail+PROPERTIES OF ROT BAND,GRPH	
Spect (n,γ)	2.0+3	INL	Expt	Jour NP/A 252 260	Nov 75 Greenwood+TBL E+INT,LVL SCH OF 172YB	
				Conf 69Montreal 662	Aug 69 - +LOW-SPIN STATES.NDG.	
(n,2n)	Fiss	CRC	Eval	Rept CRC-1003	Dec 60 Roy+,ESTIMATED AVG SIG=29.5MB	
(n,2n)	1.5+7	DEB	Eval	Jour REA 11 1 153	Mar 73 Boedy+ RECOMM.VALUE FROM N-Z SYSTEM.	
(n,2n)	1.5+7	KFI	Theo	Rept KFKI-73-68	Dec 73 Jeki.NEW FIT,CALC SIG CFD OTHERS,TBL	
(n,p)	Fiss	CRC	Eval	Rept CRC-1003	Dec 60 Roy+,ESTIMATED AVG SIG=0.03MB	
(n,p)	Maxwl	IFU	Theo	Rept ICD-4 20	67 Dadakina+ PENETR COEFF CALC,TABLE	
(n,α)	Fiss	CRC	Eval	Rept CRC-1003	Dec 60 Roy+,ESTIMATED AVG SIG=0.0054MB	
(n,α)	Maxwl	CCP	Expt	Jour YF 1 252	Feb 65 Andreev.IONIZ-CHAMBER,SIG=M.04MB	+
				Jour SNP 1 177	Aug 65 TRANSLATN.*	
(n,α)	Maxwl	LYO	Expt	Jour NP/A 231 437	Oct 74 Emsallem+ILL HF REACTOR,SIG+GRPH+TBL	+
	2.5-2			Data EXFOR20564.007	Sep 75 1PNT.SIGMA.	
(n,α)	Fast	DUB	Expt	Conf 75Kiev 4 60	May 75 Balabanov+ FOR ALF-WID.SIG NOT GIVEN	
	+0 1.0+2			Rept JINR-P3-8653	Mar 75 - + CORREL N-,A-WIDS,CFD THEO	
(n,α)	1.4+7 1.8+7	IBJ	Expt	Jour NP/A 262 205	May 75 Glowacka+ALPHA SPECT. SIGMA(E).	+
				Prog INR-1502 4	May 75 - + ALPHA SPECTR AT 2 ES,TABLE	
	1.4+7			Data EXFOR30298.	May 75 DOUBLE DIFFSIG(36 PTS)+ANGDIST(1 PT)	
	1.8+7			Data EXFOR30299.	May 75 DOUBLE DIFFSIG(44 PTS)+ANGDIST(1 PT)	

70 Ytterbium 171

Quantity	Energy (ev) Min	Max	Lab	Type	Documentation Ref Vol Page	Author, Comments Date	Data
Reson Params	8.0+0	2.1+2	ANL Expt	Rept	ANL-6589 88	Aug 62 Carpenter. EOS,RES. PAR., SPECTRA	+
	8.1+0	2.1+2		Data	EXFOR12048.008	Jun 76 . 16RES,E0J,	
	1.4+1			Data	EXFOR12048.007	Jun 76 . 1 RES E0J,WT,WN,PCS	
Reson Params	7.9+0	1.5+2	DUB Expt	Jour	YF 3 48	Jan 66 Wang+ TOF, TRNS, TBL, 22 RES	+
				Rept	INDSWG-126	66 .	
				Conf	65Antwerp 187	Jul 65 .SEE ALSO	
				Rept	JINR-P-2158	Jun 65 Wang+ 16RES, TBL, GWN, AVG D	
				Jour	SNP 3 34	Jul 66 .ENGL TRANSL	
	7.9+0	1.5+2		Data	EXFOR40030.	Aug 70 N-WIDTH AT 22RES, TOT-WID,CAPT-WID,D	
Reson Params		1.0+6	AUA Theo	Jour	AUJ 20 477	Oct 67 Cook. TBL OF AVG LVL SPACING D,L=0,1	
Reson Params	7.9+0	2.3+2	BNL Expt	Jour	PR 174 1400	Oct 68 Mughabghab+ TRN 27ES 2G WN+AVG D.3WG	+
	7.9+0	2.3+2		Data	EXFOR12130.014	Jun 76 . 27 RES,E0,WN,WN0,WG	
Reson Params	7.9+0	3.5+2	BNL Expt	Jour	PR/C 1 1850	May 70 Mughabghab+, AVG WG=73+-5	+
Reson Params	-		AUA Theo	Rept	AAEC/E-211	Nov 70 Musgrove. CALCULTD D+GAM WIDTH GIVEN	
Reson Params	7.4+0	1.3+2	CJD Eval	Rept	YK-7	71 Zakharova+ SURVEY+SYSTEMATICS,GW,TBL	
				Rept	INDC(CCP)-27	Nov 72 .ENGLISH TRANSLATION OF YK-7 /71	
Reson Params	None		DUB Theo	Jour	YF 13 240	Feb 71 Malecki+G-WID,THEO CFD EXPT.TBL,GRPH	
				Jour	SNP 13 133	Aug 71 - + ENGL OF YF 13 240.	
Reson Params	7.9+0	1.3+2	BNL Expt	Prog	NCSAC-38 23	May 71 Chrien+. J PI FOR 20RESON FROM CAPT	
Reson Params	7.9+0	1.7+3	COL Expt	Jour	PR/C 7 823	Feb 73 Liou+.TOF.G*WN WG J VALUES GIVN,D	+
	7.9+0	3.5+2		Rept	NYO-72-190	68 - .TOF.G*WN,WG,J.AVGD	
	8.0+0	1.7+3		Data	EXFOR10081.	Jan 78 . 168 RES WN*G,37RES WG,J GVN.D GVN.	
Reson Params	Fast		DUB Expt	Conf	75Kiev 4 60	May 75 Balabanov+ AVG ALF-WIDTHS.TABLE	
	+0	1.0+2		Rept	JINR-P3-8653	Mar 75 - + CORREL N-,A-WIDS,CFD THEO	
	None			Rept	YFI-17 30	Aug 74 Karzhavina+ SPIN OF NEUT-RES	
	+0	+3		Conf	73Kiev 2 337	May 73 - + SPIN IDENT,G-MULTIP MTHD	
Strnth Fnctn	5.0+0	1.5+2	DUB Expt	Jour	YF 3 48	Jan 66 Wang+ TOF, TRNS, TBL, 22 RES	
				Rept	INDSWG-126	66 .	
				Conf	65Antwerp 187	Jul 65 .SEE ALSO	
				Rept	JINR-P-2158	Jun 65 Wang+ 16RES, TBL, GWN, AVG D	
				Jour	SNP 3 34	Jul 66 .ENGL TRANSL	
	7.9+0	1.5+2		Data	EXFOR40030.008	Aug 70 STRENGTH-FUNCTION, S-WAVE	
Strnth Fnctn	7.9+0	3.5+2	BNL Expt	Jour	PR 174 1400	Oct 68 Mughabghab+ STF=1.59+-0.31 FROM RES.	
		+4		Jour	PL/B 24 573	May 67 Chrien+ FROM RES+UNRESOLVED REGIONS	
		5.0+3		Conf	65Antwerp 69	Jul 65 - +TOTSIG SLOPE SWAVE STF1.20+-	
Strnth Fnctn	7.9+0	3.5+2	BNL Expt	Jour	PR/C 1 1850	May 70 Mughabghab+,STF FROM RESON+SIGMA	+
Strnth Fnctn	-		AUA Theo	Rept	AAEC/E-211	Nov 70 Musgrove. SMOOTHED S0,S1 AND S2 GIVN	
Strnth Fnctn	None		COL Expt	Jour	NSE 48 219	Jun 72 Rahn+. AVG WG=76.5MEV OVER 44RESON	
Strnth Fnctn	7.9+0	1.7+3	COL Expt	Jour	PR/C 7 823	Feb 73 Liou+.TOF.S0=1.86+-0.16	+
	7.9+0	3.5+2		Rept	NYO-72-190	68 - .TOF.S0=(1.49+-.4)-4	
		+3		Abst	BAP 12 650	May 67 Havens+ 1.76+-.45 FROM RES	
	7.9+0	1.7+3		Data	EXFOR10081.037	Jan 78 . 1PT.S0=(1.86+-.16)-4	
Strnth Fnctn	None		AUA Eval	Rept	AAEC/E-277	Mar 73 Musgrove.TBLS EXPTL DATA+BEST VALUES	
Strnth Fnctn	5.0+3	8.0+4	FEI Expt	Jour	YF 20 1092	Dec 74 Shorin+ AVG S0,S1,S2,S-GAM BY (N,G)	
Strnth Fnctn	None		COL Revw	Conf	75Wash. 780	Mar 75 Hacken+ NEVIS TOF S-WAVE STF	
Lvl Density	3.0+0	1.5+2	DUB Expt	Jour	YF 3 1 48	Jan 66 Van Nai Yang+ CHOPPER.LVL-DENSITY.	+
	4.5+0	1.3+2		Rept	JINR-P-2158	Jun 65 Van-Nai-Yang+	
	3.0+0	1.5+2		Jour	SNP 3 34	Jul 66 Van Nai Yang+ ENGL OF YF 3 48.	
	7.9+0	1.5+2		Data	EXFOR40030.009	Aug 70 LEVEL-DENSITY PARAMETER	
Lvl Density	+6		MIL Theo	Jour	EN 15 1 54	Jan 68 Facchini+ LDL PARS FROM LOW EN RES	
Lvl Density	None		AUWTheo	Conf	70Madurai 2 267	Dec 70 Ramamurty+ A-PARAMETER GVN,LANG'S-TH	
Lvl Density	None		MUNTheo	Jour	NP/A 217 269	Dec 73 Dilg+ A,DELTA. BACK SHIFTED FERMIGAS	
Lvl Density	None		ROC Theo	Jour	NP/A 223 589	May 74 Huizenga+ EXP CFD MICROSC TH AX SYMM	

70 Ytterbium 172

Quantity	Energy (ev) Min	Max	Lab	Type	Documentation Ref Vol Page	Author, Comments Date	Data
Total		2.5-2	BNL Expt	Jour	PR 174 1400	Oct 68 Mughabghab+ TRANS, SIG=10.2+-1.5B	+
				Conf	68Wash. § E28	Mar 68 .SUPERSEDED	
		2.5-2		Data	EXFOR12130.005	Jun 76 . 1 PT. SIGMA	
Total	1.0+0	2.0+4	COL Expt	Jour	PR/C 7 823	Feb 73 Liou+TRNS.TOF.RES PAR ANAL.NO CS GVN	+
	3.5+2	1.1+3		Rept	NYO-72-190	68 - . TOF, TRANS, CURVE	
	None			Data	EXFOR10081.067	Jan 78 .RAW DATA GVN UPON REQUEST TO NNDC.	
Total	1.4+7		LIN Expt	Conf	75Kiev 4 140	May 75 Djumin+ SIG GIVEN.OPTMOD ANAL,RADIUS	
Elastic		2.5-2	IJI Eval	Conf	75Kiev 1 169	May 75 Fedorova+ EVAL 2200M/S SIG,TABLE	
Potntl Scat	None		BNL Expt	Jour	PL/B 24 573	May 67 Chrien+ FROM ANALYSIS OF RESONANCES	
Thermal Scat		2.5-2	BNL Expt	Jour	PR 174 1400	Oct 68 Mughabghab+ PARAMAGN SIG=5.5+-1.7B	

70 Ytterbium 172

Quantity	Energy (ev) Min	Max	Lab	Type	Documentation Ref Vol Page	Date	Author, Comments	Data
Scattering	2.5−2		BNL	Expt	Jour PR 174 1400	Oct 68	Mughabghab+ TRANS SIG=4.3+ −0.9B.	
Absorption	2.5−2		BNL	Expt	Jour PR 174 1400	Oct 68	Mughabghab+ TRANS SIG=0.38+ −0,05B.	
Absorption	Maxwl	Pile	SGA	Expt	Jour JMS 6 435	71	Dobrozemsky+ CHANGE OF ABUND.TBL SIG	+
					Rept SGAE−PH−104	71	− + MASS−SPEC METHOD	
	Pile				Conf 66Paris 1 495	Oct 66	− +PPR82 MASS−SPEC VAL GIVN	
	Maxwl	Pile			Rept AEC−TR−7574	74	− + ENGLISH OF JMS 6 435	
	2.5−2				Data EXFOR20637.024	Sep 76	1PNT.SIGMA.	
Absorption	2.5−2		IJI	Eval	Conf 75Kiev 1 169	May 75	Fedorova+ EVAL 2200M/S SIG,TABLE	
Res Int Abs	1.4+2	8.2+2	BNL	Expt	Jour PR 174 1400	Oct 68	Mughabghab+ TRANS 23.5B FROM RES.	
					Conf 68Wash. § E28	Mar 68	.SUPERSEDED	
Res Int Abs	5.5−1		SGA	Expt	Jour JMS 6 435	71	Dobrozemsky+ EFF ABS RES INT GIVEN.	+
					Prog SGAE−PH−104	71	− +MASS−SPECTROMETRIC	
					Rept AEC−TR−7574	74	. ENGLISH OF JMS 6 415	
	5.5−1				Data EXFOR20637.025	Sep 76	1PNT.	
Res Int Abs	5.0−1		COL	Expt	Jour NSE 48 219	Jun 72	Rahn+. RI=26.2+ −6.0B	
Res Int Abs	5.0−1		IJI	Eval	Conf 75Kiev 1 169	May 75	Fedorova+ EVAL+CALC RI GIVEN,TABLE	
(n,γ)	Maxwl		MCM	Expt	Diss WALKER	May 56	Walker. SIGMA=9+ −6 B.	+
	Maxwl				Data EXFOR12127.023	Jun 76	. 1 PT. SIGMA	
(n,γ)	5.0+3	1.0+5	AUA	ExTh	Rept AAEC/E−198	May 69	Musgrove.S+P+D WAVE SIGMAS CALC,TBL	+
(n,γ)	3.0+4		AUA	Theo	Rept AAEC/E−211	Nov 70	Musgrove. SIGMA GIVEN AND CFD OTHER	
(n,γ)	8.1+0	2.0+2	NRL	Expt	Jour NP/A 173 477	Oct 71	Ritter+ LINAC TOF. TOF SPECTRUM.	
(n,γ)	1.0+5	1.0+7	BOL	Eval	Data BENZI−DFN 800.	May 72	40 PNTS	+
(n,γ)	Pile		ROS	ExTh	Prog ZFK−243 93	Sep 72	Mohsen+ NG−SYSTEMAT. FOR RARE EARTHS	
(n,γ)	5.0+3	8.0+4	FEI	Expt	Jour YF 20 1092	Dec 74	Shorin+ SIG(E)GRPH CFD H−F.RES−PARS	+
					Jour SNP 20 572	Jun 75	. ENGLISH OF YF 20,1092	
	5.0+3	8.4+4			Data EXFOR40274.003	Mar 75	SIGMA AT 32 E−RANGES GIVEN	
	2.0+3	2.0+5	FEI	Theo	Rept YK−20/1 29	75	Bychkov+ H−F,SIG(E) CURVES	
Spect (n,γ)	+0	+4	COL	Expt	Prog WASH−1124 31	Nov 68	Camarda+ MOXON−RAE DET TBC NO DATA	
Spect (n,γ)	Maxwl		NRL	Expt	Jour PR 183 983	Jul 69	Namenson+,GE(LI) DET,+ −3KEV ERROR	
Spect (n,γ)	Pile		CTH	Expt	Jour NP/A 161 209	Jan 71	Alenius+ PAIR,ANTICO SPEC. 36 LINES.	
Spect (n,γ)	1.4+2	2.0+2	NRL	Expt	Jour NP/A 173 477	Oct 71	Ritter+ LINAC TOF.4N RES. 6EG.	
(n,2n)	Fiss		CRC	Eval	Rept CRC−1003	Dec 60	Roy+,ESTIMATED AVG SIG=3.6MB	
(n,2n)	1.5+7		DEB	Eval	Rept REA 11 1 153	Mar 73	Boedy+ RECOMM.VALUE FROM N−Z SYSTEM.	
(n,2n)	1.5+7		KFI	Theo	Rept KFKI−73−68	Dec 73	Jeki.NEW FIT,CALC SIG CFD OTHERS,TBL	
(n,p)	Fiss		CRC	Eval	Rept CRC−1003	Dec 60	Roy+,ESTIMATED AVG SIG=0.006MB	
(n,p)	1.4+7	1.5+7	ARK	ExTh	Prog ORO−3235−29	Jan 67	Koch+,STAT MODEL CALC CFD EXPTS	
(n,p)	1.4+7		HLS	Expt	Jour PS 5 183	May 72	Tuurnala+ .MEASURED ACTIVATION GAMMA	
(n,α)	Fiss		CRC	Eval	Rept CRC−1003	Dec 60	Roy+,ESTIMATED AVG SIG=0.0001MB	
(n,α)	Maxwl		CCP	Expt	Jour YF 1 252	Feb 65	Andreev.IONIZ−CHAMBER,SIG=M.03MB	+
					Jour SNP 1 177	Aug 65	TRANSLATN.*	
(n,α)	Maxwl		LYO	Expt	Jour NP/A 231 437	Oct 74	Emsallem+ILL HF REACTOR,SIG+GRPH+TBL	+
	2.5−2				Data EXFOR20564.008	Sep 75	1PNT.SIGMA.	
Reson Params	1.4+2		DUB	Expt	Jour INDSWG−126 41	66	Van−Naj−Jan'.RES 141EV. PUBL.DUB2158	+
	3.0+0	1.5+2			Conf 65Antwerp § 187	Jul 65	Wang Nai Yang+ TRANS.1RES.	
	None				Rept JINR−P−2158	Jun 65	Wang Nai−Yang+ 1RES,TBL	
Reson Params	1.4+2	8.2+2	BNL	Expt	Jour PR 174 1400	Oct 68	Mughabghab+ TRANS 12ES WN+AVERAGE D	+
	1.4+2	8.2+2			Data EXFOR12130.011	Jun 76	. 12 RES E0,WN,WN0	
Reson Params	−		AUA	Theo	Rept AAEC/E−211	Nov 70	Musgrove. CALCULTD D+GAM WIDTH GIVEN	
Reson Params	−		DUB	Theo	Rept JINR−E4−5711	Apr 71	Soloviev. AVG LVL SPACING, EXPTS TBD	
Reson Params	1.4+2	1.0+4	COL	Expt	Jour PR/C 7 823	Feb 73	Liou+.TOF.G*WN FOR MANY,WG FOR 3,D	+
					Conf 71Albany 205	Aug 71	Camarada+D,WG GVN.TBP PR.	
	1.4+2	2.7+3			Rept NYO−72−190	68	Liou+TOF.WN FOR 20 ES.AVG D.WG.	
	1.4+2	9.9+3			Data EXFOR10081.	Jan 78	. 100 RES WN RED GVN,3RES WG.D GVN.	
Strnth Fnctn	1.4+2	8.2+2	BNL	Expt	Jour PR 174 1400	Oct 68	Mughabghab+ STF=.84+ −.34 FROM RES	
		+4			Jour PL/B 24 573	May 67	Chrien+ FROM RES+UNRESOLVED REGIONS	
		5.0+3			Conf 65Antwerp 69	Jul 65	− + TOT SIG SWAVE STF 1.55+ −.4	
Strnth Fnctn	1.4+2	8.2+2	BNL	Expt	Jour PR/C 1 1850	May 70	Mughabghab+,STF FROM RESON+SIGMA	
Strnth Fnctn	−		AUA	Theo	Rept AAEC/E−211	Nov 70	Musgrove. SMOOTHED S0,S1 AND S2 GIVN	
Strnth Fnctn	None		COL	Expt	Jour NSE 48 219	Jun 72	Rahn+. AVG WG=72 MEV OVER 4 RESON	
Strnth Fnctn	1.4+2	1.0+4	COL	Expt	Jour PR/C 7 823	Feb 73	Liou+.TOF.S0=1.68+ −0.20	+
					Conf 71Albany 205	Aug 71	Camarada+S0 GVN	
	1.4+2	2.7+3			Rept NYO−72−190	68	Liou.S0=(.99+ −.36)−4	
	1.4+2	1.0+4			Data EXFOR10081.040	Jan 78	. 1PT.S0=(1.68+ −.2)−4	
Strnth Fnctn	None		AUA	Eval	Rept AAEC/E−277	Mar 73	Musgrove.TBLS EXPTL DATA+BEST VALUES	
Strnth Fnctn	5.0+3	8.0+4	FEI	Expt	Jour YF 20 1092	Dec 74	Shorin+ AVG S0,S1,S2,S−GAM BY (N,G)	
					Jour SNP 20 572	Jun 75	. ENGLISH OF YF 20,1092	
Strnth Fnctn	2.5−2		COL	Theo	Conf 75Wash. 335	Mar 75	Felvinci+MOD ERICSON CALC CFD EXPT.	
Strnth Fnctn	None		COL	Revw	Conf 75Wash. 779	Mar 75	Hacken+ NEVIS TOF S−WAVE STF	

70 Ytterbium 172

Quantity	Energy (ev) Min	Max	Lab	Type	Documentation Ref Vol Page	Date	Author, Comments	Data
Lvl Density	+6		MIL	Theo Jour	EN 15 1 54	Jan 68	Facchini+ LDL PARS FROM LOW EN RES	
Lvl Density	None		CCP	Theo Jour	YF 11 1028	May 70	Rubchenya. DENSITY+A+TEMP GIVEN,GRPH	
				Jour	SNP 11 571	Nov 70	. ENGL OF YF 11 571.	
Lvl Density	None		AUW	Theo Conf	70Madurai 2 267	Dec 70	Ramamurty+ A – PARAMETER GVN,LANG'S – TH	
Lvl Density	None		CCP	Theo Jour	YF 13 43	Jan 71	Bravin+.DEFORM PAR,CALC,TBL,CFD EXPT	
Lvl Density	None		MUN	Theo Jour	NP/A 217 269	Dec 73	Dilg+ A,DELTA. BACK SHIFTED FERMIGAS	
Lvl Density	None		DUB	Theo Jour	NP/A 224 396	May 74	Malov+ 1/2 MICROSC.MODEL. DEFORM NUC	
Lvl Density	None		ROC	Theo Jour	NP/A 223 589	May 74	Huizenga+ EXP CFD MICROSC TH AX SYMM	
Lvl Density	+0	4.0+3	JAE	ExTh Jour	JPJ 37 581	Sep 74	Ideno.LVL SPACING CORRELATIONS.TBL.	
	1.0+0	4.0+3		Rept	JAERI – M – 5490	Nov 73	– .LEVEL SPACING CORRELATIONS.TBL	

70 Ytterbium 173

Quantity	Energy (ev) Min	Max	Lab	Type	Documentation Ref Vol Page	Date	Author, Comments	Data
Total	9.8+5		SHE	Theo Jour	NP 54 417	Jun 64	Maddison.OPTMOD FIT TO TOWLE GILBOY	
Total	2.5–2		BNL	Expt Jour	PR 174 1400	Oct 68	Mughabghab+ SIG=28+ – 2B.	+
				Conf	68Wash. § E28	Mar 68	.SUPERSEDED	
	2.5–2			Data	EXFOR12130.006	Jun 76	. 1 PT. SIGMA	
Total	1.0+0	2.0+4	COL	Expt Jour	PR/C 7 823	Feb 73	Liou+TRNS.TOF.RES PAR ANAL.NO CS GVN	+
	7.5+1	1.5+2		Rept	NYO – 72 – 190	68	. TOF, TRANS, CURVE.	
	None			Data	EXFOR10081.068	Jan 78	.RAW DATA GVN UPON REQUEST TO NNDC.	
Total	1.4+7		LIN	Expt Conf	75Kiev 4 140	May 75	Djumin+ SIG GIVEN.OPTMOD ANAL,RADIUS	
Elastic	2.5–2		IJI	Eval Conf	75Kiev 1 169	May 75	Fedorova+ EVAL 2200M/S SIG,TABLE	
Diff Elastic	7.0+6		LRL	Theo Rept	UCRL – 4927	Jul 57	Bjorklund+ OPTMDL CALC 6 – PARAM FIT	
Diff Elastic	9.8+5		SHE	Theo Jour	NP 54 417	Jun 64	Maddison.OPTMOD FIT TO TOWLE GILBOY	
Potntal Scat	None		BNL	Expt Jour	PL/B 24 573	May 67	Chrien+ FROM ANALYSIS OF RESONANCES	
Thermal Scat	2.5–2		BNL	Expt Jour	PR 174 1400	Oct 68	Mughabghab+ PARAMAGN SIG=5.2+ – 0.9B.	
Scattering	2.5–2		BNL	Expt Jour	PR 174 1400	Oct 68	Mughabghab+ TRANS SIG=3.8+0.6B.	
Absorption	2.5–2		BNL	Expt Jour	PR 174 1400	Oct 68	Mughabghab+ TRANS SIG=19+ – 2B.	
Absorption	Maxwl	Pile	SGA	Expt Jour	JMS 6 435	71	Dobrozemsky+ CHANGE OF ABUND.TBL SIG	+
				Rept	SGAE – PH – 104	71	– + MASS – SPEC METHOD	
	Pile			Conf	66Paris 1 495	Oct 66	– +PPR82 MASS – SPEC VAL GIVN	
	Maxwl	Pile		Rept	AEC – TR – 7574	74	– + ENGLISH OF JMS 6 435	
	2.5–2			Data	EXFOR20637.026	Sep 76	1PNT.SIGMA.	
Absorption	2.5–2		IJI	Eval Conf	75Kiev 1 169	May 75	Fedorova+ EVAL 2200M/S SIG,TABLE	
Res Int Abs	4.5+0	4.9+2	BNL	Expt Jour	PR 174 1400	Oct 68	Mughabghab+ TRANS 394B FROM RES.	
				Conf	68Wash. § E28	Mar 68	.SUPERSEDED	
Res Int Abs	5.5–1		SGA	Expt Jour	JMS 6 435	71	Dobrozemsky+ EFF ABS RES INT GIVEN.	+
				Prog	SGAE – PH – 104	71	– +MASS – SPECTROMETRIC	
				Rept	AEC – TR – 7574	74	. ENGLISH OF JMS 6 415	
	5.5–1			Data	EXFOR20637.027	Sep 76	1PNT.	
Res Int Abs	5.0–1		IJI	Eval Conf	75Kiev 1 169	May 75	Fedorova+ EVAL+CALC RI GIVEN,TABLE	
(n,γ)	Maxwl		MCM	Expt Diss	WALKER	May 56	Walker. SIGMA = 41+ – 8 B.	+
	Maxwl			Data	EXFOR12127.024	Jun 76	. 1 PT. SIGMA	
(n,γ)	5.0+3	1.0+5	AUA	ExTh Rept	AAEC/E – 198	May 69	Musgrove.S+P+D WAVE SIGMAS CALC,TBL	
(n,γ)	3.0+4		AUA	Theo Rept	AAEC/E – 211	Nov 70	Musgrove. SIGMA GIVEN AND CFD OTHER	
(n,γ)	1.0+3	1.0+7	BOL	Eval Jour	BENZI – DFN 801.	May 72	40 PNTS	
	1.0+3	1.0+7		Data	BENZI – DFN 839.	May 72	40 PNTS	
(n,γ)	5.0+3	8.0+4	FEI	Expt Jour	YF 20 1092	Dec 74	Shorin+ SIG(E)GRPH CFD H – F.RES – PARS	+
				Jour	SNP 20 572	Jun 75	. ENGLISH OF YF 20,1092	
	5.0+3	8.4+4		Data	EXFOR40274.004	Mar 75	SIGMA AT 32 E – RANGES GIVEN	
(n,γ)	2.0+3	2.0+5	FEI	Theo Rept	YK – 20/1 29	75	Bychkov+ H – F,SIG(E) CURVES	
Spect (n,γ)	+0	+4	COL	Expt Prog	WASH – 1124 31	Nov 68	Camarda+ MOXON – RAE DET TBC NO DATA	
Spect (n,γ)	Maxwl		NRL	Expt Jour	PR 183 983	Jul 69	Namenson+,GE(LI) DET,+ – 3KEV ERROR	
Spect (n,γ)	Pile		ANL	Expt Conf	69Studsvik 601	Aug 69	Smither+ NO DATA GVN,TB CFD STATMOD	
Spect (n,γ)	Maxwl		RIS	Expt Conf	69Studsvik 65	Aug 69	Koch+AUTMTD – CURVD – CRYST – SPEC,NDG+TBP	
Spect (n,γ)	Pile		CTH	Expt Jour	PS 3 55	71	Alenius+ GE(LI) PAIR+ANTICOINC	+
	Pile			Data	EXFOR20244.004	May 74	94PTS.	
Spect (n,γ)	Maxwl	2.0+3	MTR	Expt Rept	ANCR – 1016 29	Oct 71	Greenwood+.2ES TBLS GAMMA ES+INTENST	
Spect (n,γ)	7.6+4	1.2+6	MUN	Expt Jour	ZN/A 28 226	Feb 73	Wimmer. TBL, LVL – SCH OF YB – 174	
Spect (n,γ)	4.5+2	1.8+1	BNL	Expt Jour	PR/C 8 1035	Sep 73	Casten+.GAM SPECT AT 2 RESON ES	
	None			Conf	72Budapest 214	Aug 72	Mughabghab+ G – RAY SPECTRA ,GRPH	
Spect (n,γ)			MUN	Expt Jour	ZP 269 407	Sep 74	Loebner+ G – RAY – SPEC. OF YB – 174 GIVEN	
Spect (n,γ)	1.5+1	5.5+2	DUB	Expt Rept	JINR – P3 – 8511	Jan 75	Kharzavina+ GAMMA – SPECTRUM,GRAPH	
Spect (n,γ)	1.7+1	7.8+2	ORL	Expt Conf	76Lowell 1294	Jul 76	Mughabghab+G SPEC.SPINS FOR 56 RES.	
(n,2n)	Fiss		CRC	Eval Rept	CRC – 1003	Dec 60	Roy+,ESTIMATED AVG SIG=42.0MB	
(n,2n)	1.5+7		DEB	Eval Jour	REA 11 1 153	Mar 73	Boedy+ RECOMM.VALUE FROM N – Z SYSTEM.	

70 Ytterbium 173

Quantity	Energy (ev) Min	Max	Lab	Type	Documentation Ref Vol Page	Date	Author, Comments	Data
(n,2n)	1.5+7		KFI	Theo Rept	KFKI-73-68	Dec 73	Jeki.NEW FIT,CALC SIG CFD OTHERS,TBL	
(n,p)	Fiss		CRC	Eval Rept	CRC-1003	Dec 60	Roy+,ESTIMATED AVG SIG=0.007MB	
(n,p)	1.4+7	1.5+7	ARK	ExTh Prog	ORO-3235-29	Jan 67	Koch+,STAT MODEL CALC CFD EXPTS	
(n,p)	1.4+7		HLS	Expt Jour	PS 5 183	May 72	Tuurnala+.MEASURED ACTIVATION GAMMA	
(n,p)	1.5+7		KYU	Expt Jour	NST 12 681	Nov 75	Sato+.ACTIVATION SIG=13.5+-2.8 MB	+
	1.5+7			Data	EXFOR20595.005	Aug 76	1PNT.SIGMA.	
(n,α)	Fiss		CRC	Eval Rept	CRC-1003	Dec 60	Roy+,ESTIMATED AVG SIG=0.0014MB	
(n,α)	Maxwl		LYO	Expt Jour	NP/A 231 437	Oct 74	Emsallem+ILL HF REACTOR,SIG+GRPH+TBL	+
	2.5-2			Data	EXFOR20564.009	Sep 75	1PNT.SIGMA.	
(n,α)	1.4+7	1.8+7	IBJ	Expt Jour	NP/A 262 205	May 76	Glowacka+ALPHA SPECT. SIGMA(E).	+
				Prog	INR-1502 4	May 75	- + ALPHA SPECTR AT 2 ES,TABLE	
	1.4+7			Data	EXFOR30298.	May 75	DOUBLE DIFFSIG(31 PTS)+ANGDIST(1 PT)	
	1.8+7			Data	EXFOR30299.	May 75	DOUBLE DIFFSIG(38 PTS)+ANGDIST(1 PT)	
Reson Params	4.6+0	1.6+2	ANL	Expt Rept	ANL-6589 88	Aug 62	Carpenter. EOS, RES. PAR., SPECTRA	+
	3.3+1	1.6+2		Data	EXFOR12048.009	Jun 76	. 6 RES,E0,J	
	4.6+0	1.8+1		Data	EXFOR12048.010	Jun 76	. 2 RES,E0,J,WT,WN,PCS	
Reson Params	4.5+0	1.3+2	DUB	Expt Jour	YF 3 48	Jan 66	Wang+ TOF, TRNS, TBL, 22 RES	+
				Rept	INDSWG-126	66	.	
				Conf	65Antwerp 187	Jul 65	.SEE ALSO	
				Rept	JINR-P-2158	Jun 65	Wang+ 16RES, TBL, GWN, AVG D	
				Jour	SNP 3 34	Jul 66	.ENGL TRANSL	
	4.5+0	1.3+2		Data	EXFOR40030.	Aug 70	N-WIDTH AT 16RES, TOT-WID,CAPT-WID,D	
Reson Params		1.0+6	AUA	Theo Jour	AUJ 20 477	Oct 67	Cook. TBL OF AVG LVL SPACING D,L=0,1	
Reson Params	4.5+0	2.1+2	BNL	Expt Jour	PR 174 1400	Oct 68	Mughabghab+ 24ES 2G*WN+AVG D.4 WG	+
	4.5+0	2.1+2		Data	EXFOR12130.015	Jun 76	. 24 RES,E0,WN,WN0,WG	
Reson Params	-		AUA	Theo Rept	AAEC/E-211	Nov 70	Musgrove. CALCULTD D+GAM WIDTH GIVEN	
Reson Params	4.5+0	1.3+2	CJD	Eval Jour	YK-7	71	Zakharova+ SURVEY+SYSTEMATICS,GW,TBL	
				Rept	INDC(CCP)-27	Nov 72	.ENGLISH TRANSLATION OF YK-7 /71	
Reson Params	None		DUB	Theo Jour	YF 13 240	Feb 71	Malecki+G-WID,THEO CFD EXPT.TBL,GRPH	
				Jour	SNP 13 133	Aug 71	- + ENGL OF YF 13 240.	
Reson Params	4.5+0	1.1+2	BNL	Expt Prog	NCSAC-38 21	May 71	Chrien+. J FOR 14RESON FROM CAPTURE	
Reson Params	4.5+0	1.8+3	COL	Expt Jour	PR/C 7 823	Feb 73	Liou+.TOF.G*WN WG J VALUES GVN,D	+
	1.8+1	3.7+2		Rept	NYO-72-190	68	- .TOF.G*WN,WG,J.AVG D.	
	4.5+0	5.5+3		Data	EXFOR10081.	Jan 78	. 160RES.WN RED*G GVN,33RES WG.D GVN	
Reson Params	+0	+3	KUR	Theo Conf	73Kiev 2 301	May 73	Daneljan. CORREL N+G-WID+PARTL G-WID	
Reson Params	7.4+6		DUB	Theo Conf	74Petten 175	Sep 74	Malov+ DOBS,SEMI-MICROSCOPIC CALC.	
Reson Params	+0		DUB	Theo Jour	YF 21 40	Jan 75	Voronov+ MEAN D,WITH ROTAT.CFD EXPT	
				Jour	SNP 21 20	Jul 75	. ENGLISH OF YF 21,40	
Reson Params	1.8+1	6.2+2	DUB	Expt Rept	JINR-P3-8511	Jan 75	Kharzavina+ GAM-ANALYS,RES-SPINS TBL	
	+0	+3		Conf	73Kiev 2 337	May 73	Karzhavina+ SPIN IDENT,G-MULTIP MTHD	
Reson Params	1.7+1	7.8+2	ORL	Expt Conf	76Lowell 1294	Jul 76	Mughabghab+G SPEC.SPINS FOR 56 RES.	+
	1.8+1	7.7+2		Data	EXFOR10781.002	Nov 78	. 56 RES ESJ GVN.	
Strnth Fnctn	+3		BNL	Expt Jour	PRL 1 461	Dec 58	Hughes+ FC 1.2+-0.4	
Strnth Fnctn	5.0+0	1.5+2	DUB	Expt Jour	YF 3 48	Jan 66	Wang+ TOF, TRNS, TBL, 22 RES	+
				Rept	INDSWG-126	66	.	
				Conf	65Antwerp 187	Jul 65	.SEE ALSO	
				Rept	JINR-P-2158	Jun 65	Wang+ 16RES, TBL, GWN, AVG D	
				Jour	SNP 3 34	Jul 66	.ENGL TRANSL	
	4.5+0	1.3+2		Data	EXFOR40030.016	Aug 70	STRENGTH-FUNCTION, S-WAVE	
Strnth Fnctn	4.5+0	4.9+2	BNL	Expt Jour	PR 174 1400	Oct 68	Mughabghab+ STF=1.62+-.30 FROM RES	
		+4		Jour	PL/B 24 573	May 67	Chrien+ FROM RES+UNRESOLVED REGIONS	
		5.0+3		Conf	65Antwerp 69	Jul 65	- +TOT SIG SWAVE STF1.76+-.21	
Strnth Fnctn	4.5+0	4.9+2	BNL	Expt Jour	PR/C 1 1850	May 70	Mughabghab+,STF FROM RESON+SIGMA	+
Strnth Fnctn	-		AUA	Theo Rept	AAEC/E-211	Nov 70	Musgrove. SMOOTHED S0,S1 AND S2 GIVN	
Strnth Fnctn	4.5+0	1.8+3	COL	Expt Jour	PR/C 7 823	Feb 73	Liou+.TOF.S0=1.60+-0.28	
	1.8+1	3.7+2		Rept	NYO-72-190	68	- .S0=(1.64+-.45)-4	
	4.5+0	1.8+3		Data	EXFOR10081.043	Jan 78	. 1PT.S0=(1.60+-.28)-4	
Strnth Fnctn	None		AUA	Eval Rept	AAEC/E-277	Mar 73	Musgrove.TBLS EXPTL DATA+BEST VALUES	
Strnth Fnctn	5.0+3	8.0+4	FEI	Expt Jour	YF 20 1092	Dec 74	Shorin+ AVG S0,S1,S2,S-GAM BY (N,G)	
				Jour	SNP 20 572	Jun 75	. ENGLISH OF YF 20,1092	
Strnth Fnctn	1.8+1	6.2+2	DUB	Expt Rept	JINR-P3-8511	Jan 75	Kharzavina+ GAM-ANALYS,S0(I=+,-1/2)	
Strnth Fnctn	None		COL	Revw Conf	75Wash. 780	Mar 75	Hacken+ NEVIS TOF S-WAVE STF	
Lvl Density	3.0+0	1.5+2	DUB	Expt Jour	SNP 3 34	Jul 66	.TRANSLATN.*	+
				Jour	YF 3 1 48	Jan 66	Rdtv.CPTR,BETHE PRMTR,LVL DNSTY=2.5	
	4.5+0	1.3+2		Rept	JINR-P-2158	Jun 65	Van-Nai-Yang+	
	4.5+0	1.3+2		Data	EXFOR40030.017	Aug 70	LEVEL-DENSITY PARAMETER	
Lvl Density	+6		MIL	Theo Jour	EN 15 1 54	Jan 68	Facchini+ LDL PARS FROM LOW EN RES	
Lvl Density	None		AUW	Theo Conf	70Madurai 2 267	Dec 70	Ramamurty+ A-PARAMETER GVN,LANG'S-TH	

70 Ytterbium 173

Quantity	Energy (ev) Min	Max	Lab	Type	Documentation Ref Vol Page	Date	Author, Comments	Data
Lvl Density	None		MUN	Theo Jour	NP/A 217 269	Dec 73	Dilg+ A,DELTA. BACK SHIFTED FERMIGAS	
Lvl Density	None		DUB	Theo Jour	NP/A 224 396	May 74	Malov+ 1/2 MICROSC.MODEL. DEFORM NUC	
Lvl Density	None		ROC	Theo Jour	NP/A 223 589	May 74	Huizenga+ EXP CFD MICROSC TH AX SYMM	
Lvl Density	+7		FEI	Theo Jour	YF 21 485	Mar 75	Ignatjuk+ LVL DENS PARAMS,GRAPH	

70 Ytterbium 174

Quantity	Energy (ev) Min	Max	Lab	Type	Documentation Ref Vol Page	Date	Author, Comments	Data
Total	2.5−2		BNL	Expt Jour	PR 174 1400	Oct 68	Mughabghab+ TRANS SIG=142+−5B.	+
				Conf	68Wash. § E28	Mar 68	.SUPERSEDED	
	2.5−2			Data	EXFOR12130.007	Jun 76	. 1 PT. SIGMA	
Total	1.0+0	2.0+4	COL	Expt Jour	PR/C 7 823	Feb 73	Liou+TRNS.TOF.RES PAR ANAL.CURV.	+
	1.7+1	4.6+3		Rept	NYO−72−190	68	− .TOF.TRNS.SELF INDIC.	
	None			Data	EXFOR10081.069	Jan 78	.RAW DATA GVN UPON REQUEST TO NNDC.	
Total	1.4+7		LIN	Expt Conf	75Kiev 4 140	May 75	Djumin+ SIG GIVEN.OPTMOD ANAL,RADIUS	
Elastic	8.0+4	3.0+5	FEI	Theo Rept	YK− 20/1 29	75	Bychkov+ H−F,CALC SIG(E) CURVES	
Elastic	2.5−2		IJI	Eval Conf	75Kiev 1 169	May 75	Fedorova+ EVAL 2200M/S SIG,TABLE	
Potntal Scat	None		BNL	Expt Jour	PL/B 24 573	May 67	Chrien+ FROM ANALYSIS OF RESONANCES	
Tot Inelastc	8.0+4	3.0+5	FEI	Theo Rept	YK− 20/1 29	75	Bychkov+ H−F,CALC SIG(E) CURVES	
Diff Inelast	1.4+7		LRL	Theo Rept	UCRL−50181	Feb 67	Lutz+.CALC ANG DIST FOR FIRST 2+ LVL	
Thermal Scat	2.5−2		BNL	Expt Jour	PR 174 1400	Oct 68	Mughabghab+ PARAMAGN SIG=5.2+ −0.9B.	
Scattering	2.5−2		BNL	Expt Jour	PR 174 1400	Oct 68	Mughabghab+ TRANS SIG=72+ −5B	
Absorption	2.5−2		BNL	Expt Jour	PR 174 1400	Oct 68	Mughabghab+ TRANS SIG=65+ −5B	
Absorption	2.5−2		IJI	Eval Conf	75Kiev 1 169	May 75	Fedorova+ EVAL 2200M/S SIG,TABLE	
Res Int Abs	3.4+2	9.1+2	BNL	Expt Jour	PR 174 1400	Oct 68	Mughabghab+ TRANS 33.8B FROM RES	
				Conf	68Wash. § E28	Mar 68	.SUPERSEDED	
Res Int Abs	5.5−1		CPO	Expt Jour	JIN 32 2839	Oct 70	Sims+(N,G).CD CUT−OFF,VAL GVN.	+
	5.5−1			Data	EXFOR10608.	Aug 76	2PTS.MAXW SPEC MEAS AND 1/V REMOVED	
Res Int Abs	5.0−1		OSL	Expt Prog	INDC(NOR)−1 1	May 72	Alstad+ REDUCED CAPTINTEG REL AU,TBL	+
				Priv	PAPPAS	Nov 70	Pappas. ACT. POWD,LIQ SOLUT.TBP JIN	
	0.0+0	1.0+6		Data	EXFOR20094.007	Sep 71	1PNT.CAPTURE.	
Res Int Abs	5.0−1		COL	Expt Jour	NSE 48 219	Jun 72	Rahn+. RI=26+ −6B	
Res Int Abs	5.0−1		KJL	Expt Jour	JIN 34 2699	Sep 72	Steinnes. ACT. AU MONITOR	+
	5.0−1			Data	EXFOR20188.027	May 74	1PNT.CAPTURE.	
Res Int Abs	5.0−1		GHT	Expt Jour	JRC 20 695	74	Van Der Linden+ BY(N,G).CFD OTHS,TBL	+
	5.5−1			Conf	73Paris 2 241	Mar 73	− + ACT,REL THR+GOLD,TBL	
	5.5−1			Data	EXFOR20645.034	Jul 76	1PNT.CAPTURE.	
Res Int Abs	5.0−1		IJI	Eval Conf	75Kiev 1 169	May 75	Fedorova+ EVAL+CALC RI GIVEN,TABLE	
(n,γ)	Maxwl		OHO	Expt Jour	PR 53 437	Mar 38	Pool+ BETAS,CLOUDCH,RATIO YB176(N,G)	
(n,γ)	Maxwl		MCM	Expt Diss	WALKER	May 56	Walker. SIGMA = 72+ − 6 B.	+
	Maxwl			Data	EXFOR12127.025	Jun 76	. 1 PT, SIG	
(n,γ)	Maxwl		ROS	Expt Jour	ADP 12 225	63	Alexander+ ACTIV,SIG TO ISOM GIVEN	
				Rept	ZFK−RN−16	Sep 62	Brinckmann+VAL GVN,PRODCTN OF YB175M	
				Rept	RFP−TRANS−78	71	. ENGLISH OF ADP 12 225	
(n,γ)	Maxwl		ROS	Revw Rept	ZFK−RN−23	Sep 64	Albert. SIGMA (N,G) GVN,UNPUBLISHED	
(n,γ)	−		IEA	Comp Rept	IEA−INF− 10	Aug 68	Atalla. TABLES OF HL,SIG AND GAMM−E	
(n,γ)	5.0+3	1.0+5	AUA	ExTh Rept	AAEC/E−198	May 69	Musgrove.S+P+D WAVE SIGMAS CALC,TBL	+
(n,γ)	Maxwl		CPO	Expt Jour	JIN 32 2839	Oct 70	Sims+ CD CUT−OFF,REL CO59,SIG GIVEN	+
	Maxwl			Data	EXFOR10608.	Aug 76	2PTS.EFFECTIVE CS AND MAXW SPEC CALC	
(n,γ)	3.0+4		AUA	Theo Rept	AAEC/E−211	Nov 70	Musgrove. SIGMA GIVEN AND CFD OTHER	
(n,γ)	Maxwl		KFI	Comp Jour	JRC 7 365	Jun 71	Nagy+ SIGS,GAM+XRAY+BETA+ELECTR ES	
(n,γ)	1.0+3	1.0+7	BOL	Eval Data	BENZI−DFN 802.	May 72	40 PNTS	+
(n,γ)	Maxwl		OSL	Expt Prog	INDC(NOR)−1 1	May 72	Alstad+ ACTIVATION REL AU−197,TABLE	+
				Priv	PAPPAS	Nov 70	Pappas. ACT. POWD,LIQ SOLUT.TBP JIN	
	Maxwl			Data	EXFOR20094.006	Sep 71	1PNT.SIG.	
(n,γ)	2.5+4		AUW	Expt Jour	JP/A 5 877	Jun 72	Siddappa+ ACT. S,P−WAVE CS GIVEN	+
				ExTh Conf	70Madurai 2 29	Dec 70	Sriramachandra Murty+.S+P WAVE SIGMA	
	2.5+4			Expt Data	EXFOR30248.008	Jun 73	SIGMA CAPTURE VALUE	
(n,γ)	Pile		ROS	ExTh Prog	ZFK−243 93	Sep 72	Mohsen+ NG−SYSTEMAT. FOR RARE EARTHS	
(n,γ)	5.0+3	8.0+4	FEI	Expt Jour	YF 20 1092	Dec 74	Shorin+ SIG(E)GRPH CFD H−F.RES− PARS	+
				Jour	SNP 20 572	Jun 75	. ENGLISH OF YF 20,1092	
	5.0+3	8.4+4		Data	EXFOR40274.005	Mar 75	SIGMA AT 32 E− RANGES GIVEN	
(n,γ)	2.0+3	2.0+5	FEI	Theo Rept	YK− 20/1 29	75	Bychkov+ H−F,SIG(E) CURVES	
Spect (n,γ)	Maxwl		IFL	Expt Jour	NP/A 102 577	Oct 67	Bondarenko+.GE(LI)4ET=45U4354−CVENT2	
Spect (n,γ)	Maxwl		NRL	Expt Jour	PR 183 983	Jul 69	Namenson+,GE(LI) DET,+ −3KEV ERROR	
Spect (n,γ)	Maxwl		MUN	Expt Jour	ZN/A 26 3715	Mar 71	Breitig. LVL SCH OF YB 175	
Spect (n,γ)	Maxwl		KFI	Comp Jour	JRC 7 365	Jun 71	Nagy+ SIGS,GAM+XRAY+BETA+ELECTR ES	

70   Ytterbium   174

Quantity	Energy (ev) Min	Max	Lab	Type	Documentation Ref Vol Page	Author, Comments Date	Data
Spect (n,γ)	Pile		CTH	Expt	Jour PS 4 35	Oct 71 Alenius+.GE – PAIR SPEC.TBLE 126E,I. Q	+
	Pile				Data EXFOR20246.002	May 74 126PTS.	
Spect (n,γ)	Maxwl		IFL	Expt	Book PROKOFJEV	73 . TBL GAM,CONV ELECTR ES+INT,LVL SCH	
Inelastic γ	2.0+3	2.0+5	FEI	Theo	Rept YK– 20/1 29	75 Bychkov+ H–F	
(n,2n)	Fiss		CRC	Eval	Rept CRC – 1003	Dec 60 Roy+,ESTIMATED AVG SIG=6.1MB	
(n,2n)	1.5+7		DEB	Eval	Jour REA 11 1 153	Mar 73 Boedy+ RECOMM.VALUE FROM N–Z SYSTEM.	
(n,2n)	1.5+7		KFI	Expt	Rept KFKI – 73 – 68	Dec 73 Jeki.NEW FIT,CALC SIG CFD OTHERS,TBL	
(n,p)	Fiss		CRC	Eval	Rept CRC – 1003	Dec 60 Roy+,ESTIMATED AVG SIG=0.002MB	
(n,p)	1.4+7		SAH	Comp	Jour NP 60 273	Nov 64 Chatterjee.MEAN OF EXPT CFD SHELLMOD	
(n,p)	1.5+7		SAH	Expt	Jour IJP 41 667	67 Gujrathi+	+
					Prog AEET – 267 51	Aug 66 – + SIG GVN,DECAY SCHEME	
	1.5+7				Data EXFOR31069.002	Mar 73 .SIG GVN	
(n,p)	1.4+7	1.5+7	ARK	ExTh	Prog ORO – 3235 – 29	Jan 67 Koch+,STAT MODEL CALC CFD EXPTS	
(n,p)	1.5+7		ARK	Expt	Abst DA/B 32 5091	Mar 72 Bari. GE(LI) DET. ACT. SIG GIVEN	+
	1.5+7				Data EXFOR10431.018	Aug 75 1PT,SIGMA	
(n,p)	1.4+7		HLS	Expt	Jour PS 5 183	May 72 Tuurnala+.MEASURED ACTIVATION GAMMA	
(n,α)	Fiss		CRC	Eval	Rept CRC – 1003	Dec 60 Roy+,ESTIMATED AVG SIG=BELO 0.0001MB	
(n,α)	Maxwl		CCP	Expt	Jour YF 1 252	Feb 65 Andreev.IONIZ – CHAMBER,SIG=M.02MB	+
					Jour SNP 1 177	Aug 65 TRANSLATN.*	
(n,α)	1.4+7		HLS	Expt	Jour PS 5 183	May 72 Tuurnala+.MEASURED ACTIVATION GAMMA	
(n,α)	1.5+7		KYU	Expt	Jour NST 12 681	Nov 75 Sato+.ACTIVATION SIG=1.22+ – 0.23 MB	+
	1.5+7				Data EXFOR20595.006	Aug 76 1PNT.SIGMA.	
Reson Params	None		DUB	Expt	Jour JINR – P – 2158	Jun 65 Wang Nai – Yang+ 1RES,TBL	
Reson Params	3.5+2	8.9+2	BNL	Expt	Jour PR 174 1400	Oct 68 Mughabghab+ TRANS 2 ES WN+AVERAGE D	+
	3.5+2	8.9+2			Data EXFOR12130.012	Jun 76 . 2 RES,E0,WN,WN0	
Reson Params	–		AUA	Theo	Rept AAEC/E – 211	Nov 70 Musgrove. CALCULTD D+GAM WIDTH GIVEN	
Reson Params	–		DUB	Theo	Rept JINR – E4 – 5711	Apr 71 Soloviev. AVG LVL SPACING, EXPTS TBD	
Reson Params	3.4+2	2.0+4	COL	Expt	Rept PR/C 7 823	Feb 73 Liou+.TOF.G*WN FOR MANY,WG FOR 2,D	+
					Conf 71Albany 205	Aug 71 Camarada+D GVN FOR S LVLS.TBP PR	
	3.4+2	3.3+3			Rept NYO – 72 – 190	68 Liou.TOF.WN 10ES.AVG D.AVG WG.	
	3.4+2	2.0+4			Data EXFOR10081.	Jan 78 . 78RES WN RED GVN.2RES WG.D GVN.	
Strnth Fnctn		+4	BNL	Expt	Jour PL/B 24 573	May 67 Chrien+ FROM RES+UNRESOLVED REGIONS	
Strnth Fnctn	–		AUA	Theo	Rept AAEC/E – 211	Nov 70 Musgrove. SMOOTHED S0,S1 AND S2 GIVN	
Strnth Fnctn	None		COL	Expt	Jour NSE 48 219	Jun 72 Rahn+. AVG WG=80 MEV OVER 3 RESON	
Strnth Fnctn	3.4+2	2.0+4	COL	Expt	Jour PR/C 7 823	Feb 73 Liou+.TOF.SO=1.62+ – 0.21	+
					Conf 71Albany 205	Aug 71 Camarada+S0 GVN	
	3.4+2	3.3+3			Rept NYO – 72 – 190	68 Liou.TOF S0=(.89+ – .43) – 4	
	3.4+2	2.0+4			Data EXFOR10081.046	Jan 78 . 1PT.S0=(1.62+ – .21) – 4	
Strnth Fnctn	None		AUA	Eval	Rept AAEC/E – 277	Mar 73 Musgrove.TBLS EXPTL DATA+BEST VALUES	
Strnth Fnctn	5.0+3	8.0+4	FEI	Expt	Jour YF 20 1092	Dec 74 Shorin+ AVG S0,S1,S2,S – GAM BY (N,G)	
					Jour SNP 20 572	Jun 75 . ENGLISH OF YF 20,1092	
Strnth Fnctn	None		COL	Revw	Conf 75Wash. 780	Mar 75 Hacken+ NEVIS TOF S – WAVE STF	
Lvl Density	+6		MIL	Theo	Jour EN 15 1 54	Jan 68 Facchini+ LDL PARS FROM LOW EN RES	
Lvl Density	None		CCP	Theo	Jour YF 11 1028	May 70 Rubchenya. DENSITY+A+TEMP GIVEN	
					Jour SNP 11 571	Nov 70 . ENGL OF YF 11 571.	
Lvl Density	None		AUWTheo		Conf 70Madurai 2 267	Dec 70 Ramamurty+ A – PARAMETER GVN,LANG'S – TH	
Lvl Density	None		CCP	Theo	Jour YF 13 43	Jan 71 Bravin+.DEFORM PAR,CALC,TBL,CFD EXPT	
Lvl Density	None		MUNTheo		Jour NP/A 217 269	Dec 73 Dilg+ A,DELTA. BACK SHIFTED FERMIGAS	
Lvl Density	None		DUB	Theo	Jour NP/A 224 396	May 74 Malov+ 1/2 MICROSC.MODEL. DEFORM NUC	
Lvl Density	None		ROC	Theo	Jour NP/A 223 589	May 74 Huizenga+ EXP CFD MICROSC TH AX SYMM	
Lvl Density	+0	1.0+4	JAE	ExTh	Jour JPJ 37 581	Sep 74 Ideno.LVL SPACING CORRELATIONS.TBL.	
	1.0+0	1.0+4			Rept JAERI – M – 5490	Nov 73 – .LEVEL SPACING CORRELATIONS.TBL	
	+0	3.5+3			Jour JPJ 30 620	Mar 71 – + RES SPACING CORRELATION ANAL	

70   Ytterbium   175

Quantity	Energy (ev) Min	Max	Lab	Type	Documentation Ref Vol Page	Author, Comments Date	Data
Reson Params	–		AUA	Theo	Rept AAEC/E – 211	Nov 70 Musgrove. CALCULTD D+GAM WIDTH GIVEN	
Strnth Fnctn	–		AUA	Theo	Rept AAEC/E – 211	Nov 70 Musgrove. SMOOTHED S0,S1 AND S2 GIVN	
Lvl Density	+6		MIL	Theo	Jour EN 15 1 54	Jan 68 Facchini+ LDL PARS FROM LOW EN RES	
Lvl Density	None		MUNTheo		Jour NP/A 217 269	Dec 73 Dilg+ A,DELTA. BACK SHIFTED FERMIGAS	
Lvl Density	None		DUB	Theo	Jour NP/A 224 396	May 74 Malov+ 1/2 MICROSC.MODEL. DEFORM NUC	
Lvl Density	None		ROC	Theo	Jour NP/A 223 589	May 74 Huizenga+ EXP CFD MICROSC TH AX SYMM	

70 Ytterbium 176

Quantity	Energy (ev) Min	Max	Lab	Type	Documentation Ref Vol Page	Author, Comments Date	Data
Total	2.5−2		BNL	Expt Jour	PR 174 1400	Oct 68 Chrien+ TRANS SIG=14.9+ −1.0B	+
				Conf	68Wash. 875	Mar 68 Mughabghab.	
	2.5−2			Data	EXFOR12130.008	Jun 76 . 1 PT. SIGMA	
Total	1.0+0	2.0+4	COL	Expt Jour	PR/C 7 823	Feb 73 Liou+TRNS.TOF.RES PAR ANAL.NO CS GVN	+
	5.4+1	4.6+3		Rept	NYO−72−190	68 − .TOF.TRNS.SELF INDIC.	
	None			Data	EXFOR10081.070	Jan 78 .RAW DATA GVN UPON REQUEST TO NNDC.	
Total	1.4+7		LIN	Expt Conf	75Kiev 4 140	May 75 Djumin+ SIG GIVEN.OPTMOD ANAL,RADIUS	
Elastic	2.5−2		IJI	Eval Conf	75Kiev 1 169	May 75 Fedorova+ EVAL 2200M/S SIG,TABLE	
Potntal Scat	None		BNL	Expt Jour	PL/B 24 573	May 67 Chrien+ FROM ANALYSIS OF RESONANCES	
Tot Inelastc	1.5+7		DEB	ExTh Jour	AHP 25 91	Oct 68 Peto+ RATIO (NN')/(N2N) FROM THEORY	+
Tot Inelastc	1.4+7		KFI	Comp Jour	JRC 7 365	Jun 71 Nagy+ SIGMA, GAMMA+XRAY ES,HALF−LIFE	
Diff Inelast	1.4+7		ARK	Expt Jour	PL 2 293	Oct 62 Kantele. 5+ −2MB TO YB176M T=11.7SEC	+
				Data	EXFOR12105.002	Jun 76 . 1 PT. DSIGMA	
Thermal Scat	2.5−2		BNL	Expt Jour	PR 174 1400	Oct 68 Mughabghab+ PARAMAGN SIG=5.2+ −1.6B.	
Scattering	2.5−2		BNL	Expt Jour	PR 174 1400	Oct 68 Mughabghab+ TRANS SIG=4.2+ −0.8B	
Absorption	2.5−2		IJI	Eval Conf	75Kiev 1 169	May 75 Fedorova+ EVAL 2200M/S SIG,TABLE	
Res Int Abs	1.5+2	5.8+3	BNL	Expt Jour	PR 174 1400	Oct 68 Mughabghab+ TRANS 7.6B FROM RES	
				Conf	68Wash. § E28	Mar 68 .SUPERSEDED	
Res Int Abs	5.0−1		OSL	Expt Prog	INDC(NOR)−1 1	May 72 Alstad+ REDUCED CAPTINTEG REL AU,TBL	+
				Priv	PAPPAS	Nov 70 Pappas. ACT. POWD,LIQ SOLUT.TBP JIN	
	0.0+0	1.0+6		Data	EXFOR20094.009	Sep 71 1PNT.CAPTURE.	
Res Int Abs	5.0−1		COL	Expt Jour	NSE 48 219	Jun 72 Rahn+. RI=8+ −2B	
Res Int Abs	5.0−1		GHT	Expt Jour	JRC 20 695	74 Van Der Linden+ BY(N,G).CFD OTHS,TBL	+
	5.5−1			Conf	73Paris 2 241	Mar 73 − + ACT,REL THR+GOLD,TBL	
	5.5−1			Data	EXFOR20645.035	Jul 76 1PNT.CAPTURE.	
Res Int Abs	5.0−1		IJI	Eval Conf	75Kiev 1 169	May 75 Fedorova+ EVAL+CALC RI GIVEN,TABLE	
Res Int Abs	5.0−1		KJL	Expt Jour	JIN 37 1591	Aug 75 Steinnes. CD−RAT+ACTIV INTEG,CFD,TBL	+
	5.0−1			Data	EXFOR20635.011	Aug 76 1PNT.CAPTURE.	
(n,γ)	Maxwl		MCM	Expt Diss	WALKER	May 56 Walker. SIGMA APPRX 0.	+
	Maxwl			Data	EXFOR12127.026	Jun 76 . 1 PT. SIGMA	
(n,γ)	None		GOE	Expt Jour	ZP 160 201	Oct 60 Hoffman+ ACTIVATION,REL CU63	
(n,γ)	3.6+3	1.9+6	ANL	Expt Jour	JNE 22 267	May 68 Stupegia+ ACT REL U235 NF,TABLE 20ES	+
				Rept	INDC−156	67 .FULL TEXT OF PAPERS51	
				Conf	66Paris 1 520	Oct 66 .SUPERSEDED	
				Prog	ANL−7125 237	May 66 .SUPERSEDED	
				Rept	ANL−7175 212	Apr 66 .SUPERSEDED	
	3.6+3	1.9+6		Data	EXFOR11624.012	Jun 76 . 20 PTS. SIGMA	
(n,γ)	−		IEA	Comp Rept	IEA−INF− 10	Aug 68 Atalla. TABLES OF HL,SIG AND GAMM−E	
(n,γ)	5.0+3	1.0+5	AUA	ExTh Rept	AAEC/E−198	May 69 Musgrove.S+P+D WAVE SIGMAS CALC,TBL	+
(n,γ)	1.0+3	1.0+6	GA	Theo Conf	70Helsinki 2 281	Jun 70 Fricke+44. SIG(E) GRAPH,STATMOD CALC	
(n,γ)	3.0+4		AUA	Theo Rept	AAEC/E−211	Nov 70 Musgrove. SIGMA GIVEN AND CFD OTHER	
(n,γ)	Maxwl		KFI	Comp Jour	JRC 7 365	Jun 71 Nagy+ SIGMA,GAM+XRAY+ELECTR ES GIVEN	
(n,γ)	1.0+3	1.0+7	BOL	Eval Data	BENZI−DFN 803.	May 72 40 PNTS	+
(n,γ)	Maxwl		OSL	Expt Prog	INDC(NOR)−1 1	May 72 Alstad+ ACTIVATION REL AU−197,TABLE	+
				Priv	PAPPAS	Nov 70 Pappas. ACT. POWD,LIQ SOLUT.TBP JIN	
	Maxwl			Data	EXFOR20094.008	Sep 71 1PNT.SIG.	
(n,γ)	2.5+4		AUW	Expt Jour	JP/A 5 877	Jun 72 Siddappa+ ACT. S,P−WAVE CS GIVEN	+
				ExTh Conf	70Madurai 2 29	Dec 70 Sriramachandra Murty+.S+P WAVE SIGMA	
	2.5+4			Expt Data	EXFOR30248.009	Jun 73 SIGMA CAPTURE VALUE	
(n,γ)	Pile		ROS	ExTh Prog	ZFK−243 93	Sep 72 Mohsen+ NG−SYSTEMAT. FOR RARE EARTHS	
(n,γ)	5.0+3	8.0+4	FEI	Expt Jour	YF 20 1092	Dec 74 Shorin+ SIG(E)GRPH CFD H−F.RES−PARS	+
				Jour	SNP 20 572	Jun 75 . ENGLISH OF YF 20 1092	
	5.0+3	8.4+4		Data	EXFOR40274.006	Mar 75 SIGMA AT 32 E−RANGES GIVEN	
(n,γ)	1.5+7		OUL	Expt Rept	JU−RR−1/1976	Mar 76 Valkonen.(THESIS).ACTIV.TBL. 14.5MEV	+
				Data	EXFOR20673.034	Nov 76 1PNT.SIGMA.	
Spect (n,γ)	Maxwl		AMS	Expt Jour	PL 12 238	Oct 64 Loebner+ RABBIT,6S ISOMDECAY,HL LVL1	+
Spect (n,γ)	Maxwl		CTH	Expt Jour	NP/A 186 209	May 72 Alenius+ PAIR,ANTI−CO SPEC. 78 E(G)	+
	Pile			Data	EXFOR20224.	May 74 78PTS.	
Spect (n,γ)	−		HLS	Expt Jour	ZP 252 283	Jun 72 Pursiheimo+, LVL SCHM OF TM173	
Spect (n,γ)	Maxwl		IFL	Expt Book	PROKOFJEV	73 . TBL GAM,CONV ELECTR ES+INT	
Inelastic γ	1.5+7		IRK	Expt Jour	AK 9 277	Oct 67 Bornemsisza+.VAL CFD REFS	+
	1.4+7	1.5+7		ExTh Jour	OAWS 176 227	68 Bornemsisza+ CFD STATMOD	
	1.5+7			Expt Data	EXFOR20082.004	Sep 71 1PNT.SIGMA.	
Inelastic γ	1.4+7		KFI	Comp Jour	JRC 7 365	Jun 71 Nagy+ SIGMA, GAMMA+XRAY ES,HALF−LIFE	
Nonelastic γ	1.4+7		HLS	Expt Jour	PS 2 163	Nov 70 Tuurnala+. E+I TM176 AND YB176M DCAY	
(n,2n)	1.5+7		ARK	Expt Jour	PR 118 242	Apr 60 Wille+ MEAS ACT SIG = 430+ −100MB	+
	1.5+7			Data	EXFOR12033.050	Jun 76 . 1 PT. SIGMA	

70 Ytterbium 176

Quantity	Energy (ev) Min	Max	Lab	Type	Documentation Ref Vol Page	Date	Author, Comments	Data
(n,2n)	Fiss		CRC	Eval Rept	CRC - 1003	Dec 60	Roy+,ESTIMATED AVG SIG=9.3MB	
(n,2n)	1.5+7		MUA	Expt Jour	NP 28 560	Dec 61	Khurana+ ACTIV,CFD STATMOD	+
	1.5+7			Data	EXFOR31247.020	Mar 73	.SIG GVN	
(n,2n)	1.5+7		IRK	Expt Jour	NP 51 329	Feb 64	Spenke.ACTIVATION,ABS BETA COUNT	+
	1.5+7			Data	EXFOR20058.004	Sep 71	1PNT.SIG.	
(n,2n)	1.4+7		HAM	Comp Jour	NP 65 257	Mar 65	Bormann. 3EXPT VALS.CFD SHELL EFFECT	
(n,2n)	1.5+7		DEB	ExTh Jour	AHP 25 91	Oct 68	Peto+ RATIO (NN')/(N2N) FROM THEORY	+
(n,2n)	1.5+7		DEB	Comp Jour	REA 7 4 93	Dec 69	Csikai+ SIG+HL COMPILTN,N-ACTIV-ANAL	
(n,2n)	1.4+7	1.5+7	JYV	Eval Rept	JU-RR-3/1970	Jun 70	Leppaemaeki+ TABLE OF EVAL AVG SIG	
(n,2n)	+7		KFI	Theo Rept	KFKI-71-8	Feb 71	Jeki. CALCULATED CFD EXPTL SIG VALUE	
(n,2n)	1.4+7		KFI	Comp Jour	JRC 7 365	Jun 71	Nagy+ SIGMA, GAMMA+ELECTRON ES GIVEN	
(n,2n)	1.4+7		ITJ	Expt Jour	JRC 14 201	73	Janczyszyn+ TO ISO,ACTIV.CFD OTH,TBL	+
	1.4+7			Data	EXFOR30322.016	Feb 76	1 PNT.	
(n,2n)	1.5+7		DEB	Eval Jour	REA 11 1 153	Mar 73	Boedy. COMPILATION+RECOMM.VALUE,TBL	
				Rept	IAEA-153 173	73	- . RECOMM. VALUE ONLY	
(n,2n)	1.5+7		TAT	Theo Jour	JP/A 7 1457	Aug 74	Kondaiah. CALC ON STAT MODEL	
(n,2n)	1.4+7		MNZ	Expt Jour	RCA 22 11	75	Weigel+ TOT SIG, ACT METHOD	
(n,2n)	1.5+7		JUL	Expt Jour	NP/A 224 319	May 74	Qaim. ACT.GE(LI)	+
				Jour	RRL 25 335	May 76	- + SIG IN GRPH. SYST VS (N-Z)/A	
	1.5+7			Data	EXFOR20541.053	Apr 76	1PNT.SIGMA.	
(n,p)	Fiss		CRC	Eval Rept	CRC - 1003	Dec 60	Roy+,ESTIMATED AVG SIG=0.0005MB	
(n,p)	1.5+7		SAH	Expt Jour	AEET-267 52	Aug 66	Gujrathi+ SIG GVN,DECAY SCHEME	
(n,p)	1.4+7	1.5+7	ARK	ExTh Prog	ORO-3235-29	Jan 67	Koch+,STAT MODEL CALC CFD EXPTS	
(n,p)	1.4+7		HLS	Expt Jour	PS 5 183	May 72	Tuurnala+.MEASURED ACTIVATION GAMMA	
(n,α)	Fiss		CRC	Eval Rept	CRC - 1003	Dec 60	Roy+,ESTIMATED AVG SIG=BELO 0.0001MB	
(n,α)	1.5+7		ARK	Expt Jour	PR 166 1173	Feb 68	Ihochi+ SIG=0.20+-0.05MB	+
	1.5+7			Data	EXFOR12121.002	Jun 76	. 1 PT. SIGMA	
(n,α)	1.4+7		HLS	Expt Jour	PS 5 183	May 72	Tuurnala+.MEASURED ACTIVATION GAMMA	
(n,α)	Maxwl		LYO	Expt Jour	NP/A 231 437	Oct 74	Emsallem+ILL HF REACTOR,SIG+GRPH+TBL	+
	2.5-2			Data	EXFOR20564.010	Sep 75	1PNT.SIGMA.	
Reson Params	None		DUB	Expt Rept	JINR-P-2158	Jun 65	Wang Nai-Yang+ 1RES,TBL	
Reson Params	1.5+2	2.2+3	BNL	Expt Jour	PR 174 1400	Oct 68	Mughabghab+ TRANS 7 ES WN+AVERAGE D	+
	1.5+2	2.2+3		Data	EXFOR12130.013	Jun 76	. 7 RES,E0,WN,WN0	
Reson Params	-		AUA	Theo Rept	AAEC/E-211	Nov 70	Musgrove. CALCULTD D+GAM WIDTH GIVEN	
Reson Params	-		DUB	Theo Rept	JINR-E4-5711	Apr 71	Soloviev. AVG LVL SPACING, EXPTS TBD	
Reson Params	9.8+1	2.0+4	COL	Expt Jour	PR/C 7 823	Feb 73	Liou+.TOF.G*WN FOR 68RESON,D	+
				Conf	71Albany 205	Aug 71	Camarada+D GVN FOR S LVLS.TBP PR	
	9.8+1	3.2+3		Rept	NYO-72-190		68 Liou.TOF.WN 12 ES.AVG D.	
	9.8+1	2.0+4		Data	EXFOR10081.	Jan 78	. 68RES WN RED GVN.D GVN.	
Strnth Fnctn	1.5+2	5.8+3	BNL	Expt Jour	PR/C 1 1850	May 70	Mughabghab+,STF FROM RESON=1.7+-0.5	
				Jour	PR 174 1400	Oct 68	- + STF=1.70+-.54 FROM RES	
		+4		Jour	PL/B 24 573	May 67	Chrien+ FROM RES+UNRESOLVED REGIONS	
Strnth Fnctn	-		AUA	Theo Rept	AAEC/E-211	Nov 70	Musgrove. SMOOTHED S0,S1 AND S2 GIVN	
Strnth Fnctn	None		COL	Expt Jour	NSE 48 219	Jun 72	Rahn+. AVG WG=82 MEV OVER 1 RESON	
Strnth Fnctn	9.8+1	2.0+4	COL	Expt Jour	PR/C 7 823	Feb 73	Liou+.TOF.SO=2.29+-0.32	+
				Conf	71Albany 205	Aug 71	Camarada+S0 GVN	
	9.8+0	1.2+4		Data	EXFOR10081.049	Jan 78	. 1PT.S0=(2.29+-.32)-4	
Strnth Fnctn	None		AUA	Eval Rept	AAEC/E-277	Mar 73	Musgrove.TBLS EXPTL DATA+BEST VALUES	
Strnth Fnctn	5.0+3	8.0+4	FEI	Expt Jour	YF 20 1092	Dec 74	Shorin+ AVG S0,S1,S2,S-GAM BY (N,G)	
				Jour	SNP 20 572	Jun 75	. ENGLISH OF YF 20,1092	
Strnth Fnctn	None		COL	Revw Conf	75Wash. 780	Mar 75	Hacken+TBL.AVG WG,STF GVN.	
Lvl Density	None		AUW	Theo Conf	70Madurai 2 267	Dec 70	Ramamurty+ A-PARAMETER GVN,LANG'S-TH	
Lvl Density	None		CCP	Theo Jour	YF 13 43	Jan 71	Bravin+.DEFORM PAR,CALC,TBL,CFD EXPT	
Lvl Density	+0	1.0+4	JAE	ExTh Jour	JPJ 37 581	Sep 74	Ideno.LVL SPACING CORRELATIONS.TBL.	
	1.0+0	1.0+4		Rept	JAERI-M-5490	Nov 73	- .LEVEL SPACING CORRELATIONS.TBL	

70 Ytterbium 177

Quantity	Energy (ev) Min	Max	Lab	Type	Documentation Ref Vol Page	Date	Author, Comments	Data
Reson Params	-		AUA	Theo Rept	AAEC/E-211	Nov 70	Musgrove. CALCULTD D+GAM WIDTH GIVEN	
Strnth Fnctn	-		AUA	Theo Rept	AAEC/E-211	Nov 70	Musgrove. SMOOTHED S0,S1 AND S2 GIVN	
Lvl Density	+6		MIL	Theo Jour	EN 15 1 54	Jan 68	Facchini+ LDL PARS FROM LOW EN RES	
Lvl Density	None		MUN	Theo Jour	NP/A 217 269	Dec 73	Dilg+ A,DELTA. BACK SHIFTED FERMIGAS	
Lvl Density	None		DUB	Theo Jour	NP/A 224 396	May 74	Malov+ 1/2 MICROSC.MODEL. DEFORM NUC	
Lvl Density	None		ROC	Theo Jour	NP/A 223 589	May 74	Huizenga+ EXP CFD MICROSC TH AX SYMM	

71 Lutetium

Quantity	Energy (ev) Min	Max	Lab	Type	Documentation Ref Vol Page	Author, Comments Date	Data
Total	Maxwl		COL Expt	Jour	PR 48 265	Aug 35 Dunning+ IONCH,TRANS,RA-BE/PARAFIN	N
Total	3.0-1	3.5+1	BNL Expt	Jour	PR 92 656	Nov 53 Foote+ CRYSTLSPECT. CURV. RES ABS.	+
	5.4-2	3.1+0		Data	EXFOR12107.004	Jun 76 . 64 PTS.	
Total	2.7+0	3.4+2	BNL Expt	Jour	PR 99 10	Jul 55 Harvey+ FC. TRNS. CURVS. RES ANAL.	+
	2.7+0	3.4+2		Data	EXFOR11912.039	Jun 76 . 401 PTS. CS DATA	
Total	1.4-1	2.6+0	BNL Expt	Jour	PR 100 1414	Dec 55 Landon.SIG ZERO FOR 3 RESONANCE ES	
Total	1.2-0	1.0+0	HAR Expt	Jour	JNEA 13 35	Oct 60 Baston+ TRANSM NAT+ENRICHED SAMPLES	+
Total	7.4-2		IOW Expt	Jour	PR 121 610	Jan 61 Atoji. TRANSMISSION 105+ -2 B	
Total	8.2-3	2.9-1	BSP Expt	Conf	66Paris 1 53	Oct 66 Zimmerman+,P.129 , SIG(E)GRAPH	+
				Jour	NP/A 95 683	Apr 67 SEE ALSO *	
	8.2-3	2.9-1		Data	EXFOR30224.	Dec 72 SIG AT 57ES, SIG AT 0.025 EV,PRIVCOM	
Total	2.0-2	1.0+0	IFU Expt	Prog	YFI-4 38	May 67 Vertebnyj+.,TBL,CURVES,TBP UFZ	
				Rept	INDC-187E	67 . ENGL OF YFI-4 38	
Total	1.0-2	1.0+1	WUR Expt	Rept	EIR-123	Jul 67 Brunner+.TOF TRANS CFD OTHER EXPTS	+
				Conf	66Paris 1 61	Oct 66 - + PPR 20. PRELIM DATA.	
Total	1.0-4	3.0-3	MUN Expt	Jour	AKE 16 49	70 Knorr+ TRANS EXPT, TBL	
Total	2.5+6	1.5+7	BNW Expt	Jour	PR/C 3 576	Feb 71 Foster+,TRANS,CURVS,CFD OTHERS+TH	+
	3.0+6	1.5+7		Jour	PRL 22 139	Jan 69 - + TOF CURVE CFD P-B TBP SOON	
	2.5+6	1.5+7		Jour	NIM 36 1	Sep 65 .EXPT DETAILS	
	2.3+6	1.5+7		Data	EXFOR10047.075	Aug 73 . 236 PTS.	
Total	1.3+7	1.5+7	DEB Eval	Rept	IAEA-153 173	73 Boedy+ MOST PROBABLE VAL OF SIG,TBL	
				Rept	AHP 30 115	Oct 71 Angeli+ AVG SIG,CFD CALC.TBLS.GRAPH	
Total	-3	1.9+0	THS Theo	Rept	IKE-6 89 65	Jun 75 Keinert. DATA LIBRARY	
Elastic	7.4-2		IOW Expt	Jour	PR 121 610	Jan 61 Atoji. DIFFRACTION TBL.	+
	7.4-2			Data	EXFOR12113.	Jun 76 . 2 PTS. COH SCT CS, AMP GVN.	
Elastic	2.5-2		ANL Expt	Jour	JCP 35 1950	Dec 61 Atoji. DIFF. SCT. AMPL. INT. TBL.	
Elastic	1.0-2	1.0+1	IFU Expt	Jour	UFZ 13 605	Apr 68 Vertebnyi+ GRPH SIG(E),NO MAGN CONTR	
				Jour	UPJ 13 425	Oct 68 TRANSLATN.*	
Thermal Scat	1.0-2	1.0+1	IFU Expt	Jour	UFZ 13 605	Apr 68 Vertebnyi+ GRPH SIG(E),NO MAGN CONTR	
				Jour	UPJ 13 425	Oct 68 TRANSLATN.*	
Thermal Scat	1.0-4	1.0+3	MUN Revw	Jour	EEN 80 1	77 Koester. SCAT LENGTH,FREE SIG	
Scattering	7.4-2		IOW Expt	Jour	PR 121 610	Jan 61 Atoji. DIFFRACTION. CS GVN.	+
	7.4-2			Data	EXFOR12113.009	Jun 76 . 1 PT. SCT CS = 13+ -2B.	
Scattering	2.5-2		BSP Expt	Conf	66Paris 1 53	Oct 66 Amaral+,P.129,THR SIG(.025EV)GIVEN	+
				Jour	NP/A 95 683	Apr 67 SEE ALSO *	
	2.5-2			Data	EXFOR30224.023	Dec 72 DEDUCED SIGMA	
Scattering	2.0-2	3.0+1	IFU Expt	Conf	68Riga	Jan 68 Gnidak+ ABST,TOF,4PI-GEOMETRY	
Scattering	2.0-2	3.0-2	IFU Expt	Conf	70Helsinki 1 651	Jun 70 Vertebnij+ 2200M/SEC SIGMA GIVEN,TBL	
				Rept	BNL-TR-495	Jul 72 . ENGLISH OF 70HELSIN 1 651	
Absorption	1.0-4	3.0-3	MUN Theo	Jour	AKE 16 49	70 Knorr+ FROM TOT SIG EXPT CALC ,TBL	
Res Int Abs	5.0-1	1.0+6	CCP Expt	Conf	55Geneva 5 91	Aug 55 Spivak+.VAL GVN CFD REF,PPR659	
Res Int Abs	5.0-1		MTR Expt	Rept	IN- 1195	May 68 Scoville+ REACTIV COEF MEAS.	+
				Jour	ANS 10 259	Jun 67 .SUPERSEDED	
	5.0-1			Data	EXFOR11820.016	Jun 76 . 1 PT. RIA=840+ -25B.	
(n,γ)	Maxwl		ORL Expt	Jour	PR 83 643	Aug 51 Pomerance. LOCAL OSC REL AU ABS 95 B	+
	Maxwl			Data	EXFOR11047.055	Jun 76 . 1 PT. CS=108+ -6 B.	
(n,γ)	2.0+2	8.0+3	ORL Expt	Conf	61Saclay 203	Sep 61 Block+ LIQ. SCINT. 25 ELEMENTS.	+
				Conf	61Vienna 1 95	Aug 61 Neiler.	
	2.0+2	1.0+4		Conf	61Vienna 1 95	Aug 61 - .PPR73,TABLE FOR SOME ES,GRAPH	
	2.1+2	5.8+3		Data	EXFOR11935.019	Jun 76 . 44 PTS.	
(n,γ)	3.0+4	6.5+4	ORL Expt	Jour	PR 129 2695	Mar 63 Macklin+ LIQ SCINT,2.52 AND 1.20B	+
	6.5+3	2.0+5		Jour	PR 122 182	Apr 61 Gibbons+ TOF. 49 ELEMENTS. RES ANAL.	
	3.0+6	6.5+4		Conf	61Vienna 1 95	Aug 61 Neiler.	
	6.5+3	2.0+5		Data	EXFOR11329.	Jun 76 . 79 PTS, SIG	
(n,γ)	8.0-2	3.0+4	LEB Comp	Rept	INDSWG-64 43	64 Konks. GRAPH SIG(E)	
(n,γ)	3.0+4		LEB Expt	Conf	JINR-1845 100	Jun 64 Konks+ PB-SLOWDOWN-TIME, NDG	
(n,γ)	2.5-2		BSP Expt	Conf	66Paris 1 53	Oct 66 Zimmerman+,P.129,DEDUCED SIG(.025EV)	+
				Jour	NP/A 95 683	Apr 67 SEE ALSO *	
	2.5-2			Data	EXFOR30224.024	Dec 72 DEDUCED SIGMA	
(n,γ)	-1	5.0+4	DUB Expt	Jour	YF 7 493	Mar 68 Konks+ SIG(NEUT-E) GRPH,PB-SLOW-DOWN	
				Jour	SNP 7 310	Sep 68 - + ENGL OF YF 7 493.	
(n,γ)	2.5+1	1.0+4	LAS Expt	Conf	68Wash. § E22	Mar 68 Harlow+ TOF BOMB SOURCE CURVE	+
	None			Data	EXFOR10324.	Dec 73 0 PTS DATA WITHDRAWN	
(n,γ)	2.5-2	2.5-2	AE Expt	Jour	NUK 6 245	Sep 68 Sokolowski+.PILE OSC. FAST CHOPPER.	+
	Pile			Data	EXFOR20077.012	Sep 71 1PNT.SIG.	
(n,γ)	+3	+7	FEI Revw	Conf	70Helsinki 2 245	Jun 70 Abramov. PPR114.REVW OF DATA STATUS	
(n,γ)	3.0+4		AUA Theo	Rept	AAEC/E-211	Nov 70 Musgrove. SIGMA GIVEN AND CFD OTHER	

71 Lutetium

Quantity	Energy (ev) Min	Max	Lab	Type	Documentation Ref Vol Page	Author, Comments Date	Data
(n,γ)	1.0+2	1.0+6	LRL	Expt Prog	USNDC-1 94	May 72 Czirr+. TO BE COMPLETED. NO DATA GVN	
(n,γ)	3.0+4	3.0+5	USP	Expt Jour	NP/A 196 83	Nov 72 Lepine+ LI7-P NS.TOF.M-R. REL TO IN	+
	3.0+4	3.0+5		Data	EXFOR30233.010	Mar 73 NDS,RELATIVE TO IN,ABSOLUTE ERROR	
(n,γ)	None		MUN	Theo Diss	GRYNTAKIS	Mar 76 Gryntakis.,CALC.OF WESTCOTTS G-FUNCT	
				Jour	RCA 22 128	Mar 75 - +,EQUIVALENT TO THESIS	
(n,γ)	1.0-2	1.0+1	WUR	Expt Jour	NSE 60 53	May 76 Widder.TOF.CS VS.E GRPHS.2200M/S CS	+
	9.9-3	9.3+0		Rept	EIR-217	Apr 75 - . POWDER SAMPLE	
				Conf	74Petten 757	Sep 74 - . M-R DET,ABS.EXP.,NDG	
	1.0-2	9.3+0		Priv	SWISS PH S	Oct 71 - . TOF+MOXON-RAE.CURVS CFD SIGT	
	9.9-3	9.3+0		Data	EXFOR20437.009	Nov 75 387PTS.SIGMA.	
Spect (n,γ)	Maxwl		ARF	Expt Prog	ARF-1193-6	Apr 62 Greenwood. CRYST SPEC.LOW-E GAMMAS	
Spect (n,γ)	Maxwl		CAS	Expt Jour	NC 27 538	Jan 63 Giannini+ NAI(TL),E+INTENSTY,TO.35MV	+
Spect (n,γ)	1.4+7	1.5+7	HLS	Expt Jour	ZP 204 456	Aug 67 Kantele+,LU-OXYD IRRADIATED	
Spect (n,γ)	+0	+4	COL	Expt Prog	WASH-1124 31	Nov 68 Camarda+ MOXON-RAE DET TBC NO DATA	
Spect (n,γ)	2.5-2		MIT	Comp Rept	MITNE-85	Jan 69 Rasmussen+TBL G INT.=AFCRL-69-0071	
Spect (n,γ)	None		BNL	Expt Prog	WASH-1127 21	Apr 69 Chrien+ANAL TO BE COMPLETED,NO DATA	
Spect (n,γ)	Maxwl		ATI	Expt Jour	AKE 15 269	70 Fleck+ 36 GS, HL OF LU 177 ISOM	
Spect (n,γ)	2.0+3		MTR	Expt Prog	NCSAC-31 76	May 70 Greenwood+,ANAL TO BE COMPL,NO DATA	
Spect (n,γ)	None		PEL	Expt Prog	INIS-MF-310 31	71 .SHORT NOTE,LIFE-TIME VS GAM-E,NDG	
Spect (n,γ)	Maxwl		UPP	Expt Jour	ZP 254 89	Aug 72 Hoegberg+,INT CONVERSION SPEC	
Spect (n,γ)	Pile		MUN	Expt Jour	ZP 258 315	Mar 73 Henkelmann. E + INT OF GS GIVEN	+
	2.5-2			Data	EXFOR20606.018	Jun 76 9PTS.	
(n,2n)	1.5+7		DEB	Eval Jour	REA 11 1 153	Mar 73 Boedy+ RECOMM.VALUE FROM N-Z SYSTEM.	
(n,α)	1.5+7	1.5+7	CIS	Expt Jour	NP 46 51	Jul 63 Marcazzan. = 1 DATA INDEX LINES	+
Reson Params	4.4+0	1.3+2	BNL	Expt Jour	PR 99 10	Jul 55 Harvey+.FC TRANSM. 32 RES. AREA ANAL	+
	4.4+0	1.3+2		Data	EXFOR11912.055	Jun 76 . 32 RES, E0,WN,WN0	
Reson Params	1.6+0		BNL	Expt Jour	PR 100 1414	Dec 55 Landon.ALSO 1.57EV WT WG ISOT ASSGND	+
	1.6+0			Data	EXFOR12178.008	Jun 76 . 1 RES, E0,WT,WG,PCS	
Reson Params	+0	+2	BNL	Expt Prog	WASH-745 9	Nov 57 Hughes+FC.TOT CS MEAS.RES ANAL.NDG.	
Strnth Fnctn	+0	+5	BNL	Expt Prog	WASH-745 9	Nov 57 Hughes. FC ANAL P AVG. NDG.	
Strnth Fnctn	1.0+4	2.0+5	ORL	Expt Jour	PR 122 182	61 Gibbons+ CAPT MEAS. S0, S1, GVN.	+
	1.0+4	2.0+5		Data	EXFOR11329.	Jun 76 . 4 PTS, S0,S1,D,AVE WG	
Strnth Fnctn	8.0-1	5.0+4	LEB	Expt Conf	JINR-1845 100	Jun 64 Konks+ PB-SLOWDOWN-TIME, TABLE	
Strnth Fnctn		5.0+4	RI	Expt Jour	YFI-5 59	Oct 67 Konks+ TABLE	
				Rept	INDC-232E	Jan 69 . ENGL OF YFI-5 59	
Strnth Fnctn	-1	5.0+4	DUB	Expt Jour	YF 7 493	Mar 68 Konks+ TABLE OF S0+S1 VALS,CFD OTHER	
	+3	+5		Conf	65Antwerp	Jul 65 - .DUBNA.S0,S1	
	-1	5.0+4		Jour	SNP 7 310	Sep 68 - + ENGL OF YF 7 493.	
Lvl Density	None		SAC	Expt Jour	NP/A 133 417	Aug 69 Bergere+NUCL TEMP,A PARAM,FROM NG	
(γ,n)	5.0+6	3.5+7	SAC	Expt Jour	NP/A 133 417	Aug 69 Bergere+LORENTZ LINE PARAM,GRPHS,TBL	

71 Lutetium 167

Quantity	Energy (ev) Min	Max	Lab	Type	Documentation Ref Vol Page	Author, Comments Date	Data
Reson Params	-		AUA	Theo Rept	AAEC/E-211	Nov 70 Musgrove. CALCULTD D+GAM WIDTH GIVEN	
Strnth Fnctn	-		AUA	Theo Rept	AAEC/E-211	Nov 70 Musgrove. SMOOTHED S0,S1 AND S2 GIVN	

71 Lutetium 168

Quantity	Energy (ev) Min	Max	Lab	Type	Documentation Ref Vol Page	Author, Comments Date	Data
Reson Params	-		AUA	Theo Rept	AAEC/E-211	Nov 70 Musgrove. CALCULTD D+GAM WIDTH GIVEN	
Strnth Fnctn	-		AUA	Theo Rept	AAEC/E-211	Nov 70 Musgrove. SMOOTHED S0,S1 AND S2 GIVN	

71 Lutetium 169

Quantity	Energy (ev) Min	Max	Lab	Type	Documentation Ref Vol Page	Author, Comments Date	Data
(n,p)	Maxwl		IFU	Theo Rept	ICD-4 20	67 Dadakina+ PENETR COEFF CALC,TABLE	
Reson Params	-		AUA	Theo Rept	AAEC/E-211	Nov 70 Musgrove. CALCULTD D+GAM WIDTH GIVEN	
Strnth Fnctn	-		AUA	Theo Rept	AAEC/E-211	Nov 70 Musgrove. SMOOTHED S0,S1 AND S2 GIVN	

71 Lutetium 170

Quantity	Energy (ev) Min	Max	Lab	Type	Documentation Ref Vol Page	Date	Author, Comments	Data
(n,p)	Maxwl		IFU	Theo Rept	ICD – 4 20	67	Dadakina+ PENETR COEFF CALC,TABLE	
Reson Params	–		AUA	Theo Rept	AAEC/E – 211	Nov 70	Musgrove. CALCULTD D+GAM WIDTH GIVEN	
Strnth Fnctn	–		AUA	Theo Rept	AAEC/E – 211	Nov 70	Musgrove. SMOOTHED S0,S1 AND S2 GIVN	

71 Lutetium 171

Quantity	Energy (ev) Min	Max	Lab	Type	Documentation Ref Vol Page	Date	Author, Comments	Data
(n,p)	Maxwl		IFU	Theo Rept	ICD – 4 20	67	Dadakina+ PENETR COEFF CALC,TABLE	
Reson Params	–		AUA	Theo Rept	AAEC/E – 211	Nov 70	Musgrove. CALCULTD D+GAM WIDTH GIVEN	
Strnth Fnctn	–		AUA	Theo Rept	AAEC/E – 211	Nov 70	Musgrove. SMOOTHED S0,S1 AND S2 GIVN	

71 Lutetium 172

Quantity	Energy (ev) Min	Max	Lab	Type	Documentation Ref Vol Page	Date	Author, Comments	Data
(n,p)	Maxwl		IFU	Theo Rept	ICD – 4 20	67	Dadakina+ PENETR COEFF CALC,TABLE	
Reson Params	–		AUA	Theo Rept	AAEC/E – 211	Nov 70	Musgrove. CALCULTD D+GAM WIDTH GIVEN	
Strnth Fnctn	–		AUA	Theo Rept	AAEC/E – 211	Nov 70	Musgrove. SMOOTHED S0,S1 AND S2 GIVN	

71 Lutetium 173

Quantity	Energy (ev) Min	Max	Lab	Type	Documentation Ref Vol Page	Date	Author, Comments	Data
(n,p)	Maxwl		IFU	Theo Rept	ICD – 4 20	67	Dadakina+ PENETR COEFF CALC,TABLE	
Reson Params	–		AUA	Theo Rept	AAEC/E – 211	Nov 70	Musgrove. CALCULTD D+GAM WIDTH GIVEN	
Strnth Fnctn	–		AUA	Theo Rept	AAEC/E – 211	Nov 70	Musgrove. SMOOTHED S0,S1 AND S2 GIVN	

71 Lutetium 174

Quantity	Energy (ev) Min	Max	Lab	Type	Documentation Ref Vol Page	Date	Author, Comments	Data
(n,p)	Maxwl		IFU	Theo Rept	ICD – 4 20	67	Dadakina+ PENETR COEFF CALC,TABLE	
Reson Params	–		AUA	Theo Rept	AAEC/E – 211	Nov 70	Musgrove. CALCULTD D+GAM WIDTH GIVEN	
Reson Params	–		DUB	Theo Rept	JINR – E4 – 5711	Apr 71	Soloviev.RESONANCE STRUCTURE STUDY	
Strnth Fnctn	–		AUA	Theo Rept	AAEC/E – 211	Nov 70	Musgrove. SMOOTHED S0,S1 AND S2 GIVN	

71 Lutetium 175

Quantity	Energy (ev) Min	Max	Lab	Type	Documentation Ref Vol Page	Date	Author, Comments	Data
Total	+0	+3	ORL	Expt Conf	60Vienna 535	Oct 60	Block+.NDG,EXPT DESCRIBED	
		4.3+1		Abst	BAP 3 364	Nov 58	Harvey+,TRANS,12E0S SEEN,NO DATA	
Total	1.2 – 2	1.0+0	HAR	Expt Jour	JNEA 13 35	Oct 60	Baston+ TRANSM SC+CS.GRAPH SIGT – 5.5B	+
				Rept	TNCC(UK) – 49	Aug 59	Lisle.TOF CHOPPER	
Total	3.0+6	1.5+7	KFK	Revw Conf	70Helsinki 2 219	Jun 70	Cierjacks.113. SIG(E) GRPH CFD OPTMD	
Total	Maxwl		MTR	Expt Prog	NCSAC – 33 89	Dec 70	Young.FAST CHOPPER,VALUE GIVEN	
Total	1.0+0	3.0+3	COL	Expt Jour	PR/C 11 1231	Apr 75	Liou+ANAL.FOR RES,STF,AVG D.TBLS.	+
	None			Data	EXFOR10488.005	Jun 75	. 0 PTS DATA UNOBTAINABLE.	
Total		– 3	THS	Theo Rept	IKE – 6 89 65	Jun 75	Keinert. DATA LIBRARY	
Elastic	2.5 – 2	1.9+0	IJI	Eval Conf	75Kiev 1 169	May 75	Fedorova+ EVAL 2200M/S SIG,TABLE	
Potntl Scat	1.2 – 2	1.0+0	HAR	Expt Jour	JNEA 13 35	Oct 60	Baston+. 3.8 TO 5.5 B FROM TOF DATA	
Absorption	1.2 – 2	1.0+0	HAR	Expt Jour	JNEA 13 35	Oct 60	Baston+ SIGTOT – 5.5B,=23+ – 3B AT THR	
Absorption	2.5 – 2		IJI	Eval Conf	75Kiev 1 169	May 75	Fedorova+ EVAL 2200M/S SIG,TABLE	
Res Int Abs	5.5 – 1		MOL	Theo Rept	BLG – 421	Sep 67	Damle+,EVAL ACT R.I. = 638+ – 100,TO MS	
Res Int Abs	5.5 – 1		MOL	Eval Rept	BLG – 421	Sep 67	Damle+,EVAL ACT R.I. = 638+ – 100,TO MS	
Res Int Abs	5.0 – 1		MTR	Expt Rept	IN – 1195	May 68	Scoville+ REACTIVITY MEAS. TBL.	+
				Jour	ANS 10 259	Jun 67	.SUPERSEDED	
	5.0 – 1			Data	EXFOR11820.017	Jun 76	. 1 PT. RIA=885+ – 30B.	
Res Int Abs	5.0 – 1		COL	Expt Jour	NSE 48 219	Jun 72	Rahn+ CAPT.TRNS. RI=1158+ – 280B.	
Res Int Abs		– 1	CAI	ExTh Rept	AREAEE – 165	73	Abul – Ela+ EPITHRML RI VS THEO,TBL	+
	4.5 – 1			Expt Data	EXFOR30376.002	Feb 77	EPICADMIUM RI.	
Res Int Abs	5.5 – 1		RCN	Revw Conf	73Paris 2 271	Mar 73	Zijp.ACT,RECOMM FROM LITERATURE,TBL	
Res Int Abs	5.0 – 1		GHT	Expt Jour	JRC 20 695	74	Van Der Linden+ BY(N,G).CFD OTHS,TBL	+
	5.5 – 1			Conf	73Paris 2 241	Mar 73	– + ACT,REL THR+GOLD,TBL	
	5.5 – 1			Data	EXFOR20645.036	Jul 76	1PNT.CAPTURE.	
Res Int Abs	5.0 – 1		IJI	Eval Conf	75Kiev 1 169	May 75	Fedorova+ EVAL+CALC RI GIVEN,TABLE	

71 Lutetium 175

Quantity	Energy (ev) Min	Max	Lab	Type	Documentation Ref Vol Page	Date	Author, Comments	Data
Res Int Abs	5.0−1		KJL	Expt	Jour JIN 37 1591	Aug 75	Steinnes. CD−RAT+ACTIV INTEG,CFD,TBL	+
	5.0−1				Data EXFOR20635.012	Aug 76	1PNT.CAPTURE.	
Res Int Abs		2.0+2	NIR	Expt	Conf 76Lowell 1253	Jul 76	Belanova+TRNS.RIA CALC.CFD.NDG	
(n,γ)	2.0+4	7.0+5	OXF	Expt	Jour PRSA 170 513	Apr 39	Griffiths.RA−BE PHOTONEUT ACTIVATION	
	Pile		ANL	Expt	Jour PR 72 888	Nov 47	Seren+ THR IRRAD. ACT. CS GVN.	+
	Pile				Data EXFOR11447.109	Jun 76	1 PT. CS=15.9B+−20 PCT.	
(n,γ)	Fiss		ANL	Expt	Jour PR 78 632	Jun 50	Hughes+ REL SIG(THERMAL). HL GVN.	+
	Fiss				Data EXFOR11596.017	Jun 76	1 PT. CS=.158B HL=3.7HR.	
(n,γ)	Fiss		BNL	Expt	Jour PR 91 1423	Sep 53	Hughes+.ALSO LVL SPACINGS AT EXCIT E	
(n,γ)	1.5+7		ARK	Expt	Jour PR 118 242	Apr 60	Wille+ ACT. TBL. CFD STAT TH.	+
	1.5+7				Data EXFOR12033.051	Jun 76	1 PT. CS=2.+−1B.	
(n,γ)	5.0+3	9.0+4	ORL	Theo	Jour RMP 37 166	Jan 65	Macklin+.CALC FOR KT=5TO90KEV	
(n,γ)	1.0−2	6.0+1	MOL	Eval	Rept BLG−421	66	Damle+. CURVE RECOMMENDED SIGS	
(n,γ)	1.0+3	1.0+4	LAS	Theo	Rept LA−3463	Jan 66	Bell. TH CAPTURE OF RARE EARTHS	
(n,γ)	3.0+4	2.0+5	ORL	Expt	Jour PR 159 1007	Jul 67	Macklin+ TOF.TOT EN DET.TBL 8ES,ABSL	+
	3.0+4	2.0+5			Data EXFOR11679.020	Jun 76	8 PTS. CS DATA.	
(n,γ)	Maxwl	Pile	MOL	Eval	Rept BLG−421	68	Damle+ TBP THRSIG RESINTG GIVEN	
(n,γ)	Maxwl	Pile	MOL	Eval	Rept BLG−421	68	Damle+ TBP THRSIG RESINTG GIVEN	
(n,γ)	Fiss		MOL	Expt	Conf 68Wash. 2 1263	Mar 68	Fabry+ ACT 185+−10MB TO LU176M	+
	Fiss				Data EXFOR20264.005	May 74	1PNT.SIGMA.	
(n,γ)	1.4+5	3.1+6	ANL	Expt	Jour JNE 22 267	May 68	Stupegia+ CS AT 18 ES GVN,REL U235NF	+
	1.0+4	3.0+6			Conf 66Paris 1 520	Oct 66	−+ CURVE, CFD STAT MODEL	
	1.4+5	3.1+6			Data EXFOR11624.013	Jun 76	18 PTS.	
(n,γ)	−		IEA	Comp	Rept IEA−INF−10	Aug 68	Atalla. TABLES OF HL,SIG AND GAMM−E	
(n,γ)	2.4+4		MUA	Theo	Jour IJP 42 567	Sep 68	Chaubey+ METHD OF BOOTH,VAL CFD XPT	+
				Expt	Jour NP 66 267	May 65	−+,SB−BE,ACT BETA−DET REL I127	
	2.4+4				Data EXFOR30063.010	Dec 70	SIGMA FOR 3.7 H HALF−LIFE	
(n,γ)	Maxwl		MOL	Expt	Prog EANDC(E)115U	Mar 69	Fabry+JACQUEMIN, REL TO AU(N,G)	
	2.5−2				Data EXFOR20186.003	May 74	1PNT.SIGMA.	
(n,γ)	3.0+3	3.0+5	LRL	Theo	Prog NCSAC−31 108	May 70	Gardner+,OPTMDL CALCULATION,CURVE	
(n,γ)	1.0+3	1.0+6	GA	Theo	Conf 70Helsinki 2 281	Jun 70	Fricke+44. SIG(E) GRAPH,STATMOD CALC	
(n,γ)	3.0+4		AUA	Theo	Rept AAEC/E−211	Nov 70	Musgrove. SIGMA GIVEN AND CFD OTHER	
(n,γ)	Maxwl		MTR	Expt	Prog NCSAC−33 89	Dec 70	Young.FAST CHOPPER,VALUE GIVEN	
(n,γ)	1.5+7		MUA	Expt	Prog BARC−553 19	Aug 71	Hasan+ SIG EXPT,CFD TH,ABST ONLY,NDG	
					Conf 70Madurai 2 36	Dec 70	. SAME ABSTRACT ONLY	
(n,γ)	2.4+4		MUA	Theo	Jour IJP 46 114	Mar 72	Chaubey+ P−WAVE STRENGTH FUNCT,TABLE	
(n,γ)	1.0+3	1.0+7	BOL	Eval	Data BENZI−DFN 840.	May 72	40 PNTS	+
	1.0+3	1.0+7			Data BENZI−DFN 804.	May 72	40 PNTS	
(n,γ)	2.5−2		RCN	Revw	Conf 73Paris 2 271	Mar 73	Zijp.RECOMMENDED FROM LITERATURE,TBL	
	+6		II	Expt	Conf 73Kiev 4 312	May 73	Lakosi+ ACTIV BY PHOTONEUTRONS,TABLE	+
	+6				Data EXFOR30268.015	Jul 74	LU−175(INL)+LU−176(NG),1 POINT	
(n,γ)	1.0+0	3.0+3	COL	Expt	Jour PR/C 11 1231	Apr 75	Liou+ANAL.FOR AVG WG.	
(n,γ)	1.0−2	1.0+1	WUR	Expt	Jour NSE 60 53	May 76	Widder.TOF.CS VS.E GRPHS.2200M/S CS	+
	1.0−2	1.1+1			Rept EIR−217	Apr 75	− . POWDER SAMPLE	
					Conf 74Petten 757	Sep 74	− . M−R DET,ABS.EXP.,NDG	
	1.0−2	1.1+1			Data EXFOR20437.010	Nov 75	232PTS.SIGMA.	
(n,γ)	None		RCN	Revw	Rept ECN−2	Sep 76	Zijp+ INTERCOMP. INTEGRAL SIG SAND−2	
Spect (n,γ)	1.5+0		YAL	Expt	Abst BAP 4 35	Jan 59	Springer+,NAI(TL),GAMMA MULTIPLICITY	
Spect (n,γ)	Pile		CTH	Expt	Jour NP 39 286	Dec 62	Hardell+. PRECISION E DET OF ISOM LV	
Spect (n,γ)	Maxwl		RIS	Expt	Jour ZP 184 153	Apr 65	Maier. GAMMAS FROM 39 TO 524 KEV	
Spect (n,γ)	None		OSU	Expt	Abst DA 25 7339	Jun 65	Staehle. REL INTENSITY 3GS GIVEN.	
Spect (n,γ)	Maxwl		ANL	Expt	Conf 69Studsvik 15	Aug 69	Bolotin.SHERA. G−G−COINC−SPECS,GE−LI	
Spect (n,γ)	Maxwl		LAS	Expt	Jour PR 187 1516	Nov 69	Shera+,GE(LI) SI(LI) DET,152 GAMMAS	
Spect (n,γ)	Maxwl		FRS	Expt	Jour HPA 42 917	Dec 69	Michaud+ PAIR+ANTICOMPTON−SPEC,GRPH	
Spect (n,γ)	Maxwl		SAC	Expt	Prog EANDC(E)127U	Apr 70	Audias+,GE(LI) DET	
Spect (n,γ)	2.6+0	1.5+2	BNL	Expt	Jour PR/C 2 675	Aug 70	Wasson+,GE(LI) DET,RESONANT CAPTURE	
Spect (n,γ)	Maxwl		CAS	Expt	Jour NC/A 8 748	Apr 72	Fubini+ GELI.TBL GAMMA ES+INTS.	+
	Maxwl				Data EXFOR20441.002	Nov 75	53PTS.	
Spect (n,γ)	Maxwl		IFL	Expt	Book PROKOFJEV	73	. TBL GAM,CONV ELECTR ES+INT,LVL SCH	
	Pile				Jour NP/A 194 305	Oct 72	Balodis+ DR−3 RISO CRYSTSP. 193 GS.	
					Jour ZP 180 298	64	. SEE ALSO	
Spect (n,γ)	Pile		GRN	Expt	Jour ZP 259 45	Mar 73	Van Der Werf.BETA DECAY LU−176−ISOM	
Spect (n,γ)	None		ROS	Expt	Prog ZFK−262 86	Sep 73	Seidel+ PROMPT+DELAYED SPEC,GAMS,TBL	
Spect (n,γ)	2.6+0	3.0+2	NRL	Expt	Jour NP/A 237 45	Jan 75	Namenson+ GAM−SPEC GRAPH,FOR RESPARS	
Spect (n,γ)	Maxwl		FRS	Expt	Jour NP/A 251 305	Oct 75	Geinoz+ ANTI−COMPT,TBL OF EN+INTENS	
Inelastic γ	6.0+5	2.2+6	TUL	Expt	Abst BAP 18 582	Apr 73	Sperry+ GE(LI) DET, 8 NEW GAMMAS	
(n,2n)	1.5+7		ARK	Expt	Jour PR 118 242	Apr 60	Wille.MEAS ACT SIG.TBL.CFD STAT TH.	+
	1.5+7				Data EXFOR12033.052	Jun 76	1 PT. CS=1.600+−.300B	

71 Lutetium 175

Quantity	Energy (ev) Min	Energy (ev) Max	Lab	Type	Documentation Ref Vol Page	Date	Author, Comments	Data
(n,2n)	Fiss		CRC	Eval Rept	CRC-1003	Dec 60	Roy+,ESTIMATED AVG SIG=4.0MB	
(n,2n)	1.4+7		HAM	Comp Jour	NP 65 257	Mar 65	Bormann. 1EXPT VALS.CFD SHELL EFFECT	
(n,2n)	1.3+7	1.5+7	BNL	Theo Jour	NSE 23 238	Nov 65	Pearlstein.3ES.STAT MDL CALC.TBL CS.	
(n,2n)	Fiss		BNL	Theo Jour	NSE 23 238	Nov 65	Pearlstein.STATMDL CALC.SPEC AVG.TBL	
(n,2n)	1.4+7		ALD	Expt Rept	AWRE-O-76/66	Dec 66	Vallis. SIG FOR METASTABLE AND GND.	+
	1.5+7			Data	EXFOR20347.	Sep 74	2PTS.SIGMA.	
(n,2n)	1.5+7		MUN	Expt Jour	NP/A 118 9	Sep 68	Dilg+ ACTIV.REL AL(N,A) .TO G,METAST	+
	1.5+7			Data	EXFOR20802.	Dec 78	2PTS.SIGMA.	
(n,2n)	1.5+7		DEB	Comp Jour	REA 7 4 93	Dec 69	Csikai+ SIG+HL COMPILTN,N-ACTIV-ANAL	
(n,2n)	1.4+7	1.5+7	JYV	Eval Rept	JU-RR-3/1970	Jun 70	Leppaemaeki+ TABLE OF EVAL AVG SIG	
(n,2n)	+7		KFI	Theo Rept	KFKI-71-8	Feb 71	Jeki. CALCULATED CFD EXPTL SIG VALUE	
(n,2n)	1.4+7	1.5+7	IRK	ExTh Jour	APA 33 285	Jul 71	Winiwarter+ ISOMERIC RATIO	
(n,2n)	1.4+7	1.5+7	LRL	Expt Jour	NP/A 190 635	Aug 72	Nethaway. D-T NS.TO GROUND+METAST.	+
	1.4+7			Data	EXFOR10312.008	May 75	. 8 PTS. SIGMA.	
(n,2n)	1.5+7		DEB	Eval Jour	REA 11 1 153	Mar 73	Boedy. COMPILATION+RECOMM.VALUE,TBL	
			TAT	Eval Rept	IAEA-153 173	73	- . RECOMM. VALUE ONLY	
(n,2n)	1.5+7		TAT	Theo Jour	JP/A 7 147	Aug 74	Kondaiah. CALC ON STAT MODEL	
(n,2n)	Fast		GOE	Expt Jour	ZP/A 272 287	Mar 75	Kirschner+ INTCONVERS.OF LU-174 ISOM	
(n,2n)	8.6+6	2.8+7	LAS	Expt Jour	PR/C 12 451	Aug 75	Bayhurst+E715MEV.DERV.FRM.ISMR.RATIO	+
	8.5+6	2.8+7		Data	EXFOR10536.	Apr 76	. 14 PTS.	
(n,2n)	Thrsh	2.0+6	BRC	Eval Prog	CEA-N-1875 126	Apr 76	Philis+	
(n,2n)	1.5+7		JUL	Expt Jour	NP/A 224 319	May 74	Qaim. ACT.GE(LI).TO GRND, METAST	+
				Jour	RRL 25 335	May 76	- + SIG IN GRPH. SYST VS (N-Z)/A	
	1.5+7			Data	EXFOR20541.	Apr 76	4PTS.SIGMA.	
(n,2n)	8.4+6	1.5+7	BRC	Expt Jour	NIM 135 511	Jun 76	Frehaut.GD LOADED SCIN.EXPT DETAILS.	+
				Conf	75Kiev 4 303	May 75	- + LIQSCIN.SIG(E),CFD.GRPH+TBL	
				Conf	75Wash. 855	Mar 75	- + TBL.GRPH.REL 238U(N,F)	
				Rept	CEA-R-4627	Nov 74	- + LARGE LIQ SCINT METH10 VAL	
	8.4+6	1.5+7		Data	EXFOR20416.015	Jul 75	14PTS.SIGMA.	
(n,2n)	Thrsh	1.5+7	BRC	Expt Conf	76Lowell 1350	Jul 76	Cindro+EXCIT FN CALC.CFD EXPT.NDG.	
(n,2n)	8.0+6	2.4+7	LAS	Eval Prog	LA-6560 2	Nov 76	Arthur+CALC CFD EXPT.CURVS	
	None			Conf	76Lowell 1452	Jul 76	- +STATMDL CALC CS,SPEC.CFD.NDG	
(n,xn) x>2	Fiss		BNL	Theo Jour	NSE 23 238	Nov 65	Pearlstein.SPEC AVG STATMDL CALC N3N	
(n,xn) x>2	2.6+7	2.8+7	LAS	Expt Jour	PR/C 12 451	Aug 75	Bayhurst+N3N,N4N.TBL,GRPH.CFD CALC.	+
	1.5+7	2.8+7		Data	EXFOR10536.	Apr 76	. 11 PTS. N3N. 2 PTS N4N.	
(n,xn) x>2	Thrsh	2.0+6	BRC	Eval Prog	CEA-N-1875 126	Apr 76	Philis+N3N	
(n,xn) x>2	8.0+6	2.4+7	LAS	Eval Prog	LA-6560 2	Nov 76	Arthur+CALC CFD EXPT.CURVS	
	None			Conf	76Lowell 1452	Jul 76	- +STATMDL CS,SPEC.N3N.CFD.NDG	
(n,p)	1.4+7		ALD	Expt Jour	PPS 73 215	Feb 59	Coleman+. ACT. CFD DIRECT INTERACTN	+
(n,p)	Fiss		CRC	Eval Rept	CRC-1003	Dec 60	Roy+,ESTIMATED AVG SIG=0.01MB	
(n,p)	1.5+7		SAH	Comp Jour	NUC 23 8 112	Aug 65	Chatterjee. TABLE WITH REFS.	
	1.4+7			Jour	NP 60 273	Nov 64	- .MEAN OF EXPT CFD SHELLMOD	
(n,p)	Maxwl		IFU	Expt Rept	ICD-4 20	67	Dadakina+ PENETR COEFF CALC,TABLE	
(n,p)	1.4+7	1.5+7	ARK	Theo Prog	ORO-3235-29	Jan 67	Koch+,STAT MODEL CALC CFD EXPTS	
(n,p)			DEB	Comp Jour	REA 7 4 93	Dec 69	Csikai+ SIG+HL COMPILTN,N-ACTIV-ANAL	
(n,p)	1.4+7	1.5+7	JYV	Eval Rept	JU-RR-3/1970	Jun 70	Leppaemaeki+ TABLE OF EVAL AVG SIG	
(n,p)	1.4+7		KFI	Comp Jour	JRC 7 365	Jun 71	Nagy+ SIGMA,GAM+ELECTRON ES, HALF-L	
(n,p)	1.4+7	1.5+7	KAZ	Theo Jour	YF 18 705	Oct 73	Levkovsky.AVERAGED SIG,CALC,TBL	
				Jour	SNP 18 361	Apr 74	. ENGLISH OF YF 18,705	
(n,p)	1.5+7		KYU	Expt Jour	NST 12 681	Nov 75	Sato+ .ACTIVATION SIG=18.5+-2.2 MB	+
	1.5+7			Data	EXFOR20595.007	Aug 76	1PNT.SIGMA.	
(n,p)	1.5+7		JUL	Expt Jour	RRL 25 335	May 76	Qaim+ ACTIV,GELI.CFD OTHERS,TBL+GRPH	+
	1.5+7			Data	EXFOR20716.015	Jun 77	1PNT.SIGMA.	
(n,α)	Fiss		CRC	Eval Rept	CRC-1003	Dec 60	Roy+,ESTIMATED AVG SIG=BELO 0.0001MB	
(n,α)	1.5+7		CIS	Expt Jour	NP 46 51	Jul 63	Marcazzan+.DIFF.SIG-AT 30DEG MEASURE	+
(n,α)	Maxwl		CCP	Expt Jour	YF 1 252	Feb 65	Andreev.IONIZ-CHAMBER,SIG=M.06MB	+
				Jour	SNP 1 177	Aug 65	TRANSLATN.*	
(n,α)	1.4+7		TIT	Expt Jour	NP/A 149 513	Jul 70	Kitazawa. S SPEC 0 DEG+SIGMA+ANDISTR	+
	1.5+7			Data	EXFOR20336.005	Jul 74	17PTS.D/DA.DE.	
(n,α)	1.4+7	1.5+7	CIS	Theo Jour	NP/A 210 297	Aug 73	Milazzo-Colli+ ALPHA E-DISTN CFD XPT	
	1.4+7			Jour	PL/B 38 155	Feb 72	Colli-Milazzo+ A-SPECT CALC CFD EXPT	
Reson Params	5.3+0	3.1+1	BNL	Expt Jour	PR 92 656	Nov 53	Foote+ AREA ANAL. TBL.	+
	5.3+0	3.1+1		Data	EXFOR12107.007	Jun 76	. 5 RES, E0,WT**2/PCS	
Reson Params	2.6+0	5.7+1	ORL	Expt Prog	ORNL-2718 26	Jun 59	Block+ TRNS. RES ANAL. TBL.	+
	2.6+0	5.7+1		Data	EXFOR11349.003	Jun 76	. 16 RES, E0,WN	
Reson Params	2.6+0	5.7+1	MOL	Eval Rept	BLG-421	66	Damle+ .RECOMMENDED PARAMS 6 RESON	
Reson Params	2.6+0		WUR	Expt Rept	EIR-123	Jul 67	Brunner+ .SHAPE ANAL CFD OTHER EXPTS	+
				Conf	66Paris 1 61	Oct 66	- + PPR 20. PRELIM DATA.	

71 Lutetium 175

Quantity	Energy (ev) Min	Max	Lab	Type	Documentation Ref Vol Page	Author, Comments Date	Data
Reson Params	+3	+5	AUA	ExTh Rept	AAEC/E-198	May 69 Musgrove.RES PARS +STF FROM (NG)FIT	+
Reson Params	2.6+0	4.1+1	BNL	Expt Jour	PR/C 2 675	Aug 70 Wasson+,J FOR 11 RESON FROM N,G	+
	2.6+0	4.1+1		Data	EXFOR10053.002	May 71 . 11 PTS. EO, J.	
Reson Params	–		AUA	Theo Rept	AAEC/E-211	Nov 70 Musgrove. CALCULTD D+GAM WIDTH GIVEN	
Reson Params	2.6+0	4.2+1	CJD	Eval Rept	YK-7	71 Zakharova+ SURVEY+SYSTEMATICS,GW,TBL	
				Rept	INDC(CCP)-27	Nov 72 .ENGLISH TRANSLATION OF YK-7 /71	
Reson Params	None		DUB	Theo Jour	YF 13 240	Feb 71 Malecki+G-WID,THEO CFD EXPT.TBL,GRPH	
				Jour	SNP 13 133	Aug 71 – + ENGL OF YF 13 240.	
Reson Params	2.6+0	2.7+2	NRL	Expt Jour	NP/A 237 45	Jan 75 Namenson+ (N,G).SPINS+AVG N-WID,TBL	+
				Conf	74Petten 313	Sep 74 – + SPINS,AVG WN	
	2.6+0	2.7+2		Data	EXFOR10466.002	Jan 75 . 57 RES, J.	
Reson Params	2.6+1	3.0+3	COL	Expt Jour	PR/C 11 1231	Apr 75 Liou+TBL.E0,GWN0,AVG WG,AVG D,S0.	+
	None			Conf	75Wash. 780	Mar 75 Hacken+ TBL AVG WG,STF,NUMBER GWN,WG	
				Jour	NSE 48 219	Jun 72 Rahn+.AVG WG=60 MEV OVER 8 RESONANCS	
	2.6+0	3.0+3		Data	EXFOR10491.	Jun 75 . 446 RES, RED WN,AVG WG, D GVN	
Strnth Fnctn	+3		BNL	Expt Jour	PRL 1 461	Dec 58 Hughes+ FC. 1.7+-0.2=STF	
Strnth Fnctn	+0	+2	MOL	Eval Rept	BLG-421	66 Damle+. RECOMMENDED S0=1.65+-0.7META	
Strnth Fnctn	+3	+5	AUA	ExTh Rept	AAEC/E-198	May 69 Musgrove.S+P+D STF FROM (NG)FIT,TBL	+
Strnth Fnctn	–		AUA	Theo Rept	AAEC/E-211	Nov 70 Musgrove. SMOOTHED S0,S1 AND S2 GIVN	
Strnth Fnctn	2.4+4		MUA	Theo Jour	IJP 46 114	Mar 72 Chaubey+ P-WAVE.FOR A-SYSTEMTIC,GRPH	
Strnth Fnctn	None		AUA	Eval Rept	AAEC/E-277	Mar 73 Musgrove.TBLS EXPTL DATA+BEST VALUES	
Strnth Fnctn	2.6+0	2.7+2	NRL	Expt Conf	74Petten 313	Sep 74 Namenson+ S-NEUTRON STF FOR J=3,4	
Strnth Fnctn	2.6+1	3.0+3	COL	Expt Jour	PR/C 11 1231	Apr 75 Liou+S0=(1.83+-0.12)-4	+
	None			Conf	75Wash. 780	Mar 75 Hacken+ NEVIS TOF S-WAVE STF	
	2.0+0	3.0+3		Data	EXFOR10491.003	Jun 75 . 1 PT.	
Lvl Density	–		COP	Theo Jour	NP 6 62	Mar 58 Ericson. LVL DENSITY FORM CFD EXP	
Lvl Density	–		FEI	Eval Rept	FEI-36	66 Kapchigashev+.TBL OF RELATD QUANTTYS	+
		5.0+4		Jour	YF 4 686	Sep 66 .TABLE.SHORT VERSION OF FEI-36	
	–			Prog	YFI-3 3	66 .ABSTRACT.TABLE LDL+NUCL.EXCIT.E	
		5.0+4		Jour	SNP 4 486	67 .ENGLISH OF YF 4.FROM(N,GAMMA).TABLE	
				Prog	INDC-E-140 3	66 .ENGLISH TRANSL OF YFI-3	
Lvl Density	None		AUW	Theo Conf	70Madurai 2 267	Dec 70 Ramamurty+ A-PARAMETER GVN,LANG'S-TH	
Lvl Density	None		DUB	Theo Jour	JINR-P4-8102	Jul 74 Malov+ SEMI-MICROSC CALC OKS XPT,TBL	
				Rept	UCRL-TR-10845	Apr 75 . ENGL OF JINR-P4-8102	

71 Lutetium 176

Quantity	Energy (ev) Min	Max	Lab	Type	Documentation Ref Vol Page	Author, Comments Date	Data
Evaluation	Pile		CRC	Eval Rept	CRRP-960	Nov 60 Westcott.G,S FACTORS EFFECTIVE CAPT.	
Total	+0	+3	ORL	Expt Conf	60Vienna 535	Oct 60 Block+.NDG,EXPT DESCRIBED	
		4.3+1		Abst	BAP 3 364	Nov 58 Harvey+,TRANS,14E0S SEEN,9E0S GIVEN	
Total	2.0-2	2.5-1	BNL	Expt Jour	NSE 7 502	Jun 60 Roberge+ CS CURV, CFD BREIT-WIGNER	+
	1.9-2	5.0-1		Data	EXFOR12096.002	Jun 76 . 46 PTS, SIG	
Total	1.2-2	1.0+0	HAR	Expt Jour	JNEA 13 35	Oct 60 Baston+ TRNS SL CHOP.GRAPH SIGT-5.5B	+
				Rept	TNCC(UK)-49	Aug 59 Lisle.TOF CHOPPER .14EV RESON PARAMS	
Total	Maxwl		MTR	Expt Prog	NCSAC-33 89	Dec 70 Young.FAST CHOPPER,VALUE GIVEN	
Total	-3	1.9+0	THS	Theo Rept	IKE-6 89 65	Jun 75 Keinert. DATA LIBRARY	
Diff Inelast	+6		II	Expt Conf	73Kiev 4 312	May 73 Lakosi+ ACTIV BY PHOTONEUTRONS,TABLE	+
	+6			Data	EXFOR30268.015	Jul 74 LU-175(INL)+LU-176(NG),1 POINT	
Absorption	1.2-2	1.0+0	HAR	Expt Jour	JNEA 13 35	Oct 60 Baston+ SIGTOT-5.5B,=2100+-150B THR	
Absorption	2.5-2		ROS	Expt Jour	KE 10 25	Jan 67 Albert.VAL 2200M/SEC GVN,LOCAL OSCIL	
Absorption	Maxwl		ROS	Expt Rept	ZFK-132 19	Dec 67 Faehrmann. CFD WITH OTHER AUTHORS	
Absorption	2.5-2		IJI	Eval Conf	75Kiev 1 169	May 75 Fedorova+ EVAL 2200M/S SIG,TABLE	
Res Int Abs	5.5-1		MOL	Theo Rept	BLG-421	Sep 67 Damle+,EVAL ACT R.I.=2400+-250B,TO G	
Res Int Abs	5.5-1		MOL	Eval Rept	BLG-421	Sep 67 Damle+,EVAL ACT R.I.=2400+-250B,TO G	
Res Int Abs	5.0-1		MTR	Expt Rept	IN-1195	May 68 Scoville+ REACTIVITY MEAS.	+
				Jour	ANS 10 259	Jun 67 .SUPERSEDED	
	5.0-1			Data	EXFOR11820.018	Jun 76 . 1 PT. CS=1160+-35 B.	
Res Int Abs	6.3-1		CAS	Eval Jour	NSE 40 51	70 Gibello+,EVAL.CAPT RES INT=978B	
Res Int Abs	-1		CAI	ExTh Rept	AREAEE-165	73 Abul-Ela+ EPITHRML RI VS THEO,TBL	+
	4.5-1			Expt Data	EXFOR30376.003	Feb 77 EPICADMIUM RI.	
Res Int Abs	5.5-1		RCN	Revw Conf	73Paris 2 271	Mar 73 Zijp.ACT,RECOMM FROM LITERATURE,TBL	
Res Int Abs	5.0-1		GHT	Expt Jour	JRC 20 695	74 Van Der Linden+ BY(N,G).CFD OTHS,TBL	+
	5.5-1			Conf	73Paris 2 241	Mar 73 – + ACT,REL THR+GOLD,TBL	
	5.5-1			Data	EXFOR20645.037	Jul 76 1PNT.CAPTURE.	
Res Int Abs		2.0+2	NIR	Expt Conf	76Lowell 1253	Jul 76 Belanova+TRNS.RIA CALC.CFD.NDG	

71 Lutetium 176

Quantity	Energy (ev) Min	Energy (ev) Max	Lab	Type	Documentation Ref Vol Page	Author, Comments Date	Data
(n,γ)	Pile		ANL	Expt Jour	PR 72 888	Nov 47 Seren+ THR IRRAD. ACT. CS GVN.	+
	Pile			Data	EXFOR11447.110	Jun 76 . 1 PT. CS=3640B+ −20 PCT.	
(n,γ)	Fiss		ANL	Expt Jour	PR 78 632	Jun 50 Hughes+ REL SIG(THERMAL). HL GVN.	+
	Fiss			Data	EXFOR11596.018	Jun 76 . 1 PT. CS=.33 B.	
(n,γ)	Fiss		BNL	Expt Jour	PR 91 1423	Sep 53 Hughes+.ALSO LVL SPACINGS AT EXCIT E	
(n,γ)	Maxwl		HAR	Expt Jour	JNEA 10 157	Sep 59 Price.ACT REL MN IN C PILE,18−99DEGC	
(n,γ)	2.5−2		COP	Expt Jour	PL 1 321	Jul 62 Jorgensen+. LU2O3 ACT TO 155D METAST	+
	Pile			Data	EXFOR20096.002	Sep 71 1PNT.SIG.	
(n,γ)	1.4+7		ROM	Expt Jour	NCS 370	Sep 63 Giannini+LVLS.EXCITED IN CAPTURE NDG	
(n,γ)	Maxwl		ROS	Expt Jour	NP 70 415	Aug 65 Heiser+160MICROSEC ISOMER 315+ −60B	
(n,γ)	1.0−2	5.0+1	MOL	Eval Rept	BLG−421	66 Damle+. CURVE RECOMMENDED SIGS	
(n,γ)	1.0+3	1.0+4	LAS	Theo Rept	LA−3463	Jan 66 Bell. TH CAPTURE OF RARE EARTHS	
(n,γ)	Maxwl		LRL	Expt Jour	JIN 29 865	67 Nethaway+ ACT. HL, CS GVN.	+
	Maxwl			Data	EXFOR12088.002	Jun 76 . 1 PT. CS=7+ −2B.	
(n,γ)	3.0+4	2.0+5	ORL	Expt Jour	PR 159 1007	Jul 67 Macklin+ TOF, TOT EN DET .8ES.	+
	3.0+4	2.0+5		Data	EXFOR11679.021	Jun 76 . 8 PTS.	
(n,γ)	Maxwl		ROS	Expt Jour	KE 10 306	Oct 67 Albert+ ACT CS,VAL CFD REFS,IN GERMN	
(n,γ)	Maxwl	Pile	MOL	Eval Rept	BLG−421	68 Damle+ TBP THRSIG RESINTG GIVEN	
(n,γ)	Maxwl	Pile	MOL	Eval Rept	BLG−421	68 Damle+ TBP THRSIG RESINTG GIVEN	
(n,γ)	Maxwl		AUA	Theo Jour	NSE 31 234	Feb 68 Cook+ STATISTICAL CALC CFD EXPT	
(n,γ)	−		IEA	Comp Rept	IEA−INF− 10	Aug 68 Atalla. TABLES OF HL,SIG AND GAMM−E	
(n,γ)	1.0−4	1.8+7	BNW	Eval Rept	BNWL−1312	May 70 Simons+ GRPH. TBL.	
(n,γ)	3.0+4		AUA	Theo Rept	AAEC/E−211	Nov 70 Musgrove. SIGMA GIVEN AND CFD OTHER	
(n,γ)	Maxwl		MTR	Expt Prog	NCSAC−33 89	Dec 70 Young.FAST CHOPPER,VALUE GIVEN	
(n,γ)	Maxwl	1.0+6	KFI	Comp Jour	JRC 7 365	Jun 71 Nagy+ SIGMA,GAMMA−E, HALF−LIVES GIVN	
(n,γ)	1.0+3	1.0+7	BOL	Eval Data	BENZI−DFN 805.	May 72 40 PNTS	+
(n,γ)	1.4−1		BSP	Expt Prog	INDC(SEC)−28	Sep 72 . P34,ABST.SIG−0 AT 0.141EV−RES GIVN	
(n,γ)	Fast		DUB	Expt Jour	JINR−P12−6810	Nov 72 Ngo Quoc Buu+ ACT ANALYS, CD−RATIOS	
(n,γ)	Maxwl		RCN	Revw Rept	INDC(NDS)−56	Sep 73 Zijp.PG103,FOR DOSIMETRY,SIG GIVEN	
	2.5−2			Conf	73Paris 2 271	Mar 73 − .RECOMMENDED FROM LITERATURE,TB	
(n,γ)	1.0−2	2.0+0	WUR	Expt Jour	NSE 60 53	May 76 Widder.TOF.CS VS.E GRPHS.2200M/S CS	+
				Rept	EIR−217	Apr 75 − . TOF	
				Conf	74Petten 757	Sep 74 − . M−R DET,ABS.EXP.,NDG	
	1.0−2	2.0+0		Data	EXFOR20437.011	Nov 75 277PTS.SIGMA.	
(n,γ)	None		RCN	Revw Rept	ECN−2	Sep 76 Zijp+ INTERCOMP. INTEGRAL SIG SAND−2	
Res Int Capt	None		ROS	Revw Rept	ZFK−RN−23	Sep 64 Albert. VAL GVN,UNPUBLISHED	
Spect (n,γ)	1.4−1	2.6+0	YAL	Expt Abst	BAP 4 35	Jan 59 Springer+,NAI(TL),GAMMA MULTIPLICITY	
Spect (n,γ)	Pile		UPP	Expt Jour	NP 40 329	Jan 63 Marklund+.E DETERM. NO INTENS MEAS.	
Spect (n,γ)	Maxwl		RIS	Expt Jour	ZP 184 153	Apr 65 Maier.TBL OF GS TO 1.3MEV,LU177−LVLS	
Spect (n,γ)	Maxwl		IFL	Expt Jour	YF 3 199	Feb 66 Balodis.GAMMAS AND CONVERSION−ELCTRN	
				Book	PROKOFJEV	73 . TBL GAM,CONV ELECTR ES+INT,LVL SCH	
	Pile			Jour	IZV 35 759	Apr 71 Beitin'+ LEVELS OF LU−177, GRAPH,TBL	
	Maxwl			Jour	SNP 3 141	Aug 66 TRANSLATN.*	
	Pile			Jour	BAS 35 699	Apr 72 . ENGLISH OF IZV 35 759 4/71	
Spect (n,γ)	Maxwl		ATI	Expt Jour	AKE 15 269	70 Fleck+ HALF LIFE OF 458KEV ISOMER	
Spect (n,γ)	Maxwl		LAS	Expt Jour	PR/C 3 766	Feb 71 Jurney+,GE(LI)+SI(LI) DET,TBL+CURVS	
Spect (n,γ)	Maxwl	1.0+6	KFI	Comp Jour	JRC 7 365	Jun 71 Nagy+ SIGMA,GAMMA−E, HALF−LIVES GIVN	
Spect (n,γ)	Maxwl		FRS	Expt Jour	HPA 45 93	Jun 72 Michaud+ LVLSCH	+
				Jour	HPA 42 917	Dec 69 − + PAIR+ANTICOMPTON−SPEC,GRPH	
	Maxwl			Data	EXFOR20518.	Apr 76 163PTS.	
Spect (n,γ)	5.0+5	2.0+6	CAS	Expt Conf	72Budapest 228	Aug 72 Fubini+ CORRELATION (N,G)−(D,P),NDG	+
				Jour	NCL 4 1003	Aug 72 − .CORR BETWEEN N,G AND D,P	
	Maxwl			Data	EXFOR20443.002	Nov 75 45PTS.	
Spect (n,γ)	Maxwl		ROS	Expt Conf	72Budapest 98	Aug 72 Andrejtscheff+ LIFETIME OF EX.STATE	
	None			Prog	ZFK−223 51	Sep 71 − + NS TIME DEPEND'T SPEC	
Spect (n,γ)	Pile		ROS	Expt Jour	NP/A 194 561	Oct 72 Manfrass+ GE−LI. +LU177 LVL 1/2LIFE	
				Jour	NP/A 172 298	Sep 71 − + SPEC 337EG + CONV+COINC.	
	None			Conf	69Studsvik 161	Aug 69 − + GAM−E TBL,(N,G)+(N,E−) XPT	
Spect (n,γ)	None		ANL	Expt Prog	ERDA−NDC−2 28	May 75 Wilson+G−RAY SPC.	
Spect (n,γ)	Maxwl		FRS	Expt Jour	NP/A 251 305	Oct 75 Geinoz+ BAND−FILTER,TBL OF EN+INTENS	
(n,2n)	Fiss		CRC	Eval Rept	CRC−1003	Dec 60 Roy+,ESTIMATED AVG SIG=52.0MB	
(n,2n)	1.3+7	1.5+7	BNL	Theo Jour	NSE 23 238	Nov 65 Pearlstein.3ES.STAT MDL CALC.TBL CS.	
(n,2n)	Fiss		BNL	Theo Jour	NSE 23 238	Nov 65 Pearlstein.STATMDL CALC.SPEC AVG.TBL	
(n,xn) x>2	Fiss		BNL	Theo Jour	NSE 23 238	Nov 65 Pearlstein.SPEC AVG STATMDL CALC N3N	
(n,xn) x>2	1.4+7	1.5+7	LRL	Eval Jour	ND/A 11 792	Jul 73 Alley+ (N,3N) CURVE BEST ESTIMATE	
(n,p)	Fiss		CRC	Eval Rept	CRC−1003	Dec 60 Roy+,ESTIMATED AVG SIG=0.5MB	
(n,α)	Fiss		CRC	Eval Rept	CRC−1003	Dec 60 Roy+,ESTIMATED AVG SIG=0.0014MB	
(n,α)	1.5+7	1.5+7	CIS	Expt Jour	NP 46 51	Jul 63 Marcazzan. = 1 DATA INDEX LINES	+

71 Lutetium 176

Quantity	Energy (ev) Min	Max	Lab	Type	Documentation Ref Vol Page	Author, Comments Date	Data
(n,α)	Maxwl		CCP	Expt	Jour YF 1 252	Feb 65 Andreev.IONIZ – CHAMBER,SIG=M2MB	+
					Jour SNP 1 177	Aug 65 TRANSLATN.*	
(n,α)	1.5+7		KYU	Expt	Jour NST 12 681	Nov 75 Sato+.ACTIVATION SIG=2.30+ – 0.57 MB	+
	1.5+7			Data	EXFOR20595.008	Aug 76 1PNT.SIGMA.	
Reson Params	1.4–1	4.8+0	BNL	Expt	Jour PR 92 656	Nov 53 Foote+ CRYSTSPEC. AREA ANAL. TBL.	+
	1.4–1	4.8+0		Data	EXFOR12107.008	Jun 76 . 4 RES, E0,WT**2/PCS	
Reson Params	1.4–1	4.8+0	BNL	Expt	Jour PR 96 1014	Nov 54 Sailor+ CRYSTSPEC. TBL RES ES	
Reson Params	2.6+0		BNL	Expt	Jour PR 100 1414	Dec 55 Landon+ AREA ANAL. TBL.	+
	2.6+0			Data	EXFOR12178.007	Jun 76 . 1 RES, E0,WT,WN,WG,PCS	
Reson Params	1.6+0	4.7+1	ORL	Expt	Prog ORNL–2718 26	Jun 59 Block+ TRNS. RES ANAL. TBL.	+
	1.6+0	4.7+1		Data	EXFOR11349.004	Jun 76 . 20 RES, E0,WN	
Reson Params	1.4–1		BNL	Expt	Jour NSE 7 502	Jun 60 Roberge. WT WG 2GWN OTHER PARAMETERS	+
	1.4–1			Data	EXFOR12096.003	Jun 76 . 1 RES, E0,WT,WN,WG	
Reson Params	1.5–1		BSP	Expt	Conf 66Paris 1 53	Oct 60 Zimmerman+,P.129 GAMMA+N WIDTH	+
					Jour NP/A 95 683	Apr 67 SEE ALSO *	
	1.5–1				EXFOR30224.	Dec 76 GAMMA + REDUCED NEUTRON WIDTH	
Reson Params	1.4–1		HAR	Expt	Jour JNEA 13 35	Oct 60 Baston+ WG=60+ – 2MV,2GWN=.088+ – .005MV	
	1.2–2	1.0+0			Rept TNCC(UK)–49	Aug 59 LISLE SINGLE RES .142EV	
Reson Params	1.4–1	4.7+1	MOL	Eval	Rept BLG–421	66 Damle+. RECOMMENDED PARAMS 21RESON	
Reson Params	1.4–1	1.6+0	WUR	Expt	Rept EIR–123	Jul 67 Brunner+.SHAPE ANAL CFD OTHER EXPTS	+
					Conf 66Paris 1 61	Oct 66 – + PPR 20. PRELIM DATA.	
Reson Params		1.0+6	AUA	Theo	Jour AUJ 20 477	Oct 67 Cook. TBL OF AVG LVL SPACING D,L=0,1	
Reson Params	–		AUA	Theo	Rept AAEC/E–211	Nov 70 Musgrove. CALCULTD D+GAM WIDTH GIVEN	
Reson Params	1.4–1	1.6+0	CJD	Eval	Rept YK–7	71 Zakharova+ SURVEY+SYSTEMATICS,GW,TBL	
					Rept INDC(CCP)–27	Nov 72 .ENGLISH TRANSLATION OF YK–7 /71	
Reson Params	6.9+6		DUB	Theo	Conf 74Petten 175	Sep 74 Malov+ DOBS,SEMI–MICROSCOPIC CALC.	
Reson Params	+0		DUB	Theo	Jour YF 21 40	Jan 75 Voronov+ MEAN D,WITH ROTAT.CFD EXPT	
					Jour SNP 21 20	Jul 75 . ENGLISH OF YF 21,40	
Strnth Fnctn	+0	+2	MOL	Eval	Rept BLG–421	66 Damle+. RECOMMENDED S0=1.85+ – 0.7 GND	
Strnth Fnctn	–		AUA	Theo	Rept AAEC/E–211	Nov 70 Musgrove. SMOOTHED S0,S1 AND S2 GIVN	
Strnth Fnctn	None		AUA	Eval	Rept AAEC/E–277	Mar 73 Musgrove.TBLS EXPTL DATA+BEST VALUES	
Lvl Density	–		COP	Theo	Jour NP 6 62	Mar 58 Ericson. LVL DENSITY FORM CFD EXP	
Lvl Density	+6		MIL	Theo	Jour EN 15 1 54	Jan 68 Facchini+ LDL PARS FROM LOW EN RES	
Lvl Density	None		MUN	Theo	Jour NP/A 217 269	Dec 73 Dilg+ A,DELTA. BACK SHIFTED FERMIGAS	
Lvl Density	None		COP	Theo	Jour NP/A 222 493	Apr 74 Dossing+COLL ROTAT.SPAC. ACCUR ESTIM	
Lvl Density	None		ROC	Theo	Jour NP/A 223 589	May 74 Huizenga+ EXP CFD MICROSC TH AX SYMM	
Lvl Density	+0		DUB	Theo	Conf 75Kiev 3 23	May 75 Voronov. LVL SPACING OF LU177.TABLE	

71 Lutetium 177

Quantity	Energy (ev) Min	Max	Lab	Type	Documentation Ref Vol Page	Author, Comments Date	Data
(n,γ)	1.4+7		ROM	Expt	Jour NCS 370	Sep 63 Giannini+LVLS.EXCITED IN CAPTURE NDG	
Spect (n,γ)	None		ANL	Expt	Prog ERDA–NDC–2 28	May 75 Wilson+G–RAY SPC.	
Reson Params	–		AUA	Theo	Rept AAEC/E–211	Nov 70 Musgrove. CALCULTD D+GAM WIDTH GIVEN	
Reson Params	–		DUB	Theo	Rept JINR–E4–5711	Apr 71 Soloviev.RESONANCE STRUCTURE STUDY	
Strnth Fnctn	–		AUA	Theo	Rept AAEC/E–211	Nov 70 Musgrove. SMOOTHED S0,S1 AND S2 GIVN	
Lvl Density	+6		MIL	Theo	Jour EN 15 1 54	Jan 68 Facchini+ LDL PARS FROM LOW EN RES	
Lvl Density	None		MUN	Theo	Jour NP/A 217 269	Dec 73 Dilg+ A,DELTA. BACK SHIFTED FERMIGAS	
Lvl Density	None		COP	Theo	Jour NP/A 222 493	Apr 74 Dossing+COLL ROTAT.SPAC. ACCUR ESTIM	
Lvl Density	None		DUB	Theo	Jour NP/A 224 396	May 74 Malov+ 1/2 MICROSC.MODEL. DEFORM NUC	
Lvl Density	None		ROC	Theo	Jour NP/A 223 589	May 74 Huizenga+ EXP CFD MICROSC TH AX SYMM	

71 Lutetium 178

Quantity	Energy (ev) Min	Max	Lab	Type	Documentation Ref Vol Page	Author, Comments Date	Data
Reson Params	–		AUA	Theo	Rept AAEC/E–211	Nov 70 Musgrove. CALCULTD D+GAM WIDTH GIVEN	
Strnth Fnctn	–		AUA	Theo	Rept AAEC/E–211	Nov 70 Musgrove. SMOOTHED S0,S1 AND S2 GIVN	
Lvl Density	–		CIS	Eval	Jour NP 51 460	Feb 64 Facchini+SMALL A.TA181(NA)ALPHA SPEC	

71 Lutetium 179

Quantity	Energy (ev) Min	Max	Lab	Type	Documentation Ref Vol Page	Author, Comments Date	Data
Reson Params	–		AUA	Theo	Rept AAEC/E–211	Nov 70 Musgrove. CALCULTD D+GAM WIDTH GIVEN	
Strnth Fnctn	–		AUA	Theo	Rept AAEC/E–211	Nov 70 Musgrove. SMOOTHED S0,S1 AND S2 GIVN	

72 Hafnium

Quantity	Energy (ev) Min	Max	Lab	Type	Documentation Ref Vol Page	Author, Comments Date	Data
Evaluation	Maxwl		GEN	Eval Rept	APEX - 467	Jun 58 Tralli+.68 - 3000DEG F SCT NG	
Evaluation	3.2 - 2	1.0 + 7	GEN	Eval Rept	APEX - 467	Jun 58 Tralli+.18GROUPS AS IN IN + SNE,TOT	
Evaluation	5.0 + 5	1.5 + 7	LRL	Eval Rept	UCRL - 5351	Nov 58 Howerton. CURVES	
Evaluation	Pile		CRC	Eval Rept	CRRP - 960	Nov 60 Westcott.G,S FACTORS EFFECTIVE CAPT.	
Evaluation	2.5 - 2	1.0 + 7	KFK	Eval Rept	KFK - 352	Aug 65 Schmidt+.TOT SEL DEL SNE SIN NG	
Evaluation	1.0 - 3	1.5 + 7	KAP	Eval Rept	KAPL - 3327	Aug 67 Reynolds+TOT RES ELAS INEL NP NG N2N	
Evaluation	1.0 - 5	2.0 + 7	SAI	Eval Rept	EPRI - 250	Nov 76 Drake+ENDF/B5.TBLS,GRPHS.CFD.	
Total	3.0 - 2	1.5 + 0	ORL	Expt Jour	PR 87 487	Aug 52 Bernstein+	+
	3.0 - 2	1.5 + 0		Data	EXFOR11745.	Jun 76 . 18 PTS.	
Total	1.0 - 3	1.0 - 1	HAR	Expt Rept	AERE - N/R - 1147	Apr 53 Egelstaff.GIVES ABS.+SCATTERNG XSECT	
Total	9.5 - 1	8.6 + 3	ANL	Expt Jour	PR 92 1527	Dec 53 Bollinger.	+
	9.5 - 1	8.6 + 3		Data	EXFOR12108.002	Jun 76 . 190 DATA POINTS.	
Total	6.0 + 4	3.0 + 6	WIS	Expt Jour	PR 93 461	Feb 54 Okazaki+ TRANS AVG OVER RESON OKS TH	+
	5.0 + 4	3.0 + 6		Data	EXFOR12061.006	Jun 76 . 23 PTS.	
Total	1.4 + 7		ANL	Expt Prog	ANL - 5497 48	Mar 55 Jaffey+ SIG = 5.72B.	
Total	5.1 + 0	3.9 + 3	BNL	Expt Jour	PR 99 10	Jul 55 Harvey+	+
	5.1 + 0	3.9 + 3		Data	EXFOR11912.040	Jun 76 . 338 DATA PTS.	
Total	5.0 - 1	7.0 + 0	BNL	Expt Jour	PR 101 726	Jan 56 Igo+,CS+TRNS CRV PARS FOR 1.1,2.4EV	
Total	1.8 - 2	3.3 - 1	BNL	Expt Priv	SCHERMER	Oct 61 Schermer.	+
	1.8 - 2	3.3 - 1		Data	EXFOR12124.002	Jun 76 . 34 DATA PTS.	
Total	1.0 + 6		ANL	Theo Jour	PR 124 826	Nov 61 Sokoloff.HARMONIC OSCILLAT POT CURVE	
Total	2.4 - 2	3.5 + 0	MTR	Expt Jour	NSE 11 298	Nov 61 Joki+,XTAL SPEC CURVE	+
	4.0 - 2	1.0 + 1		Rept	MTR - L - 54 - 53	Jun 54 - + CRYST SPEC 2RESONANCES MEASD	
	2.4 - 2	3.5 + 0		Data	EXFOR11635.	Jun 76 . 439 DATA PTS.	
Total	3.0 + 4	6.5 + 5	DKE	Expt Prog	WASH - 1034 10	Dec 61 Seth+5,10KEV STEPS.5 PC ACC.	+
	3.0 + 4	6.5 + 5		Data	EXFOR11936.004	Jun 76 . 102 DATA PTS.	
Total	1.0 + 4	1.0 + 7	KFK	Eval Rept	KFK - 352	Aug 65 Schmidt.GRAPHS+TABULATED DATA(NO.12)	
Total	1.4 + 7		ANL	Expt Abst	DA/B 28 3835	Mar 68 Haugsnes. SIG = 5.37+ - .02B, CFD OPTMDL	
				Rept	ANL - 5609	Nov 56 .SEE ALSO	
				Rept	ANL - 5554	Aug 56 .SEE ALSO	
	1.4 + 7			Data	EXFOR11733.010	Jun 76 . 1 PT.	
Total	None		DKE	Expt Abst	DA/B 28 3834	Mar 68 Divadeenam.TRNS.AVG CS CFD OPTMDL.	+
	1.2 + 5	6.4 + 5		Data	EXFOR10523.012	Jan 78 . 27 PTS, CS DATA	
Total	1.0 + 5	1.5 + 6	ANL	Expt Jour	NSE 39 67	Jan 70 Sherwood+,TOF,CFD OPTICAL MODEL	+
				Rept	ANL - 7567	May 69 - +DATA PTS IN APPENDIX.	
	1.0 + 5	1.5 + 6		Data	EXFOR10007.	May 75 . 444 DATA PTS.	
Total	2.5 + 6	1.5 + 7	BNW	Expt Jour	PR/C 3 576	Feb 71 Foster+,TRANS,CURVS,CFD OTHERS+TH	+
				Jour	NIM 36 1	Sep 65 .EXPT DETAILS	
	2.3 + 6	1.5 + 7		Data	EXFOR10047.076	Aug 73 . 258 PTS.	
Total	8.0 + 6		AE	Theo Rept	AE - 430	Sep 71 Holmqvist+ CALC FROM OPTMOD PARAMS	
	8.1 + 6			Conf	70Helsinki 2 341	Jun 70 - + OPTMOL ANALYSIS. 8 MEV	
Total	2.7 + 3		MUN	Expt Prog	EANDC(E)150U	Oct 72 Dilg+ AVERAGE TOT XSECT+S0	+
				Conf	71Albany 327	Aug 71 - +TRNS.AVG CS GVN.31 ELEMENT GRP	
	2.7 + 3			Data	EXFOR20583.025	Jun 76 1PNT.	
Total	1.3 + 7	1.5 + 7	DEB	Eval Rept	IAEA - 153 173	73 Boedy+ MOST PROBABLE VAL OF SIG,TBL	
				Jour	AHP 30 115	Oct 71 Angeli+ AVG SIG,CFD CALC.TBLS.GRAPH	
Total	5.0 + 5	1.0 + 7	BET	Expt Rept	WAPD - TM - 1073	Apr 73 Green+.CF252 SOURCE.TOF.CURV.CFDENDF	+
	5.0 + 5	9.9 + 7		Data	EXFOR10225.	Aug 73 . 697 PTS. SIGMA	
Total	3.8 - 2	1.5 + 0	KIL	Expt Jour	AKE 22 69	Sep 73 Priesmeyer+ TOF TRANS EXPT, CURVE	
Total	2.0 + 2	1.0 + 5	HAR	Expt Prog	NEANDC(UK)160	Jul 74 Uttley+ TOF LINAC.OKS MOXON <2.5KEV	
	2.0 + 1	1.0 + 5		Prog	AERE - PR/NP21	Mar 74 - +LINAC.TOF 60M+120M.FOR RES.	
Total	2.5 + 5	1.5 + 7	JAE	Theo Conf	JAERI - M - 5984	Feb 75 Tanaka.OPTMDL/COUPLD CH.GRPH CFD EXP	
Total	5.0 + 0	3.0 + 1	HAR	Expt Prog	UKNDC(75)P71	Jul 75 Moxon+ MULTI - SAMPLE TRANSMISSION TOF	
	7.0 + 0	1.0 + 4		Prog	NEANDC(UK)160	Jul 74 - + TOF LINAC 8 SAMPLES GRPH	
Total	6.0 - 4	4.0 - 1	KAP	Expt Abst	BAP 6 70	Feb 61 Moore.TRANS,1/V OVER FULL RANGE	+
	6.0 - 4	4.0 - 1		Data	EXFOR12083.004	Jun 76 . 37 DATA PTS.	
Elastic	1.0 + 6		WIS	Expt Jour	PR 93 1062	Mar 54 Walt.	+
	1.0 + 6			Data	EXFOR11637.059	Jun 76 . 1 DATA PT.	
Elastic	7.2 - 2	4.6 - 1	ANL	Expt Jour	ACR 17 1087	Aug 64 Atoji. COH SCAT SIG = 7.59+ - 0.27 B	+
	7.2 - 2	4.6 - 1		Data	EXFOR12076.	Jun 76 . 2 PTS, COH, COH AMP	
Elastic	1.0 + 6		AGN	Eval Rept	TID - 21629	Dec 64 Perkins+ UCRL - 5573 DATA	
Elastic	1.0 + 4	1.0 + 7	KFK	Eval Rept	KFK - 352	Aug 65 Schmidt.GRAPHS+TABULATED DATA(NO.12)	
Elastic	3.0 + 5	1.5 + 6	ANL	Expt Jour	NSE 39 67	Jan 70 Sherwood+. INTEGRATED SIG,CURVE	+
				Abst	DA 30 3211	Jan 70 -	
				Rept	ANL - 7567	May 69 - +CALC CS AND LEG COEFS GVN.	
	3.0 + 5	1.5 + 6		Data	EXFOR10007.002	May 75 . 42 PTS. CALC CS GVN.	

72 Hafnium

Quantity	Energy (ev) Min	Max	Lab	Type	Documentation Ref Vol Page	Date	Author, Comments	Data
Elastic	8.0+6		AE Expt	Rept	AE– 430	Sep 71	Holmqvist+ INTEGRATED ANGDIST VALUES	+
				Conf	70Helsinki 2 341	Jun 70	– + OPTMOD ANALYSIS. 8 MEV	
	8.1+6			Data	EXFOR20162.020	May 74	1PNT.	
Elastic	9.5+5		ANL Expt	Rept	ANL– 7935	Jun 72	COX+ 4 PI B(O)	+
	9.5+5			Data	EXFOR10332.120	Jun 74	. 1 PT.	
Elastic	7.0+6		AE Expt	Rept	AE– 482	Dec 73	Etemad. INTEGRATED.	+
	7.0+6			Data	EXFOR20346.014	Sep 74	1PNT.	
Diff Elastic	1.0+6		WIS Expt	Jour	PR 93 1062	Mar 54	Walt+ HE COUNTER 30–150DEG LAB CURVE	+
	1.0+6			Data	EXFOR11637.061	Jun 76	. 9 PTS, DSIG	
Diff Elastic	1.0+6		ANL Theo	Jour	PR 124 826	Nov 61	Sokoloff.HARM OSC POT CFD EXPT CURVE	
Diff Elastic	1.0+6		AGN Eval	Rept	TID– 21629	Dec 64	Perkins+ LEG COEF FRM OTHER DATA	
Diff Elastic	1.0+6		LAS Theo	Prog	WASH– 1064 84	Oct 65	Rosen+, OPTMDL+ CPD ELST CFD WIS XPT	
Diff Elastic	3.0+5	1.5+6	ANL Expt	Jour	NSE 39 67	Jan 70	Sherwood+,TOF,CFD OPTMDL+ENDF/B	+
				Abst	DA/B 30 3211	Jan 70	– .	
				Rept	ANL– 7567	May 69	– +DIN VS ANG AT 1MEV.	
	3.0+5	1.5+6		Data	EXFOR10007.003	May 75	. 187 PTS. LEG COEFS GVN.	
Diff Elastic	8.0+6		AE Expt	Rept	AE– 430	Sep 71	Holmqvist+ TBLS + GEN OPTMOD FITS	+
				Jour	NP/A 188 24	Jun 72	– + OPTMOD ANAL OF 8MEV DATA	
	8.1+6			Rept	AE– 452	May 72	Salama.VDG TOF CURVES TABLES	
	8.0+6			Conf	70Helsinki 2 341	Jun 70	Holmqvist+ OPTMOD ANALYSIS. 8 MEV	
	8.1+6			Data	EXFOR20162.	May 74	32PTS.D/DA,LEG.FIT.	
Diff Elastic	9.5+5		ANL Expt	Rept	ANL– 7935	Jun 72	Cox+. CFD OPTMOD,HAUSER– FESHBACH	+
	9.5+5			Data	EXFOR10332.027	Jun 74	. 8 PTS.	
Diff Elastic	7.0+6		AE Expt	Rept	AE– 482	Dec 73	Etemad. VDG. TOF.	+
	7.0+6			Data	EXFOR20346.	Sep 74	30PTS.D/DA,LEG.FIT.	
Diff Elastic	8.0+6		JAE Theo	Conf	JAERI–M– 5984	Feb 75	Tanaka.OPTMDL/COUPLD CH CFD EXPTS.	
Polarization	9.1+5		ANL Expt	Rept	ANL– 7935	Jun 72	Cox+. CFD OPTMOD,HAUSER– FESHBACH	+
	9.1+5			Data	EXFOR10332.061	Jun 74	. 8 PTS.	
Potntal Scat		6.5+5	DKE ExTh	Jour	PL 13 70	Nov 64	Seth+ SIG TOT AV 3–650KEV	
Potntal Scat	None		DKE Expt	Abst	DA/B 28 3834	Mar 68	Divadeenam.TRNS.EFFECTIVE RADIUS	
Tot Inelastc	1.0+4	1.0+7	KFK Eval	Rept	KFK– 352	Aug 65	Schmidt.GRAPHS+TABULATED DATA(NO.12)	
Diff Inelast	3.2+5	1.5+6	ANL Expt	Jour	NSE 39 67	Jan 70	Sherwood+,TOF,CFD OPTMDL+ENDF/B	+
				Abst	DA/B 30 3211	Jan 70	– .	
				Rept	ANL– 7567	May 69	– +DIN VS ANG AT 1MEV	
	3.2+5	1.5+6		Data	EXFOR10007.004	Nov 75	.146 PTS. CALC CS GVN.	
Thermal Scat	1.0–4	1.0+3	MUN Revw	Jour	EEN 80 1	77	Koester. SCAT LENGTH	
Scattering	2.5–2		ORL Expt	Jour	PR 87 487	52	Bernstein+	+
	2.5–2			Data	EXFOR11745.010	Jun 76	. 1 PT.	
Scattering	Maxwl		HAR Expt	Rept	AERE–N/R– 1147	Apr 53	Egelstaff.FROM SLOW SIGMA TOT	
Nonelastic	1.0+6		WIS Expt	Jour	PR 93 1062	Mar 54	Walt.	+
	1.0+6			Data	EXFOR11637.060	Jun 76	. 1 PT.	
Nonelastic	1.0+4	1.0+7	KFK Eval	Rept	KFK– 352	Aug 65	Schmidt.GRAPHS+TABULATED DATA(NO.12)	
Absorption	Pile		HAR Expt	Jour	PPSA 63 1175	Oct 50	Colmer+ LITTLER.PILE OSC REL HAR B	+
				Rept	AERE–N/R– 527	Jun 50	– + PILE OSC.	
Absorption	Maxwl		HAR Expt	Rept	AERE–N/R– 1147	Apr 53	Egelstaff.FROM SLOW SIGMA TOT	
Absorption	2.0–2	2.4–1	CUW Theo	Rept	CWR– 400– 1	Sep 57	Roberts.MAXWELL– BOLTZMANN AVGD SIGS.	
Absorption	2.5–2		HAR Expt	Jour	JNEA 12 32	May 60	Tattersall+. PILE OSCILLATOR	+
				Rept	AERE–R– 2887	Aug 59	– . PILE OSC.REL BORON	
	2.5–2			Data	EXFOR20638.054	Jul 76	1PNT.SIGMA.	
Absorption	2.5–2		FAR Expt	Conf	66Paris 1 479	Oct 66	Carre+ OSCILLATOR MEHTOD.	+
	2.5–2			Data	EXFOR20658.024	Jul 76	1PNT.SIGMA.	
Absorption	8.1+6		AE Theo	Conf	70Helsinki 2 341	Jun 70	Holmqvist+55. OPTMODEL CALC SIGMA	
Res Int Abs	5.0–1		ANL Expt	Jour	PR 79 11	Jul 50	Harris+ EPI–CD,REL THERMAL ACT. B–W	+
	5.0–1			Data	EXFOR11343.028	Jun 76	. 1 PT. RI	
Res Int Abs	Pile		FAR Expt	Jour	CR 234 2448	Jun 52	Netter+. PILE OSC. REL B.	
Res Int Abs	5.0–1	1.0+6	CCP Expt	Conf	55Geneva 5 91	Aug 55	Spivak+.VAL GVN CFD REF,PPR659	
Res Int Abs	None		ORL Revw	Conf	55Geneva 5 96	Aug 55	Macklin+.TABLE,EXPT CFD THEORY,P833	
Res Int Abs	–		CCP Expt	Jour	AE 3 507	Dec 57	Klimentov+.EPI CD REACTIVITY REL LI	+
				Jour	JNE 9 20	Jun 59	TRANSLATN.*	
				Jour	SJA 3 1387	57	TRANSLATN.*	
Res Int Abs	5.0–1		HAR Expt	Jour	JNE 12 32	May 60	Tattersall+ ABOVE 1/V,OSCIL,REL B+AU	+
				Rept	AERE–R– 2887	Aug 59	– . PILE OSC.REL BORON	
				Conf	58Geneva 16 34	Sep 58	Rose+ SUPERSEDED	
	6.7–1			Data	EXFOR20638.055	Jul 76	1PNT.	
Res Int Abs	5.5–1		KAP Expt	Prog	KAPL– 2000– 16	Dec 61	Feiner+	+
	5.5–1			Data	EXFOR11454.004	Jun 76	. 1 PT, RI	
Res Int Abs	Pile		SAC Theo	Conf	64Geneva § 102	May 64	Carre+CF CALC VAL+EXP BY TATTERSAL	

72 Hafnium

Quantity	Energy (ev) Min	Max	Lab	Type	Documentation Ref Vol Page	Date	Author, Comments	Data
Res Int Abs	5.0−1		STF	Expt	Conf 66S.Diego 2 175	Feb 66	Le−Sage+	+
	5.0−1				Data EXFOR11754.010	Jun 76	. 1 PT. RI	
Res Int Abs	5.0−1		FAR	Expt	Conf 66Paris 1 479	Oct 66	Carre+ OSCILLATOR METHOD.	+
					Conf 66Paris 2 371	Oct 66	Vidal+.PPR73,RES INT,E ABOVE 1EV	
					Rept CEA−R−2486	Jul 64	− + PILE OSC REL B AND AU	
	5.5−1				Data EXFOR20658.025	Jul 76	1PNT.	
Res Int Abs	5.0−1		KAP	Expt	Conf 68Wash. § E20	Mar 68	Fulmer+ PILE OSC 2040+ − 110B REL AU	
Res Int Abs	5.0−1		MTR	Expt	Jour NSE 33 350	Sep 68	Rogers+ REACTIVITY METHOD REL TO AU	+
					Prog IDO−16977 7	Dec 63	Scoville+. AVG OF 3 INDEPEND MEASTS.	
	5.0−1				Data EXFOR12104.	68	. 2 PTS, RI	
Res Int Abs	5.0−1	1.9+1	JUL	Expt	Jour AKE 25 271	75	Jonas+ EXPT CFD THEORY	
					Rept JUEL−1164	Feb 75	− + EQUIVALENT TO AKE 25 271	
		1.0+1			Jour ATW 16 532	Oct 71	Demmeler+,2280+− 180 B	
Res Int Abs	5.0−1	7.8+0	JUL	Expt	Jour AKE 28 2 104	76	Kloth+ LEAD−SPECT EXPT, 2 TEMP	
(n,γ)	Pile		ANL	Expt	Jour PR 80 342	Nov 50	Harris+.PILE OSC.REL TO BORON.	+
	Pile				Data EXFOR11528.040	Jun 76	. 1 DATA PT.	
(n,γ)	Maxwl		ORL	Expt	Jour PR 83 641	Aug 51	Pomerance+ OSCILLATOR REL AU ABS 95B	+
	Maxwl				Data EXFOR11047.056	Jun 76	. 1 PT.	
(n,γ)	2.5−2		ANL	Expt	Jour NSE 9 132	Sep 61	Meadows+PULSED SOURCE.TBL	+
	2.5−2				Data EXFOR11028.023	Sep 76	. 1 PT. CS=101.4B	
(n,γ)	2.0+2	8.0+3	ORL	Expt	Conf 61Saclay 203	Sep 61	Block+.LIQUID SCINTILLATOR	+
					Conf 61Vienna 1 95	Aug 61	Neiler.PPR73,GRAPH,FAST CHOPPER	
	2.0+2	8.0+3			Data EXFOR11935.020	Jun 76	. 43 PTS.	
(n,γ)	3.0+4	6.5+4	ORL	Expt	Jour PR 129 2695	Mar 63	Macklin+ LIQ SCINT,510 AND 330MB	+
	3.0+4	6.5+4			Data EXFOR11331.027	63	. 2 PTS.	
(n,γ)	Maxwl		MTR	Expt	Prog WASH−1053 78	Oct 64	Scoville+ 124+ − 8B.REL AU AND DY	
(n,γ)	5.0+3	9.0+4	ORL	Theo	Jour RMP 37 166	Jan 65	Macklin+.CALC FOR KT=5TO90KEV	
(n,γ)	1.0+4	1.0+7	KFK	Eval	Jour KFK−352	Aug 65	Schmidt.GRAPHS+TABULATED DATA(NO.12)	
(n,γ)	1.0+4	1.5+5	KFK	Expt	Jour NP/A 133 513	Aug 69	Kompe.VDG.LIQ SCINT. REL AU MEAS.	+
					Rept KFK−1071	Aug 69	−". REPRINT OF NP/A 133 513	
					Rept EANDC(E)89U3	Feb 68	−. RENORMAL OF 66PARIS,GRAPH	
					Rept KFK−635	Oct 67	Poenitz+ RENORMALISED TO NEW AU VAL	
					Conf 66Paris 1 513	Oct 66	Kompe. LARGE LIQ SCIN. SUPERSEDED.	
	1.2+4	1.5+5			Data EXFOR20358.023	Sep 74	68PTS.SIGMA.	
(n,γ)	3.0+4		AUA	Theo	Rept AAEC/E−211	Nov 70	Musgrove. SIGMA GIVEN AND CFD OTHER	
(n,γ)		1.0+1	JUL	Expt	Jour ATW 16 532	Oct 71	Demmeler+,SIG−CURVE NOT CALIBRATED	
(n,γ)	5.0−1	3.0+1	HAR	Expt	Prog UKNDC(75)P71	Jul 75	Moxon+ MULTI−SAMPLE CAPTURE TOF	
(n,γ)	1.0+0	8.0+3	JUL	Expt	Jour AKE 28 2 104	76	Kloth+ LEAD−SPECT, DOPPLER RATIOS	
(n,γ)	Fast		RCN	Expt	Rept ECN−1	Oct 76	Veenema+ STEK REACTIVITY WORTHS TBL.	
Spect (n,γ)	Pile		PAR	Expt	Diss CEA−177 187	53	Ballini+.GRAPH. LEVELS IN TA 181	
Spect (n,γ)	Pile		CRC	Expt	Jour CJP 35 1361	Dec 57	Bartholomew+CRYST SPEC 6ES	
Spect (n,γ)	Maxwl		GEA	Eval	Rept DC−58−1−30	Jan 58	Deloume.BY APPROXIMATION CURV+TABLE	
Spect (n,γ)	Maxwl		KUR	Expt	Jour AE 4 5	Jan 58	Groshev+ SPEC+LINES 0.3−6.39MEV	
					Jour JNE 9 50	Jun 59	. ENGL OF AE 4 5	
					Jour SJA 4 1	58	. ENGL OF AE 4 5	
Spect (n,γ)	Maxwl		YAL	Expt	Jour PR 114 268	Apr 59	Draper.SC SPECTR,GAM E 0 TO 600 KEV	
Spect (n,γ)	Maxwl		ARF	Expt	Prog ARF−1193−17	Dec 62	Greenwood+ GAMMAS .0280−1.177MEV	
Spect (n,γ)	Maxwl		CAS	Expt	Jour NC 29 977	Aug 63	Giannini+ NAI, E+INTENSITY,TO 322KEV	+
Spect (n,γ)	Pile		ANL	Expt	Jour PR 146 844	Jun 66	Namenson+ LI−GE DET. GS5.5−7.6 MEV	
					Conf 65Antwerp 49	Jul 65	.SUPERSEDED	
Spect (n,γ)	2.5−2		MIT	Comp	Rept MITNE−85	Jan 69	Rasmussen+TBL G INT.=AFCRL−69−0071	
Spect (n,γ)	Pile		ANL	Expt	Prog WASH−1127 10	Apr 69	Bollinger+ LVL STRUCTRE ONLY,TBC,NDG	
Spect (n,γ)	Maxwl		KFI	Revw	Jour YF 10 907	Nov 69	Kecskemeti+ AVG GAM−MULTIPLICITY,TBL	
					Jour SNP 10 524	May 70	TRANSLATN.*	
Spect (n,γ)	2.0+3		MTR	Expt	Prog NCSAC−31 76	May 70	Greenwood+,ANAL TO BE COMPL,NO DATA	
Spect (n,γ)	Maxwl		WAL	Eval	Rept WANL−TME−2713	Jul 70	Fody.GAM YLDS FOR WANL POINT LIBRARY	
Spect (n,γ)	Pile		CAI	Expt	Jour ZP 265 313	Nov 73	Bashandy+,INT CONVERSION IN HF−180	
Inelastic γ	3.0+5	2.0+6	MIT	Expt	Jour PR 101 1516	Mar 56	Guernsey+,CS 230−KEV LEVEL	+
	3.3+5	1.9+6			Data EXFOR11691.004	Jun 76	. 20 PTS.	
(n,2n)	1.5+7		DEB	Eval	Jour REA 11 1 153	Mar 73	Boedy+ RECOMM.VALUE FROM N−Z SYSTEM.	
Reson Params	7.0+1	4.0+2	ORL	Expt	Jour NYA 25 522	Mar 63	Russell+ORNL N,G XPT. 6ES, IA UNSURE	
Reson Params	1.1+0	3.0+1	HAR	Expt	Prog UKNDC(75)P71	Jul 75	Moxon+ RESON PARAM ALL ISOTOPES TO30	
	2.4+0	6.0+0			Prog AERE−PR/NP21	Mar 74	− +MULTILVL ANAL.TOT.NG.TBLS PARS	
Strnth Fnctn	+3		BNL	Expt	Jour PRL 1 461	Dec 58	Hughes+FC, 1.1+ − 0.3	
Strnth Fnctn		6.5+5	DKE	ExTh	Jour PL 13 70	Nov 64	Seth+S,P,D STF FRM SIG TOT 3−650KEV	+
				Expt	Conf 64Paris 2 916	Jul 64	.SUPERSEDED	
	3.0+3	6.5+5			Data EXFOR11665.025	Jun 76	. 3 PTS.	

72 Hafnium

Quantity	Energy (ev) Min	Max	Lab	Type	Documentation Ref Vol Page	Date	Author, Comments	Data
Strnth Fnctn	None		DKE Expt	Abst	DA/B 28 3834	Mar 68	Divadeenam.S,P,D WAVES.CFD POT MDLS.	
Strnth Fnctn	1.0+4	1.5+5	KFK Expt	Jour	NP/A 133 513	Aug 69	Kompe. S1,S2,S(GAMMA)LEAST SQ NG FIT	+
				Rept	KFK – 1071	Aug 69	– . REPRINT OF NP/A 133 513	
	1.0+4	1.5+5		Data	EXFOR20358.	Sep 74	3PTS.GAMMA STF.	
Strnth Fnctn	2.7+3		MUNExpt	Conf	71Albany 327	Aug 76	Dilg+TRNS.S0 STF GVN.31 ELEMENT GRPH	
Lvl Density	None		FEI Theo	Jour	YF 11 1213	Jun 70	Ignatyuk+ SPIN DEPENDENCE OF DENSITY	
				Jour	SNP 11 674	Dec 70	. ENGL OF YF 11 1213	

72 Hafnium 166

Quantity	Energy (ev) Min	Max	Lab	Type	Documentation Ref Vol Page	Date	Author, Comments	Data
Lvl Density	None		CCP Theo	Jour	YF 13 43	Jan 71	Bravin+.DEFORM PAR,CALC,TBL,CFD EXPT	

72 Hafnium 168

Quantity	Energy (ev) Min	Max	Lab	Type	Documentation Ref Vol Page	Date	Author, Comments	Data
Lvl Density	None		CCP Theo	Jour	YF 13 43	Jan 71	Bravin+.DEFORM PAR,CALC,TBL,CFD EXPT	

72 Hafnium 170

Quantity	Energy (ev) Min	Max	Lab	Type	Documentation Ref Vol Page	Date	Author, Comments	Data
Lvl Density	None		CCP Theo	Jour	YF 13 43	Jan 71	Bravin+.DEFORM PAR,CALC,TBL,CFD EXPT	

72 Hafnium 172

Quantity	Energy (ev) Min	Max	Lab	Type	Documentation Ref Vol Page	Date	Author, Comments	Data
Lvl Density	None		CCP Theo	Jour	YF 13 43	Jan 71	Bravin+.DEFORM PAR,CALC,TBL,CFD EXPT	

72 Hafnium 174

Quantity	Energy (ev) Min	Max	Lab	Type	Documentation Ref Vol Page	Date	Author, Comments	Data
Evaluation	1.0–3	1.5+7	KAP Eval	Rept	KAPL – 3327	Aug 67	Reynolds+TOT RES ELAS INEL NP NG N2N	
Evaluation	1.0–5	2.0+7	SAI Eval	Rept	EPRI – 250	Nov 76	Drake+ENDF/B5.TBLS,GRPHS.CFD.	
Total	2.5–2		JAE Expt	Rept	JAERI – M – 4301	71	Okamoto. TRANSM, ENRICHED SAMPLES	+
	Maxwl			Data	EXFOR20318.002	Jun 74	1PNT.	
Total	2.0–2	5.0–1	IJI Expt	Rept	YFI – 18 36	Aug 74	Vertebny+ TOF,SIG GVN IN TBL	+
	2.5–2			Conf	73Kiev 2 114	May 73	– + SIG=650+ – 20 B	
	6.0–2	5.0–1		Conf	73Kiev 2 114	May 73	– + SIG(NEUT-E),GRAPH	
				Rept	INDC(CCP) – 49	Feb 75	+ (ENGL).TRANS,TOTSIG(E) TBL	
	2.0–2	5.0–1		Data	EXFOR40279.012	Apr 75	.SIGMA FOR 32 ES GVN	
Scattering	2.5–2		IJI Expt	Rept	YFI – 18 36	Aug 74	Vertebny+ TOF,SIG GVN IN TBL	+
				Conf	73Kiev 2 114	May 73	– + SIG=15+ – 3 B	
				Rept	INDC(CCP) – 49	Feb 75	– +(ENGL). 4PI – GEOM.VALUE GIVN	
	2.5–2			Data	EXFOR40279.007	May 75	.SIGMA GVN	
Absorption	2.5–2		IJI Expt	Rept	YFI – 18 36	Aug 74	Vertebny+ TOF,SIG GVN IN TBL	+
				Conf	73Kiev 2 114	May 73	– + SIG=635+ – 20 B	
				Rept	INDC(CCP) – 49	Feb 75	– +(ENGL).BY LSQ – FIT TO TOTSIG	
	2.5–2			Data	EXFOR40279.002	Apr 75	.SIGMA GVN	
Res Int Abs	5.0–1		GHT Expt	Rept	JRC 20 695	74	Van Der Linden+ BY(N,G).CFD OTHS,TBL	+
	5.5–1			Conf	73Paris 2 241	Mar 73	– + ACT,REL THR+GOLD,TBL	
	5.5–1			Data	EXFOR20645.038	Jul 76	1PNT.CAPTURE.	
(n,γ)	Maxwl		ORL Expt	Jour	PR 88 412	Oct 52	Pomerance.PILE OSC.ESTIM.ERROR 100PC	+
	Maxwl			Data	EXFOR11507.084	Jun 76	. 1 PT.	
(n,γ)	–		IEA Comp	Rept	IEA – INF – 10	Aug 68	Atalla. TABLES OF HL,SIG AND GAMM – E	
(n,γ)	5.0+3	1.0+5	AUA ExTh	Rept	AAEC/E – 198	May 69	Musgrove.S+P+D WAVE SIGMAS CALC,TBL	+
(n,γ)	3.0+4		AUA Theo	Rept	AAEC/E – 211	Nov 70	Musgrove. SIGMA GIVEN AND CFD OTHER	
(n,γ)	1.0+3	1.0+7	BOL Eval	Data	BENZI – DFN 806.	May 72	40 PNTS	+
(n,γ)	2.0–2	9.0–2	IJI Expt	Conf	75Kiev 3 171	May 75	Pavlenko+ SIG(E),GRPH.SIG(.02EV),TBL	
(n,γ)	Maxwl		KAP Expt	Abst	BAP 6 70	Feb 61	Esch+.SIG=390+ – 55B REL AU,ACTIVATION	+
	Maxwl			Data	EXFOR11989.004	Jun 76	. 1 PT.	
Spect (n,γ)	Pile		UPP Expt	Jour	AF 21 49	May 62	Bashandy+. COINC. K,L CONV COEFFS.	
Spect (n,γ)	Pile		CTH Expt	Jour	NP/A 161 209	Jan 71	Alenius+ PAIR,ANTICO SPEC. 34 LINES.	

72 Hafnium 174

Quantity	Energy (ev) Min	Max	Lab	Type	Documentation Ref Vol Page	Author, Comments Date	Data
(n,2n)	Fiss		CRC Eval	Rept	CRC – 1003	Dec 60 Roy+,ESTIMATED AVG SIG=1.9MB	
(n,2n)	1.5+7		BNL Expt	Jour	JIN 31 909	Apr 69 Hillman+,ACTIV	
				Rept	BNL – 11506	Jun 67 – + 860+ –60MB REL AL(NA) TBP NP	
	1.5+7			Data	EXFOR12092.002	Jun 76 . 1 PT.	
(n,2n)	1.5+7		DEB Comp	Jour	REA 7 4 93	Dec 69 Csikai+ SIG+HL COMPILTN,N – ACTIV – ANAL	
(n,2n)	1.4+7	1.5+7	JYV Eval	Rept	JU – RR – 3/1970	Jun 70 Leppaemaeki+ TABLE OF EVAL AVG SIG	
(n,2n)	1.5+7		DEB Eval	Rept	REA 11 1 153	Mar 73 Boedy+ RECOMM.VALUE FROM N – Z SYSTEM.	
(n,2n)	1.5+7		TAT Theo	Jour	JP/A 7 1457	Aug 74 Kondaiah. CALC ON STAT MODEL	
(n,2n)	1.5+7		JUL Expt	Jour	NP/A 224 319	May 74 Qaim. ACT.GE(LI)	+
				Jour	RRL 25 335	May 76 – + SIG IN GRPH. SYST VS (N – Z)/A	
	1.5+7			Data	EXFOR20541.058	Apr 76 1PNT.SIGMA.	
(n,p)	Fiss		CRC Eval	Rept	CRC – 1003	Dec 60 Roy+,ESTIMATED AVG SIG=0.05MB	
(n,p)	Maxwl		IFU Theo	Rept	ICD – 4 20	67 Dadakina+ PENETR COEFF CALC,TABLE	
(n,α)	Fiss		CRC Eval	Rept	CRC – 1003	Dec 60 Roy+,ESTIMATED AVG SIG=0.0009MB	
Reson Params	3.1+1		BNL Expt	Jour	PR 99 10	Jul 55 Harvey+.FC TRANSM. 1 RES. AREA ANAL	+
	3.1+1			Data	EXFOR11912.056	Jun 76 . 1 RES, E0, WN, WN0	
Reson Params	4.3+0	2.1+2	ORL Expt	Prog	ORNL – 3778 38	May 65 Fuketa+FC+TOF,WN+AVG D FOR 10 RES	+
	4.3+0	2.1+2		Data	EXFOR11372.002	Jun 76 . 10 RES, E0, WN	
Reson Params		1.0+6	AUA Theo	Jour	AUJ 20 477	Oct 67 Cook. TBL OF AVG LVL SPACING D,L=0,1	
Reson Params	–		AUA Theo	Rept	AAEC/E – 211	Nov 70 Musgrove. CALCULTD D+GAM WIDTH GIVEN	
Strnth Fnctn	4.3+0	2.1+2	ORL Expt	Prog	ORNL – 3778 38	May 65 Fuketa+FC+TOF,S – WAVE 2.8+ – 1.0	+
	4.3+0	2.1+2		Data	EXFOR11372.002	Jun 76 . 1 PT.	
Strnth Fnctn	–		AUA Theo	Rept	AAEC/E – 211	Nov 70 Musgrove. SMOOTHED S0,S1 AND S2 GIVN	
Strnth Fnctn	None		AUA Eval	Rept	AAEC/E – 277	Mar 73 Musgrove.TBLS EXPTL DATA+BEST VALUES	
Lvl Density	None		CCP Theo	Jour	YF 13 43	Jan 71 Bravin+.DEFORM PAR,CALC,TBL,CFD EXPT	

72 Hafnium 175

Quantity	Energy (ev) Min	Max	Lab	Type	Documentation Ref Vol Page	Author, Comments Date	Data
(n,p)	Maxwl		IFU Theo	Rept	ICD – 4 20	67 Dadakina+ PENETR COEFF CALC,TABLE	
Reson Params	–		AUA Theo	Rept	AAEC/E – 211	Nov 70 Musgrove. CALCULTD D+GAM WIDTH GIVEN	
Strnth Fnctn	–		AUA Theo	Rept	AAEC/E – 211	Nov 70 Musgrove. SMOOTHED S0,S1 AND S2 GIVN	
Lvl Density	+6		MIL Theo	Jour	EN 15 1 54	Jan 68 Facchini+ LDL PARS FROM LOW EN RES	
Lvl Density	None		MUN Theo	Jour	NP/A 217 269	Dec 73 Dilg+ A,DELTA. BACK SHIFTED FERMIGAS	
Lvl Density	None		COP Theo	Jour	NP/A 222 493	Apr 74 Dossing+COLL ROTAT.SPAC. ACCUR ESTIM	
Lvl Density	None		ROC Theo	Jour	NP/A 223 589	May 74 Huizenga+ EXP CFD MICROSC TH AX SYMM	

72 Hafnium 176

Quantity	Energy (ev) Min	Max	Lab	Type	Documentation Ref Vol Page	Author, Comments Date	Data
Evaluation	1.0–3	1.5+7	KAP Eval	Rept	KAPL – 3327	Aug 67 Reynolds+TOT RES ELAS INEL NP NG N2N	
Evaluation	1.0–5	2.0+7	SAI Eval	Rept	EPRI – 250	Nov 76 Drake+ENDF/B5.TBLS,GRPHS.CFD.	
Total	+2		ORL Expt	Prog	WASH – 1071 174	Nov 66 Fuketa.LINAC,NDG,NEARLY COMPLETE	
Total	1.5–2	6.0–1	RPI Expt	Abst	BAP 14 496	Apr 69 Conrad. ABST AH16	+
	1.0–2	1.0+0		Prog	RPI – 328 – 148	Dec 68 – + LINAC TRANS VALUE GIVEN	
	1.5–2	6.0–1		Data	EXFOR12085.002	Jun 76 . 20 PTS.	
Total	2.5–2		JAE Expt	Rept	JAERI – M – 4301	71 Okamoto. TRANSM, ENRICHED SAMPLES	+
	Maxwl			Data	EXFOR20318.003	Jun 74 1PNT.	
Total	7.0–2	1.0+4	HAR Expt	Prog	NEANDC(UK)160	Jul 74 Moxon+ TOF LINAC	
Total	2.0–2	5.0–1	IJI Expt	Rept	YFI – 18 36	Aug 74 Vertebny+ SIG(NEUT – E),TBL	+
	2.5–2			Conf	73Kiev 2 114	May 73 – + SIG=19+ – 15 B	
	6.0–2	5.0–1		Conf	73Kiev 2 114	May 73 – + SIG(NEUT – E),TBL	
				Rept	INDC(CCP) – 49	Feb 75 – + (ENGL).TRANS,TOTSIG(E) TBL	
	2.5–2	5.0–1		Data	EXFOR40279.013	Apr 75 .SIGMA FOR 31 ES GVN	
Total	1.4+7		LIN Expt	Conf	75Kiev 4 140	May 75 Djumin+ SIG GIVEN.OPTMOD ANAL,RADIUS	
Scattering	2.5–2		IJI Expt	Rept	YFI – 18 36	Aug 74 Vertebny+ TOF,SIG GVN IN TBL	+
				Conf	73Kiev 2 114	May 73 – + SIG=5.6+ – 0.3B	
				Rept	INDC(CCP) – 49	Feb 75 – +(ENGL).BY LSQ – FIT TO TOTSIG	
	2.5–2			Data	EXFOR40279.008	May 75 .SIGMA GVN	
Absorption	2.5–2		IJI Expt	Rept	YFI – 18 36	Aug 74 Vertebny+ TOF,SIG GVN IN TBL	+
				Conf	73Kiev 2 114	May 73 – + SIG=16+ – 15 B	
				Rept	INDC(CCP) – 49	Feb 75 – +(ENGL).BY LSQ – FIT TO TOTSIG	
	2.5–2			Data	EXFOR40279.003	Apr 75 .SIGMA GVN	
Res Int Abs	5.0–1		KAP Expt	Conf	68Wash. § E20	Mar 68 Fulmer+ PILE OSC 640+ – 3B REL AU	+
	5.0–1			Data	EXFOR12140.002	Jun 76 . 1 PT. RI	

72 Hafnium 176

Quantity	Energy (ev) Min	Max	Lab	Type	Documentation Ref Vol Page	Date	Author, Comments	Data
Res Int Abs	5.0-1	+6	MTR	Expt Jour	NSE 33 350	Sep 68	Rogers+ REACTIVITY METHOD REL TO AU	+
	5.0-1			Prog	IDO-16977 7	Dec 63	Scoville+. VALUE GIVEN.	
	5.0-1			Data	EXFOR12104.004	Jun 76	. 1 PT, RI	
(n,γ)	Maxwl		ORL	Expt Jour	PR 88 412	Oct 52	Pomerance.PILE OSC.ESTIM.ERROR 100PC	+
	Maxwl			Data	EXFOR11507.085	Jun 76	. 1 PT.	
(n,γ)	1.0+2	1.0+3	ORL	Expt Abst	BAP 9 31	Jan 64	Russell+ CA4, NO DATA GIVEN.	
(n,γ)	Maxwl		MTR	Expt Prog	WASH-1053 78	Oct 64	Scoville+21,5+-3.5B, REL AU AND DY	
(n,γ)	2.5+4		FEI	ExTh Prog	YFI-4 22	May 67	Shorin+.,TBLS GIVEN,TBP YF	
				Rept	INDC-187E	67	. ENGL OF YFI-4 22	
(n,γ)	None		RPI	Expt Prog	WASH-1127 182	Apr 69	Kirouac+ NDG	
(n,γ)	5.0+3	1.0+5	AUA	ExTh Rept	AAEC/E-198	May 69	Musgrove.S+P+D WAVE SIGMAS CALC,TBL	+
(n,γ)	3.0+4		AUA	Theo Rept	AAEC/E-211	Nov 70	Musgrove. SIGMA GIVEN AND CFD OTHER	
(n,γ)	1.0+3	1.0+7	BOL	Eval Data	BENZI-DFN 807.	May 72	40 PNTS	+
(n,γ)	7.0-3	1.0+5	HAR	Expt Prog	NEANDC(UK)160	Jul 74	Moxon+ TOF LINAC	
(n,γ)	2.5-2		IJI	Expt Conf	75Kiev 3 171	May 75	Pavlenko+ TOF+M-R DET.SIGMA GIVEN	
Spect (n,γ)	Pile		ANL	Expt Jour	PR 158 1206	Jun 67	Bolotin+ GE-LI DET, 5762KEV GAM, INT	
Spect (n,γ)	7.8+0		HAR	Expt Rept	NEANDC(UK)160	Jul 74	Thomas+ GAMMA SPECTRUM. TOF.	
(n,2n)	Fiss		CRC	Eval Rept	CRC-1003	Dec 60	Roy+,ESTIMATED AVG SIG=3.2MB	
(n,2n)	Fiss		BNL	Theo Jour	NSE 23 238	Nov 65	Pearlstein.STATMDL CALC.SPEC AVG.TBL	
(n,2n)	1.3+7	1.5+7	BNL	Theo Jour	NSE 23 238	Nov 65	Pearlstein.3ES.STAT MDL CALC.TBL CS.	
(n,2n)	1.5+7		BNL	Expt Jour	JIN 31 909	Apr 69	Hillman+,ACTIV	+
				Rept	BNL-11506	Jun 67	-+ 2000MB REL AL(N,A) TBP NP	
	1.5+7			Data	EXFOR12092.003	Jun 76	. 1 PT.	
(n,2n)	1.5+7		MUN	Expt Jour	NP/A 118 9	Sep 68	Dilg+ ACTIV.REL AL(N,A)	+
				Jour	OAWS 177 323	69	Winkler+(IRK) ACTIVATION.	
	1.5+7			Data	EXFOR20802.014	Dec 78	1PNT.SIGMA.	
(n,2n)	1.5+7		DEB	Comp Jour	REA 7 4 93	Dec 69	Csikai+ SIG+HL COMPILTN,N-ACTIV-ANAL	
(n,2n)	1.4+7	1.5+7	CCP	Comp Rept	ICD-6 215	70	Sluchevskaja.SIG FROM 2 REFERENC,TBL	
(n,2n)	1.4+7	1.5+7	JYV	Eval Rept	JU-RR-3/1970	Jun 70	Leppaemaeki+ TABLE OF EVAL AVG SIG	
(n,2n)	+7		KFI	Theo Rept	KFKI-71-8	Feb 71	Jeki. CALCULATED CFD EXPTL SIG VALUE	
(n,2n)	1.5+7		DEB	Eval Jour	REA 11 1 153	Mar 73	Boedy. COMPILATION+RECOMM.VALUE,TBL	
				Rept	IAEA-153 173	73	-. RECOMM. VALUE ONLY	
(n,2n)	1.5+7		TAT	Theo Jour	JP/A 7 1457	Aug 74	Kondaiah. CALC ON STAT MODEL	
(n,2n)	1.5+7		JUL	Expt Jour	NP/A 224 319	May 74	Qaim. ACT.GE(LI)	+
				Jour	RRL 25 335	May 76	-+ SIG IN GRPH. SYST VS (N-Z)/A	
	1.5+7			Data	EXFOR20541.059	Apr 76	1PNT.SIGMA.	
(n,xn) x>2	Fiss		BNL	Theo Jour	NSE 23 238	Nov 65	Pearlstein.SPEC AVG STATMDL CALC N3N	
(n,p)	Fiss		CRC	Eval Rept	CRC-1003	Dec 60	Roy+,ESTIMATED AVG SIG=0.08MB	
(n,p)	1.4+7	1.5+7	ARK	Theo Prog	ORO-3235-29	Jan 67	Koch+,STAT MODEL CALC CFD EXPTS	
(n,α)	Fiss		CRC	Eval Rept	CRC-1003	Dec 60	Roy+,ESTIMATED AVG SIG=0.0002MB	
Reson Params	4.8+0	2.0+2	ORL	Expt Prog	ORNL-3778 38	May 65	Fuketa+FC+FOF,WN+AVG D FOR 6 RES	+
	4.8+0	2.0+2		Data	EXFOR11372.003	Jun 76	. 6 RES, E0,WN	
Reson Params	2.0+2	1.1+3	ORL	Expt Prog	WASH-1064 158	Oct 65	Hockenbury+,TRNS,WN FOR 16 RES,TABLE	
Reson Params	None		RPI	Expt Prog	WASH-1127 182	Apr 69	Kirouac+ TRANS+CAPT MEASTS,NO DATA	
Reson Params	-		AUA	Theo Rept	AAEC/E-211	Nov 70	Musgrove. CALCULTD D+GAM WIDTH GIVEN	
Reson Params	7.8+1		HAR	Expt Diss	HASTE	74	Haste+(OXF)CAPT GAMMAS IDENTIFICATN.	
Reson Params	8.0+0	2.6+2	HAR	Expt Prog	NEANDC(UK)160	Jul 74	Moxon+ WN FROM TRANS+CAPT DATA TBC	
Strnth Fnctn	4.8+0	2.0+2	ORL	Expt Prog	ORNL-3778 38	May 65	Fuketa+FC+TOF,S-WAVE 1.4+-.6	+
	+0	+2		Prog	WASH-1056 71	Mar 65	-.S-WAVE,1.4+-.6,TBP ORNL PR	
Strnth Fnctn	-		AUA	Theo Rept	AAEC/E-211	Nov 70	Musgrove. SMOOTHED S0,S1 AND S2 GIVN	
Strnth Fnctn	None		AUA	Eval Rept	AAEC/E-277	Mar 73	Musgrove.TBLS EXPTL DATA+BEST VALUES	
Lvl Density	None		CCP	Theo Jour	YF 13 43	Jan 71	Bravin+.DEFORM PAR,CALC,TBL,CFD EXPT	

72 Hafnium 177

Quantity	Energy (ev) Min	Max	Lab	Type	Documentation Ref Vol Page	Date	Author, Comments	Data
Evaluation	2.5-2	1.0+7	KFK	Eval Rept	KFK-352	Aug 65	Schmidt+.RES	
Evaluation	1.0-3	1.5+7	KAP	Eval Rept	KAPL-3327	Aug 67	Reynolds+TOT RES ELAS INEL NP NG N2N	
Evaluation	1.0-5	2.0+7	SAI	Eval Rept	EPRI-250	Nov 76	Drake+ENDF/B5.TBLS,GRPHS.CFD.	
Total	1.0+2	1.0+3	ORL	Expt Prog	WASH-1071 174	Nov 66	Fuketa.LINAC,NDG,NEARLY COMPLETE	
Total	1.5-2	8.0-1	RPI	Expt Abst	BAP 14 496	Apr 69	Conrad+ AH16.	+
	1.0-2	1.0+0		Prog	RPI-328-148	Dec 68	-+ LINAC TRANS VALUE GIVEN	
	1.5-2	8.0-1		Data	EXFOR12085.003	Jun 76	. 21 PTS.	
Total	2.5-2		JAE	Expt Rept	JAERI-M-4301	71	Okamoto. TRANSM, ENRICHED SAMPLES	+
	Maxwl			Data	EXFOR20318.004	Jun 74	1PNT.	
Total	7.0-2	1.0+4	HAR	Expt Prog	NEANDC(UK)160	Jul 74	Moxon+TOF LINAC	

72 Hafnium 177

Quantity	Energy (ev) Min	Max	Lab	Type	Documentation Ref Vol Page	Date	Author, Comments	Data
Total	2.0−2	5.0−1	IJI	Expt Rept	YFI−18 36	Aug 74	Vertebny+ SIG(NEUT−E),TBL	+
	6.0−2	5.0−1		Conf	73Kiev 2 114	May 73	− + SIG(NEUT−E),TBL	
	2.5−2			Conf	73Kiev 2 114	May 73	− + SIG=380+−10B	
	6.0−2	5.0−1		Rept	INDC(CCP)−49	Feb 75	− + (ENGL).TRANS,TOTSIG(E) TBL	
	2.0−2	5.0−1		Data	EXFOR40279.014	Apr 75	.SIGMA FOR 32 ES GVN	
Total	1.4+7		LIN	Expt Conf	75Kiev 4 140	May 75	Djumin+ SIG GIVEN.OPTMOD ANAL,RADIUS	
Total	3.0+0	7.0+2	COL	Expt Jour	PR/C 11 2022	Jun 75	Liou+ NEVIS,TBL RES PAR	+
	None			Data	EXFOR10520.008	Jan 76	UNCORRECTED DATA AVAILABLE	
Scattering	2.5−2		IJI	Expt Rept	YFI−18 36	Aug 74	Vertebny+ TOF,SIG GVN IN TBL	
				Conf	73Kiev 2 114	May 73	− + SIG=0+−0.2 B	
				Rept	INDC(CCP)−49	Feb 75	− +(ENGL).BY LSQ−FIT TO TOTSIG	
Absorption	Maxwl		ANL	Expt Jour	PR 92 1527	Dec 53	Bollinger+	+
	Maxwl			Data	EXFOR12108.003	Jun 76	. 1 PT.	
Absorption	2.5−2		IJI	Expt Rept	YFI−18 36	Aug 74	Vertebny+ TOF,SIG GVN IN TBL	
				Rept	INDC(CCP)−49	Feb 75	− +(ENGL).BY LSQ−FIT TO TOTSIG	
Res Int Abs	None		KAP	Expt Abst	BAP 7 22	Jan 62	Feiner+ F4, RESON PARAMS	
Res Int Abs	5.0−1		KAP	Expt Conf	68Wash. § E20	Mar 68	Fulmer+ PILE OSC 7380+−500B REL AU	+
	5.0−1			Data	EXFOR12140.003	Jun 76	. 1 PT.	
Res Int Abs	5.0−1		MTR	Expt Jour	NSE 33 350	Sep 68	Rogers+ REACTIVITY METHOD REL TO AU	+
				Prog	IDO−16977 7	Dec 63	Scoville+. VALUE GIVEN.	
	5.0−1			Data	EXFOR12104.005	Jun 76	. 1 PT.	
(n,γ)	Maxwl		ORL	Expt Jour	PR 88 412	Oct 52	Pomerance.PILE OSC.	+
	Maxwl			Data	EXFOR12085.003	Jun 76	. 1 PT.	
(n,γ)	Maxwl		ROS	Expt Jour	NP 32 482	May 62	Alexander+ SIGMA (N,G)M GVN	
(n,γ)	2.5+2	1.0+3	ORL	Expt Jour	NYA 25 522	Mar 63	Russell+ PRELIM ORNL EXPT	
(n,γ)	Maxwl		MTR	Expt Prog	WASH−1053 78	Oct 64	Scoville+389+−27B,REL AU AND DY	
(n,γ)	1.0+3	1.0+4	LAS	Theo Rept	LA−3463	Jan 66	Bell. TH CAPTURE OF RARE EARTHS	
(n,γ)	Maxwl		MIL	Expt Jour	EN 14 4 228	Apr 67	FOGLIO PARA+.SIG GS+ISOM CFD THEORY.	
(n,γ)	−		IEA	Comp Rept	IEA−INF−10	Aug 68	Atalla. TABLES OF HL,SIG AND GAMM−E	
(n,γ)	None		RPI	Expt Prog	WASH−1127 182	Apr 69	Kirouac+ NDG	
(n,γ)	5.0+3	1.0+5	AUA	ExTh Rept	AAEC/E−198	May 69	Musgrove.S+P+D WAVE SIGMAS CALC,TBL	+
(n,γ)	3.0+4		AUA	Theo Rept	AAEC/E−211	Nov 70	Musgrove. SIGMA GIVEN AND CFD OTHER	
(n,γ)	Maxwl		KFI	Expt Jour	JRC 7 365	Jun 71	Nagy+ SIGMA,GAM+XRAY+ELECTR ES GIVEN	
(n,γ)	1.0+3	1.0+7	BOL	Eval Data	BENZI−DFN 808.	May 72	40 PNTS	+
(n,γ)	Maxwl		INL	Expt Jour	NP/A 211 1	Aug 73	Helmer+ SIG TO 2ND 178HF ISOMER	+
	Maxwl			Data	EXFOR10354.002	Jul 74	1 PT	
(n,γ)	7.0−3	1.0+5	HAR	Expt Prog	NEANDC(UK)160	Jul 74	Moxon+ TOF LINAC	
(n,γ)	2.0−2	9.0−2	IJI	Expt Conf	75Kiev 3 171	May 75	Pavlenko+ SIG(E),GRPH.SIG(.02EV),TBL	
(n,γ)	None		GEL	Expt Prog	NEANDC(E)172 3	Feb 76	Rohr+LINAC TOF	
		3.0+2		Prog	NEANDC(E)−161U	Aug 74	− +	
Spect (n,γ)	Maxwl		CCP	Expt Jour	AE 4 22	Jan 58	Sklyarevskii+.EGS+INTENS BELOW .3MEV	
Spect (n,γ)	Maxwl		KUR	Expt Conf	58Geneva 15 138	Sep 58	Groshev+ PPR2029.CURV,COMPTON−SPEC	
Spect (n,γ)	1.1+0	2.4+0	YAL	Expt Jour	NP 10 386	Apr 59	Fenstermacher+.GRAPH.2NES.NAT SAMPLE	
Spect (n,γ)	1.1+0	2.4+0	YAL	Expt Jour	NP 14 693	Jan 60	Draper+REL GAMMA WIDTHS,2RES.CRYSPEC	
Spect (n,γ)	Maxwl		ANL	Expt Jour	PR 129 1691	Feb 63	Smither+217 GAMMAS .05 TO 1.6 MEV	
Spect (n,γ)	1.1+0		JAE	Expt Rept	JAERI−1073	Mar 65	Kawarasaki. RES CAPT.LINAC.TOF.E,INT	+
				Rept	INDSWG−90 6	Jul 65	− . TABLE E,INTS GIVEN.	
	1.1+0			Data	EXFOR20277.017	Jun 74	4PTS.	
Spect (n,γ)	Maxwl	2.4+1	FEI	Expt Jour	INDSWG−74	Jul 65	BRODER ET AL.3 ES.	+
Spect (n,γ)	1.1+0	2.4+0	NRL	Expt Jour	NP 82 441	Jul 66	Vogt. AT RES, NAT TARGET	
Spect (n,γ)	Pile		ANL	Expt Jour	PR 158 1206	Jun 67	Bolotin+ GE−LI DET,5.3−7.5MEV GS,TBL	
				Jour	PR 146 844	Jun 66	Namenson+ DATA	
				Conf	65Antwerp 49	Jul 65	.SUPERSEDED	
Spect (n,γ)	+0	+4	COL	Expt Prog	WASH−1124 31	Nov 68	Camarda+ MOXON−RAE DET TBC NO DATA	
Spect (n,γ)	6.0−2	8.8+0	MTR	Expt Jour	NP/A 123 616	Jan 69	Faler+ GE(LI).AT 6RES. 5.8TO7.6MEVGS	
Spect (n,γ)	Pile		ANL	Expt Conf	69Studsvik 601	Aug 69	Smither+ NO DATA GVN,OKS STATMOD	
				Conf	JINR−D−3893	May 68	Bollinger+ ABSTRACT,NO DATA GIVEN	
Spect (n,γ)	Maxwl		CCP	Expt Jour	IZV 33 1655	Oct 69	Prokofjev+ CONV−ELEC.G−E+INT,LVL SCH	
	Pile			Jour	IZV 33 1655	69	− + CONV−EL SPEC TABL,LVL SCH	
	Maxwl			Jour	BAS 33 1518	Oct 70	.ENGLISH OF IZV 33 1655	
	Pile			Rept	ANL−TRANS−815	Mar 70	. ENGLISH OF IZV 33 1655	
Spect (n,γ)	Maxwl		KFI	Revw Jour	YF 10 907	Nov 69	Kecskemeti+ AVG GAM−MULTIPLICITY,TBL	
				Jour	SNP 10 524	May 70	TRANSLATN.*	
Spect (n,γ)	Maxwl		KFI	Comp Jour	JRC 7 365	Jun 71	Nagy+ SIGMA,GAM+XRAY+ELECTR ES GIVEN	
Spect (n,γ)	Maxwl		UPP	Expt Jour	NP/A 171 353	Aug 71	Fogelberg+ G+COINC+CONV ELECTR SPEC.	
				Conf	69Studsvik 155	Aug 69	− + SPEC GRPHS=GAM+ELEC,COINC	
Spect (n,γ)	+3	1.0+5	KUR	Expt Prog	INDC(SEC)−28	Sep 72	. SAME AS INDC(HUN)−9 15	
Spect (n,γ)	Maxwl		IFL	Expt Book	PROKOFJEV	73	. TBL GAM,CONV ELECTR ES+INT,LVL SCH	

72 Hafnium 177

Quantity	Energy (ev) Min	Max	Lab	Type	Documentation Ref Vol Page	Date	Author, Comments	Data
Spect (n,γ)	Maxwl	2.0+3	MTR Expt	Abst	BAP 18 592	Apr 73	Greenwood+ 2ES,NO DATA GIVEN	
Spect (n,γ)	Maxwl		KFI Expt	Prog	KFKI – YB – 72 31	May 73	Kardon+ VERY BRIEF,G – SPECT,G – WID,NDG	
Spect (n,γ)	Maxwl		CCP Theo	Jour	ZET 65 12	Jul 73	Nosov+ THERMODYN CALC CFD EXPT,GRAPH	
				Jour	JET 38 6	Jan 74	. ENGLISH OF ZET 65 6	
Spect (n,γ)	1.1+1	6.6+1	GEL Expt	Jour	NP/A 218 61	Jan 74	Coceva+TOF,GE(LI) EG,INT,POPL RATIOS	
	+0	+3		Prog	EANDC(E)157U I	Mar 73	– + HIGH ENERGY GAMMAS IN RESON	
(n,2n)	Fiss		CRC Eval	Rept	CRC – 1003	Dec 60	Roy+,ESTIMATED AVG SIG = 38.0MB	
(n,2n)	Fiss		BNL Theo	Jour	NSE 23 238	Nov 65	Pearlstein.STATMDL CALC.SPEC AVG.TBL	
(n,2n)	1.3+7	1.5+7	BNL Theo	Jour	NSE 23 238	Nov 65	Pearlstein.3ES.STAT MDL CALC.TBL CS.	
(n,2n)	1.5+7		DEB Eval	Jour	REA 11 1 153	Mar 73	Boedy+ RECOMM.VALUE FROM N – Z SYSTEM.	
(n,2n)	1.5+7		KFI Expt	Rept	KFKI – 73 – 68	Dec 73	Jeki.NEW FIT,CALC SIG CFD OTHERS,TBL	
(n,xn) x > 2	Fiss		BNL Theo	Jour	NSE 23 238	Nov 65	Pearlstein.SPEC AVG STATMDL CALC N3N	
(n,p)	Fiss		CRC Eval	Rept	CRC – 1003	Dec 60	Roy+,ESTIMATED AVG SIG = 0.02MB	
(n,p)	Maxwl		CCP Theo	Rept	ICD – 4 20	67	Dadakina+PENETRATION COEF CALC,TABLE	
(n,α)	Fiss		CRC Eval	Rept	CRC – 1003	Dec 60	Roy+,ESTIMATED AVG SIG = 0.0038MB	
(n,α)	– 1	+2	DUB Expt	Rept	JINR – P3 – 5875	71	Popov+ GRPH ALF VS EN.RES – E,SIG GIVN	
(n,α)	Maxwl		LYO Expt	Prog	LYCEN/75 – 01 27	74	Emsallem+ABST,NDG	
(n,α)	None		DUB Expt	Conf	76Lowell 1250	Jul 76	Antonov+TOT ALPHA WIDS OF N – RES.NDG	
	1.1+0	1.4+1		Rept	JINR – P3 – 7376	Sep 73	Balabanov+ RES – PARS+TOF SPEC,TBL,GRF	
	+2	1.0+3		Conf	73Kiev 2 148	May 73	– + TOT ALF – WID,CFD OPTMDL	
Reson Params	1.1+0	1.4+1	ANL Expt	Jour	PR 92 1527	Dec 53	Bollinger+ TRANS 6RESON WT+STRENGTH	+
	1.1+0	1.4+1		Data	EXFOR12108.006	Jun 76	. 6RES, E0, WT, PCS,WT**2/PCS	
Reson Params	5.9+0	1.1+2	BNL Expt	Jour	PR 99 10	Jul 55	Harvey+.FC TRANSM. 28 RES. AREA ANAL	+
	5.9+0	1.1+2		Data	EXFOR11912.057	Jun 76	. 28 RES, E0, WN, WN0	
Reson Params	1.1+0	2.4+0	BNL Expt	Jour	PR 101 726	Jan 56	Igo+,2ES WT WN WG OTHER PARS GIVEN	+
Reson Params	2.4+0	6.5+0	BNL Expt	Jour	PR 101 1328	Feb 56	Levin+,TWO LEVELS	
Reson Params	1.1+0	1.0+2	KAP Eval	Rept	KAPL – M – JBN – 9	Jul 56	Nims+21 ES WN SOME WG BEST VALUES.	
Reson Params	1.1+0	2.4+0	YAL Expt	Jour	NP 10 386	Apr 59	Fenstermacher.	+
	1.1+0	2.4+0		Data	EXFOR11171.003	Jun 76	. 2 RES, E0	
Reson Params	1.1+0	2.4+0	MTR Expt	Jour	NSE 11 298	Nov 61	Joki+,XTAL SPEC WT = .068EV GWN = .163EV	+
				Rept	MTR – L – 54 – 53	Jun 54	– + CRYST SPEC 2RESON B – W PARAMS	
	1.1+0	2.4+0		Data	EXFOR11635.009	Jun 76	. 2 RES, E0, WN, WG	
Reson Params	5.5+1	5.0+2	ORL Expt	Jour	NYA 25 522	Mar 63	Russell+ FROM ORNL (N,G). 65RES ES.	
	3.2+1	3.8+2		Prog	WASH – 1056 19	Mar 65	Fuketa.TRNS,AVGD DATA,71 RES,GWN	
Reson Params	1.1+0	2.2+1	ANL Expt	Conf	64Paris 2 673	Jul 64	Bollinger+SPIN OF FEW LVLS	+
				Prog	ANL – 6589	Aug 62	Carpenter.	
	1.1+0	2.2+1		Data	EXFOR12043.006	Jun 76	. 9 RES, J	
Reson Params	1.1+0	2.4+0	MOL Expt	Jour	NP 62 641	Feb 65	Ceulemans+J = 3,J = 4 FROM GAMMA N/GAMMA	+
				Rept	EANDC(E)76U	Jan 67	Poortmans. AGREE WITH NP 62	
	2.4+0			Data	EXFOR20180.	May 74	. 2PTS.J,WN/WT.	
	1.1+0	2.4+0		Data	EXFOR20208.	May 74	4PTS.J,WN/WT.	
Reson Params	1.1+0	1.8+2	ORL Expt	Prog	ORNL – 3778 38	May 65	Fuketa+FC+TOF,WN+AVG D FOR 46 RES	+
	5.0+1	5.0+2		Prog	ORNL – 3425 64	63	Block+HF02 ONLY LVLS AND D DISTRIB	
	1.1+0	1.8+2		Data	EXFOR11372.	Jun 76	. 48 RES, E0, WT, WN, WG	
Reson Params	–		KFK Eval	Rept	KFK – 352	Aug 65	Schmidt.AVERAGE S – WAWE RES PAR(TAB19	
Reson Params	1.1+0	2.4+0	ITE Expt	Conf	66Paris 1 71	Oct 66	PPR104,KALEBIN+.E – VAL AT 2ES,CHOPPER	
Reson Params	1.1+0	2.4+0	BNL Expt	Prog	WASH – 1071 24	Nov 66	Sailor+,J FOR 2 RESONANCES MEASURED	
Reson Params		1.0+6	AUA Theo	Jour	AUJ 20 477	Oct 67	Cook. TBL OF AVG LVL SPACING D,L = 0,1	
Reson Params	1.1+0	2.1+2	ISP Expt	Jour	NP/A 117 586	Sep 68	Coceva+.SPIN ASSIGN 46 RES.FROM N – G	+
	1.1+0	3.0+2		Rept	RT/FI – 70 55	Dec 70	– +. J FOR 97 RESONANCES	
	1.1+0	3.0+2		Data	EXFOR20375.002	Oct 74	97PTS.J.	
Reson Params	None		RPI Expt	Prog	WASH – 1127 182	Apr 69	Kirouac+ TRANS+CAPT MEASTS,NO DATA	
Reson Params	1.1+0	8.9+0	ANL Expt	Jour	PR/C 1 1501	Apr 70	Wetzel+J FROM CAPT MEAS.TBL GVN.	+
	1.1+0	8.9+0		Data	EXFOR10080.006	Feb 76	. 4 PTS. J, E0	
Reson Params	–		AUA Theo	Rept	AAEC/E – 211	Nov 70	Musgrove. CALCULTD D+GAM WIDTH GIVEN	
Reson Params	1.1+0	6.6+0	CJD Eval	Rept	YK – 7	71	Zakharova+ SURVEY+SYSTEMATICS,GW,TBL	
				Rept	INDC(CCP) – 27	Nov 72	.ENGLISH TRANSLATION OF YK – 7 /71	
Reson Params	None		DUB Theo	Jour	YF 13 240	Feb 71	Malecki+G – WID,THEO CFD EXPT.TBL,GRPH	
				Jour	SNP 13 133	Aug 71	– + ENGL OF YF 13 240.	
Reson Params	None		CCP Expt	Jour	IZV 37 1129	May 73	Danelyan.I = 4,GAMS FROM 13 LEVELS,NDG	
				Jour	BAS 37 5 190	May 73	.ENGLISH OF IZV 37 1129	
Reson Params	+0	+3	KUR Theo	Conf	73Kiev 2 301	May 73	Daneljan. CORREL N+G – WID+PARTL G – WID	
Reson Params	1.1+0	1.4+1	DUB Expt	Rept	JINR – P3 – 7376	Sep 73	Balabanov+ RES – E,ALF – WID,SPIN,TABLE	
	+2	1.0+3		Conf	73Kiev 2 148	May 73	– + TOT ALF – WID,CFD OPTMDL	
	1.0+0	3.0+2		Conf	72Budapest 140	Aug 72	– + ALPHA – WIDTHS ,TBL	
	1.1+0	8.9+0		Rept	JINR – P3 – 5875	71	Popov+ FROM (N,A),A – WIDTH,D GIVN.TBL	
Reson Params		+3	HAR Expt	Diss	HASTE	74	Haste+(OXF) SPIN ASSGNS FROM GAMMAS	
Reson Params	1.1+0	3.3+1	HAR Expt	Prog	NEANDC(UK)160	Jul 74	Moxon+ WG WN FROM TRANS+CAPT DATA	

72 Hafnium 177

Quantity	Energy (ev) Min	Max	Lab	Type	Documentation Ref Vol Page	Date	Author, Comments	Data
Reson Params	7.6+6		DUB Theo	Conf	74Petten 175	Sep 74	Malov+ DOBS,SEMI-MICROSCOPIC CALC.	
Reson Params	+0		DUB Theo	Jour	YF 21 40	Jan 75	Voronov+ MEAN D,WITH ROTAT.CFD EXPT	
				Jour	SNP 21 20	Jul 75	. ENGLISH OF YF 21,40	
Reson Params	5.9+0	7.0+2	COL Expt	Jour	PR/C 11 2022	Jun 75	Liou+ TBL E0,GWN0,SOME WG.176 LEVELS	+
	1.1+0	7.0+2		Data	EXFOR10520.	Jan 76	.204PTS.(RED WN)G=178PTS.WG=25PTS.D	
Reson Params	Maxwl		KUK Theo	Conf	76Ahmedabd 2 1	Dec 76	Sharma+AVG S-WAVE REDUCED N-WID ANAL	
Strnth Fnctn	+3		BNL Expt	Jour	PRL 1 461	Dec 58	Hughes+ FC 2.2+-0.4	
Strnth Fnctn	1.1+0	1.8+2	ORL Expt	Prog	ORNL-3778 38	May 65	Harvey.FC+TOF,S-WAVE 2.8+-.4	+
Strnth Fnctn	1.1+0	2.1+2	ISP Expt	Jour	NP/A 117 586	Sep 68	Coceva+.S.WAVE STRFUNCT(J) VARIATION	
Strnth Fnctn	–		DUB Revw	Jour	YF 11 111	Jan 70	Malecki+ VALUES FOR TWO SPIN STATES	
				Jour	SNP 11 61	Jul 70	- + ENGL OF YF 11 61.	
Strnth Fnctn	–		AUA Theo	Rept	AAEC/E-211	Nov 70	Musgrove. SMOOTHED S0,S1 AND S2 GIVN	
Strnth Fnctn	1.0+0	3.0+2	GEL Expt	Rept	RT/FI-70 55	Dec 70	Coceva+	+
	1.0+0	3.0+2		Data	EXFOR20375.003	Oct 74	2PTS.L=0.	
Strnth Fnctn	None		AUA Eval	Rept	AAEC/E-277	Mar 73	Musgrove.TBLS EXPTL DATA+BEST VALUES	
Strnth Fnctn	0.0+0	3.0+2	BOL Expt	Conf	JINR-D3-7991	Apr 74	Coceva.P266.S-WAVE,STF(I=3,I=4),GRPH	
Strnth Fnctn	3.0+0	7.0+2	COL Expt	Jour	PR/C 11 2022	Jun 75	Liou+S WAVE. GRPH.	+
	5.9+0	7.0+2		Data	EXFOR10520.005	Jan 76	. 1 PT. S0=(2.7+-.25)-4	
Strnth Fnctn	0.0+0	3.0+2	GEL Expt	Conf	76Lowell 1258	Jul 76	Rohr.STF E DEP OVER 2 E RANGES.	
	1.0+1	3.0+2		Jour	NP/A 264 93	Jun 76	- + TBL.100EV RANGES FROM RES PAR	
	0.0+0	3.0+2		Conf	73Munich 1 524	Aug 73	- J=3,4.AVG FOR 3 E-INTERVLS,TB	
	1.0+1	3.0+2		Conf	72Budapest 52	Aug 72	- + S-WAVE STRENGTH FUNCTION GIVE	
Lvl Density	–		COP Theo	Jour	NP 6 62	Mar 58	Ericson. LVL DENSITY FORM CFD EXP	
Lvl Density	+6		MIL Theo	Jour	EN 15 1 54	Jan 68	Facchini+ LDL PARS FROM LOW EN RES	
Lvl Density	1.1+0	2.1+2	ISP Expt	Jour	NP/A 117 586	Sep 68	Coceva+.LOWER LIMIT CUTOFF PARAM.	
Lvl Density	None		AUW Theo	Conf	70Madurai 2 267	Dec 70	Ramamurty+ A-PARAMETER GVN,LANG'S-TH	
Lvl Density	None		MUN Theo	Jour	NP/A 217 269	Dec 73	Dilg+ A,DELTA. BACK SHIFTED FERMIGAS	
Lvl Density	None		ROC Theo	Jour	NP/A 223 589	May 74	Huizenga+ EXP CFD MICROSC TH AX SYMM	
Lvl Density	1.0+1	3.0+2	GEL Expt	Jour	NP/A 264 93	Jun 76	Rohr+ TBL.LEVEL SPACING ANALYSIS.	

72 Hafnium 178

Quantity	Energy (ev) Min	Max	Lab	Type	Documentation Ref Vol Page	Date	Author, Comments	Data
Evaluation	1.0-3	1.5+7	KAP Eval	Rept	KAPL-3327	Aug 67	Reynolds+TOT RES ELAS INEL NP NG N2N	
Evaluation	1.0-5	2.0+7	SAI Eval	Rept	EPRI-250	Nov 76	Drake+ENDF/B5.TBLS,GRPHS.CFD.	
Total	+2		ORL Expt	Prog	WASH-1071 174	Nov 66	Fuketa.LINAC,NDG,NEARLY COMPLETE	
Total	1.5-2	8.0-1	RPI Expt	Abst	BAP 14 496	Apr 69	Conrad. AH16	+
	1.0-2	1.0+0		Prog	RPI-328-148	Dec 68	- + LINAC TRANS VALUE GIVEN	
	1.5-2	8.0-1		Data	EXFOR12085.004	Jun 76	. 21 PTS.	
Total	2.5-2		JAE Expt	Rept	JAERI-M-4301	71	Okamoto. TRANSM, ENRICHED SAMPLES	+
	Maxwl			Data	EXFOR20318.005	Jun 74	1PNT.	
Total	7.0-2	1.0+4	HAR Expt	Prog	NEANDC(UK)160	Jul 74	Moxon+ TOF LINAC	
Total	2.0-2	5.0-1	IJI Expt	Rept	YFI-18 36	Aug 74	Vertebny+ TOF,SIG GVN IN TBL	+
	6.0-2	5.0-1		Conf	73Kiev 2 114	May 73	- + SIG(NEUT-E),TBL	
	2.5-2			Conf	73Kiev 2 114	May 73	- + SIG=99+-4 B	
	6.0-2	5.0-1		Rept	INDC(CCP)-49	Feb 75	- (ENGL).TRANS,TOTSIG(E) TBL	
	2.5-2	5.0-1		Data	EXFOR40279.015	Apr 75	.SIGMA FOR 25 ES GVN	
Total	1.4+7		LIN Expt	Conf	75Kiev 4 140	May 75	Djumin+ SIG GIVEN.OPTMOD ANAL,RADIUS	
Scattering	2.5-2		IJI Expt	Rept	YFI-18 36	Aug 74	Vertebny+ TOF,SIG GVN IN TBL	+
				Conf	73Kiev 2 114	May 73	- + SIG=4.5+-0.2 B	
				Rept	INDC(CCP)-49	Feb 75	- +(ENGL).BY LSQ-FIT TO TOTSIG	
	2.5-2			Data	EXFOR40279.009	May 75	.SIGMA GVN	
Absorption	Pile		ANL Expt	Jour	PR 92 1527	Dec 53	Bollinger+	+
	Pile			Data	EXFOR12108.004	Jun 76	. 1 PT.	
Absorption	2.5-2		IJI Expt	Rept	YFI-18 36	Aug 74	Vertebny+ TOF,SIG GVN IN TBL	+
				Conf	73Kiev 2 114	May 73	- + SIG=51.4+-4 B	
				Rept	INDC(CCP)-49	Feb 75	- +(ENGL).BY LSQ-FIT TO TOTSIG	
	2.5-2			Data	EXFOR40279.004	Apr 75	.SIGMA GVN	
Res Int Abs	None		KAP Expt	Abst	BAP 7 22	Jan 62	Feiner+OKS PUBLISHED RES PARAMS	
Res Int Abs	5.0-1		KAP Expt	Conf	68Wash. § E20	Mar 68	Fulmer+ PILE OSC 1950+-120B REL AU	+
	5.0-1			Data	EXFOR12140.004	Jun 76	. 1 PT.	
Res Int Abs	5.0-1		MTR Expt	Jour	NSE 33 350	Sep 68	Rogers+ REACTIVITY METHOD REL TO AU	+
				Prog	IDO-16977 7	Dec 63	Scoville+. VALUE GIVEN.	
	5.0-1			Data	EXFOR12104.006	Jun 76	. 1 PT.	
Res Int Abs	5.0-1		GHT Expt	Jour	JRC 23 113	74	Van Der Linden+ (N,G).CD-RATIO,TABLE	
(n,γ)	Maxwl		ORL Expt	Jour	PR 88 412	Oct 52	Pomerance.PILE OSC.	+
	Maxwl			Data	EXFOR11507.087	Jun 76	. 1 PT.	

72 Hafnium 178

Quantity	Energy (ev) Min	Max	Lab	Type	Documentation Ref Vol Page	Date	Author, Comments	Data
(n,γ)	Maxwl		ROS Expt	Jour	NP 32 482	May 62	Alexander+ SIGMA (N,G)M GVN	
(n,γ)	2.5+2	1.0+3	ORL Expt	Jour	NYA 25 522	Mar 63	Russell+ PRELIM XPT. ROUGH REL CRV	
(n,γ)	Maxwl		MTR Expt	Prog	WASH - 1053 78	Oct 64	Scoville +86+ - 7B,REL AU AND DY	
(n,γ)	Maxwl		MIL Expt	Jour	EN 14 4 228	Apr 67	FOGLIO PARA+.SIG GS+ISOM CFD THEORY.	
(n,γ)	-		IEA Comp	Rept	IEA - INF- 10	Aug 68	Atalla. TABLES OF HL,SIG AND GAMM - E	
(n,γ)	None		RPI Expt	Rept	WASH - 1127 182	Apr 69	Kirouac+ NDG	
(n,γ)	5.0+3	1.0+5	AUA ExTh	Rept	AAEC/E - 198	May 69	Musgrove.S+P+D WAVE SIGMAS CALC,TBL	+
(n,γ)	3.0+4		AUA Theo	Rept	AAEC/E - 211	Nov 70	Musgrove. SIGMA GIVEN AND CFD OTHER	
(n,γ)	Maxwl		KFI Comp	Jour	JRC 7 365	Jun 71	Nagy+ SIGMA,GAM+XRAY+ELECTR ES GIVEN	
(n,γ)	1.0+3	1.0+7	BOL Eval	Data	BENZI - DFN 841.	May 72	40 PNTS	+
	1.0+3	1.0+7		Data	BENZI - DFN 809.	May 72	40 PNTS	
(n,γ)	2.5+4		AUW Expt	Jour	JP/A 5 877	Jun 72	Siddappa+ ACT.	+
			ExTh	Conf	70Madurai 2 29	Dec 70	Sriramachandra Murty+.S+P WAVE SIGMA	
	2.5+4		Expt	Data	EXFOR30248.011	Jun 73	SIGMA CAPTURE TO THE MS STATE	
(n,γ)	Pile		ROS ExTh	Prog	ZFK - 243 93	Sep 72	Mohsen+ NG - SYSTEMAT. FOR RARE EARTHS	
(n,γ)	7.0-3	1.0+5	HAR Expt	Prog	NEANDC(UK)160	Jul 74	Moxon+ TOF LINAC	
(n,γ)	2.5-2		IJI Expt	Conf	75Kiev 3 171	May 75	Pavlenko+ TOF+M - R DET.SIGMA GIVEN	
Spect (n,γ)	1.1+0	2.4+0	YAL Expt	Conf	57Col.Univ 266	Sep 57	Schultz+. NA(TL). 2 RESON ES. CURVE.	
Spect (n,γ)	Maxwl		AMS Expt	Jour	PL 12 238	Oct 64	Loebner+ RABBIT,18S ISOM FOR HL LVL1	+
Spect (n,γ)	7.8+0		JAE Expt	Rept	JAERI - 1073	Mar 65	Kawarasaki. RES CAPT.LINAC.TOF.E,INT	+
				Rept	INDSWG - 90 6	Jul 65	- . TABLE E,INTS GIVEN.	
	7.8+0			Data	EXFOR20277.018	Jun 74	4PTS.	
Spect (n,γ)	7.8+0		MTR Expt	Conf	66Argonne 514	Nov 66	Faler+,GE(LI),SPECT 4.3 - 6.2MEV GAMS	
Spect (n,γ)	Pile		ANL Expt	Jour	PR 158 1206	Jun 67	Bolotin+ GE - LI DET,4.3 - 5.7MEV GS,TBL	
				Jour	PR 146 844	Jun 66	Namenson+	
				Conf	65Antwerp 49	Jul 65	.SUPERSEDED	
Spect (n,γ)	Maxwl		ROS Expt	Jour	NP/A 102 563	Oct 67	Manfrass+. GE(LI)DET.DEDUCED LEVELS	
Spect (n,γ)	Maxwl	4.9+0	BNL Expt	Rept	WASH - 1093 16	Apr 68	Chrien+ SPECTRA SHOWN	
Spect (n,γ)	None		ORL Theo	Jour	NSE 36 220	May 69	Yost+ CALCULAT BY GAMMA CASCADE MDL	
Spect (n,γ)	Maxwl		KFI Comp	Jour	JRC 7 365	Jun 71	Nagy+ SIGMA,GAM+XRAY+ELECTR ES GIVEN	
Spect (n,γ)	Maxwl		MUN Expt	Prog	EANDC(E)140U	Aug 71	VAN ASSCHE+, MEASURED AT RISO	
Spect (n,γ)	Maxwl		CTH Expt	Jour	NP/A 186 209	May 72	Alenius+ PAIR,ANTI - CO SPEC. 66 E(G)	+
	Pile			Data	EXFOR20224.	May 74	131PTS.	
Spect (n,γ)	Maxwl	1.0+2	KUR Expt	Conf	72Budapest 254	Aug 72	Danelyan+ RATIOS OF TRANSITIONS,TBL	
Spect (n,γ)	7.8+0		BNL Expt	Jour	PR/C 7 419	Jan 73	Casten+.GE(LI) DET.TABLE+CURVE	
Spect (n,γ)	Pile		CCP Expt	Jour	IZV 37 1813	Sep 73	Beitin+ TBL GAM - ES+INTENS,GRPH LVLS	
				Jour	BAS 37 9 21	Sep 73	.ENGLISH OF IZV 37 1813	
Spect (n,γ)	None		ROS Expt	Prog	ZFK - 262 89	Sep 73	Seidel+ DELAYED GAMMAS,E+INTENS,TBL	
Spect (n,γ)	Maxwl		ROS Expt	Jour	NP/A 225 300	Jun 74	Andrejtscheff+ 179HF DEDUCED LVL,TI/2	
Spect (n,γ)	Maxwl		IFL Expt	Jour	NP/A 262 273	May 76	Beitins+G+B SPEC,RISO.GE - LI. LVL SCM	
				Book	PROKOFJEV	73	. TBL GAM,CONV ELECTR ES+INT,LVL SCH	
Inelastic γ	None		KFI Comp	Jour	JRC 7 365	Jun 71	Nagy+ GAMMA+XRAY+ELECTR ES,HALF - LIFE	
Inelastic γ	1.5+7		SMU Expt	Conf	75Wash. 712	Mar 75	Salaita+ CS PROD 178M +(N,2N) 179HF	+
				Conf	74Columbia 95	Jul 74	- + ACT.SIG TO SHORTLIV ISO.TBL	
	1.5+7			Data	EXFOR10356.006	Sep 76	.1PT=1452+ - 116MB=PROD178+(N,2N)179HF	
Inelastic γ	2.8+6		CCP Expt	Conf	76Lowell 1334	Jul 76	Andreev+DIRECT EXCIT EFFECTS.NDG	
(n,2n)	Fiss		CRC Eval	Rept	CRC - 1003	Dec 60	Roy+,ESTIMATED AVG SIG=6.3MB	
(n,2n)	Fiss		BNL Theo	Jour	NSE 23 238	Nov 65	Pearlstein.STATMDL CALC.SPEC AVG.TBL	
(n,2n)	1.3+7	1.5+7	BNL Theo	Jour	NSE 23 238	Nov 65	Pearlstein.3ES.STAT MDL CALC.TBL CS.	
(n,2n)	1.5+7		DEB Eval	Jour	REA 11 1 153	Mar 73	Boedy+ RECOMM.VALUE FROM N - Z SYSTEM.	
(n,2n)	1.5+7		KFI Theo	Rept	KFKI - 73 - 68	Dec 73	Jeki.NEW FIT,CALC SIG CFD OTHERS,TBL	
(n,xn) x>2	Fiss		BNL Theo	Jour	NSE 23 238	Nov 65	Pearlstein.SPEC AVG STATMDL CALC N3N	
(n,p)	Fiss		CRC Eval	Rept	CRC - 1003	Dec 60	Roy+,ESTIMATED AVG SIG=0.004MB	
(n,p)	1.5+7		ARK Expt	Jour	RCA 6 26	Aug 66	Meason+.SIG FOR 16MIN + 30MIN 178LU	
(n,p)	1.4+7	1.5+7	ARK ExTh	Rept	ORO - 3235 - 29	Jan 67	Koch+,STAT MODEL CALC CFD EXPTS	
(n,p)	1.4+7	1.5+7	JYV Eval	Rept	JU - RR - 3/1970	Jun 70	Leppaemaeki+ TABLE OF EVAL AVG SIG	
(n,α)	1.4+7		ALD Expt	Jour	PPS 73 215	Feb 59	Coleman+. ACTIVATION	+
(n,α)	Fiss		CRC Eval	Rept	CRC - 1003	Dec 60	Roy+,ESTIMATED AVG SIG=BELO 0.0001MB	
(n,α)	1.4+7		CIS Expt	Jour	NP 51 460	Feb 64	Facchini+STATMOD SIG XPT/CALC=16 - 20	
(n,α)	1.5+7		DEB Comp	Jour	REA 7 4 93	Dec 69	Csikai+ SIG+HL COMPILTN,N - ACTIV - ANAL	
(n,α)	1.4+7	1.5+7	JYV Eval	Rept	JU - RR - 3/1970	Jun 70	Leppaemaeki+ TABLE OF EVAL AVG SIG	
(n,α)	1.4+7		KFI Comp	Jour	JRC 7 365	Jun 71	Nagy+ SIGMA,GAM+ELECTR ES,HALF - LIFE	
(n,α)	Maxwl		LYO Expt	Prog	LYCEN/75 - 01 27	74	Emsallem+ABST,NDG	
(n,α)	1.5+7		RBZ Expt	Jour	ASL 28 207	76	Caplar+ A - SPEC AT ODEG,GRPH.DIFF CS	+
Reson Params	7.6+0		ANL Expt	Jour	PR 92 1527	Dec 53	Bollinger+ TRANS STRENGTH	
	7.6+0			Data	EXFOR12108.007	Jun 76	. 1 RES, E0, WT**2/PCS	
Reson Params	7.8+0		BNL Expt	Jour	PR 99 10	Jul 55	Harvey+.FC TRANSM. 1 RES. AREA ANAL	+
	7.8+0			Data	EXFOR11912.058	Jun 76	. 1 RES, E0,WN,WN0	

72 Hafnium 178

Quantity	Energy (ev) Min	Max	Lab	Type	Documentation Ref Vol Page	Date	Author, Comments	Data
Reson Params	7.8+0		KAP Eval	Rept	KAPL−M−JBN−9	Jul 56	Nims+ WN 55MV WT82MVQ BEST VALUE	
Reson Params	1.0+2	4.5+2	ORL Expt	Jour	NYA 25 522	Mar 63	Russell. FROM ORNL (N,G). 8 ES ONLY	
	1.1+2	3.8+2		Prog	WASH−1056 99	Mar 65	Fuketa.TRNS,AVGD DATA,6 RES,WN	
	5.0+2	8.6+2		Prog	RPI−63	63	Russell.	
Reson Params	7.8+0	1.6+2	ORL Expt	Prog	ORNL−3778 38	May 65	Fuketa+FC+TOF,WN+AVG D FOR 3 RES	+
	+0	+2		Prog	WASH−1056 71	Mar 65	− .AVG D 60+−20 EV,TBP ORNL PR	
	5.0+1	5.0+2		Prog	ORNL−3425 64	63	Block+ HF02 ONLY LVLS AND D DISTRIB	
	7.8+0	1.6+2		Data	EXFOR11372.005	Jun 76	. 3 RES, EO, WN	
Reson Params	7.8+0		ITE Expt	Conf	66Paris 1 71	Oct 66	PPR104,KALEBIN+.E−VAL AT 1E ,CHOPPER	
Reson Params		1.0+6	AUA Theo	Jour	AUJ 20 477	Oct 67	Cook. TBL OF AVG LVL SPACING D,L=0,1	
Reson Params	None		RPI Expt	Prog	WASH−1127 182	Apr 69	Kirouac+ TRANS+CAPT MEASTS,NO DATA	
Reson Params	−		AUA Theo	Rept	AAEC/E−211	Nov 70	Musgrove. CALCULTD D+GAM WIDTH GIVEN	
Reson Params	1.0+2	2.1+3	HAR Expt	Prog	AERE−PR/NP21	Mar 74	Moxon+ RES PARS FROM TOTAL+CAPT SIG	+
	1.0+2	2.1+3		Data	EXFOR20689.002	Jun 77	23PTS.E0,WN,WG.	
Reson Params	7.8+0	7.2+2	COL Expt	Jour	PR/C 11 2022	Jun 75	Liou+ TBL E0,WN0.12 LEVELS	+
	7.8+0	7.2+2		Data	EXFOR10520.004	Jan 76	. 12 PTS. RED WN.	
Strnth Fnctn	7.8+0	1.6+2	ORL Expt	Prog	ORNL−3778 38	May 65	Harvey.FC+TOF,S−WAVE 1.1+−.7	+
	+0	+2		Prog	WASH−1056 71	Mar 65	Fuketa.S−WAVE,1.1+−.7,TBP ORNL PR	
Strnth Fnctn	−		AUA Theo	Rept	AAEC/E−211	Nov 70	Musgrove. SMOOTHED S0,S1 AND S2 GIVN	
Strnth Fnctn	None		AUA Eval	Rept	AAEC/E−277	Mar 73	Musgrove.TBLS EXPTL DATA+BEST VALUES	
Strnth Fnctn	7.8+0	7.2+2	COL Expt	Jour	PR/C 11 2022	Jun 75	Liou+S WAVE.GRPH	+
	7.7+0	7.2+2		Data	EXFOR10520.007	Jan 76	. 1 PT. S0=(1.9+−.8)−4	
Lvl Density	+6		MIL Theo	Jour	EN 15 1 54	Jan 68	Facchini+ LDL PARS FROM LOW EN RES	
Lvl Density	None		CCP Theo	Jour	YF 11 1028	May 70	Rubchenya. DENSITY+A+TEMP GIVEN	
				Jour	SNP 11 571	Nov 70	. ENGL OF YF 11 571.	
Lvl Density	None		AUW Theo	Conf	70Madurai 2 267	Dec 70	Ramamurty+ A−PARAMETER GVN,LANG'S−TH	
Lvl Density	1.0+0	3.0+2	GEL Expt	Jour	RT/FI−70 55	Dec 70	Coceva+	+
	1.0+0	3.0+2		Data	EXFOR20375.004	Oct 74	1PNT.SP.CUT.	
Lvl Density	None		CCP Theo	Jour	YF 13 43	Jan 71	Bravin+.DEFORM PAR,CALC,TBL,CFD EXPT	
Lvl Density	None		MUN Theo	Jour	NP/A 217 269	Dec 73	Dilg+ A,DELTA. BACK SHIFTED FERMIGAS	
Lvl Density	None		COP Theo	Jour	NP/A 222 493	Apr 74	Dossing+COLL ROTAT.SPAC. ACCUR ESTIM	
Lvl Density	None		DUB Theo	Jour	NP/A 224 396	May 74	Malov+ 1/2 MICROSC.MODEL. DEFORM NUC	
Lvl Density	None		ROC Theo	Jour	NP/A 223 589	May 74	Huizenga+ EXP CFD MICROSC TH AX SYMM	

72 Hafnium 179

Quantity	Energy (ev) Min	Max	Lab	Type	Documentation Ref Vol Page	Date	Author, Comments	Data
Evaluation	2.5−2	1.0+7	KFK Eval	Rept	KFK−352	Aug 65	Schmidt+.RES	
Evaluation	1.0−3	1.5+7	KAP Eval	Rept	KAPL−3327	Aug 67	Reynolds+TOT RES ELAS INEL NP NG N2N	
Evaluation	1.0−5	2.0+7	SAI Eval	Rept	EPRI−250	Nov 76	Drake+ENDF/B5.TBLS,GRPHS.CFD.	
Total	+2		RPI Expt	Prog	WASH−1071 174	Nov 66	Fuketa.LINAC,NDG,NEARLY COMPLETE	
Total	1.5−2	8.0−1	RPI Expt	Abst	BAP 14 496	Apr 69	Conrad+ AH16	+
	1.0−2	1.0+1		Prog	RPI−328−148	Dec 68	− + LINAC TRANS VALUE GIVEN	
	1.5−2	8.0−1		Data	EXFOR12085.005	Jun 76	. 21 PTS.	
Total	2.5−2		JAE Expt	Rept	JAERI−M−4301	71	Okamoto. TRANSM, ENRICHED SAMPLES	+
	Maxwl			Data	EXFOR20318.006	Jun 74	1PNT.	
Total	7.0−2	1.0+4	HAR Expt	Prog	NEANDC(UK)160	Jul 74	Moxon+ TOF LINAC	
Total	2.0−2	5.0−1	IJI Expt	Rept	YFI−18 36	Aug 74	Vertebny+ TOF,SIG GVN IN TBL	+
	2.5−2			Conf	73Kiev 2 114	May 73	− + SIG=65+−2.5 B	
	6.0−2	5.0−1		Conf	73Kiev 2 114	May 73	− + SIG(NEUT−E),TBL	
				Rept	INDC(CCP)−49	Feb 75	− + (ENGL).TRANS,TOTSIG(E) TBL	
	2.5−2	5.0−1		Data	EXFOR40279.016	Apr 75	.SIGMA FOR 25 ES GVN	
Diff Elastic	1.0+6		LAS Eval	Rept	LA−2016	Jun 56	Longley+,TBL ANG DIST 3−DEG STEPS	
Tot Inelastc	2.0+6		KFI Comp	Jour	JRC 7 365	Jun 71	Nagy+ SIGMA,GAM+XRAY+ELECTR ES GIVEN	
Scattering	2.5−2		IJI Expt	Rept	YFI−18 36	Aug 74	Vertebny+ SIG GVN IN TBL	+
				Conf	73Kiev 2 114	May 73	− + SIG=7.0+−0.3 B	
				Rept	INDC(CCP)−49	Feb 75	− +(ENGL).BY LSQ−FIT TO TOTSIG	
	2.5−2			Data	EXFOR40279.010	May 75	.SIGMA GVN	
Absorption	Pile		ANL Expt	Jour	PR 92 1527	Dec 53	Bollinger+	+
	Pile			Data	EXFOR12108.005	Jun 76	. 1 PT.	
Absorption	2.5−2		IJI Expt	Rept	YFI−18 36	Aug 74	Vertebny+ TOF,SIG GVN IN TBL	+
				Conf	73Kiev 2 114	May 73	− + SIG=58+−2 B	
				Rept	INDC(CCP)−49	Feb 75	− +(ENGL).BY LSQ−FIT TO TOTSIG	
	2.5−2			Data	EXFOR40279.005	Apr 75	.SIGMA GVN	
Res Int Abs	None		KAP Expt	Abst	BAP 7 22	Jan 62	Feiner+ F4, RESON PARAMS	
Res Int Abs	5.0−1		KAP Expt	Conf	68Wash. § E20	Mar 68	Fulmer+ PILE OSC 660+−30B REL AU	+
	5.0−1			Data	EXFOR12140.005	Jun 76	. 1 PT. RI	

72 Hafnium 179

Quantity	Energy (ev) Min	Max	Lab	Type	Documentation Ref Vol Page	Date	Author, Comments	Data
Res Int Abs	5.0-1		MTR	Expt Jour	NSE 33 350	Sep 68	Rogers+ REACTIVITY METHOD REL TO AU	+
				Prog	IDO-16977 7	Dec 63	Scoville+. VALUE GIVEN.	
	5.0-1			Data	EXFOR12104.007	Jun 76	. 1 PT.	
Res Int Abs	5.0-1		GHT	Expt Jour	JRC 20 695	74	Van Der Linden+ BY(N,G).CFD OTHS,TBL	+
	5.5-1			Conf	73Paris 2 241	Mar 73	- + ACT,REL THR+GOLD,TBL	
	5.5-1			Data	EXFOR20645.039	Jul 76	1PNT.CAPTURE.	
(n,γ)	Maxwl		ORL	Expt Jour	PR 88 412	Oct 52	Pomerance.PILE OSC.	+
	Maxwl			Data	EXFOR11507.088	Jun 76	. 1 PT.	
(n,γ)	Pile		FTI	ExTh Jour	NP 6 561	Apr 58	Gvozdev+. SIGMA FOR HF180M.	
(n,γ)	Maxwl		MTR	Expt Prog	WASH-1053 78	Oct 64	Scoville+38+-3B,REL AU AND DY	
(n,γ)	1.0+3	1.0+4	LAS	Theo Rept	LA-3463	Jan 66	Bell. TH CAPTURE OF RARE EARTHS	
(n,γ)	Maxwl		BNL	Expt Jour	PR 158 1105	Jun 67	Goldhaber.	+
	Maxwl			Data	EXFOR12119.002	Jun 76	. 1 PT.	
(n,γ)	-		IEA	Comp Rept	IEA-INF- 10	Aug 68	Atalla. TABLES OF HL,SIG AND GAMM-E	
(n,γ)	None		RPI	Expt Prog	WASH-1127 182	Apr 69	Kirouac+ NDG	
(n,γ)	5.0+3	1.0+5	AUA	ExTh Jour	AAEC/E-198	May 69	Musgrove.S+P+D WAVE SIGMAS CALC,TBL	+
(n,γ)	3.0+5		AUA	Theo Rept	AAEC/E-211	Nov 70	Musgrove. SIGMA GIVEN AND CFD OTHER	
(n,γ)	1.0+3	1.0+7	BOL	Eval Data	BENZI-DFN 810.	May 72	40 PNTS	+
(n,γ)	2.5+4		AUW	Expt Jour	JP/A 5 877	Jun 72	Siddappa+ ACT.	+
				ExTh Conf	70Madurai 2 29	Dec 70	Sriramachandra Murty+.S+P WAVE SIGMA	
	2.5+4			Expt Data	EXFOR30248.012	Jun 73	SIGMA CAPTURE TO THE MS STATE	
(n,γ)	7.0-3	1.0+5	HAR	Expt Prog	NEANDC(UK)160	Jul 74	Moxon+ TOF LINAC	
(n,γ)	Maxwl		MUN	Expt Jour	ZP/A 272 273	Mar 75	Mannhart+0.4326 B TO HF-180 ISOM	+
				Diss	MANNHART	Jul 74	- . 0.4326+- 0.0024 B	
	2.5-2			Data	EXFOR20610.005	May 76	1PNT.SIGMA.	
Spect (n,γ)	Pile		FTI	Expt Jour	NP 6 561	Apr 58	Gvozdev+. GRAPH. INTERNAL CONV STUDY	
Spect (n,γ)	Pile		ANL	Expt Jour	PR 146 844	Jun 66	Namenson+LI-GE DET,GS5,8-7,1MEV, TBL	+
				Conf	65Antwerp 47	Jul 65	.SUPERSEDED	
Spect (n,γ)	Pile		ANL	Expt Conf	69Studsvik 601	Aug 69	Smither+ NO DATA GVN,OKS STATMOD	
Spect (n,γ)	4.2+0	7.8+0	BNL	Expt Abst	BAP 17 17	Jan 72	Casten+. 3NEUT ES. NO DATA GIVEN	
Spect (n,γ)	Maxwl		BON	Expt Jour	ZP 263 395	Sep 73	Schmidt+,POLRZ 501-KEV-GS OF HF180	
Spect (n,γ)	Pile		ANL	Expt Jour	PR/C 10 2483	Dec 74	Bushnell+ CRYST.DIFF+GELI.COINC.NAI	
Inelastic γ	2.8+6		REN	Expt Jour	ARI 18 279	May 67	Broadhead+ ACTIV 19SEC ISOMER 422MB	+
	2.8+6			Data	EXFOR11850.010	Jun 76	. 1 PT.	
Inelastic γ	2.0+6		KFI	Comp Jour	JRC 7 365	Jun 71	Nagy+ SIGMA,GAM+XRAY+ELECTR ES GIVEN	
(n,2n)	Fiss		CRC	Eval Rept	CRC-1003	Dec 60	Roy+,ESTIMATED AVG SIG=60.0MB	
(n,2n)	Fiss		BNL	Theo Jour	NSE 23 238	Nov 65	Pearlstein.STATMDL CALC.SPEC AVG.TBL	
(n,2n)	1.3+7	1.5+7	BNL	Theo Jour	NSE 23 238	Nov 65	Pearlstein.3ES.STAT MDL CALC.TBL CS.	
(n,2n)	1.5+7		MUA	Expt Jour	NP 88 349	Nov 66	Prasad+,T-D NEUT ACT REL TO FE56(NP)	+
	1.5+7			Data	EXFOR30015.006	May 70	PARTIAL SIGMA(METASTABLE)	
(n,2n)	1.5+7		DEB	Comp Jour	REA 7 4 93	Dec 69	Csikai+ SIG+HL COMPILTN,N-ACTIV-ANAL	
(n,2n)	1.4+7	1.5+7	JYV	Eval Rept	JU-RR-3/1970	Jun 70	Leppaemaeki+ TABLE OF EVAL AVG SIG	
(n,2n)	None		KFI	Comp Jour	JRC 7 365	Jun 71	Nagy+ GAMMA+XRAY+ELECTR ES,HALF-LIFE	
(n,2n)	1.5+7		DEB	Eval Jour	REA 11 1 153	Mar 73	Boedy+ RECOMM.VALUE FROM N-Z SYSTEM.	
(n,2n)	1.5+7		SMU	Expt Conf	75Wash. 712	Mar 75	Salaita+SHORT-LIVED ISOMER PROD.TBL.	+
				Conf	74Columbia 95	Jul 74	- + ACT.SIG TO SHORTLIV ISO.TBL	
	1.5+7			Data	EXFOR10356.006	Sep 75	. 1 PT.	
(n,xn) x>2	Fiss		BNL	Theo Jour	NSE 23 238	Nov 65	Pearlstein.SPEC AVG STATMDL CALC N3N	
(n,p)	Fiss		CRC	Eval Rept	CRC-1003	Dec 60	Roy+,ESTIMATED AVG SIG=0.004MB	
(n,p)	1.4+7	1.5+7	ARK	Theo Prog	ORO-3235-29	Jan 67	Koch+ STAT MODEL CALC CFD EXPTS	
(n,α)	Fiss		CRC	Eval Rept	CRC-1003	Dec 60	Roy+,ESTIMATED AVG SIG=0.001MB	
Reson Params	1.1+0	2.2+0	HAR	Expt Jour	NAT 167 896	Jun 51	Egelstaff. RES PARAMS GIVEN.	+
Reson Params	5.6+0		ANL	Expt Jour	PR 92 1527	Dec 53	Bollinger+ TRANS STRENGTH	+
	5.6+0			Data	EXFOR12108.008	Jun 76	. 1 RES, EO, WT**2/PCS	
Reson Params	5.7+0	1.1+2	BNL	Expt Jour	PR 99 10	Jul 55	Harvey+.FC TRANSM. 26 RES. AREA ANAL	+
	5.7+0	1.1+2		Data	EXFOR11912.059	Jun 76	. 26 RES. EO, WN, WNO	
Reson Params	5.7+0	4.3+1	KAP	Eval Rept	KAPL-M-JBN-9	Jul 56	Nims+ 8ES WN WG70MV ASSUMED	
Reson Params	5.5+1	4.9+2	ORL	Expt Jour	NYA 25 522	Mar 63	Russell. PREL RPT 47ES ONLY	
	3.1+1	3.9+2		Prog	WASH-1056 99	Mar 65	Fuketa.TRNS,AVGD DATA,45 RES,GWN	
Reson Params	5.7+0	1.9+2	ORL	Expt Prog	ORNL-3778 38	May 65	Fuketa+FC+TOF,WN+AVG D FOR 33 RES	+
	+0	+2		Prog	WASH-1056 71	Mar 65	- .AVG D 9.0+-1.3 EV,TBP ORNL PR	
	5.0+1	5.0+2		Prog	ORNL-3425 64	63	Block+HF02 ONLY LVLS AND D DISTRIB	
	5.7+0	1.9+2		Data	EXFOR11372.006	Jun 76	. 33 RES. E0, WN	
Reson Params	-		KFK	Eval Rept	KFK-352	Aug 65	Schmidt.AVERAGE S-WAWE RES PAR(TAB19	
Reson Params	1.9+1	4.8+1	ITE	Expt Conf	66Paris 1 71	Oct 66	PPR104,KALEBIN+.E-VAL AT 5ES,CHOPPER	
Reson Params		1.0+6	AUA	Theo Jour	AUJ 20 477	Oct 67	Cook. TBL OF AVG LVL SPACING D,L=0,1	
Reson Params	None		RPI	Expt Prog	WASH-1127 182	Apr 69	Kirouac+ TRANS+CAPT MEASTS,NO DATA	
Reson Params	-		AUA	Theo Rept	AAEC/E-211	Nov 70	Musgrove. CALCULTD D+GAM WIDTH GIVEN	

PAGE 1315

72 Hafnium 179

Quantity	Energy (ev) Min	Max	Lab	Type	Documentation Ref Vol Page	Date	Author, Comments	Data
Reson Params	5.7+0	2.0+2	GEL	Expt Rept	RT/FI – 70 55	Dec 70	Coceva+	+
	5.7+0	2.0+2		Data	EXFOR20375.005	Oct 74	44PTS.J.	
Reson Params	–		DUB	Theo Rept	JINR – E4 – 5711	Apr 71	Soloviev.RESONANCE STRUCTURE STUDY	
Reson Params		+3	HAR	Expt Diss	HASTE	74	Haste+(OXF) SPIN ASSGNS FROM GAMMAS	
Reson Params	5.7+0	3.1+1	HAR	Expt Prog	NEANDC(UK)160	Jul 74	Moxon+ WG WN FROM TRANS+CAPT DATA	
Reson Params	7.3+6		DUB	Theo Conf	74Petten 175	Sep 74	Malov+ DOBS,SEMI – MICROSCOPIC CALC.	
Reson Params	Maxwl		KUK	Theo Conf	76Ahmedabd 2 1	Dec 76	Sharma+AVG S – WAVE REDUCED N – WID ANAL	
Strnth Fnctn	+3		BNL	Expt Jour	PRL 1 461	Dec 58	Hughes+ FC 1.3+ – 0.3	
Strnth Fnctn	5.7+0	1.9+2	ORL	Expt Prog	ORNL – 3778 38	May 65	Harvey.FC+TOF,S – WAVE 2.1+ – .4	+
Strnth Fnctn	–		AUA	Theo Rept	AAEC/E – 211	Nov 70	Musgrove. SMOOTHED S0,S1 AND S2 GVN	
Strnth Fnctn	1.0+0	2.0+2	GEL	Expt Rept	RT/FI – 70 55	Dec 70	Coceva+	+
	1.0+0	2.0+2		Data	EXFOR20375.006	Oct 74	2PTS.L=0.	
Strnth Fnctn	None		AUA	Eval Rept	AAEC/E – 277	Mar 73	Musgrove.TBLS EXPTL DATA+BEST VALUES	
Lvl Density	–		COP	Theo Jour	NP 6 62	Mar 58	Ericson. LVL DENSITY FORM CFD EXP	
Lvl Density	+6		MIL	Theo Jour	EN 15 1 54	Jan 68	Facchini+ LDL PARS FROM LOW EN RES	
Lvl Density	None		AUW	Theo Conf	70Madurai 2 267	Dec 70	Ramamurty+ A – PARAMETER GVN,LANG'S – TH	
Lvl Density	None		MUN	Theo Jour	NP/A 217 269	Dec 73	Dilg+ A,DELTA. BACK SHIFTED FERMIGAS	
Lvl Density	None		COP	Theo Jour	NP/A 222 493	Apr 74	Dossing+COLL ROTAT.SPAC. ACCUR ESTIM	
Lvl Density	None		DUB	Theo Jour	NP/A 224 396	May 74	Malov+ 1/2 MICROSC.MODEL. DEFORM NUC	
Lvl Density	None		ROC	Theo Jour	NP/A 223 589	May 74	Huizenga+ EXP CFD MICROSC TH AX SYMM	

72 Hafnium 180

Quantity	Energy (ev) Min	Max	Lab	Type	Documentation Ref Vol Page	Date	Author, Comments	Data
Evaluation	1.0 – 3	1.5+7	KAP	Eval Rept	KAPL – 3327	Aug 67	Reynolds+TOT RES ELAS INEL NP NG N2N	
Evaluation	1.0 – 5	2.0+7	SAI	Eval Rept	EPRI – 250	Nov 76	Drake+ENDF/B5.TBLS,GRPHS.CFD.	
Total	+2		ORL	Expt Rept	WASH – 1071 174	Nov 66	Fuketa.LINAC,NDG,NEARLY COMPLETE	
Total	1.5 – 2	8.0 – 1	RPI	Expt Abst	BAP 14 496	Apr 69	Conad+ AH16	+
	1.0 – 1	1.0+0		Prog	RPI – 328 – 148	Dec 68	Conrad+ LINAC TRANS VALUE GIVEN	
	1.5 – 2	8.0 – 1		Data	EXFOR12085.006	Jun 76	. 21 PTS.	
Total	2.5 – 2		JAE	Expt Rept	JAERI – M – 4301	71	Okamoto. TRANSM, ENRICHED SAMPLES	+
	Maxwl			Data	EXFOR20318.007	Jun 74	1PNT.	
Total	7.0 – 2	1.0+4	HAR	Expt Prog	NEANDC(UK)160	Jul 74	Moxon+ TOF LINAC	
Total	2.0 – 2	5.0 – 1	IJI	Expt Rept	YFI – 18 36	Aug 74	Vertebny+ SIG(NEUT – E),TBL	+
	6.0 – 2	5.0 – 1		Conf	73Kiev 2 114	May 73	– + SIG(NEUT – E),TBL	
	2.5 – 2			Conf	73Kiev 2 114	May 73	– + SIG=51+ – 4 B	
	6.0 – 2	5.0 – 1		Rept	INDC(CCP) – 49	Feb 75	– +(ENGL).TRANS,TOTSIG(E) TBL	
	2.5 – 2	5.0 – 1		Data	EXFOR40279.017	Apr 75	.SIGMA FOR 25 ES GVN	
Total	1.4+7		LIN	Expt Conf	75Kiev 4 140	May 75	Djumin+ SIG GIVEN.OPTMOD ANAL,RADIUS	
Tot Inelastc	1.5+7		BNL	Expt Jour	JIN 31 909	Apr 69	Hillman+,ACTIV OF ISOM STATE	+
				Rept	BNL – 11506	Jun 67	– + 12.4+ – .5MB REL AL(NA)TBP NP	
	1.5+7			Data	EXFOR12092.004	Jun 76	. 1 PT.	
Tot Inelastc	1.4+7	1.5+7	JYV	Eval Rept	JU – RR – 3/1970	Jun 70	Leppaemaeki+ TABLE OF EVAL AVG SIG	
Diff Inelast	1.4+7		LRL	Theo Rept	UCRL – 50181	Feb 67	Lutz+.CALC ANG DIST FOR FIRST 2+ LVL	
Scattering	2.5 – 2		IJI	Expt Rept	YFI – 18 36	Aug 74	Vertebny+ SIG GVN IN TBL	+
				Conf	73Kiev 2 114	May 73	– + SIG = 18.0+ – 0.5B	
				Rept	INDC(CCP) – 49	Feb 75	– +(ENGL).BY LSQ – FIT TO TOTSIG	
	2.5 – 2			Data	EXFOR40279.011	May 75	.SIGMA GVN	
Absorption	2.5 – 2		IJI	Expt Rept	YFI – 18 36	Aug 74	Vertebny+ TOF,SIG GVN IN TBL	+
				Conf	73Kiev 2 114	May 73	– + SIG=29+ – 3 B	
				Rept	INDC(CCP) – 49	Feb 75	– +(ENGL).BY LSQ – FIT TO TOTSIG	
	2.5 – 2			Data	EXFOR40279.006	Apr 75	.SIGMA GVN	
Res Int Abs	5.0 – 1		ANL	Expt Jour	PR 79 11	Jul 50	Harris+ EPI – CD,REL THERMAL ACT. B – W	+
	5.0 – 1			Data	EXFOR11343.027	Jun 76	. 1 PT.	
Res Int Abs	None		ORL	Revw Conf	55Geneva 5 96	Aug 55	Macklin+.TABLE,EXPT CFD THEORY,P833	
Res Int Abs	5.0 – 1		KAP	Expt Conf	68Wash. § E20	Mar 68	Fulmer+ PILE OSC 43+ – 8B REL AU	+
	5.0 – 1			Data	EXFOR12140.006	Jun 76	. 1 PT.	
Res Int Abs	5.0 – 1		MTR	Expt Jour	NSE 33 350	Sep 68	Rogers+ REACTIVITY METHOD REL TO AU	
				Prog	IDO – 16977 7	Dec 63	Scoville+. VALUE GIVEN.	
	5.0 – 1			Data	EXFOR12104.008	Jun 76	. 1 PT.	
Res Int Abs	5.0 – 1		CNE	Expt Jour	CJP 47 2031	Oct 69	Ricabarra+ RATIO TO ACTIVAT SIG,TBL	+
				Conf	70Helsinki 2 589	Jun 70	. *SAME+MORE DATA TABLES	
				Rept	CNEA – 282	70	*	
	6.0 – 1			Data	EXFOR30128.009	Dec 72	RES INTEG AND RATIO TO THR – ABS SIGM.	
Res Int Abs	5.0 – 1		KJL	Expt Jour	JIN 34 2699	Sep 72	Steinnes. ACT. AU MONITOR	+
	5.0 – 1			Data	EXFOR20188.028	May 74	1PNT.CAPTURE.	

72 Hafnium 180

Quantity	Energy (ev) Min	Max	Lab	Type	Documentation Ref Vol Page	Date	Author, Comments	Data
Res Int Abs	5.0−1		MUN	Expt Jour	JRC 15 535	73	Alian+CAPT CD−R, 30.8B INCL 1/V	+
	5.0−1			Data	EXFOR20644.016	Jun 76	1PNT.CAPTURE.	
Res Int Abs	5.0−1		GHT	Expt Jour	JRC 20 695	74	Van Der Linden+ BY(N,G).CFD OTHS,TBL	+
	5.5−1			Conf	73Paris 2 241	Mar 73	− + ACT,REL THR+GOLD,TBL	
	5.5−1			Data	EXFOR20645.040	Jul 76	1PNT.CAPTURE.	
(n,γ)	Pile		ANL	Expt Jour	PR 72 888	Nov 47	Seren+.ACT METHOD.PILE IRRAD.	+
(n,γ)	Pile			Data	EXFOR11447.111	Jun 76	. 1 PT.	
(n,γ)	Maxwl		ORL	Expt Jour	PR 88 412	Oct 52	Pomerance.PILE OSC.	+
	Maxwl			Data	EXFOR11507.089	Jun 76	.	
(n,γ)	2.4+4		ORL	Expt Jour	PR 107 504	Jul 57	Macklin+.SB−BE NS,441+−66MB,.482MEVG	+
				Conf	58Geneva 671	Sep 58	.SUPERSEDED	
	2.4+4			Data	EXFOR11399.044	Jun 76	. 1 PT.	
(n,γ)	3.2+4	4.0+6	LRL	Expt Jour	PR 128 2717	Dec 62	Miskel+3, TABLE OF SIG AT 15ES. ACT	+
				Rept	UCRL−5454	Jan 59	.SUPERSEDED	
	3.2+4	4.0+6		Data	EXFOR12115.002	Jun 76	. 15 PTS.	
(n,γ)	1.0+2	1.0+3	ORL	Expt Abst	BAP 9 31	Jan 64	Russell+ NDG	
(n,γ)	Maxwl		MTR	Expt Prog	WASH−1053 78	Oct 64	Scoville+11+−2B,REL AU AND DY	
(n,γ)	Maxwl		BNL	Expt Jour	PR 158 1105	Jun 67	Goldhaber.	+
	Maxwl			Data	EXFOR12119.003	Jun 76	. 1 PT.	
(n,γ)	−		IEA	Comp Rept	IEA−INF−10	Aug 68	Atalla. TABLES OF HL,SIG AND GAMM−E	
(n,γ)	None		RPI	Expt Prog	WASH−1127 182	Apr 69	Kirouac+ NDG	
(n,γ)	3.0+4		AUA	Theo Rept	AAEC/E−211	Nov 70	Musgrove. SIGMA GIVEN AND CFD OTHER	
(n,γ)	2.4+4		MUA	Theo Jour	IJP 46 114	Mar 72	Chaubey+ P−WAVE STRENGTH FUNCT,TABLE	
(n,γ)	1.0+3	1.0+7	BOL	Eval Data	BENZI−DFN 811.	May 72	40 PNTS	+
(n,γ)	Pile		ROS	ExTh Prog	ZFK−243 93	Sep 72	Mohsen+ NG−SYSTEMAT. FOR RARE EARTHS	
(n,γ)	3.5+4		AUW	Expt Jour	NC/A 18 48	Nov 73	Sidappa+ ACTIVATION CROSS−SECT.	
(n,γ)	7.0−3	1.0+5	HAR	Expt Prog	NEANDC(UK)160	Jul 74	Moxon+ TOF LINAC	
(n,γ)	Maxwl		MUN	Expt Jour	ZP/A 272 273	Mar 75	Mannhart+13.04 +− 0.07 B	+
				Diss	MANNHART	Jul 74	− . 13.04+−0.07 B	
	2.5−2			Data	EXFOR20610.006	May 76	1PNT.SIGMA.	
(n,γ)	None		STR	Expt Diss	BOUSSAHA	May 76	Boussaha.MODIF OF STRUCT IN CMP	
Spect (n,γ)	2.5+4		ORL	Expt Conf	58Geneva 15 68	Sep 58	Macklin.PPR671,SIGMA+G−ENERGY GVN	
Spect (n,γ)	None		ROS	Expt Rept	ZFK−PHA−20 34	Feb 66	Meiling+ LVL SCH OF TA 181	
Spect (n,γ)	Pile		ANL	Expt Jour	PR 158 1206	Jun 67	Bolotin+ GE−LI DET,4.0−5.7MEV GS,TBL	
				Jour	PR 146 844	Jun 66	Namenson+ DATA	
				Conf	65Antwerp 49	Jul 65	.SUPERSEDED	
Spect (n,γ)	Maxwl	7.5+1	BNL	Expt Prog	WASH−1093 16	Apr 68	Chrien+ SPECTRA SHOWN	
Spect (n,γ)		+3	KFT	Expt Jour	IZV 33 714	Apr 69	Kljucharev+ CONV−EL SPECTRUM	
				Jour	BAS 33 4 657	70	. ENGL OF IZV 33 714	
Spect (n,γ)	None		ORL	Theo Jour	NSE 36 220	May 69	Yost+ CALCULAT BY GAMMA CASCADE MDL	
Spect (n,γ)	Maxwl	2.0+3	MTR	Expt Conf	69Studsvik 607	Aug 69	Greenwood+ NDG,THR+2KEV RES−N−CAPTUR	
Spect (n,γ)	Pile		CTH	Expt Jour	PS 3 105	Aug 71	Alenius+.Q−VAL.E+INT 138GS.GRPH+TBLS	+
	Pile			Data	EXFOR20243.	May 74	137PTS.	
Spect (n,γ)	Maxwl		BON	Expt Jour	ZP 255 368	Nov 72	Bodenstedt+,ANG−CORR MEAS. OF TA−181	
(n,2n)	Fiss		CRC	Eval Rept	CRC−1003	Dec 60	Roy+,ESTIMATED AVG SIG=8.0MB	
(n,2n)	Fiss		BNL	Theo Jour	NSE 23 238	Nov 65	Pearlstein.STATMDL CALC.SPEC AVG.TBL	
(n,2n)	1.3+7	1.5+7	BNL	Theo Jour	NSE 23 238	Nov 65	Pearlstein.3ES.STAT MDL CALC.TBL CS.	
(n,2n)	1.5+7		MUA	Expt Jour	NP 88 349	Nov 66	Prasad+,T−D NEUT ACT REL TO FE56(NP)	+
	1.5+7			Data	EXFOR30015.007	May 70	PARTIAL SIGMA(METASTABLE)	
(n,2n)	1.5+7		TUR	Theo Jour	NC 56 18 201	Jul 68	Minetti+THEOR ISOM RATIO SPIN CO PAR	
(n,2n)	1.5+7		DEB	Comp Jour	REA 7 4 93	Dec 69	Csikai+ SIG+HL COMPILTN,N−ACTIV−ANAL	
(n,2n)	1.4+7	1.5+7	JYV	Eval Rept	JU−RR−3/1970	Jun 70	Leppaemaeki+ TABLE OF EVAL AVG SIG	
(n,2n)	1.5+7		IBJ	Expt Jour	APPB 1 415	Dec 70	Rurarz+ NA−I,SIG TO ISOM GVN,CFD OTH	+
				Jour	APPB 1 415	70	− + ACTIV,NAI,SIG(M)+ISORATIO	
	1.5+7			Data	EXFOR30154.	Feb 72	PAR SIG,ISOM RATIO,SPIN CUT−OFF FACT	
(n,2n)	None		KFI	Comp Jour	JRC 7 365	Jun 71	Nagy+ GAMMA+XRAY+ELECTR ES,HALF−LIFE	
(n,2n)	1.5+7		DEB	Eval Jour	REA 11 1 153	Mar 73	Boedy+ RECOMM.VALUE FROM N−Z SYSTEM.	
(n,2n)	1.5+7		KFI	Theo Rept	KFKI−73−68	Dec 73	Jeki.NEW FIT,CALC SIG CFD OTHERS,TBL	
(n,xn) x>2	Fiss		BNL	Theo Jour	NSE 23 238	Nov 65	Pearlstein.SPEC AVG STATMDL CALC N3N	
(n,p)	Fiss		CRC	Eval Rept	CRC−1003	Dec 60	Roy+,ESTIMATED AVG SIG=0.001MB	
(n,p)	1.4+7		SAH	Comp Jour	NP 60 273	Nov 64	Chatterjee.MEAN OF EXPT CFD SHELLMOD	
(n,p)	1.4+7	1.5+7	ARK	Theo Prog	ORO−3235−29	Jan 67	Koch+ STAT MODEL CALC CFD EXPTS	
(n,α)	Fiss		CRC	Eval Rept	CRC−1003	Dec 60	Roy+,ESTIMATED AVG SIG=BELO 0.0001MB	
(n,α)	1.5+7		BNL	Expt Jour	JIN 31 909	Apr 69	Hillman+,ACTIV	+
				Rept	BNL−11506	Jun 67	− + 2.2+−.2MB REL AL(NA) TBP NP	
				Prog	WASH−1071 25	Nov 66	.SUPERSEDED	
	1.5+7			Data	EXFOR12092.005	Jun 76	. 1 PT.	
(n,α)	1.5+7		DEB	Comp Jour	REA 7 4 93	Dec 69	Csikai+ SIG+HL COMPILTN,N−ACTIV−ANAL	

72 Hafnium 180

Quantity	Energy (ev) Min	Energy (ev) Max	Lab	Type	Documentation Ref Vol Page	Author, Comments Date	Data
(n,α)	1.4+7	1.5+7	JYV	Eval Rept	JU-RR-3/1970	Jun 70 Leppaemaeki+ TABLE OF EVAL AVG SIG	
(n,α)	None		KFI	Comp Jour	JRC 7 365	Jun 71 Nagy+ GAMMA+XRAY+ELECTR ES,HALF-LIFE	
(n,α)	Pile		MUA	Expt Prog	INDC(SEC)-35	Sep 73 Alam+ P101.ACTIV,SHORT NOTE,NDG	+
				Jour	NP/A 205 614	May 73 − + RATIO TO NG SIGMA,HALF LIVES	
	Pile			Data	EXFOR30249.002	Jul 73 RATIO TO NG-SIGMA,HALF-LIVES	
(n,α)	1.5+7		ARK	Expt Abst	DA/B 34 1934	Nov 73 Rao.ISOMERIC XSECTION RATIOS	
(n,α)	1.5+7		RBZ	Expt Jour	ASL 26 207	76 Caplar+ A-SPEC AT ODEG,GRPH.DIFF CS	
Reson Params	7.4+1		BNL	Expt Jour	PR 99 10	Jul 55 Harvey+.FC TRANSM. 1 RES. AREA ANAL	+
	7.4+1			Data	EXFOR11912.060	Jun 76 . 1 RES. E0, WN, WN0	
Reson Params	7.2+1	4.8+2	ORL	Expt Jour	NYA 25 522	Mar 63 Russell. PREL RPT 4 ES ONLY	
	7.3+1	1.7+2		Prog	WASH-1056 99	Mar 65 Fuketa.TRNS,AVGD DATA,2 RES,WN	
	8.0+2	9.1+2		Prog	RPI-63	63 Russell.	
Reson Params	7.3+1	1.7+2	ORL	Expt Jour	ORNL-3778 38	May 65 Fuketa+FC+TOF,WN+AVG D FOR 2 RES	+
	+0	+2		Prog	WASH-1056 71	Mar 65 − .AVG D 100+−40 EV,TBP ORNL PR	
	5.0+1	5.0+2		Prog	ORNL-3425 64	63 Block+ HF02 ONLY LVLS AND D DISTRIB	
	7.3+1	1.7+2		Data	EXFOR11372.007	Jun 76 . 2 RES. E0, WN.	
Reson Params		1.0+6	AUA	Theo Jour	AUJ 20 477	Oct 67 Cook. TBL OF AVG LVL SPACING D,L=0,1	
Reson Params	None		RPI	Expt Prog	WASH-1127 182	Apr 69 Kirouac+ TRANS+CAPT MEASTS,NO DATA	
Reson Params	−		AUA	Theo Rept	AAEC/E-211	Nov 70 Musgrove. CALCULTD D+GAM WIDTH GIVEN	
Reson Params	None		DUB	Theo Jour	ZEP 14 194	Aug 71 Solovev.LARGE N−WID G−WID CORREL.NDG	
	−			Rept	JINR-E4-5711	Apr 71 Soloviev.RESONANCE STRUCTURE STUDY	
	None			Jour	JEL 14 129	Aug 71 − . ENGL OF ZEP 14 194.	
Reson Params	7.2+1	1.1+4	HAR	Expt Prog	AERE-PR/NP21	Mar 74 Moxon+ RES PARS FROM TOTAL+CAPT SIG	+
	7.2+1	1.1+4		Data	EXFOR20689.003	Jun 77 30PTS.E0,WN,WG.	
Strnth Fnctn	7.3+1	1.7+2	ORL	Expt Prog	ORNL-3778 38	May 65 Harvey.FC+TOF,S−WAVE 0.7+−.5	+
	+0	+2		Prog	WASH-1056 71	Mar 65 Fuketa.S−WAVE,.7+−.5,TBP IN ORNL PR	
Strnth Fnctn	−		AUA	Theo Rept	AAEC/E-211	Nov 70 Musgrove. SMOOTHED S0,S1 AND S2 GIVN	
Strnth Fnctn	2.4+4		MUA	Theo Jour	IJP 46 114	Mar 72 Chaubey+ P−WAVE.FOR A−SYSTEMTIC,GRPH	
Strnth Fnctn	None		AUA	Eval Jour	AAEC/E-277	Mar 73 Musgrove.TBLS EXPTL DATA+BEST VALUES	
Lvl Density	+6		MIL	Theo Jour	EN 15 1 54	Jan 68 Facchini+ LDL PARS FROM LOW EN RES	
Lvl Density	None		CCP	Theo Jour	YF 11 1028	May 70 Rubchenya. DENSITY+A+TEMP GIVEN	
				Jour	SNP 11 571	Nov 70 . ENGL OF YF 11 571.	
Lvl Density	None		AUW	Theo Conf	70Madurai 2 267	Dec 70 Ramamurty+ A−PARAMETER GVN,LANG'S−TH	
Lvl Density	1.0+0	2.0+2	GEL	Expt Jour	RT/FI-70 55	Dec 70 Coceva+	+
	1.0+0	2.0+2		Data	EXFOR20375.007	Oct 74 1PNT.SP.CUT.	
Lvl Density	None		CCP	Theo Jour	YF 13 43	Jan 71 Bravin+.DEFORM PAR,CALC,TBL,CFD EXPT	
Lvl Density	None		MUN	Theo Jour	NP/A 217 269	Dec 73 Dilg+ A,DELTA. BACK SHIFTED FERMIGAS	
Lvl Density	None		COP	Theo Jour	NP/A 222 493	Apr 74 Dossing+COLL ROTAT.SPAC. ACCUR ESTIM	
Lvl Density	None		DUB	Theo Jour	NP/A 224 396	May 74 Malov+ 1/2 MICROSC.MODEL. DEFORM NUC	
Lvl Density	None		ROC	Theo Jour	NP/A 223 589	May 74 Huizenga+ EXP CFD MICROSC TH AX SYMM	

72 Hafnium 181

Quantity	Energy (ev) Min	Energy (ev) Max	Lab	Type	Documentation Ref Vol Page	Author, Comments Date	Data
(n,γ)	Pile		ANL	Expt Jour	PR 123 1354	61 Wing+	+
	Pile			Data	EXFOR12114.002	Jun 76 . 1 PT.	
Reson Params	−		AUA	Theo Rept	AAEC/E-211	Nov 70 Musgrove. CALCULTD D+GAM WIDTH GIVEN	
Reson Params	None		DUB	Theo Rept	JINR-E4-5880	Jul 71 Soloviev.N−GAM−WIDS CORR.SHORT NOTE	
Strnth Fnctn	−		AUA	Theo Rept	AAEC/E-211	Nov 70 Musgrove. SMOOTHED S0,S1 AND S2 GIVN	
Lvl Density	+6		MIL	Theo Jour	EN 15 1 54	Jan 68 Facchini+ LDL PARS FROM LOW EN RES	
Lvl Density	None		MUN	Theo Jour	NP/A 217 269	Dec 73 Dilg+ A,DELTA. BACK SHIFTED FERMIGAS	
Lvl Density	None		COP	Theo Jour	NP/A 222 493	Apr 74 Dossing+COLL ROTAT.SPAC. ACCUR ESTIM	
Lvl Density	None		ROC	Theo Jour	NP/A 223 577	May 74 Huizenga+ EXP CFD MICROSC TH SPH NUC	
Lvl Density	None		ROC	Theo Jour	NP/A 223 589	May 74 Huizenga+ EXP CFD MICROSC TH AX SYMM	

72 Hafnium 182

Quantity	Energy (ev) Min	Energy (ev) Max	Lab	Type	Documentation Ref Vol Page	Author, Comments Date	Data
Reson Params	−		AUA	Theo Rept	AAEC/E-211	Nov 70 Musgrove. CALCULTD D+GAM WIDTH GIVEN	
Strnth Fnctn	−		AUA	Theo Rept	AAEC/E-211	Nov 70 Musgrove. SMOOTHED S0,S1 AND S2 GIVN	

73 Tantalum 175

Quantity	Energy (ev) Min	Max	Lab	Type	Documentation Ref Vol Page	Author, Comments Date	Data
Reson Params	–		AUA	Theo Rept	AAEC/E – 211	Nov 70 Musgrove. CALCULTD D+GAM WIDTH GIVEN	
Strnth Fnctn	–		AUA	Theo Rept	AAEC/E – 211	Nov 70 Musgrove. SMOOTHED S0,S1 AND S2 GIVN	

73 Tantalum 177

Quantity	Energy (ev) Min	Max	Lab	Type	Documentation Ref Vol Page	Author, Comments Date	Data
(n,p)	Maxwl		IFU	Theo Rept	ICD – 4 20	67 Dadakina+ PENETR COEFF CALC,TABLE	
Reson Params	–		AUA	Theo Rept	AAEC/E – 211	Nov 70 Musgrove. CALCULTD D+GAM WIDTH GIVEN	
Strnth Fnctn	–		AUA	Theo Rept	AAEC/E – 211	Nov 70 Musgrove. SMOOTHED S0,S1 AND S2 GIVN	

73 Tantalum 178

Quantity	Energy (ev) Min	Max	Lab	Type	Documentation Ref Vol Page	Author, Comments Date	Data
Reson Params	–		AUA	Theo Rept	AAEC/E – 211	Nov 70 Musgrove. CALCULTD D+GAM WIDTH GIVEN	
Strnth Fnctn	–		AUA	Theo Rept	AAEC/E – 211	Nov 70 Musgrove. SMOOTHED S0,S1 AND S2 GIVN	

73 Tantalum 179

Quantity	Energy (ev) Min	Max	Lab	Type	Documentation Ref Vol Page	Author, Comments Date	Data
(n,p)	Maxwl		IFU	Theo Rept	ICD – 4 20	67 Dadakina+ PENETR COEFF CALC,TABLE	
Reson Params	–		AUA	Theo Rept	AAEC/E – 211	Nov 70 Musgrove. CALCULTD D+GAM WIDTH GIVEN	
Strnth Fnctn	–		AUA	Theo Rept	AAEC/E – 211	Nov 70 Musgrove. SMOOTHED S0,S1 AND S2 GIVN	

73 Tantalum 180

Quantity	Energy (ev) Min	Max	Lab	Type	Documentation Ref Vol Page	Author, Comments Date	Data
Total	2.5 – 2	8.2 + 1	MTR	Expt Jour	PR 97 565	Jan 55 Evans+ 0.43EV RESONANCE OBSERVED.	+
Total	3.0 – 2	2.0 + 2	ORL	Expt Prog	ORNL – 5025 122	May 75 Harvey+TRNS.GRPH.RES PARS DRVD	
(n,γ)	–		IEA	Comp Rept	IEA – INF – 10	Aug 68 Atalla. TABLES OF HL,SIG AND GAMM – E	
(n,γ)	3.0 + 4		AUA	Theo Rept	AAEC/E – 211	Nov 70 Musgrove. SIGMA GIVEN AND CFD OTHER	
Spect (n,γ)	None		KFI	Comp Jour	JRC 7 365	Jun 71 Nagy+ GAMMA+XRAY ENERGIES, HALF – LIFE	
Spect (n,γ)	Maxwl		LRL	Expt Conf	74Petten 578	Sep 74 Mann+ GG – COINC, ROT.BANDS IN TA – 181	
(n,2n)	Fiss		CRC	Eval Rept	CRC – 1003	Dec 60 ROY+ ESTIMATED AVG SIG=43.5MB	
(n,p)	Fiss		CRC	Eval Rept	CRC – 1003	Dec 60 ROY+ ESTIMATED AVG SIG=0.34B	
(n,α)	Fiss		CRC	Eval Rept	CRC – 1003	Dec 60 ROY+ ESTIMATED AVG SIG=0.0047MB.	
Reson Params	4.3 – 1		MTR	Expt Jour	PR 97 565	Jan 55 Evans+ WT, G*WN GIVN.ALSO ABUNDANCE	+
	4.3 – 1			Data	EXFOR12183.003	Jun 76 . 1 RES E0, WN, WT AND TOT PCS.	
Reson Params		1.1 + 1	ORL	Expt Abst	BAP 3 364	Nov 58 Harvey+ TRANS,2.13 5.96EV NEW,1 OLD	
Reson Params	4.3 – 1	6.0 + 0	ORL	Expt Prog	ORNL – 2718 26	Jun 59 Block+	+
	4.3 – 1	6.0 + 0		Data	EXFOR11349.002	Jun 76 . 3 RES E0,WG, AND WN.	
Reson Params		1.0 + 6	AUA	Theo Jour	AUJ 20 477	Oct 67 Cook.TBL OF AVG LVL SPACING D,L=0,1	
Reson Params	–		AUA	Theo Rept	AAEC/E – 211	Nov 70 Musgrove. CALCULTD D+GAM WIDTH GIVEN	
Reson Params	7.6 + 6		DUB	Theo Conf	74Petten 175	Sep 74 Malov+ DOBS,SEMI – MICROSCOPIC CALC.	
Reson Params	+0		DUB	Theo Jour	YF 21 40	Jan 75 Voronov+ MEAN D,WITH ROTAT.CFD EXPT	
				Jour	SNP 21 20	Jul 75 . ENGLISH OF YF 21,40	
Reson Params	3.0 – 1	2.0 + 2	ORL	Expt Prog	ORNL – 5025 122	May 75 Harvey+DRVD PARS TO 20EV.TBL	+
	4.3 – 1	1.0 + 2		Data	EXFOR10526.	Apr 76 . 60RES ES WT,WG,(WN,WN RED)2G.D GVN	
Strnth Fnctn	–		AUA	Theo Rept	AAEC/E – 211	Nov 70 Musgrove. SMOOTHED S0,S1 AND S2 GIVN	
Strnth Fnctn	None		AUA	Eval Rept	AAEC/E – 277	Mar 73 Musgrove.TBLS EXPTL DATA+BEST VALUES	
Strnth Fnctn	1.0 + 1	3.1 + 1	ORL	Expt Prog	ORNL – 5025 122	May 75 Harvey+GRPH.TRANS.DATA.AVG.LVL.SPC.	+
	4.0 – 1	1.0 + 2		Data	EXFOR10526.	Apr 76 . 1 PT. S0=(2.4+ – .4) – 4	

73 Tantalum 181

Quantity	Energy (ev) Min	Max	Lab	Type	Documentation Ref Vol Page	Author, Comments Date	Data
Evaluation	5.0 + 2	1.0 + 7	ANL	Eval Book	FRC	60 Yftah+ 16E GROUPS,FAST REACTOR DATA	
Evaluation	2.5 – 2	1.1 + 7	FEI	Eval Book	ABAGJAN	64 26 GROUP CONST,TOT,CAPT,INEL,EL,ETC	
Evaluation	1.0 – 3	1.5 + 7	GEN	Eval Rept	GEMP – 448	Nov 66 Henderson+ TOT NG SIN N2N NP ENDF/B	
Evaluation	1.0 – 5	1.7 + 7	AI	Eval Rept	AI – AEC – 12990	Sep 71 Ottewitte+. CURVES.EVAL FOR ENDF/B	
Evaluation	None		LAS	Eval Prog	LA – 5570 – PR	Apr 74 Foster+ ABSTRACT	
Evaluation	1.0 – 5	2.0 + 7	LRL	Eval Rept	UCRL – 51306	Feb 75 Howerton+ ENDF – 4 EVAL.	
	5.0 + 5	1.5 + 7		Rept	UCRL – 5351	Nov 58 – . CURVES.	

73 Tantalum 181

Quantity	Energy (ev) Min	Max	Lab	Type	Documentation Ref Vol Page	Author, Comments Date	Data
Total	Maxwl		COL	Expt Jour	PR 48 265	Aug 35 Dunning+ IONCH,TRANS,RA – BE/PARAFIN N	
Total	2.5−2	5.0+3	COL	Expt Jour	PR 71 165	Feb 47 Havens+ TOF TRSM	
Total	1.2+2	3.0+2	ANL	Expt Jour	PR 76 100	Jul 49 Hibdon+TRNS.10PC RSLN.CO,MN SCT DET.	
Total	1.2+4	1.5+6	WIS	Expt Jour	PR 76 277	Jul 49 Bockelman+CFD STATIST THEO	+
	1.2+4	1.5+6		Data	EXFOR11881.007	Jun 76 . 33 PTS, SIGMA	
Total	1.0+5	1.5+6	MIT	Theo Jour	PR 76 1550	Dec 49 Feshbach+ AVERAGE OVER RESON,CF EXPT	
Total	4.2+7		BRK	Expt Jour	PR 80 842	Dec 50 Hildebrand+ BE – D NS.TRANSM. C DETECT	+
	4.2+7			Data	EXFOR11039.028	Jun 76 . 1 PT. SIGMA	
Total	5.0+4	3.2+6	WIS	Expt Jour	PR 88 83	Oct 52 Miller+20KEVSPREAD TRNSM	+
	1.0+6	3.2+6		Data	EXFOR11712.020	Jun 76 . 14 PTS, SIGMA	
Total	1.4+7		LAS	Expt Jour	PR 88 562	Nov 52 Coon+GOOD GEOM USING D – T REACTION.	+
	1.4+7			Data	EXFOR11056.048	Jun 76 . 1 PT. SIGMA.	
Total	3.5+7	1.9+8	BRK	Expt Rept	UCRL – 2337	Aug 53 Ragent.	+
	3.5+7	1.9+8		Data	EXFOR11338.005	Jun 76 . 30 PTS. SIGMA	
Total	3.8+1	3.1+3	COL	Expt Jour	PR 92 702	Nov 53 Melkonian+	+
	3.8+1	3.1+3		Data	EXFOR11670.008	Jun 76 . 32 PTS, SIGMA.	
Total	2.7−1	5.0+1	BNL	Expt Jour	PR 92 1509	Dec 53 Christensen.CRYST SPEC 7RESON SEEN	+
	2.7−1	1.0+1		Data	EXFOR12169.002	Jun 76 . 69 PTS. SIGMA	
Total	2.7+6	1.3+7	LAS	Expt Jour	PR 94 1678	Jun 54 Nereson+ RSLN 10 PERCENT	+
	2.7+6	1.3+7		Data	EXFOR11308.021	Jun 76 . 29 PTS. SIGMA	
Total	2.5−2	8.2+1	MTR	Expt Jour	PR 97 565	Jan 55 Evans+ CRYSTLSPECT HI RESOLUTION	+
	5.0−2	1.0+2		Rept	IDO – 16120	Apr 55 - .CRYSTLSPECT 5MMSAMPLE TBC	
	2.5−2	8.2+1		Data	EXFOR12183.002	Jun 76 . 503 PTS SIGMA	
Total	4.0+0	1.1+1	BNL	Expt Priv	SAILOR	Mar 55 Sailor.	+
	4.0+0	1.1+1		Data	EXFOR12075.003	Jun 76 . 32 PTS SIGMA	
Total	4.1+6		LAS	Expt Jour	PR 98 677	May 55 Walt+ TRANSMISSION EXPT 6.4B CFD TH	+
	4.1+6			Data	EXFOR11215.040	Jun 76 . 1 PT. SIGMA	
Total	9.3+0	1.8+1	BNL	Expt Jour	PR 99 10	Jul 55 Harvey+ BNL FAST CHOPPER	+
	9.3+0	1.8+1		Data	EXFOR11912.041	Jun 76 . 41 PTS SIGMA	
Total	8.0+0	1.0+4	CCP	Expt Conf	55Geneva 4 22	Aug 55 Vladimirski+.P641,CURVE,CHOPPER,TOF	+
Total	1.4+7		NRL	Theo Rept	NRL – 4666	Nov 55 Mcgarry+ CFD COMPLEX SQUARE WELL	
Total	1.0+1	3.6+3	MTR	Expt Jour	PR 103 1778	Sep 56 Fluharty+ TRNS+FC 4RES SIGS	
Total	3.0+0	5.0+2	AMS	Expt Jour	PHY 22 1131	Nov 56 Radkevich+ABSTRACT,FAST CHOPPER. NDG	
Total	3.5+1	1.0+4	CCP	Expt Jour	AE 1 5 55	Nov 56 Radkevich+.TOF TRANSM. CS CURVE	+
				Jour	JNE 5 92	Jul 57 TRANSLATN.*	
				Jour	SJA 1 5 727	56 TRANSLATN.*	
Total	3.0−1	2.0+1	BNL	Expt Jour	PR 104 1425	Dec 56 Wood.TRNS+CS CRV 25000B AT 4.28EVRES	
Total	5.0+4	1.8+7	LAS	Theo Rept	LA – 2099	Dec 56 Beyster+,OPTMDL CALC CFD EXPT,CURVE	
Total	5.0+2	5.8+3	DKE	Expt Jour	PR 105 198	Jan 57 Newson+TRNS CURV 12.5B FLAT	+
	5.0+2	5.8+3		Data	EXFOR11569.012	Jun 76 . 20 PTS. SIGMA	
Total	2.0+1	1.1+2	HAR	Expt Jour	NP 9 198	58 Firk. TOF.TRANSMISSION.	+
Total	1.3+7	1.6+7	LAS	Expt Jour	PR 109 1268	Feb 58 Conner.TRNS SC 6ES 5.45BMAX 5.27BMIN	+
				Conf	58Geneva 15 11	Sep 58 Coon+.PPR666,SIGMA FOR 6ES,TOF	
	1.3+7	1.6+7		Data	EXFOR11320.012	Jun 76 . 6 PTS. SIGMA	
Total	7.1+6	1.4+7	LRL	Expt Jour	PR 110 927	May 58 Bratenahl+SC TRNS 5ES, 5.28B+ – 2PC	+
				Conf	58Geneva 14 109	Sep 58 - +.P1881,TBL,CURV,CFD OPTMDL	
	7.1+6	1.4+7		Data	EXFOR11155.026	Jun 76 . 5 PTS. SIGMA.	
Total		1.0+3	COL	Expt Abst	BAP 3 267	Jun 58 Desjardins+ TOF SO+RESON PARAMETERS	
Total	4.0+2	1.8+7	HAR	Theo Jour	PPS 71 910	Jun 58 Egelstaff.FLUCTUATIONS CFD THEORY	+
	1.0+3	3.2+4		Expt	PPSA 70 51	Jan 57 Gayther+ FC THICK SAMPLE,AVSIG CF TH	
	8.0+2	2.4+4		Priv	EGELSTAFF5	Jun 56 Egelstaff+ NUMERICAL DATA	
Total	+0	+3	ORL	Expt Prog	ORNL – 2718 26	Jun 59 Block+ 3 RES SEEN	
				Conf	60Vienna 535	Oct 60 - +.NDG,EXPT DESCRIBED	
Total	2.0−3	2.8−1	MTR	Expt Jour	NSE 7 193	Feb 60 Schmunk+ SCINT TRANS CURVE	+
	2.0−3	2.8−1		Data	EXFOR11634.005	Jun 76 . 93 PTS. SIGMA	
Total	Cold		KJL	Revw Conf	60Vienna 169	Oct 60 Riste.NDG,TBP	
Total	1.7+7	2.8+7	LRL	Expt Jour	PR 120 521	Oct 60 Peterson+ TRANS 4ES CURV CFD OPTMDL	+
				Conf	58Geneva 14 109	Sep 58 Bratenahl+ TBL,CURVE,CFD OPTMDL	
	1.7+7	2.8+7		Data	EXFOR11108.034	Jun 76 . 4 PTS. SIGMA	
Total	9.8+5		SHE	Theo Jour	NP 54 417	Jun 64 Maddison.OPTMOD FIT TO TOWLE GILBOY	
Total	5.0+4	3.0+6	BNL	Theo Jour	PR/B 135 895	Aug 64 Auerbach+LCL OPTMDL 2SETS PAR CF XPT	
Total	2.1−3	2.3−1	CAI	Expt Jour	JNE 21 425	May 67 Adib+,TOF SPECT,SIG(E) GRAPH,CHOPPER	+
	2.1−3	2.3−1		Data	EXFOR30123.002	Mar 71 124 DATA LINES	
Total	4.5+6	7.7+6	WIS	Expt Jour	PR 158 1142	Jun 67 Carlson+VDG, CURV,50KEV RESOL	+
				Abst	DA/B 28 1084	Sep 67 - . THESIS CFD WITH THEORY	
				Conf	65Antwerp 101	Jul 65 - +	
	4.5+6	7.7+6		Data	EXFOR11497.027	Jun 76 . 64 PTS. SIGMA	

73 Tantalum 181

Quantity	Energy (ev) Min	Max	Lab	Type	Documentation Ref Vol Page	Author, Comments Date	Data
Total	4.1+6		IFU	Theo Jour	UFZ 13 51	Jan 68 Kashuba+ TBL,SIG-VAL,EXPT CFD OPTMOD	
				Jour	UPJ 13 33	Jul 68 TRANSLATN.*	
Total	7.0+6	1.5+7	OHO	Theo Jour	NC/B 53 2 363	Feb 68 Cassola+OPTMOD CALC CFD EXPT	
Total	6.0+5	2.5+7	RPI	ExTh Abst	DA/B 28 3435	Feb 68 Martin.TOF, OKS DEFORMED NUCL OPTMOD	+
	7.0+5	1.5+7		Expt Data	EXFOR12159.002	Jun 76 . 565 PTS, SIGMA.	
Total	1.4+7		ANL	Expt Abst	DA/B 28 3835	Mar 68 Haugsnes.SIG=5.02+-0.03B CFD OPTMODS	+
				Rept	ANL-5609 52	Nov 56 Casson+ SIG=4.99+-0.08B	
				Rept	ANL-5554 51	Aug 56 - + SIG=4.96B TENTATIVE	
	1.4+7			Data	EXFOR11733.012	Jun 76 . 1 PT. SIGMA	
Total	None		DKE	Expt Abst	DA/B 28 3834	Mar 68 Divadeenam.TRNS.AVG SIG CFD OPTMDL.	+
	1.2+5	6.4+5		Data	EXFOR10523.013	Jan 76 . 27 PTS. CS DATA	
	1.0+5	6.5+5	ANL	Expt Jour	PR 168 1344	Apr 68 Smith+TRNS.GRPH.OPTMDL CALC.CFD.	+
				Rept	ANL-7363	Aug 67 - + TOF 2-KEV RESOL TABLE+CURVE	
	1.0+5	6.5+5		Data	EXFOR10631.011	Apr 77 . 538 PTS SIGMA.	
Total	3.3+6	5.1+6	JNE	Expt Jour	ARS 66 27	Feb 70 Manero. VDG. TRANSMISSION	+
	3.3+6	5.1+6		Data	EXFOR20171.003	May 74 . 67PTS.	
Total	2.0+7	3.0+7	AMS	Expt Prog	EANDC(E)127U	Apr 70 Rethmeier+,AVF CYCLOTRON,TOF	
Total		1.0+2	MOL	Expt Prog	EANDC(E)127U	Apr 70 Poortmans+,CBNM LINAC TOF	
Total	7.0-2	8.4-1	BNL	Expt Jour	NIM 86 83	Sep 70 Malik+HIGH FLUX BEAM REACTOR USED.	+
	7.0-2	8.4-1		Data	EXFOR10501.009	May 75 . 4 PTS. SIGMA	
Total	2.5+6	1.5+7	BNW	Expt Jour	PR/C 3 576	Feb 71 Foster+,TRANS,CURVS,CFD OTHERS+TH	+
				Jour	NIM 36 1	Sep 65 .EXPT DETAILS	
	2.3+6	1.5+7		Data	EXFOR10047.077	Aug 73 . 243PTS SIGMA	
Total	2.5+6	8.0+6	AE	Theo Rept	AE-430	Sep 71 Holmqvist+ CALC FROM OPTMOD PARAMS	
	3.0+6			Eval Conf	71Knoxvill 184	Mar 71 - +,OPTICAL MODEL ANALYSIS	
Total	1.0+6	2.0+6	DAC	Comp Rept	AECD/EP-18	Dec 70 Ameen+ EXPTL DATA FROM DAC,TABLES	+
	1.0+6	2.0+6		Expt Data	EXFOR30134.009	Nov 71 SIGMA-TOT AT 100 ES,PRIVATE COMM.	
Total	2.7+3		MUN	Expt Prog	EANDC(E)150U	Oct 72 Dilg+ AVERAGE TOT XSECT+S0	
				Conf	71Albany 327	Aug 71 - +TRNS.AVG CS GVN.31 ELEMENT GRP	
	2.7+3			Data	EXFOR20583.026	Jun 76 1PNT.	
Total	1.3+7	1.5+7	DEB	Eval Rept	IAEA-153 173	73 Boedy+ MOST PROBABLE VAL OF SIG,TBL	
				Jour	AHP 30 115	Oct 71 Angeli+ AVG SIG,CFD CALC.TBLS.GRAPH	
	1.0+3	1.0+5	RPI	Expt Jour	COO-3058-34 7	Mar 73 Byoun+CFD ANALYTICAL CALC.GRPHS.	+
	2.0+2	1.0+5		Conf	71Knoxvill 895	Mar 71 - +TRNS,SELF INDIC.3TEMPS.GRAPH	
	2.0+2	1.0+5		Data	EXFOR10577.	Nov 76 . 345PT.CS=-LOG(TRNS.VAL/SAMPL THICK	
Total	1.0-4	1.5+7	UK	Eval Data	UKNDL-DFN 328B	Mar 73 1705 PNTS	+
Total	1.0+6	2.0+6	DAC	Theo Jour	NP/A 209 202	Jul 73 Islam+ FLUCTUATION ANALYSIS,OWN DATA	+
				Expt Jour	NP/A 209 189	Jul 73 - + VDG,TRANS,CFD OPTICAL MODEL	
Total	1.0+6	2.0+6	RAM	Eval Jour	NSPB 6 59	Oct 73 Enayetullah+ SIG(E),LSQ-FIT,TBL+GRPH	
Total	2.5+5	1.5+7	JAE	Theo Conf	JAERI-M-5984	Feb 75 Tanaka.OPTMDL/COUPLD CH.GRPH CFD EXP	
Total	4.3+0	1.0+2	CCP	Expt Conf	75Kiev	May 75 Kalebin+ TOT SIG	
Total	4.3+0	6.3+1	NIR	Expt Jour	AE 38 430	Jun 75 Belanova+ TOTSIG FOR EACH RES.TABLE	+
				Jour	SJA 38 553	Dec 75 . ENGL OF AE 38 430	
	7.8+0	7.1+1		Data	EXFOR40430.004	Jan 76 1559 PNTS	
Total	1.8-3	5.0+5	CAI	Expt Jour	AJN 9 155	Feb 76 Adib+ TRANS.B-W ANALYS,GRAPH TOTSIG	
Total	3.0+4	6.5+5	DKE	Expt Abst	BAP 7 23	Jan 62 Tabony+AVG CS MEAS.CFD CALC.NDG.	+
	3.0+4	6.5+5		Data	EXFOR11936.005	Jun 76 . 102 PTS. SIGMA	
Elastic		+5	ANL	Expt Jour	PR 79 11	Jul 50 Harris+ EPI-CD,RES INT SCAT,B-W TH	
Elastic	2.5-2		ORL	Expt Jour	PR 81 527	Feb 51 Shull+ COH SCATTERING PROPERTIES	+
	2.5-2			Data	EXFOR11043.	Jun 76 . 1 PT. BAS, COH, AND COH AMP.	
Elastic	1.0+6		WIS	Expt Jour	PR 93 1062	Mar 54 Walt+ MSD FROM 30DEG TO 150 DEG	+
	1.0+6			Data	EXFOR11637.062	Jun 76 . 1 PT. SIGMA	
Elastic	4.1+6		LAS	Expt Jour	PR 98 677	May 55 Walt+ CFD WITH THEORY	+
	4.1+6			Data	EXFOR11215.038	Jun 76 . 1 PT. SIGMA	
Elastic	6.0-1	1.4+1	BNL	Expt Jour	PR 104 1425	Dec 56 Wood.CURVE CFD BREIT-WIGNER	
Elastic	1.5+7		VIR	Expt Jour	PR 128 1271	Nov 62 Hudson+, 2.63+-.20B,INTEGRAL OF DIFF	+
	1.5+7			Data	EXFOR12180.002	Jun 76 . 1 PT. SIGMA	
Elastic	1.0+6		ALD	Expt Jour	NP 42 86	Apr 63 Gilboy+.SIG=5.60B+-3PC	+
Elastic	3.0+5	1.5+6	ANL	Expt Rept	EANDC(US)-62	Jun 64 Smith+TOF,TBL.50KEV STEPS,20KEV RSLN	+
				Rept	ANL-6727	May 63 - + TOF 20KEV RESOLUTION	
	3.0+5	1.5+6		Data	EXFOR12175.003	Jun 76 . 25 PTS, SIGMA.	
Elastic	1.0+5	1.4+7	AGN	Eval Rept	TID-21629	Dec 64 Perkins+ELASTIC SCATTERING CURVES	
Elastic	2.0+6		FEI	Expt Rept	EANDC-50 200	Jul 65 Kazakova+ EXPT,TABLE CFD OPTMODEL	+
				Prog	YFI-3 6	Sep 66 .TABLE	
				Prog	INDC-E-140 6	Sep 66 .ENGLISH TRANSL OF YFI-3 6 9/66	
Elastic	1.5+6		IFU	Expt Prog	YFI-5 42	Oct 67 Korzh+ TBL OPTMDL PARAMS + TOTELAST	
				Rept	INDC-232E	67 . ENGL OF YFI-5 42	

73 Tantalum 181

Quantity	Energy (ev) Min	Max	Lab	Type	Documentation Ref Vol Page	Date	Author, Comments	Data
Elastic	1.5+6		IFU	Comp	Jour YF 7 277	Feb 68	Korzh+ OPTMOD PARS-FIT TO EXPTL-SIG	
					Jour SNP 7 2 190	Aug 68	TRANSLATN.*	
Elastic	7.0+6	1.5+7	OHO	Theo	Jour NC/B 53 2 363	Feb 68	Cassola+ OPTMOD CALC CFD EXPT	
Elastic	3.0+5	1.5+6	ANL	Expt	Jour PR 168 1344	Apr 68	Smith+ TOF FROM ANG DIST TBL+CURVE	+
					Rept ANL-7363	Aug 67	- + SUPERSEDED.	
	3.0+5	1.5+6			Data EXFOR10631.002	Apr 77	. 96PTS.SEL+6KEV INL EXCTD STATE	
Elastic	2.5+6	8.0+6	AE	Expt	Rept AE- 366	Jun 69	Holmqvist+.VDG.TOF.20-160DEG.+LEGNDR	+
					Rept AE- 430	Sep 71	- + INTEGRATED ANGDIST VALUES	
	3.0+6				Conf 71Knoxvill 184	Mar 71	- +. OPTICAL MODEL ANALYSIS	
	2.5+6	8.0+6			Jour NP/A 150 105	Jul 70	- + INTEGRATED ANGDIST.OPTMOD	
	2.5+6	8.1+6			Data EXFOR20019.198	Sep 71	7PTS.	
Elastic	1.5-3		MUN	Expt	Jour ZN/A 26 391	Mar 71	Koester+ SMALL ANGLE SCT.COH AMPLTDE	+
	2.5-2				Data EXFOR20758.008	Jun 78	1PNT.COH.SC.AMP.	
Elastic	8.7+5		ANL	Expt	Rept ANL-7935	Jun 72	COX+ 4 PI B(O)	+
	8.7+5				Data EXFOR10332.122	Jun 74	. 1 PT. SIGMA.	
Elastic	1.0-4	1.5+7	UK	Eval	Data UKNDL-DFN 328B	Mar 73	1705 PNTS	+
Elastic	1.0+5	1.5+7	CCP	Eval	Data SOKRATOR-1035	76	50 PTS	+
Elastic	9.0+5		CSE	Expt	Abst BAP 6 61	Feb 61	Rogers. ABST TA7 MSD AT 90 DEG	+
	9.0+5				Data EXFOR11269.005	Jun 76	. 1 PT. SIGMA	
Diff Elastic	1.0+6		WIS	Expt	Jour PR 93 1062	Mar 54	Walt+ HE COUNTER 30-150DEG LAB CURVE	+
	1.0+6				Data EXFOR11637.064	Jun 76	. 9 PTS, DSIGMA.	
Diff Elastic	1.0+6		WIS	Expt	Jour PR 96 836	Nov 54	Darden+ SMALL ANGLE SCATTERING NDG	
Diff Elastic	4.1+6		LAS	Expt	Jour PR 98 677	May 55	Walt+ BIASED SCINT ANG DISTR CFD TH	+
	4.1+6				Data EXFOR11215.041	Jun 76	. 13 PTS. DSIGMA	
Diff Elastic	5.0+5	1.6+6	WIS	Expt	Jour PR 100 1315	Dec 55	Darden+,ALSO1MEV100KEVRSLN CF OPTMDL	+
	5.0+5	1.6+6			Data EXFOR11638.009	Jun 76	. 8 PTS, DSIGMA	
Diff Elastic	1.4+7		NRL	Expt	Jour PR 101 684	Jan 56	Elliott.5-55DEG CYL GEOMETRY SCINT	+
					Abst PR 98 1147	56	Elliot. ABST A3 SUPERSEDED	
	1.4+7				Data EXFOR11568.005	Jun 76	. 11 PTS.DSIGMA	
Diff Elastic	1.0+6	7.0+6	LAS	Eval	Rept LA- 2016	Jun 56	Longley+,4 ES ANG DIST 3-DEG STEPS	
Diff Elastic	3.3+6		ETH	Expt	Jour HPA 29 545	Dec 56	Remond.30-150DEG CURV.ABS CF FPW CCB	+
Diff Elastic	2.5+6	7.0+6	LAS	Expt	Jour PR 104 1319	Dec 56	Beyster+ 12 TO 160 DEG CURVE	+
	2.5+6	7.0+6			Data EXFOR11220.027	Jun 76	. 30 PTS, DSIGMA	
Diff Elastic	1.0+6	1.8+7	LAS	Theo	Rept LA- 2099	Dec 56	Beyster+ 21ES, OPTMDL CALC CFD EXPT	
Diff Elastic	1.4+7		LRL	Theo	Rept UCRL- 4926	Jul 57	Bjorklund+ OPTMDL CALC 6-PARAM FIT	
Diff Elastic	1.4+7		LAS	Expt	Jour PR 107 824	Aug 57	Rosen+ NUCLEAR EMULSION DETECTION	+
					Rept LA- 2099	Dec 56	Beyster. OPTMDL CALC.	
	1.4+7				Data EXFOR11223.005	Jun 76	. 8 PTS, DSIGMA	
Diff Elastic	7.0+6		LRL	Theo	Jour RMP 30 414	Apr 58	Fernbach.TH CURVE AND EXPTL PTS	
					Jour PR 109 1295	Feb 58	Bjorklund+ OPTMDL FIT XPT,CURV.POLRZ	
					Rept UCRL-4927	Jul 57	- + OPTMDL CALC 6-PARAM FIT	
Diff Elastic	1.4+7		MOS	Theo	Jour NP 8 325	Oct 58	Lukyanov+CFD OTHERS,EXPT DATA.CURVES	
Diff Elastic	7.0+6		LRL	Theo	Jour PR 113 900	Feb 59	Schey.OPTMDL CALCS,CFD C EXPT	
Diff Elastic	1.5+7		CRC	Expt	Jour NP 15 155	Feb 60	Cross+.25ANGLES 8-80DEG SMALL SAMPLE	+
					Jour PR 99 621	Jul 55	- + MIN AT 30 DEGREES	
	1.5+7				Data EXFOR11465.008	Jun 76	. 23 PTS, DSIGMA.	
Diff Elastic	1.0+6	7.0+6	ORL	Theo	Jour NP 32 353	May 62	Perey+ 3ES,OPTICALMOD FITTED XPT	
Diff Elastic	1.5+7		VIR	Expt	Jour PR 128 1271	Nov 62	Hudson+ TOF.RSLN1.8MEV. CFD OPTMDL	+
					Abst BAP 6 251	62	- + ALSO SEE DA 23 4393,DA24	
	1.5+7				Data EXFOR12180.003	Jun 76	. 38 PTS, DSIGMA	
Diff Elastic	7.0+6		LAS	Expt	Jour PR 129 1649	Feb 63	Thomson. SIG AT 90DEG	+
	7.0+6				Data EXFOR11495.044	Jun 76	. 1 PT. DSIGMA	
Diff Elastic	1.0+6		ALD	Expt	Jour NP 42 86	Apr 63	Gilboy+30TO137DEG.COMP.WITH OPTICMOD	+
Diff Elastic	3.0+5	1.5+6	ANL	Expt	Rept EANDC(US)-62	Jun 64	Smith+TOF,TBL.50KEV STEPS,20KEV RSLN	
					Rept ANL-6727	May 63	- +TOF 20KEV RESOL CURVS CFD TH	
	3.0+5	1.5+6			Data EXFOR12175.002	Jun 76	. 127 PTS, DSIGMA	
	3.0+5	1.5+6			Data EXFOR12175.004	May 63	. 125 PTS. LEGENDRE COEFFICIENTS	
Diff Elastic	9.8+5		SHE	Theo	Jour NP 54 417	Jun 64	Maddison.OPTMOD FIT TO TOWLE GILBOY	
Diff Elastic	3.5+5	1.1+6	BNL	Theo	Jour PR/B 135 895	Aug 64	Auerbach+LCL OPTMDL FIT, TBL BNL818	
Diff Elastic	1.0+5	1.4+7	AGN	Eval	Rept TID-21629	Dec 64	Perkins+. LEG COEF FRM OTHERS	
Diff Elastic	3.3+6	7.0+6	ITY	Theo	Priv IANEVA	May 65	Cnen.OPTMDL+APPROX FOR DEFORM. CFXPT	
Diff Elastic	1.4+7		KYU	Expt	Rept INDSWG-90 24	Jun 65	Yoshimura+ TOF. REL H.	+
	1.4+7				Data EXFOR20266.006	Jun 74	7PTS D/DA.	
Diff Elastic	3.0+4	1.5+7	AI	Eval	Rept NAA-SR-11980	Jul 65	Campbell+ LEG COEFS TBL+CURVS C-MSYS	
Diff Elastic	3.3+6	1.5+7	BOL	Theo	Conf 65Antwerp § 32	Jul 65	Kazakova+ OPT.MOD ADIABATIC APPROX.	
Diff Elastic	2.0+6		FEI	Expt	Rept EANDC-50 200	Jul 65	Kazakova+ EXPT,CURVE CFD OPTMODEL	+
					Prog ICD-2 112	Jul 65	.CURVE	
					Prog INDSWG-101E	65	.ENGLISH TRANSL OF ICD-2 112 7/65	

73 Tantalum 181

Quantity	Energy (ev) Min	Max	Lab	Type	Documentation Ref Vol Page	Date	Author, Comments	Data
Diff Elastic	1.4+7		RPI	Expt Abst	DA/B 26 438	Jul 65	Pearlstein.STUDY OF ENERGY SPECTRA.	+
	1.4+7			Data	EXFOR10234.006	May 73	. 1 PT. DSIGMA PT 90 DEG	
Diff Elastic	1.0+6		LAS	Theo Prog	WASH – 1064 84	Oct 65	Rosen+, OPTMDL+ CPD ELST CFD WIS XPT	
Diff Elastic	1.0+3	1.4+7	GEN	Eval Rept	GEMP – 388	Nov 65	Prince.OPTMDL FIT WITH COMPETITION	
				Jour	ANS 8 457	Nov 65	– .ABACUS II CALCULATIONS	
Diff Elastic	4.0+5	1.0+6	HAR	ExTh Jour	NP 76 369	Feb 66	Ferguson+ OPTMDL PARS TO FIT POLARIZ	+
Diff Elastic	5.0+6		DKE	Expt Jour	ZP 196 103	Sep 66	Buccino+ 20 – 140DEG,CFD OPTMOD. TABLE	+
				Abst	DA 24 4251	Apr 64	Hollandsworth.CFD OPTMDL CALCS.	
	5.0+6			Data	EXFOR11877.008	Jun 76	. 13 PTS. DSIGMA	
Diff Elastic	3.2+6		BCM	Expt Jour	NP 89 154	Dec 66	Becker+ 12 ANGLES GRAPH CFD OPTMDL	+
	3.2+6			Data	EXFOR11511.032	Jun 76	. 12 PTS, DSIGMA.	
Diff Elastic	4.4+6	5.5+6	WIS	ExTh Jour	NP/A 95 193	Mar 67	Mahajan.POLARIZATION OPTMDL ANALYSIS	
				Abst	DA/B 28 1093	Sep 67	– . THESIS	
Diff Elastic	7.0+6		SAF	Eval Jour	AP 42 262	Apr 67	Engelbrecht+ OPTMDL CALCS CFD EXPTS	
Diff Elastic	4.1+6		IFU	Theo Jour	UFZ 13 51	Jan 68	Kashuba+ GRPH,EXPT CFD OPTMOD – CALC	
				Jour	UPJ 13 33	Jul 68	TRANSLATN.*	
Diff Elastic	1.5+6		IFU	Comp Jour	YF 7 277	Feb 68	Korzh+ GRPH SIG(ANG),OPTMOD PARS – FIT	
				Jour	SNP 7 2 190	Aug 68	TRANSLATN.*	
Diff Elastic	1.5+7		OHO	Theo Jour	NC/B 53 2 363	Feb 68	Cassola+ OPTMOD CALC CFD EXPT	
Diff Elastic	3.0+5	1.5+6	ANL	Expt Jour	PR 168 1344	Apr 68	Smith+ TOF ANG DIST LEG COEF CURVES	+
				Rept	ANL – 7363	Aug 67	.SUPERSEDED	
	3.0+5	1.5+6		Data	EXFOR10631.003	Apr 77	. 480PTS.LEG COEFS.6KEV INEL INCLUDE	
Diff Elastic	2.0+6	5.0+6	SCU	Theo Rept	ICD – 6 236	69	Averyanov+CALC ANGDIST CFD EXPT,GRPH	
Diff Elastic	2.5+6	8.1+6	AE	Expt Jour	NP/A 150 105	Jul 70	Holmqvist+ OKS NON – SPHERICAL OPT POT	+
				Rept	AE – 366	Jun 70	– + DATA TBLS GIVEN.	
				ExTh Conf	69Montreal 749	Aug 69	– +OPTMDL+DEFORM THRY CFD XPT	
	2.5+6	8.0+6		Rept	AE – FFN – 94	Oct 68	Benzi – Holmqvist+. 7 ES.CFD NSPH OPTM	
	2.5+6	8.1+6		Expt Data	EXFOR20019.	Sep 71	209PTS.D/DA,LEG.FIT.	
Diff Elastic	7.0+6		CCP	Theo Jour	IZV 35 118	Jan 71	Sirotkin+ DIFFSIG,CFD OPTMOD,GRAPH	
				Jour	BAS 35 108	Jan 71	*ENGL OF IZV 35 118	
Diff Elastic	2.0+6		ANL	Expt Prog	NCSAC – 42 10	Nov 71	Cox. NO DATA GIVEN.	
Diff Elastic	0.0+0	1.5+7	FEI	Eval Book	NIKOLAEV 156	72	.LEG COEFFS+ANG DISTRIBUTS,GRAPH	
Diff Elastic	8.7+5		ANL	Expt Rept	ANL – 7935	Jun 72	Cox+. CFD OPTMOD,HAUSER – FESHBACH	+
	8.7+5			Data	EXFOR10332.028	Jun 74	. 8 PTS, DSIGMA	
Diff Elastic	1.0 – 4	1.5+7	UK	Eval Data	UKNDL – DFN 328B	Mar 73	14 PNTS,C.M.	+
Diff Elastic	1.5+7		ALB	Expt Jour	NP/A 212 147	Sep 73	Benenson+ 1.5 – 10DEG SCAT CFD OPTMODL	+
	1.5+7			Data	EXFOR10370.005	May 74	. 8 PTS. DSIGMA.	
Diff Elastic	4.6+3	6.5+6	FEI	Theo Rept	YK – 8/2 3	Sep 72	Bazazjants+ ANISOTR GROUP – PARAMS,TBL	
				Rept	INDC(CCP) – 39	Jul 74	.P1. ENGLISH OF YK – 8/2 3	
Diff Elastic	8.0+6		JAE	Theo Conf	JAERI – M – 5984	Feb 75	Tanaka.OPTMDL/COUPLD CH CFD EXPTS.	
Diff Elastic	1.4+7	1.5+7	JAE	Theo Conf	JAERI – M – 5984	Feb 75	Tanaka.OPTMDL/COUPLD CH.GRPH CFD EXP	
Diff Elastic	1.0+5	2.0+7	ORL	Expt Abst	BAP 20 166	Feb 75	Dickens+ ORELA NDG 75WASH	
Diff Elastic	1.0+5	1.5+7	CCP	Eval Data	SOKRATOR – 1035	76	50 PTS	+
Diff Elastic	7.1+5	9.0+5	CSE	Expt Abst	BAP 6 61	Feb 61	Rogers+ NDG OKS OTHERS'	+
	4.2+5	9.0+5		Data	EXFOR11269.	Jun 76	. 26 PTS, DSIGMA.	
Polarization	4.0+5		WIS	Expt Jour	PR 96 503	Oct 54	Adair+ POL FOR 50DEG NEUTS CFD TH	
Polarization	3.8+5	9.8+5	WIS	ExTh Jour	NP 6 177	Mar 58	Clement+. POLARIZATION. CFD OPT MDL	
				Expt Rept	AECU – 3628	57	– +.LI7(P,N) SOURCE. 3ANGLES.	
Polarization	2.0+6		ANL	Expt Prog	NCSAC – 42 10	Nov 71	Cox. NO DATA GIVEN	
Polarization	8.8+5		ANL	Expt Rept	ANL – 7935	Jun 72	COX+ CFD OPTMOD,HAUSER – FESHBACH	+
	8.8+5			Data	EXFOR10332.062	Jun 74	. 8 PTS.	
Potntal Scat	1.2+2	3.0+2	ANL	Expt Jour	PR 76 100	Jul 49	Hibdon+ TRNSM MN CO SCATT DETCTRS	
	1.2+2	3.0+2		Data	EXFOR11261.030	Jun 76	. 2 PTS SIGMA POTENTIAL.	
Potntal Scat	1.7+1	5.4+1	MTR	Expt Jour	PR 103 1778	Sep 56	Fluharty+ TRNS+FC 9.1+ – 1B CFD 8.5 TH	
Potntal Scat	4.3+0		BNL	Expt Jour	PR 104 1425	Dec 56	Wood.SIG=7.0+ – 1.0B	
Potntal Scat	+4		HAR	Expt Jour	PPSA 70 51	Jan 57	Gayther+ FROM AVG SIGTOT. FC TRANSM	
Potntal Scat	+0	2.0+3	BNL	Expt Jour	PR 110 692	May 58	Seth+ 8.5+ – 0.8B CALCTD FROM TOT SIG	+
				Rept	ORNL – 2309	Jun 57	Block+ SUPERSEDED	
	1.0+3	2.0+3		Data	EXFOR11788.005	Jun 76	. 1 PT, SIGMA POTENTIAL.	
Potntal Scat		6.5+5	DKE	ExTh Jour	PL 13 70	Nov 64	Seth+0,1PHASE FRM SIG TOT AV 3 – 650KV	
Potntal Scat	7.0 – 2	2.3 – 1	CAI	Expt Jour	JNE 21 425	May 67	Adib+ FROM MEAS TOTAL.CHOPPER.	+
Potntal Scat	None		DKE	Expt Abst	DA/B 28 3834	Mar 68	Divadeenam.TRNS.EFFECTIVE RADIUS	
Potntal Scat	1.0+3	1.0+6	GA	Expt Conf	71Knoxvill 252	Mar 71	Fricke+. SIG=8.5B	
Potntal Scat	1.8 – 3	5.0+0	CAI	Expt Jour	AJN 9 155	Feb 76	Adib+ FROM TOTSIG – RES SIG.TBL+GRPH	
Tot Inelastc	1.5+6		LAS	Expt Jour	PR 72 881	Nov 47	Barschall+ BIASED DETECTOR	
Tot Inelastc	4.0+5	1.2+6	FEI	Expt Jour	AE 15 416	63	Glazkov+ SPHER GEOM	
				Jour	JNE 18 656	64	. ENGL OF AE 15 416	
				Jour	SJA 15 1173	63	. ENGL OF AE 15 416	

73 Tantalum 181

Quantity	Energy (ev) Min	Max	Lab	Type	Documentation Ref Vol Page	Date	Author, Comments	Data
Tot Inelastc	+6		BNL Theo	Conf	65Antwerp 25	Jul 65	Auerbach+NDG COMPLEX POTENTIAL MODL	
	Thrsh	1.6+6		Jour	PR/B 135 895	Aug 64	- + LCL OPTMDL CALC, CF XPT	
Tot Inelastc	5.0+6	7.0+6	ALD Expt	Jour	NP/A 112 337	May 68	Owens+.3ES.FROM N SPECT 90DEG.	+
Tot Inelastc	1.7+5	1.3+6	FEI Expt	Conf	70Helsinki 2 295	Jun 70	Broder+81. SIG(E) TABLE,INEL-GAM-XPT	
Tot Inelastc	6.3+3	1.5+7	UK Eval	Data	UKNDL-DFN 328B	Mar 73	67 PNTS	+
Tot Inelastc	1.5+7		TUD Expt	Prog	ZFK-262 28	Sep 73	Hermsdorf+ DEDUCED FROM N-EMIS,TABLE	
Diff Inelast	2.5+6	6.3+6	LAS Expt	Rept	ORNL-2309	Jun 57	Levin+TOF 3ES 3D4MEV TS CFS MXWLCURV	
Diff Inelast	1.4+7		LAS Expt	Jour	PR 107 824	Aug 57	Rosen+NUCLEAR EMULSION DETECTION	+
				Conf	58Geneva 15 11	Sep 58	Coon+.PPR666,EXPT DESCRIBED,TOF	
	1.4+7			Data	EXFOR11223.003	Jun 76	. 18 PTS DSIGMA	
	1.4+7			Data	EXFOR11223.006	Jun 76	. 1 PT, SIG	
Diff Inelast	1.3+7	1.7+7	PCF Expt	Jour	NC 9 664	Aug 58	Remy+NN N2N TOF SPECTRA RELATIV.ONLY	
Diff Inelast	1.4+7		ISL Theo	Jour	PR 118 781	May 60	DOSTROVSKY MONTE CARLO CALC CFD EXP	
Diff Inelast	1.5+7		JAE Expt	Priv	TSUKADA	62	Tsukada.T-D NS.TOF.	+
	1.5+7			Data	EXFOR20323.004	Jun 74	22PTS.D/DA.	
Diff Inelast	2.4+6	7.0+6	RIC Expt	Rept	SCR-466	Feb 62	Ewing+ ALSO 5MEV,E SPECT+NUCL TEMP.	
Diff Inelast	4.0+5	1.2+6	FEI Expt	Jour	AE 15 416	63	Glazkov+ SPHER GEOM,5 ENERGIES	
				Jour	JNE 18 656	64	. ENGL OF AE 15 416	
				Jour	SJA 15 1173	63	. ENGL OF AE 15 416	
Diff Inelast	7.0+6		LAS Expt	Jour	PR 129 1649	Feb 63	Thomson+ 90DEG TEMP FOR NS TO 5MEV	+
	7.0+6			Data	EXFOR11495.047	Jun 76	. 1 PT SIGMA	
	7.0+6			Data	EXFOR11495.043	Jun 76	. 2 PTS, DSIGMA.	
Diff Inelast	3.0+5	1.5+6	ANL Expt	Rept	ANL-6727	May 63	Smith.TOF.20KEV RSLN CURVS.CFD TH	
Diff Inelast	7.1+5		BNL Theo	Jour	PR/B 135 895	Aug 64	Auerbach+LCL OPTMDL CALC SEE BNL818	
Diff Inelast	4.0+6	6.5+6	DKE Expt	Jour	NP 60 17	Nov 64	Buccino+N SPEC MEASURED 4ES+NUC TEMP	
				Abst	DA 24 4251	Apr 64	Hollandsworth.TOF.EN SPEC.NUCL T.	
Diff Inelast	1.4+7		KYU Expt	Rept	INDSWG-90 24	Jul 65	Yoshimura+ TOF. REL H	+
	1.4+7			Data	EXFOR20266.007	Jun 74	14PTS.D/DA.	
Diff Inelast	1.4+7		RPI Expt	Jour	JNAB 19 497	Jul 65	Pearlstein+.INEL SPECTRUM 6-14 MEV	
				Abst	DA 26 438	Jul 65	- .EXCIT OF COLLECTIVE LEVEL	
	1.4+7			Data	EXFOR10234.002	May 73	. 1 PT. DSIGMA PT 90 DEG	
Diff Inelast	2.5+6	1.5+7	FEI Theo	Jour	NP 76 232	Feb 66	Malyshev+ SPEC ANALYSED FOR TEMP	
Diff Inelast	3.5+6	8.5+6	JAE ExTh	Jour	NP 78 369	Apr 66	Tsukada+ SPECTRA CFD FERMI GAS MDL	+
	3.6+6	8.5+6		Expt	NP/A 131 145	Jun 69	Maruyama. E DEPENDENCE,PARAM,TH FIT	
Diff Inelast	1.4+7		FEI Expt	Jour	YF 4 1154	Dec 66	Sal'Nikow+ SPEC OF SECNDARY NS,CURVE	
				Jour	SNP 4 831	Jun 67	.ENGLISH TRANSL OF YF 4 1154 12/66	
	1.4+7			Data	EXFOR40134.015	Feb 73	N-SPECTRUM AT 92 DEG, 54EN'	
Diff Inelast	4.5+5	1.5+6	ANL Expt	Jour	PR 168 1344	Apr 68	Smith+ TOF SIGS FOR 6LVLS TBLS+CURVS	+
				Rept	ANL-7363	Aug 67	.SUPERSEDED	
	3.0+5	1.5+6		Data	EXFOR10631.	Apr 77	. 626PTS.480PTS SEL.146PTS DIN DATA.	
Diff Inelast	5.0+6	7.0+6	ALD Expt	Jour	NP/A 112 337	May 68	Owens+.3ES.FROM N SPECT 90DEG NDG.	
				Conf	65Antwerp 547	Jul 65	- + PPR122.ABST.SPECT N' AT 90DEG	
Diff Inelast	1.7+5	2.9+6	FEI Expt	Conf	70Helsinki 2 295	Jun 70	Broder+81. EXCITATN OF LEVELS DERIVD	
				Rept	FEI-155	69	- + EXCIT 5 LVLS,TABLE	
Diff Inelast	2.4+5	1.8+6	MIT Expt	Jour	NSE 45 297	Sep 71	Rogers+.LVL EXCIT FNCTS FROM GAM PRO	+
				Jour	NP/A 142 100	Feb 70	.SUPERSEDED	
	2.4+5	1.8+6		Data	EXFOR10146.	Dec 72	. 79 PTS. DSIGMA	
Diff Inelast	1.4+7		TUD Expt	Prog	ZFK-223 28	Sep 71	Hantzsch+ TOF,DIFFSIG TO BE CALC,NDG	
Diff Inelast	1.4+7		KFI Theo	Jour	KFKI-72-17	Feb 72	Kluge+ CALC N-SPEC INEL+N2N,TBL,GRPH	
Diff Inelast	1.5+6	1.4+7	TUD Expt	Prog	ZFK-243 23	Sep 72	Hermsdorf+ DOUBLE-DIFF,5 ANGS,GRAPH	
Diff Inelast	1.2+6	1.5+7	UK Eval	Data	UKNDL-DFN 328B	Mar 73	.TO CONTINUUM.34 PTS.E DIST.ANGDIST.	+
	6.3+3	1.9+6		Data	UKNDL-DFN 328B	Mar 73	1ST- 8TH LVL,ANGDIST	
Diff Inelast	1.4+7		TUD Expt	Conf	73Kiev 1 269	May 73	Seeliger+ TOF,DOUBLDIFF.GRAPH(1 ANG)	
				Rept	BNL-TR-586	74	. ENGLISH OF 73KIEV 1,P.269	
Diff Inelast	1.4+7		TUD Expt	Jour	KE 16 252	Aug 73	Hermsdorf+ SIG+SPEC PARAMETRISATION	
				Conf	73Kiev 1 258	May 73	- + DESCRIPN OF N-SPEC,GRAPH	
				Prog	ZFK-243 20	Sep 72	- + PRE-EQUIL STAT MDL ANALYS	
Diff Inelast	1.4+7		FEI Expt	Rept	YK-15 129	74	Sal'Nikov+ TOF,SPEC OF SECOND-NS,TBL	+
	1.4+7			Data	EXFOR40238.	Nov 76	.MB/SR/MEV FOR 5 ANGLES AND 50ES GVN	
Diff Inelast	1.4+7		CIS Theo	Jour	ZFK-271 39	Feb 74	Braga-Marcazzan+ CALC N-E-SPEC,GRPH	
Diff Inelast	1.4+7		KYU Expt	Jour	NST 11 523	Dec 74	Akiyoshi+.TOF,E-SPECTRA AT 7 ANGLES	
Diff Inelast	1.4+7		DUB Theo	Jour	YF 21 260	Feb 75	Gudima+ EQU+PRE-EQU MDL,SPEC CFD OTH	
				Jour	SNP 21 138	Aug 75	. ENGLISH OF YF 21 260	
Diff Inelast	1.4+7		FEI Eval	Conf	75Kiev 4 128	May 75	Luk'Janov+ DIR,INDIR SIG,TEMP.TABLE	
Diff Inelast	4.2+5	9.9+5	CSE Expt	Abst	BAP 6 61	Feb 61	Rogers+ TO 133 AND 303KEV LEVELS	+
	7.1+5	9.0+5		Data	EXFOR11269.008	Jun 76	. 3 PTS, SIGMA.	
	4.2+5	9.9+5		Data	EXFOR11269.	Jun 76	. 40 PTS, DSIGMA.	
Thermal Scat	Cold		CRC ExTh	Jour	PR/A 136 781	Nov 64	Woods.XTAL SPECT,FREQ SPECT DEDUCED	

73 Tantalum 181

Quantity	Energy (ev) Min	Energy (ev) Max	Lab	Type	Documentation Ref Vol Page	Date	Author, Comments	Data
Thermal Scat	None		TKU	Theo Jour	AAF 6 321	Jul 69	Laehteenkorva. DISPERSION CURVES GVN	
Thermal Scat	1.8−3	5.0+0	CAI	Expt Jour	AJN 9 155	Feb 76	Adib+ COH SCAT AMP,BY TOTSIG.VAL GVN	
Thermal Scat	1.0−4	1.0+3	MUN	Revw Jour	EEN 80 1	77	Koester. SCAT LENGTH,FREE+INCOH SIG	
Scattering	Maxwl		CAV	Expt Jour	PRSA 162 127	Sep 37	Goldhaber+.ABOUT 10B REL 4.83B FOR C	
Scattering	2.0+5	3.0+6	LAS	Expt Jour	PR 72 881	Nov 47	Barschall+ POOR GEOM+BACKSCT.BIAS DET	
Scattering	3.0+4	1.4+6	ANL	Expt Jour	PR 107 1077	Aug 57	Langsdorf+,LEGENDRE COEFS CURVES	+
				Rept	ANL−5567	Oct 61	− +LEGENDRE EXPANSION DATA	
	3.0+4	1.4+6		Data	EXFOR11224.054	Jun 76	. 18 PTS. SIGMA	
	3.0+4	1.4+6		Data	EXFOR11224.055	Jun 76	. 90 PTS, DSIG.	
Scattering	Maxwl		GEN	Eval Rept	XDC−61−4−35	Apr 61	Jacob+TRANSFER MATRIX 68 TO 4500 F	
Scattering	2.5−2	1.0+7	GEN	Eval Rept	XDC−61−4−35	Apr 61	Jacob+ .19,25GROUPS+TRANSFER MATRIX	
Scattering	2.0−2	2.0+0	IFU	Expt Prog	INDSWG−120 27	65	Vertebnyj.GRAPH,TOF,SIG(0.025)=2.9	
Scattering	8.0+1	1.0+5	HAR	Expt Prog	AERE−PR/NP11 4	Oct 66	Asami+ EXP COMPLETE.ANALYSIS IN PROG	
Scattering		1.0+2	MOL	Expt Prog	EANDC(E)127U	Apr 70	Poortmans+,CBNM LINAC TOF	
Scattering	3.0+2		AI	Theo Jour	NSE 49 450	72	Levitt. MTE−CRLO,PROBABILTY TBLS.TBL	
				Conf	BNL−50387 79	Apr 73	− . SIMILAR NSE 49,LESS DETAILED	
Scattering	None		SAC	Expt Jour	PRL 33 102	Jul 74	Roubeau+ SLOW N SPIN−DEP SCT LENGTH	
Nonelastic	1.0+6		WIS	Expt Jour	PR 93 1062	Mar 54	Walt. MSD FROM 30−150 DEG.	+
	1.0+6			Data	EXFOR11637.063	Jun 76	. 1 PT SIGMA	
Nonelastic	4.1+6		LAS	Expt Jour	PR 98 677	May 55	Walt+ 2.7+−0.2B FROM TOT MINUS ELAST	+
	4.1+6			Data	EXFOR11215.039	Jun 76	. 1 PT SIGMA	
Nonelastic	2.5+6	7.0+6	LAS	Expt Jour	PR 104 1319	Dec 56	Beyster+ SPH TRNS 2ES+TOT−EL 2ES	+
	2.5+6	7.0+6		Data	EXFOR11220.026	Jun 76	. 2 PTS SIGMA	
Nonelastic	5.0+4	1.8+7	LAS	Theo Rept	LA−2099	Dec 56	Beyster+ OPTMDL CALC CFD EXPT,CURVE	
Nonelastic	1.4+7		LAS	Expt Jour	PR 107 824	Aug 57	Rosen+ NUCLEAR EMULSION DETECTION	+
	1.4+7			Data	EXFOR11223.007	Jun 76	. 1 PT, SIGMA.	
Nonelastic	7.0+7	1.4+7	LRL	Revw Rept	UCRL−5345	Sep 58	Howerton.RVN EXP,+TBP BJORKLUND CCB	
Nonelastic	1.4+7		GHT	Expt Jour	ACA 64 187	73	Vandecasteele+ FLUX−ATTENUAT,SIG GVN	
Nonelastic	1.4+7		TUD	Theo Conf	ZFK−271 63	Nov 73	Seeliger+ N−SPEC,NDG.INTEG−SIG SHOWN	
				Jour	KE 16 252	Aug 73	Hermsdorf+ FIT,TBL SIG,GRPH DIFFSIG	
Absorption	Pile		HAR	Expt Jour	PPSA 63 1175	Oct 50	Colmer+LITTLER.PILE OSC REL HAR B	+
				Rept	AERE−N/R−527	Jun 50	− + PILE OSCILLATOR.	
Absorption	Pile		ANL	Expt Jour	PR 80 342	Nov 50	Harris+.PILE OSC.REL TO BORON.	+
	Pile			Data	EXFOR11528.041	Jun 76	. 1 PT, SIGMA	
Absorption	Maxwl		HAR	Expt Rept	AERE−R/R−2516	Mar 58	Jowitt+ PILE OSC.REL BORON.293DEGK.	
Absorption	2.5−2		HAR	Expt Jour	JNEA 12 32	May 60	Tattersall+ PILE OSCILLATOR.	+
	2.5−2			Data	EXFOR20638.056	Jul 76	1PNT.SIGMA.	
Absorption	Maxwl		GEN	Eval Rept	XDC−61−4−35	Apr 61	Jacob+.10 TEMPS 68 TO 4500 F	
Absorption	2.5−2	1.0+7	GEN	Eval Rept	XDC−61−4−35	Apr 61	Jacob+.19,25GROUPS	
Absorption	2.0+4	8.6+5	ATI	Expt Prog	EANDC(OR)117L	Aug 72	Bensch+ TBL FOR 4 ENERGIES. TBP	
Absorption	Fiss		BET	Expt Jour	NSE 58 361	Dec 75	Green.252CF FISS NEUT SPECT AVG.	
Res Int Abs	5.0−1		ANL	Expt Jour	PR 79 11	Jul 50	Harris+ EPI−CD,REL THERMAL ACT.B−W	+
	5.0−1			Data	EXFOR11343.029	Jun 76	. 1 PT, RI	
Res Int Abs	None		ORL	Revw Conf	55Geneva 5 96	Aug 55	Macklin+.TABLE,EXPT CFD THEORY,P833	
Res Int Abs	−		CCP	Expt Jour	AE 3 507	Dec 57	Klimentov+.EPI CD REACTIVITY REL LI	+
				Jour	JNE 9 20	Jun 59	TRANSLATN.*	
				Jour	SJA 3 1387	57	TRANSLATN.*	
Res Int Abs	5.0−1		HAR	Expt Jour	JNE 12 32	May 60	Tattersall+ ABOVE 1/V,OSCIL,REL B+AU	+
				Rept	AERE−R−2887	Aug 59	− . PILE OSC.REL BORON	
				Conf	58Geneva 16 34	Sep 58	Rose+ SUPERSEDED	
	6.7−1			Data	EXFOR20638.057	Jul 76	1PNT.	
Res Int Abs	5.0−1	5.0−1	MUN	Expt Jour	NUK 2 255	Dec 60	Wolf+ CAPTURE INTEGRAL CFD OTHERS	+
	5.0−1			Data	EXFOR20651.007	Oct 76	1PNT.CAPTURE.	
Res Int Abs	−		WIN	Expt Jour	JNAB 16 335	Jul 62	Moore+.CD TUBED OSC. NOT INF DILUTE	
				Rept	AEEW−R−57	Aug 61	− + EQU TO JNE(A+B)16 335	
Res Int Abs		1.0+5	LEB	Expt Jour	ZET 46 80	Jan 64	Konks.TBL 3E−RANGES.ENGL JET 19 59	
Res Int Abs	5.0−1		STF	Expt Conf	66S.Diego 2 175	Feb 66	Lesage+	+
	5.0−1			Data	EXFOR11754.011	Jun 76	. 1 PT, RI.	
Res Int Abs	5.0−1		BGK	Expt Rept	THAI−AEC−10	Oct 67	. CD−RATIO REL AU.TO GRND,META.TABLE	+
	5.0−1			Data	EXFOR30368.	Jan 77	REL AU, PRELM. TO TA−182M AND −182G	
Res Int Abs	5.0−1		MTR	Expt Rept	IN−1195	May 68	Scoville+REACTIVITY MEASUREMENTS	+
				Jour	ANS 10 259	Jun 67	Rogers+ SUPERSEDED.	
	5.0−1			Data	EXFOR11820.019	Jun 76	. 1 PT, RI.	
Res Int Abs	Pile		IBJ	Expt Jour	NKA 13 881	Aug 68	Latek+ PILE OSC,REL AU(NG),TBL	
Res Int Abs	5.0−1		MTR	Expt Rept	IN−1296	May 69	Schuman+. PILE ACT. 640+−60B. 1/V	+
	5.0−1			Data	EXFOR11687.007	Jun 76	. 1 PT, SIGMA.	
Res Int Abs	5.0−1		LRC	Expt Rept	NASA−TN−D−5628	70	Pierce.	+
	5.0−1			Data	EXFOR10260.002	Aug 72	. 1 PT. SIGMA	

73 Tantalum 181

Quantity	Energy (ev) Min	Max	Lab	Type	Documentation Ref Vol Page	Date	Author, Comments	Data
Res Int Abs	Maxwl		BKB	Expt Jour	BKN 22 1	Sep 71	Markovic. PILE OSCI,RES INT REL AU	+
	−1			Data	EXFOR30289.005	Jun 75	INFINITE DILUTION RI WITHOUT 1/V	
Res Int Abs	5.0−1		KJL	Expt Jour	JIN 34 2699	Sep 72	Steinnes. ACT. AU MONITOR	+
	5.0−1			Data	EXFOR20188.029	May 74	1PNT.CAPTURE.	
Res Int Abs	5.0−1		MUN	Expt Jour	JRC 15 535	73	Alian+CAPT CD−R, 564 B INCL 1/V	+
	5.0−1			Data	EXFOR20644.017	Jun 76	1PNT.CAPTURE.	
Res Int Abs	5.0−1		GHT	Expt Jour	JRC 20 695	74	Van Der Linden+ BY(N,G).CFD OTHS,TBL	+
	5.5−1			Conf	73Paris 2 241	Mar 73	− + ACT,REL THR+GOLD,TBL	
	5.5−1			Data	EXFOR20645.	Jul 76	2PTS.CAPTURE.	
Res Int Abs	5.0−1		VIP	Expt Abst	ANS 23 501	Jun 76	Sage+CD RATIO TECHNIQUE.TBL.	+
	5.0−1				EXFOR10637.016	Apr 77	. 1 PT.RIA=1.86+−1.25B	
(n,γ)	Maxwl		JAP	Expt Jour	SCP 38 167	Jan 41	Sinma+.LI+D.RELATIVE SIG MEASUREMENT	
(n,γ)	Pile		ANL	Expt Jour	PR 72 888	Nov 47	Seren+.THR IRRAD. TO16.2MIN,117D ISO	+
	Pile			Data	EXFOR11447.	Jun 76	. 2 PTS, MS AND GND SIGMA.	
(n,γ)	Maxwl		ANL	Expt Jour	PR 76 531	Aug 49	Kubitscheck+ YIELD CFD SIG.G−M COINC	
(n,γ)	Maxwl		ORL	Expt Jour	PR 83 643	Aug 51	Pomerance.LOCAL OSC REL AU ABS 95 B	+
	Maxwl			Data	EXFOR11047.057	Jun 76	. 1 PT, SIGMA.	
(n,γ)	Fiss		BNL	Expt Jour	PR 91 1423	Sep 53	Hughes+.ALSO LVL SPACINGS AT EXCIT E	+
	Fiss			Data	EXFOR11562.015	Jun 76	. 1 PT, SIGMA.	
(n,γ)	8.0+0	9.9+1	KAP	Expt Rept	KAPL−1084	54	Gaerttner+ USING KAPL BETATRON.	
(n,γ)		1.0+2	BNL	Expt Prog	WASH−190 9	Feb 56	Draper.NDG CYCL TOF NGAMMA SELFIND.	
(n,γ)	7.5+1	2.5+2	COL	Expt Conf	ORNL−2309	Jun 57	Rainwater+ TOF, NEVIS, CURV	
	7.5+1	2.6+2		Rept	AERE−NP/R−2076	Jan 57	− +TOF SELFINDICATION NOT ABS	
	3.1+1	2.6+2		Rept	CU− 155	Dec 56	Grimm. REL FOR RES PAR ONLY CF HGR	
(n,γ)	Fast		HAR	Expt Jour	JNE 5 4	Jul 57	Rose. SAME DATA AS 55GENEVA 5,331,55	
				Revw Conf	55Geneva 5 331	Aug 55	Holmes+.P404,VAL GVN,THEORET DISCUSS	
	2.0+5		KUR	Expt Conf	58Geneva 15 50	Sep 58	Leipunskij+.PPR2219,VAL GVN,ACTIVATN	
(n,γ)	2.5+4		LRL	Expt Jour	PR 112 226	Oct 58	Booth+ SB−BE REL I+THR,ACT 112D HL	+
				Abst	BAP 2 268	Jun 57	− + ABST L6 ALSO WASH190,192,194	
	2.5+4			Data	EXFOR11429.026	Jun 76	. 1 PT. SIGMA.	
(n,γ)	2.5−2		MTR	Expt Jour	NSE 7 193	Feb 60	Schmunk+ 20+−0.09B FROM 1/V FIT	
	2.5−2			Data	EXFOR11634.006	Jun 76	. 1 PT SIGMA.	
(n,γ)	1.8+5	1.0+6	LAS	Expt Jour	PR 120 556	Oct 60	Diven.SC−T.	+
	1.8+5	1.0+6		Data	EXFOR11616.024	Jun 76	. 7 PTS, SIGMA.	
(n,γ)	None		ANL	Theo Jour	PR 120 1305	Nov 60	Huizenga+ ISOMER RATIO,TH CFD EXPT	
(n,γ)	Maxwl	Pile	ORL	Expt Jour	NSE 8 378	Nov 60	Lyon. ACTIVATION, 2 SIGMA VALUES GVN	+
	Maxwl	Pile		Data	EXFOR11625.	Jun 76	. 2 PTS, SIG	
(n,γ)	Fast		LAS	Expt Jour	NSE 8 608	Dec 60	Byers. GODIVA ACTIVATION CS GIVEN	
(n,γ)	Maxwl		MUN	Expt Jour	NUK 2 255	Dec 60	Wolf. CS GVN,CFD RESULTS OTHERS	+
				Revw Conf	60Vienna 63	Oct 60	Maierleibnitz. TABLE,ACCURATE VALUES	
	2.5−2			Expt Data	EXFOR20651.006	Oct 76	1PNT.SIGMA.	
(n,γ)	Maxwl		BNL	Expt Jour	PR 121 1158	Feb 61	Sunyar+ STUDY OF TA182M DECAY.	+
	Maxwl			Data	EXFOR12172.002	Jun 76	. 3 PTS. GND,META,ISOMER RATIO	
(n,γ)	2.1+2	8.0+3	ORL	Expt Conf	61Saclay 203	Sep 61	Block+.LIQUID SCINTILLATOR	+
	2.0+2	1.0+4		Conf	61Vienna 1 95	Aug 61	Neiler.PPR73,TABLE FOR SOME ES,GRAPH	
	2.1+2	7.0+3		Data	EXFOR11935.021	Jun 76	. 49 PTS, SIGMA.	
(n,γ)	3.2+4	4.0+6	LRL	Expt Jour	PR 128 2717	Dec 62	Miskel+3, TABLE OF SIG AT 26ES. ACT	
	3.2+4	4.0+6		Data	EXFOR12115.	Jun 76	. 26 PTS (TWO MEASUREMENTS)	
(n,γ)	3.0+4	3.0+5	FOA	Expt Jour	AF 23 425	Mar 63	Bergqvist.TOF 5 ES.NAI.REL AG. GRAPH	
	3.5+4	3.0+5		Data	EXFOR20024.003	Sep 71	5PTS.SIG.	
(n,γ)	3.0+3	8.0+5	ORL	Expt Jour	PR 122 182	Apr 61	Gibbons+ CURVE CFD THEORY REPL BNL65	+
	3.0+4	6.5+4		Jour	PR 129 2695	Mar 63	Macklin+ LIQ SCINT,735 AND 440MB	
	3.0+4	1.7+5		Conf	61Vienna 1 95	Aug 61	Neiler.	
	6.5+3	1.7+5		Data	EXFOR11329.	Jun 76	. 51 PTS, SIGMA.	
(n,γ)	3.0+4		ORL	Expt Jour	NP 43 353	May 63	Macklin+.SIG=630MB+−20PC	+
	3.0+4			Data	EXFOR11380.010	Jun 76	. 1 PT SIGMA	
(n,γ)	1.2+5	1.8+6	ANL	Expt Jour	PR/B 133 378	Jan 64	COX.CURVS NORM TO THR.16.4H,115D ACT	+
	1.2+5	1.6+6		Data	EXFOR11835.	Jun 76	. 25 PTS, MS SIGMA, 14 PTS GND SIGMA	
(n,γ)	3.0+4	6.0+5	LEB	Expt Jour	ZET 46 80	Jan 64	Konks.PB−SLOW−DOWN,GRAPH SIG(E)	+
				Jour	JET 19 59	Jul 64	TRANSLATN.*	
(n,γ)	9.7+0	1.0+2	HAR	Expt Priv	MOXON1	Apr 64	Moxon+ M−R DET. NUMERICAL DAT1§	+
	1.0+2	1.5+4		Jour	NIM 24 445	Oct 63	− +RAE TOF.SCINT DET DESCRIBED	
				Rept	AERE−NP/GEN 30	Feb 63	− DETECTOR DESCRIBED.	
(n,γ)	1.0+3	1.4+7	GEN	Eval Jour	ANS 7 244	Nov 64	Prince. THEORY OF LANE AND LYNN	
(n,γ)	Maxwl		UCB	Expt Rept	NYO−10175	Dec 64	Arino+ACT.TBLS.GRAPHS.PRODUCT HL.	+
	Maxwl			Data	EXFOR11817.015	Jun 76	. 1 PT, SIGMA.	
(n,γ)	5.0+3	9.0+4	ORL	Theo Jour	RMP 37 166	Jan 65	Macklin+.CALC FOR KT=5TO90KEV	
(n,γ)	+2	+4	LAS	Expt Prog	WASH−1056 2	Mar 65	Glass.BOMB SOURCE,NDG MOXON−RAE DET	

73 Tantalum 181

Quantity	Energy (ev) Min	Max	Lab	Type	Documentation Ref Vol Page	Date	Author, Comments	Data
(n,γ)	3.3+4	1.6+5	FEI	Expt	Jour AE 19 457	Nov 65	Kononov+ TOF,SCIN-TANK,PLSD C-W,GRPH	+
					Jour SNP 4 209	Feb 67	*	
					Conf 66Paris 1 469	Oct 66	*PPR99.GRPH CFD OTHER	
					Jour YF 4 282	Aug 66	*	
					Jour SJA 19 1428	May 66	* ENGL OF AE 19 457	
					Jour EAF 19 5 74	May 66	*FRENCH OF AE 19 457	
					Jour JNE 20 1049	66	* ENGL OF AE 19 457	
	2.9+4	1.7+5			Data EXFOR40076.003	Jul 71	SIG AT 15 ENERGIES FROM PRIV COMMUN	
(n,γ)	3.0+4	3.1+5	ORL	Expt	Abst BAP 11 167	Feb 66	Macklin+OKS PR 122,182(1961)	+
	2.0+2	8.0+5			Jour RMP 37 166	Jan 65	- +ORNL LIQ SC-T	
	3.0+4	3.1+5			Data EXFOR12158.002	Jun 76	. 4 PTS, SIGMA.	
(n,γ)	7.5+3	3.0+4	KFK	Expt	Conf 66Paris 1 502	Oct 66	Miessner+ ABST.NDG. EFF CAPT SIG.	
(n,γ)	4.3+0		TRM	Expt	Conf 67Kanpur 409	Feb 67	Chandramoleswar. WG= 37+ - 4 MICRO S	
					Prog AEET-267 4	Aug 66	- + VALUE GIVEN,CFD BNL	
(n,γ)	Pile		FRK	Expt	Conf 67Juelich 65	Apr 67	Hanle+ CHANNEL VS COMPD NUC,4.3EVRES	
(n,γ)	2.0+2	1.0+4	KFK	Expt	Conf 67Karlsrhe 1 77	Nov 67	Seufert+,HOT-TO-COLD CAPTURE RATIO	
(n,γ)	-		KFK	Revw	Conf IAEA-107 150	68	Poenitz.SIG PROPOSED AS STANDARD	
					Conf 67Brussels	May 67	- . PPR 10. EQU TO IAEA-107	
	1.0+3	1.0+6		Eval	Conf 66Paris 1 277	Oct 66	- . TBL EVAL+RENORMAL TO AU	
(n,γ)	3.0+4	5.0+6	WWA	Expt	Conf JINR-D3893 131	May 68	Brzosko+ EXPTL SIG(E) GRAPH,STATMOD	
(n,γ)	-		IEA	Comp	Rept IEA-INF- 10	Aug 68	Atalla. TABLES OF HL,SIG AND GAMM-E	
	1.0+6	1.0+7	IBJ	Theo	Rept INR-967	Dec 68	Brzosko+,WG-MEAN LVL DIST,PIGMY RES	
	3.5+4	5.2+6	WWA	Expt	Jour APP 35 417	Mar 69	Brzosko+ACTIVATION,THEORY,TABLE,GRPH	+
					Jour NP/A 123 603	Jan 69	SEE ALSO *SHORTENED	
					Rept INR-940	Aug 68	EQUIVALENT*	
					Rept INDC-230 48	May 68	SEE ALSO *PROG REPT	
	3.5+4	5.2+6			Data EXFOR30024.002	Jun 70	SIGMA AT 38 ES.	
(n,γ)	2.0+3		MTR	Expt	Prog WASH-1127 72	Apr 69	Schuman+ FILTERED BEAM,RELATVE CURVS	
(n,γ)	1.0+4	1.5+5	KFK	Expt	Jour NP/A 133 513	Aug 69	Kompe.VDG.LIQ SCINT. REL AU MEAS.	+
					Rept KFK-1071	Aug 69	- . REPRINT OF NP/A 133 513	
					Rept EANDC(E)89U3	Feb 68	- . RENORMAL OF 66PARIS	
	1.5+4	1.5+5			Conf 67Karlsrhe 1 67	Nov 67	Beckurts+,RE-EVALUATED REL AU(N,GAM)	
	1.0+4	1.5+5			Rept KFK-635	Oct 67	Poenitz+ RENORM TO NEW AU VALUE.	
					Conf 66Paris 1 513	Oct 66	Kompe. LARGE LIQ SCIN.GRPH.SUPERSEDD	
	1.3+4	1.6+5			Data EXFOR20358.026	Sep 74	66PTS.SIGMA.	
(n,γ)	2.0+5		MUA	Theo	Conf 69Roorke 2 129	Dec 69	Chaubey+ SIG VALUE GIVEN, STATIST-TH	
(n,γ)	1.0-4	1.8+7	BNW	Eval	Rept BNWL-1312	May 70	Simons+.	
(n,γ)	+2	+7	HAR	Revw	Conf 70Helsinki 1 267	Jun 70	James.107. ACCURACY CFD REACTOR COST	
	3.3-2	8.3-1	BNL	Expt	Jour NIM 86 83	Sep 70	Malik+ MOXON RAE DET RELATIVE TO AU	+
	7.0-2	8.4-1			Data EXFOR10501.008	May 75	. 4 PTS. SIGMA	
(n,γ)	-		CCP	Revw	Jour AE 29 187	Sep 70	Sukhoruchkin. (D,P GAM) CFD (N,GAM)	
					Jour SJA 29 896	Sep 70	TRANSLATN.*	
	1.0+3	1.0+6	GA	Revw	Conf 70ANL 285	Oct 70	Carlson. STATUS AS STANDARD SIG,CURV	
(n,γ)	3.0+4		AUA	Theo	Rept AAEC/E-211	Nov 70	Musgrove. SIGMA GIVEN AND CFD OTHER	
(n,γ)	Fast		MTR	Expt	Abst ANS 13 755	Nov 70	Scoville+.CFRMF MEAST.VALUE GIVEN.	
					Prog IN-1407 29	Jun 70	- +.ACT.FAST SPEC.VALUE GIVEN.	
(n,γ)	1.0-2	1.0+2	HAR	Expt	Prog AERE-PR/NP17	Dec 70	Moxon+ TOF LINAC ANAL TBC	
	3.0+4	1.5+6	WWA	Expt	Jour APPB 2 489	71	Brzosko+ PARTIAL,TOTAL SIG CFD THEO	+
					Rept INDC(SEC)-18	Aug 71	* PAGE 120 =INR-1318	
					Rept INR-1318 28	Apr 71	*SHORT REPORT,DATA GIV	
					Rept INR-1224	Sep 70	*	
					Rept INR-1197 26	May 70	*SHORTER THAN INR-1224	
					Jour CJP 47 2849	Dec 69	*TH.CALCULATIONS OF SIG	
	3.4+2	1.3+6			Data EXFOR30159.021	Apr 72	PARTIAL SIGMA FOR 8 NEUTRON ENERGIES	
	4.0+5				Data EXFOR30159.	Apr 72	PARTIAL,TOTAL SIGMAS GIVEN	
(n,γ)	1.0+3	1.0+6	GA	Expt	Conf 71Knoxvill 252	Mar 71	Fricke+,ABSOL AVG SIG,CURVE	+
					Rept N-70-41999	Jun 70	Friesenhahn+ TOF ABSOL SIG(E) MEASD	
				ExTh	Conf 70Helsinki 2 265	Jun 70	Fricke+ TOF	
	9.6+2	1.1+6		Expt	Data EXFOR10049.004	Jul 71	. 95PTS, SIGMA	
(n,γ)	Maxwl		BKB	Expt	Jour BKN 22 1	Sep 71	Markovic. PILE OSCI,REL B-10,SIG GVN	+
	Maxwl				Data EXFOR30289.004	Jun 75	1 POINT	
(n,γ)	1.4+7		LAS	Expt	Jour PL/B 36 557	Oct 71	Drake+ SPECTRUM SUMMED CFD PB208 NG	+
	1.4+7				Data EXFOR10193.004	Jun 72	. 1 PT. SIGMA	
	3.0+2		AI	Theo	Jour NSE 49 450	72	Levitt. MTE-CRLO,PROBABILTY TBLS.TBL	
					Conf BNL-50387 79	Apr 73	- . SIMILAR NSE 49,LESS DETAILED	
(n,γ)	2.4+4		MUA	Theo	Jour IJP 46 114	Mar 72	Chaubey+ P-WAVE STRENGTH FUNCT,TABLE	
(n,γ)	1.0+3	1.0+7	BOL	Eval	Data BENZI-DFN 812.	May 72	40 PNTS	+
(n,γ)	3.0+4		AUA	Expt	Prog INDC(SEC)-28	Sep 72	Stroud+P285. VDG, SIG MEASURED,NDG	

73 Tantalum 181

Quantity	Energy (ev) Min	Max	Lab	Type	Documentation Ref Vol Page	Date	Author, Comments	Data
(n,γ)	2.4+4		RPI	Expt Conf	72Kiamesha 2 1107	Sep 72	Block+.FE-FILTERED BEAM.RELATV MEAST	+
	2.4+4			Data	EXFOR10594.004	Aug 76	. 1 PT REL TOAU. CS=.96B	
(n,γ)	Fast		DUB	Expt Rept	JINR-P12-6810	Nov 72	Ngo Quoc Buu+ ACT ANALYS, CD-RATIOS	
(n,γ)	3.0+4	3.0+5	USP	Expt Jour	NP/A 196 83	Nov 72	Lepine+ LI7-P NS.TOF.M-R. REL TO IN	+
	3.0+4	3.0+5		Data	EXFOR30233.011	Mar 73	NDS,RELATIVE TO IN,ABSOLUTE ERROR	
(n,γ)	3.0+4	1.5+6	AE	Expt Jour	JNE 27 71	Feb 73	Hellstroem. TOF. LIQ SCINT. REL AU	+
				Rept	AE- 443	Dec 71	Hellstrom+ SIG REL AU	
	3.0+4	1.8+5		Rept	AE- 441	Nov 71	- + SIG REL AU	
	3.0+4	1.5+6		Data	EXFOR20194.	May 74	28PTS.SIGMA.	
(n,γ)	1.5+3	1.0+5	RPI	Expt Prog	COO-3058-34 7	Mar 73	Byoun+SELF INDIC RATIO VS E GRPH.	+
				Conf	71Knoxvill 895	Mar 71	- +TRNS,SELF INDIC.NDG	
	2.0+2	1.0+5		Data	EXFOR10577.	Nov 76	345PT.CS=-LOG(SELF-INDIC RATIO/SAMP)	
(n,γ)	2.5+4		AUW	Expt Jour	NC/A 18 48	Nov 73	Sidappa+ ACTIV SIG,CFD.TABLE	
(n,γ)	+3	3.0+4	JAE	Expt Prog	NEANDC(J)36L 4	Sep 74	Mizumoto+.LINAC,TOF.LIQ-SCINT.NDG	
(n,γ)	Maxwl		MUA	Theo Jour	NP/A 235 307	Dec 74	Alam+ STATMDL,CALC SIG REL PR,HF,W	
(n,γ)	Fast		INL	Expt Abst	BAP 20 173	Feb 75	Anderl+SIG FOR GD ST,M1 ST. 75WASH	
(n,γ)	1.4-2	2.0+1	WUR	Expt Conf	EIR-217	Apr 75	Widder. METAL SAMPLE	+
				Conf	74Petten 757	Sep 74	- . M-R DET,ABS.EXP.,NDG	
	1.4-2	2.0+1		Data	EXFOR20437.012	Nov 75	226PTS.SIGMA.	
(n,γ)	3.0+5	3.0+6	ANL	Expt Rept	ANL-NDM-15	Jun 75	Poenitz. TBL,GRPH CFD OPT MODEL CALC	+
	2.0+4	3.5+6		Conf	AERE-R-8082	Jul 75	-.ABSTR LIQ SCINT,REL AU	
	3.0+5	3.0+6		Data	EXFOR10401.003	Feb 76	. 14 PTS. SIGMA.	
(n,γ)	+0	+6	LRL	Expt Jour	NIM 133 35	Feb 76	Marion+ 3-XTL SPECTROMETER. YLD GIVN	
	1.0+0	1.0+2		Prog	UCID-16514 9	Jun 74	Stelts+ GRPH.	
(n,γ)	1.2+5	2.8+6	LRL	Expt Jour	NSE 59 381	Apr 76	Linder+REL U235NF.TBL,GRPHS.CFD ENDF	+
	1.2+5	2.7+6		Data	EXFOR10221.	Aug 75	. 31 PTS, SIGMA	
(n,γ)	None		RCN	Revw Rept	ECN-2	Sep 76	Zijp+ INTERCOMP. INTEGRAL SIG SAND-2	
(n,γ)	1.3+4	1.6+5	CAD	Expt Rept	CEA-R-4788	Nov 76	Le Rigoleur+ VDG,TOF,WEIGHTING METH	
				Conf	75Wash. 953	Mar 75	- + GRAPH CFD ENDF/B-4	
	1.3+4	1.6+5		Data	EXFOR20572.	Feb 76	226PTS.SIGMA.	
(n,γ)	1.5+4	6.5+4	CAD	Expt Rept	CEA-R-4788	Nov 76	Le Rigoleur+ VDG.TOF.WEIGHTING METH	
(n,γ)	1.5+7		IRK	Expt Priv	WAGNER	77	Wagner+	+
	1.4+7			Rept	INDC(SEC)-51	Oct 75	- + ABST PAGE 3	
	1.5+7			Data	EXFOR20718.	Jan 76	2PTS.SIGMA.	
Spect (n,γ)	Maxwl		CRC	Expt Jour	CJP 31 1025	Nov 53	Bartholomew+ PAIR SP,140KV LINEWIDTH	
Spect (n,γ)	Maxwl		CCP	Expt Jour	AE 4 22	Jan 58	Sklyarevskii+.EGS+INTENS BELOW .3MEV	
				Jour	JNE 9 69	Jun 59	TRANSLATN.*	
				Jour	SJA 4 19	58	TRANSLATN.*	
Spect (n,γ)	Maxwl		GEA	Eval Rept	DC-58-1-3	Jan 58	Deloume.BY APPROXIMATION TABLE	
Spect (n,γ)	Maxwl		KUR	Expt Conf	58Geneva 15 138	Sep 58	Groshev+ PPR2029.CURV,COMPTON-SPEC	
				Jour	AE 4 5	Jan 58	- + SPECTRUM+LINES 0.3-6.04MEV	
				Jour	JNE 9 50	Jun 59	. ENGL OF AE 4 5	
				Jour	SJA 4 1	58	. ENGL OF AE 4 5	
Spect (n,γ)	+0		KAP	Expt Prog	WASH-1006	Oct 58	Yeater. TOF CRYST SPEC NO DATA GIVEN	
Spect (n,γ)	Maxwl		YAL	Expt Jour	PR 114 268	Apr 59	Draper.SC SPECTR,GAM E 0 TO 600 KEV	
Spect (n,γ)	Maxwl		CCP	Expt Jour	JNE 9 50	Jun 59	TRANSLATN.*	
				Rept	AEC-TR-3515	58	SEE ALSO *	
				Jour	SJA 4 1	58	TRANSLATN.*	
Spect (n,γ)	3.0+4		ORL	Expt Conf	61Saclay 213	Jul 61	Firk+,TOF, GRPHS COUNTS/CHANNEL	
Spect (n,γ)	Maxwl		ARF	Expt Prog	ARF-1193-12	Jul 62	Greenwood+,CRYST SPEC,LOW-E GAMMAS	
Spect (n,γ)	Maxwl	3.0+5	FOA	ExTh Jour	NP 39 353	Dec 62	Bergqvist+.5 ES.GRAPH. CFD STAT THEO	
				Conf	61Saclay	61	- + SUPERSEDED	
Spect (n,γ)	Maxwl		CAS	Expt Jour	NC 27 1032	Feb 63	Giannini+ NA-I,E+INTENSITY TO270 KEV	+
Spect (n,γ)	4.8+0		JAE	Expt Rept	JAERI-1073	Mar 65	Kawarasaki. RES CAPT.LINAC.TOF.E,INT	+
				Rept	INDSWG-90 6	Jul 65	- . TABLE E,INTS GIVEN.	
	4.8+0			Data	EXFOR20277.019	Jun 74	4PTS.	
Spect (n,γ)	3.0+5	4.2+6	FOA	ExTh Jour	NP 67 321	May 65	Lundberg+ XPT CFD STAT THEORY	
				Rept	FOA4-A4382	64	- + SUPERSEDED.	
				Rept	ANL-6797 220	63	- + SUPERSEDED.	
Spect (n,γ)	None		ROS	Expt Rept	ZFK-PHA-20 38	Feb 66	Meiling+ LVL SCH OF W 182	
Spect (n,γ)	Pile		AE	Expt Jour	AF 35 51	Jan 68	Hoejeberg+. DECAY OF TA182M.TBL+GRPH	
Spect (n,γ)	1.0+5	1.5+6	FEI	Expt Conf	68Riga	Jan 68	Broder+ ABST,GE 100-511 KEV,GE-LI	
Spect (n,γ)	Pile		CCP	Expt Jour	IZV 32 307	Feb 68	Metskhvarishvili+ CONVERSN-EL-SPECS	
				Jour	BAS 32 281	69	TRANSLATN.*NO 2	
Spect (n,γ)	Maxwl		ANL	Expt Conf	JINR-D-3893	May 68	Burson. ABSTRACT,GAM+CONV E XPT,NDG	
Spect (n,γ)	Pile		ANL	Expt Conf	JINR-D-3893	May 68	Bollinger+ ABSTRACT,NO DATA GIVEN	
Spect (n,γ)	+0	+4	COL	Expt Prog	WASH-1124 31	Nov 68	Camarda+ MOXON-RAE DET TBC NO DATA	
Spect (n,γ)	Maxwl		UPP	Expt Jour	NP/A 120 561	Nov 68	Nilsson+.INT CONVERSION. PURE E2 TR.	

73 Tantalum 181

Quantity	Energy (ev) Min	Energy (ev) Max	Lab	Type	Documentation Ref Vol Page	Date	Author, Comments	Data
Spect (n,γ)	Maxwl		UPP Expt	Jour	NP/A 120 569	Nov 68	Hoegberg+ M INT CONVERSION. PURE E2.	
Spect (n,γ)	Maxwl		CCP Expt	Jour	IZV 32 1990	Dec 68	Alksnis+ TABLE OF CONVERSN-ELECTR-ES	
				Jour	BAS 32 1833	69	. ENGL OF IZV 32 1990	
Spect (n,γ)	2.5-2		MIT Comp	Rept	MITNE-85	Jan 69	Rasmussen+TBL G INT.=AFCRL-69-0071	
Spect (n,γ)	Maxwl		BNL Expt	Prog	WASH-1127 18	Apr 69	Chrien+ GROUND-STATE GAMMA E GIVEN	
Spect (n,γ)	Pile		ANL Expt	Conf	69Studsvik 601	Aug 69	Smither+ NO DATA GVN,OKS STATMOD	
Spect (n,γ)	Maxwl		KFI Revw	Jour	YF 10 907	Nov 69	Kecskemeti+ AVG GAM-MULTIPLICITY,TBL	
				Jour	SNP 10 524	May 70	TRANSLATN.*	
Spect (n,γ)	5.0+1	5.0+3	WWA Theo	Jour	CJP 47 2849	Dec 69	Brzosko+,COMPOUND NUCL CALC CFD EXPT	
Spect (n,γ)	Pile		CCP Expt	Jour	IZV 34 89	Jan 70	Burgov+ RES NS CAPTURE,LVL SCH,CURVS	
				Jour	BAS 34 85	Jan 70	*	
Spect (n,γ)	Maxwl		WAL Eval	Rept	WANL-TME-2713	Jul 70	Fody.GAM YLDS FOR WANL POINT LIBRARY	
Spect (n,γ)	Maxwl		MUN Expt	Prog	EANDC(OR)95L	Aug 70	Baader+ BENT CRYSTAL SPEC. (RISO)	
Spect (n,γ)	1.4+7		LAS Expt	Conf	71Knoxvill 266	Mar 71	Bergqvist+,NO DATA,ABSTRACT ONLY	
Spect (n,γ)	Maxwl	+2	ANL Expt	Prog	NCSAC-38 13	May 71	Erskine+. NO DATA GIVEN,TO BE COMPLT	
Spect (n,γ)	Pile		KFK Expt	Rept	KFK-1401	Jun 71	Djadali.AVG POLRZ G EXPT,CFD T,SPIN	
	Maxwl			Jour	NP/A 147 150	May 70	Eichler+ POL NS.CIRC POL GS+ASSYMTRY	
Spect (n,γ)	Maxwl		MTR Expt	Jour	NP/A 168 449	Jun 71	Helmer+ 74EG 3883-6063,49EG48-252KEV	
				Abst	ANS 12 927	Nov 69	Greenwood+.GRAPH 2KEV+THR NEUT E CFD	
				Conf	69Studsvik 607	Aug 69	- +.GRAPH 2KEV+THR NEUT E CFD	
Spect (n,γ)	2.0+3		MTR Expt	Jour	NP/A 168 449	Jun 71	Helmer+ GE(LI). 70EG 4619-6065 KEV.	
Spect (n,γ)	4.0+5		WWA Expt	Prog	APPB 2 489	Aug 71	Brzosko+ GAMMA-EN = 3 TO 7 MEV,GRAPH	
	+5	+7		Prog	INR-1197/I/PL	May 70	Brosko+ 3 TO 6.5MEV GAMMA E,SPECTRUM	
Spect (n,γ)	Maxwl	9.1+5	PUR ExTh	Jour	NSE 47 209	Feb 72	Yost+.CAPTURE GAMMA YLDS.TBLS+CURVS.	
			Expt	Abst	ANS 13 867	Nov 70	- +.TABL CAPT GAM YLDS 1-7 MEV	
				Prog	ORNL-4592 44	Sep 70	- +.CAPTURE GAMMA YLDS.TABLE.	
Spect (n,γ)	2.4+4		RPI Expt	Prog	COO-3058-20 16	Jun 72	Block+. CURVE PULSE-HEIGHT SPECTRA	
Spect (n,γ)	1.0+7		WWA Theo	Jour	NP/A 189 545	Jul 72	Brzosko+ CMPD NUCL DECAY.PARTIAL WG	
Spect (n,γ)	4.3+0	2.0+2	HAR Expt	Jour	NP/A 198 430	Dec 72	Axmann+LOW EN GAMMAS IN RES CAPTURE	
Spect (n,γ)	Maxwl		IFL Expt	Book	PROKOFJEV	73	. TBL GAM,CONV ELECTR ES+INT,LVL SCH	
Spect (n,γ)	+0	+2	IFB Theo	Conf	73Pacif.Gr 2 1071	Mar 73	Rudak+ GRAPH STATMOD-CALC CFD G-SPEC	
Spect (n,γ)	2.4+4		BNL Expt	Prog	USNDC-7 36	Jun 73	Wasson+. GE(LI) DET. NO DATA GIVEN	
Spect (n,γ)	Maxwl		CCP Theo	Jour	ZET 65 12	Jul 73	Nosov+ THERMODYN CALC CFD EXPT,GRAPH	
				Jour	JET 38 6	Jan 74	. ENGLISH OF ZET 65 6	
Spect (n,γ)	Maxwl		ROS Expt	Prog	ZFK-262 95	Sep 73	Andrejtscheff+ DELAYED GAMS,TBL,GRPH	
				Prog	ZFK-243 86	Sep 72	Seidel+ DELAY G-SPECT,GG-COINC,GRPHS	
Spect (n,γ)	1.4+7		NJS Expt	Priv	CVELBAR	Oct 73	.INTEGRAL EXPT,SCINT PAIR SPECTRMTR	+
	1.4+7			Data	EXFOR30185.017	Oct 73	PROMPT GAMMA-RAY SPECT,25 DATA LINES	
Spect (n,γ)	Pile		CAI Expt	Jour	ZP 265 313	Nov 73	Bashandy+,INT CONVERSION IN TA-182	
Spect (n,γ)	Maxwl		LVN Expt	Rept	RCN-203 57	Dec 73	Van Den Gruyce+ G RAYS 40 TO 1300KEV	
				Conf	73Munich 1 153	Aug 73	Van Den Cruyce+ ROTAT BANDS CONFIGUR	
Spect (n,γ)	1.0+3		BNL Expt	Prog	USNDC-11 47	Jun 74	Rimawi+LI6 FILTER USED, NDG.	
Spect (n,γ)	7.0+5	2.6+6	CRC Expt	Jour	CJP 52 989	Jun 74	Earle+ STRENGTH FUNCTS	
				Conf	72Budapest 262	Aug 72	Lone+ G-RAY INTENSITIES, NDG	
				Prog	AECL-4147 48	Feb 72	Earle+. 2ES. NO DATA GIVEN.	
	None			Prog	AECL-4068 80	Sep 71	Lone+. RESON CAPTURE. NO DATA GIVEN	
		3.0+6		Prog	AECL-3912 64	Mar 71	Bartholomew+.NAI DET.PRELIM. NO DATA	
Spect (n,γ)	1.0+6	1.0+7	CRC Revw	Conf	74Petten 119	Sep 74	Bartholomew+ PHOTON STRF GRPH	
Spect (n,γ)	Maxwl	Pile	SGA ExTh	Jour	APA 41 4 338	75	Korn+ SPEC SHAPE	
				Rept	SGAE-PH-174	Nov 74	- + SPEC SHAPE	
Spect (n,γ)	2.0+6	2.0+7	IRT Expt	Abst	BAP 20 141	Feb 75	Harris+TOF,75WASH,NDG	
Spect (n,γ)	Maxwl		LAS Eval	Conf	75Wash. 149	Mar 75	Young. GA MEAS CFD CALC	
Spect (n,γ)	None		LRL Theo	Prog	ERDA-NDC-2 73	May 75	Gardner.MDL.CALC.NDG.	
Spect (n,γ)	Maxwl		ATI ExTh	Conf	INDC(SEC)-51	Oct 75	Korn+ ABST ON PAGE 2 SHAPE G-SPECT	
Spect (n,γ)	Maxwl		IFL Expt	Conf	76Lowell 1439	Jul 76	Balodis+ LVL ES(PI=+1) CALC+EXPT,TBL	
Inelastic γ	3.2+6		NRL Expt	Jour	PR 96 386	Oct 54	Sherrer+ NAI(TL) DETECTOR.	+
	3.2+6			Data	EXFOR11672.013	Jun 76	. 2 PTS. INELASTIC GAMMAS.	
Inelastic γ	1.4+5	1.8+6	MIT Expt	Jour	PR 101 1516	Mar 56	Guernsey+,CS 137-KEV LEVEL CFD TH	+
				Abst	PR 98 1147	May 55	- + ABST A1 (SUPERSEDED)	
	2.7+5	1.8+6		Data	EXFOR11691.005	Jun 76	. 19 PTS, INELASTIC GAMMAS.	
Inelastic γ	2.6+6		LAS Expt	Jour	PR 102 767	Apr 56	Day.VALUES AT 4 GAMMA ES AT 95 DEG	+
				Conf	55Geneva 2 9	Aug 55	DAY.P581,ONLY TBL G-ES,RING GEOMETRY	
	2.6+6			Data	EXFOR11218.028	Jun 76	. 4 PTS, DSIGMA.	
Inelastic γ	3.0+6		FEI Expt	Jour	AE 9 403	Nov 60	Androsenko+ TABLE OF GAMMA-ENERGIES	
				Jour	SJA 9 945	Sep 61	. ENGL OF AE 9 403	
				Jour	KE 4 510	Jun 61	. GERMAN OF AE 9 403	
				Jour	KE 4 510	Jun 61	. GERMAN OF AE 9 403	

73 Tantalum 181

Quantity	Energy (ev) Min	Energy (ev) Max	Lab	Type	Documentation Ref Vol Page	Author, Comments Date	Data
Inelastic γ	2.0+5	3.5+6	CLU	Expt Jour	AP 12 485	Mar 61 Lind. SIG(94DEG) FOR 0.482MEV GAMMA	+
	4.4+5	1.6+6		Data	EXFOR11188.013	Jun 76 . 34 PTS, DSIGMA.	
Inelastic γ	3.0+6		RI	Expt Jour	ZET 42 349	Feb 62 Graudynya+.SPECT FROM .35 TO 3 MEV	
				Jour	JET 15 2 240	Aug 62 TRANSLATN.*	
Inelastic γ	5.5+6	7.5+6	ALD	Expt Jour	NP 63 526	Mar 65 PERKIN STARFELT CFD CALC SPECTRA	
Inelastic γ	5.8+6	7.5+6	FOA	Expt Jour	NP 80 198	May 66 Bergqvist+CFD SPEC IN CAPT.AT 0.1MEV	
				Conf	65Antwerp 505	Jul 65 - + ABST.NDG.PPR28	
Inelastic γ	1.0+6		TNC	Expt Prog	ORO - 2791 - 79	Aug 67 Morgan+ NAI(TL)+GE-LI NDG TBC	
Inelastic γ	5.0+6	7.0+6	ALD	Expt Jour	NP/A 112 337	May 68 Owens+.3ES.TOF SPECT 90 DEG. NDG.	+
Inelastic γ	None		FEI	Expt Jour	YFI - 7 4	Apr 69 Broder+ PRODUCTION SIG FOR 5 GAMMAS	
				Rept	INDC(CCP) - 7U5	Feb 70 TRANSLATN.*	
	1.7+5	2.9+6		Prog	YFI - 11 12	70 Broder+ ABST,GE - LI,GAM - SPECS(EN),NDG	
Inelastic γ	1.7+5	2.9+6	FEI	Expt Conf	70Helsinki 2 295	Jun 70 Broder+81. SIG FOR 0.1 - 0.5MEV GAMMAS	+
				Rept	FEI - 155	69 - + 5 LVLS, 39 ES, TABLE,GRAPH	
	5.1+5	2.9+6		Data	EXFOR40095.046	Sep 74 .PARTIAL CS FOR INL GAMMA PROD	
	1.7+5	1.5+6		Data	EXFOR40036.	Aug 70 SIGMA AT 30 EN FOR PROD OF 4 GAMMAS	
Inelastic γ	2.4+5	1.8+6	MIT	Expt Jour	NSE 45 297	Sep 71 Rogers+.GAM PROD SIGS+LVL EXCIT FNCT	+
	1.0+6	2.0+6		Conf	67Tokyo § 4.114	Sep 67 Beghian+ LI - GE,TIMEGATE.12LVLS+DECAY	
	2.4+5	1.8+6		Data	EXFOR10146.	Dec 72 . 94PTS, DSIGMA	
Inelastic γ	1.4+7		LAS	Eval Conf	75Wash. 149	Mar 75 Young.ORELA MEAS CFD ENDF AT 125 DEG	
Inelastic γ	1.0+5	2.0+7	LRL	Theo Conf	75Wash. 651	Mar 75 Gardner.CFD ORNL EXPT.GRPH.	
Inelastic γ	1.0+5	2.0+7	LRL	Theo Jour	NSE 57 1	May 75 Perkins+ GRPHS G - RAY PROD CFD EXPT	
Inelastic γ	None		ORL	Expt Prog	ERDA - NDC - 2 138	May 75 Dickens+LVL.STRUCT.NDG.	
Inelastic γ	2.5+6		FEI	Expt Rept	YK - 22 21	76 Bezotosnyj+ SIG(10EGAM - INTERVLS),TBL	
Inelastic γ	3.3+6		SBL	Expt Jour	NIM 134 545	76 Habbani+ 90 DEG TBL	+
	3.3+6			Data	EXFOR20667.022	Oct 76 1PNT.D/DA.	
Nonelastic γ		1.0+7	GEN	Eval Rept	GEMP - 360	Aug 65 Edwards. 15 - GROUP GAM PRODUCTN SIGS	
Nonelastic γ	1.4+7		KUR	Expt Conf	75Kiev 4 133	May 75 Bezotosnyj+ NA - I.SIG(.5 - .8MEV) GIVEN	
(n,2n)	1.5+7		CRC	Expt Jour	CJP 31 267	Feb 53 Paul+.BETA ACT.CFD TH. HL= 70M+8H	+
	1.5+7			Data	EXFOR11271.093	Jun 76 . 1 PT, SIGMA.	
(n,2n)	1.4+7		LAS	Expt Jour	PR 107 824	Aug 57 Rosen+ 1.8+ - 0.3B	+
	1.4+7			Data	EXFOR11223.004	Jun 76 . 1 PT, SIGMA.	
	1.4+7			Data	EXFOR11223.003	Jun 76 . 18 PTS. DSIG	
(n,2n)	1.4+7		LRL	Expt Jour	PR 111 616	Jul 58 Ashby+,SC 2.64+ - 0.20B	+
				Conf	58Geneva 15 3	Sep 58 Benveniste.PPR2494,VAL GVN,TOF	
	1.4+7			Data	EXFOR11097.021	Jun 76 . 1 PT (RENORMALIZED)	
(n,2n)	1.3+7	1.7+7	PCF	Expt Jour	NC 9 664	Aug 58 Remy+ NN AND N2N.TOF.N SPECTRA.	
	1.4+7			Jour	CR 246 1410	Mar 58 - +TOF+NSPECT+RESD GROUPS 1+1.3ME	
(n,2n)	1.5+7		ARK	Expt Jour	JIN 13 196	Jun 60 Poularikas. ACTIVATION	+
	1.5+7			Data	EXFOR11957.004	Jun 76 . 1 PT SIGMA	
(n,2n)	Fiss		CRC	Eval Rept	CRC - 1003	Dec 60 Roy+,ESTIMATED AVG SIG = 6.5MB	
(n,2n)	1.4+7	2.0+7	LAS	Expt Jour	PR 121 1438	Mar 61 Prestwood+ SUMMARY OF DATA	+
				Rept	LA - 2493	Dec 60 Bayhurst+,ACT EXCITATION CURVE	
	1.4+7	2.0+7		Data	EXFOR11645.024	Jun 76 . 8 PTS, SIGMA.	
(n,2n)	1.4+7		HAM	Comp Jour	NP 65 257	Mar 65 Bormann. 5EXPT VALS.CFD SHELL EFFECT	
(n,2n)	1.3+7	1.5+7	DEB	Expt Conf	65Antwerp § 102	Jul 65 Csikai.ACTIV,EXC FUNC,REL VALUES,GRV	+
				Jour	MFF 16 123	Feb 66 - .THESIS,IN HUNGARIAN,EXPT,GRPH	
				Jour	AK 8 79	66 - . THESIS ABSTR(ENGLISH),GRAPH	
	1.3+7	1.5+7		Data	EXFOR30032.009	Nov 70 REL VAL'S EXCIT FUNC,PRIV COM CSIKAI	
(n,2n)	1.3+7	1.5+7	BNL	Theo Jour	NSE 23 238	Nov 65 Pearlstein.3ES.STAT MDL CALC.TBL CS.	
(n,2n)	Fiss		BNL	Theo Jour	NSE 23 238	Nov 65 Pearlstein.STATMDL CALC.SPEC AVG.TBL	
(n,2n)	1.2+7	1.8+7	IBJ	Expt Rept	INR - 795	Jun 67 Brzosko+ SIG(E) TO ISOM CFD TH,TABLE	+
				Jour	NP/A 123 603	Jan 69 * SIG(E) CFD TH,GRAPH	
				Rept	JINR - D3893	Jul 68 *PAGE 131,SIG(E) CFD TH	
	1.2+7	1.8+7		Data	EXFOR30110.	Apr 72 SIGMA TO ISOM STATE, 23 DATA LINES	
(n,2n)	1.3+7	1.5+7	MUN	Expt Conf	68Wash. 2 885	Mar 68 Vonach+ ACT EXCITATION FUNCTION	+
	1.3+7	1.5+7		Data	EXFOR20815.023	Oct 78 11PTS.RELATIVE SIGMA.	
(n,2n)	1.3+7	1.8+7	HAM	Expt Jour	NP/A 115 309	Jul 68 Bormann+VDG.TO META.CFD STAT+OPTMDL	
	1.5+7		TUR	Theo Jour	NC 56 18 201	Jul 68 Minetti+THEOR ISOM RATIO SPIN CO PAR	
(n,2n)	7.7+6	2.0+7	CRC	Expt Prog	EANDC(CAN) - 40	Sep 69 Santry+ EXCIT CRVS MEASURD,TBC,NDG.	
(n,2n)	8.0+6	2.0+7	AUA	Theo Rept	AAEC/TM - 522	Nov 69 Bertram. CALC SIG(E)GRAPHS CFD EXPTS	
(n,2n)	1.5+7		DEB	Comp Jour	REA 7 4 93	Dec 69 Csikai+ SIG+HL COMPILTN,N - ACTIV - ANAL	
(n,2n)	1.4+7	1.5+7	JYV	Eval Rept	JU - RR - 3/1970	Jun 70 Leppaemaeki+ TABLE OF EVAL AVG SIG	
(n,2n)	+7		KFI	Theo Rept	KFKI - 71 - 8	Feb 71 Jeki. CALCULATED CFD EXPTL SIG VALUE	
(n,2n)	1.4+7	1.5+7	IRK	ExTh Jour	APA 33 285	Jul 71 Winiwarter+ ISOMERIC RATIO	
(n,2n)	1.4+7		KFI	Theo Rept	KFKI - 72 - 17	Feb 72 Kluge+ CALC N - SPEC INEL+N2N,TBL,GRPH	
(n,2n)	1.4+7		HAM	Expt Jour	AKE 19 107	Apr 72 Mogharrab+ACT EXPT,SIG REL AL27(N,A)	

73 Tantalum 181

Quantity	Energy (ev) Min	Max	Lab	Type	Documentation Ref Vol Page	Author, Comments Date	Data
(n,2n)	1.5+7		DEB	Eval	Jour REA 11 1 153	Mar 73 Boedy. COMPILATION+RECOMM.VALUE,TBL	
					Rept IAEA-153 173	73 - . RECOMM. VALUE ONLY	
(n,2n)	7.6+6	1.5+7	UK	Eval	Data UKNDL-DFN 328B	Mar 73 .14 PTS.E DIST.ANG DIST.	
(n,2n)	1.4+7		LOU	Expt	Prog INR-1464 12	May 73 Araminowicz+BRIEF,ACTIV,TABLE,GRAPH	+
	1.4+7				Data EXFOR30264.041	Nov 73 SIGMA AT 14.6 MEV	
(n,2n)	7.0+6	2.0+7	IFL	Eval	Rept YK-15 63	Aug 73 Bondars+ SHORT. GRAPH OF EVAL DATA	
(n,2n)	1.4+7		AUW	Expt	Conf 75Calcutta 2 31	Dec 75 Lakshmandas+1096+ - 88 MB ACTIVATION	
(n,2n)	8.4+6	1.5+7	BRC	Expt	Jour NIM 135 511	Jun 76 Frehaut.GD LOADED SCIN.EXPT DETAILS.	+
					Conf 75Kiev 4 303	May 75 - + LIQSCIN.SIG(E),CFD.GRPH+TBL	
					Conf 75Wash. 855	Mar 75 - + TBL.GRPH.REL 238U(N,F)	
					Rept CEA-R-4627	Nov 74 - + LARGE LIQ SCINT METH10 VAL	
	8.4+6	1.5+7			Data EXFOR20416.016	Jul 75 14PTS.SIGMA.	
(n,2n)	Thrsh	1.5+7	BRC	Expt	Conf 76Lowell 1350	Jul 76 Cindro+EXCIT FN CALC.CFD EXPT.NDG.	
(n,2n)	8.0+6	2.4+7	LAS	Theo	Prog LA-6560 2	Nov 76 Arthur+CALC CFD EXPT.CURVS.	
(n,xn) x>2	Fiss		BNL	Theo	Jour NSE 23 238	Nov 65 Pearlstein.SPEC AVG STATMDL CALC N3N	
(n,xn) x>2	1.4+7	1.5+7	LRL	Eval	Jour ND/A 11 796	Jul 73 Alley+ (N,3N) CURVE BEST ESTIMATE	
(n,xn) x>2	8.0+6	2.4+7	LAS	Theo	Prog LA-6560 2	Nov 76 Arthur+CALC CFD EXPT.CURVS.	
n Emission	1.4+7		LAS	Expt	Jour PR 107 824	Aug 57 Rosen+ SIGMA GVN	+
					Conf 58Geneva 15 11	Sep 58 Coon+.PPR666,VAL GVN,EXPT DESCRIBED	
	1.4+7				Data EXFOR11223.003	Jun 76 . 18 PTS, DSIGMA	
n Emission	1.4+7		TUD	Theo	Prog ZFK-262 25	Sep 73 Hermsdorf+ CALC N-SPEC CFD EXPT,NDG	
n Emission	1.4+7		FEI	Expt	Jour YF 20 852	Nov 74 Sal'Nikov+ TOF,TBL DOUBLDIFF+INTEGRL	+
					Jour SNP 20 454	May 75 . ENGLISH OF YF 20 852	
	5.0+5	1.4+7			Data EXFOR40333.	Feb 76 .DATA IN MB/SR AT 5EN RANGES+4 ANGLS	
n Emission	1.5+7		TUD	Expt	Jour KE 19 241	Aug 76 Hermsdorf+ ABSOL DOUBDIF,FIG.TOT,TBL	+
					Rept ZFK-277(U)	Aug 75 - + DIFFSIG AT 5ANGS,TBL+GRPH	
	1.5+7				Data EXFOR30397.027	May 77 49 PTS. ANGLE INT.N-EMISS.SPECT.	
	1.5+7				Data EXFOR30275.	Apr 74 DOUBLDIF(5ANG,499PTS)+PARTIAL ANGDIS	
(n,p)	1.4+7		CIS	Expt	Jour NC 7 400	Feb 58 Colli+ P-SPECT.	+
(n,p)	1.4+7		LRL	Expt	Prog WASH-1127 96	Apr 69 Lindner. REVISED WASH-1018 VALUE	+
					Prog WASH-1018 63	Mar 59 - +. ACTIVATION.ALSO EUR 122E	
	1.4+7				Data EXFOR12185.002	Jun 76 . 1 PT, SIGMA.	
(n,p)	Fiss		CRC	Eval	Rept CRC-1003	Dec 60 Roy+,ESTIMATED AVG SIG=0.008MB	
(n,p)	1.4+7		SAH	Expt	Conf 63Bombay 244	Feb 63 Mukherjee+.VAL GVN,ACTIVATION METHOD	+
	1.4+7				Data EXFOR31330.009	Sep 72 .SIG GVN	
(n,p)	1.4+7	1.5+7	SAH	Comp	Jour NUC 23 8 112	Aug 65 Chatterjee. TABLE WITH REFS.	
	1.4+7				Jour NP 60 273	Nov 64 - .MEAN OF EXPT CFD SHELLMOD	
(n,p)	1.3+7	1.8+7	WWA	Expt	Conf JINR-D3893 131	May 68 Brzosko+ SIG(E) GRAPH CFD COMP-MODEL	+
	1.3+7	1.8+7			Data EXFOR30017.002	Jul 70 SIGMA AT 10 ES.	
(n,p)	1.5+7		DEB	Comp	Jour REA 7 4 93	Dec 69 Csikai+ SIG+HL COMPILTN,N-ACTIV-ANAL	
(n,p)	1.4+7	1.5+7	JYV	Eval	Rept JU-RR-3/1970	Jun 70 Leppaemaeki+ TABLE OF EVAL AVG SIG	
(n,p)	1.4+7		CIS	Theo	Jour PR/C 6 1398	Oct 72 Braga-Marcazzan+. PRE-EQUILIBR MODEL	
(n,p)	1.4+7	1.5+7	KAZ	Theo	Jour YF 18 705	Oct 73 Levkovsky.AVERAGED SIG,CALC,TBL	
					Jour SNP 18 361	Apr 74 . ENGLISH OF YF 18,705	
(n,p)	Fiss		GHT	Expt	Jour RCA 19 3 102	Dec 73 Regge+ MEAN FISS NEUT XSECT	
(n,p)	1.4+7		TUD	Theo	Conf ZFK-271 80	Feb 74 Herrmann+ CALC P-E-SPEC CFD EXP,GRPH	
					Conf ZFK-271 63	Nov 73 Seeliger+ P-EMISSION SPEC,TH CFD XPT	
(n,t)	2.3+7		JUL	Expt	Jour JIN 36 3639	Dec 74 Qaim+ (NT)+(NNT), 4.5+-0.7 MB	+
	2.3+7				Data EXFOR20524.011	Apr 76 1PNT§+NNT	
(n,nt)	2.3+7		JUL	Expt	Jour JIN 36 3639	Dec 74 Qaim+ (NT)+(NNT), 4.5+-0.7 MB	+
	2.3+7				Data EXFOR20524.011	Apr 76 1PNT.+NT.	
(n,He3)	1.5+7		ARK	Expt	Prog ORO-3235-11	Jul 70 Bari.TO BE COMPLETED,NO DATA GIVEN	
(n,He3)	1.5+7		JUL	Expt	Jour JIN 36 2 239	Feb 74 Qaim. ACTIVATION	+
					Jour JRC 21 395	74 - + CHEM SEPAR,SIG VS Z SYSTEMATI	
	1.5+7				Data EXFOR20523.008	Apr 76 1PNT.SIGMA.	
(n,α)	+5	+7	KJL	Expt	Conf 57Paris 1 48	Sep 57 Samsahl.SAELAN. EXPTL VALUE OF 1954	
(n,α)	Fiss		GES	Revw	Jour NUC 17 1 54	Jan 59 Rochlin.47 ISOTOPES.ACT.RVS.TBL	
(n,α)	Fiss		CRC	Eval	Rept CRC-1003	Dec 60 Roy+,ESTIMATED AVG SIG=0.0001MB	
(n,α)	Pile		CRC	Expt	Jour CJP 39 381	Mar 61 Glentworth+19MIN LU178 PRODUCED	
(n,α)	1.4+7		SAH	Expt	Conf 63Bombay 244	Feb 63 Mukherjee+.VAL GVN,ACTIVATION METHOD	+
	1.4+7				Data EXFOR31330.008	Sep 72 .SIG GVN	
(n,α)	1.5+7		CIS	Expt	Jour NP 46 51	Jul 63 Marcazzan+.DIFF.SIG-AT 30DEG MEASURE	+
					Jour PL 1 6	Apr 62 SUPERSEDED*SIG FWD VS BACK	
(n,α)	1.4+7		IBJ	Expt	Jour NP 66 361	May 65 Osakiewicz+ RELATED TO NUCL SURFACE	
(n,α)	1.4+7		FRK	Expt	Conf 65Antwerp 542	Jul 65 Breuer+. SPECTRUM +ANG.DISTR. EMULS	
(n,α)	1.5+7		DEB	Expt	Jour AK 8 79	Jun 66 Csikai.RATIO FORWARD/BACKWARD RECOIL	
(n,α)	1.5+7		ARK	Expt	Jour RCA 6 26	Aug 66 Meason+.SIG FOR 16MIN + 30MIN 178LU	

73 Tantalum 181

Quantity	Energy (ev) Min	Max	Lab	Type	Documentation Ref Vol Page	Date	Author, Comments	Data
(n,α)	1.2+7	2.3+7	FRK	Expt Jour	NP 85 606	Sep 66	Rubbino+ZUBKE ANGLE+ENERGY SPECTRA	
				Abst	BSI 46 43	Nov 65	- +(2B5).E SPEC,ANGDST ANAL.NDG	
(n,α)	1.5+7		DEB	Comp Jour	REA 7 4 93	Dec 69	Csikai+ SIG+HL COMPILTN,N-ACTIV-ANAL	
(n,α)	1.4+7	1.5+7	JYV	Eval Rept	JU-RR-3/1970	Jun 70	Leppaemaeki+ TABLE OF EVAL AVG SIG	
(n,α)	1.4+7		TIT	Expt Jour	NP/A 149 513	Jul 70	Kitazawa. S SPEC 0 DEG+SIGMA+ANDISTR	+
	1.5+7			Data	EXFOR20336.006	Jul 74	13PTS.D/DA.DE.	
(n,α)	1.4+7	1.5+7	CIS	Theo Jour	NP/A 210 297	Aug 73	Milazzo-Colli+ ALPHA E-DISTN CFD XPT	
	1.4+7			Jour	PL/B 38 155	Feb 72	Colli-Milazzo+ A-SPECT CALC CFD EXPT	
(n,α)	1.4+7		TUD	Theo Conf	ZFK-271 63	Nov 73	Seeliger+ A-EMISSION SPEC, NDG	
(n,α)	Maxwl		MUA	ExTh Jour	NP/A 235 307	Dec 74	Alam+ TO META+GND,CALC DIFFSIG GRAPH	
(n,α)	1.4+7		AUW	Expt Conf	75Calcutta 2 31	Dec 75	Lakshmandas+1.8+-0.3 MB ACTIVATION	
Reson Params	4.1+0	3.0+2	COL	Expt Jour	PR 71 165	Feb 47	Havens+TOF TRNSM STRGTH FOR 5 RES	+
	4.1+0	3.0+3		Data	EXFOR12184.004	Jun 76	. 7RES E0 AND WT**2/PCS	
Reson Params	6.1+0	3.8+1	COL	Expt Jour	PR 92 702	Nov 53	Melkonian+WT,WN,SIG FROM AREA METHOD	+
	6.1+0	3.8+1		Data	EXFOR11670.009	Jun 76	. 7RES E0 AND WT**2/PCS	
Reson Params	4.3+0	3.9+1	BNL	Expt Jour	PR 92 1509	Dec 53	Christensen.7RESON WN+SIG+STRENGTH	+
	4.3+0	3.9+1		Data	EXFOR12169.003	Jun 76	. 7 RES EO, PCS,WT**2/PCS	
Reson Params	1.0+1	3.9+1	KAP	Expt Rept	KAPL-1084	54	Gaerttner. LEVEL PARAMETERS	+
	1.0+1	3.9+1		Data	EXFOR11659.010	Jun 76	. 7 RES E0 AND WG**2/PCS	
Reson Params	1.0+1	1.3+2	BNL	Expt Jour	PR 99 10	Jul 55	Harvey+.FC TRANSM. 19 RES. AREA ANAL	+
				Abst	PR 99 611	Jul 55	Pilcher+ ABST B8	
	1.0+1	1.3+2		Data	EXFOR11912.061	Jun 76	. 19 RES E0, WN, AND WN0.	
Reson Params	1.4+1	1.5+2	MTR	Expt Jour	PR 103 1778	Sep 56	Fluharty+ TRNS+FC 23RES ES WN WG	+
				Abst	PR 99 610	Jul 55	Simpson+ ABST B5(SUPERSEDED)	
	1.4+1	1.5+2		Data	EXFOR11946.010	Jun 76	. 23 RES E0, WN, WN0, WG, AND PCS.	
Reson Params	1.0+0		AMS	Expt Jour	PHY 22 1131	Nov 56	Radkevich+GAMMA N,G.DIST NOT EXPONTL	
Reson Params	1.0+1	2.8+2	CCP	Expt Jour	AE 1 5 55	Nov 56	Radkevich+. 24 RES, WG, WN. D PLOT	+
				Jour	JNE 5 92	Jul 57	TRANSLATN.*	
				Jour	SJA 1 5 727	56	TRANSLATN.*	
Reson Params	4.3+0		BNL	Expt Jour	PR 104 1425	Dec 56	Wood.WT=.053 WN=.0039 WG=.049EV J=4	+
	4.3+0			Data	EXFOR11947.004	Jun 76	. 1 RES. E0,WT,WN,WG, AND PCS	
Reson Params	3.0+1	4.0+1	CCP	Expt Jour	AE 5 69	Jul 58	Vladimirskii+ 35EV RES NOT DOUBLET	
				Jour	JNEA 10 64	Jul 59	TRANSLATN.*	
				Jour	SJA 5 883	58	TRANSLATN.*	
Reson Params	2.0+1	1.0+2	HAR	Expt Jour	NP 9 198	Dec 58	Firk.TOF 20RES D=8+-2EV	+
Reson Params	4.3+0	6.3+1	HAR	Expt Jour	NP 9 205	Dec 58	Evans+TOF WG AND WN GIVEN	+
Reson Params	4.2+0	3.3+2	COL	Expt Jour	PR 120 2214	Dec 60	Desjardins+ TOF, 62 RESONANCES	+
	7.7+1	3.3+2		Data	EXFOR11948.008	Jun 76	. 62 RES E0, WN, WN0, AND WG	
Reson Params	-		FOA	ExTh Jour	NP 39 353	Dec 62	Bergqvist+.AVERAGE GAMMA WIDTH.EXPTH	
Reson Params	4.3+0		TRM	Expt Prog	AEET-267 4	Aug 66	Chandramoleswar+TABLE WN,WT, CFD BNL	+
	4.3+0			Data	EXFOR30408.005	Aug 77	N-,TOT-WIDTHS, PEAK SIG.	
Reson Params	4.3+0	1.0+1	NRL	Expt Jour	PR 155 1330	Mar 67	Stolovy. 2RES J=4,3. TRNS POLARZD NS	+
	4.3+0	1.0+1		Data	EXFOR11995.003	Jun 76	. 2 RES E0 AND J	
Reson Params	2.4+1		MOL	Expt Jour	NP/A 97 657	May 67	Poortmans+ FROM RESON SCATTERING XPT	+
	2.4+1			Data	EXFOR20213.	May 74	2PTS.J,WN/WT.	
Reson Params		1.0+6	AUA	Theo Jour	AUJ 20 477	Oct 67	Cook.TBL OF AVG LVL SPACING D,L=0,1	
Reson Params	+0	+2	ANL	Expt Prog	WASH-1124 8	Nov 68	Jackson+ WN+PARTIAL WG CORRELATN NDG	
Reson Params	+3	+5	AUA	ExTh Rept	AAEC/E-198	May 69	Musgrove.RES PARS+STF FROM (NG)FIT	+
Reson Params	-1	3.5+2	BNL	Expt Jour	NP/A 132 161	Jul 69	Wasson+ FAST CHOP GE(LI) EG 4.7MEVUP	
Reson Params	None		BNL	Comp Conf	69Studsvik 627	Aug 69	Chrien. WG/WN-CORREL,WG CFD P-T,TBLS	
Reson Params	None		ANL	Expt Prog	WASH-1136 11	Sep 69	Poenitz+ J FROM OCCUPATN PROB RATIOS	
Reson Params	2.0+5		MUA	Theo Conf	69Roorke 2 129	Dec 69	Chaubey+ D/GAM-WIDTH RATIO, STATMOD	
Reson Params	-		AUA	Theo Rept	AAEC/E-211	Nov 70	Musgrove. CALCULTD D+GAM WIDTH GIVEN	
Reson Params	4.3+0	2.2+2	CJD	Eval Rept	YK-7	71	Zakharova+ SURVEY+SYSTEMATICS,GW,TBL	
				Rept	INDC(CCP)-27	Nov 72	.ENGLISH TRANSLATION OF YK-7 /71	
Reson Params	None		DUB	Theo Jour	YF 13 240	Feb 71	Malecki+G-WID,THEO CFD EXPT.TBL,GRPH	
				Jour	SNP 13 133	Aug 71	- + ENGL OF YF 13 240.	
Reson Params	1.0+3	1.0+6	GA	Expt Conf	71Knoxvill 252	Mar 71	Fricke+,AVG WG AND D GIVEN	
Reson Params	+3	+5	AUA	Expt Prog	AAEC/PR-36P 11	Mar 72	Allen+ ORELA.DATA TO BE ANALYZED,NDG	
Reson Params	4.3+0	9.9+1	HAR	Expt Prog	AERE-PR/NP18	Mar 72	Thomas+ J ASSIGNED FROM CAPT GS.TBL	+
	4.3+0	9.9+1		Data	EXFOR20451.005	Jan 76	20PTS.J.	
Reson Params	4.3+0	2.0+2	HAR	Expt Jour	NP/A 198 430	Dec 72	Riehs+. LINAC. GE(LI)	+
	4.3+0	2.0+2		Data	EXFOR20473.002	Jan 76	25PTS.J.	
Reson Params	1.0+4	1.0+5	RPI	Expt Conf	COO-3058-34 7	Mar 73	Byoun+D,WG.TBL.FROM TRNS,SELF INDIC.	+
				Conf	71Knoxvill 895	Mar 71	- +WN0,WG,D.TBL.TBC	
	1.0+4	1.0+5		Data	EXFOR10577.040	Nov 76	. 4PTS D,WG GVN FOR S AND P WAVE	
Reson Params	4.0-1	2.5+4	WIN	Eval Prog	EANDC(UK) 151	Aug 73	James+ GENEX EVAL BASED ON ENDF/B	
Reson Params	4.3+0	1.0+2	CCP	Expt Conf	75Kiev	May 75	Kalebin+ RESONANCE NEUT-S,STF,LVLWID	

73 Tantalum 181

Quantity	Energy (ev) Min	Energy (ev) Max	Lab	Type	Documentation Ref Vol Page	Date	Author, Comments	Data
Reson Params	4.3+0	6.3+1	NIR	Expt Jour	AE 38 430	Jun 75	Belanova+ TOF,PARAM OF RES,TBL	+
	4.2+0	6.3+1		Conf	75Kiev 3 205	May 75	- + BY TOTSIG.N,TOT WIDS,TABLE	
	4.3+0	6.3+1		Jour	SJA 38 553	Dec 75	. ENGL OF AE 38 430	
	4.3+0	6.3+1		Data	EXFOR40430.	Jan 76	G*WN, TOT PK CS, WG	
Strnth Fnctn	1.7+1	5.2+1	MTR	Expt Jour	PR 103 1778	Sep 56	Fluharty+ TRNS+FC STF=1.70+-0.30	
Strnth Fnctn	3.0+0	5.0+2	AMS	Expt Jour	PHY 22 1131	Nov 56	Radkevich+ABSTRACT,NDG	
Strnth Fnctn	1.0+1	6.3+1	CCP	Expt Jour	AE 1 5 55	Nov 56	Radkevich+. S0=2.17+-0.22	
				Jour	JNE 5 92	Jul 57	TRANSLATN.*	
				Jour	SJA 1 5 727		56 TRANSLATN.*	
Strnth Fnctn	+4		HAR	Expt Jour	PPSA 70 51	Jan 57	Gayther+ FROM AVG SIGTOT. FC TRANSM	
Strnth Fnctn	2.0+1	1.0+3	MTR	Expt Abst	BAP 3 176	May 58	Simpson+ FAST CHOPPER STF=2.00+-0.24	
Strnth Fnctn	+3		BNL	Expt Jour	PRL 1 461	Dec 58	Hughes. FC 1.9+-0.2	
Strnth Fnctn	None		COL	Expt Jour	PR 120 2214	Dec 60	Havens.TOF 1.84	
	4.3+1	3.3+2		Rept	CU- 189	May 59	Desjardins. TOF. 1.9+-0.3	
Strnth Fnctn	1.0+4	2.0+5	ORL	Expt Jour	PR 122 182	Apr 61	Gibbons+ TOF LIQUID SCINTILLATOR	+
	1.0+4	2.0+5		Data	EXFOR11329.	Jun 76	. 1 PT, STF,D,AVE WG	
Strnth Fnctn	+3	+5	BOL	Theo Conf	61Vienna 1 179	Aug 61	Benzi+.PPR11,TABLE CFD EXPERIMENT	
Strnth Fnctn		6.0+4	LEB	Expt Jour	ZET 46 80	Jan 64	Konks.PB - SLOW - DOWN,VALUE GIVEN	
				Jour	JET 19 59	Jul 64	TRANSLATN.*	
Strnth Fnctn	3.0+3	6.5+5	DKE	ExTh Jour	PL 13 70	Nov 64	Seth+S,P,D STF FRM SIG TOT 3-650KEV	+
	5.0+4	1.5+5		Expt Conf	64Paris 2 916	Jul 64	- +S0,S1,S2 R PRIME/R DUKE U.	
	3.0+3	6.5+5		Data	EXFOR11665.026	Jun 76	. 3 PTS, STF.	
Strnth Fnctn	+6		FOA	Theo Jour	NP 67 321	May 65	Lundberg+ RED GAMMA RAY STF CALC	
Strnth Fnctn	None		DKE	Expt Abst	DA/B 28 3834	Mar 68	Divadeenam.S,P,D WAVES.CFD POT MDLS.	
Strnth Fnctn	+3	+5	AUA	ExTh Rept	AAEC/E-198	May 69	Musgrove.S+P+D STF FROM (NG)FIT,TBL	+
Strnth Fnctn	1.0+4	1.5+5	KFK	Expt Jour	NP/A 133 513	Aug 69	Kompe. S1,S2,S(GAMMA)LEAST SQ NG FIT	+
				Rept	KFK-1071	Aug 69	- . REPRINT OF NP/A 133 513	
	1.0+4	1.5+5		Data	EXFOR20358.	Sep 74	3PTS.GAMMA STF.	
Strnth Fnctn	-		AUA	Theo Rept	AAEC/E-211	Nov 70	Musgrove. SMOOTHED S0,S1 AND S2 GIVN	
Strnth Fnctn	1.0+3	1.0+6	GA	Expt Conf	71Knoxvill 252	Mar 71	Fricke+, S0 AND S1 GIVEN	
Strnth Fnctn	2.4+4		MUA	Theo Jour	IJP 46 114	Mar 72	Chaubey+ P-WAVE.FOR A-SYSTEMTIC,GRPH	
Strnth Fnctn	None		AUA	Eval Rept	AAEC/E-277	Mar 73	Musgrove.TBLS EXPTL DATA+BEST VALUES	
Strnth Fnctn	1.0+4	1.0+5	RPI	Expt Prog	COO-3058-34 7	Mar 73	Byoun+S0,S1 TBL.CFD PREVIOUS MEAS.	+
	1.0+4	1.0+5		Data	EXFOR10577.040	Nov 76	2PT.S0=(1.6+.3-.2)-4S1=(.4+.3-.2)-4	
Strnth Fnctn	5.0+3	8.0+4	FEI	Expt Jour	YK- 19 57	May 75	Shorin+ RADIAT+P-NEUT STRENGTH FUNCT	
Strnth Fnctn	2.7+3		MUN	Expt Conf	71Albany 327	Aug 76	Dilg+TRNS.S0 STF GVN.31 ELEMENT GRPH	
Lvl Density	-		COP	Theo Jour	NP 6 62	Mar 58	Ericson. LVL DENSITY FORM CFD EXP	
Lvl Density	2.4+6	7.0+6	RIC	Expt Rept	SCR-466	Feb 62	Ewing+,PARAM A FROM INELASTIC,3 ES	
Lvl Density	7.0+6		ISL	Theo Conf	64Geneva § 511	May 64	Szwarcbaum+.T FROM 3 FORMLS CFD EXPS	
Lvl Density	1.4+7		FEI	Theo Conf	64Paris 2 762	Jul 64	Malushev+.THERMOD T VERSUS XPT+FMGAS	
Lvl Density	1.4+7		FEI	Expt Rept	FEI-30	Dec 65	Anufrienko+.PARAMS FROM NONELASTIC	+
Lvl Density	-		FEI	Eval Rept	FEI-36		66 Kapchigashev+.TBL OF RELATD QUANTTYS	+
		5.0+4		Jour	YF 4 686	Sep 66	.TABLE.SHORT VERSION OF FEI-36	
	-			Prog	YFI-3 3		66 .ABSTRACT.TABLE LDL+LVL.EXCIT.E	
		5.0+4		Jour	SNP 4 486		67 .ENGLISH OF YF 4.FROM(N,GAMMA).TABLE	
				Prog	INDC-E-140 3		66 .ENGLISH TRANSL OF YFI-3	
Lvl Density	-		JAE	ExTh Jour	NP 78 369	Apr 66	Tsukada+ FOR 2-8MEV EXCIT E TEMPS+A	+
	3.6+6	8.5+6		Expt Jour	NP/A 131 145	Jun 69	Maruyama. E DEPENDENCE,PARAM,TH FIT	
	-			ExTh Conf	67Tokyo 373	Sep 67	- + PPR8.127. ABST	
Lvl Density	None		LRL	Expt Jour	NP/A 93 648	Mar 67	Chodil+ P,N+P,2N GIVES SMALL A=A/25	
Lvl Density	5.0+6	7.0+6	ALD	Expt Jour	NP/A 112 337	May 68	Owens+.LVL DENS VERSUS EXCIT.MEAN T	+
				Conf	65Antwerp 547	Jul 65	- + PPR122.ABST	
Lvl Density	+6	+7	AUA	Theo Rept	AAEC/TM-522	Nov 69	Bertram. FORMULAE+PARS IN(N,2N)-ANAL	
Lvl Density	1.4+7		BAS	Expt Jour	HPA 43 559	Nov 70	Sobottka+ LVL DENS,NUCL TEMP,TOF	
Lvl Density	1.5+6	1.4+7	TUD	Expt Prog	ZFK-243 25	Sep 72	Hermsdorf+ T+LVD DENS PARAM,TBL+GRPH	
Lvl Density	None		COP	Theo Jour	NP/A 222 493	Apr 74	Dossing+COLL ROTAT.SPAC. ACCUR ESTIM	
Lvl Density	None		DUB	Theo Rept	JINR-P4-8102	Jul 74	Malov+ SEMI-MICROSC CALC OKS XPT,TBL	
				Jour	NP/A 224 396	May 74	- + 1/2 MICROSC.MODEL. DEFORM NUC	
				Rept	UCRL-TR-10845	Apr 75	. ENGL OF JINR-P4-8102	
Lvl Density	2.0+6	4.5+6	AE	Expt Jour	AE- 503	Apr 75	Almen Ramstrom+ NUCL TEMP,LVL DENSTY	+
	2.0+6	4.5+6		Data	EXFOR20788.	Dec 78	4PTS.NUCL TEMP,4PTS.DENSITY.	
(γ,n)	+7		BSP	Revw Conf	55Geneva 2 169	Aug 55	Souza-Santos+.P897,THRESHOLD VAL GVN	
(γ,n)	8.0+6	3.0+7	SAC	Expt Jour	NP/A 121 463	Dec 68	Bergere+LORENTZ LINE PARAM,GRPHS,TBL	
(γ,n)	7.0+6	3.0+7	MOS	Expt Jour	ZEP 10 80	Jul 69	Ishkhakov+ GRPHS SIG(GAM-E) CFD TH	
				Jour	JEL 10 51	Jul 69	. ENGL OF ZEP 10 80	

73 Tantalum 182

Quantity	Energy (ev) Min	Max	Lab	Type	Documentation Ref Vol Page	Author, Comments Date	Data
Evaluation	1.0−2	4.0+0	AI	Eval Rept	AI−AEC−12990	Sep 71 Ottewitte+. CURVES.EVAL FOR ENDF/B	
Total	1.0−2	1.0+3	MTR	Expt Jour	NSE 33 16	Jul 68 Stokes+ FAST CHOPPER 8200+−600B=THR	+
				Rept	IDO−16956	Apr 64 − + TBLS	
	9.1−3	3.3+0		Data	EXFOR10407.	Apr 75 . 1266 PTS, SIGMA	
Res Int Abs	1.0−2	1.0+3	MTR	Expt Jour	NSE 33 16	Jul 68 Stokes+ FAST CHOPPER 943+−50B	+
Res Int Abs	5.5−1		MUN	Expt Diss	GRYNTAKIS	Mar 76 Gryntakis.ACT CD−RATIO,912 B,EX 1/V	
Res Int Abs	5.5−1		MUN	Comp Diss	GRYNTAKIS	Mar 76 Gryntakis. 912 B,CALC.FROM RES.PAR.	
(n,γ)	Maxwl		BNL	Expt	BNL−1437	52 Mihelich.MINIMUM SIG=180KILOBARNS	
(n,γ)	Pile		BNL	Expt Jour	PR 97 1023	Feb 55 Der−Mateosian.BETA ACTIVITY CFD.	+
	Pile			Data	EXFOR12171.002	Jun 76 . 1 PT. SIGMA.	
(n,γ)	Pile		CAL	Expt Jour	PR 97 1007	Feb 55 Murray+ IRRAD AT MTR. (13+−4)KILOBRN	+
				Jour	PR 92 202	Oct 53 Dumond+ OKS PR 91 427	
	Pile			Data	EXFOR12170.002	Jun 76 . 1 PT, SIGMA.	
(n,γ)	Pile		MTR	Expt Rept	IDO−16238	Sep 55 Smith+.ACTIVATION. 15+−2KILOBARNS	+
	Pile			Data	EXFOR12160.002	Jun 76 . 1 PT. SIGMA.	
(n,γ)	2.5−2		UCB	Expt Rept	NYO−10175	Dec 64 Arino+ACT.TBLS.GRAPHS.PRODUCT HL.	+
	2.5−2			Data	EXFOR11817.016	Jun 76 . 1 PT, SIGMA.	
(n,γ)	Maxwl		MTR	Expt Rept	IN−1296	May 69 Schuman+ PILE ACT.	+
	Maxwl			Data	EXFOR11687.008	Jun 76 . 1 PT, SIGMA	
(n,γ)	1.0−4	1.8+7	BNW	Eval Rept	BNWL−1312	May 70 Simons+.	
(n,γ)	Maxwl		MUN	ExTh Diss	GRYNTAKIS	Mar 76 Gryntakis.,ACT.MEAS.,CALC OF G−FUNCT	+
	None			Theo Jour	RCA 22 128	Mar 75 − +,CALC WESTCOTTS G−FUNCTION	
	2.5−2			Expt Data	EXFOR20625.032	Aug 76 1PNT.SIGMA.	
Reson Params	1.5−1	8.8+1	MTR	Expt Jour	NSE 33 16	Jul 68 Stokes+ FAST CHOPPER 18ES,WG 2G*WN	+
	1.4−1	3.3+1		Data	EXFOR10407.	Apr 75 . 8 RES, WN, 3RES WG	
Reson Params	−		AUA	Theo Rept	AAEC/E−211	Nov 70 Musgrove. CALCULTD D+GAM WIDTH GIVEN	
Reson Params	1.5−1	6.0+0	CJD	Eval Rept	YK−7	71 Zakharova+ SURVEY+SYSTEMATICS,GW,TBL	
				Rept	INDC(CCP)−27	Nov 72 .ENGLISH TRANSLATION OF YK−7 /71	
Reson Params	1.5−1	9.5+1	NIR	Expt Conf	75Kiev 3 205	May 75 Belanova+ BY TOTSIG.2G*GN,TABLE	
Strnth Fnctn	1.0−2	1.0+3	MTR	Expt Jour	NSE 33 16	Jul 68 Stokes+ FAST CHOPPER S0=1+−0.1	
Strnth Fnctn	−		AUA	Theo Rept	AAEC/E−211	Nov 70 Musgrove. SMOOTHED S0,S1 AND S2 GIVN	
Lvl Density	+6		MIL	Theo Jour	EN 15 1 54	Jan 68 Facchini+ LDL PARS FROM LOW EN RES	
Lvl Density	None		MUN	Theo Jour	NP/A 217 269	Dec 73 Dilg+ A,DELTA. BACK SHIFTED FERMIGAS	
Lvl Density	None		COP	Theo Jour	NP/A 222 493	Apr 74 Dossing+COLL ROTAT.SPAC. ACCUR ESTIM	
Lvl Density	None		ROC	Theo Jour	NP/A 223 577	May 74 Huizenga+ EXP CFD MICROSC TH SPH NUC	
Lvl Density	None		ROC	Theo Jour	NP/A 223 589	May 74 Huizenga+ EXP CFD MICROSC TH AX SYMM	

73 Tantalum 183

Quantity	Energy (ev) Min	Max	Lab	Type	Documentation Ref Vol Page	Author, Comments Date	Data
Reson Params	−		AUA	Theo Rept	AAEC/E−211	Nov 70 Musgrove. CALCULTD D+GAM WIDTH GIVEN	
Strnth Fnctn	−		AUA	Theo Rept	AAEC/E−211	Nov 70 Musgrove. SMOOTHED S0,S1 AND S2 GIVN	

73 Tantalum 184

Quantity	Energy (ev) Min	Max	Lab	Type	Documentation Ref Vol Page	Author, Comments Date	Data
Reson Params	−		AUA	Theo Rept	AAEC/E−211	Nov 70 Musgrove. CALCULTD D+GAM WIDTH GIVEN	
Strnth Fnctn	−		AUA	Theo Rept	AAEC/E−211	Nov 70 Musgrove. SMOOTHED S0,S1 AND S2 GIVN	

73 Tantalum 185

Quantity	Energy (ev) Min	Max	Lab	Type	Documentation Ref Vol Page	Author, Comments Date	Data
Reson Params	−		AUA	Theo Rept	AAEC/E−211	Nov 70 Musgrove. CALCULTD D+GAM WIDTH GIVEN	
Strnth Fnctn	−		AUA	Theo Rept	AAEC/E−211	Nov 70 Musgrove. SMOOTHED S0,S1 AND S2 GIVN	

74 Tungsten

Quantity	Energy (ev) Min	Max	Lab	Type	Documentation Ref Vol Page	Date	Author, Comments	Data
Evaluation	2.5−2	1.0+7	UNC	Eval Rept	NDA−57−27	Sep 56	Monroe+ TOT,ABS.TABLE+CURVE	
Evaluation	5.0+5	1.5+7	LRL	Eval Rept	UCRL−5351	Nov 58	Howerton. CURVES	
Evaluation	2.5−2	2.6+2	LAS	Eval Rept	LA−2289	May 59	Devaney+ TOT,SCT,NG,FNCT TARGET TEMP	
Evaluation	9.8+3	1.4+7	AI	Eval Rept	NAA−SR−TDR6545	Jun 61	Alter.TABLES.TOT,SEL,SIN.MTCARLO DEL	
Evaluation	2.5−2	1.0+7	GEN	Eval Rept	APEX−704	Nov 61	Cooper+ CONTENT OF C−FINE TAPES	
Evaluation	2.5−2	1.3+7	GEN	Eval Rept	GEMP−223	Jun 63	Zwick+ NG,SCT,DEL,SIN.9,16GROUP+TABL	
Evaluation	2.5−2	1.1+7	FEI	Eval Book	ABAGJAN	64	26 GROUP CONST,TOT,CAPT,INEL,EL,ETC	
Evaluation	3.7−2	1.8+7	UNC	Eval Rept	UNC−5099	Dec 64	Troubetzkoy+	
Evaluation	1.0+3	1.4+7	GEN	Eval Rept	GEMP−388	Nov 65	Prince.OPTMDL WITH CHANNEL COMPETIT	
Evaluation	1.0−2	1.5+7	GEN	Eval Rept	GEMP−448	Nov 66	Henderson+ TOT NG FOR ENDF/B	
Total	Maxwl		COL	Expt Jour	PR 48 265	Aug 35	Dunning+ IONCH,TRANS,SIG SLOW+FAST N	
Total	4.0+0	1.0+4	COL	Expt Jour	PR 71 165	Feb 47	Havens+ TOF TRSM.	+
	1.5+2	3.0+4		Data	EXFOR12184.002	Jun 76	. 33 PTS.	
Total	2.4+4	8.3+5	ANL	Expt Jour	PR 71 508	Apr 47	Fields+GN SOURCES 6ES POWDER SCATT	+
	2.4+4	8.3+5		Data	EXFOR11260.021	Jun 76	. 6 PTS.	
Total	1.0+5	1.5+6	MIT	Theo Jour	PR 76 1550	Dec 49	Feshbach+ AVERAGE OVER RESON,CF EXPT	
Total	3.5+4	1.3+6	WIS	Expt Jour	PR 77 748	50	Adair. ABST.H9.	+
	3.5+4	1.3+6		Data	EXFOR11636.006	Jun 76	. 17 PTS.	
Total	2.7+8		BRK	Expt Jour	PR 80 27	Oct 50	Dejuren. BE(P,N) NS, BI FISS COUNTER	+
	2.7+8			Data	EXFOR11176.009	Jun 76	. 1 PT.	
Total	4.2+7		BRK	Expt Jour	PR 80 842	Dec 50	Hildebrand+ BE−D NS.TRANSM. C DETECT	+
	4.2+7			Data	EXFOR11039.	Jun 76	. 1 PT.	
Total	3.3+0	1.3+1	ANL	Expt Jour	PR 84 869	Dec 51	Selove.	+
	3.3+0	1.3+1		Data	EXFOR12168.002	Jun 76	. 34 PTS.	
Total	5.0+4	3.2+6	WIS	Expt Jour	PR 88 83	Oct 52	Miller+ 20KEVSPREAD TRNSM	+
	8.4+5	3.2+6		Data	EXFOR11712.021	Jun 76	. 15 PTS.	
Total	1.4+7		ANL	Expt Jour	PR 88 686	Nov 52	Goodman+ T−D NEUTS 4.8+−0.3B	+
	1.4+7			Data	EXFOR11057.019	Jun 76	. 1 PT.	
Total	1.4+7		LAS	Expt Jour	PR 88 562	Nov 52	Coon+	+
	1.4+7			Data	EXFOR11056.049	Jun 76	. 1 PT.	
Total	2.7+6	1.3+7	LAS	Expt Jour	PR 94 1678	Jun 54	Nereson+ RSLN 10 PERCENT	+
	2.7+6	1.3+7		Data	EXFOR11308.022	Jun 76	. 29 PTS.	
Total	4.1+6		LAS	Expt Jour	PR 98 677	May 55	Walt+ TRANSMISSION EXPT 6.4B	+
	4.1+6			Data	EXFOR11215.044	Jun 76	. 1 PT.	
Total	5.9+8		CCP	Expt Jour	ZET 29 369	Sep 55	Dzhelepov.EXPRMNTL SIG CFD GEOMETRCL	
				Jour	JET 2 349	Mar 56	TRANSLATN.*	
Total	2.7+0	8.1+2	BNL	Expt Abst	BAP 1 187	Apr 56	Schwartz+ ABST. K3	+
	2.7+0	8.1+2		Data	EXFOR12152.002	Jun 76	. 234 PTS.	
Total	8.0+2	2.4+4	HAR	Expt Priv	EGELSTAFF5	Jun 56	Egelstaff. = 1 DATA INDEX LINES	
	1.4+2	2.9+5		Priv	EGELSTAFF4	Jun 55	−. = 1 DATA INDEX LINES	
Total	1.0+3	3.2+4	HAR	Expt Jour	PPSA 70 51	Jan 57	Gayther+ FC THICK SAMPLE,AVSIG CF TH	
Total	1.8+1	4.9+1	BNL	Expt Abst	BAP 3 19	Jan 58	Chrien+ ABST. F8.	+
	1.8+1	4.9+1		Data	EXFOR12153.002	Jun 76	. 75 PTS.	
Total	1.8+1	1.5+2	ORL	Expt Abst	BAP 3 177	Apr 58	Harvey. ABST. F11	
	1.8+1	1.5+2		Data	EXFOR12154.004	Jun 76	. 248 PTS.	
Total	7.1+6	1.4+7	LRL	Expt Jour	PR 110 927	May 58	Bratenahl+SC TRN 5ES 5.37 5.40N+−1PC	+
				Conf	58Geneva 14	Sep 58	−+ TBL,CURV,CFD OPTMDL	
	7.1+6	1.4+7		Data	EXFOR11155.027	Jun 76	. 5 PTS.	
Total	2.5+1	2.0+2	HAR	Expt Jour	NP 12 552	Sep 59	Firk+ TOF 9RES W183,1RES W182,4,6.	
				Rept	AERE−NP/GEN 11	Apr 59	−+ RESONANCE ANALYSIS.	
Total	2.0−3	2.9−1	MTR	Expt Jour	NSE 7 193	Feb 60	Schmunk+ SCINT TRANS CURVE	+
	2.0−3	2.9−1		Data	EXFOR11634.007	Jun 76	. 93 PTS.	
Total	Cold		KJL	Revw Conf	60Vienna 169	Oct 60	Riste.NDG,TBP	
Total	1.7+7	2.9+7	LRL	Expt Jour	PR 120 521	Oct 60	Peterson+ TRANS 4ES CURV CFD OPTMDL	+
				Conf	58Geneva 14 109	Sep 58	Bratenahl+ P1881,TBL,CURV,CFD OPTMDL	
	1.7+7	2.9+7		Data	EXFOR11108.035	Jun 76	. 4 PTS. SIG	
Total	7.6+0		SAC	Expt Jour	CR 255 1913	Oct 62	LE PIPEC+ CRYST BINDING EFF ON RES	
				Theo Jour	JPR 24 176	Mar 63	Le Pipec. THEORY	
Total	3.7−2	1.8+7	UNC	Comp Rept	UNC−PH/M−2813	Dec 62	Celnick. COMPILED MANY SOURCES	
Total	2.1+0	4.7+3	CCP	Eval Rept	INDSWG−64 274	64	Nikolaev.TABLE OF CHARACTRSTC PARAMS	
Total	2.2+1	4.7+3	FEI	Expt Conf	JINR−1845 108	Jun 64	Nikolaev+ TABLE,SIG OF E−GROUPS,TOF	
Total	3.0+5	1.5+6	ANL	Expt Abst	BAP 9 651	Oct 64	Whalen+RESOLUTION 1−10KEV NDG	+
	8.1+5	1.5+6		Data	EXFOR12176.002	Jun 76	. 70 PTS.	
Total	4.1+0		BNL	Expt Abst	DA 25 6010	Apr 65	Bernabei.AROUND 4.1EV RES,4−825DEG K	
Total	1.0−2	2.0+1	GA	Expt Prog	WASH−1064 43	Oct 65	Friesenhahn+ SIG ANAL .025EV S GIVN	
Total	1.0−3	1.0+2	WES	Eval Rept	WANL−TME−1472	Jul 66	Gibson+ CURVE CALC FROM RES	

74 Tungsten

Quantity	Energy (ev) Min	Max	Lab	Type	Documentation Ref Vol Page	Author, Comments Date	Data
Total	1.0+5	6.5+5	ANL Expt	Prog	ANL-7210 16	Dec 66 Whalen.SHORT NOTE,GRAPH ONLY	+
	None			Jour	NIM 39 185	Jan 66 - +COMPUTER EXPT.NDG,CF BAP 9 6	
	1.0+5	6.5+5		Data	EXFOR11540.008	Jun 76 . 270 PTS.	
Total	5.3+6	6.3+6	THU Expt	Jour	CHP 5 43	Oct 67 Kao+.TOF-TRNSM,VDG,CURVE+TABLE	+
	5.3+6	6.3+6		Data	EXFOR30050.003	Dec 70 SIG TOT AT 24 ES., NUCL RADIUS	
Total	4.1+6		IFU Theo	Jour	UFZ 13 51	Jan 68 Kashuba+ TBL,SIG-VAL,EXPT CFD OPTMOD	
				Jour	UPJ 13 33	Jul 68 TRANSLATN.*	
Total	1.2+5	6.4+5	DKE Expt	Abst	DA/B 28 3834	Mar 68 Divadeenam.TRNS.AVG SIG CFD OPTMDL.	+
	1.2+5	6.4+5		Data	EXFOR10523.014	Jan 76 . 27 PTS. CS DATA	
Total	2.0+3	2.0+6	GA Expt	Conf	68Wash. 61	Mar 68 Froehner+ TRANS CURVS AT 293 755DEGK	
Total	2.5+4	9.0+4	FEI Expt	Conf	68Dubna § 17	Jun 68 Filippov+VDG,TRANS.TBL,GRPH.FLUCTUAT	+
				Rept	INDC(CCP)-16	Jul 71 .PAGE 67.ENGLISH TRANSL OF 68DUBNA	
	2.5+4	9.0+4		Data	EXFOR40082.019	Nov 71 SIGMA AT 5 ES	
Total	+9		MHG Expt	Jour	PL/B 27 328	Aug 68 Jones+	+
	+9			Data	EXFOR11206.006	Jun 76 . 1 PT.	
Total	2.5+6	1.5+7	BNW Expt	Jour	PR/C 3 576	Feb 71 Foster+ TRANS,CURVES,CFD OTHERS+TH	+
				Jour	NIM 36 1	Sep 65 .EXPT DETAILS	
	2.3+6	1.5+7		Data	EXFOR10047.078	Aug 73 . 246 PTS.	
Total	2.0+4	2.2+7	LAS Eval	Rept	LA-4928	Jun 72 Devaney+ SMOOTH SIG CURVES	
Total	+9		NYU Theo	Jour	PR/C 6 748	Sep 72 Franco. GLAUBER APPROX. CFD EXPT	
Total	2.7+3		MUN Expt	Prog	EANDC(E)150U	Oct 72 Dilg+ AVERAGE TOT XSECT+S0	+
				Conf	71Albany 327	Aug 71 - +TRNS.AVG CS GVN.31 ELEMENT GRP	
	2.7+3			Data	EXFOR20583.027	Jun 76 1PNT.	
Total	+9		MHG Expt	Abst	DA/B 33 2271	Nov 72 Mccorriston. OKS GLAUBER TH. NDG	
Total	1.3+7	1.5+7	DEB Eval	Rept	IAEA-153 173	73 Boedy+ MOST PROBABLE VAL OF SIG,TBL	
				Jour	AHP 30 115	Oct 71 Angeli+ AVG SIG,CFD CALC.TBLS.GRAPH	
Total	1.0+2	2.4+3	COL Expt	Jour	PR/C 8 1813	Nov 73 Camarda+ BETWEEN LVL SIG VS.E SHOWN	+
	1.0+2	2.4+3		Data	EXFOR10507.010	Jun 76 .UNCORRECTED DATA AVAILABLE.	
Total	+9		MHG Expt	Jour	NP/B 92 269	Jun 75 Murthy+ 34GEV/C TO 273 GEV/C	+
				Jour	PRL 33 1440	Dec 74 Jones+ TBL. 30 GEV/C TO 270 GEV/C	
	+9			Data	EXFOR10403.009	Dec 74 . 7 PTS,SIGMA	
Total	-3	1.9+0	THS Theo	Rept	IKE-6 89 65	Jun 75 Keinert. DATA LIBRARY	
Total	3.0+4	6.5+5	DKE Expt	Abst	BAP 7 23	Jan 62 Tabony+S,P,D STF FROM TOT.NDG	+
	3.0+4	6.5+5		Data	EXFOR11936.006	Jun 76 . 101 PTS.	
Elastic	2.5-2		ORL Expt	Jour	PR 81 527	Feb 51 Shull+ COH.SCAT.LENGTH	+
	2.5-2			Data	EXFOR11043.	Jun 76 . 3 PTS. BAS,COH,COH AMP	
Elastic	1.0+6		WIS Expt	Jour	PR 93 1062	Mar 54 Walt+	+
	1.0+6			Data	EXFOR11637.065	Jun 76 . 1 PT.	
Elastic	4.1+6		LAS Expt	Jour	PR 98 677	May 55 Walt.	+
	4.1+6			Data	EXFOR11215.042	Jun 76 . 1 PT.	
Elastic	3.7-2	1.8+7	UNC Comp	Rept	UNC-PH/M-2813	Dec 62 Celnick. COMPILED MANY SOURCES	
Elastic	3.0+5	1.5+6	ANL Expt	Rept	EANDC(US)-62	Jun 64 Smith.TOF,TBL.50KEV STEPS,20KEV RSLN	+
	3.0+5	1.5+6		Data	EXFOR12156.004	Jun 76 . 27 PTS. SIG	
Elastic	1.0+5	1.4+7	AGN Eval	Rept	TID-21629	Dec 64 Perkins+CALC FR BNL400,UCRL5573,CRV	
Elastic	2.0+6		FEI Expt	Rept	EANDC-50 200	Jul 65 Kazakova+ EXPT,TABLE CFD OPTMODEL	+
				Prog	YFI-3 6	Sep 66 .TABLE	
				Prog	INDC-E-140 6	Sep 66 .ENGLISH TRANSL OF YFI-3 6 9/66	
Elastic	3.0+5	8.0+5	IFU ExTh	Jour	AE 20 8	Jan 66 Korzh+ SUMMARY OF SEVERAL YRS WORK	+
				Jour	UFZ 9 929	May 64 .	
	5.0+5	8.0+5		Jour	SJA 20 8	Jul 66 .ENGLISH TRANSL OF AE 20 8 1/66	
	3.0+5	8.0+5		Rept	INDSWG-101 112	65 .=UFZ9.ENGL NO GRPHS.RUSS LARGER GPH	
Elastic	1.0-3	1.0+2	WES Eval	Rept	WANL-TME-1472	Jul 66 Gibson+ CURVE CALC FROM RES	
Elastic	None		RPI Expt	Abst	BAP 12 512	Apr 67 Block+3.LI6 SC+SC-T FOR WEAK RES	
Elastic	1.5+6		IFU Expt	Prog	YFI-5 42	Oct 67 Korzh+ TBL OPTMDL PARAMS + TOTELAST	
				Rept	INDC-232E	67 . ENGL OF YFI-5 42	
Elastic	1.5+1	2.6+2	ANL Expt	Jour	NIM 57 82	Dec 67 Garnsworthy+BRIGHT LINE TECHNIQUE	
Elastic	1.5+6		IFU Comp	Jour	YF 7 277	Feb 68 Korzh+ OPTMOD PARS-FIT TO EXPTL-SIG	
				Jour	SNP 7 2 190	Aug 68 TRANSLATN.*	
Elastic	Cold		MUN Expt	Jour	ZP 219 300	Jan 69 Koester+,SCAT AMPLITUDE=4.77+-0.05 F	+
	Cold			Data	EXFOR20812.004	Dec 78 1PNT.COHERENT SCT AMPLITUDE.	
Elastic	8.7+5		ANL Expt	Rept	ANL-7935	Jun 72 COX+ 4 PI B(O)	+
	8.7+5			Data	EXFOR10332.124	Jun 74 . 1 PT.	
Elastic	4.3+6	8.6+6	ORL Expt	Rept	ORNL-4803	May 73 Kinney+. ANGLE-INTEGRATED SIGS SHOWN	+
				Conf	75Wash. 883	Mar 75 - +26NUCLIDES ELAS,INEL CS RVW.	
	4.3+6	8.6+6		Data	EXFOR10284.005	Jan 76 . 5 PTS, SIGMA	
Elastic	1.0+5	1.5+7	CCP Eval	Data	SOKRATOR-1036	76 50 PTS	+
Diff Elastic	2.5+6		HAR Expt	Jour	PM 44 1398	Dec 53 Poole.AT 97DEG 130+-40MB/SR,P RECOIL	

74 Tungsten

Quantity	Energy (ev) Min	Max	Lab	Type	Documentation Ref Vol Page	Date	Author, Comments	Data
Diff Elastic	1.0+6		WIS	Expt Jour	PR 93 1062	Mar 54	Walt+ HE COUNTER 30-150DEG LAB CURVE	+
	1.0+6			Data	EXFOR12156.003	Jun 76	. 1 PT.	
Diff Elastic	4.1+6		LAS	Expt Jour	PR 98 677	May 55	Walt+ BIASED SCINT ANG DISTR CURVE	+
	4.1+6			Data	EXFOR11215.045	Jun 76	. 1 PT.	
Diff Elastic	1.4+7	1.4+7	GRN	Expt Jour	NP 2 124	Oct 56	Nauta. GRAPH.20-90 DEG.RING GEOMETRY	+
	1.4+7			Data	EXFOR20199.005	May 74	15PTS.D/DA.	
Diff Elastic	7.0+6		LRL	Theo Rept	UCRL-4927	Jul 57	Bjorklund+ OPTMDL CALC 6-PARAM FIT	
Diff Elastic	1.4+7		LRL	Theo Rept	UCRL-4926	Jul 57	Bjorklund+ OPTMDL CALC 6-PARAM FIT	
Diff Elastic	5.0+6		WES	Expt Jour	PR 109 2105	Mar 58	Hill.SC 30-150DEG ABS CRV CFD OPTMDL	+
	5.0+6			Data	EXFOR11321.010	Jun 76	. 13 PTS.	
Diff Elastic	4.1+6		LRL	Expt Jour	RMP 30 414	Apr 58	Fernbach.TH CURVE AND EXPTL PTS	
Diff Elastic	1.3+5	2.0+7	GEA	Eval Rept	TID-12742	Feb 61	Gerardo. FROM BNL-400+OTHER SOURCES	
Diff Elastic	3.7-2	1.8+7	UNC	Comp Rept	UNC-PH/M-2813	Dec 62	Celnick. COMPILED MANY SOURCES	
Diff Elastic	1.4+7		FTI	Expt Jour	ZET 44 130	Jan 63	Dukarevich+ GRAPH ANGL=3-20 DEG	+
				Jour	JET 17 89	Jul 63	TRANSLATN.*	
	1.4+7			Data	EXFOR40078.002	Oct 71	DIFF SIG AT 9 ANGLES	
Diff Elastic	7.0+6		LAS	Expt Jour	PR 129 1649	Feb 63	Thomson. SIG AT 90DEG	+
	7.0+6			Data	EXFOR11495.046	Jun 76	. 1 PT.	
Diff Elastic	3.5+5	5.0+6	AI	Eval Rept	NAA-SR-M-9027	Sep 63	Alter+ MT CARLO LEAST SR ANAL BNL400	
Diff Elastic	3.0+5	8.0+5	IFU	Expt Jour	UFZ 9 929	May 64	Korzh.GRAPHS SIG(COS),TBL DERIVD VAL	+
				Jour	AE 20 8	Jan 66	- + SUMMARY OF SEVERAL YRS WORK	
				Rept	INDSWG-101 112	65	.=UFZ9.ENGL NO GRPHS.RUSS LARGER GPH	
	5.0+5	8.0+5		ExTh Jour	SJA 20 8	Jul 66	.ENGLISH TRANSL OF AE 20 8 1/66	
Diff Elastic	3.0+5	1.5+6	ANL	Expt Rept	EANDC(US)-62	Jun 64	Smith.TOF,TBL.50KEV STEPS,20KEV RSLN	+
	5.5+5	1.3+6		Conf	61Vienna 1 29	Aug 61	- .CURVE,ANGL N-DISTRIB AT 4 N-ES	
	3.0+3	1.5+6		Data	EXFOR12156.003	Jun 76	. 135 PTS, LEG. COEFS AT 27ES	
	3.5+5	1.3+6		Data	EXFOR12156.002	Jun 76	. 115 PTS, DSIG	
Diff Elastic	1.0+5	1.4+7	AGN	Eval Rept	TID-21629	Dec 64	Perkins+LEGCOEF CAL FR OTHER DAT,CRV	
Diff Elastic	8.0+5		IFU	Theo Jour	UFZ 10 6 586	Jun 65	Korzh.OPTMDL GRAPH SIG,CFD XPT	
				Jour	IZV 29 862	May 65	.	
Diff Elastic	2.0+6		FEI	Expt Rept	EANDC-50 200	Jul 65	Kazakova+ EXPT,CURVE CFD OPTMODEL	+
				Prog	ICD-2 112	Jul 65	.CURVE	
				Prog	INDSWG-101E	65	.ENGLISH TRANSL OF ICD-2 112 7/65	
Diff Elastic	8.0+5		IFU	Theo Conf	65Antwerp § 193	Jul 65	Pasechnic+. OPT.MOD.PARAMETERS	
Diff Elastic	1.4+7		RPI	Expt Abst	DA 26 438	Jul 65	Pearlstein+	+
	1.4+7			Data	EXFOR10234.007	May 73	. 1 PT. DSIGMA AT 90DEG	
Diff Elastic	1.0+6		LAS	Theo Prog	WASH-1064 84	Oct 65	Rosen+ OPTMDL+ CPD ELST CFD WIS XPT	
Diff Elastic	4.0+5	1.0+6	HAR	ExTh Jour	NP 76 369	Feb 66	Ferguson+ OPTMDL PARS TO FIT POLARIZ	+
Diff Elastic	3.2+6		BCM	Expt Jour	NP 89 154	Dec 66	Becker+ 12 ANGLES GRAPH CFD OPTMDL	+
	3.2+6			Data	EXFOR11511.033	Jun 76	. 12 PTS.	
Diff Elastic	4.4+6	5.5+6	WIS	ExTh Jour	NP/A 95 193	Mar 67	Mahajan.POLARIZATION OPTMDL ANALYSIS	
				Abst	DA/B 28 1093	Sep 67	.SEE ALSO	
Diff Elastic	3.5+5	1.4+7	AI	Eval Rept	NAA-SR-11980	Apr 67	Campbell+ LEG COEFS TBL+CURVS C-MSYS	
Diff Elastic	4.0+0	4.8+1	RPI	Expt Jour	NIM 52 321	Jun 67	King+ LI-GLASS/LIQSCINT,(NG) OUT.NDG	
Diff Elastic	4.1+6		IFU	Theo Jour	UFZ 13 51	Jan 68	Kashuba+ GRPH,EXPT CFD OPTMOD-CALC	
				Jour	UPJ 13 33	Jul 68	TRANSLATN.*	
Diff Elastic	1.5+6		IFU	Comp Jour	YF 7 277	Feb 68	Korzh+ GRPH SIG(ANG),OPTMOD PARS-FIT	
				Jour	SNP 7 2 190	Aug 68	TRANSLATN.*	
Diff Elastic	8.4+5	1.2+6	ANL	Expt Jour	PR 176 1405	Dec 68	Kuchnir+ VDG+SCINT 3ES 1.75-15DEG	+
	8.4+5	1.2+6		Data	EXFOR11977.003	Jun 76	. 18 PTS. DSIG	
Diff Elastic	2.0+6	4.0+6	SCU	Theo Rept	ICD-6 236	69	Averyanov+CALC ANGDIST CFD EXPT,GRPH	
Diff Elastic	1.4+6	2.0+6	JAE	Expt Jour	NP/A 125 641	Mar 69	Tsukada+. TOF. CFD OPTMDL,H-F,MOLDAU	+
	1.4+6	2.0+6		Data	EXFOR20304.020	Jun 74	24PTS.D/DA.	
Diff Elastic	1.4+6	2.0+6	CCP	Comp Rept	ICD-6 50	70	Bazajanc+ ANGDIST EXPTS,GRPH AT 2ES	
Diff Elastic	2.0+6		ANL	Expt Prog	NCSAC-42 10	Nov 71	Cox. NO DATA GIVEN.	
Diff Elastic	0.0+0	1.5+7	FEI	Eval Book	NIKOLAEV 162	72	.LEG COEFFS+ANG DISTRIBUTS,GRAPH	
Diff Elastic	8.7+5		ANL	Expt Rept	ANL-7935	Jun 72	COX+ CFD OPTMOD,HAUSER-FESHBACH	+
	8.7+5			Data	EXFOR10332.029	Jun 74	. 8 PTS.	
Diff Elastic	3.2+6		AMS	Theo Jour	NP/A 222 93	Apr 74	Zijp+ LEG.COEFF COMPOUND ELASTIC.H-F	
Diff Elastic	4.6+3	6.5+6	FEI	Theo Rept	YK-8/2 3	Sep 72	Bazajants+ ANISOTR GROUP-PARAMS,TBL	
				Rept	INDC(CCP)-39	Jul 74	.P1. ENGLISH OF YK-8/2 3	
Diff Elastic	7.6+6		BRL	Expt Rept	BRL-R-1764	Mar 75	Hollandsworth+6ANGS.DATA GIVEN	+
	7.6+6			Data	EXFOR10319.008	May 75	.6PTS.ANG=2.68-14.16DEG.EN=7.55MEV.	
Diff Elastic	4.3+6	8.6+6	ORL	Expt Rept	ORNL-4803	May 73	Kinney+ TOF. VDG. 5ES. TABLES+CURVES	+
				Conf	75Wash. 883	Mar 75	+26NUCLIDES ELAS,INEL CS RVW.	
	4.3+6	8.6+6		Data	EXFOR10284.002	Apr 75	. 94 PTS. DSIGMA AT 5 ENERGIES	
Diff Elastic	7.6+6	1.4+7	BRL	Expt Prog	ERDA-NDC-2 212	May 75	Bucher+EN=7.55MEV.SMALL ANG.EL.SCT.	

74 Tungsten

Quantity	Energy (ev) Min	Max	Lab	Type	Documentation Ref Vol Page	Date	Author, Comments	Data
Diff Elastic	1.0+5	1.5+7	CCP	Eval Data	SOKRATOR – 1036	76	50 PTS	+
Polarization	4.0+5		WIS	Expt Jour	PR 96 503	Oct 54	Adair+ POL FOR 50DEG NEUTS CFD TH	
Polarization	3.8+5	9.8+5	WIS	ExTh Jour	NP 6 177	Mar 58	Clement+. POLARIZATION. CFD OPT MDL	
				Expt Rept	AECU – 3628	57	– +.LI7(P,N) SOURCE. 3ANGLES.	
Polarization	1.5+6		DKE	Expt Rept	TID – 19051	62	Olness+ TOF 51.5DEG POLARIZ MEASD	
Polarization	8.4+5	1.2+6	ANL	Expt Jour	PR 176 1405	Dec 68	Kuchnir+ VDG+SCINT 3ES 1.75 – 15DEG	
Polarization	2.0+6		ANL	Expt Prog	NCSAC – 42 10	Nov 71	Cox. NO DATA GIVEN	
Polarization	8.7+5		ANL	Expt Rept	ANL – 7935	Jun 72	Cox+. CFD OPTMOD,HAUSER – FESHBACH	+
	8.7+5			Data	EXFOR10332.063	Jun 74	. 8 PTS.	
Polarization	3.2+6		AMS	Expt Jour	NP/A 222 93	Apr 74	Zijp+ TABLES,GRAPHS. CFD NON – SPH POT	+
				Conf	75Zurich 189	Aug 75	– + GRPH OF DATA IN REVIEW.	
				Conf	72Budapest 170	Aug 72	– + POLARIZTN,EXPT CFD OPTMOD,GRP	
	3.2+6			Data	EXFOR20777.018	Apr 78	4PTS.	
Potntal Scat	1.2+2	3.0+2	ANL	Expt Jour	PR 76 100	Jul 49	Hibdon+TRNS.10PC RSLN.CO,MN SCT DET.	+
	1.2+2	3.0+2		Data	EXFOR11261.031	Jun 76	. 2 PTS.	
Potntal Scat	+4		HAR	Expt Jour	PPSA 70 51	Jan 57	Gayther+ FROM AVG SIGTOT. FC TRANSM	
Potntal Scat		6.5+5	DKE	ExTh Jour	PL 13 70	Nov 64	Seth+0,1PHASE FRM SIG TOT AV 3 – 650KV	
Potntal Scat	5.4+6	6.3+6	THU	Expt Jour	CHP 5 43	Oct 67	KAO+ CALC FROM TOTSIG,VALUE GIVEN	
Potntal Scat	None		DKE	Expt Abst	DA/B 28 3834	Mar 68	Divadeenam.TRNS.EFFECTIVE RADIUS	
Tot Inelastc	1.5+6	3.0+6	LAS	Expt Jour	PR 72 881	Nov 47	Barschall+POOR GEOM+BACKSCT.BIAS DET	
Tot Inelastc	1.5+6	3.0+6	MIT	Theo Jour	PR 75 1115	Apr 49	Feld.FEW – LVL VS STATMOD FOR LAS DATA	
Tot Inelastc	2.9+5	1.0+6	CCP	Expt Jour	ZET 30 1017	Jun 56	Poze.SIG AT 3ES GIVEN,AV E OF SCT NS	
	3.0+5	1.0+6		Jour	ADP 20 3	Jul 57	Pose+,MEASURED AT 3 E – POINTS,TBL	
	2.9+5	1.0+6		Jour	JET 3 745	Dec 56	TRANSLATN.*	
Tot Inelastc	2.5+6		IFU	Expt Jour	JET 4 769	Jun 57	.ENGLISH OF ZET 31 907	
				Jour	ZET 31 907	Nov 56	Strizhak. SPHERE METHOD,TABLE	
Tot Inelastc	1.4+7		LRL	Expt Conf	58Paris § NS609	Jul 58	Mcgregor.FROM SNE 9AND14MEV CUTOFF	+
	1.4+7			Data	EXFOR11205.020	Jun 76	. 1 PT.	
Tot Inelastc	Fiss		KUR	Revw Conf	60Vienna 159	Oct 60	Bondarenko+.TABLE,EXPT DESCRIBED	
Tot Inelastc	3.7-2	1.8+7	UNC	Comp Rept	UNC – PH/M – 2813	Dec 62	Celnick. COMPILED MANY SOURCES	
Tot Inelastc	4.0+5	1.0+6	CCP	Expt Jour	AE 14 400	Apr 63	SPH 60KEVRSLN 4ES+SPECTRA3ES GLAZKOV	+
Tot Inelastc	8.0+5	4.0+6	IFU	Expt Prog	INDSWG – 126 22	66	Pasechnik. AT 5 ES, TBP IN AE	
	2.5+6	1.4+7		Conf	55Geneva 2 3	Aug 55	– . INTEGR SIGMA,2ES,TABLE	
Tot Inelastc	5.0+6	7.0+6	ALD	Expt Jour	NP/A 112 337	May 68	Owens+.3ES.FROM N SPECT 90DEG.	+
Tot Inelastc	1.4+7		TUD	Expt Prog	ZFK – 262 39	Sep 73	Goebel+ INTEGRATED DIFFSIG,TB DONE	
Diff Inelast	4.3+6		BAR	Expt Jour	PR 86 861	Jun 52	Mandeville+ VDG D – D NEUTS E DIST CRV	
Diff Inelast	2.5+6		HAR	Expt Jour	PM 44 1398	Dec 53	Poole.AT 97DEG 100+ – 40MB/SR,P RECOIL	
Diff Inelast	2.5+6	6.3+6	LAS	Expt Conf	ORNL – 2309	Jun 57	Levin+TOF 3ES 3D4MEV TS CFD MXWCUR	
Diff Inelast	1.4+7		CCP	Expt Jour	AE 3 540	Dec 57	Zamyatnin+.P RECOIL, T=0.62+ – 0.05MEV	
				Jour	JNE 9 41	Jun 59	TRANSLATN.*	
				Jour	SJA 3 1427	57	TRANSLATN.*	
Diff Inelast	1.5+7		TNC	Expt Rept	AFSWC – TR – 60 – 30	Jun 60	Prudhomme+	+
	1.5+7			Data	EXFOR11183.015	Jun 76	. 10 PTS.	
Diff Inelast	1.5+7		JAE	Expt Priv	TSUKADA	62	Tsukada. T – D NS. TOF.	+
	1.5+7			Data	EXFOR20323.005	Jun 74	22PTS.D/DA.	
Diff Inelast	2.4+6	7.0+6	RIC	Expt Rept	SCR – 466	Feb 62	Ewing+ ALSO 5MEV,E SPECT+NUCL TEMP	
Diff Inelast	3.7-2	1.8+7	UNC	Comp Rept	UNC – PH/M – 2813	Dec 62	Celnick. COMPILED MANY SOURCES	
Diff Inelast	7.0+6		LAS	Expt Jour	PR 129 1649	Feb 63	Thomson+. 90DEG TEMP FOR NS TO 5MEV	+
	7.0+6			Data	EXFOR11495.048	Jun 76	. 1 PT. SIG.	
	7.0+6			Data	EXFOR11495.045	Jun 76	. 2 PTS. DSIG	
Diff Inelast	4.0+5	1.0+6	CCP	Expt Jour	AE 14 400	Apr 63	SPH 60KEVRSLN 4ES+SPECTRA3ES GLAZKOV	
Diff Inelast	3.0+5	1.2+6	ANL	Expt Prog	WASH – 1044	Aug 63	Reitmann+TOF.XCITN CURVS.NDG	
	1.2+5	1.1+6		Conf	61Vienna 1 29	Aug 61	Smith.CURVE,N – SPECT FOR 6INCDNT N – ES	
Diff Inelast	4.0+6	6.5+6	DKE	Expt Jour	NP 60 17	Nov 64	Buccino+N SPEC MEASURED 6ES+NUC TEMP	
				Abst	DA 24 4251	Apr 64	Hollandsworth.TOF.EN SPEC.NUCL T.	
Diff Inelast	1.4+7		FEI	Expt Rept	FEI – 4	65	Anufrienko+ SPEC OF SECONDARY NEUTNS	+
				Prog	YFI – 1 11	65	.	
				Prog	INDSWG – 120E 8	65	.ENGLISH TRANSL OF YFI – 1 11 /65	
	1.4+7			Data	EXFOR40133.022	Feb 73	N – SPECTRUM AT 92 DEG	
Diff Inelast	1.4+7		RPI	Expt Jour	JNAB 19 497	Jul 65	Pearlstein+.INEL SPECTRUM 6 – 14 MEV	+
				Abst	DA 26 438	Jul 65	– .SIGMA+INEL EN SPECTRA.NDG	
	1.4+7			Data	EXFOR10234.003	May 73	. 1 PT. DSIGMA AT 90DEG	
Diff Inelast	3.0+5	8.0+5	IFU	Expt Prog	INDSWG – 126 22	66	Pasechnik. AT 3 ES, TBP IN AE	
Diff Inelast	2.5+6	1.5+7	FEI	Theo Jour	NP 76 232	Feb 66	Malyshev+ SPEC ANALYSED FOR TEMP	
Diff Inelast	1.5+7		TNC	Expt Jour	PR 186 1038	Oct 69	Mathur+TOF,DIST INEL SCT NEUTS	+
				Rept	NDL – TR – 86	Jan 67	– +TBLS.ANG=90DEG.EXPT DETAILS	
	1.5+7			Data	EXFOR10043.	Jun 72	. 72 PTS.D/DA	

74 Tungsten

Quantity	Energy (ev) Min	Max	Lab	Type	Documentation Ref Vol Page	Author, Comments Date	Data
Diff Inelast	5.0+6	7.0+6	ALD	Expt	Jour NP/A 112 337	May 68 Owens+.3ES.FROM N SPECT 90DEG NDG.	+
					Conf 65Antwerp 547	Jul 65 − + PPR122.ABST.SPECT N' AT 90DEG	
Diff Inelast	6.9+5	2.0+6	JAE	Expt	Jour NP/A 125 641	Mar 69 Tsukada+. TOF. CFD OPTMDL,H−F,MOLDAU	+
	6.9+5	2.2+6			Data EXFOR20304.	Jun 74 58PTS.D/DA.	
Diff Inelast	1.4+6	2.0+6	CCP	Comp	Rept ICD−6 106	70 Sluchevskaja.SIG(ANG) TO LVLS,GRAPHS	
Diff Inelast	1.4+7		FEI	Expt	Prog YFI−11 11	70 Lovchikova+ ABST,TOF,DIFFSIG,NDG	
					Prog INDC(CCP)−31	Dec 72 .PAGE 9,ENGLISH OF YFI−11 11	
Diff Inelast	1.4+7		FEI	Expt	Jour AE 29 395	Nov 70 .ABSTRACT FRANCO−SOV SEMINAR DUBNA	
					Conf 70Helsinki 2 359	Jun 70 Salnikov+79. SIG(ANG,N') TABLE, TOF	
					Rept FEI−39	Jan 66 .TOF SPECTRA,RING GEOM,E−SPECTRA	
					Rept BNL−TR−545	Jul 73 . ENGLISH OF 70HELSIN 2 359	
					Jour SJA 29 1156	Nov 70 .ENGLISH TRANSL OF AE 29 395 11/70	
Diff Inelast	1.4+7		TUD	Expt	Prog ZFK−262 39	Sep 73 Goebel+ DOUBLEDIFFSIG,IN PROGRESS	
Diff Inelast	1.4+7		KYU	Expt	Jour NST 11˜523	Dec 74 Akiyoshi+.TOF,E−SPECTRUM AT 100 DEG	
Diff Inelast	6.4+6	8.6+6	ORL	Expt	Rept ORNL−4803	May 73 Kinney+. TOF. VDG. 5ES. TABLES+CURVS	+
					Conf 75Wash. 883	Mar 75 +26NUCLIDES ELAS,INEL CS RVW.	
	6.4+6	8.6+6			Data EXFOR10284.004	Apr 75 . 314 PTS. DBL DIFF AT 5 ENERGIES	
Diff Inelast	1.4+7		FEI	Eval	Conf 75Kiev 4 128	May 75 Luk'Janov+ DIR,INDIR SIG,TEMP.TABLE	
Thermal Scat	Maxwl		UJV	Theo	Rept UJV−2275	69 Krivy. DEBYE TEMP,BRAGG+OTHER EXPTS	
Thermal Scat	None		TKU	Theo	Jour AAF 6 321	Jul 69 Laehteenkorva. DISPERSION CURVES GVN	
Thermal Scat	1.0−4	1.0+3	MUN	Revw	Jour EEN 80 1	77 Koester. SCAT LENGTH,FREE+INCOH SIG	
Scattering	Maxwl		CAV	Expt	Jour PRSA 162 127	Sep 37 Goldhaber+. 7.8B REL 4.83B FOR C	
Scattering	Maxwl		JAP	Expt	Jour SCP 36 153	Jul 39 Kimura.SIG=9.3 PM 2B	
Scattering	Slow		JAP	Expt	Jour JPJO 25 481	Jul 43 Kimura.SIG + CURVE GIVN	
Scattering	2.0+5	3.0+6	LAS	Expt	Jour PR 72 881	Nov 47 Barschall+POOR GEOM+BACKSCT.BIAS DET	
Scattering	6.0+4	1.8+6	ANL	Expt	Jour PR 107 1077	Aug 57 Langsdorf+,LEGENDRE COEFS CURVES	+
					Rept ANL−5567	Oct 61 .REVISED DATA	
	6.0+4	1.0+6			Data EXFOR11224.056	Jun 76 . 13 PTS, SIG	
	6.0+4	1.0+6			Data EXFOR11224.057	Jun 76 . 65 PTS, DSIG	
Scattering	2.5−2	2.6+2	LAS	Eval	Rept LA−2289	May 59 Devaney+.TABLES.T=.025TO100EV,MAXWLN	
Scattering	+0	+3	ORL	Revw	Conf 60Vienna 535	Oct 60 Block+.NDG,EXPT DESCRIBED	
Scattering	Fast		FEI	Expt	Jour AE 18 409	Apr 65 Gusejnov+ ANGL DIST,TH(N,F)DETECTOR	
					Jour JNE 20 700	Aug 66 . ENGL OF AE 18 409	
					Jour SJA 18 526	Apr 65 . ENGL OF AE 18 409	
					Jour EAF 18 4 134	Apr 65 . FRENCH OF AE 18 409	
Nonelastic	1.0+6		WIS	Expt	Jour PR 93 1062	Mar 54 Walt+	+
	1.0+6				Data EXFOR11637.066	Jun 76 . 1 PT.	
Nonelastic	4.1+6		LAS	Expt	Jour PR 98 677	May 55 Walt+ 2.4+−0.3B FROM TOT MINUS ELAST	+
	4.1+6				Data EXFOR11215.043	Jun 76 . 1 PT.	
Nonelastic	4.0+6	4.5+6	LAS	Expt	Jour PR 98 1216	Jun 55 Beyster+ SPH TRNS 2ES 2.60 AND 2.60B	+
					Jour PR 97 563	Jan 55 .SUPERSEDED.(LETTER)	
	4.0+6	4.5+6			Data EXFOR11216.014	Jun 76 . 2 PTS.	
Nonelastic	2.5+6	1.4+7	CCP	Expt	Conf 55Geneva 2 3	Aug 55 Pasechnik.SPH MEAS SPEC OF SCT N	+
Nonelastic	1.4+7				Jour AE 1 4 155	Sep 56 Flerov+.SPHERE TRANSM, 2480+−30MB	+
					Jour JNE 4 529	Apr 57 TRANSLATN.*	
					Jour SJA 1 4 617	56 TRANSLATN.*	
Nonelastic	1.0+6	7.0+6	LAS	Expt	Jour PR 104 1319	Dec 56 Beyster+,SPH TRNS 2.25−2.45B 3ES	+
	1.0+6	7.0+6			Data EXFOR11220.029	Jun 76 . 3 PTS.	
Nonelastic	1.4+7		IFU	Expt	Jour AE 2 68	Jan 57 Strizhak.SPHERE TRANSMISS 2.35+−.14B	+
					Jour JNE 5 253	Nov 57 TRANSLATN.*	
					Jour SJA 2 72	57 TRANSLATN.*	
Nonelastic	Fiss		LAS	Expt	Jour JNE 4 147	Feb 57 Bethe+.SPH TRNSM,POOR RSLN DETECTORS	+
					Rept LA−1429	Dec 55 .SUPERSEDED	
	Fiss				Data EXFOR11461.	Jun 76 . 3 PTS. SIG FOR 3 DETECTORS	
Nonelastic	1.4+7		LRL	Expt	Jour PR 108 726	Nov 57 Macgregor+ SPH TRNS CFD OPTMDL+EXPTS	+
					Conf 58Geneva 14 109	Sep 58 Ball+.PPR1881,SPHERE TRANSM−METHOD	
	1.4+7				Data EXFOR11226.020	Jun 76 . 1 PT.	
Nonelastic	7.0+6	1.4+7	LRL	Revw	Rept UCRL−5345	Sep 58 Howerton.RVN EXP,+TBP BJORKLUND CCB	
Nonelastic	1.0+6	1.5+7	LOK	Theo	Conf 60Kingston 146	Aug 60 Walt+.CURVE,OPTMDL FIT CFD EXPT	
Nonelastic	8.0+5	2.5+6	IFU	ExTh	Jour AE 20 8	Jan 66 Korzh+ SUMMARY OF SEVERAL YRS WORK	+
					Jour UFZ 9 929	May 64 .	
					Jour SJA 20 8	Jul 66 .ENGLISH TRANSL OF AE 20 8 1/66	
	8.0+5	2.0+6			Rept INDSWG−101 112	65 .=UFZ9.ENGL NO GRPHS.RUSS LARGER GPH	
Nonelastic	1.5+7		BOS	Expt	Jour PR 161 1181	Sep 67 Chatterjee+ SPHERE .2.44+−.06B	+
	1.5+7				Data EXFOR30337.009	Jun 76 1 PNT	
Nonelastic	1.4+7		GHT	Expt	Jour ACA 64 187	73 Vandecasteele+ FLUX−ATTENUAT,SIG GVN	
Nonelastic	1.4+7		BOS	ExTh	Conf 74Calcutta 44	Nov 74 PAL+ SPHER TRANS.SIG GVN,OPTMOD ANAL	

74 Tungsten

Quantity	Energy (ev) Min	Max	Lab	Type	Documentation Ref Vol Page	Author, Comments Date	Data
Absorption	Pile		HAR	Expt	Jour PPSA 63 1175	Oct 50 Colmer+LITTLER.PILE OSC REL HAR B	+
					Rept AERE-N/R-527	Jun 50 - + PILE OSCILLATOR.	
Absorption	Fiss		WAD	Expt	Rept WADC-TR-58 266	Jan 58 Schamberger.REMOVL CS,SIG EFFECT GVN	
Absorption	2.5+4	8.3+5	FEI	Expt	Jour ZET 34 574	Mar 58 Belanova. VALUES GIVEN AT 3ES	+
					Jour JET 7 397	Sep 58 TRANSLATN.*	
Absorption	2.5+4		KUR	Expt	Conf 58Geneva 15 50	Sep 58 Leipunskij+.PPR2219,VAL GVN,ACTIVATN	
Absorption	2.5-2		HAR	Expt	Jour JNEA 12 32	May 60 Tattersall+. PILE OSCILLATOR	+
					Rept AERE-R-2887	Aug 59 - . PILE OSC.REL BORON	
	2.5-2				Data EXFOR20638.058	Jul 76 1PNT.SIGMA.	
Absorption	8.3+5		FEI	Expt	Jour AE 8 549	Jun 60 Belanova.VAL FOR 3ES,SPHERE TRNSMISS	
					Jour SJA 8 462	Jul 61 TRANSLATN.*GERMAN KE4 147 2/61	
Absorption	3.0+6	1.5+7	FEI	Expt	Book SPN 205	61 .ENGL TRANSL OF NEJTRONFIZ 278	
					Book NEJTRONFIZ 278	61 Kukhtevich+ SIGMA AT 2ES	
Absorption	2.4+4		FEI	Expt	Jour AE 19 3	Jul 65 Belanova+ 2 METHODS,ABSOL EXPT,TABLE	+
					Jour JNE 20 411	66 .ENGLISH TRANSL OF AE 19 3 7/65	
					Jour SJA 19 858	65 .ENGLISH TRANSL OF AE 19 3 7/65	
					Jour EAF 19 1 11	65 . FRENCH TRANSL OF AE 19 3 7/65	
	2.4+4				Data EXFOR40072.013	Jul 71 SIGMA AT 24 KEV AS PUBLISHED	
Res Int Abs	5.0-1	1.0+6	CCP	Expt	Conf 55Geneva 5 91	Aug 55 Spivak+.VAL GVN CFD REF,PPR659	
Res Int Abs	-		CCP	Expt	Jour AE 3 507	Dec 57 Klimentov+.EPI CD REACTIVITY REL LI	+
					Jour JNE 9 20	Jun 59 TRANSLATN.*	
					Jour SJA 3 1387	57 TRANSLATN.*	
Res Int Abs	5.0-1		HAR	Expt	Jour JNE 12 32	May 60 Tattersall+. ABOVE 1/V. OSC. CF CALC	+
					Rept AERE-R-2887	Aug 59 - . PILE OSC.REL BORON	
	6.7-1				Data EXFOR20638.059	Jul 76 1PNT.	
Res Int Abs	-		WIN	Expt	Jour JNAB 16 335	Jul 62 Moore+.CD TUBED OSC. NOT INF DILUTE	
					Rept AEEW-R-57	Aug 61 - + EQU TO JNE(A+B)16 335	
Res Int Abs	5.0-1		MTR	Expt	Abst ANS 5 377	Nov 62 Scoville.	+
	5.0-1				Data EXFOR12080.003	Jun 76 . 1 PT.	
Res Int Abs	5.0-1		LEB	ExTh	Jour AE 15 120	Aug 63 Kapchigashev+ 325 +- 20 B	
					Jour SJA 15 808	Aug 63 . ENGL OF AE 15 120	
Res Int Abs	4.1-1	1.5+7	GA	Eval	Rept GA-5885	Nov 64 Joanou+CALC FROM EVAL RES PARAM	
Res Int Abs	5.0-1		AE	Expt	Rept AE-RFT-113	Feb 65 Quensel. NON 1/V .026+- .006B REL B10	
Res Int Abs	None		WES	Eval	Rept WANL-TME-1472	Jul 66 Gibson+. CFD OTHERS	
Res Int Abs	5.0-1	1.2+2	AUS	Expt	Jour AKE 20 135	Nov 72 Heimel+ EFFECTIVE RESONINTEG,CFD TH	
(n,γ)	2.2+5		PCF	Expt	Jour NAT 142 392	Aug 38 Halban+ ACT CS GIVEN	
(n,γ)	Maxwl		ANL	Expt	Jour PR 75 531	Aug 49 Kubitscheck+ YIELD CFD SIG.G-M COINC	
(n,γ)	Pile		ANL	Expt	Jour PR 80 342	Nov 50 Harris+.PILE OSC.REL TO BORON.	+
	Pile				Data EXFOR11528.042	Jun 76 . 1 PT.	
(n,γ)	Maxwl		ORL	Expt	Jour PR 83 643	Aug 51 Pomerance.LOCAL OSC REL AU ABS 95 B	+
	Maxwl				Data EXFOR11047.058	Jun 76 . 1 PT.	
(n,γ)		1.0+2	BNL	Prog	WASH-190	Feb 56 Draper.NDG CYCL TOF SELFIND	
(n,γ)	1.5+7		HAR	Expt	Conf 57Col.Univ § 2B5	Sep 57 Lynn.UNPUBL EXPT. 4.0 MB	
(n,γ)	2.0+5		KUR	Expt	Conf 58Geneva 15 50	Sep 58 Leipunskij+.PPR2219,VAL GVN,ACTIVATN	
(n,γ)	Maxwl		MTR	Expt	Jour NSE 7 193	Feb 60 Schmunk+ 18+8+ -0.8B FROM 1/V FIT	+
	Maxwl				Data EXFOR11634.008	Jun 76 . 1 PT.	
(n,γ)	1.8+5	1.0+6	LAS	Expt	Jour PR 120 556	Oct 60 Diven.SC-T.	+
					Conf 58Geneva 15 60	Sep 58 .SUPERSEDED	
	1.8+5	1.0+6			Data EXFOR11616.025	Jun 76 . 7 PTS.	
	5.0+4	1.2+6	FEI	Expt	Book NEJTRONFIZ 310	61 Stavisskij. GRPH. ENGL TRNSL=SPN227	+
	5.0+4	1.0+6			Rept AEC-TR-3946	59 - + CA-F2 CRYS DET,+ -3TO6 PC	
(n,γ)	1.2+4	1.8+5	ORL	Expt	Jour PR 122 182	Apr 61 Gibbons.CURVE CFD THEORY REPL BNL653	+
	3.0+4	6.5+4			Jour PR 129 2695	Mar 63 Macklin+ LIQ SCINT,270 AND 190MB	
					Conf 61Vienna 1 95	Aug 61 Neiler.	
	1.2+4	1.8+5			Data EXFOR11329.	Jun 76 . 57 PTS.	
(n,γ)	2.0+2	8.0+3	ORL	Expt	Conf 61Saclay 203	Sep 61 Block+.LIQUID SCINTILLATOR	+
	2.0+2	1.0+4			Conf 61Vienna 1 95	Aug 61 Neiler.PPR73,TABLE FOR SOME ES,GRAPH	
	2.0+2	8.0+3			Data EXFOR11935.022	Jun 76 . 42 PTS.	
(n,γ)	Maxwl		MHG	Expt	Jour NP 34 623	Jun 62 Treado+ SIG=1.8B.SPECTRA OF GAMMAS	
(n,γ)	3.7-2	1.8+7	UNC	Comp	Rept UNC-PH/M-2813	Dec 62 Celnick. COMPILED MANY SOURCES	
(n,γ)	5.0+1	1.1+3	FEI	Expt	Rept FEI-	63 Shapar'+ SIGMA(N,GAMMA) TABL	
(n,γ)	1.8+4	3.0+5	FOA	Expt	Jour AF 23 425	Mar 63 Bergqvist.TOF 8 ES.NAI.REL AG. GRAPH	+
	1.9+4	3.0+5			Data EXFOR20024.004	Sep 71 8PTS.SIG.	
(n,γ)	3.0+4		ORL	Expt	Jour NP 43 353	May 63 Macklin+.SIG=184MB+ -21PC	+
	3.0+4				Data EXFOR11380.011	Jun 76 . 1 PT.	

74 Tungsten

Quantity	Energy (ev) Min	Max	Lab	Type	Documentation Ref Vol Page	Date	Author, Comments	Data
(n,γ)	Maxwl	5.0+4	CCP	ExTh	Jour AE 15 120	Aug 63	Kapchigashev+.PB SLOWING-DOWN CURVE	+
					Jour SJA 15 808	64	- +. ENGLISH	
					Jour EAF 15 2 2	Aug 63	- + FRENCH TRANSLATION	
(n,γ)	1.0+4	4.0+6	CJD	Comp Rept	INDSWG-64 43	64	. GRAPH VARIOUS EXPERIMENTS	
(n,γ)	None		LAS	Expt Prog	WASH-1048 56	Jun 64	Glass.TOF,PULSED DETONTNS SOURCE,TBC	
(n,γ)	5.0+3	9.0+4	ORL	Theo Jour	RMP 37 166	Jan 65	Macklin+.CALC FOR KT=5TO90KEV	
(n,γ)	1.0-3	1.0+2	WES	Eval Rept	WANL-TME-1472	Jul 66	Gibson+.CURVE CALC FROM RES	
(n,γ)	3.3+4	1.7+5	FEI	Expt Jour	YF 4 282	Aug 66	Kononov+ TOF,SCIN-TANK,GRPH CFD THEO	+
				Conf	66Paris 1 469	Oct 66	* GRAPH CFD OTHERS	
				Rept	EANDC-50 199	Jul 65	* GRPH EXPT CFD THEO	
				Jour	SNP 4 204	Feb 67	.ENGLISH TRANSL OF YF 4 282 8/66	
	2.9+4	1.7+5		Data	EXFOR40076.004	Jul 71	SIG AT 16 ENERGIES FROM PRIV COMMUN	
(n,γ)	1.0+3	1.0+6	KFK	Eval Conf	66Paris 1 277	Oct 66	Poenitz. TBL EVAL+RENORMAL TO AU	
(n,γ)	1.0-2	1.0+1	GA	Expt Jour	NSE 26 487	Dec 66	Friesenhahn+THR 18.3+ -.5 LIQ SCIN	+
				Conf	66Wash. 182	Mar 66	.SUPERSEDED	
				Rept	GA-6886	Jan 66	.SUPERSEDED	
	1.0-2	1.0+1		Data	EXFOR12167.	Jun 76	. 36 PTS.	
(n,γ)	1.3+5	2.2+5	ORL	Expt Jour	PR 159 1007	Jul 67	Macklin+ TOF,TOTAL-E DET, 4ES,ABSL	+
	1.3+5	2.2+5		Data	EXFOR11679.022	Jun 76	. 4 PTS.	
(n,γ)	2.0+2	1.0+4	KFK	Expt Conf	67Karlsrhe 1 77	Nov 67	Seufert+,HOT-TO-COLD CAPTURE RATIO	
(n,γ)	4.0+0	3.8+2	SAC	Expt Jour	NP/A 123 581	Jan 69	Samour+ GE(LI). TOTAL AMPLITUDE SPEC	
				Rept	CEA-R-3776	Apr 69	- . (THESIS) DATA GIVEN	
(n,γ)	1.0+4	1.5+5	KFK	Expt Jour	NP/A 133 513	Aug 69	Kompe.VDG.LIQ SCINT. REL AU MEAS.	+
				Rept	KFK-1071	Aug 69	- . REPRINT OF NP/A 133 513	
				Rept	EANDC(E)89U3	Feb 68	- . RENORMAL OF 66PARIS	
				Rept	KFK-635	Oct 67	Ponitz+ SUPERSEEDED BY NP/A 133	
				Conf	66Paris 1 513	Oct 66	Kompe. LARGE LIQ SCIN.GRPH.SUPERSEDD	
	1.2+4	1.5+5		Data	EXFOR20358.029	Sep 74	68PTS.SIGMA.	
(n,γ)	1.0+3	1.0+6	GA	Theo Conf	70Helsinki 2 281	Jun 70	Fricke+44. SIG(E) GRAPH,OPTMOD CALC	
	1.0+3	7.0+5		Jour	PL/B 29 393	Jun 69	- +G STRENTH FN AS FN EXCIT E	
(n,γ)	3.0+4		AUA	Theo Rept	AAEC/E-211	Nov 70	Musgrove. SIGMA GIVEN AND CFD OTHER	
(n,γ)	1.0+3	1.0+6	GA	Expt Conf	71Knoxvill 252	Mar 71	Fricke+,ABSOL AVG SIG,NO DATA GIVEN	+
				ExTh	70Helsinki 2 265	Jun 70	- + TOF	
	1.0+3	6.4+5		Expt Rept	GA-10114	May 70	- +	
	1.0+3	6.4+5		Data	EXFOR10049.005	Jul 71	. 92 PTS, SIGMA	
(n,γ)	None		LAS	Theo Jour	PRL 29 1567	Dec 72	Devaney. MULTIPLE-REACTION CORRCTN	
(n,γ)	5.0+3	2.0+7	LAS	Eval Rept	LA-5221	May 73	Devaney+. ENDF/B LISTING. CURVES	+
(n,γ)	1.4+7		NJS	Expt Jour	NP/A 213 525	Oct 73	Potokar+ INTEGRATED FROM SPECTRUM	
				Priv	CVELBAR	Oct 72	.INTEG SIG	
	1.4+7			Data	EXFOR30185.008	Oct 72	1 DATA LINE	
(n,γ)	Fast		RCN	Expt Rept	ECN-10	Oct 76	Veenema+ STEK REACTIVITY WORTHS TBL.	
Spect (n,γ)	Maxwl		ANL	Expt Jour	PR 76 531	Aug 49	Kubitscheck+ MAX E.G-M COINC+ABSORBR	
Spect (n,γ)	Maxwl		ANL	Expt Jour	PR 80 415	Nov 50	Hamermesh.FOTOPLATE,GAMMAS ABVE 3MEV	
				Rept	ANL-4437 48	Apr 50	.SUPERSEDED	
Spect (n,γ)	Maxwl		CRC	Expt Jour	CJP 31 1051	Nov 53	Kinsey+ PAIR SPECT,LINE WIDTH=100KEV	
Spect (n,γ)	Fast		CNE	Expt Jour	ZN/A 11 679	Aug 56	Gatti+ HF183(HL=64MIN)PRODUCED	
Spect (n,γ)	Maxwl		GEA	Eval Rept	DC-58-1-30	Jan 58	Deloume.BY APPROXIMATION CURV+TABLE	
Spect (n,γ)	Maxwl		ARF	Expt Prog	ARF-1193-17	Dec 62	Greenwood+NAI(TL) SPEC 4GAMMAS	
				Prog	ARF-1193-12	Jul 62	- +,CRYST SPEC,LOW-E GAMMAS	
Spect (n,γ)	Maxwl	3.0+5	FOA	ExTh Jour	NP 39 353	Dec 62	Bergqvist+.5 ES.GRAPH. CFD STAT THEO	
				Conf	61Saclay	61	- + SUPERSEDED	
Spect (n,γ)	3.7-2	1.8+7	UNC	Comp Rept	UNC-PH/M-2813	Dec 62	Celnick. COMPILED MANY SOURCES	
Spect (n,γ)	9.0+1	5.6+2	ORL	Expt Prog	ORNL-3425 64	63	Block+TOF SPECTRUM REL	
Spect (n,γ)	Maxwl		CAS	Expt Jour	NC 29 977	Aug 63	Giannini+ NAI, E+INTENSITY,TO 271KEV	+
Spect (n,γ)	7.6+0	4.0+1	ITE	Expt Jour	ZET 45 875	Oct 63	Ignat'Ev.GRAPH G-SPEC FROM 3RES,J=1	
				Jour	JET 18 602	Mar 64	TRANSLATN.*	
Spect (n,γ)	6.0-2	1.0+4	BNL	Expt Jour	NIM 53 108	Jul 67	Chrien+ GE-LI FAST CHOPPER	
	+0	+2		Conf	66Argonne 459	Nov 66	- +,GE(LI),1.8-7.7 MEV GAMMAS	
Spect (n,γ)	+0	+4	COL	Expt Prog	WASH-1124 31	Nov 68	Camarda+ MOXON-RAE DET TBC NO DATA	
Spect (n,γ)	2.5-2		MIT	Comp Rept	MITNE-85	Jan 69	Rasmussen+TBL G INT.=AFCRL-69-0071	
Spect (n,γ)	Maxwl		SAC	Expt Jour	NP/A 123 581	Jan 69	Samour+ GE(LI). 34LINES 4098-7413KEV	
				Rept	CEA-R-3776	Apr 69	- . (THESIS) DATA GIVEN	
Spect (n,γ)	Pile		ANL	Expt Prog	WASH-1127 10	Apr 69	Bollinger+ LVL STRUCTRE ONLY,TBC,NDG	
Spect (n,γ)	None		GA	Expt Conf	69Studsvik 117	Aug 69	Orphan+ NDG,GE(LI)-NAI,LINAC,TBP NIM	
	2.0-2	1.0+2		Jour	NIM 72 254	Mar 69	- +RESONANCE CAPTURE	
Spect (n,γ)	Maxwl		KFI	Expt Jour	YF 10 907	Nov 69	Kecskemeti+ AVG GAM-MULTIPLICITY,TBL	
				Jour	SNP 10 524	May 70	TRANSLATN.*	

74 Tungsten

Quantity	Energy (ev) Min	Max	Lab	Type	Documentation Ref Vol Page	Date	Author, Comments	Data
Spect (n,γ)	Maxwl		WAL	Eval	Rept WANL-TME-2713	Jul 70	Fody.GAM YLDS FOR WANL POINT LIBRARY	
Spect (n,γ)	1.4+7		NJS	Expt	Jour NP/A 213 525	Oct 73	Potokar+ D-T NS. PAIR SPECTROMETER.	+
				Priv	CVELBAR	Oct 72	.PROMPT GAMMA-RAY SPECTRUM	
	1.4+7			Data	EXFOR30185.009	Oct 72	25 DATA LINES	
Spect (n,γ)	1.0+6	1.0+7	CRC	Revw	Conf 74Petten 119	Sep 74	Bartholomew+ PHOTON STRF GRPH	
Spect (n,γ)	2.4+4		ATH	Expt	Prog INDC(SEC)-51	Dec 75	Dritsa+ GELI,ANALYS IN PROGRESS,NDG	
Inelastic γ	1.2+5	1.7+6	MIT	Expt	Jour PR 101 1516	Mar 56	Guernsey+ CS 115-KEV LEVEL	+
					Rept AECU-3021	Feb 55	.SUPERSEDED	
	3.0+5	1.7+6			Data EXFOR11691.006	Jun 76	. 15 PTS, SIG	
Inelastic γ	2.6+6		NRL	Expt	Rept NRL-4937	Jun 57	Shapiro+. NAI SCINT SPEC,GAM SP GIVN	
Inelastic γ	3.0+6		FEI	Expt	Jour AE 7 268	Sep 59	Androsenko+ GRAPH+TABLE OF G-ENERGS	
					Jour SJA 7 763	Mar 61	. ENGL OF AE 7 268	
					Jour JNEA 12 136	Jun 60	. ENGL OF AE 7 268	
					Jour KE 3 565	Jun 60	. GERMAN OF AE 7 268	
Inelastic γ	3.7-2	1.8+7	UNC	Comp	Rept UNC-PH/M-2813	Dec 62	Celnick. COMPILED MANY SOURCES	
Inelastic γ	5.8+6	7.5+6	FOA	Expt	Jour NP 80 198	May 66	Bergqvist+CFD SPEC IN CAPT.AT 0.1MEV	
					Conf 65Antwerp 505	Jul 65	- + PPR28.ABST.NDG.	
Inelastic γ	5.0+6	7.0+6	ALD	Expt	Jour NP/A 112 337	May 68	Owens+.3ES.TOF SPECT 90 DEG. NDG.	+
Inelastic γ	5.0+6	1.1+7	TNC	Expt	Rept DASA-2333	Jul 69	Tucker+VDG.GAMS DIFF CS.TBLS,GRPHS.	+
	5.0+6	1.1+7			Data EXFOR10091.	Dec 75	. 80PTS.G PROD CS.	
Inelastic γ	8.7+6		BRC	Expt	Conf 69Studsvik 119	Aug 69	Haouat+ SPEC-GRPH,RESON+ISOT IDENTFD	
Inelastic γ	4.0+6	7.5+6	LAS	Expt	Jour NSE 40 294	May 70	Drake+,TOF,NAI(TL) DET,DIFFNTL SIGS	+
					Conf 66Paris 1 419	Oct 66	Conde+SUPERSEDED.	
	3.5+6	7.5+6			Conf 66Wash. 2 735	Mar 66	+SUPERSEDED.	
	4.0+6	7.5+6			Data EXFOR10025.019	Jul 74	. 46 PTS.	
Inelastic γ	3.0+5	1.0+6	TNC	Expt	Prog NCSAC-31 214	May 70	Nellis+,TO BE COMPLETED,NO DATA GIVN	
Inelastic γ	3.0+5	1.5+7	TNC	Expt	Rept ORO-2791-32	Feb 71	Buchanan+.5NEUT ES,55-DEG SIGS	
	1.0+6				Prog ORO-2791-84	Aug 67	Morgan+ DIFF SIG(55DEG).062-.904MEVG	
	4.1+6	1.5+7			Rept TID-20658	Sep 63	- +,GAMMA SPEC+PROD SIGS,90DEG	
Inelastic γ	Pile		FEI	Expt	Prog YFI-12 14	72	Bakov+ AVG SIG OF GAM YLD,ABST,NDG	
					Prog INDC(CCP)-30	Dec 72	.PG 11,ENGLISH OF YFI-12 14	
Inelastic γ	1.0+6	1.5+6	LAS	Eval	Conf 75Wash. 149	Mar 75	Young.ORELA MEAS CFD ENDF AT 125 DEG	
Inelastic γ	2.5+6		FEI	Expt	Rept YK-22 21		76 Bezotosnyj+ SIG(10EGAM-INTERVLS),TBL	
Nonelastic γ	2.1+6	2.8+6	OSA	Expt	Jour JMJ 21 232		39 Aoki.SIG GIVN	
	2.4+6				Jour JMJ 21 75		39 Kikuchi+.D-P LI-D N,SIG GIVN	
		2.4+6			Jour JPJO 19 369		37 Aoki.D+D NEUTRON.RELATIV SIG GIVN	
Nonelastic γ	4.4+6		WES	Expt	Jour PR 107 1306	Sep 57	Sinclair.XTL SPEC REL CRV 100KEV G	
					Rept AECU-3387	55	. PHS+2 GAM ES GIVN.NAI(TL)	
Nonelastic γ	3.5+6	8.5+6	ALD	Expt	Jour NP 60 561	Dec 64	Perkin.TABLE OF G PROD SIG GIVN.	+
Nonelastic γ		1.0+7	GEN	Eval	Rept GEMP-360	Aug 65	Edwards. 15-GROUP GAM PRODUCTN SIGS	
Nonelastic γ	4.1+6	1.5+7	LRL	Theo	Jour NSE 32 178	May 68	Howerton+ 3ES CALCTD SIGS CFD EXPTS	
Nonelastic γ	1.4+7		LAS	Expt	Prog USNDC-7 128	Jun 73	Drake+. NO DATA GIVEN. TO BE COMPLTD	
Nonelastic γ	1.4+7		KUR	Expt	Conf 75Kiev 4 133	May 75	Bezotosnyj+ NA-I.SIG(.5-7.0MEV) GIVN	
(n,2n)	1.4+7		LRL	Expt	Conf 58Geneva 15 3	Sep 58	Ashby+PPR2494,VAL GVN,TOF	+
	1.4+7				Data EXFOR11632.012	Jun 76	. 1 PT.	
(n,2n)	1.5+7		TNC	Expt	Rept AFSWC-TR-60-30	60	Prudhomme+	+
	1.5+7				Data EXFOR11183.015	Jun 76	. 10 PTS, DSIG	
(n,2n)	3.7-2	1.8+7	UNC	Comp	Rept UNC-PH/M-2813	Dec 62	Celnick. COMPILED MANY SOURCES	
(n,2n)	1.4+7		FEI	Expt	Conf 70Helsinki 2 359	Jun 70	Salnikov+79.(N,2N)+(N,N') TOF EXPT	
					Rept BNL-TR-545	Jul 73	. ENGLISH OF 70HELSIN 2 359	
(n,2n)	1.5+7		DEB	Eval	Jour REA 11 1 153	Mar 73	Boedy+ RECOMM.VALUE FROM N-Z SYSTEM.	
n Emission	1.5+7		TNC	Expt	Jour PR 186 1038		69 Mathur+TOF.90 DEG.MULTISCAT CORRC.	+
					Rept NDL-TR-86	Jan 67	- +EXPT+MULTISCAT CORRC DETAILS.	
	1.5+7				Data EXFOR10090.021	May 73	.2PTS.NEM.CS=271.53,148.61 MB/SR	
n Emission	1.4+7		FEI	Expt	Rept YK-7 102	Mar 72	Salnikov+	+
					Conf 70Helsinki 2 359	Jun 70	- +79. EXPTL+OTHER'S SIGMA GVN	
					Rept BNL-TR-545	Jul 73	. ENGLISH OF 70HELSIN 2 359	
	1.4+7				Data EXFOR40037.	Aug 72	5 SUBENT,DIFF+DOUBLE DIFF N-EMISS CS	
n Emission	1.5+7		TUD	Expt	Jour KE 19 241	Aug 76	Hermsdorf+ ABSOL DOUBDIF,FIG.TOT,TBL	+
					Rept ZFK-277(U)	Aug 75	- + DIFFSIG AT 5ANGS,TBL+GRPH	
					Conf ZFK-271 94	Nov 73	Goebel+ N-EMISSION SPEC,TOF.SUMMARY	
	1.5+7				Data EXFOR30397.028	May 77	51 PTS. ANGLE INT.N-EMISS.SPECT.	
	1.5+7				Data EXFOR30275.	Apr 74	DOUBLDIF(5ANG,473PTS)+PARTIAL ANGDIS	
Fission	1.4+7		LAS	Expt	Jour PR 75 919	Mar 49	Phillips+ UPPER LIM REL U238.PHOTOPL	
Reson Params	4.0+0	1.8+2	COL	Expt	Jour PR 71 165	Feb 47	Havens+ TRANSM.TOF.APPROX STRFNC 5E0	+
	4.0+0	1.8+2			Data EXFOR12184.005	Jun 76	. 5 RES, EO,WT**2/PCS	

74 Tungsten

Quantity	Energy (ev) Min	Max	Lab	Type	Documentation Ref Vol Page	Author, Comments Date	Data
Reson Params	7.6+0	1.6+2	ORL	Expt Abst	BAP 3 177	Apr 58 Harvey. ABST. F11. EN. J.	+
	7.6+0	1.6+2		Data	EXFOR12154.006	Jun 76 . 7 RES, EO,J	
Reson Params	6.5+1	5.9+3	SAC	Expt Jour	CR 249 413	Jul 59 Corge+ E0 ONLY FOR 61RES.	+
	6.5+1	5.9+3		Data	EXFOR20678.	Sep 77 59PTS.E0,MEAN LVL SPACING.	
Reson Params	7.6+0		SAC	Theo Jour	JPR 24 176	Mar 63 Le Pipec+NDG LATTICE BINDING EFFECTS	
				Expt Jour	CR 255 1913	Oct 62 - +DOPPLER BROADENING CFD TH.	
Reson Params	4.1+0		BNL	ExTh Rept	BNL - 860	Apr 64 Bernabei.DOPPLER BROADENING STUDY	
				Abst	DA 25 6010	Apr 65 .THESIS ABST	
Reson Params	None		RPI	Expt Abst	DA/B 30 3819	Feb 70 King.LINAC.LI6 SCIN.RES PARAMS.SPIN.	
	4.0+0	4.8+1		Jour	NIM 52 321	Jun 67 - + LI - GLASS/LIQSCINT,G FOR 7 RES	
Reson Params	4.1+0	1.6+3	JAE	Expt Priv	OHKUBO	Nov 76 Ohkubo+ TABLE NUMERICAL DATA.	+
				Rept	JAERI - M - 5624	Feb 74 - + PARAMETERS FOR W - 182,183,4,6	
	4.1+0	1.6+3		Data	EXFOR20818.002	Mar 79 100PTS.RED.2G*WN,WT,WG.	
Strnth Fnctn	+4		HAR	Expt Jour	PPSA 70 51	Jan 57 Gayther+ FROM AVG SIGTOT. FC TRANSM	
Strnth Fnctn	+3	+5	MTR	Expt Prog	WASH - 1013	Nov 58 Simpson+ NDG FC TBC	
Strnth Fnctn	+3		BNL	Expt Jour	PRL 1 461	Dec 58 Hughes.FC 3.0+ - 1.0	
Strnth Fnctn	3.0+3	6.5+5	DKE	Expt Jour	PL 13 70	Nov 64 Seth+S,P,D STF FROM SIG TOT.	+
	5.0+4	1.5+5		Conf	64Paris 2 916	Jul 64 - +S0,S1,S2 R PRIME/R DUKE U.	
	3.0+3	6.5+5		Data	EXFOR11665.027	Jun 76 . 3 PTS.	
Strnth Fnctn	None		DKE	Expt Abst	DA/B 28 3834	Mar 68 Divadeenam.S,P,D WAVES.CFD POT MDLS.	
Strnth Fnctn	1.0+4	1.5+5	KFK	Expt Jour	NP/A 133 513	Aug 69 Kompe. S1,S2,S(GAMMA)LEAST SQ NG FIT	+
				Rept	KFK - 1071	Aug 69 - REPRINT OF NP/A 133 513	
	1.0+4	1.5+5		Data	EXFOR20358.	Sep 74 3PTS.GAMMA STF.	
Strnth Fnctn	2.7+3		MUN	Expt Conf	71Albany 327	Aug 76 Dilg+TRNS.S0 STF GVN.31 ELEMENT GRPH	
Lvl Density	6.0+6		DKE	Expt Rept	AD - 299005	62 Seth+,NUCL TEMP+FERMI LVL DENS COEFF	
Lvl Density	2.4+6	7.0+6	RIC	Expt Rept	SCR - 466	Feb 62 Ewing+,PARAM A FROM INELAST,3 ES	
Lvl Density	1.4+7		FEI	Theo Conf	64Paris 2 762	Jul 64 Malushev+.THERMOD T VERSUS XPT+FMGAS	
Lvl Density	1.4+7		FEI	Expt Jour	YF 2 826	Nov 65 Anufrienko+.PARAMS FROM NONELASTIC	+
				Rept	FEI - 30	Dec 65 .	
				Rept	EANDC - 50 197	Jul 65 .FULL PAPER FROM 65ANTWERP	
				Rept	FEI - 4	65 .	
				Jour	SNP 2 589	May 66 .ENGLISH TRANSL OF YF 2 826 11/65	
Lvl Density	5.0+6	7.0+6	ALD	Expt Jour	NP/A 112 337	May 68 Owens+.LVL DENS VERSUS EXCIT.MEAN T	+
				Conf	65Antwerp 547	Jul 65 - + PPR122. TBL FERMI GAS CONST.	
Lvl Density	1.5+7		TNC	Expt Jour	PR 186 1038	Oct 69 Mathur+,FERMI GAS LVL DENSITY COEF	
				Rept	NDL - TR - 86	Jan 67 - +EXPT+MULTISCAT CORRC DETAILS.	
	1.5+7			Data	EXFOR10090.037	May 73 . 2 PTS. NUCLEAR T=.72, .29 MEV.	
Lvl Density	1.4+7		FEI	Expt Conf	70Helsinki 2 359	Jun 70 Salnikov+79. TEMP GVN,(N,N'+2N) EXPT	
				Rept	BNL - TR - 545	Jul 73 . ENGLISH OF 70HELSIN 2 359	
(γ,n)	+7		BNL	Expt Jour	PR 79 539	Aug 50 Poss.N INTENSITY 0/90DEG,BY AL(NP)	

74 Tungsten 172

Quantity	Energy (ev) Min	Max	Lab	Type	Documentation Ref Vol Page	Author, Comments Date	Data
Lvl Density	None		CCP	Theo Jour	YF 13 43	Jan 71 Bravin+.DEFORM PAR,CALC,TBL,CFD EXPT	

74 Tungsten 174

Quantity	Energy (ev) Min	Max	Lab	Type	Documentation Ref Vol Page	Author, Comments Date	Data
Lvl Density	None		CCP	Theo Jour	YF 13 43	Jan 71 Bravin+.DEFORM PAR,CALC,TBL,CFD EXPT	

74 Tungsten 176

Quantity	Energy (ev) Min	Max	Lab	Type	Documentation Ref Vol Page	Author, Comments Date	Data
Lvl Density	None		CCP	Theo Jour	YF 13 43	Jan 71 Bravin+.DEFORM PAR,CALC,TBL,CFD EXPT	

74 Tungsten 178

Quantity	Energy (ev) Min	Max	Lab	Type	Documentation Ref Vol Page	Author, Comments Date	Data
Lvl Density	None		CCP	Theo Jour	YF 13 43	Jan 71 Bravin+.DEFORM PAR,CALC,TBL,CFD EXPT	

74 Tungsten 179

Quantity	Energy (ev) Min	Max	Lab	Type	Documentation Ref Vol Page	Author, Comments Date	Data
Reson Params	–		AUA	Theo Rept	AAEC/E – 211	Nov 70 Musgrove. CALCULTD D+GAM WIDTH GIVEN	
Strnth Fnctn	–		AUA	Theo Rept	AAEC/E – 211	Nov 70 Musgrove. SMOOTHED S0,S1 AND S2 GIVN	

74 Tungsten 180

Quantity	Energy (ev) Min	Max	Lab	Type	Documentation Ref Vol Page	Author, Comments Date	Data
(n,γ)	Maxwl		ORL	Expt Jour	PR 88 412	Oct 52 Pomerance.PILE OSC.ESTIM.ERROR 400PC	+
	Maxwl			Data	EXFOR11507.090	Aug 76 . 1 PT.	
(n,γ)	–		IEA	Comp Rept	IEA – INF – 10	Aug 68 Atalla. TABLES OF HL,SIG AND GAMM – E	
(n,γ)	3.0+4		AUA	Theo Rept	AAEC/E – 211	Nov 70 Musgrove. SIGMA GIVEN AND CFD OTHER	
(n,γ)	1.0+3	1.0+7	BOL	Eval Data	BENZI – DFN 813.	May 72 40 PNTS	+
Inelastic γ	None		KFI	Comp Jour	JRC 7 365	Jun 71 Nagy+ MAX GAMMA – E AND HALF – LIFE GIVN	
(n,2n)	Fiss		CRC	Eval Rept	CRC – 1003	Dec 60 Roy+,ESTIMATED AVG SIG=2.7MB	
(n,2n)	1.5+7		DEB	Eval Jour	REA 11 1 153	Mar 73 Boedy+ RECOMM.VALUE FROM N – Z SYSTEM.	
(n,2n)	1.5+7		JUL	Expt Jour	NP/A 242 317	Apr 75 Qaim+ SIG MEASURED BY ACT,VS (N – Z)/A	+
	1.5+7			Data	EXFOR20668.	Oct 76 2PTS.SIGMA.	
(n,p)	Fiss		CRC	Eval Rept	CRC – 1003	Dec 60 Roy+,ESTIMATED AVG SIG=0.09MB	
(n,p)	Maxwl		IFU	Theo Rept	ICD – 4 20	67 Dadakina+ PENETR COEFF CALC,TABLE	
(n,p)	1.5+7		JUL	Expt Jour	NP/A 242 317	Apr 75 Qaim+ SIG MEASURED BY ACT,VS (N – Z)/A	+
	1.5+7			Data	EXFOR20668.004	Oct 76 1PNT.SIGMA.	
(n,α)	Fiss		CRC	Eval Rept	CRC – 1003	Dec 60 Roy+,ESTIMATED AVG SIG=0.0006MB	
Reson Params	1.6+1		ANL	Expt Jour	PR 132 1640	Nov 63 Bollinger.	+
Reson Params	1.6+1		RPI	Expt Prog	WASH – 1048 71	Jun 64 Block.ANL XPT ASSIGNED TO W180	
Reson Params	–		AUA	Theo Rept	AAEC/E – 211	Nov 70 Musgrove. CALCULTD D+GAM WIDTH GIVEN	
Reson Params	1.6+1	8.7+1	ORL	Expt Prog	ORNL – 3924 3	May 66 Jung+	+
	1.6+1	8.7+1		Data	EXFOR12161.002	Jun 76 . 5 RES,E0,WN	
Strnth Fnctn	–		AUA	Theo Rept	AAEC/E – 211	Nov 70 Musgrove. SMOOTHED S0,S1 AND S2 GIVN	
Lvl Density	None		CCP	Theo Jour	YF 13 43	Jan 71 Bravin+.DEFORM PAR,CALC,TBL,CFD EXPT	

74 Tungsten 181

Quantity	Energy (ev) Min	Max	Lab	Type	Documentation Ref Vol Page	Author, Comments Date	Data
Spect (n,γ)	Maxwl	9.1+5	PUR	ExTh Jour	NSE 47 209	Feb 72 Yost+. CAPTURE GAMMA YLDS.TBLS+CURVS	
(n,p)	Maxwl		IFU	Theo Rept	ICD – 4 20	67 Dadakina+ PENETR COEFF CALC,TABLE	
Reson Params	–		AUA	Theo Rept	AAEC/E – 211	Nov 70 Musgrove. CALCULTD D+GAM WIDTH GIVEN	
Strnth Fnctn	–		AUA	Theo Rept	AAEC/E – 211	Nov 70 Musgrove. SMOOTHED S0,S1 AND S2 GIVN	
Lvl Density	+6		MIL	Theo Jour	EN 15 1 54	Jan 68 Facchini+ LDL PARS FROM LOW EN RES	
Lvl Density	None		MUN	Theo Jour	NP/A 217 269	Dec 73 Dilg+ A,DELTA. BACK SHIFTED FERMIGAS	
Lvl Density	None		ROC	Theo Jour	NP/A 223 577	May 74 Huizenga+ EXP CFD MICROSC TH SPH NUC	

74 Tungsten 182

Quantity	Energy (ev) Min	Max	Lab	Type	Documentation Ref Vol Page	Author, Comments Date	Data
Evaluation	1.0–3	1.5+7	GA	Eval Rept	GA – 5885	Nov 64 Joanou+ TOT STF SEL SNE SIN N2N ETC.	
Evaluation	1.0+3	1.4+7	GEN	Eval Rept	GEMP – 388	Nov 65 Prince.OPTMDL WITH CHANNEL COMPETIT	
				Jour	ANS 8 457	Nov 65 .SUPERSEDED	
Evaluation	1.0–2	1.5+7	GEN	Eval Rept	GEMP – 448	Nov 66 Henderson+ TOT NG SIN N2N NP ENDF/B	
Evaluation	1.0–4	2.0+7	AI	Eval Rept	TI – 707 – 130 – 26	Jul 73 Rose+	
Total	3.3+0	5.2+5	ANL	Expt Jour	PR 84 869	Dec 51 Selove.	+
	3.3+0	2.1+5		Data	EXFOR12166.003	Jun 76 . 76 PTS.	
Total	4.1+0		BNL	Expt Jour	PR 100 1414	Dec 55 Landon.5050+ – 200B AT 4.14+ – 0.03EV	+
	4.1+0			Data	EXFOR12178.003	Jun 76 . 1 PT.	
Total	3.0+5	1.5+6	AI	Eval Rept	NAA – SR – 11973	Jul 66 Dunford.NONSPHERICAL OPTMDL 1TABLE	
Total	1.0+5	6.5+5	ANL	Expt Prog	ANL – 7210 16	Dec 66 Whalen.SHORT NOTE,GRAPH ONLY	+
	1.0+5	6.5+5		Data	EXFOR11540.009	Jun 76 . 266 PTS.	
Total	6.0+5	2.5+7	RPI	ExTh Abst	DA/B 28 3435	Feb 68 Martin.TOF.OKS DEFORMED NUCL OPTMOD	+
	7.0+5	1.5+7		Expt Data	EXFOR12159.003	Jun 76 . 547 PTS.	
Total	1.5+2	1.0+5	RPI	Expt Jour	NSE 37 137	Jul 69 Bartolome+LINAC,RES PARS FROM TRNS.	
	1.5+2	2.0+4		Abst	DA/B 30 679	Aug 69 – .RES PARS FROM TRNS.	
				Conf	68Wash. 795	Mar 68 – .RES PARS FROM TRNS,TBP,NDG	
Total	2.5+6	1.5+7	BNW	Expt Jour	PR/C 3 576	Feb 71 Foster+,TRANS,CURVS,CFD OTHERS+TH	+
				Jour	NIM 36 1	Sep 65 .EXPT DETAILS	
	2.3+6	1.5+7		Data	EXFOR10047.105	Aug 73 . 252PTS,DSIGMA	
Total	1.0+5	2.0+7	LAS	Eval Rept	LA – 4928	Jun 72 Devaney+EVAL.SMOOTH SIG CURVES.	

74 Tungsten 182

Quantity	Energy (ev) Min	Max	Lab	Type	Documentation Ref Vol Page	Date	Author, Comments	Data
Total	1.3+7	1.5+7	DEB	Eval	Rept IAEA – 153 173	73	Boedy+ MOST PROBABLE VAL OF SIG,TBL	
					Jour AHP 30 115	Oct 71	Angeli+ AVG SIG,CFD CALC.TBLS.GRAPH	
Total	None		SAC	Theo	Jour JPR 35 4	Sep 74	Lagrange+OPTMDL FOR EVEN ISO.DEFORMT	
Total	2.5+5	1.5+7	JAE	Theo	Conf JAERI – M – 5984	Feb 75	Tanaka.OPTMDL/COUPLD CH.GRPH CFD EXP	
Total	1.4+7		LIN	Expt	Conf 75Kiev 4 140	May 75	Djumin+ SIG GIVEN.OPTMOD ANAL,RADIUS	
Total	–3	1.9+0	THS	Theo	Rept IKE – 6 89 65	Jun 75	Keinert. DATA LIBRARY	
Elastic	3.0+5	1.5+6	AI	Eval	Rept NAA – SR – 11973	Jul 66	Dunford. NONSPH OPTMDL TABLE+ CURVES	
Elastic	3.3+5	1.4+6	ANL	Expt	Jour PR 162 1077	Oct 67	Lister+TOF.INTEGRATED DIFF SIG.	+
					Rept ANL – 7288	Jan 67	– + TOF 55ES TABLE+CURVE CFD TH	
	3.3+5	1.4+6			Data EXFOR12174.003	Jun 76	. 55 PTS.	
Elastic	3.4–2		DUB	Expt	Prog YFI – 7 58	Apr 69	Alexandrov+ SCAT – LENGTH GIVEN, TBP	
					Jour YF 10 328	Aug 69	Aleksandrov+ SCAT LENGTH GIVEN	
					Rept JINR – P3 – 4121	Oct 68	Alexandrov+ SCATTERING LENGTH, TBP	
					Jour SNP 10 189	Feb 70	. ENGL OF YF 10 328	
					Rept INDC(CCP) – 7U62	Feb 70	Alexandrov+ ENGL OF YFI – 7 58.	
Diff Elastic	3.0+5	1.5+6	AI	Eval	Rept NAA – SR – 11973	Jul 66	Dunford.NONSPH OPTMDL TABLE+CURVES	
Diff Elastic	4.1–1	1.0+7	WES	Eval	Rept WANL – TME – 1472	Jul 66	Gibson+.68GROUP P0 P1 MATRIX	
Diff Elastic	3.0+5	1.5+6	ANL	Expt	Jour PR 162 1077	Oct 67	Lister+ FAST TOF 27 – 150DEG CURVES	+
					Rept ANL – 7288	Jan 67	.SEE ALSO	
	3.3+5	1.4+6			Data EXFOR12175.002	Jun 76	. 275 LEG COEFS. AT 55ES	
Tot Inelastc	3.0+5	1.5+6	AI	Eval	Rept NAA – SR – 11973	Jul 66	Dunford.NONSPH OPTMDL TABLE+CURVES	
Diff Inelast	4.1–1	1.0+7	WES	Eval	Rept WANL – TME – 1472	Jul 66	Gibson+.68GROUP MATRIX	
Diff Inelast	3.0+5	1.5+6	ANL	Expt	Jour PR 162 1077	Oct 67	Lister+ FAST TOF 2STATES CRVS CFD TH	+
					Rept ANL – 7288	Jan 67	.SEE ALSO	
	3.0+5	1.5+6			Data EXFOR12174.004	Jun 76	. 81 PTS, SIG	
Diff Inelast	+6	+7	BRC	Expt	Conf 69Studsvik 119	Aug 69	Haouat+ NDG,SIG+ANGDIST,STRONG TRANS	
Nonelastic	None		CCP	Theo	Conf 68Riga	Jan 68	Gordeev+ ABST,EXCITATION FN CALCUL	
Res Int Abs	5.0–1		COL	Expt	Jour NSE 48 219	Jun 72	Rahn+. RI=592+ – 60B	
(n,γ)	Maxwl		ORL	Expt	Rept PR 88 412	Oct 52	Pomerance.PILE OSC.	+
(n,γ)	Maxwl				Data EXFOR11507.091	Jun 76	. 1 PT.	
(n,γ)	+0	1.5+3	HAR	Expt	Jour NP 3 553	Jun 57	Bowey. TOF. CAPT GAM YLD CURVE	
(n,γ)	Maxwl		MHG	Expt	Jour NP 34 623	Jun 62	Treado+ SIG=20.0B.SPECTRA OF GAMMAS	
(n,γ)	Maxwl	+5	FOA	Expt	Jour NP 39 353	Dec 62	Bergqvist+. IN PER CENT OF NAT ELEMT	
(n,γ)			LEB	Comp	Rept INDSWG – 64 43	64	Konks. GRAPH SIG(E)	
(n,γ)	1.0–3	1.0+7	WES	Eval	Rept WANL – TME – 1472	Jul 66	Gibson+.68GROUPS .4EV UP+CURVE – 100EV	
(n,γ)	3.3+4	1.7+5	FEI	Expt	Jour YF 4 282	Aug 66	Kononov+ TOF,SCIN – TANK,GRPH CFD THEO	+
					Conf 66Paris 1 469	Oct 66	* GRAPH CFD OTHERS	
					Rept EANDC – 50 199	Jul 65	* GRPH EXPT CFD THEO	
					Jour SNP 4 204	Feb 67	.ENGLISH TRANSL OF YF 4 282 8/66	
	2.9+4	1.7+5			Data EXFOR40076.005	Jul 71	SIG AT 15 ENERGIES FROM PRIV COMMUN	
(n,γ)	1.0–2	1.0+1	GA	Expt	Jour NSE 26 487	Dec 66	Friesenhahn+THR 20.7+ – .5 LIQ SCIN	+
					Conf 66Wash. 182	Mar 66	.SUPERSEDED	
					Rept GA – 6882	Jan 66	.SUPERSEDED	
	1.0–2	1.0+1			Data EXFOR12167.	Jun 76	. 35 PTS.	
(n,γ)	–		IEA	Comp	Rept IEA – INF – 10	Aug 68	Atalla. TABLES OF HL,SIG AND GAMM – E	
(n,γ)	1.5+2	1.0+5	RPI	Expt	Jour NSE 37 137	Jul 69	Bartolome+CAPT AREA,NO CS GVN.	
	1.5+2	2.0+4			Abst DA/B 30 679	Aug 69	– +LINAC,RES PARS FROM DATA.	
					Conf 68Wash. 795	Mar 68	– +AVG CAPT CS GRPHS.	
	4.0+2	8.0+3			Conf 66Wash. 404	Mar 66	Gibbons.RPI LINAC+SC(T)CURVE	
	3.5+1	1.0+4			Prog ORNL – 3778 53	May 65	Block.LINAC,SC,NUMEROUS RES,CRVS	
(n,γ)	3.0+4		AUA	Theo	Rept AAEC/E – 211	Nov 70	Musgrove. SIGMA GIVEN AND CFD OTHER	
(n,γ)	Maxwl		KFI	Comp	Jour JRC 7 365	Jun 71	Nagy+ SIGMA,GAM+XRAY+ELECTR ES GIVEN	
(n,γ)	1.0+3	1.0+7	BOL	Eval	Data BENZI – DFN 814.	May 72	40 PNTS	+
(n,γ)	Pile		ROS	ExTh	Prog ZFK – 243 93	Sep 72	Mohsen+ NG – SYSTEMAT. FOR RARE EARTHS	
(n,γ)	5.0+3	2.0+7	LAS	Eval	Rept LA – 5221	May 73	Devaney+. ENDF/B LISTING. CURVES	
Spect (n,γ)	Maxwl		KJL	Expt	Jour NP 2 664	Feb 57	Trumpy.CIRCULAR POL OF 6.18 MEV GAM.	
Spect (n,γ)	4.1+0	1.9+1	HAR	Expt	Conf 58Geneva 14 294	Sep 58	Bird.CURVE,PPR35,NAI(TL) – DETECTOR	
Spect (n,γ)	4.2+0	2.1+1	ORL	Expt	Conf 61Saclay 203	Sep 61	Block+.AT 4.2 21 EV.LIQUID SCINTILTR	
Spect (n,γ)	4.1+0		BNL	Expt	Conf 63ANL 324	Oct 63	Moore+ SPECTRA FOR 4.14EV RESON NAI	
Spect (n,γ)	4.1+0	2.1+1	ITE	Expt	Conf ZET 45 870	Oct 63	Ratynskil.G – SPEC FROM 2 N – RES COMPRD	
					Jour JET 18 598	Mar 64	TRANSLATN.*	
Spect (n,γ)	4.1+0		ITE	Expt	Conf JINR – 1845 140	Jun 64	Beljaev+ TOF,TBL,E – GAMM=5.05 MEV	
Spect (n,γ)	Maxwl		ORL	Expt	Abst BAP 11 336	Apr 66	Martin+ (D,P) EXPTS.	
Spect (n,γ)	4.1+0		NRL	Expt	Jour NP 82 441	Jul 66	Vogt+ AT RESONANCE NATURAL TARGET	
Spect (n,γ)	4.1+0	1.1+2	BNL	Expt	Conf 66Argonne 459	Nov 66	Chrien+,GE(LI),30GAMS 3.6 – 6.2MEV	
					Jour NIM 53 108	Jul 67	.SEE ALSO	
					Jour NIM 53 93	Jul 67	.SEE ALSO	
Spect (n,γ)	6.0–2	4.1+0	MTR	Expt	Jour PR 155 1368	Mar 67	Spencer+0.06EV+1RES 4 – 6MEV GS. X ABS	

74 Tungsten 182

Quantity	Energy (ev) Min	Energy (ev) Max	Lab	Type	Documentation Ref Vol Page	Author, Comments Date	Data
Spect (n,γ)	4.1+0	1.1+2	RPI	Expt	Jour PR 155 1301	Mar 67 Rae+,3RES,4LINES 5.2-6.2MEV, ABS INT	
Spect (n,γ)	Maxwl	2.2+2	ANL	Expt	Jour PR 160 1038	Aug 67 Cote+ TOF,INT 3TRANS FOR THR + 4RES	
Spect (n,γ)	+0	+4	COL	Expt	Prog WASH-1124 31	Nov 68 Camarda+ MOXON-RAE DET TBC NO DATA	
Spect (n,γ)	4.0+0	1.1+2	SAC	Expt	Jour NP/A 123 581	Jan 69 Samour+ GE(LI).3RES. 3690TO8450 KEV	
					Rept CEA-R-3776	Apr 69 - . (THESIS) DATA GIVEN	
Spect (n,γ)	2.5+1	6.0+1	GA	Expt	Jour NIM 72 254	Mar 69 Orphan+RESONANCE CAPTURE	
Spect (n,γ)	None		BNL	Expt	Conf 69Studsvik 627	Aug 69 Chrien. WG/WN-CORREL,WG CFD P-T,TBLS	
Spect (n,γ)	4.1+0	4.9+2	HAR	Expt	Rept 69Studsvik 579	Aug 69 Murray+ GAM INTENS TBL VS GAM-E,N-E	
Spect (n,γ)	Pile		IBJ	Expt	Rept INR-1262/IA/PL	Feb 71 Ratynski.G CIRC POLARIZ,POLARIZED NS	
Spect (n,γ)	Maxwl		INL	Expt	Prog NCSAC-38 86	May 71 Greenwood+. 2ES. CURVES	
Spect (n,γ)	Maxwl		KFI	Comp	Jour JRC 7 365	Jun 71 Nagy+ SIGMA,GAM+XRAY+ELECTR ES GIVEN	
Spect (n,γ)	Maxwl		RCN	Expt	Jour NP/A 181 250	Feb 72 Stecher-Rasmussen+GAM CIRC POL.SPINS	
					Rept RCN-152	Jun 71 - + (THESIS)	
Spect (n,γ)	4.1+0		BNL	Expt	Jour PR/C 7 419	Jan 73 Casten+. GE(LI) DET. TABLE+CURVE.	
Spect (n,γ)	2.4+4		BNL	Expt	Prog USNDC-9 52	Dec 73 Rimawi+. NO DATA GIVEN.	
Spect (n,γ)	2.8+6		KGU	Expt	Conf 76Lowell 1334	Jul 76 Andreev+DIRECT EXCIT EFFECTS.NDG	
Inelastic γ	2.6+6		NRL	Expt	Rept NRL-4937	Jun 57 Shapiro+. NAI SCINT SPEC.GAM SP GIVE	
Inelastic γ	5.0+5	1.5+6	WES	Expt	Jour PR 107 1306	Sep 57 Sinclair.XTL SPEC REL CURV 100KEV G	
Inelastic γ	8.7+6		BRC	Expt	Conf 69Studsvik 119	Aug 69 Haouat+ SPEC-GRPH,RESON IDENTIFIED	
Inelastic γ	1.0+6		TNC	Expt	Rept ORO-2791-32	Feb 71 Buchanan+.55-DEG SIGS TABULATED	
Inelastic γ	1.0+7		CCP	Expt	Conf 74Kharkov 146	Feb 74 Demidov+ ABST,GE-LI,GAMMA-SPEC	
Inelastic γ	2.8+6		CCP	Expt	Conf 76Lowell 1334	Jul 76 Andreev+DIRECT EXCIT EFFECTS.NDG	
Nonelastic γ	1.0-5	2.0+7	LAS	Eval	Rept LA-5793	Apr 75 Young. GAMMA PROD CS FOR ENDF	
(n,2n)	Fiss		CRC	Eval	Rept CRC-1003	Dec 60 Roy+,ESTIMATED AVG SIG=5.5MB	
(n,2n)	1.3+7	1.5+7	BNL	Theo	Jour NSE 23 238	Nov 65 Pearlstein.3ES.STAT MDL CALC.TBL CS.	
(n,2n)	Fiss		BNL	Theo	Jour NSE 23 238	Nov 65 Pearlstein.STATMDL CALC.SPEC AVG.TBL	
(n,2n)	4.1-1	1.0+7	WES	Eval	Rept WANL-TME-1472	Jul 66 Gibson+.68GROUP MATRIX	
(n,2n)	1.5+7		CCP	Expt	Jour YF 4 515	Sep 66 Druzhinin+.ACTIVATION METHOD,VAL GVN	+
					Jour SNP 4 366	Mar 67 . ENGL OF YF 4 515	
(n,2n)	1.4+7		IRK	Expt	Diss WINKLER	68 Winkler.(THESIS)	
(n,2n)	1.5+7		MUN	Expt	Jour NP/A 118 9	Sep 68 Dilg+ ACTIV.REL AL(N,A)	+
					Jour OAWS 177 323	69 Winkler+(IRK) ACTIVATION.	
	1.5+7				Data EXFOR20802.015	Dec 78 1PNT.SIGMA.	
(n,2n)	1.4+7	1.5+7	IRK	Comp	Jour OAWS 177 469	69 Hille.	
(n,2n)	1.5+7		DEB	Comp	Jour REA 7 4 93	Dec 69 Csikai+ SIG+HL COMPILTN,N-ACTIV-ANAL	
(n,2n)	1.4+7	1.5+7	JYV	Eval	Rept JU-RR-3/1970	Jun 70 Leppaemaeki+ TABLE OF EVAL AVG SIG	
(n,2n)	+7		KFI	Theo	Rept KFKI-71-8	Feb 71 Jeki. CALCULATED CFD EXPTL SIG VALUE	
(n,2n)	1.4+7		CCP	Expt	Rept YK-9 50	72 Maslov+ REL CU65(N,2N),NA-I,SIG GIVN	+
					Rept INDC(CCP)-42	Aug 74 .P10.ENGLISH OF YK-9	
	1.4+7				Data EXFOR40136.019	Feb 73 .1 DATA LINE	
(n,2n)	1.5+7		DEB	Eval	Jour REA 11 1 153	Mar 73 Boedy. COMPILATION+RECOMM.VALUE,TBL	
					Rept IAEA-153 173	73 - . RECOMM. VALUE ONLY	
(n,2n)	None		LAS	Eval	Prog LA-5570-PR	Apr 74 Foster+ ABSTRACT	
(n,2n)	1.5+7		TAT	Theo	Jour JP/A 7 1457	Aug 74 Kondaiah. CALC ON STAT MODEL	
(n,2n)	1.5+7		JUL	Expt	Jour NP/A 242 317	Apr 75 Qaim+ SIG MEASURED BY ACT,VS (N-Z)/A	+
	1.5+7				Data EXFOR20668.005	Oct 76 1PNT.SIGMA.	
(n,2n)	1.4+7		LRL	Expt	Prog WASH-1018 63	Apr 59 Lindner+	+
	1.4+7				Data EXFOR12185.004	Jun 76 . 1 PT. SIG	
(n,xn) x>2	Fiss		BNL	Theo	Jour NSE 23 238	Nov 65 Pearlstein.SPEC AVG STATMDL CALC N3N	
(n,xn) x>2	None		LAS	Eval	Prog LA-5570-PR	Apr 74 Foster+N3N.ISOTR ANG DIST.ENDF4.NDG.	
(n,p)	Fiss		CRC	Eval	Rept CRC-1003	Dec 60 Roy+,ESTIMATED AVG SIG=0.02MB	
(n,p)	1.4+7		SAH	Comp	Jour NUC 23 8 112	Aug 65 Chatterjee. TABLE WITH REFS.	
(n,p)	Fiss		GRE	Expt	Jour RCA 8 196	Dec 67 Rivier+ 3.8+-.6 MICROB	+
	Fiss				Data EXFOR20737.002	Apr 77 1PNT.SIGMA.	
(n,p)	1.4+7		LRL	Expt	Prog WASH-1127 96	Apr 69 Lindner+ REVISED VALUE GIVEN	+
	1.4+7				Data EXFOR12185.003	Jun 76 . 1 PT.	
(n,p)	1.5+7		DEB	Comp	Jour REA 7 4 93	Dec 69 Csikai+ SIG+HL COMPILTN,N-ACTIV-ANAL	
(n,p)	1.4+7	1.5+7	JYV	Eval	Rept JU-RR-3/1970	Jun 70 Leppaemaeki+ TABLE OF EVAL AVG SIG	
(n,p)	1.5+7		JUL	Expt	Jour NP/A 242 317	Apr 75 Qaim+ SIG MEASURED BY ACT,VS (N-Z)/A	+
	1.5+7				Data EXFOR20668.	Oct 76 2PTS.SIGMA.	
(n,np)	None		LAS	Eval	Prog LA-5570-PR	Apr 74 Foster+ ABSTRACT	
(n,α)	Fiss		CRC	Eval	Rept CRC-1003	Dec 60 Roy+,ESTIMATED AVG SIG=0.0001MB	
(n,α)	None		KFI	Comp	Jour JRC 7 365	Jun 71 Nagy+ GAMMA+XRAY+ELECTR ES,HALF-LIFE	
(n,α)	1.5+7		JUL	Expt	Jour NP/A 242 317	Apr 75 Qaim+ SIG MEASURED BY ACT,VS (N-Z)/A	+
	1.5+7				Data EXFOR20668.008	Oct 76 1PNT.SIGMA.	
Reson Params	4.1+0		ANL	Expt	Jour PR 84 869	Dec 51 Selove.	+
	4.1+0				Data EXFOR12168.007	Jun 76 . 1 RES,WT,PCS	

74 Tungsten 182

Quantity	Energy (ev) Min	Max	Lab	Type	Documentation Ref Vol Page	Date	Author, Comments	Data
Reson Params	4.1+0		BNL Expt	Jour	PR 100 1414	Dec 55	Landon.WT=.047 WN=.00143 WG=.046EV	+
	4.1+0			Data	EXFOR12178.003	Jun 76	. 1 RES, E0,WT,WN,WG,PCS	
Reson Params	4.1+0	3.8+2	BNL Expt	Abst	BAP 1 187	Apr 56	Schwartz+ ABST. K3	
	4.1+0	3.8+2		Data	EXFOR12152.003	Jun 76	. 7 RES,E0,WN,WG	
Reson Params	2.1+1	2.6+2	HAR Expt	Jour	NP 3 553	Jun 57	Bowey.TOF.3ES FROM CAPT GAMMA YIELDS	
Reson Params	4.1+0		BNL Expt	Jour	PR 110 1472	Jun 58	FOX+SLOW NEUTRON CAPTURE SPINS	+
Reson Params	1.1+2		HAR Expt	Jour	NP 12 552	Sep 59	Firk+ TOF 1RES.114EV	+
				Rept	AERE-NP/GEN 11	Apr 59	- + TOF. RES SPINS ASSIGNED.	
Reson Params	4.1+0	1.1+2	HAR Expt	Jour	NP 12 563	Sep 59	Waters+ WN WG J GIVEN FOR 3 RES	+
Reson Params	-		FOA ExTh	Jour	NP 39 353	Dec 62	Bergqvist+.AVERAGE GAMMA WIDTH.EXPTH	
Reson Params	1.2+2		RPI Expt	Prog	ORNL-3425 64	63	Block+ SIG WG WN FROM SNG	
Reson Params	4.2+0	2.1+1	ORL Expt	Conf	66Wash. 31	Mar 66	Harvey.2ES,PARS BY AREA ANALYSIS	+
	4.0+0	2.2+1		Conf	66S.Diego 2 103	Feb 66	. .PARAM FOR LVL AT 4.16AND21EV	
	4.2+0	2.1+1		Prog	ORNL-3582 58	Jun 64	Paya+	
	4.2+0	2.1+1		Data	EXFOR11238.003	Jun 76	. 2 RES,E0,WT,WN,WG	
Reson Params	-.3+2		GA ExTh	Jour	NSE 26 487	Dec 66	Friesenhahn+NEG ENERGY RES	+
				Rept	GA-6832	66	.SUPERSEDED	
	-.3+2			Expt Data	EXFOR12167.012	Jun 76	. 1 RES,E0,WN0,WG	
Reson Params	4.2+0		JAE Expt	Prog	EANDC(J)7L8	Jan 67	Ideno+ LINAC. WN,WT GIVEN AT 4.15EV	+
	4.2+0			Data	EXFOR20267.	Jun 74	2PTS.WN,WT.	
Reson Params	2.1+1	2.1+1	SAC Expt	Jour	CR 248 2330	Apr 59	Huynh+ SPINS GIVEN.	+
	1.2+1	7.0+2		Conf	67Bordeaux	Mar 67	Samour+G(GAMMA).NAT W,GE DET. FP JPR	
	2.1+1			Data	EXFOR20677.002	Sep 77	1PNT.E0.	
Reson Params		1.0+6	AUA Theo	Jour	AUJ 20 477	Oct 67	Cook. TBL OF AVG LVL SPACING D,L=0,1	
Reson Params	+3	+5	AUA ExTh	Rept	AAEC/E-198	May 69	Musgrove.RES PARS +STF FROM (NG)FIT	+
Reson Params	2.1+2	3.6+3	RPI Expt	Jour	NSE 37 137	Jul 69	Bartolome+LINAC RES PARS TO 2.4KEV.	+
	1.5+2	2.0+4		Abst	DA/B 30 679	Aug 69	- .RES PARS FROM TRANS,CAPT	
				Conf	68Wash. 795	Mar 68	- +RES PARS BY CAPT,TRNS,TBD.	
	2.3+2	2.4+3		Data	EXFOR10002.	Jan 78	. 33 RES ES.WN,WG,D GVN.	
Reson Params	4.1+0	4.9+2	HAR ExTh	Conf	69Studsvik 579	Aug 69	Murray+CORRELATION WN+WG,CFD STATMOD	
Reson Params	-		AUA Theo	Rept	AAEC/E-211	Nov 70	Musgrove. CALCULTD D+GAM WIDTH GIVEN	
Reson Params	-.3+2	2.3+3	CJD Eval	Rept	YK-7	71	Zakharova+ SURVEY+SYSTEMATICS,GW,TBL	
				Rept	INDC(CCP)-27	Nov 72	.ENGLISH TRANSLATION OF YK-7 /71	
Reson Params	None		DUB Theo	Jour	YF 13 240	Feb 71	Malecki+G-WID,THEO CFD EXPT.TBL,GRPH	
				Jour	SNP 13 133	Aug 71	- + ENGL OF YF 13 240.	
Reson Params	None		DUB Theo	Jour	ZEP 14 194	Aug 71	Solovev.LARGE N-WID G-WID CORREL.NDG	
				Rept	JINR-E4-5880	71	Soloviev.N-GAM-WIDS CORR.SHORT NOTE	
				Jour	JEL 14 129	Aug 71	- . ENGL OF ZEP 14 194.	
Reson Params	2.1+1	1.3+4	COL Expt	Jour	PR/C 8 1813	Nov 73	Camarda+. WN+AVG D FOR MANY RESON	+
	None			Conf	75Wash. 780	Mar 75	Hacken+19 ELEMENT RVW.TBLS,GRPHS.	
	2.1+1	1.3+4		Conf	71Albany 205	Aug 71	Camarada+D GVN FOR S LVLS.TBP PR	
	4.2+0	1.3+5		Data	EXFOR10507.	Apr 76	. 142 PTS. WN,D VAL GVN	
Reson Params	4.0+0	1.2+3	JAE Expt	Rept	JAERI-M-5624	Feb 74	Ohkubo.LINAC,TOF.WT,WN IN TABLE	
Reson Params	2.5-2		COL Expt	Conf	75Wash. 335	Mar 75	Felvinci+MOD ERICSON CALC CFD EXPT.	
Reson Params	Maxwl		KUK Theo	Conf	76Ahmedabd 2 1	Dec 76	Sharma+AVG S-WAVE REDUCED N-WID ANAL	
Strnth Fnctn	None		BNL Expt	Abst	BAP 1 187	Apr 56	Schwartz+ 2.0+-1.0 FIRST 4 LEVELS	
Strnth Fnctn	1.0+4		ANL Theo	Jour	PR 162 1077	Oct 67	Lister+ OPTMDL CALC S,P,AND D WAVE	
				Rept	ANL-7288	Jan 67	.SUPERSEDED	
Strnth Fnctn	+3	+5	AUA ExTh	Rept	AAEC/E-198	May 69	Musgrove.S+P+D STF FROM (NG)FIT,TBL	+
Strnth Fnctn	2.1+2	2.4+3	RPI Expt	Jour	NSE 37 137	Jul 69	Bartolome+S0=2.60+-.54S1=2.8+.52-.15	+
				Abst	DA/B 30 679	Aug 69	- .S,P STF CFD OPT,SPH MDLS.	
	2.1+2	2.4+3		Data	EXFOR10002.025	Jan 78	.S0=(2.60+-.54)-4 S1=(.28+.52-.15)-4	
Strnth Fnctn	-		AUA Theo	Rept	AAEC/E-211	Nov 70	Musgrove. SMOOTHED S0,S1 AND S2 GIVN	
Strnth Fnctn	None		COL Expt	Jour	NSE 48 219	Jun 72	Rahn+. AVG WG=75 MEV OVER 2 RESON	
Strnth Fnctn	None		AUA Eval	Rept	AAEC/E-277	Mar 73	Musgrove.TBLS EXPTL DATA+BEST VALUES	
Strnth Fnctn	+1	+4	COL Expt	Jour	PR/C 8 1813	Nov 73	Camarda+ S WAVE.GRPH,TBL	+
	None			Conf	75Wash. 780	Mar 75	Hacken+19 ELEMENT RVW.TBLS,GRPHS.	
	2.1+1	1.3+4		Conf	71Albany 205	Aug 71	Camarada+S0 GVN	
	0.0+0	1.3+4		Data	EXFOR10507.002	Apr 76	. 1 PT. S0=(2.40+-.31)-4	
Lvl Density	-		COP Theo	Jour	NP 6 62	Mar 58	Ericson. LVL DENSITY FORM CFD EXP	
Lvl Density	+7		MIL Theo	Jour	NC/A 51 4 1074	Oct 67	Gadioli+THEOR EVAL EVAPORATION SPECT	
Lvl Density	0.0+0	1.0+4	ITE Theo	Conf	72Budapest 268	Aug 72	Belyaev+ GROUPINGS OF LVL SPACNG,TBL	

74 Tungsten 183

Quantity	Energy (ev) Min	Max	Lab	Type	Documentation Ref Vol Page	Date	Author, Comments	Data
Evaluation	1.0-3	1.5+7	GA Eval	Rept	GA-5885	Nov 64	Joanou+ TOT STF SEL SNE SIN N2N ETC.	

74 Tungsten 183

Quantity	Energy (ev) Min	Max	Lab	Type	Documentation Ref Vol Page	Date	Author, Comments	Data
Evaluation	1.0+3	1.4+7	GEN	Eval	Rept GEMP – 388	Nov 65	Prince.OPTMDL WITH CHANNEL COMPETIT	
Evaluation	1.0–2	1.5+7	GEN	Eval	Rept GEMP – 448	Nov 66	Henderson+ TOT NG SIN N2N NP ENDF/B	
Evaluation	1.0–4	2.0+7	AI	Eval	Rept TI– 707–130–26	Jul 73	Rose+	
Total	3.3+0	2.3+5	ANL	Expt	Jour PR 84 869	Dec 51	Selove+ TRANS	+
	3.3+0	2.3+5			Data EXFOR12168.004	Jun 76	. 75 PTS, SIG	
Total	6.0+5	2.5+7	RPI	Expt	Abst DA/B 28 3435	Feb 68	Martin+TOF, OKS DEFORMED NUCL OPTMOD	
Total	1.5+2	1.0+5	RPI	Expt	Jour NSE 37 137	Jul 69	Bartolome+LINAC,RES PARS FROM TRNS.	
	1.5+2	2.0+4			Abst DA/B 30 679	Aug 69	– .RES PARS FROM TRNS.	
					Conf 68Wash. 795	Mar 68	– +RES PARS FROM TRNS,TBP,NDG	
Total	1.0+5	2.0+7	LAS	Eval	Rept LA– 4928	Jun 72	Devaney+EVAL.SMOOTH SIG CURVS.	
Total	–3	1.9+0	THS	Theo	Rept IKE–6 89 65	Jun 75	Keinert. DATA LIBRARY	
Elastic	2.0+1	1.5+2	ORL	Expt	Abst BAP 3 177	May 58	Harvey+,TOF,CFD SNEL FOR J	
Elastic	3.4–2		DUB	Expt	Jour JINR–P3–4121	Oct 68	Alexandrov+ SCATTERING LENGTH, TBP	
Elastic	3.4–2		DUB	Expt	Prog YFI– 7 58	Apr 69	Alexandrov+ SCAT–LENGTH GIVEN, TBP	
					Jour YF 10 328	Aug 69	Aleksandrov+ SCAT LENGTH GIVEN	
					Jour SNP 10 189	Feb 70	. ENGL OF YF 10 328	
					Rept INDC(CCP)–7U62	Feb 70	Alexandrov+ ENGL OF YFI–7 58.	
Diff Elastic	4.1–1	1.0+7	WES	Eval	Rept WANL–TME–1472	Jul 66	Gibson+.68GROUP P0 P1 MATRIX	
Diff Inelast	4.1–1	1.0+7	WES	Eval	Rept WANL–TME–1472	Jul 66	Gibson+.68GROUP MATRIX	
Diff Inelast	1.4+7		ITJ	Expt	Jour JRC 14 201	73	Janczyszyn+ ISO–PROD BY NAT–W ACTIV	+
	1.4+7				Data EXFOR30322.017	Feb 76	MEAN OF W183(N,N')+W184(N,2N)	
Diff Inelast	Thrsh	Up	CAI	Theo	Jour AKE 28 3 201	76	Abboud. EXCITATION–FN,STATMOD	
Res Int Abs	None		WES	Eval	Rept WANL–TME–1472	Jul 66	Gibson+. CFD OTHERS	
Res Int Abs	5.0–1		COL	Expt	Jour NSE 48 219	Jun 72	Rahn+. RI=371+ –42B	
(n,γ)	Maxwl		ORL	Expt	Jour PR 88 412	Oct 52	Pomerance.PILE OSC.	+
	Maxwl				Data EXFOR11507.092	Jun 76	. 1 PT.	
(n,γ)	+0	1.5+3	HAR	Expt	Jour NP 3 553	Jun 57	Bowey. TOF. CAPT GAM YLD CURVE	
(n,γ)	6.6+1	5.9+3	SAC	Expt	Jour CR 249 413	Jul 59	Corge+ MANY RESONANCES PROB.J=1	+
(n,γ)	Maxwl	+5	FOA	Theo	Jour NP 39 353	Dec 62	Bergqvist+. IN PER CENT OF NAT ELEMT	
(n,γ)	5.0+3	5.0+4	LEB	Comp	Rept INDSWG–64 43	64	Konks. GRAPH SIG(E)	
(n,γ)	1.2+1	1.5+4	LEB	Expt	Conf JINR–1845 104	Jun 64	Kapchigashev+ OKS OTHER EXPTS, NDG	
(n,γ)	1.0–3	1.0+7	WES	Eval	Rept WANL–TME–1472	Jul 66	Gibson+.68GROUPS .4EV UP+CURVE–100EV	
(n,γ)	3.3+4	1.7+5	FEI	Expt	Jour YF 4 282	Aug 66	Kononov+ BY SUBTR FROM NAT W,GRAPH	+
					Conf 66Paris 1 469	Oct 66	*GRPH EXPT CFD OTHERS	
					Rept EANDC–50 199	Jul 65	*GRPH EXPT CFD THEO	
					Rept FEI–29	65	.	
					Jour SNP 4 204	Feb 67	.ENGLISH TRANSL OF YF 4 282 8/66	
(n,γ)	1.0–2	1.0+1	GA	Expt	Jour NSE 26 487	Dec 66	Friesenhahn.THR 10.0+ – .3 LIQ SCIN	+
					Conf 66Wash. 182	Mar 66	.SUPERSEDED	
					Rept GA– 6882	Jan 66	.SUPERSEDED	
	1.0–2	1.0+1			Data EXFOR12167.	Jun 76	. 33 PTS.	
(n,γ)	1.5+2	1.0+5	RPI	Expt	Jour NSE 37 137	Jul 69	Bartolome+LINAC,CAPT AREAS,AVG CS.	
	1.5+2	2.0+4			Abst DA/B 30 679	Aug 69	– .LINAC RES PARS FROM DATA.	
					Conf 68Wash. 795	Mar 68	– +AVG CAPT CS GRPHS.	
	4.0+2	8.0+3			Conf 66Wash. 404	Mar 66	Gibbons.RPI LINAC+SC(T),CURVE	
(n,γ)	3.0+4		AUA	Theo	Rept AAEC/E–211	Nov 70	Musgrove. SIGMA GIVEN AND CFD OTHER	
(n,γ)	1.0+3	1.0+7	BOL	Eval	Data BENZI–DFN 815.	May 72	40 PNTS	+
(n,γ)	5.0+3	2.0+7	LAS	Eval	Rept LA– 5221	May 73	Devaney+. ENDF/B LISTING. CURVES	
Spect (n,γ)	7.6+0	1.1+2	HAR	Expt	Conf 58Geneva 14 294	Sep 58	Bird.CURVE,PPR35,NAI(TL)– DETECTOR	+
Spect (n,γ)	+0	+2	BNL	Expt	Jour PRL 2 505	Jun 59	Hughes+. LANDON METHOD FOR J	
Spect (n,γ)	7.7+0	4.7+1	ORL	Expt	Conf 61Saclay 203	Sep 61	Block+.AT7.7 27 47 EV.LIQUID SCINTIL	
Spect (n,γ)	7.6+0	4.8+1	BNL	Expt	Conf 63ANL 324	Oct 63	Moore+ SPECTRA FOR 4 RESONANCES NAI	
Spect (n,γ)	7.6+0	2.7+1	ITE	Expt	Jour ZET 45 870	Oct 63	Ratynskil.G–SPEC FROM 2 N–RES COMPRD	
					Jour JET 18 598	Mar 64	TRANSLATN.*	
Spect (n,γ)	8.0+0	6.5+1	ANL	Expt	Jour PR 132 1640	Nov 63	Bollinger+FC.E–LVLS OF COMP–NUCL.PT.	
					Jour PRL 3 377	Oct 60	.SUPERSEDED	
Spect (n,γ)	Maxwl		ORL	Expt	Prog WASH–1068 149	Mar 66	Martin+,LI–GE DET,TBL 31 G ES,TBC	
Spect (n,γ)	7.6+1	2.2+2	BNL	Expt	Conf 66Argonne 459	Nov 66	Chrien+,GE(LI),47GAMMAS SEEN	
Spect (n,γ)	6.0–2	7.6+0	MTR	Expt	Jour PR 155 1368	Mar 67	Spencer+0.06EV+1RES 4–7MEV GS, X ABS	
Spect (n,γ)	7.6+0	2.7+1	RPI	Expt	Jour PR 155 1301	Mar 67	Rae+,2RES,9LINES 5.6–7.4MEV,ABS INT	
Spect (n,γ)	Maxwl	1.9+1	ANL	Expt	Jour PR 160 1038	Aug 67	Cote+ TOF,INT 3TRANS FOR THR + 1RES	
	Maxwl				Conf 68DUBSY 317	Jul 68	Bollinger.ANAL.RAD. TRANSITIONS.	
Spect (n,γ)	7.6+0		MTR	Expt	Prog WASH–1124 77	Nov 68	Faler+ TO BE PUBLISHED IN PHYS REV	
Spect (n,γ)	7.6+0	3.6+2	SAC	Expt	Jour NP/A 123 581	Jan 69	Samour+ GE(LI),J,PI=1 – ;7302– 7413CORR	
					Rept CEA–R–3776	Apr 69	– . (THESIS) DATA GIVEN	
					Conf 65Antwerp 532	Jul 65	– + PPR89.ABST.NDG.	
					Rept CEA–R–2810	Jun 65	Huynh.NAI DETS. SUPERSEDED.	
Spect (n,γ)	6.0+1	9.9+1	GA	Expt	Jour NIM 72 254	Mar 69	Orphan+ RESONANCE CAPTURE	

74 Tungsten 183

Quantity	Energy (ev) Min	Max	Lab	Type	Documentation Ref Vol Page	Date	Author, Comments	Data
Spect (n,γ)	Pile		ANL Expt	Conf	69Studsvik 601	Aug 69	Smither+ NO DATA GVN,TB CFD STATMOD	
Spect (n,γ)	None		BNL Expt	Conf	69Studsvik 627	Aug 69	Chrien. WG – DISTR CFD PORTER – THOM,TBL	
Spect (n,γ)	None		RPI Expt	Prog	WASH – 1136 148	Sep 69	Tatarczuk+,GE(LI) DET,NO DATA GIVEN	
Spect (n,γ)	Pile		IBJ Expt	Rept	INR – 1262/IA/PL	Feb 71	Ratynski.G CIRC POLARIZ,POLARIZED NS	
Spect (n,γ)	Maxwl		RCN Expt	Jour	NP/A 181 250	Feb 72	Stecher – Rasmussen+GAM CIRC POL.SPINS	
				Rept	RCN – 152	Jun 71	– + (THESIS)	
Spect (n,γ)	7.6+0		BNL Expt	Jour	PR/C 7 419	Jan 73	Casten+. GE(LI) DET. TABLE+CURVE.	
Spect (n,γ)	Maxwl		INL Expt	Jour	NP/A 223 66	Apr 74	Greenwood+ GE(LI). TABLES.	
	2.0+3			Jour	NP/A 223 66	Apr 74	– + GE(LI). TABLES.	
	Maxwl			Abst	ANS 14 905	Oct 71	– . 2ES. ABSOL GAM SPEC SHOWN	
Spect (n,γ)	None		INL Expt	Prog	USNDC – 11 9	Jun 74	Greenwood+ LVL STUDY OF W – 184	
Spect (n,γ)	Maxwl		NIU Expt	Jour	PR/C 11 1401	Apr 75	Bushell+ GRPHS,TBL	
Spect (n,γ)	+0		NIU Expt	Jour	PR/C 11 1401	Apr 75	Bushell+ RES CAPT. GRPHS,TBL	
Spect (n,γ)	Maxwl		RCN Expt	Conf	75Kiev 3 254	May 75	Abrahams+ POLARZD NS,POLAR GAMS,TABL	
Spect (n,γ)	Maxwl	7.6+0	BNL Expt	Jour	PR/C 12 821	Sep 75	Casten+ SPECT AT 2 ES.ROT BAND	
				Jour	PL/B 58 39	Aug 75	Macphail+GE – LI.ROT BAND POPS	
Inelastic γ	5.0+5	1.5+6	WES Expt	Jour	PR 107 1306	Sep 57	Sinclair.XTL SPEC REL CURV 99KEV G	
Inelastic γ	None		KFI Comp	Jour	JRC 7 365	Jun 71	Nagy+ GAMMA+XRAY+ELECTR ES,HALF – LIFE	
Nonelastic γ	1.0–5	2.0+7	LAS Eval	Rept	LA – 5793	Apr 75	Young. GAMMA PROD CS FOR ENDF	
(n,2n)	Fiss		CRC Eval	Rept	CRC – 1003	Dec 60	Roy+,ESTIMATED AVG SIG = 19.3MB	
(n,2n)	1.3+7	1.5+7	BNL Theo	Jour	NSE 23 238	Nov 65	Pearlstein.3ES.STAT MDL CALC.TBL CS.	
(n,2n)	Fiss		BNL Theo	Jour	NSE 23 238	Nov 65	Pearlstein.STATMDL CALC.SPEC AVG TBL	
(n,2n)	4.1–1	1.0+0	WES Eval	Rept	WANL – TME – 1472	Jul 66	Gibson+.68GROUP MATRIX	
(n,2n)	1.5+7		DEB Eval	Jour	REA 11 1 153	Mar 73	Boedy+ RECOMM.VALUE FROM N – Z SYSTEM.	
(n,2n)	1.5+7		KFI Theo	Rept	KFKI – 73 – 68	Dec 73	Jeki.NEW FIT,CALC SIG CFD OTHERS,TBL	
(n,2n)	None		LAS Eval	Prog	LA – 5570 – PR	Apr 74	Foster+ ABSTRACT	
(n,xn) x>2	Fiss		BNL Theo	Jour	NSE 23 238	Nov 65	Pearlstein.SPEC AVG STATMDL CALC N3N	
(n,xn) x>2	1.4+7	1.5+7	LRL Expt	Jour	ND/A 11 798	Jul 73	Alley+ (N,3N) CURVE BEST ESTIMATE	
(n,xn) x>2	None		LAS Eval	Prog	LA – 5570 – PR	Apr 74	Foster+N3N.ISOTR ANG DIST.ENDF4.NDG.	
(n,p)	Fiss		CRC Eval	Rept	CRC – 1003	Dec 60	Roy+,ESTIMATED AVG SIG = 0.008MB	
(n,p)	1.4+7		SAH Comp	Jour	NUC 23 8 112	Aug 65	Chatterjee. TABLE WITH REFS.	
(n,p)	Fiss		GRE Expt	Jour	RCA 8 196	Dec 67	Rivier+ 2.8+ – .5 MICROB	+
	Fiss			Data	EXFOR20737.003	Apr 77	1PNT.SIGMA.	
(n,p)	1.5+7		DEB Comp	Jour	REA 7 4 93	Dec 69	Csikai+ SIG+HL COMPILTN,N – ACTIV – ANAL	
(n,p)	1.4+7	1.5+7	JYV Eval	Rept	JU – RR – 3/1970	Jun 70	Leppaemaeki+ TABLE OF EVAL AVG SIG	
(n,p)	1.5+7		JUL Expt	Jour	NP/A 242 317	Apr 75	Qaim+ SIG MEASURED BY ACT,VS (N – Z)/A	+
	1.5+7			Data	EXFOR20668.009	Oct 76	1PNT.SIGMA.	
(n,p)	1.4+7		LRL Expt	Prog	WASH – 1127 96	Apr 69	Lindner+ REVISED VALUE GIVEN	+
	1.4+7			Data	EXFOR12185.005	Jun 76	. 1 PT.	
(n,np)	None		LAS Eval	Prog	LA – 5570 – PR	Apr 74	Foster+ ABSTRACT	
(n,α)	Fiss		CRC Eval	Rept	CRC – 1003	Dec 60	Roy+,ESTIMATED AVG SIG = 0.0001MB	
(n,α)	1.5+7		JUL Expt	Jour	NP/A 242 317	Apr 75	Qaim+ SIG MEASURED BY ACT,VS (N – Z)/A	+
	1.5+7			Data	EXFOR20668.011	Oct 76	1PNT.SIGMA.	
Reson Params	7.8+0	4.9+1	ANL Expt	Jour	PR 84 869	Dec 51	Selove.	
	7.8+0	4.9+1		Data	EXFOR12168.004	Jun 76	. 75 PTS.	
Reson Params	7.6+0	3.5+2	BNL Expt	Abst	BAP 1 187	Apr 56	Schwartz+ ABST. K3	+
	7.6+0	3.5+2		Data	EXFOR12152.004	Jun 76	. 13 RES,E0,WN,WG	
Reson Params	2.7+1	1.6+2	HAR Expt	Jour	NP 3 553	Jun 57	Bowey.TOF.5ES FROM CAPT GAMMA YIELDS	
Reson Params	2.7+1	4.6+1	BNL Expt	Abst	BAP 3 19	Jan 58	Chrien. ABST. F8,RES J.	+
	2.7+1	4.6+1		Data	EXFOR12153.003	Jun 76	. 2 RES, J	
Reson Params	2.7+1	1.0+2	MTR Expt	Abst	BAP 3 176	May 58	Simpson+	+
Reson Params	7.6+0	2.7+1	BNL Expt	Jour	PR 110 1472	Jun 58	FOX+SLOW NEUT.CAPTURE,SPINS.	
Reson Params	2.7+1	1.0+2	ORL Expt	Prog	WASH – 1006 24	Oct 58	Harvey+ 4E0S FROM SCAT EXP	
Reson Params	1.0+2		BNL Expt	Abst	BAP 4 271	Apr 59	FOX+ 102 EV RES J=1	
Reson Params	7.6+0	6.6+1	BNL Expt	Jour	PRL 2 505	Jun 59	Hughes+ TRANS PROB+WN J1 LEVELS	
Reson Params	2.7+1	1.7+2	HAR Expt	Jour	NP 12 552	Sep 59	Firk+ TOF 9RES. J=0,1 STF CALC.	+
				Rept	AERE – NP/GEN 11	Apr 59	– + TOF. RES SPINS ASSIGNED.	
Reson Params	4.1+0	1.1+2	HAR Expt	Jour	NP 12 563	Sep 59	Waters+ WN WG J GIVEN FOR 5 RES.	+
Reson Params	7.6+0	4.6+1	ANL Expt	Jour	PRL 3 376	Oct 59	Bollinger+,PARTIAL WG FLUCTUATES,J	
Reson Params	–		FOA ExTh	Jour	NP 39 353	Dec 62	Bergqvist+.AVERAGE GAMMA WIDTH.EXPTH	
Reson Params	1.2+2	1.7+2	RPI Expt	Prog	ORNL – 3425 64	63	Block+SIG WG WN 4LVLS FROM SNG	
Reson Params	7.6+0	1.0+2	CCP ExTh	Jour	ZET 45 875	Oct 63	Ignat'Ev.3RES	+
Reson Params	7.6+0	4.6+1	ANL Expt	Jour	PR 132 1640	Nov 63	Bollinger.	+
	7.6+0	4.6+1		Data	EXFOR12195.002	Jun 76	. 4 RES, J	
Reson Params	7.7+0	2.7+1	ORL Expt	Conf	66Wash. 31	Mar 66	Harvey.2ES,PARS BY AREA ANALYSIS	+
	4.0+0	2.2+1		Conf	66S.Diego 2 103	Feb 66	– +PARAM FOR LEVEL AT 7.67 EV	
	7.7+0	2.7+1		Prog	ORNL – 3582 58	Jun 64	Paya+	
	7.7+0	2.7+1		Data	EXFOR11238.	Jun 76	. 2 RES, E0,WT,WN,WG	

74 Tungsten 183

Quantity	Energy (ev) Min	Max	Lab	Type	Documentation Ref Vol Page	Date	Author, Comments	Data
Reson Params	7.6+0		JAE Expt	Prog	EANDC(J)7L8	Jan 67	Ideno+ LINAC, W + WN GIVEN AT 7.64EV	+
	7.6+0			Data	EXFOR20267.	Jun 74	2PTS.WN,WT.	
Reson Params		1.0+6	AUA Theo	Jour	AUJ 20 477	Oct 67	Cook. TBL OF AVG LVL SPACING D,L=0,1	
Reson Params	2.7+1	1.6+2	SAC Expt	Jour	JPR 21 426	May 60	Corge+.WN WG WT E0 SIGMA0.1LVL FIT	+
	7.0+0	3.6+2		Conf	68DUBSY 361	Jul 68	Samour. GAM – WIDTH DISTRIBUTION GRAPH	
	2.7+1	1.5+3		ExTh Conf	JINR – D3893 119	May 68	– + 13RESONANCES,GAM WIDTH ANAL	
				Expt Conf	68Wash. 867	Mar 68	Morgenstern.WG VS.A,AVERAGE WG GIVEN	
				Conf	68Wash. 783	Mar 68	Alves+	
				Conf	65Antwerp 525	Jul 65	De Barros+ PPR73.ABST.NDGJ=1 LEVELS	
	7.6+0			Jour	CR 255 1913	Oct 62	Le Pipec+ DOPPLER EFFECT.	
	2.7+1	1.6+2		Jour	JPR 21 423	May 60	Corge+ LINAC.TOF.8 RESONANCES.	
	1.5+3			Jour	CR 249 413	Jul 59	– +.E0 FOR J=1 20RES	
	6.6+1	1.5+3		Jour	CR 248 2330	Apr 59	Huynh+ J FOR 6 RES	
	7.7+0	6.6+1		Data	EXFOR20679.	Sep 77	32PTS.E0,WG,AVG WG,WN,WT,J,PAR,– –	
	0.0+0	1.5+3						
Reson Params	+3	+5	AUA ExTh	Rept	AAEC/E – 198	May 69	Musgrove.RES PARS +STF FROM (NG)FIT	+
Reson Params	1.5+2	1.4+3	RPI Expt	Jour	NSE 37 137	Jul 69	Bartolome+LINAC,WN RES PARS TO 760EV	+
	1.5+2	2.0+4		Abst	DA/B 30 679	Aug 69	– .RES PARS FROM TRNS,CAPT.	
				Conf	68Wash. 795	Mar 68	– +RES PARS BY CAPT,TRNS,TBD.	
	1.8+2	7.6+2		Data	EXFOR10002.	Jan 78	. 47 RES ES.WN,WG,D GVN.	
Reson Params	None		ANL Expt	Prog	WASH – 1136 11	Sep 69	Poenitz+ J FROM OCCUPATN PROB RATIOS	
Reson Params	None		RPI Expt	Prog	WASH – 1136 148	Sep 69	Tatarczuk+,J FROM CAPT SPEC,NDG,TBC	
Reson Params	2.7+1	1.0+2	ANL Expt	Jour	PR/C 1 1501	Apr 70	Wetzel+J FROM CAPT MEAS.TBL GVN.	+
	2.7+1	1.0+2		Data	EXFOR10080.002	Feb 76	. 5 PTS. J,E0.	
Reson Params	–	–	AUA Theo	Rept	AAEC/E – 211	Nov 70	Musgrove. CALCULTD D+GAM WIDTH GIVEN	
Reson Params	7.7+0	7.7+2	CJD Eval	Rept	YK – 7	71	Zakharova+ SURVEY+SYSTEMATICS,GW,TBL	
				Rept	INDC(CCP) – 27	Nov 72	.ENGLISH TRANSLATION OF YK – 7 /71	
Reson Params	None		DUB Theo	Jour	YF 13 240	Feb 71	Malecki+G – WID,THEO CFD EXPT.TBL,GRPH	
				Jour	SNP 13 133	Aug 71	– + ENGL OF YF 13 240.	
Reson Params	7.6+0		COL Expt	Jour	NSE 51 1196	Jun 73	Wynchank+. E0 ONLY FOR 1 RESON	
Reson Params	7.6+0	2.6+3	COL Expt	Jour	PR/C 8 1813	Nov 73	Camarda+. G*WN+AVG D FOR MANY RESON	+
	None			Conf	75Wash. 780	Mar 75	Hacken+19 ELEMENT RVW.TBLS,GRPHS.	
	7.6+0	2.6+3		Data	EXFOR10507.	Apr 76	. 94 PTS. WN,D VAL GVN.	
Reson Params	4.0+0	1.2+3	JAE Expt	Rept	JAERI – M – 5624	Feb 74	Ohkubo.LINAC,TOF.WT,WN IN TABLE	
Strnth Fnctn	+3		BNL Expt	Jour	PRL 1 461	Dec 58	Hughes.FC 1.4+ – 0.5	
Strnth Fnctn	2.5+1	2.0+2	HAR Expt	Jour	NP 12 552	Sep 59	Firk+ 9RES. APPROX STF FOR J=0 AND1	+
Strnth Fnctn		1.6+2	SAC Expt	Jour	JPR 21 426	May 60	Corge+.S – WAVE	
Strnth Fnctn	1.0+3	6.0+4	LEB Expt	Conf	65Antwerp § 182	Jul 65	Bergman.LEBEDEV.S1=.7+ – .3.ALSO DO	
Strnth Fnctn	+3	+5	AUA ExTh	Rept	AAEC/E – 198	May 69	Musgrove.S+STF FROM (NG)FIT,TBL	+
Strnth Fnctn	1.5+2	7.6+2	RPI Expt	Jour	NSE 37 137	Jul 69	Bartolome+,S0=2.41+ – 0.48	+
				Abst	DA/B 30 679	Aug 69	– .S STF CFD OPT,SPH MDLS.	
	1.5+2	7.6+2		Data	EXFOR10002.026	Jan 78	. 1PT.S0=(2.41)+ – .48	
Strnth Fnctn	–		DUB Revw	Jour	YF 11 111	Jan 70	Malecki+ VALUES FOR TWO SPIN STATES	
				Jour	SNP 11 61	Jul 70	– + ENGL OF YF 11 61.	
Strnth Fnctn	–		AUA Theo	Rept	AAEC/E – 211	Nov 70	Musgrove. SMOOTHED S0,S1 AND S2 GIVN	
Strnth Fnctn	None		AUA Eval	Rept	AAEC/E – 277	Mar 73	Musgrove.TBLS EXPTL DATA+BEST VALUES	
Strnth Fnctn	+1	+4	COL Expt	Jour	PR/C 8 1813	Nov 73	Camarda+S WAVE,GRPH TBL.	+
	None			Conf	75Wash. 780	Mar 75	Hacken+19ELEMENTS RVW.TBLS,GRPHS.	
	0.0+0	2.6+3		Data	EXFOR10507.003	Apr 76	. 1 PT. S0=(1.65+ – .32) – 4	
Lvl Density	–		COP Theo	Jour	NP 6 62	Mar 58	Ericson. LVL DENSITY FORM CFD EXP	
Lvl Density	–		FEI Eval	Rept	FEI – 36	66	Kapchigashev+.TBL OF RELATD QUANTTYS	+
		5.0+4		Jour	YF 4 686	Sep 66	.TABLE.SHORT VERSION OF FEI – 36	
	–			Prog	YFI – 3 3	66	.ABSTRACT.TABLE LDL+NUCL.EXCIT.E	
		5.0+4		Jour	SNP 4 486	67	.ENGLISH OF YF 4.FROM(N,GAMMA).TABLE	
				Prog	INDC – E – 140 3	66	.ENGLISH TRANSL OF YFI – 3	
Lvl Density	+6		MIL Theo	Jour	EN 15 1 54	Jan 68	Facchini+ LDL PARS FROM LOW EN RES	
Lvl Density	None		MUN Theo	Jour	NP/A 217 269	Dec 73	Dilg+ A,DELTA. BACK SHIFTED FERMIGAS	
Lvl Density	None		COP Theo	Jour	NP/A 222 493	Apr 74	Dossing+COLL ROTAT.SPAC. ACCUR ESTIM	
Lvl Density	None		ROC Theo	Jour	NP/A 223 577	May 74	Huizenga+ EXP CFD MICROSC TH SPH NUC	

74 Tungsten 184

Quantity	Energy (ev) Min	Max	Lab	Type	Documentation Ref Vol Page	Date	Author, Comments	Data
Evaluation	1.0 – 3	1.5+7	GA Eval	Rept	GA – 5885	Nov 64	Joanou+ TOT STF SEL SNE SIN N2N ETC.	
Evaluation	1.0+3	1.4+7	GEN Eval	Rept	GEMP – 388	Nov 65	Prince.OPTMDL FITTING WITH COMPETIT	
Evaluation	1.0 – 2	1.5+7	GEN Eval	Rept	GEMP – 448	Nov 66	Henderson+ TOT NG SIN N2N NP ENDF/B	
Evaluation	1.0 – 4	2.0+7	AI Eval	Rept	TI – 707 – 130 – 26	Jul 73	Rose+	
Total	7.6+0	6.6+1	BNL Expt	Jour	PRL 2 505	May 59	Hughes.	+

74 Tungsten 184

Quantity	Energy (ev) Min	Energy (ev) Max	Lab	Type	Documentation Ref Vol Page	Author, Comments Date	Data
Total	5.0+4	3.0+6	BNL ExTh	Jour	PR/B 135 895	Aug 64 Auerbach+LCL OPTMDL FITS TO OLD, ANL	+
Total	2.2+6	1.5+7	BNW Expt	Jour	NIM 36 1	Sep 65 Foster+ VDG,TOF,LIQ SCINT. NO DATA	+
	2.3+6	1.5+7		Data	EXFOR10047.106	Aug 73 . 246 PTS. SIGMA	
Total	3.0+5	1.5+6	AI Eval	Rept	NAA-SR-11973	Jul 66 Dunford. NONSPHERICAL OPTMDL 1TABLE	
Total	2.0+6	1.6+7	LAS Theo	Rept	LA- 3538	Sep 66 Agee+ OPTICAL MODEL CALCULATION	
Total	1.0+5	6.5+5	ANL Expt	Prog	ANL-7210 16	Dec 66 Whalen.SHORT NOTE,GRAPH ONLY	+
	1.0+5	6.5+5		Data	EXFOR11540.010	Jun 76 . 268 PTS.	
Total	6.0+5	2.5+7	RPI ExTh	Abst	DA/B 28 3435	Feb 68 Martin. TOF, OKS DEFORMED NUCL OPTMO	+
	7.0+5	1.5+7	Expt	Data	EXFOR12159.004	Jun 76 . 558 PTS.	
Total	1.5+2	1.0+5	RPI Expt	Jour	NSE 37 137	Jul 69 Bartolome+LINAC,RES PARS FROM TRNS.	
	1.5+2	2.0+4		Abst	DA/B 30 679	Aug 69 - .RES PARS FROM TRNS.	
				Conf	68Wash. 795	Mar 68 - +RES PARS FROM TRNS,TBP,NDG	
Total	5.7+9		MHG Expt	Jour	PL/B 31 250	Feb 70 Parker+GRPHS,RESULTS CFD OTHERS.	+
				Rept	UNIV-MI-3028-3	Nov 69 - +TBLS,DATA GVN,OPT MDL FIT.	
	5.7+9			Data	EXFOR10043.011	Aug 71 . 1 PT. CS=2970+ - 70MB.	
Total	1.0+5	2.0+7	LAS Eval	Rept	LA- 4928	Jun 72 Devaney+EVAL.SMOOTH SIG CURVS.	
Total	1.4+7		LIN Expt	Conf	75Kiev 4 140	May 75 Djumin+ SIG GIVEN.OPTMDL ANAL,RADIUS	
Elastic	3.0+5	1.5+6	ANL Expt	Jour	ZP 175 242	Oct 63 Smith.SEPARATED FROM INELAST.LEG-FIT	+
				Conf	64Paris 2 772	Jul 64 .SUPERSEDED	
				Rept	EANDC(US)-62	Jun 64 .SUPERSEDED	
Elastic	3.0+5	1.5+6	AI Eval	Rept	NAA-SR-11973	Jul 66 Dunford.NONSPH OPTMDL TABLE+CURVES	
Elastic	2.0+6	1.6+7	LAS Theo	Rept	LA- 3538	Sep 66 Agee+ OPTMDL MODEL+H-F FOR COMP	
Elastic	3.3+5	1.5+6	ANL Expt	Jour	PR 162 1077	Oct 67 Lister+TOF.INTEGRTD DIFF SIG	
				Rept	ANL-7288	Jan 67 - + TOF 59ES TABLE+CURVE CFD TH	+
	3.3+5	1.5+6		Data	EXFOR12174.006	Jun 76 . 59 PTS.	
Elastic	1.5+6		IFU Expt	Prog	YFI-5 42	Oct 67 Korzh+ TBL OPTMDL PARAMS + TOTELAST	
				Rept	INDC-232E	67 . ENGL OF YFI-5 42	
Elastic	1.5+6		IFU Comp	Jour	YF 7 277	Feb 68 Korzh+ OPTMDL PARS-FIT TO EXPTL-SIG	
				Jour	SNP 7 2 190	Aug 68 TRANSLATN.*	
Elastic	3.4-2		DUB Expt	Prog	YFI-7 58	Apr 69 Alexandrov+ SCAT-LENGTH GIVEN, TBP	
				Rept	JINR-P3-4121	Oct 68 - + SCATTERING LENGTH, TBP	
				Rept	INDC(CCP)-7U62	Feb 70 - + ENGL OF YFI-7 58.	
Elastic	3.4-2		DUB Expt	Jour	YF 10 328	Aug 69 Aleksandrov+ SCAT LENGTH GIVEN	
				Jour	SNP 10 189	Feb 70 . ENGL OF YF 10 328	
Diff Elastic	1.0+6	4.1+6	LAS Eval	Rept	LA- 2016	Jun 56 Longley+,2ES ANG DIST 3-DEG STEPS	
Diff Elastic	3.0+5	1.5+6	ANL Expt	Jour	ZP 175 242	Oct 63 Smith.SEPARATED FROM INELAST.LEG-FIT	+
				Rept	EANDC(US)-62	Jun 64 - +TOF,TBL.50KEV STEPS,20KEV RSLN	
Diff Elastic	3.5+5	1.3+6	BNL Theo	Jour	PR/B 135 895	Aug 64 Auerbach+LCL OPTMDL FIT ANL XPT	
Diff Elastic	3.0+5	1.5+6	AI Eval	Rept	NAA-SR-11973	Jul 66 Dunford.NONSPH OPTMDL TABLD+CURVES	
Diff Elastic	4.1-1	1.0+7	WES Eval	Rept	WANL-TME-1472	Jul 66 Gibson+.68GROUP P0 P1 MATRIX	
Diff Elastic	2.0+6	1.6+7	LAS Theo	Rept	LA- 3538	Sep 66 Agee+ OPTMDL MODEL+H-F FOR COMP	
Diff Elastic	2.0+6	1.6+7	LAS Theo	Rept	LA- 3788	67 Beery+.OPTMOD CALC POLARIZ ANG DISTR	
Diff Elastic	2.0+6	1.4+7	THS Theo	Rept	BMWF-FBK67-46	May 67 Buhler+OPTMO DEF OPTICAL POTENTIAL	
Diff Elastic	3.0+5	1.5+6	ANL Expt	Jour	PR 162 1077	Oct 67 Lister+ FAST TOF 27-150DEG CURVES	+
				Rept	ANL-7288	Jan 67 .SEE ALSO	
				Prog	ANL-7210 11	Dec 66 Smith+ TOF,ANGDIST,REL C EL,GRPH,TBP	
	3.3+5	1.5+6		Data	EXFOR12174.005	Jun 76 . 295 LEG COEFS AT 59ES	
Diff Elastic	1.5+6		IFU Comp	Jour	YF 7 277	Feb 68 Korzh+ GRPH SIG(ANG),OPTMOD PARS-FIT	
				Jour	SNP 7 2 190	Aug 68 TRANSLATN.*	
Diff Elastic	0.0+0	1.5+7	FEI Eval	Book	NIKOLAEV 169	72 .LEG COEFFS+ANG DISTRIBUTS,GRAPH	
Polarization	2.0+6	1.6+7	LAS Theo	Rept	LA- 3788	67 Beery+.OPTMOD CALC COS(THETA) DISTR	
Tot Inelastc	3.0+5	1.5+6	ANL Eval	Jour	ZP 175 242	Oct 63 Smith.BY DIRECT SUMMING.C-STANDARD.	
Tot Inelastc	+6		BNL Theo	Conf	65Antwerp 25	Jul 65 Auerbach+NDG COMPLEX POTENTIAL MODL	
	1.1+5	1.6+6		Jour	PR/B 135 895	Aug 64 - +LCL OPTMDL CALC 6LVLS.	
Tot Inelastc	3.0+5	1.5+6	AI Eval	Rept	NAA-SR-11973	Jul 66 Dunford. NONSPH OPTMDL TABLE+CURVES	
Diff Inelast	6.3+5	9.5+5	ANL Revw	Conf	61Vienna 1 29	Aug 61 Smith.CURVE,N-SPECTRUM,TOF,REFS GVN	
Diff Inelast	3.0+5	1.5+6	ANL Expt	Jour	ZP 175 242	Oct 63 Smith.6 XCIT-LVLS.MEAS.AT 9 AS.ISOT	
Diff Inelast	5.0+5		BNL Theo	Jour	PR/B 135 895	Aug 64 Auerbach+LCL OPTMDL CAL 2LVLS ISOT	
Diff Inelast	3.0+5	1.5+6	AI Eval	Rept	NAA-SR-11973	Jul 66 Dunford.NONSPH OPTMDL TABLE+CURVES	
Diff Inelast	4.1-1	1.0+7	WES Eval	Rept	WANL-TME-1472	Jul 66 Gibson+.68GROUP MATRIX	
Diff Inelast	1.4+7		LRL Theo	Rept	UCRL-50181	Feb 67 Lutz+.CALC ANG DIST FOR FIRST 2+ LVL	
Diff Inelast	3.0+5	1.5+6	ANL Expt	Jour	PR 162 1077	Oct 67 Lister+ FAST TOF 5STATES CRVS CFD TH	+
				Rept	ANL-7288	Jan 67 .SEE ALSO	
	3.5+5	1.5+6		Data	EXFOR12174.007	Jun 76 . 159 PTS, SIGMA	
Diff Inelast	+6	+7	BRC Expt	Conf	69Studsvik 119	Aug 69 Haouat+ NDG,SIG+ANGDIST,STRONG TRANS	
Diff Inelast	6.0+5	1.1+6	CCP Comp	Rept	ICD-6 106	70 Sluchevskaja.SIG(ANG) TO LVLS,GRAPHS	
Res Int Abs	5.0-1		MTR Expt	Abst	ANS 5 377	Nov 62 Scoville.	+
	5.0-1			Data	EXFOR12080.004	Jun 76 . 1 PT.	

74 Tungsten 184

Quantity	Energy (ev) Min	Max	Lab	Type	Documentation Ref Vol Page	Date	Author, Comments	Data
Res Int Abs	5.0-1		ORL Expt	Jour	NSE 25 31	May 66	Khan+ RIA=12B	
Res Int Abs	None		WES Eval	Rept	WANL-TME-1472	Jul 66	Gibson+. CFD OTHERS	
Res Int Abs	5.0-1	+2	LRC Expt	Jour	NSE 31 431	Mar 68	Pierce+ ACTIV 14.9+-1.6B REL AU	
Res Int Abs	5.0-1		COL Expt	Jour	NSE 48 219	Jun 72	Rahn+. RI=14.1+-1.5B	
Res Int Abs	5.0-1		GHT Expt	Jour	JRC 20 695	74	Van Der Linden+ BY(N,G).CFD OTHS,TBL	+
	5.5-1			Conf	73Paris 2 241	Mar 73	- + ACT,REL THR+GOLD,TBL	
	5.5-1			Data	EXFOR20645.043	Jul 76	1PNT.CAPTURE.	
(n,γ)	Maxwl		JAP Expt	Jour	SCP 42 139	Jan 44	Minakawa.CYC,ACTIVATION.SIG NDG	
(n,γ)	Pile		ANL Expt	Jour	PR 72 888	Nov 47	Seren+.ACT METHOD.PILE IRRAD.METAL.	+
	Pile			Data	EXFOR11447.114	Jun 76	. 1 PT.	
(n,γ)	Maxwl		ORL Expt	Jour	PR 88 412	Oct 52	Pomerance.PILE OSC.	+
	Maxwl			Data	EXFOR11507.093	Jun 76	. 1 PT.	
(n,γ)	+0	1.5+3	HAR Expt	Jour	NP 3 553	Jun 57	Bowey. TOF. CAPT GAM YLD CURVE	
(n,γ)	2.5+4		LRL Expt	Jour	PR 112 226	Oct 58	Booth+ SB-BE REL I+THR,ACT 74D HL	+
	2.5+4			Data	EXFOR11429.027	Jun 76	. 1 PT.	
(n,γ)	2.7+1	1.6+2	SAC Expt	Jour	JPR 21 426	May 60	Corge+ DATA FOR RESONANCE ANALYSIS.	+
(n,γ)	Pile		ORL Expt	Jour	NSE 8 378	Nov 60	Lyon. ACTIVATION,SIGMA GIVEN	+
	Pile			Data	EXFOR11625.030	Jun 76	. 1 PT.	
(n,γ)	Maxwl		MHG Expt	Jour	NP 34 623	Jun 62	Treado+ SIG=2.0B. SPECTRA OF GAMMAS	
(n,γ)	Maxwl		MUA Expt	Jour	NP 36 542	Aug 62	Mangal+ SCINT SPECT,REL TO AU197,TBL	
				Conf	62Madras 95	Feb 62	- +	
(n,γ)	Maxwl	+5	FOA Theo	Jour	NP 39 353	Dec 62	Bergqvist+. IN PER CENT OF NAT ELEMT	
(n,γ)	1.5+3	4.0+4	LEB Comp	Rept	INDSWG-64 43	64	Konks. GRAPH SIG(E)	
(n,γ)	Maxwl		ANL Comp	Jour	NP 60 241	Nov 64	Bishop+EXP AND TH ISOMER RATIOS CFD	
(n,γ)	1.0-3	1.0+7	WES Eval	Rept	WANL-TME-1472	Jul 66	Gibson+.68GROUPS .4EV UP+CURVE-100EV	
(n,γ)	3.3+4	1.7+5	FEI Expt	Jour	YF 4 282	Aug 66	Kononov+ TOF,SCIN-TANK,GRPH CFD THEO	+
				Conf	66Paris 1 469	Oct 66	* GRAPH CFD OTHERS	
				Jour	SNP 4 204	Feb 67	.ENGLISH TRANSL OF YF 4 282 8/66	
				Prog	INDSWG-152 108	66	.ENGLISH TRANSL OF ICD-3	
	2.9+4	1.7+5		Data	EXFOR40076.006	Jul 71	SIG AT 15 ENERGIES FROM PRIV COMMUN	
(n,γ)	Fiss		CCP Expt	Jour	YF 4 515	Sep 66	Druzhinin+.ACTIVATION METHOD,VAL GVN	+
				Jour	SNP 4 366	Mar 67	. ENGL OF YF 4 515	
(n,γ)	1.0-2	1.0+1	GA Expt	Jour	NSE 26 487	Dec 66	Friesenhahn.THR 1.7+-.1 LIQ SCIN	+
				Conf	66Wash. 182	Mar 66	.SUPERSEDED	
				Rept	GA-6882	Jan 66	.SUPERSEDED	
	1.0-2	2.4+0		Data	EXFOR12167.	Jun 76	. 29 PTS.	
(n,γ)	-		IEA Comp	Rept	IEA-INF-10	Aug 68	Atalla. TABLES OF HL,SIG AND GAMM-E	
(n,γ)	1.5+2	1.0+5	RPI Expt	Jour	NSE 37 137	Jul 69	Bartolome+CAPT AREAS,AVG CS.	
	1.5+2	2.0+4		Abst	DA/B 30 679	Aug 69	- .LINAC,RES PARS FROM DATA.	
				Conf	68Wash. 795	Mar 68	- +AVG CAPT CS GRPHS.	
	4.0+2	8.0+3		Conf	66Wash. 404	Mar 66	Gibbons.RPI LINAC+SC(T),CURVE	
	3.5+1	1.0+4		Prog	ORNL-3778 53	May 65	Block.LINAC,SC,NUMEROUS RES,CRVS	
(n,γ)	3.0+4		AUA Theo	Rept	AAEC/E-211	Nov 70	Musgrove. SIGMA GIVEN AND CFD OTHER	
(n,γ)	2.4+4		MUA Theo	Jour	IJP 46 114	Mar 72	Chaubey+ P-WAVE STRENGTH FUNCT,TABLE	
(n,γ)	1.0+3	1.0+7	BOL Eval	Data	BENZI-DFN 816.	May 72	40 PNTS	+
(n,γ)	1.0+3	1.0+7	BOL Eval	Data	BENZI-DFN 842.	May 72	40 PNTS	+
(n,γ)	Pile		ROS ExTh	Prog	ZFK-243 93	Sep 72	Mohsen+ NG-SYSTEMAT. FOR RARE EARTHS	
(n,γ)	5.0+3	2.0+7	LAS Eval	Rept	LA-5221	May 73	Devaney+. ENDF/B LISTING. CURVES	+
(n,γ)	Maxwl		UCB Expt	Abst	BAP 8 71	Jan 63	Kramer+ACT.CS DETERMINED	+
	Maxwl			Data	EXFOR12157.002	Jun 76	. 1 PT.	
Spect (n,γ)	Maxwl		ORL Expt	Prog	WASH-1064 123	Oct 65	Harvey+,LI-GE DET,RSLN 10KEV AT 6MEV	
Spect (n,γ)	Maxwl		ORL Expt	Abst	BAP 11 336	Apr 66	Martin+CFD (D,P)EXPTS.ABST.DB13.	
Spect (n,γ)	None		BNL Expt	Abst	BAP 12 105	Jan 67	Chrien+5. 120 GS WITH E P 3.4 MEV	
Spect (n,γ)	+0	+4	COL Expt	Prog	WASH-1124 31	Nov 68	Camarda+ MOXON-RAE DET TBC NO DATA	
Spect (n,γ)	1.8+2		SAC Expt	Jour	NP/A 123 581	Jan 69	Samour+ GE(LI). 1RES. 3690TO8450 KEV	
				Rept	CEA-R-3776	Apr 69	- . (THESIS) DATA GIVEN	
Spect (n,γ)	1.8+2	4.3+2	HAR Expt	Conf	69Studsvik 579	Aug 69	Murray+ GAM INTENS TBL VS GAM-E,N-E	
Spect (n,γ)	Pile		AE Expt	Jour	AF 40 247	Feb 70	Malmskog+.E+INT FOR W185M GS. SPINS	
				Rept	AE-349	Feb 69	- . LOW EN LVLS IN W-185	
Spect (n,γ)	Maxwl		IFL Expt	Conf	72Kiev 1 155	Jan 72	Beitin'+ ABSTR.GAM-ES,LVL SCH GIVEN	
Spect (n,γ)	Maxwl		IFL Expt	Book	PROKOFJEV	73	. TBL GAM,CONV ELECTR ES+INV,LVL SCH	
Spect (n,γ)	Maxwl		ROS Expt	Rept	ZFK-260	Jul 73	.FULL PAPER, TABLES	+
				Prog	ZFK-243 89	Sep 72	Prade+ HIGH-E G-SPECT,GE-LI,LVL GRPH	
	Maxwl			Data	EXFOR30276.	Oct 74	LOW+HIGH ENRGY PARTS OF SPEC,97 PTS	
Spect (n,γ)	2.8+6		KGU Expt	Conf	76Lowell 1334	Jul 76	Andreev+DIRECT EXCIT EFFECTS.NDG	
Inelastic γ	2.6+6		NRL Expt	Rept	NRL-4937	Jun 57	Shapiro+. NAI SCINT SPEC.GAM SP GIVE	
Inelastic γ	5.0+5	1.5+6	WES Expt	Jour	PR 107 1306	Sep 57	Sinclair.XTL SPEC REL CURV 112KEV G	
Inelastic γ	8.7+6		BRC Expt	Conf	69Studsvik 119	Aug 69	Haouat+ SPEC-GRPH,RESON IDENTIFIED	

74 Tungsten 184

Quantity	Energy (ev) Min	Max	Lab	Type	Documentation Ref Vol Page	Date	Author, Comments	Data
Inelastic γ	1.0+6		TNC	Expt Rept	ORO-2791-32	Feb 71	Buchanan+.55-DEG SIGS TABULATED	
Inelastic γ	2.8+6		CCP	Expt Conf	76Lowell 1334	Jul 76	Andreev+DIRECT EXCIT EFFECTS.NDG	
Nonelastic γ	1.0-5	2.0+7	LAS	Eval Rept	LA- 5793	Apr 75	Young. GAMMA PROD CS FOR ENDF	
(n,2n)	Fiss		CRC	Eval Rept	CRC-1003	Dec 60	Roy+,ESTIMATED AVG SIG=7.5MB	
(n,2n)	1.3+7	1.5+7	BNL	Theo Jour	NSE 23 238	Nov 65	Pearlstein.3ES.STAT MDL CALC.TBL CS.	
(n,2n)	Fiss		BNL	Theo Jour	NSE 23 238	Nov 65	Pearlstein.STATMDL CALC.SPEC AVG.TBL	
(n,2n)	4.1-1	1.0+7	WES	Eval Rept	WANL-TME-1472	Jul 66	Gibson+.68GROUP MATRIX	
(n,2n)	1.5+7		MUA	Expt Jour	NP 88 349	Nov 66	Prasad+,T-D NEUT ACT REL TO FE56(NP)	+
	1.5+7			Data	EXFOR30015.008	May 70	PARTIAL SIGMA(METASTABLE)	
(n,2n)	1.5+7		TUR	Theo Jour	NC 56 18 201	Jul 68	Minetti+THEOR ISOM RATIO SPIN CO PAR	
(n,2n)	1.5+7		DEB	Comp Jour	REA 7 4 93	Dec 69	Csikai+ SIG+HL COMPILTN,N-ACTIV-ANAL	
(n,2n)	1.4+7	1.5+7	JYV	Eval Jour	JU-RR-3/1970	Jun 70	Leppaemaeki+ TABLE OF EVAL AVG SIG	
(n,2n)	None		KFI	Comp Jour	JRC 7 365	Jun 71	Nagy+ GAMMA+XRAY+ELECTR ES,HALF-LIFE	
(n,2n)	1.4+7		ITJ	Expt Jour	JRC 14 201	73	Janczyszyn+ ISO-PROD BY NAT-W ACTIV	+
	1.4+7			Data	EXFOR30322.017	Feb 76	MEAN OF W183(N,N')+W184(N,2N)	
(n,2n)	1.5+7		DEB	Eval Jour	REA 11 1 153	Mar 73	Boedy+ RECOMM.VALUE FROM N-Z SYSTEM.	
(n,2n)	1.5+7		KFI	Expt Rept	KFKI-73-68	Dec 73	Jeki.NEW FIT,CALC SIG CFD OTHERS,TBL	
(n,xn) x>2	Fiss		BNL	Theo Jour	NSE 23 238	Nov 65	Pearlstein.SPEC AVG STATMDL CALC N3N	
(n,p)	1.4+7		ALD	Expt Jour	PPS 73 215	Feb 59	Coleman+. ACT. CFD DIRECT INTERACTN	+
(n,p)	1.5+7		ARK	Expt Rept	A-ARK-60 4	Jan 60	Poularikas+	+
	1.5+7			Data	EXFOR12181.002	Jun 76	. 1 PT.	
(n,p)	Fiss		CRC	Eval Rept	CRC-1003	Dec 60	Roy+,ESTIMATED AVG SIG=0.003MB	
(n,p)	1.4+7		SAH	Expt Conf	63Bombay 244	Feb 63	Mukherjee+.VAL GVN,ACTIVATION METHOD	+
	1.4+7			Data	EXFOR31330.010	Sep 72	.SIG GVN	
(n,p)	1.4+7	1.5+7	SAH	Comp Jour	NUC 23 8 112	Aug 65	Chatterjee. TABLE WITH REFS.	
	1.4+7			Jour	NP 60 273	Nov 64	- .MEAN OF EXPT CFD SHELLMOD	
(n,p)	1.4+7	1.5+7	NAP	Comp Rept	INFN/BE-67-10	Jul 67	Cuzzocrea+ AVERAGED CHOSEN DATA.	
(n,p)	1.5+7		DEB	Comp Jour	REA 7 4 93	Dec 69	Csikai+ SIG+HL COMPILTN,N-ACTIV-ANAL	
(n,p)	1.4+7	1.5+7	JYV	Eval Jour	JU-RR-3/1970	Jun 70	Leppaemaeki+ TABLE OF EVAL AVG SIG	
(n,p)	1.4+7	1.5+7	KAZ	Theo Jour	YF 18 705	Oct 73	Levkovsky.AVERAGED SIG,CALC,TBL	
				Jour	SNP 18 361	Apr 74	. ENGLISH OF YF 18,705	
(n,p)	1.5+7		JUL	Expt Jour	NP/A 242 317	Apr 75	Qaim+ SIG MEASURED BY ACT,VS (N-Z)/A	+
	1.5+7			Data	EXFOR20668.012	Oct 76	1PNT.SIGMA.	
(n,np)	1.5+7		SAH	Expt Conf	63Bombay 240	Feb 63	Ganguly+ VAL GVN,ACTIVATION METHOD	+
	1.5+7			Data	EXFOR31329.005	Sep 72	.SIG (NNP)+(ND) GVN	
(n,d)	1.5+7		SAH	Expt Conf	63Bombay 240	Feb 63	Ganguly+.VAL GVN, ACTIVATION METHOD	+
	1.5+7			Data	EXFOR31329.005	Sep 72	.SIG (NNP)+(ND) GVN	
(n,α)	1.4+7		LRL	Expt Prog	WASH-1018 63	Apr 59	Lindner+	+
	1.4+7			Data	EXFOR12185.006	Jun 76	. 1 PT.	
(n,α)	Fiss		CRC	Eval Rept	CRC-1003	Dec 60	Roy+,ESTIMATED AVG SIG=BELO 0.0001MB	
(n,α)	Fiss		GRE	Expt Jour	RCA 8 196	Dec 67	Rivier+ .19+-.4 MICROB	+
	Fiss			Data	EXFOR20737.004	Apr 77	1PNT.SIGMA.	
(n,α)	1.5+7		JUL	Expt Jour	NP/A 242 317	Apr 75	Qaim+ SIG MEASURED BY ACT,VS (N-Z)/A	+
	1.5+7			Data	EXFOR20668.014	Oct 76	1PNT.SIGMA.	
Reson Params	1.0+2	2.0+2	ANL	Expt Jour	PR 84 869	Dec 51	Selove.	+
Reson Params	1.9+2	3.2+2	BNL	Expt Abst	BAP 1 187	Apr 56	Schwartz+ ABST. K3,WN.	
	1.9+2	3.2+2		Data	EXFOR12153.003	Jun 76	. 2 RES, E0, WN	
Reson Params	1.8+2		HAR	Expt Jour	NP 3 553	Jun 57	Bowey.TOF.1 E FROM CAPT GAMMA YIELDS	
Reson Params	1.8+2		HAR	Expt Jour	NP 12 552	Sep 59	Firk+ TOF 1RES.185EV	+
				Rept	AERE-NP/GEN 11	Apr 59	- + TOF. RES SPINS ASSIGNED.	
Reson Params	+0	+3	ORL	Revw Conf	60Vienna 535	Oct 60	Block+.NDG,EXPT DESCRIBED	
Reson Params	+1	+2	ANL	Expt Prog	WASH-1048 9	Jun 64	Bollinger. JS FROM G CASCADES. NDG	
Reson Params	1.0+2	2.1+3	ORL	Expt Jour	NSE 25 31	May 66	Khan+	+
	1.0+2	2.1+3		Data	EXFOR12182.002	Jun 76	. 16 RES,E0,WN	
Reson Params	-.1+3		GA	ExTh Jour	NSE 26 487	Dec 66	Friesenhahn. NEG ENERGY RESON.	+
				Rept	GA- 6882	Jan 66	.SUPERSEDED	
	-.1+3			Expt Data	EXFOR12167.013	Jun 76	. 1 RES, E0, WN0,NG	
Reson Params	1.0+4	2.0+6	FEI	ExTh Jour	YF 5 129	Jan 67	Kononov.Lσ2 N CAPTURE,TBL,CURVES GVN	+
				Jour	SNP 5 89	Jul 67	TRANSLATN.*	
Reson Params		1.0+6	AUA	Theo Jour	AUJ 20 477	Oct 67	Cook. TBL OF AVG LVL SPACING D,L=0,1	
Reson Params	+0	+2	LRC	Expt Jour	NSE 31 431	Mar 68	Pierce+ ACTIV AVG WG=0.062+-0.007EV	
Reson Params	+3	+5	AUA	ExTh Rept	AAEC/E-198	May 69	Musgrove.RES PARS +STF FROM (NG)FIT	+
Reson Params	1.6+2	4.2+3	RPI	Expt Jour	NSE 37 137	Jul 69	Bartolome+LINAC,RES PARS TO 2.6KEV.	+
	1.5+2	2.0+4		Abst	DA/B 30 679	Aug 69	- .RES PARS FROM TRNS,CAPT.	
				Conf	68Wash. 795	Mar 68	+RES PARS BY CAPT,TRNS,TBD.	
	1.7+2	2.6+3		Data	EXFOR10002.	Jan 78	. 26 RES ES.WN,WG,D GVN.	
Reson Params	1.8+2	4.3+3	HAR	ExTh Conf	69Studsvik 579	Aug 69	Murray+CORRELATION WN+WG,TBLS GVN	
Reson Params	-		AUA	Theo Rept	AAEC/E-211	Nov 70	Musgrove. CALCULTD D+GAM WIDTH GIVEN	

74 Tungsten 184

Quantity	Energy (ev) Min	Max	Lab	Type	Documentation Ref Vol Page	Date	Author, Comments	Data
Reson Params	−.1+3	2.6+3	CJD	Eval	Rept YK− 7	71	Zakharova+ SURVEY+SYSTEMATICS,GW,TBL	
					Rept INDC(CCP)−27	Nov 72	.ENGLISH TRANSLATION OF YK−7 /71	
Reson Params	None		DUB	Theo	Jour YF 13 240	Feb 71	Malecki+G−WID,THEO CFD EXPT.TBL,GRPH	
					Jour SNP 13 133	Aug 71	− + ENGL OF YF 13 240.	
Reson Params	1.0+2	1.6+4	COL	Expt	Jour PR/C 8 1813	Nov 73	Camarda+. WN+AVG D FOR MANY RESON	+
	None				Conf 75Wash. 780	Mar 75	Hacken+19ELEMENTS RVW.TBLS,GRPHS.	
	1.0+2	1.6+4			Conf 71Albany 205	Aug 71	Camarada+D GVN FOR S LVLS.TBP PR	
	1.0+2	1.6+4			Data EXFOR10507.	Apr 76	.127 PTS. WN,D VAL GVN.	
Reson Params	4.0+0	1.2+3	JAE	Expt	Rept JAERI−M−5624	Feb 74	Ohkubo.LINAC,TOF.WT,WN IN TABLE	
Strnth Fnctn	1.0+3	6.0+4	LEB	Expt	Conf 65Antwerp § 182	Jul 65	Bergman.LEBEDEV.S1=2+−.5.ALSO DO	
Strnth Fnctn		1.0+4	ORL	Expt	Jour NSE 25 31	May 66	Khan+ S0,D	
Strnth Fnctn	1.0+4	2.0+6	FEI	ExTh	Rept YF 5 129	Jan 67	Kononov.Lσ2 N CAPTURE,TBL,CURVES GVN	+
					Jour SNP 5 89	Jul 67	TRANSLATN.*	
	1.0+4	2.0+6		Expt	Data EXFOR40013.004	Mar 73	.VALUE GIVEN	
Strnth Fnctn	1.0+4		ANL	Theo	Jour PR 162 1077	Oct 67	Lister+ OPTMDL CALC S,P,AND D WAVE	
					Rept ANL−7288	Jan 67	.SUPERSEDED	
Strnth Fnctn	+3	+5	AUA	ExTh	Rept AAEC/E−198	May 69	Musgrove.S+P+D STF FROM (NG)FIT,TBL	+
Strnth Fnctn	1.6+2	2.6+3	RPI	ExTh	Jour NSE 37 137	Jul 69	Bartolome+S0=3.0+−.6,S1=.28+.52−.15	+
					Abst DA/B 30 679	Aug 69	− .S,P STF CFD OPT,SPH MDLS.	
	1.7+2	2.6+3			Data EXFOR10002.027	Jan 78	.S0=(3.0+−.6)−4,S1=(.28+.52−.15)−4	
Strnth Fnctn	−		AUA	Theo	Rept AAEC/E−211	Nov 70	Musgrove. SMOOTHED S0,S1 AND S2 GIVN	
Strnth Fnctn	2.4+4		MUA	Theo	Jour IJP 46 114	Mar 72	Chaubey+ P−WAVE.FOR A−SYSTEMATIC,GRPH	
Strnth Fnctn	None		AUA	Eval	Rept AAEC/E−277	Mar 73	Musgrove.TBLS EXPTL DATA+BEST VALUES	
Strnth Fnctn	+1	+4	COL	Expt	Jour PR/C 8 1813	Nov 73	Camarda+S WAVE,GRPH,TBL.	+
	None				Conf 75Wash. 780	Mar 75	Hacken+19ELEMENTS RVW.TBLS,GRPHS.	
	1.0+1	9.9+4			Conf 71Albany 205	Aug 71	Camarada+S0 GVN	
	0.0+0	1.6+4			Data EXFOR10507.004	Apr 76	. 1 PT. S0=(2.35+−.24)−4	
Lvl Density	7.0+6		ISL	Theo	Conf 64Geneva § 511	May 64	Szwarcbaum+.T FROM 3 FORMLS CFD EXPS	
Lvl Density	−		FEI	Eval	Rept FEI−36	66	Kapchigashev+.TBL OF RELATD QUANTTYS	+
		5.0+4			Jour YF 4 686	Sep 66	.TABLE.SHORT VERSION OF FEI−36	
	−				Prog YFI−3 3	66	.ABSTRACT.TABLE LDL+NUCL.EXCIT.E	
		5.0+4			Jour SNP 4 486	67	.ENGLISH OF YF 4.FROM(N,GAMMA).TABLE	
					Prog INDC−E−140 3	66	.ENGLISH TRANSL OF YFI−3	
Lvl Density	+6		MIL	Theo	Jour EN 15 1 54	Jan 68	Facchini+ LDL PARS FROM LOW EN RES	
Lvl Density	None		CCP	Theo	Jour YF 11 1028	May 70	Rubchenya. DENSITY+A+TEMP GIVEN	
					Jour SNP 11 571	Nov 70	. ENGL OF YF 11 571.	
Lvl Density	None		AUW	Theo	Conf 70Madurai 2 267	Dec 70	Ramamurty+ A−PARAMETER GVN,LANG'S−TH	
Lvl Density	0.0+0	1.0+4	ITE	Theo	Conf 72Budapest 268	Aug 72	Belyaev+ GROUPINGS OF LVL SPACNG,TBL	
Lvl Density	None		MUN	Theo	Jour NP/A 217 269	Dec 73	Dilg+ A,DELTA. BACK SHIFTED FERMIGAS	
Lvl Density	None		COP	Theo	Jour NP/A 222 493	Apr 74	Dossing+COLL ROTAT.SPAC. ACCUR ESTIM	
Lvl Density	None		DUB	Theo	Jour NP/A 224 396	May 74	Malov+ 1/2 MICROSC.MODEL. DEFORM NUC	
Lvl Density	None		ROC	Theo	Jour NP/A 223 577	May 74	Huizenga+ EXP CFD MICROSC TH SPH NUC	
Lvl Density	None		ROC	Theo	Jour NP/A 223 589	May 74	Huizenga+ EXP CFD MICROSC TH AX SYMM	
Lvl Density	Maxwl		COL	Theo	Conf 75Wash. 335	Mar 75	Felvinci+MOD ERICSON CALC CFD EXP	

74 Tungsten 185

Quantity	Energy (ev) Min	Max	Lab	Type	Documentation Ref Vol Page	Date	Author, Comments	Data
Spect (n,γ)	Maxwl		ANL	Theo	Conf 68DUBSY 317	Jul 68	Bollinger.ANAL.RAD. TRANSITIONS.	
Reson Params	−		AUA	Theo	Rept AAEC/E−211	Nov 70	Musgrove. CALCULTD D+GAM WIDTH GIVEN	
Strnth Fnctn	−		AUA	Theo	Rept AAEC/E−211	Nov 70	Musgrove. SMOOTHED S0,S1 AND S2 GIVN	
Lvl Density	−		COP	Theo	Jour NP 6 62	Mar 58	Ericson. LVL DENSITY FORM CFD EXP	
Lvl Density	+6		MIL	Theo	Jour EN 15 1 54	Jan 68	Facchini+ LDL PARS FROM LOW EN RES	
Lvl Density	None		MUN	Theo	Jour NP/A 217 269	Dec 73	Dilg+ A,DELTA. BACK SHIFTED FERMIGAS	
Lvl Density	None		COP	Theo	Jour NP/A 222 493	Apr 74	Dossing+COLL ROTAT.SPAC. ACCUR ESTIM	
Lvl Density	None		ROC	Theo	Jour NP/A 223 577	May 74	Huizenga+ EXP CFD MICROSC TH SPH NUC	
Lvl Density		+3	DUB	Theo	Conf 75Kiev 3 23	May 75	Voronov. LVL SPACING.TABLE.	
	None				Jour NP/A 224 396	May 74	Malov+ 1/2 MICROSC.MODEL. DEFORM NUC	

74 Tungsten 186

Quantity	Energy (ev) Min	Max	Lab	Type	Documentation Ref Vol Page	Date	Author, Comments	Data
Evaluation	1.0−3	1.5+7	GA	Eval	Rept GA−5885	Nov 64	Joanou+ TOT STF SEL SNE SIN N2N ETC.	
Evaluation	1.0+3	1.4+7	GEN	Eval	Rept GEMP−388	Nov 65	Prince.OPTMDL WITH CHANNEL COMPETIT	
Evaluation	1.0−2	1.5+7	GEN	Eval	Rept GEMP−448	Nov 66	Henderson+ TOT NG SIN N2N NP ENDF/B	
Evaluation	1.0−4	2.0+7	AI	Eval	Rept TI−707−130−26	Jul 73	Rose+	

74 Tungsten 186

Quantity	Energy (ev) Min	Max	Lab	Type	Documentation Ref Vol Page	Date	Author, Comments	Data
Total	3.3+0	5.2+5	ANL	Expt	Jour PR 84 869	Dec 51	Selove.	+
	3.3+0	5.2+5			Data EXFOR12168.006	Jun 76	. 72 PTS.	
Total	3.0+5	1.5+6	AI	Eval	Rept NAA−SR−11973	Jul 66	Dunford.NONSPHERICAL OPTMDL 1TABLE	
Total	1.0+5	6.5+5	ANL	Expt	Prog ANL−7210 16	Dec 66	Whalen.SHORT NOTE,GRAPH ONLY	+
	1.0+5	6.5+5			Data EXFOR11540.011	Jun 76	. 272 PTS.	
Total	6.0+5	2.5+7	RPI	ExTh	Abst DA/B 28 3435	Feb 68	Martin.TOF, OKS DEFORMED NUCL OPTMOD	+
	7.0+5	1.5+7			Expt EXFOR12159.005	Jun 76	. 547 PTS.	
Total	1.5+2	1.0+5	RPI	Expt	Jour NSE 37 137	Jul 69	Bartolome+LINAC,RES PARS FROM TRNS.	
	1.5+2	2.0+4			Abst DA/B 30 679	Aug 69	− +RES PARS FROM TRNS.	
					Conf 68Wash. 795	Mar 68	− +RES PARS FROM TRNS,TBP,NDG	
Total	2.5+6	1.5+7	BNW	Expt	Jour PR/C 3 576	Feb 71	Foster+,TRANS,CURVS,CFD OTHERS+TH	+
					Jour NIM 36 1	Sep 65	.EXPT DETAILS	
	2.3+6	1.5+7			Data EXFOR10047.107	Aug 73	.250PTS.SIGMA	
Total	1.0+5	2.0+7	LAS	Eval	Rept LA− 4928	Jun 72	Devaney+EVAL.SMOOTH SIG CURVS.	
Total	1.3+7	1.5+7	DEB	Eval	Rept IAEA−153 173	73	Boedy+ MOST PROBABLE VAL OF SIG,TBL	
					Jour AHP 30 115	Oct 71	Angeli+ AVG SIG,CFD CALC.TBLS.GRAPH	
Total	1.4+7		LIN	Expt	Conf 75Kiev 4 140	May 75	Djumin+ SIG GIVEN.OPTMOD ANAL,RADIUS	
Total	−3	1.9+0	THS	Theo	Rept IKE−6 89 65	Jun 75	Keinert. DATA LIBRARY	
Elastic		+5	ANL	Expt	Jour PR 79 11	Jul 50	Harris+ EPI−CD,RES INT SCAT,B−W TH	
Elastic	3.0+5	1.5+6	AI	Eval	Rept NAA−SR−11973	Jul 66	Dunford.NONSPH OPTMDL TABLE+CURVES	
Elastic	3.3+5	1.5+6	ANL	Expt	Jour PR 162 1077	Oct 67	Lister+TOF.INTEGRTD DIFF SIG.	+
					Rept ANL−7288	Jan 67	− TOF 59ES TABLE+CURVE CFD TH	
	3.3+5	1.5+6			Data EXFOR12174.009	Jun 76	. 59 PTS.	
Elastic	3.4−2		DUB	Expt	Prog YFI−7 58	Apr 69	Alexandrov+ SCAT−LENGTH GIVEN, TBP	
					Jour YF 10 328	Aug 69	Aleksandrov+ SCAT LENGTH+COHER.SIG	
					Rept JINR−P3−4121	Oct 68	Alexandrov+ SCATTERING LENGTH, TBP	
					Rept INDC(CCP)−7U62	Feb 70	+ ENGL OF YFI−7 58.	
					Jour SNP 10 189	Feb 70	. ENGL OF YF 10 328	
Elastic	3.7−4	6.3−2	MUN	Expt	Rept JINR−E3−5371	Oct 70	Alexandrov+ COHERENT SCAT.AMPL.GIVEN	
Diff Elastic	3.0+5	1.5+6	AI	Eval	Rept NAA−SR−11973	Jul 66	Dunford. NONSPH OPTMDL TABLE+CURVES	
Diff Elastic	4.1−1	1.0+7	WES	Eval	Rept WANL−TME−1472	Jul 66	Gibson+.68GROUP P0 P1 MATRIX	
Diff Elastic	3.0+5	1.5+6	ANL	Expt	Jour PR 162 1077	Oct 67	Lister+ FAST TOF 27−150DEG CURVES	+
					Rept ANL−7288	Jan 67	.SEE ALSO.	
	3.3+5	1.5+6			Data EXFOR12174.008	Jun 76	. 295 LEG COEFS AT 59 ES	
Diff Elastic	3.0+6		BRC	Theo	Conf IAEA−190 251	76	Delaroche+ ANGDIS,COUPL−CHANNEL,GRPH	
Tot Inelastc	2.0+5	+6	CCP	Theo	Jour ZET 30 141	Jan 56	HAUSER CALC 1ST LVL XCTN .6 B	
					Jour JET 3 98	Aug 56	TRANSLATN.*	
Tot Inelastc	3.0+5	1.5+6	AI	Eval	Rept NAA−SR−11973	Jul 66	Dunford. NONSPH OPTMDL TABLE+CURVES	
Diff Inelast	7.5+5	9.5+5	ANL	Revw	Conf 61Vienna 1 29	Aug 61	Smith.CURVE,N−SPECTRUM,TOF,REFS GVN	
Diff Inelast	4.1−1	1.0+7	WES	Eval	Rept WANL−TME−1472	Jul 66	Gibson+.68GROUP MATRIX	
Diff Inelast	3.0+5	1.5+6	ANL	Expt	Jour PR 162 1077	Oct 67	Lister+ FAST TOF 6STATES CRVS CFD TH	+
					Rept ANL−7288	Jan 67	.SEE ALSO	
	3.5+5	1.6+6			Data EXFOR12174.010	Jun 76	. 159 PTS, SIGMA	
Diff Inelast	3.0+6		BRC	Theo	Conf IAEA−190 251	76	Delaroche+ ANGDIS(1ST EXC STATE)GRPH	
Res Int Abs	5.0−1		ANL	Expt	Jour PR 79 11	Jul 50	Harris+ EPI−CD,REL THERMAL ACT. B−W	+
	5.0−1				Data EXFOR11343.030	Jun 76	. 1 PT.	
Res Int Abs	None		ORL	Revw	Conf 55Geneva 5 96	Aug 55	Macklin+.TABLE,EXPT CFD THEORY,P833	
Res Int Abs	5.0−1		MTR	Expt	Abst ANS 5 377	Nov 62	Scoville+	+
	5.0−1				Data EXFOR12080.005	Jun 76	. 1 PT.	
Res Int Abs	6.2−1		SRL	Expt	Rept DP− 817	Jan 63	Baumann.CD COV FOIL,/ AU,NO1/V, 476B	+
	6.2−1				Data EXFOR11376.009	Jun 76	. 1 PT.	
Res Int Abs	5.0−1		NSW	Eval	Rept AAEC/TM−191	Apr 63	Connolly+ CALC RES INT=456B	
Res Int Abs	5.2−1		LRC	Expt	Abst ANS 8 284	Jun 65	Shook+ OKS CALC VALUE	
Res Int Abs	None		WES	Eval	Rept WANL−TME−1472	Jul 66	Gibson+. CFD OTHERS	
Res Int Abs	Maxwl		ORL	Expt	Prog ORNL−4013 5	Sep 66	Gillette.RESONANCE INTEGRAL=318B	
Res Int Abs	5.0−1		MOL	Expt	Prog EANDC(E)76U107	Jan 67	Damle+ ACT. W−AL ALLOY	+
	5.0−1				Data EXFOR20184.003	May 74	1PNT.CAPTURE.	
Res Int Abs	2.0−1	1.0+5	JUL	Expt	Rept JUEL−503−RX	Sep 67	Borchardt.SELF−SHIELD−CORRC,CFD TH	+
	5.0−1				Data EXFOR20647.006	Jul 76	1PNT.CAPTURE.	
Res Int Abs	5.5−1		MOL	Theo	Rept BLG−421	Sep 67	Damle+,EVAL ACT R.I.=509+−50B,INC 1/V	
Res Int Abs	5.5−1		MOL	Eval	Rept BLG−421	Sep 67	Damle+,EVAL ACT R.I.=509+−50B,INC 1/V	
Res Int Abs	7.8−1		AI	Expt	Rept NAA−SR−12500	Oct 67	Beller+ ACTIV 450+−36B REL AU	+
	7.8−1				Data EXFOR12164.002	Jun 76	. 1 PT.	
Res Int Abs	5.0−1		BGK	Expt	Rept THAI−AEC−10	Oct 67	. ACTIV(NA−I),CD−RATIO,REL AU. TABLE	+
	5.0−1				Data EXFOR30368.029	Jan 77	REL AU, PRELM.	
Res Int Abs	5.0−1	+2	LRC	Expt	Jour NSE 31 431	Mar 68	Pierce+ ACTIV 441+−22B REL AU 1575B	
Res Int Abs	5.5−1		GHT	Expt	Jour JRC 9 9	71	De Corte+CAPT CD−R,290 B INCL 1/V	+
Res Int Abs	5.0−1		COL	Expt	Jour NSE 48 219	Jun 72	Rahn+. 486+−50B	

74 Tungsten 186

Quantity	Energy (ev) Min	Max	Lab	Type	Documentation Ref Vol Page	Date	Author, Comments	Data
Res Int Abs	5.0−1		GER Revw	Conf	73Paris 2 193	Mar 73	Krivan.EVALUATED DATA CFD,ACTIV,TBL	
Res Int Abs	5.5−1		RCN Revw	Conf	73Paris 2 271	Mar 73	Zijp.ACT,RECOMM FROM LITERATURE,TBL	
	−1	+3		Rept	STI/DOC/10−107	May 70	− .CH 4. (NG) VAL TBL,TECHNIQ−REV	
Res Int Abs	5.0−1		GHT Expt	Jour	JRC 20 695	74	Van Der Linden+ .BY(N,G).CFD OTHS,TBL	+
	5.5−1			Conf	73Paris 2 241	Mar 73	− + ACT,REL THR+GOLD,TBL	
	5.5−1			Data	EXFOR20645.044	Jul 76	1PNT.CAPTURE.	
Res Int Act	Pile		AUA Expt	Rept	AAEC/TM−466	Jul 68	Wall. VAL GVN,CFD OTHER EXPT,TBL	
(n,γ)	Maxwl		JAP Expt	Jour	SCP 38 167	Jan 41	Sinma+.LI+D.RELATIVE SIG MEASUREMENT	
(n,γ)	Pile		ANL Expt	Jour	PR 72 888	Nov 47	Seren+.THR IRRAD. TO16.2MIN,METAL.	+
	Pile			Data	EXFOR11447.115	Jun 76	. 1 PT.	
(n,γ)	2.2+5	9.0+5	OXF Expt	Jour	NAT 161 727	May 48	Allen+ ACTIVATION RATIO	
(n,γ)	Fiss		ANL Expt	Jour	PR 75 1781	Jun 49	Hughes+ REL SIG(THERMAL),FOIL ACTIVN	+
	Fiss			Data	EXFOR11450.035	Jun 76	. 1 PT.	
(n,γ)	Maxwl		ORL Expt	Jour	PR 88 412	Oct 52	Pomerance.PILE OSC.	+
	Maxwl			Data	EXFOR11507.094	Jun 76	. 1 PT.	
(n,γ)	2.5+4		ANL Expt	Jour	PR 89 1306	Mar 53	Kimball+	
				Rept	AECU−2394	Jan 53	− + ACT SB−BE PHOTONEUTS 119MB	
(n,γ)	Fiss		BNL Expt	Jour	PR 91 1423	Sep 53	Hughes+.ALSO LVL SPACINGS AT EXCIT E	
(n,γ)	+0	1.5+3	HAR Expt	Jour	NP 3 553	Jun 57	Bowey. TOF. CAPT GAM YLD CURVE	
(n,γ)	2.4+4		ORL Expt	Jour	PR 107 504	Jul 57	Macklin+.SB−BE NS,294+ −44MB,.686MEVG	+
				Conf	58Geneva 671	Sep 58	.SUPERSEDED	
	2.4+4			Data	EXFOR11399.045	Jun 76	. 1 PT.	
(n,γ)	2.5+6	4.0+6	IFU Expt	Conf	58Geneva 15 18	Sep 58	Pasechnik+.PPR2030,SIGMA AT 3ES	+
(n,γ)	2.5+6	4.0+6	KUR Expt	Conf	58Geneva 15 50	Sep 58	Leipunskij+.PPR2219,TBL AT 4ES	+
(n,γ)	1.4+7		ALD Expt	Jour	PPS 72 505	Oct 58	Perkin+ACT ANAL 4.0MB+ −20PC, B−W TH	
(n,γ)	2.5+4		LRL Expt	Jour	PR 112 226	Oct 58	Booth+ SB−BE REL I+THR,ACT 24.1H HL	+
	2.5+4			Data	EXFOR11429.028	Jun 76	. 1 PT.	
(n,γ)	2.5+4		FEI Expt	Jour	AE 5 564	Nov 58	Kononov+ ACT CS REL TO I127(N,G) GVN	
				Jour	JNEA 11 46	59	.TRANSLATION	
				Jour	SJA 5 1483	58	.TRANSLATION	
(n,γ)	2.0+5		ORL Expt	Jour	PR 114 1619	Jun 59	Lyon+.ABS GAMMA COUNT 100+ −20MB ACT	+
	2.0+5			Data	EXFOR11407.030	Jun 76	. 1 PT.	
(n,γ)	1.0+5	1.0+6	COL Theo	Jour	PR 116 937	Nov 59	Troubetzkoy+.TH CFD EXPT. CURVES.	
(n,γ)	1.5+5	3.0+6	WIS Expt	Jour	PR 116 927	Nov 59	Johnsrud+ SC CFD OTHERS SIG VS E	+
	1.5+5	2.6+6		Data	EXFOR11675.025	Jun 76	. 22 PTS.	
(n,γ)	3.0+4	1.4+6	CCP Expt	Jour	AE 9 401	Nov 60	Stavisskij+.GRAPH,REL I127,ACTIVTN	+
				Jour	SJA 9 942	Sep 61	TRANSLATN.*JNE AB16 496 0/62	
				Jour	KE 4 508	Jun 61	TRANSLATN	
(n,γ)	Maxwl	Pile	ORL Expt	Jour	NSE 8 378	Nov 60	Lyon. ACTIVATION, 2 SIGMA VALUES GVN	+
	Maxwl			Data	EXFOR11625.	Jun 76	. 2 PTS, SIG	
(n,γ)	5.0+4	1.0+6	CCP	Jour	AE 11 56	Jul 61	CCB THEORY CFD DATA	
				Jour	SJA 11 691	Mar 62	TRANSLATN.*	
(n,γ)	Maxwl		MHG Expt	Jour	NP 34 623	Jun 62	Treado+ SIG=36.0B.SPECTRA OF GAMMAS	
(n,γ)	Maxwl	+5	FOA Theo	Jour	NP 39 353	Dec 62	Bergqvist+. IN PER CENT OF NAT ELEMT	
(n,γ)	3.2+4	4.0+6	LRL Expt	Jour	PR 128 2717	Dec 62	Miskel+3, TABLE OF SIG AT 26ES. ACT	+
				Rept	UCRL−5454	Jan 59	.SUPERSEDED	
	3.2+4	4.0+6		Data	EXFOR12115.	Jun 76	. 26 PTS.	
(n,γ)	1.0−1	6.0+4	LEB Comp	Rept	INDSWG−64 43	64	Konks. GRAPH SIG(E)	
(n,γ)	1.0−1	2.1+1	MOL Eval	Rept	BLG−421	66	Damle+. CURVE RECOMMENDED SIGS	
(n,γ)	Maxwl		UJV Expt	Rept	UJV−1368	66	Slunecko+.SIG ACTIVATION GIVEN	
(n,γ)	1.0−3	1.0+7	WES Eval	Rept	WANL−TME−1472	Jul 66	Gibson+.68GROUPS .4EV UP+CURVE−100EV	
(n,γ)	4.6+4	1.7+5	FEI Expt	Jour	YF 4 282	Aug 66	Kononov+ TOF,SCIN−TANK,GRPH CFD THEO	+
				Conf	66Paris 1 469	Oct 66	* GRAPH CFD OTHERS	
				Rept	EANDC−50 199	Jul 65	* GRPH EXPT CFD THEO	
				Jour	SNP 4 204	Feb 67	.ENGLISH TRANSL OF YF 4 282 8/66	
	2.9+4	1.7+5		Data	EXFOR40076.007	Jul 71	SIG AT 14 ENERGIES FROM PRIV COMMUN	
(n,γ)	Fiss		CCP Expt	Jour	YF 4 515	Sep 66	Druzhinin+.ACTIVATION METHOD,VAL GVN	
				Jour	SNP 4 366	Mar 67	. ENGL OF YF 4 515	
(n,γ)	Maxwl		ORL Expt	Prog	ORNL−4013 5	Sep 66	Friesenhahn.SIG=33B	
(n,γ)	1.0−2	1.0+1	GA Expt	Jour	NSE 26 487	Dec 66	Friesenhahn.THR 37.8+ −1.2 LIQ SCIN	+
				Conf	66Wash. 182	Mar 66	.SUPERSEDED	
				Rept	GA−6882	Jan 66	.SUPERSEDED	
	1.0−2	1.0+1		Data	EXFOR12167.	Jun 76	. 35 PTS.	
(n,γ)	2.4+4		MUA Expt	Jour	PR 152 1055	Dec 66	Chaubey+ BETA−DET,SIG REL I−127,TBL	+
			Theo	Jour	IJP 42 567	Sep 68	− + METHD OF BOOTH,VAL CFD XPT	
	2.4+4		Expt	Data	EXFOR30079.035	Dec 70	SIGMA FOR 24. H HALF−LIFE	
(n,γ)	2.5−2		MOL Expt	Prog	EANDC(E)76U107	Jan 67	Damle+ ACT. H−L MEASURED	+
	2.5−2			Data	EXFOR20184.002	May 74	1PNT.SIGMA.	

74 Tungsten 186

Quantity	Energy (ev) Min	Max	Lab	Type	Documentation Ref Vol Page	Date	Author, Comments	Data
(n,γ)	2.3+5	3.2+6	IFU Expt	Prog	YFI−6 103	68	Zaikin+. TABLE SIG(E) REL U−235(NF)	
				Rept	INDC−260E	69	. ENGL OF YFI−6 103	
(n,γ)	Maxwl	Pile	MOL Eval	Rept	BLG−421	68	Damle+ THRESHOLD RES INTG. TBP	
(n,γ)	Maxwl	Pile	MOL Eval	Rept	BLG−421	68	Damle+ THRESHOLD RES INTG. TBP	
(n,γ)	Maxwl		AUA Theo	Jour	NSE 31 234	Feb 68	Cook+ STATISTICAL CALC CFD EXPT	
(n,γ)	−		IEA Comp	Rept	IEA−INF− 10	Aug 68	Atalla. TABLES OF HL,SIG AND GAMM−E	
(n,γ)	2.0+5	3.1+6	IFU Expt	Jour	AE 25 526	Dec 68	Zaikin+ GRPH SIG(NEUT−E) GVN	+
				Jour	SJA 25 1362	Jun 69	.ENGLISH TRANSL OF AE 25 526	
				Jour	EAF 25 6 112	Dec 68	.FRENCH TRANSL OF AE 25 526	
	2.3+5	3.1+6		Data	EXFOR40248.004	Oct 74	.SIGMA AT 17 ES GIVEN	
(n,γ)	1.5+2	1.0+5	RPI Expt	Jour	NSE 37 137	Jul 69	Bartolome+CAPT AREAS,AVG CS.	
	1.5+2	2.0+4		Abst	DA/B 30 679	Aug 69	− +LINAC,RES PARS FROM DATA.	
				Conf	68Wash. 795	Apr 68	− +AVG CAPT CS GRPHS.	
	4.0+2	8.0+3		Conf	66Wash. 404	Mar 66	Gibbons.RPI LINAC+SC(T),CURVE	
	3.5+1	1.0+4		Prog	ORNL−3778 53	May 65	Block.LINAC,SC,NUMEROUS RES,CRVS	
(n,γ)	2.0+5		MUA Theo	Conf	69Roorke 2 129	Dec 69	Chaubey+ SIG VALUE GIVEN, STATIST−TH	
(n,γ)	3.0+6		DEB Expt	Jour	AHP 28 257	Jan 70	Diksic+ SIG+ −ERROR,REL AU197(N,G)	+
	3.0+6			Data	EXFOR30023.012	Jun 70	SIGMA CAPT	
(n,γ)	Maxwl		MTR Expt	Prog	IN− 1317 53	Jan 70	Hogg+ ACTIVATION,VALUE GIVEN	+
	Maxwl			Data	EXFOR12602.007	Jun 76	. 1 PT, SIGMA.	
(n,γ)	3.0+4		AUA Theo	Rept	AAEC/E−211	Nov 70	Musgrove. SIGMA GIVEN AND CFD OTHER	
(n,γ)	Fast		MTR Expt	Abst	ANS 13 755	Nov 70	Scoville+ .CFRMF MEAST.VALUE GIVEN.	
				Prog	IN− 1407 29	Jun 70	− +.ACT.FAST SPEC.VALUE GIVEN.	
(n,γ)	2.4+4		MUA Theo	Jour	IJP 46 114	Mar 72	Chaubey+ P−WAVE STRENGTH FUNCT,TABLE	
(n,γ)	1.0+3	1.0+7	BOL Eval	Data	BENZI−DFN 817.	May 72	40 PNTS	+
(n,γ)	Pile		ROS ExTh	Prog	ZFK−243 93	Sep 72	Mohsen+ NG−SYSTEMAT. FOR RARE EARTHS	
(n,γ)	Fast		DUB Expt	Rept	JINR−P12−6810	Nov 72	Ngo Quoc Buu+ ACT ANALYS, CD−RATIOS	
(n,γ)	5.0+3	2.0+7	LAS Eval	Rept	LA−5221	May 73	Devaney+. ENDF/B LISTING. CURVES	
(n,γ)	Maxwl		RCN Revw	Rept	INDC(NDS)−56	Sep 73	Zijp.PG103,FOR DOSIMETRY,SIG GIVEN	
	2.5−2			Conf	73Paris 2 271	Mar 73	− .RECOMMENDED FROM LITERATURE,TB	
(n,γ)	1.5+7		OUL Expt	Rept	JU−RR−1/1976	Mar 76	Valkonen.(THESIS).ACTIV.TBL. 14.5MEV	+
	1.5+7			Data	EXFOR20673.035	Nov 76	1PNT.SIGMA.	
(n,γ)	1.2+5	2.7+6	LRL Expt	Jour	NSE 59 381	Apr 76	Lindner+ REL U235NF,TBL,GRPH	+
	1.0+5	3.0+6		Conf	71Knoxvill 259	Mar 71	.SUPERSEDED	
	1.2+5	2.7+6		Data	EXFOR10221.	Aug 75	. 23 PTS. SIGMA	
(n,γ)	1.4+7		IRK Expt	Jour	NP/A 264 105	Jun 76	Schwerer+ GE−LI.ACT SIG=2.2+ −0.5MB	+
	1.5+7			Prog	EANDC(OR)117L	Aug 72	Rohatsch+ TBL SIG GIVEN. ABST.	
	1.5+7			Data	EXFOR20670.016	Oct 76	1PNT.SIGMA.	
Spect (n,γ)	4.1+0	1.9+1	HAR Expt	Conf	58Geneva 14 294	Sep 58	Bird.CURVE,PPR35,NAI(TL)−DETECTOR	
Spect (n,γ)	2.5+4		ORL Expt	Conf	58Geneva 15 68	Sep 58	Macklin.PPR671,SIGMA+G−ENERGY GVN	
Spect (n,γ)	Pile		CAL Expt	Jour	NP 19 18	Sep 60	Gallagher+. TABLE. LEVELS IN RE 187	
Spect (n,γ)	Pile		MSU Expt	Jour	NP 19 634	Dec 60	Arns+. TABLE 25 GAMMAS. RE187 LEVELS	
Spect (n,γ)	1.9+1		ORL Expt	Conf	61Saclay 203	Sep 61	Block+.DIFF PULSE−HEIGHT.LIQUIDSCINT	
Spect (n,γ)	Pile		UPP Expt	Jour	NP 40 329	Jan 63	Marklund+ .E DETERM. NO INTENS MEAS.	
Spect (n,γ)	1.8+1		BNL Expt	Conf	63ANL 324	Oct 63	Moore+ SPECTRA FOR 18EV RESON NAI	
Spect (n,γ)	1.9+1		ITE Expt	Conf	JINR−1845 140	Jun 64	Beljaev+ TOF,TBL,E−GAMM=5.22 MEV	
Spect (n,γ)	Maxwl		ORL Expt	Abst	BAP 11 336	Apr 66	Martin+ (D,P) EXPTS.	
Spect (n,γ)	1.9+1			Conf	66Argonne 459	Nov 66	Chrien+,GE(LI),28GAMS 3.7−5.5MEV	
Spect (n,γ)	6.0−2	1.9+1	MTR Expt	Jour	PR 155 1368	Mar 67	Spencer+0.06EV+1RES 4−5MEV GS, X ABS	
Spect (n,γ)	+0	+4	COL Expt	Prog	WASH−1124 31	Nov 68	Camarda+ MOXON−RAE DET TBC NO DATA	
Spect (n,γ)	4.0+1	2.0+3	RPI Expt	Abst	BAP 13 1392	Nov 68	Tatarczuk+ GE(LI) LINAC NO DATA GIVN	
Spect (n,γ)	1.8+1	2.9+2	SAC Expt	Jour	NP/A 123 581	Jan 69	Samour+ GE(LI). 3RES. 3690TO8450 KEV	
				Rept	CEA−R−3776	Apr 69	− . (THESIS) DATA GIVEN	
Spect (n,γ)	Maxwl		ANL Expt	Conf	69Studsvik 389	Aug 69	Bolotin+ SINGLE+COINC SPECS,GRPH+TBL	
Spect (n,γ)	None		BNL Expt	Conf	69Studsvik 627	Aug 69	Chrien. WG/WN−CORREL,WG CFD P−T,TBLS	
Spect (n,γ)	1.9+1	5.1+2	HAR Expt	Conf	69Studsvik 579	Aug 69	Murray+ GAM SPEC GRPHS+TBL,5 N−RESON	
Spect (n,γ)	Pile		IBJ Expt	Rept	INR−1262/IA/PL	Feb 71	Ratynski.G CIRC POLARIZ,POLARIZED NS	
Spect (n,γ)	Maxwl		RCN Expt	Jour	NP/A 181 250	Feb 72	Stecher−Rasmussen+GAM CIRC POL.SPINS	
				Rept	RCN−152	Jun 71	− + (THESIS)	
Spect (n,γ)	Pile		ROS Expt	Rept	ZFK−228	Feb 72	Gabriel. W−187 LVLS,351KEV HL,GE−LI	
Spect (n,γ)	Maxwl		ROS Expt	Conf	72Budapest 98	Aug 72	Andrejtscheff+ LIFETIME OF EX.STATE	
Spect (n,γ)	Maxwl		IFL Expt	Book	PROKOFJEV	73	. TBL GAM−ES+INTS(60−5470KEV), GE−LI	
Spect (n,γ)	Maxwl		CCP Theo	Jour	ZET 65 12	Jul 73	Nosov+ THERMODYN CALC CFD EXPT,GRAPH	
				Jour	JET 38 6	Jan 74	. ENGLISH OF ZET 65 6	
Spect (n,γ)	Maxwl		ROS Expt	Rept	ZFK−260	Jul 73	.FULL PAPER, TABLES	+
	None			Prog	ZFK−223 63	Sep 71	Manfrass+ GE−LI,GAM−E,LVL−SCHEME,NDG	
	Maxwl			Data	EXFOR30276.	Oct 74	LOW +HIGH ENRGY PARTS OF SPEC,168PNTS	
Spect (n,γ)	2.4+4		BNL Expt	Prog	USNDC−11 55	Jun 74	Casten+ GRPHS.	

74 Tungsten 186

Quantity	Energy (ev) Min	Max	Lab	Type	Documentation Ref Vol Page	Date	Author, Comments	Data
Spect (n,γ)	Maxwl	2.4+4	BNL Expt	Jour	NP/A 228 493	Aug 74	Casten+ GE−LI,2E(N),W187 LVLSCH,THEO	
Spect (n,γ)	Maxwl		BNL Expt	Conf	74Petten 271	Sep 74	Cole+ DIRECT CAPT.COMP. TBL	
Spect (n,γ)	None		NOT Expt	Jour	ZP 271 339	Dec 74	Funk+.72.KEV−GAMMA−RAY OBSERVED	
Spect (n,γ)	2.8+6		KGU Expt	Conf	76Lowell 1334	Jul 76	Andreev+DIRECT EXCIT EFFECTS.NDG	
Inelastic γ	5.0+5	1.5+6	WES Expt	Jour	PR 107 1306	Sep 57	Sinclair.XTL SPEC REL CURV 124KEV G	
Inelastic γ	8.7+6		BRC Expt	Jour	69Studsvik 119	Aug 69	Haouat+ SPEC−GRPH,RESON IDENTIFIED	
Inelastic γ	1.0+6		TNC Expt	Rept	ORO−2791−32	Feb 71	Buchanan+ 55−DEG SIGS TABULATED	
Inelastic γ	2.8+6		CCP Expt	Conf	76Lowell 1334	Jul 76	Andreev+DIRECT EXCIT EFFECTS.NDG	
Nonelastic γ	1.0−5	2.0+7	LAS Eval	Rept	LA−5793	Apr 75	Young. GAMMA PROD CS FOR ENDF	
(n,2n)	+6		JAP Expt	Jour	SCP 42 139	Jan 44	Minakawa.CYC,ACTIVATION.SIG NDG	
(n,2n)	1.5+7		ARK Expt	Rept	A−ARK−60 4	Jan 60	Poularikas+	+
	1.5+7			Data	EXFOR12181.006	Jun 76	. 1 PT.	
(n,2n)	Fiss		CRC Eval	Rept	CRC−1003	Dec 60	Roy+,ESTIMATED AVG SIG=12.0MB	
(n,2n)	1.3+7	1.5+7	BNL Theo	Jour	NSE 23 238	Nov 65	Pearlstein.3ES.STAT MDL CALC.TBL CS.	
(n,2n)	Fiss		BNL Theo	Jour	NSE 23 238	Nov 65	Pearlstein.STATMDL CALC.SPEC AVG.TBL	
(n,2n)	4.1−1	1.0+7	WES Eval	Rept	WANL−TME−1472	Jul 66	Gibson+.68GROUP MATRIX	
(n,2n)	+6		CCP Expt	Jour	YF 4 515	Sep 66	Druzhinin. SIG FOR 15MEV AND FISS NS	+
				Jour	SNP 4 366	Mar 67	.ENGL OF YF 4 515	
(n,2n)	1.5+7		MUA Expt	Jour	NP 88 349	Nov 66	Prasad+,T−D NEUT ACT REL TO FE56(NP)	+
	1.5+7			Data	EXFOR30015.009	May 70	PARTIAL SIGMA(METASTABLE)	
(n,2n)	1.5+7		TUR Theo	Jour	NC/B 56 1 201	Jul 68	Minetti+THEOR ISOM RATIO SPIN CO PAR	
(n,2n)	1.5+7		SAH Expt	Prog	BARC−401 23	69	Pathak+ DECAY OF METASTABLE 185−W	
	1.4+7			Conf	68Bombay 2 293	Dec 68	− + GAM SPEC GRPH+TBL,LVL SCHEME	
(n,2n)	1.5+7		DEB Comp	Jour	REA 7 4 93	Dec 69	Csikai+ SIG+HL COMPILTN,N−ACTIV−ANAL	
(n,2n)	1.4+7	1.5+7	JYV Eval	Rept	JU−RR−3/1970	Jun 70	Leppaemaeki+ TABLE OF EVAL AVG SIG	
(n,2n)	+7		KFI Theo	Rept	KFKI−71−8	Feb 71	Jeki. CALCULATED CFD EXPTL SIG VALUE	
(n,2n)	1.4+7	1.5+7	IRK ExTh	Jour	APA 33 285	Jul 71	Winiwarter+ ISOMERIC RATIO	
(n,2n)	1.5+7		IBJ Expt	Jour	APPB 2 553	71	Rurarz+ ACTIV,GELI+NAI,CFD THEO,TABL	+
	1.5+7			Data	EXFOR30156.	Feb 72	SIGMA TO METASTABLE STATE GIVEN	
(n,2n)	1.5+7		DEB Eval	Jour	REA 11 1 153	Mar 73	Boedy. COMPILATION+RECOMM.VALUE,TBL	
				Rept	IAEA−153 173	73	−. RECOMM. VALUE ONLY	
(n,2n)	None		LAS Eval	Prog	LA−5570−PR	Apr 74	Foster+ ABSTRACT	
(n,2n)	1.5+7		JUL Expt	Jour	NP/A 242 317	Apr 75	Qaim+ SIG MEASURED BY ACT,VS (N−Z)/A	+
	1.5+7			Data	EXFOR20668.	Oct 76	2PTS.SIGMA.	
(n,2n)	1.5+7		WKU Expt	Abst	BAP 20 700	May 75	KAO+ ACT CS TO ISOMER	+
	1.5+7			Data	EXFOR10486.005	May 75	. 1 PT.SIGMA	
(n,2n)	1.4+7		LRL Expt	Prog	WASH−1018 63	Apr 59	Lindner+	+
	1.4+7			Data	EXFOR12185.007	Jun 76	. 1 PT, SIG	
(n,xn) x>2	Fiss		BNL Theo	Jour	NSE 23 238	Nov 65	Pearlstein.SPEC AVG STATMDL CALC N3N	
(n,xn) x>2	None		LAS Eval	Prog	LA−5570−PR	Apr 74	Foster+N3N.ISOTR ANG DIST.ENDF4.NDG.	
(n,p)	1.4+7	2.1+7	ALD Expt	Jour	PPS 74 632	Nov 59	Barry+ACT.6ES SIG=1+−0.2−13.6+−2.7MB	+
				Jour	PPS 73 215	Feb 59	− + ACTIVATION.SUPERSEDED.	
(n,p)	1.5+7		ARK Expt	Rept	A−ARK−60 4	Jan 60	Poularikas+	+
	1.5+7			Data	EXFOR12181.004	Jun 76	. 1 PT.	
(n,p)	Fiss		CRC Eval	Rept	CRC−1003	Dec 60	Roy+,ESTIMATED AVG SIG=0.0008MB	
(n,p)	1.4+7		SAH Expt	Conf	63Bombay 244	Feb 63	Mukherjee+.VAL GVN,ACTIVATION METHOD	+
	1.4+7			Data	EXFOR31330.012	Sep 72	.SIG GVN	
(n,p)	1.4+7	1.5+7	SAH Comp	Jour	NUC 23 8 112	Aug 65	Chatterjee. TABLE WITH REFS.	
(n,p)	1.4+7	1.5+7	NAP Comp	Rept	INFN/BE−67−10	Jul 67	Cuzzocrea+ AVERAGED CHOSEN DATA.	
(n,p)	1.5+7		DEB Comp	Jour	REA 7 4 93	Dec 69	Csikai+ SIG+HL COMPILTN,N−ACTIV−ANAL	
(n,p)	1.4+7	1.5+7	JYV Eval	Rept	JU−RR−3/1970	Jun 70	Leppaemaeki+ TABLE OF EVAL AVG SIG	
(n,p)	1.4+7	1.5+7	KAZ Theo	Jour	YF 18 705	Oct 73	Levkovsky.AVERAGED SIG,CALC,TBL	
				Jour	SNP 18 361	Apr 74	. ENGLISH OF YF 18,705	
(n,p)	1.5+7		JUL Expt	Jour	NP/A 242 317	Apr 75	Qaim+ SIG MEASURED BY ACT,VS (N−Z)/A	+
	1.5+7			Data	EXFOR20668.017	Oct 76	1PNT.SIGMA.	
(n,np)	1.5+6		LON Expt	Jour	NP 1 278	Mar 56	Cohen+. ACT METHOD. UPPER LIMIT	
(n,np)	1.4+7	2.1+7	ALD Expt	Jour	PPS 74 632	Nov 59	Barry+ACT.6ES SIG=0.04TO17.1+−3MB	+
(n,np)	1.5+7		ARK Expt	Rept	A−ARK−60 4	Jan 60	Poularikas+	+
	1.5+7			Data	EXFOR12181.005	Jun 76	. 1 PT. INCL ND	
(n,np)	1.4+7		OSM Theo	Jour	PHY 27 1113	Dec 61	Hyder. DIRECT INTERACT,NUMER VALUES	
(n,np)	1.4+7		SAH Expt	Conf	63Bombay 240	Feb 63	Ganguly+ VAL GVN,ACTIVATION METHOD	+
	1.5+7			Data	EXFOR31329.006	Sep 72	.SIG (NNP)+(ND) GVN	
(n,np)	1.4+7	1.5+7	JYV Eval	Rept	JU−RR−3/1970	Jun 70	Leppaemaeki+ TABLE OF EVAL AVG SIG	
(n,np)	None		LAS Eval	Prog	LA−5570−PR	Apr 74	Foster+ ABSTRACT	
(n,d)	1.5+7		ARK Expt	Rept	A−ARK−60 4	Jan 60	Poularikas+	+
	1.5+7			Data	EXFOR12181.005	Jun 76	. 1 PT. INCL NNP.	
(n,d)	1.5+7		SAH Expt	Conf	63Bombay 240	Feb 63	Ganguly+.VAL GVN, ACTIVATION METHOD	+
	1.5+7			Data	EXFOR31329.006	Sep 72	.SIG (NNP)+(ND) GVN	

74 Tungsten 186

Quantity	Energy (ev) Min	Energy (ev) Max	Lab	Type	Documentation Ref Vol Page	Date	Author, Comments	Data
(n,d)	1.4+7	1.5+7	SAH	Comp Jour	NUC 23 8 112	Aug 65	Chatterjee. TABLE WITH REFS.	
(n,α)	1.5+7		ARK	Expt Rept	A-ARK-60 4	Jan 60	Poularikas+	+
	1.5+7			Data	EXFOR12181.003	Jun 76	. 1 PT.	
(n,α)	Fiss		CRC	Eval Rept	CRC-1003	Dec 60	Roy+,ESTIMATED AVG SIG=BELO 0.0001MB	
(n,α)	1.4+7		SAH	Expt Conf	63Bombay 244	Feb 63	Mukherjee+.VAL GVN,ACTIVATION METHOD	+
	1.4+7			Data	EXFOR31330.011	Sep 72	.SIG GVN	
(n,α)	1.5+7		DEB	Comp Jour	REA 7 4 93	Dec 69	Csikai+ SIG+HL COMPILTN,N-ACTIV-ANAL	
(n,α)	1.4+7	1.5+7	JYV	Eval Rept	JU-RR-3/1970	Jun 70	Leppaemaeki+ TABLE OF EVAL AVG SIG	
(n,α)	1.5+7		JUL	Expt Jour	NP/A 242 317	Apr 75	Qaim+ SIG MEASURED BY ACT,VS (N-Z)/A	+
	1.5+7			Data	EXFOR20668.019	Oct 76	1PNT.SIGMA.	
Reson Params	1.9+1		ANL	Expt Jour	PR 84 869	Dec 51	Selove.	+
	1.9+1			Data	EXFOR12168.005	Jun 76	. 1 RES,PCS	
Reson Params	1.9+1	4.1+2	BNL	Expt Abst	BAP 1 187	Apr 56	Schwartz+ ABST. K3,EN,WN,WG.	+
	1.9+1	4.1+2		Data	EXFOR12153.006	Jun 76	. 5 RES,E0,WN,WG.	
Reson Params	1.9+1	2.2+2	HAR	Expt Jour	NP 3 553	Jun 57	Bowey.TOF.2ES FROM CAPT GAMMA YIELDS	
Reson Params	1.9+1		SAC	Expt Jour	CR 248 2330	Apr 59	Huynh+ E0=18,8 ONLY	
	1.9+1			Data	EXFOR20677.003	Sep 77	1PNT.E0.	
Reson Params	1.7+2		HAR	Expt Jour	NP 12 552	Sep 59	Firk+ TOF 1RES.171EV	+
				Rept	AERE-NP/GEN 11	Apr 59	- + TOF. RES SPINS ASSIGNED.	
Reson Params	4.1+0	1.1+2	HAR	Expt Jour	NP 12 563	Sep 59	Waters+ WN WG J GIVEN FOR 1 RES.	+
Reson Params	-		FOA	ExTh Rept	NP 39 353	Dec 62	Bergqvist+.AVERAGE GAMMA WIDTH.EXPTH	
Reson Params	1.9+1	2.2+2	MOL	Eval Rept	BLG-421	66	Damle+.RECOMMENDED PARAMS 6 RESON	
Reson Params	1.0-2	1.0+1	GA	Expt Rept	GA-6882	Jan 66	Haddad.PARM FOR 18.8 EV LEVEL TBP	
Reson Params	1.9+1		ORL	Expt Conf	66Wash. 31	Mar 66	Harvey.E=18.84+-2EV,AREA+SHAPE ANAL	+
				Conf	66S.Diego 2 103	Feb 66	- +PARAM FOR LEVEL AT 18.8 EV	
	1.9+1			Data	EXFOR11238.	Jun 76	. 1 RES, E0,WT,WN,WG	
Reson Params	1.0+4	2.0+6	FEI	ExTh Jour	YF 5 129	Jan 67	Kononov.Lσ2 N CAPTURE,TBL,CURVES GVN	+
				Jour	SNP 5 89	Jul 67	TRANSLATN.*	
Reson Params	1.9+1		MOL	Expt Prog	EANDC(E)76U107	Jan 67	Damle+ DERIVED FROM (NG) SIG+RES INT	+
	1.9+1			Data	EXFOR20184.	May 74	3PTS.WG,WN,WT.	
Reson Params	1.9+1		LRC	Expt Jour	NSE 31 431	Mar 68	Pierce+ ACTIV WG=0.041+-0.003EV	
Reson Params	1.9+1	2.1+3	KFK	Expt Rept	KFK-718	Apr 68	Schmidt+ RESOLVED+AVG RES PARAM(S,P)	
Reson Params	+3	+5	AUA	ExTh Rept	AAEC/E-198	May 69	Musgrove.RES PARS +STF FROM (NG)FIT	+
Reson Params	1.7+2	4.5+3	RPI	Expt Jour	NSE 37 137	Jul 69	Bartolome+LINAC RES PARS TO 3.4 KEV.	+
	1.5+2	2.0+4		Abst	DA/B 30 679	Aug 69	- .RES PARS FROM TRNS,CAPT.	
				Conf	68Wash. 795	Mar 68	- +RES PARS BY CAPT,TRANS,TBD	
	2.0+2	3.4+3		Data	EXFOR10002.	Jan 78	. 25 RES ES.WN,WG,D GVN.	
Reson Params	1.9+1	5.1+2	HAR	ExTh Conf	69Studsvik 579	Aug 69	Murray+CORRELATION WN+WG,CFD STATMOD	
Reson Params	2.0+5		MUA	Theo Conf	69Roorke 2 129	Dec 69	Chaubey+ D/GAM-WIDTH RATIO, STATMOD	
Reson Params	1.9+1	2.1+3	KFK	Comp Rept	KFK-1233	Jul 70	Mueller. ES,WN,WG,G OF 27 RESON	
Reson Params	-		AUA	Theo Rept	AAEC/E-211	Nov 70	Musgrove. CALCULTD D+GAM WIDTH GIVEN	
Reson Params	1.9+1	3.4+3	CJD	Eval Rept	YK-7	71	Zakharova+ SURVEY+SYSTEMATICS,GW,TBL	
				Rept	INDC(CCP)-27	Nov 72	.ENGLISH TRANSLATION OF YK-7 /71	
Reson Params	None		DUB	Theo Jour	YF 13 240	Feb 71	Malecki+G-WID,THEO CFD EXPT.TBL,GRPH	
				Jour	SNP 13 133	Aug 71	- + ENGL OF YF 13 240.	
Reson Params	1.9+1	1.7+4	COL	Expt Jour	PR/C 8 1813	Nov 73	Camarda+. WN+AVG D FOR MANY RESON	+
	None			Conf	75Wash. 780	Mar 75	Hacken+19 ELEMENTS RVW.TBLS,GRPHS	
	1.9+2	1.7+4		Data	EXFOR10507.	Apr 76	. 103 PTS. WN,D VAL GVN.	
Reson Params	4.0+0	1.2+3	JAE	Expt Rept	JAERI-M-5624	Feb 74	Ohkubo.LINAC,TOF.WT,WN IN TABLE	
Strnth Fnctn	None		GA	Eval Rept	GA-5885	Nov 64	Joanou+S=3.1-4 P=.5-4 D=2-4 F=.2-4	
Strnth Fnctn	1.0+3	6.0+4	LEB	Expt Conf	65Antwerp § 182	Jul 65	Bergman.LEBEDEV.S1=.76+-.30.ALSO DO	
Strnth Fnctn	+0	+2	MOL	Eval Rept	BLG-421	66	Damle+. RECOMMENDED S0=1.8+-0.5	
Strnth Fnctn	1.0+4	2.0+6	FEI	ExTh Jour	YF 5 129	Jan 67	Kononov.Lσ2 N CAPTURE,TBL,CURVES GVN	
				Jour	SNP 5 89	Jul 67	TRANSLATN.*	
	1.0+4	2.0+6		Expt Data	EXFOR40013.005	Mar 73	.VALUE GIVEN	
Strnth Fnctn	1.0+4		ANL	Theo Jour	PR 162 1077	Oct 67	Lister+ OPTMDL CALC S,P,AND D WAVE	
				Rept	ANL-7288	Jan 67	.SUPERSEDED	
Strnth Fnctn	+3	+5	AUA	ExTh Rept	AAEC/E-198	May 69	Musgrove.S+P+D STF FROM (NG)FIT,TBL	+
Strnth Fnctn	1.7+2	3.4+3	RPI	Expt Jour	NSE 37 137	Jul 69	Bartolome+S0=30+-.6,S1=.28+.52-.15.	+
				Abst	DA/B 30 679	Aug 69	- .S,P STF CFD OPT,SPH MDLS.	
	1.7+2	3.4+3		Data	EXFOR10002.028	Jan 78	.S0=(2.15+-.46)-4 S1=(.28+.52-.15)-4	
Strnth Fnctn	-		AUA	Theo Rept	AAEC/E-211	Nov 70	Musgrove. SMOOTHED S0,S1 AND S2 GIVN	
Strnth Fnctn	2.4+4		MUA	Theo Jour	IJP 46 114	Mar 72	Chaubey+ P-WAVE.FOR A-SYSTEMATIC,GRPH	
Strnth Fnctn	None		AUA	Eval Rept	AAEC/E-277	Mar 73	Musgrove.TBLS EXPTL DATA+BEST VALUES	
Strnth Fnctn	+1	+4	COL	Expt Jour	PR/C 8 1813	Nov 73	Camarda+S WAVE,GRPH,TBL.	+
	4.1-1	+6		Prog	COO-2176-1 1	Jun 72	Rainwater+. AVG WG GIVEN	
	None			Jour	NSE 48 219	Jun 72	Rahn+. AVG WG=47 MEV OVER 3 RESON	
	0.0+0	1.7+4		Data	EXFOR10507.005	Apr 76	. 1 PT. S0=(2.23+-.27)-4	

74 Tungsten 186

Quantity	Energy (ev) Min	Energy (ev) Max	Lab	Type	Documentation Ref Vol Page	Date	Author, Comments	Data
Lvl Density	–		FEI	Eval Rept	FEI – 36	66	Kapchigashev+ .TBL OF RELATD QUANTTYS	+
		5.0+4		Jour	YF 4 686	Sep 66	.TABLE.SHORT VERSION OF FEI – 36	
	–			Prog	YFI – 3 3	66	.ABSTRACT.TABLE LDL+NUCL.EXCIT.E	
		5.0+4		Jour	SNP 4 486	67	.ENGLISH OF YF 4.FROM(N,GAMMA).TABLE	
				Prog	INDC – E – 140 3	66	.ENGLISH TRANSL OF YFI – 3	
Lvl Density	0.0+0	1.0+4	ITE	Theo Conf	72Budapest 268	Aug 72	Belyaev+ GROUPINGS OF LVL SPACNG,TBL	

74 Tungsten 187

Quantity	Energy (ev) Min	Energy (ev) Max	Lab	Type	Documentation Ref Vol Page	Date	Author, Comments	Data
Res Int Abs	Maxwl		ORL	Expt Prog	ORNL – 4013 5	Sep 66	Gillette.RESONANCE INTEGRAL=2760B	
(n,γ)	Maxwl		ORL	Expt Prog	ORNL – 4013 5	Sep 66	Gillette.SIG=64B	
Spect (n,γ)	Maxwl		ANL	Theo Conf	68DUBSY 317	Jul 68	Bollinger.ANAL.RAD. TRANSITIONS.	
(n,2n)	None		LAS	Eval Prog	LA – 5570 – PR	Apr 74	Foster+ ABSTRACT	
(n,xn) x>2	None		LAS	Eval Prog	LA – 5570 – PR	Apr 74	Foster+N3N.ISOTR ANG DIST.ENDF4.NDG.	
(n,np)	None		LAS	Eval Prog	LA – 5570 – PR	Apr 74	Foster+ ABSTRACT	
Reson Params	–		AUA	Theo Rept	AAEC/E – 211	Nov 70	Musgrove. CALCULTD D+GAM WIDTH GIVEN	
Strnth Fnctn	–		AUA	Theo Rept	AAEC/E – 211	Nov 70	Musgrove. SMOOTHED S0,S1 AND S2 GIVN	
Lvl Density	+6		MIL	Theo Jour	EN 15 1 54	Jan 68	Facchini+ LDL PARS FROM LOW EN RES	
Lvl Density	None		MUN	Theo Jour	NP/A 217 269	Dec 73	Dilg+ A,DELTA. BACK SHIFTED FERMIGAS	
Lvl Density	None		COP	Theo Jour	NP/A 222 493	Apr 74	Dossing+COLL ROTAT.SPAC. ACCUR ESTIM	
Lvl Density	None		ROC	Theo Jour	NP/A 223 577	May 74	Huizenga+ EXP CFD MICROSC TH SPH NUC	

75 Rhenium

Quantity	Energy (ev) Min	Max	Lab	Type	Documentation Ref Vol Page	Date	Author, Comments	Data
Evaluation	2.5-2	1.1+7	FEI Eval	Book	ABAGJAN	64	26 GROUP CONST,TOT,CAPT,INEL,EL,ETC	
Evaluation	1.0+2	1.5+7	GEN Eval	Rept	GEMP - 587	67	Henderson+ NG,DEL,SEL,TOT,SIN,N2+N3N	
Total	Maxwl		COL Expt	Jour	PR 48 265	Aug 35	Dunning+ IONCH,TRANS,RA - BE/PARAFIN N	
Total	1.3+0	1.0+6	COL Expt	Jour	PR 92 702	Nov 53	Melkonian+ TRANS. CURV.	+
	3.0-3	7.4-1		Data	EXFOR11670.010	Jun 76	. 30 PTS.	
Total	1.0+0	1.3+1	BNL Expt	Jour	PR 100 1338	Dec 55	IGO+ CURVE	
Total	2.4+3	1.9+6	ANL Expt	Priv	STUPEGIA	Jun 65	Stupegia+100E PTS,DELTA E 2-90KEV	+
	2.4+3	1.9+6		Data	EXFOR12125.004	Jun 76	. 110 PTS.	
Total	5.0-3	2.0+4	IFU Expt	Jour	AE 19 250	Sep 65	Vertebny+ TOF,SMALL GRAPH RES ES	+
				Jour	SJA 19 1162	Sep 65	TRANSLATN.*	
				Jour	EAF 19 3 28	Sep 65	TRANSLATN.*	
				Rept	INDSWG - 120 22	65	SUPERSEDED*	
	2.9+0	1.7+4		Data	EXFOR40060.002	Mar 71	TRANSMISSION AT 744 CHANNEL - NUMBERS	
Total	2.5-2	1.8+1	NRL Expt	Jour	PR 155 1330	Mar 67	Stolovy. TRANS. CURV.	
Total	3.0+4	6.5+5	DKE Expt	Jour	AP 46 401	Feb 68	Tabony+ TRANS CURV DERIVES S0,S1,S2	+
	3.0+4	6.5+5		Data	EXFOR11953.008	Jun 76	. 102 PTS.	
Total	5.4+5	1.5+6	ANL Expt	Jour	PR 168 1344	Apr 68	Smith+TRNS.GRPH.OPTMDL CALC.CFD	+
	1.0+5	6.5+5		Rept	ANL - 7363	Aug 67	- + TOF 5 - KEV RESOL TABLE+CURVE	
	None			Jour	NIM 39 185	Jan 66	Whalen+COMPUTER EXPT.NDG,	
	5.4+5	1.5+6		Data	EXFOR10631.	Apr 77	. 146 PTS.	
Total	1.0-2	3.0+4	GA Expt	Jour	JNE 22 191	Apr 68	Friesenhahn+ CURVS .01 - 10EV,.1 - 20KEV	+
	1.2-2	1.0+1		Data	EXFOR12163.	Jun 76	. 92 PTS, SIG	
Total	2.0+4	7.0+6	FEI Expt	Conf	68Dubna § 17	Jun 68	Filippov+VDG,TRANS.TBL,GRPH.FLUCTUAT	
	2.5+4	9.0+6		Prog	ICD - 3 102	Oct 66	.GRAPH CFD REFS.VDG	
	2.0+4	7.0+6		Rept	INDC(CCP) - 16	Jul 71	.PAGE 67.ENGLISH TRANSL OF 68DUBNA	
	2.5+4	9.0+6		Prog	INDSWG - 152E	66	.PAGE 102. ENGLISH TRANSL OF ICD - 3	
Total	3.0+0	3.3+2	JAE Expt	Prog	EANDC(J)10L5	Nov 68	Ideno+.TOF,P100LVLS,DOPPLER IN 4EV	
Total	2.5+5	1.5+7	BNW Expt	Jour	PR/C 3 576	Feb 71	Foster+ TRANS,CURVS, CFD OTHERS+TH	+
				Jour	NIM 36 1	Sep 65	.EXPT DETAILS	
	2.3+6	1.5+7		Data	EXFOR10047.082	Aug 73	. 245 PTS.	
Total	2.7+3		MUN Expt	Prog	EANDC(E)150U	Oct 72	Dilg+ AVERAGE TOT XSECT+S0	+
				Conf	71Albany 327	Aug 71	- +TRNS.AVG CS GVN.31 ELEMENT GRP	
	2.7+3			Data	EXFOR20583.028	Jun 76	1PNT.	
Total	1.3+7	1.5+7	DEB Eval	Rept	IAEA - 153 173	73	Boedy+ MOST PROBABLE VAL OF SIG,TBL	
				Jour	AHP 30 115	Oct 71	Angeli+ AVG SIG,CFD CALC.TBLS.GRAPH	
Elastic		+5	ANL Expt	Jour	PR 79 11	Jul 50	Harris+ EPI - CD,RES INT SCAT,B - W TH	
Elastic	3.0+5	1.5+6	ANL Expt	Jour	PR 168 1344	Apr 68	Smith+ TOF FROM ANG DIST TABLE+CURVE	+
				Rept	ANL - 7363	Aug 67	.SUPERSEDED	
	3.0+5	1.5+6		Data	EXFOR10631.004	Apr 77	. 97 PTS. SEL CS DATA.	
Diff Elastic	3.0+5	1.5+6	ANL Expt	Jour	PR 168 1344	Apr 68	Smith+ TOF ANG DIST LEG COEF CURVES	+
				Rept	ANL - 7363	Aug 67	.SUPERSEDED	
	3.0+5	1.5+6		Data	EXFOR10631.005	Apr 77	. 490 PTS. LEG COEFS	
Potntal Scat	1.2+2	3.0+2	ANL Expt	Jour	PR 76 100	Jul 49	Hibdon+TRNS.10PC RSLN.MN SCT DET.	+
	1.2+2	3.0+2		Data	EXFOR11261.032	Jun 76	. 2 PTS.	
Potntal Scat		6.5+5	DKE ExTh	Jour	PL 13 70	Nov 64	Seth+0,1PHASE FRM SIG TOT AV 3 - 650KV	
Potntal Scat	2.5-2		GA Expt	Jour	JNE 22 191	Apr 68	Friesenhahn+ 9.5+ - 0.5B FROM SIGTOT	+
	2.5-2			Data	EXFOR12163.003	Jun 76	. 1 PT, SIG	
Diff Inelast	3.8+5	1.5+6	ANL Expt	Jour	PR 168 1344	Apr 68	Smith+ TOF SIGS FOR 11LVLS CFD THEOR	+
				Rept	ANL - 7363	Aug 67	.SUPERSEDED	
	3.8+5	1.6+6		Data	EXFOR10631.009	Apr 77	. 167 PTS.	
Thermal Scat	1.0-4	1.0+3	MUN Revw	Jour	EEN 80 1	77	Koester. SCAT LENGTH	
Scattering	4.0-2	1.0+0	IFU Expt	Prog	INDSWG - 120 27	65	Vertebnyj.GRAPH,TOF	
Scattering	2.5-2		IFU Expt	Jour	YFI - 10 43	May 71	Koloty+ 2200M/SEC SIG REL V,POWDER	
				Rept	INDC(CCP) - 15	Dec 71	*P48 ENG OF YFI - 10	
				Conf	70Helsinki 1 651	Jun 70	*DETAILS OF METHOD	
				Rept	BNL - TR - 495	Jul 72	. ENGLISH OF 70HELSIN 1 651	
Absorption	Pile		ANL Expt	Jour	PR 80 342	Nov 50	Harris+.PILE OSC.REL TO BORON.	+
				Jour	PR 79 11	Jul 50	- + TBP.	
	Pile			Data	EXFOR11528.023	Jun 76	. 1 PT.	
Res Int Abs	5.0-1		FLA Expt	Rept	AD - 402668	Mar 63	Karam+	+
				Conf	66Wash. 171	Mar 66	- + RIG=657+ - 28B EXCL 1/V REL AU	
	5.0-1			Data	EXFOR12179.006	Jun 76	. 1 PT, RI	
Res Int Abs	5.0-1		STF Expt	Jour	ANS 9 248	66	Sher+	+
	5.0-1			Data	EXFOR12194.007	Jun 76	. 1 PT, RI	
Res Int Abs	5.0-1		LRC Expt	Rept	NASA - TN - D - 4938	Dec 68	Pierce+	+
	5.0-1			Data	EXFOR12165.002	Jun 76	. 1 PT, RI	

75 Rhenium

Quantity	Energy (ev) Min	Max	Lab	Type	Documentation Ref Vol Page	Author, Comments Date	Data
(n,γ)	Maxwl		ORL	Expt	Jour PR 83 643	Aug 51 Pomerance. OSC REL AU	+
	Maxwl			Data	EXFOR11047.067	Jun 76 . 1 PT.	
(n,γ)	2.0+2	8.0+3	ORL	Expt	Conf 61Saclay 203	Sep 61 Block+.LIQUID SCINTILLATOR	+
	2.0+2	1.0+4			Conf 61Vienna 1 95	Aug 61 Neiler.PPR73,GRAPH,FAST CHOPPER	
	2.1+2	9.5+3			Data EXFOR11935.023	Jun 76 . 51 PTS.	
(n,γ)	2.5−2		FLA	Expt	Rept AD− 402668	Mar 63 Karam+	
(n,γ)	3.0+4	6.5+4	ORL	Expt	Jour PR 129 2695	Mar 63 Macklin+ LIQ SCINT,900 AND 525MB	+
	3.0+4	6.5+4			Data EXFOR11331.028	Jun 76 . 2 PTS.	
(n,γ)	2.0−1	4.0+4	LEB	Comp	Rept INDSWG−64 43	64 Konks. GRAPH SIG(E)	
(n,γ)	3.0+4	9.0+4	ORL	Theo	Jour RMP 37 166	Jan 65 Macklin+ CALC FOR KT=5TO90KEV. MAXW	
(n,γ)	2.0+4	9.0+5	FEI	Expt	Jour AE 19 42	Jul 65 Staviski+ CAF2 SCINTILLATOR REL I127	+
					Jour EAF 19 1 63	Jul 65 TRANSLATN.*	
					Jour SJA 19 905	Jul 65 TRANSLATN.*	
(n,γ)	2.9+4	1.7+5	FEI	Expt	Jour AE 19 457	Nov 65 Kononov+ TOF,SCIN−TANK,PLSD C−W,GRPH	+
					Jour SNP 4 209	Feb 67 *	
					Conf 66Paris 1 469	Oct 66 *PPR99.GRPH CFD OTHER	
					Jour YF 4 282	Aug 66 *	
					Jour EAF 19 5 74	May 66 *FRENCH OF AE 19 457	
					Jour SJA 19 1428	May 66 * ENGL OF AE 19 457	
					Jour JNE 20 1049	66 * ENGL OF AE 19 457	
	2.9+4	1.7+5			Data EXFOR40076.002	Jul 71 1 DATA POINT(130KEV)	
(n,γ)	Fiss	1.5+7	CCP	Expt	Jour YF 5 18	Jan 67 Druzhinin+.TBL,ACTIVATION METHOD	+
					Jour SNP 5 13	Jul 67 .ENGL OF YF 5 18	
(n,γ)	1.0−2	3.0+4	GA	Expt	Jour JNE 22 191	Apr 68 Friesenhahn+ NDG, SEE RE185,RE187	+
	2.5−2				Data EXFOR12163.002	Jun 76 . 1 PT.	
(n,γ)	1.0+4	1.5+5	KFK	Expt	Jour NP/A 133 513	Aug 69 Kompe.VDG.LIQ SCINT. REL AU MEAS.	+
					Rept KFK−1071	Aug 69 − . REPRINT OF NP/A 133 513	
					Rept EANDC(E)89U3	Feb 68 − . RENORMAL OF 66PARIS	
					Rept KFK−635	Oct 67 Ponitz+ SUPERSEEDED BY NP/A 133	
					Conf 66Paris 1 513	Oct 66 Kompe. LARGE LIQ SCIN.GRPH.SUPERSEDD	
	1.2+4	1.6+5			Data EXFOR20358.032	Sep 74 72PTS.SIGMA.	
(n,γ)	+3	+7	FEI	Revw	Conf 70Helsinki 2 245	Jun 70 Abramov. PPR114.REVW OF DATA STATUS	
(n,γ)	1.0+3	1.0+6	GA	Revw	Conf 70ANL 285	Oct 70 Carlson. STATUS AS STANDARD SIG,CURV	
(n,γ)	3.0+4		AUA	Theo	Rept AAEC/E−211	Nov 70 Musgrove. SIGMA GIVEN AND CFD OTHER	
(n,γ)	1.0+3	1.0+6	GA	Expt	Conf 71Knoxvill 252	Mar 71 Fricke+ ABSOL AVG SIG, NO DATA GIVEN	+
				ExTh	Conf 70Helsinki 2 265	Jun 70 − + TOF	
	1.0+3	6.4+5		Expt	Data EXFOR10049.006	Jul 71 92PTS,SIGMA	
(n,γ)	1.0−1	5.0+1	LEB	Expt	Conf 71Kiev	May 71 Bergman+ SIG(NEUT−E),GRAPH,CFD OTHER	
Spect (n,γ)	Maxwl		YAL	Expt	Jour PR 114 268	Apr 59 Draper.SC SPECTR,GAM E 0 TO 600 KEV	
Spect (n,γ)	Maxwl		ARF	Expt	Prog ARF−1193−9	Apr 62 Greenwood+,CRYST SPEC,LOW−E GAMMAS	
Spect (n,γ)	2.5−2		MIT	Comp	Rept MITNE−85	Jan 69 Rasmussen+TBL G INT.=AFCRL−69−0071	
Spect (n,γ)	Maxwl		KFI	Revw	Jour YF 10 907	Nov 69 Kecskemeti+ AVG GAM−MULTIPLICITY,TBL	
					Jour SNP 10 524	May 70 TRANSLATN.*	
Spect (n,γ)	None		CRC	Expt	Prog AECL−3865 56	Dec 70 Lone+.RESONANCE CAPT, NO DATA GIVEN	
Inelastic γ	1.0+5	1.9+6	MIT	Expt	Jour PR 101 1516	Mar 56 Guernsey+,CS 135−KEV LEVEL CFD TH	+
					Rept AECU−3021	Feb 55 .SUPERSEDED	
	1.1+5	1.9+6			Data EXFOR11691.007	Jun 76 . 15 PTS.	
Inelastic γ	1.0+6	1.0+7	KUR	Expt	Jour 75Kiev 4 191	May 75 Savin+ SIG(E) TO 8 GAM−E GROUPS.GRPH	
(n,2n)	1.5+7		DEB	Eval	Jour REA 11 1 153	Mar 73 Boedy+ RECOMM.VALUE FROM N−Z SYSTEM.	
(n,t)	2.3+7		JUL	Expt	Jour JIN 36 3639	Dec 74 Qaim+ (NT)+(NNT), 4.1+−0.7 MB	+
	2.3+7				Data EXFOR20524.012	Apr 76 1PNT§=NNT	
(n,nt)	2.3+7		JUL	Expt	Jour JIN 36 3639	Dec 74 Qaim+ (NT)+(NNT), 4.1+−0.7 MB	+
	2.3+7				Data EXFOR20524.012	Apr 76 1PNT.+NT.	
Reson Params		+5	ANL	Expt	Jour PR 79 11	Jul 50 Harris+ EPI−CD,B−W SINGLE RES.E+GN/G	
Reson Params	5.9+0	2.1+1	COL	Expt	Jour PR 92 702	Nov 53 Melkonian+	+
	5.9+0	2.1+1			Data EXFOR11670.011	Jun 76 . 5 RES, E0,WT**2/PCS	
Reson Params	1.0+0	1.4+1	BNL	Expt	Abst PR 99 610	Jul 55 IGO+	
Strnth Fnctn	3.0+4	6.5+5	DKE	Expt	Jour AP 46 401	Feb 68 Tabony+ TRANS DERIVES S0, S1, S2	+
					Jour PL 13 70	Nov 64 .SUPERSEDED	
	5.0+4	1.5+5			Conf 64Paris 2 916	Jul 64 Seth+S0,S1,S2 R PRIME/R	
	3.0+3	6.5+5			Data EXFOR11665.028	Jun 76 . 3 PTS.	
Strnth Fnctn	None		GA	Expt	Jour JNE 22 191	Apr 68 Friesenhahn+ FROM RES PARS,AV SIGTOT	+
Strnth Fnctn	1.0+4	1.5+5	KFK	Expt	Jour NP/A 133 513	Aug 69 Kompe. S1,S2,S(GAMMA)LEAST SQ NG FIT	+
					Rept KFK−1071	Aug 69 − . REPRINT OF NP/A 133 513	
	1.0+4	1.5+5			Data EXFOR20358.	Sep 74 3PTS.GAMMA STF.	
Strnth Fnctn	2.7+3		MUN	Expt	Conf 71Albany 327	Aug 76 Dilg+TRNS.S0 STF GVN.31 ELEMENT GRPH	

75 Rhenium 181

Quantity	Energy (ev) Min	Max	Lab	Type	Documentation Ref Vol Page	Date	Author, Comments	Data
Reson Params	–		AUA	Theo Rept	AAEC/E–211	Nov 70	Musgrove. CALCULTD D+GAM WIDTH GIVEN	
Strnth Fnctn	–		AUA	Theo Rept	AAEC/E–211	Nov 70	Musgrove. SMOOTHED S0,S1 AND S2 GIVN	

75 Rhenium 182

Quantity	Energy (ev) Min	Max	Lab	Type	Documentation Ref Vol Page	Date	Author, Comments	Data
(n,p)	Maxwl		IFU	Theo Rept	ICD–4 20	67	Dadakina+ PENETR COEFF CALC,TABLE	
Reson Params	–		AUA	Theo Rept	AAEC/E–211	Nov 70	Musgrove. CALCULTD D+GAM WIDTH GIVEN	
Strnth Fnctn	–		AUA	Theo Rept	AAEC/E–211	Nov 70	Musgrove. SMOOTHED S0,S1 AND S2 GIVN	

75 Rhenium 183

Quantity	Energy (ev) Min	Max	Lab	Type	Documentation Ref Vol Page	Date	Author, Comments	Data
Spect (n,γ)	2.5+4	4.0+5	CCP	Expt Conf	76Baku 128	Feb 76	Avchukhov+.ABST,GE–LI,ES+INTENS,TBL	
(n,p)	Maxwl		IFU	Theo Rept	ICD–4 20	67	Dadakina+ PENETR COEFF CALC,TABLE	
Reson Params	–		AUA	Theo Rept	AAEC/E–211	Nov 70	Musgrove. CALCULTD D+GAM WIDTH GIVEN	
Strnth Fnctn	–		AUA	Theo Rept	AAEC/E–211	Nov 70	Musgrove. SMOOTHED S0,S1 AND S2 GIVN	

75 Rhenium 184

Quantity	Energy (ev) Min	Max	Lab	Type	Documentation Ref Vol Page	Date	Author, Comments	Data
(n,p)	Maxwl		IFU	Theo Rept	ICD–4 20	67	Dadakina+ PENETR COEFF CALC,TABLE	
Reson Params	–		AUA	Theo Rept	AAEC/E–211	Nov 70	Musgrove. CALCULTD D+GAM WIDTH GIVEN	
Reson Params	–		DUB	Theo Rept	JINR–E4–5711	Apr 71	Soloviev.RESONANCE STRUCTURE STUDY	
Strnth Fnctn	–		AUA	Theo Rept	AAEC/E–211	Nov 70	Musgrove. SMOOTHED S0,S1 AND S2 GIVN	

75 Rhenium 185

Quantity	Energy (ev) Min	Max	Lab	Type	Documentation Ref Vol Page	Date	Author, Comments	Data
Total	1.0+0	1.3+1	BNL	Expt Jour	PR 100 1338	Dec 55	Igo.CS 12300+–200B AT 2.156+–0.004EV	
Total		5.0+2	IFU	Expt Jour	AE 19 250	Sep 65	Vertebny+ TOF,GRAPH 118+–2B AT THR	+
				Jour	SJA 19 1162	Sep 65	TRANSLATN.*	
				Jour	EAF 19 3 28	Sep 65	TRANSLATN.*	
				Rept	INDSWG–120 22	65	SUPERSEDED*	
				Conf	JINR–1845 150	Jun 64	.	
	4.9–3	1.2+0		Data	EXFOR40060.003	Mar 71	SIG AT 81ES, = AE 19 250 FIG3	
Res Int Abs	5.0–1		ANL	Expt Jour	PR 79 11	Jul 50	Harris+ EPI–CD,REL THERMAL ACT. B–W	+
	5.0–1			Data	EXFOR11343.031	Jun 76	. 1 PT. RIG.	
Res Int Abs	None		ORL	Revw Conf	55Geneva 5 96	Aug 55	Macklin+TBL.RIG EXPT CFD THEORY,P833	
Res Int Abs	5.0–1		STF	Expt Jour	ANS 5 375	62	Brown+RIG.DISAGREE NORDHEIM CALC.	+
				Abst	DA/B 27 1244	Oct 66	– . 1666+–83B,DISAGREE OTHER DATA	
	5.0–1			Data	EXFOR11830.003	Jun 76	. 1 PT. RIG	
Res Int Abs	5.0–1		STF	Expt Jour	ANS 9 248	66	Sher+	+
	5.0–1			Data	EXFOR12194.002	Jun 76	. 1 PT. RIG	
Res Int Abs	5.0–1		GA	Expt Jour	JNE 22 191	Apr 68	Friesenhahn+. 1726+–68B FROM RES PAR	+
Res Int Abs	5.0–1		LRC	Expt Rept	NASA–TN–D–4938	Dec 68	Pierce+ RIG.	+
	5.0–1			Data	EXFOR12165.003	Jun 76	. 1 PT.	
Res Int Abs	5.0–1		GHT	Expt Jour	JRC 20 695	74	Van Der Linden+ BY (N,G).CFD OTH,TBL	+
	5.5–1			Conf	73Paris 2 241	Mar 73	– + ACT,REL THR+GOLD,TBL	
	5.5–1			Data	EXFOR20645.045	Jul 76	1PNT.CAPTURE.	
(n,γ)	Maxwl		JAP	Expt Jour	SCP 38 167	Jan 41	Sinma+.LI+D.RELATIVE SIG MEASUREMENT	
(n,γ)	Pile		ANL	Expt Jour	PR 72 888	Nov 47	Seren+ THR IRRAD. TO16.2MIN,METAL.	+
	Pile			Data	EXFOR11447.116	Jun 76	. 1 PT.	
(n,γ)	Maxwl		ORL	Expt Jour	PR 88 412	Oct 52	Pomerance.PILE OSC.	
	Maxwl			Data	EXFOR11507.095	Jun 76	. 1 PT.	
(n,γ)	Fiss		BNL	Expt Jour	PR 91 1423	Sep 53	Hughes+.ALSO LVL SPACINGS AT EXCIT E	+
	Fiss			Data	EXFOR11562.018	Jun 76	. 1 PT.	
(n,γ)	2.4+4		ORL	Expt Jour	PR 107 504	Jul 57	Macklin+ SB–BE NS.2650+–500MB,ACT	+
	2.4+4			Data	EXFOR11399.046	Jun 76	. 1 PT.	
(n,γ)	Maxwl		ORL	Expt Jour	NSE 8 378	Nov 60	Lyon. ACTIVATION, SIGMA THR GIVEN	+
	Maxwl			Data	EXFOR11625.033	Jun 76	. 1 PT.	
(n,γ)	Fast		LAS	Expt Jour	NSE 8 608	Dec 60	Byers. GODIVA ACTIVATION CS GIVEN	

75 Rhenium 185

Quantity	Energy (ev) Min	Max	Lab	Type	Documentation Ref Vol Page	Date	Author, Comments	Data
(n,γ)	2.5−2		FLA	Expt Rept	AD− 402668	Mar 63	Karam+	+
	2.5−2			Data	EXFOR12179.004	Jun 76	. 1 PT.	
(n,γ)	4.6+3	2.6+6	ANL	Expt Jour	JNE 19 767	Oct 65	Stupegia+ CS AT 33 ES REL SIGF U235	+
	4.0+3	2.0+6		Prog	ANL−7020 228	Jul 65	− + SIG REL U235 NF,28 ES,GRPH	
	4.6+3	2.6+6		Data	EXFOR12162.002	Jun 76	. 33 PTS.	
(n,γ)	2.4+4		MUA	Expt Jour	PR 152 1055	Dec 66	Chaubey+ BETA−DET,SIG REL I−127,TBL	+
				Theo Jour	IJP 42 567	Sep 68	− + METHD OF BOOTH,VAL CFD XPT	
	2.4+4			Expt Data	EXFOR30079.036	Dec 70	SIGMA FOR 89. H HALF−LIFE	
(n,γ)	Fiss		CCP	Expt Jour	YF 5 18	Jan 67	Druzhinin+.TBL,ACTIVATION METHOD	+
				Jour	SNP 5 13	Jul 67	.ENGL OF YF 5 18	
(n,γ)	1.0−2	3.0+4	GA	Expt Jour	JNE 22 191	Apr 68	Friesenhahn+ CURVS .01−10EV,.4−30KEV	
	1.0−2	4.0+4		Data	EXFOR12163.	Jun 76	. 1 PT TH.30PTS(10−2−9.9).11PTS(400)	
(n,γ)	−		IEA	Comp Rept	IEA−INF−10 6	Aug 68	Atalla. TABLES OF HL,SIG AND GAMM−E	
(n,γ)	2.5+4		MTR	Expt Prog	IN− 1407 31	Jun 70	Tromp.ACT,FE FILTRD BEAM,VALUE GIVEN	
(n,γ)	3.0+4		AUA	Theo Rept	AAEC/E−211	Nov 70	Musgrove. SIGMA GIVEN AND CFD OTHER	
(n,γ)	1.0−1	5.0+1	LEB	Expt Conf	71Kiev	May 71	Bergman+ SIG(NEUT−E),GRAPH,CFD OTHER	
(n,γ)	2.4+4		MUA	Theo Jour	IJP 46 114	Mar 72	Chaubey+ P−WAVE STRENGTH FUNCT,TABLE	
(n,γ)	1.0+3	1.0+7	BOL	Eval Data	BENZI−DFN 818.	May 72	40 PNTS	+
(n,γ)	2.0+4	3.0+4	TAT	Expt Prog	BARC−831 20	75	Anand+ GAM−ACTIV(GELI),REL THERM,NDG	
(n,γ)	1.2+5	2.7+6	LRL	Expt Jour	NSE 59 381	Apr 76	Linder+REL U235NF,TBL,GRPHS.CFD ENDF	+
	1.2+5	2.7+6		Data	EXFOR10221.	Aug 75	. 16 PTS. MAXWL	
Spect (n,γ)	2.5+4		ORL	Expt Conf	58Geneva 15 68	Sep 58	Macklin. SIGMA+G−ENERGY GVN	
Spect (n,γ)	Pile		UPP	Expt Jour	NP 40 329	Jan 63	Marklund+.E DETERM. NO INTENS MEAS.	
Spect (n,γ)	Pile		RIS	Expt Prog	EANDC(OR)32L	Jun 64	Gruber+	
	Maxwl			Prog	EANDC(OR)22U	Sep 63	Maier+. AROUND 140 LINES	
Spect (n,γ)	None		IFU	Expt Prog	INDSWG−120 32	65	Berestovoj.TABLE OF 5 G−ES AND HL	
Spect (n,γ)	Pile		CCP	Expt Jour	IZV 30 209	Feb 66	Berestovoj+.CURVES,LIVETIMEEXPTH ENGL TRANS SEE BAS90 215 (2/66)	
Spect (n,γ)	Maxwl		LAS	Expt Prog	WASH−1074 82	Apr 67	Jurney+GE(LI) NAI SPECTROMETER NDG	
Spect (n,γ)	Maxwl	Pile	ORL	Expt Prog	WASH−1093 106	Apr 68	Campbell+ NDG	
Spect (n,γ)	Maxwl		DEL	Expt Abst	DA/B 30 3819	Feb 70	Koekstra. GELI DET.CALIB CL−35(N,G)	
Spect (n,γ)	2.2+0	3.6+2	NRL	Expt Jour	PR/C 4 1466	Oct 71	Stolovy+. RESONANCE CAPTURE SPECTRA	
Spect (n,γ)	1.0+7		WWA	Theo Jour	NP/A 189 545	Jul 72	Brzosko+ CMPD NUCL DECAY.PARTIAL WG	
Spect (n,γ)	2.5+0	2.7+1	CRC	Expt Prog	INDC(CAN)−13 8	Oct 73	Lone+ LVL STUDIES FRM G−SPECT,NDG	
Spect (n,γ)	Maxwl		MUN	Expt Jour	ZP 265 335	Nov 73	Glatz. LVL SCHEME OF RE−186	
Spect (n,γ)	2.4+1	2.0+3	ORL	Expt Jour	NP/A 266 83	Aug 76	Namenson+TOF SPEC.1,4MEV G THRS.WN.	
(n,2n)	Fiss		CRC	Eval Rept	CRC−1003	Dec 60	Roy+,ESTIMATED AVG SIG=5.5MB	
(n,2n)	1.4+7		FLA	Expt Rept	AD−402668	Mar 63	Karam+ 1.91+−.6B,1.12+−.4B TO META	+
				Rept	NP−11874	Jul 62	− +	
	1.4+7			Data	EXFOR12179.	Jun 76	. 1 PT, EACH. GND + META	
(n,2n)	1.4+7		HAM	Comp Jour	NP 65 257	Mar 65	Bormann. 1EXPT VALS.CFD SHELL EFFECT	
(n,2n)	Fiss	1.5+7	CCP	Expt Jour	YF 5 18	Jan 67	Druzhinin+.TBL,ACTIVATION METHOD	+
(n,2n)	1.5+7		DEB	Comp Jour	REA 7 4 93	Dec 69	Csikai+ HL COMPILTN,N−ACTIV−ANAL	
(n,2n)	1.4+7	1.5+7	JYV	Eval Rept	JU−RR−3/1970	Jun 70	Leppaemaeki+ TABLE OF EVAL AVG SIG	
(n,2n)	Fiss		KJL	Expt Jour	RCA 13 169	Jun 70	Steinnes.AVERAGE FISS NEUT CROSS−SEC	+
	Fiss			Data	EXFOR20109.	Sep 71	2PTS.SIG.	
(n,2n)	+7		KFI	Theo Rept	KFKI−71−8	Feb 71	Jeki. CALCULATED CFD EXPTL SIG VALUE	
(n,2n)	1.4+7	1.5+7	IRK	ExTh Jour	APA 33 285	Jul 71	Winiwarter+ ISOMERIC RATIO	
(n,2n)	1.5+7		DEB	Eval Rept	REA 11 1 153	Mar 73	Boedy. COMPILATION+RECOMM.VALUE,TBL	
				Rept	IAEA−153 173	73	− . RECOMM. VALUE ONLY	
(n,p)	Fiss		CRC	Eval Rept	CRC−1003	Dec 60	Roy+,ESTIMATED AVG SIG=0.03MB	
(n,p)	Maxwl		IFU	Theo Rept	ICD−4 20	67	Dadakina+ PENETR COEFF CALC,TABLE	
(n,α)	Fiss		CRC	Eval Rept	CRC−1003	Dec 60	Roy+,ESTIMATED AVG SIG=0.0002MB	
Reson Params	2.2+0		COL	Expt Jour	PR 92 702	Nov 53	Melkonian+FRM AREA METHOD DOPPLCORR	+
	2.2+0			Data	EXFOR11670.012	Jun 76	. 1 RES, EO,WT**2/PCS	
Reson Params	2.2+0		BNL	Expt Jour	PR 100 1338	Dec 55	Igo.CS WT=.059EV WG=.0557EV AT2.16EV	
Reson Params	2.2+0	2.2+1	IFU	Expt Jour	AE 19 250	Sep 65	Vertebny+.TOF,TBL,8 RES−ES + WIDTHS	
				Prog	INDSWG−120	65	.SUPERSEDED BY AE 19 250 9/65	
				Jour	SJA 19 1162	Mar 66	.ENGLISH TRANSL OF AE 19 250 9/65	
				Jour	EAF 19 3 28	Sep 65	. FRENCH TRANSL OF AE 19 250 9/65	
	2.1+0	1.1+2		Data	EXFOR40060.	Mar 71	N−WID AT 7 ES, AND MORE RES−ENERGIES	
Reson Params	2.2+0	1.3+1	NRL	Expt Jour	PR 155 1330	Mar 67	Stolovy.J FOR 4RES,TRNSMSN POLARZ NS	+
	2.2+0	1.3+1		Data	EXFOR11995.004	Jun 76	. 4 RES, E0,J	
Reson Params	2.2+0		MOL	Expt Jour	NP/A 97 657	May 67	Poortmans+.FROM RES SCATTERING EXPT.	
	2.2+0			Data	EXFOR20213.	May 74	2PTS.J,WN/WT.	
Reson Params		1.0+6	AUA	Theo Jour	AUJ 20 477	Oct 67	Cook. TBL OF AVG LVL SPACING D,L=0,1	
Reson Params	−.7+1	5.0+2	GA	Expt Jour	JNE 22 191	Apr 68	Friesenhahn+ 96ER,30WN,11WG,CF OTHER	+
	−.7+1	5.0+2		Data	EXFOR12163.	Jun 76	. 96 RES, E0,WN,WN0,WG	

75 Rhenium 185

Quantity	Energy (ev) Min	Max	Lab	Type	Documentation Ref Vol Page	Author, Comments Date	Data
Reson Params	+3	+5	AUA ExTh	Rept	AAEC/E-198	May 69 Musgrove.RES PARS +STF FROM (NG)FIT	+
Reson Params	-		AUA Theo	Rept	AAEC/E-211	Nov 70 Musgrove. CALCULTD D+GAM WIDTH GIVEN	
Reson Params	2.1+0	6.7+1	CJD Eval	Rept	YK-7	71 Zakharova+ SURVEY+SYSTEMATICS,GW,TBL	
				Rept	INDC(CCP)-27	Nov 72 .ENGLISH TRANSLATION OF YK-7 /71	
Reson Params	None		DUB Theo	Jour	YF 13 240	Feb 71 Malecki+G-WID,THEO CFD EXPT.TBL,GRPH	
				Jour	SNP 13 133	Aug 71 - + ENGL OF YF 13 240.	
Reson Params	2.2+0	3.8+2	NRL Expt	Jour	PR/C 4 1466	Oct 71 Stolovy+. RESON ENERGIES GIVEN	+
	2.2+0	3.8+2		Data	EXFOR10041.002	Jul 72 . 86 RES, EO	
Reson Params	3.0+0	1.2+2	JAE Expt	Jour	NST 9 261	May 72 Ideno+.TOF.RES-PARM IN TABLES	+
	+0	1.2+2		Prog	EANDC(J)13L5	Aug 69 - +.AGREE WITH FRIESENHAHN+.TBP	
	5.9+0	1.0+2		Data	EXFOR20702.002	Jun 77 28PTS.E0,WG,2G*WN.	
Reson Params	2.4+1	2.0+3	ORL Expt	Jour	NP/A 266 83	Aug 76 Namenson+TOF.S,P WAVE.2G*WN.TBL.CFD	+
	2.2+0	2.0+3		Data	EXFOR10630.002	Nov 76 . 488 RES, E0, WN	
Strnth Fnctn	+3		BNL Expt	Jour	PRL 1 461	Dec 58 Hughes+ FC, 2.1+ - 0.2	
Strnth Fnctn	-		IFU Expt	Jour	AE 19 250	Sep 65 Vertebny+ MOST PROB VALUE 0.00018	+
				Jour	EAF 19 3 28	Sep 65 TRANSLATN.*	
				Jour	SJA 19 1162	Sep 65 TRANSLATN.*	
				Rept	INDSWG-120 22	65 SUPERSEDED*	
	2.0+0	2.2+1		Data	EXFOR40060.008	Mar 71 STRENGTH-FUNCTION	
Strnth Fnctn	None		GA Expt	Jour	JNE 22 191	Apr 68 Friesenhahn+ S0=1.8+ -.5,S1=2.04+ -1.0	+
Strnth Fnctn	+3	+5	AUA ExTh	Rept	AAEC/E-198	May 69 Musgrove.S+P+D STF FROM (NG)FIT,TBL	+
Strnth Fnctn	-		AUA Theo	Rept	AAEC/E-211	Nov 70 Musgrove. SMOOTHED S0,S1 AND S2 GIVN	
Strnth Fnctn	2.4+4		MUA Theo	Jour	IJP 46 114	Mar 72 Chaubey+ P-WAVE.FOR A-SYSTEMTIC,GRPH	
Strnth Fnctn		7.1+1	JAE Expt	Jour	NST 9 261	May 72 Ideno+ TBL. FROM RES ANALYSIS.	+
	0.0+0	7.1+1		Data	EXFOR20702.003	Jun 77 1PNT.	
Strnth Fnctn	None		AUA Eval	Rept	AAEC/E-277	Mar 73 Musgrove.TBLS EXPTL DATA+BEST VALUES	
Strnth Fnctn	2.2+0	4.2+2	ORL Expt	Jour	NP/A 266 83	Aug 76 Namenson+	+
		3.0+3		Prog	USNDC-7 157	Jun 73 Stolovy+ LINAC. CAPT MEAST NO DATA	
	2.2+0	4.2+2		Data	EXFOR10630.004	Oct 76 . 5 PTS, D	
Lvl Density	None		DUB Theo	Rept	JINR-P4-8102	Jul 74 Malov+ SEMI-MICROSC CALC OKS XPT,TBL	
				Rept	UCRL-TR-10845	Apr 75 . ENGL OF JINR-P4-8102	
Lvl Density	+0		DUB Theo	Conf	75Kiev 3 23	May 75 Voronov. LVL SPACING OF RE186.TABLE	

75 Rhenium 186

Quantity	Energy (ev) Min	Max	Lab	Type	Documentation Ref Vol Page	Author, Comments Date	Data
(n,γ)	1.0+3	1.0+7	BOL Eval	Data	BENZI-DFN 843.	May 72 40 PNTS	+
(n,p)	Maxwl		IFU Theo	Rept	ICD-4 20	67 Dadakina+ PENETR COEFF CALC,TABLE	
Reson Params	-		AUA Theo	Rept	AAEC/E-211	Nov 70 Musgrove. CALCULTD D+GAM WIDTH GIVEN	
Strnth Fnctn	-		AUA Theo	Rept	AAEC/E-211	Nov 70 Musgrove. SMOOTHED S0,S1 AND S2 GIVN	
Lvl Density	Fiss		BNL Expt	Jour	PR 91 1423	Sep 53 Hughes+ FROM NG.	
Lvl Density	+6		MIL Theo	Jour	EN 15 1 54	Jan 68 Facchini+ LDL PARS FROM LOW EN RES	
Lvl Density	None		MUN Theo	Jour	NP/A 217 269	Dec 73 Dilg+ A,DELTA. BACK SHIFTED FERMIGAS	
Lvl Density	None		COP Theo	Jour	NP/A 222 493	Apr 74 Dossing+COLL ROTAT.SPAC. ACCUR ESTIM	
Lvl Density	None		ROC Theo	Jour	NP/A 223 577	May 74 Huizenga+ EXP CFD MICROSC TH SPH NUC	

75 Rhenium 187

Quantity	Energy (ev) Min	Max	Lab	Type	Documentation Ref Vol Page	Author, Comments Date	Data
Total	1.0+0	1.3+1	BNL Expt	Jour	PR 100 1338	Dec 55 Igo.CS 1560+ -50B AT 4.416+ -.008EV	
Total		5.0+2	IFU Expt	Jour	AE 19 250	Sep 65 Vertebny+ TOF,GRAPH 90+ -2B AT THR	+
				Jour	EAF 19 3 28	Sep 65 TRANSLATN.*	
				Jour	SJA 19 1162	Sep 65 TRANSLATN.*	
				Rept	INDSWG-120 22	65 SUPERSEDED*DUB 1845 P50	
	4.9-3	1.2+0		Data	EXFOR40060.004	Mar 71 SIG AT 81ES, = AE 19 250 FIG3	
Res Int Abs	5.0-1		ANL Expt	Jour	PR 79 11	Jul 50 Harris+ EPI-CD,REL THERMAL ACT. B-W	+
	5.0-1			Data	EXFOR11343.032	Jun 76 . 1 PT, RI	
Res Int Abs	None		ORL Revw	Conf	55Geneva 5 96	Aug 55 Macklin+TBL.RIG.EXPT CFD THEORY.	
Res Int Abs	5.0-1		STF Expt	Jour	ANS 9 248	66 Sher+	+
	5.0-1			Data	EXFOR12194.004	Jun 76 . 1 PT. RIG	
Res Int Abs	5.0-1		GA Expt	Jour	JNE 22 191	Apr 68 Friesenhahn+.292+ -42B FROM RES PARS	+
Res Int Abs	Pile		LRC Expt	Rept	NASA-TN-D-4938	Dec 68 Pierce+	+
	5.0-1			Data	EXFOR12163.004	Jun 76 . 1 PT.	
Res Int Abs	5.0-1		GHT Expt	Jour	JRC 20 695	74 Van Der Linden+ BY (N,G).CFD OTH,TBL	+
	5.5-1			Conf	73Paris 2 241	Mar 73 - + ACT,REL THR+GOLD,TBL	
	5.5-1			Data	EXFOR20645.	Jul 76 2PTS.CAPTURE.	

75 Rhenium 187

Quantity	Energy (ev) Min	Max	Lab	Type	Documentation Ref Vol Page	Date	Author, Comments	Data
(n,γ)	Maxwl		JAP	Expt	Jour SCP 38 167	Jan 41	Sinma+.LI+D.RELATIVE SIG MEASUREMENT	
(n,γ)	2.5−2		ANL	Expt	Jour PR 72 888	Nov 47	Seren+.ACT METHOD.THR IRRAD.METAL.	+
	Pile				Data EXFOR11447.117	Jun 76	. 1 PT.	
(n,γ)	Maxwl		ORL	Expt	Jour PR 88 412	Oct 52	Pomerance.PILE OSC.	+
	Maxwl				Data EXFOR11507.096	Jun 76	. 1 PT.	
(n,γ)	Fiss		BNL	Expt	Jour PR 91 1423	Sep 53	Hughes+.ALSO LVL SPACINGS AT EXCIT E	+
	Fiss				Data EXFOR11562.017	Jun 76	. 1 PT.	
(n,γ)	2.4+4		ORL	Expt	Jour PR 107 504	Jul 57	Macklin+.SB−BE NS,970+−200MB,ACT	+
	2.4+4				Data EXFOR11399.047	Jun 76	. 1 PT.	
(n,γ)	Maxwl		ORL	Expt	Jour NSE 8 378	Nov 60	Lyon. ACTIVATION, SIGMA THR GIVEN	+
	Maxwl				Data EXFOR11625.034	Jun 76	. 1 PT.	
(n,γ)	Fast		LAS	Expt	Jour NSE 8 608	Dec 60	Byers. GODIVA ACTIVATION CS GIVEN	
(n,γ)	Pile		KSU	Expt	Rept TID−22165	62	Simons.ISOMERIC SIG RATIOS CFD TH	
	Pile				Data EXFOR12631.	Jun 76	. 2 PTS , SIG FOR GND + META	
(n,γ)	2.5−2		FLA	Expt	Rept AD−402668	Mar 63	Karam+	+
	2.5−2				Data EXFOR12179.003	Jun 76	. 1 PT.	
(n,γ)	Maxwl		BNL	Expt	Jour PR/B 136 18	Oct 64	Takahashi+	+
	Maxwl				Data EXFOR12173.002	Jun 76	. 2 PTS, ISM RATIO + META SIG	
(n,γ)	4.0+3	2.0+6	ANL	Expt	Prog ANL−7055 230	Oct 65	Stupegia+ REL U235 NF,RE188M+G,GRAPH	+
	4.6+3	2.6+6			Jour JNE 19 767	Oct 65	− + CS FOR 2 RE188 ISOM,33 ES	
	4.0+3	2.0+6			Prog ANL−7020 228	Jul 65	− + REL U235 NF,RE188M+G,GRAPH	
					Prog ANL−6900 332	Aug 64	− + REL U235 NF, ES ,GRAPH	
	4.6+3	2.6+6			Data EXFOR12162.004	Jun 76	. 33 PTS.	
(n,γ)	Maxwl		KFI	Expt	Jour KFI 14 85	Apr 66	Kardon. IN HUN,ISOMERIC RATIO GIVEN	+
					Conf 64Paris 2 703	Jul 64	Gulyas+ISOMER RATIO.SEE ALSO LDL	
	Maxwl				Data EXFOR30341.005	Sep 76	ISOMERIC RATIO, 1 PNT	
(n,γ)	2.4+4		MUA	Expt	Jour PR 152 1055	Dec 66	Chaubey+ SIG(17 HRS) REL I−127,TBL	
				Theo	Jour IJP 42 567	Sep 68	− + METHOD OF BOOTH,VAL CFD XPT	
	2.4+4			Expt	Data EXFOR30079.037	Dec 70	SIGMA FOR 17. H HALF−LIFE	
(n,γ)	Fiss		CCP	Expt	Jour YF 5 18	Jan 67	Druzhinin+.TBL,ACTIVATION METHOD	+
					Jour SNP 5 13	Jul 67	.ENGL OF YF 5 18	
(n,γ)	1.0−2	3.0+4	GA	Expt	Jour JNE 22 191	Apr 68	Friesenhahn+ CURVS .01−10EV,.4−30KEV	+
	2.5−2	4.0+4			Data EXFOR12163.	Jun 76	.1PT(TH).16PTS(10−2).11PTS(GT400	
(n,γ)	−		IEA	Comp	Rept IEA−INF−10 6	Aug 68	Atalla. TABLES OF HL,SIG AND GAMM−E	
(n,γ)	Pile		MUN	Revw	Conf 69Studsvik 127	Aug 69	Egidy.PART'L SIGS OF CONV LINES,GRPH	
(n,γ)	3.0+4		AUA	Theo	Rept AAEC/E−211	Nov 70	Musgrove. SIGMA GIVEN AND CFD OTHER	
(n,γ)	1.0−1	5.0+1	LEB	Expt	Conf 71Kiev	May 71	Bergman+ SIG(NEUT−E),GRAPH,CFD OTHER	
(n,γ)	2.4+4		MUA	Theo	Jour IJP 46 114	Mar 72	Chaubey+ P−WAVE STRENGTH FUNCT,TABLE	
(n,γ)	1.0−3	1.0+7	BOL	Eval	Data BENZI−DFN 819.	May 72	40 PNTS	
(n,γ)	1.5+7		IRK	Expt	Prog EANDC(OR)117L	Aug 72	Rohatsch+ TBL SIG TO GS AND MS.	
	1.4+7	1.5+7			Jour OAWA 107 136	Apr 70	Leithner+ ISOMER	
(n,γ)	2.0+4	3.0+4	TAT	Expt	Prog BARC−831 20	75	Anand+ GAM−ACTIV(GELI),REL THERM,NDG	
(n,γ)	1.2+5	2.7+6	LRL	Expt	Jour NSE 59 381	Apr 76	Linder+REL U235NF.TBL,GRPHS.CFD ENDF	+
	1.2+5	2.7+6			Data EXFOR10221.	Aug 75	16PTS,SIGMA	
Spect (n,γ)	2.5+4		ORL	Expt	Conf 58Geneva 15 68	Sep 58	Macklin. SIGMA+G−ENERGY GVN	
Spect (n,γ)	Pile		CTH	Expt	Jour NP 39 286	Dec 62	Hardell+. PRECISION E DET OF ISOM LV	
Spect (n,γ)	Pile		UPP	Expt	Jour NP 40 329	Jan 63	Marklund+.E DETERM. NO INTENS MEAS.	
Spect (n,γ)	Pile		RIS	Expt	Prog EANDC(OR)32L	Jun 64	Gruber+	
Spect (n,γ)	Maxwl		KFI	Expt	Conf 64Paris 2 703	Jul 64	Gulyas+ALSO LEVEL SCHEME	
Spect (n,γ)	None		IFU	Expt	Jour INDSWG−120 32	65	Berestovoj.TABLE OF 5 G−ES AND HL	
Spect (n,γ)	Pile		CCP	Expt	Jour IZV 30 209	Feb 66	Berestovoi+.CURVES,LIVETIMEEXPTH	
					−		ENGL TRANS SEE BAS90 215 (2/66)	
Spect (n,γ)	Maxwl		LAS	Expt	Prog WASH−1074 82	Apr 67	Jurney+GE(LI) NAI SPECTROMETER NDG	
Spect (n,γ)	Maxwl		MUN	Expt	Jour NP/A 107 417	Jan 68	Suarez+INTCONVERSN.53LINES 8TO300KEV	
					Conf 67Juelich 56	Apr 67	− + SUPERSEDED.	
Spect (n,γ)	Maxwl	Pile	ORL	Expt	Prog WASH−1093 106	Apr 68	Campbell+ NDG	
Spect (n,γ)	Maxwl	4.4+0	IFU	Expt	Jour UFZ 13 2082	Dec 68	Vertebnyj+ G−SPEC,'POS'+'NEG' RESON	
					Jour UPJ 13 1489	Jun 69	TRANSLATN.*	
Spect (n,γ)	Maxwl		DEL	Expt	Abst DA/B 30 3819	Feb 70	Koekstra. GELI DET.CALIB CL−35(N,G)	
Spect (n,γ)	4.4+0	3.6+2	NRL	Expt	Jour PR/C 4 1466	Oct 71	Stolovy+. RESONANCE CAPTURE SPECTRA	
Spect (n,γ)	Maxwl		LAS	Expt	Prog USNDC−1 118	May 72	Shera. NO DATA GIVEN	
Spect (n,γ)	Maxwl		CCP	Theo	Jour ZET 65 12	Jul 73	Nosov+ THERMODYN CALC CFD EXPT,GRAPH	
					Jour JET 38 6	Jan 74	. ENGLISH OF ZET 65 6	
Spect (n,γ)	Maxwl		ROS	Expt	Prog ZFK−262 100	Sep 73	Schilling+ DELAYED GS,LVL−E+HL GIVEN	
Spect (n,γ)	4.4+0	1.9+1	CRC	Expt	Prog INDC(CAN)−13 8	Oct 73	Lone+ LVL STUDIES FRM G−SPECT,NDG	
Spect (n,γ)	Maxwl		LSU	Expt	Jour ZP/A 272 213	Feb 75	Hawk+ G−SPEC,LVLSCH OF RE−188 GIVEN	
Spect (n,γ)	2.4+1	2.0+3	ORL	Expt	Jour NP/A 266 83	Aug 76	Namenson+TOF SPEC.1,4MEV G THRS.WN.	
(n,2n)	Fiss		CRC	Eval	Rept CRC−1003	Dec 60	Roy+,ESTIMATED AVG SIG=5.0MB	

75 Rhenium 187

Quantity	Energy (ev) Min	Max	Lab	Type	Documentation Ref Vol Page	Author, Comments Date	Data
(n,2n)	1.5+7		MUA	Expt Jour	NP 28 560	Dec 61 Khurana+HANS.ACTIVATION CFD STAT MOD	+
	1.5+7			Data	EXFOR31247.021	Mar 73 .SIG GVN	
(n,2n)	1.4+7		FLA	Expt Prog	AD- 402668	Mar 63 Karam+ 1.44+ −0.41B	+
	1.4+7			Data	EXFOR12179.008	Jun 76 . 1 PT.	
(n,2n)	1.4+7		HAM	Comp Jour	NP 65 257	Mar 65 Bormann. 2EXPT VALS.CFD SHELL EFFECT	+
(n,2n)	Fiss	1.5+7	CCP	Expt Jour	YF 5 18	Jan 67 Druzhinin+.TBL,ACTIVATION METHOD	+
	Fiss			Jour	SNP 5 13	Jul 67 .ENGL OF YF 5 18	
(n,2n)	1.5+7		DEB	Comp Jour	REA 7 4 93	Dec 69 Csikai+ SIG+HL COMPILTN,N−ACTIV−ANAL	
(n,2n)	1.4+7	1.5+7	JYV	Eval Rept	JU−RR−3/1970	Jun 70 Leppaemaeki+ TABLE OF EVAL AVG SIG	
(n,2n)	+7		KFI	Theo Rept	KFKI−71−8	Feb 71 Jeki. CALCULATED CFD EXPTL SIG VALUE	
(n,2n)	1.5+7		DEB	Eval Jour	REA 11 1 153	Mar 73 Boedy. COMPILATION+RECOMM.VALUE,TBL	
				Rept	IAEA−153 173	73 − . RECOMM. VALUE ONLY	
(n,2n)	1.5+7		TAT	Theo Jour	JP/A 7 1457	Aug 74 Kondaiah. CALC ON STAT MODEL	
(n,p)	1.4+7		ALD	Expt Jour	PPS 73 215	Feb 59 Coleman+. ACT. CFD DIRECT INTERACTN	+
(n,p)	Fiss		CRC	Eval Rept	CRC−1003	Dec 60 Roy+,ESTIMATED AVG SIG=0.007MB	
(n,p)	1.5+7		SAH	Comp Jour	NUC 23 8 112	Aug 65 Chatterjee. TABLE WITH REFS.	
	1.4+7			Jour	NP 60 273	Nov 64 − .MEAN OF EXPT CFD SHELLMOD	
(n,p)	1.5+7		DEB	Comp Jour	REA 7 4 93	Dec 69 Csikai+ SIG+HL COMPILTN,N−ACTIV−ANAL	
(n,p)	1.4+7	1.5+7	JYV	Eval Rept	JU−RR−3/1970	Jun 70 Leppaemaeki+ TABLE OF EVAL AVG SIG	
(n,p)	1.4+7	1.5+7	KAZ	Theo Jour	YF 18 705	Oct 73 Levkovsky.AVERAGED SIG,CALC,TBL	
				Jour	SNP 18 361	Apr 74 . ENGLISH OF YF 18,705	
(n,He3)	1.5+7		RBZ	Expt Jour	JIN 36 477	74 Diksic+ ACTIV,GE(LI),TABLES	+
	1.4+7			Data	EXFOR30152.015	Apr 72 1 DATA LINE	
(n,α)	1.4+7		ALD	Expt Jour	PPS 73 215	Feb 59 Coleman+. ACTIVATION	+
(n,α)	Fiss		CRC	Eval Rept	CRC−1003	Dec 60 Roy+,ESTIMATED AVG SIG=BELO 0.0001MB	
(n,α)	1.4+7		CIS	Theo Jour	NP 51 460	Feb 64 Facchini+STATMOD SIG XPT/CALC3.4−4.7	
(n,α)	1.5+7		MUA	Expt Jour	NP 69 153	Jul 65 Khurana+	
(n,α)	1.5+7		DEB	Comp Jour	REA 7 4 93	Dec 69 Csikai+ SIG+HL COMPILTN,N−ACTIV−ANAL	
(n,α)	1.4+7	1.5+7	JYV	Eval Rept	JU−RR−3/1970	Jun 70 Leppaemaeki+ TABLE OF EVAL AVG SIG	
(n,α)	1.4+7	1.5+7	KAZ	Theo Jour	YF 18 705	Oct 73 Levkovsky.AVERAGED SIG,CALC,TBL	
				Jour	SNP 18 361	Apr 74 . ENGLISH OF YF 18,705	
(n,α)		7.5+8	IOW	Expt Jour	PR/C 12 1978	Dec 75 Hill+750EV P ON CU LAMPF	
Reson Params	4.4+0	1.1+1	COL	Expt Jour	PR 92 702	Nov 53 Melkonian+FRM AREA METHOD DOPPLCORR	+
	4.4+0	1.1+1		Data	EXFOR11670.013	Jun 76 . 2 RES, E0,WT**2/PCS	
Reson Params	4.4+0		BNL	Expt Jour	PR 100 1338	Dec 55 Igo.CS WT=.045EV WG=.045EV AT4.416EV	+
Reson Params	4.4+0	1.9+1	IFU	Expt Jour	AE 19 250	Sep 65 Vertebny+.TOF,TBL,5 RES−ES + WIDTHS	+
				Prog	INDSWG−120	65 .SUPERSEDED BY AE 19 250 9/65	
				Jour	SJA 19 1162	Mar 66 .ENGLISH TRANSL OF AE 19 250 9/65	
				Jour	EAF 19 3 28	Sep 65 . FRENCH TRANSL OF AE 19 250 9/65	
	4.4+0	1.1+2		Data	EXFOR40060.	Mar 71 N−WID AT 5 ES, AND MORE RES−ENERGIES	
Reson Params	4.4+0	1.1+1	NRL	Expt Jour	PR 155 1330	Mar 67 Stolovy.2RES J=3,2. TRNSMN POLARZ NS	+
	4.4+0	1.1+1		Data	EXFOR11995.005	Jun 76 . 2 RES, E0,J	
Reson Params	1.0+6		AUA	Theo Jour	AUJ 20 477	Oct 67 Cook. TBL OF AVG LVL SPACING D,L=0,1	
Reson Params	−.3+1	4.9+2	GA	Expt Jour	JNE 22 191	Apr 68 Friesenhahn+ 76ER,24WN,15WG,CF OTHER	+
	−.2+2	4.9+2		Data	EXFOR12163.	Jun 76 . 76 RES, E0,WN,WN0,WG	
Reson Params	4.4+0	6.2+1	KFK	Eval Rept	KFK−718	Apr 68 Schmidt+ RESOLVED+AVG RES PARAM(S,P)	
Reson Params	+3	+5	AUA	ExTh Rept	AAEC/E−198	May 69 Musgrove.RES PARS +STF FROM (NG)FIT	+
Reson Params	4.4+0	9.2+1	KFK	Comp Rept	KFK−1233	Jul 70 Mueller. ES,WN,WG,G OF 23 RESON	
Reson Params	−		AUA	Theo Rept	AAEC/E−211	Nov 70 Musgrove. CALCULTD D+GAM WIDTH GIVEN	
Reson Params	4.4+0	8.6+1	CJD	Eval Rept	YK−7	71 Zakharova+ SURVEY+SYSTEMATICS,GW,TBL	
				Rept	INDC(CCP)−27	Nov 72 .ENGLISH TRANSLATION OF YK−7 /71	
Reson Params	None		DUB	Theo Jour	YF 13 240	Feb 71 Malecki+G−WID,THEO CFD EXPT.TBL,GRPH	
				Jour	SNP 13 133	Aug 71 − + ENGL OF YF 13 240.	
Reson Params	4.4+0	3.6+2	NRL	Expt Jour	PR/C 4 1466	Oct 71 Stolovy+. RESON ENERGIES GIVEN	
	4.4+0	3.3+2		Jour	NIM 95 595	Dec 70 Godlove+EXPT DATA AQUISITION SYSTEM	
	4.4+0	3.6+2		Data	EXFOR10041.003	Jul 72 . 76 RES, E0	
Reson Params	3.0+0	1.2+2	JAE	Expt Jour	NST 9 261	May 72 Ideno+.TOF,RES−PARM IN TABLES	+
	+0	1.2+2		Prog	EANDC(J)13L5	Aug 69 − +.AGREE WITH FRIESENHAHN+.TBP	
	4.4+0	1.2+2		Data	EXFOR20702.004	Jun 77 26PTS.E0,WG,2G*WN.	
Reson Params	2.4+1	2.0+3	ORL	Expt Jour	NP/A 266 83	Aug 76 Namenson+TOF.S,P WAVE.2G*WN.TBL.CFD	+
		3.0+3		Prog	ORNL−4844 87	Apr 73 Harvey+SUPERSEDED	
	2.5+1	2.0+3		Data	EXFOR10630.003	Oct 76 . 393 RES, E0,WN	
Strnth Fnctn	−		IFU	Expt Jour	AE 19 250	Sep 65 Vertebny+ MOST PROB VALUE 0.00009	+
				Jour	EAF 19 3 28	Sep 65 TRANSLATN.*	
				Jour	SJA 19 1162	Sep 65 TRANSLATN.*	
				Rept	INDSWG−120 22	65 SUPERSEDED*	
	4.0+0	2.0+1		Data	EXFOR40060.009	Mar 71 STRENGTH−FUNCTION	
Strnth Fnctn	None		GA	Expt Jour	JNE 22 191	Apr 68 Friesenhahn+ S0=2.3+ −.7,S1=1.96+ −1.0	+

75 Rhenium 187

Quantity	Energy (ev) Min	Energy (ev) Max	Lab	Type	Documentation Ref Vol Page	Author, Comments Date	Data
Strnth Fnctn	+3	+5	AUA	ExTh Rept	AAEC/E-198	May 69 Musgrove.S+P+D STF FROM (NG)FIT,TBL	+
Strnth Fnctn	-		AUA	Theo Rept	AAEC/E-211	Nov 70 Musgrove. SMOOTHED S0,S1 AND S2 GIVN	
Strnth Fnctn	2.4+4		MUA	Theo Jour	IJP 46 114	Mar 72 Chaubey+ P-WAVE.FOR A-SYSTEMTIC,GRPH	
Strnth Fnctn		9.6+1	JAE	Expt Jour	NST 9 261	May 72 Ideno+ TBL. FROM RES ANALYSIS.	+
	0.0+0	9.6+1		Data	EXFOR20702.005	Jun 77 1PNT.	
Strnth Fnctn	None		AUA	Eval Rept	AAEC/E-277	Mar 73 Musgrove.TBLS EXPTL DATA+BEST VALUES	
Strnth Fnctn	4.4+0	4.2+2	ORL	Expt Jour	NP/A 266 83	Aug 76 Namenson+	+
	3.0+3			Prog	USNDC-7 157	Jun 73 Stolovy+ LINAC, CAPT MEAST NO DATA	
	4.4+0	4.2+2		Data	EXFOR10630.005	Oct 76 . 5 PTS, D	
Lvl Density	Maxwl		KFI	Expt Conf	64Paris 2 703	Jul 64 Gulyas+DISPERS.PAR=1TO3 FROM ISOMRAT	

75 Rhenium 188

Quantity	Energy (ev) Min	Energy (ev) Max	Lab	Type	Documentation Ref Vol Page	Author, Comments Date	Data
(n,γ)	Maxwl		MTR	Expt Jour	JIN 3 157	Oct 56 Smith.SIG IS SMALL OR RE189 HL POOR	
(n,γ)	1.5+7		IRK	Expt Priv	WAGNER	77 Wagner+	+
	1.5+7			Data	EXFOR20718.	Jan 76 2PTS.SIGMA.	
Reson Params	-		AUA	Theo Rept	AAEC/E-211	Nov 70 Musgrove. CALCULTD D+GAM WIDTH GIVEN	
Strnth Fnctn	-		AUA	Theo Rept	AAEC/E-211	Nov 70 Musgrove. SMOOTHED S0,S1 AND S2 GIVN	
Lvl Density	Fiss		BNL	Expt Jour	PR 91 1423	Sep 53 Hughes+ FROM NG	
Lvl Density	+0	+3	IFU	Expt Conf	67Kharkov 171	Feb 67 Vertebny.TRANSMISSION EXPT	
Lvl Density	+6		MIL	Theo Jour	EN 15 1 54	Jan 68 Facchini+ LDL PARS FROM LOW EN RES	
Lvl Density	None		MUN	Theo Jour	NP/A 217 269	Dec 73 Dilg+ A,DELTA. BACK SHIFTED FERMIGAS	
Lvl Density	None		COP	Theo Jour	NP/A 222 493	Apr 74 Dossing+COLL ROTAT.SPAC. ACCUR ESTIM	
Lvl Density	None		ROC	Theo Jour	NP/A 223 577	May 74 Huizenga+ EXP CFD MICROSC TH SPH NUC	

75 Rhenium 189

Quantity	Energy (ev) Min	Energy (ev) Max	Lab	Type	Documentation Ref Vol Page	Author, Comments Date	Data
Reson Params	-		AUA	Theo Rept	AAEC/E-211	Nov 70 Musgrove. CALCULTD D+GAM WIDTH GIVEN	
Strnth Fnctn	-		AUA	Theo Rept	AAEC/E-211	Nov 70 Musgrove. SMOOTHED S0,S1 AND S2 GIVN	

75 Rhenium 190

Quantity	Energy (ev) Min	Energy (ev) Max	Lab	Type	Documentation Ref Vol Page	Author, Comments Date	Data
Reson Params	-		AUA	Theo Rept	AAEC/E-211	Nov 70 Musgrove. CALCULTD D+GAM WIDTH GIVEN	
Strnth Fnctn	-		AUA	Theo Rept	AAEC/E-211	Nov 70 Musgrove. SMOOTHED S0,S1 AND S2 GIVN	

76 Osmium

Quantity	Energy (ev) Min	Max	Lab	Type	Documentation Ref Vol Page	Author, Comments Date	Data
Evaluation	5.0+5	1.5+7	LRL	Eval	Rept UCRL-5351	Nov 58 Howerton+ CURVES	
Total	Maxwl		COL	Expt	Jour PR 48 265	Aug 35 Dunning+ IONCH,TRANS,RA-BE/PARAFIN N	
Total	1.0-2	+4	COL	Expt	Jour PR 71 174	Feb 47 WU+ SLOW N SOURCE.TOF.TRANSM.	+
	8.3-3	9.2-1			Data EXFOR11751.007	Jun 76 . 29 PTS. SIGMA.	
Total	4.0+0	1.0+4	CCP	Expt	Conf 55Geneva 4 22	Aug 55 Vladimirski+.P641,CURVE,CHOPPER,TOF	+
Total	3.0+0	5.0+2	AMS	Expt	Jour PHY 22 1131	Nov 56 Radkevich+ABSTRACT,FAST CHOPPER. NDG	
Total	6.5+0	6.9+0	ANL	Expt	Jour PR 127 461	Jul 62 Jackson+ METAL AT 105,297DEG K.	
Total	None		DKE	Expt	Abst DA/B 28 3834	Mar 68 Divadeenam.TRNS.AVG SIG CFD OPTMDL.	+
	1.2+5	6.4+5			Data EXFOR10523.015	Jan 76 . 27 PTS. CS DATA.	
Total	2.0+4	7.0+6	FEI	Expt	Conf 68Dubna § 17	Jun 68 Filippov+VDG,TRANS.TBL,GRPH.FLUCTUAT	
	2.5+4	7.0+6			Prog ICD-3 102	Oct 66 .GRAPH CFD REFS.VDG	
	2.0+4	7.0+6			Rept INDC(CCP)-16	Jul 71 .PAGE 67.ENGLISH TRANSL OF 68DUBNA	
	2.5+4	7.0+6			Prog INDSWG-152E	66 .PAGE 102. ENGLISH TRANSL OF ICD-3	
Total	2.5+6	1.5+7	BNW	Expt	Jour PR/C 3 576	Feb 71 Foster+,TRANS,CURVS,CFD OTHERS+TH	+
					Jour NIM 36 1	Sep 65 .EXPT DETAILS	
	2.3+6	1.5+7			Data EXFOR10047.083	Aug 73 . 243 PTS.	
Total	1.3+7	1.5+7	DEB	Eval	Rept IAEA-153 173	73 Boedy+ MOST PROBABLE VAL OF SIG,TBL	
					Jour AHP 30 115	Oct 71 Angeli+ AVG SIG,CFD CALC.TBLS.GRAPH	
Total	3.6-1	1.6+5	BNL	Expt	Prog WASH-1013 16	Nov 58 Chrien.	+
	3.6-1	1.6+5			Data EXFOR12177.002	Jun 76 . 489 PTS. SIGMA.	
Total	3.0+4	6.5+5	DKE	Expt	Abst BAP 7 23	Jan 62 Tabony+AVG CS MEAS.CFD.NDG	+
	3.0+4	6.5+5			Data EXFOR11936.007	Jun 76 . 92 PTS. SIGMA.	
Elastic	5.2-1		ANL	Expt	Jour PR 105 216	Jan 57 Heaton+,COH=15.2B,BOUND NUCL=15.36B	
Elastic	2.5-2		ANL	Expt	Conf 63ANL 393	Oct 63 Mueller+ COHER SCAT SIG BY NEUT DIFF	+
	2.5-2				Data EXFOR11508.	Jun 76 . 2 PTS, COH, COH AMP	
Potntal Scat		6.5+5	DKE	ExTh	Jour PL 13 70	Nov 64 Seth+0,1PHASE FRM SIG TOT AV 3-650KV	
Potntal Scat	None		DKE	Expt	Abst DA/B 28 3834	Mar 68 Divadeenam.TRNS.EFFECTIVE RADIUS	
Thermal Scat	Cold		ANL	Expt	Jour JAP 30 1323	Sep 59 Sidhu+ 14.5BCOH SCAT BY NEUT DIFFR	
					Conf 58Geneva 14 212	Sep 58 - +.PPR680,TBL OF SIGMA-COHERENT	
Thermal Scat	7.0-2	3.0-1	IJI	Expt	Prog YFI-12 66	72 Vertebny+ ABST,TOT SCAT SIG GIVEN	
					Prog INDC(CCP)-30	Sep 72 .PAGE 57,ENGLISH OF YFI-12 66	
Thermal Scat	1.0-4	1.0+3	MUN	Revw	Jour EEN 80 1	77 Koester. SCAT LENGTH	
Scattering	Maxwl		CAV	Expt	Jour PRSA 162 127	Sep 37 Goldhaber+. 10.8B REL 4.83B FOR C	
Res Int Abs	—		CCP	Expt	Jour AE 3 507	Dec 57 Klimentov+.EPI CD REACTIVITY REL LI	+
					Jour JNE 9 20	Jun 59 TRANSLATN.*	
					Jour SJA 3 1387	57 TRANSLATN.*	
Res Int Abs	5.0-1		MTR	Expt	Rept IN-1195	May 68 Scoville+	+
					Jour ANS 10 259	Jun 67 .SUPERSEDED	
	5.0-1				Data EXFOR11820.020	Jun 76 . 1 PT.	
(n,γ)	Maxwl		ORL	Expt	Jour PR 83 643	Aug 51 Pomerance. LOCAL OSC REL AU ABS.	+
	Maxwl				Data EXFOR11047.068	Jun 76 . 1 PT.	
(n,γ)	2.0+2	8.0+3	ORL	Expt	Conf 61Saclay 203	Sep 61 Block+.LIQUID SCINTILLATOR	+
	2.0+2	1.0+4			Conf 61Vienna 1 95	Aug 61 Neiler.PPR73,GRAPH,FAST CHOPPER	
	2.1+2	7.2+3			Data EXFOR11935.024	Jun 76 . 49 PTS.	
(n,γ)	3.0+4	6.5+4	ORL	Expt	Jour PR 129 2695	Mar 63 Macklin+ LIQ SCINT,300 AND 175MB	+
	3.0+4	6.5+5			Data EXFOR11331.029	Jun 76 . 2 PTS.	
(n,γ)	5.0+3	9.0+4	ORL	Theo	Jour RMP 37 166	Jan 65 Macklin+.CALC FOR KT=5TO90KEV	
(n,γ)	3.0+4		AUA	Theo	Rept AAEC/E-211	Nov 70 Musgrove. SIGMA GIVEN AND CFD OTHER	
Spect (n,γ)	Maxwl		CAS	Expt	Jour NC 29 977	Aug 63 Giannini+ NAI, E+INTENSITY,TO 366KEV	
Spect (n,γ)	Pile		UJV	Expt	Rept UJV-1909	67 Plajner+.GRAPH,DECAY OF OS193	
Spect (n,γ)	2.5-2		MIT	Comp	Rept MITNE-85	Jan 69 Rasmussen+TBL G INT.=AFCRL-69-0071	
Spect (n,γ)	Pile		ANL	Expt	Prog WASH-1127 10	Apr 69 Bollinger+ LVL STRUCTRE ONLY,TBC,NDG	
Spect (n,γ)	None		BNL	Expt	Prog WASH-1127 24	Apr 69 Kane+ TO BE COMPLETED,NO DATA GIVEN	
(n,2n)	1.5+7		DEB	Eval	Rept REA 11 1 153	Mar 73 Boedy+ RECOMM.VALUE FROM N-Z SYSTEM.	
Reson Params	6.5+0	8.4+1	COL	Expt	Jour PR 71 174	Feb 47 WU+ 6E0. APPROX STRENGTH GIVEN.	+
	6.5+0	8.4+1			Data EXFOR11751.011	Jun 76 . 6 RES, E0,WT**2/PCS	
Reson Params	1.0+0		AMS	Expt	Jour PHY 22 1131	Nov 56 Radkevich+ABSTRACT,NDG.GAMMA(N),(G)	
Reson Params	6.7+0	3.3+2	CCP	Expt	Jour AE 1 5 55	Nov 56 Radkevich+. 22 RES, WG=67MV AV,3 WTS	+
					Jour JNE 5 92	Jul 57 TRANSLATN.*	
					Jour SJA 1 5 727	56 TRANSLATN.*	
Reson Params	1.2+1	4.5+1	ANL	Expt	Jour PR 124 1142	Nov 61 Jackson.	+
	1.2+1	4.5+1			Data EXFOR11992.010	Jun 76 . 6 RES, E0	
Reson Params	6.7+0		ANL	Expt	Jour PR 127 461	Jul 62 Jackson+LYNN.FIT TO RES IN METAL	+
	6.7+0				Data EXFOR11373.002	Jun 76 . 1 RES, EO,WT,WNO	
Reson Params	5.0+1	3.2+2	ITE	Expt	Prog INDSWG-120 19	65 Ignat'Ev.TOF,TABLE OF 19 RES ES	
Reson Params	+0	+3	IFU	Expt	Conf 67Kharkov 171	Feb 67 Vertebny.PARAMETERS FROM TRNSMISSN	

76 Osmium

Quantity	Energy (ev) Min	Max	Lab	Type	Documentation Ref Vol Page	Author, Comments Date	Data
Reson Params	3.9+1	8.0+1	CJD	Eval	Rept YK- 7	71 Zakharova+ SURVEY+SYSTEMATICS,GW,TBL	
					Rept INDC(CCP)-27	Nov 72 .ENGLISH TRANSLATION OF YK-7 /71	
Reson Params	6.7+0	7.9+1	BNL	Expt	Prog WASH-1013 1	58 Chrien+ E0,WN FOR 7,W,WG FOR 4 LEVLS	+
	6.7+0	7.9+1			Data EXFOR12177.003	Jun 76 . 7 RES, E0,WT,WG	
Strnth Fnctn	3.0+0	5.0+2	AMS	Expt	Jour PHY 22 1131	Nov 56 Radkevich+ABSTRACT,NDG	
Strnth Fnctn	+3		BNL	Expt	Jour PRL 1 461	Dec 58 Hughes. FC 1.9+-0.3	
Strnth Fnctn		6.5+5	DKE	ExTh	Jour PL 13 70	Nov 64 Seth+S,P,D STF FRM SIG TOT 3-650KEV	+
	5.0+4	1.5+5		Expt	Conf 64Paris 2 916	Jul 64 - +S0,S1,S2 R PRIME/R DUKE U.	
	3.0+3	6.5+5			Data EXFOR11665.029	Jun 76 . 3 PTS.	
Strnth Fnctn	None		DKE	Expt	Abst DA/B 28 3834	Mar 68 Divadeenam.S,P,D WAVES.CFD POT MDLS.	
Lvl Density	None		FEI	Theo	Jour YF 11 1213	Jun 70 Ignatyuk+ SPIN DEPENDENCE OF DENSITY	
					Jour SNP 11 674	Dec 70 . ENGL OF YF 11 1213	

76 Osmium 178

Quantity	Energy (ev) Min	Max	Lab	Type	Documentation Ref Vol Page	Author, Comments Date	Data
Lvl Density	None		CCP	Theo	Jour YF 13 43	Jan 71 Bravin+.DEFORM PAR,CALC,TBL,CFD EXPT	

76 Osmium 180

Quantity	Energy (ev) Min	Max	Lab	Type	Documentation Ref Vol Page	Author, Comments Date	Data
Lvl Density	None		CCP	Theo	Jour YF 13 43	Jan 71 Bravin+.DEFORM PAR,CALC,TBL,CFD EXPT	

76 Osmium 182

Quantity	Energy (ev) Min	Max	Lab	Type	Documentation Ref Vol Page	Author, Comments Date	Data
Reson Params	-		AUA	Theo	Rept AAEC/E-211	Nov 70 Musgrove. CALCULTD D+GAM WIDTH GIVEN	
Strnth Fnctn	-		AUA	Theo	Rept AAEC/E-211	Nov 70 Musgrove. SMOOTHED S0,S1 AND S2 GIVN	
Lvl Density	None		CCP	Theo	Jour YF 13 43	Jan 71 Bravin+.DEFORM PAR,CALC,TBL,CFD EXPT	

76 Osmium 183

Quantity	Energy (ev) Min	Max	Lab	Type	Documentation Ref Vol Page	Author, Comments Date	Data
Reson Params	-		AUA	Theo	Rept AAEC/E-211	Nov 70 Musgrove. CALCULTD D+GAM WIDTH GIVEN	
Strnth Fnctn	-		AUA	Theo	Rept AAEC/E-211	Nov 70 Musgrove. SMOOTHED S0,S1 AND S2 GIVN	

76 Osmium 184

Quantity	Energy (ev) Min	Max	Lab	Type	Documentation Ref Vol Page	Author, Comments Date	Data
Res Int Abs	5.5-1		GHT	Expt	Jour RCA 9 61	Aug 68 KIM+ CD-RATIO,0.38+-0.02 WITHUOT 1/V	+
	5.0-1				Data EXFOR20656.009	Jun 76 1PNT.CAPTURE.	
Res Int Abs	5.0-1		GHT	Expt	Jour JRC 20 695	74 Van Der Linden+ BY (N,G).CFD OTH,TBL	+
	5.5-1				Conf 73Paris 2 241	Mar 73 - + ACT,REL THR+GOLD,TBL	
	5.5-1				Data EXFOR20645.048	Jul 76 1PNT.CAPTURE.	
(n,γ)	2.5-2		GHT	Expt	Jour RCA 9 61	Aug 68 KIM+ ACTIV,REL AU,CD-RATIO.SIG GIVEN	+
	2.5-2				Data EXFOR20656.008	Jun 76 1PNT.SIGMA.	
(n,γ)	-		IEA	Comp	Rept IEA-INF-10 6	Aug 68 Atalla. TABLES OF HL,SIG AND GAMM-E	
(n,γ)	3.0+4		AUA	Theo	Rept AAEC/E-211	Nov 70 Musgrove. SIGMA GIVEN AND CFD OTHER	
(n,γ)	1.0+3	1.0+7	BOL	Eval	Data BENZI-DFN 820.	May 72 40 PNTS	+
Spect (n,γ)	Maxwl		HAM	Expt	Jour ZP 234 171	May 70 Sturm+ G-G-ANG-CORR MEASUREMENTS	
Spect (n,γ)	Maxwl		IFL	Expt	Conf 74Kharkov 149	Feb 74 Prokof'Ev+ ABST,GE-LI,ES+INTENS,TBL	
					Jour IZV 38 2135	74 - + TBL CONV-ELS,GRPH LVL SCH	
					Jour BAS 38 10 104	74 . ENGL OF IZV 38,2135	
(n,2n)	Fiss		CRC	Eval	Rept CRC-1003	Dec 60 Roy+,ESTIMATED AVG SIG=2.6MB	
(n,2n)	1.5+7		DEB	Eval	Jour REA 11 1 153	Mar 73 Boedy+ RECOMM.VALUE FROM N-Z SYSTEM.	
(n,α)	Fiss		CRC	Eval	Rept CRC-1003	Dec 60 Roy+,ESTIMATED AVG SIG=0.0028MB	
(n,α)	Maxwl		CCP	Expt	Jour YF 1 252	Feb 65 Andreev.IONIZ-CHAMBER,SIG=M10MB	+
					Jour SNP 1 177	Aug 65 TRANSLATN.*	
Reson Params	-		AUA	Theo	Rept AAEC/E-211	Nov 70 Musgrove. CALCULTD D+GAM WIDTH GIVEN	
Strnth Fnctn	-		AUA	Theo	Rept AAEC/E-211	Nov 70 Musgrove. SMOOTHED S0,S1 AND S2 GIVN	
Lvl Density	None		CCP	Theo	Jour YF 13 43	Jan 71 Bravin+.DEFORM PAR,CALC,TBL,CFD EXPT	

76 Osmium 185

Quantity	Energy (ev) Min	Max	Lab	Type	Documentation Ref Vol Page	Date	Author, Comments	Data
(n,p)	Maxwl		IFU	Theo	Rept ICD-4 20	67	Dadakina+ PENETR COEFF CALC,TABLE	
Reson Params	–		AUA	Theo	Rept AAEC/E-211	Nov 70	Musgrove. CALCULTD D+GAM WIDTH GIVEN	
Strnth Fnctn	–		AUA	Theo	Rept AAEC/E-211	Nov 70	Musgrove. SMOOTHED S0,S1 AND S2 GIVN	

76 Osmium 186

Quantity	Energy (ev) Min	Max	Lab	Type	Documentation Ref Vol Page	Date	Author, Comments	Data
Elastic	2.0-2	3.0+3	IJI	Expt	Jour YF 22 674	Oct 75	Vertebny+ TRANS,TOF.AVG SCATSIG,TABL	
					Jour SNP 22 348	Oct 75	. ENGL OF YF 22,674	
Thermal Scat	7.0-2	3.0-1	IJI	Expt	Prog YFI-12 66	72	Vertebny+ ABST,TOT SCAT SIG GIVEN	
					Prog INDC(CCP)-30	Sep 72	.PAGE 57,ENGLISH OF YFI-12 66	
(n,γ)	2.5+4		FEI	ExTh	Prog YFI-4 22	May 67	Shorin+.,TBLS GIVEN,TBP YF	
					Rept INDC-187E	67	. ENGL OF YFI-4 22	
(n,γ)	5.0+3	5.0+4	CCP	Expt	Jour YF 6 769	Oct 67	Shorin+VAL+GRPH,25KEV +SIG(5TO50KEV)	
(n,γ)	3.0+4		AUA	Theo	Rept AAEC/E-211	Nov 70	Musgrove. SIGMA GIVEN AND CFD OTHER	
(n,γ)	1.0+3	1.0+7	BOL	Eval	Data BENZI-DFN 821.	May 72	40 PNTS	+
(n,γ)	2.5+4		IJI	Expt	Jour YF 22 674	Oct 75	Vertebny+ TRANS.SIG(L=0,1),TABLE	
					Conf 73Kiev 2 95	May 73	- + SIG GVN FOR 3L,TBL	
	7.0-2	3.0-1			Prog YFI-12 66	72	+ ABST,SIG GIVEN	
	2.5+4				Jour SNP 22 348	Oct 75	. ENGL OF YF 22,674	
	7.0-2	3.0-1			Prog INDC(CCP)-30	Sep 72	.PAGE 57,ENGLISH OF YFI-12 66	
(n,γ)	2.0-2	3.0+3	IJI	Expt	Jour YF 22 674	Oct 75	Vertebny+ TOF,SIG AT 2200 M/SEC,TBL	
					Jour SNP 22 348	Oct 75	. ENGL OF YF 22,674	
(n,γ)		1.5+5	LRL	Expt	Jour NAT 262 197	Jul 76	Browne+CS VS E GRPH.AGE OF UNIVERSE	
(n,γ)	2.5+4		NBS	Expt	Jour PR/C 14 1287	Aug 76	Browne+25KEV OS186/187.UNIVERSE AGE	+
	2.5+4				Data EXFOR10638.002	Apr 77	.1PT.RATIO OS186NG/OS187NG=.41+-.04	
Spect (n,γ)	Maxwl		IFL	Expt	Conf 74Kharkov 151	Feb 74	Nejburg+ ABST,GE-LI,ES+INTENS,TBL	
					Jour IZV 38 2135	74	Prokof'Ev+ OS187 LVL SCH DEDUCD,GRPH	
					Jour BAS 38 10 104	74	. ENGL OF IZV 38,2135	
Spect (n,γ)	Maxwl		IJI	Expt	Rept YFI-18 28	Aug 74	Barchuk+ GE-LI,ES+INTENSITIES,TBL	+
					Rept INDC(CCP)-49	Feb 75	- + ENGLISH OF YFI-18 22	
	2.5-2				Data EXFOR40267.002	Feb 75	GAMMA/100NEUT AT 26 GAM ES GVN	
(n,2n)	Fiss		CRC	Eval	Rept CRC-1003	Dec 60	Roy+,ESTIMATED AVG SIG=40.0MB	
(n,2n)	1.5+7		DEB	Eval	Jour REA 11 1 153	Mar 73	Boedy+ RECOMM.VALUE FROM N-Z SYSTEM.	
(n,2n)	1.5+7		KFI	Theo	Rept KFKI-73-68	Dec 73	Jeki.NEW FIT,CALC SIG CFD OTHERS,TBL	
(n,p)	Fiss		CRC	Eval	Rept CRC-1003	Dec 60	Roy+,ESTIMATED AVG SIG=0.04MB	
(n,α)	Fiss		CRC	Eval	Rept CRC-1003	Dec 60	Roy+,ESTIMATED AVG SIG=0.0004MB	
(n,α)	Maxwl		CCP	Expt	Jour YF 1 252	Feb 65	Andreev.IONIZ-CHAMBER,SIG=M.1MB	+
					Jour SNP 1 177	Aug 65	TRANSLATN.*	
(n,α)	None		KFI	Comp	Jour JRC 7 365	Jun 71	Nagy+ GAMMA+XRAY+ELECTR ES,HALF-LIFE	
Reson Params	2.5+4		FEI	ExTh	Prog YFI-4 22	May 67	Shorin+.,TBLS GIVEN,TBP YF	
					Rept INDC-187E	67	. ENGL OF YFI-4 22	
Reson Params	–		AUA	Theo	Rept AAEC/E-211	Nov 70	Musgrove. CALCULTD D+GAM WIDTH GIVEN	
Reson Params	2.2+1	2.7+2	IJI	Expt	Conf 71Moscow	Feb 71	Vertebny+.ABST,TOF,WN,WG,D,D-CORREL	
Reson Params	None		DUB	Theo	Jour ZEP 14 194	Aug 71	Solovev.LARGE N-WID G-WID CORREL.NDG	
					Rept JINR-E4-5880	71	Soloviev.N-GAM-WIDS CORR.SHORT NOTE	
					Jour JEL 14 129	Aug 71	- . ENGL OF ZEP 14 194.	
Reson Params	2.2+1	2.7+2	IJI	Expt	Prog YFI-12 70	72	Vertebny+ ABSTRACT,TBL RES-E+N-WID,D	
					Prog INDC(CCP)-30	Sep 72	.PAGE 60,ENGLISH OF YFI-12 70	
Reson Params	2.2+1	2.7+2	IFU	Expt	Prog YFI-12 70	Jun 72	Vertebny+	+
	2.2+1	2.7+2			Data EXFOR40127.	Jan 73	6 RES, RED N-WIDTH, D	
Reson Params	3.9+0	3.0+2	NIR	Expt	Jour AE 37 437	Nov 74	Belanova+ TOF,RES LVLS,TBLS	+
					Jour SJA 37 1204	May 75	.ENGLISH OF AE 37 437	
	1.9+1	2.8+2			Data EXFOR40330.002	Sep 76	.13 EN-RES GVN	
Reson Params	2.2+1	4.4+1	IJI	Expt	Jour YF 22 674	Oct 75	Vertebny+ G-WIDS(2RES),D-OBS,D0.TABL	
					Jour SNP 22 348	Oct 75	. ENGL OF YF 22,674	
Strnth Fnctn	–		AUA	Theo	Rept AAEC/E-211	Nov 70	Musgrove. SMOOTHED S0,S1 AND S2 GIVN	
Strnth Fnctn	2.2+1	2.7+2	IFU	Expt	Prog YFI-12 70	Jun 72	Vertebny+	+
	2.2+1	2.7+2			Data EXFOR40127.024	Jan 73	STRENGTH-FUNCTION, S	
Strnth Fnctn	None		IJI	Expt	Jour YF 22 674	Oct 75	Vertebny+ TOF,S0 VAL,TBL	
	2.5+4				Conf 73Kiev 2 95	May 73	- + 5.6X10-4,TBL	
	2.2+1	2.7+2			Prog YFI-12 70	72	+ ABSTRACT,VALUE GIVEN	
					Prog INDC(CCP)-30	Sep 72	.PAGE 60,ENGLISH OF YFI-12 70	
Lvl Density	None		CCP	Theo	Jour YF 13 43	Jan 71	Bravin+.DEFORM PAR,CALC,TBL,CFD EXPT	

76 Osmium 187

Quantity	Energy (ev) Min	Max	Lab	Type	Documentation Ref Vol Page	Date	Author, Comments	Data
Total	6.0−3	2.8−1	IFU	Expt	Rept IF− 69 4	69	Vertebny+ GRPH SIG(E) +2200M/SEC VAL	+
	5.8−2	2.8−1			Data EXFOR40094.002	Mar 72	SIG TOT AT 120 EN.	
Total	5.8−3	2.8−1	IFU	Expt	Prog YFI−7 39	Apr 69	Vertebny+ SIG(E) TABLE,NEGATIVE LVLS	
					Rept INDC(CCP)−7U42	Feb 70	TRANSLATN.*	
Elastic	2.0−2	3.0+3	IJI	Expt	Jour YF 22 674	Oct 75	Vertebny+ TRANS,TOF.AVG SCATSIG,TABL	
					Jour SNP 22 348	Oct 75	. ENGL OF YF 22,674	
Thermal Scat	7.0−2	3.0−1	IJI	Expt	Prog YFI−12 66	72	Vertebny+ ABST,TOT SCAT SIG GIVEN	
					Prog INDC(CCP)−30	Sep 72	.PAGE 57,ENGLISH OF YFI−12 66	
(n,γ)	2.5+4		FEI	ExTh	Prog YFI−4 22	May 67	Shorin+.,TBLS GIVEN,TBP YF	
					Rept INDC−187E	67	. ENGL OF YFI−4 22	
(n,γ)	5.0+3	5.0+4	CCP	Theo	Jour YF 6 769	Oct 67	Shorin+VAL+GRPH,25KEV +SIG(5T050KEV)	
					Jour SNP 6 558	Apr 68	TRANSLATN.*	
(n,γ)	5.0+3	1.0+5	AUA	ExTh	Rept AAEC/E−198	May 69	Musgrove.S+P+D WAVE SIGMAS CALC,TBL	+
(n,γ)	3.0+4		AUA	Theo	Rept AAEC/E−211	Nov 70	Musgrove. SIGMA GIVEN AND CFD OTHER	
(n,γ)	1.0+3	1.0+7	BOL	Eval	Data BENZI−DFN 822.	May 72	40 PNTS	+
(n,γ)	Maxwl		BNL	Expt	Jour PL/B 58 39	Aug 75	Macphail+SYSTEMATICS ROTATIONAL BAND	
(n,γ)	2.5+4		IJI	Expt	Jour YF 22 674	Oct 75	Vertebny+ TRANS.SIG(L=0,1),TABLE	
					Conf 73Kiev 2 95	May 73	− + SIG GVN FOR 3L,TBL	
	7.0−2	3.0−1			Prog YFI−12 66	72	− + ABST,SIG GIVEN	
	2.5+4				Jour SNP 22 348	Oct 75	. ENGL OF YF 22,674	
	7.0−2	3.0−1			Prog INDC(CCP)−30	Sep 72	.PAGE 57,ENGLISH OF YFI−12 66	
(n,γ)	2.0−2	3.0+3	IJI	Expt	Jour YF 22 674	Oct 75	Vertebny+ TOF,SIG AT 2200 M/SEC,TBL	
					Jour SNP 22 348	Oct 75	. ENGL OF YF 22,674	
(n,γ)		1.5+5	LRL	Expt	Jour NAT 262 197	Jul 76	Browne+CS VS E GRPH.AGE OF UNIVERSE	
(n,γ)	2.5+4		NBS	Expt	Jour PR/C 14 1287	Aug 76	Browne+25KEV OS186/187.UNIVERSE AGE	+
	2.5+4				Data EXFOR10638.002	Apr 77	.1PT.RATIO OS186NG/OS187NG=.41+−.04	
Spect (n,γ)	6.0+0	6.1+1	ANL	Expt	Jour PR 124 1142	Nov 61	Jackson+ FAST CHOPPER LOW E GAMMAS.	
Spect (n,γ)	1.0+2	+5	ANL	Expt	Conf 69Studsvik 601	Aug 69	Smither+ NO DATA GVN,OKS STATMOD	
Spect (n,γ)	2.6+0	3.0+2	NRL	Expt	Jour NP/A 237 45	Jan 75	Namenson+ GAM−SPEC GRAPH,FOR RESPARS	
Spect (n,γ)	Maxwl		BNL	Expt	Jour PL/B 58 39	Aug 75	Macphail+GE−LI.ROT BAND POPS	
Spect (n,γ)	5.0+0	3.5+2	LRL	Expt	Jour PR/C 14 965	Aug 76	Stolovy+LINAC,TOF.G INT GRPHS.	
(n,2n)	Fiss		CRC	Eval	Rept CRC−1003	Dec 60	Roy+,ESTIMATED AVG SIG=42.0MB	
(n,2n)	1.5+7		DEB	Eval	Jour REA 11 1 153	Mar 73	Boedy+ RECOMM.VALUE FROM N−Z SYSTEM.	
(n,2n)	1.5+7		KFI	Theo	Rept KFKI−73−68	Dec 73	Jeki.NEW FIT,CALC SIG CFD OTHERS,TBL	
(n,p)	Fiss		CRC	Eval	Rept CRC−1003	Dec 60	Roy+,ESTIMATED AVG SIG=0.025MB	
(n,p)	Maxwl		IFU	Theo	Rept ICD−4 20	67	Dadakina+ PENETR COEFF CALC,TABLE	
(n,α)	Fiss		CRC	Eval	Rept CRC−1003	Dec 60	Roy+,ESTIMATED AVG SIG=0.0009MB	
(n,α)	Maxwl		CCP	Expt	Jour YF 1 252	Feb 65	Andreev.IONIZ−CHAMBER,SIG=M.1MB	+
					Jour SNP 1 177	Aug 65	TRANSLATN.*	
(n,α)	9.5+0	2.0+1	DUB	Expt	Rept JINR−P3−7376	Sep 73	Balabanov+ RES−E,ALF−WID,SPIN,TABLE	
Reson Params	6.0+0	6.1+1	ANL	Expt	Jour PR 124 1142	Nov 61	Jackson+ FAST CHOPPER EO, WT, WN	+
	9.5+0	4.8+1			Data EXFOR11992.011	Jun 76	. 3 RES, E0	
Reson Params	−2		IFU	Expt	Conf 67Kharkov	Feb 67	Vertebnyj+. TBP IN IZV	
Reson Params	+0	+3	IFU	Expt	Conf 67Kharkov 171	Feb 67	Vertebny.PARAMETERS FROM TRNSMISSN	
Reson Params	2.5+4		FEI	ExTh	Prog YFI−4 22	May 67	Shorin+.,TBLS GIVEN,TBP YF	
					Rept INDC−187E	67	. ENGL OF YFI−4 22	
Reson Params	4.0−3	3.0+2	IFU	Expt	Prog YFI−4 34	May 67	Vertebnyj+.,TBL GIVEN	
					Rept INDC−187E	67	. ENGL OF YFI−4 34	
Reson Params	9.5+0	6.5+1	IFU	Expt	Rept IF− 69 4	69	Vertebny+ TBL RESON−E CFD OTHER,D	+
	9.5+0	6.5+1			Data EXFOR40094.	Mar 72	G*N−WIDTH 1RES., E−RES FOR 8 RES.	
Reson Params	9.5+0	1.3+1	ANL	Expt	Jour PR/C 1 1501	Apr 70	Wetzel+J FROM CAPT MEAS. TBL GVN.	+
	9.5+0	1.3+1			Data EXFOR10080.007	Feb 76	. 2 PTS. J,E0.	
Reson Params	−		AUA	Theo	Rept AAEC/E−211	Nov 70	Musgrove. CALCULTD D+GAM WIDTH GIVEN	
Reson Params	9.5+0	3.1+2	IJI	Expt	Conf 71Moscow	Feb 71	Vertebny+.ABST,TOF,WN,WG,D,D−CORREL	
Reson Params	9.4+0	4.8+1	DUB	Expt	Rept JINR−P3−6092	Nov 71	Karzhavina.GS MULTIPLICITY,SPINS,TBL	
Reson Params	9.6+0	1.2+2	IJI	Expt	Prog YFI−12 70	72	Vertebny+ ABSTRACT,TBL RES−E+N−WID,D	
					Prog INDC(CCP)−30	Sep 72	.PAGE 60,ENGLISH OF YFI−12 70	
Reson Params	2.2+1	2.7+2	IFU	Expt	Prog YFI−12 70	Jun 72	Vertebny+	+
	9.5+0	1.2+2			Data EXFOR40127.	Jan 73	10 RES, RED N−WIDTH, D	
Reson Params	9.5+0	2.0+1	DUB	Expt	Rept JINR−P3−7376	Sep 73	Balabanov+ RES−E,ALF−WID,SPIN,TABLE	
Reson Params	3.9+0	3.0+2	NIR	Expt	Jour AE 37 437	Nov 74	Belanova+ TOF,RES LVLS,TBLS	+
					Jour SJA 37 1204	May 75	.ENGLISH OF AE 37 437	
	9.4+0	2.5+2			Data EXFOR40330.003	Sep 76	.18 EN−RES GVN	
Reson Params	9.5+0	3.0+2	NRL	Expt	Jour NP/A 237 45	Jan 75	Namenson+ SPINS OF (N,G)RES,TBL	
	9.5+0	2.9+2			Prog USNDC−11 178	Jun 74	− + RES EN. SPINS	
	9.5+0	3.0+2			Data EXFOR10466.003	Jan 75	. 44 RES. J	

76 Osmium 187

Quantity	Energy (ev) Min	Max	Lab	Type	Documentation Ref Vol Page	Date	Author, Comments	Data
Reson Params	9.5+0	2.0+1	IJI	Expt	Jour YF 22 674	Oct 75	Vertebny+ G-WIDS(3RES),D-OBS,D0.TABL	
					Jour SNP 22 348	Oct 75	. ENGL OF YF 22,674	
Reson Params	9.5+0	1.3+2	LRL	Expt	Jour PR/C 14 965	Aug 76	Stolovy+G SPEC,I ASSIGNED.CFD OTH.	+
	9.5+0	2.5+2		Data	EXFOR10659.	Nov 77	. 51RES ES.J ASSIGN GVN.D FOR 34 RES	
Strnth Fnctn	–		AUA	Theo	Rept AAEC/E-211	Nov 70	Musgrove. SMOOTHED S0,S1 AND S2 GIVN	
Strnth Fnctn	2.2+1	2.7+2	IFU	Expt	Prog YFI-12 70	Jun 72	Vertebny+	+
	9.5+0	1.2+2		Data	EXFOR40127.027	Jan 73	STRENGTH-FUNCTION	
Strnth Fnctn	None		IJI	Expt	Jour YF 22 674	Oct 75	Vertebny+ TOF,S0 VAL,TBL	
	2.5+4				Conf 73Kiev 2 95	May 73	– + 2.0X10-4,TBL	
	9.6+0	1.2+2			Prog YFI-12 70	72	– + ABSTRACT,VALUE GIVEN	
					Prog INDC(CCP)-30	Sep 72	.PAGE 60,ENGLISH OF YFI-12 70	
Lvl Density	9.5+0	6.5+1	IFU	Expt	Rept IF-69-4	Apr 69	Vertebny+	+
	9.5+0	6.5+1		Data	EXFOR40094.008	Mar 72	AVERAGE LEVEL SPACING	
Lvl Density	None		MUN	Theo	Jour NP/A 217 269	Dec 73	Dilg+ A,DELTA. BACK SHIFTED FERMIGAS	
Lvl Density	None		ROC	Theo	Jour NP/A 223 577	May 74	Huizenga+ EXP CFD MICROSC TH SPH NUC	

76 Osmium 188

Quantity	Energy (ev) Min	Max	Lab	Type	Documentation Ref Vol Page	Date	Author, Comments	Data
Elastic	2.5-2		ANL	Expt	Conf 63ANL 393	Oct 63	Mueller+ COHER SCAT SIG BY NEUT DIFF	+
	2.5-1			Data	EXFOR11508.	Jun 76	. 2 PTS, COH, COH AMP	
Elastic	2.0-2	3.0+3	IJI	Expt	Jour YF 22 674	Oct 75	Vertebny+ TRANS,TOF.AVG SCATSIG,TABL	
					Jour SNP 22 348	Oct 75	. ENGL OF YF 22,674	
(n,γ)	–		IEA	Comp	Rept IEA-INF-10 6	Aug 68	Atalla. TABLES OF HL,SIG AND GAMM-E	
(n,γ)	3.0+4		AUA	Theo	Rept AAEC/E-211	Nov 70	Musgrove. SIGMA GIVEN AND CFD OTHER	
(n,γ)	1.0+3	1.0+7	BOL	Eval	Data BENZI-DFN 823.	May 72	40 PNTS	+
(n,γ)	2.0+0	3.0+5	LRL	Expt	Prog ERDA-NDC-2 75	May 75	Browne+TBC.NDG.	
(n,γ)	2.0-2	3.0+3	IJI	Expt	Jour YF 22 674	Oct 75	Vertebny+ TOF,SIG AT 2200 M/SEC,TBL	
					Jour SNP 22 348	Oct 75	. ENGL OF YF 22,674	
Spect (n,γ)	Maxwl	1.0+1	BNL	Expt	Jour PL/B 58 39	Aug 75	Macphail+GE-LI.ROT BAND POPS	
(n,2n)	Fiss		CRC	Eval	Rept CRC-1003	Dec 60	Roy+,ESTIMATED AVG SIG=5.0MB	
(n,2n)	1.5+7		DEB	Expt	Jour REA 11 1 153	Mar 73	Boedy+ RECOMM.VALUE FROM N-Z SYSTEM.	
(n,2n)	1.5+7		KFI	Theo	Jour KFKI-73-68	Dec 73	Jeki.NEW FIT,CALC SIG CFD OTHERS,TBL	
(n,p)	Fiss		CRC	Eval	Rept CRC-1003	Dec 60	Roy+,ESTIMATED AVG SIG=0.011MB	
(n,p)	1.5+7		AMS	Expt	Jour PHY 31 1091	Jul 65	Nagel+.REL FE56(NP)	+
					Diss NAGEL	Dec 66	– .D-T NS.ACT.FINAL	
	1.5+7				Data EXFOR20198.023	May 74	1PNT.SIGMA.	
(n,p)	1.4+7		DEB	Expt	Jour NP/A 91 222	Jan 67	Csikai+ ACTIV, VALUE AT 14.7MEV,TBL	+
					Jour MFF 16 123	Feb 68	SEE ALSO *THESIS HUNG	
	1.5+7				Data EXFOR30115.010	Jan 71	SIGMA AT 14.7 MEV FROM NP A91 222	
(n,p)	1.4+7	1.5+7	NAP	Comp	Rept INFN/BE-67-10	Jul 67	Cuzzocrea+ AVERAGED CHOSEN DATA.	
	1.5+7		DEB	Expt	Jour REA 7 4 93	Dec 69	Csikai+ SIG+HL COMPILTN,N-ACTIV-ANAL	
(n,p)	1.4+7	1.5+7	JYV	Eval	Rept JU-RR-3/1970	Jun 70	Leppaemaeki+ TABLE OF EVAL AVG SIG	
(n,p)	1.4+7	1.5+7	KAZ	Theo	Jour YF 18 705	Oct 73	Levkovsky.AVERAGED SIG,CALC,TBL	
					Jour SNP 18 361	Apr 74	. ENGLISH OF YF 18,705	
(n,α)	Fiss		CRC	Eval	Rept CRC-1003	Dec 60	Roy+,ESTIMATED AVG SIG=0.0003MB	
(n,α)	Maxwl		CCP	Expt	Jour YF 1 252	Feb 65	Andreev.IONIZ-CHAMBER,SIG=M.03MB	+
					Jour SNP 1 177	Aug 65	TRANSLATN.*	
(n,α)	1.5+7	1.5+7	AMS	Expt	Priv NAGEL	Dec 66	Nagel. = 1 DATA INDEX LINES	+
Reson Params	-2		IFU	Expt	Conf 67Kharkov	Feb 67	Vertebnyj+. TBP IN IZV	
Reson Params	+0	+3	IFU	Expt	Conf 67Kharkov 171	Feb 67	Vertebny.PARAMETERS FROM TRNSMISSN	
Reson Params	4.0-3	3.0+2	IFU	Expt	Prog YFI-4 34	May 67	Vertebnyj+.,TBL GIVEN	
					Rept INDC-187E		67 . ENGLISH OF YFI-4 34	
Reson Params	3.9+1	8.3+1	IFU	Expt	Rept IF-69 4	69	Vertebny+ TBL RESON-E CFD OTHER,D	+
	3.9+1	8.3+1			Data EXFOR40094.005	Mar 72	2G*N-WIDTH FOR 2 RESONANCES	
Reson Params	–		AUA	Theo	Rept AAEC/E-211	Nov 70	Musgrove. CALCULTD D+GAM WIDTH GIVEN	
Reson Params	3.8+1	7.8+1	IJI	Expt	Conf 71Moscow	Feb 71	Vertebnyj+.ABST,TOF,WN,WG,D,D-CORREL	
Reson Params	3.8+1	3.9+2	IJI	Expt	Prog YFI-12 70	72	– + ABSTRACT,TBL RES-E+N-WID,D	
					Prog INDC(CCP)-30	Sep 72	.PAGE 60,ENGLISH OF YFI-12 70	
Reson Params	2.2+1	2.7+2	IFU	Expt	Prog YFI-12 70	Jun 72	Vertebny+	+
	3.8+1	3.9+2			Data EXFOR40127.	Jan 73	7 RES, RED N-WIDTH, D	
Reson Params	3.9+0	3.0+2	NIR	Expt	Jour AE 37 437	Nov 74	Belanova+ TOF,RES LVLS,TBLS	+
					Jour SJA 37 1204	May 75	.ENGLISH OF AE 37 437	
	2.5+1	2.8+2			Data EXFOR40330.004	Sep 76	.11 EN-RES GVN	
Reson Params	3.8+1		IJI	Expt	Jour YF 22 674	Oct 75	Vertebny+ G-WIDS(1RES),D-OBS,D0.TABL	
					Jour SNP 22 348	Oct 75	. ENGL OF YF 22,674	

76 Osmium 188

Quantity	Energy (ev) Min	Max	Lab	Type	Documentation Ref Vol Page	Date	Author, Comments	Data
Strnth Fnctn	–		AUA Theo	Rept	AAEC/E – 211	Nov 70	Musgrove. SMOOTHED S0,S1 AND S2 GIVN	
Strnth Fnctn	2.2+1	2.7+2	IFU Expt	Jour	YFI – 12 70	Jun 72	Vertebny+	+
	3.8+1	3.9+2		Data	EXFOR40127.025	Jan 73	STRENGTH – FUNCTION, S – WAVE	
Strnth Fnctn	None		IJI Expt	Jour	YF 22 674	Oct 75	Vertebny+ TOF,S0 VAL,TBL	
	3.8+1	3.9+2		Prog	YFI – 12 70	72	– + ABSTRACT,VALUE GIVEN	
				Prog	INDC(CCP) – 30	Sep 72	.PAGE 60,ENGLISH OF YFI – 12 70	
Lvl Density	+0	+3	IFU Expt	Conf	67Kharkov 171	Feb 67	Vertebny.TRANSMISSION EXPT	
Lvl Density	+6		MIL Expt	Jour	EN 15 1 54	Jan 68	Facchini+ LDL PARS FROM LOW EN RES	
Lvl Density	None		CCP Theo	Jour	YF 11 1028	May 70	Rubchenya. DENSITY+A+TEMP GIVEN	
				Jour	SNP 11 571	Nov 70	. ENGL OF YF 11 571.	
Lvl Density	None		MUN Theo	Jour	NP/A 217 269	Dec 73	Dilg+ A,DELTA. BACK SHIFTED FERMIGAS	
Lvl Density	None		ROC Theo	Jour	NP/A 223 577	May 74	Huizenga+ EXP CFD MICROSC TH SPH NUC	
Lvl Density	None		ROC Theo	Jour	NP/A 223 589	May 74	Huizenga+ EXP CFD MICROSC TH AX SYMM	

76 Osmium 189

Quantity	Energy (ev) Min	Max	Lab	Type	Documentation Ref Vol Page	Date	Author, Comments	Data
Elastic	2.5 – 2		ANL Expt	Conf	63ANL 393	Oct 63	Mueller+ COHER SCAT SIG BY NEUT DIFF	+
	2.5 – 2			Data	EXFOR11508.	Jun 76	. 2 PTS, COH, COH AMP	
Elastic	2.0 – 2	3.0+3	IJI Expt	Jour	YF 22 674	Oct 75	Vertebny+ TRANS,TOF.AVG SCATSIG,TABL	
				Jour	SNP 22 348	Oct 75	. ENGL OF YF 22,674	
Res Int Abs	5.0 – 1		GHT Expt	Jour	JRC 20 695	74	Van Der Linden+ BY (N,G).CFD OTH,TBL	+
	5.5 – 1			Conf	73Paris 2 241	Mar 73	– + ACT,REL THR+GOLD,TBL	
	5.5 – 1			Data	EXFOR20645.049	Jul 76	1PNT.CAPTURE.	
(n,γ)	Maxwl		MUA Expt	Jour	NP 20 183	Oct 60	Hans+ CS OF OS189(NG)OS190M GIVEN	+
	Maxwl			Data	EXFOR31246.012	Sep 72	.SIG TO MS – STATE GVN	
(n,γ)	Maxwl		MUA Expt	Jour	NP 36 542	Aug 62	Mangal+ SCINT SPECT,REL TO AU197,TBL	+
				Conf	62Madras 95	Feb 62	– +	
	Maxwl			Data	EXFOR31248.014	Apr 73	.SIG TO MS – STATE GVN	
(n,γ)	Maxwl		UCB Expt	Rept	NYO – 10175	Dec 64	Arino+ACT.TBLS.GRAPHS.PRODUCT HL.	+
	Maxwl			Data	EXFOR11817.017	Jun 76	. 1 PT.	
(n,γ)	None		LOK Expt	Prog	WASH – 1071 109	Nov 66	Grench+ TO OS190M,TBD	
(n,γ)	–		IEA Comp	Rept	IEA – INF – 10 6	Aug 68	Atalla. TABLES OF HL,SIG AND GAMM – E	
(n,γ)	5.0+3	1.0+5	AUA ExTh	Rept	AAEC/E – 198	May 69	Musgrove.S+P+D WAVE SIGMAS CALC,TBL	
(n,γ)	3.0+4		AUA Theo	Rept	AAEC/E – 211	Nov 70	Musgrove. SIGMA GIVEN AND CFD OTHER	
(n,γ)	1.0+3	1.0+7	BOL Eval	Data	BENZI – DFN 824.	May 72	40 PNTS	+
(n,γ)	2.0+0	3.0+5	LRL Expt	Prog	ERDA – NDC – 2 75	May 75	Browne+TBC.NDG.	
(n,γ)	Maxwl		BNL Expt	Jour	PL/B 58 39	Aug 75	Macphail+SYSTEMATICS ROTATIONAL BAND	
				Prog	ERDA – NDC – 2 46	May 75	– +POP.ROTA.BANDS.DEF.NUC.GRPH	
(n,γ)	2.0 – 2	3.0+3	IJI Expt	Jour	YF 22 674	Oct 75	Vertebny+ TOF,SIG AT 2200 M/SEC,TBL	
				Jour	SNP 22 348	Oct 75	. ENGL OF YF 22,674	
Spect (n,γ)	6.0+0	6.1+1	ANL Expt	Jour	PR 124 1142	Nov 61	Jackson+ FAST CHOPPER LOW E GAMMAS.	
Spect (n,γ)	Maxwl		BNL Expt	Rept	BNL – 11426	May 67	Kane+ GE(LI) 46GAMMAS 0.161 – 7.79MEV	
Spect (n,γ)	Pile		ANL Expt	Conf	69Studsvik 601	Aug 69	Smither+ NO DATA GVN,OKS STATMOD	
Spect (n,γ)	6.7+0		BNL Expt	Conf	69Studsvik 105	Aug 69	Kane+ GRPH GAM – SPEC,NEUT – MONOCHROMTR	
Spect (n,γ)	Maxwl		FRK Expt	Conf	69Studsvik 403	Aug 69	Boehm+ SPEC GRPH+TBL,DECAY SCH GVN	
Spect (n,γ)	Maxwl		KFK Expt	Conf	72Budapest 70	Aug 72	Heck+ RATIOS FOR DEPOPULATION ,TBL	
				Rept	KFK – 1604	Mar 72	– + ANTI – COMPT GE – LI SPECT,LVL SC	
Spect (n,γ)	2.6+0	3.0+2	NRL Expt	Jour	NP/A 237 45	Jan 75	Namenson+ GAM – SPEC GRAPH,FOR RESPARS	
Spect (n,γ)	Maxwl	1.0+1	BNL Expt	Jour	PL/B 58 39	Aug 75	Macphail+PROPERTIES OF ROT BAND,GRPH	
Spect (n,γ)	5.0+0	3.5+2	LRL Expt	Jour	PR/C 14 965	Aug 76	Stolovy+LINAC,TOF.G INT GRPHS.	
(n,2n)	Fiss		CRC Eval	Rept	CRC – 1003	Dec 60	Roy+,ESTIMATED AVG SIG=49.0MB	
(n,2n)	1.5+7		DEB Eval	Jour	REA 11 1 153	Mar 73	Boedy+ RECOMM.VALUE FROM N – Z SYSTEM.	
(n,2n)	1.5+7		KFI Expt	Jour	KFKI – 73 – 68	Dec 73	Jeki.NEW FIT,CALC SIG CFD OTHERS,TBL	
(n,p)	Fiss		CRC Eval	Rept	CRC – 1003	Dec 60	Roy+,ESTIMATED AVG SIG=0.005MB	
(n,α)	Fiss		CRC Eval	Rept	CRC – 1003	Dec 60	Roy+,ESTIMATED AVG SIG=0.11MB	
(n,α)	Maxwl		CCP Expt	Jour	YF 1 252	Feb 65	Andreev.IONIZ – CHAMBER,SIG=M.01MB	+
				Jour	SNP 1 177	Aug 65	TRANSLATN.*	
(n,α)	6.8+0	2.2+1	DUB Expt	Jour	JINR – P3 – 7376	Sep 73	Balabanov+ RES – E,ALF – WID,SPIN,TABLE	
Reson Params	None		ANL Expt	Jour	NP 21 66	Nov 60	Carpenter+D=4.3EV+ – 20PC WG=85+ – 10MV	
Reson Params	6.7+0	6.1+1	ANL Expt	Jour	PR 124 1142	Nov 61	Jackson+ FAST CHOPPER E0, WT, WN	+
	6.7+0	6.1+1		Data	EXFOR11992.012	Jun 76	. 13 RES, E0	
Reson Params	– 2		IFU Expt	Conf	67Kharkov	Feb 67	Vertebnyj+. TBP IN IZV	
Reson Params	+0	+3	IFU Expt	Conf	67Kharkov 171	Feb 67	Vertebny.PARAMETERS FROM TRNSMISSN	
Reson Params	4.0 – 3	3.0+2	IFU Expt	Prog	YFI – 4 34	May 67	Vertebnyj+.,TBL GIVEN	
				Rept	INDC – 187E	67	. ENGL OF YFI – 4 34	
Reson Params		1.0+6	AUA Theo	Jour	AUJ 20 477	Oct 67	Cook. TBL OF AVG LVL SPACING D,L=0,1	

76 Osmium 189

Quantity	Energy (ev) Min	Max	Lab	Type	Documentation Ref Vol Page	Date	Author, Comments	Data
Reson Params	6.7+0	2.8+1	IFU	Expt	Rept IF- 69 4	69	Vertebny+ TBL RESON-E CFD OTHER	+
	6.7+0	2.8+1			Data EXFOR40094.	Mar 72	2G*N-WIDTH 1RES., E-RES FOR 5 RES.	
Reson Params	6.7+0	6.1+1	ANL	Expt	Jour PR/C 1 1501	Apr 70	Wetzel+J FROM CAPT MEAS. TBL GVN.	+
	6.7+0	6.1+1			Data EXFOR10080.008	Feb 76	. 12 PTS. J, E0.	
Reson Params	–		AUA	Theo	Rept AAEC/E-211	Nov 70	Musgrove. CALCULTD D+GAM WIDTH GIVEN	
Reson Params	6.7+0	2.2+1	CJD	Eval	Rept YK- 7	71	Zakharova+ SURVEY+SYSTEMATICS,GW,TBL	
					Rept INDC(CCP)-27	Nov 72	.ENGLISH TRANSLATION OF YK-7 /71	
Reson Params	None		DUB	Theo	Jour YF 13 240	Feb 71	Malecki+G-WID,THEO CFD EXPT.TBL,GRPH	
					Jour SNP 13 133	Aug 71	– + ENGL OF YF 13 240.	
Reson Params	6.7+0	6.3+1	IJI	Expt	Conf 71Moscow	Feb 71	Vertebny+.ABST,TOF,WN,WG,D,D-CORREL	
Reson Params	6.8+0	3.2+2	IJI	Expt	Prog YFI-12 70	72	Vertebny+ ABSTRACT,TBL RES-E+N-WID,D	
					Prog INDC(CCP)-30	Sep 72	.PAGE 60,ENGLISH OF YFI-12 70	
Reson Params	2.2+1	2.7+2	IFU	Expt	Prog YFI-12 70	Jun 72	Vertebny+	+
	6.8+0	3.2+2			Data EXFOR40127.	Jan 73	35 RES, RED N-WIDTH, D	
Reson Params	+0	+3	DUB	Expt	Conf 73Kiev 2 337	May 73	Karzhavina+ SPIN IDENT,G-MULTIP MTHD	
	6.7+0	6.1+1			Rept JINR-P3-6092	Nov 71	– .GS MULTIPLICITY,SPINS,TBL	
Reson Params	6.8+0	2.2+1	DUB	Expt	Rept JINR-P3-7376	Sep 73	Balabanov+ RES-E,ALF-WID,SPIN,TABLE	
Reson Params	3.9+0	3.0+2	NIR	Expt	Jour AE 37 437	Nov 74	Belanova+ TOF,RES LVLS,TBLS	+
					Jour SJA 37 1204	May 75	.ENGLISH OF AE 37 437	
	7.0+0	2.9+2			Data EXFOR40330.005	Sep 76	.38 EN-RES GVN	
Reson Params	6.6+0	1.9+2	NRL	Expt	Jour NP/A 237 45	Jan 75	Namenson+ (N,G).SPINS+AVG N-WID,TBL	+
	6.6+0	1.9+2			Data EXFOR10466.004	Jan 75	. 38 RES. J.	
Reson Params	6.7+0	2.8+1	IJI	Expt	Jour YF 22 674	Oct 75	Vertebny+ G-WIDS(5RES),D-OBS,D0.TABL	
					Jour SNP 22 348	Oct 75	. ENGL OF YF 22,674	
Reson Params	6.7+0	2.7+1	LRL	Expt	Jour PR/C 14 965	Aug 76	Stolovy+G SPEC,I ASSIGNED.CFD OTH.	+
	6.7+0	2.7+2			Data EXFOR10659.	Nov 77	. 63RES ES.J ASSIGN GVN, D FOR 35 RE	
Strnth Fnctn	None		ANL	Expt	Jour PR 124 1142	Nov 61	Jackson+ FAST CHOPPER.	
Strnth Fnctn	–		AUA	Theo	Rept AAEC/E-211	Nov 70	Musgrove. SMOOTHED S0,S1 AND S2 GIVN	
Strnth Fnctn	2.2+1	2.7+2	IFU	Expt	Prog YFI-12 70	Jun 72	Vertebny+	+
	6.8+0	3.2+2			Data EXFOR40127.028	Jan 73	STRENGTH-FUNCTION, S-WAVE	
Strnth Fnctn	None		AUA	Eval	Rept AAEC/E-277	Mar 73	Musgrove.TBLS EXPTL DATA+BEST VALUES	
Strnth Fnctn	None		IJI	Expt	Jour YF 22 674	Oct 75	Vertebny+ TOF,S0 VAL,TBL	
	6.8+0	3.2+2			Prog YFI-12 70	72	– + ABSTRACT,VALUE GIVEN	
					Prog INDC(CCP)-30	Sep 72	.PAGE 60,ENGLISH OF YFI-12 70	
Lvl Density	+0	+3	IFU	Expt	Conf 67Kharkov 171	Feb 67	Vertebny.TRANSMISSION EXPT	
Lvl Density	-1	+6	MIL	Theo	Jour EN 15 54	Jan 68	Facchini+ LDL PARS FROM LOW EN RES	
Lvl Density	6.7+0	2.8+1	IFU	Expt	Rept IF- 69-4	Apr 69	Vertebny+	+
	6.7+0	2.8+1			Data EXFOR40094.009	Mar 72	AVERAGE LEVEL SPACING	

76 Osmium 190

Quantity	Energy (ev) Min	Max	Lab	Type	Documentation Ref Vol Page	Date	Author, Comments	Data
Elastic	2.5-2		ANL	Expt	Conf 63ANL 393	Oct 63	Mueller+ COHER SCAT SIG BY NEUT DIFF	+
	2.5-2				Data EXFOR11508.	Jun 76	. 2 PTS, COH, COH AMP	
Elastic	2.0-2	3.0+3	IJI	Expt	Jour YF 22 674	Oct 75	Vertebny+ TRANS,TOF.AVG SCATSIG,TABL	
					Jour SNP 22 348	Oct 75	. ENGL OF YF 22,674	
Tot Inelastc	Pile		FEI	Comp	Rept ICD-4 57	67	Sluchevskaja.SELECTIV COMPIL ,TABLE	
Tot Inelastc	Fast		MUN	Expt	Rept NUK 10 181	Oct 67	Koehler+H2O MODER REACT. .1MEVCUTOFF	
					Rept FRM-81	Aug 66	– + SUPERSEDED.	
Diff Inelast	2.5-2		UCB	Expt	Rept NYO-10175	Dec 64	Arino+ACT.TBLS.GRAPHS.PRODUCT HL.	+
	2.5-2				Data EXFOR11817.018	Jun 76	. 1 PT.	
Diff Inelast	2.8+6		DEB	Expt	Jour AK 10 112	Jul 68	Bornemisza+ UPPER LIMIT OF SIGMA GVN	+
	2.8+6				Data EXFOR30338.009	Aug 76	TO ISOM. UPPER LIMIT. 1 PNT	
Diff Inelast	+6		LOK	Expt	Prog WASH-1136 107	Sep 69	Grench+,TO ISOMER,TBC,XOKS H-F,NDG	
Diff Inelast	1.5+7		IBJ	Expt	Jour APPB 2 553	71	Rurarz+ ACTIV,GELI+NAI,CFD THEO,TABL	+
	1.5+7				Data EXFOR30156.	Feb 72	SIGMA TO METASTABLE STATE GIVEN	
Thermal Scat	7.0-2	3.0-1	IJI	Expt	Prog YFI-12 66	72	Vertebny+ ABST,TOT SCAT SIG GIVEN	
					Prog INDC(CCP)-30	Sep 72	.PAGE 57,ENGLISH OF YFI-12 66	
Res Int Abs	5.0-1		GHT	Expt	Jour RCA 9 61	Aug 68	KIM+. OVER 1/V. CALC FROM SIG(NG).	+
	5.0-1				Data EXFOR20656.011	Jun 76	1PNT.CAPTURE.	
Res Int Abs	5.0-1		GHT	Expt	Jour JRC 20 695	74	Van Der Linden+ BY (N,G).CFD OTH,TBL	+
	5.5-1				Conf 73Paris 2 241	Mar 73	– + ACT,REL THR+GOLD,TBL	
	5.5-1				Data EXFOR20645.	Jul 76	2PTS.CAPTURE.	
(n,γ)	Pile		ANL	Expt	Jour PR 72 888	Nov 47	Seren+.ACT METHOD.PILE IRRAD.METAL.	+
	Pile				Data EXFOR11447.119	Jun 76	. 1 PT.	

76 Osmium 190

Quantity	Energy (ev) Min	Max	Lab	Type	Documentation Ref Vol Page	Date	Author, Comments	Data
(n,γ)	2.4+4		ORL	Expt	Jour PR 107 504	Jul 57	Macklin+.SB – BE NS,886+ – 130MB,ACT	+
				Conf	58Geneva 671	Sep 58	.SUPERSEDED	
	2.4+4			Data	EXFOR11399.048	Jun 76	. 1 PT.	
(n,γ)	2.0+5		ORL	Expt	Jour PR 114 1619	Jun 59	Lyon+.ABS GAMMA COUNT 200+ – 30MB ACT	+
	2.0+5			Data	EXFOR11407.031	Jun 76	. 1 PT. SIGMA.	
(n,γ)	Maxwl		MUA	Expt	Jour NP 20 183	Oct 60	Hans+ 2ISOM PROD,SIGMA GIVEN	+
	Maxwl			Data	EXFOR31246.013	Sep 72	.SIG GVN	
(n,γ)	Maxwl		MUA	ExTh	Jour NP 41 372	Mar 63	Mangal+ (N,G)M SIGMA GVN,TH CFD EXPT	
(n,γ)	–2		IAN	Expt	Rept IAN – E – 1	Sep 64	Carrillo+,ISOMERIC RATIO 191M TO 191	+
	Maxwl			Data	EXFOR30216.002	Nov 72	ISOM RATIO 191M TO 191 GROUND	
(n,γ)	Maxwl		ANL	Comp	Jour NP 60 241	Nov 64	Bishop+EXP AND TH ISOMER RATIOS CFD	
(n,γ)	Pile		GHT	Expt	Jour RCA 9 61	Aug 68	Kim+. ACT, CD FILTER REL AU	+
	2.5–2			Data	EXFOR20656.010	Jun 76	1PNT.SIGMA.	
(n,γ)	–		IEA	Comp	Rept IEA – INF – 10 6	Aug 68	Atalla. TABLES OF HL,SIG AND GAMM – E	
(n,γ)	3.0+4		AUA	Theo	Rept AAEC/E – 211	Nov 70	Musgrove. SIGMA GIVEN AND CFD OTHER	
(n,γ)	7.0–2	3.0–1	IJI	Expt	Prog YFI – 12 66	72	Vertebny+ ABST,SIG GIVEN	
					Prog INDC(CCP) – 30	Sep 72	.PAGE 57,ENGLISH OF YFI – 12 66	
(n,γ)	1.0+3	1.0+7	BOL	Eval	Data BENZI – DFN 825.	May 72	40 PNTS	+
	1.0+3	1.0+7			Data BENZI – DFN 844.	May 72	40 PNTS	
(n,γ)	2.5+4		AUW	Expt	Jour NC/A 18 48	Nov 73	Sidappa+ ACTIV SIG,CFD.TABLE	
(n,γ)	2.5–2		BRK	Theo	Jour NP/A 237 3 419	Jan 75	Nardi+ ISOM RATIO,MTE – CARLO,CFD XPT	
(n,γ)	Maxwl		BNL	Expt	Prog ERDA – NDC – 2 50	May 75	Macphail+G – DECAY OF 0+ AND 2+ STATES	
(n,γ)	2.0+0	3.0+5	LRL	Expt	Prog ERDA – NDC – 2 75	May 75	Browne+TBC.NDG	
(n,γ)	2.0–2	3.0+3	IJI	Expt	Jour YF 22 674	Oct 75	Vertebny+ TOF,SIG AT 2200 M/SEC,TBL	
					Jour SNP 22 348	Oct 75	. ENGL OF YF 22,674	
Spect (n,γ)	Pile		IFL	Expt	Conf 73Tbilisi 114	Feb 73	Nejburg+ ABST,GE – LI,TABLE ES + INTENS	
Spect (n,γ)	Pile		HEI	Expt	Jour ZP 259 61	Mar 73	Loeweneck+ K – CONVER. COEF OF OS – 191	
Inelastic γ	2.5+4		ORL	Expt	Conf 58Geneva 15 68	Sep 58	Macklin.PPR671,SIGMA+G – ENERGY GVN	
Inelastic γ	1.5+7		IBJ	Expt	Prog INR – 1318 43	Apr 71	Rurarz+ OS190M, GAMMA SPECTRUM	
(n,2n)	Fiss		CRC	Eval	Rept CRC – 1003	Dec 60	Roy+,ESTIMATED AVG SIG = 7.0MB	
(n,2n)	1.5+7		KFI	Theo	Rept KFKI – 73 – 68	Dec 73	Jeki.NEW FIT,CALC SIG CFD OTHERS,TBL	
(n,p)	Fiss		CRC	Eval	Rept CRC – 1003	Dec 60	Roy+,ESTIMATED AVG SIG = 0.003MB	
(n,p)	1.4+7		DEB	Expt	Jour NP/A 91 222	Jan 67	Csikai+ ACTIV, VALUE AT 14.7MEV,TBL	+
					Jour MFF 16 123	Feb 68	SEE ALSO *THESIS HUNG	
	1.5+7				Data EXFOR30115.011	Jan 71	SIGMA AT 14.7 MEV FROM NP A91 222	
(n,p)	1.5+7		DEB	Comp	Jour REA 7 4 93	Dec 69	Csikai+ SIG+HL COMPILTN,N – ACTIV – ANAL	
(n,p)	1.4+7	1.5+7	JYV	Eval	Rept JU – RR – 3/1970	Jun 70	Leppaemaeki+ TABLE OF EVAL AVG SIG	
(n,p)	1.5+7		IBJ	Expt	Jour APPB 3 195	72	Rurarz+ SIG TO GND STATE OF RE – 190	+
					Prog INR – 1318 43	Apr 71	– + SIG TO GND OF RE – 190 = 1.95MB	
	1.5+7				Data EXFOR30157.	Feb 72	SIG TO GND OF RE – 190 GIVEN	
(n,p)	1.4+7	1.5+7	KAZ	Theo	Jour YF 18 705	Oct 73	Levkovsky.AVERAGED SIG,CALC,TBL	
					Jour SNP 18 361	Apr 74	. ENGLISH OF YF 18,705	
(n,α)	1.4+7		ALD	Expt	Jour PPS 73 215	Feb 59	Coleman+. ACTIVATION	
(n,α)	Fiss		CRC	Eval	Rept CRC – 1003	Dec 60	Roy+,ESTIMATED AVG SIG = 0.0013MB	
(n,α)	1.4+7		CIS	Theo	Jour NP 51 460	Feb 64	Facchini+STATMOD SIG XPT/CALC130 – 170	
(n,α)	Maxwl		CCP	Expt	Jour YF 1 252	Feb 65	Andreev.IONIZ – CHAMBER,SIG = M.02MB	+
					Jour SNP 1 177	Aug 65	TRANSLATN.*	
(n,α)	1.5+7		AMS	Expt	Jour PHY 31 1091	Jul 65	Nagel+.REL FE56(NP)	
					Diss NAGEL	Dec 66	– .D – T NS.ACT.FINAL	
	1.5+7				Data EXFOR20198.024	May 74	1PNT.SIGMA.	
(n,α)	1.4+7	1.5+7	NAP	Comp	Rept INFN/BE – 67 – 11	Sep 67	Cuzzocrea+ AVERAGED CHOSEN DATA.	
(n,α)	1.5+7		DEB	Comp	Jour REA 7 4 93	Dec 69	Csikai+ SIG+HL COMPILTN,N – ACTIV – ANAL	
(n,α)	1.4+7	1.5+7	JYV	Eval	Rept JU – RR – 3/1970	Jun 70	Leppaemaeki+ TABLE OF EVAL AVG SIG	
(n,α)	1.4+7	1.5+7	KAZ	Theo	Jour YF 18 705	Oct 73	Levkovsky.AVERAGED SIG,CALC,TBL	
					Jour SNP 18 361	Apr 74	. ENGLISH OF YF 18,705	
Reson Params	–		DUB	Expt	Conf 68DUBSY 283	Jul 68	Shapiro.AVERAGE ALFA WIDTH,LVL SPAC.	
Reson Params	–		AUA	Theo	Rept AAEC/E – 211	Nov 70	Musgrove. CALCULTD D+GAM WIDTH GIVEN	
Reson Params	1.1+1	3.2+2	IJI	Expt	Conf 71Moscow	Feb 71	Vertebny+.ABST,TOF,WN,WG,D,D – CORREL	
Reson Params	1.1+1	5.6+2	IJI	Expt	Prog YFI – 12 70	72	Vertebny+ ABSTRACT,TBL RES – E+N – WID,D	
					Prog INDC(CCP) – 30	Sep 72	.PAGE 60,ENGLISH OF YFI – 12 70	
Reson Params	2.2+1	2.7+2	IFU	Expt	Prog YFI – 12 70	Jun 72	Vertebny+	+
	1.1+1	5.6+2			Data EXFOR40127.	Jan 73	6 RES, RED N – WIDTH, D	
Reson Params	3.9+0	3.0+2	NIR	Expt	Jour AE 37 437	Nov 74	Belanova+ TOF,RES LVLS,TBLS	+
					Jour SJA 37 1204	May 75	.ENGLISH OF AE 37 437	
	1.1+1	1.6+2			Data EXFOR40330.006	Sep 76	. 5 EN – RES GVN	
Reson Params	2.0–2	3.0+3	IJI	Expt	Jour YF 22 674	Oct 75	Vertebny+ TRANS,TOF,AUG D – OBS,D0.TBL	
					Jour SNP 22 348	Oct 75	. ENGL OF YF 22,674	
Strnth Fnctn	–		AUA	Theo	Rept AAEC/E – 211	Nov 70	Musgrove. SMOOTHED S0,S1 AND S2 GIVN	

76 Osmium 190

Quantity	Energy (ev) Min	Max	Lab	Type	Documentation Ref Vol Page	Author, Comments Date	Data
Lvl Density	+0	+3	IFU	Expt Conf	67Kharkov 171	Feb 67 Vertebny.TRANSMISSION EXPT	
Lvl Density	None		CCP	Theo Jour	YF 11 1028	May 70 Rubchenya. DENSITY+A+TEMP GIVEN,GRPH	
				Jour	SNP 11 571	Nov 70 . ENGL OF YF 11 571.	
Lvl Density	None		MUN	Theo Jour	NP/A 217 269	Dec 73 Dilg+ A,DELTA. BACK SHIFTED FERMIGAS	
Lvl Density	None		ROC	Theo Jour	NP/A 223 577	May 74 Huizenga+ EXP CFD MICROSC TH SPH NUC	

76 Osmium 191

Quantity	Energy (ev) Min	Max	Lab	Type	Documentation Ref Vol Page	Author, Comments Date	Data
Reson Params	–		AUA	Theo Rept	AAEC/E – 211	Nov 70 Musgrove. CALCULTD D+GAM WIDTH GIVEN	
Strnth Fnctn	–		AUA	Theo Rept	AAEC/E – 211	Nov 70 Musgrove. SMOOTHED S0,S1 AND S2 GIVN	

76 Osmium 192

Quantity	Energy (ev) Min	Max	Lab	Type	Documentation Ref Vol Page	Author, Comments Date	Data
Elastic	2.5 – 2		ANL	Expt Conf	63ANL 393	Oct 63 Mueller+ COHER SCAT SIG BY NEUT DIFF	+
	2.5 – 2			Data	EXFOR 11508.	Jun 76 . 2 PTS, COH, COH AMP	
Elastic	2.0 – 2	3.0 + 3	IJI	Expt Jour	YF 22 674	Oct 75 Vertebny+ TRANS,TOF.AVG SCATSIG,TABL	
				Jour	SNP 22 348	Oct 75 . ENGL OF YF 22,674	
Diff Inelast	1.4 + 7		LRL	Theo Rept	UCRL – 50181	Feb 67 Lutz+.CALC ANG DIST FOR FIRST 2+ LVL	
Thermal Scat	7.0 – 2	3.0 – 1	IJI	Expt Prog	YFI – 12 66	72 Vertebny+ ABST,TOT SCAT SIG GIVEN	
				Prog	INDC(CCP) – 30	Sep 72 .PAGE 57,ENGLISH OF YFI – 12 66	
Res Int Abs	5.0 – 1		GHT	Expt Jour	RCA 9 61	Aug 68 KIM +. OVER 1/V. CALC FROM SIG(NG).	+
	5.0 – 1			Data	EXFOR 20656.013	Jun 76 1PNT.CAPTURE.	
Res Int Abs	5.0 – 1		GHT	Expt Jour	JRC 20 695	74 Van Der Linden+ BY (N,G).CFD OTH,TBL	+
	5.5 – 1			Conf	73Paris 2 241	Mar 73 – + ACT,REL THR+GOLD,TBL	
	5.5 – 1			Data	EXFOR 20645.052	Jul 76 1PNT.CAPTURE.	
(n,γ)	Pile		ANL	Expt Jour	PR 72 888	Nov 47 Seren+.ACT METHOD.PILE IRRAD.METAL.	+
	Pile			Data	EXFOR 11447.118	Jun 76 . 1 PT.	
(n,γ)	3.0 + 6		DEB	Expt Jour	JNE 21 797	Oct 67 Peto+ACTIV,SIGMA REL TO AU(N,G)	+
	3.0 + 6			Data	EXFOR 30031.027	Aug 70 SINGLE VALUE	
(n,γ)	2.0 + 5	3.2 + 6	FEI	Expt Prog	YFI – 5 13	Oct 67 Tolstikov+ TABLE SIGMA AT 19 ES	
	1.0 + 5	2.6 + 6		Jour	AE 23 566	Dec 67 – + GRPH SIG(E),CFD OPTMOD	
	2.0 + 5	3.0 + 6		Rept	BNL – TR – 240	Oct 68 . ENGLISH OF AE 23 576	
	1.0 + 5	2.6 + 6		Jour	EAF 23 6 114	Jun 68 . FRENCH OF AE 23 566	
				Jour	SJA 23 1347	Jun 68 . ENGL OF AE 23 566	
	2.0 + 5	3.2 + 6		Rept	INDC – 232E	67 . ENGL OF YFI – 5 13	
(n,γ)	1.1 + 4	3.5 + 5	FEI	Expt Prog	YFI – 6 11	68 Dovbenko+. TABLE. TO BE PUBL IN AE	+
	1.0 + 4	4.0 + 5		Jour	SJA 27 1185	Nov 69 .ENGL. TRANSL. OF AE 27 406	
				Jour	EAF 27 41	Nov 69 .FRENCH TRANSL. OF AE 27 406	
				Jour	AE 27 406	Nov 69 Dovbenko+ SIG(E)GRPH,CFD OTHR+OPTMOD	
	1.1 + 4	3.5 + 5		Prog	INDC(CCP) – 3U	Mar 69 .ENGLISH TRANSL OF YFI – 6 11 /68	
	1.1 + 4	3.4 + 5		Data	EXFOR 40331.008	Jan 76 SIG(E) AT 8 ES	
(n,γ)	1.0 + 4	3.2 + 6	FEI	Expt Prog	YFI – 6 5	68 Kolesov+. CURVE	
				Prog	INDC(CCP) – 3U	Mar 69 .ENGLISH TRANSL OF YFI – 6 5 /68	
(n,γ)	Pile		GHT	Expt Jour	RCA 9 61	Aug 68 Kim+. ACT, CD FILTER REL AU	+
	2.5 – 2			Data	EXFOR 20656.012	Jun 76 1PNT.SIGMA.	
(n,γ)	–		IEA	Comp Rept	IEA – INF – 10 6	Aug 68 Atalla. TABLES OF HL,SIG AND GAMM – E	
(n,γ)	Maxwl		AAU	Expt Jour	NP/A 125 305	Feb 69 MAACK BISGARD+ ISOM RATIO,BETA CONV.	
(n,γ)	3.0 + 4		AUA	Theo Rept	AAEC/E – 211	Nov 70 Musgrove. SIGMA GIVEN AND CFD OTHER	
(n,γ)	7.0 – 2	3.0 – 1	IJI	Expt Jour	YFI – 12 66	72 Vertebny+ ABST,SIG GIVEN	
				Prog	INDC(CCP) – 30	Sep 72 .PAGE 57,ENGLISH OF YFI – 12 66	
(n,γ)	1.0 + 3	1.0 + 7	BOL	Eval Data	BENZI – DFN 826.	May 72 40 PNTS	+
(n,γ)	2.5 + 4		AUW	Expt Jour	JP/A 5 877	Jun 72 Siddappa+ ACT. S,P CS GIVN.	+
				ExTh Conf	70Madurai 2 29	Dec 70 Sriramachandra Murty+.S+P WAVE SIGMA	
	2.5 + 4			Expt Data	EXFOR 30248.014	Jun 73 SIGMA CAPTURE VALUE	
(n,γ)	1.5 + 7		DEB	Expt Prog	INDC(SEC) – 50	Jan 76 Kovacs+ P108,ABST. SIGMA GIVEN	+
	1.5 + 7			Data	EXFOR 30290.002	May 75 1 POINT	
(n,γ)	2.0 + 0	3.0 + 5	LRL	Expt Prog	ERDA – NDC – 2 74	May 75 Browne+TBC.NDG.	
(n,γ)	2.0 – 2	3.0 + 3	IJI	Expt Jour	YF 22 674	Oct 75 Vertebny+ TOF,SIG AT 2200 M/SEC,TBL	
				Jour	SNP 22 348	Oct 75 . ENGL OF YF 22,674	
Spect (n,γ)	Pile		IPS	Expt Jour	AF 3 47	Aug 51 Kondaiah. B,B – G COINC.HL.DEC SCHEME	
				Jour	AF 4 81	Aug 52 SEE ALSO *	
Spect (n,γ)	Pile		LND	Expt Jour	AF 3 533	Aug 52 Johansson. NAI(TL). E. K – CONV COEFF.	
Spect (n,γ)	–		AUW	Expt Prog	BARC – 401 25	69 Rao+ ABSTR,ANG – CORRELATN 193OS DECAY	
Spect (n,γ)	Pile		IFL	Expt Rept	JINR – 7094 139	Jun 73 Nejburg+ ABST,GE – LI,TABLE ES+INTENS	

76 Osmium 192

Quantity	Energy (ev) Min	Max	Lab	Type	Documentation Ref Vol Page	Author, Comments Date	Data
(n,2n)	Fiss		CRC	Eval Rept	CRC – 1003	Dec 60 Roy+,ESTIMATED AVG SIG=9.3MB	
(n,2n)	1.5+7		RBZ	Expt Jour	JIN 27 2471	Dec 65 Kolar+ ISOMERIC SIG RATIO,CFD THEORY	+
	1.5+7			Data	EXFOR31077.005	May 78 ISOMERIC RATIO AT 14.6 MEV	
(n,2n)	1.2+7	1.8+7	HAM	Expt Jour	NP/A 157 481	Nov 70 Bormann+ ACT. CFD STATIST TH.	
(n,2n)	1.5+7		IRK	Expt Jour	NP/A 158 77	Dec 70 Winiwarter.ACT.GE(LI).GRNDST,METAST.	+
	1.4+7	1.5+7		ExTh Jour	APA 33 285	Jul 71 – + ISOMERIC RATIO	
	1.5+7			Expt Data	EXFOR20071.	Sep 71 4PTS.SIG.	
(n,2n)	1.4+7		GIT	Expt Jour	NP/A 180 157	Jan 72 Hankla+ ACT,GE(LI),MIXED POWDER.	+
				Abst	DA/B 32 293	Nov 71 – . ACT METHOD, CFD THEORY.	
	1.4+7			Data	EXFOR10244.002	Jun 74 . 1 PT. SIGMA.	
(n,2n)	1.5+7		DEB	Eval Rept	REA 11 1 153	Mar 73 Boedy. COMPILATION+RECOMM.VALUE,TBL	
(n,2n)	1.5+7		KFI	Theo Rept	KFKI – 73 – 68	Dec 73 Jeki.NEW FIT,CALC SIG CFD OTHERS,TBL	
(n,2n)	1.5+7		TAT	Theo Jour	JP/A 7 1457	Aug 74 Kondaiah. CALC ON STAT MODEL	
(n,p)	Fiss		CRC	Eval Rept	CRC – 1003	Dec 60 Roy+,ESTIMATED AVG SIG=0.0009MB	
(n,p)	1.4+7		SAH	Comp Jour	NP 60 273	Nov 64 Chatterjee.MEAN OF EXPT CFD SHELLMOD	
(n,p)	None		KFI	Comp Jour	JRC 7 365	Jun 71 Nagy+ GAMMA+BETA ES AND HALF–L GIVEN	
(n,p)	1.4+7		ITJ	Expt Jour	JRC 14 201	73 Janczyszyn+ BY ACTIV.SIG CFD OTH,TBL	+
	1.4+7			Data	EXFOR30322.018	Feb 76 1 PNT.	
(n,α)	Fiss		CRC	Eval Rept	CRC – 1003	Dec 60 Roy+,ESTIMATED AVG SIG=BELO 0.0001MB	
(n,α)	Maxwl		CCP	Expt Jour	YF 1 252	Feb 65 Andreev.IONIZ – CHAMBER,SIG=M.01MB	+
				Jour	SNP 1 177	Aug 65 TRANSLATN.*	
(n,α)	1.5+7		DEB	Expt Prog	INDC(SEC) – 50	Jan 76 Kovacs+ P108,ABST. SIGMA GIVEN	+
	1.5+7			Data	EXFOR30290.008	May 75 1 POINT	
Reson Params	1.0+5	2.6+6	FEI	Expt Jour	AE 23 566	Dec 67 Tolstikov+ MEAN WG,OPTMOD OKS EXPT	
				Jour	EAF 23 6 114	Jun 68 . FRENCH OF AE 23 566	
				Jour	SJA 23 1347	Jun 68 . ENGL OF AE 23 566	
Reson Params	–		AUA	Theo Rept	AAEC/E – 211	Nov 70 Musgrove. CALCULTD D+GAM WIDTH GIVEN	
Reson Params	2.0+1	7.2+2	IJI	Expt Conf	71Moscow	Feb 71 Vertebny+ .ABST,TOF,WN,WG,D,D – CORREL	
Reson Params	2.0+1	7.3+2	IJI	Expt Prog	YFI – 12 70	72 Vertebny+ ABSTRACT,TBL RES – E+N – WID,D	
				Prog	INDC(CCP) – 30	Sep 72 .PAGE 60,ENGLISH OF YFI – 12 70	
Reson Params	2.2+1	2.7+2	IFU	Expt Prog	YFI – 12 70	Jun 72 Vertebny+	+
	2.0+1	7.2+2		Data	EXFOR40127.005	Jan 73 6 RES, RED N – WIDTH, D	
Reson Params	3.9+0	3.0+2	NIR	Expt Jour	AE 37 437	Nov 74 Belanova+ TOF,RES LVLS,TBLS	+
				Jour	SJA 37 1204	May 75 .ENGLISH OF AE 37 437	
	2.0+1	1.3+2		Data	EXFOR40330.007	Sep 76 . 7 EN – RES GVN	
Reson Params	2.0–2	3.0+3	IJI	Expt Jour	YF 22 674	Oct 75 Vertebny+ TRANS,TOF,AUG D – OBS,D0.TBL	
				Jour	SNP 22 348	Oct 75 . ENGL OF YF 22,674	
Strnth Fnctn	–		AUA	Theo Rept	AAEC/E – 211	Nov 70 Musgrove. SMOOTHED S0,S1 AND S2 GIVN	
Strnth Fnctn	2.2+1	2.7+2	IFU	Expt Prog	YFI – 12 70	Jun 72 Vertebny+	+
	2.0+1	7.2+2		Data	EXFOR40127.026	Jan 73 STRENGTH – FUNCTION, S	
Strnth Fnctn	None		IJI	Expt Jour	YF 22 674	Oct 75 Vertebny+ TOF,S0 VAL,TBL,D,WG	
	2.0+1	7.3+2		Prog	YFI – 12 70	72 – + ABSTRACT,VALUE GIVEN	
				Prog	INDC(CCP) – 30	Sep 72 .PAGE 60,ENGLISH OF YFI – 12 70	

76 Osmium 193

Quantity	Energy (ev) Min	Max	Lab	Type	Documentation Ref Vol Page	Author, Comments Date	Data
Reson Params	–		AUA	Theo Rept	AAEC/E – 211	Nov 70 Musgrove. CALCULTD D+GAM WIDTH GIVEN	
Strnth Fnctn	–		AUA	Theo Rept	AAEC/E – 211	Nov 70 Musgrove. SMOOTHED S0,S1 AND S2 GIVN	

76 Osmium 194

Quantity	Energy (ev) Min	Max	Lab	Type	Documentation Ref Vol Page	Author, Comments Date	Data
Reson Params	–		AUA	Theo Rept	AAEC/E – 211	Nov 70 Musgrove. CALCULTD D+GAM WIDTH GIVEN	
Strnth Fnctn	–		AUA	Theo Rept	AAEC/E – 211	Nov 70 Musgrove. SMOOTHED S0,S1 AND S2 GIVN	

77 Iridium

Quantity	Energy (ev) Min	Max	Lab	Type	Documentation Ref Vol Page	Author, Comments Date	Data
Total	Maxwl		COL Expt	Jour	PR 48 265	Aug 35 Dunning+ IONCH,TRANS,RA - BE/PARAFIN N	
Total	5.3-1	+3	COL Expt	Jour	PR 71 65	Jan 47 Rainwater+ CURV.TOF. 11MUSECR SLN.	+
	2.4-2	6.3+0		Data	EXFOR11685.005	Jun 76 . 52 PTS.	
Total	5.0-2	1.6+0	ORL Expt	Jour	PR 72 109	Jul 47 Sawyer+ CURV. BENT CRYSTAL SPECTR.	
Total	2.5+0	1.0+4	CCP Expt	Conf	55Geneva 4 22	Aug 55 Vladimirski+.P641,CURVE,CHOPPER,TOF	+
Total	4.5-1	6.2+0	BNL Expt	Jour	PR 100 1414	Dec 55 Landon.ALSO 1.30EV SIG ZERO AT 3RES	+
	4.6-1	1.5+0		Data	EXFOR12178.002	Jun 76 . 127 PTS.	
Total	3.0+0	5.0+2	AMS Expt	Jour	PHY 22 1131	Nov 56 Radkevich+ABSTRACT,FAST CHOPPER. NDG	
Total	4.5+0	1.3+1	CCP Expt	Jour	AE 1 5 55	Nov 56 Radkevich+.TOF TRANSM. CS CURVE	
				Jour	JNE 5 92	Jul 57 TRANSLATN.*	
				Jour	SJA 1 5 727	56 TRANSLATN.*	
Total	2.0-3	2.4-2	SAC Expt	Priv	HUBERT	Mar 58 Hubert. = 1 DATA INDEX LINES	+
Total	2.5-3	4.8-3	HAN Expt	Prog	HW - 55879 3	Apr 58 Seppi+ CRYSTSPEC.SIG REL .1EV.TABLE	+
	2.5-3	1.0-1		Data	EXFOR11791.003	Jun 76 . 11 PTS, SIG	
Total	2.0-2	1.0+4	MTR Expt	Prog	WASH - 1013	Nov 58 Brice.NDG TBC ES FOR 27RES LT 2KEV.	
Total	1.0-2	1.8+1	WUR Expt	Rept	EIR - 123	Jul 67 Brunner+.TOF TRANS.CFD OTHERS EXPTS	+
				Conf	66Paris 1 61	Oct 66 - + PPR 20. PRELIM DATA.	
Total	2.0+4	7.0+6	FEI Expt	Conf	68Dubna § 17	Jun 68 Filippov+VDG,TRANS.TBL,GRPH.FLUCTUAT	
	2.5+4	7.0+6		Prog	ICD-3 102	Oct 66 .GRAPH CFD REFS.VDG	
	2.0+4	7.0+6		Rept	INDC(CCP) - 16	Jul 71 .PAGE 67.ENGLISH TRANSL OF 68DUBNA	
	2.5+4	7.0+6		Prog	INDSWG - 152E	66 .PAGE 102. ENGLISH TRANSL OF ICD-3	
Total	3.0+6	1.5+7	KFK Revw	Conf	70Helsinki 2 219	Jun 70 Cierjacks.113. SIG(E) GRPH CFD OPTMD	
Total	2.5+6	1.5+7	BNW Expt	Jour	PR/C 3 576	Feb 71 Foster+ TRANS.CURVS.CFD OTHERS+TH	+
				Jour	PRL 22 139	Jan 69 .SUPERSEDED	
				Jour	NIM 36 1	Sep 65 .EXPT DETAILS	
	2.3+6	1.5+7		Data	EXFOR10047.084	Aug 73 . 243 PTS.	
Total	5.5-1	7.5-1	IEA ExTh	Rept	IEA - 255	Dec 71 Fulfaro.TE - FILTR,TRANS,CALC CFD EXPT	+
	5.6-1	7.5-1		Expt	Data EXFOR30215.002	Nov 72 TOTSIG AT 20 ES,PRIV COMMUNICATION	
	1.3+7	1.5+7	DEB Eval	Rept	IAEA - 153 173	73 Boedy+ MOST PROBABLE VAL OF SIG,TBL	
				Jour	AHP 30 115	Oct 71 Angeli+ AVG SIG,CFD CALC.TBLS.GRAPH	
Total	None		DKE Expt	Prog	USNDC - 11 226	Jun 74 Pineo+NDG.TBP IN AP	+
	1.2+5	6.4+5		Data	EXFOR10523.016	Jan 76 . 27 PTS.	
Total	3.0+4	6.5+5	DKE Expt	Abst	BAP 7 23	Jan 62 Tabony+	+
	3.0+4	6.5+5		Data	EXFOR11936.008	Jun 76 . 102 PTS.	
Elastic	Maxwl		ANL Expt	Jour	JAP 30 1323	Sep 59 Sidhu+ 1.6B COH SCAT BY NEUT DIFFR	
				Conf	58Geneva 14 212	Sep 58 - + TBL OF SIGMA - COHERENT	
Elastic	2.5-2		ANL Expt	Conf	63ANL 393	Oct 63 Mueller+ COHER SCAT SIG BY NEUT DIFF	+
	2.5-2			Data	EXFOR11528.	Jun 76 . 1 PT. EACH, COH.SCT.+COH.AMP.	
Potntl Scat	3.0+3	6.5+6	DKE ExTh	Jour	PL 13 70	Nov 64 Seth+0,1PHASE FRM SIG TOT AV 3 - 650KV	
Potntl Scat	7.0+0	7.0+0	MOL Expt	Jour	NP/A 97 657	May 67 Poortmans+ VALUE BETWEEN RESONANCES.	+
Potntl Scat	None		DKE Expt	Abst	DA/B 28 3834	Mar 68 Divadeenam.TRNS.EFFECTIVE RADIUS	
Thermal Scat	5.7-1	7.6-1	IEA Expt	Rept	IEA - 150	Oct 67 Fulfaro+DOPPLER BROADNG RES - PEAK,CVS	
Thermal Scat	1.0-4	1.0+3	MUN Revw	Jour	EEN 80 1	77 Koester. SCAT LENGTH,FREE SIG	
Scattering	Fast		FEI Expt	Jour	AE 18 409	Apr 65 Gusejnov+ ANGL DIST,TH(N,F)DETECTOR	
				Jour	JNE 20 700	Aug 66 . ENGL OF AE 18 409	
				Jour	SJA 18 526	Apr 65 . ENGL OF AE 18 409	
				Jour	EAF 18 4 134	Apr 65 . FRENCH OF AE 18 409	
Absorption	Pile		ANL Expt	Jour	PR 80 342	Nov 50 Harris+.PILE OSC.REL TO BORON.APPROX	+
	Pile			Data	EXFOR11528.044	Jun 76 . 1 PT.	
Absorption	2.0-2	2.4-1	CUW Theo	Rept	CWR - 400 - 1	Sep 57 Roberts.MAXWELL - BOLTZMANN AVGD SIGS.	
Res Int Abs	-		CCP Expt	Jour	AE 3 507	Dec 57 Klimentov+.EPI CD REACTIVITY REL LI	+
				Jour	JNE 9 20	Jun 59 TRANSLATN.*	
				Jour	SJA 3 1387	57 TRANSLATN.*	
Res Int Abs	5.0-1		MTR Expt	Rept	IN - 1195	May 68 Scoville+	+
	5.0-1			Data	EXFOR11820.021	Jun 76 . 1 PT.	
(n,γ)	Maxwl		ANL Expt	Jour	PR 76 531	Aug 49 Kubitscheck+ YIELD CFD SIG.G - M COINC	
(n,γ)	Maxwl		ORL Expt	Jour	PR 83 643	Aug 51 Pomerance. LOCAL OSC REL AU ABS 95 B	+
	Maxwl			Data	EXFOR11047.069	Jun 76 . 1 PT.	
(n,γ)	Maxwl		ETH Expt	Jour	ZP 156 293	Oct 59 Knoepfel+ PAIR SP,SUM INTENS 8GAMMAS	
(n,γ)	Pile		CRC Eval	Rept	CRRP - 960	Nov 60 Westcott.G,S FACTORS EFFECTIVE CAPT.	
(n,γ)	2.0+2	8.0+3	ORL Expt	Conf	61Saclay 203	Sep 61 Block+.LIQUID SCINTILLATOR	+
	2.0+2	1.0+4		Conf	61Vienna 1 95	Aug 61 Neiler. GRAPH, FAST CHOPPER	
	2.0+2	9.5+3		Data	EXFOR11935.025	Jun 76 . 50 PTS.	
(n,γ)	1.0-1	4.0+4	LEB Expt	Jour	ZET 42 988	Apr 62 Popov.PB - SLO - DOWN,GRPH SG(E)CFD OTHR	+
				Jour	JET 15 683	Oct 62 TRANSLATN.*	
(n,γ)	1.0+3	1.0+5	DUB Expt	Jour	ZET 43 2000	Dec 62 Exp.COMP.WITH THEORY	
				Jour	JET 16 1409	Jun 63 TRANSLATN.*	

77 Iridium

Quantity	Energy (ev) Min	Max	Lab	Type	Documentation Ref Vol Page	Author, Comments Date	Data
(n,γ)	3.0+4	6.5+4	ORL Expt	Jour	PR 129 2695	Mar 63 Macklin+ LIQ SCINT,795 AND 450MB	+
	3.0+4	6.5+4		Data	EXFOR11331.030	Jun 76 . 2 PTS.	
(n,γ)	3.0+4	9.0+4	ORL Theo	Jour	RMP 37 166	Jan 65 Macklin+ CALC FOR KT=5T090KEV.MAXW.	
(n,γ)	5.7−1	7.6−1	IEA Expt	Rept	IEA−150	Oct 67 Fulfaro+CRYST−SPEC,RES−CV CORRCTD=TH	
(n,γ)	−		CCP Revw	Jour	AE 29 187	Sep 70 Sukhoruchkin. (D,P GAM) CFD (N,GAM)	
				Jour	SJA 29 896	Sep 70 TRANSLATN.*	
(n,γ)	1.0+3	1.0+6	GA Revw	Conf	70ANL 285	Oct 70 Carlson. STATUS AS STANDARD SIG,CURV	
(n,γ)	3.0+4		AUA Theo	Rept	AAEC/E−211	Nov 70 Musgrove. SIGMA GIVEN AND CFD OTHER	
(n,γ)	1.0+6	1.0+7	CRC Revw	Conf	74Petten 119	Sep 74 Bartholomew+ PHOTON STRF GRPH	
(n,γ)	None		MUNTheo	Diss	GRYNTAKIS	Mar 76 Gryntakis.,CALC.OF WESTCOTTS G−FUNCT	
				Jour	RCA 22 128	Mar 75 − +,EQUIVALENT TO THESIS	
Spect (n,γ)	Maxwl		ANL Expt	Jour	PR 76 531	Aug 49 Kubitschek+ MAX E.G−M COINC+ABSORBR	
Spect (n,γ)	Maxwl		YAL Expt	Jour	PR 114 268	Apr 59 Draper.SC SPECTR,GAM E 0 TO 600 KEV	
Spect (n,γ)	Pile		ETH Expt	Abst	HPA 32 264	Oct 59 Balzer+.PAIR SPEC. GS 4 TO 6MEV	
	Maxwl			Jour	ZP 156 293	Oct 59 Knoepfel+ PAIR SP,12GS 4.5−6MV,E+INT	
				Jour	NC 11 609	Jan 59 Balzer+ LINE ENS ONLY.CRYSTALSPEC.	
Spect (n,γ)	Maxwl		KUR Expt	Jour	NP 16 645	Jun 60 Groshev+ COMPTON SPEC,+THEOR DISCUSS	
Spect (n,γ)	Pile		MHG Expt	Prog	TID−6709 1	Aug 60 Treado+ CRYST SPEC 6 NEW GAMMAS	
Spect (n,γ)	Maxwl		ARF Expt	Prog	ARF−1193−17	Dec 62 Greenwood+ NAI(TL) SPEC, 11 GAMMAS	
Spect (n,γ)	2.5−2		MIT Expt	Rept	MITNE−37	Aug 63 Neill+LOW ENRG GAMMAS.=AFCRL−63−341	
Spect (n,γ)	−2	1.0+4	YAL Expt	Jour	NP 78 576	Apr 66 Wasson+DRAPER G−RAY INT IS FUNC OF E	
Spect (n,γ)	Maxwl		BUC Expt	Jour	RRP 12 561	Jun 67 Dorcioman+,TBL,CRVS,LVL,GE−LI DETECT	+
	Maxwl			Data	EXFOR30208.004	Nov 72 INTENSITIES OF 11 SPECTRUM LINES	
Spect (n,γ)	2.5−2		MIT Comp	Rept	MITNE−85	Jan 69 Rasmussen+TBL G INT.=AFCRL−69−0071	
Spect (n,γ)	2.0+3		MTR Expt	Prog	NCSAC−31 76	May 70 Greenwood+,ANAL TO BE COMPL,NO DATA	
Spect (n,γ)	None		CRC Expt	Prog	AECL−3865 56	Dec 70 Lone+.RESONANCE CAPT, NO DATA GIVEN	
Spect (n,γ)	Pile		FRS Expt	Prog	EANDC(OR)116L	Jun 72 Gasser+ PAIR+ANTICOMPT−SPECTR	
Spect (n,γ)	Maxwl		FRS Expt	Prog	NEANDC(OR)142L	Jun 75 Beer+ LVL IR192,IR194,CRYST SPEC	
				Rept	IPF−SP−006	75 Raemy+ ENRICHED TGTS. TBL EN+INTS.	
Inelastic γ	3.0+6		FEI Expt	Jour	AE 7 268	Sep 59 Androsenko+ GRAPH+TABLE OF G−ENERGS	
				Jour	SJA 7 763	Mar 61 . ENGL OF AE 7 268	
				Jour	KE 3 565	Jun 60 . GERMAN OF AE 7 268	
				Jour	JNEA 12 136	Jun 60 . ENGL OF AE 7 268	
(n,2n)	1.5+7		DEB Eval	Jour	REA 11 1 153	Mar 73 Boedy+ RECOMM.VALUE FROM N−Z SYSTEM.	
(n,α)	1.2+7	2.3+7	FRK Expt	Jour	NP 85 606	Sep 66 Rubbino+ZUBKE ANGLE+ENERGY SPECTRA	
				Abst	BSI 46 43	Nov 65 − +(2B5).E SPEC,ANGDST ANAL.NDG	
Fission	1.4+7		LAS Expt	Jour	PR 75 919	Mar 49 Phillips+ UPPER LIM REL U238.PHOTOPL	
Reson Params	6.4−1	8.7+0	COL Expt	Jour	PR 71 65	Jan 47 Rainwater+ 4LVLS FROM AREA.	+
	6.4−1	2.5+1		Data	EXFOR11685.011	Jun 76 . 5 RES. E0.	
Reson Params	6.3−1	6.0+0	ANL Expt	Jour	PR 71 757	Jun 47 Sturm. CRYSTLSPECT TRNSM.	+
	6.3−1	6.0+0		Data	EXFOR12136.003	Jun 76 . 3 RES,E0,WT,PCS	
Reson Params	6.2−1	1.3+0	ORL Expt	Jour	PR 72 109	Jul 47 Sawyer+ WT FROM BR−WIGN FIT.(UPPLIM)	+
	6.2−1	1.3+0		Data	EXFOR11982.002	Jun 76 . 2 RES. E0. PCS, WT.	
Reson Params	6.5−1	5.4+0	BNL Expt	Jour	PR 100 1414	Dec 55 Landon.ALSO 1.30EV WT WG ISOT ASSGND	+
	6.1+0	9.9+0		Data	EXFOR12178.006	Jun 76 . 3 RES. E0.	
Reson Params	1.0+0		AMS Expt	Jour	PHY 22 1131	Nov 56 Radkevich+ABSTRACT,NDG.GAMMA(N),(G)	
Reson Params	5.4+0	9.4+1	CCP Expt	Jour	AE 1 5 55	Nov 56 Radkevich+. 20 RES, WG=44MV, D PLOT	+
	5.4+0	9.5+1		Jour	JNE 5 92	Jul 57 TRANSLATN.*	
	5.4+0	9.4+1		Jour	SJA 1 5 727	56 TRANSLATN.*	
Reson Params	1.9+1	2.3+2	MTR Expt	Prog	WASH−1013 59	Nov 58 Brice. TRANS. ES ONLY 27 RESON.	
Reson Params	1.9+1	4.2+2	ITE Expt	Prog	INDSWG−120 19	65 Ignat'Ev.TOF,TABLE OF 58 RES ES	
Reson Params	None		TRM Expt	Conf	68Madras 1 288	Feb 68 Ramakrishna+ PPRN36.ABST ONLY,NDG	
Strnth Fnctn	3.0+0	5.0+2	AMS Expt	Jour	PHY 22 1131	Nov 56 Radkevich+ABSTRACT,NDG	
Strnth Fnctn	5.4+0	9.4+1	CCP Expt	Jour	AE 1 5 55	Nov 56 Radkevich+. S0=0.57+−0.14 ISOTOPE AV	
	5.4+0	9.5+1		Jour	JNE 5 92	Jul 57 TRANSLATN.*	
	5.4+0	9.4+1		Jour	SJA 1 5 727	56 TRANSLATN.*	
Strnth Fnctn	+3	+5	MTR Expt	Prog	WASH−1013 59	Nov 58 Brice. NDG FC TBC.	
Strnth Fnctn	+3		BNL Expt	Jour	PRL 1 461	Dec 58 Hughes. FC, 2.2+−0.2	
Strnth Fnctn	1.0+3	1.5+4	DUB Expt	Rept	JINR−P−1010	62 Popov+. P−WAVE STF CFD OTHERS+OPTMDL	
Strnth Fnctn	3.0+3	6.5+5	DKE ExTh	Jour	PL 13 70	Nov 64 Seth+S,P,D STF FRM SIG TOT 3−650KEV	+
	5.0+4	1.5+5		Conf	64Paris 2 916	Jul 64 − +S0,S1,S2 R PRIME/R	
	3.0+3	6.5+5		Data	EXFOR11665.030	Jun 76 . 3 PTS.	
Strnth Fnctn	None		DKE Expt	Prog	USNDC−11 226	Jun 74 Pineo+NDG.TBP IN AP	

77   Iridium   186

Quantity	Energy (ev) Min	Max	Lab	Type	Documentation Ref Vol Page	Author, Comments Date	Data
Reson Params	–		AUA	Theo Rept	AAEC/E-211	Nov 70 Musgrove. CALCULTD D+GAM WIDTH GIVEN	
Strnth Fnctn	–		AUA	Theo Rept	AAEC/E-211	Nov 70 Musgrove. SMOOTHED S0,S1 AND S2 GIVN	

77   Iridium   187

Quantity	Energy (ev) Min	Max	Lab	Type	Documentation Ref Vol Page	Author, Comments Date	Data
Reson Params	–		AUA	Theo Rept	AAEC/E-211	Nov 70 Musgrove. CALCULTD D+GAM WIDTH GIVEN	
Strnth Fnctn	–		AUA	Theo Rept	AAEC/E-211	Nov 70 Musgrove. SMOOTHED S0,S1 AND S2 GIVN	

77   Iridium   188

Quantity	Energy (ev) Min	Max	Lab	Type	Documentation Ref Vol Page	Author, Comments Date	Data
(n,p)	Maxwl		IFU	Theo Rept	ICD-4 20	67 Dadakina+ PENETR COEFF CALC,TABLE	
Reson Params	–		AUA	Theo Rept	AAEC/E-211	Nov 70 Musgrove. CALCULTD D+GAM WIDTH GIVEN	
Strnth Fnctn	–		AUA	Theo Rept	AAEC/E-211	Nov 70 Musgrove. SMOOTHED S0,S1 AND S2 GIVN	

77   Iridium   189

Quantity	Energy (ev) Min	Max	Lab	Type	Documentation Ref Vol Page	Author, Comments Date	Data
(n,p)	Maxwl		IFU	Theo Rept	ICD-4 20	67 Dadakina+ PENETR COEFF CALC,TABLE	
Reson Params	–		AUA	Theo Rept	AAEC/E-211	Nov 70 Musgrove. CALCULTD D+GAM WIDTH GIVEN	
Strnth Fnctn	–		AUA	Theo Rept	AAEC/E-211	Nov 70 Musgrove. SMOOTHED S0,S1 AND S2 GIVN	

77   Iridium   190

Quantity	Energy (ev) Min	Max	Lab	Type	Documentation Ref Vol Page	Author, Comments Date	Data
(n,p)	Maxwl		IFU	Theo Rept	ICD-4 20	67 Dadakina+ PENETR COEFF CALC,TABLE	
Reson Params	–		AUA	Theo Rept	AAEC/E-211	Nov 70 Musgrove. CALCULTD D+GAM WIDTH GIVEN	
Strnth Fnctn	–		AUA	Theo Rept	AAEC/E-211	Nov 70 Musgrove. SMOOTHED S0,S1 AND S2 GIVN	

77   Iridium   191

Quantity	Energy (ev) Min	Max	Lab	Type	Documentation Ref Vol Page	Author, Comments Date	Data
Total	2.5-2	1.0+2	BNL	Expt Abst	BAP 4 271	Apr 59 Bolotin+ RES PAR. STR FCTN TBG.	+
	2.5-2			Data	EXFOR12155.002	Jun 76 . 1 PT.	
Diff Inelast	Fiss		UCB	Expt Rept	NYO-10175	Dec 64 Arino+ACT.TBLS,GRPHS.PRODUCT HL.	+
	Fiss			Data	EXFOR11817.019	Jun 76 . 1 PT, SIG	
Diff Inelast	2.8+6		DEB	Expt Jour	AK 10 112	Jul 68 Bornemisza+ TBL HL+SIGMA FOR IR191M	+
	2.8+6			Data	EXFOR30338.003	Aug 76 TO ISOM. 1 PNT	
Res Int Abs	5.0-1		ANL	Expt Jour	PR 79 11	Jul 50 Harris+ EPI-CD,REL THERMAL ACT. B-W	+
	5.0-1			Data	EXFOR11343.023	Jun 76 . 1 PT. RIG.	
Res Int Abs	None		ORL	Revw Conf	55Geneva 5 96	Aug 55 Macklin+ TABLE,EXPT CFD THEORY.	
Res Int Abs	5.5-1		MOL	Theo Rept	BLG-421	Sep 67 Damle+,EVAL ACT R.I=3590+-400B,GND	
Res Int Abs	5.5-1		MOL	Eval Rept	BLG-421	Sep 67 Damle+,EVAL ACT R.I=3590+-400B,GND	
Res Int Abs	5.0-1		CPO	Expt Jour	JIN 30 349	Feb 68 Sims+ 4800+-240 REL TO CO59=69.9 B	+
	5.0-1			Data	EXFOR11658.	Jun 76 . 2 PTS, RI FOR GND AND META	
Res Int Abs	5.5-1	1.0+2	MUN	Expt Jour	NUK 12 197	Aug 69 Koehler+RES INTEG+SELF-SHIELDG CORRC	+
	6.2-1			Data	EXFOR20655.	Jun 76 2PTS.CAPTURE.	
Res Int Abs	5.5-1		GHT	Expt Jour	JRC 20 695	74 Van Der Linden+ BY (N,G).CFD OTH,TBL	+
	5.5-1			Conf	73Paris 2 241	Mar 73 - + ACT,REL THR+GOLD,TBL	
	5.5-1			Data	EXFOR20645.053	Jul 76 1PNT.CAPTURE.	
(n,γ)	Maxwl		JAP	Expt Jour	SCP 38 167	Jan 41 Sinma+.LI+D.RELATIVE SIG MEASUREMENT	
(n,γ)	Pile		ANL	Expt Jour	PR 72 888	Nov 47 Seren+.ACT METHOD.TO1.5MIN,70D ISOM.	+
	Pile			Data	EXFOR11447.	Jun 76 . 2 PTS, SIG FOR GND AND META	
(n,γ)	None		ANL	Theo Jour	PR 120 1305	Nov 60 Huizenga+ ISOMER RATIO,TH CFD EXPT	
(n,γ)	Maxwl		MTR	Expt Jour	PR 129 769	Jan 63 Keisch. ACT,ISM RATIO FOR 3 SPECT	+
	Maxwl			Data	EXFOR11748.	Jun 76 . 3 PTS, SIG FOR GND, META, RATIO	
(n,γ)	Maxwl		ANL	Comp Jour	NP 60 241	Nov 64 Bishop+EXP AND TH ISOMER RATIOS CFD	
(n,γ)	Maxwl		UCB	Expt Rept	NYO-10175	Dec 64 Arino+ACT.TBLS,GRPHS.PRODUCT HL.	+
	Maxwl			Data	EXFOR11817.	Jun 76 . 2 PTS, SIG FOR GND AND META	
(n,γ)	1.0-2	1.0+2	MOL	Eval Rept	BLG-421	66 Damle+. CURVE RECOMMENDED SIGS	

77 Iridium 191

Quantity	Energy (ev) Min	Max	Lab	Type	Documentation Ref Vol Page	Date	Author, Comments	Data
(n,γ)	Maxwl		FEI	Theo	Jour YF 6 1174	Dec 67	Malyshev.STATMOD ISOM SIG,HIGH+LOW L	
					Jour SNP 6 853	Jun 68	.TRANSLATION	
(n,γ)	Maxwl	Pile	MOL	Eval	Rept BLG – 421	68	Damle+ TBP THRSIG RESINTG GIVEN	
(n,γ)	Maxwl	Pile	MOL	Eval	Rept BLG – 421	68	Damle+ TBP THRSIG RESINTG GIVEN	
(n,γ)	Maxwl		CPO	Expt	Jour JIN 30 349	Feb 68	Sims+ 1120+ – 25 REL TO CO59=37.5 B	+
	Maxwl			Data	EXFOR11658.	Jun 76	. 2 PTS, SIG FOR GND AND META	
(n,γ)	–		IEA	Comp	Rept IEA – INF – 10 6	Aug 68	Atalla. TABLES OF HL,SIG AND GAMM – E	
(n,γ)	2.0+3		MTR	Expt	Prog WASH – 1127 72	Apr 69	Schuman+ FILTERED BEAM,RELATVE CURVS	
(n,γ)	5.0+3	1.0+5	AUA	ExTh	Rept AAEC/E – 198	May 69	Musgrove.S+P+D WAVE SIGMAS CALC,TBL	+
(n,γ)	2.5+4		MTR	Expt	Prog IN – 1407 31	Jun 70	Tromp.ACT,FE FILTRD BEAM,VALUE GIVEN	
(n,γ)	3.0+4		AUA	Theo	Rept AAEC/E – 211	Nov 70	Musgrove. SIGMA GIVEN AND CFD OTHER	
(n,γ)	2.5+4		AUW	ExTh	Conf 70Madurai 2 29	Dec 70	Sriramachandra Murty+.S+P WAVE SIGMA	+
	2.5+4			Expt	Data EXFOR30248.013	Jun 73	SIGMA CAPTURE TO THE GND STATE	
(n,γ)	None		KFI	Comp	Jour JRC 7 365	Jun 71	Nagy+ GAMMA – E AND HALF – LIFE GIVEN	
(n,γ)	1.0+3	1.0+7	BOL	Eval	Data BENZI – DFN 827.	May 72	40 PNTS	+
(n,γ)	8.3+5		II	Expt	Conf 73Kiev 4 312	May 73	Lakosi+ FOTO – N,REL AU197(N,G	+
	+6				Data EXFOR30268.016	Jul 74	1 POINT	
(n,γ)	None		MUN	Theo	Diss GRYNTAKIS	Mar 76	Gryntakis.,CALC.OF WESTCOTTS G – FUNCT	
					Jour RCA 22 128	Mar 75	– +,EQUIVALENT TO THESIS	
(n,γ)	1.2+5	2.8+6	LRL	Expt	Jour NSE 59 381	Apr 76	Lindner+U235NF.TBL.GRPHS.CFD ENDF.	+
	1.2+5	2.8+6			Data EXFOR10221.	Aug 75	. 16 PTS. SIGMA.	
Spect (n,γ)	Maxwl		KUR	Expt	Conf 58Geneva 15 138	Sep 58	Groshev+ PPR2029.CURV,COMPTON – SPEC	
Spect (n,γ)	Pile		UPP	Expt	Jour AF 17 125	Apr 60	Bergvall.DECAY GS E+INT.CRVD CRYSTAL	
Spect (n,γ)	Pile		VBT	Expt	Jour AF 22 485	Nov 62	Hamilton+. E+INT OF PT192 GAMMAS	
Spect (n,γ)	Pile		UPP	Expt	Jour NP 40 329	Jan 63	Marklund+.E DETERM. NO INTENS MEAS.	
Spect (n,γ)	Pile		FRK	Expt	Conf 69Studsvik 411	Aug 69	Krueger+THR+EPITH CAPT CFD,DECAY SCH	
Spect (n,γ)	Maxwl		KFI	Revw	Jour YF 10 907	Nov 69	Kecskemeti+ AVG GAM – MULTIPLICITY,TBL	
					Jour SNP 10 524	May 70	TRANSLATN.*	
Spect (n,γ)	Pile		CAI	Expt	Jour ZN/A 26 1109	Jul 71	Bashandy. PART OF G – SPEC FROM IR – 192	
Spect (n,γ)	Pile		KFK	Expt	Jour NP/A 169 363	Jul 71	Krueger+ GE(LI) – NAI(TL). 153 LINES.	
Spect (n,γ)	None		KUR	Expt	Conf 72Kiev 1 157	Jan 72	Bondarenko+ ABSTR,NDG.G+CONV – E SPEC	
Spect (n,γ)	Pile		FRS	Expt	Prog EANDC(OR)116L	Jun 72	Gasser+ PAIR+ANTICOMPT – SPECTR	
Spect (n,γ)	1.0+7		WWA	Theo	Jour NP/A 189 545	Jul 72	Brzosko+ CMPD NUCL DECAY.PARTIAL WG	
Spect (n,γ)	Maxwl		IFL	Expt	Book PROKOFJEV	73	. TBL GAM – ES + INTS(80 – 1015KEV), GE – LI	
Spect (n,γ)	+0	+2	IFB	Theo	Conf 73Pacif.Gr 2 1071	Mar 73	Rudak+ GRAPH STATMOD – CALC CFD G – SPEC	
Spect (n,γ)	None		GEL	Expt	Prog NEANDC(E)162 3	Feb 75	Coceva+LINAC TOF	
Spect (n,γ)	Pile		FRS	Expt	Jour HPA 49 4 645	Aug 76	Raemy+ LVL SCHEME IR192	
	Maxwl				Rept IPF – SP – 006	75	– + ENRICHED TGTS. TBL EN+INTS.	
Inelastic γ	2.8+6		REN	Expt	Jour ARI 18 279	May 67	Broadhead+ ACTIV 4.9SEC ISOMER 510MB	+
	2.8+6				Data EXFOR11850.011	Jun 76	. 1 PT.	
Inelastic γ	None		KFI	Comp	Jour JRC 7 365	Jun 71	Nagy+ GAM+XRAY+ELECTR ES, HALF – LIFE	
(n,2n)	Fiss		CRC	Eval	Rept CRC – 1003	Dec 60	Roy+,ESTIMATED AVG SIG=9.0MB	
(n,2n)	1.5+7		MUA	Expt	Jour NP 28 560	Dec 61	Khurana+ ACTIV,CFD STATMOD	+
	1.5+7				Data EXFOR31247.022	Mar 73	.SIG GVN	
(n,2n)	1.4+7		HAM	Comp	Jour NP 65 257	Mar 65	Bormann. 1EXPT VALS.CFD SHELL EFFECT	
(n,2n)	1.5+7		MUN	Expt	Jour NP/A 118 9	Sep 68	Dilg+ ACTIV.REL AL(N,A).TO GROUNDST.	+
	1.5+7				Data EXFOR20802.016	Dec 78	1PNT.SIGMA.	
(n,2n)	1.5+7		DEB	Expt	Jour REA 7 4 93	Dec 69	Csikai+ SIG+HL COMPILTN,N – ACTIV – ANAL	
(n,2n)	1.4+7	1.5+7	JYV	Eval	Jour JU – RR – 3/1970	Jun 70	Leppaemaeki+ TABLE OF EVAL AVG SIG	
(n,2n)	1.4+7		BRL	Expt	Rept BRL – 1491	Aug 70	Temperley. ACT, GND AND META	+
	1.4+7				Data EXFOR10214.	Oct 73	. 2 PTS. SIGMA. GND AND META.	
(n,2n)	1.2+7	1.8+7	HAM	expt	Jour NP/A 157 481	Nov 70	Bormann+ ACT. CFD STATIST TH.	
(n,2n)	+7		KFI	Theo	Rept KFKI – 71 – 8	Feb 71	Jeki. CALCULATED CFD EXPTL SIG VALUE	
(n,2n)	1.5+7		JUL	Expt	Jour NP/A 185 614	May 72	Qaim. ACT,GE(LI). CFD TH+OTHR.+ISOMR	+
	1.5+7				Data EXFOR20536.	Apr 76	4PTS.SIGMA.	
(n,2n)	1.4+7		HFA	Expt	Jour PR/C 6 315	Jul 72	Maor Zellermayer+ ISOM RATIO CFD TH	+
	1.4+7				Data EXFOR30182.	Jun 73	ISOMERIC RATIOS, 11+,7+ AND GND	
(n,2n)	1.5+7		DEB	Eval	Jour REA 11 1 153	Mar 73	Boedy. COMPILATION+RECOMM.VALUE,TBL	+
					Rept IAEA – 153 173	73	– . RECOMM. VALUE ONLY	
(n,2n)	1.5+7		TAT	Theo	Jour JP/A 7 1457	Aug 74	Kondaiah. CALC ON STAT MODEL	
(n,2n)	8.6+6	2.4+7	LAS	Expt	Jour PR/C 12 451	Aug 75	Bayhurst+TBL,GRPH	+
	8.6+6	2.4+7			Data EXFOR10536.	Apr 76	. 11 PTS.	
(n,xn) x>2	1.6+7	2.8+7	LAS	Expt	Jour PR/C 12 451	Aug 75	Bayhurst+ N3N,N4N.TBL GRPH CFD CALC.	+
	1.6+7	2.8+7			Data EXFOR10536.	Apr 76	11 PTS. N3N, 1 PT.N4N.	
(n,p)	Fiss		CRC	Eval	Rept CRC – 1003	Dec 60	Roy+,ESTIMATED AVG SIG=0.02MB	
(n,p)	Maxwl		BNL	Expt	Jour NP 41 604	Apr 63	Harbottle+	+
	Maxwl				Data EXFOR12166.002	Jun 76	. 1 PT, SIG	
(n,p)	Maxwl		IFU	Theo	Rept ICD – 4 20	67	Dadakina+ PENETR COEFF CALC,TABLE	

77 Iridium 191

Quantity	Energy (ev) Min	Max	Lab	Type	Documentation Ref Vol Page	Author, Comments Date	Data
(n,α)	1.4+7		ALD Expt	Jour	PPS 73 215	Feb 59 Coleman+. ACTIVATION	+
(n,α)	Fiss		CRC Eval	Rept	CRC – 1003	Dec 60 Roy+,ESTIMATED AVG SIG=0.0009MB	
(n,α)	1.4+7		CIS Theo	Jour	NP 51 460	Feb 64 Facchini+STATMOD SIG XPT/CALC=33–43	
(n,α)	1.5+7		DEB Comp	Jour	REA 7 4 93	Dec 69 Csikai+ SIG+HL COMPILTN,N–ACTIV–ANAL	
(n,α)	1.4+7	1.5+7	JYV Eval	Rept	JU–RR–3/1970	Jun 70 Leppaemaeki+ TABLE OF EVAL AVG SIG	
(n,α)	1.4+7	1.5+7	KAZ Theo	Jour	YF 18 705	Oct 73 Levkovsky.AVERAGED SIG,CALC,TBL	
				Jour	SNP 18 361	Apr 74 . ENGLISH OF YF 18,705	
Reson Params	6.5–1	5.4+0	BNL Expt	Jour	PR 100 1414	55 Landon.	+
	6.5–1	5.4+0		Data	EXFOR12178.004	Jun 76 . 2 RES, E0,WT,WN,WG,PCS	
Reson Params	5.4+0	6.5+1	HAR Expt	Jour	NP 5 294	Jan 58 Bowey+. 9 RESONANCE ES GVN. LINAC	+
Reson Params	9.1+0	1.0+2	BNL Expt	Abst	BAP 4 271	Apr 59 Bolotin+	+
	9.1+0	1.0+2		Data	EXFOR12155.004	Jun 76 . 19 RES, E0,WN0	
Reson Params	5.4+0	5.1+1	BNL Expt	Jour	NP 42 676	Apr 63 Bolotin+.WG,WN GIVEN FOR 4 RESONANCE	+
	5.4+0	5.1+1		Data	EXFOR11922.008	Jun 76 . 4 RES E0,WN0,WG	
Reson Params	6.5–1	1.0+2	MOL Eval	Rept	BLG–421	66 Damle+. RECOMMENDED PARAMS 23RESON	
Reson Params	5.4+0	5.1+1	CRC Expt	Jour	CJP 44 399	Feb 66 Bhat.5EV SPIN 2.30 AND 51EV SPINS 1	+
	5.4+0	5.1+1		Data	EXFOR11374.002	Jun 76 . 3 RES, J	
Reson Params	6.5–1	9.1+0	NRL Expt	Jour	PR 155 1330	Mar 67 Stolovy.3RES,ALL J=2. TRNSM POLRZ NS	+
	6.5–1	9.1+0		Data	EXFOR11995.006	Jun 76 . 3 RES, E0,J	
Reson Params	6.5–1	9.1+0	MOL Expt	Jour	NP/A 97 657	May 67 Poortmans+ FROM RESON SCATTERING XPT	+
	6.5–1	9.1+0		Data	EXFOR20213.	May 74 8PTS.WT,J,TOT(RES),WN/WT.	
Reson Params	6.5–1		WUR Expt	Jour	EIR–123	Jul 67 Brunner+.SHAPE ANAL CFD OTHER EXPTS	+
				Conf	66Paris 1 61	Oct 66 – + PPR 20. PRELIM DATA.	
Reson Params		1.0+6	AUA Theo	Jour	AUJ 20 477	Oct 67 Cook. TBL OF AVG LVL SPACING D,L=0,1	
Reson Params	6.5–1	5.1+1	KFK Eval	Rept	KFK–718	Apr 68 Schmidt+ RESOLVED+AVG RES PARAM(S,P)	
Reson Params	6.5–1	5.1+1	KFK Comp	Rept	KFK–1233	Jul 70 Mueller. ES,WN,WG,G OF 15 RESON	
Reson Params	–		AUA Theo	Rept	AAEC/E–211	Nov 70 Musgrove. CALCULTD D+GAM WIDTH GIVEN	
Reson Params	6.5–1	5.1+1	CJD Eval	Rept	YK–7	71 Zakharova+ SURVEY+SYSTEMATICS,GW,TBL	
				Comp Rept	INDSWG–64 19	64 . TABL OF 3RES FROM 3 REFERENCES	
				Eval Rept	INDC(CCP)–27	Nov 72 .ENGLISH TRANSLATION OF YK–7 /71	
Reson Params	None		DUB Theo	Jour	YF 13 240	Feb 71 Malecki+G–WID,THEO CFD EXPT.TBL,GRPH	
				Jour	SNP 13 133	Aug 71 – + ENGL OF YF 13 240.	
Reson Params	1.9+1	2.3+2	DUB Expt	Rept	RCN–203 269	Dec 73 Lason+ G * WN,D	+
				Rept	JINR–P3–6545	Jun 72 Lason'+ G*N–WIDTH,55 RES,TOF,TBL	
	1.9+1	2.3+2		Data	EXFOR40119.	Nov 72 E–RES FOR 55RES, N–WIDTH AT 39RES,D	
Strnth Fnctn	None		BNL Expt	Prog	WASH–1021 10	Jun 59 Hughes+	
Strnth Fnctn	+0	+2	MOL Eval	Rept	BLG–421	66 Damle+. RECOMMENDED S0=2.0+–0.8 GND	
Strnth Fnctn	–		AUA Theo	Rept	AAEC/E–211	Nov 70 Musgrove. SMOOTHED S0,S1 AND S2 GIVN	
Strnth Fnctn	None		AUA Eval	Rept	AAEC/E–277	Mar 73 Musgrove.TBLS EXPTL DATA+BEST VALUES	
Lvl Density	–		FEI Eval	Rept	FEI–36	66 Kapchigashev+.TBL OF RELATD QUANTTYS	+
		5.0+4		Jour	YF 4 686	Sep 66 .TABLE.SHORT VERSION OF FEI–36	
				Prog	YFI–3 3	66 .ABSTRACT.TABLE LDL+NUCL.EXCIT.E	
		5.0+4		Jour	SNP 4 486	67 .ENGLISH OF YF 4.FROM(N,GAMMA).TABLE	
				Prog	INDC–E–140 3	66 .ENGLISH TRANSL OF YFI–3	
Lvl Density	2.4+1	3.9+2	DUB Expt	Rept	JINR–P3–6545	Jul 72 Lason'+	+
	0.0+0	1.8+2		Data	EXFOR40119.005	Nov 72 LEVEL–DENSITY PARAMETER	

77 Iridium 192

Quantity	Energy (ev) Min	Max	Lab	Type	Documentation Ref Vol Page	Author, Comments Date	Data
(n,γ)	Pile		CAL Expt	Jour	PR 105 974	Feb 57 Boehm+,ACT 1500B	
(n,γ)	1.0+3	1.0+7	BOL Eval	Data	BENZI–DFN 845.	May 72 40 PNTS	+
(n,p)	Maxwl		IFU Theo	Jour	ICD–4 20	67 Dadakina+ PENETR COEFF CALC,TABLE	
Reson Params	–		AUA Theo	Rept	AAEC/E–211	Nov 70 Musgrove. CALCULTD D+GAM WIDTH GIVEN	
Strnth Fnctn	–		AUA Theo	Rept	AAEC/E–211	Nov 70 Musgrove. SMOOTHED S0,S1 AND S2 GIVN	
Lvl Density	+6		MIL Theo	Jour	EN 15 1 54	Jan 68 Facchini+ LDL PARS FROM LOW EN RES	
Lvl Density	None		MUN Theo	Jour	NP/A 217 269	Dec 73 Dilg+ A,DELTA. BACK SHIFTED FERMIGAS	
Lvl Density	None		COP Theo	Jour	NP/A 222 493	Apr 74 Dossing+COLL ROTAT.SPAC. ACCUR ESTIM	
Lvl Density	None		ROC Theo	Jour	NP/A 223 577	May 74 Huizenga+ EXP CFD MICROSC TH SPH NUC	

77 Iridium 193

Quantity	Energy (ev) Min	Max	Lab	Type	Documentation Ref Vol Page	Author, Comments Date	Data
Total	2.5–2	1.0+2	BNL Expt	Abst	BAP 4 271	Apr 59 Bolotin+ RES PAR. STR FCTN TBG.	+
	2.5–2			Data	EXFOR12155.003	Jun 76 . 1 PT.	

77 Iridium 193

Quantity	Energy (ev) Min	Max	Lab	Type	Documentation Ref Vol Page	Author, Comments Date	Data
Tot Inelastc	7.6+6	1.5+7	LAS	Expt Jour	PR/C 12 451	Aug 75 Bayhurst+ TBL,GRPH	+
	7.6+6	1.5+7		Data	EXFOR10536.051	Apr 76 . 4 PTS.	
Res Int Abs	5.0-1		ANL	Expt Jour	PR 79 11	Jul 50 Harris+ EPI-CD,REL THERMAL ACT. B-W	+
	5.0-1			Data	EXFOR11343.034	Jun 76 . 1 PT. RIG.	
Res Int Abs	None		ORL	Revw Conf	55Geneva 5 96	Aug 55 Macklin+.TABLE,EXPT CFD THEORY,P833	
Res Int Abs	5.5-1		MOL	Theo Rept	BLG-421	Sep 67 Damle+,EVAL ACT R.I=1370+-150B,GND	
Res Int Abs	5.5-1		MOL	Eval Rept	BLG-421	Sep 67 Damle+,EVAL ACT R.I=1370+-150B,GND	
Res Int Abs	5.0-1		GHT	Expt Jour	JRC 20 695	74 Van Der Linden+ BY (N,G).CFD OTH,TBL	+
	5.5-1			Conf	73Paris 2 241	Mar 73 - + ACT,REL THR+GOLD,TBL	
	5.5-1			Data	EXFOR20645.054	Jul 76 1PNT.CAPTURE.	
(n,γ)	2.0+4	7.0+5	OXF	Expt Jour	PRSA 170 513	Apr 39 Griffiths.RA-BE PHOTONEUT ACTIVATION	
(n,γ)	Maxwl		JAP	Expt Jour	SCP 38 167	Jan 41 Sinma+.LI+D.RELATIVE SIG MEASUREMENT	
(n,γ)	Pile		ANL	Expt Jour	PR 72 888	Nov 47 Seren+.ACT METHOD.THR IRRAD.METAL.	+
	Pile			Data	EXFOR11447.122	Jun 76 . 1 PT.	
(n,γ)	Fast		LAS	Expt Jour	NSE 8 608	Dec 60 Byers. GODIVA JEZEBEL ACT CS GIVEN	
(n,γ)	Maxwl		MTR	Expt Jour	PR 129 769	Jan 63 Keisch.ACT,97+-10B,SPECTRUM NOT GIVN	+
	Maxwl			Data	EXFOR11748.024	Jun 76 . 1 PT.	
(n,γ)	Maxwl		UCB	Expt Rept	NYO-10175	Dec 64 Arino+ACT.TBLS,GRPHS.PRODUCT HL.	+
	Maxwl			Data	EXFOR11817.022	Jun 76 . 1 PT.	
(n,γ)	1.0-2	1.0+2	MOL	Eval Rept	BLG-421	66 Damle+. CURVE RECOMMENDED SIGS	
(n,γ)	1.7+5	3.1+6	FEI	Expt Conf	66Paris 1 473	Oct 66 PPR103,TOLSTIKOV+.CURVE CFD U235,VDG	+
(n,γ)	1.5+5	3.2+6	FEI	Expt Jour	AE 23 151	Aug 67 Dovbenko+.GRAPH,ACTIVATION METHOD	+
				Jour	EAF 23 88	Aug 67 . FRENCH TRANSL OF AE 23 151 8/67	
	1.0+4	3.1+6		Data	EXFOR40004.004	Jul 70 SIGMA AT 21 ENERGIES	
(n,γ)	3.0+6		DEB	Expt Jour	JNE 21 797	Oct 67 Peto+ACTIV,SIGMA REL TO P-31(N,P)	+
	3.0+6			Data	EXFOR30031.028	Aug 70 SINGLE VALUE	
(n,γ)	1.0+4	3.8+5	FEI	Expt Prog	YFI-6 11	68 Dovbenko+. TABLE. TO BE PUBL IN AE	+
	1.0+4	4.0+5		Jour	AE 27 406	Nov 69 - + SIG(E)GRPH,CFD OTHR+OPTMOD	
				Jour	EAF 27 41	Nov 69 .FRENCH TRANSL. OF AE 27 406	
				Jour	SJA 27 1185	Nov 69 .ENGL. TRANSL. OF AE 27 406	
				Prog	INDC(CCP)-3U	Mar 69 .ENGLISH TRANSL OF YFI-6 11 /68	
	1.0+4	3.8+5		Data	EXFOR40331.010	Jan 76 SIG(E) AT 7 ES	
(n,γ)	Maxwl	Pile	MOL	Eval Rept	BLG-421	68 Damle+ TBP THRSIG RESINTG GIVEN	
(n,γ)	Maxwl	Pile	MOL	Eval Rept	BLG-421	68 Damle+ TBP THRSIG RESINTG GIVEN	
(n,γ)	-		IEA	Comp Rept	IEA-INF-10 6	Aug 68 Atalla. TABLES OF HL,SIG AND GAMM-E	
(n,γ)	2.4+4		MUA	Theo Jour	IJP 42 567	Sep 68 Chaubey+ METHD OF BOOTH,VAL CFD XPT	+
				Expt Jour	PR 152 1055	Dec 66 - + SIG TO GND REL I-127,TABLE	
	2.4+4			Data	EXFOR30079.038	Dec 70 SIGMA FOR 19. H HALF-LIFE	
(n,γ)	2.0+3		MTR	Expt Prog	WASH-1127 72	Apr 69 Schuman+ FILTERED BEAM,RELATVE CURVS	
(n,γ)	5.0+3	1.0+5	AUA	ExTh Rept	AAEC/E-198	May 69 Musgrove.S+P+D WAVE SIGMAS CALC,TBL	+
(n,γ)	2.5+4		MTR	Expt Prog	IN-1407 31	Jun 70 Tromp.ACT,FE FILTRD BEAM,VALUE GIVEN	
(n,γ)	3.0+4		AUA	Theo Rept	AAEC/E-211	Nov 70 Musgrove. SIGMA GIVEN AND CFD OTHER	
(n,γ)	2.4+4		MUA	Theo Jour	IJP 46 114	Mar 72 Chaubey+ P-WAVE STRENGTH FUNCT,TABLE	
(n,γ)	1.0+3	1.0+7	BOL	Eval Data	BENZI-DFN 828.	May 72 40 PNTS	+
(n,γ)	1.5+7		KOS	Expt Rept	IAEA-R-596	May 72 Csikai. FOR SYSTEMATICS,IN PROGR,NDG	
(n,γ)	8.3+5		II	Expt Conf	73Kiev 4 312	May 73 Lakosi+ FOTO-N,REL AU197(N,G	+
	+6			Data	EXFOR30268.017	Jul 74 1 POINT	
(n,γ)	None		MUN	Theo Diss	GRYNTAKIS	Mar 75 Gryntakis.,CALC.OF WESTCOTTS G-FUNCT	
				Jour	RCA 22 128	Mar 75 - +,EQUIVALENT TO THESIS	
(n,γ)	1.2+5	2.8+6	LRL	Expt Jour	NSE 59 381	Apr 76 Lindner+U235NF.TBL.GRPHS.CFD ENDF.	+
	1.2+5	2.8+6		Data	EXFOR10221.	Aug 75 . 16 PTS. SIGMA.	
Spect (n,γ)	Pile		UPP	Expt Jour	NP 19 461	Nov 60 Kern+. 32 TRANSITIONS TABLE	
Spect (n,γ)	Pile		UPP	Expt Jour	NP 40 329	Jan 65 Marklund+.E DETERM. NO INTENS MEAS.	
Spect (n,γ)	Maxwl		ROS	Expt Jour	ZFK-150 81	Jun 68 Heiser+ RE-EXPT GE-LI,ACT SIG CALC	
Spect (n,γ)	Pile		FRK	Expt Conf	69Studsvik 411	Aug 69 Krueger+ 4.9-6.1KEV GAM-E GRPH,PAIR	
Spect (n,γ)	Pile		CAI	Expt Jour	ZN/A 26 1109	Jul 71 Bashandy. PART OF G-SPEC FROM IR-194	
Spect (n,γ)	Pile		KFK	Expt Jour	NP/A 169 363	Jul 71 Krueger+ GE(LI)-NAI(TL). 141 LINES.	
Spect (n,γ)	Maxwl		IFL	Expt Book	PROKOFJEV	73 . TBL GAM-ES+INTS(80-835KEV),LVL SCH	
Spect (n,γ)	None		GEL	Expt Prog	NEANDC(E)162 3	Feb 75 Coceva+LINAC TOF	
Spect (n,γ)	Pile		FRS	Expt Rept	HPA 49 4 645	Aug 76 Raemy+ LVL SCHEME IR194	
	Maxwl			Rept	IPF-SP-006	75 - + ENRICHED TGTS. TBL EN+INTS.	
(n,2n)	Fiss		CRC	Eval Rept	CRC-1003	Dec 60 Roy+,ESTIMATED AVG SIG=5.6MB	
(n,2n)	1.4+7		BRL	Expt Rept	BRL-1491	Aug 70 Temperley. ACT	+
	1.4+7			Data	EXFOR10214.019	Oct 73 . 1 PT. SIGMA. INCL.	
(n,2n)	1.5+7		CCP	Expt Jour	YF 14 682	Oct 71 Druzhinin+ NAI,ABSOL,TBL CFD OTHERS	
				Jour	SNP 14 383	Apr 72 *ENGL OF YF 14 682	
(n,2n)	1.5+7		JUL	Expt Jour	NP/A 185 614	May 72 Qaim. ACT,GE(LI). CFD TH+OTHR.	+
	1.5+7			Data	EXFOR20536.025	Apr 76 1PNT.SIGMA.	

77 Iridium 193

Quantity	Energy (ev) Min	Max	Lab	Type	Documentation Ref Vol Page	Author, Comments Date	Data
(n,2n)	1.5+7		DEB Eval	Jour	REA 11 1 153	Mar 73 Boedy+ RECOMM.VALUE FROM N-Z SYSTEM.	
(n,2n)	1.5+7		KFI Theo	Rept	KFKI-73-68	Dec 73 Jeki.NEW FIT,CALC SIG CFD OTHERS,TBL	
(n,2n)	1.5+7		TAT Theo	Jour	JP/A 7 1457	Aug 74 Kondaiah. CALC ON STAT MODEL	
(n,2n)	8.6+6	2.1+7	LAS Expt	Jour	PR/C 12 451	Aug 75 Bayhurst+ TBL,GRPH	+
	8.6+6	2.1+7		Data	EXFOR10536.	Apr 76 . 9 PTS.	
(n,p)	1.4+7		ALD Expt	Jour	PPS 73 215	Feb 59 Coleman+. ACT. CFD DIRECT INTERACTN	+
(n,p)	Fiss		CRC Eval	Rept	CRC-1003	Dec 60 Roy+,ESTIMATED AVG SIG=0.005MB	
(n,p)	1.5+7		SAH Comp	Jour	NUC 23 8 112	Aug 65 Chatterjee. TABLE WITH REFS.	
	1.4+7			Jour	NP 60 273	Nov 64 - .MEAN OF EXPT CFD SHELLMOD	
(n,p)	1.5+7		DEB Comp	Jour	REA 7 4 93	Dec 69 Csikai+ SIG+HL COMPILTN,N-ACTIV-ANAL	
(n,p)	1.4+7	1.5+7	JYV Eval	Rept	JU-RR-3/1970	Jun 70 Leppaemaeki+ TABLE OF EVAL AVG SIG	
(n,p)	1.4+7	1.5+7	KAZ Theo	Jour	YF 18 705	Oct 73 Levkovsky.AVERAGED SIG,CALC,TBL	
				Jour	SNP 18 361	Apr 74 . ENGLISH OF YF 18,705	
(n,α)	1.4+7		MUAExpt	Conf	60Waltair 297	Feb 60 Khurana+.VAL GVN REL FE056(N,P),C-W	+
	1.4+7			Data	EXFOR30403.026	Jul 77 1 PNT. REL TO FE56(N,P)= 110 MB	
(n,α)	Fiss		CRC Eval	Rept	CRC-1003	Dec 60 Roy+,ESTIMATED AVG SIG=0.0001MB	
(n,α)	1.5+7		DEB Comp	Jour	REA 7 4 93	Dec 69 Csikai+ SIG+HL COMPILTN,N-ACTIV-ANAL	
(n,α)	1.4+7	1.5+7	JYV Eval	Rept	JU-RR-3/1970	Jun 70 Leppaemaeki+ TABLE OF EVAL AVG SIG	
Reson Params	1.3+0		BNL Expt	Jour	PR 100 1414	55 Landon.	+
	1.3+0			Data	EXFOR12178.005	Jun 76 . 1 RES, E0,WT,WN,WG,PCS	
Reson Params	9.0+0	7.7+1	HAR Expt	Jour	NP 5 294	Jan 58 Bowey+. 7 RESONANCE ES GVN. LINAC	+
Reson Params	9.1+0	2.2+2	BNL Expt	Abst	BAP 4 271	Apr 59 Bolotin+	+
	9.1+0	2.2+2		Data	EXFOR12155.005	Jun 76 . 18 RES, E0,WN0	
Reson Params	4.3+1		BNL Expt	Jour	NP 42 676	Apr 63 Bolotin+.WG,WN GIVEN FOR 1 RESONANCE	+
	4.3+1			Data	EXFOR11922.009	Jun 76 . 1 RES, E0,WN0,WG	
Reson Params	1.3+0	1.2+2	MOLEval	Rept	BLG-421	66 Damle+. RECOMMENDED PARAMS 15RESON	
Reson Params	1.3+0		NRL Expt	Jour	PR 155 1330	Mar 67 Stolovy.3J=2,BY TRANSMISS POLARZD NS	+
	1.3+0			Data	EXFOR11995.007	Jun 76 . 1 RES, E0, J	
Reson Params	1.3+0	9.1+0	MOLExpt	Jour	NP/A 97 657	May 67 Poortmans+ FROM RESON SCATTERING XPT	+
	1.3+0	9.1+0		Data	EXFOR20213.	May 74 6PTS.WT,J,TOT(RES),WN/WT.	
Reson Params	1.3+0		WURExpt	Rept	EIR-123	Jul 67 Brunner+.SHAPE ANAL CFD OTHER EXPTS	+
				Conf	66Paris 1 61	Oct 66 - + PPR 20. PRELIM DATA.	
Reson Params		1.0+6	AUA Theo	Jour	AUJ 20 477	Oct 67 Cook. TBL OF AVG LVL SPACING D,L=0,1	
Reson Params	-		AUA Theo	Rept	AAEC/E-211	Nov 70 Musgrove. CALCULTD D+GAM WIDTH GIVEN	
Reson Params	1.3+0	4.3+1	CJD Eval	Rept	YK-7	71 Zakharova+ SURVEY+SYSTEMATICS,GW,TBL	
				Rept	INDC(CCP)-27	Nov 72 .ENGLISH TRANSLATION OF YK-7 /71	
Reson Params	None		DUB Theo	Jour	YF 13 240	Feb 71 Malecki+G+ WID,THEO CFD EXPT.TBL,GRPH	
				Jour	SNP 13 133	Aug 71 - + ENGL OF YF 13 240.	
Reson Params	-		DUB Theo	Rept	JINR-E4-5711	Apr 71 Soloviev.RESONANCE STRUCTURE STUDY	
Reson Params	2.4+1	3.9+2	DUB Expt	Rept	RCN-203 269	Dec 73 Lason+ G * WN,D	+
	2.5+1	3.9+2		Rept	JINR-P3-6545	Jun 72 Lason'+ G*N-WIDTH,51 RES,TOF,TBL	
	2.4+1	3.9+2		Data	EXFOR40119.	Nov 72 E-RES FOR 51RES, N-WIDTH AT 37RES,D	
Strnth Fnctn	None		BNL Expt	Prog	WASH-1021 10	Jun 59 Hughes+	
Strnth Fnctn	+0	+2	MOLEval	Rept	BLG-421	66 Damle+. RECOMMENDED S0=1.9+-0.5 GND	
Strnth Fnctn	-		AUA Theo	Rept	AAEC/E-211	Nov 70 Musgrove. SMOOTHED S0,S1 AND S2 GIVN	
Strnth Fnctn	2.4+4		MUATheo	Jour	IJP 46 114	Mar 72 Chaubey+ P-WAVE.FOR A-SYSTEMTIC,GRPH	
Strnth Fnctn	None		AUA Eval	Rept	AAEC/E-277	Mar 73 Musgrove.TBLS EXPTL DATA+BEST VALUES	
Lvl Density	-		FEI Eval	Rept	FEI-36	66 Kapchigashev+.TBL OF RELATD QUANTTYS	+
		5.0+4		Jour	YF 4 686	Sep 66 .TABLE.SHORT VERSION OF FEI-36	
	-			Prog	YFI-3 3	66 .ABSTRACT.TABLE LDL+NUCL.EXCIT.E	
		5.0+4		Jour	SNP 4 486	67 .ENGLISH OF YF 4.FROM(N,GAMMA).TABLE	
				Prog	INDC-E-140 3	66 .ENGLISH TRANSL OF YFI-3	
Lvl Density	0.0+0	3.9+2	DUB Expt	Rept	JINR-P3-6545	Jul 72 Lason'+	+
	0.0+0	3.9+2		Data	EXFOR40119.008	Nov 72 LEVEL-DENSITY PARAMETER	

77 Iridium 194

Quantity	Energy (ev) Min	Max	Lab	Type	Documentation Ref Vol Page	Author, Comments Date	Data
Reson Params	-		AUA Theo	Rept	AAEC/E-211	Nov 70 Musgrove. CALCULTD D+GAM WIDTH GIVEN	
Strnth Fnctn	-		AUA Theo	Rept	AAEC/E-211	Nov 70 Musgrove. SMOOTHED S0,S1 AND S2 GIVN	
Lvl Density	+6		MIL Theo	Jour	EN 15 1 54	Jan 68 Facchini+ LDL PARS FROM LOW EN RES	
Lvl Density	None		MUNTheo	Jour	NP/A 217 269	Dec 73 Dilg+ A,DELTA. BACK SHIFTED FERMIGAS	
Lvl Density	None		COP Theo	Jour	NP/A 222 493	Apr 74 Dossing+COLL ROTAT.SPAC. ACCUR ESTIM	
Lvl Density	None		ROC Theo	Jour	NP/A 223 577	May 74 Huizenga+ EXP CFD MICROSC TH SPH NUC	

77   Iridium   195

Quantity	Energy (ev) Min Max	Lab	Type	Documentation Ref Vol Page	Author, Comments Date	Data
Reson Params	–	AUA	Theo Rept	AAEC/E-211	Nov 70 Musgrove. CALCULTD D+GAM WIDTH GIVEN	
Strnth Fnctn	–	AUA	Theo Rept	AAEC/E-211	Nov 70 Musgrove. SMOOTHED S0,S1 AND S2 GIVN	

77   Iridium   196

Quantity	Energy (ev) Min Max	Lab	Type	Documentation Ref Vol Page	Author, Comments Date	Data
(n,p)	Maxwl	IFU	Theo Rept	ICD-4 20	67 Dadakina+ PENETR COEFF CALC,TABLE	
Reson Params	–	AUA	Theo Rept	AAEC/E-211	Nov 70 Musgrove. CALCULTD D+GAM WIDTH GIVEN	
Strnth Fnctn	–	AUA	Theo Rept	AAEC/E-211	Nov 70 Musgrove. SMOOTHED S0,S1 AND S2 GIVN	

77   Iridium   197

Quantity	Energy (ev) Min Max	Lab	Type	Documentation Ref Vol Page	Author, Comments Date	Data
Reson Params	–	AUA	Theo Rept	AAEC/E-211	Nov 70 Musgrove. CALCULTD D+GAM WIDTH GIVEN	
Strnth Fnctn	–	AUA	Theo Rept	AAEC/E-211	Nov 70 Musgrove. SMOOTHED S0,S1 AND S2 GIVN	

78 Platinum

Quantity	Energy (ev) Min	Max	Lab	Type	Documentation Ref Vol Page	Date	Author, Comments	Data
Evaluation	5.0+5	1.5+7	LRL	Eval	Rept UCRL-5351	Nov 58	Howerton. CURVES	
Total	Maxwl			COL Expt	Jour PR 48 265	Aug 35	Dunning+ IONCH,TRANS,RA-BE/PARAFIN N	
Total	Maxwl			CAV Expt	Jour PRSA 162 127	Sep 37	Goldhaber+BRIGGS.TRANSMISSION 21.5B	
Total	4.0-3	1.0+4		COL Expt	Jour PR 71 165	Feb 47	Havens+ TOF TRSM	+
	4.0-3	1.0+4			Data EXFOR12184.003	Jun 76	. 80 PTS.	
Total	1.4+7			LAS Expt	Jour PR 88 562	Nov 52	Coon+	+
	1.4+7				Data EXFOR11056.050	Jun 76	. 1 PT.	
Total	9.0+4	3.0+6		WIS Expt	Jour PR 89 1271	Mar 53	Walt+ GRAPH, ZR-T AND LI TARGETS	+
	1.1+5	3.0+6			Data EXFOR11746.007	Jun 76	. 18 PTS.	
Total	9.2+0	2.0+2		BNL Expt	Priv CARTER	Mar 55	Carter.	+
	9.2+0	2.0+2			Data EXFOR11897.006	Jun 76	. 147 PTS.	
Total	1.0+3	3.2+4		HAR Expt	Jour PPSA 70 51	Jan 57	Gayther+ FC THICK SAMPLE,AVSIG CF TH	
Total	8.3+0	1.7+2		BNL Expt	Priv SETH	58	Seth+	+
	8.3+0	1.7+2			Data EXFOR11879.002	Jun 76	. 378 PTS.	
Total	6.8+6	1.4+7		LRL Expt	Jour PR 110 927	May 58	Bratenahl+SC TRNS 5ES 5.73 5.38B+-1P	+
					Conf 58Geneva 14 109	Sep 58	- +P1881,TBL,CURV,CFD OPTMDL	
	6.8+6	1.4+7			Data EXFOR11155.028	Jun 76	. 5 PTS.	
Total	4.0+2	2.0+3		HAR Theo	Jour PPS 71 910	Jun 58	Egelstaff.FLUCTUATIONS CFD THEORY	+
	1.4+2	2.9+5		Expt	Priv EGELSTAFF4	Jun 55	- . NUMERICAL DATA.	
Total	6.5+1	1.5+2		ANL Expt	Prog WASH-1026 8	Oct 59	Thomas+FC 10RES SEEN,NOT 6RPTD CORGE	
Total	Cold			KJL Revw	Conf 60Vienna 169	Oct 60	Riste.NDG,TBP	
Total	1.7+7	2.9+7		LRL Expt	Jour PR 120 521	Oct 60	Peterson+ TRANS 4ES CURV CFD OPTMDL	+
					Conf 58Geneva 14 109	Sep 58	Bratenahl+ TBL,CURV,CFD OPTMDL	
	1.7+7	2.9+7			Data EXFOR11108.036	Jun 76	. 4 PTS.	
Total	2.0-3	6.4-2		TRM Expt	Conf 62Madras 369	Feb 62	Duggal+ .CURVE,TRANSM-METHOD	+
	2.0-3	6.1-2			Data EXFOR31092.003	Feb 71	.SIG AT 46 ES GVN	
Total	3.0+3	6.5+5		DKE ExTh	Jour PL 16 306	Jun 65	Seth.AV CS 8-10KEV RSN INT RES OBSV	+
	5.0+4	6.4+5		Expt	Data EXFOR11781.018	Jun 76	. 95 PTS.	
Total	1.0+5	3.0+6		FEI Expt	Rept ICD-3 102	Oct 66	Filippov+ .GRAPH CFD REFS,VDG	
					Prog INDSWG-152E		66 .PAGE 102. ENGLISH TRANSL OF ICD-3	
Total	1.0+5	6.5+5		ANL Expt	Prog ANL-7210 16	Dec 66	Whalen.SHORT NOTE,GRAPH ONLY	+
	1.0+5	6.5+5			Data EXFOR11540.012	Jun 76	. 265 PTS.	
Total	4.0+0	8.3+2		SAC Expt	Jour NP/A 131 305	Jun 69	De Barros+ LINAC.TRANS.NDG.SEE RES.	+
	4.0+0	8.3+2			Data EXFOR20685.	Jul 77	0PTS. SEE RESONANCE PARAMETERS.	
Total	2.5+6	1.5+7		BNW Expt	Jour PR/C 3 576	Feb 71	Foster+TRANS,CURVS,CFD OTHERS+TH	+
					Jour NIM 36 1	Sep 65	.EXPT DETAILS	
	2.3+6	1.5+7			Data EXFOR10047.085	Aug 73	272PTS.	
Total	1.3+7	1.5+7		DEB Eval	Rept IAEA-153 173	73	Boedy+ MOST PROBABLE VAL OF SIG,TBL	
					Jour AHP 30 115	Oct 71	Angeli+ AVG SIG,CFD CALC.TBLS.GRAPH	
Total	2.7+3			MUN Expt	Conf 71Albany 327	Aug 76	Dilg+ TRANSMISSION.	+
					Prog EANDC(E)150U	Oct 72	- + AVERAGE TOT XSECT+S0	
	2.7+3				Data EXFOR20583.029	Jun 76	1PNT.	
Elastic	2.5-2			ORL Expt	Jour PR 81 527	Feb 51	Shull+	+
	2.5-2				Data EXFOR10431.	Jun 76	. 3 PTS, BAS, COH, COH AMP	
Elastic	1.5+6			IFU Expt	Prog YFI-5 42	Oct 67	Korzh+ TBL OPTMDL PARAMS + TOTELAST	
					Rept INDC-232E	67	. ENGL OF YFI-5 42	
Elastic	1.5+6			IFU Comp	Jour YF 7 277	Feb 68	Korzh+ OPTMOD PARS-FIT TO EXPTL-SIG	
					Jour SNP 7 2 190	Aug 68	TRANSLATN.*	
Elastic	3.0+5	1.5+6		ANL Expt	Jour PR 168 1344	Apr 68	Smith+ TOF FROM ANG DIST TABLE+CURVE	+
					Rept ANL-7363	Aug 67	.SUPERSEDED,TBLS.	
					Rept EANDC(US)-62	Jun 64	Smith+TOF,TBL.50KEV STEPS,20KEV RSLN	
	3.0+5	1.6+6			Data EXFOR10631.006	Apr 77	. 105 PTS. SEL CS DATA	
Diff Elastic	7.0+6			LRL Theo	Rept UCRL-4927	Jul 57	Bjorklund+ OPTMDL CALC 6-PARAM FIT	
Diff Elastic	1.4+7			LRL Theo	Rept UCRL-4926	Jul 57	Bjorklund+ OPTMDL CALC 6-PARAM FIT	
Diff Elastic	1.5+6			IFU Comp	Jour YF 7 277	Feb 68	Korzh+ GRPH SIG(ANG),OPTMOD PARS-FIT	
					Jour SNP 7 2 190	Aug 68	TRANSLATN.*	
Diff Elastic	3.0+5	1.5+6		ANL Expt	Jour PR 168 1344	Apr 68	Smith+ TOF ANG DIST LEG COEFF CURVES	+
					Rept ANL-7363	Aug 67	.SUPERSEDED,TBLS.	
					Rept EANDC(US)-62	Jun 64	Smith+TOF,TBL.50KEV STEPS,20KEV RSLN	
	3.0+5	1.6+6			Data EXFOR10631.007	Apr 77	525PTS.LEG COEFS	
Polarization	1.5+6			DKE Expt	Rept TID-19051		62 Olness+ TOF 51.5DEG POLARIZ MEASD	
Potntal Scat	1.2+2	3.4+2		ANL Expt	Jour PR 79 747	Sep 50	Hibdon. REL MN+CO RESON SCAT. METAL	
Potntal Scat	+4			HAR Expt	Jour PPSA 70 51	Jan 57	Gayther+ FROM AVG SIGTOT. FC TRANSM	
Potntal Scat	+0	+5		BNL Expt	Prog WASH-1006 5	Oct 58	Hughes+ NDG	
Potntal Scat		6.5+6		DKE ExTh	Jour PL 13 70	Nov 64	Seth+0,1PHASE FRM SIG TOT AV 3-650KV	
Diff Inelast	6.0+6			DKE Expt	Rept AD-299005		62 Seth+ NUCL TEMP+FERMI LVL DENS COEFF	

78 Platinum

Quantity	Energy (ev) Min	Max	Lab	Type	Documentation Ref Vol Page	Date	Author, Comments	Data
Diff Inelast	4.0+6	6.5+6	DKE	Expt	Jour NP 60 17	Nov 64	Buccino+N SPEC MEASURED 4ES+NUC TEMP	
					Abst DA 24 4251	Apr 64	Hollandsworth.TOF.EN SPEC.NUCL T.	
Diff Inelast	4.5+5	1.5+6	ANL	Expt	Jour PR 168 1344	Apr 68	Smith+ TOF SIGS FOR 10LVLS CFD THEOR	+
					Rept ANL-7363	Aug 67	.SUPERSEDED	
	4.5+5	1.6+6			Data EXFOR10631.010	Apr 77	155PTS.	
Thermal Scat	Maxwl		UJV	Theo	Rept UJV-2275	69	Krivy. DEBYE TEMP,BRAGG+OTHER EXPTS	
Thermal Scat	None		TKU	Theo	Jour AAF 6 321	Jul 69	Laehteenkorva. DISPERSION CURVES GVN	
Thermal Scat	1.0-4	1.0+3	MUN	Revw	Jour EEN 80 1	77	Koester. SCAT LENGTH,FREE+INCOH SIG	
Scattering	Maxwl		CAV	Expt	Jour PRSA 162 127	Sep 37	Goldhaber+. 8.3B REL 4.83B FOR C	
Scattering	3.1+6		LAS	Expt	Jour PR 70 602	Nov 46	Manley+	
Scattering	6.0+4	1.8+6	ANL	Expt	Jour PR 107 1077	Aug 57	Langsdorf+ LEGENDRE COEFS CURVES	+
					Rept ANL-5567	Oct 61	.REVISED DATA	
	1.4+4	1.4+6			Data EXFOR11224.059	Jun 76	. 75 PTS, DSIG AT 15 ES	
	1.4+4	1.4+6			Data EXFOR11224.058	Jun 76	. 15 PTS, SIG	
Scattering	+0	+3	ORL	Revw	Conf 60Vienna 535	Oct 60	Block+.NDG,EXPT DESCRIBED	
Absorption	Pile		HAR	Expt	Jour PPSA 63 1175	Oct 50	Colmer+LITTLER.PILE OSC REL HAR B	+
					Rept AERE-N/R-527	Jun 50	- + PILE OSCILLATOR.	
Absorption	2.5-2		HAR	Expt	Jour JNEA 12 32	May 60	Tattersall+. PILE OSCILLATOR	+
					Rept AERE-R-2887	Aug 59	-. PILE OSC.REL BORON	
	Maxwl				Rept AERE-R/R-2516	Mar 58	Jowitt+ PILE OSC.REL BORON.293DEGK.	
	2.5-2				Data EXFOR20638.060	Jul 76	1PNT.SIGMA.	
Absorption	1.0+3		RPI	Expt	Rept AERE-R-4131 1	Sep 62	Block.ELAST.LIN.ACCELERATOR NDC	
Res Int Abs	5.0-1		HAR	Expt	Jour JNE 12 32	May 60	Tattersall+ ABOVE 1/V,PILE OSC,ONE	+
					Rept AERE-R-2887	Aug 59	-. PILE OSC.REL BORON	
					Conf 58Geneva 16 34	Sep 58	Rose+ SUPERSEDED	
	6.7-1				Data EXFOR20638.061	Jul 76	1PNT.	
Res Int Abs	-		WIN	Expt	Jour JNAB 16 335	Jul 62	Moore+.CD TUBED OSC. NOT INF DILUTE	
					Rept AEEW-R-57	Aug 61	+ EQU TO JNE(A+B)16 335	
Res Int Abs	5.0-1		STF	Expt	Conf 66S.Diego 2 175	Feb 66	Sage.	+
	5.0-1				Data EXFOR11754.012	Jun 76	. 1 PT.	
(n,γ)	None		PAR	Expt	Jour CR 200 391	Jan 35	Sosnowski+	
					Jour CR 200 446	Feb 35	- +	
(n,γ)	Maxwl		ANL	Expt	Jour PR 76 531	Aug 49	Kubitscheck+ YIELD CFD SIG.G-M COINC	
(n,γ)	Pile		ANL	Expt	Jour PR 80 342	Nov 50	Harris+.PILE OSC.REL TO BORON.	+
	Pile				Data EXFOR11528.045	Jun 76	. 1 PT.	
(n,γ)	Maxwl		ORL	Expt	Jour PR 83 643	Aug 51	Pomerance.LOCAL OSC REL AU ABS 95 B	+
	Maxwl				Data EXFOR11047.059	Jun 76	. 1 PT.	
(n,γ)	1.8+5	1.0+6	LAS	Expt	Jour PR 120 556	Oct 60	Diven.SC-T.	+
					Conf 58Geneva 15 60	Sep 58	.SUPERSEDED	
	1.8+5	1.0+6			Data EXFOR11616.026	Jun 76	. 7 PTS.	
(n,γ)	2.5+2	6.0+5	ORL	Revw	Conf 61RPI 64	May 61	Harvey. CURVE	
(n,γ)	2.0+2	8.0+3	ORL	Expt	Conf 61Saclay 203	Sep 61	Block+ LIQUID SCINTILLATOR	+
	2.0+2	1.0+4			Conf 61Vienna 1 95	Aug 61	Neiler.PPR73,TABLE FOR SOME ES,GRAPH	
	2.0+2	9.6+3			Data EXFOR11935.027	Jun 76	. 51 PTS.	
(n,γ)	6.5+3	1.7+5	ORL	Expt	Jour PR 122 182	Apr 61	Gibbons+	+
	3.0+4	6.5+4			Jour PR 129 2695	Mar 63	Macklin+ SIGMA=330 AND 234MB,SCINT	
					Conf 61Vienna 1 95	Aug 61	Neiler.	
	6.5+3	1.7+5			Data EXFOR11329.	Jun 76	. 56 PTS, SIG	
(n,γ)	3.0+4		ORL	Expt	Jour NP 43 353	May 63	Macklin+ SIG=321MB+ -23PC	+
	3.0+4				Data EXFOR11380.012	Jun 76	. 1 PT.	
(n,γ)	5.0+3	9.0+4	ORL	Theo	Jour RMP 37 166	Jan 65	Macklin+.CALC FOR KT=5TO90KEV	
(n,γ)	Maxwl		KUR	Expt	Jour YF 7 937	May 68	Groshev+ OTHER SIG VALUE GIVEN	
					Jour SNP 7 563	Nov 68	. ENGL OF YF 7 937	
(n,γ)	-		CCP	Revw	Jour AE 29 187	Sep 70	Sukhoruchkin. (D,P GAM) CFD (N,GAM)	
					Jour SJA 29 896	Sep 70	TRANSLATN.*	
(n,γ)	3.0+4		AUA	Theo	Rept AAEC/E-211	Nov 70	Musgrove. SIGMA GIVEN AND CFD OTHER	
(n,γ)	1.0+6	1.0+7	CRC	Revw	Conf 74Petten 119	Sep 74	Bartholomew+ PHOTON STRF GRPH	
(n,γ)	1.0+3	3.0+6	BRC	Eval	Prog CEA-N-1875 121	Apr 76	Bertrand-Lepage+RECOMMENDED VALUES	
Res Int Capt	None		ORL	Revw	Conf 55Geneva 5 96	Aug 55	Macklin+.TABLE,EXPT CFD THEORY,P833	
Spect (n,γ)	Maxwl		CRC	Expt	Jour CJP 31 1051	Nov 53	Kinsey+ PAIR SPECT,LINE WIDTH=100KEV	
Spect (n,γ)	Maxwl		GEA	Eval	Rept DC-58-1-30	Jan 58	Deloume.BY APPROXIMATION CURV+TABLE	
Spect (n,γ)	Maxwl		YAL	Expt	Jour PR 114 268	Apr 59	Draper.SC SPECTR,GAM E 0 TO 600 KEV	
Spect (n,γ)	4.7+1	6.0+2	HAR	Expt	Jour NP 14 212	Dec 59	Bird+HARD GAMMAS OBSERVED	
					Rept AERE-NP/GEN12	Aug 59	- +TBL RES EN.ISOTOPE ASSGN.GAMMA	
Spect (n,γ)	Maxwl		KUR	ExTh	Conf 68Riga	Jan 68	Groshev+ ABST,G ES,INT,COMPTON SPECT	

78 Platinum

Quantity	Energy (ev) Min	Max	Lab	Type	Documentation Ref Vol Page	Author, Comments Date	Data
Spect (n,γ)	Maxwl		KUR	Expt	Jour SNP 7 563	Nov 68 .TRANSLATION OF YF 7 937	+
					Jour YF 7 937	May 68 Groshev+ TBL,GRPH,GAM−INT(GAM−E)	
					Conf 67Tokyo § 4.112	Sep 67 − + 40GS PT196(7.9−4.9MEV)3OTHR	
	2.5−2				Data EXFOR40224.002	May 74 .43 GAMMA ES AND GAM/100N GIVEN	
Spect (n,γ)	1.0+1	7.0+2	SAC	Expt	Jour NP/A 121 65	Dec 68 Samour+ GE(LI).+NEW LVL SCH. 193,7,9	
					Conf 67Bordeaux	Mar 67 − + ABST.SUPERSEDED.	
Spect (n,γ)	2.5−2		MIT	Comp	Rept MITNE−85	Jan 69 Rasmussen+TBL G INT.=AFCRL−69−0071	
Spect (n,γ)	2.0+3		MTR	Expt	Prog NCSAC−31 76	May 70 Greenwood+,ANAL TO BE COMPL,NO DATA	
Spect (n,γ)	Maxwl		CCP	Revw	Jour AE 29 187	Sep 70 Sukhoruchkin. GAM−SPEC,DOORWAY−STATE	
					Jour SJA 29 896	Sep 70 TRANSLATN.*	
Spect (n,γ)	2.4+4		BNL	Expt	Prog USNDC−7 36	Jun 73 Wasson+. GE(LI) DET. CURVE.	
Inelastic γ	3.3+5	1.8+6	MIT	Expt	Jour PR 101 1516	Mar 56 Guernsey+,CS 330−KEV LEVEL CFD TH	+
	4.0+5	1.8+6			Data EXFOR11691.008	Jun 76 . 12 PTS, SIG	
Inelastic γ	3.0+6		FEI	Expt	Jour AE 9 403	Nov 60 Androsenko+ TABLE OF GAMMA−ENERGIES	
					Jour SJA 9 945	Sep 61 . ENGL OF AE 9 403	
					Jour KE 4 510	Jun 61 . GERMAN OF AE 9 403	
(n,2n)	1.5+7		DEB	Eval	Jour REA 11 1 153	Mar 73 Boedy+ RECOMM.VALUE FROM N−Z SYSTEM.	
(n,2n)	7.9+6	1.5+7	BRC	Expt	Jour NIM 135 511	Jun 76 Frehaut.GD LOADED SCIN.EXPT DETAILS.	+
					Conf 75Kiev 4 303	May 75 − + LIQSCIN.SIG(E),CFD.GRPH+TBL	
					Conf 75Wash. 855	Mar 75 − + TBL.GRPH.REL 238U(N,F)	
	7.9+6	1.5+7			Data EXFOR20416.018	Jul 75 15PTS.SIGMA.	
Reson Params	1.2+1	1.8+1	COL	Expt	Jour PR 71 165	Feb 47 Havens+TOF TRNSM APPROX STRGTH 2 RES	+
	1.2+1	1.0+3			Data EXFOR12184.006	Jun 76 . 4 RES, E0,WT**2/PCS	
Reson Params	3.3+1	1.5+2	BNL	Expt	Priv ZIMMERMAN	Jan 58 Zimmerman.	+
	3.3+1	1.5+2			Data EXFOR12494.002	Jun 76 . 7 RES, E0,WN0	
Reson Params	6.7+1	1.5+2	ANL	Expt	Prog ANL−6072 4	59 Bollinger+ 10 ES	+
	6.7+1	1.5+2			Data EXFOR12479.002	Jun 76 . 10 RES, E0	
Reson Params	4.7+1	5.7+2	HAR	Expt	Jour NP 14 212	Dec 59 Bird+ASSIGNMENT OF RES.TO ISOTOPES	+
Reson Params	5.4+1	5.9+3	SAC	Expt	Jour JPR 21 426	May 60 Corge+ E0 AND LEVEL SPACING.	+
					Jour CR 249 413	Jul 59 − + E0 ONLY.72RES. DATA.	
	5.4+1	5.9+3			Data EXFOR20679.	Sep 77 95PTS.E0,MEAN LVL SPACING.	
Reson Params	1.6+2		ANL	Expt	Prog WASH−1044	Aug 63 Cote+FC,NO INTRFRNC SHOWS J 0,NOT 1	
Reson Params	1.2+1	2.0+1	ITE	Expt	Jour ZET 45 875	Oct 63 Ignat'Ev. 2RES BY RES−SCATTERING	
					Jour JET 18 602	Mar 64 TRANSLATN.*	
Reson Params	9.8+1	8.2+2	SAC	Expt	Jour NP/A 131 305	Jun 69 DE BARROS+ LINAC.36E0,SOME WN,WN0	+
					Rept CEA−R−3385	Feb 68 Julien.(THESIS).DATA GIVEN.	
					Rept CEA−R−3077	Dec 67 De Barros.TBL WN,WG,W,. SEE PT195.	
					Conf 66Paris 1 193	Oct 66 − + CURVES.LVL SPACING.	
	9.8+1	8.2+2			Data EXFOR20685.013	Jul 77 32PTS.E0,WT,J,A*G*WN.	
Strnth Fnctn	+4		HAR	Expt	Jour PPSA 70 51	Jan 57 Gayther+ FROM AVG SIGTOT. FC TRANSM	
Strnth Fnctn	+3		BNL	Expt	Jour PRL 1 461	Dec 58 Hughes. FC 1.4+−0.3	
Strnth Fnctn		6.5+6	DKE	ExTh	Jour PL 13 70	Nov 64 Seth+S,P,D STF FRM SIG TOT 3−650KEV	+
		6.5+6		Expt	Data EXFOR11665.031	Jun 76 . 3 PTS.	
Strnth Fnctn	2.7+3		MUN	Expt	Conf 71Albany 327	Aug 76 Dilg+TRNS.S0 STF GVN.31 ELEMENT GRPH	
Lvl Density	6.0+6		DKE	Expt	Rept AD−299005	62 Seth+,NUCL TEMP+FERMI LVL DENS COEFF	
Lvl Density	None		FEI	Theo	Jour YF 11 1213	Jun 70 Ignatyuk+ SPIN DEPENDENCE OF DENSITY	
					Jour SNP 11 674	Dec 70 . ENGL OF YF 11 1213	

78 Platinum 188

Quantity	Energy (ev) Min	Max	Lab	Type	Documentation Ref Vol Page	Author, Comments Date	Data
(n,p)	Maxwl		IFU	Theo	Rept ICD−4 20	67 Dadakina+ PENETR COEFF CALC,TABLE	
Reson Params	−		AUA	Theo	Rept AAEC/E−211	Nov 70 Musgrove. CALCULTD D+GAM WIDTH GIVEN	
Strnth Fnctn	−		AUA	Theo	Rept AAEC/E−211	Nov 70 Musgrove. SMOOTHED S0,S1 AND S2 GIVN	
Lvl Density	−3	+0	IFU	Theo	Jour UFZ 13 700	Apr 68 Pisanko+ LEVEL SPACING CALC,TBL	
					Jour UPJ 13 498	Oct 68 TRANSLATN.*	

78 Platinum 189

Quantity	Energy (ev) Min	Max	Lab	Type	Documentation Ref Vol Page	Author, Comments Date	Data
Reson Params	−		AUA	Theo	Rept AAEC/E−211	Nov 70 Musgrove. CALCULTD D+GAM WIDTH GIVEN	
Strnth Fnctn	−		AUA	Theo	Rept AAEC/E−211	Nov 70 Musgrove. SMOOTHED S0,S1 AND S2 GIVN	

78 Platinum 190

Quantity	Energy (ev) Min	Max	Lab	Type	Documentation Ref Vol Page	Author, Comments Date	Data
Elastic	2.0−2	3.0+3	IJI	Expt	Jour YF 22 674	Oct 75 Vertebny+ TRANS,TOF.AVG SCATSIG,TABL	
					Jour SNP 22 348	Oct 75 . ENGL OF YF 22,674	
Scattering	2.5−2	1.0+0	IJI	Expt	Conf 73Kiev 2 95	May 73 Vertebny+ TOF,10B,TBL	
	2.5−2				Rept INDC(CCP)−49	Feb 75 − + ENGLISH OF 73KIEV 2 95	
Scattering	2.5−2		IJI	Expt	Rept YFI−18 32	Aug 74 Vertebny+ VAL GVN IN TBL	
Absorption	2.5−2		IJI	Expt	Rept YFI−18 32	Aug 74 Vertebny+ VAL GVN IN TBL	
(n,γ)	Maxwl		ORL	Expt	Prog ORNL−1879 50	55 Pomerance.	+
	Maxwl				Data EXFOR11885.003	Jun 76 . 1 PT.	
(n,γ)	Maxwl		KUR	Expt	Jour YF 7 937	May 68 Groshev+ OTHER SIG VALUE GIVEN	
					Jour SNP 7 563	Nov 68 . ENGL OF YF 7 937	
(n,γ)	−		IEA	Comp	Rept IEA−INF−10 6	Aug 68 Atalla. TABLES OF HL,SIG AND GAMM−E	
(n,γ)	3.0+4		AUA	Theo	Rept AAEC/E−211	Nov 70 Musgrove. SIGMA GIVEN AND CFD OTHER	
(n,γ)	2.5−2	1.0+0	IJI	Expt	Conf 73Kiev 2 95	May 73 Vertebny+ TOF,800+−70B,TBL	
	0.0+0	2.0+3			Rept INDC(CCP)−49	Feb 75 − + ENGLISH OF 73KIEV 2 95	
(n,γ)	2.0−2	3.0+3	IJI	Expt	Jour YF 22 674	Oct 75 Vertebny+ TOF,SIG AT 2200 M/SEC,TBL	
					Jour SNP 22 348	Oct 75 . ENGL OF YF 22,674	
(n,2n)	Fiss		CRC	Eval	Rept CRC−1003	Dec 60 ROY+ ESTIMATED AVG SIG=0.04MB	
(n,2n)	1.5+7		DEB	Eval	Jour REA 11 1 153	Mar 73 Boedy+ RECOMM.VALUE FROM N−Z SYSTEM.	
(n,2n)	1.5+7		KFI	Theo	Rept KFKI−73−68	Dec 73 Jeki.NEW FIT,CALC SIG CFD OTHERS,TBL	
(n,p)	Fiss		CRC	Eval	Rept CRC−1003	Dec 60 Roy+,ESTIMATED AVG SIG=0.04MB	
(n,α)	Fiss		CRC	Eval	Rept CRC−1003	Dec 60 ROY+ ESTIMATED AVG SIG=0.004MB	
(n,α)	Maxwl		CCP	Expt	Jour YF 1 252	Feb 65 Andreev.IONIZ−CHAMBER,SIG=M8MB	+
					Jour SNP 1 177	Aug 65 TRANSLATN.*	
Reson Params	−		AUA	Theo	Rept AAEC/E−211	Nov 70 Musgrove. CALCULTD D+GAM WIDTH GIVEN	
Reson Params	None		DUB	Theo	Jour ZEP 14 194	Aug 71 Solovev.LARGE N−WID G−WID CORREL.NDG	
					Rept JINR−E4−5880	71 Soloviev.N−GAM−WIDS CORR.SHORT NOTE	
					Jour JEL 14 129	Aug 71 − . ENGL OF ZEP 14 194.	
Reson Params	2.8+1		IJI	Expt	Conf 73Kiev 2 95	May 73 Vertebny+ WN,WG,TBL,TOF	
					Rept INDC(CCP)−49	Feb 75 − + ENGLISH OF 73KIEV 2 95	
Reson Params	0.0+0	2.0+3	IJI	Expt	Rept YFI−18 32	Aug 74 Vertebny+ TOF,WN,D,AVG D,TBL	
Strnth Fnctn	−		AUA	Theo	Rept AAEC/E−211	Nov 70 Musgrove. SMOOTHED S0,S1 AND S2 GIVN	

78 Platinum 191

Quantity	Energy (ev) Min	Max	Lab	Type	Documentation Ref Vol Page	Author, Comments Date	Data
(n,p)	Maxwl		IFU	Theo	Rept ICD−4 20	67 Dadakina+ PENETR COEFF CALC,TABLE	
Reson Params	−		AUA	Theo	Rept AAEC/E−211	Nov 70 Musgrove. CALCULTD D+GAM WIDTH GIVEN	
Strnth Fnctn	−		AUA	Theo	Rept AAEC/E−211	Nov 70 Musgrove. SMOOTHED S0,S1 AND S2 GIVN	

78 Platinum 192

Quantity	Energy (ev) Min	Max	Lab	Type	Documentation Ref Vol Page	Author, Comments Date	Data
Elastic	2.0−2	3.0+3	IJI	Expt	Jour YF 22 674	Oct 75 Vertebny+ TRANS,TOF.AVG SCATSIG,TABL	
					Jour SNP 22 348	Oct 75 . ENGL OF YF 22,674	
Potntal Scat		5.8+2	SAC	Expt	Jour NP/A 123 561	Jan 69 Morgenstern+ RADIUS FROM RES ANAL	+
					Rept CEA−R−3609	Sep 68 − + (THESIS) RADIUS.	
	0.0+0	5.8+2			Data EXFOR20685.016	Jul 77 1PNT.RADIUS.	
Scattering	2.5−2	1.0+0	IJI	Expt	Conf 73Kiev 2 95	May 73 Vertebny+ TOF,12.3+−1.2B,TBL	
	2.5−2				Rept INDC(CCP)−49	Feb 75 − + ENGLISH OF 73KIEV 2 95	
Scattering	2.5−2		IJI	Expt	Rept YFI−18 32	Aug 74 Vertebny+ VAL GVN IN TBL	
Absorption	2.5−2		IJI	Expt	Rept YFI−18 32	Aug 74 Vertebny+ VAL GVN IN TBL	
(n,γ)	Pile		NOT	Expt	Priv HALDAR	Jan 53 Haldar.	+
	Pile				Data EXFOR12244.002	Jun 76 . 1 PT.	
(n,γ)	Maxwl		ORL	Expt	Prog ORNL−1879 50	55 Pomerance.	+
	Maxwl				Data EXFOR11885.004	Jun 76 . 1 PT.	
(n,γ)	Maxwl		BNL	Expt	Jour PR 128 761	Oct 62 Sehgal.ACT,2.2+−0.8B(4.7DAY)	+
	Maxwl				Data EXFOR11994.010	Jun 76 . 1 PT.	
(n,γ)	Maxwl		MUA	ExTh	Jour NP 41 372	Mar 63 Mangal+ (N,G)M SIGMA GVN,TH CFD EXPT	+
	Maxwl			Expt	Data EXFOR31249.009	Sep 72 .SIG GVN	
(n,γ)	2.5+4		FEI	ExTh	Prog YFI−4 22	May 67 Shorin+.,TBLS GIVEN,TBP YF	
				Theo	Jour YF 6 769	Oct 67 − + VALUE GIVEN,STATIST THEORY	
					Jour SNP 6 558	Apr 68 . ENGL OF YF 6 769	
				ExTh	Prog INDC−187E	67 . ENGL TRANSL OF YFI−4 22	
(n,γ)	Maxwl		KUR	Expt	Jour YF 7 937	May 68 Groshev+ OTHER UPPER LIMIT GIVEN	
					Jour SNP 7 563	Nov 68 . ENGL OF YF 7 937	

78 Platinum 192

Quantity	Energy (ev) Min	Max	Lab	Type	Documentation Ref Vol Page	Author, Comments Date	Data
(n,γ)	–		IEA	Comp Rept	IEA – INF – 10 6	Aug 68 Atalla. TABLES OF HL,SIG AND GAMM – E	
(n,γ)	3.0+4		AUA	Theo Rept	AAEC/E – 211	Nov 70 Musgrove. SIGMA GIVEN AND CFD OTHER	
(n,γ)	1.0+3	1.0+7	BOL	Eval Data	BENZI – DFN 829.	May 72 40 PNTS	+
(n,γ)	2.5+4		IJI	Expt Jour	YF 22 674	Oct 75 Vertebny+ TRANS.SIG(L=0,1),TABLE	
	2.5–2	1.0+0		Conf	73Kiev 2 95	May 73 – + TOF,10+ – 2.5B,TBL	
	2.5+4			Conf	73Kiev 2 95	May 73 – + SIG GVN FOR 3L,TBL	
				Jour	SNP 22 348	Oct 75 . ENGL OF YF 22,674	
	0.0+0	2.0+3		Rept	INDC(CCP) – 49	Feb 75 Vertebny+ ENGLISH OF 73KIEV 2 95	
(n,γ)	2.0–2	3.0+3	IJI	Expt Jour	YF 22 674	Oct 75 Vertebny+ TOF,SIG AT 2200 M/SEC,TBL	
				Jour	SNP 22 348	Oct 75 . ENGL OF YF 22,674	
Spect (n,γ)	3.0+1	6.0+2	HAR	Expt Jour	NP 14 212	Dec 59 Bird+RES CAPT SPECTRA.G INTS.TBL.	
				Rept	AERE – NP/GEN12	Aug 59 – + RES CAPT GAMMA SPECS.GRPH.	
Spect (n,γ)	Pile		BKB	Expt Jour	BKP 18 9	Oct 67 Kukoc+.GRAPH,SPIN DETERMINATION	
Spect (n,γ)	1.2+1	7.0+2	SAC	Expt Jour	NP/A 121 65	Dec 68 Samour+ RES CAPT.LVL SCHEME PT – 193	
				Rept	CEA – R – 3776	Apr 69 – . THESIS	
				Conf	67Bordeaux	Mar 67 – +G(GAMMA).NAT PT,GE DET.FP JPR	
				Rept	INDC – 156	67 Jackson+FULL PAPER OF 66PARIS.	
				Conf	66Paris 1 564	Oct 66 – +SPECT FROM 2 RES CAPTS.	
Spect (n,γ)	Pile		GIT	Expt Jour	ZP/A 279 27	76 Saleh+ INT CONVERSION 135.5 KEV	
Inelastic γ	2.0+5	6.0+5	LEB	Expt Conf	77Kiev	77 Konobeevsky+ GE – LI,SIG(NEUT – E),GRAPH	
(n,2n)	Fiss		CRC	Eval Rept	CRC – 1003	Dec 60 ROY+ ESTIMATED AVG SIG=6.7MB	
(n,2n)	1.4+7		GIT	Expt Jour	NP/A 180 157	Jan 72 Hankla+ – ACT,GE(LI),MIXED POWDER.	+
				Abst	DA/B 32 293	Nov 71 – . ACT METHOD, CFD THEORY.	
	1.4+7			Data	EXFOR10244.003	Jun 74 1PT SIGMA	
(n,2n)	1.5+7		JUL	Expt Jour	NP/A 185 614	May 72 Qaim. ACT,GE(LI). CFD TH+OTHR.	+
	1.5+7			Data	EXFOR20536.026	Apr 76 1PNT.SIGMA.	
(n,2n)	1.5+7		DEB	Eval Jour	REA 11 1 153	Mar 73 Boedy. COMPILATION+RECOMM.VALUE,TBL	
(n,2n)	1.5+7		KFI	Theo Rept	KFKI – 73 – 68	Dec 73 Jeki.NEW FIT,CALC SIG CFD OTHERS,TBL	
(n,2n)	1.5+7		TAT	Theo Jour	JP/A 7 1457	Aug 74 Kondaiah. CALC ON STAT MODEL	
(n,p)	Fiss		CRC	Eval Rept	CRC – 1003	Dec 60 ROY+ ESTIMATED AVG SIG=0.02MB	
(n,α)	Fiss		CRC	Eval Rept	CRC – 1003	Dec 60 ROY+ ESTIMATED AVG SIG=0.0005MB	
(n,α)	Maxwl		CCP	Expt Jour	YF 1 252	Feb 65 Andreev.IONIZ – CHAMBER,SIG=M.2MB	+
				Jour	SNP 1 177	Aug 65 TRANSLATN.*	
Reson Params	4.7+1		HAR	Expt Jour	NP 14 212	Dec 59 Bird+RES EN FROM TOF.ISTPE ASGN BY G	
				Rept	AERE – NP/GEN12	Aug 59 – +TBL RES EN.ISOTOPE ASSGN.GAMMA	
Reson Params	2.5+4		FEI	ExTh Prog	YFI – 4 22	May 67 Shorin+.,TBLS GIVEN,TBP YF	
				Prog	INDC – 187E	67 . ENGL TRANSL OF YFI – 4 22	
Reson Params		1.0+6	AUA	Expt Jour	AUJ 20 477	Oct 67 Cook. TBL OF AVG LVL SPACING D,L=0,1	
Reson Params	4.7+1	5.8+2	SAC	Expt Jour	NP/A 131 305	Jun 69 DE BARROS+ LINAC.WN,WN0,WG,WT,J,6RES	+
				Conf	68Wash. 867	Mar 68 Morgenstern.WG VS.A,AVERAGE WG GIVEN	
				Rept	CEA – R – 3385	Feb 68 Julien. (THESIS) DATA GIVEN.	
				Conf	66Paris 1 559	Oct 66 Huynh+ ABST.NDG. SEE INDC – 156	
	0.0+0	8.3+2		Data	EXFOR20685.	Jul 77 7PTS.E0,WG,AVG WG,WN,WT,J,G*WN.	
Reson Params	1.0+1	8.3+2	RIO	Expt Jour	NDF 15 167	Aug 69 Barros+ 5RESON,WT+WN+WG+SPIN TABLE	
Reson Params	–		AUA	Theo Rept	AAEC/E – 211	Nov 70 Musgrove. CALCULTD D+GAM WIDTH GIVEN	
Reson Params	4.7+1	3.9+2	CJD	Eval Rept	YK – 7	71 Zakharova+ SURVEY+SYSTEMATICS,GW,TBL	
				Rept	INDC(CCP) – 27	Nov 72 .ENGLISH TRANSLATION OF YK – 7 /71	
Reson Params	None		DUB	Theo Jour	YF 13 240	Feb 71 Malecki+G – WID,THEO CFD EXPT.TBL,GRPH	
				Jour	SNP 13 133	Aug 71 – + ENGL OF YF 13 240.	
Reson Params	2.2+1	9.0+2	IJI	Expt Conf	73Kiev 2 95	May 73 Vertebny+ TOF,WN,WG,D,TBL	
				Rept	INDC(CCP) – 49	Feb 75 – + ENGLISH OF 73KIEV 2 95	
Reson Params	0.0+0	2.0+3	IJI	Expt Jour	YFI – 18 32	Aug 74 Vertebny+ TOF,WN,D,AVG D,TBL	
Reson Params	2.2+1		IJI	Expt Jour	YF 22 674	Oct 75 Vertebny+ G – WID(1RES),D – OBS,D0.TABLE	
				Jour	SNP 22 348	Oct 75 . ENGL OF YF 22,674	
Strnth Fnctn		5.8+2	SAC	Expt Rept	CEA – R – 3609	Sep 68 Morgenstern. S – WAVE, RADIUS	+
				Conf	68Wash. 867	Mar 68 – +	
	0.0+0	5.8+2		Data	EXFOR20685.017	Jul 77 1PNT.L=0.	
Strnth Fnctn	–		AUA	Theo Rept	AAEC/E – 211	Nov 70 Musgrove. SMOOTHED S0,S1 AND S2 GIVN	
Strnth Fnctn	None		AUA	Eval Rept	AAEC/E – 277	Mar 73 Musgrove.TBLS EXPTL DATA+BEST VALUES	
Strnth Fnctn	9.6+1	1.3+3	IJI	Expt Conf	73Kiev 2 95	May 73 Vertebny+ STF GVN IN TBL	
	2.5+4			Conf	73Kiev 2 95	May 73 – + 3.6X10 – 4,TBL	
Strnth Fnctn	None		IJI	Expt Jour	YF 22 674	Oct 75 Vertebny+ TOF,S0 VAL,TBL,D,WG	
				Rept	YFI – 18 32	Aug 74 – + VAL GVN IN TBL	

78 Platinum 193

Quantity	Energy (ev) Min	Max	Lab	Type	Documentation Ref Vol Page	Date	Author, Comments	Data
Reson Params	–		AUA	Theo Rept	AAEC/E – 211	Nov 70	Musgrove. CALCULTD D+GAM WIDTH GIVEN	
Strnth Fnctn	–		AUA	Theo Rept	AAEC/E – 211	Nov 70	Musgrove. SMOOTHED S0,S1 AND S2 GIVN	
Lvl Density	+6		MIL	Theo Jour	EN 15 1 54	Jan 68	Facchini+ LDL PARS FROM LOW EN RES	
Lvl Density	None		COP	Theo Jour	NP/A 222 493	Apr 74	Dossing+COLL ROTAT.SPAC. ACCUR ESTIM	
Lvl Density	None		ROC	Theo Jour	NP/A 223 577	May 74	Huizenga+ EXP CFD MICROSC TH SPH NUC	

78 Platinum 194

Quantity	Energy (ev) Min	Max	Lab	Type	Documentation Ref Vol Page	Date	Author, Comments	Data
Total	7.0+6	1.4+7	CJD	Theo Rept	ICD – 5 20	68	Averjanov+ VIBRATION MDL,AT 4ES,TBL	
Elastic	7.0+6	1.4+7	CJD	Theo Rept	ICD – 5 20	68	Averjanov+ VIBRATION MDL,AT 4ES,TBL	
Elastic	2.0–2	3.0+3	IJI	Expt Jour	YF 22 674	Oct 75	Vertebny+ TRANS,TOF.AVG SCATSIG,TABL	
Potntal Scat		7.0+2	SAC	Expt Jour	NP/A 123 561	Jan 69	Morgenstern+ RADIUS FROM RES ANAL	+
				Rept	CEA – R – 3609	Sep 68	– + (THESIS) RADIUS.	
	0.0+0	7.0+2		Data	EXFOR20685.020	Jul 77	1PNT.RADIUS.	
Tot Inelastc	7.0+6	1.4+7	CJD	Theo Rept	ICD – 5 20	68	Averjanov+ VIBRATION MDL,AT 4ES,TBL	
Diff Inelast	1.4+7		LRL	Theo Rept	UCRL – 50181	Feb 67	Lutz+ CALC ANG DIST FOR FIRST 2+ LVL	
Diff Inelast	7.0+6	1.4+7	CJD	Theo Rept	ICD – 5 20	68	Averjanov+ TO 1ST LVL,ANGDIST,GRAPH	
Scattering	2.5–2	1.0+0	IJI	Expt Conf	73Kiev 2 95	May 73	Vertebny+ TOF,14.0+ – 0.2 B,TBL	
	2.5–2			Rept	INDC(CCP) – 49	Feb 75	– + ENGLISH OF 73KIEV 2 95	
Scattering	2.5–2		IJI	Expt Rept	YFI – 18 32	Aug 74	Vertebny+ VAL GVN IN TBL	
Absorption	2.5–2		IJI	Expt Rept	YFI – 18 32	Aug 74	Vertebny+ VAL GVN IN TBL	
(n,γ)	Maxwl		ORL	Expt Prog	ORNL – 1879 50	55	Pomerance.	+
	Maxwl			Data	EXFOR11885.005	Jun 76	. 1 PT.	
(n,γ)	Maxwl		BNL	Expt Jour	PR 128 761	Oct 62	Sehgal.ACT,87+ – 13MB(3.8DAY)REL AU197	+
	Maxwl			Data	EXFOR11994.011	Jun 76	. 1 PT	
(n,γ)	Maxwl		MUA	ExTh Jour	NP 41 372	Mar 63	Mangal+ (N,G)M SIGMA GVN,TH CFD EXPT	+
	Maxwl			Expt Data	EXFOR31249.010	Sep 72	.SIG GVN	
(n,γ)	Maxwl		KUR	Expt Jour	YF 7 937	May 68	Groshev+ OTHER SIG VALUE GIVEN	
				Jour	SNP 7 563	Nov 68	. ENGL OF YF 7 937	
(n,γ)	–		IEA	Comp Rept	IEA – INF – 10 6	Aug 68	Atalla. TABLES OF HL,SIG AND GAMM – E	
(n,γ)	3.0+4		AUA	Theo Rept	AAEC/E – 211	Nov 70	Musgrove. SIGMA GIVEN AND CFD OTHER	
(n,γ)	1.0+3	1.0+7	BOL	Eval Data	BENZI – DFN 830.	May 72	40 PNTS	+
(n,γ)	2.5–2	1.0+0	IJI	Expt Conf	73Kiev 2 95	May 73	Vertebny+ TOF,1.2+ – 0.4 B,TBL	
	0.0+0	2.0+3		Rept	INDC(CCP) – 49	Feb 75	– + ENGLISH OF 73KIEV 2 95	
(n,γ)	2.0–2	3.0+3	IJI	Expt Jour	YF 22 674	Oct 75	Vertebny+ TOF,SIG AT 2200 M/SEC,TBL	
				Jour	SNP 22 348	Oct 75	. ENGL OF YF 22,674	
Spect (n,γ)	3.8+2		SAC	Expt Jour	NP/A 121 65	Dec 68	Samour+ RES CAPT. 6109KEV G ONLY.	
	1.1+1	6.8+2		Rept	CEA – R – 3776	Apr 69	– .THESIS,GE – LI,LINAC	
Inelastic γ	1.7+6		LAS	Expt Conf	ORNL – 2309	Jun 57	DAY. TOF PHS D29D33D62MEVGS	
(n,2n)	Fiss		CRC	Eval Rept	CRC – 1003	Dec 60	ROY+ ESTIMATED AVG SIG = 4.0MB	
(n,2n)	1.3+7	1.5+7	BNL	Theo Jour	NSE 23 238	Nov 65	Pearlstein.3ES.STAT MDL CALC.TBL CS.	
(n,2n)	Fiss		BNL	Theo Jour	NSE 23 238	Nov 65	Pearlstein.STATMDL CALC.SPEC AVG.TBL	
(n,2n)	1.5+7		DEB	Eval Jour	REA 11 1 153	Mar 73	Boedy+ RECOMM.VALUE FROM N – Z SYSTEM.	
(n,2n)	1.5+7		KFI	Theo Rept	KFKI – 73 – 68	Dec 73	Jeki.NEW FIT,CALC SIG CFD OTHERS,TBL	
(n,xn) x>2	Fiss		BNL	Theo Jour	NSE 23 238	Nov 65	Pearlstein.SPEC AVG STATMDL CALC N3N	
(n,p)	1.4+7		ALD	Expt Jour	PPS 73 215	Feb 59	Coleman+. ACT. CFD DIRECT INTERACTN	+
(n,p)	Fiss		CRC	Eval Rept	CRC – 1003	Dec 60	ROY+ ESTIMATED AVG SIG = 0.008MB	
(n,p)	1.5+7		SAH	Comp Jour	NUC 23 8 112	Aug 65	Chatterjee. TABLE WITH REFS.	
(n,p)	1.5+7		DEB	Comp Jour	REA 7 4 93	Dec 69	Csikai+ SIG+HL COMPILTN,N – ACTIV – ANAL	
(n,p)	1.4+7	1.5+7	JYV	Eval Rept	JU – RR – 3/1970	Jun 70	Leppaemaeki+ TABLE OF EVAL AVG SIG	
(n,p)	1.4+7		KFI	Comp Jour	JRC 7 365	Jun 71	Nagy+ SIGMA, GAMMA – E AND HALF – L GIVN	
(n,p)	1.4+7		GIT	Expt Jour	NP 180 157	Jan 72	Hankla+ ACT,GE(LI),MIXED POWDER.	+
				Abst	DA/B 32 293	Nov 71	– . ACT METHOD, CFD THEORY.	
	1.4+7			Data	EXFOR10244.021	Jun 74	1PT SIGMA	
(n,p)	1.4+7	1.5+7	KAZ	Theo Jour	YF 18 705	Oct 73	Levkovsky.AVERAGED SIG,CALC,TBL	
				Jour	SNP 18 361	Apr 74	. ENGLISH OF YF 18,705	
(n,α)	1.4+7		ALD	Expt Jour	PPS 73 215	Feb 59	Coleman+. ACTIVATION	+
(n,α)	Fiss		CRC	Eval Rept	CRC – 1003	Dec 60	ROY+ ESTIMATED AVG SIG = BELO 0.0001MB	
(n,α)	1.4+7		CIS	Theo Jour	NP 51 460	Feb 64	Facchini+STATMOD SIG XPT/CALC = 58 – 86	
(n,α)	Maxwl		CCP	Expt Jour	YF 1 252	Feb 65	Andreev.IONIZ – CHAMBER,SIG = M.005MB	+
				Jour	SNP 1 177	Aug 65	TRANSLATN.*	
(n,α)	1.5+7		DEB	Comp Jour	REA 7 4 93	Dec 69	Csikai+ SIG+HL COMPILTN,N – ACTIV – ANAL	
(n,α)	1.4+7	1.5+7	JYV	Eval Rept	JU – RR – 3/1970	Jun 70	Leppaemaeki+ TABLE OF EVAL AVG SIG	
(n,α)	1.4+7	1.5+7	KAZ	Theo Jour	YF 18 705	Oct 73	Levkovsky.AVERAGED SIG,CALC,TBL	
				Jour	SNP 18 361	Apr 74	. ENGLISH OF YF 18,705	

78 Platinum 194

Quantity	Energy (ev) Min	Energy (ev) Max	Lab	Type	Documentation Ref Vol Page	Date	Author, Comments	Data
Reson Params	3.8+2	7.0+2	SAC	Expt	Jour NP/A 131 305	Jun 69	DE BARROS+ LINAC.WN,WN0,WG,WT,J,4RES	+
					Conf 68Wash. 867	Mar 68	Morgenstern.WG VS.A,AVERAGE WG GIVEN	
					Rept CEA-R-3385	Feb 68	Julien+ (THESIS) DATA GIVEN.	
					Rept CEA-R-3077	Dec 67	De Barros.ISOTOPIC ASS.TBL WN,WG.	
					Conf 66Paris 1 559	Oct 66	Huynh+ ABST.NDG. SEE INDC-156	
	2.6+2	3.1+2			Jour CR 254 4287	Jun 62	Corge+ TOF.TRANSMISSION. SUPERSEDED.	
	0.0+0	8.3+2			Data EXFOR20685.	Jul 77	5PTS.E0,WG,AVG WG,WN,WT,J,G*WN.	
Reson Params	1.0+1	8.3+2	RIO	Expt	Jour NDF 15 167	Aug 69	Barros+ 3RESON,WT+WN+WG+SPIN TABLE	
Reson Params	–		AUA	Theo	Rept AAEC/E-211	Nov 70	Musgrove. CALCULTD D+GAM WIDTH GIVEN	
Reson Params	3.8+2	4.9+2	CJD	Eval	Rept YK-7	71	Zakharova+ SURVEY+SYSTEMATICS,GW,TBL	
					Rept INDC(CCP)-27	Nov 72	.ENGLISH TRANSLATION OF YK-7 /71	
Reson Params	None		DUB	Theo	Jour YF 13 240	Feb 71	Malecki+G-WID,THEO CFD EXPT.TBL,GRPH	
					Jour SNP 13 133	Aug 71	– + ENGL OF YF 13 240.	
Reson Params	None		DUB	Theo	Jour ZEP 14 194	Aug 71	Solovev.LARGE N-WID G-WID CORREL.NDG	
					Rept JINR-E4-5880	71	Soloviev.N-GAM-WIDS CORR.SHORT NOTE	
					Jour JEL 14 129	Aug 71	– . ENGL OF ZEP 14 194.	
Reson Params	3.7+2	2.5+3	IJI	Expt	Jour 73Kiev 2 95	May 73	Vertebny+ TOF,WN,D,TBL	
					Rept INDC(CCP)-49	Feb 75	– + ENGLISH OF 73KIEV 2 95	
Reson Params	None		DUB	Theo	Rept JINR-P4-7499	Oct 73	Soloviev+ CALC D CFD EXPTS,TABLE	
Reson Params	0.0+0	2.0+3	IJI	Expt	Rept YFI-18 32	Aug 74	Vertebny+ TOF,WN,D,AVG D,TBL	
Reson Params	2.0-2	3.0+3	IJI	Expt	Jour YF 22 674	Oct 75	Vertebny+ TRANS,TOF.AVG D-OBS,D0.TBL	
					Jour SNP 22 348	Oct 75	. ENGL OF YF 22,674	
Strnth Fnctn		7.0+2	SAC	Expt	Jour NP/A 123 561	Jan 69	Morgenstern+ FROM RES ANALYSIS.	+
					Rept CEA-R-3609	Sep 68	– . S-WAVE,RADIUS	
					Conf 68Wash. 867	Mar 68	– +	
					Conf 66Paris 1 183	Oct 66	– + PPR65.ABST.NDG.INDC-156	
	0.0+0	7.0+2			Data EXFOR20685.021	Jul 77	1PNT.L=0.	
Strnth Fnctn	–		AUA	Theo	Rept AAEC/E-211	Nov 70	Musgrove. SMOOTHED S0,S1 AND S2 GIVN	
Strnth Fnctn	None		AUA	Eval	Rept AAEC/E-277	Mar 73	Musgrove.TBLS EXPTL DATA+BEST VALUES	
Strnth Fnctn	9.6+1	1.3+3	IJI	Expt	Conf 73Kiev 2 95	May 73	Vertebny+ STF GVN IN TBL	
Strnth Fnctn	None		IJI	Expt	Jour YF 22 674	Oct 75	Vertebny+ TOF,S0 VAL,TBL,D,WG	
					Rept YFI-18 32	Aug 74	– + VAL GVN IN TBL	
Lvl Density	None		AUW	Theo	Conf 70Madurai 2 267	Dec 70	Ramamurty+ A-PARAMETER GVN,LANG'S TH	

78 Platinum 195

Quantity	Energy (ev) Min	Energy (ev) Max	Lab	Type	Documentation Ref Vol Page	Date	Author, Comments	Data
Elastic	2.0-2	3.0+3	IJI	Expt	Jour YF 22 674	Oct 75	Vertebny+ TRANS,TOF.AVG SCATSIG,TABL	
Potntal Scat		8.2+2	SAC	Expt	Jour NP/A 123 561	Jan 69	Morgenstern+ RADIUS FROM RES ANAL	+
					Rept CEA-R-3609	Sep 68	– + (THESIS) RADIUS.	
	0.0+0	8.2+2			Data EXFOR20685.024	Jul 77	1PNT.RADIUS.	
Scattering	2.5-2	1.0+0	IJI	Expt	Conf 73Kiev 2 95	May 73	Vertebny+ TOF,10.1+ -0.2 B,TBL	
Scattering	2.5-2		IJI	Expt	Rept YFI-18 32	Aug 74	Vertebny+ VAL GVN IN TBL	
Absorption	2.5-2		IJI	Expt	Rept YFI-18 32	Aug 74	Vertebny+ VAL GVN IN TBL	
(n,γ)	Maxwl		ORL	Expt	Prog ORNL-1879 50	55	Pomerance.	+
	Maxwl				Data EXFOR11885.006	Jun 76	. 1 PT.	
(n,γ)	Maxwl		KUR	Expt	Jour YF 7 937	May 68	Groshev+ OTHER SIG VALUE GIVEN	
					Jour SNP 7 563	Nov 68	. ENGL OF YF 7 937	
(n,γ)	4.6+2	4.9+2	RIO	Expt	Jour NDF 15 167	Aug 69	Barros+ TOF TRANSM GRAPH,5 RESONANCS	
(n,γ)	3.0+4		AUA	Theo	Rept AAEC/E-211	Nov 70	Musgrove. SIGMA GIVEN AND CFD OTHER	
(n,γ)	1.0+3	1.0+7	BOL	Eval	Data BENZI-DFN 831.	May 72	40 PNTS	+
(n,γ)	2.5-2	1.0+0	IJI	Expt	Conf 73Kiev 2 95	May 73	Vertebny+ TOF,3.0+ -1.2B,TBL	
(n,γ)	2.0-2	3.0+3	IJI	Expt	Jour YF 22 674	Oct 75	Vertebny+ TOF,SIG AT 2200 M/SEC,TBL	
					Jour SNP 22 348	Oct 75	. ENGL OF YF 22,674	
Spect (n,γ)	None		YAL	Expt	Abst BAP 1 296	Jun 56	Bennett+ LOW E LINES ONLY LINAC+SCIN	
Spect (n,γ)	Maxwl		KUR	Expt	Conf 58Geneva 15 138	Sep 58	Groshev+ PPR2029.CURV,COMPTON-SPEC	
Spect (n,γ)	*		CCP		Abst BAP 4 34	Jan 59	BRUSSL PHS J1 12EV J0 19D6 68EV	
Spect (n,γ)	3.0+1	6.0+2	HAR	Expt	Jour NP 14 212	Dec 59	Bird+RES CAPT SPECTRA.G INTS.TBL.	
					Rept AERE-NP/GEN12	Aug 59	– + RES CAPT GAMMA SPECS.GRPH.	
Spect (n,γ)	1.2+1	2.0+1	YAL	Expt	Jour NP 14 693	Jan 60	Draper+REL GAMMA WIDTHS,2RES.CRYSPEC	
Spect (n,γ)	6.7+1		ANL	Expt	Jour PR 124 1142	Nov 61	Jackson+ FAST CHOPPER LOW E GAMMAS	
Spect (n,γ)	1.2+1	3.0+2	BNL	Expt	Jour PR 127 1680	Sep 62	Chrien+,REL INT OF 3GS AT 12 RES	
Spect (n,γ)	1.2+1	6.9+1	ITE	Expt	Jour ZET 45 870	Oct 63	Ratynskij.G-SPEC FROM 3 N-RES COMPRD	
					Jour JET 18 598	Mar 64	TRANSLATN.*	
Spect (n,γ)	1.2+1	1.9+2	ANL	Expt	Jour PR 132 1640	Nov 63	Bollinger+ FC.E-LVLS OF COMP-NUCL.PT	

78 Platinum 195

Quantity	Energy (ev) Min	Energy (ev) Max	Lab	Type	Documentation Ref Vol Page	Date	Author, Comments	Data
Spect (n,γ)	1.2+1		JAE	Expt Rept	JAERI – 1073	Mar 65	Kawarasaki. RES CAPT.LINAC.TOF.E,INT	+
				Rept	INDSWG – 90 6	Jul 65	– . TABLE E,INTS GIVEN.	
	1.2+1			Data	EXFOR20277.020	Jun 74	2PTS.	
Spect (n,γ)	1.2+1	6.7+1	ANL	Expt Conf	66Argonne 501	Nov 66	Cote+,3 RESON ES,GE(LI),CURVES	
Spect (n,γ)	1.2+1	6.8+1	CRC	Expt Abst	BAP 13 722	Apr 68	Bartholomew+2. STRONG GS NEAR5.5MEV	
Spect (n,γ)	Maxwl		KUR	Expt Jour	YF 7 937	May 68	Groshev+ GAM – E,INTS.DECAY SCHEME	
				ExTh Jour	NP 16 645	Jun 60	– + COMPTON SPEC,+THEOR DISCUSS	
				Expt Jour	SNP 7 563	Nov 68	. ENGL OF YF 7 937	
Spect (n,γ)	1.0+1	7.0+2	SAC	Expt Jour	NP/A 121 65	Dec 68	Samour+ GE(LI).WG(I) 22LVLS OKS P – T.	+
				Conf	JINR – D3893 52	May 68	Alves+LINAC,LVL SCH,30RESONANCES	
				Conf	68Wash. § E2	Mar 68	Samour+ FOR PARTIAL GAMMA WIDTHS.	
				Conf	66Paris 1 175	Oct 66	– + PPR60.	
				Conf	66Paris 1 564	Oct 66	Jackson+CAPT IN 22RES.NDG.	
				Jour	PRL 17 656	Sep 66	– + FOR PARTIAL WG. SUPERSEDED	
				Rept	CEA – R – 2810	Jun 65	Huynh.NAI DETS. SUPERSEDED.	
				Jour	CR 254 4162	Jun 62	Julien+TOF RES ISOTOPIC ATTRIBUTION	
Spect (n,γ)	Pile		ANL	Expt Conf	69Studsvik 601	Aug 69	Smither+ NO DATA GVN,OKS STATMOD	
				Conf	68DUBSY 317	Jul 68	Bollinger.ANAL.RAD. TRANSITIONS.	
				Conf	JINR – D – 3893	May 68	– + ABSTRACT,NO DATA GIVEN	
Spect (n,γ)	Maxwl	+3	CRC	Revw Conf	69Studsvik 553	Aug 69	Bartholomev. GRPH GVN, '5.5MEV BUMP'	
Spect (n,γ)		1.9+1	RIO	Expt Jour	NDF 15 167	Aug 69	Barros+ 350KEV GAMMA PEAK,GRPH	
Spect (n,γ)	Maxwl		KFI	Revw Jour	YF 10 907	Nov 69	Kecskemeti+ AVG GAM – MULTIPLICITY,TBL	
				Jour	SNP 10 524	May 70	TRANSLATN.*	
Spect (n,γ)	1.2+1		BNL	Expt Prog	NCSAC – 33 16	Dec 70	Chrien+,ABSOL GAMMA INTENSITY REL AU	
Spect (n,γ)	1.0+7		WWA	Theo Jour	NP/A 189 545	Jul 72	Brzosko+ CMPD NUCL DECAY.PARTIAL WG	
(n,2n)	Fiss		CRC	Eval Rept	CRC – 1003	Dec 60	Roy+,ESTIMATED AVG SIG=37.5MB	
(n,2n)	1.3+7	1.5+7	BNL	Theo Jour	NSE 23 238	Nov 65	Pearlstein.3ES.STAT MDL CALC.TBL CS.	
(n,2n)	Fiss		BNL	Theo Jour	NSE 23 238	Nov 65	Pearlstein.STATMDL CALC.SPEC AVG.TBL	
(n,2n)	1.5+7		DEB	Eval Jour	REA 11 1 153	Mar 73	Boedy+ RECOMM.VALUE FROM N – Z SYSTEM.	
(n,2n)	1.5+7		KFI	Theo Rept	KFKI – 73 – 68	Dec 73	Jeki.NEW FIT,CALC SIG CFD OTHERS,TBL	
(n,xn) x>2	Fiss		BNL	Theo Jour	NSE 23 238	Nov 65	Pearlstein.SPEC AVG STATMDL CALC N3N	
(n,p)	1.4+7		ALD	Expt Jour	PPS 73 215	Feb 59	Coleman+. ACT. CFD DIRECT INTERACTN	+
(n,p)	Fiss		CRC	Eval Rept	CRC – 1003	Dec 60	Roy+,ESTIMATED AVG SIG=0.001MB	
(n,p)	1.5+7		SAH	Comp Jour	NUC 23 8 112	Aug 65	Chatterjee. TABLE WITH REFS.	
	1.4+7			Jour	NP 60 273	Nov 64	– .MEAN OF EXPT CFD SHELLMOD	
(n,p)	1.5+7		DEB	Comp Jour	REA 7 4 93	Dec 69	Csikai+ SIG+HL COMPILTN,N – ACTIV – ANAL	
(n,p)	1.4+7	1.5+7	JYV	Eval Rept	JU – RR – 3/1970	Jun 70	Leppaemaeki+ TABLE OF EVAL AVG SIG	
(n,p)	1.4+7	1.5+7	KAZ	Theo Jour	YF 18 705	Oct 73	Levkovsky.AVERAGED SIG,CALC,TBL	
				Jour	SNP 18 361	Apr 74	. ENGLISH OF YF 18,705	
(n,α)	Fiss		CRC	Eval Rept	CRC – 1003	Dec 60	Roy+,ESTIMATED AVG SIG=0.0001MB	
(n,α)	Maxwl		CCP	Expt Jour	YF 1 252	Feb 65	Andreev.IONIZ – CHAMBER,SIG=M.005MB	+
				Jour	SNP 1 177	Aug 65	TRANSLATN.*	
Reson Params	1.2+1	1.5+2	BNL	Expt Jour	PR 108 353	57	Stolovy+	+
	1.2+1	1.5+2		Data	EXFOR11866.013	Jun 76	. 5 RES, EO,WT,WN,WG	
Reson Params	1.2+1		BNL	Expt Jour	PR 108 353	Oct 57	Harvey+,FC,TRNS WT WN WG	+
Reson Params	1.2+0	6.8+1	CCP	Expt Abst	BAP 4 34	Jan 59	BRUSSL PHS +19D6EV J1 J0 J0	+
Reson Params	3.2+1	1.5+2	BNL	Expt Prog	WASH – 1026 11	Oct 59	Zimmerman+ PART RAD WIDTHS	+
	1.2+1	6.7+1		Data	EXFOR12494.003	Jun 76	. 3 RES, EO,WN	
Reson Params	6.9+1	3.1+2	HAR	Expt Jour	NP 14 212	Dec 59	Bird+RES EN FROM TOF.ISTPE ASGN BY G	
				Rept	AERE – NP/GEN12	Aug 59	– +TBL RES EN.ISOTOPE ASSGN.GAMMA	
Reson Params	1.2+1	2.0+1	YAL	Expt Jour	NP 14 693	Jan 60	Draper.	+
	1.2+1	2.0+1		Data	EXFOR12498.002	Jun 76	. 2 RES, J	
Reson Params	1.2+1	1.6+2	ORL	Expt Conf	60Vienna 535	Oct 60	Block+.NDG,EXPT DESCRIBED	
Reson Params	1.2+1	6.8+1	RPI	Expt Jour	PR 120 2090	Dec 60	Waters.TOF,GIVES G,WN,WG	+
Reson Params	6.7+1		ANL	Expt Jour	PR 124 1142	Nov 61	Jackson+ FAST CHOPPER E0	+
				Jour	PRL 6 695	61	Cote.	
Reson Params	1.2+1	3.0+2	BNL	Expt Jour	PR 127 1680	Sep 62	Chrien+,J FOR 12RES FROM NGAMMA SPEC	
Reson Params	1.2+1	6.7+1	CCP	ExTh Jour	ZET 45 875	Oct 63	Ignat'Ev.3RES,MORE DATA INDSWG64 P19	+
Reson Params	1.2+1	1.9+2	ANL	Expt Jour	PR 132 1640	Nov 63	Bollinger+	+
	1.2+1	6.8+1		Jour	PRL 3 376	Oct 59	– +,PARTIAL WG FLUCTUATES,J	
	6.7+1	1.5+2		Prog	ANL – 6072 4	59	Thomas.	
	1.2+1	1.6+2		Data	EXFOR12195.003	Jun 76	. 4 RES, E0,J	
Reson Params		1.0+6	AUA	Theo Jour	AUJ 20 477	Oct 67	Cook. TBL OF AVG LVL SPACING D,L=0,1	

78 Platinum 195

Quantity	Energy (ev) Min	Max	Lab	Type	Documentation Ref Vol Page	Date	Author, Comments	Data
Reson Params	1.2+1	8.4+2	SAC	Expt	Jour NP/A 131 305	Jun 69	De Barros+LINAC SAME DATA CEA-R3385	+
	1.2+1	8.3+2			Jour NP/A 132 129	Jul 69	Julien+LINAC. WG J=0,1 28E0	
	1.2+1	6.8+2			Rept CEA-R-3602	Jul 69	Alves. (THESIS)	
	1.2+1	8.3+2			Rept CEA-R-3776	Apr 69	Samour. (THESIS) DATA GIVEN	
					Jour NP/A 121 65	Dec 68	- + TBL LVLS,WG,WN.	
					Conf 68DUBSY 361	Jul 68	- .WG=DISTRIBUTION+INTERFERENCE	
				ExTh	Conf JINR-D3893 119	May 68	+GAM WITDTH ANALYSIS,GRAPHS	
				Expt	Conf 68Wash. 867	Mar 68	Morgenstern.WG VS.A,AVERAGE WG GIVEN	
					Rept CEA-R-3385	Feb 68	Julien.WN WN0 WG WT J 42 E0 THESIS	
					Conf 66Paris 1 559	Oct 66	Huynh+ ABST.NDG. SEE INDC-156	
					Rept CEA-R-3077	Apr 66	De Barros+ SUPERSEDED. NAITL. J=1	
					Conf 65Antwerp 525	Jul 65	- + PPR73.ABST.NDG	
					Jour PL 3 67	Dec 62	Corge+ SUPERSEDED	
					Jour CR 254 4287	Jun 62	- + SUPERSEDED	
	1.2+1	1.5+2			Jour JPR 22 722	Oct 61	- +TOF NAI(TL) WG PARTIAL 8PARAM	
	1.2+1	8.3+2			Jour JPR 21 426	May 60	- + SUPERSEDED	
	6.9+1	8.3+2			Jour CR 249 413	Jul 59	- + E0 ONLY 22RES J=1	
	0.0+0	8.3+2			Data EXFOR20685.	Jul 77	46PTS.E0,WG,AVG WG,WN,WT,J,G*WN.	
Reson Params	+3	+5	AUA	ExTh	Rept AAEC/E-198	May 69	Musgrove.RES PARS +STF FROM (NG)FIT	+
Reson Params	None		BNL	Expt	Conf 69Studsvik 627	Aug 69	Chrien. WG-DISTR CFD PORTER-THOM,TBL	
Reson Params	1.0+1	8.3+2	RIO	Expt	Jour NDF 15 167	Aug 69	Barros+ 44RESON,WT,WG,WN,D,SPIN TBL	
Reson Params	-		AUA	Theo	Rept AAEC/E-211	Nov 70	Musgrove. CALCULTD D+GAM WIDTH GIVEN	
Reson Params	1.2+1	7.9+2	CJD	Eval	Rept YK-7	71	Zakharova+ SURVEY+SYSTEMATICS,GW,TBL	
					Rept INDC(CCP)-27	Nov 72	.ENGLISH TRANSLATION OF YK-7 /71	
Reson Params	None		DUB	Theo	Jour YF 13 240	Feb 71	Malecki+G-WID,THEO CFD EXPT.TBL,GRPH	
					Jour SNP 13 133	Aug 71	- + ENGL OF YF 13 240.	
Reson Params	-		DUB	Theo	Rept JINR-E4-5711	Apr 71	Soloviev.RESONANCE STRUCTURE STUDY	
Reson Params	None		DUB	Theo	Rept JINR-P4-7499	Oct 73	Soloviev+ CALC D CFD EXPTS,TABLE	
Reson Params	1.2+1	1.9+1	IJI	Expt	Jour YF 22 674	Oct 75	Vertebny+ G-WIDTHS AT 2RES,TABLE	
					Jour SNP 22 348	Oct 75	. ENGL OF YF 22,674	
Reson Params	Maxwl		KUK	Theo	Conf 76Ahmedabd 2 1	Dec 76	Sharma+AVG S-WAVE REDUCED N-WID ANAL	
Strnth Fnctn	5.0+4	1.5+5	DKE	Expt	Conf 64Paris 2 916	Jul 64	Seth+S0,S1,S2 R PRIME/R DUKE U.	
Strnth Fnctn	1.2+1	8.3+2	SAC	Expt	Jour NP/A 131 305	Jun 69	De Barros+SAME DATA IN CEA-R-3385	+
					Jour NP/A 123 561	Jan 69	Morgenstern+ FROM RES ANALYSIS.	
					Rept CEA-R-3609	Sep 68	- . (THESIS) S-WAVE. RADIUS	
					Conf 68Wash. 867	Mar 68	- + PPR E27.	
					Rept CEA-R-3385	Feb 68	Julien.S-WAVE,J=0,1. THESIS	
					Rept CEA-R-3077	Dec 67	De Barros.S+P WV.S0=1.7+-0.5(10-4)	
					Conf 66Paris 1 205	Oct 66	Julien+ PPR64.ABST.NDG. SEE INDC-156	
					Jour NP 66 433	May 65	- +S0 IN TBL.DATA EQU PL 3 1963.	
					Jour PL 10 86	May 64	- +S0 IN TBL.EQU PL 3 67,1963.	
					Jour PL 3 67	Dec 62	- +S0+S1 FROM RESPARS.SUPERSEDED	
					Jour JPR 21 426	May 60	Corge+ SUPERSEDED	
	0.0+0	8.2+2			Data EXFOR20685.025	Jul 77	1PNT.L=0.	
Strnth Fnctn	+3	+5	AUA	ExTh	Rept AAEC/E-198	May 69	Musgrove.S+P+D STF FROM (NG)FIT,TBL	+
Strnth Fnctn	1.0+1	8.3+2	RIO	Expt	Jour NDF 15 167	Aug 69	Barros+ S0 VALUE +- ERROR GVN	
Strnth Fnctn	-		DUB	Revw	Jour YF 11 111	Jan 70	Malecki+ VALUES FOR TWO SPIN STATES	
					Jour SNP 11 61	Jul 70	- + ENGL OF YF 11 61.	
Strnth Fnctn	-		AUA	Theo	Rept AAEC/E-211	Nov 70	Musgrove. SMOOTHED S0,S1 AND S2 GIVN	
Strnth Fnctn	None		AUA	Eval	Rept AAEC/E-277	Mar 73	Musgrove.TBLS EXPTL DATA+BEST VALUES	
Strnth Fnctn	9.6+1	1.3+3	IJI	Expt	Conf 73Kiev 2 95	May 73	Vertebny+ STF GVN IN TBL	
Strnth Fnctn	None		IJI	Expt	Jour YF 22 674	Oct 75	Vertebny+ TOF,S0 VAL,TBL,D,WG	
					Rept YFI-18 32	Aug 74	- + VAL GVN IN TBL	
Lvl Density	None		AUW	Theo	Conf 70Madurai 2 267	Dec 70	Ramamurty+ A-PARAMETER GVN,LANG'S TH	
Lvl Density	None		DUB	Theo	Jour NP/A 224 411	May 74	Soloviev+ 1/2 MICROSC MDL. SPH NUCL.	

78 Platinum 196

Quantity	Energy (ev) Min	Max	Lab	Type	Documentation Ref Vol Page	Date	Author, Comments	Data
Elastic Scattering	2.0-2	3.0+3	IJI	Expt	Jour YF 22 674	Oct 75	Vertebny+ TRANS,TOF.AVG SCATSIG,TABL	
	2.5-2	1.0+0	IJI	Expt	Conf 73Kiev 2 95	May 73	Vertebny+ TOF,12.3+- 0.2 B,TBL	
Scattering	2.5-2				Rept INDC(CCP)-49	Feb 75	- + ENGLISH OF 73KIEV 2 95	
Scattering	2.5-2		IJI	Expt	Rept YFI-18 32	Aug 74	Vertebny+ VAL GVN IN TBL	
Absorption	Maxwl		UK	Expt	Jour BJAS 5 71	56	Macrae+INSTRUMENTATION OF REACTORS	
Absorption	2.5-2		IJI	Expt	Rept YFI-18 32	Aug 74	Vertebny+ VAL GVN IN TBL	

78 Platinum 196

Quantity	Energy (ev) Min	Max	Lab	Type	Documentation Ref Vol Page	Date	Author, Comments	Data
Res Int Abs	5.0−1		NPL Expt	Jour	JNE 25 129	Mar 71	Ryves+REL AU.LESS 1/V PART.ACT EXPT.	+
				Conf	71Canterby 139	Sep 71	− .REDUCED CAPT RES INTEGRAL,TBL	
	5.0−1			Data	EXFOR20791.018	Dec 78	1PNT.REDUCED CAPT INTGRL.	
Res Int Abs	5.0−1		GHT Expt	Jour	JRC 20 695	74	Van Der Linden+ BY (N,G).CFD OTH,TBL	+
	5.5−1			Conf	73Paris 2 241	Mar 73	− + ACT,REL THR+GOLD,TBL	
	5.5−1			Data	EXFOR20645.055	Jul 76	1PNT.CAPTURE.	
(n,γ)	Pile		ANL Expt	Jour	PR 72 888	Nov 47	Seren+ ACT TO 1.5MIN,18HR,70D ISOMRS	
	Pile			Data	EXFOR11447.	Jun 76	. 2 PTS, SIG FOR 2 ISOMERS	
(n,γ)	Maxwl		ORL Expt	Prog	ORNL−1879 50	55	Pomerance.	+
	Maxwl			Data	EXFOR11885.007	Jun 76	. 1 PT.	
(n,γ)	Maxwl		ORL Expt	Conf	55ANS 203	Dec 55	Brookshank.	+
	Maxwl			Data	EXFOR11426.014	Jun 76	. 1 PT.	
(n,γ)	Pile		ORL Expt	Prog	WASH−191	Jun 56	Lyon+ ACTIVATION,SIGMA GIVEN	
(n,γ)	2.5+4		LRL Expt	Jour	PR 112 226	Oct 58	Booth+ SB − BE REL I+THR,ACT 19H HL	+
				Abst	BAP 2 268	Sep 57	. ABST L6	
	2.5+4			Data	EXFOR11429.029	Jun 76	. 1 PT.	
(n,γ)	1.1+2	3.0+2	SAC Expt	Jour	JPR 21 426	May 60	Corge+ DATA FOR RESONANCE ANALYSIS.	+
(n,γ)	Maxwl		MUAExpt	Jour	NP 36 542	Aug 62	Mangal+ SCINT SPECT,REL TO AU197,TBL	+
	Maxwl			Data	EXFOR31248.013	Apr 73	.SIG GVN	
(n,γ)	Maxwl		BNL Expt	Jour	PR 128 761	Oct 62	Sehgal.ACT,50+ − 10MB(86MIN) REL AU197	+
	Maxwl			Data	EXFOR11994.	Jun 76	. 2 PTS, SIG AND ISM RATIO	
(n,γ)	Maxwl		ANL Comp	Jour	NP 60 241	Nov 64	Bishop+EXP AND TH ISOMER RATIOS CFD	
(n,γ)	Maxwl		UCB Expt	Rept	NYO−10175	Dec 64	Arino+ACT.TBLS,GRPHS.PRODUCT HL.	+
	Maxwl			Data	EXFOR11817.023	Jun 76	. 1 PT.	
(n,γ)	2.4+4		MUAExpt	Jour	PR 152 1055	Dec 66	Chaubey+ SIG(18 HRS) REL I−127,TBL	+
	2.4+4			Data	EXFOR30079.039	Dec 70	SIGMA FOR 18. H HALF−LIFE	
(n,γ)	Maxwl		KUR Expt	Jour	YF 7 937	May 68	Groshev+ OTHER SIG VALUE GIVEN	
				Jour	SNP 7 563	Nov 68	. ENGL OF YF 7 937	
(n,γ)	−		IEA Comp	Rept	IEA−INF−10 6	Aug 68	Atalla. TABLES OF HL,SIG AND GAMM−E	
(n,γ)	3.0+4		AUA Theo	Rept	AAEC/E−211	Nov 70	Musgrove. SIGMA GIVEN AND CFD OTHER	
(n,γ)	2.5+4		AUWExpt	Conf	70Madurai 2 19	Dec 70	Lakshmana Rao+. HIGH+LOW SPIN SIGMAS	+
	2.5+4			Data	EXFOR30246.	Jun 73	.SIG TO GROUND AND META.ISOM RATIO	
(n,γ)	2.5−2		NPL Expt	Jour	JNE 25 129	Mar 71	Ryves Rel Au.SIG=0.74+ − .08B.ACT EXPT	
				Conf	71Canterby 139	71	Ryves. VDG,GRAPHITE MODERATOR.ACTIVN	
	2.5−2			Data	EXFOR20791.017	Dec 78	1PNT.SIGMA.	
(n,γ)	1.0+3	1.0+7	BOL Eval	Data	BENZI−DFN 832.	May 72	40 PNTS	+
(n,γ)	2.5+4		AUWExpt	Jour	NCL 5 16 1025	Dec 72	Lakshmana−Rao+ TO M,G,ISORAT	
(n,γ)	2.5−2	1.0+0	IJI Expt	Conf	73Kiev 2 95	May 73	Vertebny+ TOF,0.3−+ −0.2B,TBL	
	0.0+0	2.0+3		Rept	INDC(CCP)−49	Feb 75	− + ENGLISH OF 73KIEV 2 95	
(n,γ)	2.5−2		BRK Theo	Jour	NP/A 237 3 419	Jan 75	Nardi+ ISOM RATIO,MTE−CARLO,CFD XPT	
(n,γ)	2.0−2	3.0+3	IJI Expt	Jour	YF 22 674	Oct 75	Vertebny+ TOF,SIG AT 2200 M/SEC,TBL	
				Jour	SNP 22 348	Oct 75	. ENGL OF YF 22,674	
Spect (n,γ)	Maxwl		ANL Theo	Conf	68DUBSY 317	Jul 68	Bollinger.ANAL.RAD. TRANSITIONS.	
Spect (n,γ)	1.2+1	7.0+2	SAC Expt	Jour	NP/A 121 65	Dec 68	Samour+ RES CAPT.LVL SCH PT−197	
				Conf	67Bordeaux	Mar 67	− +G(GAMMA).NAT PT,GE DET.FP JPR	
				Conf	66Paris 1 564	Oct 66	Jackson+ 18 LVLS. SUPERSEDED.	
				Jour	PRL 17 656	Sep 66	− + 22 LVLS.RES CAPT	
Spect (n,γ)	Pile		HAMExpt	Jour	ZP 230 72	Dec 69	Gerdau+ LVL SCH OF PT−197 CF	
(n,2n)	Fiss		CRC Eval	Rept	CRC−1003	Dec 60	ROY+ ESTIMATED AVG SIG=5.7MB	
(n,2n)	1.3+7	1.5+7	BNL Theo	Jour	NSE 23 238	Nov 65	Pearlstein.3ES.STAT MDL CALC.TBL CS.	
(n,2n)	Fiss		BNL Theo	Jour	NSE 23 238	Nov 65	Pearlstein.STATMDL CALC.SPEC AVG.TBL	
(n,2n)	1.4+7		GIT Expt	Jour	NP/A 180 157	Jan 72	Hankla+ ACT,GE(LI),MIXED POWDER.	+
				Abst	DA/B 32 293	Nov 71	− . ACT METHOD, CFD THEORY.	
	1.4+7			Data	EXFOR10244.004	Jun 74	1PT,SIGMA,META,INCL PT195 SIN.	
(n,2n)	1.5+7		DEB Eval	Jour	REA 11 1 153	Mar 73	Boedy+ RECOMM.VALUE FROM N−Z SYSTEM.	
(n,2n)	1.5+7		KFI Theo	Rept	KFKI−73−68	Dec 73	Jeki.NEW FIT,CALC SIG CFD OTHERS,TBL	
(n,xn) x>2	Fiss		BNL Theo	Jour	NSE 23 238	Nov 65	Pearlstein.SPEC AVG STATMDL CALC N3N	
(n,p)	Fiss		CRC Eval	Rept	CRC−1003	Dec 60	ROY+ ESTIMATED AVG SIG=0.002MB	
(n,p)	1.4+7		IRK Expt	Jour	APA 23 185	May 66	Vonach. ACTIVATION.	
	1.4+7			Data	EXFOR20031.002	Sep 71	1PNT.SIG.	
(n,p)	1.4+7		MUNExpt	Jour	ZP 195 343	Aug 66	Vonach+ FROM G+BETA SPECT 50SEC ACT	
				Jour	APA 23 185	May 66	− +	
(n,p)	1.4+7		GIT Expt	Jour	NP/A 180 157	Jan 72	Hankla+ ACT,GE(LI),MIXED POWDER.	+
				Abst	DA/B 32 293	Nov 71	− . ACT METHOD, CFD THEORY.	
	1.4+7			Data	EXFOR10244.022	Jun 74	1PT SIGMA	
(n,α)	1.4+7		ALD Expt	Jour	PPS 73 215	Feb 59	Coleman+. ACTIVATION	+
(n,α)	Fiss		CRC Eval	Rept	CRC−1003	Dec 60	ROY+ ESTIMATED AVG SIG=BELO 0.0001MB	
(n,α)	1.4+7		CIS Theo	Jour	NP 51 460	Feb 64	Facchini+STATMOD SIG XPT/CALC3.1−5.6	

78 Platinum 196

Quantity	Energy (ev) Min	Max	Lab	Type	Documentation Ref Vol Page	Date	Author, Comments	Data
(n,α)	1.5+7		DEB	Comp	Jour REA 7 4 93	Dec 69	Csikai+ SIG+HL COMPILTN,N−ACTIV−ANAL	
(n,α)	1.4+7	1.5+7	JYV	Eval	Rept JU−RR−3/1970	Jun 70	Leppaemaeki+ TABLE OF EVAL AVG SIG	
(n,α)	1.4+7	1.5+7	KAZ	Theo	Jour YF 18 705	Oct 73	Levkovsky.AVERAGED SIG,CALC,TBL	
Reson Params	+0	+3	ORL	Revw	Conf 60Vienna 535	Oct 60	Block+ NDG,EXPT DESCRIBED	
Reson Params	−.1+0	6.7+2	ANL	Expt	Jour PRL 6 695	Jun 61	Cote. MULTILVL FIT TO NG	
Reson Params	None		ANL	Expt	Abst BAP 12 27	Jan 67	Jackson. INVITED PAPER TITLE. NDG	
Reson Params	Maxwl	+3	AUA	Revw	Jour NSP 3 2 64	Oct 67	Allen.TABLE OF PARTIAL WIDTHS	
Reson Params	5.7+2		SAC	Expt	Jour NP/A 131 305	Jun 69	De Barros+ LINAC.WN,WN0,WG,WT,J,	+
					Conf 68Wash. 867	Mar 68	Morgenstern.WG VS A,AVERAGE WG GIVEN	
					Rept CEA−R−3385	Feb 68	Julien. (THESIS)	
	2.6+2	3.1+2			Rept CEA−R−3077	Dec 67	De Barros.ISOTOPIC ASS.TBL WN,WG.	
					Conf 66Paris 1 559	Oct 66	Huynh+ ABST.NDG. SEE INDC−156	
		6.8+2			Jour PRL 17 656	Sep 66	Jackson+ PARTIAL WG P−T	
	2.6+2	3.1+2			Jour CR 254 4287	Jun 62	Julien+TRANSMISSION TOF METHOD	
					Jour JPR 21 423	May 60	Corge+ SUPERSEDED	
					Jour JPR 21 426	May 60	− + SUPERSEDED	
					Jour CR 249 413	Jul 59	− + SUPERSEDED	
	0.0+0	8.2+2			Data EXFOR20685.	Jul 77	4PTS.E0,WG,AVG WG,WN,WT,J,G*WN.	
Reson Params	1.0+1	8.3+2	RIO	Expt	Jour NDF 15 167	Aug 69	Barros+ 3RESON,WT+WN+WG+SPIN TABLE	
Reson Params	−		AUA	Theo	Rept AAEC/E−211	Nov 70	Musgrove. CALCULTD D+GAM WIDTH GIVEN	
Reson Params	3.0+2	5.6+2	CJD	Eval	Rept YK−7	71	Zakharova+ SURVEY+SYSTEMATICS,GW,TBL	
					Rept INDC(CCP)−27	Nov 72	.ENGLISH TRANSLATION OF YK−7 /71	
Reson Params	None		DUB	Theo	Jour ZEP 14 194	Aug 71	Solovev.LARGE G−WID G−WID CORREL.NDG	
					Jour JEL 14 129	Aug 71	Soloviev. ENGL OF ZEP 14 194.	
Reson Params	1.9+1	2.5+3	IJI	Expt	Conf 73Kiev 2 95	May 73	Vertebny+ TOF,WN,WG,D,TBL	
					Rept INDC(CCP)−49	Feb 75	− + ENGLISH OF 73KIEV 2 95	
Reson Params	None		DUB	Theo	Rept JINR−P4−7499	Oct 73	Soloviev+ CALC D CFD EXPTS,TABLE	
Reson Params	0.0+0	2.0+3	IJI	Expt	Rept YFI−18 32	Aug 74	Vertebny+ TOF,WN,D,AVG D,TBL	
Reson Params	1.9+1	3.1+2	IJI	Expt	Rept YF 22 674	Oct 75	Vertebny+ G−WIDS(2RES),D−OBS,D0.TABL	
					Jour SNP 22 348	Oct 75	. ENGL OF YF 22,674	
Strnth Fnctn	6.9+1	1.5+3	SAC	Expt	Jour JPR 21 426	May 60	Corge+. CALCULATED FROM RES	
Strnth Fnctn	−		AUA	Theo	Rept AAEC/E−211	Nov 70	Musgrove. SMOOTHED S0,S1 AND S2 GIVN	
Strnth Fnctn	9.6+1	1.3+3	IJI	Expt	Conf 73Kiev 2 95	May 73	Vertebny+ STF GVN IN TBL	
Strnth Fnctn	None		IJI	Expt	Jour YF 22 674	Oct 75	Vertebny+ TOF,S0 VAL,TBL,D,WG	
					Rept YFI−18 32	Aug 74	− + VAL GVN IN TBL	
Lvl Density	6.9+1	1.5+3	SAC	Expt	Jour CR 249 413	Jul 59	Corge+. FOR SPIN1 LVLS CFD WIGNER TH	
Lvl Density	+6		MIL	Theo	Jour EN 15 1 54	Jan 68	Facchini+ LDL PARS FROM LOW EN RES	
Lvl Density	2.5+4		AUW	Expt	Conf 70Madurai 2 19	Dec 70	Lakshmana.EXPTL SPIN−CUT−OFF CFD TH	+
	2.5+4				Data EXFOR30246.033	Jun 73	SPIN CUT−OFF FACTOR FROM NG REACTION	
Lvl Density	None		AUW	Theo	Conf 70Madurai 2 267	Dec 70	Ramamurty+ A−PARAMETER GVN,LANG'S−TH	
Lvl Density	None		MUN	Theo	Jour NP/A 217 269	Dec 73	Dilg+ A,DELTA. BACK SHIFTED FERMIGAS	
Lvl Density	None		COP	Theo	Jour NP/A 222 493	Apr 74	Dossing+COLL ROTAT.SPAC. ACCUR ESTIM	
Lvl Density	None		ROC	Theo	Jour NP/A 223 577	May 74	Huizenga+ EXP CFD MICROSC TH SPH NUC	
Lvl Density	None		ROC	Theo	Jour NP/A 223 589	May 74	Huizenga+ EXP CFD MICROSC TH AX SYMM	

78 Platinum 197

Quantity	Energy (ev) Min	Max	Lab	Type	Documentation Ref Vol Page	Date	Author, Comments	Data
Reson Params	−		AUA	Theo	Rept AAEC/E−211	Nov 70	Musgrove. CALCULTD D+GAM WIDTH GIVEN	
Strnth Fnctn	−		AUA	Theo	Rept AAEC/E−211	Nov 70	Musgrove. SMOOTHED S0,S1 AND S2 GIVN	
Lvl Density	None		DUB	Theo	Jour NP/A 224 411	May 74	Soloviev+ 1/2 MICROSC MDL. SPH NUCL.	

78 Platinum 198

Quantity	Energy (ev) Min	Max	Lab	Type	Documentation Ref Vol Page	Date	Author, Comments	Data
Elastic	2.0−2	3.0+3	IJI	Expt	Jour YF 22 674	Oct 75	Vertebny+ TRANS,TOF.AVG SCATSIG,TABL	
Scattering	2.5−2	1.0+0	IJI	Expt	Conf 73Kiev 2 95	May 73	Vertebny+ TOF,7.7+−0.2 B,TBL	
	2.5−2				Rept INDC(CCP)−49	Feb 75	− + ENGLISH OF 73KIEV 2 95	
Scattering	2.5−2		IJI	Expt	Rept YFI−18 32	Aug 74	Vertebny+ VAL GVN IN TBL	
Absorption	2.5−2		IJI	Expt	Rept YFI−18 32	Aug 74	Vertebny+ VAL GVN IN TBL	
Res Int Abs	5.0−1		NSW	Eval	Rept AAEC/TM−191	Apr 63	Connolly+ CD−RATIOS,53B,REL AU 197	
Res Int Abs	5.0−1		BGK	Expt	Rept THAI−AEC−10	Oct 67	. ACTIV(NA−I),CD−RATIO,REL AU. TABLE	+
	5.0−1				Data EXFOR30368.030	Jan 77	REL AU, PRELM.	
Res Int Abs	5.0−1		CRC	Expt	Jour NAP 4 190	Mar 68	De−Lange+ ACT, 50+−6B EXCL 1/V	+
	5.0−1				Data EXFOR12600.005	Jun 76	. 1 PT, RI	

78 Platinum 198

Quantity	Energy (ev) Min	Max	Lab	Type	Documentation Ref Vol Page	Date	Author, Comments	Data
Res Int Abs	5.0-1		NPL	Expt Jour	JNE 25 129	Mar 71	Ryves+REL AU.LESS 1/V PART.ACT EXPT.	+
				Conf	71Canterby 139	Sep 71	- .REDUCED CAPT RES INTEGRAL,TBL	
	5.0-1			Data	EXFOR20791.020	Dec 78	1PNT.REDUCED CAPT INTGRL.	
Res Int Abs	5.0-1		GHT	Expt Jour	JRC 20 695	74	Van Der Linden+ BY (N,G)CFD OTH,TBL	+
				Jour	JRC 23 113	74	- + (N,G).CD-RATIO,TABLE	
	5.5-1			Conf	73Paris 2 241	Mar 73	- + ACT,REL THR+GOLD,TBL	
	5.5-1			Data	EXFOR20645.056	Jul 76	1PNT.CAPTURE.	
(n,γ)	Slow		JAP	Expt Jour	SCP 38 167	Jan 41	Sinma+.LI+D.RELATIVE SIG MEASUREMENT	
(n,γ)	Pile		ANL	Expt Jour	PR 72 888	Nov 47	Seren+.ACT METHOD.PILE IRRAD.METAL.	+
	Pile			Data	EXFOR11447.125	Jun 76	. 1 PT.	
(n,γ)	2.2+5	9.0+5	OXF	Expt Jour	NAT 161 727	May 48	Allen+ ACTIVATION RATIO	
(n,γ)	Fiss		ANL	Expt Jour	PR 75 1781	Jun 49	Hughes+ REL SIG(THERMAL),FOIL ACTIVN	+
	Fiss			Data	EXFOR11450.036	Jun 76	. 1 PT.	
(n,γ)	2.4+4		ANL	Expt Jour	PR 82 69	Apr 51	Hummel+ SB-BE PHOTONEUTS. ACTIVATION	+
	2.4+4			Data	EXFOR11010.015	Jun 76	. 1 PT.	
(n,γ)	Fiss		BNL	Expt Jour	PR 91 1423	Sep 53	Hughes+.ALSO LVL SPACINGS AT EXCIT E	
(n,γ)	Maxwl		ORL	Expt Prog	ORNL-1879 50	55	Pomerance.	+
	Maxwl			Data	EXFOR11885.008	Jun 76	. 1 PT.	
(n,γ)	1.4+7		ALD	Expt Jour	PPS 72 505	Oct 58	Perkin+ACT ANAL 1.7MB+-20PC, B-W TH	+
(n,γ)	2.5+4		LRL	Expt Jour	PR 112 226	Oct 58	Booth+ SB-BE REL I+THR,ACT 30M HL	+
	2.5+4			Data	EXFOR11429.030	Jun 76	. 1 PT.	
(n,γ)	1.5+3	3.0+5	DKE	Expt Jour	AP 10 455	Aug 60	Bilpuch.GRPH SIG(E).BETA ACTIVATION	+
	1.5+3	5.0+5		Data	EXFOR11187.007	Jun 76	. 17 PTS.	
(n,γ)	Fiss		KUR	Revw Conf	60Vienna 159	Oct 60	Bondarenko+.TABLE FOR 1E ,EXPT DSCRB	
(n,γ)	Maxwl		UCB	Expt Rept	NYO-10175	Dec 64	Arino+ACT.TBLS,GRPHS.PRODUCT HL.	+
	Maxwl			Data	EXFOR11817.	Jun 76	. 2 PTS, SIG FOR 2 ISOMERS	
(n,γ)	2.4+4		MUA	Expt Jour	PR 152 1055	Dec 66	Chaubey+ SIG(30 MIN) REL I-127,TBL	+
				Theo Jour	IJP 42 567	Sep 68	- + METHD OF BOOTH,VAL CFD XPT	
	2.4+4			Expt Data	EXFOR30079.040	Dec 70	SIGMA FOR 30. MIN HALF-LIFE	
(n,γ)	Maxwl		KUR	Expt Jour	YF 7 937	May 68	Groshev+ OTHER SIG VALUE GIVEN	
(n,γ)	-		IEA	Comp Rept	IEA-INF-10 6	Aug 68	Atalla. TABLES OF HL,SIG AND GAMM-E	
(n,γ)	3.0+4		AUA	Theo Rept	AAEC/E-211	Nov 70	Musgrove. SIGMA GIVEN AND CFD OTHER	
(n,γ)	2.5-2		NPL	Expt Jour	JNE 25 129	Mar 71	Ryves Rel Au.SIG=3.66+-.19B.ACT EXPT	+
				Conf	71Canterby 139	71	Ryves. VDG,GRAPHITE MODERATOR.ACTIVN	
	2.5-2			Data	EXFOR20791.019	Dec 78	1PNT.SIGMA.	
(n,γ)	Maxwl		KFI	Comp Jour	JRC 7 365	Jun 71	Nagy+ SIGMA, GAM+BETA ES, HALF-LIFE	
(n,γ)	2.4+4		MUA	Theo Jour	IJP 46 114	Mar 72	Chaubey+ P-WAVE STRENGTH FUNCT,TABLE	
(n,γ)	1.0+3	1.0+7	BOL	Eval Data	BENZI-DFN 833.	May 72	40 PNTS	+
(n,γ)	1.4+7		DEB	Expt Jour	AK 15 3 161	Mar 73	Uray. ACTIV, PARTIAL+TOTAL SIGMAS	+
	1.4+7			Data	EXFOR30282.	Nov 74	ISOM SIG, TOT SIG, ISOM RATIO GIVEN	
(n,γ)	2.5-2	1.0+0	IJI	Expt Conf	73Kiev 2 95	May 73	Vertebny+ TOF,4.2+-0.3 B,TBL	
	0.0+0	2.0+3		Rept	INDC(CCP)-49	Feb 75	- + ENGLISH OF 73KIEV 2 95	
(n,γ)	2.0-2	3.0+3	IJI	Expt Jour	YF 22 674	Oct 75	Vertebny+ TOF,SIG AT 2200 M/SEC,TBL	
				Jour	SNP 22 348	Oct 75	. ENGL OF YF 22,674	
(n,γ)	1.4+7		IRK	Expt Jour	NP/A 264 105	Jun 76	Schwerer+ GE-LI.ACT SIG=0.6+-0.4MB	+
	1.5+7			Data	EXFOR20670.017	Oct 76	1PNT.SIGMA.	
Spect (n,γ)	3.0+1	6.0+2	HAR	Expt Jour	NP 14 212	Dec 59	Bird+RES CAPT SPECTRA.G INTS.TBL.	
				Rept	AERE-NP/GEN12	Aug 59	- + RES CAPT GAMMA SPECS.GRPH.	
Spect (n,γ)	9.6+1		SAC	Expt Rept	CEA-R-3776	Apr 69	Samour.THESIS	
				Jour	NP/A 121 65	Dec 68	- + RES CAPT. LVL SCHEME PT-199	
				Rept	INDC-156	67	Jackson+ FULL PAPER OF 66PARIS.	
				Conf	66Paris 1 564	Oct 66	- +.PPR66,CURVE,LINAC,GE-DETECT	
	1.9+1			Jour	CR 254 4162	Jun 62	Julien+TOF RES ISOTOPIC ATTRIBUTION	
Spect (n,γ)	Maxwl		KFI	Comp Jour	JRC 7 365	Jun 71	Nagy+ SIGMA, GAM+BETA ES, HALF-LIFE	
(n,2n)	1.5+7		CRC	Expt Jour	CJP 31 267	Feb 53	Paul+.BETA ACT.CFD TH. HL=70M+18H	+
	1.5+7			Data	EXFOR11274.094	Jun 76	. 1 PT.	
(n,2n)	Fiss		CRC	Eval Rept	CRC-1003	Dec 60	Roy+,ESTIMATED AVG SIG=6.0MB	
(n,2n)	1.4+7		HAM	Comp Jour	NP 65 257	Mar 65	Bormann. 1EXPT VALS.CFD SHELL EFFECT	
(n,2n)	1.5+7		MUA	Expt Jour	NP 69 158	Jul 65	Mangal+ 1.138 TO 88M LVL,2.3B TO GND	+
	1.5+7			Data	EXFOR31254.	Mar 73	.SIG POPULATING MS+GND-STATE GVN	
(n,2n)	1.3+7	1.5+7	BNL	Theo Jour	NSE 23 238	Nov 65	Pearlstein.3ES.STAT MDL CALC.TBL CS.	
(n,2n)	Fiss		BNL	Theo Jour	NSE 23 238	Nov 65	Pearlstein.STATMDL CALC.SPEC AVG.TBL	
(n,2n)	1.5+7		DEB	Comp Jour	REA 7 4 93	Dec 69	Csikai+ SIG+HL COMPILTN,N-ACTIV-ANAL	
(n,2n)	1.4+7	1.5+7	JYV	Eval Rept	JU-RR-3/1970	Jun 70	Leppaemaeki+ TABLE OF EVAL AVG SIG	
(n,2n)	1.2+7	1.8+7	HAM	Expt Jour	NP/A 157 481	Nov 70	Bormann+ ACT. CFD STATIST TH.+ISOM R	
(n,2n)	+7		KFI	Theo Rept	KFKI-71-8	Feb 71	Jeki. CALCULATED CFD EXPTL SIG VALUE	

78 Platinum 198

Quantity	Energy (ev) Min	Max	Lab	Type	Documentation Ref Vol Page	Author, Comments Date	Data
(n,2n)	1.5+7	1.5+7	IRK	Expt Jour	NP/A 158 77	Dec 70 Winiwarter.	+
	1.4+7	1.5+7		ExTh Jour	APA 33 285	Jul 71 - + ISOMERIC RATIO	
				Expt Jour	OAWA 107 150	May 70 - .ACTIV METHOD ISOM RATIO	
	1.5+7			Data	EXFOR20071.	Sep 71 4PTS.SIG.	
(n,2n)	1.4+7		GIT	Expt Jour	NP/A 180 157	Jan 72 Hankla+ ACT,GE(LI),MIXED POWDER.G,M.	+
				Abst Jour	DA/B 32 293	Nov 71 - . ACT METHOD, CFD THEORY.	
	1.4+7			Data	EXFOR10244.	Jun 74 2PTS,TOTAL AND META.	
(n,2n)	1.5+7		JUL	Expt Jour	NP/A 185 614	May 72 Qaim. ACT,GE(LI). CFD TH+OTHR.+ISOMR	+
	1.5+7			Data	EXFOR20536.	Apr 76 4PTS.SIGMA.	
(n,2n)	1.5+7		DEB	Eval Jour	REA 11 1 153	Mar 73 Boedy. COMPILATION+RECOMM.VALUE,TBL	
				Rept	IAEA-153 173	73 - . RECOMM. VALUE ONLY	
(n,2n)	1.5+7		NPL	Expt Jour	JNE 27 531	Aug 73 Robertson+ SIG=2091MB.REL FE056 NP	+
	1.5+7			Data	EXFOR20799.018	Oct 78 1PNT.SIGMA.	
(n,2n)	1.5+7		TAT	Theo Jour	JP/A 7 1457	Aug 74 Kondaiah. CALC ON STAT MODEL	
(n,2n)	8.0+6	2.0+7	IRK	Theo Conf	IAEA-190 2 361	76 UHL. STATMOD+PREEQ CFD XPTL DATA.FIG	
(n,2n)	1.5+7		SLO	Expt Jour	ASL 26 64	76 Hlavac+ ACTIV.TO GRND,META.CFD,TABLE	+
	1.5+7			Data	EXFOR30286.	Apr 75 SIG TO ISOMR,TOTSIG,ISOMERIC RATIO	
(n,xn) x>2	Fiss		BNL	Theo Jour	NSE 23 238	Nov 65 Pearlstein.SPEC AVG STATMDL CALC N3N	
(n,p)	Fiss		CRC	Eval Rept	CRC-1003	Dec 60 ROY+ ESTIMATED AVG SIG=0.002MB	
(n,p)	None		KFI	Comp Jour	JRC 7 365	Jun 71 Nagy+ GAM+BETA ENERGIES,HALF-L GIVEN	
(n,p)	1.4+7		DEB	Expt Jour	AK 15 3 161	Mar 73 Uray. ACTIV, PARTIAL SIGMA,TBL,GRAPH	+
				Jour	RRL 14 2 135	73 Szalay+ EVIDENCE FOR IR-198,ACTIV	
	1.4+7			Data	EXFOR30282.007	Nov 74 PARTIAL SIGMA FOR THE 407.8 KEV LINE	
(n,np)	1.4+7		DEB	Expt Prog	INDC(HUN)-11	Sep 73 Uray.P 14,VERY BRIEF,ACTIV,NDG	
(n,d)	1.4+7		DEB	Expt Jour	AK 15 3 161	Mar 73 Uray. ACTIV, UPPER LIMIT OF SIG,TBL	+
	1.4+7			Data	EXFOR30282.005	Nov 74 UPPER LIMIT OF SIGMA GIVEN	
(n,α)	Fiss		CRC	Eval Rept	CRC-1003	Dec 60 ROY+ ESTIMATED AVG SIG=BELO 0.0001MB	
(n,α)	1.4+7		DEB	Expt Jour	AK 15 3 161	Mar 73 Uray. ACTIV, UPPER LIMIT OF SIG,TBL	+
	1.4+7			Data	EXFOR30282.006	Nov 74 UPPER LIMIT OF SIGMA GIVEN	
Reson Params	9.5+1		BNL	Expt Priv	ZIMMERMAN	Jan 58 Zimmerman.	+
	9.5+1			Data	EXFOR12494.004	Jun 76 . 1 PT	
Reson Params	9.6+1		ANL	Expt Prog	ANL-6072 4	59 Thomas.	+
Reson Params	9.8+1		HAR	Expt Jour	NP 14 212	Dec 59 Bird+RES EN FROM TOF.ISTPE ASGN BY G	
				Rept	AERE-NP/GEN12	Aug 59 - + TBL RES ENS.ISOTOPIS ASSGN.	
Reson Params	9.6+1		RPI	Expt Jour	PR 120 2090	Dec 60 Waters.TOF,GIVES G,WN,WG	+
Reson Params		1.0+6	AUA	Theo Jour	AUJ 20 477	Oct 67 Cook. TBL OF AVG LVL SPACING D,L=0,1	
Reson Params	9.7+1		SAC	Expt Jour	NP/A 131 305	Jun 69 De Barros+ LINAC.WN,WN0,WG,WT,J,	+
				Conf	68Wash. 867	Mar 68 Morgenstern.WG VS.A,AVERAGE WG GIVEN	
	9.6+1			Rept	CEA-R-3385	Feb 68 Julien (THESIS)	
	1.2+1	7.0+2		Conf	67Bordeaux	Mar 67 Samour+G(GAMMA).NAT PT,GE DET.FP JPR	
	1.2+1	7.1+2		Conf	66Paris 1 559	Oct 66 Huynh+ ABST.NDG. SEE INDC-156	
				Conf	65Antwerp 525	Jul 65 De Barros+ PPR73.ABST.NDG	
	2.6+2	3.1+2		Jour	CR 254 4287	Jun 62 Julien+ TRANSMISSION TOF METHOD	
	9.6+1	6.6+2		Data	EXFOR20685.028	Jul 77 2PTS.E0,WG,WN,WT,G*WN.	
Reson Params	9.6+1	3.1+2	KFK	Eval Rept	KFK-718	Apr 68 Schmidt+ RESOLVED+AVG RES PARAM(S,P)	
Reson Params	1.0+1	8.3+2	RIO	Expt Jour	NDF 15 167	Aug 69 Barros+ ONE RESON RESOLVD,I+WN+WT+WG	
Reson Params	9.6+1	3.1+2	KFK	Comp Rept	KFK-1233	Jul 70 Mueller. ES,WN,WG,G OF 3 RESON	
Reson Params	-		AUA	Theo Rept	AAEC/E-211	Nov 70 Musgrove. CALCULTD D+GAM WIDTH GIVEN	
Reson Params	9.7+1		CJD	Eval Rept	YK-7	71 Zakharova+ SURVEY+SYSTEMATICS,GW,TBL	
				Rept	INDC(CCP)-27	Nov 72 .ENGLISH TRANSLATION OF YK-7 /71	
Reson Params	9.6+1	1.3+3	IJI	Expt Conf	73Kiev 2 95	May 73 Vertebny+ TOF,WN,WG,D,TBL	
				Rept	INDC(CCP)-49	Feb 75 - + ENGLISH OF 73KIEV 2 95	
Reson Params	None		DUB	Theo Rept	JINR-P4-7499	Oct 73 Soloviev+ CALC D CFD EXPTS,TABLE	
Reson Params	0.0+0	2.0+3	IJI	Expt Rept	YFI-18 32	Aug 74 Vertebny+ TOF,WN,D,AVG D,TBL	
Reson Params	9.6+1		IJI	Expt Jour	YF 22 674	Oct 75 Vertebny+ G-WID(1 RES),D-OBS,D0.TABL	
				Jour	SNP 22 348	Oct 75 . ENGL OF YF 22,674	
Strnth Fnctn	-		AUA	Theo Rept	AAEC/E-211	Nov 70 Musgrove. SMOOTHED S0,S1 AND S2 GIVN	
Strnth Fnctn	2.4+4		MUA	Theo Jour	IJP 46 114	Mar 72 Chaubey+ P-WAVE.FOR A-SYSTEMTIC,GRPH	
Strnth Fnctn	9.6+1	1.3+3	IJI	Expt Conf	73Kiev 2 95	May 73 Vertebny+ STF GVN IN TBL	
Strnth Fnctn	None		IJI	Expt Jour	YF 22 674	Oct 75 Vertebny+ TOF,S0 VAL,TBL,D,WG	
				Rept	YFI-18 32	Aug 74 - + VAL GVN IN TBL	

78 Platinum 199

Quantity	Energy (ev) Min	Max	Lab	Type	Documentation Ref Vol Page	Author, Comments Date	Data
(n,γ)	Pile		CRC	Expt Jour	PR 105 1337	Feb 57 ROY+ NRX APPROXIMATELY 15B	
Inelastic γ	None		KFI	Comp Jour	JRC 7 365	Jun 71 Nagy+ GAM+XRAY+ELECTR ES, HALF-LIFE	

78 Platinum 199

Quantity	Energy (ev) Min Max	Lab	Type	Documentation Ref Vol Page	Date	Author, Comments	Data
Reson Params	–	AUA	Theo Rept	AAEC/E-211	Nov 70	Musgrove. CALCULTD D+GAM WIDTH GIVEN	
Strnth Fnctn	–	AUA	Theo Rept	AAEC/E-211	Nov 70	Musgrove. SMOOTHED S0,S1 AND S2 GIVN	
Lvl Density	None	COP	Theo Jour	NP/A 222 493	Apr 74	Dossing+COLL ROTAT.SPAC. ACCUR ESTIM	
Lvl Density	None	DUB	Theo Jour	NP/A 224 411	May 74	Soloviev+ 1/2 MICROSC MDL. SPH NUCL.	

78 Platinum 200

Quantity	Energy (ev) Min Max	Lab	Type	Documentation Ref Vol Page	Date	Author, Comments	Data
Reson Params	–	AUA	Theo Rept	AAEC/E-211	Nov 70	Musgrove. CALCULTD D+GAM WIDTH GIVEN	
Strnth Fnctn	–	AUA	Theo Rept	AAEC/E-211	Nov 70	Musgrove. SMOOTHED S0,S1 AND S2 GIVN	

79 Gold 190

Quantity	Energy (ev) Min	Max	Lab	Type	Documentation Ref Vol Page	Author, Comments Date	Data
Reson Params	–		AUA	Theo Rept	AAEC/E – 211	Nov 70 Musgrove. CALCULTD D+GAM WIDTH GIVEN	
Strnth Fnctn	–		AUA	Theo Rept	AAEC/E – 211	Nov 70 Musgrove. SMOOTHED S0,S1 AND S2 GIVN	

79 Gold 191

Quantity	Energy (ev) Min	Max	Lab	Type	Documentation Ref Vol Page	Author, Comments Date	Data
Reson Params	–		AUA	Theo Rept	AAEC/E – 211	Nov 70 Musgrove. CALCULTD D+GAM WIDTH GIVEN	
Strnth Fnctn	–		AUA	Theo Rept	AAEC/E – 211	Nov 70 Musgrove. SMOOTHED S0,S1 AND S2 GIVN	

79 Gold 192

Quantity	Energy (ev) Min	Max	Lab	Type	Documentation Ref Vol Page	Author, Comments Date	Data
Reson Params	–		AUA	Theo Rept	AAEC/E – 211	Nov 70 Musgrove. CALCULTD D+GAM WIDTH GIVEN	
Strnth Fnctn	–		AUA	Theo Rept	AAEC/E – 211	Nov 70 Musgrove. SMOOTHED S0,S1 AND S2 GIVN	

79 Gold 193

Quantity	Energy (ev) Min	Max	Lab	Type	Documentation Ref Vol Page	Author, Comments Date	Data
Reson Params	–		AUA	Theo Rept	AAEC/E – 211	Nov 70 Musgrove. CALCULTD D+GAM WIDTH GIVEN	
Strnth Fnctn	–		AUA	Theo Rept	AAEC/E – 211	Nov 70 Musgrove. SMOOTHED S0,S1 AND S2 GIVN	

79 Gold 194

Quantity	Energy (ev) Min	Max	Lab	Type	Documentation Ref Vol Page	Author, Comments Date	Data
(n,p)	Maxwl		IFU	Theo Rept	ICD – 4 20	67 Dadakina+ PENETR COEFF CALC,TABLE	
Reson Params	–		AUA	Theo Rept	AAEC/E – 211	Nov 70 Musgrove. CALCULTD D+GAM WIDTH GIVEN	
Strnth Fnctn	–		AUA	Theo Rept	AAEC/E – 211	Nov 70 Musgrove. SMOOTHED S0,S1 AND S2 GIVN	

79 Gold 195

Quantity	Energy (ev) Min	Max	Lab	Type	Documentation Ref Vol Page	Author, Comments Date	Data
(n,p)	Maxwl		IFU	Theo Rept	ICD – 4 20	67 Dadakina+ PENETR COEFF CALC,TABLE	
Reson Params	–		AUA	Theo Rept	AAEC/E – 211	Nov 70 Musgrove. CALCULTD D+GAM WIDTH GIVEN	
Strnth Fnctn	–		AUA	Theo Rept	AAEC/E – 211	Nov 70 Musgrove. SMOOTHED S0,S1 AND S2 GIVN	

79 Gold 196

Quantity	Energy (ev) Min	Max	Lab	Type	Documentation Ref Vol Page	Author, Comments Date	Data
(n,p)	Maxwl		IFU	Theo Rept	ICD – 4 20	67 Dadakina+ PENETR COEFF CALC,TABLE	
Reson Params	–		AUA	Theo Rept	AAEC/E – 211	Nov 70 Musgrove. CALCULTD D+GAM WIDTH GIVEN	
Strnth Fnctn	–		AUA	Theo Rept	AAEC/E – 211	Nov 70 Musgrove. SMOOTHED S0,S1 AND S2 GIVN	
Lvl Density	8.0+6	1.5+7	ANL	Eval Rept	ANL – 75 – 34	Jun 75 Davey+N2NEVAL.CONSTANT T,LVL DEN FIT	

79 Gold 197

Quantity	Energy (ev) Min	Max	Lab	Type	Documentation Ref Vol Page	Author, Comments Date	Data
Evaluation	Maxwl		GEN	Eval Rept	APEX – 467	Jun 58 Tralli+.68 – 3000DEG F SCT ABS	
Evaluation	3.2 – 2	1.0+7	GEN	Eval Rept	APEX – 467	Jun 58 Tralli+.18GROUPS AS IN AG + N2N	
Evaluation	5.0+5	1.5+7	LRL	Eval Rept	UCRL – 5351	Nov 58 Howerton. CURVES.	
Evaluation	None		UK	Eval Prog	NEANDC(UK)160	Jul 74 Story+(WIN).UKNDL EVL TBC.	
Evaluation	1.0 – 5	2.0+7	BNL	Eval Rept	BNL – 50439	Oct 74 Mughabghab+ ENDF – 4 EVAL.	
Total	Maxwl		COL	Expt Jour	PR 48 265	Aug 35 Dunning+ IONCH,TRANS,RA – BE/PARAFIN N	
Total	Maxwl		COL	Expt Jour	PR 49 453	Mar 36 Mitchell. TRANSM. CD STOPPED+EPI CD	
Total	4.0+0	9.0+0	COL	Expt Jour	PR 71 165	Feb 47 Havens+ TOF TRSM	
Total	4.0 – 2	8.0+0	ANL	Expt Jour	PR 71 757	Jun 47 Sturm. TRNSM APPROX RES PARAMS	
Total	4.0 – 3	1.6 – 1	ANL	Expt Jour	PR 72 585	Oct 47 Brill+.ROTATING SHUTTER. TRANSM.	
Total	1.0 – 2	3.0 – 1	LAS	Expt Jour	PR 72 729	Oct 47 Mcdaniel+ D – BE NS.TOF.TRANSMISSION.	
Total	2.2 – 2	1.2+1	COL	Expt Jour	PR 83 746	Aug 51 Tittman+ LOW E TOTAL.SCAT/TOT.TRANS	+
	7.1 – 2	1.2+1		Data	EXFOR12203.	Jun 76 . 37 PTS. SIGMA.	

79 Gold 197

Quantity	Energy (ev) Min	Max	Lab	Type	Documentation Ref Vol Page	Author, Comments Date	Data
Total	4.5+0	5.4+0	COL Expt	Jour	PR 83 1123	Sep 51 Havens+.TOF.TRANSMISSION CURVE.	+
	4.5+0	5.4+0		Data	EXFOR11732.007	Jun 76 . 8 PTS. SIGMA.	
Total	1.4+7		LAS Expt	Jour	PR 88 562	Nov 52 Coon+ SCINT.DET.	+
	1.4+7			Data	EXFOR11056.051	Jun 76 . 1 PT. SIGMA.	
Total	1.4+7		ROM Expt	Jour	NC 10 281	Mar 53 Ageno+LI TARGET TRANSMIS.5.06+ −0.14B	
Total	9.5+4	3.0+6	WIS Expt	Jour	PR 89 1271	Mar 53 Walt+. GRAPH. ZR−T AND LI TARGETS	+
	9.5+4	3.0+6		Data	EXFOR11746.008	Jun 76 . 18 PTS. SIGMA.	
Total	1.0+5	7.2+5	BAR Expt	Jour	PR 90 615	May 53 Snowdon. 40KEVRSLN NO RES	+
	9.8+4	7.2+5		Data	EXFOR11559.004	Jun 76 . 84 PTS. SIGMA.	
Total	1.2−3	3.9−2	BNL Expt	Jour	PR 92 716	Nov 53 Carter+	+
	1.2−3	3.9−2		Data	EXFOR11211.004	Jun 76 . 70 PTS. SIGMA.	
Total	2.8+6	1.3+7	LAS Expt	Jour	PR 94 1678	Jun 54 Nereson+ WHITE SOURCE, RSLN 10 PC.	+
	2.8+6	1.3+7		Data	EXFOR11308.023	Jun 76 . 31 PTS. SIGMA.	
Total	3.0+0	3.0+2	BNL Expt	Jour	PR 95 476	Jul 54 Seidl+ TRANSM CURVE RES PARMS.	+
	5.6+1	1.1+2		Data	EXFOR11671.012	Jun 76 . 22 PTS. SIGMA.	
Total	1.4−3	1.5−1	HAR Expt	Jour	JNE 1 57	Aug 54 Egelstaff.SC.REVISED JNE 5 41 REFS.	+
				Rept	AERE−N/R−1131	Apr 53 .SEE ALSO	
Total	5.0−3	8.0−2	ORL Expt	Jour	PR 96 1297	Dec 54 Allen+ CRYSTAL SPECTR	+
				Rept	TID−14868	Jun 53 − .TRNS CRYST SPEC 106B AT .025EV	
	5.0−3	8.0−2		Data	EXFOR11762.005	Jun 76 . 16 PTS. SIGMA.	
Total	5.7+1	6.3+1	ANL Expt	Priv	BOLLINGER	Jan 55 Bollinger.	+
	5.7+1	6.3+1		Data	EXFOR12231.002	Jun 76 . 15 PTS. SIGMA.	
Total	1.0+0	1.5+1	BNL Expt	Jour	PR 98 639	Jan 55 Wood+	+
	1.0+0	1.5+1		Data	EXFOR12241.002	Jun 76 . 67 PTS. SIGMA.	
Total	4.1+6		LAS Expt	Jour	PR 98 677	May 55 Walt+ TRANSMISSION EXPT 7.1B	+
	4.1+6			Data	EXFOR11215.048	Jun 76 . 1 PT. SIGMA.	
Total	4.0+4	1.8+7	LAS Theo	Rept	LA−2099	Dec 56 Beyster+,OPTMDL CALC CFD EXPT,CURVE	
Total	1.0+3	4.0+4	DKE Expt	Jour	PR 105 198	Jan 57 Newson+.TRNS 12.0B AVGD 12−21KEV	
Total	1.0+0	1.5+1	COL Expt	Rept	CU−165	Jun 57 Moore.TRANS. RATIO S(SCT)/S(TOT) MSD	
Total	1.3+7	1.6+7	LAS Expt	Jour	PR 109 1268	Feb 58 Conner.TRNS SC 6ES 5.52BMAX 5.34BMIN	+
				Conf	58Geneva 15 11	Sep 58 Coon+.PPR666,SIGMA FOR 6ES,TOF	
	1.3+7	1.6+7		Data	EXFOR11320.013	Jun 76 . 6 PTS. SIGMA.	
Total	3.1+1	5.1+2	ORL Expt	Prog	ORNL−2501 26	Mar 58 Slaughter+	+
	3.1+1	5.1+2		Data	EXFOR11446.007	Jun 76 . 310 PTS. SIGMA.	
Total	7.3+0	5.4+1	BNL Expt	Jour	PR 110 692	May 58 Seth+	+
	7.3+0	5.4+1		Data	EXFOR11788.017	Jun 76 . 31 PTS. SIGMA.	
Total	7.0+6	1.4+7	LRL Expt	Jour	PR 110 927	May 58 Bratenahl+ SC TRNS 5ES	+
	7.1+6	1.4+7		Conf	58Geneva 14 109	Sep 58 − +.P1881,TBL,CURV,CFD OPTMDL	
	7.1+6	1.4+7		Data	EXFOR11155.029	Jun 76 . 5 PTS. SIGMA.	
Total	1.0+5	1.5+7	BNL Comp	Conf	58Geneva 16 8	Sep 58 Hughes.PPR2483,CURVE,MANY REFS	
Total	3.0+5	5.0+5	ANL Expt	Prog	ANL−5937 28	Nov 59 Monahan+ 7.6 TO 6.5 B MONOT DECRSNG.	
Total	1.7+7	2.9+7	LRL Expt	Jour	PR 120 521	Oct 60 Peterson+ TRANS 5ES CURV CFD OPTMDL	+
				Conf	58Geneva 14 109	Sep 58 Bratenahl+ TBL,CURV,CFD OPTMDL.	
	1.7+7	2.9+7		Data	EXFOR11108.037	Jun 76 . 5 PTS. SIGMA.	
Total	3.0+1	4.0+2	ORL Expt	Conf	60Vienna 535	Oct 60 Block+.CURVE,EXPT DESCRIBED,FAST CH	+
Total	6.2−4	3.3−3	COL Expt	Jour	NSE 8 453	Dec 60 Gould+,CS TABLE+CURVE	+
	6.2−4	3.3−3		Data	EXFOR11198.003	Jun 76 . 13 PTS. SIGMA.	
Total	Maxwl		MTR Expt	Jour	PR 126 29	Apr 62 Brugger.FC TRNS, 106.9+ −1.0B	
Total	7.8+1		SAC Expt	Jour	JPR 24 176	Mar 63 Le Pipec+ RESONANCE ANALYSIC.77DEG K	
				Jour	CR 255 1913	Oct 62 LE PIPEC+ CRYST BINDING EFF ON RES	
Total	3.0−4	1.1+1	RIS Expt	Jour	PR/B 133 925	Feb 64 Als−Nielsen+ OKS EARLIER DATA.	+
				Rept	RISO−61	63 − + DATA GIVEN.	
	3.0−4	1.1+1		Data	EXFOR20105.007	Sep 71 18PTS.	
Total	5.0+4	3.0+6	BNL Theo	Jour	PR/B 135 895	Aug 64 Auerbach+ LCL OPTMDL CALC X FIT XPT.	
Total	5.3−3	2.5−2	IEA Expt	Rept	IEA−78	Nov 64 Bianchini+ XTAL SPECT+VEL SELECT,GRF	
	5.3−3	2.5−2		Data	EXFOR30164.	Apr 72 DATA AT 8 ES, PRIV COM FROM FULFARO	
Total	1.4+0		ORL Expt	Jour	NP 61 381	Jan 65 Rayburn+ IN RES 1.44EV 30.9B	+
	1.4+0			Data	EXFOR11026.	Jun 76 . 2 PTS. SIGMA.	
Total	7.0−2	2.0−1	CAS Expt	Jour	NIM 33 229	Mar 65 Antonini+.SLOW CHOPPER.GRAPH. TRNSM	
Total	5.0+3	6.5+5	DKE ExTh	Jour	PL 16 306	Jun 65 Seth. AV CS 8−10KEV RSN INT RES OBSV	+
	5.0+3	6.5+5		Expt	EXFOR11781.019	Jun 76 . 94 PTS. SIGMA.	
Total	5.0+5	4.1+6	LAS Expt	Priv	DAY	Jul 65 DAY.	+
	5.0+5	4.1+6		Data	EXFOR12191.002	Jun 76 . 4 PTS. SIGMA.	
Total	2.0−2	8.0−2	MTR Eval	Conf	66Paris 2 50	Oct 66 Smith. PPR50,CURVS,LEAST SQUARES FIT	
Total	1.0+5	6.5+5	ANL Expt	Prog	ANL−7210 16	Dec 66 Whalen.SHORT NOTE,GRAPH ONLY	+
	1.0+5	6.5+5		Data	EXFOR11540.013	Jun 76 . 66 PTS. SIGMA.	
Total	1.6−3	8.8−2	IEA Expt	Rept	IEA−136	Feb 67 Herdade+ TOF,TABLE,GRAPH	+
	1.6−3	8.8−2		Data	EXFOR30166.	Apr 72 SIG VERSUS LAMBDA, 150 DATA POINTS	

79 Gold 197

Quantity	Energy (ev) Min	Max	Lab	Type	Documentation Ref Vol Page	Author, Comments Date	Data
Total	7.0+3	7.0+6	HAR	Expt Prog	AERE – PR/NP12	Aug 67 Diment+LINAC.TOF.GRPH CFD TH.STF.	
Total	None		ANL	Expt Abst	BAP 12 1187	Dec 67 Mooring+. SELF – INDICATION FOR AV SIG	
Total	4.0+6		IFU	Theo Jour	UFZ 13 51	Jan 68 Kashuba+ TBL,SIG – VAL,EXPT CFD OPTMOD	
				Jour	UPJ 13 33	Jul 68 TRANSLATN.*	
Total	2.5−2	1.0+0	IEA	Expt Jour	CEC 20 2 130	Jun 68 Stasiulevius+	+
	2.5−2	1.0+0		Data	EXFOR30165.	Apr 72 DATA AT 71 ES, PRIV COM FROM FULFARO	
Total	1.0+3	2.1+3	SAC	Expt Jour	NP/A 131 450	Jun 69 Alves+LINAC.TRANSM.	+
	1.0+1	1.0+3		Jour	NP 76 391	Feb 66 Julien+TRANSMISSION ANAL TO GIVE RP	
	1.0+1	3.1+3		Data	EXFOR20686.	Aug 77 0PTS. SEE RESONANCE PARAMETERS.	
Total	3.0+6	1.5+7	KFK	Revw Conf	70Helsinki 2 219	Jun 70 Cierjacks.113. SIG(E) GRPH CFD OPTMOD	
Total	1.0+0	2.0+2	AUA	Theo Jour	AUJ 23 823	Dec 70 Clayton. R – MATRIX ANALYSIS,SIG – GRAPH	
Total	2.5+6	1.5+7	BNW	Expt Jour	PR/C 3 576	Feb 71 Foster+,TRANS,CURVS,CFD OTHERS+TH	+
				Jour	PRL 22 139	Jan 69 .SUPERSEDED	
				Jour	NIM 36 1	Sep 65 Foster+ EXPT DETAILS	
	2.3+6	1.5+7		Data	EXFOR10047.086	Aug 73 . 251 PTS. SIGMA.	
Total	1.0−2	1.0+0	IFU	Expt Prog	YFI – 12 79	Jun 71 Vertebny+	+
	1.0−2	1.0+0		Data	EXFOR40109.005	Dec 72 SIGMA AT 31 ES	
Total	8.0+6		AE	Theo Rept	AE – 430	Sep 71 Holmqvist+ CALC FROM OPTMOD PARAMS	
	8.1+6			Conf	70Helsinki 2 341	Jun 70 – + OPTMOD ANALYSIS. 8 MEV	
Total	1.0−2	1.0+0	IJI	Expt Prog	YFI – 12 74	72 Vertebny+ ABSTRACT,TBL SIG(N – E)	
	1.0−2	3.0−1		Prog	INDC(CCP) – 30	Sep 72 .PAGE 64,ENGLISH OF YFI – 12 74	
	1.4+4	5.8+4	KFK	Expt Rept	KFK – 1519	Feb 72 Schneider.T=11+800C,MONTE – CARLO TH	
	1.0+4	6.0+4		Rept	KFK – 1229	Jun 70 Froehner+ TRANS EXPT,T – DEPEND,CFD TH	
				Conf	70Helsinki 1 201	Jun 70 Schneider+10. TEMPERATURE+TRANSMISSN	
Total	2.0−7	2.0−3	MUN	Expt Jour	ZP 250 166	Feb 72 Steyerl+, TOF TRANS AT 80+299 DEG K	+
	1.0−7	6.0−5		Jour	PL/B 29 33	Mar 69 – + SUPERSEDED	
Total	None		COL	Expt Prog	USNDC – 1 40	May 72 Rainwater+. ANAL TO BE COMPL.NO DATA	
Total	2.7+3		MUN	Expt Prog	EANDC(E)150U	Oct 72 Dilg+AVERAGE TOT XSECT+S0	+
				Conf	71Albany 327	Aug 71 – +TRNS.AVG CS GVN.31 ELEMENT GRP	
	2.7+3			Data	EXFOR20583.030	Jun 76 1PNT.SIGMA.	
Total	1.3+7	1.5+7	DEB	Eval Rept	IAEA – 153 173	73 Boedy+ MOST PROBABLE VAL OF SIG,TBL	
				Jour	AHP 30 115	Oct 71 Angeli+ AVG SIG,CFD CALC.TBLS.GRAPH	
Total	4.0−5	3.5−3	MUN	Expt Jour	ZP 264 427	73 Dilg+ CHOPPER,TOF,TBL.	+
				Conf	JINR – D3 – 7991	Apr 74 Steyerl+ P42. CURVE.	
				Jour	PL/A 44 165	73 Dilg+ TOF SPECTROMETER.	
	4.0−5	3.5−3		Data	EXFOR20823.002	Mar 79 21PTS.SIGMA.	
Total	Maxwl		MUN	Expt Jour	ZP 264 427	73 Dilg+ DERIVED FROM LOW VELOCITY DATA	+
				Jour	PL/A 44 165	73 – + TOF SPECTROMETER.	
	Maxwl			Data	EXFOR20823.003	Mar 79 1PNT.DERIVED SIGMA.	
Total	9.3−3	2.0−2	IEA	Expt Prog	INDC – 6 15	Jun 70 Fulfaro. SHORT PROGR REPORT,NDG	+
	9.3−3	2.0−2		Data	EXFOR30232.002	Jan 73 SIG TOT AT 8 ES, DATA FROM PRIVCOM	
Total	1.0+3	6.0+5	NBS	Expt Jour	PR/C 9 28	Jan 74 Camarda.LINAC.TOF.GRPH.TRANS.MEAS.S1	
Total	2.5−2		KAP	Expt Jour	NSE 54 286	Apr 74 Eiland+	+
	2.5−2			Data	EXFOR10147.014	Aug 75 . 1 PT. SIGMA.	
Total	None		NRL	Expt Prog	USNDC – 11 182	Jun 74 Stolovy+ THIN FILM TRNSM, GRPH.	+
Total	2.5+5	1.5+7	JAE	Theo Conf	JAERI – M – 5984	Feb 75 Tanaka.OPTMDL/COUPLD CH.GRPH CFD EXP	
Total	−3	1.9+0	THS	Theo Rept	IKE – 6 89 65	Jun 75 Keinert. DATA LIBRARY	
Total	+6		IJI	Expt Conf	77Kiev	77 Trofimova+ SIG	
	2.0+3			Conf	76Lowell 1244	Jul 76 Vertebnyi+ TRANSM VS THICKNESS,NDG	
Elastic	4.8+0		ANL	Expt Jour	PR 79 11	Jul 50 Harris+ SCT,NEAR RES.ABS.	
Elastic	2.5−2		ORL	Expt Jour	PR 81 527	Feb 51 Shull+ COH SCATT, DIFFRACTION.	+
	2.5−2			Data	EXFOR11043.	Jun 76 . 3 PTS, BAS,COH,COH AMP	
Elastic	3.2+1	5.0+2	COL	Expt Jour	PR 83 746	Aug 51 Tittman+THICK TARGET SCATT REL TO C	+
	7.1−1	1.2+1		Data	EXFOR12203.	Jun 76 . 37 PTS.	
Elastic	2.5−2		ORL	Expt Rept	TID – 14868	Jun 53 Allen.TRNS CRYST SPEC 11.17+ – 1.07B	
Elastic	1.0+6		WIS	Expt Jour	PR 93 1062	Mar 54 Walt+ ANG DIST.	+
	1.0+6			Data	EXFOR11637.068	Jun 76 . 1 PT.	
Elastic	4.1+6		LAS	Expt Jour	PR 98 677	May 55 Walt+ SCINT.	+
	4.1+6			Data	EXFOR11215.046	Jun 76 . 1 PT.	
Elastic	5.0+5		LAS	Expt Jour	PR 104 731	Nov 56 Allen+,5.4B+ – 10 TO 15PC	+
	5.0+5			Data	EXFOR12207.002	Jun 76 . 1 PT.	
Elastic	4.5+0	5.4+0	BNL	Expt Jour	PR 104 1425	Dec 56 Wood.CURVE CFD BREIT – WIGNER	
Elastic	1.0+6		CCP	Theo Jour	ZET 32 1143	May 57 CALCULATED 2B	
				Jour	JET 5 932	Dec 57 TRANSLATN.*	
Elastic	1.0+5	1.4+7	AGN	Eval Rept	TID – 21629	Dec 64 Perkins+ CALCTD BNL400,UCRL5573.	
Elastic	1.4+0		ORL	ExTh Jour	NP 61 381	Jan 65 Rayburn+ TOTAL – ABS XSECTS AT 1.44EV	+
	1.4+0			Expt Data	EXFOR11026.028	Jun 76 . 1 PT. SIGMA.	

79 Gold 197

Quantity	Energy (ev) Min	Max	Lab	Type	Documentation Ref Vol Page	Author, Comments Date	Data
Elastic	3.0+5	1.5+6	ANL	Expt	Jour ZP 183 323	Mar 65 Devilliers+TOF.TBL.CFD OPT MDL.	+
					Conf 64Paris 2 772	Jul 64 .SUPERSEDED	
					Rept EANDC(US)-62	Jun 64 .SUPERSEDED	
	3.0+5	1.5+6			Data EXFOR12240.003	Jun 76 . 26 PTS. SIGMA.	
Elastic	5.3+1	7.5+2	HAR	Expt	Jour NIM 39 68	Jan 66 Asghar+ LI-6 GLASS DETS	
	5.0+1	7.5+2			Rept AERE-NP/GEN40	Jan 65 - +MATEHED LI-6 DET.LINAC.GRPH	
	3.6+2	7.5+2			Jour NIM 28 205	Jun 64 Firk.YLD DATA IN LINAC EXPT REVIEW	
Elastic	1.5+6		IFU	Expt	Prog YFI-5 42	Oct 67 Korzh+ TBL OPTMDL PARAMS + TOTELAST	
					Rept INDC-232E	67 . ENGL OF YFI-5 42	
Elastic	1.5+6		IFU	Comp	Jour YF 7 277	Feb 68 Korzh+ OPTMOD PARS-FIT TO EXPTL-SIG	
					Jour SNP 7 2 190	Aug 68 TRANSLATN.*	
Elastic	1.5+2	7.0+2	SAC	Expt	Jour NIM 72 307	Dec 68 TROCHON B10 LOADED LIQUID SCINTILL	
Elastic	1.0+0	2.0+2	AUA	Theo	Jour AUJ 23 823	Dec 70 Clayton. MULTILEVEL ANALYSIS	
Elastic	8.0+6		AE	Expt	Rept AE-430	Sep 71 Holmqvist+ INTEGRATED ANGDIST VALUES	+
					Conf 70Helsinki 2 341	Jun 70 - + OPTMOD ANALYSIS. 8 MEV	
	8.1+6				Data EXFOR20162.023	May 74 1PNT.	
Elastic	8.8+5		ANL	Expt	Rept ANL-7935	Jun 72 COX+ 4 PI B(O)	+
	8.8+5				Data EXFOR10332.126	Jun 74 . 1 PT.	
Elastic	7.0+6		AE	Expt	Rept AE-482	Dec 73 Etemad. INTEGRATED.	+
	7.0+6				Data EXFOR20346.017	Sep 74 1PNT.	
Diff Elastic	2.5+6		HAR	Expt	Jour PM 44 1398	Dec 53 Poole.AT 97DEG 200+-50MB/SR,P RECOIL	
Diff Elastic	1.0+6		WIS	Expt	Jour PR 93 1062	Mar 54 Walt+ HE COUNTER 30-150DEG LAB CURVE	+
	1.0+6				Data EXFOR11637.070	Jun 76 . 9 PTS. DSIGMA.	
Diff Elastic	4.1+6		LAS	Expt	Jour PR 98 677	May 55 Walt+ BIASED SCINT ANG DISTR CURVE	+
	4.1+6				Data EXFOR11215.049	Jun 76 . 13 PTS. DSIGMA.	
Diff Elastic	1.0+6	4.1+6	LAS	Eval	Rept LA-2016	Jun 56 Longley+,2ES ANG DIST 3-DEG STEPS	
Diff Elastic	5.0+5		LAS	Expt	Jour PR 104 731	Nov 56 Allen+,CURVE ABSOLUTE 25-130DEG	+
	5.0+5				Data EXFOR12207.004	Jun 76 . 9 PTS. DSIGMA.	
Diff Elastic	1.0+5	1.8+7	LAS	Theo	Rept LA-2099	Dec 56 Beyster+,21ES,OPTMDL CALC CFD EXPT	
Diff Elastic	7.0+6		LRL	Theo	Rept UCRL-4927	Jul 57 Bjorklund+ OPTMOD CALC 6-PARAM FIT	
Diff Elastic	1.4+7		LRL	Theo	Rept UCRL-4926	Jul 57 Bjorklund+ OPTMOD CALC 6-PARAM FIT	
Diff Elastic	1.6+8		UPP	ExTh	Jour NP 21 383	Dec 60 Johansson+ ANGDST SCAT PS.CFD OPTMDL	
Diff Elastic	1.0+6		ANL	Theo	Jour PR 124 826	Nov 61 Sokoloff+ OSC POT CFD EXPT CURVE.	
Diff Elastic	4.0+6	7.0+6	LAS	Expt	Jour PR 129 1649	Feb 63 Thomson. SIG AT 90DEG	+
	4.0+6	7.0+6			Data EXFOR11495.050	Jun 76 . 2 PTS. DSIGMA.	
Diff Elastic	5.0+5	1.6+6	BNL	Theo	Jour PR/B 135 895	Aug 64 Auerbach+ LCL OPTMDL PAR TO FIT XPT.	
Diff Elastic	1.0+5	1.4+7	AGN	Eval	Rept TID-21629	Dec 64 Perkins+ LEGENDRE COEF CALCULATED.	
Diff Elastic	3.0+5	1.5+6	ANL	Expt	Jour ZP 183 323	Mar 65 Devilliers+TOF.TBL.CFD OPT MDL.GRPHS	+
					Jour PL 11 331	Aug 64 Vonach+EXPT CFD OPT MDL AT 800KEV.	
					Rept EANDC(US)-62	Jun 64 Smith+TOF.TBL.50KEV STEPS,20KEV RSLN	
	3.0+5	1.5+6			Data EXFOR12240.002	Jun 76 . 130 PTS. DSIGMA.	
Diff Elastic	5.0+5	2.5+6	LAS	Expt	Priv DAY	Jul 65 DAY.	+
	5.0+5	2.5+6			Data EXFOR12191.003	Jun 76 . 71 PTS. DSIGMA.	
Diff Elastic	1.0+6		LAS	Theo	Prog WASH-1064 84	Oct 65 Rosen+, OPTMDL+ CPD ELST CFD WIS XPT	
Diff Elastic	5.0+6		DKE	Expt	Jour ZP 196 103	Sep 66 Buccino+ 20-140DEG,CFD OPTMOD. TABLE	+
					Abst DA 24 4251	Apr 64 Hollandsworth+ CFD OPTMOD CALCS.	
	5.0+6				Data EXFOR11877.009	Jun 76 . 13 PTS. DSIGMA.	
Diff Elastic	5.0+5	4.1+6	AI	Eval	Jour NAA-SR-11980	Apr 67 Campbell+ LEG COEFS TBL+CURVS C-MSYS	
Diff Elastic	4.1+6		IFU	Theo	Jour UFZ 13 51	Jan 68 Kashuba+ GRPH,EXPT CFD OPTMOD-CALC	
					Jour UPJ 13 33	Jul 68 TRANSLATN.*	
Diff Elastic	1.5+6		IFU	Comp	Jour YF 7 277	Feb 68 Korzh+ GRPH SIG(ANG),OPTMOD PARS-FIT	
					Jour SNP 7 2 190	Aug 68 TRANSLATN.*	
Diff Elastic	6.0+5	1.6+6	ANL	Expt	Jour PR 176 1405	Dec 68 Kuchnir+ VDG+SCINT 5ES 1.75-15DEG	+
	6.0+5	1.6+6			Data EXFOR11977.004	Jun 76 . 31 PTS. DSIGMA.	
Diff Elastic	4.0+6	5.0+6	SCU	Theo	Rept ICD-6 236	69 Averyanov+CALC ANGDIST CFD EXPT,GRPH	
Diff Elastic	8.0+6		AE	Expt	Rept AE-430	Sep 71 Holmqvist+ TBLS + GEN OPTMOD FITS	+
					Jour NP/A 188 24	Jun 72 - + OPTMOD ANAL OF 8MEV DATA	
	8.1+6				Rept AE-452	May 72 Salama.VDG TOF CURVES TABLES	
	8.0+6				Conf 70Helsinki 2 341	Jun 70 Holmqvist+ OPTMOD ANALYSIS. 8 MEV	
	8.1+6				Data EXFOR20162.	May 74 . 32PTS.D/DA,LEG.FIT.	
Diff Elastic	8.7+5	2.0+6	ANL	Expt	Prog ANL-7910 20	Jan 72 COX. 2 ES. CURVES	
Diff Elastic	8.8+5		ANL	Expt	Rept ANL-7935	Jun 72 Cox+. CFD OPTMOD,HAUSER-FESHBACH	+
	8.8+5				Data EXFOR10332.030	Jun 74 . 8 PTS.	
Diff Elastic	8.0+6	1.1+7	BRC	Expt	Prog EANDC(E)-15702	May 73 Haouat+, BETWEEN 20 AND 160 DEGREES	
Diff Elastic	1.5+6		SCU	Comp	Rept YK-15 153	Aug 73 Aver'Janov+ H-F,OPTMOD,DIFFSIG,GRAPH	
Diff Elastic	7.0+6		AE	Expt	Rept AE-482	Dec 73 Etemad. VDG. TOF.	+
	7.0+6				Data EXFOR20346.	Sep 74 31PTS.D/DA,LEG.FIT.	

79 Gold 197

Quantity	Energy (ev) Min	Max	Lab	Type	Documentation Ref Vol Page	Date	Author, Comments	Data
Diff Elastic	3.5+1	2.8+6	LAS Expt	Rept	LA- 5552	Oct 74	Hoffman+ TBL.GRPH.40-90DEG.PHYSICS-8	+
	2.5+1	1.0+6		Conf	71Knoxvill 868	Mar 71	- +.NUCLEAR SHOT,CURVE	
	3.5+1	2.8+6		Data	EXFOR10264.	Apr 75	. 41300 PTS. DSIGMA AT 2 ANGLES.	
Diff Elastic	8.0+6		JAE Theo	Conf	JAERI-M-5984	Feb 75	Tanaka.OPTMDL/COUPLD CH CFD EXPTS.	
Polarization	1.5+6		DKE Expt	Rept	TID-19051	62	Olness+ TOF 51.5DEG POLARIZ MEASD	
Polarization	6.0+5	1.6+6	ANL Expt	Jour	PR 176 1405	Dec 68	Kuchnir+ VDG+SCINT 5ES 1.75-15DEG	
Polarization	8.7+5	2.0+6	ANL Expt	Prog	ANL-7910 20	Jan 72	COX. 2 ES. POLARIZING POWER. CURVES	
Polarization	8.8+5		ANL Expt	Jour	ANL-7935	Jun 72	Cox+. CFD OPTMOD,HAUSER-FESHBACH	+
	8.8+5			Data	EXFOR10332.064	Jun 74	. 8 PTS.	
Potntal Scat	1.2+2	3.0+2	ANL Expt	Jour	PR 76 100	Jul 49	Hibdon+ TRNSM. MN CO SCATT DETCTRS.	+
	1.2+2	3.0+2		Data	EXFOR11261.033	Jun 76	. 2 PTS.	
Potntal Scat	4.9+0		COL Expt	Jour	PR 80 903	Dec 50	Tittman+ FROM TRANSM, B-W FIT.	
Potntal Scat	2.5-2		ORL Expt	Jour	PR 81 527	Feb 51	Shull+	+
	2.5-2			Data	EXFOR11043.175	Jun 76	. 1 PT.	
Potntal Scat	4.9+1		COL Theo	Jour	PR 99 154	Jul 55	Kofoed-Hansen.THEORY 9.2+-.3B CFD BW	
Potntal Scat	4.9+0		BNL Expt	Jour	PR 104 1425	Dec 56	Wood.SIG=11.1+-0.8B	
Potntal Scat	+0	+3	BNL Expt	Jour	PR 110 692	May 58	Seth+ 11.2+-0.3B CALCTD FROM TOT SIG	+
	3.1+1			Data	EXFOR11788.016	Jun 76	. 1 PT.	
Potntal Scat		6.5+6	DKE ExTh	Jour	PL 13 70	Nov 64	Seth+0,1PHASE FRM SIG TOT AV 3-650KV	
Potntal Scat	2.4+4		LRC Theo	Conf	66Paris 1 503	Oct 66	Bogart. VAL GVN, BETHE ANALYSIS	
Potntal Scat		1.0+3	SAC Expt	Jour	NP/A 123 561	Jan 69	Morgenstern+ RADIUS FROM RES ANAL	+
				Rept	CEA-R-3609	Sep 68	- + (THESIS). RADIUS.	
	0.0+0	1.0+3		Data	EXFOR20686.004	Aug 77	1PNT.RADIUS.	
Potntal Scat	1.0+3	1.0+6	GA Expt	Conf	71Knoxvill 252	Mar 71	Fricke+. SIG=9.5B	
Potntal Scat	2.0+3		IJI Expt	Conf	76Lowell 1244	Jul 76	Vertebnyi+ SCT-LNGTH GVN,FRM TOT+SCT	
Tot Inelastc	3.0+6		LAS Expt	Jour	PR 72 881	Nov 47	Barschall+POOR GEOM+BACKSCT.BIAS DET	
Tot Inelastc	1.4+7		LAS Expt	Jour	PR 97 1205	Mar 55	Graves+ LESS THAN 1.22+-0.04 B.	
Tot Inelastc	1.4+7		LRL Expt	Conf	58Paris § NS609	Jul 58	Macgregor. FROM SNE 9,14 MEV CUTOFF.	+
	1.4+7			Data	EXFOR11205.021	Jun 76	. 1 PT.	
Tot Inelastc	Fiss		AE Theo	Rept	AE- 102	May 63	Konijn.ISOMER PROD CALC FOR LA FSPEC	
Tot Inelastc	7.7+4	1.6+6	BNL Theo	Jour	PR/B 135 895	Aug 64	Auerbach+ LCL OPTMDL 5LVL X FIT.TBL.	
	+6			Conf	65Antwerp 25	Jul 65	- +NDG COMPLEX POTENTIAL MODL	
Tot Inelastc	Pile		FEI Comp	Rept	ICD-4 57	67	Sluchevskaja.SELECTIV COMPIL ,TABLE	
Tot Inelastc	1.3+7	1.6+7	FEI Comp	Rept	ICD-4 57	67	Sluchevskaja.SELECTIV COMPIL ,TABLE	
Tot Inelastc	Fast		MUN Expt	Jour	NUK 10 181	Oct 67	Koehler+H2O MODER REACT. .1MEVCUTOFF	
				Rept	FRM-81	Aug 66	- + SUPERSEDED.	
Tot Inelastc	1.5+7		DEB ExTh	Jour	AHP 25 91	Oct 68	Peto+ REL PR141(N,2N) CFD THEORY	+
	1.5+7		Expt	Data	EXFOR30069.004	Dec 70	SIG REL PR-141(N2N)	
Tot Inelastc	Fiss		MUN Expt	Jour	JNE 22 632	Oct 68	Durrani+ AVERAGE XSECT,FAST SPECT.HL	
Tot Inelastc	2.8+6	1.5+7	CCP Comp	Rept	ICD-6 106	70	Sluchevskaja.ALSO FISS,TABLE OF SIGS	
Tot Inelastc	8.0+4	2.0+6	GA Theo	Conf	70Helsinki 2 281	Jun 70	Fricke+44. SIG(E) GRAPH,STATMOD CALC	
Tot Inelastc	1.4+7	1.5+7	JYV Eval	Rept	JU-RR-3/1970	Jun 70	Leppaemaeki+ TABLE OF EVAL AVG SIG	
Tot Inelastc	2.5+6	3.0+6	KFI Comp	Jour	JRC 7 365	Jun 71	Nagy+ SIGMA,GAM+XRAY+ELECTR ES GIVEN	
Tot Inelastc	1.5+7		TUD Expt	Prog	ZFK-262 28	Sep 73	Hermsdorf+ DEDUCED FROM N-EMIS,TABLE	
Tot Inelastc	1.4+7		KYU Expt	Jour	NST 13 334	Jun 76	Irie+.CFD C PRE-COMPOUND MODEL	
Diff Inelast	2.5+6		HAR Expt	Jour	PM 44 1398	Dec 53	Poole.AT 97DEG 70+-30MB/STR,P RECOIL	
Diff Inelast	5.0+5	5.5+6	LAS Expt	Jour	PR 93 199	Jan 54	Martin+ AU197M EXCITATION CURVE	+
	4.3+5	5.3+6		Data	EXFOR11985.003	Jun 76	. 46 PTS. DSIGMA.	
Diff Inelast	5.3+5	2.0+6	MIT Expt	Jour	PR 93 197	Jan 56	Ebel+ AU197M EXCITATION CURVE	
Diff Inelast	2.4+6		LAS Expt	Jour	PR 103 343	Jul 56	Cranberg+,TOF CURVE 90 160DEG	
Diff Inelast	2.5+6	6.3+6	LAS Expt	Conf	ORNL-2309	Jun 57	Levin+ TOF. 3 ES CFD MAXWL. CURVE.	
Diff Inelast	4.0+6	7.0+6	LAS Expt	Jour	PR 129 1649	Feb 63	Thomson+ 90DEG TEMP FOR NS TO 3MEV	+
	4.0+6	7.0+6		Data	EXFOR11495.049	Jun 76	. 2 PTS. DSIGMA.	
Diff Inelast	4.0+6		BNL Theo	Jour	PR/B 135 895	Aug 64	Auerbach+OPTMDL CALC 3LVLS,NRLY ISOT	
Diff Inelast	4.0+6	6.5+6	DKE Expt	Jour	NP 60 17	Nov 64	Buccino+N SPEC MEASURED 4ES+NUC TEMP	
				Abst	DA 24 4251	Apr 64	Hollandsworth.TOF.EN SPEC.NUCL T.	
	6.0+6			Rept	AD- 299005	62	Seth+,NUCL TEMP+FERMI LVL DENS COEFF	
Diff Inelast	Fiss		UCB Expt	Rept	NYO-10175	Dec 64	Arino+ACT.TBLS,GRPHS.PRODUCT HL.	+
	Fiss			Data	EXFOR11817.026	Jun 76	. 1 PT.	
Diff Inelast	3.0+5	1.5+6	ANL Expt	Jour	ZP 183 323	Mar 65	Devilliers+ EXC CURVS, 8 LVLS.	
	3.0+5	1.5+6		Data	EXFOR12240.	Jun 76	. 112 PTS. SIGMA.	
Diff Inelast	Fiss		IIT Comp	Conf	65IAEA 251	Mar 65	Barrall+CALC AVG SIGS OF 3FISS-SPECS	
Diff Inelast	1.4+7		KYU Expt	Prog	INDSWG-90 24	Jul 65	Yoshimura.TIME OF FLIGHT, TBC	
Diff Inelast	2.5+6	1.5+7	FEI Theo	Jour	NP 76 232	Feb 66	Malyshev+ SPEC ANALYSED FOR TEMP	
Diff Inelast	3.5+6	8.5+6	JAE ExTh	Jour	NP 78 369	Apr 66	Tsukada+ SPECTRA CFD FERMI GAS MDL	
	3.6+6	8.5+6	Expt	Jour	NP/A 131 145	Jun 69	Maruyama. E DEPENDENCE,PARAM,TH FIT	
Diff Inelast	1.3+7	1.6+7	HAM Expt	Prog	EANDC(E)76U	Jan 67	Bormann+ TABLE	+

79 Gold 197

Quantity	Energy (ev) Min	Max	Lab	Type	Documentation Ref Vol Page	Author, Comments Date	Data
Diff Inelast	1.3+5	1.5+6	PEL Expt	Jour	NP/A 107 612	Jan 68 Barnard+.VDG+TOF. AT90DEG. 16LEVELS	+
	1.0+5	1.6+6		Conf	67Tokyo § 4.92	Sep 67 - + SIG 90DEG,EXCIT FNS 10LEVLS	
				Jour	ZP 183 323	Mar 65 - + CURVS+DATA GVN,SEE NP/A 167	
	1.2+5	1.5+6		Data	EXFOR30010.	Mar 70 SCATTERING FROM MANY LEVELS	
Diff Inelast	-		BHU Theo	Conf	68Madras 1 291	Feb 68 Sharma+ PPRN39.CALCS TB ANALYSED,NDG	
Diff Inelast	2.8+6		DEB Expt	Jour	AK 10 112	Jul 68 Bornemisza+ TBL HL+SIGMA FOR AU197M	+
	2.8+6			Data	EXFOR30338.002	Aug 76 TO ISOM. 1 PNT	
Diff Inelast	1.4+7		TUD Expt	Prog	ZFK-223 28	Sep 71 Hantzsch+ TOF,DIFFSIG TO BE CALC,NDG	
Diff Inelast	1.4+7		VNV Expt	Rept	CEA-N-4279	Mar 72 Clayeux+ TOF,DIF NTS .1 TO 7 MEV	
				Conf	71Knoxvill 196	Mar 71 Voignier+SIG VS.E(PRIME) 90DEG CRV	
Diff Inelast	1.4+7		TUD Theo	Prog	ZFK-243 20	Sep 72 Hermsdorf+ PRE-EQUIL STAT MDL ANALYS	
Diff Inelast	1.5+6	1.4+7	TUD Expt	Prog	ZFK-243 23	Sep 72 Hermsdorf+ DOUBLE-DIFF,5 ANGS,GRAPH	
Diff Inelast	1.4+7		ITJ Expt	Jour	JRC 14 201	73 Janczyszyn+ TO ISO,ACTIV.CFD OTH,TBL	+
	1.4+7			Data	EXFOR30322.019	Feb 76 1 PNT.	
Diff Inelast	+6		KOS Expt	Jour	AHP 33 363	73 Peto+ SIG TO ISOM FOR PU-BE NS,TABLE	+
	+6			Data	EXFOR30265.018	Feb 74 1 DATA LINE	
Diff Inelast	8.0+6	1.1+7	BRC Expt	Prog	EANDC(E)-15702	May 73 Haouat+, BETWEEN 20 AND 160 DEGREES	
Diff Inelast	1.4+7		TUD Theo	Conf	73Kiev 1 258	May 73 Hermsdorf+ DESCRIPN OF N-SPEC	
Diff Inelast	1.4+7		KYU Expt	Jour	NST 11 523	Dec 74 Akiyoshi+.TOF,E-SPECTRUM AT 100 DEG	
Diff Inelast	Thrsh	Up	CAI Theo	Jour	AKE 28 3 201	76 Abboud. EXCITATION-FN,STATMOD	
Diff Inelast	+7		CCP Expt	Rept	YK-23 4	76 Brodskaja+ ACTIV,AVG SIG,TBL	
Diff Inelast	1.4+7		KYU Expt	Jour	NST 13 334	Jun 76 Irie+.E-SPECTRA 20 TO 150 DEG. NDG	
Thermal Scat	Maxwl		UJV Theo	Rept	UJV-2275	69 Krivy. DEBYE TEMP,BRAGG+OTHER EXPTS	
Thermal Scat	1.0-4	1.0+3	MUNRevw	Jour	EEN 80 1	77 Koester. SCAT LENGTH,INCOH SIG	
Scattering	3.1+6		LAS Expt	Jour	PR 70 602	Nov 46 Manley+ BACK SCATT, (DD).	
Scattering	2.0+5	3.0+6	LAS Expt	Jour	PR 72 881	Nov 47 Barschall+POOR GEOM+BACKSCT.BIAS DET	
Scattering	Maxwl		COL Expt	Rept	CR-1765	Sep 56 Havens+	
Scattering	1.0+0	1.5+1	COL Expt	Rept	CU-165	Jun 57 Moore.TRANS. CURVE:ALSO RATIO TO TOT	
Scattering	6.0+4	1.8+6	ANL Expt	Jour	PR 107 1077	Aug 57 Langsdorf+,LEGENDRE COEFS CURVES	+
				Rept	ANL-5567	Oct 61 .REVISED DATA	
	6.0+4	1.8+6		Data	EXFOR11224.061	Jun 76 . 65 PTS. DSIGMA.	
	6.0+4	1.8+6		Data	EXFOR11224.060	Jun 76 . 13 PTS, SIGMA	
Scattering	2.4+4		LRC Theo	Conf	66Paris 1 503	Oct 66 Bogart. VAL GVN, BETHE ANALYSIS	
Scattering	-3		JUL Expt	Conf	75Wash. 823	Mar 75 Schmatz+INCOH SC LT 500+-50MB REL VA	
Scattering	2.0+3		IJI Expt	Conf	76Lowell 1244	Jul 76 Vertebnyi+ SCT-SIG VS THICKNESS,NDG	
Nonelastic	1.4+7		LAS Expt	Jour	PR 88 600	Nov 52 Phillips+ INEL. CROSS.	+
	1.4+7			Data	EXFOR11210.009	Jun 76 . 1 PT.	
Nonelastic	1.4+7		LAS Expt	Jour	PR 89 343	Jan 53 Graves+ 2.1+ -0.5. CFD LA-1532.	+
	1.4+7			Data	EXFOR11304.010	Jun 76 . 1 PT.	
Nonelastic	1.0+6		WIS Expt	Jour	PR 93 1062	Mar 54 Walt+ DIFF.EL.SCATT.	+
	1.0+6			Data	EXFOR11637.069	Jun 76 . 1 PT.	
Nonelastic	1.4+7		LAS Expt	Jour	PR 97 1205	Mar 55 Graves+ 2.44+ -.02B.CFD PR88 600 1952	+
	1.4+7			Data	EXFOR11310.010	Jun 76 . 1 PT.	
Nonelastic	4.1+6		LAS Expt	Jour	PR 98 677	May 55 Walt+ 2.7+ -0.3B FROM TOT MINUS ELAST	+
	4.1+6			Data	EXFOR11215.047	Jun 76 . 1 PT.	
Nonelastic	1.0+6	4.5+6	LAS Expt	Jour	PR 98 1216	Jun 55 Beyster+	+
	1.0+6	4.5+6		Data	EXFOR11216.015	Jun 76 . 3 PTS.	
Nonelastic	5.0+5		LAS Expt	Jour	PR 104 731	Nov 56 Allen. ANG.DIST.	+
	5.0+5			Data	EXFOR12207.003	Jun 76 . 1 PT.	
Nonelastic	4.0+4	1.8+7	LAS Theo	Rept	LA-2099	Dec 56 Beyster+,OPTMDL CALC CFD EXPT,CURVE	
Nonelastic	1.0+6	7.0+6	LAS Expt	Jour	PR 104 1319	Dec 56 Beyster+,SPH TRNS 1.75-2.50B 5ES	+
	1.0+6	7.0+6		Data	EXFOR11220.030	Jun 76 . 5 PTS.	
Nonelastic	Fiss		LAS Expt	Jour	JNE 4 147	Feb 57 Bethe+.SPH TRNSM,POOR RSLN DETECTORS	+
				Rept	LA-1429	Dec 55 - +	
	Fiss			Data	EXFOR11461.	Jun 76 . 3 PTS. SIGMA FOR 3 DETECTORS.	
Nonelastic	1.4+7		LRL Expt	Jour	PR 108 726	Nov 57 Macgregor+,SPH TRNS CFD OPTMDL+XPTS	+
				Conf	58Geneva 14 109	Sep 58 Ball+.PPR1881,SPHERE TRANSM-METHOD	
	1.4+7			Data	EXFOR11226.021	Jun 76 . 1 PT.	
Nonelastic	1.0+6	1.5+7	BNL Comp	Conf	58Geneva 16 8	Sep 58 Hughes.PPR2483,CURVE,MANY REFS	
Nonelastic	1.0+6	1.5+7	LOK Expt	Conf	60Kingston 146	Aug 60 Walt+.CURVE,OPTMDL FIT CFD EXPT	
Nonelastic	1.4+7		TUD Theo	Rept	ZFK-271 63	Nov 73 Seeliger+ N-SPEC,NDG.INTEG-SIG SHOWN	
				Jour	KE 16 252	Aug 73 Hermsdorf+ INTEG FITTED DIFFSIG,TBL	
Nonelastic	1.4+7	1.5+7	ANL Eval	Rept	ANL-75-34	Jun 75 Davey+CORRC APPLIED TO N2N CS.TBLS.	
Absorption	Slow		OSA Expt	Jour	JPJO 18 188	36 Kikuchi+.SIG AND G-ENERGY DETERMIN	
Absorption	Maxwl		HAR Expt	Jour	JNE 1 57	Aug 54 Egelstaff.REL TO B STANDARD.	
	2.5-2	2.5-2		Jour	JNE 5 41	Jul 57 - .REVISED BORON STANDARD.	

79 Gold 197

Quantity	Energy (ev) Min	Max	Lab	Type	Documentation Ref Vol Page	Author, Comments Date	Data
Absorption	Maxwl		HAR Expt	Rept	AERE – R/R – 2516	Mar 58 Jowitt+ PILE OSC.REL BORON.293DEGK.	+
	2.5 – 2	2.5 – 2		Rept	AERE – R/R – 2333	57 Cummins+ PILE OSCILLATOR.	
	Maxwl			Jour	JNE 1 144	Dec 54 Green+. LOCAL PILE OSC REL B AND AG	
Absorption	2.5 – 2		HAR Expt	Jour	JNEA 12 32	May 60 Tattersall+ PILE OSCILLATOR.	+
	2.5 – 2			Data	EXFOR20638.062	Jul 76 1PNT.SIGMA.	
Absorption	2.4+4	8.3+5	FEI Expt	Jour	AE 8 549	Jun 60 Belanova.VAL FOR 3ES,SPHERE TRNSMISS	
				Jour	SJA 8 462	Jul 61 TRANSLATN.*GERMAN KE4 147 2/61	
Absorption	Cold	2.5 – 2	COL Expt	Jour	NSE 8 453	Dec 60 Gould+,CS SIG=98.8+ – 0.3B AT .0253EV	+
Absorption	4.1 – 1	1.0+7	GA Eval	Rept	GA – 2451	Aug 61 Joanou+.68GROUP DATA FOR GAM – I	
Absorption	2.5 – 1		WWA Expt	Conf	61Bucharst 623	Nov 61 Bouzyk+ PILE OSC,REL B.PRELIMIN.TBL	+
	Maxwl			Data	EXFOR30412.010	Aug 77 1 PNT.	
Absorption	Maxwl		ROS Expt	Jour	KE 6 336	Jan 63 Huettel+.VAL GVN,PILE OSCILL METHOD	+
	Maxwl			Data	EXFOR31311.007	Sep 72 .SIG GVN	
Absorption	2.5 – 2	2.5 – 2	FAR Expt	Rept	CEA – R – 2486	64 Vidal+ 2 VALUES.FOR NORMALISATION	+
Absorption	2.5 – 2		RIS Expt	Jour	PR/B 133 925	Feb 64 Als – Nielsen+ 98.6+ – 2B FROM TOTAL SIG	+
	2.5 – 2			Data	EXFOR20105.006	Sep 71 1PNT.SIG.	
Absorption	2.4+4		FEI Expt	Jour	AE 19 3	Jul 65 Belanova+ 2 METHODS,ABSOL EXPT,TABLE	+
				Jour	JNE 20 411	66 .ENGLISH TRANSL OF AE 19 3 7/65	
				Jour	SJA 19 858	65 .ENGLISH TRANSL OF AE 19 3 7/65	
				Jour	EAF 19 1 11	65 . FRENCH TRANSL OF AE 19 3 7/65	
	2.4+4			Data	EXFOR40072.014	Jul 71 SIGMA AT 24 KEV AS PUBLISHED	
Absorption	8.1+6		AE Theo	Conf	70Helsinki 2 341	Jun 70 Holmqvist+55. OPTMODEL CALC SIGMA	
Absorption	2.5 – 2		MUN Expt	Prog	EANDC(E)157U	Mar 73 Dilg+FRM.CHOPPER.SIG=98.68+ – 0.10B	
Absorption	Fiss		BET Expt	Jour	NSE 58 361	Dec 75 Green. 252CF FISS NEUT SPECT AVG	+
	Fiss			Data	EXFOR10557.002	Apr 76 . 1 PT. SIGMA.	
Res Int Abs	5.0 – 1		ANL Expt	Jour	PR 79 11	Jul 50 Harris+. EPI – CD REL THERMAL ACT.B – W	
Res Int Abs	None		ORL Revw	Conf	55Geneva 5 96	Aug 55 Macklin+.TABLE,EXPT CFD THEORY,P833	
Res Int Abs	5.0 – 1	5.0 – 1	AE Expt	Jour	JNE 11 101	Jan 60 Popovic+.	+
	5.0 – 1			Data	EXFOR20048.002	Sep 71 1PNT.CAPTURE.	
Res Int Abs	None		MTR Expt	Prog	WASH – 1039 36	May 62 Schuman. VARIOUS THICKNESSES	
Res Int Abs	–		WIN Expt	Jour	JNAB 16 335	Jul 62 Moore+.CD TUBED OSC. NOT INF DILUTE	
				Rept	AEEW – R – 57	Aug 61 – + EQU TO JNE(A+B)16 335	
Res Int Abs	– 3	+3	DGE Eval	Conf	62Harwell 2 11	Dec 62 Delattre+ RECOMM TOT RES – INTGRL GIVN	
Res Int Abs	– 3	+2	FAR Theo	Conf	62Harwell 1 181	Dec 62 Brisbois.CAPT RES INTS DISCUSSED	
Res Int Abs	5.0 – 1		NSW Eval	Rept	AAEC/TM – 191	Apr 63 Connolly+ CALC RES INT=1566B	
Res Int Abs	Pile		DKE Expt	Abst	DA 23 4719	Jun 63 Furr.RES INTEG REL TO I127.NDG	
Res Int Abs	7.0 – 1		WIN Expt	Rept	AEEW – R – 217	Aug 63 Hardiman+ CD RATIOS,E – CD VALUES CALC	
		1.0+5	LEB Expt	Jour	ZET 46 80	Jan 64 Konks.TBL 3E – RANGES.ENGL JET 19 59	
Res Int Abs	5.0 – 1		KFK Expt	Jour	NSE 19 244	Jun 64 Brose. RI=1461.8B. TBP NUK STANDARD	
Res Int Abs	4.0 – 1		AUA Eval	Rept	AAEC/TM – 270	Oct 64 Doherty.TBL.EFFECT OF SPEC,RESPARAMS	
Res Int Abs	4.0 – 1	1.8+7	IIT Comp	Conf	65IAEA 251	Mar 65 Barrall+ RECOMENDED VAL,LITER – SURVEY	
Res Int Abs	5.0 – 1		AE Expt	Diss	GOTHENBURG	Feb 66 Johansson.ACT.NOTE LATER MEASUREMET	+
				Conf	66S.Diego 2 151	Feb 66 – + ACTIV. SUPERSEDED.	
				Jour	JNEA 11 101	Feb 60 Jirlow+ VAL CHANGED,NOT 1/V.AT SEV.	
	5.0 – 1			Data	EXFOR20048.002	72 1PT. ACTIVATION. FROM JIRLOW.	
Res Int Abs	5.0 – 1		AE Revw	Conf	66S.Diego 2 161	Feb 66 Hellstrand.REVW CAPT MEAS AND CALC R	
Res Int Abs	2.0 – 1	1.0+5	JUL Expt	Rept	JUEL – 503 – RX	Sep 67 Borchardt.SELF – SHIELD – CORRC,CFD TH	
Res Int Abs	5.5 – 1		MOL Theo	Rept	BLG – 421	Sep 67 Damle+,EVAL ACT R.I=1550+ – 50B,INC1/V	
Res Int Abs	5.5 – 1		MOL Eval	Rept	BLG – 421	Sep 67 Damle+,EVAL ACT R.I=1550+ – 50B,INC1/V	
Res Int Abs	5.0 – 1		AUA Expt	Rept	AAEC/TM – 466	Jul 68 Wall. VAL GVN,CFD OTHER EXPT,TBL	
Res Int Abs	6.3 – 1		CAS Eval	Jour	NSE 40 51	70 Gibello+,EVAL. CAPT RES INT=1567B	
Res Int Abs	– 4	+7	BNW Eval	Rept	BNWL – 1312	May 70 Simons+ RI = 1585. B	
Res Int Abs	5.6 – 1	1.8+7	JUL Theo	Rept	JUEL – 814 – RX	Dec 71 Borchardt.ACTIV.FOR DIFF 1/E SP	
Res Int Abs	5.5 – 1		RCN Revw	Conf	73Paris 2 271	Mar 73 Zijp.ACT,RECOMM FROM LITERATURE,TBL	
	– 1	+3		Rept	STI/DOC/10 – 107	May 70 – .CH 4. (NG) VAL TBL,TECHNIQ – REV	
Res Int Abs	5.0 – 1		GHT Comp	Jour	JRC 20 695	74 Van Der Linden+ CAPT.NORMALISATION.	
Res Int Act	–		ISL Expt	Jour	JNAB 16 291	Jun 62 Ben – David+. 1607B. SEE IA612 1961	
(n,γ)	Maxwl		PAR Expt	Jour	JPR 7 511	Dec 36 Pontecorvo. PO – BE	
(n,γ)	2.2+5		PCF Expt	Jour	NAT 142 392	Aug 38 Halban+ ACT CS GIVEN	
(n,γ)	2.0+4	7.0+5	OXF Expt	Jour	PRSA 170 513	Apr 39 Griffiths.RA – BE PHOTONEUT ACTIVATION	
(n,γ)	Maxwl		JAP Expt	Jour	SCP 38 167	Jan 41 Sinma+.LI+D.RELATIVE SIG MEASUREMENT	
(n,γ)	4.0+4	7.7+5	LAS Expt	Rept	LA – 467	Jul 46 Linenberger+ TBL,GRPH. REL TO H001.	
(n,γ)	Pile		ANL Expt	Jour	PR 72 888	Nov 47 Seren+.ACT METHOD.TO1.5MIN,70D ISOM.	+
	Pile			Data	EXFOR11447.126	Jun 76 . 1 PT.	
(n,γ)	2.2+5	9.0+5	OXF Expt	Jour	NAT 161 727	May 48 Allen+ ACTIVATION RATIO	
(n,γ)	Fiss		ANL Expt	Jour	PR 75 1781	Jun 49 Hughes+ REL SIG(THERMAL),FOIL ACTIVN	+
	Fiss			Data	EXFOR11450.037	Jun 76 . 1 PT.	
(n,γ)	Maxwl		ANL Expt	Jour	PR 76 531	Aug 49 Kubitscheck+ YIELD CFD SIG.G – M COINC	

79 Gold 197

Quantity	Energy (ev) Min	Max	Lab	Type	Documentation Ref Vol Page	Author, Comments Date	Data
(n,γ)	Pile		ANL	Expt Jour	PR 80 342	Nov 50 Harris+.PILE OSC.REL TO BORON.APPROX	+
	Pile			Data	EXFOR11528.046	Jun 76 . 1 PT.	
(n,γ)	2.4+4		ANL	Expt Jour	PR 82 67	Apr 51 Hummel+ SB – BE PHOTONEUTS. ACTIVATION	+
	2.4+4			Data	EXFOR11010.016	Aug 76 . 1 PT. SIG=1.5 B.	
(n,γ)	Fiss		BNL	Expt Jour	PR 91 1423	Sep 53 Hughes+.ALSO LVL SPACINGS AT EXCIT E	
(n,γ)	1.0–3	2.5–2	BNL	Expt Jour	PR 92 716	Nov 53 Carter+ 1PC ERSLN. SLOWCHOPP. OKS TH	+
	2.5–2			Data	EXFOR11211.005	Jun 76 . 1 PT.	
(n,γ)	Maxwl		ORL	Expt Jour	PR 96 1267	Dec 54 Allen+	+
				Rept	TID – 14868	Jun 53 – .TRNS CRYST SPEC 94.55+ – 0.78B	
	Maxwl			Data	EXFOR12636.002	Jun 76 . 1 PT, SIGMA.	
(n,γ)	2.5–2		BNL	Comp Conf	55Geneva 4 147	Aug 55 Harvey.VAL 2200M/SEC,PPR832	
(n,γ)		1.0+2	BNL	Prog	WASH – 190	Feb 56 Draper+ NDG,TOF,CYCL,SELF IND	
(n,γ)	6.2–4	3.3–3	COL	Expt Rept	CR – 1765	Sep 56 Havens.LINEAR 1/V FIT.HENCE SIG(THR)	
(n,γ)	Maxwl		SRL	Expt Rept	DP – 207	Feb 57 Wade.	+
	Maxwl			Data	EXFOR11777.003	Jun 76 . 1 PT.	
(n,γ)	Fast		HAR	Expt Jour	JNE 5 4	Jul 57 Rose. ACT CS GVN,ZEPHYR,TH DISCUSS	
				Rept	AERE – R/R – 2151	57 Absalom+ ZEPHYR+TH ENVELOPE.	
				Revw Conf	55Geneva 5 331	Aug 55 Holmes+P404,SAME DATA AS JNE 5,4,57	
(n,γ)	2.5+4		ORL	Expt Jour	PR 107 504	Jul 57 Macklin+.SB – BE NS. 1120+ – 110MB	+
				Conf	58Geneva 671	Sep 58 .SUPERSEDED.	
	2.5+4			Data	EXFOR11399.049	Jun 76 . 1 PT.	
(n,γ)	1.0+3		NDA	Theo Rept	NDA – 2093 – 7	May 58 Kalos. STAT TH CALC CFD EXPT CURVES	
(n,γ)	1.0+3	6.0+6	BNL	Comp Conf	58Geneva 16 8	Sep 58 Hughes.PPR2483,CURVE,MANY REFS	
(n,γ)	2.5+4	2.0+5	KUR	Expt Conf	58Geneva 15 50	Sep 58 Leipunskij+.PPR2219,VAL GVN,ACTIVATN	
(n,γ)	2.5+4		LRL	Expt Jour	PR 112 226	Oct 58 Booth+ SB – BE REL I+THR,ACT 2.7D HL	+
	2.5+4			Data	EXFOR11429.031	Jun 76 . 1 PT.	
(n,γ)	2.5+4		FEI	Expt Jour	AE 5 564	Nov 58 Kononov+ ACT CS REL TO I127(N,G) GVN	
				Jour	JNEA 11 46	59 .TRANSLATION	
				Jour	SJA 5 1483	58 .TRANSLATION	
(n,γ)	1.8+5		LAS	Expt Jour	PR 113 256	Jan 59 Bame+,ACT 310+ – 20MB	+
	1.8+5			Data	EXFOR11405.004	Jun 76 . 1 PT.	
(n,γ)	3.2–2	1.0+7	GEA	Eval Rept	XDC – 60 – 8 – 81	Jun 59 Roberts.19 – GROUP – AVGD SIGS	
(n,γ)	2.0+5		ORL	Expt Jour	PR 114 1619	Jun 59 Lyon+ ABS GAMMA COUNT 320+ – 20MB ACT.	+
	2.0+5			Data	EXFOR11407.032	Jun 76 . 1 PT.	
(n,γ)	1.5+5	1.0+6	HAR	Expt Jour	JNEA 10 19	Jul 59 Ferguson+ SIG AT 3ES REL SIGSCAT H	
(n,γ)	5.0+1	2.0+4	LEB	Expt Conf	59Tashkent 1 64	Sep 59 Isakov.PB – SLOW – DOWN, GRAPH SIG(E)	
				Rept	AEC – TR – 6398	64 .VOL 1,P70 .ENGL OF 59TASHKE 1 64	
(n,γ)	3.0+5	5.0+5	ANL	Expt Jour	ANL – 5937 28	Nov 59 Monahan. OKS DIVEN SELF DETECTION.	
(n,γ)	1.0+5	1.0+6	COL	Theo Jour	PR 116 937	Nov 59 Troubetzkoy+.TH CFD EXPT. CURVES.	
(n,γ)	1.5+5	6.0+6	WIS	Expt Jour	PR 116 927	Nov 59 Johnsrud+ SC CFD OTHERS SIG VS E.	+
	1.5+5	5.4+6		Data	EXFOR11675.026	Jun 76 . 21 PTS. SIGMA.	
(n,γ)	5.0+1	3.0+4	LEB	Expt Jour	ZET 38 989	Mar 60 Isakov.GRAPH SIG(E).ENGL= JET 11 712	
(n,γ)	1.5+3	2.0+5	DKE	Expt Jour	AP 10 455	Aug 60 Bilpuch.GRPH SIG(E),S – P – WAVE COMPONT	+
	1.5+3	2.0+5		Data	EXFOR11187.004	Jun 76 . 13 PTS. SIGMA.	
(n,γ)	1.8+5	1.0+6	LAS	Expt Jour	PR 120 556	Oct 60 Diven.SC – T.	
				Conf	58Geneva	Sep 58 .SUPERSEDED.	
	1.8+5	1.0+6		Data	EXFOR11616.027	Jun 76 . 7 PTS. SIGMA.	
(n,γ)	Maxwl		MUN	Revw Conf	60Vienna 63	Oct 60 Maierleibnitz. TABLE,ACCURATE VALUES	
(n,γ)	2.4+4		ORL	Expt Jour	NP 20 202	Oct 60 Schmitt.SHELL TRANSMISSION 585+ – 60MB	+
				Prog	EANDC – 33 41	Sep 63 . + REVISED NP 20 202.	
	2.4+4			Data	EXFOR11778.013	Jun 76 . 1 PT. SIGMA.	
(n,γ)	Pile		CRC	Eval Rept	CRRP – 960	Nov 60 Westcott.G,S FACTORS EFFECTIVE CAPT.	
				Rept	CRRP – 862	Aug 59 .SUPERSEDED.	
				Rept	CRRP – 787	Sep 58 .SUPERSEDED.	
				Rept	CRRP – 680	Jan 57 .SUPERSEDED	
(n,γ)	1.0+3	1.0+6	CCP	Expt Jour	ZET 39 1737	Dec 60 .OPTMDL FIT,S CURVES P PAR	
				Jour	JET 12 1213	Jun 61 .TRANSLATN.	
(n,γ)	Fast		LAS	Expt Jour	NSE 8 608	Dec 60 Byers. GODIVA JEZEBEL ACT CS GIVEN	
(n,γ)	2.5–2		ANL	Expt Jour	NSE 9 132	Feb 61 Meadows+.PULSED NEUTS. SIG =98.2+ – .5B	+
	2.5–2			Data	EXFOR11028.024	Sep 76 . 1 PT. SIG=98.2 B.	
(n,γ)	9.0+3	1.7+5	ORL	ExTh Jour	PR 122 182	Apr 61 Gibbons.GRPH XPTL POINTS,TH CRV	+
	3.0+4	6.5+4		Expt Jour	PR 129 2695	Mar 63 Macklin+ LIQ SCINT,515 AND 332MB	
	3.0+4	1.7+5		Conf	61Vienna 1 95	Aug 61 Neiler.	
	9.4+3	1.7+5		Data	EXFOR11329.	Jun 76 . 64 PTS.	
(n,γ)	7.3+4	1.5+6	ANL	Expt Jour	PR 122 1280	May 61 Cox.TBL AND GRAPHS SIG(E),CFD OTHERS	+
(n,γ)	2.0+4	2.0+6	ANL	Revw Conf	61Vienna 1 29	Aug 61 Smith.PPR76,CURVE CFD REFERENCES	

79 Gold 197

Quantity	Energy (ev) Min	Max	Lab	Type	Documentation Ref Vol Page	Author, Comments Date	Data
(n,γ)	2.5−2	2.5−2	KUR	Expt Conf	61Vienna 3 315	Aug 61 Leipunskij+,TBL WITH SIG GIVEN.	
	Pile			Conf	58Geneva 12 3	Sep 58 − +.PPR2038,VAL U238/PU239	
	2.5−2	2.5−2		Rept	ANL−TR−9	62 .ENGLISH TRANSLATION.	
(n,γ)	3.0+4	6.4+4	ORL	Expt Jour	PR 123 948	Aug 61 Weston+ 0.767+−0.06,0.456+−0.04B	+
				Jour	PRL 6 656	Jun 61 .SUPERSEDED.	
	3.0+4	6.4+4		Data	EXFOR12214.002	Jun 76 . 2 PTS.	
(n,γ)	2.3+2	7.6+3	ORL	Expt Conf	61Saclay 203	Sep 61 Block+.LIQUID SCINTILLATOR	+
	2.0+2	1.0+4		Conf	61Vienna 1 95	Aug 61 Neiler.PPR73,TABLE FOR SOME ES,GRAPH	
	2.3+2	7.6+3		Data	EXFOR11935.026	Jun 76 . 42 PTS. SIGMA.	
(n,γ)	2.5+4		DKE	Expt Rept	TID−16059	62 Furr.ACT 0.80+−0.28B REL I127 0.78B	
(n,γ)	1.1−3	2.5−3	BUC	Expt Jour	NUK 4 165	Jun 62 Teutsch+ TOF,SIG(E) AND FIT2200M/SEC	+
	1.1−3	2.5−3		Data	EXFOR30018.	Dec 70 TOF AT 21ES AND FITTED VALUE 2200M/S	
(n,γ)	1.0+3		RPI	Expt Rept	AERE−R−4131 1	Sep 62 Block. ELAST.LIN.ACCELERATOR. NDG.	
(n,γ)	1.0+4	6.0+5	ORL	Expt Abst	BAP 7 553	Nov 62 Harris+ SPHERE OK. ORNL SHAPE.	
(n,γ)	2.5−2		DGE	Eval Conf	62Harwell 2 11	Dec 62 Delattre+ RECOMM ACT−SIG+ACCURCY GVN	
(n,γ)	1.8+4	3.0+5	FOA	Expt Jour	AF 23 425	Mar 63 Bergqvist.TOF 8 ES.NAI.REL AG. GRAPH	+
	2.0+3	3.0+5		Theo Jour	NP 39 353	Dec 62 − +. GRAPH. STATISTICAL MODEL	
	1.8+4	3.0+5		Expt	EXFOR20024.005	Sep 71 8PTS.SIG.	
(n,γ)	3.2+4	4.0+6	LRL	Expt Jour	PR 128 2717	Dec 62 Miskel+ TABLE OF SIG AT 26 ES. ACT.	+
				Rept	UCRL−5454	Jan 59 .SUPERSEDED	
	3.2+4	4.0+6		Data	EXFOR12115.	Jun 76 . 26 PTS.	
(n,γ)	2.5−2		MTR	Expt Prog	IDO−16827 18	Jan 63 Berreth+ THER CS GIVEN	
(n,γ)	1.0+3	1.0+5	UK	Expt Rept	NRDC−138 17	Jan 63 CURVE	
(n,γ)	3.0+4		ORL	Expt Jour	NP 43 353	May 63 Macklin+.SIG=513MB+−20PC	+
	3.0+4			Data	EXFOR11380.013	Jun 76 . 1 PT.	
(n,γ)		2.0+5	DKE	Theo Abst	DA/B 23 4719	Jun 63 Furr.CS PREDICTED FROM RES PARS.NDG	
(n,γ)	1.8+4	4.0+6	CJD	Comp Rept	INDSWG−64 43	64 . GRAPH VARIOUS EXPERIMENTS	
(n,γ)	1.8−1	2.0+4	LEB	Expt Jour	ZET 46 80	Jan 64 Konks.PB−SLOW−DOWN,GRAPH SIG(E)	+
				Jour	JET 19 59	Jul 64 TRANSLATN.*	
(n,γ)	2.5−2	2.5−2	CRC	Expt Rept	CRRP−1183	Feb 64 Bigham.	+
(n,γ)	Maxwl		KFK	Expt Jour	NSE 19 244	Jun 64 Brose. SIG(EFF)=99.3B. TBP NUK	
(n,γ)	Pile		CCP	Expt Jour	AE 17 113	Aug 64 Bondarenko+VAL GVN REL TO U−235(N,F)	+
				Jour	SJA 17 821	Aug 64 TRANSLATN.*	
(n,γ)	1.2+5	7.6+6	ALD	Expt Jour	JNE 18 491	Sep 64 Barry.+ −5PC REL NP SCAT.CFD OTHERS	+
(n,γ)	Pile		CCP	Expt Jour	AE 17 294	Oct 64 Batyrbekov+VAL GVN REL TO PU239(N,F)	+
				Jour	SJA 17 1025	Oct 64 TRANSLATN.*	
(n,γ)	1.0−2	3.0+4	GA	Expt Jour	NIM 31 125	Dec 64 Haddad+ BIG LIQUID SC.OKS(NG),NOT−ACT	+
	1.0−2	1.0+5		Jour	NIM 28 205	Jun 64 Firk.PRELIM DATA IN LINAC EXPT REVW	
	2.0−2	2.0+4		Rept	GA−3874	Mar 63 Haddad.LINAC.TOF.LIQ SC−T.CRVE ONLY	
	1.0−2	8.0+0		Data	EXFOR12196.	Jun 76 . 173 PTS. SIGMA.	
(n,γ)	1.4+5	1.2+6	LOK	Expt Prog	EANDC(US)−79	65 Grench+ PG.72.	+
	1.4+5	1.2+6		Data	EXFOR12192.002	Jun 76 . 12 PTS. SIGMA.	
(n,γ)	5.0+3	9.0+4	ORL	Theo Jour	RMP 37 166	Jan 65 Macklin+.CALC FOR KT=5TO90KEV	
(n,γ)	Fiss		IIT	Comp Conf	65IAEA 251	Mar 65 Barrall+CALC AVG SIGS OF 3FISS−SPECS	
(n,γ)	Pile		CCP	Expt Jour	AE 18 469	May 65 Golubev+VAL GVN REL TO PU−239(N,F)	
				Jour	SJA 18 608	May 65 TRANSLATN.*	
(n,γ)	1.3+4	6.8+5	LOK	Expt Jour	NP 69 37	Jul 65 Harris.ACT.TBL,GRPH.=WASH−1056,38	+
	1.3+4	6.8+5		Data	EXFOR12197.002	Jun 76 . 15 PTS.	
(n,γ)	Maxwl	+2	FEI	Expt Jour	AE 19 292	Sep 65 Stavisskij+ REL TO PU−239(N,F)	
				Jour	SJA 19 1210	Sep 65 . ENGL OF AE 19 292	
(n,γ)	1.0−2	1.0+2	MOL	Eval Rept	BLG−421	66 Damle+. CURVE RECOMMENDED SIGS	
(n,γ)	1.0+4	6.0+6	ALD	Comp Conf	66Berkeley 384	Sep 66 BATCHELOR EXPTS DISAGREE TO 200KEV	
(n,γ)	3.0+4	6.4+4	KFK	Expt Jour	JNE 20 825	Oct 66 Poenitz.2 ENS.TWO METHODS.ABS VALUES	+
	3.0+4			Conf	66Paris 1 277	Oct 66 − . PPRG ABS XPT FOR NORMALIZTN	
				Rept	KFK−454	Oct 66 − . REPRINT OF 66PARIS	
				Rept	KFK−505	Oct 66 − . EQU TO JNE 20 825	
				Rept	EANDC−33U164	Sep 63 − . LI−7(P,N) THRES.REL TO BE−7	
				Rept	EANDC−33U87	Sep 63 − + REPORT OF MN5O4 BATH EXPT	
(n,γ)	1.0−2	8.0+0	GA	Expt Jour	NSE 26 487	Dec 66 Friesenhahn+,TOF, 1 PC ACCURACY.	
				Rept	GA−6832	Jan 65 − .	
(n,γ)	4.9+0		TRM	Expt Conf	67Kanpur 409	Feb 67 Chandramoleswar. WG=41+−4 MICRO S	
				Prog	AEET−267 4	Aug 66 − + VALUE GIVEN,CFD BNL	
(n,γ)	Pile		FRK	Expt Conf	67Juelich 65	Apr 67 Hanle+ CHANNEL VS COMPD NUC,4.9EVRES	
(n,γ)	1.3+5	1.8+5	ORL	Expt Jour	PR 159 1007	Jul 67 Macklin+ TOF,TOTAL−E DET, 3ES,ABSL	+
	1.3+5	1.8+5		Data	EXFOR11679.023	Jun 76 . 3 PTS. SIGMA.	
(n,γ)	3.0+4		KFK	Eval Jour	JNE 21 643	Aug 67 Knoll+ WEIGHTED AV OF POST 1960 DATA	
				Rept	EANDC(E)74S	Nov 66 − + SAME AS JNE 21 643	
				Conf	66Paris 1 277	Oct 66 Poenitz. BEST VAL FROM POST 60 DATA	

79 Gold 197

Quantity	Energy (ev) Min	Max	Lab	Type	Documentation Ref Vol Page	Author, Comments Date	Data
(n,γ)	3.0+6		DEB	Expt Jour	JNE 21 797	Oct 67 Peto+ACTIV,SIGMA REL TO P−31(N,P)	+
	3.0+6			Data	EXFOR30031.029	Aug 70 SINGLE VALUE	
(n,γ)	Pile		FEI	Expt Jour	AE 23 396	Nov 67 Lejpunskij.RATIO REL U235(N,F),PILE	
				Jour	SJA 23 1150	Nov 67 .ENGLISH TRANSL OF AE 23 396 11/67	
				Jour	EAF 23 5 21	Nov 67 . FRENCH TRANSL OF AE 23 396 11/67	
(n,γ)	1.0+6	1.0+6	MOL	Expt Jour	NUK 10 280	Nov 67 Fabry.CFD FISS SPEC CALC.TBL.−A9M T	+
	Fiss			Data	EXFOR20229.006	May 74 1 PNT. SIGMA.	
(n,γ)	None		ANL	Expt Abst	BAP 12 1187	Dec 67 Mooring+. AVERAGE OVER 8KEV	
(n,γ)	Maxwl		KFK	Expt Conf	IAEA−107 150	68 Poenitz.PREL VAL GVN,SURVEY OF EXPTS	
				Conf	67Brussels	May 67 − . PPR10. SAME AS IAEA−107	
(n,γ)	Maxwl	Pile	MOL	Eval Rept	BLG−421	68 Damle+ TBP THRSIG RESINTG GIVEN	
(n,γ)	Maxwl	Pile	MOL	Eval Rept	BLG−421	68 Damle+ TBP THRSIG RESINTG GIVEN	
(n,γ)	Fiss		BNW	Theo Rept	BNWL−SA−1794	Apr 68 Mcelroy. SAND 2 CALCULATN.	
(n,γ)	2.5−2		GA	Expt Jour	JNE 22 191	Apr 68 Friesenhahn+ .292.	+
	2.5−2			Data	EXFOR12163.	Jun 76 . 1 PT.	
(n,γ)	+3	+6	WWA	Theo Conf	JINR−D3893 131	May 68 Brzosko+ ABSTRACT,SIG CALCULATED,NDG	
(n,γ)	1.0+3	1.0+5	HAR	Expt Rept	NP−17644	Jul 68 Moxon.THESIS.MOXON−RAE DET.AVG SIG	
				Jour	NIM 24 445	Oct 63 − +RAE TOF.SCINT DET DESCRIBED	
	1.0+2	5.0+4		Rept	AERE−NP/GEN 30	Feb 63 − . DETECTOR DESCRIBED.	
(n,γ)	−		IEA	Comp Rept	IEA−INF−10 6	Aug 68 Atalla. TABLES OF HL,SIG AND GAMM−E	
(n,γ)	2.5+4	5.0+5	KFK	Expt Jour	JNE 22 505	Aug 68 Poenitz+DATA TBL.CURVE.NORM AT 30KEV	
				Conf	67Karlsrhe 1 67	Nov 67 Beckurts+,ABSOLUTE AT 30KEV,GRAPH	
				Rept	KFK−635	Oct 67 Poenitz+GREY DET. GRPH.NORM AT 30KEV	
(n,γ)	2.4+4		MU	ATheo Jour	IJP 42 567	Sep 68 Chaubey+ METHD OF BOOTH,VAL CFD XPT	+
				Expt Jour	NP 66 267	May 65 − +,SB−BE,ACT BETA−DET REL I127	
	2.4+4			Data	EXFOR30063.011	Dec 70 SIGMA FOR 2.7 D HALF−LIFE	
(n,γ)	Pile		CCP	Expt Jour	AE 25 292	Oct 68 Golubev+EXPTL+CALC MEAN SIG VAL GVN	
				Jour	EAF 25 4 37	Oct 68 TRANSLATN.*	
(n,γ)	1.5+4	5.6+4	PEL	Expt Jour	NP/A 121 655	Dec 68 Spitz+ TOF,SIG PEL TO IN,GRAPHS	+
	1.5+4	5.6+4		Data	EXFOR30114.007	Mar 71 T−O−F, 18 DATA LINES,PRIV COMM	
(n,γ)	1.0+6	1.0+7	WWA	Theo Rept	INR−967	Dec 68 Brzosko+ WG−MEAN LVL DIST,PIGMY RES	
(n,γ)	5.8+5		LOK	Expt Prog	WASH−1127 116	Apr 69 Grench+ NEUT E BEING RECALBRTD NDG	
(n,γ)	9.7+5		NPL	Expt Jour	JNE 23 205	Apr 69 Robertson+ ABSOL.EXPT.SIG=96.2+−2.MB	+
(n,γ)	1.4+7		STF	Expt Prog	WASH−1127 117	Apr 69 Depangher+ ACT, TBC, NDG	
(n,γ)	1.0+0	4.0+3	SAC	Expt Jour	NP/A 131 450	Jun 69 De Barros+ RESONANCE ANALYSIS.	+
	1.0+1	1.0+3		Jour	NP 76 391	Feb 66 Julien+ ANALYSED TO GIVE RES PARS	
	1.0+0	4.0+3		Data	EXFOR20686.	Aug 77 0PTS. SEE RESONANCE PARAMETERS	
(n,γ)	1.0+4	1.5+5	KFK	Expt Jour	NP/A 133 513	Aug 69 Kompe.VDG.REL B10,LI6(N,A)	+
				Jour	JNE 22 505	Aug 68 Ponitz+ TABL,CURV,NORMAL AT 30 KEV	
				Rept	EANDC(E)89U3	Feb 68 Kompe. RENORMAL OF 66PARIS	
				Conf	67Karlsrhe 1 67	Nov 67 Beckurts+ RENORM SHAPE. FIG 3	
				Rept	KFK−635	Oct 67 Poenitz+TOF.LARGE L SCN.SHAPE ONLY.	
				Conf	66Paris 1 513	Oct 66 Kompe.SHAPE MEAS NORM AT 30KEV(P277)	
	1.0+4	1.6+5		Data	EXFOR20358.035	Sep 74 72PTS.SIGMA.	
(n,γ)	Pile		MUN	Revw Conf	69Studsvik 127	Aug 69 Egidy.PART'L SIGS OF CONV LINES,GRPH	
(n,γ)	Fiss		MTR	Expt Prog	WASH−1136 55	Sep 69 Schuman+ ACTIVATION, VALUE GIVEN.	
(n,γ)	2.0+5		MUA	Theo Conf	69Roorke 2 129	Dec 69 Chaubey+ SIG VALUE GIVEN, STATIST−TH	
(n,γ)	5.0+1	6.0+3	WWA	Theo Jour	CJP 47 2849	Dec 69 Brzosko+,COMPOUND NUCL CALC CFD EXPT	
(n,γ)	Pile		ANL	Expt Prog	ANL−7629	May 70 Dudey+.EBR−2 SPECTRUM−AVGD SIGS MEAS	
(n,γ)	1.0−4	2.0+7	BNW	Eval Rept	BNWL−1312	May 70 Simons+ TABLE, CURVE.	
(n,γ)	1.3+1	6.9+2	LOK	Eval Prog	NCSAC−31 118	May 70 Grench+,RE−EVAL OF EARLIER DATA	
(n,γ)	1.0+4	2.0+5	FEI	Revw Conf	70Helsinki 2 245	Jun 70 Abramov.114. DATA STATUS, SIG(E) CRV	
(n,γ)	1.0+3	1.0+6	GA	Theo Conf	70Helsinki 2 281	Jun 70 Fricke+44. SIG(E) GRAPH,STAT+OPTMOD	
	1.0+3	7.0+5		Jour	PL/B 29 393	Jun 69 − +G STRENTH FN AS FN EXCIT E	
(n,γ)		1.5+6	GEL	Revw Conf	70Helsinki 1 127	Jun 70 Deruytter.106. DISCUSSED AS STANDARD	
(n,γ)	1.0+4	1.0+6	JAE	Revw Conf	70Helsinki 2 805	Jun 70 Nishimura+28. USED AS STANDARD,GRAPH	
(n,γ)	2.4+4		KFK	Theo Rept	KFK−1228	Jun 70 Froehner.CALC FROM SHELL TRANS DATA	
				Conf	70Helsinki 1 209	Jun 70 − + SEE FIGURE A.	
(n,γ)	−		CCP	Revw Jour	AE 29 187	Sep 70 Sukhoruchkin. (D,P GAM) CFD (N,GAM)	
				Jour	SJA 29 896	Sep 70 TRANSLATN.*	
(n,γ)	2.0+4	1.0+6	ANL	Revw Conf	70ANL 320	Oct 70 Poenitz. REVIEW ABSOL MEASTS,CURVE	
				Conf	70Helsinki 2 3	Jun 70 − .111. REL+ABSOL SIG(E) GRAPHS	
(n,γ)	1.0+3	1.0+6	GA	Revw Conf	70ANL 285	Oct 70 Carlson. STATUS AS STANDARD SIG,CURV	
(n,γ)	3.0+4		AUA	Theo Rept	AAEC/E−211	Nov 70 Musgrove. SIGMA GIVEN AND CFD OTHER	
(n,γ)	2.5+4		MTR	Expt Prog	NCSAC−33 100	Dec 70 Tromp. ACTIVATION,NDG,GRAPH	
	2.0+3	2.5+4		Prog	WASH−1127 72	Apr 69 Schuman+ FILTERED BEAM,RELATVE CURVS	

79 Gold 197

Quantity	Energy (ev) Min	Max	Lab	Type	Documentation Ref Vol Page	Date	Author, Comments	Data
(n,γ)	3.0+4	1.5+6	WWA	Expt	Jour APPB 2 489	71	Brzosko+ PARTIAL,TOTAL SIG CFD THEO	+
					Rept INR-1318 28	Apr 71	*SHORT REPORT,DATA GIV	
					Jour CJP 47 2849	Dec 69	*TH.CALCULATIONS OF SIG	
	4.0+5				Data EXFOR30159.	Apr 72	PARTIAL,TOTAL SIGMAS GIVEN	
	3.2+2	1.3+6			Data EXFOR30159.024	Apr 72	PARTIAL SIGMA FOR 9 NEUTRON ENERGIES	
(n,γ)	2.0+5	8.1+5	MUA	Theo	Jour IJP 45 88	Feb 71	Gupta+ STATISTICAL THEORY, CFD EXPT	
(n,γ)	1.0+3	1.0+6	GA	Expt	Conf 71Knoxvill 252	Mar 71	Fricke+,ABSOL AVG SIG,CURVE	+
				ExTh	Conf 70Helsinki 2 265	Jun 70	- + TOF	
	9.6+2	1.1+6		Expt	Data EXFOR10049.007	Jul 71	. 95 PTS. SIGMA.	
(n,γ)	1.0+4	5.4+6	LOK	Eval	Conf 71Knoxvill 430	Mar 71	Vaughn+.LEAST-SQUARES FIT,TBL+CURVE	
(n,γ)	Pile		MTR	Expt	Conf 71Knoxvill 79	Mar 71	Scoville.RATIO TO U238 NG,U235 NF	+
(n,γ)	Fast		KUR	Expt	Jour AE 30 369	Apr 71	Ivanova+ AU-198 BETAS,SCINT.SIG GIVN	
					Jour SJA 30 452	Nov 71	. ENGL OF AE 30 369	
(n,γ)	Pile		ORL	Expt	Abst ANS 14 381	Jun 71	Jenkins+. EFFECTIVE SIG=120MB	
(n,γ)	2.0+3	2.4+4	WIS	Expt	Abst DA/B 32 336	Jul 71	Bohl. ACT. SC AND FE FILTD BEAMS	
(n,γ)	2.4+4	9.7+5	ATI	Expt	Prog EANDC(OR)105L	Aug 71	Bensch+,PHOTO-NEUTRON SOURCES	
(n,γ)	1.0-1	4.0+4	FEI	Expt	Jour AE 31 107	Aug 71	Stavisskij+ RELB10(N,A)+REL THR.GRPH	
	+3	5.0+4			Prog YFI-11 9	70	Stavissky+ ABST,SLOWING DOWN,NDG	
					Prog INDC(CCP)-31	Dec 72	.PAGE 7,ENGLISH OF YFI-11 9	
	1.0-1	4.0+4			Jour SJA 31 814	Mar 72	. ENGL OF AE 31 107	
(n,γ)	1.0+3	1.0+6	HED	Theo	Rept HEDL-TME-71106	Aug 71	Schmittroth. H-F CALCULATION	
(n,γ)	Fiss		AMS	Expt	Jour JNE 25 457	Sep 71	Pauw+ CF252 SPEC,SIG=95.5+-2.3MB	
	2.2+4				Prog EANDC(E)127U	Apr 70	.SB-BE SOURCE	
	1.4+7		LAS	Expt	Jour PL/B 36 557	Oct 71	Drake+ SPECTRUM SUMMED CFD PB208 NG	+
	1.4+7				Data EXFOR10193.005	Jun 72	. 1 PT. SIGMA.	
(n,γ)	2.4+4		NPL	Expt	Jour JNE 25 557	Nov 71	Ryves+.SB-BE NEUTS SPECTRUM AVERAGE	+
					Jour JNE 20 249	Apr 66	- + SUPERSEDED.	
(n,γ)	2.3+4		NPL	Expt	Jour JNE 25 557	Nov 71	RYVES RE-EVAL OF RECENT EXPT	
(n,γ)	Maxwl	1.0+5	IAE	Revw	Rept INDC(NDS)-47	72	Vlasov+ REVIEW DATA STATUS ,TBL+GRPH	
(n,γ)	1.0+3	1.0+6	FEI	Theo	Rept FEI-293	Jan 72	Dovbenko+ STAT-TH,CALC CFD EXPT,GRPH	
(n,γ)	+3	+5	AUA	Expt	Prog AAEC/PR-36P 11	Mar 72	Allen+ ORELA.DATA TO BE ANALYZED,NDG	
(n,γ)	2.4+4		LRC	Theo	Jour JNE 27 185	Mar 72	Semler.CAL AV SIG,SEP/MERGED SPINS.	
					Rept N-69-24826	May 69	- . ANAL OF SPH TRANS EXPTS	
(n,γ)	2.4+4		MUA	Theo	Jour IJP 46 114	Mar 72	Chaubey+ P-WAVE STRENGTH FUNCT,TABLE	
(n,γ)	1.0+3	1.0+7	BOL	Eval	Data BENZI-DFN 834.	May 72	40 PNTS	+
(n,γ)	1.5+7		KOS	Expt	Rept IAEA-R-596	May 72	Csikai. FOR SYSTEMATICS,IN PROGR,NDG	
(n,γ)	1.0+6		MOL	Eval	Rept BLG-465	May 72	Fabry. SIGMA GIVEN	
	1.0+6	1.0+6			Conf 70Helsinki 2 535	Jun 70	- .RECOMMENDED DATA,TABLES,CRVS.	
(n,γ)	1.5+7		IRK	Expt	Prog EANDC(OR)117L	Aug 72	Rohatsch+ TBL ABST	
	1.4+7	1.5+7			Jour OAWA 107 136	Apr 70	Leithner+	
(n,γ)	2.4+4		RPI	Expt	Conf 72Kiamesha 2 1107	Sep 72	Block+.FE-FILTERED BEAM.RELATV MEAST	+
	2.4+4				Data EXFOR10594.	Aug 76	. 1 PT CS=.67B. IN,TA181,U238 REL.	
(n,γ)	2.0+2	3.5+4	FEI	Expt	Prog YFI-13 6	Oct 72	Chelnokov+ ABSTRACT,TBL SIGMA VS N-E	+
					Prog INDC(CCP)-32	Apr 73	.PAGE 8.ENGLISH OF YFI-13 6	
	2.0+2	3.5+4			Data EXFOR40105.006	Jun 72	SIGMA AT 26 ES, ABSOL + REL U235NF	
(n,γ)	Fast		DUB	Expt	Rept JINR-P12-6810	Nov 72	Ngo Quoc Buu+ ACT ANALYS, CD-RATIOS	
(n,γ)	+6		KOS	Expt	Jour AHP 33 363	73	Peto+ AVERAGE SIG FOR ALF-BE N,TABLE	+
	+6				Data EXFOR30265.019	Feb 74	SIG FOR PU-BE AND PO-BE NEUTRONS	
(n,γ)	3.0+4	1.5+6	AE	Expt	Jour JNE 27 71	Feb 73	Hellstrom.TOF,LIQ SCINT.	
(n,γ)	Fiss		RCN	Revw	Conf 73Paris 2 271	Mar 73	Zijp.RECOMM INTEG CFD DIFF CALC,TBLS	
	2.5-2				Conf 73Paris 2 271	Mar 73	- .RECOMMENDED FROM LITERATURE,TB	
	1.0+0	5.0+2			Rept STI/DOC/10-107	May 70	- .PAGE95. SIG(E)-GRPH,TECHNQ-REV	
(n,γ)	+3	+7	TUD	Theo	Prog ZFK-262 133	Sep 73	Hoehn+ CALC SIG CFD EXP,GRPH AT 1MEV	
(n,γ)	4.0-5	3.6-3	MUN	expt	Jour ZP 264 427	Oct 73	Dilg+,2200-XSEC=98.68+-0.12 B	
(n,γ)	2.5+4		AUW	Expt	Jour NC/A 18 48	Nov 73	Sidappa+ ACTIV SIG,CFD.TABLE	
(n,γ)	1.7+2	6.0+5	LRL	Expt	Jour NSE 52 299	Nov 73	Czirr+. ABSOL+RELATIVE MEASTS	+
	6.9+3	2.5+5			Data EXFOR10305.003	Nov 75	. 15 PTS. SIGMA.	
(n,γ)	7.0+5	2.6+6	CRC	Expt	Jour CJP 52 989	Jun 74	Earle+ STRENGTH FUNCTS	
					Conf 74Petten 119	Sep 74	Bartholomew+ PHOTON STRF GRPH	
(n,γ)	2.5+4		TRM	Expt	Conf 74Bombay 2 106	Dec 74	Anand+ ANOMALY IN SPECIF ACTIV,GRAPH	
(n,γ)	5.0+3	8.0+4	FEI	Expt	Rept YK-19 57	75	Shorin+ SIG(NEUT-E),TBL,GRAPH	+
	5.0+3	8.4+4			Rept YFI-17 9	Aug 74	- + SIG+ERRORS GVN IN TBL,32 PTS	
					Jour YF 19 5	Jan 74	- + TOF,SIG(NEUT-E),GRAPHS	
	5.0+3	7.0+4			Conf 73Kiev 2 206	May 73	Kononov+ TOF,SIG(NEUT-E),GRAPH	
	5.0+3	8.4+4			Rept INDC(CCP)-48	Feb 75	. P.5.ENGLISH OF YFI-17 9	
	5.0+3	8.4+4			Data EXFOR40222.002	Mar 74	.SIGMA FOR 32 EN-RANGES GVN	
(n,γ)	1.5+7		KOS	Expt	Jour ASL 25 185	75	Peto+ ACTIV,GE-LI.SIG TO ISOMER GIVN	+
	1.5+7				Data EXFOR30310.004	Oct 75	1 PNT.	

79 Gold 197

Quantity	Energy (ev) Min	Max	Lab	Type	Documentation Ref Vol Page	Author, Comments Date	Data
(n,γ)	+2	+3	COL Expt	Abst	BAP 20 139	Feb 75 Arbo+ 75WASH NDG.	
(n,γ)	1.0+4	5.0+5	CAD Expt	Conf	75Wash. 957	Mar 75 Fort+ TBL.ACTIVATION.CFD OTHER EXPT.	+
	1.0+4	5.0+5		Data	EXFOR20573.002	Feb 76 10PTS.SIGMA.	
(n,γ)	Fiss		HED Expt	Conf	75Wash. 189	Mar 75 Mcelroy.235U THERM FISS SPECT AVG CS	
(n,γ)	2.4+4		KTO Expt	Conf	75Wash. 802	Mar 75 Yamamuro+ N.FLUX=B10(N,AG).CS=0.68B	+
	2.4+4			Data	EXFOR20432.006	Jul 75 1PNT.SIGMA.	
(n,γ)	1.0+3	6.0+5	LRL Theo	Conf	75Wash. 651	Mar 75 Gardner.CFD ORNL + LLL EXPT.GRPH.	
	1.0+3	4.0+6		Prog	USNDC-3 103	Oct 72 - +. OPTMOD CALCULATN. CURVE	
(n,γ)	Fiss		MOL Expt	Conf	75Wash. 254	Mar 75 Fabry+INTEG CS REL U238NF=.287+-.014	
(n,γ)	1.0+3	1.0+6	NBS Revw	Conf	75Wash. 293	Mar 75 Carlson. GRPHS EXP CFD ENDF-4 EVAL.	
(n,γ)	3.0+3	5.5+5	ORL Expt	Jour	PR/C 11 1270	Apr 75 Macklin+GRPHS.TBLS.RES PARS.	+
	2.8+3	5.5+5		Data	EXFOR10432.	Oct 74 . 850 PTS. SIGMA.	
(n,γ)	3.5+5	9.0+5	CCP Expt	Conf	75Kiev	May 75 Bajkalov+ SIG,COINC METH	
(n,γ)	5.9+5	6.0+5	FEI Expt	Conf	75Kiev 4 9	May 75 Davletshin+ ACT,GE-LI, TBL	+
	5.9+5	6.0+5		Data	EXFOR40402.002	Oct 76 SIGMA AT 2 ES	
(n,γ)	1.0+3	5.0+6	FEI Expt	Conf	75Kiev 4 99	May 75 Davletshin+ ACTIV,GELI.SIGMA GIVEN	
(n,γ)	2.5-2		IJI Expt	Conf	75Kiev 3 171	May 75 Pavlenko+ TOF+M-R DET.SIGMA GIVEN	
(n,γ)	5.8+1	4.7+4	SAC Expt	Diss	CEA-N-1806	May 75 Alix.MAIER-LEIBNITZ DETECT,TOF,GRPH	+
	5.8+1	4.7+4		Data	EXFOR20580.	May 76 0PTS. SEE RESONANCE PARAMETERS.	
(n,γ)	2.4+4		BNL Expt	Conf	AERE-R-8082	Jul 75 Rimawi+ABSTR,IRON FILTER TECHN,NDG	+
				Conf	75Wash. 920	Mar 75 - + CS=630+-17MB.CFD OTHER EXPT	
	2.4+4			Data	EXFOR10434.002	Oct 74 . 1 PT. SIGMA.	
(n,γ)	2.0+5	3.0+6	GEL Expt	Jour	AKE 26 2 80	75 Paulsen+ ACTIVATION METHOD	+
	2.0+5	3.0+6		Data	EXFOR20419.002	Jul 75 19PTS.SIGMA.	
(n,γ)	4.0+5	3.5+6	ANL Expt	Jour	NSE 57 300	Aug 75 Poenitz.ABS MEAS	+
				Conf	AERE-R-8082	Jul 75 - . ABSTR ABS SIG,7010 ACC,NDG	
	4.0+5	3.5+6		Data	EXFOR10421.004	Apr 75 . 18 PTS. SIGMA.	
(n,γ)	5.0+4	1.0+5	LAS Eval	Prog	LA-6164-PR 2	Dec 75 Stewart.NDG.DISCREPANCY IN NF CS.	
(n,γ)	None		MUN Theo	Diss	GRYNTAKIS	Mar 76 Gryntakis.,CALC.OF WESTCOTTS G-FUNCT	
				Jour	RCA 22 128	Mar 75 - +,EQUIVALENT TO THESIS	
(n,γ)	1.0+4	3.5+6	FEI Eval	Rept	INDC(CCP)-82	Apr 76 Vinogradov+ EVAL CURV GVN,CF ENDF/B4	
	1.0+3	1.0+5		Rept	YK-21 106	76 Tolstikov+ SIG(E,MDLPARAMS),TBL+GRPH	
	1.0+4	3.5+6		Conf	75Kiev 1 165	May 75 Vinogradov+ EVAL DESCRIBED,GRAPH.	
(n,γ)	1.2+5	2.7+6	LRL Expt	Jour	NSE 59 381	Apr 76 Linder+REL U235NF.TBL,GRPHS.CFD ENDF	+
	1.2+5	2.7+6		Data	EXFOR10221.	Aug 75 . 23 PTS. SIGMA.	
(n,γ)	3.0+4	1.5+6	ANL Expt	Prog	WASH-1068 5	Mar 66 Cox.SIG RELATIV TO U235 NF,TABLE	+
	3.0+4	1.5+6		Data	EXFOR12213.002	Jun 76 . 21 PTS.	
(n,γ)	2.5-2		COL Expt	Abst	BAP 2 42	Feb 57 Gould+ SIG=98.8+-0.03B FROM SIG TOT	+
	2.5-2			Data	EXFOR11198.004	Jun 76 1 PT.	
(n,γ)	1.4+7		IRK Expt	Jour	NP/A 264 105	Jun 76 Schwerer+ GE-LI.ACT SIG=2.1+-1.2MB	+
	1.5+7			Data	EXFOR20670.018	Oct 76 1PNT.SIGMA.	
(n,γ)		1.0+3	KUK Eval	Conf	76Lowell 1280	Jul 76 Malik+VARIOUS CAPT DATA CFD AND ANAL	
(n,γ)	Fast		LON Expt	Prog	NEANDC(E)172 8	Aug 76 Hannan+ RATIO TO U235(N,F)	
(n,γ)	7.5+4	5.5+5	CAD Expt	Rept	CEA-R-4788	Nov 76 Le Rigoleur+ RENORMALISED.	+
				Rept	KFK-2046 53	May 75 - + E WEIGTING EXPT	
				Rept	CEA-N-1662	Aug 73 - +VDG,TABLES+GRAPHS	
				Conf	73Kiev 3 3	May 73 . TOT-E-WEIGHTING. CFD OTHERS,GRAPH	
	7.5+4	5.4+5		Data	EXFOR20558.	Feb 76 322PTS.SIGMA.	
(n,γ)	1.2+4	1.6+5	CAD Expt	Rept	CEA-R-4788	Nov 76 Le Rigoleur+ VDG.LI SCIN.RENORMALISD	+
	1.0+4	5.0+5		Conf	75Wash. 953	Mar 75 Fort+TBL,GRPHS CFD ENDF-4,OTHER EXPT	
	1.2+4	1.6+5		Prog	NEANDC(E)161U	Aug 74 Leroy+ LI-SCIN.	
	1.2+4	1.6+5		Data	EXFOR20573.	Feb 76 431PTS.SIGMA.	
Spect (n,γ)	None		PAR Expt	Jour	CR 207 856	Nov 38 Pontecorvo.ABOUT SMOOTH GAMMA RAY	
Spect (n,γ)	Maxwl		ANL Expt	Jour	PR 75 531	Aug 49 Kubitscheck+ MAX E.G-M COINC+ABSORBR	
Spect (n,γ)	Maxwl		ANL Expt	Jour	PR 80 415	Nov 50 Hamermesh. FOTOPLATE, GS ABOVE 3MEV.	
Spect (n,γ)	Maxwl		CRC Expt	Jour	CJP 31 1025	Nov 53 Bartholomew+ PAIR SP,100KV LINEWIDTH	
Spect (n,γ)	2.5+6		ANL Expt	Abst	PR 98 224	Apr 55 Hibdon+ CASCADES AT .98 1.38 1.98MEV	
Spect (n,γ)	Maxwl		BNL Expt	Jour	PR 100 1302	Dec 55 Reier+,XTL SPEC 0.248MEV GAMMA SEEN	
Spect (n,γ)	Maxwl		MOS Expt	Jour	ZET 32 979	May 57 Estulin+ SCINT SPEC 50-500KEV GAMMAS	
				Jour	JET 5 801	Dec 57 TRANSLATN.*	
Spect (n,γ)	Maxwl		MOS Expt	Jour	NP 4 91	Aug 57 Estulin+. INTESITY OF 4 SOFT GAMMAS	
Spect (n,γ)	Maxwl		GEA Eval	Rept	DC-58-1-30	Jan 58 Deloume. BY APPROXIMATION.TABLE+CURV	
Spect (n,γ)	Maxwl		KUR Expt	Conf	58Geneva 15 138	Sep 58 Groshev+ PPR2029.CURV,COMPTON-SPEC	
Spect (n,γ)	2.5+4		ORL Expt	Conf	58Geneva 15 68	Sep 58 Macklin.PPR671,SIGMA+G-ENERGY GVN	
Spect (n,γ)	+0	+2	KAP Expt	Prog	WASH-1006	Oct 58 Yeater. R TOF CS PRELIM NDG	
Spect (n,γ)	4.9+0		YAL Expt	Abst	BAP 4 35	Jan 59 Springer+,NAI(TL),GAMMA MULTIPLICITY	
Spect (n,γ)	Maxwl		YAL Expt	Jour	PR 114 268	Apr 59 Draper.SC SPECTR,GAM E 0 TO 600 KEV	

79 Gold 197

Quantity	Energy (ev) Min	Max	Lab	Type	Documentation Ref Vol Page	Author, Comments Date	Data
Spect (n,γ)	Maxwl		ANL	Expt	Jour AP 13 284	May 61 Hamermesh+ CRYST SPEC 122GAMMA ES	
					Conf 60Vienna 135	Oct 60 Cote+.GRAPH,EXPT DESCRIBED	
					Jour RSI 28 238	Apr 57 Hamermest+ CPT NEW CS P50LINES. TBC.	
Spect (n,γ)	Maxwl	3.0+4	ORL	Expt	Conf 61Saclay 213	Jul 61 Firk+,TOF, GRPHS COUNTS/CHANNEL	
Spect (n,γ)	Maxwl		ARF	Expt	Prog ARF-1193-9	Apr 62 Greenwood+,CRYST SPEC,LOW-E GAMMAS	
Spect (n,γ)	Maxwl	3.0+5	FOA	ExTh	Jour NP 39 353	Dec 62 Bergqvist+.5 ES.GRAPH. CFD STAT THEO	
	7.5+6			Expt	Conf 65Antwerp 550	Jul 65 - + NAI. ABST.NDG.SHAPE ONLY.	
	1.0+5				Jour NP 22 513	Feb 61 - +CRYSTSPEC,SPEC CFD THERMAL	
	Maxwl	3.0+5		ExTh	Conf 61Saclay	61 - + SUPERSEDED	
Spect (n,γ)	4.9+0	6.1+1	ITE	Expt	Jour ZET 45 870	Oct 63 Ratynskil.G - SPEC FROM 2 N-RES COMPRD	
					Jour JET 18 598	Mar 64 TRANSLATN.*	
Spect (n,γ)	4.9+0		UJV	Expt	Rept UJV-1088	64 Skrivanek+ TOF.GAMS TIME SPEC.GRPH	
Spect (n,γ)	1.2+5		FOA	Theo	Jour NP 53 397	Apr 64 Starfelt. GIANT RES E1+M1 TO FIT TH.	
					Rept FOA4-A4355 411	Feb 64 Bergqvist+ M1 GIANT RES (=ANL-6797)	
Spect (n,γ)	+0		DUB	ExTh	Jour ZET 46 1578	May 64 RESONANCE CAPTURE SPECTRUM	
					Jour JET 19 1067	Nov 64 TRANSLATN.*	
Spect (n,γ)	4.9+0		JAE	Expt	Rept JAERI-1073	Mar 65 Kawarasaki. RES CAPT.LINAC.TOF.E,INT	+
					Rept INDSWG-90 6	Jul 65 - . TABLE E,INTS GIVEN.	
	4.9+0				Data EXFOR20277.021	Jun 74 4PTS.	
Spect (n,γ)	3.0+5	4.2+6	FOA	ExTh	Jour NP 67 321	May 65 Lundberg+ XPT CFD STAT THEORY	
					Rept FOA4-A4382	64 - + SUPERSEDED	
					Rept ANL-6797 220	63 - + SUPERSEDED	
Spect (n,γ)	Maxwl		KUR	Expt	Jour IZV 29 766	May 65 Groshev+.TBL + GRAPH. ENGL BAS29 769	
Spect (n,γ)	Fast		GOE	Expt	Jour ZP 191 1	Feb 66 Smend+SPECTRUM CFD TH.ISOMER7.5+-.2S	
Spect (n,γ)	Maxwl		IFL	Expt	Jour YF 3 193	Feb 66 Bondarenko.GAMMAS AND CONVERSION-ELS	
					Jour SNP 3 135	Aug 66 TRANSLATN.*	
Spect (n,γ)	Maxwl		MCM	Expt	Jour NP 84 113	Aug 66 Johnson+ 80GAMMAS REDUCED WIDTHS CAL	
Spect (n,γ)	Maxwl		MUN	Expt	Jour ZP 195 489	Aug 66 Egidy+.INTCONVERSN.130LINES1KEV-7MEV	
					Conf 67Juelich 56	Apr 67 Koehler+ SUPERSEDED.	
Spect (n,γ)	Maxwl		YAL	Expt	Jour NP/A 92 696	Feb 67 Wetzel+ GE(LI) DETECTOR 33 LINES	
					Abst DA/B 27 569	Aug 66 - .HI RSLN HARD GAM.SAME THR 5EV	
Spect (n,γ)	Pile		FRK	Expt	Conf 67Juelich 65	Apr 67 Hanle+ GE-LI, +3CRYST-NAI,INTERN TGT	
					Conf 65Antwerp § 44	Jul 65 Fiebiger+. +-BORON ABSORBER	
Spect (n,γ)	None		LRL	Expt	Prog WASH-1079 81	Oct 67 Auchampaugh+ LINAC, GE-LI, NDG	
Spect (n,γ)	Maxwl		KUR	Expt	Jour YF 7 937	May 68 Groshev+ GAM-E,INTS.DECAY SCHEME	
				ExTh	Jour NP 16 645	Jun 60 - + COMPTON SPEC,+THEOR DISCUSS	
				Expt	Jour SNP 7 563	Nov 68 . ENGL OF YF 7 937	
Spect (n,γ)	+3		AUA	Expt	Rept AAEC/TM-462	Jul 68 Allen. GAM-SPEC,FULL EXPT-DESCRIPTN	
Spect (n,γ)	Maxwl	4.0+2	BNL	Expt	Jour PR 173 1170	Sep 68 Wasson+ GE(LI) VARIATION OF G INTENS	
Spect (n,γ)	2.5-2		MIT	Comp	Rept MITNE-85	Jan 69 Rasmussen+TBL G INT.=AFCRL-69-0071	
Spect (n,γ)	1.0+0	1.0+3	HAR	Expt	Prog AERE-PR/NP15	May 69 Axmann+LINAC.NAI RES SPECS.ANAL TBC.	
					Prog EANDC(OR)86L	Jan 69 - +LINAC.NDG.TBC.	
Spect (n,γ)	4.9+3	1.1+5	SAC	Expt	Jour NP/A 130 353	Jun 69 Samour+LINAC,GE(LI).AT 5RES E .AREAS	
	5.8-2				Jour NP/A 130 353	Jun 69 - +LINAC,GE(LI).65LINES.INT,J,PI	
	4.9+3	1.1+5			Rept CEA-R-3776	Apr 69 - . (THESIS) DATA GIVEN	
	5.8-2				Rept CEA-R-3776	Apr 69 - . (THESIS) DATA GIVEN	
	Maxwl				Rept CEA-R-2810	Jun 65 Huynh.3TO7 MEV GAMMA SPECT.	
	4.9+0	6.0+2			Rept CEA-R-2810	Jun 65 - .DET=2 NAI(TL)COAXIAL CRYSTALS	
Spect (n,γ)	Pile		ANL	Expt	Conf 69Studsvik 601	Aug 69 Smither+ NO DATA GVN,TB CFD STATMOD	
Spect (n,γ)	Maxwl	+3	CRC	Revw	Conf 69Studsvik 553	Aug 69 Bartholomew. GRPH GVN.'5.5MEV BUMP'.	
Spect (n,γ)	Pile		SGA	Expt	Conf 69Studsvik 307	Aug 69 Gryksa+ THR+EPITHR CAPT CFD,TBP NP	
					Prog EANDC(OR)86L	Jan 69 - +,GE(LI) DET	
Spect (n,γ)	Maxwl		KFI	Expt	Jour YF 10 907	Nov 69 Kecskemeti+ AVG GAM-MULTIPLICITY,TBL	
					Jour SNP 10 524	May 70 TRANSLATN.*	
Spect (n,γ)	5.0+1	6.0+3	WWA	Theo	Jour CJP 47 2849	Dec 69 Brzosko+,COMPOUND NUCL CALC CFD EXPT	
Spect (n,γ)	Pile		CCP	Expt	Jour IZV 34 89	Jan 70 Burgov+ RES NS CAPTURE,LVL SCH,CURVS	
					Jour BAS 34 85	Jan 70 *	
Spect (n,γ)	Maxwl		NRL	Expt	Abst BAP 15 549	Apr 70 Stolovy.GAMMA CIRCULAR POLARIZATION	
Spect (n,γ)	2.0+3		MTR	Expt	Prog NCSAC-31 76	May 70 Greenwood+,ANAL TO BE COMPL,NO DATA	
Spect (n,γ)	Maxwl		WAL	Eval	Rept WANL-TME-2713	Jul 70 Fody.GAM YLDS FOR WANL POINT LIBRARY	
Spect (n,γ)	Maxwl		CCP	Revw	Jour AE 29 187	Sep 70 Sukhoruchkin. GAM-SPEC,DOORWAY-STATE	
					Jour SJA 29 896	Sep 70 TRANSLATN.*	
Spect (n,γ)	4.9+0		TOR	Expt	Jour NIM 86 25	Sep 70 ING+ LINEAC TIME OF FLIGHT.	
Spect (n,γ)	1.4+7		LAS	Expt	Conf 71Knoxvill 266	Mar 71 Bergqvist+,NO DATA,ABSTRACT ONLY	
Spect (n,γ)	Pile		MRY	Expt	Jour ZP 245 198	Apr 71 Elkady+, LI DRIFTED GE DET	
Spect (n,γ)	Pile		CAI	Expt	Jour ZP 245 198	Aug 71 Flkady+ NEW LEVELS BELOW 5 MEV	
Spect (n,γ)	4.0+5		WWA	Expt	Jour APPB 2 489	Aug 71 Brzosko+ GAMMA-EN = 3 TO 7 MEV,GRAPH	
	+5	+7			Prog INR-1197/I/PL	May 70 Brosko+ 3 TO 6.5MEV GAMMA E,SPECTRUM	

79 Gold 197

Quantity	Energy (ev) Min	Max	Lab	Type	Documentation Ref Vol Page	Author, Comments Date	Data
Spect (n,γ)	Maxwl	4.9+0	BNL Expt	Prog	NCSAC – 42 57	Nov 71 Kane. E+I FOR 2 NEUT ES TABULATED	
Spect (n,γ)	2.4+4		RPI Expt	Prog	COO – 3058 – 20 16	Jun 72 Block+. CURVE PULSE – HEIGHT SPECTRA	
Spect (n,γ)	1.0+7		WWA Theo	Jour	NP/A 189 545	Jul 72 Brzosko+ CMPD NUCL DECAY.PARTIAL WG	
Spect (n,γ)	7.0+5	2.6+6	CRC Expt	Conf	72Budapest 262	Aug 72 Lone+ G – RAY INTENSITIES ,NDG	
Spect (n,γ)	+0	+2	IFB Theo	Conf	73Pacif.Gr 2 1071	Mar 73 Rudak+ GRAPH STATMOD – CALC CFD G – SPEC	
Spect (n,γ)	Pile		ANL Expt	Jour	NIM 121 581	74 Loper+ ABSOLUTE INT.G.RAYS AU198	
Spect (n,γ)	1.0+0	6.0+2	SAC Expt	Jour	NP/A 223 509	May 74 Jain+GRAPHS,HIGH/LOW EG,WIDTH CORR	
	1.0+0	4.0+2		Jour	JPR 34 123	Feb 73 Lottin+TOF SPINS BY MULTIPOLARITY	
				ExTh Rept	CEA – N – 1600	Sep 71 Jain. SEARCH FOR MICRO RES.	
Spect (n,γ)	4.5+5		AUA Expt	Rept	INDC – 17 7	Oct 74 Kenny+ NA – I GAM – SPEC,GRAPH	
Spect (n,γ)	3.5+4	1.5+5	UPP Expt	Prog	INIS – MF – 1634	Jan 75 Earle+ VDG,NA – I.TO INVESTIG BUMP,NDG	
Spect (n,γ)	Maxwl		MUN Expt	Jour	ZP/A 272 175	Feb 75 Loebner+ G – RAY – SPEC,LVLSCH OF AU – 198	+
				Conf	73Munich 1 234	Aug 73 Mirza+ G – G – COINC,IMPROVD LVL SCH,NDG	
				Conf	69Studsvik 65	Aug 69 Koch+AUT CURVD CRYST SPEC.NDG.TBP	
	2.5 – 2			Data	EXFOR20608.002	Jun 76 451PTS.	
Spect (n,γ)	2.4+2		HAR Expt	Prog	AERE – PR/NP22	Mar 75 Gayther+LINAC.RES CAPT.LIQ SCIN SPEC	
Spect (n,γ)	None		LRL Theo	Prog	ERDA – NDC – 2 72	May 75 Gardner.MDL.CALC.GRPH.	
	Maxwl			Conf	75Wash. 651	Mar 75 - .CFD ORPHAN DATA.GRPH.	
Spect (n,γ)	3.0+4	2.5+6	LND Revw	Conf	76Lowell 99	Jul 76 Bergqvist.3 ES,.03,1.2,2.5MEV.GRPHS	
Inelastic γ	+5	1.3+6	NOT Expt	Jour	PR 68 1	Jul 45 Wiedenbeck. EXCITN FN 1.22MEV LEVEL.	
Inelastic γ	3.7+6		BAR Expt	Jour	PR 100 83	Oct 55 Rothman+,NO GAMMAS SIG=M.02B AT90DEG	+
	3.7+6			Data	EXFOR11478.006	Jun 76 . 1 PT. DSIGMA.	
Inelastic γ	2.5+6		NRL Expt	Priv	SCHERRER	Oct 55 Scherrer+	+
	2.5+6			Data	EXFOR11500.007	Jun 76 . 6 PTS. DSIGMA.	
Inelastic γ	2.7+5	1.6+6	MIT Expt	Jour	PR 101 1516	Mar 56 Guernsey+,CS 270 – KEV LEVEL CFD TH	+
	4.1+5	1.7+6		Data	EXFOR11691.009	Jun 76 . 11 PTS. SIGMA.	
Inelastic γ	3.0+6		FEI Expt	Jour	AE 9 403	Nov 60 Androsenko+ TABLE OF GAMMA – ENERGIES	
				Jour	SJA 9 945	Sep 61 . ENGL OF AE 9 403	
				Jour	KE 4 510	Jun 61 . GERMAN OF AE 9 403	
Inelastic γ	2.0+5	3.5+6	LAS Expt	Jour	AP 12 485	Mar 61 Lind. SIG(94DEG) FOR 5 GAMMAS.	+
	4.5+5	1.5+6		Data	EXFOR11188.014	Jun 76 . 48 PTS. DSIGMA.	
Inelastic γ	5.5+6	7.5+6	ALD Expt	Jour	NP 63 526	Mar 65 Perkin+ CFD CALC SPECTRA.	
Inelastic γ	3.0+5	1.5+6	ANL Expt	Jour	ZP 183 323	Mar 65 Devilliers+ VDG.TOF. GRPHS+TBLS.	
Inelastic γ	4.0+5	1.2+6	LAS Expt	Conf	65Antwerp § 29	Jul 65 DAY+GE – DET 5 – 7KEV RSLN.+GS FROM N,G	
Inelastic γ	5.8+6	7.5+6	FOA Expt	Jour	NP 80 198	May 66 Bergqvist+CFD SPEC IN CAPT.AT 0.1MEV	
				Conf	65Antwerp 505	Jul 65 - + PPR28.ABST.NDG.	
Inelastic γ	1.0+6		TNC Expt	Jour	ORO – 2791 – 79	Aug 67 Morgan+ NAI(TL)+GE – LI NDG TBC	
Inelastic γ	1.4+7	1.5+7	IRK ExTh	Jour	OAWS 176 227	68 Bornemisza+ CFD STATMOD	+
	1.5+7			Jour	AK 9 477	67 – +	
	1.5+7			Expt Data	EXFOR20082.005	Sep 71 1PNT.SIGMA.	
Inelastic γ	2.0+5	2.2+6	TUL Expt	Jour	PR/C 3 307	Jan 71 Nelson+,GE(LI),GAM SPEC+95DEG SIG	+
	2.2+5	2.2+6		Abst	DA/B 30 3332	Jan 70 - . PRODUCTION SIGS.	
	1.0+6	2.2+6		Data	EXFOR10153.002	Aug 74 . 149 PTS. DSIGMA, MANY GS.	
Inelastic γ	2.5+6	3.0+6	KFI Comp	Jour	JRC 7 365	Jun 71 Nagy+ SIGMA,GAM+XRAY+ELECTR ES GIVEN	
Inelastic γ	4.0+5	1.3+6	PEL Expt	Jour	NP/A 167 511	Jun 71 Barnard+ VDG.TOF.37EG 418 – 1242 KEV.	
Inelastic γ	4.0+6	6.5+6	LRL Theo	Conf	75Wash. 651	Mar 75 Gardner.GRAPH GAMMA PROD	
Nonelastic γ		2.4+6	OSA Expt	Jour	JMJ 19 369	37 Aoki.D+D NEUTRON.RELATIV SIG GIVN	
	Slow			Jour	JPJO 18 115	36 Kikuchi+.REL SIG GIVN FOR G – EMISSION	
				Jour	JMJ 17 369	35 - +.GAMMAS DETECT.REL SIG GIVN	
Nonelastic γ	4.0+5	7.0+5	PUC Theo	Conf	64Chandgrh 91	Feb 64 Singhal+.GRAPH CFD EXPT,DISCUSSION	
Nonelastic γ	5.0+6	8.7+6	VNV Expt	Rept	CEA – R – 4047	Apr 70 Bertin.AT THREE ENERGIES	
	5.0+6	1.4+7		Prog	EANDC(E)89U	Jan 68 Delobeau.TOF	
	2.5+6	1.4+7		Prog	EANDC(E)89U	Jan 68 Haouat+.ANGDIST.	
Nonelastic γ	1.4+7		LAS Expt	Prog	USNDC – 7 128	Jun 73 Drake+. NO DATA GIVEN. TO BE COMPLTD	
(n,2n)	1.5+7		CRC Expt	Jour	CJP 31 267	Feb 53 Paul+.BETA ACT.CFD TH. HL= 70M+5.5D	+
	1.5+7			Data	EXFOR11274.095	Jun 76 . 1 PT.	
(n,2n)	1.4+7		LAS Expt	Jour	PR 97 1205	Mar 55 Graves. BETWEEN 1.22 AND 1.83 B.	
(n,2n)	1.4+7		LRL Expt	Jour	PR 111 616	Jul 58 Ashby+,SC 2.60+ – 0.20B APP=NONELASTIC	+
				Conf	58Geneva 15 3	Sep 58 Benveniste.PPR2494,VAL GVN,TOF	
	1.4+7			Data	EXFOR11097.024	Jun 76 . 1 PT.	
(n,2n)	8.4+6	1.5+7	LRL Expt	Rept	UCRL – 6028	Jun 60 Tewes.ACT 16ES,TO GND AND XCIT LVL	+
	8.4+6	1.5+7		Data	EXFOR11504.017	Jun 76 . 16 PTS.	
(n,2n)	1.4+7		CCP Expt	Jour	IZV 24 818	Jul 60 Bak+. EFFECTIVE SIG=1800+ – 500MB	
(n,2n)	Fiss		CRC Eval	Rept	CRC – 1003	Dec 60 Roy+,ESTIMATED AVG SIG=5.1MB	
(n,2n)	1.2+7	2.0+7	LAS Expt	Jour	PR 121 1438	Mar 61 Prestwood+ EXC.FUN, CHEM.	+
				Rept	LA – 2493	Dec 60 Bayhurst+ EXCITATION CURVE.	
	1.2+7	2.0+7		Data	EXFOR11645.026	Jun 76 . 10 PTS.	
(n,2n)	1.2+7	1.6+7	ANL Theo	Jour	NP 60 70	Nov 64 Vonach+ISOMERIC SIG RATIOS CFD EXPT	

79 Gold 197

Quantity	Energy (ev) Min	Max	Lab	Type	Documentation Ref Vol Page	Author, Comments Date	Data
(n,2n)	1.4+7		HAM	Comp Jour	NP 65 257	Mar 65 Bormann. 4EXPT VALS.CFD SHELL EFFECT	
(n,2n)	1.5+7		MUA	Expt Jour	NP 69 158	Jul 65 Mangal+ 1.72B TO GRND,0.23B TO 9.6HR	+
	1.5+7			Data	EXFOR31254.	Mar 73 .SIG POPULATING MS-AND GND-STATE GVN	
(n,2n)	1.3+7	1.5+7	BNL	Theo Jour	NSE 23 238	Nov 65 Pearlstein.3ES.STAT MDL CALC.TBL CS.	
(n,2n)	Fiss		BNL	Theo Jour	NSE 23 238	Nov 65 Pearlstein.STATMDL CALC.SPEC AVG.TBL	
	1.4+7		ALD	Expt Priv	MATHER	Nov 66 Mather+	
(n,2n)	1.3+7	1.5+7	MUN	Expt Conf	68Wash. 2 885	Mar 68 Vonach+ ACTIV.EXCITATION FUNCTION.	+
	1.3+7	1.5+7		Data	EXFOR20815.025	Oct 78 11PTS.RELATIVE SIGMA.	
(n,2n)	1.5+7		MUN	Expt Conf	68Wash. 2 885	Mar 68 Vonach+ ACTIVATION. REL AL-27(N,A)	+
				Rept	EANDC(E)89U 37	Feb 68 - + ABST.TBL.	
	1.5+7			Data	EXFOR20815.024	Oct 78 1PNT.RATIO.	
(n,2n)	1.5+7		MUN	Expt Jour	NP/A 118 9	Sep 68 Dilg+ ACTIV.REL AL(N,A).TO G,METAST.	
	1.5+7			Data	EXFOR20802.	Dec 78 2PTS.SIGMA.	
(n,2n)	1.5+7		DEB	ExTh Jour	AHP 25 91	Oct 68 Peto+ RATIO (NN')/(N2N) FROM THEORY	+
(n,2n)	1.5+7		DEB	ExTh Jour	NP/A 122 234	Dec 68 Karolyi.ISOMERIC RATIO,HUIZ-VANDENB.	+
	1.5+7			Expt Data	EXFOR30101.015	Feb 71 ISOMERIC RATIO	
(n,2n)	1.5+7		STF	Expt Rept	AFWL-TR-68-134	Mar 69 Barrall.	+
	1.5+7			Data	EXFOR10022.022	Nov 72 . 1 PT. SIGMA.	
(n,2n)	Fiss		MTR	Expt Prog	WASH-1136 55	Sep 69 Schuman+,ACTIVATION,VALUE GIVEN	
(n,2n)	1.5+7		DEB	Comp Jour	REA 7 4 93	Dec 69 Csikai+ SIG+HL COMPILTN,N-ACTIV-ANAL	
(n,2n)	1.4+7	1.5+7	CCP	Comp Rept	ICD-6 215	70 Sluchevskaja.SIGS GND+ISOM,RATIO,TBL	
(n,2n)	0.0+0	1.5+7	LAS	Expt Jour	NSE 40 136	Apr 70 Menlove. DELAYED N YIELD.	+
(n,2n)	Pile		ANL	Expt Jour	ANL-7629	May 70 Dudey+.EBR-2 SPECTRUM-AVGD SIGS MEAS	
(n,2n)	8.0+6	1.4+7	AUA	Theo Rept	AAEC/TM-542	May 70 Bertram. CALC SIG(E) CFD EXPTS,GRPHS	
	8.0+6	2.0+7		Rept	AAEC/TM-522	Nov 69 - . CALC SIG(E)GRAPHS CFD EXPTS	
(n,2n)	1.4+7	1.5+7	JYV	Eval Rept	JU-RR-3/1970	Jun 70 Leppaemaeki+ TABLE OF EVAL AVG SIG	
(n,2n)	1.4+7	1.5+7	JYV	Eval Rept	JU-RR-3/1970	Jun 70 Leppaemaeki+ (N,3N) UPPER LIMIT,TBL	
(n,2n)	+7		KFI	Theo Rept	KFKI-71-8	Feb 71 Jeki. CALCULATED CFD EXPTL SIG VALUE	
(n,2n)	1.4+7	1.5+7	IRK	ExTh Jour	APA 33 285	Jul 71 Winiwarter+ ISOMERIC RATIO	
(n,2n)	Fiss		AMS	Expt Jour	JNE 25 457	Sep 71 Pauw+ CF252 SPEC,SIG=4.93+-.14MB	
(n,2n)	1.4+7		CCP	Expt Rept	YK-9 50	72 Maslov+ REL CU65(N,2N),NA-I,SIG GIVN	+
				Rept	INDC(CCP)-42	Aug 74 .P10.ENGLISH OF YK-9	
	1.4+7			Data	EXFOR40136.020	Feb 73 .1 DATA LINE	
(n,2n)	1.4+7		GIT	Expt Jour	NP/A 180 157	Jan 72 Hankla+ ACT,GE(LI),MIXED POWDER.G,M.	+
				Abst	DA/B 32 293	Nov 71 - . ACT METHOD, CFD THEORY.	
	1.4+7			Data	EXFOR10244.	Jun 74 . 2 PTS. TOTAL AND METASTABLE.	
(n,2n)	1.5+7		JUL	Expt Jour	NP/A 185 614	May 72 Qaim. ACT,GE(LI). CFD TH+OTHR. GRND.	+
	1.5+7			Data	EXFOR20536.031	Apr 76 1PNT.SIGMA.	
(n,2n)	1.4+7		HFA	Expt Jour	PR/C 6 315	Jul 72 Maor Zellermayer+ ISOM RATIO CFD TH	
	1.4+7			Data	EXFOR30182.	Jun 73 ISOMERIC RATIOS, 12-,5+ AND GND	
(n,2n)	1.4+7	1.5+7	LRL	Expt Jour	NP/A 190 635	Aug 72 Nethaway. D-T NS.TO METST.+-5PC ACCU	+
	1.4+7	1.5+7		Data	EXFOR10312.009	May 75 . 10 PTS. SIGMA.	
(n,2n)	1.2+7	1.4+7	ALD	Expt Rept	AWRE-O-72/72	Nov 72 Mather+ REL U-238.LARGE LIQ SCIN.	+
	1.2+7	1.4+7		Data	EXFOR20795.008	Oct 78 2PTS.SIGMA.	
(n,2n)	1.3+7	1.8+7	IBJ	Theo Rept	INR-1475/1/PL	73 Marcinkowski. SIG(GND)/SIG(META),FIG	
(n,2n)	1.5+7		DEB	Eval Jour	REA 11 1 153	Mar 73 Boedy. COMPILATION+RECOMM.VALUE,TBL	
				Rept	IAEA-153 173	73 - . RECOMM. VALUE ONLY	
(n,2n)	Fiss		KOS	Eval Jour	AK 16 351	74 Boedy. U238,MAXW-SPC.AVG CFD XPT,TBL	
(n,2n)	1.5+7		TAT	Theo Jour	JP/A 7 1457	Aug 74 Kondaiah. CALC ON STAT MODEL	
(n,2n)	1.0+7	2.0+7	GEL	Expt Jour	AKE 26 1 34	75 Paulsen+ EXCIT FN BY ACT METHOD	+
	1.0+7	2.0+7		Data	EXFOR20486.005	Mar 76 28PTS.SIGMA.	
(n,2n)	Fiss		KOS	Eval Conf	75Karlsrhe 29	Apr 75 Csikai. CF252,MAXW-SPC.AVG FOR 2TEMP	
(n,2n)	8.0+6	1.5+7	ANL	Eval Rept	ANL-75-34	Jun 75 Davey+CONSTANT T MDL,LVL DEN MDL FIT	
(n,2n)	8.7+6	2.8+7	LAS	Expt Jour	PR/C 12 451	Aug 75 Bayhurst+ TBL,GRPH	+
	8.7+6	2.8+7		Data	EXFOR10536.	Apr 76 . 17 PTS. SIGMA.	
(n,2n)	+7		CCP	Expt Rept	YK-23 4	76 Brodskaja+ ACTIV,AVG SIG,TBL	
(n,2n)	8.4+6	1.5+7	BRC	Expt Jour	NIM 135 511	Jun 76 Frehaut.GD LOADED SCIN.EXPT DETAILS.	+
				Conf	75Kiev 4 303	May 75 - + LIQSCIN.SIG(E),CFD.GRPH+TBL	
				Conf	75Wash. 855	Mar 75 - + TBL.GRPH.REL 238U(N,F)	
				Rept	CEA-R-4627	Nov 74 - + LARGE LIQ SCINT METH10 VAL	
	8.4+6	1.5+7		Data	EXFOR20416.019	Jul 75 14PTS.SIGMA.	
(n,2n)	Thrsh	1.5+7	BRC	Expt Conf	76Lowell 1350	Jul 76 Cindro+EXCIT FN CALC.CFD EXPT.NDG.	
(n,2n)	8.0+6	2.8+7	TUD	Theo Rept	TU-05-41-76	Jul 76 Meister+ PREEQU-STATMOD CFD XPT,GRPH	
(n,xn) x>2	Pile		CRC	Expt Jour	CJP 37 815	Jul 59 Eastwood+N3N.EFF CS=.3MICROB	
(n,xn) x>2	1.5+7		ARK	Expt Jour	PR 131 2649	Sep 63 Bramlitt+N3N.LESS THAN .1MB.REL AL.	+
				Rept	TID-16949	62 .THESIS	
	1.5+7			Data	EXFOR11590.077	Jun 76 . 1 PT.	
(n,xn) x>2	Fiss		BNL	Theo Jour	NSE 23 238	Nov 65 Pearlstein.SPEC AVG STATMDL CALC N3N	

79 Gold 197

Quantity	Energy (ev) Min	Max	Lab	Type	Documentation Ref Vol Page	Author, Comments Date	Data
(n,xn) x>2	1.4+7		GIT	Expt Jour	NP/A 180 157	Jan 72 Hankla+N3N.ACT,GE(LI).MIXED POWDER.	+
				Abst	DA/B 32 293	Nov 71 - . ACT METHOD, CFD THEORY.	
	1.4+7			Data	EXFOR10244.020	Jun 74 . 1 PT. SIGMA.	
(n,xn) x>2	1.6+7	2.8+7	LAS	Expt Jour	PR/C 12 451	Aug 75 Bayhurst+N3N,N4N.TBL,GRPH.CFD CALC.	+
	1.6+7	2.8+7		Data	EXFOR10536.	Apr 76 . 9 PTS N3N, 3 PTS N4N.	
n Emission	1.4+7		TUD	Theo Prog	ZFK - 262 25	Sep 73 Hermsdorf+ CALC N - SPEC CFD EXPT,NDG	
n Emission	1.5+7		TUD	Expt Jour	KE 19 241	Aug 76 Hermsdorf+ ABSOL DOUBDIF,FIG.TOT,TBL	+
				Rept	ZFK - 277(U)	Aug 75 - + DIFFSIG AT 5ANGS,TBL+GRPH	
	1.5+7			Data	EXFOR30397.029	May 77 31 PTS. ANGLE INT.N - EMISS.SPECT.	
	1.5+7			Data	EXFOR30275.	Apr 74 DOUBLDIF(5ANG,186PTS)+PARTIAL ANGDIS	
(n,p)	1.4+7		BRN	Expt Jour	PR 106 965	Jun 57 Peck.FOTOPL THETA = 10 - 45DEG 20.5MB	+
	1.4+7			Data	EXFOR12208.013	Jun 76 . 1 PT. SIGMA.	
	1.4+7			Data	EXFOR12208.	Jun 76 . 39 PTS. DSIGMA.	
(n,p)	1.4+7		CIS	Expt Jour	NC 7 400	Feb 58 Colli+ P - SPECT.	+
(n,p)	1.4+7		ALD	Expt Jour	PPS 73 215	Feb 59 Coleman+. ACT. CFD DIRECT INTERACTN	+
(n,p)	1.2+7	1.4+7	LRL	Expt Rept	UCRL - 6028	Jun 60 Tewes+ ACT,TBC,VALS GVN.ALSO 12.8MEV	
	1.2+7	1.4+7		Data	EXFOR11504.016	Jun 76 . 3 PTS.	
(n,p)	Fiss		CRC	Eval Rept	CRC - 1003	Dec 60 Roy+,ESTIMATED AVG SIG = 0.007MB	
(n,p)	7.0+6	2.0+7	LAS	Expt Jour	JIN 23 173	Dec 61 Bayhurst+.18ES.FROM BETA ACTIVITY	+
				Rept	LA - 2493	Dec 60 - + SEE ALSO FOR EXCITN CURVE.	
	1.2+7	2.0+7		Data	EXFOR11462.019	Jun 76 . 15 PTS.	
(n,p)	1.5+7		MUA	Expt Jour	NP 47 473	Sep 63 Hans+.CURVE P - SPECTRUM AT 0 DEGREE	+
	1.5+7			Data	EXFOR30055.005	Jun 71 PROTON SPECT AT 0 DEG.(=NP47,FIG4)	
(n,p)	1.4+7		RBZ	Expt Conf	64Paris 2 934	Jul 64 Paic.GRPHS A - DSTB OF P FOR 4 P - GRPS	
(n,p)	1.4+7		SAH	Comp Jour	NUC 23 8 112	Aug 65 Chatterjee. TABLE WITH REFS.	
					NP 60 273	Nov 64 - .MEAN OF EXPT CFD SHELLMOD	
(n,p)	1.4+7	1.5+7	NAP	Comp Rept	INFN/BE - 67 - 10	Jul 67 Cuzzocrea+ AVERAGED CHOSEN DATA.	
(n,p)	1.5+7		DEB	Comp Jour	REA 7 4 93	Dec 69 Csikai+ SIG+HL COMPILTN,N - ACTIV - ANAL	
(n,p)	1.4+7	1.5+7	JYV	Eval Rept	JU - RR - 3/1970	Jun 70 Leppaemaeki+ TABLE OF EVAL AVG SIG	
(n,p)	1.4+7		CIS	Theo Jour	PR/C 6 1398	Oct 72 Braga - Marcazzan+. PRE - EQUILIBR MODEL	
(n,p)	1.4+7		KUK	Theo Jour	IPA 11 61	Jan 73 Manocha+ P - SPEC,OPTMDL+SQU - POT,GRPHS	
(n,p)	1.4+7	1.5+7	KAZ	Theo Jour	YF 18 705	Oct 73 Levkovsky.AVERAGED SIG,CALC,TBL	
				Jour	SNP 18 361	Apr 74 . ENGLISH OF YF 18,705	
(n,p)	1.4+7		TUD	Theo Conf	ZFK - 271 63	Nov 73 Seeliger+ P - EMISSION SPEC, NDG	
(n,p)	+7		CCP	Expt Rept	YK - 23 4	76 Brodskaja+ ACTIV,AVG SIG,TBL	
(n,np)		7.5+8	IOW	Expt Jour	PR/C 12 1978	Dec 75 Hill+ ES TO 750 MEV.(N,2PN) REACTION	
(n,d)	1.4+7		RBZ	ExTh Jour	PR/B 139 331	Jul 65 Valkovic+ C - W.UPPLIM SIG(FORWRD DEUT	
(n,t)	Fiss		ETH	Expt Jour	NSA 17 1243	Mar 63 Tanner. NDG 1962 51P.	
(n,t)	1.5+7		JUL	Expt Jour	JRC 21 395	74 Qaim+ DIRECT GAMS,SIG VS Z SYSTEMATC	+
				Jour	JIN 35 19	Jan 73 - +ACTIVATION	
				Conf	72Budapest 50	Aug 72 - . ACTIVATION ,GRP	
				Conf	71Canterby 121	Sep 71 - + PRELIM RESULT. SEE JIN 35 19	
	1.5+7			Data	EXFOR20522.013	Apr 76 1PNT.SIGMA.	
(n,t)	2.3+7		JUL	Expt Jour	JIN 36 3639	Dec 74 Qaim+ (NT)+(NNT) 3.9+ - 0.9 MB	+
	2.3+7			Data	EXFOR20524.013	Apr 76 1PNT.SIGMA.	
(n,nt)	2.3+7		JUL	Expt Jour	JIN 36 3639	Dec 74 Qaim+ (NT)+(NNT), 3.9+ - 0.9 MB	
	2.3+7			Data	EXFOR20524.013	Apr 76 1PNT.+NT.	
(n,He3)	1.5+7		ARK	Expt Jour	PR 131 2649	Sep 63 Bramlitt+ LESS THAN 0.020MB	+
				Rept	TID - 16949	62 - . THESIS.	
	1.5+7			Data	EXFOR11590.078	Jun 76 . 1 PT. SIGMA.	
(n,He3)	1.4+7	1.5+7	JYV	Eval Rept	JU - RR - 3/1970	Jun 70 Leppaemaeki+ UPPER LIMIT,AVG SIG,TBL	
(n,α)	1.4+7		ALD	Expt Jour	PPS 73 215	Feb 59 Coleman+. ACTIVATION	+
(n,α)	Fiss		CRC	Eval Rept	CRC - 1003	Dec 60 Roy+,ESTIMATED AVG SIG = BELO 0.0001MB	
(n,α)	7.0+6	2.0+7	LAS	Expt Jour	JIN 23 173	Dec 61 Bayhurst+.18ES FROM BETA ACTIVITY	+
				Rept	LA - 2493	Dec 60 - + SEE ALSO FOR EXCITN CURVE.	
	7.0+6	2.0+7		Data	EXFOR11462.018	Jun 76 . 15 PTS.	
(n,α)	1.5+7	1.5+7	CIS	Expt Jour	NP 46 51	Jul 63 Marcazzan. = 1 DATA INDEX LINES	+
(n,α)	5.0-1	2.5+2	YAL	Expt Jour	PL 6 350	Oct 63 Wasson+ G PULSERATE VS E.TH ANAL.	
(n,α)	1.4+7		CIS	Theo Jour	NP 51 460	Feb 64 Facchini+STATMOD SIG XPT/CALC3.9 - 4.7	
				Jour	NP 46 51	Jul 63 - + SI DETECTOR AT 30DEG.	
				Jour	PL 1 6	Apr 62 - + FWD VS BACK ANGLES	
(n,α)			IBJ	Expt Jour	NP 66 361	May 65 Osakiewicz+ RELATED TO NUCL SURFACE	
(n,α)	1.5+7		MUA	Expt Jour	NP 69 153	Jul 65 Khurana+	
(n,α)	1.2+7	2.3+7	FRK	Expt Jour	NP 85 606	Sep 66 Rubbino+ZUBKE ANGLE+ENERGY SPECTRA	
				Abst	BSI 46 43	Nov 65 - +(2B5).E SPEC,ANGDST ANAL.NDG	
(n,α)	1.4+7	1.5+7	NAP	Comp Rept	INFN/BE - 67 - 11	Sep 67 Cuzzocrea+ AVERAGED CHOSEN DATA.	
(n,α)	1.5+7		DEB	Comp Jour	REA 7 4 93	Dec 69 Csikai+ SIG+HL COMPILTN,N - ACTIV - ANAL	
(n,α)	1.4+7	1.5+7	JYV	Eval Rept	JU - RR - 3/1970	Jun 70 Leppaemaeki+ TABLE OF EVAL AVG SIG	

79 Gold 197

Quantity	Energy (ev) Min	Energy (ev) Max	Lab	Type	Documentation Ref Vol Page	Documentation Date	Author, Comments	Data
(n,α)	1.4+7		TIT	Expt Jour	NP/A 149 513	Jul 70	Kitazawa. S SPEC 0 DEG+SIGMA+ANDISTR	+
	1.5+7			Data	EXFOR20336.007	Jul 74	14PTS.D/DA.DE.	
(n,α)	1.4+7		KFI	Comp Jour	JRC 7 365	Jun 71	Nagy+ SIGMA, GAMM-E AND HALF-L GIVEN	
(n,α)	9.0+6	2.0+7	CIS	Theo Jour	NP/A 210 297	Aug 73	Milazzo-Colli+ CALC EXCIT FN CFD XPT	
	1.4+7	2.1+7		Jour	PL/B 38 155	Feb 72	Colli-Milazzo+ A-SPECT+EXCIT FN CALC	
(n,α)	1.4+7	1.5+7	KAZ	Theo Jour	YF 18 705	Oct 73	Levkovsky.AVERAGED SIG,CALC,TBL	
				Jour	SNP 18 361	Apr 74	. ENGLISH OF YF 18,705	
(n,α)	1.6+7		RAM	Expt Jour	NSPB 6 45	Oct 73	ALI+ SI-DET.GRAPH ALFA-SPECTRUM	+
	1.6+7			Data	EXFOR30294.004	Oct 75	26 PTS, YIELD OF ALPHA SPECTRA.	
(n,α)	1.4+7		TUD	Theo Conf	ZFK-271 63	Nov 73	Seeliger+ A-EMISSION SPEC, NDG	
(n,α)	Fiss		HED	Eval Conf	75Wash. 375	Mar 75	Lippincott+ TBL MEAS CFD ENDF4	
(n,α)		7.5+8	IOW	Expt Jour	PR/C 12 1978	Dec 75	Hill+ ES TO 750 MEV.	
(n,α)	+7		CCP	Expt Rept	YK- 23 4	76	Brodskaja+ ACTIV,AVG SIG,TBL	
(n,nα)	1.5+7		ARK	Expt Jour	PR 131 2649	Sep 63	Bramlitt+ LESS THAN 0.040MB	+
				Rept	TID-16949	62	-. THESIS.	
	1.5+7			Data	EXFOR11590.079	Jun 76	. 1 PT.	
(n,nα)	1.4+7	1.5+7	JYV	Eval Rept	JU-RR-3/1970	Jun 70	Leppaemaeki+ TABLE OF EVAL AVG SIG	
Fission	1.4+7		LAS	Expt Jour	PR 75 919	Mar 49	Phillips+ UPPER LIM REL U238.PHOTOPL	
Reson Params	2.6+0		LUQ	Expt Jour	PR 61 469	Apr 42	Feeny+ G(TOT) BY ACTIVN+SELFSCREENNG	
Reson Params	4.8+0		COL	Expt Jour	PR 70 154	Aug 46	Havens+	+
	4.8+0			Data	EXFOR11139.009	Jun 76	. 1 RES, E0.	
Reson Params	4.8+0		COL	Expt Jour	PR 71 165	Feb 47	Havens+ TOF, TRNSM.	+
Reson Params	4.8+0		LAS	Expt Jour	PR 72 729	Oct 47	Mcdaniel+ WT FROM BREIT-WIGNER FIT.	
Reson Params	4.9+0		COL	Expt Jour	PR 83 746	Aug 51	Tittman+WN,WG,WT,R,SIG0,E0. J=1OR2	+
				Jour	PR 80 903	Dec 50	- + WN,WT FROM TRANSM. B-W FIT.	
	4.9+0			Data	EXFOR12203.	Jun 76	. 1 RES, E0,WT,WN.	
Reson Params	4.9+0		COL	Expt Jour	PR 83 1123	Sep 51	Havens+	+
	4.9+0			Data	EXFOR11732.012	Jun 76	. 1 RES, E0,WT,PCS,WT**2/PCS.	
Reson Params	4.9+0		BNL	Expt Jour	PR 93 1030	Mar 54	Landon+ RSLN, 12EV SIGMA.	+
	4.9+0			Data	EXFOR12029.006	Jun 76	. 1 RES, E0,WT,PCS.	
Reson Params	4.9+0	1.9+2	BNL	Expt Jour	PR 95 476	Jul 54	Seidl+ RSLN .04TO6EV. ASSUMED WG.	+
	4.9+0	1.9+2		Data	EXFOR11671.011	Jun 76	. 7 RES, E0,WN,WT**2/PCS.	
Reson Params	5.8+1	6.0+1	ANL	Expt Priv	BOLLINGER	Apr 55	Bollinger+	+
	5.8+1	6.0+1		Data	EXFOR12231.004	Jun 76	. 2 RES, E0.	
Reson Params	4.9+0	6.1+1	BNL	Expt Jour	PR 101 1328	56	Levin+	+
	4.9+0	6.1+1		Data	EXFOR12274.	Jun 76	. 1 RES, WT,WN,WG. 1 RES, WG.	
Reson Params	4.6+1		BNL	Expt Priv	ZIMMERMAN	Oct 56	Zimmerman.	+
	4.6+1			Data	EXFOR12499.002	Jun 76	. 1 RES, E0,WN0,WN.	
Reson Params	4.9+0		BNL	Expt Jour	PR 104 1425	Dec 56	Wood.WT=.140 WN=.0156 WG=.124EV J=2	+
	4.9+0			Data	EXFOR12241.003	Jun 76	. 1 RES, E0,WT,PCS,WT**2/PCS.	
Reson Params	4.7+1		BNL	Expt Jour	PR 110 692	May 58	Seth+ NEW 46.5EV RWN 0.00002 FC	+
	4.7+1			Data	EXFOR11788.038	Jun 76	. 1 RES, E0,WN0.	
Reson Params	6.1+1	2.7+2	ORL	Expt Prog	ORNL-2501	Jun 58	Slaughter+ 10 RES, FAST CHOPPR,G*WN.	
	6.1+1	2.7+2		Data	EXFOR11446.006	Jun 76	. 10 RES, E0,WN,WN0.	
Reson Params	4.9+0	9.4+2	COL	Expt Jour	PR 120 2214	Dec 60	Desjardins+ TOF, 55 RESONANCES.	+
	4.7+1	9.4+2		Data	EXFOR11948.009	Jun 76	. 55 RES, E0,J,WN,WN0,WG.	
Reson Params	-		FOA	ExTh Jour	NP 39 353	Dec 62	Bergqvist+.AVERAGE GAMMA WIDTH.EXPTH	
Reson Params	7.8+1		SAC	Expt Jour	JPR 24 176	Mar 63	Le Pipec+ RESONANCE ANALYSIC.77DEG K	
				Jour	CR 255 1913	Oct 62	- + CRYSTAL BINDING EFFECT.	
Reson Params	4.9+0	1.1+2	MOL	Eval Rept	BLG-421	66	Damle+.RECOMMENDED PARAMS 6 RESON	
Reson Params	5.3+1	7.5+2	HAR	Expt Jour	NIM 39 68	Jan 66	Asghar+LI-6 DET. FOR RES ANALYSIS.	+
	4.6+1	5.5+2		Conf	65Antwerp 552	Jul 65	- .GIVE WN WG J COMPAR WITH OTHR	
	5.0+1	7.5+2		Rept	AERE-NP/GEN40	Jun 65	- +LI-6 DET. SCAT EXPT.FOR RES	
Reson Params	6.0+1	2.4+2	SAC	Expt Jour	CR 262 507	Feb 66	Trochon+AREA,J,G FROM SCATT+TRANSM	+
Reson Params	4.9+0		TRM	Expt Prog	AEET-267 4	Aug 66	Chandramoleswar+TABLE WN,WT, CFD BNL	+
	4.9+0			Data	EXFOR30408.003	Aug 77	N-,TOT-WIDTHS, PEAK SIG.	
Reson Params	2.4+4		LRC	Theo Conf	66Paris 1 503	Oct 66	Bogart. VAL GVN, BETHE ANALYSIS	
		1.0+6	AUA	Theo Jour	AUJ 20 477	Oct 67	Cook. TBL OF AVG LVL SPACING D,L=0,1	
Reson Params	4.9+0	9.9+2	KFK	Eval Rept	KFK-718	Apr 68	Schmidt+ RESOLVED+AVG RES PARAM(S,P)	
Reson Params	1.0+3	1.0+5	HAR	Expt Rept	NP-17644	Jul 68	Moxon.THESIS. AVG D,WG,AND WG/D	
Reson Params	+3	+5	AUA	ExTh Rept	AAEC/E-198	May 69	Musgrove.RES PARS +STF FROM (NG)FIT	+
Reson Params	None		BNL	Eval Conf	69Studsvik 627	Aug 69	Chrien. WG-DISTR CFD PORTER-THOM,TBL	

79 Gold 197

Quantity	Energy (ev) Min	Max	Lab	Type	Documentation Ref Vol Page	Author, Comments Date	Data
Reson Params	4.9+0	3.1+3	SAC	Expt	Jour NP/A 131 450	Jun 69 De Barros+ TBL.TOTAL AND CAPT.LINAC	+
	4.9+0				Rept CEA−N−1230	Oct 69 Tellier+TOF TRANSMISSION,SHAPE ANA	
	4.9+0	2.6+3		Priv	ALVES	Jul 69 Alves+,NEUT+GAM WIDTH,SPIN,LINAC,TOF	
	1.0+3	3.1+3		Conf	CEA−R−3602	May 68 − . (THESIS) TBL.	
	4.9+0	3.1+3		ExTh Conf	JINR−D3893 120	May 68 Julien+130RES,WG+D ANALYSIS GRAPHS	
	4.9+0	2.6+3		Expt Conf	68Wash. 867	Mar 68 Morgenstern.WG VS.A,AVERAGE WG GIVEN	
				Rept	CEA−R−3385	Feb 68 Julien. (THESIS)	
				Conf	66Paris 1 193	Oct 66 Huynh+ ALSO PAGE 559	
				Jour	NP 76 391	Feb 66 − + SUPERSEDED.	
				Conf	65Antwerp 525	Jul 65 De Barros+ PPR73.ABST.NDG	
	0.0+0	3.1+3		Data	EXFOR20686.	Aug 77 175PTS.E0,WG,AVG WG,WN,WT,J,G*WN.	
Reson Params	2.0+5		MUA Theo	Conf	69Roorke 2 129	Dec 69 Chaubey+ D/GAM−WIDTH RATIO, STATMOD	
Reson Params	2.4+4		KFK Eval	Conf	70Helsinki 1 197	Jun 70 Froehner.8. S WAVE, D + GAM WIDTH	
Reson Params	1.0+4	6.0+4	KFK Expt	Conf	70Helsinki 1 201	Jun 70 Schneider+10. RES ANALYSIS+TEMP INFL	
Reson Params	4.9+0	1.0+3	KFK Comp	Rept	KFK−1233	Jul 70 Mueller. ES,WN,WG,G OF 50 RESON	
Reson Params	−		AUA Theo	Rept	AAEC/E−211	Nov 70 Musgrove. CALCULTD D+GAM WIDTH GIVEN	
Reson Params	1.0+0	2.0+2	AUA Theo	Jour	AUJ 23 823	Dec 70 Clayton.MULTILEVEL ANALYS,ELAST SCAT	
Reson Params	4.9+0	2.1+3	CJD Eval	Rept	YK− 7	71 Zakharova+ SURVEY+SYSTEMATICS,GW,TBL	
				Rept	INDC(CCP)−27	Nov 72 .ENGLISH TRANSLATION OF YK−7 /71	
Reson Params	None		DUB Theo	Jour	YF 13 240	Feb 71 Malecki+G−WID,THEO CFD EXPT.TBL,GRPH	
				Jour	SNP 13 133	Aug 71 − + ENGL OF YF 13 240.	
Reson Params	1.0+3	1.0+6	GA Expt	Conf	71Knoxvill 252	Mar 71 Fricke+,AVG WG AND D GIVEN	
Reson Params	5.3+2	4.8+3	LAS Expt	Conf	71Knoxvill 868	Mar 71 Hoffman+. G*WN(SQUARED)/WT,TABLE	
Reson Params	+3	+5	AUA Expt	Prog	AAEC/PR−36P 11	Mar 72 Allen+ ORELA.DATA TO BE ANALYZED,NDG	
Reson Params	9.1+1	1.0+3	SAC Expt	Conf	72Budapest 32	Aug 72 Lottin+ SPIN ASSIGNM OF LEVELS ,GRPH	
Reson Params	None		SAC Expt	Conf	74Petten 165	Sep 74 Jain+ NO WIDTH CORRELATIONS OBSERVED	
Reson Params	+2	+3	COL Expt	Abst	BAP 20 139	Feb 75 Arbo+ 75WASH NDG.	
Reson Params	2.6+3	4.8+3	ORL Expt	Jour	PR/C 11 1270	Apr 75 Macklin+ TBL E0,G(WG)WN/WT	+
	2.6+3	4.8+3		Data	EXFOR10432.004	Oct 74 . 115 RES. G*WN*WG/WT.	
Reson Params	5.8+1	2.6+3	SAC Expt	Diss	CEA−N−1806	May 75 Alix. EN,WG,SPIN GIVEN (129 RES)	+
	5.8+1	2.6+3		Data	EXFOR20580.	May 76 127PTS.E0,AVG WG.	
Reson Params	Maxwl		KUK Theo	Jour	76Ahmedabd 2 1	Dec 76 Sharma+AVG S−WAVE REDUCED N−WID ANAL	
Strnth Fnctn	+3	+5	MTR Expt	Prog	WASH−1013 59	Nov 58 Simpson+ NDG. FC. TBC.	
Strnth Fnctn	+3		BNL Expt	Jour	PRL 1 461	Dec 58 Hughes+ FC, 1.2+−0.3.	
Strnth Fnctn	1.0+3	2.0+5	DKE Expt	Jour	AP 10 455	60 Bilpuch+	+
	1.0+3	2.0+5		Data	EXFOR11187.008	Jun 76 . 1 PT.	
Strnth Fnctn	None		DKE Eval	Jour	AP 10 477	Aug 60 Weston+ CALC FROM CAPT SIG L=1	
Strnth Fnctn	3.0+1	4.0+2	ORL Expt	Conf	60Vienna 535	Oct 60 Block+.VAL GVN,EXPT DESCRIBED	
Strnth Fnctn	None		COL Expt	Jour	PR 120 2214	Dec 60 Havens.TOF 1.5	
Strnth Fnctn	1.0+4	2.0+5	ORL Expt	Jour	PR 122 182	61 Gibbons+	+
	1.0+4	2.0+5		Data	EXFOR11329.	Jun 76 . 4 PTS. STF,D,AVE WG.	
Strnth Fnctn	+3	+5	BOL Theo	Conf	61Vienna 1 179	Aug 61 Benzi+.PPR11,TABLE CFD EXPERIMENT	
Strnth Fnctn	+3	+4	DKE Expt	Rept	TID−16059	62 Furr.ACT S,P FNCTS FOR N,G AVG	
	None			Abst	DA 23 4719	Jun 63 − .S,P WAVE.G,N STF CALC.NDG.	
Strnth Fnctn		2.0+4	LEB Expt	Jour	ZET 46 80	Jan 64 Konks.PB−SLOW−DOWN,VALUE GIVEN	
				Jour	JET 19 59	Jul 64 TRANSLATN.*	
Strnth Fnctn	3.0+3	6.5+5	DKE ExTh	Jour	PL 13 70	Nov 64 Seth+S,P,D STF FRM SIG TOT 3−650KEV	+
	5.0+4	1.5+5		Expt Conf	64Paris 2 916	Jul 64 − + S0,S1,S2 R PRIME/R.	
	3.0+3	6.5+5		Data	EXFOR11665.032	Jun 76 . 3 PTS.	
Strnth Fnctn	+6		FOA Theo	Jour	NP 67 321	May 65 Lundberg+ RED GAMMA RAY STF CALC	
Strnth Fnctn	+0	+2	MOL Eval	Rept	BLG−421	66 Damle+. RECOMMENDED S0=1.5+−0.3	
Strnth Fnctn	2.4+4		LRC Theo	Conf	66Paris 1 503	Oct 66 Bogart. VAL GVN, BETHE ANALYSIS	
Strnth Fnctn	−		HAR Expt	Prog	AERE−PR/NP12	Aug 67 Diment+ VALUES SO SI GIVEN	
Strnth Fnctn	None		ANL Expt	Abst	BAP 12 1187	Dec 67 Mooring+. FROM AV,VARIANCE OF SIG	
Strnth Fnctn	1.0+3	1.0+5	HAR Expt	Rept	NP−17644	Jul 68 Moxon.THESIS.MOXON−RAE DET.S+P+DWAVE	
Strnth Fnctn	8.0+3	3.0+4	PEL Expt	Jour	NP/A 121 655	Dec 68 Spitz+ FROM SIG(N,G)	+
	8.0+3	3.0+4		Data	EXFOR30114.015	Mar 71 P−WAVE STRENGTH FUNCTION.	
Strnth Fnctn	4.9+0	1.0+3	SAC Expt	Jour	NP/A 123 561	Jan 69 Morgenstern+ TBL. FROM RES ANALYSIS	+
				Rept	CEA−R−3609	Sep 68 − . S−WAVE, RADIUS	
				Rept	CEA−R−3602	Jul 69 Alves. (THESIS)	
				Conf	68Wash. 867	Mar 68 Morgenstern+	
				Rept	CEA−R−3385	Feb 68 Julien. (THESIS).SEE ALSO.S0 VS J.	
				Conf	66Paris 1 183	Oct 66 Morgenstern+ PPR65.ABST.NDG.INDC−156	
				Jour	NP 76 391	Feb 66 Julien+ SUPERSEDED.	
				Conf	65Antwerp 531	Jul 65 Morgenstern+ PPR87.ABST.NDG.	
	0.0+0	1.0+3		Data	EXFOR20686.005	Aug 77 1PNT.L=0.	
Strnth Fnctn	+3	+5	AUA ExTh	Rept	AAEC/E−198	May 69 Musgrove.S+P+D STF FROM (NG)FIT,TBL	+

79 Gold 197

Quantity	Energy (ev) Min	Max	Lab	Type	Documentation Ref Vol Page	Author, Comments Date	Data
Strnth Fnctn	1.0+4	1.5+5	KFK	Expt Jour	NP/A 133 513	Aug 69 Kompe. S1,S2,S(GAMMA)LEAST SQ NG FIT	+
				Rept	KFK-1071	Aug 69 - . REPRINT OF NP/A 133 513	
	1.0+4	1.5+5		Data	EXFOR20358.	Sep 74 3PTS.GAMMA STF.	
Strnth Fnctn	-		DUB	Revw Jour	YF 11 111	Jan 70 Malecki+ VALUES FOR TWO SPIN STATES	
				Jour	SNP 11 61	Jul 70 - + ENGL OF YF 11 61.	
Strnth Fnctn	2.4+4		KFK	Eval Conf	70Helsinki 1 197	Jun 70 Froehner.8. ANALYSIS OF S0 VALUES	
Strnth Fnctn			AUA	Theo Rept	AAEC/E-211	Nov 70 Musgrove. SMOOTHED S0,S1 AND S2 GIVN	
Strnth Fnctn	1.0+3	1.0+6	GA	Expt Conf	71Knoxvill 252	Mar 71 Fricke+, S0 AND S1 GIVEN	
Strnth Fnctn		1.0+5	VIP	Expt Abst	DA/B 32 2932	Nov 71 Lindsay. GAMMA,S,P WAVE.	
Strnth Fnctn	2.4+4		MUA	Theo Jour	IJP 46 114	Mar 72 Chaubey+ P-WAVE.FOR A-SYSTEMTIC,GRPH	
Strnth Fnctn			AUA	Eval Rept	AAEC/E-277	Mar 73 Musgrove.TBLS EXPTL DATA+BEST VALUES	
Strnth Fnctn	1.0+3	6.0+5	NBS	Expt Jour	PR/C 9 28	Jan 74 Camarda.LINAC.TRANS. S1 MEASURED.	+
	1.0+3	7.0+5		Prog	USNDC-7 147	Jun 73 - . LINAC. S1 MEASD. NO DATA	
	1.0+3	6.0+5		Data	EXFOR10765.012	Nov 78 . 1PT.S1=(0.4+.4-.3)-4	
Strnth Fnctn	2.6+3	4.8+3	ORL	Expt Jour	PR/C 11 1270	Apr 75 Macklin+ S =(2.0+-0.2)E-4. 115 RES	+
	2.6+3	4.8+3		Data	EXFOR10432.005	May 76 . 3 PTS. S,P,D WAVE.	
Strnth Fnctn	5.0+3	8.0+4	FEI	Expt Jour	YK- 19 57	May 75 Shorin+ RADIAT+P-NEUT STRENGTH FUNCT	
Strnth Fnctn	2.0+6	8.0+6	LND	Revw Conf	76Lowell 99	Jul 76 Bergqvist. GRPH	
Strnth Fnctn	2.7+3		MUN	Expt Conf	71Albany 327	Aug 76 Dilg+TRNS.S0 STF GVN.31 ELEMENT GRPH	
Lvl Density	1.4+7		LAS	Expt Jour	PR 89 343	Jan 53 Graves. TEMP GIVEN CF LA-1532	
Lvl Density	6.0+6		DKE	Expt Rept	AD- 299005	62 Seth+,NUCL TEMP+FERMI LVL DENS COEFF	
Lvl Density	4.0+6	7.0+6	ISL	Theo Conf	64Geneva § 511	May 64 Szwarcbaum+.T FROM 3 FORMLS CFD EXPS	
Lvl Density	1.4+7		FEI	Theo Conf	64Paris 2 762	Jul 64 Malushev+.THERMOD T VERSUS XPT+FMGAS	
Lvl Density	None		ANL	Theo Jour	NP 60 70	Nov 64 Vonach+NUCL TEMP CFD ANGDIST INEL N	
Lvl Density	-		FEI	Eval Rept	FEI-36	66 Kapchigashev+.TBL OF RELATD QUANTTYS	+
		5.0+4		Jour	YF 4 686	Sep 66 .TABLE.SHORT VERSION OF FEI-36	
				Prog	YFI-3 3	66 .ABSTRACT.TABLE LDL+NUCL.EXCIT.E	
		5.0+4		Jour	SNP 4 486	67 .ENGLISH OF YF 4.FROM(N,GAMMA).TABLE	
				Prog	INDC-E-140 3	66 .ENGLISH TRANSL OF YFI-3	
Lvl Density	-		JAE	ExTh Jour	NP 78 369	Apr 66 Tsukada+ FOR 2-8MEV EXCIT E TEMPS+A	+
	3.6+6	8.5+6		Expt Jour	NP/A 131 145	Jun 69 Maruyama. E DEPENDENCE,PARAM,TH FIT	
	-			ExTh Conf	67Tokyo 373	Sep 67 - + PPR8.127. ABST	
Lvl Density	None		LRL	Expt Jour	NP/A 93 648	Mar 67 Chodil+ P,N+P,2N GIVES SMALL A=A/25	
Lvl Density	-1	+6	MIL	Theo Jour	EN 15 54	Jan 68 Facchini+ LDL PARS FROM LOW EN RES	
Lvl Density	+7		DEB	ExTh Jour	NP/A 122 234	Dec 68 Karolyi+ SPIN CUTOFF,M OF INERT,N2N	+
	+7			Expt Data	EXFOR30101.032	Feb 71 CUT-OFF PARAMETER,MAX EXC EN=9.4 MEV	
Lvl Density	+6	+7	AUA	Theo Rept	AAEC/TM-522	Nov 69 Bertram. FORMULAE+PARS IN(N,2N)-ANAL	
Lvl Density	None		AUW	Theo Conf	70Madurai 2 267	Dec 70 Ramamurty+ A-PARAMETER GVN,LANG'S-TH	
Lvl Density	1.5+6	1.4+7	TUD	Expt Prog	ZFK-243 25	Sep 72 Hermsdorf+ T+LVD DENS PARAM,TBL+GRPH	
Lvl Density	+7		FEI	Theo Jour	YF 21 485	Mar 75 Ignatjuk+ LVL DENS PARAMS,GRAPH	
(γ,n)	+7		BSP	Revw Conf	55Geneva 2 169	Aug 55 Souza-Santos+.P897,THRESHOLD VAL GVN	
Photo-Fissn		1.0+8	FTI	Expt Conf	67Kharkov § SP	Feb 67 Sanin+. TBP IN IZV	

79 Gold 198

Quantity	Energy (ev) Min	Max	Lab	Type	Documentation Ref Vol Page	Author, Comments Date	Data
Total	2.5-2		MTR	Expt Abst	ANS 6 43	Jun 63 Simpson+ 25600+-1280 B.	+
	1.0-2	5.0-1		Conf	61Saclay 85	Jul 61 - +,GRAPH SIG(E)GIVEN WITH 199	
	2.5-2			Data	EXFOR12786.002	Jun 76 . 1 PT.	
Res Int Abs	5.0-1		MTR	Expt Prog	WASH-1033 38	Aug 61 Schuman.	
Res Int Abs	5.5-1		MUN	Expt Diss	GRYNTAKIS	Mar 76 Gryntakis.ACT,31031+-10941B,EXCL 1/V	+
	5.5-1			Data	EXFOR20625.034	Aug 76 1PNT.CAPTURE.	
(n,γ)	None		UI	Expt Jour	PR 79 275	Jul 50 Hill+DOUBLE CAPT	
(n,γ)	Maxwl		UI	Expt Jour	PR 83 1097	Sep 51 Sherk+ BETA SPECTRA.	+
	Maxwl			Data	EXFOR12204.002	Jun 76 . 1 PT.	
(n,γ)	Pile		IPS	Expt Jour	AF 4 223	Aug 52 Siegbahn. FROM AU198/AU199 CONV GAM	
(n,γ)	Pile		UBC	Expt Jour	CJP 33 25	Jan 55 Bedford+ 17800B CF NSA9 2524	
				Jour	CJP 33 492	Aug 55 - CORRECTED TO 26400 B.	
(n,γ)	Maxwl		CRC	Expt Jour	CJP 33 457	Aug 55 Bell+ 26000+-1200B REL AU197 99B	+
	Maxwl			Data	EXFOR12245.002	Jun 76 . 1 PT.	
(n,γ)	Maxwl		BNL	Expt Abst	PR 99 1646	Sep 55 Graham+ SIGMA=26000+-1200 B.	
(n,γ)	Maxwl		HAR	Expt Rept	AERE-R-6384	May 70 Cabell+ TBL.SIG=25102+-371B. T=70C	+
	Pile			Jour	JIN 31 1229	May 69 - +,CALIB GAM SPECT	
	Maxwl			Data	EXFOR20457.002	Jan 76 1PNT.SIGMA.	
(n,γ)	Maxwl		MIS	Expt Jour	NAP 9 622	Nov 70 Serment+	+
	Maxwl			Data	EXFOR12601.002	Jun 76 . 1 PT, SIGMA.	
(n,γ)	2.0+4	3.0+4	TAT	Expt Prog	BARC-831 21	75 Anand+ ACTIV.ANOMALY EXPLAINED,NDG	

79 Gold 198

Quantity	Energy (ev) Min Max	Lab	Type	Documentation Ref Vol Page	Author, Comments Date	Data
(n,γ)	Maxwl 2.5−2	MUN	Expt Data	Diss GRYNTAKIS EXFOR20625.033	Mar 76 Gryntakis.,ACT.,26736+ − 850B, REL.AU Aug 76 1PNT.SIGMA.	+
Res Int Capt	5.0−1	HAR	Expt Rept	AERE − R − 6384	May 70 Cabell+ REDUCED VAL= − 41240+ − 4190TBL	
Spect (n,γ)	Maxwl Maxwl	MUN	Expt Jour Data	ZN/A 26 1928 EXFOR20260.002	Nov 71 Breitig. LEVEL − SCHEME OF AU − 199 73 54PTS.	+
Spect (n,γ)	Maxwl	ANL	Expt Prog	USNDC − 1 18	May 72 Thomas+. ABSOL GAMMA INTENSITY MEASD	
(n,2n)	1.0+7 2.0+7	IRK	Theo Jour	APA 31 258	Jul 70 UHL+ STATMDL CALC+ISOM RATIO.	
(n,p)	Maxwl	IFU	Theo Rept	ICD − 4 20	67 Dadakina+ PENETR COEFF CALC,TABLE	
Reson Params	−	AUA	Theo Rept	AAEC/E − 211	Nov 70 Musgrove. CALCULTD D+GAM WIDTH GIVEN	
Strnth Fnctn	−	AUA	Theo Rept	AAEC/E − 211	Nov 70 Musgrove. SMOOTHED S0,S1 AND S2 GIVN	
Lvl Density	+6	MIL	Theo Jour	EN 15 1 54	Jan 68 Facchini+LDL PARS FROM LOW EN RES	
Lvl Density	None	MUN	Theo Jour	NP/A 217 269	Dec 73 Dilg+ A,DELTA. BACK SHIFTED FERMIGAS	
Lvl Density	None	COP	Theo Jour	NP/A 222 493	Apr 74 Dossing+COLL ROTAT.SPAC. ACCUR ESTIM	
Lvl Density	None	ROC	Theo Jour	NP/A 223 577	May 74 Huizenga+ EXP CFD MICROSC TH SPH NUC	

79 Gold 199

Quantity	Energy (ev) Min Max	Lab	Type	Documentation Ref Vol Page	Author, Comments Date	Data
(n,γ)	Pile	MTR	Expt Prog	AECD − 3691 11	Oct 55 Passell+,MTR IRRAD,SIG=30B (ROUGH)	
Reson Params	−	AUA	Theo Rept	AAEC/E − 211	Nov 70 Musgrove. CALCULTD D+GAM WIDTH GIVEN	
Strnth Fnctn	−	AUA	Theo Rept	AAEC/E − 211	Nov 70 Musgrove. SMOOTHED S0,S1 AND S2 GIVN	

79 Gold 200

Quantity	Energy (ev) Min Max	Lab	Type	Documentation Ref Vol Page	Author, Comments Date	Data
Reson Params	−	AUA	Theo Rept	AAEC/E − 211	Nov 70 Musgrove. CALCULTD D+GAM WIDTH GIVEN	
Strnth Fnctn	−	AUA	Theo Rept	AAEC/E − 211	Nov 70 Musgrove. SMOOTHED S0,S1 AND S2 GIVN	

79 Gold 201

Quantity	Energy (ev) Min Max	Lab	Type	Documentation Ref Vol Page	Author, Comments Date	Data
Reson Params	−	AUA	Theo Rept	AAEC/E − 211	Nov 70 Musgrove. CALCULTD D+GAM WIDTH GIVEN	
Strnth Fnctn	−	AUA	Theo Rept	AAEC/E − 211	Nov 70 Musgrove. SMOOTHED S0,S1 AND S2 GIVN	

79 Gold 202

Quantity	Energy (ev) Min Max	Lab	Type	Documentation Ref Vol Page	Author, Comments Date	Data
Reson Params	−	AUA	Theo Rept	AAEC/E − 211	Nov 70 Musgrove. CALCULTD D+GAM WIDTH GIVEN	
Strnth Fnctn	−	AUA	Theo Rept	AAEC/E − 211	Nov 70 Musgrove. SMOOTHED S0,S1 AND S2 GIVN	

80 Mercury

Quantity	Energy (ev) Min	Max	Lab	Type	Documentation Ref Vol Page	Author, Comments Date	Data
Evaluation	5.0+5	1.5+7	LRL Eval	Rept	UCRL-5351	Nov 58 Howerton.CURVS TOT SEL SNE SIN N2N	
Total	Maxwl		COL Expt	Jour	PR 48 265	Aug 35 Dunning+ IONCH,TRANS,SIG SLOW+FAST N	
Total	2.9+6		COL Expt	Jour	PR 56 260	Aug 39 Zinn+ D-D FRWRD NS +-40KEV RSLN	+
	2.9+6			Data	EXFOR11136.023	Jun 76 . 1 PT. SIG	
Total	2.5+7		HRV Expt	Jour	PR 68 240	Dec 45 Sherr.LIDN NS C DTECTOR 10PC ERROR	+
	2.5+7			Data	EXFOR11138.009	Jun 76 . 1 PT, SIG	
Total	2.0-2	4.1+0	COL Expt	Jour	PR 70 154	Aug 46 Havens.	+
	2.0-2	4.1+0		Data	EXFOR11139.005	Jun 76 . 46 PTS, SIG	
Total	2.7+8		BRK Expt	Jour	PR 80 23	Oct 50 Fox+ BE(P,N) NS,SCINTILLATION COUNT.	+
	2.7+8			Data	EXFOR11175.011	Jun 76 . 1 PT. SIG	
Total	4.2+7		BRK Expt	Jour	PR 80 842	Dec 50 Hildebrand+ BE-D NS.TRANSM. C DETECT	+
	4.2+7			Data	EXFOR11039.030	Jun 76 . 1 PT. SIG	
Total	1.4+7		LAS Expt	Jour	PR 88 562	Nov 52 Coon+ GOOD GEOM	+
	1.4+7			Data	EXFOR11056.052	Jun 76 . 1 PT, SIG	
Total	4.0+0	1.1+4	HAR Expt	Jour	PPSA 65 992	Dec 52 Hodgson+.TOF.	+
Total	3.4+5	3.4+6	ORL Expt	Prog	ORNL-1365 1	Jan 53 Johnson+	+
	3.4+5	3.4+6		Data	EXFOR11292.006	Jun 76 . 33 PTS, SIG	
Total	1.4+7		ROM Expt	Jour	NC 10 281	Mar 53 Ageno+LI TARGET TRANSMIS.5.34+-0.11B	
Total	9.0+4	3.0+6	WIS Expt	Jour	PR 89 1271	Mar 53 Walt+. GRAPH. ZR-T AND LI TARGETS	+
	1.8+5	2.8+6		Data	EXFOR11746.009	Jun 76 . 17 PTS, SIG	
Total	2.8+6	1.3+7	LAS Expt	Jour	PR 94 1678	Jun 54 Nereson+ RSLN 10 PERCENT	+
	2.8+6	1.3+7		Data	EXFOR11308.024	Jun 76 . 30 PTS, SIG	
Total	1.3+7	1.6+7	UMX Expt	Jour	AIF 1 69	55 Mazari+ GRAPH GIVEN,TRANSMISSION	+
				Jour	PR 100 972	Nov 55 .SHORT ABSTRACT	
	1.3+7	1.6+7		Data	EXFOR30037.012	Sep 70 7 DATA POINTS,PRIV COMM FROM MAZARI	
Total	1.2+1	1.6+3	BNL Expt	Priv	CARTER	Mar 55 Carter.	+
	1.2+1	1.6+3		Data	EXFOR11897.007	Jun 76 . 231 PTS, SIG	
Total	6.1+7	1.1+8	HRV Expt	Jour	PR 99 740	Aug 55 Culler.	+
	6.1+7	1.1+8		Data	EXFOR11088.012	Jun 76 . 12 PTS, SIG.	
Total	1.6+1	1.3+3	ANL Expt	Jour	PR 102 228	Apr 56 Palmer+,TRNS,ISOTOPIC ASSGNMENT 7RES	+
	1.6+1	7.4+3		Data	EXFOR11804.018	Jun 76 . 91 PTS, SIG	
Total	3.0+1	2.0+3	HAR Expt	Jour	NP 13 525	Nov 59 Bird+TOF RESULTS CFD TRANS.MEAS=GOOD	+
Total	4.1+6		TNC Expt	Rept	WADD-TR-60-217	Apr 60 Vincent.TOF 6.8+-0.1B	
	4.1+6			Data	EXFOR11621.028	Jun 76 . 1 PT, SIG	
Total	1.0+1	3.0+4	ANL Expt	Jour	NP 21 66	Nov 60 Carpenter+FC TRANSMISSION	+
	1.8+1	3.5+4		Data	EXFOR12236.002	Jun 76 . 932 PTS, SIG.	
Total	2.8+7		LVN Expt	Jour	JPR 22 652	Oct 61 Deconninck+TRANSMISS.5.23B AT 28.4MV	+
	2.8+7			Data	EXFOR20195.017	May 74 1PNT.	
Total	1.0+5	6.5+5	ANL Expt	Prog	ANL-7210 16	Dec 66 Whalen.SHORT NOTE,GRAPH ONLY	+
	1.0+5	6.5+5		Data	EXFOR11540.014	Jun 76 . 336 PTS, SIG.	
Total	3.0+4	6.5+5	DKE Expt	Jour	AP 46 401	Feb 68 Tabony+ TRANS CURV DERIVES S0,S1,S2	+
	4.0+4	6.5+5		Data	EXFOR11953.009	Jun 76 . 101 PTS, SIG	
Total	2.5+6	1.5+7	BNW Expt	Jour	PR/C 3 576	Feb 71 Foster+,TRANS,CURVS,CFD OTHERS+TH	+
				Jour	NIM 36 1	Sep 65 .EXPT DETAILS	
	2.3+6	1.5+7		Data	EXFOR10047.087	Aug 73 243PTS.	
Total	2.7+3		MUN Expt	Prog	EANDC(E)150U	Oct 72 Dilg+ AVERAGE TOT XSECT+S0	+
				Conf	71Albany 327	Aug 71 - +TRNS.AVG CS GVN.31 ELEMENT GRP	
	2.7+3			Data	EXFOR20585.031	Jun 76 1PNT.	
Total	1.3+7	1.5+7	DEB Eval	Rept	IAEA-153 173	73 Boedy+ MOST PROBABLE VAL OF SIG,TBL	
				Jour	AHP 30 115	Oct 71 Angeli+ AVG SIG,CFD CALC.TBLS.GRAPH	
Total	1.0+6	2.0+6	DAC Expt	Jour	NP/A 209 189	Jul 73 Islam+ VDG,TRANS,CFD OPTICAL MODEL	+
			Theo	Jour	NP/A 209 202	Jul 73 - + FLUCTUATION ANALYSIS,OWN DATA	
Total	1.6+7	1.9+7	RAM Expt	Prog	INDC(SEC)-35	Sep 73 Husain+ P25.TRANS,100 KEV STEPS,NDG	
	4.0+6	6.0+6		Prog	INDC(SEC)-35	Sep 73 - + P25.TRANS,100 KEV STEPS,NDG	
Total	1.0+6	2.0+6	DAC Eval	Jour	NSPB 6 59	Oct 73 Enayetullah+ SIG(E),LSQ-FIT,TBL+GRPH	
	1.0+6	1.8+7	Comp	Rept	AECD/EP-18	Dec 70 Ameen+ EXPTL DATA FROM DAC,TABLES	
	1.0+6	1.8+7	Expt	Data	EXFOR30134.010	Nov 71 SIGMA-TOT AT 100 ES,PRIVATE COMM.	
Total	1.5+4	6.0+5	DKE Expt	Jour	AP 84 165	May 74 Pineo+TRNS.AVG CS TBLS,GRPHS.OPTMDL	+
	1.0+5	6.5+5		Abst	DA/B 31 6821	May 71 .2 EN RANGE AVGS CFD OPTMOD	
	1.5+4	6.0+5		Diss	PINEO	70 .AVG CS.GRPHS.CFD.STF CALC.TBL.CFD.	
	1.5+4	6.0+5		Data	EXFOR10542.025	Jan 79 . DATA UNOBTAINABLE FROM AUTHORS.	
Total	4.4-4	1.0+1	CAB Expt	Jour	AKE 28 228	76 Granada+ ABST. TOF,GRAPH SIG(E)	+
	4.4-4	1.0+1		Data	EXFOR30349.002	Sep 76 144 PTS, TOT AT 20+-0.5 DEG-C.	
Elastic	Maxwl	+2	JAP Expt	Jour	JPJO 24 569	42 Kimura.SIG CURVE GIVN	
Elastic	2.5-2		ANL Expt	Jour	PR 82 560	May 51 Hibdon+	+
	2.5-2			Data	EXFOR11202.	Jun 76 . 2 PTS, SIG, COH	

80 Mercury

Quantity	Energy (ev) Min	Max	Lab	Type	Documentation Ref Vol Page	Date	Author, Comments	Data
Elastic	1.0+6		WIS	Expt	Jour PR 93 1062	Mar 54	Walt+ INTEG ANG DIST	+
	1.0+6				Data EXFOR11637.071	Jun 76	. 1 PT, SIG	
Elastic	4.1+6		TNC	Expt	Rept WADD−TR−60−217	Apr 60	Vincent.TOF INT20−135DEG 4.2+−0.4B	+
	4.1+6				Data EXFOR11621.026	Jun 76	. 1 PT, SIG	
Elastic	1.0−3		MUN	Expt	Jour ZAP 14 738	Dec 62	MAIER−LEIBNIZ.COH.SCAT.LGTH.REFRAKT	+
Elastic	1.0+6	4.1+6	AGN	Eval	Rept TID−21629	Dec 64	Perkins+CALC FROM BNL400,UCRL5573	
Elastic	1.5−4	4.0−3	MUN	Expt	Jour ZP 182 328	Jan 65	Koester.SIGMA(COHERENT)=20.25+−.05B	
					Conf 67Juelich 80	Apr 67	− + COH SCAT AMP.	
Elastic	2.5−2	2.5−2	MUN	Expt	Rept EANDC(E)57 2	Feb 65	Triftshauser. = 2 DATA INDEX LINES	+
Elastic	3.0+5	1.5+6	ANL	Expt	Jour ZP 183 323	Mar 65	Devilliers+TOF.TBL.CFD OPT MDL.	+
					Rept EANDC(US)−62	Jun 64	Smith+TOF,TBL.50KEV STEPS,20KEV RSLN	
	3.0+5	1.5+6			Data EXFOR12240.008	Jun 76	. 25 PTS, SIG	
Elastic	2.0+6		FEI	Expt	Rept EANDC−50 200	Jul 65	Kazakova+ EXPT,TABLE CFD OPTMODEL	+
					Prog YFI−3 6	Sep 66	.TABLE	
					Prog INDC−E−140 6	Sep 66	.ENGLISH TRANSL OF YFI−3 6 9/66	
Elastic	3.0+5	8.0+5	IFU	ExTh	Jour AE 20 8	Jan 66	Korzh+ SUMMARY OF SEVERAL YRS WORK	+
					Jour UFZ 8 389		63 .650KEV SEE P1323.300KEV SEE P1389	
					Jour SJA 20 8	Jul 66	.ENGLISH TRANSL OF AE 20 8 1/66	
Elastic	1.5+6		IFU	Expt	Prog YFI−5 42	Oct 67	Korzh+ TBL OPTMDL PARAMS + TOTELAST	+
					Rept INDC−232E		67 . ENGL OF YFI−5 42	
Elastic	1.5+6		IFU	Comp	Jour YF 7 277	Feb 68	Korzh+ OPTMOD PARS−FIT TO EXPTL−SIG	
					Jour SNP 7 2 190	Aug 68	TRANSLATN.*	
Elastic	Maxwl		LRL	Expt	Jour PR 175 313	Oct 68	Bartolini+ COH. MIRROR REFL. METHOD	+
	Maxwl				Data EXFOR11125.008	Jun 76	. 1 PT, COH AMP	
Elastic	8.8+5		ANL	Expt	Rept ANL−7935	Jun 72	COX+ 4 PI B(O)	+
	8.8+5				Data EXFOR10332.128	Jun 74	1 PT	
Diff Elastic	1.0+6		WIS	Expt	Jour PR 93 1062	Mar 54	Walt+ HE COUNTER 30−150DEG LAB CURVE	+
	1.0+6				Data EXFOR11637.073	Jun 76	. 9 PTS, DSIG	
Diff Elastic	1.4+7		GRN	Expt	Jour NP 2 124	Oct 56	Nauta. GRAPH 20−110 DEG LAB.RING GEO	+
	1.4+7				Data EXFOR20199.006	May 74	16PTS.D/DA.	
Diff Elastic	2.8+6		IFU	Expt	Conf 58Geneva 15 18	Sep 58	Pasechnik+.PPR2030,CURV,N−ANGL−DISTR	+
Diff Elastic	2.8+6		IFU	ExTh	Conf 59Tashkent 1 103	Sep 59	Pasechnik. XPT AND OPTMDL−TH,GRAPH	
					Rept AEC−TR−6398		64 .VOL 1,P120.ENGL OF 59TASHKE 1 103	
Diff Elastic	4.1+6		TNC	Expt	Rept WADD−TR−60−217	Apr 60	Vincent.TOF 20−135DEG.CURVE+TABLE	+
	4.1+6				Data EXFOR11621.029	Jun 76	. 16 PTS, DSIG	
Diff Elastic	1.4+7		IFU	Expt	Jour UFZ 5 702	Oct 60	Strizhak+ SCINT−COUNTR,GRAPH SIG(ANG	
Diff Elastic	1.5+7		IFU	Expt	Jour ZET 40 725	Mar 61	Strizhak.GRAPHS SIG(ANGL) CFD OPTMDL	+
					Jour JET 13 506	Sep 61	TRANSLATN.*	
Diff Elastic	1.0+6	4.1+6	AGN	Eval	Rept TID−21629	Dec 64	Perkins+ LEGNDR COEF FROM OTHERDAT	
Diff Elastic	3.0+5	1.5+6	ANL	Expt	Jour ZP 183 323	Mar 65	Devilliers+TOF.TBL.CFD OPT MDL.GRPHS	+
					Jour PL 11 331	Aug 64	Vonach+EXPT CFD OPT MDL AT 800KEV.	
					Rept EANDC(US)−62	Jun 64	Smith+TOF,TBL.50KEV STEPS,20KEV RSLN	
	3.0+5	1.5+6			Data EXFOR12240.007	Jun 76	. 125 LEG COEFS AT 25 ES	
	8.0+5		IFU	Theo	Jour UFZ 10 6 586	Jun 65	Korzh.OPTMDL GRAPH SIG,CFD XPT	
					Jour IZV 29 862	May 65	.	
Diff Elastic	2.0+6		FEI	Expt	Rept EANDC−50 200	Jul 65	Kazakova+ EXPT,CURVE CFD OPTMODEL	+
					Prog ICD−2 112	Jul 65	.CURVE	
					Prog INDSWG−101E		65 .ENGLISH TRANSL OF ICD−2 112 7/65	
Diff Elastic	8.0+5		IFU	Theo	Conf 65Antwerp § 193	Jul 65	Pasechnic+. OPT.MOD.PARAMETERS	
Diff Elastic	1.0+6		LAS	Theo	Prog WASH−1064 84	Oct 65	Rosen+, OPTMDL+ CPD ELST CFD WIS XPT	
Diff Elastic	3.0+5	8.0+5	IFU	ExTh	Jour AE 20 8	Jan 66	Korzh+ SUMMARY OF SEVERAL YRS WORK	+
	3.0+5			Expt	Rept BNL−TR−232	Sep 68	− + ANGDIS(30−140DEG),GRPH+TBL	
	5.0+5	8.0+5			Jour AE 16 207	Mar 64	Pasechnik+ SPH,30−140 DEGREES	
	3.0+5	8.0+5		ExTh	Jour UFZ 8 389		63 .650KEV SEE P1323.300KEV SEE P1389	
	6.5+5			Expt	Rept BNL−TR−242	Sep 68	Korzh+ ANGDIST(30−140DEG),GRAPH+TABL	
	3.0+5	8.0+5		ExTh	Jour SJA 20 8	Jul 66	.ENGLISH TRANSL OF AE 20 8 1/66	
	5.0+5	8.0+5		Expt	Jour JNE 19 278		65 . ENGL OF AE 16 207	
					Jour SJA 16 246	Sep 64	. ENGL OF AE 16 207	
Diff Elastic	3.2+6		BCM	Expt	Jour NP 89 154	Dec 66	Becker+ 12 ANGLES GRAPH CFD OPTMDL	+
	3.2+6				Data EXFOR11511.034	Jun 76	. 12 PTS, DSIG	
Diff Elastic	4.4+6	5.5+6	WIS	ExTh	Jour NP/A 95 193	Mar 67	Mahajan.POLARIZATION OPTMDL ANALYSIS	
					Abst DA/B 28 1093	Sep 67	.SEE ALSO	
Diff Elastic	1.0+6	1.4+7	AI	Eval	Rept NAA−SR−11980	Apr 67	Campbell+ LEG COEFS TBL+CURVS C−MSYS	
Diff Elastic	1.5+6		IFU	Comp	Jour YF 7 277	Feb 68	Korzh+ GRPH SIG(ANG),OPTMOD PARS−FIT	
					Jour SNP 7 2 190	Aug 68	TRANSLATN.*	
Diff Elastic	2.0+6	3.2+6	SCU	Theo	Rept ICD−6 236		69 Averyanov+CALC ANGDIST CFD EXPT,GRPH	

80 Mercury

Quantity	Energy (ev) Min	Max	Lab	Type	Documentation Ref Vol Page	Date	Author, Comments	Data
Diff Elastic	8.8+5		ANL	Expt Rept	ANL-7935	Jun 72	Cox+. CFD OPTMOD,HAUSER-FESHBACH	+
	8.8+5			Data	EXFOR10332.031	Jun 74	8 PTS	
Diff Elastic	8.0+5		SCU	Comp Rept	YK- 15 153	Aug 73	Aver'Janov+ H-F,OPTMOD,DIFFSIG,GRAPH	
Diff Elastic	1.5+7		ALB	Expt Jour	NP/A 212 147	Sep 73	Benenson+ 1.5-10DEG SCAT CFD OPTMODL	+
	1.5+7			Data	EXFOR10370.004	May 74	11 PTS	
Polarization	3.8+5	9.8+5	WIS	ExTh Jour	NP 6 177	Mar 58	Clement+. POLARIZATION. CFD OPT MDL	
				Expt Rept	AECU-3628	57	- +.LI7(P,N) SOURCE. 3ANGLES.	
Polarization	1.5+6		DKE	Expt Rept	TID-19051	62	Olness+ TOF 51.5DEG POLARIZ MEASD	
Polarization	2.0+5	1.7+6	AE	Expt Prog	EANDC(OR)59L	Dec 66	Aspelund. POLARISED NEUTRONS.	
Polarization	8.8+5		ANL	Expt Rept	ANL-7935	Jun 72	Cox+. CFD OPTMOD,HAUSER-FESHBACH	+
	8.8+5			Data	EXFOR10332.065	Jun 74	8 PTS	
Potntal Scat	1.2+2	3.0+2	ANL	Expt Jour	PR 76 100	Jul 49	Hibdon+TRNS.10PC RSLN.CO,MN SCT DET.	+
	1.2+2	3.0+2		Data	EXFOR11261.034	Jun 76	. 2 PTS, SIG	
Potntal Scat		6.5+6	DKE	ExTh Jour	PL 13 70	Nov 64	Seth+0,1PHASE FRM SIG TOT AV 3-650KV	
Potntal Scat	3.0+3	6.5+5	DKE	Expt Jour	AP 84 165	May 74	Pineo+TRNS.S WAVE SCT LENGTH.TBL.CFD	
				Abst	DA/B 31 6821	May 71	.THESIS ABST.	
				Diss	PINEO	70	.TBL.GRPHS.CFD TO 3 COLLECTIVE MDLS.	
Tot Inelastc	2.9+5	1.0+6	CCP	Expt Jour	ZET 30 1017	Jun 56	Poze.SIG AT 3ES GIVEN,AV E OF SCT NS	
	3.0+5	1.0+6		Jour	ADP 20 3	Jul 57	Pose+,MEASURED AT 3 ENERGIES,TBL	
	2.9+5	1.0+6		Jour	JET 3 745	Dec 56	TRANSLATN.*	
Tot Inelastc	2.5+6		IFU	Expt Jour	JET 4 769	Jun 57	.ENGLISH OF ZET 31 907	
				Jour	ZET 31 907	Nov 56	Strizhak. SPHERE METHOD,TABLE	
Tot Inelastc	1.4+7		LRL	Expt Conf	58Paris § NS609	Jul 58	Mcgregor.FROM SNE 9AND14MEV CUTOFF	+
	1.4+7			Data	EXFOR11205.022	Jun 76	. 1 PT, SIG	
Tot Inelastc	Fiss		KUR	Revw Conf	60Vienna 159	Oct 60	Bondarenko+.TABLE,EXPT DESCRIBED	
Tot Inelastc	4.0+5	1.0+6	CCP	Expt Jour	AE 14 400	Apr 63	SPH 60KEVRSLN 4ES+SPECTRA GLAZKOV	+
Tot Inelastc	8.0+5	4.0+6	IFU	Expt Prog	INDSWG-126 22	66	Pasechnik. AT 5 ES, TBP IN AE	
	2.5+6	1.4+7		Conf	55Geneva 2 3	Aug 55	- . INTEGR SIGMA,3ES,TABLE	
Tot Inelastc	1.4+7		TUD	Expt Prog	ZFK-262 39	Sep 73	Goebel+ INTEGRATED DIFFSIG,TB DONE	
Diff Inelast	1.4+7		CCP	Expt Jour	AE 3 540	Dec 57	Zamyatnin+.P RECOIL, T=0.6+-0.05 MEV	
				Jour	JNE 9 41	Jun 59	TRANSLATN.*	
				Jour	SJA 3 1427	57	TRANSLATN.*	
Diff Inelast	4.1+6		TNC	Expt Rept	WADD-TR-60-217	Apr 60	Vincent.TOF ISOTROPIC 20-135DEG	+
	4.1+6			Data	EXFOR11621.031	Jun 76	. 1 PT, SIG	
	4.1+6			Data	EXFOR11621.	Jun 76	. 22 PTS, DSIG	
Diff Inelast	6.0+6		DKE	Expt Rept	AD- 299005	62	Seth+,NUCL TEMP+FERMI LVL DENS COEFF	
Diff Inelast	4.0+5	1.0+6	CCP	Expt Jour	AE 14 400	Apr 63	SPH 60KEVRSLN 4ES+SPECTRA GLAZKOV	
Diff Inelast	1.4+7		BAS	Expt Jour	PL 5 202	Jul 63	Huber+ GRAPH OF INELASTIC N SPECTRUM	
				Jour	HPA 34 520	Aug 61	Niklaus+.NUC.TEMP.0.87MEV	
				Jour	HPA 36 1059	Dec 59	Huber+.T=0.98MEV	
Diff Inelast	4.0+6	6.5+6	DKE	Expt Jour	NP 60 17	Nov 64	Buccino+N SPEC MEASURED 4ES+NUC TEMP	
				Abst	DA 24 4251	Apr 64	Hollandsworth.TOF.EN SPEC.NUCL T.	
Diff Inelast	3.0+5	1.5+6	ANL	Expt Jour	ZP 183 323	Mar 65	Devilliers+.EXCITAT CURVS 6 LEVELS	+
	5.5+5	1.5+6		Data	EXFOR11240.	Jun 76	. 45 PTS, SIG	
Diff Inelast	3.0+5	8.0+5	IFU	Expt Prog	INDSWG-126 22	66	Pasechnik. AT 3 ES, TBP IN AE	
Diff Inelast	7.5+6	8.0+6	AE	Expt Prog	EANDC(OR)44L	Mar 66	Bergqvist+ TBC.VDG TOF	
Diff Inelast	1.4+7		FEI	Expt Jour	YF 4 1154	Dec 66	Sal'Nikow+ SPEC OF SECNDARY NS,CURVE	+
				Rept	FEI-39	Jan 66	Sal'Nikov+TOF SPECT,RING GEOM,E-SPEC	
				Prog	YFI-2 11	66	.ABSTRACT	
				Rept	FEI-30	Dec 65	.SAME CURVE,SIMILAR TEXT AS YF 4	
				Jour	SNP 4 831	Jun 67	.ENGLISH TRANSL OF YF 4 1154 12/66	
				Prog	INDSWG-126E 10	66	.ABSTRACT.ENGLISH TRANSL OF YFI-2	
	1.4+7			Data	EXFOR40134.016	Feb 73	N-SPECTRUM AT 92 DEG, 53EN'	
Diff Inelast	1.4+7		KGU	Theo Jour	UFZ 14 342	Feb 69	Strizhak+ ANGDIST,OPTMOD FIT,GRAPH	
Diff Inelast	1.4+7		KFI	Theo Rept	KFKI-72-17	Feb 72	Kluge+ CALC N-SPEC INEL+N2N,TBL,GRPH	
Diff Inelast	1.4+7		TUD	Expt Prog	ZFK-262 39	Sep 73	Goebel+ DOUBLEDIFFSIG,IN PROGRESS	
Diff Inelast	1.4+7		KYU	Expt Jour	NST 11 523	Dec 74	Akiyoshi+.TOF,E-SPECTRUM AT 100 DEG	
Thermal Scat	1.0-4	1.0+3	MUN	Revw Jour	EEN 80 1	77	Koester. SCAT LENGTH,FREE+INCOH SIG	
Scattering	Maxwl		NYU	Expt Jour	PR 48 653	Oct 35	Mitchell+ RA-BE/PARAF NS.VAL REL ABS	
Scattering	Maxwl		NYU	Expt Jour	PR 50 133	Jul 36	Mitchell+ RA-BE+PARAFF NS. FILTERED.	
Scattering	Maxwl		JAP	Expt Jour	SCP 36 153	Jul 39	Kimura.SIG=12.0 PM 1B	
Scattering	Slow		JAP	Expt Jour	JPJO 22 391	May 40	Kimura.RN+BE.SIG=12 TO 28 B	
Scattering	Slow		JAP	Expt Jour	JPJO 25 481	Jul 43	Kimura.SIG + CURVE GIVN	
Scattering	Fast		FEI	Expt Jour	AE 18 409	Apr 65	Gusejnov+ ANGL DIST,TH(N,F)DETECTOR	
				Jour	JNE 20 700	Aug 66	. ENGL OF AE 18 409	
				Jour	SJA 18 526	Apr 65	. ENGL OF AE 18 409	
				Jour	EAF 18 4 134	Apr 65	. FRENCH OF AE 18 409	

80 Mercury

Quantity	Energy (ev) Min	Max	Lab	Type	Documentation Ref Vol Page	Date	Author, Comments	Data
Nonelastic	1.0+6		WIS	Expt	Jour PR 93 1062	Mar 54	Walt+	+
	1.0+6			Data	EXFOR11637.072	Jun 76	. 1 PT, SIG	
Nonelastic	1.4+7		CCP	Expt	Jour AE 1 4 155	Sep 56	Flerov+.SPHERE TRANSM, 2650+ − 40MB	+
					Jour JNE 4 529	Apr 57	TRANSLATN.*	
					Jour SJA 1 4 617	56	TRANSLATN.*	
Nonelastic	1.4+7		IFU	Expt	Jour AE 2 68	Jan 57	Strizhak.SPHERE TRANSMISS 2.8 + − .3 B	+
					Jour JNE 5 253	Nov 57	TRANSLATN.*	
					Jour SJA 2 72	57	TRANSLATN.*	
Nonelastic	1.4+7		LRL	Expt	Jour PR 108 726	Nov 57	Macgregor+,SPH TRNS CFD OPTMDL+XPTS	+
					Conf 58Geneva 14 109	Sep 58	Ball+.PPR1881,SPHERE TRANSM − METHOD	
	1.4+7			Data	EXFOR11226.022	Jun 76	. 1 PT, SIG	
Nonelastic	1.4+7		CCP	Expt	Jour AE 5 522	Nov 58	Lebedev+ SPH GEOM,TR DET, 2.46+ − .1B	+
					Jour JNEA 11 39	59	TRANSLATN.*	
					Jour SJA 5 1431	58	TRANSLATN.*	
Nonelastic	4.1+6		TNC	Expt	Rept WADD−TR−60−217	Apr 60	Vincent+	+
	4.1+6			Data	EXFOR11621.027	Jun 76	. 1 PT, SIG	
Nonelastic	8.0+5	4.1+6	IFU	ExTh	Jour AE 20 8	Jan 66	Korzh+ SUMMARY OF SEVERAL YRS WORK	+
					Jour AE 16 207	64	.	
					Jour UFZ 8 389	63	.	
					Jour SJA 20 8	Jul 66	.ENGLISH TRANSL OF AE 20 8 1/66	
Absorption	Slow		OSA	Expt	Jour JMJ 19 799	37	Aoki.SIG MEASURED	
					Jour JPJO 18 188	36	Kikuchi+.SIG AND G−ENERGY DETERMIN	
Absorption	+7		BRK	Expt	Jour PR 53 795	May 38	Grahame+ RA−BE,TRANS,CU+PB(NNG)DETS	
Absorption	Maxwl		JAP	Expt	Jour SCP 36 153	Jul 39	Kimura.SIG=5 B	
Absorption	Maxwl	+2	JAP	Expt	Jour JPJO 24 569	42	Kimura.SIG CURVE GIVN	
Absorption	Slow		JAP	Expt	Jour JPJO 25 481	Jul 43	Kimura.SIG + CURVE GIVN	
Absorption	Maxwl	1.4+7	AUS	Expt	Jour APA 3 352	Mar 50	Lintner. RA−BE SOURCE	
					Jour OAWS 158 135	Nov 49	− .	
Absorption	Maxwl		FAR	Expt	Rept CEA− 137	Mar 52	Ailloud+.PILE OSCILLATOR 354BARNS	+
	Pile				Jour JPR 13 171	Mar 52	− +.PILE OSC.CFD OTHER EXPTS	
	2.5−2				Jour CR 232 2089	Jun 51	Grimeland+. PILE OSC. REL TO BORON.	
					Rept CEA−81	Jun 51	− + PILE OSC.	
Absorption	2.5+4	8.3+5	FEI	Expt	Jour ZET 34 574	Mar 58	Belanova. VALUES GIVEN AT 3ES	
	2.4+4	8.3+5			Jour SJA 8 462	Jul 61	.TRANSLATN.*GERMAN KE4 147 2/61	
					Jour AE 8 549	Jun 60	Belanova.VAL FOR 3ES,SPHERE TRNSMISS	
	2.5+4	8.3+5			Jour JET 7 397	Sep 58	TRANSLATN.*	
Absorption	2.5+4		KUR	Expt	Conf 58Geneva 15 50	Sep 58	Leipunskij+.PPR2219,VAL GVN,ACTIVATN	
Absorption	2.4+4		FEI	Expt	Jour AE 19 3	Jul 65	Belanova+ 2 METHODS,ABSOL EXPT,TABLE	+
					Jour JNE 20 411	66	.ENGLISH TRANSL OF AE 19 3 7/65	
					Jour EAF 19 1 11	65	. FRENCH TRANSL OF AE 19 3 7/65	
					Jour SJA 19 858	65	.ENGLISH TRANSL OF AE 19 3 7/65	
	2.4+4			Data	EXFOR40072.015	Jul 71	SIGMA AT 24 KEV AS PUBLISHED	
Res Int Abs	Pile		FAR	Expt	Jour CR 234 2448	Jun 52	Netter+. PILE OSC. REL B.	
Res Int Abs	5.0−1	1.0+6	CCP	Expt	Conf 55Geneva 5 91	Aug 55	Spivak+.VAL GVN CFD REF,PPR659	
Res Int Abs	None		ORL	Revw	Conf 55Geneva 5 96	Aug 55	Macklin+.TABLE,EXPT CFD THEORY,P833	
Res Int Abs	−		CCP	Expt	Jour AE 3 507	Dec 57	Klimentov+.EPI CD REACTIVITY REL LI	+
					Jour JNE 9 20	Jun 59	TRANSLATN.*	
					Jour SJA 3 1387	57	TRANSLAN.*	
(n,γ)	Maxwl		COL	Expt	Jour PR 50 738	Oct 36	Fink. RATE OF ABSORPTION+SIGMA	
(n,γ)	Slow		JAP	Expt	Jour JPJO 21 594	39	Nonaka.SIG GIVN	
(n,γ)	Maxwl		ANL	Expt	Jour PR 76 531	Aug 49	Kubitscheck+ YIELD CFD SIG.G−M COINC	
(n,γ)	Pile		ANL	Expt	Jour PR 80 342	Nov 50	Harris+.PILE OSC.REL TO BORON.APPROX	+
	Pile			Data	EXFOR11528.047	Jun 76	. 1 PT, SIG	
(n,γ)	Pile		ORL	Expt	Jour PR 82 276	Apr 51	Lyon. ACT TO 46.5D/5.6MIN(HG202/205)	
(n,γ)	Maxwl		ORL	Expt	Jour PR 83 643	Aug 51	Pomerance. OSC REL AU	
	Maxwl			Data	EXFOR11047.060	Jun 76	. 1 PT, SIG	
(n,γ)	2.0+5		KUR	Expt	Conf 58Geneva 15 50	Sep 58	Leipunskij+.PPR2219,VAL GVN,ACTIVATN	
(n,γ)	5.0+3	5.8+3	SAC	Expt	Jour CR 249 413	Jul 59	Corge+ 3 RESONANCES	+
(n,γ)	2.4+4		ORL	Expt	Jour NP 20 202	Oct 60	Schmitt.SHELL TRANSMISS.380+ − 100MB	+
	2.4+4			Data	EXFOR11778.015	Jun 76	. 1 PT, SIG	
(n,γ)	Pile		CRC	Eval	Rept CRRP−960	Nov 60	Westcott.G,S FACTORS EFFECTIVE CAPT.	
(n,γ)	2.5−2		ANL	Expt	Jour NSE 9 132	Feb 61	Meadows+.PULSED NEUTS.SIG=374+ − 5B	+
	2.5−2			Data	EXFOR11028.025	Jun 76	. 1 PT, SIG	
(n,γ)	3.0+4	6.5+4	ORL	Expt	Jour PR 122 182	Apr 61	Gibbons+ 295, 103 MB	+
					Conf 61Vienna 1 95	Aug 61	Neiler.PPR73,TABLE FOR SOME ES,GRAPH	
	3.0+4	6.5+4			Data	EXFOR11329.069	Jun 76	. 2 PTS, SIG

80 Mercury

Quantity	Energy (ev) Min	Max	Lab	Type	Documentation Ref Vol Page	Date	Author, Comments	Data
(n,γ)	3.4+4	3.0+5	FOA Expt	Jour	AF 23 425	Mar 63	Bergqvist.VDG TOF NAI SCINT REL AG	+
	3.5+4	3.0+5		Data	EXFOR20024.006	Sep 71	5PTS.SIG.	
(n,γ)	2.3+4	8.0+5	CJD Comp	Rept	INDSWG – 64 43	64	. GRAPH VARIOUS EXPERIMENTS	
(n,γ)	5.0+3	9.0+9	ORL Theo	Jour	RMP 37 166	Jan 65	Macklin+.CALC FOR KT=5TO90KEV	
(n,γ)	1.5+1	4.2+2	SAC Expt	Jour	NP/A 135 241	Oct 69	Alves+ LINAC GE(LI)+TO 4 E(G) INTERV	
(n,γ)	3.0+4		AUA Theo	Rept	AAEC/E – 211	Nov 70	Musgrove. SIGMA GIVEN AND CFD OTHER	
(n,γ)	1.0+6	1.0+7	CRC Revw	Conf	74Petten 119	Sep 74	Bartholomew+ PHOTON STRF GRPH	
Spect (n,γ)	Maxwl		JAP Expt	Jour	JPJO 22 551	Jul 40	Nonaka.0.82 G – QUANTA REL TO CD(N,G)	
Spect (n,γ)	Maxwl		ANL Expt	Jour	PR 76 531	Aug 49	Kubitscheck+ MAX E.G – M COINC+ABSORBR	
Spect (n,γ)	Maxwl		ANL Expt	Jour	PR 80 415	Nov 50	Hamermesh.FOTOPLATE,GAMMAS ABVE 3MEV	
	None			Prog	ANL – 4437 48	Apr 50	– .CURVE 2.8 TO 10.0MEV GAMS	
Spect (n,γ)	Maxwl		CRC Expt	Jour	CJP 31 1051	Nov 53	Kinsey+ PAIR SPECT,LINE WIDTH=100KEV	
Spect (n,γ)	Maxwl		CCP Expt	Conf	55Moscow 270	Jul 55	Adjasevich+. CURVES AND DISCUSSION	
				Rept	AEC – TR – 2435	55	. PAGE 195,ENGL OF 55MOSCOW 270	
Spect (n,γ)	Maxwl		CCP		Rept	AEC – TR – 2435PT1	56	.USSR PAGE 199
Spect (n,γ)	Maxwl		CCP		Rept	AEC – 5554	Aug 56	.COINC SC NEW ON AEC TR2435 USSR
Spect (n,γ)	2.3+1	3.1+2	HAR Expt	Jour	PR 107 1333	Sep 57	Landon+,CS PHS 2.4TO8MEV GS 34EV RES	
Spect (n,γ)	Maxwl		GEA Eval	Rept	DC – 58 – 1 – 30	Jan 58	Deloume. BY APPROXIMATION CURV+TABLE	
Spect (n,γ)	Maxwl		HAR Expt	Jour	NP 13 525	Nov 59	Bird+SPECTRA+GAMMA INTENSITY	
Spect (n,γ)	3.0+5		TNC Expt	Prog	TID – 20657 40	62	Nellis+.PRELIMINARY.COUNTS/CHANNEL.	
Spect (n,γ)	Maxwl		ARF Expt	Prog	ARF – 1193 – 17	Dec 62	Greenwood.NAI(TL) SPEC 12GAMMAS	
				Prog	ARF – 1193 – 12	Jul 62	– +,CRYST SPEC,LOW – E GAMMAS	
Spect (n,γ)	Maxwl	3.0+5	FOA ExTh	Jour	NP 39 353	Dec 62	Bergqvist+.5 ES.GRAPH. CFD STAT THEO	
				Conf	61Saclay	61	– + SUPERSEDED	
Spect (n,γ)	None		UJV Expt	Rept	UJV – 1088	64	Skrivanek+ FAST CHOPPER.TOF.NDG	
Spect (n,γ)	+3		AUA Expt	Jour	NSP 3 64	Oct 67	Allen.CURVE,PRELIM RESULTS,TBC	
Spect (n,γ)	2.5 – 2		MIT Comp	Rept	MITNE – 85	Jan 69	Rasmussen+TBL G INT.=AFCRL – 69 – 0071	
Spect (n,γ)	Pile		ANL Expt	Prog	WASH – 1127 10	Apr 69	Bollinger+ LVL STRUCTRE ONLY,TBC,NDG	
Spect (n,γ)	Maxwl		SAC Expt	Jour	NP/A 135 241	Oct 69	Alves+ LINAC GE(LI) 4368 – 5146KEV GAM	
				Rept	CEA – R – 3602	Jul 69	– . THESIS	
Spect (n,γ)	2.0+3		MTR Expt	Prog	NCSAC – 31 76	May 70	Greenwood+,ANAL TO BE COMPL,NO DATA	
Spect (n,γ)	Maxwl		ITE Revw	Jour	AE 29 187	Sep 70	Sukhoruchkin. GAM – SPEC,DOORWAY STATE	
				Jour	SJA 29 896	Sep 70	. ENGL OF AE 29 187	
Spect (n,γ)	7.0+5	2.6+6	CRC Expt	Conf	72Budapest 262	Aug 72	Lone+ G – RAY INTENSITIES ,NDG	
				Prog	AECL – 4147 48	Feb 72	Earle+. 3ES NO DATA GIVEN.	
Spect (n,γ)	1.4+7		JYV Expt	Jour	ZP 254 98	Aug 72	Helppi+DECAY OF AU .GAM ES GIVN	
Spect (n,γ)	1.4+7		SF Expt	Jour	ZP 254 98	Aug 72	Helppi+,DECAY OF AU – 121,GAM – ES GIVN	
Spect (n,γ)	Pile		MUN Expt	Jour	ZP 258 315	Mar 73	Henkelmann. E + INT OF GS GIVEN	+
	2.5 – 2			Data	EXFOR20606.019	Jun 76	2PTS.	
Inelastic γ	Fast		BRK Expt	Jour	PR 52 408	Sep 37	Seaborg+ INELASTIC SCAT SHOWN.SIG(G)	
Inelastic γ	5.8+6	7.5+6	FOA Expt	Jour	NP 80 198	May 66	Bergqvist+CFD SPEC IN CAPT.AT 0.1MEV	
				Conf	65Antwerp 505	Jul 65	– + PPR28.ABST.NDG.	
Nonelastic γ	Slow		OSA Expt	Jour	JMJ 19 295	37	Wakatsuki.BE+RA,3.8B	
Nonelastic γ	2.4+6		OSA Expt	Jour	JMJ 21 75	39	Kikuchi+.D – P LI – D N,SIG GIVN	
	2.1+6	2.8+6		Jour	JMJ 21 232	39	Aoki.SIG GIVN	
	2.4+6			Jour	SCP 34 865	Aug 38	Kikuchi+ D+D,G – M.SIG=4.1B	
		2.4+6		Jour	JMJ 19 369	37	Aoki.D+D NEUTRON.RELATIV SIG GIVN	
	Slow			Jour	JPJO 18 115	36	Kikuchi+.REL SIG GIVN FOR G – EMISSION	
				Jour	JMJ 17 369	35	– +.GAMMAS DETECT	
Nonelastic γ	3.2+6		NRL Expt	Jour	PR 96 386	Oct 54	Scherrer+ C – W+CRYST SPEC 5 PEAKS	
(n,2n)	5.0+6	1.4+7	AUS Expt	Jour	APA 3 352	Mar 50	Lintner. RA – BE SOURCE	
				Jour	OAWS 158 135	Nov 49	– .	
(n,2n)	1.4+7		CCP Expt	Jour	AE 5 522	Nov 58	Lebedev+ N2N+2(N3N) – REM=2.02+ – 0.2B	
(n,2n)	1.4+7		KFI Theo	Rept	KFKI – 72 – 17	Feb 72	Kluge+ CALC N – SPEC INEL+N2N,TBL,GRPH	
(n,2n)	1.5+7		DEB Eval	Rept	REA 11 1 153	Mar 73	Boedy+ RECOMM.VALUE FROM N – Z SYSTEM.	
n Emission	1.4+7		CCP Expt	Jour	AE 5 522	Nov 58	Lebedev+ SPH GEOM,N COUNT,ETA GIVEN	
				Jour	JNEA 11 39	59	.TRANSLATION	
				Jour	SJA 5 1431	58	.ENGL OF AE 5 522 NOV58	
n Emission	1.5+7		TUD Expt	Jour	KE 19 241	Aug 76	Hermsdorf+ ABSOL DOUBDIF,FIG.TOT,TBL	+
				Rept	ZFK – 277(U)	Aug 75	– + DIFFSIG AT 5ANGS,TBL+GRPH	
				Conf	ZFK – 271 94	Nov 73	Goebel+ N – EMISSION SPEC,TOF.SUMMARY	
	1.5+7			Data	EXFOR30397.030	May 77	49 PTS. ANGLE INT.N – EMISS.SPECT.	
	1.5+7			Data	EXFOR30275.	Apr 74	DOUBDIF(5ANG,474PTS)+PARTIAL ANGDIS	
(n,p)	1.0+7		HRV Expt	Jour	PR 60 473	Oct 41	Sherr+ SEVERAL AU ACTIVITIES SHOWN	
(n,α)	1.0+7		HRV Expt	Jour	PR 60 473	Oct 41	Sherr+ SEVERAL PT ACTIVITIES SHOWN	
Fission	2.5+7	8.4+7	BRK Expt	Jour	PR 73 1135	May 48	Kelly+ RELATIVE TO THORIUM.	
Fission	1.4+7		LAS Expt	Jour	PR 75 919	Mar 49	Phillips+ UPPER LIM REL U238.PHOTOPL	

80 Mercury

Quantity	Energy (ev) Min	Max	Lab	Type	Documentation Ref Vol Page	Author, Comments Date	Data
Reson Params	-.1+0		JAP	Expt Jour	PR 60 688	Nov 41 Kimura. NEG E RES,FITS SCAT.	
Reson Params	-.2+1		ANL	Expt Jour	PR 82 560	May 51 Hibdon+ RESONANCE NS	+
	-.2+1			Data	EXFOR12202.004	Jun 76 . 1 RES, WT, WN, WG	
Reson Params	2.3+1	3.5+2	HAR	Expt Jour	PPSA 65 992	Dec 52 Hodgson+ FROM TOTAL,TOF MEASUREMENT.	
Reson Params	1.3+2	2.1+2	ANL	Expt Jour	PR 102 228	Apr 56 Palmer+	+
	1.3+2	2.1+2		Data	EXFOR11804.019	Jun 76 . 2 RES, E0	
Reson Params	3.3+1	2.1+2	HAR	Expt Jour	NP 13 525	Nov 59 Bird+E0 SIG0 WT WN WG J ISOT ASSIGNE	
Reson Params	2.3+1	7.8+3	ANL	Expt Jour	NP 21 66	Nov 60 Carpenter+EO WN WG J ISOT ASSIGNED	+
	7.1+1	7.8+3		Conf	60Vienna 135	Oct 60 Cote+.RESONANCES DER FROM TRSM-CURVE	
	2.7+2	6.5+2		Data	EXFOR12236.009	Jun 76 . 4 RES, E0, WT, WN, PCS	
Reson Params	-		FOA	Theo Jour	NP 39 353	Dec 62 Bergqvist+.AVERAGE GAMMA WIDTH.	
Reson Params	3.4+1	1.8+2	RPI	Expt Prog	WASH-1068 184	Mar 66 Rae+,LI-GE DET+TOF,4 RES ES,NDG,TBC	
Reson Params	4.3+1	3.1+2	BNL	Expt Prog	WASH-1026 11	Oct 59 Zimmerman+ PART RAD WIDTHS	+
	4.3+1	3.1+2		Data	EXFOR12494.005	Jun 76 . 2 RES, E0, WN0	
Strnth Fnctn	+3		BNL	Expt Jour	PRL 1 461	Dec 58 Hughes. FC 1.1+ -0.2	
Strnth Fnctn	3.0+4	6.5+5	DKE	Expt Jour	AP 46 401	Feb 68 Tabony+ TRANS DERIVES S0, S1, S2	+
				Jour	PL 13 70	Nov 64 .SUPERSEDED	
	5.0+4	1.5+5		Conf	64Paris 2 916	Jul 64 Seth+S0,S1,S2 R PRIME/R	
Strnth Fnctn	3.0+3	6.5+5	DKE	Expt Abst	DA/B 31 6821	May 71 Pineo.S,P,D WAVE.THESIS ABST	
				Diss	PINEO	70 .S0,S1.TBL.GRPHS.CFD CALC,OTH EXPTS.	
Strnth Fnctn	2.7+3		MUN	Expt Conf	71Albany 327	Aug 76 Dilg+TRNS.S0 STF GVN.31 ELEMENT GRPH	
Lvl Density	6.0+6		DKE	Expt Rept	AD- 299005	62 Seth+,NUCL TEMP+FERMI LVL DENS COEFF	
Lvl Density	1.4+7		BAS	Expt Jour	PL 5 202	Jul 63 Huber+TBL OF NUC TEMP AND LVL DENSTY	
				Jour	HPA 36 1059	Dec 63 Plattner+TOF TBL12ELEM.CFD TH	
Lvl Density	1.4+7		FEI	Expt Rept	FEI-30	Dec 65 Anufrienko+.PARAMS FROM NONELASTIC	+

80 Mercury 192

Quantity	Energy (ev) Min	Max	Lab	Type	Documentation Ref Vol Page	Author, Comments Date	Data
Reson Params	-		AUA	Theo Rept	AAEC/E-211	Nov 70 Musgrove. CALCULTD D+GAM WIDTH GIVEN	
Strnth Fnctn	-		AUA	Theo Rept	AAEC/E-211	Nov 70 Musgrove. SMOOTHED S0,S1 AND S2 GIVN	

80 Mercury 193

Quantity	Energy (ev) Min	Max	Lab	Type	Documentation Ref Vol Page	Author, Comments Date	Data
Reson Params	-		AUA	Theo Rept	AAEC/E-211	Nov 70 Musgrove. CALCULTD D+GAM WIDTH GIVEN	
Strnth Fnctn	-		AUA	Theo Rept	AAEC/E-211	Nov 70 Musgrove. SMOOTHED S0,S1 AND S2 GIVN	

80 Mercury 194

Quantity	Energy (ev) Min	Max	Lab	Type	Documentation Ref Vol Page	Author, Comments Date	Data
(n,p)	Maxwl		IFU	Theo Rept	ICD-4 20	67 Dadakina+ PENETR COEFF CALC,TABLE	
Reson Params	-		AUA	Theo Rept	AAEC/E-211	Nov 70 Musgrove. CALCULTD D+GAM WIDTH GIVEN	
Reson Params	None		DUB	Theo Jour	ZEP 14 194	Aug 71 Soloviev.LARGE N-WID G-WID CORREL.NDG	
				Rept	JINR-E4-5880	71 Soloviev.N-GAM-WIDS CORR.SHORT NOTE	
				Jour	JEL 14 129	Aug 71 - . ENGL OF ZEP 14 194.	
Strnth Fnctn	-		AUA	Theo Rept	AAEC/E-211	Nov 70 Musgrove. SMOOTHED S0,S1 AND S2 GIVN	
Lvl Density	-3	+0	IFU	Theo Jour	UFZ 13 700	Apr 68 Pisanko+ LEVEL SPACING CALC,TBL	
				Jour	UPJ 13 498	Oct 68 TRANSLATN.*	

80 Mercury 195

Quantity	Energy (ev) Min	Max	Lab	Type	Documentation Ref Vol Page	Author, Comments Date	Data
Reson Params	-		AUA	Theo Rept	AAEC/E-211	Nov 70 Musgrove. CALCULTD D+GAM WIDTH GIVEN	
Strnth Fnctn	-		AUA	Theo Rept	AAEC/E-211	Nov 70 Musgrove. SMOOTHED S0,S1 AND S2 GIVN	

80 Mercury 196

Quantity	Energy (ev) Min	Max	Lab	Type	Documentation Ref Vol Page	Author, Comments Date	Data
Res Int Abs	5.0-1		GHT	Expt Jour	RCA 8 165	Dec 67 KIM+ ACT. 413B,58.9B ISOM. REL AU	+
	5.0-1			Data	EXFOR20254.	May 74 2PTS.CAPTURE.	

80 Mercury 196

Quantity	Energy (ev) Min	Max	Lab	Type	Documentation Ref Vol Page	Date	Author, Comments	Data
Res Int Abs	5.0−1		GHT	Expt Jour	JRC 20 695	74	Van Der Linden+ BY (N,G).CFD OTH,TBL	+
	5.5−1			Conf	73Paris 2 241	Mar 73	− + ACT,REL THR+GOLD,TBL	
	5.5−1			Data	EXFOR20645.	Jul 76	2PTS.CAPTURE.	
(n,γ)	Pile		ANL	Expt Jour	PR 71 562	Apr 47	Ingraham+FROM ISOT COMPOS IRRAD HG.	
(n,γ)	Maxwl		MUA	Expt Jour	NP 12 261	Jul 59	Sehgal+420+ − 80B ISOMER.880+ − 175B TOT	+
	Maxwl			Data	EXFOR31244.	Jun 78	SIG TO GND AND MS − STATE GVN	
(n,γ)	Maxwl		ANL	ExTh Jour	PR 120 1313	Nov 60	Vandenbosch+ ISOMER RATIO HG197,CFD	+
	Maxwl			Expt Data	EXFOR11994.014	Jun 76	. 1 PT, ISOMER RATIO	
(n,γ)	Maxwl		BNL	Expt Jour	PR 128 761	Oct 62	Sehgal.ACT,RATIO 24 TO 65HR=36+ − 6	+
	Maxwl			Data	EXFOR11994.014	Jun 76	. 1 PT, ISOMER RATIO	
(n,γ)	Maxwl		MUA	ExTh Jour	NP 41 372	Mar 63	Mangal+ (N,G)M SIGMA GVN,TH CFD EXPT	+
	Maxwl			Expt Data	EXFOR31249.	Sep 72	.SIG GVN	
(n,γ)	Maxwl		ANL	Comp Jour	NP 60 241	Nov 64	Bishop+EXP AND TH ISOMER RATIOS CFD	
(n,γ)	Maxwl		IIT	Theo Jour	NP/A 90 665	Jan 67	Sperber. ISOMERIC RATIO CALC	
(n,γ)	Maxwl		GHT	Expt Jour	RCA 8 165	Dec 67	KIM+ TO GS+MS. REL TO AU − 197.TBL	+
	2.5−2			Data	EXFOR20254.	May 74	2PTS.SIGMA.	
(n,γ)	Maxwl		UCS	Expt Jour	NSE 31 545	Mar 68	Tilbury+ ACTIV TO GND AND ISOM	+
				Rept	NYO − 10175	Dec 64	Arino+ACT.TBLS,GRPHS.PRODUCT HL.	
	Maxwl			Data	EXFOR11927.	Jun 76	. 2 PTS, SIG FOR 2 ISOMERS	
(n,γ)	−		IEA	Comp Rept	IEA − INF − 10 6	Aug 68	Atalla. TABLES OF HL,SIG AND GAMM − E	
(n,γ)	3.0+4		AUA	Theo Rept	AAEC/E − 211	Nov 70	Musgrove. SIGMA GIVEN AND CFD OTHER	
(n,γ)	Maxwl		IAE	Revw Rept	STI/DOC/10 − 137	Jul 72	Guinn.P87.SIG TBL FOR ACTIV ANALYSIS	
(n,γ)	3.0+3	5.0+5	ORL	Expt Prog	USNDC − 3 148	Oct 72	Macklin+. ANAL TBC.NO DATA GVN.ORELA	
(n,γ)	2.5−2		BRK	Theo Jour	NP/A 237 3 419	Jan 75	Nardi+ ISOM RATIO,MTE − CARLO,CFD XPT	
Spect (n,γ)	Pile		UPP	Expt Jour	NP 40 329	Jan 63	Marklund+.E DETERM. NO INTENS MEAS.	
Spect (n,γ)	Pile		HAM	Expt Jour	ZP 230 72	Dec 69	Gerdau+ LVL SCH OF HG − 197 CF	
(n,2n)	Fiss		CRC	Eval Rept	CRC − 1003	Dec 60	Roy+,ESTIMATED AVG SIG=6.0MB	
(n,2n)	1.4+7		NDL	Expt Jour	PR 178 1904	Feb 69	Temperley.ACT,1060+ − 70MB TO META	+
	1.4+7			Data	EXFOR12219.	Jun 76	. 2 PTS, SIG FOR 2 ISOMERS	
(n,2n)	1.5+7		DEB	Comp Jour	REA 7 4 93	Dec 69	Csikai+ SIG+HL COMPILTN,N − ACTIV − ANAL	
(n,2n)	1.4+7	1.5+7	JYV	Eval Rept	JU − RR − 3/1970	Jun 70	Leppaemaeki+ TABLE OF EVAL AVG SIG	
(n,2n)	1.4+7	1.5+7	IRK	ExTh Rept	APA 33 285	Jul 71	Winiwarter+ ISOMERIC RATIO	
(n,2n)	1.4+7		GIT	Expt Jour	NP/A 180 157	Jan 72	Hankla+ ACT,GE(LI),MIXED POWDER.G,M.	+
				Abst	DA/B 32 293	Nov 71	− . ACT METHOD, CFD THEORY.	
	1.4+7			Data	EXFOR10244.	Jun 74	2PTS,GND AND META.	
(n,2n)	1.5+7		DEB	Eval Jour	REA 11 1 153	Mar 73	Boedy. COMPILATION+RECOMM.VALUE,TBL	
(n,2n)	1.5+7		KFI	Theo Rept	KFKI − 73 − 68	Dec 73	Jeki.NEW FIT,CALC SIG CFD OTHERS,TBL	
(n,2n)	1.5+7		TAT	Theo Rept	JP/A 7 1457	Aug 74	Kondaiah. CALC ON STAT MODEL	
(n,p)	Fiss		CRC	Eval Rept	CRC − 1003	Dec 60	Roy+,ESTIMATED AVG SIG=0.04MB	
(n,p)	Maxwl		IFU	Theo Rept	ICD − 4 20	67	Dadakina+ PENETR COEFF CALC,TABLE	
(n,α)	Fiss		CRC	Eval Rept	CRC − 1003	Dec 60	Roy+,ESTIMATED AVG SIG=BELO 0.0001MB	
Reson Params	9.4+1		ANL	Expt Jour	NP 21 66	Nov 60	Carpenter+EO WN WG J ISOT ASSIGNED	+
	9.4+1			Data	EXFOR12236.003	Jun 76	. 1 RES, E0, J, WT, WN, WG, PCS	
Reson Params	−		AUA	Theo Rept	AAEC/E − 211	Nov 70	Musgrove. CALCULTD D+GAM WIDTH GIVEN	
Reson Params	9.4+1		CJD	Eval Rept	YK − 7	71	Zakharova+ SURVEY+SYSTEMATICS,GW,TBL	
				Rept	INDC(CCP) − 27	Nov 72	.ENGLISH TRANSLATION OF YK − 7 /71	
Reson Params	None		DUB	Theo Jour	ZEP 14 194	Aug 71	Solovev.LARGE N − WID G − WID CORREL.NDG	
				Rept	JINR − E4 − 5880	71	Soloviev.N − GAM − WIDS CORR.SHORT NOTE	
				Jour	JEL 14 129	Aug 71	− . ENGL OF ZEP 14 194.	
Strnth Fnctn	−		AUA	Theo Rept	AAEC/E − 211	Nov 70	Musgrove. SMOOTHED S0,S1 AND S2 GIVN	
Lvl Density	+6	+7	FEI	Expt Conf	75Kiev 3 18	May 75	Ignatjuk+ FISS LVL DENS PAR VS EXC − E	

80 Mercury 197

Quantity	Energy (ev) Min	Max	Lab	Type	Documentation Ref Vol Page	Date	Author, Comments	Data
(n,p)	Maxwl		IFU	Theo Rept	ICD − 4 20	67	Dadakina+ PENETR COEFF CALC,TABLE	
Reson Params	−		AUA	Theo Rept	AAEC/E − 211	Nov 70	Musgrove. CALCULTD D+GAM WIDTH GIVEN	
Strnth Fnctn	−		AUA	Theo Rept	AAEC/E − 211	Nov 70	Musgrove. SMOOTHED S0,S1 AND S2 GIVN	
Lvl Density	None		PTN	Expt Jour	PR 81 51	Jan 51	Gugelot. REL LVL DENS VS EXC.T GIVEN	

80 Mercury 198

Quantity	Energy (ev) Min	Max	Lab	Type	Documentation Ref Vol Page	Date	Author, Comments	Data
Potntal Scat		4.2+2	SAC	Expt Jour	NP/A 123 561	Jan 69	Morgenstern+ RADIUS FROM RES ANAL	+
				Rept	CEA − R − 3609	Sep 68	− + (THESIS) RADIUS.	
	0.0+0	4.2+2		Data	EXFOR20687.040	Aug 77	1PNT.RADIUS.	

80 Mercury 198

Quantity	Energy (ev) Min	Max	Lab	Type	Documentation Ref Vol Page	Author, Comments Date	Data
Diff Inelast	Thrsh	Up	LEB Expt	Jour	IZV 37 1714	Aug 73 .SIG OF EXCIT 1-ST LVL	+
				Conf	73Tbilisi 156	Feb 73 Konobeevsky+ ABST,CFD,STAT MODL,NDG	
	4.2+5	7.3+5		Data	EXFOR40215.002	Jun 74 .SIGMA FOR 28 ES GIVEN,1 E-LVL	
Res Int Abs	5.0-1		GHT Expt	Jour	JRC 20 695	74 Van Der Linden+ BY (N,G).CFD OTH,TBL	+
	5.5-1			Conf	73Paris 2 241	Mar 73 - + ACT,REL THR+GOLD,TBL	
	5.5-1			Data	EXFOR20645.059	Jul 76 1PNT.CAPTURE.	
(n,γ)	Maxwl		MUA Expt	Jour	NP 12 261	Jul 59 Sehgal+0.018+ -0.004B METASTABLE	+
	Maxwl			Data	EXFOR31244.013	Jun 78 SIG TO ISOMER	
(n,γ)	Maxwl	+5	FOA Theo	Jour	NP 39 353	Dec 62 Bergqvist+. IN PER CENT OF NAT ELEMT	
(n,γ)	2.5+4		FEI ExTh	Prog	YFI-4 22	May 67 Shorin+.,TBLS GIVEN,TBP YF	
			Theo	Jour	YF 6 769	Oct 67 - + VALUE GIVEN,STATIST THEORY	
				Jour	SNP 6 558	Apr 68 . ENGL OF YF 6 769	
			ExTh	Prog	INDC-187E	67 . ENGL TRANSL OF YFI-4 22	
(n,γ)	-		IEA Comp	Rept	IEA-INF-10 6	Aug 68 Atalla. TABLES OF HL,SIG AND GAMM-E	
(n,γ)	5.0+3	1.0+5	AUA ExTh	Rept	AAEC/E-198	May 69 Musgrove.S+P+D WAVE SIGMAS CALC,TBL	+
(n,γ)	3.0+5		AUA Theo	Rept	AAEC/E-211	Nov 70 Musgrove. SIGMA GIVEN AND CFD OTHER	
(n,γ)	Maxwl		IAE Revw	Rept	STI/DOC/10-137	Jul 72 Guinn.P87.SIG TBL FOR ACTIV ANALYSIS	
(n,γ)	+6		KOS Expt	Jour	AHP 33 363	73 Peto+ HG-199(INL)+HG-198(N,G)HG-199M	+
	+6			Data	EXFOR30265.017	Feb 74 AVERAGE SIG FOR PU-BE NEUTRONS	
(n,γ)	Fiss		KOS Expt	Conf	75Karlsrhe 29	Apr 75 Csikai. CF252.+199(N,N')META.SIG GVN	+
	1.4+6			Data	EXFOR30400.052	Oct 78 1 PNT. HG198(N,G)+HG199(N,N')HG199M	
(n,γ)	0.0+0	2.2+2	CRC Expt	Jour	NP/A 243 413	May 75 Lone+ TOF,FAST CHOPPER,GE-LI	
Spect (n,γ)	Maxwl		BNL Expt	Abst	BAP 3 176	May 58 Bollinger+,TOF LANDON METHOD FOR J	
Spect (n,γ)	2.3+1		ANL Revw	Conf	60Vienna 135	Oct 60 Cote+.GRAPH,EXPT DESCRIBED	
Spect (n,γ)	2.3+1	9.0+1	ITE Expt	Jour	ZET 45 870	Oct 63 Ratynskil.G-SPEC FROM 2 N-RES COMPRD	
				Jour	JET 18 598	Mar 64 TRANSLATN.*	
Spect (n,γ)	2.3+1	9.0+1	SAC Expt	Rept	CEA-R-2810	Jun 65 Huynh+DET=2 NAI(TL)COAXIAL CRYSTALS	
				Rept	CEA-R-3602	Jul 69 Alves. (THESIS)	
				Jour	NIM 36 29	Jul 65 Huynh+ DATA GIVEN.	
Spect (n,γ)	2.3+1	9.0+1	RPI Expt	Jour	PR 155 1301	Mar 67 Rae+,2RES,12LINES 4.4-6.7MEV,+HG204Q	
Spect (n,γ)	2.0+1	5.0+2	HAR Expt	Prog	AERE-PR/NP15	May 69 Thomas+ GE DET GRAPHS TABLE 5 RES	
Spect (n,γ)	0.0+0	2.2+2	CRC Expt	Jour	NP/A 243 413	May 75 Lone+ G-RAYS INT TBL,SPECT,LVL CHEME	
	2.3+1	9.0+1		Prog	AECL-3865 56	Dec 70 - +.2 RESON ES.GAM INTENSITIES GV	
Inelastic γ	4.2+5	7.3+5	LEB Expt	Jour	IZV 37 1714	Aug 73 Konobeevskij+ SIG TO 1ST LEVEL,GRAPH	+
	4.1+5	7.0+5		Jour	BAS 37 8 129	Aug 73 . ENGL OF IZV 37 1714	
	4.2+5	7.3+5		Data	EXFOR40215.002	Jun 74 .SIGMA FOR 28 ES GIVEN,1 E-LVL	
(n,2n)	1.4+7		ANL ExTh	Jour	PR 120 1313	Nov 60 Vandenbosch+ ISOMER RATIO HG197,CFD	+
	1.4+7		Expt	Data	EXFOR12212.002	Jun 76 . 1 PT, ISOMER RATIO	
(n,2n)	Fiss		CRC Eval	Rept	CRC-1003	Dec 60 Roy+,ESTIMATED AVG SIG=9.5MB	
(n,2n)	1.5+7		MUN Expt	Jour	NP/A 118 9	Sep 68 Dilg+ ACTIV.REL AL(N,A)	+
	1.5+7			Data	EXFOR20802.019	Dec 78 1PNT.SIGMA.	
(n,2n)	1.4+7		NDL Expt	Jour	PR 178 1904	Feb 69 Temperley.ACT, 90DMB META,940MB GND	+
	1.4+7			Data	EXFOR12219.	Jun 76 . 2 PTS, FOR 2 ISOMERS	
(n,2n)	1.4+7		DEB Comp	Jour	REA 7 4 93	Dec 69 Csikai+ SIG+HL COMPILTN,N-ACTIV-ANAL	
(n,2n)	1.4+7	1.5+7	CCP Comp	Rept	ICD-6 215	70 Sluchevskaja.SIGS ISOM,SUM (G+M),TBL	
(n,2n)	1.4+7	1.5+7	JYV Eval	Rept	JU-RR-3/1970	Jun 70 Leppaemaeki+ TABLE OF EVAL AVG SIG	
(n,2n)	1.4+7	1.5+7	IRK ExTh	Jour	APA 33 285	Jul 71 Winiwarter+ ISOMERIC RATIO	
(n,2n)	1.4+7		GIT Expt	Jour	NP/A 180 157	Jan 72 Hankla+ ACT,GE(LI),MIXED POWDER.G,M.	+
				Abst	DA/B 32 293	Nov 71 - . ACT METHOD, CFD THEORY.	
	1.4+7			Data	EXFOR10244.	Jun 74 3PTS,TOTAL GND AND META.	
(n,2n)	1.5+7		JUL Expt	Jour	NP/A 185 614	May 72 Qaim. ACT,GE(LI). CFD TH+OTHR.+ISOMR	+
	1.5+7			Data	EXFOR20536.	Apr 76 4PTS.SIGMA.	
(n,2n)	1.5+7		DEB Eval	Rept	REA 11 1 153	Mar 73 Boedy. COMPILATION+RECOMM.VALUE,TBL	
(n,2n)	1.5+7		KFI Theo	Rept	KFKI-73-68	Dec 73 Jeki.NEW FIT,CALC SIG CFD OTHERS,TBL	
	+7			Rept	KFKI-71-8	Feb 71 - . CALCULATED CFD EXPTL SIG VALU	
(n,2n)	1.5+7		TAT Theo	Jour	JP/A 7 1457	Aug 74 Kondaiah. CALC ON STAT MODEL	
(n,p)	Fiss		CRC Eval	Rept	CRC-1003	Dec 60 Roy+,ESTIMATED AVG SIG=0.02MB	
(n,p)	1.4+7		NDL Expt	Jour	PR 178 1904	Feb 69 Temperley.ACT,4.7+ -0.3MB REL FE56 NP	+
	1.4+7			Data	EXFOR12219.006	Jun 76 . 1 PT, SIG	
(n,p)	1.4+7	1.5+7	JYV Eval	Rept	JU-RR-3/1970	Jun 70 Leppaemaeki+ TABLE OF EVAL AVG SIG	
(n,p)	1.4+7		GIT Expt	Jour	NP/A 180 157	Jan 72 Hankla+ ACT,GE(LI),MIXED POWDER.	+
				Abst	DA/B 32 293	Nov 71 - . ACT METHOD, CFD THEORY.	
	1.4+7			Data	EXFOR10244.023	Jun 74 1PT,SIGMA	
(n,p)	1.4+7	1.5+7	KAZ Theo	Rept	YF 18 705	Oct 73 Levkovsky.AVERAGED SIG,CALC,TBL	
				Jour	SNP 18 361	Apr 74 . ENGLISH OF YF 18,705	
(n,α)	Fiss		CRC Eval	Rept	CRC-1003	Dec 60 Roy+,ESTIMATED AVG SIG=BELO 0.0001MB	
Reson Params	2.3+1		BNL Expt	Jour	PR 101 1328	Feb 56 Levin+,23.3EV WG=145+ -20MV,WN=5.8MV	+
	2.3+1			Data	EXFOR12274.009	Jun 76 . 1 RES, E0, WT, WN, WG, PCS	

80 Mercury 198

Quantity	Energy (ev) Min	Max	Lab	Type	Documentation Ref Vol Page	Author, Comments Date	Data
Reson Params	2.3+1	3.1+2	ANL	Expt Jour	PR 102 228	Apr 56 Palmer+	+
	2.3+1	3.1+2		Data	EXFOR11804.020	Jun 76 . 3 RES, E0	
Reson Params	2.3+1		BNL	Expt Priv	ZIMMERMAN	Oct 56 Zimmerman+	+
	2.3+1			Data	EXFOR12494.006	Jun 76 . 1 RES, E0, WN	
Reson Params	9.0+1		HAR	Expt Jour	NP 13 525	Nov 59 Bird+E0 SIG0 WT WN WG TOF+GAMMA SPEC	+
Reson Params	2.3+1	4.2+2	ANL	Expt Jour	NP 21 66	Nov 60 Carpenter+EO WN WG J ISOT ASSIGNED	
	9.0+1	9.7+2		Conf	60Vienna 135	Oct 60 Cote+.RESONS DERIVED FROM TRNSM−CURV	
	3.4+1	4.2+2		Data	EXFOR12236.004	Jun 76 . 5 RES, E0, WT, WN, WG, PCS	
Reson Params	−		FOA	Theo Jour	NP 39 353	Dec 62 Bergqvist+.AVERAGE GAMMA WIDTH.	
Reson Params	2.3+1	9.1+1	BNL	Expt Jour	NP 42 676	Apr 63 Bolotin+.WG,WN GIVEN FOR 2 RESONANCE	+
	2.3+1	9.1+1		Data	EXFOR11922.010	Jun 76 . 2 RES, E0, WT, WN, WG	
Reson Params	2.5+4		FEI	ExTh Prog	YFI−4 22	May 67 Shorin+.,TBLS GIVEN,TBP YF	
				Prog	INDC−187E	67 . ENGL TRANSL OF YFI−4 22	
Reson Params		1.0+6	AUA	Theo Jour	AUJ 20 477	Oct 67 Cook. TBL OF AVG LVL SPACING D,L=0,1	
Reson Params	2.3+1	4.2+2	SAC	Expt Jour	NP/A 132 129	Jul 69 Julien+ TABLE	+
				Rept	CEA−R−3602	Jul 69 Alves. (THESIS).SEE ALSO	
				Rept	CEA−R−3385	Feb 68 Julien.PARS.	
				Conf	66Paris 1 559	Oct 66 Huynh+ ABST.NDG. SEE INDC−156	
				Conf	65Antwerp 525	Jul 65 De Barros+ PPR73.ABST.NDG	
	0.0+0	4.2+2		Data	EXFOR20687.	Aug 77 6PTS.E0,WG,AVG WG,WN,WT,J,G*WN.	
Reson Params	−		AUA	Theo Rept	AAEC/E−211	Nov 70 Musgrove. CALCULTD D+GAM WIDTH GIVEN	
Reson Params	2.3+1	4.2+2	CJD	Eval Rept	YK−7	71 Zakharova+ SURVEY+SYSTEMATICS,GW,TBL	
				Rept	INDC(CCP)−27	Nov 72 .ENGLISH TRANSLATION OF YK−7 /71	
Reson Params	None		DUB	Theo Jour	YF 13 240	Feb 71 Malecki+G−WID,THEO CFD EXPT.TBL,GRPH	
				Jour	SNP 13 133	Aug 71 − + ENGL OF YF 13 240.	
Reson Params	None		DUB	Theo Jour	ZEP 14 194	Aug 71 Solovev.LARGE N−WID G−WID CORREL.NDG	
				Rept	JINR−E4−5880	71 Soloviev.N−GAM−WIDS CORR.SHORT NOTE	
				Jour	JEL 14 129	Aug 71 − . ENGL OF ZEP 14 194.	
Reson Params	None		DUB	Theo Jour	JINR−P4−7499	Oct 73 Soloviev+ CALC D CFD EXPTS,TABLE	
Strnth Fnctn	2.3+1	4.2+2	ANL	Expt Jour	NP 21 66	Nov 60 Carpenter+.7+−80PC	
Strnth Fnctn	2.3+1	4.2+2	SAC	Expt Jour	NP/A 123 561	Jan 69 Morgenstern+ TBL. FROM RES ANALYSIS	+
				Rept	CEA−R−3609	Sep 68 − . (THESIS) S−WAVE.RADIUS	
				Conf	68Wash. 867	Mar 68 − +	
				Rept	CEA−R−3385	Feb 68 Julien. (THESIS).SEE ALSO.S0 VS J.	
				Conf	66Paris 1 183	Oct 66 Morgenstern+ PPR65.ABST.NDG.INDC−156	
	0.0+0	4.2+2		Data	EXFOR20687.041	Aug 77 1PNT.L=0.	
Strnth Fnctn	−		AUA	Theo Rept	AAEC/E−211	Nov 70 Musgrove. SMOOTHED S0,S1 AND S2 GIVN	
Strnth Fnctn	None		AUA	Eval Rept	AAEC/E−277	Mar 73 Musgrove.TBLS EXPTL DATA+BEST VALUES	
Lvl Density	None		AUW	Theo Conf	70Madurai 2 267	Dec 70 Ramamurty+ A−PARAMETER GVN,LANG'S−TH	
Lvl Density	+6	+7	FEI	Expt Conf	75Kiev 3 18	May 75 Ignatjuk+ FISS LVL DENS PAR VS EXC−E	

80 Mercury 199

Quantity	Energy (ev) Min	Max	Lab	Type	Documentation Ref Vol Page	Author, Comments Date	Data
Polarization	Maxwl		KFK	Expt Jour	NP/A 147 150	May 70 Eichler+ POL NS.CIRC POL GS+ASYMMETR	
Potntal Scat		7.0+2	SAC	Expt Jour	NP/A 123 561	Jan 69 Morgenstern+ RADIUS FROM RES ANAL	+
				Rept	CEA−R−3609	Sep 68 − + (THESIS) RADIUS.	
	0.0+0	7.0+2		Data	EXFOR20687.044	Aug 77 1PNT.RADIUS.	
Tot Inelastc	1.4+7	1.5+7	JYV	Eval Rept	JU−RR−3/1970	Jun 70 Leppaemaeki+ TABLE OF EVAL AVG SIG	
Diff Inelast	2.8+6		DEB	Expt Jour	AK 10 112	Jul 68 Bornemisza+ TBL HL+SIGMA FOR HG199M	+
	2.8+6			Data	EXFOR30338.004	Aug 76 TO ISOM. 1 PNT	
Diff Inelast	1.4+7		GIT	Expt Jour	NP/A 180 157	Jan 72 Hankla+ ACT,GE(LI),MIXED POWDER.MST.	+
				Abst	DA/B 32 293	Nov 71 − . ACT METHOD, CFD THEORY.	
	1.4+7			Data	EXFOR10244.014	Jun 74 1PT,SIGMA,META.	
Diff Inelast	+6		KOS	Expt Jour	AHP 33 363	73 Peto+ HG−199(INL)+HG−198(N,G)HG−199M	+
	+6			Data	EXFOR30265.017	Feb 74 AVG SIG FOR PU−BE NEUTRONS	
Diff Inelast	Fiss		KOS	Expt Conf	75Karlsrhe 29	Apr 75 Csikai. CF252.+198(N,G)META. SIG GVN	+
	1.4+7			Data	EXFOR30400.052	Oct 78 1 PNT. HG198(N,G)+HG199(N,N')HG199M	
Diff Inelast	1.4+7		NDL	Expt Jour	PR 178 1904	Feb 69 Temperley+	+
	1.4+7			Data	EXFOR12219.007	Jun 76 . 1 PT, SIG	
(n,γ)	Pile		ANL	Expt Jour	PR 71 562	Apr 47 Ingraham+FROM ISOT COMPOS IRRAD HG.	
(n,γ)	Maxwl	+5	FOA	Theo Jour	NP 39 353	Dec 62 Bergqvist+. IN PER CENT OF NAT ELEMT	
(n,γ)	5.0+3	1.0+5	AUA	ExTh Rept	AAEC/E−198	May 69 Musgrove.S+P+D WAVE SIGMAS CALC,TBL	+
(n,γ)	3.0+4		AUA	Theo Rept	AAEC/E−211	Nov 70 Musgrove. SIGMA GIVEN AND CFD OTHER	
(n,γ)	Maxwl		IAE	Revw Rept	STI/DOC/10−137	Jul 72 Guinn.P87.SIG TBL FOR ACTIV ANALYSIS	
(n,γ)	0.0+0	2.2+2	CRC	Expt Jour	NP/A 243 413	May 75 Lone+ TOF,FAST CHOPPER,GE−LI	
Spect (n,γ)	Pile		ANL	Expt Jour	PR 88 943	Nov 52 Hibdon+ INTERNAL CONVERSION,GAMMA ES	

80 Mercury 199

Quantity	Energy (ev) Min	Max	Lab	Type	Documentation Ref Vol Page	Author, Comments Date	Data
Spect (n,γ)	Maxwl		MOS Expt	Jour	ZET 32 979	May 57 Estulin+ SCINT SPEC 50-500KEV GAMMAS	
				Jour	JET 5 801	Dec 57 TRANSLATN.*	
Spect (n,γ)	Maxwl		MOS Expt	Jour	NP 4 91	Aug 57 Estulin+. INTESITY OF 2 SOFT GAMMAS	
Spect (n,γ)	Maxwl		KUR Expt	Conf	58Geneva 15 138	Sep 58 Groshev+ PPR2029.CURV,COMPTON-SPEC	
Spect (n,γ)	Maxwl		BNL Expt	Prog	WASH-1013 16	Nov 58 Chrien+ INT GND ST TRANS. NDG	
Spect (n,γ)	Maxwl		CSR Expt	Jour	CZJ 9 544	Aug 59 Urbanec+ CURVES,ABSOLUTE INTENSITIES	
Spect (n,γ)	3.4+1	1.8+2	ANL Expt	Jour	PRL 3 376	Oct 59 Bollinger+,PHS FOR 2 RESONANCES	
Spect (n,γ)	3.3+1	1.7+2	HAR Expt	Jour	NP 13 525	Nov 59 Bird+ GAMMA SPEC FROM CAPT EXPT.	
	3.3+1	2.7+2		Conf	58Geneva 14 294	Sep 58 - .CURVE,PPR35,NAI(TL)-DETECTOR	
Spect (n,γ)	Slow		CCP	Jour	NSA 14 1134	May 60 BLG-39 VERVIER,BRUSSELS	
Spect (n,γ)	3.4+1		ANL Revw	Conf	60Vienna 135	Oct 60 Cote+.GRAPH,EXPT DESCRIBED	
Spect (n,γ)	2.0+0	1.8+2	ITE Expt	Jour	ZET 45 870	Oct 63 Ratynskil.G-SPEC FROM 4 N-RES COMPRD	
				Jour	JET 18 598	Mar 64 TRANSLATN.*	
Spect (n,γ)	None		CRC Expt	Jour	NP 50 209	Jan 64 Bartholomew+.GAM.SPEC.E LVLS HG200	
	Maxwl			Jour	CJP 45 1517	Apr 67 - + GE(LI) DET .66-7.7MEV G	
				Conf	65Antwerp § 43	Jul 65 - +HG200 LVLS GS MULTIP	
Spect (n,γ)	5.0-2		BUC Expt	Rept	IFA-NR-21	May 65 Cojocaru+,ANGCORRCOEF,CURVS,TBL,LVLS	
Spect (n,γ)	Maxwl		RIS Expt	Jour	ZP 185 478	May 65 Maier.TBL OF GS TO 1.7MEV,HG200-LVLS	
Spect (n,γ)	Maxwl	1.8+2	RPI Expt	Jour	PR 155 1301	Mar 67 Rae+,THR+3RES,28LINES 4.7-8.0MEV,ABS	
Spect (n,γ)	Maxwl		CRC Expt	Jour	CJP 45 2063	Jun 67 Bartholomew+ POLARIZ CORRELAT MEASTS	
Spect (n,γ)	-2	+2	BNL Expt	Jour	PR 164 1548	Dec 67 Schult+ GE(LI) DET 150-8040KEV GAMS	
Spect (n,γ)	Maxwl		KUR Expt	Jour	YF 7 937	May 68 Groshev+ OTHER XPTAL GAM-INT(GAM-E)	
				Jour	SNP 7 563	Nov 68 . ENGL OF YF 7 937	
Spect (n,γ)	Maxwl		MUNExpt	Jour	ZP 226 13	Jul 69 Loebner+ SPIN-MEAS. OF 1-029KEV-LVL	
Spect (n,γ)	3.3+1	1.8+2	SAC Expt	Rept	CEA-R-3602	Jul 69 Alves. (THESIS)	
				Jour	NIM 36 29	Jul 65 Huynh+ DATA GIVEN.	
				Rept	CEA-R-2810	Jun 65 - + NAI COAXIAL DETECTORS	
Spect (n,γ)	1.0+2	+5	ANL Expt	Conf	69Studsvik 601	Aug 69 Smither+ NO DATA GVN,TB CFD STATMOD	
Spect (n,γ)	Maxwl		SAC Expt	Jour	NP/A 135 241	Oct 69 Alves+LINAC GE(LI) 4674-6458KEV GAM	
				Conf	JINR-D3893 52	May 68 - +LINAC LEVEL SCHEME GIVEN	
				Rept	IEA-96	Jun 65 Abreu.GAMMA-CASCADES,TABLE,GRAPH	
Spect (n,γ)	Maxwl		KFI Expt	Jour	YF 10 907	Nov 69 Kecskemeti+ AVG GAM-MULTIPLICITY,TBL	
				Jour	SNP 10 524	May 70 TRANSLATN.*	
Spect (n,γ)	9.0+5	8.0+6	MUNExpt	Jour	ZN/A 26 405	Mar 71 Nampe+ INT CONVERSION,LVL SCH HG200	
	Maxwl			Theo Conf	69Studsvik 541	Aug 69 Egidy. STATMOD CALC GRPHS CFD EXPT	
				Expt Jour	ZP 218 95	Dec 68 Schult+,CONVERSION-ELECTRON SPEC	
Spect (n,γ)	Pile		KFK Expt	Rept	KFK-1401	Jun 71 Djadali.AVG POLRZ G EXPT,CFD T,SPIN	
	Maxwl			Jour	NP/A 147 150	May 70 Eichler+ POL NS.CIRC POL GS+ASYMMETR	
Spect (n,γ)	1.4+7		JYV Expt	Jour	ZP 255 385	Nov 72 Helppi+,DECAY-SCHEME OF AU-200 GIVEN	
Spect (n,γ)	+0	+2	IFB Theo	Conf	73Pacif.Gr 2 1071	Mar 73 Rudak+ GRAPH STATMOD-CALC CFD G-SPEC	
Spect (n,γ)	Maxwl	1.8+2	BNL Expt	Jour	PR/C 9 366	Jan 74 Breitig+.THR+3 RESON ES.	
	3.3+1	1.7+2		Conf	73Munich 1 236	Aug 73 Casten+ AT 3 RES-ES,FOR LEVEL-SCHEME	
	Maxwl			Conf	73Munich 1 236	Aug 73 - + GE-LI,LVL SCHEME. NO DETAILS	
Spect (n,γ)	Pile		FRK Expt	Jour	ZP 271 97	Dec 74 Schumann+.INT PAIR CONVERSION	
Spect (n,γ)	0.0+0	2.2+2	CRC Expt	Jour	NP/A 243 413	May 75 Lone+ G-RAYS INT TBL,SPECT,LVL CHEME	
Inelastic γ	3.7+5	2.2+6	BAR Expt	Jour	PR 100 1329	Dec 55 Swann+	+
	3.7+5	2.2+6		Data	EXFOR11862.004	Jun 76 . 22 PTS, SIG	
Inelastic γ	2.8+6		REN Expt	Jour	ARI 18 279	May 67 Broadhead+ ACTIV 44MIN ISOMER 95MB	+
	2.8+6			Data	EXFOR11850.012	Jun 76 . 1 PT, SIG	
(n,2n)	Fiss		CRC Eval	Rept	CRC-1003	Dec 60 Roy+,ESTIMATED AVG SIG=18.0MB	
(n,2n)	1.5+7		DEB Eval	Jour	REA 11 1 153	Mar 73 Boedy+ RECOMM.VALUE FROM N-Z SYSTEM.	
(n,2n)	1.5+7		KFI Theo	Rept	KFKI-73-68	Dec 73 Jeki.NEW FIT,CALC SIG CFD OTHERS,TBL	
(n,p)	Fiss		CRC Eval	Rept	CRC-1003	Dec 60 Roy+,ESTIMATED AVG SIG=0.009MB	
(n,p)	Maxwl		IFU Theo	Rept	ICD-4 20	67 Dadakina+ PENETR COEFF CALC,TABLE	
(n,p)	1.4+7		NDL Expt	Jour	PR 178 1904	Feb 69 Temperley.ACT,4.6+-0.6MB REL FE56 NP	+
	1.4+7			Data	EXFOR12219.008	Jun 76 . 1 PT, SIG	
(n,p)	1.4+7	1.5+7	JYV Eval	Rept	JU-RR-3/1970	Jun 70 Leppaemaeki+ TABLE OF EVAL AVG SIG	
(n,p)	1.4+7		GIT Expt	Jour	NP/A 180 157	Jan 72 Hankla+ ACT,GE(LI),MIXED POWDER.	+
				Abst	DA/B 32 293	Nov 71 - . ACT METHOD, CFD THEORY.	
	1.4+7			Data	EXFOR10244.024	Jun 74 1PT,SIGMA	
(n,p)	1.4+7	1.5+7	KAZ Theo	Jour	YF 18 705	Oct 73 Levkovsky.AVERAGED SIG,CALC,TBL	
				Jour	SNP 18 361	Apr 74 . ENGLISH OF YF 18,705	
(n,np)	1.4+7	1.5+7	JYV Eval	Rept	JU-RR-3/1970	Jun 70 Leppaemaeki+ TABLE OF EVAL AVG SIG	
(n,d)	1.4+7		GIT Expt	Jour	NP/A 180 157	Jan 72 Hankla+ ND+NNP+NPN,ACT,GE(LI).	+
				Abst	DA/B 32 293	Nov 71 - . ACT METHOD, CFD THEORY.	
	1.4+7			Data	EXFOR10244.026	Jun 74 1PT,SIGMA,INCLUDES NNP	
(n,α)	Fiss		CRC Eval	Rept	CRC-1003	Dec 60 Roy+,ESTIMATED AVG SIG=BELO 0.0001MB	

80 Mercury 199

Quantity	Energy (ev) Min	Max	Lab	Type	Documentation Ref Vol Page	Author, Comments Date	Data
Reson Params	3.4+1		BNL Expt	Jour	PR 101 1328	Feb 56 Levin+,WG DEPENDS ON J WT=360+ −40MV	+
	3.4+1			Data	EXFOR12274.010	Jun 76 . 1 RES, E0, WT, WN, WG, PCS	
Reson Params	3.4+1	1.8+2	ANL Expt	Jour	PR 102 228	Apr 56 Palmer+	+
	3.4+1	1.8+2		Data	EXFOR11804.021	Jun 76 . 3 RES, E0	
Reson Params	3.3+1		BNL Expt	Priv	ZIMMERMAN	Jan 58 Zimmerman+	+
	3.3+1			Data	EXFOR12494.007	Jun 76 . 1 RES, E0, WN	
Reson Params	3.4+1		BNL Expt	Prog	WASH−1013 16	Nov 58 Chrien+J=1 FROM N GAM SPEC	
Reson Params	3.4+1		CCP	Abst	BAP 4 34	Jan 59 BRUSSL PHS J1 OKS PR110 1472	
Reson Params	−.2+1	1.8+2	ANL Expt	Jour	PR 132 1640	Nov 63 Bollinger+	+
				Conf	61Saclay 199	Jul 61 − +.L FROM 2 STEP.CASCADE.NDG	
				Jour	PRL 3 376	Oct 59 − +,PARTIAL WG FLUCTUATES,J	
	−.2+1	1.8+2		Data	EXFOR12195.004	Jun 76 . 4 RES, J	
Reson Params	3.3+1	1.7+2	HAR Expt	Jour	NP 13 525	Nov 59 Bird+E0 SIG0 WT WN WG J TOF+GAM.SPEC	+
	3.4+1			Rept	ORNL−2309	Aug 57 Landon. AERE JJ FROM NGSPEC	
Reson Params	3.4+1	8.8+2	ANL Expt	Jour	NP 21 66	Nov 60 Carpenter+EO WN WG J ISOT ASSIGNED	+
	1.3+2	1.1+3		Conf	60Vienna 135	Oct 60 Cote+.RESONS DERIVED FROM TRNSM−CURV	
	3.4+1	8.8+2		Data	EXFOR12236.005	Jun 76 . 8 RES, E0, J, WT, WN, WG, PCS	
Reson Params	−		FOA ExTh	Jour	NP 39 353	Dec 62 Bergqvist+.AVERAGE GAMMA WIDTH.EXPTH	
Reson Params	3.4+1	1.3+2	BNL Expt	Jour	NP 42 676	Apr 63 Bolotin+.WG,WN GIVEN FOR 2 RESONANCE	+
	3.4+1	1.3+2		Data	EXFOR11922.011	Jun 76 . 2 RES, E0, WT	
Reson Params	−.2+1		CRC Expt	Jour	NP 50 209	Jan 64 Bartholomew+	+
	−.2+1			Data	EXFOR12501.002	Jun 76 . 1 RES, J	
Reson Params		1.0+6	AUA Theo	Jour	AUJ 20 477	Oct 67 Cook. TBL OF AVG LVL SPACING D,L=0,1	
Reson Params	3.3+1	6.9+2	SAC Expt	Jour	NP/A 132 129	Jul 69 Julien+ TABLE	+
				Rept	CEA−R−3602	Jul 69 Alves. (THESIS).SEE ALSO	
				Conf	68Wash. 867	Mar 68 Morgenstern.WG VS.A,AVERAGE WG GIVEN	
				Conf	68Wash. 783	Mar 68 Alves+ SEE THESIS	
				Rept	CEA−R−3385	Feb 68 Julien. (THESIS).TBL	
				Conf	66Paris 1 559	Oct 66 Huynh+ ABST.NDG. SEE INDC−156	
				Conf	65Antwerp 525	Jul 65 De Barros+ PPR73.ABST.NDG	
	0.0+0	7.0+2		Data	EXFOR20687.	Aug 77 9PTS.E0,WG,AVG WG,WN,WT,J,G*WN.	
Reson Params	−		AUA Theo	Rept	AAEC/E−211	Nov 70 Musgrove. CALCULTD D+GAM WIDTH GIVEN	
Reson Params	−.2+1	8.9+2	CJD Eval	Rept	YK−7	71 Zakharova+ SURVEY+SYSTEMATICS,GW,TBL	
				Rept	INDC(CCP)−27	Nov 72 .ENGLISH TRANSLATION OF YK−7 /71	
Reson Params	None		DUB Theo	Rept	JINR−P4−7499	Oct 73 Soloviev+ CALC D CFD EXPTS,TABLE	
Strnth Fnctn	3.3+1	8.8+2	ANL Expt	Jour	NP 21 66	Nov 60 Carpenter+2.7+−40PC	
Strnth Fnctn	3.3+1	6.9+2	SAC Expt	Jour	NP/A 123 561	Jan 69 Morgenstern+ TBL. FROM RES ANALYSIS	+
				Rept	CEA−R−3609	Sep 68 − . (THESIS) S−WAVE.RADIUS	
				Conf	68Wash. 867	Mar 68 − +	
				Rept	CEA−R−3385	Feb 68 Julien. (THESIS).SEE ALSO.S0 VS J.	
				Conf	66Paris 1 183	Oct 66 Morgenstern+ PPR65.ABST.NDG.INDC−156	
				Conf	65Antwerp 531	Jul 65 − + PPR87.ABST.NDG.	
	0.0+0	7.0+2		Data	EXFOR20687.045	Aug 77 1PNT.L=0.	
Strnth Fnctn	−		AUA Theo	Rept	AAEC/E−211	Nov 70 Musgrove. SMOOTHED S0,S1 AND S2 GIVN	
Strnth Fnctn	None		AUA Eval	Rept	AAEC/E−277	Mar 73 Musgrove.TBLS EXPTL DATA+BEST VALUES	
Lvl Density	+6		MIL Theo	Jour	EN 15 1 54	Jan 68 Facchini+ LDL PARS FROM LOW EN RES	
Lvl Density	None		AUW Theo	Conf	70Madurai 2 267	Dec 70 Ramamurty+ A−PARAMETER GVN,LANG'S−TH	
Lvl Density	None		MUN Theo	Jour	NP/A 217 269	Dec 73 Dilg+ A,DELTA. BACK SHIFTED FERMIGAS	
Lvl Density	None		COP Theo	Jour	NP/A 222 493	Apr 74 Dossing+COLL ROTAT.SPAC. ACCUR ESTIM	
Lvl Density	None		DUB Theo	Jour	NP/A 224 411	May 74 Soloviev+ 1/2 MICROSC MDL. SPH NUCL	
Lvl Density	None		ROC Theo	Jour	NP/A 223 577	May 74 Huizenga+ EXP CFD MICROSC TH SPH NUC	
Lvl Density	+6	+7	FEI Expt	Conf	75Kiev 3 18	May 75 Ignatjuk+ FISS LVL DENS PAR VS EXC−E	

80 Mercury 200

Quantity	Energy (ev) Min	Max	Lab	Type	Documentation Ref Vol Page	Author, Comments Date	Data
Diff Inelast	Thrsh	Up	LEB Expt	Jour	IZV 37 1714	Aug 73 .SIG OF EXCIT 1−ST LVL	+
				Conf	73Tbilisi 156	Feb 73 Konobeevsky+ ABST,CFD,STAT MODL,NDG	
	3.8+5	7.3+5		Data	EXFOR40215.003	Jun 74 .SIGMA FOR 28 ES GIVEN,1 E−LVL	
(n,γ)	Maxwl	+5	FOA Theo	Jour	NP 39 353	Dec 62 Bergqvist+. IN PER CENT OF NAT ELEMT	
(n,γ)	5.0+3	1.0+5	AUA ExTh	Rept	AAEC/E−198	May 69 Musgrove.S+P+D WAVE SIGMAS CALC,TBL	+
(n,γ)	3.0+4		AUA Theo	Rept	AAEC/E−211	Nov 70 Musgrove. SIGMA GIVEN AND CFD OTHER	
(n,γ)	Maxwl		IAE Revw	Rept	STI/DOC/10−137	Jul 72 Guinn.P87.SIG TBL FOR ACTIV ANALYSIS	
Spect (n,γ)	None		MUN Expt	Prog	EANDC(E)140U	Aug 71 Egidy+. INT.CONVERSION(R,L,M)	
Spect (n,γ)	Pile		FRK Expt	Prog	IKF−32 30	74 Waldschmidt+ PAIR PRODUCTION	

80 Mercury 200

Quantity	Energy (ev) Min	Max	Lab	Type	Documentation Ref Vol Page	Author, Comments Date	Data
Inelastic γ	3.8+5	7.3+5	LEB Expt	Jour	IZV 37 1714	Aug 73 Konobeevskij+ SIG TO 1ST LEVEL,GRAPH	+
	3.7+5	7.0+5		Jour	BAS 37 8 129	Aug 73 . ENGL OF IZV 37 1714	
	3.8+5	7.3+5		Data	EXFOR40215.003	Jun 74 .SIGMA FOR 28 ES GIVEN,1 E−LVL	
(n,2n)	Fiss		CRC Eval	Rept	CRC−1003	Dec 60 Roy+,ESTIMATED AVG SIG=5.5MB	
(n,2n)	1.4+7		NDL Expt	Jour	PR 178 1904	Feb 69 Temperley.ACT,880+−60MB TO META	+
(n,2n)	1.4+7			Data	EXFOR12219.009	Jun 76 . 1 PT, SIG	
(n,2n)	1.5+7		DEB Comp	Jour	REA 7 4 93	Dec 69 Csikai+ SIG+HL COMPILTN,N−ACTIV−ANAL	
(n,2n)	1.4+7	1.5+7	JYV Eval	Rept	JU−RR−3/1970	Jun 70 Leppaemaeki+ TABLE OF EVAL AVG SIG	
(n,2n)	1.4+7		GIT Expt	Jour	NP/A 180 157	Jan 72 Hankla+ ACT,GE(LI),MIXED POWDER.MST.	+
				Abst	DA/B 32 293	Nov 71 − . ACT METHOD, CFD THEORY.	
	1.4+7			Data	EXFOR10244.015	Jun 74 1PT,SIGMA,META.	
(n,2n)	1.5+7		DEB Eval	Jour	REA 11 1 153	Mar 73 Boedy+ RECOMM.VALUE FROM N−Z SYSTEM.	
(n,2n)	1.5+7		KFI Theo	Rept	KFKI−73−68	Dec 73 Jeki.NEW FIT,CALC SIG CFD OTHERS,TBL	
(n,2n)	1.4+7		TUD Theo	Conf	75Kiev 4 149	May 75 Seidel+ PREEQ−EFF ON CALC SIG.TABLE	
(n,p)	1.4+7		ALD Expt	Jour	PPS 73 215	Feb 59 Coleman+. ACT. CFD DIRECT INTERACTN	+
(n,p)	Fiss		CRC Eval	Rept	CRC−1003	Dec 60 Roy+,ESTIMATED AVG SIG=0.005MB	
(n,p)	1.5+7		SAH Comp	Jour	NUC 23 8 112	Aug 65 Chatterjee. TABLE WITH REFS.	
	1.4+7			Jour	NP 60 273	Nov 64 − .MEAN OF EXPT CFD SHELLMOD	
(n,p)	1.4+7		NDL Expt	Jour	PR 178 1904	Feb 69 Temperley. ACT REL FE56 NP	+
	1.4+7			Data	EXFOR12219.011	Jun 76 . 1 PT, SIG	
(n,p)	1.5+7		DEB Comp	Jour	REA 7 4 93	Dec 69 Csikai+ SIG+HL COMPILTN,N−ACTIV−ANAL	
(n,p)	1.4+7	1.5+7	JYV Eval	Rept	JU−RR−3/1970	Jun 70 Leppaemaeki+ TABLE OF EVAL AVG SIG	
(n,p)	1.4+7	1.5+7	KAZ Theo	Jour	YF 18 705	Oct 73 Levkovsky.AVERAGED SIG,CALC,TBL	
				Jour	SNP 18 361	Apr 74 . ENGLISH OF YF 18,705	
(n,np)	1.4+7		NDL Expt	Jour	PR 178 1904	Feb 69 Temperley. ACT REL FE56 NP	+
	1.4+7			Data	EXFOR12219.012	Jun 76 . 1 PT, SIG INCL ND	
(n,np)	1.4+7		TUD Theo	Conf	75Kiev 4 149	May 75 Seidel+ (NNP),(NPN).PREEQ−EFF.TABLE	
(n,d)	1.4+7		NDL Expt	Jour	PR 178 1904	Feb 69 Temperley. ACT REL FE56 NP	+
	1.4+7			Data	EXFOR12219.012	Jun 76 . 1 PT, SIG INCL NND	
(n,α)	1.4+7		ALD Expt	Jour	PPS 73 215	Feb 59 Coleman+. ACTIVATION	+
(n,α)	Fiss		CRC Eval	Rept	CRC−1003	Dec 60 Roy+,ESTIMATED AVG SIG=BELO 0.0001MB	
(n,α)	1.4+7		CIS Theo	Jour	NP 51 460	Feb 64 Facchini+STATMOD SIG XPT/CALC286−420	
(n,α)	1.4+7		NDL Expt	Jour	PR 178 1904	Feb 69 Temperley.ACT,0.2+−0.1MB REL FE56 NP	+
	1.4+7			Data	EXFOR12219.010	Jun 76 . 1 PT, SIG	
(n,α)	1.5+7		DEB Comp	Jour	REA 7 4 93	Dec 69 Csikai+ SIG+HL COMPILTN,N−ACTIV−ANAL	
(n,α)	1.4+7	1.5+7	JYV Eval	Rept	JU−RR−3/1970	Jun 70 Leppaemaeki+ TABLE OF EVAL AVG SIG	
(n,α)	1.4+7	1.5+7	KAZ Theo	Jour	YF 18 705	Oct 73 Levkovsky.AVERAGED SIG,CALC,TBL	
				Jour	SNP 18 361	Apr 74 . ENGLISH OF YF 18,705	
Reson Params	1.3+3	7.8+3	ANL Expt	Jour	NP 21 66	Nov 60 Carpenter+EO WN WG J ISOT ASSIGNED	+
	1.3+3	7.8+4		Conf	60Vienna 135	Oct 60 Cote+.RESONS DERIVED FROM TRNSM−CURV	
	1.3+3	7.8+3		Data	EXFOR12236.006	Jun 76 . 6 RES, E0, WT, WN, WG, PCS	
Reson Params	−		FOA Theo	Jour	NP 39 353	Dec 62 Bergqvist+.AVERAGE GAMMA WIDTH.	
Reson Params		1.0+6	AUA Theo	Jour	AUJ 20 477	Oct 67 Cook. TBL OF AVG LVL SPACING D,L=0,1	
Reson Params	−		AUA Theo	Rept	AAEC/E−211	Nov 70 Musgrove. CALCULTD D+GAM WIDTH GIVEN	
Reson Params	None		DUB Theo	Jour	ZEP 14 194	Aug 71 Solovev.LARGE N−WID G−WID CORREL.NDG	
				Rept	JINR−E4−5880	71 Soloviev.N−GAM−WIDS CORR.SHORT NOTE	
				Jour	JEL 14 129	Aug 71 − . ENGL OF ZEP 14 194.	
Reson Params	None		DUB Theo	Rept	JINR−P4−7499	Oct 73 Soloviev+ CALC D CFD EXPTS,TABLE	
Strnth Fnctn	1.3+3	7.8+3	ANL Expt	Jour	NP 21 66	Nov 60 Carpenter+2.1+−60PC	
Strnth Fnctn	−		AUA Theo	Rept	AAEC/E−211	Nov 70 Musgrove. SMOOTHED S0,S1 AND S2 GIVN	
Lvl Density	+6		MIL Theo	Jour	EN 15 1 54	Jan 68 Facchini+ LDL PARS FROM LOW EN RES	
Lvl Density	−		FEI Theo	Conf	70Helsinki 2 885	Jun 70 Ignatjuk+76. SUPERFLUID CFD FERMI−TH	
Lvl Density	None		AUW Theo	Conf	70Madurai 2 267	Dec 70 Ramamurty+ A−PARAMETER GVN,LANG'S−TH	
Lvl Density	None		MUN Theo	Jour	NP/A 217 269	Dec 73 Dilg+ A,DELTA. BACK SHIFTED FERMIGAS	
Lvl Density	None		COP Theo	Jour	NP/A 222 493	Apr 74 Dossing+COLL ROTAT.SPAC. ACCUR ESTIM	
Lvl Density	None		ROC Theo	Jour	NP/A 223 577	May 74 Huizenga+ EXP CFD MICROSC TH SPH NUC	
Lvl Density	+6	+7	FEI Expt	Conf	75Kiev 3 18	May 75 Ignatjuk+ FISS LVL DENS PAR VS EXC−E	

80 Mercury 201

Quantity	Energy (ev) Min	Max	Lab	Type	Documentation Ref Vol Page	Author, Comments Date	Data
Diff Elastic	1.0+6		LAS Eval	Rept	LA−2016	Jun 56 Longley+,TBL ANG DIST 3−DEG STEPS	
Potntal Scat	7.0+2		SAC Expt	Jour	NP/A 123 561	Jan 69 Morgenstern+ RADIUS FROM RES ANAL	+
				Rept	CEA−R−3609	Sep 68 − + (THESIS) RADIUS.	
	0.0+0	7.0+2		Data	EXFOR20687.048	Aug 77 1PNT.RADIUS.	
(n,γ)	Maxwl	+5	FOA Theo	Jour	NP 39 353	Dec 62 Bergqvist+. IN PER CENT OF NAT ELEMT	
(n,γ)	4.3+1	7.1+1	SAC Expt	Prog	EANDC(E)49L 52	Oct 63 Bianchi+ DATA FOR RESONANCE ANALYSIS	+

80 Mercury 201

Quantity	Energy (ev) Min	Max	Lab	Type	Documentation Ref Vol Page	Author, Comments Date	Data
(n,γ)	5.0+3	1.0+5	AUA	ExTh Rept	AAEC/E – 198	May 69 Musgrove.S+P+D WAVE SIGMAS CALC,TBL	+
(n,γ)	3.0+4		AUA	Theo Rept	AAEC/E – 211	Nov 70 Musgrove. SIGMA GIVEN AND CFD OTHER	
(n,γ)	Maxwl		IAE	Revw Rept	STI/DOC/10 – 137	Jul 72 Guinn.P87.SIG TBL FOR ACTIV ANALYSIS	
(n,γ)	0.0+0	2.2+2	CRC	Expt Jour	NP/A 243 413	May 75 Lone+ TOF,FAST CHOPPER,GE – LI	
	7.0+5	2.6+6		Jour	CJP 52 989	Jun 74 Earle+ STRENGTH FUNCTS	
Spect (n,γ)	4.3+1	2.1+2	ANL	Expt Jour	NP 21 66	Nov 60 Carpenter+ABS INTENS.OF7HARD G(3RES)	
	4.3+1			Conf	60Vienna 135	Oct 60 Cote+.GRAPH,EXPT DESCRIBED	
Spect (n,γ)	4.3+1	2.1+2	SAC	Expt Rept	CEA – R – 2810	Jun 65 Huynh+DET=2 NAI(TL)COAXIAL CRYSTALS	
				Rept	CEA – R – 3602	Jul 69 Alves. (THESIS)	
				Jour	NIM 36 29	Jul 65 Huynh+ DATA GIVEN.	
Spect (n,γ)	1.0+2	+5	ANL	Expt Conf	69Studsvik 601	Aug 69 Smither+ NO DATA GVN,TB CFD STATMOD	
Spect (n,γ)	4.3+1	5.6+2	HAR	Expt Prog	AERE – PR/NP17	Dec 70 Thomas+ TBL TRANSITION STRENGTH 5RES	
Spect (n,γ)	Maxwl	2.1+2	BNL	Expt Conf	74Petten 316	Sep 74 Breitig+ THR+RES CAPT.HG 202 DECAY	
Spect (n,γ)	0.0+0	2.2+2	CRC	Expt Jour	NP/A 243 413	May 75 Lone+ G – RAYS INT TBL,SPECT,LVL CHEME	
(n,2n)	Fiss		CRC	Eval Rept	CRC – 1003	Dec 60 Roy+,ESTIMATED AVG SIG=29.0MB	
(n,2n)	1.5+7		DEB	Eval Jour	REA 11 1 153	Mar 73 Boedy+ RECOMM.VALUE FROM N – Z SYSTEM.	
(n,2n)	1.5+7		KFI	Theo Rept	KFKI – 73 – 68	Dec 73 Jeki.NEW FIT,CALC SIG CFD OTHERS,TBL	
(n,p)	1.4+7		ALD	Expt Jour	PPS 73 215	Feb 59 Coleman+. ACT. CFD DIRECT INTERACTN	+
(n,p)	Fiss		CRC	Eval Rept	CRC – 1003	Dec 60 Roy+,ESTIMATED AVG SIG=0.06MB	
(n,p)	1.5+7		SAH	Comp Jour	NUC 23 8 112	Aug 65 Chatterjee. TABLE WITH REFS.	
(n,p)	1.4+7		NDL	Expt Jour	PR 178 1904	Feb 69 Temperley.ACT,1.5+ – 0.7MB REL FE56 NP	+
	1.4+7			Data	EXFOR12219.013	Jun 76 . 1 PT, SIG	
(n,p)	1.5+7		DEB	Comp Jour	REA 7 4 93	Dec 69 Csikai+ SIG+HL COMPILTN,N – ACTIV – ANAL	
(n,p)	1.4+7	1.5+7	JYV	Eval Rept	JU – RR – 3/1970	Jun 70 Leppaemaeki+ TABLE OF EVAL AVG SIG	
(n,p)	1.4+7	1.5+7	KAZ	Theo Jour	YF 18 705	Oct 73 Levkovsky.AVERAGED SIG,CALC,TBL	
				Jour	SNP 18 361	Apr 74 . ENGLISH OF YF 18,705	
(n,np)	1.4+7		NDL	Expt Jour	PR 178 1904	Feb 69 Temperley. ACT REL FE56 NP	+
	1.4+7			Data	EXFOR12219.014	Jun 76 . 1 PT, SIG INCL ND	
(n,d)	1.4+7		NDL	Expt Jour	PR 178 1904	Feb 69 Temperley. ACT REL FE56 NP	+
	1.4+7			Data	EXFOR12219.014	Jun 76 . 1 PT, SIG INCL NNP	
(n,α)	Fiss		CRC	Eval Rept	CRC – 1003	Dec 60 Roy+,ESTIMATED AVG SIG=BELO 0.0001MB	
Reson Params	4.3+1		ANL	Expt Rept	PR 102 228	Apr 56 Palmer+	+
	4.3+1			Data	EXFOR11804.022	Jun 76 . 1 RES, E0	
Reson Params	4.3+1	2.1+2	HAR	Expt Jour	NP 13 525	Nov 59 Bird+E0 SIG0 WT WN WG TOF+GAMMA SPEC	
Reson Params	4.3+2	6.9+2	ANL	Expt Jour	NP 21 66	Nov 60 Carpenter+EO WN WG J ISOT ASSIGNED	+
	7.1+1	6.9+2		Conf	60Vienna 135	Oct 60 Cote+.RESONS DERIVED FROM TRNSM – CURV	
	4.3+1	6.9+2		Data	EXFOR12236.007	Jun 76 . 7 RES, E0, J, WT, WN, WG, PCS	
Reson Params	None		ANL	Expt Conf	61Saclay 199	Jul 61 Bollinger+.L FROM 2 STEP.CASCADE.NDG	
Reson Params	–		FOA	Theo Jour	NP 39 353	Dec 62 Bergqvist+.AVERAGE GAMMA WIDTH.	
Reson Params	4.3+1	7.2+1	BNL	Expt Jour	NP 42 676	Apr 63 Bolotin+.WG,WN GIVEN FOR 2 RESONANCE	+
	4.3+1	7.2+1		Data	EXFOR11922.012	Jun 76 . 2 RES, E0, WT	
Reson Params		1.0+6	AUA	Theo Jour	AUJ 20 477	Oct 67 Cook. TBL OF AVG LVL SPACING D,L=0,1	
Reson Params	4.3+1	6.9+2	SAC	Expt Jour	NP/A 132 129	Jul 69 Julien+ TABLE	+
				Rept	CEA – R – 3602	Jul 69 Alves. (THESIS).SEE ALSO	
				Conf	68Wash. 867	Mar 68 Morgenstern.WG VS.A AVERAGE WG GIVEN	
				Rept	CEA – R – 3385	Feb 68 Julien. (THESIS) TBL.	
				Conf	66Paris 1 559	Oct 66 Huynh+ ABST.NDG. SEE INDC – 156	
				Conf	65Antwerp 525	Jul 65 De Barros+ PPR73.ABST.NDG	
	0.0+0	7.0+2		Data	EXFOR20687.	Aug 77 9PTS.E0,WG,AVG WG,WN,WT,J,G*WN.	
Reson Params	–		AUA	Theo Rept	AAEC/E – 211	Nov 70 Musgrove. CALCULTD D+GAM WIDTH GIVEN	
Reson Params	4.3+1	6.8+2	CJD	Eval Rept	YK – 7	71 Zakharova+ SURVEY+SYSTEMATICS,GW,TBL	
				Rept	INDC(CCP) – 27	Nov 72 .ENGLISH TRANSLATION OF YK – 7 /71	
Reson Params	None		DUB	Theo Rept	JINR – P4 – 7499	Oct 73 Soloviev+ CALC D CFD EXPTS,TABLE	
Strnth Fnctn	4.8+2	6.9+2	ANL	Expt Jour	NP 21 66	Nov 60 Carpenter+1.8+ – 60PC	
Strnth Fnctn	4.3+1	6.9+2	SAC	Expt Jour	NP/A 123 561	Jan 69 Morgenstern+ TBL. FROM RES ANALYSIS	+
				Rept	CEA – R – 3609	Sep 68 – . (THESIS) S – WAVE.RADIUS	
				Conf	68Wash. 867	Mar 68 – +	
				Rept	CEA – R – 3385	Feb 68 Julien. (THESIS).SEE ALSO.S0 VS J.	
				Conf	66Paris 1 183	Oct 66 Morgenstern+ PPR65.ABST.NDG.INDC – 156	
				Conf	65Antwerp 531	Jul 65 – + PPR87.ABST.NDG.	
	0.0+0	7.0+2		Data	EXFOR20687.049	Aug 77 1PNT.L=0.	
Strnth Fnctn	–		AUA	Theo Rept	AAEC/E – 211	Nov 70 Musgrove. SMOOTHED S0,S1 AND S2 GIVN	
Strnth Fnctn	None		AUA	Eval Rept	AAEC/E – 277	Mar 73 Musgrove.TBLS EXPTL DATA+BEST VALUES	
Lvl Density	+6		MIL	Theo Jour	EN 15 1 54	Jan 68 Facchini+ LDL PARS FROM LOW EN RES	
Lvl Density	None		AUW	Theo Conf	70Madurai 2 267	Dec 70 Ramamurty+ A – PARAMETER GVN,LANG'S – TH	
Lvl Density	None		MUN	Theo Jour	NP 217 269	Dec 73 Dilg+ A,DELTA. BACK SHIFTED FERMIGAS	
Lvl Density	None		COP	Theo Jour	NP/A 222 493	Apr 74 Dossing+COLL ROTAT.SPAC. ACCUR ESTIM	
Lvl Density	None		DUB	Theo Jour	NP/A 224 411	May 74 Soloviev+ 1/2 MICROSC MDL. SPH NUCL.	

80 Mercury 201

Quantity	Energy (ev) Min	Max	Lab	Type	Documentation Ref Vol Page	Date	Author, Comments	Data
Lvl Density	None		ROC	Theo	Jour NP/A 223 577	May 74	Huizenga+ EXP CFD MICROSC TH SPH NUC	

80 Mercury 202

Quantity	Energy (ev) Min	Max	Lab	Type	Documentation Ref Vol Page	Date	Author, Comments	Data
Total	7.0+6	1.4+7	CJD	Theo	Rept ICD-5 20	68	Averjanov+ VIBRATION MDL,AT 4ES,TBL	
Total	+3		DKE	Expt	Jour AP 84 165	May 74	Pineo+ N STRENGTH FUNC, TBLS, GRPHS.	
Elastic	7.0+6	1.4+7	CJD	Theo	Rept ICD-5 20	68	Averjanov+ VIBRATION MDL,AT 4ES,TBL	
Tot Inelastc	7.0+6	1.4+7	CJD	Theo	Rept ICD-5 20	68	Averjanov+ VIBRATION MDL,AT 4ES,TBL	
Diff Inelast	7.0+6	1.4+7	CJD	Theo	Rept ICD-5 20	68	Averjanov+ TO 1ST LVL,ANGDIST,GRAPH	
Diff Inelast	Thrsh	Up	LEB	Expt	Jour IZV 37 1714	Aug 73	.SIG OF EXCIT 1-ST LVL	+
					Conf 73Tbilisi 156	Feb 73	Konobeevsky+ ABST,CFD,STAT MODL,NDG	
	4.5+5	7.3+5			Data EXFOR40215.004	Jun 74	.SIGMA FOR 23 ES GIVEN,1 E-LVL	
Res Int Abs	5.0-1		AE	Expt	Jour JNE 17 350	Apr 63	Brune+ ACTIV. CD RATIO.NON 1/V.	+
	6.0+2				Data EXFOR20050.005	Sep 71	1PNT.CAPTURE.	
Res Int Abs	5.0-1		GHT	Expt	Jour RCA 8 165	Dec 67	KIM+. ACT. 4.99 B. REL TO AU	+
	5.0-1				Data EXFOR20254.007	May 74	1PNT.CAPTURE.	
Res Int Abs	5.0-1		CPO	Expt	Jour JIN 30 349	Feb 68	Sims+ 3.94+-0.08 REL TO CO59=69.9 B	+
	5.0-1				Data EXFOR11658.	Jun 76	2 RI FOR 2 ISOMERS	
Res Int Abs	5.0-1		GHT	Expt	Jour JRC 20 695	74	Van Der Linden+ BY (N,G).CFD OTH,TBL	+
	5.5-1				Conf 73Paris 2 241	Mar 73	- + ACT,REL THR+GOLD,TBL	
	5.5-1				Data EXFOR20645.060	Jul 76	1PNT.CAPTURE.	
(n,γ)	Pile		ANL	Expt	Jour PR 72 888	Nov 47	Seren+.ACT METHOD.PILE IRRAD.HGO.	+
	Pile				Data EXFOR11447.128	Jun 76	1 PT, SIG	
(n,γ)	Pile		ORL	Expt	Jour PR 82 276	Apr 51	Lyon. ACT TO 46.5 D	+
	Pile				Data EXFOR12201.002	Jun 76	1 PT, SIG	
(n,γ)	2.4+4		ORL	Expt	Jour PR 107 504	Jul 57	Macklin.SB - BE NS,57+-13MB,0.279MEVG	+
					Conf 58Geneva 671	Sep 58	.SUPERSEDED	
	2.4+4				Data EXFOR11399.050	Jun 76	1 PT, SIG	
(n,γ)	2.0+5		ORL	Expt	Jour PR 114 1619	Jun 59	Lyon+.ABS GAMMA COUNT 32+-5MB ACT	+
	2.0+5				Data EXFOR11407.033	Jun 76	1 PT, SIG	
(n,γ)	Maxwl		BNL	Expt	Jour PR 128 761	Oct 62	Sehgal. SIG = 4.6+-.7B(REL AU197=97B	+
	Maxwl				Data EXFOR11994.015	Jun 76	1 PT, SIG	
(n,γ)	Maxwl	+5	FOA	Theo	Jour NP 39 353	Dec 62	Bergqvist+. IN PER CENT OF NAT ELEMT	
(n,γ)	Maxwl		GHT	Expt	Jour RCA 8 165	Dec 67	Kim+ 5.04 B REL TO AU197	+
	2.5-2				Data EXFOR20254.006	May 74	1PNT.SIGMA.	
(n,γ)	Maxwl		CPO	Expt	Jour JIN 30 349	Feb 68	Sims+ 4.87+-0.05 REL TO CO59=37.5 B	+
	Maxwl				Data EXFOR11658.	Jun 76	2 PTS, SIG FOR 2 ISOMERS	
(n,γ)	-		IEA	Comp	Rept IEA-INF-10 6	Aug 68	Atalla. TABLES OF HL,SIG AND GAMM-E	
(n,γ)	3.0+4		AUA	Theo	Rept AAEC/E-211	Nov 70	Musgrove. SIGMA GIVEN AND CFD OTHER	
(n,γ)	2.4+4		MUA	Theo	Jour IJP 46 114	Mar 72	Chaubey+ P-WAVE STRENGTH FUNCT,TABLE	
(n,γ)	Maxwl		IAE	Revw	Rept STI/DOC/10-137	Jul 72	Guinn.P87.SIG TBL FOR ACTIV ANALYSIS	
(n,γ)	Maxwl		GER	Revw	Conf 73Paris 2 193	Mar 73	Krivan.EVALUATED DATA CFD,TABLE	
(n,γ)	2.5+4		AUW	Expt	Jour NC/A 18 48	Nov 73	Sidappa+ ACTIV SIG,CFD.TABLE	
Spect (n,γ)	Pile		LND	Expt	Jour AF 3 533	Aug 52	Johansson. NAI(TL). E. K-CONV COEFF.	
Spect (n,γ)	Pile		IPS	Expt	Jour AF 7 239	Mar 54	Thulin+. K,K/(L+M). NAI(TL)	
Spect (n,γ)	2.4+4		ORL	Expt	Conf 58Geneva 15 68	Sep 58	Macklin.PPR671,SIGMA+G-ENERGY GVN	
Inelastic γ	4.5+5	7.3+5	LEB	Expt	Jour IZV 37 1714	Aug 73	Konobeevskij+ SIG TO 1ST LEVEL,GRAPH	+
	4.3+5	7.0+5			Jour BAS 37 8 129	Aug 73	. ENGL OF IZV 37 1714	
	4.5+5	7.3+5			Data EXFOR40215.004	Jun 74	.SIGMA FOR 23 ES GIVEN,1 E-LVL	
(n,2n)	Fiss		CRC	Eval	Rept CRC-1003	Dec 60	Roy+,ESTIMATED AVG SIG=7.5MB	
(n,2n)	1.5+7		DEB	Eval	Jour REA 11 1 153	Mar 73	Boedy+ RECOMM.VALUE FROM N-Z SYSTEM.	
(n,2n)	1.5+7		KFI	Theo	Rept KFKI-73-68	Dec 73	Jeki.NEW FIT,CALC SIG CFD OTHERS,TBL	
(n,p)	Fiss		CRC	Eval	Rept CRC-1003	Dec 60	Roy+,ESTIMATED AVG SIG=0.003MB	
(n,p)	None		KFI	Comp	Jour JRC 7 365	Jun 71	Nagy+ HALF LIFE GIVEN	
(n,α)	1.4+7		ALD	Expt	Jour PPS 73 215	Feb 59	Coleman+. ACTIVATION	+
(n,α)	Fiss		CRC	Eval	Rept CRC-1003	Dec 60	Roy+,ESTIMATED AVG SIG=BELO 0.0001MB	
(n,α)	1.4+7		NDL	Expt	Jour PR 178 1904	Feb 69	Temperley. ACT REL FE56 NP	+
	1.4+7				Data EXFOR12219.015	Jun 76	1 PT, SIG	
(n,α)	1.5+7		DEB	Comp	Jour REA 7 4 93	Dec 69	Csikai+ SIG+HL COMPILTN,N-ACTIV-ANAL	
(n,α)	1.4+7	1.5+7	JYV	Eval	Rept JU-RR-3/1970	Jun 70	Leppaemaeki+ TABLE OF EVAL AVG SIG	
(n,α)	1.4+7		KFI	Comp	Jour JRC 7 365	Jun 71	Nagy+ SIGMA, GAM+XRAY+ELECTR ES GIVN	
(n,α)	1.4+7	1.5+7	KAZ	Theo	Jour YF 18 705	Oct 73	Levkovsky.AVERAGED SIG,CALC,TBL	
					Jour SNP 18 361	Apr 74	. ENGLISH OF YF 18,705	
Reson Params	1.7+3	4.1+3	ANL	Expt	Jour NP 21 66	Nov 60	Carpenter+EO WN WG J ISOT ASSIGNED	
					Conf 60Vienna 135	Oct 60	Cote+.RESONS DERIVED FROM TRNSM-CURV	
	1.7+3	4.1+3			Data EXFOR12236.008	Jun 76	. 2 RES, E0, J, WT, WN, PCS	

80 Mercury 202

Quantity	Energy (ev) Min	Max	Lab	Type	Documentation Ref Vol Page	Date	Author, Comments	Data
Reson Params	–		FOA	Theo Jour	NP 39 353	Dec 62	Bergqvist+.AVERAGE GAMMA WIDTH.	
Reson Params		1.0+6	AUA	Theo Jour	AUJ 20 477	Oct 67	Cook. TBL OF AVG LVL SPACING D,L=0,1	
Reson Params	–		AUA	Theo Rept	AAEC/E-211	Nov 70	Musgrove. CALCULTD D+GAM WIDTH GIVEN	
Reson Params	None		DUB	Theo Rept	JINR-P4-7499	Oct 73	Soloviev+ CALC D CFD EXPTS,TABLE	
Strnth Fnctn	+0	+3	ANL	Expt Jour	NP 21 66	Nov 60	Carpenter+1.7+ –200PC	
Strnth Fnctn	–		AUA	Theo Rept	AAEC/E-211	Nov 70	Musgrove. SMOOTHED S0,S1 AND S2 GIVN	
Strnth Fnctn	2.4+4		MUA	Expt Jour	IJP 46 114	Mar 72	Chaubey+ P–WAVE.FOR A–SYSTEMTIC,GRPH	
Lvl Density	+6		MIL	Theo Jour	EN 15 1 54	Jan 68	Facchini+ LDL PARS FROM LOW EN RES	
Lvl Density	–		FEI	Theo Conf	70Helsinki 2 885	Jun 70	Ignatjuk+76. SUPERFLUID CFD FERMI–TH	
Lvl Density	None		AUW	Theo Conf	70Madurai 2 267	Dec 70	Ramamurty+ A–PARAMETER GVN,LANG'S–TH	
Lvl Density	None		MUN	Theo Jour	NP/A 217 269	Dec 73	Dilg+ A,DELTA. BACK SHIFTED FERMIGAS	
Lvl Density	None		COP	Theo Jour	NP/A 222 493	Apr 74	Dossing+COLL ROTAT.SPAC. ACCUR ESTIM	
Lvl Density	None		ROC	Theo Jour	NP/A 223 577	May 74	Huizenga+ EXP CFD MICROSC TH SPH NUC	

80 Mercury 203

Quantity	Energy (ev) Min	Max	Lab	Type	Documentation Ref Vol Page	Date	Author, Comments	Data
Reson Params	–		AUA	Theo Rept	AAEC/E-211	Nov 70	Musgrove. CALCULTD D+GAM WIDTH GIVEN	
Strnth Fnctn	–		AUA	Theo Rept	AAEC/E-211	Nov 70	Musgrove. SMOOTHED S0,S1 AND S2 GIVN	
Lvl Density	None		COP	Theo Jour	NP/A 222 493	Apr 74	Dossing+COLL ROTAT.SPAC. ACCUR ESTIM	
Lvl Density	None		DUB	Theo Jour	NP/A 224 411	May 74	Soloviev+ 1/2 MICROSC MDL. SPH NUCL.	
Lvl Density	None		ROC	Theo Jour	NP/A 223 577	May 74	Huizenga+ EXP CFD MICROSC TH SPH NUC	

80 Mercury 204

Quantity	Energy (ev) Min	Max	Lab	Type	Documentation Ref Vol Page	Date	Author, Comments	Data
Res Int Abs	5.0-1		GHT	Expt Jour	JRC 20 695	74	Van Der Linden+ BY (N,G).CFD OTH,TBL	+
	5.5-1			Conf	73Paris 2 241	Mar 73	– + ACT,REL THR+GOLD,TBL	
	5.5-1			Data	EXFOR20645.061	Jul 76	1PNT.CAPTURE.	
(n,γ)	Pile		ANL	Expt Jour	PR 72 888	Nov 47	Seren+.ACT METHOD.TO1.5MIN,7HGO.	+
	Pile			Data	EXFOR11447.127	Jun 76	. 1 PT, SIG	
(n,γ)	Fiss		ANL	Expt Jour	PR 75 1781	Jun 49	Hughes+ REL SIG(THERMAL),FOIL ACTIVN	+
	Fiss			Data	EXFOR11450.038	Jun 76	. 1 PT, SIG	
(n,γ)	Pile		ORL	Expt Jour	PR 82 276	Apr 51	Lyon. ACT TO 5.6 MIN	+
	Pile			Data	EXFOR12201.003	Jun 76	. 1 PT, SIG	
(n,γ)	Fiss		BNL	Expt Jour	PR 91 1423	Sep 53	Hughes+.ALSO LVL SPACINGS AT EXCIT E	
(n,γ)	2.0+5	4.0+6	KUR	Expt Conf	58Geneva 15 50	Sep 58	Leipunskij+.PPR2219,TBL AT 3ES	+
(n,γ)	Maxwl	+5	FOA	Theo Jour	NP 39 353	Dec 62	Bergqvist+. IN PER CENT OF NAT ELEMT	
(n,γ)	2.4+4		MUA	Expt Jour	PR 152 1055	Dec 66	Chaubey+ BETA–DET,SIG REL I–127,TBL	+
	2.4+4			Data	EXFOR30079.041	Dec 70	SIGMA FOR 5.6 MIN HALF–LIFE	
(n,γ)	–		IEA	Comp Jour	IEA–INF–10 6	Aug 68	Atalla. TABLES OF HL,SIG AND GAMM–E	
(n,γ)	Maxwl		IAE	Revw Rept	STI/DOC/10-137	Jul 72	Guinn.P87.SIG TBL FOR ACTIV ANALYSIS	
Spect (n,γ)	2.3+1		RPI	Expt Jour	PR 155 1301	Mar 67	Rae+ 6LINES 4.4–5.3MEV,MAY BE HG198	
(n,2n)	Fiss		CRC	Eval Rept	CRC-1003	Dec 60	Roy+,ESTIMATED AVG SIG=8.6MB	
(n,2n)	1.5+7		DEB	Expt Jour	AHP 25 91	Oct 68	Peto+ REL Y89(N,2N), ACTIVATION	+
	1.5+7			Data	EXFOR30069.008	Dec 70	SIG REL Y–089(N2N)	
(n,2n)			MUN	Expt Jour	OAWS 177 323	69	Winkler+(IRK) ACTIVATION.	+
				Jour	NP/A 118 9	Sep 68	Dilg+ ACTIV.REL AL(N,A)	
	1.5+7			Data	EXFOR20802.020	Dec 78	1PNT.SIGMA.	
(n,2n)	1.4+7		NDL	Expt Jour	PR 178 1904	Feb 69	Temperley.ACT,2060+ –190MB REL FE56NP	+
	1.4+7			Data	EXFOR12219.016	Jun 76	. 1 PT, SIG	
(n,2n)	1.5+7		DEB	Comp Jour	REA 7 4 93	Dec 69	Csikai+ SIG+HL COMPILTN,N–ACTIV–ANAL	
(n,2n)	1.4+7	1.5+7	FEI	Comp Rept	ICD-6 215	70	Sluchevskaja. SIG FROM 3 REFS,TABLE	
(n,2n)	1.4+7	1.5+7	JYV	Eval Rept	JU–RR–3/1970	Jun 70	Leppaemaeki+ TABLE OF EVAL AVG SIG	
(n,2n)	+7		KFI	Theo Rept	KFKI-71-8	Feb 71	Jeki. CALCULATED CFD EXPTL SIG VALUE	
(n,2n)	1.4+7		GIT	Expt Jour	NP/A 180 157	Jan 72	Hankla+ ACT,GE(LI),MIXED POWDER.	+
				Abst	DA/B 32 293	Nov 71	– . ACT METHOD, CFD THEORY.	
	1.4+7			Data	EXFOR10244.016	Jun 74	1PT,SIGMA	
(n,2n)	1.5+7		JUL	Expt Jour	NP/A 185 614	May 72	Qaim. ACT,GE(LI). CFD TH+OTHR.	+
	1.5+7			Data	EXFOR20536.036	Apr 76	1PNT.SIGMA.	
(n,2n)	1.5+7		DEB	Eval Jour	REA 11 1 153	Mar 73	Boedy. COMPILATION+RECOMM.VALUE,TBL	
				Rept	IAEA-153 173	73	– . RECOMM. VALUE ONLY	
(n,2n)	1.5+7		TAT	Theo Rept	JP/A 7 1457	Aug 74	Kondaiah. CALC ON STAT MODEL	
(n,2n)	1.3+7	1.8+7	HAM	Expt Jour	ZP 277 2 203	May 76	Bormann+ SIG + EXCIT–FN	+
	1.3+7	1.8+7		Data	EXFOR20614.013	Jun 76	9PTS.SIGMA.	
(n,p)	Fiss		CRC	Eval Rept	CRC-1003	Dec 60	Roy+,ESTIMATED AVG SIG=0.001MB	

80 Mercury 204

Quantity	Energy (ev) Min Max	Lab	Type	Documentation Ref Vol Page	Date	Author, Comments	Data
(n,d)	1.5+7	BUC	Expt Jour	RCA 18 4 192	Dec 72	Bunus.ACTIV DETERM 203AU	
(n,α)	Fiss	CRC	Eval Rept	CRC-1003	Dec 60	Roy+,ESTIMATED AVG SIG=BELO 0.0001MB	
(n,α)	Fiss	TAT	Expt Jour	NC 30 14	Oct 63	Gopinathan+ ACTIV,SIGMA GIVEN	
Reson Params	None	ANL	Revw Conf	60Vienna 135	Oct 60	Cote+.RESONS DERIVED FROM TRNSM-CURV	

81 Thallium

Quantity	Energy (ev) Min	Max	Lab	Type	Documentation Ref Vol Page	Author, Comments Date	Data
Evaluation	5.0+5	1.5+7	LRL	Eval Rept	UCRL-5351	Nov 58 Howerton.	
Total	Maxwl		COL	Expt Jour	PR 48 265	Aug 35 Dunning+ IONCH,TRANS,RA-BE/PARAFIN	N
Total	1.0-2	+4	COL	Expt Jour	PR 71 174	Feb 47 WU+ SLOW N SOURCE.TOF.TRANSM.	+
	1.5-2	2.9+3		Data	EXFOR11751.008	Jun 76 . 46 PTS. SIGMA	
Total	1.4+7		LAS	Expt Jour	PR 88 562	Nov 52 Coon+	+
	1.4+7			Data	EXFOR11056.053	Jun 76 . 1 PT. SIGMA	
Total	2.8+6	1.3+7	LAS	Expt Jour	PR 94 1678	Jun 54 Nereson+ RSLN 10 PERCENT	+
	2.8+6	1.3+7		Data	EXFOR11308.025	Jun 76 . 31 PTS. SIGMA	
Total	8.4+1	5.4+2	BNL	Expt Priv	HUGHES	Mar 55 Hughes.	+
	8.4+1	5.4+2		Data	EXFOR12233.002	Jun 76 . 65 PTS. SIGMA	
Total	1.0+3	5.5+4	ANL	Expt Abst	PR 98 224	Apr 55 Hibdon+ NDG RESONANCES CFD,NEW RES	
Total	1.0+2	8.0+4	DKE	Expt Jour	PR 105 198	Jan 57 Newson+,TRNS CURV ABS ISOT ASSGN PKS	+
	1.5+2	8.1+4		Data	EXFOR11569.	Jun 76 . 163 PTS. SIGMA	
Total	3.0+0	6.0+2	BNL	Expt Jour	PR 108 353	Oct 57 Stolovy+ FC, TRANS	
Total	2.0+0	8.0+3	BNL	Expt Jour	PR 110 692	May 58 Seth+.ABSOLUTE CURVE.FAST CHOPPER	+
	1.3+1	3.9+3		Data	EXFOR11788.034	Jun 76 . 42 PTS. SIGMA	
Total	7.2+6	1.4+7	LRL	Expt Jour	PR 110 927	May 58 Bratenahl+ SC TRNS 5ES	+
				Conf	58Geneva 14 109	Sep 58 - + P1881,TBL,CURVE,CFD OPTMD	
	7.2+6	1.4+7		Data	EXFOR11155.030	Jun 76 . 5 PTS. SIGMA	
Total	1.8+7	2.9+7	LRL	Expt Jour	PR 120 521	Oct 60 Peterson+	+
				Conf	58Geneva 14 109	Sep 58 Bratenahl+.P1881,TBL,CURV,CFD OPTMDL	
	1.8+7	2.9+7		Data	EXFOR11108.038	Jun 76 . 4 PTS. SIGMA	
Total	1.5+7	1.6+7	UMX	Expt Conf	58Geneva 15 28	Sep 58 Mazari+.PPR1088,VAL AT 2ES GVN,VDG	+
	1.5+7	1.6+7		Data	EXFOR30037.013	Sep 70 2 DATA POINTS,FROM TABLE IN 58GENEVA	
Total	1.9+1	7.9+6	ANL	Expt Priv	CARPENTER	Aug 62 Carpenter+	+
	1.9+1	1.0+4		Data	EXFOR12189.002	Jun 76 . 523 PTS. SIGMA	
Total	1.4+7		CCP	ExTh Jour	ZET 46 1496	Apr 64 5.48+-.02B,CFD OPTMDL,SHELL.SEP ISOQ	
				Jour	JET 19 1013	Oct 64 TRANSLATN.*	
Total	1.4+7		FTI	Expt Conf	64Paris 2 811	Jul 64 Kaminker.	
Total	3.0+3	6.5+5	DKE	ExTh Jour	PL 16 306	Jun 65 Seth+AV CS 8-10KEV RSN INT RES OBSV	+
	6.0+3	1.9+5		Expt Data	EXFOR11781.020	Jun 76 . 44 PTS.	
Total	5.0+5	4.1+6	LAS	Expt Priv	DAY	Jul 65 DAY.	+
	5.0+5	4.1+6		Data	EXFOR12191.004	Jun 76 . 4 PTS. SIGMA	
Total	1.4+7		CCP	ExTh Jour	IZV 31 217	Feb 67 Dukarevich+.TBL,CURVES,CFD OPTMDL TH	
				Jour	BAS 31 197	Feb 67 TRANSLATN.*	
Total	1.4+7		FTI	Expt Jour	NP/A 92 433	Feb 67 Dukarevich+ 5.36+-0.03B	
Total	None		DKE	Expt Abst	DA/B 28 3834	Mar 68 Divadeenam.TRNS.AVG SIG CFD OPTMDL.	+
	1.1+5	6.5+5		Data	EXFOR10523.017	Jan 76 . 110 PTS.	
Total	2.5+6	1.5+7	BNW	Expt Jour	PR/C 3 576	Feb 71 Foster+,TRANS,CURVS,CFD OTHERS+TH	+
				Jour	NIM 36 1	Sep 65 .EXPT DETAILS	
	2.3+6	1.5+7		Data	EXFOR10047.088	Aug 73 . 243 PTS.	
Total	1.3+7	1.5+7	DEB	Eval Rept	IAEA-153 173	73 Boedy+ MOST PROBABLE VAL OF SIG,TBL	
				Jour	AHP 30 115	Oct 71 Angeli+ AVG SIG,CFD CALC.TBLS.GRAPH	
Total	5.0+5	4.0+7	KFK	ExTh Conf	JAERI-M-5984	Feb 75 Newstead+P230.OPTMDL/C-C CFD TOF GRP	+
	1.0+6	3.9+7		Revw Conf	70Helsinki 2 219	Jun 70 Cierjacks.113. SIG(E) GRPH CFD OPTMD	
	5.0+5	3.0+7		Expt Rept	KFK-1000	Jun 68 - + GRPH TOF HIGH RESOL EXPT	
				Conf	68Wash. 2 743	Mar 68 - + PPR E9. FLUCTUATIONS OBS	
	4.2+5	3.2+7		Data	EXFOR20010.008	Mar 71 5633PTS.	
Total	1.5+1	2.5+5	COL	Expt Jour	PR/C 12 102	Jul 75 Liou+TOF.GRPH.RES PAR TBL.	+
	1.5+1	2.5+5		Data	EXFOR10535.013	Mar 76 .UNCORRECTED CS DATA AVAILABLE.	
Elastic	2.5-2		ANL	Expt Jour	PR 75 975	May 49 Winsberg+	+
	2.5-2			Data	EXFOR12625.005	Jun 76 . 1 PT, SIGMA.	
Elastic		+5	ANL	Expt Jour	PR 79 11	Jul 50 Harris+ EPI-CD,RES INT SCAT,B-W TH	
Elastic	5.2-1		ANL	Expt Jour	PR 105 216	Jan 57 Heaton+,COH=10.04B,BOUND NUCL=10.14B	
Elastic	Maxwl		ANL	Expt Jour	JAP 30 1323	Sep 59 Sidhu+ COH SCAT BY NEUT DIFFR	
				Conf	58Geneva 14 212	Sep 58 - +.PPR680,TBL OF SIGMA-COHERENT	
Elastic	3.0+5	1.5+6	ANL	Expt Jour	ZP 183 323	Mar 65 Devilliers+TOF.TBL.CFD OPT MDL.	+
				Rept	EANDC(US)-62	Jun 64 Smith+TOF,TBL.50KEV STEPS,20KEV RSLN	
	3.0+5	1.5+6		Data	EXFOR12240.013	Jun 76 . 25 PTS. SIGMA	
Elastic	1.5+6		IFU	Expt Prog	YFI-5 42	Oct 67 Korzh+ TBL OPTMDL PARAMS + TOTELAST	
				Rept	INDC-232E	67 . ENGL OF YFI-5 42	
Elastic	1.5+6		IFU	Comp Jour	YF 7 277	Feb 68 Korzh+ OPTMOD PARS-FIT TO EXPTL-SIG	
				Jour	SNP 7 2 190	Aug 68 TRANSLATN.*	
Diff Elastic	4.0+6	7.0+6	LAS	Expt Jour	PR 129 1649	Feb 63 Thomson. SIG AT 90DEG	+
	4.0+6	7.0+6		Data	EXFOR11495.052	Jun 76 . 4 PTS. DSIGMA	
Diff Elastic	1.4+7		RPI	Expt Abst	DA 26 438	Jul 63 Pearlstein.	+
	1.4+7			Data	EXFOR10234.008	May 73 1PT,DSIGMA AT 90DEG	

81 Thallium

Quantity	Energy (ev) Min	Max	Lab	Type	Documentation Ref Vol Page	Date	Author, Comments	Data
Diff Elastic	3.0+5	1.5+6	ANL	Expt	Jour ZP 183 323	Mar 65	Devilliers+TOF.TBL.CFD OPT MDL.GRPHS	+
					Jour PL 11 331	Aug 64	Vonach+EXPT CFD OPT MDL AT 800KEV.	
					Rept EANDC(US)-62	Jun 64	Smith+TOF,TBL.50KEV STEPS,20KEV RSLN	
	3.0+5	1.5+6			Data EXFOR12240.012	Jun 76	. 125 LEG COEFS. AT 25ES.	
Diff Elastic	5.0+6		DKE	Expt	Jour ZP 196 103	Sep 66	Buccino+ 20-140DEG,CFD OPTMOD. TABLE	+
					Abst DA 24 4251	Apr 64	Hollandsworth.CFD OPTMDL CALCS.	
	5.0+6				Data EXFOR11877.010	Jun 76	. 13 PTS. DSIGMA	
Diff Elastic	3.2+6		BCM	Expt	Jour NP 89 154	Dec 66	Becker+ 12 ANGLES GRAPH CFD OPTMDL	+
	3.2+6				Data EXFOR11511.035	Jun 76	. 12 PTS. DSIGMA	
Diff Elastic	1.5+6		IFU	Comp	Jour YF 7 277	Feb 68	Korzh+ GRPH SIG(ANG),OPTMOD PARS-FIT	
					Jour SNP 7 2 190	Aug 68	TRANSLATN.*	
Diff Elastic	3.2+6	5.0+6	SCU	Theo	Rept ICD-6 236	69	Averyanov+CALC ANGDIST CFD EXPT,GRPH	
Diff Elastic	3.2+6		AMS	Theo	Jour NP/A 222 93	Apr 74	Zijp+ LEG.COEFF COMPOUND ELASTIC.H-F	
Polarization	9.8+5		WIS	ExTh	Jour NP 6 177	Mar 58	Clement+. POLARIZATION. TABLE,GRAPH	
				Expt	Rept AECU-3628	57	- +.LI7(P,N) SOURCE.	
Polarization	3.2+6		AMS	Expt	Jour NP/A 222 93	Apr 74	Zijp+ TABLES,GRAPHS. CFD NON-SPH POT	+
					Conf 75Zurich 189	Aug 75	- + GRPH OF DATA IN REVIEW.	
					Conf 72Budapest 170	Aug 72	- + POLARIZTN,EXPT CFD OPTMOD,GRP	
	3.2+6				Data EXFOR20777.019	Apr 78	4PTS.	
Potntal Scat	1.2+2	3.0+2	ANL	Expt	Jour PR 76 100	Jul 49	Hibdon+TRNS.10PC RSLN.MN SCT DET.	+
	1.2+2	3.0+2			Data EXFOR11261.035	Jun 76	. 2 PTS. SIG	
Potntal Scat	+0	+3	BNL	Expt	Jour PR 110 692	May 58	Seth+,11.5+-0.8B CALCTD FROM TOT SIG	+
	+0	+4			Conf ORNL-2309	Jun 57	- +	
	1.9+3				Data EXFOR11788.018	Jun 76	. 1 PT. SIG	
Potntal Scat		6.5+6	DKE	ExTh	Jour PL 13 70	Nov 64	Seth+0,1PHASE FRM SIG TOT AV 3-650KV	
Potntal Scat	None		DKE	Expt	Abst DA/B 28 3834	Mar 68	Divadeenam.TRNS.EFFECTIVE RADIUS	
Tot Inelastc	2.5+6	1.4+7	IFU	Expt	Conf 58Geneva 15 18	Sep 58	Pasechnik+.PPR2030,NDG,EXPT DESCRIBD	
Diff Inelast	4.0+6	7.0+6	LAS	Expt	Jour PR 129 1649	Feb 63	Thomson+ 90DEG TEMP FOR NS TO 5	+
	4.0+6	7.0+6			Data EXFOR11495.051	Jun 76	. 6 PTS. DSIG	
	5.0+6	6.0+6			Data EXFOR11495.055	Jun 76	. 2 PTS. SIG	
Diff Inelast	4.0+6	6.5+6	DKE	Expt	Jour NP 60 17	Nov 64	Buccino+N SPEC MEASURED 4ES+NUC TEMP	
					Abst DA 24 4251	Apr 64	Hollandsworth.TOF.EN SPEC.NUCL T.	
Diff Inelast	3.0+5	1.5+6	ANL	Expt	Jour ZP 183 323	Mar 65	Devilliers+ EXC CURVS 6 LVLS	+
	5.0+5	1.5+6			Data EXFOR12240.	Jun 76	. 68 PTS. SIG	
Diff Inelast	1.4+7		RPI	Expt	Jour JNAB 19 497	Jul 65	Pearlstein+ INEL SPECTRUM 6-14 MEV	+
					Abst DA 26 438	Jul 65	- .SIGMA+INEL EN SPECTRA.NDG	
	1.4+7				Data EXFOR10234.004	May 73	1PT,DSIGMA AT 90DEG	
Diff Inelast	1.4+7		KYU	Expt	Jour NST 11 523	Dec 74	Akiyoshi+ .TOF,E-SPECTRUM AT 100 DEG	
Thermal Scat	Maxwl		HAR	Expt	Jour JP/C 1 1075	Aug 68	North+ STRUCTURE FACTOR FOR LIQUIDS	
Thermal Scat	Cold		MUN	Expt	Prog EANDC(E)150U	Oct 72	Koester+ COH SCATT AMPL	+
	4.5-4				Data EXFOR20581.008	Jun 76	1PNT.COH.SC.AMP.	
Thermal Scat	1.0-4	1.0+3	MUN	Revw	Jour EEN 80 1	77	Koester. SCAT LENGTH,FREE SIG	
Scattering	Maxwl		CAV	Expt	Jour PRSA 162 127	Sep 37	Goldhaber+. 14.2B REL 4.83B FOR C	
Scattering	6.0+4	1.8+6	ANL	Expt	Jour PR 107 1077	Aug 57	Langsdorf+,LEGENDRE COEFS CURVES	+
					Rept ANL-5567	Oct 61	.REVISED DATA	
	6.0+4	1.8+6			Data EXFOR11224.062	Jun 76	. 22 PTS. SIG	
	6.0+4	1.8+6			Data EXFOR11224.063	Jun 76	. 110 PTS. DSIG	
Absorption	Maxwl	1.4+7	AUS	Expt	Jour APA 3 352	Mar 50	Lintner. RA-BE SOURCE	
					Jour OAWS 158 135	Nov 49	- .	
Absorption	Pile		ANL	Expt	Jour PR 80 342	Nov 50	Harris+.PILE OSC.REL TO BORON.	+
	Pile				Data EXFOR11528.048	Jun 76	. 1 PT. SIGMA	
Res Int Abs	1.0+1	4.0+4	LEB	Expt	Jour ZET 47 795	Sep 64	RIA=12+-2 BARNS,CFD OTHER EXPT 38.4B	
					Jour JET 20 531	Mar 65	TRANSLATN.*	
Res Int Abs	Pile		ROS	Expt	Jour KE 14 73	Mar 71	Huettel.VALUES GIVEN VS ATOM DENSITY	+
	Pile				Data EXFOR30137.006	Nov 71	INF DILUTE RES-INT	
(n,γ)	2.2+5		PCF	Expt	Jour NAT 142 392	Aug 38	Halban+ ACT CS GIVEN	
(n,γ)	Maxwl		ORL	Expt	Jour PR 83 643	Aug 51	Pomerance.LOCAL OSC REL AU ABS 95 B	+
	Maxwl				Data EXFOR11047.020	Jun 76	. 1 PT. SIG	
(n,γ)	1.5+7		HAR	Expt	Conf 57Col.Univ § 2B5	Sep 57	Lynn.UNPUBL EXPT. 2.0 MB	
(n,γ)	2.0+5		KUR	Expt	Conf 58Geneva 15 50	Sep 58	Leipunskij+.PPR2219,VAL GVN,ACTIVATN	
(n,γ)	3.0+4	6.5+4	ORL	Expt	Jour PR 122 182	Apr 61	Gibbons+	+
					Jour PR 129 2695	Mar 63	Macklin+ LIQ SCINT,71 AND 35MB	
					Conf 61Vienna 1 95	Aug 61	Neiler.	
	3.0+4	6.5+4			Data EXFOR11329.070	Jun 76	. 2 PTS. SIG	
(n,γ)	8.0+0	7.0+4	LEB	Comp	Rept INDSWG-64 43	64	Konks. GRAPH SIG(E), (FIAN A-25 1964	
(n,γ)	1.0+1	4.0+4	LEB	Expt	Jour ZET 47 795	Sep 64	NORMALIZED TO AU,BR,TA AVERAGE,CURVE	+
					Jour JET 20 531	Mar 65	TRANSLATN.*	

81 Thallium

Quantity	Energy (ev) Min	Max	Lab	Type	Documentation Ref Vol Page	Author, Comments Date	Data
(n,γ)	1.0+4	2.0+5	KFK	Expt	Jour NP/A 141 602	Jan 70 Kompe+ VDG.REL TO AU.ALSO MAXWELL AV	
					Rept KFK-1165	Feb 70 - + EQU TO NP/A 141 602.	
(n,γ)	-		CCP	Revw	Jour AE 29 187	Sep 70 Sukhoruchkin. (D,P GAM) CFD (N,GAM)	
					Jour SJA 29 896	Sep 70 TRANSLATN.*	
(n,γ)	3.0+4		AUA	Theo	Rept AAEC/E-211	Nov 70 Musgrove. SIGMA GIVEN AND CFD OTHER	
(n,γ)	4.0+5		WWA	Expt	Jour APPB 2 489	71 Brzosko+ PARTIAL,TOTAL SIG CFD THEO	+
					Rept INR-1318 28	Apr 71 *SHORT REPORT,DATA GIV	
					Jour CJP 47 2849	Dec 69 *TH.CALCULATIONS OF SIG	
	4.0+5				Data EXFOR30159.	Apr 72 PARTIAL,TOTAL SIGMAS GIVEN	
Spect (n,γ)	Maxwl		CRC	Expt	Jour CJP 31 1025	Nov 53 Bartholomew+ PAIR SP,140KV LINEWIDTH	
Spect (n,γ)	Maxwl		GEA	Eval	Jour DC-58-1-30	Jan 58 Deloume. BY APPROXIMATION CURV+TABLE	
Spect (n,γ)	Maxwl		ARF	Expt	Prog ARF-1193-17	Dec 62 Greenwood+NAI(TL) SPEC 10GAMMAS	
Spect (n,γ)	2.5-2		MIT	Comp	Rept MITNE-85	Jan 69 Rasmussen+TBL G INT.=AFCRL-69-0071	
Spect (n,γ)	2.0+3		MTR	Expt	Prog NCSAC-31 76	May 70 Greenwood+,ANAL TO BE COMPL,NO DATA	
Spect (n,γ)	Maxwl		CCP	Revw	Jour AE 29 187	Sep 70 Sukhoruchkin. GAM-SPEC,DOORWAY-STATE	
					Jour SJA 29 896	Sep 70 TRANSLATN.*	
Spect (n,γ)	4.0+5		WWA	Expt	Jour APPB 2 489	Aug 71 Brzosko+ GAMMA-EN = 3 TO 7 MEV,GRAPH	
Spect (n,γ)	7.0+5	2.6+6	CRC	Expt	Conf 72Budapest 262	Aug 72 Lone+ G-RAY INTENSITIES ,GRPH	
					Prog AECL-4147 48	Feb 72 Earle+. 3ES. NO DATA GIVEN.	
		3.0+6			Prog AECL-4068 80	Sep 71 - +. NO DATA GIVEN	
					Prog AECL-3912 64	Mar 71 Bartholomew+.NAI DET.PRELIM. NO DATA	
Spect (n,γ)	1.4+7		NJS	Expt	Priv CVELBAR	Oct 73 .INTEGRAL EXPT,SCINT PAIR SPECTRMTR	+
	1.4+7				Data EXFOR30185.019	Oct 73 1 DATA LINE	
Spect (n,γ)	1.0+6	1.0+7	CRC	Revw	Conf 74Petten 119	Sep 74 Bartholomew+ PHOTON STRF GRPH	
Spect (n,γ)	4.5+5		AUA	Expt	Rept INDC-17 7	Oct 74 Kenny+ NA-I GAM-SPEC,GRAPH	
Inelastic γ	1.5+6		LAS	Expt	Jour AP 12 485	Mar 61 Lind+ SIG(94DEG) FOR 3 GAMMAS	+
	1.5+6				Data EXFOR11188.015	Jun 76 . 3 PTS. DSIG	
Inelastic γ	5.0+5	1.5+6	ANL	Expt	Jour ZP 183 323	Mar 65 Devilliers+VDG.TOF,GRPHS	
Inelastic γ	1.0+6		TNC	Expt	Prog ORO-2791-79	Aug 67 Morgan+ NAI(TL)+GE-LI NDG TBC	
Inelastic γ	1.0+5	2.2+6	ARK	Expt	Abst DA/B 36 1785	Oct 75 Cottles.G PROD THRS,ANG DISTR,SIGS.	
Nonelastic γ		2.4+6	OSA	Expt	Jour JPJO 19 369	37 Aoki.D+D NEUTRON.RELATIV SIG GIVN	
(n,2n)	5.0+6	1.4+7	AUS	Expt	Jour APA 3 352	Mar 50 Lintner. RA-BE SOURCE	
					Jour OAWS 158 135	Nov 49 - .	
(n,2n)	1.5+7		DEB	Eval	Jour REA 11 1 153	Mar 73 Boedy+ RECOMM.VALUE FROM N-Z SYSTEM.	
					Rept IAEA-153 173	73 - + DATA SUPERSEDED	
Fission	2.5+7	8.4+7	BRK	Expt	Jour PR 73 1135	May 48 Kelly+ RELATIVE TO THORIUM.	
Reson Params	2.7+2	1.1+3	COL	Expt	Jour PR 71 174	Feb 47 WU+ 2E0. APPROX STRENGTH GIVEN 270EV	+
	2.7+2	1.1+3			Data EXFOR11751.012	Jun 76 . 2 RES, E0,WT**2/PCS	
Reson Params	-.4+1	1.1+3	BNL	Expt	Jour PR 110 692	May 58 Seth+,2 RESONANCES FC	+
	-.4+1				Data EXFOR11788.039	Jun 76 . 1 RES, E0,WN0	
Reson Params	2.4+2		ITE	Expt	Prog INDSWG-120 19	65 Ignat'Ev.TOF,RES AT 238.8 EV	
Reson Params	2.1+4	1.0+5	COL	Expt	Jour PR/C 12 102	Jul 75 Liou+TOF.TBL.SINGLE LVL SHAPE ANAL.	+
	2.1+4	1.0+5			Data EXFOR10535.	Mar 76 . 54 RES. ES.WT,WN AG VALS GVN.	
Strnth Fnctn		6.5+5	DKE	ExTh	Jour PL 13 70	Nov 64 Seth+S,P,D STF FRM SIG TOT 3-650KEV	+
	5.0+4	1.5+5		Expt	Conf 64Paris 2 916	Jul 64 - +S0,S1,S2 R PRIME/R DUKE U.	
	3.0+3	6.5+5			Data EXFOR11665.033	Jun 76 . 3 PTS.	
Strnth Fnctn	None		DKE	Expt	Abst DA/B 28 3834	Mar 68 Divadeenam.S,P,D WAVES.CFD POTMDLS.	

81 Thallium 194

Quantity	Energy (ev) Min	Max	Lab	Type	Documentation Ref Vol Page	Author, Comments Date	Data
Reson Params	-		AUA	Theo	Rept AAEC/E-211	Nov 70 Musgrove. CALCULTD D+GAM WIDTH GIVEN	
Strnth Fnctn	-		AUA	Theo	Rept AAEC/E-211	Nov 70 Musgrove. SMOOTHED S0,S1 AND S2 GIVN	

81 Thallium 195

Quantity	Energy (ev) Min	Max	Lab	Type	Documentation Ref Vol Page	Author, Comments Date	Data
Reson Params	-		AUA	Theo	Rept AAEC/E-211	Nov 70 Musgrove. CALCULTD D+GAM WIDTH GIVEN	
Strnth Fnctn	-		AUA	Theo	Rept AAEC/E-211	Nov 70 Musgrove. SMOOTHED S0,S1 AND S2 GIVN	

81 Thallium 196

Quantity	Energy (ev) Min	Max	Lab	Type	Documentation Ref Vol Page	Author, Comments Date	Data
Reson Params	-		AUA	Theo	Rept AAEC/E-211	Nov 70 Musgrove. CALCULTD D+GAM WIDTH GIVEN	

81 Thallium 196

Quantity	Energy (ev) Min	Max	Lab	Type	Documentation Ref Vol Page	Date	Author, Comments	Data
Strnth Fnctn	-		AUA	Theo Rept	AAEC/E-211	Nov 70	Musgrove. SMOOTHED S0,S1 AND S2 GIVN	

81 Thallium 197

Quantity	Energy (ev) Min	Max	Lab	Type	Documentation Ref Vol Page	Date	Author, Comments	Data
Reson Params	-		AUA	Theo Rept	AAEC/E-211	Nov 70	Musgrove. CALCULTD D+GAM WIDTH GIVEN	
Strnth Fnctn	-		AUA	Theo Rept	AAEC/E-211	Nov 70	Musgrove. SMOOTHED S0,S1 AND S2 GIVN	

81 Thallium 198

Quantity	Energy (ev) Min	Max	Lab	Type	Documentation Ref Vol Page	Date	Author, Comments	Data
Reson Params	-		AUA	Theo Rept	AAEC/E-211	Nov 70	Musgrove. CALCULTD D+GAM WIDTH GIVEN	
Strnth Fnctn	-		AUA	Theo Rept	AAEC/E-211	Nov 70	Musgrove. SMOOTHED S0,S1 AND S2 GIVN	

81 Thallium 199

Quantity	Energy (ev) Min	Max	Lab	Type	Documentation Ref Vol Page	Date	Author, Comments	Data
Reson Params	-		AUA	Theo Rept	AAEC/E-211	Nov 70	Musgrove. CALCULTD D+GAM WIDTH GIVEN	
Strnth Fnctn	-		AUA	Theo Rept	AAEC/E-211	Nov 70	Musgrove. SMOOTHED S0,S1 AND S2 GIVN	

81 Thallium 200

Quantity	Energy (ev) Min	Max	Lab	Type	Documentation Ref Vol Page	Date	Author, Comments	Data
Reson Params	-		AUA	Theo Rept	AAEC/E-211	Nov 70	Musgrove. CALCULTD D+GAM WIDTH GIVEN	
Strnth Fnctn	-		AUA	Theo Rept	AAEC/E-211	Nov 70	Musgrove. SMOOTHED S0,S1 AND S2 GIVN	

81 Thallium 201

Quantity	Energy (ev) Min	Max	Lab	Type	Documentation Ref Vol Page	Date	Author, Comments	Data
Reson Params	-		AUA	Theo Rept	AAEC/E-211	Nov 70	Musgrove. CALCULTD D+GAM WIDTH GIVEN	
Strnth Fnctn	-		AUA	Theo Rept	AAEC/E-211	Nov 70	Musgrove. SMOOTHED S0,S1 AND S2 GIVN	

81 Thallium 202

Quantity	Energy (ev) Min	Max	Lab	Type	Documentation Ref Vol Page	Date	Author, Comments	Data
(n,2n)	7.8+6	1.4+7	LAS	Eval Prog	LA-5546-PR	Apr 74	Muir. ABSTRACT	
(n,p)	Maxwl		IFU	Theo Rept	ICD-4 20	67	Dadakina+ PENETR COEFF CALC,TABLE	
Reson Params	-		AUA	Theo Rept	AAEC/E-211	Nov 70	Musgrove. CALCULTD D+GAM WIDTH GIVEN	
Strnth Fnctn	-		AUA	Theo Rept	AAEC/E-211	Nov 70	Musgrove. SMOOTHED S0,S1 AND S2 GIVN	
Lvl Density	8.0+6	1.5+7	ANL	Eval Rept	ANL-75-34	Jun 75	Davey+N2NEVAL.CONSTANT T,LVL DEN FIT	

81 Thallium 203

Quantity	Energy (ev) Min	Max	Lab	Type	Documentation Ref Vol Page	Date	Author, Comments	Data
Total	5.0+3	5.5+4	DKE	Expt Jour	AP 14 346	Jul 61	Newson+TRNS RATIOS.CURV.LVL SPACING.	+
	4.0+3	3.0+4		Data	EXFOR11888.014	Jun 76	. 66 PTS. SIG	
Total	1.0+1	3.0+5	ORL	Expt Prog	ORNL-4743 54	Dec 71	Harvey+.ORELA.TRANS. NO DATA GIVEN	
Total	1.5+1	1.6+5	COL	Expt Jour	PR/C 12 102	Jul 75	Liou+ GRPH,RES PAR TBL	+
	1.5+1	2.1+4		Data	EXFOR10535.014	Mar 76	UNCORRECTED CS DATA AVAILABLE.	
Diff Inelast	1.5+6	3.2+6	ALA	Expt Jour	PR/C 11 869	Mar 75	Ahmed+ TBL,GRPH LEVEL EXCITATIONS	+
	1.1+6	2.9+6		Rept	ALBERTA-67	May 74	Gill+ TABLE, INEGRAL SIGMA, 15 LEVLS	
	1.2+6	2.9+6		Data	EXFOR10367.002	Jan 75	103 PTS	
Nonelastic	1.4+7	1.5+7	ANL	Eval Rept	ANL-75-34	Jun 75	Davey+CORRC APPLIED TO N2N CS.TBLS.	
Res Int Abs	5.0-1		ANL	Expt Jour	PR 79 11	Jul 50	Harris+ EPI-CD,REL THERMAL ACT. B-W	+
	5.0-1			Data	EXFOR11343.035	Jun 76	. 1 PT. RI	
Res Int Abs	None		ORL	Revw Conf	55Geneva 5 96	Aug 55	Macklin+.TABLE,EXPT CFD THEORY,P833	
Res Int Abs	1.0+1	4.0+4	LEB	Expt Jour	ZET 47 795	Sep 64	RIA=40+-5B,CFD OTHER EXPT 129B	
				Jour	JET 20 531	Mar 65	TRANSLATN.*	
Res Int Abs	5.5-1		CPO	Expt Jour	JIN 32 2839	Oct 70	Sims+ (N,G).CD CUT-OFF,VALUE GIVEN	+
	5.5-1			Data	EXFOR10608.	Aug 76	2PTS.MAXW SPEC MEAS AND 1/V REMOVED	
(n,γ)	None		PAR	Expt Jour	CR 201 722	Oct 35	Preiswerk+	

81 Thallium 203

Quantity	Energy (ev) Min	Energy (ev) Max	Lab	Type	Documentation Ref Vol Page	Author, Comments Date	Data
(n,γ)	Maxwl		JAP	Expt Jour	SCP 38 167	Jan 41 Sinma+.LI+D.RELATIVE SIG MEASUREMENT	
(n,γ)	Maxwl		UI	Expt Jour	PR 59 102	Jan 41 O−Neal+ ACTIVATION. REL TO MN.	
(n,γ)	Pile		ANL	Expt Jour	PR 72 888	Nov 47 Seren+.ACT METHOD.PILE IRRADTLNO3	+
	Pile			Data	EXFOR11447.130	Jun 76 . 1 PT. SIG	
(n,γ)	Maxwl		ORL	Expt Jour	PR 88 412	Oct 52 Pomerance.PILE OSC.	+
	Maxwl			Data	EXFOR11507.097	Jun 76 . 1 PT. SIG	
(n,γ)	1.0+0	4.0+4	LEB	Comp Rept	INDSWG−64 43	64 Konks. GRAPH SIG(E), (FIAN A−25 1964	
(n,γ)	1.0+1	4.0+4	LEB	Expt Jour	ZET 47 795	Sep 64 NORMALIZED TO AU,BR,TA AVERAGE,CURVE	+
				Jour	JET 20 531	Mar 65 TRANSLATN.*	
(n,γ)	Pile		ORL	Expt Prog	ORNL−4306 2	May 68 Druschel+,VALUE GIVEN	
(n,γ)	−		IEA	Comp Rept	IEA−INF−10 6	Aug 68 Atalla. TABLES OF HL,SIG AND GAMM−E	
(n,γ)	Maxwl		CRC	Expt Prog	AECL−3742 41	Sep 70 Merritt+,ACT,SIG REL TO TL205 GIVEN	+
	Maxwl			Data	EXFOR10606.002	Aug 76 1PT=(1.1+−.3)+2.ACT RATIO TL203/205	
(n,γ)	Maxwl		CPO	Expt Jour	JIN 32 2839	Oct 70 Sims+ CD CUT−OFF,REL CO59,SIG GIVEN	+
	Maxwl			Data	EXFOR10608.	Aug 76 2PTS.EFFECTIVE CS AND MAXW SPEC CALC	
(n,γ)	3.0+4		AUA	Theo Rept	AAEC/E−211	Nov 70 Musgrove. SIGMA GIVEN AND CFD OTHER	
(n,γ)	2.0+6	7.0+6	MCME	ExTh Jour	CJP 52 1217	Jul 74 Colenbrander+ INT OF TRANSITIONS,TBL	
(n,γ)	1.5+1	1.0+5	COL	Expt Jour	PR/C 12 102	Jul 75 Liou+ GRPH,RES PAR TBL	
Spect (n,γ)	Maxwl		KUR	Expt Conf	58Geneva 15 138	Sep 58 Groshev+ PPR2029.CURV,COMPTON−SPEC	
Spect (n,γ)	Pile		MCM	Expt Jour	PR/B 140 1562	Dec 65 Prestwich+ GE−LI DET	+
Spect (n,γ)	Maxwl		ORL	Expt Abst	BAP 12 922	Aug 67 Harvey+3 (Y10). SOME NEW G ES	
Spect (n,γ)	Maxwl		KUR	Expt Jour	YF 7 937	May 68 Groshev+ OTHER XPTAL GAM−INT(GAM−E)	
				Jour	SNP 7 563	Nov 68 . ENGL OF YF 7 937	
	Maxwl		KFK	Expt Rept	KFK−1099	Aug 69 Weitkamp+REPRINT FROM 69STUDSVIK	
				Conf	69Studsvik 421	Aug 69 − + GRPH 2−5MEV GAM,DECAY SCH	
Spect (n,γ)	Maxwl		CAS	Expt Jour	NCL 2 992	Nov 71 Fubini+ PAIR SPECT.	+
				Conf	69Studsvik 317	Aug 69 − + EXPTAL DETAILS	
	Maxwl			Data	EXFOR20442.002	Nov 75 20PTS.	
Spect (n,γ)	1.0+7		WWA	Theo Jour	NP/A 189 545	Jul 72 Brzosko+ CMPD NUCL DECAY.PARTIAL WG	
Spect (n,γ)	Pile		CAS	Expt Jour	NC/A 18 711	Dec 73 Fubini+ G SPECT ANAL,TL204 LVLS DRVD	+
	Pile			Data	EXFOR20357.002	Sep 74 127PTS.	
Spect (n,γ)	Maxwl		MUN	Expt Conf	74Petten 584	Sep 74 Rabenstein+ DECAY SCHEME TL−204	
Inelastic γ	6.0+5	1.6+6	PEL	Expt Jour	NP/A 157 130	Nov 70 Barnard+ VDG TOF GE(LI) NDG.LVL SCHM	
Inelastic γ	2.8+6		MUN	Expt Jour	ZP 245 13	Jul 71 Feicht+ D−D NS,GE(LI) PROD C.S.+LVLS	
				Rept	INIS−MF−3775	76 Hegewisch. THESIS.G−ES+INTS,LVL SCH	
Inelastic γ	1.1+6	3.2+6	ALA	Expt Jour	PR/C 11 869	Mar 75 Ahmed+ LVL PROD CS.GRPHS.LVL SCHEMES	
Inelastic γ	1.0+5	2.2+6	ARK	Expt Abst	DA/B 36 1785	Oct 75 Cottles.G PROD THRS,ANG DISTR,SIGS.	
Inelastic γ	1.3+6		ALA	Expt Jour	NIM 134 291	76 Davidson+ ANG DIST GRPH I FOR 1.1MEV	
(n,2n)	1.2+7	1.8+7	LAS	Expt Jour	PR 86 565	May 52 Martin+ ACT ENERGY DEPENDENCE CURVE	
				Rept	AECU−2650	53 Bame+T−D NEUTS EXCITATION FUNCTION	
(n,2n)	Pile		CRC	Expt Rept	CRC−852	Jul 59 Roy+ ACTIVATION IN NRX FLUX	
(n,2n)	1.5+7		ARK	Expt Prog	A−ARK−60	Jan 60 Poularikas+	+
	1.5+7			Data	EXFOR12181.008	Jun 76 . 1 PT. SIG	
(n,2n)	8.4+6	1.5+7	LRL	Expt Rept	UCRL−6028	Jun 60 Tewes.ACT,14ES 15MB TO 1.7B +−20PC	+
	8.4+6	1.5+7		Data	EXFOR11504.018	Jun 76 . 14 PTS. SIG	
(n,2n)	Fiss		CRC	Eval Rept	CRC−1003	Dec 60 Roy+,ESTIMATED AVG SIG=2.3MB	
(n,2n)	1.2+7	2.0+7	LAS	Expt Jour	PR 121 1438	Mar 61 Prestwood+ INCL N3N	+
				Rept	LA−2493	Dec 60 Bayhurst+ EXCITATION CURVE	
	1.2+7	2.0+7		Data	EXFOR11645.027	Jun 76 . 10 PTS. SIG	
(n,2n)	1.4+7		HAM	Comp Jour	NP 65 257	Mar 65 Bormann. 2EXPT VALS.CFD SHELL EFFECT	
(n,2n)	1.3+7	1.5+7	BNL	Theo Jour	NSE 23 238	Nov 65 Pearlstein.3ES.STAT MDL CALC.TBL CS.	
(n,2n)	Fiss		BNL	Theo Jour	NSE 23 238	Nov 65 Pearlstein.STATMDL CALC.SPEC AVG.TBL	
(n,2n)	1.4+7		GRE	Expt Rept	CEA−R−2900	Dec 65 Monnand. SIGMA TO ISOM.STATE GIVEN	
(n,2n)	1.5+7		ALD	Expt Rept	AWRE−O−76/66	Dec 66 Vallis. ACTIV. AL27(N,ALPHA) STANDRD	
	1.5+7			Data	EXFOR20347.010	Sep 74 1PNT.SIGMA.	
(n,2n)	1.4+7		IRK	Expt Jour	NP/A 102 534	Oct 67 Scheimbauer+.ISOM RATIO.HL.NAT.TARGT	+
				Jour	OAWS 175 163	Apr 66 − + TO GS AND MS.	
	1.4+7			Data	EXFOR20062.	Sep 71 3PTS.SIG.	
(n,2n)	Fiss		CCP	Expt Jour	DOK 180 836	Jun 68 Nasyrov.(AVG+EFFECTIV)THRESH−SIG−TBL	
				Jour	SPD 13 6 559	Dec 68 TRANSLATN.*	
				Jour	EAF 25 5 125	Nov 68 .TRANSLATN.*	
				Jour	AE 25 437	Nov 68 Nasyrov.(AVG+EFFECTIV)THRESH−SIG−TBL	
				Jour	SJA 25 1251	Nov 68 . ENGL OF AE 25 437	
(n,2n)	1.5+7		DEB	Expt Jour	AHP 25 91	Oct 68 Peto+ REL Y89(N,2N), ACTIVATION	+
	1.5+7			Data	EXFOR30069.007	Dec 70 SIG REL Y−089(N2N)	
(n,2n)	1.5+7		MUN	Expt Jour	OAWS 177 323	69 Winkler+(IRK) ACTIVATION.	+
				Jour	NP/A 118 9	Sep 68 Dilg+ ACTIV.REL AL(N,A)	
	1.5+7			Data	EXFOR20802.021	Dec 78 1PNT.SIGMA.	

81 Thallium 203

Quantity	Energy (ev) Min	Max	Lab	Type	Documentation Ref Vol Page	Author, Comments Date	Data
(n,2n)	1.5+7		DEB Comp	Jour	REA 7 4 93	Dec 69 Csikai+ SIG+HL COMPILTN,N−ACTIV−ANAL	
(n,2n)	1.4+7	1.5+7	CCP Comp	Rept	ICD−6 215	70 Sluchevskaja.ALSO FISS,4REFS,TBL	
(n,2n)	8.0+6	1.3+7	AUA Theo	Rept	AAEC/TM−542	May 70 Bertram. CALC SIG(E) CFD EXPT,GRAPHS	
	8.0+6	2.0+7		Rept	AAEC/TM−522	Nov 69 − . CALC SIG(E)GRAPHS CFD EXPTS	
(n,2n)	1.4+7	1.5+7	JYV Eval	Rept	JU−RR−3/1970	Jun 70 Leppaemaeki+ TABLE OF EVAL AVG SIG	
(n,2n)	1.4+7	1.5+7	JYV Eval	Rept	JU−RR−3/1970	Jun 70 Leppaemaeki+ (N,3N) UPPER LIMIT,TBL	
(n,2n)	+7		KFI Theo	Rept	KFKI−71−8	Feb 71 Jeki. CALCULATED CFD EXPTL SIG VALUE	
(n,2n)	1.4+7		KFI Comp	Jour	JRC 7 365	Jun 71 Nagy+ SIGMA, GAMMA−E AND HALF−L GIVN	
(n,2n)	1.4+7	1.5+7	IRK ExTh	Jour	APA 33 285	Jul 71 Winiwarter+ ISOMERIC RATIO	
(n,2n)	Fast		JUL Expt	Conf	71Canterby 121	Sep 71 Qaim+EFFECTIVE SIGMA.ACTIV,GAMMA DET	+
	Fast			Data	EXFOR20554.013	Apr 76 1PNT.SIGMA.	
(n,2n)	1.5+7		CCP Expt	Jour	YF 14 682	Oct 71 Druzhinin+ NAI,ABSOL,TBL CFD OTHERS	
				Jour	SNP 14 383	Apr 72 *ENGL OF YF 14 682	
(n,2n)	1.4+7		GIT Expt	Jour	NP/A 180 157	Jan 72 Hankla+ ACT,GE(LI),MIXED POWDER.	+
				Abst	DA/B 32 293	Nov 71 − . ACT METHOD, CFD THEORY.	
	1.4+7			Data	EXFOR10244.017	Jun 74 1PT,SIGMA	
(n,2n)	1.5+7		DEB Eval	Jour	REA 11 1 153	Mar 73 Boedy. COMPILATION+RECOMM.VALUE,TBL	
				Rept	IAEA−153 173	73 − . RECOMM. VALUE ONLY	
(n,2n)	1.4+7		LOU Expt	Prog	INR−1464 12	May 73 Araminowicz+ BRIEF,ACTIV,TABLE,GRAPH	+
	1.4+7			Data	EXFOR30264.042	Nov 73 SIGMA AT 14.6 MEV	
(n,2n)	8.0+6	2.0+7	IFL Eval	Rept	YK− 15 63	Aug 73 Bondars+ SHORT. GRAPH OF EVAL DATA	
(n,2n)	Fiss		KOS Eval	Jour	AK 16 351	74 Boedy. U238,MAXW−SPC.AVG CFD XPT,TBL	
(n,2n)	1.5+7		TAT Theo	Jour	JP/A 7 1457	Aug 74 Kondaiah. CALC ON STAT MODEL	
(n,2n)	Fiss		KOS Eval	Conf	75Karlsrhe 29	Apr 75 Csikai. CF252,MAXW−SPC.AVG FOR 2TEMP	
(n,2n)	1.5+7		SMU Expt	Jour	JIN 37 1121	May 75 Eapen+ TO GND,META.RATIO CFD TH,TBLS	+
				Conf	75Wash. 712	Mar 75 Salaita+SHORT−LIVED ISOMER PROD.TBL.	
				Conf	74Columbia 95	Jul 74 − + ACT.SIG TO GROUND+META.TABL	
	1.5+7			Data	EXFOR10493.	May 75 3 PTS. ISOM,GND ST PROD CS + RATIO	
(n,2n)	8.0+6	1.5+7	ANL Eval	Rept	ANL−75−34	Jun 75 Davey+CONSTANT T MDL,LVL DEN MDL FIT	
(n,2n)	2.4+7	2.8+7	LAS Expt	Jour	PR/C 12 451	Aug 75 Bayhurst+TBL,GRPH.	+
	1.6+7	2.8+7		Data	EXFOR10536.	Apr 76 16PTS.	
(n,2n)	Fiss		CNE Expt	Jour	JIN 38 1386	Jul 76 Gerbino+ ACTIV.TABLE SIG VS STANDARD	+
	Fiss			Data	EXFOR30339.002	Aug 76 1 DATA PNT	
(n,xn) x>2	1.7+7	2.0+7	LAS Expt	Jour	PR 121 1438	Mar 61 Prestwood+VDG+COCKROFT WALTON.TBL	+
	1.7+7	2.0+7		Data	EXFOR11645.028	Jun 76 . 3 PTS. SIG N3N	
(n,xn) x>2	1.5+7		ARK Expt	Jour	PR 131 2649	Sep 63 Bramlitt+N3N.LESS THAN 10MB.HL GVN	
				Rept	TID−16949	Jan 63 .THESIS	
	1.5+7			Data	EXFOR11590.080	Jun 76 . 1 PT. SIG,N3N	
(n,xn) x>2	Fiss		BNL Theo	Rept	NSE 23 238	Nov 65 Pearlstein.SPEC AVG STATMDL CALC N3N	
(n,xn) x>2	1.5+7	2.8+7	LAS Expt	Jour	PR/C 12 451	Aug 75 Bayhurst+N3N,N4N.TBL,GRPH.CFD CALC.	+
	1.5+7	2.8+7		Data	EXFOR10536.	Apr 76 11PTSN3N.3PTS N4N	
(n,p)	Fiss		HAR Expt	Rept	AERE−I/R−2630	Jul 58 Mellish+ SIG VAL GIVEN,ACTIVATION	
				Conf	57Paris 1 35	57 − +ACTIVATION.	
(n,p)	Fiss		GES Revw	Jour	NUC 17 1 54	Jan 59 Rochlin.47 ISOTOPES.ACT.RVS.TBL	
(n,p)	1.5+7		ARK Expt	Prog	A−ARK−604	Jan 60 Poularikas+	+
	1.5+7			Data	EXFOR12181.007	Jun 76 . 1 PT. SIG	
(n,p)	Fiss		CRC Eval	Rept	CRC−1003	Dec 60 Roy+,ESTIMATED AVG SIG=0.007MB	
(n,p)	1.5+7		SAH Comp	Jour	NUC 23 8 112	Aug 65 Chatterjee. TABLE WITH REFS.	
(n,p)	Maxwl		IFU Theo	Rept	ICD−4 20	67 Dadakina+ PENETR COEFF CALC,TABLE	
(n,p)	1.5+7		DEB Comp	Jour	REA 7 4 93	Dec 69 Csikai+ SIG+HL COMPILTN,N−ACTIV−ANAL	
(n,p)	1.4+7	1.5+7	JYV Eval	Rept	JU−RR−3/1970	Jun 70 Leppaemaeki+ TABLE OF EVAL AVG SIG	
(n,α)	1.4+7		ALD Expt	Jour	PPS 73 215	Feb 59 Coleman+. ACTIVATION	+
(n,α)	Fiss		CRC Eval	Rept	CRC−1003	Dec 60 Roy+,ESTIMATED AVG SIG−BELO 0.0001MB	
(n,α)	1.5+7		DEB Comp	Jour	REA 7 4 93	Dec 69 Csikai+ SIG+HL COMPILTN,N−ACTIV−ANAL	
(n,α)	1.4+7	1.5+7	JYV Eval	Rept	JU−RR−3/1970	Jun 70 Leppaemaeki+ TABLE OF EVAL AVG SIG	
(n,α)	1.4+7		GIT Expt	Jour	NP/A 180 157	Jan 72 Hankla+ ACT,GE(LI),MIXED POWDER.	+
				Abst	DA/B 32 293	Nov 71 − . ACT METHOD, CFD THEORY.	
	1.4+7			Data	EXFOR10244.027	Jun 74 1PT,SIGMA	
(n,α)	Pile		MUA Expt	Prog	INDC(SEC)−35	Sep 73 Alam+ P101.ACTIV,SHORT NOTE,NDG	
				Jour	NP/A 205 614	May 73 − + RATIO TO NG SIGMA,HALF LIVES	
	Pile			Data	EXFOR30249.003	Jul 73 RATIO TO NG−SIGMA,HALF−LIVES	
(n,nα)	1.5+7		ARK Expt	Jour	PR 131 2649	Sep 63 Bramlitt+ LESS THAN 0.012MB	
				Rept	TID−16949	Jan 62 .THESIS	
	1.5+7			Data	EXFOR11590.081	Jun 76 . 1 PT, SIG	
(n,nα)	1.4+7	1.5+7	JYV Eval	Rept	JU−RR−3/1970	Jun 70 Leppaemaeki+ TABLE OF EVAL AVG SIG	
(n,nα)	1.5+7		ARK Expt	Prog	ORO−3235−11	Jul 70 Bari.TO BE COMPLETED,NO DATA GIVEN	
Reson Params	2.4+2		BNL Expt	Jour	PR 101 1328	Feb 56 Levin+,FROM THR J=1 WG=0.8EV WT=5EV	

81 Thallium 203

Quantity	Energy (ev) Min	Max	Lab	Type	Documentation Ref Vol Page	Author, Comments Date	Data
Reson Params	2.4+2		BNL	Expt Jour	PR 108 353	Oct 57 Stolovy+FC,TRNS WT=4.9EV IF WG=0.4EV	+
	2.4+2			Data	EXFOR11866.044	Jun 76 . 1 RES. E0,J,WT	
Reson Params	5.0+3	5.5+4	DKE	Expt Jour	AP 14 346	Jul 61 Newson+ D=2+−1 KEV FOR L=0	+
Reson Params	2.4+2		CCP	Comp Rept	INDSWG−64 19	64 Popov. 1 RES WN WG	
Reson Params	1.0+1	4.0+4	LEB	Expt Jour	ZET 47 795	Sep 64 AVERAGE D=5+−2KEV	+
				Jour	JET 20 531	Mar 65 TRANSLATN.*	
Reson Params	2.4+2		DUB	Comp Rept	INDSWG−101 25	65 1 RES ONLY, SEE ALSO ZET 47 795	
Reson Params		1.0+6	AUA	Theo Jour	AUJ 20 477	Oct 67 Cook. TBL OF AVG LVL SPACING D,L=0,1	
Reson Params	2.9+2		MTR	Expt Prog	NCSAC−31 70	May 70 Watanabe+ TRANS,REDUCED WN GIVEN	
Reson Params	−		AUA	Theo Rept	AAEC/E−211	Nov 70 Musgrove. CALCULTD D+GAM WIDTH GIVEN	
Reson Params	2.4+1		CJD	Eval Rept	YK−7	71 Zakharova+ SURVEY+SYSTEMATICS,GW,TBL	
				Rept	INDC(CCP)−27	Nov 72 .ENGLISH TRANSLATION OF YK−7 /71	
Reson Params	3.8+1		ANL	Expt Jour	NP/A 193 643	Oct 72 Thomas+ SWN,WG,D FIT TO TRANSM CURVE	
Reson Params	3.8+1	1.9+4	COL	Expt Jour	PR/C 12 102	Jul 75 Liou+ 36 RES.GWN,J,L,E0	+
	3.8+1	1.0+5		Data	EXFOR10535.	Mar 76 58RES ES.WN*G,WT,WG,D,J,L VALS GVN.	
Reson Params	3.5+3	3.5+4	ORL	Expt Abst	AJ 208 812	Sep 76 Macklin+PARS DRVD FROM CAPT DATA.TBL	+
	3.6+3	3.5+4		Data	EXFOR10602.	Nov 76 122RES ES.G*(WN)(WG)/WT,WG,G*WN,J.	
Strnth Fnctn	−		AUA	Theo Rept	AAEC/E−211	Nov 70 Musgrove. SMOOTHED S0,S1 AND S2 GIVN	
Strnth Fnctn	3.8+1	1.9+4	COL	Expt Jour	PR/C 12 102	Jul 75 Liou+GRPH.S0,S1 GVN.	+
	2.0+4			Data	EXFOR10535.011	Mar 76 2PTS. S,P WAVE STF	
Lvl Density	−		FEI	Eval Rept	FEI−36	66 Kapchigashev+.TBL OF RELATD QUANTTYS	+
		5.0+4		Jour	YF 4 686	Sep 66 .TABLE.SHORT VERSION OF FEI−36	
				Prog	YFI−3 3	66 .ABSTR.TABLE SHOULD READ TL(NOT TE).	
		5.0+4		Jour	SNP 4 486	67 .ENGLISH OF YF 4.FROM(N,GAMMA).TABLE	
				Prog	INDC−E−140 3	66 .ENGLISH TRANSL OF YFI−3	
Lvl Density	None		AUW	Theo Conf	70Madurai 2 267	Dec 70 Ramamurty+ A−PARAMETER GVN,LANG'S−TH	
(γ,n)		2.0+7	CCP	Expt Jour	IZV 34 116	Jan 70 Antropov+ GAM−EMAX 7−20MEV,TBL,GRAPH	
				Jour	BAS 34 108	Jan 71 * ENGL OF IZV 34 116	

81 Thallium 204

Quantity	Energy (ev) Min	Max	Lab	Type	Documentation Ref Vol Page	Author, Comments Date	Data
Total	2.0−1	1.0+3	MTR	Expt Conf	68Wash. 2 893	Mar 68 Watanabe+.TRANS.FC.2 RESON ALALYZED	+
Diff Elastic	5.0+3	2.5+6	LAS	Expt Priv	DAY	Jul 65 DAY.	+
	5.0+3	2.5+6		Data	EXFOR12191.005	Jun 76 . 66 PTS. DSIG	
(n,γ)	Pile		ORL	Expt Prog	ORNL−4306 2	May 68 Druschel+,VALUE GIVEN	
(n,γ)	7.0+5	2.6+6	CRC	Expt Jour	CJP 52 989	Jun 74 Earle+ STRENGTH FUNCTS	
(n,2n)	Fiss		CRC	Eval Rept	CRC−1003	Dec 60 Roy+,ESTIMATED AVG SIG=21.0MB	
(n,p)	Fiss		CRC	Eval Rept	CRC−1003	Dec 60 Roy+,ESTIMATED AVG SIG=0.15MB	
(n,p)	Maxwl		IFU	Theo Rept	ICD−4 20	67 Dadakina+ PENETR COEFF CALC,TABLE	
(n,α)	Fiss		CRC	Eval Rept	CRC−1003	Dec 60 Roy+,ESTIMATED AVG SIG=BELO 0.0001MB	
Reson Params	1.2+2	8.0+2	MTR	Expt Conf	68Wash. 2 893	Mar 68 Watanabe+.TRANS 2ES SIG0*GAM SQUARED	+
	1.2+2	8.0+2		Data	EXFOR12506.002	Jun 76 . 2 RES, E0,WT**2/PCS	
Lvl Density	4.0+6	7.0+6	ISL	Theo Conf	64Geneva § 511	May 64 Szwarcbaum+.T FROM 3 FORMLS CFD EXPS	
Lvl Density	+6		MIL	Theo Jour	EN 15 1 54	Jan 68 Facchini+ LDL PARS FROM LOW EN RES	
Lvl Density	None		MUN	Theo Jour	NP/A 217 269	Dec 73 Dilg+ A,DELTA. BACK SHIFTED FERMIGAS	
Lvl Density	None		COP	Theo Jour	NP/A 222 493	Apr 74 Dossing+COLL ROTAT.SPAC. ACCUR ESTIM	
Lvl Density	None		ROC	Theo Jour	NP/A 223 577	May 74 Huizenga+ EXP CFD MICROSC TH SPH NUC	

81 Thallium 205

Quantity	Energy (ev) Min	Max	Lab	Type	Documentation Ref Vol Page	Author, Comments Date	Data
Total	3.9+3	5.7+4	DKE	Expt Jour	AP 14 346	Jul 61 Newson+ TRANS	+
	3.9+3	5.7+4		Data	EXFOR11888.015	Jun 76 . 86 PTS. SIG	
Total	1.5+1	1.6+5	COL	Expt Jour	PR/C 12 102	Jul 75 Liou+ GRPH, RES PAR TBL	+
	1.5+1	2.1+4		Data	EXFOR10535.015	Mar 76 UNCORRECTED CS DATA AVAILABLE.	
Total		1.0+5	ORL	Expt Conf	76Lowell 1260	Jul 76 Winters+RES PARS FROM TOT,CAPT.NDG	
Diff Inelast	1.5+6	3.2+6	ALA	Expt Jour	PR/C 11 869	Mar 75 Ahmed+ TBL,GRAPH LEVEL EXCITATIONS	+
	1.1+6	2.9+6		Rept	ALBERTA−67	May 74 Gill+ TABLE, INEGRAL SIGMA, 10 LEVLS	
	1.2+6	2.8+6		Data	EXFOR10367.003	Jan 75 62 PTS	
Res Int Abs	5.0−1		ANL	Expt Jour	PR 79 11	Jul 50 Harris+ EPI−CD,REL THERMAL ACT. B−W	+
	5.0−1			Data	EXFOR11343.036	Jun 76 . 1 PT. RI	
Res Int Abs	None		ORL	Revw Conf	55Geneva 5 96	Aug 55 Macklin+.P833 ,EXPT CFD THEORY,TABLE	
Res Int Abs	1.0+1	4.0+4	LEB	Expt Jour	ZET 47 795	Sep 64 RIA=0.7+−0.1B,CFD OTHER EXPT 0.5B	
				Jour	JET 20 531	Mar 65 TRANSLATN.*	
(n,γ)	None		PAR	Expt Jour	CR 201 722	Oct 35 Preiswerk+	

81 Thallium 205

Quantity	Energy (ev) Min	Max	Lab	Type	Documentation Ref Vol Page	Date	Author, Comments	Data
(n,γ)	2.0+4	7.0+5	OXF Expt	Jour	PRSA 170 513	Apr 39	Griffiths.RA – BE PHOTONEUT ACTIVATION	
(n,γ)	Pile		ANL Expt	Jour	PR 72 888	Nov 47	Seren+.ACT METHOD.PILE IRRAD.TLNO3.	+
	Pile			Data	EXFOR11447.129	Jun 76	. 1 PT. SIG	
(n,γ)	Maxwl		ORL Expt	Jour	PR 88 412	Oct 52	Pomerance.PILE OSC.	+
	Maxwl			Data	EXFOR11507.098	Jun 76	. 1 PT. SIG	
(n,γ)	2.5+6	4.0+6	IFU Expt	Conf	58Geneva 15 18	Sep 58	Pasechnik+.PPR2030,SIGMA AT 3ES	
(n,γ)	2.5+4	2.0+5	KUR Expt	Conf	58Geneva 15 50	Sep 58	Leipunskij+.PPR2219,VAL GVN,ACTIVATN	
(n,γ)	1.4+7		ALD Expt	Jour	PPS 72 505	Oct 58	Perkin+ACT ANAL 2.0MB+ – 20PC, B – W TH	+
(n,γ)	2.5+4		FEI Expt	Jour	AE 5 564	Nov 58	Kononov+ ACT CS REL TO I127(N,G) GVN	
				Jour	JNEA 11 46	59	.TRANSLATION	
				Jour	SJA 5 1483	58	.TRANSLATION	
(n,γ)	2.7+4	2.7+6	CCP Expt	Jour	AE 9 401	Nov 60	Stavisskij+.GRAPH,REL I127,ACTIVTN	+
				Jour	SJA 9 942	Sep 61	TRANSLATN.*JNE AB16 496 0/62	
				Jour	KE 4 508	Jun 61	.TRANSLATN	
(n,γ)	Fast		LAS Expt	Jour	NSE 8 608	Dec 60	Byers. GODIVA ACTIVATION CS GIVEN	
(n,γ)	1.0+1	4.0+4	LEB Comp	Rept	INDSWG – 64 43	64	Konks. GRAPH SIG(E), (FIAN A – 25 1964	
(n,γ)	1.0+1	4.0+4	LEB Expt	Jour	ZET 47 795	Sep 64	NORMALIZED to AU,BR,TA AVERAGE,CURVE	+
				Jour	JET 20 531	Mar 65	TRANSLATN.*	
(n,γ)	–		IEA Comp	Rept	IEA – INF – 10 6	Aug 68	Atalla. TABLES OF HL,SIG AND GAMM – E	
(n,γ)	2.4+4		MUAExpt	Jour	NC/B 58 402	Dec 68	Hasan+,SB – BE,ACT BETA – DET REL I – 127.	+
	2.4+4			Data	EXFOR30077.020	Dec 70	SIGMA FOR 4.3 MIN HALF LIFE GIVEN	
(n,γ)	Maxwl		CRC Expt	Prog	AECL – 3742 41	Sep 70	Merritt+,ACT,SIG REL TO TL203 GIVEN	+
	Maxwl			Data	EXFOR10606.002	Aug 76	1PT=(1.1 + – .3)+2.ACT RATIO TL203/205	
(n,γ)	Pile		CAS Expt	Jour	NC/A 19 294	Jan 74	Oliva+ GAMMAS FROM N CAPTURE ANAL.	
(n,γ)	1.5+1	1.0+5	COL Expt	Jour	PR/C 12 102	Jul 75	Liou+ GRPH, RES PAR TBL	
Spect (n,γ)	Maxwl		KFK Expt	Conf	69Studsvik 421	Aug 69	Weitkamp+ GRPH 2 – 5MEV GAM,LVL CFD TH	
				Rept	KFK – 1099	Aug 69	– +REPRINT FROM 69STUDSVIK	
Spect (n,γ)	2.5 – 2	3.0+3	CRC Expt	Abst	BAP 15 550	Apr 70	Bartholomew+,GE(LI) DET,RESON CAPT	
Spect (n,γ)	Maxwl		ORL Expt	Prog	NCSAC – 42 187	Nov 71	Earle+. 5.5 – MEV GAMMA ANOMALY. CURVE	
Spect (n,γ)	4.5+1		ORL Expt	Prog	AECL – 4205	Mar 72	Earle+. P – WAVE CAPTURE	
Inelastic γ	6.0+5	1.6+6	PEL Expt	Jour	NP/A 157 130	Nov 70	Barnard+ VDG TOF GE(LI) NDG.LVL SCHM	
Inelastic γ	2.8+6		MUNExpt	Jour	ZP 245 13	Jul 71	Feicht+ D – D NS,GE(LI) PROD C.S. +LVLS	
				Rept	INIS – MF – 3775	76	Hegewisch. THESIS.G – ES+INTS,LVL SCH	
Inelastic γ	1.1+6	3.2+6	ALA Expt	Jour	PR/C 11 869	Mar 75	Ahmed+ LVL PROD CS.GRPHS.LVL SCHEMES	
Inelastic γ	1.0+5	2.2+6	ARK Expt	Abst	DA/B 36 1785	Oct 75	Cottles.G PROD THRS,ANG DISTR,SIGS.	
(n,2n)	Fiss		CRC Eval	Rept	CRC – 1003	Dec 60	Roy+,ESTIMATED AVG SIG=8.0MB	
(n,2n)	1.5+7		IRK Expt	Jour	NP 51 329	Feb 64	Spenke.ACTIVATION,ABS BETA COUNT	+
				Jour	OAWA 100 197	Jun 63	– . SUPERSEDED	
	1.5+7			Data	EXFOR20058.005	Sep 71	1PNT.SIG.	
(n,2n)	1.4+7		HAMComp	Jour	NP 65 257	Mar 65	Bormann. 1EXPT VALS.CFD SHELL EFFECT	
(n,2n)	1.3+7	1.5+7	BNL Theo	Jour	NSE 23 238	Nov 65	Pearlstein.3ES.STAT MDL CALC.TBL CS.	
(n,2n)	Fiss		BNL Theo	Jour	NSE 23 238	Nov 65	Pearlstein.STATMDL CALC.SPEC AVG.TBL	
(n,2n)	1.4+7		GRE Expt	Rept	CEA – R – 2900	Dec 66	Monnand. SIGMA TO ISOM.STATE GIVEN	
(n,2n)	1.5+7		ALD Expt	Rept	AWRE – O – 76/66	Dec 66	Vallis. ACTIV. AL27(N,ALPHA) STANDRD	+
	1.5+7			Data	EXFOR20347.011	Sep 74	1PNT.SIGMA.	
(n,2n)	1.5+7		DEB Comp	Jour	REA 7 4 93	Dec 69	Csikai+ SIG+HL COMPILTN,N – ACTIV – ANAL	
(n,2n)	1.4+7	1.5+7	JYV Eval	Rept	JU – RR – 3/1970	Jun 70	Leppaemaeki+ TABLE OF EVAL AVG SIG	
(n,2n)	+7		KFI Theo	Rept	KFKI – 71 – 8	Feb 71	Jeki. CALCULATED CFD EXPTL SIG VALUE	
(n,2n)	1.5+7		DEB Eval	Jour	REA 11 1 153	Mar 73	Boedy. COMPILATION+RECOMM.VALUE,TBL	
				Rept	IAEA – 153 173	73	– . RECOMM. VALUE ONLY	
(n,2n)	1.5+7		TAT Theo	Jour	JP/A 7 1457	Aug 74	Kondaiah. CALC ON STAT MODEL	
(n,2n)	1.5+7		SMU Expt	Jour	JIN 35 2139	Jul 73	Salaita+ CYCLIC ACTIV, ISOM STATES	+
				Conf	75Wash. 712	Mar 75	– +SHORT – LIVED ISOMER PROD.TBL.	
				Conf	74Columbia 95	Jul 74	– + ACT.SIG TO SHORTLIV ISO.TBL	
	1.5+7			Data	EXFOR10361.	Jun 74	1 PT M – ST.	
(n,xn) x>2	Fiss		BNL Theo	Jour	NSE 23 238	Nov 65	Pearlstein.SPEC AVG STATMDL CALC N3N	
(n,xn) x>2	2.4+7	2.8+7	LAS Expt	Jour	PR/C 12 451	Aug 75	Bayhurst+.N4N.TBL.4ES.CFD CALC.	+
	2.3+7	2.8+7		Data	EXFOR10536.	Apr 76	. 4 PTS. N3N, 4 PTS. N4N	
(n,p)	1.5+7		CRC Expt	Jour	CJP 31 267	Feb 53	Paul+ BETA ACT.CFD TH HL=6M	+
	1.5+7			Data	EXFOR11274.096	Jun 76	. 1 PT. SIG	
(n,p)	1.5+7		GLS Theo	Jour	PM 2 473	Apr 57	Brown+ COMPNUCL NIL, DIRECT 3MB	
(n,p)	1.4+7		ALD Expt	Jour	PPS 73 215	Feb 59	Coleman+. ACT. CFD DIRECT INTERACTN	+
(n,p)	1.5+7		ARK Expt	Prog	A – ARK – 60 4	Jan 60	Poularikas+	+
	1.5+7			Data	EXFOR12181.010	Jun 76	. 1 PT. SIG	
(n,p)	Fiss		CRC Eval	Rept	CRC – 1003	Dec 60	Roy+,ESTIMATED AVG SIG=0.0014MB	
(n,p)	1.4+7		FRK Theo	Jour	ZP 171 379	Dec 62	Lindner.STATMOD,CF CJP 31 267,TH+XPT	
(n,p)	1.4+7	1.5+7	SAH Comp	Jour	NUC 23 8 112	Aug 65	Chatterjee. TABLE WITH REFS.	
	1.4+7			Jour	NP 60 273	Nov 64	– .MEAN OF EXPT CFD SHELLMOD	

81 Thallium 205

Quantity	Energy (ev) Min	Max	Lab	Type	Documentation Ref Vol Page	Author, Comments Date	Data
(n,p)	1.4+7	1.5+7	NAP Comp	Rept	INFN/BE – 67 – 10	Jul 67 Cuzzocrea+ AVERAGED CHOSEN DATA.	
(n,p)	1.5+7		DEB Comp	Jour	REA 7 4 93	Dec 69 Csikai+ SIG+HL COMPILTN,N – ACTIV – ANAL	
(n,p)	1.4+7	1.5+7	JYV Eval	Rept	JU – RR – 3/1970	Jun 70 Leppaemaeki+ TABLE OF EVAL AVG SIG	
(n,p)	1.4+7		GIT Expt	Jour	NP/A 180 157	Jan 72 Hankla+ ACT,GE(LI),MIXED POWDER	
				Abst	DA/B 32 293	Nov 71 – . ACT METHOD, CFD THEORY.	
(n,np)	1.5+7		GLS Theo	Jour	PM 2 473	Apr 57 Brown+ N,PN* COMPNUCL NIL,DIRECT NIL	
(n,He3)	1.5+7		ARK Expt	Jour	PR 131 2649	Sep 63 Bramlitt+ LESS THAN 0.070MB	+
	1.5+7			Data	EXFOR11590.082	Jun 76 . 1 PT. SIG	
(n,He3)	1.4+7	1.5+7	JYV Eval	Rept	JU – RR – 3/1970	Jun 70 Leppaemaeki+ UPPER LIMIT,AVG SIG,TBL	
(n,α)	1.5+7		ARK Expt	Prog	A – ARK – 60 4	Jan 60 Poularikas+	+
	1.5+7			Data	EXFOR12181.009	Jun 76 . 1 PT. SIG.	
(n,α)	1.4+7		FRK Theo	Jour	ZP 171 379	Dec 62 Lindner.STATMOD,INC PAIR+SHELL TERMS	
(n,α)	1.5+7		DEB Comp	Jour	REA 7 4 93	Dec 69 Csikai+ SIG+HL COMPILTN,N – ACTIV – ANAL	
(n,α)	1.4+7		KFI Comp	Jour	JRC 7 365	Jun 71 Nagy+ SIGMA AND HALF LIFE GIVEN	
Reson Params	5.0+3	5.5+4	DKE Expt	Jour	AP 14 346	Jul 61 Newson+ 3 EOS	+
Reson Params	1.0+1	4.0+4	LEB Expt	Jour	ZET 47 795	Sep 64 AVERAGE D GREATER THAN 15 KEV	
				Jour	JET 20 531	Mar 65 TRANSLATN.*	
Reson Params		1.0+6	AUA Theo	Jour	AUJ 20 477	Oct 67 Cook. TBL OF AVG LVL SPACING D,L=0,1	
Reson Params	2.4+4		MUA ExTh	Jour	NC/B 58 402	Dec 68 Hasan+ AVERAGE LEVEL SPACING D GIVEN	+
	2.4+4			Expt Data	EXFOR30091.015	Dec 70 ESTIMATED AVERAGE LEVEL SPACING D	
Reson Params	3.0+3		CJD Eval	Rept	YK – 7	71 Zakharova+ SURVEY+SYSTEMATICS,GW,TBL	
				Rept	INDC(CCP) – 27	Nov 72 .ENGLISH TRANSLATION OF YK – 7 /71	
Reson Params	4.5+1		ANL Expt	Jour	NP/A 193 643	Oct 72 Thomas+ SWN,WG,D FIT TO TRANSM CURVE	
Reson Params	+0	4.5+5	ORL Expt	Prog	INDC(CAN) – 13 6	Oct 73 Earle+ EXPT EXTENDED,WIDTHS+D,NDG	
Reson Params	4.5+1	1.9+4	COL Expt	Jour	PR/C 12 102	Jul 75 Liou+ 11 RES. GWN,J,L,E0	+
	4.5+1	9.3+4		Data	EXFOR10535.	Mar 76 18RES ES.WN*G,WT,WG,J,L VALS GVN.	
Reson Params		1.0+5	ORL Expt	Conf	76Lowell 1260	Jul 76 Winters+WG,PI DRVD FROM TOT,CAPT.	+
	5.1+4	5.4+4		Data	EXFOR10602.004	Nov 76 2 RES ES GVN.	
Strnth Fnctn	5.0+3	5.5+4	DKE Expt	Jour	AP 14 346	Jul 61 Newson+ D=10+ – 3	
Strnth Fnctn	3.5+6	7.5+6	CCP Expt	Jour	IZV 37 1904	Sep 73 Earle+ FROM EL GAM – SCAT,GRAPH	
				Jour	BAS 37 9 92	Sep 73 .ENGLISH OF IZV 37 1904	
Strnth Fnctn	3.8+1	1.9+4	COL Expt	Jour	PR/C 12 102	Jul 75 Liou+GRPH.S0,S1 GVN.	+
	2.0+4			Data	EXFOR10535.012	Mar 76 2PTS. S,P WAVE STF	
Strnth Fnctn	0.0+0	1.0+5	ORL Expt	Conf	76Lowell 1260	Jul 76 Winters+S0,S1 GVN.GRPHS.	
Lvl Density	–		FEI Eval	Rept	FEI – 36	66 Kapchigashev+.TBL OF RELATD QUANTTYS	+
		5.0+4		Jour	YF 4 686	Sep 66 .TABLE.SHORT VERSION OF FEI – 36	
	–			Prog	YFI – 3 3	66 .ABSTR.TABLE SHOULD READ TL(NOT TE).	
		5.0+4		Jour	SNP 4 486	67 .ENGLISH OF YF 4.FROM(N,GAMMA).TABLE	
				Prog	INDC – E – 140 3	66 .ENGLISH TRANSL OF YFI – 3	
Lvl Density	None		AUW Theo	Conf	70Madurai 2 267	Dec 70 Ramamurty+ A – PARAMETER GVN,LANG'S – TH	
(γ,n)		2.0+7	CCP Expt	Jour	IZV 34 116	Jan 70 Antropov+ GAM – EMAX 7 – 20MEV,TBL,GRAPH	
				Jour	BAS 34 108	Jan 71 * ENGL OF IZV 34 116	

81 Thallium 206

Quantity	Energy (ev) Min	Max	Lab	Type	Documentation Ref Vol Page	Author, Comments Date	Data
Lvl Density	+6		MIL Theo	Jour	EN 15 1 54	Jan 68 Facchini+ LDL PARS FROM LOW EN RES	
Lvl Density	None		MUN Theo	Jour	NP/A 217 269	Dec 73 Dilg+ A,DELTA. BACK SHIFTED FERMIGAS	
Lvl Density	None		COP Theo	Jour	NP/A 222 493	Apr 74 Dossing+COLL ROTAT.SPAC. ACCUR ESTIM	
Lvl Density	None		ROC Theo	Jour	NP/A 223 577	May 74 Huizenga+ EXP CFD MICROSC TH SPH NUC	

82 Lead

Quantity	Energy (ev) Min	Max	Lab	Type	Documentation Ref Vol Page	Date	Author, Comments	Data
Evaluation	2.5−2	1.0+7	UNC	Eval	Rept NDA−57−27	Sep 56	Monroe+.TOT,ABS.TABLE+CURVE	
Evaluation	2.5−2	1.4+7	PCT	Eval	Rept NP− 8216	Oct 58	Lamarsh+ ALL DATA. CURVS. TBL	
Evaluation	5.0+5	1.5+7	LRL	Eval	Rept UCRL−5351	Nov 58	Howerton.CURVS,COMP AND EVAL.	
Evaluation	5.0+2	1.0+7	ANL	Eval	Book FRC	60	Yftah+.16E GROUPS.FAST REACTOR DATA	
Evaluation	1.0+5	1.4+7	GA	Eval	Rept GA− 2156	61	Joanou+.ALL DATA XCEPT SECONDARY ES	
Evaluation	1.0−4	1.5+7	UK	Eval	Rept AWRE−O−28/60	Mar 61	Buckingham.(ALD).EVAL ABOVE 1EV	
Evaluation	2.5−2	1.1+7	FEI	Eval	Book ABAGJAN	64	26 GROUP CONST,TOT,CAPT,INEL,EL,ETC	
Evaluation	1.0−4	1.5+7	UK	Eval	Rept AEEW−R−351	Feb 64	Barrington+(WIN).UKNDL LOW EN REVISN	
Evaluation	3.7−2	1.8+7	UNC	Eval	Rept UNC−5099	Dec 64	Troubetzkoy+ALL DATA.TBLS.(NDL−TR−5)	
Evaluation		2.0+7	TRM	Eval	Conf 69Roorke 2 106	Dec 69	Garg+INDIAN EVALUATN ACTIVITIES, NDG	
Evaluation	1.0−5	2.0+7	ORL	Eval	Rept ORNL−4765	Mar 72	FU+ ENDF 3. N AND G PROD CS. CURVS.	
Evaluation	1.0−5	2.0+7	ORL	Eval	Jour ND/A 16 409	Nov 75	FU+RECOMMENDED FOR ENDF4.TBLS,GRPHS	
Total	Maxwl		COL	Expt	Jour PR 48 265	Aug 35	Dunning+ IONCH,TRANS,SIG SLOW+FAST N	
Total	Maxwl		CAV	Expt	Jour PRSA 162 127	Sep 37	Goldhaber+BRIGGS.TRANSMISSION 12.5B	
Total	2.9+6		COL	Expt	Jour PR 56 260	Aug 39	Zinn+D−D NS. 90 DEG.40KEV RSLN.	+
	2.9+6			Data	EXFOR11136.024	Jun 76	. 1 PT. CS=6.74+−.24 B	
Total	1.0−5	1.8+5	ITY	Expt	Jour PR 56 881	Nov 39	Amaldi+ TRANSM.C−D NS. AVERAGE ES.	
Total	9.0−1		COL	Expt	Jour PR 59 489	Mar 41	Hanstein.RES FILTER. 9.6+−.8B	
	5.0−1	1.0+0		Abst	PR 57 565	Mar 40	− +INDIUM RES NS. PRELIM. VAL	
Total	9.0+5		UI	Expt	Jour PR 59 917	May 41	Good+ 7ELEMENTS.TBL. CFD OTH.	+
	9.0+5			Data	EXFOR11178.007	Jun 76	. 1 PT. CS=6.83+−.40B	
Total	Maxwl		NYU	Expt	Jour PR 60 155	Aug 41	Whitaker+ RA−BE,PARAFIN. 10.0B	
Total	2.4+4	8.3+5	ANL	Expt	Jour PR 71 508	Apr 47	Fields+ GN SOURCES. TBL. 6ES.	+
	2.4+4	8.3+5		Data	EXFOR11260.022	Jun 76	. 6 PTS. CS DATA	
Total	8.3+7		BRK	Expt	Jour PR 75 7	Jan 49	Cook+ TRNS. 15 ELEMENTS. TBL.	+
	8.3+7			Data	EXFOR11146.014	Jun 76	. 1 PT. CS=4.53+−.09 B.	
Total	1.2+2	3.0+2	ANL	Expt	Jour PR 76 100	Jul 49	Hibdon+TRNS. 2ES. 10 PCT RSLN.TBL.	
	1.2+2	3.0+2		Data	EXFOR11261.036	Jun 76	. 2 PTS. CS GVN AT EACH E.	
Total	2.0+4	1.6+6	WIS	Expt	Jour PR 76 277	Jul 49	Bockelman+TRNS.GRPH.CFD STAT TH.	+
	7.9+5	1.5+6		Data	EXFOR11881.008	Jun 76	. 15 PTS. CS DATA	
Total	2.0+4	7.5+5	WIS	Expt	Jour PR 76 1146	Oct 49	Barschall+ 10KV RSLN,3RESON/5KV RSLN	+
	1.8+4	7.6+5		Data	EXFOR12228.002	Jun 76	. 105 PTS. CS DATA	
Total	1.0+5	1.5+6	MIT	Theo	Jour PR 76 1550	Dec 49	Feshbach+ AVERAGE OVER RESON,CF EXPT	
Total	8.4+7		BRK	Expt	Jour PR 77 597	Mar 50	Bratenahl+TRNS EXPT. CFD.	+
	8.4+7			Data	EXFOR11472.007	Jun 76	. 1 PT. CS=4.53+−.09 B.	
Total	6.1+5	2.3+6	MIT	Expt	Priv WILLARD	Sep 50	Willard. SIGS GVN	+
	6.1+5	2.4+6		Data	EXFOR12239.002	Jun 76	. 31 PTS. CS DATA	
Total	6.9+5	7.5+5	WIS	Expt	Jour PR 79 935	Sep 50	Peterson+GRPHS. 3 TO 10KEV RSLN.	+
	2.9+6	7.5+5		Data	EXFOR12200.	Jun 76	. 112 PTS. SIGMA.	
Total	2.7+8		BRK	Expt	Jour PR 80 27	Oct 50	Dejuren. BE(P,N) NS, BI FISS COUNTER	+
	9.5+7	2.7+8		Rept	AECD−2987	Aug 50	− +. SIG VARIATION WITH E.	
	9.5+7			Jour	PR 77 606	Mar 50	− + BI FISSION CH,R CALC FR TH	
	9.5+7			Data	EXFOR11174.014	Jun 76	. 1 PT. CS=4.48+−.03B	
	2.7+8			Data	EXFOR11176.010	Jun 76	. 1 PT. CS=2.84+−.03B	
Total	2.7+8		BRK	Expt	Jour PR 80 23	Oct 50	Fox+ BE(P,N) NS,SCINTILLATION COUNT.	+
	2.7+8			Data	EXFOR11175.012	Jun 76	. 1 PT. CS=2.89+−.03 B	
Total	4.2+7		BRK	Expt	Jour PR 80 842	Dec 50	Hildebrand+ BE−D NS.TRANSM. C DETECT	+
	4.2+7			Data	EXFOR11039.031	Jun 76	. 1 PT. CS=4.44+−.05B	
Total	1.4+7		CAR	Expt	Jour PR 81 139	Jan 51	Lasday.MEAN E GOOD GEOM RADII GIVEN	+
	1.4+7			Data	EXFOR11041.008	Jun 76	. 1 PT. CS=4.97+−.27 B	
Total	1.1+8	2.4+8	BRK	Expt	Jour PR 81 919	Mar 51	Dejuren+ P−BE NS. TRNS.TBL. CFD	+
	1.8+8	2.4+8		Data	EXFOR11177.007	Jun 76	. 4 PTS. CS AT 4ES	
Total	2.0+6	6.0+6	CAV	Expt	Jour PPSA 64 388	Apr 51	Stafford.DATA IN SMALL GRAPH	+
Total	3.1−3	3.0+2	COL	Expt	Priv HAVENS	52	Havens. TOT CS DATA.	+
	3.1−3	3.0+2		Data	EXFOR11361.009	Jun 76	. 55 PTS.	
Total	3.0+8		BRK	Eval	Rept UCRL−1938	Aug 52	Ball+ TOT=INTEG. EL.+INL.	
Total	5.0+4	3.2+6	WIS	Expt	Jour PR 88 83	Oct 52	Miller+TRNS. 23ELEMENTS.GRPH.	+
	1.0+6	3.2+6		Data	EXFOR11712.022	Jun 76	. 16 PTS. CS DATA	
Total	1.4+7		ANL	Expt	Jour PR 88 686	Nov 52	Goodman. T−D NS. 21 ISOTPS.TBL.CFD	+
	1.4+7			Data	EXFOR11057.020	Jun 76	. 1 PT. CS=5.1+−.4B	
Total	1.4+7		LAS	Expt	Jour PR 88 562	Nov 52	Coon+TRNS. 54 ELEMS. TBL, CURVS	+
	1.4+7			Data	EXFOR11056.054	Jun 76	. 1 PT. CS= 5.48+−.11 B.	
Total	3.0+7	1.5+8	HAR	Expt	Jour PM 44 95	Jan 53	Taylor+WOOD.TABLE,14 ES	+
	1.6+8			Jour	PM 42 751	Jul 51	− +. 3499+−26MB AT 156+−3MEV	
Total	2.9+6	1.3+7	LAS	Expt	Jour PR 89 775	Feb 53	Nereson+AVG CS.CURV. CFD. 10PCT.ACC.	+
				Prog	LA− 1655	Apr 54	− +SURVEY 41 ELEMENTS CS	
	2.9+6	1.3+7		Data	EXFOR11060.011	Jun 76	. 33 PTS. CS DATA	

PAGE 1446

82 Lead

Quantity	Energy (ev) Min	Max	Lab	Type	Documentation Ref Vol Page	Author, Comments Date	Data
Total	1.4+7		ROM	Expt	Jour NC 10 281	Mar 53 Ageno+LI TARGET TRANSMIS.5.82+-0.17B	
Total	6.0+7	1.5+8	HAR	Theo	Jour PM 44 1028	Sep 53 Mandl+.SQUARE WELL OPT MODEL CFD XPT	
Total	3.7+6		BAR	Expt	Jour PR 92 114	Oct 53 Whitehead+ TRANS. CFD OTH.	+
	3.7+6				Data EXFOR11475.006	Jun 76 . 1 PT. CS= 7.60B	
Total	1.9+7		LAS	Expt	Jour PR 92 358	Oct 53 DAY+ TRANS. 13 ELEMENTS.TBL.	+
	1.9+7				Data EXFOR11068.012	Jun 76 . 1 PT. CS=5.96+-3.0B	
Total	4.8+7	8.8+7	HRV	Expt	Jour PR 96 115	Oct 54 Hillman+ TRNS. TBL. 2ES.	+
	4.8+7	8.8+7			Data EXFOR11081.011	Jun 76 . 2 PTS. CS DATA.	
Total	1.3+7	1.6+7	UMX	Expt	Jour AIF 1 69	55 Mazari+,GRAPH GIVEN,TRANSMISSION	+
					Jour PR 100 972	Nov 55 ABSTRACT *	
					Jour PR 97 985	Feb 55 SEE ALSO *+RMF 4 52 1/55	
	1.3+7	1.6+7			Data EXFOR30037.014	Sep 70 10DATA POINTS,PRIV COMM FROM MAZARI	
Total	1.1+1	1.7+2	BNL	Expt	Priv CARTER	Mar 55 Carter+ SIGS GVN.	+
	1.1+1	1.7+2			Data EXFOR11897.008	Jun 76 . 17 PTS. CS DATA.	
Total	4.1+6		LAS	Expt	Jour PR 98 677	May 55 Walt+ TRANS.EXPT.TBL.CFD TH	+
	4.1+6				Data EXFOR11215.052	Jun 76 . 1 PT. CS=7.8B	
Total	1.4+9		BNL	Expt	Jour PR 98 1369	Jun 55 Coor+ TRNS. OPTMDL PARS. TBL	+
	1.4+9				Data EXFOR11087.015	Jun 76 . 1 PT. CS=3.210B +-3 PCT	
Total	1.8-4	5.9-3	BNL	Expt	Abst PR 99 611	Jul 55 Palevsky+TRNS.VARIATION WITH TEMP.	+
	1.8-4	5.9-3			Data EXFOR11782.007	Jun 76 . 60 PTS. CS DATA	
Total	6.1+7	1.1+8	HRV	Expt	Jour PR 99 740	Aug 55 Culler+TRNS.GRPH.TBL.CFD	+
	6.1+7	1.1+8			Data EXFOR11088.013	Jun 76 . 12 PTS. CS DATA.	
Total	5.9+8		CCP	Expt	Jour ZET 29 369	Sep 55 Dzhelepov.EXPRMNTL SIG CFD GEOMETRCL	
					Jour JET 2 349	Mar 56 TRANSLATN.*	
Total	3.4+8	3.4+8	AML	Theo	Jour PPSA 69 365	May 56 Nohr+OPTMDL CFD BORN APPROX.	
Total	2.0+3	8.0+4	DKE	Expt	Jour PR 102 1580	Jun 56 Newson+,ABS CURV ISOTOPIC ASSIGNMENT	+
	4.5+3	8.2+4			Data EXFOR11834.009	Jun 76 . 130 PTS. CS DATA	
Total	1.0+6	5.0+6	CCP	Theo	Jour ZET 31 159	Jul 56 TH CURVS SML A POL SC CFD SCHWINGER	
					Jour JET 4 259	Mar 57 TRANSLATN.*	
Total	1.0+6	5.0+6	ITE	Theo	Jour PHY 22 1180	Nov 56 Baz.ABSTRACT,COMPLEX NUCLEUS MODEL	
Total	1.0+0	1.0+1	BNL	Expt	Jour PR 104 1425	Dec 56 Wood.CURVE 11.3+-0.3B GRAPHITE STD	+
Total	1.5+7		CCP		Jour SPD 6 129	Apr 57 KHLTSKI SC 5D28PMD15B COINC MTD	
Total	3.5+8		LVP	Expt	Jour PPSA 70 745	Oct 57 Ashmore+. 2828+-14MB AT 351.5+-2MEV	
Total	1.3+7	1.6+7	LAS	Expt	Jour PR 109 1268	Feb 58 Conner.TRNS SC 6ES 5.61BMAX 5.38BMIN	+
					Conf 58Geneva 15 11	Sep 58 Coon. PPR666,SIGMA FOR 6ES,TOF	
	1.3+7	1.6+7			Data EXFOR11320.014	Jun 76 . 6 PTS. CS DATA	
Total	2.0+4	3.4+4	ORL	Expt	Jour PR 109 926	Feb 58 Good+,TOF+SC 10.2B+-10PC	+
	None				Data EXFOR11402.024	Jun 76 .DATA UNOBTAINABLE FROM AUTHORS	
Total	7.7+8		BIR	Expt	Jour PPS 71 293	Mar 58 Booth+ 3106MB AT 765MEV,CFD OPTMODEL	
Total		3.0+7	LRL	Theo	Rept UCRL-5028	Mar 58 Bjorklund. CCB OKS EXPT DEL.	
Total	1.4+7	1.5+7	LVN	Expt	Jour NP 6 260	Mar 58 Vervier+ TRANSMISSION,CFD OPTICALMOD	+
	1.4+7	1.5+7			Data EXFOR20204.007	May 74 19PTS.	
Total	4.0+6	8.1+6	COL	Expt	Jour PR 110 466	Apr 58 Weil+ D-D NS.VDG.TRNS CFD OTHER	+
	4.0+6	8.1+6			Data EXFOR11482.008	Jun 76 . 40 PTS. CS DATA	
Total	2.5+2	2.1+4	BNL	Expt	Jour PR 110 692	May 58 Seth+TRNS.NO RES.SEEN.FAST CHOPPER	+
	2.1+2	2.1+4			Data EXFOR11788.035	Jun 76 . 89 PTS. CS DATA	
Total	7.2+6	1.4+7	LRL	Expt	Jour PR 110 927	May 58 Bratenahl+SC,TRNS. 5ES. TBL	+
	7.1+6	1.4+7			Conf 58Geneva 14 109	Sep 58 Macgregor. P1881,TBL,CURV, CFD OPTMD	
	7.2+6	1.4+7			Data EXFOR11155.031	Jun 76 . 5 PTS.	
Total	1.0+4	1.0+8	BNL	Comp	Conf 58Geneva 16 8	Sep 58 Hughes.PPR2483,CURVE,MANY REFS	
Total	2.1+6	3.0+6	LVN	Expt	Jour BCS 44 851	58 Deconnink+ VDG. TRANSMISSION	+
					Conf 58Geneva 15 30	Sep 58 Vervier+PPR1699.CURVE.EXPT DESCRBD.	
	2.1+6	3.0+6			Data EXFOR20172.005	May 74 9PTS.	
Total	1.7+7	2.9+7	LRL	Expt	Jour PR 120 521	Oct 60 Peterson+ TRANS 4ES CURV CFD OPTMDL	+
					Conf 58Geneva 14 109	Apr 58 Macgregor. TBL,CURV,CFD OPTMDL	
	1.7+7	2.9+7			Data EXFOR11108.039	Jun 76 . 4 PTS. CS DATA	
Total	2.0+5	1.0+6	DKE	Expt	Jour PR 121 1150	Feb 61 Wilenzick+TOF.CURVS.MULTILVL FIT	
	3.0+5	7.5+5			Data EXFOR11327.006	Jun 76 . 153 PTS.	
Total	1.5+7	1.2+8	HAR	Expt	Jour NP 22 640	Feb 61 Bowen+.TOF 64ES CFD OPTICAL MODEL	
Total	3.0+8	5.0+9	LON	Theo	Jour NP 23 681	Mar 61 Elton. SEMI-CLASSICAL ANALYSIS.	
Total	Cold		CAV	Expt	Jour PM 6 485	Apr 61 Collins+.TEMP VARIATION 290-840DEG K	
Total	4.7+4	2.0+5	DKE	Expt	Jour AP 14 387	Jul 61 Bilpuch+. NATURAL,ALSO RADIOGENIC	+
	None				Data EXFOR11599.047	Jun 76 . DATA UNOBTAINABLE FROM AUTHORS.	
Total	5.0+9		BRK	Expt	Jour PR 123 1850	Sep 61 Atkinson+TRNS.GOOD,POOR GEOM.CFD	
	5.0+9				Data EXFOR11112.018	Jun 76 . 1 PT. CS=2.534+-.105 B	
Total	1.4+7		BOS	Expt	Conf 62Madras 61	Feb 62 Mitra.VAL GVN CFD REFS,CORR FOR SCAT	+
	1.4+7				Data EXFOR31318.003	Feb 71 .SIG GVN	

82 Lead

Quantity	Energy (ev) Min	Max	Lab	Type	Documentation Ref Vol Page	Author, Comments Date	Data
Total	7.7−4	2.5−3	BUC	Expt Jour	SCF 13 477	May 62 Teutsch+ TOF. 2 PC E−RESOLUTION	
Total	1.0+6		ALD	Expt Jour	NP 42 86	Apr 63 Gilboy+.BY TRANSMISSION SIG=4.33B	+
Total	1.4+6		LSU	Expt Jour	PR 132 1211	Nov 63 Haas+CS FOR ORDINARY+RADIO PB GIVEN	+
	1.4+6			Data	EXFOR11794.004	Jun 76 . 1 PT. CS=5.27+−.07B	
Total	4.0+2	3.0+3	CCP	Eval Jour	AE 15 493	Dec 63 Nikolaev.TABLE OF CHARACTRSTC PARAMS	
				Rept	INDSWG−64 274	64 .SEE ALSO	
					−	FR EAF15 6 68 ENG SJA15 1281 JNE18	
Total	1.0−4	1.0−1	UK	Eval Rept	AEEW−R−351	Feb 64 Barrington+(WIN).UKNDL LOW EN REVISN	+
	1.0−4	1.5+7		Data	UKNDL−DFN 26C	Mar 73 162 PNTS	
Total	1.0+6	1.4+7	HAR	Theo Rept	AERE−R−4649	Jun 64 Wilmore.OPTMDL TH.TBLS,CURVES.PM10PC	
Total	1.4+7		FTI	Expt Conf	64Paris 2 811	Jul 64 Kaminker.SIG VERSUS MASS NUMBER	
Total	+2	+5	COL	Expt Prog	WASH−1053 21	Oct 64 Garg+ TOF.NEVIS.LO RSLN.NDG.TBC.	
Total	4.0+6		KUR	Expt Rept	IAE−1053	65 Gorlov+,SIG GIVEN,TBL	
				ExTh Jour	DOK 174 60	Jul 67 − + SMALL ANGL EXPT,POLARZ GIVEN	
				Jour	SPD 12 451	Nov 67 . ENGL OF DOK 174	
				Expt Rept	ANL−TRANS−371	66 . ENGL OF IAE−1053	
Total	1.4+0		ORL	Expt Jour	NP 61 381	Jan 65 Rayburn+TRNS INDIUM RES 1.44EV.TBL	+
	1.4+0			Data	EXFOR11026.031	Jun 76 . 1 PT. CS=11.31+−.06B	
Total	2.2+6	1.5+7	BNW	Expt Jour	NIM 36 1	Sep 65 Foster+ VDG,TOF,LIQ SCINT. NO DATA	+
	2.5+6	1.5+7		Data	EXFOR10047.089	Aug 73 . 231 PTS. SIGMA	
Total	4.5+5	4.5+7	RPI	Expt Prog	WASH−1068 185	Mar 66 Yergin+,TOF,NDG,TBC	
Total	4.0+6	5.0+6	JAE	ExTh Jour	NP 83 274	Aug 66 Tsukada+LEE AV SIGMA 3.95,4.70 MEV	
				Jour	PL 11 141	Jul 64 − + SUPERSEDED.	
Total	2.0+6	1.0+7	CSE	Expt Rept	COO−1573−6	Sep 66 Galloway+ TOF TO +−1PC,CFD OTHERS	+
				Abst	DA/B 28 1087	Sep 67 .THESIS ABST.	
	2.0+6	1.0+7		Data	EXFOR11522.009	Jun 76 . 347 PTS. CS DATA	
Total	1.4+7		CCP	ExTh Jour	IZV 31 217	Feb 67 Dukarevich+.TBL,CURVES,CFD OPTMDL TH	
				Jour	BAS 31 197	Feb 67 TRANSLATN.*	
Total	1.4+7		FTI	Expt Jour	NP/A 92 433	Feb 67 Dukarevich+ FROM ISOTOPES+DIRECT	
Total	3.0+6	1.4+8	SAF	Eval Jour	AP 42 262	Apr 67 Engelbrecht+ OPTMDL CALCS CFD EXPTS	
Total	6.0+5	1.2+6	BRC	Expt Rept	CEA−R−3279	Jun 67 Cabe. RES+INT STR S5AR3H.3O6=N−49SCR	+
	6.0+5	1.2+6		Data	EXFOR20479.004	Feb 76 175PTS.	
Total	2.5+6	7.5+6	WIS	Expt Jour	PR 158 1142	Jun 67 Carlson+ VDG,CURV,20−50KEV RESOL, TH	+
				Abst	DA/B 28 1084	Sep 67 .THESIS ABST.	
	2.5+6	7.5+6		Data	EXFOR11497.028	Jun 76 . 167 PTS. CS DATA	
Total	4.0+6		IFU	Theo Jour	UFZ 13 51	Jan 68 Kashuba+ TBL,SIG−VAL,EXPT CFD OPTMOD	
				Jour	UPJ 13 33	Jul 68 TRANSLATN.*	
Total	8.4+7	9.6+7	CCP	Theo Jour	YF 7 283	Feb 68 Aver'Yanov+ OPTMOD−CALCTD SIG GVN	
				Jour	SNP 7 2 193	Aug 68 TRANSLATN.*	
Total	1.4+7		OHO	Theo Jour	NC/B 53 2 363	Feb 68 Fontannaz.OPTMOD CALC CFD EXPT	
Total	1.4+7		ANL	Expt Abst	DA/B 28 3835	Mar 68 Haugsnes. TRNS. CFD OPTMODS	+
				Diss	HAUGSNES	67 − . GOOD GEOM.	
	1.4+7			Data	EXFOR11733.013	Jun 76 . 1 PT. CS=5.40+−.04B	
Total	1.0+5	6.6+5	DKE	Expt Abst	DA/B 28 3834	Apr 68 Divadeenam. VDG. OPTMDL	+
	1.0+5	6.6+5		Data	EXFOR10523.023	Jan 76 . 30 PTS.	
Total	1.4+7		CCP	Theo Jour	YF 7 1221	Jun 68 Aver'Yanov+SIG VAL,GENERALIZD OPTMOD	
				Jour	SNP 7 728	Dec 68 TRANSLATN.*	
Total	4.6+5	3.0+6	FEI	Expt Conf	68Dubna § 17	Jun 68 Filippov+VDG,TRANS.TBL,GRPH.FLUCTUAT	+
				Rept	INDC(CCP)−16	Jul 71 .PAGE 67.ENGLISH TRANSL OF 68DUBNA	
	4.6+5	3.0+6		Data	EXFOR40082.020	Nov 71 SIGMA AT 11 ES	
Total	1.0+8	9.0+9	MHG	Expt Jour	PL/B 27 328	Aug 68 Jones+ GOOD GEOM. ATTEN. TBL.	+
	1.0+8	9.0+9		Data	EXFOR11206.007	Jun 76 . 1 PT. CS=2.630+−.120B	
Total	5.3+6	6.3+6	THU	Expt Jour	CHP 6 74	Oct 68 Yang+.TOF−TRNSM VDG,CURVES,CFD OTHRS	+
	5.3+6	6.3+6		Data	EXFOR30049.003	Dec 70 SIG TOT AT 21 ES.	
Total	1.0+8	1.5+8	USA	Expt Jour	NP/A 119 197	Oct 68 Schneider+	+
				Abst	DA/B 31 2182	Oct 70 − . 1 PC ACCURACY, 1 MEV RSLN	
	9.9+7	1.5+8		Data	EXFOR11514.005	Jun 76 . 6 PTS. CS DATA	
Total	1.0+7		IJE	Comp Jour	REA 6 4 3	Dec 68 Konshin+ SIG(NEUT−E)+−ERROR GVN,GRPH	
Total	4.0+6		KUR	Expt Jour	YF 8 1086	Dec 68 Gorlov+.SMALL ANG SCAT EXPERIMENT	
				ExTh Jour	YF 6 910	Nov 67 − + POLRZD INC N.CFD OPTMOD.	
Total	1.5+7		ORL	Expt Jour	AJP 37 482	May 69 Robinson+TOF EXPT FOR UNDERGRAD LAB.	+
	1.5+7			Data	EXFOR10020.005	Jan 70 . 1 PT.CS=5.11B.	
Total	1.5+7	1.2+8	PEL	Theo Jour	NP/A 128 673	May 69 Fiedeldey+ E DEPEND OPTMDL POT. FITS	
Total	8.9+6		ORL	Expt Jour	AJP 37 649	Jun 69 Minor+ UNDER GRAD EXPT.TBL.	+
	8.9+6			Data	EXFOR11505.006	Jun 76 . 1 PT CS=7.39+−.27B	
Total	5.0+5	1.7+7	FEI	Expt Jour	AE 27 141	Aug 69 Kukhtevich+ TRANSMISSN+RES SHIELDING	
				Jour	SJA 27 852	69 . ENGL OF AE 27 141	

82 Lead

Quantity	Energy (ev) Min	Max	Lab	Type	Documentation Ref Vol Page	Date	Author, Comments	Data
Total	8.0+5	1.5+6	ANL	Expt Prog	ANL-7610 14	Jan 70	Whalen+. CURVE	
Total	9.9+8		STF	Expt Jour	PL/B 31 677	May 70	Lakin+ 3.8 GEV/C. TBL. CFD OPTMDL.	+
	9.9+8			Data	EXFOR10196.005	Jul 72	. 1 PT. 3.8 GEV/C=3071+ −79MB	
Total	8.0+6		AE	Theo Rept	AE- 430	Sep 71	Holmqvist+ CALC FROM OPTMOD PARAMS	
	8.1+6			Conf	70Helsinki 2 341	Jun 70	− + OPTMOD ANALYSIS. 8 MEV	
Total	1.3+2		MUN	Expt Jour	ZN/A 26 442	Mar 71	Dilg+TRANS EXPT,COH SCAT LENGTH CALC	
Total	2.1+1	3.9+2	KUR	Expt Conf	71Kiev	May 71	Muradjan+.SIG(NEUT−E),TBL	+
	2.1+1	4.0+2		Data	EXFOR40167.002	Nov 73	.SIGMA AT 10 ES GIVEN	
Total	1.0+5	1.0+7	TRM	Eval Prog	INDC(IND)-12 2	Jul 71	Garg.FIT TO EXPTL DATA+THEO CALC,NDG	
Total	2.7+3		MUN	Expt Conf	71Albany 327	Aug 71	Dilg+TRNS.AVG CS GVN.31 ELEMENT GRPH	
Total	1.4+7		KOS	Expt Jour	AHP 30 115	Oct 71	Angeli+EXPT,DATA TABLE,LITER. SURVEY	+
	1.4+7			Data	EXFOR30141.015	Jan 72	SIGMA AT 14.7 MEV GIVEN	
Total	2.0+7	9.1+9	MCG	Theo Jour	CJP 50 1609	Jul 72	Best. GLAUBER THEORY CALCULATN.CURVE	
Total	+9		NYU	Theo Jour	PR/C 6 748	Sep 72	Franco. GLAUBER APPROX. CFD EXPT	
Total	+9		MHG	Expt Abst	DA/B 33 2271	Nov 72	Mccorriston. OKS GLAUBER TH. NDG	
Total	1.3+7	1.5+7	DEB	Eval Rept	IAEA-153 173	73	Boedy+ MOST PROBABLE VAL OF SIG,TBL	
Total	3.8+8	1.7+9	PTN	Expt Jour	PR/C 7 248	Jan 73	Schimmerling+.TOF. TRANS.TABLE 15ES	+
				Jour	PL/B 37 177	Nov 71	.SUPERSEDED	
	3.8+8	1.7+9		Data	EXFOR10082.011	Dec 75	. 15 PTS. TOT CS DATA.	
Total	2.4+6		PAD	Expt Jour	NC/A 13 867	Feb 73	Drigo+	+
	2.4+6			Data	EXFOR20664.004	Oct 76	1PNT.	
Total	5.0+5	1.0+7	BET	Expt Rept	WAPD-TM-1073	Apr 73	Green+.CF252 SOURCE.TOF.CURV.CFDENDF	+
	1.0+6	8.1+6		Data	EXFOR10225.	Aug 73	. 434 PTS, SIGMA	
Total	3.0+6		EDG	Expt Jour	NP/A 212 182	Sep 73	Galloway+ POLRZD NS.	+
	3.0+6			Data	EXFOR20359.007	Sep 74	1PNT.	
Total	4.8+5	1.5+7	NBS	Expt Rept	NBS-MONO-138	Jan 74	Schwartz+LINAC,TOF,GRPHS.	+
	7.0+5	4.4+6		Conf	68Wash. § E12	Mar 68	− + LINAC+TOF CURVE CFD OTHERS	
	4.7+5	1.5+7		Data	EXFOR10069.002	Aug 71	. 3454 PTS.	
Total	None		DKE	Expt Prog	ERDA-NDC-2 177	May 75	Clement+NDG.	
Total	+9		MHG	Expt Jour	NP/B 92 269	Jun 75	Murthy+ 34GEV/C TO 273 GEV/C	+
				Jour	PRL 33 1440	Dec 74	Jones+ TBL. 30 GEV/C TO 270 GEV/C	
	+9			Data	EXFOR10403.010	Dec 74	. 7 PTS,SIGMA	
Total	1.3+0	5.2+0	MUN	Expt Jour	ZN/A 31 115	Feb 76	Waschkowski+ TRANS. RH,AG RES DET.	+
				Jour	PRL 36 1021	Apr 76	Koester+TRNS.TBL.N−E INT EVALUATION	
	1.3+0	5.2+0		Data	EXFOR20603.006	Jun 76	2PTS.	
Total	1.0+8	9.0+9	NAL	Expt Jour	PRL 36 1004	Apr 76	Biel+TRNS.GRPH.TBL.NOVEL DET SYSTEM.	+
	1.0+8	9.0+9		Data	EXFOR10603.005	Aug 76	. 8 PTS. AVG CS DATA 8ES	
Total	2.2+6	2.7+6	TEX	Expt Abst	BAP 2 232	Apr 57	Bennett+FAST COINC DETECT. NDG	
	2.3+6	2.7+6		Data	EXFOR11265.008	Jun 76	. 14 PTS. CS DATA.	
Total	2.5−2		KTO	Expt Jour	NSE 60 230	Jul 76	Kanda+TRNS.TAR CS AND T DEP.GRPHS.	+
	1.0−3	5.0−1		Data	EXFOR20756.	Dec 77	445PTS.	
Elastic	Maxwl	+2	JAP	Expt Jour	JPJO 24 569	42	Kimura.SIG CURVE GIVN	
Elastic	2.5+6		PTN	Expt Jour	PR 61 129	Feb 42	Barschall+ HE ION CH,CFD ESTIM INEL	
Elastic	3.6+6	3.6−2	ANL	Expt Jour	PR 71 666	May 47	Fermi+ SCATT LENGTH+SIGN FROM INTERF	+
	3.6−2			Data	EXFOR12593.019	Jun 76	. 1 PT, SIGMA.	
Elastic	2.5−2		ORL	Expt Jour	PR 81 527	Feb 51	Shull+POWDER DIFFRACTION TECH.TBL.	+
	2.5−2			Data	EXFOR11043.	Jun 76	. 3 PTS. COH,BAS SCT CS. AMP.	
Elastic	2.5−2		BNL	Expt Priv	WEISS	52	Weiss. PILE FILTERED BEAM.	+
	2.5−2			Data	EXFOR12246.002	Jun 76	. 1 PT. BOUND ATOM SCT CS.=11.2+−.5B	
Elastic	3.0+8		BRK	Expt Rept	UCRL-1938	Aug 52	Ball. THESIS. RING GEOM.	+
	3.0+8			Data	EXFOR11503.009	Jun 76	. 1 PT. CS=1.339B.	
Elastic	3.7+6		BAR	Expt Jour	PR 92 114	Oct 53	Whitehead+ INTEG.ANG.DIST.	+
	3.7+6			Data	EXFOR11475.005	Jun 76	. 1 PT. CS=5.17 B	
Elastic	3.7+6		BIR	Expt Jour	PR 92 114	Oct 53	Whitehead. = 1 DATA INDEX LINE	+
Elastic	1.0+6		WIS	Expt Jour	PR 93 1062	Mar 54	Walt+ INTEG.ANG.DIST.	+
	1.0+6			Data	EXFOR11637.074	Jun 76	. 1 PT. CS=4.7B	
Elastic	1.0+6	1.2+7	SPN	Theo Jour	ARS 50 107	Jun 54	.ELAST SPEC RA−BE SOURCE,MONTECARLO	
Elastic	4.1+6		LAS	Expt Jour	PR 98 677	May 55	Walt+INTEG. FROM DEL DATA.	+
	4.1+6			Data	EXFOR11215.050	Jun 76	. 1 PT. CS=5.9+−.3 B	
Elastic	1.0+6	1.5+7	TEX	Expt Jour	PR 98 1300	Jun 55	Rhein. INTEG. ANG. DIST. TBL	+
	1.0+6	1.5+7		Data	EXFOR12206.002	Jun 76	. 4 PTS. 4ES.	
Elastic	1.3+8		OXF	Expt Jour	PM 1 1003	Nov 56	Vanzyl+ FROM DIFF ELAST,CFD STOT−SNE	
Elastic	2.9+6		CCP	Expt Jour	AE 3 498	Dec 57	Popov.INTEGRAL ANG DISTRIB 5.9+−0.2B	+
				Jour	JNE 9 9	Jun 59	TRANSLATN.*	
				Jour	SJA 3 1379	57	TRANSLATN.*	
Elastic	−		HAR	Expt Jour	NAT 181 643	Mar 58	Mccallum+ TOF.INCOH.SIG=.05+−.03B	

82 Lead

Quantity	Energy (ev) Min	Max	Lab	Type	Documentation Ref Vol Page	Author, Comments Date	Data
Elastic	1.5+7		LAS	Expt Jour	PR 111 250	Jul 58 Coon+RING GEOM.INTEG ANG DIST.	+
	1.5+7			Data	EXFOR11322.022	Jun 76 . 1 PT. CS=2.83+−.14B	
Elastic	3.7+6	4.7+6	TNC	Expt Rept	WADC−TN−59−31	Feb 59 Bostrom+ INTEGR ANG DIST CURVES	+
	3.7+6	4.7+6		Data	EXFOR11341.009	Jun 76 . 3 PTS.	
Elastic	2.2+5		FEI	Expt Jour	ZET 38 1434	May 60 Lovchikova+ INTEGRATD ANGDIS,=8.79B	
				Jour	JET 11 1036	Nov 60 . ENGL OF ZET 38 1434	
Elastic	1.0+6		ALD	Expt Jour	NP 42 86	Apr 63 Gilboy+.SIG=4.32B+−3PC	
Elastic	6.5+5		IFU	Expt Jour	UFZ 8 1323	Dec 63 Korzh.INTEGRATD FROM ANGDSTRB 5.85	+
Elastic	1.0−4	1.0−1	UK	Eval Rept	AEEW−R−351	Feb 64 Barrington+(WIN).UKNDL LOW EN REVISN	+
	1.0−4	1.5+7		Data	UKNDL−DFN 26C	Mar 73 162 PNTS	
Elastic	3.0+5	1.5+6	ANL	Expt Rept	EANDC(US)−62	Jun 64 Smith.TOF,TBL.50KEV STEPS,20KEV RSLN	+
	3.0+5	1.5+6		Data	EXFOR12039.007	Jun 76 . 25 PTS. CS DATA.	
Elastic	1.0+6	1.6+7	HAR	Theo Jour	NP 55 673	Jul 64 Wilmore+OPTMOD SHAPE ELASTIC ONLY	
Elastic	4.0+6		KUR	Expt Jour	DOK 158 574	Sep 64 Gorlov+	+
	4.0+6			Data	EXFOR40221.033	May 74 .1 DATA LINE	
Elastic	1.0+5	1.4+7	AGN	Eval Rept	TID−21629	Dec 64 Perkins+EL.SCT.TBLS.CURVS.	
Elastic	4.0+6		KUR	Expt Rept	IAE−1053	65 Gorlov+,SIG ELASTIC AT 0 DEG,TBL	
				Rept	ANL−TRANS−371	66 . ENGL OF IAE−1053	
Elastic	1.4+0		ORL	Expt Jour	NP 61 381	65 Rayburn+TRNS CS AT 1.44EV.	+
	1.4+0			Data	EXFOR11026.030	Jun 76 . 1 PT.CS=11.28B.	
Elastic	3.0+5	8.0+5	IFU	ExTh Jour	AE 20 8	Jan 66 Korzh+ SUMMARY OF SEVERAL YRS WORK	+
				Jour	AE 16 207	64 .	
				Jour	UFZ 9 577	64 .	
				Jour	SJA 20 8	Jul 66 .ENGLISH TRANSL OF AE 20 8 1/66	
				Rept	INDSWG−101 112	65 . =UFZ9.ENGL NO GRPHS.RUSS LARGER GPH	
Elastic	6.0−1		JUL	Expt Jour	ZP 190 295	Jan 66 Niklaus+ FREE + INCOHERENT SCAT	
				Rept	JUEL−353−NP	66 − + REPRINT OF ZP 190 295	
Elastic	Cold		MUN	Expt Jour	ZP 190 295	Jan 66 Niklaus+ SIG(FREE)+SIG(INCOHERENT)	+
				Conf	67Juelich 80	Apr 67 Simson+ INCOHERENT SCAT,COOLED TGT.	
Elastic	1.5+6		IFU	Expt Prog	YFI−5 42	Oct 67 Korzh+ TBL OPTMDL PARAMS + TOTELAST	
				Rept	INDC−232E	67 . ENGL OF YFI−5 42	
Elastic	1.5+6		IFU	Comp Jour	YF 7 277	Feb 68 Korzh+ OPTMOD PARS−FIT TO EXPTL−SIG	
				Jour	SNP 7 2 190	Aug 68 TRANSLATN.*	
Elastic	1.4+7		OHO	Theo Jour	NC/B 53 2 363	Feb 68 Fontannaz. OPTMOD CALC CFD EXPT	
Elastic	−3	+1	IFU	Expt Jour	UFZ 13 605	Apr 68 Vertebnyi+ GRPH,EXPTL SIG=NUCL+MAGN	
				Jour	UPJ 13 425	Oct 68 TRANSLATN.*	
Elastic	1.4+7		CCP	Theo Jour	YF 7 1221	Jun 68 Aver'Yanov+SIG VAL,GENERALIZD OPTMOD	
				Jour	SNP 7 728	Dec 68 TRANSLATN.*	
Elastic	4.0−4	1.3−3	JUL	Expt Rept	NUK 12 4	Dec 68 Scherm. INCOHERENT SCAT SIG EXPT	
				Conf	67Juelich 83	Apr 67 − . PRELIMINARY DATA.	
Elastic	4.0+6		KUR	Expt Jour	YF 8 1086	Dec 68 Gorlov+ SIG VAL GVN,SMALL−ANG−SCATNG	
				Jour	SNP 8 630	Jun 69 TRANSLATN.*	
Elastic	2.0+3		MTR	Expt Prog	NCSAC−31 75	May 70 Smith+,ANAL TO BE COMPLETED,NO DATA	
Elastic	+5	+7	GEL	Revw Conf	70Helsinki 1 127	Jun 70 Deruytter.106. DISCUSSED AS STANDARD	
Elastic	1.0+5	1.0+7	TRM	Eval Prog	INDC(IND)−12 2	Jul 71 Garg.FIT TO EXPTL DATA+THEO CALC,NDG	
Elastic	8.1+6		AE	Expt Rept	AE−430	Sep 71 Holmqvist+ INTEGRATED ANGDIST VALUES	+
	8.0+6			Conf	70Helsinki 2 341	Jun 70 − + OPTMOD ANALYSIS. 8 MEV	
	8.1+6			Data	EXFOR20162.029	May 74 . 1PNT RADIOGENIC LEAD	
	8.1+6			Data	EXFOR20162.026	May 74 1PNT.	
Elastic	1.1+6		ANL	Expt Rept	ANL−7935	Jun 72 COX+ 4 PI B(O)FROM LST SQ FIT.	+
	1.1+6			Data	EXFOR10332.130	Jun 74 . 1 PT. CS=4.8306B	
Elastic	7.0+6		AE	Expt Rept	AE−482	Dec 73 Etemad. INTEGRATED.	+
	7.0+6			Data	EXFOR20346.020	Sep 74 1PNT.	
Elastic	1.5+6	8.5+6	AE	Theo Rept	AE−485	Feb 74 Etemad. OPT MOD CALC COMPARED EXPT	
Elastic	1.0+5	1.5+7	CCP	Eval Data	SOKRATOR−1037	76 74 PTS	+
Elastic	1.3+0	5.2+0	MUN	Expt Jour	ZN/A 31 115	Feb 76 Waschkowski. FREE SCAT SIGMA.	+
				Jour	PRL 36 1021	Apr 76 Koester+MIRROR REFLECT.COHSCT LENGTH	
	0.0+0	0.0+0		Data	EXFOR20603.005	Jun 76 1PNT.FREE ATOM AT ZERO ENERGY	
Diff Elastic	2.5+5		PTN	Expt Jour	PR 61 129	Feb 42 Barschall+ HE ION CH, 45 + 100 DEG	
Diff Elastic	8.4+7		BRK	Expt Rept	PR 77 597	Mar 50 Bratenahl+2.5−25DEG,C12(N2N)ACT DET.	+
	8.4+7			Data	EXFOR11472.004	Jun 76 . 12 PTS.	
Diff Elastic	3.0+8		BRK	Expt Rept	UCRL−1938	Aug 52 Ball. THESIS. RING GEOM.	+
	3.0+8			Data	EXFOR11503.004	Jun 76 . 14 PTS. ANG DIST.	
Diff Elastic	3.7+6		BAR	Expt Jour	PR 92 114	Oct 53 Whitehead+ 13 TO 140 DEG. GRPH.	+
	3.7+6			Data	EXFOR11475.007	Jun 76 . 36 PTS. ANG.DIST.	
Diff Elastic	1.0+6		WIS	Expt Jour	PR 93 1062	Mar 54 Walt+ HE COUNTER 30−150DEG LAB CURVE	+
	1.0+6			Data	EXFOR11637.076	Jun 76 . 9 PTS. ANG. DIST.	

82 Lead

Quantity	Energy (ev) Min	Max	Lab	Type	Documentation Ref Vol Page	Author, Comments Date	Data
Diff Elastic	4.1+6		LAS	Expt	Jour PR 98 677	May 55 Walt+ BIASED SCINT ANG DISTR CFD TH	+
	4.1+6				Data EXFOR11215.053	Jun 76 . 11 PTS.	
Diff Elastic	1.0+6	1.5+7	TEX	Expt	Jour PR 98 1300	Jun 55 Rhein.4ES RING GEOM.ANG DIST CURVS	+
	1.0+6	1.5+7			Data EXFOR12206.003	Jun 76 . 57 PTS.	
Diff Elastic	6.0+5	1.4+7	LAS	Revw	Conf 55Geneva 2 18	Aug 55 Walt.P588,CURV,DISCUS OF RESULTS	
Diff Elastic	3.5+8		CAR	Expt	Jour PR 100 437	Oct 55 Siegel. 16 PCT. POL BEAM.ANG DIST.	
Diff Elastic	1.0+6	1.6+6	WIS	Expt	Jour PR 100 1315	Dec 55 Darden+ 100 KEV RSLN. CFD OPTMDL	+
	1.0+6	1.6+6			Data EXFOR11638.015	Jun 76 . 3 PTS.	
Diff Elastic	1.4+7		LRL	Theo	Jour PR 101 1047	Feb 56 Culler+,OPTMDL CALC ANG DISTR CFDXPT	
Diff Elastic	3.4+8		AML	Theo	Jour PPSA 69 365	May 56 Mohr+ OPTMDL CFD BORN APPROX + EXPT	
Diff Elastic	1.4+7		GRN	Expt	Jour NP 2 124	Oct 56 Nauta. GRAPH 20-125 DEG LAB.RING GEO	+
	1.4+7				Data EXFOR20199.007	May 74 15PTS.D/DA.	
Diff Elastic	3.0+6	4.0+6	LEB	Theo	Jour ZET 31 726	Oct 56 SML A SHWNGR ABSCURV COULOMB EFF	
					Jour JET 4 612	May 57 TRANSLATN.*	
Diff Elastic	1.0+6	5.0+6	ITE	Theo	Jour PHY 22 1180	Nov 56 Baz.ABSTRACT,LESS 30DEG COMPLEX MOD.	
Diff Elastic	1.4+8		OXF	Expt	Jour PM 1 1003	Nov 56 Vanzyl+ TABLE 0-17DEG.THEO PAGE 1013	+
Diff Elastic	3.3+6		ETH	Expt	Jour HPA 29 545	Dec 56 Remond.30-150DEG CURV.ABS CF FPW CCB	+
	3.4+6				Jour HPA 28 331	Aug 55 Brugger+.30DEG TO150DEG SHORT NOTICE	
Diff Elastic	2.0+4	1.4+7	WES	Theo	Jour PR 104 1399	Dec 56 Emmerich+,LEG POLY XPNSN CRV CFD XPT	
Diff Elastic	9.0+5		FEI	Expt	Jour AE 2 174	Feb 57 Lovchikova. 40-140DEG,(GN)SOURCE	
					Jour SJA 2 197	Feb 57 . ENGL OF AE 2 174	
Diff Elastic	1.4+7		CCP	Expt	Jour SPD 6 152	Apr 57 . ABS CURVE. 10-90DEG, + -15PERCENT	
Diff Elastic	2.0+6		KUR	Expt	Jour ZET 33 294	Jul 57 Aleksandrov.HE4-CHAMBR,4-25DEG,GRAPH	
					Jour JET 6 228	Jan 58 TRANSLATN.*	
Diff Elastic	2.3+6		FEI	Expt	Jour AE 3 106	Aug 57 Salnikov. TABLE AT 6 ANGS,30-135DEG	
					Jour JNE 9 9	Jun 59 . ENGL OF AE 3 106	
					Jour SJA 3 869	57 . ENGL OF AE 3 106	
Diff Elastic	3.0+6		VIR	Expt	Jour PR 108 116	Oct 57 Hereford+,D-D NS,ANG DISTR OF POLARZ	
Diff Elastic	2.9+6		CCP	Expt	Jour AE 3 498	Dec 57 Popov.RING GEOM. 6 ANGLES 30-150DEGS	+
Diff Elastic	4.1+6	1.4+7	LRL	Theo	Jour PR 109 1295	Feb 58 Bjorklund+,OPTMDL FIT XPT,CRV POLRZ	
					Rept UCRL-5028	Mar 58 .SUPERSEDED	
Diff Elastic	1.5+7		VIR	Expt	Jour NP 6 210	Mar 58 Berko+ TOF. GRAPH. 10-110 DEG.	
					Abst BAP 1 339	Nov 58 Dolan+ 17-140DEG 3DEG STEPS NDG	
Diff Elastic	5.0+6		WES	Expt	Jour PR 109 2105	Mar 58 Hill.SC 30-150DEG ABS CRV CFD OPTMDL	+
	5.0+6				Data EXFOR11321.011	Jun 76 . 13 PTS.	
Diff Elastic	1.4+7		LRL	Theo	Jour RMP 30 414	Apr 58 Fernbach.TH CURVE AND EXPTL PTS	
					Rept UCRL-4926	Jul 57 Bjorklund+ OPTMDL CALC 6-PARAM FIT	
Diff Elastic	1.5+7		LRL	Expt	Jour PR 110 160	Apr 58 Anderson+,TOF 90-167DEG 5AS CURVE	+
					Conf 58Geneva 15 3	Sep 58 Benveniste.PPR2494,CURVE CFD THEORY	
	1.5+7				Data EXFOR11716.006	Jun 76 . 19 PTS.	
Diff Elastic	3.5+8		LVP	ExTh	Jour PPS 71 552	Apr 58 Ashmore+ 1-8 DEG. BROWN+ CFD OPTMDL	+
Diff Elastic	1.4+7	1.5+7	LAS	Expt	Jour PR 111 250	Jul 58 Coon+,SC,5-150DEG ABSCURV CFD CCB	+
	1.4+7				Conf 58Geneva 15 11	Sep 58 .SUPERSEDED	
	1.4+7	1.5+7			Data EXFOR11322.	Jun 76 . 21 PTS. 14MEV,28 PTS. 14.5MEV.	
Diff Elastic	4.1+6	1.4+7	BRK	Theo	Conf 58Geneva 14 24	Sep 58 Bjorklund+.PPR649,CURVE CFD EXPT	
Diff Elastic	2.2+5	2.8+6	IFU	Expt	Conf 58Geneva 15 18	Sep 58 Pasechnik+.PPR2030,CURV,N-ANGL-DISTR	+
Diff Elastic	1.4+7		MOS	Theo	Jour NP 8 325	Oct 58 Lukyanov+CFD OTHERS,EXPT DATA.CURVES	
Diff Elastic	1.4+7	1.5+7	KON	Expt	Jour JPJ 13 1248	Nov 58 Yuasa.ANG.DIST.CFD OPTMOD THEORY	+
	1.4+7				Data EXFOR20281.004	Jun 74 9PTS.D/DA.	
Diff Elastic	3.7+6	4.7+6	TNC	Expt	Rept WADC-TR-59-31	Feb 59 Bostrom+TOF. TBLS. GRPH.CFD	
	3.7+6	4.7+6			Data EXFOR11341.010	Jun 76 . 30 PTS. ANG DIST.	
Diff Elastic	2.8+6		IFU	ExTh	Conf 59Tashkent 1 103	Sep 59 Pasechnik. XPT AND OPTMDL-TH,GRAPH	
					Rept AEC-TR-6398	64 .VOL 1,P120.ENGL OF 59TASHKE 1 103	
Diff Elastic	4.2+6		TNC	Expt	Jour PR 116 986	Nov 59 Okhuysen+ TOF. CFD TH.GRPHS.	+
					Rept WADC-TN-59 107	Feb 59 .SUPERSEDED	
	4.2+6				Data EXFOR12211.002	Jun 76 . 13 PTS.	
Diff Elastic	1.4+7		ANL	Expt	Jour PR 116 1571	Dec 59 Rayburn.MONTE CARLO CORRECT,CFD TH	+
	1.4+7				Data EXFOR11806.005	Jun 76 . 28 PTS.	
Diff Elastic	2.2+5		FEI	Expt	Jour ZET 38 1434	May 60 Lovchikova+ GRAPH SIG(COS),30-150DEG	
					Jour JET 11 1036	Nov 60 . ENGL OF ZET 38 1434	
Diff Elastic	9.6+7		OXF	Expt	Jour NP 21 15	Nov 60 Salmon.EFFECTIVE E. 1 TO 10 DEG CM.	+
				ExTh	Jour NP 21 21	Nov 60 Hodgson. OPTMDL FIT TO DATA 3 REFS.	
Diff Elastic	1.4+7		LVN	Expt	Jour ASS 75 102	61 Deconninck+ SMALL ANGLE SCATTERING.	
Diff Elastic	5.0+4	2.3+6	ANL	Expt	Jour AP 12 135	Feb 61 Lane+,7ES,LEG COEF GIVEN	+
					Rept ANL-6172	Oct 60 . + TABULATED DATA	
	5.0+4	2.3+6			Data EXFOR10415.016	Jul 74 . 248 PTS. DSIGMA	
Diff Elastic	1.3+5	2.0+7	GEA	Eval	Rept TID-12742	Feb 61 Gerardo.FROM BNL-400+OTHER SOURCES	

82 Lead

Quantity	Energy (ev) Min	Max	Lab	Type	Documentation Ref Vol Page	Author, Comments / Date	Data
Diff Elastic	1.5+7		CCP		Jour AE 11 395	Oct 61 RING CFD BJ–F 10–120 DEG OK	
					Jour SJA 11 1041	61 . ENGL OF AE 11 395	
Diff Elastic	1.0+6		ANL	Theo	Jour PR 124 826	Nov 61 Sokoloff.HARM OSC POT.CFD EXPT.CURVE	
Diff Elastic	7.0+6	1.4+7	ORL	Theo	Jour NP 32 353	May 62 Perey+2ES OPTMDL FITTED XPT.	
Diff Elastic	1.2+6	3.2+6	ORL	Expt	Jour PR 127 2192	Sep 62 Fowler+50 KEV SPREAD.GRPH.CFD.	+
	1.2+6	3.2+6			Data EXFOR12215.002	Jun 76 . 31 PTS. ANG DIST.	
Diff Elastic	2.4+7		LRL	Expt	Jour PR 128 2339	Dec 62 Wong+ 20–70DEG 5DEG STEPS OKS OPTMDL	
Diff Elastic	1.4+7		FTI	Expt	Jour ZET 44 130	Jan 63 Dukarevich+ GRAPH ANGL=3–20 DEG	+
					Jour JET 17 89	Jul 63 TRANSLATN.*	
	1.4+7				Data EXFOR40078.003	Oct 71 DIFF SIG AT 9 ANGLES	
Diff Elastic	1.0+6		ALD	Expt	Jour NP 42 86	Apr 63 Gilboy+30TO137DEG.COMP.WITH OPTICMOD	+
Diff Elastic	6.5+5		IFU	Expt	Jour UFZ 8 1323	Dec 63 Korzh+ CURV TBL SPH GEOM	+
					Rept BNL–TR–242	Sep 68 . + ANGDIST(30–140DEG),GRAPH+TABL	
Diff Elastic	1.0–4	1.0–1	UK	Eval	Rept AEEW–R–351	Feb 64 Barrington+(WIN).UKNDL LOW EN REVISN	+
	1.0–4	1.5+7			Data UKNDL–DFN 26C	Mar 73 6 RNGS,C.M.	
Diff Elastic	3.0+5		IFU	Expt	Jour UFZ 9 577	May 64 Korzh.GRAPH SIG(COS),TBL DERIVD VALS	+
					Rept INDSWG–101 112	65 .=UFZ9.ENGL NO GRPHS.RUSS LARGER GPH	
Diff Elastic	3.0+5	1.5+6	ANL	Expt	Rept EANDC(US)–62	Jun 64 Smith.TOF,TBL LEGEND COEF LAB SYSTEM	+
	3.0+5	1.5+6			Data EXFOR12039.006	Jun 76 . 125 PTS. LEG COEFS.	
Diff Elastic	1.0+6	1.4+7	HAR	Theo	Jour NP 55 673	Jul 64 Wilmore+OPTMOD SHAPE + COMP.ELASTIC	
					Rept AERE–R–4649	Jun 64 – + OPTICAL MODEL	
Diff Elastic	4.0+6		KUR	Expt	Jour DOK 158 574	Sep 64 Gorlov+,POLRZ NS,TBL SIG VS COS	+
					Jour SPD 9 806	Mar 65 . ENGL OF DOK 158 574	
					Rept INDSWG–101 112	65 . LARGE GRPH.ALSO AVAILABLE IN ENGL.	
	4.0+6				Data EXFOR40221.032	May 74 .SIGMA IN MB/SR AT 17 ANGLES GIVEN	
Diff Elastic	2.0+6	1.4+7	THS	Expt	Jour AKE 9 321	Sep 64 Buhler+2MEV STEPS COMP DEL.LEG COEFF	
Diff Elastic	1.0+5	1.4+7	AGN	Eval	Rept TID–21629	Dec 64 Perkins+LEG.COEF.CALC.FROM OTH.DATA.	
Diff Elastic	4.0+6		KUR	Expt	Rept IAE–1053	65 Gorlov+,POLRZ EFFECTS,2–6DEG,TBL	
					Rept ANL–TR–371	66 TRANSLATN.*	
Diff Elastic	8.0+5		IFU	Theo	Jour UFZ 10 6 586	Jun 65 Korzh.OPTMDL GRAPH SIG,CFD XPT	
					Jour IZV 29 862	May 65 .	
Diff Elastic	1.4+7		ORL	ExTh	Jour NP 68 97	Jun 65 Stelson+ XPT CFD DIST OPTMDL CALC	+
	1.4+7			Expt	Data EXFOR11527.024	Jun 76 . 10 PTS.	
Diff Elastic	1.4+7		RPI	Expt	Jour NE 19 497	Jun 65 Pearlstein+ 90DEG. SPEC. GRPH.	+
					Abst DA 26 438	Jul 65 – +ASSOC. PART. COINC. TECH.	
	1.4+7				Data EXFOR10234.009	May 73 . 1 PT. CS AT 90DEG =16+ –2MB/SR	
Diff Elastic	1.3+6	8.4+6	FEI	ExTh	Conf 65Antwerp § 574	Jul 65 Anikin+ 2–24DEG,4ENERGIES,NOT=OPTMOD	
Diff Elastic	8.0+5		IFU	Theo	Conf 65Antwerp § 193	Jul 65 Pasechnic+. OPT.MOD.PARAMETERS	
Diff Elastic	9.5+4		FOA	Expt	Jour NP 71 511	Sep 65 Stroemberg+, TOF. ESTIMATED REL U238	+
Diff Elastic	1.0+6		LAS	Theo	Prog WASH–1064 84	Oct 65 Rosen+ OPTMDL+CPD ELST CFD EXPT.GRPH	
Diff Elastic	1.0+3	2.5+4	DUB	Expt	Rept JINR–P–2764	66 Aleksandrov+,TOF,ANGDIST30–150DEG,	+
	1.0+3	4.0+4			Rept JINR–P3–4354	Mar 69 – + PHASE–SHIFT FROM ANGDIS	
	1.0+0	2.5+4			Jour ZEP 4 196	Sep 66 – + TOF.	
	1.0+3	2.5+4			Rept ANL–TR–378	Sep 66 TRANSLATN.*	
					Prog YFI–3 22	Sep 66 .SEE ALSO	
	4.6+2	2.6+4			Data EXFOR40044.	Aug 70 REL ANG DSTRB	
Diff Elastic	3.0+5	8.0+5	IFU	ExTh	Jour AE 20 8	Jan 66 Korzh+SJA 20 8 SUM OF SEV YRS WORK	+
	5.0+5	8.0+5		Expt	Jour AE 16 207	Mar 64 Pasechnik+ SPH,30–140 DEGREES	
					Jour JNE 19 278	65 . ENGL OF AE 16 207	
					Jour SJA 16 246	Sep 64 . ENGL OF AE 16 207	
Diff Elastic	4.0+5	1.0+6	HAR	ExTh	Jour NP 76 369	Feb 66 Ferguson+ OPTMDL PARS TO FIT POLARIZ	+
Diff Elastic		3.0+4	CCP	Expt	Conf 66Gatlinbg § 3.35	Sep 66 Aleksandrov+,TOF,FIRST LEG COEF,CRVS	
Diff Elastic	5.0+6		DKE	Expt	Jour ZP/A 196 103	Sep 66 Buccino+RADIO.PB.20 TO 140 DEG.TBL	+
					Abst DA 24 4251	Apr 64 Hollandsworth.CFD OPTMDL CALCS.	
	5.0+6				Data EXFOR11877.011	Jun 76 . 13 PTS	
Diff Elastic	3.2+6		BCM	Expt	Jour NP 89 154	Dec 66 Becker+ 12 ANGLES GRAPH CFD OPTMDL	+
	3.2+6				Data EXFOR11511.036	Jun 76 . 12 PTS.	
Diff Elastic	5.0+4	1.4+7	AI	Eval	Rept NAA–SR–11980	Apr 67 Campbell+ LEG COEFS TBL+CURVS C–MSYS	
Diff Elastic	1.4+7	2.4+7	SAF	Eval	Rept AP 42 262	Apr 67 Engelbrecht+ OPTMDL CALCS CFD EXPTS	
Diff Elastic	4.0+6		KUR	Expt	Jour PL/B 25 197	Aug 67 Gorlov+,2 TO 170DEG.CFD OPTMODEL	
					Jour YF 6 910	Nov 67 – + SCAT POLRZ N,OPTMOD CFD,CURV	
					Rept ANL–TR–462	Apr 67 SEE ALSO *	
					Jour ZEP 5 131	Feb 67 Gorlov+ COULOMB+NUCL SIG(ANG),GRAPHS	
				ExTh	Conf 67Kharkov 175	Feb 67 – .POLRSD NS,ANGLES=10–170 DEGRS	
				Expt	Jour JEL 5 106	Feb 67 . ENGL OF ZEP 5 131	
Diff Elastic	4.0+6		IFU	Theo	Jour UFZ 13 51	Jan 68 Kashuba+ GRPH,EXPT CFD OPTMOD–CALC	
					Jour UPJ 13 33	Jul 68 TRANSLATN.*	

82 Lead

Quantity	Energy (ev) Min	Max	Lab	Type	Documentation Ref Vol Page	Date	Author, Comments	Data
Diff Elastic	8.4+7	9.6+7	CCP	Theo	Jour YF 7 283	Feb 68	Aver'Yanov+ OPTMOD SIG(ANG) CFD EXPT	
					Jour SNP 7 2 193	Aug 68	TRANSLATN.*	
Diff Elastic	1.5+6		IFU	Comp	Jour YF 7 277	Feb 68	Korzh+ GRPH SIG(ANG),OPTMOD PARS – FIT	
					Jour SNP 7 2 190	Aug 68	TRANSLATN.*	
Diff Elastic	1.4+7		CCP	Theo	Jour YF 7 1221	Jun 68	Aver'Yanov+ GENERALIZD OPTMOD CALC	
					Jour SNP 7 728	Dec 68	TRANSLATN.*	
Diff Elastic	4.6+6		UBC	Expt	Jour CJP 46 1883	Sep 68	Tripard+ 5DEG STEPS 10–40DEG TBL+CRV	+
	4.6+6				Data EXFOR12190.002	Jun 76	. 7 PTS.	
Diff Elastic	8.4+5		ANL	Expt	Jour PR 176 1405	Dec 68	Kuchnir+ VDG+SCINT 1.75–15DEG	+
	8.4+5				Data EXFOR11977.005	Jun 76	. 6 PTS.	
Diff Elastic	4.0+6		KUR	Expt	Jour YF 8 1086	Dec 68	Gorlov+ SIG–GRPH,SPIN–ORBIT–ASSYMTRY	+
				ExTh	Jour IZV 34 138	Jan 70	– + OPTMOD,2–21DEG.CURVES,TABLE	
				Expt	Jour SNP 8 630	Jun 69	TRANSLATN.*	
				ExTh	Rept IAE – 1653	68	Gorlov+ ANGDIST 2–21 DEG,SIG, GRPH	
					Conf 67Kharkov 175	Feb 67	– .POLRSD NS,ANGLES=2–21 DEGREES	
					Jour BAS 34 126	Jan 70	. ENGL OF IZV 34 138	
	4.0+6			Expt	Data EXFOR40307.008	Nov 76	DIFF CS 2–21 DEG(8 ANGLES)	
Diff Elastic	+6	+7	CCP	Revw	Jour AE 28 310	Apr 70	Lebedeva+ ANOMALOUS SIG(ANG) GRAPHS	
					Jour EAF 28 4 35	Apr 70	. FRENCH OF AE 28 310	
Diff Elastic	4.0+6		KUR	Expt	Jour ZEP 12 181	Aug 70	Morozov+ SIG(ANG=140 TO 180) GRAPH	
					Jour JEL 12 125	Aug 70	. ENGL OF ZEP 12 181	
Diff Elastic	1.3+6	8.4+6	FEI	Expt	Rept FEI – 244	Apr 71	Anikin+ SCAT AT 17ANGS,GRPH SIG(ANG)	+
	5.8+5	8.4+6			Data EXFOR40080.	Nov 71	ANGDIST 2.5–24DEG AT 5 ES,TBL YFI–10	
Diff Elastic	+3		RPI	Expt	Prog NCSAC–38 172	May 71	Zuhr+.TOF. TO BE COMPLETED.NO DATA	
Diff Elastic	1.0+5	1.0+7	TRM	Eval	Prog INDC(IND)–12 2	Jul 71	Garg.ANGDIST FIT FOR OPTMOD PARS,NDG	
Diff Elastic	8.0+6		AE	Expt	Rept AE – 430	Sep 71	Holmqvist+ TBLS + GEN OPTMOD FITS	+
					Jour NP/A 188 24	Jun 72	– + OPTMOD ANAL OF 8MEV DATA	
	8.1+6				Rept AE – 452	May 72	Salama. VDG. TOF. CURVES, TABLES	
					Rept AE – 430	Sep 71	Holmqvist+ TBLS + GEN OPTMOD FITS	
	8.0+6				Conf 70Helsinki 2 341	Jun 70	– + OPTMOD ANALYSIS. 8 MEV	
	8.1+6				Data EXFOR20162.	May 74	32PTS.D/DA,LEG.FIT.	
	8.1+6				Data EXFOR20162.	May 74	31PTS.D/DA,LEG.FIT.	
Diff Elastic	2.0+6		ANL	Expt	Prog NCSAC–42 10	Nov 71	COX. NO DATA GIVEN.	
Diff Elastic	0.0+0	1.5+7	FEI	Eval	Book NIKOLAEV 169	72	.LEG COEFFS+ANG DISTRIBUTS,GRAPH	
Diff Elastic	1.4+7		LEB	Expt	Jour LEB 63 0	72	Belovitskij+ ANGDIS CFD OTH+THEO,FIG	
					Jour LEB 63 0	72	– + NUC EMULS.CFD OTH,GRAPH	
					Rept AD – A009563	Jun 74	Skobeltsyn – editr. PG231,ENGL OF LEB	
					Rept AD – A009 – 563	Jun 74	. PAGE 231.ENGL OF LEB 63	
Diff Elastic	1.1+6		ANL	Expt	Rept ANL – 7935	Jun 72	Cox+. CFD OPTMOD,HAUSER–FESHBACH	+
	1.1+6				Data EXFOR10332.032	Jun 74	. 8 PTS.	
Diff Elastic	3.7+6		WSU	Expt	Jour CJP 51 121	Jan 73	Gupta+.THETA=10,180DEG.CFD OPTMOD	+
					Abst DA/B 33 6013	Jun 73	– .THETA=180DEG.SIG GIVN.CFD TH.	
	3.7+6				Data EXFOR10307.003	Jun 74	. 2 PTS. 3.65 MEV ENERGY.	
Diff Elastic	1.4+7	1.5+7	CCP	Expt	Conf 73Tbilisi 154	Feb 73	Benecky+ ABST,SCAT AT 65,70 DEG,CFD	
Diff Elastic	2.5+6		PAD	Expt	Jour NC/A 13 867	Feb 73	Drigo+ SMALL ANGLE SCATTERING	+
	2.4+6				Data EXFOR20664.002	Oct 76	3PTS.D/DA.	
Diff Elastic	1.4+7		LRL	Expt	Abst DA/B 33 4954	Apr 73	Kammerdiener.TOF.20 – 160DEG.NO DATA.	
					Rept UCRL – 51232	Jul 72	– . RING GEOM.ANG DISTR	
Diff Elastic	1.5+6		SCU	Comp	Rept YK – 15 153	Aug 73	Aver'Janov+ H–F,OPTMOD,DIFFSIG,GRAPH	
	8.0+5				Rept YK – 15 153	Aug 73	– + H–F,OPTMOD,DIFFSIG,GRAPH	
Diff Elastic	1.5+7		ALB	Expt	Jour NP/A 212 147	Sep 73	Benenson+ .35–10DEG SCAT CFD OPTMODL	+
	1.5+7				Data EXFOR10370.003	May 74	. 16 PTS.	
Diff Elastic	3.0+6		EDG	Expt	Jour NP/A 212 182	Sep 73	Galloway+ POLARISED NS.ANGDIST.	+
	3.0+6				Data EXFOR20359.005	Sep 74	5PTS.D/DA.	
Diff Elastic	3.2+6		AMS	Theo	Jour NP/A 222 93	Apr 74	Zijp+ LEG.COEFF COMPOUND ELASTIC.H–F	
Diff Elastic	4.6+3	6.5+6	FEI	Theo	Rept YK – 8/2 3	Sep 72	Bazazjants+ ANISOTR GROUP–PARAMS,TBL	
					Rept INDC(CCP) – 39	Jul 74	.P1. ENGLISH OF YK – 8/2 3	
Diff Elastic	7.0+6		AE	Expt	Jour NP/A 232 436	Nov 74	Corcalciuc+ ANGDIST,GRAPH,TABLE.	+
					Rept AE – 482	Dec 73	Etemad. VDG. TOF.	
					Conf 73Kiev 3 87	May 73	Holmqvist+ SHORT DESCRIPTION.OPTMDL	
	7.0+6				Data EXFOR20346.	Sep 74	31PTS.D/DA,LEG.FIT.	
Diff Elastic	+7		BUC	Expt	Prog INDC(SEC) – 42	Dec 74	Corcalciuc+ FORWARD ANGDIST,NDG	
Diff Elastic	1.5+7		UFT	Theo	Rept KHFTI – 75 – 15	75	Berezhnoj+ GRPH,CFD EXPT.NUCL RADIUS	
Diff Elastic	1.4+7	1.5+7	JAE	Theo	Conf JAERI – M – 5984	Feb 75	Tanaka.OPTMDL/COUPLD CH.GRPH CFD EXP	
Diff Elastic	1.8+6		KUR	ExTh	Conf 75Kiev 3 175	May 75	Zareckij+ FILTRD,UNFILTRD.CFD TH.FIG	

82 Lead

Quantity	Energy (ev) Min	Max	Lab	Type	Documentation Ref Vol Page	Date	Author, Comments	Data
Diff Elastic	4.3+6		UBC	Expt	Jour CJP 51 2197	73	Martin+3ANGS.TBL OPTMDL PARS.GRPH.	+
					Abst DA/B 35 5580	May 75	Mcfadden.5TO15DEG.CFD OPT MDL.AGREE.	
	4.3+6				Data EXFOR10375.	Apr 76	. DATA UNOBTAINABLE FROM AUTHORS	
Diff Elastic	7.0+6	1.5+7	BRL	Expt	Jour PRL 35 1419	Nov 75	Bucher+ GRPHS CFD OPT MDL+OTHER EXPT	+
	7.0+6	1.4+7			Jour PL/B 58 277	Sep 75	- +SMALL ANGLE SCATT,GRAPH	
					Conf 75Wash. 946	Mar 75	.SUPERSEDED	
	7.6+6				Jour NIM 111 237	Aug 73	Bucher+EXPT DETAILS	
	7.0+6	1.4+7			Data EXFOR10510.002	Jul 75	. 9 ES,5ANGS. 39 DATA POINTS.	
Diff Elastic	8.0+6		AE	Theo	Conf IAEA-190 2 205	76	Wiedling+ ANGDIS,OPTMOD.CFD XPT,CURV	
	1.5+6	8.5+6			Rept AE- 485	Feb 74	Etemad.OPT MOD CALC COMP.WITH EXPT	
Diff Elastic	1.6+6		KFI	Expt	Prog INDC(SEC)-50	Jan 56	Hrehuss+ P63,ABST.SMALL ANGL,TBC,NDG	
Diff Elastic	1.4+7		BRN	Expt	Abst BAP 1 56	Jan 56	Melhorn+ 90 TO 150 DEG.	+
	1.4+7				Data EXFOR12187.002	Jun 76	. 7 PTS. ANG DIST.	
Diff Elastic	5.0+6		WES	Expt	Abst BAP 1 174	Apr 56	Hill. SCINT 10-45DEG CFD TH NDG	+
	5.0+6				Data EXFOR11300.006	Jun 76	. 6 PTS.	
Diff Elastic	4.4+6		WES	Expt	Abst BAP 1 339	Nov 56	Weddell. P RECOIL NUCL EMULSION	
	4.4+6				Data EXFOR11695.008	Jun 76	. 1 PT. 90 DEG CS=125+ -25MB	
Diff Elastic	6.0+5	2.2+6	ORE	Expt	Abst DA/B 37 307	Jul 76	YU.3 SMALL ANGS.CFD OPTMDL CALC.	+
	6.0+5	2.3+6			Data EXFOR10570.003	Jun 76	54PTS.SMALL ANGLE CS DATA	
Diff Elastic	3.4+6		TUD	Expt	Prog ZFK-315 12	Aug 76	Abdel-Harit+ ABST.ANAL COMPLETED,NDG	+
	3.4+6				Data EXFOR30464.	Jan 79	DIFF.CS + LEGENDRE-COEF.	
Polarization	3.5+8		CAR	Expt	Jour PR 100 437	55	Siegel. 16PC POL BEAM.2ANGS.TBL.	
Polarization	3.0+6		VIR	Expt	Jour PR 108 116	Oct 57	Hereford+ EL SCT POL.TBL.GRPHS.CFD	
Polarization	1.4+7		LRL	Theo	Jour PR 109 1295	Feb 58	Bjorklund+ PREDICTED PCT POL.CURV.	
Polarization	1.7+4		OSU	Theo	Jour NP 22 498	Feb 61	Margolis. POL(THETA) CALCULATED.	
Polarization	1.5+6		DKE	Expt	Rept TID-19051	62	Olness+ TOF.51.5DEG POL.CFD OPTMDL.	
Polarization	1.0+6	2.0+6	AE	Expt	Conf 65KFK 470	Sep 65	Aspelund+.12ES 8AS.GRAPHS NH/NL 3 AS	
Polarization	4.0+6		KUR	Expt	Jour ZEP 5 131	Feb 67	Gorlov+ SCHWINGER(COUL)+NUC SCAT CFD	+
					Jour DOK 158 574	Sep 64	- +	
					Jour JEL 5 106	Feb 67	. ENGL OF ZEP 5 131	
	4.0+6				Data EXFOR40221.034	May 74	.DIFF POLARZ OF EL SCAT,DATA AT17ANG	
Polarization	4.4+6	5.5+6	WIS	ExTh	Jour NP/A 95 193	Mar 67	Mahajan. 3ANGS.TBL.CURV CFD OPTMDL	
					Abst DA/B 28 1093	Sep 67	.THESIS ABST.	
Polarization	8.4+5		ANL	Expt	Jour PR 176 1405	Dec 68	Kuchnir+ VDG+SCINT 1.75-15DEG	
Polarization	4.0+6		KUR	Expt	Jour YF 8 1086	Dec 68	Gorlov+ GRPH POLARIZ-EFF(0 TO 7 DEG)	+
					Jour SNP 8 630	Jun 69	TRANSLATN.*	
	4.0+6				Data EXFOR40307.009	Nov 76	DIF.ASYM. 2-21 DEG(8 ANGLES)	
Polarization	4.0+6		KUR	Expt	Jour ZEP 12 181	Aug 70	Morozov+ POLARIZ(ANG=140 - 180) GRPH	
					Jour JEL 12 125	Aug 70	. ENGL OF ZEP 12 181	
Polarization	1.3+6	8.4+6	FEI	Expt	Rept FEI-244	Apr 71	Anikin+ POLARIZABILITY OF N ESTIMATD	
Polarization	2.0+6		ANL	Expt	Prog NCSAC-42 10	Nov 71	COX. NO DATA GIVEN	
Polarization	1.1+6		ANL	Expt	Rept ANL-7935	Jun 72	Cox+. CFD OPTMOD,HAUSER-FESHBACH	+
	1.1+6				Data EXFOR10332.066	Jun 74	. 8 PTS.	
Polarization	2.4+6		PAD	Expt	Jour NC/A 13 867	Feb 73	Drigo+ ANGULAR DISTRIBUTION	+
	2.5+6				Prog NP-18698 39	69	- +. CURVE POLARIZATN ANG DISTR	
	2.4+6				Data EXFOR20664.003	Oct 76	3PTS.	
Polarization	3.0+6		EDG	Expt	Jour NP/A 212 182	Sep 73	Galloway+ POLARISATION ANGDIST.	+
	3.0+6				Data EXFOR20359.006	Sep 74	5PTS.D/DA.ASSYM.	
Polarization	3.2+6		AMS	Expt	Jour NP/A 222 93	Apr 74	Zijp+ TABLES,GRAPHS. CFD NON-SPH POT	+
					Conf 75Zurich 189	Aug 75	- + GRPH OF DATA IN REVIEW.	
					Conf 72Budapest 170	Aug 72	- + POLARIZTN,EXPT CFD OPTMOD,GRP	
	3.2+6				Data EXFOR20777.020	Apr 78	4PTS.	
Potntal Scat	2.0+4	3.4+4	ORL	Expt	Jour PR 109 926	Feb 58	Good+ TOF+SC 10.2B	
Potntal Scat	+0	+3	BNL	Expt	Jour PR 110 692	May 58	Seth+ CALCTD FROM TOT SIG	
	+0	+4			Rept ORNL-2309	Jun 57	.SUPERSEDED	
	1.0+4				Data EXFOR11788.019	Jun 76	. 1 PT. POT= 11.3+ -.5 B	
Potntal Scat	1.0+6	1.4+7	HAR	Theo	Rept AERE-R-4649	Jun 64	Wilmore.OPTMDL TH.TBLS,CURVES.PM10PC	
Potntal Scat	4.0+6		KUR	Expt	Jour YF 8 1086	Dec 68	Gorlov+NUCL+COUL(SPIN-ORB)POT SCATNG	
					Jour SNP 8 630	Jun 69	TRANSLATN.*	
Tot Inelastc	None		BRK	Expt	Jour PR 51 590	Apr 37	Grahame+ EVIDENCE FOR INELASTIC SCAT	
Tot Inelastc	2.2+6	3.0+6	KYU	Theo	Jour SCP 40 351	Apr 43	Muto.OPTMDL CALCULATION,CFD EXPT	
Tot Inelastc	1.5+6	3.0+6	LAS	Expt	Jour PR 72 881	Nov 47	Barschall+ POOR GEOM+BACKSCT.BIAS DET	
Tot Inelastc	1.5+6	3.0+6	MIT	Theo	Jour PR 75 1115	Apr 49	Feld.FEW-LVL VS STATMOD FOR LAS DATA	
Tot Inelastc	1.4+7		LAS	Expt	Jour PR 75 1610	May 49	Gittings+ SPHERE GEOM,AL+CU63 DETS	
Tot Inelastc	9.5+6		BRK	Expt	Jour PR 77 606	Mar 50	Dejuren+ REL SIG(TOT),VALS MAYBE LOW	
Tot Inelastc	1.4+7		CAN	Expt	Jour PR 92 654	Nov 53	Whitmore.PHOTOGRAPH EMULS.CFD.OTH.	
Tot Inelastc	1.0+6	1.2+7	SPN	Theo	Jour ARS 50 107	Jun 54	.INEL SPECT RA-BE SOURCE,MONTECARLO	

82 Lead

Quantity	Energy (ev) Min	Max	Lab	Type	Documentation Ref Vol Page	Author, Comments Date	Data
Tot Inelastc	1.4+7		LAS	Expt Jour	PR 97 1205	Mar 55 Graves.BETWEEN 0.00 AND 0.73+ - 0.06B	
Tot Inelastc	5.5+7	1.4+8	HAR	Expt Jour	NAT 175 1027	Jun 55 Wilson.NDG.SIG HAS SMALL ENERGY VAR.	
Tot Inelastc	Cold		TRM	Theo Conf	55Geneva 2 56	Aug 55 Singwi+.P870,CURVE REL TEMP,CFD EXPT	
Tot Inelastc	2.9+5	1.0+6	CCP	Expt Jour	ZET 30 1017	Jun 56 Poze.SIG AT 3ES GIVEN,AV E OF SCT NS	
	7.7+5	1.0+6		Jour	ADP 20 3	Jul 57 Pose+,MEASURED AT 2 ENERGIES,TBL	
	2.9+5	1.0+6		Jour	JET 3 745	Dec 56 TRANSLATN.*	
Tot Inelastc	Cold		TRM	Theo Jour	PM 1 560	Jun 56 Kothari+ MELTING ENTROPY EFFECT	
Tot Inelastc	2.5+6		IFU	Expt Jour	JET 4 769	Jun 57 .ENGLISH OF ZET 31 907	
				Jour	ZET 31 907	Nov 56 Strizhak. SPHERE METHOD,TABLE	
Tot Inelastc	1.5+7		LAS	Expt Jour	PR 111 250	Jul 58 Coon+INTEG 9 - 14MEV,40 - 180DEG.	+
	1.5+7			Data	EXFOR11322.023	Jun 76 . 1 PT. CS=88+ - 30MB	
Tot Inelastc	1.4+7		LRL	Expt Conf	58Paris § NS609	Jul 58 Macgregor.FROM SNE 9AND14MEV CUTOFF	+
	1.4+7			Data	EXFOR11205.023	Jun 76 . 1 PT. CS=.17+ - .05B	
Tot Inelastc	2.5+6	1.4+7	IFU	Expt Conf	58Geneva 15 18	Sep 58 Pasechnik+.PPR2030,NDG,EXPT DESCRIBD	
				Conf	55Geneva 2 3	Aug 55 - . INTEGR SIGMA,3ES,TABLE	
Tot Inelastc	Fiss		KUR	Revw Conf	60Vienna 159	Oct 60 Bondarenko+.TABLE,EXPT DESCRIBED	
Tot Inelastc	1.4+7		CCP	Expt Jour	AE 11 398	Oct 61 TOF, 1.8 PM .3 B	+
				Jour	SJA 11 1044	61 . ENGL OF AE 11 398	
Tot Inelastc	8.0+5	4.0+6	IFU	Expt Prog	INDSWG - 126 22	66 Pasechnik. AT 5 ES, TBP IN AE	
Tot Inelastc	1.4+7		CCP	Theo Jour	SNP 7 728	Dec 68 .TRANSLATN.*	
				Jour	YF 7 1221	Jun 68 Aver'Yanov+SIG VAL,GENERALIZD OPTMOD	
				Rept	ICD - 4 158	67 Averjanov+OPTMOD CALC	
Tot Inelastc	2.8+6		IFU	Expt Jour	UFZ 14 330	Feb 69 Prokopesc+ TRANS,SCINT FOR NS,TABLE	+
	2.8+6			Data	EXFOR40050.006	Aug 70 SIGMA	
Tot Inelastc	1.5+7		LND	Expt Jour	AF 39 295	Sep 69 Joensson+. MEASURED NONEL GAMMAS	+
	1.5+7	1.6+7		Data	EXFOR20164.029	May 74 1PNT.SIGMA.	
Tot Inelastc	None		FEI	Theo Jour	AE 29 395	Nov 70 Popov.ABST FRANC - SOV SEM DUBNA 6/70	
				Jour	SJA 29 1159	Nov 70 . ENGL OF AE 29 395	
Tot Inelastc	1.0+5	1.0+7	TRM	Eval Prog	INDC(IND) - 12 2	Jul 71 Garg.FIT TO EXPTL DATA+THEO CALC,NDG	
Tot Inelastc	2.0+6	4.5+6	AE	Expt Rept	AE - 481	73 Etemad.TOF,AT 125 DEG,REL.TO H,TBLS	
Tot Inelastc	3.8+8	1.7+9	PTN	Expt Jour	PR/C 7 248	Jan 73 Schimmerling+.TOF. TRANS.TABLE 15ES	+
				Jour	PL/B 37 177	Nov 71 .SUPERSEDED	
	3.8+8	1.7+9		Data	EXFOR10082.023	Dec 75 . 15 PTS.SIN CS DATA	
Tot Inelastc	1.4+7		TUD	Expt Prog	ZFK - 262 39	Sep 73 Goebel+ INTEGRATED DIFFSIG,TB DONE	
Tot Inelastc	4.1+6	5.2+6	NAG	Expt Jour	NST 13 343	Jul 76 Bhoraskar+	+
	4.1+6	5.2+6		Data	EXFOR20703.003	Nov 76 5PTS.SIGMA.	
Diff Inelast	2.5+6		RIC	Expt Jour	PR 60 693	Nov 41 Dunlap+ E SPECT CFD LIQUID DROP C - N	
Diff Inelast	1.5+7		MIT	Expt Jour	PR 82 69	Apr 51 Stelson+ SPECT INEL NS.EMULS.	
Diff Inelast	3.0+8		BRK	Expt Rept	UCRL - 1938	Aug 52 Ball+ INTEG CS GVN	
Diff Inelast	3.5 - 1		CRC	Expt Jour	PR 88 542	Nov 52 Brockhouse+CD FILTER NEUT ENERGY DST	
Diff Inelast	1.4+7		LAS	Expt Jour	PR 89 343	Jan 53 Graves. TEMP GIVEN.	
Diff Inelast	1.5+7		COR	Expt Jour	PR 95 1235	Sep 54 Oneill+ TOF. E SPECT,ANG.DIST	
Diff Inelast	1.5+6	3.2+6	ORL	Expt Jour	PR 97 1222	Mar 55 Stelson+ EXCIT.OF METASTABLE GRPH	+
	1.5+6	3.2+6		Data	EXFOR12242.002	Jun 76 . 30 PTS. SIGMA.	
Diff Inelast	4.3+6		WES	Expt Abst	BAP 1 175	Apr 56 Smith.TOF NEUT SPEC AT 90DEG NDG	+
Diff Inelast	2.3+6		FEI	Expt Jour	AE 3 106	Aug 57 Salnikov. EXCIT 805+890KEV,ANISOTRPY	
				Jour	JNE 9 9	Jun 59 . ENGL OF AE 3 106	
				Jour	SJA 3 869	57 . ENGL OF AE 3 106	
Diff Inelast	2.9+6		CCP	Expt Jour	AE 3 498	Dec 57 Popov.EXCIT LEVELS ABOUT 0.8MEV	
				Jour	JNE 9 9	Jun 59 TRANSLATN.*	
				Jour	SJA 3 1379	57 TRANSLATN.*	
Diff Inelast	1.4+7		CCP	Expt Jour	AE 3 540	Dec 57 Zamyatnin+.P RECOIL, T=0.73+ - 0.05MEV	
Diff Inelast	1.5+7		LAS	Expt Jour	PR 111 250	Jul 58 Coon+,SC,35 - 145DEG NS +9MEV ABSCURV	+
				Conf	58Geneva 15 11	Sep 58 - +.PPR666,CURVE,EXPT DESCRIBED	
	1.5+7			Data	EXFOR11322.024	Jun 76 . 26 PTS. ANG DIST.	
Diff Inelast	3.7+6	1.5+7	TNC	Expt Jour	PR 118 1059	May 60 Prudhomme+REL ANG.DIST. 5ES	
				Rept	AD - 154995	Feb 58 .SUPERSEDED	
Diff Inelast	1.4+7		CCP	Jour	AE 11 398	Oct 61 TOF, TEMP. 0.75PM.08 MEV	
				Jour	SJA 11 1044	61 . ENGL OF AE 11 398	
Diff Inelast	1.4+7		BAS	Expt Jour	PL 5 202	Jul 63 Huber+ GRAPH OF INELASTIC N SPECTRUM	
				Jour	HPA 34 520	Aug 61 Niklaus+.NUC.TEMP.1.06MEV	
				Jour	HPA 36 1059	Dec 59 Huber+.T=1.28MEV	
Diff Inelast	1.4+7		ORL	ExTh Jour	NP 68 97	Jun 65 Stelson+TOF.GRPHS.CFD DWBA MDL CALCS	+
	1.4+7			Expt Data	EXFOR11527.025	Jun 76 . 17 PTS.	
Diff Inelast	1.4+7		RPI	Expt Jour	JNAB 19 497	Jul 65 Pearlstein+.INEL SPECTRUM 6 - 14 MEV	+
				Abst	DA 26 438	Jul 65 - .SIGMA+INEL EN SPECTRA.NDG	
	1.4+7			Data	EXFOR10234.005	May 73 . 1 PT. DSIGMA AT 90DEG	

82 Lead

Quantity	Energy (ev) Min	Max	Lab	Type	Documentation Ref Vol Page	Date	Author, Comments	Data
Diff Inelast	1.4+7		FEI	Expt	Jour YF 2 826	Nov 65	Anufrienko+ SPEC OF SECONDARY NS,CRV	+
					Rept ICD-1 249	Aug 64	.	
					Rept ANL-TRANS-168	Apr 67	.PAGE 249.ENGLISH TRANSL OF ICD-1	
					Jour SNP 2 589	May 66	.ENGLISH TRANSL OF YF 2 826 11/65	
					Prog INDSWG-64E	64	.ENGLISH TRANSL OF ICD-1	
	1.4+7				Data EXFOR40133.023	Feb 73	N-SPECTRUM AT 92 DEG	
Diff Inelast	3.0+5	8.0+5	IFU	Expt	Prog INDSWG-126 22	66	Pasechnik. AT 3 ES, TBP IN AE	
Diff Inelast	1.4+7		FEI	Expt	Rept FEI-39	Jan 66	Sal'Nikov+TOF SPECT,RING GEOM,E-SPEC	
Diff Inelast	8.0+6		LAS	Expt	Jour PR 142 775	Feb 66	Cranberg+ VDG.TOF.EXCIT 2.6MEV LVL	+
	8.0+6				Data EXFOR12216.002	Jun 76	. 13 PTS.	
Diff Inelast	1.4+7		LRL	ExTh	Jour NP 77 241	Mar 66	Schectman+ SPEC AT 3 ANGLES CFD STAT	+
	1.4+7			Expt	Data EXFOR11698.007	Jun 76	. 1 PT. CS=255.MB/SR+-20PCT	
Diff Inelast	1.5+7		TNC	Expt	Jour PR 186 1038	Oct 69	Mathur+TOF,DIST INEL SCT NEUTS	+
					Rept NDL-TR-86	Jan 67	- +TBLS.ANG=90DEG.EXPT DETAILS	
	1.5+7				Data EXFOR10043.	Jun 72	. 15 PTS. D/DA	
Diff Inelast	1.4+7		CCP	Theo	Rept SNP 7 728	Dec 68	.TRANSLATN.*	
					Jour YF 7 1221	Jun 68	Aver'Yanov+ SIG-GRPH,OPTMOD OKS EXPT	
					Rept ICD-4 158	67	Averjanov+OPTMOD CALC CFD EXPT	
Diff Inelast	+3		RPI	Expt	Prog NCSAC-33 208	Dec 70	Zuhr+,SCINT DET,TOF SPECT GIVEN,TBC	
Diff Inelast	1.4+7		VNV	Expt	Rept CEA-N-4279	Mar 72	Clayeux+ TOF,DIF NTS .1 TO 7 MEV	
					Conf 71Knoxvill 196	Mar 71	Voignier+SIG,VS.E(PRIME) 90DEG CRV	
					Rept CEA-R-3807	Aug 69	Clayeux+	
Diff Inelast	1.4+7		KFI	Theo	Conf 72Budapest 202	Aug 72	Kluge+ CALCULATED EN-SPECTRA ,GRPH	
					Rept KFKI-72-17	Feb 72	- + CALC N-SPEC INEL+N2N,TBL,GRPH	
Diff Inelast	5.7+5	1.5+7	UK	Eval	Data UKNDL-DFN 26C	Mar 73	.TO CONTINUUM.54 PTS.E DIST.ANGDIST.	
Diff Inelast	1.4+7		LRL	Expt	Abst DA/B 33 4954	Apr 73	Kammerdiener.TOF.20-160DEG.NO DATA.	
					Rept UCRL-51232	Jul 72	- . RING GEOM.ANG DISTR	
Diff Inelast	1.4+7		TUD	Expt	Prog ZFK-262 39	Sep 73	Goebel+ DOUBLEDIFFSIG,IN PROGRESS	
Diff Inelast	1.4+7		FEI	Expt	Rept YK-15 129	74	Sal'Nikov+ TOF,SPEC OF SECOND-NS,TBL	+
	1.4+7				Data EXFOR40238.	Nov 74	.MB/SR/MEV FOR 5 ANGLES AND 50ES GVN	
Diff Inelast	1.4+7		KYU	Expt	Jour NST 11 523	Dec 74	Akiyoshi+.TOF,E-SPECTRUM AT 100 DEG	
Diff Inelast	2.0+6	4.5+6	AE	Expt	Conf 75Wash. 871	Mar 75	Etemad. TO LVLS,125DEG.CFD THEO,GRPH	
Diff Inelast	1.4+7		FEI	Eval	Conf 75Kiev 4 128	May 75	Luk'Janov+ DIR,INDIR SIG,TEMP.TABLE	
Diff Inelast	4.4+6		WES	Expt	Abst BAP 1 339	Nov 56	Weddell. 90DEG. FOR SCT NS GT .8 MEV	+
	4.4+6				Data EXFOR11695.009	Jun 76	. 1 PT. CS=68+-23MB/SR	
Diff Inelast	3.4+6		TUD	Expt	Prog ZFK-315 12	Aug 76	Abdel-Harit+ ABST.ANAL COMPLETED,NDG	
Diff Inelast	4.7+6		RI	Expt	Conf 77Kiev	77	Lebedev+ TOF,SIG(NEUT-E),TBL	
Thermal Scat	Cold		LUQ	Expt	Jour PR 58 321	Aug 40	Rasetti. CS(SCAT)VS CRYSTL STRUCTURE	
Thermal Scat	Pile		ANL	Expt	Jour PR 72 408	Sep 47	Fermi+. SPIN DEPENDENCE.	
Thermal Scat	1.3-3	2.0-2	BNL	Expt	Jour PR 91 1368	Sep 53	Mcreynolds.TRANS,80+295DEGK,TOT,INEL	
					Rept BNL-1568	53	- .TRANS,80+295DEGK,OKS TH	
Thermal Scat	-1		SAC	Expt	Conf 55Geneva 5 77	Aug 55	Jacrot+NDG,SLOW CHOPPER,PPR357	
Thermal Scat	1.2-3		TAT	Expt	Jour PRSA 231 293	Sep 55	Kothari+.XTAL,THEOR SIGTOT CFD EXPT	
Thermal Scat	4.4-1	1.1+2	HAR	Expt	Jour NAT 181 643	Mar 58	Mccallum+TOF MEAN FREE PATH OF PHON.	
Thermal Scat	Cold		BNL	Expt	Prog WASH-1028 13	Apr 60	Palevsky+ TBC. DIFFUSIVE SCT.NDG.	
Thermal Scat	2.5-2	2.5-2	HAR	Theo	Conf 60Vienna 75	Oct 60	Marshall+COHERENT SCAT VS TEMP,TBL	
Thermal Scat	Maxwl		OXF	Theo	Jour PPS 77 353	Feb 61	Chudley+.JUMP DIFFUSION MOD CFD EXPT	
Thermal Scat	5.0-3		KRK	Expt	Jour PF 12 473	Aug 61	SPEC OF NS AT ANGL=90DEG,TEMP=462CGR	
Thermal Scat	None		ANL	Theo	Conf 62Chalk R. 1 215	Sep 62	Singwi+,FREQUENCY SPECT AT 620DEGK	
Thermal Scat	Cold		HAR	ExTh	Rept AERE-R-4101	Sep 62	Egelstaff.SOLID+LIQUID SCAT CFD.	
	0.0+0	1.0+0		Theo	Conf 62Chalk R. 1 203	Sep 62	- .SIG CFD TH FOR LIQUID LEAD	
Thermal Scat	-2		WWA	Expt	Jour NKA 9 523	Jul 64	Buras. DIFFRACTN-PATTERN BY TOF,GRPH	
Thermal Scat	Cold		BNL	Expt	Abst BAP 10 436	Apr 65	Mozer+VIB. EXCIT.SPEC.POLY CRYSTL	
Thermal Scat		2.0-2	DUB	Expt	Conf 66Dubna 161	Jul 66	Golikov+,GRAPH,INEL N,SOLID+LIQUID	
Thermal Scat	Cold		MHG	ExTh	Abst DA/B 27 508	Aug 66	Werner.MOSAIC XTAL,SECONDRY EXTINCTN	
Thermal Scat	1.5-2	2.0-2	MTR	Expt	Jour PR 152 99	Dec 66	Randolph+ 352DEG C,3ES, CURVS S(A,B)	
Thermal Scat	2.0-4		MUN	Expt	Jour PRL 36 1021	Apr 76	Koester+ COH SCAT AMP. BOUND,REFLECT	+
					Conf 67Juelich 80	Apr 67	- + SUPERSEDED.	
	2.0-4	5.2+0			Data EXFOR20598.	Jun 76	3PNTS.COH.SCAT.AMP.	
Thermal Scat	3.0-2	5.0-2	MTR	Expt	Rept IN-1115	Aug 67	Randolph+350DEGC 2ES 12AS PHASED CHP	
	1.5-2	2.5-2			Rept IN-1094	Jun 67	- +350DEG. 6ES.NO KOHN EFFECT	
Thermal Scat		-3	+1	IFU	Expt Jour UFZ 13 605	Apr 68	Vertebnyi+ GRPH SIG(E),MAGN CONTRIB	
					Jour UPJ 13 425	Oct 68	TRANSLATN.*	
Thermal Scat	2.0-3	2.0-2	KTH	Revw	Conf 68Copenhgn 1 397	May 68	Larsson.PPR200.SIG(E'),LIQUID STATE	
		+0			Conf 64Bombay 2 3	Dec 64	- LIQUID DYNAMICS AND N SCAT	

82 Lead

Quantity	Energy (ev) Min	Max	Lab	Type	Documentation Ref Vol Page	Author, Comments Date	Data
Thermal Scat	Maxwl		HAR	Expt	Jour JP/C 1 1075	Aug 68 North+ STRUCTURE FACTOR FOR LIQUIDS	
	2.0−3				Conf 68Copenhgn 1 463	May 68 Cocking.PPR115.SIG(E'),PHON−T,LIQUID	
					Jour AIP 16 189	Apr 67 Cooking.SPEC SCAT NEUTS,LIQUID+SOLID	
Thermal Scat	Maxwl		UJV	Theo	Rept UJV−2275	69 Krivy. DEBYE TEMP,BRAGG+OTHER EXPTS	
Thermal Scat	−3	−1	UMX	Revw	Diss MEXICO	69 Lonngi. LIQUID STATE,REVIEW	
Thermal Scat	Maxwl		TOR	Theo	Jour PR 180 299	Apr 69 Desai+ S(A,B) CURVES,CFD EXPT,LIQUID	
Thermal Scat	None		TKU	Theo	Jour AAF 6 321	Jul 69 Laehteenkorva. DISPERSION CURVES GVN	
Thermal Scat	1.3−3	9.2−3	CCP	Expt	Jour AE 27 511	Dec 69 Khrushchev+ SIG(LAMBDA,TEMP) GRAPHS	
					Jour EAF 27 6 24	Dec 69 . FRENCH OF AE 27 511	
Thermal Scat	None		BUC	Theo	Jour SCF 23 699	71 Trepadus.GAUSS APPROX.CRVS CFD EXPT	
Thermal Scat	4.4−3	5.0−3	KFK	ExTh	Conf 72Grenoble 137	Mar 72 Gompf+ COH.INEL SCAT ,TOF,2ES ,GRPH	
Thermal Scat	Pile		JUL	Comp	Rept JUEL−875−RX	Aug 72 Scharenberg. DATA ON USE AS N−FILTER	
Thermal Scat	1.0−4	1.0+3	MUN	Revw	Jour EEN 80 1	77 Koester. SCAT LENGTH,FREE+INCOH SIG	
Scattering	Maxwl		NYU	Expt	Jour PR 48 653	Oct 35 Mitchell+ RA−BE/PARAF NS.VAL REL ABS	
Scattering	Maxwl		NYU	Expt	Jour PR 50 133	Jul 36 Mitchell+ RA−BE+PARAFF NS. FILTERED.	
Scattering	2.0−2	8.0+1	NYU	Expt	Jour PR 52 282	Aug 37 Mitchell+ RA−BE+PARAF,ACTIVN DETECTR	
Scattering	Maxwl		CAV	Expt	Jour PRSA 162 127	Sep 37 Goldhaber+. 12.9B REL 4.83B FOR C	
Scattering	Maxwl		JAP	Expt	Jour SCP 36 153	Jul 39 Kimura.SIG=9.8 PM 0.8B	
Scattering	Maxwl		NYU	Expt	Jour PR 60 155	Aug 41 Whitaker+ 9.0B ,SIG(CAPT) DEDUCED	
Scattering	3.1+6		LAS	Expt	Jour PR 70 602	Nov 46 Manley+CS FOR BACK SCATTERING	
Scattering	2.0+5	3.0+6	LAS	Expt	Jour PR 72 881	Nov 47 Barschall+ POOR GEOM+BACKSCT.BIAS DET	
Scattering	7.0−4	1.0−1	CAV	Expt	Jour NAT 161 282	Feb 48 Latham+. 0.6+−0.3B BELOW 0.001EV	
Scattering	9.0+7		BRK	Theo	Jour PR 75 1352	May 49 Fernbach+ EXPT CFD OPAQUE SPH MODEL	
Scattering	1.3+7	1.6+7	UMX	Expt	Jour RMF 4 52	Jan 55 Bonner+ BROAD MAXIMUM AT 16 MEV	
Scattering	6.0+4	1.8+6	ANL	Expt	Jour PR 107 1077	Aug 57 Langsdorf+,LEGENDRE COEFS CURVES	+
					Rept ANL−5567	Oct 61 .REVISED DATA	
	3.0+4	1.5+6			Data EXFOR11224.064	Jun 76 . 20 PTS. SIGMA.	
	3.0+4	1.5+6			Data EXFOR11224.065	Jun 76 . 100 PTS,DSIGMA.	
Scattering	Fast		FEI	Expt	Jour AE 18 409	Apr 65 Gusejnov+ ANGL DIST,TH(N,F)DETECTOR	
					Jour JNE 20 700	Aug 66 . ENGL OF AE 18 409	
					Jour SJA 18 526	Apr 65 . ENGL OF AE 18 409	
					Jour EAF 18 4 134	Apr 65 . FRENCH OF AE 18 409	
Scattering	8.2−4	8.2−2	NYB	Expt	Abst DA/B 28 1107	Sep 67 Edwards.FORWARD COH SCT AMPL VS TEMP	
Scattering	2.0−2	1.5+7	IFU	Expt	Prog YFI−6 108	68 Vertebnyj+. SIGMA GIVEN. TBP UFZ	
					Rept INDC−260E	69 . ENGL OF YFI−6 108	
Scattering	1.0+0	1.0+1	TRM	Expt	Jour JNE 22 261	Apr 68 Navalkar+ NEUT DECAY TIME IN PB PILE	
Scattering	2.0−2	3.0−2	IFU	Expt	Conf 70Helsinki 1 651	Jun 70 Vertebnij+ 2200M/SEC SIGMA GIVEN,TBL	
					Rept BNL−TR−495	Jul 72 . ENGLISH OF 70HELSIN 1 651	
Scattering	−3		JUL	Expt	Conf 75Wash. 823	Mar 75 Schmatz+INCOH SC=2.0+−1.0MB.REL VA	
Nonelastic	+7		BRK	Expt	Jour PR 53 795	May 38 Grahame+ RA−BE,TRANS,BY FE56+AL(N,P)	
Nonelastic	1.4+7		WWA	Expt	Jour NAT 142 252	Aug 38 Soltan.WIDE−ANGLE TRNSM,ACTVN DETECT	
Nonelastic	3.1+6		OSA	Expt	Jour JPJO 22 142	40 Kikuchi+.D+D.ANGDIST IN FIG	
	3.1+6	1.4+7			Jour JMJ 22 430	40 Wakatsuki.D+D,LI+D ANGDIST IN FIGS	
	3.1+6				Jour PR 55 1264	Jun 39 Kikuchi+ DIFF SIG.23−55DEG,RING SCT	
Nonelastic	None		CHI	Expt	Jour PR 73 1307	Jun 48 Szilard+ RA−BE, B SPHERE	
Nonelastic	1.4+7		LAS	Expt	Jour PR 88 600	Nov 52 Phillips+ SPHERE TRNS. 5 MEV RSLN.	+
	1.4+7				Data EXFOR11210.010	Jun 76 . 1 PT. CS=2.56+−.05 B	
Nonelastic	1.4+7		LAS	Expt	Jour PR 89 343	Jan 53 Graves+ SPHERE TRANS. .7MEV RSLN.	+
	1.4+7				Data EXFOR11304.011	Jun 76 . 1 PT. CS=3.3+−.8B	
Nonelastic	1.0+6		WIS	Expt	Jour PR 93 1062	Mar 54 Walt+ SNE=TOT−SEL	+
	1.0+6				Data EXFOR11637.075	Jun 76 . 1 PT. CS=.3+−.7 B	
Nonelastic	1.4+7		LAS	Expt	Jour PR 97 1205	Mar 55 Graves+ SPHERE MULT+TRNS. CFD.	+
	1.4+7				Data EXFOR11310.011	Jun 76 . 1 PT. CS=2.49+−.02B	
Nonelastic	8.0+5	1.6+6	LAS	Expt	Priv ALLEN	Mar 55 Allen.SPHERICAL TRNS.	
	8.0+5	1.6+6			Data EXFOR11693.003	Jun 76 . 8 PTS. CS DATA	
Nonelastic	4.1+6		LAS	Expt	Jour PR 98 677	May 55 Walt+ FROM TOT MINUS ELAST	+
	4.1+6				Data EXFOR11215.051	Jun 76 . 1 PT. CS=1.9+−.3 B.	
Nonelastic	1.0+6	4.5+6	LAS	Expt	Jour PR 98 1216	Jun 55 Beyster+ SPH TRNS 3ES 2ND IS 4.0MEV	+
					Jour PR 97 563	Jan 55 .SUPERSEDED.(LETTER)	
	1.0+6	4.5+6			Data EXFOR11216.016	Jun 76 . 3 PTS.	
Nonelastic	2.5+6	4.1+6	IFU	Expt	Conf 55Geneva 2 3	Aug 55 Pasechnik.SPH MEAS SPEC OF SCT N	+
					Conf 56Kiev 102	56 .	
Nonelastic	1.0+6	1.5+7	LAS	Revw	Conf 55Geneva 2 18	Aug 55 Walt.P588, CURVE,DISCUSSN OF RESULTS	
Nonelastic	3.5+6	1.4+7	RIC	Expt	Jour PR 100 174	Oct 55 Taylor+,SPHERE TRNS	+
	3.5+6	1.4+7			Data EXFOR11217.012	Jun 76 . 5 PTS.	
Nonelastic	5.5+7	1.4+8	OXF	ExTh	Jour PR/A 236 41	Jul 56 Voss+WILSON.EXPT+OPT MODEL THEORY	+
					Jour PR/A 236 52	Jul 56 − + OPTICAL MODEL.	

82 Lead

Quantity	Energy (ev) Min	Max	Lab	Type	Documentation Ref Vol Page	Author, Comments Date	Data
Nonelastic	1.4+7		CCP	Expt	Jour AE 1 4 155	Sep 56 Flerov+.SPHERE TRANSM, 2540+ − 50MB	+
					Jour SJA 1 4 617	56 TRANSLATN.*	
Nonelastic	5.0+5	2.0+6	HAR	Expt	Jour PHY 22 1135	Nov 56 Morrison.0.4,0.6,1B AT 1.2,1.6,2MEV	
Nonelastic	2.5+6	7.0+6	LAS	Expt	Jour PR 104 1319	Dec 56 Beyster+,SPH TRNS 0.71−2.38B 2ES	+
	2.5+6	7.0+6			Data EXFOR11220.031	Jun 76 . 2 PTS.	
Nonelastic	1.4+7		IFU	Expt	Jour AE 2 68	Jan 57 Strizhak.SPHERE TRANSMISS 2.42+ − .08B	+
					Jour JNE 5 253	Nov 57 TRANSLATN.*	
					Jour SJA 2 72	57 TRANSLATN.*	
Nonelastic	Fiss		LAS	Expt	Jour JNE 4 147	Feb 57 Bethe+.SPH TRNSM,POOR RSLN DETECTORS	+
					Rept LA− 1429	Dec 55 − +SPHERE TRANS. FISS SPECT	
	Fiss				Data EXFOR11461.	Jun 76 . 3 PTS. 3 THRESHOLD DETECT	
Nonelastic	1.4+7		LRL	Expt	Jour PR 108 726	Nov 57 Macgregor+,SPH TRNS CFD OPTMDL+XPTS	+
	1.4+7				Data EXFOR11226.023	Jun 76 . 1 PT. CS=2.56+ − .03 B	
Nonelastic	3.6+6		IFU	Expt	Jour UFZ 3 185	Feb 58 Batalin+SPH TR DET EXPT DETAIL	+
Nonelastic		3.0+7	LRL	Theo	Rept UCRL−5028	Mar 58 Bjorklund. CCB OKS EXPT DEL.	
Nonelastic	1.0+6	1.0+8	BNL	Comp	Conf 58Geneva 16 8	Sep 58 Hughes.PPR2483,CURVE,MANY REFS	
Nonelastic	2.1+7	2.9+7	LRL	Expt	Jour PR 111 1155	Aug 58 Macgregor+ SPH TRNS. 3ES.	+
					Conf 58Geneva 14 109	Sep 58 Ball+.PPR1881,TBL AT 4ES GVN,C−W	
	2.1+7	2.9+7			Data EXFOR11230.011	Jun 76 . 3 PTS.	
Nonelastic	1.4+7		CCP	Expt	Jour AE 5 522	Nov 58 Lebedev+ SPH GEOM,TR DET, 2.46+ − .1B	+
					Jour JNEA 11 39	Nov 59 TRANSLATN.*	
					Jour SJA 5 1431	58 TRANSLATN.*	
Nonelastic	8.2+6	1.8+7	RIC	Expt	Jour PR 113 1088	Feb 59 Bonner+,SPH TRANSMISSION,2.74TO2.35B	+
					Jour PRL 2 186	Feb 59 .SUPERSEDED	
	8.2+6	1.9+7			Data EXFOR11793.005	Jun 76 . 5 PTS.	
Nonelastic	1.4+7		ALD	Expt	Rept AWRE−NR/P−3 60	Oct 60 White.2.0+ − 0.2 NEUTRONS PER NON−ELAS	
Nonelastic	5.0+9		BRK	Expt	Jour PR 123 1850	Sep 61 Atkinson+ TRNS GOOD+POOR GEOM.	+
	5.0+9				Data EXFOR11112.017	Jun 76 . 1 PT. CS=1.670+ − .079B	
Nonelastic	1.3+7	2.0+7	CCP	Expt	Jour AE 11 397	Oct 61 SPH,4ES, 2.62PM.1 2.56PM.06	
					Jour SJA 11 1043	61 . ENGL OF AE 11 397	
Nonelastic	1.4+6		LSU	Expt	Jour PR 132 1211	Nov 63 Haas+SPHERE TRNS. TBL. CFD	+
					Abst DA 24 4747	May 64 .ABST. ORDINARY AND RADIO PB	
	1.4+6				Data EXFOR11794.003	Jun 76 . 1 PT. CS=2.53+ − .05B	
Nonelastic	1.0+6	1.6+7	HAR	Theo	Jour NP 55 673	Jul 64 Wilmore+OPTMOD INCLUDES COMP.ELASTIC	
Nonelastic	4.0+6	3.6+7	LAS	Theo	Prog WASH−1056 1	Mar 65 Rosen.CRV CALCTD FROM OPTMDL,CFD EXP	
Nonelastic	8.1+6		CCP	Expt	Jour AE 19 456	Nov 65 Degtjarev.SPHERE TRANSM, 2.28+ − .08B	+
					Jour JNE 20 818	Sep 66 TRANSLATN.*	
					Jour EAF 19 5 72	Nov 65 TRANSLATN.*	
					Jour SJA 19 1426	Nov 65 TRANSLATN.*	
Nonelastic	2.5+6	4.1+6	IFU	ExTh	Jour AE 20 8	Jan 66 Korzh+SJA 20 8 SUM OF SEV YRS WORK	+
Nonelastic	1.7+6	2.1+6	MIT	Expt	Conf 66Wash. 726	Mar 66 Beghian+ TOF. GRPH. CFD OTH	+
	1.7+6	2.1+6			Data EXFOR12235.002	Jun 76 . 2 PT. CS AT 2ES.	
Nonelastic	5.5+6	1.4+7	FEI	Comp	Rept ICD−4 57	67 Sluchevskaya.SELECTIV COMPIL ,TABLE	
Nonelastic	3.0+6	1.4+8	SAF	Eval	Jour AP 42 262	Apr 67 Engelbrecht+ OPTMDL CALCS CFD EXPTS	
Nonelastic	1.5+7		BOS	Expt	Jour PR 161 1181	Sep 67 Chatterjee+ SPHERE .2.50+ − .05B	+
	1.5+7				Data EXFOR30337.010	Jun 76 1 PNT	
Nonelastic	8.4+7	9.6+7	CCP	Theo	Jour YF 7 283	Feb 68 Aver'Yanov+ OPTMOD−CALCTD SIG GVN	
					Jour SNP 7 2 193	Aug 68 TRANSLATN.*	
Nonelastic	1.0+7		IJE	Comp	Jour REA 6 4 3	Dec 68 Konshin+ SIG(NEUT−E)+ − ERROR GVN,GRPH	
Nonelastic	4.0+6		KUR	ExTh	Jour YF 6 910	Nov 70 Gorlov+ POLRZ INC N,OPTMOD CFD.1.79B	
Nonelastic	1.4+7		GHT	Expt	Jour ACA 64 187	73 Vandecasteele+ FLUX−ATTENUAT,SIG GVN	
Nonelastic	1.0−4	1.5+7	UK	Eval	Data UKNDL−DFN 26C	Mar 73 162 PNTS	+
Nonelastic	1.4+7		BOS	ExTh	Conf 74Calcutta 44	Nov 74 PAL+ SPHER TRANS.SIG GVN,OPTMOD ANAL	+
				Expt	Conf 72Bombay 2 33	Feb 72 Bharati+ REPROCICAL SPHR TRANS,TBL	
	1.4+7				Data EXFOR30335.002	May 76 1 PNT	
Nonelastic	1.4+7		BOS	ExTh	Conf 74Calcutta 44	Nov 74 PAL+ SPHER TRANS.SIG GVN,OPTMOD ANAL	
Nonelastic	1.5+7	1.8+7	NAG	Expt	Jour NST 13 343	Jul 76 Bhoraskar+ SIG IN TBL FOR MS.ACTIV.	+
	1.5+7	1.8+7			Data EXFOR20703.004	Nov 76 2PTS.SIGMA.	
Absorption	+7		BRK	Expt	Jour PR 53 795	May 38 Grahame+ RA−BE,TRANS,CU+PB(NNG)DETS	
Absorption	Maxwl	+2	JAP	Expt	Jour JPJO 24 569	42 Kimura.SIG CURVE GIVN	
Absorption	Maxwl	1.4+7	AUS	Expt	Jour APA 3 352	Mar 50 Lintner. RA−BE SOURCE	
		7.0+5			Jour OAWS 158 123	Nov 49 − .RN−BE−SOURCE SPHER DEVICE	
	Maxwl	1.4+7			Jour OAWS 158 135	Nov 49 − .	
Absorption	Pile		HAR	Expt	Jour PPSA 63 1175	Oct 50 Colmer+LITTLER.PILE OSC REL HAR B	+
					Rept AERE−N/R−527	Jun 50 − + PILE OSCILLATOR.	
Absorption	Pile		ANL	Expt	Jour PR 80 342	Nov 50 Harris+.PILE OSC.REL TO BORON.	+
	Pile				Data EXFOR11528.049	Jun 76 . 1 PT. CS=.16B+ − 5PCT.	

82 Lead

Quantity	Energy (ev) Min	Max	Lab	Type	Documentation Ref Vol Page	Author, Comments Date	Data
Absorption	Pile		HAR	Expt	Jour PPSA 65 761	Sep 52 Aitken+.PILE OSC REL HAR B	
Absorption	Maxwl		KRK	Expt	Jour BPP 1 60	Jan 53 Wielowiejska.RA+BE SOURCE,EMULS METH	
					Jour APP 12 8	Jun 53 CONTINUED *	
Absorption	1.4+9		BNL	Expt	Jour PR 98 1369	Jun 55 Coor+ TRANS. OPTMDL PARS. TBL	+
	1.4+9				Data EXFOR11087.014	Jun 76 . 1 PT. CS=1.730B+ − 5 PCT	
Absorption	7.7+8		BIR	Expt	Jour PPS 29 293	Mar 58 Booth+ FROM SIGTOT, CFD OPTICALMODEL	
Absorption	2.5+4	8.3+5	FEI	Expt	Jour ZET 34 574	Mar 58 Belanova. VALUES GIVEN AT 3ES	+
					Jour JET 7 397	Sep 58 TRANSLATN.*	
Absorption	Maxwl		HAR	Expt	Rept AERE−R/R−2516	Mar 58 Jowitt+ PILE OSC.REL BORON.293DEGK.	
Absorption	3.5+8		LVP	Expt	Jour PPS 71 552	Apr 58 Ashmore+ FROM SIGTOT − DIFFRACTION 0CT	
Absorption	8.0+5	1.0+7	FAR	Expt	Conf 58Geneva 13 31	Sep 58 Bourgeois+ PPR1190,CURVE,REMOVAL SIG	
Absorption	2.5+4		KUR	Expt	Conf 58Geneva 15 50	Sep 58 Leipunskij+.PPR2219,VAL GVN,ACTIVATN	
Absorption	2.9+6		CCP	Expt	Jour AE 5 565	Nov 58 Kukhtevich+ "REMOVAL"SIGMA GIVEN	
					Jour SJA 5 1484	Nov 58 TRANSLATN.*	
Absorption	3.6+9		USA	Expt	Rept AFOSR−59−15	Dec 58 Barrett+. TRANS. SIG=1930+ −300MB	
Absorption	2.5−2		HAR	Expt	Jour JNEA 12 32	May 60 Tattersall+ PILE OSCILLATOR.	+
	2.5−2				Data EXFOR20638.063	Jul 76 1PNT.SIGMA.	
Absorption	4.0+6	1.5+7	FEI	Expt	Book SPN 194	61 .ENGL TRANSL OF NEJTRONFIZ 263	
					Book NEJTRONFIZ 263	61 Broder+ REMOVAL CS, GRAPH CFD	
	3.0+6	1.5+7			Book NEJTRONFIZ 278	61 Kukhtevich+ SIGMA AT 2ES,GRAPH CF TH	
					Book SPN 205	61 .ENGL TRANSL OF NEJTRONFIZ 278	
Absorption	3.0+8	5.0+9	LON	Theo	Jour NP 23 681	Mar 61 Elton. SEMI−CLASSICAL ANALYSIS.	
Absorption	Pile		BUC	Revw	Rept IFA−FR−37	Sep 63 Purica. PILE OSC,TBL,SIG	
Absorption	1.0+6	1.4+7	HAR	Theo	Rept AERE−R−4649	Jun 64 Wilmore.OPTMDL TH.TBLS,CURVES.PM10PC	
Absorption	2.4+4		FEI	Expt	Jour AE 19 3	Jul 65 Belanova+ 2 METHODS,ABSOL EXPT,TABLE	+
					Jour JNE 20 411	66 .ENGLISH TRANSL OF AE 19 3 7/65	
					Jour EAF 19 1 11	65 . FRENCH TRANSL OF AE 19 3 7/65	
					Jour SJA 19 858	65 .ENGLISH TRANSL OF AE 19 3 7/65	
	2.4+4				Data EXFOR40072.016	Jul 71 SIGMA AT 24 KEV AS PUBLISHED	
Absorption	8.1+6		AE	Theo	Conf 70Helsinki 2 341	Jun 70 Holmqvist+55. OPTMODEL CALC SIGMA	
Res Int Abs	None		ORL	Revw	Conf 55Geneva 5 96	Aug 55 Macklin+.P833 ,EXPT CFD THEORY,TABLE	
Res Int Abs	5.0−1		HAR	Expt	Jour JNE 12 32	May 60 Tattersall+PILE OSC.LESS 1/V BKD.	+
					Rept AERE−R−2887	Aug 59 − . PILE OSC.REL BORON	
	6.7−1				Data EXFOR20638.064	Jul 76 1PNT.	
(n,γ)	Maxwl		COL	Expt	Jour PR 50 738	Oct 36 Fink. RATE OF ABSORPTION ONLY	
(n,γ)	None		BRK	Expt	Jour PR 51 370	Mar 37 Gibson+. RA−BE SOURCE.FIRST EXPERMNT	
(n,γ)	2.2+6	2.9+6	JAP	Expt	Jour PR 59 681	Apr 41 NONAKA GEIGERCOUNTER+PB,ABST+FIG.TBP	
(n,γ)	Maxwl		UI	Expt	Jour PR 69 411	May 46 Coltman+ POWDERED SAMPLE+C. REL TO B	+
	Maxwl				Data EXFOR12616.020	Jun 76 . 1 PT, SIGMA.	
(n,γ)	Maxwl		ANL	Expt	Jour PR 76 531	Aug 49 Kubitscheck+ YIELD CFD SIG.G−M COINC	
(n,γ)	Maxwl		ORL	Expt	Jour PR 83 641	Aug 51 Pomerance.LOCAL OSC REL AU. THR SPEC	+
	Maxwl				Data EXFOR11047.071	Jun 76 . 1 PT. CS=.19B+ −5PCT	
(n,γ)	Maxwl		CRC	Expt	Jour BJAS 5 54	56 Laurence.OF SHIELDING FOR REACT	
(n,γ)	4.0+2	2.0+4	LEB	Expt	Jour ZET 33 9	Jul 57 SLO DWN T SPECMR	
					Jour JET 6 6	Jan 58 TRANSLATN.*	
(n,γ)	+2	+4	CCP	Revw	Conf 58Geneva 15 309	Sep 58 Vladimirsky+.PPR2221,NDG	
(n,γ)	2.0+5		KUR	Expt	Conf 58Geneva 15 50	Sep 58 Leipunskij+.PPR2219,VAL GVN,ACTIVATN	
(n,γ)	3.2−2	1.0+7	GEA	Eval	Rept XDC−60−8−81	Jun 59 Roberts.6.734+7.380MEV GAMMAS,19GPS	
(n,γ)	1.8+5	1.0+6	LAS	Expt	Jour PR 120 556	Oct 60 Diven+ SCINT.REL U235. 7ES.TBL	+
					Conf 58Geneva 15 60	Sep 58 .SUPERSEDED	
	1.8+5	1.0+6			Data EXFOR11616.028	Jun 76 . 7 PTS.	
(n,γ)	2.4+4		ORL	Expt	Jour NP 20 202	Oct 60 Schmitt.SHELL TRAN. PHOTO NS.	+
	2.4+4				Data EXFOR11778.016	Jun 76 . 1 PT. CS=3+ −9MB	
(n,γ)	2.0+2	6.5+4	ORL	Revw	Conf 61Vienna 1 95	Aug 61 Neiler.PPR73,TABLE FOR SOME ES,GRAPH	
(n,γ)	2.5−2		BUC	Expt	Conf 61Bucharst 553	Nov 61 Stefanescu+ PILE OSCILLATOR, TABLE	+
	2.5−2				Data EXFOR30073.008	Oct 71 PILE OSCILLATOR METHOD	
(n,γ)	3.0+4	6.5+4	ORL	Expt	Jour PR 129 2695	Mar 63 Macklin+SCINT.TBL.MANY ELEMENTS	
	3.0+4	6.5+7			Jour PR 122 182	Apr 61 Gibbons+AVG.CS.TOF. 2ES.TBL.	
	3.0+4	6.5+4			Data EXFOR11329.071	Jun 76 . 2 PTS. .3+ −.3 AND 1+ −2MB	
(n,γ)	1.0−4	1.0−1	UK	Eval	Rept AEEW−R−351	Feb 64 Barrington+(WIN).UKNDL LOW EN REVISN	+
	1.0−4	1.5+7			Data UKNDL−DFN 26C	Mar 73 162 PNTS	
(n,γ)	3.0+4		KFK	Expt	Conf 66Paris 1 502	Oct 66 Miessner+ ABST.RES−SHLD SIG.	
					Jour NSE 26 573	Dec 66 − + TECHNICAL NOTE. TBL	
					Rept INDC−156 8	Oct 66 − + EQU TO NSE 26 573	
					Rept KFK−451	Oct 66 − + EFF SIG. REPRINT OF 66PAR.	
					Rept KFK−540	Aug 66 − + EFF CAPT+TRANSPORT SIG.	
					Jour NUK 8 428	66 − + NEUT DECAY IN PB.	

82 Lead

Quantity	Energy (ev) Min	Max	Lab	Type	Documentation Ref Vol Page	Date	Author, Comments	Data
(n,γ)	1.5+4	6.0+4	AML	Expt	Jour NP/A 121 329	Dec 68	Broomhall+. REL YIELDS 3 E(G)INTERV.	
(n,γ)	1.3+3	1.3+5	RPI	Expt	Prog WASH – 1127 173	Apr 69	Hockenbury+CAPT YLDS TBL RES PARS	
(n,γ)	Maxwl		LRL	Expt	Jour NP/A 169 95	Jun 71	Cranston+ CALIBRATION EXPT.REL TO AU	
(n,γ)	Maxwl		ORL	Eval	Rept ORNL – TM – 3910	Aug 72	Ford.GAM YLDS FROM ENDF/B – 3 CFD XPT	
(n,γ)	1.0+5	7.0+6	IBJ	Theo	Rept INR – 1475/1/PL	73	Marcinkowski. SIG(E) CFD STATMOD,FIG	
	1.0+6	1.0+7			Jour NP/A 194 380	Oct 72	Decowski+. G – DECAY UNBOUND ST CFD XPT	
(n,γ)	1.4+7		NJS	Expt	Jour NP/A 213 525	Oct 73	Potokar+ INTEGRATED FROM SPECTRUM	+
					Jour FIZS 4 53	Dec 72	Cvelbar+ INTEG SIG OF DIR G, GRAPH	
	1.4+7				Data EXFOR30185.010	Oct 72	1 DATA LINE	
Spect (n,γ)	Maxwl		CRC	Expt	Jour PR 82 380	May 51	Kinsey+ PAIR SPEC,POOR RESOLUTION	
					Rept PR 78 77	Apr 50	.SUPERSEDED	
Spect (n,γ)	Maxwl		CCP	Expt	Conf 55Moscow 270	Jul 55	Adjasevich+. CURVES AND DISCUSSION	
					Rept AEC – TR – 2435	55	. PAGE 195,ENGL OF 55MOSCOW 270	
Spect (n,γ)	Maxwl		CCP		Rept AEC – TR – 2435PT1	56	.USSR PAGE 200	
Spect (n,γ)	Maxwl		GEA	Eval	Rept DC – 58 – 1 – 30	Jan 58	Deloume. BY APPROXIMATION.TABLE	
Spect (n,γ)	9.0+4	9.7+5	TNC	Expt	Rept AD – 154995	Feb 58	Bostrom+ SIGS FOR 6.0 AND 8.0MEV GS	
Spect (n,γ)	None		YAL	Expt	Abst BAP 5 17	Jan 60	Draper+ ANTICOINCIDENCE. NO DATA GVN	
Spect (n,γ)	3.0+4		ORL	Expt	Jour PL 1 262	Jul 62	Bird+ RELATIVE SPECTRUM GIVEN	
Spect (n,γ)	4.5+4	1.5+5	FOA	ExTh	Jour NP 39 353	Dec 62	Bergqvist+.2 ES. CFD THR RESULT.	
					Conf 61Saclay	61	– + SUPERSEDED	
	7.4+6		FOA	Expt	Jour PL 19 670	Jan 66	Bergqvist+ CFD COMPOUND NUC SPECT	
					Conf 65Antwerp 550	Jul 65	– + PPR130.ABST. NAI.	
Spect (n,γ)	2.5 – 2		MIT	Comp	Rept MITNE – 85	Jan 69	Rasmussen+TBL G INT. = AFCRL – 69 – 0071	
Spect (n,γ)	Maxwl		WAL	Eval	Rept WANL – TME – 2713	Jul 70	Fody.GAM YLDS FOR WANL POINT LIBRARY	
Spect (n,γ)		3.0+6	CRC	Expt	Prog AECL – 3912 64	Mar 71	Bartholomew+.NAI DET.PRELIM. NO DATA	
Spect (n,γ)	1.0+4	6.0+4	ORL	Comp	Rept ORNL – TM – 3379	Apr 71	Bird+.VDG. NAI CRYST. CURVES	
Spect (n,γ)	Maxwl		BNL	Expt	Jour PR/C 5 178	Jan 72	Mariscotti+. GE(LI) DET	
Spect (n,γ)	1.5+7		CCP	Expt	Conf 73Tbilisi 159	Feb 73	Kravtsov+ ABST,GE – LI,G – SPEC AT 90DEG	
Spect (n,γ)	2.4+4		BNL	Expt	Prog USNDC – 7 36	Jun 73	Wasson+. GE(LI) DET. TBL PARTIAL SIG	
Spect (n,γ)	1.4+7		NJS	Expt	Jour NP/A 213 525	Oct 73	Potokar+ D – T NS. PAIR SPECTROMETER.	+
					Priv CVELBAR	Oct 72	.PROMPT GAMMA – RAY SPECTRUM	
	1.4+7				Data EXFOR30185.011	Oct 72	25 DATA LINES	
Spect (n,γ)	7.0+6		LAS	Expt	Prog A – WAU – 76 91	Jun 76	Arthur+ASYMMETRIC RADIATIONS.NDG	
Inelastic γ	Fast		BRK	Expt	Jour PR 52 408	Sep 37	Seaborg+ INELASTIC SCAT SHOWN.SIG(G)	
Inelastic γ	1.4+7		NRL	Expt	Jour PR 91 1476	Sep 53	Scherrer+.SPECTRUM+GAMMA PROD SIGMA.	+
	1.4+7				Data EXFOR11306.	Jun 76	. 3 PTS. SIGMA.	
Inelastic γ	3.9+6		BAR	Expt	Jour PR 93 796	Feb 54	Rothman+ VDG+CRYST SPEC 2 PEAKS	
Inelastic γ	8.0 – 1	2.7+6	LRL	Expt	Jour PR 95 751	Aug 54	Shapiro+ .805MEV LVL EXCITED CURVE	
Inelastic γ	3.2+6		NRL	Expt	Jour PR 96 386	Oct 54	Scherrer+ CS FOR 6G ES. TBL.	+
	3.2+6				Data EXFOR11672.014	Jun 76	. 6 PTS, SIGMA.	
Inelastic γ	4.5+6		WES	Expt	Jour PR 98 579	May 55	Griffith. 0.79,1.36,2.70MEV GAMMAS	
Inelastic γ	2.6+6		LAS	Expt	Jour PR 102 767	Apr 56	Day.VALUES AT 7 GAMMA ES AT 95 DEG	+
					Conf 55Geneva 2 9	Aug 55	DAY.P581,ONLY TBL G – ES,RING GEOM.	
	2.6+6				Data EXFOR11218.029	Jun 76	. 7 PTS, DSIGMA.	
Inelastic γ	3.5+6	4.2+6	TNC	Expt	Rept WADC – TN – 59 – 31	Feb 59	Bostrom+ NAI(TL) SPECT,TABLE+CURVES	+
	3.5+6	4.6+6			Data EXFOR11341.	Jun 76	. 17 PTS. DSIGMA.	
Inelastic γ	5.0+5	1.0+7	GEA	Eval	Rept XDC – 60 – 8 – 81	Jun 59	Roberts.13GAMMAS 6GROUPS	
Inelastic γ	1.4+7		LRL	Expt	Rept UCRL – 5768	Aug 59	Hallet+SPEC. 2.61MEV G STUDY.	+
	1.4+7				Data EXFOR12222.002	Jun 76	. 1 PT. CS = 25.5 + – 4.6 MB	
	1.4+7				Data EXFOR12222.003	Jun 76	. 5 PTS. DSIGMA.	
Inelastic γ	None		RIC	Expt	Prog WASH – 1028 60	Apr 60	Hall+G RAD FROM INEL SCT. NDG	
Inelastic γ	3.0+6		FEI	Expt	Jour AE 9 403	Nov 60	Androsenko+ TABLE OF GAMMA – ENERGIES	
					Jour SJA 9 945	Sep 61	. ENGL OF AE 9 403	
Inelastic γ	4.0+6	1.5+7	TNC	Expt	Jour TID – 20689	Feb 62	Nellis+. GAM SPECT+PROD SIGS 90 DEG	
Inelastic γ	1.4+7		CCP	Expt	Jour YF 3 861	May 66	Bezotosnyj+.SIG FOR PROD OF 8 GAMMAS	+
					Jour SNP 3 632	Nov 66	TRANSLATN.*	
Inelastic γ	5.8+6	7.5+6	FOA	Expt	Jour NP 80 198	May 66	Bergqvist+CFD SPEC IN CAPT.AT 0.1MEV	
Inelastic γ	1.0+6		TNC	Expt	Prog ORO – 2791 – 84	Aug 67	Morgan+ NDG TBC	
Inelastic γ	7.0+6		AE	Expt	Prog EANDC(OR)73L	Jan 68	BERGQVIST +CALIBR GE – LI TOF	
Inelastic γ	Fast		CCP	Expt	Jour AE 29 338	Nov 70	Barkov+ AVG SIG FOR GAM PROD.TBLS	
					Jour SJA 29 1080	Nov 70	TRANSLATN.*	
Inelastic γ	Fiss		FEI	Expt	Jour AE 29 338	Nov 70	Bakov+	+
	Fiss				Data EXFOR40131.012	Jan 73	PRODUCTION OF 3 GAMMA – LINES	
	Pile		FEI	Expt	Prog YFI – 12 14	72	Bakov+ AVG SIG OF GAM YLD,ABST,NDG	
					Prog INDC(CCP) – 30	Dec 72	.PG 11,ENGLISH OF YFI – 12 14	
Inelastic γ	1.9+6	3.9+6	KUR	Expt	Conf 73Kiev 3 120	May 73	Degtjarev+ GE – LI,VDG,SIG(NEUT – E),TBL	+
	1.9+6	3.9+6			Data EXFOR40266.004	Feb 75	.SIGMA AT 6 ES TO VARIOUS LVLS GVN	

82 Lead

Quantity	Energy (ev) Min	Max	Lab	Type	Documentation Ref Vol Page	Author, Comments Date	Data
Inelastic γ	4.9+6	1.6+7	FEI	Expt Rept	FEI – 584	75 Gonchar+ GELI G – SPEC.G – PROD SIG,TABL	
Inelastic γ	1.4+7		CCP	Expt Rept	YK – 23 120	76 Sukhanov+ GROUP SIGS OF G – RAYS,TBLS	
Inelastic γ	2.5+6		FEI	Expt Rept	YK – 22 21	76 Bezotosnyj+ GELI+NAI.SIG(EGAM),TABLE	
Inelastic γ	3.3+6		SBL	Expt Jour	NIM 134 545	76 Habbani+ 90 DEG TBL	+
	3.3+6			Data	EXFOR20667.023	Oct 76 2PTS.D/DA.	
Inelastic γ	None		LAS	Expt Prog	A – WAU – 76 91	Jun 76 Arthur+4.4MEV LVL.NDG	
Nonelastic γ	Slow		OSA	Expt Jour	JMJ 19 295	37 Wakatsuki.BE+RA,3.9B	
				Jour	JPJO 18 297	36 Kikuchi+.BE+RA.SIG AGRE WITH D+D SIG	
Nonelastic γ	2.4+6		OSA	Expt Jour	JMJ 21 75	39 Kikuchi+.D – D P LI – D N,SIG GIVN	
	2.1+6	2.8+6		Jour	JMJ 21 232	39 Aoki.SIG GIVN	
	2.4+6			Jour	SCP 34 865	Aug 38 Kikuchi+ D+D,G – M.SIG=5.0B	
		2.4+6		Jour	JMJ 19 369	37 Aoki.D+D NEUTRON.RELATIV SIG GIVN	
	Slow			Jour	JMJ 18 115	36 Kikuchi+.REL SIG GIVN FOR G – EMISSION	
				Jour	JMJ 18 188	36 – +.SIG GIVN BY D+D NEUTRON	
				Jour	JMJ 17 369	35 – +.GAMMAS DETECT	
				Jour	JPJO 17 189	35 – +.LESS THAN 1.2B	
Nonelastic γ	2.3+6	2.9+6	JAP	Expt Jour	JPJO 23 925	41 Nonaka.SIG CURVE GIVN	+
	2.3+6	2.9+6		Data	EXFOR20297.008	Jun 74 7PTS.SIGMA.	
Nonelastic γ	1.4+7		LAS	Expt Rept	LA – 1507	Jan 53 Battat+ PROPORT COUNTER SIG GIVEN	
Nonelastic γ	4.4+6		WES	Expt Rept	AECU – 3387	55 Sinclair. PHS+4 GAM ES GIVN.NAI(TL)	
Nonelastic γ	8.0+5	+6	BNL	Comp Conf	58Geneva 16 8	Sep 58 Hughes.PPR2483,CURVE,MANY REFS	
Nonelastic γ	1.4+7		ALD	Expt Jour	PPS 75 855	Jun 60 Deuchars+ TABLE RESOLVED GAMS GIVEN	
Nonelastic γ	1.4+7		LRL	Expt Rept	UCID – 4619	Oct 63 Beneveniste+ G PROD. SPEC.	+
	1.4+7			Data	EXFOR11537.008	Jun 76 . 1 PT. CS=3.2B	
Nonelastic γ	3.5+6	8.5+6	ALD	Expt Jour	NP 60 561	Dec 64 Perkin.TABLE OF G PROD SIG GIVEN.	+
Nonelastic γ	1.5+7		NRD	Expt Jour	JNE 21 487	Jun 67 Engesser+ SIGMAS FOR RESOLVED GAMMAS	+
				Rept	USNRDL – TR – 1043	66 .SUPERSEDED	
	1.5+7			Data	EXFOR11423.006	Jun 76 . 11 PTS. DIFF. DATA	
Nonelastic γ	4.1+6	1.5+7	LRL	Theo Jour	NSE 32 178	May 68 Howerton+ 3ES CALCTD SIGS CFD EXPTS	
Nonelastic γ	1.4+7		FR	Expt Prog	EANDC(E)115U	Mar 69 Perrin. GE(LI) DET	
Nonelastic γ	1.6+7		LND	Expt Jour	PS 2 277	Dec 70 Joensson. 120 DEG. LI(GE).	+
	1.5+7			Jour	AF 39 295	Sep 69 – +. GE(LI). 80 DEGREES	
				Rept	LU – NP – 6804	Mar 68 – + EQUIVALENT TO AF 39 295	
	1.5+7	1.6+7		Data	EXFOR20164.028	May 74 12PTS.D/DA.	
Nonelastic γ	1.4+7		LAS	Expt Prog	USNDC – 7 128	Jun 73 Drake+. NO DATA GIVEN. TO BE COMPLTD	
Nonelastic γ	1.4+7		KUR	Expt Conf	75Kiev 4 133	May 75 Bezotosnyj+ NA – I.SIG(.5 – 12.0MEV) GVN	
(n,2n)	5.0+6	1.4+7	AUS	Expt Jour	APA 3 352	Mar 50 Lintner. RA – BE SOURCE	
				Jour	OAWS 158 135	Nov 49 – .	
(n,2n)	1.4+7		LAS	Expt Jour	PR 97 1205	Mar 55 Graves+BETWEEN 1.76 AND 2.12B LIMITS	
(n,2n)	1.4+7		LRL	Expt Jour	PR 111 616	Jul 58 Ashby+APPROX=SNE.NUCL TEMP CALC	+
				Conf	58Geneva 15 3	Sep 58 Beneviste.PPR2494,VAL GVN,TOF	
				Data	EXFOR11097.025	Jun 76 . 1 PT. RENORM CS=2.65+ – .19B	
(n,2n)	1.4+7		CCP	Expt Jour	AE 5 522	Nov 58 Lebedev+ N2N+2(N3N) – REM=2.18+ – 0.2B	
				Jour	JNEA 11 39	Nov 59 TRANSLATN.*	
				Jour	SJA 5 1431	58 TRANSLATN.*	
(n,2n)	1.4+7		CCP	Expt Jour	AE 5 657	Dec 58 Flerov+ (N,EM) – (N,X)=2.30+ – 0.19BARNS	+
				Jour	JNEA 11 174	Feb 60 TRANSLATN.*	
				Jour	SJA 5 1601	58 TRANSLATN.*	
(n,2n)	1.4+7		KFI	Expt Jour	NP 49 489	Dec 63 Adam+MECHANISM OF (N,2N) REACTION	+
	1.4+7			Data	EXFOR30107.002	Oct 71 MECHANISM OF THE (N,2N) REACTION	
(n,2n)	1.4+7		HAM	Comp Jour	NP 65 257	Mar 65 Bormann.1EXPT VALUE.CFD SHELL EFFECT	
(n,2n)	1.4+7		KGU	Expt Conf	68Riga	Jan 68 Vojtenko+ ABST,ANGULAR CORRELATIONS	
(n,2n)	1.4+7		KGU	Expt Jour	YF 9 9	Jan 69 Voitenko+.NEUTRONS ANG CORR,CURVE	
(n,2n)	1.4+7		KGU	Expt Jour	YF 9 9	Jan 69 Voitenko+ GRPH,ANG DIST OF NEUTRONS	
				Jour	SNP 9 5	Jul 69 TRANSLATN.*	
(n,2n)	1.4+7		ALD	Expt Rept	AWRE – O – 47/69	Aug 69 Mather+PAIN LARGE LIQUID SCINT	+
	1.4+7			Data	EXFOR20794.012	Oct 78 1PNT.SIGMA.	
(n,2n)	1.5+7		LND	Expt Jour	AF 39 295	Sep 69 Joensson+. MEASURED NONEL GAMMAS	+
	1.5+7	1.6+7		Data	EXFOR20164.030	May 74 1PNT.SIGMA.	
(n,2n)	1.4+7		KGU	Expt Jour	YF 10 699	Oct 69 Prokopets+ NEUT DOUBLE ANGDIST,GRPHS	
				Jour	SNP 10 403	Apr 70 TRANSLATN.*	
				Jour	UFZ 14 865	May 69 Prokopec+ ANG CORR BETWEEN NS,GRAPH	
(n,2n)	1.4+7		CCP	Expt Rept	YK – 9 50	72 Maslov+ FROM TRANSMISSION,SIG GIVEN	+
				Rept	INDC(CCP) – 42	Aug 74 .P10.ENGLISH OF YK – 9	
	1.4+7			Data	EXFOR40136.025	Feb 73 .1 DATA LINE	
(n,2n)	1.4+7		VNV	Expt Prog	EANDC(E)150U	May 72 Voignier.DOUBLE TOF	
				Conf	71Knoxvill 306	Mar 71 – +TOF,COINC.SPECT+DIFF SIGS	

82 Lead

Quantity	Energy (ev) Min	Max	Lab	Type	Documentation Ref Vol Page	Author, Comments Date	Data
(n,2n)	1.4+7		KFI	Theo Conf	72Budapest 202	Aug 72 Kluge+ CALCULATED EN-SPECTRA ,GRPH	
				Rept	KFKI-72-17	Feb 72 - + CALC N-SPEC INEL+N2N,TBL,GRPH	
(n,2n)	1.2+7		ALD	Expt Rept	AWRE-O-72/72	Nov 72 Mather+ REL U-238.LARGE LIQ SCINT.	+
	1.2+7			Data	EXFOR20795.009	Oct 78 1PNT.SIGMA.	
(n,2n)	1.5+7		DEB	Eval Jour	REA 11 1 153	Mar 73 Boedy+ RECOMM.VALUE FROM N-Z SYSTEM.	
(n,2n)	6.7+6	1.5+7	UK	Eval Data	UKNDL-DFN 26C	Mar 73 .22 PTS.E DIST.ANG DIST,LAB.	
(n,2n)	1.4+7		BRC	Expt Conf	73Kiev 3 227	May 73 Voignier. ANG-CORREL,GRPH 1ST RESLTS	
(n,2n)	1.4+7		BRC	ExTh Prog	CEA-N-1875 60	Apr 76 Frehaut+ SYSTEMATIC LAWS SEARCH	+
	9.4+6	1.5+7		Expt Conf	75Gothenbg	Jun 75 - +	
	9.4+6	1.5+7		Data	EXFOR20571.022	Mar 76 10PTS.SIGMA.	
(n,xn) x>2	1.4+7		BRC	ExTh Prog	CEA-N-1875 60	Apr 76 Frehaut+N3N.SYSTEMATIC LAWS SEARCH	
n Emission	1.4+7		CCP	Expt Jour	AE 5 522	Nov 58 Lebedev+ SPH GEOM,N COUNT,ETA GIVEN	
				Jour	JNEA 11 39	59 .TRANSLATION	
				Jour	SJA 5 1431	58 .ENGL OF AE 5 522 NOV58	
n Emission	1.4+7		CCP	Expt Jour	AE 5 657	Dec 58 Flerov+ SPHERE TRANSM, ETA=1.91+-.08	
				Jour	JNEA 11 174	Feb 60 TRANSLATN.*	
				Jour	SJA 5 1601	58 TRANSLATN.*	
n Emission	1.5+7		TNC	Expt Jour	PR 186 1038	69 Mathur+TOF.90 DEG.MULTISCAT CORRC.	+
				Rept	NDL-TR-86	Jan 67 - +EXPT+MULTISCAT CORRC DETAILS.	
	1.5+7			Data	EXFOR10090.022	May 73 . 2 PTS. NEM CS=102.24,259.87 MB/SR	
n Emission	1.4+7		FEI	Expt Jour	YF 20 852	Nov 74 Sal'Nikov+ TOF,TBL DOUBLDIFF+INTEGRL	+
				Jour	SNP 20 454	May 75 . ENGLISH OF YF 20 852	
	5.0+5	1.4+7		Data	EXFOR40333.	Feb 76 .DATA IN MB/SR AT 5EN RANGES+4 ANGLS	
n Emission	1.5+7		TUD	Expt Jour	KE 19 241	Aug 76 Hermsdorf+ ABSOL DOUBDIF,FIG.TOT,TBL	+
				Rept	ZFK-277(U)	Aug 75 - + DIFFSIG AT 5ANGS,TBL+GRPH	
				Conf	ZFK-271 94	Nov 73 Goebel+ N-EMISSION SPEC,TOF.SUMMARY	
	1.5+7			Data	EXFOR30397.031	May 77 49 PTS. ANGLE INT.N-EMISS.SPECT.	
	1.5+7			Data	EXFOR30275.	Apr 74 DOUBLDIF(5ANG,472PTS)+PARTIAL ANGDIS	
(n,p)	9.0+8		BRK	Expt Jour	PR 80 345	Nov 50 Hadley+ BE-D NS. DBLE DIFF AT 4ANGLS	
(n,p)	1.0-4	1.0-1	UK	Eval Rept	AEEW-R-351	Feb 64 Barrington+(WIN).UKNDL LOW EN REVISN	
(n,p)	1.4+7		RBZ	Expt Conf	64Paris 2 934	Jul 64 Paic.ANG DSTRB OF PROTONS,SHORT NOTE	
(n,d)	9.0+8		BRK	Expt Jour	PR 80 345	Nov 50 Hadley+ BE-D NS. DBLE DIFF AT 4ANGLS	
(n,α)	1.0-4	1.0-1	UK	Eval Rept	AEEW-R-351	Feb 64 Barrington+(WIN).UKNDL LOW EN REVISN	
Fission		1.6+7	EDG	Expt Jour	NAT 158 871	Dec 46 Broda+UPPER LIM.REL U-238.RADCH+EMUL	
Fission	2.5+7	8.4+7	BRK	Expt Jour	PR 73 1135	May 48 Kelly+ RELATIVE TO THORIUM.	
Fission	1.4+7		LAS	Expt Jour	PR 75 919	Mar 49 Phillips+ UPPER LIM REL U238.PHOTOPL	
Fission	Spont		DUB	Expt Jour	AE 26 520	Jun 69 Flerov+ HALF-LIFE MEASUREMENT	
				Rept	JINR-D6-4554	Jun 69 - + PROPORT COUNT,HL GIVEN	
				Jour	SJA 26 603	Jun 69 .TRANSLATN.*	
Fission	1.4+7		TRM	Expt Prog	BARC-872 107	76 Iyer+ ABST.REL U238,SIG=2.9X10E-7 B	
Reson Params	3.5+5	7.2+5	WIS	Expt Jour	PR 76 1146	Oct 49 Barschall+ 3 RESON,5KV RSLN.L IF 208	
Reson Params	3.2+6		CAV	Expt Jour	PPSA 64 388	Apr 51 Stafford.WIDTH ABOUT 1MEV	
Reson Params	1.6+5		WIS	Expt Jour	PR 99 748	Aug 55 Darden.TRANSMISSION,STRENGTH FN DATA	
Reson Params	+3		CCP	Expt Conf	58Geneva 15 309	Sep 58 Vladimirsky+.PPR2221,PARAMS GVN	
Reson Params	1.2+5	1.5+5	DKE	Expt Jour	AP 14 387	Jul 61 Bilpuch+TBL RES PARS AREA ANAL	+
	1.2+5	1.5+5		Data	EXFOR11599.049	Jun 76 . 3 RES. E0.	
Reson Params	1.7+3	2.4+4	HAR	ExTh Prog	WASH-1048 71	Jun 64 Block.ISOTOPIC ASSIGNMENTS.TBL.	
Reson Params	1.6+4	1.3+5	RPI	Expt Prog	RPI-328-87 24	67 Bartolome+	+
	1.6+4	1.3+5		Data	EXFOR12588.002	Jun 76 . 11 RES, WT,WN,WG	
Reson Params	1.0+3	1.4+5	RPI	Expt Prog	WASH-1074 97	Apr 67 Hockenbury+ 29RES 6NEW N,GAMMA EXPT	
Reson Params	None		DKE	Expt Prog	ERDA-NDC-2 181	May 75 Divadeenam.SHELL MDL +VIBR.DOORWAY	
Strnth Fnctn	4.0+6	5.0+6	JAE	Expt Jour	PL 11 141	Jul 64 Tsukada+ FROM FLUCT, COMPD FORM SIG	
Lvl Density	None		PTN	Expt Jour	PR 81 51	Jan 51 Gugelot. REL LVL DENS VS EXC.T GIVEN	
Lvl Density	1.5+7		MIT	Expt Jour	PR 82 69	Apr 51 Stelson+ NUCL TEMP FROM INEL SPEC+TH	
Lvl Density	6.0+6		DKE	Expt Rept	AD-299005	62 Seth+,NUCL TEMP+FERMI LVL DENS COEFF	
Lvl Density	1.4+7		BAS	Expt Jour	PL 5 202	Jul 63 Huber+TBL OF NUC TEMP AND LVL DENSTY	
				Jour	HPA 36 1059	Dec 63 Plattner+TOF TBL12ELEM.CFD TH	
Lvl Density	1.4+7		FEI	Expt Jour	YF 2 826	Nov 65 Anufrienko+.PARAMS FROM NONELASTIC	+
				Rept	FEI-30	Dec 65 .	
				Rept	EANDC-50 197	Jul 65 .FULL PAPER FROM 65ANTWERP	
				Rept	FEI-4	65 .	
				Jour	SNP 2 589	May 66 .ENGLISH TRANSL OF YF 2 826 11/65	
Lvl Density	1.5+7		TNC	Expt Jour	PR 186 1038	Oct 69 Mathur+,FERMI GAS LVL DENSITY COEF	+
				Rept	NDL-TR-86	Jan 67 - +EXPT+MULTISCAT CORRC DETAILS.	
	1.5+7			Data	EXFOR10090.038	May 73 . 2 PTS.NUCLEAR T=1.04,.58 MEV.	
Lvl Density	None		FEI	Theo Jour	YF 11 1213	Jun 70 Ignatyuk+ SPIN DEPENDENCE OF DENSITY	
				Jour	SNP 11 674	Dec 70 . ENGL OF YF 11 1213	

82 Lead

Quantity	Energy (ev) Min	Max	Lab	Type	Documentation Ref Vol Page	Date	Author, Comments	Data
Lvl Density		8.0+7	IEA	Expt Prog	IEA – INF – 22 3	Aug 72	Goldemberg. RESON SCAT,TO BE DONE	
(γ,n)	+7		BNL	Expt Jour	PR 79 539	Aug 50	Poss.N INTENSITY 0/90DEG.BY AL(NP)	
(γ,n)	2.4+7		BSP	Expt Conf	55Geneva 2 169	Aug 55	Souza – Santos +.P897,THRESHOLD	
Photo – Fissn	5.0+6		TOR	Expt Abst	DA/B 29 3041	Feb 69	Hussain.YLD,ANG DIST FAST NTNS.	
Photo – Fissn	None		LND	Expt Rept	INIS – MF – 427	Jun 72	Kroon.PRR5.7,ABST,FRAG ANGDIST,NDG	

82 Lead 196

Quantity	Energy (ev) Min	Max	Lab	Type	Documentation Ref Vol Page	Date	Author, Comments	Data
Reson Params	–		AUA	Theo Rept	AAEC/E – 211	Nov 70	Musgrove. CALCULTD D+GAM WIDTH GIVEN	
Strnth Fnctn	–		AUA	Theo Rept	AAEC/E – 211	Nov 70	Musgrove. SMOOTHED S0,S1 AND S2 GIVN	

82 Lead 197

Quantity	Energy (ev) Min	Max	Lab	Type	Documentation Ref Vol Page	Date	Author, Comments	Data
Reson Params	–		AUA	Theo Rept	AAEC/E – 211	Nov 70	Musgrove. CALCULTD D+GAM WIDTH GIVEN	
Strnth Fnctn	–		AUA	Theo Rept	AAEC/E – 211	Nov 70	Musgrove. SMOOTHED S0,S1 AND S2 GIVN	

82 Lead 198

Quantity	Energy (ev) Min	Max	Lab	Type	Documentation Ref Vol Page	Date	Author, Comments	Data
Polarization	1.4+7		IJI	Theo Jour	YF 18 1203	Dec 73	Ivanjuk+ SHELL CORR, POL(ANG),GRAPH	
				Jour	SNP 18 616	Jun 74	.ENGLISH OF YF 18, 1203.	
Fiss Yield	None		TRM	Theo Conf	72Bombay 2 201	Feb 72	Ramamurthy.FRAG MASS AS FUNCT T,CURV	
				Prog	BARC – 633 64	72	– . FRAG MASS DISTRIB ,GRPH	
Reson Params	–		AUA	Theo Rept	AAEC/E – 211	Nov 70	Musgrove. CALCULTD D+GAM WIDTH GIVEN	
Strnth Fnctn	–		AUA	Theo Rept	AAEC/E – 211	Nov 70	Musgrove. SMOOTHED S0,S1 AND S2 GIVN	

82 Lead 199

Quantity	Energy (ev) Min	Max	Lab	Type	Documentation Ref Vol Page	Date	Author, Comments	Data
Reson Params	–		AUA	Theo Rept	AAEC/E – 211	Nov 70	Musgrove. CALCULTD D+GAM WIDTH GIVEN	
Strnth Fnctn	–		AUA	Theo Rept	AAEC/E – 211	Nov 70	Musgrove. SMOOTHED S0,S1 AND S2 GIVN	

82 Lead 200

Quantity	Energy (ev) Min	Max	Lab	Type	Documentation Ref Vol Page	Date	Author, Comments	Data
Polarization	1.4+7		IJI	Theo Jour	YF 18 1203	Dec 73	Ivanjuk+ SHELL CORR, POL(ANG),GRAPH	
				Jour	SNP 18 616	Jun 74	.ENGLISH OF YF 18, 1203.	
Reson Params	–		AUA	Theo Rept	AAEC/E – 211	Nov 70	Musgrove. CALCULTD D+GAM WIDTH GIVEN	
Strnth Fnctn	–		AUA	Theo Rept	AAEC/E – 211	Nov 70	Musgrove. SMOOTHED S0,S1 AND S2 GIVN	

82 Lead 201

Quantity	Energy (ev) Min	Max	Lab	Type	Documentation Ref Vol Page	Date	Author, Comments	Data
Reson Params	–		AUA	Theo Rept	AAEC/E – 211	Nov 70	Musgrove. CALCULTD D+GAM WIDTH GIVEN	
Strnth Fnctn	–		AUA	Theo Rept	AAEC/E – 211	Nov 70	Musgrove. SMOOTHED S0,S1 AND S2 GIVN	

82 Lead 202

Quantity	Energy (ev) Min	Max	Lab	Type	Documentation Ref Vol Page	Date	Author, Comments	Data
Polarization	1.4+7		IJI	Theo Jour	YF 18 1203	Dec 73	Ivanjuk+ SHELL CORR, POL(ANG),GRAPH	
				Jour	SNP 18 616	Jun 74	.ENGLISH OF YF 18, 1203.	
Reson Params	–		AUA	Theo Rept	AAEC/E – 211	Nov 70	Musgrove. CALCULTD D+GAM WIDTH GIVEN	
Reson Params	–		DUB	Theo Rept	JINR – E4 – 5711	Apr 71	Soloviev.RESONANCE STRUCTURE STUDY	
Strnth Fnctn	–		AUA	Theo Rept	AAEC/E – 211	Nov 70	Musgrove. SMOOTHED S0,S1 AND S2 GIVN	
Lvl Density	–3	+0	IFU	Theo Jour	UFZ 13 700	Apr 68	Pisanko+ LEVEL SPACING CALC,TBL	
				Jour	UPJ 13 498	Oct 68	TRANSLATN.*	

82 Lead 203

Quantity	Energy (ev) Min	Max	Lab	Type	Documentation Ref Vol Page	Author, Comments Date	Data
(n,γ)	–		IEA	Comp Rept	IEA – INF – 10 6	Aug 68 Atalla. TABLES OF HL,SIG AND GAMM – E	
(n,p)	Maxwl		IFU	Theo Rept	ICD – 4 20	67 Dadakina+ PENETR COEFF CALC,TABLE	
Reson Params	–		AUA	Theo Rept	AAEC/E – 211	Nov 70 Musgrove. CALCULTD D+GAM WIDTH GIVEN	
Strnth Fnctn	–		AUA	Theo Rept	AAEC/E – 211	Nov 70 Musgrove. SMOOTHED S0,S1 AND S2 GIVN	
Lvl Density	8.5+6	1.5+7	ANL	Eval Rept	ANL – 75 – 34	Jun 75 Davey+N2NEVAL.CONSTANT T,LVL DEN FIT	

82 Lead 204

Quantity	Energy (ev) Min	Max	Lab	Type	Documentation Ref Vol Page	Author, Comments Date	Data
Total	1.4+7		CCP	ExTh Jour	ZET 46 1496	Apr 64 5.54+ – .05B,CFD OPTMDL,SHELL.SEP ISOQ	
				Jour	JET 19 1013	Oct 64 TRANSLATN.*	
Total	1.4+7		FEI	Expt Prog	INDSWG – 126 33	66 Dukarevich.SIG=5.43+ – 0.06B	
Total	5.0+3	8.0+4	ORL	Expt Jour	PR 153 1356	Jan 67 Gibbons+ VDG TOF, CURV,22 RES,SOME P	
				Abst	BAP 10 10	Apr 65 .ABST. HB51	
Total	1.4+7		CCP	ExTh Jour	IZV 31 217	Feb 67 Dukarevich+.TBL,CURVES,CFD OPTMDL TH	
				Jour	BAS 31 197	Feb 67 TRANSLATN.*	
Total	1.4+7		FTI	Expt Jour	NP/A 92 433	Feb 67 Dukarevich+ CFD OPTMDL 5.43+ – 0.06B	+
Total	1.3+7	1.5+7	DEB	Eval Jour	AHP 30 115	Oct 71 Angeli+ AVG SIG,CFD CALC.TBLS.GRAPH	
Total	1.3+7	1.5+7	DEB	Eval Rept	IAEA – 153 173	73 Boedy+ MOST PROBABLE VAL OF SIG,TBL	
Total	1.0+3	4.0+5	ORL	Expt Prog	USNDC – 7 172	Jun 73 Good+. TRANS. LINAC. NO DATA GIVEN.	
Polarization	1.4+7		IJI	Theo Jour	YF 18 1203	Dec 74 Ivanjuk+ SHELL CORR, POL(ANG),GRAPH	
				Jour	SNP 18 616	Jun 74 .ENGLISH OF YF 18, 1203.	
Tot Inelastc	Pile		FEI	Comp Rept	ICD – 4 57	67 Sluchevskaja.SELECTIV COMPIL ,TABLE	
Tot Inelastc	1.5+7		DEB	Expt Jour	AHP 23 87	May 67 Csikai+ ACTIV,SIGMA AT 14.7MEV,TABLE	+
				Jour	MFF 16 123	Feb 68 SEE ALSO *THESIS IN HUNG	
	1.5+7			Data	EXFOR30119.009	Feb 71 SIGMA AT 14.7 MEV REL CU – 65(N,2N)	
Tot Inelastc	Fast		MUN	Expt Jour	NUK 10 181	Oct 67 Koehler+H2O MODER REACT. .1MEVCUTOFF	
				Rept	FRM – 81	Aug 66 – + SUPERSEDED.	
Tot Inelastc	1.5+7		DEB	ExTh Jour	AHP 25 91	Oct 68 Peto+ RATIO (NN')/(N2N) FROM THEORY	+
Tot Inelastc	Fast		KTO	Expt Jour	NST 8 59	Feb 71 Kimura+.MEAN S=18.9+ – 2.0 MB,ISOM	+
				Conf	71Vienna 113	Aug 71 – + ACTIVATION,TBL CFD OTHERS	
	Fast			Data	EXFOR20317.018	Jun 74 1PNT.SIGMA.	
Tot Inelastc	1.4+7		GIT	Expt Jour	NP/A 180 157	Jan 72 Hankla+ ACT,GE(LI),MIXED POWDER.MST.	+
				Abst	DA/B 32 293	Nov 71 – . ACT METHOD, CFD THEORY.	
	1.4+7			Data	EXFOR10244.018	Jun 74 . 1 PT,SIGMA, META.	
Tot Inelastc	1.3+7	1.8+7	IBJ	Expt Conf	72Budapest 190	Aug 72 Decowski+ ACTIVATION,CFD THEORY,GRPH	
	1.2+7	1.8+7		Rept	INP – 702/PS	Jun 70 – + GAMMA – N COMPETITN CFD THEO	
Tot Inelastc	None		ANL	Expt Prog	ERDA – NDC – 3 26	May 76 Smith+NDG.PRELIM MEAS FOR ISOM REAC.	
Tot Inelastc		2.0+7	BRC	Theo Conf	76Lowell 365	Jul 76 Frehaut.SYST.NT.CASCADE REACTIONS.	
Diff Inelast	2.2+6	1.9+7	AMS	Expt Jour	PHY 30 1609	Aug 64 Heertje+EXCIT.LONG – LIVED METAST.STAT	
Diff Inelast	2.8+6		DEB	Expt Jour	AK 10 112	Jul 68 Bornemisza+ UPPER LIMIT OF SIGMA GVN	+
	2.8+6			Data	EXFOR30338.010	Aug 76 TO ISOM. UPPER LIMIT. 1 PNT	
Diff Inelast	Pile		SEO	Expt Conf	IAEA – 132 24	71 LEE+ ABSTR.AVG SIG TO META=20MB	
Diff Inelast	1.4+7		CCP	Expt Rept	YK – 9 50	72 Maslov+ TO ISOMER,NA – I,SIG GIVEN	+
				Rept	INDC(CCP) – 42	Aug 74 .P10.ENGLISH OF YK – 9	
	1.4+7	1.5+7		Data	EXFOR40136.021	Sep 74 .SIGMA AT 2 ES GIVEN	
Diff Inelast	+6		KOS	Expt Jour	AHP 33 363	73 Peto+ SIG TO ISOM FOR ALF – BE N,TABLE	+
	+6			Data	EXFOR30265.020	Feb 74 1 DATA LINE	
Diff Inelast	1.3+7	1.8+7	IBJ	Expt Jour	NP/A 204 1 21	Apr 73 Decowski+ NA – I.SIG TO ISOM,FINAL PPR	+
				Prog	INR – 1197 18	May 70 – + SIGMA AT 10 ES,GRAPH+TABLE	
	1.3+7	1.8+7		Data	EXFOR30151.003	Jan 72 SIGMA TO METASTABLE STATE AT 10 ES	
Diff Inelast	Fiss		KOS	Expt Conf	75Karlsrhe 29	Apr 75 Csikai. CF252.TO META,ACTIV. SIG GVN	+
	1.4+6			Data	EXFOR30400.053	Oct 78 1 PNT. PB204(N,N')PB204 – M.	
Diff Inelast	+7		CCP	Expt Rept	YK – 23 4	76 Brodskaja+ ACTIV,AVG SIG,TBL	
Diff Inelast	None		LAS	Theo Prog	LA – 6472 10	Sep 76 Arthur+ACT CS GNASH CODE CALC.NDG	
Thermal Scat	7.9 – 2		NRI	Expt Prog	INDC(SEC) – 50	Jan 76 Aladdin+ COH SCAT.SIG FREE,BOUND GVN	
Nonelastic	None		FR	Theo Jour	APA 7 102	Apr 53 Hittmair.ANGDIST NUCL REACTIONS	
Nonelastic	1.4+7	1.5+7	ANL	Eval Rept	ANL – 75 – 34	Jun 75 Davey+CORRC APPLIED TO N2N CS.TBLS.	
Res Int Abs	2.6+3	1.6+5	ORL	Expt Jour	PR/C 8 1504	Oct 73 Allen+RES INTEGRAL FOR CAPT GVN.	+
	2.6+3	1.6+5		Data	EXFOR10155.012	Jan 78 . 1PT.RIA=726+ – 22MB.	
(n,γ)	Maxwl		ORL	Expt Jour	PR 88 412	Oct 52 Pomerance.PILE OSC.TBL 100 ISOTOPES	+
	Maxwl			Data	EXFOR11507.099	Jun 76 . 1 PT. CS=.9B+ – 70PCT.	
(n,γ)	Pile		ANL	Expt Jour	PR 111 590	Jul 58 Wing+ MTR NS, CS GVN. CFD OTH.	+
	Pile			Data	EXFOR12210.002	Jun 76 . 1 PT. CS=700+ – 20MB	
(n,γ)	Maxwl	+5	FOA	Theo Jour	NP 39 353	Dec 62 Bergqvist+. IN PER CENT OF NAT ELEMT	

82 Lead 204

Quantity	Energy (ev) Min	Max	Lab	Type	Documentation Ref Vol Page	Author, Comments Date	Data
(n,γ)	Maxwl		LAS	Expt Conf	63ANL 236	63 Jurney+CAPT G SPECT.REL PB207	+
	Maxwl			Data	EXFOR11133.009	Jun 76 . 1 PT. RATIO=.94+−.07	
(n,γ)	5.0+3	9.0+4	ORL	Theo Jour	RMP 37 166	Jan 65 Macklin+.CALC FOR KT=5TO90KEV	
(n,γ)	Maxwl		LAS	Expt Jour	NP/A 94 351	Mar 67 Jurney+ G SPEC. REL N−14	+
				Prog	WASH−1071 137	Nov 66 − . PB205 LEVEL SCHEME	
	Maxwl			Data	EXFOR12237.002	Jun 76 . 1 PT. CS=661+−70MB	
(n,γ)	2.5+4		FEI	ExTh Prog	YFI−4 22	May 67 Shorin+.,TBLS GIVEN,TBP YF	
				Rept	INDC−187E	67 . ENGL OF YFI−4 22	
(n,γ)	3.0+4	1.6+5	ORL	Expt Jour	PR 159 1007	Jul 67 Macklin+ TOF,TOTAL−E DET, 2ES,ABSL	+
	3.0+4	1.6+5		Data	EXFOR11679.024	Jun 76 . 5 PTS.	
(n,γ)	−		IEA	Comp Jour	IEA−INF−10 6	Aug 68 Atalla. TABLES OF HL,SIG AND GAMM−E	
(n,γ)	Maxwl		KFI	Comp Jour	JRC 7 365	Jun 71 Nagy+ SIGMA, GAM+XRAY ES,HALF−L GIVN	
(n,γ)	2.0+3		MTR	Expt Jour	PR/C 4 2249	Dec 71 Greenwood+FROM PRIMARY CAPT LINES	+
	2.0+3			Data	EXFOR10243.003	Nov 72 . 1 PT. SIGMA=1.8+−.5B	
(n,γ)	2.5+3	6.0+5	ORL	Expt Jour	PR/C 8 1504	Oct 73 Allen+CAPT YLD CURVES.RES PAR ANAL.	
(n,γ)	None		LAS	Theo Prog	LA−6472 10	Sep 76 Arthur+ACT CS GNASH CODE CALC.NDG	
Spect (n,γ)	Maxwl		LAS	Expt Jour	NP/A 94 351	Mar 67 Jurney+ ENRICHED TARGET LI(GE) DET	
Spect (n,γ)	Maxwl		CCP	Expt Jour	YF 7 937	May 68 Groshev+ OTHER EXPTL GAM−INT(GAM−E)	
				Jour	SNP 7 563	Nov 68 TRANSLATN.*	
Spect (n,γ)	None		ORL	Theo Jour	NSE 36 220	May 69 Yost+ CALCULAT BY GAMMA CASCADE MDL	
Spect (n,γ)	Maxwl		KFI	Comp Jour	JRC 7 365	Jun 71 Nagy+ SIGMA, GAM+XRAY ES,HALF−L GIVN	
Spect (n,γ)	2.0+3		MTR	Expt Jour	PR/C 4 2249	Dec 71 Greenwood+. TABLE HIGH−ENERGY GAMMAS	+
	2.0+3			Data	EXFOR10243.002	Nov 72 . 18 PTS. DSIGMA	
(n,2n)	Pile		CRC	Expt Rept	CRC−852	Jul 59 Roy+ ACTIVATION IN NRX FLUX	
(n,2n)	1.0+7	1.4+7	LRL	Expt Rept	UCRL−6028	Jun 60 Tewes.ACT 6ES .5 TO 1.5B +−40PC,TBC	+
	1.0+7	1.4+7		Data	EXFOR11504.019	Jun 76 . 5 PTS.	
(n,2n)	Fiss		CRC	Eval Rept	CRC−1003	Dec 60 Roy+,ESTIMATED AVG SIG=2.9MB	
(n,2n)	1.2+7	1.9+7	LOK	Expt Priv	VAUGHN	Sep 63 Vaughn. ACTIVATION	+
	1.2+7	1.9+7		Data	EXFOR12223.002	Jun 76 . 13 PTS. CS DATA.	
(n,2n)	Fast		AMS	Expt Jour	PHY 30 1762	Sep 64 Heertje+COMPARE WITH OTHER EXPTS	
(n,2n)	1.3+7	1.5+7	BNL	Theo Jour	NSE 23 238	Nov 65 Pearlstein.3ES.STAT MDL CALC.TBL CS.	
(n,2n)	Fiss		BNL	Theo Jour	NSE 23 238	Nov 65 Pearlstein.STATMDL CALC.SPEC AVG.TBL	
(n,2n)	1.3+7	1.7+7	HAM	Expt Prog	EANDC(E)76U	Jan 67 Bormann+ TABLE.ISOM.STATE	+
(n,2n)	1.5+7		DEB	Expt Jour	AHP 23 87	May 67 Csikai+ ACTIV,SIGMA AT 14.7MEV,TABLE	+
				Jour	MFF 16 123	Feb 68 SEE ALSO *THESIS IN HUNG	
	1.5+7			Data	EXFOR30119.008	Feb 71 SIGMA AT 14.7 MEV REL CU−65(N,2N)	
(n,2n)	1.5+7		MUN	Expt Jour	NP/A 118 9	Sep 68 Dilg+ ACTIV.REL AL(N,A)	+
				Jour	OAWS 177 323	69 Winkler+(IRK) ACTIVATION.	
	1.5+7			Data	EXFOR20802.022	Dec 78 1PNT.SIGMA.	
(n,2n)	1.5+7		DEB	ExTh Jour	AHP 25 91	Oct 68 Peto+ REL PR141(N,2N) CFD THEORY	+
	1.5+7			Expt Data	EXFOR30069.006	Dec 70 SIG REL PR−141(N2N)	
(n,2n)	1.5+7		DEB	Expt Jour	NP/A 122 234	Dec 68 Karolyi+,ACT,D−T NS,ISOM RAT,CFD TH	+
	1.5+7			Data	EXFOR30101.016	Feb 71 ISOMERIC RATIO	
(n,2n)	1.5+7		DEB	Comp Jour	REA 7 4 93	Dec 69 Csikai+ SIG+HL COMPILTN,N−ACTIV−ANAL	
(n,2n)	1.5+7		CCP	Comp Rept	ICD−6 215	70 Sluchevskaja.SIGS GND+ISOM,RATIO,TBL	
(n,2n)	1.2+7	1.8+7	IBJ	Expt Rept	INP−702/PS	Jun 70 Decowski+ GAMMA−N COMPETITION CFD TH	
(n,2n)	1.4+7	1.5+7	JYV	Eval Rept	JU−RR−3/1970	Jun 70 Leppaemaeki+ TABLE OF EVAL AVG SIG	
(n,2n)	Pile		SEO	Expt Conf	IAEA−132 24	71 LEE+ ABSTR.AVG SIG=6.2MILLIBARN	
(n,2n)	+7		KFI	Theo Rept	KFKI−71−8	Feb 71 Jeki. CALCULATED CFD EXPTL SIG VALUE	
(n,2n)	Fast		KTO	Expt Jour	NST 8 59	Feb 71 Kimura+.MEAN S=1.90+−0.18 MILLI−B	+
				Conf	71Vienna 113	Aug 71 − + ACTIVATION,TBL CFD OTHERS	
	Fast			Data	EXFOR20317.019	Jun 74 1PNT.SIGMA.	
(n,2n)	1.4+7		KFI	Comp Jour	JRC 7 365	Jun 71 Nagy+ SIGMA, GAMMA+ELECTR ES, HALF−L	
(n,2n)	1.4+7	1.5+7	IRK	ExTh Jour	APA 33 285	Jul 71 Winiwarter+ ISOMERIC RATIO	
(n,2n)	Fast		JUL	Expt Conf	71Canterby 121	Sep 71 Qaim+EFFECTIVE SIGMA.ACTIV,GAMMA DET	+
	Fast			Data	EXFOR20554.014	Apr 76 1PNT.SIGMA.	
(n,2n)	1.5+7		CCP	Expt Jour	YF 14 682	Oct 71 Druzhinin+ NAI,ABSOL,TBL CFD OTHERS	
				Jour	SNP 14 383	Apr 72 *ENGL OF YF 14 682	
(n,2n)	1.4+7		CCP	Expt Rept	YK−9 50	72 Maslov+ REL CU65(N,2N),NA−I,SIG GIVN	
				Rept	INDC(CCP)−42	Aug 74 .P10.ENGLISH OF YK−9	
	1.4+7	1.5+7		Data	EXFOR40136.022	Sep 74 .SIGMA AT 2 ES GIVEN	
(n,2n)	1.4+7		GIT	Expt Jour	NP/A 180 157	Jan 72 Hankla+ ACT,GE(LI),MIXED POWDER.	+
				Abst	DA/B 32 293	Nov 71 − . ACT METHOD, CFD THEORY.	
	1.4+7			Data	EXFOR10244.019	Jun 74 .PT.SIGMA=1.737+−.140B	
(n,2n)	1.5+7		IBJ	Expt Jour	APPB 2 553	71 Rurarz+ ACTIV,NAI,CFD THEO,TABLES	+
	1.5+7			Data	EXFOR30156.	Feb 72 SIGMA TO METASTABLE STATE GIVEN	
(n,2n)	8.0+6	1.9+7	IBJ	Theo Rept	INR−1475/1/PL	73 Marcinkowski. SIG(E) CFD STATMOD,FIG	

82 Lead 204

Quantity	Energy (ev) Min	Max	Lab	Type	Documentation Ref Vol Page	Author, Comments Date	Data
(n,2n)	1.4+7		ITJ	Expt	Jour JRC 14 201	73 Janczyszyn+ TO ISO,ACTIV.CFD OTH,TBL	+
	1.4+7			Data	EXFOR30322.020	Feb 76 1 PNT.	
(n,2n)	1.5+7		DEB	Eval	Jour REA 11 1 153	Mar 73 Boedy. COMPILATION+RECOMM.VALUE,TBL	
				Rept	IAEA-153 173	73 - . RECOMM. VALUE ONLY	
(n,2n)	1.3+7	1.8+7	IBJ	Expt	Jour NP/A 204 1 21	Apr 73 Decowski+ NA-1.TOTSIG(E),FINAL PAPER	+
				Conf	72Budapest 190	Aug 72 - + ACTIVATION,CFD THEORY,GRPH	
				Prog	INR-1197 18	May 70 - + SIGMA AT 10 ES,GRAPH+TABLE	
	1.3+7	1.8+7		Data	EXFOR30151.004	Jan 72 TOTAL SIGMA AT 9 ENERGIES	
(n,2n)	1.4+7		LOU	Expt	Prog INR-1464 12	May 73 Araminowicz+BRIEF,ACTIV,TABLE,GRAPH	+
	1.4+7			Data	EXFOR30264.043	Nov 73 SIGMA AT 14.6 MEV	
(n,2n)	Fiss		KOS	Eval	Jour AK 16 351	74 Boedy. U238,MAXW-SPC.AVG CFD XPT,TBL	
(n,2n)	1.5+7		TAT	Theo	Jour JP/A 7 1457	Aug 74 Kondaiah. CALC ON STAT MODEL	
(n,2n)	Fiss		KOS	Eval	Conf 75Karlsrhe 29	Apr 75 Csikai. CF252,MAXW-SPC.AVG FOR 2TEMP	
(n,2n)	8.5+6	1.5+7	ANL	Eval	Rept ANL-75-34	Jun 75 Davey+CONSTANT T MDL,LVL DEN MDL FIT	
(n,2n)	+7		CCP	Expt	Rept YK-23 4	76 Brodskaja+ ACTIV,AVG SIG,TBL	
(n,2n)		2.0+7	BRC	Theo	Rept 76Lowell 365	Jul 76 Frehaut.SYST.NT.CASCADE REACTIONS.	
(n,xn) x>2	Fiss		BNL	Theo	Jour NSE 23 238	Nov 65 Pearlstein.SPEC AVG STATMDL CALC N3N	
(n,xn) x>2	None		LAS	Theo	Prog LA-6472 10	Sep 76 Arthur+ACT CS GNASH CODE CALC.NDG	
(n,p)	Fiss		CRC	Eval	Rept CRC-1003	Dec 60 Roy+,ESTIMATED AVG SIG=0.03MB	
(n,p)	Fast		GHT	Expt	Jour RCA 4 32	May 65 Op-De-Beeck+ ACT. REL S32(N,P)	+
	Fast			Data	EXFOR20250.002	May 74 1PNT.SIGMA.	
(n,p)	Maxwl		CCP	Theo	Rept ICD-4 20	67 Dadakina+PENETRATION COEF CALC,TABLE	
(n,p)	+7		CCP	Expt	Rept YK-23 4	76 Brodskaja+ ACTIV,AVG SIG,TBL	
(n,p)	None		LAS	Theo	Prog LA-6472 10	Sep 76 Arthur+ACT CS GNASH CODE CALC.NDG	
(n,t)	1.5+7		JUL	Expt	Jour NP/A 257 233	Feb 76 Qaim+ACT,TBL,GRPH,CFD OTHER ISOTOPE	+
	1.5+7			Data	EXFOR20669.010	Oct 76 1PNT.SIGMA.	
(n,α)	Fiss		CRC	Eval	Rept CRC-1003	Dec 60 Roy+,ESTIMATED AVG SIG=BELO 0.0001MB	
(n,α)	+7		CCP	Expt	Rept YK-23 4	76 Brodskaja+ ACTIV,AVG SIG,TBL	
Fission	1.4+7		LAS	Expt	Jour PR 75 919	Mar 49 Phillips+ UPPER LIM REL U238.PHOTOPL	
Reson Params	1.7+3	2.4+4	HAR	ExTh	Prog WASH-1048 71	Jun 64 Block.ANAL OF TRANSM DATA.TBL	
Reson Params	1.7+3	2.4+4	ORL	ExTh	Prog WASH-1048 71	Jun 64 Block.ANALYZ OF HARWELL TRNSDATA,TBL	
Reson Params	1.7+3	1.3+4	CCP	Comp	Rept INDSWG-101 25	65 DATA OF 5 RES LISTED WITHOUT REFERNC	
Reson Params	1.3+3	2.7+4	RPI	Expt	Prog RPI-328-87 24	67 Bartolome+ LINAC+TOF,E0,G*WN*WG/WT	
Reson Params	6.5+3	5.9+4	ORL	Expt	Jour PR 153 1356	Jan 67 Gibbons+ TRNS.E0,WN,L.D.AREA ANAL	+
	6.5+3	5.9+4		Data	EXFOR12218.003	Jun 76 . 24 RES. E0,WN,L GVN.	
Reson Params	1.3+3	2.7+4	RPI	Expt	Prog WASH-1074 97	Apr 67 . SUPERSEDED	
Reson Params	1.3+3	2.7+4	RPI	Expt	Abst BAP 12 512	Apr 67 .ABST DH13	
Reson Params	1.3+3	2.7+4	RPI	Expt	Prog WASH-1079 139	Oct 67 . SUPERSEDED	
Reson Params	1.3+3	2.7+4	RPI	Expt	Prog WASH-1127 173	Apr 69 Wolfe+ CAPT TBL,E0,WN,G*WN*WG/WT	
Reson Params	1.7+3	1.3+4	CJD	Eval	Rept YK-7	71 Zakharova+ SURVEY+SYSTEMATICS,GW,TBL	
				Rept	INDC(CCP)-27	Nov 72 .ENGLISH TRANSLATION OF YK-7 /71	
Reson Params	None		DUB	Theo	Jour JINR-P4-7499	Oct 73 Soloviev+ CALC D CFD EXPTS,TABLE	
Reson Params	2.6+3	1.3+4	ORL	Expt	Jour PR/C 8 1504	Oct 73 Allen+ ORELA.CAPT.WT G*WG D.4 ES.	+
	2.6+3	1.6+5		Data	EXFOR10155.	Jan 78 . 5RES.WT,WG G,D,WG AVG,G STF.	
Reson Params	1.3+3	2.7+4	RPI	Expt	Data EXFOR12588.003	Jun 76 . 14 RES, WT,WN,WG	+
Strnth Fnctn		6.0+4	ORL	Expt	Jour PR 153 1356	Jan 67 Gibbons+ =.55+-.2, FROM 10 L=0 RES	
	6.5+3	5.9+4			Jour PR 153 1356	Jan 67 - + TRNS. S0=(.55)-4	
Strnth Fnctn	None		AUA	Eval	Rept AAEC/E-277	Mar 73 Musgrove.TBLS EXPTL DATA+BEST VALUES	
Lvl Density	+7		DEB	ExTh	Jour NP/A 122 234	Dec 68 Karolyi+ SPIN CUTOFF,M OF INERT,N2N	+
	1.5+7			Expt	Data EXFOR30101.020	Jun 72 CUTOFF PARAMETER	

82 Lead 205

Quantity	Energy (ev) Min	Max	Lab	Type	Documentation Ref Vol Page	Author, Comments Date	Data
Inelastic γ	1.5+7		LND	Expt	Jour AF 39 295	Sep 69 Joensson+. 80 DEG. 1 TRANSITION	
(n,p)	Maxwl		CCP	Theo	Rept ICD-4 20	67 Dadakina+PENETRATION COEF CALC,TABLE	
Lvl Density	+6		MIL	Theo	Jour EN 15 1 54	Jan 68 Facchini+ LDL PARS FROM LOW EN RES	
Lvl Density	None		MUN	Theo	Jour NP/A 217 269	Dec 73 Dilg+ A,DELTA. BACK SHIFTED FERMIGAS	
Lvl Density	None		DUB	Theo	Jour NP/A 224 411	May 74 Soloviev+ 1/2 MICROSC MDL. SPH NUCL.	
Lvl Density	None		ROC	Theo	Jour NP/A 223 577	May 74 Huizenga+ EXP CFD MICROSC TH SPH NUC	

82 Lead 206

Quantity	Energy (ev) Min	Max	Lab	Type	Documentation Ref Vol Page	Author, Comments Date	Data
Evaluation	3.2-2	1.0+7	GEA	Eval	Rept XDC-60-8-81	Jun 59 Roberts.ACT+GAM PROD SIGS,GP AVGD	
Evaluation	1.0-5	2.0+7	ORL	Eval	Rept ORNL-4765	Mar 72 FU+ ENDF 3. CALCS CFD EXPT.	

82 Lead 206

Quantity	Energy (ev) Min	Max	Lab	Type	Documentation Ref Vol Page	Author, Comments Date	Data
Total	1.5+4	7.5+5	WIS	Expt	Jour PR 79 935	Sep 50 Peterson. 3-10KEVRSLN 88/100 PURE	+
	1.3+4	7.4+5		Data	EXFOR12200.004	Jun 76 . 245 PTS.	
Total	5.0+4	3.2+6	WIS	Expt	Jour PR 88 83	Oct 52 Miller+TRNS. 20KEV SPREAD. GRPH.	+
	8.4+5	3.2+6		Data	EXFOR11712.023	Jun 76 . 15 PTS. CS DATA.	
Total	1.4+7		LAS	Expt	Jour PR 88 562	Nov 52 Coon+SCIN CRYSTAL.GOOD GEOM	+
	1.4+7			Data	EXFOR11056.055	Jun 76 . 1 PT. CS=5.40+−.11 B	
Total	3.6+4	6.6+5	DKE	Expt	Priv BILPUCH	61 Bilpuch. TABULATED DATA	+
	3.6+4	6.6+5		Data	EXFOR11011.006	Jun 76 . 1252 PTS.	
Total	8.5+4	2.0+5	DKE	Expt	Jour AP 14 387	Jul 61 Bilpuch+RADIO GENIC PB GRPH.RES ANAL	+
	1.0+4	3.5+5		Data	EXFOR11599.048	Jun 76 . DATA UNOBTAINABLE FROM AUTHORS.	
Total	1.4+6		LSU	Expt	Jour PR 132 1211	Nov 63 Haas+TRNS. MULT SCT CORREC. CFD	
	1.4+6			Data	EXFOR11794.	Jun 76 . 2 PTS.	
Total	1.4+7		CCP	ExTh	Jour ZET 46 1496	Apr 64 5.47+−.03B,CFD OPTMDL,SHELL.SEP ISOQ	
					Jour JET 19 1013	Oct 64 TRANSLATN.*	
Total	1.0+4	9.0+4	ORL	Expt	Jour PR/B 136 695	Nov 64 Macklin. TOF.TRNS.CURV.	+
	1.0+4	8.5+4		Data	EXFOR11575.017	Jun 76 . 137 PTS. CS DATA	
Total	1.2+5	8.4+5	DKE	ExTh	Jour PL 17 286	Jul 65 Farrell+ .5 KEV INTERVALS 2-3KEV RES	
Total	5.0+5	4.1+6	LAS	Expt	Priv DAY	Jul 65 DAY. TABULATED DATA.	+
	5.0+5	4.1+6		Data	EXFOR12191.006	Jun 76 . 4 PTS. CS DATA FOR 4 ES.	
Total	1.4+7		FEI	Expt	Prog INDSWG-126 33	66 Dukarevich.SIG=5.37+−0.04B	
Total	1.4+7		CCP	ExTh	Jour IZV 31 217	Feb 67 Dukarevich+.TBL,CURVES,CFD OPTMDL TH	
					Jour BAS 31 197	Feb 67 TRANSLATN.*	
Total	1.4+7		FTI	Expt	Jour NP/A 92 433	Feb 67 Dukarevich+ CFD OPTMDL 5.37+−0.04B	+
Total	2.5+6	7.5+6	WIS	Expt	Jour PR 158 1142	Jun 67 Carlson+ VDG,CURV,88PERCENT PB206	+
					Abst DA/B 28 1084	Sep 67 .THESIS ABST.	
	2.5+6	7.5+6			Data EXFOR11497.031	Jun 76 . 164 PTS.	
Total	5.0+5	2.5+6	BNL	Theo	Rept BNL-50151	Oct 68 Moore.ALSO 1MEV.OPTMDL FIT TO DATA	
Total	1.3+6	1.9+6	DKE	Expt	Prog NCSAC-33 230	Dec 70 Malan+,C12(D,N) SOURCE,ANAL TBC,NDG	
Total	2.5+6	1.5+7	BNW	Expt	Jour PR/C 3 576	Feb 71 Foster+,TRANS,CURVS,CFD OTHERS+TH	+
					Jour NIM 36 1	Sep 65 .EXPT DETAILS	
	2.3+6	1.5+7			Data EXFOR10047.	Aug 73 . 502 PTS.	
Total	1.3+7	1.5+7	DEB	Eval	Rept IAEA-153 173	73 Boedy+ MOST PROBABLE VAL OF SIG,TBL	
					Jour AHP 30 115	Oct 71 Angeli+ AVG SIG,CFD CALC.TBLS.GRAPH	
Total	1.3+7	1.7+7	CCP	Expt	Jour YF 17 21	Jan 73 Benecky+ SIG(NEUT−E)	
					Jour SNP 17 10	Jul 73 .ENGLISH TRANSLATION	
Total	1.9+5	4.3+5	ORL	Expt	Conf JINR-D-37991	Apr 74 Harvey.P157.PLAST SCINT,SIG(E) PLOT	
Total	1.5+7	1.8+7	IJI	Theo	Conf 77Kiev	77 Benecky+ OPTMOD, NDG,CALCULATION	
Elastic	1.0+6		WIS	Expt	Jour PR 93 1062	Mar 54 Walt+ INTEG ANG DIST	+
	1.0+6			Data	EXFOR11637.077	Jun 76 . 1 PT. CS=4.6B	
Elastic	2.2+6		BNL	Expt	Jour PR 112 1192	Nov 58 Landon+INTEG ANG DIST	+
	2.2+6			Data	EXFOR11717.012	Jun 76 . 1 PT. CS=4.68B	
Elastic	4.2+6		TNC	Expt	Rept WADC-TN-59-107	59 Bostrom+ INTEG ANG DIST	
	4.2+6			Data	EXFOR11130.024	Jun 76 . 1 PT. CS=4.4+−.7 B	
Elastic	1.0+6	4.2+6	AGN	Eval	Rept TID-21629	Dec 64 Perkins+3E CALC. FROM BNL400,UCRL557	
Elastic	7.0+6		AE	Expt	Rept AE-482	Dec 73 Etemad. INTEGRATED.	+
	7.0+6			Data	EXFOR20346.	Sep 74 2PTS.	
Elastic	1.0+5	1.2+7	WAY	Theo	Jour PR/C 10 1223	Sep 74 LEV+ S-WAVE,IMAGIN OPT-POT CALC,CURV	
Elastic	3.4+6		TUD	Expt	Prog ZFK-315 13	Aug 76 Abdel-Harith+ ABST, NDG	+
	3.4+6			Data	EXFOR30464.018	Jan 79 1 PNT	
Diff Elastic	1.0+6		WIS	Expt	Jour PR 93 1062	Mar 54 Walt+ HE COUNTER 30-150DEG 88PC 206	+
	1.0+6			Data	EXFOR11637.079	Jun 76 . 9 PTS.	
Diff Elastic	2.2+6		BNL	Expt	Jour PR 112 1192	Nov 58 Landon+,TOF,CURVE GIVEN	+
	2.2+6			Data	EXFOR11717.010	Jun 76 . 14 PTS. ANG DIST.	
Diff Elastic	4.2+6		TNC	Expt	Rept WADC-TN-59-107	59 Bostrom+ ANG DIST. H STANDARD	
	4.2+6			Data	EXFOR11130.029	Jun 76 . 13 PTS.	
Diff Elastic	4.2+6		TNC	Expt	Jour PR 116 986	Nov 59 Okhuysen+ TOF CFD THEORY 88 PC PB206	+
	4.2+6			Data	EXFOR12211.003	Jun 76 . 13 PTS.	
Diff Elastic	4.0+6	7.0+6	LAS	Expt	Jour PR 129 1649	Feb 63 Thomson. SIG AT 90DEG	+
	4.0+6	7.0+6		Data	EXFOR11495.054	Jun 76 . 2 PTS.	
Diff Elastic	1.5+6	4.2+6	TEX	Expt	Abst DA 23 3938	Apr 63 Brandenberger. 4ES.	
Diff Elastic	1.0+6		IFU	Theo	Jour UFZ 9 251	Mar 64 Ol'Khovskij. TH GRAPH CFD PR 93 1062	
					Jour IZV 29 319	Feb 65 .	
					Jour BAS 29 322	Feb 66 .ENGLISH TRANSL OF IZV 29 319 2/65	
Diff Elastic	1.0+6	4.2+6	AGN	Eval	Rept TID-21629	Dec 64 Perkins+ 3ES LEG COEF CALC FROM OTH	
Diff Elastic	7.0+6		LAS	Expt	Jour PRL 14 913	May 65 Zafiratos. 20-165DEG. OPTMDL	+
	7.0+6			Data	EXFOR12220.002	Jun 76 . 30 PTS.	
Diff Elastic	5.0+5	2.5+6	LAS	Expt	Priv DAY	Jul 65 DAY. ANG DIST DATA	+
	5.0+5	2.5+6		Data	EXFOR12191.007	Jun 76 . 72 PTS.	

82 Lead 206

Quantity	Energy (ev) Min	Max	Lab	Type	Documentation Ref Vol Page	Author, Comments Date	Data
Diff Elastic	3.1+6		TEX Expt	Abst	DA 26 1112	Aug 65 Spahn.TOF METHOD.NDG	
Diff Elastic	8.0+5	4.5+6	ORL Theo	Rept	ORNL-TM-1238	Sep 65 Smith.H-F ANALYSIS GOOD AGREEMENT	
Diff Elastic	1.0+6		LAS Theo	Prog	WASH-1064 84	Oct 65 Rosen+, OPTMDL+ CPD ELST CFD WIS XPT	
Diff Elastic	5.0+6		ORL Expt	Prog	WASH-1064 121	Oct 65 Dickens+,TOF,THETA=30-130DEG,TBC NDG	
Diff Elastic	3.2+6	5.0+6	SCU Theo	Rept	ICD-6 236	69 Averyanov+CALC ANGDIST CFD EXPT,GRPH	
Diff Elastic	1.4+7		CCP Expt	Conf	69Erevan	Feb 69 Belovickij+.ABST,45-138 DEGS,EMULS	
Diff Elastic	1.4+7		IJI Expt	Conf	72Budapest 164	Aug 72 Belovickij+ PHOTOEMULS,ANGDIST,GRAPH	+
				Jour	YF 15 662	Apr 72 Belovitskij+ ANGDIST CFD OPTMOD,GRPH	
				Jour	SNP 15 369	Oct 72 .ENGLISH OF YF 15 662	
	1.4+7			Data	EXFOR40288.002	Apr 75 .DATA IN MB/SR AT 7 ANGLS GVN	
Diff Elastic	7.0+6		AE Expt	Rept	AE-482	Dec 73 Etemad. VDG. TOF. +RADIOGENIC LEAD	+
	7.0+6			Data	EXFOR20346.	Sep 74 51PTS.D/DA,LEG.FIT.	
Diff Elastic	3.4+6		TUD Expt	Prog	ZFK-315 12	Aug 76 Abdel-Harith+ ABST, NDG	+
	3.4+6			Data	EXFOR30464.019	Jan 79 LEGENDRE-COEF.	
Polarization	1.4+7		IJI Theo	Jour	YF 18 1203	Dec 73 Ivanjuk+ SHELL CORR, POL(ANG),GRAPH	
				Jour	SNP 18 616	Jun 74 .ENGLISH OF YF 18, 1203.	
Tot Inelastc	1.6+7		LND Expt	Jour	PS 2 277	Dec 70 Joensson.LIMITS FROM NAT+RADIOPB GS	
Tot Inelastc	2.5+6	3.0+6	KFI Comp	Jour	JRC 7 365	Jun 71 Nagy+ SIGMA, GAMMA-E AND HALF-L GIVN	
Diff Inelast	1.0+6	2.1+6	BNL ExTh	Rept	BNL-273	Dec 53 Oleksa.HAUSER-FESHB CALC,TBLS,CURVES	+
Diff Inelast	2.5+6		LAS Expt	Jour	PR 103 343	Jul 56 Cranberg+,TOF 90DEG .8 1.4 1.7MEVLVL	+
	2.5+6			Data	EXFOR11396.024	Jun 76 . 3 PTS.	
Diff Inelast	-		JAP	Jour	PA 60 6581	Jul 57 JAP TH CFD XPT PTPJ15 586 0656	
Diff Inelast	2.2+6		BNL Expt	Jour	PR 112 1192	Nov 58 Landon+,TOF,SCATTER FROM 3 LEVELS	+
	2.2+6			Data	EXFOR11717.013	Jun 76 . 1 PT. CS=.86 B	
	2.2+6			Data	EXFOR11717.011	Jun 76 . 11 PTS. DSIG	
Diff Inelast	3.0+6		LAS Expt	Conf	60Kingston 357	Aug 60 Cranberg+.CURVE,DIFF SIGMA(ANGLE)	
Diff Inelast	4.0+6	7.0+6	LAS Expt	Jour	PR 129 1649	Feb 63 Thomson+ 90DEG TEMP FOR NS TO 5	+
	4.0+6	7.0+6		Data	EXFOR11495.053	Jun 76 . 4 PTS. DSIG	
	7.0+6			Data	EXFOR11495.056	Jun 76 . 1 PT. CS=2.39+-.24B	
Diff Inelast	1.4+7		BAS Expt	Jour	PL 5 202	Jul 63 Huber+ GRAPH OF INELASTIC N SPECTRUM	
				Jour	HPA 34 520	Aug 61 Niklaus+.NUC.TEMP.0.98MEV	
				Jour	HPA 36 1059	Dec 59 Huber+.T=1.11MEV	
Diff Inelast	4.0+6	6.5+6	DKE Expt	Jour	NP 60 17	Nov 64 Buccino+N SPEC MEASURED 4ES+NUC TEMP	
				Abst	DA 24 4251	Apr 64 Hollandsworth.TOF.EN SPEC.NUCL T.	
Diff Inelast	8.0+5	4.5+6	ORL Theo	Rept	ORNL-TM-1238	Sep 65 Smith.H-F ANALYSIS GOOD AGREEMENT	
Diff Inelast	5.0+6		ORL Expt	Prog	WASH-1064 121	Oct 65 Dickens+,TOF,THETA=30-130DEG,TBC NDG	
Diff Inelast	8.0+6		LAS Expt	Jour	PR 142 775	Feb 66 Cranberg+.VDG+TOF 3ES 2.6MEV COLLLVL	+
				Conf	63Houston 94	Feb 63 - - GRPH EX FN 9LVLS AT 50 DEG	
	8.0+6			Data	EXFOR12216.	Jun 76 . 36 PTS.	
Diff Inelast	2.0+6	8.0+6	LAS Expt	Jour	PR 159 969	Jul 67 Cranberg+.EXC FN TO 4.5MEV ANG DIST	
				Jour	PRL 11 341	Oct 63 .SUPERSEDED	
	2.5+6	8.0+6		Conf	63Houston 99	Feb 63 .GRPH ANGDIST FOR 8LVLS.=BAP8.SPSDED	
Diff Inelast	-		BHU Theo	Conf	68Madras 1 291	Feb 68 Sharma+ PPRN39.CALC SIG,5 LVLS,GRPHS	
Diff Inelast	2.5+6		BNL Eval	Rept	BNL-50151	Oct 68 Moore.OPTICAL MODEL ANALYSIS	
Diff Inelast		1.5+7	FEI Eval	Rept	INDC-257	Oct 68 Popov+ 120EVALD PARAMS FOR INEL SCAT	
				Rept	INDC-257E	68 . ENGL OF INDC-257	
Diff Inelast	2.5+6		CCP Comp	Rept	ICD-6 106	70 Sluchevskaja.SIG(ANG) TO LVLS,GRAPHS	
Diff Inelast	2.5+6		SCU Theo	Rept	ICD-6 236	70 Averyanov+CALC ANGDIST CFD EXPT,GRPH	
Diff Inelast	1.3+7	1.4+7	IJI Expt	Conf	72Kiev 2 14	Jan 72 Belovickij+ ABST,NDG.N-SPEC AT 2 ES	
Diff Inelast	1.4+7		CCP Expt	Jour	YF 15 666	Apr 72 Belovitskij+ N-SPEC,ANGDIST,GRAPHS	
				Jour	SNP 15 372	Oct 72 *ENGL OF YF 15 666	
				Conf	72Budapest 166	Aug 72 Belovitzky+ PHOTOEMULSN,ANGDIST,GRPH	
Diff Inelast	Thrsh	Up	LEB Expt	Jour	IZV 37 1714	Aug 73 .SIG OF EXCIT 1-ST LVL	+
				Conf	73Tbilisi 156	Feb 73 Konobeevsky+ ABST,CFD,STAT MODL,NDG	
	8.1+5	1.1+6		Data	EXFOR40215.005	Jun 74 .SIGMA FOR 25 ES GIVEN,1 E-LVL	
Diff Inelast	5.5+6	8.5+6	ORL Expt	Rept	ORNL-4909	Jun 74 Kinney+ CFD PREVIOUS RESULTS,OTH.	+
				Conf	75Wash. 883	Mar 75 - +26NUCLIDES ELAS,INEL CS RVW.	
	6.0+6	8.5+6		Data	EXFOR10412.002	Sep 74 13PTS,DSIGMA AT 5ENERGIES	
Diff Inelast	None		LAS Theo	Prog	LA-6472 10	Aug 76 Arthur+ACT CS GNASH CODE CALC.NDG.	
Diff Inelast	3.4+6		TUD Expt	Prog	ZFK-315 13	Aug 76 Abdel-Harith+ ABST, NDG	+
	3.4+6			Data	EXFOR30464.	Jan 79 PARTIAL,DIFF.PARTL.CS (2 LEVELS)	
Thermal Scat	Cold		LUQ Expt	Jour	PR 58 321	Aug 40 Rasetti. SCATTERING AS POR NATURL PB	
Thermal Scat	7.9-2		NRI Expt	Prog	INDC(SEC)-50	Jan 76 Aladdin+ COH SCAT.SIG FREE,BOUND GVN	
Nonelastic	1.0+6		WIS Expt	Jour	PR 93 1062	Mar 54 Walt+ SNE=TOT-SEL	+
	1.0+6			Data	EXFOR11637.078	Jun 76 . 1 PT. CS=.2+-.7B	
Nonelastic	4.2+6		TNC Expt	Rept	WADC-TN-59-107	59 Bostrom+ SNE=TOT-SEL	+
	4.2+6			Data	EXFOR11130.025	Jun 76 . 1 PT. CS=4.2+-.9B	
Nonelastic	8.0+5	3.0+6	DLH Theo	Conf	62Madras 86	Feb 62 Nath.GRAPH CFD EXPT,SHELLMODEL	

82 Lead 206

Quantity	Energy (ev) Min	Max	Lab	Type	Documentation Ref Vol Page	Author, Comments Date	Data
Absorption	Pile		HAR	Expt Jour	PPSA 65 761	Sep 52 Aitken+.PILE OSC REL HAR B	+
Absorption	1.0+5	1.2+7	WAY	Theo Jour	PR/C 10 1223	Sep 74 LEV+ INTERMED STRUCT,OPTMDL.SIG–CURV	
Res Int Abs	3.4+3	2.0+5	ORL	Expt Jour	PR/C 8 1504	Oct 73 Allen+RES INTEGRAL FOR CAPT GVN.	+
	3.4+3	2.0+5		Data	EXFOR10155.014	Jan 78 . 1PT.RIG=86+−6MB.	
(n,γ)	Maxwl		ORL	Expt Jour	PR 88 412	Oct 52 Pomerance.PILE OSC.TBL 100 ISOTOPES.	+
	Maxwl			Data	EXFOR11507.100	Jun 76 . 1 PT. CS=.1+−100 PCT	
(n,γ)	3.2−2	1.0+7	GEA	Eval Rept	XDC−60−8−81	Jun 59 Roberts.6.734MEV GAMMA 19GROUPS	
(n,γ)	2.5−2	+5	FOA	Theo Jour	NP 39 353	Dec 62 Bergqvist+ IN NAT ELEMENT ABONDANCE	
(n,γ)	Maxwl		LAS	Expt Conf	63ANL 236	Nov 63 Jurney+CAPT. G SPEC. REL PB 207	+
	Maxwl			Data	EXFOR11133.007	Jun 76 . 1 PT. CS RATIO=.043+−.001	
(n,γ)	1.4+4	5.8+4	ORL	Expt Jour	PR/B 136 695	Nov 64 Macklin. TOF. CURV SEVERAL CAPT RES	+
	1.0+4	5.8+4		Conf	63Houston 193	Feb 63 Gibbons. RELATIVE GAMMAS 2−4 MEV	
	1.4+4	5.8+4		Data	EXFOR11575.014	Jun 76 . 42 PTS.	
(n,γ)	5.0+3	9.0+4	ORL	Theo Jour	RMP 37 166	Jan 65 Macklin+.CALC FOR KT=5TO90KEV	
(n,γ)	2.5−3		CCP	Theo Conf	66Moscow	Feb 66 .TBL GIVEN	
(n,γ)	−		IEA	Comp Rept	IEA−INF−10 6	Aug 68 Atalla. TABLES OF HL,SIG AND GAMM−E	
(n,γ)	None		LRL	Expt Prog	WASH−1136 83	Sep 69 Bowman+,INVERSE REACT,DOORWAY STATE	
(n,γ)	1.5+6	8.5+6	FOA	Expt Jour	NP/A 153 553	Sep 70 Bergqvist+ AT 90DEG.TO 3 1−PARICL ST	+
				Conf	69Studsvik 569	Aug 69 − + SUPERSEDED	
	1.6+6	8.5+6		Data	EXFOR20070.	Sep 71 25PTS.SIG.	
(n,γ)	2.5+3	6.0+5	ORL	Expt Jour	PR/C 8 1504	73 Allen+CAPT YLD CURVES RES PAR ANAL	
(n,γ)	2.0+4	3.0+5	FEI	Expt Rept	INDC(CCP)−44	Jun 74 Abramov. P55.INV,TOF,SIG(N−E),GRAPH	
(n,γ)		2.0+6	WAY	Theo Jour	PR/C 13 2585	Jun 76 LEV+S WAV CS CALC.DOORWAY EFFECT.	
Spect (n,γ)	Maxwl		CCP	Theo Jour	ZET 29 60 866	Dec 55 TH WITHOUT COMPOUND NUCL,LEVEL SCHEM	
				Jour	JET 2 753	Jun 56 . ENGL OF ZET 29 866	
Spect (n,γ)	Maxwl		LAS	Expt Conf	63ANL 236	Oct 63 Jurney+ CS FROM CAPT. SPEC.	
Spect (n,γ)	1.0+4	1.0+5	ORL	Expt Jour	PR 154 1136	Feb 67 Good+ TOF+NAI XTL,5RES,FEW PARTIAL W	
				Conf	65Antwerp 68	Jul 65 .SUPERSEDED	
Spect (n,γ)	Maxwl		LAS	Expt Prog	WASH−1127 144	Apr 69 Shera+ TO BE DONE WITH 6CC GE(LI)DET	
Spect (n,γ)	1.6+4	7.0+4	AUA	Revw Rept	AAEC/TM−565	Sep 70 Allen.4 RES GAMSPEC GRPH,TOF	
				−		FULL TEXT OF PAPER AT 70CHICAGO (APS	
Spect (n,γ)	1.5+6	8.5+6	FOA	Expt Jour	NP/A 153 553	Sep 70 Bergqvist+ TOF.NAITL.	
				Conf	69Studsvik 569	Aug 69 − + SUPERSEDED	
Spect (n,γ)		3.0+6	CRC	Expt Prog	AECL−3912 64	Mar 71 Bartholomew+.NAI DET.PRELIM. NO DATA	
Spect (n,γ)	1.6+4	7.5+4	ORL	Comp Rept	ORNL−TM−3379	Apr 71 Bird+SPEC. GRPHS.TBL.COMPILATION.	
Spect (n,γ)	None		KFI	Comp Jour	JRC 7 365	Jun 71 Nagy+ GAMMA+ELECTR ES AND HALF−LIFE	
Spect (n,γ)	5.7+6		OHO	Expt Prog	ERDA−NDC−2 165	May 75 Brient+NAICRYS.SPECT.NDG	
Inelastic γ	1.2+6	2.7+6	MIT	Expt Jour	PR 95 989	Aug 54 Kiehn+ 20KEV RSLN. GRPHS. CFD H−F.	+
	1.2+6	2.7+6		Data	EXFOR11477.008	Jun 76 . 27 PTS. SIGMA	
Inelastic γ	2.6+6		LAS	Expt Jour	PR 102 767	Apr 56 Day.VALUES AT 5 GAMMA ES AT 95 DEG	+
	2.6+6			Data	EXFOR11218.030	Jun 76 . 5 PTS, DSIG	
Inelastic γ	1.0+6		TNC	Expt Rept	WADC−TN−59−107	59 Bostrom. RADIO LEAD RING GEOM.	+
	1.0+6			Data	EXFOR11130.026	Jun 76 . 1 PT. CS=31.+−7MB, DSIG	
Inelastic γ		2.3+7	LOK	Theo Conf	60Kingston 146	Aug 60 Walt+.CURVE,OPTMDL FIT CFD EXPT	
Inelastic γ	2.0+5	3.5+6	LAS	Expt Jour	AP 12 485	Mar 61 Lind+SIG(94DEG) FOR 7 GAMMAS	+
	7.0+5	3.1+6		Data	EXFOR11188.016	Jun 76 . 233 PTS,DSIG	
Inelastic γ	+6		PSU	Expt Jour	PR 128 1231	Nov 62 Donahue. EXCITATION OF LVLS GROM GS	
Inelastic γ	4.1+6		ETH	Theo Jour	RMP 38 143	Jan 66 .THEOR CALC OF GAM−RAY ANGL DISTR	
Inelastic γ	6.0+5	4.0+6	IND	Theo Jour	IJP 42 408	Jul 68 Gupta. DIFF INELAST SIG ,H−F TH	
Inelastic γ	1.5+7		LND	Expt Jour	AF 39 295	Sep 69 Joensson+. 80 DEG. 4 TRANSITIONS	+
				Rept	LU−NP−6804	Mar 68 − + EQUIVALENT TO AF 39 295	
	1.5+7	1.6+7		Data	EXFOR20164.	May 74 2PTS.D/DA.	
Inelastic γ	2.9+6		KTY	Expt Jour	PR 124 1531	Dec 61 Boring+, E,THETA DIST OF GAM CFD TH	+
				Abst	DA/B 31 2874	Nov 70 − .PROD SIG.ANGDIST.CFD STATMOD	
	2.9+6			Data	EXFOR11489.009	Jun 76 . 2 PTS. TOT DNG. 10 PTS. DIF DNG.	
Inelastic γ	1.0+6	1.5+7	TNC	Expt Rept	ORO−2791−32	Feb 71 Buchanan+.11NEUT ES,DIFF SIGS TABULT	
	3.0+6	4.1+6		Conf	65Antwerp 34	Jul 65 Morgan+G SPEC. NDG	
	4.1+6	1.5+7		Prog	TID−20658	Sep 63 − +,GAMMA SPEC+PROD SIGS,90DEG	
	4.0+6			Prog	TID−20657 36	62 Nellis+.CURVE OF GAMMA ANGULAR DISTR	
	1.0+6	1.5+7		Rept	AD−154995	Feb 58 Bostrom+ 7NEUT ES GAMMA PRODUCT SIGS	
Inelastic γ	2.5+6	3.0+6	KFI	Comp Jour	JRC 7 365	Jun 71 Nagy+ SIGMA, GAMMA−E AND HALF−L GIVN	
Inelastic γ	8.1+5	1.1+6	LEB	Expt Jour	IZV 37 1714	Aug 73 Konobeevskij+ SIG TO 1ST LEVEL,GRAPH	+
	8.0+5	1.1+6		Jour	BAS 37 8 129	Aug 73 . ENGL OF IZV 37 1714	
	8.1+5	1.1+6		Data	EXFOR40215.005	Jun 74 .SIGMA FOR 25 ES GIVEN,1 E−LVL	
Inelastic γ	1.5+7		SMU	Expt Jour	JIN 35 2139	Jul 73 Salaita+CYCLIC ACTIV,ISOM STATES.TBL	+
				Conf	75Wash. 712	Mar 75 Salatia+CYCLIC ACT.TBL.CFD.	
				Conf	74Columbia 95	Jul 74 Salaita+ ACT.SIG TO SHORTLIV ISO.TBL	
	1.5+7			Data	EXFOR10361.004	Sep 76 1PT=1017+−92MB=PROD206M+(N,2N)207PB.	

82 Lead 206

Quantity	Energy (ev) Min	Max	Lab	Type	Documentation Ref Vol Page	Date	Author, Comments	Data
Inelastic γ	1.0+6	1.0+7	KUR Expt	Conf	77Kiev	77	Savin+ SIG(NEUT–E),GRAPH	
Nonelastic γ	1.5+7		ARK Expt	Prog	A–ARK–61	Jan 61	Chittenden+ TOF. G PROD.CS.	+
	1.5+7			Data	EXFOR11132.	Jun 76	. 14 PTS. DIFF CS.	
Nonelastic γ	4.9+6	8.0+6	ORL Expt	Prog	NCSAC–42 194	Nov 71	Dickens. GE(LI) DET. GAMMA SPECTRA	
(n,2n)	1.5+7		CCP Expt	Jour	ZET 36 1046	Apr 59	Glagolev.G OF SHORT–LIVED ISOMERES	
				Jour	JET 9 742	Oct 59	TRANSLATN.*	
(n,2n)	1.4+7		CCP Expt	Jour	ZET 39 1621	Dec 60	$S=1.1+-0.2B$	
				Jour	JET 12 1131	Jun 61	TRANSLATN.*	
(n,2n)	Fiss		CRC Eval	Rept	CRC–1003	Dec 60	Roy+,ESTIMATED AVG SIG=4.9MB	
(n,2n)	1.3+7	1.5+7	BNL Theo	Jour	NSE 23 238	Nov 65	Pearlstein.3ES.STAT MDL CALC.TBL CS.	
(n,2n)	Fiss		BNL Theo	Jour	NSE 23 238	Nov 65	Pearlstein.STATMDL CALC.SPEC AVG.TBL	
(n,2n)	1.4+7		GRE Expt	Jour	CEA–R–2900	Dec 65	Monnand. SIGMA TO ISOM.STATE GIVEN	
(n,2n)	1.5+7		DEB Comp	Jour	REA 7 4 93	Dec 69	Csikai+ SIG+HL COMPILTN,N–ACTIV–ANAL	
(n,2n)	1.4+7	1.5+7	CCP Comp	Rept	ICD–6 215	70	Sluchevskaja.SIG TO PB205M,2REFS,TBL	
(n,2n)	1.4+7	1.5+7	JYV Eval	Rept	JU–RR–3/1970	Jun 70	Leppaemaeki+ TABLE OF EVAL AVG SIG	
(n,2n)	1.6+7		LND Expt	Jour	PS 2 277	Dec 70	Joensson.LIMITS FROM NAT+RADIOPB GS	
(n,2n)	Maxwl	1.4+7	KFI Expt	Jour	JRC 7 365	Jun 71	Nagy+ SIGMAS, GAM+XRAY ES, HALF–LIFE	
(n,2n)	1.4+7	1.5+7	IRK ExTh	Jour	APA 33 285	Jul 71	Winiwarter+ ISOMERIC RATIO	
(n,2n)	1.5+7		DEB Eval	Jour	REA 11 1 153	Mar 73	Boedy+ RECOMM.VALUE FROM N–Z SYSTEM.	
(n,2n)	1.5+7		KFI Theo	Rept	KFKI–73–68	Dec 73	Jeki.NEW FIT,CALC SIG CFD OTHERS,TBL	
(n,2n)	1.5+7		SMU Expt	Jour	JIN 35 2139	Jul 73	Salaita+ CYCLIC ACTIV, ISOM STATES	+
				Revw Conf	75Wash. 712	Mar 75	– +SHORT–LIVED ISOMER PROD.TBL.	
				Expt Conf	74Columbia 95	Jul 74	– + ACT.SIG TO SHORTLIV ISO.TBL	
	1.5+7			Data	EXFOR10361.	Sep 76	. 1 PT. M–ST CS=866+–69MB.	
(n,2n)	None		LAS Theo	Prog	LA–6472 10	Aug 76	Arthur+ACT CS GNASH CODE CALC.NDG.	
(n,xn) x>2	1.7+7	2.8+7	AMS Expt	Jour	PHY 30 1609	Aug 64	Heertje+EXCIT.LONG–LIVED METAST.STAT	
(n,xn) x>2	Fiss		BNL Theo	Jour	NSE 23 238	Nov 65	Pearlstein.SPEC AVG STATMDL CALC N3N	
(n,xn) x>2	1.4+7		AUWExpt	Conf	75Calcutta 2 31	Dec 75	Lakshmandas+ACT.(N,3N).SIG=1.2+–.6MB	
(n,xn) x>2	None		LAS Theo	Prog	LA–6472 10	Sep 76	Arthur+ACT CS GNASH CODE CALC.NDG	
(n,p)	Fiss		CRC Eval	Rept	CRC–1003	Dec 60	Roy+,ESTIMATED AVG SIG=0.01MB	
(n,p)	1.3+7	1.5+7	JIA Expt	Conf	75Kiev 4 209	May 75	Belovitskij+.SIG,ENERGY DEPEND,E–LVL	+
				Conf	75Leningrd 348	Jan 75	Belovicikij+ ABST. SIG(14.5MEV)=1.8MB	
	1.4+7			Data	EXFOR40347.002	Dec 77	SIG AT 14.5MEV,REL BI–209.1 PNT	
(n,p)	None		LAS Theo	Prog	LA–6472 10	Aug 76	Arthur+ACT CS GNASH CODE CALC.NDG.	
(n,α)	Fiss		CRC Eval	Rept	CRC–1003	Dec 60	Roy+,ESTIMATED AVG SIG=BELO 0.0001MB	
(n,α)	1.4+7		IIT Expt	Jour	NP/A 98 451	Jun 67	YU+ ACTIV. REL AL27 NA	+
				ExTh Abst	DA/B 27 4267	Jun 67	YU+ ACT CFD STATIST MOD	
	1.4+7			Data	EXFOR11583.020	Jun 76	. 1 PT. CS=2.7MB+–15PCT	
(n,α)	1.4+7	1.5+7	JYV Eval	Rept	JU–RR–3/1970	Jun 70	Leppaemaeki+ TABLE OF EVAL AVG SIG	
(n,α)	1.4+7		CCP Expt	Rept	YK–9 50	72	Maslov+ REL CU65(N,2N),NA–I,SIG GIVN	+
				Rept	INDC(CCP)–42	Aug 74	.P10.ENGLISH OF YK–9	
	1.4+7	1.5+7		Data	EXFOR40136.023	Feb 73	.SIGMA AT 2 ES GIVEN	
(n,α)	None		LAS Theo	Prog	LA–6472 10	Aug 76	Arthur+ACT CS GNASH CODE CALC.NDG.	
Fission	2.5+7	8.4+7	BRK Expt	Jour	PR 73 1135	May 48	Kelly+ RELATIVE TO THORIUM.	
Fission	1.4+7		LAS Expt	Jour	PR 75 919	Mar 49	Phillips+ UPPER LIM REL U238.PHOTOPL	
Reson Params	8.5+4	2.0+5	DKE Expt	Jour	AP 14 387	Jul 61	Bilpuch+. WN,WN(P)STF(P) ASSIGNED P	+
	1.5+4	5.0+4		Jour	AP 14 346	Jul 61	Newson+ LVL SEP S,P NEUTS=70,40KEV	
	8.5+4	2.0+5		Data	EXFOR11599.050	Jun 76	. 5 RES. E0,L,WN,WN0	
Reson Params	8.0+5	3.0+6	DLH Theo	Conf	62Madras 86	Feb 62	Nath.ENERGY LEVEL DIAGRAM GVN	
Reson Params	3.4+3	2.5+4	HAR ExTh	Prog	WASH–1048 71	Jun 64	Block.ANAL OF TRANSM DATA.TBL.	
Reson Params	3.4+3	2.5+4	ORL ExTh	Prog	WASH–1048 71	Jun 64	Block.ANALYZ OF HARWELL TRNSDATA,TBL	
Reson Params	1.2+4	7.5+4	ORL Expt	Jour	PR/B 136 695	Nov 64	Macklin+ 7RES FROM N,G. L,WT,WG GVN	+
	1.2+4	7.5+4		Data	EXFOR11575.	Jun 76	. 8 RES. E0,WN,L,WG/WT. 13 RES.WG.	
Reson Params	3.4+3	6.6+4	RPI Expt	Prog	RPI–328–87 24	67	Bartolome+ LINAC+TOF,E0,G*WN*WG/WT	
Reson Params	3.4+3	6.6+4	RPI Expt	Prog	WASH–1074 97	Apr 67	. SUPERSEDED	
Reson Params	3.4+3	6.6+4	RPI Expt	Abst	BAP 12 512	Apr 67	.ABST DH13	
Reson Params		1.0+6	AUA Theo	Jour	AUJ 20 477	Oct 67	Cook. TBL OF AVG LVL SPACING D,L=0,1	
Reson Params	3.4+3	6.6+4	RPI Expt	Prog	WASH–1079 139	Oct 67	. SUPERSEDED	
Reson Params	3.4+3	6.6+4	RPI Expt	Prog	WASH–1127 173	Apr 69	Wolfe+ CAPT TBL,E0,WN,G*WN*WG/WT	
Reson Params	2.1+5	6.2+5	CCP Theo	Jour	IZV 34 2183	Oct 70	Kolomiets.CALC T–WID,J,GIANT RES,TBL	
				Jour	BAS 34 1947	Oct 70	*ENGL OF IZV 34 2183	
Reson Params	3.3+3	4.6+4	CJD Eval	Rept	YK–7	71	Zakharova+ SURVEY+SYSTEMATICS,GW,TBL	
				Rept	INDC(CCP)–27	Nov 72	.ENGLISH TRANSLATION OF YK–7 /71	
Reson Params	1.0+3	4.0+5	ORL Expt	Jour	USNDC–7 172	Jun 73	Good+ TRANS. LINAC. NDG	
Reson Params	None		DUB Theo	Jour	JINR–P4–7499	Oct 73	Soloviev+ CALC D CFD EXPTS,TABLE	
Reson Params	3.4+3	2.0+5	ORL Expt	Jour	PR/C 8 1504	Oct 73	Allen+.ORELA.TED DET.WT G*WG D.29ES.	+
	3.4+3	2.0+5		Data	EXFOR10155.	Jan 78	. 30PTS.WT,WG*G,WG AVG,D,G STF.	
Reson Params	None		DKE Theo	Prog	USNDC–11 231	Jun 74	Divadeenam+ SHELL MDL CALC, NDG	

82 Lead 206

Quantity	Energy (ev) Min	Max	Lab	Type	Documentation Ref Vol Page	Author, Comments Date	Data
Reson Params	3.4+3	6.6+4	RPI Expt	Data	EXFOR12588.004	Jun 76 . 10 RES, WT,WN,WG	+
Strnth Fnctn	3.0+4	1.5+5	DKE Expt	Jour	AP 14 387	Jul 61 Bilpuch+. P WAVE	
Strnth Fnctn	None		AUA Eval	Rept	AAEC/E – 277	Mar 73 Musgrove.TBLS EXPTL DATA+BEST VALUES	
Lvl Density	Fast		ANL Expt	Jour	NP 25 511	Jun 61 Vandenbosh+LVL DENS.FROM OTHER REACT	
Lvl Density	1.4+7		BAS Expt	Jour	PL 5 202	Jul 63 Huber+TBL OF NUC TEMP AND LVL DENSTY	
					HPA 36 1059	Dec 63 Plattner+TOF TBL12ELEM.CFD TH	
Lvl Density	7.0+6		ISL Theo	Conf	64Geneva § 511	May 64 Szwarcbaum+.T FROM 3 FORMLS CFD EXPS	
Lvl Density	None		AUWTheo	Conf	70Madurai 2 267	Dec 70 Ramamurty+ A – PARAMETER GVN,LANG'S – TH	
Lvl Density	5.5+6	8.5+6	ORL Expt	Prog	ORNL – 4909	Jun 74 Kinney+NUC TEMP FROM LEAST SQ FIT.	+
	5.5+6	8.5+6		Data	EXFOR10412.030	Apr 76 . 3 PTS. NUCLEAR TEMPERATURES.	

82 Lead 207

Quantity	Energy (ev) Min	Max	Lab	Type	Documentation Ref Vol Page	Author, Comments Date	Data
Evaluation	3.2-2	1.0+7	GEA Eval	Rept	XDC – 60 – 8 – 81	Jun 59 Roberts.ACT+GAM PROD SIGS,GP AVGD	
Evaluation	1.0-5	2.0+7	ORL Eval	Rept	ORNL – 4765	Mar 72 FU+ ENDF 3. CALC CFD. EXP.	
Total	7.2+4	1.4+5	DKE Expt	Jour	AP 14 387	Jul 61 Bilpuch+ GRPH. RES PAR ANAL.	+
	1.5+4	5.0+4		Jour	AP 14 346	Jul 61 Newson+ TRNS. 4 RESONANCES SEEN	
	3.3+4	6.3+5		Data	EXFOR11011.007	Jun 76 . 1157 PTS.	
Total	1.4+7		CCP ExTh	Jour	ZET 46 1496	Apr 64 5.38+ – .03B,CFD OPTMDL,SHELL.SEP ISOQ	
				Jour	JET 19 1013	Oct 64 TRANSLATN.*	
Total	1.0+4	6.0+4	ORL Expt	Jour	PR/B 136 695	Nov 64 Macklin.TOF TRNS.CURV.3 RES CFD.	+
	1.1+4	5.9+4		Data	EXFOR11575.016	Jun 76 . 143 PTS.	
Total	1.0+5	7.0+5	DKE ExTh	Jour	PL 17 286	Jul 65 Farrell+ .5 KEV INTERVALS 2 – 3KEV RES	
Total	5.0+5	4.1+6	LAS Expt	Priv	DAY	Jul 65 DAY. TABULATED DATA	+
	5.0+5	4.1+6		Data	EXFOR12191.008	Jun 76 . 4 PTS.	
Total	1.4+7		FEI Expt	Prog	INDSWG – 126 33	66 Dukarevich.SIG=5.30+ – 0.05B	
Total	1.4+7		CCP ExTh	Jour	IZV 31 217	Feb 67 Dukarevich+.TBL,CURVES,CFD OPTMDL TH	
				Jour	BAS 31 197	Feb 67 TRANSLATN.*	
Total	1.4+7		FTI Expt	Jour	NP/A 92 433	Feb 67 Dukarevich+ CFD OPTMDL 5.30+ – 0.05B	+
Total	5.0+5	2.5+6	BNL Theo	Rept	BNL – 50151	Oct 68 Moore.ALSO 1MEV.OPTMDL FIT TO DATA	
Total	5.7+9		MHGExpt	Jour	PL/B 31 250	Feb 70 Parker+ GRPHS,RESULTS.CFD OTHERS.	
				Rept	UNIV – MI – 3028 – 3	Nov 69 – +TBLS,DATA GVN,OPT MDL FIT.	
	5.7+9			Data	EXFOR10043.012	Aug 71 . 1 PT. CS=3240+ – 50	
Total	1.5+7	1.7+7	IJI Expt	Conf	72Kiev 2 12	Jan 72 Beneckij+ ABST,NDG.RES – BEHAVIOUR	
Total	1.3+7	1.4+7	IJI Expt	Conf	72Kiev 2 12	Jan 72 Beneckij+ ABST,NDG.SIG(E)	
Total	3.0+5	5.8+5	DKE Theo	Jour	AP 69 451	Feb 72 Seibel+. R – MATRIX ANALYSIS. CURVES.	+
	3.3+5	5.8+5		Expt Data	EXFOR10727.003	Jul 78 . DATA UNOBTAINABLE FROM AUTHOR.	
Total	1.3+5	1.5+7	DEB Eval	Rept	IAEA – 153 173	73 Boedy+ MOST PROBABLE VAL OF SIG,TBL	
				Jour	AHP 30 115	Oct 71 Angeli+ AVG SIG,CFD CALC.TBLS.GRAPH	
Total	1.3+7	1.7+7	CCP Expt	Jour	YF 17 21	Jan 73 Benecky+ SIG(NEUT – E)GRAPH	
				Conf	72Budapest 194	Aug 72 Beneckij+ TOTAL SIG ,GRPH	
				Jour	SNP 17 10	Jul 73 .ENGLISH TRANSLATION	
Total	4.0+4		LRL Expt	Jour	PR/C 9 407	Jan 74 Phillips+STUDY.40.8KEV.RES	
Total	1.6+7	1.7+7	LRL Expt	Jour	YF 19 943	May 74 Anderson+ SIG(E) GRPH,NO RES FOUND	
				Jour	SNP 19 483	Nov 74 . ENGLISH OF YF 19 943	
Total	1.1+7	2.0+7	ORL Expt	Prog	ORNL – 4937 193	May 74 Harvey+GRPH.	
Total	1.6+7	1.8+7	DUB Expt	Jour	JINR – P3 – 9047	Jul 75 Beneckij+ 16.8MEV – RES CONFIRMED,GRPH	
Total	1.5+7	1.8+7	IJI Theo	Conf	77Kiev	77 Benecky+ OPTMOD, NDG,CALCULATION	
Elastic	1.4+6	3.6+6	JAE ExTh	Rept	JAERI – M – 5418	Oct 73 Tomita+GRPH.EXP CFD OPTMOD. 125DEG	
Diff Elastic	1.0+6	2.0+7	LAS Eval	Rept	LA – 2016	Jun 56 Longley+,18ES,ANG DIST 3 – DEG STEPS	
Diff Elastic	1.4+7		LRL Theo	Jour	NP/A 169 385	Jul 61 Canfield+ WOODS – SAX POT A=.207.	
Diff Elastic	4.5+6		FEI Expt	Prog	INDSWG – 120 9	65 Anikin. A=2.5 – 24DEG, NDG	
Diff Elastic	5.0+5	2.5+6	LAS Expt	Priv	DAY	Jul 65 DAY. ANG.DIST.DATA	+
	5.0+5	2.5+6		Data	EXFOR12191.009	Jun 76 . 51 PTS.	
Diff Elastic	5.0+6		ORL Expt	Prog	WASH – 1064 121	Oct 65 Dickens+,TOF,THETA=30 – 130DEG,TBC NDG	
Diff Elastic	1.4+7		RAMTheo	Jour	AP 49 320	Sep 68 Rahman+ STRONG ABSORPTION MODEL,GRPH	
Diff Elastic	1.4+7		CCP Expt	Conf	69Erevan	Feb 69 Belovickij+.ABST,45 – 138 DEGS,EMULS	
Diff Elastic	2.5+6		HEI Theo	Jour	NP/A 135 481	Oct 69 Dover+ RANDOM PHASE APPROX.CURVE.	
Diff Elastic	1.4+7		IJI Expt	Conf	72Budapest 164	Aug 72 Belovickij+ PHOTOEMULS.ANGDIST,GRAPH	+
				Jour	YF 15 662	Apr 72 Belovitskij+ ANGDIST CFD OPTMOD,GRPH	
				Jour	SNP 15 369	Oct 72 .ENGLISH OF YF 15 662	
	1.4+7			Data	EXFOR40288.003	Apr 75 .DATA IN MB/SR AT 5 ANGLS GVN	
Diff Elastic	1.5+6	3.6+6	JAE ExTh	Rept	JAERI – M – 5418	Oct 73 Tomita+GRPH.5 ENS.ANGDISTS CFD CALC	
	1.4+6	3.6+6		Expt Prog	EANDC(J)30L 6	Sep 73 – +.VDG,TOF.CFD C OPTMDL,FIGS	
	1.4+6	3.6+6		Data	EXFOR20340.	Jul 74 193PTS.D/DA,LEG.FIT.	
Diff Elastic	1.7+7		CCP Expt	Conf	74Kharkov 355	Feb 74 Benecky+ ABST,SIG(NEUT – E) AT 7ANGS	

82 Lead 207

Quantity	Energy (ev) Min	Max	Lab	Type	Documentation Ref Vol Page	Author, Comments Date	Data
Diff Elastic	1.0+5	1.5+7	CCP	Eval Data	SOKRATOR – 1037	76 74 PTS	+
Tot Inelastc	1.4+7		LRL	Expt Jour	NIM 15 74	Feb 62 Ruby+A FAST NEUTRON ACTIV DETECTOR	
Tot Inelastc	1.5+7		DEB	Expt Jour	AHP 25 91	Oct 68 Peto+ SUM PB207(NN')+PB208(N2N)	+
	1.5+7			Data	EXFOR30069.005	Dec 70 SUM PB – 207(NN')+PB – 208(N2N)	
Tot Inelastc	1.6+7		LND	Expt Jour	PS 2 277	Dec 70 Joensson.LIMITS FROM NAT+RADIOPB GS	
Tot Inelastc	2.5+6	1.4+7	KFI	Comp Jour	JRC 7 365	Jun 71 Nagy+ SIGMA,GAMMA+ELECTR ES,HALF – LIF	
Tot Inelastc	1.4+6	3.6+6	JAE	ExTh Rept	JAERI – M – 5418	Oct 73 Tomita+GRPH.3 LVLS EXCIT FN CFD CALC	
Tot Inelastc	None		LRL	Theo Jour	PR/C 11 1298	Apr 75 Brown+ CORE POLARIZATION EFFECTS	
Diff Inelast	1.0+6	2.1+6	BNL	ExTh Rept	BNL – 273	Dec 53 Oleksa.HAUSER – FESHB CALC,TBLS,CURVES	+
Diff Inelast	5.0+6	1.0+7	CUW	Eval Rept	CWR – 4040	Jun 58 Kavanagh+,H – F CURVE	
Diff Inelast	2.0+6	8.0+6	LAS	Expt Jour	PR 159 969	Jul 67 Cranberg+ SOME EXCIT FNS, ANG DIST	
	2.5+6	8.0+6		Conf	63Houston 98	Feb 63 .GRPH ANGDIST FOR 3LVLS.SIMILAR BAP	
Diff Inelast	–		BHU	Theo Conf	68Madras 1 291	Feb 68 Sharma+ PPRN39.CALC SIG CFD EXPT,NDG	
Diff Inelast	2.5+6		BNL	Eval Rept	BNL – 50151	Oct 68 Moore.OPTICAL MODEL ANALYSIS	
Diff Inelast		1.5+7	FEI	Eval Rept	INDC – 257	Oct 68 Popov+ 120EVALD PARAMS FOR INEL SCAT	
				Rept	INDC – 257E	68 . ENGL OF INDC – 257	
Diff Inelast	2.5+6		HEI	Theo Jour	NP/A 135 481	Oct 69 Dover+ RANDOM PHASE APPROX.CURVES.	
Diff Inelast	2.5+6		CCP	Comp Rept	ICD – 6 106	70 Sluchevskaja.SIG(ANG) TO LVLS,GRAPHS	
Diff Inelast	1.3+7	1.4+7	IJI	Expt Conf	72Kiev 2 14	Jan 72 Belovickij+ ABST,NDG.N – SPEC AT 2 ES	
Diff Inelast	1.4+7		CCP	Expt Jour	YF 15 666	Apr 72 Belovitskij+ N – SPEC,ANGDIST,GRAPHS	
				Jour	SNP 15 372	Oct 72 *ENGL OF YF 15 666	
				Conf	72Budapest 166	Aug 72 Belovitzky+ PHOTOEMULSN,ANGDIST,GRPH	
Diff Inelast	1.4+7		ITJ	Expt Jour	JRC 14 201	73 Janczyszyn+ ISO – PROD BY NAT – PB ACTIV	+
	1.4+7			Data	EXFOR30322.021	Feb 76 MEAN OF PB207(N,N')+PB208(N,2N)	
Diff Inelast	1.5+6	3.6+6	JAE	ExTh Rept	JAERI – M – 5418	Oct 73 Tomita+GRPH.5 ENS.ANGDISTS CFD CALC	+
	1.4+6	3.6+6		Expt Prog	EANDC(J)30L 6	Sep 73 – +.VDG,TOF.FIGS GIVEN	
				Priv	TOMITA	73 – NUMERICAL VALUES.	
	1.4+6	3.6+6		Data	EXFOR20340.	Jul 74 482PTS.D/DA,LEG.FIT.	
Diff Inelast	5.5+6	8.5+6	ORL	Expt Rept	ORNL – 4909	Jun 74 Kinney+ CFD PREVIOUS RESULTS,OTH.	+
				Conf	75Wash. 883	Mar 75 – +26NUCLIDES ELAS,INEL CS RVW.	
	5.5+6	8.5+6		Data	EXFOR10412.	Sep 74 . 61 PTS. DSIGMA	
Diff Inelast	None		LAS	Theo Prog	LA – 6472 10	Aug 76 Arthur+ACT CS GNASH CODE CALC.NDG	
Diff Inelast	3.4+6		TUD	Expt Prog	ZFK – 315 13	Aug 76 Abdel – Harith+ ABST, NDG	
	3.4+6			Data	EXFOR30464.	Jan 79 PARTIAL,DIFF.PARTL.CS (2 LEVELS)	
Thermal Scat	7.9 – 2		NRI	Expt Prog	INDC(SEC) – 50	Jan 76 Aladdin+ COH SCAT.SIG FREE,BOUND GVN	
Scattering	None		HEI	Theo Jour	NP/A 111 392	Apr 68 Dietrich+.NUMERICL CALC TBD.SEE MANY	
Nonelastic	2.6+6		DLH	Theo Conf	62Madras 86	Feb 62 Nath.VAL FOR SOME EXCITAT LVLS GVN	
Absorption	Pile		HAR	Expt Prog	PPSA 65 761	Sep 52 Aitken+.PILE OSC REL HAR B	+
Res Int Abs	3.1+3	1.8+5	ORL	Expt Jour	PR/C 8 1504	Oct 73 Allen+RES INTEGRAL FOR CAPT GVN.	+
	3.1+3	1.8+5		Data	EXFOR10155.017	Jan 78 . 1PT.RIA=381+ – 23 MB.	
(n,γ)	Maxwl		ORL	Expt Jour	PR 88 412	Oct 52 Pomerance. PILE OSC. TBL.100 ISOTOP.	+
	Maxwl			Data	EXFOR11507.101	Jun 76 . 1 PT. CS=.70+ – 10 PCT.	
(n,γ)	Maxwl		LEB	Expt Jour	PHY 22 1142	Nov 56 Kliger+ LOW LVLS P SNG THR NO COMPNCL	
(n,γ)	3.2 – 2	1.0+7	GEA	Eval Rept	XDC – 60 – 8 – 81	Jun 59 Roberts.7.38MEV GAMMA 19GROUPS	
(n,γ)	Maxwl	+5	FOA	Theo Jour	NP 39 353	Dec 62 Bergqvist+. IN PER CENT OF NAT ELEMT	
(n,γ)	Maxwl		LAS	Expt Conf	63ANL 236	Oct 63 Jurney+CS FROM CAPT SPEC.	+
	Maxwl			Data	EXFOR11133.008	Jun 76 . 1 PT. CS=709+ – 10MB.	
(n,γ)	1.4+4	5.8+4	ORL	Expt Jour	PR/B 136 695	Nov 64 Macklin. TOF CURV SEVERAL CAPT. RES	+
	1.4+4	5.8+4		Data	EXFOR11575.015	Jun 76 . 38 PTS.	
(n,γ)	Maxwl		ORL	Theo Jour	RMP 37 166	Jan 65 Macklin+ CALC FOR KT=5 TO 90 KEV	
(n,γ)	1.5+4	6.0+4	AML	Expt Jour	NP/A 121 329	Dec 68 Broomhall+. REL YIELD 7.41 MEV GAM	
(n,γ)	4.1+4		AUA	Revw Rept	AAEC/TM – 565	Sep 70 Allen.SIG GIVN,CFD G – N SIG AND THEO	
	4.7+4			Expt Prog	AAEC/PR – 40P 34	Jul 74 – + INTERFERENCE EFF STUDIED,NDG	
	4.1+4			Revw		FULL TEXT OF PAPER AT 70CHICAGO (APS	
(n,γ)	–		CCP	Revw Jour	AE 29 187	Sep 70 Sukhoruchkin. (D,P GAM) CFD (N,GAM)	
				Jour	SJA 29 896	Sep 70 TRANSLATN.*	
(n,γ)	4.0+6	1.0+7	COP	Theo Jour	PL/B 33 205	Oct 70 Zimanyi+ IMPROVED SEMIDIRECT CAPT TH	
(n,γ)	2.0+3		MTR	Expt Jour	PR/C 4 2249	Dec 70 Greenwood+ FROM PRIMARY CAPT LINES	+
				Rept	IN – 1407 46	Jun 70 .SUPERSEDED	
	2.0+3			Data	EXFOR10243.004	Nov 72 . 1 PT,SIGMA CS=3.2+ – 1.2B	
(n,γ)	1.8+7		BGN	Expt Rept	BUP – 49	73 Vold+ DP STRIP DIFFSIG VDG	
(n,γ)	2.5+3	6.0+5	ORL	Expt Jour	PR/C 8 1504	73 Allen+RES PAR ANAL,CAPT YLD CURVES	+
	3.0+3	6.4+5		Conf	71Knoxvill 764	Mar 71 Macklin+.LINAC+TOTAL ENERGY DETECTRS	
	3.0+3	2.0+5		Jour	PRL 25 1675	Dec 70 +REL I.TBP.41KEV CAPT. YLD.	
(n,γ)	4.1+4		BNL	Expt Prog	USNDC – 7 36	Jun 73 Wasson+CS DEDUCED FROM ANAL. CFD	
	2.4+4			Prog	USNDC – 7 36	Jun 73 – + REL AU. CS=1.1+ – .3MB.	
(n,γ)	2.5+5	5.0+5	AUA	Expt Rept	AAEC/E – 302	May 74 Broomhall+ NA – I.PARTIAL SIG,GRAPH.	
(n,γ)	1.4+7		LAS	Expt Prog	USNDC – 11 151	Jun 74 Arthur+ ANG DISTR GAMMAS, NDG.	+

82 Lead 207

Quantity	Energy (ev) Min	Max	Lab	Type	Documentation Ref Vol Page	Author, Comments Date	Data
Spect (n,γ)	Maxwl		CCP Theo	Jour	ZET 29 60 866	Dec 55 TH WITHOUT COMPOUND NUCL,LEVEL SCHEM	
				Jour	JET 2 753	Jun 56 . ENGL OF ZET 29 866	
Spect (n,γ)	Maxwl		LAS Expt	Conf	63ANL 236	Oct 63 Jurney+ CS FROM CAPT SPEC	
Spect (n,γ)	1.0+4	1.0+5	ORL Expt	Jour	PR 154 1136	Feb 67 Good+ TOF+NAI XTL,SPECT VAR WITH EN	
				Conf	65Antwerp 68	Jul 65 .SUPERSEDED. PAPER 68.	
Spect (n,γ)	Maxwl		LAS Expt	Prog	WASH – 1127 144	Apr 69 Shera+ GE(LI),TO BE DONE	
Spect (n,γ)	Maxwl		RCN Expt	Jour	NP/A 124 34	Feb 69 Abrahams+GE(LI).BETTER J'S .POLRZ NS	
				Rept	RCN – 105	May 69 – + POL GS.	
				Conf	65Antwerp 510	Jul 65 – + PPR41. CIRC POL GS.	
				Conf	65Antwerp 511	Jul 65 – + PPR42.PARITY CONSEVATION.	
Spect (n,γ)	1.5+4	6.0+4	AUA Expt	Prog	AAEC/PR – 33P 8	70 Broomhall+ TOF+NAI EXPERIMENT, NDG	
Spect (n,γ)	Maxwl		MUN Expt	Jour	ZP 236 440	Oct 70 Egidy+, INTERNAL CONVERSION	
Spect (n,γ)	1.7+4	4.2+4	ORL Comp	Rept	ORNL – TM – 3379	Apr 71 Bird+ SPEC GRPHS. TBL. COMPILATION	
Spect (n,γ)	2.0+3		MTR Expt	Jour	PR/C 4 2249	Dec 71 Greenwood+ CS FROM PRIMARY LINES.	
Spect (n,γ)	Maxwl		BNL Expt	Jour	PR/C 5 178	Jan 72 Mariscotti+. GE(LI) DET	
Spect (n,γ)	Pile		UTR Expt	Jour	NP/A 180 569	Jan 72 Op – Den – Kamp+. E(G) +AS STRONG BACKGR	
Spect (n,γ)	2.4+4		BNL Expt	Prog	USNDC – 7 36	Jun 73 Wasson+ GE(LI). GRPH GND STATE G.	
Spect (n,γ)	None		LIE Theo	Jour	NP/A 222 525	Apr 74 Baudinet – Robinet.STAT CORR PART WID	
Spect (n,γ)	5.7+6		OHO Expt	Prog	ERDA – NDC – 2 165	May 75 Brient+NAICRYS.SPECT.NDG.	
Spect (n,γ)	3.0+6	1.9+7	NJS Theo	Jour	FIZ 7 157	Dec 75 Likar+ SEMIDIR ANGDIS CFD EXPT,CURVE	
Inelastic γ	1.4+6	3.1+6	ORL Theo	Jour	PR 97 1222	Mar 55 Stelson+ 1.6MEVTO3.1MEV LEV ONLY CFD	
Inelastic γ	2.6+6		LAS Expt	Jour	PR 102 767	Apr 56 Day.VALUES AT 2 GAMMA ES AT 95 DEG	+
	2.6+6			Data	EXFOR11218.031	Jun 76 . 2 PTS. DSIG	
Inelastic γ	1.5+7		CCP Expt	Jour	ZET 36 1046	Apr 59 Glagolev. G – SPEC, DISCUSSN OF ISOMRS	
				Jour	JET 9 742	Oct 59 TRANSLATN.*	
Inelastic γ	5.0+5	1.0+7	GEA Eval	Rept	XDC – 60 – 8 – 81	Jun 59 Roberts.7GAMMAS 6GROUPS	
Inelastic γ	4.1+6		ETH Theo	Jour	RMP 38 143	Jan 66 .THEOR CALC OF GAM – RAY ANGL DISTR	
Inelastic γ	6.0+5	4.0+6	IND Theo	Jour	IJP 42 408	Jul 68 Gupta. DIFF INELAST SIG ,H – F TH	
Inelastic γ	1.5+7		LND Expt	Jour	AF 39 295	Sep 69 Joensson+. 80 DEG. 4 TRANSITIONS	+
				Rept	LU – NP – 6804	Mar 68 – + EQUIVALENT TO AF 39 295	
	1.5+7	1.6+7		Data	EXFOR20164.	May 74 4PTS.D/DA.	
Inelastic γ	1.0+6	1.5+7	TNC Expt	Jour	ORO – 2791 – 32	Feb 71 Buchanan+.12NEUT ES,DIFF SIGS TABULT	
	None			ExTh Conf	65Antwerp 34	Jul 65 Morgan+TOF.CFD TH.NDG	
	1.5+6	5.3+6	Expt	Prog	WASH – 1056 123	Mar 65 Nellis.ANG DISTR OF INTENSE GS,NDG	
	4.1+6	1.5+7		Rept	TID – 20658	Sep 63 Morgan+ANG DIST. SPEC, PROD CS.	
	4.0+6			Prog	TID – 20657 36	62 Nellis+.CURVE OF GAMMA ANGULAR DISTR	
	1.0+6	1.5+7		Rept	AD – 154995	Feb 58 Bostrom+ 7NEUT ES GAMMA PRODUCT SIGS	
Inelastic γ	2.5+6	1.4+7	KFI Comp	Jour	JRC 7 365	Jun 71 Nagy+ SIGMA,GAMMA+ELECTR ES,HALF – LIF	
Inelastic γ	1.8+6	1.4+7	LAS Expt	Abst	BAP 7 334	Apr 62 Shunk+ NAI. TBL. 8PCT ACC.	+
	1.8+6	1.4+7		Data	EXFOR12188.002	Jun 76 . 11 PTS. SIGMA	
Inelastic γ	1.0+6	1.0+7	KUR Expt	Conf	77Kiev	77 Savin+ SIG(NEUT – E),GRAPH	
Nonelastic γ	1.5+7		ARK Expt	Prog	A – ARK – 61 1	Jan 61 Chittenden+ TOF. G PROD CS.	+
	1.5+7			Data	EXFOR11132.	Jun 76 . 14 PTS.	
Nonelastic γ	4.9+6	8.0+6	ORL Expt	Prog	NCSAC – 42 194	Nov 71 Dickens. GE(LI) DET. GAMMA SPECTRA	
(n,2n)	Fiss		CRC Eval	Rept	CRC – 1003	Dec 60 Roy+,ESTIMATED AVG SIG =21.0MB	
(n,2n)	1.3+7	1.5+7	BNL Theo	Jour	NSE 23 238	Nov 65 Pearlstein.3ES.STAT MDL CALC.TBL CS.	
(n,2n)	Fiss		BNL Theo	Jour	NSE 23 238	Nov 65 Pearlstein.STATMDL CALC.SPEC AVG.TBL	
(n,2n)	1.4+7		GRE Expt	Rept	CEA – R – 2900	Dec 65 Monnand. SIGMA TO ISOM.STATE GIVEN	
(n,2n)	1.6+7		LND Expt	Jour	PS 2 277	Dec 70 Joensson.LIMITS FROM NAT+RADIOPB GS	+
	1.5+7			Jour	AF 39 295	Sep 69 – +. 80 DEG. 1 GAMMA.ESTIMATE.	
				Rept	LU – NP – 6804	Mar 68 – + EQUIVALENT TO AF 39 295	
	1.5+7	1.6+7		Data	EXFOR20164.035	May 74 1PNT.D/DA.	
(n,2n)	1.4+7		KFI Comp	Jour	JRC 7 365	Jun 71 Nagy+ SIGMA, GAMMA – E AND HALF – L GIVN	
(n,2n)	1.5+7		DEB Eval	Rept	REA 11 1 153	Mar 73 Boedy+ RECOMM.VALUE FROM N – Z SYSTEM.	
(n,2n)	1.5+7		KFI Theo	Rept	KFKI – 73 – 68	Dec 73 Jeki.NEW FIT,CALC SIG CFD OTHERS,TBL	
(n,2n)	1.5+7		SMU Expt	Jour	JIN 35 2139	Jul 73 Salaita+ CYCLIC ACTIV, ISOM STATES	+
				Conf	75Wash. 712	Mar 75 – +SHORT – LIVED ISOMER PROD.TBL.	
				Conf	74Columbia 95	Jul 74 – + ACT.SIG TO SHORTLIV ISO.TBL	
	1.5+7			Data	EXFOR10361.	Jun 74 1 PT INCLUDES INELAS SCAT ON PB – 206	
(n,2n)	2.0+6	2.0+7	LAS Theo	Prog	LA – 6472 10	Aug 76 Arthur+ACT CS GNASH CODE CALC.CURV	
(n,xn) x>2	Fiss		BNL Theo	Jour	NSE 23 238	Nov 65 Pearlstein.SPEC AVG STATMDL CALC N3N	
(n,xn) x>2	None		LAS Theo	Prog	LA – 6472 10	Aug 76 Arthur+ACT CS GNASH CODE CALC.NDG.	
(n,p)	Fiss		CRC Eval	Rept	CRC – 1003	Dec 60 Roy+,ESTIMATED AVG SIG =0.002MB	
(n,p)	1.3+7	1.5+7	JIA Expt	Jour	75Kiev 4 209	May 75 Belovitskij+ .SIG,ENERGY DEPEND,E – LVL	+
				Conf	75Leningrd 348	Jan 75 Belovickij+ ABST. SIG(14.5MEV)=1.5MB	
	1.4+7			Data	EXFOR40347.003	Dec 77 SIG AT 14.5MEV,REL BI – 209.1 PNT	
(n,p)	None		LAS Theo	Prog	LA – 6472 10	Aug 76 Arthur+ACT CS GNASH CODE CALC.NDG	
(n,np)	None		LAS Theo	Prog	LA – 6472 10	Aug 76 Arthur+ACT CS GNASH CODE CALC.NDG	

82 Lead 207

Quantity	Energy (ev) Min	Max	Lab	Type	Documentation Ref Vol Page	Author, Comments Date	Data
(n,α)	Fiss		CRC	Eval Rept	CRC - 1003	Dec 60 Roy+,ESTIMATED AVG SIG=BELO 0.0001MB	
Fission	2.5+7	8.4+7	BRK	Expt Jour	PR 73 1135	May 48 Kelly+ RELATIVE TO THORIUM.	
Fission	1.4+7		LAS	Expt Jour	PR 75 919	Mar 49 Phillips+ UPPER LIM REL U238.PHOTOPL	
Reson Params	2.0+4	1.4+5	DKE	Expt Jour	AP 14 387	Jul 61 Bilpuch+. WN(S,P) STF(S)	+
	1.5+4	5.0+4		Jour	AP 14 346	Jul 61 Newson+ LVL SEP, S,P NEUTS=19,70KEV	
	2.0+4	1.4+5		Data	EXFOR11599.051	Jun 76 . 7 RES. EO,L,WN.	
Reson Params	-		FOA	Theo Jour	NP 39 353	Dec 62 Bergqvist+.AVERAGE GAMMA WIDTH.	
Reson Params	3.1+3	2.4+4	HAR	ExTh Prog	WASH - 1048 71	Jun 64 Block.ANAL OF TRANSM DATA.TBL.	
Reson Params	3.1+3	2.4+4	ORL	Theo Prog	WASH - 1048 71	Jun 64 Block.ANALYZ OF HARWELL TRNSDATA,TBL	
Reson Params	1.7+4	4.1+4	ORL	Expt Jour	PR/B 136 695	Nov 64 Macklin+ 4RES FROM N,G.DATA	+
	1.2+4	4.1+4		Data	EXFOR11575.	Jun 76 . 5 RES. EO,J,L,WG. 13 RES WT.	
Reson Params	3.0+3	4.1+4	RPI	Expt Prog	RPI - 328 - 87 24	67 Bartolome+ LINAC+TOF,E0,G*WN*WG/WT	
Reson Params	4.1+4		ORL	Expt Jour	PR 153 1356	Jan 67 Gibbons+ VDG. TOF.	+
Reson Params	3.0+3	4.1+4	RPI	Expt Prog	WASH - 1074 97	Apr 67 . SUPERSEDED	
Reson Params	3.0+3	4.1+4	RPI	Expt Abst	BAP 12 512	Apr 67 .ABST DH13	
Reson Params		1.0+6	AUA	Theo Jour	AUJ 20 477	Oct 67 Cook. TBL OF AVG LVL SPACING D,L=0,1	
Reson Params	3.0+3	4.1+4	RPI	Expt Prog	WASH - 1079 139	Oct 67 . SUPERSEDED	
Reson Params	3.0+3	4.1+4	RPI	Expt Prog	WASH - 1127 173	Apr 69 Wolfe+ CAPT TBL,E0,WN,G*WN*WG/WT	
Reson Params	3.1+3	4.3+4	CJD	Eval Rept	YK - 7	71 Zakharova+ SURVEY+SYSTEMATICS,GW,TBL	
				Rept	INDC(CCP) - 27	Nov 72 .ENGLISH TRANSLATION OF YK-7 /71	
Reson Params	9.0+4	9.0+5	LRL	Expt Abst	BAP 18 539	Apr 73 Phillips+. TOF. NO DATA GIVEN.	
Reson Params	3.1+3	1.8+5	ORL	Expt Jour	PR/C 8 1504	Oct 73 Allen+.ORELA.TED DET.WT G*WG D.11ES.	+
	3.1+3	7.0+5		Conf	71Knoxvill 764	Mar 71 - + FROM CAPTURE MEAS.	
	3.1+3	7.0+5		Data	EXFOR10155.	Jan 78 .152 PTS.WG*G*WN/WT,D,G,STF,J,PI.	
Reson Params	None		LIE	Theo Jour	NP/A 222 525	Apr 74 Baudinet - Robinet.STAT CORR PART WID	
Reson Params	3.0+4	4.9+4	AUA	Expt Rept	AAEC/E - 302	May 74 Broomhall+ NA - I,VDG.CAPT RES - ES GIVN	
Reson Params	1.1+7	2.0+7	ORL	Expt Prog	ORNL - 4937 193	May 74 Harvey+STUDY 16.8MEV RES.	
Reson Params	3.0+3	4.1+4	RPI	Expt Data	EXFOR12588.005	Jun 76 . 6 RES, WT,WN,WG	+
Strnth Fnctn	3.0+4	1.5+5	DKE	Expt Jour	AP 14 387	Jul 61 Bilpuch+. S,P WAVE	
Strnth Fnctn	None		AUA	Eval Rept	AAEC/E - 277	Mar 73 Musgrove.TBLS EXPTL DATA+BEST VALUES	
Strnth Fnctn	3.1+3	7.0+5	ORL	Expt Jour	PR/C 8 1504	Oct 73 Allen+CAPT MEAS.G STF,STF GVN.	+
				Conf	71Knoxvill 764	Mar 71 - +S,P WAVE STF.CAPT STF CFD TRNS	
	3.1+3	7.0+5		Data	EXFOR10155.	Jan 78 . 2PTS.S0=(.15+ - .8)-4,S1=(1.1+ - 1)-4	
Lvl Density	+6		MIL	Theo Jour	EN 15 1 54	Jan 68 Facchini+ LDL PARS FROM LOW EN RES	
Lvl Density	None		AUW	Theo Conf	70Madurai 2 267	Dec 70 Ramamurty+ A - PARAMETER GVN,LANG'S - TH	
Lvl Density	None		MUN	Theo Jour	NP/A 217 269	Dec 73 Dilg+ A,DELTA. BACK SHIFTED FERMIGAS	
Lvl Density	None		COP	Theo Jour	NP/A 222 493	Apr 74 Dossing+COLL ROTAT.SPAC. ACCUR ESTIM	
Lvl Density	None		DUB	Theo Jour	NP/A 224 411	May 74 Soloviev+ 1/2 MICROSC MDL. SPH NUCL.	
Lvl Density	None		ROC	Theo Jour	NP/A 223 577	May 74 Huizenga+ EXP CFD MICROSC TH SPH NUC	
Lvl Density	5.5+6	8.5+6	ORL	Expt Prog	ORNL - 4909	Jun 74 Kinney+NUC TEMP FROM LEAST SQ FIT.	+
	5.5+6	8.5+6		Data	EXFOR10412.031	Apr 76 4 PTS.NUCLEAR TEMPERATURES.	
(γ,n)	2.5+4	3.5+5	AUA	Revw Rept	AAEC/TM - 565	Sep 70 Allen.GRPH.EXPT CONFIRMD ASYM.CFD TH	
				-		FULL TEXT OF PAPER AT 70CHICAGO (APS	

82 Lead 208

Quantity	Energy (ev) Min	Max	Lab	Type	Documentation Ref Vol Page	Author, Comments Date	Data
Evaluation	2.2+6	1.0+7	GEA	Eval Rept	XDC - 60 - 8 - 81	Jun 59 Roberts.ACT+GAM PROD SIGS,GP AVGD	
Evaluation	1.0 - 5	2.0+7	ORL	Eval Rept	ORNL - 4765	Mar 72 FU+ ENDF 3 CALC CFD EXPT.	
Total	3.5+5	7.2+5	DKE	Expt Jour	PR 121 1150	Feb 61 Wilenzick+ TOF. RES. PARS.	+
Total	8.0+4	1.2+5	DKE	Expt Jour	AP 14 387	Jul 61 Bilpuch+ RES.PAR. ANAL.	+
Total	7.2+5	1.9+6	ORL	Expt Jour	PR 127 2192	Sep 62 Fowler+, TRNS,FIGS+RES PARS.3KV RSLN	+
	5.5+5	4.3+6		Conf	60Kingston 474	Aug 60 - .CURVE,T(P,N) NEUTRON SOURCE	
	7.2+5	1.9+6		Data	EXFOR12215.003	Jun 76 . 536 PTS.	
Total	4.0+4	1.0+6	DKE	Expt Priv	BILPUCH	Nov 62 Bilpuch. TABULATED DATA	+
	4.0+4	1.0+6		Data	EXFOR11011.008	Jun 76 . 1292 PTS.	
Total	1.4+7		CCP	ExTh Jour	ZET 46 1496	Apr 64 5.33+ - .04B,CFD OPTMDL,SHELL.SEP ISOQ	
				Jour	JET 19 1013	Oct 64 TRANSLATN.*	
Total	9.8+5		SHE	Theo Jour	NP 54 417	Jun 64 Maddison.OPTMOD FIT TO TOWLE GILBOY	
Total	7.0+5	3.0+6	BNL	Theo Jour	PR/B 135 895	Aug 64 Auerbach+ OPTMDL CFD EXPT	
Total	1.0+5	7.0+5	DKE	ExTh Jour	PL 17 286	Jul 65 Farrell+ .5 KEV INTERVALS 2 - 3KEV RES	
Total	5.0+5	4.1+6	LAS	Expt Priv	DAY	Jul 65 DAY. TABULATED DATA.	+
	5.0+5	4.1+6		Data	EXFOR12191.010	Jun 76 . 4 PTS.	
Total	1.4+7		FEI	Expt Prog	INDSWG - 126 33	66 Dukarevich.SIG=5.26+ - 0.04B	
Total	2.6+4	8.4+4	ORL	Expt Jour	PR 153 1356	Jan 67 Gibbons+ VDG TOF, CURV,2RES 70,77KEV	+
				Prog	WASH - 1048 76	Jun 64 .SUPERSEDED	
	2.4+4	8.8+4		Data	EXFOR12218.002	Jun 76 . 120 PTS.	

82 Lead 208

Quantity	Energy (ev) Min	Energy (ev) Max	Lab	Type	Documentation Ref Vol Page	Author, Comments Date	Data
Total	1.4+7		CCP	ExTh	Jour IZV 31 217	Feb 67 Dukarevich+.TBL,CURVES,CFD OPTMDL TH	
					Jour BAS 31 197	Feb 67 TRANSLATN.*	
Total	1.4+7		FTI	Expt	Jour NP/A 92 433	Feb 67 Dukarevich+ CFD OPTMDL 5.26+ −0.04B	+
Total	1.0+6	1.0+7	TRM	Theo	Conf 67Karlsrhe 1 95	Nov 67 Garg+ OPTMOD CALC,CFD EXPT,TBL+GRPH	
Total	5.0+5	2.5+6	BNL	Theo	Rept BNL−50151	Oct 68 Moore.ALSO 1MEV.OPTMDL FIT TO DATA	
Total	2.5+6	1.5+7	BNW	Expt	Jour PR/C 3 576	Feb 71 Foster+,TRANS,CURVS,CFD OTHERS+TH	+
					Jour NIM 36 1	Sep 65 .EXPT DETAILS	
	2.5+6	1.5+7			Data EXFOR10047.092	Aug 73 . 231 PTS.	
Total	1.3+7	1.4+7	IJI	Expt	Conf 72Kiev 2 12	Jan 72 Beneckij+ ABST,NDG.SIG(E)	
Total	1.3+7	1.5+7	DEB	Eval	Rept IAEA−153 173	73 Boedy+ MOST PROBABLE VAL OF SIG,TBL	
					Jour AHP 30 115	Oct 71 Angeli+ AVG SIG,CFD CALC.TBLS.GRAPH	
	1.3+7	1.7+7	CCP	Expt	Jour YF 17 21	Jan 73 Benecky+ SIG(NEUT−E)	
					Jour SNP 17 10	Jul 73 .ENGLISH TRANSLATION	
Total	1.0+3	4.0+5	ORL	Expt	Prog USNDC−7 172	Jun 73 Good+. TRANS. LINAC. NO DATA GIVEN.	
	+3	+6			Prog ORNL−4844 47	Apr 73 − +ORELA.NDG	
Total	4.0+6		KUR	Expt	Jour YF 21 945	May 75 Morozov+ FILTERD+UNFILT ANGDIS,GRPHS	
					Jour SNP 21 485	May 75 .ENGLISH OF YF 21 945	
Total	2.0+5	6.0+5	LRL	Theo	Jour PR/C 12 713	Aug 75 Ferguson. TOT.FOR.S,D WAVES SHOWN	
Total	7.0+5	1.5+6	ORL	Expt	Abst BAP 20 537	Apr 76 Fowler+TRNS.TOF.100 RES OBS.NDG	
Elastic	Maxwl		GER	Theo	Jour PA 60 7 57	Jan 57 Hunger+ APPROX SOL Z ASTROPHYS 39 4	
Elastic	4.0+6	1.6+7	LAS	Theo	Rept LA−3538	Sep 66 Agee+ OPTMDL MODEL+H−F FOR COMP	
Elastic	1.0+5	3.0+6	KTY	Theo	Jour NP/A 225 61	Jun 74 Mackellar+ LOCAL EQUIV TO NONCOC POT	
Elastic	1.0+5	1.2+7	WAY	Theo	Jour PR/C 10 1223	Sep 74 LEV+ S−WAVE,IMAGIN OPT−POT CALC,CURV	
	0.0+0	1.2+7			Jour PR/C 9 2416	Jun 74 LEV+ COMPLEX OPTMDL POT FOR N−SCAT	
Diff Elastic	1.0+6		LAS	Eval	Rept LA−2016	Jun 56 Longley+,TBL ANG DIST 3−DEG STEPS	
Diff Elastic	1.2+6	3.2+6	ORL	Expt	Jour PR 127 2192	Sep 62 Fowler+,ALSO2.2MEV 50KEV RSLN	
Diff Elastic	1.5+6	4.2+6	TEX	Expt	Abst DA 23 3938	Apr 63 Brandenberger.CFD PB206 FOR CPD.DEL6	
Diff Elastic	3.5+6	4.1+6	ALD	Expt	Jour NP 44 256	Jun 63 Towle+,TOF,TOT ELASTIC BY INT.,GRAPH	
Diff Elastic	9.8+5		SHE	Theo	Jour NP 54 417	Jun 64 Maddison.OPTMOD FIT TO TOWLE GILBOY	
Diff Elastic	1.2+6	2.2+6	BNL	Theo	Jour PR/B 135 895	Aug 64 Auerbach+ OPTMDL CFD EXPT.	
Diff Elastic	5.0+5	2.5+6	LAS	Expt	Priv DAY	Jul 65 DAY. ANG DIST. DATA	+
	5.0+5	2.5+6			Data EXFOR12191.011	Jun 76 . 111 PTS.	
Diff Elastic	3.1+6		TEX	Expt	Abst DA 26 1112	Aug 65 Spahn.TOF METHOD.NDG	
Diff Elastic	8.0+5	4.5+6	ORL	Theo	Rept ORNL−TM−1238	Sep 65 Smith. H−F ANALYSIS GOOD AGREEMENT	
Diff Elastic	7.2+5	1.8+6	ORL	Expt	Jour PR 147 870	Jul 66 Fowler. ABS CURVS 29ES,PHASE SHIFTS	+
	7.2+5	1.8+6			Data EXFOR12217.002	Jun 76 . 306 PTS.	
Diff Elastic	1.5+7		CCP	Theo	Jour IZV 30 1357	Aug 66 Docenko+.GRAPH,NONLOCAL OPT POTNTIAL	
					Jour BAS 30 1416	66 . ENGL OF IZV 30 1357	
Diff Elastic	4.0+6	1.6+7	LAS	Theo	Rept LA−3538	Sep 66 Agee+ OPTMDL MODEL+H−F FOR COMP	
Diff Elastic	3.1+6	1.6+7	LAS	Theo	Rept LA−3788	67 Beery+.OPTMOD CALC POLARIZ ANG DISTR	
Diff Elastic	1.4+7		LEB	Expt	Jour IZV 32 2044	Dec 68 Belovitskij+ ANGDIST GRPH,CFD OPTMOD	
					Jour BAS 32 1880	Dec 69 . ENGL OF IZV 32 2044	
Diff Elastic	7.0+6	1.4+7	ALA	Expt	Jour PR 178 1647	Feb 69 Dotsenko.CURVE OPTMDL ANAL,CFD EXPT	
Diff Elastic	1.4+7		CCP	Expt	Conf 69Erevan	Feb 69 Belovickij+.ABST,45−138 DEGS,EMULS	
Diff Elastic	1.4+7		OSP	Expt	Prog EANDC(J)13L36	Aug 69 Azuma+. VDG,TOF	
Diff Elastic	2.2+6	4.1+6	AUA	Theo	Rept AAEC/TM−545	Jul 70 Bertram. SIG(ANG) GRAPHS AT 3 N−ES	
Diff Elastic	1.8+6		CCP	Expt	Jour ZEP 14 137	Jul 71 Morozov+ DIFFSIG 12 TO 168 DEG.GRAPH	
					Jour JEL 14 91	Jul 71 . ENGL OF ZEP 14 137	
Diff Elastic	5.5+6	8.5+6	ORL	Expt	Rept ORNL−4909	Jun 74 Kinney+ CFD PREVIOUS RESULTS,OTH.3ES	+
					Conf 75Wash. 883	Mar 75 − +26NUCLIDES ELAS,INEL CS RVW.	
	5.5+6	8.5+6			Data EXFOR10412.	Sep 74 66PTS,DSIGMA. LEG COEF AT 3 ENERG	
Diff Elastic	4.0+6		KUR	Expt	Jour SNP 21 485	May 75 .ENGLISH OF YF 21 945 (NO DATA GIVN)	
Diff Elastic	1.8+6		KUR	ExTh	Conf 75Zurich 609	Aug 75 Morozov+ GRPH EXPT CFD OPTMOD CALC	+
				Expt	Prog YFI−12 37	72 − + ABST,SIG AT 12−168 DEG,TBL	
					Prog YFI−14 8	72 − + SIG(ANG),TBL,SCAT AT 17ANGS	
					Conf 71Kiev 1 267	May 71 − +	
					Prog INDC(CCP)−30	Sep 72 .PAGE 33,ENGLISH OF YFI−12 37	
	1.8+6				Data EXFOR40075.004	Jul 73 .17SIG(ANG) GVN	
Diff Elastic	1.3+7	1.5+7	CCP	Expt	Rept YK−23 114	76 Belovicky+ OPTMOD,SIG(ANG),GRAPHS	
Diff Elastic	1.3+7	1.5+7	IJI	Expt	Rept YK−23 128	76 Belovickij+ OPTMOD,SIG(ANG),GRAPHS	+
	1.4+7				Conf 72Budapest 164	Aug 72 − + PHOTOEMULS.ANGDIST,GRAPH	
					Jour YF 15 662	Apr 72 Belovitskij+ ANGDIST CFD OPTMOD,GRPH	
					Jour SNP 15 369	Oct 72 .ENGLISH OF YF 15 662	
	1.4+7				Data EXFOR40288.004	Apr 75 .DATA IN MB/SR AT 12 ANGLS GVN	
Diff Elastic	1.4+7		LIE	Theo	Jour FIZS 9 3 79	77 Lejeune. OPTMOD ANALYSIS.GRAPH	
Polarization	3.1+6	1.6+7	LAS	Theo	Rept LA−3788	67 Beery+.OPTMOD CALC COS(THETA) DISTR	
Polarization	4.0+6		IJI	Theo	Jour YF 13 1026	May 71 Pasechnik+ POLRZ(ANG) CFD EXPT,GRAPH	
					Jour SNP 13 589	Nov 71 . ENGL OF YF 13 1026	

82 Lead 208

Quantity	Energy (ev) Min	Max	Lab	Type	Documentation Ref Vol Page	Author, Comments Date	Data
Polarization	1.4+7		IJI Theo	Jour	YF 18 1203	Dec 73 Ivanjuk+ SHELL CORR, POL(ANG),GRAPH	
				Jour	SNP 18 616	Jun 74 .ENGLISH OF YF 18, 1203.	
Polarization	1.8+6		KUR ExTh	Conf	75Zurich 609	Aug 75 Morozov+ GRPH EXPT CFD OPTMOD CALC	
			Expt	Prog	YFI- 14 8	72 - + POLARIZATION GVN,TBL	
Potntl Scat		8.4+4	ORL Expt	Jour	PR 153 1356	Jan 67 Gibbons+ EFFECTIVE RADIUS =8.4+ -.3F	
Potntl Scat	1.0+6	1.0+7	TRM Theo	Conf	67Karlsrhe 1 95	Nov 67 Garg+ OPTMOD CALC,TBL	
Tot Inelastc	4.0+6	1.8+7	OSU Theo	Jour	NP 33 626	Jun 62 Payne+EXCITATION OF2.62MEV LVL	
Tot Inelastc	3.2+6	4.5+6	ALD Expt	Jour	NP 44 256	Jun 63 Towle+ TOF.INT OF 55DEG MEAS.T.3LVLS	+
Tot Inelastc	2.6+6	4.6+6	BNL Theo	Jour	PR/B 135 895	Aug 64 Auerbach+ OPTMDL CALC. CFD EXPT.	
	+6			Conf	65Antwerp 25	Jul 65 Auerbach+NDG COMPLEX POTENTIAL MODL	
Tot Inelastc	3.1+6		TNC ExTh	Rept	ORO – 2791 – 23	Feb 67 Mathur+,WIDTH - FLUCTUATION CORRECTION	
Tot Inelastc	1.0+6	1.0+7	TRM Theo	Conf	67Karlsrhe 1 95	Nov 67 Garg+ H - F THEO CFD MOLDAUER THEO.NDG	
Tot Inelastc	1.0+5	7.0+6	AUA Theo	Prog	AAEC/PR – 31P 9	Apr 69 Bertram. H - F CALCULTN CFD XPTS,N47	
Tot Inelastc	1.6+7		LND Expt	Jour	PS 2 277	Dec 70 Joensson.LIMITS FROM NAT+RADIOPB GS	
Diff Inelast	5.0+6	1.0+7	CUWEval	Rept	CWR – 4040	Jun 58 Kavanagh+,H - F CURVE	
Diff Inelast	3.2+6	4.5+6	ALD Expt	Jour	NP 44 256	Jun 63 Towle+TO 2.6,3.2,3.5MEV.	+
				Rept	AERE – R – 4131 27	Sep 62 - +TOF.ANG DIST,2.6MEV.OTHER LVLS	
Diff Inelast	4.0+6		BNL Theo	Jour	PR/B 135 895	Aug 64 Auerbach+ OPTMDL CALC. CFD EXPT.	
Diff Inelast	7.4+6		FOA Expt	Conf	65Antwerp 504	Jul 65 Bergqvist+ N' SPECT +G SPECT.PPR27.	
Diff Inelast	8.0+5	4.5+6	ORL Theo	Rept	ORNL – TM – 1238	Sep 65 Smith. H - F ANALYSIS GOOD AGREEMENT	
Diff Inelast	3.2+6	4.5+6	BNL Eval	Rept	BNL – 50151	Oct 68 Moore.OPTMDL ANAL,2.6,3.2,3.5MEV LVL	
Diff Inelast		1.5+7	FEI Eval	Rept	INDC – 257	Oct 68 Popov+ 120EVALD PARAMS FOR INEL SCAT	
				Rept	INDC – 257E	68 . ENGL OF INDC – 257	
Diff Inelast	1.4+7		LEB Expt	Jour	IZV 32 2044	Dec 68 Belovitskij+ ANG+E SPEC GRPHS,OPTMOD	
				Jour	BAS 32 1880	Dec 69 . ENGL OF IZV 32 2044	
Diff Inelast	1.4+7		OSP Expt	Prog	EANDC(J)13L36	Aug 69 Azuma+.VDG,TOF SIG AT 35DEG GIVEN	
Diff Inelast	2.0+6	5.0+6	AUA Theo	Rept	AAEC/TM – 545	Jul 70 Bertram. SIG(E) GRAPHS FOR SOME LVLS	
Diff Inelast	1.3+7	1.4+7	IJI Expt	Conf	72Kiev 2 14	Jan 72 Belovickij+ ABST,NDG.N - SPEC AT 2 ES	
Diff Inelast	1.4+7		CCP Expt	Jour	YF 15 666	Apr 72 Belovitskij+ N - SPEC,ANGDIST,GRAPHS	
				Jour	SNP 15 372	Oct 72 *ENGL OF YF 15 666	
				Conf	72Budapest 166	Aug 72 Belovitzky+ PHOTOEMULSN,ANGDIST,GRPH	
Diff Inelast	5.5+6	8.5+6	ORL Expt	Rept	ORNL – 4909	Jun 74 Kinney+ CFD PREVIOUS RESULTS,OTH.	+
				Conf	75Wash. 883	Mar 75 +26NUCLIDES ELAS,INEL CS RVW.	
	5.5+6	8.5+6		Data	EXFOR10412.	Sep 74 . 254 PTS.DSIGMA	
Nonelastic	4.1+6		DLH Theo	Conf	62Madras 86	Feb 62 Nath.VAL FOR SOME EXCITAT LVLS GVN	
Nonelastic	1.4+6		LSU Expt	Jour	PR 132 1211	Nov 63 Haas+ SPH TRANS SIG=2.58+ – 0.09	+
				Abst	DA 24 4747	May 64 - . SPHERE TRANS.SIG,RAD CFD PB20	
	1.4+6			Data	EXFOR11794.005	Jun 76 . 1 PT.	
Absorption	2.5-2	2.5-2	FAR Expt	Rept	EANDC(E)49 8	Oct 63 Cabe. PILE OSCILLATOR. 1 VALUE GIVEN	+
Absorption	1.0+5	1.2+7	WAYTheo	Jour	PR/C 10 1223	Sep 74 LEV+ INTERMED STRUCT,OPTMDL.SIG - CURV	
Res Int Abs	2.5+3	7.8+4	ORL Expt	Jour	PR/C 8 1504	Oct 73 Allen+RES INTEGRAL FOR CAPT GVN.	+
	2.5+3	7.8+4		Data	EXFOR10155.019	Jan 78 . 1PT.RIA=2.8+ – .3 MB.	
(n,γ)	Fiss		ANL Expt	Jour	PR 75 1781	Jun 49 Hughes+ REL SIG(THERMAL),FOIL ACTIVN	
	Fiss			Data	EXFOR11450.039	Jun 76 . 1 PT.	
(n,γ)	Maxwl		ORL Expt	Jour	PR 88 412	Oct 52 Pomerance.PILE OSC.100 ISOTOPES.TBL	+
	Maxwl			Data	EXFOR11507.102	Jun 76 . 1 PT. CS=0(+.03)	
(n,γ)	Fiss		BNL Expt	Jour	PR 91 1423	Sep 53 Hughes+.ALSO LVL SPACINGS AT EXCIT E	
(n,γ)	-		LEB Expt	Jour	PHY 22 1142	Nov 56 Kliger+,LOW LVLS P SNG THR NO COMPNCL	
(n,γ)	2.0+5	4.0+6	KUR Expt	Conf	58Geneva 15 50	Sep 58 Leipunskij+.PPR2219,TBL AT 3ES	+
(n,γ)	1.4+7		ALD Expt	Jour	PPS 72 505	Oct 58 Perkin+ACT ANAL 3.05MB+ – 15PC,B - W TH	+
(n,γ)	Fiss		KUR Revw	Conf	60Vienna 159	Oct 60 Bondarenko+.TABLE FOR 1E ,EXPT DSCRB	
(n,γ)	Maxwl	+5	FOA Theo	Jour	NP 39 353	Dec 62 Bergqvist+. IN PER CENT OF NAT ELEMT	
(n,γ)	Maxwl		LAS Expt	Prog	WASH – 1044	Aug 63 Carter+ FROM STR CAPT GS .3MB	
(n,γ)	2.5-3		CCP Theo	Conf	66Moscow	Feb 66 .TBL GIVEN	
(n,γ)	5.0+6	2.5+7	HEB Theo	Jour	NP 79 257	Apr 66 Gutfreund+DIRECT CAPTURE SIG CALCUL.	
(n,γ)	2.4+4		MUAExpt	Jour	PR 152 1055	Dec 66 Chaubey+ BETA - DET,SIG REL I - 127,TBL	+
			Theo	Jour	IJP 42 567	Sep 68 - + METHD OF BOOTH,VAL CFD XPT	
	2.4+4		Expt	Data	EXFOR30079.042	Dec 70 SIGMA FOR 3.3 H HALF - LIFE	
(n,γ)	7.0+6	7.7+4	ORL Expt	Jour	PR 159 1007	Jul 67 Macklin+ TOF,SIG - AREA 2RES=CA375B - EV	
(n,γ)	+6	+7	LOK Expt	Prog	WASH – 1079 94	Oct 67 Grench+ TBD	
(n,γ)	+7		BOL Theo	Jour	NC/B 52 2 539	Dec 67 Longo+DIR AND COLLECTIVE TH OKS EXPT	
(n,γ)	1.3+7	1.5+7	DEB Expt	Jour	MFF 16 123	Feb 68 Csikai+,ACTIV,SIG(E)/SIG(14.7),GRAPH	+
				Jour	NP/A 95 229	Mar 67 EQUIVALENT*	
	1.5+7			Data	EXFOR30067.018	Nov 70 VALUE AT 14.7 MEV,(=NP/A 95,TBL 1)	
	1.3+7	1.5+7		Data	EXFOR30074.007	Nov 70 SIGMA AT 8ES REL VALUE AT 14.7 MEV	
(n,γ)	-		IEA Comp	Rept	IEA – INF – 10 6	Aug 68 Atalla. TABLES OF HL,SIG AND GAMM - E	
(n,γ)	Maxwl		ORL Expt	Prog	ORNL – 4343 71	Dec 68 Emery.	+
	Maxwl			Data	EXFOR12632.003	Jun 76 . 1 PT, SIGMA.	

82 Lead 208

Quantity	Energy (ev) Min	Max	Lab	Type	Documentation Ref Vol Page	Date	Author, Comments	Data
(n,γ)	1.0+4	2.0+5	ORL Expt	Jour	PR 181 1639	May 69	Macklin+ ACTIVATN,MAXWELL-AVGD SIGS	+
	3.1+4	1.9+5		Data	EXFOR10019.002	Nov 70	. 10 PTS.AREA.	
(n,γ)	2.5+5	3.1+5	IRK Expt	Jour	OAWA 106 153	Jun 69	Colditz+	
(n,γ)	1.3+7	1.5+7	DEB Comp	Jour	REA 7 4 93	Dec 69	Csikai+ COMP SIG+HL,GRPH,ACTIV-ANAL	
(n,γ)	2.0+5		MUA Theo	Conf	69Roorke 2 129	Dec 69	Chaubey+ SIG VALUE GIVEN, STATIST-TH	
(n,γ)	1.4+7		LAS Expt	Jour	PL/B 36 557	Oct 71	Drake+ CAPT. SPEC. CS GVN	+
	1.4+7			Data	EXFOR10193.006	Jun 72	. 1 PT. SIGMA	
(n,γ)	1.4+7		GRE Theo	Jour	NP/A 189 334	Jul 72	Boisson+.DIR,COLLECT.CURV. DEFORMNUC	
(n,γ)	6.2+6	1.5+7	LAS Expt	Jour	NP/A 191 641	Sep 72	Bergqvist+ TO SINGL PARTCL LVLS.	+
	6.0+6	1.5+7		Conf	72Budapest 244	Aug 72	- + TOF,NAI-ANTICOMPTON ,NDG	
				Conf	71Knoxvill 266	Mar 71	- +,NO DATA,ABSTRACT ONLY	
	7.2+6	1.5+7		Data	EXFOR10226.002	Jun 74	. 8 PTS.SIGMA	
(n,γ)	None		FEI Theo	Prog	YFI-13 4	Oct 72	Dovbenko+ ABSTRACT ONLY,NDG	
				Prog	INDC(CCP)-32	Apr 73	.PAGE 16.ENGLISH OF YFI-13 14	
(n,γ)	2.5+3	6.0+5	ORL Expt	Jour	PR/C 8 1504	73	Allen+CAPT YLD CURVES RES PAR ANAL	+
	2.5+3	6.0+5		Data	EXFOR10454.009	Dec 74	0PTS, DATA UNOBTAINABLE	
(n,γ)	2.3+6	7.3+6	HEI Theo	Jour	ZP 264 405	Oct 73	Mantzouranis.MODIFIED H-F-TH	
	2.2+6	7.3+6		Conf	73Munich 1 639	Aug 73	- . DIRCT+COMP,GRPH TOTSIG	
(n,γ)	1.5+7		JYV Comp	Rept	JU-RR-1/1976	Mar 76	Valkonen.(THESIS).EXPTS CFD DSD MODL	
(n,γ)	2.2+6		BOL Theo	Conf	76Lowell 1284	Jul 76	Longo+ISOVECTOR QUADRUPOLE CS.NDG	
(n,γ)	9.0-3		CRC Expt	Conf	76Lowell 777	Jul 76	Earle+DOUBLY RADIATIVE CAPTURE	
(n,γ)	None		LAS Theo	Prog	LA-6472 10	Aug 76	Arthur+ACT CS GNASH CODE CALC.NDG.	
(n,γ)	5.0+6	2.0+7	TIT Expt	Jour	JPJ 41 1102	Oct 76	Kitazawa+.GIANT E1+E2 CAPT.FIG GIVEN	
				Conf	JAERI-M-5984	Feb 75	- +PART-VIB COUPLING. CURVES	
	5.0+6	2.1+7		Prog	EANDC(J)30L 64	Sep 73	- +.SEMI-DIRECT CAPT FIG GIVEN	
(n,γ)	Maxwl		CRC Theo	Jour	PL/B 65 201	Nov 76	LEE+SIG FOR DOUBLE RADIATIVE CAPT	
Spect (n,γ)	Maxwl		LAS Expt	Prog	WASH-1048 52	Jun 64	Motz.TOT-E SCINT-SPECTROM,TBL SIG(E)	
Spect (n,γ)	Maxwl		LAS Expt	Prog	WASH-1127 144	Apr 69	Shera+ GE(LI),TO BE DONE	
Spect (n,γ)	1.4+7		LAS Expt	Jour	PL/B 36 557	Oct 71	Drake+ SPECTRUM CFD HO AND U238	
Spect (n,γ)	1.4+7		NJS Theo	Conf	72Budapest 250	Aug 72	Potokar+ CALC SPECTRA CFD EXPTS,GRPH	
Spect (n,γ)	6.2+6	1.5+7	LAS Expt	Jour	NP/A 191 641	Sep 72	Bergqvist+VDG TEST OF 1/2DIRECT NG	
	6.0+6	1.5+7		Conf	72Budapest 244	Aug 72	- + TOF,NAI-ANTICOMPTON ,NDG	
	9.2+6	1.3+7		Jour	PRL 27 269	Aug 71	- +. VDG. 3ES. CURVES	
				Conf	71Knoxvill 266	Mar 71	.SUPERSEDED	
Spect (n,γ)	1.4+7		BOR Expt	Conf	73Pacif.Gr 2 953	Mar 73	Rigaud+ HIGH-E G-SPEC CFD THEO,GRAPH	
Spect (n,γ)	9.0+6	1.5+7	LND ExTh	Conf	74Petten 199	Sep 74	Bergqvist+FAST N CAPT EXP AND CALC.	+
	9.2+6	1.5+7		Theo Jour	NKA 19 411	May 74	- .SEMIDIRECT TH CFD EXP,GRPH	
Spect (n,γ)	1.1+7		LAS Expt	Conf	75Wash. 923	Mar 75	Drake+ GRPH COUNTS VS CHANNEL	
Spect (n,γ)	5.7+6		OHO Expt	Prog	ERDA-NDC-2 165	May 75	Brient+NAICRYS.SPECT.NDG.	
Spect (n,γ)	Fiss		BOL Theo	Conf	IAEA-190 191	76	Longo+ AVG DIFFSIG(GAM-E) CALC,GRAPH	
	4.0+6	1.5+7		Conf	IAEA-190 191	76	- + AVG DIFFSIG(GAM-E) CALC,GRAPH	
	1.1+7	1.3+7		Conf	75Wash. 346	Mar 75	- +2 EN.G SPECT 10-18MEV CFD EXP	+
Inelastic γ	3.3+6	4.6+6	TNC Expt	Rept	WADC-TR-59-31	59	Bostrom.	
	3.3+6	4.6+6		Data	EXFOR11341.012	Jun 76	. 10 PTS,DSIG	
Inelastic γ	2.2+6	1.0+7	GEA Eval	Rept	XDC-60-8-81	Jun 59	Roberts.6GAMMAS 3GROUPS	
Inelastic γ	None		PEN Expt	Jour	PR 124 224	Oct 61	Donahue. ANG DISTR OF 2.6MEV GAMMA	
Inelastic γ	2.6+6	4.5+6	ALD Expt	Jour	NP 44 256	Jun 63	Towle+.SIG FOR2.61,3.20,3.48MEV LVLS	
Inelastic γ	4.1+6		ETH Theo	Jour	RMP 38 143	Jan 66	.THEOR CALC OF GAM-RAY ANGL DISTR	
Inelastic γ	1.0+6	5.0+6	TNC Theo	Jour	NP 81 468	Jun 66	Mathur+ OKS SATCHLER SIGMAS GIVEN	
Inelastic γ	3.1+6		TNC Theo	Jour	PR 160 816	Aug 67	Mathur+ WIDTH FLUCT EFFECT 2.61MEV G	
				Rept	ORO-2791-23	Feb 67	.SUPERSEDED	
Inelastic γ	1.5+7		LND Expt	Jour	AF 39 295	Sep 69	Joensson+. 80 DEG. 3 TRANSITIONS	+
	1.5+7	1.6+7		Data	EXFOR20164.	May 74	4PTS.D/DA.	
Inelastic γ	1.0+5	3.4+6	KUR Expt	Jour	IZV 35 2341	Nov 71	Degtjarev+ GE-LI,SIG(NEUT-E),GRAPH	+
				Jour	BAS 35 2123	Nov 72	.ENGLISH OF IZV 35 2341 N/71	
	3.0+6	3.4+6		Data	EXFOR40278.008	Apr 75	.SIGMA AT 2 ES TO ONE LVL GVN	
Inelastic γ	3.1+6	5.2+6	TNC Expt	Jour	PR/C 9 1972	May 74	Nellis+. GAMMA PRODUCTION SIGS MEASD	+
	3.0+6	4.1+6		ExTh Conf	65Antwerp § 34	Jul 65	Morgan+TOF.CFD TH.FROM 2.61MEV-LVL	
				Expt Abst	DA 25 568	Jul 64	Nellis. ANG.DISTRIB CFD SATCHLER TH	
	4.1+6			Conf	63Houston 127	Feb 63	.GRPH ANGDIST 2.62-MEV GAMMA	
	3.1+6	5.3+6		Data	EXFOR10485.	May 75	. 40 PTS,DSIGMA, 9 G-RAYS	
Inelastic γ	1.5+7		SMU Expt	Conf	75Wash. 712	Mar 75	Salaita+CYCLIC ACT.TBL.CFD	+
	1.5+7			Conf	74Columbia 95	Jul 74	Salaita+ ACT.SIG TO SHORTLIV ISO.TBL	
				Data	EXFOR10361.004	Sep 76	1PT=1310+-116MB=PROD207M+(N,2N)PB208	
Inelastic γ	1.0+6	1.0+7	KUR Expt	Conf	77Kiev	77	Savin+ SIG(NEUT-E),GRAPH	
Nonelastic γ	1.5+7		ARK Expt	Prog	A-ARK-61 1	Jan 61	Chittenden+ TOF. G PROD CS.	+
	1.5+7			Data	EXFOR11132.	Jun 76	. 11 PTS, DSIG.	
Nonelastic γ	1.6+7		LND Expt	Jour	PS 2 277	Dec 70	Joensson.(N,2NG),(N,N'G) AT 120 DEG.	

82 Lead 208

Quantity	Energy (ev) Min	Energy (ev) Max	Lab	Type	Documentation Ref Vol Page	Date	Author, Comments	Data
(n,2n)	1.5+7		CCP	Expt	Jour ZET 36 1046	Apr 59	Glagolev.G OF SHORT-LIVED ISOMERES	
					Jour JET 9 742	Oct 59	TRANSLATN.*	
(n,2n)	1.4+7		CCP	Theo	Jour ZET 38 1824	Jun 60	TH N ANG DISTR,STRIPPING REACTION	
					Jour JET 11 1312	Dec 60	. ENGL OF ZET 38 1824	
(n,2n)	Fiss		CRC	Eval	Rept CRC-1003	Dec 60	Roy+,ESTIMATED AVG SIG=11.0MB	
(n,2n)	1.5+7		CCP	Expt	Jour ZET 40 743	Mar 61	S FOR ACT.OF B1207META 1.7+−.3B	
					Jour JET 13 520	Sep 61	TRANSLATN.*	
(n,2n)	1.4+7		LRL	Expt	Jour NIM 15 74	Feb 62	Ruby+A FAST NEUTRON ACTIV.DETECTOR	
(n,2n)	1.4+7		HAM	Comp	Jour NP 65 257	Mar 65	Bormann. 2EXPT VALS.CFD SHELL EFFECT	
(n,2n)	1.3+7	1.5+7	BNL	Theo	Jour NSE 23 238	Nov 65	Pearlstein.3ES.STAT MDL CALC.TBL CS.	
(n,2n)	Fiss		BNL	Theo	Jour NSE 23 238	Nov 65	Pearlstein.STATMDL CALC.SPEC AVG.TBL	
(n,2n)	1.4+7		GRE	Expt	Rept CEA-R-2900	Dec 65	Monnand. SIGMA TO ISOM.STATE GIVEN	
(n,2n)	1.5+7		MUA	Expt	Jour NP 88 349	Nov 66	Prasad+,T-D NEUT ACT REL TO FE56(NP)	+
	1.5+7				Data EXFOR30015.010	May 70	PARTIAL SIGMA(METASTABLE)	
(n,2n)	1.4+7		KGU	Expt	Prog YFI-6 117	68	Vojtenko+. TABLE SIG AT 10 ANGLES	
					Rept INDC-260E	69	. ENGL OF YFI-6 117	
(n,2n)	1.5+7		TUR	Theo	Jour NC/B 56 1 201	Jul 68	Minetti+THEOR ISOM RATIO SPIN CO PAR	
(n,2n)	1.5+7		DEB	Expt	Jour AHP 25 91	Oct 68	Peto+ SUM PB207(NN')+PB208(N2N)	+
	1.5+7				Data EXFOR30069.005	Dec 70	SUM PB-207(NN')+PB-208(N2N)	
(n,2n)	1.5+7		DEB	Expt	Jour NP/A 122 234	Dec 68	Karolyi+,ACT,D-T NS,ISOM RAT,CFD TH	+
	1.5+7				Data EXFOR30101.017	Feb 71	ISOMERIC RATIO	
(n,2n)	1.4+7		CCP	Theo	Conf 69Erevan	Feb 69	Ezhov+.ABST,ANGL CORRELATION FUNCT	
(n,2n)	1.5+7		DEB	Comp	Jour REA 7 4 93	Dec 69	Csikai+ SIG+HL COMPILTN,N-ACTIV-ANAL	
(n,2n)	1.4+7		CCP	Comp	Rept ICD-6 215	70	Sluchevskaja.SIGS GND+ISOM,RATIO,TBL	
(n,2n)	1.4+7		KGU	Theo	Jour YF 11 122	Jan 70	Ezhov+ DOUBLEDIFF SIG(E)GRPH CFD XPT	
					Jour SNP 11 68	Jul 70	TRANSLATN.*	
(n,2n)	1.4+7	1.5+7	JYV	Eval	Rept JU-RR-3/1970	Jun 70	Leppaemaeki+ TABLE OF EVAL AVG SIG	
(n,2n)	1.6+7		LND	Expt	Jour PS 2 277	Dec 70	Joensson.LIMITS FROM NAT+RADIOPB GS	+
	1.5+7				Jour AF 39 295	Sep 69	−+. 80 DEG. 2 GAMMAS.ESTIMATE	
					Rept LU-NP-6804	Mar 68	−+ EQUIVALENT TO AF 39 295	
	1.5+7	1.6+7			Data EXFOR20164.038	May 74	1PNT.D/DA.	
(n,2n)	1.4+7		KFI	Comp	Jour JRC 7 365	Jun 71	Nagy+ SIGMA,GAMMA+ELECTR ES,HALF-LIF	
(n,2n)	1.4+7		ITJ	Expt	Jour JRC 14 201	73	Janczyszyn+ ISO-PROD BY NAT-PB ACTIV	+
	1.4+7				Data EXFOR30322.021	Feb 76	MEAN OF PB207(N,N')+PB208(N,2N)	
(n,2n)	1.5+7		DEB	Eval	Jour REA 11 1 153	Mar 73	Boedy+ RECOMM.VALUE FROM N-Z SYSTEM.	
(n,2n)	1.5+7		KFI	Theo	Rept KFKI-73-68	Dec 73	Jeki.NEW FIT,CALC SIG CFD OTHERS,TBL	
(n,2n)	1.5+7		SMU	Expt	Jour JIN 35 2139	Jul 73	Salaita+ CYCLIC ACTIV, ISOM STATES	+
					Conf 75Wash. 712	Mar 75	−+SHORT-LIVED ISOMER PROD.TBL.	
					Conf 74Columbia 95	Jul 74	−+ ACT.SIG TO SHORTLIV ISO.TBL	
	1.5+7				Data EXFOR10361.	Jun 74	1 PT INCLUDES INELAS SCAT ON PB-207	
(n,2n)	1.4+7		TUD	Theo	Conf 75Kiev 4 149	May 75	Seidel+ PREEQ-EFF ON CALC SIG.TABLE	
(n,2n)	8.0+6	1.4+7	LAS	Expt	Abst BAP 7 334	Apr 62	Shunk+ 1.064 MEV G. TBL. 5ES	+
	8.0+6	1.4+7			Data EXFOR12188.003	Jun 76	. 5 PTS.	
(n,xn) x>2	Fiss		BNL	Theo	Jour NSE 23 238	Nov 65	Pearlstein.SPEC AVG STATMDL CALC N3N	
(n,xn) x>2	None		LAS	Theo	Prog LA-6472 10	Aug 76	Arthur+ACT CS GNASH CODE CALC.NDG	
(n,p)	1.5+7		CRC	Expt	Jour CJP 31 267	Feb 53	Paul+ BETA ACT. CFD TH HL=3.1M	+
	1.5+7				Data EXFOR11274.097	Jun 76	. 1 PT.	
(n,p)	1.5+7		GLS	Theo	Jour PM 2 473	Apr 57	Brown+ COMPNUCL NIL, DIRECT 0.3MB	
(n,p)	Fiss		CRC	Eval	Rept CRC-1003	Dec 60	Roy+,ESTIMATED AVG SIG=0.0001MB	
(n,p)	1.4+7		FRK	Theo	Jour ZP 171 379	Dec 62	Lindner.STATMOD,CF CJP 31 267,TH+XPT	
(n,p)	1.5+7		SAH	Comp	Jour NUC 23 8 112	Aug 65	Chatterjee. TABLE WITH REFS.	
	1.4+7				Jour NP 60 273	Nov 64	−.MEAN OF EXPT CFD SHELLMOD	
(n,p)	1.4+7	1.8+7	FRK	Expt	Prog EANDC(E)89U58	Feb 68	Bass+ NDG,BUT COMPLETE, 17−18.4AND14	
(n,p)	1.5+7		DEB	Comp	Jour REA 7 4 93	Dec 69	Csikai+ SIG+HL COMPILTN,N-ACTIV-ANAL	
(n,p)	1.4+7	1.5+7	JYV	Eval	Rept JU-RR-3/1970	Jun 70	Leppaemaeki+ TABLE OF EVAL AVG SIG	
(n,p)	1.4+7		CCP	Expt	Rept YK-9 50	72	Maslov+ REL CU65(N,2N),NA-I,SIG GIVN	+
					Rept INDC(CCP)-42	Aug 74	.P10.ENGLISH OF YK-9	
	1.5+7				Data EXFOR40136.024	Feb 73	.1 DATA LINE	
(n,p)	1.4+7		GIT	Expt	Jour NP/A 180 157	Jan 72	Hankla+ ACT,GE(LI),MIXED POWDER.	+
					Abst DA/B 32 293	Nov 71	−. ACT METHOD, CFD THEORY.	
	1.4+7				Data EXFOR10244.025	Jun 74	. 1 PT.SIGMA=.46+−.06 MB	
(n,p)	1.6+7	1.9+7	VIP	Expt	Jour CJP 52 599	Apr 74	Long+. ACTIVATION. VDG. CURVE.	
(n,p)	1.3+7	1.5+7	JIA	Expt	Conf 75Kiev 4 209	May 75	Belovitskij+.SIG,ENERGY DEPEND,E-LVL	+
					Conf 75Leningrd 348	Jan 75	Belovickij+ ABST. SIG(14.5MEV)=.5 MB	
					Data EXFOR40347.004	Dec 77	SIG AT 14.5MEV,REL BI-209.1 PNT	
(n,p)	1.4+7		AUW	Expt	Conf 75Calcutta 2 31	Dec 75	Lakshmandas+0.52+−.07MB ACTIVATION	
(n,p)	None		LAS	Theo	Prog LA-6472 10	Aug 76	Arthur+ACT CS GNASH CODE CALC.NDG.	
(n,np)	1.5+7		GLS	Theo	Jour PM 2 473	Apr 57	Brown+ N,PN* COMPNUCL NIL,DIRECT NIL	

82 Lead 208

Quantity	Energy (ev) Min	Max	Lab	Type	Documentation Ref Vol Page	Author, Comments Date	Data
(n,np)	1.4+7		TUD	Theo Conf	75Kiev 4 149	May 75 Seidel+ (NNP),(NPN).PREEQ-EFF.TABLE	
(n,α)	1.4+7		ALD	Expt Jour	PPS 73 215	Feb 59 Coleman+. ACTIVATION	+
(n,α)	Fiss		CRC	Eval Rept	CRC-1003	Dec 60 Roy+,ESTIMATED AVG SIG=BELO 0.0001MB	
(n,α)	1.4+7		FRK	Theo Jour	ZP 171 379	Dec 62 Lindner.STATMOD,CF CJP 31 267,TH+XPT	
(n,α)	1.5+7		DEB	Comp Jour	REA 7 4 93	Dec 69 Csikai+ SIG+HL COMPILTN,N-ACTIV-ANAL	
(n,α)	1.4+7	1.5+7	JYV	Eval Rept	JU-RR-3/1970	Jun 70 Leppaemaeki+ TABLE OF EVAL AVG SIG	
(n,α)	Pile		MUA	Expt Prog	INDC(SEC)-35	Sep 73 Alam+ P101.ACTIV,SHORT NOTE,NDG	+
	Maxwl			Jour	NP/A 205 614	May 73 - + ACTIVATION REL (N,G).UPPER LI	
	Pile			Jour	NP/A 205 614	May 73 - + RATIO TO NG SIGMA,HALF LIVES	
	Pile			Data	EXFOR30249.004	Jul 73 RATIO TO NG-SIGMA,HALF-LIVES	
(n,α)	None		LAS	Theo Prog	LA-6472 10	Aug 76 Arthur+ACT CS GNASH CODE CALC.NDG.	
Fission	2.5+7	8.4+7	BRK	Expt Jour	PR 73 1135	May 48 Kelly+ RELATIVE TO THORIUM.	
Fission	1.4+7		LAS	Expt Jour	PR 75 919	Mar 49 Phillips+ UPPER LIM REL U238.PHOTOPL	
Fission	-		TPI	Theo Jour	YF 9 102	Jan 69 Korostova+ CV,SHELL CORR,LIQU-DROP-E	
				Jour	SNP 9 62	Jul 69 TRANSLATN.*	
Reson Params	3.5+5	7.2+5	WIS	Expt Jour	PR 79 935	Sep 50 Peterson+ TRNS. PB208 RES.	+
Reson Params	3.5+5	7.2+5	DKE	Expt Jour	PR 121 1150	Feb 61 Wilenzick+AREA ANAL.WN 4 LVLS.TBL.	+
	3.5+5	7.2+5		Data	EXFOR11327.007	Jun 76 . 4 RES. E0,WN,WN0	
Reson Params	8.0+4	1.2+5	DKE	Expt Jour	AP 14 387	Jul 61 Bilpuch+. WN(P)STF(P) ASSIGNED P	+
	1.5+4	5.0+4		Jour	AP 14 346	Jul 61 Newson+ LVL SEP S,P NEUTS=350,70KEV	
	8.0+4	1.2+5		Data	EXFOR11599.052	Jun 76 . 3 RES E0,L,WN,WN0	
Reson Params	7.2+5	1.9+6	ORL	Expt Jour	PR 127 2192	Sep 62 Fowler+,24RES+E0,WT,J FROM SIG TOT	+
				Abst	BAP 6 251	Apr 61 .SUPERSEDED	
	7.2+5	1.9+6		Data	EXFOR12215.004	Jun 76 . 24 RES.E0,J,WT.	
Reson Params	1.2+4	2.4+4	ORL	Theo Prog	WASH-1048 71	Jun 64 Block.ANALYZ OF HARWELL TRNSDATA,TBL	
Reson Params	7.2+5	1.8+6	ORL	Expt Jour	PR 147 870	Jul 66 Fowler. J,PARITY,W 21RES,FROM DEL	+
				Conf	65Antwerp	Jul 65 .SUPERSEDED	
	7.2+5	1.8+6		Data	EXFOR12217.003	Jun 76 . 21 RES. E0,J,WT.	
Reson Params	7.0+4	7.7+4	ORL	Expt Jour	PR 153 1356	Jan 67 Gibbons+ FROM TOT,2RES,BOTH P, WN	+
	7.0+4	7.7+4		Data	EXFOR12218.004	Jun 76 . 4 RES. E0,WN,L.	
Reson Params	7.2+5	1.2+6	BRC	Expt Rept	CEA-R-3279	Jun 67 Cabe+ NAT TGT,J(7RESON)CF PR127 2192	
Reson Params	7.0+4	7.7+4	ORL	Expt Jour	PR 159 1007	Jul 67 Macklin+ FROM (N,G),2RES, WG=CA2.2EV	
Reson Params		1.0+6	AUA	Theo Jour	AUJ 20 477	Oct 67 Cook. TBL OF AVG LVL SPACING D,L=0,1	
Reson Params	1.2+4	1.2+5	ORL	Expt Jour	PR 181 1639	May 69 Macklin+ G*WG AT 4 RESON FROM N,G	+
	1.2+4	1.2+5		Data	EXFOR10019.003	Nov 70 5PTS.E0,G TIMES WG GVN.	
Reson Params	2.0+5		MUA	Theo Conf	69Roorke 2 129	Dec 69 Chaubey+ D/GAM-WIDTH RATIO, STATMOD	
Reson Params	5.4+5	2.1+6	CCP	Theo Jour	IZV 34 2183	Oct 70 Kolomiets.CALC T-WID,J,GIANT RES,TBL	
				Jour	BAS 34 1947	Oct 70 *ENGL OF IZV 34 2183	
Reson Params	None		FEI	Theo Conf	71Kiev	May 71 Ignatjuk+.AVG WG,SUPERFLUID-MDL,GRPH	
Reson Params	7.8+4		ORL	Expt Jour	PR/C 8 1504	Oct 73 Allen+ ORELA,TED DET,WT G*WG.	+
	2.5+3	7.7+4		Data	EXFOR10155.	Jan 78 . 2PTS.G STF,D,WG AVG.77KEV WT,WG*G.	
Reson Params	None		DKE	Theo Prog	USNDC-11 231	Jun 74 Divadeenam+ SHELL MDL CALC, NDG	
Reson Params	2.0+5	6.0+5	LRL	Theo Jour	PR/C 12 713	Aug 75 Ferguson. TOT FOR S,D WAVES.	
Reson Params	7.0+5	1.5+6	ORL	Expt Prog	ERDA-NDC-3 181	May 76 Fowler+SPINS,PI,RED WID.TBD.NDG.	
Strnth Fnctn	3.0+4	1.5+5	DKE	Expt Jour	AP 14 387	Jul 61 Bilpuch+. P WAVE	
Strnth Fnctn	None		AUA	Eval Rept	AAEC/E-277	Mar 73 Musgrove.TBLS EXPTL DATA+BEST VALUES	
Lvl Density	Fast		ANL	Expt Jour	NP 25 511	Jun 61 Vandenbosh+LVL DENS.FROM OTHER REACT	
Lvl Density	+6		MIL	Theo Jour	EN 15 1 54	Jan 68 Facchini+ LDL PARS FROM LOW EN RES	
Lvl Density	+7		DEB	ExTh Jour	NP/A 122 234	Dec 68 Karolyi+ SPIN CUTOFF,M OF INERT,N2N	+
	1.5+7			Expt Data	EXFOR30101.021	Jun 72 CUTOFF PARAMETER	
Lvl Density	None		CCP	Theo Jour	YF 11 1028	May 70 Rubchenya.INFL.OF QADRUPOL-DEFORMATN	
				Jour	SNP 11 571	Nov 70 . ENGL OF YF 11 571.	
Lvl Density	+6	+7	FEI	Theo Jour	YF 11 1012	May 70 Ignatyuk+ DENSITY+A+TEMP VS EXCIT-E	
	+6			Rept	INDC(CCP)-7U5	Feb 70 .TRANSLATN.*	
				Prog	YFI-7 7	Apr 69 Ignatyuk+ TEMP+DENS+A VS EXCIT-E,CRV	
	+6	+7		Jour	SNP 11 563	Nov 70 . ENGL OF YF 11 1012	
Lvl Density	None		AUW	Theo Conf	70Madurai 2 267	Dec 70 Ramamurty+ A-PARAMETER GVN,LANG'S-TH	
Lvl Density		6.0+7	ROC	Theo Jour	NP/A 187 225	Jun 72 Williams+ A,COMBIN+STATIST+SHELLCORR	
Lvl Density	None		MUN	Theo Jour	NP/A 217 269	Dec 73 Dilg+ A,DELTA. BACK SHIFTED FERMIGAS	
Lvl Density	None		COP	Theo Jour	NP/A 222 493	Apr 74 Dossing+COLL ROTAT.SPAC. ACCUR ESTIM	
Lvl Density	None		ROC	Theo Jour	NP/A 223 577	May 74 Huizenga+ EXP CFD MICROSC TH SPH NUC	
Lvl Density	5.5+6	8.5+6	ORL	Expt Prog	ORNL-4909	Jun 74 Kinney+NUC TEMP FROM LEAST SQ FIT.	+
	5.5+6	8.5+6		Data	EXFOR10412.032	Apr 76 1PTS.NUCLEAR TEMPERATURES.	
Lvl Density	+7		FEI	Theo Jour	YF 21 485	Mar 75 Ignatjuk+ LVL DENS PARAMS,GRAPH	
	-			Conf	70Helsinki 2 885	Jun 70 - +76. SUPERFLUID CFD FERMI-TH	
(γ,n)	7.0+6	1.7+7	MOS	Expt Jour	YF 12 682	Oct 70 Ishkhanov+ SIG(GAM-E) GRAPHS+TABLES	
				Jour	SNP 12 370	71 . ENGL OF YF 12 682	

82 Lead 208

Quantity	Energy (ev) Min	Max	Lab	Type	Documentation Ref Vol Page	Author, Comments Date	Data
(γ,n)	+6	+7	CCP	Theo Jour	YF 12 965	Nov 70 Dubovoi. TABLE OF FINE STRUCTURE	
				Jour	SNP 12 526	May 71 TRANSLATN.*	
(γ,n)	9.0+6		ANL	Expt Conf	75Zurich 759	Aug 75 Holt+ POLARISATION OF PHOTONEUTRONS	

82 Lead 209

Quantity	Energy (ev) Min	Max	Lab	Type	Documentation Ref Vol Page	Author, Comments Date	Data
(n,2n)	1.5+7		TAT	Theo Jour	JP/A 7 1457	Aug 74 Kondaiah. CALC ON STAT MODEL	
Lvl Density	+6		MIL	Theo Jour	EN 15 1 54	Jan 68 Facchini+ LDL PARS FROM LOW EN RES	
Lvl Density	None		MUN	Theo Jour	NP/A 217 269	Dec 73 Dilg+ A,DELTA. BACK SHIFTED FERMIGAS	
Lvl Density	None		COP	Theo Jour	NP/A 222 493	Apr 74 Dossing+COLL ROTAT.SPAC. ACCUR ESTIM	
Lvl Density	None		ROC	Theo Jour	NP/A 223 577	May 74 Huizenga+ EXP CFD MICROSC TH SPH NUC	
Lvl Density	+7		FEI	Theo Jour	YF 21 485	Mar 75 Ignatjuk+ LVL DENS PARAMS,GRAPH	
(γ,n)	None		KUR	Theo Conf	68Riga	Jan 68 Bunatjan+ ABST,FERMI-SIST EFF POTENT	

82 Lead 210

Quantity	Energy (ev) Min	Max	Lab	Type	Documentation Ref Vol Page	Author, Comments Date	Data
Polarization	1.4+7		IJI	Theo Jour	YF 18 1203	Dec 73 Ivanjuk+ SHELL CORR, POL(ANG),GRAPH	
				Jour	SNP 18 616	Jun 74 . ENGLISH OF YF 18, 1203.	

82 Lead 212

Quantity	Energy (ev) Min	Max	Lab	Type	Documentation Ref Vol Page	Author, Comments Date	Data
Polarization	1.4+7		IJI	Theo Jour	YF 18 1203	Dec 73 Ivanjuk+ SHELL CORR, POL(ANG),GRAPH	
				Jour	SNP 18 616	Jun 74 . ENGLISH OF YF 18, 1203.	

82 Lead 213

Quantity	Energy (ev) Min	Max	Lab	Type	Documentation Ref Vol Page	Author, Comments Date	Data
Fiss Yield	None		TRM	Theo Prog	BARC-614 7	72 Ramamurthy. MASS-DISTR CFD XPT,NDG.	

82 Lead 214

Quantity	Energy (ev) Min	Max	Lab	Type	Documentation Ref Vol Page	Author, Comments Date	Data
Polarization	1.4+7		IJI	Theo Jour	YF 18 1203	Dec 73 Ivanjuk+ SHELL CORR, POL(ANG), GRAPH	
				Jour	SNP 18 616	Jun 74 . ENGLISH OF YF 18, 1203.	

82 Lead 216

Quantity	Energy (ev) Min	Max	Lab	Type	Documentation Ref Vol Page	Author, Comments Date	Data
Polarization	1.4+7		IJI	Theo Jour	YF 18 1203	Dec 73 Ivanjuk+ SHELL CORR, POL(ANG), GRAPH	
				Jour	SNP 18 616	Jun 74 . ENGLISH OF YF 18, 1203.	

83 Bismuth 205

Quantity	Energy (ev) Min	Max	Lab	Type	Documentation Ref Vol Page	Date	Author, Comments	Data
(n,p)	Maxwl		IFU	Theo Rept	ICD-4 20	67	Dadakina+ PENETR COEFF CALC,TABLE	

83 Bismuth 206

Quantity	Energy (ev) Min	Max	Lab	Type	Documentation Ref Vol Page	Date	Author, Comments	Data
(n,p)	Maxwl		IFU	Theo Rept	ICD-4 20	67	Dadakina+ PENETR COEFF CALC,TABLE	

83 Bismuth 207

Quantity	Energy (ev) Min	Max	Lab	Type	Documentation Ref Vol Page	Date	Author, Comments	Data
(n,p)	Maxwl		IFU	Theo Rept	ICD-4 20	67	Dadakina+ PENETR COEFF CALC,TABLE	

83 Bismuth 208

Quantity	Energy (ev) Min	Max	Lab	Type	Documentation Ref Vol Page	Date	Author, Comments	Data
(n,2n)	Fiss		CRC	Eval Rept	CRC-1003	Dec 60	Roy+,ESTIMATED AVG SIG=17.0MB	
(n,p)	Fiss		CRC	Eval Rept	CRC-1003	Dec 60	Roy+,ESTIMATED AVG SIG=3.5MB	
(n,p)	Maxwl		IFU	Theo Rept	ICD-4 20	67	Dadakina+ PENETR COEFF CALC,TABLE	
(n,α)	Fiss		CRC	Eval Rept	CRC-1003	Dec 60	Roy+,ESTIMATED AVG SIG=0.0001MB	

83 Bismuth 209

Quantity	Energy (ev) Min	Max	Lab	Type	Documentation Ref Vol Page	Date	Author, Comments	Data
Evaluation	5.0+5	1.5+7	LRL	Eval Rept	UCRL-5351	Nov 58	Howerton. CURVES.	
Evaluation	5.0+2	1.0+7	ANL	Eval Book	FRC	60	Yftah+.16E GROUPS.FAST REACTOR DATA	
Evaluation	+4	1.4+7	GA	Eval Rept	GA-2156	61	Joanou+.ALL DATA XCEPT SECONDARY ES	
Evaluation	2.5-2	1.1+7	FEI	Eval Book	ABAGJAN	64	26 GROUP CONST,TOT,CAPT,INEL,EL,ETC	
Total	Maxwl		COL	Expt Jour	PR 48 265	Aug 35	Dunning+ IONCH,TRANS,RA-BE/PARAFIN N	
Total	Maxwl		CAV	Expt Jour	PRSA 162 127	Sep 37	Goldhaber+BRIGGS.TRANSMISSION 8.9B	
Total	1.0+5	1.8+5	ITY	Expt Jour	PR 56 881	Nov 39	Amaldi+ TRANSM.C-D NS. AVERAGE ES.	
Total	9.0-1		COL	Expt Jour	PR 59 489	Mar 41	Hanstein.RESONANCE FILTER METH.(IN)	
	5.0-1	1.0+0		Abst	PR 57 565	Mar 40	- + RESONANCE FILTER METHOD.	
Total	Maxwl		CHI	Expt Jour	PR 70 815	Dec 46	Anderson+ C-FILTERED NS TO 18DEG K.	
Total	2.4+4	8.3+5	ANL	Expt Jour	PR 71 508	Apr 47	Fields+ GN SOURCES 6ES FIELDS+.	+
	2.4+4	8.3+5		Data	EXFOR11260.023	Jun 76	. 5 PTS. SIGMA.	
Total	1.0+4	1.4+6	WIS	Expt Jour	PR 73 659	Apr 48	Barschall+ TRANSM. 20,150KEV RESOL.	+
	5.2+5	1.4+6		Data	EXFOR11227.002	Jun 76	. 11 PTS. SIGMA.	
Total	1.3-2	1.0+4	COL	Expt Jour	PR 73 963	May 48	Havens+ SLOW TRANSMISSION. TOF.	+
	1.8-1	2.4+1		Data	EXFOR11361.010	Jun 76	. 18 PTS. SIGMA.	
Total	1.6-3		ANL	Expt Jour	PR 75 1098	Apr 49	Krueger+ CHOPPER	
Total	1.2+2	3.0+2	ANL	Expt Jour	PR 76 100	Jul 49	Hibdon+ 10PC ERSLN TRANSM MN. CO.	+
	1.2+2	3.0+2		Data	EXFOR11261.037	Jun 76	. 2 PTS. SIGMA.	
Total	2.0+4	5.2+5	WIS	Expt Jour	PR 76 1146	Oct 49	Barschall+10KEV RSLN,NO RESON.CF PBD	+
	8.5+5	5.3+5		Data	EXFOR12228.003	Jun 76	. 43 PTS. SIGMA.	
Total	1.0+5	1.5+6	MIT	Theo Jour	PR 76 1550	Dec 49	Feshbach+ AVERAGE OVER RESON,CF EXPT	
Total	4.2+7		BRK	Expt Jour	PR 80 842	Dec 50	Hildebrand+ BE-D NS.TRANSM. C DETECT	+
	4.2+7			Data	EXFOR11039.032	Jun 76	. 1 PT. SIGMA.	
Total	5.0+4	3.2+6	WIS	Expt Jour	PR 88 83	Oct 52	Miller+ 20KEVSPREAD TRNSM.	+
	1.0+6	3.2+6		Data	EXFOR11712.024	Jun 76	. 14 PTS. SIGMA.	
Total	1.4+7		ANL	Expt Jour	PR 88 686	Nov 52	Goodman+ T-D NEUTS 5.2+-0.5B	+
	1.4+7			Data	EXFOR11057.021	Jun 76	. 1 PT. SIGMA.	
Total	1.4+7		LAS	Expt Jour	PR 88 562	Nov 52	Coon+	+
	1.4+7			Data	EXFOR11056.056	Jun 76	. 1 PT. SIGMA.	
Total	3.0+6	1.3+7	LAS	Expt Jour	PR 89 775	Feb 53	Nereson+ FAST NEUTS. 10PCT. RESOL.	+
				Prog	LA-1655	Apr 54	- . E RESOL 10PC	
	3.0+6	1.3+7		Data	EXFOR11060.012	Jun 76	. 34 PTS. SIGMA.	
Total	1.4+7		ROM	Expt Jour	NC 10 281	Mar 53	Ageno+LI TARGET TRANSMIS.5.35+-0.12B	
Total	Maxwl		HAR	Expt Rept	AERE-N/R-1131	Apr 53	Egelstaff.GRAPH,EXPT DESCRIBED	
				Rept	AERE-N/R-1147	Apr 53	- .GIVES ABS.+SCAT XSECT	
Total	1.9+7		LAS	Expt Jour	PR 92 358	Oct 53	Day+ TRANS 5.69B AT 19.00MEV	+
	1.9+7			Data	EXFOR11068.013	Jun 76	. 1 PT. SIGMA.	
Total	4.6+7	1.6+8	LRL	Expt Jour	PR 92 835	Nov 53	Angell.	+

83 Bismuth 209

Quantity	Energy (ev) Min	Energy (ev) Max	Lab	Type	Documentation Ref Vol Page	Author, Comments Date	Data
Total	1.7−4	4.1−3	BNL	Expt Jour	PR 92 1206	Dec 53 Hughes+	+
	1.7−4	4.1−3		Data	EXFOR12243.002	Jun 76 . 105 PTS. SIGMA.	
Total	4.6+7	1.6+8	BRK	Expt Jour	PR 92 835	Dec 53 Linlor+	+
	4.6+7	1.6+8		Data	EXFOR12205.002	Jun 76 . 10 PTS. SIGMA.	
Total	3.7+6		BAR	Expt Jour	PR 94 1267	Jun 54 Snowden.	+
	3.7+6			Data	EXFOR11965.010	Jun 76 . 1 PT. SIGMA.	
Total	1.3+7	1.6+7	UMX	Expt Jour	AIF 1 69	55 Mazari+,GRAPH GIVEN,TRANSMISSION	+
				Jour	PR 100 972	Nov 55 ABSTRACT *	
	1.3+7	1.6+7		Data	EXFOR30037.015	Sep 70 7 DATA POINTS,PRIV COMM FROM MAZARI	
Total	1.0+3	5.5+4	ANL	Expt Abst	PR 98 224	Apr 55 Hibdon+ NDG RESONANCES CFD	+
	1.2+4	5.1+4		Data	EXFOR11244.009	Jun 76 . 34 PTS,SIGMA.	
Total	4.9+0		BNL	Expt Priv	SAILOR	Apr 55 Sailor.	+
	4.9+0			Data	EXFOR11344.003	Jun 76 . 1 PT. SIGMA.	
Total	4.1+6		LAS	Expt Jour	PR 98 677	May 55 Walt+ TRANSMISSION EXPT 7.9B	+
	4.1+6			Data	EXFOR11215.056	Jun 76 . 1 PT. SIGMA.	
Total	1.4+9		BNL	Expt Jour	PR 98 1369	Jun 55 Coor+	+
	1.4+9			Data	EXFOR11087.017	Jun 76 . 1 PT. SIGMA.	
Total	1.4+2	2.9+5	HAR	Expt Priv	EGELSTAFF4	Jun 55 Egelstaff. 1 DATA INDEX LINE *	
Total	2.0+0	2.0+4	ANL	Expt Jour	PR 100 126	Oct 55 Bollinger+,TOF 2RES ANALYZED CURVE	+
	1.5+0	9.9+3		Data	EXFOR11690.006	Jun 76 . 67 PTS. SIGMA.	
Total	1.4+7		NRL	ExTh Rept	NRL−4666	Nov 55 Mcgarry+ 5.33+−.10B CFD SQUARE WELL	
Total	1.0+3	3.0+4	SAH	Expt Jour	IJP 30 99	Mar 56 Patro+ TOF.TRANSMISSN CURVES ONLY	
Total	3.5+2	8.0+4	DKE	Expt Jour	PR 102 1574	Jun 56 Gibbons.ABSOLUTE CURVE TRANSMISSION	+
	7.0+2	8.0+4		Data	EXFOR11864.004	Jun 76 . 128 PTS. SIGMA.	
Total	1.8+6	7.0+6	LAS	Expt Jour	PR 104 1319	Dec 56 Beyster+,TRNS CURVE CFD CCB	+
	1.8+6	7.0+6		Data	EXFOR11220.034	Jun 76 . NO DATA POINTS.	
Total	4.0+4	1.8+7	LAS	Theo Rept	LA−2099	Dec 56 Beyster+,OPTMDL CALC CFD EXPT,CURVE	
Total	1.0+3	3.2+4	HAR	Expt Jour	PPSA 70 51	Jan 57 Gayther+ FC THICK SAMPLE,AVSIG CF TH	
Total	1.5+7		CCP	Expt Jour	SPD 6 129	Apr 57 . COINC METHOD, 5.33 +− 0.08 BARN	
Total	None		COL	Expt Prog	WASH−745	Nov 57 Rustad. LIQ NDG CS.	
Total	2.2+3	2.6+3	ORL	Expt Jour	PR 109 926	Feb 58 Good+,TOF+SC ABS RES CURVE	+
	2.0+3	3.8+3		Conf	ORNL−2309	Jun 57 − + TOF ABS CURV.	
	2.2+3	2.6+3		Data	EXFOR11402.025	Jun 76 . 18 PTS. SIGMA.	
Total	2.6+1	1.7+3	BNL	Expt Jour	PR 110 692	May 58 Seth.	+
	2.6+1	1.7+3		Data	EXFOR11788.020	Jun 76 . 36 PTS. SIGMA.	
Total	7.0+6	1.4+7	LRL	Expt Jour	PR 110 927	May 58 Bratenahl+ SC TRNS 6.02 5.44B+−1PC.	+
	7.1+6	1.4+7		Conf	58Geneva 14 109	Sep 58 − +.P1881,TBL,CURV,CFD OPTMDL	
	7.1+6	1.4+7		Data	EXFOR11155.032	Jun 76 . 5 PTS. SIGMA.	
Total	2.3+6	3.0+6	LVN	Expt Conf	58Geneva 15 30	Sep 58 Vervier+.PPR1699,CURVE,EXPT DESCRIBD	+
	2.2+6	3.1+6		Data	EXFOR20172.006	May 74 5PTS.	
Total	1.0+4	1.4+5	DKE	Expt Jour	AP 8 250	Oct 59 Nichols+ TRANS DATA CURVE TOTAL SIG	
Total	1.0+5	3.0+5	ANL	Expt Prog	ANL−6111 21	Feb 60 Lane. CURVE	
Total	1.7+7	2.9+7	LRL	Expt Jour	PR 120 521	Oct 60 Peterson+ TRANS 4ES CURV CFD OPTMDL	+
				Conf	58Geneva 14 109	Sep 58 Bratenahl+ TBL,CURV,CFD OPTMDL.	
	1.7+7	2.9+7		Data	EXFOR11108.040	Jun 76 . 4 PTS. SIGMA.	
Total	3.2+6	4.6+6	CCP	Expt Book	NEJTRONFIZ 298	61 Zubov. NO VALUES GIVEN. ENGL.=SPN219	
Total	2.0−1	1.0+7	B+W	Eval Rept	BAW−158	Jun 61 Roach+ AVERAGED SIG 40 GROUPS	
Total	9.0+3	1.9+4	HAR	Expt Jour	NP 44 431	Jul 63 Firk+ TOF.MEASURED BELOW 9KEV,BUTNDG	
	1.0+4	2.0+4		Jour	NIM 3 309	Dec 58 − +HIGH RESOL N TOF EXPERIMENTS	
	3.0+2	4.0+3		Jour	NP 7 613	Aug 58 Lynn+TOF TRANSM.+ABS.CURV 2RESONANCE	
Total	4.0+2	2.7+3	CCP	Eval Jour	AE 15 493	Dec 63 Nikolaev.TABLE OF CHARACTRSTC PARAMS	
				Rept	INDSWG−64 274	64 SEE ALSO *	
				−		EAF15 6 68 ENG SJA15 1281 JNE18 4	
Total	2.0+2	1.5+5	COL	Expt Rept	CR−1860	64 Garg+TRNS.TBLS.CURVS.CFD.	+
	None			Jour	RSI 36 48	Jan 65 .EXPT SPECT.297 AND 77 DEG K CURV.	
	2.0+2	1.5+5		Jour	RSI 35 263	Mar 64 Rainwater+ EXPT DETAILS.	
				Rept	EANDC(US)−54L	64 .EQUIVALENT TO TID−21144,CR−1860	
	5.0+2	1.5+5		Data	EXFOR11646.021	Jun 76 . 2726 PTS. SIGMA.	
Total	1.4+7		CCP	ExTh Jour	ZET 46 1496	Apr 64 5.41+−.03B,CFD OPTMDL,SHELL.SEP ISOQ	
				Jour	JET 19 1013	Oct 64 TRANSLATN.*	
Total	1.0+6	2.0+7	UEN	Theo Jour	ZN/A 19 406	Apr 64 Krell.OPTMOD RECURSION FORM FOR INT	
Total	1.4+7		FTI	Expt Conf	64Paris 2 811	Jul 64 Kaminker.	
Total	5.0+4	3.0+6	BNL	Theo Jour	PR/B 135 895	Aug 64 Auerbach+ OPTMDL PAR,TBL IN BNL818	
Total	1.4+0		ORL	Expt Jour	NP 61 381	Jan 65 Rayburn+ IN RES 1.44EV 9.10B.	+
	1.4+0			Data	EXFOR11026.032	Jun 76 . 1 PT. SIGMA.	
Total	3.2+6	5.2+6	JNE	Expt Jour	NP 65 419	Mar 65 Manero.TRAMSMISS RES 30KEV BROAD RES	+
				ExTh Jour	NP/A 119 356	Oct 68 − +.FLUCT ANAL OF NP65 419	
	3.2+6	5.2+6		Expt Data	EXFOR20209.005	May 74 37PTS.	

83 Bismuth 209

Quantity	Energy (ev) Min	Max	Lab	Type	Documentation Ref Vol Page	Date	Author, Comments	Data
Total	+1		MUN	ExTh Jour	ZP 186 23	Jun 65	Triftshauser.N – SPC MAX 10EV,SIGTOT,	
Total	5.0+5	4.1+6	LAS	Expt Priv	DAY	Jul 65	DAY.	+
	5.0+5	4.1+6		Data	EXFOR12191.012	Jun 76	. 4 PTS. SIGMA.	
Total	1.4+7		FEI	Expt Prog	INDSWG – 126 33	66	Dukarevich.SIG = 5.33 + – 0.04B	
Total	4.0+6	6.0+6	LAS	Theo Rept	LA – 3538	Sep 66	Agee+ OPTICAL MODEL CALCULATION	
Total	2.4+7		ORL	Theo Jour	NP/A 91 75	Jan 67	Satchler. OPTMDL CFD EXPT	
Total	4.3+5	5.7+5	RPI	Expt Jour	PL/B 24 33	Jan 67	Martin+ FINE STRUCTURE AS FOR PB ISO	
Total	1.4+7		CCP	ExTh Jour	IZV 31 217	Feb 67	Dukarevich+.TBL,CURVES,CFD OPTMDL TH	
				Jour	BAS 31 197	Feb 67	TRANSLATN.*	
Total	1.4+7		FTI	Expt Jour	NP/A 92 433	Feb 67	Dukarevich+ CFD OPTMDL 5.33 + – 0.04B	+
Total	1.0+5	6.0+5	DKE	Expt Prog	WASH – 1074 36	Apr 67	Seibel+ 38 RESONANCES SEEN NDG	
Total	2.5+6	7.5+6	WIS	Expt Jour	PR 158 1142	Jun 67	Carlson+ VDG,CURV,20 – 50KEV RESOL, TH	+
				Abst	DA/B 28 1084	Sep 67	.SUPERSEDED	
				Conf	65Antwerp 101	Jul 65	.SUPERSEDED	
	2.5+6	7.5+6		Data	EXFOR11497.032	Jun 76	. 164 PTS. SIGMA.	
Total	4.0+6		IFU	Theo Jour	UFZ 13 51	Jan 68	Kashuba+ TBL,SIG – VAL,EXPT CFD OPTMOD	
				Jour	UPJ 13 33	Jul 68	TRANSLATN.*	
Total	2.5+6	2.4+7	CCP	Theo Jour	YF 7 283	Feb 68	Aver'yanov+ OPTMOD – CALCTD SIG GVN	
				Jour	SNP 7 2 193	Aug 68	TRANSLATN.*	
Total	1.2+6	1.2+6	MUN	Expt Rept	EANDC(E)89 4	Feb 68	Koester. = 1 DATA INDEX LINES	+
Total	6.0+6	1.5+7	OHO	Theo Jour	NC/B 53 2 363	Feb 68	Cassola+ OPTMOD CALC CFD EXPT.	
Total	None		DKE	Expt Abst	DA/B 28 3834	Mar 68	Divadeenam.TRANS, AV SIG CFD OPTMDL	+
	1.1+5	6.5+5		Data	EXFOR10523.020	Jan 76	. 109 PTS. SIGMA.	
Total	4.0+5	2.5+6	BNL	Eval Rept	BNL – 50151	Oct 68	Moore.OPTMDL FIT TO BNL – 325 DATA	
Total	4.0+6		KUR	Expt Jour	YF 8 1086	Dec 68	Gorlov+.SMALL ANG SCAT EXPERIMENT	
				ExTh Jour	YF 6 910	Nov 67	– + POLRZ INC N,OPTMOD CFD.7.52B	
Total	4.0+3	7.0+4	SAC	Expt Jour	NP/A 123 561	Jan 69	Morgenstern+LINAC .26 – .19NS/M NDG	+
	4.0+3	7.0+4		Data	EXFOR20684.	Jul 77	0PTS. SEE RESONANCE PARAMETERS.	
Total	6.0+5	2.0+6	RAM	Expt Prog	INDC(PAK) – 1 1	May 69	. EXPT TO BE DONE,NO DATA GIVEN	
Total	2.6 – 2	9.2 – 1	UJV	Expt Rept	UJV – 2488	70	Mikula+ BI AS FILTER,TRANSMISSN VS E	
Total	2.0+7	3.0+7	AMS	Expt Prog	EANDC(E)127U	Apr 70	Rethmeier+,AVF CYCLOTRON,TOF	
Total	2.1+5	1.4+6	ANL	Expt Jour	NSE 41 63	Jul 70	Smith+,TRANS,RESOL BELOW 3KEV,CURVE	+
				Rept	ANL – 7636	Nov 69	+DATA PTS IN APPENDIX.	
	5.0+5	1.4+6		Data	EXFOR10010.	Mar 76	. 1062 PTS. TOF. AND MONO E RESOL.	
Total	3.0+6	3.0+7	KOS	Theo Jour	NP/A 158 389	Dec 70	Angeli+ RAMSAUER EFFECT OKS EXPT.	
Total	2.5+6	1.5+7	BNW	Expt Jour	PR/C 3 576	Feb 71	Foster+,TRANS,CURVS,CFD OTHERS+TH	+
				Jour	NIM 36 1	Sep 65	.EXPT DETAILS	
	2.4+6	1.5+7		Data	EXFOR10047.093	Aug 73	. 236 PTS. SIGMA.	
Total	1.3+2		MUN	Expt Jour	ZN/A 26 442	Mar 71	Dilg+TRANS EXPT,COH SCAT LENGTH CALC	
Total	6.1+6	8.0+6	AE	Theo Rept	AE – 430	Sep 71	Holmqvist+ CALC FROM OPTMOD PARAMS	
	8.1+6			Conf	70Helsinki 2 341	Jun 70	– + OPTMOD ANALYSIS. 8 MEV	
Total	1.4+7		KOS	Expt Jour	AHP 30 115	Oct 71	Angeli+EXPT,DATA TABLE,LITER. SURVEY	+
	1.4+7			Data	EXFOR30141.016	Jan 72	SIGMA AT 14.7 MEV GIVEN	
Total	1.0+1	3.0+5	ORL	Expt Prog	ORNL – 4743 54	Dec 71	Harvey+.ORELA. TRANS.NO DATA GIVEN	
Total	1.5+7		AMS	Expt Jour	NP/A 181 545	Feb 72	Kuijper+ TRANSMISSION	+
	1.5+7			Data	EXFOR20223.011	May 74	1PNT.	
Total	+9		NYU	Theo Jour	PR/C 6 748	Sep 72	Franco. GLAUBER APPROX. CFD EXPT	
Total	1.3+7	1.5+7	DEB	Eval Rept	IAEA – 153 173	73	Boedy+ MOST PROBABLE VAL OF SIG,TBL	
Total	3.8+8	1.7+9	PTN	Expt Jour	PR/C 7 248	Jan 73	Schimmerling+.TOF.TRANS.TABLE 15 ES	+
				Jour	PL/B 37 177	Nov 71	.SUPERSEDED	
	3.8+8	1.7+9		Data	EXFOR10082.012	Dec 75	15PTS.TOT CS DATA.	
Total	2.4+6		PAD	Expt Jour	NC/A 13 867	Feb 73	Drigo+	+
	2.4+6			Data	EXFOR20664.007	Oct 76	1PNT.	
Total	1.0+6	5.0+6	SHI	Expt Jour	NSF 11 179	Dec 74	C F Ai+ TOF,TRANS.GRPH CFD OTH+OPTMOD	+
	1.0+6	5.0+6		Data	EXFOR30297.004	Jul 75	33 PTS.SIGMA	
Total	2.5+5	1.5+7	JAE	Theo Conf	JAERI – M – 5984	Feb 75	Tanaka.OPTMDL/COUPLD CH.GRPH CFD EXP	
Total	5.0+5	4.0+7	KFK	ExTh Conf	JAERI – M – 5984	Feb 75	Newstead+P230.OPTMDL/C – C CFD TOF GRP	+
	1.0+6	3.9+7		Revw Conf	70Helsinki 2 219	Jun 70	Cierjacks.113. SIG(E) GRPH CFD OPTMD	
	5.0+5	3.0+7		Expt Rept	KFK – 1000	Jun 68	– + GRPH TOF HIGH RESOL EXPT	
				Conf	68Wash. 2 743	Mar 68	– + PPR E9. FLUCTUATIONS OBS	
	4.2+5	3.2+7		Data	EXFOR20010.009	Mar 71	5632PTS.	
Total	1.2+0	5.2+0	MUN	Expt Jour	ZN/A 31 115	Feb 76	Waschkowski+ TRANS RH,AG RES T§	+
				Jour	PRL 36 1021	Apr 76	Koester+ N – E INT EVALUATION.	
	1.3+0	5.2+0		Data	EXFOR20603.008	Jun 76	2PTS.	
Total	2.2+5		ANL	Expt Prog	WASH – 1013	Nov 58	Kimball+ VDG ST NDG.	
	2.2+5			Data	EXFOR12234.002	Jun 76	. 1 PT. SIGMA.	
Total	1.8+7	2.2+7	CNM	Expt Rept	INIS – MF – 1743	May 75	Maggi. THESIS.TRANS,SCIN – DET,GRAPH	+
	1.8+7	2.2+7		Data	EXFOR30378.004	Feb 77	11 PTS, READ FROM CURVE.	

83 Bismuth 209

Quantity	Energy (ev) Min	Max	Lab	Type	Documentation Ref Vol Page	Date	Author, Comments	Data
Elastic	2.5−2		ORL	Expt Jour	PR 81 527	Feb 51	Shull+	+
	2.5−2			Data	EXFOR11043.	Jun 76	. 3 PTS. BAS,COH,COH AMP.	
Elastic	2.5−2		BNL	Expt Jour	PR 83 379	Jul 51	Weiss.	+
	2.5−2			Data	EXFOR11580.008	Jun 76	. 1 PT, COH	
Elastic	2.5−2		BNL	Expt Priv	HARVEY	Dec 52	Harvey+	+
	2.5−2			Data	EXFOR12226.002	Jun 76	. 1 PT. BAS	
Elastic	2.5−2		BNL	Expt Priv	HUGHES	53	Hughes.	+
	2.5−2			Data	EXFOR12243.004	Jun 76	. 1 PT. COH	
Elastic	1.0+6		WIS	Expt Jour	PR 93 1062	Mar 54	Walt.	+
	1.0+6			Data	EXFOR11637.080	Jun 76	. 1 PT. SIGMA.	
Elastic	3.7+6		BAR	Expt Jour	PR 94 1267	Jun 54	Snowden+	+
	3.7+6			Data	EXFOR11965.008	Jun 76	. 1 PT. SIGMA.	
Elastic	4.1+6		LAS	Expt Jour	PR 98 677	May 55	Walt+	+
	4.1+6			Data	EXFOR11215.054	Jun 76	. 1 PT. SIGMA.	
Elastic	1.5+7		LRL	Theo Jour	PR 101 1833	Mar 56	Bjorklund+,OPTMDL CALC SIG=3.4 B	
Elastic	5.0+5		LAS	Expt Jour	PR 104 731	Nov 56	Allen+,6.3B+−10 TO 15PC	+
	5.0+5			Data	EXFOR12207.005	Jun 76	. 1 PT. SIGMA.	
Elastic	2.9+6		CCP	Expt Jour	AE 3 498	Dec 57	Popov.INTEGRAL ANG DISTRIB 5.9+−0.2B	+
				Jour	JNE 9 9	Jun 59	TRANSLATN.*	
				Jour	SJA 3 1379	57	TRANSLATN.*	
Elastic	4.2+6		TNC	Expt Rept	WADC−TR−59−107	Feb 59	Bostrom+ INTEG ANG DIST CURVES	+
	4.2+6			Data	EXFOR11130.023	Jun 76	. 1 PT. SIGMA.	
Elastic	1.5+7		CRC	Expt Jour	NP 15 155	Feb 60	Cross+,SMALL SAMPLE,CFD TOT−NONELAST	+
	1.5+7			Data	EXFOR11465.009	Jun 76	. 1 PT. SIGMA.	
Elastic	2.2+5		FEI	Expt Jour	ZET 38 1434	May 60	Lovchikova+ INTEGRATD ANGDIS,=8.23B	
				Jour	JET 11 1036	Nov 60	. ENGL OF ZET 38 1434	
Elastic	1.5+7		VIR	Expt Jour	PR 128 1271	Nov 62	Hudson+, 2.64+−.20B,INTEGRAL OF DIFF	+
	1.5+7			Data	EXFOR12180.004	Jun 76	. 1 PT. SIGMA.	
Elastic	1.0−3		MUN	Expt Jour	ZAP 14 738	Dec 62	MAIER−LEIBNIZ.COH.SCAT.LGTH.REFRAKT	+
Elastic	2.5−2	2.5−2	MUN	Expt Jour	ZN/A 19 354	63	Scherm+ INTEGRATED DIFF EL. 12MB.	+
Elastic	1.0+6	2.0+7	UEN	Theo Jour	ZN/A 19 406	Apr 64	Krell.OPTMOD RECURSION FORM FOR INT	
Elastic	4.0+6		KUR	Expt Jour	DOK 158 574	Sep 64	Gorlov+	+
	4.0+6			Data	EXFOR40221.036	May 74	.1 DATA LINE	
Elastic	1.0+5	1.4+7	AGN	Eval Rept	TID−21629	Dec 64	Perkins+CALCTD FROM BNL400,UCRL5573.	
Elastic	9.4+0	9.4+0	MUN	Expt Jour	ZP 186 23	65	Triftshauser. N−SPEC MAX 10EV.	+
Elastic	6.0+6		DKE	Expt Jour	NP 62 511	Feb 65	Wilenzick.CS=3.4+−.5B	+
	6.0+6			Data	EXFOR11287.046	Jun 76	. 1 PT. SIGMA.	
Elastic	2.0+6		FEI	Expt Rept	EANDC−50 200	Jul 65	Kazakova+ EXPT,TABLE CFD OPTMODEL	+
				Prog	YFI−3 6	Sep 66	.TABLE	
				Prog	INDC−E−140 6	Sep 66	.ENGLISH TRANSL OF YFI−3 6 9/66	
Elastic	3.0+5	8.0+5	IFU	ExTh Jour	AE 20 8	Jan 66	Korzh+ SUMMARY OF SEVERAL YRS WORK	+
				Jour	UFZ 9 577	64	.	
				Jour	AE 16 207	64	.	
				Jour	SJA 20 8	Jul 66	.ENGLISH TRANSL OF AE 20 8 1/66	
				Rept	INDSWG−101 112	65	.=UFZ9.ENGL NO GRPHS.RUSS LARGER GPH	
Elastic	4.0+6	6.0+6	LAS	Theo Rept	LA−3538	Sep 66	Agee+ OPTMDL MODEL+H−F FOR COMP.	
Elastic	2.4+7		ORL	Theo Jour	NP/A 91 75	Jan 67	Satchler. OPTMDL CFD EXPT	
Elastic	1.5+6		IFU	Expt Prog	YFI−5 42	Oct 67	Korzh+ TBL OPTMDL PARAMS + TOTELAST	
				Rept	INDC−232E	67	. ENGL OF YFI−5 42	
Elastic	1.3+0		MUN	Expt Prog	EANDC(E)−89	Jan 68	Fehsenfeld+ FREE SCAT SIGMA.	
Elastic	1.5+6		IFU	Comp Jour	YF 7 277	Feb 68	Korzh+ OPTMOD PARS−FIT TO EXPTL−SIG	
				Jour	SNP 7 2 190	Aug 68	TRANSLATN.*	
Elastic	6.0+6	1.5+7	OHO	Theo Jour	NC/B 53 2 363	Feb 68	Cassola+ OPTMOD CALC CFD EXPT.	
Elastic	4.0−4	1.3−3	JUL	Expt Jour	NUK 12 4	Dec 68	Scherm. INCOHERENT SCAT SIG EXPT	+
				Conf	67Juelich 83	Apr 67	−. PRELIMINARY DATA.	
	4.0−4	1.8−3		Rept	JUEL−430−NP	Mar 64	−. INCOHERENT SCATTERING.	
				Jour	ZN/A 19 354	Mar 64	−. INCOHERENT SCAT. SUPERSEDED	
Elastic	4.0+6		KUR	Expt Jour	YF 8 1086	Dec 68	Gorlov+ SIG VAL GVN,SMALL−ANG−SCATNG	
				Jour	SNP 8 630	Jun 69	TRANSLATN.*	
Elastic	6.1+6	8.0+6	AE	Expt Rept	AE−366	Jun 69	Holmqvist+.VDG.TOF.20−160DEG.+LEGNDR	+
				Rept	AE−430	Sep 71	−+ INTEGRATED ANGDIST VALUES	
				Conf	70Helsinki 2 341	Jun 70	−+ OPTMOD ANALYSIS. 8 MEV	
				Jour	AF 38 403	Nov 68	−+ INTEG ANGDIST.OPTMOD ANAL	
				Conf	68Wash. 845	Mar 68	−+ ANGDIST.GRPH+OPTMOD ANAL	
	6.1+6	8.1+6		Data	EXFOR20019.213	Sep 71	3PTS.	
Elastic	2.5+6		BRC	Theo Prog	EANDC(E)127U	Apr 70	Rolard+	

83 Bismuth 209

Quantity	Energy (ev) Min	Max	Lab	Type	Documentation Ref Vol Page	Date	Author, Comments	Data
Elastic	3.0+5	1.5+6	ANL	Expt	Jour NSE 41 63	Jul 70	Smith+RESULTS CFD OPT MDL,STAT CALCS	+
					Rept ANL-7636	Nov 69	- +INTEGRATED CS,LEG COEFS.TBLS	
					Rept EANDC(US)-62	Jun 64	- .TOF,TBL.50KEV STEPS,20KEV RSLN	
	3.0+5	1.5+6		Data	EXFOR10010.002	Mar 76	96PTS.INTEGRATED CS GVN.	
Elastic	8.9+5		ANL	Expt	Rept ANL-7935	Jun 72	COX+ 4 PI B(O)	+
	8.9+5			Data	EXFOR10332.132	Jun 74	1 PT	
Elastic	5.0+4	1.5+7	CCP	Eval	Data SOKRATOR-1038	76	60 PTS	+
Elastic	1.2+0	5.2+0	MUN	Expt	Jour ZN/A 31 115	Feb 76	Waschkowski. FREE SCAT SIGMA.	+
	1.3+0	5.2+0			Jour PRL 36 1021	Apr 76	Koester+COH SCT LENGTH RE-CALC.	
	0.0+0	0.0+0			Data EXFOR20603.007	Jun 76	1PNT.FREE ATOM AT ZERO ENERGY	
	1.3+0	5.2+0			Data EXFOR20598.004	Jun 76	2PTS.COH.SC.AMP.	
Elastic	1.5+6		KTY	Expt	Abst BAP 20 1195	Sep 75	Brandenberger+DIFF MEAS.CFD ANL.NDG	+
	1.5+6				Data EXFOR10578.005	Nov 76	1PT=4596+ -59MB FROM LEG COEFS.	
Diff Elastic	2.5+6		HAR	Expt	Jour PM 44 1398	Dec 53	Poole.AT 97DEG 230+ -40MB/SR,P RECOIL	
Diff Elastic	1.0+6		WIS	Expt	Jour PR 93 1062	Mar 54	Walt+ HE COUNTER 30-150DEG LAB CURVE	+
	1.0+6				Data EXFOR11637.082	Jun 76	. 9 PTS. DSIGMA.	
Diff Elastic	3.7+6		BAR	Expt	Jour PR 94 1267	Jun 54	Snowdon+ D-D NS RING GEOM.	+
	3.7+6				Data EXFOR11965.009	Jun 76	. 19 PTS. DSIGMA.	
Diff Elastic	4.1+6		LAS	Expt	Jour PR 98 677	May 55	Walt+ BIASED SCINT ANG DISTR CURVE	+
	4.1+6				Data EXFOR11215.057	Jun 76	. 12 PTS. DSIGMA.	
Diff Elastic	1.5+7		CRC	Expt	Jour PR 99 621	Jul 55	Cross+ MIN AT 27 AND 57 DEGREES	
Diff Elastic	2.5+6		LAS	Revw	Conf 55Geneva 2 18	Aug 55	Walt.P588,CURV,DISCUS OF RESULTS	
Diff Elastic	5.0+5	1.6+6	WIS	Expt	Jour PR 100 1315	Dec 55	Darden+,ALSO1MEV100KEVRSLN CF OPTMDL	+
	5.0+5	1.6+6			Data EXFOR11638.010	Jun 76	. 8 PTS. DSIGMA.	
Diff Elastic	1.4+7		NRL	Expt	Jour PR 101 684	Jan 56	Elliott.5-55DEG CYL GEOMETRY SCINT	+
	1.4+7				Data EXFOR11568.006	Jun 76	. 12 PTS. DSIGMA.	
Diff Elastic	1.4+7		LRL	Theo	Jour PR 101 1047	Feb 56	Culler+,OPTMDL CALC ANG DISTR CFDXPT	
Diff Elastic	1.0+6	7.0+6	LAS	Eval	Rept LA-2016	Jun 56	Longley+,4ES,ANG DIST 3-DEG STEPS	
Diff Elastic	5.0+5		LAS	Expt	Jour PR 104 731	Nov 56	Allen+,CURV ABSOLUTE 25 TO 130DEG	+
	5.0+5				Data EXFOR12207.016	Jun 76	. 9 PTS. DSIGMA.	
Diff Elastic	4.4+6		WES	Expt	Jour PR 104 1069	Nov 56	Weddell.FOTOPLATE.82DEG 185+ -40MB.	+
	4.4+6				Data EXFOR11479.007	Jun 76	. 1 PT. DSIGMA.	
Diff Elastic	3.3+6		ETH	Expt	Jour HPA 29 545	Dec 56	Remond.30-150DEG CURV.ABS CF FPW CCB	+
	3.4+6				Jour HPA 28 331	Aug 55	Brugger+.30DEG TO150DEG SHORT NOTICE	
Diff Elastic	2.5+6	1.5+7	LAS	Theo	Jour PR 104 1319	Dec 56	Beyster+,THEORY CFD XPTS CURVES	
	1.0+5	1.8+7			Rept LA-2099	Dec 56	- +,21ES,OPTMDL CALC CFD EXPT	
Diff Elastic	2.5+6	7.0+6	LAS	Expt	Jour PR 104 1319	Dec 56	Beyster+,12 TO 160DEG CURVES	+
	2.5+6	7.0+6			Data EXFOR11220.033	Jun 76	. 33 PTS. DSIGMA.	
Diff Elastic	2.0+4	2.0+7	WES	Theo	Jour PR 104 1399	Dec 56	Emmerich+,LEG POLY XPNSN CRV CFD XPT	
Diff Elastic	9.0+5		FEI	Expt	Jour AE 2 174	Feb 57	Lovchikova. 40-140DEG,(GN)SOURCE	
					Jour SJA 2 197	Feb 57	. ENGL OF AE 2 174	
Diff Elastic	2.0+6		KUR	Expt	Jour ZET 33 294	Jul 57	Aleksandrov.HE4-CHAMBR,4-25DEG,GRAPH	
					Jour JET 6 228	Jan 58	TRANSLATN.*	
Diff Elastic	1.4+7		LAS	Expt	Jour PR 107 824	Aug 57	Rosen+	+
	1.4+7				Data EXFOR11223.011	Jun 76	. 4 PTS.DSIGMA.	
Diff Elastic	2.9+6		CCP	Expt	Jour AE 3 498	Dec 57	Popov.RING GEOM. 6 ANGLES 30-150DEGS	+
					Jour JNE 9 9	Jun 59	TRANSLATN.*	
					Jour SJA 3 1379	57	TRANSLATN.*	
Diff Elastic	None		CUW	Expt	Rept CWR-400-7	58	Snowdon. TO BE PUBLISHED.	
Diff Elastic	5.0+4	1.0+5	DKE	Expt	Jour PR 109 1620	Mar 58	Block+ 180/90DEG 0.94AVG	
Diff Elastic	1.5+7		VIR	Expt	Jour NP 6 210	Mar 58	Berko+. TOF. GRAPH. 10-110 DEG.	
Diff Elastic	4.1+6	1.5+7	LRL	Theo	Jour RMP 30 414	Apr 58	Fernbach. TH CURVE AND EXPTL POINTS	
	7.0+6				Rept UCRL-4927	Jul 57	Bjorklund+ OPTMDL CALC 6-PARAM FIT	
	1.4+7				Rept UCRL-4926	Jul 57	- + OPTMDL CALC 6-PARAM FIT	
	1.5+7				Jour PR 101 1833	Mar 56	- +,OPTMDL ANG DISTR CFD EXPT	
Diff Elastic	2.8+6		KTY	Expt	Abst BAP 3 268	Jun 58	Kern. TOF C-W	
Diff Elastic	4.1+6	1.4+7	BRK	Theo	Conf 58Geneva 14 24	Sep 58	Bjorklund+.PPR649,CURVE CFD EXPT	
Diff Elastic	2.2+5	2.8+6	IFU	Expt	Conf 58Geneva 15 18	Sep 58	Pasechnik+.PPR2030,CURV,N-ANGL-DISTR	+
	2.5+6		LAS	Prog	Rept WASH-1006	Oct 58	Cranberg. OKS BEYSTER	
Diff Elastic	1.4+7	1.5+7	MOS	Theo	Jour NP 8 325	Oct 58	Lukyanov+CFD OTHERS,EXPT DATA.CURVES	
Diff Elastic	1.4+7	1.5+7	KON	Expt	Jour JPJ 13 1248	Nov 58	Yuasa.ANG.DIST.CFD OPTMOD THEORY	+
	1.4+7				Data EXFOR20281.005	Jun 74	11PTS.D/DA.	
Diff Elastic	4.2+6		TNC	Expt	Rept WADC-TR-59-107	Feb 59	Bostrom+ TOF CURVE+TABLE 20-140DEG	+
	4.2+6				Data EXFOR11130.028	Jun 76	. 13 PTS. DSIGMA.	
Diff Elastic	2.8+6		IFU	ExTh	Conf 59Tashkent 1 103	Sep 59	Pasechnik. XPT AND OPTMDL-TH,GRAPH	
					Rept AEC-TR-6398	64	.VOL 1,P120.ENGL OF 59TASHKE 1 103	
Diff Elastic	1.4+7		ANL	Expt	Jour PR 116 1571	Dec 59	Rayburn.MONTE CARLO CORRECT,CFD TH	+
	1.4+7				Data EXFOR11806.006	Jun 76	. 26 PTS. DSIGMA.	

83 Bismuth 209

Quantity	Energy (ev) Min	Max	Lab	Type	Documentation Ref Vol Page	Date	Author, Comments	Data
Diff Elastic	1.5+7		CRC	Expt	Jour NP 15 155	Feb 60	Cross+.25ANGLES8–130DEG SMALL SAMPLE	+
	1.5+7			Data	EXFOR11465.010	Jun 76	. 34 PTS. DSIGMA.	
Diff Elastic	2.2+5		FEI	Expt	Jour ZET 38 1434	May 60	Lovchikova+ GRAPH SIG(COS),30–150DEG	
					Jour JET 11 1036	Nov 60	. ENGL OF ZET 38 1434	
Diff Elastic	2.4+7		LOK	Theo	Conf 60Kingston 146	Aug 60	Walt+.CURVE,OPTMDL FIT CFD EXPT	
Diff Elastic	1.4+7		LVN	Expt	Jour ASS 75 102	61	Deconninck+ SMALL ANGLE SCATTERING.	
Diff Elastic	1.5+7		IFU	Expt	Jour ZET 40 725	Mar 61	Strizhak.GRAPHS SIG(ANGL) CFD OPTMDL	+
					Jour JET 13 506	Sep 61	TRANSLATN.*	
Diff Elastic	2.4+7		LRL	Expt	Jour PR 125 276	Jan 62	Stuart+ 15–90DEG. OKS OPTMDL	+
					Rept UCRL–6277	62	.SUPERSEDED	
	2.4+7				Data EXFOR11490.005	Jun 76	. 43 PTS. DSIGMA.	
Diff Elastic	1.0+6	2.4+7	ORL	Theo	Jour NP 32 353	May 62	Perey+BUCK 5ES,OPTICALMOD FITTED XPT	
Diff Elastic	1.5+7		VIR	Expt	Jour PR 128 1271	Nov 62	Hudson+ TOF.RSLN1.8MEV. CFD OPTMDL	+
					Abst DA/B 23 4393	62	. THESIS ABST	
	1.5+7				Data EXFOR12180.009	Jun 76	. 29 PTS. DSIGMA.	
Diff Elastic	2.4+7		LRL	Expt	Jour PR 128 2339	Dec 62	Wong+ 20–70DEG 5DEG STEPS OKS OPTMDL	
Diff Elastic	1.4+7		FTI	Expt	Jour ZET 44 130	Jan 63	Dukarevich+ GRAPH ANGL=3–20 DEG	+
					Jour JET 17 89	Jul 63	TRANSLATN.*	
	1.4+7				Data EXFOR40078.004	Oct 71	DIFF SIG AT 13 ANGLES	
Diff Elastic	4.0+6	7.0+6	LAS	Expt	Jour PR 129 1649	Feb 63	Thomson. SIG AT 90DEG	+
	4.0+6	7.0+6			Data EXFOR11495.057	Jun 76	. 2 PTS. DSIGMA.	
Diff Elastic	2.5+6	8.0+6	LAS	Expt	Conf 63Houston 96	Feb 63	Cranberg+ GRPH DIFFSIG,CFD H–F CALC	
Diff Elastic	4.0–4	1.8–3	MUN	Expt	Jour ZN/A 19 354	Mar 64	Scherm+ISOTROP INCOHER.SCAT SIG=12MB	+
Diff Elastic	3.0+5		IFU	Expt	Jour UFZ 9 577	May 64	Korzh.GRAPH SIG(COS),TBL DERIVD VALS	+
					Rept INDSWG–101 112	65	.=UFZ9.ENGL NO GRPHS.RUSS LARGER GPH	
Diff Elastic	1.0+5	3.0+6	BNL	Theo	Jour PR/B 135 895	Aug 64	Auerbach+ OPTMDL PAR,TBL IN BNL818	
Diff Elastic	4.0+6		KUR	Expt	Jour DOK 158 574	Sep 64	Gorlov+,POLRZ NS,TBL SIG VS COS	+
					Jour SPD 9 806	Mar 65	. ENGL OF DOK 158 574	
					Rept INDSWG–101 112	65	. LARGE GRPH.ALSO AVAILABLE IN ENGL.	
	4.0+6				Data EXFOR40221.035	May 74	.SIGMA IN MB/SR AT 17 ANGLES GIVEN	
Diff Elastic	1.0+5	1.4+7	AGN	Eval	Rept TID–21629	Dec 64	Perkins+ LEGNDR COEF CALC FROM DAT.	
Diff Elastic	6.0+6		DKE	Expt	Jour NP 62 511	Feb 65	Wilenzick+ 20–150D CFD OPTMDL CALCS	–
	6.0+6				Data EXFOR11287.047	Jun 76	. 12 PTS. DSIGMA.	
Diff Elastic	8.5+4	7.0+5	HAR	Expt	Jour NIM 34 29	Apr 65	Barnard+.75 DEG GRPH.CONT SPEC LI(PN	
Diff Elastic	7.0+6	2.4+7	LAS	Theo	Jour NAT 206 284	Apr 65	Rosen+ OPTMOD+SPIN–ORBIT POT. 2+7MEV	
Diff Elastic	7.0+6		LAS	Expt	Jour PRL 14 913	May 65	Zafiratos+ 15–165DEG. CF OPTMDL.	+
	7.0+6				Data EXFOR12220.003	Jun 76	. 30 PTS. DSIGMA.	
Diff Elastic	8.0+5		IFU	Theo	Jour UFZ 10 6 586	Jun 65	Korzh.OPTMDL GRAPH SIG,CFD XPT	
					Jour IZV 29 862	May 65	.	
Diff Elastic	1.4+7		ORL	ExTh	Jour NP 68 97	Jun 65	Stelson+ XPT CFD DIST OPTMDL CALC	+
	1.4+7			Expt	Data EXFOR11527.026	Jun 76	. 6 PTS. DSIGMA.	
Diff Elastic	2.0+6		FEI	Expt	Rept EANDC–50 200	Jul 65	Kazakova+ EXPT,CURVE CFD OPTMODEL	+
					Prog ICD–2 112	Jul 65	.CURVE	
					Prog INDSWG–101E	65	.ENGLISH TRANSL OF ICD–2 112 7/65	
Diff Elastic	8.0+5		IFU	Theo	Conf 65Antwerp § 193	Jul 65	Pasechnic+. OPT.MOD.PARAMETERS	
Diff Elastic	5.0+5	1.0+6	LAS	Expt	Priv DAY	Jul 65	DAY.	+
	5.0+5	1.0+6			Data EXFOR12191.013	Jun 76	. 30 PTS. DSIGMA.	
Diff Elastic	8.0+5	4.5+6	ORL	Theo	Rept ORNL–TM–1238	Sep 65	Smith. H–F ANALYSIS GOOD AGREEMENT.	
Diff Elastic	1.0+6		LAS	Theo	WASH–1064 84	Oct 65	Rosen+, OPTMDL+ CPD ELST CFD WIS XPT	
Diff Elastic	5.0+6		ORL	Expt	Prog WASH–1064 121	Oct 65	Dickens+,TOF,THETA=30–130DEG,TBC NDG	
Diff Elastic	3.0+5	8.0+5	IFU	ExTh	Jour AE 20 8	Jan 66	Korzh+SJA 20 8 SUM OF SEV YRS WORK	+
	5.0+5	8.0+5		Expt	Jour AE 16 207	Mar 64	Pasechnik+ SPH,30–140 DEGREES	
					Jour JNE 19 278	65	. ENGL OF AE 16 207	
					Jour SJA 16 246	Sep 64	. ENGL OF AE 16 207	
					Jour EAF 16 3 2	Mar 64	. FRENCH OF AE 16 207	
Diff Elastic	4.0+5	1.0+6	HAR	ExTh	Jour NP 76 369	Feb 66	Ferguson+ OPTMDL PARS TO FIT POLARIZ	+
Diff Elastic	4.0+6	6.7+6	LAS	Expt	Prog WASH–1068 114	Mar 66	Hopkins+,ANAL TBD,NDG	
Diff Elastic	4.0+6	6.0+6	LAS	Theo	Rept LA–3538	Sep 66	Agee+ OPTMDL MODEL+H–F FOR COMP	
Diff Elastic	3.2+6		BCM	Expt	Jour NP 89 154	Dec 66	Becker+ 12 ANGLES GRAPH CFD OPTMDL	+
	3.2+6				Data EXFOR11511.037	Jun 76	. 13 PTS. DSIGMA.	
Diff Elastic	4.0+6		LAS	Theo	Rept LA–3788	67	Beery+.OPTMOD CALC POLARIZ ANG DISTR	
Diff Elastic	1.0+6	2.5+6	JAE	Theo	Rept JAERI–1126 1	Jan 67	Kawai+IGARASI.OPT MDL CAL C ELIESE–2	
Diff Elastic	2.4+7		ORL	Theo	Jour NP/A 91 75	Jan 67	Satchler. OPTMDL CFD XPT	
Diff Elastic	4.4+6	5.5+6	WIS	ExTh	Jour NP/A 95 193	Mar 67	Mahajan.POLARIZATION OPTMDL ANALYSIS	
					Abst DA/B 28 1093	Sep 67	.SEE ALSO	
Diff Elastic	3.0+4	1.4+7	AI	Eval	Rept NAA–SR–11980	Apr 67	Campbell+ LEG COEFS TBL+CURVS C–MSYS	
Diff Elastic	7.0+6	2.4+7	SAF	Eval	Jour AP 42 262	Apr 67	Engelbrecht+ OPTMDL CALCS CFD EXPTS	
Diff Elastic	2.5+6		LAS	Expt	Jour PR 159 969	Jul 67	Cranberg+ TOF,CURV,T0+–3PC,CF OPTMDL	

83 Bismuth 209

Quantity	Energy (ev) Min	Max	Lab	Type	Documentation Ref Vol Page	Date	Author, Comments	Data
Diff Elastic	4.0+6		KUR	Expt	Jour PL/B 25 197	Aug 67	Gorlov+,2 TO 170DEG.CFD OPTMODEL	
					Jour YF 6 910	Nov 70	− + SCAT POLRZ N,OPTMOD CFD,CURV	
					Rept ANL−TR−462	Apr 67	SEE ALSO *	
				ExTh	Conf 67Kharkov 175	Feb 67	Gorlov.POLRSD NS,ANGLES=10−170 DEGRS	
				Expt	Jour ZEP 5 131	Feb 67	− + COULOMB+NUCL SIG(ANG),GRAPHS	
					Jour JEL 5 106	Feb 67	. ENGL OF ZEP 5 131	
Diff Elastic	1.4+7		CNE	Theo	Jour NP/A 105 569	Dec 67	Erramuspe. OPTMOD. ISOSP COEFF CALC.	
Diff Elastic	4.0+6		IFU	Theo	Jour UFZ 13 51	Jan 68	Kashuba+ GRPH,EXPT CFD OPTMOD−CALC	
					Jour UPJ 13 33	Jul 68	TRANSLATN.*	
Diff Elastic	2.5+6	2.4+7	CCP	Theo	Jour YF 7 283	Feb 68	Aver'Yanov+ OPTMOD SIG(ANG) CFD EXPT	
					Jour SNP 7 2 193	Aug 68	TRANSLATN.*	
Diff Elastic	1.5+6		IFU	Comp	Jour YF 7 277	Feb 68	Korzh+ GRPH SIG(ANG),OPTMOD PARS−FIT	
					Jour SNP 7 2 190	Aug 68	TRANSLATN.*	
Diff Elastic	1.5+7		OHO	Theo	Jour NC/B 53 2 363	Feb 68	Cassola+ OPTMOD CALC CFD EXPT.	
Diff Elastic	5.0+5	2.5+6	BNL	Eval	Rept BNL−50151	Oct 68	Moore.OPTMDL FIT TO DATA,ALSO 1 MEV	
Diff Elastic	4.0+6		KUR	Expt	Jour YF 8 1086	Dec 68	Gorlov+ SIG−GRPH,SPIN−ORBIT−ASSYMTRY	+
				ExTh	Jour IZV 34 138	Jan 70	− + OPTMOD,2−21DEG.CURVES,TABLE	
				Expt	Jour SNP 8 630	Jun 69	TRANSLATN.*	
				ExTh	Rept IAE−1653	68	Gorlov+ ANGDIST 2−21 DEG,SIG, GRPH	
					Conf 67Kharkov 175	Feb 67	− .POLRSD NS,ANGLES=2−21 DEGREES	
					Jour BAS 34 126	Jan 70	. ENGL OF IZV 34 138	
	4.0+6			Expt	Data EXFOR40307.010	Nov 76	DIFF CS 2−21 DEG(8 ANGLES)	
Diff Elastic	2.0+6	6.0+6	SCU	Theo	Rept ICD−6 236	69	Averyanov+CALC ANGDIST CFD EXPT,GRPH	
Diff Elastic	5.0+5	2.4+7	BAT	Theo	Jour PR 177 1706	Jan 69	Hogan+ OPTMDL CALC WITH MAGN INTERCT	
Diff Elastic	6.8+6		KGU	Theo	Jour YF 9 190	Jan 69	Ol'Khovskij+DELAY−T(ANG) GRPH,OPTMOD	
					Jour SNP 9 114	Jul 69	TRANSLATN.*	
Diff Elastic	6.1+6	8.0+6	AE	Expt	Rept AE−366	Jun 69	Holmqvist+.VDG.TOF.20−160DEG.+LEGNDR	+
					Jour NP/A 188 24	Jun 72	− + OPTMOD ANAL OF 8MEV DATA	
					Rept AE−430	Sep 71	− + TBLS + GEN OPTMOD FITS	
					Conf 70Helsinki 2 341	Jun 70	− + OPTMOD ANALYSIS. 8 MEV	
					Jour AF 38 403	Nov 68	− + SYSTEMATICS OF OPT PARAMS	
					Jour PL/B 26 620	Apr 68	− + SYMMETRY TERM IN OPTMOD	
					Conf 68Wash. 845	Mar 68	− + ANGDIST.GRPH+OPTMOD ANAL	
	6.1+6	8.1+6			Data EXFOR20019.	Sep 71	96PTS.D/DA,LEG.FIT.	
Diff Elastic	6.1+6	8.1+6	CCP	Comp	Rept ICD−6 50	70	Bazazjanc+ ANGDIST EXPTS,GRPH AT 3ES	
Diff Elastic	1.1+6		ANL	Expt	Prog ANL−7610 9	Jan 70	Cox+. CURVE. CFD OPTMOD.	
Diff Elastic	4.0+6		CCP	Revw	Jour AE 28 310	Apr 70	Lebedeva+ ANOMALOUS SIG(ANG) GRAPH	
					Jour EAF 28 4 35	Apr 70	. FRENCH OF AE 28 310	
Diff Elastic	1.4+6		ISS	Expt	Jour JPJ 28 1116	May 70	Katori+.DEPOLRZ IN FIG.OPT−MDL ANAL	
					Conf 70Madison 638	Sep 70	− + POLRZD NS,DEPOLARIZATN MEAST	
Diff Elastic	3.0+5	1.5+6	ANL	Expt	Jour NSE 41 63	Jul 70	Smith+,TOF,20KEV RESOL,CURVES	+
					Rept ANL−7636	Nov 69	− +LEG COEFS IN APPENDIX.	
				ExTh	Jour PL 11 331	Aug 64	.TOF 10AS 20−145LAB XPT CFD OPTMDL	
				Expt	Rept EANDC(US)−62	Jun 64	Smith+TOF.TBL.50KEV.STEPS.20KEV RSLN	
	3.0+5	1.5+6			Data EXFOR10010.003	Mar 76	428PTS.LEG COEFS GVN.	
Diff Elastic	4.0+6		KUR	Expt	Jour ZEP 12 181	Aug 70	Morozov+ SIG(ANG=140 TO 180) GRAPH	
					Jour JEL 12 125	Aug 70	. ENGL OF ZEP 12 181	
Diff Elastic	0.0+0	1.5+7	FEI	Eval	Book NIKOLAEV 176	72	.LEG COEFFS+ANG DISTRIBUTS,GRAPH	
Diff Elastic	1.5+6	3.6+6	JAE	Expt	Jour NP/A 179 513	Jan 72	Tanaka+ ANGDIST CFD OPTMOD,C−CHANNEL	+
	1.4+6	3.6+6			Priv TANAKA	Aug 71	− . TOF.REL H(NN). +LEGENDRE FIT	
	1.5+6	3.6+6			Data EXFOR20337.	Jul 74	105PTS.D/DA,LEG.FIT.	
Diff Elastic	1.4+7		KGU	Expt	Conf 72Kiev 2 16	Jan 72	Gurtovoj+ ABST,NDG.DIFFSIG 30−130DEG	
Diff Elastic	1.5+7		AMS	Expt	Jour NP/A 181 545	Feb 72	Kuijper+ LIQUID SCINT. 8AS 23−120LAB	+
	1.4+7				Jour NIM 77 55	Jun 69	− .PLURAL NEUTRON SCATTERING	
	1.5+7				Data EXFOR20223.009	May 74	8PTS.D/DA.	
Diff Elastic	8.9+5		ANL	Expt	Rept ANL−7935	Jun 72	Cox+. CFD OPTMOD,HAUSER−FESHBACH	+
	8.9+5				Data EXFOR10332.033	Jun 74	8 PTS	
Diff Elastic	6.2−2		BUC	Expt	Prog INDC(SEC)−28	Sep 72	.SAME AS INDC(RUM)−3 16	
Diff Elastic	1.4+7		KYU	Expt	Jour NP/A 204 129	Apr 73	Matoba+ TOF, 10−160DEG, OPTMODEL	+
	1.4+7				Data EXFOR20308.002	Jun 74	25PTS.D/DA.	
Diff Elastic	8.0+5		SCU	Comp	Rept YK−15 153	Aug 73	Aver'Janov+ H−F,OPTMOD,DIFFSIG,GRAPH	
Diff Elastic	3.2+6		AMS	Theo	Jour NP/A 222 93	Apr 74	Zijp+ LEG.COEFF COMPOUND ELASTIC.H−F	
Diff Elastic	4.6+3	6.5+6	FEI	Theo	Rept INDC(CCP)−39	Jul 74	.Pl. ENGLISH OF YK−8/2 3	
					Rept YK−8/2 3	Sep 72	Bazazjants+ ANISOTR GROUP−PARAMS,TBL	
	7.0+6		AE	Expt	Jour NP/A 232 436	Nov 74	Corcalciuc+ ANGDIST,GRAPH.TABLE.	
					Conf 73Kiev 3 87	May 73	Holmqvist+ SHORT DESCRIPTION.OPTMOD.	
Diff Elastic	+7		BUC	Expt	Prog INDC(SEC)−42	Dec 74	Corcalciuc+ FORWARD ANGDIST,NDG	
Diff Elastic	2.4+7		UFT	Theo	Rept KHFTI−75−15	75	Bereznhoj+ GRPH,CFD EXPT.NUCL RADIUS	

83 Bismuth 209

Quantity	Energy (ev) Min	Max	Lab	Type	Documentation Ref Vol Page	Date	Author, Comments	Data
Diff Elastic	1.4+7	1.5+7	JAE	Theo Conf	JAERI – M – 5984	Feb 75	Tanaka.OPTMDL/COUPLD CH.GRPH CFD EXP	
Diff Elastic	4.4+6		FEI	Expt Rept	YK – 19 66	May 75	Trykova+ SIG(ANG),TBL,GRAPH	+
	4.4+6			Data	EXFOR40338.007	Jan 76	.DATA IN B/SR AT 14ANGLS GVN	
Diff Elastic	4.3+6		UBC	Expt Jour	CJP 51 2197	73	Martin+3ANGS.TBL OPTMDL PARS.GRPH.	+
				Abst	DA/B 35 5580	May 75	Mcfadden.5TO15DEG.CFD OPT MDL.AGREE.	
	4.3+6			Data	EXFOR10375.	Apr 76	DATA UNOBTAINABLE FROM AUTHORS	
Diff Elastic	1.5+7		ALB	Expt Prog	A – ALB – 75 27	Jun 75	Benenson+TOF.3ANG.2.6,4.2,5.5MEV LVL	
Diff Elastic	7.5+6	1.4+7	BRL	Expt Jour	PL/B 58 277	Sep 75	Bucher+VDG D(D,N).SMALL ANG SCAT.	+
	7.6+6	1.4+7		Jour	PL/B 58 277	Sep 75	– +3ES.SMALL ANG SCT.GRPHS.	
	1.1+7	1.4+7		Data	EXFOR10556.002	Jul 78	. 8PTS.2ES.ANGDIST	
Diff Elastic	5.0+4	1.5+7	CCP	Eval Data	SOKRATOR – 1038	76	60 PTS	+
Diff Elastic	2.5+6		PAD	Expt Jour	NIM 135 483	76	Giordano+ SCATT+POL. 1TO10 DEGR GRPH	+
				Jour	NC/A 13 867	Feb 73	Drigo+ SMALL ANGLE SCATTERING	
	2.4+6			Data	EXFOR20664.005	Oct 76	3PTS.D/DA.	
Diff Elastic	9.7+6		AE	Expt Prog	KDK – 12 9	Apr 76	Corcalciuc+.TOF 20 TO 160 DEGREES	
				Prog	S – 501 23	Sep 75	– +.TOF 20 TO 160 DEGREES	
Diff Elastic	2.6+7		OHO	Expt Prog	USNDC – 11 209	May 76	Carlson+ TBC.	
Diff Elastic	6.4+6		PAR	Expt Jour	JPR 37 6 651	Jun 76	Ramstein+ ANGDIST.5,130DEG.OPTMDL.	
				Diss	FRNC – TH – 418	Mar 73	– . ORSAY.VDG.	
Diff Elastic	7.0+6		LAS	Expt Conf	76Lowell 1461	Jul 76	Ramstrom+SPIN – ORB.ANG DISTR CFD CALC	
Diff Elastic	1.5+6		KTY	Expt Abst	BAP 20 1195	Sep 75	Brandenberger+CFD ANL MEAS.NDG	+
	1.5+6			Data	EXFOR10578.004	Nov 76	5PTS.LEG COEFS	
Diff Elastic	1.1+7		LIE	Theo Jour	FIZS 9 3 79	77	Lejeune. OPTMOD ANALYSIS.GRAPH	
Polarization	4.0+5		WIS	Expt Jour	PR 96 503	Oct 54	Adair+ POL FOR 50DEG NEUTS CFD TH	
Polarization	3.8+5	9.8+5	WIS	ExTh Jour	NP 6 177	Mar 58	Clement+. POLARIZATION. CFD OPT MDL	
				Expt Rept	AECU – 3628	57	– +.LI7(P,N) SOURCE. 3ANGLES.	
Polarization	1.5+6		DKE	Expt Rept	TID – 19051	62	Olness+ TOF 51.5DEG POLARIZ MEASD	
Polarization	1.0+6	1.9+6	AE	Expt Conf	65KFK 470	Sep 65	Aspelund+.11ES 8AS.GRAPHS NH/NL 3 AS	
Polarization	4.0+6		LAS	Theo Rept	LA – 3788	67	Beery+.OPTMOD CALC COS(THETA) DISTR	
Polarization	4.0+6		KUR	Expt Jour	ZEP 5 131	Feb 67	Gorlov+ SCHWINGER(COUL)+NUC SCAT CFD	+
				Jour	DOK 158 574	Sep 64	– +	
				Jour	JEL 5 106	Feb 67	. ENGL OF ZEP 5 131	
	4.0+6			Data	EXFOR40221.037	May 74	.DIFF POLARZ OF EL SCAT,DATA AT17ANG	
Polarization	4.0+6		KUR	Expt Jour	YF 8 1086	Dec 68	Gorlov+ GRPH POLARIZ – EFF(0 TO 7 DEG)	+
				Jour	SNP 8 630	Jun 69	TRANSLATN.*	
	4.0+6			Data	EXFOR40307.011	Nov 76	DIF.ASYM. 2 – 21 DEG(8 ANGLES)	
Polarization	5.0+5	2.4+7	BAT	Theo Jour	PR 177 1706	Jan 69	Hogan+ OPTMDL CALC WITH MAGN INTERCT	
Polarization	1.1+6		ANL	Expt Prog	ANL – 7610 9	Jan 70	Cox+. CURVE. CFD OPTMOD.	
Polarization	4.0+6		KUR	Expt Jour	ZEP 12 181	Aug 70	Morozov+ POLARIZ(ANG = 140 – 180) GRPH	
				Jour	JEL 12 125	Aug 70	. ENGL OF ZEP 12 181	
Polarization	4.0+6		IJI	Theo Jour	YF 13 1026	May 71	Pasechnik+ POLRZ(ANG) CFD EXPT,GRAPH	
				Jour	SNP 13 589	Nov 71	. ENGL OF YF 13 1026	
Polarization	9.2+5		ANL	Expt Rept	ANL – 7935	Jun 72	Cox+. CFD OPTMOD,HAUSER – FESHBACH	+
	9.2+5			Data	EXFOR10332.067	Jun 74	. 8 PTS.	
Polarization	2.4+6		PAD	Expt Jour	NC/A 13 867	Feb 73	Drigo+	+
	2.4+6			Data	EXFOR20664.006	Oct 76	3PTS.	
Polarization	3.2+6		AMS	Expt Jour	NP/A 222 93	Apr 74	Zijp+ TABLES,GRAPHS. CFD NON – SPH POT	+
				Conf	75Zurich 189	Aug 75	– + GRPH OF DATA IN REVIEW.	
				Conf	72Budapest 170	Aug 72	– + POLARIZTN,EXPT CFD OPTMOD,GRP	
	3.2+6			Data	EXFOR20777.021	Apr 78	9PTS.	
Polarization	1.0-2		ATI	ExTh Conf	76Lowell 1027	Jul 76	Rauch+N INTFEROMETER.POL EFFECT.GRPH	
Potntal Scat	+4		HAR	Expt Jour	PPSA 70 51	Jan 57	Gayther+ FROM AVG SIGTOT. FC TRANSM	
Potntal Scat	+0	+3	BNL	Expt Jour	PR 110 692	May 58	Seth+,10.2+ – 0.2B CALCTD FROM TOT SIG	+
				Rept	ORNL – 2309	Jun 57	.SUPERSEDED	
	2.6+1	1.7+3		Data	EXFOR11788.026	Jun 76	. 1 PT. SIGMA.	
Potntal Scat	1.0+1	3.0+3	HAR	Expt Jour	NP 7 613	Aug 58	Lynn+TOF MEAN = 9.5B TRUE = 10.4+ – 0.4B	
Potntal Scat	Pile		WWA	Expt Rept	INR – 103	Aug 59	Ratynski.TRNSMISSIONMETHOD,VAL GIVEN	
				Jour	BPP 7 527	Aug 59	SEE ALSO BPP7 527 (8/59)	
Potntal Scat	None		WWA	Expt Jour	NKA 5 467	Aug 60	Wilhelmi.GEN REVIEW,CFD FPW THEORY	
Potntal Scat	-1		WWA	Expt Jour	NKA 9 511	Jul 64	Aleksandrowicz+ BRIEF.EFF RADIUS,NDG	
Potntal Scat	None		DKE	Expt Abst	DA/B 28 3834	Mar 68	Divadeenam.TRNS.EFFECTIVE RADIUS	
Potntal Scat	4.0+6		KUR	Expt Jour	YF 8 1086	Dec 68	Gorlov+NUCL+COUL(SPIN – ORB)POT SCATNG	
				Jour	SNP 8 630	Jun 69	TRANSLATN.*	
Potntal Scat	6.8+6		KGU	Theo Jour	YF 9 190	Jan 69	Ol'Khovskij+GRPH POT – PARAM(SCAT – ANG)	
				Jour	SNP 9 114	Jul 69	TRANSLATN.*	

83 Bismuth 209

Quantity	Energy (ev) Min	Max	Lab	Type	Documentation Ref Vol Page	Date	Author, Comments	Data
Potntal Scat		+5	SAC Expt	Jour	NP/A 123 561	Jan 69	Morgenstern+ RADIUS.RES SHAPE ANAL.	+
		+6		Rept	CEA-R-3609	Sep 68	- .(THESIS).DATA GIVEN	
		+5		Conf	68Wash. 867	Mar 68	- + PPR E27	
	0.0+0	7.0+4		Data	EXFOR20684.029	Jul 77	1PNT.RADIUS.	
Potntal Scat	Cold		MUNExpt	Jour	ZP 227 152	Sep 69	Nuecker.POT SCAT LENGTH=9.47+-0.005F	
Tot Inelastc	2.5+6	2.5+6	OXF Expt	Jour	PR 94 144	Apr 54	Eliot. = 1 DATA INDEX LINES	+
Tot Inelastc	1.4+7		LAS Expt	Jour	PR 97 1205	Mar 55	Graves. BETWEEN 0.00 AND 0.67+-0.04B	
Tot Inelastc	8.0+5	1.4+7	BNL Eval	Rept	BNL-3341	Sep 55	Oleksa. FROM SNE-N2N.ALSO 2 FIRST LV	
Tot Inelastc	2.9+5	1.0+6	CCP Expt	Jour	ZET 30 1017	Jun 56	Poze.SIG AT 3ES GIVEN,AV E OF SCT NS	
				Jour	JET 3 745	Dec 56	TRANSLATN.*	
Tot Inelastc	2.5+6		IFU Expt	Jour	JET 4 769	Jun 57	.ENGLISH OF ZET 31 907	
				Jour	ZET 31 907	Nov 56	Strizhak. SPHERE METHOD,TABLE	
Tot Inelastc	1.4+7		LAS Expt	Jour	PR 107 824	Aug 57	Rosen+ 0.17+-0.03B.	+
	1.4+7			Data	EXFOR11223.009	Jun 76	. 1 PT. SIGMA.	
Tot Inelastc	1.4+7		LRL Expt	Jour	PR 108 726	Nov 57	Macgregor.	+
				Conf	58Paris § NS609	Jul 58	Mcgregor.FROM SNE 9AND14MEV CUTOFF	
	1.4+7			Data	EXFOR11205.024	Jun 76	. 1 PT. SIGMA.	
Tot Inelastc	2.5+6	1.4+7	IFU Expt	Conf	58Geneva 15 18	Sep 58	Pasechnik+.PPR2030,NDG,EXPT DESCRIBD	
				Conf	55Geneva 2 3	Aug 55	- . INTEGR SIGMA,4ES,TABLE	
Tot Inelastc	Fiss		KUR Revw	Conf	60Vienna 159	Oct 60	Bondarenko+.TABLE,EXPT DESCRIBED	
Tot Inelastc	1.4+6	1.0+7	B+WEval	Rept	BAW-158	Jun 61	Roach+ AVERAGED SIG 7 GROUPS	
Tot Inelastc	1.5+7		NED Expt	Conf	62Padua 563	Sep 62	NDG DIFFERENCE BETWEEN N AND P SCATT	
Tot Inelastc	9.0+5	2.9+6	BNL Theo	Jour	PR/B 135 895	Aug 64	Auerbach+ OPTMDL 2LVLS TBL BNL818	
	+6			Conf	65Antwerp 25	Jul 65	- +NDG COMPLEX POTENTIAL MODL	
Tot Inelastc	8.0+5	4.0+6	IFU Expt	Prog	INDSWG-126 22	66	Pasechnik. AT 5 ES, TBP IN AE	
Tot Inelastc	1.0+6	3.5+6	CCP ExTh	Conf	66Moscow	Feb 66	.TBL AND CURVES GIVEN	
Tot Inelastc	5.0+5	4.0+6	FEI ExTh	Jour	IZV 31 327	Feb 67	Broder+.EXPT CFD H-F,TBL,CURVES GVN	
				Jour	BAS 31 311	Feb 67	TRANSLATN.*	
Tot Inelastc	1.4+6	3.8+6	CCP Expt	Jour	AE 23 6 568	Nov 67	Degtjarev+	+
	1.4+6	3.8+6		Data	EXFOR40047.011	Aug 70	PARTIAL SIGMA AT 7 EN, 4LEVELS	
Tot Inelastc	6.0+6	7.0+6	ALD Expt	Jour	NP/A 112 337	May 68	Owens+.2ES.FROM N SPECT 90DEG.	+
Tot Inelastc	1.5+7		LND Expt	Jour	AF 39 295	Sep 69	Joensson+. MEASURED NONEL GAMMAS	+
				Rept	LU-NP-6804	Mar 68	- + EQUIVALENT TO AF 39 295	
	1.5+7	1.6+7		Data	EXFOR20164.040	May 74	1PNT.SIGMA.	
Tot Inelastc	None		NZWExpt	Prog	AEC(NZ)-347 70	Sep 70	.TOF.IN PROGRESS,PRELIM RESULTS,NDG	
Tot Inelastc	3.8+8	1.7+9	PTN Expt	Jour	PR/C 7 248	Jan 73	Schimmerling+.TOF.TRANS.TABLE 15 ES	+
				Jour	PL/B 37 177	Nov 71	.SUPERSEDED	
	3.8+8	1.7+9		Data	EXFOR10082.024	Dec 75	15PTS.SIN CS DATA.	
Tot Inelastc	1.4+7		TUD Expt	Prog	ZFK-262 39	Sep 73	Goebel+ INTEGRATED DIFFSIG,TB DONE	
Diff Inelast	1.4+7		LAS Expt	Jour	PR 89 343	Jan 53	Graves. TEMP GIVEN CF LA-1532	
Diff Inelast	2.5+6		HAR Expt	Jour	PM 44 1398	Dec 53	Poole.AT 97DEG 60,25MB/SR TO EX 1,2	
Diff Inelast	2.6+6	2.6+6	OXF Expt	Jour	PR 94 144	Apr 54	Eliot. = 1 DATA INDEX LINES	+
Diff Inelast	1.4+7		LAS Theo	Jour	PR 99 1052	Aug 55	Rosen+ STAT TH OF NUCLEAR REACTIONS	
Diff Inelast	Thrsh	2.8+6	BNL Theo	Rept	BNL-3341	Sep 55	Oleksa. TO .895,1.56 MEV LEVELS	
	1.0+6	2.5+6		Rept	BNL-3344	Jan 54	Oleksa+,SIGS FOR SEVERAL LVLS CALCTD	
Diff Inelast	4.3+6		WES Expt	Abst	BAP 1 175	Apr 56	Smith+TOF NEUT SPEC AT 90DEG NDG	
Diff Inelast	2.5+6		LAS Expt	Jour	PR 103 343	Jul 56	Cranberg+,TOF 90DEG .93 1.65MEV LVLS	+
	2.5+6			Data	EXFOR11396.025	Jun 76	. 2 PTS. DSIGMA.	
Diff Inelast	4.4+6		WES Expt	Jour	PR 104 1069	Nov 56	Weddell.FOTOPLATE 82DEG 135MB	+
	4.4+6			Data	EXFOR11479.008	Jun 76	. 2 PTS. DSIGMA.	
Diff Inelast	1.4+7		GLS Theo	Jour	PM 2 473	Apr 57	Brown+ THEORY OKS XPT FOR E*=4-12MEV	
Diff Inelast	4.3+6		ORL Expt	Conf	ORNL-2309	Jun 57	West.ELVLS D9Q 1D8MEV DATA CFD	
Diff Inelast	1.4+7		LAS Expt	Jour	PR 107 824	Aug 57	Rosen+	+
				Conf	58Geneva 15 11	Sep 58	Coon+.PPR666,EXPT DESCRIBED,TOF	
				Conf	55Geneva 4 97	Aug 55	Rosen.P582,CURVE,EXPT DESCRIBED	
	1.4+7			Data	EXFOR11223.012	Jun 76	. 21 PTS. DSIGMA.	
Diff Inelast	1.4+7		LRL Expt	Conf	57Col.Univ § 4C4	Sep 57	Nakada. TOF.	
Diff Inelast	2.9+6		CCP Expt	Jour	AE 3 498	Dec 57	Popov.EXCIT 900 AND 1560KEV LEVELS	+
				Jour	JNE 9 9	Jun 59	TRANSLATN.*	
				Jour	SJA 3 1379		57 TRANSLATN.*	
Diff Inelast	1.4+7		CCP Expt	Jour	AE 3 540	Dec 57	Zamyatnin+.P RECOIL, T=0.9+-0.08 MEV	
				Jour	JNE 9 41	Jun 59	TRANSLATN.*	
				Jour	SJA 3 1427		57 TRANSLATN.*	
Diff Inelast	2.5+6		WLY Expt	Jour	PR 110 915	May 58	Boley+,SC RATIO PLOT G SPECTRUM	
Diff Inelast	2.8+6		KTY Expt	Abst	BAP 3 268	Jun 58	Kern. 90DEG 0.9 1.6MEV LVLS 26 22MB	
Diff Inelast	2.8+6		LAS Expt	Prog	WASH-1006	Oct 58	Cranberg. D9 1D6MEVLVLS ANISM1/5	
Diff Inelast	2.8+6		LAS Expt	Abst	BAP 3 365	Nov 58	Thomson+,0.90 1.56MEV LVLS,30PC ANIS	
Diff Inelast	1.4+7		ANL Expt	Prog	WASH-1021 2	Jun 59	Casson. TOF,NDG	

83 Bismuth 209

Quantity	Energy (ev) Min	Max	Lab	Type	Documentation Ref Vol Page	Date	Author, Comments	Data
Diff Inelast	1.4+7		VBT	Expt Abst	BAP 5 104	Mar 60	Arnold+.OKS TEMP.5 – 4MEV,T=0.95MEV	
Diff Inelast	1.4+7		ISL	Theo Jour	PR 118 781	May 60	Dostrovsky.MONTE CARLO CALC CFD EXPT	
Diff Inelast	3.2+6		SAC	Expt Jour	JPR 21 384	May 60	Naggiar+ ABST.SCAT BY 1ST EXCT LVL	
Diff Inelast	1.5+7		AMS	Expt Jour	NIM 17 273	Dec 62	Rethmeier+.E SPEC,ANGDIST Q=–7.6MEV	+
				Jour	NP 38 222	Oct 62	– + 4AS,10–40DEG,FROM 7.65MEV	
	1.5+7			Data	EXFOR20200.004	May 74	6PTS.D/DA.	
Diff Inelast	4.0+6	7.0+6	LAS	Expt Jour	PR 129 1649	Feb 63	Thomson+ 90DEG TEMP FOR NS TO 5	+
	7.0+6			Data	EXFOR11495.058	Jun 76	. 1 PT. SIGMA.	
	4.0+6	7.0+6		Data	EXFOR11495.059	Jun 76	. 3 PTS. DSIGMA.	
Diff Inelast	1.4+7		BAS	Expt Jour	PL 5 202	Jul 63	Huber+ GRAPH OF INELASTIC N SPECTRUM	
				Jour	HPA 36 1059	Dec 59	– +.T=1.26MEV	
Diff Inelast	3.8+6		ALD	Expt Conf	64Paris 2 690	Jul 64	Gilboy+TOF CFD H–F AND BUCK	
Diff Inelast	2.5+6		BNL	Theo Jour	PR/B 135 895	Aug 64	Auerbach+ OPTMDL 2LVLS.	
Diff Inelast	4.0+6	6.5+6	DKE	Expt Jour	NP 60 17	Nov 64	Buccino+N SPEC MEASURED 4ES+NUC TEMP	
				Abst	DA 24 4251	Apr 64	Hollandsworth.TOF.EN SPEC.NUCL T.	
Diff Inelast	6.0+6		DKE	Expt Jour	NP 62 511	Feb 65	Wilenzick+ TO LVLS IN 0.5 – 4.0MEV AD	+
	6.0+6			Data	EXFOR11287.048	Jun 76	. 1 PT. SIGMA.	
	6.0+6			Data	EXFOR11287.049	Jun 76	. 9 PTS. DSIGMA.	
Diff Inelast	1.4+7		ORL	ExTh Jour	NP 68 97	Jun 65	Stelson+TOF.GRPHS.CFD DWBA MDL CALCS	+
	1.4+7			Expt Data	EXFOR11527.027	Jun 76	. 12 PTS. DSIGMA.	
Diff Inelast	2.5+6	4.1+6	LAS	Expt Conf	65Antwerp § 29	Jul 65	DAY+GE–DET 5–7KEV RSLN.OKS OTHERS	
Diff Inelast	8.0+5	4.5+6	ORL	Theo Rept	ORNL–TM–1238	Sep 65	Smith. H–F ANALYSIS,GOOD AGREEMENT.	
Diff Inelast	5.0+6		ORL	Expt Prog	WASH–1064 121	Oct 65	Dickens+,TOF,THETA=30–130DEG,TBC NDG	
Diff Inelast	1.4+7		FEI	Expt Jour	YF 2 826	Nov 65	Anufrienko+ SPEC OF SECONDARY NS,CRV	+
				Rept	ICD–1 250	Aug 64	.	
				Rept	ANL–TRANS–168	Apr 67	.PAGE 250.ENGLISH TRANSL OF ICD–1	
				Jour	SNP 2 589	May 66	.ENGLISH TRANSL OF YF 2 826 11/65	
	1.4+7			Data	EXFOR40133.024	Feb 73	N–SPECTRUM AT 92 DEG	
Diff Inelast	3.0+5	8.0+5	IFU	Expt Prog	INDSWG–126 22	66	Pasechnik. AT 3 ES, TBP IN AE	
Diff Inelast	1.4+7		FEI	Expt Rept	FEI–39	Jan 66	Sal'Nikov+TOF SPECT,RING GEOM,E–SPEC	
Diff Inelast	2.5+6	1.5+7	FEI	Theo Jour	NP 76 232	Feb 66	Malyshev+ SPEC ANALYSED FOR TEMP	
Diff Inelast	6.0+6	8.0+6	LAS	Expt Jour	PR 142 775	Feb 66	Cranberg+ VDG+TOF XCIT 2.6MEV.	+
	2.5+6	8.0+6		Conf	63Houston 96	Feb 63	– + GRPH DIFFSIG 2LVLS.CFD H–F	
Diff Inelast	4.0+6	6.7+6	LAS	Expt Prog	WASH–1068 114	Mar 66	Hopkins+,ANAL TBD,NDG	
Diff Inelast	1.4+7		LRL	ExTh Jour	NP 77 241	Mar 66	Schectman+ SPEC AT 3 ANGLES CFD STAT	+
	1.4+7			Expt Data	EXFOR11698.008	Jun 76	. 1 PT. DSIGMA.	
Diff Inelast	2.5+6		LAS	Expt Jour	PR 159 969	Jul 67	Cranberg+ ANG DIST .90,1.61MEV LEVLS	
Diff Inelast	1.4+6	3.8+6	CCP	Expt Jour	AE 23 568	Dec 67	Degtiarev+ LOW–LVL SIG–TBL,N'–SPECS	
					–		(FRENCH EAF 23 118,ENGL SJA 23 1350)	
Diff Inelast	–		BHU	Theo Conf	68Madras 1 291	Feb 68	Sharma+ PPRN39.CALC LVL EXCIT,NDG	
Diff Inelast	1.3+6	3.8+6	KUR	Expt Jour	IZV 32 706	Apr 68	Degtyarev+ SIG(N,N') GRPH+TABLE,VDG	
				Jour	BAS 32 651		69 TRANSLATN.*NO 4	
							ABSTRACT,67KHARKOV 173 2/67	
Diff Inelast	5.0+6	7.0+6	ALD	Expt Jour	NP/A 112 337	May 68	Owens+.3ES.FROM N SPECT 90DEG NDG.	+
				Conf	65Antwerp 547	Jul 65	– + PPR122.ABST.SPECT N' AT 90DEG	
Diff Inelast	2.5+6		BNL	Eval Rept	BNL–50151	Oct 68	Moore.OPTMDL ANAL,1.6 0.894MEV LVLS	
Diff Inelast	1.4+7		KGU	Theo Jour	UFZ 14 342	Feb 69	Strizhak+ ANGDIST,OPTMOD FIT,GRAPH	
Diff Inelast	3.6+6	8.5+6	JAE	Expt Jour	NP/A 131 145	Jun 69	Maruyama. E DEPENDENCE,PARAM,TH FIT	
	4.2+6	8.5+6		Priv	MARUYAMA	Jul 68	– . N(EN')/EN',EN'.55TO1.95MEV	
Diff Inelast	1.5+7	1.6+7	LND	Expt Jour	AF 39 295	Sep 69	Joensson+ DERIVED FROM NON–ELASTIC G	+
	1.5+7	1.6+7		Data	EXFOR20164.041	May 74	1PNT.D/DA.	
Diff Inelast	1.4+7		FEI	Expt Prog	YFI–11 11	70	Lovchikova+ ABST,TOF,DIFFSIG,NDG	
				Prog	INDC(CCP)–31	Dec 72	.PAGE 9,ENGLISH OF YFI–11 11	
Diff Inelast	2.5+6		BRC	Theo Rept	EANDC(E)127U	Apr 70	Rolard+	
Diff Inelast	1.0+6	1.5+6	PEL	Expt Prog	INDC(SAF)–2G	Apr 70	Barnard+ EXCITATION CURVE,TBP NSE	
Diff Inelast	1.0+6	1.5+6	ANL	Expt Jour	NSE 41 63	Jul 70	Smith+,TOF,896+–1KEV STATE CURVE	+
				Rept	ANL–7636	Nov 69	– +DIN TBL FOR AS.Q=896 KEV.	
	1.0+6	1.5+6		Data	EXFOR10010.	Mar 76	162PTS.DIN 90DEG,OTHER AS.LEG COEFS	
Diff Inelast	1.4+7		FEI	Expt Conf	71Kiev	May 71	Sal'Nikov+.SIG(COS),GRPH,31–151 DEG	
				Prog	YFI–11 10		70 Salnikov+ ABST,N–SPEC 30–150DEG,NDG	
				Prog	INDC(CCP)–31	Dec 72	.PAGE 8,ENGLISH OF YFI–11 10	
Diff Inelast	1.5+6	3.5+6	JAE	Expt Jour	NP/A 179 513	Jan 72	Tanaka+. ANGDIST CFD OPTMDL,C–CHANNL	+
	1.4+6	3.6+6		Priv	TANAKA	Aug 71	– . TOF.REL H(NN). +LEGENDRE FIT	
	1.4+6	3.6+6		Data	EXFOR20337.	Jul 74	187PTS.D/DA,LEG.FIT.	
Diff Inelast	1.4+7		KGU	Expt Conf	72Kiev 2 16	Jan 72	Gurtovoj+ ABST,NDG.DIFFSIG 60–90DEG	
Diff Inelast	1.5+7		AMS	Expt Jour	NP/A 181 545	Feb 72	Kuijper+ LIQ SC. 3LVLS.8AS 23–120	+
	1.5+7			Data	EXFOR20223.010	May 74	24PTS.D/DA.	

83 Bismuth 209

Quantity	Energy (ev) Min	Max	Lab	Type	Documentation Ref Vol Page	Author, Comments Date	Data
Diff Inelast	1.4+7		VNV Expt	Rept	CEA-N-4279	Mar 72 Clayeux+ TOF,DIF NTS .1 TO 7 MEV	
				Conf	71Knoxvill 196	Mar 71 Voignier+SIG VS.E(PRIME) 90DEG CRV	
Diff Inelast	1.4+7		KFI Theo	Conf	72Budapest 202	Aug 72 Kluge+ CALCULATED EN-SPECTRA ,GRPH	
				Rept	KFKI-72-17	Feb 72 - + CALC N-SPEC INEL+N2N,TBL,GRPH	
Diff Inelast	1.4+7		KYU Expt	Jour	NP/A 204 129	Apr 73 Matoba+ TOF, 20-140DEG, 3LVLS,OPTMOD	+
	1.4+7			Data	EXFOR20308.003	Jun 74 37PTS.D/DA.	
Diff Inelast	1.4+7		TUD Expt	Prog	ZFK-262 39	Sep 73 Goebel+ DOUBLEDIFFSIG,IN PROGRESS	
Diff Inelast	9.1+6		FEI Expt	Jour	YF 19 1190	Jun 74 Birjukov+ TOF,NEUT-E SPEC,GRAPH	+
				Jour	SNP 19 608	Dec 74 . ENGLISH OF YF 19 1190	
	9.2+6			Data	EXFOR40287.020	Apr 75 .DATA IN MB/SR/MEV AT 49 ES GVN	
Diff Inelast	1.4+7		KYU Expt	Jour	NST 11 523	Dec 74 Akiyoshi+.TOF,E-SPECTRA AT 7 ANGLES	
Diff Inelast	1.4+7	1.5+7	JAE Theo	Conf	JAERI-M-5984	Feb 75 Tanaka.OPTMDL/COUPLD CH.2.6-6MEV LVL	
Diff Inelast	2.0+6	4.5+6	AE Expt	Conf	75Wash. 871	Mar 75 Etemad. TO LVLS,125DEG.CFD THEO,GRPH	
Diff Inelast	1.4+7		FEI Eval	Conf	75Kiev 4 128	May 75 Luk'Janov+ DIR,INDIR SIG,TEMP.TABLE	
Diff Inelast	4.4+6		FEI Expt	Rept	YK-19 66	May 75 Trykova+ SIG(ANG),TBL,GRAPH	+
	4.4+6			Data	EXFOR40338.	Jan 76 .DATA AT 3 E-LVL AND 5 ANGLS GVN	
Diff Inelast	1.5+7		ELU Expt	Prog	INDC(SEC)-50	Jan 76 Deak+ P125,ABST. +(N,2N),E-SPEC.NDG	
Thermal Scat	Cold		LUQ Expt	Jour	PR 58 321	Aug 40 Rasetti. SIG(SCAT)VS CRYSTL STRUCT.	
Thermal Scat	Pile		ANL Expt	Jour	PR 72 408	Sep 47 Fermi+. SPIN DEPENDENCE.	
Thermal Scat	3.0-4	6.0-3	BNL Expt	Jour	PR 99 611	Jul 55 Palevsky+ TOF,SAMPLE100-1000DEGK,NDG	
Thermal Scat	-1		SAC Expt	Conf	55Geneva 5 77	Aug 55 Jacrot+,NDG,SLOW CHOPPER,PPR357	
Thermal Scat	-2		TRM Expt	Conf	61Bombay 431	Feb 61 Iyengar+.DIFF SIGMA OF LIQUID BI	
Thermal Scat	Maxwl		ISP Expt	Conf	62Chalk R. 1 139	Sep 62 Menardi+,XTAL AT LIQUID NITROGEN T	
Thermal Scat		5.2-3	HLT Expt	Conf	68Copenhgn 1 431	May 68 Tunkelo+PPR27.SIG(E'),6ANGS,LIQ+SOLD	
Thermal Scat	Maxwl		HAR Expt	Jour	JP/C 1 1075	Aug 68 North+ STRUCTURE FACTOR FOR LIQUIDS	
	2.0-3			Jour	AIP 16 189	Apr 67 Cocking.SPEC SCAT NEUTS,LIQUID+SOLID	
Thermal Scat	2.0-4		MUNExpt	Jour	ZP 227 152	Sep 69 Nuecker+, COH SCAT AMP.TOT REFL.BOUND	
				Jour	PRL 36 1021	Apr 76 Koester+ COH SCAT AMP. BOUND,REFLECT	
				Conf	67Juelich 80	Apr 67 - + SUPERSEDED.	
Thermal Scat	-3	-2	BUC Expt	Jour	SCF 22 733	Jul 70 Mateescu.THESIS,LIQUID,S(K,E)-GRAPHS	
Thermal Scat	-3	-1	BUC Expt	Jour	SCF 23 517	May 71 Teutsch. LIQUID, S(K,OMEGA) GRAPHS	
		-3		Conf	68Copenhgn 1 439	May 68 Mateescu+PPR56.EXPT AT 6ANGS,LIQUID	
Thermal Scat	Pile		JUL Comp	Rept	JUEL-875-RX	Aug 72 Scharenberg. DATA ON USE AS N-FILTER	
Thermal Scat	1.0-4	1.0+3	MUNRevw	Jour	EEN 80 1	77 Koester. SCAT LENGTH,FREE+INCOH SIG	
Scattering	Maxwl		NYU Expt	Jour	PR 50 133	Jul 36 Mitchell+ RA-BE+PARAFF NS. FILTERED.	
Scattering	Maxwl		CAV Expt	Jour	PRSA 162 127	Sep 37 Goldhaber+. 8.9B REL 4.83B FOR C	
Scattering	3.1+6		OSA Expt	Jour	JPJO 21 410	39 Kikuchi+.ANG DIST GIVN	
Scattering	Maxwl		JAP Expt	Jour	SCP 36 153	Jul 39 Kimura.SIG=16 PM 1B	
Scattering	Maxwl		HAR Expt	Rept	AERE-N/R-1147	Apr 53 Egelstaff.SCT AND COH FROM STOT	
Scattering	6.0+4	1.8+6	ANL Expt	Jour	PR 107 1077	Aug 57 Langsdorf+,LEGENDRE COEFS CURVES	+
				Rept	ANL-5567	Oct 61 .REVISED DATA	
	3.0+4	1.4+6		Data	EXFOR11224.066	Jun 76 . 18 PTS. SIGMA.	
	3.0+4	1.4+6		Data	EXFOR11224.082	Jun 76 . 90 PTS. DSIGMA.	
Scattering	2.0-4	8.0-4	TAT Theo	Jour	PM 3 798	Aug 58 Bhandari+ 1-PHONON MOD DISAGREES XPT	
Scattering	6.0+6		DKE Expt	Jour	NP 62 511	Feb 65 Wilenzick+ INTEGRATED ELAST+INELAST.	
Scattering	Fast		FEI Expt	Jour	AE 18 409	Apr 65 Gusejnov+ ANGL DIST,TH(N,F)DETECTOR	
				Jour	JNE 20 700	Aug 66 . ENGL OF AE 18 409	
				Jour	EAF 18 4 134	Apr 65 . FRENCH OF AE 18 409	
				Jour	SJA 18 526	Apr 65 . ENGL OF AE 18 409	
Scattering	8.2-4	8.2-2	NYB Expt	Abst	DA/B 28 1107	Sep 67 Edwards.FORWARD COH SCT AMPL VS TEMP	
Scattering	5.0+5	2.4+7	OSU Theo	Abst	DA/B 29 1802	Nov 68 Hogan.ELECTROMAG.SCAT.IN OPTMOD CALS	
Scattering	-3		JUL Expt	Conf	75Wash. 823	Mar 75 Schmatz+INCOH SC LT 10+-2MB.REL VA	
Nonelastic	+7		BRK Expt	Jour	PR 53 795	May 38 Grahame+ RA-BE,TRANS,BY FE56+AL(N,P)	
Nonelastic	1.4+7		WWAExpt	Jour	NAT 142 252	Aug 38 Soltan.WIDE-ANGLE TRNSM,ACTVN DETECT	
Nonelastic	None		CHI Expt	Jour	PR 73 1307	Jun 48 Szilard+ RA-BE,B SPH	
Nonelastic	1.4+7		LAS Expt	Jour	PR 88 600	Nov 52 Phillips+	+
	1.4+7			Data	EXFOR11210.011	Jun 76 . 1 PT. SIGMA.	
Nonelastic	1.4+7		LAS Expt	Jour	PR 89 343	Jan 53 Graves+ 3.9+-1.0B CF LA-1532	+
	1.4+7			Data	EXFOR11304.012	Jun 76 . 1 PT. SIGMA.	
Nonelastic	1.0+6		WIS Expt	Jour	PR 93 1062	Mar 54 Walt.	+
	1.0+6			Data	EXFOR11637.081	Jun 76 . 1 PT. SIGMA.	
Nonelastic	1.4+7		LAS Expt	Jour	PR 97 1205	Mar 55 Graves+2.53+-0.02B CFD PR88 600 1952	+
	1.4+7			Data	EXFOR11310.012	Jun 76 . 1 PT. SIGMA.	
Nonelastic	4.1+6		LAS Expt	Jour	PR 98 677	May 55 Walt+ 2.2+-0.3B FROM TOT MINUS ELAST	+
	4.1+6			Data	EXFOR11215.055	Jun 76 . 1 PT. SIGMA.	
Nonelastic	1.0+6	4.5+6	LAS Expt	Jour	PR 98 1216	Jun 55 Beyster+ SPH TRNS 3ES 2ND IS 4.0MEV	+
				Jour	PR 97 563	Jan 55 .SUPERSEDED.(LETTER)	
	1.0+6	4.5+6		Data	EXFOR11216.017	Jun 76 . 3 PTS. SIGMA.	

83 Bismuth 209

Quantity	Energy (ev) Min	Max	Lab	Type	Documentation Ref Vol Page	Author, Comments Date	Data
Nonelastic	1.0+6	1.4+7	BNL	Eval Rept	BNL-3341	Sep 55 Oleksa.FROM TOT(BNL-325)-SEL	
Nonelastic	3.5+6	1.4+7	RIC	Expt Jour	PR 100 174	Oct 55 Taylor+,SPHERE TRNS	+
	3.5+6	1.4+7		Data	EXFOR11217.013	Jun 76 . 5 PTS. SIGMA.	
Nonelastic	1.5+7		LRL	Theo Jour	PR 101 1833	Mar 56 Bjorklund+,OPTMDL CALC SIG=2.3 B	
Nonelastic	1.4+7		CCP	Expt Jour	AE 1 4 155	Sep 56 Flerov+.SPHERE TRANSM, 2590+ - 30MB	+
				Jour	JNE 4 529	Apr 57 TRANSLATN.*	
				Jour	SJA 1 4 617	56 TRANSLATN.*	
Nonelastic	6.0+5	1.6+6	LAS	Expt Jour	PR 104 731	Nov 56 Allen+	+
	6.0+5	1.6+6		Data	EXFOR11693.004	Jun 76 . 11 PTS. SIGMA.	
Nonelastic	1.8+6	7.0+6	LAS	Expt Jour	PR 104 1319	Dec 56 Beyster+,SPH TRNS 4ES+TOT-EL 2ES	+
	1.8+6	7.0+6		Data	EXFOR11220.032	Jun 76 . 4 PTS. SIGMA.	
Nonelastic	4.0+4	1.8+6	LAS	Theo Rept	LA-2099	Dec 56 Beyster+,OPTMDL CALC CFD EXPT,CURVE	
Nonelastic	1.4+7		IFU	Expt Jour	AE 2 68	Jan 57 Strizhak.SPHERE TRANSMISS 2.40+ - .99B	+
				Jour	JNE 5 253	Nov 57 TRANSLATN.*	
				Jour	SJA 2 72	57 TRANSLATN.*	
Nonelastic	Fiss		LAS	Expt Jour	JNE 4 147	Feb 57 Bethe+.SPH TRNSM,WIDE GRP-GRP SIGMAS	+
				Rept	LA-1429	Dec 55 .SUPERSEDED	
	Fiss			Data	EXFOR11461.	Jun 76 . 3 PTS. SIGMA. 3 DETECTORS	
Nonelastic	1.4+7		LAS	Expt Jour	PR 107 824	Aug 57 Rosen+	+
	1.4+7			Data	EXFOR11223.008	Jun 76 . 1 PT. SIGMA.	
Nonelastic	1.4+7		LRL	Expt Jour	PR 108 726	Nov 57 Macgregor+,SPH TRNS CFD OPTMDL+XPTS	+
	1.4+7			Data	EXFOR11226.024	Jun 76 . 1 PT. SIGMA.	
Nonelastic	7.2+6	1.4+7	LRL	Expt Jour	PR 110 1392	Jun 58 Ball+,SPH TRNS 7ES 2.42 TO 2.59 B	+
				Conf	58Geneva 14 109	Sep 58 - +.PPR1881,TBL AT 9ES GVN,C-W	
	7.2+6	1.4+7		Data	EXFOR11257.009	Jun 76 . 6 PTS. SIGMA.	
Nonelastic	2.6+7		LRL	Expt Jour	PR 111 1155	Aug 58 Macgregor+,SPH TRNS	+
	2.6+7			Data	EXFOR11230.012	Jun 76 . 1 PT. SIGMA.	
Nonelastic	7.0+6	1.4+7	LRL	Revw Rept	UCRL-5345	Sep 58 Howerton.RVN EXP,+TBP BJORKLUND CCB	
Nonelastic	1.4+7		CCP	Expt Jour	AE 5 522	Nov 58 Lebedev+ SPH GEOM,TR DET, 2.58+ - .1B	+
				Jour	JNEA 11 39	59 TRANSLATN.*	
				Jour	SJA 5 1431	58 TRANSLATN.*	
Nonelastic	8.2+6	1.9+7	RIC	Expt Jour	PR 113 1088	Feb 59 Bonner+,SPH TRANSMISSION,2.60TO2.36B	+
				Jour	PRL 2 186	Feb 59 .SUPERSEDED	
	8.2+6	1.9+7		Data	EXFOR11793.006	Jun 76 . 5 PTS. SIGMA.	
Nonelastic	1.0+6	2.7+7	LOK	Theo Conf	60Kingston 146	Aug 60 Walt+.CURVE,OPTMDL FIT CFD EXPT	
Nonelastic	1.4+7		LSU	Expt Jour	PR 132 1211	Nov 63 Haas+ SPH TRANS SIG=2.53+ - 0.05	+
	1.4+7			Data	EXFOR11794.008	Jun 76 . 1 PT. SIGMA.	
Nonelastic	2.4+7		SAC	Theo Jour	NP 68 153	Jun 65 Picard. OPTMDL CALCS CFD XPT VALUES.	
Nonelastic	2.5+6	3.6+6	IFU	ExTh Jour	AE 20 8	Jan 66 Korzh+ SUMMARY OF SEVERAL YRS WORK	+
				Jour	AE 16 207	64 .	
				Jour	UFZ 3 185	58 .	
				Jour	SJA 20 8	Jul 66 .ENGLISH TRANSL OF AE 20 8 1/66	
Nonelastic	2.5+6	2.4+7	CCP	Theo Jour	YF 7 283	Feb 68 Aver'Yanov+ OPTMOD-CALCTD SIG GVN	
				Jour	SNP 7 2 193	Aug 68 TRANSLATN.*	
Nonelastic	4.0+6		KUR	ExTh Jour	YF 6 910	Nov 70 Gorlov+ POLRZ INC N,OPTMOD CFD.1.79B	
Nonelastic	1.4+7		GHT	Expt Jour	ACA 64 187	73 Vandecasteele+ FLUX-ATTENUAT,SIG GVN	
Absorption	+7		BRK	Expt Jour	PR 53 795	May 38 Grahame+ RA-BE,TRANS,PB(NNGAMMA) DET	
Absorption	Maxwl		JAP	Expt Jour	SCP 36 153	Jul 39 Kimura.SIG=5.6 B	
Absorption	Maxwl	1.4+7	AUS	Expt Jour	APA 3 352	Mar 50 Lintner. RA-BE SOURCE	
				Jour	OAWS 158 135	Nov 49 - .	
Absorption	Pile		ANL	Expt Jour	PR 80 342	Nov 50 Harris+.PILE OSC.REL TO BORON.	+
	Pile			Data	EXFOR11528.050	Jun 76 . 1 PT. SIGMA.	
Absorption	Pile		HAR	Expt Jour	PPSA 66 700	Aug 53 Littler+.OSC,30.8+ - 2.2MB REL B 710B	
				Rept	AERE-N/R-527	Jun 50 Colmer+ PILE OSCILLATOR.	
Absorption	Pile		BNL	Expt Jour	PR 92 120	Dec 53 Hughes+	+
	Pile			Data	EXFOR12243.003	Jun 76 .1PT, SIG.	
Absorption	1.4+9		BNL	Expt Jour	PR 98 342	Jun 55 Coor+	+
	1.4+9			Data	EXFOR11087.016	Jun 76 . 1 PT. SIGMA.	
Absorption	Fiss		WAD	Expt Rept	WADC-TR-58 266	Jan 58 Schamberger.REMOVL CS,SIG EFFECT GVN	
Absorption	Maxwl		HAR	Expt Rept	AERE-R/R-2516	Mar 58 Jowitt+ PILE OSC.REL BORON.293DEGK.	
Absorption	1.0+5	3.0+5	ANL	Expt Rept	ANL-6111 21	Feb 60 Lane+ TOO SMALL TO READ	
Absorption	2.5-2		HAR	Expt Jour	JNEA 12 32	May 60 Tattersall+ PILE OSCILLATOR.	+
	2.5-2			Data	EXFOR20638.065	Jul 76 1PNT.SIGMA.	
Absorption	Maxwl		BNL	Expt Rept	BNL-719 1034	61 Starr+	+
	Maxwl			Data	EXFOR11272.003	Jun 76 . 1 PT. SIGMA.	
Absorption	3.0+6	1.5+7	FEI	Expt Book	NEJTRONFIZ 278	61 Kukhtevich+ SIGMA AT 2ES	
				Book	SPN 205	61 .ENGL TRANSL OF NEJTRONFIZ 278	
Absorption	2.0-1	1.0+7	B+W	Eval Rept	BAW-158	Jun 61 Roach+ AVERAGED SIG 40 GROUPS	

83 Bismuth 209

Quantity	Energy (ev) Min	Max	Lab	Type	Documentation Ref Vol Page	Author, Comments Date	Data
Absorption	2.4+4		FEI	Expt	Jour AE 19 3	Jul 65 Belanova+ 2 METHODS,ABSOL EXPT,TABLE	+
					Jour JNE 20 411	66 .ENGLISH TRANSL OF AE 19 3 7/65	
					Jour EAF 19 1 11	65 . FRENCH TRANSL OF AE 19 3 7/65	
					Jour SJA 19 858	65 .ENGLISH TRANSL OF AE 19 3 7/65	
	2.4+4			Data	EXFOR40072.017	Jul 71 SIGMA AT 24 KEV AS PUBLISHED	
Absorption	8.1+6		AE	Theo	Conf 70Helsinki 2 341	Jun 70 Holmqvist+55. OPTMODEL CALC SIGMA	
Res Int Abs	None		ORL	Revw	Conf 55Geneva 5 96	Aug 55 Macklin+.P833 ,EXPT CFD THEORY,TABLE	
Res Int Abs	5.0−1		HAR	Expt	Jour JNE 12 32	May 60 Tattersall+ ABOVE 1/V,OSCIL,REL B+AU	+
					Rept AERE−R−2887	Aug 59 − . PILE OSC.REL BORON	
					Conf 58Geneva 16 34	Sep 58 Rose+ SUPERSEDED	
	6.7−1			Data	EXFOR20638.066	Jul 76 1PNT.	
(n,γ)	Slow		JAP	Expt	Jour JPJO 21 594	39 Nonaka.SIG GIVN	
(n,γ)	Maxwl		UI	Expt	Jour PR 59 102	Jan 41 O'Neal+ ACTIVATION. REL TO MN.	
(n,γ)	Pile		ANL	Expt	Jour PR 72 888	Nov 47 Seren+.ACT METHOD.PILE IRRAD.METAL.	+
	Pile			Data	EXFOR11447.131	Jun 76 . 1 PT. SIGMA.	
(n,γ)	Fiss		ANL	Expt	Jour PR 75 1781	Jun 49 Hughes+ REL SIG(THERMAL),FOIL ACTIVN	+
	Fiss			Data	EXFOR11450.040	Jun 76 . 1 PT. SIGMA.	
(n,γ)	Pile		HAR	Expt	Jour PPSA 63 1175	Oct 50 Colmer+ PO210,ALPHA,ACT,REL NA,BETA	
					Rept AERE−N/R−527	Jun 50 − + ACTIVATION.	
(n,γ)	Fiss		BNL	Expt	Jour PR 91 1423	Sep 53 Hughes+.ALSO LVL SPACINGS AT EXCIT E	
(n,γ)	Pile		HAR	Expt	Jour JNE 6 41	Dec 57 Horsley.REFINED COMMERCIAL,38−39MB	
(n,γ)	2.0+5		KUR	Expt	Conf 58Geneva 15 50	Sep 58 Leipunskij+.PPR2219,VAL GVN,ACTIVATN	
(n,γ)	1.4+7		ALD	Expt	Jour PPS 72 505	Oct 58 Perkin+ACT ANAL 1.45MB+−12PC,B−W TH	+
(n,γ)	2.5+4		LRL	Expt	Jour PR 112 226	Oct 58 Booth+ SB−BE REL I+THR,ACT 5D HL	+
	2.5+4			Data	EXFOR11429.032	Jun 76 . 1 PT. SIGMA.	
(n,γ)	1.5+7		ARK	Expt	Jour PR 115 989	Aug 59 Poularikas. C−W BELOW 1.7MB	+
					Jour PRL 3 253	Sep 59 .SUPERSEDED	
	1.5+7			Data	EXFOR11484.016	Jun 76 . 1 PT. SIGMA.	
(n,γ)	Fiss		KUR	Revw	Conf 60Vienna 159	Oct 60 Bondarenko+.TABLE FOR 1E ,EXPT DSCRB	
(n,γ)	4.0+5		LRL	Expt	Jour PR 120 556	Oct 60 Diven.SC−T.	+
	4.0+5			Data	EXFOR11616.029	Jun 76 . 1 PT. SIGMA.	
(n,γ)	Fast		LAS	Expt	Jour NSE 8 608	Dec 60 Byers. GODIVA ACTIVATION CS GIVEN	
(n,γ)	−		ROS	Expt	Jour NP 40 639	Feb 63 Schlintmeister+.SEARCH FOR DIR BETA	
(n,γ)	3.0+4	6.5+4	ORL	Expt	Jour PR 122 182	Apr 61 Gibbons.	+
					Jour PR 129 2695	Mar 63 Macklin+ LIQ SCINT,1+−4 AND 4+−3MB	
					Conf 61Vienna 73	Aug 61 − +	
	3.0+4	6.5+4		Data	EXFOR11329.072	Jun 76 . 2 PTS. SIGMA.	
(n,γ)	1.0+6	1.5+7	AMS	Revw	Jour PHY 30 2290	Dec 64 Heertje+ USE AS N MONITOR DISCUSSED	
(n,γ)	5.0+3	9.0+4	ORL	Theo	Jour RMP 37 166	Jan 65 Macklin+.CALC FOR KT=5TO90KEV	
(n,γ)	1.5+7		DEB	Expt	Jour NP/A 95 229	Mar 67 Csikai+,ACTIV,THEORY SIG=F(N),TABLE	+
					Jour MFF 16 123	Feb 68 − .THESIS,IN HUNGARIAN,EXPT,GRPH	
					Jour AK 8 79	Jun 66 ABSTRACT *THESIS, VALUE GIVEN	
	1.5+7			Data	EXFOR30067.017	Nov 70 VALUE AT 14.7 MEV, (= NP A95 TBL 1)	
(n,γ)	−		IEA	Comp	Rept IEA−INF−10 6	Aug 68 Atalla. TABLES OF HL,SIG AND GAMM−E	
(n,γ)	4.7+6	8.3+6	FOA	ExTh	Jour NP/A 120 161	Nov 68 Bergqvist+ FROM N−G SPEC.Q=4−4.6 MEV	+
	4.7+6	8.3+6		Expt Data	EXFOR20065.004	Sep 71 5PTS.SIG.	
(n,γ)	3.0+6		DEB	Expt	Jour AHP 28 257	Jan 70 Diksic+ SIG,REL S32(N,P),BETA−ACTVTY	+
	3.0+6			Data	EXFOR30023.013	Jun 70 SIGMA CAPT TO GND STATE	
(n,γ)	1.4+7	1.5+7	JYV	Eval	Rept JU−RR−3/1970	Jun 70 Leppaemaeki+ TABLE OF EVAL AVG SIG	
(n,γ)	2.4+4		MUA	Theo	Jour IJP 46 114	Mar 72 Chaubey+ P−WAVE STRENGTH FUNCT,TABLE	
(n,γ)	+3	+7	TUD	Theo	Prog ZFK−262 133	Sep 73 Hoehn+ CALC SIG CFD EXP,GRPH AT 1MEV	
(n,γ)	1.4+7		NJS	Expt	Jour NP/A 213 525	Oct 73 Potokar+ INTEGRATED FROM SPECTRUM	+
					Jour FIZS 4 53	Dec 72 Cvelbar+ INTEG SIG OF DIR G, GRAPH	
	1.4+7			Data	EXFOR30185.012	Oct 72 1 DATA LINE	
(n,γ)	2.2+5		ANL	Expt	Prog WASH−745	Nov 57 Kimball+ NEW MTHD 21P48M21MB.	+
	2.2+5			Data	EXFOR12234.003	Jun 76 . 1 PT. SIGMA.	
Spect (n,γ)	Maxwl		CRC	Expt	Jour PR 82 380	May 51 Kinsey+ PAIR SPEC,POOR RESOLUTION	
					Jour PR 78 77	Apr 50 .SUPERSEDED.	
Spect (n,γ)	None		LAS	Expt	Jour WASH−1034 121	Dec 61 Motz+ 325,678,785,1180,1335KEV.	
Spect (n,γ)	Maxwl		ETH	Expt	Jour ZMP 13 117	62 Jarczyk. G G COINC WITH 4MEV GS	
					Abst HPA 34 457	Aug 61 − .GAM GAM CINCIDENCE	
					Jour ZP 156 293	Oct 59 Knoeppel+ 4.0 TO 4.2MEV GAMMAS	
Spect (n,γ)	Maxwl		ORL	Expt	Prog ORNL−3778 44	May 65 Harvey.FC+LI−GE DET,CFD D,P REACTION	
Spect (n,γ)	7.5+6		FOA	Expt	Jour NP/A 120 161	Nov 68 Bergqvist+ VDG TOF.CFD 1/2DIRECT NG	
					Jour PL 19 670	Jan 66 − + CFD COMPOUND NUCL SPECT	
					Conf 65Antwerp 550	Jul 65 − + NAI. ABST.NDG.SHAPE ONLY.	
Spect (n,γ)	2.5−2		MIT	Comp	Rept MITNE−85	Jan 69 Rasmussen+TBL G INT.=AFCRL−69−0071	
Spect (n,γ)	Maxwl		ANL	Expt	Conf 69Studsvik 15	Aug 69 Bolotin.SHERA. G−G−COINC−SPECS,GE−LI	

83 Bismuth 209

Quantity	Energy (ev) Min	Max	Lab	Type	Documentation Ref Vol Page	Date	Author, Comments	Data
Spect (n,γ)	2.0+3		MTR	Expt Prog	NCSAC-31 76	May 70	Greenwood+,ANAL TO BE COMPL,NO DATA	
Spect (n,γ)		3.0+6	CRC	Expt Prog	AECL-3912 64	Mar 71	Bartholomew+.NAI DET.PRELIM. NO DATA	
Spect (n,γ)	2.0+4	6.0+4	ORL	Expt Rept	ORNL-TM-3379	Apr 71	Bird+.VDG. NAI CRYST. CURVE	
Spect (n,γ)	Maxwl		LAS	Expt Prog	NCSAC-38 123	May 71	Jurney.0.04-2.9MEV GAMS.BI210 LVLS	
Spect (n,γ)	1.5+7		CCP	Expt Conf	73Tbilisi 159	Feb 73	Kravtsov+ ABST,GE-LI,G-SPEC AT 90DEG	
Spect (n,γ)	1.4+7		NJS	Expt Jour	NP/A 213 525	Oct 73	Potokar+ D-T NS. PAIR SPECTROMETER.	+
				Priv	CVELBAR	Oct 72	.PROMPT GAMMA-RAY SPECTRUM	
	1.4+7			Data	EXFOR30185.013	Oct 72	25 DATA LINES	
Spect (n,γ)	Maxwl		CCP	Expt Conf	75Leningrd 350	Jan 75	Begzhanov+ G-SPEC	
Inelastic γ	3.9+6		BAR	Expt Jour	PR 93 796	Feb 54	Rothman+ VDG+CRYST SPEC 4 PEAKS	
Inelastic γ	8.0-1	2.7+6	LRL	Expt Jour	PR 95 751	Aug 54	Shapiro+ .895 1.56MEV LVLS EXC CURVS	
Inelastic γ	8.9+5	2.7+6	MIT	Expt Jour	PR 95 989	Aug 54	Kiehn+	+
	8.9+5	2.7+6		Data	EXFOR11477.009	Jun 76	. 36 PT. DSIGMA	
Inelastic γ	3.2+6		NRL	Expt Jour	PR 96 386	Oct 54	Scherrer+	+
	3.2+6			Data	EXFOR11672.015	Jun 76	. 4 PTS. DSIGMA	
Inelastic γ	1.3+7		RIC	Expt Prog	WASH-188	May 55	Hall+ SPHERE ONLY 5 PC OF AL TO FE.	
Inelastic γ	2.6+6		LAS	Expt Jour	PR 102 767	Apr 56	Day.VALUES AT 2 GAMMA ES AT 95 DEG	+
				Conf	55Geneva 2 9	Aug 55	DAY.P581, EXCITATN 0.895+1.56 LVL	
Inelastic γ	3.0+6		YOK	Expt Jour	JPJ 14 699	Jun 59	Hosoe+.E(GAMMA)TO2.2MEV.CFD TH	+
	3.0+6			Data	EXFOR20286.010	Jun 74	2PTS.D/DA.	
Inelastic γ	3.0+6		FEI	Expt Jour	AE 7 268	Sep 59	Androsenko+ GRAPH+TABLE OF G-ENERGS	
				Jour	SJA 7 763	Mar 61	. ENGL OF AE 7 268	
				Jour	KE 3 565	Jun 60	. GERMAN OF AE 7 268	
				Jour	JNEA 12 136	Jun 60	. ENGL OF AE 7 268	
Inelastic γ	4.2+6		TNC	Expt Jour	PR 118 1059	May 60	Morgan. ISOTROPIC TO +-15 PERCENT	
				Prog	WADC-TN-107	Feb 59	Bostrom+ NAI(TL) SPECT,TABLE+CURVES	
Inelastic γ	None		JAE	Expt Rept	JAERI-4016 86	Jun 61	Nishimura+ EXCIT CURVES CFD H-F MODL	
Inelastic γ	3.0+6		CCP	Expt Prog	IZV 25 1280	Oct 61	Graudynya+,OKS OTHERS EXCEPT 1.25MEV	
Inelastic γ	2.5+6	4.1+6	LAS	Expt Conf	65Antwerp § 29	Jul 65	DAY+GE-DET 5-7KEV RSLN.OKS OTHERS	
				Rept	LA-DC-7096	64	.EQUIVALENT	
Inelastic γ	4.1+6		ETH	Theo Jour	RMP 38 143	Jan 66	.THEOR CALC OF GAM-RAY ANGL DISTR	
Inelastic γ	5.8+6	7.5+6	FOA	Expt Jour	NP 80 198	May 66	Bergqvist+CFD SPEC IN CAPT.AT 0.1MEV	
Inelastic γ	1.4+7		FEI	Expt Rept	ICD-4 47	67	Bakov+ GAMMA RAY SPECTRA,CURVES	
Inelastic γ	1.0+6	3.5+6	FEI	ExTh Jour	IZV 31 327	Feb 67	Broder+.CRYST SPEC,CURVE CFD STAT TH	+
				Jour	BAS 31 311	Feb 67	TRANSLATN.*	
	1.0+6	3.5+6		Expt Data	EXFOR40161.	Mar 73	.FOR 3 E-LVL TABLES OF SIG-(EN) GVN	
Inelastic γ	1.1+6	2.0+6	BHU	ExTh Conf	67Tokyo § 8.87	Sep 67	Nath+ HARWELL-VDG,ANGDIST OF GAMMAS	+
	1.1+6	2.0+6		Expt Data	EXFOR30056.	Nov 70	ANGDIST OF 0.89+1.6 MEV G AT 3EN	
Inelastic γ	3.0+5	3.2+6	ALD	Expt Prog	AWRE-CNRPR/10	Apr 68	Gilboy+RING SCAT.EXCIT.FUNCT.	
Inelastic γ	5.0+6	7.0+6	ALD	Expt Jour	NP/A 112 337	May 68	Owens+.3ES.TOF SPECT 90 DEG. NDG.	+
Inelastic γ	1.0+6		STF	Expt Abst	DA/B 28 4715	May 68	Torop.GAM ADIST NR THRSHLD CF THEORY	
Inelastic γ	2.8+6		NRD	Expt Prog	WASH-1127 158	Apr 69	Engesser+ 3GAM ES AT 70DEG,TBP SOON	
Inelastic γ	Fast		CCP	Expt Jour	AE 29 338	Nov 70	Barkov+ AVG SIG FOR GAM PROD.TBLS	
				Jour	SJA 29 1080	Nov 70	TRANSLATN.*	
Inelastic γ	Fiss		FEI	Expt Jour	AE 29 338	Nov 70	Bakov+	+
	Fiss			Data	EXFOR40131.013	Jan 73	PRODUCTION OF 4 GAMMA-LINES	
Inelastic γ	1.0+6	1.5+7	TNC	Expt Rept	ORO-2791-32	Feb 71	Buchanan+.13NEUT ES,DIFF SIGS TABULT	
	2.6+6	4.1+6		Prog	TID-20658	Sep 63	Morgan+.GAMMA SPEC+PROD SIGS,90 DEG.	
Inelastic γ	1.0+6	9.0+6	SAC	Expt Conf	71Knoxvill 318	Mar 71	Lucas+,LINAC,.9 AND 1.6MEV GAMS,CRVS	
Inelastic γ	8.0+6		BRC	Expt Rept	EANDC(E)140U	Aug 71	Lachkar+,ANG.DISTRIBUTION	
Inelastic γ	1.0+6	1.0+7	VNV	Expt Rept	CEA-N-1476	Aug 71	Bertin+LINAC TOF G-SPECTRUM	
	5.0+6	8.7+6		Rept	CEA-R-3808	Jul 69	- +VDG,NAI(TL),	
Inelastic γ	1.0+6	3.4+6	KUR	Expt Jour	IZV 35 2341	Nov 71	Degtjarev+ GE-LI,SIG(NEUT-E),GRAPH	+
				Jour	BAS 35 2123	Nov 72	.ENGLISH OF IZV 35 2341 N/71	
	1.4+6	3.4+6		Data	EXFOR40278.009	Apr 75	.SIGMA AT 6 ES TO VARIOUS LVLS GVN	
Inelastic γ	Pile		FEI	Expt Prog	YFI-12 14	72	Bakov+ AVG SIG OF GAM YLD,ABST,NDG	
				Prog	INDC(CCP)-30	Dec 72	.PG 11,ENGLISH OF YFI-12 14	
Inelastic γ	4.9+6	1.6+7	FEI	Expt Rept	FEI-584	75	Goncharv+ GELI G-SPEC.G-PROD SIG,TABL	
Inelastic γ	3.3+6		SBL	Expt Jour	NIM 134 545	76	Habbani+ 90 DEG TBL	+
	3.3+6			Data	EXFOR20667.024	Oct 76	2PTS.D/DA.	
Nonelastic γ	2.4+6		OSA	Expt Jour	JMJ 21 75	39	Kikuchi+.D-D P LI-D N,SIG GIVN	
	2.1+6	2.8+6		Jour	JMJ 21 232	39	Aoki.SIG GIVN	
	2.4+6			Jour	SCP 34 865	Aug 38	Kikuchi+ D+D,G-M.SIG=5.5B	
			2.4+6	Jour	JMJ 19 369	37	Aoki.D+D NEUTRON.RELATIV SIG GIVN	
	Slow			Jour	JPJO 18 115	36	Kikuchi+.REL SIG GIVN FOR G-EMISSION	
				Jour	JMJ 18 188	36	- +.SIG GIVN BY D+D NEUTRON	
Nonelastic γ	2.3+6	2.9+6	JAP	Expt Jour	JPJO 26 66	44	Nonaka.D+D,ANGDIST 0 TO 135 DEG	+
	2.3+6	2.9+6		Data	EXFOR20298.004	Jun 74	7PTS.SIGMA.	

83 Bismuth 209

Quantity	Energy (ev) Min	Energy (ev) Max	Lab	Type	Documentation Ref Vol Page	Author, Comments Date	Data
Nonelastic γ	2.5+6	1.5+7	ARK	Expt Prog	A−ARK−61 1	Jan 61 Chittenden+	+
	2.5+6	1.5+7		Data	EXFOR11132.	Jun 76 . 28 PTS. SIGMA.	
Nonelastic γ	1.5+7		LND	Expt Jour	AF 39 295	Sep 69 Joensson+. GE(LI). 80 DEGREES	+
				Rept	LU−NP−6804	Mar 68 − + EQUIVALENT TO AF 39 295	
	1.5+7	1.6+7		Data	EXFOR20164.039	May 74 5PTS.D/DA.	
Nonelastic γ	1.4+7		MUN	Expt Jour	ZP 245 13	Jul 71 Feicht+ D−D NS,GE(LI) PROD C.S.+LVLS	
Nonelastic γ	1.0+6	1.0+7	SAC	Expt Rept	CEA−N−1476	Sep 71 Bertin. AT 90 DEGREES	
Nonelastic γ	6.0+6		ORL	Expt Prog	NCSAC−42 195	Nov 71 Dickens+. NO DATA GIVEN	
(n,2n)	5.0+6	1.4+7	AUS	Expt Jour	APA 3 352	Mar 50 Lintner. RA−BE SOURCE	
				Jour	OAWS 158 135	Nov 49 − .	
(n,2n)	1.4+7		LAS	Expt Jour	PR 97 1205	Mar 55 Graves. BETWEEN 1.86 AND 2.19B	
(n,2n)	Thrsh	1.4+7	BNL	Eval Rept	BNL−3341	Sep 55 Oleksa.FROM SNE+14MEV VALUE+CALC	
(n,2n)	1.4+7		LAS	Expt Jour	PR 107 824	Aug 57 Rosen+ 2.3+−0.3B	+
	1.4+7			Data	EXFOR11223.010	Jun 76 . 1 PT. SIGMA.	
	1.4+7			Data	EXFOR11223.012	Jun 76 . 21 PTS. DSIGMA.	
(n,2n)	1.4+7		LRL	Expt Jour	PR 111 616	Jul 58 Ashby+,SC 2.60+−0.19B APP=NONELASTIC	+
				Conf	58Geneva 15 3	Sep 58 Benveniste.PPR2494,VAL GVN,TOF	
	1.4+7			Data	EXFOR11097.027	Jun 76 . 1 PT. SIGMA.	
(n,2n)	1.4+7		CCP	Expt Jour	AE 5 522	Nov 58 Lebedev+ N2N+2(N3N)−REM=2.18+−0.2B	
				Jour	JNEA 11 39	59 TRANSLATN.*	
				Jour	SJA 5 1431	58 TRANSLATN.*	
(n,2n)	1.4+7		CCP	Expt Jour	AE 5 657	Dec 58 Flerov+ (N,EM)−(N,X)=2.42+−0.20BARNS	+
				Jour	JNEA 11 174	Feb 60 TRANSLATN.*	
				Jour	SJA 5 1601	58 TRANSLATN.*	
(n,2n)	1.5+7		CCP	Expt Jour	ZET 36 1046	Apr 59 Glagolev.G OF SHORT−LIVED ISOMERES	
				Jour	JET 9 742	Oct 59 TRANSLATN.*	
(n,2n)	Fiss		CRC	Eval Rept	CRC−1003	Dec 60 Roy+,ESTIMATED AVG SIG=10.4MB	
(n,2n)	1.5+7		CCP	Expt Jour	ZET 40 743	Mar 61 S FOR ACT.OF BI208META .66+−.12B	
				Jour	JET 13 520	Sep 61 TRANSLATN.*	
(n,2n)	Maxwl		ORL	Expt Prog	ORNL−3320 7	62 Halperin.	+
	Maxwl			Data	EXFOR12199.002	Jun 76 . 1 PT. SIGMA.	
(n,2n)	1.4+7		PCF	Expt Jour	NP 47 225	Aug 63 Jeremie.TOF	
(n,2n)	1.4+7		KFI	Expt Jour	NP 49 489	Dec 63 Adam+MECHANISM OF (N,2N) REACTION	+
	1.4+7			Data	EXFOR30107.003	Oct 71 MECHANISM OF THE (N,2N) REACTION	
(n,2n)	Pile		MND	Expt Abst	BAP 8 634	Dec 63 Lange. NDG	
(n,2n)	1.4+7		HAM	Comp Jour	NP 65 257	Mar 65 Bormann. 2EXPT VALS.CFD SHELL EFFECT	
(n,2n)	1.3+7	1.5+7	BNL	Theo Jour	NSE 23 238	Nov 65 Pearlstein.3ES.STAT MDL CALC.TBL CS.	
(n,2n)	Fiss		BNL	Theo Jour	NSE 23 238	Nov 65 Pearlstein.STATMDL CALC.SPEC AVG.TBL	
(n,2n)	1.4+7	1.4+7	GRE	Expt Jour	CR 265 712	Sep 66 Monnand. = 1 DATA INDEX LINES	+
				Rept	CEA−R−2900	Dec 65 − .SIG ISOM.PRODUCT+HALF LIFE	
(n,2n)	1.4+7		MUN	Expt Jour	NUK 10 58	Jul 67 Feicht+ FERMI−WATER−TANK METHOD	+
(n,2n)	1.4+7		KGU	Expt Prog	YFI−6 117	68 Vojtenko+. TABLE SIG AT 10 ANGLES	
				Rept	INDC−260E	69 . ENGL OF YFI−6 117	
(n,2n)	1.4+7		KGU	Expt Conf	68Riga	Jan 68 Vojtenko+ ABST,ANGULAR CORRELATIONS	
(n,2n)	1.4+7		KGU	Expt Jour	YF 9 9	Jan 69 Voitenko+.NEUTRONS ANG CORR,CURVE	
(n,2n)	1.4+7		KGU	Expt Jour	YF 9 9	Jan 69 Voitenko+ GRPH,ANG DIST OF NEUTRONS	
				Jour	SNP 9 5	Jul 69 TRANSLATN.*	
(n,2n)	1.4+7		CCP	Theo Conf	69Erevan	Feb 69 Ezhov+.ABST,ANGL CORRELATION FUNCT	
(n,2n)	1.4+7		KGU	Expt Jour	YF 10 699	Oct 69 Prokopets+ NEUT DOUBLE ANGDIST,GRPHS	
				Jour	SNP 10 403	Apr 70 TRANSLATN.*	
				Jour	UFZ 14 865	May 69 Prokopec+ ANG CORR BETWEEN NS,GRAPH	
				Jour	UFZ 14 687	Apr 69 − + ANG CORREL BETWEEN NEUTS	
(n,2n)	1.5+7		DEB	Comp Jour	REA 7 4 93	Dec 69 Csikai+ SIG+HL COMPILTN,N−ACTIV−ANAL	
(n,2n)	1.3+7	1.4+7	CCP	Comp Rept	ICD−6 215	70 Sluchevskaja.SIGS ISOM,SUM (G+M),TBL	
(n,2n)	1.4+7		KGU	Theo Jour	YF 11 122	Jan 70 Ezhov+ DOUBLEDIFF SIG(E)GRPH CFD XPT	
				Jour	SNP 11 68	Jul 70 TRANSLATN.*	
(n,2n)	1.4+7	1.5+7	JYV	Eval Rept	JU−RR−3/1970	Jun 70 Leppaemaeki+ TABLE OF EVAL AVG SIG	
(n,2n)	+7		KFI	Theo Rept	KFKI−71−8	Feb 71 Jeki. CALCULATED CFD EXPTL SIG VALUE	
(n,2n)	Maxwl	1.4+7	KFI	Comp Jour	JRC 7 365	Jun 71 Nagy+ SIGMAS,GAMMA−E AND HALF−L GIVN	
(n,2n)	1.4+7		KFI	Theo Conf	72Budapest 202	Aug 72 Kluge+ CALCULATED EN−SPECTRA ,GRPH	
				Rept	KFKI−72−17	Feb 72 − + CALC N−SPEC INEL+N2N,TBL,GRPH	
(n,2n)	1.5+7		DEB	Eval Jour	REA 11 1 153	Mar 73 Boedy. COMPILATION+RECOMM.VALUE,TBL	
				Rept	IAEA−153 173	73 − . RECOMM. VALUE ONLY	
(n,2n)	1.5+7		ELU	Expt Jour	AHP 38 209	75 Deak+ E−SPC OF THE 2NS,GAM−COMPETITN	+
	1.5+7			Data	EXFOR30333.003	May 76 1 PNT.	

83 Bismuth 209

Quantity	Energy (ev) Min	Max	Lab	Type	Documentation Ref Vol Page	Author, Comments Date	Data
(n,2n)	1.5+7		SMU	Expt Conf	75Wash. 712	Mar 75 Salaita+SHORT-LIVED ISOMER PROD.TBL.	+
				Conf	74Columbia 95	Jul 74 - + ACT.SIG TO SHORTLIV ISO.TBL	
				Jour	JIN 35 2139	Jul 73 - + CYCLIC ACTIV, ISOM STATES	
	1.5+7			Data	EXFOR10361.	Jun 74 1 PT M-ST	
(n,2n)	1.4+7		TUD	Theo Conf	75Kiev 4 149	May 75 Seidel+ PREEQ-EFF ON CALC SIG.TABLE	
(n,2n)	7.9+6	1.5+7	BRC	Expt Jour	NIM 135 511	Jun 76 Frehaut.GD LOADED SCIN.EXPT DETAILS.	+
				Conf	75Kiev 4 303	May 75 - + LIQSCIN.SIG(E),CFD.GRPH+TBL	
				Conf	75Wash. 855	Mar 75 - + TBL.GRPH.REL 238U(N,F)	
				Rept	CEA-R-4627	Nov 74 - + LARGE LIQ SCINT METH11 VAL	
	7.9+6	1.5+7		Data	EXFOR20416.020	Jul 75 15PTS.SIGMA.	
(n,2n)	Thrsh	1.5+7	BRC	Expt Jour	76Lowell 1350	Jul 76 Cindro+EXCIT FN CALC.CFD EXPT.NDG.	
(n,2n)	8.0+6	2.4+7	LAS	Theo Prog	LA-6560 2	Nov 76 Arthur+CALC CFD EXPT.CURVS.	
(n,xn) x>2	Pile		CRC	Expt Jour	CJP 37 815	Jul 59 Eastwood+N3N.EFF CS=.3MICROB	
(n,xn) x>2	Pile		MND	Expt Abst	BAP 8 634	Dec 63 Lange+N3N.RADIOCHEM YLDS MEAS.NDG	
(n,xn) x>2	Fiss		BNL	Theo Jour	NSE 23 238	Nov 65 Pearlstein.SPEC AVG STATMDL CALC N3N	
n Emission	1.4+7		LAS	Expt Jour	PR 107 824	Aug 57 Rosen+ SIGMA GIVEN	+
				Conf	58Geneva 15 11	Sep 58 Coon+.PPR666,VAL GVN,EXPT DESCRIBED	
	1.4+7			Data	EXFOR11223.012	Jun 76 . 21 PTS. SIGMA.	
n Emission	1.4+7		CCP	Expt Jour	AE 5 522	Nov 58 Lebedev+ SPH GEOM,N COUNT,ETA GIVEN	
				Jour	JNEA 11 39	59 .TRANSLATION	
				Jour	SJA 5 1431	58 .ENGL OF AE 5 522 NOV58	
n Emission	1.4+7		CCP	Expt Jour	AE 5 657	Dec 58 Flerov+ SPHERE TRANSM, ETA=1.93+-.08	
				Jour	JNEA 11 174	Feb 60 TRANSLATN.*	
				Jour	SJA 5 1601	58 TRANSLATN.*	
n Emission	1.4+7		FEI	Expt Rept	YK-7 102	Mar 72 Salnikov+	+
	1.4+7			Data	EXFOR40037.	Aug 72 6 SUBENT,DIFF+DOUBLE DIFF N-EMISS CS	
n Emission	1.5+7		TUD	Expt Jour	KE 19 241	Aug 76 Hermsdorf+ ABSOL DOUBDIF,FIG.TOT,TBL	+
				Rept	ZFK-277(U)	Aug 75 - + DIFFSIG AT 5ANGS,TBL+GRPH	
				Conf	ZFK-271 94	Nov 73 Goebel+ N-EMISSION SPEC,TOF.SUMMARY	
	1.5+7			Data	EXFOR30397.032	May 77 49 PTS. ANGLE INT.N-EMISS.SPECT.	
	1.5+7			Data	EXFOR30275.	Apr 74 DOUBLDIF(5ANG,473PTS)+PARTIAL ANGDIS	
(n,p)	1.4+7		ALD	Expt Jour	PPS 73 215	Feb 59 Coleman+. ACT. CFD DIRECT INTERACTN	+
(n,p)	1.5+7		ARK	Expt Jour	PR 115 989	Aug 59 Poularikas+ C-W. 83+-.4 MB.	+
				Jour	PRL 3 253	Sep 59 .SUPERSEDED	
	1.5+7			Data	EXFOR11484.014	Jun 76 . 1 PT. SIGMA.	
(n,p)	Fiss		CRC	Eval Rept	CRC-1003	Dec 60 Roy+,ESTIMATED AVG SIG=0.005MB	
(n,p)	1.5+7		SAH	Expt Jour	PPS 77 508	Feb 61 Mukherjee+0.7MB+-15PC FOR 3.3HR ACT	+
	1.4+7			Conf	60Waltair 289	Feb 60 - +.VAL GVN REL AL(N,A),VDG	
(n,p)	1.4+7		FRK	Theo Jour	ZP 171 379	Dec 62 Lindner.STATMOD,INC PAIR+SHELL TERMS	
(n,p)	1.4+7	1.5+7	SAH	Comp Jour	NUC 23 8 112	Aug 65 Chatterjee. TABLE WITH REFS.	
	1.4+7			Jour	NP 60 273	Nov 64 - .MEAN OF EXPT CFD SHELLMOD	
(n,p)	Maxwl		IFU	Theo Rept	ICD-4 20	67 Dadakina+ PENETR COEFF CALC,TABLE	
(n,p)	1.4+7	1.5+7	NAP	Comp Rept	INFN/BE-67-10	Jul 67 Cuzzocrea+ AVERAGED CHOSEN DATA.	
(n,p)	1.5+7		DEB	Comp Jour	REA 7 4 93	Dec 69 Csikai+ SIG+HL COMPILTN,N-ACTIV-ANAL	
(n,p)	1.4+7	1.5+7	JYV	Eval Rept	JU-RR-3/1970	Jun 70 Leppaemaeki+ TABLE OF EVAL AVG SIG	
(n,p)	1.3+7	1.5+7	JIA	Expt Conf	75Kiev 4 209	May 75 Belovitskij+.SIG,ENERGY DEPEND,E-LVL	+
	1.4+7			Data	EXFOR40347.005	Dec 77 SIG AT 14.5MEV,REL BI209(N,A).1 PNT	
(n,p)	None		DAV	Expt Conf	76Lowell 1273	Jul 76 Brady+FOR BIO-MED APPLICATIONS.NDG	
(n,p)	4.3+7	6.4+7	DAV	Expt Conf	76Lowell 1344	Jul 76 King+3ES.ANG DISTR.ISOVECTOR RES.NDG	
(n,np)	1.4+7		TUD	Theo Conf	75Kiev 4 149	May 75 Seidel+ (NNP),(NPN).PREEQ-EFF.TABLE	
(n,np)	None		DAV	Expt Conf	76Lowell 1273	Jul 76 Brady+FOR BIO-MED APPLICATIONS.NDG	
(n,d)	None		DAV	Expt Conf	76Lowell 1273	Jul 76 Brady+FOR BIO-MED APPLICATIONS.NDG	
(n,d)	4.3+7	6.4+7	DAV	Expt Conf	76Lowell 1344	Jul 76 King+3ES.P HOLE STRENGTHS.CFD.NDG	
(n,nd)	None		DAV	Expt Conf	76Lowell 1273	Jul 76 Brady+FOR BIO-MED APPLICATIONS.NDG	
(n,t)	2.3+7		JUL	Expt Jour	JIN 36 3639	Dec 74 Qaim+ (NT)+(NNT), 3.7+-0.7 MB	+
	2.3+7			Data	EXFOR20524.014	Apr 76 1PNT.+NNT	
(n,t)	None		DAV	Expt Conf	76Lowell 1273	Jul 76 Brady+FOR BIO-MED APPLICATIONS.NDG	
(n,nt)	2.3+7		JUL	Expt Jour	JIN 36 3639	Dec 74 Qaim+ (NT)+(NNT), 3.7+-0.7 MB	+
	2.3+7			Data	EXFOR20524.014	Apr 76 1PNT.+NT.	
(n,nt)	None		DAV	Expt Conf	76Lowell 1273	Jul 76 Brady+FOR BIO-MED APPLICATIONS.NDG	
(n,He3)	None		DAV	Expt Conf	76Lowell 1273	Jul 76 Brady+BIO-MED APPLICATIONS.TBD.NDG	
(n,α)	1.5+7		CRC	Expt Jour	CJP 31 267	Feb 53 Paul+ BETA ACT. CFD TH. HL=4M	+
	1.5+7			Data	EXFOR11274.098	Jun 76 . 1 PT. SIGMA.	
(n,α)	1.4+7		ALD	Expt Jour	PPS 73 215	Feb 59 Coleman+. ACTIVATION	+
(n,α)	1.5+7		ARK	Expt Jour	PR 115 989	Aug 59 Poularikas+ C-W. 1.1+-.3 MB.	+
				Jour	PRL 3 253	Sep 59 .SUPERSEDED	
	1.5+7			Data	EXFOR11484.015	Jun 76 . 1 PT. SIGMA.	
(n,α)	Fiss		CRC	Eval Rept	CRC-1003	Dec 60 Roy+,ESTIMATED AVG SIG=0.0001MB	

83 Bismuth 209

Quantity	Energy (ev) Min	Max	Lab	Type	Documentation Ref Vol Page	Date	Author, Comments	Data
(n,α)	1.5+7		SAH	Expt Jour	PPS 77 508	Feb 61	Mukherjee+0.6MB+−15PC FOR 4.4MIN ACT	+
	1.4+7			Conf	60Waltair 289	Feb 60	− +.VAL GVN REL AL(N,A),VDG	
(n,α)	1.4+7		FRK	Theo Jour	ZP 171 379	Dec 62	Lindner.STATMOD,CF CJP 31 267,TH+XPT	
(n,α)	1.4+7		CIS	Theo Jour	NP 51 460	Feb 64	Facchini+STATMOD SIG XPT/CALC0.8−1.4	
(n,α)	1.5+7		RBZ	Expt Jour	NP 73 548	Nov 65	Kulisic.E+ANGDIST+SIGTOT.CFD TH.CURV	+
				Rept	EANDC−50S148	Jul 65	. FULL PAPER PRESENTD AT 65ANTWERP	
				Conf	64Paris 2 769	Jul 64	.	
	1.5+7			Data	EXFOR30127.	Mar 71	SIGMA, ANG−DISTR, ALFA−SPECTR(0DEG)	
(n,α)	1.2+7	2.3+7	FRK	Expt Jour	NP 85 606	Sep 66	Rubbino+ZUBKE ANGLE+ENERGY SPECTRA	
				Abst	BSI 46 43	Nov 65	− +(2B5).E SPEC,ANGDST ANAL.NDG	
				Conf	65Antwerp 548	Jul 65	− + ABST.PPR124. 14MEV.	
(n,α)	1.4+7	1.5+7	NAP	Comp Rept	INFN/BE−67−11	Sep 67	Cuzzocrea+ AVERAGED CHOSEN DATA.	
(n,α)	1.5+7		DEB	Comp Jour	REA 7 4 93	Dec 69	Csikai+ SIG+HL COMPILTN,N−ACTIV−ANAL	
(n,α)	1.4+7	1.5+7	JYV	Eval Rept	JU−RR−3/1970	Jun 70	Leppaemaeki+ TABLE OF EVAL AVG SIG	
(n,α)	1.4+7		RBZ	Theo Conf	72Budapest 168	Aug 72	Caplar+ ANALYSIS OF SPECTRA,GRAPH	
(n,α)	Maxwl		MUA	Expt Jour	NP/A 205 614	May 73	Alam+ ACTIVATION REL (N,GAMMA)	+
	Pile			Jour	NP/A 205 614	May 73	− + RATIO TO NG SIGMA,HALF LIVES	
	Pile			Data	EXFOR30249.005	Jul 73	RATIO TO NG−SIGMA,HALF−LIVES	
(n,α)	1.4+7	1.5+7	CIS	Theo Jour	NP/A 210 297	Aug 73	Milazzo−Colli+ ALPHA E−DISTN CFD XPT	
	1.4+7	2.3+7		Jour	PL/B 38 155	Feb 72	Colli−Milazzo+ A−SPECT+EXCIT FN CALC	
(n,α)	1.5+6		CCP	Expt Conf	75Leningrd 348	Jan 75	Belovicky+ ABST,SIG	
(n,α)	Maxwl		ILL	Expt Prog	BLG−520	77	Wagemans+ PRELIM.ABST.NDG.	
Fission		1.6+7	EDG	Expt Jour	NAT 158 871	Dec 46	Broda+UPPER LIM.REL U−238.RADCH+EMUL	
Fission	2.5+7	8.4+7	BRK	Expt Jour	PR 73 1135	May 48	Kelly+ RELATIVE TO THORIUM.	
Fission	1.4+7		LAS	Expt Jour	PR 75 919	Mar 49	Phillips+ UPPER LIM REL U238.PHOTOPL	
Fission	1.5+7		ARK	Expt Jour	RCA 4 113	Jun 65	Ganapathy+ FROM RU105 YIELD	+
	1.5+7			Data	EXFOR12221.002	Jun 76	. 1 PT. SIGMA.	
Fission	1.5+7		ARK	Expt Abst	DA/B 29 319	Jul 68	Ganapathy. SIG=(35+−10)NANOBARNS	
Fission	1.4+7		TRM	Expt Prog	BARC−872 107	76	Iyer+ ABST.REL U238,SIG=5.6X10E−7 B	
Frag Spectra	9.0+7		BRK	Expt Jour	PR 76 1112	Oct 49	Jungerman+ PROMPT NS TAKE SURPLUS E	
Reson Params	1.2+4		ANL	Expt Jour	PR 98 223	Apr 55	Hibdon+	+
				Prog	ANL−5498 52	Jun 56	− . GT BY 2 METHODS.	
	1.2+4			Data	EXFOR11244.	Jun 76	. 1 RES. E0,WT**2	
Reson Params	8.1+2	2.4+3	ANL	Expt Jour	PR 100 126	Oct 55	Bollinger+,TOF PARS FOR 2RES ES	+
				Abst	PR 95 645	Jul 54	.ABSTRACT RA10	
	8.1+2	2.4+3		Data	EXFOR11690.007	Jun 76	. 2 RES. E0,WT	
Reson Params	8.1+2	2.4+3	BNL	Expt Jour	PR 101 1328	Feb 56	Levin+,IF 2LVLS ADD THR GIVES WG44MV	
Reson Params	1.0+3	7.0+3	DKE	Expt Jour	PR 102 1574	Jun 56	Gibbons.ALSO 3 13 34 47KEV ONE J L=0	
Reson Params	2.3+3	3.3+4	ORL	Expt Jour	PR 109 926	Feb 58	Good+,TOF+SC 4EOS WT=24EV 1ST EO	+
	2.3+3	3.3+4		Data	EXFOR11402.	Jun 76	. 4 RES. E0,WT	
Reson Params	8.0+2	3.1+3	CCP	Expt Jour	AE 5 69	Jul 58	Vladimirskii+ 3RES,WT WN WG AT 800EV	+
				Jour	SJA 5 883	58	TRANSLATN.*	
				Jour	JNEA 10 64	Jul 54	TRANSLATN.*	
Reson Params	7.8+2	2.2+3	HAR	Expt Jour	NP 7 613	Aug 58	Lynn+ TOF J§4,5 WG,WT 3 RESONANCES	
	7.8+2	1.2+3		Conf	58Paris 496	Jul 58	− .	
Reson Params	1.2+4	1.3+5	DKE	Expt Jour	AP 8 250	Oct 59	Nichols+ 18 RESON ES+WN GIVEN	+
	1.2+4	1.3+5		Data	EXFOR11587.002	Jun 76	. 15 RES. E0,WN,WN0	
Reson Params	7.8+2	1.5+4	HAR	Expt Jour	NP 44 431	Jul 63	Firk+ 5RESONANCES.SPINS GIVEN.	
				Rept	AERE−NP/GEN 16	Aug 60	Lynn+ TEXT OF 60KINGSTON	
Reson Params	8.0+2	1.5+5	COL	Expt Rept	CR−1860	64	Garg+,49RESON ES,AVG D=3.1+−.3KEV	+
	8.0+2	1.5+5		Data	EXFOR11646.022	Jun 76	. 49 RES.E0	
Reson Params		1.0+6	AUA	Theo Jour	AUJ 20 477	Oct 67	Cook. TBL OF AVG LVL SPACING D,L=0,1	
Reson Params	3.2+6	5.2+6	JNE	ExTh Jour	NP/A 119 356	Oct 68	Manero+.AVERAGE WT FROM FLUCT ANAL.	
Reson Params	4.4+3	7.0+4	SAC	Expt Jour	NP/A 123 561	Jan 69	Morgenstern+ LINAC E0,J,WN	+
				Rept	CEA−R−3609	Sep 68	− . THESIS	
				Jour	CR 265 506	Jul 67	− + PARAMS FOR MANY RES	
	7.8+2	7.0+4		Data	EXFOR20684.028	Jul 77	46PTS.E0,WN,J,L,G*WN.	
Reson Params	7.9+2		CJD	Eval Rept	YK−7	71	Zakharova+ SURVEY+SYSTEMATICS,GW,TBL	
				Rept	INDC(CCP)−27	Nov 72	.ENGLISH TRANSLATION OF YK−7 /71	
Reson Params	None		ORL	Expt Prog	NCSAC−42 183	Nov 71	Harvey+. TRANS. ANAL TBC. NO DATA	
Strnth Fnctn	8.0+4	1.6+5	WIS	Expt Jour	PR 99 748	Aug 55	Darden. STF FROM TRANSMISSION MEAS.	
Strnth Fnctn	+2	+5	DKE	Expt Jour	AP 8 250	Oct 59	Nichols+ STF,D FROM RESON PARAMS	
	1.0+2	9.9+5		Jour	AP 14 346	Jul 61	Newson+ QUOTES AP 8 250	
Strnth Fnctn	None		DKE	Expt Abst	DA/B 28 3834	Mar 68	Divadeenam. S P D WAVES, CFD OPTMDLS	

83 Bismuth 209

Quantity	Energy (ev) Min	Max	Lab	Type	Documentation Ref Vol Page	Author, Comments Date	Data
Strnth Fnctn		7.0+4	SAC	Expt	Jour NP/A 123 561	Jan 69 Morgenstern+ S,P WAVE.	+
					Rept CEA-R-3609	Sep 68 - .(THESIS).DATA GIVEN	
					Conf 68Wash. 867	Mar 68 - +	
					Jour CR 265 506	Jul 67 - + PRELIM VALUES	
	0.0+0	7.0+4			Data EXFOR20684.030	Jul 77 2PTS.	
Strnth Fnctn	-		DUB	Revw	Jour YF 11 111	Jan 70 Malecki+ VALUES FOR TWO SPIN STATES	
					Jour SNP 11 61	Jul 70 - + ENGL OF YF 11 61.	
Strnth Fnctn	2.4+4		MUA	Theo	Jour IJP 46 114	Mar 72 Chaubey+ P-WAVE.FOR A-SYSTEMTIC,GRPH	
Strnth Fnctn	1.5+2	6.5+2	SAC	ExTh	Diss FRNC-TH-450	Oct 72 Delaroche.OPTICAL MODEL PARAMETERS	
Strnth Fnctn	None		AUA	Eval	Rept AAEC/E-277	Mar 73 Musgrove.TBLS EXPTL DATA+BEST VALUES	
Strnth Fnctn		+5	KFK	Theo	Rept JAERI-M-5984	Feb 75 Newstead.P230.TBL S0,S1 CFD EXP.	
Lvl Density	Fast		ANL	Expt	Jour NP 25 511	Jun 61 Vandenbosh+LVL DENS.FROM OTHER REACT	
Lvl Density	6.0+6		DKE	Expt	Rept AD-299005	62 Seth+,NUCL TEMP+FERMI LVL DENS COEFF	
Lvl Density	1.4+7		BAS	Expt	Jour PL 5 202	Jul 63 Huber+TBL OF NUC TEMP AND LVL DENSTY	
					Jour HPA 36 1059	Dec 63 Plattner+TOF TBL12ELEM.CFD TH	
Lvl Density	5.0+6	7.0+6	ISL	Theo	Conf 64Geneva § 511	May 64 Szwarcbaum+.T FROM 3 FORMLS CFD EXPS	
Lvl Density	1.4+7		FEI	Expt	Jour YF 2 826	Nov 65 Anufrienko+.PARAMS FROM NONELASTIC	+
					Rept FEI-30	Dec 65 .	
					Rept EANDC-50 197	Jul 65 .FULL PAPER FROM 65ANTWERP	
					Rept FEI-4	65 .	
					Jour SNP 2 589	May 66 .ENGLISH TRANSL OF YF 2 826 11/65	
Lvl Density	5.0+6	7.0+6	ALD	Expt	Jour NP/A 112 337	May 68 Owens+.LVL DENS VERSUS EXCIT.MEAN T	+
					Conf 65Antwerp 547	Jul 65 - + PPR122. TBL FERMI GAS CONST.	
Lvl Density	3.6+6	8.5+6	JAE	Expt	Jour NP/A 131 145	Jun 69 Maruyama. E DEPENDANCE,PARAM,TH FIT.	
Lvl Density	+6	+7	FEI	Theo	Jour YF 11 1012	May 70 Ignatyuk+ DENSITY+A+TEMP VS EXCIT-E	
	+6				Rept INDC(CCP)-7U5	Feb 70 .TRANSLATN.*	
					Prog YFI-7 7	Apr 69 Ignatyuk+ TEMP+DENS+A VS EXCIT-E,CRV	
	+6	+7			Jour SNP 11 563	Nov 70 . ENGL OF YF 11 1012	
Lvl Density	None		AUW	Theo	Conf 70Madurai 2 267	Dec 70 Ramamurty+ A-PARAMETER GVN,LANG'S-TH	
Lvl Density	1.4+7		FEI	Expt	Conf 71Kiev	May 71 Sal'Nikov+.FERMI LDLDEN+NUC TEMP,TBL	
Lvl Density	9.1+6		FEI	Expt	Jour YF 19 1190	Jun 74 Birjukov+ TOF,LVL DEN LAW,T,TBL	+
					Jour SNP 19 608	Dec 74 . ENGLISH OF YF 19 1190	
	9.2+6				Data EXFOR40287.	Apr 75 .NUCL TEMP,LVL DENSITY PARAM	
(γ,n)		+7	BNL	Expt	Jour PR 79 539	Aug 50 Poss. N INTENSITY 0/90DEG,BY AL(NP)	
(γ,n)		+7	BSP	Revw	Conf 55Geneva 2 169	Aug 55 Souza-Santos+.P897,THRESHOLD VAL GVN	
(γ,n)		2.9+7	CCP	Expt	Jour YF 11 266	Feb 70 Lazareva+ ANG+E SPECS OF NEUTS,GRPHS	
					Jour SNP 11 149	Aug 70 TRANSLATN.*NO 2	
(γ,n)	9.0+6		MCM	Expt	Jour PL/B 55 369	Mar 75 Mcfee+ HE3 SPECTRO,GRPH,TBL	
Photo-Fissn	None		CHI	Expt	Jour PR 79 532	Aug 50 Sugarman. HIGH E,YIELDS GE-BA.	
Photo-Fissn		1.0+8	FTI	Expt	Conf 67Kharkov	Feb 67 Sanin+. TBP IN IZV	
Photo-Fissn	7.0+8	1.1+9	LND	Expt	Jour NP/A 143 449	Mar 70 Schroder+ MASS-YIELD DIST. TH MODEL.	

83 Bismuth 210

Quantity	Energy (ev) Min	Max	Lab	Type	Documentation Ref Vol Page	Author, Comments Date	Data
Res Int Abs	5.0-1		ORL	Expt	Rept ORNL-3320 2	62 Halperin+	+
	5.0-1				Data EXFOR12198.003	Jun 76 . 1 PT. SIGMA.	
(n,γ)	Maxwl		ORL	Expt	Rept ORNL-3320 2	62 Halperin.	+
	Maxwl				Data EXFOR12198.002	Jun 76 . 1 PT. SIGMA.	
(n,2n)	Fiss		CRC	Eval	Rept CRC-1003	Dec 60 Roy+,ESTIMATED AVG SIG=185.0MB	
(n,p)	Fiss		CRC	Eval	Rept CRC-1003	Dec 60 Roy+,ESTIMATED AVG SIG=0.08MB	
(n,p)	Maxwl		IFU	Theo	Rept ICD-4 20	67 Dadakina+ PENETR COEFF CALC,TABLE	
(n,α)	Fiss		CRC	Eval	Rept CRC-1003	Dec 60 Roy+,ESTIMATED AVG SIG=0.01MB	
Lvl Density	+6		MIL	Theo	Jour EN 15 1 54	Jan 68 Facchini+ LDL PARS FROM LOW EN RES	
	+7				Jour NC/A 51 4 1074	Oct 67 Gadioli+THEOR EVAL EVAPORATION SPECT	
Lvl Density	None		MUN	Theo	Jour NP/A 217 269	Dec 73 Dilg+ A,DELTA. BACK SHIFTED FERMIGAS	
Lvl Density	None		COP	Theo	Jour NP/A 222 493	Apr 74 Dossing+COLL ROTAT.SPAC. ACCUR ESTIM	

84 Polonium 206

Quantity	Energy (ev) Min Max	Lab	Type	Documentation Ref Vol Page	Author, Comments Date	Data
(n,p)	Maxwl	IFU	Theo Rept	ICD-4 20	67 Dadakina+ PENETR COEFF CALC,TABLE	
Lvl Density	-3 +0	IFU	Theo Jour	UFZ 13 700	Apr 68 Pisanko+ LEVEL SPACING CALC,TBL	
			Jour	UPJ 13 498	Oct 68 TRANSLATN.*	

84 Polonium 208

Quantity	Energy (ev) Min Max	Lab	Type	Documentation Ref Vol Page	Author, Comments Date	Data
(n,p)	Maxwl	IFU	Theo Rept	ICD-4 20	67 Dadakina+ PENETR COEFF CALC,TABLE	
Lvl Density	-3 +0	IFU	Theo Jour	UFZ 13 700	Apr 68 Pisanko+ LEVEL SPACING CALC,TBL	
			Jour	UPJ 13 498	Oct 68 TRANSLATN.*	

84 Polonium 209

Quantity	Energy (ev) Min Max	Lab	Type	Documentation Ref Vol Page	Author, Comments Date	Data
(n,p)	Maxwl	IFU	Theo Rept	ICD-4 20	67 Dadakina+ PENETR COEFF CALC,TABLE	

84 Polonium 210

Quantity	Energy (ev) Min Max	Lab	Type	Documentation Ref Vol Page	Author, Comments Date	Data
Diff Elastic	7.0+6	LRL	Theo Rept	UCRL-4927	Jul 57 Bjorklund+ OPTMDL CALC 6-PARAM FIT	
(n,γ)	Maxwl	ORL	Expt Jour	NSE 15 217	Feb 63 Halperin+,M30MB .52SEC,M.5MB 25SEC	+
Spect (n,γ)	None	KFI	Comp Jour	JRC 7 365	Jun 71 Nagy+ GAMMA+ELECTR ES AND HALF-LIFE	
(n,2n)	Pile	MND	Expt Abst	BAP 8 634	Dec 63 Lange. NDG	
(n,2n)	1.3+7 1.5+7	BNL	Theo Jour	NSE 23 238	Nov 65 Pearlstein.3ES.STAT MDL CALC.TBL CS.	
(n,2n)	Fiss	BNL	Theo Jour	NSE 23 238	Nov 65 Pearlstein.STATMDL CALC.SPEC AVG.TBL	
(n,xn) x>2	Pile	MND	Expt Abst	BAP 8 634	Dec 63 Lange+N3N RADIOCHEM YLDS MEAS.NDG.	
(n,xn) x>2	Fiss	BNL	Theo Jour	NSE 23 238	Nov 65 Pearlstein.SPEC AVG STATMDL CALC N3N	
(n,p)	Maxwl	IFU	Theo Rept	ICD-4 20	67 Dadakina+ PENETR COEFF CALC,TABLE	
(n,d)	6.0+6 2.2+7	ANL	Expt Jour	PR 114 154	Apr 59 Ramler+,INV PROC .2-20MB CURVE	
(n,α)	Maxwl	CCP	Expt Jour	YF 1 252	Feb 65 Andreev.IONIZ-CHAMBER,SIG=M2MB	+
			Jour	SNP 1 177	Aug 65 TRANSLATN.*	
(n,α)	Maxwl	LEB	Expt Conf	65Antwerp § 176	Jul 65 Andreev+ CFD TH NDG	
Fission	-	TPI	Theo Jour	YF 9 102	Jan 69 Korostova+ CV,SHELL CORR,LIQU-DROP-E	
			Jour	SNP 9 62	Jul 69 TRANSLATN.*	
Fiss Yield	None	BAS	Theo Jour	PL/B 34 264	Mar 71 Pauli+ FRAG MASS RATIO AS STRUTINSKY	
Fiss Yield	Maxwl	JUL	Theo Rept	JUEL-844-KP	Apr 72 Slavov. DEFORM-E+FRAG MASS YLD CALC	
	0.0+0 1.0+0		Jour	PL/B 37 483	Dec 71 - + ASYMMETRY BY 2-CENTRE SHELL	
Lvl Density	-3 +0	IFU	Theo Jour	UFZ 13 700	Apr 68 Pisanko+ LEVEL SPACING CALC,TBL	
			Jour	UPJ 13 498	Oct 68 TRANSLATN.*	
Lvl Density	+6 +7	FEI	Expt Conf	75Kiev 3 18	May 75 Ignatjuk+ FISS LVL DENS PAR VS EXC-E	

84 Polonium 211

Quantity	Energy (ev) Min Max	Lab	Type	Documentation Ref Vol Page	Author, Comments Date	Data
Fiss Yield	-	TRM	Theo Conf	69Vienna 41	Jul 69 Ramamurthy+PPR15. CALCTD GRPH YLD(A)	

84 Polonium 212

Quantity	Energy (ev) Min Max	Lab	Type	Documentation Ref Vol Page	Author, Comments Date	Data
Fiss Yield	-	FEI	Theo Prog	YFI-4 14	May 67 Ignatjuk.CURVES GIVEN	
	None		Jour	YF 7 1043	May 68 - . SHELL-TH OKS FRAG-A RATIO	
			Jour	SNP 7 626	Nov 68 . ENGL OF YF 7 1043	
	-		Rept	INDC-187E	67 . ENGL OF YFI-4 14	
Frag Spectra	None	FEI	Theo Jour	YF 7 1043	May 68 Ignatjuk. E-KIN(FRAG-A),SHELL-THEORY	
			Jour	SNP 7 626	Nov 68 . ENGL OF YF 7 1043	

85 Astatine 212

Quantity	Energy (ev) Min	Max	Lab	Type	Documentation Ref Vol Page	Author, Comments Date	Data
(n,α)	1.5+7	2.6+7	BRK	Expt Abst	DA 25 4206	Jan 65 Jones. INVERSE REACTION	
Fission	None		BRK	Revw Jour	NP 81 1	Jun 66 Myers+ TABLE 2, FISS BARRIER	

85 Astatine 213

Quantity	Energy (ev) Min	Max	Lab	Type	Documentation Ref Vol Page	Author, Comments Date	Data
Fiss Yield	None		TRM	Theo Conf Prog	72Bombay 2 201 BARC-633 64	Feb 72 Ramamurthy.FRAG MASS AS FUNCT T,CURV 72 - . FRAG MASS DISTRIB ,GRPH	

86 Radon 222

Quantity	Energy (ev) Min Max	Lab	Type	Documentation Ref Vol Page	Date	Author, Comments	Data
Diff Inelast	1.4+7	LRL	Theo Rept	UCRL-50181	Feb 67	Lutz+.CALC ANG DIST FOR FIRST 2+ LVL	
(n,γ)	Pile	CRC	Expt Jour	PR 90 1121	Jun 53	Baerg+	+
	Pile		Data	EXFOR12238.002	Jun 76	. 1 PT, SIG	
Fission	–	TPI	Theo Jour	YF 9 102	Jan 69	Korostova+ CV,SHELL CORR,LIQU-DROP-E	
			Jour	SNP 9 62	Jul 69	TRANSLATN.*	

88 Radium

Quantity	Energy (ev) Min	Max	Lab	Type	Documentation Ref Vol Page	Author, Comments Date	Data
Fission	Spont		KTO	Theo Jour	PL/B 47 227	Nov 73 Ohnishi. SPON FISS VS STELLAR TEMP	

88 Radium 223

Quantity	Energy (ev) Min	Max	Lab	Type	Documentation Ref Vol Page	Author, Comments Date	Data
(n,γ)	Pile		BNL	Expt Jour	JIN 1 253	Oct 55 Harbottle. SIG = 125 + − 15B	+
	Pile			Data	EXFOR12258.002	Jun 76 . 1 PT, SIG	
Fission	Pile		ANL	Expt Book	TRANSU.EL.	49 Peterson+	+
	Pile			Data	EXFOR12249.002	Jun 76 . 1 PT, SIG	
Fission	Pile		TRM	Expt Jour	JIN 29 267	Jan 67 Jain+ ESTIMATE BY SR−91 ACT CFD U235	+
	Pile			Data	EXFOR30142.002	Nov 71 ESTIMATE OF SIG FOR PILE+EPICAD NEUT	

88 Radium 224

Quantity	Energy (ev) Min	Max	Lab	Type	Documentation Ref Vol Page	Author, Comments Date	Data
Fission	Spont		CCP	Expt Jour	YF 16 438	Aug 72 Kuks+ SPONT FISS ISOMER FROM N,N'	
				Jour	SNP 16 244	Feb 73 . ENGLISH OF YF 16 438 8/72	
Fission	2.5−2		JUL	Theo Jour	ZP 257 389	Dec 72 Mcminn. 2.01 E−5 B	
Lvl Density	−3	+0	IFU	Theo Jour	UFZ 13 700	Apr 68 Pisanko+ LEVEL SPACING CALC,TBL	
				Jour	UPJ 13 498	Oct 68 TRANSLATN.*	

88 Radium 225

Quantity	Energy (ev) Min	Max	Lab	Type	Documentation Ref Vol Page	Author, Comments Date	Data
Fission	Spont		CCP	Expt Jour	YF 16 438	Aug 72 Kuks+ SPONT FISS ISOMER FROM N,3N	
				Jour	SNP 16 244	Feb 73 . ENGLISH OF YF 16 438 8/72	

88 Radium 226

Quantity	Energy (ev) Min	Max	Lab	Type	Documentation Ref Vol Page	Author, Comments Date	Data
Total	2.2−2	5.0+1	CCP	Expt Jour	AE 1 4 67	Sep 56 Pevzner+.SLOW CHOPPER.RES AT 0.537EV	
				Jour	JNE 4 366	Mar 57 TRANSLATN.*	
				Jour	SJA 1 4 517	56 TRANSLATN.*	
Total	2.0−2	1.0+2	FEI	Expt Priv	KALEBIN	Oct 66 SHORT ABSTRACT NDG (CN−23)	
Total	2.2−2	3.3+2	ITE	ExTh Jour	YF 14 22	Jul 71 Kalebin+ SAME AS ITE−801	+
	2.2−2	3.0+2		Expt Rept	ITE−801	70 − + CHOPPER.7 RES,GRPH.	
	2.2−2	3.3+2		ExTh Jour	SNP 14 13	Jan 72 . ENGLISH OF YF 14 22	
	2.2−2	3.3+2		Expt Data	EXFOR40170.013	Dec 73 .203 DATA LINES	
Total	1.0−2	1.0+0	MOL	Expt Conf	72Budapest 100	Aug 72 Ceulemans+ RES AT 0.54EV FOUND,GRAPH	
	1.5−1	1.7+0			EANDC(E)150U	May 72 − +,BR2 R3 CRYST SPECT	
Total	5.4−1	8.0+2	CCP	Expt Conf	75Kiev	May 75 Kalebin+ TOT SIG	
Total	2.0+1	2.0+3	NIR	Expt Conf	75Kiev 3 205	May 75 Belanova+ TOTSIG(E),GRAPH.RESPARS	
Total		2.5+3	GEL	Expt Prog	BLG−515	76 Ceulemans. TRANSM. ABST.NDG.	
Total	1.0+1	6.0+2	MOL	Expt Prog	NEANDC(E)172 3	Feb 76 Ceulemans+ LINAC.TOF.GEEL	
Elastic	+1	+6	GEL	Expt Prog	INDC(SEC)−26	May 72 Theobald+ NUC EXPLOSION,EXPT PROPOSD	
Diff Elastic	1.0+6		LAS	Eval Rept	LA−2016	Jun 56 Longley.,TBL ANG DIST 3−DEG STEPS	
Potntal Scat	2.5−2		ITE	ExTh Jour	YF 14 22	Jul 71 Kalebin+ SAME AS ITE−801	
				Expt Rept	ITE−801	70 − + CALC FROM RES PARS.	
				ExTh Jour	SNP 14 13	Jan 72 . ENGLISH OF YF 14 22	
Potntal Scat	1.5+1		ITE	Expt Data	EXFOR40170.002	Dec 73 .1 DATA LINE,SIGMA GIVEN	+
Diff Inelast	1.4+7		LRL	Theo Rept	UCRL−50181	Feb 67 Lutz+.CALC ANG DIST FOR FIRST 2+ LVL	
Nonelastic	1.5+7		CCP	Expt Jour	YF 16 438	Aug 72 Kuks+ NO SPONT−FISS RA−ISOMERS FOUND	
				Jour	SNP 16 244	Feb 73 .ENGLISH TRANSL OF YF 16 438	
Absorption	Maxwl		CCP	Expt Jour	AE 1 4 67	Sep 56 Pevzner+. 13.5 +− 1.5B FROM 0.54EV RES	
				Jour	JNE 4 366	Mar 57 TRANSLATN.*	
				Jour	SJA 1 4 517	56 TRANSLATN.*	
Res Int Abs	5.0−1	3.0+2	ITE	ExTh Jour	YF 14 22	Jul 71 Kalebin+ SAME AS ITE−801	+
				Expt Rept	ITE−801	70 − + CALC FROM RES PARS.	
				ExTh Jour	SNP 14 13	Jan 72 . ENGLISH OF YF 14 22	
	5.4−1	2.9+2		Expt Data	EXFOR40170.	Dec 73 .7 DATA LINES,PARTIAL AND TOTAL	
(n,γ)	Pile		ANL	Expt Book	TRANSU.EL.	49 Peterson+ PAPER 19.9	+
	Pile			Data	EXFOR12282.002	Jun 76 . 1 PT, SIG	

88 Radium 226

Quantity	Energy (ev) Min	Max	Lab	Type	Documentation Ref Vol Page	Author, Comments Date	Data
(n,γ)	Pile		ANL	Expt	Jour ACS 72 768	50 Hagemann.	+
	Pile				Data EXFOR11727.002	Jun 76 . 1 PT, SIG	
(n,γ)	Pile		CRC	Expt	Jour PR 91 1219	Sep 53 Butler+ NRX 23B	+
					Jour NAT 170 832	Nov 52 − + SUPERSEDED	
	Pile				Data EXFOR12262.002	Jun 76 . 1 PT, SIG	
(n,γ)	2.5−2		ITE	ExTh	Jour YF 14 22	Jul 71 Kalebin+ SAME AS ITE−801	
				Expt	Rept ITE−801	70 − + CALC FROM RES PARS.	
				ExTh	Jour SNP 14 13	Jan 72 . ENGLISH OF YF 14 22	
(n,γ)	+1	+6	GEL	Expt	Prog INDC(SEC)−26	May 72 Theobald+ NUC EXPLOSION,EXPT PROPOSD	
(n,γ)	+1	+6	MOL	Expt	Prog INDC(SEC)−26	May 72 Ceulemans.M− R DET, BOMB SHOT,PROPOSD	
(n,γ)	2.5−2		ITE	Expt	Data EXFOR40170.003	Dec 73 .SIGMA(N,G) AND SIG(TOT−POTENT) GVN	+
(n,γ)	None		MUN	Theo	Diss GRYNTAKIS	Mar 76 Gryntakis.,CALC.OF WESTCOTTS G−FUNCT	
					Jour RCA 22 128	Mar 75 − +,EQUIVALENT TO THESIS	
(n,2n)	1.4+7		ALD	Expt	Jour JIN 13 5	Apr 60 Oconnor+SIG=1.6+ −0.2B	+
(n,2n)	1.3+7	1.5+7	BNL	Theo	Jour NSE 23 238	Nov 65 Pearlstein.3ES.STAT MDL CALC.TBL CS.	
(n,2n)	Fiss		BNL	Theo	Jour NSE 23 238	Nov 65 Pearlstein.STATMDL CALC.SPEC AVG.TBL	
(n,2n)	1.5+7		DEB	Eval	Jour REA 11 1 153	Mar 73 Boedy. COMPILATION+RECOMM.VALUE,TBL	
					Rept IAEA−153 173	73 − . RECOMM. VALUE ONLY	
(n,xn) x>2	1.4+7		ALD	Expt	Jour JIN 13 5	Apr 60 Oconnor+ N3N SIG=0.63+ −0.07B	+
(n,xn) x>2	Fiss		BNL	Theo	Jour NSE 23 238	Nov 65 Pearlstein.SPEC AVG STATMDL CALC N3N	
(n,p)	1.4+7		SAH	Comp	Jour NP 60 273	Nov 64 Chatterjee.MEAN OF EXPT CFD SHELLMOD	
Fission	Pile		ANL	Expt	Book TRANSU.EL.	49 Ames+	+
	Pile				Data EXFOR12248.002	Jun 76 . 1 PT, SIG	
Fission	2.0+6	2.3+7	LAS	Expt	Jour NP 5 211	Jan 58 Nobles+.9 ES. GRPH. .5MB TO 37MB	+
					Conf 58Geneva 15 344	Sep 58 Hemmendinger.SUPERSEDED	
	2.1+6	2.3+7			Data EXFOR12264.002	Jun 76 . 10 PTS, SIG	
Fission	Spont		DUB	Theo	Rept JINR−P−2265	Jul 65 Mekhedov. FISS+ALPH HLS ESTIMATED	
Fission	3.0+6	1.5+7	RI	Expt	Prog YFI−5 50	Oct 67 Babenko+ TABLE SIGMA AT 18 ENERGIES	+
					Rept INDC−232E	Jan 69 . ENGL OF YFI−5 50	
					Jour SNP 7 2 186	Aug 68 . ENGL OF YF 7 269	
	3.0+6	1.5+7			Data EXFOR40069.002	Jun 71 SIGMA AT 18 ENERGIES	
Fission	3.0+6	1.5+7	RI	Expt	Jour YF 7 269	Feb 68 Babenko+ GRPH SIG(NEUT−E),ANG−ANISOT	
Fission	3.6+6	9.5+6	CCP	Expt	Jour YF 10 233	Aug 69 Babenko+ SIG(E) CRV,OLD DATA INCLUDD	
Fission	3.6+6	9.5+6	RI	Expt	Jour YF 10 233	Aug 69 Babenko+ SIG(E) CURV,OLD DATA INCLUD	+
					Jour SNP 10 133	Feb 70 . ENGL OF YF 10 233	
	3.6+6	9.5+6			Data EXFOR40395.002	Nov 76 SIG AT 18 EN GIVEN	
Fission	1.2+7	2.0+7	RI	Expt	Jour YF 11 1006	May 70 Babenko+ SIG(NEUT−E),GRAPH	
					Jour SNP 11 560	Nov 70 . ENGL OF YF 11 1006	
Fission	+1	+6	GEL	Expt	Prog INDC(SEC)−26	May 72 Theobald+ NUC EXPLOSION,EXPT PROPOSD	
Fission	2.5−2		JUL	Theo	Jour ZP 257 389	Dec 72 Mcminn. 2.43 E−6 B	
Fission	None		FRK	Theo	Jour NP/A 207 225	Jun 73 Albrecht. 2CENTRE SHELLMOD,DEF−E MAP	
Fission	5.8+6	9.5+6	RI	Expt	Prog YFI−16 11	Jun 73 Zhagrov+ TABLE SIG AT 7 ES TBP IN NP	
Fission	5.0+6	1.5+7	RI	Expt	Jour 73 Kiev 2 213 436	Oct 73 Zhagrov+REL U238 NEW MEAS+SYM,ASSYM.	
Fission	3.6+6	9.0+6	ORU	Theo	Jour PR/C 10 697	Aug 74 Groening+ H−F FIT,GRPH.LVLS DEDUCED	
	3.6+6	9.7+6			Conf 73Rochestr 1 39	Aug 73 − + H−F,FIT TO EXPTL DATA,GRPH	
Fission	Maxwl		RI	Expt	Conf 75Kiev 5 216	May 75 Selickij. THERMAL SIG=5 MILLIBARN	
Fission	Maxwl		KTO	Expt	Jour JIN 38 203	Feb 76 Nakahara+ SURFAC−BARR−DET,SIG=7MICRO	+
					Jour JIN 36 487	Mar 74 − + TRACK DET,SIG=460MICROBARN	
	Pile				Data EXFOR20525.002	Apr 76 1PNT.SIGMA.	
Fiss Yield	None		KFK	Theo	Conf 69Vienna 25	Jul 69 Dickmann+PPR45. MASS−RATIO VAL GVN	
Fiss Yield	Maxwl		KTO	Expt	Jour JIN 36 487	Mar 74 Nakahara+	
Fiss Yield	4.0+6	1.5+7	RI	Eval	Conf 75Kiev 5 216	May 75 Selickij. REL SYM YLD VS EXC−E.GRAPH	
Frag Spectra	3.3+6	2.2+7	LAS	Expt	Jour NP 5 211	Jan 58 Nobles+.7 ES. FRAG KIN EN GRPH.XE−SC	
	3.3+6	1.5+7			Conf 58Geneva 15 344	Sep 58 Hemmendinger.SUPERSEDED	
Frag Spectra	6.0+6	1.4+7	LAS	Expt	Prog WASH−1003 34	Nov 58 Blumberg+ WORK PLANNED	
Frag Spectra	6.7+6	1.5+7	RI	Expt	Prog YFI−5 50	Oct 67 Babenko+ TBL ANGDIST OF FPROD AT 7ES	+
					Jour YF 7 269	Feb 68 − + GRPH ANG−ANISOTR FISS−PROD	
					Rept INDC−232E	Jan 69 . ENGL OF YFI−5 50	
					Jour SNP 7 2 186	Aug 68 . ENGL OF YF 7 269	
	6.7+6	1.5+7			Data EXFOR40069.003	Jun 71 ANG DISTRIB OF FRAGMENTS AT 7 EN	
Frag Spectra	1.4+7	1.6+7	CCP	Expt	Conf 69Vienna 960	Jul 69 Babenko+PPR148.ANOMALUS FRAG ANGDIST	
Frag Spectra	3.6+6	9.5+6	CCP	Expt	Jour YF 10 233	Aug 69 Babenko+ ANGDIS(E)CRVS,THIS+OLD XPT	
Frag Spectra	3.6+6	9.5+6	RI	Expt	Jour YF 10 233	Aug 69 Babenko+ ANGDIS(E)CURVS,THIS+OLD XPT	+
	4.0+6	9.0+6			Conf 69Vienna 961	Jul 69 − + PPR149.FRAG ANGDIS(NEUT−E)	
	3.6+6	9.5+6			Jour SNP 10 133	Feb 70 . ENGL OF YF 10 233	
	3.6+6	7.1+6			Data EXFOR40395.	Nov 76 ANGDIST OF FISS−FRAGMENTS	
Frag Spectra	1.2+7	2.0+7	CCP	Expt	Jour YF 11 1006	May 70 Babenko+ FRAG−ANGDIST AT 8 ES,GRAPHS	
					−	= ENGLISH $SNP 11 560 N/70$	

88 Radium 226

Quantity	Energy (ev) Min	Max	Lab	Type	Documentation Ref Vol Page	Author, Comments Date	Data
Frag Spectra	1.2+7	2.0+7	RI	Expt	Jour YF 11 1006	May 70 Babenko+ FRAG ANGDIST AT 8 ES,GRAPHS	
					Jour SNP 11 560	Nov 70 . ENGL OF YF 11 1006	
Frag Spectra	4.0+6	1.0+7	RI	Expt	Jour YF 14 939	Nov 71 Ippolitov+ ANGDIST GRAPH,LEG COEFS	
					Jour SNP 14 526	May 72 * ENGL OF YF 14 939	
					Jour SNP 10 133	Feb 70 *ENGL OF YF 10 233	
					Jour YF 10 233	Aug 69 *+OTHER REF,EARLIER EXPT	
Frag Spectra	1.1+7	1.4+7	CCP	Expt	Conf 73Kiev 3 267	May 73 Kuks+ NO ANISOTR-ASYMM CORREL FOUND	
Frag Spectra	5.0+6	1.5+7	RI	Expt	Jour NP/A 213 436	Oct 73 Zhagrov+ FRAGM KIN-E DISTR,SI-DET	
					Prog YFI-16 11	Jun 73 - + FRAG KIN EN DISTR TBP IN NP	
					Conf 73Kiev 3 256	May 73 - + FRAG KE-SPEC,GRAPH	
Frag Spectra	7.9+6	9.7+6	RI	Expt	Data EXFOR40195.	Nov 73 .7 ANG DIST AT 3ES	
	8.0+6	9.8+6			Prog YFI-12 97	72 Ippolitov+ ABST,ANG-ANISOTR,TBL,GRPH	
					Prog INDC(CCP)-30	Sep 72 .PAGE 84,ENGLISH OF YFI-12 97	
Frag Spectra	3.6+6	9.7+6	ORU	Theo	Jour PR/C 10 697	Aug 74 Groening+ H-F,FIT TO ANGDIST,GRAPHS	
					Conf 73Rochestr 1 39	Aug 73 - + H-F,FIT TO EXPTL DATA,GRPH	
Frag Spectra	7.1+6	1.4+7	FEI	Expt	Rept YK-19 16	75 Vorob'Eva+ E-KIN OF FRAGMENTS,TBL	
Frag Spectra	8.0+6		RI	Expt	Jour YF 24 17	Jul 76 D'Jachenko+ EKIN DIST AT 0,90DEG.FIG	
					Jour SNP 24 8	Jul 76 . ENGL OF YF 24,17.	
Reson Params	5.4-1		CCP	Expt	Jour AE 1 4 67	Sep 56 Pevzner+.WT29MV,WN.021MV,SIGPOT6.5B	+
					Conf 58Geneva § 2221	Sep 58 .SEE ALSO. WN IN ERROR	
					Jour JNE 4 366	Mar 57 TRANSLATN.*	
					Jour SJA 1 4 517	56 TRANSLATN.*	
Reson Params	2.0-2	1.0+2	FEI	Expt	Priv KALEBIN	Oct 66 SHORT ABSTRACT NDG (CN-23)	
Reson Params	5.4-1	2.9+2	ITE	ExTh	Jour YF 14 22	Jul 71 Kalebin+ SAME AS ITE-801	+
				Expt	Rept ITE-801	70 - + AVG D,G-WID.REDUC N-WID.TBL	
				ExTh	Jour SNP 14 13	Jan 72 . ENGLISH OF YF 14 22	
	5.4-1	2.9+2		Expt	Data EXFOR40170.	Dec 73 .GAMMA,NEUTRON-WIDTH,6 SUBENTRIES	
Reson Params	5.4-1	8.0+2	CCP	Expt	Conf 75Kiev	May 75 Kalebin+ RESONANCE NEUT-S,STF,LVLWID	
Reson Params	5.4-1	6.8+2	NIR	Expt	Conf 75Kiev 3 205	May 75 Belanova+ BY TOTSIG.G,N-WIDS,TABLE	
Reson Params	5.3-1	5.2+2	MOL	Expt	Rept NEANDC(E)172	Feb 76 Ceulemans.TBL ES AND N-WIDS.	+
	2.4+1	5.2+2			Prog INDC(SEC)-51	Dec 75 - .P63. ES+N-WIDS(19RES),TABL	
	4.0+1	6.8+2			Prog INDC(SEC)-43	Dec 74 - +RES,ES,N-WID GIVEN	
	5.4-1				Conf 72Budapest 100	Aug 72 - + EN RES, TOT WIDTH	
	5.3-1	5.2+2			Data EXFOR20712.	Sep 77 41PTS.WN,WN0,MEAN LVLSP.	
Strnth Fnctn	None		AI	Theo	Rept NAA-SR-M-12538	Oct 67 Gigas.OPTMDL CALC AVG SO,S1,S2	
Strnth Fnctn	5.4-1	2.9+2	ITE	ExTh	Jour YF 14 22	Jul 71 Kalebin+ SAME AS ITE-801	+
				Expt	Rept ITE-801	70 - + P-WAVE,VALUE GVN.	
				ExTh	Jour SNP 14 13	Jan 72 . ENGLISH OF YF 14 22	
	5.4-1	2.9+2		Expt	Data EXFOR40170.012	Dec 73 .1 DATA LINE	
Strnth Fnctn	None		AUA	Eval	Rept AAEC/E-277	Mar 73 Musgrove.TBLS EXPTL DATA+BEST VALUES	
Lvl Density	None		FEI	Theo	Jour YF 11 1213	Jun 70 Ignatjuk+ SPIN DEPENDENCE OF DENSITY	
					Jour SNP 11 674	Dec 70 .ENGL TRANSL OF YF 11 1213	
Lvl Density	3.6+6	7.0+6	ORU	Theo	Jour PR/C 10 697	Aug 74 Groening+ SINGL-PART MDL CFD XPT,GRF	
	3.6+6	9.7+6			Conf 73Rochestr 1 39	Aug 73 - + H-F,LVL DENSITY PAR,GRAPH	
Photo-Fissn	8.3+6	2.6+7	RI	Expt	Prog YFI-5 52	Oct 67 Zhagrov+ ANISOTROPY OF FISPROD, TBL	
	8.3+6	2.5+7			Jour YF 7 264	Feb 68 - + GRPH YLD(G-E)REL U238,THRSH	
	8.3+6	2.6+7			Rept INDC-232E	Jan 69 . ENGL OF YFI-5 52	
	8.3+6	2.5+7			Jour SNP 7 183	Aug 68 . ENGL OF YF 7 264	
Photo-Fissn	1.0+7		FR	Expt	Conf 69Vienna 915	Jul 69 Tamain+PPR84. FRAGMENT ANGDISTRIBUTN	
Photo-Fissn	9.0+6	2.0+7	LEB	Expt	Conf 71Moscow	Feb 71 Zhagrov+.ABST,SIG(GAM-E),TBL GVN	
Photo-Fissn	9.0+6	2.0+7	LEB	Expt	Jour YF 13 934	May 71 Zmagrov+ GRPH SIG(G-E),N-WID/F-WID	
					Jour SNP 13 537	Nov 71 . ENGL OF YF 13 934	
Photo-Fissn	1.0+7	2.8+7	RI	Eval	Conf 75Kiev 5 216	May 75 Selickij. REL SYM YLD,ANISOTR.GRAPHS	
Photo-Fissn	1.1+7	2.8+7	RI	Expt	Jour YF 22 36	Jul 75 Bazhanov+ SYM,ASYM YLD,FRAG-SPEC.FIG	
	1.1+7	1.5+7			Jour ZEP 20 220	Aug 74 Zhagrov+ ANG ANISOTROPY OF YLD ,GRPH	
	1.5+7	2.8+7			Conf 73Kiev 3 264	May 73 - + SYMM YIELD(G-E,ANG).GRAPH	
	1.1+7	2.8+7			Jour SNP 22 17	Jul 75 . ENGL OF YF 22 36	

88 Radium 228

Quantity	Energy (ev) Min	Max	Lab	Type	Documentation Ref Vol Page	Author, Comments Date	Data
(n,γ)	Pile		CRC	Expt	Jour PR 85 499	Feb 52 Depocas+ NRX UNDER CADMIUM	+
	Pile				Data EXFOR12308.002	Jun 76 . 1 PT, SIG	
Fission	Pile		ANL	Expt	Book TRANSU.EL.	49 Peterson+P19.4,CS LT 2.B,NO CNTS DET	+
	Pile				Data EXFOR12249.004	Jun 76 . 1 PT, SIG	
Fission	2.5-2		JUL	Theo	Jour ZP 257 389	Dec 72 Mcminn. 1.82 E-6 B	
Fiss Yield	None		BAS	Theo	Jour PL/B 34 264	Mar 71 Pauli+ FRAG MASS RATIO AS STRUTINSKY	

89 Actinium 223

Quantity	Energy (ev) Min	Max	Lab	Type	Documentation Ref Vol Page	Date	Author, Comments	Data
Fission	2.5 – 2		JUL	Theo Jour	ZP 257 389	Dec 72	Mcminn. 3.31 E – 3 B	

89 Actinium 225

Quantity	Energy (ev) Min	Max	Lab	Type	Documentation Ref Vol Page	Date	Author, Comments	Data
(n,p)	Maxwl		IFU	Theo Rept	ICD – 4 20	67	Dadakina+ PENETR COEFF CALC,TABLE	
Fission	2.5 – 2		JUL	Theo Jour	ZP 257 389	Dec 72	Mcminn. 3.27 E – 4 B	

89 Actinium 226

Quantity	Energy (ev) Min	Max	Lab	Type	Documentation Ref Vol Page	Date	Author, Comments	Data
(n,p)	Maxwl		IFU	Theo Rept	ICD – 4 20	67	Dadakina+ PENETR COEFF CALC,TABLE	

89 Actinium 227

Quantity	Energy (ev) Min	Max	Lab	Type	Documentation Ref Vol Page	Date	Author, Comments	Data
Total	+1	+6	MOL	Expt Prog	INDC(SEC) – 26	May 72	Ceulemans.TRANS AT BOMB SHOT,PROPOSD	
Elastic	+1	+6	GEL	Expt Prog	INDC(SEC) – 26	May 72	Theobald+ NUC EXPLOSION,EXPT PROPOSD	
Res Int Abs	5.0 – 1		MOL	Expt Jour	JIN 37 1841	Sep 75	Monsecour+ CAPT,GELI.TBL CD – RATIO,RI	+
	5.0 – 1			Data	EXFOR20636.003	Aug 76	1PNT.CAPTURE.	
(n,γ)	Maxwl		ORL	Expt Prog	ORNL – 1415 15	Feb 53	Pomerance.SIG = 500 + – 35 B.PILE OSC	+
	Maxwl			Data	EXFOR12307.002	Jun 76	. 1 PT, SIG	
(n,γ)	Maxwl		ANL	Expt Rept	ANL – 5263	May 54	Sjoblom+ PILE ACT,FROM TH228/TH227	+
	Maxwl			Data	EXFOR12250.002	Jun 76	. 1 PT, SIG	
(n,γ)	Pile		MND	Expt Jour	PR 102 1140	May 56	Kirby+ PILE OSC. 495 + – 35B HL = 22 YRS	+
	Pile			Data	EXFOR12275.	Jun 76	. 2 PTS, SIG TO GND + META	
(n,γ)	Pile		CRC	Expt Jour	CJC 37 1094	Jun 59	Cabell+ ACT 814 + – 13B REL CO 36.5B	+
	Pile			Data	EXFOR12254.003	Jun 76	. 1 PT, SIG	
(n,γ)	+1	+6	GEL	Expt Prog	INDC(SEC) – 26	May 72	Theobald+ NUC EXPLOSION,EXPT PROPOSD	
(n,γ)	+1	+6	MOL	Expt Prog	INDC(SEC) – 26	May 72	Ceulemans.M – R DET, BOMB SHOT,PROPOSD	
(n,γ)	2.5 – 2		IJI	Eval Conf	73Kiev 1 197	May 73	Fedorova. SIG 2200M/S = 830 + – 20 B	
(n,γ)	Maxwl		MOL	Expt Jour	JIN 37 1841	Sep 75	Monsecour+ GELI,REL CO59,TBL RESULTS	+
	2.5 – 2			Data	EXFOR20636.002	Aug 76	1PNT.SIGMA.	
Res Int Capt	5.0 – 1		CRC	Expt Jour	CJC 37 1094	Jun 59	Cabell+ ACT,1177 + – 19B REL CO 48.6B	+
	5.0 – 1			Data	EXFOR12254.002	Jun 76	. 1 PT, RI	
Fission	Pile		ANL	Expt Book	TRANSU.EL.	49	Peterson+P19.4,CS LT 2.B,NO CNTS DET	+
	Pile			Data	EXFOR12249.003	Jun 76	. 1 PT, SIG	
Fission	+6		FOA	Expt Prog	EANDC(OR)99 32	Aug 70	Holmberg+. IN PROGRESS.THRSHLD STUDY	
Fission	+1	+6	GEL	Expt Prog	INDC(SEC) – 26	May 72	Theobald+ NUC EXPLOSION,EXPT PROPOSD	
Fission	Spont		CCP	Expt Jour	YF 16 438	Aug 72	Kuks+ SPONT FISS ISOMER FROM D,2N	
				Jour	SNP 16 244	Feb 73	. ENGLISH OF YF 16 438 8/72	
Fission	2.5 – 2		JUL	Theo Jour	ZP 257 389	Dec 72	Mcminn. 3.39 E – 5 B	
Fission	Maxwl		MOL	Expt Jour	JIN 35 4323	Dec 73	Del Marmol+ TRACK DETECTOR	+
	Maxwl			Data	EXFOR20351.002	Sep 74	1PNT.SIGMA.	
Nu	Thrsh	Up	SAH	Theo Conf	70Madurai 2 619	Dec 70	Sarkar+ CALC NU VS A OF FRAGS.GRAPH	
Fiss Yield	Fiss		TRM	Expt Conf	65Salzburg 439	Mar 65	Iyer.YLD OF VARIOUS ISOTOPS,TBL,GRPH	
Fiss Yield	–		CCP	Theo Jour	YF 7 832	Apr 68	Shigin.YLD(FRAG – A,EXCIT – E),LVL DEN	
				Jour	SNP 7 4 506	Oct 68	TRANSLATN.*	
Fiss Yield	–		TRM	Theo Conf	69Vienna 41	Jul 69	Ramamurthy+PPR15. CALCTD GRPH YLD(A)	
Fiss Yield	Pile		HAR	Eval Conf	73Paris 1 393	Mar 73	Crouch.EXPTL DATA+EVAL CHAIN YLD,TBL	
	Maxwl			Rept	AERE – R – 7209	Jan 73	– .12 CHAIN YLDS RECOMMENDED TBL	
Fiss Yield	Maxwl		AUA	Theo Rept	AAEC/E – 386	Mar 76	Cook+ 3 – GAUSS FIT,PARAMS GIVEN	
Frag Spectra	+6		FOA	Expt Prog	EANDC(OR)99 32	Aug 70	Holmberg+.A – DIST.IN PROGR.THRSH STUD	
Lvl Density	–		CCP	Theo Jour	YF 7 832	Apr 68	Shigin.GRPH LVL DEN(FISS – FRAG – A),YLD	
				Jour	SNP 7 4 506	Oct 68	TRANSLATN.*	
Lvl Density	None		FEI	Theo Jour	YF 11 1213	Jun 70	Ignatyuk+ SPIN DEPENDENCE OF DENSITY	
				Jour	SNP 11 674	Dec 70	. ENGL OF YF 11 1213	

89 Actinium 229

Quantity	Energy (ev) Min	Max	Lab	Type	Documentation Ref Vol Page	Date	Author, Comments	Data
Fission	2.5 – 2		JUL	Theo Jour	ZP 257 389	Dec 72	Mcminn. 1.55 E – 5 B	

89 Actinium 231

Quantity	Energy (ev) Min Max	Lab	Type	Documentation Ref Vol Page	Date	Author, Comments	Data
Fission	2.5 – 2	JUL	Theo Jour	ZP 257 389	Dec 72	Mcminn.	2.31 E – 6 B

90 Thorium 224

Quantity	Energy (ev) Min	Max	Lab	Type	Documentation Ref Vol Page	Date	Author, Comments	Data
Fission	2.5−2		JUL	Theo Jour	ZP 257 389	Dec 72	Mcminn. 2.19 E−1 B	

90 Thorium 226

Quantity	Energy (ev) Min	Max	Lab	Type	Documentation Ref Vol Page	Date	Author, Comments	Data
Fission	Spont		CCP	Comp Jour	AE 26 436	May 69	Romanov. HALF−LIFE VAL ESTIMATD,GRPH	
				Jour	EAF 26 48	69	. FRENCH OF AE 26 436.	
				Jour	SJA 26 498	69	. ENGL OF AE 26 436.	
Fission	2.5−2		JUL	Theo Jour	ZP 257 389	Dec 72	Mcminn. 1.01 E−2 B	
Strnth Fnctn	None		AI	Theo Rept	NAA−SR−M−12538	Oct 67	Gigas.OPTMDL CALC AVG S0,S1,S2	

90 Thorium 227

Quantity	Energy (ev) Min	Max	Lab	Type	Documentation Ref Vol Page	Date	Author, Comments	Data
(n,p)	Maxwl		IFU	Theo Rept	ICD−4 20	67	Dadakina+ PENETR COEFF CALC,TABLE	
Fission	Maxwl		TRM	Revw Conf	66Bombay 1	Feb 66	Ramanna.VALS CFD TH,SIG,BINDING,DEF.	
Fission	Maxwl		WUR	Expt Jour	JIN 32 3441	Dec 70	Von Gunten+ REL TO U−235 + ABSOLUTE	+
				Rept	EIR−190	Dec 70	− + FISS COUNTERS	
				Conf	69Vienna 731	Jul 69	Flynn+PPR1. PREL NEW SIG VAL GVN	
	Maxwl			Data	EXFOR20438.002	Nov 75	1PNT.SIGMA.	
Fission	Maxwl		MOL	Expt Jour	JIN 35 4323	Dec 73	Del Marmol+ TRACK DETECTOR	+
	Maxwl			Data	EXFOR20351.003	Sep 74	1PNT.SIGMA.	
Nu	Maxwl		WUR	Expt Conf	69Vienna 731	Jul 69	Flynn+PPR1. VAL ESTIMATED IN YLD XPT	+
Fiss Yield	Maxwl		WUR	Expt Conf	69Vienna 731	Jul 69	Flynn+PPR1. YLD(FRAG−A,Z) GRPH + TBL	+
				Rept	EIR−157	Jun 69	− + MASS AND CHARGE DISTR.	
Fiss Yield	Maxwl		HAR	Eval Conf	73Paris 1 393	Mar 73	Crouch.EXPTL DATA+EVAL CHAIN YLD,TBL	
				Rept	AERE−R−7209	Jan 73	− .27 CHAIN YLDS RECOMMENDED TBL	
Fiss Yield	Maxwl		AUA	Theo Rept	AAEC/E−386	Mar 76	Cook+ 3−GAUSS FIT,PARAMS GIVEN	
Frag Charge	Maxwl		WUR	Expt Conf	69Vienna 731	Jul 69	Flynn+PPR1. YLD OF 30ISOTOPES,TABLE	
				Rept	EIR−157	Jun 69	− + MASS AND CHARGE YIELDS.	
Frag Charge	Maxwl		LRL	Comp Rept	UCRL−51640	Jul 74	Nethaway. TBL.	

90 Thorium 228

Quantity	Energy (ev) Min	Max	Lab	Type	Documentation Ref Vol Page	Date	Author, Comments	Data
Total	1.8+0	8.0+0	MTR	Expt Jour	NSE 29 423	Sep 67	Simpson+ FC CURVS NEAR TWO RES ES	+
				Rept	IN−1040	Dec 66	.SUPERSEDED	
	1.8+0	8.0+0		Data	EXFOR12268.	Jun 76	. 50 PTS.	
Elastic	+1	+6	GEL	Expt Prog	INDC(SEC)−26	May 72	Theobald+ NUC EXPLOSION,EXPT PROPOSD	
Absorption	2.5−2		IJI	Eval Conf	73Kiev 1 197	May 73	Fedorova. SIG 2200M/S=120+−15 B	
(n,γ)	+1	+6	GEL	Expt Prog	INDC(SEC)−26	May 72	Theobald+ NUC EXPLOSION,EXPT PROPOSD	
Fission	Spont		DUB	Theo Rept	JINR−P−2265	Jul 65	Mekhedov. FISS+ALPH HLS ESTIMATED	
Fission	Spont		CCP	Comp Jour	AE 26 436	May 69	Romanov. HALF−LIFE VAL ESTIMATD,GRPH	
				Jour	EAF 26 48	69	. FRENCH OF AE 26 436.	
				Jour	SJA 26 498	69	. ENGL OF AE 26 436.	
Fission	1.9+5	5.0+6	KUR	Expt Prog	YFI−14 6	72	Vorotnikov+ SIGMA(E),TBL	+
	1.9+5	1.0+6		Data	EXFOR40155.002	May 73	SIGMA AT 9 ENERGIES	
Fission	+1	+6	GEL	Expt Prog	INDC(SEC)−26	May 72	Theobald+ NUC EXPLOSION,EXPT PROPOSD	
Fission	1.6+5	5.0+6	KUR	Expt Jour	YF 16 916	Nov 72	Vorotnikov+ ACCEL,GLASS DET,GRAPH	
				Jour	SNP 16 505	May 73	.ENGLISH OF YF 16 916	
Fission	2.5−2		JUL	Theo Jour	ZP 257 389	Dec 72	Mcminn. 2.23 E−3 B	
Fission	2.5−2		IJI	Eval Conf	73Kiev 1 197	May 73	Fedorova. SIG 2200M/S=0.3 B	
Reson Params	1.9+0	7.6+0	MTR	Expt Jour	NSE 29 423	Sep 67	Simpson+ FC WN WG 2ES FROM TOTAL SIG	+
				Rept	IN−1040	Dec 66	.SUPERSEDED	
	1.9+0	7.6+0		Data	EXFOR12268.002	Jun 76	. 2 RES E0, WN0, WG	
Reson Params	1.9+0	7.6+0	CCP	Theo Rept	YK−16 121	74	Gorbachev+ G+N−WIDTHS,TABLE	
Strnth Fnctn	None		AI	Theo Rept	NAA−SR−M−12538	Oct 67	Gigas.OPTMDL CALC AVG S0,S1,S2	
Lvl Density	−3	+0	IFU	Theo Jour	UFZ 13 700	Apr 68	Pisanko+ LEVEL SPACING CALC,TBL	
				Jour	UPJ 13 498	Oct 68	TRANSLATN.*	

90 Thorium 229

Quantity	Energy (ev) Min	Max	Lab	Type	Documentation Ref Vol Page	Author, Comments Date	Data
Total	3.9−1	3.1+1	ANL Expt	Abst	BAP 6 417	Nov 61 Cote+ 14RESON SEEN 0.6−15.2EV	+
	3.9−1	3.1+1		Data	EXFOR12298.006	Jun 76 . 231 PTS.	
Elastic	+1	+6	GEL Expt	Prog	INDC(SEC)−26	May 72 Theobald+ NUC EXPLOSION,EXPT PROPOSD	
(n,γ)	+1	+6	GEL Expt	Prog	INDC(SEC)−26	May 72 Theobald+ NUC EXPLOSION,EXPT PROPOSD	
(n,γ)	None		MUN Theo	Diss	GRYNTAKIS	Mar 76 Gryntakis.,CALC.OF WESTCOTTS G−FUNCT	
				Jour	RCA 22 128	Mar 75 − +,EQUIVALENT TO THESIS	
Fission	Pile		ANL Expt	Rept	CF− 3809	47 Studier+	+
	Pile			Data	EXFOR12296.002	Jun 76 . 1 PT.	
Fission	6.0+3	1.2+6	KUR Expt	Conf	59Tashkent 1 57	Sep 59 Gokhberg.VDG,RSLN 2−20KEV, GRAPH	
				Rept	AEC−TR−6398	64 .VOL 1,P59 .ENGL OF 59TASHKE 1 57	
Fission	1.6−2	8.0−1	KUR Expt	Jour	AE 8 47	Jan 60 Konakhovich+ CRYST SP,GRAPH,3 RES	+
				Jour	SJA 8 39	Apr 61 TRANSLATN.*	
Fission	Maxwl		ANL Expt	Jour	JIN 15 1	Sep 60 Gindler+30.5+−3B REL SIG U233,PU239	+
	Maxwl			Data	EXFOR12259.003	Jun 76 . 2 PTS, SIG REL U233, PU239	
Fission	4.0+0	1.0+2	HAR Expt	Jour	NIM 28 205	Jun 64 Firk.EXPT BY BOLLINGER MENTIOND(HAR)	
Fission	Maxwl		TRM Revw	Conf	66Bombay 1	Feb 66 Ramanna.VALS CFD TH,SIG,BINDING,DEF.	
Fission	−		BER Theo		69Vienna 197	Jul 69 Krappe+PPR96. 1+2 FISSN BARRIER TBL	
Fission	3.6−2	+1	COL Expt	Prog	NCSAC−38 66	May 71 Flevinci+ TOF, SIG CURV 1−5.8EV	
	6.1−1	5.8+0		Prog	NYO−73−340 40	Dec 70 Felvinci+.NEVIS.CURVE.TBL 5RES SIGS.	
Fission	+1	+6	GEL Expt	Prog	INDC(SEC)−26	May 72 Theobald+ NUC EXPLOSION,EXPT PROPOSD	
Fission	2.5−2		IJI Eval	Conf	73Kiev 1 197	May 73 Fedorova. SIG 2200M/S=32+−2 B	
Fission	None		COL Expt	Rept	ERDA−NDC−3 63	May 76 Luers+ NEW MEAS FOR BETTER STATS.TBC	
Res Int Fiss	−		KUR Expt	Jour	AE 8 47	Jan 60 Konakhovich+ CD RATIO, 240B REL THR	
				Jour	SJA 8 39	Apr 61 TRANSLATN.*	
Nu	Maxwl		CCP Expt	Jour	ZET 35 535	Aug 58 REL TO U235,2.13+−.03	+
				Jour	JET 8 370	Feb 59 . ENGL OF ZET 35 535	
Nu	Pile		CCP Expt	Jour	YF 8 695	Oct 68 Borisova+ RADIOCHEM ESTIMATD VAL GVN	
				Jour	SNP 8 404	Apr 69 TRANSLATN.*	
Nu	Maxwl	1.5+7	HAR Revw	Conf	70Helsinki 2 195	Jun 70 Colvin.PPR99. REPORT ON DATA STATUS	
Nu	Maxwl		NIR Expt	Jour	AE 29 95	Aug 70 Kroshkin+ NU BAR +− 3.0 PERCENT GIVN	+
				Jour	SJA 29 790	Aug 70 . ENGL OF AE 29 95	
	2.5−2			Data	EXFOR40064.006	Sep 73 .1 DATA LINE	
Nu	Maxwl		CUA Theo	Abst	DA/B 32 5980	Apr 72 Lee. CALC OF AVG PROMPT NU	
Nu	Maxwl		IAE Eval	Jour	REA 10 637	Dec 72 Manero+ EXTENSIVE SURVEY,TBL,AVG VAL	
Nu	2.5−2		ANL Expt	Conf	73Rochestr 2 19	Aug 73 Unik+NU TOTAL VS MASS 13 NUCLIDES.	
Nu	Maxwl		AUA Revw	Conf	IAEA−169 2 163	74 Musgrove+ TOTAL NU−BAR,GRAPH	
Nu	Maxwl		ANL Expt	Prog	ANL−6600 124	61 Jaffey+ NUBAR=2.32+−0.06	+
	Maxwl			Data	EXFOR12251.002	Jun 76 . 1 PT.	
Spect Fiss n	Maxwl		TRM Expt	Conf	66Bombay 28	Feb 66 Zaghloul.GRPH,REL TO U235,TBC	
Spect Fiss n	Maxwl		NIR Expt	Jour	AE 29 95	Aug 70 Kroshkin+ AVG FISSN NEUT E +SPEC CRV	+
				Jour	SJA 29 790	Aug 70 . ENGL OF AE 29 95	
	2.5−2			Data	EXFOR40064.012	Sep 73 .1 DATA LINE	
Spect Fiss n	Maxwl		ANL Revw	Conf	71Vienna 3	Aug 71 Smith. MEAN−E OF NEUTS,EXPTS CFD,TBL	
Fiss Yield	Maxwl		ANL Expt	Jour	JIN 28 921	Apr 66 Ravindran+.25 MASS CHAINS.RADIOCHEM.	
Fiss Yield	Maxwl		MCM Expt	Jour	CJP 44 1011	May 66 Harvey+REL+ABS CUMUL YLDS BY M.SPECT	
Fiss Yield	Pile		CCP Expt	Jour	YF 8 695	Oct 68 Borisova+ RADIOCHEM METHD,GRPH+TBL	
				Jour	SNP 8 404	Apr 69 TRANSLATN.*	
Fiss Yield			HAR Eval	Conf	73Paris 1 393	Mar 73 Crouch.EXPTL DATA+EVAL CHAIN YLD,TBL	
				Rept	AERE−R−7209	Jan 73 − .49 CHAIN YLDS RECOMMENDED TBL	
Fiss Yield	Maxwl		ANL Expt	Conf	73Rochestr 2 19	Aug 73 Unik+ PROMPT YLDS,MASS DISTRIB,GRPHS	
Fiss Yield	Maxwl		AUA Revw	Conf	IAEA−169 2 163	74 Musgrove+ PROMPT,EVEN−Z POSITN,GRAPH	
Fiss Yield	1.0+7	2.5+7	RI Eval	Conf	75Kiev 5 216	May 75 Selickij. REL SYM YLD VS EXC−E.GRAPH	
Fiss Yield	Maxwl		AUA Theo	Rept	AAEC/E−386	Mar 76 Cook+ 3−GAUSS FIT,PARAMS GIVEN	
Fiss Yield	2.5−2	1.4+7	LAS Eval	Rept	LA−6430	Jul 76 Madland+PAIR EFFECT ON INDEP YLD TBL	
Frag Spectra	Maxwl		TRM Expt	Conf	66Bombay 28	Feb 66 Zaghloul.PRELIM DATA,TO BE CONTINUED	
Frag Spectra	−		SAH Theo	Prog	BARC−401 21	69 Sarkar+ FRAGS EXCIT+KIN E OKS EXPTS	
Frag Spectra	Maxwl		CUA Theo	Abst	DA/B 32 5980	Apr 72 Lee. CALC OF TOT FRAG KE DISTRIBUTS	
Frag Spectra	Maxwl		ANL Expt	Conf	73Rochestr 2 19	Aug 73 Unik+ TOTAL KIN−E OF FRAGS,GRPH	
Frag Spectra	Maxwl		AUA Revw	Conf	IAEA−169 2 163	74 Musgrove+ AVG FRAG MASS,GRAPH	
Frag Charge	Maxwl		OSL Revw	Conf	69Vienna 669	Jul 69 Pappas+PPR206. REVW OF EXPTS+METHODS	
Frag Charge	Maxwl		LRL Comp	Rept	UCRL−51640	Jul 74 Nethaway. TBL.	
Reson Params	2.4−1	7.3−1	KUR Expt	Jour	AE 8 47	Jan 60 Konakhovich+ 3ER, 2AREAS FROM SIGF	+
				Jour	SJA 8 39	Apr 61 TRANSLATN.*	
Reson Params	6.1−1	5.0+1	COL Expt	Prog	NYO−73−340 40	Dec 70 Felvinci+ NEVIS,TABLE,SO*WF,WF	+
	6.1−1	5.1+1		Data	EXFOR10198.002	Jun 74 . 29RES, S0*WF, 5RES, WF	
Reson Params	2.4−1	2.9+1	CCP Theo	Rept	YK−16 121	74 Gorbachev+ TOT+N+G−WIDTHS,TBL	
Reson Params	None		COL Expt	Abst	BAP 20 149	Feb 75 Cacuci+LVL DENSITY CALC CFD EXPT.	

90 Thorium 229

Quantity	Energy (ev) Min	Max	Lab	Type	Documentation Ref Vol Page	Date	Author, Comments	Data
Reson Params	2.4−1	3.0+1	ANL	Expt Prog	WASH−1034 1	Dec 61	Cote.FROM SIG TOTAL 22E0S WG=0.038EV	+
	6.1−1	1.7+1		Data	EXFOR12298.	Jun 76	. 17RES, WT, WN, NN0, PCS	
Reson Params	6.1−1	1.7+1	ANL	Expt Abst	BAP 8 370	Apr 63	Bollinger+ ABST RA15	+
	6.1−1	1.7+1		Data	EXFOR12281.002	Jun 76	. 18 RES, E0	
Strnth Fnctn	None		AUA	Eval Rept	AAEC/E−277	Mar 73	Musgrove.TBLS EXPTL DATA+BEST VALUES	
Lvl Density		1.0+1	KUR	Theo Jour	YF 9 303	Feb 69	Vorotnikov.LVL DEN(EXCIT−E),TBL GRPH	
				Jour	SNP 9 179	Aug 69	TRANSLATN.*	
Lvl Density	+6		DUB	Theo Rept	JINR−E4−9236	Nov 75	Komov+ AVG LVL−SPAC,SEMIMICRO CFD XP	

90 Thorium 230

Quantity	Energy (ev) Min	Max	Lab	Type	Documentation Ref Vol Page	Date	Author, Comments	Data
Total	2.2−2	5.0+1	ITE	Expt Conf	66Paris 1 71	Oct 66	PPR104.KALEBIN+.FC.CURVE+RES ANALYS	+
	2.2−2	5.0+1		Data	EXFOR40093.002	Mar 72	SIGMA AT 221 ENERGIES	
Total	1.4−2	1.0+0	ITE	Expt Jour	AE 24 243	Mar 68	Kalebin+ GRAPH SIG(E) GIVEN	
	1.2−2	1.2+0			−		ENGL TRANSL INDC−232E	
	1.4−2	1.0+0		Jour	SJA 24 296	68	. ENGL OF AE 24 243	
	1.2−2	1.2+0		Rept	INDC−232E	67	. ENGL OF YFI−5 26	
Total	2.0−2	5.0+1	ITE	Expt Prog	YFI−4 29	May 67	Kalebin+.,CURVES,TBL GIVEN	
				Rept	INDC−E−187	68	. ENGL OF YFI−4 29	
Total	2.5−2		ITE	Expt Prog	YFI−6 82	68	Kalebin+ VALUE GIVEN	
				Conf	68Dubna § 18	Jun 68	SEE ALSO *−	
				Rept	INDC−260E	69	. ENGL OF YFI−6 82	
Total	5.0−2	5.0+2	ANL	Expt Jour	PR 176 1421	Dec 68	Cote+ TRANS SIGS 3ES,PARAMS 20ES	
Total	1.1−2	6.0+2	CCP	Expt Jour	AE 26 507	Jun 69	Kalebin+ EXPTL SIG GRPH(NEUT−E),TOF	+
				Jour	SJA 26 588	Jun 69	.TRANSLATN.*	+
Elastic	8.0+0		ITE	Expt Conf	68Dubna	68	Kalebin+	
	8.0+0			Data	EXFOR40093.005	Mar 72	SIGMA	
Elastic	+1	+6	GEL	Expt Prog	INDC(SEC)−26	May 72	Theobald+ NUC EXPLOSION,EXPT PROPOSD	
Scattering	2.5−2		IJI	Eval Conf	73Kiev 1 197	May 73	Fedorova. SIG 2200M/S=15+−2 B	
Absorption	1.4−2	1.0+0	ITE	Expt Rept	ITE−546	67	Kalebin+ CHOPPER.SEVERAL ES.GRPH	
Absorption	8.0+0		ITE	Expt Conf	68Dubna	68	Kalebin+	+
	2.5−2			Data	EXFOR40093.009	Mar 72	SIGMA	
Absorption	2.5−2		IJI	Eval Conf	73Kiev 1 197	May 73	Fedorova. SIG 2200M/S=26+−2 B	
Res Int Abs	8.0+0		ITE	Expt Conf	68Dubna	68	Kalebin+ CAPTURE	+
	1.4+0	5.6+2		Data	EXFOR40093.008	Mar 72	CAPTURE RES−INT, S−WAVE	
Res Int Abs	1.4+0	5.6+2	CCP	Expt Jour	AE 26 507	Jun 69	Kalebin+ VAL GVN,S−NEUTRONS	
				Jour	SJA 26 588	Jun 69	.TRANSLATN.*	
(n,γ)	Pile		ANL	Expt Prog	ANL−4183	Aug 48	Hyde.	+
	Pile			Data	EXFOR12292.002	Jun 76	. 1 PT.	
(n,γ)	Pile		ANL	Expt Prog	ANL−4249	49	Jaffey.	+
	Pile			Data	EXFOR12293.002	Jun 76	. 1 PT.	
(n,γ)	Maxwl		ORL	Expt Prog	ORNL−1620 4	Dec 53	Pomerance. 26+−2B REL AU=95B	+
	Maxwl			Data	EXFOR12303.002	Jun 76	. 1 PT.	
(n,γ)	Maxwl		CRC	Expt Jour	CJP 40 194	Feb 62	Attree+ 22.7+−0.6B REL CO 36.5B	+
				Jour	CJP 36 989	Aug 58	Cabell.REV. VAL IN CJP 40, 194	
	Maxwl			Data	EXFOR12297.005	Jun 76	. 1 PT. FROM CJP 36, 989 (1958)	
(n,γ)	2.5−2		CCP	Expt Jour	AE 26 507	Jun 69	Kalebin+ THR SIG VAL GVN,CFD ACTIVTN	
				Jour	SJA 26 588	Jun 69	TRANSLATN.*	
(n,γ)	+1	+6	GEL	Expt Prog	INDC(SEC)−26	May 72	Theobald+ NUC EXPLOSION,EXPT PROPOSD	
Res Int Capt	5.0−1		CRC	Expt Jour	CJP 40 194	Feb 62	Attree+ 996+−40B REL CO 74B	+
				Jour	CJP 36 989	Aug 58	Cabell. REV. VALUE IN CJP 40, 194	
	5.0−1			Data	EXFOR12297.003	Jun 76	. 1 PT. FROM CJP 36,989 (1958)	
Res Int Capt	5.0−2	5.0+2	ANL	Expt Jour	PR 176 1421	Dec 68	Cote+ TRANS 1020+−30B	
(n,α)	1.4+7		CIS	Theo Jour	NP 51 460	Feb 64	Facchini+STATMOD SIG XPT/CALC=900	
(n,α)	1.4+7	1.5+7	JYV	Eval Rept	JU−RR−3/1970	Jun 70	Leppaemaeki+ TABLE OF EVAL AVG SIG	
Fission	6.7+5	1.2+6	KUR	Expt Conf	59Tashkent 1 57	Sep 59	Gokhberg.VDG,RSLN 2−20KEV, GRAPH	
				Book	NEJTRONFIZ 211	61	Otroshchenko. GRPH SIG(E)CFD ANISOTR	
				Rept	AEC−TR−6398	64	.VOL 1,P59 .ENGL OF 59TASHKE 1 57	
				Book	SPN 155	61	. ENGL TRANSL OF NEJTRONFIZ 211	
Fission	2.5+6	1.5+7	CCP	Expt Jour	AE 8 139	Feb 60	Kazarinova+ 0.41+−.08B, 0.72+−.15B	+
				Jour	SJA 8 125	May 61	TRANSLATN.*	
Fission	6.7+5	1.2+6	KUR	Expt Rept	IAE−817	65	Dubrovina+,PARTIAL FISSSIG(E) K−BAND	
				Rept	ANL−TRANS−242	65	. ENGL OF IAE−817	
Fission	−2	+2	HAR	ExTh Conf	65Salzburg 187	Mar 65	RAE.REVIEW,SOME CALCULATIONS CFD XPT	
Fission	6.7+5	3.0+6	ORL	Expt Prog	WASH−1056 68	Mar 65	Lamphere.5PKS 740−2300KEV,REL U235	

90 Thorium 230

Quantity	Energy (ev) Min	Max	Lab	Type	Documentation Ref Vol Page	Author, Comments Date	Data
Fission	6.9+5	1.2+6	KUR	ExTh Jour	YF 5 295	Feb 67 Vorotnikov+ CURVE CFD REFS,VDG	
				Jour	SNP 5 207	Aug 67 . ENGL OF YF 5 295	
Fission	+5	+6	KUR	Theo Jour	YF 7 1228	Jun 68 Vorotnikov. F-BARRIER,QUASISTABLE TH	
				Jour	SNP 7 732	Dec 68 . ENGL OF YF 7 1228	
Fission	-		COP	Theo Conf	68DUBSY 431	Jul 68 Strutinsky+,INTERM. STATES IN FISS.	
Fission	+5	+6	CCP	Theo Jour	YF 9 535	Mar 69 Gejlikman. SIG MAXIMA+QUASISTAT LVLS	
				Jour	SNP 9 306	Sep 69 TRANSLATN.*	
Fission	Spont		CCP	Comp Jour	AE 26 436	May 69 Romanov. HALF-LIFE VAL ESTIMATD,GRPH	
				Jour	SJA 26 498	69 . ENGL OF AE 26 436.	
				Jour	EAF 26 48	69 . FRENCH OF AE 26 436.	
Fission	6.0+5	1.2+6	COP	Revw Conf	69Vienna 155	Jul 69 Strutinsky+PPR203. SIG(E),VIBR-RESON	
Fission	3.0+5	3.0+6	LAS	Expt Conf	71Knoxvill 292	Mar 71 Muir+,0.6NS/M RESOL,15PC ACCURACY	+
	3.0+5	3.0+6		Data	EXFOR10223.003	Dec 74 . 181PTS,SIGMA	
Fission	6.8+5	7.5+5	ROC	ExTh Jour	NP/A 171 614	Aug 71 Yuen+DATA FIT CHECKS VIBR K IN 2HUMP	+
	6.8+5	7.2+5		Expt Data	EXFOR10255.	Jan 73 . 32 PTS. D/DA.	
Fission	+1	+6	GEL	Expt Prog	INDC(SEC)-26	May 72 Theobald+ NUC EXPLOSION,EXPT PROPOSD	
Fission	6.2+5	1.4+6	HAR	Expt Jour	NP/A 189 225	Jul 72 James+VDG 2TO5KEV RESL.CF VIBRAT RES	+
	6.0+5	1.4+6		Revw Rept	AERE-R-2505	Dec 71 Lynn.GRPH. 2-HUMP STRUCT.ANGDISTS.	
	6.2+5	1.4+6		Expt Rept	AERE-R-6901	Oct 71 - + EQU TO NP/A 189 225.	
	6.7+5	8.5+5		Conf	70Helsinki 1 267	Jun 70 James.107. SIG(E) GRAPH, RESON ANAL	
	6.5+5	9.0+5		Revw Conf	69Vienna 249	Jul 69 Lynn.TBL=2HUMPED FISS-BARRIER PARS	
	6.8+5	1.4+6		Expt Conf	69Vienna 911	Jul 69 Earwaker+PPR61.SIG(E),IBIS-ACCELERTR	
	6.0+5	1.4+6		Prog	AERE-PR/NP16	Apr 69 - +5KEV RESOL.IBIS.GRPH W-RES	
	6.2+5	1.4+6		Revw Rept	AERE-R-5891	Sep 68 Lynn.STRUCTURE IN FISS.DISCUSSED.NDG	
	6.3+5	1.4+6		Expt Data	EXFOR20472.002	Jan 76 50PTS.SIGMA.	
Fission	2.5-2		JUL	Theo Jour	ZP 257 389	Dec 72 Mcminn. 2.41 E-4 B	
Fission	2.5-2		IJI	Eval Conf	73Kiev 1 197	May 73 Fedorova. SIG(2200M/S)=0.001 MB	
Fission	None		BSP	Theo Jour	NP/A 256 271	Jan 75 Bhandari+ 3-HUMPED BARRIER	
Fission	6.2+5	2.0+6	JAE	Revw Conf	IAEA-186 3 1	76 Igarasi. REVW AVAIL DATA,GRPH+BIBLIO	
	6.0+5	2.0+6		Rept	JAERI-M-6315	Nov 75 - +GRPHS DATA TO 1972 COMPARED	
Fission	6.0+5	1.4+6	BRC	Revw Conf	76Lowell 641	Jul 76 Michaudon.VIBRAT.RESON.IN NF.	
Nu	7.1+5	1.9+6	AUA	Expt Prog	AAEC/PR-42P 25	Sep 76 Boldeman+ NUBAR(5ES),TBL.NO BARR-EFF	+
	7.0+5	2.0+6		Jour	PL/B 62 149	May 76 - +5 ES REL TO CF-252	
	7.0+5	1.9+6		Data	EXFOR30370.002	Jan 77 5 PTS, PROMPT NUBAR, PRELIM.	
Fiss Yield	6.7+5	2.3+6	ORL	Expt Prog	WASH-1056 120	Mar 65 Lamphere.FRAG ANG ANISOTROPY	
Fiss Yield	-		FEI	Theo Prog	YFI-4 14	May 67 Ignatjuk.CURVES GIVEN	
	None			Jour	YF 7 1043	May 68 - . SHELL-TH OKS FRAG-A RATIO	
				Jour	SNP 7 626	Nov 68 . ENGL OF YF 7 1043	
	-			Rept	INDC-187E	67 . ENGL OF YFI-4 14	
Fiss Yield	1.2+7	1.7+7	RI	Eval Conf	75Kiev 5 216	May 75 Selickij. REL SYM YLD VS EXC-E.GRAPH	
Frag Spectra	Maxwl		ANL	Expt Conf	58Geneva 15 392	Sep 58 Smith+ ENERGY OF FRAGMENTS	
Frag Spectra	7.0+5	1.2+6	KUR	Expt Conf	59Tashkent 1 57	Sep 59 Gokhberg.VDG,GRPH FISS-ANISTRPY VS E	
	6.9+5	1.2+6		ExTh Jour	YF 5 295	Feb 67 Vorotnikov. ANGDIST OF FRAGMENTS	
	6.7+5	1.2+6		Expt Book	NEJTRONFIZ 211	61 Otroshchenko. GRPH FISS-ANISOTROPY	
	6.9+5	1.2+6		ExTh Jour	SNP 5 207	Aug 67 . ENGL OF YF 5 295	
	7.0+5	1.2+6		Expt Rept	AEC-TR-6398	64 ,VOL 1,P59 .ENGL OF 59TASHKE 1 57	
	6.7+5	1.2+6		Book	SPN 155	61 . ENGL TRANSL OF NEJTRONFIZ 211	
Frag Spectra	1.0+6	9.2+6	LAS	Expt Jour	PR 120 198	Oct 60 Simmons+ FRAGMENT ANGULAR DIST	
Frag Spectra	5.0+4	1.4+6	KUR	Expt Jour	IAE-817	65 Dubrovina+,ANG DIST FRAGMENTS,GRAPHS	
				Rept	ANL-TR-242	65 TRANSLATN.*	
Frag Spectra	6.0+5	3.0+6	ORL	ExTh Conf	65Salzburg 63	Mar 65 Lamphere.ANISTRPY OF FRGS,TH CFD XPT	
Frag Spectra	6.9+5	1.2+6	KUR	ExTh Jour	YF 5 295	Feb 67 Vorotnikov+ FRAG ANGDIST	
	1.0+5	1.2+6		Expt Conf	65Salzburg 157	Mar 65 - .A-DSTRB,GRAPHS	
	6.9+5	1.2+6		ExTh Jour	SNP 5 207	Aug 67 . ENGL OF YF 5 295	
Frag Spectra	-		FEI	Theo Prog	YFI-4 14	May 67 Ignatjuk.CURVES GIVEN	
	None			Jour	YF 7 1043	May 68 - . E-KIN(FRAG-A),SHELL-THEORY	
				Jour	SNP 7 626	Nov 68 . ENGL OF YF 7 1043	
	-			Rept	INDC-187E	67 . ENGL OF YFI-4 14	
Frag Spectra	5.0+5	1.0+6	COP	Revw Conf	69Vienna 155	Jul 69 Strutinsky+GRPH ANG ANISTRPY (E)	
Frag Spectra	3.0+5	2.9+6	LAS	Expt Conf	71Knoxvill 292	Mar 71 Muir+ FRG ANG DIST	+
	3.0+5	2.9+6		Data	EXFOR10223.	Sep 75 . 360PTS. DSIGMA AT 2 ANG	
Frag Spectra	3.0+5	2.9+6	LAS	Eval Rept	LA-4648-MS	Jun 71 Muir. FRAG ANG DIST POWER SERIES FIT	
Frag Spectra	6.8+5	1.0+6	ROC	Expt Jour	NP/A 171 614	Aug 71 Yuen+ 6ES 5-20KEV RESOL.ANGDIS +FITS	+
	6.8+5	1.0+6		Data	EXFOR10255.	Jan 73 . 96PTS, DSIGMA AT 8 E0	
Frag Spectra	6.9+5	1.2+6	HAR	Expt Jour	NP/A 189 225	Jul 72 James+VDG 18 KEV RESOL.CF VIBRAT RES	
	6.9+5	9.5+5		ExTh Conf	70Helsinki 1 267	Jun 70 - .107. FIT TO EXPTL FRAG ANGDIST	
Frag Charge	None		FEI	Theo Jour	YF 7 1043	May 68 Ignatjuk. CHARG(FRAG-A),SHELL-THEORY	
				Jour	SNP 7 626	Nov 68 . ENGL OF YF 7 1043	

90 Thorium 230

Quantity	Energy (ev) Min	Max	Lab	Type	Documentation Ref Vol Page	Author, Comments Date	Data
Reson Params	1.1+0	4.8+1	ITE	Expt Conf	66Paris 1 71	Oct 66 PPR104,KALEBIN+.VAL WG WN AT 9ES GVN	+
Reson Params	2.0−2	5.0+1	ITE	Expt Prog	YFI−4 29	May 67 Kalebin+.,CURVES,TBL GIVEN	
				Rept	INDC−187E	67 . ENGL OF YFI−4 29	
Reson Params	−.8−1	5.7+2	ITE	Expt Prog	YFI−6 82	68 Kalebin+ TABLE 29 RES	+
	−.8−1	5.6+2		Jour	AE 26 507	Jun 69 − + VAL CFD TH−232,S−NEUTS	
	−.8−2	5.7+2		Conf	68Dubna § 18	Jun 68 SEE ALSO *−	
	−.8−1	5.6+2		Jour	SJA 26 588	Jun 69 . ENGL OF AE 26 507	
	−.8−1	5.7+2		Rept	INDC−E−260	69 . ENGLISH TRANSLATION	
	1.4+0	5.6+2		Data	EXFOR40093.	Mar 72 N−WIDTH AT 28 RES, CAPT−WIDTH, D	
Reson Params	+5	+6	KUR	Theo Jour	YF 7 1228	Jun 68 Vorotnikov+ GRPHS D,WF.QUASISTABL TH	
	6.9+5	1.2+6		ExTh Jour	YF 5 295	Feb 67 − + CHANNEL ANALYS,FISS−WIDS	
	+5	+6		Theo Jour	SNP 7 732	Dec 68 . ENGL OF YF 7 1228	
	6.9+5	1.2+6		ExTh Jour	SNP 5 207	Aug 67 . ENGL OF YF 5 295	
Reson Params	1.4+0	2.9+2	ANL	Expt Jour	PR 176 1421	Dec 68 Cote+ TRANS 20RESON SEEN WT WN WG D	+
	1.4+0	2.9+2		Data	EXFOR12280.	Jun 76 . 3 RES(E0),20(WN),3(WG,WT, PCS)	
Reson Params	6.0+5	1.2+6	COP	Revw Conf	69Vienna 155	Jul 69 Strutinsky+PPR203. 'VIBRATION−RESON'	
Reson Params	None		DUB	Theo Jour	YF 13 240	Feb 71 Malecki+G− WID,THEO CFD EXPT.TBL,GRPH	
				Jour	SNP 13 133	Aug 71 − + ENGL OF YF 13 240.	
Reson Params	7.2+5		HAR	Revw Rept	AERE−R−2505	Dec 71 Lynn.GRPHS.ANGDISTS AT RES.	
Reson Params	1.1+0	4.8+1	CCP	Theo Rept	YK− 16 121	74 Gorbachev+ G+N−WIDTHS, TBL	
Reson Params	7.2+5		BRC	Revw Conf	76Lowell 641	Jul 76 Michaudon.VIB.RES.3−HUMPED FIS.BAR.	
Strnth Fnctn	2.0−2	5.0+1	ITE	Expt Prog	YFI−4 29	May 67 Kalebin+.,CURVES,TBL GIVEN	
				Rept	INDC−187E	67 . ENGL OF YFI−4 29	
Strnth Fnctn	None		AI	Theo Rept	NAA−SR−M−12538	Oct 67 Gigas.OPTMDL CALC AVG S0,S1,S2	
Strnth Fnctn		+2	ITE	Expt Prog	YFI−6 82	68 Kalebin+ VALUE GIVEN	+
	−.8−1	5.6+2		Jour	AE 26 507	Jun 69 − + VAL CFD TH−232,S−NEUTS	
		+2		Conf	68Dubna § 18	Jun 68 SEE ALSO *−	
	−.8−1	5.6+2		Jour	SJA 26 588	Jun 69 . ENGL OF AE 26 507	
		+2		Rept	INDC−260E	69 . ENGL OF YFI−6 82	
	1.4+0	5.6+2		Data	EXFOR40093.006	Mar 72 STRENGTH−FUNCTION, S−WAVE	
Strnth Fnctn	5.0−2	5.0+2	ANL	Expt Jour	PR 176 1421	Dec 68 Cote+ TRANS S0=1.3+0.6−0.3	+
	1.4+0	2.4+2		Data	EXFOR12280.004	Jun 76 . 1 PT. D	
Strnth Fnctn	None		AUA	Eval Rept	AAEC/E−277	Mar 73 Musgrove.TBLS EXPTL DATA+BEST VALUES	
Lvl Density	+6		MIL	Theo Jour	EN 15 1 54	Jan 68 Facchini+ LDL PARS FROM LOW EN RES	
Lvl Density	−3	+0	IFU	Theo Jour	UFZ 13 700	Apr 68 Pisanko+ LEVEL SPACING CALC,TBL	
				Jour	UPJ 13 498	Oct 68 TRANSLATN.*	
Lvl Density	−.8−1	5.6+2	CCP	ExTh Jour	AE 26 507	Jun 69 Kalebin+ FORMULA GVN,AVG D CFD EXPT	
				Jour	SJA 26 588	Jun 69 .TRANSLATN.*	
Lvl Density	None		MUN	Theo Jour	NP/A 217 269	Dec 73 Dilg+ A,DELTA. BACK SHIFTED FERMIGAS	
Lvl Density	None		COP	Theo Jour	NP/A 222 493	Apr 74 Dossing+COLL ROTAT.SPAC. ACCUR ESTIM	
Lvl Density	None		ROC	Theo Jour	NP/A 223 589	May 74 Huizenga+ EXP CFD MICROSC TH AX SYMM	
Lvl Density	+6		DUB	Theo Rept	JINR−E4−9236	Nov 75 Komov+ AVG LVL−SPAC,SEMIMICRO CFD XP	
Photo−Fissn		2.2+7	LAS	Expt Jour	PR 81 342	Feb 51 Mcelhinney+ SIGMA REL TO GF(U238)	

90 Thorium 231

Quantity	Energy (ev) Min	Max	Lab	Type	Documentation Ref Vol Page	Author, Comments Date	Data
Fission	Maxwl		CCP	Comp Jour	AE 26 436	May 69 Romanov. UPPER SIG LIMIT ESTIMATED	
				Jour	SJA 26 498	69 . ENGL OF AE 26 436.	
				Jour	EAF 26 48	69 . FRENCH OF AE 26 436.	
Fission	5.0+5	2.0+6	LAS	Theo Jour	NSE 41 177	Aug 70 Cramer+,SIG FROM(T,P+FISS)+H−F CALC	
Fission	−		GEL	Revw Jour	AKE 18 229	Nov 71 Theobald+ SUB−BARRIER FISS EXPTS,TH	
Fission	2.5−2		IJI	Eval Conf	73Kiev 1 197	May 73 Fedorova. SIG 2200M/S=580 B	
Nu	Maxwl		IAE	Eval Jour	REA 10 637	Dec 72 Manero+ CALC,SYSTEMATICS,TBL	
Reson Params		+7	CCP	Theo Jour	AE 17 479	Dec 64 Usachev+ FISS CHANNEL THRESHOLDS EST	
				Jour	SJA 17 1242	Dec 64 TRANSLATN.*	
Lvl Density	+6		MIL	Theo Jour	EN 15 1 54	Jan 68 Facchini+ LDL PARS FROM LOW EN RES	
Lvl Density	None		MUN	Theo Jour	NP/A 217 269	Dec 73 Dilg+ A,DELTA. BACK SHIFTED FERMIGAS	
Lvl Density	None		ROC	Theo Jour	NP/A 223 589	May 74 Huizenga+ EXP CFD MICROSC TH AX SYMM	
Lvl Density	6.5+6	1.2+7	ANL	Eval Rept	ANL−75−34	Jun 75 Davey+N2NEVAL.CONSTANT T,LVL DEN FIT	

90 Thorium 232

Quantity	Energy (ev) Min	Max	Lab	Type	Documentation Ref Vol Page	Author, Comments Date	Data
Evaluation	5.0+5	1.5+7	LRL	Eval Rept	UCRL−5351	Nov 58 Howerton+CURVS.SAME AS TL+NG,N3N,NF	
Evaluation	6.7+4	1.0+7	ANL	Eval Book	FRC	60 Yftah+.9 E GROUPS+NUCL TEMPS,TRANSFR	

90 Thorium 232

Quantity	Energy (ev) Min	Max	Lab	Type	Documentation Ref Vol Page	Author, Comments Date	Data
Evaluation	−2	1.4+7	UNC	Eval	Rept NDA−2134−2	Sep 60 Kalos+.N2N NG DIN NU SEL SIN	
Evaluation	2.5−2	1.0+3	LAS	Eval	Rept LA− 2525	Jul 61 Devaney+.TOT,SCT,NG.FNCT TARGET TEMP	
Evaluation	4.1−1	1.0+7	GA	Eval	Rept GA− 2451	Aug 61 Joanou+ 68 GROUP DATA FOR GAM−I.	
Evaluation	2.5−2	1.0+7	GEN	Eval	Rept APEX−704	Nov 61 Cooper+. CONTENT OF C−FINE TAPES	
Evaluation	2.5−2	1.1+7	FEI	Eval	Book ABAGJAN	64 26 GROUP CONST,TOT,FISS,NU,CAPT,SCAT	
Evaluation	1.0−3	1.4+7	UK	Eval	Rept AEEW−R−351	Feb 64 Barrington+(WIN).UKNDL LOW EN REVISN	
Evaluation	4.0−1	1.0+7	JUL	Eval	Rept JUEL−214−RG	Dec 64 Jung.68GROUP GAM1 ABS+FISS+N2N	
Evaluation	1.0+3	1.4+7	UK	Eval	Rept AHSB(S)R−124	May 67 Hart.(RLY).UK−DFN 332.UPDATES NSE 26	
	1.0−3	1.4+7			Rept AWRE−O−28/60	Mar 61 Buckingham.(ALD).EVAL ABOVE 1EV	
Evaluation	−		CCP	Eval	Jour AE 23 6	Jul 67 Kirpitchnikov.RESON PARAMS,MANY REFS	
					Jour SJA 23 669	Jul 67 TRANSLATN.*	
Evaluation		2.0+7	TRM	Eval	Conf 69Roorke 2 106	Dec 69 Garg+INDIAN EVALUATN ACTIVITIES, NDG	
Evaluation	Maxwl	1.5+5	SAC	Eval	Conf NEANDC(E)163U	Jan 75 Derrien+ENDFB FORMAT MAT 445	
Total	Maxwl		COL	Expt	Jour PR 48 265	Aug 35 Dunning+. IONCH,TRANS,RA−BE/PARAFIN N	
Total	1.0+5	1.8+5	ITY	Expt	Jour PR 56 881	Nov 39 Amaldi+ TRANSM.C−D NS. AVERAGE ES.	
Total	4.2+7		BRK	Expt	Jour PR 80 842	Dec 50 Hildebrand+ BE−D NS.TRANSM. C DETECT	+
	4.2+7				Data EXFOR11039.033	Jun 76 . 1 PT.	
Total	1.4+7		CAR	Expt	Rept AECD−3018	Sep 50 Lasday.TRANS,RECOIL METH,6.11+−0.33B	
					Abst NSA 5 140	51 .REPORT GIVEN IN ENTIRITY.	
Total	1.4+7		LAS	Expt	Jour PR 88 562	Nov 52 Coon+5.69+−0.11B. GOOD GEOM.	+
	1.4+7				Data EXFOR11056.057	Jun 76 . 1 PT.	
Total	2.5+0	1.7+3	HAR	Expt	Jour PPSA 65 992	Dec 52 Hodgson+.TOF.	
Total	9.0+4	3.0+6	WIS	Expt	Jour PR 89 1271	Mar 53 Walt+ GRAPH./VDG.ZR−T AND LI SOURCES	+
	1.1+5	3.0+6			Data EXFOR11746.010	Jun 76 . 18 PTS.	
Total	1.1+3	1.6+5	ANL	Expt	Prog ANL−5175 7	Feb 54 Hibdon+ NO INDICATION OF PROM. RES.	+
	6.7+2	1.6+5			Data EXFOR11002.004	Jun 76 . 133 PTS.	
Total	1.7+1	2.2+2	BNL	Expt	Jour PR 95 476	Jul 54 Seidl. FASTS CHOPPER. TOF	+
	1.7+1	2.3+2			Data EXFOR11671.014	Jun 76 . 128 PTS.	
Total	1.9−3	2.5+0	HAR	Expt	Priv EGELSTAFF3	Dec 54 Egelstaff. NUMERICAL DATA.TRANS.	+
Total	2.1+1	5.8+2	BNL	Expt	Priv PILCHER	Jan 55 Pilcher.	+
	2.1+1	5.8+2			Data EXFOR12290.002	Jun 76 . 139 PTS.	
Total	6.6+2	3.7+3	BNL	Expt	Priv CARTER	Mar 55 Carter.	+
	6.6+2	3.7+3			Data EXFOR12310.002	Jun 76 . 12 PTS.	
Total	3.0+0	5.0+2	AMS	Expt	Jour PHY 22 1131	Nov 56 Radkevich+ABSTRACT,FAST CHOPPER. NDG	
Total	1.8+1	4.5+2	CCP	Expt	Jour AE 1 5 55	Nov 56 Radkevich+.TOF TRANSM. CS CURVE	
					Jour JNE 5 92	Jul 57 TRANSLATN.*	
					Jour SJA 1 5 727	56 TRANSLATN.*	
Total	4.0+4	1.0+7	LAS	Theo	Rept LA− 2099	Dec 56 Beyster+,OPTMDL CALC CFD EXPT,CURVE	
Total		7.0+1	BNL	Expt	Jour PR 110 692	May 58 Seth+,ABSOLUTE CURVE FC	+
	5.3−1	5.4+1			Data EXFOR11788.022	Jun 76 . 21 PTS.	
Total	3.4+6	5.1+6	JAE	Expt	Jour JPJ 15 1994	Nov 60 Tsukada+TRANS.D−D NS. TH02	
	3.4+6	5.1+6			Data EXFOR20288.007	Jun 74 89PTS.	
Total	1.9+6	8.0+6	CCP	Expt	Book NEJTRONFIZ 258	61 Averchenkov.TOF,PO−BE SOURCE, GRAPH	
					Book SPN 191	61 . ENGL TRANSL OF NEJTRONFIZ 258	
Total	2.0−1	1.0+7	B+W	Eval	Rept BAW−158	Jun 61 Roach+ AVERAGED SIG 40 GROUPS	
Total	2.8+7		LVN	Expt	Jour JPR 22 652	Oct 61 Deconninck+TRANSMISS.5.49B AT 28.4MV	+
	2.8+7				Data EXFOR20195.018	May 74 1PNT.	
Total	1.0−3	1.0+7	AI	Eval	Rept NAA−SR−M−8904	Aug 63 Alter+ CURVE GIVEN	
Total	2.0+6	1.0+7	SAC	Expt	Jour JPR 24 826	Nov 63 Leroy+TOF OKS PREVIOUS EXPERIMENTS	+
Total	1.0+1	3.7+2	CCP	Eval	Rept INDSWG−64 274	64 Nikolaev.TABLE OF CHARACTRSTC PARAMS	
Total	1.0−3	1.0+0	UK	Eval	Rept AEEW−R−351	Feb 64 Barrington+(WIN).UKNDL LOW EN REVISN	+
	1.0−4	1.5+7			Data UKNDL−DFN 930.	Mar 73 224 PNTS	
Total	9.0+1	4.0+3	COL	Expt	Jour PR/B 134 985	Jun 64 Garg+ TOF,CURVES,TRANS.	+
	8.2+1	4.0+3			Data EXFOR12278.002	Jun 76 . 5877 PTS.	
Total	1.0+5	3.0+6	BNL	Theo	Jour PR/B 135 895	Aug 64 Auerbach+LOC OM CALC.POT PAR.TBL	
Total	1.0+4	1.5+7	FEI	Theo	Jour AE 17 304	Oct 64 Marchuk+ OPTMOD,GRPH SIG(E) CFD XPTS	
					Jour JNE 20 77	Jan 66 . ENGL OF AE 17 304	
					Jour EAF 17 4 103	Oct 64 . FRENCH OF AE 17 304	
					Jour SJA 17 1038	Oct 64 . ENGL OF AE 17 304	
Total	1.4+0		ORL	Expt	Jour NP 61 381	Jan 65 Rayburn+ IN RES 1.44EV 13.28B	+
	1.4+0				Data EXFOR11026.034	Jun 76 . 1 PT.	
Total	2.0+6	7.0+6	ALD	Expt	Jour NP 65 236	Mar 65 Batchelor+ TRMNS CFD SUN OF PARTIALS	+
Total	5.7+5	1.5+7	BOL	Theo	Conf 65Antwerp 556	Jun 65 Baldoni+ROT.OPT.MOD.	
Total	4.0+0	1.0+3	HAR	Expt	Jour NP 76 196	Feb 66 Asghar+ TRNS.TOF.GRPH TO 350EV.RES P	+
	8.0+0	1.0+2			Prog AERE−PR/NP8 11	May 65 Pattenden+ OKS SMALL RESONS (PL8 45)	
Total	1.0+6	5.0+6	LAS	Theo	Rept LA− 3538 2	Sep 66 Agee+ OPTICAL MODEL CALCULATION	
Total	4.0+6		IFU	Theo	Jour UFZ 13 51	Jan 68 Kashuba+ TBL,SIG−VAL,EXPT CFD OPTMOD	
					Jour UPJ 13 33	Jul 68 TRANSLATN.*	

90 Thorium 232

Quantity	Energy (ev) Min	Energy (ev) Max	Lab	Type	Documentation Ref Vol Page	Date	Author, Comments	Data
Total	None		DKE	Expt	Abst DA/B 28 3834	Mar 68	Divadeenam.TRNS.AVG SIG CFD OPTMDL.	+
	1.5+5	6.0+5			Data EXFOR10523.018	Jan 76	10PTS.	
Total	2.0−2	1.5−1	ITE	Expt	Jour AE 24 243	Mar 68	Kalebin+ GRAPH SIG(E) GIVEN	
					Jour SJA 24 296	68	. ENGL OF AE 24 243	
Total	1.0+5	6.5+5	ANL	Expt	Prog WASH−1093 4	Apr 68	Whalen+ NDG	
Total	2.0+4	3.5+5	FEI	Expt	Conf 68Dubna § 17	Jun 68	Filippov+VDG,TRANS.TBL,GRPH.FLUCTUAT	+
					Rept INDC(CCP)−16	Jul 71	.PAGE 67.ENGLISH TRANSL OF 68DUBNA	
	2.0+4	3.5+5			Data EXFOR40082.021	Nov 71	SIGMA AT 8 ES	
Total	3.3+6	5.2+6	JNE	Expt	Jour ARS 64 373	Dec 68	Manero.30KEV RESOL,1.4PC,BROAD RES	+
	3.3+6	5.1+6			Data EXFOR20169.005	May 74	60PTS.	
Total	2.1+2	1.1+4	SAC	Expt	Rept CEA−N−1149	Jan 69	Ribon. TOF, TRANSMISSION. +SCATTERNG	+
					Priv RIBON	Jan 70	− + DATA FOR COMPILATION.	
					Conf 65Antwerp 565	Jul 65	− + LINAC. 0.6NS/M. THICK TGT.	
	2.1+2	1.1+4			Data EXFOR20149.	May 73	4118PTS.	
Total	3.0+6	1.5+7	KFK	Revw	Conf 70Helsinki 2 219	Jun 70	Cierjacks.113. SIG(E) GRPH CFD OPTMD	
Total	1.5+6	8.5+6	PAD	Expt	Jour NP/A 151 369	Aug 70	Fasoli+ VDG TRANSM 2PC STATISTERROR	+
	1.5+6	8.6+6			Data EXFOR20500.002	Mar 76	139PTS.	
Total	7.0+5	1.5+6	ANL	Expt	Prog ANL−7710 12	Jan 71	Whalen+. CURVE.	+
	1.0+5	1.5+6			Data EXFOR10374.002	Mar 74	. 513 PTS.	
Total	2.5+6	1.5+7	BNW	Expt	Jour PR/C 3 576	Feb 71	Foster+ TRANS.CURVS.CFD OTHERS+TH	+
					Jour PRL 22 139	Jan 69	.SUPERSEDED BY PR/C 3,604	
					Jour NIM 36 1	Sep 65	.EXPT DETAILS	
	2.3+6	1.5+7			Data EXFOR10047.094	Aug 73	. 242 PTS.	
Total	2.5+6	1.5+7	BNW	Theo	Jour PR/C 3 604	Feb 71	Glasgow+ SPHER. NON−LOC. OM CFD EXPT	
Total	1.0+1	1.0+4	COL	Expt	Jour PR/C 6 1854	Nov 72	Rahn+ TRANS.	
Total	1.3+7	1.5+7	DEB	Eval	Rept IAEA−153 173	73	Boedy+ MOST PROBABLE VAL OF SIG,TBL	
					Jour AHP 30 115	Oct 71	Angeli+ AVG SIG,CFD CALC.TBLS.GRAPH	
Total	5.0+5	1.0+7	BET	Expt	Rept WAPD−TM−1073	Apr 73	Green+.CF252 SOURCE.TOF.CURV.CFDENDF	+
	5.0+5	9.6+6			Data EXFOR10225.	Aug 73	636PTS,SIGMA	
Total	1.0+6	2.0+7	AUW	Theo	Prog BARC−770 36	74	Satyanarayana+ STRONG ABSORP MDL,NDG	
Total	1.0+3	6.0+5	NBS	Expt	Jour PR/C 9 28	Jan 74	Camarda.LINAC.TOF.GRPH.TRANS.MEAS.S1	
Total	1.0+5	2.0+7	TRM	Eval	Conf 74Calcutta 70	Nov 74	Garg+ OPTMOD FIT TO XPTS,SIG(E) TABL	
Total	2.5+5	1.5+7	JAE	Theo	Conf JAERI−M−5984	Feb 75	Tanaka.OPTMDL/COUPLD CH.GRPH CFD EXP	
Total	−3	1.9+0	THS	Theo	Rept IKE−6 89 51	Jun 75	Keinert. DATA LIBRARY	
Total	9.7+0	2.3+3	ANL	Expt	Abst PR 98 223	Apr 55	Bollinger+ NEW STRUCTURE ABOVE 100EV	+
	9.7+0	2.3+3			Data EXFOR12304.002	Jun 76	. 286 PTS.	
Total	8.2−3	2.1+4	COL	Expt	Rept CUD−90	Apr 51	Havens+ TRNSM DIPS 23 84 +300EV	+
	8.2−3	2.1+4			Data EXFOR12247.002	Jun 76	. 101 PTS.	
Total	3.0+4	6.5+5	DKE	Expt	Abst BAP 7 23	Jan 62	Tabony+AVG CS MEAS.CFD OTH.NDG	
	3.0+4	6.5+5			Data EXFOR11936.009	Jun 76	. 102 PTS.	
Total	8.0+0	5.5+3	ORL	Expt	Prog ORNL−1620 42	53	Pawlicki+	+
	8.0+0	5.5+3			Data EXFOR11773.005	Jun 76	. 53 PTS.	
Total	2.0+3		IJI	Expt	Conf 76Lowell 1244	Jul 76	Vertebnyi+ TRANSM VS THICKNESS,NDG	
					Conf 75Kiev 3 151	May 75	Vertebnyj+ RES−NEUT FILTRAT.SIG GIVN	
Total	1.0+4	2.5+5	FEI	Expt	Rept YK−26 5	77	Filippov. TRANS.TOTSIG(E),GRAPH+TABL	
Elastic	2.5−2		ANL	Expt	Rept ANL−4680	51	Hibdon+	+
	2.5−2				Data EXFOR11434.004	Jun 76	. 1 PT, SIG	
Elastic	2.5−2		ORL	Expt	Jour PR 81 527	Feb 51	Shull+	+
	2.5−2				Data EXFOR11043.	Jun 76	. 1 PT. EACH. BAS. COH.SCT,AND AMP	
Elastic	1.0+6		WIS	Expt	Jour PR 93 1062	Mar 54	Walt+ ANGLE INTEGRATED	+
	1.0+6				Data EXFOR11637.083	Jun 76	. 1 PT.	
Elastic	4.2−2		LAS	Expt	Jour ACR 15 351	62	Roof+	+
	4.2−2				Data EXFOR11435.003	Jun 76	. 1 PT, COH. AMP.	
Elastic	5.7+5	1.5+6	ANL	Expt	Jour PR 126 718	Apr 62	Smith.TBL INTEG OF ELASTIC DSTR	+
	5.7+5	1.5+6			Data EXFOR12277.004	Jun 76	. 6 PTS.	
Elastic	1.5+7		VIR	Expt	Jour PR 128 1271	Nov 62	Hudson+ 3.13+−.25B,INTEGRAL OF DIFF	+
	1.5+7				Data EXFOR12180.005	Jun 76	. 1 PT.	
Elastic	Maxwl		HAR	Expt	Jour PRSA 274 122	Jun 63	Willis.COH NEUT DIFFRACTION BY THO2	
Elastic	1.0+1	1.0+2	BET	Eval	Rept WAPD−T−1630	Oct 63	Harris+ MULTILEVEL EFFECTS	
Elastic	1.0−3	1.0+0	UK	Eval	Rept AEEW−R−351	Feb 64	Barrington+(WIN).UKNDL LOW EN REVISN	+
	1.0−4	1.5+7			Data UKNDL−DFN 930.	Mar 73	224 PNTS	
Elastic	3.0+5	1.5+6	ANL	Expt	Rept EANDC(US)−62	Jun 64	Smith+ TOF,TBL.50KEV STEPS,20KEV RSL	+
	3.0+5	1.5+6			Data EXFOR12039.009	Jun 76	. 16 PTS.	
Elastic	1.0+5	1.4+7	AGN	Eval	Rept TID−21629	Dec 64	Perkins+CALCTD FRM BNL400, UCRL557	
Elastic	1.4+0		ANL	Expt	Jour NP 61 381	65	Rayburn+	+
	1.4+0				Data EXFOR11026.033	Jun 76	. 1 PT.	
Elastic	2.0+6	7.0+6	ALD	Expt	Jour NP 65 236	Mar 65	Batchelor+ BY INT OF DIFF CROSS SECT	+

90 Thorium 232

Quantity	Energy (ev) Min	Max	Lab	Type	Documentation Ref Vol Page	Author, Comments Date	Data
Elastic	2.0+6		FEI	Expt	Rept EANDC-50 200	Jul 65 Kazakova+ EXPT,TABLE CFD OPTMODEL	+
					Prog YFI-3 6	Sep 66 .TABLE	
					Prog INDC-E-140 6	Sep 66 .ENGLISH TRANSL OF YFI-3 6 9/66	
Elastic	1.0+6	5.0+6	LAS	Theo	Rept LA-3538	Sep 66 Agee+ OPTMDL MODEL+H-F FOR COMP	
Elastic	5.6+5	3.0+6	TRM	Eval	Rept BARC-279	May 67 Garg+ CALC FROM TOTSCAT-INEL SIG.TBL	
Elastic	1.5+6		IFU	Expt	Prog YFI-5 42	Oct 67 Korzh+ TBL OPTMDL PARAMS + TOTELAST	
					Rept INDC-232E	67 . ENGL OF YFI-5 42	
Elastic	1.5+6		IFU	Comp	Jour YF 7 277	Feb 68 Korzh+ OPTMOD PARS-FIT TO EXPTL-SIG	
					Jour SNP 7 2 190	Aug 68 TRANSLATN.*	
Elastic	0.0+0	7.0+2	SAC	Expt	Rept CEA-N-1149	Jan 69 Ribon.	+
		7.0+2			Data EXFOR20149.062	May 73 1PNT.RADIUS.	
Elastic	8.7+5		ANL	Expt	Rept ANL-7935	Jun 72 COX+ 4 PI B(O)	+
	8.7+5				Data EXFOR10332.134	Jun 74 . 1 PT.	
Elastic	2.5-2		BET	Expt	Jour NSE 54 18	May 74 Green+ AVE SIG=12.78+-0.30B REL V	+
					Rept WAPD-TM-1132	Mar 74 - +	
	2.5-2				Data EXFOR10388.002	Jun 74 . 1 PT.	
Elastic	1.0+5	2.0+7	TRM	Eval	Conf 74Calcutta 70	Nov 74 Garg+ OPTMOD FIT TO XPTS,SIG(E) TABL	
Elastic	5.0+4	1.5+7	CCP	Eval	Data SOKRATOR-1039	76 51 PTS	+
Diff Elastic	1.0+6		WIS	Expt	Jour PR 93 1062	Mar 54 Walt+ HE COUNTER 30-150DEG LAB CURVE	+
	1.0+6				Data EXFOR11637.085	Jun 76 . 9 PTS, DSIG	
Diff Elastic	6.5+5	1.6+6	WIS	Expt	Jour PR 100 1315	Dec 55 Darden+,ALSO1MEV100KEVRSLN CF OPTMDL	+
	5.0+5	1.6+6			Data EXFOR11638.011	Jun 76 . 8 PTS, DSIG	
Diff Elastic	1.0+5	1.0+7	LAS	Theo	Rept LA-2099	Dec 56 Beyster+,16ES,OPTMDL CALC CFD EXPT	
Diff Elastic	7.0+6		LRL	Theo	Rept UCRL-4927	Jul 57 Bjorklund+ OPTMDL CALC 6-PARAM FIT	
Diff Elastic	1.3+6	1.6+6	ALD	Expt	Jour PPS 73 193	59 Batchelor+ ANGULAR DIST.	+
Diff Elastic	8.0+5	2.8+6	KUR	Expt	Jour ZET 40 1878	Jun 61 Aleksandrov.SMALL ANG SCAT INCREASED	+
					Jour JET 13 1319	Dec 61 TRANSLATN.*	
Diff Elastic	1.0+6		ANL	Theo	Jour PR 124 826	Nov 61 Sokoloff.HARM OSC POT CFD EXPT CURVE	
Diff Elastic	5.7+5	1.5+6	ANL	Expt	Jour PR 126 718	Apr 62 Smith. CURVES+LEGENDRE COEFFS,TOF	
	5.5+5	1.5+6			Conf 61Vienna 1 29	Aug 61 - .CURVE,ANGL N-DISTRIBUTION,TOF	
	5.6+5	1.5+6			Data EXFOR12277.012	Jun 76 . 41 PTS, DSIG	
Diff Elastic	1.5+7		VIR	Expt	Jour PR 128 1271	Nov 62 Hudson+ TOF, 16 PC RES.	+
	1.5+7				Data EXFOR12180.006	Jun 76 . 32 PTS, DSIG	
Diff Elastic	1.4+7		FTI	Expt	Jour ZET 44 130	Jan 63 Dukarevich+ GRAPH ANGL=3-20 DEG	+
					Jour JET 17 89	Jul 63 TRANSLATN.*	
	1.4+7				Data EXFOR40078.005	Oct 71 DIFF SIG AT 12 ANGLES	
Diff Elastic	5.0+5	1.5+6	AI	Eval	Rept NAA-SR-M-9024	Sep 63 Alter+ MT CARLO LEAST SQ ANAL BNL400	
Diff Elastic	3.1+6		CCP	Comp	Rept INDSWG-64 118	64 Popov. GRAPH SIG(COS)	
				Expt	Book NEJTRONFIZ 306	61 - . GRAPH. ENGL TRNSL=SPN 224	
Diff Elastic	1.0-3	1.0+0	UK	Eval	Rept AEEW-R-351	Feb 64 Barrington+(WIN).UKNDL LOW EN REVISN	+
	1.0-4	1.5+7			Data UKNDL-DFN 930.	Mar 73 19 RNGS,C.M.	
Diff Elastic	5.6+5		IFU	Theo	Jour UFZ 9 251	Mar 64 Ol'Khovskij. TH GRAPH CFD PR 126 718	
					Jour IZV 29 319	Feb 65 .	
					Jour BAS 29 322	Feb 66 .ENGLISH TRANSL OF IZV 29 319 2/65	
Diff Elastic	3.0+5	1.5+6	ANL	Expt	Rept EANDC(US)-62	Jun 64 Smith+TOF,TBL LEGEND COEF LAB SYSTEM	+
	3.0+5	1.5+6			Data EXFOR12039.008	Jun 76 . 80 PTS. LEG. POLY. COEF.	
Diff Elastic	5.6+5	1.0+6	BNL	Theo	Jour PR/B 135 895	Aug 64 Auerbach+LOC OM CALC.POT PART.TBL	
Diff Elastic	1.0+5	1.4+7	AGN	Eval	Rept TID-21629	Dec 64 Perkins+LEGNDR COEF CALC FRM OTH	
Diff Elastic	2.0+6	7.0+6	CJD	Comp	Rept INDSWG-101 112	65 . GRAPHS FROM 2 REFERENCES AT 4 ES	
Diff Elastic	4.5+6		FEI	Expt	Prog INDSWG-120 9	65 Anikin. A=2.5-24DEG, NDG	
Diff Elastic	2.0+6	7.0+6	ALD	Expt	Jour NP 65 236	Mar 65 Batchelor+ CFD OPTMDL CALCS	+
					Rept INDSWG-101 112	64 - + CFD OTHER DATA.	
Diff Elastic	5.7+5	1.5+7	BOL	Theo	Conf 65Antwerp 556	Jun 65 Baldoni+ROT.OPT.MOD.PARAMS GIVEN	
	+6		KAP	Theo	Abst BAP 10 576	Jun 65 Dunford+OPTMDL ROTOR + H=F OKS XPT	
Diff Elastic	2.0+6		FEI	Expt	Rept EANDC-50 200	Jul 65 Kazakova+ EXPT,CURVE CFD OPTMODEL	+
					Conf 65Antwerp 576	Jul 65 .ABSTRACT ONLY OF EANDC-50	
					Prog ICD-2 112	Jul 65 .CURVE	
					Prog INDSWG-101E	65 .ENGLISH TRANSL OF ICD-2 112 7/65	
Diff Elastic	5.0+6		DKE	Expt	Jour ZP 196 103	Sep 66 Buccino+ 20-140DEG,CFD OPTMOD. TABLE	+
					Abst DA 24 4251	Apr 64 Hollandsworth.CFD OPTMDL CALCS.	
	5.0+6				Data EXFOR11877.012	Jun 76 . 13 PTS, DSIG	
Diff Elastic	1.0+6	5.0+6	LAS	Theo	Rept LA-3538	Sep 66 Agee+ OPTMDL MODEL+H-F FOR COMP	
Diff Elastic	5.6+5	2.5+6	TRM	Eval	Rept BARC-279	May 67 Garg+ OPTMOD FIT TO EXPTL DATA.TBL	
Diff Elastic	6.0+4	1.5+7	AI	Eval	Rept NAA-SR-11980	Aug 67 Campbell+ LEG COEFS TBL+CURVS C-MSYS	
Diff Elastic	4.0+3	1.5+7	GA	Eval	Rept GA-7462	Sep 67 Drake+ TABLE LEGENDRE COEFS MANY PTS	
Diff Elastic	4.0+6		IFU	Theo	Jour UFZ 13 51	Jan 68 Kashuba+ GRPH,EXPT CFD OPTMOD-CALC	
					Jour UPJ 13 33	Jul 68 TRANSLATN.*	

90 Thorium 232

Quantity	Energy (ev) Min	Max	Lab	Type	Documentation Ref Vol Page	Date	Author, Comments	Data
Diff Elastic	1.5+6		IFU	Comp	Jour YF 7 277	Feb 68	Korzh+ GRPH SIG(ANG),OPTMOD PARS – FIT	
					Jour SNP 7 2 190	Aug 68	TRANSLATN.*	
Diff Elastic	6.0+5	1.6+6	ANL	Expt	Jour PR 176 1405	Dec 68	Kuchnir+ VDG+SCINT 5ES 1.75 – 15DEG	+
	6.0+5	1.6+6			Data EXFOR11077.002	Jun 76	. 31 PTS, DSIG	
Diff Elastic	2.0+6	5.0+6	SCU	Theo	Rept ICD – 6 236	69	Averyanov+CALC ANGDIST CFD EXPT,GRPH	
Diff Elastic	+5	1.5+6	ANL	Expt	Prog WASH – 1127 2	Apr 69	Smith+ TBC,SELECTED ES,NO DATA GIVEN	
Diff Elastic	+6	+7	CCP	Revw	Jour AE 28 310	Apr 70	Lebedeva+ ANOMALOUS SIG(ANG) GRAPHS	
					Jour EAF 28 4 35	Apr 70	. FRENCH OF AE 28 310	
Diff Elastic	1.0+3	4.0+4	DUB	Expt	Jour YF 11 1152	Jun 70	Samosvat.LEGENDRECOEF(E) GRPH,OPTMOD	+
					Rept JINR – P3 – 4724	Oct 69	– . ASSYMMETRY,0+180DEG ANG	
					Jour SNP 11 639	Dec 70	– . ENGL OF YF 11 1152.	
	1.6+3	3.9+4			Data EXFOR40285.010	Apr 75	.LEGEND – COEF FOR 10 ES GVN	
Diff Elastic	2.0+6	7.0+6	PAD	ExTh	Jour NP/A 151 369	Aug 70	Fasoli+ OPTMDL PARAMS FROM TOT ANAL	
Diff Elastic	1.5+7		KFI	Theo	Jour PL/B 35 477	Jul 71	Palla. OPTMOD CALC,SMALL ANGLE SCAT	
Diff Elastic	1.0+5	1.0+7	TRM	Eval	Prog INDC(IND) – 12 2	Jul 71	Garg.ANGDIST FIT FOR OPTMOD PARS,NDG	
Diff Elastic	0.0+0	1.5+7	FEI	Eval	Book NIKOLAEV 181	72	.LEG COEFFS+ANG DISTRIBUTS,GRAPH	
Diff Elastic	8.7+5		ANL	Expt	Rept ANL – 7935	Jun 72	Cox+. CFD OPTMOD,HAUSER – FESHBACH	+
	8.7+5				Data EXFOR10332.034	Jun 74	. 8 PTS.	
Diff Elastic	1.5+5		SCU	Comp	Rept YK – 15 153	Aug 73	Aver'Janov+ H – F,OPTMOD,DIFFSIG,GRAPH	
Diff Elastic	4.6+3	6.5+6	FEI	Theo	Rept YK – 8/2 3	Sep 72	Bazajants+ ANISOTR GROUP – PARAMS,TBL	
					Rept INDC(CCP) – 39	Jul 74	.P1. ENGLISH OF YK – 8/2 3	
Diff Elastic	None		AUW	Theo	Prog BARC – 831 34	75	Satyanarayana+ STRONG ABSORP MDL,NDG	
Diff Elastic	1.5+7		BRC	Eval	Conf JAERI – M – 5984	Feb 75	Lagrange.COUPLD CHANL MDL.4 GRPHS.	
Diff Elastic	1.4+7	1.5+7	JAE	Theo	Conf JAERI – M – 5984	Feb 75	Tanaka.OPTMDL/COUPLD CH.GRPH CFD EXP	
Diff Elastic	5.0+4	1.5+7	CCP	Eval	Data SOKRATOR – 1039	76	51 PTS	+
Polarization	1.0+6		WIS	Expt	Abst PR 96 836	Nov 54	Okazaki+ NDG.	
Polarization	3.1+6		VIR	Expt	Jour PR 108 116	Oct 57	Mc – Cormac+D – D NS,ANG DISTR OF POLARZ	
Polarization	6.0+5	1.6+6	ANL	Expt	Jour PR 176 1405	Dec 68	Kuchnir+ VDG+SCINT 5ES 1.75 – 15DEG	
Polarization	0.0+0		ANL	Expt	Rept ANL – 7935	Jun 72	Cox+. CFD OPTMOD,HAUSER – FESHBACH	+
	8.7+5				Data EXFOR10332.068	Jun 74	. 8 PTS.	
Potntal Scat	+0	+3	BNL	Expt	Jour PR 110 692	May 58	Seth+,12.0+ – 0.3B CALCTD FROM TOT SIG	+
	+0	+4			Rept ORNL – 2309	Jun 57	.SUPERSEDED	
	5.2 – 1	5.4+1			Data EXFOR11788.021	Jun 76	. 1 PT.	
Potntal Scat	–		UK		Rept NRDC – 138 26	Jan 63	10.6PM.3B FOR E APPROACHING ZERO	
Potntal Scat	5.6+5	2.5+6	TRM	Eval	Rept BARC – 279	May 67	Garg+ TOT – EL AND COMPOUND – EL SIG TBL	
Potntal Scat	None		DKE	Expt	Abst DA/B 28 3834	Mar 68	Divadeenam.TRNS.EFFECTIVE RADIUS	
		6.5+6		ExTh	Jour PL 13 70	Nov 64	Seth+0,1PHASE FRM SIG TOT AV 3 – 650KV	
Potntal Scat	0.0+0	7.0+2	SAC	Expt	Rept CEA – N – 1149	Jan 69	Ribon.	+
		7.0+2			Data EXFOR20149.062	May 73	1PNT.RADIUS.	
Potntal Scat	Maxwl		SAC	Eval	Conf NEANDC(E)163U	Jan 75	Derrien+RECOMMENDED VALUE 11.7+ – 0.3B	
Potntal Scat	1.0+4		BRC	Eval	Conf JAERI – M – 5984	Feb 75	Lagrange.COUPLD CHANL MDL.TBL SIG	
Potntal Scat	2.0+3		IJI	Expt	Conf 76Lowell 1244	Jul 76	Vertebnyi+ SCT – LNGTH GVN,FRM TOT+SCT	
Tot Inelastc	9.9+5	1.0+7	B+W	Eval	Rept BAW – 158	Jun 61	Roach+ AVERAGED SIG 8 GROUPS	
Tot Inelastc	4.0+5	1.0+6	CCP	Expt	Jour AE 14 400	Apr 63	SPH 60KEVRSLN 4ES+SPECTRA2ES GLAZKOV	+
Tot Inelastc	1.4+7		ALD	Expt	Jour JNAB 17 437	Dec 63	Mctaggart+ 390+ – 180MB BY DIFFERENCE	
Tot Inelastc	5.0+4	1.6+6	BNL	Theo	Jour PR/B 135 895	Aug 64	Auerbach+LOC OM CALC 6LVLS TBL	
	+6				Conf 65Antwerp 25	Jul 65	– +NDG COMPLEX POTENTIAL MODL	
Tot Inelastc	2.0+6	7.0+6	ALD	Expt	Jour NP 65 236	Mar 65	Batchelor+ BY INT OVER ENERGY	+
Tot Inelastc	5.6+5	3.0+6	TRM	Eval	Rept BARC – 279	May 67	Garg+ STATMOD FIT TO LVL – PARS.TBL	
Tot Inelastc	1.0+5	2.0+7	TRM	Eval	Conf 74Calcutta 70	Nov 74	Garg+ OPTMOD FIT TO XPTS,SIG(E) TABL	
Diff Inelast	1.4+7		CCP	Expt	Jour AE 4 337	Apr 58	Zamiatnin+ FISS+EVAP SPECTR FIT DATA	
					Jour JNE 9 194	Jun 59	TRANSLATN.*	
					Jour SJA 4 443	58	TRANSLATN.*	
Diff Inelast	7.4+5	1.6+6	ALD	Expt	Jour PPS 73 193	Feb 59	Batchelor+ TOF,6 LVLS 0.05 – 1.09MEV	+
Diff Inelast	3.0+5	1.6+6	ANL	Expt	Jour PR 126 718	Apr 62	Smith. XCIT OF 7LVLS,ANG DSTR FOR 2	+
	5.0+4	1.5+6			Conf 61Vienna 1 29	Aug 61	– .CURVE,N – SPECTRA FOR LVLEXCITNS	
	5.7+5	1.5+6			Data EXFOR12277.005	Jun 76	. 6 PTS, SIGMA	
	5.6+5				Data EXFOR12277.003	Jun 76	. 20 PTS, D SIGMA	
Diff Inelast	4.0+5	1.0+6	CCP	Expt	Jour AE 14 400	Apr 63	SPH 60KEVRSLN 4ES+SPECTRA2ES GLAZKOV	
Diff Inelast	3.0+5	1.2+6	ANL	Expt	Prog WASH – 1044 5	Aug 63	Reitman+TOF ABS XCITN CURVS.NDG	
Diff Inelast	5.6+5		IFU	Theo	Jour UFZ 9 251	Mar 64	Ol'Khovskij. TH GRAPH CFD PR 126 718	
					Jour IZV 29 319	Feb 65	.	
					Jour BAS 29 322	Feb 66	.ENGLISH TRANSL OF IZV 29 319 2/65	
Diff Inelast	5.6+5		BNL	Theo	Jour PR/B 135 895	Aug 64	Auerbach+ LOC OM CLC2 LVLS CF ANL XPT	
Diff Inelast	5.0+4	1.2+6	FEI	Theo	Jour AE 17 304	Oct 64	Marchuk+ H – F THEORY CFD EXPTL DATA	
					Jour JNE 20 77	66	. ENGL OF AE 17 304	
					Jour SJA 17 1038	Oct 64	. ENGL OF AE 17 304	

90 Thorium 232

Quantity	Energy (ev) Min	Max	Lab	Type	Documentation Ref Vol Page	Author, Comments Date	Data
Diff Inelast	4.0+6	6.5+6	DKE Expt	Jour	NP 60 17	Nov 64 Buccino+N SPEC MEASURED 4ES+NUC TEMP	
				Abst	DA 24 4251	Apr 64 Hollandsworth.TOF.EN SPEC.NUCL T.	
Diff Inelast	2.0+6	7.0+6	ALD Expt	Jour	NP 65 236	Mar 65 Batchelor+ SPECTRA ANALYSED	
Diff Inelast	5.7+5	1.5+7	BOL Theo	Conf	65Antwerp 556	Jun 65 Baldoni+ROT.OPT.MOD.2+ STATE	
Diff Inelast	1.4+7		LRL Theo	Rept	UCRL-50181	Feb 67 Lutz+.CALC ANG DIST FOR FIRST 2+ LVL	
Diff Inelast	5.6+6	2.5+6	TRM Eval	Rept	BARC-279	May 67 Garg+ STATMOD FIT TO LVL-PARS.TBL	
Diff Inelast	1.4+7		FEI Expt	Prog	YFI-6 16	68 Sal'Nikov+. TABLE, 5 ANGLES	
				Prog	INDC(CCP)-003	Mar 69 .ENGLISH TRANSL OF YFI-6 16 /68	
Diff Inelast	+5	1.5+6	ANL Expt	Prog	WASH-1127 2	Apr 69 Smith+ TBC,SELECTED ES,NO DATA GIVEN	
Diff Inelast	1.0+6	2.2+6	FOA Expt	Jour	NP/A 127 149	Apr 69 Holmberg+VDG.SPEC100DEG.SIG TO3GROUP	+
	1.1+6	2.2+6		Data	EXFOR20066.	Sep 71 36PTS. PARTIAL SIGS TO 3 LVLS	
Diff Inelast	5.0+4	2.0+6	KUR Expt	Jour	AE 29 48	Jul 70 Vorotnikov. SIG(E)CURVS,OPTMOD+EXPTS	
				Jour	SJA 29 735	Jul 70 . ENGL OF AE 29 48	
Diff Inelast	9.2+6		FEI Expt	Conf	71Kiev	May 71 Zhuravlev+.TOF,SPEC OF SECOND NS	
Diff Inelast	4.5+4	1.5+7	UK Eval	Data	UKNDL-DFN 930.	Mar 73 .TO CONTINUUM.72 PTS.E DIST.ANGDIST.	
Diff Inelast	None		AUW Theo	Prog	BARC-831 34	75 Satyanarayana+ STRONG ABSORP MDL,NDG	
Thermal Scat	2.0-2	3.5+2	AUA Expt	Rept	AAEC/TM-497	Apr 69 Dalton. LATTICE,N-SPEC OKS DATA-SETS	
Thermal Scat	1.0-4	1.0+3	MUN Revw	Jour	EEN 80 1	77 Koester. SCAT LENGTH,FREE+INCOH SIG	
Scattering	6.0+4	1.8+6	ANL Expt	Jour	PR 107 1077	Aug 57 Langsdorf+ LEGENDRE COEFS CURVES	+
				Rept	ANL-5567	Oct 61 .REVISED DATA	
	6.0+4	1.4+6		Data	EXFOR11224.079	Jun 76 . 68 LEG COEF.	
	6.0+4	1.4+6		Data	EXFOR11224.078	Jun 76 . 85 PTS, DSIG	
	6.0+4	1.4+6		Data	EXFOR11224.077	Jun 76 . 17 PTS. SIGMA.	
Scattering	Fast		CCP Expt	Jour	AE 13 62	Jul 62 Kozlova+ E+ANGL DIST SEC N	
				Jour	SJA 13 649	Mar 63 .ENGL TRANSLATION OF AE 13 62 JUL62	
Scattering	Fast		FEI Expt	Jour	AE 18 409	Apr 65 Gusejnov+. ANGDIST,TH(N,F)DETECTOR	
				Jour	JNE 20 700	Aug 66 . ENGL OF AE 18 409	
				Jour	SJA 18 526	Apr 65 . ENGL OF AE 18 409	
				Jour	EAF 18 4 134	Apr 65 . FRENCH OF AE 18 409	
Scattering	1.0+1	4.5+2	HAR Expt	Jour	NP 76 196	Feb 66 Asghar+LI-6.GRPH YLD.TBL RES PARS.	
	1.5+1	4.0+2		Jour	NIM 39 68	Jan 66 - + LI6 GLASS DETECTORS.	
	1.0+1	4.0+2		Rept	AERE-NP/GEN40	Jun 65 - +MATEHED LI-6 DET.LINAC.GRPH	
Scattering	5.6+5	4.0+6	TRM Eval	Rept	BARC-279	May 67 Garg+ OPTMOD FIT TO EXPTL DATA.TBL	
Scattering	2.5-2		IJI Eval	Conf	73Kiev 1 197	May 73 Fedorova. SIG 2200M/S=12.29+-0.13 B	
Scattering	2.0+3		IJI Expt	Conf	76Lowell 1244	Jul 76 Vertebnyi+ SCT-SIG VS THICKNESS,NDG	
Nonelastic	1.0+6		WIS Expt	Jour	PR 93 1062	Mar 54 Walt+	+
	1.0+6			Data	EXFOR11637.084	Jun 76 . 1 PT.	
Nonelastic	4.0+4	1.0+7	LAS Theo	Rept	LA-2099	Dec 56 Beyster+,OPTMDL CALC CFD EXPT,CURVE	
Nonelastic	1.4+7		ALD Expt	Rept	AWRE-NR/P-3 60	Oct 60 White.2.4+-0.3 NEUTRONS PER NON-ELAS	
Nonelastic	1.4+7		ALD Expt	Jour	JNAB 17 437	Dec 63 Mctaggart+. 2.77+-.09B SHELL TRANSMIS	+
Nonelastic	3.0+6	7.0+6	ALD	Jour	NP 65 236	Mar 65 Batchelor+EXPT+OTHER DATA,DEDUCED.	+
Nonelastic	None		CCP Theo	Conf	68Riga	Jan 68 Gordeev+ ABST,EXCITATION FN CALCUL	
Nonelastic	1.0-4	1.5+7	UK Eval	Data	UKNDL-DFN 930.	Mar 73 224 PNTS	+
Nonelastic	2.0+3		IJI Expt	Conf	75Kiev 3 151	May 75 Vertebnyj+ RES-NEUT FILTRAT.SIG GIVN	
Nonelastic	1.4+7		ANL Eval	Rept	ANL-75-34	Jun 75 Davey+CORRC APPLIED TO N2N CS.TBLS.	
Absorption	Pile		HAR Expt	Rept	AERE-N/R-527	Jun 50 Colmer+LITTLER.PILE OSC REL HAR B	
Absorption	Maxwl		HAR Expt	Jour	JNE 1 319	Jun 55 Small. LOCAL PILE OSC REL MNSO4	+
Absorption	Maxwl		SRL Expt	Rept	DP-207	Feb 57 Wade.7.55+-0.25B,FE AU CU STANDARDS	+
Absorption	2.5+4	8.3+5	FEI Expt	Jour	ZET 34 574	Mar 58 Belanova. VALUES GIVEN AT 3ES	+
				Jour	JET 7 397	Sep 58 TRANSLATN.*	
Absorption	2.5-2	1.0+7	AI Eval	Rept	NAA-SR-M-3013	Aug 58 Kistler. 32-GROUP SIGS TABULATED	
Absorption	2.5+4		KUR Expt	Conf	58Geneva 15 50	Sep 58 Leipunskij+.PPR2219,VAL GVN,ACTIVATN	
Absorption	2.5-2		HAR Expt	Jour	JNEA 12 32	May 60 Tattersall+. PILE OSCILLATOR	+
				Rept	AERE-R-2887	Aug 59 - . PILE OSC.REL BORON	
	2.5-2			Data	EXFOR20638.067	Jul 76 1PNT.SIGMA.	
Absorption	2.2+5		FEI Expt	Jour	AE 8 549	Jun 60 Belanova.VAL FOR 3ES,SPHERE TRNSMISS	
				Jour	SJA 8 462	Jul 61 TRANSLATN.*GERMAN KE4 147 2/61	
Absorption	5.0-3	2.5+0	GA Eval	Rept	GA-2113	Jun 61 Wikner+.TABLE 100 E POINTS	
Absorption	2.5-2		BEP Revw	Jour	KE 8 625	Jan 65 Wenzel.VAL GVN,MANY REFERENCES	
Absorption	2.4+4		FEI Expt	Jour	AE 19 3	Jul 65 Belanova+ 2 METHODS,ABSOL EXPT,TABLE	+
				Jour	JNE 20 411	66 .ENGLISH TRANSL OF AE 19 3 7/65	
				Jour	SJA 19 858	65 .ENGLISH TRANSL OF AE 19 3 7/65	
				Jour	EAF 19 1 11	65 . FRENCH TRANSL OF AE 19 3 7/65	
	2.4+4			Data	EXFOR40072.018	Jul 71 SIGMA AT 24 KEV AS PUBLISHED	
Absorption	2.4+4		FEI Expt	Jour	AE 20 431	May 66 Koroleva+ ABSOL EXPT,TBL CFD OTHERS	
				Jour	SJA 20 493	Nov 66 .ENGLISH TRANSL OF AE 20 431 5/66	
	2.4+4			Data	EXFOR40074.004	Jul 71 SIGMA AS PUBLISHED,GAMMAS DETECTED	

90 Thorium 232

Quantity	Energy (ev) Min	Energy (ev) Max	Lab	Type	Documentation Ref Vol Page	Date	Author, Comments	Data
Absorption	2.5−2		FAR	Expt Conf	66Paris 1 479	Oct 66	Carre+ OSCILLATOR MEHTOD.	+
	2.5−2			Data	EXFOR20658.026	Jul 76	1PNT.SIGMA.	
Absorption	6.2−1	1.0+7	SRL	Theo Conf	71Knoxvill 714	Mar 71	Mccrosson. SPECTRUM−AVERAGED SIG	
Absorption	1.0−3	2.0+0	JUL	Theo Rept	JUEL−746−RG 49	Apr 71	Bonka.KUGEL−THERMOS−LIBR,T=300K,CURV	
Absorption	2.5−2		IJI	Eval Conf	73Kiev 1 197	May 73	Fedorova. SIG 2200M/S=7.4+−0.1 B	
Absorption	Fiss		BET	Expt Jour	NSE 58 361	Dec 75	Green. 252CF FISS NEUT.SPECT AVG	+
	Fiss			Data	EXFOR10557.003	Apr 76	2PTS. ABS CS. TH232/AU197 CS RATIO.	
Absorption	2.5−2		BET	Expt Rept	WAPD−TM−1279	Nov 76	Green+WSCOTT G=.993+−.004.TBL.CFD.	
Res Int Abs	None		ORL	Theo Jour	NSE 1 68	Mar 56	Dresner.EFF RIA CALCTD FROM RES PARS	
Res Int Abs	None		ITE	Expt Jour	AE 2 22	Jan 57	Myasishcheva+ RELATIVE AU,IN,U235	
				Jour	JNE 5 230	Nov 57	.TRANSLATION	
				Jour	SJA 2 21	57	.TRANSLATION	
Res Int Abs	−		CCP	Expt Jour	AE 3 507	Dec 57	Klimentov+.EPI CD REACTIVITY REL LI	+
				Jour	JNE 9 20	Jun 59	TRANSLATN.*	
				Jour	SJA 3 1387	57	TRANSLATN.*	
Res Int Abs	None		AI	Theo Jour	NSE 4 649	Nov 58	Chernick+,ABS INT CALC FROM RES PARS	
Res Int Abs	5.0−1		HAR	Expt Jour	NE 12 32	May 60	Tattersall+. ABOVE 1/V. OSC. CF CALC	+
				Rept	AERE−R−2887	Aug 59	−. PILE OSC.REL BORON	
	6.7−1			Data	EXFOR20638.068	Jul 76	1PNT.	
Res Int Abs	5.0−1	5.0−1	GER	Expt Rept	EANDC(E)23 5	Feb 62	Brose. = 1 DATA INDEX LINES	+
Res Int Abs	3.5−1	+6	WIN	Expt Rept	AEEW−R−163	Mar 62	Tiren+. 83+−6B REL.AU 1510B NO 1/V	+
	5.0−1			Data	EXFOR20622.002	Oct 76	1PNT.CAPTURE.	
	5.0−1		WIN	Expt Jour	JNAB 16 335	Jul 62	Moore+.CD TUBED OSC. RANGE OF S/M	
				Rept	AEEW−R−57	Aug 61	− + EQU TO JNE(A+B)16 335	
Res Int Abs	4.4−1		ANL	Theo Abst	ANS 6 39	Jun 63	Persiani+RNEGCRESRCONTRIB.INFNITLDIL	
Res Int Abs	−		SAC	Revw Conf	64Geneva § 102	May 64	Carre+CF CALC VAL+EXP BY TATTERSAL	
Res Int Abs	4.0−1		AUA	Eval Rept	AAEC/TM−270	Oct 64	Doherty.TBL.EFFECT OF SPEC,RESPARAMS	
Res Int Abs	5.0−1		GA	Expt Abst	ANS 8 216	Jun 65	Nordheim. CALC CFD XPT	
Res Int Abs	5.0+0		HAR	ExTh Jour	NP 76 196	Feb 66	Asghar+CALC FROM RES PARS.79+−4B.	
Res Int Abs	5.0−1		FAR	Expt Conf	66Paris 1 479	Oct 66	Carre+ OSCILLATOR METHOD.	+
				Conf	66Paris 2 371	Oct 66	Vidal+.PPR73,RES INT,E ABOVE 1EV	
				Rept	CEA−R−2486	Jul 64	− + PILE OSC REL B AND AU	
	5.5−1			Data	EXFOR20658.027	Jul 76	1PNT.	
Res Int Abs	Pile		AUA	Theo Rept	AAEC/E−168	Dec 66	Keane+ EFFECTIV INTEGRL,TEMP+DOPPLER	
				Rept	AAEC/E−164	Oct 66	Kletzmayr. LUBRA CODE USED	
				Rept	AAEC/TM−343	Sep 66	.BIBLIOGRAPHY OF CODES	
				Eval Rept	AAEC/E−150	Apr 66	Keane.-COMPARISON-WITH-GYMEA-CODE---	
				Theo Rept	AAEC/E−147	Mar 66	−. COMPARISON WITH GYMEA CODE	
				Rept	AAEC/E−49	Jun 60	SUPERSEDED* KEANE	
Res Int Abs	−		AUA	Theo Rept	AAEC/TM−362	Dec 66	Cook+ TWO RESONANCE CALCULATNS CFD	
				Rept	AAEC/TM−343	Sep 66	.BIBLIOGRAPHY OF CODES	
				−			SEE AAEC/E−119,E−126 AND E−163	
Res Int Abs	5.0−1		BNL	Theo Jour	PR 155 1362	Mar 67	Bhat+ USING BNL RES PARS,=86+−6B	
	None			Abst	ANS 6 41	Jun 63	Sehgal. CALC FROM DATA OTHERS.	
Res Int Abs	5.0−1		GFK	Expt Jour	AKE 15 83	70	Breitenhuber+.SAME GEOM AS RIR8 EXPT	+
	2.5−2	1.0+6		Data	EXFOR20029.006	Sep 71	1PNT.	
Res Int Abs	None		DEL	Expt Abst	DA/B 30 3817	Feb 70	DEKKER LOCAL REACTOR OSCL.300−900K	
Res Int Abs	5.0−1		MUN	Expt Jour	JRC 15 535	73	Alian+CAPT CD−R, 86.0B INCL 1/V	+
	5.0−1			Data	EXFOR20644.018	Jun 76	1PNT.CAPTURE.	
Res Int Abs	5.0−1		SGA	Comp Conf	73Paris 1 233	Mar 73	Eder+ REDUCED RES INTEG CAPTURE,TBL	
				Rept	SGAE−PH−141	Feb 73	.SAME AS 73PARIS,NO DETAILS,TBP	
Res Int Abs	5.0−1		GHT	Expt Jour	JRC 20 695	74	Van Der Linden+ BY (N,G).CFD OTH,TBL	+
	5.5−1			Conf	73Paris 2 241	Mar 73	− + ACT,REL THR+GOLD,TBL	
	5.5−1			Data	EXFOR20645.062	Jul 76	1PNT.CAPTURE.	
Res Int Abs	2.2+1	2.3+1	TRM	Theo Jour	AKE 28 3 189	76	Menon+ OVERLAP 2 RESON,T−DEPENDENCE	
(n,γ)	−		PAR	Expt Jour	JPR 6 361	Sep 35	Curie+RN−BE STUDY OF RADIO−PRODUCTS	
(n,γ)	2.0−1	3.5+0	IPS	Expt Jour	PR 60 58	Jul 41	MEITNER IN,RH,AU RES NS.TH RES CA2EV	
(n,γ)	Pile		MON	Expt Rept	MC−70	44	Grumitt+	+
	Pile			Data	EXFOR12040.003	Jun 76	. 1 PT.	
(n,γ)	Pile		ANL	Expt Abst	CP−2376	Nov 44	Seren+	+
(n,γ)	1.9+5	1.2+6	LAS	Expt Rept	LA−467	Jan 46	Linenberger+	+
	1.9+5	1.2+6		Data	EXFOR11945.011	Jun 76	. 8 PTS.	
(n,γ)	Maxwl		LAS	Expt Rept	LA−467	Jan 46	Linenberger+	+
	Maxwl			Data	EXFOR11945.011	Jun 76	. 1 PT. SIGMA.	
(n,γ)	Maxwl		ORL	Expt Jour	PR 88 412	Oct 52	Pomerance.PILE OSC.	+
	Maxwl			Data	EXFOR11507.103	Jun 76	. 1 PT.	
(n,γ)	2.5−2	2.5−2	HAR	Expt Jour	JNE 1 319	55	Small. PILE OSCILLATOR.	+

90 Thorium 232

Quantity	Energy (ev) Min	Max	Lab	Type	Documentation Ref Vol Page	Date	Author, Comments	Data
(n,γ)	Maxwl		HAR	Expt Jour	JNE 1 234	Feb 55	Crocker. ACT CS REL AU – 197 GIVEN	
				Rept	AERE – RP/R – 1511	Oct 54	Cocker+ ACTIVATION.	
(n,γ)	2.5 – 2	2.5 – 2	HAR	Expt Rept	NRDC – 84 1	Dec 55	Egelstaff. = 1 DATA INDEX LINES	+
(n,γ)	Fast		HAR	Expt Rept	AERE – R/R – 2151	57	Absalom+ ZEPHYR+TH ENVELOPE.	
(n,γ)	Pile		SRL	Expt Rept	DP – 207	57	Wade.	+
	Pile			Data	EXFOR11777.004	Jun 76	. 1 PT.	
(n,γ)	Maxwl		ITE	Expt Jour	AE 2 22	Jan 57	Myasishcheva+ ACT CS REL AU,IN,U235	
				Jour	JNE 5 230	Nov 57	.TRANSLATION	
				Jour	SJA 2 21	57	.TRANSLATION	
(n,γ)	2.4 + 4		ORL	Expt Jour	PR 107 504	Jul 57	Macklin+ SB – BE NS,500+ – 100MB	+
				Conf	58Geneva 671	Sep 58	.SUPERSEDED	
	2.4 + 4			Data	EXFOR11399.051	Jun 76	. 1 PT.	
(n,γ)	1.0 + 4	1.0 + 6	HAR	Theo Jour	PPSA 70 557	Aug 57	Lane+.THEORY AGREES WITH EXPER.DATA	
(n,γ)	2.5 – 2		SAC	Expt Rept	TID – 7547 3	Sep 57	Hubert. = 1 DATA INDEX LINES	+
(n,γ)	Fiss		ANL	Expt Jour	JNE 7 205	Sep 58	Hasse+ RATIO NG/N2N=11.3+ – 0.3 ACTIVN	
(n,γ)	2.0 + 5	4.0 + 6	KUR	Expt Conf	58Geneva 15 50	Sep 58	Leipunskij+.PPR2219,TBL AT 3ES	+
(n,γ)	1.4 + 7		ALD	Expt Jour	PPS 72 505	Oct 58	Perkin+ACT ANAL 5.2MB+ – 15PC, B – W TH	+
(n,γ)	1.0 + 5	1.2 + 6	HAR	Expt Jour	JNE 8 197	Jan 59	Hanna+ BETA ACTIV,REL AU(NG) THERMAL	+
				Jour	JNE 9 310	Apr 59	– + ERRATUM. SEE ALSO	
(n,γ)	Pile		ORL	Eval Jour	NSE 6 100	Aug 59	Stoughton+,BEST VALUE .025EV=7.45B	
				Conf	58Geneva 16 64	Sep 58	Halperin+PPR1072,VAL GVN,MANY REFS	
(n,γ)	3.0 + 5	1.2 + 6	ALD	Expt Rept	PPS 74 685	Dec 59	Barry+. ACTIVATION.	
(n,γ)	Fiss		ALD	Eval Rept	AWRE – O – 02/60	Apr 60	Hinves+AWRE EVAL DATA CFD XPT	
(n,γ)	+ 0	+ 3	ORL	Expt Conf	60Vienna 535	Oct 60	Block+.NDG,EXPT DESCRIBED	
(n,γ)	3.0 + 4	9.5 + 5	CCP	Expt Jour	AE 10 508	May 61	Stavisskii+ GRAPH,ACT REL I127 + THR	+
				Jour	JNE 17 579	Dec 63	TRANSLATN.*	
	3.0 + 4	9.6 + 5		Jour	SJA 10 498	Mar 62	TRANSLATN.*	
(n,γ)	Pile		CRC	Eval Rept	CRRP – 960	Jan 62	Westcott+EFF SIG TABLE 20 – 130DEG	
(n,γ)	3.2 + 4	4.0 + 6	LRL	Expt Jour	PR 128 2717	Dec 62	Miskel+ TABLE OF SIG AT 26ES.27.4D	+
	3.2 + 4	5.8 + 6		Data	EXFOR12115.	Jun 76	. 33 PTS.	
(n,γ)	1.9 + 5	1.1 + 6	ANL	Expt Jour	JIN 25 627	Jun 63	Stupegia+SLIGHT RISE IN CURV.AT0.8MV	+
	1.9 + 5	1.2 + 6		Data	EXFOR12260.002	Jun 76	. 22 PTS.	
(n,γ)	1.0 + 6	8.0 + 6	ORL	Expt Prog	WASH – 1044	Aug 63	Gibbons+TOF.MXN – RAE DETECT.TBC,NDG	
(n,γ)	1.0 + 1	1.0 + 2	BET	Eval Jour	WAPD – T – 1630	Oct 63	Harris+MULTILEVEL EFFECTS	
(n,γ)	5.0 + 3	2.0 + 5	FEI	Expt Jour	AE 15 414	Nov 63	Tolstikov+ ACTIV,CFD B10(N,A) CURVE	
				Jour	SJA 15 1170	63	. ENGL OF AE 15 414	
(n,γ)	1.0 – 3	1.0 + 0	UK	Eval Rept	AEEW – R – 351	Feb 64	Barrington+(WIN).UKNDL LOW EN REVISN	+
	1.0 – 4	1.5 + 7		Data	UKNDL – DFN 930.	Mar 73	224 PNTS	
(n,γ)	Pile		CCP	Expt Jour	AE 17 294	Oct 64	Batyrbekov+VAL GVN REL TO PU239(N,F)	+
				Jour	SJA 17 1025	Oct 64	TRANSLATN.*	
(n,γ)	6.5 + 2	1.2 + 6	FEI	Theo Jour	AE 17 304	Oct 64	Marchuk+ H – F THEORY CFD EXPTL DATA	
				Jour	JNE 20 77	65	. ENGL OF AE 17 304	
				Jour	SJA 17 1038	Oct 64	. ENGL OF AE 17 304	
(n,γ)	– 3	+ 6	TRM	Revw Rept	AEET – 234	65	SHANKAR SINGH.DATA REVWD,SIG(T) – TBLS	
(n,γ)	5.0 + 4	9.0 + 4	ORL	Theo Jour	RMP 37 166	Jan 65	Macklin+.CALC FOR KT=5TO90KEV	
(n,γ)	2.0 + 6	7.0 + 6	ALD	Expt Jour	NP 65 236	Mar 65	Batchelor. = 1 DATA INDEX LINES	+
(n,γ)	Fiss		IIT	Comp Conf	65IAEA 251	Mar 65	Barrall+CALC AVG SIGS OF 3FISS – SPECS	
(n,γ)	2.1 + 1	2.2 + 2	GA	Expt Jour	PR/B 140 50	Oct 65	Haddad+SC – T.RES AREA.CF RES PARAM	
(n,γ)	3.0 + 1	1.5 + 4	TRM	Comp Rept	AEET – 272	66	SHANKAR SINGH+ GROUP SIGS,TEMPERATUR	
(n,γ)	Maxwl		AUA	Theo Jour	NSE 31 234	Feb 68	Cook+ STATISTICAL CALC CFD EXPT	
(n,γ)	9.8 – 2	3.4 + 0	UPP	Expt Jour	NUK 11 61	May 68	Lundgren. R1 CHOPPER.REL CU.TBL+GRPH	+
				Rept	AE – 304	Nov 67	– . ENERGY DEPENDENCE	
	9.8 – 2	3.4 + 0		Data	EXFOR20006.002	Nov 70	47PTS.SIG.	
(n,γ)	1.0 + 3	1.0 + 5	HAR	Expt Rept	NP – 17644	Jul 68	Moxon.THESIS.MOXON – RAE DET.AVG SIG	
	1.5 + 0	1.0 + 3		Jour	NP 76 196	Feb 66	Asghar+ MOXON – RAE DETECTOR TOF	
(n,γ)	–		IEA	Comp Rept	IEA – INF – 10 6	Aug 68	Atalla. TABLES OF HL,SIG AND GAMM – E	
(n,γ)	2.4 + 4		MUA	Theo Jour	IJP 42 567	Sep 68	Chaubey+ METHD OF BOOTH,VAL CFD XPT	+
				Expt Jour	NP 66 267	May 65	– +,SB – BE,ACT BETA – DET REL I127	
	2.4 + 4			Data	EXFOR30063.012	Dec 70	SIGMA FOR 23. MIN HALF – LIFE	
(n,γ)	2.0 + 3		MTR	Expt Prog	WASH – 1127 72	Apr 69	Schuman+ FILTERED BEAM,RELATVE CURVS	
(n,γ)	Fiss		MTR	Expt Prog	WASH – 1136 55	Sep 69	Schuman+,ACTIVATION,VALUE GIVEN	
(n,γ)	2.0 + 5		MUA	Theo Conf	69Roorke 2 129	Dec 69	Chaubey+ SIG VALUE GIVEN,STATIST – TH	
(n,γ)	1.0 – 4	1.8 + 7	BNW	Eval Rept	BNWL – 1312	May 70	Simons+.	
(n,γ)	1.0 – 2	1.0 + 7	ORL	Revw Jour	REA 8 473	Sep 70	Kasten. REVIEW,SIG(NEUT – E) GRAPH	
(n,γ)		1.5 + 7	BET	Eval Rept	WAPD – TM – 971	Dec 70	Steen.PARAMETERIZED REPRESENT OF SIG	
(n,γ)	+ 3		COL	Expt Prog	NCSAC – 33 44	Dec 70	Rahn+MOXON – RAE.ANAL TBC,NO DATA	

90 Thorium 232

Quantity	Energy (ev) Min	Max	Lab	Type	Documentation Ref Vol Page	Date	Author, Comments	Data
(n,γ)	1.0+4	1.5+7	FEI Eval	Rept	FEI-234	Apr 71	Davletshin+ SIG(NEUT-E),TBL,MANY REF	
	1.2+4	1.5+7		Rept	INDC(CCP)-15	Dec 71	.*ENGL OF YFI-10 3	
	1.0+4	1.5+7		Conf	71Kiev	May 71	SUPERSEDED*	
	1.2+4	1.5+7		Prog	YFI-10 3	May 71	Davletshin+ RECOMMEND SIG,25 ES,TBL	
	1.0+4	1.5+7		Rept	LIB/TRANS-380	Jan 72	. ENGLISH OF FEI-234 .	
(n,γ)	1.0+6		FEI Expt	Conf	71Kiev 1 325	May 71	Ivanov+ RATIO TH232(NG)/U238(NG) GVN	+
	1.0+6			Data	EXFOR40153.003	Apr 74	.1 DATA LINE	
(n,γ)	2.0+1	3.0+4	LAS Expt	Jour	PRL 27 117	Jul 71	Forman+TOF.AVG CS.CALC.CAPT YLD CURV	+
				Conf	71Knoxvill 735	Mar 71	- +NUCLEAR SHOT.CS MEAS.NDG	
	2.0+3	3.0+4		Data	EXFOR10250.004	Jan 78	. 28PTS.AVG NG CS DATA.	
(n,γ)	1.0-1	4.0+4	FEI Expt	Jour	AE 31 107	Aug 71	Stavisskij+ REL AU-197,AG.GRPH CFD	
	+3	5.0+4		Prog	YFI-11 9	70	Stavissky+ ABST,SLOWING DOWN,NDG	
				Prog	INDC(CCP)-31	Dec 72	.PAGE 7,ENGLISH OF YFI-11 9	
	1.0-1	4.0+4		Jour	SJA 31 814	Mar 72	. ENGL OF AE 31 107	
(n,γ)	2.4+4		MUA Theo	Jour	IJP 46 114	Mar 72	Chaubey+ P-WAVE STRENGTH FUNC,TABLE	
(n,γ)	2.0+2	3.5+4	FEI Expt	Prog	YFI-13 6	Oct 72	Chelnokov+ ABSTRACT,TBL SIGMA VS N-E	+
				Prog	INDC(CCP)-32	Apr 73	.PAGE 8.ENGLISH OF YFI-13 6	
	2.0+2	3.5+4		Data	EXFOR40105.007	Jun 72	SIG AT 26ES,ABSOL+REL U235NF,PU239NF	
(n,γ)	Fast		DUB Expt	Rept	JINR-P12-6810	Nov 72	Ngo Quoc Buu+ ACT ANALYS, CD-RATIOS	
(n,γ)	Maxwl	Fiss	SGA Comp	Conf	73Paris 1 233	Mar 73	Eder+ DATA FROM EXPTS+EVALS,TABLE	
				Rept	SGAE-PH-141	Feb 73	.SAME AS 73PARIS,NO DETAILS	
(n,γ)	Maxwl		KTO Expt	Prog	NEANDC(J)36L40	Sep 74	Kobayashi. ACTIV METHOD.7.35+-0.21B	+
	2.5-2			Data	EXFOR20691.002	Nov 76	1PNT.SIGMA.	
(n,γ)	1.4+4	2.5+6	KYU Expt	Prog	NEANDC(J)36L60	Sep 74	Kawamura+.STATISTIC MDL CALC.IN FIG	
(n,γ)	Maxwl		SAC Eval	Conf	NEANDC(E)163U	Jan 75	Derrien+RECOMMENDED SIG(2200)=7.40B	
(n,γ)	3.0+3	1.5+5	SAC Eval	Conf	NEANDC(E)163U	Jan 75	Derrien+ENDFB FORMAT MAT 445	
(n,γ)	2.3+1		ORL Expt	Prog	ORNL-5101 10	Jan 76	Halperin+22EV DOUBLET.WN*G	
(n,γ)	1.2+5	2.7+6	LRL Expt	Jour	NSE 59 381	Apr 76	Lindner+REL U235NF.TBL.GRPHS.CFDENDF	+
	1.2+5	2.7+6		Data	EXFOR10221.	Aug 75	. 30 PTS. SIGMA.	
(n,γ)	Maxwl		LAS Expt	Prog	ERDA-NDC-3 93	May 76	Jurney+G SPEC.THR CS=7.1+-.6B.GRPH.	
(n,γ)	+7		FEI Theo	Rept	YK-21 3	Oct 76	Blokhin+ SIG(NEUT-E),GRAPH	
(n,γ)	Pile		FEI Expt	Rept	YK-24 48		77 Andrijakhina+ AVG SIG AT DIFF POSITS	
(n,γ)	Maxwl		TRM Expt	Prog	BARC-897 16		77 Jain+ ABST,NDG.TO BE DONE.	
Res Int Capt	5.0-1		ORL Expt	Jour	JNE 2 243	Jun 56	Macklin+. 67+-5B REL.AU AND U238	+
				Conf	55Geneva 5 96	Aug 55	- +EXPT CFD THEORY,TABLE	
	5.0-1			Data	EXFOR12261.004	Jun 76	. 1 PT.	
Res Int Capt	5.0-1	1.0+6	ORL Eval	Jour	NSE 6 100	Aug 59	Stoughton+ BEST VALUE 85+-10B	
	3.0-1	+6		Conf	58Geneva 16 64	Sep 58	Halperin+.PPR1072,VAL GVN,MANY REFS	
Res Int Capt	5.0-1		ORL Expt	Jour	JNEA 11 95	Feb 60	Johnston+ SIG REL AU197 + THR ACT	+
	5.0-1			Data	EXFOR11739.003	Jun 76	. 1 PT.	
Res Int Capt	5.0-1		GA Expt	Rept	GA-3069	Sep 62	Sampson. 84 B REL AV INCL 1/E.	
	5.0-1			Data	EXFOR11655.005	Jun 76	. 1 PT.	
Res Int Capt	Pile		KFK Expt	Jour	NSE 19 244	Jun 64	Brose. RI=82.7+-1.8B REL AU(1461.8B)	+
	5.0-1			Data	EXFOR20650.002	Oct 76	1PNT.CAPTURE.	
Res Int Capt	5.0-1		TRM Revw	Rept	AEET-234		65 SHANKAR SINGH.CFD CALCS FROM RESPARS	
Res Int Capt	4.0-1	1.8+7	IIT Comp	Conf	65IAEA 251	Mar 65	Barrall+ RECOMENDED VAL,LITER-SURVEY	
Res Int Capt	5.0-1		MTR ExTh	Jour	NSE 21 406	Mar 65	Foell+ MEAS 81.2+-3.4, CALC 82.3	+
	5.0-1			Expt	EXFOR12266.002	Jun 76	. 1 PT.	
Res Int Capt	5.0-1		BET Expt	Jour	NSE 22 121	May 65	Hardy. 82.5+-3.0 B	
	5.0-1			Data	EXFOR12283.002	Jun 76	. 1 PT.	
Res Int Capt	5.0-1		AE Revw	Conf	66S.Diego 2 161	Feb 66	Hellstrand.REVW MEAS AND CALC R.INT.	
Res Int Capt	5.0-1		UPP Expt	Jour	NUK 11 61	May 68	Lundgren. 1/V-PART FROM NEGATIVE RES	+
	5.0-1	6.0-1		Data	EXFOR20006.003	Nov 70	2PTS.	
Res Int Capt	5.0-1		GFK Expt	Jour	AKE 15 83		70 Breitenhuber+ACTIV.GEOM AS RIA5 EXPT	
	5.0-1	1.0+6		Data	EXFOR20029.005	Sep 71	1PNT.ACTIVATION.	
Res Int Capt		1.4+3	BET Eval	Rept	WAPD-TM-971	Dec 70	Steen.RI=85.24B	
Res Int Capt	5.0-1		KJL Expt	Jour	JIN 34 2699	Sep 72	Steinnes. ACT. AU MONITOR	+
	5.0-1			Data	EXFOR20188.030	May 74	1PNT.	
Res Int Capt	1.0+0	3.0+3	SAC Eval	Conf	NEANDC(E)163U		75 Greneche. EXPT RES INTGR EVAL	
				Diss	FRNC-TH-??	Nov 73	- .	
Res Int Capt	0.0+0	1.0+6	SAC Eval	Conf	NEANDC(E)163U	Jan 75	Derrien+RI=84.8+-1.8B	
Res Int Capt	None		WUR Eval	Conf	NEANDC(E)-163U	Jan 75	Ottewitte. PROBABLE RANGE 84-90B	
Spect (n,γ)	Maxwl		CCP Expt	Conf	58Geneva 15 138	Sep 58	Groshev+.PPR2029,CURVE,COMPTON-SPECT	
Spect (n,γ)	2.5+4		ORL Expt	Conf	58Geneva 15 68	Sep 58	Macklin. SIGMA+G-ENERGY GVN	
Spect (n,γ)	Maxwl		UEN Expt	Conf	67Juelich 50	Apr 67	Kernbach+ GE-LI,LVLS TO 1.3MV,COINCS	
Spect (n,γ)	-2	6.9+1	BNL Expt	Conf	68Wash. § E3	Mar 68	Wasson+ FC 31GAMMA LINES PARTIAL WG	
Spect (n,γ)	None		BNL Eval	Conf	69Studsvik 627	Aug 69	Chrien. WG-DISTR CFD PORTER-THOM,TBL	
Spect (n,γ)	None		LAS Expt	Prog	WASH-1136 114	Sep 69	Harlow+,PHYSICS -8 SHOT,ANAL TBC	

90 Thorium 232

Quantity	Energy (ev) Min	Max	Lab	Type	Documentation Ref Vol Page	Date	Author, Comments	Data
Spect (n,γ)	Maxwl		KFI Expt	Jour	YF 10 907	Nov 69	Kecskemeti+ AVG GAM-MULTIPLICITY,TBL	
				Jour	SNP 10 524	May 70	TRANSLATN.*	
Spect (n,γ)	Maxwl		DEL Expt	Abst	DA/B 30 3819	Feb 70	Koekstra. GELI DET.CALIB CL-35(N,G)	
Spect (n,γ)	2.0+3		MTR Expt	Prog	NCSAC-31 76	May 70	Greenwood+,ANAL TO BE COMPL,NO DATA	
Spect (n,γ)	Maxwl		MIT Expt	Abst	ANS 14 418	Jun 71	Hukai+. 66 GAMMA ES TABULATED	
Spect (n,γ)	None		SRL Expt	Abst	ANS 14 807	Oct 71	Ahlfeld+.AL CAPTURE GAMS. SIG GIVEN	
Spect (n,γ)	-1	+2	ANL Expt	Jour	PR/C 6 266	Jul 72	Von-Egidy+ MANY LINES RESOLVED	
				Rept	EANDC(OR)-95	Aug 70	.SUPERSEDED	
Spect (n,γ)	Maxwl		KFK Expt	Prog	EANDC(E)157U I	Mar 73	Fanger+	
Spect (n,γ)	4.6+5		AUA Expt	Prog	AAEC/PR-39P 44	Jan 74	Allen+ NA-I,GAMMA YIELD.FIGURE ONLY	
Spect (n,γ)	Maxwl		FRS Expt	Jour	PR/C 10 1554	Oct 74	Kern+ LVL STUDY,GRAPHS AND TBLS.	
Spect (n,γ)	2.0+3		KFK Expt	Prog	KFK-1980 2 2	Oct 74	Matussek+ ABSL INTENS OF 19 GS	
Spect (n,γ)	Maxwl		ILL Expt	Abst	75Harwell 39	Mar 75	Borner+CURVD CRYST. NDG. TBC.	
Spect (n,γ)	Pile		AAU Expt	Jour	NP/A 248 406	Sep 75	Hornshoj+ E+INT OF GAM+CONV ELECT	
Spect (n,γ)	Maxwl		LAS Expt	Prog	ERDA-NDC-3 93	May 76	Jurney+G SPEC MEAS.GRPHS.	
Inelastic γ		1.9+6	SUN Expt	Jour	ZP 253 289	Aug 72	Mcmurray+ LVL SCHEME OF TH-232	
	7.0+5	1.9+6		Conf	72Budapest 10	Aug 72	- + LVLS,G-ES,BRANCH RATIO,TBL	
Inelastic γ	1.5+5	2.1+6	KUR Expt	Conf	75Leningrd 157	Jan 75	Demidov+ ABST,ES+INTENSITIES,TBL	+
	Fast			Data	EXFOR40317.002	Oct 75	.GAM/100N FOR 76 GAM-E AT 90 DEG GVN	
Inelastic γ	7.5+5	2.1+6	SUN Expt	Conf	76Lowell 1329	Jul 76	Mcmurray+ LVL STRUCT,DECAY PAR.H-F.	
(n,2n)	1.5+7	1.5+7	HAR Expt	Rept	AERE-NP/R-2033	56	= 1 DATA INDEX LINES	+
(n,2n)	Fiss		HAR Expt	Jour	JNE 7 215	Sep 58	Phillips.ACT REL S32(N,P),12.4+-.6MB	+
				Rept	AERE-R/R-2366	Aug 57	- . ACT METHOD.	
(n,2n)	7.0+6	8.2+6	ORL Expt	Prog	WASH-1006 25	Oct 58	Halperin+ PRELIMINARY SIGMA 3 ES	
(n,2n)	7.0+6	1.6+7	LAS Expt	Prog	WASH-1013 34	Nov 58	Coohran+.28,.48B,ALSO OTHER ES.NDG	+
	7.0+6	1.6+7		Data	EXFOR12305.002	Jun 76	. 2 PTS.	
(n,2n)	Fiss		GES Revw	Jour	NUC 17 1 54	Jan 59	Rochlin.47 ISOTOPES.ACT.RVS.TBL	
(n,2n)	Pile		CRC Expt	Rept	CRC-852	Jul 59	Roy+ ACTIVATION IN NRX FLUX	
(n,2n)	Fiss		ALD Eval	Rept	AWRE-O-02/60	Apr 60	Hinves+AWRE EVAL DATA CFD XPT.	
(n,2n)	1.5+7		CCP Expt	Jour	AE 8 360	Apr 60	Zisin+.ACTIVATION 650+-150 MB	+
				Jour	JNAB 16 121	Feb 62	TRANSLATN.*	
				Jour	SJA 8 310		61 TRANSLATN.*	
(n,2n)	8.4+6	1.5+7	LRL Expt	Rept	UCRL-6028	Jun 60	Tewes+ACT 13ES+-20PC, TO BE COMPLETD	+
	8.4+6	1.5+7		Data	EXFOR11504.020	Jun 76	. 13 PTS.	
(n,2n)	6.5+6	2.0+7	CRC Expt	Jour	CJC 39 689	Mar 61	Butler+ACTIV.CURV+DATA REL S32(N,P)	+
	6.5+6	2.0+7		Data	EXFOR12255.	Jun 76	. 18 PTS.	
(n,2n)	1.2+7	1.6+7	LAS Expt	Jour	PR 121 1438	Mar 61	Prestwood.TBL.	+
				Rept	LA-2493	Dec 60	Bayhurst+ ACT EXCITATION CURVE ONLY	
	1.2+7	1.7+7		Data	EXFOR11645.029	Jun 76	. 13 PTS.	
(n,2n)	1.4+7		ALD Expt	Jour	JNAB 14 69	May 61	Perkin+ ABSOLUTE ACTIVN 1.20+-0.05B	+
(n,2n)	Thrsh	1.9+7	ANL Theo	Jour	NP 25 511	Jun 61	Vandenbosh+EVAPORATION TH CFD DATA	
(n,2n)	Fiss		TRM Theo	Conf	63Bombay 232	Feb 63	Singh.VAL COMPUTD BY SEMIEMP FORMULA	
(n,2n)	7.0+6	7.0+6	ALD Expt	Jour	NP 65 236	Mar 65	Batchelor+ N SPECTRUM.	+
(n,2n)	1.4+7		HAMComp	Jour	NP 65 257	Mar 65	Bormann. 5EXPT VALS.CFD SHELL EFFECT	
(n,2n)	Fiss		BNL Theo	Jour	NSE 23 238	Nov 65	Pearlstein.STATMDL CALC.SPEC AVG.TBL	
(n,2n)	1.3+7	1.5+7	BNL Theo	Jour	NSE 23 238	Nov 65	Pearlstein.3ES. STAT MDL CALC.TBL CS.	
(n,2n)	1.4+7		FEI Expt	Prog	YFI-7 3	Apr 69	Salnikov+ SPECTRUM OF 2ND NEUT, NDG	
				Rept	INDC(CCP)-7 3		69 . ENGL OF YFI-7 3	
(n,2n)	Fiss		MTR Expt	Prog	WASH-1136 55	Sep 69	Schuman+,ACTIVATION,VALUE GIVEN	
(n,2n)	1.5+7		DEB Comp	Jour	REA 7 4 93	Dec 69	Csikai+ SIG+HL COMPILTN,N-ACTIV-ANAL	
(n,2n)	6.5+6	1.1+7	AUA Theo	Rept	AAEC/TM-542	May 70	Bertram. CALC SIG(E) CFD EXPT,GRAPHS	
	6.0+6	1.7+7		Rept	AAEC/TM-522	Nov 69	- . CALC SIG(E)GRAPHS CFD EXPTS	
(n,2n)	1.4+7	1.5+7	JYV Eval	Rept	JU-RR-3/1970	Jun 70	Leppaemaeki+ TABLE OF EVAL AVG SIG	
	+7		KFI Theo	Rept	KFKI-71-8	Feb 71	Jeki. CALCULATED CFD EXPTL SIG VALUE	
(n,2n)	1.0+6		FEI Expt	Conf	71Kiev 1 325	May 71	Ivanov+ RATIO TH232(N2N)/TH232(NG)	+
	1.0+6			Data	EXFOR40153.007	Apr 74	.1 DATA LINE	
(n,2n)	1.5+7		DUB Expt	Jour	AE 31 156	Aug 71	Gangrskij+ UPPER LIMIT FOR SPON-ISOM	
	+6	+7		Rept	JINR-P3-5528	Jan 71	- + GND+ISOM FISSN STATE SIGS	
	1.5+7			Jour	SJA 31 874	Mar 72	. ENGL OF AE 31 156	
(n,2n)	Fast		KTO Expt	Jour	NST 8 492	Sep 71	Kobayashi+.ACTIV,AVG S=12.5+-0.84MB	+
				Conf	71Vienna 113	Aug 71	Kimura+ ACTIVATION,TBL CFD OTHERS	
	Fast			Data	EXFOR20592.002	Aug 76	1PNT.SIGMA.	
(n,2n)	1.5+7		DUB Expt	Jour	IJP 47 232		73 Belov+ SIG TO SPONFIS GIVN,FRAGM-DET	
				Rept	JINR-E15-6807	Nov 72	+ SPON FISS ISOMER PRODUCTN,TBL	
(n,2n)	1.5+7		KFI Expt	Jour	MFF 21 555		73 Nagy. THESIS,HUNG. TO FISS ISO,GRND	
(n,2n)	1.5+7		DEB Eval	Jour	REA 11 1 153	Mar 73	Boedy. COMPILATION+RECOMM.VALUE,TBL	
				Rept	IAEA-153 173		73 - . RECOMM. VALUE ONLY	
(n,2n)	6.3+6	1.5+7	UK Eval	Data	UKNDL-DFN 930.	Mar 73	.19 PTS.E DIST.ANG DIST,LAB.	

90 Thorium 232

Quantity	Energy (ev) Min	Max	Lab	Type	Documentation Ref Vol Page	Date	Author, Comments	Data
(n,2n)	Fiss		IFL	Eval	Book LAPENAS	75	Lapenas. EVAL DATA AVGD,VALUE GIVEN	+
	6.6+6	1.8+7			Book LAPENAS	75	- . FULL DOCUM OF EVAL,TABLES	
	Fiss				Rept YK- 15 63	Aug 73	Bondars+ SHORT. AVG VALUE GIVEN	
	5.0+6	2.0+7			Rept YK- 15 63	Aug 73	- + SHORT. GRAPH OF EVAL DATA	
	6.6+6	1.8+7			Data VIEN-V0002.017	Nov 75	SIGMA AT 111 ENERGIES	
	Fiss				Data VIEN-V0003.017	Nov 75	WATT-SPECTRUM, 1 POINT	
(n,2n)	6.5+6	1.2+7	ANL	Eval	Rept ANL-75-34	Jun 75	Davey+CONSTANT T MDL,LVL DEN MDL FIT	
(n,2n)	1.3+7	1.8+7	HAM	Expt	Prog NEANDC(E)172 5	Jul 76	Karius+P.45. TBL 9 DATA	
(n,xn) x>2	1.4+7		ALD	Expt	Jour JNAB 17 437	Dec 63	Mctaggart+ N3N SIG=850+-150MB. *	+
(n,xn) x>2	Fiss		BNL	Theo	Jour NSE 23 238	Nov 65	Pearlstein.SPEC AVG STATMDL CALC N3N	
(n,xn) x>2	1.1+7	1.5+7	UK	Eval	Data UKNDL-DFN 930.	Mar 73	.8 PTS. E DIST.ANG DIST,LAB.N3N.	
n Emission	1.4+7		FEI	Expt	Jour IZV 32 653	Apr 68	Salnikov+ E SPECS OF SECONDARY NEUTS	+
					Rept FEI-441	73	- + DOUBLEDIFFSIG,TBL+GRAPHS	
					Jour BAS 32 600	69	.ENGLISH TRANSL OF IZV 32 653 4/68	
	1.4+7				Data EXFOR40332.004	Feb 76	DOUBLE-DIFF CS AT 92DEG, 43 PNTS	
(n,p)	1.4+7		SAH	Comp	Jour NP 60 273	Nov 64	Chatterjee.MEAN OF EXPT CFD SHELLMOD	
(n,t)	2.0+6	7.0+6	ALD	Expt	Jour NP 65 236	Mar 65	Batchelor. = 1 DATA INDEX LINES	+
(n,α)	1.4+7		ALD	Expt	Jour PPS 73 215	Feb 59	Coleman+.ACTIVATION	+
(n,α)	1.0-3	1.0+0	UK	Eval	Rept AEEW-R-351	Feb 64	Barrington+(WIN).UKNDL LOW EN REVISN	
(n,α)	1.5+7		DEB	Comp	Jour REA 7 4 93	Dec 69	Csikai+ SIG+HL COMPILTN,N-ACTIV-ANAL	
(n,α)	1.4+7	1.5+7	JYV	Eval	Rept JU-RR-3/1970	Jun 70	Leppaemaeki+ TABLE OF EVAL AVG SIG	
(n,α)	Maxwl		ILL	Expt	Prog BLG-520	77	Wagemans+ PRELIM.ABST.NDG.	
(n,α)	+6		TRM	Expt	Prog BARC-897 16	77	Jain+ PRELIM,NDG.LI7(P,N)NEUTS.TBL.	
Fission	1.3+5	5.0+5	CAW	Expt	Jour PR 55 416	Feb 39	Roberts+ RELEASE 75-150MEV,ION CH	
Fission	2.4+6		JHU	Expt	Jour PR 55 417	Feb 39	Fowler+ ION CHAMBER	
Fission	Spont		BRK	Expt	Jour PR 55 1269	Jun 39	Libby. 10(14)YR LOWER LIM ON T1/2	
Fission	2.1+6	3.1+6	PTN	Expt	Jour PR 56 168	Jul 39	Ladenburg+.D-D NS.25PC UNCERTAINTY	
Fission	None		PAR	Expt	Jour JPR 10 495	Dec 39	Curie+RN-BE FISSION PRODUCTS	
					Jour JPR 10 159	Mar 39	Joliot+RN-BE	
	Maxwl				Jour CR 208 341	Jan 39	- .PROOF OF EXPLOSION EXISTENCE	
Fission	+6	+7	COP	Theo	Jour PR 58 864	Nov 40	Bohr. PROB INC ABOV 10MV BY N ESCAPE	
Fission	+5	+6	ITY	Expt	Jour PR 60 67	Jul 41	Ageno+ FISS RATE REL U,D/LI+D/BE NS.	
Fission	1.4+7		LAS	Expt	Rept LAMS-774	Sep 48	Phillips+ PHOTOPLATE VDG REL U238	+
	1.4+7				Data EXFOR12495.002	Jun 76	. 1 PT.	
Fission	3.4+6	5.9+6	LAS	Expt	Rept LA-520	50	Williams.	+
	3.4+6	5.9+6			Data EXFOR12312.002	Jun 76	. 3 PTS.	
Fission	1.4+7		LAS	Expt	Rept LAMS-938	Jun 50	Nyer+ FISS CHAMBER RELATIVE TO U238	+
	1.4+7				Data EXFOR12306.002	Jun 76	. 1 PT.	
Fission	Spont		CCP	Expt	Jour ZET 28 503	Apr 55	Podgurskaja.SHORT REVW,HL MEASURED	
					Jour JET 1 392	Sep 55	TRANSLATN.* AEERE-L/T-569	
Fission	Pile		HAR	Revw	Conf 55Geneva 5 331	Aug 55	Holmes+.P404,RATIO PU239/TH232 GVN	
Fission	1.0+6	7.0+6	PTN	Expt	Conf 55Geneva 2 155	Aug 55	Wheeler. CURVE, THEORET DISCUSSN	
Fission	1.4+7		HAR	Expt	Rept AERE-NP/R-1996	Jun 56	Uttley+.BACK TO BACK FISS CHAMBER	+
Fission	Fast		HAR	Expt	Rept AERE-R/R-2151	57	Absalom+ ZEPHYR+TH ENVELOPE.	
Fission	1.2+6	3.0+6	UK		Rept A- 8 21	Jan 57	.REVIEW CURV ABS FROM UNPUB 1955	
Fission	1.1+6	9.0+6	LAS	Expt	Rept LA- 2122	Mar 57	Henkel.	+
	1.2+6	9.5+6			Data EXFOR12257.003	Jun 76	. 209 PTS.	
Fission	Spont		CCP	Expt	Jour DOK 118 69	58	Flerov+SEE ALSO(PA 61 3388 6/58)	
Fission	1.5+7		CCP	Expt	Jour AE 4 190	Feb 58	Protopopov+ 350+-20MB, T(DN)HE COUNT	+
					Jour JNE 9 157	Jun 59	TRANSLATN.*	
					Jour SJA 4 256	58	TRANSLATN.*	
Fission	3.0+6	1.1+7	KUR	Expt	Conf 58Geneva 16 136	Sep 58	Kalinin+.PPR2149,CURVE,CYCLOTRON	+
Fission	1.5+7		CCP	Expt	Jour AE 5 659	Dec 58	Berezin+ (1952 WORK) 370+-20MB	+
					Jour JNEA 11 175	Feb 60	TRANSLATN.*	
					Jour SJA 5 1604	58	TRANSLATN.*	
Fission	Maxwl		CCP	Expt	Jour ZET 37 41	Jul 59	ION CHAMBER,0.06+- -0.02 MB	
					Jour JET 10 29	Jan 60	TRANSLATN.*	
Fission	+5	+7	GEA	Revw	Conf 60S-Vienna 383	Jun 60	Moteff+ THRS-SIG-TBL FOR DOSIMETRY	
Fission	1.0+7	2.1+7	CCP	Expt	Jour AE 9 399	Nov 60	Pankratov+ TOF,FISS CH,NORM AT 14MEV	+
					Jour JNAB 16 494	Oct 62	TRANSLATN.*	
					Jour SJA 9 939	Sep 61	TRANSLATN.*	
Fission	1.4+7	1.5+7	KYU	Expt	Priv KATASE	61	Katase. C-W. PPL.SIG AT 3 ENERGIES.	+
	1.4+7	1.5+7			Data EXFOR20299.002	Jun 74	3PTS.SIGMA.	
Fission	1.4+7		B+W	Eval	Rept BAW-158	Jun 61	Roach+ AVERAGED SIG 7 GROUPS	
Fission	1.0+6	1.0+7	ANL	Revw	Conf 61Vienna 1 29	Aug 61	Smith.P76,CURVE,MANY REFS GVN	
Fission	1.1+6	1.8+7	BET	Expt	Priv BABCOCK	Oct 61	Babcock.	+
	1.1+6	1.8+7			Data EXFOR12294.	Jun 76	. 7 PTS.(11+6-19+6).5PTS.(13+7-18+7)	
Fission	Fiss		AI	Eval	Conf 62Harwell 2 385	Dec 62	Strominger. SIG IN VARIOUS CORES,TBL	

90 Thorium 232

Quantity	Energy (ev) Min	Max	Lab	Type	Documentation Ref Vol Page	Author, Comments Date	Data
Fission	1.0+6	1.0+7	ISP	Revw Conf	62Harwell 1 27	Dec 62 Bresesti+ SIG(E) GRAPH,THRESHOLD−DET	
Fission	3.0+6	3.7+7	CCP	ExTh Jour	AE 14 177	Feb 63 Pancratov+.TOF SC CURVE GIVEN	+
				Jour	SJA 14 167	63 . ENGL OF AE 14 177	
Fission	1.0+6	1.0+7	AI	Eval Rept	NAA−SR−M−8904	Aug 63 Alter+ CURVE GIVEN	
Fission	1.2+6	1.6+6	ORL	Expt Rept	ORNL−P−1082	64 Lamphere.FISS CHAMB.ANG ANISOT.	
Fission	Pile		CCP	Expt Jour	AE 17 113	Aug 64 Bondarenko+VAL GVN REL TO U−235(N,F)	+
				Jour	SJA 17 821	Aug 64 TRANSLATN.*	
Fission	Pile		CCP	Expt Jour	AE 17 294	Oct 64 Batyrbekov+VAL GVN REL TO PU239(N,F)	+
				Jour	SJA 17 1025	Oct 64 TRANSLATN.*	
Fission	2.0+6	7.0+6	ALD	Expt Jour	NP 65 236	Mar 65 Batchelor+ CFD OTHER DATA	+
Fission	Fiss		IIT	Comp Conf	65IAEA 251	Mar 65 Barrall+CALC AVG SIGS OF 3FISS−SPECS	
Fission	Pile		CCP	Expt Jour	AE 18 469	May 65 Golubev+VAL GVN REL TO PU−239(N,F)	+
				Jour	SJA 18 608	May 65 TRANSLATN.*	
Fission	None		BRK	Revw Jour	NP 81 1	Jun 66 Myers+ TABLE 2 FISS BARRIER	
Fission	6.0+5	3.0+6	FEI	Expt Prog	YFI−3 13	Sep 66 Smirenkin. VERY SHORT NOTE	
Fission	1.0+3	1.4+7	ANL	Eval Jour	NSE 26 149	Oct 66 Davey. EVALUATION	
Fission	1.0+3	1.4+7	UK	Eval Rept	AHSB(S)R−124	May 67 Hart.(RLY).UK−DFN 332.UPDATES NSE 26	+
	1.0−3	1.0+0		Rept	AEEW−R−351	Feb 64 Barrington+(WIN).UKNDL LOW EN REVISN	
	1.0+6	1.5+7		Data	UKNDL−DFN 930.	Mar 73 54 PNTS	
Fission	1.2+7	1.8+7	NRD	Expt Jour	HP 13 654	Jun 67 Rago+ REL U238(NF),TABLE.TRACK COUNT	+
	1.3+7	1.8+7		Data	EXFOR12284.002	Jun 76 . 16 PTS, SIG AND RATIO TO U238	
Fission	5.0+5	3.0+6	FEI	Theo Jour	AE 23 20	Jul 67 Ermagambetov+.ANGULAR DEPENDANCE	
	6.0+5	3.0+6		Expt Prog	YFI−4 8	May 67 .CURVES GIVEN	
				ExTh Jour	YF 5 257	Feb 67 .ANGULAR ANISOTROPY.GRAPH	
	5.0+5	3.0+6		Expt Conf	66Paris 2 146	Oct 66 .PAPER 127.ABSTRACT ONLY.CURVES	
	6.0+5	1.3+6		Prog	ICD−3 5	Oct 66 .VDG.TABLE,GRAPH	
	5.0+5	3.0+6		Rept	INDC−156	66 .FULL PAPER FROM 66PARIS	
	6.0+5	3.0+6		ExTh Jour	SNP 5 181	Aug 67 .ENGLISH TRANSL OF YF 4 257 2/67	
	5.0+5	3.0+6		Theo Jour	SJA 23 683	Jul 67 .ENGLISH TRANSL OF AE 23 20 7/67	
				Jour	EAF 23 27	Jul 67 . FRENCH TRANSL OF AE 23 20 7/67	
	6.0+5	3.0+6		Expt Prog	INDC−E−187	67 .ENGLISH TRANSL OF YFI−4	
	6.0+5	1.3+6		Prog	INDC−E−152 5	67 .ENGLISH TRANSL OF ICD−3	
Fission		1.4+7	SOR	Revw Conf	IAEA−107 57	68 Ben−David.GRPH THRS−SIG(NEUT−E) GVN	
Fission	Maxwl		MOL	Expt Conf	68Wash. 611	Mar 68 Neve+ MAKROFOL DET. 39+−4MICRO B.	+
	Maxwl			Data	EXFOR20263.002	May 74 1PNT.SIGMA.	
Fission	1.2+6	4.0+6	FEI	Expt Jour	YF 7 778	Apr 68 Sergachev+ OTHER SIG(E)+ANG ASYMM(E)	
				Jour	SNP 7 475	Oct 68 . ENGL OF YF 7 778	
Fission	1.2+6	1.6+6	ANL	Expt Jour	NP/A 118 65	Sep 68 Behkami+ RESIN DET.REL U236. 3ES	+
				Prog	NYO−3938−1	Jun 68 − + 3ES ANG DIST CURVES	
	1.2+6	1.6+6		Data	EXFOR12289.002	Jun 76 . 3 PTS.	
Fission	−		TPI	Theo Jour	YF 9 102	Jan 69 Korostova+ CV,SHELL CORR,LIQU−DROP−E	
				Jour	SNP 9 62	Jul 69 TRANSLATN.*	
Fission	1.0+3	1.7+3	KUR	Expt Rept	IAE−1806	Mar 69 Vorotnikov+ SIG(N,FISSION) ,GRPH	
Fission	1.5+7		STF	Expt Rept	AFWL−TR−68−134	Mar 69 Barrall.	+
	1.5+7			Data	EXFOR10022.	Nov 72 . 2 PTS. SIGMA.	
Fission	1.0+6	1.8+6	FOA	Theo Jour	NP/A 127 149	Apr 69 Holmberg+.DOUBLE HUMP BARRIER MODEL	
Fission	Spont		BER	Theo Conf	69Vienna 197	Jul 69 Krappe+SINGLE+DOUBLE BARRIER.TBL.	
Fission	Spont		COP	Revw Conf	69Vienna 155	Jul 69 Strutinsky+PPR203. HL GVN,'SHELL−TH'	
Fission	−		FEI	Theo Conf	69Vienna 337	Jul 69 Gaj+PPR132. 2HUMPD−BARR−CALC,TBL	
Fission	Spont		FR	Expt Conf	69Vienna 952	Jul 69 Monnin+PPR83. SPON FISSN HALF−LIFE	
Fission	0.0+0	1.0+7	HAR	Theo Conf	69Vienna 249	Jul 69 Lynn.TBL 2 HUMP FISS BARRIER PARAMS.	
				Revw Rept	AERE−R−5891	Sep 68 − .STRUCTURE IN FISS.DISCUSSED.ND	
				Theo Conf	68DUBSY 463	Jul 68 − .REVIEW,STRUCT EFFECTS IN FISS.	
Fission	1.4+7		TRM	Expt Conf	69Roorke 2 289	Dec 69 Iyer+ SIGMA RELATIVE TO U238	+
				Rept	BARC/I−79 55	70 . SIMILAR TO 69ROORKE	
	1.4+7			Data	EXFOR30035.002	Dec 72 ONE VALUE	
Fission	8.0+5	1.0+7	TRM	Eval Rept	BARC/I−96	70 Kapil. 5 GROUP SIG,2 N−SPECS,TABLES	
Fission	1.0−4	1.8+7	BNW	Eval Rept	BNWL−1312	May 70 Simons+.	
Fission	+6	+7	HAR	Revw Rept	STI/DOC/10−107	May 70 Wright. PAGE37,THRESHOLD DETECT DATA	
Fission		1.4+7	VLD	Expt Jour	ARS 66 195	May 70 Valle+,MICA,SIGMA=0.28PM0.02 B	
Fission	3.2+5	2.5+6	TRM	Expt Conf	70Madurai 2 67	Dec 70 Iyengar+ SIGMA EXPT TB CONT'D, NDG	
Fission	+6	+7	DUB	Expt Rept	JINR−P3−5528	Jan 71 Gangrskij+ TH232(N,2N)ISOM FISSN SIG	
Fission	6.0+5	3.0+6	LAS	Expt Conf	71Knoxvill 292	Mar 71 Muir+,0.6NS/M RESOL,15PC ACCURACY	+
	6.0+5	3.0+6		Data	EXFOR10223.004	Dec 74 . 104PTS,SIGMA	
Fission	Fiss		IAE	Eval Jour	KNS 3 77	Jun 71 Bak+ RECOMMENDED AVG SIG CFD OTHERS	
	1.0+5	1.8+7		Jour	KNS 3 77	Jun 71 BAK+ FIT TO EXPTS,POINT SIG TBL+GRPH	
Fission	Pile		ORL	Expt Abst	ANS 14 381	Jun 71 Jenkins+. EFFECTIVE SIG=57.7MB	

90 Thorium 232

Quantity	Energy (ev) Min	Max	Lab	Type	Documentation Ref Vol Page	Date	Author, Comments	Data
Fission	Fast		KTO	Expt	Conf 71Vienna 113	Aug 71	Kimura+ ACTIVATION,TBL CFD OTHERS	+
					Prog EANDC(J)19L37	Aug 70	Kobayashi+.AVG SIG=67PM7 MILLI-B	
	Fast				Data EXFOR20272.002	Jun 74	1PNT.SIGMA.	
Fission	Fiss		IAE	Revw	Rept INDC(NDS)-47	72	Vlasov+ REVIEW DATA STATUS ,TBL+GRPH	
Fission	1.3+7	1.5+7	FEI	Expt	Jour ZEP 15 323	Mar 72	Shpak+ RATIO TO PU238(N,F),GRAPH	+
					Jour JET 15 228	Mar 72	. ENGL OF ZEP 15 323	
	1.3+7	1.5+7			Data EXFOR40111.003	Aug 72	SIGMA REL PU238NF AT 10 ES	
Fission	Fiss		MOL	Eval	Rept BLG-465	May 72	Fabry.83+ - 3.5MB	
					Conf 70Helsinki 2 535	Jun 70	- +39. RECOMMENDED DATA,TABLES	
Fission	1.1+6	1.9+6	MUN	Expt	Jour ZP 251 400	May 72	Konecny+,REL SIG,8KEV RESOL	
Fission	4.5+6	1.4+7	VLD	Expt	Jour ARS 69 71	Jan 73	.SAME AS 70BARCELNA 2 489 7/70	
					Conf 70Barcelona 489	Jul 70	Casanova+ SIGMA AT 2 ENERGIES,MICA	
Fission	Fiss		SGA	Eval	Conf 73Paris 1 233	Mar 73	Eder+ FISS SPEC REL U238(N,F),TBLS	
					Rept SGAE-PH-141	Feb 73	.SAME AS 73PARIS,NO DETAILS,TBP	
Fission	1.0+6	1.4+7	CCP	Eval	Conf 73Kiev 1 227	May 73	Borisov+ SIG(NEUT-E),TBL,CFD OTHERS	
Fission	2.5-2		IJI	Eval	Conf 73Kiev 1 197	May 73	Fedorova. EVAL SIG(2200 M/S) GIVEN	
Fission	None		FRK	Theo	Jour NP/A 207 225	Jun 73	Albrecht. 2CENTRE SHELLMOD,DEF-E MAP	
Fission	Thrsh	2.0+7	RCN	Comp	Rept RCN-196	Oct 73	Zijp+COMPIL.EVAL.CS.FAST N.METROLOGY	
	Fiss			Revw	Rept INDC(NDS)-56	Sep 73	- .PG103, USE FOR DOSIMETRY,NDG	
					Conf 73Paris 2 271	Mar 73	- .RECOMM INTEG CFD DIFF CALC,TBL	
Fission	1.0+6	2.0+7	AUW	Theo	Prog INDC(SEC)-42	Dec 74	Satyanarayana+ ABS-MDL,CFD XPT,NDG	
Fission	Fiss		IFL	Eval	Book LAPENAS	75	Lapenas. EVAL DATA AVGD,VALUE GIVEN	+
	1.0+6	1.8+7			Book LAPENAS	75	- . FULL DOCUM OF EVAL,TABLES	
	1.0+6	1.8+7			Data VIEN-V0002.006	Nov 75	SIGMA AT 167 ENERGIES	
	Fiss				Data VIEN-V0003.006	Nov 75	WATT-SPECTRUM, 1 POINT	
Fission	Fiss		PTB	Eval	Rept PTB-FMRB-60	Feb 75	Alberts. CF252-SPC,EVAL DATA AVG,TBL	
Fission	Fiss		HED	Eval	Conf 75Wash. 189	Mar 75	Mc-Elroy.235U THERM FISS SPECT AVG	
Fission	1.2+6	2.0+7	CRC	Eval	Jour NSE 58 377	Dec 75	Cross+EMPIRICAL FIT TO DATA	
Fission	7.2+5		LAS	Expt	Prog ERDA-NDC-3 93	May 76	Veeser+2.7KEV RESOL.SOME STRUCT.NDG	
Fission	Maxwl		MOL	Expt	Jour NP/A 259 423	Mar 76	Wagemans+ HFR-ILL(GRE) SIG<4 MICRO B	+
					Rept BLG-514	Jun 76	- + SIG < 4 MICRO B.	
	2.5-2				Data EXFOR20587.002	Aug 76	2PTS.SIGMA.	
Fission	1.2+6	2.0+6	BRC	Revw	Conf 76Lowell 641	Jul 76	Michaudon.VIBRAT.RESON.IN NF.	
Fission	Fast		KTO	Expt	Jour NST 13 531	Oct 76	Kobayashi+ ACT.SIG=78.6+ - 3.9MB.	+
					Rept NEANDC(J)42L31	76	- +	
	Fast				Data EXFOR20693.014	Nov 76	1PNT.SIGMA.	
Res Int Fiss	5.0-1	+6	COR	Expt	Jour NSE 46 31	Oct 71	Draper.INTEGRAL SIG TIMES E.4 SPECTR	
	+0	+1			Abst DA/B 31 1466	Sep 70	- .EXPT FOR 4 SPEC,GOOD CFD CALC	
Res Int Fiss	Fiss		TEX	Expt	Rept UMO-74-24,841	May 74	Chromik. THESIS. CF252-NEUTRONS	
Alpha	0.0+0	6.0+6	FEI	Eval	Prog YFI-11 13	70	Vorobyeva+ ABST,TBL VALUE FOR 1.7MEV	
					Prog INDC(CCP)-31	Dec 72	.PAGE 12,ENGLISH OF YFI-11 13	
Eta	1.4+7		ALD	Expt	Jour JNAB 17 437	Dec 63	Mctaggart+ 2.34+ - .08B SHELL TRANS	+
Eta	2.5-1	1.0+6	BEP	Revw	Jour KE 8 625	Jan 65	Wenzel. VAL FOR 3ES GIVN,MANY REFS	
Eta	2.0+6	7.0+6	ALD	Expt	Jour NP 65 236	Mar 65	Batchelor+ CONSISTENT VALUES GIVEN	
Nu	Spont		HAR	Expt	Jour PPSA 65 73	Jan 52	Barclay+.RATIO TO NAT U 1.07+ - 0.10	
Nu	2.0+6	1.4+7	LAS	Theo	Rept LA-1863	Dec 54	Leachman.AVG NU+NEUT EMISSION PROBAB	
Nu	Fiss		FEI	Expt	Jour AE 4 187	Feb 58	Kuz'Minov+ PROMPT NS,REL U235 THERM	
					Jour JNE 9 153	Jun 59	. ENGL OF AE 4 187	
					Jour SJA 4 250	58	. ENGL OF AE 4 187	
Nu	1.4+7	1.4+7	FR	Expt	Conf 58Geneva 16 10	Sep 58	Billaud. = 1 DATA INDEX LINES	+
Nu	1.4+6		ANL	Expt	Jour PR 115 1242	Sep 59	Smith+REL.TO 2 STANDARDS	+
	1.4+6				Data EXFOR12276.002	Jun 76	. 2 PTS. REL. TO 2 STANDARDS.	
Nu	Fiss		CCP	Theo	Jour AE 8 409	May 60	Zysin+.VAL CALCD FROM FRGMNT-DISTRBS	
					Jour SJA 8 343	Jun 61	TRANSLATN.*JNE AB17 41 1/61	
					Jour KE 4 40	Jan 61	.TRANSLATN	
Nu	1.4+7		SAC	Expt	Jour JPR 21 617	Aug 60	Leroy. 4.64+ - 0.2 REL TO U235 THERMAL	+
					Conf 58Geneva 16 106	Sep 58	- . REL U-235.SUPERSEDED.	
					Jour CR 247 200	Feb 58	- . SEE JPR 21.	
Nu	2.3+6	1.6+7	FEI	Expt	Book NEJTRONFIZ 241	61	Kuz'Minov. AVG NU AT 3ES.GRPH+TABLE	
					Rept AEC-TR-3944	59	- . AVG NU VS E AT 3 ES	
					Book SPN 177	61	. ENGL TRANSL OF NEJTRONFIZ 241	
Nu	1.6+6		ANL	Expt	Prog WASH-1033 2	Aug 61	Meadows+REL NU THR U235	
Nu		1.5+7	ANL	Revw	Conf 61Vienna 1 29	Aug 61	Smith. CURVE MANY REFS	
Nu	3.6+6	1.5+7	FOA	Expt	Prog BNL-694 3	Oct 61	Conde+NU=1.877+0.17E LST SQ FIT	
Nu	3.6+6	1.5+7	FOA	Expt	Jour NSE 11 397	Dec 61	Conde+ CCW.LIQ SCINT. REL CF-252 SP	+
					Conf 65Salzburg 2 57	Mar 65	- + SEE NSE 11 397	
	3.6+6	1.5+7			Data EXFOR20072.002	Sep 71	2PTS.PROMPT	
Nu	Fiss		REH	Theo	Rept IA-757	Jul 62	Sieger+ CALC FRM CHAIN-Y,CFD OTH.TBL	

90 Thorium 232

Quantity	Energy (ev) Min	Max	Lab	Type	Documentation Ref Vol Page	Date	Author, Comments	Data
Nu	Fast		FOA	Comp	Rept NP - 16440	Mar 63	ASPLUND - NILSSON. REVIEW. TABLE.	
Nu	1.0+6	1.0+7	AI	Eval	Rept NAA - SR - M - 8904	Aug 63	Alter+ CURVE GIVEN	
Nu	3.5+6	6.5+6	ANL	Expt	Prog WASH - 1048 12	Jun 64	Meadows+ PRMPT REL TO CF252,.5PCT ACC	
Nu	1.4+6	4.0+6	ALD	Expt	Jour NP 66 149	Apr 65	Mather+ PROMPT SC-T LEAST SQ FIT	+
Nu	1.5+6	3.3+6	FEI	Expt	Prog YFI - 5 6	Oct 67	Prokhorova+ TABLE NU - BAR AT 7 ES	+
					Jour YF 7 961	May 68	- + TBL,GRPH.+OTHER EXPTS	
					Rept FEI - 107	Oct 67	.REL MEAS BASED ON THERMAL NU U - 235	
	1.6+6	3.2+6			Prog YFI - 4 11	May 67	.CURVES GIVEN	
	1.5+6	3.2+6			Conf 66Paris 2 67	Oct 66	.PAPER 95.TABLE+CURVES.VDG	
	1.6+6	2.8+6			Prog YFI - 1	65	.TABLE NU AT 4 ES	
	1.5+6	3.3+6			Prog INDC(CCP) - 1	Jan 69	.ENGLISH TRANSL OF YFI - 5 6 8/67	
					Jour SNP 7 579	Nov 68	. ENGL OF YF 7 961	
					Rept LA - TR - 68 - 20	Jul 68	.ENGLISH TRANSL OF FEI - 107	
	1.6+6	3.2+6			Prog INDC - E - 187	67	.ENGLISH TRANSL OF YFI - 4 11 5/67	
	1.5+6	3.3+6			Data EXFOR40132.003	Feb 73	PROMPT NU - BAR AT 7 ES REL U - 235	
Nu	Thrsh	1.5+7	AI	Eval	Jour JNE 22 79	Feb 68	Fillmore.DATA TBL,GRAPH.LEAST SQ FIT	
Nu	1.4+6	4.0+6	FEI	Expt	Jour YF 7 778	Apr 68	Sergachev+ OTHER AVG NU(E),GRAPH	
					Jour SNP 7 475	Oct 68	. ENGL OF YF 7 778	
Nu	Maxwl	1.5+7	HAR	Revw	Conf 70Helsinki 2 195	Jun 70	Colvin.PPR99. REPORT ON DATA STATUS	
Nu	1.5+6	6.0+6	FEI	Theo	Jour AE 29 130	Aug 70	Vorobeva+ RECOMMENDED NU(E) GRAPH	
					Conf 70Helsinki 2 177	Jun 70	.SAME AS AE 29 130 8/70	
	0.0+0	6.0+6		Eval	Prog YFI - 11 13	70	Vorobyeva+ ABST,TBL VALUE FOR 1.7MEV	
					Prog INDC(CCP) - 31	Dec 72	.PAGE 12,ENGLISH OF YFI - 11 13	
	1.5+6	6.0+6		Theo	Jour SJA 29 835	Aug 70	.ENGLISH TRANSL OF AE 29 130 8/70	
Nu		1.5+7	ANL	Eval	Jour NSE 44 345	Jun 71	Davey. PROMPT NEUTS PER FISSION	
Nu	Spont		IAE	Eval	Jour REA 10 637	Dec 72	Manero+ EXTENSIVE SURVEY,TBL,AVG VAL	
	1.4+6	1.5+7			Jour REA 10 637	Dec 72	- + SURVEY,TBLS+GRPHS,RECOMM VAL	
Nu	1.0+6	1.5+7	UK	Eval	Data UKNDL - DFN 930.	Mar 73	. 50 POINTS + FISS N ANGDIST, LAB CS	+
Nu	1.4+6	1.5+7	FOA	Expt	Jour AF 29 33	Nov 65	Conde+ 7 ES.LIQ SCIN.CFD OTHS,TBL+GR	+
					Conf 73Kiev 4 130	May 73	- . SUMMARY OF NUBAR(EN),NO VALUE	
	1.4+6	1.5+7			Data EXFOR20112.002	Sep 71	9PTS.PROMPT.	
Nu	5.0+6	1.7+7	LRL	Expt	Jour UCID - 16514 6	Jun 74	Alvarez+	
Nu	1.4+7		MIF	Theo	Jour IVU 17 7 7	Jul 74	Koldobskij+ NU(A)CALC CFD EXPT.GRAPH	
Nu	1.4+7		GRE	Expt	Rept FRNC - TH - 584	75	Feu Alvim. THESIS.FROM PEAK - MASS,TBL	
Nu	1.0+6	2.0+6	HED	Theo	Abst ANS 21 518	Jun 75	Schenter+ TBL CALC FROM ENDF FP FILE	
Nu	0.0+0	1.5+7	BRC	Eval	Rept CEA - R - 4791	Oct 76	Bois+NUBAR VS EN,CALC CFD EXP,TABLES	
Delayd Neuts	None		CAW	Expt	Jour PR 55 664	Apr 39	Roberts+ PERIOD CA 12.5SEC.CF PAG510	
Delayd Neuts	None		OHO	Expt	Jour PR 76 946	Oct 49	Creveling+ LI - D NS,REL YLDS FOR 5H - L	
Delayd Neuts	+7		WES	Expt	Jour PR 79 3	Jul 50	Sun+ DELAYED NEUTRON YIELDS CFD OTHR	
Delayd Neuts	Fiss		LAS	Expt	Jour NUC 13 10 49	Oct 55	Paxton+	
Delayd Neuts	Fiss		ANL	Expt	Jour NSE 1 174	May 56	Brunson+,EBR NUD=3.09+ - .78 REL U235	
Delayd Neuts	Fast		HAR	Expt	Jour JNE 4 141	Jun 57	Rose+ ZEPHYR. 5 GROUPS.TBL YLD+FRACT	+
Delayd Neuts	Fast		LAS	Expt	Jour PR 107 1044	Aug 57	Keepin+,0.0496+ - 0.0020 N/FISS 6GRPS	
					Jour JNE 6 1	Dec 57	- + SAME DATA AS PR107,1044	
					Rept LA - 1970	Oct 55	- . NEUT YLDS+SPECTR,CURVS+TABLS	
					Conf 55Geneva 4 162	Aug 55	.SUPERSEDED	
Delayd Neuts	None		LAS	Theo	Jour JNE 7 13	Aug 58	Keepin.THEOR DEL NEUT PRECURSRS,YLDS	
					Jour AE 4 250	Mar 58	.SEE ALSO JNE 7,13(1958)	
					Jour SJA 4 339	Mar 58	.TRANSLATION OF AE 4, 250	
Delayd Neuts	2.4+6	1.5+7	FEI	Expt	Jour ZET 35 815	Sep 58	Maksjutenko. YLD OF 5GROUPS AT 3ES	+
					Jour AE 7 474	Nov 59	.YLD AT 3ES REL U235 THERMAL NU	
					Jour JET 8 565	Mar 59	TRANSLATN.*	
					Jour SJA 7 943	Mar 61	.ENGLISH TRANSL OF AE 7 474 11/59	
					Jour JNE 12 141	Jun 60	.SECTION A.ENGL OF AE 7 474 11/59	
Delayd Neuts	Maxwl		OSL	Expt	Conf 58Geneva 15 373	Sep 58	Pappas+.PPR583,TBL CFD THEORIE	
Delayd Neuts	None		LAS	Expt	Abst BAP 4 31	Jan 59	Fisher+SCINT. NDG.	
Delayd Neuts	1.5+7		RI	Expt	Jour AE 11 539	Dec 61	Shpakov+ T(D,N)SOURCE,BORON COUNTERS	+
					Jour SJA 11 1190	May 62	TRANSLATN.*	
Delayd Neuts	2.0+6		LAS	Revw	Jour NUC 20 8 150	Aug 62	Keepin.	
Delayd Neuts	1.3+6	1.7+6	ANL	Expt	Prog WASH - 1041 4	Oct 62	COX.YLD INCREASES NEAR THRESHOLD	
Delayd Neuts	1.6+6	7.8+6	FEI	Expt	Jour YF 4 526	Aug 66	Maksjutenko. YIELD AT 4ES,TABLE,CURV	+
					Jour YF 5 529	Mar 67	.TABLE,CONTINUATION OF YF 4 526 8/66	
					Conf 66Paris 2 45	Oct 66	.SIMILAR TO YF 4 526 8/66	
					Rept FEI - 26	65	.SAME TEXT AS YF 4 526 8/66	
					Jour SNP 5 375	Sep 67	.ENGLISH-TRANSL-OF-YF 5 529 3/67	
					Jour SNP 4 374	Mar 67	.ENGLISH TRANSL OF YF 4 526 8/66	
					Rept LA - TR - 66 - 34	66	.ENGLISH-TRANSL-OF-FEI - 26	
Delayd Neuts		+7	HFA	Revw	Conf 67Vienna 23	Apr 67	Yiftah+ TBL OF YLD+HL,REACTR DYNAMIC	

90 Thorium 232

Quantity	Energy (ev) Min	Max	Lab	Type	Documentation Ref Vol Page	Date	Author, Comments	Data
Delayd Neuts	1.4+7		MNZ	Expt Conf	67Vienna 147	Apr 67	Herrmann+,ABS NEUT YLD REL U235(THR)	
Delayd Neuts	Fiss	1.4+7	SOR	Expt Conf	67Vienna 115	Apr 67	Amiel+ DEL-N PRECURSORS,TBL=XPT+COMP	
				Rept	IA- 1190 95	Jul 69	- + NEW INFORMATION	
Delayd Neuts	Fiss		MNZ	Theo Jour	AF 36 453	Nov 67	Patzelt+.FROM DERIVED N-EMISS PROB.	
Delayd Neuts	1.4+7		CCP	Comp Jour	YF 7 670	Mar 69	Krisyuk+ DEL NEUT YLD FROM BR+I ISOT	
				Jour	SNP 9 3 387	Sep 69	TRANSLATN.*	
Delayd Neuts	3.1+6	1.5+7	LAS	Expt Jour	NSE 36 202	May 69	Masters+ 2ES RELATIVE+ABSOL MEASTS	+
	Thrsh	1.5+7		Conf	69Vienna 647	Jul 69	East+PPR109. YLD TABLE,REVW,SAFGUARD	
	3.1+6	1.5+7		Rept	LA-DC-9403	65	.SUPERSEDED	
	3.1+6	1.5+7		Data	EXFOR12288.	Jun 76	. 2 PTS.	
Delayd Neuts	5.0+6	7.2+6	FEI	Expt Conf	69Vienna 939	Jul 69	Maksjutenko+PPR136. REL GROUP YLDS	
	5.0+6	8.0+6		Conf	67Vienna 191	Apr 67	.REL YLDS FOR 5 GROUPS	
	5.0+6	7.8+6		Jour	YF 5 529	Mar 67	Maksjutenko+ GRPH+TABLE FOR 4 GROUPS	
				Jour	SNP 5 375	Sep 67	. ENGL OF YF 5 529.	
Delayd Neuts	1.4+7		SOR	Expt Prog	IA- 1190 95	Jul 69	Notea.TOTAL+RELAT YIELD FOR 5 GROUPS	+
	1.4+7			Data	EXFOR30238.	May 73	.TOTL DELAYED NEUT YLD FOR 5 GROUPS.	
Delayd Neuts	1.8+7	2.1+7	FEI	Expt Rept	ICD-6 272	70	Maksyutenko+ YLDS 11GROUPS.TBL,GRPHS	
				Rept	FEI-115	Oct 68	Makcyutenko+ REL.YIELD DEL.NEUT.,TBL	
Delayd Neuts	1.2+6	1.8+6	ANL	Expt Prog	ANL-7610 45	Jan 70	COX+ CURVE DELAYED NEUTRON YIELD	
	Thrsh	2.4+6		Prog	ANL-7410 27	Jan 69	COX+ YLD, PERIOD CURVES	
Delayd Neuts	1.4+7		KOS	Expt Prog	INDC(HUN)-1G	Apr 70	.PROG REPORT.NEUT-SPEC,PREL EXPT TBD	
Delayd Neuts			KEN	Expt Jour	RCA 15 109	Apr 71	Brown+ YIELDS+HALFLIVES,FOUR GROUPS.	
Delayd Neuts	1.5+6	1.5+7	HAR	Eval Rept	AERE-R-6993	Feb 72	TOMLINSON TOTAL+GROUP YLDS SPEC TBL	
Delayd Neuts	1.5+7		MNZ	Expt Jour	RCA 17 1 61	Feb 72	Benedict+ REL TO THR FISS OF 235U	
Delayd Neuts	1.0+5	1.5+7	IAE	Eval Jour	REA 10 637	Dec 72	Manero+ SURVEY,AVERAGE YLD,TBL+GRPHS	
Delayd Neuts	Fast		HFA	Expt Jour	NSE 51 52	May 73	Shalev+ HE-3 DET. NEUT ENERGY DISTR	
Delayd Neuts	1.0+5	1.5+7	LAS	Revw Conf	IAEA-169 377	74	Evans. TBL YLD,AT 3 ES+FAST FISSION	
Delayd Neuts	Fiss	1.5+7	SOR	Revw Conf	IAEA-169 2 33	74	Amiel.ALL YLDS,DEL-N SPECS,TBL,GRPHS	
Delayd Neuts	3.5+6	1.5+7	ANL	Eval Rept	ANL-NDM-5	Apr 74	COX. REL YLD, HL, GRPH	
Delayd Neuts	1.1+7	1.7+7	LRL	Expt Prog	UCID-16514 6	Jun 74	Alvarez+	
Delayd Neuts	1.3+6	1.5+7	AI	Eval Jour	NSE 56 37	Jan 75	Tuttle.TBL.GRPH.RVW MEAS.CFD REC VAL	
	2.5-2			Prog	AI-AEC-13025	May 72	Springer+ VALUE=0.0545+-.0021	
Delayd Neuts	1.0+6	2.0+6	HED	Theo Abst	ANS 21 518	Jun 75	Schenter+ TBL CALC FROM ENDF FP FILE	
Delayd Neuts	Fast		CSR	Revw Jour	JE 23 9 345	77	Tinka. REVW GROUP-SPEC,PARAMS.TABLES	
Frag Neuts	1.4+7		TOR	Expt Conf	69Vienna 939	Jul 69	Sharma+PPR142. RADIOCHEM YLD(FRAG-A)	
Spect Fiss n	1.4+7		CCP	Expt Jour	AE 4 337	Apr 58	Zamiatnin+ FISS+EVAP SPECTR FIT DATA	
				Jour	JNE 9 194	Jun 59	TRANSLATN.*	
				Jour	SJA 4 443	58	TRANSLATN.*	
Spect Fiss n	3.0+6	7.0+6	ALD	Expt Jour	NP 65 236	Mar 65	Batchelor+ DEDUCED FROM SNE3 SPEC	
Spect Fiss n	1.4+7		HAR	Eval Jour	NP 71 228	Sep 65	Barnard+ CORRELATED WITH NU BAR	
Spect Fiss n	1.4+7		FEI	Expt Jour	IZV 32 653	Apr 68	Salnikov+ FISSN+OTHER NEUT SPECS,CRV	
				Jour	BAS 32 600	69	.ENGLISH TRANSL OF IZV 32 653 4/68	
Spect Fiss n	1.4+7		ANL	Revw Conf	71Vienna 3	Aug 71	Smith. MEAN-E OF NEUTS,EXPTS CFD,TBL	
Spect Fiss n	1.0+6	1.5+7	UK	Eval Data	UKNDL-DFN 930.	Mar 73	1 RANGES	+
Spect Fiss γ	None		GA	Expt Rept	GA-6445	May 65	Walton.DELAYD G(S) FROM PHOTO FISS	
Spect Fiss γ	1.4+7		KFI	Expt Jour	KFI 18 13	Feb 70	Jeki+ GAM-ANISOTROPY-COEFFICIENT GVN	
Spect Fiss γ	2.5-2	1.4+7	LAS	Theo Prog	LA-6018-PR 25	Jul 75	Stamatelatos+FPG SPEC CALC.	
Fiss Prod γ	None		LAS	Theo Rept	LA-2811	Dec 62	Griffin.BETA+GAMMA DECAY CALUCLATNS	
Fiss Prod γ	None		GA	Expt Jour	PR/B 134 824	May 64	Walton+LINAC.G-FIS.E SPECT.T.1MS-10S	
Fiss Prod γ	Fast		LAS	Expt Jour	PR/B 134 796	May 64	Fisher+GODIVA NS.GS TO6MEV.T=.2TO45S	
Fiss Prod γ	Pile		SOR	Comp Conf	67Vienna 115	Apr 67	Amiel+ GRAPH SPEC,FOR DEL-NEUTS-EXPT	
Fiss Prod γ	1.0+6	2.0+7	SOR	Revw Conf	IAEA-107 57	68	Ben-David.NEW THRS-REACT TBD,GE-DET	
Fiss Prod γ	Pile		MCM	Expt Jour	CJC 46 2911	Sep 68	Clarke+ FAST REACTOR GE-LI DET	
Fiss Prod γ	Pile		HFA	Expt Conf	69Vienna 947	Jul 69	Notea+PPR36. GAM SPECS FOR CHAIN YLD	
Fiss Prod γ	1.4+7		KFI	Expt Jour	KFI 18 13	Feb 70	Jeki+ GAM-ANISOTROPY-COEFFICIENT GVN	
Fiss Prod γ	1.4+7		KOS	Expt Prog	INDC(HUN)-1G	Apr 70	.PROG REPORT. GAM FOR YLD,TB CONTIND	
Fiss Prod γ	-		WIN	Theo Jour	JNE 25 513	Oct 71	James.MEAN EN OF DELAYD GAMS,BETAS.	
Fiss Prod γ	Fast		CEG	Eval Rept	RD/B/M-2669	Jun 73	Tobias. BETA GAMMA DECAY SCH ALL FP	
Fiss Prod γ	None		MIP	Expt Jour	EN 12 691	Dec 73	Brasca+	
Fiss Yield	None		JHU	Expt Jour	PR 55 880	May 39	Dodson+ 2 I ISOTOPES, 1 BROMINE	
Fiss Yield	9.0+6		BRK	Expt Jour	PR 56 205	Jul 39	Langsdorf. EVIDENCE FOR KR88 YIELD.	
Fiss Yield		2.0+6	IRK	Expt Jour	OAWS 151 147	Jun 40	Jentschke.TH-IONIUM FISS.PROD 1,2,7	
Fiss Yield	1.7+7		BRK	Expt Jour	PR 59 212	Jan 41	Segre+ PROD OF PD111,2,RU,AG OBSERVD	
Fiss Yield	Pile		ANL	Expt Rept	AECD-2862	Jun 50	Niday+,RADIOCHEM YLDS 21 FRAGS,REL S	
Fiss Yield	2.5+6		CBR	Expt Jour	PR 83 1076	Sep 51	Titterton.PROBABLE EMISSION OF BE8.	
				Jour	PR 83 673	Aug 51	- .EMISS OF LONG RANGE FRAGM.	
Fiss Yield	2.6+6		ANL	Expt Jour	PR 84 52	Oct 51	Turkevich+RADIOCHEM.YLD CFD OTHE.NUC	
Fiss Yield	+6	+7	CHI	Expt Jour	PR 89 552	Feb 53	Turkevich+ LI-D NEUTS RADIOCHEM MANY	

90 Thorium 232

Quantity	Energy (ev) Min	Max	Lab	Type	Documentation Ref Vol Page	Date	Author, Comments	Data
Fiss Yield	Spont		CHI	Expt Jour	PR 92 907	Nov 53	Wetherill.XE+KR REL YLDS ORE SAMPLES	
Fiss Yield	Fast		ANL	Revw Conf	55Geneva 7 3	Aug 55	Steinberg+ P614.EXPTL YLD TBL+GRPH	
Fiss Yield	7.2+6		CCP	Theo Jour	AE 2 508	Jun 57	Strutinsky.ANG DN,STATIST TH CFD EXP	
				Jour	JNE 7 239	Sep 58	TRANSLATN.*	
				Jour	SJA 2 621	57	TRANSLATN.*	
Fiss Yield	Fiss		MCM	Expt Jour	CJP 35 969	Aug 57	Kennett+ KR+XE ISOT ABSOL+REL YLDS	
				Jour	CJP 35 1401	Dec 57	.CORRECTION	
Fiss Yield		1.9+7	MIT	Expt Jour	PR 108 1274	Dec 57	Alexander+A=82-140MASS YLDS REL SR89	
Fiss Yield	Pile		HAR	Comp Rept	AERE-R-3209	Jan 60	Croall.COMP OF INDP YLDS(NSA 14 1397	
Fiss Yield	1.5+7		RI	Expt Jour	ZET 38 384	Feb 60	Protopopov. GRAPHSYLD VS MASS RATIO	
				Jour	JET 11 279	Aug 60	TRANSLATN.*	
Fiss Yield	1.5+6	1.6+6	ANL	Expt Rept	ANL-6247	Nov 60	Smith+ 1475+1600MEV FRAG MASS DIST	
Fiss Yield	Fast		BNL	Eval Jour	NUC 18 11 201	Nov 60	Katcoff.RECOMMENDED YLD-SET,TBL	
				Jour	NUC 16 4 78	Apr 58	.SUPERSEDED	
Fiss Yield	1.4+7		CCP	Expt Book	NEJTRONFIZ 235	61	Vlasov. GRAPH+TABLE YLD OF MANY NUCL	
				Book	SPN 172	61	+AEC-TR-4665,ENGL OF NEJTRONFIZ 235	
Fiss Yield	1.4+7	1.5+7	KYU	Expt Priv	KATASE	61	Katase. AD OF FF.PPL.TBLS + FIGS GVN	
Fiss Yield	2.8+6		DKE	Theo Jour	PR 122 1224	May 61	Newson.MASS DIST ASYMMETRIC+SYMMETR	
Fiss Yield	1.4+7		CCP	Jour	NSA 16 297	Jan 62	AEC-TR-4665 USSR	
Fiss Yield	Pile		IOW	Expt Rept	IS- 558	63	Crook+ RADCHEM YLD,9 NUCL REL BA-140	
Fiss Yield	Pile		TRM	Expt Jour	JIN 25 465	May 63	Iyer+ RADIOCHEM YLDS 30NUCS REL U235	
Fiss Yield	3.0+6	1.5+7	ARK	Expt Jour	PR/B 133 874	Feb 64	Broom.2ES,RADCHEM YLDS REL MO99,TBL	
				Abst	DA 24 5476	Jun 64	- .	
Fiss Yield	Fiss	9.0+6	CER	Theo Jour	NP 58 177	Sep 64	Faissner+ ASSYMETRIC,CLUSTER MOD.2ES	
				Jour	PL 2 212	Oct 62	- + SUPERSEDED	
Fiss Yield	1.5+7		DUR	Expt Jour	RCA 3 80	Oct 64	Lyle+RADIOCHEM YIELD.14NUCL.E=14.7MV	
Fiss Yield	1.4+7		TRM	Comp Rept	AEET-209	65	Rangarajan+ YLDS+PRODUCTN RATIO,TBLS	
	Fiss			Rept	AEET-209	65	- + YLDS+PRODUCTN RATIO,TBLS	
Fiss Yield	1.4+7		CCP	Expt Jour	RAK 7 96	Jan 65	BR86,87,88,89-90 I136,137,138 YIELDS	
				Jour	SRA 7 94	Feb 65	. ENGL OF RAK 7 96	
Fiss Yield	9.1+6	1.8+7	LAS	ExTh Jour	PR/B 137 826	Feb 65	Ford+YLDS FOR4-5 NUCLEI,CFD STATSTCL	
	5.1+6	1.5+7		Jour	PR/B 137 817	Feb 65	Leachman+REL ANG DIS FIS-FRAG.CF OM	
Fiss Yield	Pile		WUR	Expt Conf	65Salzburg 415	Mar 65	Wyttenbach. YLD OF 10 ISOTOPES, TBLS	+
				Rept	EIR- 77	Feb 65	- . 6 FISS PROD YLDS	
				Jour	RCA 3 118	Nov 64	- . EQUIVALENT TO EIR-77	
Fiss Yield	1.5+7		ARK	Expt Jour	PR 151 960	Nov 66	Ganapathy+YLD 5.3H ISOM OF MO103=.03	
Fiss Yield	1.5+7		ARK	Expt Jour	JIN 28 3071	May 67	Ganapathy+ MO YIELD	
Fiss Yield	Pile		ISP	Expt Jour	JIN 29 1189	Sep 67	Bresesti+ RADCHEM,GE-LI,YLD OF 9NUCL	
Fiss Yield	1.3+6	5.6+6	FEI	Expt Prog	YFI-5 8	Oct 67	Sergachev+ CURVE MASS AND E SPECTRA	+
				Prog	INDC(CCP)-1	Jan 69	.ENGLISH TRANSL OF YFI-5 8 10/67	
	1.4+6	5.6+6		Jour	SNP 7 475	Oct 68	.ENGL OF YF 7 4 778	
				Jour	YF 7 778	Apr 68	Sergachev+ GRAPHS YLD(FRAG-A,NEUT-E)	
				Rept	FEI-109	67	.YIELD(MASS,NEUT E).GRAPHS	
	1.6+6	5.8+6		Data	EXFOR40173.	Nov 73	.6 SUBENT FOR 6 ES,EACH 42 LINES	
Fiss Yield	1.0+6	2.0+7	SOR	Revw Conf	IAEA-107 57	68	Ben-David.NEW THRS-REACT TBD,GE-DET	
Fiss Yield	Fast		HAR	Eval Rept	AERE-R-5086	Jan 68	Croall.RECOMMENDED CUMULAT YLDS,TBL	
Fiss Yield	1.4+7		RI	ExTh Conf	68Riga	Jan 68	Adamov+ ABST,LONG-RANGE PARTICLES YL	
Fiss Yield	1.5+7		ARK	Expt Jour	JIN 30 345	Feb 68	Ganapathy+YLD FOR 7 NUCLIDES	
				Abst	DA/B 29 319	Jul 68	- .RADIOCHEM 10YLDS A=99-115	
Fiss Yield	2.5+6	1.4+7	KFI	Expt Jour	YF 8 443	Sep 68	Nagy+DOUB/TERN FISS GVN,LONG-R-ALPHA	
	-2	1.4+7		Jour	KFI 15 85	Apr 67	- + TERN,ALFA PROBABILITY,TBL	
	2.5+6	1.4+7		Jour	SNP 8 257	Mar 69	TRANSLATN.*	
Fiss Yield	Fast		MCM	Expt Jour	CJC 46 2911	Sep 68	Clarke+ FAST SPECTRUM MASS SP+GE-LI	
Fiss Yield	1.5+7		ARK	Expt Jour	JIN 30 1145	Jun 68	Thein+ RARE EARTH REGION	
				Abst	DA/B 29 1809	Nov 68	- .CUMUL.YLDS.A BETWEEN 141,157.	
Fiss Yield	Maxwl		MIT	Expt Prog	MIT-905-133 17	Dec 68	. TABLE YIELDS A=85 TO 149.CFD OTHRS	
Fiss Yield	2.9+6		IFJ	Expt Jour	APP 35 67	Jan 69	Benisz.TERNARY TOT K-E,E-MASS CORREL	
				Jour	APP 32 485	Sep 67	*EXPTL DETAILS+CALCS	
				Rept	INP-547	Jun 67	*	
Fiss Yield	1.4+6	5.3+6	FEI	Expt Jour	YF 9 296	Feb 69	Vorobeva+ GRPHS YLD(FRAG-A,2NEUT-ES)	
				Jour	SNP 9 175	Aug 69	TRANSLATN.*	
Fiss Yield	None		MCM	Theo Jour	CJP 47 525	Feb 69	Thind+,CALCTD CUMULATIVE YIELDS,CURV	
Fiss Yield	1.5+7		ARK	Expt Jour	JIN 31 591	Mar 69	RAO+,INDEP YLD OF 124,126SB+136CS	
Fiss Yield	1.0+6	1.0+6	HAR	Theo Rept	AERE-R-6056	Mar 69	Crouch.CALC FRACT IND YLDS.TBL.	
Fiss Yield	1.4+7		CCP	Expt Jour	YF 9 732	Apr 69	Adamov+ LONG RANGE PARTICLE YLD GIVN	
				Jour	SNP 9 424	Oct 69	TRANSLATN.*NO4	
Fiss Yield	1.5+7		LRL	Expt Jour	PR 182 1251	Jun 69	Nethaway+ MASS YLD DIST=GAUSSIAN	
Fiss Yield	Maxwl		EDG	Revw Conf	69Vienna 83	Jul 69	Feather.PPR201. SURVEY,TERNARY-YIELD	

90 Thorium 232

Quantity	Energy (ev) Min	Max	Lab	Type	Documentation Ref Vol Page	Date	Author, Comments	Data
Fiss Yield	Maxwl	1.6+7	FEI	Expt	Conf 69Vienna 923	Jul 69	Vorob'Eva+PPR133. FRAG YLD+E(NEUT-E)	
Fiss Yield	1.4+7		FTI	Expt	Conf 69Vienna 900	Jul 69	Adamov+PPR146.LONG-RANGE-YLD VAL GVN	
					Jour YF 9 732	Apr 69	- + LONG RANGE PARTICLE YLD GIVN	
					Jour SNP 9 424	Oct 69	. ENGL OF YF 9 732	
Fiss Yield	Pile		HFA	Expt	Conf 69Vienna 947	Jul 69	Notea+PPR36. CHAIN YLDS VS TIME,GELI	
Fiss Yield	3.0+6	1.5+7	KEN	Expt	Jour RCA 12 43	Jul 69	Lyle+,FINE STRUCT YLD MASS 131-135	
					Jour RCA 9 90	Jul 68	- + 2ES,RADCHEM YLDS,9 NUCL REL 9	
Fiss Yield	+5	+7	OSL	Revw	Conf 69Vienna 669	Jul 69	Pappas+PPR206.REVW,INITIAL MASS DIST	
Fiss Yield	1.4+7		IFJ	Expt	Jour APP 36 707	Oct 69	Benisz+ TERNARY FISSION	
Fiss Yield	1.7+6	3.0+6	FEI	Expt	Rept FEI-195	70	Maksyutenko. 5 ES, TABLE	
Fiss Yield	7.0+6	1.9+7	CCP	Revw	Jour IZV 34 438	Feb 70	Soloveva.ALF-EMISSN PROBABILITY,GRPH	
					Jour BAS 34 378	Jan 71	.ENGL TRANSL OF IZV 34 438	
Fiss Yield	1.4+7		TOR	Expt	Jour CJC 48 641	Feb 70	Gevaert+ RADIOCHEM YLDS 10 FRAGMENTS	
					Abst DA/B 32 3838	Jan 72	- . RADIOCHEM. A=99-125 YLDS	
					Conf 69Vienna 939	Jul 69	Sharma+ RADIOCHEMICAL YLD(A)	
Fiss Yield	None		BLA	Expt	Prog INDC(BUL)-1G	Apr 70	Kashukeev+ PRELIMIN EXPT,NDG	
Fiss Yield	Pile		KTO	Expt	Prog EANDC(J)19L37	Aug 70	Kobayashi+.5 NUCLIDES REL TO BA-140	+
	Fast				Data EXFOR20272.003	Jun 74	5PTS.	
Fiss Yield	1.4+7		CCP	Theo	Jour YF 12 471	Sep 70	Bogdanov+ TERN FISSN,EXPT+THEORY CFD	
					Jour SNP 12 257	Mar 71	TRANSLATN.*	
Fiss Yield	8.0+6	1.4+7	ANL	Eval	Rept ANL-7749	Dec 70	Flynn+ ALSO FISS SPEC NEUTS TBL+CURV	
Fiss Yield	1.5+7		ARK	Expt	Jour JIN 33 651	Mar 71	Swindle+ YLD FOR 5 MASS CH. A=73-81	
	3.0+6				Jour JIN 333 643	Nov 71	- + MASS DISTR A=77-93/141-156	
	2.9+6				Prog ORO-3235-14	Jul 70	- +,A=73-81,141-156YLDS,TBC,NDG	
Fiss Yield	None		BAS	Theo	Jour PL/B 34 264	Mar 71	Pauli+ FRAG MASS RATIO AS STRUTINSKY	
Fiss Yield	1.9+6	4.8+6	TUE	Expt	Jour NP/A 171 631	Aug 71	Holubarsch+ MASS YIELD.FINE STRUCT.	
	4.8+6	1.4+7			Jour ZP 240 403	Dec 70	Pfeiffer. PRIMARY MASS DISTRIBUTION	
	1.9+6	4.8+6			Conf 69Vienna 944	Jul 69	Goennewein+PPR25.YLD(A,NEUT+FRAG E)	
	None			Revw	Conf 69Bochum 175	Jul 69	- + CLUSTER MODEL,YLD GRAPH	
	1.5+7			Expt	Jour ZP 207 209	Oct 67	Pfeiffer+,CURVE OF MASS-DISTRIBUTION	
Fiss Yield	Fast		GA	Eval	Rept GA-12071	Sep 71	Mathews+. RECOMMENDED VALUES	
Fiss Yield	+0	1.5+7	MNZ	Expt	Jour JIN 33 11 3649	Nov 71	Denschlag+ INDEP YLD 133,134,135I	
	1.4+7				Conf 71Canterby 51	Sep 71	Qaim+ DIRECT YLD I-133-135,XE135,TBL	
	Fast				Conf 71Canterby 51	Sep 71	- + DIRECT YLD I-133,134,135,TABL	
Fiss Yield	1.5+7		ARK	Expt	Jour PR/C 5 171	Jan 72	Rao. INDEP YLDS 7FRAGS+CHAIN YLDS	
					Abst DA/B 34 1934	Nov 73	RAO.INDEP YLDS 13 FRAGS+CHAIN YLDS	
Fiss Yield	Fiss		GEV	Eval	Rept NEDO-12154	Jan 72	Meek+TABULATED RECOMMENDED YIELDS	
Fiss Yield	1.5+7		ARK	Expt	Jour JIN 34 8 2405	Aug 72	RAO. ISOM YLD RATIO 115CD	
Fiss Yield	Maxwl	1.5+7	LRL	Comp	Rept UCRL-51458	73	Nethaway+.ALSO FISS SPEC. 111 FRAGS.	
Fiss Yield	4.5+6	1.4+7	VLD	Expt	Jour ARS 69 71	Jan 73	.SAME AS 70BARCELNA 2 489 7/70	
					Conf 70Barcelna 489	Jul 70	Casanova+ MASS DISTRIBUTION,GRAPH	
Fiss Yield	Fast		SGA	Eval	Conf 73Paris 1 505	Mar 73	Lammer+ EVAL DISCUSSN,TBL ALL A YLDS	
Fiss Yield	1.5+7		ARK	Expt	Jour JIN 35 1443	May 73	RAO+ INDEP FISS YLDS 117IN+I-ISOTES	
Fiss Yield	1.5+6	1.8+7	KUR	Expt	Prog YFI-16 19B	Jun 73	Dubrovina+ 7FRAG REL SR89, AT 9 ES	+
					Jour YF 17 470	Mar 73	- + REL PEAK/VALLEY YLDS,TBL	
					Jour SNP 17 240	Sep 73	.ENGLISH OF YF 17 470, GRAPH AT 3 ES	
	1.5+6	1.8+7			Data EXFOR40193.	Mar 74	.9 SUBENT FOR 9 ES	
Fiss Yield	1.5+7		ARK	Expt	Jour JIN 35 9 3075	Sep 73	Battles+ YLD OF 66,67,72,73,77 CHAIN	
Fiss Yield	1.4+7		GRE	Expt	Diss FRNC-TH-470	Sep 73	Chauvin.CHEMICAL METHODS (98PAGES)	
					Jour NP/A 189 556	Jul 72	Bocquet+ON-LINE ISOT SEPAR.INDEP,CUM	
					Conf 71Canterby 13	Sep 71	.GE(LI) G-SPECTRA ANAL.CUMUL YLD,TBL	
Fiss Yield	1.5+7		IEN	Expt	Prog INDC(SEC)-35	Sep 73	Santos+ P53.AG115 YLD,SHORT NOTE,TBL	
Fiss Yield	Fast	1.4+7	HAR	Revw	Conf IAEA-169 1 353	74	Cuninghame.FAST+N-E DEPEND,TBLS,GRPH	
					Rept AERE-R-7548	Sep 73	.SAME AS 73BOLOGNA, EVALUATIONS CFD	
Fiss Yield	Fast		IAE	Eval	Conf IAEA-169 3 245	74	Lammer. XPTS+DISCUSS,CRITIC EVAL,TBL	
Fiss Yield		7.5+6	VLD	Expt	Jour ARS 70 199	Apr 74	Casanova+,TRACK DET,GRAPHS	
Fiss Yield	Pile		HAR	Eval	Rept AERE-R-7680	May 74	Crouch. FRACTIONAL INDEPENDENT YLD	
					Conf 73Paris 1 393	Mar 73	- .EXPTL DATA+EVAL CHAIN YLD,TBL	
					Rept AERE-R-7209	Jan 73	- .37 CHAIN YLDS RECOMMENDED TBL	
Fiss Yield	1.4+7		MIF	Theo	Jour IVU 17 7 7	Jul 74	Koldobskij+ CUM YLDSI135 CFD XPT.TBL	
Fiss Yield	1.4+7		GRE	Expt	Prog NEANDC(E)161U	Aug 74	Blachot+ MASS DISTRIBUTION	
	Fiss				Prog NEANDC(E)161U	Aug 74	- + MASS DISTRIBUTION	
	1.4+7				Jour JRC 7 309	71	- + GE-LI.10 ISOTOPS,TBL,PRELIM	
Fiss Yield	+6	+7	TUE	Expt	Rept ORO-4856-26	75	Holubarsch+ P.591,ABSTRACT.	
Fiss Yield	Fast	1.4+7	HAR	Eval	Rept AERE-R-8152	Jan 76	Crouch. ADJUSTED FISSION YIELD,TABLE	
	1.0+6	1.0+6			Rept AERE-R-7785	Feb 75	- .CHAIN+IND YLDS.TBL.	
					Rept AERE-R-7394	Mar 73	- .CHAIN YLDS.RECOMMENDED.TBL.	

90 Thorium 232

Quantity	Energy (ev) Min	Max	Lab	Type	Documentation Ref Vol Page	Author, Comments Date	Data
Fiss Yield	2.0+6	1.4+7	AUA	Theo	Jour AUJ 29 125	Jun 76 Cook+ 2ES.GAUSSFIT PARAMS VS E.TBLS	
					Rept AAEC/E-386	Mar 76 - + 3 - GAUSS FIT,PARAMS GIVEN	
Fiss Yield	Fast		GA	Expt	Abst ANS 24 458	Nov 76 Buzzelli+TRITIUM FAST FISS YLD.TBL	
Fiss Yield	1.3+6	1.3+7	KUR	Expt	Jour YF 24 1089	Dec 76 Lisin+ YLD 11 FRAGS REL SR89, TBL	
					Jour SNP 24 572	Dec 76 .ENGLISH OF YF 24	
Fiss Yield	1.4+7		TIL	Expt	Rept YK - 27 42	77 Petrzhak+ YLD XE - 131,132,134,136,TBL	
Frag Spectra	4.5+7	9.0+7	BRK	Expt	Jour PR 76 1112	Oct 49 Jungerman+ PROMPT NS TAKE SURPLUS E	
Frag Spectra	1.4+7		LAS	Expt	Jour PR 94 640	May 54 Brolley+ FRAG ANGULAR DISTRIBUTION	
Frag Spectra	1.4+6	2.0+7	LAS	Expt	Jour PR 103 1292	Sep 56 Henkel+FRAG AND ANISOTROPY 0/90 CRV	
Frag Spectra	1.6+6		LAS	Theo	Jour PR 103 1296	Sep 56 Wilets+FRAG ANG DIST BOHR TH CFDXPT	
Frag Spectra	+6		LAS	Revw	Conf 58Geneva 15 344	Sep 58 Hemmendinger+ CURVE REL ANGLE	
Frag Spectra	2.0+6	1.8+7	LAS	Theo	Jour PR 116 107	Oct 59 Griffin.ANISOTROPY OF FRAGS BOHR TH	
Frag Spectra	6.0+6	2.0+7	CRC	Expt	Jour CJP 37 1418	Dec 59 Baerg+ PHOTO-FIS FRAG ANG DIST ANISOT	
Frag Spectra	1.5+7		RI	Expt	Jour ZET 38 384	Feb 60 Protopopov. GRAPHS E AND MASS DSTRB	
					Jour JET 11 279	Aug 60 TRANSLATN.*	
Frag Spectra	1.6+6		ATI	Theo	Jour NP 18 346	Aug 60 Hittmair. ANG DISTR CFD PR 103,1292	
Frag Spectra	1.5+6	1.6+6	ANL	Expt	Rept ANL-6247	Nov 60 Smith+ 1475+1600MEV KE DIST	
Frag Spectra	1.4+7	1.5+7	KYU	Expt	Priv KATASE	61 Katase. AD OF FF.PPL.TBLS + FIGS GVN	
Frag Spectra	Pile		FEI	Expt	Jour ZET 42 105	Jan 62 Kuz'Minov. E - SPEC,ANISOTROPY.GRAPHS	
					Jour JET 15 75	Jul 62 . ENGL OF ZET 42 105	
Frag Spectra	-		CCP	Expt	Jour AE 15 320	Oct 63 Kovalenko+.KINETIC E OF FISS FRAGM	
					Jour SJA 15 1039	63 . ENGL OF AE 15 320	
Frag Spectra	1.4+7		FTI	Expt	Jour DOK 152 858	Oct 63 Bochagov+ CURVES,ANGLR DSTR OF FFRGM	
					Jour SPD 8 978	63 .ENGLISH OF DOK 152 858	
Frag Spectra	1.5+6	5.0+6	FEI	Expt	Conf 65Salzburg 611	Mar 65 Kuz'Minov.GRPH MASS - E - SPCT AT A=0,90	
					Rept ANL-TR-611	65 .ENGL.TRANS*	
Frag Spectra	5.4+6	6.9+6	FEI	Expt	Conf 65Salzburg 1 135	Mar 65 Rabotnov+,ANG DIST FOTO FISS FRAGMTS	
					Rept ANL-TRANS-245	65 . ENGL OF 65SALZBURG 1 135	
Frag Spectra	1.2+6	4.0+6	ORL	ExTh	Conf 65Salzburg 63	Mar 65 Lamphere.ANISTRPY OF FRGS,TH CFD XPT	
Frag Spectra	1.7+6	5.3+6	CAT	Expt	Jour NP/A 96 617	Apr 67 Lo Nigro+ ANGULAR DIST OF FRAGS.	+
Frag Spectra	1.3+6	5.6+6	FEI	Expt	Prog YFI-5 8	Oct 67 Sergachev+ CURVE MASS AND E SPECTRA	+
					Prog INDC(CCP)-1	Jan 69 .ENGLISH TRANSL OF YFI-5 8 10/67	
	1.4+6	5.6+6			Jour SNP 7 475	Oct 68 .ENGL OF YF 7 4 778	
					Jour YF 7 778	Apr 68 Sergachev+ KIN - E - SPEC(FRAG - A,NEUT - E)	
					Rept FEI-109	67 .YIELD(FRAG KIN E).GRAPHS	
	1.6+6	5.8+6			Data EXFOR40173.	Nov 73 .6 SUBENT FOR 6 ES,EACH 42 LINES	
Frag Spectra	1.2+6	1.6+6	ANL	Expt	Jour NP/A 118 65	Sep 68 Behkami+ RESIN DET. 3ES. CFD TH.	
Frag Spectra	1.3+6	1.6+6	CAT	Expt	Jour NP/A 118 461	Oct 68 Lo Nigro+,ANG DISTR FRAGM.LEGENDRFIT	+
Frag Spectra	None		SAH	Theo	Conf 68Bombay 2 122	Dec 68 RATNA SARKAR+ EXCIT+KIN E(A),GRAPHS	
Frag Spectra	2.9+6		IFJ	Expt	Jour APP 35 67	Jan 69 Benisz.TERNARY FISS,MASS YLDS,GRAPHS	
					Jour APP 32 485	Sep 67 *EXPTL DETAILS+CALCS	
					Rept INP-547	Jun 67 *	
Frag Spectra	1.4+6		FEI	Expt	Jour YF 9 296	Feb 69 Vorobeva+ E - SPEC DEVIATN,STATMOD	
					Jour SNP 9 175	Aug 69 TRANSLATN.*	
Frag Spectra		1.0+6	COP	Revw	Conf 69Vienna 155	Jul 69 Strutinsky+GRPH ANG ANISOTRPY (E)	
Frag Spectra	Maxwl	1.6+7	FEI	Expt	Conf 69Vienna 923	Jul 69 Vorob'Eva+ PPR133. FRAG YLD+E(NEUT - E)	
Frag Spectra	None		BLA	Expt	Prog INDC(BUL)-1G	Apr 70 Kashukeev+ PRELIMIN EXPT,NDG	
Frag Spectra	9.5+5	2.3+6	FEI	Expt	Jour YFI 11 1164	Jun 70 Ermagambetov+ ANISOTROPY+LEGCOEF,TBL	+
					Rept YFI-10 20	May 71 *	
					Conf 69Vienna 419	Jul 69 *PPR134.ANISOTR,GRAPHS	
	5.0+5	3.0+6		ExTh	Jour AE 23 20	Jul 67 .CHANNEL ANALYSIS,CURVES	
	6.0+5	3.0+6		Expt	Prog YFI-4 8	May 67 .CURVES GIVEN	
	1.2+6	1.6+6		ExTh	Jour YF 5 257	Feb 67 .ANGULAR ANISOTROPY.GRAPH	
	1.6+6				Jour ZEP 5 39	Jan 67 .CURVES GIVEN	
				Expt	Rept FEI-45	66 .ANG DISTRIBUTION CFD THEORY.CURVES	
	9.5+5	2.3+6			Rept INDC(CCP)-15	Dec 71 .ENGLISH TRANSL OF YFI-10 20 5/71	
					Jour SNP 11 646	Dec 70 .ENGLISH TRANSL OF YF 11 1164 6/70	
	1.2+6	1.6+6		ExTh	Jour SNP 5 181	Aug 67 .ENGLISH TRANSL OF YF 4 257 2/67	
	5.0+5	3.0+6			Jour EAF 23 27	Jul 67 . FRENCH TRANSL OF AE 23 20 7/67	
					Jour SJA 23 683	Jul 67 .ENGLISH TRANSL OF AE 23 20 7/67	
	6.0+5	3.0+6		Expt	Prog INDC-E-187	67 .ENGLISH TRANSL OF YFI-4	
	1.6+6				Rept ANL-TRANS-407	Nov 66 .ENGLISH TRANSL OF FEI-45	
	9.5+5	2.3+6			Data EXFOR40014.	Aug 70 LEG - COEFS+ANISOTROPY AT 18 ENERGIES	
Frag Spectra	Thrsh	+6	FEI	Expt	Jour AHP 29 357	Aug 70 Androsenko+ ANGDIST CFD 2-HUMPD-BARR	
Frag Spectra	1.5+6	6.0+6	FEI	Theo	Jour AE 29 130	Aug 70 Vorobeva+ AVG KIN - E(NEUT - E) CFD NU	
					Conf 70Helsinki 2 177	Jun 70 .SAME AS AE 29 130 8/70	
					Jour SJA 29 835	Aug 70 .ENGLISH TRANSL OF AE 29 130 8/70	

90 Thorium 232

Quantity	Energy (ev) Min	Max	Lab	Type	Documentation Ref Vol Page	Author, Comments Date	Data
Frag Spectra	Pile		TRM	Expt	Conf 70Madurai 2 79	Dec 70 Prakash+ KIN-E VS MASS RATIO, GRAPHS	
					Jour JIN 31 1217	May 69 - + KINETIC E OF FRAGMENTS	
					Conf 68Madras § 46	Feb 68 - +.RANGES+E OF FISSFRGMNTS	
Frag Spectra	1.4+7		CCP	Theo	Jour IZV 35 169	Jan 71 Bochagov+ ANALYS,DROP MODL,FRAG KINE	
					Jour BAS 35 152	Jan 71 *ENGL OF IZV 35 169	
Frag Spectra	5.9+5	2.9+6	LAS	Expt	Conf 71Knoxvill 292	Mar 71 Muir+ FRG ANG DIST	+
	5.9+5	2.9+6			Data EXFOR10223.	Sep 75 . 201PTS, DSIGMA AT 2 ANG	
Frag Spectra	5.9+5	2.9+6	LAS	Eval	Rept LA- 4648-MS	Jun 71 Muir. FRAG ANG DIST POWER SERIES FIT	
Frag Spectra	Maxwl	+7	CRC	Theo	Prog INDC(CAN)-9 4	Jul 71 Walker. THR+FAST FISSN,ENERGY-BALANC	
Frag Spectra	1.9+6	4.8+6	TUE	Expt	Jour NP/A 171 631	Aug 71 Holubarsch+ EK VS PRIM MASS+AVERGED	
	4.8+6	1.4+7			Jour ZP 240 403	Dec 70 Pfeiffer. ENERGY + ANG DISTRIBUTION	
	1.9+6	4.8+6			Conf 69Vienna 944	Jul 69 Goennenwein+PPR25.YLD(A,NEUT+FRAG E)	
	None			Theo	Conf 69Bochum 175	Jul 69 - + ANGDIST VS A,CLUSTER-TH	
Frag Spectra	1.4+7		KOS	Expt	Jour NP/A 173 571	Oct 71 Barutcugil+ TRACK DET.SIG(THETAFRAG)	+
	1.4+7				Data EXFOR30117.002	Feb 71 ANG DISTRB OF FISFRAGMNTS AT 21ANGLS	
Frag Spectra	1.6+7		TRM	Expt	Prog BARC-628 94	72 Iyer+ ANGULAR ANISOTROPY OF FRAG,TBL	+
	1.4+7	1.6+7			Conf 70Madurai 2 57	Dec 70 - + ANGDISTR,GRAPH+TABLE,TRACK-DE	
	1.6+7				Data EXFOR30235.	Jul 73 COS.COEF.OF ANG.DIST. OF FIS.FRAGM.	
Frag Spectra	1.3+7	1.5+7	FEI	Expt	Prog YFI-13 4	Oct 72 Shpak+ ANG ANISOTR OF FRAGMTS,TBL	+
					Jour ZEP 15 323	Mar 72 - + ANG ANISOTR AT 11 ES,GRAPH	
					Prog INDC(CCP)-32	Apr 73 .PAGE 4.ENGLISH OF YFI-13 4	
					Jour JET 15 228	Mar 72 . ENGL OF ZEP 15 323	
	1.3+7	1.5+7			Data EXFOR40111.002	Aug 72 ANG DSTRB OF FRGMNTS AT 11ES,COS-FIT	
Frag Spectra	1.2+7	1.8+7	CAT	Expt	Jour NP/A 199 186	Jan 73 Emma+ ANG DIST.FRAG.GLASS DETECTOR	+
Frag Spectra	1.5+6	5.6+6	FEI	Expt	Rept YK- 12 1 3	Jan 73 Sergachev+ DATA TABLES AND CURVES	+
	1.5+6	5.6+6			Data EXFOR40210.	Jun 74 .SPECTR OF FISFRAG AT 2EN,AVER KIN-E	
Frag Spectra	4.5+6	1.4+7	VLD	Expt	Jour ARS 69 71	Jan 73 .SAME AS 70BARCELNA 2 489 7/70	
					Conf 70Barcelna 489	Jul 70 Casanova+ E-DISTRB OF FRAGMENTS,GRPH	
Frag Spectra	7.5+5	1.1+6	FEI	Expt	Jour ZEP 19 355	Mar 74 Androsenko+ ANISOT CFD FIS-SIG,GRAPH	
					Jour JEL 19 199	Mar 74 . ENGL OF ZEP 19 355	
Frag Spectra		7.5+6	VLD	Expt	Jour ARS 70 199	Apr 74 Casanova+,TRACK DET,GRAPHS	
Frag Spectra	Maxwl		AUA	Expt	Prog AAEC/PR-41P 35	75 Boldeman+ NDG.SYSTEMAT ERROR FOUND.	
Frag Spectra	+6	+7	TUE	Expt	Rept ORO-4856-26	75 Holubarsch+ P.591,ABSTR.EKIN-DISTRIB	
Frag Spectra	5.0+6	1.0+7	FOA	Expt	Prog INIS-MF-1634	Jan 75 Conde+ ANGDIST AT 4ES,IN PROGRSS,NDG	
Frag Spectra	Fiss		KOS	Expt	Conf 75Karlsrhe 29	Apr 75 Csikai. CF52-NS.SSTR,W(0)/W(ANG)CURV	
Frag Spectra	5.0+6	1.0+7	UPP	Expt	Conf 75Gothenbg	Jun 75 Nordborg+ABSTR,SCT CHAMBER,MACROFOL	
Frag Spectra	1.2+6	5.0+6	SAC	Expt	Jour PRL 35 1749	Dec 75 Blons+ ANGULAR ANISOTROPY GRPHS	
Frag Charge	Fast		ANL	Eval	Conf 55Geneva 7 3	Aug 55 Steinberg+ P614.CHARGE DISPERSN,GRPH	
Frag Charge		1.9+7	MIT	Expt	Jour PR 108 1274	Dec 57 Alexander+A=82-140 CHARGE DISTRIBUTN	
Frag Charge	3.0+6	1.5+7	ARK	Expt	Jour PR/B 133 874	Feb 64 Broom.CHARGE DISPERSN,A=131-136,TBLS	
Frag Charge	Maxwl		CNA	Theo	Jour PR/B 134 972	Jun 64 Talat+ N,CHARGE DIST IN FISS PRODS.	
				ExTh	Rept CNAEM-12	63 - + TBL AVERAGE CHARGE/NUCLEON	
	Fast		HAR	Theo	Rept AERE-R-6056	Mar 69 Crouch.CALC CHARGE DISPERSION,ZP,TBL	
Frag Charge	1.4+7		OSL	Revw	Conf 69Vienna 669	Jul 69 Pappas+PPR206. REVW OF EXPTS+METHODS	
Frag Charge	1.4+7		MNZ	Expt	Conf 71Canterby 51	Sep 71 Qaim+WIDTH CHG DISPERSION,MASS 135.	
	Pile				Conf 69Vienna 945	Jul 69 Denschlag+PPR26. CHARGE DISPERSION	
Frag Charge	1.5+7		ARK	Expt	Abst DA/B 34 1934	Nov 73 RAO.CHG DIST CFD SEVERAL TH MODELS	
					Jour PR/C 5 171	Jan 72 Rao. CHG DIST CFD SEVERAL TH DIST	
Frag Charge	Fiss		LRL	Comp	Rept UCRL-51640	Jul 74 Nethaway.TBL.AVG E FOR FISS=1.8MEV	
Reson Params	2.3+1		COL	Expt	Prog AECD-3288	Apr 51 Havens+STRENGTH=35B/EV SQ ROUGHLY	
					Rept CUD-90	51 - + SAME AS AECD-3288	
Reson Params	2.2+1	1.3+2	BNL	Expt	Jour PR 95 476	Jul 54 Seidl+	+
	2.2+1	1.3+2			Data EXFOR11671.013	Jun 76 . 7 RES. E0,WN,WT**2/PCS.	
Reson Params	2.2+1	3.1+2	BNL	Expt	Priv PILCHER	Jan 55 Pilcher.	+
	2.2+1	3.1+2			Data EXFOR12290.003	Jun 76 . 16 RES WN	
Reson Params	2.2+1	2.4+1	BNL	Expt	Jour PR 101 1328	Feb 56 Levin+,2 LEVELS WG=30+ -10MV	+
	2.2+1	2.4+1			Data EXFOR12274.003	Jun 76 . 2 RES, WN,WG	
Reson Params	1.0+0		AMS	Expt	Jour PHY 22 1131	Nov 56 Radkevich+ABSTRACT,NDG.GAMMA(N),(G)	
Reson Params	2.2+1	3.5+2	CCP	Expt	Jour AE 1 5 55	Nov 56 Radkevich+. 16 RES, WG, WN. D PLOT	+
					Jour JNE 5 92	Jul 57 TRANSLATN.*	
					Jour SJA 1 5 727	56 TRANSLATN.*	
Reson Params	-.7+0		BNL	Expt	Jour PR 110 692	May 58 Seth+ RWN 0.0055 EV CALC FC	+
	-.7+0				Data EXFOR11788.040	Jun 76 . 1 RES, E0, WN0	
Reson Params	-.4+1		GA	Expt	Abst ANS 4 271	61 Cooper+	+
	-.4+1				Data EXFOR12285.002	Jun 76 . 1 RES WN0, WG.	
Reson Params	8.3+0	1.0+2	ANL	Expt	Jour PL 8 45	Jan 64 Bollinger+P RES P WG LESS THAN0.06EV	+
	8.3+0	1.0+2			Data EXFOR12271.002	Jun 76 . 11 RES E0, WN	

90 Thorium 232

Quantity	Energy (ev) Min	Energy (ev) Max	Lab	Type	Documentation Ref Vol Page	Author, Comments Date	Data
Reson Params	8.2+0	8.7+2	BNL	Expt Abst	BAP 9 20	Jan 64 Palevsky+	+
	8.2+0	8.7+2		Data	EXFOR12270.	Jun 76 . 46 RES. E0,WN,WG.	
Reson Params	6.9+1	4.0+3	COL	Expt Jour	PR/B 134 985	Jun 64 Garg+ MANY LEVELS,WN,SOME WG	+
		2.3+3		Conf	61RPI 91	May 61 Havens. MORE TBD	
	1.1+2	4.0+3		Data	EXFOR12278.	Jun 76 . 220 E0, WN0	
Reson Params	-.5+1	4.0+3	CJD	Comp Rept	INDSWG - 101 25	65 .TBL OF 220RES FROM VARIOUS SOURCES	
Reson Params	-3	+6	TRM	Revw Rept	AEET - 234	65 SHANKAR SINGH.STATUS OF DATA REVIEWD	
Reson Params	-.3+1		JAE	Theo Jour	NST 2 39	Jan 65 Iizumi. E + RWN FROM ABS S + WG	
Reson Params	2.1+1	2.2+2	GA	Expt Jour	PR/B 140 50	Oct 65 Haddad+LINAC.SC - T,WG,WN,11RES.	+
	2.2+1	2.2+2		Data	EXFOR12279.002	Jun 76 . 11 RES E0, WN0, WG	
Reson Params	None		GA	Eval Abst	BAP 11 101	Jan 66 Frohner+LST - SQ ANALYSIS TECH	
Reson Params	8.2+0	8.7+2	HAR	Expt Jour	NP 76 196	Feb 66 Asghar+TBL WN,WG FROM TRNS,CAPT,SCT.	
	1.0+1	4.0+2		Rept	AERE - NP/GEN40	Jun 65 - +LI - 6 DET. SCAT EXPT.FOR RES	
	2.2+1	4.6+2		Priv	RAE	64 RAE+ DATA FOR 4RES.	
	2.2+1	3.4+2		Rept	AERE - M - 1223	Mar 63 Uttley+ TBL WG,WT.	
	5.9+1	1.2+2		Rept	NRDC - 138 10	Jan 63 - + 4RES,WG,WT.ALSO P17 AVG VALS	
	3.3+2	1.3+3		Rept	AERE - R - 3929	62 - . TBL AS IN PR/NP2	
	3.0+2	1.3+3		Conf	61Saclay 109	Jul 61 - +45 RES.NDG.AVERAGE WN ONLY.	
Reson Params	2.2+1	6.9+1	BNL	Expt Jour	PR 155 1362	Mar 67 Bhat+ WN,WG FOR 4RES FROM TRANSMISSN	+
Reson Params	-		CCP	Eval Jour	AE 23 6	Jul 67 Kirpitchnikov.FISS - ,N - WIDTH,STRNTH - F	
				Jour	SJA 23 669	Jul 67 TRANSLATN.*	
Reson Params	5.0+5	3.0+6	FEI	ExTh Jour	AE 23 20	Jul 67 Ermagambetov+.,CHANNEL ANALYSIS,CRVS	
				Jour	EAF 23 27	Jul 67 . FRENCH TRANSL OF AE 23 20 7/67	
				Jour	SJA 23 683	Jul 67 .ENGLISH TRANSL OF AE 23 20 7/67	
Reson Params		1.0+6	AUA	Theo Jour	AUJ 20 477	Oct 67 Cook. TBL OF AVG LVL SPACING D,L=0,1	
Reson Params	7.5+1	1.5+6	SUN	Expt Prog	INDC - 282 2	68 Mcmurray+ LVL - ANALYSIS,WORK CONT'D	
Reson Params	8.4+0	6.9+2	ANL	Expt Abst	BAP 13 722	Apr 68 Bollinger+2.FROM SIG TOT.4S,2P RESON	
Reson Params	-.5+1	2.5-2	UPP	Expt Jour	NUK 11 61	May 68 Lundgren. ERES,WN0,SCAT XSECT,G - FACT	+
	-.5+0			Data	EXFOR20006.004	Nov 70 1PNT.WN0.	
Reson Params	+5	+6	KUR	Theo Jour	YF 7 1228	Jun 68 Vorotnikov+ D,XPT CFD DEGEN - FERMIGAS	
	4.0+6	7.0+6		Jour	SNP 5 728	Nov 67 . ENGL OF YF 5 728	
	4.5+6	7.0+6		ExTh Jour	YF 5 728	May 67 Vorotnikov. GRAPH N+GAMMA FISSWIDTH	
	+5	+6		Theo Jour	SNP 7 732	Dec 68 . ENGL OF YF 7 1228	
Reson Params	1.0+3	1.0+5	HAR	Expt Rept	NP - 17644	Jul 68 Moxon.THESIS. AVG D,WG,AND WG/D	
Reson Params		1.0+6	AUA	Theo Rept	AAEC/TM - 467	Sep 68 Musgrove.GRAPH GAMMA - WIDTH(E)	
Reson Params	+2	+6	FEI	Theo Jour	YF 10 542	Sep 69 Gai+ TABLE OF RESON+FAST FISSN WIDTH	
	None			Rept	FEI - 158	Feb 69 GAJ+ FISSN WIDTH,2HUMPED - BARR - CALCUL	
	+2	+6		Jour	SNP 10 311	Mar 70 . ENGL OF YF 10 542	
Reson Params	2.0+5		MUA	Theo Conf	69Roorke 2 129	Dec 69 Chaubey+ D/GAM - WIDTH RATIO, STATMOD	
Reson Params	-.2+3	1.4+3	BET	Eval Rept	WAPD - TM - 971	Dec 70 Steen.G WG WF WN,S AND P WAVE RESON	
Reson Params	None		DUB	Theo Jour	YF 13 240	Feb 71 Malecki+G - WID,THEO CFD EXPT.TBL,GRPH	
				Jour	SNP 13 133	Aug 71 - + ENGL OF YF 13 240.	
Reson Params	5.0+2	4.0+3	SAC	ExTh Conf	71Knoxvill 438	Mar 71 Ribon+.DISCREPANCIES AMONG WN DATA	+
	2.1+1	2.7+3		Conf	70Helsinki 1 571	Jun 70 - .108 EVALUATION PROBLEMS,TABLE	
	8.3+0	3.0+3		Expt Priv	RIBON	Jan 70 - + VALUES FOR COMPILATION.	
	8.4+0	3.0+3		Rept	CEA - N - 1149	Jan 69 . 6EXPTS;3 TOF PATHS,TRANS.	
	8.3+0	3.0+3		Conf	67Bordeaux	Mar 67 - + 300RES.N WIDTH DISTN NOT=P - T	
				Conf	65Antwerp 565	Jul 65 - + ABST. 265 WN,20 WG.	
				Conf	64Paris 2 744	Jul 64 - + ABST. LINAC.	
	5.0+2	6.0+2		Revw Jour	NIM 28 205	Jun 64 Michaudon+(QUOTE) E(N).TRANS,77DEG K	
	2.2+1	6.9+1		Expt Rept	CEA - R - 2228	62 Nifenecker.WG 3.9MEV (7E0),5MEV(4E0)	
	8.3+0	3.0+3		Data	EXFOR20149.	May 73 663PTS.E0,WG,AVG WG,WT,L,G*WN.	
Reson Params	6.2-1	5.0+4	SRL	Expt Conf	71Knoxvill 714	Mar 71 Mccrosson. STAT CALCULATN AVG PARAMS	
Reson Params		3.8+3	HAR	Theo Jour	NP/A 170 309	Jul 71 James.DISTRIB FREE STATIST ANAL WN	
				ExTh Rept	AERE - R - 6633	71 - . DISTRIB - FREE STRUCT ANALYSIS.	
				Prog	AERE - PR/NP17	Dec 70 - + NO MEDT IN RED WN TEST WALD+	
				Revw Conf	70Helsinki 1 267	Jun 70 - .107. REDUCED FISSN - W(E) GRAPH	
Reson Params	+0		KUR	Theo Jour	AE 31 18	Jul 71 Vorotnikov. S+P,FISS - WIDTHS DERIVED	
				Jour	SJA 31 706	Feb 72 . ENGL OF AE 31 18	
Reson Params	2.0+1	2.0+3	LAS	Expt Jour	PRL 27 117	Jul 71 Forman+TOF.G*WN FROM CAPT.GRPH.	+
	3.7+1	2.0+3		Conf	71Knoxvill 735	Mar 71 - +. NUCLEAR SHOT WG+G*WN TABLE	
	6.0+0	2.0+3		Data	EXFOR10250.002	Jan 78 . 66 RES ES WG GVN.	
Reson Params	+1	+4	CCP	Revw Jour	AE 31 595	Dec 71 Sukhoruchkin.ACCURACY G+N - WIDS,GRPH	
				Jour	SJA 31 1380	Jun 72 *ENGL OF AE 31 595	
Reson Params	+0	+3	BOR	Theo Jour	JPRC 33 13	Aug 72 Doan+ TBL 8 VALS GVN	

90 Thorium 232

Quantity	Energy (ev) Min	Max	Lab	Type	Documentation Ref Vol Page	Date	Author, Comments	Data
Reson Params	2.2+1	4.0+3	COL	Expt	Jour PR/C 6 1854	Nov 72	Rahn+WN WG G*WN L=0.1.ALSO P-T DIST	+
	2.2+1	4.4+3			Conf 71Albany 205	Aug 71	Camarada+D,WG GVN.TBP PR.	
	2.0+1	4.0+3			Prog NYO-73-340 3	Dec 70	Rahn+	
	2.2+1	4.0+3			Data EXFOR10274.	Feb 75	240RES,RED N-WID.	
Reson Params	4.0-1	2.5+4	WIN	Eval	Prog EANDC(UK) 151	Aug 73	James+ GENEX EVAL BASED ON ENDF/B	
Reson Params	None		SAC	Eval	Diss FRNC-TH-	Nov 73	Greneche.EVAL FOR REACTOR CALCULATN	
Reson Params	7.0+0	3.6+3	CCP	Theo	Rept YK- 16 121	74	Gorbachev+ TOT+G+N-WIDTHS, TBL	
Reson Params	8.0+0	3.0+3	SAC	Eval	Conf NEANDC(E)163U	Jan 75	Derrien+ENDFB FORMAT MAT 445	
	2.1+1	7.0+1			Conf NEANDC(E)163U	Jan 75	- +EVALUATION OF 4 S-WAVE RES	
Reson Params	1.6+3	3.6+3	SAC	Eval	Conf NEANDC(E)163U	Jan 75	Derrien. SHAPE ANAL OF VARIOUS DATA	
Reson Params	None		WUR	Eval	Conf NEANDC(E)-163U	Jan 75	Ottewitte. AVG G-WID 25-29B	
Reson Params	2.5-2		COL	Theo	Conf 75Wash. 335	Mar 75	Felvinci+MOD ERICSON CALC CFD EXPT.	
Reson Params	2.2+1		ORL	Expt	Prog ERDA-NDC-2 141	May 75	Halperin+EL/WID*G=3.72+-0.11 MILLIEV	
Reson Params	2.0+3	2.4+4	BNL	Expt	Prog ERDA-NDC-3 47	May 76	Greenwood+TH233 SPIN,PI ASSIGNED.TBP	
Reson Params	7.2+5		LAS	Expt	Prog ERDA-NDC-3 93	May 76	Veeser+J AND PI ANAL TBD.NDG	
Reson Params	2.2+1	6.9+1	ANL	Expt	Abst PR 98 223	Apr 55	Bollinger+ NDG 3RESONANCES	+
	2.2+1	2.6+2			Data EXFOR12304.003	Jun 76	. 13 RES E0, WT, WN, WG, PCS	
Reson Params	1.4+6	1.7+6	BRC	Revw	Conf 76Lowell 641	Jul 76	Michaudon.VIB.RES.3 - HUMPED FIS.BAR.	
Reson Params	+7		FEI	Theo	Rept YK- 21 3	Oct 76	Blokhin+ D,WG,WG/D,TBL	
Strnth Fnctn	3.0+0	5.0+2	AMS	Expt	Jour PHY 22 1131	Nov 56	Radkevich+ABSTRACT,NDG	
Strnth Fnctn	1.0+0		BNL	Revw	Jour PHY 22 994	Nov 56	Hughes.DISTRIBUTN OF LEVEL SPACINGS	
Strnth Fnctn	2.2+1	1.4+2	CCP	Expt	Jour AE 1 5 55	Nov 56	Radkevich+. S0=1.06+-0.3	+
					Jour JNE 5 92	Jul 57	TRANSLATN.*	
					Jour SJA 1 5 727	56	TRANSLATN.*	
Strnth Fnctn	+3		BNL	Expt	Jour PRL 1 461	Dec 58	Hughes+ FC 0.8+-0.2	
Strnth Fnctn	3.0+3	5.0+4	HAR	Theo	Jour PPS 82 903	Dec 63	Lynn.S1=2.4+-.36 MULTILVL ANAL TRNSM	
Strnth Fnctn	+1	+3	COL	Expt	Jour PR/B 134 985	Jun 64	Garg+ S0 ONLY	
	2.0+3			Theo	Jour PL 12 240	Oct 64	- .LVL SPACING DIST TH232+U238	
Strnth Fnctn	-3	+6	TRM	Revw	Rept AEET-234	65	SHANKAR SINGH.S-,P-WAVE DERIVED,TBL	
Strnth Fnctn	-		KUR	Theo	Jour NP 68 549	Jul 65	Muradyan+PROB DISTN OF VALUE CFT XPT	
Strnth Fnctn	8.2+0	1.0+5	HAR	Expt	Jour NP 76 196	Feb 66	Asghar+ S0=.8+-.17E-4.S1 FROM 64PARIS	+
	5.0+5	5.0+5			Conf 66Paris 1 165	Oct 66	Uttley.2 ENERGY RNGS.S0,S1 *	
	1.0+3	1.0+5			Conf 64Paris 2 700	Jul 64	- .S0.S1.RADIUS	
	3.0+2	5.0+3			Conf 61Saclay 109	Jul 61	- +,TOF,AVG S0 FOR 13 E-RANGES	
Strnth Fnctn	None		AI	Theo	Rept NAA-SR-M-12538	Oct 67	Gigas.OPTMDL CALC AVG S0,S1,S2	
Strnth Fnctn	1.4+0	2.9+2	ANL	Expt	Jour PR 176 1421	68	Cote+	+
	1.0+2				Jour PL 8 45	Jan 64	Bollinger.P STF .5P.6M.2 10 MINUS4	
	1.4+0	2.9+2			Data EXFOR12280.004	Jun 76	. 1 PT.	
Strnth Fnctn	1.0+3	1.0+5	HAR	Expt	Rept NP- 17644	Jul 68	Moxon.THESIS.MOXON-RAE DET.S+P+DWAVE	
Strnth Fnctn		1.0+6	AUA	Theo	Rept AAEC/TM-467	Sep 68	Musgrove.GRAPH S-0(E), D(E)	
Strnth Fnctn	8.3+0	3.0+3	SAC	Expt	Rept CEA-N-1149	Jan 69	Ribon. TOF,TRANS + SCATTERING.	+
					Conf 65Antwerp 565	Jul 65	- + ABST.PPR166.RES ANAL	
	5.0+2	3.0+3			Data EXFOR20149.	May 73	2PTS.L=0,L=1.	
Strnth Fnctn		1.4+3	BET	Eval	Rept WAPD-TM-971	Dec 70	Steen.50 AND 51 GIVEN FROM N,G	
Strnth Fnctn	2.4+4		MUA	Theo	Jour IJP 46 114	Mar 72	Chaubey+ P-WAVE.FOR A-SYSTEMTIC,GRPH	
Strnth Fnctn	2.2+1	4.0+3	COL	Expt	Jour PR/C 5 1854	Nov 72	Rahn+. S0=0.84+-0.08,S1=0.9 APPROX	+
	2.2+1	4.4+3			Conf 71Albany 205	Aug 71	Camarada+S0 GVN	
		4.0+3			Data EXFOR10274.009	Feb 75	. 4 PTS.	
Strnth Fnctn	None		AUA	Eval	Rept AAEC/E-277	Mar 73	Musgrove.TBLS EXPTL DATA+BEST VALUES	
Strnth Fnctn	+3	+4	BET	Theo	Jour NSE 52 461	Dec 73	Goldsmith.OPTMOD CALC. S1 GIVN.	
Strnth Fnctn	1.0+3	6.0+5	NBS	Expt	Jour PR/C 9 2085	Jan 74	Camarda.LINAC.TRANS. S1 MEASURED.	+
	1.0+3	6.0+5			Data EXFOR10765.013	Nov 78	. 1PT.S1=(1.5+-0.4)	
Strnth Fnctn	8.0+0	3.0+3	SAC	Eval	Conf NEANDC(E)163U	Jan 75	Derrien+S0,S1 FROM RES PARAM	
Strnth Fnctn	1.0+6		BRC	Eval	Conf JAERI-M-5984	Feb 75	Lagrange.COUPLD CHANL MDL.TBL S0,S1	
Strnth Fnctn	None		COL	Revw	Conf 75Wash. 780	Mar 75	Hacken+ TBL AVG WG,STF,NUMBER GWN,WG	
Strnth Fnctn	3.0+3	6.5+3	DKE	ExTh	Jour PL 13 70	Nov 64	Seth+S,P,D STF FRM SIG TOT 3-650KEV	+
	5.0+4	1.5+5			Conf 64Paris 2 916	Jul 64	- +S0,S1,S2 R PRIME/R	
	3.0+3	6.5+3			Data EXFOR11788.022	Jun 76	. 3 PTS.	
Strnth Fnctn	2.0+3		IJI	Expt	Conf 76Lowell 1244	Jul 76	Vertebnyi+ S0 GVN.FROM TOT,SCAT-DATA	
					Conf 75Kiev 3 151	May 75	Vertebnyj+ RES-NEUT FILTRAT.SIG GIVN	
Lvl Density	-		COP	Theo	Jour NP 6 62	Mar 58	Ericson. LVL DENSITY FORM CFD EXP	
Lvl Density	1.4+7		FEI	Expt	Jour IZV 32 653	Apr 68	Salnikov+ A+TEMP GVN,LE COUTEUR EXPT	+
					Prog YFI-4 21	May 67	.DENSITY+NUCLEAR TEMP.TABLE	
					Conf 67Kharkov 173	Feb 67	.ABSTRACT	
					Jour BAS 32 600	69	.ENGLISH TRANSL OF IZV 32 653 4/68	
					Prog INDC-E-187 29	67	.ENGLISH TRANSL OF YFI-4	
	1.4+7				Data EXFOR40332.	Feb 76	TEMP(.005),LVL DENS PARAM(.006)	

90 Thorium 232

Quantity	Energy (ev) Min	Max	Lab	Type	Documentation Ref Vol Page	Date	Author, Comments	Data
Lvl Density	0.0+0	3.0+3	SAC	Expt	Rept CEA – N – 1149	Jan 69	Ribon.	+
		3.0+3			Conf 65Antwerp 565	Jul 65	– + ABST.PPR166.RES ANAL 00640126	
		3.0+3			Data EXFOR20149.065	May 73	1PNT.SP.CUT(0).	
Lvl Density		4.0+2	KUR	Theo	Jour YF 9 303	Feb 69	Vorotnikov.LVL DEN(EXCIT – E),TBL GRPH	
	None				Jour IZV 36 175	Jan 72	– + LVL DENS(EXCIT – E),GRAPH	
		4.0+2			Jour SNP 9 179	Aug 69	TRANSLATN.*	
	None				Jour BAS 36 165	73	. ENGL OF IZV 36 175	
Lvl Density	1.4+7		BAS	Expt	Jour HPA 42 225	Apr 69	Boschung+.NUCL TEMP TOF CFD TH+EXP	
Lvl Density	9.2+6		FEI	Expt	Conf 71Kiev	May 71	Zhuravlev+.TOF,TEMP AND LVL DEN,TBL	
Lvl Density	+6		DUB	Theo	Rept JINR – E4 – 9236	Nov 75	Komov+ AVG LVL – SPAC,SEMIMICRO CFD XP	
(γ,n)	9.0+6	1.6+7	SAC	Expt	Prog NEANDC(E)161U	Aug 74	Bergere+ ALSO (G,2N)	
(γ,n)	None		LRL	Expt	Prog ERDA – NDC – 2 74	May 75	Alvarez+TBC.NDG.	
(γ,n)	5.0+6	2.0+7	CCP	Expt	Rept YK – 23 117	76	Antropov+ SIG(E – GAMMA),GRAPH	
Photo – Fissn	–		KTO	Expt	Jour JPJO 23 440	41	Arakatsu+.SIGS FOR LI(P.G)+F(P,G)	
Photo – Fissn	6.3+6		WES	Expt	Jour PR 59 57	Jan 41	Haxby+ P – F GAMMAS.	
					Jour PR 58 92	40	.SUPERSEDED	
Photo – Fissn	5.2+6	6.1+6	UI	Expt	Jour PR 77 329	Feb 50	Koch+ FISS COUNTS PER ROENTGN / E(G)	
Photo – Fissn		2.2+7	LAS	Expt	Jour PR 81 342	Feb 51	Mcelhinney+ SIGMA REL TO GF(U238)	
Photo – Fissn	1.6+7		MIT	Expt	Jour PR 87 1139	Sep 52	Winhold+ FRAG ANG DIST 5 ANGLES	
Photo – Fissn	1.6+7		MIT	Expt	Jour PR 94 733	May 54	Fairhall+ LINAC FRAG ANGULAR ANISOTR	
Photo – Fissn	1.2+7	2.0+7	ANL	Expt	Jour PR 95 1009	Aug 54	Huizenga+ 3ES RELATIVE FISS YIELDS	
Photo – Fissn		1.9+7	LEB	Expt	Jour ZET 29 274	Sep 55	Lazareva.DELAYED NS FROM FOTOFISSION	
					Jour JET 2 301	Mar 56	TRANSLATN.*	
	5.0+6	2.5+7			Conf 55Moscow 306	Jul 55	Lazareva. N – YILD IN FOTOFIS,CURV+TBL	
					Rept AEC – TR – 2435	56	. P 217. ENGL TRANSL OF 55MOSCOW 306	
Photo – Fissn		1.9+7	LEB	Expt	Jour ZET 29 280	Sep 55	Baluev.NUMBER OF NS PER FOTOFISSION	
					Jour JET 2 106	Jan 56	TRANSLATN.*	
Photo – Fissn	1.5+7		CCP	Expt	Jour SPD 2 106	Jan 56	NEUTRONS FROM FOTOFISSION	
Photo – Fissn	6.0+6	1.9+7	ANL	Expt	Jour PR 104 425	Oct 56	Gindler+,RADIOCHEM BETATRON EXC FNCT	
					Jour PR 104 425	Oct 56	– +RADIOCHEM BETATRON EXC FNCT	
Photo – Fissn	4.5+6	1.0+7	UI	Expt	Jour PR 105 1277	Feb 57	Schmitt+,ACTVTN FN SYM/ASYM FISS	
Photo – Fissn	–		TRM	Revw	Conf 59Calcutta 152	Feb 59	Ramanna. REVW.MASS VS ANGANISOT,GRPH	
Photo – Fissn	6.0+6	2.0+7	CRC	Expt	Jour CJP 37 1418	Dec 59	Baerg+. FRAG ANG DIST ANISOTROPIC	
Photo – Fissn	7.0+6		FEI	Expt	Jour AE 8 457	May 60	Prokhorava+ REL U235,F – 19(P,AG)O – 16	
					Jour SJA 8 390	Jun 61	. ENGL OF AE 8 457	
					Jour KE 4 74	Jan 61	. GERMAN OF AE 8 457	
Photo – Fissn	1.2+7	2.0+7	USP	Expt	Jour PR 126 1098	May 62	Moscati+.DELAYED NEUT YLD.TBL+CURVES	
	2.2+7				Jour PR 126 1098	May 62	– +. DELAYED NEUT YLDS	
Photo – Fissn	7.0+6		ANL	Expt	Jour NP 34 439	Jun 62	Huizenga+ 6.91+7.12MEV GAMMAS.	
	6.1+6	7.0+6			Rept ANL – 5853	Jul 58	Clarke.2 GAMMA ES IONIZATION CHAMBER	
Photo – Fissn	6.6+6		ROM	Expt	Jour NC 25 534	Aug 62	Manfredini+,SIG GVN,EMULSIONS USED	+
					Jour NC 29 463	Jul 63	De Carvalho+ANG.DIST.OF FRAGMENTS	
Photo – Fissn	1.2+7		RIO	Expt	Jour NDF 10 12	63	Ballariny.ANG DIST FIS FRAG,EMULSION	+
					Abst BAP 8 483	62	.ABSTRACT	
Photo – Fissn	5.2+6	9.3+6	FEI	Expt	Prog INDSWG – 120 4	65	Soldatov.A – DSTR FOTOFFRGM, TBP, NDG	
Photo – Fissn		7.8+6	MIT	Expt	Jour PR/B 137 89	Jan 65	Sargent+TOF.SPECT.PROMPT NEUTRONS	
Photo – Fissn	1.5+7		CCP	Expt	Jour AE 20 268	Mar 66	Nikotin+.DELAYED NEUT YIELD,6 GROUPS	
					Jour SJA 20 300	66	. ENGL OF AE 20 268	
Photo – Fissn	7.7+6		ARK	Expt	Prog ORO – 3235 – 18	Jan 67	Meason+,NDG XE MASS YLDS TO BE MEASD	
Photo – Fissn	1.5+7		MNZ	Theo	Jour AF 36 453	Nov 67	Patzelt+.FROM DERIVED N – EMISS PROB.	
Photo – Fissn	8.3+6	1.7+7	CCP	Expt	Jour YF 7 264	Feb 68	Zhagrov+ANISOTR – COEF(G – E),CFD RA – 226	
					Jour SNP 7 2 183	Aug 68	TRANSLATN.*	
Photo – Fissn		8.0+6	IFP	ExTh	Jour ZEP 9 128	Jan 69	Kapitza+SIG ANGDIST CV,2 – HUMP – BARIER	
					Jour JEL 9 2 73	Jan 69	.ENGLISH TRANSL OF ZEP 9 128 1/69	
					Rept ANL – TRANS – 639	69	.ENGLISH TRANSL OF ZEP 9 128 1/69	
Photo – Fissn	–		CCP	Theo	Jour YF 9 535	Mar 69	Gejlikman. SIG MAXIMA+QUASISTAT LVLS	
					Jour SNP 9 306	Sep 69	TRANSLATN.*	
Photo – Fissn	5.0+7	9.0+7	FEI	ExTh	Prog YFI – 7 21	Apr 69	Rabotnov+ SIG+YLD+ANGDIST VS E GRPHS	
	+6	+7		Expt	Jour SNP 11 285	Sep 70	.TRANSLATN.*0,NO 3	
					Jour YF 11 508	Mar 70	Rabotnov+ ANGDIST+YLD+SIG,GRPHS+TBLS	
	5.0+7	9.0+7		ExTh	Rept INDC(CCP) – 7U24	Feb 70	TRANSLATN.*	
Photo – Fissn	None		GA	Expt	Prog WASH – 1127 53	Apr 69	Rundquist+ GE(LI),FRAG GAM SPECT,NDG	
Photo – Fissn	5.4+6	9.0+6	MES	Expt	Jour NP/A 127 687	Apr 69	Manfredini+ AT 12 E(G). EMULSION	

90 Thorium 232

Quantity	Energy (ev) Min	Energy (ev) Max	Lab	Type	Documentation Ref Vol Page	Date	Author, Comments	Data
Photo – Fissn	5.0+6	8.0+6	FEI	ExTh Conf	69Vienna 419	Jul 69	Androsenko+ PPR134. XPTL ANGDIST + TH	
				Expt Jour	PL/B 26 4 218	Jan 68	Rabotnov+ ANGDIST FISS FRAG AT THRES	
				Prog	YFI – 4 12	May 67	.CURVES GIVEN	
	5.0+6	9.0+6		ExTh Conf	67Kharkov 216	Feb 67	.ANG DISTRIB,CHANNEL EFFECTS	
	5.4+6	6.9+6		Expt Conf	65Salzburg 1 135	Mar 65	.ANG DISTRIB FOTO FISS FRAGMENTS	
	5.0+6	8.0+6		Prog	INDC – E – 187	67	.ENGLISH TRANSL OF YFI–4 12 5/67	
	5.4+6	6.9+6		Rept	ANL – TRANS – 245	65	.ENGLISH TRANSL OF 65SALZBG	
Photo – Fissn	–		FR	Expt Conf	69Vienna 915	Jul 69	Tamain+ PPR84. FRAGMENT ANGDISTRIBUTN	
Photo – Fissn	Thrsh	5.4+6	IFP	Expt Conf	69Vienna 925	Jul 69	Kapica+ PPR135.SIG+ANGDIST,STRUTINSKY	
Photo – Fissn	2.5+7		TOR	Expt Jour	CJC 48 652	Feb 70	Gevaert+,RADIOCHEM YLDS 9 FRAGMENTS	
	3.3+7			Conf	69Vienna 939	Jul 69	Sharma+ YIELD+NU VS FRAG MASS	
Photo – Fissn	2.8+7		DEB	Expt Jour	AHP 28 169	Mar 70	Medveczky+ TBL=TERN+BINARY FISSN CFD	
		2.8+7		Conf	69Vienna 897	Jul 69	– +PPR95.SYMMETRIC TERN FISSN	
Photo – Fissn	2.0+8	9.0+8	LND	Expt Jour	NP/A 158 433	Dec 70	Methasiri.GLASS DET.RESON AT 350MEV	
Photo – Fissn	Thrsh	Up	ITY	Expt Jour	NC/A 4 2 421	Jul 71	Manfredini+ ANGDIST FISS FRAG	
Photo – Fissn	None		BLA	Expt Prog	INDC(SEC) – 18	Aug 71	Kashukeev+ PG21.FRAG MEAN–E DIST,TBL	
Photo – Fissn	5.6+6	8.5+6	IFP	Expt Jour	ZET 61 1284	Oct 71	Ignatyuk+ SIG,FRAG ANGDIST,TBL,GRPHS	
				Jour	JET 34 684	Apr 72	*ENGL OF ZET 61 1284	
Photo – Fissn	5.0+6	8.3+6	CRC	Expt Jour	NP/A 179 333	Jan 72	Khan+(N,G) – SOURCE,GRPH ABSOL SIG	
	5.0+6	9.0+6		Jour	IZV 34 1627	Aug 70	.SAME EXP+RES.AS NP/A179,333	
				Jour	BAS 34 1445	Aug 71	.ENGL OF IZV 34 1627	
Photo – Fissn	5.4+6	9.0+6	IEA	Expt Jour	NP/A 186 110	May 72	Mafra+ MONOENERGET GAMS,SIG,TBL,GRPH	
				Rept	IEA – 324	Jan 74	– + 12 CAPT–GAMS,TBL,CFD OTH GRPH	
				Jour	AAB 43 57	Dec 71	*	
				Rept	INDC(SEC) – 18	Aug 71	* PG 16.SHORT NOTE,NDG	
				Rept	INDC – 6 15	Jun 70	*	
				Rept	IEA – 211	May 70	EQUIVALENT*	
				Rept	INDC(BZL) – 2	May 69	*EXPT DESCRIBED,NDG	
Photo – Fissn	3.0+8	6.0+9	LND	Expt Rept	INIS – MF – 427	Jun 72	Schroeder.PPR23.3,ABST,MASS YLDS,NDG	
	3.0+8	1.1+9		Jour	NP/A 143 449	Mar 70	Schroder+ MASS–YIELD DIST. TH MODEL.	
	6.1+6			Jour	NP 70 209	Aug 65	Albertsson+FRAG.ANGULAR DISTRIBUTION	
Photo – Fissn		1.5+7	IAE	Eval Jour	REA 10 637	Dec 72	Manero+ DELAYED NEUTRON YIELD,TBL	
Photo – Fissn	9.0+6	1.6+7	SAC	Expt Jour	NP 199 45	Jan 73	Veyssiere+ MONOCHROMAT.NEW ANAL TECH	
Photo – Fissn	5.0+6	8.0+6	IOW	Expt Jour	NP/A 206 593	May 73	Yester+ COMPTON GS,SIG FROM YLD,TBL	
				Abst	DA/B 33 4955	Apr 73	– . STRUCTURE SEEN. NO DATA GVN	
				Rept	IS – T – 543	Nov 72	– .STRUCTURE SEEN.SIG MEASD.	
Photo – Fissn		6.0+6	IRT	Expt Conf	73Rochestr 2 501	Aug 73	Gozani. ABST,DEL+PROMPT–N YLD/FISYLD	
	5.3+6	8.0+6		Conf	73Pacif.Gr 1 649	Mar 73	– + PROMPT,DELAY N–YLDS,GRAPHS	
	4.5+6	1.5+7		Rept	GULF – RT – 10538	Feb 71	Bramblett+ CURVS SIG,PROMPT,DELAY NU	
Photo – Fissn	8.0+6	1.2+7	LAS	Expt Conf	73Rochestr 1 431	Aug 73	Caldwell+ PROMPT+DELAYED–N YLDS,TBLS	
				Conf	73Pacif.Gr 1 651	Mar 73	– + PROMPT,DELAY NS,GN/GF,TBL	
				Rept	LA – UR – 73 – 968	73	– +.PROMPT AND DELAYD NEUT YLD	
Photo – Fissn	None		CAN	Expt Jour	RRL 15 335	Nov 73	Parsons+ YIELDS BY GAM–SPECTROSC,NDG	
Photo – Fissn	6.0+6	9.0+6	IEA	Expt Jour	NP/A 236 1	Dec 74	Mafra+ CFD SIG(G,N),GRAPH	
Photo – Fissn	5.0+6	1.2+7	TIL	Expt Rept	YK – 19 42	75	Ivanov+ YIELD OF FRAGS,CFD,GRAPH+TBL	
				Rept	INDC(CCP) – 65	Dec 74	.P10.ENGL ABSTR OF YK–19	
Photo – Fissn	None		BSP	Theo Jour	NP/A 256 271	Jan 75	Bhandari+ 3–HUMPED BARRIER	
Photo – Fissn	6.4+6	8.1+6	LAS	Expt Jour	NSE 56 179	Feb 75	Caldwell+ TBL,GRPH NU PROMPT+DELAYED	
Photo – Fissn	5.2+6	1.8+7	LAS	Expt Abst	BAP 20 582	Apr 75	Dowdy+ ENERGY DEP NUBAR + WN/WF	
Photo – Fissn	5.0+6	1.2+7	CCP	Expt Rept	YK – 19 42	May 75	Ivanov+ FISS FRAG YLD,SIG,TBL,GRAPHS	
	5.0+5	1.2+7		Jour	AE 36 404	May 74	– + INTEG YLD/INTG U238–YLD,GRPH	
				Jour	SJA 36 515	Nov 74	. ENGLISH OF AE 36 404	
Photo – Fissn	+7		BLA	Expt Conf	75Kiev 6 146	Jun 75	Dragnev+ SIG(E–GAMMA),GRAPHS	
	6.4+6	9.0+6		Prog	INDC(SEC) – 42	Dec 74	– + ABST.8CAPT–GAMS,TBL SIG(E)	
Photo – Fissn	3.8+6	5.5+6	IFP	Expt Jour	ZEP 22 225	Aug 75	Zhuchko+ SIG(E),GRPH.DOUBL–HUMP MODL	
				Jour	JEL 22 118	Aug 75	. ENGL OF ZEP 22 225	
Photo – Fissn	5.0+6	8.0+6	UI	Expt Jour	PRL 35 501	Aug 75	Dickey+ GRPHS GF,GN,GF+GN.TBL PARAM	
				Abst	DA/B 36 297	Jul 75	– .G,F CS.NS,G DETECTED.STRUCT	
Photo – Fissn		1.7+7	IJI	Expt Rept	KIYAI – 76 – 40	76	Aleksandrov+ DELAY NS,GROUPS INT+HL	
Photo – Fissn	5.0+6	1.2+7	TIL	Expt Rept	YK – 22 83	76	Ivanov+ SIG TH32/U38 VS EGAM,TBL+FIG	
Photo – Fissn	1.2+7	3.0+7	USP	Expt Prog	INDC(SEC) – 50	Jan 76	Miyao+ P32.VERY BRIEF.DELAY NEUT.NDG	
Photo – Fissn	None		CRC	Expt Abst	BAP 21 776	May 76	Pich+MONOCHROMATIC PHOTONS.NDG	

90 Thorium 233

Quantity	Energy (ev) Min	Energy (ev) Max	Lab	Type	Documentation Ref Vol Page	Date	Author, Comments	Data
Total	1.0+5	2.0+7	TRM	Theo Conf	74Calcutta 70	Nov 74	Garg+ OPTMOD CALC, SIG(E) TABLE	

90 Thorium 233

Quantity	Energy (ev) Min	Max	Lab	Type	Documentation Ref Vol Page	Date	Author, Comments	Data
Elastic	1.0+5	2.0+7	TRM	Theo Conf	74Calcutta 70	Nov 74	Garg+ OPTMOD CALC.SHAP,COMP SIG.TABL	
Absorption	2.5-2		IJI	Eval Conf	73Kiev 1 197	May 73	Fedorova. SIG 2200M/S=1450+ - 100 B	
Res Int Abs	5.0-1		ORL	Expt Jour	JNE 11 95	Feb 60	Johnston+ SIG REL AU197 + THR ACT	+
	5.0-1			Data	EXFOR11739.005	Jun 76	. 1 PT.	
(n,γ)	Pile		ORL	Eval Jour	NSE 6 100	Aug 59	Stoughton+,BEST VALUE .025EV=1450B	
(n,γ)	Maxwl		ORL	Expt Jour	JNE 11 95	Feb 60	Johnston+ SIGMA GVN	+
	Maxwl			Data	EXFOR11739.004	Jun 76	. 1 PT.	
(n,γ)	1.0+5	2.0+7	TRM	Theo Conf	74Calcutta 70	Nov 74	Garg+ OPTMOD CALC. SIG(E) TABLE	
(n,γ)	Pile		ANL	Expt Prog	ANL-4165	Jun 48	Hyde+	+
	Pile			Data	EXFOR12291.002	Jun 76	. 1 PT.	
Res Int Capt	5.0-1	1.0+6	ORL	Eval Jour	NSE 6 100	Aug 59	Stoughton+ BEST VALUE 400+ - 100B	
Fission	1.0+6	1.6+6	WES	Expt Jour	PR 75 785	Mar 49	Shoupp+ EXCIT FN FOR FISS THRESHOLD	
Fission	Maxwl		LRL	Expt Prog	WASH-190	Feb 56	Crane+ 15+ -2 B.	
Fission	Maxwl		ANL	Expt Jour	NSE 2 33	Feb 57	Fields+,MTR SIG UPPER LIMIT=20B	
Fission	5.0+5	2.0+6	LAS	Theo Jour	NSE 41 177	Aug 70	Cramer+,SIG FROM(T,P+FISS)+H-F CALC	
Fission	2.5-2		IJI	Eval Conf	73Kiev 1 197	May 73	Fedorova. SIG 2200M/S=15+ -2 B	
Fission	1.0+5	2.0+7	TRM	Theo Conf	74Calcutta 70	Nov 74	Garg+ OPTMOD CALC. SIG(E) TABLE	
Lvl Density	+6		MIL	Theo Jour	EN 15 1 54	Jan 68	Facchini+ LDL PARS FROM LOW EN RES	
Lvl Density	None		MUN	Theo Jour	NP/A 217 269	Dec 73	Dilg+ A,DELTA. BACK SHIFTED FERMIGAS	
Lvl Density	None		COP	Theo Jour	NP/A 222 493	Apr 74	Dossing+COLL ROTAT.SPAC. ACCUR ESTIM	
Lvl Density	None		ROC	Theo Jour	NP/A 223 589	May 74	Huizenga+ EXP CFD MICROSC TH AX SYMM	
Lvl Density	None		COL	Expt Abst	BAP 20 149	Feb 75	Cacuci+LVL DENSITY CAL CFD EXPT.	

90 Thorium 234

Quantity	Energy (ev) Min	Max	Lab	Type	Documentation Ref Vol Page	Date	Author, Comments	Data
Fission	2.2+5	3.0+6	ORL	Expt Rept	ORNL-P-1082	64	Lamphere+FISS CHAMB,ANG ANISOT	
Fission	2.5-2		JUL	Theo Jour	ZP 257 389	Dec 72	Mcminn. 8.29 E-6 B	
Strnth Fnctn	None		AI	Theo Rept	NAA-SR-M-12538	Oct 67	Gigas.OPTMDL CALC AVG SO,S1,S2	

90 Thorium 236

Quantity	Energy (ev) Min	Max	Lab	Type	Documentation Ref Vol Page	Date	Author, Comments	Data
Fission	4.0+5	8.5+5	ORL	Expt Rept	ORNL-P-1082	64	Lamphere+FISS CHAMB.ANG ANISOT	

91 Protactinium 223

Quantity	Energy (ev) Min – Max	Lab	Type	Documentation Ref Vol Page	Date	Author, Comments	Data
Fission	2.5 – 2	JUL	Theo	Jour ZP 257 389	Dec 72	Mcminn. 4.49 E – 4 B	

91 Protactinium 225

Quantity	Energy (ev) Min – Max	Lab	Type	Documentation Ref Vol Page	Date	Author, Comments	Data
Fission	2.5 – 2	JUL	Theo	Jour ZP 257 389	Dec 72	Mcminn. 3.37 E + 1 B	

91 Protactinium 227

Quantity	Energy (ev) Min – Max	Lab	Type	Documentation Ref Vol Page	Date	Author, Comments	Data
Fission	2.5 – 2	JUL	Theo	Jour ZP 257 389	Dec 72	Mcminn. 4.88 E – 1 B	

91 Protactinium 229

Quantity	Energy (ev) Min – Max	Lab	Type	Documentation Ref Vol Page	Date	Author, Comments	Data
(n,p)	Maxwl	IFU	Theo	Rept ICD – 4 20	67	Dadakina+ PENETR COEFF CALC,TABLE	
Fission	2.5 – 2	JUL	Theo	Jour ZP 257 389	Dec 72	Mcminn. 6.67 E – 2 B	

91 Protactinium 230

Quantity	Energy (ev) Min – Max	Lab	Type	Documentation Ref Vol Page	Date	Author, Comments	Data
(n,p)	Maxwl	IFU	Theo	Rept ICD – 4 20	67	Dadakina+ PENETR COEFF CALC,TABLE	
Fission	Maxwl	LRL	Expt	Book ACT.EL	54	Ghiorso+ SIG = 1500 + – 250 B	
				Rept RL – 4 – 14 – 52	46	– + SUPERSEDED	
Fission	Maxwl	TRM	Revw	Conf 66Bombay 1	Feb 66	Ramanna.VALS CFD TH,SIG,BINDING,DEF.	

91 Protactinium 231

Quantity	Energy (ev) Min – Max	Lab	Type	Documentation Ref Vol Page	Date	Author, Comments	Data
Evaluation	1.0 – 3 1.5 + 7	GA	Eval	Rept GA – 7462	Sep 67	Drake+ TOT N2N N3N SIN SEL NF NG SNE	
Evaluation	2.5 – 2 1.0 + 7	KFK	Eval	Rept KFK – 1186	Jul 70	Hinkelmann.RES,STF,N2N,NF,NU,NG,R.I.	
				Conf 70Helsinki 2 721	Jun 70	– . DESCRIPTION.ALL QUANTITY	
Total	1.0 – 2 2.0 + 3	MTR	Expt	Jour NSE 12 243	Feb 62	Simpson+,FC+TRNS CURVE RES PARAMS	+
	1.5 – 2 2.0 + 3			Rept IDO – 16698	Jan 62	– + TABULATED DATA	
	1.5 – 2 2.1 + 3			Data EXFOR12265.	Jun 76	. 1343 PTS, SIG	
Total	4.0 – 2 2.0 + 2	ORL	Expt	Prog ORNL – 3268 47	Jun 62	Patterson+ TRANS.	
Total	2.5 – 2	IJI	Eval	Conf 73Kiev 1 197	May 73	Fedorova. SIG 2200M/S = 211 + – 2 B	
Elastic	+1 +6	GEL	Expt	Prog INDC(SEC) – 26	May 72	Theobald+ NUC EXPLOSION,EXPT PROPOSD	
Absorption	6.2 – 1 1.0 + 7	SRL	Theo	Conf 71Knoxvill 714	Mar 71	Mccrosson. SPECTRUM – AVERAGED SIG	
Absorption	2.5 – 2	IJI	Eval	Conf 73Kiev 1 197	May 73	Fedorova. SIG 2200M/S = 200 + – 5 B	
Res Int Abs	1.0 – 1	MTR	Expt	Jour NSE 12 243	Feb 62	Simpson+ RIA = 1560 + – 55B.BW FIT RES.	+
Res Int Abs	4.0 – 1	RI	Expt	Jour AE 32 2 178	Feb 72	Aleksandrov+ DATA GVN,REL NP237	+
	5.0 – 1			Prog YFI – 12 88	72	– + ABST,ACTIV,SIG GIVEN	
				Prog INDC(CCP) – 30	Sep 72	.PAGE 77,ENGLISH OF YFI – 12 88	
	4.0 – 1			Jour SJA 32 203	Aug 72	.ENGLISH OF AE 32 178 2/72	
	4.0 – 1			Data EXFOR40163.003	May 73	.1 DATA LINE	
(n,γ)	Maxwl	ANL	Expt	Jour PR 90 102	Apr 53	Elson+ ACT HANFORD PILE 293 + – 15PC	+
	Maxwl			Data EXFOR12272.002	Jun 76	. 1 PT.	
(n,γ)	Maxwl	MTR	Expt	Jour PR 101 1053	Feb 56	Smith+ SIG = 200 + – 15B,(REL CO = 37.0B)	+
	Maxwl			Data EXFOR12273.002	Jun 76	. 1 PT.	
(n,γ)	2.5 – 2	MTR	Expt	Jour NSE 12 243	Feb 62	Simpson+ SIG = 200 + – 5B (TOT – SCAT)	+
(n,γ)	Maxwl	AUA	Theo	Jour NSE 31 234	Feb 68	Cook+ STATISTICAL CALC CFD EXPT	
(n,γ)	2.5 – 2	KFK	Eval	Rept KFK – 1186	Jul 70	Hinkelmann. RECOMMENDED 200 B	
(n,γ)	2.5 – 2	RI	Expt	Jour AE 32 2 178	Feb 72	Aleksandrov+ DATA GVN,REL NP237	+
	Maxwl			Prog YFI – 12 88	72	– + ABST,ACTIV,SIG GIVEN	
				Prog INDC(CCP) – 30	Sep 72	.PAGE 77,ENGLISH OF YFI – 12 88	
	2.5 – 2			Jour SJA 32 203	Aug 72	.ENGLISH OF AE 32 178 2/72	
	2.5 – 2			Data EXFOR40163.002	May 73	.1 DATA LINE	
(n,γ)	+1 +6	GEL	Expt	Prog INDC(SEC) – 26	May 72	Theobald+ NUC EXPLOSION,EXPT PROPOSD	
(n,γ)	Maxwl	KTO	Expt	Prog NEANDC(J)36L40	Sep 74	Kobayashi. ACTIV METHOD.201 + – 6 BARNS	+
	2.5 – 2			Data EXFOR20691.003	Nov 76	1PNT.SIGMA.	

91 Protactinium 231

Quantity	Energy (ev) Min	Max	Lab	Type	Documentation Ref Vol Page	Author, Comments Date	Data
(n,γ)	Maxwl		MUN	ExTh	Diss GRYNTAKIS	Mar 76 Gryntakis.,ACT.MEAS.,CALC OF G-FUNCT	+
	None			Theo	Jour RCA 22 128	Mar 75 - +,CALC WESTCOTTS G-FUNCTION	
	Maxwl			Expt	Jour JIN 36 1447	Jul 74 - +,THER CROSS SEC MEASUR.	
	2.5-2			Data	EXFOR20634.002	Jul 76 2PTS.SIGMA.	
(n,γ)	1.0+5	2.0+7	TRM	Theo	Conf 76Ahmedabd 2 17	Dec 76 Garg. ABST,NDG.CALC WITH'FISPRO'CODE	
Res Int Capt	4.7-1	1.0+7	KFK	Eval	Rept KFK-1186	Jul 70 Hinkelmann. INFIN DILUTION RES INTEG	
Res Int Capt	5.5-1		MUN	Expt	Diss GRYNTAKIS	Mar 76 Gryntakis. ACT.MEAS.WITHOUT CD-FILT.	+
					Jour JIN 36 1447	Jul 74 - +ACTIV.EQUIVALENT TO THESIS	
	2.0-1	5.1-1		Data	EXFOR20634.003	Jul 76 2PTS.CAPTURE.	
(n,2n)	8.0+5	1.0+7	KFK	Eval	Rept KFK-1186	Jul 70 Hinkelmann.AVG SIG FOR THR+FAST SPEC	
(n,p)	1.4+7		SAH	Comp	Jour NP 60 273	Nov 64 Chatterjee.MEAN OF EXPT CFD SHELLMOD	
(n,p)	Maxwl		IFU	Theo	Rept ICD-4 20	67 Dadakina+ PENETR COEFF CALC,TABLE	
Fission	+6	+7	COP	Theo	Jour PR 58 864	Nov 40 Bohr. PROB INC ABOV 10MV BY N ESCAPE	
Fission	Pile		ANL	Expt	Book TRANSU.EL.	49 Ghiorso.	+
					Prog CS-3471 2	Apr 46 Seaborg. SIG=0.01+-0.005B	
	Pile			Data	EXFOR12287.002	Jun 76 . 1 PT.	
Fission	4.3+5	3.0+6	LAS	Expt	Rept LA-150	Oct 44 Williams. GRPH 15 PTS.REL U235	
					Rept LA-1714	Aug 54 Barschall+ RENORM LA-150	
	4.3+5	3.0+6		Data	EXFOR12300.002	Jun 76 . 15 PTS.	
Fission	4.5+5		PTN	Revw	Conf 55Geneva 2 155	Aug 55 Wheeler. THEORY CFD EXP	
Fission	3.0-1	1.5+0	HAN	Expt	Rept HW-67219	Oct 60 Leonard+FISSION IN 4 RESONANCES	+
	3.7-1	5.2-1		Data	EXFOR12286.004	Jun 76 . 20 PTS, SIG	
Fission	1.5+5	1.7+6	KUR	Expt	Jour DOK 157 561	Jul 64 Dubrovina+,CURVE SIG VS E,3 MAXIMA	+
					Jour SPD 9 579	Jan 65 TRANSLATN.*ANL-TR-176 7/64	
Fission	-2	+2	HAR	ExTh	Conf 65Salzburg 187	Mar 65 RAE.REVIEW,SOME CALCULATIONS CFD XPT	
Fission	2.5-2	5.7+6	BRK	Revw	Jour NP 81 1	Jun 66 Myers+ TABLE2, FISS BARRIER	
Fission		1.0+6	KUR	Theo	Jour YF 9 538	Mar 69 Vorotnikov. OTHER SIG GRPH,FISS-ANAL	
Fission	2.0+5	1.0+6	KUR	Theo	Jour YF 9 538	Mar 69 Vorotnikov.WF FOR S- AND P-NS,CURVS	
Fission	-		FEI	Theo	Conf 69Vienna 337	Jul 69 Gaj+PPR132. 2HUMPD-BARR-CALC,TBL	
Fission	1.5+6	1.7+6	HAR	Revw	Conf 69Vienna 249	Jul 69 Lynn.TBL DOUBLE HUMPED FISS BAR PARS	
	1.0+5	3.0+6			Rept AERE-R-2505	Dec 71 - .GRPH. 2-HUMP STRUCTURE IN FISS	
	1.5+6	1.7+6			Rept AERE-R-5891	Sep 68 - .STRUCTURE IN FISS.DISCUSSED.ND	
					Conf 68DUBSY 463	Jul 68 - .REV.STRUCT EFFECTS IN FISS.	
Fission	1.5+5	1.4+6	KUR	Expt	Jour YF 10 488	Sep 69 Vorotnikov+ SIG(E) GRAPH, OLD EXPT	
					Jour SNP 10 280	Mar 70 . ENGL OF YF 10 488	
Fission	2.5-2	1.0+7	KFK	Eval	Rept KFK-1186	Jul 70 Hinkelmann.5-GROUP SIG,THR+FAST SPEC	
Fission	1.0+5	3.0+6	LAS	Expt	Conf 71Knoxvill 292	Mar 71 Muir+,0.6NS/M RESOL,15PC ACCURACY	+
	1.0+5	3.0+6		Data	EXFOR10223.002	Dec 74 . 374PTS,SIGMA	
Fission	Maxwl	1.4+7	TRM	Expt	Prog BARC-628 94	72 Iyer+ THR+14MEV VALUES GIVEN	
Fission	+1	+6	GEL	Expt	Prog INDC(SEC)-26	May 72 Theobald+ NUC EXPLOSION,EXPT PROPOSD	
Fission	Thrsh		FOA	Expt	Prog EANDC(OR)115L	Jul 72 Holmberg+, MAKROFOL TECHNIQUE	
Fission	2.5-2		IJI	Eval	Conf 73Kiev 1 197	May 73 Fedorova. SIG 2200M/S=10+-5 B	
Fission	2.1+6	7.6+6	KTO	Expt	Rept KURRI-TR-8	Mar 75 Kobayashi+ VDG IN115 INEL STANDARD	+
	3.6+6	4.9+6			Prog NEANDC(J)36L36	Sep 74 - +.VDG.SIG IN FIG.	
	2.1+6	7.6+6			Data EXFOR20562.002	Dec 75 10PTS.SIGMA.	
Fission	+5	6.3+6	LAS	Theo	Conf 75Wash. 218	Mar 75 Wilhelmy+CALC USING TH232(HE3,TF)	
Fission	1.0+5	3.0+6	JAE	Revw	Conf IAEA-186 3 1	76 Igarasi. REVW AVAIL DATA,GRPH+BIBLIO	
					Rept JAERI-M-6315	Nov 75 - +GRPH. 3 DATA SETS COMPARED.	
Fission	5.0+5	2.5+6	TRM	Expt	Prog BARC-872 106	76 Iyer+ ABST.REL U235.SIG(E) TABLE	
Fission	Maxwl		MOL	Theo	Jour NP/A 259 423	Mar 76 Wagemans+ CALC FOR DOUBLE HUMP + IH0	
Fission	Maxwl		MUN	ExTh	Diss GRYNTAKIS	Mar 76 Gryntakis.,ACT.MEAS.,CALC OF G-FUNCT	+
	None			Theo	Jour RCA 22 128	Mar 75 - +,CALC WESTCOTTS G-FUNCTION	
	2.5-2			Expt	Data EXFOR20625.035	Aug 76 1PNT.SIGMA.	
Fission	1.3+5	1.3+6	BOR	Expt	Rept CEN(BG)-76 03	May 76 Sicre.ANG DIST,FIS BARRIER ANALYSIS	
					Rept CEN(BG)-75 06	75 Caitucoli. TH,SIG FIS BY FAST NEUTRS	
	1.0+5	1.3+6			Conf 73Rochestr 1 71	Aug 73 Sicre+ SIG(E) REL U-235,U-238 GRAPH	
Res Int Fiss	4.7-1	1.0+7	KFK	Eval	Rept KFK-1186	Jul 70 Hinkelmann. INFIN DILUTION RES INTEG	
Res Int Fiss	5.5-1		MUN	Expt	Diss GRYNTAKIS	Mar 76 Gryntakis.,CD,0.049+-0.013B,INCL 1/V	+
	5.5-1				Data EXFOR20625.036	Aug 76 1PNT.	
Nu	4.7+4	8.0+5	KFK	Eval	Rept KFK-1186	Jul 70 Hinkelmann.AVG VALUE OF MEAN NUMBER	
Delayd Neuts	-		ATH	Expt	Jour JNE 24 157	Jun 70 Chrysochoides+ BR I137 YLDS REL U235	
					Rept IAEA-124 27	Feb 70 *DISCUSSION,NDG	
Delayd Neuts		1.5+7	KEN	Expt	Jour RCA 15 109	Apr 71 Brown+ YIELDS+HALFLIVES,FOUR GROUPS.	
Delayd Neuts	1.4+7	1.5+7	IAE	Eval	Jour REA 10 637	Dec 72 Manero+ SURVEY,AVERAGE YLD,TBL+GRPHS	
Delayd Neuts	Pile		ATH	Expt	Rept RCA 20 118	73 Anoussis+ DELAYED N YIELDS	
Fiss Yield	+6	1.4+7	CHI	Expt	Jour PR 56 382	Aug 39 Grosse+ DET 138CS/88RB=2	
Fiss Yield	Fiss		TRM	Expt	Conf 65Salzburg 439	Mar 65 Iyer.YLD OF VARIOUS ISOTOPS,TBL,GRPH	
Fiss Yield	1.5+7		KEN	Expt	Jour RCA 6 16	Aug 66 Brown+ 11 MASS YIELDS,RECOIL METHOD	

91   Protactinium   231

Quantity	Energy (ev) Min	Max	Lab	Type	Documentation Ref Vol Page	Author, Comments Date	Data
Fiss Yield	Fiss		LAS Expt	Jour	PR 156 1277	Apr 67 Bennett+ GRPH YLD VS A,E VS A.SI DET	
Fiss Yield	Pile		TRM Expt	Jour	JIN 30 2305	Sep 68 Namboodini+ YLD OF 20 NUCLIDE	
Fiss Yield	3.0+6		KEN Expt	Jour	RCA 11 108	Apr 69 Birgul+,CUMULATIVE YLD OF 10 NUCL	
Fiss Yield	+5	+7	OSL Revw	Conf	69Vienna 669	Jul 69 Pappas+PPR206.REVW,INITIAL MASS DIST	
Fiss Yield	1.5+7		KEN Expt	Jour	RCA 12 66	Aug 69 Birgul+,FINE STRUCT YLD MASS 131–135	
Fiss Yield	Pile		MUN Expt	Jour	RCA 13 4 181	Jun 70 Kemmer+ MASS 85–149 YIELDS	
Fiss Yield	3.0+6		KEN Expt	Jour	RCA 16 2 103	Apr 71 Birgul+ CUM YLDS AT MASS CHAIN 129	
Fiss Yield	Pile		HAR Eval	Conf	73Paris 1 393	Mar 73 Crouch.EXPTL DATA+EVAL CHAIN YLD,TBL	
				Rept	AERE–R–7209	Jan 73 - .28 CHAIN YLDS RECOMMENDED TBL	
Fiss Yield	3.0+6	1.4+7	HAR Eval	Rept	AERE–R–7394	May 73 Crouch.CHAIN YLDS.RECOMMENDED.TBL.	
Fiss Yield	6.0+6	8.0+6	RI Eval	Conf	75Kiev 5 216	May 75 Selickij. REL SYM YLD VS EXC–E.GRAPH	
Frag Spectra	Spont		CCP Expt	Conf	55Moscow 226	Jul 55 Goldin+.ALFA SPECTRUM.EXPT FROM 1955	
				Rept	AEC–TR–2435	56 . P 167.ENGL TRANSL OF 55MOSCOW 226	
Frag Spectra	Fiss		LAS Expt	Jour	PR 156 1277	Apr 67 Bennett+ TBL.GRPHS EN VS A	
Frag Spectra	Fiss		ORL Theo	Conf	69Vienna 67	Jul 69 Schmitt.GRPH EKIN VS A	
Frag Spectra	1.4+5	1.3+6	KUR Expt	Jour	YF 10 488	Sep 69 Vorotnikov+ FRAG(ANG,NEUT–E) GRAPHS	+
				Jour	SNP 10 280	Mar 70 . ENGL OF YF 10 488	
	1.4+5	1.3+6		Data	EXFOR40228.	May 75 .DATA FOR 17 ES AT 4 ANGLES GVN	
Frag Spectra	1.4+5	4.0+6	LAS ExTh	Rept	LA–4648–MS	Jun 71 Muir. FRAG ANG DIST POWER SERIES FIT	+
	1.0+5	3.0+6	Expt	Conf	71Knoxvill 292	Mar 71 - + FRG ANG DIST	
	1.0+5	3.0+6		Data	EXFOR10223.	Sep 75 538PTS,DSIGMA AT 2 ANG	
Frag Spectra	Thrsh		FOA Expt	Prog	EANDC(OR)115L	Jul 72 Holmberg+. MAKROFOL TECHNIQUE	
Frag Spectra	1.0+5	1.3+6	BOR Expt	Conf	73Rochestr 1 71	Aug 73 Sicre+ ANG DISTRIBTN OF FRAGS, GRAPH	
Frag Charge	1.8+6		LRL Comp	Rept	UCRL–51640	Jul 74 Nethaway. TBL.	
Reson Params	4.0–1	1.2+0	HAN Expt	Rept	HW–67219	Oct 60 Leonard+FISSION IN 4 RESONANCES	+
	4.0–1	1.2+0		Data	EXFOR12286.	Jun 76 . 4 RES, WF,PCS – FISSION	
Reson Params	–.3+0	1.1+1	MTR Expt	Jour	NSE 12 243	Feb 62 Simpson+,FC+TRNS B–W FIT+AREA ANAL	+
	–.3–2	1.1+1		Data	EXFOR12265.006	Jun 76 . 25 RES,E0,WN0,WG	
Reson Params	4.0–1	9.9+1	ORL Expt	Prog	ORNL–3268 47	Jun 62 Patterson+ TBL GRPH WG D GWN	+
	4.0–1	2.0+2		Data	EXFOR12269.	Jun 76 . 118 RES, E0,WN0,WG	
Reson Params		1.0+6	AUA Theo	Jour	AUJ 20 477	Oct 67 Cook. TBL OF AVG LVL SPACING D,L=0,1	
Reson Params		1.0+6	KUR Theo	Jour	YF 9 538	Mar 69 Vorotnikov. W–FISS GRPH IN FISS–ANAL	
				Jour	SNP 9 308	Sep 69 TRANSLATN.*	
	4.5+6	7.0+6	ExTh	Jour	YF 5 728	May 67 Vorotnikov. GRAPH N+GAMMA FISSWIDTH	
	4.0+6	7.0+6	Theo	Jour	SNP 5 728	Nov 67 . ENGL OF YF 5 728	
Reson Params	+2	+6	FEI Theo	Jour	YF 10 542	Sep 69 Gai+ TABLE OF RESON+FAST FISSN WIDTH	
	None			Rept	FEI–158	Feb 69 GAJ+ FISSN WIDTH,2HUMPED–BARR–CALCUL	
	+2	+6		Jour	SNP 10 311	Mar 70 . ENGL OF YF 10 542	
Reson Params	1.0+3	4.6+4	KFK Eval	Rept	KFK–1186	Jul 70 Hinkelmann. AVG.WG,WF LVL SPACING	
Reson Params	None		DUB Theo	Jour	YF 13 240	Feb 71 Malecki+G–WID,THEO CFD EXPT.TBL,GRPH	
				Jour	SNP 13 133	Aug 71 - + ENGL OF YF 13 240.	
Reson Params	6.2–1	5.0+4	SRL Theo	Conf	71Knoxvill 714	Mar 71 Mccrosson. STAT CALCULATN AVG PARAMS	
Reson Params	+0		KUR Theo	Jour	AE 31 18	Jul 71 Vorotnikov. S+P,FISS–WIDTHS DERIVED	
				Jour	SJA 31 706	Feb 72 . ENGL OF AE 31 18	
Reson Params	+0	+3	BOR Theo	Jour	JPRC 33 13	Aug 72 Doan+ TBL 7 VALS GVN	
Reson Params	3.2–1	1.1+1	CCP Theo	Rept	YK–16 121	74 Gorbachev+ G+F+N–WIDTHS, TBL	
Strnth Fnctn	4.0–1	1.1+1	MTR Expt	Jour	NSE 12 243	Feb 62 Simpson+ B–W CFD EST IN KEV	+
	4.0–1	1.1+1		Data	EXFOR12265.	Jun 76 . 2 PTS, STF,D	
Strnth Fnctn	4.0–1	9.9+1	ORL Expt	Prog	ORNL–3268 47	Jun 62 Patterson+ (.85+ –.10)–4,118 RES.	
Strnth Fnctn	1.0+3	4.6+4	KFK Eval	Rept	KFK–1186	Jul 70 Hinkelmann. SO=0.60 SI=2.	
Strnth Fnctn	None		AUA Eval	Rept	AAEC/E–277	Mar 73 Musgrove.TBLS EXPTL DATA+BEST VALUES	
Lvl Density		1.3+1	KUR Theo	Jour	YF 9 303	Feb 69 Vorotnikov.LVL DEN(EXCIT–E),TBL GRPH	
				Jour	SNP 9 179	Aug 69 TRANSLATN.*	
Lvl Density	+6		DUB Theo	Rept	JINR–E4–9236	Nov 75 Komov+ AVG LVL–SPAC,SEMIMICRO CFD XP	

91   Protactinium   232

Quantity	Energy (ev) Min	Max	Lab	Type	Documentation Ref Vol Page	Author, Comments Date	Data
Absorption	2.5–2		IJI Eval	Conf	73Kiev 1 197	May 73 Fedorova. SIG 2200M/S=760+ –100 B	
Res Int Abs	5.5–1		MUN Expt	Diss	GRYNTAKIS	Mar 76 Gryntakis.ACT.CD–R,90+ –53 B,EXCL 1/V	+
	5.5–1			Data	EXFOR20625.038	Aug 76 1PNT.CAPTURE.	
(n,γ)	Pile		ANL Expt	Jour	PR 90 102	Apr 53 Elson+ ACT HANFORD PILE 40+40–20B	+
	Pile			Data	EXFOR12272.003	Jun 76 . 1 PT.	
(n,γ)	Maxwl		MTR Expt	Jour	PR 101 1053	Feb 56 Smith+ SIG=760+ –100B, REL 233PA=130B	+
	Maxwl			Data	EXFOR12273.003	Jun 76 . 1 PT.	
(n,γ)	Maxwl		MUN Expt	Diss	GRYNTAKIS	Mar 76 Gryntakis.,ACT.,464+ –95 B , REL. AU	+
	2.5–2			Data	EXFOR20625.037	Aug 76 1PNT.SIGMA.	

91 Protactinium 232

Quantity	Energy (ev) Min	Max	Lab	Type	Documentation Ref Vol Page	Date	Author, Comments	Data
(n,p)	Maxwl		IFU	Theo Rept	ICD – 4 20	67	Dadakina+ PENETR COEFF CALC,TABLE	
Fission	Maxwl		TRM	Revw Conf	66Bombay 1	Feb 66	Ramanna.VALS CFD TH,SIG,BINDING,DEF.	
Fission	–		GEL	Revw Jour	AKE 18 229	Nov 71	Theobald+ SUB – BARRIER FISS EXPTS,TH	
Frag Spectra		2.0+6	COP	Revw Conf	69Vienna 155	Jul 69	Strutinsky+PPR203. GRPH ANGANISTR(E)	
Lvl Density	+6		MIL	Theo Jour	EN 15 1 54	Jan 68	Facchini+ LDL PARS FROM LOW EN RES	
Lvl Density	None		COP	Theo Jour	NP/A 222 493	Apr 74	Dossing+COLL ROTAT.SPAC. ACCUR ESTIM	
Lvl Density	None		ROC	Theo Jour	NP/A 223 589	May 74	Huizenga+ EXP CFD MICROSC TH AX SYMM	

91 Protactinium 233

Quantity	Energy (ev) Min	Max	Lab	Type	Documentation Ref Vol Page	Date	Author, Comments	Data
Evaluation	–1	1.0+7	UNC	Eval Rept	NDA – 2134 – 2	Sep 60	Kalos+.TOT SNE SIN DIN N2N NF NG LVL	
Evaluation	2.5–2		TRM	Eval Rept	AEET – 257	Aug 66	Singh.NG(BNL 325 SUPPL NO.2)	
Evaluation	5.0+2	3.7+6	TRM	Eval Rept	AEET – 257	Aug 66	Singh.16GROUPS SIN DIN NF NU NG	
Evaluation	1.0–3	1.5+7	GA	Eval Rept	GA – 7462	Sep 67	Drake+ TOT N2N N3N SIN SEL NF NG SNE	
Total	1.0–2	1.0+4	MTR	Expt Rept	NSE 28 133	Apr 67	Simpson+ 55+ – 3B AT 2200M/S	+
				Rept	IN – 1014	Jul 66	– + TABULATED DATA	
				Conf	66Wash. 67	Mar 66	– . SUPERSEDED	
	1.0–2	1.0+0		Jour	NSE 20 235	Aug 64	– + SUPERSEDED	
	1.0–2	1.0+4		Conf	61Saclay 85	Jul 61	– + SUPERSEDED	
	1.0–2	1.1+4		Data	EXFOR12263.	Jun 76	. 1327 PTS, SIG	
Total	1.0–4	1.0+7	UK	Eval Data	UKNDL – DFN 86A	Mar 73	592 PNTS	+
Total	2.5–2		IJI	Eval Conf	73Kiev 1 197	May 73	Fedorova. SIG 2200M/S = 55+ – 3 B	
Elastic	1.0–4	1.0+7	UK	Eval Data	UKNDL – DFN 86A	Mar 73	592 PNTS	+
Diff Elastic	1.0–4	1.0+7	UK	Eval Data	UKNDL – DFN 86A	Mar 73	1 RNGS,C.M.	+
Tot Inelastc	4.1+4	3.7+6	TRM	Eval Rept	AEET – 257	Aug 66	Singh.10GROUPS FROM HAUSER – FESHBACH	
Tot Inelastc	3.0+4	1.0+7	KYU	Eval Jour	NST 10 583	Sep 73	Ohta+.RESULTS IN FIG.	
Diff Inelast	4.1+4	3.7+6	TRM	Eval Rept	AEET – 257	Aug 66	Singh.10GROUPS J – J+K MATRIX K = 0TO9	
Diff Inelast	2.0+4	1.0+7	UK	Eval Data	UKNDL – DFN 86A	Mar 73	.TO CONTINUUM.45 PTS.E DIST.ANGDIST.	
Scattering	2.5–2		IJI	Eval Conf	73Kiev 1 197	May 73	Fedorova. SIG 2200M/S = 10+ – 5 B	
Nonelastic	1.0–4	1.0+7	UK	Eval Data	UKNDL – DFN 86A	Mar 73	592 PNTS	+
Absorption	6.2–1	1.0+7	SRL	Theo Rept	71Knoxvill 714	Mar 71	Mccrosson. SPECTRUM – AVERAGED SIG	
Absorption	1.0–3	2.0+0	JUL	Theo Rept	JUEL – 746 – RG 49	Apr 71	Bonka.KUGEL – THERMOS – LIBR,T = 300K,CURV	
Absorption	2.5–2		IJI	Eval Conf	73Kiev 1 197	May 73	Fedorova. SIG 2200M/S = 44+ – 3 B	
Absorption	None		MUN	Theo Diss	GRYNTAKIS	Mar 76	Gryntakis.,CALC.OF WESTCOTTS G – FUNCT	
				Jour	RCA 22 128	Mar 75	– +,EQUIVALENT TO THESIS	
Res Int Abs	5.5–1		MTR	Expt Rept	TNCC – 3	Aug 56	Smith+ SUPERSEDED	
Res Int Abs	5.0–1		TRM	Revw Rept	AEET – 234		65 SHANKAR SINGH.CFD CALCS FROM RESPARS	
Res Int Abs	4.0–1		MTR	Expt Jour	NSE 28 133	Apr 67	Simpson+ 901+ – 45B SEP.ISOTOPE	
Res Int Abs	5.0–1		SGA	Comp Conf	73Paris 1 233	Mar 73	Eder+ REDUCED RES INTEG CAPTURE,TBL	
				Rept	SGAE – PH – 141	Feb 73	.SAME AS 73PARIS,NO DETAILS,TBP	
(n,γ)	Pile		ANL	Expt Prog	CP – 3630	Sep 46	Katzin. SIG = 37+ – 14B REACT.SPECT	+
	Pile			Data	EXFOR12295.002	Jun 76	. 1 PT.	
(n,γ)	Pile		ANL	Expt Priv	KATZIN	53	Katzin.	+
	Pile			Data	EXFOR12309.002	Jun 76	. 1 PT.	
(n,γ)	Maxwl	Pile	MTR	Expt Rept	IDO – 16226	Oct 55	Smith+ UX2 = 43+ – 5B,UZ = 25+ – 4B	+
	Maxwl			Data	EXFOR12299.	Jun 76	. 6 PTS, SIG FOR DIFF SAMPLES	
(n,γ)	Maxwl		ORL	Expt Rept	NSE 1 1	Mar 56	Halperin+,LITR SIG = 140+ – 20B	
				Conf	55Geneva 7 258	Aug 55	.SUPERSEDED	
	Maxwl			Data	EXFOR12301.	Jun 76	. 3 PTS, SIG TO GND,META, AND TOTAL	
(n,γ)	2.5–1		ORL	Eval Jour	NSE 6 100	Aug 59	Stoughton+ REC VAL CFD MANY	
	2.5–2			Conf	58Geneva 16 64	Sep 58	Halperin+ REC VALUE CFD MANY REF	
(n,γ)	Maxwl		CRC	Expt Jour	CJP 38 751	Jun 60	Eastwood+ 2 ISOM STATES 20+ – 4,19+ – 3B	+
	Maxwl			Data	EXFOR12256.	Jun 76	. 2 PTS, SIG FOR 2 ISOMERS	
(n,γ)	Maxwl		ORL	Expt Priv	STOUGHTON	Dec 64	Halperin+CORRC ORNL3320 FOR0.4EV RES	+
				Prog	ORNL – 3320 1	Dec 62	– + SUPERSEDED.1/V DEP WRONG	
	Maxwl			Data	EXFOR12302.	Jun 76	. 3 PTS, SIG TO GND,META, AND TOTAL	
(n,γ)		+6	TRM	Revw Rept	AEET – 234		65 SHANKAR SINGH.STATUS OF DATA REVIEWD	
(n,γ)	2.0+1	3.0+2	LAS	Expt Rept	LA – DC – 7864	Aug 66	Brown. TBD DIVEN SEEGER BOMB N(S)	
(n,γ)	5.0+2	3.7+6	TRM	Eval Rept	AEET – 257	Aug 66	Singh.16GROUPS CALC FROM NDA 2134 – 2	
(n,γ)	Maxwl		AUA	Theo Jour	NSE 31 234	Feb 68	Cook+ STATISTICAL CALC CFD EXPT	
(n,γ)	2.5–2		BET	Eval Rept	WAPD – TM – 814	Dec 69	Harris. REC AV DIFF + INTEGRAL DATA	
(n,γ)	Maxwl		BET	Expt Rept	WAPD – TM – 837	Jun 70	Connor.SIG = 31.4+ – 1.0B,+0.025EV SIG	+
	Maxwl			Data	EXFOR10083.	Sep 72	. 2 PTS, SIG FOR 2 ISOMERS	
(n,γ)	1.0–2	+6	ORL	Revw Jour	REA 8 473	Sep 70	Kasten. REVIEW,SIG(NEUT – E) GRAPH	
(n,γ)	Maxwl		SGA	Comp Conf	73Paris 1 233	Mar 73	Eder+ DATA FROM EXPTS+EVALS,TABLE	
				Rept	SGAE – PH – 141	Feb 73	.SAME AS 73PARIS,NO DETAILS	

91 Protactinium 233

Quantity	Energy (ev) Min	Max	Lab	Type	Documentation Ref Vol Page	Date	Author, Comments	Data
(n,γ)	1.0−4	1.0+7	UK Eval	Data	UKNDL−DFN 86A	Mar 73	592 PNTS	+
(n,γ)	1.0+5	2.0+7	TRM Theo	Conf	76Ahmedabd 2 17	Dec 76	Garg. ABST,NDG.CALC WITH'FISPRO'CODE	
Res Int Capt	5.5−1		MTR Expt	Rept	IDO−16226	Oct 55	Smith+ UX2=400B,UZ=270B	+
	5.5−1			Data	EXFOR12299.	Jun 76	. 3 PTS, RI FOR DIFF SAMPLES	
Res Int Capt	5.0−1	1.0+6	ORL Eval	Jour	NSE 6 100	Aug 59	Stoughton+ REC VALUE CFD MANY REF	
	4.0−1	1.0+6		Conf	58Geneva 16 64	Sep 58	Halperin+ REC VALUE CFD REF	
Res Int Capt	5.0−1		CRC Expt	Jour	CJP 38 751	Jun 60	Eastwood+2 ISOM,470+ −90B,460+ −100B	+
	5.0−1			Data	EXFOR12256.	Jun 76	. 2 PTS, RI FOR GND AND META	
Res Int Capt	5.0−1		ORL Expt	Prog	ORNL−3320 1	Dec 62	Halperin+ GD(.2EV)+CD(.55EV)	+
	5.0−1			Data	EXFOR12302.004	Jun 76	. 1 PT, RI	
Res Int Capt	5.0−1		BET Expt	Jour	NSE 29 408	Sep 67	Conner+	+
	5.0−1			Data	EXFOR12427.	Jun 76	. 2 PTS, SIG TO GND AND META	
Res Int Capt	5.0−1		BET Eval	Rept	WAPD−TM−814	Dec 69	Harris. REC AV DIFF + INTEGRAL DATA	
Res Int Capt	5.0−1		BET Expt	Rept	WAPD−TM−837	Jun 70	Connor.RI=857+ −35B INCLUDING 1/V	+
	5.0−1			Data	EXFOR10083.002	Sep 72	. 1 PT. CADMIUM CVR,REACTOR SPECTRUM	
(n,2n)	7.5+6	1.0+7	UK Eval	Data	UKNDL−DFN 86A	Mar 73	.6 PTS. E DIST,ANG DIST,LAB.	+
	7.5+6	1.0+7		Data	UKNDL−DFN 86A	Mar 73	ANGULAR DISTRIBUTION, 1 RNGS,LAB.	
	7.5+6	1.0+7		Data	UKNDL−DFN 86A	Mar 73	ENERGY DISTRIBUTION, 1 RANGES	
Fission	8.2+5	3.7+6	TRM Eval	Rept	AEET−257	Aug 66	Singh. 4GROUPS TAKEN=TO U238	
Fission	Fiss		WUR Expt	Jour	NSE 27 85	Jan 67	Von Gunten+ AVG VALUE=775+ −190MB.	+
				Rept	EIR−112	Mar 67	− + EQUIVALENT.	
Fission	Thrsh	Up	LAS Expt	Prog	WASH−1124 99	Nov 68	Codding+ BOMB NEUTS TBC NO DATA GIVN	
Fission	+5	+7	ORL Revw	Jour	REA 8 473	Sep 70	Kasten. REVIEW,SIG(NEUT−E) GRAPH	
Fission	Fiss		SGA Eval	Conf	73Paris 1 233	Mar 73	Eder+ FISS SPEC REL U238(N,F),TBLS	
				Rept	SGAE−PH−141	Feb 73	.SAME AS 73PARIS,NO DETAILS,TBP	
Fission	2.0+5	1.0+7	UK Eval	Data	UKNDL−DFN 86A	Mar 73	34 PNTS	+
Fission	2.5−2		IJI Eval	Conf	73Kiev 1 197	May 73	Fedorova. SIG 2200M/S=775+ −10 B	
Nu	8.2+5	3.7+6	TRM Eval	Rept	AEET−257	Aug 66	Singh. 4GROUPS TAKEN=TO U238	
Nu	2.0+5	1.0+7	UK Eval	Data	UKNDL−DFN 86A	Mar 73	. 34 POINTS + FISS N ANGDIST, LAB CS	+
Spect Fiss n	2.0+5	1.0+7	UK Eval	Data	UKNDL−DFN 86A	Mar 73	1 RANGES	+
Reson Params	−.1+1	1.7+1	MTR Expt	Jour	NSE 28 133	Apr 67	Simpson+ 28 RESONANCES, SEP.ISO	+
	1.4+0	3.4+0		Conf	66Wash. 67	Mar 66	− + SUPERSEDED	
	1.4+0	4.3+0		Conf	61Saclay 85	Jul 61	− + SUPERSEDED	
	−.1+1	1.7+1		Data	EXFOR12263.005	Jun 76	. 28 RES, E0,WN0,WG	
Reson Params		1.0+6	AUA Theo	Jour	AUJ 20 477	Oct 67	Cook. TBL OF AVG LVL SPACING D,L=0,1	
Reson Params	None		DUB Theo	Jour	YF 13 240	Feb 71	Malecki+G−WID,THEO CFD EXPT.TBL,GRPH	
				Jour	SNP 13 133	Aug 71	− + ENGL OF YF 13 240.	
Reson Params	6.2−1	5.0+4	SRL Expt	Conf	71Knoxvill 714	Mar 71	Mccrosson. STAT CALCULATN AVG PARAMS	
Reson Params	7.9−1	1.8+1	CCP Expt	Rept	YK−16 121	74	Gorbachev+ G+F+N−WIDTHS, TBL	
Lvl Density		1.3+1	KUR Theo	Jour	YF 9 303	Feb 69	Vorotnikov.LVL DEN(EXCIT−E),TBL GRPH	
				Jour	SNP 9 179	Aug 69	TRANSLATN.*	
Lvl Density	+6		DUB Theo	Rept	JINR−E4−9236	Nov 75	Komov+ AVG LVL−SPAC,SEMIMICRO CFD XP	

91 Protactinium 234

Quantity	Energy (ev) Min	Max	Lab	Type	Documentation Ref Vol Page	Date	Author, Comments	Data
(n,γ)	2.0+4		GSF Theo	Jour	AF 36 509	Nov 67	Truran+.STAT MODEL. TWO MASS FORMLS	
Lvl Density	+6		MIL Theo	Jour	EN 15 1 54	Jan 68	Facchini+ LDL PARS FROM LOW EN RES	
Lvl Density	None		COP Theo	Jour	NP/A 222 493	Apr 74	Dossing+COLL ROTAT.SPAC. ACCUR ESTIM	
Lvl Density	None		ROC Theo	Jour	NP/A 223 589	May 74	Huizenga+ EXP CFD MICROSC TH AX SYMM	

91 Protactinium 235

Quantity	Energy (ev) Min	Max	Lab	Type	Documentation Ref Vol Page	Date	Author, Comments	Data
(n,γ)	2.0+4		GSF Theo	Jour	AF 36 509	Nov 67	Truran+.STAT MODEL. TWO MASS FORMLS	
Fission	2.5−2		JUL Theo	Jour	ZP 257 389	Dec 72	Mcminn. 9.58 E−5 BARNS	

91 Protactinium 236

Quantity	Energy (ev) Min	Max	Lab	Type	Documentation Ref Vol Page	Date	Author, Comments	Data
(n,γ)	2.0+4		GSF Theo	Jour	AF 36 509	Nov 67	Truran+.STAT MODEL. TWO MASS FORMLS	
Fission	Spont		DUB Theo	Rept	JINR−E−2515	Dec 65	Malov+ SPON FISSN ISOMER, LIFE−TIME	

91 Protactinium 237

Quantity	Energy (ev) Min Max	Lab	Type	Documentation Ref Vol Page	Author, Comments Date	Data
(n,γ)	2.0+4	GSF	Theo Jour	AF 36 509	Nov 67 Truran+.STAT MODEL. TWO MASS FORMLS	
Fission	2.5−2	JUL	Theo Jour	ZP 257 389	Dec 72 Mcminn. 7.96 E−6 BARNS	

91 Protactinium 238

Quantity	Energy (ev) Min Max	Lab	Type	Documentation Ref Vol Page	Author, Comments Date	Data
(n,γ)	2.0+4	LAS	Theo Jour	PR/B 139 1207	Sep 65 Bell.STATISTCL TH CALC CF WEAPON XPT	
(n,γ)	2.0+4	GSF	Theo Jour	AF 36 509	Nov 67 Truran+.STAT MODEL. TWO MASS FORMLS	
Fiss Yield	1.4+7	WUR	Expt Abst	HPA 49 2 187	May 76 Baertschi+ MUOV FISS U238 FISS PROB	

91 Protactinium 239

Quantity	Energy (ev) Min Max	Lab	Type	Documentation Ref Vol Page	Author, Comments Date	Data
(n,γ)	2.0+4	LAS	Theo Jour	PR/B 139 1207	Sep 65 Bell.STATISTCL TH CALC CF WEAPON XPT	
(n,γ)	2.0+4	GSF	Theo Jour	AF 36 509	Nov 67 Truran+.STAT MODEL. TWO MASS FORMLS	

91 Protactinium 240

Quantity	Energy (ev) Min Max	Lab	Type	Documentation Ref Vol Page	Author, Comments Date	Data
(n,γ)	2.0+4	LAS	Theo Jour	PR/B 139 1207	Sep 65 Bell.STATISTCL TH CALC CF WEAPON XPT	
(n,γ)	2.0+4	GSF	Theo Jour	AF 36 509	Nov 67 Truran+.STAT MODEL. TWO MASS FORMLS	

91 Protactinium 241

Quantity	Energy (ev) Min Max	Lab	Type	Documentation Ref Vol Page	Author, Comments Date	Data
(n,γ)	2.0+4	LAS	Theo Jour	PR/B 139 1207	Sep 65 Bell.STATISTCL TH CALC CF WEAPON XPT	
(n,γ)	2.0+4	GSF	Theo Jour	AF 36 509	Nov 67 Truran+.STAT MODEL. TWO MASS FORMLS	

91 Protactinium 242

Quantity	Energy (ev) Min Max	Lab	Type	Documentation Ref Vol Page	Author, Comments Date	Data
(n,γ)	2.0+4	LAS	Theo Jour	PR/B 139 1207	Sep 65 Bell.STATISTCL TH CALC CF WEAPON XPT	
(n,γ)	2.0+4	GSF	Theo Jour	AF 36 509	Nov 67 Truran+.STAT MODEL. TWO MASS FORMLS	

91 Protactinium 243

Quantity	Energy (ev) Min Max	Lab	Type	Documentation Ref Vol Page	Author, Comments Date	Data
(n,γ)	2.0+4	LAS	Theo Jour	PR/B 139 1207	Sep 65 Bell.STATISTCL TH CALC CF WEAPON XPT	
(n,γ)	2.0+4	GSF	Theo Jour	AF 36 509	Nov 67 Truran+.STAT MODEL. TWO MASS FORMLS	

91 Protactinium 244

Quantity	Energy (ev) Min Max	Lab	Type	Documentation Ref Vol Page	Author, Comments Date	Data
(n,γ)	2.0+4	LAS	Theo Jour	PR/B 139 1207	Sep 65 Bell.STATISTCL TH CALC CF WEAPON XPT	
(n,γ)	2.0+4	GSF	Theo Jour	AF 36 509	Nov 67 Truran+.STAT MODEL. TWO MASS FORMLS	

91 Protactinium 245

Quantity	Energy (ev) Min Max	Lab	Type	Documentation Ref Vol Page	Author, Comments Date	Data
(n,γ)	2.0+4	LAS	Theo Jour	PR/B 139 1207	Sep 65 Bell.STATISTCL TH CALC CF WEAPON XPT	
(n,γ)	2.0+4	GSF	Theo Jour	AF 36 509	Nov 67 Truran+.STAT MODEL. TWO MASS FORMLS	

91 Protactinium 246

Quantity	Energy (ev) Min Max	Lab	Type	Documentation Ref Vol Page	Author, Comments Date	Data
(n,γ)	2.0+4	LAS	Theo Jour	PR/B 139 1207	Sep 65 Bell.STATISTCL TH CALC CF WEAPON XPT	
(n,γ)	2.0+4	GSF	Theo Jour	AF 36 509	Nov 67 Truran+.STAT MODEL. TWO MASS FORMLS	

91 Protactinium 247

Quantity	Energy (ev) Min Max	Lab	Type	Documentation Ref Vol Page	Author, Comments Date	Data
(n,γ)	2.0+4	LAS	Theo Jour	PR/B 139 1207	Sep 65 Bell.STATISTCL TH CALC CF WEAPON XPT	
(n,γ)	2.0+4	GSF	Theo Jour	AF 36 509	Nov 67 Truran+.STAT MODEL. TWO MASS FORMLS	

91 Protactinium 248

Quantity	Energy (ev) Min Max	Lab	Type	Documentation Ref Vol Page	Author, Comments Date	Data
(n,γ)	2.0+4	LAS	Theo Jour	PR/B 139 1207	Sep 65 Bell.STATISTCL TH CALC CF WEAPON XPT	
(n,γ)	2.0+4	GSF	Theo Jour	AF 36 509	Nov 67 Truran+.STAT MODEL. TWO MASS FORMLS	

91 Protactinium 249

Quantity	Energy (ev) Min Max	Lab	Type	Documentation Ref Vol Page	Author, Comments Date	Data
(n,γ)	2.0+4	LAS	Theo Jour	PR/B 139 1207	Sep 65 Bell.STATISTCL TH CALC CF WEAPON XPT	
(n,γ)	2.0+4	GSF	Theo Jour	AF 36 509	Nov 67 Truran+.STAT MODEL. TWO MASS FORMLS	

91 Protactinium 250

Quantity	Energy (ev) Min Max	Lab	Type	Documentation Ref Vol Page	Author, Comments Date	Data
(n,γ)	2.0+4	LAS	Theo Jour	PR/B 139 1207	Sep 65 Bell.STATISTCL TH CALC CF WEAPON XPT	
(n,γ)	2.0+4	GSF	Theo Jour	AF 36 509	Nov 67 Truran+.STAT MODEL. TWO MASS FORMLS	

91 Protactinium 251

Quantity	Energy (ev) Min Max	Lab	Type	Documentation Ref Vol Page	Author, Comments Date	Data
(n,γ)	2.0+4	LAS	Theo Jour	PR/B 139 1207	Sep 65 Bell.STATISTCL TH CALC CF WEAPON XPT	
(n,γ)	2.0+4	GSF	Theo Jour	AF 36 509	Nov 67 Truran+.STAT MODEL. TWO MASS FORMLS	

91 Protactinium 252

Quantity	Energy (ev) Min Max	Lab	Type	Documentation Ref Vol Page	Author, Comments Date	Data
(n,γ)	2.0+4	LAS	Theo Jour	PR/B 139 1207	Sep 65 Bell.STATISTCL TH CALC CF WEAPON XPT	
(n,γ)	2.0+4	GSF	Theo Jour	AF 36 509	Nov 67 Truran+.STAT MODEL. TWO MASS FORMLS	

91 Protactinium 253

Quantity	Energy (ev) Min Max	Lab	Type	Documentation Ref Vol Page	Author, Comments Date	Data
(n,γ)	2.0+4	LAS	Theo Jour	PR/B 139 1207	Sep 65 Bell.STATISTCL TH CALC CF WEAPON XPT	
(n,γ)	2.0+4	GSF	Theo Jour	AF 36 509	Nov 67 Truran+.STAT MODEL. TWO MASS FORMLS	

91 Protactinium 254

Quantity	Energy (ev) Min Max	Lab	Type	Documentation Ref Vol Page	Author, Comments Date	Data
(n,γ)	2.0+4	LAS	Theo Jour	PR/B 139 1207	Sep 65 Bell.STATISTCL TH CALC CF WEAPON XPT	
(n,γ)	2.0+4	GSF	Theo Jour	AF 36 509	Nov 67 Truran+.STAT MODEL. TWO MASS FORMLS	

91 Protactinium 255

Quantity	Energy (ev) Min Max	Lab	Type	Documentation Ref Vol Page	Author, Comments Date	Data
(n,γ)	2.0+4	LAS	Theo Jour	PR/B 139 1207	Sep 65 Bell.STATISTCL TH CALC CF WEAPON XPT	
(n,γ)	2.0+4	GSF	Theo Jour	AF 36 509	Nov 67 Truran+.STAT MODEL. TWO MASS FORMLS	

91 Protactinium 256

Quantity	Energy (ev) Min Max	Lab	Type	Documentation Ref Vol Page	Author, Comments Date	Data
(n,γ)	2.0+4	LAS	Theo Jour	PR/B 139 1207	Sep 65 Bell.STATISTCL TH CALC CF WEAPON XPT	
(n,γ)	2.0+4	GSF	Theo Jour	AF 36 509	Nov 67 Truran+.STAT MODEL. TWO MASS FORMLS	

91 Protactinium 257

Quantity	Energy (ev) Min Max	Lab	Type	Documentation Ref Vol Page	Date	Author, Comments	Data
(n,γ)	2.0+4	LAS	Theo Jour	PR/B 139 1207	Sep 65	Bell.STATISTCL TH CALC CF WEAPON XPT	
(n,γ)	2.0+4	GSF	Theo Jour	AF 36 509	Nov 67	Truran+.STAT MODEL. TWO MASS FORMLS	

91 Protactinium 258

Quantity	Energy (ev) Min Max	Lab	Type	Documentation Ref Vol Page	Date	Author, Comments	Data
(n,γ)	2.0+4	GSF	Theo Jour	AF 36 509	Nov 67	Truran+.STAT MODEL. TWO MASS FORMLS	

91 Protactinium 259

Quantity	Energy (ev) Min Max	Lab	Type	Documentation Ref Vol Page	Date	Author, Comments	Data
(n,γ)	2.0+4	GSF	Theo Jour	AF 36 509	Nov 67	Truran+.STAT MODEL. TWO MASS FORMLS	

91 Protactinium 260

Quantity	Energy (ev) Min Max	Lab	Type	Documentation Ref Vol Page	Date	Author, Comments	Data
(n,γ)	2.0+4	GSF	Theo Jour	AF 36 509	Nov 67	Truran+.STAT MODEL. TWO MASS FORMLS	

91 Protactinium 261

Quantity	Energy (ev) Min Max	Lab	Type	Documentation Ref Vol Page	Date	Author, Comments	Data
(n,γ)	2.0+4	GSF	Theo Jour	AF 36 509	Nov 67	Truran+.STAT MODEL. TWO MASS FORMLS	

91 Protactinium 262

Quantity	Energy (ev) Min Max	Lab	Type	Documentation Ref Vol Page	Date	Author, Comments	Data
(n,γ)	2.0+4	GSF	Theo Jour	AF 36 509	Nov 67	Truran+.STAT MODEL. TWO MASS FORMLS	

91 Protactinium 263

Quantity	Energy (ev) Min Max	Lab	Type	Documentation Ref Vol Page	Date	Author, Comments	Data
(n,γ)	2.0+4	GSF	Theo Jour	AF 36 509	Nov 67	Truran+.STAT MODEL. TWO MASS FORMLS	

91 Protactinium 264

Quantity	Energy (ev) Min Max	Lab	Type	Documentation Ref Vol Page	Date	Author, Comments	Data
(n,γ)	2.0+4	GSF	Theo Jour	AF 36 509	Nov 67	Truran+.STAT MODEL. TWO MASS FORMLS	

92 Uranium

Quantity	Energy (ev) Min	Max	Lab	Type	Documentation Ref Vol Page	Date	Author, Comments	Data
Total	Maxwl		COL	Expt Jour	PR 48 265	Aug 35	Dunning+ IONCH,TRANS,RA – BE/PARAFIN	N
Total	Maxwl		NYU	Expt Jour	PR 55 793	Apr 39	Whitaker+ U METAL 23B,CF DUNNING UO2	
Total	1.0+5	1.8+5	ITY	Expt Jour	PR 56 881	Nov 39	Amaldi+ TRANSM.C – D NS. AVERAGE ES.	
Total	3.3–2	7.4–1	COL	Expt Rept	MDDC – 103	44	Havens+	+
	3.3–2	7.4–1		Data	EXFOR12386.002	Jun 76	. 11 PTS, SIGMA.	
Total	8.3+7		BRK	Expt Jour	PR 75 7	Jan 49	Cook+ GOOD GEOM ATTENUATION MEAS.	+
	8.3+7			Data	EXFOR11146.015	Jun 76	. 1 PT. SIGMA.	
Total	1.2+2	3.5+2	ANL	Expt Rept	ANL – 4277 39	Apr 49	Hibdon. CS MEAS OVER CO+MN RESONANCE	
Total	2.7+8		BRK	Expt Jour	PR 80 27	Oct 50	Dejuren. BE(P,N) NS, BI FISS COUNTER	+
	9.5+7	2.7+8		Rept	AECD – 2987	Aug 50	– +. SIG VARIATION WITH E.	
	9.5+7			Jour	PR 77 606	Mar 50	– + BI FISSION CH,R CALC FR TH	
	9.5+7			Data	EXFOR11174.015	Jun 76	. 1 PT. FROM PR,77,606	
	2.7+8			Data	EXFOR11176.011	Jun 76	. 1 PT. FROM PR,80,27.	
Total	2.7+8		BRK	Expt Jour	PR 80 23	Oct 50	Fox+ BE(P,N) NS,SCINTILLATION COUNT.	+
	2.7+8			Data	EXFOR11175.013	Jun 76	. 1 PT.	
Total	4.2+7		BRK	Expt Jour	PR 80 842	Dec 50	Hildebrand+ BE – D NS.TRANSM. C DETECT	+
	4.2+7			Data	EXFOR11039.034	Jun 76	. 1 PT.	
Total	1.9+8		BRK	Expt Jour	PR 81 919	Mar 51	Dejuren+ P – BE NS. TRANSM	+
	1.9+8			Data	EXFOR11177.008	Jun 76	. 1 PT.	
Total	1.4+7		LAS	Expt Jour	PR 88 562	Nov 52	Coon+	+
	1.4+7			Data	EXFOR11056.058	Jun 76	. 1 PT.	
Total	3.7+0	1.0+3	AE	Expt Jour	AF 6 57	Jan 53	Hellstrand+. TOF.CYCLTRN. RES PARAMS	
Total	2.9+6	1.3+7	LAS	Expt Jour	PR 89 775	Feb 53	Nereson+ APP 10 PCT. RESOL.	+
				Prog	LA – 1655	Apr 54	– . E RESOL 10PC	
	2.9+6	1.3+7		Data	EXFOR11060.013	Jun 76	. 13 PTS.	
Total	1.8+7	2.0+7	LAS	Expt Jour	PR 92 358	Oct 53	Day+ TRANS 3ES 6.14,5.94,6.29B	+
	1.8+7	2.0+7		Data	EXFOR11068.014	Jun 76	. 3 PTS.	
Total	4.6+7	1.6+8	BRK	Expt Jour	PR 92 835	Nov 53	Linlor+	+
	4.6+7	1.6+8		Data	EXFOR12205.003	Jun 76	. 10 PTS.	
Total	1.9–3	7.9–1	CIS	Expt Jour	NC 11 262	Mar 54	= 1 DATA INDEX LINES	+
Total	2.0+4	2.0+7	LAS	Expt Jour	PR 94 141	Apr 54	Henkel+,15 – 200KEV RESOL,GAP7.6 – 17MEV	+
				Rept	AECD – 3598	Nov 53	.SUPERSEDED	
				Rept	AECD – 3500	Jan 53	.SUPERSEDED	
				Rept	LA – 1493	Nov 52	.SUPERSEDED	
	7.1+4	2.0+7		Data	EXFOR12377.002	Jun 76	. 54 PTS.	
Total	5.7–3	6.0–1	HAR	Expt Jour	JNE 1 92	Aug 54	Egelstaff. EXPT 1951. NAT+235ENRICHD	+
	1.0–3	1.2–3		Priv	EGELSTAFF3	Dec 54	– . = 1 DATA INDEX LINES	
	1.1–3	3.1–3		Priv	EGELSTAFF2	52	– . = 1 DATA INDEX LINES	
Total	1.5+5	2.2+6	HAR	Expt Rept	AERE – NP/R – 1643	May 55	Meads. NEUTRONS FROM LI7(PN)+T(PN)	
Total	1.4+9		BNL	Expt Jour	PR 98 1369	Jun 55	Coor.	+
	1.4+9			Data	EXFOR11087.018	Jun 76	. 1 PT. SIGMA.	
Total	3.7+0	2.7+2	BNL	Expt Jour	PR 99 10	Jul 55	Harvey+	+
				Rept	BNL – 221	Jan 53	– + DECL JUL 1955 NEW VAL.	
	3.7+0	2.7+2		Data	EXFOR11912.042	Jun 76	. 245 PTS. SIGMA	
Total	3.0–4	1.0+0	BNL	Revw Conf	55Geneva 4 3	Aug 55	Hughes.P576,CURVE,MANY REFERENCES	
Total	–3	2.0+0	SAC	Expt Conf	55Geneva 4 235	Aug 55	Auclair.GRAPH,CRYSTAL – SPECTR, P354	+
				Priv	AUCLAIR	Jan 55	– .DATA 0.01 – 1EV.	
Total	5.9+8		CCP	Expt Jour	ZET 29 369	Sep 55	Dzhelepov.EXPRMNTL SIG CFD GEOMETRCL	
				Jour	JET 2 349	Mar 56	TRANSLATN.*	
Total	1.0+6	2.5+6	LAS	Expt Jour	PR 104 1319	Dec 56	Beyster+,TRNS	
Total	4.0+4	1.0+7	LAS	Theo Rept	LA – 2099	Dec 56	Beyster+,OPTMDL CALC CFD EXPT,CURVE	
Total	1.5+7		CCP	Expt Jour	SPD 6 129	Apr 57	. COINC METHOD, 5.64 + – 0.1 BARN	
Total	2.7+2	3.1+4	HAR	Expt Priv	LYNN	58	Lynn. = 1 DATA INDEX LINES	
Total	1.4+7	1.5+7	LVN	Expt Jour	NP 6 260	Mar 58	Vervier+ TRANSMISSION,CFD OPTICALMOD	+
				Jour	PR 109 947	Feb 58	– + SUPERSEDED.	
	1.4+7	1.5+7		Data	EXFOR20204.008	May 74	22PTS.	
Total	1.0+4	1.0+7	BNL	Comp Conf	58Geneva 16 8	Sep 58	Hughes.PPR2483,CURVE,MANY REFS	
Total	2.0+5	1.5+7	CCP	Theo Book	NEJTRONFIZ 314	61	Ermakov.GRPH SCHROEDINGER – TH CFD XPT	
				Book	SPN 231	61	. ENGL TRANSL OF NEJTRONFIZ 314	
Total	1.5+7	1.2+8	HAR	Expt Jour	NP 22 640	Feb 61	Bowen+.TOF 64ES CFD OPTICAL MODEL	+
				Prog	BNL – 653	Feb 61	– . SUPERSEDED.	
Total	2.8+7		LVN	Expt Jour	JPR 22 652	Oct 61	Deconninck+TRANSMISS.6.00B AT 28.4MV	+
	2.8+7			Data	EXFOR20195.019	May 74	1PNT.	
Total	1.4+7		SAC	Expt Jour	JPRA 22 149	Nov 61	Didier+ A – ASSOCIATED + NON ELASTIC	
Total	2.0+6	1.0+7	SAC	Expt Jour	JPR 24 826	Nov 63	Leroy+TOF OKS PREVIOUS EXPERIMENTS	+
Total	4.6+0	3.3+5	CCP	Eval Rept	INDSWG – 64 274	64	Nikolaev.TABLE OF CHARACTRSTC PARAMS	
Total	1.0+6	1.4+7	HAR	Theo Rept	AERE – R – 4649	Jun 64	Wilmore.OPTMDL TH.TBLS,CURVES.PM10PC	

92 Uranium

Quantity	Energy (ev) Min	Max	Lab	Type	Documentation Ref Vol Page	Date	Author, Comments	Data
Total	8.2+5	1.5+6	ANL Expt	Prog	ANL-7110 1	Dec 65	Smith+	
Total	None		ANL Expt	Jour	NIM 39 185	Jan 66	Whalen+COMPUTER EXPT.NDG,CF BAP 9 6	
Total	2.0+4	3.0+6	CCP Expt	Conf	66Moscow	Feb 66	.CURVES GIVEN	
Total	4.5-3	2.8-2	AE Expt	Rept	AE-222	Mar 66	Beshai.TOF.CALC BRAGG EDGES.20 DEG	+
	5.0-3	2.8-2		Data	EXFOR20161.003	May 74	64PTS.	
Total	4.0+6		IFU Theo	Jour	UFZ 13 51	Jan 68	Kashuba+ TBL,SIG-VAL,EXPT CFD OPTMOD	
				Jour	UPJ 13 33	Jul 68	TRANSLATN.*	
Total	7.0+6	1.5+7	OHOTheo	Jour	NC/B 53 2 363	Feb 68	Cassola+ OPTMOD CALC CFD EXPT.	
Total	None		DKE Expt	Abst	DA/B 28 3834	Mar 68	Divadeenam.TRNS.AVG SIG CFD OPTMDL.	+
	1.5+5	6.0+5		Data	EXFOR10523.019	Jan 76	10PTS.	
Total	1.0+4	3.0+5	FEI Expt	Conf	68Dubna § 17	Jun 68	Filippov+VDG,TRANS.TBL,GRPH.FLUCTUAT	+
	2.0+4	6.3+5		Prog	ICD-3 93	Oct 66	.TABLE.VDG.THEORETICAL FIT	
	1.0+4	3.0+5		Rept	INDC(CCP)-16	Jul 71	.PAGE 67.ENGLISH TRANSL OF 68DUBNA	
	2.0+4	6.3+5		Prog	INDSWG-152E 93	66	.ENGLISH TRANSL OF ICD-3	
	1.0+4	2.9+5		Data	EXFOR40082.022	Nov 71	SIGMA AT 14 ES	
Total	1.0+7		IJE Comp	Jour	REA 6 4 3	Dec 68	Konshin+ SIG(NEUT-E)+ - ERROR GVN,GRPH	
Total	4.0+6		KUR Expt	Jour	YF 8 1086	Dec 68	Gorlov+.SMALL ANG SCAT EXPERIMENT	
				Jour	DOK 174 60	Jul 67	- + SMALL ANGLS,POLARIZATN GIVEN	
				Rept	IAE-1053	65	- +,SIG GIVEN, TBL	
			ExTh	Jour	SPD 12 451	Nov 67	. ENGL OF DOK 174 60	
			Expt	Rept	ANL-TR-371	66	. ENGLISH TRANS	
	3.3+6	5.1+6	JNE Expt	Jour	ARS 66 27	Feb 70	Manero. TRANSM 25-30KEV STEPS,D-D NS	+
	3.3+6	5.1+6		Data	EXFOR20171.004	May 74	60PTS.	
Total	5.0+5	4.5+6	KFK Expt	Conf	70Helsinki 2 39	Jun 70	Kopsch+12. SIG(E) GRAPHS CFD OTHER	+
	5.0+5	4.4+6		Rept	KFK-1199	May 70	- +. 5-GROUP SIG,THR+FAST SPEC	
	5.0+5	4.4+6		Data	EXFOR20016.002	Mar 71	3162PTS.	
Total	9.9+7	1.5+8	USA Expt	Abst	DA/B 31 2182	Oct 70	Schneider. ACCURACY 1PC. 1 MEV RSL.	+
	9.9+7	1.5+8		Data	EXFOR11514.006	Jun 76	. 6 PTS.	
Total	None		COL Expt	Prog	NCSAC-42 61	Nov 71	Hacken+ TRANS. ANAL TBC. NDG.	
Total	+9		NYU Theo	Jour	PR/C 6 748	Sep 72	Franco. GLAUBER APPROX. CFD EXPT	
Total	2.7+3		MUN Expt	Prog	EANDC(E)150U	Oct 72	Dilg+ AVERAGE TOT XSECT+S0	+
				Conf	71Albany 327	Aug 71	- +TRNS.AVG CS GVN.31 ELEMENT GRP	
	2.7+3			Data	EXFOR20583.032	Jun 76	1PNT.	
Total	1.3+7	1.5+7	DEB Eval	Rept	IAEA-153 173	73	Boedy+ MOST PROBABLE VAL OF SIG,TBL	
				Jour	AHP 30 115	Oct 71	Angeli+ AVG SIG,CFD CALC.TBLS.GRAPH	
Total	3.8+8	1.7+9	PTN Expt	Jour	PR/C 7 248	Jan 73	Schimmerling+.TOF.TRANS.TABLE 15 ES	+
				Jour	PL/B 37 177	Nov 71	.SUPERSEDED	
	3.8+8	1.7+9		Data	EXFOR10082.013	Dec 75	15PTS. TOT CS DATA.	
Total	3.0+6		EDG Expt	Jour	NP/A 212 182	Sep 73	Galloway+ POLRZD NS.	+
	3.0+6			Data	EXFOR20359.010	Sep 74	1PNT.	
Total	1.2+1	3.0+4	JAE Expt	Prog	NEANDC(J)36L 1	Sep 74	Nakajima+.LINAC,TRANSMISSION.IN FIG	
Total	2.5+5	1.5+7	JAE Theo	Conf	JAERI-M-5984	Feb 75	Tanaka.OPTMDL/COUPLD CH.GRPH CFD EXP	
Total	+9		MHG Expt	Jour	NP/B 92 269	Jun 75	Murthy+ 34GEV/C TO 273 GEV/C	
				Jour	PRL 33 1440	Dec 74	Jones+ TBL. 30 GEV/C TO 270 GEV/C	
	+9			Data	EXFOR10403.011	Dec 74	7PTS,SIGMA	
Total	6.7+2	1.5+5	ANL Expt	Prog	ANL-5175 7	Feb 54	Hibdon.	+
	6.7+2	1.5+5		Data	EXFOR11002.007	Jun 76	. 135 PTS.	
Total	2.3-4	2.7-2	BNL Expt	Priv	PALEVSKY	52	Palevsky.	+
	2.3-4	2.7-2		Data	EXFOR12376.	Jun 76	. 94 PTS.	
Total	3.0+4	6.5+5	DKE Expt	Prog	WASH-1034 10	Dec 61	Bilpuch+STEPS	+
	3.0+4	6.5+5		Data	EXFOR11936.010	Jun 76	. 102 PTS.	
Total	9.0+5		UI Expt	Abst	PR 59 917	May 41	Good+ ABST. 19	+
	9.0+5			Data	EXFOR11178.008	Jun 76	. 1 PT. SIGMA.	
Total	1.0+4	2.5+5	FEI Expt	Rept	YK-26 5	77	Filippov. TRANS.TOTSIG(E),GRAPH+TABL	
Elastic	Maxwl		NYU Expt	Jour	PR 55 793	Apr 39	Whitaker+ U METAL, AG ACTIVATION DET	
Elastic	2.5-2		ORL Expt	Jour	PR 81 527	Feb 51	Shull+	+
	2.5-2			Data	EXFOR11043.	Jun 76	. 2 PTS. BAS, COH.	
Elastic	1.0+6		WIS Expt	Prog	TID-5157	53	Walt. CALC. FROM D SIGMA.	+
	1.0+6			Data	EXFOR12381.053	Jun 76	. 1 PT. SIGMA.	
Elastic	1.0-3	2.0-1	HAR Expt	Jour	JNE 1 92	Aug 54	Egelstaff. 8.6+ -.3B CALC FROM SIGTOT	+
Elastic	5.5+5	2.0+6	LAS Expt	Jour	PR 109 2063	Mar 58	Cranberg+	+
	5.5+5	2.0+6		Data	EXFOR12378.004	Jun 76	. 2 PTS. SIGMA.	
Elastic	1.4+7		LAS Expt	Jour	PR 111 250	Jul 58	Coon+,SC,2.73+ -.14B ONLY TO 50 DEG	+
	1.4+7			Data	EXFOR11322.025	Jun 76	. 1 PT. SIGMA.	
Elastic	7.3-2		ANL Expt	Jour	JCP 35 1950	Dec 61	Atoji+	+
	7.3-2			Data	EXFOR11606.008	Jun 76	. 1 PT. COH AMP.	

92 Uranium

Quantity	Energy (ev) Min	Max	Lab	Type	Documentation Ref Vol Page	Author, Comments Date	Data
Elastic	4.2−2		LAS	Expt Jour	ACR 15 351	62 Roof+	+
	4.2−2			Data	EXFOR11435.004	Jun 76 . 1 PT. COH AMP.	
Elastic	1.5+7		VIR	Expt Jour	PR 128 1271	Nov 62 Hudson+ 3.21+ −.24B,INTEGRAL OF DIFF	+
	1.5+7			Data	EXFOR12180.007	Jun 76 . 1 PT. SIGMA.	
Elastic	9.8+5		ALD	Expt Jour	NP 42 86	Apr 63 Gilboy+ BY INTEGRATION + −3PC	
Elastic	3.0+5	1.5+6	ANL	Expt Jour	NP 47 633	Sep 63 Smith.TOF.	+
				Rept	EANDC(US)−62	Jun 64 − .TOF,TBL.50KEV STEPS,20KEV RSLN	
	3.0+5	1.5+6		Data	EXFOR12382.003	Jun 76 . 30 PTS. SIGMA.	
Elastic	1.0+5	1.4+7	AGN	Eval Rept	TID−21629	Dec 64 Perkins+ CALCTD FROM BNL400,UCRL5573	
Elastic	4.0+6		KUR	Expt Rept	IAE−1053	65 Gorlov+,SIG ELASTIC AT 0 DEG,TBL	
				Rept	ANL−TRANS−371	66 . ENGL OF IAE−1053	
Elastic	3.0+5	8.0+5	IFU	ExTh Jour	AE 20 8	Jan 66 Korzh+SJA 20 8 SUM OF SEV YRS WORK	+
Elastic	7.0+6	1.5+7	OHO	Theo Jour	NC/B 53 2 363	Feb 68 Cassola+ OPTMOD CALC CFD EXPT.	
Elastic	4.0+6		KUR	Expt Jour	YF 8 1086	Dec 68 Gorlov+ NATURAL U,VAL GVN	
				Jour	SNP 8 630	Jun 69 TRANSLATN.*	
Elastic	8.7+5		ANL	Expt Rept	ANL−7935	Jun 72 COX+ 4 PI B(O)	+
	8.7+5			Data	EXFOR10332.136	Jun 74 1 PT	
Diff Elastic	1.0+6		WIS	Expt Rept	TID−5157	53 Walt+ CURVE	+
	1.0+6			Data	EXFOR12381.003	Jun 76 . 9 PTS. D SIGMA.	
Diff Elastic	8.0+4		HAR	Expt Jour	PPSA 68 940	Oct 55 Allen+.ANG DIST 60−150DEG NEAR ISOTR	
Diff Elastic	2.5+6	7.0+6	LAS	Expt Rept	LA−2061	56 Walt.	+
	2.5+6	7.0+6		Data	EXFOR12371.	Jun 76 . 47 PTS. DSIGMA.	
Diff Elastic	1.0+5	1.0+7	LAS	Theo Rept	LA−2099	Dec 56 Beyster+,16ES,OPTMDL CALC CFD EXPT	
Diff Elastic	1.4+7		LAS	Expt Rept	LA−2111	57 Rosen+	+
	1.4+7			Data	EXFOR12372.002	Jun 76 . 9 PTS. D SIGMA.	
Diff Elastic	2.0+6		KUR	Expt Jour	ZET 33 294	Jul 57 Aleksandrov.HE4−CHAMBR,4−25DEG,GRAPH	
				Jour	JET 6 228	Jan 58 TRANSLATN.*CTD ZET 40 1878	
Diff Elastic	5.5+5	2.0+6	LAS	Expt Jour	PR 109 2063	Mar 58 Cranberg+,TOF SC ABS CRVS	+
	5.5+5	2.0+6		Data	EXFOR12378.	Jun 76 . 30 PTS. DSIGMA.	
Diff Elastic	1.4+7		LAS	Expt Jour	PR 111 250	Jul 58 Coon+,SC,5−55DEG ABSCURV CFD CCB	+
				Conf	58Geneva 15 11	Sep 58 − +.PPR666,CURVE CFD OPTMDL CALCU	
	1.4+7			Data	EXFOR11322.026	Jun 76 . 13 PTS. D SIGMA.	
Diff Elastic	1.4+7		LRL	Expt Rept	UCRL−4926	Jul 57 Walt+ SC 3−18DEG. GIVES TOP E−POLRZB	
				Conf	58Geneva 15 3	Sep 58 Benveniste.PPR2494,CURVE CFD THEORY	
Diff Elastic	1.3+6	1.6+6	ALD	Expt Jour	PPS 73 193	59 Batchelor. = 1 DATA INDEX LINES	+
Diff Elastic	9.6+7		OXF	Expt Jour	NP 21 15	Nov 60 Salmon.EFFECTIVE E. 1 TO 10 DEG CM.	+
				ExTh Jour	NP 21 21	Nov 60 Hodgson. OPTMDL FIT TO DATA 3 REFS.	
Diff Elastic	1.0+6		CCP	Theo Book	NEJTRONFIZ 314	61 Ermakov.GRPH SCHROEDINGER−TH CFD XPT	
				Book	SPN 231	61 . ENGL TRANSL OF NEJTRONFIZ 314	
Diff Elastic	5.0+4	2.3+6	ANL	Expt Jour	AP 12 135	Feb 61 Lane+ MOD TANK DET	+
				Rept	ANL−6172	Oct 60 − + TABULATED DATA	
	5.0+4	2.3+6		Data	EXFOR10415.017	Jul 74 248PTS,DSIGMA	
Diff Elastic	8.0+5	2.8+6	KUR	Expt Jour	JET 40 1878	Jun 61 Aleksandrov.SMALL ANG SCAT INCREASED	+
				Jour	JET 13 1319	Dec 61 TRANSLATN.*	
Diff Elastic	5.5+5		ANL	Expt Conf	61Vienna 1 29	Aug 61 Smith.P76,CURVE,MANY REFS GVN	
Diff Elastic	1.5+7		VIR	Expt Jour	PR 128 1271	Nov 62 Hudson+ TOF.RSLN1.8MEV. CFD OPTMDL	+
	1.5+7			Data	EXFOR12180.008	Jun 76 . 32 PTS. D SIGMA.	
Diff Elastic	1.4+7		FTI	Expt Jour	ZET 44 130	Jan 63 Dukarevich+ GRAPH ANGL=3−20 DEG	+
				Jour	JET 17 89	Jul 63 TRANSLATN.*	
	1.4+7			Data	EXFOR40078.006	Oct 71 DIFF SIG AT 13 ANGLES	
Diff Elastic	1.8+7	1.2+8	HAR	Expt Jour	NP 40 186	Jan 63 Bowen+.DSIG+POL AT 1,2.5,4.5 DEGREES	+
Diff Elastic	9.8+5		ALD	Expt Jour	NP 42 86	Apr 63 Gilboy+ 30 TO 137DEG.CFD OPTICAL MOD	+
Diff Elastic	3.0+5	1.5+6	ANL	Expt Jour	NP 47 633	Sep 63 Smith.TOF.CFD C DIFF ELAST.20−145DEG	+
				Rept	EANDC(US)−62	Apr 67 − .TOF,TBL LEGEND COEF LAB SYSTEM	
	3.0+5	1.5+6		Data	EXFOR12382.002	Jun 76 . 150 PTS. LEG COEFS.	
	3.5+5	1.3+6		Data	EXFOR12382.004	Jun 76 . 121 PTS. D SIGMA.	
Diff Elastic	3.0+5	5.0+5	IFU	Expt Jour	UFZ 9 929	May 64 Korzh.GRPHS SIG(COS),TBL DERIVD VALS	
				Rept	INDSWG−101 112	65 .=UFZ9.ENGL NO GRPHS.RUSS LARGER GPH	
Diff Elastic	1.0+6	1.4+7	HAR	Theo Rept	AERE−R−4649	Jul 64 Wilmore+OPTMOD SHAPE + COMP.ELASTIC	
						Jun 64 − . OPTMOD. TBLS.CURVES.	
Diff Elastic	1.0+5	1.4+7	AGN	Eval Rept	TID−21629	Dec 64 Perkins+ LEG COEF CALC FROM DAT.CRV	
Diff Elastic	5.7+5		LMS	Expt Jour	PR/B 137 629	Feb 65 Walt+ SC 3−18 DEG CONST.	+
	5.7+5			Data	EXFOR12379.002	Jun 76 . 7 PTS. SIGMA.	
Diff Elastic	8.0+5		IFU	Theo Jour	UFZ 10 6 586	Jun 65 Korzh.OPTMDL GRAPH SIG,CFD XPT	
				Jour	IZV 29 862	May 65 .	

92 Uranium

Quantity	Energy (ev) Min	Max	Lab	Type	Documentation Ref Vol Page	Author, Comments Date	Data
Diff Elastic	8.0+5		IFU	Theo	Conf 65Antwerp § 193	Jul 65 Pasechnic+. OPT.MOD.PARAMETERS	
					Jour AE 16 207	Mar 64 Rasechnik+ SPH 30–140 DEGREES	
					Jour JNE 19 278	Apr 65 . ENGL OF AE 16 207	
					Jour SJA 16 246	Mar 64 . ENGL OF AE 16 207	
Diff Elastic	3.0+5	8.0+5	IFU	ExTh	Jour AE 20 8	Jan 66 Korzh+SJA 20 8 SUM OF SEV YRS WORK	+
Diff Elastic	8.3+5		ANL	ExTh	Jour PR 142 758	Feb 66 Elwyn+ 1.6–149DEG. LO A SCAT.	+
	8.3+5			Expt	Data EXFOR12380.003	Jun 76 . 4 PTS. D SIGMA.	
Diff Elastic	5.0+6		DKE	Expt	Jour ZP 196 103	Sep 66 Buccino+ 20–140DEG,CFD OPTMOD. TABLE	+
					Abst DA 24 4251	Apr 64 Hollandsworth. CFD.OPTMOD CALCS.	
	5.0+6				Data EXFOR11877.013	Jun 76 . 12 PTS. D SIGMA.	
Diff Elastic	4.0+6		CCP	Expt	Jour ZEP 5 131	Feb 67 Gorlov+ COULOMB+NUCL SIG(ANG) GRAPHS	
					-	= ENGLISH $JEL 5 106 2/67$	
Diff Elastic	4.0+6		IFU	Theo	Jour UFZ 13 51	Jan 68 Kashuba+ GRPH,EXPT CFD OPTMOD–CALC	
					Jour UPJ 13 33	Jul 68 TRANSLATN.*	
Diff Elastic	1.4+7		SAC	Expt	Prog EANDC(E)89U	Jan 68 Delobeau.TOF	
					Prog EANDC(E)57U	Feb 65 .TOF.ANGL DISTR 20–100DGR,TBC	
Diff Elastic	1.5+7		OHO	Theo	Jour NC/B 53 2 363	Feb 68 Cassola+ OPTMOD CALC CFD EXPT.	
Diff Elastic	1.0+5	1.5+7	FEI	Eval	Conf 68Dubna § 9	Jun 68 Nikolaev+.ANGDIST VS COS,COEFF VS E	
Diff Elastic	1.5+7		KFI	Expt	Jour YF 8 439	Sep 68 Adam+ CV SIG(0TO 100DEG) OKS OPTMOD	
					Jour SNP 8 255	Mar 69 TRANSLATN.*	
Diff Elastic	6.0+5	1.6+6	ANL	Expt	Jour PR 176 1405	Dec 68 Kuchnir+ VDG+SCINT 5ES 1.75–15DEG	+
	6.0+5	1.6+6			Data EXFOR11977.007	Jun 76 . 31 PTS. D SIGMA.	
Diff Elastic	4.0+6		KUR	Expt	Jour YF 8 1086	Dec 68 Gorlov+ SIG(ANG),ASSYM,INC N POLRZD	+
					Jour IZV 34 138	Jan 70 – + OPTMOD,2–21DEGS.CURVES,TABLE	
					Jour SNP 8 630	Jun 69 TRANSLATN.*	
				ExTh	Rept IAE–1653	68 Gorlov+ ANGDIST 2–21 DEG,SIG, GRPH	
				Expt	Jour PL/B 25 197	Aug 67 – +,SMALL ANGLES,CFD OPTMOD	
					Rept ANL–TR–462	Apr 67 .SEE ALSO *	
					Jour ZEP 5 131	Feb 67 Gorlov+ COUL+NUCL SIG(ANG),GRAPHS	
					Rept IAE–1053	65 – +,POLRZ EFFECTS,2–6 DEGS,TBL	
					Jour BAS 34 126	Jan 70 . ENGL OF IZV 34 138	
					Jour JEL 5 106	Feb 67 . ENGL OF ZEP 5 131	
					Rept ANL–TRANS–371	66 . ENGL OF IAE–1053	
	4.0+6				Data EXFOR40307.012	Nov 76 DIFF CS 2–21 DEG(8 ANGLES)	
Diff Elastic	2.0+6	5.0+6	SCU	Theo	Rept ICD–6 236	69 Averyanov+CALC ANGDIST CFD EXPT,GRPH	
Diff Elastic	+6	+7	CCP	Revw	Jour AE 28 310	Apr 70 Lebedeva+ ANOMALOUS SIG(ANG) GRAPHS	
					Jour EAF 28 4 35	Apr 70 . FRENCH OF AE 28 310	
Diff Elastic	4.0+6		KUR	Expt	Jour ZEP 12 181	Aug 70 Morozov+ SIG(ANG=140 TO 180) GRAPH	
					Jour JEL 12 125	Aug 70 . ENGL OF ZEP 12 181	
Diff Elastic	1.3+6	8.4+6	FEI	Expt	Rept FEI–244	Apr 71 Anikin+ SCAT AT 17ANGS,GRPH SIG(ANG)	+
					Jour SNP 12 614	Jun 71 *ENGL OF YF 12 1121	
					Jour YF 12 1121	Dec 70 *REPLACED BY FEI–244	
	5.7+5	8.4+6		ExTh	Conf 65Antwerp	Jul 65 Anikin. 6 ES. AS 2.5–23.8. CF OPTMDL	
	5.8+5	8.4+6		Expt	Data EXFOR40080.	Nov 71 ANGDIST 2.5–24DEG AT 5 ES,TBL YFI–10	
Diff Elastic	8.7+5		ANL	Expt	Rept ANL–7935	Jun 72 Cox+. CFD OPTMOD,HAUSER–FESHBACH	+
	8.7+5				Data EXFOR10332.035	Jun 74 8 PTS	
Diff Elastic	2.0+6		ANL	Expt	Prog ANL–8010 13	Jun 72 COX.25 ELEMENT STUDY.16 ANG.ANAL TBC	
Diff Elastic	8.0+5		SCU	Comp	Rept YK– 15 153	Aug 73 Aver'Janov+ H–F,OPTMOD,DIFFSIG,GRAPH	
Diff Elastic	1.5+7		ALB	Expt	Jour NP/A 212 147	Sep 73 Benenson+0.35–10DEG.CFD SCAT.CFD OPTMODL	+
	1.5+7				Data EXFOR10370.002	May 74 10 PTS	
Diff Elastic	3.0+6		EDG	Expt	Jour NP/A 212 182	Sep 73 Galloway+ POLRZD NS.	+
	3.0+6				Data EXFOR20359.008	Sep 74 . 5PTS.D/DA.	
Diff Elastic	1.4+7	1.5+7	JAE	Theo	Conf JAERI–M–5984	Feb 75 Tanaka.OPTMDL/COUPLD CH.GRPH CFD EXP	+
						73 Martin+3ANGS.TBL OPTMDL PARS.GRPH.	
Diff Elastic	4.3+6		UBC	Expt	Jour CJP 51 2197	May 75 Mcfadden.5TO15DEG.CFD OPT MDL.AGREE.	
					Abst DA/B 35 5580		
	4.3+6				Data EXFOR10375.	Apr 76 DATA UNOBTAINABLE FROM AUTHORS	
Polarization	3.0+6		VIR	Expt	Jour PR 108 116	Oct 57 Hereford+,D–D NS,ANG DISTR OF POLARZ	
Polarization	3.8+5	9.8+5	WIS	ExTh	Jour NP 6 177	Mar 58 Clement+. POLARIZATION. CFD OPT MDL	
				Expt	Rept AECU–3628	57 – +.LI7(P,N) SOURCE. 3ANGLES.	
Polarization	1.5+6		DKE	Expt	Rept TID–19051	62 Olness+ TOF 51.5DEG POLARIZ MEASD	
Polarization	6.0+5	1.6+6	ANL	Expt	Jour PR 176 1405	Dec 68 Kuchnir+ VDG+SCINT 5ES 1.75–15DEG	
Polarization	4.0+6		KUR	Expt	Jour YF 8 1086	Dec 68 Gorlov+ GRPH POLARIZ–EFF(0 TO 7 DEG)	+
					Jour SNP 8 630	Jun 69 TRANSLATN.*	
					Jour ZEP 5 131	Feb 67 Gorlov+ SCHWINGER(COUL)+NUC SCAT CFD	
					Jour JEL 5 106	Feb 67 . ENGL OF ZEP 5 131	
	4.0+6				Data EXFOR40307.013	Nov 76 DIF.ASYM. 2–21 DEG(8 ANGLES)	

92 Uranium

Quantity	Energy (ev) Min	Max	Lab	Type	Documentation Ref Vol Page	Author, Comments Date	Data
Polarization	5.7+5	4.0+6	CCP	Revw	Jour AE 28 310	Apr 70 Lebedeva+ POLARIZ(ANG),ANOMALOUS – SCAT	
					Jour EAF 28 4 35	Apr 70 . FRENCH OF AE 28 310	
Polarization	4.0+6		KUR	Expt	Jour ZEP 12 181	Aug 70 Morozov+ NO DATA GIVEN,HIGH BACKGRND	
					Jour JEL 12 125	Aug 70 . ENGL OF ZEP 12 181	
Polarization	1.3+6	8.4+6	FEI	Expt	Rept FEI – 244	Apr 71 Anikin+ POLARIZABILITY OF N ESTIMATD	
Polarization	8.7+5		ANL	Expt	Rept ANL – 7935	Jun 72 Cox+. CFD OPTMOD,HAUSER – FESHBACH	+
	8.7+5				Data EXFOR10332.069	Jun 74 8 PTS	
Polarization	2.0+6		ANL	Expt	Prog ANL – 8010 13	Jun 72 COX.25 ELEMENT STUDY.16 ANG.ANAL TBC	
Polarization	3.2+6		AMS	Expt	Conf 72Budapest 170	Aug 72 Zijp+ POLARIZTN,EXPT CFD OPTMOD,GRPH	
Polarization	3.0+6		EDG	Expt	Jour NP/A 212 182	Sep 73 Galloway+ 2 – 8DEG DIFF SCAT CFD TH.	+
	3.0+6				Data EXFOR20359.009	Sep 74 5PTS.ASSYM.	
Potntal Scat	2.0+1	8.0+1	BNL	Expt	Jour PR 110 692	May 58 Seth+,10.7+ – 0.3B CALCTD FROM TOT SIG	+
					Jour RMP 30 442	Apr 58 – . SIG = 10.7+ – 0.4 B.	
					Jour PHY 22 994	Nov 56 Hughes.10.7B+ – 0.4B RECT FOR INTERFER	
	2.0+1	8.0+1			Data EXFOR11788.023	Jun 76 . 1 PT.	
Potntal Scat	1.0+6	1.6+7	HAR	Theo	Jour NP 55 673	Jul 64 Wilmore+ OPTMOD. SHAPE ELASTIC ONLY.	
	1.0+6	1.4+7			Rept AERE – R – 4649	Jun 64 – .OPTMDL TH.TBLS,CURVES.PM10PC	
Potntal Scat	None		DKE	Expt	Abst DA/B 28 3834	Mar 68 Divadeenam.TRNS.EFFECTIVE RADIUS	
Potntal Scat	4.0+6		KUR	Expt	Jour YF 8 1086	Dec 68 Gorlov+ NUCL+ COUL(SPIN – ORB)POT SCATNG	
					Jour SNP 8 630	Jun 69 TRANSLATN.*	
Tot Inelastc	5.0+5	1.0+6	HAR	Expt	Jour PPSA 69 214	Mar 56 Batchelor. HE3 SPECTROMETER	
					Rept AERE – NP/R – 1629	Feb 55 – . TO 1.3MEV	
Tot Inelastc	2.9+5	1.0+6	CCP	Expt	Jour ZET 30 1017	Jun 56 Poze.SIG AT 3ES GIVEN,AV E OF SCT NS	
	3.0+5	1.0+6			Jour ADP 20 3	Jul 57 Pose+,MEASURED AT 3 E – POINTS,TBL	
	2.9+5	1.0+6			Jour JET 3 745	Dec 56 TRANSLATN.*	
Tot Inelastc	1.4+7		ALD	Eval	Jour JNAB 14 100	May 61 Allen+ LESS THAN 0.3B	
Tot Inelastc	4.0+5	1.0+6	CCP	Expt	Jour AE 14 400	Apr 63 SPH 60KEVRSLN 4ES+SPECTRA GLAZKOV	+
Tot Inelastc	8.0+5	4.0+6	IFU	Expt	Prog INDSWG – 126 22	66 Pasechnik. AT 5 ES, TBP IN AE	
Tot Inelastc	3.8+8	1.7+9	PTN	Expt	Jour PR/C 7 248	Jan 73 Schimmerling+.TOF.TRANS.TABLE 15 ES	+
					Jour PL/B 37 177	Nov 71 .SUPERSEDED	
	3.8+8	1.7+9			Data EXFOR10082.025	Dec 75 15PTS. SIN CS DATA.	
Diff Inelast	5.0+5	1.0+6	HAR	Expt	Jour PPSA 69 214	Mar 56 Batchelor. HE3 SPECTROMETER	
					Rept AERE – NP/R – 1629	Feb 55 – . TO 1.3MEV	
Diff Inelast	5.5+5	2.0+6	LAS	Expt	Jour PR 109 206	Mar 58 Cranberg+	+
	5.5+5	2.0+6			Data EXFOR12378.	Jun 76 . 30 PTS, DSIGMA	
Diff Inelast	1.3+6	1.6+6	ALD	Expt	Jour PPS 73 193	59 Batchelor. = 1 DATA INDEX LINES	
Diff Inelast	9.8+5		LAS	Expt	Rept LA – 2177	Jan 59 Cranberg.	+
	9.8+5				Data EXFOR12373.002	Jun 76 . 15 PTS. D SIGMA.	
	9.8+5				Data EXFOR12373.003	Jun 76 . 1 PT. SIGMA.	
Diff Inelast	1.4+7		CRC	Expt	Jour CJP 39 957	Jul 61 Clarke.2MEV UP AT 90D,9MEV UP 30+60D	+
	1.4+7				Data EXFOR12385.002	Jun 76 . 1 PT.	
Diff Inelast	4.0+5	1.0+6	CCP	Expt	Jour AE 14 400	Apr 63 SPH 60KEVRSLN 4ES+SPECTRA GLAZKOV	
Diff Inelast	4.0+6	6.5+6	DKE	Expt	Jour NP 60 17	Nov 64 Buccino+N SPEC MEASURED 4ES+NUC TEMP	
					Abst DA 24 4251	Apr 64 Hollandsworth. TOF. EN SPEC.NUCL T.	
Diff Inelast	1.4+7		SAC	Expt	Prog EANDC(E)57U	Feb 65 .TOF.SPECT OF SCAT NS GIVEN,TBC	
Diff Inelast	3.0+5	8.0+5	IFU	Expt	Prog INDSWG – 126 22	66 Pasechnik. AT 3 ES, TBP IN AE	
Diff Inelast	1.5+7		KFI	Expt	Jour YF 8 439	Sep 68 Adam+'ANOMALOS – EL – FORW – SCAT'EXPLAIND	
					Jour SNP 8 255	Mar 69 TRANSLATN.*	
Diff Inelast	1.0+4	1.0+7	HEB	Theo	Priv NISSIMOV	69 Nissimov+MICROSC SIG CHECK BY N – SPEC	
Diff Inelast	4.0+5	1.0+7	KFK	Expt	Rept KFK – 1968	May 74 Pieroni. SIG CHECK BY N – SPEC EXPT	
Thermal Scat	1.0+4	1.0+7	HEB	Theo	Priv NISSIMOV	69 Nissimov+MICROSC SIG CHECK BY N – SPEC	
Thermal Scat	1.0 – 4	1.0+3	MUN	Revw	Jour EEN 80 1	77 Koester. SCAT LENGTH	
Scattering	9.0+7		BRK	Theo	Jour PR 75 1352	May 49 Fernbach+ EXPT CFD OPAQUE SPH MODEL	
Scattering	6.0+4	1.8+6	ANL	Expt	Jour PR 107 1077	Aug 57 Langsdorf+,LEGENDRE COEFS CURVES	+
					Rept ANL – 5567	Oct 61 .REVISED DATA	
	1.4+5	1.4+6			Data EXFOR11224.074	Jun 76 . 16 PTS. SIGMA.	
	1.4+5	1.4+6			Data EXFOR11224.075	Jun 76 . 80 PTS. D SIGMA.	
	1.4+5	1.4+6			Data EXFOR11224.073	Jun 76 . 6 PTS. LEG. COEFFS.	
Scattering	Fast		CCP	Expt	Jour AE 13 62	Jul 62 Kozlova+ E+ANGL DIST SEC N	
					Jour SJA 13 649	Mar 63 .ENGL TRANSLATION OF AE 13 62 JUL62	
Scattering	8.3+5		ANL	Expt	Jour PR 142 758	Feb 65 Elwyn+	+
				ExTh	Conf 65Antwerp 150	Jul 65 Monahan+. 1.6TO23DEGR. ALSO POLARIZ.	
	8.3+5			Expt	Data EXFOR12380.004	Jun 76 . 12 PTS. DSIGMA.	
Scattering	Fast		FEI	Expt	Jour AE 18 409	Apr 65 Gusejnov+ ANGDIST,TH(N,F)DETECTOR	
					Jour JNE 20 700	Aug 66 . ENGL OF AE 18 409	
					Jour EAF 18 4 134	Apr 65 . FRENCH OF AE 18 409	
					Jour SJA 18 526	Apr 65 . ENGL OF AE 18 409	

92 Uranium

Quantity	Energy (ev) Min	Max	Lab	Type	Documentation Ref Vol Page	Author, Comments Date	Data
Nonelastic	7.0+6		LAS	Expt Rept	LA – 2061	56 Walt+	+
	7.0+6			Data	EXFOR12371.005	Jun 76 . 1 PT. SIGMA.	
Nonelastic	1.0+6	2.5+6	LAS	Expt Jour	PR 104 1319	Dec 56 Beyster+,SPH TRNS 2ES+TOT – EL 1E	+
	1.0+6	2.5+6		Data	EXFOR11220.035	Jun 76 . 2 PTS. SIGMA.	
Nonelastic	4.0+4	1.0+7	LAS	Theo Rept	LA – 2099	Dec 56 Beyster+,OPTMDL CALC CFD EXPT,CURVE	
Nonelastic	1.0+6	1.0+7	BNL	Comp Conf	58Geneva 16 8	Sep 58 Hughes.PPR2483,CURVE,MANY REFS	
Nonelastic	7.0+6	1.4+7	LRL	Revw Rept	UCRL – 5345	Sep 58 Howerton.RVN EXP,+TBP BJORKLUND CCB	
Nonelastic	1.4+7		CCP	Expt Jour	AE 5 522	Nov 58 Lebedev+ SPH GEOM,TR DET, 2.91+ – .14B	+
				Jour	JNEA 11 39	59 TRANSLATN.*	
				Jour	SJA 5 1431	58 TRANSLATN.*	
Nonelastic	1.3+7	1.9+7	ALD	Expt Jour	JNAB 14 180	Jul 61 Cohen.SPH TRNS,TABLE. 2.89B AT 14MEV	+
Nonelastic	1.4+7	1.5+7	SAC	Expt Rept	EANDC(E)49L85	Oct 63 DIDIER 2.80 B + – 0.08	+
Nonelastic	1.0+6	1.6+7	HAR	Theo Jour	NP 55 673	Jul 64 Wilmore+OPTMOD INCLUDES COMP ELASTIC	
Nonelastic	8.0+5		IFU	ExTh Jour	AE 20 8	Jan 66 Korzh+SJA 20 8 SUM OF SEV YRS WORK	+
Nonelastic	1.0+7		IJE	Comp Jour	REA 6 4 3	Dec 68 Konshin+ SIG(NEUT – E)+ – ERROR GVN,GRPH	
Absorption	+5		COL	Expt Jour	PR 55 798	Apr 39 Anderson+ WATER BATH,SIG CA 5BN	
Absorption	–		LIE	Expt Jour	ASS 65 125	Dec 51 GUEBEN 5.5+ – 1B RABESOURCE PARFMOD	
Absorption	3.7+0	1.0+3	AE	Expt Jour	AF 6 57	Jan 53 Hellstrand+. TOF.CYCLTRN. RES PARAMS	
Absorption	1.4+9		BNL	Expt Jour	PR 98 13	Jun 55 Coor+	+
	1.4+9			Data	EXFOR11087.019	Jun 76 . 1 PT, SIGMA.	
Absorption	2.5+4	8.3+5	FEI	Expt Jour	ZET 34 574	Mar 58 Belanova. VALUES GIVEN AT 3ES	+
	2.4+4	8.3+5		Jour	SJA 8 462	Jul 61 .TRANSLATN.*GERMAN KE4 147 2/61	
				Jour	AE 8 549	Jun 60 Belanova.VAL FOR 3ES,SPHERE TRNSMISS	
	2.5+4	8.3+5		Jour	JET 7 397	Sep 58 TRANSLATN.*	
Absorption	2.5+4		KUR	Expt Conf	58Geneva 15 50	Sep 58 Leipunskij+.PPR2219,VAL GVN,ACTIVATN	
Absorption	Pile		BUC	Revw Rept	IFA – FR – 37	Sep 63 Purica. PILE OSC,TBL,SIG	
Absorption	1.0+6	1.4+7	HAR	Theo Jour	AERE – R – 4649	Jun 64 Wilmore.OPTMDL TH.TBLS,CURVES.PM10PC	
Absorption	2.4+4		FEI	Expt Conf	66Paris 1 455	Oct 66 Belanova+ 2METHODS,ABSOL EXPT,TABLE	
				Rept	INDSWG – 74 5	Jul 65 *ALSO ENGL,SUPERSEDED	
Absorption	+1	+4	TOK	Expt Conf	67Tokai 127	Oct 67 Akira – Sekiguchi+ PB – SLOW DOWN,TBD	
Res Int Abs	Pile		FAR	Expt Jour	CR 234 2448	Jun 52 Netter+. PILE OSC. REL B.	
Res Int Abs	None		ORL	Theo Jour	NSE 1 501	Dec 56 Dresner.TH EXPRESSN FOR GEOM EFFECTS	
Res Int Abs	–		CCP	Expt Jour	AE 3 507	Dec 57 Klimentov+.EPI CD REACTIVITY REL LI	
				Jour	JNE 9 20	Jun 59 TRANSLATN.*	
				Jour	SJA 3 1387	57 TRANSLATN.*	
Res Int Abs	None		DEL	Expt Abst	DA/B 30 3817	Feb 70 DEKKER LOCAL REACTOR OSCL.300 – 900K	
(n,γ)	Maxwl		NYU	Expt Jour	PR 55 793	Apr 39 Whitaker+ U METAL, AG ACTIVATION DET	
(n,γ)	Maxwl		PAR	Expt Jour	CR 208 1396	May 39 Halban+ALSO RES.NEUTRONS	
(n,γ)	2.5–2	2.5–2	HAR	Expt Jour	JNE 1 319	55 Small. = 1 DATA INDEX LINES	+
(n,γ)	2.5–2		BUC	Expt Conf	61Bucharst 553	Nov 61 Stefanescu+ PILE OSCILLATOR, TABLE	+
	2.5–2			Data	EXFOR30073.009	Oct 71 PILE OSCILLATOR METHOD	
(n,γ)	1.8+4	3.0+5	FOA	Expt Jour	AF 23 425	Mar 63 Bergqvist.TOF 8 ES.NAI.REL AG. GRAPH	+
	1.8+4	3.0+5		Data	EXFOR20024.007	Sep 71 8PTS.SIG.	
(n,γ)	2.0+4		CCP	Theo Jour	AE 23 319	Oct 67 Zagrafov+ CURV(N,G)VS MASS,A=237 – 275	
				Jour	EAF 23 4 62	Oct 67 . FRENCH OF AE 23 319	
(n,γ)	+3	3.0+4	JAE	Expt Prog	NEANDC(J)36L 4	Sep 74 Mizumoto+.LINAC,TOF.LIQ – SCINT.NDG	
Spect (n,γ)	7.5+6		FOA	Expt Conf	65Antwerp 550	Jul 65 Bergqvist+ NAI. ABST.NDG.SHAPE ONLY.	
Spect (n,γ)	2.0+3		MTR	Expt Jour	NCSAC – 31 76	May 70 Greenwood+,ANAL TO BE COMPL,NO DATA	
Inelastic γ	None		DEB	Expt Prog	INDC(SEC) – 18	Aug 71 PG36.PROMPT GAMSPEC,SHORT NOTE,NDG	
Nonelastic γ	5.0+6	1.4+7	SAC	Expt Prog	EANDC(E)89U	Jan 68 DELOBEAU TOF	
(n,2n)	1.5+7		DEB	Eval Jour	REA 11 1 153	Mar 73 Boedy+ RECOMM.VALUE FROM N – Z SYSTEM.	
				Rept	IAEA – 153 173	73 – + DATA SUPERSEDED	
(n,xn) x>2	1.4+7		ALD	Eval Jour	JNAB 14 100	May 61 Allen+ N3N SIG BETWEEN 0.8 AND 1.1B	
(n,α)	Maxwl		CIS	Expt Jour	PR 81 475	Feb 51 Facchini+ ALPHA,SPECTRUMIONCH.TBP NC	
				Jour	PR 82 555	51 – + ERRATUM. LINE 11: 0.3PC.	
Fission	None		PAR	Expt Jour	CR 206 1643	May 38 Curie+ABOUT A FISSION PRODUCT	
Fission	Maxwl		PAR	Expt Jour	CR 208 341	Jan 39 Joliot.PROOF OF EXPLOSION EXISTENCE	
Fission	Maxwl		BRK	Expt Jour	PR 55 417	Feb 39 Green+ ION CH,DELAY LESSTHAN 3MILLIS	
Fission	1.3+5	5.0+5	CAW	Expt Jour	PR 55 416	Feb 39 Roberts+. E RELEASE 75 – 150MEV,ION CH	
Fission	2.4+6		JHU	Expt Jour	PR 55 417	Feb 39 Fowler+ ION CH,INCREASE BY PARAF MOD	
Fission	Maxwl		PAR	Expt Jour	CR 208 652	Feb 39 Thibaud+STUDY OF FISSION FRAGMENTS	
Fission	–2	+2	PTN	Theo Jour	PR 55 418	Feb 39 Bohr.FISS IN 235,CAPT 238.DROP MODEL	
Fission	None		BRK	Expt Jour	PR 55 509	Mar 39 Corson+ CLOUDCH PHOTO OF HEAVY FRAGS	
Fission	Maxwl		COL	Expt Jour	PR 55 511	Mar 39 Anderson+ SIG CA 2B,FOLLOWS 1/V LAW	
Fission	None		PAR	Expt Jour	JPR 10 159	Mar 39 Joliot+RN – BE	
Fission	Fast		PAR	Expt Jour	CR 208 742	Mar 39 Magnan.ALSO TARGET=AU,BI,HG	
Fission	Maxwl		PAR	Expt Jour	CR 208 744	Mar 39 Thibaud+STUDY OF ENERGY	

92 Uranium

Quantity	Energy (ev) Min	Max	Lab	Type	Documentation Ref Vol Page	Date	Author, Comments	Data
Fission	None		PAR	Expt Jour	CR 208 898	Mar 39	Haenny+WE CAN USE NUCLEAR ENERGY	
Fission	Maxwl		PAR	Expt Jour	CR 208 995	Mar 39	Dode. PROOF(NU>1,CHAIN REACTION)	
Fission	–		PAR	Expt Jour	CR 208 1084	Apr 39	Beck+EVIDENCE FOR DISSYMETRY	
Fission	None		PAR	Expt Jour	CR 208 1218	Apr 39	Magnan.NEUTRONS EMITTED	
Fission	Spont		BRK	Expt Jour	PR 55 1269	Jun 39	Libby. 10(14)YR LOWER LIM ON T1/2	
Fission	2.1+6	3.1+6	PTN	Expt Jour	PR 56 168	Jul 39	Ladenburg+.D–D NS.25PC UNCERTAINTY	
Fission	None		PAR	Expt Jour	JPR 10 477	Aug 39	Golstein+PO–BE	
Fission	None		PAR	Expt Jour	JPR 10 388	Aug 39	Thibaud+MANY FISS PRODUCTS AVAILABLE	
Fission	None		PAR	Expt Jour	JPR 10 495	Dec 39	Curie+RN–BE FISSION PRODUCTS	
Fission	Maxwl	+7	BRN	Expt Jour	PR 59 834	May 41	Haynes.TOTAL DECAY CURVES VS E(N)	
Fission	+5	+6	ITY	Expt Jour	PR 60 67	Jul 41	Ageno+ REL FISS RATE,DIFFT N SPECTRA	
Fission	Maxwl		PAR	Expt Jour	CR 223 986	46	TSIEN SAN TSIANG+TERNARY FISSION	
Fission	Maxwl		LAU	Expt Jour	HPA 22 609	Dec 49	Haenny+. REL TO B. FOTOPLATE 4.1B	
Fission	Maxwl		CIS	Expt Jour	HPA 23 556	Sep 50	Facchini+.FISS CHAMBER REL LI 3.97B	
Fission	Maxwl	Pile	SAC	Expt Jour	CR 235 159	Jul 52	Cohen+ PILE,REL PU239.OKS FISS CHAMB	
				Jour	CR 234 2355	Jun 52	– + SUPERSEDED.	
Fission	Pile		HAR	Revw Conf	55Geneva 5 331	Aug 55	Holmes+.P404,RATIO PU239/U GVN	
Fission	9.0+5	5.0+6	PTN	Expt Conf	55Geneva 2 155	Aug 55	Wheeler.P593,CURVE,THEORET DISCUSSN	
Fission	Fast		HAR	Expt Rept	AERE–R/R–2151	57	Absalom+ ZEPHYR+TH ENVELOPE.	
Fission	1.4+7		DEB	Expt Jour	AK 9 297	Dec 67	Somogyi.TERNARY+BINARY FISS–PROBALTY	
Fission	Spont		KTO	Theo Jour	PL/B 47 227	Nov 73	Ohnishi. SPON FISS VS STELLAR TEMP	
Fission	1.4+7		TRM	Expt Rept	BARC–768 53	74	Mehta+ SIG DELAYD FIS,TRACK DET,NDG	
Eta	+6		COL	Expt Jour	PR 55 798	Apr 39	Anderson+ WATER BATH,RA–BE NEUTS	
Eta	None		COL	Expt Jour	PR 56 284	Aug 39	Anderson.FERMI+ EMISSION EXCEEDS ABS	
Eta	Maxwl		CCP	Expt Conf	55Geneva 4 305	Aug 55	Burgov.P660,VAL GVN,EXPT DESCRIBED	
Eta	Maxwl		CCP	Expt Conf	55Geneva 4 295	56	Spivak+SIG=1.337+–0.017	+
Eta	1.4+7		CCP	Expt Jour	AE 5 522	Nov 58	Lebedev+ SPH GEOM,N COUNT, 2.8+–.25	+
				Jour	JNEA 11 39	59	TRANSLATN.*	
				Jour	SJA 5 1431	58	TRANSLATN.*	
Eta	1.2+7	1.9+7	ALD	Expt Jour	JNE 16 261	May 62	White+ SPHERE METHOD.TABLE 3.1–4.1	
				Jour	JNE 14 100	May 61	– + SUPERSEDED	
Nu	Maxwl		COL	Expt Jour	PR 55 799	Apr 39	Szilard+ ABOUT 2. FEW FAST DELAYD NS	
Nu	Maxwl		NYU	Expt Jour	PR 56 619	Oct 39	Zinn+ RA–BE SOURCE. RECOIL H	
Nu	None		PTN	ExTh Jour	PR 57 334	Feb 40	Turner. CALC FROM HALBAN+JOLIOT+XPT	
Nu	Spont		CAN	Expt Jour	CJP 32 498	Aug 54	Geiger+. AVG NU=2.3+–0.2	
Nu	Spont		CBR	Expt Jour	AUJ 9 429	Dec 56	Edge. 0.0156+–0.0012 NS/SEC.G	
Nu	Spont		HAR	Expt Jour	JNEA 11 34	Nov 59	Littler. 15.2+–0.5N/SEC KG.	
				Jour	PPSA 65 203	Mar 52	– .SUPERSEDED.	
Nu	Spont		UK	Expt Jour	JIN 11 1	Nov 59	Waltner+NEUTRONS/SEC/GM=1.532+–.061	
Delayd Neuts	None		CAW	Expt Jour	PR 55 664	Apr 39	Roberts+ PERIOD CA 12.5SEC,4X10(–2)B	
Delayd Neuts		5.0–1	COL	Expt Jour	PR 55 876	May 39	Booth+ ABOUT 1/60 OF PROMPT	
Delayd Neuts	Cold		CHI	Expt Jour	PR 72 541	47	Snell+. YLD OF DELAYED NEUTRONS	
Delayd Neuts	Maxwl		CHI	Expt Jour	PR 72 541	Oct 47	Snell+ 5 PERIODS, INTENSITY.VS T	
Delayd Neuts	Pile		BNL	Expt Jour	PR 91 594	Aug 53	Kunstadter+ LONG–LIVED EMITTERS	
Delayd Neuts	Pile		UK	Expt Jour	BJAS 5 71	56	Macrae+INSTRUMENTATION OF REACTORS	
Delayd Neuts	–		CCP	Expt Jour	YF 7 670	Mar 69	Krisyuk+ XE+KR AS DEL–N–PRECURSORS	
				Jour	SNP 9 3 387	Sep 69	TRANSLATN.*	
Delayd Neuts	None		OSA	Expt Prog	NEANDC(J)42L51	Sep 75	Fukuda.8 SHOULDERS IN N–SPECTRUM	
Frag Neuts	Maxwl		KJL	Expt Conf	55Geneva 2 185	Aug 55	Skarsvag.P884,CURV+TABELS CFD THEORY	
Spect Fiss n	Maxwl		NYU	Expt Jour	PR 56 619	Oct 39	Zinn+ RA–BE SOURCE, RECOIL H	
Spect Fiss n	1.4+7		CAN	Expt Abst	BAP 4 258	Apr 59	Clarke. TOF,E DIST SEC N AT 90 DEG	
Spect Fiss n	1.0+4	1.0+7	HEB	Theo Priv	NISSIMOV	69	Nissimov+MICROSC SIG CHECK BY N–SPEC	
Spect Fiss γ	Maxwl		BRK	Expt Jour	PR 55 877	May 39	Kennedy+ NO HIGH E BETAS,FEW PROMPT	
Spect Fiss γ		5.0–1	COL	Expt Jour	PR 55 876	May 39	Booth+ DECAY PERIODS CA. 10S AND 40S	
Spect Fiss γ	None		PTN	Expt Jour	PR 55 989	May 39	Barschall+ RELATIVLY V FEW HARD BETA	
Spect Fiss γ	2.5+6		DKE	Expt Jour	PR 56 238	Aug 39	Mouzon+ E(G)VERSUS NO TRACKS	
Fiss Prod γ	2.5+6		DKE	Expt Jour	PR 56 238	Aug 39	Mouzon+ E(G)VERSUS NO TRACKS AT.5SEC	
Fiss Prod γ	Pile		CCP	Expt	–		ENGLISH SRA 7 122 1–2/65	
				Jour	SRA 7 122	Feb 65	. ENGL OF RAK 7 120	
Fiss Prod γ	Pile		SOR	Comp Conf	67Vienna 115	Apr 67	Amiel+ GRAPH SPEC,FOR DEL–NEUTS–EXPT	
Fiss Prod γ	Maxwl		HAR	Expt Conf	69Vienna 637	Jul 69	Large+PPR59. E–GAM=MEV,HLS=MIN TO H	
Fiss Prod γ	Maxwl		PEL	Expt Rept	PEL–194	Oct 69	Steyn+ GAM–SPECS,FISS–PRODCT–RELEASE	
Fiss Prod γ	Pile		BRK	Expt Jour	PL/B 38 22	Jan 72	Slaughter+ G,N COMPETITION BY BR+KR	
Fiss Yield	Maxwl		BRK	Expt Jour	PR 55 670	Apr 39	Abelson.SB+TE+I ACTS.CF PR55,418+876	
Fiss Yield	None		COL	Expt Jour	PR 55 982	May 39	Glasoe+ 2 GAS SERIES DETECTD. KR,XE	
Fiss Yield	2.5+6		JHU	Expt Jour	PR 55 880	May 39	Dodson+ 2 I ISOTOPES, 1 BROMINE	

92 Uranium

Quantity	Energy (ev) Min	Max	Lab	Type	Documentation Ref Vol Page	Date	Author, Comments	Data
Fiss Yield	+5		JHU Expt	Jour	PR 57 966	Jun 40	Dodson+ STUDY OF I,XE PRODUCTS	
				Jour	PR 55 880	May 39	− + CONTINUED	
Fiss Yield	None		COL Expt	Jour	PR 58 1	Jul 40	Glasoe+ RB+CS CHAINS OBS.G−M COUNTER	
Fiss Yield	1.7+7		BRK Expt	Jour	PR 59 212	Jan 41	Segre+ PROD OF PD111,2,RU,AG OBSERVD	
Fiss Yield	+6		JAP Expt	Jour	PR 59 677	Apr 41	Nishina+ RH AND RU OBSERVED	
				Jour	PR 59 323	Feb 41	SUPERSEDED*	
				Jour	PR 58 660	Oct 40	SEE ALSO * PD,AG,CD,IN.	
	+7			Jour	SCP 37 457	Jul 40	Yasaki.LI+D.ACTIVITY OF PD,AG,CD,IN	
Fiss Yield	Maxwl		IRK Expt	Jour	OAWS 151 323	Dec 42	Jentschke.RANGE SPECT.	
Fiss Yield	−		COP Expt	Jour	PR 71 281	Mar 47	Boggild+CLOUDCH DIFFERENT GASES.NDG.	
Fiss Yield	Maxwl		CHI Expt	Jour	PR 72 545	Oct 47	Snell+ CHEM.ISOLATION OF I, BR.	
Fiss Yield	Maxwl		CAV Expt	Jour	PRSA 191 428	Dec 47	Cassels+.DETECT TERNARY FISS,1943−5	
Fiss Yield	+0	+6	CAV Expt	Jour	PCP 44 124	Jan 48	Broda+ RATIO OF BA139 FAST TO SLOW F	
Fiss Yield	None		ANL Expt	Jour	PR 76 1717	Dec 49	Inghram+ REL YLDS CS133−137.MASSSPEC	
Fiss Yield	Maxwl		LAS Expt	Jour	PR 89 570	Feb 53	Sugarman. RADIOCHEM GE77+78,AS77+78.	
Fiss Yield	Pile		HAR Expt	Jour	PR 92 1072	Nov 53	Hardwick.RU−103,106 YLDS.GAM DET.	
Fiss Yield	1.5+6	1.4+7	LAS Expt	Abst	PR 92 1091	Nov 53	Sugarman. RADIOCHEM GE77+78,AS7+78.	
Fiss Yield	Maxwl		USA Expt	Jour	PR 96 1614	Dec 54	Petrow+ SM153 EU156 GD159 TB161 YLDS	
Fiss Yield	2.5−2	2.5−2	HAR Expt	Conf	55Geneva 5 141	Aug 55	Littler.TBL,FISSYLDS+SIGTOT,P432.	
Fiss Yield	Fast		MCM Expt	Jour	CJP 33 541	Sep 55	Wanless+ MASS−SPEC,XE+KR REL YIELDS	
Fiss Yield	Pile		MCM Expt	Jour	CJP 33 541	Sep 55	Wanless+ MASS−SPEC,XE+KR EPICD YLDS	
Fiss Yield	Maxwl		CIS Expt	Jour	EN 2 519	Oct 55	Mongini+	
Fiss Yield	Pile		HAR Expt	Jour	JIN 1 248	Oct 55	Brown.YLD FOR CS137/BA140 CFD OTHERS	
Fiss Yield	1.4+7		LEB Expt	Jour	ZET 29 537	Nov 55	EMISSION CHARGED PARTICLES RARE	
				Jour	JET 2 493	May 56	TRANSLATN.*	
Fiss Yield	Pile		UK Expt	Jour	BJAS 5 71	56	Macrae+INSTRUMENTATION OF REACTORS	
Fiss Yield	Pile		OSL Expt	Jour	JIN 2 69	Feb 56	Pappas+NEW RADIOCHEM.;NEW ISOT.OF SN	
Fiss Yield	Pile		DUR Expt	Jour	CJC 34 293	Mar 56	Purkayastha+ I129 0.5 AND 0.9PC NRX	
Fiss Yield	None		MNZ Expt	Jour	ZN/A 11 946	Nov 56	Herrmann+BE−D N;1.2MEV CASCADE ACCEL	
Fiss Yield	1.4+7		CCP Expt	Jour	AE 5 175	Aug 58	Perfilov+.RANGE+ANG DIS ASSOC ALPHAS	
				Jour	JNEA 10 89	Jul 59	TRANSLATN.*	
				Jour	SJA 5 1017	58	TRANSLATN.*	
Fiss Yield	None		SRL Expt	Jour	NUC 18 9 100	Sep 60	Albenesius+YIELD TRITONS+TRANSURANI	
Fiss Yield	1.4+7		CCP Expt	Jour	RAK 4 587	Oct 62	PARTIAL YLDS OF A=139 ISOBARS,CURVE	
				Jour	SRA 4 515	Oct 62	TRANSLATN.*	
Fiss Yield	Spont		MNZ Expt	Rept	NP−13995	63	Menke.THESIS.I131−135 CUMULAT YLDS	
Fiss Yield	1.5+7		DUR Expt	Jour	RCA 3 80	Oct 64	Lyle+RADIOCHEM YIELD.19NUCL.E=14.7MV	
Fiss Yield	Pile		TRM Revw	Rept	AEET−235	65	Methasiri.TERNRY FISS EXPTS,TBL	
Fiss Yield	Pile		CCP Expt	Jour	RAK 7 120	Jan 65	SC,BA140YLD MEASD,NO.FISSNS CALCTD	
				Jour	SRA 7 122	Feb 65	. ENGL OF RAK 7 120	
Fiss Yield	Fast		ANL Expt	Prog	ANL−7375 179	Oct 67	Meyer+ YLD RATIO PR141/CS137 GIVEN	
Fiss Yield	Maxwl		SAH Expt	Conf	68Bombay 2 216	Dec 68	RAMA RAO. CLOUD−CHAMBR,TERNARY FISSN	
Fiss Yield	Pile		GRE Expt	Conf	69Vienna 803	Jul 69	Blachot+PPR88. YLD,NB+SB+I ISOTOPS	
Fiss Yield	Pile		MCM Expt	Jour	CJP 47 1409	Jul 69	Laeter+ MASS SPEC,SN117−126 REL YLDS	
Fiss Yield	1.5+7		RI Expt	Jour	YF 11 1178	Jun 70	Petrzhak+ YIELD OF XE−ISOTOPES GIVEN	
				Jour	SNP 11 654	Dec 70	. ENGL OF YF 11 1178	
Fiss Yield	Pile		TRM Expt	Rept	BARC−690 137	73	Bhargava+ TABLE+GRAPH. +CD−WRAP,TABL	
Fiss Yield	Pile		TRM Expt	Jour	PR/C 9 1506	Apr 74	RAO+. SEARCH FOR LOW−YIELD FRAGS.	
				Conf	72Bombay 2 53	Feb 72	RAO+ TBL YLDS MASS 66,67,172,175,177	
				Prog	BARC−628 87	72	RAO+ ASYMMETRIC BINARY FISS,TBL+GRPH	
Frag Spectra	None		BRK Expt	Jour	PR 55 510	Mar 39	Mcmillan.ACT OF THIN STACKED FOILS	
Frag Spectra	Maxwl		COL Expt	Jour	PR 55 981	May 39	Booth+ AR IONCH,DOUBLE PEAK N/E CURV	
				Jour	PR 55 982	May 39	− + RANGE DISTRBN IN AIR	
Frag Spectra	Spont		COP Expt	Jour	PR 58 651	Oct 40	Brostrom+ RAVGE+V DIST IN CLOUD CH	
				Jour	PR 58 839	Nov 40	Bostrom+ PART III	
				Jour	PR 58 654	Oct 40	− + PART II	
Frag Spectra	Maxwl		PTN Expt	Jour	PR 58 774	Nov 40	Henderson.HEAT OF FISS BY CALORIMETR	
Frag Spectra	+6		PUR Expt	Jour	PR 60 156	Aug 41	Lark−Horovitz+ ION CH. TERNARY FISS.	
Frag Spectra	None		PAR Expt	Jour	CR 214 110	Jan 42	Magnan.BIPARTITION STUDY	
Frag Spectra	−		COP Expt	Jour	PR 70 577	Nov 46	Lassen. IONISATION LOSSES IN AR.	
Frag Spectra	−		COP Expt	Jour	PR 71 281	Mar 47	Boggild+CLOUDCH DIFFERENT GASES.NDG.	
Frag Spectra	None		ORL Expt	Jour	PR 72 447	Sep 47	Wollan+ ALPHA A,E DISTR. EMULSION.	
Frag Spectra	Spont		HAR Expt	Rept	AERE−N/R−483	Jan 50	Whitehouse+ CFD.U235 THR.FISSN SPECT	
Frag Spectra	Pile		SAC Expt	Rept	CEA−237	Nov 53	DE LABOULAYE+.TRACK LGTH DIST IN AR	
Frag Spectra	+7		CCP Expt	Jour	ZET 31 716	Oct 56	Ostrounov.ANG DSTRB,GRAPH	
Frag Spectra	Maxwl		PSU Expt	Conf	58Geneva 15 404	Sep 58	ROY.PPR694,ANGLE+E−DISTRIBS OF FRAGM	
Frag Spectra	Maxwl		AGN ExTh	Jour	NSE 23 8	Sep 65	Kahn+ INCLUDES RANGE−ENERGY RELATION	

92 Uranium

Quantity	Energy (ev) Min	Max	Lab	Type	Documentation Ref Vol Page	Date	Author, Comments	Data
Frag Charge	0.0+0	1.0+0	COP Expt	Conf	55Geneva 2 214	Aug 55	Lassen.P913,CURVE,EXPT DESCRIBED	
				Jour	PR 69 137	Mar 46	- .MOST PROB.VALUE TOTAL FRG CHG	
Frag Charge	Pile		GRE Expt	Conf	69Vienna 803	Jul 69	Blachot+PPR88. YLD,NB+SB+I ISOTOPS	
Reson Params	6.6+0	6.0+2	AE Expt	Jour	AF 6 57	Jan 53	Hellstrand+. 6.6,20,38EV PARAMS. TOF	
Reson Params	6.7+0	2.0+2	BNL Revw	Conf	55Geneva 5 215	Aug 55	Chernik.P603,TOTAL+N-WIDTH FOR 8RESN	
Reson Params	2.7+2	4.1+3	HAR Expt	Priv	LYNN	58	Lynn. = 1 DATA INDEX LINES	+
Reson Params		1.2+3	UK	Rept	NRDC-138 17	Jan 63	WG IS 23.2PM1.1MV AVERAGE	
Reson Params	2.0+4	3.0+6	CCP Expt	Conf	66Moscow	Feb 66	.INTERMEDIATE FLUCT OF SECTION	
Reson Params	8.5+5	8.5+5	HAR Expt	Jour	NP 80 46	May 66	Barnard. = 1 DATA INDEX LINES	+
Strnth Fnctn	None		DKE Expt	Abst	DA/B 28 3834	Mar 68	Divadeenam.S,P,D WAVES.CFD POT MDLS.	
Strnth Fnctn	2.7+3		MUNExpt	Conf	71Albany 327	Aug 76	Dilg+TRNS.S0 STF GVN.31 ELEMENT GRPH	
Lvl Density	1.4+7		BAS Expt	Abst	HPA 40 345	Jul 67	Boschung+. NUCL T FROM NSPEC TOF TBC	
Lvl Density	None		FEI Theo	Jour	YF 11 1213	Jun 70	Ignatyuk+ SPIN DEPENDENCE OF DENSITY	
				Jour	SNP 11 674	Dec 70	. ENGL OF YF 11 1213	
Lvl Density	None		IBJ Revw	Jour	PF 23 561	Sep 72	Jastrzebski. SPONTAN.FISSION ISOMERS	
(γ,n)		2.5+8	LEB Expt	Jour	ZET 28 623	May 55	Gol'Danskii.MAX FOTO-NS-YLD MEASURED	
				Jour	JET 1 580	Nov 55	TRANSLATN.*	
(γ,n)	6.0+6	2.7+7	LEB Expt	Jour	ZET 30 855	May 56	Gavrilov.GRAPH SIG(E) CFD OTHER XPTS	
				Jour	JET 3 871	Jan 57	TRANSLATN.*	
(γ,n)	+7		CCP Expt	Jour	ZET 46 1906	May 64	Glazunov.GRPH PHOTONEUTRON-E-DSTRB	
				Jour	JET 19 1284	Nov 64	TRANSLATN.*	
Photo-Fissn	None		WES Expt	Jour	PR 58 759	Oct 40	Langer+ BA+SR FRAGS IN BOTH N+G FISS	
Photo-Fissn	-		KTO Expt	Jour	JPJO 23 440	41	Arakatsu+.SIGS FOR LI(P,G)+F(P,G)	
Photo-Fissn	6.3+6		WES Expt	Jour	PR 59 57	Jan 41	Haxby+ P-F GAMMA2=	
	None			Jour	PR 58 92	Jul 40	- + F(P,GAMMA),SIG ESTIM 1/50BARN	
Photo-Fissn		1.9+7	LEB Expt	Jour	ZET 29 274	Sep 55	Lazareva.DELAYED NS FROM FOTOFISSION	
				Jour	JET 2 301	Mar 56	TRANSLATN.*	
Photo-Fissn		1.9+7	LEB Expt	Jour	ZET 29 280	Sep 55	Baluev.NUMBER OF NS PER FOTOFISSION	
				Jour	JET 2 106	Jan 56	TRANSLATN.*	
Photo-Fissn	1.5+7		CCP Expt	Jour	SPD 2 106	Jan 56	NEUTRONS FROM FOTOFISSION	
Photo-Fissn	9.4+6	2.7+7	LEB Expt	Jour	ZET 33 53	Jul 57	Bannik.ANG-DSTRB OF PHOTOFISSFRGMTS	
				Jour	JET 6 39	Jan 58	TRANSLATN.*	
Photo-Fissn	6.1+6	2.0+7	LND Expt	Jour	NP 20 136	Oct 60	Forman+ BREMSTR+ F-P GS. ANGDISTR.	
Photo-Fissn	5.4+6	9.0+6	IEA Expt	Jour	NP/A 186 110	May 72	Mafra+ MONOENERGET GAMS,SIG,TBL,GRPH	
	5.4+6	9.1+6		Jour	AAB 43 57	Dec 71	.SAME EXPERIMENT,TABLE+GRAPH	
	5.4+6	9.0+6		Rept	INDC(BZL)-2	May 69	*EXPT DESCRIBED,NDG	
Photo-Fissn	1.0+7	5.5+7	USP Expt	Conf	73Pacif.Gr 1 653	Mar 73	Nascimento+ SIG(G,F)/SIG(E,F),GRAPH	
Photo-Fissn	8.0+6	1.6+7	BUC Expt	Rept	INDC(SEC)-50	Jan 76	Galateanu+ DELAY GAMS VS INCOM E,TBL	

92 Uranium 230

Quantity	Energy (ev) Min	Max	Lab	Type	Documentation Ref Vol Page	Date	Author, Comments	Data
(n,p)	Maxwl		IFU Theo	Rept	ICD-4 20	67	Dadakina+ PENETR COEFF CALC,TABLE	
Fission	Pile		ANL Expt	Rept	CC-3699 6	46	Bentley+	+
	Pile			Data	EXFOR12384.002	Jun 76	. 1 PT. SIGMA	
Fission	Spont		DUB Theo	Jour	JINR-P-2265	Jul 65	Mekhedov. FISS+ALPH HLS ESTIMATED	
Fission	Spont		CCP Comp	Jour	AE 26 436	May 69	Romanov. HALF-LIFE VAL ESTIMATD,GRPH	
				Jour	EAF 26 48	69	. FRENCH OF AE 26 436.	
				Jour	SJA 26 498	69	. ENGL OF AE 26 436.	
Frag Spectra	None		SAH Theo	Prog	BARC-401	69	RATNA SARKAR+,FERMI-SURFACE MODL,ABS	
				Prog	BARC-401 21	69	Sarkar+ FRAGS EXCIT+KIN E OKS EXPTS	
Strnth Fnctn	None		AI	Rept	NAA-SR-M-12538	Oct 67	Gigas.OPTMDL CALC AVG S0,S1,S2	
Lvl Density	-3	+0	IFU Theo	Jour	UFZ 13 700	Apr 68	Pisanko+ LEVEL SPACING CALC,TBL	
				Jour	UPJ 13 498	Oct 68	TRANSLATN.*	

92 Uranium 231

Quantity	Energy (ev) Min	Max	Lab	Type	Documentation Ref Vol Page	Date	Author, Comments	Data
(n,p)	Maxwl		IFU Theo	Rept	ICD-4 20	67	Dadakina+ PENETR COEFF CALC,TABLE	
Fission	Pile		ANL Expt	Rept	CC-3699 6	46	Bentley+	+
	Pile			Data	EXFOR12384.003	Jun 76	. 1 PT.	
Fission	Maxwl		TRM Theo	Conf	66Bombay 1	Feb 66	Ramanna.VALS CFD TH,SIG,BINDING,DEF.	

92 Uranium 232

Quantity	Energy (ev) Min	Energy (ev) Max	Lab	Type	Documentation Ref Vol Page	Author, Comments Date	Data
Evaluation	–		CCP	Eval	Jour AE 23 6	Jul 67 Kirpitchnikov.RESON PARAMS,MANY REFS	
					Jour SJA 23 669	Jul 67 TRANSLATN.*	
Evaluation	1.0 – 3	1.5 + 7	GA	Eval	Rept GA – 7462	Sep 67 Drake+ TOT N2N N3N SIN SEL NF NG SNE	
Evaluation	2.5 – 2	1.0 + 7	KFK	Eval	Rept KFK – 1186	Jul 70 Hinkelmann.RES,STF,N2N,NF,NU,NG,R.I.	
					Conf 70Helsinki 2 721	Jun 70 – + DESCRIPTION OF EVL.	
Total	1.0 – 2	1.0 + 4	MTR	Expt	Jour NSE 29 415	Sep 67 Simpson+ FC 6RES BELOW 30EV ANALYZED	+
					Rept IN – 1015	Dec 66 – +	
					Jour ANS 6 44	Jun 63 – +	
	1.0 – 2	9.3 + 3			Data EXFOR12375.002	Jun 76 . 931 PTS. SIGMA.	
Total	1.0 + 0	3.1 + 1	MTR	Expt	Prog WASH – 1127 60	Apr 69 Simpson+ REICH – MOORE MULTILEVEL FIT	
Total	2.5 – 2		IJI	Eval	Conf 73Kiev 1 197	May 73 Fedorova. SIG 2200M/S = 163 + – 10 B	
Elastic	4.5 + 5		ANL	Expt	Jour PRL 16 525	Mar 66 Smith.	+
Diff Elastic	4.7 + 5	7.0 + 5	ANL	Expt	Jour PRL 16 525	Mar 66 Smith.	+
Diff Inelast	3.0 + 3	1.0 + 6	BRC	Eval	Rept CEA – R – 4631	Nov 74 Thomet. STAT MDL ANAL TBLS GRPHS	
Scattering	1.3 + 5		ANL	Expt	Jour PR 107 1077	Aug 57 Langsdorf.	+
Scattering	2.5 – 2		IJI	Eval	Conf 73Kiev 1 197	May 73 Fedorova. SIG 2200M/S = 8 + – 5 B	
Absorption	Maxwl		HAR	Expt	Conf 71Canterby 161	Sep 71 Cabell+ ACT	
	Maxwl				Data EXFOR20477.005	Jan 76 1PNT.SIGMA.	
Absorption	None		MUN	Theo	Diss GRYNTAKIS	Mar 76 Gryntakis.,CALC.OF WESTCOTTS G – FUNCT	
					Jour RCA 22 128	Mar 75 – +,EQUIVALENT TO THESIS	
Res Int Abs	5.0 – 1		ORL	Expt	Jour NSE 21 257	Feb 65 Halperin. 280 + – 15B FROM CO IRRADTN	+
	5.0 – 1				Data EXFOR12374.004	Jun 76 . 1 PT. RI	
(n,γ)	Maxwl		ANL	Expt	Jour PR 89 320	Jan 53 Elson+	+
	Maxwl				Data EXFOR12387.003	Jun 76 . 1 PT.	
(n,γ)	Maxwl		ORL	Expt	Jour NSE 21 257	Feb 65 Halperin+78+ – 4B.NEG E RES	+
	Maxwl	Pile			Data EXFOR12374.002	Jun 76 . 2 PTS. SIGMA.	
(n,γ)	Maxwl		AUA	Theo	Jour NSE 31 234	Feb 68 Cook+ STATISTICAL CALC CFD EXPT	
(n,γ)	2.5 – 2	1.0 + 7	KFK	Eval	Rept KFK – 1186	Jul 70 Hinkelmann.5 – GROUP SIG,THR + FAST SPEC	
	2.5 – 2				Rept KFK – 1186	Jul 70 – . RECOMMENDED 78 B	
(n,γ)	Maxwl		HAR	Expt	Conf 71Canterby 161	Sep 71 Cabell+ ACT	+
	Maxwl				Data EXFOR20477.002	Jan 76 1PNT.SIGMA.	
(n,γ)	2.5 – 2		IJI	Eval	Conf 73Kiev 1 197	May 73 Fedorova. SIG 2200M/S = 78 + – 4 B	
(n,γ)	3.0 + 3	1.0 + 6	BRC	Eval	Rept CEA – R – 4631	Nov 74 Thomet. STAT MDL ANAL TBLS GRPHS	
(n,γ)	None		MUN	Theo	Diss GRYNTAKIS	Mar 76 Gryntakis.,CALC.OF WESTCOTTS G – FUNCT	
					Jour RCA 22 128	Mar 75 – +,EQUIVALENT TO THESIS	
Res Int Capt	4.7 – 1	1.0 + 7	KFK	Eval	Rept KFK – 1186	Jul 70 Hinkelmann. INFIN DILUTION RES INTEG	
(n,2n)	8.0 + 5	1.0 + 7	KFK	Eval	Rept KFK – 1186	Jul 70 Hinkelmann.AVG SIG FOR THR + FAST SPEC	
(n,2n)	2.0 + 6	1.5 + 7	BRC	Eval	Rept CEA – R – 4647	Jan 75 Jary. EVAL,STAT MDL, 15 VALS	
(n,xn) x > 2	2.0 + 6	1.5 + 7	BRC	Eval	Rept CEA – R – 4647	Jan 75 Jary. EVAL,STAT MDL, 15 VALS	
Fission	Pile		ANL	Expt	Rept CS – 3471 2	Apr 46 Seaborg.	+
	Pile				Data EXFOR12287.002	Jun 76 . 1 PT. SIGMA.	
Fission	Maxwl		ANL	Expt	Jour PR 89 320	Jan 53 Elson+ BY PA231 IRRADIATION 83 + – 15B	+
	Maxwl				Data EXFOR12387.002	Jun 76 . 1 PT. SIGMA.	
Fission	Pile		LRL	Expt	Prog WASH – 1033 28	Aug 61 Hulet. 50 B	
Fission	4.0 + 0	4.0 + 2	HAR	Expt	Jour NP 55 517	Jul 64 James.GRAPH4 – 100EV,8RES.CF PR112 191	+
	4.0 + 0	1.0 + 2			Jour NIM 28 205	Jun 64 Firk.(JAMES).GAS SCIN DATA IN REVIEW	
	4.0 + 0	4.0 + 2			Rept AERE – M – 1339	Jan 64 James. RESONANCE PARAMETERS GIVEN	
Fission	Maxwl		TRM	Revw	Conf 66Bombay 1	Feb 66 Ramanna.VALS CFD TH,SIG,BINDING,DEF.	
Fission	None		BRK	Revw	Jour NP 81 1	Jun 66 Myers+ TABLE2 FISS BARRIER	
Fission	Pile		FEI	Expt	Jour AE 23 396	Nov 67 Lejpunskij.RATIO REL U235(N,F),PILE	
					Jour EAF 23 5 21	Nov 67 . FRENCH TRANSL OF AE 23 396 11/67	
					Jour SJA 23 1150	Nov 67 .ENGLISH TRANSL OF AE 23 396 11/67	
Fission	5.0 + 0	1.9 + 3	LRL	Expt	Jour NP/A 112 329	May 68 Auchampaugh+.SPARK CH DTECT.REL MTR	+
					Rept UCRL – 70920	Feb 68 .SUPERSEDED	
	4.0 + 0	1.0 + 3			Conf 66Paris 2 149	Oct 66 Bowman+PPR38,NDG.LINAC,SPARKCHAMBER	
	5.1 + 0	1.9 + 3			Data EXFOR12383.003	Jun 76 . 707 PTS. SIGMA.	
Fission	Spont		COP	Revw	Conf 69Vienna 155	Jul 69 Strutinsky+PPR203. HL GVN,'SHELL – TH'	
Fission	Spont		FR	Revw	Conf 69Vienna 952	Jul 69 Monnin+PPR83. SPON FISSN HALF – LIFE	
Fission	4.0 + 1	2.1 + 4	LAS	Expt	Rept LA – 4420	Apr 70 Farrell.NUCL SHOT,TOF,TABLES + CURVES	+
	4.0 + 1	2.0 + 4			Data EXFOR10055.002	May 71 2199PTS.	
Fission	2.5 – 2		KFK	Eval	Rept KFK – 1186	Jul 70 Hinkelmann. RECOMMENDED 77 B	
	2.5 – 2	1.0 + 7			Rept KFK – 1186	Jul 70 – .5 – GROUP SIG,THR + FAST SPEC	
Fission	1.3 + 5	1.5 + 6	KUR	Expt	Jour YF 12 474	Sep 70 Vorotnikov+ REL U FISS,SIG(N – E),GRPH	+
					Rept INDC(CCP) – 15	Dec 71 *P32,ENG OF YFI – 10	
					Rept YFI – 10 30	May 71 *	
					Jour SNP 12 259	Mar 71 *ENGL OF YF 12 474	
	1.2 + 5	1.5 + 6			Data EXFOR40057.002	Mar 71 SIGMA AT 22 ENERGIES	

92 Uranium 232

Quantity	Energy (ev) Min	Max	Lab	Type	Documentation Ref Vol Page	Date	Author, Comments	Data
Fission	Spont		MRY	Theo	Prog ORO-4028-28	71	Jackson+. SPON FISSION HALF-LIFE GVN	
Fission	Maxwl		HAR	Expt	Conf 71Canterby 161	Sep 71	Cabell+ ACT	+
	Maxwl				Data EXFOR20477.003	Jan 76	1PNT.SIGMA.	
Fission	2.5-2		IJI	Eval	Conf 73Kiev 1 197	May 73	Fedorova. SIG 2200M/S=77+-10 B	
Fission	3.0+3	1.0+6	BRC	Eval	Rept CEA-R-4631	Nov 74	Thomet. STAT MDL ANAL TBLS GRPHS	
Fission	3.0+6	5.0+6	LAS	Theo	Conf 75Wash. 129	Mar 75	Moore.GRPH R MATR STAT CALC CFD EXP	
Fission	1.0+1	1.5+6	JAE	Revw	Conf IAEA-186 3 1	76	Igarasi. REVW AVAIL DATA,GRPH+BIBLIO	
	1.0+4	1.5+6			Rept JAERI-M-6315	Nov 75	- +GRPH. 2 DATA SETS COMPARED.	
Fission	Maxwl		MUN	Expt	Diss GRYNTAKIS	Mar 76	Gryntakis.,ACT.MEAS.,CALC OF G-FUNCT	+
				ExTh	Jour RCA 22 128	Mar 75	- +,CALC WESTCOTTS G-FUNCTION	
	2.5-2				Expt Data EXFOR20625.039	Aug 76	1PNT.SIGMA.	
Res Int Fiss	4.7-1	1.0+7	KFK	Eval	Rept KFK-1186	Jul 70	Hinkelmann. INFIN DILUTION RES INTEG	
Res Int Fiss	5.5-1		MUN	Expt	Diss GRYNTAKIS	Mar 76	Gryntakis.,CD-RAT.,378+-116B,INC 1/V	+
	5.5-1				Data EXFOR20625.040	Aug 76	1PNT.	
Alpha	Maxwl		HAR	Expt	Conf 71Canterby 161	Sep 71	Cabell+ FROM ACTIVATION.	+
	Maxwl				Data EXFOR20477.004	Jan 76	1PNT.	
Nu	2.5-2		ANL	Expt	Jour NP/A 145 1	Apr 70	Jaffey+REL TO U STANDARDS.	+
					Rept ANL-7625	Nov 69	- +COMPLETE DATA GVN.	
	2.5-2				Data EXFOR10125.009	May 72	1PT.PROMPT N YLD=3.130+-.060.	
Nu	2.5-2	1.0+7	KFK	Eval	Rept KFK-1186	Jul 70	Hinkelmann. VERSUS E ,TABLE,GRAPH	
Nu	Maxwl		IAE	Eval	Jour REA 10 637	Dec 72	Manero+ EXTENSIVE SURVEY,TBL,AVG VAL	
Nu	Maxwl		ANL	Expt	Prog ANL-6600 124	61	Jaffey.COINC TECH.NU=3.07+-.06	+
	Maxwl				Data EXFOR12251.003	Jun 76	. 1 PT.	
Fiss Yield	Spont		FR	Expt	Conf 69Vienna 952	Jul 69	Monnin+PPR83. YLD(A)+HALF LIFE EXPT	
Fiss Yield	Pile		MUU	Expt	Jour RCA 15 113	Mar 71	Kemmer+ 16 CHAIN YLDS A=85-147	
Fiss Yield	Pile		HAR	Eval	Conf 73Paris 1 393	Mar 73	Crouch.EXPTL DATA+EVAL CHAIN YLD,TBL	
					Rept AERE-R-7209	Jan 73	- .15 CHAIN YLDS RECOMMENDED TBL	
Fiss Yield	Pile		TRM	Expt	Prog BARC-872 101	76	Manohar+ 4 MORE ISOT.MASS-Y,TBL+GRPH	
	Maxwl				Conf 75Calcutta 2 138	Dec 75	- + MASS DISTRIBUTION,GRAPHS	
	Pile				Prog BARC-821 183	75	- + TBL MASS-YLDS(115,127 NEW)	
					Rept BARC-690 132	73	- + REL U-235,G-SPEC+CHEM,TABLE	
Frag Spectra	1.3+5	1.5+6	KUR	Expt	Jour YF 12 474	Sep 70	Vorotnikov+ ANISOTROPY VS N-E,GRAPH	+
					Rept INDC(CCP)-15	Dec 71	*P32,ENG OF YFI-10	
					Rept YFI-10 30	May 71	*	
					Jour SNP 12 259	Mar 71	*ENGL OF YF 12 474	
	1.2+5	1.5+6			Data EXFOR40057.003	Mar 71	ANISOTROPY OF FRAGMENTS AT 22 ES	
Frag Spectra	Maxwl		TRM	Expt	Conf 74Bombay 2 140	Dec 74	Nadkarni+ FRGM MASS-ENERGY CORREL	
Frag Spectra	Pile		TRM	Expt	Prog BARC-821 174	75	Ramaswami+ TOT EKIN(HEAVY FRGS),GRPH	
					Conf 73Bangalor 2 5	Dec 73	Manohar+TOTAL KINETIC E DISTRB GRAPH	
					Rept BARC-690 132	73	- + FRGM-RANGE IN AL,GE-LI+CHEM	
Reson Params	4.3+1	1.9+2	MTR	Expt	Prog IDO-16917 19	Nov 63	Simpson+	+
	1.9+0	4.7+1			Prog IDO-16898 9	Aug 63	- +	
	4.3+1	1.9+2			Data EXFOR12375.	Jun 76	. 12 RES, E0	
Reson Params	4.0+0	4.0+2	HAR	Expt	Jour NP 55 517	Jul 64	James.17RES,4-400EV,G+F+N WIDTHS OF8	+
					Rept AERE-M-1339	Jan 64	- . 17RES. WG,WF,WN	
Reson Params	-		CCP	Eval	Jour AE 23 6	Jul 67	Kirpitchnikov.FISS-,N-WIDTH,STRNTH-F	
					Jour SJA 23 669	Jul 67	TRANSLATN.*	
Reson Params	-.6+0	2.8+1	MTR	Expt	Jour NSE 29 415	Sep 67	Simpson+ WN WF1 WF2 6RES FROM TOT,FC	+
					Rept IN-1015	Dec 66	- +	
	-.6-2	2.8+1			Data EXFOR12375.003	Jun 76	. 12 RES. WN,WF.	
Reson Params		1.0+6	AUA	Theo	Jour AUJ 20 477	Oct 67	Cook. TBL OF AVG LVL SPACING D,L=0,1	
Reson Params	-.6+0	7.4+1	LRL	Expt	Jour NP/A 112 329	May 68	Auchampaugh+.14E0 WN WF MULTILVL FIT	+
					Rept UCRL-70920	Feb 68	.SUPERSEDED	
	-.6-2	7.4+1			Data EXFOR12383.002	Jun 76	. 14 RES. E0, WN, WF	
Reson Params	+5	+6	KUR	Theo	Jour YF 7 1228	Jun 68	Vorotnikov+ D,XPT CFD DEGEN-FERMIGAS	
					Jour SNP 7 732	Dec 68	. ENGL OF YF 7 1228	
Reson Params	6.0+0	2.8+1	MTR	Eval	Prog WASH-1127 60	Apr 69	Simpson+ WN+WF 5ES FROM REICH-MOORE	
Reson Params	None		HAR	Revw	Conf 69Vienna 249	Jul 69	Lynn.TBL STRUTINSKY PARS,FISS+CAPT	
Reson Params	6.5+1	2.2+2	LAS	Eval	Conf 69Vienna 921	Jul 69	Farrell. PPE105. RES ANAL,WN+WF.	
Reson Params	1.0+3	4.6+4	KFK	Eval	Rept KFK-1186	Jul 70	Hinkelmann. AVG.WG,WF,WN,LVL SPACING	
Reson Params	5.9+0	2.6+2	CCP	Theo	Rept YK-16 121	74	Gorbachev+ G+F+N-WIDTHS, TBL	
Strnth Fnctn	6.0+0	7.6+1	HAR	Expt	Jour NP 55 517	Jul 64	James.(1.0)10-4 FROM 8RES UP TO 75EV	+
Strnth Fnctn	None		AI	Theo	Rept NAA-SR-M-12538	Oct 67	Gigas.OPTMDL CALC AVG SO,S1,S2	
Strnth Fnctn	1.0+3	4.6+4	KFK	Eval	Rept KFK-1186	Jul 70	Hinkelmann. SO=1.0 SI=2.	
Strnth Fnctn	None		AUA	Eval	Rept AAEC/E-277	Mar 73	Musgrove.TBLS EXPTL DATA+BEST VALUES	
Lvl Density	-3	+0	IFU	Theo	Jour UFZ 13 700	Apr 68	Pisanko+ LEVEL SPACING CALC,TBL	
					Jour UPJ 13 498	Oct 68	TRANSLATN.*	

92 Uranium 232

Quantity	Energy (ev) Min	Max	Lab	Type	Documentation Ref Vol Page	Date	Author, Comments	Data
Lvl Density		1.0+2	KUR Theo	Jour	YF 9 303	Feb 69	Vorotnikov.LVL DEN(EXCIT−E),TBL GRPH	
				Jour	SNP 9 179	Aug 69	TRANSLATN.*	
Lvl Density	+6		DUB Theo	Rept	JINR−E4−9236	Nov 75	Komov+ AVG LVL−SPAC,SEMIMICRO CFD XP	

92 Uranium 233

Quantity	Energy (ev) Min	Max	Lab	Type	Documentation Ref Vol Page	Date	Author, Comments	Data
Evaluation	5.0+5	1.5+7	LRL Eval	Rept	UCRL−5351	Nov 58	Howerton. CRVS SAME AS TL +NG,N3N,NF	
Evaluation	5.0+2	1.0+7	ANL Eval	Book	FRC 29	60	Yiftah+ 16E GROUPS,FAST REACT DATA.	
Evaluation	2.5−2		MTR Eval	Jour	NSE 8 66	Jul 60	Evans+TOT,SCT,ABS,ALFA,NF,NG,ETA,NU	+
				Rept	IDO−16554	59	−+	
Evaluation	−2	1.0+7	UNC Eval	Rept	NDA−2134−2	Sep 60	Kalos+.DIN N2N NF ETA LVL SEL SIN	
Evaluation	4.1−1	1.0+7	GA Eval	Rept	GA−2451	Aug 61	Joanou+ 68 GROUP DATA FOR GAM−I	
Evaluation	1.0−3	1.0+7	AI Eval	Rept	NAA−SR−M−8904	Aug 63	Alter+.SAME AS MO +NF NU N2N.RES GAP	
Evaluation	2.5−2	1.1+7	FEI Eval	Book	ABAGJAN	64	26 GROUP CONST,TOT,FISS,NU,CAPT,INEL	
Evaluation	2.5−2		BNL Eval	Rept	BNL−918	Mar 65	Sher+. SIGS,FISSN DATA LEAST SQ ANAL	
				Rept	BNL−722	Jun 62	.SUPERSEDED	
Evaluation	1.0−4	1.0+7	B+W Eval	Rept	BAW−393−5	Apr 66	Snidow.TOT SEL ABS SNE NF NG ALF ETA	
Evaluation	2.5−2		TRM Eval	Rept	AEET−257	Aug 66	Singh.NG NF ABS ALF ETA RIF(BNL32552	
Evaluation	1.0−3	1.5+7	GA Eval	Rept	GA−7076	Sep 66	Drake.TOT ABS NF NG ETA ALF NU DEL	
Evaluation	5.0−1	1.0+4	INA Eval	Conf	66Paris 2 333	Oct 66	Hennies.PPR5.RES INT CAPT+FISS,ALPHA	
				Rept	NAA−SR−11980 5	May 67	−. RECOMMENDED DATA.IMPROVED	
Evaluation	1.0+3	1.4+7	UK Eval	Rept	AHSB(S)R−124	May 67	Hart.(RLY).UK−DFN 333.UPDATES NSE 26	
	4.0+6	1.5+7		Rept	AWRE−O−100/64	Jan 65	Douglas+(ALD).UKNDL−DFN 202	
	2.5−2	1.5+7		Rept	AWRE−O−28/60	Mar 61	Buckingham.(ALD).EVAL FOR UKNDL	
	4.0+6	1.5+7		Rept	AWRE−O−28/60	61	−.(ALD).EVAL FOR UKNDL.SPDD	
Evaluation	−		CCP Eval	Jour	AE 23 6	Jul 67	Kirpitchnikov.RESON PARAMS,MANY REFS	
				Jour	SJA 23 669	Jul 67	TRANSLATN.*	
Evaluation		1.4+7	BET Eval	Rept	WAPD−TM−691	Dec 69	Steen.NU,NG,NF EVALTN FOR ENDF/B	
Evaluation	0.0+0	6.0+0	KAP Eval	Rept	KAPL−M−7323	Jun 73	Reynolds+ REICH−MOORE MULTILVL ANAL	
Evaluation	Maxwl		IAE Eval	Conf	75Wash. 286	Mar 75	Lemmel. 3RD IAEA−EVAL BY LSQ FIT	
				Jour	REA 7 4 3	Dec 69	Hanna+ SUPERSEDED	
Total	3.4−2	2.3+3	ANL Expt	Prog	ANL−4983 4	Nov 52	Bollinger+	+
	3.4−2	2.3+3		Data	EXFOR12346.002	Jun 76	. 45 PTS. SIGMA.	
Total	Pile		BNL Expt	Rept	BNL−221	Jan 53	Harvey+ DECL JUL1955 NEW VALUE.	
Total	1.0+1	1.2+2	BNL Expt	Priv	CARTER	Jun 54	Carter.	+
	1.0+1	1.2+2		Data	EXFOR12366.002	Jun 76	. 73 PTS. SIGMA.	
Total	1.5+5	2.2+6	HAR Expt	Rept	AERE−NP/R−1643	May 55	Meads. NEUTRONS FROM LI7(PN)+T(PN)	
Total	2.5−2	2.5−2	HAR Expt	Conf	55Geneva 4 210	Aug 55	Price. (LYNN) = 2 DATA INDEX LINES	+
Total	6.0−1	3.0+1	HAR Revw	Conf	55Geneva 4 238	Aug 55	Lynn+TRANS.RESOL=2PC 18RES OBSERVED	+
		1.0+0		Conf	55Geneva 4 238	Aug 55	−+TRANS.RESOL=5PC TOF SCALE	
Total	1.0−2	1.0+2	ITE Expt	Conf	55Geneva 4 224	Aug 55	Nikitin+ P646. PULSED CYCL, CURVES	+
				Conf	55Moscow 87	Jul 55	SEE ALSO *AEC−TR−2435 81	
Total	1.0−1	1.1+1	BNL Expt	Conf	58Geneva 15 111	Sep 58	Sailor. GRAPH CFD MTR.	+
				Rept	AERE−NP/R−2076	Jul 56	−. CRYSTAL SPECTROMETER, CURVES	
	3.0−1	1.1+1		Data	EXFOR12363.004	Jun 76	. 248 PTS. SIGMA.	
Total	1.5−3	1.2+1	HAR Expt	Jour	JNE 3 28	Aug 56	Pattenden.SLOCHOP,CRYSTSPEC,CURVES	+
				Rept	AERE−NP/R−2104	57	. ABST. DATA GIVEN.	
				Jour	JNE 2 187	Mar 56	−. SLOW CHOPPER.OXI+METAL.	
				Rept	NRDC−81	55	−. DATA	
Total	6.5+0	3.6+2	CCP Expt	Jour	AE 2 129	Feb 57	Sokolovsky+.FAST CHOP,TRANSMIS CURVE	+
				Jour	JNE 5 389	Nov 57	TRANSLATN.*	
				Jour	SJA 2 147	57	TRANSLATN.*	
Total	2.0+2	8.0+3	KAP Expt	Prog	KAPL−1770 65	Apr 57	Yeater+ TRANSMISSION, TOF	+
	9.0+1	1.6+4		Data	EXFOR11681.003	Jun 76	. 222 PTS. SIGMA.	
Total	2.5−2	1.0+2	CCP Expt	Conf	58Geneva 15 309	Sep 58	Vladimirsky+.PPR2221,NDG,BF3−DETECTR	
Total	−2	1.0+3	MTR Revw	Conf	58Geneva 15 111	Sep 58	Fluharty+.PPR645,CURVE,MANY REFS	
Total	None		MTR Eval	Rept	IDO−16579	Dec 59	Moore+ MULTILEVEL ANALYSIS CURVES	
Total	2.0−2	8.0−2	MTR Expt	Jour	NSE 7 187	Feb 60	Simpson+,FC TRNS 587+−6B AT.0253EV	+
Total	8.1−4	8.2−2	COL Expt	Jour	PR 118 799	May 60	Safford+ CRYSTSPEC,LIQUID+METL SAMPLS	+
				Conf	60Vienna 203	60	−+	
	8.2−4	8.2−2		Data	EXFOR12362.	Jun 76	. 33 PTS. SIGMA.	

92 Uranium 233

Quantity	Energy (ev) Min	Energy (ev) Max	Lab	Type	Documentation Ref Vol Page	Date	Author, Comments	Data
Total	2.0 – 2	2.0 + 2	MTR	Expt	Jour PR 118 714	May 60	Moore+ GRAPHS.	+
	2.5 – 2	5.5 + 0			Conf 61RPI 35	May 61	Fluharty.	
	2.0 – 2	2.0 + 2			Jour NSE 7 187	Feb 60	– +	
					Jour PRL 4 260	Jan 60	.SUPERSEDED	
					Rept IDO – 16576	59	.SUPERSEDED	
					Conf 58Geneva 645	Sep 58	Fluharty+	
	2.0 – 2	2.2 + 2			Data EXFOR12341.003	Jun 76	. 1071 PTS. SIGMA.	
Total	1.8 – 2	9.6 – 2	ORL	Expt	Jour NSE 8 112	Aug 60	Block+ FAST CHOPR,TBL,FIT(0.0253EV)	+
					Conf 61RPI 64	May 61	.SEE ALSO	
	2.5 – 2				Conf 60Vienna 535	Oct 60	Block+.VAL(2200M/SEC) GVN,EXPT DESCR	
	1.8 – 2	9.6 – 2			Data EXFOR12024.005	Jun 76	. 41 PTS. SIGMA.	
Total	5.6 – 3	9.9 – 2	BNL	Expt	Rept AEEW – R – 125 15	Apr 61	Muether+ SLOW CHOP	+
					Jour JNE 3 177	56	– +	
	5.7 – 3	1.1 – 1			Data EXFOR12324.002	Jun 76	. 35 PTS. SIGMA.	
Total	Maxwl		HAN	Eval	Conf 61RPI 3	May 61	Leonard.	
Total	2.0 – 1	1.0 + 7	B+W	Eval	Rept BAW – 158	Jun 61	Roach+ AVERAGED SIG 40 GROUPS	
Total	3.4 + 3	1.6 + 6	ANL	Expt	Jour JNAB 16 201	Apr 62	Stupegia.TABLE 17 – 6.4B.RSLN 1.2 – 8KEV	+
	3.4 + 3	1.6 + 6			Data EXFOR12323.002	Jun 76	. 45 PTS. SIGMA.	
Total	2.5 – 3	7.5 – 2	BNL	Revw	Rept BNL – 722	Jun 62	Sher+ REVIEW CURVE GIVEN	
Total	7.2 – 2	8.8 + 3	ORL	Expt	Jour NSE 17 404	Nov 63	Pattenden+	+
					Rept ORNL – TM – 556	Apr 63	– +HARVEY,FC,TOF,TBL GIVEN	
	7.2 – 2	+ 2			Conf 60Kingston 882	Aug 60	– +.NDG,EXPT DESCRIBED	
	7.2 – 2	8.8 + 3			Data EXFOR12333.002	Jun 76	. 1512 PTS. SIGMA.	
Total	– 3	+ 6	TRM	Revw	Rept AEET – 234	65	SHANKAR SINGH.ACCURACY OF DATA GIVEN	
Total	4.0 + 6	1.5 + 7	UK	Eval	Rept AWRE – O – 100/64	Jan 65	Douglas+(ALD).UKNDL – DFN 202	+
	1.0 – 4	1.5 + 7			Data UKNDL – DFN 87B	Mar 73	1063 PNTS	
Total	1.0 – 2	1.0 + 0	MTR	Expt	Conf 66Wash. 840	Mar 66	Moore+,MULTILEVEL ANAL CURVE CFD XPT	
Total	4.0 – 2	1.1 + 1	HAR	Expt	Rept AERE – M – 1709	Sep 66	Brooks+ TOF LINAC GRAPH TBL	+
	3.5 – 1	1.0 + 1			Data EXFOR20623.007	Dec 76	10PTS.	
Total	4.7 + 1	1.0 + 4	INA	Eval	Conf 66Paris 2 333	Oct 66	Hennies.PPR5.TBL RECOM DATA CFD OTHR	
					Rept NAA – SR – 11980 5	May 67	– . RECOMMENDED DATA.IMPROVED	
Total		6.2 + 1	WAL	Eval	Conf 68Wash. 615	Mar 68	Schneider. CURVE 1 – LVL B – W FIT.	
Total	7.0 – 1	3.2 + 2	GEL	Expt	Conf 70Helsinki 1 387	Jun 70	Kolar+16. EXPTL+FITTED SIG(E) GRAPHS	+
	6.8 – 1	7.5 + 2			Data EXFOR20114.	Jul 72	11454PTS.	
Total	+ 0	3.0 + 1	ORL	Theo	Conf 70Helsinki 2 757	Jun 70	Desaussure+94.SIG(E)CRV,MULTILVL FIT	
		3.0 + 1			Rept ORNL – TM – 2745	Nov 69	– . MULTILVL ANAL+LEAST SQ.	
Total	2.0 – 2	1.0 + 0	ORL	Expt	Prog ORNL – 4592 11	Sep 70	Weston+,LINAC,NO DATA GIVEN,TBC	
Total	2.5 + 6	1.5 + 7	BNW	Expt	Jour PR/C 3 576	Feb 71	Foster+,TRANS,CURVS,CFD OTHERS+TH	+
					Jour NIM 36 1	Sep 65	.EXPT DETAILS	
	2.3 + 6	1.5 + 7			Data EXFOR10047.095	Aug 73	. 244 PTS. SIGMA.	
Total	None		DUB	Expt	Jour YF 13 457	Mar 71	Ryabov+ TOF,2 METHODS,SCINT,NDG	
	– 1	+ 1			Rept JINR – P3 – 4992	Apr 70	Rjabov+ PULSD REACTOR,TOF,LIQ SCINT	
	None				Jour SNP 13 255	Sep 71	. ENGL OF YF 13 457	
Total	5.0 + 5	1.0 + 7	BET	Expt	Rept WAPD – TM – 1073	Apr 73	Green+.CF252 SOURCE.TOF.CURV.CFDENDF	+
	5.0 + 5	9.9 + 6			Data EXFOR10225.	Aug 73	. 696 PTS. SIGMA.	
Total	2.5 – 2		IJI	Eval	Conf 73Kiev 1 197	May 73	Fedorova. SIG 2200M/S = 586.3 + – 1.7 B	
Total	3.2 – 2	9.4 – 1	IJI	Expt	Prog YFI – 16 8	Jun 73	Vertebnyj+ TOF,SIGMA(E), TABLE	+
	3.1 – 2	9.3 – 1			Data EXFOR40191.002	Apr 74	.SIG AT 29 EN GVN	
Total	1.0 + 5	2.0 + 7	TRM	Eval	Conf 74Calcutta 70	Nov 74	Garg+ OPTMOD FIT TO XPTS,SIG(E) TABL	
Total	2.5 – 2		IAE	Eval	Conf 75Wash. 286	Mar 75	Lemmel. TBL LSQ ANAL CFD OTHER EVAL	
Total	– 3	1.9 + 0	THS	Theo	Rept IKE – 6 89 52	Jun 75	Keinert. DATA LIBRARY	
Total	2.0 + 3		IJI	Expt	Conf 76Lowell 1244	Jul 76	Vertebnyi+ TRANSM VS THICKNESS,NDG	
					Conf 75Kiev 3 151	May 75	Vertebnyj+ RES – NEUT FILTRAT.SIG GIVN	
Elastic	2.7 – 1	3.3 + 0	BNL	Expt	Jour PR 109 1645	Mar 58	Oleksa.11ES SIG ALMOST CONST = 12.5B	+
	2.7 – 1	3.3 + 0			Data EXFOR12340.002	Jun 76	. 11 PTS.	
Elastic	Maxwl		HAN	Eval	Conf 61RPI 3	May 61	Leonard.	
Elastic	1.8 + 0	1.8 + 1	MTR	Expt	Jour NSE 13 18	May 62	Moore+,FC,XPT DESCR,CFD TH,GRAPHS	+
					Conf 58Geneva 645	Sep 58	.SUPERSEDED.	
	1.7 + 0	1.9 + 1			Data EXFOR12332.002	Jun 76	. 55 PTS.	
Elastic	4.0 + 6	1.5 + 7	UK	Eval	Rept AWRE – O – 100/64	Jan 65	Douglas+(ALD).UKNDL – DFN 202	+
	1.0 – 4	1.5 + 7			Data UKNDL – DFN 87B	Mar 73	1063 PNTS	
Elastic	1.0 + 0	3.1 + 1	LRL	Expt	Jour PR 174 1413	Oct 68	Sauter+ LINAC+SCINT CURVE	+
					Conf 68Wash. 541	Mar 68	.SUPERSEDED	
	1.0 + 0	2.2 + 1			Prog UCRL – 50001 2	Sep 66	Sauter+. CURVE.	
	1.0 + 0	3.1 + 1			Data EXFOR12344.002	Jun 76	. 192 PTS.	
Elastic		3.0 + 6	CCP	Theo	Jour YF 12 293	Aug 70	Zhmailo. U233(D,P NEUT)GRAPH CFD XPT	
					Jour SNP 12 160	Feb 71	TRANSLATN.*	

92 Uranium 233

Quantity	Energy (ev) Min	Max	Lab	Type	Documentation Ref Vol Page	Date	Author, Comments	Data
Elastic	5.0−1	1.9+2	MTR	Expt Jour	NP/A 164 34	Mar 71	Simpson+ POOR RESOL DATA,LINAC,CRVS	+
	5.0−1	1.9+2		Data	EXFOR10132.004	Jan 73	. DATA UNAVAILABLE.	
Elastic	9.7−2	4.6−1	IJI	Expt Prog	YFI−16 8	Jun 73	Vertebnyj+ TOF,REL V AND PB, TABLE	
Elastic	2.5−2		BET	Expt Jour	NSE 54 18	May 74	Green+. SIG=12.30+−0.70B REL V	+
				Rept	WAPD−TM−1132	Mar 74	− +	
	2.5−2			Data	EXFOR10388.003	Jun 74	. 1 PT.	
Elastic	1.0+5	2.0+7	TRM	Eval Conf	74Calcutta 70	Nov 74	Garg+ OPTMOD FIT TO XPTS,SIG(E) TABL	
Elastic	2.5−2		IAE	Eval Conf	75Wash. 286	Mar 75	Lemmel. TBL LSQ ANAL CFD OTHER EVAL	
Diff Elastic	1.0−4	1.5+7	UK	Eval Data	UKNDL−DFN 87B	Mar 73	17 PNTS,C.M.	+
Potntal Scat	4.7+1	1.0+4	INA	Eval Conf	66Paris 2 333	Oct 66	Hennies.PPR5.TBL RECOM DATA CFD OTHR	
				Rept	NAA−SR−11980 5	May 67	− . RECOMMENDED DATA.IMPROVED	
Potntal Scat	2.5−2		IAE	Revw Jour	REA 7 4 3	Dec 69	Hanna+WESTCOTT+ DISCUSSION	
Potntal Scat	2.0+3		IJI	Expt Conf	76Lowell 1244	Jul 76	Vertebnyi+ SCT−LNGTH GVN,FRM TOT+SCT	
Tot Inelastc	4.0+6	1.5+7	UK	Eval Rept	AWRE−O−100/64	Jan 65	Douglas+(ALD).UKNDL−DFN 202	
Tot Inelastc	1.0+5	2.0+7	TRM	Eval Conf	74Calcutta 70	Nov 74	Garg+ OPTMOD FIT TO XPTS,SIG(E) TABL	
Tot Inelastc	None		AUA	Theo Prog	AAEC/PR−41P 65	75	Bertram+ NDG.MULTILVL R−MATR OKS XPT	
Diff Inelast	1.4+7		CCP	Expt Jour	AE 4 337	Apr 58	Zamiatnin+ FISS+EVAP SPECTR FIT DATA	
				Jour	JNE 9 194	Jun 59	TRANSLATN.*	
				Jour	SJA 4 443	58	TRANSLATN.*	
Diff Inelast	None		CCP		Jour AE 13 321	Oct 62	HF CALCULATION NDG	
					Jour SJA 13 931	62	. ENGL OF AE 13 321	
Diff Inelast	4.0+4	1.5+7	UK	Eval Data	UKNDL−DFN 87B	Mar 73	.TO CONTINUUM.75 PTS.E DIST.ANGDIST.	
Thermal Scat	2.5−2	2.0−1	ANL	Theo Jour	ACR 20 587	Apr 66	Atoji. E DEPNDNCE RE(SAM),IM(SAM).	
Thermal Scat	2.0−2	3.5+2	AUA	Expt Rept	AAEC/TM−497	Apr 69	Dalton. LATTICE,N−SPEC OKS DATA−SETS	
Scattering	1.7+6	2.0+7	BNL	Eval Prog	BNL−694 2	Oct 61	Moore+ POT SCAT=12.6 B USED.	
Scattering	4.0+6	1.5+7	UK	Eval Rept	AWRE−O−100/64	Jan 65	Douglas+(ALD).UKNDL−DFN 202	
Scattering	2.5−2		ANL	Eval Conf	71Knoxvill 560	Mar 71	Devolpi.ABS NF NG ALFA ETA NU GIVEN	
Scattering	Maxwl		BET	Eval Rept	WAPD−TM−1052	Sep 72	Steen. EVAL WITH,WITHOUT U235 RATIO	
Scattering	2.5−2		IJI	Eval Conf	73Kiev 1 197	May 73	Fedorova. SIG 2200M/S=10.7+−1.8 B	
Scattering	9.7−2	4.6−1	IJI	Expt Prog	YFI−16 8	Jun 73	Vertebnyj+	+
	9.7−2	4.6−1		Data	EXFOR40191.004	Apr 74	.SIG AT 11 EN GVN	
Scattering	2.0+3		IJI	Expt Conf	76Lowell 1244	Jul 76	Vertebnyi+ SCT−SIG VS THICKNESS,NDG	
Nonelastic	1.5+6	1.6+6	LAS	Expt Priv	TASCHEK	55	Taschek.	+
	1.5+6	1.6+6		Data	EXFOR12364.002	Jun 76	. 2 PTS. SIGMA.	
Nonelastic	4.0+6	1.5+7	UK	Eval Rept	AWRE−O−100/64	Jan 65	Douglas+(ALD).UKNDL−DFN 202	
Nonelastic	2.0+3		IJI	Expt Conf	75Kiev 3 151	May 75	Vertebnyj+ RES−NEUT FILTRAT.SIG GIVN	
Absorption	Pile		ANL	Expt Conf	CF−3651	Oct 46	Zinn.	+
	Pile			Data	EXFOR12319.003	Jun 76	. 1 PT.	
Absorption	Pile		CCP	Expt Conf	55Geneva 4 230	Aug 55	Kukavadse+.VAL GVN,MASSPECTROM,P644	+
Absorption	Maxwl		CCP	Expt Conf	55Geneva 4 230	Aug 55	Kukavadse+ P644. REL LI−6(N,ALFA)	+
Absorption	2.5−2		IAE	Revw Conf	55Geneva 4 287	Aug 55	Worldvalue+ERROR GVN (2200M/SEC)	
				Eval Jour	NAT 176 619	Oct 55	.SEE ALSO *	
				Revw Jour	JET 2 271	55	.SAME ARTICLE,RUSSIAN ZET 29 1455	
Absorption	2.5−2		FR	Eval Jour	CR 241 669	Sep 55	Perrin.QUOTES WORLD SIGMA =593+−8B	
Absorption	Maxwl		HAR	Revw Jour	NAT 176 619	Oct 55	Gaunt+593+−8B WORLD AVG VALUES	
Absorption	Maxwl		KAP	Expt Rept	KAPL−1464	Dec 55	Mcmillan+ FROM TTRSPECT AVG 599 B.	
Absorption	4.4+3	1.2+4	ORL	Expt Jour	PR 102 797	May 56	Macklin+	+
				Rept	ORNL−2022	Feb 56	− + 2 ES USELESS FOR ALPHA.	
	4.4+3	1.2+4		Data	EXFOR12334.003	Jun 76	. 2 PTS.	
Absorption	2.5−2	6.5−2	ORL	Expt Prog	ORNL−56 41	Jun 56	Harvey.AVERAGED OVER MAXWELLIAN,4ES	
Absorption	2.5−2		BNL	Eval Rept	BNL−325 1	Jan 57	Hughes+ WORLD CONSIST.VAL.=588+−7 B.	
Absorption	Maxwl		HAR	Comp Rept	AERE−NP/R−2104	Mar 57	Egelstaff.EXPT METHODS FOR HAR VALUE	
Absorption	2.5−2		HAR	Expt Jour	JNE 4 409	Apr 57	Green+ CLINTON OSCILLATOR,SIG REL AU	+
Absorption	2.0−2	2.4−1	CUW	Theo Rept	CWR−400−1	Sep 57	Roberts.MAXWELL−BOLTZMANN AVGD SIGS.	
Absorption	Maxwl		HAR	Eval Rept	AERE−NP/R−2140	Dec 57	Egelstaff+ CONSISTENT VALUES 2200M/S	
Absorption	Maxwl		BNL	Comp Conf	58Geneva 16 8	Sep 58	Hughes.PPR2483,VAL V=2200M/SEC GVN	
Absorption	Pile		ORL	Eval Jour	NSE 6 100	Aug 59	Stoughton+,BEST VALUE .025EV=580B	
Absorption	2.5−2		AE	Comp Rept	AE−11	Apr 60	Story+,DISCUSSION+TABULATN OF MEASTS	
Absorption		1.0+0	MTR	Revw Jour	NSE 8 66	Jul 60	Evans+ MANY VALUES, GRAPHS.	
Absorption	Maxwl		ORL	Expt Jour	NSE 8 112	Aug 60	Block+,FC 576+−4B SIG(TOT)−SIG(SCT)	+
	Maxwl			Data	EXFOR12024.004	Jun 76	. 1 PT. SIGMA.	
Absorption	Maxwl		HAN	Eval Conf	61RPI 3	May 61	Leonard.	
Absorption	2.0−1	1.0+7	B+W	Eval Rept	BAW−158	Jun 61	Roach+ AVERAGED SIG 40 GROUPS	
Absorption	5.0−1	2.5+0	GA	Eval Rept	GA−2113	Jun 61	Wikner+.TABLE+CURVE.100 E POINTS	
Absorption	Maxwl		CRC	Expt Conf	61Saclay 57	Jul 61	Westcott. 2200METRE/SEC SIG GIVEN	
Absorption	4.1−1	1.0+7	GA	Eval Prog	GA−2451 1	Aug 61	Joanou+.68GROUP DATA FOR GAM−I	
Absorption	Pile		CRC	Eval Rept	CRRP−960	Jan 62	Westcott. EFF SIG TBL 20−1300 DEG C.	
Absorption	5.0−3	7.5−2	BNL	Revw Rept	BNL−722	Jun 62	Sher+ REVIEW CURVE GIVEN	

92 Uranium 233

Quantity	Energy (ev) Min	Max	Lab	Type	Documentation Ref Vol Page	Date	Author, Comments	Data
Absorption	Pile		CJD	Eval	Rept INDSWG – 64 285	64	Galanin. TBL EFF SIG FOR MANY SPECTR	
Absorption	2.5 – 2		BEP	Revw	Jour KE 8 625	Jan 65	Wenzel. VAL GVN, MANY REFERENCES	
Absorption	4.0+6	1.5+7	UK	Eval	Rept AWRE – O – 100/64	Jan 65	Douglas+(ALD).UKNDL – DFN 202	
Absorption	1.0 – 2	5.0 – 1	MTR	Eval	Conf 66Wash. 985	Mar 66	Fluharty+, COEF OF SIG EXPANSN CALCTD	
Absorption	2.0 – 2	5.0 – 1	MTR	Eval	Conf 66Paris 2 50	Oct 66	Smith+ TBL+CURV, LSTSQ FIT. PPR50.	
					Rept INDC – 15	Sep 66	– + FULL PAPER.	
Absorption	Maxwl		ITE	Theo	Rept ICD – 4 385	67	Birzgal+.AVERAGING OVER MAXWELL SPEC	
Absorption	Maxwl		UFP	Expt	Rept CCEN – 17	Dec 70	CLEMENTE REL TO U235, FISSION CHAMB.	+
					Conf 70Helsinki 1 295	Jun 70	.SEE ALSO *	
	2.5 – 2				Data EXFOR20552.004	Apr 76	1PNT.SIGMA.	
Absorption	2.5 – 2		ANL	Eval	Conf 71Knoxvill 560	Mar 71	Devolpi. ADJUSTED VALUE GIVEN.	
Absorption	6.2 – 1	1.0+7	SRL	Theo	Conf 71Knoxvill 714	Mar 71	Mccrosson. SPECTRUM – AVERAGED SIG	
Absorption	1.0 – 3	2.0+0	JUL	Theo	Rept JUEL – 746 – RG 49	Apr 71	Bonka.KUGEL – THERMOS – LIBR, T=300K, CURV	
Absorption	2.5 – 2		IFB	Eval	Rept YK – 9 34	72	Morogovsky. COMPUTR RE – EVAL, DATA GVN	
					Rept INDC(CCP) – 42	Aug 74	.Pl.ENGLISH OF YK – 9	
Absorption	Maxwl		BET	Eval	Rept WAPD – TM – 1052	Sep 72	Steen. EVAL WITH, WITHOUT U235 RATIO	
Absorption	2.5 – 2		IJI	Eval	Conf 73Kiev 1 197	May 73	Fedorova. SIG 2200M/S=578.4+ – 1.8 B	
Absorption	None		MUN	Theo	Diss GRYNTAKIS	Mar 76	Gryntakis., CALC.OF WESTCOTTS G – FUNCT	
					Jour RCA 22 128	Mar 75	– +, EQUIVALENT TO THESIS	
Res Int Abs	None		MTR	Eval	Conf 57Col.Univ 98	Sep 57	Evans. FC. 927+ – 30 B INC 1/V.	
Res Int Abs	5.0 – 1	1.0+6	ORL	Eval	Jour NSE 6 100	Aug 59	Stoughton+, BEST VALUE 1200+ – 200B	
Res Int Abs	None		ORL	Expt	Prog WASH – 1033 33	Aug 61	Halperin+ INC FISS. MASS SPEC.	
Res Int Abs	5.0 – 1		GA	Eval	Rept GA – 8854	Aug 68	Boroughs+ ENDF/B DATA	
Res Int Abs	4.1 – 1	1.2+3	COL	Expt	Prog COO – 2176 – 1 7	Jun 72	Felvinci+. TABLE. CFD OTHERS	
Res Int Abs	5.0 – 1		SGA	Comp	Conf 73Paris 1 233	Mar 73	Eder+ INCLUDING 1/V PART, CAPTURE, TBL	
					Rept SGAE – PH – 141	Feb 73	.SAME AS 73PARIS, NO DETAILS, TBP	
Res Int Abs	0.0+0	6.0+1	NSU	Theo	Prog INDC(SEC) – 42	Dec 74	CHI+ ADL – ADL CALC OKS XPT. TBP KNS	
(n,γ)	Maxwl		ANL	Expt	Rept CF – 3651	Oct 46	Zinn.	+
	Maxwl				Data EXFOR12319.006	Jun 76	. 1 PT. SIGMA.	
(n,γ)	Pile		ANL	Expt	Conf 55Geneva 4 105	Aug 55	Inghram+ P596, VAL GVN.MASS – SPECTRM.	+
					Prog ANL – 4515 15	Oct 50	– +	
	Pile				Data EXFOR12351.002	Jun 76	. 1 PT. SIGMA.	
(n,γ)	Pile		CCP	Expt	Conf 55Geneva 4 230	Aug 55	Kukavadse+.VAL GVN, MASSPECTROM, P644	
(n,γ)	None		KAP	Expt	Prog WASH – 745	Nov 57	Yeater. CS CAPT/TOT TBD.	
(n,γ)	2.5 – 2		ORL	Comp	Conf 58Geneva 16 64	Sep 58	Halperin+.PPR1072, VAL GVN, MANY REFS	
(n,γ)	Pile		ORL	Eval	Jour NSE 6 100	Aug 59	Stoughton+, BEST VALUE .025EV=52+ – 5B	
	Maxwl	Pile	ORL	Expt	Prog ORNL – 3320 1	61	Halperin+	+
					Prog ORNL – 3176 1	61	– .	
	Maxwl	Pile			Data EXFOR12335.	Jun 76	. 2 PTS. SIGMA.	
(n,γ)	Maxwl		MCM	Expt	Jour CJC 39 628	Mar 61	Bidinosti+ MASS – SPEC, MASS – PEAK YLDS	
					Conf 58Geneva 15 459	Sep 58	.SUPERSEDED P/201.	
(n,γ)	Maxwl		HAN	Eval	Conf 61RPI 3	May 61	Leonard.	
(n,γ)	2.5 – 2	5.5+0	MTR	Eval	Jour PR 118 718	May 60	Moore. SIG FIT FROM MEAS TOT + FISS	
					Conf 61RPI 35	May 61	Fluharty.	
	None				Rept IDO – 16579	Dec 59	Moore+ MULTILEVEL ANALYSIS CURVES	
(n,γ)	5.0 – 3	2.5+0	GA	Eval	Rept GA – 2113	Jun 61	Wikner+.NFISSION, ALPHA GIVEN 100 ES	
(n,γ)	Fast		HFA	Expt	Rept IA – 642	Jul 61	Yiftah. 16 – GROUP SIGS	
(n,γ)	Pile		CRC	Expt	Rept CRRP – 960	Jan 62	Westcott. EFF SIG TBL 20 – 1300 DEG C.	
(n,γ)	3.0+4	1.0+6	LAS	Expt	Jour NSE 12 169	Feb 62	Hopkins+. CALCULATED FROM ALPHA(XPT)	+
	3.0+4	1.0+6			Data EXFOR12331.003	Jun 76	. 9 PTS. SIGMA.	
(n,γ)	– 3	+6	TRM	Revw	Rept AEET – 234	65	SHANKAR SINGH.NO DIRECT EXPTS SO FAR	
(n,γ)	4.0+6	1.5+7	UK	Eval	Rept AWRE – O – 100/64	Jan 65	Douglas+(ALD).UKNDL – DFN 202	+
	1.0 – 4	2.4+6			Data UKNDL – DFN 87B	Mar 73	1028 PNTS	
(n,γ)	1.0 – 0	1.0+0	MTR	Eval	Conf 66Wash. 840	Mar 66	Moore+, MULTILEVEL ANAL CURVE CFD XPT	
(n,γ)	3.5 – 1	1.0+1	HAR	Expt	Rept AERE – M – 1709	Sep 66	Brooks+ LINAC.GRPH.TBL.	+
	3.5 – 1	1.0+1			Data EXFOR20623.002	Dec 76	10PTS.SIGMA.	
(n,γ)	5.0 – 1	1.0+4	INA	Eval	Conf 66Paris 2 333	Oct 66	Hennies.PPR5.TBL RECOM DATA CFD OTHR	
					Rept NAA – SR – 11980 5	May 67	– . RECOMMENDED DATA.IMPROVED	
(n,γ)	Maxwl		ARK	Expt	Jour JIN 29 257	May 67	Ganapathy+ RADCHEM, 15 YLDS REL MO99	
					Abst DA 29 319	Jul 68	.THESIS ABST.	
(n,γ)	2.0+1	1.0+6	LAS	Expt	Prog WASH – 1079 98	Oct 67	Psangaree. BOMB SHOT TBD SPR68.	
(n,γ)	Maxwl		AUA	Theo	Jour NSE 31 234	Feb 68	Cook+ STATISTICAL CALC CFD EXPT	
(n,γ)		6.2+1	WAL	Eval	Conf 68Wash. 615	Mar 68	Schneider. CURVE 1 – LVL B – W FIT.	
(n,γ)	2.0+3		MTR	Expt	Prog WASH – 1093 61	Apr 68	Simpson+ TBD	
(n,γ)	1.0 – 2	1.0+5	GA	Eval	Rept GA – 8854	Aug 68	Boroughs+ ENDF/B DATA CURVES	

92 Uranium 233

Quantity	Energy (ev) Min	Energy (ev) Max	Lab	Type	Documentation Ref Vol Page	Author, Comments Date	Data
(n,γ)	4.0−1	2.0+3	ORL	Expt	Jour NSE 34 1	Oct 68 Weston+ RPI LINAC+SCINT NF+NG SIMULT	+
					Rept ORNL−TM−2140	Apr 68 .SUPERSEDED	
					Conf 66Paris 2 233	Oct 66 Desaussure+ SUPERSEDED.	
	4.0−1	2.0+3			Data EXFOR12336.005	Jun 76 . 3423 PTS. SIGMA.	
(n,γ)	Maxwl	2.6−2	FAR	Expt	Conf 70Helsinki 1 295	Jun 70 Vidal+97. VALUE GIVEN,EXPT REL U−235	
(n,γ)	+0	6.0+1	ORL	Theo	Conf 70Helsinki 2 757	Jun 70 Desaussure+ 94.SIG(E)CRV,MULTILVLFIT	
	1.0−2	6.0+1			Rept ORNL−TM−2745	Nov 69 − . MULTILVL ANAL+LEAST SQ.	
(n,γ)		7.0+3	SDC	Theo	Conf 70Helsinki 2 799	Jun 70 Garrison.DISCUSSN. RESONANCE ANAL	
(n,γ)	2.0−2	1.0+0	ORL	Expt	Jour NSE 42 143	Nov 70 Weston+,RPI LINAC+SCINT.NF+NG SIMULT	+
	1.7−2	1.1+0			Rept ORNL−TM−2353	Feb 69 .SUPERSEDED	
					Data EXFOR10100.003	Aug 71 . 50 PTS. E**1/2.	
(n,γ)	1.0+2	1.0+5	GA	Theo	Jour NP/A 159 305	Dec 70 Garrison.AVERAGE C.S.=NO RES INTERF	
(n,γ)	2.5−2		ANL	Eval	Conf 71Knoxvill 560	Mar 71 Devolpi. ADJUSTED VALUE GIVEN.	
(n,γ)	Maxwl		HAR	Expt	Jour JIN 33 11 3972	Nov 71 Cabell+	+
	2.5−2				Data EXFOR20459.002	Jan 76 1PNT.SIGMA.	
(n,γ)	Maxwl		BET	Eval	Rept WAPD−TM−1052	Sep 72 Steen. EVAL WITH,WITHOUT U235 RATIO	
					Conf 71Knoxvill 566	Mar 71 − . BEST VALUE=45.8+−0.4B	
(n,γ)	2.5−2		IJI	Eval	Conf 73Kiev 1 197	May 73 Fedorova. SIG 2200M/S=47.0+−0.9 B	
(n,γ)	0.0+0	6.0+1	NSU	Theo	Prog INDC(SEC)−42	Dec 74 CHI+ ADL−ADL CALC OKS XPT. TBP KNS	
(n,γ)	None		AUA	Theo	Prog AAEC/PR−41P 65	75 Bertram+ NDG.MULTILVL R−MATR OKS XPT	
(n,γ)	None		MUN	Theo	Diss GRYNTAKIS	Mar 76 Gryntakis.,CALC.OF WESTCOTTS G−FUNCT	
					Jour RCA 22 128	Mar 75 − +,EQUIVALENT TO THESIS	
(n,γ)	1.0+5	2.0+7	TRM	Theo	Conf 76Ahmedabd 2 17	Dec 76 Garg. ABST,NDG.CALC WITH'FISPRO'CODE	
(n,γ)	Pile		FEI	Expt	Rept YK−24 48	77 Andrijakhina+ AVG SIG AT DIFF POSITS	
Res Int Capt	5.0−1	1.0+6	ORL	Eval	Jour NSE 6 100	Aug 59 Stoughton+ BEST VALUE 300+−100B	
	3.0−1			Comp	Conf 58Geneva 16 64	Sep 58 Halperin+ VAL CFD MANY REFS	
Res Int Capt	5.4−1		ORL	Expt	Prog ORNL−3320 1	61 Halperin+	+
	5.4−1				Data EXFOR12335.	Jun 76 . 1 PT.	
Res Int Capt	5.0−1		KAP	Expt	Abst ANS 7 272	Nov 64 Esch+ RI=138+−10B. MASS SPECTRMTR.	+
Res Int Capt	5.0−1		KAP	Comp	Conf 66S.Diego 2 299	Feb 66 Feiner+.COMPIL PREV RESULTS+RECOMMND	
Res Int Capt	4.0−1	7.5+0	HAR	Expt	Rept AERE−M−1709	Sep 66 Brooks+ TOF.LINAC.SC PSD.GRPH.TBL	+
	3.5−1	1.0+1			Data EXFOR20623.003	Dec 76 10PTS.CAPTURE.	
Res Int Capt	5.0−1	1.0+4	INA	Eval	Conf 66Paris 2 333	Oct 66 Hennies.PPR5.TBL RECOM DATA CFD OTHR	
					Rept NAA−SR−11980 5	May 67 − . RECOMMENDED DATA.IMPROVED	
Res Int Capt	5.0−1		ORL	Expt	Abst ANS 10 220	Jun 67 Weston+ RPI LINAC+SCINT 140+−13B CFD	
Res Int Capt	5.0−1		BET	Expt	Jour NSE 29 1	Jul 67 Conway+ 135+−8B	+
					Rept WAPD−TM−613	Jun 67 .SUPERSEDED	
	5.0−1				Data EXFOR12313.002	Jun 76 . 1 PT.	
Res Int Capt	5.0−1		BET	Revw	Rept WAPD−TM−760	Aug 68 Gunst+. CURVES. 40 REFERENCES	
Res Int Capt	5.0−1		GA	Eval	Rept GA−8854	Aug 68 Boroughs+ ENDF/B DATA	
Res Int Capt	None		TRM	Eval	Prog BARC−418 1	69 Singh+ CALC FROM RES PARS.NDG.TBP	
Res Int Capt	5.0−1		KAP	Expt	Jour NSE 44 180	May 71 Eiland+ CD AND CD−RH FILTERS	+
	5.0−1				Data EXFOR10143.	Aug 73 . 4 PTS.	
Spect (n,γ)	None		COL	Expt	Prog NCSAC−31 56	May 70 Felvinci+,TO BE DONE	
Spect (n,γ)	Maxwl		KFK	Expt	Priv WIETKAMP	73 Weitkamp. SPECTRA FOR COMPILATION	
Nonelastic γ	2.5−2		IFB	Eval	Rept YK−9 34	72 Morogovsky. SIG G−PROD EVAL,DATA GVN	
					Rept INDC(CCP)−42	Aug 74 .P1.ENGLISH OF YK−9	
(n,2n)	Fiss		ALD	Eval	Rept AWRE−O−02/60	Apr 60 Hinves+AWRE EVAL DATA CFD XPT	
(n,2n)	Thrsh	1.5+7	UK	Eval	Rept AWRE−O−100/64	Jan 65 Douglas+(ALD).UKNDL−DFN 202	
	5.9+6	1.5+7			Data UKNDL−DFN 87B	Mar 73 .26 PTS.E DIST.ANG DIST,LAB.	
(n,2n)	Fiss		BNL	Theo	Jour NSE 23 238	Nov 65 Pearlstein.STATMDL CALC.SPEC AVG TBL	
(n,2n)	1.3+7	1.5+7	BNL	Theo	Jour NSE 23 238	Nov 65 Pearlstein.3ES.STAT MDL CALC.TBL CS.	
(n,2n)	Pile		ORL	Expt	Prog ORNL−4306 1	May 68 Halperin+, PRELIMINARY VALUE GIVEN	
(n,2n)	1.5+7		KFI	Expt	Jour MFF 21 555	73 Nagy. THESIS,HUNG. TO FISS ISO,GRND	
(n,2n)	Fiss		KTO	Expt	Jour NST 10 668	Nov 73 Kobayashi+.AVERAGE SIG 4.08+−0.30 MB	+
	1.5+6				Data EXFOR20594.002	Jul 76 1PNT.SIGMA.	
(n,2n)	2.0+6	1.5+7	BRC	Eval	Rept CEA−R−4647	Jan 75 Jary. EVAL,STAT MDL, 15 VALS	
(n,xn) x>2	Thrsh	1.5+7	ALD	Eval	Rept AWRE−O−100/64	Jan 65 Douglas.UKAEA DFN−202. N3N.	
(n,xn) x>2	Fiss		BNL	Theo	Jour NSE 23 238	Nov 65 Pearlstein.SPEC AVG STATMDL CALC N3N	
(n,xn) x>2	1.3+7	1.5+7	UK	Eval	Rept UKNDL−DFN 87B	Mar 73 .5 PTS. E DIST.ANG DIST,LAB.N3N.	
(n,xn) x>2	2.0+6	1.5+7	BRC	Eval	Rept CEA−R−4647	Jan 75 Jary. EVAL,STAT MDL, 15 VALS	
(n,p)	Maxwl		IFU	Theo	Rept ICD−4 20	67 Dadakina+ PENETR COEFF CALC,TABLE	
Fission	2.2−2	4.6−1	LAS	Expt	Rept LA−190	44 Anderson+	+
	2.2−2	4.6−1			Data EXFOR12359.002	Jun 76 . 12 PTS. SIGMA.	
Fission	3.4+6	5.9+6	LAS	Expt	Rept LA−520	Mar 46 Williams.	+
	3.4+6	5.9+6			Data EXFOR12312.	Jun 76 . 3 PTS. SIGMA.	
Fission	Maxwl		ANL	Expt	Rept CF−3651	Oct 46 Zinn+	+
	Maxwl				Data EXFOR12319.	Jun 76 . 2 PTS. SIGMA,AND RATIO U235 NF.	

92 Uranium 233

Quantity	Energy (ev) Min	Max	Lab	Type	Documentation Ref Vol Page	Date	Author, Comments	Data
Fission	None		BRK	Expt Jour	PR 71 378	Mar 47	Seaborg+1942LETTER.FISSION OBSERVED.	
Fission	1.4+7		LAS	Expt Rept	LAMS-938	Jun 50	Nyer+ FISS CHAMBER RELATIVE TO U238	+
	1.4+7			Data	EXFOR12306.	Jun 76	. 1 PT.	
Fission	1.0-2	4.9+1	CRC	Expt Rept	CRGP-458	51	Tunnicliffe.EARLY DATA,SHORT TBL	+
Fission	Fast		LAS	Expt Rept	LA-1250	May 51	Jurney. FAST REACT SPEC AVG SIG.	
Fission	Pile		ANL	Expt Prog	ANL-5411 1	53	Sellers+	+
	Pile			Data	EXFOR12352.	Jun 76	. 1 PT.	
Fission	Pile	2.5-2	HAR	Expt Rept	NRDC-51	Oct 54	Raffle.BEPO CORE+THR COL+TOF 2200M/S	+
	Maxwl	Pile		Rept	AERE-R-2998	Jul 59	- .SIG AT 0.025EV=515+ -15B	
Fission	Maxwl		KJL	Expt Jour	JNE 1 286	Jun 55	Popovic. REL NA ACTIVATION	+
	Maxwl			Data	EXFOR20047.	Sep 71	3PTS.	
Fission	1.0-2	1.0+2	CCP	Expt Conf	55Moscow 87	Jul 55	Nikitin+.SIMULTAN ABS AND FISS,CURVE	
				Rept	AEC-TR-2435 81	56	. ENGL TRANSL OF 55MOSCOW 87	
Fission	Pile		ANL	Expt Conf	55Geneva 4 105	Aug 55	Ingham+.P596,VAL GVN,MASS-SPECTRM	+
	Pile			Data	EXFOR12352.002	Jun 76	. 1 PT.	
Fission	Pile		HAR	Revw Conf	55Geneva 5 331	Aug 55	Holmes+.P404,RATIO PU239/U233 GVN	
Fission	2.5-2		IAE	Revw Conf	55Geneva 4 287	Aug 55	Worldvalue+ERROR GVN (2200M/SEC)	
				Eval Jour	NAT 176 619	Oct 55	.SEE ALSO *	
				Revw Jour	JET 2 271	55	.SAME ARTICLE,RUSSIAN ZET 29 1455	
Fission	1.0-2	5.0+2	KUR	Expt Conf	55Geneva 4 216	Aug 55	Adamchuk+.P645,GRAPHS,FC,DISCUSSN	+
Fission	+3	1.3+6	SAC	Expt Conf	55Geneva 4 245	Aug 55	Szteinsznaider+.GRAPH+TBL REL U238	
				Jour	NKA 1 2 95	Sep 65	- +	
Fission	-3	1.0+3	SAC	Expt Jour	JNE 1 306	Jun 55	Auclair+ SLOW NEUTRONS.	+
				Conf	55Geneva 4 235	Aug 55	- .GRAPH,CRYST-SPECTR,TOF,P/354	
				Jour	JPRS 16 50	Jul 55	- + REL PU-239.	
	Maxwl			Jour	CR 240 2306	Jun 55	- +SIG U233/SIG PU239 NSA9 6044	
Fission	2.5-2		FR	Eval Jour	CR 241 669	Sep 55	Perrin.QUOTES WORLD SIGMA =524+ -8B	
Fission	Maxwl		HAR	Revw Jour	NAT 176 619	Oct 55	Gaunt+524+ -8B WORLD AVG VALUES	
Fission	Maxwl		KAP	Expt Rept	KAPL-1464	Dec 55	Mcmillan+,AVERAGE SIG=533B REL U235	
Fission	1.0-3	1.0+0	CCP	Expt	-		ENGL TRANSL AEC-TR-2435 PAGE 1	
				Rept	AEC-TR-2435 1	56	. ENGL OF 55MOSCOW 15	
Fission	1.4+7		HAR	Expt Rept	AERE-NP/R-1996	Jun 56	Uttley+.BACK TO BACK FISS CHAMBER	+
Fission	1.2-1	3.8+0	MTR	Expt Abst	BAP 1 247	Jun 56	Miller+ ABST. C5.	+
	1.2-1	3.8+0		Data	EXFOR12315.002	Jun 76	. 75 PTS. SIGMA.	
Fission	2.5-2	6.5-2	ORL	Expt Prog	ORNL-56 41	Jun 56	Harvey.AVERAGED OVER MAXWELLIAN,4ES	
Fission	7.0+5	3.4+6	SAC	Expt Jour	JPR 17 565	Jul 56	Netter+VDG SIG=2.3TO1.6B 0.6TO3.4MEV	+
Fission	4.0+3	3.0+6	ORL	Expt Jour	PR 104 1654	Dec 56	Lamphere.CRV MD SAVE NR.2MEV+MAX NR2	+
	4.9+3	3.0+6		Data	EXFOR12338.002	Jun 76	. 96 PTS. RATIO TO U235 NF.	
Fission	Fast		HAR	Expt Rept	AERE-R/R-2151	57	Absalom+ ZEPHYR+TH ENVELOPE.	
Fission	2.5-2		BNL	Eval Rept	BNL-325 1	Jan 57	Hughes+ WORLD CONSIST.VAL=532+ -6 B.	
Fission	3.0+3	5.0+6	CCP	Expt Jour	AE 2 10	Jan 57	Dorofeev+.REL+ABS DATA, 5 GN SOURCES	+
				Jour	JNE 5 217	Nov 57	TRANSLATN.*	
				Jour	SJA 2 9	57	TRANSLATN.*	
Fission	1.0+5	7.0+6	LAS	Expt Jour	LA-2122	Jun 57	Henkel.CURV,REPLACES LA-1714	+
	3.0+4	1.7+6		Rept	LA-2114	Feb 57	- + ABSOL CURV REVIEWS ALL DATA	
	1.0+5	7.0+6		Data	EXFOR12321.002	Jun 76	. 49 PTS. SIGMA.	
Fission	3.0+4	3.0+6	HAR	Expt Jour	PPSA 70 573	Aug 57	Allen+.SIGF TO + -3PERCENT,AND RATIOS	+
				Conf	55Geneva 2 228	Aug 55	- + SUPERSEDED	
				Conf	55Geneva 4 291	Aug 55	- + SUPERSEDED	
Fission	1.0-2	2.0+1	ANL	Expt Conf	57Col.Univ 85	Sep 57	Bollinger+ SUMM CURV. NO PTS. FC.	
Fission	2.0-2	2.4-1	CUW	Theo Rept	CWR-400-1	Sep 57	Roberts.MAXWELL-BOLTZMANN AVGD SIGS.	
Fission	Maxwl		HAR	Eval Rept	AERE-NP/R-2140	Dec 57	Egelstaff+ CONSISTENT VALUES 2200M/S	
				Comp Rept	AERE-NP/R-2104	Mar 57	- .EXPT METHODS FOR HAR VALUE	
Fission	9.0-3	2.4+1	HAR	Expt Jour	JNE 6 114	Dec 57	Sanders+.GRAPH,RELATIVE TO B(NA)	+
	1.0-2	2.5+1		Revw	55Geneva 4 210	Aug 55	Lynn+ NORM TO 515B AT 0.025EV	
Fission	2.6-2	3.0+1	CCP	Expt Jour	AE 5 69	Jul 58	Vladimirskii+ SEE 58GENEVA15 309	+
				Jour	JNEA 10 64	Jul 59	TRANSLATN.*	
	2.5-2	1.0+2		Conf	58Geneva 15 309	Sep 58	Vladimirsky+.PPR2221,CURVE,BF3-DETCT	
	2.6-2	3.0+1		Jour	SJA 5 883		58 TRANSLATN.*	
Fission	3.0+4	1.0+7	BNL	Comp Conf	58Geneva 16 8	Sep 58	Hughes.PPR2483,CURVE,MANY REFS	
Fission	Pile		KUR	Expt Conf	58Geneva 12 3	Sep 58	Leipunskij+.PPR2038,VAL U233/PU239	
Fission	3.0+6	8.0+6	KUR	Expt Conf	58Geneva 16 136	Sep 58	Kalinin+.PPR2149,CURVE,CYCLOTRON	+
Fission	1.0+4	1.0+7	LAS	Revw Conf	58Geneva 15 344	Sep 58	Hemmendinger.PPR663,CURVE,MANY REFS	
Fission	Thrsh	Up	LAS	Expt Prog	WASH-1006	Oct 58	Leachman. AD V MRATIO TBD	

92 Uranium 233

Quantity	Energy (ev) Min	Max	Lab	Type	Documentation Ref Vol Page	Author, Comments Date	Data
Fission	3.4+3	7.7+5	CCP	Expt	Jour AE 6 453	Apr 59 Gorlov+ VDG,FISS CHAMBER,ABSOL,GRAPH	+
					Jour SJA 6 317	Nov 60 *ENGL OF AE 6 453	
					Jour KE 3 222	Mar 60 *	
					Rept AEC-TR-3913	59 . ENGL OF AE 6 453	
	3.4+3	7.7+5		Data	EXFOR40055.003	Sep 70 SIG AT 24 ES,PRIVATE COMM AUG 1970	
Fission	Pile		ORL	Eval	Jour NSE 6 100	Aug 59 Stoughton+,BEST VALUE .025EV=530B	
Fission	Maxwl		CRC	Expt	Jour NSE 6 379	Nov 59 Bigham.DEPEND ON MOD TEMP 0 TO 100C	+
					Jour NSE 59 50	Jan 76 - +CS OF 1958 WORK.REVISED	
					Conf 58Geneva 16 125	Sep 58 - + PAPER 204	
					Rept AERE-NP/R-2076	Jan 57 Hanna. RATIO TO U235 = .927+- .9PC	
	Maxwl			Data	EXFOR12356.	Jun 76 . 3 PTS. SIGMA, RATIO TO U239,U235.	
Fission	3.0-1	1.1+1	MTR	Eval	Rept IDO-16579	Dec 59 Moore+ MULTILEVEL ANALYSIS CURVES	
Fission	2.5-2		AE	Comp	Rept AE-11	Apr 60 Story+,DISCUSSION+TABULATN OF MEASTS	
Fission	Fiss		ALD	Eval	Rept AWRE-O-02/60	Apr 60 Hinves+AWRE EVAL DATA CFD XPT.	
Fission	2.0-2	1.0+3	MTR	Expt	Jour PR 118 714	May 60 Moore+	+
	2.5-2	5.5+0			Conf 61RPI 35	May 61 Fluharty.	
	2.0-2	1.0+3			Jour NSE 7 187	Feb 60 - +	
					Rept IDO-16576	Dec 59 Moore+	
	-2	1.0+3			Conf 58Geneva 15 111	Sep 58 Fluharty+.PPR645,CURVE,MANY REFS	
	1.9-2	9.6+2			Data EXFOR12341.002	Jun 76 . 953 PTS. SIGMA.	
Fission	2.0-2	1.0+0	MTR	Expt	Jour NSE 8 66	Jul 60 Evans+ DATA, GRAPHS.	
	4.0-2	5.0+0			Rept AERE-NP/R-2076	Jan 57 - .FIGS 1D10 1D11 CS	
Fission	Fiss		KUR	Revw	Conf 60Vienna 159	Oct 60 Bondarenko+.TABLE,EXPT DESCRIBED	
Fission	1.0+0	3.0+1	MTR	Revw	Conf 60Vienna 93	Oct 60 Evans+.CURVE,CRYSTAL SPECTR	
Fission	Maxwl		KUR	Expt	Jour AE 10 372	Apr 61 Mostovaja. TERN FISS PROB REL U235	
					Jour JNAB 17 424	Nov 63 . ENGL OF AE 10 372	
					Jour SJA 10 359	Jan 62 . ENGL OF AE 10 372	
					Jour KE 4 986	Dec 61 . GERMAN OF AE 10 372	
Fission	Maxwl		HAN	Eval	Conf 61RPI 3	May 61 Leonard.	
Fission	2.0-1	1.0+7	B+W	Eval	Rept BAW-158	Jun 61 Roach+ AVERAGED SIG 40 GROUPS	
Fission	5.0-3	2.5+0	GA	Eval	Rept GA-2113	Jun 61 Wikner+.TABLE+CURVE.100 E POINTS	
Fission	Maxwl		CRC	Expt	Conf 61Saclay 57	Jul 61 Westcott. 2200METRE/SEC SIG GIVEN	
Fission	4.0+3	1.0+7	ANL	Revw	Conf 61Vienna 1 29	Aug 61 Smith.P76,CURVE,MANY REFS GVN	
Fission	Pile		CRC	Eval	Rept CRRP-960	Jan 62 Westcott. EFF SIG TBL 20-1300 DEG C.	
Fission	2.5-3	7.5-2	BNL	Revw	Rept BNL-722	Jun 62 Sher+ REVIEW CURVE GIVEN	
Fission	1.0+0	1.0+1	CCP	Expt	Jour ZET 43 847	Sep 62 Prob. OF TERNARY FISSION MEASURED	
					Jour JET 16 599	Mar 63 TRANSLATN.*	
Fission	Fiss		AI	Eval	Conf 62Harwell 2 385	Dec 62 Strominger. SIG IN VARIOUS CORES,TBL	
Fission	-2	3.0+7	KFI	Revw	Rept MFF 11 325	Jan 63 Szabo.REVIEW,GRAPHS TABLES MANY REFS	
Fission	3.0+6	2.2+7	CCP	ExTh	Jour AE 14 177	Feb 63 Pancratov+.TOF SC CURVE GIVEN	+
					Jour SJA 14 167	63 . ENGL OF AE 14 177	
Fission	Pile		CJD	Eval	Rept INDSWG-64 285	64 Galanin. TBL EFF SIG FOR MANY SPECTR	+
Fission	Maxwl		CRC	Expt	Rept CRRP-1183	64 Bigham.	+
	Maxwl				Data EXFOR12230.	Jun 76 . 1 PT.	
Fission	Pile		ICD	Eval	Rept INDSWG-64 285	64 Galanin.TBL EFF SIG FOR MANY SPECTRA	
Fission	Pile		CCP	Expt	Jour AE 17 113	Aug 64 Bondarenko+VAL GVN REL TO U-235(N,F)	+
					Jour SJA 17 821	Aug 64 TRANSLATN.*	
Fission	Pile		CCP	Expt	Jour AE 17 294	Oct 64 Batyrbekov+VAL GVN REL TO PU239(N,F)	+
					Jour SJA 17 1025	Oct 64 TRANSLATN.*	
Fission	Spont		RI	Expt	Prog INDSWG-120 35	65 Aleksandrov.T=1.2 X 10EXP17 YEARS	
Fission	-3	+6	TRM	Revw	Rept AEET-234	65 SHANKAR SINGH.ACCURACY OF DATA GIVEN	
Fission	2.5-2		BEP	Revw	Jour KE 8 625	Jan 65 Wenzel.VAL GVN,MANY REFERENCES	
Fission	+0	+3	CAI	Theo	Jour NP 62 667	Feb 65 Stavinsky+(N,GF)PROB ABOUT=(N,GAMMA)	
Fission	4.0+4	5.0+5	ALD	Expt	Conf 65Salzburg 1 219	Mar 65 White+ 6 ENERGIES.TBL. REL TO U235.	
Fission	1.7+0	3.5+1	SAC	Expt	Jour JPR 24 264	Apr 63 Nifenecker+ LINAC,TOF.FOR RES ANAL.	
					Conf 65Salzburg 245	Mar 65 - + LINAC,TOF.	
					Jour JPR 25 877	Oct 64 - + RESONANCE PARAM ANALYSIS	
	1.7+0	3.5+1			Data EXFOR20814.002	Mar 78 1020PTS.SIGMA(RTE)	
Fission	2.4+4		ALD	Expt	Jour JNE 19 423	Jun 65 Perkin+.CALIB SB-BE SRCE. 2.73+- .11B	+
	2.4+4				Data EXFOR20584.002	Jul 76 1PNT.SIGMA.	
Fission	+0	+1	HAR	Theo	Jour PL 18 31	Aug 65 LYNN SLOW (N,GAMMA F) REACTION CALCD	
Fission	1.0+2	6.5+6	LRL	Expt	Jour PR 142 778	Feb 66 Albert+ HI-ALT BOMB,AVG SIG REL U235	+
	3.3+1	7.8+6			Data EXFOR12343.	Jun 76 . 708 PTS. SIGMA.	
Fission	Maxwl		TRM	Revw	Conf 66Bombay 1	Feb 66 Ramanna.VALS CFD TH,SIG,BINDING,DEF.	
Fission	1.0-2	1.0+0	MTR	Eval	Conf 66Wash. 840	Mar 66 Moore+,MULTILEVEL ANAL CURVE CFD XPT	
Fission	1.0-2	5.0-1	MTR	Eval	Conf 66Wash. 985	Mar 66 Fluharty+,COEF OF SIG EXPANSN CALCTD	
Fission	None		BRK	Revw	Jour NP 81 1	Jun 66 Meyers+ TABLE 2 FISS BARRIER.	

92 Uranium 233

Quantity	Energy (ev) Min	Max	Lab	Type	Documentation Ref Vol Page	Date	Author, Comments	Data
Fission	4.0−2	1.1+1	HAR	Expt	Rept AERE−M−1709	Sep 66	Brooks+ TOF LINAC SC PSD GRAPH TBL	+
	3.5−1	1.0+1			Data EXFOR20623.004	Dec 76	10PTS.SIGMA.	
Fission	2.0−2	5.0−1	MTR	Eval	Conf 66Paris 2 50	Oct 66	Smith. PPR50.TBL+CURV,LSTSQ FIT.	
					Rept INDC−15	66	−.	
Fission	Maxwl		ITE	Theo	Rept ICD−4 385	67	Birzgal+.AVERAGING OVER MAXWELL SPEC	
Fission	1.0+0	2.5+4	HAR	Expt	Prog AERE−PR/NP11 1	Apr 67	James+ LINAC,REL CURVS ONLY. FLUCTS.	
					Conf 66ANL 16	Oct 66	− + LINAC	
Fission	1.0+3	1.4+7	UK	Eval	Rept AHSB(S)R−124	May 67	Hart.(RLY).UK − DFN 333.UPDATES NSE 26	+
	4.0+6	1.5+7			Rept AWRE−O−100/64	Jan 65	Douglas+(ALD).UKNDL − DFN 202	
	1.0−4	1.5+7			Data UKNDL−DFN 87B	Mar 73	1063 PNTS	
Fission	Pile		WIN	Expt	Rept AEEW−R−526	Jun 67	Stevenson+.FISS RATIO TO U235.ZEBRA	+
Fission	1.0+6	1.4+7	ALD	Expt	Jour JNE 21 671	Aug 67	White+ 4ES REL U235. CFD OTHER DATA	+
Fission	Pile		FEI	Expt	Jour AE 23 396	Nov 67	Lejpunskij.RATIO REL U235(N,F),PILE	
					Jour SJA 23 1150	Nov 67	.ENGLISH TRANSL OF AE 23 396 11/67	
					Jour EAF 23 5 21	Nov 67	. FRENCH TRANSL OF AE 23 396 11/67	
Fission	3.0+5	2.5+6	FEI	Expt	Jour AE 24 185	Feb 68	Nesterov+ SIG U233/U235 RATIO	+
					Prog YFI−5 4	Oct 67	Smirenkin+ CURVE SIGMA RATIO 233/235	
	3.5+5	2.6+6			Rept ICD−4 339	67	− +.MEAS OF RATIO SIG U3/U5	
	3.0+5	2.5+6			Rept INDSWG−64 260	64	. TABULATED DATA	
					Jour AE 13 366	Oct 62	Smirenkin+ E − STEPS 30KEV.CFD OTHERS	
					Jour SJA 24 101	68	. ENGL OF AE 24 185	
					Rept INDC−232E	67	. ENGL OF YFI−5 4	
					Jour EAF 13 4 82	Oct 62	. FRENCH OF AE 13 366	
	4.8+5	2.5+6			Data EXFOR40309.003	Oct 75	SIG U−233/235 FOR 4 EN GIVEN	
	3.3+5	2.5+6			Data EXFOR40027.	Oct 72	RATIO U−233/U−235, 43 EN, VDG, REAC.	
Fission	2.0+1	1.0+6	LAS	Expt	Jour PR 166 1178	Feb 68	Bergen+ BOMB TOF 1LVL+MULTILVL FITS	+
					Abst DA/B 28 4244	Apr 68	−. TOF,PETREL EVENT JUNE65.	
					Rept LA−DC−8946	67	.SUPERSEDED	
	1.0+1	1.0+7			Conf 66Paris 2 219	Oct 66	Hemmendinger.DETONATION TOF	
	2.0+1	1.0+6			Conf 66Wash. 895	Mar 66	.SUPERSEDED	
	2.0+1	9.8+5			Data EXFOR12360.	Jun 76	. 3047 PTS. SIGMA.	
Fission		6.2+1	WAL	Eval	Conf 68Wash. 615	Mar 68	Schneider. CURVE 1 − LVL B − W FIT.	
Fission	9.1+5	1.0+7	ANL	Eval	Jour NSE 32 35	Apr 68	Davey. RE − EVALUATION OF DATA.	
	1.0+3	1.0+7			Jour NSE 26 149	Oct 66	−. EVALUATION.	
Fission	2.0+3		MTR	Expt	Prog WASH−1093 61	Apr 68	Simpson+ VALUE GIVN CFD OTHERS TBC	
Fission	Maxwl		ALD	Expt	Jour JNE 22 477	Aug 68	Keith+ REL.TO CAPT XSEC CO59	
Fission	1.0−2	1.0+7	GA	Eval	Rept GA−8854	Aug 68	Boroughs+ ENDF/B DATA CURVES	
Fission	4.0−1	2.0+3	ORL	Expt	Jour NSE 34 1	Oct 68	Weston+ RPI LINAC+SCINT NF+NG SIMULT	+
					Rept ORNL−TM−2140	Apr 68	.TABLES.	
					Rept ORNL−TM−1751	Apr 67	.SUPERSEDED	
					Conf 66Paris 2 233	Oct 66	.SUPERSEDED.	
					Rept RPI−328−68 20	Jun 66	.SUPERSEDED	
					Rept RPI−328−56 45	Mar 66	.SUPERSEDED	
	4.0−1	2.0+3			Data EXFOR12336.004	Jun 76	. 3416 PTS. SIGMA.	
Fission	+5	+6	LAS	Expt	Prog WASH−1124 110	Nov 68	Smith+ TO BE PUBLISHED IN NSE NDG	
Fission	−		SUK	Theo	Conf 68Bombay 2 170	Dec 68	Narayana. FISSN − MODEL,4 − POLE − MOMENT	
Fission	1.0+1	2.0+4	HAR	Comp	Rept AERE−M−2157	Jan 69	James+ TBL AVG SIGF DATA FROM SCISRS	
Fission	Pile		AUA	ExTh	Rept AAEC/TM−496	Apr 69	Cripps.MARKS.FISS − RATIO CFD SIG − SETS	
Fission	8.0+6	9.5+6	CCP	Expt	Jour IZV 33 726	Apr 69	Andreev+ (D,PF),E=DEUT−E	
					Jour BAS 33 668	70	. ENGLISH OF IZV 33 726	
Fission	2.2+6	5.5+6	ANL	Expt	Conf 69Vienna 457	Jul 69	Elwyn.DISCUSSN.'DELAYED + PROMPT'FISSN	
Fission	Spont		FR	Expt	Conf 69Vienna 952	Jul 69	Monnin+PPR83. SPON FISSN HALF − LIFE	
Fission	−		HAR	Revw	Conf 69Vienna 249	Jul 69	Lynn. TBL=2HUMPED FISS − BARRIER PARS	
Fission	1.4+7		TRM	Expt	Conf 69Roorke 2 289	Dec 69	Iyer+ SIGMA RELATIVE TO U238	+
	1.4+7				Data EXFOR30035.003	Dec 72	ONE VALUE	
Fission	1.0+3	1.0+7	TRM	Eval	Rept BARC/I−96	70	Kapil.14 GROUP SIG,2 N − SPECS,TABLES	
Fission	2.4+2	2.4+4	ANL	Expt	Jour NSE 39 361	Mar 70	Lehto.FISS CS RATIO TO U235.TBL GVN.	+
	2.4+2	2.4+4			Data EXFOR10084.003	Jul 71	. 26 PTS. FISS CS RATIO TO U235.	
Fission	Pile		FTI	Expt	Jour AE 28 359	Apr 70	BAK+.CD FILTERS USED,U235 − RATIO,TABL	+
					Jour SJA 28 460	Apr 70	.ENGLISH OF AE 28 359	
					Jour EAF 28 4 112	Apr 70	. FRENCH OF AE 28 359	
	Pile				Data EXFOR40349.006	Dec 77	SIG(N,F)U − 233/SIG(N,F)U − 235, 1 PNT	
Fission	1.0+1	2.8+6	LAS	Expt	Rept LA−4420	Apr 70	Bergen. NUCL SHOT,TOF,TABLES+CURVES	+
	1.0+1	2.8+6			Data EXFOR10056.002	Apr 71	. 2911 PTS. SIGMA.	
Fission	1.5+2	1.0+5	TOK	Theo	Jour NST 7 157	Apr 70	Kikuchi+.CALC USING SPIN DEPENDNT WF	
Fission	1.0+4	6.0+6	ANL	Revw	Conf 70Helsinki 2 3	Jun 70	Poenitz. RELATIVE SIG(E) GRAPHS.	
Fission	Maxwl	2.6−2	CRC	Expt	Conf 70Helsinki 1 287	Jun 70	Lounsbury+THR FLUX,CS RATIO/U235 GVN	+
	Maxwl				Data EXFOR10013.007	Sep 72	. 1 PT. CS RATIO/U235 GIVEN.	

92 Uranium 233

Quantity	Energy (ev) Min	Max	Lab	Type	Documentation Ref Vol Page	Date	Author, Comments	Data
Fission	Maxwl	2.6−2	FAR	Expt	Conf 70Helsinki 1 295	Jun 70	Vidal+97. VAL GVN,EXPT RELATIV U−235	+
	2.5−2				Data EXFOR20552.002	Apr 76	1PNT.SIGMA.	
Fission	+5	+7	GEL	Revw	Conf 70Helsinki 1 127	Jun 70	Deruytter.106. PROPOSED AS STANDARD	
Fission	1.8−2	3.0+3	GEL	Expt	Jour JNE 24 111	Jun 70	Cao+ MULTLVL FIT TO RES BELOW 65EV	+
	1.8−1	3.0+3			Conf 70Helsinki 1 419	Jun 70	CAO+PPR19. SIG(E) GRAPHS,SPARK+SCINT	
	1.8−2	3.0+3			Data EXFOR20003.	Nov 70	5386PTS.	
Fission	5.5+5	2.2+6	HAR	Expt	Jour NP/A 148 337	Jun 70	Elwyn+ STUDY OF SHORT LIVED ISOMERS.	
					Prog AERE−PR/NP17	Dec 70	− + SPON FISS ISOMS HL 32 NS	
Fission	5.0+3	1.0+6	KFK	Expt	Rept KFK−1240	Jun 70	Kaeppeler+ SIG RATIO /U235,TOF EXPT	+
					Jour NSE 40 375	Jun 70	− + EQU TO KFK−1240	
	5.2+3	1.0+6			Data EXFOR20363.002	Sep 74	49PTS.SIGMA.	
Fission	+0	6.0+1	ORL	Eval	Conf 70Helsinki 2 757	Jun 70	Desaussure+ 94.SIG(E)CRV,MULTLVL FIT	
	1.0−2	6.0+1			Rept ORNL−TM−2745	Nov 69	− + MULTILVL ANAL + LEAST SQ	
Fission		7.0+3	SDC	Theo	Conf 70Helsinki 2 799	Jun 70	Garrison.DISCUSSN. RESONANCE ANAL	
Fission		3.0+6	CCP	Theo	Jour YF 12 293	Aug 70	Zhmailo. U233(D,P FISSN)GRPH CFD XPT	
					Jour SNP 12 160	Feb 71	TRANSLATN.*	
Fission	2.0+6	7.0+6	TRM	Theo	Jour NP/A 151 532	Aug 70	Sood+ CORREL ANAL OF INTERM STRUCTUR	
	−				Prog BARC−471 5	70 −	+ CORREL ANAL,D CLASS II VAL GV	
Fission	2.0−2	1.0+0	ORL	Expt	Jour NSE 42 143	Nov 70	Weston+ RPI LINAC, NF + NG SIMUL	+
	1.0+0	2.0+2			Prog ORNL−4592 11	Sep 70	− +. LINAC.PRELIM CURV SHOWN.TBC	
	1.7−2	1.1+0			Data EXFOR10100.002	Aug 71	. 50 PTS, E**1/2.	
Fission	1.0+2	1.0+5	GA	Theo	Jour NP/A 159 305	Dec 70	Garrison.AVERAGE C.S.=NO RES INTERF	
Fission	3.2+5	2.5+6	TRM	Expt	Conf 70Madurai 2 67	Dec 70	Iyengar+ SIGMA EXPT TB CONT'D, NDG	
Fission	Maxwl		UFP	Expt	Rept CCEN−17	Dec 70	Clemente. REL TO U235,FISSION CHAMB.	
					Conf 70Helsinki 1 295	Jun 70	.SEE ALSO *	
Fission	2.5−2		ANL	Eval	Conf 71Knoxvill 560	Mar 71	Devolpi. ADJUSTED VALUE GIVEN.	
Fission	8.0−1	1.0+2	COL	Expt	Conf 71Knoxvill 855	Mar 71	Felvinci+. CURVES	
	6.0−1	4.0+4			Prog NYO−73−340 37	Dec 70	− +.NEVIS. CURVES.	
	+0	+4			Conf 69Vienna 922	Jul 69	Melkonian+PPR117. CHANNEL ANAL	
Fission	1.0−3	2.0+0	JUL	Theo	Rept JUEL−746−RG 50	Apr 71	Bonka.KUGEL−THERMOS−LIBR,T=300K,CURV	
	2.5−2		IFB	Eval	Rept YK−9 34	72	Morogovsky. COMPUTR RE−EVAL,DATA GVN	
					Rept INDC(CCP)−42	Aug 74	.P1.ENGLISH OF YK−9	
Fission	Maxwl		BET	Eval	Rept WAPD−TM−1052	Sep 72	Steen. EVAL WITH,WITHOUT U235 RATIO	
					Conf 71Knoxvill 566	Mar 71	− . BEST VALUE=524.0+− 5.0B	
Fission	None		CRC	Expt	Priv WALKER	Nov 72	Walker. VAL IN AECL−3477 IS FINAL.	
					Prog EANDC(CAN)−40	Sep 69	Durham. PAGE6. HALFLIFE GIVEN.	
Fission	Fiss		SGA	Eval	Conf 73Paris 1 233	Mar 73	Eder+ FISS SPEC REL U238(N,F),TBLS	
					Rept SGAE−PH−141	Feb 73	.SAME AS 73PARIS,NO DETAILS,TBP	
Fission	2.5−2		IJI	Eval	Conf 73Kiev 1 197	May 73	Fedorova. SIG 2200M/S=530.6+− 1.9 B	
Fission	6.0+0	1.2+2	SAC	Expt	Jour NSE 54 116	Jun 74	Nizamuddin+ SINGLE LEVEL ANALYSIS	+
	6.0+0	3.0+4			Jour NSE 51 130	Jun 73	Blons. HIGH RESOL. LINAC. CURVES	
	3.0+1	2.0+2			Conf 71Knoxvill 829	Mar 71	− +.CURVE	
	6.0+0	3.0+4			Data EXFOR20446.002	Oct 75	7534PTS.SIGMA.	
Fission	Maxwl	5.0+1	GEL	Expt	Jour NSE 54 423	Aug 74	Deruytter+ NORM TO 2200M/S CS,TBLS.	+
	1.8−2	3.0+7			Priv DERUYTTER	Jun 74	− .	
	1.8−2	3.0+7			Data EXFOR20411.002	Apr 75	1359PTS.SIGMA.	
Fission	8.0+0	2.5+1	COL	Expt	Abst ANS 19 420	Oct 74	Felvinci+ ORELA.PULSE.HEIGHT.EFFECTS	
Fission	1.0−2	3.0+1	GEL	Expt	Prog INDC(SEC)−43	Dec 74	Wagemans+ STAND FIS−INTEGRL SUGGESTD	
Fission	0.0+0	6.0+1	NSU	Theo	Rept INDC(SEC)−42	Dec 74	CHI+ ADL−ADL CALC OKS XPT. TBP KNS	
Fission	1.5+3	2.0+3	FEI	Expt	Jour AE 38 43	Jan 75	Dvukhsherstnov+ SIGU−233/SIGU−235	+
	2.0+3				Jour SJA 38 49	Jul 75	. ENGLISH OF AE 38,43	
	1.5+3	2.0+3			Data EXFOR40321.003	Feb 76	.RATIO U−239 TO U235 GVN	
Fission	3.0+6	5.0+6	LAS	Theo	Conf 75Wash. 129	Mar 75	Moore.GRPH R MATR STAT CALC CFD EXP	
Fission	1.5+4	2.0+6	FEI	Expt	Jour YF 21 704	Apr 75	Shpak+ SIG U233/SIG U235 VS EN,GRAPH	
					Jour SNP 21 363	Apr 75	. ENGLISH OF YF 21 704	
	1.5+4	2.0+6			Data EXFOR40361.003	Feb 75	SIG U233/SIG U235 AT 70 ENERGIES	
Fission	1.0+4	6.0+5	AUA	Theo	Conf 75Kiev 5 191	May 75	Bertram+ NEW STATMOD,CURVE CFD DATA	
Fission	2.0+3	2.4+4	FEI	Expt	Conf 75Kiev	May 75	Zhuravlev+ SIG,COMPARATIV EVALUATION	
Fission	2.5−2		MAG	Eval	Rept EPRI−NP−163	Dec 75	Beer+ MONTECARLO ANAL 70HELSINKI P287	
Fission	4.0+5	7.0+6	FEI	Expt	Rept YK−23 102	76	Maksjutenko+ REACT N,NF+DELYD NSGRP	
Fission	Maxwl		MUN	Expt	Diss GRYNTAKIS	Mar 76	Gryntakis.,ACT.MEAS.,CALC OF G−FUNCT	+
			ExTh		Jour RCA 22 128	Mar 75	− +,CALC WESTCOTTS G−FUNCTION	
	2.5−2			Expt	Data EXFOR20625.042	Aug 76	1PNT.SIGMA.	
Fission	1.0+1	7.0+4	LRL	Expt	Prog ERDA−NDC−3 66	May 76	Czirr+TOF.CS REL LI6.ANAL TBD.NDG	
Fission	1.0+5	7.5+6	ANL	Expt	Jour NSE 54 317	Jul 74	Meadows. U233/U235 FISS RATIO C−SECT	+
	1.0+5	1.0+7			Conf 76ANL 73	Jun 76	− .U233/U235 RATIO.GRPH.CFD OTH	
	1.4+5	7.4+6			Data EXFOR10236.002	Apr 74	. 20 PTS. RATIO TO U235 NF.	
Fission	1.0+4	1.0+7	ANL	Revw	Conf 76ANL	Jun 76	Poenitz+SUPPLEMENT TO CONF.DATA FILE	

92 Uranium 233

Quantity	Energy (ev) Min	Energy (ev) Max	Lab	Type	Documentation Ref Vol Page	Date	Author, Comments	Data
Fission	2.0+6	1.0+7	LAS	Expt Abst	BAP 2 196	Apr 57	Smith+,DBL ION CHAMBER,+ − 5PC	+
	2.0+6	1.0+7		Data	EXFOR12316.002	Jun 76	. 19 PTS. SIGMA.	
Fission	1.0−2	3.0+4	LRL	Expt Conf	76ANL 47	Jun 76	Behrens+CFD THR E NF CS RATIOS.TBL.	
Fission	1.0+4	1.0+6	AUA	Theo Jour	NP/A 265 337	Jul 76	Boldeman+CFD EVAL DATA ANE,1,409,75	
Fission	Maxwl		PAH	ExTh Conf	76Lowell 725	Jul 76	Hooshyar+STATMDL APLD TO EXPT.DATA	
	7.0+6	1.6+7		Conf	76Lowell 725	Jul 76	− + 2ES.STATMD CFD XPT	
Fission	+7		RI	Expt Conf	77Kiev	77	Adamov+ COINC,SIG = 1947+ − 31 MB	
Res Int Fiss	None		ORL	Revw Conf	55Geneva 5 96	Aug 55	Macklin+.P833 ,EXPT CFD THEORY,TABLE	
Res Int Fiss	5.0−1	1.0+6	ORL	Eval Jour	NSE 6 100	Aug 59	Stoughton+,BEST VALUE 900+ − 100B	
Res Int Fiss	Pile		ORL	Expt Conf	60Vienna 239	Oct 60	Stoughton+.VAL GVN CFD OTHERS	
Res Int Fiss	7.3−1		WIN	Expt Rept	AEEW − R − 217	Aug 63	Hardiman+.CD RATIOS.E − CD VALUES CALC	
Res Int Fiss	Pile		CRC	Expt Rept	CRRP − 1183	Feb 64	Bigham. NRX,REL IN,B,LI,AU 761+ − 17B	+
	Pile			Data	EXFOR12230.003	Jun 76	. 1 PT.	
Res Int Fiss	5.0−1		KAP	Expt Abst	ANS 7 272	Nov 64	Esch+ RI 820PM65 MASS SPECT P RADCHM	+
Res Int Fiss	5.0−1		BET	Expt Jour	NSE 22 121	May 65	Hardy. 798+ − 26 B OTHER CUTOFFS ALSO	+
	5.0−1			Data	EXFOR12283.003	Jun 76	. 1 PT.	
Res Int Fiss	5.0−1		JAE	Expt Jour	NST 2 532	Dec 65	Yasuno. AT 3 CD − CUTOFF ES,REL TO AU	+
	5.0−1			Data	EXFOR20309.002	Jun 74	1PNT.	
Res Int Fiss	5.0−1		KAP	Comp Conf	66S.Diego 2 299	Feb 66	Feiner+.COMPIL PREV RESLT+RECOM VAL	
Res Int Fiss	4.0−1	7.5+0	HAR	Expt Rept	AERE − M − 1709	Sep 66	Brooks+ TOF.LINAC.SC PSD.GRPH.TBL	+
	3.5−1	1.0+1		Data	EXFOR20623.005	Dec 76	10PTS.	
Res Int Fiss	5.0−1	1.0+4	INA	Eval Conf	66Paris 2 333	Oct 66	Hennies.PPR5.TBL RECOM DATA CFD OTHR	
				Rept	NAA − SR − 11980 5	May 67	− . RECOMMENDED DATA.IMPROVED	
Res Int Fiss	5.0−1		ORL	Expt Abst	ANS 10 220	Jun 67	Weston+ RPI LINAC+SCINT 735+ − 15B CFD	
Res Int Fiss	5.0−1	+6	BET	Expt Jour	NSE 29 1	Jul 67	Conway+ 771+ − 49B	+
				Rept	WAPD − TM − 613	Jun 67	.SUPERSEDED	
	5.0−1	+6		Data	EXFOR12313.003	Jun 76	. 1 PT.	
Res Int Fiss	5.0−1		BET	Revw Rept	WAPD − TM − 760	Aug 68	Gunst+. CURVES. 40 REFERENCES	
Res Int Fiss	5.0−1		GA	Eval Rept	GA − 8854	Aug 68	Boroughs+ ENDF/B DATA	
Res Int Fiss	1.0+1	2.0+4	HAR	Comp Rept	AERE − M − 2157	Jun 69	James+ TBL RES INTEG SCISRS DATA	
Res Int Fiss	Pile		RI	Expt Prog	YFI − 8 17	Dec 69	Bak+ REL EXPT TO U − 235,VALUES GIVEN	
				Rept	INDC(CCP) − 8U22	Dec 70	TRANSLATN.*	
		+7		Jour	AE 28 359	Apr 70	BAK+ INTEGRAL VALUE GIVEN,CFD OTHER	
				Jour	EAF 28 4 112	Apr 70	. FRENCH OF AE 28 359	
Res Int Fiss	Maxwl		FTI	Expt Jour	AE 28 359	Apr 70	BAK+ INTEGRAL VALUE GIVEN,CFD OTHER	+
				Jour	EAF 28 4 112	Apr 70	. FRENCH OF AE 28 359	
				Jour	SJA 28 460	Apr 70	.ENGLISH OF AE 28 359	
	Maxwl			Data	EXFOR40349.002	Dec 77	CD − DIFF,REL U235. 1 DATAPNT	
Res Int Fiss	5.3−1	3.0+3	GEL	Expt Jour	JNE 24 111	Jun 70	CAO+ FROM LINAC.TOF. RES PARAMS.	+
	4.1−1	1.2+3		Conf	70Helsinki 1 419	Jun 70	CAO+PPR19. 30E − RANGES CFD OTHER DATA	
	5.3−1	3.0+3		Data	EXFOR20003.	Nov 70	48PTS.	
Res Int Fiss	4.1−1	1.2+3	HAR	Expt Conf	70Helsinki 1 267	Jun 70	James.107. SIG AT 24RANGES,CFD OTHER	
Res Int Fiss	5.0−1	+6	KAP	Expt Jour	NSE 44 180	May 71	Eiland+ CD AND CD − RH FILTERS	+
	5.0−1			Data	EXFOR10143.	Aug 73	. 2 PTS.	
Res Int Fiss	5.0−1	+6	COR	Expt Jour	NSE 46 31	Oct 71	Draper.INTEGRAL SIG TIMES E.4 SPECTR	
	+0	+1		Abst	DA/B 31 1466	Sep 70	− .EXPT FOR 4 SPEC,GOOD CFD CALC	
Res Int Fiss	4.1−1	1.2+3	COL	Expt Prog	COO − 2176 − 1 7	Jun 72	Felvinci+. TABLE.CFD OTHERS	
Res Int Fiss	5.0−1		SGA	Comp Conf	73Paris 1 233	Mar 73	Eder+ INCLUDING 1/V PART OF SIG,TBL	
				Rept	SGAE − PH − 141	Feb 73	.SAME AS 73PARIS,NO DETAILS,TBP	
Res Int Fiss	8.3+0	1.2+3	SAC	Expt Jour	NSE 51 130	Jun 73	Blons. TABLE. CFD OTHER EXPERIMENTS	
Res Int Fiss	Maxwl	5.0+1	GEL	Expt Jour	NSE 54 423	Aug 74	Deruytter+ TBL.	
Res Int Fiss	5.5−1		MUN	Expt Diss	GRYNTAKIS	Mar 76	Gryntakis.,CD − RAT.,812+ − 90B,INCL 1/V	+
	5.5−1			Data	EXFOR20625.043	Aug 76	1PNT.	
Alpha	Maxwl		ANL	Expt Rept	CF − 3651	Oct 46	Zinn.	+
	Maxwl			Data	EXFOR12319.005	Jun 76	. 1 PT.	
Alpha	Maxwl		KAP	Expt Rept	KAPL − 511	Aug 51	Sampson. EMP DEPND QUALITAT VALUE.	
Alpha	Pile		ANL	Expt Conf	55Geneva 4 105	Aug 55	Inghram+.P596,VAL GVN,MASS − SPECTRM	+
				Prog	ANL − 4515 15	Oct 50	− +	
	Pile			Data	EXFOR12351.003	Jun 76	. 1 PT.	
Alpha	Maxwl		CCP	Expt Conf	55Geneva 4 230	Aug 55	Kukavadse+ P644. ABSOLUTE VALUE	+
Alpha	Maxwl	5.0+5	ORL	Revw Conf	55Geneva 3 19	Aug 55	Weinberg.P862,VAL FOR 2ES GVN,REFS	
Alpha	Pile		KAP	Expt Prog	BNL − 433 33	Sep 56	Mcmillan+.4ALFA MEASTS.3SHIELDS+NONE	
Alpha	1.0−2	1.0−1	BNL	Eval Jour	JNE 3 177	Oct 56	Palevsky+ CALC FROM ETA,IF NU CONST	
				Revw Conf	55Geneva 4 311	Aug 55	− .GRAPH,EXPT DESCRIBED,P587	
Alpha	1.1+0	2.2+0	HAR	Expt Jour	JNE 5 186	57	Sanders+ CRYSTAL SPECTR DATA.	+
Alpha	1.8+0	1.0+1	BNL	Expt Rept	AERE − NP/R − 2076	Jan 57	Sailor.CS FOR 5BIG RES 5WEAK SEEN	
Alpha	2.5−2		BNL	Eval Rept	BNL − 325 1	Jan 57	Hughes+ WORLD CONSIST.VAL = .105+ − .007	
Alpha	1.1−3		MTR	Expt Rept	AERE − NP/R − 2076	Jan 57	Cocking. D113PMD019	

92 Uranium 233

Quantity	Energy (ev) Min	Max	Lab	Type	Documentation Ref Vol Page	Date	Author, Comments	Data
Alpha	Maxwl		HAR	Eval Rept	AERE−NP/R−2140	Dec 57	Egelstaff+ CONSISTENT VALUES 2200M/S	
				Comp Rept	AERE−NP/R−2104	Mar 57	− .EXPT METHODS FOR HAR VALUE	
				Revw Conf	55Geneva 4 307	Aug 55	− +.VAL GVN,EXPT DESCRBD,P425	
Alpha	1.1−3		HAR	Expt Jour	JNE 6 285	May 58	Cocking.FILTER NEUTS,ALFA=.113+−.018	+
Alpha	Maxwl		BNL	Revw Conf	58Geneva 16 8	Sep 58	Hughes.PPR2483,VAL V=2200M/SEC GVN	
Alpha	2.5−2		AE	Comp Rept	AE− 11	Apr 60	Story+,DISCUSSION+TABULATN OF MEASTS	
Alpha	1.0+0	8.2+2	RPI	Expt Jour	NSE 9 105	Feb 61	Yeater.	+
Alpha	Maxwl		HAN	Eval Conf	61RPI 3	May 61	Leonard.	
Alpha	5.0−3	2.5+0	GA	Eval Rept	GA− 2113	Jun 61	Wikner+.TABLE 100 E POINTS	
Alpha	Maxwl		CRC	Expt Conf	61Saclay 57	Jul 61	Westcott. 2200METRE/SEC SIG GIVEN	
Alpha	+4	1.0+6	ANL	Revw Conf	61Vienna 1 29	Aug 61	Smith.P76,CURVE,MANY REFS GVN	
Alpha	2.5−2	1.0+6	ROS	Revw Jour	KE 5 701	Jan 62	Falkenberg.VAL GVN,REFERENCES	
Alpha	3.0+4	1.0+6	LAS	Expt Jour	NSE 12 169	Feb 62	Hopkins+ TABLE+CURVE CFD OTHER EXPTS	+
				Conf	61Vienna 1 111	Aug 61	− +.PPR55,GRAPH CFD REFS	
				Conf	61Saclay 407	Jul 61	Diven+,CURVE ALFA VS E GIVEN	
	3.0+4	1.0+6		Data	EXFOR12331.002	Jun 76	9 PTS.	
Alpha	Pile		ORL	Expt Jour	NSE 16 245	Jun 63	Halperin+,ALPHA=0.170+−0.017	
Alpha	5.0−1		KAP	Expt Abst	ANS 7 272	Nov 64	Esch+ AVG 1/E SPECT P.SEV.	+
	5.0−1			Data	EXFOR12314.002	Jun 76	1 PT. RATIO OF RI.	
Alpha	Maxwl		CRC	Expt Rept	AECL−2148	Dec 64	Okazaki+ CHEM/MASS ANAL IRRAD U.	+
	Maxwl			Data	EXFOR12350.003	Jun 76	1 PT.	
Alpha	−3	+6	TRM	Revw Rept	AEET−234	65	SHANKAR SINGH.NO DATA BELOW 30 KEV	
Alpha	Fast		ANL	Expt Jour	NSE 21 179	Feb 65	Crouthamel+ FST REACT.CFD DIVEN,ANL.	
Alpha	Pile		MTR	ExTh Conf	66Wash. 919	Mar 66	Smith+,REACTVTY MEASTS+SPECTRAL CORR	
Alpha	3.5−2	1.1+1	HAR	Expt Priv	BROOKS3	Aug 66	Brooks. = 1 DATA INDEX LINES	+
Alpha	Maxwl		HAR	Expt Jour	JNE 16 195	Apr 62	Cabell+ 0.0942+−.0016, MASS SPECTR	+
				Conf	66Paris 2 3	Oct 66	− + PPR21, MASS−SPEC VAL GIVEN	
				Jour	RST 16 195	62	− + MASS SPEC.	
				Rept	AERE−R−3775	Jul 61	− + 2PC ACCURACY OKS PREV.BEST	
Alpha	5.0−1	1.0+4	INA	Eval Conf	66Paris 2 333	Oct 66	Hennies.PPR5.TBL RECOM DATA CFD OTHR	
				Rept	NAA−SR−11980 5	May 67	− . RECOMMENDED DATA.IMPROVED	
Alpha	1.0+0	1.0+3	ORL	Expt Conf	66Paris 2 233	Oct 66	Desaussure+ TBD,CAPT+FIS SIMULTN.	
Alpha	1.0+4	2.0+4	LAS	Theo Jour	PR 158 1127	Jun 67	Bell. PREDICT 10−20KEV BY SYSTEMATCS	
Alpha	5.0−1	+6	BET	Expt Jour	NSE 29 1	Jul 67	Conway+ ALFA=0.175+−0.006 1/E SPECT	
				Rept	WAPD−TM−613	Jun 67	.SUPERSEDED	
Alpha	3.0+1	6.3+1	LAS	Expt Jour	PR 166 1178	Feb 68	Bergen+ BOMB TOF CURVES	
				Rept	LA−DC−8946	67	.SUPERSEDED	
				Rept	LA− 3676	Dec 66	.SUPERSEDED	
Alpha	Maxwl	+3	RPI	Expt Prog	WASH−1093 113	Apr 68	Weinstein+ LINAC ANAL TBC NDG	
Alpha	5.0−1		BET	Revw Rept	WAPD−TM−760	Aug 68	Gunst+. CURVES. 40 REFERENCES	
Alpha	1.0+4	1.0+7	GA	Eval Rept	GA− 8854	Aug 68	Boroughs+ ENDF/B DATA	
Alpha	1.5+2	1.0+5	TOK	Theo Jour	NST 7 157	Apr 70	Kikuchi+.CALC USING SPIN DEPENDNT WF	
Alpha	2.5−2		CRC	Expt Conf	70Helsinki 1 287	Jun 70	Lounsbury+THR FLUX.VAL AT 2200M/S.	+
	2.5−2			Data	EXFOR10013.002	Sep 72	1 PT. VAL AT 2200 M/S.	
Alpha	2.5−2		ANL	Eval Conf	71Knoxvill 560	Mar 71	Devolpi. ADJUSTED VALUE GIVEN.	
Alpha	5.0−1		KAP	Expt Jour	NSE 44 180	May 71	Eiland+ CD AND CD−RH FILTERS	
				Conf	KAPL−P−3438	Jun 68	− + 0.184 INCLUDING 1/E,PRELIMIN	
Alpha	Fast		ANL	Expt Jour	NSE 45 37	Jul 71	Kato+.FAST REACTOR SPEC. INTEG MEAST	
Alpha	2.5−2		IFB	Eval Rept	YK− 9 34	72	Morogovsky. COMPUTR RE−EVAL,DATA GVN	
				Rept	INDC(CCP)−42	Aug 74	.P1.ENGLISH OF YK−9	
Alpha	Maxwl		BET	Eval Rept	WAPD−TM−1052	Sep 72	Steen. EVAL WITH,WITHOUT U235 RATIO	
				Conf	71Knoxvill 566	Mar 71	− . BEST VALUE=0.0874+−0.0006	
Alpha	Pile		ANL	Expt Jour	NSE 53 9	Jan 74	Dudey+. INTEGRAL MEASTS IN EBR−2.	
				Rept	ANL−7791	Jul 71	Heinrich+. INTEGRAL MEAST IN EBR−2	
Alpha	2.5−2		MAG	Eval Rept	EPRI−NP−163	Dec 75	Beer+MONTECARLO ANAL 70HELSINKI P287	
				Abst	ANS 23 509	Jun 76	− +MONTCARLO ANAL CRC DATA.TBL.CF	
Eta	Maxwl		ANL	Expt Rept	CF− 3651	Oct 46	Zinn.	+
	Maxwl			Data	EXFOR12319.007	Jun 76	1 PT. RATIO TO U235.	
Eta	Pile		CRC	Expt Rept	CRP− 378	48	Cruikshank+	+
	Pile			Data	EXFOR12347.002	Jun 76	.1PT, SIGMA	
Eta	Pile		ANL	Expt Prog	ANL−4746 17	Dec 51	Harris+.PILE OSCILLATOR. ETA=2.31	
Eta	Maxwl		ANL	Revw Conf	55Geneva 3 198	Aug 55	Zinn.VAL 2200M/SEC GVN,	
Eta	Maxwl		CCP	Expt Conf	55Geneva 4 295	Aug 55	Spivak+.VAL GVN,EXPT DESCRIBED,P657	+
Eta	Maxwl		CCP	Expt Conf	55Geneva 4 301	Aug 55	Alichanov+.VAL GVN,EXPT DESCRBD,P658	
Eta	Maxwl		HAR	Revw Conf	55Geneva 4 307	Aug 55	Egelstaff+.VAL GVN,EXPT DESCRBD,P425	
Eta	Maxwl		ORL	Revw Conf	55Geneva 3 19	Aug 55	Weinberg.P862,VAL GVN,DISCUSSION	

92 Uranium 233

Quantity	Energy (ev) Min	Max	Lab	Type	Documentation Ref Vol Page	Date	Author, Comments	Data
Eta	Maxwl 1.3+2		CCP	Expt	Jour AE 1 3 13	Jun 56	Spivak+.AVERAGES IN 6 BROAD SPECTRA	
					Jour JNE 4 70	Jan 57	TRANSLATN.*	
					Jour NE 1 101	Jun 56	SEE ALSO *	
					Jour SJA 1 3 295	56	TRANSLATN.*	
Eta	3.0+4	9.0+5	CCP	Expt	Jour AE 1 3 21	Jun 56	Spivak+.DATA AT 4 ENERGIES	+
					Jour JNE 4 79	Jan 57	TRANSLATN.*	
					Jour NE 1 101	Jun 56	SEE ALSO *	
					Jour SJA 1 3 303	56	TRANSLATN.*	
Eta	1.0−2	1.0−1	BNL	Expt	Jour JNE 3 177	Oct 56	Palevsky+ SC GRAPH,ETA NEARLY CONST	+
					Conf 55Geneva 4 311	Aug 55	− .GRAPH,EXPT DESCRIBED,P587	
	1.0−2	9.9−2			Data EXFOR12322.002	Jun 76	. 14 PTS.	
Eta	1.0−1	8.0+0	MTR	Expt	Rept IDO − 16366	Nov 56	Magleby+. ETA ENERGY DEPENDENCE GUN	+
	2.2−2	1.1+1			Data EXFOR12317.002	Jun 76	. 154 PTS.	
Eta	Maxwl 2.5−2		HAR	Expt	Rept AERE − NP/R − 2104	57	Richmond. REL U − 235. ABST. DATA.	
	Maxwl				Rept AERE − R/M − 63	Aug 55	− . CFD U235	
Eta	Pile		ORL	Expt	Jour NSE 1 20	Mar 56	Thomas+,CRITICAL SOLUTION 2.31+ − 0.03	+
					Jour NSE 2 253	57	Frances+ RECALCULATION.	
	Pile				Data EXFOR12348.003	Jun 76	. 1 PT. FROM NSE 2,253.	
Eta	2.5−2		BNL	Eval	Rept BNL − 325 1	Jan 57	Hughes+ WORLD CONSIST.VAL.=2.28+ − .02	
Eta	Maxwl		HAR	Expt	Rept AERE − NP/R − 2104	Mar 57	Littler+ CITED.PILE OSC,CALC IMPTNCE	
					Conf 55Geneva 4 351	56	− + PILE OSC.	
Eta	2.5−2	2.2+0	HAR	Expt	Jour JNE 5 186	Nov 57	Sanders+.CRYSTAL SPECTR.DATA	+
					Rept AERE − NP/R − 2076	Jan 57	− + SUPERSEDED	
					Rept UK/C − 5/2	57	− + SUPERSEDED	
Eta	Maxwl		HAR	Eval	Rept AERE − NP/R − 2140	Dec 57	Egelstaff+ CONSISTENT VALUES 2200M/S	
Eta	Maxwl		KAP	Expt	Jour NSE 3 758	Jun 58	Gaerttner+,2.231+ − .034 SUBCADMIUM TH	+
					Rept KAPL − 1468	Feb 56	.SUPERSEDED	
					Rept KAPL − 1464	Dec 55	.SUPERSEDED	
	Maxwl				Data EXFOR12327.002	Jun 76	. 2 PTS. ETA AND RATIO TO U235.	
Eta	Maxwl		BNL	Comp	Conf 58Geneva 16 8	Sep 58	Hughes.PPR2483,VAL V=2200M/SEC GVN	
Eta	−2	1.0+3	MTR	Revw	Conf 58Geneva 15 111	Sep 58	Fluharty+.PPR645,CURVE,MANY REFS	
Eta	−2	+0	ORL	Revw	Conf 59ANL 253	59	Desaussure.SUMMARY OF ORNL MEASTS.	
Eta	2.5−2		ORL	Expt	Jour NSE 5 49	Jan 59	Desaussure. SILVER REL TO U − 235.	
Eta	Maxwl		ANL	Expt	Jour NSE 5 225	Apr 59	Muehlhause.OSC 2.25+ − 0.03	+
	Maxwl				Data EXFOR12361.005	Jun 76	. 1 PT.	
Eta	Maxwl 2.5−1		MTR	Expt	Prog IDO − 16561 23	Nov 59	Fluharty.ABSOLUTE VALUE VS E. NDG	
Eta	2.5−2		AE	Comp	Rept AE − 11	Apr 60	Story+,DISCUSSION+TABULATN OF MEASTS	
Eta	Maxwl		HAR	Expt	Rept TNCC(UK)−77	Aug 60	Cabell+ PILE OSC.REL.U235	
					Conf 58Geneva 16 34	Sep 58	Rose+.PPR14,VAL REL TO U235,PILEOSCL	
					Rept AERE − R/R − 2457	Feb 58	− + RATIO TO U235. PILE OSC METHO	
Eta	2.5−2		ORL	Expt	Jour NSE 8 210	Sep 60	Macklin+ .MN BATH,ETA=2.296+ − 0.010	+
	2.5−2				Data EXFOR12349.002	Jun 76	. 1 PT.	
Eta	1.0−1	3.0+0	ORL	Expt	Conf 60Vienna 535	Oct 60	Block+.CURVE EXPT DESCRIBED	
Eta	1.4+7		CCP	Expt	Jour AE 10 68	Jan 61	Flerov+.VAL GVN,GRAPHIT − PRISMA DTCTR	
					Jour SJA 10 65	Nov 61	TRANSLATN.*JNE17 423 N/63	
					Jour KE 4 574	Jul 61	.TRANSLATN	
Eta	1.0+0	8.2+2	RPI	Expt	Jour NSE 9 105	Feb 61	Yeater+,ANALYSIS DESCR,GRAPHS+TABLES	+
	1.0+0	3.3+1			Prog KAPL − 1770 65	Apr 57	− + EXPERIMENT IN PREPARATION	
	1.0+0	8.2+2			Data EXFOR12330.002	Jun 76	. 155 PTS.	
Eta	Maxwl		HAN	Eval	Conf 61RPI 3	May 61	Leonard.	
Eta	5.0−3	2.5+0	GA	Eval	Rept GA − 2113	Jun 61	Wikner+.TABLE 100 E POINTS	
Eta	Maxwl		CRC	Expt	Conf 61Saclay 57	Jul 61	Westcott. 2200METRE/SEC SIG GIVEN	
Eta	2.5−2	1.1+1	BNL	Eval	Conf 61Vienna 1 435	Aug 61	Chernick+.CURVE(E=2−11EV)+VAL 2200M	
Eta	1.0+4	5.0+5	ORL	Expt	Prog WASH − 1034 25	Dec 61	Desaussure+ TBD.	
Eta	Pile		CRC	Eval	Rept CRRP − 960	Jan 62	Westcott. EFF SIG TBL 20 − 1300 DEG C.	
Eta	2.5−2	1.0+6	ROS	Revw	Jour KE 5 701	Jan 62	Falkenberg.VAL GVN,REFERENCES	
Eta	Maxwl		ORL	Expt	Jour NSE 12 364	Mar 62	Gwin+ CRIT SOLTN 2.292+ − .015.	+
					Jour NSE 44 266	May 71	Magnuson.RE − ANAL GWIN − MAGNUSON DATA	
Eta		1.0+1	UK		Rept NRDC − 138 23	Jan 63	NDG	
Eta	Pile		CJD	Eval	Rept INDSWG − 64 285	64	Galanin. TBL EFF ETA FOR MANY SPECTR	
Eta	2.5−2	1.0+6	BEP	Revw	Jour KE 8 625	Jan 65	Wenzel. VAL FOR 3ES GVN,MANY REFS	
Eta	2.5−2	5.7−2	MTR	Expt	Rept IDO − 17083	Feb 66	Smith+,MONOCHROM NEUTS.MNSO4 BATH	+
	2.5−2	5.7−2			Data EXFOR12318.	Jun 76	. 2 PTS. RATIO TO U235, PU239.	
Eta		1.1+1	MTR	Eval	Conf 66Wash. 919	Mar 66	Smith+,MN BATH+MTR REL MEASTS,CFD TH	
Eta	1.0−2	1.0+0	MTR	Eval	Conf 66Wash. 840	Mar 66	Moore+.MULTILEVEL ANAL.CURVE CFD XPT	
Eta	4.0−2	1.1+1	HAR	Expt	Rept AERE − M − 1709	Sep 66	Brooks+ TOF LINAC SC PSD GRAPH TBL	+
					Conf 66S.Diego 2 193	Feb 66	− . SEE ALSO	
	3.5−1	1.0+1			Data EXFOR20623.006	Dec 76	10PTS.	

92 Uranium 233

Quantity	Energy (ev) Min	Max	Lab	Type	Documentation Ref Vol Page	Date	Author, Comments	Data
Eta	2.0−2	5.0−1	MTR	Eval	Conf 66Paris 2 50	Oct 66	Smith+ TBL+CURV,LSTSQ FIT. PPR50.	
					Rept INDC−15	66	− + FULL PAPER.	
Eta	1.0−2	1.0+0	GA	Eval	Rept GA− 8854	Aug 68	Boroughs+ ENDF/B DATA CURVES	
Eta	2.5−2		BET	Eval	Rept WAPD−TM−772	Sep 68	Emert+ MONTE CARLO ANAL 2.298+−0.009	
Eta	Maxwl	2.6−2	FAR	Expt	Conf 70Helsinki 1 295	Jun 70	Vidal+97. VAL GVN,OSCILLATN METHOD	+
	2.5−2				Data EXFOR20552.003	Apr 76	1PNT.	
Eta	+0	1.0+1	ORL	Eval	Conf 70Helsinki 2 757	Jun 70	Desaussure+ 94.ETA(E)CRVMLTILVL FIT.	
	1.0−2	1.0+1			Rept ORNL−TM−2745	Nov 69	− + MULTILVL ANAL + LEAST SQ	
Eta	1.0−2	1.0+7	ORL	Revw	Jour REA 8 473	Sep 70	Kasten. REVIEW,ETA(E)+AVG ETA,GRAPHS	
Eta	1.7−2	1.1+0	ORL	Expt	Jour NSE 42 143	Nov 70	Weston+.	+
	1.7−2	1.1+0			Data EXFOR10100.004	Aug 71	. 50 PTS.	
Eta	Maxwl		UFP	Expt	Rept CCEN−17	Dec 70	CLEMENTE REL TO U235,OSCILLAT.METH.	
					Conf 70Helsinki 1 295	Jun 70	.SEE ALSO *	
Eta	2.5−2		ANL	Eval	Conf 71Knoxvill 560	Mar 71	Devolpi. ADJUSTED VALUE GIVEN.	
Eta	2.5−2		BET	Eval	Conf 71Knoxvill 605	Mar 71	Mitchell+.MONTE CARLO ANAL OKS SMITH	
Eta	Maxwl		ORL	Expt	Jour NSE 44 266	May 71	Magnuson.RE−ANAL GWIN−MAGNUSON DATA	+
	Maxwl				Data EXFOR10207.013	Dec 71	. 1 PT.	
Eta	2.5−2		IFB	Eval	Rept YK− 9 34	72	Morogovsky. COMPUTR RE−EVAL,DATA GVN	
					Rept INDC(CCP)−42	Aug 74	.P1.ENGLISH OF YK−9	
Eta	Maxwl		BET	Eval	Rept WAPD−TM−1052	Sep 72	Steen. EVAL WITH,WITHOUT U235 RATIO	
					Conf 71Knoxvill 566	Mar 71	− . BEST VALUE=2.2978+−0.007	
Eta	6.0−2	2.6−1	MTR	Expt	Prog IN−1407 39	Jun 70	Smith+4ES,MN BATH,TBL.CURVE.	
	None				Prog ERDA−NDC−2 7	May 75	− .REANAL.DATA.ETA=2.295+−0.009	
Eta	2.5−2		BET	Eval	Jour NSE 60 239	Jul 76	Ullo+MONTE CARLO ANAL SMITH EXPT.TBL	
					Rept WAPD−TM−1217	Apr 75	.SUPERSEDED	
					Conf 75Wash. 553	Mar 75	.SUPERSEDED	
Eta	2.5−2		BET	Eval	Jour NSE 60 251	Jul 76	Goldsmith+MONTECARLO ANAL ORNL EXPT.	
					Rept WAPD−TM−1218	Apr 75	.SUPERSEDED	
					Conf 75Wash. 557	Mar 75	.SUPERSEDED	
Nu	Maxwl		ANL	Expt	Rept CF−3651	Oct 46	Zinn.	+
	Maxwl				Data EXFOR12319.004	Jun 76	. 1 PT.	
Nu	−.7+6	1.4+7	LAS	Theo	Rept LA−1863	Dec 54	Leachman.AVG NU+NEUT EMISSION PROBAB	
Nu	Maxwl		CCP	Expt	Conf 55Moscow 156	Jul 55	Kalashnikova+.RATIOS+ABSOLUTE VALUES	
					Rept AEC−TR−2435	56	. P 123. ENGL TRANSL OF 55MOSCOW 156	
Nu	2.0−1	1.0+2	CCP	Expt	Conf 55Moscow 369	Jul 55	Erozolimsky+. TABLE NU−EFF REL THR	
					Rept AEC−TR−2435	56	. P 255. ENGL TRANSL OF 55MOSCOW 369	
Nu	2.5−2	1.3+2	CCP	Expt	Conf 55Geneva 5 172	Aug 55	Spivak+.VAL GVN CFD REF,PPR659	
Nu	None		ORL	Revw	Conf 55Geneva 3 19	Aug 55	Weinberg.P862,VAL GVN,DISCUSSION	
Nu	Pile		KAP	Expt	Rept KAPL−1464	Dec 55	Mcmillan+,NU=2.502+−0.063 REL U235	+
	Pile				Data EXFOR12357.	Jun 76	. 2 PTS. NU AND RATIO U235.	
Nu	Maxwl		CCP	Expt	Rept AEC−TR−2435PT1	56	. USSR,PAGE 131. NU=2.6+−0.1	
Nu	8.0+4		LAS	Expt	Jour PR 101 1012	Feb 56	Diven+,LIQ SCINT,+PROB EMISS	+
					Conf 55Geneva 2 193	Aug 55	Leachman.P592,CURVE,EXPT DESCRIBED	
	8.0+4				Data EXFOR12337.002	Jun 76	. 1 PT.	
Nu	Maxwl		HAR	Expt	Jour JNE 2 247	Jun 56	Sanders.PROMPT NEUTS. REL+ABS VALUES	+
					Rept AERE−RP/R−1627	Mar 55	− + SUPERSEDED.	
Nu	2.5−2		BNL	Eval	Rept BNL−325 1	Jan 57	Hughes+ WRLD CONSIST.VAL.=2.52+−0.03	
Nu	Maxwl	Fiss	CCP	Expt	Jour AE 2 18	Jan 57	Kalashnikova+.FAST/THR=1.075+−0.01	+
Nu	Maxwl	9.0+5	CCH	Expt	Rept NP−TR−440	Sep 57	Saunders. NDG NSA 14 2213 9/60	
Nu	Maxwl		HAR	Eval	Rept AERE−NP/R−2140	Dec 57	Egelstaff+ CONSISTENT VALUES 2200M/S	
			Comp	Rept	AERE−NP/R−2104	Mar 57	− .EXPT METHODS FOR HAR VALUE	
			Revw	Conf	55Geneva 4 307	Aug 55	− +.VAL GVN,EXPT DESCRBD,P425	
Nu	4.0+6		FEI	Expt	Jour AE 4 188	Feb 58	Smirenkin+ REL THERMAL,PROMPT NEUTS	
					Jour JNE 9 155	Jun 59	. ENGL OF AE 4 188	
					Jour SJA 4 253	58	. ENGL OF AE 4 188	
Nu	1.5+7		CCP	Expt	Jour AE 5 71	Jul 58	Protopopov+ 4.4+−0.45 REL THR,PROMPT	+
					Jour JNEA 10 65	Jul 59	TRANSLATN.*	
					Jour SJA 5 885	58	TRANSLATN.*	
Nu	Maxwl		BNL	Revw	Conf 58Geneva 16 8	Sep 58	Hughes.PPR2483,VAL V=2200M/SEC GVN	
Nu	−2	1.5+7	CCP	Expt	Conf 58Geneva 15 353	Sep 58	Bondarenko+.PPR2187,CURVE CFD REFS	
Nu	Pile		LAS	Expt	Conf 58Geneva 15 331	Sep 58	Leachman.PPR665,VAL REL TO U235 GVN	
Nu	Maxwl		ORL	Expt	Jour NSE 5 49	59	Desaussure.	+
					Conf 57ANS 37	Oct 57	− + U233,PU239,PU241 RATIOS.	
	Maxwl				Data EXFOR12328.002	Jun 76	. 1 PT. RATIO TO U235.	
Nu	Maxwl		ANL	Expt	Jour JNEA 11 21	Nov 59	Jaffey+ NU.SIGF REL U235 PU239 PU241	
Nu	2.5−2		AE	Comp	Rept AE−11	Apr 60	Story+,DISCUSSION+TABULATN OF MEASTS	

92 Uranium 233

Quantity	Energy (ev) Min Max	Lab	Type	Documentation Ref Vol Page	Author, Comments Date	Data
Nu	Maxwl	CCP	Theo	Jour AE 8 409	May 60 Zysin+.VAL CALCD FROM FRGMNT-DISTRBS	
				Jour SJA 8 343	Jun 61 TRANSLATN.*JNE AB17 41 1/61	
				Jour KE 4 40	Jan 61 .TRANSLATN	
Nu	1.4+7	CCP	Expt	Jour AE 10 68	Jan 61 Flerov+.VAL GVN,GRAPHIT-PRISMA DTCTR	
				Jour SJA 10 65	Nov 61 TRANSLATN.*JNE17 423 N/63	
				Jour KE 4 574	Jul 61 .TRANSLATN	
Nu	Maxwl	HAN	Eval	Conf 61RPI 3	May 61 Leonard.	
Nu	Maxwl	CRC	Expt	Conf 61Saclay 57	Jul 61 Westcott. 2200METRE/SEC SIG GIVEN	
Nu	1.5+7	ANL	Revw	Conf 61Vienna 1 29	Aug 61 Smith.PPR76,CURVE MANY REFS	
Nu	-	CCP	Theo	Jour ZET 42 180	Jan 62 Blinov.GRAPH NUCL-SHELL-TH CFD XPTS	
				Jour JET 15 130	Jul 62 TRANSLATN.*	
Nu	2.5-2 1.0+6	ROS	Revw	Jour KE 5 701	Jan 62 Falkenberg.VAL GVN,REFERENCES	
Nu	Maxwl	REH	Theo	Rept IA- 757	Jul 62 Sieger+ CALC FRM CHAIN-Y,CFD OTH.TBL	
Nu	Maxwl	CCP	Expt	Jour ZET 43 2053	Dec 62 .AVG.NU=2.50.COMP.WITH THEORY	
				Jour JET 16 1451	Jun 63 .TRANSLATN.	
Nu	-2 +7	FOA	Comp	Rept NP- 16440	Mar 63 ASPLUND-NILSSON. REVIEW. TABLES.	
Nu	1.4+7	CCP		Jour NSA 17 2527	Jun 63 ABSTR 19394 USSR NU IS 4.2PM.3	
Nu	2.5-2 3.9+6	LAS	Expt	Jour NP 48 433	Oct 63 Hopkins+SCINT TANK,RELAT TO CF252	+
				Conf 61Vienna 1 149	Aug 61 .SUPERSEDED	
	2.5-2 3.9+6			Data EXFOR12326.	Jun 76 . 6 PTS.	
Nu	Maxwl	YAM	Theo	Jour JPJ 18 1697	Nov 63 Honda.CALC E FISSFRAGS VS A.TBCFD NU	
Nu	Thrsh 1.5+7	LRL	Expt	Jour JNAB 18 125	Mar 64 Schuster+ E DEPENDNCE THEOR,CFD EXPT	
Nu	Maxwl 1.0+6	FEI	ExTh	Jour NP 52 648	Apr 64 Blyumkina+DATA OF AE 2 18 CFD FRAG E	
Nu	Maxwl	HAR	Expt	Conf 65Salzburg 2 25	Mar 65 Colvin+PPR44.BORONPILE.RATIO/U-235	+
				Prog AERE-PR/NP8 9	Feb 65 - +TBL.NU=2.433+-0.021.ABS.	
Nu	None	LAS	Revw	Conf 65Salzburg 3	Mar 65 Terrell.XPTL WORK CFD THEORY.GRAPHS	
Nu	Maxwl 4.0+6	ALD	Expt	Jour NP 66 149	Apr 65 Mather+ PROMPT SC-T LEAST SQ FIT	
Nu	Maxwl	KUR	Expt	Jour NP 71 553	Sep 65 Apalin+NU VERSUS FRAGMENT MASS	
Nu	4.0+5 7.0+6	FEI	Expt	Conf 66Paris 2 85	Oct 66 PPR110,D'JACHENKO+. NU GVN AT 6ES	
Nu	8.0+4 7.0+5	FEI	Expt	Conf 66Paris 2 75	Oct 66 PPR97.KUZNECOV+.NU-BAR(E) REL THERML	+
	8.0+4 1.0+6			Prog YFI-4 18	May 67 .ALSO P19.TABLE,CURVES	
	8.0+4 7.0+5			Rept FEI- 48	Jul 66 .VDG,REL MEASUREMENT NU VS E	
				Rept FEI- 47	Jul 66 .E YLD FROM NU+FISS FRAG KINETIC E	
				Prog INDC-E-187	67 .ENGLISH TRANSL OF YFI-4 5/67	
				Rept INDSWG-152E 51	67 .ENGLISH TRANSL OF ICD-3 51 11/66	
	8.0+4 7.0+5			Data EXFOR40217.003	Jun 74 .DATA AT 7 ES GIVEN	
	8.0+4 7.0+5			Data EXFOR40158.005	Mar 73 SAME DATA AS EXFOR 40217.003	
Nu	Fiss	LRL	Expt	Jour PR 152 1046	Dec 66 Fultz+ ROUGH VALUE, 2.54+-.04	+
				Conf 66Paris 2 149	Oct 66 .SUPERSEDED	
	Fiss			Data EXFOR12345.002	Jun 76 . 1 PT.	
Nu	8.0+4 7.0+5	CCP	Expt	Jour AE 22 401	May 67 Kuznetsov+.TABLE,FISSCHMBR TH232	
				Jour SJA 22 500	May 67 TRANSLATN.*	
Nu	Maxwl 1.5+7	AI	Eval	Jour JNE 22 79	Feb 68 Fillmore. DATA TBL,GRPH,LSTSQ FIT.	
Nu	1.0-5 1.5+7	GA	Eval	Rept GA- 8854	Aug 68 Boroughs+ ENDF/B DATA	
Nu	Maxwl	CUA	Theo	Abst DA/B 30 2222	Nov 69 Rogers.	
Nu	1.0-2 5.5+0	RPI	Expt	Conf 69Vienna 477	Jul 69 Weinstein+PPR113. NU(NEUT-E) GRPH	
	None			Abst DA/B 30 3823	Feb 70 - + LINAC.VAR WITH NTN ENERGY	
Nu	Maxwl	AE	Comp	Conf 70Helsinki 2 93	Jun 70 Almen+57. COMPILATN AND NU-TEMP-PLOT	
Nu	Maxwl 1.5+7	HAR	Revw	Conf 70Helsinki 2 195	Jun 70 Colvin.PPR99. REPORT ON DATA STATUS	
	-3 1.4+7		Eval	Conf 69Vienna 930	Jul 69 - .PPR55. RECOMMENDATION+REVIEW	
Nu	8.0+4	TOK	Theo	Jour NST 7 635	Dec 70 Hara.CAL CFD C DIVEN EXP	
Nu	2.5-2	ANL	Eval	Conf 71Knoxvill 560	Mar 71 Devolpi. ADJUSTED VALUE GIVEN.	
Nu	1.5+7	ANL	Eval	Jour NSE 44 345	Jun 71 Davey. PROMPT NEUTS PER FISSION	
Nu	2.5-2	IFB	Eval	Rept YK- 9 34	72 Morogovsky. EVAL+RECOMM VALUE,CF OTH	
				Rept INDC(CCP)-42	Aug 74 .P1.ENGLISH OF YK-9	
Nu	Maxwl 1.6+6	FEI	Expt	Jour AE 32 83	Jan 72 Kolosov+ FROM FRAG A-KE-BALANCE,GRPH	+
	0.0+0 1.6+6		Eval	Prog YFI-11 13	70 - + ABST,ANALYSIS OF EXPTS,NDG	
				Prog INDC(CCP)-31	Dec 72 .PAGE 11,ENGLISH OF YFI-11 13	
	Maxwl 1.6+6		Expt	Jour SJA 32 92	Jul 72 . ENGL OF AE 32 83	
	7.0+4 1.6+6			Data EXFOR40130.005	Sep 72 NU-BAR AT 15 ES REL THERMAL	
Nu	Maxwl	CUA	Theo	Abst DA/B 32 5980	Apr 72 Lee. CALC OF AVG PROMPT NU	
Nu	Maxwl	BET	Eval	Rept WAPD-TM-1052	Sep 72 Steen. EVAL WITH,WITHOUT U235 RATIO	
				Conf 71Knoxvill 566	Mar 71 - . NU(P)=3.774+-0.014 REL CF252	
Nu	6.0+6	FEI	Expt	Jour YF 16 475	Sep 72 Sergachev+ FROM ENERG BALANCE EQUAT.	+
				Jour SNP 16 266	Mar 73 .ENGLISH TRANSL OF YF 16 475 9/72	
	2.5-2 2.1+6			Data EXFOR40106.003	Sep 73 .20 DATA-LINES GVN	
Nu	2.5-2	IAE	Eval	Jour REA 10 637	Dec 72 Manero+ SURVEY,TBLS+GRPHS,RECOMM VAL	+
	2.5-2 1.5+7			Rept INDC(NDS)-34	Jul 72 .REPLACED BY NEW EVALUATION	

92 Uranium 233

Quantity	Energy (ev) Min	Max	Lab	Type	Documentation Ref Vol Page	Date	Author, Comments	Data
Nu	1.0-4	1.5+7	UK Eval	Data	UKNDL-DFN 87B	Mar 73	43 PNTS	+
	1.0-4	1.5+7		Data	UKNDL-DFN 87B	Mar 73	ANGDIST OF FISS NEUT, 1 RNGS,LAB.	
Nu	2.5-2		ANL Expt	Conf	73Rochestr 2 19	Aug 73	Unik+NU TOTAL VS MASS 13 NUCLIDES.	
Nu	1.1-2	1.0+2	RPI Expt	Conf	73Rochestr 2 503	Aug 73	Reed+ ABST,NUBAR(N-E) REL .025EV,NDG	+
	2.2+0	1.1+2		Data	EXFOR10427.002	Dec 74	. 54 PTS.	
Nu	1.3+6	1.5+7	DUB Comp	Jour	YF 18 724	Oct 73	Dakovsky+ DISPERSION VS NUBAR, GRAPH	
				Jour	SNP 18 371	Apr 74	.ENGLISH OF YF 18,724	
Nu	0.0+0	1.4+6	FEI Expt	Jour	SJA 34 603	Dec 73	.ENGLISH OF AE 34 491	+
				Jour	AE 34 491	Jun 73	Nurpeisov+ NU-BAR AT 14ES,TBL,GRAPH	
	0.0+0	1.4+6		Data	EXFOR40189.	Nov 73	.REL NU-BAR CF 252	
Nu	Maxwl		AUA Revw	Conf	IAEA-169 2 163	74	Musgrove+ TOTAL NU-BAR,GRAPH	
Nu	5.0+6	1.7+7	LRL Expt	Prog	UCID-16514 6	Jun 74	Alvarez+	
Nu	-2	3.0+5	AUA Expt	Prog	AAEC/PR-40P 28	Jul 74	Boldeman+ SEARCH FOR NUBAR-MIN,TBD	
Nu	0.0+0	5.0+6	FEI Eval	Rept	YK-20/1 104	75	Prokhorova+ NUBAR(NEUT-E),GRAPH,TBL	
	5.0+4	5.0+6		Rept	INDC(CCP)-91	Jun 76	. ENGL OF YK-20 104(TBLS+GRPHS GIVN)	
Nu	Maxwl		AUA Expt	Jour	AEA 18 2 2	Apr 75	Walsh. REVW OF WORK,RESULTS GIVEN	+
				Rept	AAEC/E-172	Mar 67	Boldeman+ SUPERSEDED,EXPTL DETAILS	
	Maxwl			Data	EXFOR30046.002	Jan 73	.ABSOL THR VALUE,PRIV COMM NOV 1972	
Nu	1.0+4	1.9+6	AUA Expt	Jour	AEA 18 2 2	Apr 75	Walsh. REVW OF WORK.NUBAR(N-E),GRAPH	+
	+0	1.9+6		Jour	JNE 25 321	Aug 71	- + NU(E-N) REL CF-252,TBL,GRAPH	
	3.0+5	1.9+6		Data	EXFOR30006.003	Jan 73	. PROMPT NUBAR AT 8 ES,REL CF-252	
Nu	2.5-2		HED Theo	Abst	ANS 21 518	Jun 75	Schenter+ TBL CALC FROM ENDF FP FILE	
Nu	+6	5.0+6	FEI Expt	Jour	AE 39 199	Sep 75	Nurpeisov+ NUBAR(NEUT-E),TBL,GRAPH	
	1.0+5	5.0+6		Conf	75Kiev 5 175	May 75	- + NUBAR(E),GRPH.CFD LINEAR	
	1.0+6	5.0+6		Jour	SJA 39 807	Mar 76	. ENGLISH OF AE 39 199	
Nu	Maxwl		AUA Eval	Jour	NP/A 265 337	Jul 76	Boldeman+LINEAR FIT TO DATA.=73KIEV	
	+4	4.0+6		Expt	75Kiev 5 271	May 75	Bertram+ NUBAR CFD OTHS,LIN FIT.GRPH	
	1.5+5	4.0+6		Eval	Conf 73Kiev 4 121	May 73	Boldeman+ FRG-E SUGGEST LIN FIT.GRPH	
	Maxwl	5.0+6		Jour	JNE 25 321	Aug 71	Walsh+ 2 LINE FIT,SLOPES GIVEN,GRAPH	
Nu	0.0+0	1.5+7	BRC Eval	Rept	CEA-R-4791	Oct 76	Bois+NUBAR VS EN,CALC CFD EXP,TABLES	
Delayd Neuts	Maxwl		CCP Expt	Conf	55Geneva 4 171	Aug 55	Girshfeld.TABLE 6GROUPS,YIELD,P648	
Delayd Neuts	Maxwl		ORL Expt	Jour	NSE 1 20	Mar 56	Thomas+,CRITICAL SOL .33 X U233 YLD	
Delayd Neuts	Maxwl	Fiss	ANL Expt	Jour	NSE 1 174	May 56	Brunson+,EBR NUD=.396 .414 +-11PC	
Delayd Neuts	Pile		HAR Revw	Jour	NPW 1 114	Jul 56	Cox. YIELD+HALF LIFES OF DEL-NEUTS	
Delayd Neuts	Fast		HAR Expt	Jour	JNE 4 141	Jun 57	Rose+ ZEPHYR. 5 GROUPS.TBL YLD+FRACT	+
Delayd Neuts	Maxwl		MTR Expt	Prog	WASH-194	Jul 57	.SAME YLD PM2PC NS DELYD P15SEC.	
Delayd Neuts	Maxwl	Fiss	LAS Expt	Jour	PR 107 1044	Aug 57	Keepin+,0.0070+-0.0004 N/FISS 6GRPS	
				Jour	JNE 6 1	Dec 57	- +. SAME DATA AS PR(8/57)	
				Rept	LA-1970	Oct 55	- . NEUT YLDS+SPECTR,CURVS+TABLS	
				Conf	55Geneva 4 162	Aug 55	- +.P/831. PRELIMINARY.	
Delayd Neuts	None		LAS Theo	Jour	JNE 7 13	Aug 58	Keepin.THEOR DEL NEUT PRECURSRS,YLDS	
				Jour	SJA 4 339	Mar 58	- .	
				Jour	AE 4 250	Mar 58	- .	
Delayd Neuts	Maxwl		OSL Expt	Conf	58Geneva 15 373	Sep 58	Pappas+.PPR583,TBL CFD THEORIE	
Delayd Neuts	Maxwl		LAS Expt	Conf	61Vienna 1 149	Aug 61	Diven+.PPR56,TABLE REL TO CF252	
Delayd Neuts	Maxwl	1.6+7	LAS Revw	Jour	NUC 20 8 150	Aug 62	Keepin+	
Delayd Neuts	2.3+6	1.5+7	FEI Expt	Rept	ICD-2 161	65	Maksjutenko. YIELD OF 5GROUPS, TABLE	+
				Jour	AE 15 321	Oct 63	.MORE DATA	
				Prog	INDSWG-101 158	65	.ENGLISH TRANSL OF ICD-2 161 /65	
				Jour	SJA 15 1042	64	.ENGLISH TRANSL OF AE 15 321 /63	
				Jour	EAF 15 4 56	63	. FRENCH TRANSL OF AE 15 321 /63	
Delayd Neuts	Maxwl		LAS Expt	Prog	WASH-1068 119	Mar 66	Stein+,ANAL TBC,NDG	
Delayd Neuts		+7	HFA Revw	Conf	67Vienna 23	Apr 67	Yiftah+ TBL OF YLD+HL,REACTR DYNAMIC	
Delayd Neuts	Maxwl	1.4+6	SOR Comp	Conf	67Vienna 115	Apr 67	Amiel+ DEL-N PRECURSRS,TBL=CALC+COMP	
				Rept	IA-1190 95	Jul 69	- + NEW INFORMATION	
Delayd Neuts	5.6+6	7.3+6	FEI Expt	Jour	YF 6 22	Jul 67	Maxyutenko.FRACT YIELDS AT 6 ES	
				Jour	SNP 6 16	Jan 68	TRANSLATN.*	
	5.0+6	8.0+6		Conf	67Vienna 191	Apr 67	.REL YLDS FOR 5 GROUPS	
	5.5+6	7.3+6		Conf	67Kharkov 216	Feb 67	.SPECTRUM GIVEN	
Delayd Neuts	Maxwl		MNZ Theo	Jour	AF 36 453	Nov 67	Patzelt+.FROM DERIVED N-EMISS PROB.	
Delayd Neuts	3.1+6	1.5+7	LAS Expt	Jour	NSE 36 202	May 69	Masters+ 2ES RELATIVE+ABSOL MEASTS	+
	3.1+6	1.5+7		Data	EXFOR12288.	Jun 76	. 2 PTS.	
Delayd Neuts	Fiss	1.5+7	LAS Expt	Conf	69Vienna 647	Jul 69	East+PPR109. YLD TABLE,REVW,SAFGUARD	
Delayd Neuts	Maxwl	+7	SOR Revw	Conf	69Vienna 569	Jul 69	Amiel+.PPR205. REVW,EXPTS+TH,TABLES	
Delayd Neuts	2.5-2		SOR Expt	Prog	IA-1190 95	Jul 69	Notea.RELATIVE TO U235,CFD OTHERS	+
	2.5-2			Data	EXFOR30238.002	May 73	.TOTL DELAYED NEUT YLD FOR 5 GROUPS.	
Delayd Neuts		1.0+6	BET Eval	Rept	WAPD-TM-691	Dec 69	Steen.DELAYED NEUTS/FISS FOR ENDF/B	

92 Uranium 233

Quantity	Energy (ev) Min	Max	Lab	Type	Documentation Ref Vol Page	Date	Author, Comments	Data
Delayd Neuts	Maxwl		VIP	Expt	Abst DA/B 30 4749	Apr 70	Rambo. 5 NTN,GPS.YLD.HL,REL ABUNDS.	
					Rept TID – 25645	May 69	– .HALF – LIVES + REL ABUNDANCES	
Delayd Neuts	Maxwl		BNL	Expt	Jour NSE 44 173	May 71	Conant + DELAYED NEUT FRACTION	+
	Maxwl				Data EXFOR10144.004	Mar 72	. 1 PT.	
Delayd Neuts	1.8+7	2.1+7	FEI	Expt	Prog YFI – 10 27	May 71	Maksjutenko + ABST,YLDS REL BR87,TBL	
					Rept INDC(CCP) – 15	Dec 71	*P29,ENG OF YFI – 10	
					Jour SNP 13 163	Aug 71	.ENGLISH OF YF 13 293 FEB/71	
					Jour YF 13 293	Feb 71	Maksyutenko + 11GROUPS REL YIELD,TBL	
Delayd Neuts	Maxwl	1.5+7	HAR	Eval	Rept AERE – R – 6993	Feb 72	TOMLINSON TOTAL + GROUP YLDS SPEC TBL	
Delayd Neuts	5.0+4	6.6+6	LAS	Expt	Jour NSE 53 80	Jan 73	Evans + REVISED NUD DATA.TBLS.	+
	1.0+5	6.5+6			Jour NSE 47 311	Mar 72	Krick + SPRSDD.DATA REVISED	
	5.0+4	6.6+6			Data EXFOR10117.	Jul 74	. 25 PTS.	
Delayd Neuts	Maxwl		WAU	Expt	Prog RLO – 2225 – 4	Jul 72	Woodruff. NEUT SPEC MEASD. NO DATA	
Delayd Neuts	2.5–2	1.5+7	IAE	Eval	Jour REA 10 637	Dec 72	Manero + SURVEY,AVERAGE YIELD,TBLS	
Delayd Neuts		5.0+6	FEI	Expt	Rept YK – 12 15	Jan 73	Balakshev +	+
		5.0+6			Data EXFOR40209.	May 74	.4 SUBENT EACH 4 DATA LINES	
Delayd Neuts	Maxwl		HFA	Expt	Jour NSE 51 52	May 73	Shalev + HE – 3 DET. NEUT ENERGY DISTR	
Delayd Neuts	Maxwl		FEI	Theo	Jour YF 17 1149	Jun 73	Tarasko + TRANSFORM OF HL – GROUPS,GRPH	
					Rept FEI – 369	72	– + SAME AS YF 17 1149	
					Jour SNP 17 598	Dec 73	.ENGL OF YF 17 1149	
					Rept KFK – TR – 437	73	. GERMAN OF FEI – 370	
Delayd Neuts	Maxwl		FEI	Theo	Conf IAEA – 169 3 105	74	Maksjutenko + CALC PROBAB(H – L),GRAPHS	
Delayd Neuts	1.0+5	1.5+7	LAS	Revw	Conf IAEA – 169 3 377	74	Evans. TBL YLD,GROSS E – SPEC GRAPH	
Delayd Neuts	Maxwl	1.5+7	SOR	Revw	Conf IAEA – 169 2 33	74	Amiel.ALL YLDS,DEL – N SPECS,TBL,GRPHS	
Delayd Neuts	Maxwl		ANL	Eval	Rept ANL – NDM – 5	Apr 74	COX. REL YLD, HL, GRPH	
Delayd Neuts	4.0+5	1.1+6	FEI	Expt	Rept YFI – 18 8	Aug 74	Balakshev + YLD DELAYED NEUT,TBL GVN	+
					Rept INDC(CCP) – 49	Feb 75	– + ENGLISH OF YFI – 18 8	
	4.0+5	1.1+6			Data EXFOR40298.	Dec 75	.DATA AT 8 ES GVN	
Delayd Neuts	2.5–2	1.5+7	AI	Eval	Jour NSE 56 37	Jan 75	Tuttle.TBL.GRPH.RVW MEAS.CFD REC VAL	
	2.5–2				Prog AI – AEC – 13025	May 72	Springer + VALUE = 0.00697 + – 0.00016	
Delayd Neuts	2.5–2		IAE	Eval	Conf 75Wash. 286	Mar 75	Lemmel. TBL LSQ ANAL.CFD OTHER EVAL.	
Delayd Neuts	2.5–2		HED	Theo	Abst ANS 21 518	Jun 75	Schenter + TBL CALC FROM ENDF FP FILE	
Delayd Neuts	Fast		SOR	Expt	Jour NSE 57 117	Jun 75	Izak – Biran + PN – VALUES,GROUP – YL4b,cK3	
	Maxwl				Jour NSE 57 117	Jun 75	– + PN – VALUES,GROUP – YLUB,CK3	
Delayd Neuts	Maxwl		CSR	Revw	Jour JE 23 9 345	77	Tinka. REVW GROUP – SPEC,PARAMS.TABLES	
Frag Neuts	Maxwl		CRC	Expt	Jour PR 93 818	Feb 54	Fraser + DIST OF PROMPT NEUT EMISSION	
Frag Neuts	Maxwl		CCP	Revw	Jour AE 8 15	Jan 60	Apalin + .YIELD FOR DIFF FRAGMENTS GVN	
					Jour SJA 8 10	Apr 61	TRANSLATN.* JNE AB17 25 1/63	
					Jour KE 3 633	Jul 60	.TRANSLATN	
Frag Neuts	None		LAS	Revw	Jour PR 127 880	Aug 62	Terrell.ANALYSIS OF TOF + RADIOCHEM	
Frag Neuts	Maxwl		KUR	Expt	Rept IAE – 819	65	Apalin + GRPHS NEUT NO NU(FRAG – MASS)	
Frag Neuts	Maxwl		CRC	Expt	Conf 65Salzburg 2 39	Mar 65	Milton + . P.45 TABLES + GRAPHS GIVEN	
					Rept AECL – 2613	Feb 65	– +	
Frag Neuts	Maxwl		KUR	Expt	Conf 65Salzburg 1 587	Mar 65	Apalin + ,SYMMETRIC FISS,GRPHS,CFD XPT	
					Jour YF 1 639	Apr 65	SEE ALSO *NP 71 553 9/65,	
					Jour SNP 1 457	Oct 65	. ENGL OF YF 1 639	
Frag Neuts	None		LAS	Revw	Jour 65Salzburg 3	Mar 65	Terrell.XPTL WORK CFD THEORY.GRAPHS	
Frag Neuts	Maxwl		ITK	Theo	Conf 68Madras 1 302	Feb 68	Mukherji + CALC NU VS HEAVY MASS,GRPH	
Frag Neuts	Maxwl		MCM	Theo	Jour CJP 46 1137	May 68	Gorman + CALCULATD NEUT YLDS CFD EXPT	
Frag Neuts	Maxwl		MCM	Theo	Conf 69Vienna 845	Jul 69	Thind + PPR50. FRAG – EXCIT – E CFD NU(A)	
Frag Neuts	Maxwl		KFI	Theo	Jour PL/B 30 311	Oct 69	Kluge +	
Frag Neuts	Maxwl		SAH	Theo	Conf 70Madurai 2 619	Dec 70	Sarkar + NU VS FRAGMASS GRPH CFD EXPT	
Frag Neuts	Maxwl		AUA	Expt	Prog AAEC/PR – 40P 28	Jul 74	Boldeman + NU(FRGM – MASS),TBD	
Spect Fiss n	Maxwl		CRC	Expt	Jour PR 88 536	Nov 52	Fraser. ANGDIST CURVES CFD THEORY.	
Spect Fiss n	Maxwl		ORL	Expt	Rept ORNL – CF – 4 22	Apr 55	Henry + .CURVE 2 – 11 MEV NEUTRONS.	
Spect Fiss n	Maxwl		CCP	Expt	Jour ZET 33 1069	Oct 57	Kovalev.HARDER THAN U235,THRESHLDDET	
					Jour JET 6 825	Apr 58	TRANSLATN.*	
					-		FRENCH CEA – TR – R – 725	
Spect Fiss n	5.0+4	7.0+5	CCP	Expt	Jour ZET 34 501	Feb 58	CLOUD CHAMB,AGREES WITH WATT, T = 1MEV	
					Jour JET 7 345	Aug 58	TRANSLATN.*	
Spect Fiss n	1.4+7		CCP	Expt	Jour AE 4 337	Apr 58	Zamiatnin + FISS + EVAP SPECTR FIT DATA	
					Jour JNE 9 194	Jun 59	TRANSLATN.*	
					Jour SJA 4 443		58 TRANSLATN.*	
Spect Fiss n	Maxwl		CCP	Theo	Jour AE 5 649	Dec 58	Kovalev + THEORY COMPARED WITH EXPT	
					Jour JNEA 11 166	Feb 60	TRANSLATN.*	
					Jour SJA 5 1588		58 TRANSLATN.*	
Spect Fiss n	Maxwl		ANL	Expt	Jour PR 114 1351	Jun 59	Smith + 0.3 – 7.MEV.REL TERRELLS U235FI	
					Conf 58Geneva 15 392	Sep 58	– + .PPR690,CURVE	

92 Uranium 233

Quantity	Energy (ev) Min	Max	Lab	Type	Documentation Ref Vol Page	Date	Author, Comments	Data
Spect Fiss n	Fiss		KUR	Revw Conf	60Vienna 159	Oct 60	Bondarenko+.NDG,MEASRMNT REL TO U235	
Spect Fiss n	Maxwl		RIC	Expt Jour	NP 23 116	Feb 61	Bonner.MOD SPH SP. T=1.356+ −0.030MEV	
Spect Fiss n	1.4+7		CCP	Jour	NSA 17 2527	Jun 63	ABSTR 19394 USSR	
Spect Fiss n	Maxwl		ORL	Eval Rept	ORNL−TM−795	Feb 64	Halperin+ FISS SPEC .01−25MEV TABLE	
Spect Fiss n	Maxwl	1.4+7	HAR	Eval Jour	NP 71 228	Sep 65	Barnard+ CORRELATED WITH NU BAR	
Spect Fiss n	Maxwl		CCP	ExTh Jour	YF 4 1179	Dec 66	Blinov.TOF,CRVS GVN	
Spect Fiss n	5.5+6	7.3+6	FEI	Expt Conf	67Kharkov	Feb 67	Maksjutenko. TBP IN IZV	
Spect Fiss n	Maxwl		LAS	Expt Jour	NSE 31 191	Feb 68	Grundl. 8 ACT DET CFD.8−16MEV RANGE.	
				Abst	DA 25 6704	May 65	− . REL U235,PU239.	
				Rept	LAMS−2883	May 63	− . ACT DETECTOR 0.16−16MEV NEUT	
Spect Fiss n	Maxwl		KFI	Theo Jour	PL/B 30 311	Oct 69	Kluge+	
Spect Fiss n	Maxwl		CUA	Theo Abst	BAP 16 56	Jan 71	Lee+. THEORETICAL EXPRESSION.NO DATA	
Spect Fiss n	Maxwl	1.4+7	ANL	Revw Conf	71Vienna 3	Aug 71	Smith. MEAN−E OF NEUTS,EXPTS CFD,TBL	
Spect Fiss n	1.0−4	1.5+7	UK	Eval Data	UKNDL−DFN 87B	Mar 73	1 RANGES	+
Spect Fiss n	8.0+5	1.0+7	BET	Expt Jour	NSE 52 406	Nov 73	Green+. TOF.CURVS.CFD ENDF/B.T PARAM	
	+5			Rept	WAPD−TM−1129	Dec 73	− +. 0.8−10 MEV NEUTUTNS.CURVES.	
Spect Fiss n	2.5−2		IAE	Eval Conf	75Wash. 286	Mar 75	Lemmel. 3RD IAEA−EVAL BY LSQ FIT	
				Revw Jour	REA 7 4 3	Dec 69	Hanna+ N−SPECTRUM IN NU−BAR EXPTS	
Spect Fiss γ	Maxwl		HAR	Rept	NRDC−58	Feb 55	.ROUGH EXPT BUT VERY CLOSE TO U235	
Spect Fiss γ	Maxwl		LAS	ExTh Jour	PR/B 133 714	Feb 64	Hoffman. G−FRAG ANG CORR FITS.	
Spect Fiss γ	6.0−2	1.8+0	MTR	Expt Rept	IDO−17025	Oct 64	Moore+,GAM SPECT AT .06AND1.8EV SAME	
Spect Fiss γ	Maxwl		FTI	Expt Jour	ZET 47 2064	Nov 64	G YLDS FOR 9AS,ANISOTROPY=(13+−1)PC	
				Jour	JET 20 1387	Jun 65	TRANSLATN.*	
Spect Fiss γ	Maxwl		JUL	Revw Rept	JUEL−405−NP	65	Maier−Leibnitz+ANG CORR GAM−FISSFRAG	
				Conf	65Salzburg 2 113	Mar 65	− +	
Spect Fiss γ	Maxwl		FTI	Expt Jour	AE 18 64	Jan 65	Petrov. ANG CORREL GS−FISFRAGMENTS	
				Jour	JNE 20 91	Jan 66	TRANSLATN.*	
				Jour	EAF 18 1 107	Jan 65	TRANSLATN.*	
				Jour	SJA 18 72	Jan 65	TRANSLATN.*	
Spect Fiss γ	+0	+3	CAI	Theo Jour	NP 62 667	Feb 65	Stavinsky+(N,GF)PROB ABOUT=(N,GAMMA)	
Spect Fiss γ	+0	+1	COL	Expt Prog	WASH−1124 35	Nov 68	Felvinci+ NAI FISS+CAPT GAMMAS NDG	
Spect Fiss γ	Maxwl		CCP	Expt Jour	YF 9 29	Jan 69	Davydov.FRAG K−XRAYS REL U−235,TBL	
				Jour	SNP 9 18	Jul 69	*	
Spect Fiss γ	Maxwl		CUA	Theo Abst	DA/B 30 2222	Nov 69	Rogers.	
Spect Fiss γ	None		ITK	Theo Prog	BARC−474 54	70	Mukherji+ CALC TOTAL GAM−E OKS EXPT	
Spect Fiss γ	1.4+7		KFI	Expt Jour	KFI 18 13	Feb 70	Jeki+ GAM−ANISOTROPY−COEFFICIENT GVN	
Spect Fiss γ	2.5−2		SRC	Expt Jour	JNE 25 339	Aug 71	Scobie+ VAR.BETA EN REL RATE WTH TME	
	Pile			Expt Jour	JNE 25 1	Jan 71	− + BETA EN RELESE RATE REL U235	
Spect Fiss γ	Maxwl		KFK	Expt Priv	WIETKAMP	73	Weitkamp. SPECTRA.PROMPT+DELAYED	
Spect Fiss γ	Maxwl		ORL	Expt Jour	NP/A 213 413	Oct 73	Pleasonton. AVG NB,EG/CORR FRAG M,E	
				Conf	73Rochestr 2 494	Aug 73	− + ABST,BELOW 5 NSECS,NDG	
Spect Fiss γ	2.5−2		LAS	Expt Conf	75Wash. 193	May 75	Stamatelatos+GRPHS.G SPECT.CINDER.	
Spect Fiss γ	Maxwl		LIN	Expt Jour	YF 22 462	Sep 75	Teterev+ G−SPEC CFD U,PU,CF−FIS.GRPH	
				Conf	75Kiev 6 121	Jun 75	− + G−SPEC,YLD GAMMAS,GRAPHS	
				Jour	SNP 22 238	Sep 75	. ENGL OF YF 22 462	
Fiss Prod γ	None		LAS	Theo Rept	LA−2811	Dec 62	Griffin. BETA+GAMMA DECAY CALCLTNS.	
Fiss Prod γ	Fiss		LAS	Expt Jour	PR/B 134 796	May 64	Fisher.GDIVA NS,GS TO6MEV,T=.2 TO45S	
Fiss Prod γ	Maxwl		AUA	Expt Rept	AAEC/TM−252	Jun 64	Frost.FRAG BETA−ACTIVITY(TIME),GRPHS	
Fiss Prod γ	Pile		BET	Expt Jour	NSE 22 386	Jul 65	Klein. CD RATIO CFD FISSN XSECT.	
Fiss Prod γ	Fiss		NRD	Theo Rept	USNRDL−TR−1009	Dec 65	Turner. GROSS F PROD G SPEC CALCT.	
Fiss Prod γ	Maxwl		MIT	Expt Rept	MIT−905−68	Jul 66	Gordon+,LI−GE DET 28 PKS IDENTIFIED	
Fiss Prod γ	2.5−2		RI	Expt Prog	YFI−6 100	68	Davydov+. SUBMITTED TO YF	
	Maxwl			Jour	YF 9 29	Jan 69	− . TBL,K−RADIAT,HEAVY+L FRAGS	
				Jour	SNP 9 18	Jul 69	. ENGL OF YF 9 29	
	2.5−2			Rept	INDC−260E	69	. ENGL OF YFI−6 100	
Fiss Prod γ	Maxwl		RI	Expt Jour	IZV 33 718	Apr 69	Davydov+ FRAG'S K−X−RAY YIELD,TABLE	
				Jour	BAS 33 661	70	TRANSLATN.*NO 4	
Fiss Prod γ	Maxwl		CCP	Expt Conf	69Vienna 932	Jul 69	Smirnov+PPR152. X−RAYS OF FRAGS,REVW	
Fiss Prod γ	Maxwl		HFA	Expt Conf	69Vienna 947	Jul 69	Notea+PPR36. GAM SPECS FOR CHAIN YLD	
Fiss Prod γ	Maxwl		LAS	Expt Conf	69Vienna 647	Jul 69	East+PPR109. DELAYED G−SPEC,SAFGUARD	
Fiss Prod γ	2.5−2		IAE	Revw Jour	REA 7 4 3	Dec 69	Hanna+ DELAYD GAMMAS IN NU−BAR EXPTS	
Fiss Prod γ	1.4+7		KFI	Expt Jour	KFI 18 13	Feb 70	Jeki+ GAM−ANISOTROPY−COEFFICIENT GVN	
Fiss Prod γ	−		WIN	Theo Jour	JNE 25 513	Oct 71	James.MEAN EN OF DELAYD GAMS,BETAS.	
Fiss Prod γ	Maxwl		ANL	Expt Jour	NP/A 177 337	Dec 71	Reisdorf+SIMULT MEAS K.E. ANG G−SPEC	
				Conf	69Vienna 781	Jul 69	.PRELIMINARY.	
Fiss Prod γ	Maxwl		KFK	Expt Priv	WIETKAMP	73	Weitkamp. DELAYED SPECTS OF F PRODS	
Fiss Prod γ	Maxwl	Fiss	TRM	Theo Rept	BARC−706 149	73	Iyer+. COMPUT−PROGR G−SPC.NDG	

92 Uranium 233

Quantity	Energy (ev) Min Max	Lab	Type	Documentation Ref Vol Page	Date	Author, Comments	Data
Fiss Prod γ	Maxwl	ITK Theo	Jour	AUJ 26 279	Jun 73	Mukherji+ MEAN-E VS FRAG-MASS,GRAPH	
	None		Prog	BARC-474 54	70	- + CALC GAM-E/FRAG CFD EXPT	
Fiss Prod γ	Maxwl	ORL Expt	Conf	73Rochestr 2 494	Aug 73	Pleasonton+ ABST,AVG GAM-E(FRAG),NDG	
Fiss Prod γ	Maxwl +6	CAD Revw	Conf	IAEA-169 2 115	74	Lott.AFTERHEAT,NDG	
Fiss Prod γ	Maxwl	CAI Expt	Jour	NP/A 224 468	May 74	Kandil+ GS PER 10E6 FISS 90-180DEG L	+
	2.5-2		Data	EXFOR30411.	Oct 77	PROMPT GAMS(2E-GROUPS),5ANGS.10 PTS	
Fiss Prod γ	Maxwl	MNZ Expt	Jour	NP/A 250 13	Sep 75	Kratz+ RADIOACTIVITY OF AS80-86 FP	
Fiss Yield	None	ANL Expt	Rept	MDDC-1632	Nov 47	Steinberg+	
Fiss Yield	Pile	CRC Expt	Jour	NAT 161 520	Apr 48	Grummitt+.RADIOCHEM REL U235 NF YLDS	
Fiss Yield	None	LAS Expt	Jour	JCP 17 653	Jul 49	Stanley+ I136 YIELDS	
Fiss Yield	Maxwl	CRC Expt	Rept	CRC-470	Mar 51	Grummitt+,RADIOCHEM,YLDS 20FRAGS	
Fiss Yield	Pile	CRC Expt	Jour	PR 82 392	May 51	Allen+ NON TERNARY,SHORT-RANGE DISTR	
			Jour	PR 76 181	Jul 49	.SUPERSEDED.	
Fiss Yield	Pile	MCM Expt	Jour	CJP 32 522	54	Fleming+ MASS-SPEC,KR-,XE-,CS-YLDS	
Fiss Yield	Maxwl	ANL Expt	Jour	PR 95 867	Aug 54	Steinberg+YIELD CURVE-FINE STUCTURE	
Fiss Yield		MCM Expt	Jour	CJC 33 830	May 55	Melaika+ MASS DIST ND+SM REL YLDS	
Fiss Yield	Maxwl	AN Revw	Conf	55Geneva 7 3	Aug 55	Steinberg+ P614.EXPTL YLD TBL+GRPH	
Fiss Yield	1.0+4 3.0+6	MTR Expt	Conf	55Geneva 7 19	Aug 55	Pappas+.P881,YIELD FOR SOME FRGMNTS	
Fiss Yield		MCM Expt	Jour	CJP 33 693	Nov 55	Petruska+MASS SPECTR.YLD OF 28 CHAIN	
Fiss Yield	Maxwl	KAP Expt	Jour	NUC 13 12 30	Dec 55	Robb+PC POISONS BURNUP CURVS	
Fiss Yield	Maxwl	LAS Expt	Rept	LA-1997	Feb 56	Ford+ MO99 ABSOL YIELDS	
Fiss Yield	Maxwl	MCM Expt	Jour	PR 103 323	Jul 56	Kennett+ NRX YLDS I128,130 BR80,82.	
Fiss Yield	Maxwl	CRC Expt	Jour	JIN 5 93	57	Grummitt+INDEPEND.YLD OF LA140Y90,91	
Fiss Yield	Pile	CCP Expt	Jour	AE 2 275	Mar 57	Anikina+.SR90.REVISED AE 4 198 (1958	+
			Jour	JNE 9 167	Jun 59	.TRANSLATN.*	
	Maxwl		Conf	58Geneva 15 446	Sep 58	Anikina+.PPR2040,TBL OF MASSYIELDS	
	Pile		Jour	AE 4 198	Feb 58	- + SR88 SR90,MASS SP,ISOT DILN	
			Jour	SJA 4 270	58	.TRANSLATN.*	
			Jour	JNE 6 169	Dec 57	TRANSLATN.*	
			Jour	SJA 2 332	57	TRANSLATN.*	
Fiss Yield	Maxwl	LAS Expt	Jour	PR 108 94	Oct 57	Stein+ TOF MASS,ENERGY DISTRIBUTION.	
Fiss Yield	+0 +2	ANL Expt	Prog	WASH-745 6	Nov 57	Roeland+ MDIST THR 1D8RES P2EV SAME.	
Fiss Yield	Maxwl	CCP Expt	Jour	AE 3 546	Dec 57	Ivanov+.CS CE ND SM,MASS SP,ISOT DIL	+
			Jour	JNE 9 46	Jun 59	TRANSLATN.*	
			Jour	SJA 3 1436	57	TRANSLATN.*	
Fiss Yield	Maxwl 4.7+0	MTR Expt	Jour	PR 113 1589	Mar 59	Regier+,RADIOCHEM RELATIVE YLDS ONLY	
			Jour	PRL 2 274	Mar 59	.SUPERSEDED	
Fiss Yield	Maxwl	CRC Expt	Jour	CJC 37 660	Apr 59	Bartholomew+ BA139,140 LA141 SR89,91	
Fiss Yield	Maxwl	CCP Expt	Jour	AE 7 144	Aug 59	Gorshkov+ SR,Y,ZR,BA YLDS,MASS SPEC	
			Jour	SJA 7 649	Feb 61	TRANSLATN.*	
			Jour	JNEA 13 198	Jan 61	TRANSLATN.*	
Fiss Yield	Pile	RI Expt	Conf	59Tashkent 1 222	Sep 59	Krizhanskij.GRAPH YLD OF MANY NUCLEI	
			Rept	AEC-TR-6398	64	.VOL 1,P288.ENGL OF 59TASHKE 1 222	
Fiss Yield	-1 +1	HAR Expt	Rept	AERE-M-559	Nov 59	Wraight. SPINS OF FISSN.RESONANCES	
Fiss Yield	Maxwl	MCG Expt	Jour	CJC 38 421	Mar 60	Santry+ RADIOCHEM ABSOL YLDS 22FRAGS	
Fiss Yield	-2	RI Expt	Jour	ZET 38 998	Mar 60	Dmitriev.TRIPLE FISSION PROBABILITY	
			Jour	JET 11 718	Sep 60	TRANSLATN.*	
Fiss Yield	Maxwl	BNL Eval	Jour	NUC 18 11 201	Nov 60	Katcoff.RECOMMENDED YLD-SET,TBL,GRPH	
			Jour	NUC 16 4 78	Apr 58	.SUPERSEDED	
Fiss Yield	None	GA Revw	Rept	GA-2307	61	Fischer+TABLES OF YLD FOR A=81TO159	
Fiss Yield	Fiss 1.5+7	CCP Expt	Jour	AE 10 13	Jan 61	Bonjuskin+.ABS YIELD OF FRGMNTS,GRPH	
			Jour	SJA 10 10	Nov 61	TRANSLATN.*GERMAN KE4 553 7/61	
Fiss Yield	None	BNL Expt	Jour	NSE 9 495	Apr 61	Levine.XE135 FROM EQUAL Z DISPL.RULE	
Fiss Yield	Maxwl	DKE Theo	Jour	PR 122 1224	May 61	Newson.MASS DIST ASYMMETRIC+SYMMETR	
Fiss Yield	Pile	CRC Expt	Jour	JIN 20 6	Nov 61	Grummitt+ DIRECT YLD CS136.	
Fiss Yield	Maxwl	MIT Expt	Rept	NYO-2669-19	62	Storms+YIELDS OF XE133 XE135	
Fiss Yield	Fiss	GA Eval	Jour	NSE 12 115	Jan 62	Garrison+.(Z,A).WEIGHTD AVRAGE OTHRS	
Fiss Yield	Maxwl	HAR Expt	Jour	JIN 24 221	Mar 62	Croall+.RADIOCHEM.SE81,SE83 BA140 YLD	
			Rept	AERE-R-3879	Nov 61	- . LIMIT ON YIELD OF RH 106M	
	Pile		Jour	JIN 16 358	Feb 61	- . DIRECT YLD NB96	
Fiss Yield	Maxwl	LAS Expt	Jour	PR 126 1508	May 62	Nobles. YIELD OF LONG RANGE FFRGM	
Fiss Yield	Maxwl	WAS Expt	Jour	PR 126 1112	May 62	Wahl+, FRAC INDEPENDENT YIELD GIVEN	
Fiss Yield	Maxwl	ORL Eval	Rept	ORNL-3305	Jul 62	Ferguson+ 39REFS PREFERRED YLDS GIVN	
Fiss Yield	Maxwl 4.7+0	MTR Expt	Rept	IDO-16797	Jul 62	Burgus. RADIOCHEM ASYM/SYM YLD RATIO	
	None		Rept	AERE-M-1078 12	Aug 62	-	
Fiss Yield	Maxwl 1.4+7	NRD Eval	Rept	USNRDL-TR-633	Mar 63	Bunney. 2ES+FISSSPCT.EST OF YLD.	
Fiss Yield	Maxwl	KUR Expt	Rept	IAE-710	64	Apalin+.GRAPH,DISTRIB OF FFRGM+FPROD	
Fiss Yield	2.5-2	BNL Theo	Jour	PR/B 133 976	Feb 64	Thomas+ CF FRAG E DETLS C EMP.MASS	

92 Uranium 233

Quantity	Energy (ev) Min	Energy (ev) Max	Lab	Type	Documentation Ref Vol Page	Date	Author, Comments	Data
Fiss Yield	Maxwl		CRC	Expt Conf	64Geneva 7 430	May 64	Fraser+ DOUBLE VEL. MEAS.	
Fiss Yield	Pile		MOL	Expt Conf	64Paris § EC192	Jul 64	Deruytter.B/T RATIO+TERNR/SPECTR	
Fiss Yield	Maxwl		CER	Theo Jour	NP 58 177	Sep 64	Faissner+ASSYMETRIC,CLUSTER MODEL	
Fiss Yield	Maxwl		GEV	Expt Rept	GEAP−4716	Sep 64	Rider+MASS.SPECTRO.YIELDS OF ND ISOT	
Fiss Yield	Maxwl		TRM	Comp Rept	AEET−209	65	Rangarajan+ YLDS+PRODUCTN RATIO,TBLS	
Fiss Yield	−3	+7	TRM	Revw Rept	AEET−235	65	Methasiri.TERNRY FISS EXPTS REVWD	
Fiss Yield	9.5+6	1.2+7	LAS	ExTh Jour	PR/B 137 814	Feb 65	Leachman+ RLTV ANGDIST FISS+FRAG CFD	
Fiss Yield	Maxwl		LAS	Expt Jour	PR/B 137 929	Feb 65	Wolfberg+ K,XE ISOT.YLDS,USED Z DIST	
Fiss Yield	Maxwl		NRD	Expt Jour	JIN 27 273	Feb 65	Bunney+.RADCHEM YIELDS A=91,141−161	+
				Rept	USNRDL−TR−679	Sep 63	− . EU157GD159TB161,LOW MS YLDS.	
Fiss Yield	Maxwl		KUR	Expt Conf	65Salzburg 1 587	Mar 65	Apalin+,GRPH MASS DIST,SYMMETR FISS	
				Jour	YF 1 639	Apr 65	SEE ALSO *NP 71 553 9/65	
				Jour	SNP 1 457	Oct 65	. ENGL OF YF 1 639	
Fiss Yield	1.2+7	2.4+7	LAS	ExTh Prog	WASH−1056 4	Mar 65	Blumberg. FISSION ANISOTROPY,NDG.	
Fiss Yield	Maxwl		PTN	Expt Conf	65Salzburg 1 467	Mar 65	Thomas+ MASS YIELD CURVES	
Fiss Yield	Maxwl		WAS	Revw Conf	65Salzburg 317	Mar 65	Wahl.GRAPHS TH CFD XPTS	
Fiss Yield	Pile		SGA	Expt Conf	NUK 7 169	Apr 65	Balcarczyk+. CS,RU YIELDS REL BA140	+
Fiss Yield	Maxwl		CRC	Expt Jour	CJP 43 1036	Jun 65	Okazaki+ I135 BA140 RELU235F CF CUM	
				Rept	EANDC(CAN)−23	Apr 65	.SEE ALSO	
Fiss Yield	Fiss		NRD	Expt Jour	JIN 27 1183	Jun 65	Bunney.YIELDS 16MASSES FROM 89 TO161	
Fiss Yield	Maxwl		KAP	Expt Rept	KAPL−3113	Sep 65	Mchugh.RB86 CS132 134 136 YIELDS	
Fiss Yield	Maxwl		ORL	Expt Rept	ORNL−TM−1333	Dec 65	Niece. YLD. CHG DISP OF MASS 95.	
Fiss Yield	2.0−2	1.0+1	MTR	Expt Rept	IDO−17105	66	Miller+	
Fiss Yield	Maxwl		CRC	Expt Jour	CJP 44 237	Jan 66	Okazaki+ XE135 DRCTYLD 19.5PM1.6PC	
				Jour	CJP 49 498	Feb 71	.CORRECTED VALUE.	
Fiss Yield	Maxwl		MCM	Expt Prog	EANDC(CAN)−28	Mar 66	Tomlinson+ YLDS OF BR−87,−88,−89	
Fiss Yield	None		MTR	Expt Jour	NSE 25 93	May 66	Nisle. I135YIELD REL TO U235 .700	
Fiss Yield	Maxwl		TRM	Theo Jour	PL 21 437	Jun 66	Ramanna+ MASS DIST ON STOCHASTIC MDL	
Fiss Yield	Maxwl		SRL	Expt Jour	JIN 28 1763	Sep 66	Ondrejcin.137CS−YIELD=6.13+−.13PC	
Fiss Yield	Maxwl		MIT	Expt Jour	NUC 24 12 62	Dec 66	Gordon+ GE−LI,REL MO99,REL U235,TBL	
				Rept	MIT−905−68	Jul 66	− + LI−GE DET.REL U235.TBL+CURV	
Fiss Yield	Maxwl		ISL	Expt Prog	IA−1168 67	Jan 67	CHUL LEE+ YLD VALUES OF BR,SR,Y,MO	
Fiss Yield	−		FEI	Expt Conf	67Kharkov	Feb 67	Vorob'Eva+. TBP IN IZV	
Fiss Yield	Maxwl	1.4+7	HNS	Theo Rept	HNS−1229−77	Feb 67	Castagnola. ALSO FISS SPEC 28FRAGS	
Fiss Yield	Maxwl	7.0+6	FEI	Expt Jour	YF 5 514	Mar 67	Senchenko+.CURV FOR THERM+3 HIGH E	
	4.0+5	2.6+6		Jour	YF 6 708	Oct 67	− + YLD CURVS AT 2ES,CFD THRM	
	Maxwl			Jour	YF 6 708	Oct 67	− + YLD CURV,CFD .4,2.6MEV−NS	
	2.5−2	2.6+6		Prog	YFI−4 14	May 67	.CURVES GIVEN	
	Maxwl			Jour	SNP 6 516	Apr 68	. ENGL OF YF 6 708	
	4.0+5	2.6+6		Jour	SNP 6 516	Apr 68	. ENGL OF YF 6 708	
	Maxwl	7.0+6		Jour	SNP 5 362	Sep 67	.ENGLISH TRANSL OF YF 5 514 3/67	
	2.5−2	2.6+6		Prog	INDC−E−187	67	.ENGLISH TRANSL OF YFI−4 14 5/67	
Fiss Yield	Maxwl		BOR	Theo Jour	NP/A 96 588	Apr 67	Doan+ ALPHA YIELD CALCULATED	
Fiss Yield	−2	1.4+7	KFI	Expt Jour	KFI 15 85	Apr 67	Nagy+ TERN,ALFA PROBABILITY,TBL	
Fiss Yield	Maxwl		LAS	Expt Jour	PR 156 1277	Apr 67	Stein+ SI DETECT,CURVE YIELDS,ENERGY	
Fiss Yield	Maxwl		FLA	Expt Jour	PR 161 1266	Sep 67	Muga+ NO ALPHAS FROM BINARY FISSION	
				Conf	69Vienna 107	Jul 69	− +PPR99. BINARY+TERN+PU FISSN CF	
				Jour	PRL 18 404	Mar 67	.SUPERSEDED	
Fiss Yield	Maxwl	1.1+6	FEI	Expt Jour	YF 6 1167	Dec 67	Djachenko+ FRAG YIELD CFD THR,GRAPH	
				Jour	SNP 6 848	Jun 68	*	
Fiss Yield	Maxwl		HAR	Eval Rept	AERE−R−5086	Jan 68	Croall.RECOMMENDED CUMULAT YLDS,TBL	
				Comp Rept	AERE−R−3209	Jan 60	− .COMP OF INDP YLDS(NSA 14 1397	
			HAR	Eval Rept	AERE−R−5086	Jan 68	Croall. RECOMMENDED CUMULT YLDS.TBL.	
Fiss Yield	Fast							
Fiss Yield	1.4+7		RI	ExTh Conf	68Riga	Jan 68	Adamov+ ABST,LONG−RANGE PARTICLES YL	
Fiss Yield	1.4+7		RI	ExTh Conf	68Riga	Jan 68	Adamov+ ABST,A−PARTICLES,TRITON YLD	
Fiss Yield	1.4+7		RI	ExTh Conf	68Riga	Jan 68	Adamov+ ABST,TERNARY FISSION PROBAB	
Fiss Yield	Maxwl		MTR	Expt Jour	NSE 31 241	Feb 68	Nisle+ I135 YLD=.825+−.072 REL U235	
				Rept	IN−1096	Sep 67	.SUPERSEDED	
				Rept	IN−1048 56	Sep 66	.SUPERSEDED	
Fiss Yield	Maxwl		BOL	Comp Rept	CEC(68)−6	Jun 68	Cenacci.YLDS,DECAY CHAINS,FPROD DATA	
				Rept	RT/FI−68 4		68 .EQUIVALENT	
Fiss Yield	Maxwl		GA	Eval Rept	GA−8854	Aug 68	Boroughs+ RECOMMENDED YLDS 91 MASSES	
Fiss Yield	Maxwl		KFI	Expt Jour	YF 8 443	Sep 68	Nagy+DOUB/TERN FISS GVN,LONG−R−ALPHA	
				Jour	SNP 8 257	Mar 69	TRANSLATN.*	
Fiss Yield	Maxwl		MIS	Expt Abst	DA/B 29 927	Sep 68	Roche. YLDS,INDEP,AG112,CUMUL,PD115.	
				Rept	TID−24500	Jan 68	− .AG112 INDEP YLD+ PD115 CUM YLD	
Fiss Yield	Pile		CCP	Expt Conf	69Erevan	Feb 69	Vorobev+.ABST,LIGHT NUCLEI YIELDS	
Fiss Yield	Pile		CCP	Theo Conf	69Erevan	Feb 69	Zalite+.ABST,TERN FISS,E SPECTRA	

92 Uranium 233

Quantity	Energy (ev) Min	Max	Lab	Type	Documentation Ref Vol Page	Date	Author, Comments	Data
Fiss Yield	Maxwl		HAR	Theo Rept	AERE – R – 6056	Mar 69	Crouch. CALC FRACT INDEPEND YLD,TBLS	
				Rept	AERE – R – 5488	Mar 67	– .SUPERSEDED.	
				Rept	AERE – R – 5250	Apr 66	– .SUPERSEDED.	
Fiss Yield	Maxwl		CCP	Expt Conf	69Vienna 932	Jul 69	Smirnov+ PPR152. X – RAYS OF FRAGS,REVW	
Fiss Yield	Maxwl		EDG	Revw Conf	69Vienna 83	Jul 69	Feather.PPR201. SURVEY,TERNARY – YIELD	
Fiss Yield	+3	1.4+7	FTI	Expt Conf	69Vienna 900	Jul 69	Adamov+ PPR146.LONG – RANGE – YLD VAL GVN	
	Maxwl	1.4+7		Jour	YF 9 732	Apr 69	– + PROTON,T,D AND ALFA YLD GIVN	
				Jour	SNP 9 424	Oct 69	. ENGL OF YF 9 732	
Fiss Yield	Maxwl		HFA	Expt Conf	69Vienna 947	Jul 69	Notea+ PPR36. CHAIN YLDS VS TIME,GELI	
Fiss Yield	Maxwl		ISL	Expt Prog	IA – 1190 101	Jul 69	Isak+ 90 – Y YIELD CHEMICAL DETERMINTN	
Fiss Yield	Maxwl		MCM	Theo Conf	69Vienna 845	Jul 69	Thind+ PPR50. YLD(Z,A)+NU(A)+EXCIT E	
Fiss Yield	Maxwl		ORL	Comp Conf	69Vienna 67	Jul 69	Schmitt.PPR122. YLD GRPH,PUBL IN PR	
Fiss Yield	Maxwl		OSL	Revw Conf	69Vienna 669	Jul 69	Pappas+ PPR206. INITIAL+FINAL YLD(A)	
Fiss Yield	Maxwl	1.4+7	SAC	Comp Rept	CEA – N – 1180	Jul 69	Bessis+ CAPTURE IN FRAGMENTS	
Fiss Yield	1.5+7		ARK	Expt Jour	JIN 31 2623	Aug 69	Borden+ YLD REL TO BA – 140	
				Abst	DA/B 29 1621	Nov 68	– + A=83 – 140, CFD THR FISS.TH.	
Fiss Yield	Pile		FTI	Expt Jour	PL/B 30 332	Oct 69	Vorobiev+ EN SPEC LIGHT NUCL.D TOBE10	
Fiss Yield	Maxwl		CUA	Theo Abst	DA/B 30 2222	Nov 69	Rogers.	
Fiss Yield	Maxwl		MIS	Expt Jour	PR/C 1 312	Jan 70	Niece+ FRACT INDEPEND YLD OF ZR – 95	
				Abst	DA/B 27 1249	Oct 66	.THESIS ABST.	
Fiss Yield	Maxwl		ORL	Expt Jour	PR/C 1 316	Jan 70	Runnalls+,I132 133 134 INDEPEND YLDS	
Fiss Yield	None		CCP	Revw Jour	IZV 34 438	Feb 70	Soloveva.ALF – EMISSN PROBABILITY,GRPH	
				Jour	BAS 34 378	Jan 71	.ENGL TRANSL OF IZV 34 438	
Fiss Yield	Maxwl		SAC	Expt Prog	EANDC(E)127U	Apr 70	Signarbieux+	
				Prog	EANDC(E)115U	Mar 69	Nifenecker.SYMM FISS	
Fiss Yield	+0	+2	COL	Expt Prog	NCSAC – 31 55	May 70	Felvinci+,ANAL TO BE COMPLETED,NDG	
Fiss Yield	Maxwl		MNZ	Expt Jour	JIN 32 1767	Jun 70	Qaim+. INDEP YLD OF 133,134,135I	
Fiss Yield	Maxwl		MCM	Expt Jour	CJP 48 1708	Jul 70	Tracy+ BR80,82,I128,130 IND.YLDS.	
Fiss Yield	Pile		ANL	Expt Jour	NP/A 151 65	Aug 70	Horrocks+ TRITIUM FISS YIELD	
				Prog	ANL – 7450	Apr 68	.CALCULATED TRITIUM YIELDS.	
Fiss Yield	Maxwl		MTR	Expt Jour	NSE 42 191	Nov 70	Lisman+YLDS STABLE+LONG – LIVED FRAGS	
				Rept	IN – 1277	Jun 68	– + SUMMARIZES RESULTS	
				Rept	IDO – 14681	Feb 67	Maeck+ MASS SP.SM,KR,RU,XE,CS,CE,ND	
	None			Rept	IDO – 14676	May 66	– + RU101,102,104,106 YIELDS	
Fiss Yield	Maxwl	1.4+7	ANL	Eval Rept	ANL – 7749	Dec 70	Flynn+ ALSO FISS SPEC NEUTS TBL+CURV	
Fiss Yield	1.5+7		LRL	Expt Jour	PR/C 2 2289	Dec 70	Nethaway+,YLDS 25 FRAGS A=66 – 175	
				Prog	UCID – 15749 42	Nov 70	– + ABSOL MASS – YLD(66 – 125)GRPH	
Fiss Yield	Pile		MIS	Expt Jour	JIN 33 1	Jan 71	Harbour+ NB99M YIELD.	
	Maxwl			Abst	DA/B 30 1578	Oct 69	– . FCY NB099,HL EXPT.	
Fiss Yield	Pile		MTR	Expt Jour	JIN 33 643	Mar 71	Lisman+ YLD OF KR – 85	
Fiss Yield	Maxwl		CRC	Expt Jour	CJP 49 785	Apr 71	Hawkings+ XE135 INDEP/I135 CUMUL YLD	
				Rept	INDC(CAN) – 9 4	Jul 71	.ABSTRACT.	
				Rept	EANDC(CAN) – 32	Jan 67	.SUPERSEDED	
				Rept	EANDC(CAN) – 23	Apr 65	.SUPERSEDED	
Fiss Yield	Maxwl		ORL	Expt Jour	RCA 16 2 66	Apr 71	Roche+ INDEP YLD OF 112AG	
Fiss Yield		1.5+7	FEI	Expt Conf	71Kiev	May 71	Sergachev+.FRAG YLD,KE OF FRAG,GRPHS	
Fiss Yield	4.8+5		ANL	Expt Prog	ANL – 7824 11	Aug 71	Fluss+.PRELIM YLDS OF TRITIUM GIVEN	
Fiss Yield	Maxwl		GA	Eval Rept	GA – 12071	Sep 71	Mathews+. RECOMMENDED VALUES	
Fiss Yield	5.5+6	1.5+7	FEI	Expt Jour	YF 14 935	Nov 71	Surin+ FRAG YIELD,2 ES CFD THR,GRAPH	+
				Jour	SNP 14 523	May 72	* ENGL OF YF 14 935	
	2.5-2	1.5+7		Data	EXFOR40112.	Nov 73	.3SUBENTRIES FOR 3EN,EACH 42DATALINE	
Fiss Yield	Maxwl		ANL	Expt Jour	NP/A 177 337	Dec 71	Reisdorf+SIMULT MEAS K.E. ANG G – SPEC	
				Conf	69Vienna 781	Jul 69	.PRELIMINARY.	
Fiss Yield	None		TRM	Expt Prog	INIS – MF – 334 64	72	.RADIOCHEM+GAM – SPEC,SHORT NOTE,NDG	
Fiss Yield	Maxwl		GEV	Eval Rept	NEDO – 12154	Jan 72	Meek+.TABULATD RECOMMENDED YIELDS	
				Rept	GEAP – 5356	Sep 67	Rider+ TABULATED CHAIN YLDS 90MASSES	
Fiss Yield	+1	+6	MOL	Expt Prog	INDC(SEC) – 26	May 72	Deruytter+ TERN/BINAR,EXPLOS,PROPOSD	
Fiss Yield	1.4+7		GRE	Expt Jour	NP/A 189 556	Jul 72	Bocquet+ON – LINE ISOT SEPAR.INDEP,CUM	
				Conf	71Canterby 13	Sep 71	.GE(LI) G – SPECTRA ANAL.CUMUL YLD,TBL	
Fiss Yield	Pile		RI	Expt Jour	AE 33 709	Aug 72	Petrzhak+ XE-131,132,134,136 YLD,TBL	
Fiss Yield		6.0+7	FEI	Expt Jour	YF 16 475	Sep 72	Sergachev+ MASS+KIN – E DISTR,NU – BAR	+
	+0	6.0+7		Jour	SNP 16 266	Mar 73	.ENGLISH TRANSL OF YF 16 475 9/72	
	4.5+5	5.4+6		Data	EXFOR40106.	Sep 73	.9SUBENTRIES	
Fiss Yield	Maxwl	1.5+7	LRL	Comp Rept	UCRL – 51458	73	Nethaway+.ALSO FISS SPEC. 111 FRAGS.	
Fiss Yield	Maxwl		JAE	Expt Jour	JIN 35 2 353	Feb 73	Umezawa.INDEP ISOM YLD RATIO 148PM	
	Pile			Rept	JAERI – 1103	Feb 66	– .PM148 CHEM SEPA.INDEPT YIELD	
Fiss Yield	Maxwl		SGA	Eval Conf	73Paris 1 505	Mar 73	Lammer+ EVAL DISCUSSN,TBL ALL A YLDS	

92 Uranium 233

Quantity	Energy (ev) Min	Energy (ev) Max	Lab	Type	Documentation Ref Vol Page	Date	Author, Comments	Data
Fiss Yield	Maxwl		ANL	Expt	Jour NP/A 205 348	Apr 73	Reisdorf+ MASS DIST AT GIVEN E. CURV	
					Conf 73Rochestr 2 19	Aug 73	Unik+ PROMPT YLDS,MASS DISTRIB,GRPHS	
Fiss Yield	Maxwl		CRC	Eval	Rept AECL-3037 2	Apr 73	Walker.ALL DETAILS,CHAIN YIELDS,TBLS	
					Conf 73Paris 1 459	Mar 73	– .EVAL PROCEDURE,SELECTED TBLS	
					Conf 66Paris 1 521	Oct 66	– .EARLIER EVAL,SUPERSEDED	
					Rept AECL-2497	66	.SAME AS 66PARIS 1 521,SUPERSEDED	
					Rept AECL-2111	Nov 64	Walker. PSUEDO FPY	
					Rept CRRP-913	Mar 60	– .SUPERSEDED	
					Rept CRRP-760	Oct 58	Hurst+ CALC YLDS	
Fiss Yield	Maxwl		LIN	Expt	Conf 73Munich 1 716	Aug 73	Vorobjov+ Z=1-8 MASS-SPC,ODD-EVN,NDG	
Fiss Yield	Fast		HAR	Revw	Rept AERE-R-7548	Sep 73	Cunninghame. FAST+N-E DEPEND,TBLS,	
					Conf 73Bologna § 11B	73	– . EVALUATIONS CFD.	
Fiss Yield	Maxwl		MIS	Expt	Jour JIN 33 1543	Jul 71	Eichor+ FRACT INDEP YLD OF BA139,140	
					Abst DA/B 34 1034	Sep 73	– .BA139,140 FRACT YLDS GIVEN.	
Fiss Yield	Maxwl		MIS	Expt	Abst DA/B 34 1034	Sep 73	Berge.TE131,133 I131,133 SB131,133	
Fiss Yield	Maxwl		MCM	Expt	Prog INDC(CAN)-13	Oct 73	Delaeter+ CD-ANAL OF OLD SAMPLE, NDG	
	Maxwl Pile				Jour CJP 47 1409	Jul 69	– + MASS SPEC,SN117-126,REL YL	
Fiss Yield	Pile		NIR	Expt	Jour YF 18 710	Oct 73	Zakharova+ KE OF FRAG,NEUT-SPEC,GRPH	+
					Jour SNP 18 364	Apr 74	. ENGLISH OF YF 18,710.	
	2.5-2				Data EXFOR40398.002	Feb 77	.57 KINET.ENERGY OF FISS-FRAG GVN	
Fiss Yield	None		COL	Expt	Prog USNDC-9 72	Dec 73	Felvinci+. ORELA. TO BE DONE.	
Fiss Yield	Maxwl		AUA	Theo	Conf IAEA-169 2 163	74	Musgrove+ GAUSS FIT MASS YLDS,GRAPH	
Fiss Yield	Maxwl Pile		CRC	Revw	Conf IAEA-169 1 285	74	Walker.STATUS CHAIN+INDEP YLDS,TBLS	
					Rept AECL-4704	73	.SAME AS 73BOLOGNA,EVALS CFD,DICUSSN	
Fiss Yield	Maxwl		HAR	Revw	Conf IAEA-169 1 353	74	Cuninghame.SURVEY TRITIUM YLDS,TBL	
					Rept AERE-R-7548	Sep 73	.SAME AS 73BOLOGNA	
Fiss Yield	Pile		UBE	Expt	Jour RCA 21 200	74	Egger+ ABS YIELD OF MO 99	
Fiss Yield	Maxwl		AUA	Expt	Prog AAEC/PR-40P 28	Jul 74	Boldeman+ MASS-DISTRIBUTION,TBD	
Fiss Yield	Maxwl		MIF	Theo	Jour IVU 17 7 7	Jul 74	Koldobskij+ CUM YLDS(3ISOT)CFD EXPTS	
Fiss Yield	Maxwl		PAH	Theo	Jour PL/B 55 144	Feb 75	Hooshyar+ISOMERIC FISS,TH CFD EXPTAL	
Fiss Yield	Maxwl		SOR	Eval	Jour PR/C 11 845	Mar 75	Amiel+ IND YLDS,ODD-EVEN EFF.TBL+GRF	
Fiss Yield	Maxwl		ANL	Expt	Jour JIN 37 869	Apr 75	Flynn+ CHEM.INDEP RB84,86,CS136.TBLS	+
	Maxwl				Data EXFOR10517.002	Apr 78	. 3PTS.INDEPENDENT FISS YLDS.	
Fiss Yield	Maxwl 9.9-2		WAI	Expt	Jour CJP 53 775	Apr 75	De-Laeter+ CD YLD REL CD-116	
Fiss Yield	Maxwl		RI	Expt	Conf 75Kiev 6 97	Jun 75	Kondurov+ YLD ALPHA-PART,GRAPH,TBL	
Fiss Yield	Maxwl Pile		GRE	Expt	Prog NEANDC(E)162U	Aug 75	Blachot+ 18 YIELDS TBL	
Fiss Yield	Pile		MOL	Expt	Jour ZP/A 275 149	Nov 75	Wagemans+ YIELD OF LONGE-RANGE A	
Fiss Yield	1.5+7		ARK	Expt	Jour JIN 37 1341	Jun 75	James+ RADIOCHEM,TOT CHAIN,GRAPH+TBL	+
					Abst DA/B 36 2800	Dec 75	– +MASS YLD DISTRB VALLEY REGION.	
	1.5+7				Data EXFOR10433.002	Nov 76	. 8 PTS. TOT NFY 8 A CHAINS,HL GVN.	
Fiss Yield	Maxwl		GRE	Expt	Jour NP/A 255 461	Dec 75	Brissot+YIELDS OF RARE GAS ISOTOPES	
Fiss Yield	Maxwl		HAR	Eval	Rept AERE-R-8152	Jan 76	Crouch.ADJUSTED FISS YLD.TBL.	
					Rept AERE-R-7785	Feb 75	– .CHAIN+INDEPENDENT	
	Pile				Rept AERE-R-7680	May 74	– . FRACTIONAL INDEPENDENT YLD	
	Maxwl				Conf 73Paris 1 393	Mar 73	– .EXPTL DATA+EVAL CHAIN YLD,TBL	
					Rept AERE-R-7209	Jan 73	– .84 CHAIN YLDS RECOMMENDED TBL	
Fiss Yield	Fast		HAR	Eval	Rept AERE-R-8152	Jan 76	Crouch. ADJUSTED FISSION YIELD,TABLE	
					Rept AERE-R-7394	May 73	– .CHAIN YLDS.RECOMMENDED TBL.	
Fiss Yield	Maxwl		UBE	Expt	Jour JIN 38 205	Feb 76	Gaeggeler+ PM150,RADIOCHEM.MANY TBLS	
					Diss GAEGGELER	Dec 73	– . COMPLETE EXPT DESCRIPTION	
					Conf 73Rochestr 2 475	Aug 73	– + ABST,PM150 INDEP YLD GIVN	
Fiss Yield	Maxwl		AUA	Theo	Jour AUJ 29 125	Jun 76	Cook+ GAUSSFIT.FOR E-DEPEND OF PARAM	
	2.0+6 1.5+7				Jour AUJ 29 125	Jun 76	– + 2ES.GAUSSFIT PARAMS VS E.TBLS	
	Maxwl 1.4+7				Rept AAEC/E-386	Mar 76	– + 3-GAUSS FIT,SAME 3ES AS AUJ 2	
Fiss Yield	Maxwl		PAH	ExTh	Conf 76Lowell 725	Jul 76	Hooshyar+STATMDL APLD TO EXPT.DATA	
	7.0+6 1.6+7				Conf 76Lowell 725	Jul 76	– + 2ES.STATMD CFD XPT	
Fiss Yield	Maxwl		LIN	Theo	Jour YF 24 270	Aug 76	Val'Skii+ A=1TO20 YLD,4PARAM FORMULA	
					Jour SNP 24 140	Aug 76	. ENGLISH OF YF 24 270	
Fiss Yield	Fast		GA	Expt	Abst ANS 24 458	Nov 76	Buzzelli+TRITIUM FISS YLD.NDG. TBD.	
Fiss Yield	2.5-2		UI	Expt	Abst ANS 24 459	Nov 76	Dilorio+PHYSICAL MEAS.NDG.TBD.	
Fiss Yield	Fiss		GRE	Expt	Rept CEA-N-1979	77	Ferrieu+ ABSTRACT,TABLE GIVEN	
Fiss Yield	+7		RI	Expt	Conf 77Kiev	77	Kondurov+ YLD ALPHA-PART,GRAPH	
Frag Spectra	Maxwl		CRC	Expt	Jour PR 75 990	Mar 49	Brunton+ E-DIST VS MASS. CFD U235+PU	
Frag Spectra	Maxwl		CRC	Expt	Jour CJR 28 190	Mar 50	Brunton+. ENERGY DISTRIBUTION	
Frag Spectra	Pile		CRC	Expt	Jour PR 80 181	Oct 50	Allen+ E SPECT,FAST ALPHAS+FISSFRAGS	
Frag Spectra	None		LAS	Expt	Jour PR 87 444	Aug 52	Leachman+ TOF VELOCITY DIST CURVES	
Frag Spectra	Maxwl 1.4+7		LAS	Expt	Jour PR 94 640	May 54	Brolley+ 2ES 0 DEG/90 DEG RATIO	

92 Uranium 233

Quantity	Energy (ev) Min	Max	Lab	Type	Documentation Ref Vol Page	Date	Author, Comments	Data
Frag Spectra	Spont		CCP	Expt	Conf 55Moscow 226	Jul 55	Goldin+.ALFA SPECTRUM.EXPT FROM 1952	
					Rept AEC−TR−2435	56	. P 167.ENGL TRANSL OF 55MOSCOW 226	
Frag Spectra	Maxwl		LAS	Expt	Jour PR 108 94	Oct 57	Stein. TOF MASS,ENERGY DISTRIBUTION.	
Frag Spectra	+6	+7	LAS	Theo	Jour PR 116 107	59	Griffin.ANISOTROPY OF FRAGS.BOHR TH	
Frag Spectra	6.8+5	1.5+7	LAS	Expt	Jour PR 116 102	Oct 59	Blumberg+,ANISOTROPY OF FRAGMENTS	
Frag Spectra	6.0+6	2.0+7	CRC	Expt	Jour CJP 37 1418	Dec 59	Baerg+. FRAG ANG DIST ISOTROPIC	
Frag Spectra	Pile		RI	Expt	Jour ZET 38 1723	Jun 60	Petrzhak.GRPH+TBL FRAGMENT RANGE+E	
					Jour JET 11 1244	Dec 60	TRANSLATN.*	
Frag Spectra	5.2−5	2.3+7	LAS	Expt	Jour PR 120 198	Oct 60	Simmons+ FRAGMENT ANGULAR DIST 28ES	
Frag Spectra	1.0+5	1.0+6	KUR	Expt	Jour DOK 140 351	Sep 61	Shigin.FRAGMENT ANGULAR ANISOTROPY	
Frag Spectra	+6		LAS	Theo	Jour AP 18 274	May 62	Leachman+ CALC ANISOTROPY CFD EXPTS	
Frag Spectra	Maxwl		CRC	Expt	Jour CJP 40 1626	Nov 62	Milton+ DOUBLE VEL MEASUREMNTS.	
Frag Spectra	1.5+7		CCP	Expt	−		ENGLISH SJA15 1039 FRANCAIS EAF15 4	
					Jour SJA 15 1039	63	. ENGL OF AE 15 320	
Frag Spectra	Maxwl		CCP	ExTh	Jour AE 15 419	Nov 63	Okolovich+ AV EK REL U238. THEORY	
					Jour JNE 18 533	Sep 64	TRANSLATN.*	
					Jour SJA 15 1177	Nov 63	TRANSLATN.*	
Frag Spectra	8.0+4	1.3+6	CCP	Expt	Rept ANL−TR−179	64	Bondarenko+,ANG DIST FRAGS,GRPH	
Frag Spectra	3.0+5	4.7+6	FEI	Expt	Jour NP 52 648	Apr 64	Blyumkina+MEAN FRAG KINETICIE VS EN	+
	3.0+5	4.7+6			Data EXFOR40158.008	Mar 73	REL E−KIN OF FRGMNTS AT 13 ES	
Frag Spectra	1.5+7	2.0+7	CCP	Expt	Jour AE 16 521	Jun 64	Okolovich+MEAN KINETIC E OF FRAGMENT	
					Jour SJA 16 644		. ENGL OF AE 16 521	
Frag Spectra	Maxwl		CRC	Revw	Conf 65Salzburg 1 451	Mar 65	Fraser.P.34,DISCUSSION OF XPTS	
					Conf 64Geneva 7 430	May 64	− + NU/FRAGM.MASS.	
Frag Spectra	−2		ORL	Theo	Conf 65Salzburg 39	Mar 65	Dabbs.ANISOTROPY OF ALFAS CALCULATED	
Frag Spectra	Maxwl		PTN	Expt	Conf 65Salzburg 1 467	Mar 65	Thomas+ SINGLE FRAG E−SPECTRA	
Frag Spectra	1.0+5	2.0+6	FEI	Expt	Rept FEI−49	66	Bol'Shov+.MEAN FISS FRAG−E VS NEUT−E	
					Rept LA−TR−68−19	68	. ENGL OF FEI−49	
Frag Spectra	Maxwl		MIT	Expt	Jour CJP 47 2371	Nov 69	Nakahara+,RANGES IN ALUMINUM	
					Rept MIT−905−81	Dec 66	.SUPERSEDED	
					Rept TID−23365	Aug 66	Nakahara.FRAG RANGES+KE DEFICITS	
					Rept MIT−905−21	Dec 65	.SUPERSEDED	
Frag Spectra		2.0+6	CCP	Comp	Rept ICD−3 26	Oct 66	Bolshov+.GRAPHS CFD TH,MANY REFS	
					Rept INDC−152E	67	. ENGL OF ICD−3 26	
Frag Spectra	8.0+4	1.3+6	FEI	Expt	Jour YF 4 993	Nov 66	Nesterov+ ANG DISTRB OF FRAGMENTS	+
					Rept FEI−33	65	.FRAG ANGDIST(E),GRAPH,TABLE	
	8.0+4	6.1+6			Rept LA−TR−66−41	66	.ENGLISH TRANSL OF FEI−33 /65	
Frag Spectra	Maxwl		MIT	Expt	Jour NUC 24 12 62	Dec 66	Gordon+ GE−LI,RANGES OF FRAGS IN AL	
Frag Spectra	−		FEI	Expt	Conf 67Kharkov	Feb 67	Vorob'Eva+. TBP IN IZV	
Frag Spectra	Maxwl	7.0+6	FEI	Expt	Jour YF 5 514	Mar 67	Senchenko+.CURV KIN E REL FRGMNTMASS	
	Maxwl				Jour YF 6 708	Oct 67	− + AVG EKIN VS MASS,GRAPH	
	4.0+5	2.6+6			Jour YF 6 708	Oct 67	− + AVG EKIN VS MASS,AT 2 ES	
	4.3+5	2.6+6			Prog YFI−4 14	May 67	.CURVES GIVEN AT 2ES	
	4.0+5	2.6+6			Jour SNP 6 516	Apr 68	. ENGL OF YF 6 708	
	Maxwl				Jour SNP 6 516	Apr 68	. ENGL OF YF 6 708	
	Maxwl	7.0+6			Jour SNP 5 362	Sep 67	.ENGLISH TRANSL OF YF 5 514 3/67	
	4.3+5	2.6+6			Prog INDC−E−187	67	.ENGLISH TRANSL OF YFI−4 14 5/67	
Frag Spectra	Maxwl		FLA	Expt	Jour PRL 18 404	Mar 67	Muga+ E SPEC IN TERNARY FISSION.	
					Conf 69Vienna 107	Jul 69	− +PPR99. BINARY+TERN+PU E−KIN CF	
Frag Spectra	Maxwl		LAS	Expt	Jour PR 156 1277	Apr 67	Stein+ FRAG ENERGIES VS MASS,+ TOTAL	
Frag Spectra	5.0−2	7.0−1	MTR	Expt	Jour PR 157 1055	May 67	Moore+ YLD HIGH KE FRAG VS NEUT E	
					Rept IN−1033	Nov 66	.SEE ALSO	
Frag Spectra		1.3+6	CCP	Expt	Jour YF 6 1162	Dec 67	Bolshov+ AVG FRAG KIN−E(NEUT−E)GRAPH	
Frag Spectra	Maxwl	1.1+6	FEI	Expt	Jour YF 6 1167	Dec 67	Djachenko+ FRAG K−E REL THR,TBL,GRPH	
					Jour SNP 6 848	Jun 68	*	
Frag Spectra	Maxwl		KFK	Comp	Rept KFK−693	Dec 67	Muenzel+ RANGE DIST OF FISS FRAG	
Frag Spectra	1.4+7		RI	ExTh	Conf 68Riga	Jan 68	Adamov+ ABST,E−DIST OF A−PART,TRITON	
Frag Spectra	Maxwl		ORL	Expt	Jour PR 174 1500	Oct 68	Pleasanton+ KINETIC ENERGY DIST.	
Frag Spectra	Pile		CCP	Expt	Conf 69Erevan	Feb 69	Vorobev+.ABST,LIGHT NUCLEI E DIST	
Frag Spectra	+3	1.4+7	FTI	Expt	Conf 69Vienna 900	Jul 69	Adamov+PPR146. ALFA+TRITIUM SPECTRUM	
	Maxwl	1.4+7			Jour YF 9 732	Apr 69	− + AVG ALFA,T,P ENERGY +−SPREAD	
					Jour SNP 9 424	Oct 69	. ENGL OF YF 9 732	
Frag Spectra	Maxwl		ORL	Theo	Conf 69Vienna 67	Jul 69	Schmitt.PPR122.GRPH,(EKIN+−RMS) VS A	
Frag Spectra	Maxwl		TRM	Expt	Conf 69Vienna 741	Jul 69	Dange+PPR97.RANGES IN AL+KIN−E,TBL	
					Rept BARC/I−79 51	70	− + SAME RESULTS	
					Conf 69Chandigr 1 182	Sep 69	− + FRAG RANGE IN AL,KIN−E,TABLES	
Frag Spectra	Pile		FTI	Expt	Jour PL/B 30 332	Oct 69	Vorobiev+EN SPEC LIGHT FRAGS TOF	

92 Uranium 233

Quantity	Energy (ev) Min	Max	Lab	Type	Documentation Ref Vol Page	Author, Comments Date	Data
Frag Spectra	None		SAH	Theo	Conf 69Roorke 2 217	Dec 69 Sarkar+ E BALANCE OKS EXPTS, GRAPHS	
	Maxwl				Jour PL/B 30 313	Oct 69 − +CALC EXCIT+KE PROMPT FRAGS	
Frag Spectra	+0	8.1+5	FEI	Expt	Prog YFI−11 16	70 Smirenkin+ ABST,ANISOTROPY(N−E),GRPH	
					Prog INDC(CCP)−31	Dec 72 .PAGE 15,ENGLISH OF YFI−11 16	
Frag Spectra		7.0+5	IRE	Expt	Jour ZEP 11 489	May 70 Smirenkin+ ANG ANISOTR(NEUT−E),GRPHS	
					Jour JEL 11 333	May 70 TRANSLATN.*NO10	
Frag Spectra	1.6+7		RI	Expt	Jour YF 11 1006	May 70 Babenko+ FRAG ANGDIST, GRAPH	
					Jour SNP 11 560	Nov 70 . ENGL OF YF 11 1006	
Frag Spectra	None		COL	Expt	Conf 71Knoxvill 855	Mar 71 Felvinci+. KINETIC ENERGY DISTR	
	+0	+4			Conf 69Vienna 922	Jul 69 Melkonian+PPR117. FRAG KIN−E(NEUT−E)	
Frag Spectra	Maxwl	1.3+6	AUA	ExTh	Rept AAEC/TM−574	Apr 71 Walsh+ AVG KE VS N−E CFD EXPTS,GRAPH	
Frag Spectra	3.0+4	2.2+5	FEI	Expt	Prog YFI−10 22	May 71 Smirenkin+ ANG ANISOTROPY,TBL,GRAPH	
					Rept INDC(CCP)−15	Dec 71 *P24,ENG OF YFI−10	
Frag Spectra	5.5+6	1.5+7	FEI	Expt	Jour YF 14 935	Nov 71 Surin+ FRAG KIN−E,2 ES CFD THR,GRAPH	+
					Jour SNP 14 523	May 72 * ENGL OF YF 14 935	
	2.5−2	1.5+7			Data EXFOR40112.	Nov 73 .KIN−E AND AVERAGE KIN−E,4SUBENT	
Frag Spectra	Maxwl		ANL	Expt	Jour NP/A 177 337	Dec 71 Reisdorf+SIMULT MEAS K.E. ANG G−SPEC	
					Conf 69Vienna 781	Jul 69 .PRELIMINARY.	
Frag Spectra	7.6+5		CCP	Expt	Jour IZV 36 1 215	72 Nikolaev+	+
	7.6+5				Data EXFOR40159.005	May 73 AVERAGE E−KIN OF FRAGMENTS	
Frag Spectra	1.6+7		TRM	Expt	Prog BARC−628 94	72 Iyer+ ANGULAR ANISOTROPY OF FRAG,TBL	+
	1.4+7	1.6+7			Conf 70Madurai 2 57	Dec 70 − ANGDIST,GRAPH+TABLE,TRACK−DE	
	1.6+7				Data EXFOR30235.	Jul 73 COS.COEF.OF ANG.DIST. OF FIS.FRAGM.	
Frag Spectra	Maxwl	1.6+6	FEI	Expt	Jour AE 32 83	Jan 72 Kolosov+ FRAG AVG KIN−E REL THR,GRPH	+
	2.5−2	1.6+6			Jour AE 32 83	Jan 72 − +	
	Maxwl	1.6+6			Jour SJA 32 92	Jul 72 . ENGL OF AE 32 83	
	2.5−2	1.6+6			Data EXFOR40130.003	Sep 72 AVERAGE E−KIN OF FRAGMNTS AT 16 ES	
Frag Spectra	Maxwl		CUA	Theo	Abst DA/B 32 5980	Apr 72 Lee. CALC OF TOT FRAG KE DISTRIBUTS	
Frag Spectra	4.0−1	2.0+3	HAR	Expt	Jour NP/A 190 401	Aug 72 Kuiken+ ANGDIST ALIGNED NUC	
		2.0+3			Prog AERE−PR/NP18	Mar 72 Pattenden+ FRAG ANG DIST ALIGNED NUC	
	4.0−1	2.0+3			Rept RCN−142	Jun 71 Kuiken+ DIST FROM ALIGNED NUCL.(RCN)	
Frag Spectra	4.0−1	2.0+3	LEI	Expt	Jour NP/A 190 401	Aug 72 Kuiken+ LEGENDR COEF(2) VS E.	
Frag Spectra		6.0+7	FEI	Expt	Jour YF 16 475	Sep 72 Sergachev+ MASS+KIN−E DISTR,NU−BAR	+
	+0	6.0+7			Jour SNP 16 266	Mar 73 .ENGLISH TRANSL OF YF 16 475 9/72	
	2.5−2	5.4+6			Data EXFOR40106.	Sep 73 .KIN−E AND AVER KIN−E OF FISS FRAG	
Frag Spectra	Maxwl		TRM	Expt	Jour JIN 34 9 2685	Sep 72 Prakash+ KIN ENERGY DISTR	
	Pile				Conf 70Madurai 2 79	Dec 70 − + KIN−E VS MASS RATIO, GRAPHS	
Frag Spectra	Maxwl		ANL	Expt	Jour NP/A 205 348	Apr 73 Reisdorf+ MASS DIST AT GIVEN E. CURV	
					Conf 73Rochestr 2 19	Aug 73 Unik+ TOTAL KIN−E OF FRAGS,GRPH	
Frag Spectra	Maxwl		PAV	Expt	Rept STI/DOC/10−144	May 73 Pinelly+ LIGHT FRAG SPEC,NDG,TBP NC	
					Prog EANDC(E)140U	Aug 71 Cambiaghi+, ENERGY DISTRIB.FOR HE6	
					Jour NC/B 59 2 236	Feb 69 − + LIGHT FRAG ENERGY RANGE.	
Frag Spectra	Maxwl		ITK	Theo	Jour AUJ 26 279	Jun 73 Mukherji+ CALC KE VS FRAG−MASS,GRAPH	
	None				Conf 69Roorke 2 226	Dec 69 − + TOT−KINE(A) CRV,LIQID−DROP	
Frag Spectra	Maxwl		LIN	Expt	Conf 73Munich 1 716	Aug 73 Vorobjov+ Z=1...8 E−SPECTRUM,NDG	
Frag Spectra	Maxwl		AUA	Revw	Conf IAEA−169 2 163	74 Musgrove+ AVG FRAG MASS,GRAPH	
Frag Spectra	1.0+5	1.1+6	BIR	Revw	Jour RPP 37 951	74 Beynon+ COMPAR AVG TOT FRG−EKIN,GRPH	
Frag Spectra	3.0+4	1.9+6	WUC	Expt	Conf 74Bombay 2 93	Dec 74 Walsh+ ANGDIST+E−SPEC OF FRAGMENTS	
Frag Spectra	0.0+0	1.4+6	AUA	ExTh	Prog AAEC/PR−41P 32	75 Boldeman+ AVG TOT EKIN CALC+XPT,GRPH	
Frag Spectra	Maxwl		PAH	Theo	Jour PL/B 55 144	Feb 75 Hooshyar+ISOMERIC FISS,TH CFD EXPTAL	
Frag Spectra	1.0+4	1.9+6	AUA	Expt	Jour AEA 18 2 2	Apr 75 Walsh. W(0DEG)/W(90DEG) VS E−N,GRAP	
	3.0+4	1.9+6			Conf 74Bombay 2 92	Dec 74 − + W(0)/W(90)VS E,ANALYSIS.GRPHS	
	3.0+4	2.0+6			Prog AAEC/PR−40P 28	Jul 74 Boldeman+ W(0)/W(90) CFD OTHRS,GRPH	
Frag Spectra	1.5+4	2.0+6	FEI	Expt	Jour YF 21 704	Apr 75 Shpak+ W(0)/W(90),ANG MOMENTUM,GRAPH	+
					Jour SNP 21 363	Apr 75 . ENGLISH OF YF 21 704	
	1.5+4	2.0+6			Data EXFOR40361.002	Feb 75 ANGDIST COS COEF AT 70 ENERGIES	
Frag Spectra	Pile		TRM	Theo	Jour PR/C 11 1251	Apr 75 Dange+ FRGM−EKIN FORMUL CFD OTHS,FIG	
Frag Spectra	+3	1.4+6	AUA	Expt	Conf 75Kiev 5 191	May 75 Bertram+ AVG EKIN,W(0)/W(90).GRAPHS	
	2.6+6	1.0+6			Conf 73Kiev 4 121	May 73 Boldeman+ AVG KIN−E VS EN,GRAPH+TABL	
Frag Spectra	+7		FEI	Theo	Conf 75Kiev	May 75 Ermagambetov+ ANGANIZOTR,ANALYS,GRPH	
Frag Spectra	None		DKE	Theo	Conf 76Lowell 1403	Jul 76 Newson.EXCIT E,3−50MEV.FINE STRUC.ND	
Frag Charge	Maxwl		ANL	Eval	Conf 55Geneva 7 3	Aug 55 Steinberg+ P614.CHARGE DISPERSN,GRPH	
Frag Charge	None		MTR	Expt	Conf 55Geneva 7 19	Aug 55 Pappas+.P881,CHARGE DISTRIBTN CURVE	
Frag Charge	None		BNL	Theo	Jour NSE 9 495	Apr 61 Levine.MOST PROB Z.FROM =CHG DISPL.	
Frag Charge	Maxwl		CNA	Theo	Jour PR/B 134 972	Jun 64 Talat+ N,CHARGE DIST IN FISS PRODS.	
				ExTh	Rept CNAEM−12	63 − + TBL AVERAGE CHARGE/NUCLEON	
Frag Charge	Maxwl		WAS	Revw	Conf 65Salzburg 317	Mar 65 Wahl.GRAPHS TH CFD XPTS	
Frag Charge	Maxwl		FEI	Theo	Prog YFI−3 12	Sep 66 Ignatjvk. GRAPH	

92 Uranium 233

Quantity	Energy (ev) Min	Energy (ev) Max	Lab	Type	Documentation Ref Vol Page	Date	Author, Comments	Data
Frag Charge	Maxwl		ISL	Expt Prog	IA- 1168 67	Jan 67	CHUL LEE+ YLD VALUES OF BR,SR,Y,MO	
Frag Charge	Maxwl		HAR	Theo Rept	AERE-R-6056	Mar 69	Crouch.CALC CHARGE DISPERSION,ZP,TBL	
Frag Charge	Maxwl	1.4+7	RAM	Revw Jour	NSPA 5 43	Apr 69	Khan. REVIEW,CHARGE DISTRIBUTN EXPTS	
Frag Charge	Maxwl		RI	Expt Jour	IZV 33 718	Apr 69	Davydov+ FRAG'S K-X-RAY YIELD,TABLE	
				Jour	BAS 33 661	70	TRANSLATN.*NO 4	
Frag Charge	Maxwl		SOR	Theo Jour	PR 182 1331	Jun 69	Notea.EMPIRICAL FUNCTION DERIVED	
Frag Charge	Maxwl		ANL	Expt Conf	69Vienna 781	Jul 69	Glendenin+PPR114.CHARGE DIST,K X-RAY	
Frag Charge	Maxwl		CCP	Expt Conf	69Vienna 932	Jul 69	Smirnov+PPR152. TERNARY+BIN,FISS CFD	
Frag Charge	Maxwl		MCM	Theo Conf	69Vienna 845	Jul 69	Thind+PPR50. YLD(Z,A)+NU(A)+EXCIT E	
Frag Charge	Maxwl		MNZ	Expt Conf	69Vienna 945	Jul 69	Denschlag+PPR26. CHARGE DISPERSION	
Frag Charge	Maxwl		CUA	Theo Abst	DA/B 30 2222	Nov 69	Rogers.	
Frag Charge	Maxwl		ORL	Expt Jour	PR/C 1 316	Jan 70	Runnalls+,ZP ESTIMATED FROM I YLDS	
Frag Charge	Maxwl		ANL	Expt Abst	BAP 16 98	Jan 71	Unik.K X-RAY METHOD. NO DATA GIVEN	
Frag Charge	Maxwl		JAE	Revw Jour	NP/A 160 65	Jan 71	Umezawa+ SYSTEMATICS VS FRAG MASS	
Frag Charge	Maxwl		ANL	Expt Jour	NP/A 177 337	Dec 71	Reisdorf+SIMULT MEAS K.E. ANG G-SPEC	
				Conf	69Vienna 781	Jul 69	.PRELIMINARY.	
Frag Charge	Maxwl		MIS	Eval Jour	JIN 33 12 4327	Dec 71	Troutner.	
Frag Charge	Maxwl		MNZ	Expt Jour	JIN 34 6 1785	Jun 72	Naeumann+ CHARGE DISTR MASS CHAIN132	
Frag Charge	Maxwl		MIS	Expt Abst	DA/B 34 1034	Sep 73	Eichor.NUCLEAR CHG DISTR CFD U235	
Frag Charge	Maxwl		MIS	Expt Abst	DA/B 34 1034	Sep 73	Berge.CHG DISTR OF 131,133 MASSES	
Frag Charge	Maxwl		AUA	Revw Conf	IAEA-169 2 163	74	Musgrove+ CHARGE DISPERSN PARS,GRPHS	
Frag Charge	1.8+6	1.5+7	LRL	Comp Rept	UCRL-51640	Jul 74	Nethaway. TBL.	
	Maxwl			Rept	UCRL-51640	Jul 74	- . TBL.	
Frag Charge	Maxwl		SOR	Eval Jour	PR/C 11 845	Mar 75	Amiel+ FRACT IND,ODD-EVN EFF.TBL+GRF	
Frag Charge	Maxwl		ANL	Expt Jour	JIN 37 869	Apr 75	Flynn+ FRAC INDEP RB84,86,CS136.CURV	+
	Maxwl			Data	EXFOR10517.005	Apr 78	. 3PTS.CHARGE DISTRB DATA	
Frag Charge	Maxwl		UBE	Expt Jour	JIN 38 205	Feb 76	Gaeggeler+ ZP(A=150),GRPH Z-SYSTEMAT	
				Diss	GAEGGELER	Dec 73	- . COMPLETE EXPT DESCRIPTION	
				Conf	73Rochestr 2 475	Aug 73	- + ABST,ZP FOR A=150 GIVEN	
Reson Params	-.5+1	4.7+0	LAS	Expt Rept	LA- 520	Mar 46	Williams.	+
	-.5+1	4.7+0		Data	EXFOR12312.006	Jun 76	. 7 RES. E0,WT,WN,WF.	
Reson Params	6.7+0		BNL	Expt Priv	PILCHER	Jan 55	Pilcher.	
	6.7+0			Data	EXFOR12290.	Jun 76	. 1 RES. EP,WN,WN0.	
Reson Params	1.9+0		SAC	Expt Jour	JNE 1 306	Jun 55	Auclair+.RES E 1.85+-.15EV FROM SIGF	
Reson Params	1.0-2	1.0+2	CCP	Expt Conf	55Moscow 87	Jul 55	Nikitin+.SIMULTAN ABS AND FISS,TABLE	+
				Rept	AEC-TR-2435 81	56	. ENGL TRANSL OF 55MOSCOW 87	
Reson Params	3.6+0	3.6+0	HAR	Expt Conf	55Geneva 4 210	Aug 55	Price. (LYNN) = 9 DATA INDEX LINES	+
Reson Params	1.4+0	2.2+0	CCP		Rept	AEC-TR-2435PT1	56	.USSR ALSO 1D75EV PAGE 85	
Reson Params	1.8+0	1.0+1	BNL	Expt Rept	AERE-NP/R-2076	Jan 57	Sailor. CS WN WF FOR 5RES P WT	+
				Abst	PR 100 1249	Nov 55	- . ABSTR. I6.	
	1.8+0	1.0+1		Data	EXFOR12363.	Jun 76	. 10 RES. E0,WT,WN,WN0,WF.	
Reson Params	1.8+0	2.3+0	MTR	Expt Rept	AERE-NP/R-2076	Jan 57	Evans.2RES WT,WF IF NO INTERF.	
Reson Params	6.8+0	5.8+1	CCP	Expt Jour	AE 2 129	Feb 57	Sokolovsky+.TABLE 26 E RES,GWN,9 WT	+
				Jour	JNE 5 389	Nov 57	TRANSLATN.*	
				Jour	SJA 2 147	57	TRANSLATN.*	
Reson Params	1.8+0	3.6+0	HAR	Expt Jour	JNE 6 114	Dec 57	Sanders+. +2.3EV, WT SIGF	+
Reson Params	1.5+0	1.9+1	CCP	Expt Jour	AE 5 69	Jul 58	Vladimirskii+ SIGR.WF FOR 11 RES	+
				Jour	JNEA 10 64	Jul 59	TRANSLATN.*	
				Jour	SJA 5 883	58	TRANSLATN.*	
Reson Params	2.0-1	1.0+1	BNL	Revw Conf	58Geneva 16 8	Sep 58	Hughes.PPR2483,PARAMS FOR 15ES GVN	
Reson Params	1.5+0	2.2+1	CCP	Expt Conf	58Geneva 15 309	Sep 58	Vladimirsky+.PPR2221,PARAMS FOR 12ES	
Reson Params	1.0-1	9.0+0	CRC	Theo Jour	PR 118 724	May 60	Vogt.MULTILEVEL FIT TO BNL+MTR DATA	
Reson Params	1.5-1	1.1+1	MTR	ExTh Jour	PR 118 718	May 60	Moore.MULTILEVEL FIT TO SIGTOT +FISS	+
				Abst	BAP 5 294	60	.ABSTR. YA11.	
				Conf	58Geneva 2483	Sep 58	Moore.	
				Conf	58Geneva 645	Sep 58	- .	
	1.5-1	1.0+1		Expt Data	EXFOR12342.	Jun 76	. 20 RES. E0,J,WT,WN,WG,WF.	
Reson Params	None		BRK	Revw Conf	60Kingston 659	Aug 60	Harvey.CURVE,FISS WIDTH DISTRBUTION	
Reson Params	2.0-1	2.6+0	ORL	Expt Conf	60Kingston 882	Aug 60	Pattenden+.TABLE,GAMMA-,N-,FISSWIDTH	+
	-.1-2	1.5+1		Conf	61RPI 64	May 61	Harvey. MULTILEVEL FIT	
	2.0-1	2.6+0		Data	EXFOR12358.	Jun 76	. 28 RES. E0,WG,WF.	
Reson Params	1.5-1	1.0+1	HAR	Expt Conf	61Saclay 571	Jul 61	Pattenden.8RESONANCES CFD OTHERS	
	2.5-1	1.1+1		Jour	JNE 3 28	Aug 56	- . 7 RES ES ONLY,FROM SIGTOT	
Reson Params	-.1+1	2.0+0	CCP	Expt Jour	AE 12 408	May 62	Gordeev.MULTILVL FIT,CF VOGT	
				Jour	SJA 12 433	62	. ENGLISH	
				Jour	EAF 12 5 59	62	. FRENCH	
Reson Params	1.0+0	1.5+1	UI	Theo Abst	ANS 7 87	Jun 64	Adler+ MULTILEVEL PARAMETERS.	

92 Uranium 233

Quantity	Energy (ev) Min	Energy (ev) Max	Lab	Type	Documentation Ref Vol Page	Author, Comments Date	Data
Reson Params	+0	+2	FEI	Theo	Jour AE 17 22	Jul 64 Usachev+ MANY NARROW RES NOT SEEN	
					Jour SJA 17 709	Jul 64 . ENGL OF AE 17 22	
					Jour EAF 17 1 3	Jul 64 . FRENCH OF AE 17 22	
Reson Params	-		HAR	Theo	Jour PRL 13 412	Sep 64 Lynn. ERRORS IN 1-LVL ANAL OF WIDTH	
					Rept AERE-NP/GEN 38	Jul 64 - . RES ANAL TECHNIQUES.	
Reson Params		+7	FEI	Theo	Jour AE 17 479	Dec 64 Usachev+ FISS CHANN THRESH ESTIMATED	
					Jour JNE 19 987	Dec 65 . ENGL OF AE 17 479	
					Jour SJA 17 1242	Dec 64 . ENGL OF AE 17 479	
Reson Params	+0	+3	CAI	Theo	Jour NP 62 667	Feb 65 Stavinsky+(N,GF)PROB ABOUT=(N,GAMMA)	
Reson Params	1.8+0	3.0+1	SAC	ExTh	Jour JPR 25 877	Oct 64 Nifenecker+ BREIT WIGNER ANAL. WF.	+
					Conf 65Salzburg 245	Mar 65 - .LEAST SQU AN OF JPR24 254	
	1.8+0	3.0+1		Expt	Data EXFOR20814.	Mar 78 39PTS.EN,WT,WF,WN,AVG 2G*WN,WF	
Reson Params	1.8+0	2.6+1	AUA	Theo	Jour AUJ 20 73	Feb 67 MUSGROVE CORRTO EXPT FOR MISSED LVLS	
Reson Params	2.9-1	1.5+2	AI	Eval	Rept NAA-SR-11980 5	May 67 Hennies.WN WG WF +AVG PARS TO 10KEV	
Reson Params	-		CCP	Eval	Jour AE 23 6	Jul 67 Kirpitchnikov.FISS-,N-WIDTH,STRNTH-F	
					Jour SJA 23 669	Jul 67 TRANSLATN.*	
Reson Params		1.0+6	AUA	Theo	Jour AUJ 20 477	Oct 67 Cook. TBL OF AVG LVL SPACING D,L=0,1	
Reson Params		1.1+1	AUA	Theo	Jour AUJ 20 617	Dec 67 Musgrove.TBLS SINGL+MULTLVL RES PAR	
Reson Params	None		FEI	Theo	Jour YF 6 1313	Dec 67 GAJ+ MISSD LVLS=50PC,OKS AE 17 22/64	
					Jour SNP 6 952	Jun 68 .TRANSLATION	
Reson Params	2.0+1	6.3+1	LAS	Expt	Jour PR 166 1178	Feb 68 Bergen+ BOMB TOF 2G*WN WF FROM NF	+
					Abst DA/B 28 4244	Apr 68 - . SNGLE+MLTILVL FIT,FISS+ALPHA	
					Rept LA-DC-8946	67 .SUPERSEDED	
Reson Params	1.7-1	6.1+1	WAL	Eval	Conf 68Wash. 615	Mar 68 Schneider. WG,WF,WG*WN,1-LVL B-W FIT	
Reson Params	None		AUA	Theo	Rept AAEC/TM-463	Jul 68 Musgrove.METHOD TO FIND MISSED LVLS	
Reson Params	1.0-5	1.0+5	GA	Eval	Rept GA-8854	Aug 68 Boroughs+ ENDF/B DATA	
Reson Params	1.6+0	3.1+1	LRL	Expt	Jour PR 174 1413	Oct 68 Sauter+ LINAC 30 RESON ES+PARAMS	+
					Conf 68Wash. 541	Mar 68 .SUPERSEDED	
	1.6+0	3.1+1			Data EXFOR12344.005	Jun 76 . 30 RES. E0,WT,WN,WN**2,WG.	
Reson Params	1.8+0	3.0+1	AUA	Theo	Jour AUJ 21 779	Dec 68 Musgrove. UNRESOLVD RES,D+NEUT WIDTH	
Reson Params	-		SUK	Theo	Conf 68Bombay 2 170	Dec 68 Narayana. CALCULTD QUADRUPOLE MOMENT	
Reson Params	-		FEI	Theo	Rept FEI-157	Feb 69 Ignatjuk+ 2HUMPED-BARR-CALCUL,WN/WF	
Reson Params	2.0-1	1.0+2	CCP	Revw	Rept ICD-6 7	70 Lukyanov.N-,G-,F-WIDS OF 12 RES,TBLS	
Reson Params	None		TRM	Theo	Prog BARC-471 5	70 Sood+ CORREL ANAL,D CLASS II VAL GVN	
	2.0+1	1.0+6			Conf 69Roorke 2 198	Dec 69 - + AVG LEVL SPACING D,2-HUMPED-T	
Reson Params	1.8+0	2.1+1	DUB	Expt	Rept JINR-P3-4992	Apr 70 Rjabov+ TOT+N-WIDS FOR 13 RES GIVEN	+
					Jour SNP 13 255	Sep 71 * ENGL OF YF 13 457	
					Jour YF 13 457	Mar 71 .METHOD DESCRIBED, NO DATA	
					Prog YFI-11 27	70 Rjabov+ ABST,SAME TBL AS JINR-4992	
					Prog INDC(CCP)-31	Dec 72 .PAGE 26,ENGLISH OF YFI-11 27	
	1.8+0	2.1+1			Data EXFOR40070.	Aug 70 TOT-WIDTH+ELAS-WIDTH,13 RESONANCES	
Reson Params	1.5+0	1.0+5	TOK	Theo	Jour NST 7 157	Apr 70 Kikuchi+.CHANNEL TH,SPIN DEPENDNT WF	
Reson Params	7.0-1	3.2+2	GEL	Expt	Jour 70Helsinki 1 387	Jun 70 Kolar+16. SINGLE+MULT LEVEL PARAMS	+
	1.6+0	9.4+1			Data EXFOR20114.	Jul 72 400PTS.ADLER GT,ADLER HT,ADLER NU.	
Reson Params	-.2-1	6.5+1	GEL	Expt	Jour JNE 24 111	Jun 70 CAO+ PARAMETERS FROM (N,F) EXPT.	+
					Conf 70Helsinki 1 419	Jun 70 CAO+PPR19. MULTILEVEL RESON PARAMS	
	-.2+0	6.5+1			Data EXFOR20003.	Nov 70 216PTS.ADLER GF,ADLER HF,ADLER NU.	
Reson Params	-.3+1	6.4+1	ORL	Eval	Conf 70Helsinki 2 757	Jun 70 Desaussure. P94,MLTILVL RES PARS.	+
					Rept ORNL-TM-2745	Nov 69 - . MULTILVL, 70 RESONANCES.	
	2.0-2	6.4+1		Expt	Data EXFOR10079.002	Dec 78 . 70RES.ADLER-ADLER PARAMETERS	
Reson Params		7.0+3	SDC	Theo	Conf 70Helsinki 2 799	Jun 70 Garrison.DISCUSSN. RESONANCE ANAL	
Reson Params	None		DUB	Theo	Jour YF 13 240	Feb 71 Malecki+G-WID,THEO CFD EXPT.TBL,GRPH	
					Jour SNP 13 133	Aug 71 - ENGL OF YF 13 240	
Reson Params	6.2-1	5.0+4	SRL	Theo	Conf 71Knoxvill 714	Mar 71 Mccrosson. STAT CALCULATN AVG PARAMS	
Reson Params	None		LAS	Expt	Prog NCSAC-42 153	Nov 71 Keyworth+. J AND K TO BE MEASD.ORELA	
Reson Params	1.5+0	3.0+1	COL	Expt	Prog COO-2176-1 7	Jun 72 Felvinci+. TABLE.WT AND S0*WF	+
	+0	+4			Conf 71Knoxvill 855	Mar 71 - +. WF FOR 36 RESONANCES	
					Conf 69Vienna 922	Jul 69 Melkonian+PPR117. CHANNEL ANAL	
	1.5+0	3.0+1			Data EXFOR10200.002	Sep 73 . 36 RES. WF.	
Reson Params	2.2-1	6.0+1	KTO	Eval	Jour NST 10 709	Dec 73 Otani+.SINGLE- AND MULTI-LVL ANAL.	
Reson Params	5.0+0	9.8+1	CCP	Theo	Rept YK-16 121	74 Gorbachev+ G+F+N+TOT-WIDTHS, TBL	
Reson Params	5.9+0	1.2+2	SAC	Expt	Jour NSE 54 116	74 Blons+SINGLE LEVEL ANALYSIS	+
					Conf 73Kiev 2 239	May 73 - . AVERAGE F-WIDTH + NU-BAR GIVN	
	5.9+0	1.2+2			Data EXFOR20446.	Oct 75 172PTS.AVG.WF,WT,MEAN LVLSP.	
Reson Params	1.5-1	6.4+1	AUA	Theo	Jour AUJ 27 1	Feb 74 Rose+ ADLER RESPARS STATISTICS,TBLS	
Reson Params	None		AUA	Eval	Prog AAEC/PR-41P 64	75 Cook+ FIS+N-WID STATIST STUDIED.NDG	
Reson Params	None		COL	Expt	Abst BAP 20 149	Feb 75 Cacuci+LVL DENSITY CALC CFD EXPT.	
Strnth Fnctn	1.5+0	2.2+1	CCP	Expt	Conf 58Geneva 15 309	Sep 58 Vladimirsky+.PPR2221,VAL GVN	

92 Uranium 233

Quantity	Energy (ev) Min	Max	Lab	Type	Documentation Ref Vol Page	Date	Author, Comments	Data
Strnth Fnctn	+3		BNL	Expt	Jour PRL 1 461	Dec 58	Hughes. FC. 1.1+ − 0.2.	
Strnth Fnctn		2.0+1	MTR	Expt	Jour PR 118 714	May 60	Moore. 1.0+ − 0.2.	+
					Rept IDO − 16576	Dec 59	.SUPERSEDED	
					Conf 58Geneva 15 111	Sep 58	Fluharty+.PPR645,VAL GVN	
		2.0+1			Data EXFOR12341.004	Jun 76	. 1 PT.	
Strnth Fnctn	None		DKE	Theo	Jour NP 24 169	Apr 61	Seth. J − DEPENDENCE OF S−WAVE STRFUNC	
Strnth Fnctn	−1	+2	AUA	Eval	Jour AUJ 20 73	Feb 67	Musgrove.CORRECTIONS FOR UNRES LVLS	
Strnth Fnctn	1.0+0	2.1+1	DUB	Expt	Rept JINR − P3 − 4992	Apr 70	Rjabov+ MAXIMUM LIKELIHOOD VALUE S0	+
					Jour SNP 13 255	Sep 71	*ENGL OF YF 13 457	
					Jour YF 13 457	Mar 71	Rjabov+ S−0 GIVEN	
	1.0+0	2.1+1			Data EXFOR40070.025	Aug 70	S−WAVE STRENGTH FUNCTION S0	
Strnth Fnctn	0.0+0	3.0+1	GEL	Expt	Conf 70Helsinki 1 387	Jun 70	Kolar+ FROM TOT SIG RES PAR ANAL.	+
		3.0+1			Data EXFOR20114.012	Jul 72	1PNT.L=0.	
Strnth Fnctn		1.0+5	GA	Theo	Jour NP/A 159 305	Dec 70	Garrison. S,P−WAVE.TO FIT AVG NG,NF	
Strnth Fnctn	None		AUA	Eval	Rept AAEC/E − 277	Mar 73	Musgrove.TBLS EXPTL DATA+BEST VALUES	
Strnth Fnctn	2.0+3		IJI	Expt	Conf 76Lowell 1244	Jul 76	Vertebnyj+ S0 GVN.FROM TOT,SCAT − DATA	
					Conf 75Kiev 3 151	May 75	Vertebnyj+ RES − NEUT FILTRAT.SIG GIVN	
Lvl Density	−		COP	Theo	Jour NP 6 62	Mar 58	Ericson. LVL DENSITY FORM CFD EXP	
Lvl Density	1.8+0	3.0+1	SAC	Expt	Conf 65Salzburg 245	Mar 65	Nifenecker+ SHAPE ANALYSIS OF (N,F)	+
	1.8+0	3.0+1			Data EXFOR20814.007	Mar 78	1PNT.AVG LEVEL SPACING.	
Lvl Density	+6		MIL	Expt	EN 15 1 54	Jan 68	Facchini+ LDL PARS FROM LOW EN RES	
Lvl Density	2.1+1	6.3+1	KUR	Theo	Jour YF 9 303	Feb 69	Vorotnikov.LVL DEN(EXCIT − E),TBL GRPH	
					Jour SNP 9 179	Aug 69	TRANSLATN.*	
Lvl Density	0.0+0	3.0+1	GEL	Expt	Conf 70Helsinki 1 387	Jun 70	Kolar+.	+
		3.0+1			Data EXFOR20114.013	Jul 72	1PNT.SP.CUT(0).	
Lvl Density	None		MUN	Theo	Jour NP/A 217 269	Dec 73	Dilg+ A,DELTA. BACK SHIFTED FERMIGAS	
Lvl Density	None		COP	Theo	Jour NP/A 222 493	Apr 74	Dossing+COLL ROTAT.SPAC. ACCUR ESTIM	
Lvl Density	None		ROC	Theo	Jour NP/A 223 589	May 74	Huizenga+ EXP CFD MICROSC TH AX SYMM	
Lvl Density	+6		DUB	Theo	Rept JINR − E4 − 9236	Nov 75	Komov+ AVG LVL − SPAC,SEMIMICRO CFD XP	
Lvl Density	Maxwl		KTO	Expt	Jour NP/A 263 141	May 76	Imanishi+PRIMARY J AND SP CUT − OFF F.	
(γ,n)	None		SRL	Expt	Abst ANS 14 807	Oct 71	Ahlfeld+.AL CAPTURE GAMS. SIG GIVEN	
(γ,n)	5.0+6	1.7+7	LRL	Expt	Prog UCID − 16514 6	Jun − 74	Alvarez+	
Photo − Fissn	4.9+6	6.4+6	UI	Expt	Jour PR 77 329	Feb 50	Koch+ FISS COUNTS PER ROENTGN / E(G)	
Photo − Fissn		2.2+7	LAS	Expt	Jour PR 81 342	Feb 51	Mcelhinney+ SIGMA REL TO GF(U238)	
Photo − Fissn	1.2+7	2.0+7	ANL	Expt	Jour PR 95 1009	Aug 54	Huizenga+ 3ES RELATIVE FISS YIELDS	
Photo − Fissn	6.1+6	7.0+6	ANL	Expt	Diss ANL − 5853	Jul 58	Clarke. 2 GAMMA ES,ION CHAMBER.	
Photo − Fissn	6.0+6	2.0+7	CRC	Expt	Jour CJP 37 1418	Dec 59	Baerg+. FRAG ANG DIST ISOTROPIC	
Photo − Fissn	7.0+6		ANL	Expt	Jour NP 34 439	Jun 62	Huizenga+ 6.91+7.12MEV GAMMAS.	
Photo − Fissn		1.6+7	ANL	Expt	Rept TID − 16939	Jul 62	Vandenbosch+ CS134 ISOMER SIG RATIOS	
Photo − Fissn	None		CCP	Expt	Jour ZET 44 1950	Jun 63	FISSN TR FROM(D,PF)AND(GF)JET17 1312	
Photo − Fissn	6.7+6	1.0+7	LAS	Expt	Jour NSE 56 179	Feb 75	Caldwell+ TBL,GRPH NU PROMPT+DELAYED	
Photo − Fissn	1.0+6	2.4+7	RI	Expt	Jour AE 40 72	Jan 76	Kondratko+ REL CD,AG − YLD VS EMAX.TBL	
					Jour SJA 40 83	Jul 76	. ENGL OF AE 40,72.	

92 Uranium 234

Quantity	Energy (ev) Min	Max	Lab	Type	Documentation Ref Vol Page	Date	Author, Comments	Data
Evaluation	5.0+5	1.5+7	LRL	Eval	Rept UCRL − 5351	Nov 58	Howerton. CURVES	
Evaluation	4.1−1	1.0+7	GA	Eval	Rept GA − 2451	Aug 61	Joanou+.68GRP ABS,NF,NU,TRNSF(EL,IN)	
Evaluation	2.5−2	1.0+7	GEN	Eval	Rept APEX − 704	Nov 61	Cooper+. CONTENT OF C − FINE TAPES	
Evaluation	1.0−3	1.0+7	AI	Eval	Rept NAA − SR − M − 8904	Aug 63	Alter+.SAME AS MO +NF NU N2N.RES GAP	
Evaluation	2.5−2	1.1+7	FEI	Eval	Book ABAGJAN	64	26 GROUP CONST,TOT,FISS,NU,CAPT,SCAT	
Evaluation		+2	BNL	Eval	Rept BNL − 982	Aug 66	Pearlstein. TOT,FISS,NG(THR),RIF,RIG	
Evaluation	2.5−2		TRM	Eval	Rept AEET − 257	Aug 66	Singh.NG(BNL 325 SUPPL NO.2)	
Evaluation	5.0+2	3.7+6	TRM	Eval	Rept AEET − 257	Aug 66	Singh.16GROUPS SIN DIN NF NU NG	
Evaluation	1.0+3	1.0+7	ANL	Eval	Jour NSE 26 149	Oct 66	Davey. EVALUATION FISS SIGMA.	
Evaluation	1.0+3	1.4+7	UK	Eval	Rept AHSB(S)R − 124	May 67	Hart.(RLY).UK − DFN 334.UPDATES NSE 26	
	1.0+3	1.5+7			Rept AWRE − O − 37/64	Jul 64	Parker.(ALD).UKNDL − DFN 174	
Evaluation	None		GA	Eval	Rept GA − 8135	Sep 67	Drake + NG,SEL,TOT,RES,SNE,NF,SIN,N2N	
Evaluation	2.5−2	1.0+7	KFK	Eval	Rept KFK − 1186	Jul 70	Hinkelmann.RES,STF,N2N,NF,NU,NG,R.I.	
					Conf 70Helsinki 2 721	Jun 70	− . ALL QUANTITIES.	
Total	2.7+0	7.0+2	ORL	Expt	Jour PR 109 471	Jan 58	Harvey+.FAST CHOP,TRANSM,RESOL.3 − 2EV	+
	2.7+0	7.0+2			Data EXFOR12339.006	Jun 76	. 293 PTS. SIGMA.	
Total	1.0−2	2.0+0	HAR	Expt	Jour JNE 6 181	Apr 58	Mccallum.FC CURVE, 121+ − 8 B AT THR	+
					Rept TNCC(UK) − 13	Mar 57	− .CHOPPER TOF.SINGLE RES.	

92 Uranium 234

Quantity	Energy (ev) Min	Max	Lab	Type	Documentation Ref Vol Page	Date	Author, Comments	Data
Total	2.0−2	4.4−2	ORL	Expt Jour	NSE 8 112	Aug 60	Block+,FC SIG(.0253EV)=110+−4B TABLE	+
	2.5−2			Conf	60Vienna 535	Oct 60	− +.VAL(2200M/SEC) GVN,EXPT DESCR	
	2.0−2	4.4−2		Data	EXFOR12024.007	Jun 76	. 26 PTS. SIGMA.	
Total	5.0+6	1.6+7	LAS	Theo Rept	LA−3538	Sep 66	Agee+ OPTICAL MODEL CALCULATION	
Total	1.0+0	3.5+4	HAR	Expt Jour	NP/A 139 471	Dec 69	James+.TOF.FULL DETAILS TBP LATER.	
				Rept	AERE−R−6039	Jul 69	− EQU TO NP/A 139	
Total	2.5−2		IJI	Eval Conf	73Kiev 1 197	May 73	Fedorova. SIG 2200M/S=112+−7 B	
Total	+0	1.0+6	HAR	Expt Prog	AERE−PR/NP21	Mar 74	James+ORELA.TOF.INT STRUCT.120 RES.	
Total	5.0+2	7.5+2	ORL	Revw Conf	JINR−D−37991	Apr 74	Harvey.P157.SIG(E) PLOTTED	
Total		−3	1.9+0	THS Theo Rept	IKE−6 89 53	Jun 75	Keinert. DATA LIBRARY	
Elastic	Maxwl		HAR	Expt Jour	JNE 6 181	Apr 58	Mccallum. 17.8+−1.4B EST BY RES PAR	+
Elastic	1.0+3	1.5+7	UK	Eval Rept	AWRE−O−37/64	Jul 64	Parker.(ALD).UKNDL−DFN 174	
Elastic	5.0+6	1.6+7	LAS	Theo Rept	LA−3538	Sep 66	Agee+ OPTMDL+H−F FOR COMP	
Diff Elastic	1.0+3	1.5+7	UK	Eval Rept	AWRE−O−37/64	Jul 64	Parker.(ALD).UKNDL−DFN 174	
Diff Elastic	5.0+6	1.6+7	LAS	Theo Rept	LA−3538	Sep 66	Agee+ OPTMDL+H−F FOR COMP	
Diff Elastic	5.0+6	1.6+7	LAS	Theo Rept	LA−3788		67 Beery+.OPTMOD CALC POLARIZ ANG DISTR	
Polarization	5.0+6	1.6+7	LAS	Theo Rept	LA−3788		67 Beery+.OPTMOD CALC COS(THETA) DISTR	
Tot Inelastc	Thrsh	1.5+7	UK	Eval Rept	AWRE−O−37/64	Jul 64	Parker.(ALD).UKNDL−DFN 174	
Tot Inelastc	6.7+4	3.7+6	TRM	Eval Rept	AEET−257	Aug 66	Singh. 9GROUPS CALC FROM AWREO37/64	
Diff Inelast	Thrsh	1.5+7	UK	Eval Rept	AWRE−O−37/64	Jul 64	Parker.(ALD).UKNDL−DFN 174	
Diff Inelast	6.7+4	3.7+6	TRM	Eval Rept	AEET−257	Aug 66	Singh. 9GROUPS J−J+K MATRIX K=0TO9	
Scattering	1.0+3	1.5+7	UK	Eval Rept	AWRE−O−37/64	Jul 64	Parker.(ALD).UKNDL−DFN 174	
Scattering	2.5−2		IJI	Eval Conf	73Kiev 1 197	May 73	Fedorova. SIG 2200M/S=17.8+−1.4 B	
Nonelastic	1.0+3	1.5+7	UK	Eval Rept	AWRE−O−37/64	Jul 64	Parker.(ALD).UKNDL−DFN 174	
Absorption	Maxwl		HAR	Expt Jour	JNE 6 181	Apr 58	Mccallum. 103+−8B FROM SIGT−EST SIGS	+
				Rept	TNCC(UK)−13	Mar 57	MCCALLUM 2200M/S VALUE.	
Absorption	2.5−2	1.0+7	AI		NAA−SR−M−3013	Aug 58	Kistler. 32−GROUP SIGS TABULATED	
Absorption	Maxwl		CRC	Expt Conf	58Geneva 16 83	Sep 58	Craig+ PPR205,2200M/SEC VALUE GIVEN	+
	Maxwl			Data	EXFOR12355.003	Jun 76	. 1 PT. SIGMA.	
Absorption	2.5−2		ORL	Expt Jour	NSE 8 112	Aug 60	Block+,FC 92+−5B SIG(TOT)−SIG(SCT)	+
	2.5−2			Data	EXFOR12024.006	Jun 76	. 1 PT. SIGMA.	
Absorption	2.0−1	1.0+7	B+W	Eval Rept	BAW−158	Jun 61	Roach+ AVERAGED SIG 40 GROUPS	
Absorption	5.0−3	2.5+0	GA	Eval Rept	GA−2113	Jun 61	Wikner+.TABLE+CURVE.100 E POINTS	
Absorption	1.0+3	1.5+7	UK	Eval Rept	AWRE−O−37/64	Jul 64	Parker.(ALD).UKNDL−DFN 174	
Absorption	6.2−1	1.0+7	SRL	Theo Conf	71Knoxvill 714	Mar 71	Mccrosson. SPECTRUM−AVERAGED SIG	
Absorption	1.0−3	2.0+0	JUL	Theo Rept	JUEL−746−RG 49	Apr 71	Bonka.KUGEL−THERMOS−LIBR,T=300K,CURV	
Absorption	2.5−2		IJI	Eval Conf	73Kiev 1 197	May 73	Fedorova. SIG 2200M/S=99.7+−1.3 B	
Absorption	None		MUN	Theo Diss	GRYNTAKIS	Mar 76	Gryntakis.,CALC.OF WESTCOTTS G−FUNCT	
				Jour	RCA 22 128	Mar 75	− +,EQUIVALENT TO THESIS	
Res Int Abs	None		BNL	Expt Abst	BAP 1 187	Apr 56	Pilcher+ TRANS,710B INCLUDING 1/V	
Res Int Abs	5.0−1	1.0+6	ORL	Eval Jour	NSE 6 100	Aug 59	Stoughton+ BEST VALUE 700+−100B	
	3.0−1	+2		Conf	58Geneva 16 64	Sep 58	Halperin+.PPR1072,VAL CFD MANY REFS	
Res Int Abs	4.4−1		ANL	Theo Abst	ANS 6 39	Jun 63	Persiani+RNEGCRESRCONTRIB.INFNITLDIL	
Res Int Abs	5.5−1		BNL	Eval Prog	BNL−982 22	Aug 66	Pearlstein. 700B RECOMMENDED	
Res Int Abs	5.0−1		SGA	Comp Conf	73Paris 1 233	Mar 73	Eder+ REDUCED RES INTEG CAPTURE,TBL	
				Rept	SGAE−PH−141	Feb 73	.SAME AS 73PARIS,NO DETAILS,TBP	
(n,γ)	Pile		ANL	Expt Prog	ANL−4515 15	Oct 50	Ingham.	+
	Pile			Data	EXFOR12351.005	Jun 76	. 1 PT. SIGMA.	
(n,γ)	Maxwl		ORL	Expt Prog	ORNL−CF−51−12	Dec 51	Pomerance.	+
	Maxwl			Data	EXFOR12353.002	Jun 76	. 1 PT. SIGMA.	
(n,γ)	Pile		ORL	Eval Jour	NSE 6 100	Aug 59	Stoughton+,BEST VALUE .025EV=95+−10B	
				Conf	58Geneva 16 64	Sep 58	Halperin+.PPR1072,VAL GVN,MANY REFS	
(n,γ)	1.0+3	1.5+7	UK	Eval Rept	AWRE−O−37/64	Jul 64	Parker.(ALD).UKNDL−DFN 174	
(n,γ)	Maxwl	Pile	BNL	Eval Prog	BNL−982 22	Aug 66	Pearlstein. 94.7B,84.1B, BY RES PAR	
(n,γ)	5.0+2	3.7+6	TRM	Eval Rept	AEET−257	Aug 66	Singh.16GROUPS CALC FROM AWREO37/64	
(n,γ)	2.0+4	+6	GSF	Theo Jour	AF 36 509	Nov 67	Truran+.STAT MODEL. TWO MASS FORMLS	
(n,γ)	Maxwl		AUA	Theo Jour	NSE 31 234	Feb 68	Cook+ STATISTICAL CALC CFD EXPT	
(n,γ)	None		LAS	Expt Rept	WASH−1136 110	Sep 69	Silbert+,PHYSICS−8 SHOT,ANAL TBC	
(n,γ)	2.5−2		CRC	Expt Conf	70Helsinki 1 287	Jun 70	Lounsbury+THR FLUX.CS MULT BY G GVN.	+
	2.5−2			Data	EXFOR10013.010	Sep 72	1PT AT 2200M/S.CS MULT BY G.	
(n,γ)	2.5−2		KFK	Eval Rept	KFK−1186	Jul 70	Hinkelmann. RECOMMENDED 95 B	
(n,γ)	2.5−2	1.0+7	KFK	Eval Rept	KFK−1186	Jul 70	Hinkelmann.5−GROUP SIG,THR+FAST SPEC	
(n,γ)	1.0−2	1.0+7	ORL	Revw Jour	REA 8 473	Sep 70	Kasten. REVIEW,SIG(NEUT−E) GRAPH	
(n,γ)	Maxwl		HAR	Expt Rept	AERE−R−6761	Mar 71	Cabell+ SIG=100.5+−1.3 BY MASS SPEC	+
	Pile			Data	EXFOR20449.	Jan 76	2PTS.SIGMA.	
(n,γ)	Maxwl	Fiss	SGA	Comp Conf	73Paris 1 233	Mar 73	Eder+ DATA FROM EXPTS+EVALS,TABLE	
				Rept	SGAE−PH−141	Feb 73	.SAME AS 73PARIS,NO DETAILS	
Res Int Capt	4.7−1	1.0+7	KFK	Eval Rept	KFK−1186	Jul 70	Hinkelmann. INFIN DILUTION RES INTEG	

92 Uranium 234

Quantity	Energy (ev) Min	Max	Lab	Type	Documentation Ref Vol Page	Date	Author, Comments	Data
Spect (n,γ)	Pile		ANL	Expt	Jour NSE 1 193	Jul 56	Kaufmann+ EBR,ACT RATIO REL U235,TH	
Spect (n,γ)	Maxwl		LAS	Expt	Conf 69Studsvik 431	Aug 69	Jurney. GE+SI SPEC,GRPH+TBL,LVL SCH	
(n,2n)	Thrsh	1.5+7	UK	Eval	Rept AWRE-O-37/64	Jul 64	Parker.(ALD).UKNDL-DFN 174	
(n,2n)	1.3+7	1.5+7	BNL	Theo	Jour NSE 23 238	Nov 65	Pearlstein.3ES.STAT MDL CALC.TBL CS.	
(n,2n)	Fiss		BNL	Theo	Jour NSE 23 238	Nov 65	Pearlstein.STATMDL CALC.SPEC AVG.TBL	
(n,2n)	8.0+5	1.0+7	KFK	Eval	Rept KFK-1186	Jul 70	Hinkelmann.AVG SIG FOR THR+FAST SPEC	
(n,2n)	2.0+6	1.5+7	BRC	Eval	Rept CEA-R-4647	Jan 75	Jary. EVAL,STAT MDL, 15 VALS	
(n,xn) x>2	Thrsh	1.5+7	ALD	Eval	Rept AWRE-O-37/64	Jul 64	Parker.UKAEA DFN-174. N3N.	
(n,xn) x>2	Fiss		BNL	Theo	Jour NSE 23 238	Nov 65	Pearlstein.SPEC AVG STATMDL CALC N3N	
(n,xn) x>2	1.2+7	1.5+7	LRL	Eval	Jour ND/A 11 826	Jul 73	Alley+ (N,3N) CURVE BEST ESTIMATE	
(n,xn) x>2	2.0+6	1.5+7	BRC	Eval	Rept CEA-R-4647	Jan 75	Jary.STAT MDL, 15 VALS	
Fission	Pile		LAS	Expt	Rept LA-1250	May 51	Jurney. FAST REACTOR SPEC AVG SIGMA	
Fission	Spont		LRL	Expt	Rept UCRL-1772	Apr 52	Ghiorso+,FISSION RATE AND HALF-LIFE	
Fission	3.0+5	4.0+6	LAS	Revw	Rept LA-1714	Aug 54	Henkel+,CURVE	
Fission	3.0+5	2.0+6	PTN	Expt	Conf 55Geneva 2 155	Aug 55	Wheeler.P593,CURVE,THEORET DISCUSSN	
Fission	Pile		ANL	Expt	Jour NSE 1 193	Jul 56	Kaufmann+,EBR,CURVS REL U235,CFD TH	
Fission	2.9+5	3.0+6	ORL	Expt	Jour PR 104 1654	Dec 56	Lamphere.CURVE REL U235	+
	Thrsh	4.0+6			Jour PR 100 763	Nov 55	- +,DIPS MAY BE DUE TO RES	
	2.9+5	3.0+6			Data EXFOR12338.004	Jun 76	. 58 PTS. SIGMA.	
Fission	+4	1.5+7	LRL	Eval	Rept UCRL-5351	Nov 58	Howerton.XPTL+ASSUMED,ALSO NN'F,N2NF	
Fission	4.2+0	5.7+0	HAN	Expt	Prog HW-64866 4	Apr 60	Odegaarden.	+
	4.2+0	5.7+0			Data EXFOR12320.002	Jun 76	. 20 PTS. SIGMA.	
Fission	1.4+5	1.0+7	B+W	Eval	Rept BAW-158	Jun 61	Roach+ AVERAGED SIG 14 GROUPS	
Fission	1.0+5	6.0+6	ANL	Revw	Conf 61Vienna 1 29	Aug 61	Smith.P76,CURVE,MANY REFS GVN	
Fission	3.5+5	1.8+6	BET	Expt	Priv BABCOCK	Oct 61	Babcock. SIGMA.	+
	3.5+5	1.8+7			Data EXFOR11294.004	Jun 76	. 15 PTS.	
Fission	5.0+4	4.0+6	ORL	Expt	Jour NP 38 561	Nov 62	Lamphere.FISS SIG + FRAG.ANG.DIST.	+
	1.9+5	4.1+6			Data EXFOR12325.	Jun 76	. 164 PTS. SIGMA.	
Fission	Fiss		AI	Expt	Conf 62Harwell 2 385	Dec 62	Strominger. SIG IN VARIOUS CORES,TBL	
Fission	Spont		ALD	Expt	Jour JNE 19 33	Jan 65	White+ HALFLIFE=2.47+-0.03 10(5)Y.	
Fission	4.0+4	5.0+5	ALD	Expt	Conf 65Salzburg 1 219	Mar 65	White+ 6 ENERGIES.TBL.REL TO U235.	
Fission	2.4+4		ALD	Expt	Jour JNE 19 423	Jun 65	Perkin+.CALIB SB- BE SRCE. 15+-4MB	+
	2.4+4				Data EXFOR20584.003	Jul 76	1PNT.SIGMA.	
Fission	None		BRK	Revw	Jour NP 81 1	Jun 66	Myers+ TABLE2 FISS BARRIER.	
Fission	4.1+4	3.7+6	TRM	Eval	Rept AEET-257	Aug 66	Singh.10GROUPS CALC FROM PR104 1654	
Fission	1.0+3	1.4+7	UK	Eval	Rept AHSB(S)R-124	May 67	Hart.(RLY).UK-DFN 334.UPDATES NSE 26	
	Thrsh	1.5+7			Rept AWRE-O-37/64	Jul 64	Parker.(ALD).UKNDL-DFN 174	
Fission	Pile		WIN	Expt	Rept AEEW-R-526	Jun 67	Stevenson+.FISS RATIO TO U235.ZEBRA	
Fission	1.0+6	1.4+7	ALD	Expt	Jour JNE 21 671	Aug 67	White+ 4ES REL U235. CFD OTHER DATA	+
Fission	1.5+5	8.4+5	WAU	Theo	Jour NP/A 101 460	Sep 67	Vandenbosch. CHANNEL ANALYSIS	
					Conf 66Gatlinbg § 7.3	Sep 66	- .H-F ANAL SIG+ANG DISTR	
Fission	4.1+6	1.0+7	ANL	Eval	Jour NSE 32 35	Apr 68	Davey. RE-EVALUATION OF DATA	
	1.0+3	1.0+7			Jour NSE 26 149	Oct 66	- . EVALUATION	
Fission	2.0+5	8.4+5	ANL	Expt	Jour PR 171 1267	Jul 68	Behkami+ TOT+DIFF SIGS 7NEUT ES CRVS	
					Rept NYO-3938-1	Jun 68	.SUPERSEDED	
					Abst DA/B 28 2569	Dec 67	Behkami+	
					Jour PL/B 24 666	Jun 67	.SUPERSEDED	
Fission	4.0+0	2.0+4	HAR	Expt	Jour NP/A 118 313	Oct 68	James+.LINAC TOF	
		1.5+4			Conf 68JINR 115	Jul 68	RAE.INTERMED.STRUCT.EFFECTS IN FISS.	
	4.0+0	2.0+4			Rept AERE-M-2082	Jun 68	James. EQU TO NP/A 118 313	
	-2	+2		ExTh	Conf 65Salzburg 187	Mar 65	RAE.REVIEW,SOME CALCULATIONS CFD XPT	
Fission	+5	+6	CCP	Theo	Jour YF 9 535	Mar 69	Gejlikman. SIG MAXIMA+QUASISTAT LVLS	
					Jour SNP 9 306	Sep 69	TRANSLATN.*	
Fission	-		KUR	Theo	Jour YF 9 538	Mar 69	Vorotnikov.NEUT-ORB-MOM IN FISS-ANAL	
					Jour SNP 9 308	Sep 69	TRANSLATN.*	
	1.5+5	1.1+6			Jour YF 5 583	Mar 67	Vorotnikov+ GRPH,CHANNEL ANALYSIS	
					Jour SNP 5 415	Sep 67	. ENGL OF YF 5 583	
Fission	-		BER	Theo	Conf 69Vienna 197	Jul 69	Krappe+PPR96. 1+2 FISSN BARRIER TBL	
Fission	Spont		COP	Revw	Conf 69Vienna 155	Jul 69	Strutinsky+PPR203. HL GVN,'SHELL-TH'	
Fission	-		FEI	Theo	Conf 69Vienna 337	Jul 69	Gaj+PPR132. 2HUMPD-BARR-CALC,TBL	
Fission	Spont		HAR	Revw	Conf 69Vienna 249	Jul 69	Lynn.ISOMER.STRUTINSKY TH+EXPTS.TBL	
	None				Rept AERE-R-5891	Sep 68	- .STRUCTURE IN FISS.DISCUSSED.ND	
	None		LAS	Expt	Conf 69Vienna 918	Jul 69	Britt+PPR101.(D,P FISSN)CFD(N,FISSN)	
Fission	1.0+3	1.0+7	TRM	Eval	Rept BARC/I-96	70	Kapil.14 GROUP SIG,2 N-SPECS,TABLES	
Fission	2.2+6		HAR	Expt	Jour NP/A 148 337	Jan 70	Elwyn+ STUDY OF SHORT LIVED ISOMERS.	
					Prog AERE-PR/NP17	Dec 70	- + SPON FISS ISOMS HL 20 NS	
Fission	2.5-2	1.0+7	KFK	Eval	Rept KFK-1186	Jul 70	Hinkelmann.5-GROUP SIG,THR+FAST SPEC	
	2.5-2				Rept KFK-1186	Jul 70	- . RECOMMENDED 0 B	

92 Uranium 234

Quantity	Energy (ev) Min	Max	Lab	Type	Documentation Ref Vol Page	Date	Author, Comments	Data
Fission	7.0+5	2.0+6	ORL	Expt Prog	NCSAC-33 187	Dec 70	Rosler+,LINAC,TO BE COMPLETED,NDG	
Fission	Spont		CRC	Expt Prog	INDC(CAN)-9 3	Jul 71	Lounsbury+ EXPTL HALF-LIFE GIVEN	
Fission	Spont		MRY	Theo Jour	PL/B 38 495	Apr 72	Hooshyar+ TOTAL DELAY HALF LIFE CALC	
				Prog	ORO-4028-28	71	Jackson+. SPON FISSION HALF-LIFE GVN	
Fission	–		GEL	ExTh Jour	NP/A 187 305	Jun 72	Weigmann+ F.B.PARAMS FROM DATA ANAL.	
	0.0+0	1.0+0		Revw Jour	AKE 18 229	Nov 71	Theobald+ SUB-BARRIER FISS EXPTS,TH	
Fission	1.8+5	6.0+6	HAR	Expt Prog	AERE-PR/NP19	Sep 72	James+ TOF CYCLOTRON MEDT ANALYSED	
Fission	None		LAS	Expt Prog	USNDC-3 115	Oct 72	Silbert. NUCL SHOT. NO DATA GIVEN	
Fission	2.5-2		JUL	Theo Jour	ZP 257 389	Dec 72	Mcminn. 1.59 E-2 BARNS	
Fission	Spont		NEU	Theo Jour	HPA 45 567	Dec 72	Hooshyar+ HL GROUNDST AND FISS ISOM.	
Fission	Fiss		SGA	Eval Conf	73Paris 1 233	Mar 73	Eder+ FISS SPEC REL U238(N,F),TBLS	
				Rept	SGAE-PH-141	Feb 73	.SAME AS 73PARIS,NO DETAILS,TBP	
Fission	5.0+5	2.5+6	TUE	Expt Jour	PL/B 48 25	Jan 74	Mueller+ CFD SHAPE ISOM FISS,U235+8U	
Fission	0.0+0	1.5+3	ORL	Revw Conf	JINR-D-37991	Apr 74	Harvey.P157.SUBTHRESH-FIS,F-WID,GRPH	
Fission	3.0+6	5.0+6	LAS	Theo Conf	75Wash. 129	Mar 75	Moore.GRPH R MATR STAT CALC CFD EXP	
Fission	4.0+4	1.8+7	JAE	Revw Conf	IAEA-186 3 1	76	Igarasi. REVW AVAIL DATA,GRPH+BIBLIO	
	4.0+4	1.5+7		Rept	JAERI-M-6315	Nov 75	– +GRPH. 4 DATA SETS COMPARED.	
Fission	Maxwl		MOL	Theo Jour	NP/A 259 423	Mar 76	Wagemans+ CALC FOR DOUBLE HUMP + IH0	
Fission	2.0+5	8.4+5	ORU	Expt Jour	PL/B 61 347	Apr 76	Bouchard+FRAG ANG DISTS.GRAPHS.	
	5.0+5	8.5+5		Prog	RLO-2060-8	Mar 70	Loveland+,TO BE COMPLETED,NO DATA	
Fission	2.7+5	3.7+5	BRC	Revw Conf	76Lowell 641	Jul 76	Michaudon.STRUCTURE EFFECTS.GRPH.	
Res Int Fiss	4.7-1	1.0+7	KFK	Eval Rept	KFK-1186	Jul 70	Hinkelmann. INFIN DILUTION RES INTEG	
Eta	1.0+3	1.5+7	UK	Eval Rept	AWRE-O-37/64	Jul 64	Parker.(ALD).UKNDL-DFN 174	
Nu	–		KUR	Expt Jour	NP 41 92	Feb 63	Apalin+NU	
Nu	Thrsh	1.5+7	UK	Eval Rept	AWRE-O-37/64	Jul 64	Parker.(ALD).UKNDL-DFN 174	
Nu	1.0+6	4.0+6	ALD	Expt Jour	NP 66 149	Apr 65	Mather+ PROMPT SC-T LEAST SQ FIT	+
Nu	4.1+4	3.7+6	TRM	Expt Rept	AEET-257	Aug 66	Singh.10GROUPS CALC FROM AWREO37/64	
Nu	Thrsh	1.5+7	AI	Eval Jour	JNE 22 79	Feb 68	Fillmore.DATA TBL,GRAPH.LEAST SQ FIT	
Nu	Maxwl	1.5+7	HAR	Revw Conf	70Helsinki 2 195	Jun 70	Colvin.PPR99. REPORT ON DATA STATUS	
Nu	4.7+4	8.0+5	KFK	Eval Rept	KFK-1186	Jul 70	Hinkelmann.AVG VALUE OF MEAN NUMBER	
Nu		1.5+7	ANL	Eval Jour	NSE 44 345	Jun 71	Davey. PROMPT NEUTS PER FISSION	
Nu	+0	1.5+7	IAE	Eval Rept	REA 10 637	Dec 72	Manero+ SURVEY,TBLS+GRPHS,RECOMM VAL	
Nu	5.0+6	1.7+7	LRL	Expt Prog	UCID-16514 6	Jun 74	Alvarez+	
Nu	0.0+0	1.5+7	BRC	Eval Rept	CEA-R-4791	Oct 76	Bois+NUBAR VS EN,CALC CFD EXP,TABLES	
Spect Fiss n	Thrsh	1.5+7	UK	Eval Rept	AWRE-O-37/64	Jul 64	Parker.(ALD).UKNDL-DFN 174	
Fiss Prod γ	–		WIN	Theo Jour	JNE 25 513	Oct 71	JAMES MEAN ENGS DEL G-RAYS,BETA RAYS	
Fiss Yield	8.5+5	3.7+6	ORL	Expt Prog	WASH-745	Nov 57	Lamphere. 4AS 0/90DEGYDS NDG ORNL	
Fiss Yield	1.0+5	1.6+6	ANL	Expt Prog	WASH-1028 2	Apr 60	Butler+ NDG	
Fiss Yield	9.1+6	1.5+7	LAS	ExTh Jour	PR/B 137 824	Feb 65	Leachman+ RLTV ANG DIST FISS-FRAG.	
Fiss Yield	Maxwl		FLA	Expt Conf	69Vienna 107	Jul 69	Muga+PPR99. BINARY+TERN+PU FISSN CFD	
				Rept	ORO-2843-10	Dec 66	– +,TERNARY MASS YLD CURVS TBP PR	
Fiss Yield	None		CCP	Revw Jour	IZV 34 438	Feb 70	Soloveva.ALF-EMISSN PROBABILITY,GRPH	
				Jour	BAS 34 378	Jan 71	.ENGL TRANSL OF IZV 34 438	
Fiss Yield	8.2+5	2.3+7	ORL	Expt Prog	ORNL-4513 68	Jun 70	Schmitt+,VDG,FRAG MASS+KE DIST,CURVS	
Fiss Yield	Maxwl		JUL	Theo Rept	JUEL-844-KP	Apr 72	Slavov. DEFORM-E+FRAG MASS YLD CALC	
Fiss Yield	Spont		MRY	Theo Jour	PL/B 38 495	Apr 72	Hooshyar+ SPON AND ISOMERIC YIELDS	
Fiss Yield	1.5+7		LRL	Expt Jour	PR/C 6 1821	Nov 72	Nethaway+. 24 YLDS A=66-161	
Fiss Yield	Pile		GRE	Expt Prog	NEANDC(E)162U	Aug 75	Blachot+ 21 YIELDS	
Fiss Yield	1.5+7		AUA	Theo Rept	AAEC/E-386	Mar 76	Cook+ 3-GAUSS FIT,PARAMS GIVEN	
Fiss Yield	5.0+5	1.4+7	LAS	Eval Rept	LA-6430	Jul 76	Madland+PAIR EFFECT ON INDEP YLD.TBL	
Fiss Yield	Spont		PAH	ExTh Conf	76Lowell 725	Jul 76	Hooshyar+STATMDL APLD TO EXPT.DATA	
				Theo Jour	PL/B 55 144	Feb 75	– + TH VALUES CFD TO EXPTAL	
Fiss Yield	Fiss		GRE	Expt Rept	CEA-N-1979	77	Ferrieu+ ABSTRACT,DATA GIVEN	
Frag Spectra	Spont		CCP	Expt Conf	55Moscow 226	Jul 55	Goldin+.ALFA SPECTRUM.EXPT FROM 1952	
				Rept	AEC-TR-2435	56	. P 167.ENGL TRANSL OF 55MOSCOW 226	
Frag Spectra	6.0+0	2.0+7	CRC	Expt Jour	CJP 37 1418	Dec 59	Baerg+. FRAG ANG DIST ANISOTROPIC	
Frag Spectra	6.0-5	8.5+6	LAS	Expt Jour	PR 120 198	Oct 60	Simmons+ FRAGMENT ANGULAR DIST 18ES	
Frag Spectra	3.0+5	4.0+6	ORL	ExTh Conf	65Salzburg 63	Mar 66	Lamphere.ANISTRPY OF FRGS,TH CFD XPT	
Frag Spectra		2.0+6	CCP	Comp Rept	ICD-3 26	Oct 66	Bolshov+.GRAPHS CFD TH,MANY REFS	
				Rept	INDC-152E	67	. ENGL OF ICD-3 26	
Frag Spectra	Maxwl		FLA	Expt Rept	ORO-2843-10	Dec 66	Muga+ TERNARY FRAG KE DISTR TBP PR	
Frag Spectra	None		MIT	Theo Rept	MIT-905-81	Dec 66	Gordon+,PREDICT RB86+CS136 KE DEFICT	
Frag Spectra	3.0+5	8.4+5	WAU	Theo Jour	NP/A 101 460	Sep 67	Vandenbosch. CHANNEL ANALYSIS	
Frag Spectra	Thrsh	+7	KUR	Theo Jour	YF 7 1228	Jun 68	Vorotnikov. ANGDIST,QUASISTABLE THEO	
	1.5+5	1.1+6		Jour	YF 5 583	Mar 67	– . GRPH,ANG ANISOTROPY	
	Thrsh	+7		Jour	SNP 7 732	Dec 68	. ENGL OF YF 7 1228	
	1.5+5	1.1+6		Jour	SNP 5 415	Sep 67	. ENGL OF YF 5 583	

92 Uranium 234

Quantity	Energy (ev) Min	Max	Lab	Type	Documentation Ref Vol Page	Date	Author, Comments	Data
Frag Spectra	2.0+5	1.2+6	ANL Expt	Jour	PR 171 1267	Jul 68	Behkami+ FRAG ANG DIST 9ES CFD H-F	
				Rept	NYO-3938-1	Jun 68	.SUPERSEDED	
				Abst	DA/B 28 2569	Dec 67	.SUPERSEDED	
				Jour	PL/B 24 666	Jun 67	.SUPERSEDED	
Frag Spectra	1.2+6	3.5+6	TUE Theo	Conf	69Bochum 175	Jul 69	Goennenwein+ ANGDIST VS A,CLUSTER-TH	
Frag Spectra	8.2+5	2.3+7	ORL Expt	Prog	ORNL-4513 68	Jun 70	Schmitt+,VDG,FRAG MASS+KE DIST,CURVS	
Frag Spectra	Spont		MRY Theo	Jour	PL/B 38 495	Apr 72	Hooshyar+ KINETIC-E FN OF HEAVY MASS	
Frag Spectra	Spont		PAH Theo	Jour	PL/B 55 144	Feb 75	Hooshyar+ TH VALUES CFD TO EXPTAL	
Frag Charge	1.8+6	1.5+7	LRL Comp	Rept	UCRL-51640	Jul 74	Nethaway. TBL.	
Reson Params		2.1+2	BNL Expt	Abst	BAP 1 187	Apr 56	Pilcher+ TRANS,WN+D,ASSUMED WG	
Reson Params	1.0+0		BNL Revw	Jour	PHY 22 994	Nov 56	Hughes.LVL SPACING DIST,+TH+U236,238	
Reson Params	5.2+0	3.7+2	ORL Expt	Jour	PR 109 471	Jan 58	Harvey+.WN FROM DIP AREA.ASSUMED WG.	+
	5.2+0	3.7+2		Data	EXFOR12339.	Jun 76	. 20 RES. WN, WN0, WG.	
Reson Params	-.2+1	5.2+0	HAR Expt	Jour	JNE 6 181	Apr 58	Mccallum. - 2EV RES WN,5.2EV RES WT WN	+
Reson Params	5.2+0		HAN Expt	Rept	HW-64866 4	Apr 60	Odegaarden. WF	+
	5.2+0			Data	EXFOR12320.	Jun 76	. 1 RES. E0, WF, FISS-PCS.	
Reson Params	-.1+1		GA Expt	Abst	ANS 4 271	Nov 61	Cooper+	+
	-.1+1			Data	EXFOR12285.003	Jun 76	. 1 RES. WN0,WG	
Reson Params		1.0+6	AUA Theo	Jour	AUJ 20 477	Oct 67	Cook. TBL OF AVG LVL SPACING D,L=0,1	
Reson Params	+5	+6	KUR Theo	Jour	YF 7 1228	Jun 68	Vorotnikov+ GRPHS D,WF.QUASISTABL TH	
	4.5+6	7.0+6		ExTh Jour	YF 5 728	May 67	- . GRAPH N+GAMMA FISSWIDTH	
	1.5+5	1.1+6	Theo	Jour	YF 5 583	Mar 67	- . GRPH,CHANNEL ANALYSIS	
	+5	+6		Jour	SNP 7 732	Dec 68	. ENGL OF YF 7 1228	
	4.0+6	7.0+6		Jour	SNP 5 728	Nov 67	. ENGL OF YF 5 728	
	1.5+5	1.1+6		Jour	SNP 5 415	Sep 67	. ENGL OF YF 5 583	
Reson Params	Spont		HAR Revw	Conf	69Vienna 249	Jul 69	Lynn.FISS ISOMER.TBL STRUTINSKY PARS	
Reson Params	+2	+6	FEI Theo	Jour	YF 10 542	Sep 69	Gai+ TABLE OF RESON+FAST FISSN WIDTH	
	None			Rept	FEI-158	Feb 69	GAJ+ FISSN WIDTH,2HUMPED-BARR-CALCUL	
	+2	+6		Jour	SNP 10 311	Mar 70	. ENGL OF YF 10 542	
Reson Params	5.2+0		DUB Expt	Rept	JINR-P3-4992	Apr 70	Rjabov+ TOT+N+G-WID FOR 5.19EV GIVEN	+
				Prog	YFI-11 27	70	- + ABST,SAME TBL AS JINR-4992	
				Prog	INDC(CCP)-31	Dec 72	.PAGE 26,ENGLISH OF YFI-11 27	
	5.2+0			Data	EXFOR40070.	Aug 70	TOT-WIDTH,N-WIDTH,GAM-WIDTH,5.19EV	
Reson Params	1.0+3	4.6+4	KFK Eval	Rept	KFK-1186	Jul 70	Hinkelmann. AVG.WG,WF,WN,LVL SPACING	
Reson Params	None		DUB Theo	Jour	YF 13 240	Feb 71	Malecki+G-WID,THEO CFD EXPT.TBL,GRPH	
				Jour	SNP 13 133	Aug 71	- + ENGL OF YF 13 240.	
Reson Params	6.2-1	5.0+4	SRL Theo	Conf	71Knoxvill 714	Mar 71	Mccrosson. STAT CALCULATN AVG PARAMS	
Reson Params	5.2+0	8.2+2	HAR Expt	Jour	NP/A 139 471	Dec 69	James+.WN,SIG.WF(TO722EV),WF(TO687EV	+
	6.9+2			ExTh Jour	NP/A 170 309	Jul 71	- . DISTRIB FREE STAT ANAL WN WF	
	5.2+0	1.4+4		Rept	AERE-R-6633	71	- . DISTRIB-FREE STRUCT ANALYSIS.	
	5.0+0	1.1+3	Expt	Prog	AERE-PR/NP17	Dec 70	- + WF DIST MEDT RES 638EV GRPH	
		1.2+3		Conf	70Helsinki 1 267	Jun 70	- .107. FISSN WIDTH(E) GRAPH	
	5.2+0	8.2+2		Rept	AERE-R-6039	Jul 69	- + EQU TO NP/A 139 471	
	5.2+0	1.4+4		Jour	NP/A 118 313	Oct 68	- +.WF.FISS AREAS ONLY 367 EV UP	
				Rept	AERE-M-2082	Jun 68	- + EQU TO NP/A 118 313	
	1.0+0	3.5+4		Data	EXFOR20467.	Jan 76	159PTS.E0,WF,SIG*WF,WN,MEANLVLSP0.	
Reson Params	+0		KUR Theo	Jour	AE 31 18	Jul 71	Vorotnikov. S+P,FISS-WIDTHS DERIVED	
				Jour	SJA 31 706	Feb 72	. ENGL OF AE 31 18	
Reson Params	+0	+3	BOR Theo	Jour	JPRC 33 13	Aug 72	Doan+ TBL 7 VALS GVN	
Reson Params	2.0+0	1.4+4	CCP Theo	Rept	YK-16 121	74	Gorbachev+ G+F+N+TOT-WIDTHS, TBL	
Reson Params	2.5-2		COL Expt	Conf	75Wash. 335	Mar 75	Felvinci+MOD ERICSON CALC CFD EXPT.	
Reson Params	5.2+0		HAN Expt	Abst	BAP 6 8	Feb 61	Leonard+	+
	5.2+0			Data	EXFOR12286.005	Jun 76	. 1 RES, FISS-PCS.	
Reson Params		1.5+3	BRC Revw	Conf	76Lowell 641	Jul 76	Michaudon.EN-DEP OF WID.EX-TH COMP.	
Reson Params		1.5+3	HAR Expt	Prog	NEANDC(E)172 8	Aug 76	James+ FISSION WIDTHS,GRPH.	
				Prog	AERE-PR/NP23	Mar 76	- +FISSION WIDTH STAT ANALYSIS.	
Strnth Fnctn		2.1+2	BNL Expt	Abst	BAP 1 187	Apr 56	Pilcher+ TRANS,STF=1.2	
Strnth Fnctn		1.6+2	BNL Expt	Jour	PR 109 471	58	Harvey+	+
		1.6+2		Data	EXFOR12339.	Jun 76	. 2 PTS. STF. D	
Strnth Fnctn	+3		BNL Expt	Jour	PRL 1 461	Dec 58	Hughes. FC 1.2+-0.3	
Strnth Fnctn	None		DKE Theo	Jour	NP 24 169	Apr 61	Seth. J-DEPENDENCE OF S-WAVE STRFUNC	
Strnth Fnctn	2.6+6	4.1+6	AI Theo	Rept	NAA-SR-M-12538	Oct 67	Gigas.OPTMDL CALC AVG SO,S1,S2	
Strnth Fnctn	5.2+0	2.1+2	HAR Expt	Jour	NP/A 139 471	Dec 69	James+. S-WAVE=1.09+-.36 E-4	+
				Rept	AERE-R-6039	Jul 69	- + EQU TO NP/A 139 471	
	1.0+0	3.5+4		Data	EXFOR20467.006	Jan 76	1PNT.L=0.	
Strnth Fnctn	1.0+3	4.6+4	KFK Eval	Rept	KFK-1186	Jul 70	Hinkelmann. SO=1.2 SI=2.	
Strnth Fnctn	None		AUA Eval	Rept	AAEC/E-277	Mar 73	Musgrove.TBLS EXPTL DATA+BEST VALUES	
Strnth Fnctn	1.0+0	1.5+3	HAR Expt	Prog	AERE-PR/NP21	Mar 74	James+ ORELA.TOF.S-WAVE VALUE GIVEN.	

92 Uranium 234

Quantity	Energy (ev) Min	Max	Lab	Type	Documentation Ref Vol Page	Author, Comments Date	Data
Lvl Density	–		COP Theo	Jour	NP 6 62	Mar 58 Ericson. LVL DENSITY FORM CFD EXP	
Lvl Density	+6		MIL Theo	Jour	EN 15 1 54	Jan 68 Facchini+ LDL PARS FROM LOW EN RES	
Lvl Density		2.0+2	KUR Theo	Jour	YF 9 303	Feb 69 Vorotnikov.LVL DEN(EXCIT–E),TBL GRPH	
				Jour	SNP 9 179	Aug 69 TRANSLATN.*	
Lvl Density	None		MUN Theo	Jour	NP/A 217 269	Dec 73 Dilg+ A,DELTA. BACK SHIFTED FERMIGAS	
Lvl Density	+2	1.4+6	HAR Expt	Prog	AERE–PR/NP21	Mar 74 James+ORELA.LEVEL SPACING.CLASSI+II.	
Lvl Density	None		ROC Theo	Jour	NP/A 223 589	May 74 Huizenga+ EXP CFD MICROSC TH AX SYMM	
Lvl Density	Maxwl		COL Theo	Conf	75Wash. 335	Mar 75 Felvinci+MOD ERICSON CALC CFD EXPT.	
Lvl Density	+6		DUB Theo	Rept	JINR–E4–9236	Nov 75 Komov+ AVG LVL–SPAC,SEMIMICRO CFD XP	
(γ,n)	5.0+6	1.7+7	LRL Expt	Prog	UCID–16514 6	Jun 74 Alvarez+	
Photo–Fissn	1.2+7	2.0+7	ANL Expt	Jour	PR 95 1009	Aug 54 Huizenga+ 3ES RELATIVE FISS YIELDS	
Photo–Fissn	6.1+6	7.0+6	ANL Expt	Diss	ANL–5853	Jul 58 Clarke.2 GAMMA ES IONIZATION CHAMBER	
Photo–Fissn	6.0+6	2.0+7	CRC Expt	Jour	CJP 37 1418	Dec 59 Baerg+. FRAG ANG DIST ANISOTROPIC	
Photo–Fissn	7.0+6		ANL Expt	Jour	NP 34 439	Jun 62 Huizenga+ 6.91+7.12MEV GAMMAS.	
Photo–Fissn	None		AI Eval	Jour	NSE 56 37	Jan 75 Tuttle.TBL RVW MEAS.REC VAL DELAY N	
Photo–Fissn	6.7+6	9.5+6	LAS Expt	Jour	NSE 56 179	Feb 75 Caldwell+ TBL,GRPH NU PROMPT+DELAYED	

92 Uranium 235

Quantity	Energy (ev) Min	Max	Lab	Type	Documentation Ref Vol Page	Author, Comments Date	Data
Evaluation	6.0-2	1.0+7	LAS Eval	Jour	NSE 4 166	Aug 58 Kiehn.TOT,FISS,NG,NU,TRANSF.10GROUPS	
Evaluation	2.5-2	1.4+7	PCT Eval	Rept	NP–8216	Oct 58 Lamarsh+ ALL DATA	
Evaluation	5.0+5	1.5+7	LRL Eval	Rept	UCRL–5351	Nov 58 Howerton. CURVES.	
Evaluation	5.0+2	1.0+7	ANL Eval	Book	FRC	60 Yftah+.16E GROUPS.FAST REACT DATA	
Evaluation	1.0-3	1.0+7	GA Eval	Rept	GA–2151	Jul 61 Goodjohn+.TOT SEL SCT SIN NF ETA ALF	
				Rept	GA–2113	Jun 61 .SUPERSEDED.	
Evaluation	4.1-1	1.0+7	GA Eval	Rept	GA–2451	Aug 61 Joanou+.68GRP ABS,NF,NU,TRNSF(EL,IN)	
Evaluation	2.5-2	1.0+7	GEN Eval	Rept	APEX–704	Nov 61 Cooper+. CONTENT OF C–FINE TAPES	
Evaluation	1.0-3	1.0+7	AI Eval	Rept	NAA–SR–M–8904	Aug 63 Alter+.SAME AS MO +NF NU N2N.RES GAP	
	1.0+4	1.4+7		Rept	NAA–SR–TDR6545	Jun 61 – .TABLES.TOT,SEL,SIN.MTCARLO DEL	
	1.0+0	1.0+7		Rept	NAA–SR–TDR5861	Nov 60 – .TABULATED TOT,SEL,SIN.MTCARLO	
Evaluation	1.0-3	1.5+7	ALD Eval	Rept	AWRE–O–82/63	Dec 63 Parker.BEST XPT,TH DATA MARCH1962	
Evaluation	2.5-2	1.1+7	FEI Eval	Book	ABAGJAN	64 26 GROUP CONST,TOT,FISS,NU,CAPT,SCAT	
Evaluation	1.0-3	1.5+7	GA Eval	Rept	GA–5944	Dec 64 Joanou+.TOT SEL DEL SNE SIN DIN N2N	
Evaluation	3.7-2	1.8+7	UNC Eval	Rept	UNC–5099	Dec 64 Bertin+	
Evaluation	2.5-2		BNL Eval	Rept	BNL–918	Mar 65 Sher+. SIGS,FISSN DATA LEAST SQ ANAL	
				Rept	BNL–722	Jun 62 – + TOT ABS NF NU ETA ALF	
Evaluation	4.5-1	1.0+4	INA Eval	Conf	66Paris 2 333	Oct 66 Hennies.PPR5.RES INT CAPT+FISS,ALPHA	
				Rept	NAA–SR–11980 5	May 67 – . RECOMMENDED DATA.REVISED.	
Evaluation	1.0+3	1.4+7	UK Eval	Rept	AHSB(S)R–124	May 67 Hart.(RLY).UK–DFN 335.UPDATES NSE 26	
	1.0-4	9.0+3		Rept	AEEW–M–502	May 65 Freemantle.TOT SEL SNE NF NG RIF RIA	
				Rept	AEEW–R–351	Feb 64 Barrington+(WIN).UKNDL LOW EN REVISN	
Evaluation	–		CCP Eval	Jour	AE 23 6	Jul 67 Kirpitchnikov.RESON PARAMS,MANY REFS	
				Jour	SJA 23 669	Jul 67 TRANSLATN.*	
Evaluation	1.0+4	1.0+7	HEB Eval	Conf	67Karlsrhe 1 255	Nov 67 Rakavy+,FISSION,CAPTURE ETC,LEAST–SQ	
	6.1+6	1.4+7		Conf	66Paris 2 309	Oct 66 Pazy+ (N,F),ELAS,INEL,(N,G),NU.	
Evaluation	1.0-3	1.0+7	KFK Eval	Rept	KFK–750	Jan 68 Schmidt.TOT,SEL,SIN,DEL,NG,NP,NF ETC	
	1.0-2	1.0+7		Rept	KFK–120 1	Feb 66 – . SIG TOT,ELAS,DIFF ELAS(MU),	
				Rept	KFK–120 2	Dec 62 – .GRAPHS+TBLS,SIG TOT,ELASTIC,	
Evaluation	Fast		KFK Eval	Rept	KFK–770	Apr 68 Huschke+ 26 EGROUPS FAST REACT SPEC	
Evaluation	1.0+3	1.4+7	LAS Eval	Rept	LA–3527	Aug 68 Hunter+ TOT NG NF SIN SEL N2N N3N NU	
Evaluation		2.0+7	TRM Eval	Conf	69Roorke 2 106	Dec 69 Garg+INDIAN EVALUATN ACTIVITIES, NDG	
Evaluation	1.5+5	1.5+7	AI Eval	Rept	AI–AEC–12916	Jan 70 Alter+,RE–EVAL OF DATA FOR ENDF/B	
Evaluation	Fiss		SAC Eval	Prog	EANDC(E)127U	Apr 70 RIBON	
Evaluation	1.0+1	1.0+7	CAD Eval	Conf	70Helsinki 2 465	Jun 70 Barre+ PPR73.MICRO VS INTEGRAL DATA	
	1.0+3	1.0+7		Rept	EANDC(E)120L	Mar 69 – +RAVIER EVAL OF INTEGRAL MEAS	
Evaluation	None		LAS Eval	Prog	USNDC–9 120	Dec 73 Stewart+N FILE EVAL FOR ENDF4.	
Evaluation	1.0+2	2.0+7	HAR Eval	Jour	ANE 1 409	Jul 74 Sowerby+ LINKED EVAL U238,PU239.	
				Conf	70Helsinki 2 703	Jun 70 – +34. SIMULTAN F+GAM EVALUATN	
Evaluation	1.0+2	1.0+5	IFB Eval	Rept	YK–20/1 126	75 Ancipov+ TOT,(N,F),RES–PARS,STF,TBL	
	Thrsh	1.5+7		Rept	YK–20/1 164	75 – + DIN,LDL DEN LAW,TBL,GRAPHS	
	1.0-4	1.5+7		Rept	YK–20/2 3	75 – + G–SPEC,ALF,NUBAR,N2N,N3N	
Evaluation	Maxwl		IAE Eval	Conf	75Wash. 286	Mar 75 Lemmel. 3RD IAEA–EVAL BY LSQ FIT	
				Jour	REA 7 4 3	Dec 69 Hanna+ SUPERSEDED	
Evaluation	2.5-2	1.0+0	BNW Eval	Rept	EPRI–NP–167	Feb 76 Leonard+NF,NG,TOT,ALF,ETA,ABS.ENDF B	
Total	4.0+4	2.0+7	LAS Expt	Rept	LA–1493	Nov 52 Henkel. TRANS GAP75KEV–17MEV CURVE	+
	4.1+4	2.1+7		Data	EXFOR12396.	Jun 76 . 71 PTS.	

92 Uranium 235

Quantity	Energy (ev) Min	Max	Lab	Type	Documentation Ref Vol Page	Author, Comments Date	Data
Total	1.2−3	4.3−3	BNL	Expt Rept	BNL−222	Feb 53 Palevsky+	+
	1.2−3	4.5−3		Data	EXFOR12389.002	Jun 76 . 76 PTS.	
Total	2.5−2		COL	Expt Rept	CU− 115	Feb 53 Melkonian+	+
	2.5−2			Data	EXFOR12426.002	Jun 76 . 1 PT.	
Total	6.5+2	1.5+5	ANL	Expt Prog	ANL−5175 7	Feb 54 Hibdon+	+
	6.6+2	1.6+5		Data	EXFOR11002.005	Jun 76 . 134 PTS.	
Total	2.5−2		BNL	Expt Jour	PR 94 1088	May 54 Palevsky.	+
	2.5−2			Data	EXFOR12410.003	Jun 76 . 1 PT.	
Total	1.7−3	1.6−1	BNL	Expt Priv	PALEVSKY	Jun 55 Palevsky. PC TO NNCSC	+
	1.7−3	1.6−1		Data	EXFOR12423.002	Jun 76 . 55 PTS.	
Total	1.2−2	1.5+0	KUR	Expt Conf	55Moscow 15	Jul 55 Gerasimov+ EARLY RUSSIAN EXPT,CURVE	
				Rept	AEC−TR−2435 1	56 . ENGL TRANSL OF 55MOSCOW 15	
Total	2.0−2	1.0+5	BNL	Revw Conf	55Geneva 4 199	Aug 55 Sailor.GRAPH,SUM OF SEV EXPTS,PPR586	
Total	1.0−3	1.0+0	BNL	Revw Conf	55Geneva 4 3	Aug 55 Hughes.P576,CURVE,MANY REFERENCES	
Total	4.0+0	1.0+5	CCP	Expt Conf	55Geneva 4 22	Aug 55 Vladimirski+.CURVE,CHOPPER,TOF,P641	
Total	1.0−2	1.0+2	CCP	Expt Conf	55Geneva 4 224	Aug 55 Nikitin+.GRAPH,CYCLOTRON,TRANSM,P646	+
Total	1.0−2	8.6+1	ITE	Expt Conf	55Geneva 4 224	Aug 55 Nikitin+.TOF 10MUSEC RSLN, CURVE	+
Total	1.0−2	1.7+0	CCP	Rept	AEC−TR−2435PT1	56 .USSR CURVE PAGE 9	
Total	1.8+1	9.9+1	MTR	Expt Jour	PR 103 971	Aug 56 Simpson+	+
	9.0+0	9.9+1		Rept	IDO−16268	Nov 55 − + FAST CHOPPER 4 NEW RESON	
	9.1+0	9.9+1		Data	EXFOR12412.004	Jun 76 . 581 PTS.	
Total	1.5+0	6.0+1	BNL	Expt Jour	PR 103 1342	Sep 56 Pilcher+,TRNS+FC CURVS AREA METHOD	+
	4.5+0	3.6+1		Data	EXFOR12413.006	Jun 76 . 221 PTS.	
Total	Maxwl	5.0+0	BNL	Revw Rept	AERE−NP/R−2076	Jan 57 Sailor.FIG1D1 SAME AS BNL325Q	
Total	3.4+0	4.0+2	CCP	Expt Jour	AE 2 129	Feb 57 Sokolovsky+.FAST CHOP,TRANSMIS CURVE	+
				Jour	JNE 5 389	Nov 57 TRANSLATN.*	
				Jour	SJA 2 147	57 TRANSLATN.*	
Total	2.1+2	7.9+3	KAP	Expt Prog	KAPL−1770 65	Apr 57 Yeater+ TRANSMISSION, TOF	+
	2.1+2	7.9+3		Data	EXFOR11681.004	Jun 76 . 194 PTS. SIGMA.	
Total	5.8+2	6.1+7	KAP	Eval Rept	KAPL−1756 1	Jun 57 Baraff.TBL D25LETHARGYSTEPS	
Total	0.0+0	2.0+0	CRC	Theo Jour	PR 112 203	58 Vogt.MULTILEVEL TH CFD EXPTL DATA	
Total	1.0−1	4.0+4	COL	Expt Jour	NSE 3 435	Apr 58 Melkonian+,TOF,CURVE GIVEN	+
				Rept	CU− 163	Jun 57 .SUPERSEDED	
	1.2−2	4.8+4		Data	EXFOR12403.002	Jun 76 . 223 PTS.	
Total	2.5−3	1.0−2	HAN	Expt Prog	HW− 55879 3	Apr 58 Seppi+ REL .1EV, TABLE	+
	2.5−3	1.0−1		Data	EXFOR11791.004	Jun 76 . 11 PTS.	
Total	7.0+6	1.4+7	LRL	Expt Jour	PR 110 927	May 58 Bratenahl+	+
	7.1+6	1.4+7		Conf	58Geneva 14 109	Sep 58 − +	
	7.1+6	1.4+7		Data	EXFOR11155.034	Jun 76 . 5 PTS.	
Total	2.5−2	3.4+1	CUW	Expt Jour	NSE 4 155	Jul 58 Kavanagh.BREIT−WIGNER ANALYSIS	
Total	2.0−3	2.0+3	HAR	Theo Jour	JNE 7 35	Aug 58 EGELSTAFF CORRELATION ANAL,W+SPACING	+
	5.7−3	6.0−1		Expt Conf	55Geneva 4 214	Aug 55 Egelstaff. PPR 423	
				Jour	JNE 1 92	Aug 54 − . EXPT 1951. NAT+ENRICHED	
Total	1.0+0	1.0+4	BNL	Comp Conf	58Geneva 16 8	Sep 58 Hughes.PPR2483,CURVE,MANY REFS	
Total	2.5−2	1.0+2	CCP	Expt Conf	58Geneva 15 309	Sep 58 Vladimirsky+.PPR2221,NDG,BF3−DETECTR	
Total	1.0−1	1.0+1	BNL	Expt Jour	PR 112 191	Oct 58 Shore.CS,TRNS,ABSCRVS,MULTILVL ANAL	+
				Conf	58Geneva 15 118	Sep 58 .SUPERSEDED	
	8.8−2	6.9+0		Data	EXFOR12418.003	Jun 76 .370 PTS.	
Total	8.2−4	8.2−2	COL	Expt Jour	NSE 6 433	Nov 59 Safford+,METALLIC FOIL AND D2O SOLTN	+
	8.2−4	8.2−2		Data	EXFOR12404.	Jun 76 . 31 PTS.	
Total	2.5−2		COL	Revw Jour	NUC 17 11 134	Nov 59 Safford+. EXPTL VALUES TABULATED	
Total	2.0−2	8.0−2	MTR	Expt Jour	NSE 7 187	Feb 60 Simpson+,FC TRNS 690+ −10B AT.0253EV	+
	2.1−2	8.0−2		Data	EXFOR12329.002	Jun 76 . 115 PTS.	
Total	1.7+7	2.9+7	LRL	Expt Jour	PR 120 521	Oct 60 Peterson+	
				Conf	58Geneva 14 109	Sep 58 Bratenahl+	
Total	1.8−2	1.6−1	ORL	Expt Jour	NSE 8 112	Aug 60 Block+,FC SIG(.0253EV)=693+ −5B TABLE	+
	2.5−2			Conf	60Vienna 535	Oct 60 − +	
	1.8−1	1.6−1		Data	EXFOR12024.008	Jun 76 . 48 PTS.	
Total	4.6−3	5.6−1	ANL	Expt Jour	NSE 11 312	61 Saplakoglu+	+
	4.6−3	5.6−1		Data	EXFOR12406.	Jun 76 . 31 PTS.	
Total	1.9+6	8.0+6	CCP	Expt Book	NEJTRONFIZ 258	61 Averchenkov.TOF,PO−BE SOURCE, GRAPH	+
				Book	SPN 191	61 . ENGL TRANSL OF NEJTRONFIZ 258	
Total	Maxwl		HAN	Eval Conf	61RPI 3	May 61 Leonard.	
Total	2.0−1	1.0+7	B+W	Eval Rept	BAW−158	Jun 61 Roach+ AVERAGED SIG 40 GROUPS	
Total	4.0+0	4.0−1	TUR	Expt Jour	NSE 11 312	Nov 61 Saplakoglu.CURVE 694+ −1.5B AT.0253EV	+
Total	5.0−3	1.0−1	BNL	Revw Rept	BNL−722	Jun 62 Sher+ REVIEW CURVE GIVEN	
Total	+3	+5	DKE	Expt Prog	EANDC(US)−28 2	Sep 62 Newson+ NDG. TBD GET STF.	

92 Uranium 235

Quantity	Energy (ev) Min	Max	Lab	Type	Documentation Ref Vol Page	Date	Author, Comments	Data
Total	2.3−2	2.2+0	KUR	Expt	Jour AE 13 368	Oct 62	Gerasimov+ .TOF,MULTSCATT CORRECTN	+
					Jour SJA 13 977	Oct 62	. ENGL OF AE 13 368	
Total	2.0−2	8.0+1	ITE	Expt	Jour AE 16 110	Feb 64	Ignat'Ev+. SIGTOT+ETA EXPT, NDG	
					Rept ITE−147	63	.SIMILAR TO AE 16 110 2/64	
					Jour JNE 18 719	64	.ENGLISH TRANSL OF AE 16 110 2/64	
					Jour SJA 16 121	64	.ENGLISH TRANSL OF AE 16 110 2/64	
					Jour EAF 16 2 19	64	. FRENCH TRANSL OF AE 16 110 2/64	
					Rept INDSWG−7E	63	.ENGLISH TRANSL OF ITE−147 /63	
Total	1.3+0	2.0+4	SAC	Expt	Jour NP 69 545	Jul 65	Michaudon+ ANALYSIS+RESON PARAM	+
	7.3+2	1.0+4		Priv	DERRIEN	Sep 66	Derrien+ DATA FOR COMPILATION.	
	1.3+0	2.0+4		Diss	CEA−R−2552	May 64	Michaudon+,COMPLETE RPT,EXPT+TH,TBLS	
	7.2+2	1.0+4		Data	EXFOR20728.002	Feb 78	3982PTS.	
Total	1.0−2	1.0+6	RLY	Revw	Conf 64Vienna 56	Dec 64	Kronberger. GRPH SIG(E),+PU ISOTOPES	
Total	2.0+0	3.0+4	DUB	Expt	Conf 65Salzburg 1 287	Mar 65	VAN SHI−DI+,TOF,PULSED REACTOR,NDG	
					Rept BNL−TR−16	Jul 65	Van Shi Di+ ENGL OF 65SALZ.	
Total	1.0−4	9.0+3	UK	Eval	Rept AEEW−M−502	May 65	Freemantle.TABLE.CURVE1 TO 100EV	+
	5.0−3	5.0+0			Rept AEEW−R−351	Feb 64	Barrington+(WIN).UKNDL LOW EN REVISN	
	1.0+3	1.5+7			Rept AWRE−O−82/63	Dec 63	Parker.(ALD).UKNDL−DFN 155	
	1.0−4	1.5+7			Data UKNDL−DFN 159B	Mar 73	2065 PNTS	
Total	1.7+1	3.6+2	COL	Expt	Prog EANDC−50 95	Jul 65	Havens.SHORT NOTE (TBL 114 RES−ES)	+
					Conf 65Antwerp 95	Jul 65	Rainwater+	
	1.7+1	3.5+2			Data EXFOR11516.003	Jun 76	. 5825 PTS.	
Total	2.8+1	5.7+1	WAL	Eval	Rept WANL−TME−1228	Aug 65	Gibson+. ONLY 5.7−9.3 24−27 8EV SHWN	
Total	2.0+3	1.0+8	HAR	Expt	Prog AERE−PR/NP9 35	Oct 65	Langsford+TOF.CYCLTR.GRPH CFD EVALS	+
Total	3.0+5	1.5+6	ANL	Expt	Rept ANL−7110 15	Dec 65	Whalen+BRIEF DESCR,RSLN1−10KEV,GRAPH	+
					Jour NIM 39 185	Jan 66	− + EXP. DETAILS, NDG	
	8.1+5	1.5+6			Data EXFOR12368.002	Jun 76	. 69 PTS.	
Total	3.5−2	2.0+2	HAR	Expt	Rept AERE−M−1670	Feb 66	Brooks+ LINAC,TOF, CURVES,CFD OTHERS	+
					Conf 66S.Diego 2 193	Feb 66	− . SEE ALSO	
					Rept BNL−325	Feb 65	− . SEE FOR CURVES.	
					Rept EANDC(UK)−42	Jun 64	− .GRPH.TBL 2 MODIFD(AMENDMNT 1)	
	1.0+3	1.0+7	KFK	Eval	Rept KFK−120 1	Feb 66	Schmidt.AVERAGE CS TO21KEV+CURVE	
	1.0−2	1.0+7			Rept KFK−120 2	Dec 66	.GRAPHS AND TABULATED DATA.	
Total	1.0−2	1.0+0	MTR	Eval	Conf 66Wash. 840	Mar 66	Moore+,MULTILEVEL ANAL CURVE CFD XPT	
Total	1.0+6	1.6+7	LAS	Theo	Rept LA−3538	Sep 66	Agee+ OPTICAL MODEL CALCULATION	
Total	1.0+2	1.0+7	HAR	Expt	Conf 66Paris 1 165	Oct 66	Uttley+ PPR36.TOF.PULSED BOOSTER.NDG	+
					Prog AERE−PR/NP9	Apr 66	− +DATA CFD LANGSFORD	
	1.0+2	7.0+4			Rept AERE−M−1272	Dec 63	− .AVR TRNS TH OF POT,STF,ALPHA	
Total		6.3+1	WAL	Eval	Rept WANL−TME−1586	Mar 67	Gibson+MULTIGROUP LIBRARY+CURVE	
Total	1.0+6	1.0+7	TRM	Theo	Conf 67Karlsrhe 1 95	Nov 67	Garg+ OPTMOD CALC,CFD EXPT,TBL+GRPH	
	None				Prog BARC−418 1	69	− .TEMP DEPENDENT SIG CALC.NDG	
	1.0+6	1.0+7			Rept BARC−305 16	Oct 67	SEE ALSO *	
Total	7.5−2	2.0+2	BNL	Expt	Jour PR 167 1121	Mar 68	Schermer+ POL NEUT+NUCL J DISCUSSED	
Total	4.6−1	2.1+3	LRL	Expt	Jour NSE 35 350	Mar 69	Bramblett+ LINAC FISS CHAMBR AVG SIG	+
	4.3−1	2.1+3			Data EXFOR10134.003	Jun 72	0PTS.	
Total	2.0+3		MTR	Expt	Prog NCSAC−31 75	May 70	Smith+,ANAL TO BE COMPLETED,NO DATA	
Total	6.2+1	3.0+2	WAL	Eval	Rept WANL−TME−2705	May 70	Drawbaugh+,BREIT−WIGNER FIT,CURVES	
Total	1.0+1	1.0+2	GEL	Expt	Conf 70Helsinki 1 449	Jun 70	Poortmans+PPR70.LINAC TOF HE3 COUNTR	+
					Conf 69Vienna 911	Jul 69	− + SUPERSEDED.	
		0.0+0			Data EXFOR20145.003	Mar 73	. 0PTS. SEE RESONANCE PARAMETERS.	
Total	3.0+6	1.5+7	KFK	Revw	Conf 70Helsinki 2 219	Jun 70	Cierjacks.113. SIG(E) GRPH CFD OPTMD	
Total	+0	1.5+1	ORL	Theo	Conf 70Helsinki 2 757	Jun 70	Desaussure+ 94. CRV,MULTILVL FIT.	
Total	+0	3.5+0	SAC	Theo	Conf 70Helsinki 2 789	Jun 70	Krebs+65.SIG(E) GRAPH,RESON ANALYS	
Total		5.0+1	UI	Theo	Conf 70Helsinki 2 777	Jun 70	Adler+53. R−MATRIX CORRELATED ANAL	
	1.0+0	3.7+1			Rept TID−23396	Aug 66	− + MULTILEVEL ANAL	
Total	+3		JAE	Theo	Jour NST 7 592	Nov 70	Takano+.NUMBER OF RES TO GET AVG SIG	
Total	−1	+2	SAC	Theo	Rept CEA−N−1522	71	Barreau+ INTERMEDIATE STRC RESEARCH	
Total	2.5+6	1.5+7	BNW	Expt	Jour PR/C 3 576	Feb 71	Foster+ TRANS,CURVS,CFD OTHERS + TH	+
					Jour PRL 22 139	Jan 69	− + TOF CURVE CFD P−B TBP SOON	
					Jour NIM 36 1	Sep 65	.EXPT DETAILS	
	2.3+6	1.5+7			Data EXFOR10047.	Aug 73	. 486 PTS. SIGMA	
Total	2.2+0	4.7+0	THS	Theo	Jour AKE 17 22	Feb 71	Knapp.ONE+MULTI LVL FORMALISM CALC	
Total	None		DUB	Expt	Jour YF 13 457	Mar 71	Ryabov+ TOF,2 METHODS,SCINT,NDG	
	−1	+1			Rept JINR−P3−4992	Apr 70	Rjabov+ PULSD REACTOR,TOF,LIQ SCINT	
	None				Jour SNP 13 255	Sep 71	. ENGL OF YF 13 457	
Total	1.0+5	1.0+7	TRM	Eval	Prog INDC(IND)−12 2	Jul 71	Garg.FIT TO EXPTL DATA+THEO CALC,NDG	
Total	+0	4.0+1	CCP	Revw	Jour AE 31 595	Dec 71	Sukhoruchkin.FINE STRUCT CFD TH,GRPH	
					Jour SJA 31 1380	Jun 72	*ENGL OF AE 31 595	

92 Uranium 235

Quantity	Energy (ev) Min	Max	Lab	Type	Documentation Ref Vol Page	Date	Author, Comments	Data
Total	1.0+0	8.2+1	MTR	Eval	Rept ANCR – 1044	Dec 71	Smith+. CURVES	
Total	1.0+4	1.0+5	GEL	Expt	Jour JNE 26 91	Feb 72	Bockhoff+ TOF,REL SIG,HIGH RESOL.	+
	5.8+3	2.7+5			Data EXFOR20134.002	Mar 73	4093PTS.	
Total	1.5+6	4.0+6	ANL	Expt	Prog USNDC – 3 13	Oct 72	Guenther+. NO DATA GIVEN	
Total	1.5+6	2.3+6	GEL	Expt	Jour ZP 257 108	Dec 72	Knitter+ SUM OF EL,INEL,FISS,+NG OTH	+
	1.5+6	2.3+6			Data EXFOR20394.009	Oct 74	3PTS.	
Total	1.3+7	1.5+7	DEB	Eval	Rept IAEA – 153 173	73	Boedy+ MOST PROBABLE VAL OF SIG,TBL	
					Jour AHP 30 115	Oct 71	Angeli+ AVG SIG,CFD CALC.TBLS.GRAPH	
Total	–3	1.0+1	IKE	Theo	Rept IKE – 6 – 61/2	Jan 73	Keinert.DATA LIBRARY	
Total	5.0+5	1.0+7	BET	Expt	Rept WAPD – TM – 1073	Apr 73	Green+.CF252 SOURCE.TOF.CURV.CFDENDF	+
	5.1+5	9.9+6			Data EXFOR10225.	Aug 73	. 678 PTS,SIGMA	
Total	2.5–2		CCP	Eval	Conf 73Kiev 1 197	May 73	Fedorova.SIG = 695.6+ – 1.5B AT V=2200	
Total		1.0+5	FEI	Expt	Conf 73Kiev 2 213	May 73	Van'Kov+ TOF,SIG,TBL	
Total	4.2–2	9.4–1	IJI	Expt	Prog YFI – 16 8	Jun 73	Vertebnyj+ TOF,SIGMA(E), TABLE	+
	4.1–2	9.3–1			Data EXFOR40191.003	Apr 74	.SIG AT 27 EN GVN	
Total	1.0–2	2.0+7	LRL	Eval	Rept UCID – 16359	Jun 73	Plechaty+. ENDF/B CURVE.	
Total	5.0–1	4.6+0	KFI	Expt	Rept KFKI – 73 – 49	Sep 73	Gado+ CODE CALC TOTSIG CFD EVAL,GRPH	
Total	5.0+5	3.0+7	RPI	Expt	Prog COO – 3058 – 39 32	Sep 73	Green+P RECOIL DETC.CFD.NDG.	+
	5.0+5	3.1+7			Data EXFOR10588.002	Nov 76	. 716 PTS. CS DATA.	
Total	2.8–1	1.1+0	OSA	Theo	Jour AKE 22 143	Oct 73	Kitazoe+ RESON INTERFERENCE EFFECTS	
Total	1.0+5	6.0+6	BRC	Expt	Rept CEA – R – 4524	Nov 73	Cabe+,VDG,5 – 50KEV EN.RESOL.TABLE	+
					Conf 70Helsinki 2 31	Jun 70	– +68. SIG(E) GRAPH,TRANSMISSN,VD	
	1.1+5	6.0+6			Data EXFOR20480.	Feb 76	388PTS.	
Total	1.0+6	2.0+7	AUW	Theo	Prog BARC – 770 36	74	Satyanarayana+ STRONG ABSORP MDL,NDG	
Total	5.0+5	1.5+7	NBS	Expt	Rept NBS – MONO – 138	Jan 74	Schwartz+LINAC,TOF,GRPHS	+
					Jour NSE 54 322	Jul 74	– +CFD RPI,ENDF/B – III.	
	5.0+5	1.5+7			Data EXFOR10280.005	Dec 77	1680PTS.	
Total	8.0+5	9.0+6	GLS	Expt	Jour ANE 1 305	May 74	Syme+ TOF CFD ENDFB – 2.	+
					Jour NIM 109 3 479	Jun 73	Crawford. GRAPH GIVEN.	
	8.0+5	9.1+6			Data EXFOR20487.002	Mar 76	197PTS.	
Total	1.0–4	1.0+0	IFB	Eval	Rept YK – 20/1 126	75	Antsipov+ EVAL OF XPTAL DATA.GRAPHS	
Total	2.5+5	1.5+7	JAE	Conf	JAERI – M – 5984	Feb 75	Tanaka.OPTMDL/COUPLD CH.GRPH CFD EXP	
Total	2.0+4	2.0+7	LAS	Theo	Abst BAP 20 140	Feb 75	Moore. R MATRIX STAT CALC 75WASH	
Total	5.0+0	3.0+2	OSA	Theo	Conf JAERI – M – 5984	Feb 75	Kitazoe+HIERACHICAL MDL.GRPH CFD EXP	
	0.0+0	1.0+6			Jour AKE 22 214	Dec 73	– + INTERMEDIATE RESON MODEL	
	1.5+2	2.5+2		Eval	Jour AKE 20 13	Sep 72	– + CURVE, CFD EXPT	
Total	2.5–2		IAE	Eval	Conf 75Wash. 286	Mar 75	Lemmel. TBL LSQ ANAL.CFD OTHER EVAL.	
Total	1.0+3	2.0+6	LRL	Eval	Conf 75Wash. 651	Mar 75	Gardner.CFD ENDF + ENDL.GRPH.	
Total	–3	1.9+0	THS	Theo	Rept IKE – 6 89 54	Jun 75	Keinert. DATA LIBRARY	
Total	1.0–4	1.0+0	IJE	Eval	Rept INDC(CCP) – 78	Jan 76	Konshin+ (ENGL) BRIEF DESCRIPTION	
Total	4.7–3	1.9–1	HAN	Expt	Prog HW – 33384 33	Nov 54	Leonard+	+
	4.7–3	1.9–1			Data EXFOR12430.003	Jun 76	. 58 PTS.	
Elastic	2.5–2		ANL	Expt	Prog ANL – 4680 5	Sep 51	Hibdon.	+
	2.5–2				Data EXFOR11434.005	Jun 76	. 1 PT.	
Elastic	1.0+0		COL	Expt	Priv MELKONIAN	54	Melkonian.	+
	1.0+0				Data EXFOR12431.002	Jun 76	. 1 PT.	
Elastic	5.0+5	1.0+6	LAS	Expt	Jour NSE 2 787	Nov 57	Allen.2ES SIG=5.9 AND 4.0B	+
					Jour PR 104 731	Nov 56	.SUPERSEDED	
	5.0+5	1.0+6			Data EXFOR12207.007	Jun 76	. 2 PTS.	
Elastic	2.7–1	7.7+0	BNL	Expt	Jour PR 109 1641	Mar 58	Foote.CS ABS CRV MONOTON DECR CFD BW	+
	4.0–1	8.0+0			Rept AERE – NP/R – 2076	Jan 57	Wood. FIG1D2 DECREASE 15TO11B	
	2.5–2	7.7+0			Data EXFOR12417.	Jun 76	. 8 PTS.	
Elastic	2.5–2	3.4+1	CUW	Revw	Jour NSE 4 155	Jul 58	Kavanagh.BREIT – WIGNER ANALYSIS	
Elastic	5.5+5	2.0+6	LAS	Expt	Jour LA – 2177	Jun 59	Cranberg.	+
	5.5+5	2.0+6			Data EXFOR12373.008	Jun 76	. 3 PTS.	
Elastic	Maxwl		HAN	Eval	Conf 61RPI 3	May 61	Leonard.	
Elastic	Maxwl		HAR	Expt	Jour PRSA 274 122	Jun 63	Willis.COH NEUT DIFFRACTION BY UO2	
Elastic	3.0+5	1.5+6	ANL	Expt	Jour NSE 18 126	Jan 64	Smith+ TOF	+
					Rept EANDC(US) – 62	Jun 64	– .TOF,TBL.50KEV STEPS,20KEV RSLN	
	3.0+5	1.5+6			Data EXFOR10233.002	Sep 75	47PTS,SIGMA	
Elastic	1.0–4	9.0+3	UK	Eval	Rept AEEW – M – 502	May 65	Freemantle.TABLE.CURVE1 TO 100EV	+
	5.0–3	5.0+0			Rept AEEW – R – 351	Feb 64	Barrington+(WIN).UKNDL LOW EN REVISN	
	1.0+3	1.5+7			Rept AWRE – O – 82/63	Dec 63	Parker.(ALD).UKNDL – DFN 155	
	1.0–1	1.5+7			Data UKNDL – DFN 159B	Mar 73	2065 PNTS	
Elastic	4.0+5	1.7+7	KFK	Eval	Rept KFK – 120 1	Feb 66	Schmidt.OTHERS'XPTS + CURVE	
	1.0+3	2.1+4			Rept KFK – 120 1	Feb 66	– .TABLE OF AVERAGED CS	
	1.0–2	1.0+7			Rept KFK – 120 2	Dec 62	– .GRAPHS AND TABULATED DATA.	
Elastic	4.0+5	6.0+5	ANL	Expt	Jour PRL 16 526	Mar 66	Smith+ TOF,REL CS, RSLN 25 KEV	

92 Uranium 235

Quantity	Energy (ev) Min	Energy (ev) Max	Lab	Type	Documentation Ref Vol Page	Author, Comments Date	Data
Elastic	1.0+6	1.6+7	LAS	Theo Rept	LA- 3538	Sep 66 Agee+ OPTMDL MODEL+H-F FOR COMP	
Elastic	6.1+6	1.4+7	HEB	Eval Conf	66Paris 2 309	Oct 66 Pazy+ CORR-FACTORS BY INTEG EXPT,TBL	
Elastic	1.5+6		IFU	Expt Prog	YFI-5 42	Oct 67 Korzh+ TBL OPTMDL PARAMS + TOTELAST	
				Rept	INDC-232E	67 . ENGL OF YFI-5 42	
Elastic	1.5+6		IFU	Comp Jour	YF 7 277	Feb 68 Korzh+ OPTMOD PARS-FIT TO EXPTL-SIG	
				Jour	SNP 7 2 190	Aug 68 TRANSLATN.*	
Elastic	1.0+0	3.0+1	LRL	Expt Jour	PR 174 1413	Oct 68 Sauter+ CURVE	+
				Conf	68Wash. 541	Mar 68 .SUPERSEDED	
	1.0+0	3.0+1		Data	EXFOR12344.002	Jun 76 . 234 PTS.	
Elastic	7.4+0	1.9+2	MOL	Expt Conf	70Helsinki 1 449	Jun 70 Poortmans+20. SIG(E) GRPHS OF 5RESON	+
				Conf	69Vienna 911	Jul 69 - + HE-3 COUNTER.LINAC.TOF.	
	7.4+0	1.9+2		Data	EXFOR20145.002	Mar 73 1364PTS.	
Elastic	2.5-2		MOL	Expt Prog	EANDC(E)127U	Apr 70 Poortmans+ BR2 CRYST SPEC.	
Elastic	1.0+5	1.0+6	BOL	Theo Conf	70Helsinki § 49	Jun 70 Benzi+EXPTL SIG CFD CRIT-MASS-CALC	
Elastic	5.0-1	1.9+2	MTR	Expt Jour	NP/A 164 34	Mar 71 Simpson+ POOR RESOL DATA,LINAC,CRVS	+
	5.0-1	1.9+2		Data	EXFOR10132.005	Jan 73 0PTS,SIGMA	
Elastic	1.0-3	1.0+1	JUL	Theo Rept	JUEL-746-RG 34	Apr 71 Bonka. GAS MODEL CALC	
Elastic	2.5-2	8.0-1	MOL	Expt Conf	70Helsinki 1 461	Jun 70 Ceulmans+21. SIG(E) GRAPH,CRYST-SPEC	+
				Rept	STI/DOC/10-125	Apr 71 Ceulemans.PG46.ROLLD METAL.PREC EXPT	
	2.4-2	7.6-1		Data	EXFOR20369.	Sep 74 33PTS.	
Elastic	1.0+5	1.0+7	TRM	Eval Prog	INDC(IND)-12 2	Jul 71 Garg.FIT TO EXPTL DATA+THEO CALC,NDG	
Elastic	2.5-2		ANL	Eval Prog	NCSAC-42 29	Nov 71 Devolpi. ADJUSTED VALUE GIVEN.	
Elastic	1.5+6	2.3+6	GEL	Expt Jour	ZP 257 108	Dec 72 Knitter+ TOF,TBL+CURVE GIVEN	+
				Conf	72Budapest 184	Aug 72 - + SIG INTEG OVER ANGDIST,GRPH	
	1.5+6	2.3+6		Data	EXFOR20394.002	Oct 74 3PTS.	
Elastic	4.0+2	1.5+7	KFK	Eval Rept	KFK-1629	Jun 73 Schatz. RECOMMENDED CURVE	+
	1.0-3	1.5+7		Data	KEDAK-3	Oct 75 8096 DATA SETS	
Elastic	1.0+6		TRM	Theo Prog	INDC(SEC)-35	Sep 73 Satyanarayana+ P80.H-F,SHORTNOTE,NDG	
Elastic	2.5-2		IAE	Eval Conf	75Wash. 286	Mar 75 Lemmel. TBL LSQ ANAL.CFD OTHER EVAL.	
Elastic	1.0+3	1.0+7	LRL	Eval Conf	75Wash. 651	Mar 75 Gardner.CFD ENDF + ENDL.GRPH.	
Elastic	1.0+5	1.5+7	CCP	Eval Data	SOKRATOR-1040	76 50 PTS	+
Elastic	2.0+3		IJI	Expt Conf	77Kiev 2 223	77 Gnidak+ SIG MEASD REL PB.VALUE GIVEN	+
	2.0+3			Data	EXFOR40562.003	Dec 77 E-RESOL=.3KEV. SIG REL PB,1 PNT	
Diff Elastic	5.0+5	2.5+6	LAS	Revw Conf	55Geneva 2 18	Aug 55 Walt.P588, CURVE FOR 3 N-ES,DISCUSSN	
Diff Elastic	5.0+5	1.0+6	LAS	Expt Jour	NSE 2 787	Nov 57 Allen.2ES THETA=25-130DEG MON DECR	+
				Jour	PR 104 731	Nov 56 .SUPERSEDED	
	5.0+5	1.0+6		Data	EXFOR12207.008	Jun 76 . 18 PTS, DSIGMA.	
Diff Elastic	5.5+5	2.0+6	LAS	Expt Jour	LA- 2177	Jun 59 CRANBERG ALSO 1MEV TOF CURVES	+
	5.5+5	2.0+6		Data	EXFOR12373.	Jun 76 . 44 PTS. DSIGMA.	
Diff Elastic	1.3+5	2.0+7	GEA	Eval Rept	TID-12742	Feb 61 Gerardo. FROM BNL-400+OTHER SOURCES.	
Diff Elastic	5.5+5	2.0+6	ANL	Revw Conf	61Vienna 1 29	Aug 61 Smith.TABLE,GRAPH OF ANGL DISTRB 1E	
Diff Elastic	5.0+5	2.0+6	AI	Eval Rept	NAA-SR-M-9025	Sep 63 Alter+.MT CARLO LEAST SQ ANAL BNL400	
Diff Elastic	3.0+5	1.5+6	ANL	Expt Jour	NSE 18 126	Jan 64 Smith.TOF. 50KEV INT.LEG.COEFF.	
				Rept	EANDC(US)-62	Jun 64 - + TOF	
	3.0+5	1.5+6		Data	EXFOR10233.003	Sep 75 5 LEG COEF, 47 ENERGIES	
Diff Elastic	5.0-3	5.0+0	UK	Eval Rept	AEEW-R-351	Feb 64 Barrington+(WIN).UKNDL LOW EN REVISN	+
	1.0+3	1.5+7		Rept	AWRE-O-82/63	Dec 63 Parker.(ALD).UKNDL-DFN 155	
	1.0-4	1.5+7		Data	UKNDL-DFN 159B	Mar 73 17 PNTS,C.M.	
Diff Elastic	4.0+5	6.0+5	ANL	Expt Rept	PRL 16 526	Mar 66 Smith+ TOF	+
	4.0+5	6.0+5		Data	EXFOR12369.002	Jun 76 . 0 PTS.	
Diff Elastic	1.0+6	1.6+7	LAS	Theo Rept	LA- 3538	Sep 66 Agee+ OPTMDL MODEL+H-F FOR COMP	
Diff Elastic	2.0+5	1.8+6	HAR	Expt Conf	66Paris 1 383	Oct 66 Armitage+PPR22.CURVE CFD NSE 18 126	
	1.2+5	1.8+6		Priv	TOWLE ALD	Apr 69 + 8 ES 90D TOF 10KEV RES	
Diff Elastic	5.0+6	1.6+7	LAS	Theo Rept	LA- 3788	67 Beery+.OPTMOD CALC POLARIZ ANG DISTR	
Diff Elastic	1.5+6		IFU	Comp Jour	YF 7 277	Feb 68 Korzh+ GRPH SIG(ANG),OPTMOD PARS-FIT	
				Jour	SNP 7 2 190	Aug 68 TRANSLATN.*	
Diff Elastic	1.0+6	1.6+7	AI	Eval Rept	NAA-SR-12533	Mar 68 Campbell+,LEG COEFS,TABLE+CURVS,13ES	
	3.0+5	2.0+6		Rept	NAA-SR-11980	Apr 67 - + LEG COEFS TABLE C-M SYSTEM	
	1.5+6			Conf	66Wash. 335	Mar 66 Davis.CURVE ANG DISTRIBUTION	
Diff Elastic	2.0+6	4.0+6	ALD	Expt Rept	AWRE-O-55/69	Aug 69 Batchelor+TOF TBL CFD OTHERS	+
	2.0+6	4.0+6		Data	EXFOR20036.	Sep 71 27PTS.D/DA.	
Diff Elastic	2.0+6	4.0+6	CCP	Comp Rept	ICD-6 50	70 Bazazjanc+ ANGDIST EXPTS,GRPH AT 3ES	
Diff Elastic	1.0+5	1.0+7	TRM	Eval Prog	INDC(IND)-12 2	Jul 71 Garg.ANGDIST FIT FOR OPTMOD PARS,NDG	
Diff Elastic	0.0+0	1.5+7	FEI	Eval Book	NIKOLAEV 187	72 .LEG COEFFS+ANG DISTRIBUTS,GRAPH	
Diff Elastic	1.5+6	5.5+6	GEL	Expt Jour	ZP 257 108	Dec 72 Knitter+ TOF,DATA GIVEN AT 7 N-ENERG	+
				Conf	72Budapest 184	Aug 72 - + TOF,ANGDIST AT 3 ES,GRAPH	
	1.5+6	5.5+6		Data	EXFOR20394.003	Oct 74 137PTS.D/DA.	
Diff Elastic	-3	1.0+1	IKE	Theo Rept	IKE-6-61/2	Jan 73 Keinert.DATA LIBRARY	

92 Uranium 235

Quantity	Energy (ev) Min	Max	Lab	Type	Documentation Ref Vol Page	Date	Author, Comments	Data
Diff Elastic	1.4+7		LRL	Expt	Abst DA/B 33 4954	Apr 73	Kammerdiener.TOF.20-160DEG.NO DATA.	
					Rept UCRL-51232	Jul 72	- . RING GEOM.ANG DISTR	
Diff Elastic	1.0+4	1.5+7	KFK	Eval	Rept KFK-1629	Jun 73	Schatz. RECOMMENDED CURVES.	+
	+0	2.0+6			Rept KFK-120 1	Feb 66	Schmidt.OTHERS'XPTS+CURVE.MU ONLY	
	1.0+4	1.5+7			Data KEDAK-3	Oct 75	43 ENERGIES	
Diff Elastic	1.0+6		TRM	Theo	Prog INDC(SEC)-35	Sep 73	Satyanarayana+ P80.H-F,SHORTNOTE,NDG	
Diff Elastic	None		ANL	Expt	Prog USNDC-11 25	Jun 74	Smith. NDG	
Diff Elastic	4.6+3	6.5+6	FEI	Theo	Rept INDC(CCP)-39	Jul 74	.P1. ENGLISH OF YK-8/2 3	
					Rept YK-8/2 3	Sep 72	Bazajants+ ANISOTR GROUP-PARAMS,TBL	
Diff Elastic	5.0+6		AUW	Theo	Conf 74Bombay 2 193	Dec 74	Satyanarayana+ W/OUT STRONG ABSO,TBL	
Diff Elastic	2.0+5	5.0+5	LRL	Theo	Conf 75Wash. 651	Mar 75	Gardner.CFD ENDF + ENDL.GRPH.	
Diff Elastic	1.0+5	1.5+7	CCP	Eval	Data SOKRATOR-1040	76	50 PTS	+
Diff Elastic	5.0+5	1.5+7	IFB	Eval	Rept INDC(CCP)-78	Jan 76	Sukhovitskij+ LEG-POL CFD ANGDIS,FIG	
	5.0+4	1.5+7			Conf 75Kiev	May 75	Sukhovickij+ ANGDISTR	
	+6			Theo	Jour VBF 1975 2 23	75	- + ANGDISTR OF NEUTS,TABLS	
Polarization	5.0-1	1.6+7	LAS	Theo	Rept LA-3788	67	Beery+.OPTMOD CALC COS(THETA) DISTR	
Polarization	1.0-1	1.4+1	BNL	Expt	Jour NP/A 218 84	Jan 74	Reddingius+ TRANSM POLARIZED NS.	
Potntal Scat	2.7-1	7.7+0	BNL	Expt	Jour PR 109 1641	Mar 58	Foote.10+-1B	
Potntal Scat	1.0-1	1.0+1	BNL	Revw	Conf 58Geneva 15 118	Sep 58	Shore+.PPR648,CURVE,BREITWIGNER-FIT	
Potntal Scat	1.0+2	7.0+4	HAR	ExTh	Rept AERE-M-1272	Dec 63	Uttley.AVR TRNS..S,P WAVE,ALPHA TH	
Potntal Scat	5.0-1	1.0+1	MOL	Expt	Conf 66Paris 2 211	Oct 66	Poortmans+ FROM SCAT-RES-FISSION	
Potntal Scat	1.0+6	1.0+7	TRM	Theo	Conf 67Karlsrhe 1 95	Nov 67	Garg+ OPTMOD CALC,TBL	
					Rept BARC-305 16	Oct 67	- + SIMILAR TO 67KARLSR 1 95	
Potntal Scat	2.5-2		IAE	Revw	Jour REA 7 4 3	Dec 69	Hanna+WESTCOTT+ DISCUSSION	
Potntal Scat	7.0+0	6.0+1	MOL	Expt	Conf 70Helsinki 1 449	Jun 70	Poortmans+20. EXPT OKS GIVEN SIGMA	+
	7.0+0	6.0+1			Data EXFOR20145.009	Mar 73	1PNT.	
Tot Inelastc	6.7+4	6.1+7	KAP	Eval	Rept KAPL-1756 1	Jun 57	Baraff.TBL D25LETHARGYSTEPS	
Tot Inelastc	1.0+4	1.1+6	COL	Theo	Jour PR 112 492	Oct 58	Rae+,H-F CALC,TH CURVE CFD XPT	
					Jour PRL 1 271	Oct 58	RAE+ SUPERSEDED	
Tot Inelastc	Fiss		KUR	Revw	Conf 60Vienna 159	Oct 60	Bondarenko+.TABLE,EXPT DESCRIBED	
Tot Inelastc	Fiss	9.0+5	CCP	Expt	Book NEJTRONFIZ 287	61	Andreev.THRESH DET.SIG FOR SPEC+.9MV	+
					Book SPN 211	61	. ENGL TRANSL OF NEJTRONFIZ 287	
Tot Inelastc	2.7+5	1.0+7	B+W	Eval	Rept BAW-158	Jun 61	Roach+ AVERAGED SIG 12 GROUPS	
Tot Inelastc	2.0+4	6.0+5	ANL	Theo	Conf 61Vienna 1 171	Aug 61	Moldauer+.PPR35,CURVE BY NEW CALCLTN	
Tot Inelastc	Pile		AI	Expt	Abst ANS 5 69	Jun 62	Campise. PARTIAL RESLTS FRM SPHTRNS.	
Tot Inelastc	Thrsh	1.5+7	UK	Eval	Rept AWRE-O-82/63	Dec 63	Parker.(ALD).UKNDL-DFN 155	
Tot Inelastc	1.5+4	1.6+7	KFK	Eval	Rept KFK-120 1	Feb 66	Schmidt.CURVE+TABLE .021TO2.4MEV	
	2.5+4	1.0+7			Rept KFK-120 2	Dec 62	- .GRAPHS AND TABULATED DATA.	
Tot Inelastc	6.1+6	1.4+7	HEB	Eval	Conf 66Paris 2 309	Oct 66	Pazy+ CORR-FACTORS BY INTEG EXPT,TBL	
Tot Inelastc	2.0+6	4.0+6	ALD	Expt	Rept AWRE-O-55/69	Aug 69	Batchelor+TOF TBL CFD OTHERS	+
	2.0+6	4.0+6			Data EXFOR20036.	Sep 71	45PTS.D/DE,SIG.	
Tot Inelastc	4.0+6	7.5+6	CCP	Comp	Rept ICD-6 106	70	Sluchevskaja.ALSO 6 MEV,5 REFS,TABLE	
Tot Inelastc	1.0+5	1.0+6	BOL	Expt	Conf 70Helsinki § 49	Jun 70	Benzi+EXPTL SIG CFD CRIT-MASS-CALC	
Tot Inelastc	1.0+5	1.0+7	TRM	Eval	Prog INDC(IND)-12 2	Jul 71	Garg.FIT TO EXPTL DATA+THEO CALC,NDG	
Tot Inelastc	1.5+6	2.3+6	GEL	Expt	Jour ZP 257 108	Dec 72	Knitter+ TOF,DATA GIVEN AT 3 N-ENERG	+
					Conf 72Budapest 184	Aug 72	- + SIG INTEG OVER ANGDIST,GRPH	
	1.5+6	2.3+6			Data EXFOR20394.003	Oct 74	. 18PTS.SIGMA.	
Tot Inelastc	1.5+4	1.5+7	KFK	Eval	Rept KFK-1629	Jun 73	Schatz. RECOMMENDED CURVE	+
	2.1+4	1.5+7			Data KEDAK-3	Oct 75	131 DATA SETS + 10 EXCT LVLS	
Tot Inelastc	None		AUA	Theo	Prog AAEC/PR-41P 65	75	Bertram+ NDG.MULTILVL R-MATR OKS XPT	
Tot Inelastc	1.0+4	3.0+6	LRL	Theo	Conf 75Wash. 651	Mar 75	Gardner.CFD ENDF + ENDL.GRPH.	
Tot Inelastc	0.0+0	1.5+7	IFB	Eval	Rept INDC(CCP)-78	Jan 76	Antsipov+ STATMOD CALC CFD XPTS,GRPH	
Diff Inelast	+5	+7	TRM	Theo	Jour JNE 4 326	Mar 57	Bhandari+ CONTINUUM MODELS CFD EBR1	
Diff Inelast	1.4+7		CCP	Expt	Jour AE 4 337	Apr 58	Zamiatnin+ FISS+EVAP SPECTR FIT DATA	
					Jour JNE 9 194	Jun 59	TRANSLATN.*	
					Jour SJA 4 443	58	TRANSLATN.*	
Diff Inelast	5.5+5	2.0+6	LAS	Expt	Rept LA-2177	Jan 59	Cranberg.	+
					Conf 57Col.Univ § 4C1	Sep 57	. TOF 3ES 1MEV ROUGH SPECT.	
	5.5+5	2.0+6			Data EXFOR12373.008	Jun 76	. 3 PTS, SIG	
	5.5+5	2.0+6			Data EXFOR12373.	Jun 76	. 51 PTS. DSIGMA	
Diff Inelast	4.0+6	7.0+6	LAS	Expt	Prog WASH-1028 26	Apr 60	Thompson+ DATA BEING ANALYSED	
Diff Inelast	3.0+5	1.5+6	ANL	Expt	Prog EANDC(US)-28	Sep 62	Smith.NDG.TBD	
Diff Inelast	5.0+5		CCP		Jour AE 13 321	Oct 62	HF CALCULATION CFD DATA	
					Jour SJA 13 931	62	. ENGL OF AE 13 321	
Diff Inelast	Thrsh	1.5+7	UK	Eval	Rept AWRE-O-82/63	Dec 63	Parker.(ALD).UKNDL-DFN 155	+
	2.4+5	1.5+7			Data UKNDL-DFN 159B	Mar 73	.TO CONTINUUM.74 PTS.E DIST.ANGDIST.	
	2.0+4	1.5+6			Data UKNDL-DFN 159B	Mar 73	1ST-6TH LVL,ANGDIST	
Diff Inelast	None		ANL	Expt	Jour PL 18 149	Aug 65	Braid+ IMPT INFO ON ENERGY LEVELS	

92 Uranium 235

Quantity	Energy (ev) Min	Max	Lab	Type	Documentation Ref Vol Page	Date	Author, Comments	Data
Diff Inelast	2.1+4	2.4+6	KFK	Eval	Rept KFK – 120 1	Feb 66	Schmidt.TABLE OF 10 PARTIAL INEL CS	
	2.5+4	5.6+5			Rept KFK – 120 2	Dec 62	– .FOR 4 GROUPS OF LVLS	
Diff Inelast	1.3+5	1.5+6	HAR	Expt	Conf 66Paris 1 383	Oct 66	Armitage+PPR22.TBL,SPECT SCT NS.6ES.	+
					Conf 66Oxford	Apr 66	– +PPR44.SAME AS 66PARIS.	
Diff Inelast	1.3+5	1.5+6	FEI	Comp	Rept ICD – 4 57	67	Sluchevskaja.SELECTIV COMPIL ,TABLE	
Diff Inelast	1.0+4	1.0+7	HEB	Theo	Priv NISSIMOV	69	Nissimov+MICROSC SIG CHECK BY N – SPEC	
Diff Inelast	1.4+7		VNV	Expt	Rept 71Knoxvill 196	Mar 71	Voignier+,SIG VS.E(PRIME) 90DEG CRV	
					Rept CEA – R – 4132	Feb 71	Bertrand+EP=.1,5MEV THETA=30,135DG	
Diff Inelast	1.5+6	4.0+6	ANL	Expt	Prog USNDC – 3 13	Oct 72	Guenther+. NO DATA GIVEN	
Diff Inelast	1.4+7		LRL	Expt	Abst DA/B 33 4954	Apr 73	Kammerdiener.TOF.20 – 160DEG.NO DATA.	
					Rept UCRL – 51232	Jul 72	– . RING GEOM.ANG DISTR	
Diff Inelast	None		AUW	Theo	Prog BARC – 831 33	75	Satyanarayana+ COUPL – CHANNL CALC,NDG	
Diff Inelast		+6	CCP	Eval	Jour VBF 1975 4 20	75	Martynjuk+.H – F,SIG(NEUT – E),GRAPH	
Thermal Scat	2.5 – 2	2.0 – 1	ANL	Theo	Jour ACR 20 587	Apr 66	Atoji. E DEP. OF RE(SAM) AND IM(SAM)	
Thermal Scat	1.0+4	1.0+7	HEB	Theo	Priv NISSIMOV	69	Nissimov+MICROSC SIG CHECK BY N – SPEC	
Thermal Scat	2.0 – 2	3.5+2	AUA	Expt	Rept AAEC/TM – 497	Apr 69	Dalton. LATTICE,N – SPEC OKS DATA – SETS	
Scattering	1.0 – 1	1.0+1	BNL	Expt	Conf 55Geneva 4 199	Aug 55	Sailor.GRAPH,SUM OF SEV EXPTS,PPR586	
Scattering	2.5 – 2	3.4+1	CUW	Eval	Rept CWR – 478	Jun 57	Kavanagh.B – W ANAL PART+TOT SIGS208ES	
Scattering	None		MTR	Theo	Jour PR 111 929	Aug 58	Reich+ MULTILEVEL THEORY	
					Jour PRL 1 47	Jul 58	.SUPERSEDED	
Scattering	1.0+0	8.0+0	BNL	Comp	Conf 58Geneva 16 8	Sep 58	Hughes.PPR2483,CURVE,MANY REFS	
Scattering		1.8+0	CRC	Theo	Jour PR 112 203	Oct 58	Vogt.MULTILVL TH CFD EXP DATA	
Scattering	2.5 – 2		COL	Revw	Jour NUC 17 11 134	Nov 59	Safford+. EXPTL VALUES TABULATED	
Scattering	2.0 – 2	2.0+0	CCP	Expt	Jour AE 13 368	Oct 62	Guerassimov+.TOF,MULTSCATT CORRECTN	
					Jour SJA 13 977	Jun 63	TRANSLATN.*	
					Jour EAF 13 4 86	Oct 62	TRANSLATN.*	
Scattering	1.0+3	1.5+7	UK	Eval	Rept AWRE – O – 82/63	Dec 63	Parker.(ALD).UKNDL – DFN 155	
Scattering	2.5 – 3	1.9+1	JUL	Theo	Rept JUEL – 746 – RG 13	Apr 71	Bonka. AVG SIG CALC	
	1.0 – 3	2.0+0			Rept JUEL – 746 – RG 50	Apr 71	– .KUGEL – THERMOS – LIBR,T=300K,CURV	
Scattering	– 3	1.0+1	IKE	Theo	Rept IKE – 6 – 61/2	Jan 73	Keinert.DATA LIBRARY	
Scattering	2.5 – 2		CCP	Eval	Conf 73Kiev 1 197	May 73	Fedorova.SIG=14.6+ – ´1.5B AT V=2200	
Nonelastic	1.4+7		LAS	Expt	Rept LA – 1532	Apr 53	Graves+ NOT INCL DEST SIG	
Nonelastic	4.0+6	4.5+6	LAS	Expt	Rept LA – 1939	Aug 55	Bethe+ ALSO FISS SPEC NEUTS SPH TRNS	+
	4.0+6	4.5+6			Data EXFOR12397.003	Jun 76	. 2 PTS.	
Nonelastic	2.0+5	3.0+6	LAS	Revw	Conf 55Geneva 2 18	Aug 55	Walt.P588, CURVE,DISCUS OF RESULTS	
Nonelastic	5.0+5	1.0+6	LAS	Expt	Jour PR 104 731	Nov 56	Allen+	+
	5.0+5	1.0+6			Data EXFOR12207.006	Jun 76	. 2 PTS.	
Nonelastic	1.0+6	2.5+6	LAS	Expt	Jour PR 104 1319	Dec 56	Beyster+,SPH TRNS 2.70 3.25B 2ES	+
	1.0+6	2.5+6			Data EXFOR11220.036	Jun 76	. 2 PTS.	
Nonelastic	6.7+4	6.1+6	KAP	Eval	Rept KAPL – 1756 1	Jun 57	Baraff.TBL D25LETHARGYSTEPS	
Nonelastic	2.5+5	1.0+6	LAS	Expt	Jour NSE 2 787	Nov 57	Allen.3ES INCL .5MEV ABS+LVL EFFECTS	+
	2.5+5	1.0+6			Data EXFOR12402.002	Jun 76	. 4 PTS.	
Nonelastic	1.4+7		CCP	Expt	Jour AE 3 542	Dec 57	Vasilev+.SECONDARY SPECTRUM BY TOF	
					Jour JNE 9 43	Jun 59	TRANSLATN.*	
					Jour SJA 3 1430	57	TRANSLATN.*	
Nonelastic	1.0 – 2	2.0 – 1	SAC	Expt	Jour JPR 19 68	Jan 58	Auclair.NEUTRON E CONSISTENT 3 – FISSN	
Nonelastic	1.3+7	1.9+7	CCP	Expt	Jour AE 11 397	Oct 61	SPH, 2.64PM.06 2.74PM.07B	+
					Jour SJA 11 1043	61	. ENGL TRANSL OF AE 11 397	
Nonelastic	8.1+6	1.4+7	LRL	Expt	Jour PR 130 1471	May 63	Macgregor+ SPH TRANS ALSO 11.9MEV	+
	8.1+6	1.4+7			Data EXFOR11120.004	Jun 76	. 3 PTS.	
Nonelastic	1.0 – 4	9.0+3	UK	Eval	Rept AEEW – M – 502	May 65	Freemantle.TABLE.CURVE1 TO 100EV	+
	1.0+3	1.5+7			Rept AWRE – O – 82/63	Dec 63	Parker.(ALD).UKNDL – DFN 155	
	1.0 – 4	1.5+7			Data UKNDL – DFN 159B	Mar 73	2065 PNTS	
Nonelastic	8.1+6		CCP	Expt	Jour AE 19 456	Nov 65	Degtjarev.SPHERE TRANSM, 3.11+ – .20B	+
					Jour JNE 20 818	Sep 66	TRANSLATN.*	
					Jour EAF 19 5 72	Nov 65	TRANSLATN.*	
					Jour SJA 19 1426	Nov 65	TRANSLATN.*	
Nonelastic	1.0+3	2.1+4	KFK	Eval	Rept KFK – 120 1	Feb 66	Schmidt.TABLE OF AVERAGED CS	
	4.0+5	1.7+7			Rept KFK – 120 1	Feb 66	– .OTHERS'XPTS+CURVE	
	1.0+3	1.0+7			Rept KFK – 120 2	Dec 62	– .GRAPHS AND TABULATED DATA.	
Nonelastic	2.0+6	4.0+6	ALD	Expt	Rept AWRE – O – 55/69	Aug 69	Batchelor+ NON ELASTIC NEUTRONS.	+
	2.0+6	4.0+6			Data EXFOR20036.	Sep 71	60PTS.D/DE.	
Nonelastic	1.0+6		AUW	Theo	Conf 72Chandigr 2 213	Dec 72	Satyanarayana+ H – F CALC, NO DATA	
Nonelastic	4.0+2	1.5+7	KFK	Eval	Rept KFK – 1629	Jun 73	Schatz. RECOMMENDED CURVE	+
	1.0 – 3	1.5+7			Data KEDAK – 3	Oct 75	8428 DATA SETS	
Absorption	2.5 – 2		COL	Expt	Rept CU – 115	Feb 53	Melkonian.	+
	2.5 – 2				Data EXFOR12426.003	Jun 76	. 1 PT.	

92 Uranium 235

Quantity	Energy (ev) Min	Max	Lab	Type	Documentation Ref Vol Page	Date	Author, Comments	Data
Absorption	2.5−2		BNL	Expt Jour	PR 94 1088	May 54	Palevsky+ TRANS TOF SIG=691+ −5B	+
	2.5−2			Data	EXFOR12410.002	Jun 76	. 1 PT.	
Absorption	Maxwl		HAR	Expt Jour	JNE 1 92	Aug 54	Egelstaff. ESTIMATED FROM SIGTOT	+
Absorption	Pile		LAS	Expt Rept	LA− 512	55	Williams. REACTOR SPECTRUM	+
	Pile			Data	EXFOR12441.002	Jun 76	. 1 PT.	
Absorption	1.0−2	1.0+2	CCP	Expt Conf	55Moscow 87	Jul 55	Nikitin+.SIMULTAN ABS AND FISS,CURVE	
				Rept	AEC−TR−2435 81	56	. ENGL TRANSL OF 55MOSCOW 87	
Absorption	Cold		ANL	Revw Conf	55Geneva 5 125	Aug 55	Spinrad+.P835	
Absorption	Fast		ANL	Revw Conf	55Geneva 5 125	Aug 55	Spinrad+.P835	
Absorption	2.5−2		BNL	Comp Conf	55Geneva 4 147	Aug 55	Harvey.VAL 2200M/SEC,PPR832	
Absorption	2.5−2		IAE	Revw Conf	55Geneva 4 287	Aug 55	Worldvalue+ERROR GVN (2200M/SEC)	
				Eval Jour	NAT 176 619	Oct 55	.SEE ALSO *	
				Revw Jour	JET 2 271	55	.SAME ARTICLE,RUSSIAN ZET 29 1455	
Absorption	2.5−2		FR	Eval Jour	CR 241 669	Sep 55	Perrin.QUOTES WORLD SIGMA =698+ −10B	
Absorption	Maxwl		HAR	Revw Jour	NAT 176 619	Oct 55	Gaunt+698+ −10B WORLD AVG VALUES	
Absorption	4.4+3	4.8+4	ORL	Expt Jour	PR 102 797	May 56	Macklin+,SPH TRNS FALLS TO FLAT 2.8B	+
				Rept	ORNL−2022	Feb 56	.SUPERSEDED	
	4.4+3	4.9+4		Data	EXFOR12334.004	Jun 76	. 6 PTS.	
Absorption	2.5−2		BNL	Eval Rept	BNL−325	Jan 57	Hughes+ WORLD CONSIST. VAL. 694+ −10B	
Absorption	2.0−2	2.4−1	CUW	Theo Rept	CWR−400−1	Sep 57	Roberts.MAXWELL−BOLTZMANN AVGD SIGS.	
Absorption	Maxwl		HAR	Eval Rept	AERE−NP/R−2140	Dec 57	Egelstaff+ CONSISTENT VALUES 2200M/S	
Absorption	2.4+4	8.8+5	CCP	Expt Jour	AE 4 185	Feb 58	Andreev.ALSO AT 240KEV,SPHERE METHOD	+
				Jour	JNE 9 151	Jun 59	TRANSLATN.*	
				Jour	SJA 4 247	58	TRANSLATN.*	
Absorption	2.5−3	5.0−3	HAN	Expt Prog	WASH−1006 15	Jun 58	Seppi. NDG	
Absorption	2.5−2	3.4+1	CUW	Theo Jour	NSE 4 155	Jul 58	Kavanagh.BREIT−WIGNER ANALYSIS	
Absorption	Maxwl		BNL	Comp Conf	58Geneva 16 8	Sep 58	Hughes.PPR2483,VAL V=2200M/SEC GVN	
Absorption	Maxwl		CRC	Eval Jour	NUC 16 10 108	Oct 58	Westcott.NRX ABSOL CURVE 20−760DEGC	
Absorption	2.9−3		COL	Expt Jour	NSE 6 433	Aug 59	Safford.	+
	2.9−3			Data	EXFOR12404.004	Jun 76	. 1 PT.	
Absorption	Pile		ORL	Eval Jour	NSE 6 100	Aug 59	Stoughton+,BEST VALUE .025EV=695B	
Absorption	1.0+4	1.8+5	ORL	Expt Abst	BAP 4 414	Nov 59	Macklin+ NDG	
Absorption	2.5−2		AE	Comp Rept	AE− 11	Apr 60	Story+,DISCUSSION+TABULATN OF MEASTS	
Absorption	Maxwl		ORL	Expt Jour	NSE 8 112	Aug 60	Block+,FC 680+ −6B SIG(TOT)−SIG(SCT)	+
	Maxwl			Data	EXFOR12024.009	Jun 76	. 1 PT.	
Absorption	1.8+5	1.0+6	LAS	Eval Jour	PR 120 556	Oct 60	Diven. DERIVED FOR USE AS STD	
Absorption	Maxwl		HAN	Eval Conf	61RPI 3	May 61	Leonard.	
Absorption	2.0−1	1.0+7	B+W	Eval Rept	BAW−158	Jun 61	Roach+ AVERAGED SIG 40 GROUPS	
Absorption	5.0−3	2.5+0	GA	Eval Rept	GA− 2113	Jun 61	Wikner+.TABLE+CURVE.100 E POINTS	
Absorption	Maxwl		CRC	Revw Conf	61Saclay 57	Jul 61	Westcott. 2200METRE/SEC SIG GIVEN	
Absorption	Maxwl		ANL	Expt Jour	NSE 11 312	Nov 61	Saplakoglu.	+
	Maxwl			Data	EXFOR12406.004	Jun 76	. 1 PT.	
Absorption	Pile		CRC	Eval Rept	CRRP−1191	Jan 62	Westcott. EFF SIG.	
Absorption	5.0−3	1.0−1	BNL	Revw Rept	BNL−722	Jun 62	Sher+ REVIEW CURVE GIVEN	
Absorption	2.0−2	2.2+0	KUR	Expt Jour	AE 13 368	Oct 62	Gerasimov+.TOF,MULTSCAT CORRECTN	+
				Jour	SJA 13 977	Oct 62	. ENGL OF AE 13 368	
Absorption	Maxwl		CRC	Revw Rept	EANDC(CAN)−15	Nov 62	Hanna. COMPARES MANY VALUES	
Absorption	3.0+4	6.4+4	ORL	Expt Prog	ORNL−3360 51	Jan 63	De−Saussure+	+
	3.0+4	6.4+4		Data	EXFOR12456.002	Jun 76	. 2 PTS. SIGMA	
Absorption	1.0+2	1.0+4	HAR	ExTh Rept	AERE−M−1272	Dec 63	Uttley.AVR TRNS..S,P WAVE,ALPHA TH	
Absorption	Pile		CJD	Eval Rept	INDSWG−64 285	64	Galanin. TBL EFF SIG FOR MANY SPECTR	
Absorption	2.5−2		BEP	Revw Jour	KE 8 625	Jan 65	Wenzel.VAL GVN,MANY REFERENCES	
Absorption	2.4+4		FEI	Expt Jour	AE 19 41	Jul 65	Vankov.STAVISSKY 12.95+ −.17B	+
				Jour	JNE 20 600	Jul 65	TRANSLATN.*	
				Jour	EAF 19 1 61	Jul 65	TRANSLATN.*	
				Jour	SJA 19 903	Jul 65	TRANSLATN.*	
Absorption	4.1−1	1.0+7	WAL	Eval Rept	WANL−TME−1228	Aug 65	Gibson+.68GROUP TABLE	
	4.0−1	1.0+7		Rept	WANL−TME−1028	Nov 64	Drawbaugh+.TABLE 68 GROUPS	
Absorption	2.5−2		BNW	Theo Conf	66Wash. 75	Mar 66	Liikala+, TBLS OF LITER. VALUES	
Absorption	2.0−2	5.0−1	MTR	Eval Conf	66Paris 2 50	Oct 66	Smith. TBL+CURVE,LEAST SQUARE FIT.	
	1.0−2	5.0−1		Conf	66Wash. 985	Mar 66	Fluharty+,COEF OF SIG EXPANSN CALCTD	
Absorption	Maxwl		ITE	Theo Rept	ICD−4 385	67	Birzgal+.AVERAGING OVER MAXWELL SPEC	
Absorption	Pile		SRL	Theo Conf	68Wash. 1271	Mar 68	Hennelly. 502B CALC FOR USE AS STD	
Absorption	Maxwl		CRC	Expt Conf	CJP 47 1317	69	Bigham+	+
	Maxwl			Data	EXFOR12444.002	Jun 76	. 1 PT. SIGMA.	
Absorption	Maxwl		IFB	Theo Prog	YFI−7 45	Apr 69	Naumov+ CODES FOR EFFECTIV−SIG,TABLE	
				Rept	INDC(CCP)−7U48	Feb 70	TRANSLATN.*	
Absorption	Fast		JAE	Expt Conf	69London § 1.7	Jun 69	Kuroi+ UK,ENDF,ABBN EVALS CFD EXPT	

92 Uranium 235

Quantity	Energy (ev) Min	Energy (ev) Max	Lab	Type	Documentation Ref Vol Page	Author, Comments Date	Data
Absorption	Fiss		RCN	Eval Prog	EANDC(E)127U	Apr 70 Bustraan+	
Absorption	Pile		ROS	Theo Rept	ZFK – 201	Apr 70 Adam. EFFECTIVE SIG CALC	
Absorption	2.5 – 2	1.0+0	MOL	Expt Conf	70Helsinki 1 461	Jun 70 Ceulmans+21. DEDUCED VALUE,SCAT – EXPT	
Absorption	2.5 – 2		ANL	Eval Conf	71Knoxvill 560	Mar 71 DE VOLPI. ADJUSTED VALUE GIVEN	
Absorption	6.2 – 1	1.0+7	SRL	Theo Conf	71Knoxvill 714	Mar 71 Mccrosson. SPECTRUM – AVERAGED SIG	
Absorption	2.5 – 3	1.9+1	JUL	Theo Rept	JUEL – 746 – RG 13	Apr 71 Bonka. AVG SIG CALC	
Absorption	1.0 – 3	2.0+0	JUL	Theo Rept	JUEL – 746 – RG 49	Apr 71 Bonka.KUGEL – THERMOS – LIBR,T=300K,CURV	
Absorption	2.5 – 2		IFB	Eval Rept	YK – 9 34	72 Morogovsky. COMPUTR RE – EVAL,DATA GVN	
				Rept	INDC(CCP) – 42	Aug 74 .P1.ENGLISH OF YK – 9	
Absorption	2.5 – 2		CCP	Eval Conf	73Kiev 1 197	May 73 Fedorova.SIG=678.5+ – 1.9B AT V=2200	
Absorption	1.0+4	4.0+4	HAR	Theo Prog	AERE – PR/NP21	Mar 74 James+STAT ANL SHOWS INTRMD STR.TBL	
Absorption	1.0 – 3	1.5+7	IJE	Eval Jour	VBF 1975 1 13	75 Konshin+ SIG(NEUT – E),GRAPH,TBL	
Absorption	1.0 – 3	1.5+7	KFK	Eval Data	KEDAK – 3	Oct 75 8432 DATA SETS	+
Absorption	2.0 – 2	2.0+5	ORL	Expt Jour	NSE 59 79	Feb 76 Gwin+GRPHS,TBLS.AVG CS.CFD OTH	+
	1.0 – 2	2.0+5		Data	EXFOR10267.	Nov 75 274PTS.AVG ABS CS.1702 PTS ABS CS.	
Absorption	None		MUN	Theo Diss	GRYNTAKIS	Mar 76 Gryntakis.,CALC.OF WESTCOTTS G – FUNCT	
				Jour	RCA 22 128	Mar 75 – +,EQUIVALENT TO THESIS	
Res Int Abs	5.0 – 1	1.0+6	ORL	Eval Jour	NSE 6 100	Aug 59 Stoughton+,BEST VALUE 450+ – 100B	
Res Int Abs	Pile		CRC	Eval Rept	EANDC(CAN) – 20	Nov 62 Hanna+ CALC. CF CALCS AND EXPTS.	
Res Int Abs	4.4 – 1		ANL	Theo Abst	ANS 6 39	Jun 63 Persiani+RNEGCRESRCONTRIB.INFNITLDIL	
Res Int Abs	5.0 – 1	1.0+7	WAL	Eval Rept	WANL – TME – 1028	Nov 64 Drawbaugh+.4 PARTIAL+1.86TO49.4EV	
Res Int Abs	3.5 – 1	1.0+3	KFK	Eval Rept	KFK – 120 1	Nov 65 Schmidt. PARTIAL OVER 21 E INTERVALS	
Res Int Abs	5.0 – 1	1.0+7	BNW	Theo Conf	66Wash. 75	Mar 66 Liikala+, TBLS OF RES.INTEGRALS	
Res Int Abs	–		AUA	Theo Rept	AAEC/TM – 362	Dec 66 Cook+ TWO RESONANCE CALCULATNS CFD	
				Rept	AAEC/TM – 343	Sep 66 .BIBLIOGRAPHY OF CODES	
						SEE AAEC/E – 119,E – 126 AND E – 163	
Res Int Abs	Pile		SRL	Expt Conf	68Wash. 1271	Mar 68 Hennelly+ 380B	
Res Int Abs	Pile		UJV	Theo Rept	UJV – 2224	69 Stepanek. 7 GROUP CONSTANTS	
Res Int Abs	Maxwl	1.0+5	IAE	Revw Rept	INDC(NDS) – 47	72 Vlasov+ REVIEW DATA STATUS ,TBL+GRPH	
Res Int Abs	5.0 – 1		SGA	Comp Conf	73Paris 1 233	Mar 73 Eder+ INCLUDING 1/V PART,CAPTURE,TBL	
				Rept	SGAE – PH – 141	Feb 73 .SAME AS 73PARIS,NO DETAILS,TBP	
Res Int Abs	5.0 – 1		RPI	Expt Rept	UMO – 74 – 26,094	74 Shea. THESIS. TEMPERATURE – EFFECT	
Res Int Abs	5.0 – 1		KFI	Eval Rept	KFKI – 74 – 45	Jul 74 Gado.CAPT,PART+TOT FROM RES – PARS,TBL	
				Theo Rept	KFKI – 73 – 49	Sep 73 – + ABSORPT,CODE CALC CFD EVAL,TB	
(n,γ)	Cold		ANL	Revw Conf	55Geneva 5 125	Aug 55 Spinrad+.P835	
(n,γ)	Fast		ANL	Revw Conf	55Geneva 5 125	Aug 55 Spinrad+.P835	
(n,γ)	2.5 – 2	3.4+1	CUW	Eval Rept	CWR – 478	Jun 57 Kavanagh.B – W ANAL PART+TOT SIGS208ES	
(n,γ)	None		MTR	Theo Rept	PR 111 929	Aug 58 Reich+ MULTILEVEL THEORY.	
				Jour	PRL 1 47	Jul 58 .SUPERSEDED	
(n,γ)	1.8+5	1.0+6	LAS	Expt Jour	PR 109 144	Jan 58 Diven.	+
				Conf	58Geneva 15 60	Sep 58 – .PPR667,RATIO CAPTURE/FISSION	
(n,γ)	1.0 – 1	1.0+1	BNL	Expt Jour	PR 112 191	Oct 58 Shore.DERIVED FROM FISS+TOT SIG,B – W	
				Conf	58Geneva 15 118	Sep 58 – + CURVE FOR 3 RES	
(n,γ)	1.0+4	1.1+6	COL	Theo Jour	PR 112 492	Oct 58 Rae+,H – F CALC,TH CURVE CFD XPT	
				Jour	PRL 1 271	Oct 58 .SUPERSEDED	
(n,γ)	Pile		ORL	Eval Jour	NSE 6 100	Aug 59 Stoughton+,BEST VALUE .025EV=110B	
(n,γ)	Fiss		ALD	Eval Rept	AWRE – O – 02/60	Apr 60 Hinves+AWRE EVAL DATA CFD XPT.	
(n,γ)	Maxwl		HAN	Eval Conf	61RPI 3	May 61 Leonard.	
(n,γ)	5.0 – 3	2.5+0	GA	Eval Rept	GA – 2113	Jun 61 Wikner+.NFISSION,ALPHA GIVEN 100 ES	
(n,γ)	Pile		CRC	Eval Rept	CRRP – 1191	Jan 62 Westcott. EFF SIG.	
(n,γ)	3.0+4	1.0+6	LAS	Expt Jour	NSE 12 169	Feb 62 Hopkins+. CALCULATED FROM ALPHA(XPT)	+
	3.0+4	1.0+6		Data	EXFOR12331.004	Jun 76 . 9 PTS.	
(n,γ)	1.0 – 2	1.0+7	KFK	Eval Rept	KFK – 120 2	Dec 62 Schmidt.GRAPHS AND TABULATED DATA	+
	1.0 – 3	1.5+7		Data	KEDAK – 3	Oct 75 8381 DATA SETS	
(n,γ)	3.0 – 2	4.1+0	ITE	Expt Jour	AE 16 110	Feb 64 Ignat'Ev+ FROM TOTSIG+ETA,GRAPH	+
				Rept	ITE – 147	63 .SIMILAR TO AE 16 110 2/64	
				Jour	EAF 16 2 19	64 . FRENCH TRANSL OF AE 16 110 2/64	
				Jour	JNE 18 719	64 .ENGLISH TRANSL OF AE 16 110 2/64	
				Jour	SJA 16 121	64 .ENGLISH TRANSL OF AE 16 110 2/64	
				Rept	INDSWG – 7E	63 .ENGLISH TRANSL OF ITE – 147 /63	
(n,γ)		4.0+0	CCP	Theo Jour	AE 16 211	Mar 64 Kirpichnikov+ SIG(E) GRAPH,RES – ANAL	
				Jour	SJA 16 251	Mar 64 TRANSLATN.*NO 3	
(n,γ)	1.0 – 3	1.0+7	WAL	Eval Rept	WANL – TME – 1028	Nov 64 Drawbaugh+.CURV+TABLE.GROUP AVERAGED	
(n,γ)	Maxwl		RLY	Revw Conf	64Vienna 120	Dec 64 Raievski. TBL,AVG SIG OF 20+400DEG C	
(n,γ)	+5	+7	RLY	Revw Conf	64Vienna 56	Dec 64 Kronberger.FAST REACTOR,1 – GROUP SIGS	
(n,γ)	Maxwl		RLY	Revw Conf	64Vienna 56	Dec 64 Kronberger.ADV – G – COOLD – R,1 – GROUP – SIG	

92 Uranium 235

Quantity	Energy (ev) Min	Max	Lab	Type	Documentation Ref Vol Page	Date	Author, Comments	Data
(n,γ)	1.0+2	3.0+4	DUB	Expt	Conf 65Salzburg 1 287	Mar 65	Van – Shi – Di. TOF, TBL OF AVRGD VALUES	
					Rept JINR – P – 2024	65	Van Shi Di+ TOF.AVG VALS.	
					Rept BNL – TR – 16	Jul 65	– + ENGL OF 65SALZ.	
(n,γ)	1.0 – 4	9.0+3	UK	Eval	Rept AEEW – M – 502	May 65	Freemantle.TABLE.CURVE1 TO 100EV	+
	5.0 – 3	5.0+0			Rept AEEW – R – 351	Feb 64	Barrington+(WIN).UKNDL LOW EN REVISN	
	1.0+2	1.5+7			Rept AWRE – O – 82/63	Dec 63	Parker.(ALD).UKNDL – DFN 155	
	1.0 – 4	1.5+7			Data UKNDL – DFN 159B	Mar 73	2065 PNTS	
(n,γ)	3.2+0	2.5+1	ORL	Expt	Jour NSE 23 45	Sep 65	Desaussure. SSPD BY 1967 MEAS	+
					Rept ORNL – 3738	Apr 65	.SUPERSEDED	
(n,γ)	1.0+2	9.1+3	TRM	Comp	Rept AEET – 272	66	SHANKAR SINGH+ GROUP SIGS,TEMPERATUR	
(n,γ)	3.5 – 2	2.0+2	HAR	Expt	Rept AERE – M – 1670	Feb 66	Brooks+. LINAC,TOF, CURVES CFD OTHERS	
					Conf 66S.Diego 2 193	Feb 66	– . SEE ALSO	
					Rept EANDC(UK) – 42	Jun 64	– .FROM NF,TOT.TBL 2 SUPERSEDED	
(n,γ)	2.5 – 2		BNW	Theo	Conf 66Wash. 75	Mar 66	Liikala+, TBLS OF LITER. VALUES	
(n,γ)	1.0 – 2	1.0+0	MTR	Eval	Conf 66Wash. 840	Mar 66	Moore+,MULTILEVEL ANAL CURVE CFD XPT	
(n,γ)	4.5 – 1	1.0+4	INA	Eval	Conf 66Paris 2 333	Oct 66	Hennies.PPR5.TBL RECOM DATA CFD OTHR	
					Rept NAA – SR – 11980 5	May 67	– . RECOMMENDED DATA.REVISED	
(n,γ)	2.8+1	3.6+1	WAL	Comp	Conf 66Paris 2 251	Oct 66	Drawbaugh+ GRAPH, 3X AND 2X FIT.	
(n,γ)		6.3+1	WAL	Eval	Rept WANL – TME – 1586	Mar 67	Gibson+MULTIGROUP LIBRARY+CURVE	
(n,γ)	1.0+3	1.5+7	LAS	Eval	Prog WASH – 1074 79	Apr 67	Diven. NDG SEE EANDC(US) – 96U	
(n,γ)	1.8+5	2.6+6	IFU	Expt	Prog YFI – 4 34	May 67	Zaikin+.,TBLS GIVEN,TBP AE	
					Rept INDC – 187E	67	. ENGL OF YFI – 4 34	
(n,γ)	2.0+4	+6	GSF	Theo	Jour AF 36 509	Nov 67	Truran+.STAT MODEL. TWO MASS FORMLS	
(n,γ)	4.0 – 1	3.0+3	ORL	Expt	Rept ORNL – TM – 1804	Nov 67	Desaussure+ RPI LINAC+TOF CURVES	+
					Conf 66Paris 2 233	Oct 66	– + SUPERSEDED.	
	4.0 – 1	3.0+3			Data EXFOR10270.	Jan 73	5384PTS,SIGMA	
(n,γ)	Maxwl		RI	Revw	Jour AE 23 561	Dec 67	BAK+ OTHER SIG VAL GIVEN,TABLE	
					Jour SJA 23 1340	Dec 67	. ENGL OF AE 23 561	
(n,γ)	Maxwl		AUA	Theo	Jour NSE 31 234	Feb 68	Cook+ STATISTICAL CALC CFD EXPT	
(n,γ)	8.0+1	4.0+3	CCP	Theo	Jour YF 8 214	Jul 68	Vorotnikov. OTHER+TH SIG,FISS – MECHAN	
					Jour SNP 8 122	Jan 69	TRANSLATN.*	
(n,γ)	6.2+1	3.0+2	WAL	Eval	Rept WANL – TME – 2705	May 70	Drawbaugh+,BREIT – WIGNER FIT,CURVES	
(n,γ)	+5	+7	ANL	Revw	Conf 70Helsinki 2 119	Jun 70	Davey.112.STATUS OF DATA ABOVE RESON	
(n,γ)	1.0+1	1.0+7	CAD	Theo	Conf 70Helsinki 2 465	Jun 70	Barre+73. MICROSC CFD INTEGRAL DATA	
(n,γ)	2.5+0	5.0+3	KUR	Expt	Conf 70Helsinki 1 357	Jun 70	Muradjan.121. COUNTS VS E, GRAPHS	
(n,γ)	1.0+4	1.0+7	LAS	Eval	Conf 70Helsinki 2 517	Jun 70	Best+92. SIG(E) REVISED, INTEGRL TES	
(n,γ)	+0	1.0+2	ORL	Expt	Conf 70Helsinki 2 757	Jun 70	Desaussure. MULTILEVEL FIT	
	3.0+1	1.0+2			Prog ORNL – 4280 1	Oct 68	– + MULTILEVEL ANAL, CURV	
(n,γ)		7.0+3	SDC	Theo	Conf 70Helsinki 2 799	Jun 70	Garrison.DISCUSSN. RESONANCE ANAL	
(n,γ)		5.0+1	UI	Theo	Conf 70Helsinki 2 777	Jun 70	Adler+50. R – MATRIX CORRELATED ANAL	
(n,γ)	+3		JAE	Theo	Jour NST 7 592	Nov 70	Takano+.NUMBER OF RES TO GET AVG SIG	
(n,γ)	1.0+2		GA	Theo	Jour NP/A 159 305	Dec 70	Garrison.AVERAGE C.S.= NO RES INTERF	
(n,γ)		2.5+3	RPI	Theo	Prog NCSAC – 33 209	Dec 70	Shea.AVG SIG CALCTD,OKS EXPT,NO DATA	
(n,γ)	3.0+4		SUN	Expt	Prog INDC(SAF) – 4 14	71	Pilcher+ TO SPONFIS – ISOMER,HL	
(n,γ)	2.5 – 2		ANL	Eval	Conf 71Knoxvill 560	Mar 71	DE VOLPI. ADJUSTED VALUE GIVEN	
(n,γ)	None		DUB	Expt	Jour YF 13 457	Mar 71	Ryabov+ TOF,SELF – INDICATION METH,NDG	
	– 1	+1			Rept JINR – P3 – 4992	Apr 70	Rjabov+ PULSD REACTOR,TOF,LIQ SCINT	
	4.0+0	2.1+1			Jour PTE 8 4 63	Jul 65	– + PULSED REACTOR,CURVE SIG(E)	
	None				Jour SNP 13 255	Sep 71	. ENGL OF YF 13 457	
(n,γ)	2.5+5	4.0+6	BUC	Expt	Jour RRP 16 473	Apr 71	Boca+ SIG TO SPONFIS ISO AT 5ES.GRPH	
					Rept IFA – CRD – 42	70	– + SIG TO SPONFIS ISO.TABLE+GRAP	
(n,γ)	2.5 – 2		MOL	Expt	Rept STI/DOC/10 – 125	Apr 71	Ceulemans.PG46.DRVD FROM SCAT – EXP	
	2.5 – 2	1.0+0			Conf 70Helsinki 1 461	Jun 70	Ceulmans+21. DEDUCED VALUE,SCAT – EXPT	
(n,γ)	Maxwl		DUB	Expt	Jour YF 14 685	Oct 71	Belov+ ISOMERIC RATIO FOR U236 GIVEN	
					Jour SNP 14 385	Apr 72	*ENGL OF YF 14 685	
					Rept JINR – P7 – 5497	Jan 71	Belov+ ISOMER U236 PRODUCTN VS FISSN	
(n,γ)	1.0+2	1.0+5	ORL	Expt	Prog ORNL – 4705 10	Oct 71	Perez+.NG/NF CURV.NF CURV,TBL.CFD.	
					Conf 71Knoxvill 728	Mar 71	.SUPERSEDED	
(n,γ)	1.0+0	8.2+1	MTR	Eval	Rept ANCR – 1044	Dec 71	Smith+. CURVES	
(n,γ)	Pile		FAR	Expt	Prog EANDC(E)150U	May 72	Vidal.INTEGRAL CROSS SECTION RATIOS	
(n,γ)	2.5 – 2		CCP	Eval	Conf 73Kiev 1 197	May 73	Fedorova.SIG=98.3+ – 1.1B AT V=2200	
(n,γ)	2.5+2	6.5+3	KUR	Expt	Conf 73Kiev 4 49	May 73	Bolotskij+	+
	2.5+2	6.5+3			Data EXFOR40259.002	Feb 75	.CS U235,NG/CS U235,FISS AT 14ES GVN	
(n,γ)	0.0+0	6.0+1	ORL	Theo	Jour PR/C 7 2018	May 73	De Saussure+. MULTILEVEL ANALYSIS	
(n,γ)	6.0+4		DUB	Expt	Jour YF 18 34	Jul 73	Zen – Chang – Bom+ UPPER LIMIT TO U – 23M	
					Conf 73Kiev 3 250	May 73	Zen Chan Bom+ SIG(FIS – ISOM)/SIG(N,F)	
					Jour SNP 18 18	Jan 74	.ENGLISH OF YF 18 34	

92 Uranium 235

Quantity	Energy (ev) Min	Energy (ev) Max	Lab	Type	Documentation Ref Vol Page	Date	Author, Comments	Data
(n,γ)	8.0+0	1.0+4	ORL	Expt	Jour NSE 52 46	Sep 73	Perez+. LINAC.SIMULT NF+NG.REL B10NA	+
	8.1+0	1.0+4			Data EXFOR10249.	Jul 73	2614PTS.SIGMA,*E**1/2.	
(n,γ)	Maxwl		KFI	Expt	Rept KFKI-74-20	Apr 74	Lajtai+ UPPER LIMIT SIGMA TO U-236M	+
					Conf 73Rochestr 2 483	Aug 73	- + ABST,UPPER LIMIT SIG TO ISOM	
	Maxwl				Data EXFOR30281.002	Nov 74	UPPER LIMIT OF ISOMRC FIS/PROMPT FIS	
(n,γ)	1.0+4	4.0+4	ORL	Expt	Prog NEANDC(UK) 160	Jul 74	James+ ANAL FOR INTERMEDIATE STRUCT	
					Abst ANS 17 495	74	- +2 INTERMED STRUCT STAT TESTS	
(n,γ)	None		AUA	Theo	Prog AAEC/PR-41P 65	75	Bertram+ NDG.MULTILVL R-MATR OKS XPT	
(n,γ)	1.0+4	8.0+4	FEI	Expt	Jour AE 38 82	Feb 75	Kononov+ TOF,AVGSIG(NEUT-E),TBL	+
					Rept YK- 15 12	Aug 74	- TOF,VDG,AVGED SIG,TBL	
					Jour SJA 38 105	Aug 75	. ENGL OF AE 38 82	
	1.0+4	8.0+4			Data EXFOR40412.004	Jan 77	SIG FOR 7 E-RANGES	
(n,γ)	1.0+3	1.0+7	LRL	Theo	Conf 75Wash. 651	Mar 75	Gardner.CFD ENDF+ENDL.GRPH.	
(n,γ)	Maxwl		BNW	Eval	Abst ANS 21 507	Jun 75	Leonard+SIMULTAN FIT WITH FISS+ETA	
	-3	1.2-1			Conf 75Wash. 281	Mar 75	- .GRPH LEAST SQ EVAL CFD EXP	
(n,γ)	Fast		DOU	Expt	Rept UKNDC(75)P71	Jul 75	Davies+ IRRADIATION PFR SMALL SAMPLE	
(n,γ)	None		MUN	Theo	Diss GRYNTAKIS	Mar 76	Gryntakis.,CALC.OF WESTCOTTS G-FUNCT	
					Jour RCA 22 128	Mar 75	- +,EQUIVALENT TO THESIS	
(n,γ)	Maxwl		MTR	Expt	Prog WASH-1028 50	Apr 60	Hogg. SIG=96.6+-6.8B, U236 PROD	+
	Maxwl				Data EXFOR12438.005	Jun 76	. 1 PT. SIGMA.	
(n,γ)	Maxwl		RIS	Expt	Jour NP/A 269 338	Oct 76	Andersen+POP OF SHAPE ISOMER.	
(n,γ)	0.0+0	1.6+7	TRM	Theo	Conf 76Ahmedabd 2 116	Dec 76	Chatterjee+ DELAY/PROMPT FISS.GRAPH	
(n,γ)	2.1+1	1.0+7	CCP	Revw	Rept YK- 27 16	77	Vozjakov+ 20GROUP,5 LIBRARS CFD.TABL	
(n,γ)	Pile		FEI	Expt	Rept YK- 24 48	77	Andrijakhina+ AVG SIG AT DIFF POSITS	
Res Int Capt	5.0-1	1.0+6	ORL	Eval	Jour NSE 6 100	Aug 59	Stoughton+ BEST VALUE 150+-50B	
Res Int Capt	3.5-2	2.0+2	HAR	Expt	Rept EANDC(UK)-42	Jun 64	Brooks.FROM NF,TOT.AMENDED TBL 2	
Res Int Capt	3.9-1		KAP	Expt	Abst ANS 7 78	Jun 64	Esch+RES INT RAD CAPTURE 140PM11	
Res Int Capt	None		WAL	Eval	Rept WANL-TME-1228	Aug 65	Gibson+. CALCULATED FOR 1/E FLUX	
	5.0-1	1.0+7			Rept WANL-TME-1028	Nov 64	Drawbaugh+.4 PARTIAL(GAM TAPE 3E10)	
Res Int Capt	5.0-1		KAP	Comp	Conf 66S.Diego 2 299	Feb 66	Feiner+.COMPIL PREV RESULTS+RECOMMND	
Res Int Capt	3.5-1		WIN	Eval	Conf 66S.Diego 2 395	Feb 66	Askew. DEDUCED FROM EVAL SIGMA	
Res Int Capt	5.0-1		CRC	Expt	Conf 66Paris 2 17	Oct 66	Durham+ 143+-7B	+
	5.0-1				Data EXFOR12428.003	Jun 76	. 1 PT.	
Res Int Capt	4.5-1	1.0+4	INA	Eval	Conf 66Paris 2 333	Oct 66	Hennies.PPR5.TBL RECOM DATA CFD OTHR	
					Rept NAA-SR-11980 5	May 67	- . RECOMMENDED DATA.REVISED.	
Res Int Capt	5.0-1		BET	Expt	Jour NSE 29 1	Jul 67	Conway+ 136+-8B	+
					Rept WAPD-TM-613	Jun 67	.SUPERSEDED	
					Jour NSE 22 20	May 65	Conway. SUPERSEDED	
	5.0-1				Data EXFOR12313.004	Jun 76	. 1 PT.	
Res Int Capt		3.0+4	DUB	Expt	Prog YFI-5 61	Oct 67	Rjabov+ TABLES	
	5.0+0	2.0+4			Jour AE 24 351	Apr 68	- + VAL GIVEN,PULSED REACTOR,TOF	
	1.8+0	3.0+4			Jour AE 24 351	Apr 68	- + VAL GIVEN,PULSED REACTOR,TOF	
					Jour SJA 24 435	Apr 68	. ENGLISH OF AE 24 351	
	5.0+0	2.0+4			Jour SJA 24 435	Apr 68	. ENGLISH OF AE 24 351	
		3.0+4			Rept INDC-232E	67	. ENGL OF YFI-5 61	
Res Int Capt	None		TRM	Eval	Prog BARC-418 1	69	Singh+ CALC FROM RES PARS.NDG.TBP	
Res Int Capt	Fiss		RCN	Eval	Prog EANDC(E)127U	Apr 70	Bustraan+	
Res Int Capt	5.0-1		KAP	Expt	Jour NSE 44 180	May 71	Eiland+ CD AND CD-RH FILTERS	+
	5.0-1				Data EXFOR10143.	Aug 73	4PTS.	
Res Int Capt	5.3-1	8.2+1	MTR	Eval	Prog ANCR-1088 21	Oct 72	Smith+CALC.CFD OTH.TBL.	
					Prog ANCR-1044	Dec 71	- +CALC FROM ENDF3B.CFD OTH.TBL	
Spect (n,γ)	Maxwl		HAR		Rept NRDC-58	Feb 55	.ROUGH EXPT LIKE F GSPECT U235	
Spect (n,γ)	Maxwl		CRC	Expt	Conf 60Vienna 299	Oct 60	Bartholomew+.CURVE,EXPT DESCRIBED	
Spect (n,γ)	1.2+1		GA	Expt	Jour NIM 31 125	Dec 64	Haddad+ LIQUID SCINTILL,FISS CHAMBER	
Spect (n,γ)	8.9+0	1.2+1	SAC	Expt	Prog EANDC(E)115U	Mar 69	Asghar+, MULTIPLICITY OF CAPT GAMMAS	
	Maxwl				Jour PL/B 26 664	Apr 68	- +LOW E RES BY GAMMA YIELDS	
Spect (n,γ)	+4	+5	RPI	Expt	Prog WASH-1127 180	Apr 69	Tatarczuk+ GE(LI),NO DATA GIVEN	
Spect (n,γ)	6.4+0	3.9+1	GEL	Expt	Jour NP/A 134 535	Sep 69	Weigmann+ LINAC,GE(LI) 401-955HEVGS	+
					Conf 69Studsvik 687	Aug 69	- + GAM-INT(NEUT-E),GRPH+TBL	
	6.4+0	3.9+1			Data EXFOR20135.	Mar 73	27PTS.	
Spect (n,γ)		3.0+3	LRL	Expt	Prog WASH-1136 93	Sep 69	Bowman+,MULTIPLICIYY,ANAL TBC,NDG	
Spect (n,γ)	1.1+0	6.4+0	BNL	Expt	Jour PRL 25 953	Oct 70	Kane.HIGH-E GAMS FROM 4 RESONANCES	
	4.8+0				Conf 69Studsvik 105	Aug 69	- + TB CONTIND,CFD OTHER,N-MONOCH	
Spect (n,γ)	Maxwl		LAS	Expt	Prog NCSAC-33 152	Dec 70	Journey.PRELIM GAM ES 4.4-6.8MEV GIVN	
Spect (n,γ)	+0	+1	COL	Expt	Prog NCSAC-38 59	May 71	Derengowski+.RESON CAPT. SOME DATA	
Spect (n,γ)	None		COL	Expt	Prog NCSAC-38 60	May 71	Felvinci+. GAMMA MULTIPOL,ANAL TBC	

92 Uranium 235

Quantity	Energy (ev) Min	Energy (ev) Max	Lab	Type	Documentation Ref Vol Page	Date	Author, Comments	Data
Spect (n,γ)	Maxwl		UPP	Expt	Conf 72Budapest 6	Aug 72	Fogelberg+ CONVERSION ELECTRONS.NDG.	
					Rept INIS – MF – 427	Jun 72	– + PPR15.5,ABST,CONV EL,LVLS	
					Prog EANDC(OR)99 19	Aug 70	Baecklin+. ELECTR+GAM SPEC .5 – 1.5MEV	
					Conf 69Studsvik 141	Aug 69	– + GAM+ELECTR SPECS,GRPH+TBL	
Spect (n,γ)	Maxwl		LIN	Expt	Jour YF 17 234	Feb 73	Popeko+ GAM+CONV – EL TO U236M,GRAPHS	
					Jour SNP 17 120	Aug 73	.ENGLISH OF YF 17 234	
Spect (n,γ)	1.5+0	5.8+1	GEL	Expt	Jour NP/A 203 145	Mar 73	Corvi+ RATIO 160/642KEV. J FOR 14RES	
Spect (n,γ)	Maxwl		ATI	Expt	Jour NP/A 206 374	May 73	Schindler+ GE – LI,300 – 1300KEV.CFD CF	
					Jour AKE 21 136	Apr 73	Fleck+NEW LOW – E GAMS,SPIN+PI 1342KEV	
Spect (n,γ)	1.1+0	3.2+1	BNL	Expt	Jour PR/C 8 781	Aug 73	Graves+. RESONANCE CAPT GAMS. GE(LI)	
	– 1	+2			Abst DA/B 32 4793	Feb 72	– . EPITHERMAL NEUTS.	
					Conf 71Knoxvill 792	Mar 71	.SUPERSEDED	
	1.1+0	3.2+1			Conf 70Helsinki 1 377	Jun 70	.SUPERSEDED	
Spect (n,γ)	Maxwl		MUN	Expt	Conf 74Petten 664	Sep 74	Loebner+ PREFISSION G – RAYS	
Spect (n,γ)	Maxwl		KFK	Expt	Rept KFK – 1214	Jul 70	Matussek+ G – SPEC,GRPHS,LVL SCH U – 236	+
	2.5 – 2				Prog KFK – 1980 2 4	Oct 74	– + GE – LI,CFD FISS FRAG G – SPEC	
	Maxwl				Conf 74Petten 749	Sep 74	Weitkamp+ NONDESTR FUEL ASSAY APPL.	
					Conf 74Petten 658	Sep 74	Ottmar+ DECAY SCHEME U – 236	
					Prog EANDC(E)157U I	Mar 73	Matussek+ FR2 REACTOR	
					Priv WIETKAMP	73	Weitkamp. SPECTRA FOR COMPILATION	
					Conf 72Budapest 84	Aug 72	Matussek+ INTENSITIES ,TBL	
					Conf 69Studsvik 51	Aug 69	Michaelis+ PREL SPEC,NEUT – ANTICOINCD	
					Rept KFK – 1095	Aug 69	– + PRELIM.REPRINT OF 69STUDS	
	Maxwl				Data EXFOR20372.002	Sep 74	26PTS.	
Spect (n,γ)	+6		DUB	Expt	Rept JINR – P3 – 9274	Nov 75	Gangrskij+ GAM – SPEC TO ISOMER,GRAPH	
	Pile				Rept JINR – P15 – 6147	Nov 71	Gangrsky+ G – SPEC LEADING TO SPONFIS	
					Rept BNL – TR – 482	71	. ENGLISH OF JINR – P15 – 6147	
Spect (n,γ)	None		IJE	Eval	Rept INDC(CCP) – 78	Jan 76	Konshin+ STATMOD, NO DATA GIVEN	
Inelastic γ	4.0+6	7.5+6	LAS	Expt	Jour NP/A 133 108	Aug 69	Drake.TOF.CS CALC FROM NON – ELAS DATA	+
					Conf 66Paris 1 419	Oct 66	Conde+PPR84, NDG,VDG,TOF HIGH RESLN	
	3.5+6	7.5+6			Conf 66Wash. 735	Mar 66	– +TBC.NDG.	
	4.0+6	7.5+6			Data EXFOR10016.	May 71	. 3 PTS.CALC FROM NON – ELAS DATA	
Inelastic γ	1.1+6	1.5+7	TNC	Expt	Rept ORO – 2791 – 32	Feb 71	Buchanan+.55 – DEG SIGS,6NEUT ES	+
	1.0+6	1.5+7			Data EXFOR12408.002	Jun 76	. 6 PTS. SIGMA	
	1.0+6	1.5+7			Data EXFOR12408.005	Jun 76	. 60 PTS. ANG.DISTRIBUTION	
Inelastic γ	None		IJE	Eval	Rept INDC(CCP) – 78	Jan 76	Konshin+ STATMOD, NO DATA GIVEN	
Nonelastic γ		1.0+7	GEN	Eval	Rept GEMP – 360	Aug 65	Edwards.15 – GROUP GAMMA PRODUCTN SIGS	
Nonelastic γ	1.5+7		LRL	Theo	Jour NSE 32 178	May 68	Howerton+ 13.1B CALC,CFD EXPT 15.1B	
Nonelastic γ	4.0+6	7.5+6	LAS	Expt	Jour NP/A 133 108	Aug 69	Drake.TOF G PROD AT 4.0,6.0,7.5 MEV.	+
	3.5+6	7.5+6			Conf 66Wash. 735	Mar 66	Conde+TBC.NDG.	
	4.0+6	7.5+6			Data EXFOR10016.	May 71	. 73 PTS. G PROD CS AT 55,90DEG.3ES.	
Nonelastic γ	1.4+7		SAC	Expt	Rept CEA – R – 4132	Feb 71	Bertrand. 30 TO 130 DEGREES	
Nonelastic γ	Pile		ORL	Expt	Rept ORNL – 4691	Aug 71	Booth+. GAMMA SPEC ABOVE 1 MEV.CURVS	
Nonelastic γ	2.5 – 2		IFB	Eval	Rept YK – 9 34	72	Morogovsky. SIG G – PROD EVAL,DATA GVN	
					Rept INDC(CCP) – 42	Aug 74	.P1.ENGLISH OF YK – 9	
Nonelastic γ		2.0+7	LRL	Theo	Abst BAP 18 625	Apr 72	Gardner+ SIG + SPEC, NDG	
Nonelastic γ	1.0 – 5	2.0+7	LAS	Eval	Rept LA – 4918	Jul 72	Stewart+. GAMMA PRODUCTION SIGS	
Nonelastic γ	1.0+6	2.0+6	LAS	Expt	Rept LA – 5048	Dec 72	Drake. GAM SPEC AND PRODUCTION SIGS	+
	1.0+6	2.0+6			Data EXFOR10330.003	Sep 75	. 28 PTS.	
Nonelastic γ	1.0+6	8.0+6	LAS	Expt	Jour NSE 55 427	Dec 72	Drake. TOF,CFD EXPERIMENTS	+
	1.0+6	8.0+6			Data EXFOR10460.002	Jun 76	. 126 PTS. DSIGMA.	
Nonelastic γ	5.0+6	8.0+6	LAS	Expt	Rept LA – 5134	Feb 73	Drake.DIFF GAM PRODUCTN SIGS TABULAT	+
	5.0+6	8.0+6			Data EXFOR10329.002	Jul 74	. 97 PTS.	
Nonelastic γ	1.4+7		LAS	Expt	Rept LA – 5662 – MS	Aug 74	Drake+. 14.2MEV PLSD N – SOURCE,TBLS	+
					Conf 75Wash. 770	Mar 75	Arthur+G PROD CS.NDG	
	1.4+7				Data EXFOR10684.017	Feb 78	. 45 PTS. DSIGMA	
Nonelastic γ	1.4+7		KUR	Expt	Conf 75Kiev 4 133	May 75	Bezotosnyj+ NA – I.SIG(.5 – 8.0 MEV) GVN	
(n,2n)	Thrsh	1.5+7	UK	Eval	Rept AWRE – O – 82/63	Dec 63	Parker.(ALD).UKNDL – DFN 155	
	5.3+6	1.5+7			Data UKNDL – DFN 159B	Mar 73	.22 PTS.E DIST.ANG DIST,LAB.	
(n,2n)	1.3+7	1.5+7	BNL	Theo	Jour NSE 23 238	Nov 65	Pearlstein.3ES.STAT MDL CALC.TBL CS.	
(n,2n)	Fiss		BNL	Theo	Jour NSE 23 238	Nov 65	Pearlstein.STATMDL CALC.SPEC AVG.TBL	
(n,2n)	Thrsh	1.6+7	KFK	Eval	Rept KFK – 120 1	Feb 66	Schmidt.CURVE FROM AWRE O – 82/60	+
	5.8+6	1.0+7			Rept KFK – 120 2	Dec 62	– .GRAPHS AND TABULATED DATA	
	5.4+6	1.5+7			Data KEDAK – 3	Oct 75	60 DATA SETS	
(n,2n)	Pile		ORL	Expt	Prog ORNL – 4306 1	May 68	Halperin+ INTEGRAL MEAS, PRELM VALUE	
(n,2n)	1.5+7		DUB	Expt	Jour AE 31 156	Aug 71	Gangrskij+ UPPER LIMIT FOR SPON – ISOM	
	+6	+7			Rept JINR – P3 – 5528	Jan 71	– + GND+ISOM FISSN STATE SIGS	
	1.5+7				Jour SJA 31 874	Mar 72	. ENGL OF AE 31 156	

92 Uranium 235

Quantity	Energy (ev) Min	Max	Lab	Type	Documentation Ref Vol Page	Date	Author, Comments	Data
(n,2n)	7.0+7	1.4+7	ALD	Expt Rept	AWRE-O-72/72	Nov 72	Mather+ LARGE LIQ SCINTILLATOR.	+
	7.1+6	1.4+7		Data	EXFOR20795.010	Oct 78	4PTS.SIGMA.	
(n,2n)	1.5+7		DUB	Expt Jour	IJP 47 232	73	Belov+ SIG TO SPONFIS GIVN,FRAGM-DET	
				Rept	JINR-E15-6807	Nov 72	- + SPON FISS ISOMER PRODUCTN,TBL	
(n,2n)	1.5+7		KFI	Expt Jour	MFF 21 555	73	Nagy. THESIS,HUNG. TO FISS ISO,GRND	
(n,2n)	2.0+6	1.5+7	BRC	Eval Rept	CEA-R-4647	Jan 75	Jary. EVAL,STAT MDL, 15 VALS	
(n,2n)	Thrsh	1.5+7	BRC	Expt Rept	CEA-N-1798 34	Jun 75	Frehaut+ LARGE LIQ SCINT METH	
(n,xn) x>2	Thrsh	1.5+7	ALD	Expt Rept	AWRE-O-82/63	Dec 63	Parker.N3N.UKAEA DFN-155.	
(n,xn) x>2	Fiss		BNL	Theo Jour	NSE 23 238	Nov 65	Pearlstein.SPEC AVG STATMDL CALC N3N	
(n,xn) x>2	Thrsh	1.6+7	KFK	Eval Rept	KFKI-120	Feb 66	Schmidt.CURVE N3N OF AWRE-O-82/60	+
	1.3+7	1.5+7		Data	KEDAK-3	Oct 75	21 DATA SETS N3N.	
(n,xn) x>2	1.2+7	1.4+7	ALD	Expt Rept	AWRE-O-72/72	Nov 72	Mather+ LARGE LIQ SCINTILLATOR.(N3N)	+
	1.2+4	1.4+7		Data	EXFOR20795.011	Oct 78	2PTS.SIGMA.	
(n,xn) x>2	1.2+7	1.5+7	UK	Eval Data	UKNDL-DFN 159B	Mar 73	.7 PTS. E DIST.ANG DIST,LAB. N3N.	
(n,xn) x>2	2.0+6	1.5+7	BRC	Eval Rept	CEA-R-4647	Jan 75	Jary. EVAL,STAT MDL, 15 VALS	
(n,xn) x>2	1.0+5	1.5+7	BRC	Expt Rept	CEA-N-1798 34	Jun 75	Frehaut+ LARGE LIQ SCIN METHOD	
n Emission	1.4+7		FEI	Expt Jour	IZV 32 653	Apr 67	Salnikov+ E SPECS OF SECONDARY NEUTS	+
				Conf	67Kharkov 173	Feb 67	.ABSTRACT	
				Jour	BAS 32 600	69	.ENGLISH TRANSL OF IZV 32 653 4/68	
	1.4+7			Data	EXFOR40332.003	Feb 76	DOUBLE-DIFF CS AT 92DEG, 61 PNTS	
n Emission	1.4+7		LAS	Expt Rept	LA-5949	Jun 75	Ragan+ NEUT SPECT ORALLOY SPHERE	
(n,p)	1.4+7		ALD	Expt Rept	AWRE-O-72/72	Feb 59	Coleman+. ACT. CFD DIRECT INTERACTN	+
(n,p)	1.5+7		SAH	Comp Jour	NUC 23 8 112	Aug 65	Chatterjee. TABLE WITH REFS.	
(n,p)	1.4+7	1.5+7	JYV	Eval Rept	JU-RR-3/1970	Jun 70	Leppaemaeki+ TABLE OF EVAL AVG SIG	
(n,α)	1.4-1	8.8+0	ORL	Expt Prog	ORNL-3425 82	63	Dabbs+ANIS. AT 5RES ORIENTED NUCLEI	
(n,α)	Maxwl		IBJ	Expt Rept	ZFK-PHA-12 147	Oct 63	Dakowski+ 7-11MEV AS,NOT IDENTIFIED	
(n,α)	Pile		IBJ	Expt Jour	PL 6 321	Oct 63	Sowinsky+ ALF-SPEC ANALYSIS,TBC	
(n,α)	Maxwl		ISL	Expt Prog	IA-984 36	64	Cheifetz.DIFFERS FROM OTHER XPTS,TBC	
(n,α)	5.0-3	5.0+0	UK	Eval Rept	AEEW-R-351	Feb 64	Barrington+(WIN).UKNDL LOW EN REVISN	
(n,α)		1.0+0	NBS	Expt Prog	WASH-1053 52	Oct 64	Landon.PROPOSED XPT,XCOINC WITH FISS	
(n,α)	Maxwl		LEB	Expt Conf	65Antwerp § 176	Jul 65	Andreev+CFD TH+N,ALPHA G.	
				Jour	YF 1 252	Feb 65	- . IONIZ-CHAMBER,SIG= 2.5MB	
				Jour	SNP 1 177	Aug 65	. ENGL OF YF 1 252	
(n,α)	Maxwl		IBJ	Expt Jour	APP 35 187	Jan 69	Chwaszczewska+ A BELOW 10.7MEV,GRAPH	+
	Maxwl			Data	EXFOR30272.002	Aug 74	SIGMA UPPER LIMIT,TELESCOPE COUNTER	
(n,α)		5.8+6	ORL	Theo Prog	USNDC-3 145	Oct 72	Johnson.R-MATRIX ANALYSIS.	
(n,α)	1.0-4	1.0+0	IFB	Eval Rept	YK-20/1 126	75	Antsipov+ EVAL OF XPTAL DATA.GRAPHS	
(n,α)	1.0-4	1.0+0	IJE	Eval Rept	INDC(CCP)-78	Jan 76	Konshin+ (ENGL) BRIEF DESCRIPTION	
Fission	-		PAR	Expt Jour	JPR 8 385	Oct 37	Curie+	
				Jour	JPR 9 440	Oct 38	- +	
				Jour	JPR 9 355	Sep 38	- + HISTORICAL INTEREST.	
Fission	Maxwl		MIN	Expt Jour	PR 57 546	Mar 40	Nier+ MA2S SPECTR SEPARION OF ISOT.	
				Jour	PR 57 748	Apr 40	- . CONTINUED	
Fission	Maxwl		GES	Expt Jour	PR 57 749	Apr 40	Kingdon+ FISSION RATE U235+U234	
Fission	8.0+4	1.5+6	LAS	Expt Rept	LA-28	Oct 43	Taschek.RELATIVE TO PU 239 NF	
Fission	4.3+3	1.8+6	LAS	Expt Rept	LA-150	Oct 44	Williams.	+
	4.3+3	1.8+6		Data	EXFOR12300.003	Jun 76	. 25 PTS.	
Fission	1.4+7		LAS	Expt Rept	LAMS-774	Sep 48	Phillips+ PHOTOPLATE VDG REL U238	
	1.4+7			Data	EXFOR12495.003	Jun 76	. 1 PT.	
Fission	Maxwl	+7	KTH	Theo Jour	NAT 165 561	Apr 50	Meitner.FISSION AND NUCL SHELL MODEL	
Fission	1.4+7		LAS	Expt Rept	LAMS-938	Jun 50	Nyer+ FISS CHAMBER RELATIVE TO U238	+
	1.4+7			Data	EXFOR12306.004	Jun 76	. 1 PT.	
Fission	Maxwl		ANL	Expt Prog	ANL-5411 1	53	Sellers+ RATIO U233/,PU241/	+
	Maxwl			Data	EXFOR12352.	Jun 76	. 2 RATIOS	
Fission	8.6+5	4.2+6	ORL	Expt Rept	ORNL-1458	Feb 53	Carlson.U238/U235 RATIO,FOIL METHOD	
Fission	Pile		SAC	Expt Jour	CR 237 155	Jul 53	DE LABOULAYE+.SEARCH F LOW E ALPHAS	
				Jour	JPR 15 470	Jun 54	De Laboulaye+ FISSION ALPHAS.	
Fission	2.0-2	1.0+0	HAN	Expt Rept	HW-30128	Dec 53	Leonard. PU239/U235 RATIO.	
Fission	1.0+3	4.0+4	KAP	Expt Rept	KAPL-1109	Jun 54	Yeater. FISSION CHAMBER	+
	7.2+2	4.5+4		Data	EXFOR12422.002	Jun 76	. 28 PTS.	
Fission	Pile	2.5-2	HAR	Expt Rept	NRDC-51	Oct 54	Raffle.BEPO CORE+THR COL+TOF 2200M/S	+
	Maxwl	Pile		Rept	AERE-R-2998	Jul 59	- .SIG AT 0.025EV=582+-12B	
Fission	5.0-3	2.5+0	HAN	Expt Rept	HW-33384 33	Nov 54	Leonard+	+
	5.0-3	9.8-1		Data	EXFOR12430.002	Jun 76	. 80 PTS.	
Fission	1.0-2	2.5+1	SAC	Expt Jour	CR 239 1128	Nov 54	Galula+. PU/U235 RATIO. GRAPH.	
Fission	1.0-2	4.2-1	KJL	Expt Jour	JNE 1 170	Dec 54	Popovic.E DEPENDENCE REL B	
Fission	Fast		KJL	Expt Jour	NUC 13 2 67	Feb 55	Raisic.1D6 PM D8B AVG OVER SPECTRUM	+
	Fiss			Data	EXFOR20076.	Sep 71	2PTS.	

92 Uranium 235

Quantity	Energy (ev) Min	Energy (ev) Max	Lab	Type	Documentation Ref Vol Page	Date	Author, Comments	Data
Fission	1.0−2	1.0+2	CCP	Expt	Conf 55Moscow 87	Jul 55	Nikitin+.SIMULTAN ABS AND FISS,CURVE	
					Rept AEC−TR−2435 81	56	. ENGL TRANSL OF 55MOSCOW 87	
Fission	1.0−2	4.0+0	SAC	Expt	Jour JNE 1 306	Jun 55	Auclair. GRAPH.SLOW NEUTRONS.	
					Jour JPRS 16 50	Jul 55	− +CRYSTSPEC,CURVES,AGREES TOF	
					Conf 55Geneva § 354	Aug 55	− . SUPERSEDED	
Fission	Cold		ANL	Revw	Conf 55Geneva 5 125	Aug 55	Spinrad+.P835	
Fission	1.0+4	3.0+6	ANL	Revw	Conf 55Geneva 5 347	Aug 55	Okrent+.P609,GRAPH,NO EXPT DETAILS	
Fission	Fast		ANL	Revw	Conf 55Geneva 5 125	Aug 55	Spinrad+.P835	
Fission	2.5−2		BNL	Comp	Conf 55Geneva 4 147	Aug 55	Harvey.VAL 2200M/SEC,PPR832	
Fission	1.0−2	5.0+5	BNL	Eval	Conf 55Geneva 4 199	Aug 55	Sailor.GRAPH,SUM OF SEV EXPTS,PPR586	
Fission	Maxwl	Pile	HAR	Revw	Conf 55Geneva 4 210	Aug 55	Lynn+.ALSO VAL 2200M,GRAPH,PPR423	
Fission	Pile		HAR	Revw	Conf 55Geneva 5 331	Aug 55	Holmes+.P404,RATIO PU239/U235 GVN	
Fission	2.5−2		IAE	Revw	Conf 55Geneva 4 287	Aug 55	Worldvalue+ERROR GVN (2200M/SEC)	
				Eval	Jour NAT 176 619	Oct 55	.SEE ALSO *	
				Revw	Jour JET 2 271	55	.SAME ARTICLE,RUSSIAN ZET 29 1455	
Fission	1.1−2	9.7+2	KUR	Expt	Conf 55Geneva 4 216	Aug 55	Adamchuk+.FC,GRAPHS AND DISCUSSION	+
Fission	2.5−2		FR	Expt	Jour CR 241 669	Sep 55	Perrin.QUOTES WORLD SIGMA =590+ −15B	
Fission	Maxwl		HAR	Revw	Jour NAT 176 619	Oct 55	Gaunt+590+ −15B WORLD AVG VALUES	
Fission	5.3−3	1.5+2	HAR	Expt	Jour JNE 2 128	Dec 55	Price.TABULAR DATA IN NRDC 81 TABLE6	+
					Conf 55Geneva 4 210	Aug 55	− .(LYNN) SIG AT 9 N,F RES.	
					Rept NRDC−81	55	− . SEE FOR TBLS.	
	5.0−2	1.5+2			Rept AERE−RP/R−1389	Sep 54	− .REL B10(N,ALPHA)	
Fission	1.0−3	1.0+0	CCP	Expt	−		ENGL TRANSL AEC−TR−2435 PAGE 1	
					Rept AEC−TR−2435 1	56	. ENGL OF 55MOSCOW 15	
	4.9+3	3.0+6	ORL	Expt	Jour PR 104 1654	56	Lamphere. RATIOS U233,U234,U236,U238	+
	4.9+3	3.0+6			Data EXFOR12338.	Jun 76	. 303 RATIOS	
Fission	5.0+4	1.0+6	SAC	Expt	Conf 55Geneva 4 245	56	Szteinsznaider+.15+ −0.15B 0.7TO1MEV	+
					Jour NKA 1 2 95	Sep 65	− +	
Fission	1.4+7		HAR	Expt	Rept AERE−NP/R−1996	Jun 56	Uttley+.BACK TO BACK FISS CHAMBER	+
Fission	6.0+0	2.0+3	KAP	Expt	Jour PR 104 479	Oct 56	Yeater. FISSION CHAMBER, ABS CURVE	+
	5.0+0	2.0+3			Prog KAPL−1565	May 56	.SUPERSEDED	
	5.3+0	2.0+3			Data EXFOR12414.003	Jun 76	. 447 PTS.	
Fission	Maxwl		ORL	Expt	Prog ORNL−2081 102	Nov 56	Pratt+ RELATIVE PU239,PU240	+
	Maxwl				Data EXFOR12509.	Jun 76	. 2 RATIOS	
Fission	1.0+6	4.0+6	SAC	Expt	Abst PHY 22 1187	Nov 56	Ballini+ABSTRACT.VDG SOURCE.NDG	+
	1.0+6	3.8+6			Priv NETTER	Jun 56	Netter+ FULL DATA FOR COMPILATION.	
Fission	Fast		HAR	Expt	Rept AERE−R/R−2151	57	Absalom+ ZEPHYR+TH ENVELOPE.	
Fission	2.5−2		BNL	Eval	Rept BNL−325	Jan 57	Hughes+ WORLD CONSIST. VAL. 582+ −10B	
Fission	3.0+3	5.0+6	CCP	Expt	Jour AE 2 10	Jan 57	Dorofeev+.REL+ABS DATA, 5 GN SOURCES	+
					Jour JNE 5 217	Nov 57	TRANSLATN.*	
					Jour SJA 2 9	57	TRANSLATN.*	
Fission	2.5−2		HAN	Expt	Conf AERE−NP/R−2076	Jan 57	Leonard. P13.	+
					Prog HW−47012 50	56	Friesen+	
	2.5−2				Data EXFOR12394.002	Jun 76	. 1 PT.	
Fission	2.6−2	1.0+2	CCP	Expt	Jour AE 2 129	Feb 57	Sokolovsky+.FAST CHOPPER, NO DATA	+
					Jour JNE 5 389	Nov 57	TRANSLATN.*	
					Jour SJA 2 147	57	TRANSLATN.*	
Fission	4.0+5	1.6+6	LAS	Expt	Jour PR 105 1350	Feb 57	Diven.FLAT 1.0−1.5MEV 1.27+ −0.044B	+
	2.5+5	3.0+6			Conf 55Geneva 4 251	Aug 55	− +.GRAPH,EXPT DESCRIBED,P594	
	4.0+5	1.6+6			Data EXFOR12415.002	Jun 76	. 14 PTS.	
Fission	2.5−2	1.0−1	HAN	Expt	Rept HW−48893	Mar 57	Leonard.	+
	2.5−2	1.0−1			Data EXFOR12434.	Jun 76	. 2 PTS.	
Fission	2.0+6	2.0+7	LAS	Expt	Abst BAP 2 196	Apr 57	Smith+,XCIT CURV OK BOHR	+
	2.2+6	2.0+7			Prog WASH−1074 75	Apr 57	Hansen. REVISED 1956 VALUES, TABLE	
	1.1+4	1.0+7			Rept LA−2114	Feb 57	Henkel+ ABSOL CURV REVIEWS ALL DATA	
Fission	5.8+2	6.1+7	KAP	Eval	Rept KAPL−1756 1	Jun 57	Baraff.TBL D25LETHARGYSTEPS	
Fission	1.0+5	7.0+6	LAS	Revw	Rept LA−2122	Jun 57	Henkel.CURV,REPLACES LA−1714	
Fission	1.0+2	1.0+6	BNL	Theo	Jour JNE 5 16	Jul 57	Oleksa.THEOR AGREES XPT TO 10KEV,AVG	
Fission	3.0+4	3.0+6	HAR	Expt	Jour PPSA 70 573	Aug 57	Allen+.SIGF TO + −3PERCENT,AND RATIOS	+
Fission	2.0−2	2.4−1	CUW	Theo	Jour CWR−400−1	Sep 57	Roberts.MAXWELL−BOLTZMANN AVGD SIGS.	
Fission	2.7−3	5.1−3	HAN	Expt	Prog HW−53492 22	Nov 57	Seppi. NF*SQRT(E).	+
	2.7−3	5.1−3			Data EXFOR12400.002	Jun 76	. 10 PTS.	
Fission	3.8−3	9.5−1	ANL	Expt	Priv BOLLINGER	58	Bollinger. TOF	+
	3.8−3	9.5−1			Data EXFOR12390.002	Jun 76	. 31 PTS.	
Fission	5.0+0	2.2+1	COL	Expt	Rept CU−174	Mar 58	Havens+TOF RAW DATA NO S TBC BET RES	
Fission	1.0−1	4.0+4	COL	Expt	Jour NSE 3 435	Apr 58	Melkonian+,TOF,CURVE GIVEN	+
	1.2−2	4.0+4			Rept CU−163	Jun 57	− . TOF ABSCURVS TVLS.	
	1.1−2	4.0+4			Data EXFOR12403.003	Jun 76	. 336 PTS.	

92 Uranium 235

Quantity	Energy (ev) Min	Max	Lab	Type	Documentation Ref Vol Page	Author, Comments Date	Data
Fission	4.0−2	8.7+0	HAN Expt	Abst	BAP 3 227	May 58 Seppi. NDG, TERNARY/BINARY	
Fission	2.5−2	3.4+1	CUW Theo	Jour	NSE 4 155	Jul 58 Kavanagh.BREIT−WIGNER ANALYSIS	
				Rept	CWR−478	Jun 57 .SUPERSEDED	
Fission	5.3−3	2.0+3	HAR Theo	Jour	JNE 7 35	Aug 58 EGELSTAFF CORRELATION ANAL,W+SPACING	
	5.0+0	2.0+3		Jour	PPS 71 910	Jun 58 Egelstaff.FLUCTUATIONS CFD THEORY	
	Maxwl			Eval Rept	AERE−NP/R−2140	Dec 57 − + CONSISTENT VALUES 2200M/S	
Fission	None		MTR Theo	Jour	PR 111 929	Aug 58 Reich+ REICH MOORE MULTILEVEL THEORY	
				Jour	PRL 1 47	Jul 58 .SUPERSEDED	
Fission	2.5−2		ANL Expt	Conf	58Geneva 16 103	Sep 58 Saplakoglu.PPR1599,ABSOLUTE SIGMA	+
	2.5−2			Data	EXFOR12392.002	Jun 76 . 1 PT.	
Fission	1.0−3	1.0+0	BNL Comp	Conf	58Geneva 16 8	Sep 58 Hughes.PPR2483,CURVE,MANY REFS	
Fission	2.5−2	1.0+2	CCP Expt	Conf	58Geneva 15 309	Sep 58 Vladimirsky+.PPR2221,CURVE,BF3−DETCT	
Fission	3.0+6	8.0+6	KUR Expt	Conf	58Geneva 16 136	Sep 58 Kalinin+.PPR2149,CURVE,CYCLOTRON	+
Fission	1.0+4	1.0+7	LAS Revw	Conf	58Geneva 15 344	Sep 58 Hemmendinger.PPR663,CURVE,MANY REFS	
Fission	1.0−1	1.0+1	BNL Expt	Jour	PR 112 191	Oct 58 Shore.CS,MULTILEVEL FIT,ABS CURVES	+
				Conf	58Geneva 15 118	Sep 58 − . PPR648, CURVE	
				Conf	ORNL−2309	Jun 57 − . CS TBD.	
	1.0−1	1.0+1		Data	EXFOR12418.004	Jun 76 . 278 PTS	
Fission		2.0+0	CRC Theo	Jour	PR 112 203	Oct 58 Vogt.MULTILVL TH CFD EXP DATA	
Fission	Thrsh	Up	LAS Expt	Prog	WASH−1006 21	Oct 58 Stokes+ NDG, SLOPE AS U233,U238	
Fission	3.0+5	1.5+7	LRL Eval	Rept	UCRL−5351	Nov 58 Howerton.XPTL+ASSUMED.ALSO NN'F,N2NF	
Fission	1.5+7		CCP Expt	Jour	AE 5 659	Dec 58 Berezin+ 14.6MEV U235/U238=2.03+−.09	+
				Jour	JNEA 11 175	Feb 60 TRANSLATN.*	
				Jour	SJA 5 1604	58 TRANSLATN.*	
Fission	2.5−2		COL Expt	Jour	PR 113 1285	Mar 59 Safford+	+
				ExTh Jour	PRL 2 189	Feb 59 .SUPERSEDED	
	2.5−2			Expt Data	EXFOR12439.002	Jun 76 . 1 PT. SIGMA.	
Fission	3.4+3	7.7+5	CCP Expt	Jour	AE 6 453	Apr 59 Gorlov+ VDG,FISS CHAMBER,ABSOL,GRAPH	+
				Jour	SJA 6 317	Nov 60 *ENGL OF AE 6 453	
				Jour	KE 3 222	Mar 60 *	
				Rept	AEC−TR−3913	59 . ENGL OF AE 6 453	
	3.4+3	7.7+5		Data	EXFOR40055.002	Sep 70 SIG AT 24 ES,PRIVATE COMM AUG 1970	
Fission	Pile		ORL Eval	Jour	NSE 6 100	Aug 59 Stoughton+,BEST VALUE .025EV=580B	
Fission	2.9−3	2.5−2	COL ExTh	Jour	NSE 6 433	Nov 59 Safford+ DEDUCED FROM ALFA AND TOTAL	+
	2.5−2			Conf	60Vienna 203	Oct 60 .SEE ALSO	
	2.9−3	2.5−2		Expt Data	EXFOR12404.	Jun 76 . 2 PTS.	
Fission	2.5−2		COL Revw	Jour	NUC 17 11 134	Nov 59 Safford+. EXPTL VALUES TABULATED	
Fission	Maxwl		CRC Expt	Jour	NSE 6 379	Nov 59 Bigham. RATIO PU239, MOD TEMP DEP	+
				Jour	NSE 59 50	Jan 76 − +CS OF 1958 WORK.REVISED	
				Conf	58Geneva 16 125	Sep 58 − +,P.204,RATIO SIG U233/U235	
	Maxwl			Data	EXFOR12356.	Jun 76 . 2 RATIOS. PU/239/,U233/	
Fission	2.5−2		AE Comp	Rept	AE−11	Apr 60 Story+,DISCUSSION+TABULATN OF MEASTS	
Fission	Fiss		ALD Eval	Rept	AWRE−O−02/60	Apr 60 Hinves+AWRE EVAL DATA CFD XPT.	
Fission	Maxwl		CCP Revw	Jour	UFN 71 471	Jul 60 Perfilov+.TABLE,PROB OF COMPLEX FISS	
				Jour	SPU 3 542	Jan 61 . ENGL TRANSL OF UFN 71 471	
Fission	Fiss		KUR Revw	Conf	60Vienna 159	Oct 60 Bondarenko+.TABLE,EXPT DESCRIBED	
Fission	1.0+7	2.1+7	CCP Expt	Jour	AE 9 399	Nov 60 Pankratov+ TOF,FISS CH,NORM AT 14MEV	+
				Jour	JNAB 16 494	Oct 62 TRANSLATN.*	
				Jour	SJA 9 939	Sep 61 TRANSLATN.*	
Fission	1.3+7	1.9+7	ALD Expt	Jour	JNAB 14 85	May 61 Adams+.TABLE+CURVE.RELATIVE TO U238	+
Fission	Maxwl		HAN Eval	Conf	61RPI 3	May 61 Leonard.	
Fission	2.0−1	1.0+7	B+W Eval	Rept	BAW−158	Jun 61 Roach+ AVERAGED SIG 40 GROUPS	
Fission	5.0−3	2.5+0	GA Eval	Rept	GA−2113	Jun 61 Wikner+.TABLE+CURVE.100 E POINTS	
Fission	Maxwl		CRC Revw	Conf	61Saclay 57	Jul 61 Westcott. 2200METRE/SEC SIG GIVEN	
Fission	Maxwl		KUR Expt	Conf	61Vienna 3 315	Aug 61 Leipunskij+ SIG GIVN,TABLE	
	Pile			Conf	58Geneva 12 3	Sep 58 − +.PPR2038,VAL U235/PU239	
	Maxwl			Rept	ANL−TR−9	62 . ENGL TRANSL OF 61VIENNA 3 315	
Fission	6.5+4	1.4+7	HAR Expt	Jour	NP 27 154	Sep 61 Cuninghame+CAL.PARTIAL WAVE FISS SIG	
Fission	1.0−2	1.2−1	MOL Expt	Jour	JNE 15 165	Dec 61 Deruytter. SLOCHOP,TBL,CURV,.0253VAL	+
				Conf	60Vienna 195	Oct 60 − . BR1 SLOW CHOPPER+FISSCHMB	
	1.1−2	1.2−1		Data	EXFOR20189.002	May 74 26PTS.SIGMA.	
Fission	1.2+5		LAS Expt	Jour	PR 125 1329	Feb 62 Smith+ RATIO PU241/U235	+
	1.2+5	2.1+7		Data	EXFOR12544.002	Jun 76 . 33 PTS, RATIO	
Fission	5.0−3	1.0−1	BNL Revw	Rept	BNL−722	Jun 62 Sher+ REVIEW CURVE GIVEN	
Fission	1.4+5	1.3+6	ORL Expt	Jour	NP 38 561	Sep 62 Lamphere.	+
	1.4+5	1.3+6		Data	EXFOR12325.	Jun 76 . 73 PTS.	
Fission	Maxwl		CRC Revw	Rept	EANDC(CAN)−15	Nov 62 Hanna. COMPARES MANY VALUES.	
				Rept	EANDC(CAN)−6	Jun 60 −	

92 Uranium 235

Quantity	Energy (ev) Min	Max	Lab	Type	Documentation Ref Vol Page	Date	Author, Comments	Data
Fission	4.0+5	3.8+6	ORL	Expt Prog	ORNL-3425 72	63	Lamphere. RATIO ODEG/90DEG	
Fission	-2	3.0+7	KFI	Revw Jour	MFF 11 325	Jan 63	Szabo.REVIEW,GRAPHS TABLES MANY REFS	
Fission	3.0+6	2.7+7	CCP	ExTh Jour	AE 14 177	Feb 63	Pancratov+.TOF SC CURVE GIVEN	+
				Jour	SJA 14 167	63	. ENGL OF AE 14 177	
Fission	3.0-2	6.0+1	LRL	Expt Jour	PR 130 1482	May 63	Bowman+	+
				Rept	UCRL-7061	Feb 63	.SEE ALSO OKS UCRL-6926 NORMZT	
				Rept	UCRL-6926	Jun 62	.SUPERSEDED	
	3.2-2	6.0+1		Data	EXFOR12429.005	Jun 76	. 1438 PTS.	
Fission	2.0-3	5.0-1	MTR	Expt Jour	PR 131 1746	Aug 63	Faler+ CURVE RESONANCE AT 0.29EV	
Fission	Pile		CJD	Eval Rept	INDSWG-64 285	64	Galanin. TBL EFF SIG FOR MANY SPECTR	
Fission	Maxwl		KUR	Theo Rept	IAE-562 3	64	Geylikman+,TRIPLE FISS,E DIST CFDEXP	
				Rept	ANL-TR-68	64	TRANSLATN.*	
Fission	1.5-1	9.0+0	ORL	Expt Rept	ORNL-1067	64	Dabbs. ANISTROPY, CURVES	
	1.4-1	8.8+0		Prog	ORNL-3425 82	63	- . ANISOTROPY AT 5 RES	
Fission	Maxwl	1.4+7	CCP	Expt Jour	AE 16 144	Feb 64	Drapchinskii+ REL TERNARY FIS RATIOS	
				Jour	JNAB 19 69	Jan 65	TRANSLATN.*	
				Jour	SJA 16 164	Feb 64	TRANSLATN.*	
Fission	3.0-2	2.0+1	ITE	Expt Jour	AE 16 110	Feb 64	Ignatiev+ PULSED CYCLOTRON	+
				Jour	JNE 18 719	Nov 64	.ENGLISH TRANSL OF AE 16 110	
				Jour	EAF 16 2 19	Feb 64	. FRENCH TRANSL OF AE 16 110	
				Jour	SJA 16 121	Feb 64	.ENGLISH TRANSL OF AE 16 110	
	9.2-1	8.1+0		Data	EXFOR40156.	Mar 73	. 3 SUBENTRIES,449 DATA LINES	
Fission	2.0-2	7.0+0	CCP	Theo Jour	AE 16 211	Mar 64	Kirpichnikov+ SIG(E) GRAPHS,RES-ANAL	
				Jour	SJA 16 251	Mar 64	TRANSLATN.*NO 3	
Fission	Pile		CRC	Eval Rept	CRRP-1191	Mar 64	Westcott. EFF SIG SEE ALSO CRRP-960.	
Fission	5.0+0	1.0+2	IAE	Revw Conf	64Geneva 412	May 64	Westcott+.P717, DISCUSS PRESENT STAT	
Fission	7.0+0	1.0+4	SAC	Expt Jour	NP 69 545	Jul 65	Michaudon+ RESONANCE PARAM ANALYSIS.	+
				Rept	CEA-R-2552	May 64	- + ALSO TERNARY FISSION	
				Jour	JPR 21 429	May 60	- + SUPERSEDED.	
	4.0+0	2.0+4		Rept	CEA-R-1093	Jan 59	- +LINAC+TOF,CURVE	
Fission	1.0-2	4.5+0	HAR	Expt Jour	NIM 28 205	Jun 64	Firk.LIQ SCIN DATA IN LINAC EXPT REV	
	1.0-1	4.5+0		Conf	61Saclay 131	61	Brooks.LINAC.RAW YLD AND TRANS DATA.	
				Jour	NIM 4 151	Apr 59	- .SCINT.COUNT.N,G DISCRIMINATOR	
Fission	3.0+0	4.0+1	SAC	Expt Conf	64Paris 2 1117	Jul 64	Michaudon+TERNARY FISS FOR 22RES.	
				Jour	CR 256 1490	Feb 63	- + PRELIMINAIRES	
Fission	1.2+5	1.4+7	HAR	Expt Conf	64Geneva 2 167	Sep 64	Rae+RESULTS AGREE WITH OTHERS'EXPTS	+
Fission	Pile		CCP	Expt Jour	AE 17 294	Oct 64	Batyrbekov+VAL GVN REL TO PU239(N,F)	+
				Jour	SJA 17 1025	Oct 64	TRANSLATN.*	
Fission	Maxwl		RLY	Revw Conf	64Vienna 120	Dec 64	Raievski. TBL,AVG SIG OF 20+400DEG C	
Fission	+5	+7	RLY	Revw Conf	64Vienna 56	Dec 64	Kronberger.FAST REACTOR,1-GROUP SIGS	
Fission	Maxwl		RLY	Revw Conf	64Vienna 56	Dec 64	Kronberger.ADV-G-COOLD-R,1-GROUP-SIG	
Fission	Spont		RI	Expt Prog	INDSWG-120 35	65	Aleksandrov.T=3.5 X 10EXP17 YEARS	
Fission	Spont		ALD	Expt Jour	JNE 19 33	Jan 65	White+ HALFLIFE=7.13+-0.09 10(B)Y.	
Fission	2.5-2		BEP	Revw Jour	KE 8 625	Jan 65	Wenzel.VAL GVN,MANY REFERENCES	
Fission	+0	+3	CAI	Theo Jour	NP 62 667	Feb 65	Stavinsky+(N,GF)PROB ABOUT=(N,GAMMA)	
Fission	5.0+5	2.0+7	LAS	Theo Jour	PR/B 137 826	Feb 65	Ford+OPTMDL+STAT TH FIT TO XPTL DATA	
Fission	1.0+2	3.0+4	DUB	Expt Conf	65Salzburg 1 287	Mar 65	Van-Shi-Di+ TOF,TBL OF AVERGD VALUES	
				Rept	JINR-P-2024	65	Van Shi Di+ AREA RES ANAL.	
				Rept	BNL-TR-16	Jul 65	- + ENGL OF 65SALZ.	
Fission	Fiss		IIT	Comp Conf	65IAEA 251	Mar 65	Barrall+ CALC SIGS,3 SPECS,CFD EXPTS	
Fission	2.5-2	2.8-1	ISP	Expt Conf	65Salzburg 255	Mar 65	Fraysse.ISPRA,CS,TABLE SIG AT 4 ES	+
Fission	Maxwl		SAC	Expt Rept	CEA-R-2775	Apr 65	Fraysse+ REL BORON ABS XSECT	
Fission	4.0+4	1.4+7	ALD	Expt Jour	JNE 19 325	May 65	White. REL H SCAT TO +-2.5PERCENT	+
	4.0+4	5.0+5		Conf	65Salzburg 1 219	Mar 65	- + 6 ENERGIES.TBL.	
	4.0+4	1.4+7		Jour	JNE 19 33	Jan 65	- .TARGET ASSAY.	
Fission	Pile		CCP	Expt Jour	AE 18 469	May 65	Golubev+VAL GVN REL TO PU-239(N,F)	
				Jour	SJA 18 608	May 65	TRANSLATN.*	
Fission	Fiss		LAS	Expt Abst	DA 25 6704	May 65	Grundl. U235 SPECTRAL INDEX,REL U238	
Fission	2.1-1	3.1+4	DUB	Expt Jour	AE 19 43	Jul 65	Rjabov+.PULSED REACTOR,CURVE SIG(E)	+
	1.0+0	1.0+2		Rept	JINR-P3-3957	Jul 68	- + SPARK CHAMBER DESCRIBED,CURV	
	1.5-1	1.0+5		Jour	AE 24 351	Apr 68	- + GRPH SIG(E),PULSED REACTOR	
				Prog	YFI-5 61	Oct 67	- + CURVES	
				Rept	INDC-E-232	67	.ENG TRANSLATION	
	2.1-1	3.1+4		Jour	PTE 8 4 63	Jul 65	Rjabov+ DESCRIPTION OF EXPERIMENT	
				Conf	65Salzburg 1 287	Mar 65	.SEE ALSO	
	1.5-1	1.0+5		Jour	SJA 24 435	Apr 68	. ENGLISH OF AE 24 351	
	2.1-1	3.1+4		Jour	SJA 19 907	65	. ENGL OF AE 19 43	
	2.2-1	3.1+4		Data	EXFOR40271.	Apr 75	.SIGMA AT 2913 ES GIVEN	

92 Uranium 235

Quantity	Energy (ev) Min	Energy (ev) Max	Lab	Type	Documentation Ref Vol Page	Date	Author, Comments	Data
Fission	2.5−2		ALD	Expt	Jour PR/B 139 852	Aug 65	Maslin.FC,ANL METHOD.SIG = 572 + − 6B.	+
Fission	+0	+1	HAR	Theo	Jour PL 18 31	Aug 65	Lynn. SLOW (N,GAMMA + FISS) REACT CALC	
Fission	4.1−1	1.0+7	WAL	Eval	Rept WANL − TME − 1228	Aug 65	Gibson+.68GROUP TABLE.SOME GRAPHS	
	1.0−3	1.0+7			Rept WANL − TME − 1028	Nov 64	Drawbaugh+.CURV + TABLE.GROUP AVERAGED	
Fission	Maxwl	+2	FEI	Expt	Jour AE 19 292	Sep 65	Stavisskij + REL U238 + PU239,AU197(NG)	
					Jour SJA 19 1210	66	. ENGL OF AE 19 292	
Fission	3.2+0	2.5+1	ORL	Expt	Jour NSE 23 45	Sep 65	Desaussure+ SUPERSEDED BY 1967 MEAS.	+
Fission	1.0−2	5.0−1	MTR	Eval	Conf 66Wash. 985	66	Fluharty+	
Fission	1.0+2	9.1+3	TRM	Comp	Rept AEET − 272	66	SHANKAR SINGH+ GROUP SIGS,TEMPERATUR	
Fission	3.5−2	2.0+2	HAR	Expt	Rept AERE − M − 1670	Feb 66	Brooks+ LINAC,TOF,CURVES,CFD OTHERS	+
					Conf 66S.Diego 2 193	Feb 66	− . SEE ALSO	
					Prog AERE − PR/NP9 11	Oct 65	− + DATA RENORMALISED ABOVE 10EV	
					Rept BNL − 325	Feb 66	− + SEE FOR CURVES.	
					Rept EANDC(UK) − 42	Jun 64	− .GRPH.TBL 2 MODIFD(AMENDMNT 1)	
Fission	3.3+1	7.8+6	LRL	Expt	Jour PR 142 778	Feb 66	Albert.	+
	1.0+5	2.0+6			Jour PRL 15 15 636	Oct 65	− . BOMB DATA, STRUCT SEEN	
	3.3+1	7.8+6			Data EXFOR12343.002	Jun 76	. 636 PTS.	
Fission	1.5+5	3.4+5	ORL	Expt	Jour PRL 16 6 248	Feb 66	Macklin+ NO STRUCTURE SEEN	
Fission	Maxwl		TRM	Revw	Conf 66Bombay 1	Feb 66	Ramanna.VALS CFD TH,SIG,BINDING,DEF.	
Fission	3.8+5	6.5+5	ANL	Expt	Jour PRL 16 525	Mar 66	Smith+REL VALUES,NO STRUCT. SEEN	+
	3.8+5	6.5+5			Data EXFOR12369.003	Jun 76	. 0 PTS.	
Fission	2.5−2		BNW	Theo	Conf 66Wash. 75	Mar 66	Liikala+, TBLS OF LITER. VALUES	
Fission	2.0+1	2.0+6	LAS	Expt	Conf 66Wash. 971	Mar 66	Brown+ BOMB NEUTS TOF(= LADC − 7618)	+
					Rept LA − 3586 31	Dec 66	− . NUMERICAL DATA	
					Conf 66Paris 2 219	Oct 66	Hemmindinger.	
	2.0+1	9.8+5			Data EXFOR12432.002	Jun 76	. 3087 PTS.	
Fission	2.0−2	5.0+1	LRL	Expt	Conf 66Wash. 1004	Mar 66	Bowman+,LINAC,CFD C OTHER EXPTS	+
					Rept UCRL − 14606	Mar 66	.SUPERSEDED	
	1.3−2	8.0+1			Data EXFOR12433.	Jun 76	. 1572 PTS.	
Fission	1.0−2	1.0+0	MTR	Eval	Conf 66Wash. 840	Mar 66	Moore+,MULTILEVEL ANAL CURVE CFD XPT	
Fission	1.0−2	5.0−1	MTR	Theo	Conf 66Wash. 985	Mar 66	Fluharty+,COEF OF SIG EXPANSN CALCTD	
Fission	Maxwl	Pile	COL	Expt	Abst DA 26 6118	Apr 66	Schroder.BINARY/TERNARY F CONSTANT	
Fission	None		BRK	Revw	Jour NP 81 1	Jun 66	Myers+ TABLE 2 FISS BARRIER	
Fission	4.5+6	1.0+7	ANL	Eval	Jour NSE 32 35	Apr 68	Davey. RE − EVALUATION OF DATA.	
	1.0+3	1.0+7			Jour NSE 26 149	Oct 66	− . EVALUATION	
					Conf 66Wash. 796	Mar 66	.SUPERSEDED	
Fission	None		ANL	Theo	Conf 66Vienna 613	Oct 66	Armani.FISSION RATE,TH OF EXP,NODATA	
Fission	2.4+0	4.0+1	GA	Eval	Conf 66ANL 247	Oct 66	Cohen.NUMERICAL VS 1 − LV ANAL CURVES.	
					Rept GA − 7391	Nov 66	− .	
Fission	1.0+3	2.5+4	HAR	Expt	Conf 66ANL 16	Oct 66	JAMES TOF CFD OTHER EXPTS TABLES	
	1.0+0	3.0+4			Prog AERE − PR/NP10 4	Sep 66	James+ TOF,GAS SCINTILLATOR,TBC. NDG	
Fission	6.1+6	1.4+7	HEB	Eval	Conf 66Paris 2 309	Oct 66	Pazy+ CORR − FACTORS BY INTEG EXPT,TBL	
Fission	4.5−1	1.0+4	INA	Eval	Conf 66Paris 2 333	Oct 66	Hennies.PPR5.TBL RECOM DATA CFD OTHR	
					Rept NAA − SR − 11980 5	May 67	− . RECOMMENDED DATA.REVISED.	
Fission	9.2−1	9.0+1	ITE	Expt	Priv OBNINSK	Oct 66	KIRPICHNIKOV	+
Fission	2.0−2	5.0−1	MTR	Eval	Conf 66Paris 2 50	Oct 66	Smith. TBL+CURV, LEAST SQUARE FIT.	
Fission	2.4+4		ALD	Expt	Jour JNE 19 423	Jun 65	Perkin+.CALIB SB − BE SRCE. 2.36+ −.06B	+
					Jour JNE 20 921	Nov 66	− +DOPPLER EFF TO 770 DEG K.	
	2.4+4				Data EXFOR20584.004	Jul 76	1PNT.SIGMA.	
Fission	4.0+4	1.0+6	ANL	Eval	Prog ANL − 7210 14	Dec 66	Cox.SIG NORMALZD TO WHITES DATA,TBL	
Fission	Maxwl		ITE	Theo	Rept ICD − 4 385	67	Birzgal+.AVERAGING OVER MAXWELL SPEC	
Fission	Maxwl		SAC	Expt	Prog EANDC(E)76U	Jan 67	Audias+.SYMETRIC FISSION	
Fission	8.0−1	1.7+2	KUR	Expt	Rept IAE − 1302	Feb 67	Mostovaja. LINAC, TOF, CURVES	+
					Rept ICD − 3 10	Oct 66	EQUIVALENT*	
					Rept INDC − 152E 10	67	. ENGL OF ICD − 3 10	
	8.2−1	1.7+2			Data EXFOR40272.002	Apr 75	.SIGMA AT 1860 ES GIVEN	
Fission		6.3+1	WAL	Eval	Rept WANL − TME − 1586	Mar 67	Gibson+MULTIGROUP LIBRARY+CURVE	
Fission	1.0+3	1.5+7	LAS	Eval	Prog WASH − 1074 79	Apr 67	Diven. NDG. SEE EANDC(US) − 96U.	
Fission	1.0+3	1.4+7	RLY	Eval	Rept AHSB(S)R − 124	May 67	Hart.(RLY).UK − DFN 335.UPDATES NSE 26	
Fission	1.0+3	1.4+7	UK	Eval	Rept AHSB(S)R − 124	May 67	Hart.(RLY).UK − DFN 335.UPDATES NSE 26	+
	1.0−4	9.0+3			Rept AEEW − M − 502	May 65	Freemantle.TABLE.CURVE1 TO 100EV	
	5.0−3	5.0+0			Rept AEEW − R − 351	Feb 64	Barrington+(WIN).UKNDL LOW EN REVISN	
	1.0+3	1.5+7			Rept AWRE − O − 82/63	Dec 63	Parker.(ALD).UKNDL − DFN 155	
	1.0−4	1.5+7			Data UKNDL − DFN 159B	Mar 73	2065 PNTS	
Fission	3.0+4	6.4+4	KFK	Expt	Jour JNE 21 643	Aug 67	Knoll+ 2.19B, 1.78B REL BE7 AU ACTIV	+
					Rept KFK − 898	Aug 67	− + EQU TO JNE 21 643.	
					Rept EANDC(E)74S	Nov 66	− + SAME AS JNE 21 643	
					Jour PL 21 432	Jun 66	Gilboy+KNOLL RELATIVE NO STRUCTURE	

92 Uranium 235

Quantity	Energy (ev) Min	Max	Lab	Type	Documentation Ref Vol Page	Date	Author, Comments	Data
Fission	Pile		AE	Expt	Jour NUK 10 141	Sep 67	Tiren. RATIO U238 CAPT/U235 FISS SIG	
Fission	3.0+5	2.5+6	FEI	Expt	Prog YFI-5 4	Oct 67	Smirenkin+ CURVE RATIO /233, /PU239	+
					Rept INDSWG-64 260	64	. TABULATED DATA	
					Jour AE 13 366	Oct 62	Smirenkin+ E-STEPS 30KEV.CFD OTHERS	
					Rept INDC-232E	67	. ENGL OF YFI-5 4	
					Jour EAF 13 4 82	Oct 62	. FRENCH OF AE 13 366	
	3.3+5	2.5+6			Data EXFOR40027.	Oct 72	RATIO U-233/U-235, PU-239/U-235,43EN	
Fission	1.0-1	4.0+1	KUR	Expt	Rept IAE-1439	Oct 67	Mostovaya+ BIN+TERNARY FISSION ,GRPH	
Fission	1.1+6	8.1+6	LAS	Expt	Jour NSE 30 39	Oct 67	Grundl. DETECTOR EXCITATION MEASTS	+
	2.1+6	8.1+6			Data EXFOR10416.002	Dec 74	14PTS,SIGMA	
Fission	4.0-1	2.0+4	ORL	Expt	Rept ORNL-TM-1804	Nov 67	Desaussure+ RPI LINAC+TOF CURVES	+
					Conf 66Paris 2 233	Oct 66	- + SUPERSEDED	
	4.0-1	1.0+4			Data EXFOR10270.	Jan 73	. 5724PTS,SIGMA	
Fission	Maxwl		RI	Revw	Jour AE 23 561	Dec 67	BAK+ OTHER SIG VAL GIVEN,TABLE	
					Jour SJA 23 1340	Dec 67	. ENGL OF AE 23 561	
Fission	1.0+4		ALD	Revw	Conf IAEA-107 41	68	Batchelor.EXPTS DISCUSSD+TBD,GRPHS	
					Conf IAEA-107 51	68	- .SIG AS STANDARD,EXPTS TBD	
					Conf 67Brussels	May 67	- + PPR3.	
Fission	1.0+3	9.9+6	KFK	Expt	Conf IAEA-107 150	68	Poenitz.PREL VAL GVN,SIG AS STANDARD	
					Conf 67Brussels	May 67	- + PPR10	
	3.0+4	6.4+4			Abst BAP 12 126	Jan 67	- +ABS AT 30KEV,REL AU(N,G)64KV	
Fission	1.5+1	7.0+1	KUR	Expt	Jour YFI-6 71	68	Mostovaja+ CURVE SIG(E) AT 2 TEMPRTR	
					Conf 68Dubna § 15	Jun 68	SEE ALSO *-	
					Rept INDC-260E	69	. ENGL OF YFI-6 71	
Fission	3.0+4	1.5+6	ANL	Expt	Conf 68Wash. 503	Mar 68	Poenitz. TOF + FISS CHAMBER 14ES.	+
	3.0+4	1.5+6			Data EXFOR12401.002	Jun 76	. 14 PTS.	
Fission	1.0+6	5.0+6	LAS	Expt	Conf 68Wash. 627	Mar 68	Stein+ TOF U235/U236,/NP237,/U238	
					Rept LA-DC-9205	67	.EQUIVALENT	
					Conf 66Paris 1 419	Oct 66	.SUPERSEDED	
	1.0+6	5.0+6			Data EXFOR12452.	Jun 76	. 42 PTS,3 RATIOS	
Fission	Fiss		MOL	Expt	Conf 68Wash. 1263	Mar 68	Fabry+ FISS TRACK DET.REL IN115 INEL	+
	Fiss				Data EXFOR20264.006	May 74	1PNT.SIGMA.	
Fission	Pile		SRL	Theo	Conf 68Wash. 1271	Mar 68	Hennelly+ CALC FOR USE AS STD	
Fission	Fiss		BNW	Theo	Rept BNWL-SA-1794	Apr 68	Mcelroy. SAND 2 CALCULATION.	
Fission	6.0+0	3.0+3	GEL	Expt	Jour JNE 22 211	Apr 68	Cao+.LINAC TOF FISS NS+FRAGS DET	+
				Theo	Jour PL/B 27 409	Sep 68	CAO+AUTOCORREL EFFECTS	
				Expt	Conf 68Wash. 481	Mar 68	CAO+ TOF.FN+FFRAG DET.NDG. PPR D3	
	6.0+0	3.0+3			Data EXFOR20129.002	Mar 73	9777PTS.	
Fission	8.0+1	4.0+3	CCP	Theo	Jour YF 8 214	Jul 68	Vorotnikov. OTHER EXPTL SIG(NEUT-E)	
					Jour SNP 8 122	Jan 69	TRANSLATN.*	
Fission	Maxwl		ALD	Expt	Jour JNE 22 477	Aug 68	Keith+ REL.TO CAPT XSEC CO59	
Fission	Pile		CCP	Expt	Jour AE 25 292	Oct 68	Golubev+ EXPTL+CALC MEAN SIG VAL GVN	
					Jour EAF 25 4 37	Oct 68	TRANSLATN.*	
Fission	-		SUK	Theo	Conf 68Bombay 2 170	Dec 68	Narayana. FISSN-MODEL,4-POLE-MOMENT	
Fission	1.0+3	1.0+7	TRM	Expt	Rept BARC-421	69	Mahalingam+CRITICL-XPT CFD DAVEY-SIG	
Fission	4.6-1	2.1+3	LRL	Expt	Jour NSE 35 350	Mar 69	Bramblett+ LINAC FISS CHAMBR AVG SIG	+
	4.3-1	2.1+3			Data EXFOR10134.002	Jun 72	0PTS.SIGMA.	
Fission	2.0+3		MTR	Expt	Prog WASH-1127 72	Apr 69	Schuman+ TABLE	
Fission	Fast		KFK	Expt	Conf 69London § 1.9	Jun 69	Kiefhaber+ INTEGRL XPT CFD MICRO SIG	
Fission	-		BER	Theo	Conf 69Vienna 197	Jul 69	Krappe+PPR96. 1+2 FISSN BARRIER TBL	
Fission	Maxwl		BOR	Expt	Diss DOAN	Jul 69	Doan.TRIPARTITION	
					Diss CARLES	Jul 69	Carles.TRIPARTITION	
Fission	-		COP	Theo	Conf 69Vienna 213	Jul 69	Damgaard+PPR62. CALCULATN,'SHELL-TH'	
Fission	-		COP	Expt	Conf 69Vienna 351	Jul 69	Back+PPR74.(D,P FISSN)-REACTN,GRPHS	
Fission	5.0+1	3.0+3	DUB	Theo	Conf 69Vienna 934	Jul 69	Ryabov+PPR160. EGELSTAFF-CORR-ANALYS	
Fission	Spont		FR	Expt	Conf 69Vienna 952	Jul 69	Monnin+PPR83. SPON FISSN HALF-LIFE	
Fission	None		HAR	Revw	Conf 69Vienna 249	Jul 69	Lynn. TBL=2HUMPED FISS-BARRIER PARS	
	-			Theo	Conf 68DUBSY 463	Jul 68	- .REVIEW,STRUCT EFFECTS IN FISS.	
Fission		5.0+3	ORL	Theo	Conf 69Vienna 283	Jul 69	Perez+ SIG(E) GRPHS,INTERMED-STRUCTR	
Fission	3.0-1	1.8+2	SAC	ExTh	Conf 69Vienna 321	Jul 69	Dabbs+PPR123. SIG(E,0+90ANGDEG) GRPH	
Fission	2.0+1	1.0+3	LAS	Expt	Rept LA-4285	Oct 69	Cramer+TOF,PERSIMMON EVENT,DATA,TBLS	+
	2.0+1	1.0+3			Data EXFOR10054.002	May 71	2801PTS.SIGMA	
Fission	5.2+5	5.4+6	KUR	Expt	Prog YFI-8 12	Dec 69	Savin+ SIG REL PU239+PU240 VS NE,TBL	+
					Rept INDC(CCP)-8 16	Dec 70	*ENGL OF YFI-8 12	
	5.2+5	5.4+6			Data EXFOR40020.	Aug 70	REL PU239 35 ES,REL PU240 26 ES	
Fission	1.4+7		TRM	Expt	Conf 69Roorke 2 289	Dec 69	Iyer+ SIGMA RELATIVE TO U238	+
					Rept BARC/I-79 55	70	- + SIMILAR TO 69ROORKE	
	1.4+7				Data EXFOR30035.004	Dec 72	ONE VALUE	

92 Uranium 235

Quantity	Energy (ev) Min	Max	Lab	Type	Documentation Ref Vol Page	Date	Author, Comments	Data
Fission	1.0+4	1.5+6	KFK Revw	Jour	AKE 15 26	70	Schmidt. REVW ON EXPTS	
Fission	1.0+3	1.0+7	TRM Eval	Rept	BARC/I-96	70	Kapil.14 GROUP SIG,2 N-SPECS,TABLES	
Fission	None		ANL Expt	Rept	ANL-7610 44	Jan 70	Meadows. U234 HL,BASIC TO U235(N,F)	
Fission	1.5+4	1.5+7	ORL Eval	Rept	ORNL-TM-2797	Jan 70	Greene+,TABLE EVALUATED SIGS	
Fission	2.4+2	2.4+4	ANL Expt	Jour	NSE 39 361	Mar 70	Lehto.FISS CS RATIOS WITH U233,PU239	+
	2.4+2	2.4+4		Data	EXFOR10084.	Jul 71	52PTS.CS RATIOS WITH U233,PU239 GVN	
Fission	1.4+7		KFI Expt	Prog	INDC(HUN)-1G	Mar 70	Nagy+ HLS+SIG,SPON-FISSN-ISOMER U235	
Fission	None		ORL Theo	Jour	PL/B 31 413	Mar 70	Desaussure+AUTO-CORR INTERMED SUBTHR	
Fission	+2	+5	JAE Theo	Jour	NSE 40 25	Apr 70	Ishiguro+,STATISTICAL CALCULATN,CURV	
Fission	1.0+1	2.8+6	LAS Expt	Rept	LA-4420	Apr 70	Cramer. NUCL SHOT,TOF,TABLES+CURVES	+
	1.0+1	2.8+6		Data	EXFOR10057.002	Jul 71	3600PTS.	
Fission	Pile		ROS Theo	Rept	ZFK-201	Apr 70	Adam. EFFECTIVE SIG CALC	
Fission	1.5+2	1.0+5	TOK Theo	Jour	NST 7 157	Apr 70	Kikuchi+.CALC USING SPIN DEPENDNT WF	
Fission	1.0-4	2.0+7	BNW Eval	Rept	BNWL-1312	May 70	Simons+ TABLE+CURVE	
Fission	1.0-1	2.4+1	MOL Expt	Abst	DA/B 30 5189	May 70	Wagemans.FISS SIG BY RES NTN REL THR	
Fission	6.2+1	3.0+2	WAL Eval	Rept	WANL-TME-2705	May 70	Drawbaugh+,BREIT-WIGNER FIT,CURVES	
Fission	1.3+5	1.4+6	ANL Expt	Jour	NSE 40 383	Jun 70	Poenitz.CS RATIOS U238NG AND PU239NF	+
	1.3+5	1.4+6		Data	EXFOR10086.	Feb 72	27PTS CS RATIOS WITH U238NG,PU239NF.	
Fission	2.0+4	2.0+7	ANL Revw	Conf	70Helsinki 2 119	Jun 70	Davey.112.STATUS OF DATA, GRAPH GIVN	
Fission	3.0+3	7.0+6	ANL Revw	Conf	70Helsinki 2 3	Jun 70	Poenitz.111. ABSOLUTE+RELATIV GRAPHS	
Fission	1.0+5	1.0+6	BOL Expt	Conf	70Helsinki 2 531	Jun 70	Benzi+49. SIG(E) GRPH,CRIT ASSEMBLY	
Fission	2.0+5	1.4+6	BRC Expt	Conf	70Helsinki 2 145	Jun 70	Soleilhac+67.SIG(E) RELATIVE PU239	
Fission	1.0+4	1.0+7	CAD ExTh	Conf	70Helsinki 2 465	Jun 70	Barre+73. MICROSC CFD INTEGRAL DATA	
				Conf	69London § 1.15	Jun 69	- + INTEGRL XPT CORRECTS MICROSIG	
				Rept	EANDC(E)120L	Mar 69	- +RAVIER EVAL OF INTEGRAL MEAS	
Fission	Maxwl	2.6-2	CRC Expt	Conf	70Helsinki 1 287	Jun 70	Lounsbury+PPR2. VALUE GVN,THRML FLUX	+
	Maxwl			Data	EXFOR10013.	Sep 72	2PTS.CS RATIO/PU239,/U233 GVN.	
Fission	1.0+1	3.0+4	DUB Expt	Rept	JINR-P3-5113	Jun 70	Rjabov+ E-GROUPS AVGD SIG,TBLS+GRPH	
	-1	+1		Rept	JINR-P3-4992	Apr 70	- + PULSD REACTOR,TOF,LIQ SCINT	
	1.0+2	3.0+4		Prog	YFI-11 35	70	Kurov+ ABST,SAME TBL AS JINR-5113	
				Prog	INDC(CCP)-31	Dec 72	.PAGE 34,ENGLISH OF YFI-11 35	
Fission	1.0-2	3.0+1	GEL Revw	Conf	70Helsinki 1 127	Jun 70	Deruytter.106.INTEGRAL SIG CFD OTHER	
				Conf	70Helsinki 1 151	Jun 70	- . PPR.1.SEE ALSO.	
Fission	1.0+1	2.0+4	HAR Comp	Conf	70Helsinki 1 267	Jun 70	James.107. SIG TABLE,DATA SETS CFD	
				Rept	AERE-M-2157	Jan 69	- + TBL AVG SIGF DATA FROM SCISRS	
Fission	2.2+6		HAR Expt	Jour	NP/A 148 337	Jun 70	Elwyn+ STUDY OF SHORT-LIVED ISOMERS	
				Prog	AERE-PR/NP17	Dec 70	- + SPON FISS ISOMS HL 67 NS	
				Conf	69Vienna 457	Jul 69	- . 'DELAYED+PROMPT' FISSION	
	2.0+6			Conf	69Vienna 910	Jul 69	- +PPR54. SPON FISSN HL ESTIMATED	
Fission	2.5+0	5.0+3	KUR Expt	Conf	70Helsinki 1 357	Jun 70	Muradjan.121. COUNTS VS E, GRAPHS	
Fission	1.0+4	1.0+7	LAS Eval	Conf	70Helsinki 2 517	Jun 70	Best+92. SIG(E) REVISED.INTEGRL TEST	
Fission	1.5+3	5.0+5	LRL Expt	Conf	70Helsinki 2 65	Jun 70	Bowman+41. HIGH RESOLUTN SIG(E),GRPH	+
				Rept	UCRL-72472	May 70	- + CURVES	
	1.5+3	5.0+5		Data	EXFOR10170.002	Aug 73	0PTS.SIGMA.	
Fission	+0	1.0+2	ORL Theo	Conf	70Helsinki 2 757	Jun 70	Desaussure+ 94. CRV,MULTILVL FIT.	
	3.0+1	1.0+2		Prog	ORNL-4280 1	Oct 68	- +,MULTILEVEL ANAL,CURVE	
Fission	+1	+3	SAC Eval	Conf	70Helsinki 1 571	Jun 70	Ribon.108. EVALUATION PROBLEMS,GRPHS	
	1.0+1	5.0+1	Theo	Conf	70Helsinki 2 789	Jun 70	Krebs+65.SIG(E) GRAPH,RESON ANALYS	
Fission		7.0+3	SDC Theo	Conf	70Helsinki 2 799	Jun 70	Garrison.DISCUSSN. RESONANCE ANAL	
Fission		5.0+1	UI Theo	Conf	70Helsinki 2 777	Jun 70	Adler+50. R-MATRIX CORRELATED ANAL	
	1.0+0	3.7+1		Rept	TID-23396	Aug 66	- + MULTILEVEL ANAL.	
Fission	+6	+7	WIN Revw	Conf	70Helsinki 2 391	Jun 70	Campbell.116. MICROSCOPIC VS INTEGRL	
Fission	5.0+5	2.3+6	LAS Theo	Jour	NSE 41 177	Aug 70	Cramer+ SIG FROM (T,P+FISS)+H-F CALC	
Fission	2.0+6	7.0+6	TRM Theo	Jour	NP/A 151 532	Aug 70	Sood+ CORREL ANAL OF INTERM STRUCTUR	
	-			Prog	BARC-471 5	70	- + CORREL ANAL,D CLASS II VAL GV	
	None			Expt Prog	BARC-501 21	70	- + CLASS II LVL SPACING DETMD.ND	
Fission	7.0+5	5.0+6	CCP Expt	Jour	AE 29 218	Sep 70	Sabin+ PU239/U235,PU240/U235 GRAPHS	
				Jour	SJA 29 938	Sep 70	TRANSLATN.*	
Fission	5.0+1	3.0+4	HAR Expt	Jour	JNE 24 269	Sep 70	Patrick+ TOF.STRUCTURE IN KEV RANGE.	+
				Rept	AERE-R-6350	Mar 70	- + TOF LINAC MEDT 10-30 KEV	
	1.0+4	3.0+4		Data	EXFOR20461.	Jan 76	244PTS.SIGMA.	
Fission	5.5+5	6.4+5	ANL Expt	Conf	70ANL 281	Oct 70	Poenitz. 2ES. VDG. ASSOC ACT METHOD	+
	5.5+5	6.4+5		Data	EXFOR10296.002	Jan 73	2PTS.SIGMA.	
Fission	2.5+4	1.0+6	ANL Eval	Conf	70ANL 331	Oct 70	Poenitz. BEST VALUES FOR 17 ES	

92 Uranium 235

Quantity	Energy (ev) Min	Energy (ev) Max	Lab	Type	Documentation Ref Vol Page	Date	Author, Comments	Data
Fission	1.7+4	1.0+6	CAD	Expt	Conf 70ANL 257	Oct 70	Szabo+ ABSOLUTE EXPT.+ -3PC CFD OTHRS	+
				Rept	CEA - R - 4804	Dec 76	- + SAME AS 70ANL.	
				Conf	76ANL 208	Jun 76	- + DATA CO4PARED WITH NEW EXPT.	
				Conf	70Helsinki 1 229	Jun 70	- + ABS.SUPERSEDED.	
	1.7+4	1.0+6		Data	EXFOR20567.002	Mar 76	31PTS.SIGMA.	
Fission	2.5-2		GEL	Eval	Conf 70ANL 221	Oct 70	Deruytter. BEST VALUE=587.4+ -2.7B	
Fission	+5	+7	KFK	Revw	Rept KFK - 1303	Oct 70	Boehme+ MICROSC CFD INTEGRL DATA	
				Conf	70Helsinki 2 427	Jun 70	- + INTEGRAL TESTS.	
Fission	+3		JAE	Theo	Jour NST 7 592	Nov 70	Takano+.NUMBER OF RES TO GET AVG SIG	
Fission	4.4+5	5.3+5	KFK	Expt	Rept KFK - 1313	Nov 70	Kaeppeler. VDG EXPT, 2 SIG VALUES	+
				Conf	70ANL 272	Oct 74	- + EQU TO KFK - 1313.	
	4.4+5	5.3+5		Data	EXFOR20354.002	Sep 74	2PTS.SIGMA.	
Fission	1.0+2	1.0+5	GA	Theo	Jour NP/A 159 305	Dec 70	Garrison.AVERAGE C.S.=NO RES INTERF	
Fission	1.8+1	6.6+1	RPI	Theo	Prog NCSAC - 33 209	Dec 70	Shea.TRIPLET APPROX,OKS EXPT,NO DATA	
Fission	-1	+2	SAC	Theo	Rept CEA - N - 1522	71	Barreau+ INTERMEDIATE STRC RESEARCH	
Fission	+6	+7	DUB	Expt	Rept JINR - P3 - 5528	Jan 71	Gangrskij+ U - 235(N,2N)ISOM FISSN SIG	
Fission	Maxwl		DUB	Expt	Rept JINR - P7 - 5497	Jan 71	Belov+ ISOMER U236 PRODUCTN VS FISSN	
Fission	2.5-2		ANL	Eval	Conf 71Knoxvill 560	Mar 71	DE VOLPI. ADJUSTED VALUE GIVEN	
Fission	None		DUB	Expt	Jour YF 13 457	Mar 71	Ryabov+ TOF,SELF - INDICATION METH,NDG	
					Jour SNP 13 255	Sep 71	. ENGL OF YF 13 457	
Fission	2.0+1	1.0+5	LAS	Expt	Jour NSE 43 281	Mar 71	Lemley+,RESOL=1 NSEC/M,MUCH STRUCTRE	+
	2.0+1	1.0+5			Data EXFOR10120.002	Mar 76	6847 PTS.HIGH RESOL NF CS.	
Fission	1.2+4	3.5+5	LRL	Expt	Conf 71Knoxvill 584	Mar 71	Bowman+.TOF,LINAC,CURV,MUCH STRUCTRE	+
	1.2+4	3.5+5			Data EXFOR10419.002	Oct 74	0PTS,SIGMA	
Fission	Pile		MTR	Expt	Conf 71Knoxvill 79	Mar 71	Scoville.RATIO TO AU197 NG,U238NG,NF	
Fission	2.5+5	4.0+6	BUC	Expt	Jour RRP 16 473	Apr 71	Boca+ ISOMERIC FISS AFTER N,G. GRAPH	
				Rept	IFA - CRD - 42	70	- + U236M/U235 FIS - SIG(5ES).TABLE	
Fission	2.5-3	1.9+1	JUL	Expt	Rept JUEL - 746 - RG 13	Apr 71	Bonka. AVG SIG CALC	
	1.0-3	2.0+0			Rept JUEL - 746 - RG 50	Apr 71	.KUGEL - THERMOS - LIBR,T = 300K,CURV	
Fission	2.5-2		MOL	Expt	Rept STI/DOC/10 - 125	Apr 71	Ceulemans.PG46.DRVD FROM SCAT - SIG	
	2.5-2	1.0+0			Conf 70Helsinki 1 461	Jun 70	Ceulmans+21. DEDUCED VALUE,SCAT - EXPT	
Fission	1.1-1	4.4+4	FEI	Expt	Prog YFI - 10 4	May 71	Samsonov+ SIG AT 83 ES,TBL,TBP AE	
					Rept INDC(CCP) - 15	Dec 71	*ENGL OF YFI - 10 4	
	1.0-1	4.0+4			Jour AE 31 103	Aug 71	Samsonov+ REL B10(N,A)+ REL THR.GRPH	
					Jour SJA 31 809	Mar 72	. ENGL OF AE 31 103	
Fission		5.0+6	FEI	Theo	Rept FEI - 242	May 71	Prokhorova+ SIG(NEUT - E),GRAPH	
Fission	2.0+3	3.0+4	KFK	Eval	Prog KFK - 1271 121	May 71	Hinkelmann. AVG VALUES,VARIOUS EXPTS	
Fission	3.0+4	2.0+7	KFK	Eval	Prog KFK - 1271 121	May 71	Hinkelmann. FITTED CURVE OF EXPTS	
Fission	1.8+2	2.0+5	DUB	Theo	Rept JINR - P3 - 6239	Jun 71	Mateeva+ INTERMED.STRUCTURE OF SIG	
	+1	2.0+3			Rept KFK - TR - 406	Jun 72	.GERMAN OF JINR - P3 - 6239	
Fission	Pile		ORL	Expt	Abst ANS 14 381	Jun 71	Jenkins+. EFFECTIVE SIG=1118MB	
Fission		5.0+1	SAC	Expt	Prog EANDC(E)140U	Aug 71	Barreau+,TERNARY FISSION ONLY	
Fission	None		GEL	Expt	Conf 71Canterby 221	Sep 71	De Bievre+ U234 HL,BASIC TO U235(N,F	
Fission	1.0+0	1.0+3	BOR	Expt	Conf FRNC - TH - 165	Nov 71	Barreau.TERN.FISS 17LVLS	
Fission	-		GEL	Revw	Jour AKE 18 229	Nov 71	Theobald+ SUB - BARRIER FISS EXPTS,TH	
Fission	+1	+4	CCP	Revw	Jour AE 31 595	Dec 71	Sukhoruchkin.FINE STRUCT CFD TH,GRPH	
					Jour SJA 31 1380	Jun 72	*ENGL OF AE 31 595	
Fission	1.0+0	8.2+1	MTR	Eval	Rept ANCR - 1044	Dec 71	Smith+. CURVES	
Fission	2.5-1	5.0+4	ORL	Expt	Prog ORNL - 4743 88	Dec 71	Dabbs+. 100 - MICROGRAM SAMPLE.NO DATA	
Fission	1.0+3	1.5+7	CJD	Eval	Rept YK - 9	72	Konshin+ FIT TO ABSOL DATA,TBL+GRPHS	
					Rept INDC(CCP) - 26	Sep 72	.ENGLISH TRANSLATION OF YK - 9 172	
Fission	2.5-2	1.0+5	IAE	Revw	Rept INDC(NDS) - 47	72	Vlasov+ REVIEW DATA STATUS,TBL+GRAPH	
Fission	2.5-2		IFB	Eval	Rept YK - 9 34	72	Morogovsky. COMPUTR RE - EVAL,DATA GVN	
					Rept INDC(CCP) - 42	Aug 74	.P1.ENGLISH OF YK - 9	
Fission	1.5+1	1.0+3	LAS	Expt	Rept INDC(USA) - 44	72	Silbert+ EXPLOSION,TOF,INTEG SIG,TBL	
Fission	3.0+4		ANL	Expt	Prog ANL - 7910 22	Jan 72	Meadows. NDG, U236 CONTRIBUTION	
Fission	3.0+4	5.4+6	ANL	Expt	Jour NSE 47 228	Feb 72	Poenitz. RATIO TO PU239	+
	3.0+4	5.0+6			Prog ANL - 7910 11	Jan 72	- . RATIO TO PU239NF. CURVE	
	3.0+4	5.4+6			Data EXFOR10253.002	Sep 72	27PTS,RATIO TO PU239NF	
Fission	5.0-1	+3	COL	Expt	Abst BAP 17 441	Apr 72	Derengowski+. DELAYED/PROMPT RATIO	
Fission	1.0+3	5.0+5	GEL	Expt	Prog EANDC(E)157U I	Mar 73	Theobald+ REL TO (N,A) ON B10/LI6	
	0.0+0	1.0+0		ExTh	Jour NP/A 187 305	Jun 72	Weigmann+ F.B.PARAMS FROM DATA ANAL.	
	5.0+1	2.0+3		Expt	Prog EANDC(E)150U	May 72	Theobald+,LINAC TOF DOUBLE/TRI COINC	
Fission	None		KFK	ExTh	Jour JPRC 33 30	Aug 72	Khan+ PROMPT ELECTRONS ANAL	
Fission	2.0+6	3.0+6	ANL	Expt	Jour JNE 26 483	Sep 72	Poenitz+ REL U238.TOF,GAS SCINT.	+
	2.0+6	3.0+6			Data EXFOR10232.	May 73	6PTS, RATIOS TO U238 NF	

92 Uranium 235

Quantity	Energy (ev) Min	Max	Lab	Type	Documentation Ref Vol Page	Date	Author, Comments	Data
Fission	1.0+3	1.5+7	IJE	Eval	Rept INDC(CCP)-26	Sep 72	. ENGL OF YK-9 172	+
					Rept YK- 9 172	72	Konshin+ FIT TO ABSOL DATA,TBL+GRPHS	
					YFI-14 3	72	- + SIGMA(E),CFD OTHERS.	
	1.0+2	1.5+7			Data SOKRATOR-1043	76	163 PTS	
Fission	2.0+2	3.5+4	FEI	Expt	Prog YFI-13 6	Oct 72	Chelnokov+ ABSTRACT,TBL SIGMA VS N-E	+
					Prog INDC(CCP)-32	Apr 73	.PAGE 8.ENGLISH OF YFI-13 6	
	2.0+2	3.5+4			Data EXFOR40105.002	Jun 72	SIG AT 26ES, ABS+REL AU197NG, U238NG	
Fission	None		ORL	Expt	Prog USNDC-3 150	Oct 72	Peelle+ TBD	
Fission	1.0+6	5.0+6	ANL	Expt	Jour NSE 49 310	Nov 72	Meadows. RATIO TO U238 SIG MEASD	+
	9.0+5	5.3+6			Data EXFOR10237.	Sep 75	22PTS,RATIO TO U-238 NF	
Fission	1.0+4	6.0+6	HAR	Revw	Conf 72Vienna 357	Nov 72	Coates+ COMPILATN OF 1972-DATA,GRAPH	
Fission	1.5+6	2.3+6	GEL	Expt	Conf ZP 257 108	Dec 72	Knitter+ TOF,AT 3 N-ENERGIES	+
	1.5+6	2.3+6			Data EXFOR20394.006	Oct 74	3PTS.SIGMA.	
Fission	1.0+3	1.0+7	IAE	Eval	Jour REA 10 529	Dec 72	Byer.DEDUCED FROM PU239/U235 RATIO	
Fission	None		LAS	Theo	Jour PRL 29 1567	Dec 72	Devaney. MULTIPLE-REACTN CORRECTION	
Fission	Maxwl		TRM	Expt	Conf 72Chandigr 2 107	Dec 72	Kapoor+FISS 2 ALFAS CHANCE 10EXP-16	
Fission	2.5-2		BUC	Expt	Rept IFA-NR-47	73	Borcea+ SIG GIVN,REL B10 BRANCHRATIO	+
	2.5-2				Data EXFOR30140.	Sep 72	SIGMA WITH REVISED REFERENCE-VALUES	
Fission	Spont		UBE	Expt	Abst HPA 46 440	Feb 73	Reist+ SPON FISS HL	
Fission	Fiss		SGA	Eval	Conf 73Paris 1 233	Mar 73	Eder+ FISS SPEC REL U238(N,F),TBLS	
					Rept SGAE-PH-141	Feb 73	.SAME AS 73PARIS,NO DETAILS,TBP	
Fission	2.5-2		CCP	Eval	Conf 73Kiev 1 197	May 73	Fedorova.SIG=580.2+-1.8B AT V=2200	
Fission	Fiss		CCP	Expt	Conf 73Kiev 4 21	May 73	Adamov+ SIG=1052+-31MB AT CF-252SPON	+
	1.0+6				Data EXFOR40296.002	May 73	.DATA GVN	
Fission	2.5-2	1.1+1	GEL	Expt	Jour JNE 25 263	Jul 71	Deruytter+LINAC FISS INTGLS CALCD	+
	2.0-2	1.1+1			Conf 73Kiev 4 26	May 73	- .SEE JNE 25,NORM 2200M/S	
	1.0-2	2.1+1			Conf 68Wash. 475	Mar 68	- +LINAC,TOF,NORM TO 2200M/S	
	2.0-2	1.1+1			Data EXFOR20131.002	Mar 73	870PTS.	
Fission		6.0+1	ORL	Theo	Jour PR/C 7 2018	May 73	De Saussure+MULTILEVEL.ANAL.	
Fission	2.5+6		RI	Expt	Conf 73Kiev 4 18	May 73	Kuks+ SIG GIVEN,CFD OTHERS	
Fission	1.5+2	1.5+7	KFK	Eval	Rept KFK-1629	Jun 73	Schatz. RECOMMENDED CURVE	
Fission	1.4+4	1.1+6	KFK	Expt	Jour NSE 51 124	Jun 73	Kappeler+. 43ES. REL TO PU241 NF	+
	5.0+5	1.2+6		ExTh	Prog KFK-2223 9	Dec 75	Kaeppeler+EN-GAP OF U-236 CALC	
				Expt	Rept KFK-1772	Apr 73	- . PULSED VDG,ABS+REL VALUES	
					Conf 72Vienna 213	Nov 72	- . ABSOL+NORMLIZ REL,TBL+GRF	
	5.1+5	1.2+6			Data EXFOR20356.	Sep 74	20PTS.SIGMA.	
Fission	1.0-2	2.0+7	LRL	Eval	Rept UCID-16359	Jun 73	Plechaty+. ENDF/B CURVE.	
Fission	1.7+1	3.0+4	SAC	Expt	Jour NSE 51 130	Jun 73	Blons.HIGH RESOL.LINAC.CURVES	+
					Conf 73Kiev 2 239	May 73	- . CFD OTHERS, NDG.	
					Conf 71Knoxvill 829	Mar 71	- + CURVE.LINAC.TOF.	
					Jour AE 29 395	Nov 70	Michaudon.ABST FRANC-SOV SEM DUBNA	
					Jour SJA 29 1156	Nov 70	- .TRANSLATION	
Fission	8.0+4	1.6+6	HAR	Expt	Prog EANDC(UK) 151	Aug 73	Pearlstein+ VDG REL LONG COUNTER TBC	
					Prog AERE-PR/NP20 5	Mar 73	Pearstein+TO BE ANALYSED.	
Fission	2.5-2		GEL	Expt	Jour JNE 27 645	Sep 73	Deruytter+ SLOW CHOP.POINT+DIFF SIG.	+
	2.0-3	1.0-1			Conf 70Helsinki 1 117	Jun 70	- + 2200M/S AND VICINITY	
	2.5-2				Conf 73Kiev 4 26	May 73	- . REL B10(N-A),SIG=587.6 B	
					Conf 68Wash. 491	Mar 68	- + REL TO 10B(N-A) + -5PC	
	2.5-2				Data EXFOR20143.002	Mar 73	1PNT.	
Fission	Maxwl		LIN	Expt	Jour YF 18 492	Sep 73	Val'Skii+ SPONFIS-ISOM/INST FIS,TBL	
					Jour SNP 18 253	Apr 74	.ENGLISH OF YF 18 492	
Fission	8.0+0	1.0+4	ORL	Expt	Jour NSE 52 46	Sep 73	Perez+. LINAC.SIMULT NF+NG.REL B10NA	+
	8.1+0	1.0+4			Data EXFOR10249.	Jul 73	2629PTS,SIGMA	
Fission	Thrsh	2.0+7	RCN	Comp	Rept RCN-196	Oct 73	Zijp+COMPIL.EVAL.CS.FAST N.METROLGY	
	2.5-2			Revw	Conf 73Paris 2 271	Mar 73	- .RECOMMENDED,FROM LITERATURE,TB	
	Fiss				Conf 73Paris 2 271	Mar 73	- .RECOMM INTEG CFD DIFF CALC,TBL	
Fission	None		MUU	Theo	Jour NP/A 215 329	Nov 73	Schultheis+ AXIAL,MASS ASSYM SCISSN.	
Fission	9.6+1	1.0+3	ORL	Theo	Jour NSE 52 382	Nov 73	Desaussure+SINGL LVL+MULTI LVL CFD	
Fission	+6		KUR	Expt	Rept RCN-203 169	Dec 73	Otroschenko+ FISS ISOMER YIELD	

92 Uranium 235

Quantity	Energy (ev) Min	Max	Lab	Type	Documentation Ref Vol Page	Date	Author, Comments	Data
Fission	0.0+0	1.5+0	BUC Theo	Rept	IFA-NR-53	74	Mihailescu. MULTILVL,RANK ANNIH,GRPH	+
				Rept	IFA-NR-52	74	.MULTILVL-MULTICHANNEL CALC CFD EXPT	
	0.0+0	2.0+0		Rept	IFA-NR-51	74	Mihailescu.THEO CALCS CFD EXPT,GRPHS	
	1.0-2	1.5+0		Expt Rept	INIS-MF-1592	74	- . THESIS.TBL+GRPH,CFD THEO	
	-.1+1	6.4+0		Theo Rept	IFA-NR-48	73	- + REICH-MOORE,2 FISS-CHANL	
	0.0+0	1.5+0		Jour	RRP 18 1219	73	- + CALC SIG CFD EXPT,GRAPHS	
	-.1+1	8.8+0		Rept	IFA-NR-46	73	- + MULTILVL,RANK ANNIHILATN	
	2.0+0			Rept	IFA-NR-49	73	- . RANK ANNIHILATION METHOD	
	1.0-2	1.2-1		Expt Rept	IFA-NR-41	72	- + REL TO ABS THR VAL,GRAPH	
	1.0-2	2.0+0		Theo Rept	IFA-NR-41	72	- + MULTILEVEL CALCULATION	
	1.7-2	1.5-1		Expt	Data EXFOR30269.	Jun 74	40 PTS	
Fission	5.0+5	2.5+6	TUE Expt	Jour	PL/B 48 25	Jan 74	Mueller+ SHAPE ISOM RATIO TO PROMPT	
Fission	1.0+4	4.0+4	HAR Theo	Prog	AERE-PR/NP21	Mar 74	James+STAT ANL SHOWS INTRMD STR.TBL	
	+3			Jour	NP/A 170 309	Jul 71	- .DISTRIB FREE STATIST ANAL	
Fission	3.5+4	3.5+6	ANL Expt	Jour	NSE 53 370	Apr 74	Poenitz.RELATIVE+ABSOL MEASTS.	+
				Conf	72Vienna 189	Nov 72	- + SHAPE-SIG+NORMALIZING,GRPHS	
	3.4+4	3.5+6		Data	EXFOR10333.	Jun 74	. 136 PTS. SIGMA	
Fission	Maxwl		KFI Expt	Rept	KFKI-74-20	Apr 74	Lajtai+ SPON FISS U-236M FORMATION	+
	Maxwl			Data	EXFOR30281.002	Nov 74	UPPER LIMIT OF ISOMRC FIS/PROMPT FIS	
Fission	None		JAE Theo	Jour	PTP 51 1617	May 74	Iwamoto+.ASYM FISS BY 2-CENTRE MDL	
Fission	Fiss		TEX Expt	Rept	UMO-74-24,841	May 74	Chromik. THESIS. CF252-NEUTRONS	
Fission	3.6+0	9.0+1	KUR Expt	Priv	OBNINSK	Jun 69	Mostovaja+	+
	3.6+0	9.0+1		Data	EXFOR40218.002	Jun 74	.SIGMA AT 15 ES GIVEN	
Fission	None		LAS Expt	Prog	USNDC-11 147	Jun 74	Smith+ TELESCOPE EFF CHECK	
Fission	Maxwl		UI Expt	Abst	DA/B 34 6026	Jun 74	Withee.	
Fission	1.0+5	7.5+6	ANL Expt	Jour	NSE 54 317	Jul 74	Meadows. U233/U235 FISS RATIO C-SECT	+
	1.4+5	7.4+6		Data	EXFOR10236.002	Apr 74	20PTS,RATIO TO U-233 NF	
Fission	1.0+2	2.0+7	HAR Eval	Jour	ANE 1 409	Jul 74	Sowerby+ LSQ WITH P9 U8 ABOVE .1MEV	
				Rept	AERE-R-7273	Feb 73	- +LINKED EVAL PU239 U238 TBL	
				Rept	AERE-M-2497	Feb 72	- +LINKED EVAL PU239 U238 TBL	
				Conf	70Helsinki 2 703	Jun 70	- + PPR34.	
Fission	1.0+4	4.0+4	ORL Expt	Jour	NEANDC(UK) 160	Jul 74	James+ ANAL FOR INTERMEDIATE STRUCT	
Fission	1.0+3	1.0+7	ORL Revw	Rept	CONF-740903-7	Sep 74	De Saussure+TBLS,CURVS.CFD ENDF,OTH.	
Fission	2.0+3	1.0+5	ORL Expt	Jour	NSE 55 203	Oct 74	Perez+.TOF.GRPHS.TBLS.	+
	°1.0+2	1.0+5		Prog	ORNL-4705 10	Oct 71	- +CURVS.CFD OTHERS.TBL	
				Conf	71Knoxvill 728	Mar 71	Silver+AVG VAL NF CURV.CFD OTHERS	
	2.0+3	1.0+5		Data	EXFOR10302.002	Nov 73	1960 PTS	
Fission	1.0+6	2.0+7	AUW Theo	Prog	INDC(SEC)-42	Dec 74	Satyanarayana+ ABS-MDL,CFD XPT,NDG	
Fission	Maxwl		RIS Expt	Prog	RISO-320 69	Dec 74	Andersen+ ABST. U-236 ISOMER YLD	
				Prog	RISO-300 53	73	- + EXPERIMENTAL DETAILS	
Fission	1.0-4	1.0+0	IFB Eval	Rept	YK-20/1 126	75	Antsipov+ EVAL OF XPTAL DATA.GRAPHS	
Fission	1.0-3	1.5+7	IJE Eval	Jour	VBF 1975 1 13	75	Konshin+ SIG(NEUT-E),GRAPH,TBL	
Fission	2.5+6		CCP Expt	Data	EXFOR40258.002	Feb 75	.SIGMA GIVEN	+
Fission	1.0+4	8.0+4	FEI Expt	Jour	AE 38 82	Feb 75	Kononov+ TOF,AVGSIG(NEUT-E),TBL	+
				Rept	YK-15 12	Aug 74	- + TOF,VDG,AVGED SIG,TBL	
				Jour	SJA 38 105	Aug 75	. ENGL OF AE 38 82	
	1.0+4	8.0+4		Data	EXFOR40412.003	Jan 77	SIG FOR 7 E-RANGES	
Fission	Fast		NBS Expt	Jour	NT 25 237	Feb 75	Grundl+ RATIO TO U238,PU239, CFRMF	+
	Fast			Data	EXFOR10479.	Apr 75	2PTS,RATIO TO U238 AND PU239	
Fission	Fiss		PTB Eval	Rept	PTB-FMRB-60	Feb 75	Alberts. CF252-SPC,EVAL DATA AVG,TBL	
Fission	1.0+0	3.9+1	COL Expt	Conf	75Wash. 580	Mar 75	Felvinci+ LOW LYING RES.SPINS	
Fission	7.8+2	2.0+5	GEL Expt	Conf	75Wash. 607	Mar 75	Migneco+(CAT) STRUCTURE EFFECTS.GRPH	+
	7.5+2	1.1+6		Data	EXFOR20783.002	Mar 78	3881PTS.SIGMA.	
Fission	Fiss		HED Expt	Conf	75Wash. 189	Mar 75	Mcelroy.235U THERM FISS SPECT AVG CS	
Fission	Maxwl		IAE Eval	Conf	75Wash. 286	Mar 75	Lemmel. 3RD IAEA-EVAL BY LSQ FIT	
				Jour	REA 7 4 3	Dec 69	Hanna+ SUPERSEDED	
Fission	2.0+4	2.5+7	LAS Theo	Conf	75Wash. 129	Mar 75	Moore.GRPH R MATR STAT CALC CFD EXP	
Fission	1.0+3	2.0+6	LRL Theo	Conf	75Wash. 650	Mar 75	Gardner.CFD ENDF + ENDL.GRPH.	
Fission	1.0+5	2.0+7	NBS Revw	Conf	75Wash. 293	Mar 75	Carlson. GRPHS EXP CFD ENDF-3 EVAL	
Fission	1.0+6	3.0+6	ANL Expt	Priv	MEADOWS	Apr 75	Meadows. U238/U235 RATIO	+
	1.0+6	3.0+6		Data	EXFOR10504.002	May 75	30PTS,RATIO TO U238	
Fission	2.5-2	2.4+4	FEI Expt	Conf	75Kiev 6 67	May 75	Zhuravlev+ SIG AT 3ES.TABLE	
Fission	+3	1.5+6	KUR Theo	Conf	75Kiev 6 13	May 75	Vorotnikov+ CHANNEL ANALYSIS.GRAPHS	
Fission	1.5+1	5.0+2	KUR Expt	Conf	75Kiev 6 55	May 75	Birjukov+ TOF,TECHN DESCRIBD.NDG,TBL	
Fission	3.0+6	2.0+7	LRL Expt	Jour	NSE 57 18	May 75	Czirr+TBL,GRPH REL N-P SCAT CS.	+
				Conf	75Wash. 615	Mar 75	.SUPERSEDED	
	3.0+6	2.0+7		Data	EXFOR10428.002	Jun 75	61PTS. NF CS.	
Fission	1.0+1	1.0+4	KUR Expt	Conf	75Kiev 6 76	Jun 75	Mostovaja+ IONIZ CHAMBER	

92 Uranium 235

Quantity	Energy (ev) Min	Max	Lab	Type	Documentation Ref Vol Page	Author, Comments Date	Data
Fission	Fast		DOU	Expt Prog	UKNDC(75)P71	Jul 75 Davies+ IRRADIATION PFR SMALL SAMPLE	
Fission	Maxwl		ILL	Expt Jour	NP/A 247 74	Jul 75 Clerc+ MEASURED Z-DIST OF FP,TBL	
Fission	9.6+5		MHG	Expt Jour	ANE 2 637	Sep 75 Gilliam+ CS(964KEV) = 1.21+−0.025 B	+
				Conf	75Wash. 635	Mar 75 - +CS=1.21B+−2.1PCT.NA−BE NEUTS	
	9.6+5			Data	EXFOR10314.002	Feb 76 1 PT. 964 KEV	
Fission	1.0+5		FEI	Theo Jour	YF 22 692	Oct 75 Gonin+ CALC FROM FRGM−ANISOT,SIG.GVN	
	1.0+4	1.0+5		Expt Conf	75Kiev	May 75 - + ANALYSIS	
	1.0+5			Theo Jour	SNP 22 358	Oct 75 . ENGL OF YF 22,692	
Fission	4.0+1	2.0+2	BNL	Theo Jour	NSE 58 354	Dec 75 Pearlstein.PROB TABLE METHOD.GRPHS	
Fission	Maxwl		IBJ	Expt Jour	NP/A 255 387	Dec 75 Piasecki+P,D,T,ALF EMISSION MEASURED	
Fission	1.0+6	6.0+6	LAS	Eval Prog	LA − 6164 − PR 2	Dec 75 Stewart.NDG.DISCREPANCY IN NF CS.	
Fission	7.5+5	4.1+6	LRL	Expt Jour	NSE 58 371	Dec 75 Czirr+TBLS,GRPHS.REL NP SCATTERING.	+
				Conf	75Wash. 615	Mar 75 .SUPERSEDED	
	7.5+5	4.1+6		Data	EXFOR10558.002	Mar 76 27PTS.NF CS.	
Fission	2.5−2		MAG	Eval Rept	EPRI−NP−163	Dec 75 Beer+MONTECARLO ANAL 70HELSINKI P287	
Fission	Fiss		MOL	Expt Prog	INDC(SEC)−51	Dec 75 Fabry.P85.AVG(U35−SPEC),CFD ENDF,TBL	
				Conf	75Wash. 254	Mar 75 - +INTEG CS REL U238NF= 3.94+−.08	
Fission	0.0+0	1.0+7	CAI	Theo Jour	AKE 27 1 47	76 El Nadi+ QUASI−MOLECULAR MODEL	
Fission	Fast		FEI	Expt Rept	YK− 23 127	76 Bychkov+ SIG U38/35,FAST−THERM ASSEM	
Fission	2.0+3	1.4+5	FEI	Expt Rept	YK− 22 3	76 Zhuravlev+ SIG FOR 4ES,TABLE	
Fission	None		ANL	Expt Prog	ERDA−NDC−3 28	May 76 Poenitz+EVAL OF U235NF/LI6NT TBD.NDG	+
	6.5+4	5.5+5		Data	EXFOR10587.002	Mar 76 28PTS.U235NF/LI6NT RATIO.	
Fission	None		MUN	Theo Diss	GRYNTAKIS	Mar 76 Gryntakis.,CALC.OF WESTCOTTS G−FUNCT	
				Jour	RCA 22 128	Mar 75 - +,EQUIVALENT TO THESIS	
Fission	5.0+5	3.2+6	BRC	Expt Prog	CEA−N−1875 66	Apr 76 Cance+	
	5.0+5	2.2+6		Rept	CEA−N−1798 51	Jun 75 - + 2PI 3PI 4PI CHMBR COMP	
Fission	1.0+5	3.0+7	ANL	Eval Conf	76ANL 156	Jun 76 Poenitz+PU239,U238 REL U235 EVAL.CFD	
Fission	1.0+4	2.2+7	ANL	Revw Conf	76ANL	Jun 76 Poenitz+SUPPLEMENT TO CONF.DATA FILE	
Fission	Maxwl		ANL	Expt Rept	CF−3651	Oct 46 Zinn.	+
	Maxwl			Data	EXFOR12319.009	Jun 76 . 1 PT.	
Fission	1.0+2	2.0+7	BNL	Eval Conf	76ANL 307	Jun 76 Bhat.PRELIM EVAL ENDF5B.TBLS,GRPHS.	
Fission	1.0−5	1.0+1	BNW	Eval Conf	76ANL 281	Jun 76 Leonard.EVAL SET CFD 8 MEAS.GRPH,TBL	
	−3	3.5−2		Conf	75Wash. 281	Mar 75 - .GRPH LEAST SQ EVAL CFD EXP	
Fission	Pile		CRC	Expt Rept	CRRP−1183	Feb 64 Bigham+ RATIO U233/,PU239/,PU241/	+
	Pile			Data	EXFOR12230.	Jun 76 . 3 RATIOS	·
Fission	1.2+6	2.0+7	KFK	Expt Conf	76ANL 246	Jun 76 Levgers+REL H SCT.NORM.TBL,GRPH.CFD	
Fission	3.9+5	3.0+7	KFK	Expt Conf	76ANL 94	Jun 76 Cierjacks+ RATIO TO PU−239,U−238,TBL	+
	3.9+5	3.0+7		Data	EXFOR20621.002	Jun 76 144PTS.SIGMA.RATIO.	
Fission	3.4+6	5.9+6	LAS	Expt Rept	LA−520	Mar 46 Williams.RATIO TH232,U233,U238,PU239	
	3.4+6	5.9+6		Data	EXFOR12312.	Jun 76 . 12 PTS. RATIOS	
Fission	6.9+5	1.4+7	LAS	Expt Rept	LA−1258	May 51 Nyer.	+
	6.9+5	1.4+7		Data	EXFOR12474.002	Jun 76 . 6 PTS.	
Fission	2.5−6		LAS	Expt Rept	LA−1681	Jun 54 Wahl+ RATIOS U236/,PU239.	+
	2.5+6	1.4+7		Data	EXFOR12437.	Jun 76 . 1 PT. SIGMA, 4 PTS. RATIO.	
Fission	2.5−2	2.0+7	LRL	Revw Conf	76ANL 258	Jun 76 Carlson+STATUS RVW.3E REGIONS.TBLS.	
Fission	Maxwl		MTR	Expt Prog	WASH−1028 50	Apr 60 Hogg. SIG=552+−55B	+
	Maxwl			Data	EXFOR12438.004	Jun 76 . 1 PT.	
Fission	1.0+4	1.0+6	AUA	Theo Jour	NP/A 265 337	Jul 76 Boldeman+CFD EVAL DATA ANE,1,409,75	
Fission	None		BRC	Revw Conf	76Lowell 641	Jul 76 Michaudon.RVW FISSION PROCESSES	
				Conf	75Wash. 202	Mar 75 - . FISSION REVIEW.TH+EXPTS.	
Fission	1.6+7	2.2+7	PAH	ExTh Conf	76Lowell 725	Jul 76 Hooshyar+ 2ES.STATMD CFD XPT	
	Maxwl			Conf	76Lowell 725	Jul 76 - +STATMDL APLD TO EXPT.DATA	
Fission	+5	2.2+7	HAR	Expt Conf	NEANDC(E)172 8	Aug 76 James+ RATIO U5/U8,SYN.CYCLO,NDG	
	6.0+5	2.2+7		Conf	75Wash. 568	Mar 75 Coates+U238/U235 FISS CS RATIO	
	4.0+5	2.0+7		Prog	AERE−PR/NP20 4	Mar 73 - +RATIO U−235/U−238.GRPH−20MEV	
Fission	1.0+6	6.0+6	LAS	Expt Jour	NSE 60 369	Aug 76 Barton+REL H SCT CS.41E.TBL,GRPH.CFD	+
				Conf	76ANL 173	Jun 76 .SUPERSEDED	
				Conf	72Vienna 227	Nov 72 Diven. TBL REL SIG,TO BE RENORMALIZD	
	1.0+6	6.0+6		Data	EXFOR10346.	Mar 76 41PTS.RATIO TO H CS.41PTS NF CS ONLY	
Fission	Maxwl		LBL	Theo Jour	PL/B 63 266	Aug 76 Boneh+SINGLE PTCLE DAMPING IN FISSIO	
Fission	Maxwl		RIS	Expt Jour	NP/A 269 338	Oct 76 Andersen+FISS RATIO FOR SHAPE ISOMER	
Fission	5.0−2	4.0+4	COL	Expt Abst	ANS 15 944	Nov 72 Felvinci+CS MEAS.NDG.RES PAR TBL.	+
	5.0−2	4.0+4		Data	EXFOR10322.004	Nov 76 DATA UNOBTAINABLE FROM AUTHORS.	
Fission	5.0+0	3.0+4	GEL	Expt Jour	ANE 3 437	Nov 76 Wagemans+ LINAC.TOF.TBLS.GRAPHS.	

92 Uranium 235

Quantity	Energy (ev) Min	Max	Lab	Type	Documentation Ref Vol Page	Date	Author, Comments	Data
Fission	1.1+4	2.0+5	CAD	Expt	Rept CEA-R-4804	Dec 76	Szabo+71KNOX RENORMALIZED FACTOR1.02	+
					Conf 76ANL 208	Jun 76	- + REVISED VALS CFD NEW	
					Conf 72Vienna 175	Nov 72	- + COMPARED WITH LATER X	
					Conf 71Knoxvill 573	Mar 71	- +.TOF+IONIZAT CHAMB,15ES,CURVE	
					Jour AE 29 395	Nov 70	Leroy.ABST FRANC-SOV SEM DUBNA 6/70	
					Jour SJA 29 1156	Nov 70	- + ENGLISH TRANS OF AE 2	
	1.1+4	2.0+5			Data EXFOR20569.002	Mar 76	15PTS.SIGMA.	
Fission	2.3+6	5.5+6	CAD	Expt	Rept CEA-R-4804	Dec 76	Szabo+ NEW DATA.TABLES.GRAPHS.	+
					Conf 76ANL 208	Jun 76	- + GRAPHS TBLS.CFD REVISED VALS.	
	2.3+6	5.5+6			Data EXFOR20618.002	Jun 76	13PTS.SIGMA.	
Fission	1.7+4	2.8+6	CAD	Expt	Rept CEA-R-4804	Dec 76	Szabo+ REVISED DATA FROM 73KIEV.	+
					Conf 76ANL 208	Jun 76	- + REVISED DATA CFD NEW EXPT.	
					Conf 73Kiev 3 27	May 73	- + SUMMARY.GRAPH.TBL.CFD OTHERS.	
					Conf 72Vienna 175	Nov 72	- + COMPARED WITH EARLIER XPT.	
	1.7+4	2.8+6			Data EXFOR20570.002	Mar 76	15PTS.SIGMA.	
Fission	1.0+2	1.5+7	IJE	Eval	Rept INDC(CCP)-94	Dec 76	Konshin. REVW OF EXPTS,EVAL.TBLS+FIG	+
	1.0-4	1.0+0			Rept INDC(CCP)-78	Jan 76	- + BRIEF DESCRIPTION,IN ENGL.	
	1.0+2	2.0+7			Data VIEN-V0007.	Oct 77	179+9 PTS.	
Fission	0.0+0	1.6+7	TRM	Theo	Conf 76Ahmedabd 2 116	Dec 76	Chatterjee+ DELAY/PROMPT FISS.GRAPH	
Fission	1.5+7		TRM	Expt	Conf 76Ahmedabd 2 116	Dec 76	Chatterjee+ (N,G)DELAYDFIS.UPP LIMIT	
Fission	2.1+1	1.0+7	CCP	Revw	Rept YK-27 16	77	Vozjakov+ 20GROUP,6 LIBRARS CFD.TABL	
Res Int Fiss	5.0-1		HAN	Expt	Rept AECD-4167	Mar 55	Clayton.	
	5.0-1				Data EXFOR12388.003	Jun 76	. 1 PT. RI	
Res Int Fiss	None		ORL	Revw	Conf 55Geneva 5 96	Aug 55	Macklin+.P833 ,EXPT CFD THEORY,TABLE	
Res Int Fiss	8.0-1	1.0+2	HAR	Expt	Jour JNE 2 128	Dec 55	Price. INTEGRATES EXP.CURVE	
Res Int Fiss	5.0-1	1.0+6	ORL	Eval	Jour NSE 6 100	Aug 59	Stoughton+,BEST VALUE 300+-50B	
Res Int Fiss	5.0-1		BET	Expt	Jour NSE 9 341	Mar 61	Hardy+ 274+-11B REL AU 1535B	+
	5.0-1				Data EXFOR12405.002	Jun 76	. 1 PT.	
Res Int Fiss	6.0-1		SRL	Expt	Rept DP-817	Jan 63	Baumann./ AU,F-P ACT,INCL 1/V, 263B	+
	6.0-1				Data EXFOR11376.010	Jun 76	. 1 PT.	
Res Int Fiss	4.4-1		ANL	Theo	Abst ANS 6 39	Jun 63	Persiani+RNEGCRESRCONTRIB.INFNITLDIL	
Res Int Fiss	6.2-1		WIN	Expt	Rept AEEW-R-217	Aug 63	Hardiman+.CD RATIOS.E-CD VALUES CALC	
Res Int Fiss	Pile		CRC	Eval	Rept EANDC(CAN)-20	Oct 63	Hanna+ CALC CF CALCS AND EXPTS.	
Res Int Fiss	4.5-1		CRC	Expt	Rept CRRP-1183	Feb 64	Bigham. NRX REL IN,B,LI,AU 277+-5B.	+
	4.5-1				Data EXFOR12230.	Jun 76	. 2 PTS, 2 STANDARDS	
Res Int Fiss	3.5-2	2.0+2	HAR	Expt	Rept EANDC(UK)-42	Jun 64	Brooks.FROM NF.AMENDED TBL 2	
Res Int Fiss	3.9+1		KAP	Expt	Abst ANS 7 78	Jun 64	Esch+ RES INT 288PM18	
Res Int Fiss	5.0-1	1.0+6	AE	Expt	Rept AE-181	Apr 65	Hellstrand.CD+B FILTERS USED	+
	5.0-1	1.0+6			Data EXFOR20018.002	Sep 71	1PNT.	
Res Int Fiss	None		WAL	Eval	Rept WANL-TME-1228	Aug 65	Gibson+. CALCULATED FOR 1/E FLUX	
	5.0-1	1.0+7			Rept WANL-TME-1028	Nov 64	Drawbaugh+.4 PARTIAL(GAM TAPE 3E10)	
Res Int Fiss	3.5-1	1.0+3	KFK	Eval	Rept KFK-120 1	Nov 65	Schmidt. PARTIAL OVER 21 E INTERVALS	
Res Int Fiss	5.0-1		KAP	Comp	Conf 66S.Diego 2 299	Feb 66	Feiner+.COMPIL PREV RESULTS+RECOMMND	
Res Int Fiss	3.5-1		WIN	Eval	Conf 66S.Diego 2 395	Feb 66	Askew. DEDUCED FROM EVAL SIGMA	
Res Int Fiss	5.0-1	1.0+7	BNW	Theo	Conf 66Wash. 75	Mar 66	Liikala+, TBLS OF RES.INTEGRALS	
Res Int Fiss	4.5-1	1.0+4	INA	Eval	Conf 66Paris 2 333	Oct 66	Hennies.PPR5.TBL RECOM DATA CFD OTHR	
					Rept NAA-SR-11980 5	May 67	- . RECOMMENDED DATA.REVISED.	
Res Int Fiss	5.0-1		BET	Expt	Jour NSE 29 1	Jul 67	Conway+ 275+-16B	+
					Rept WAPD-TM-613	Jun 67	.SUPERSEDED	
					Jour NSE 22 20	May 65	Conway+SUPERSEDED	
	5.0-1				Data EXFOR12313.005	Jun 76	. 1 PT.	
Res Int Fiss			DUB	Expt	Prog YFI-5 61	Oct 67	Rjabov+ TABLES	
	1.0+2	3.0+4			Rept JINR-P3-5113	Jun 70	Ryabov+ TABLE OF VARIOUS INTEGRALS	
	1.5-1	3.0+4			Prog YFI-11 35	70	Kurov+ ABST,SAME TBL AS JINR-5113	
					Jour AE 24 351	Apr 68	Rjabov+ VAL GIVEN,PULSED REACTOR,TOP	
					Prog INDC(CCP)-31	Dec 72	.PAGE 34,ENGLISH OF YFI-11 35	
					Jour SJA 24 435	Apr 68	. ENGLISH OF AE 24 351	
			3.0+4		Jour INDC-232E	67	. ENGL OF YFI-5 61	
Res Int Fiss	None		BET	Expt	Abst ANS 10 618	Nov 67	Green. DOPPLER EFFECT 293-1100DEGK	
					Rept WAPD-TM-625	Aug 67	- . NO TEMP VARIATION TO 800 DEGC	
Res Int Fiss	5.0+0	2.0+4	GEL	Expt	Jour JNE 22 211	Apr 68	Cao+16INTERV.IONCH+LIQSCINT.CFD OTHR	+
					Conf 68Wash. 481	Mar 68	CAO+ TBL FISS INTS. 13 RANGES.	
Res Int Fiss	Pile		UJV	Theo	Rept UJV-2224	69	Stepanek. 7 GROUP CONSTANTS	
Res Int Fiss	1.0+1	2.0+4	HAR	Comp	Rept AERE-M-2157	Jan 69	James+ TBL RES INTEG SCISRS DATA	
Res Int Fiss	5.0-1	2.0+3	LRL	Expt	Jour NSE 35 350	Mar 69	Bramblett+ LINAC FISS CHAMBR 258B	
Res Int Fiss	6.3-1		CAS	Eval	Jour NSE 40 51	70	Gibello+,EVAL. RES. INT. = 251 B	
Res Int Fiss	Fiss		RCN	Eval	Prog EANDC(E)127U	Apr 70	Bustraan+	

92 Uranium 235

Quantity	Energy (ev) Min	Energy (ev) Max	Lab	Type	Documentation Ref Vol Page	Author, Comments Date	Data
Res Int Fiss		+7	RI	Expt	Jour AE 28 359	Apr 70 BAK+ INTEGRAL VALUE GIVEN,CFD OTHER	
					Jour EAF 28 4 112	Apr 70 . FRENCH OF AE 28 359	
Res Int Fiss	−4	+7	BNW	Eval	Rept BNWL−1312	May 70 Simons+ RI=289.0B	
Res Int Fiss	5.0−1		KAP	Expt	Jour NSE 44 180	May 71 Eiland+ CD AND CD−RH FILTERS	+
	5.0−1				Data EXFOR10143.	Aug 73 2PTS.	
Res Int Fiss	7.0−1	2.1+1	GEL	Expt	Jour JNE 25 263	Jul 71 Deruytter+ LINAC.TOF.	+
					Conf 68Wash. 475	Mar 68 − + 222.0+ − 2.0B − EV PRELIM	
	7.0−1	2.1+1			Data EXFOR20131.003	Mar 73 6PTS.	
Res Int Fiss	5.0−1	+6	COR	Expt	Jour NSE 46 31	Oct 71 Draper.INTEGRAL SIG TIMES E.4 SPECTR	
	+0	+1			Abst DA/B 31 1466	Sep 70 − .EXPT FOR 4 SPEC,GOOD CFD CALC	
Res Int Fiss	5.3−1	8.2+1	MTR	Eval	Rept ANCR−1044	Dec 71 Smith+CALC FROM ENDF3B.CFD OTH.TBL.	
					Prog ANCR−1088 21	Oct 72 − +CALC.CFD OTH.TBL	
Res Int Fiss	5.5−1		RCN	Revw	Conf 73Paris 2 271	Mar 73 Zijp.RECOMMENDED,FROM LITERATURE,TBL	
Res Int Fiss	5.0−1		SGA	Comp	Conf 73Paris 1 233	Mar 73 Eder+ INCLUDING 1/V PART OF SIG,TBL	
					Rept SGAE−PH−141	Feb 73 .SAME AS 73PARIS,NO DETAILS,TBP	
	5.0−1		GHT	Expt	Jour JRC 20 695	74 Van Der Linden+ CD−RATIO,RI CFD OTHS	+
	5.5−1				Data EXFOR20645.063	Jul 76 1PNT.	
Res Int Fiss	5.0−1		RPI	Expt	Rept UMO−74−26,094	74 Shea. THESIS. TEMPERATURE−EFFECT	
Res Int Fiss	5.0−1		STF	Expt	Abst DA/B 34 6026	Jun 74 Underhill. I=277.3+ − 5.4BARNS.	+
	5.0−1				Data EXFOR10448.002	Nov 74 1PT	
Res Int Fiss	5.0−1		KFI	Eval	Jour KFKI−74−45	Jul 74 Gado.PARTIAL+TOTAL FROM RES−PARS,TBL	
				Theo	Rept KFKI−73−49	Sep 73 − + ABSORPT,CODE CALC CFD EVAL,TB	
Res Int Fiss	5.0+0	2.0+2	KUR	Expt	Conf 75Kiev 6 76	Jun 75 Mostovaja+ IONIZ CHAMBER,TBL	
Res Int Fiss	7.8+0		BNL	Eval	Conf 76ANL 307	Jun 76 Bhat.PRELIM EVAL ENDF5B.TBL.	
Res Int Fiss	7.0+0	1.1+1	BNW	Eval	Conf 76ANL 281	Jun 76 Leonard.BEST VAL FOR NORM DATA SETS.	
Res Int Fiss	5.0−1	1.0+3	COL	Expt	Prog COO−2176−1 11	Jun 72 Felvinci+IDENT TO NCSAC−42 P98 N71.	+
	5.0−1	1.0+3			Data EXFOR10322.003	Nov 76 15PTS.	
Res Int Fiss	1.0+0	1.0+3	MOL	Expt	Jour ANE 3 437	Nov 76 Wagemans+CALC VAL 16.16B.KEV	
Res Int Fiss	5.0−1		MOL	Expt	Jour ANE 3 437	Nov 76 Wagemans+EPICADMIUM VAL 280+ −7B	
Alpha	Maxwl		LAS	Expt	Rept LA−512	46 Williams+	+
	Maxwl				Data EXFOR12441.003	Jun 76 . 1 PT.	
Alpha	Maxwl		LAS	Expt	Rept LA−511	Mar 46 Deutsch+	+
	Maxwl				Data EXFOR12440.002	Jun 76 . 1 PT.	
Alpha	1.0−2	1.0+6	NDA	Eval	Rept NDA−MEMO−15 1	Jul 52 Weisskopf.EXPT+THEOR PREDICTIONS	
Alpha	Pile		ANL	Revw	Conf 55Geneva 3 198	Aug 55 Zinn.P814,VAL GVN,DISCUSS OF RESULTS	
Alpha	Pile		ANL	Expt	Conf 55Geneva 4 105	Aug 55 Ingham+.P596,VAL GVN,MASS−SPECTRM	
Alpha	1.0+0	1.0+6	BNL	Revw	Conf 55Geneva 5 215	Aug 55 Chernik.P603,KAPL EXPERIMENTS,CURVE	
Alpha	Pile	1.5+6	KAP	Expt	Conf 55Geneva 4 315	Aug 55 Kanne+.TABLE FOR SEVERAL ES,PPR595	+
	Pile				Data EXFOR12421.002	Jun 76 . 1 PT.	
Alpha	Maxwl	5.0+5	ORL	Revw	Conf 55Geneva 3 19	Aug 55 Weinberg.P862,VAL FOR 6ES GVN,REFS	
Alpha	1.0−1	9.3+0	MTR	Expt	Jour PR 100 1266	Nov 55 Smith.	+
Alpha	1.5−2	7.0−1	CCP		Rept AEC−TR−2435PT1	56 .USSR CURVE OF 1OVER1PLUSALPHA P11	
Alpha	1.0−2	5.0−1	BNL	Eval	Jour JNE 3 177	Oct 56 Palevsky+ CALC FROM ETA,IF NU CONST	
					Conf 55Geneva 4 311	Aug 55 − .GRAPH,EXPT DESCRIBED,P587	
Alpha	2.5−2		BNL	Eval	Rept BNL−325	Jan 57 Hughes+ WORLD CONSIST. VAL. .192+ −.0	
Alpha	4.6+2	1.0+7	KAP	Eval	Rept KAPL−1756 1	Jun 57 Baraff.CURV REV PCALC ASU NU 2D46	
Alpha	1.0+2	1.0+6	BNL	Theo	Jour JNE 5 16	Jul 57 Oleksa.THEOR AGREES XPT TO 10KEV,AVG	
Alpha	Maxwl		HAR	Expt	Rept AERE−NP/R−2140	Dec 57 Egelstaff+ CONSISTENT VALUES 2200M/S	
				Comp	Rept AERE−NP/R−2104	Mar 57 − .EXPT METHODS FOR HAR VALUE	
				Revw	Conf 55Geneva 4 307	Aug 55 − +.VAL GVN,EXPT DESCRBD,P425	
Alpha	6.0−3	5.0+4	HAR	Expt	Jour JNE 6 212	58 Skarsgard+ REL TO THERMAL VAL.	+
Alpha	1.0+2	4.0+3	COL	Expt	Jour NSE 3 435	Apr 58 Melkonian+,TOF,CURVE GIVEN	+
	1.0+2	5.0+3			Rept CU−163	Jun 57 − . TOF D64.	
	1.0+2	4.0+3			Data EXFOR12403.008	Jun 76 . 1 PT.	
Alpha	1.1−3		HAR	Expt	Jour JNE 6 285	May 58 Cocking.FILTER NEUTS,ALFA=.172+ −.022	+
Alpha	1.0−3	1.0+0	BNL	Comp	Conf 58Geneva 16 8	Sep 58 Hughes.PPR2483,CURVE,MANY REFS	
Alpha	Pile		CRC	Expt	Conf 58Geneva 16 83	Sep 58 Craig+ PPR205,2200M/SEC VALUE GIVEN	
					Rept CRRP−622	May 57 Hurst.REVIEW.	
	Pile				Data EXFOR12355.	Jun 76 . 2 PTS, 2 ANALYSES	
Alpha	1.8+5	1.0+6	LAS	Expt	Jour PR 109 144	Jan 58 Diven.	+
					Conf 58Geneva 15 60	Sep 58 − . PPR667	
	1.8+5	1.0+6			Data EXFOR12416.002	Jun 76 . 9 PTS.	
Alpha	−2	1.1+6	LAS	Revw	Conf 58Geneva 15 344	Sep 58 Hemmendinger.PPR663,CURVE,MANY REFS	
Alpha	−.1+0	8.8+0	BNL	Eval	Jour PR 112 191	Oct 58 Shore. RES VALUE FROM FISS+TOT, B−W	
					Conf 58Geneva 15 118	Sep 58 .SUPERSEDED	
Alpha	Maxwl		MTR	Expt	Prog WASH−1006 28	Oct 58 Smith+ NDG	

92 Uranium 235

Quantity	Energy (ev) Min	Max	Lab	Type	Documentation Ref Vol Page	Date	Author, Comments	Data
Alpha	2.9 – 3		COL	Expt Jour	PR 113 1285	Mar 59	Safford+ CRYSTSPEC,SIMULTAN TOT+FIS	+
				Conf	60Vienna 203	Oct 60	.SEE ALSO	
				Jour	PRL 2 189	Feb 59	.SUPERSEDED	
	2.9 – 3			Data	EXFOR12439.003	Jun 76	. 1 PT.	
Alpha	1.0 – 1	5.0+2	HAR	Expt Rept	NRDC – 117	Aug 59	Collins+ TOF. FISSN WIDTHS OF 16 RES	+
Alpha	2.5 – 2		COL	Revw Jour	NUC 17 11 134	Nov 59	Safford+. EXPTL VALUES TABULATED	
Alpha	1.0+4	1.8+5	ORL	Theo Abst	BAP 4 414	Nov 59	Gibbons. FROM ABS DATA, NDG	
Alpha	2.5 – 2		AE	Comp Rept	AE – 11	Apr 60	Story+,DISCUSSION+TABULATN OF MEASTS	
Alpha	Pile		HAR	Expt Rept	NRDC – 129	May 60	Cornish.ACTIVATION+MASS ANALYSIS	+
Alpha	Maxwl		CRC	Expt Rept	EANDC(CAN) – 11	May 61	Jones+. MEAS. ON NRX FUEL RODS	
Alpha	Maxwl		HAN	Eval Conf	61RPI 3	May 61	Leonard.	
Alpha	5.0 – 3	2.5+0	GA	Eval Rept	GA – 2113	Jun 61	Wikner+.TABLE 100 E POINTS	
Alpha	None		KAP	Expt Abst	ANS 4 131	Jun 61	Fehr+ FN. LATTICE POSITION	
Alpha	Maxwl		CRC	Revw Conf	61Saclay 57	Jul 61	Westcott. 2200METRE/SEC SIG GIVEN	
Alpha	+4	1.0+6	ANL	Revw Conf	61Vienna 1 29	Aug 61	Smith.P76,CURVE,MANY REFS GVN	
Alpha	2.5 – 2	1.0+6	ROS	Revw Jour	KE 5 701	Jan 62	Falkenberg.VAL GVN,REFERENCES	
Alpha	3.0+4	1.0+6	LAS	Expt Jour	NSE 12 169	Feb 62	Hopkins+ TABLE+CURVE CFD OTHER EXPTS	+
				Conf	61Vienna 1 111	Aug 61	.SUPERSEDED	
				Conf	61Saclay 407	Jul 61	.SUPERSEDED	
	3.0+4	1.0+6		Data	EXFOR12331.005	Jun 76	. 9 PTS.	
Alpha	Maxwl		CRC	Revw Rept	EANDC(CAN) – 15	Nov 62	Hanna. COMPARES MANY VALUES.	
Alpha	Pile		ANL	Expt Conf	63Amsterdm 1 227	Sep 63	Armani+,ALPHAS FOR UO2 – H2O ASSEMBLY	
Alpha	1.0+2	1.0+4	HAR	ExTh Rept	AERE – M – 1272	Dec 63	Uttley.AVR TRNS..S,P WAVE,ALPHA TH	
Alpha	3.2 – 2	2.0+1	ITE	Eval Jour	AE 16 110	Feb 64	Ignat'Ev.ETA+SIGF MEAS,GRAPHS+TABLES	+
	3.0 – 2	2.0+1		Expt Jour	JNE 18 719	64	.ENGLISH TRANSL OF AE 16 110 2/64	
				Jour	EAF 16 2 19	64	. FRENCH TRANSL OF AE 16 110 2/64	
	3.2 – 2	2.0+1		Eval Jour	SJA 16 121	64	.ENGLISH TRANSL OF AE 16 110 2/64	
	3.2 – 2	2.0+1		Expt Data	EXFOR40156.007	Mar 75	.505 DATA LINES	
Alpha	Pile		CRC	Expt Rept	AECL – 1965	Apr 64	Okazaki. .1718+ – .0006 CHEM/MASS ANAL	+
	Pile			Data	EXFOR12420.003	Jun 76	. 1 PT.	
Alpha	1.2+4	6.9+5	ORL	Expt Jour	NSE 20 80	Sep 64	Weston+ 2 METHODS,TBL+CURV,CFD OTHRS	+
				Prog	EANDC – 33 64	Sep 63	.SEE ALSO +630XFORD	
	1.2+4	6.9+5		Data	EXFOR12407.002	Jun 76	. 26 PTS.	
Alpha	1.0+1	1.0+6	ORL	Revw Prog	WASH – 1053 63	Oct 64	Desaussure+ CURV ALL RECENT XPTS.	
Alpha	5.0 – 1	+6	KAP	Expt Abst	ANS 7 272	Nov 64	Esch. AVG FOR 1/E SPECT .486+ – .025	+
	5.0 – 1	+6		Data	EXFOR12314.003	Jun 76	. 1 PT.	
Alpha	1.0 – 3	1.0+7	WAL	Eval Rept	WANL – TME – 1028	Nov 64	Drawbaugh+.CURV+TABLE.GROUP AVERAGED	
Alpha	1.2+1		GA	Expt Jour	NIM 31 125	Dec 64	Haddad+ PRELIM,NDG.FISS+CAPT GAMMA CF	
Alpha	Pile		ANL	Expt Jour	NSE 21 179	Feb 65	Crouthamel+FAST REACT.CFD,WITH DIVEN	
Alpha	1.0+2	3.0+4	DUB	Expt Conf	65Salzburg 1 287	Mar 65	Van – Shi – Di. TOF, TBL OF AVRGD VALUES	
				Rept	JINR – P – 2024	65	Van Shi Di+ TOF,AVG VALS.	
				Rept	BNL – TR – 16	Jul 65	– + ENGL OF 65SALZ.	
Alpha	8.0+0	1.4+7	LAS	Expt Prog	WASH – 1056 51	Mar 65	Diven+ NDG, BOMB SOURCE, TBC	
Alpha	Maxwl		MTR	Expt Abst	ANS 8 10	Jun 65	Maeck. MASS SPECT .1716+ – .0019	+
	Maxwl			Data	EXFOR12398.002	Jun 76	. 1 PT.	
Alpha	2.0+0	5.0+1	SAC	Expt Jour	NP 69 545	Jul 65	Michaudon+ MANY RESONANCES	+
Alpha	3.2+0	1.8+4	ORL	Expt Jour	NSE 23 45	Sep 65	Desaussure+ SSPD BY 1967 MEAS	+
Alpha	3.5 – 2	2.0+2	HAR	Expt Rept	AERE – M – 1670	Feb 66	Brooks+ LINAC,TOF, CURVES CFD OTHERS	+
				Conf	66S.Diego 2 193	Feb 65	– . SEE ALSO	
				Rept	BNL – 325	Feb 65	– . CURVE GIVEN	
				Rept	EANDC(UK) – 42	Jun 64	– .TOF.FROM ETA	
Alpha	1.0+3	1.0+7	KFK	Eval Rept	KFK – 120 1	Feb 66	Schmidt.AVERAGE CS TO21KEV+CURVE	
				Conf	66S.Diego 2 223	Feb 66	– . SEE KFK – 120	
	– .1+1	1.5+2		Rept	KFK – 120 1	Nov 65	– .CALC FROM RESON PARS	
	1.0 – 2	1.0+7		Rept	KFK – 120 2 ·	Dec 62	– .GRAPHS AND TABULATED DATA	
	1.0+3	1.0+7		Conf	61Vienna 1 3	Aug 61	– . P4	
Alpha	2.5 – 2		BNW	Theo Conf	66Wash. 75	Mar 66	Liikala+, TBLS OF LITER. VALUES	
Alpha	Pile		MTR	Eval Conf	66Wash. 919	Mar 66	Smith+,REACTVTY MEASTS+SPECTRAL CORR	
Alpha	Maxwl		CRC	Expt Rept	AECL – 2615	Oct 66	.SAME	+
				Conf	66Paris 2 17	Oct 66	Durham+ XPT DESCRIBD,MASSPECTRM	
	Maxwl			Data	EXFOR12428.002	Jun 76	. 1 PT.	
Alpha	Pile		HAR	Expt Conf	66Paris 2 3	Oct 66	Cabell+ PPR21, MASS – SPEC VAL GIVEN	+
	Maxwl			Rept	AERE – R – 3986	Mar 62	– + 2PC ACCURACY OKS PREV.BEST	
	2.5 – 2			Jour	JIN 24 1493	62	– + FROM VALUES 0.178 TO 0.189	
Alpha	4.5 – 1	1.0+4	INA	Eval Conf	66Paris 2 333	Oct 66	Hennies.PPR5.TBL RECOM DATA CFD OTHR	
				Rept	NAA – SR – 11980 5	May 67	– . RECOMMENDED DATA.REVISED.	

92 Uranium 235

Quantity	Energy (ev) Min	Max	Lab	Type	Documentation Ref Vol Page	Date	Author, Comments	Data
Alpha	1.7+4	6.0+5	ORL	Expt	Conf 66Paris 2 233	Oct 66	Desaussure+PPR48.TBL,SIMULT CAPT+FIS	+
	1.0+4	6.0+5		Jour	NIM 58 143	Jan 68	Todd. NDG, INSTRUMENTATION	
	2.0+4	6.0+5		Rept	ORNL−P−2599	Dec 66	Lottin+	
				Conf	66ANL 22	Oct 66	− +	
	1.8+4	6.0+5		Data	EXFOR12409.	Jun 76	.41 PTS.	
Alpha	Pile		ANL	Expt	Jour NSE 27 34	Jan 67	Redman+AVG ALFA.217 SPECT NOT STATED	
				Rept	ANL−7143	Jan 66	.SUPERSEDED	
Alpha		6.3+1	WAL	Eval	Rept WANL−TME−1586	Mar 67	Gibson+MULTIGROUP LIBRARY+CURVE	
Alpha	1.0+4	2.0+4	LAS	Theo	Jour PR 158 1127	Jun 67	Bell. PREDICT 10−20KEV BY SYSTEMATCS	
Alpha	Pile		WIN	Expt	Abst ANS 10 231	Jun 67	Fox+ AVG ALFA=0.53+−0.06	
Alpha	5.0−1	+6	BET	Expt	Jour NSE 29 1	Jul 67	Conway+ ALFA=0.499+−0.016 1/E SPECT	
				Rept	WAPD−TM−613	Jun 67	.SUPERSEDED	
				Jour	NSE 22 20	May 65	Conway+	
				Abst	ANS 7 78	Jun 64	− +RATIO RES INT CAP TO FISS	
Alpha	1.7+0	1.0+5	DUB	Expt	Prog YFI−5 61	Oct 67	Rjabov+ CURVES	
	1.5−1	9.0+4		Jour	AE 24 351	Apr 68	+ GRPH ALFA(E),PULSED REACTOR	
				Jour	SJA 24 435	Apr 68	. ENGLISH OF AE 24 351	
	1.7+0	1.0+5		Rept	INDC−232E	67	. ENGL OF YFI−5 61	
Alpha	None		BET	Expt	Abst ANS 10 618	Nov 67	Green. DOPPLER EFFECT 293−1100DEGK.	
				Rept	WAPD−TM−625	Aug 67	− .VARIATION WITH TEMP TO 800DEGC	
Alpha	Fast			AE Expt	Prog EANDC(OR)73L	Jan 68	. RELATIVE TO B−10	
Alpha	5.0−1	+6	ANL	Expt	Jour NSE 31 247	Feb 68	Redman+ LOW−FLUX MEAST .519+−.023	+
Alpha	1.0+2	5.0+5	JAP	Theo	Jour NST 5 86	Feb 68	KIKUCHI P AN.CALC C CHANNEL THEORY	
Alpha	6.4+0	1.5+2	GEL	Expt	Jour JNE 22 211	Apr 68	CAO+ FISS N + FISS FRAG DETECTED.	+
				Conf	68Wash. 481	Mar 68	CAO+ STAT DIST OF ALF STUDIED.	
	6.4+0	1.5+2		Data	EXFOR20129.011	Mar 73	78PTS.AT RES.	
Alpha	0.0+0	6.0+6	FEI	Eval	Prog YFI−11 13	70	Vorobyeva+ ABST,TBL VALUE FOR MAXW	
				Prog	INDC(CCP)−31	Dec 72	.PAGE 12,ENGLISH OF YFI−11 13	
Alpha	Maxwl	1.0+4	ITE	Expt	Rept ITE−780	70	Belyaev+ TOF,2 METHODS,NDG	
Alpha	3.0−1	5.0+3	KUR	Expt	Rept IAE−1985	70	Muradjan+ NEW METHD TBL GRPH CFD OTH	+
				Jour	AE 29 395	Nov 70	*ABST FRANC−SOVJ SEMINAR	
				Jour	SJA 29 1156	Nov 70	*ENGL OF AE 29 395	
				Conf	70Helsinki 1 357	Jun 70	.*SAME AS IAE−1985	
	1.0+1	5.0+3		Data	EXFOR40089.002	Dec 73	.CAPT/FISS CS RATIO AT 16 E−INTERVAL	
Alpha	Pile		ANL	Expt	Jour NSE 39 368	Mar 70	Redman+,LOW−FLUX METH,0.337+−0.029	
Alpha	Pile		ANL	Expt	Jour NSE 40 132	Apr 70	Till+,NULL−REACTIVITY METHOD	
Alpha	2.9−1	5.0+1	DUB	Expt	Rept JINR−P3−4992	Apr 70	Rjabov+ ALF AT RES−E,73 RES,TBL	+
				Prog	YFI−11 27	70	− + ABST,SAME TBL AS JINR−4992	
				Prog	INDC(CCP)−31	Dec 72	.PAGE 26,ENGLISH OF YFI−11 17	
	2.9−1	5.0+1		Data	EXFOR40070.012	Aug 70	ALFA AT 78 RESONANCE ENERGIES	
Alpha	+2	+5	JAE	Theo	Jour NSE 40 25	Apr 70	Ishiguro+,STATISTICAL CALCULATN,CURV	
Alpha	Fiss		RCN	Eval	Prog EANDC(E)127U	Apr 70	Bustraan+	
Alpha	1.5+2	1.0+5	TOK	Theo	Conf NST 7 157	Apr 70	Kikuchi+.CALC USING SPIN DEPENDNT WF	
				Jour	NST 5 86	Feb 68	− + SUPERSEDED.	
Alpha	1.0+2	1.0+4	LRL	Expt	Conf UCRL−72454	May 70	Czirr+,LINAC+TOF+SCINT,ALF=0.34+−.03	+
				Conf	70Helsinki 1 331	Jun 70	.SUPERSEDED	
	4.8+1	2.8+4		Data	EXFOR12424.	Jun 76	. 31 PTS.	
Alpha	+5	+7	ANL	Revw	Conf 70Helsinki 2 119	Jun 70	Davey.112.STATUS OF DATA ABOVE RESON	
Alpha	+1	+7	CAD	Theo	Conf 70Helsinki 2 465	Jun 70	Barre+73. MICROSC CFD INTEGRAL DATA	
	4.0+2	1.0+6		Eval	Rept EANDC(E)120L	Mar 69	− +RAVIER EVAL OF INTEGRAL MEAS	
Alpha	2.5−2		CRC	Expt	Conf 70Helsinki 1 287	Jun 70	Lounsbury+THR FLUX.VAL AT 2200 M/S.−	+
	2.5−2			Data	EXFOR10013.003	Sep 72	1PT.VAL AT 2200M/S.	
Alpha	1.0+2	3.0+4	DUB	Expt	Rept JINR−P3−5113	Jun 70	Rjabov+ E−GROUPS AVGD ALF,TBLS+GRPH	+
				Jour	AE 30 258	Mar 71	Kurov+ TOF,SCINT,AVG ALFA.TABL+GRAPH	
				Conf	70Helsinki 1 345	Jun 70	Rjabov+ SAME DATA,TBL,GRAPHS.	
	1.0+2	3.0+3		Prog	YFI−11 35	70	Kurov+ ABST,SAME TBL AS JINR−5113	
	1.0+2	3.0+4		Jour	AE 24 351	Apr 68	Rjabov+ SUPERSEDED BY JINR−5113	
	1.0+2	3.0+3		Prog	INDC(CCP)−31	Dec 72	.PAGE 34,ENGLISH OF YFI−11 35	
	1.0+2	3.0+4		Jour	SJA 30 315	Oct 71	. ENGL OF AE 30 258	
				Jour	SJA 24 435	Apr 68	Rjabov+ ENGL OF AE 24 351	
				Jour	EAF 24 81	Apr 68	− + FRENCH OF AE 24 351	
	1.0+2	3.0+4		Data	EXFOR40024.002	Aug 70	ALFA AT 22 ES,JINR−P3−5113 TABLE II	
Alpha	Pile		FAR	Expt	Conf 70Helsinki 2 487	Jun 70	Bouchard+96. 2 TYPES OF INTEGRL XPTS	
				Diss	DARROUZET	Mar 70	Darrouzet.ERMINE	
Alpha	Maxwl	1.0+4	ITE	Expt	Conf 70Helsinki 1 339	Jun 70	Beljaev+89. NO DATA GIVEN	
Alpha		5.0+1	UI	Theo	Conf 70Helsinki 2 777	Jun 70	Adler+50. R−MATRIX CORRELATED ANAL	
Alpha		2.5+3	RPI	Theo	Prog NCSAC−33 209	Dec 70	Shea.AVG ALFA CALCTD,OKS EXPT,NDG	
Alpha	2.5−2		ANL	Eval	Conf 71Knoxvill 560	Mar 71	Devolpi. ADJUSTED VALUE GIVEN.	

92 Uranium 235

Quantity	Energy (ev) Min	Max	Lab	Type	Documentation Ref Vol Page	Date	Author, Comments	Data
Alpha		+7	FEI Expt	Rept	FEI – 246	Mar 71	Voropaev+ GVN ALPHA,TBL,CALC CFD EXP	
Alpha	3.0+0	+6	KAP Expt	Jour	NSE 44 180	May 71	Eiland+ CD AND CD – RH FILTERS	
				Conf	KAPL – P – 3438	Jun 68	– + 0.622 INCLUDING 1/E,PRELIMIN	
Alpha	Pile		ANL Expt	Jour	NSE 45 87	Jul 71	Bretscher+.FAST SPEC.INTEG MEAST	
Alpha	Pile		JAE Expt	Prog	EANDC(J)22L12	Aug 71	Natsume+.RAD – CHEM ANAL.MEAN – VAL GIVN	
Alpha	2.5 – 2		HAR Revw	Conf	71Canterby 65	Sep 71	Fudge+FOR BURN – UP.TABLE AVAIL DATA.	
Alpha	1.0+2	1.0+5	ORL Expt	Prog	ORNL – 4705 10	Oct 71	Perez. ORELA, AVG ALPHA CURVE, TBC	
				Conf	71Knoxvill 728	Mar 71	.SUPERSEDED	
Alpha	2.0 – 2	4.0+5	ORL Expt	Prog	ORNL – 4705 4	Oct 71	Gwin+ORELA.CURV,CFD TO ENDF/B.	
Alpha	3.1+1	4.1+1	CCP Revw	Jour	AE 31 595	Dec 71	Sukhoruchkin.FROM RESPARS,DISCREPANT	
				Jour	SJA 31 1380	Jun 72	*ENGL OF AE 31 595	
Alpha	1.2+4	1.1+6	CCP Expt	Rept	YK – 9 37	72	Kononov+ ALFA(E),LIQ SCIN DET,TBL	
				Rept	INDC(CCP) – 42	Aug 74	.P3.ENGLISH OF YK – 9	
Alpha	2.5 – 2		IFB Eval	Rept	YK – 9 34	72	Morogovsky. COMPUTR RE – EVAL,DATA GVN	
				Rept	INDC(CCP) – 42	Aug 74	.P1.ENGLISH OF YK – 9	
Alpha	5.0+3	1.3+5	KUR Expt	Prog	YFI – 12 17	72	Vorotnikov+ ALPHA(N – E),TBL,ABST	+
				Conf	71Kiev	May 71	– + ALFA(NEUT – E), TABLE	
				Prog	INDC(CCP) – 30	Dec 72	.PG 14,ENGLISH OF YFI – 12 17	
	5.0+3	1.3+5		Data	EXFOR40108.	Dec 72	ALFA AT 18 ES, 2 RUNS	
Alpha	1.0+4	1.0+6	FEI Expt	Jour	AE 32 85	Jan 72	Kononov+ TOF,SCIN – TANK,GRPH CFD OTHR	+
	1.0+4	8.0+4		Jour	AE 38 82	Feb 75	– + TOF,ALF(NEUT – E)	
				Rept	YK – 15 12	Aug 74	– + TOF,VDG,AVGED ALPH,TBL	
	1.0+4	1.0+6		Jour	SJA 32 95	Jul 72	*	
	1.2+4	1.1+6		Rept	FEI – 274	Oct 71	Kononov+ ABSOLUTE,VDG ,SC – TANK,TABLE	
	1.0+4	8.0+4		Jour	SJA 38 105	Aug 75	. ENGL OF AE 38 82	
	1.2+4	1.1+6		Data	EXFOR40412.002	Jan 77	ALFA AT 47 ENERGIES	
Alpha	+2	+5	FEI Expt	Rept	FEI – 328	Jul 72	Dvuhsherstnov+ B FILTERED SPEC,VALUE	
Alpha	Pile		FEI Expt	Prog	YFI – 13 3	Oct 72	Dvukhsherstnov+ ABST,INTEG EXPT,TBL	+
	2.0+3			Jour	AE 33 577	Jul 72	– + TABLE	
				Rept	FEI – 285	Jan 72	Dvuhsherstnov+ SC – FILTER,SCINT,VALUE	
				Conf	71Kiev	May 71	Dvukhsherstnov+ .ALPHA=0.49+ – 0.04	
	Pile			Prog	INDC(CCP) – 32	Apr 73	.PAGE 3.ENGLISH OF YFI – 13 3	
	2.0+3			Jour	SJA 33 666	Jan 73	. ENGLISH OF AE 33 577 7/72	
	2.5+4			Data	EXFOR40092.003	Dec 73	.1 DATA LINE	
	2.0+3			Data	EXFOR40092.002	Dec 73	.1 DATA LINE	
Alpha	5.3 – 1	8.2+1	MTR Eval	Rept	ANCR – 1044	Dec 72	Smith+CALC FROM ENDF3B.CFD OTH TBL	
				Prog	ANCR – 1088 21	Oct 72	– +CALC/CFD OTH.TBL.	
Alpha	1.0+4	1.0+6	SOR Revw	Prog	IA – 1282 37	73	Yiftah+ ENDF CFD USSR EXPT,DISCUSSN	
Alpha	1.5+2	1.5+7	KFK Eval	Rept	KFK – 1629	Jun 73	Schatz. RECOMMENDED CURVE	+
				Prog	KFK – 1272 1	Jun 72	– . P122 – 1,CURVE 50KEV – 1MEV	
	1.0 – 3	1.5+7		Data	KEDAK – 3	Oct 75	5248 DATA SETS	
Alpha	8.0+0	1.0+4	ORL Expt	Jour	NSE 52 46	Sep 73	Perez+. LINAC. MUCH STRUCTURE SEEN	
				Prog	USNDC – 7 176	Jun 73	.SUPERSEDED	
				Rept	ORNL – TM – 3696	Dec 72	.SUPERSEDED	
Alpha	9.0+3	6.0+4	KFK Expt	Jour	NSE 48 324	Jul 72	Bandl+VDG.TOF.DATA COMPILED.	+
	8.0+3	6.0+4		Rept	KFK – 1457	Sep 71	– + SEE ALSO	
				Conf	71Knoxvill 273	Mar 71	– + SUPERSEDED.	
	9.0+3	6.0+4		Data	EXFOR20158.002	Oct 73	21PTS.	
Alpha	5.0 – 1	1.0+2	RPI Expt	Rept	UMO – 74 – 26,094	74	Shea. THESIS. TEMPERATURE – EFFECT	
Alpha	Pile		ANL Expt	Jour	NSE 53 9	Jan 74	Dudey+. INTEGRAL MEASTS IN EBR – 2.	
				Rept	ANL – 7791	Jul 71	Heinrich+. INTEGRAL MEAST IN EBR – 2	
Alpha	1.0+2	8.0+5	FEI Eval	Rept	INDC(CCP) – 65	Dec 74	.2. ENGL OF YFI – 19,4	
Alpha	1.0 – 3	1.5+7	IJE Eval	Jour	VBF 1975 1 13	75	Konshin+ ALF(NEUT – E),TBL.	
Alpha	Fast		ITU Expt	Prog	NEANDC(E)162U	Feb 75	Cottone+ SB – 125,XE,CS,ND VOL.5.P.42.	
Alpha	1.5+2	3.2+4	GEL Expt	Conf	75Wash. 599	Mar 75	Corvi+TBL,GRPH.STAT ERROR LT + – 5PCT.	
Alpha	Fast		HAR Expt	Prog	UKNDC(75)P71	Jul 75	Crouch+ IRRADIATION DFR	
Alpha	1.5+3	1.5+5	FEI Expt	Jour	AE 39 86	Aug 75	Dvukhsherstnov+ ALF AT 3ES,CFD,TBLS	+
				Rept	YFI – 19 4	Dec 74	– + AVG OF 4E – RANGES,TBL	
	2.0+3	2.4+4		Jour	AE 33 577	Jul 72	– + ALPH GIVN,CFD OTHERS	
				Prog	YFI – 12 7	72	– + ALPHA(NEUT – E),TBL	
	1.5+3	1.5+5		Jour	SJA 39 670	Feb 76	. ENGLISH OF AE 39 86	
				Rept	INDC(CCP) – 65	Dec 74	.2. ENGL OF YFI – 19,4	
	1.5+3	1.5+5		Data	EXFOR40310.	Feb 76	.DATA FOR 3 EN – RANGES AND SPECT AVER	
Alpha	2.5 – 2		MAG Eval	Rept	EPRI – NP – 163	Dec 75	Beer+MONTECARLO ANAL 70HELSINKI P287	
				Abst	ANS 23 509	Jun 76	– +MONTCARLO ANAL CRC DATA.TBL.CF	
Alpha	1.0+2	1.0+5	IFB Eval	Rept	INDC(CCP) – 78	Jan 76	Antsipov+ EVAL XPTS CFD CALCUL,GRPHS	
Alpha	Pile		LAS Expt	Rept	LA – 102	44	Snyder.	+
	Pile			Data	EXFOR12395.005	Jun 76	. 1 PT.	

92 Uranium 235

Quantity	Energy (ev) Min	Max	Lab	Type	Documentation Ref Vol Page	Date	Author, Comments	Data
Alpha	Maxwl		MTR	Expt Prog	WASH – 1028 50	Apr 60	Hogg. MTR .171+ – .017	+
	Maxwl			Data	EXFOR12438.003	Jun 76	. 1 PT.	
Alpha	3.0+4	6.4+4	ORL	Expt Prog	ORNL – 3360 51	Jan 63	Desaussure.	+
	3.0+4	6.4+4		Data	EXFOR12456.003	Jun 76	. 2 PTS.	
Alpha	2.0+2	1.2+4	KFK	Expt Jour	NSE 61 471	Dec 76	Bluhm+ SLOWING – DOWN TIME SPECTROMTR.	+
	2.0+2	2.0+4		Rept	KFK – 2191	Sep 75	YEN. SLOWING – DOWN – TIME SPECT	
	2.0+2	1.3+4		Data	EXFOR20663.002	Oct 76	24PTS.	
Eta	Maxwl		ANL	Expt Rept	CF – 3651	Oct 46	Zinn.	+
	Maxwl			Data	EXFOR12319.007	Jun 76	. 1 PT, ETA, 1 PT. RATIO U233	
Eta	2.0–2	6.0–1	HAN	Expt Rept	HW – 33497	Oct 54	Leonard. TABLE	+
	2.5–2	4.5–1		Data	EXFOR12393.002	Jun 76	. 22 PTS.	
Eta	Maxwl		ANL	Revw Conf	55Geneva 3 198	Aug 55	Zinn.VAL 2200M/SEC GVN,	
Eta	Cold		ANL	Revw Conf	55Geneva 5 125	Aug 55	Spinrad+.P835	
Eta	Fast		ANL	Revw Conf	55Geneva 5 125	Aug 55	Spinrad+.P835	
Eta	Maxwl		CCP	Expt Conf	55Geneva 4 295	Aug 55	Spivak+.VAL GVN,EXPT DESCRIBED,P657	+
Eta	Maxwl		CCP	Expt Conf	55Geneva 4 301	Aug 55	Alichanov+.VAL GVN,EXPT DESCRBD,P658	
Eta	Maxwl		ORL	Revw Conf	55Geneva 3 19	Aug 55	Weinberg.P862,VAL GVN,REFS GVN	
Eta	4.0–2	1.0+0	MTR	Expt Abst	PR 100 1266	Nov 55	Smith+ HORNYAK BUTTON	+
				Rept	IDO – 16269	Nov 55	– +,FLAT TO 0.1EV,MAX=2.2	
Eta	Maxwl	1.3+2	CCP	Expt Jour	AE 1 3 13	Jun 56	Spivak+.AVERAGES IN 6 BROAD SPECTRA	
				Jour	JNE 4 70	Jan 57	TRANSLATN.*	
				Jour	NE 1 101	Jun 56	SEE ALSO *	
				Jour	SJA 1 3 295		56 TRANSLATN.*	
Eta	3.0+4	9.0+5	CCP	Expt Jour	AE 1 3 21	Jun 56	Spivak+.DATA AT 4 ENERGIES	+
				Jour	JNE 4 79	Jan 57	TRANSLATN.*	
				Jour	NE 1 101	Jun 56	SEE ALSO *	
				Jour	SJA 1 3 303		56 TRANSLATN.*	
Eta	1.0–2	1.7–1	BNL	Expt Jour	JNE 3 177	Oct 56	Palevsky+ SC GRAPH,WITH HANFORD DATA	+
	1.0–2	5.0–1		Conf	55Geneva 4 311	Aug 55	– .GRAPH,EXPT DESCRIBED,P587	
	1.0–2	1.7–1		Data	EXFOR12322.003	Jun 76	. 20 PTS.	
Eta	2.5–2		BNL	Eval Rept	BNL – 325	Jan 57	Hughes+ WORLD CONSIST. VAL. 2.07+ – .0	
Eta	1.0+0	4.0+1	ANL	Expt Prog	WASH – 192	Mar 57	Bollinger. REPORTS TBD	
Eta	Maxwl			Rept	AERE – NP/R – 2104	Mar 57	Littler+. CITED.PILE OSC,CALC IMPTNCE	
Eta	1.0–1	8.0+0	MTR	Expt Rept	IDO – 16373 37	Jul 57	Smith+ LONG COUNTER, CURVE	+
	1.0–1	9.3+0		Data	EXFOR12411.002	Jun 76	. 83 PTS.	
Eta	Pile		ANL	Expt Jour	NSE 2 657	Sep 57	Kafalas+,CURVS HOR VERT DISTR EBR – I	
Eta	Maxwl		HAR	Eval Rept	AERE – NP/R – 2140	Dec 57	Egelstaff+ CONSISTENT VALUES 2200M/S	
				Revw Conf	55Geneva 4 307	Aug 55	– +.VAL GVN,EXPT DESCRBD,P425	
Eta	Maxwl		KAP	Expt Rept	NSE 3 758		58 Gaerttner+ RATIO TO U233,U239,PU241	+
	Maxwl			Data	EXFOR12327.	Jun 76	. 3 RATIOS	
Eta	2.4+4	8.8+5	CCP	Expt Jour	AE 4 185	Feb 58	Andreev.ALSO AT 240KEV,SPHERE METHOD	+
				Jour	JNE 9 151	Jun 59	TRANSLATN.*	
				Jour	SJA 4 247		58 TRANSLATN.*	
Eta	2.5–3	1.0–1	HAN	Expt Rept	HW – 55879 3	Apr 58	Seppi+ CONST. MAXW VARIATION OF 2PC	
Eta	6.0–3	5.0–2	HAR	Expt Jour	JNE 6 212	Apr 58	Skarsgard+.CS CURVE REL 2.08 AT THR	+
Eta	Maxwl		BNL	Comp Conf	58Geneva 16 8	Sep 58	Hughes.PPR2483,VAL V=2200M/SEC GVN	
Eta	1.4+7		CCP	Expt Jour	AE 5 653	Dec 58	Flerov+ (1954) 2.99+ – .15 SPHERE TRNS	+
				Jour	JNEA 11 169	Feb 60	TRANSLATN.*	
				Jour	SJA 5 1593		58 TRANSLATN.*	
Eta	Pile		ANL	Expt Jour	NSE 5 227	Apr 59	Muehlhause. RECALC ETA=2.05+ – 0.03	+
				Prog	ANL – 4746 17	Dec 51	Harris+.PILE OSCILLATOR.ETA=2.10	
	Pile			Data	EXFOR12361.003	Jun 76	. 1 PT. FROM NSE,5,227.	
Eta	2.6–2		HAR	Eval Conf	59Vienna 74	Sep 59	BOLTON BEST FIT VAL+ – ERROR TO EXPTS	
Eta	2.5–2		COL	Revw Jour	NUC 17 11 134	Nov 59	Safford+. EXPTL VALUES TABULATED	
Eta	2.5–2		AE	Comp Rept	AE – 11	Apr 60	Story+,DISCUSSION+TABULATN OF MEASTS	
Eta	Maxwl		ORL	Expt Jour	NSE 8 210	Sep 60	Macklin+,MN BATH ETA=2.077+ – 0.010	+
	Maxwl			Data	EXFOR12349.003	Jun 76	. 1 PT.	
Eta	Maxwl		MTR	Expt Prog	IDO – 16710 15	Apr 61	Fast. PU239/U235 RATIO=.980+ – .009	
Eta	Maxwl		HAN	Eval Conf	61RPI 3	May 61	Leonard.	
Eta	5.0–3	2.5+0	GA	Eval Rept	GA – 2113	Jun 61	Wikner+.TABLE 100 E POINTS	
Eta	Maxwl		CRC	Revw Conf	61Saclay 57	Jul 61	Westcott. 2200METRE/SEC SIG GIVEN	
Eta	4.0+0	2.0+3	ORL	Expt Rept	TID – 19594		62 DE SAUSSURE+ RPI LINAC FISS CH+SCINT	
				Rept	EANDC(US) – 28	Sep 62	.SUPERSEDED	
Eta	Pile		CRC	Eval Rept	CRRP – 1191	Jan 62	Westcott. EFF SIG.	
Eta	2.5–2	1.0+6	ROS	Revw Jour	KE 5 701	Jan 62	Falkenberg.VAL GVN,REFERENCES	
Eta	Maxwl		ORL	Expt Jour	NSE 12 364	Mar 62	Gwin+,CRIT SOLTN ETA=2.076+ – 0.015	+
				Jour	NSE 44 266	May 71	Magnuson. RE – ANAL OF DATA	
	Maxwl			Data	EXFOR10208.006	Sep 75	. 1PT, AVE OF 13 EXPERIMENTS	

92 Uranium 235

Quantity	Energy (ev) Min	Max	Lab	Type	Documentation Ref Vol Page	Date	Author, Comments	Data
Eta	Maxwl		ORL	Expt	Jour NSE 14 101	Sep 62	Macklin+	+
	Maxwl			Data	EXFOR12508.003	Jun 76	. 1 PT.	
Eta	Maxwl		CRC	Revw	Rept EANDC(CAN) – 15	Nov 62	Hanna. COMPARES MANY VALUES.	
Eta	1.0+3	1.5+7	UK	Eval	Rept AWRE – O – 82/63	Dec 63	Parker.(ALD).UKNDL – DFN 155	
Eta	Pile		CJD	Eval	Rept INDSWG – 64 285	64	Galanin. TBL EFF ETA FOR MANY SPECTR	
Eta	3.0–2	2.0+1	ITE	Expt	Jour AE 16 110	Feb 64	Ignatiev+ PULSED CYCLOTRON	+
					Jour JNE 18 719	Nov 64	.ENGLISH TRANSL OF AE 16 110	
					Jour SJA 16 121	Feb 64	.ENGLISH TRANSL OF AE 16 110	
					Jour EAF 16 2 19	Feb 64	. FRENCH TRANSL OF AE 16 110	
	3.0–2	2.0+1			Data EXFOR40156.002	Mar 73	.ETA FOR 58 ES GIVEN	
Eta	Maxwl		WIN	Expt	Jour JNAB 18 105	Mar 64	Carter+ ETA RATIO U235/PU239 = 1.02	
					Rept AEEW – R – 201	Jan 63	– + RATIO TO PU – 239.	
Eta	2.6–2		RLY	Revw	Conf 64Vienna 120	Dec 64	Raievski.RATIO REL PU239 + – ERROR GVN	
Eta	+5	+7	RLY	Revw	Conf 64Vienna 56	Dec 64	Kronberger. VAL TABLE OF ETA+NU+SIGS	
Eta	Maxwl		RLY	Revw	Conf 64Vienna 56	Dec 64	Kronberger. AGR – REACTOR,TBL,NU+SIGS	
Eta	2.5–2	1.0+6	BEP	Revw	Jour KE 8 625	Jan 65	Wenzel. VAL FOR 3ES GVN,MANY REFS	
Eta	2.4+4		FEI	Expt	Jour AE 19 41	Jul 65	Vankov.STAVISSKY 1.79+ – .06	+
					Jour JNE 20 600	Jul 66	TRANSLATN.*	
					Jour SJA 19 903	Jul 65	TRANSLATN.*	
					Jour EAF 19 1 61	Jan 65	TRANSLATN.*	
Eta	2.0+0	5.0+1	SAC	Expt	Jour NP 69 545	Jul 65	Michaudon+ MANY RESONANCES	+
Eta	3.5–2	2.0+2	HAR	Expt	Rept AERE – M – 1670	Feb 66	Brooks+ LINAC,TOF. CURVES,CFD OTHERS	+
					Conf 66S.Diego 2 193	Feb 66	– . SEE ALSO	
					Prog AERE – PR/NP9 11	Oct 65	– +DATA RENORMALISED ABOVE 10EV	
					Rept EANDC(UK) – 42	Jun 64	. TBL 2 MODIFD(AMENDMNT 1)	
	7.0–1	5.0+1			Conf 61Saclay 131	Sep 61	– +TOF.GRAPH OF RAW DATA	
					Conf 61RPI 109	May 61	– +SAME AS 61SACLAY.	
Eta	1.0+3	2.1+4	KFK	Eval	Rept KFK – 120 1	Feb 66	Schmidt.TABLE OF AVERAGED ETA	+
	–.1+1	1.5+2			Rept KFK – 120 1	Nov 65	– .CALC FROM RESON PARS	
	1.0–2	1.0+7			Rept KFK – 120 2	Dec 62	– .GRAPHS AND TABULATED DATA	
	1.0–3	1.5+7			Data KEDAK – 3	Oct 75	5335 DATA SETS	
Eta	2.5–2	5.7–2	MTR	Expt	Rept IDO – 17083	Feb 66	Smith. MANGANESE BATH	+
					Prog IDO – 17140 30	Mar 66	–	
	2.5–2				Data EXFOR12318.	Jun 76	. 1 PT, ETA, 2 RATIOS	
Eta	2.5–2		BNW	Theo	Conf 66Wash. 75	Mar 66	Liikala+, TBLS OF LITER. VALUES	
Eta		1.0+1	MTR	Eval	Conf 66Wash. 919	Mar 66	Smith+,MN BATH+MTR REL MEASTS,CFD TH	
	2.0–2	5.0–1			Conf 66Paris 2 50	Oct 66	– . TBL+CURV LEAST SQUARE FIT.	
	1.0–2	1.0+0	MTR	Eval	Conf 66Wash. 840	Mar 66	Moore+.MULTILEVEL ANAL.CURVE CFD XPT	
Eta	3.0–2	1.2+0	ITE	Expt	Priv OBNINSK	Oct 66	KIRPICHNIKOV	+
Eta	2.9–1	5.0+1	DUB	Expt	Rept JINR – P3 – 4992	Apr 70	Rjabov+ ETA AT RES – E,73 RES,TBL	+
	2.9–1	5.0+1			Data EXFOR40070.011	Aug 70	ETA AT 78 RESONANCE ENERGIES	
Eta	Maxwl		MOL	Comp	Conf 70Helsinki 2 535	Jun 70	Fabry+39. TABLE OF DATA SETS	
Eta	2.0+3		MTR	Expt	Abst ANS 13 300	Jul 70	Smith+ MN BATH, FN SAMPLE THICKNESS	
Eta	1.0–2	1.0+7	ORL	Revw	Jour REA 8 473	Sep 70	Kasten. REVIEW,ETA(E)+AVG ETA,GRAPHS	
Eta	2.5–2		ANL	Eval	Conf 71Knoxvill 560	Mar 71	DE VOLPI. ADJUSTED VALUE GIVEN	
Eta	2.5–2		IFB	Eval	Rept YK– 9 34	72	Morogovsky. COMPUTR RE – EVAL,DATA GVN	
					Rept INDC(CCP) – 42	Aug 74	.P1.ENGLISH OF YK – 9	
Eta	1.0–4	1.0+0	IFB	Eval	Rept YK – 20/1 126	75	Antsipov+ EVAL OF XPTAL DATA.GRAPHS	
Eta	1.0–3	1.0+0	IJE	Eval	Jour VBF 1975 1 13	75	Konshin+ ETA(NEUT – E),TBL.	
Eta	None		MTR	Expt	Prog ERDA – NDC – 2 7	May 75	Smith.REANAL.DATA.ETA=2.081+ – 0.009	
Eta	Maxwl		BNW	Eval	Abst ANS 21 507	Jun 75	Leonard+SIMULTAN FIT WITH CAPT+FISS	
	–3	1.0–1			Conf 75Wash. 281	Mar 75	– .GRPH LEAST SQ EVAL CFD EXP	
Eta	1.0–4	1.0+0	IJE	Eval	Rept INDC(CCP) – 78	Jan 76	Konshin+ (ENGL) BRIEF DESCRIPTION	
Eta			MTR	Expt	Rept IN – 1060	67	Fast+ RATIO TO PU239,PU241	+
	Maxwl				Data EXFOR12505.	Jun 76	. 4 RATIOS, 2G FACTORS	
Eta	2.5–2		BET	Eval	Jour NSE 60 239	Jul 76	Ullo+MONTE CARLO ANAL SMITH EXPT.TBL	
					Rept WAPD – TM – 1217	Apr 75	.SUPERSEDED	
					Conf 75Wash. 553	Mar 75	.SUPERSEDED	
Eta	2.5–2		BET	Eval	Jour NSE 60 251	Jul 76	Goldsmith+MONTECARLO ANAL ORNL EXPT.	
					Rept WAPD – TM – 1218	Apr 75	.SUPERSEDED	
					Conf 75Wash. 557	Mar 75	.SUPERSEDED	
Nu	Pile		LAS	Expt	Rept LA – 102	Jun 44	Snyder.	+
	Pile				Data EXFOR12395.002	Jun 76	. 1 PT.	
Nu	Pile		JNE	Expt	Jour ARS 48 27	Feb 52	Keller+ RA – BE SOURCE,NU=2.49+ – 0.12	
					Rept JEN – 14	Oct 56	– + SEE ARS 48.	
Nu		1.4+7	LAS	Theo	Rept LA – 1863	Dec 54	Leachman.AVG NU+NEUT EMISSION PROBAB	
Nu	Maxwl		CCP	Expt	Conf 55Moscow 156	Jul 55	Kalashnikova+.RATIOS+ABSOLUTE VALUES	+
					Rept AEC – TR – 2435	56	. P 123. ENGL TRANSL OF 55MOSCOW 156	

92 Uranium 235

Quantity	Energy (ev) Min	Max	Lab	Type	Documentation Ref Vol Page	Date	Author, Comments	Data
Nu	2.0−1	1.0+2	CCP	Expt Conf	55Moscow 369	Jul 55	Erozolimsky+. TABLE NU−EFF REL THR	
				Rept	AEC−TR−2435	56	. P 255. ENGL TRANSL OF 55MOSCOW 369	
Nu	Pile		ANL	Revw Conf	55Geneva 3 198	Aug 55	Zinn.P814,VAL GVN,DISCUSS OF RESULTS	
Nu	2.5−2	1.3+2	CCP	Expt Conf	55Geneva 5 172	Aug 55	Spivak+.VAL GVN CFD REF,PPR659	
Nu	4.0+6	4.5+6	LAS	Expt Rept	LA−1939	Aug 55	Bethe+ ALSO FISS SPEC NEUTS SPH TRNS	+
	4.0+6	4.5+6		Data	EXFOR12397.002	Jun 76	. 2 PTS.	
Nu	8.0+4	1.3+6	LAS	Revw Conf	55Geneva 2 193	Aug 55	Leachman.P592,CURVE,EXPT DESCRIBED	
Nu	None		ORL	Revw Conf	55Geneva 3 19	Aug 55	Weinberg.P862,VAL GVN,REFS GVN	
Nu	Maxwl		CCP	Expt Rept	AEC−TR−2435PT1	56	. USSR,PAGE 131. NU=2.5+ − 4PERCENT	
Nu	2.5−2	4.0−1	HAN	Expt Abst	BAP 1 8	Jan 56	Leonard+ CONSTANT + −0.36PC, NDG	
Nu	1.2+6		HAR	Expt Rept	NRDC−86	Feb 56	Hanna.RATIO TO THR 1D05PMD02	
Nu	8.0+4		LAS	Expt Jour	PR 101 1012	Feb 56	Diven+,LIQ SCINT,+PROB EMISS	+
	8.0+4	4.8+6		Rept	TNCC(US)−7	May 56	− . CO4116 AVG PLUS FLUCT 3ES	
	8.0+4			Data	EXFOR12337.003	Jun 76	. 1 PT.	
	1.3+6	4.8+6		Data	EXFOR12436.002	Jun 76	. 2 PTS.	
Nu	Maxwl		HAR	Expt Jour	JNE 2 247	Jun 56	Sanders.PROMPT NEUTS. REL+ABS VALUES	
Nu	Pile		LAS	Expt Jour	JNE 3 64	Aug 56	Feynman+ AV NU.NU=7.8+ − .6,PILE FLUCT	
Nu	5.0+5	1.0+6	LAS	Expt Jour	PR 104 731	Nov 56	Allen+,0.77+ − 0.2 RATIO TO PU239 AVG	+
	5.0+5	1.0+6		Data	EXFOR12207.012	Jun 76	. 2 PTS.	
Nu	2.5−2		BNL	Eval Rept	BNL−325	Jan 57	Hughes+ WORLD CONSIST. VAL. 2.47+ − .0	
Nu	Maxwl	Fiss	CCP	Expt Jour	AE 2 18	Jan 57	Kalashnikova+.FAST/THR=1.000+ − 0.01	+
Nu	Fast		LAS	Expt Jour	JNE 4 38	Jan 57	Leachman.	+
				Conf	58Geneva 15 331	Sep 58	− . PILE RESULTS, HANSEN	
	Fast			Data	EXFOR12448.002	Jun 76	. 1 PT.	
Nu	Maxwl		LAS	Theo Jour	PR 105 1511	Mar 57	Leachman+,HISTOGRAM MON DECREASING	
Nu	Maxwl	9.0+5	CCH	Expt Rept	NP−TR−440	Sep 57	Saunders. NDG NSA 14 2213 9/60	
Nu	Maxwl		HAR	Eval Rept	AERE−NP/R−2140	Dec 57	Egelstaff+ CONSISTENT VALUES 2200M/S	
				Comp Rept	AERE−NP/R−2104	Mar 57	− .EXPT METHODS FOR HAR VALUE	
				Revw Conf	55Geneva 4 307	Aug 55	− +.VAL GVN,EXPT DESCRBD,P425	
Nu	Pile		CCP	Expt Jour	AE 4 187	Feb 58	Kuzminov+ FAST REACTOR SP REL NU THR	
				Jour	JNE 9 153	Jun 59	TRANSLATN.*	
				Jour	SJA 4 250		58 TRANSLATN.*	
Nu	4.0+6	1.5+7	CCP	Expt Jour	AE 4 188	Feb 58	Smirenkin+ REL NU THR,PROMPT NEUTS	+
				Jour	JNE 9 155	Jun 59	TRANSLATN.*	
				Jour	SJA 4 253		58 TRANSLATN.*	
Nu	1.5+7		CCP	Expt Jour	AE 4 374	Apr 58	Protopopov+.RATIO TO THR,PROMPT NEUT	+
				Jour	JNE 9 207	Jun 59	TRANSLATN.*	
				Jour	SJA 4 491		58 TRANSLATN.*	
Nu	1.4+7		LAS	Expt Rept	AECD−4261	Apr 58	Wahl.NU=5.2+ − 0.5 FROM FRAG CHG DISTR	
Nu	Maxwl		BNL	Comp Conf	58Geneva 16 8	Sep 58	Hughes.PPR2483,VAL V=2200M/SEC GVN	
Nu	−2	1.5+7	CCP	Expt Conf	58Geneva 15 353	Sep 58	Bondarenko+.PPR2187,CURVE CFD REFS	
Nu	+6		LAS	Revw Conf	58Geneva 15 344	Sep 58	Hemmendinger.PPR663,CURVE,MANY REFS	
Nu	1.4+7		CCP	Expt Jour	AE 5 653	Dec 58	Flerov+ (1954) 4.50+ − .32 SPHERE TRNS	+
				Jour	JNEA 11 169	Feb 60	TRANSLATN.*	
				Jour	SJA 5 1593		58 TRANSLATN.*	
Nu	Maxwl		ORL	Expt Jour	NSE 5 49	Jan 59	Desaussure+	+
				Conf	57ANS 37	Oct 57	De Saussure+U233,PU239,PU241 RATIOS	
				Data	EXFOR12328.	Jun 76	. 3 RATIOS	
Nu	Maxwl		CCP	Expt Jour	AE 7 375	Oct 59	Apalin+.VAL FOR TERNARY FISS GVN	
				Jour	SJA 7 853	Mar 61	TRANSLATN.* JNE A13 86 0/60	
				Jour	KE 3 499	May 60	.TRANSLATN	
Nu	Maxwl		ANL	Expt Jour	JNEA 11 21	Nov 59	Jaffey+ NU.SIGF REL U233 PU239 PU241	
Nu	2.5−2		COL	Revw Jour	NUC 17 11 134	Nov 59	Safford+. EXPTL VALUES TABULATED	
Nu	Spont		NCA	Expt Jour	JNE 11 1	Nov 59	Waltner+ NEUTS/SEC/GM FROM SPON FISS	+
Nu	1.4+7		CCP	Expt Jour	ZET 38 671	Mar 60	Vasil'Ev. 4.17+ − 0.30,CFD OTHER XPTS	+
				Jour	JET 11 483	Sep 60	TRANSLATN.*	
Nu	2.5−2		AE	Comp Rept	AE−11	Apr 60	Story+,DISCUSSION+TABULATN OF MEASTS	
Nu	Maxwl	Fiss	CCP	Theo Jour	AE 8 409	May 60	Zysin+.VAL CALCD FROM FRGMNT−DISTRBS	
				Jour	SJA 8 343	Jun 61	TRANSLATN.*JNE AB17 41 1/61	
				Jour	KE 4 40	Jan 61	.TRANSLATN	
Nu	1.4+7		CCP	Theo Jour	AE 8 409	May 60	Zysin+.VAL CALCD FROM FRGMNT−DISTRBS	
				Jour	SJA 8 343	Jun 61	TRANSLATN.*JNE AB17 41 1/61	
				Jour	KE 4 40	Jan 61	.GERMAN	
Nu	1.4+7		CCP	Expt Jour	AE 10 68	Jan 61	Flerov+.VAL GVN,GRAPHIT−PRISMA DTCTR	+
				Jour	SJA 10 65	Nov 61	TRANSLATN.*JNE17 423 N/63	
				Jour	KE 4 574	Jul 61	.TRANSLATN	
Nu	None		RI	Revw Jour	UFN 73 655	Apr 61	Petrzhak+ CURV,NU REL FRGM−MASSRATIO	
				Jour	SPU 4 305	Sep 61	. ENGL OF UFN 73 655	

92 Uranium 235

Quantity	Energy (ev) Min	Max	Lab	Type	Documentation Ref Vol Page	Date	Author, Comments	Data
Nu	Maxwl		HAN	Eval Conf	61RPI 3	May 61	Leonard.	
Nu	Maxwl		CRC	Revw Conf	61Saclay 57	Jul 61	Westcott. 2200METRE/SEC SIG GIVEN	
Nu		1.5+7	ANL	Revw Conf	61Vienna 1 29	Aug 61	Smith.PPR76,CURVE MANY REFS	
Nu	7.5+4	1.4+7	ALD	Expt Jour	JNAB 15 102	Oct 61	Moat+,REL CF252 SPONT FIS,SCINT TANK	+
Nu	−		CCP	Theo Jour	ZET 42 180	Jan 62	Blinov.GRAPH NUCL−SHELL−TH CFD XPTS	
Nu				Jour	JET 15 130	Jul 62	TRANSLATN.*	
Nu	2.5−2	1.0+6	ROS	Revw Jour	KE 5 701	Jan 62	Falkenberg.VAL GVN,REFERENCES	
Nu	3.0+4	1.8+6	ANL	Expt Jour	PR 126 197	Apr 62	Meadows+,NU VS E,RATIOS TO NU−CF252	+
				Conf	61Vienna 1 125	Aug 61	.SEE ALSO, GRAPH.	
	3.0+4	1.8+6		Data	EXFOR12419.	Jun 76	6 PTS. NU AND RATIO	
Nu	Maxwl		CCP	Expt Jour	ZET 43 329	Jul 62	Meas. NU VS. KINETIC ENERGY	
				Jour	JET 16 235	Jan 63	TRANSLATN.*	
Nu	Maxwl		REH	Theo Rept	IA− 757	Jul 62	Sieger+ CALC FRM CHAIN−Y,CFD OTH.TBL	
Nu	Maxwl		CRC	Revw Rept	EANDC(CAN)−15	Nov 62	Hanna. COMPARES MANY VALUES.	
Nu	5.0+5	2.5+6	HAR	Expt Prog	AERE−PR/NP4 12	Dec 62	Colvin+NU FOR 0.5,1,1.5,2,2.5MEV.NDG	
Nu	−2	+7	FOA	Comp Rept	NP− 16440	Mar 63	ASPLUND−NILSSON. REVIEW. TABLES.	
Nu	Maxwl		KJL	Expt Jour	NP 45 72	Jul 63	Skarsvag+ ANGDIST OF PROMPT NEUTRONS	
Nu	2.5−2	1.5+7	LAS	Expt Jour	NP 48 433	Oct 63	Hopkins+,SCINT TANK,RELAT TO CF−252	+
	Maxwl	1.4+7		Conf	61Vienna 1 149	Aug 61	.SUPERSEDED	
	2.5−2	1.5+7		Data	EXFOR12326.004	Jun 76	7 PTS.	
Nu	Maxwl		YAM	Theo Jour	JPJ 18 1697	Nov 63	Honda.CALC E FISSFRAGS VS A.TBCFD NU	
Nu	1.0+3	1.5+7	UK	Eval Rept	AWRE−O−82/63	Dec 63	Parker.(ALD).UKNDL−DFN 155	+
	1.0−4	1.5+7		Data	UKNDL−DFN 159B	Mar 73	85 PNTS	
	1.0−4	1.5+7		Data	UKNDL−DFN 159B	Mar 73	ANGDIST OF FISS NEUT, 1 RNGS,LAB.	
Nu	Maxwl	8.0+6	ALD	Expt Jour	PR/B 133 1403	Mar 64	Mather+ TOF.SC−T.PROMPT.19ES REL CF	
				Conf	61Vienna 1 139	Aug 61	− + GRAPH+TABLE.	
Nu	Thrsh	1.5+7	LRL	Eval Jour	JNAB 18 125	Mar 64	Schuster+ E DEPENDNCE THEOR,CFD EXPT	
Nu	Maxwl		CCP	Expt Jour	ZET 46 1197	Apr 64	NU INCREASES FOR SYMMETRICAL FISSION	
				Jour	JET 19 810	Oct 64	TRANSLATN.*	
Nu		8.0+6	IAE	Revw Conf	64Geneva 412	May 64	Westcott+.P717, DISCUSSION, CURVE	
Nu	Maxwl		KUR	Expt Jour	NP 55 249	Jun 64	Apalin+ NU VS FRAGMENT MASS	
Nu	+5	+7	RLY	Revw Conf	64Vienna 56	Dec 64	Kronberger. VAL TABLE OF ETA+NU+SIGS	
Nu	Maxwl		RLY	Revw Conf	64Vienna 56	Dec 64	Kronberger. AGR−REACTOR,TBL,ETA+SIGS	
Nu	−2	8.0+6	CRC	Revw Conf	65Salzburg 1 451	Mar 65	Fraser.P.34,NU(E) FOR MANY XPTS,GRPH	
Nu		8.0+6	FEI	Theo Conf	65Salzburg 1 127	Mar 65	Strutinskii+,GRPH NU BAR VS E,TH CFD	
				Rept	ANL−TRANS−195	65	. ENGL OF 65SALZBURG 1 127	
Nu	2.5−2		FOA	Expt Conf	65Salzburg 2 57	Mar 65	Conde+ EXTRAPOLATED FROM 60KEV.	+
	2.5−2			Data	EXFOR20112.003	Sep 71	1PNT.PROMPT.	
Nu	Maxwl		HAR	Expt Conf	65Salzburg 2 25	Mar 65	Colvin+PPR44.BORONPILE.ABSOL+RATIOS	+
				Conf	66Paris 1 307	Oct 66	− +TBLS.NU CFD OTHER TECHNIQUES	
				Prog	AERE−PR/NP8 9	Feb 65	− +TBL.NU=2.385+−0.015 ABSOLUTE	
Nu	None		LAS	Revw Conf	65Salzburg 2 3	Mar 65	Terrell.PPR.43,XPTL WORK CFD TH,GRPH	
Nu	2.5−2		FOA	Expt Jour	AF 29 293	Apr 65	Conde. EXTRAPOLATED FROM 7.5,15MEV	
	2.5−2			Data	EXFOR20025.003	Sep 71	1PNT.PROMPT.	
Nu	4.1−1	1.0+7	WAL	Eval Rept	WANL−TME−1228	Aug 65	Gibson+.68GROUP TABLE	
	4.0−1	1.0+7		Rept	WANL−TME−1028	Nov 64	Drawbaugh+.TABLE 68 GROUPS	
Nu	2.5−2		HAR	Expt Jour	NP 71 228	Sep 65	Barnard. CORRELATION WITH N−SPEC.	+
Nu	Maxwl		KUR	Expt Jour	NP 71 553	Sep 65	Apalin+NU VERSUS FRAGMENT MASS	
Nu	+0	1.5+7	KFK	Eval Rept	KFK−120 1	Feb 66	Schmidt.OTHERS'XPTS+CURVE.MU ONLY	
	1.0+3	1.0+7		Rept	KFK−120 2	Dec 62	− .PROMPT AND DELAYED NS.	
Nu	Maxwl		NIR	Expt Jour	AE 20 342	Apr 66	Nefedov+ TERN COMPARED BIN FISSION	
				Prog	INDSWG−126 39	66	− . RATIO TERNARY/BINARY FISS	
Nu	Maxwl		ALD	Revw Jour	JNAB 20 549	Jul 66	Fieldhouse+ REVISED HAR PU240 SOURCE	
Nu	Maxwl		HAR	Expt Jour	JNE 20 549	Jul 66	.VALUE RENORMALISED TO 2.370+−0.014	
				Conf	65Salzburg 2 25	Mar 65	.RENORMALISATION NU=2.363+−0.021	
				Rept	AERE−R/R−2212	Oct 58	Kenward+ 2.420+−.037	
Nu	7.5+5	1.5+7	FEI	Expt Conf	66Paris 2 85	Oct 66	PPR110,D'JACHENKO+. NU GVN AT 6ES	
Nu	6.1+6	1.4+7	HEB	Eval Conf	66Paris 2 309	Oct 66	Pazy+ CORR−FACTORS BY INTEG EXPT,TBL	

92 Uranium 235

Quantity	Energy (ev) Min	Max	Lab	Type	Documentation Ref Vol Page	Date	Author, Comments	Data
Nu	8.0+4	9.9+5	FEI	Expt	Rept ICD-3 51	Nov 66	Bljumkina+ SCINTILL DETECT, TABLE 2	+
					Prog YFI-4 19	Jun 67	.DATA OF ICD-3 NORMALIZED+SUPPLEMENT	
					Jour AE 22 401	May 67	.DATA OF ICD-3 NORMALIZED+SUPPLEMENT	
					Conf 66Paris 2 75	Oct 66	.TABLE 2	
					Jour NP 52 648	Apr 64	.TABLE 1 REVISED IN ICD-3 51 11/66	
					Jour SJA 22 500	May 67	.ENGLISH TRANSL OF AE 22 500 5/67	
					Prog INDC-E-187 26	67	.ENGLISH TRANSL OF YFI-4 19 6/67	
					Rept INDC-E-152 51	67	.ENGLISH TRANSL OF ICD-3 51 11/66	
					Jour SJA 15 725	May 64	.ENGLISH TRANSL OF AE 15 64 7/63	
					Jour EAF 15 196	64	. FRENCH TRANSL OF AE 15 64 7/63	
	8.0+4	7.0+5			Data EXFOR40217.002	Jun 74	DATA AT 7 ES GIVEN	
	8.0+4	9.9+5			Data EXFOR40158.	Mar 73	PROMPT NU AT 13 ES REL .4MEV,REL THR	
Nu	Fast		LRL	Expt	Jour PR 152 1046	Dec 66	Fultz+ ROUGH VALUE, 2.43+-.08	+
					Conf 66Paris 2 149	Oct 66	.SUPERSEDED	
	Fast				Data EXFOR12345.003	Jun 76	. 1PT.	
Nu	3.9+4	1.0+6	ANL	Expt	Jour JNE 21 157	Feb 67	Meadows+ PROMPT YLD REL CF252	+
	3.9+4	1.0+6			Data EXFOR12399.002	Jun 76	. 16 PTS, NU	
Nu	3.7+5	2.1+6	TRM	Expt	Conf 67Kanpur 325	Feb 67	Nadkarni+,NU VS E CALC,FISS FRAG KE	+
	3.7+5	2.1+6			Data EXFOR30022.002	Jun 70	NU AT 21 ES.	
Nu	4.1-1	7.8+6	WAL	Eval	Rept WANL-TME-1586	Mar 67	Gibson+AVG NU 68 GROUPS	
Nu	1.0+3	1.5+7	LAS	Eval	Prog WASH-1074 79	Apr 67	Diven. NDG. SEE EANDC(US)-96U	
Nu	Maxwl		ANL	Expt	Abst DA/B 27 4510	Jun 67	De Volpi.	
					Prog ANL-7210 21	Dec 66	- + TABLE	
					Conf 66Vienna 693	Oct 66	Porges+,NUBAR FROM FISS FRAG, CONTD	
					Conf 66Paris 1 297	Oct 66	.SUPERSEDED	
Nu	Maxwl		RI	ExTh	Conf 68Riga	Jan 68	Blinov+ ABST,NU AVG VS FRAG KIN E	
Nu	Maxwl	1.5+7	AI	Eval	Jour JNE 22 79	Feb 68	Fillmore.DATA TBL,GRAPH.LEAST SQ FIT	
Nu	1.0-2	4.0+1	RPI	Expt	Conf 68Wash. 635	Mar 68	Weinstein+ LINAC AVG NU CURVE SCINT	
	None				Abst DA/B 30 3823	Feb 70	- .	
	1.0-2	2.5+1			Conf 69Vienna 477	Jul 69	- + PPR113. GRAPH	
Nu	3.7+5	3.3+6	FEI	Expt	Jour YF 7 961	May 68	Prokhorova+ REL,PROMPT, TABLE+CURVE	+
					Jour SNP 7 579	Nov 68	.ENGLISH TRANSL OF YF 7 961 5/68	
	3.7+5	3.3+6			Data EXFOR40132.002	Feb 73	PROMPT NU-BAR AT 14 ES REL 0.37MEV	
Nu	1.0+5	1.5+7	CAD	Eval	Rept EANDC(E)120L	Mar 69	Barre+RAVIER EVAL OF INTEGRAL MEAS	
Nu	Pile		NIL	Expt	Prog INDC(PAK)-1 2	May 69	. TOF,TO BE DONE	
Nu	None		BOR	Theo	Conf 69Vienna 894	Jul 69	Doan+PPR81. CALC TERNARY NU OKS EXPT	
Nu	Maxwl		EDG	Revw	Conf 69Vienna 83	Jul 69	Feather.PPR201.REVW,CENTRAL+FRAG NU	
Nu	Maxwl		KUR	Eval	Conf 69Vienna 958	Jul 69	Blinov+PPR145. NU VS(FRAG-TOT-KIN-E)	
Nu	Maxwl		WAS	Eval	Conf 69Vienna 813	Jul 69	Wahl+PPR116.NUBAR FROM YLDS+NU(A)	
					Rept COO-1162-35	69	.EQUIVALENT	
Nu	Maxwl		CUA	Theo	Abst DA/B 30 2222	Nov 69	Rogers.	
Nu	1.2+5	1.7+6	FEI	Expt	Rept YFI-8 7	Dec 69	Djachenko+	+
		6.0+5			Conf 69Vienna 955	Jul 69	D'Jachenko+PPR137. KIN-E,Z,YIELD,NU	
	1.2+5	1.7+6			Data EXFOR40017.016	Nov 73	.10 DATA LINES	
Nu	+0	+1	DUB	Theo	Rept JINR-P3-5081	May 70	Dermendshiev+ NU CALC FROM FRAG-SPEC	
Nu	Maxwl	1.4+7	AE	Comp	Conf 70Helsinki 2 93	Jun 70	Almen+57. COMPILATN AND NU-TEMP-PLOT	
Nu	1.0+5	1.8+6	ANL	Revw	Conf 70Helsinki 2 3	Jun 70	Poenitz.111. NONLINEAR NU(E) GRAPHS	
Nu	Pile		FEI	Revw	Conf 70Helsinki 2 577	Jun 70	Veselova+75. U+BE ASSEMBLY, MEAN NU	
Nu	Maxwl	1.5+7	HAR	Revw	Conf 70Helsinki 2 195	Jun 70	Colvin.PPR99. REPORT ON DATA STATUS	
	-3	1.4+7		Eval	Conf 69Vienna 930	Jul 69	- .PPR55. RECOMMENDATION+REVIEW	
Nu	6.0+5	5.0+6	SCU	Expt	Conf 70Helsinki 2 157	Jun 70	Savin+40. NU(E) GRAPH, NEW STRUCTURE	+
	6.5+5	6.6+6			Data EXFOR40058.004	Mar 71	PROMPT NU-BAR AT 37 ENERGIES	
Nu	Maxwl	1.9+6	AUA	Expt	Jour JNE 24 191	Aug 70	Boldeman+ REL CF-252,15 ES,TBL,GRAPH	+
	Maxwl				Jour AEA 18 2 2	Apr 75	Walsh. REVW OF WORK,RESULTS GIVEN	
	Maxwl	2.0+6			Jour JNE 25 321	Aug 71	.FIT OF LINEAR E-DEPENDENCE,GRAPH	
	None				Prog AAEC/PR-34P 8	Mar 71	.7KEV RESOL,PRELIM,NO FINESTRUCT,NDG	
	Maxwl				Data EXFOR30046.003	Jan 73	.FINAL VALUE FROM PRIV COMM NOV 1972	
	1.1+5	1.9+6			Data EXFOR30006.002	Sep 70	.PROMPT NUBAR AT 15 ES AS JNE 24 191	
Nu	Maxwl	6.0+6	FEI	Theo	Jour AE 29 130	Aug 70	Vorobeva+ RECOMMENDED NU(E) GRAPH	
	2.5-2	6.0+6			Conf 70Helsinki 2 177	Jun 70	.SAME AS AE 29 130 8/70	
	0.0+0	6.0+6		Eval	Prog INDC(CCP)-31	Dec 72	.PAGE 12,ENGLISH OF YFI-11 13	
	Maxwl	6.0+6		Theo	Jour SJA 29 835	Aug 70	.ENGLISH TRANSL OF AE 29 130 8/70	
Nu	Maxwl		NIR	Expt	Jour AE 29 95	Aug 70	Kroshkin+ NU BAR +- 3.0 PERCENT GIVN	
					Jour SJA 29 790	Aug 70	. ENGL OF AE 29 95	
Nu	None		FEI	Eval	Jour AE 29 395	Nov 70	Smirenkin.ABST FRANC-SOV SEM DUBNA	
					Jour SJA 29 1156	Nov 70	. ENGL OF AE 29 395	
Nu	8.0+4	1.3+6	TOK	Theo	Jour NST 7 635	Dec 70	Hara.CAL CFD C DIVEN EXP	
Nu	2.5-2		ANL	Eval	Conf 71Knoxvill 560	Mar 71	DE VOLPI. ADJUSTED VALUE GIVEN	

92 Uranium 235

Quantity	Energy (ev) Min	Energy (ev) Max	Lab	Type	Documentation Ref Vol Page	Author, Comments Date	Data
Nu	Maxwl	1.5+6	FEI	Expt	Jour AE 30 250	Mar 71 Prokhorova+ COINC,REL CF252,TBL,GRPH	+
	+6				Conf 75Kiev	May 75 - + NUBAR(NEUT-E),TBL	
	Maxwl	1.5+6			Jour SJA 30 307	Oct 71 *ENGL OF AE 30 250	
					Rept FEI-227	Dec 70 .NUBAR(NEUT-E),TABLE,GRAPH	
		1.5+6			Conf 70Helsinki 2 167	Jun 70 Nesterov+,NU-BAR AT 13EN,REL CF252	
	0.0+0	1.5+6			Data EXFOR40115.002	Nov 72 PROMPT NU-BAR AT 13 ENERGIES	
	2.5-2	1.5+6			Data EXFOR40033.002	Aug 70 NU-BAR AT 13 ES REL CF252	
Nu	+4	1.5+7	KFK	Eval	Prog KFK-1271 121	May 71 Hinkelmann. MEAN NUMBER,GRAPHS	
Nu	6.5+5	6.6+6	KUR	Expt	Prog YFI-10 32	May 71 Savin+ TOF,LIQUID SCINT,NU VS EN,TBL	
					Rept INDC(CCP)-15	Dec 71 *P34,ENG OF YFI-10	
					Jour PTE 14 6 27	Dec 69 *TECHNIQUE DESCRIBD	
					Jour IET 14 1388	Dec 69 *ENG OF PTE 14 6 27	
Nu		1.5+7	ANL	Eval	Jour NSE 44 345	Jun 71 Davey. PROMPT NEUTS PER FISSION	
					Conf 70Helsinki 2 119	Jun 70 .SUPERSEDED.(P/112)	
Nu	+0	6.0+6	FEI	Theo	Jour YF 13 1170	Jun 71 Prokhorova+ CALC NUBAR VS N-E,GRPHS	
	0.0+0	5.0+6			Rept FEI-242	May 71 .NUBAR(NEUT-E),GRAPH	
	+0	6.0+6			Jour SNP 13 673	Dec 71 . ENGL OF YF 13 1170	
Nu	Maxwl	1.5+7	ALD	Eval	Rept AWRE-O-55/71	Aug 71 Mather+ PRE-71 DATA,SPLINE+4 ST LINE	
	Maxwl	5.0+7	AUA	Eval	Jour JNE 25 321	Aug 71 Walsh+ 2 LINE LINEAR SLOPE GIVEN	
	Maxwl	5.0+6			Rept AAEC/TM-574	Apr 71 .SAME AS JNE 25 321,FIT NUBAR VS N-E	
Nu	1.1+0	3.9+1	DUB	Expt	Jour YF 14 927	Nov 71 Ryabov+ SPIN DEPENDENCE OF NU,GRAPH	
					Prog YFI-10 38	May 71 - + ABST,SPIN DEPENDCE,TBLS,GRPH	
					Rept JINR-P3-5297	Oct 70 . *SAME AS YF 14 927	
					Rept JINR-P3-5119	Jun 70 Rjabov+ NU EXPT DESCRIBED,AVG NU GVN	
	3.1+0	1.9+1			Conf JINR-D3893 88	May 68 Ryabov+ TWO NU(NEUT-E) DATA SETS GVN	
	1.1+0	3.9+1			Jour SNP 14 519	May 72 Rjabov+ ENGL OF YF 14 927.	
					Rept BNL-TR-401	72 .ENGLISH TRANS	
					Rept INDC(CCP)-15	Dec 71 Rjabov+ ENG OF YFI-10. P42	
Nu	Pile		FEI	Expt	Prog YFI-12 13	72 Maksjutenko.ABSTRACT,NUBAR GIVEN	
					Prog INDC(CCP)-30	Dec 72 .PG10,ENGLISH OF YFI-12 13	
Nu	2.5-2		IFB	Eval	Rept YK-9 34	72 Morogovsky. EVAL+RECOMM VALUE,CF OTH	
					Rept INDC(CCP)-42	Aug 74 .P1.ENGLISH OF YK-9	
Nu	Maxwl		CUA	Theo	Abst DA/B 32 5980	Apr 72 Lee. CALC OF AVG PROMPT NU	
Nu	2.5-2		IAE	Eval	Jour REA 10 637	Dec 72 Manero+ SURVEY,TBLS+GRPHS,RECOMM VAL	+
	2.5-2	1.5+7			Rept INDC(NDS)-34	Jul 72 .REPLACED BY NEW EVALUATION	
					Rept INDC(NDS)-19	Jun 70 .REPLACED BY NEW EVALUATION	
Nu	Maxwl		BUC	Revw	Rept IFA-RN-50	73 Cristu. NU(FRAGM-E,MASS.COMP-EXCIT)	
	Fast				Rept IFA-RN-50	73 - . NU(FRAGM-E,MASS.COMP-EXCIT)	
Nu	Maxwl		KJL	Theo	Rept KR-148	Jan 73 Skarsvaag.TBL EN ANGDIST PRMPT NEUTS	
Nu	1.5+6	1.5+7	BRC	Expt	Conf 73Kiev 3 153	May 73 Frehaut+ NUBAR(E) TBL,CFD OTHS GRAPH	+
					Conf 73Kiev 3 165	May 73 . LIQ SCIN BACKGROUND ANALYSIS.	
					Conf 69Vienna 931	Jul 69 Soleilhac+PPR93.NU(NEUT-E)OKS OTHER	
					Jour JNE 23 257	May 69 - +TOF.REF.IS CF252 SPON.FISS	
	1.9+6	1.5+7			Data EXFOR20506.002	Mar 76 22PTS.PROMPT.	
Nu	7.5+6	1.5+7	FOA	Expt	Jour AF 29 293	Apr 65 Conde+ 2ENS. CFD OTHERS,FIT.	+
					Conf 73Kiev 4 130	May 73 - . SUMMARY OF NUBAR(EN).NDG.	
					Conf 65Salzburg 57	Mar 65 - . CONTINUED.	
	7.5+6	1.5+7			Data EXFOR20025.002	Sep 71 2PTS. PROMPT.	
Nu	2.0+5	1.0+6	KUR	Expt	Conf 73Kiev 4 63	May 73 Savin+ NUBAR(NEUT-E),GRAPH,CFD	
Nu	Fast		FOA	Expt	Conf 70Helsinki 2 139	Jun 70 Conde+59 PILE AVG NU AND NU(E) GIVEN	+
					Jour JNE 27 395	Jun 73 Widen+ IN 3 SPECT, CFD WITH TH SPEC	
					Conf 73Kiev 4 130	May 73 Conde+ LINEAR NUBAR(E),NO VALUES GVN	
	Fast				Data EXFOR20113.	Sep 71 .2PTS PROMPT. SPEC AVG VALUES.	
Nu	8.0+0	4.0+1	GEL	Expt	Jour JNE 27 435	Jun 73 Theobald+ VARN WITH RES.COIN TECH	
Nu	+0	1.5+7	KFK	Eval	Rept KFK-1629	Jun 73 Schatz. RECOMMENDED CURVE	+
	1.0-3	1.5+7			Data KEDAK-3	Oct 75 16 DATA SETS	
Nu	2.5-2		ANL	Expt	Conf 73Rochestr 2 19	Aug 73 Unik+NU TOTAL VS MASS 13 NUCLIDES.	
Nu	2.0+0	7.5+1	BRC	Expt	Conf 73Rochestr 2 201	Aug 73 Frehaut+ PROMPT VALUES AT RESONANCES	+
					Diss SIMON	Dec 75 Simon. (N,GAM/FIS) ANAL	
	2.0+0	7.5+1			Data EXFOR20600.002	Jul 76 52PTS.PR.AT RES.	
Nu	1.1-2	3.0+1	RPI	Expt	Conf 73Rochestr 2 503	Aug 73 Reed+ ABST,NUBAR(N-E) REL .025EV,NDG	+
	2.2+0	2.6+1			Data EXFOR10427.003	Dec 74 37PTS.	
Nu	2.0+0	4.5+1	SAC	Expt	Conf 73Rochestr 2 201	Aug 73 Frehaut+ NU(E) FOR RESON NEUTS,GRAPH	
Nu	1.3+6	1.5+7	DUB	Comp	Jour YF 18 724	Oct 73 Dakovsky+ DISPERSION VS NUBAR, GRAPH	
					Jour SNP 18 371	Apr 74 .ENGLISH OF YF 18,724	
Nu	Maxwl		AUA	Revw	Conf IAEA-169 2 163	74 Musgrove+ TOTAL NU-BAR,GRAPH	
Nu	5.0+6	1.7+7	LRL	Expt	Prog UCID-16514 6	Jun 74 Alvarez+	
Nu	1.4+7		MIF	Theo	Jour IVU 17 7 7	Jul 74 Koldobskij+ NU(A)CALC CFD EXPT.GRAPH	

92 Uranium 235

Quantity	Energy (ev) Min	Max	Lab	Type	Documentation Ref Vol Page	Author, Comments Date	Data
Nu	Maxwl		SAC	Expt Prog	NEANDC(E)161U	Aug 74 Girard+	
Nu	4.5+5	6.1+5	FEI	Expt Jour	AE 37 500	Dec 74 Seregina+ NUBAR(NEUT-E),GRAPH	+
	4.5+5	6.2+5		Jour	SJA 37 1282	Jun 75 . ENGLISH OF AE 37 500	
	4.5+5	6.1+5		Data	EXFOR40326.002	75 .TOT NU-BAR AT 9 ES GVN	
Nu	None		BRC	Revw Conf	75Wash. 202	Mar 75 Michaudon. FISSION REVIEW.TH+EXPTS.	
Nu	2.0+5	2.3+6	HAR	Expt Abst	75Harwell 56	Mar 75 Nair+ N ANGDISTS.ABST.NDG.	
Nu	8.8+5	5.7+6	KUR	Expt Conf	75Kiev 5 86	May 75 Khokhlov+ NUBAR(EN),DISPERS(EN).TABL	
Nu	Maxwl		EDG	Expt Prog	UKNDC(75)P71	Jun 75 Galloway+ SPEC FISS N ANGDIST.GRPH	
				Abst	75Harwell 55	Mar 75 - +TOF DISTS AT 9 ANGLES.NDG.	
Nu	2.5-2	1.5+7	HED	Theo Abst	ANS 21 518	Jun 75 Schenter+ TBL CALC FROM ENDF FP FILE	
Nu	Spont		HED	Eval Abst	ANS 22 673	Nov 75 Johnson. TBL,GRPH NU FROM SPON FISS	
Nu	+7		FEI	Revw Rept	YK- 22 9	76 Seregina+ REVW,MANY REFS,TBLS,GRAPH	
Nu	2.0+5	1.4+6	KFK	Expt Jour	ANE 3 31	Jan 76 Kappeler+ACCUR DATA.TOF.	+
				Prog	KFK-1274 4	May 75 Beer+ P.121-13 AS FN OF E,GRAPH,TBL	
				Conf	75Wash. 549	Mar 75 Kappeler+GRPH 22 PTS.AV E RES=3.3PCT	
	2.0+5	1.4+6		Data	EXFOR20427.002	Jul 75 22PTS.PROMPT.	
Nu	5.2-1	1.3+2	LRL	Expt Jour	PR/C 13 195	Jan 76 Howe+ TBLS,GRPHS,PROMPT NUBAR(E)	+
	5.0-1	1.0+2		Conf	73Rochester 2 495	Aug 73 - + ABST,NU VS EN,NEW METHOD,NDG	
	5.2-1	1.1+2		Data	EXFOR10574.	Nov 76 76PT.SINGLE RES,GROUP RES,GROSS RES.	
Nu	3.9+6	6.4+6	ANL	Expt Prog	WASH-1053 9	Oct 64 Meadows.TBL 7ES,TBC. RELATIVE CF252	+
	3.9+6	6.4+6		Data	EXFOR12391.002	Jun 76 . 7 PTS.	
Nu	1.0+5	4.0+6	FEI	Comp Conf	75Kiev 5 170	May 75 Prokhorova+ NU(EN),EVAL ACCURACS.TBL	
	5.0+4	5.0+6		Eval Rept	YK- 20 104	75 - + NUBAR(NEUT-E),GRAPH+TABL	
				Rept	INDC(CCP)-90	Jun 76 . ENGL OF YK- 20 104(TBLS+GRPHS GIVN)	
Nu	Pile		KAP	Expt Rept	KAPL-1464	Dec 55 Mcmillian+ RATIOS TO U233,PU239	+
	Pile			Data	EXFOR12357.	Jun 76 . 2 RATIOS	
Nu	Maxwl		LAS	Expt Rept	LA- 104	44 Dewire.	+
	Maxwl			Data	EXFOR12504.002	Jun 76 . 1 PT.	
Nu	1.4+7		NRL	Expt Abst	BAP 5 33	Jan 60 Mcgarry+	+
	1.4+7			Data	EXFOR12435.002	Jun 76 . 1 PT.	
Nu	None		GER	Theo Conf	76Lowell 1468	Jul 76 Kolb.ANAL Z114 BIN,TER FRAGMENTATION	
Nu	0.0+0	1.5+7	BRC	Eval Rept	CEA-R-4791	Oct 76 Bois+ NUBAR VS EN,CALC CFD EXP,TABLES	
Delayd Neuts	Pile		CHI	Expt Jour	PR 72 570	Oct 47 Redman+ 4 PERIODS, RELATIVE INTENSTY	
Delayd Neuts	Pile		BAS	Expt Jour	PR 73 111	Jan 48 Huber+.ENERGIES,YIELDS, 6PERIODS.	
Delayd Neuts	None		LAS	Expt Jour	PR 73 636	Mar 48 DE HOFFMANN+ RATE OF EMISS. 5PERIODS	
Delayd Neuts	Fiss		LAS	Expt Jour	PR 74 1330	Nov 48 DE HOFFMANN+. DROP EXPT. 5 PERIODS.	
Delayd Neuts	None		OHO	Expt Jour	PR 76 946	Oct 49 Creveling+ LI-D NS,CURVE ONLY,NDG	
Delayd Neuts	None		LAS	Expt Jour	PR 81 171	Jan 51 Snyder+ PERCENT OF DEL.NS.BAKER METH	
Delayd Neuts	Fiss		LAS	Expt Jour	PR 97 744	Feb 55 Bendt+ 216MSEC GROUP 0.027 DEL N YD	
Delayd Neuts	Maxwl		LAS	Expt Jour	PR 101 1514	Mar 56 Bonner+,ENERGY DISTRIBUTION CURVES	
Delayd Neuts	Maxwl	Fiss	ANL	Expt Jour	NSE 1 174	May 56 Brunson+,EBR NUD=1.017+-0.112	
Delayd Neuts	Pile		HAR	Revw Jour	NPW 1 114	Jul 56 Cox. YIELD+HALF LIFES OF DEL-NEUTS	
Delayd Neuts	Maxwl		HAR	Expt Jour	JNE 3 7	Aug 56 Batchelor+. E SPECTRA 1ST 4 PERIODS	
				Rept	AERE-NP/R- 2076	Jan 57 .SUPERSEDED	
				Conf	55Geneva 4 183	Aug 55 Batchelor+ DELAYED E SPECTRA.	
Delayd Neuts	Maxwl		ANL	Expt Rept	ANL-5609 44	Nov 56 Perlow+22 55SEC NS NBD PRELIM XPTS N	
Delayd Neuts	Fast		HAR	Expt Jour	JNE 4 141	Jun 57 Rose+ ZEPHYR. 5 GROUPS.TBL YLD+FRACT	+
Delayd Neuts	Maxwl	Fiss	LAS	Expt Jour	PR 107 1044	Aug 57 Keepin+,0.0165+-0.0005 N/FISS 6GRPS	
				Jour	JNE 6 1	Dec 57 - +. SAME DATA AS PR(8/57)	
				Jour	PR 106 1359	Jun 57 .SUPERSEDED	
				Rept	LA- 1970	Oct 55 Keepin. NEUT YLDS+SPECTR,CURVS+TABLS	
				Conf	55Geneva 4 162	Aug 55 - +.P/831. PRELIMINARY.	
Delayd Neuts	None		LAS	Theo Jour	JNE 7 13	Aug 58 Keepin.THEOR DEL NEUT PRECURSRS,YLDS	
				Jour	AE 4 250	Mar 58 .SEE ALSO	
				Jour	SJA 4 339	Mar 58 .SEE ALSO	
Delayd Neuts	Maxwl		ANL	Expt Conf	58Geneva 15 384	Sep 58 Stehney+.PPR691,TBL,EXPT DESCRIBED	
Delayd Neuts	Maxwl	1.5+7	FEI	Expt Jour	ZET 35 815	Sep 58 Maksjutenko. YLD OF 5GROUPS AT 4ES	+
	2.5-2	1.5+7			AE 7 474	Nov 59 .YIELD AT 3ES REL U235 THERMAL	
	Maxwl	1.5+7			JET 8 565	Mar 59 TRANSLATN.*	
	2.5-2	1.5+7			SJA 7 943	Mar 61 .ENGLISH TRANSL OF AE 7 474 11/59	
				Jour	JNE 12 141	Jun 60 .SECTION A.ENGL OF AE 7 474 11/59	
Delayd Neuts	Maxwl		OSL	Expt Conf	58Geneva 15 373	Sep 58 Pappas+.PPR583,TBL CFD THEORIE	
Delayd Neuts	Pile		LAS	Expt Prog	WASH-1006	Oct 58 Jurney. TO BE DONE	
Delayd Neuts	Fiss		LAS	Expt Jour	NUC 13 10 49	Oct 59 Paxton+	
Delayd Neuts	1.4+7		NRL	Expt Abst	BAP 5 33	Jan 60 Mcgarry+.DELAYED FRACTION=.022+-.005	
Delayd Neuts		2.3+6	ANL	Revw Conf	61Vienna 1 457	Aug 61 Meneghetti.MULTIGROUP DSTRBS,TABLE	
Delayd Neuts	Maxwl		LAS	Expt Conf	61Vienna 1 149	Aug 61 Diven+.PPR56,TABLE REL TO CF252	
Delayd Neuts	Maxwl	1.6+7	LAS	Revw Jour	NUC 20 8 150	Aug 62 Keepin.	

92 Uranium 235

Quantity	Energy (ev) Min	Max	Lab	Type	Documentation Ref Vol Page	Author, Comments Date	Data
Delayd Neuts	2.5+5	1.5+6	ANL Expt	Prog	WASH-1041 4	Oct 62 COX.YIELD CONSTANT OVER EXPTL RANGE	
Delayd Neuts	8.0+4	2.8+6	CCP Expt	Rept	ANL-TR-179	64 Bondarenko+,NU BAR SECONDARY NS VS E	
Delayd Neuts	2.5+6	1.5+7	FEI Expt	Rept	ICD-3 75	66 Maksjutenko.TBL REL YIELD. TBP YF	+
				Jour	AE 19 46	Jul 65 .PART OF DATA,ADDITIONAL INFORMATION	
				Prog	ICD-1 266	64 .MORE DATA	
				Rept	INDC-E-152	67 .ENGLISH TRANSL OF ICD-3 75 1966	
				Jour	JNE 20 607	Jul 66 .ENGLISH-TRANSL-OF-AE-19-46-1965----	
				Jour	EAF 19 1 70	Jul 65 . FRENCH TRANSL OF AE 19 46 1965	
				Jour	SJA 19 910	Jul 65 .ENGLISH-TRANSL-OF-AE-19-46-1965----	
				Prog	INDSWG-64E 24	64 .ENGLISH TRANSL OF ICD-1 266 1964	
Delayd Neuts	Maxwl		MIT Expt	Jour	NAP 2 256	Jun 66 Coryell+ 555 PERIOD ALL DUE TO BR87	
Delayd Neuts	Maxwl		CCP Expt	Jour	YF 4 325	Aug 66 Vorobeva+ SURFACE-BARRIER COUNTERS.	
Delayd Neuts	1.5+7		RI Expt	Prog	YFI-3 18	Sep 66 ARTEM'EV ETC. NDG, TBP IN YF	
Delayd Neuts	Pile		ANL Expt	Conf	67Vienna 229	Apr 67 Brunson+,BANDSAW EXPT(NEW METHOD)	
Delayd Neuts	5.0+6	8.0+6	FEI Expt	Conf	67Vienna 191	Apr 67 Maksiutenko.REL YLDS FOR 5GROUPS	+
Delayd Neuts		+7	HFA Revw	Conf	67Vienna 23	Apr 67 Yiftah+ TBL OF YLD+HL,REACTR DYNAMIC	
Delayd Neuts	Maxwl		SOR Expt	Conf	67Vienna 115	Apr 67 Amiel+ SPEC+PRECURSRS,GRPH+TBL,COMPL	
				Rept	IA- 1190 95	Jul 69 - + NEW INFORMATION	
Delayd Neuts	0.0+0	1.0+0	MOLExpt	Jour	JIN 29 273	May 67 Del Marmol+ GE,AS,SB PRECURSORS	
				Conf	65Salzburg 2 225	Mar 65 - +	
Delayd Neuts	1.8+7	2.1+7	FEI Expt	Prog	YFI-5 11	Oct 67 Maksjutenko+ YLD OF NS VERSUS HL	
				Rept	ICD-6 272	70 - + YLDS 11GROUPS.TBL,GRPHS	
	1.5+7	2.1+7		Conf	67Vienna 203	Apr 67 .REL YIELDS,CFD U235 AND U238	
	1.8+7	2.1+7		Prog	ICD-4 363	67 .REL NEUTRON YIELD VS HALFLIFE	
				Prog	INDC(CCP)-1	Jan 69 .ENGLISH TRANSL OF YFI-5 11 10/67	
Delayd Neuts	Maxwl		MNZTheo	Jour	AF 36 453	Nov 67 Patzelt+.FROM DERIVED N-EMISS PROB.	
Delayd Neuts	Maxwl		IOW Expt	Jour	PR 177 1805	Jan 69 Talbert+ DELAYD NEUTS VS. FRAG MASS	
Delayd Neuts	Maxwl		JUL Expt	Jour	ZP 220 101	Feb 69 Eidens+,TIME-DEPENDANT CURVES GIVEN	
				Rept	NP- 17532	Jul 68 Roeckl.TIME AND MASS DISTRIBUTION	
				Conf	67Vienna 85	Apr 67 - + DEL NEUT/MASS SEPERATED COIN	
				Conf	67Juelich 32	Apr 67 - + AS-85,BR-87,90+OTHER PRECURS	
				Rept	JUEL-463-NP 18	Mar 67 - +	
Delayd Neuts	Fiss		HAR Expt	Rept	AERE-M-2199	Apr 69 Tomlinson+ ESTIMATE YLD AL 1 MIN+	
Delayd Neuts	3.1+6	1.5+7	LAS Expt	Jour	NSE 36 202	May 69 Masters+ 2ES RELATIVE+ABSOL MEASTS	+
	2.5+5	1.5+7		Conf	69Vienna 647	Jul 69 East+PPR109.SAFEGUARD PROBL,XPT+REVW	
	3.1+6	1.5+7		Jour	ANS 11 179	Jun 68 .SUPERSEDED	
				Rept	LA-DC-9403	65 .SUPERSEDED	
	3.1+6	1.5+7		Data	EXFOR12288.	Jun 76 . 2 PTS.	
Delayd Neuts	Pile		NIL Expt	Prog	INDC(PAK)-1 2	May 69 . TOF,E-SPEC,PRECURSRS,TO BE DONE	
Delayd Neuts	Maxwl		PAR Theo	Conf	69Vienna 621	Jul 69 Gauvin+PPR85.CALC DEL-N-SPEC CFD XPT	
Delayd Neuts	Maxwl	+7	SOR Revw	Conf	69Vienna 569	Jul 69 Amiel.PPR205. REVW,EXPTS+TH,TABLES	
Delayd Neuts	Maxwl		SOR Expt	Prog	IA- 1190 104	Jul 69 Braun+ DEL-N-EMISSN-PROBAB OF BR+I	
				Jour	AF 36 169	Nov 67 Amiel+.REL IMPORTANCE BR,I IN DIF GR	
Delayd Neuts	Maxwl		WAS Expt	Conf	69Vienna 813	Jul 69 Wahl+PPR116.YLD+PRECURS+PROBABIL,TBL	+
				Rept	COO-1162-35	69 .EQUIVALENT	
Delayd Neuts	2.0+5	1.4+6	ANL Expt	Prog	ANL-7610 45	Jan 70 Cox+. CURV DELAYED NEUTRON YIELD	
	Thrsh	2.4+6		Prog	ANL-7410 27	Jan 69 COX+,YLD,PERIOD CURVES	
Delayd Neuts	None		VIP Expt	Abst	DA/B 30 4749	Apr 70 Rambo.5 NTN.GPS.YLD.HL,REL ABUNDS.	
	Maxwl			Rept	TID-25645	May 69 - .HALF-LIVES+REL ABUNDANCES	
Delayd Neuts	6.0+5	1.5+6	KFK Expt	Rept	KFK-1270 1	Jul 70 Chou+ E-SPEC DELAYED N,HL 22S,GRPH	
Delayd Neuts	Maxwl		SOR Expt	Prog	IA- 1218 96	Aug 70 Amiel+ KR+XE REGION,DEL-N,HALF-LIVES	
Delayd Neuts	Maxwl		HAR Theo	Rept	AERE-R-6596	Nov 70 Tomlinson. CALC DEL-N GROUP YLDS.TBL	
Delayd Neuts	Maxwl		MOLExpt	Jour	RCA 16 1 4	Feb 71 Del Marmol+ DELAY NEUT YLD HALOG PRC	
Delayd Neuts	Maxwl		BNL Expt	Jour	NSE 44 173	May 71 Conant+ DELAYED NEUT FRACTION	+
	Maxwl			Data	EXFOR10144.002	Mar 72 1PT	
Delayd Neuts	Pile		SRC Expt	Prog	EANDC(OR)111L	Aug 71 Shalev+. SPEC DELAYED N FROM I-137	
Delayd Neuts	Maxwl		ATH Expt	Jour	JNE 25 551	Nov 71 Chrysochoides+ EN SPEC FROM BR087,88	
	Pile			Conf	67Vienna 213	Apr 67 - +,E-DIST BY TOF+COINC	
Delayd Neuts			HAR Expt	Jour	JN 33 11 3609	Nov 71 Tomlinson+ DEL NEUT FROM SE ISOTOPES	
	2.5-2			Revw Conf	71Canterbry 239	71 - .EXP CFD CALCULATIONS.TABLE	
	Pile			Expt Conf	69Vienna 605	Jul 69 - +PPR60. LONG HLS+PHOTOFISSN	
				Jour	JIN 30 1995	Aug 68 - + SE-87 PRECURSOR	
				Jour	JIN 30 1649	Aug 68 - + SB,AS PRECURSORS	
				Jour	JIN 30 1125	Jun 68 - + SB,AS PRECURSORS	
	Maxwl			Jour	PL/B 25 545	Nov 67 - + DEL-NEUT-PRECURSOR=SB-134	
				Conf	65Salzburg 233	Mar 65 - .SB-135,AS-85 TO 87 PRECURS	
Delayd Neuts	Maxwl	1.5+7	HAR Eval	Rept	AERE-R-6993	Feb 72 TOMLINSON TOTAL+GROUP YLDS SPEC TBL	

92 Uranium 235

Quantity	Energy (ev) Min	Energy (ev) Max	Lab	Type	Documentation Ref Vol Page	Date	Author, Comments	Data
Delayd Neuts	5.0+4	6.7+6	LAS	Expt	Jour NSE 53 80	Jan 73	Evans+REVISED NUD DATA.TBLS.	+
	1.0+5	6.5+6			Jour NSE 47 311	Mar 72	Krick+SPRSDD.DATA REVISED.	
	5.0+4	6.7+6			Data EXFOR10117.	Jul 74	27PTS	
Delayd Neuts	Pile		THD	Expt	Jour ZP 254 323	Oct 72	Gremm.FERMI-AGE MEASUR. OF DELAYED N	
Delayd Neuts	Maxwl		ATH	Expt	Prog EANDC(OR)119	Nov 72	Chrysochoides+ FROM BR-87,88 PRECURS	
Delayd Neuts	2.5-2	1.5+7	IAE	Eval	Jour REA 10 637	Dec 72	Manero+ SURVEY,AVERAGE YIELD,TBLS	
Delayd Neuts	Maxwl		ISL	Expt	Jour IA- 1262 81	Dec 72	Shaanan+ RB93 DELAYED NS,E-SPEC,GRPH	
Delayd Neuts	1.4+7		KFK	Expt	Jour JNE 26 585	Dec 72	Fieg.EN SPECT,AS FN TIME AFTER FISS	
					Prog KFK-1272 1	Jun 72	- .P121-6,SPEC+MEAN ES OF 4 GROUP	
					Rept KFK-EXT-4 31	May 71	- . SPEC EXPT, 4-GROUP SPECS CALC	
			MNZ	Expt	Jour RCA 18 3 123	Dec 72	Schuessler+ 140I + 98/99Y	
					Conf 69Vienna 591	Jul 69	- +PPR22. YLD+HL+PRECURS XPT	
Delayd Neuts	Maxwl		BUC	Revw	Rept IFA-RN-50	73	Cristu. NUD(FRAGM-MASS),H-L,E-SPEC	
	Fast				Rept IFA-RN-50	73	- . NUD(FRAGM-MASS),H-L,E-SPEC	
Delayd Neuts	Maxwl		HFA	Expt	Jour NSE 51 52	May 73	Shalev+ HE-3 DET. NEUT ENERGY DISTR	
Delayd Neuts	Fast		ALD	Expt	Prog EANDC(UK) 151	Aug 73	Mctaggart.0.0174+ -0.0008 N/F TBC	
Delayd Neuts	1.5+5	1.5+7	BIR	Revw	Jour RPP 37 951	74	Beynon+ COMPAR TOT DELAYED N-YLD(E)	
	Maxwl				Jour RPP 37 951	74	- + BR88+I127,E-SPEC.EXPT CFD TH	
Delayd Neuts	Maxwl		FEI	Theo	Conf IAEA-169 3 105	74	Maksjutenko+ CALC PROBAB(H-L),GRAPHS	
					Jour YF 17 1149	Jun 73	Tarasko+ TRANSFORM OF HL-GROUPS,GRPH	
					Rept FEI-369	72	- + SAME AS YF 17 1149	
					Jour SNP 17 598	Dec 73	.ENGL OF YF 17 1149	
Delayd Neuts	1.0+5	1.5+7	LAS	Revw	Conf IAEA-169 377	74	Evans. TBL YLD,GRPH E-SPEC(HL-GROUPS	
Delayd Neuts	Maxwl	1.5+7	SOR	Revw	Conf IAEA-169 2 33	74	Amiel.ALL YLDS,DEL-N SPECS,TBL,GRPHS	
Delayd Neuts	Maxwl	1.5+7	ANL	Eval	Rept ANL-NDM-5	Apr 74	COX. REL YLD, HL, GRPH	
Delayd Neuts	1.0+6	4.0+6	ANL	Expt	Abst BAP 19 597	Apr 74	COX. 4ES. ABSOL YLD MEASD.NO DATA.	
Delayd Neuts	1.1+7	1.7+7	LRL	Expt	Prog UCID-16514 6	Jun 74	Alvarez+	
Delayd Neuts	Maxwl		VIP	Expt	Abst DA/B 35 278	Jul 74	Naeem. TBL.	
Delayd Neuts	Pile		AE	Expt	Jour NP/A 235 397	Dec 74	Roostam+ E-SPECT FROM PRECURS GRPH	
					Jour NP/A 230 153	Sep 74	Shalev+ E-SPECT FROM PRECURS+GRPH	
	Maxwl				Conf IAEA-169 3 367	74	- + PRELIM E-SPECS(BR,TE,I-ISOT)	
Delayd Neuts	Maxwl		WAU	Expt	Jour NSE 55 28	Sep 74	Sloan+ NUD SPECT.TBLS.GRPHS.	+
					Abst ANS 15 942	Nov 72	- +. CURVES NEUT ENERGY SPECTRA	
					Prog RLO-2225-4	Jul 72	Woodruff. PRELIM SPECTRA SHOWN	
	Maxwl				Data EXFOR10576.	Jun 76	139PTS.133PT NUD SPEC.6PT FRACT YLD.	
Delayd Neuts	2.5-2	1.5+7	AI	Eval	Jour NSE 56 37	Jan 75	Tuttle.TBL.GRPH.RVW MEAS.CFD REC VAL	
	2.5-2				Prog AI-AEC-13025	May 72	Springer+ VALUE=0.01682+ -0.00039	
Delayd Neuts	2.5-2		IAE	Eval	Conf 75Wash. 286	Mar 75	Lemmel. TBL LSQ ANAL.CFD OTHER EVAL.	
Delayd Neuts	1.0+5	1.2+6	KFK	Expt	Rept JUEL-1178 97	Apr 75	Bluhm+ SAME AS KFK-2000	
					Rept KFK-2200 97	Apr 75	- + EXPT METHODS DISCUSSED	
Delayd Neuts	Pile		FEI	Expt	Rept YFI-20 3	May 75	Maksyutenko+ U35/PU39-YLD BR87NS GVN	
	Maxwl				Rept INDC(CCP)-66	Feb 76	.P 1. ENGL OF YFI-20 3	
Delayd Neuts	2.5-2		HED	Theo	Abst ANS 21 518	Jun 75	Schenter+ TBL CALC FROM ENDF FP FILE	
Delayd Neuts	1.0+6	1.5+7	HED	Theo	Abst ANS 21 518	Jun 75	Schenter+ TBL CALC FROM ENDF FP FILE	
Delayd Neuts	Maxwl		SOR	Eval	Jour NSE 57 117	Jun 75	Izak-Biran+ PN-VALUES,GROUP-YLDS§TBL	
	Fast				Jour NSE 57 117	Jun 75	- + PN-VALUES,GROUP-YL4S§T23	
Delayd Neuts	Maxwl		ILL	Expt	Jour JIN 37 1563	Aug 75	Asghar+ ISOT-SEP.PN of 8PREC.TBL.	
					Jour NP/A 247 359	Aug 75	- + EMIS PROB FROM FP,GRPH,TBL	
Delayd Neuts	2.5-2		KFK	ExTh	Jour NSE 58 260	Oct 75	Fieg+ EFFECTS PB SHIELD ON SPECTRUM	
	Maxwl			Expt	Prog EANDC(E)-157 1	Mar 73	- .NEUT SPEC BY PROTON RECOIL COU	
					Jour JNE 26 585	Dec 72	- .EN SPECT.AS FN TIME AFTER FISS	
					Prog KFK-1272 1	Jun 72	- .P121-6,SPEC+MEAN ES OF 4 GROUP	
Delayd Neuts	+6		FEI	Expt	Rept YK-23 110	76	Maksjutenko+ YLD DELAYED NEUTS,GRAPH	
Delayd Neuts	Maxwl		MNZ	Expt	Conf 76Corsica 317	May 76	Shihab-Eldin+(LBL) NON STAT THEORY	+
	2.5-2				Jour ZP 263 435	Sep 73	Kratz+,DELAY.N-DECAY-PROB.FROM F-PRO	
	Maxwl				Jour PL/B 65 231	Nov 76	- + DELAYED NS CFD GAMMAS.5 ISTPS	
					Conf 76Corsica 304	May 76	- + DEL N SPECTRA.BR,AS,I,SB.	
					Jour JIN 35 1407	May 73	- + FROM 84AS, 85AS, 86AS	
	Maxwl				Data EXFOR20521.002	Apr 76	3PTS. DELAYED NS.	
Delayd Neuts	None		ALD	Expt	Prog NEANDC(E)172 8	Aug 76	Besant+ DELAYED N YIELD	
Delayd Neuts	2.5-2		IRT	Expt	Jour NSE 61 426	Nov 76	Lukens+U02,U308 DIFFERENCE IN NUD	
Delayd Neuts	Maxwl		CSR	Revw	Jour JE 23 9 345	77	Tinka. REVW GROUP-SPEC,PARAMS.TABLES	
	1.5+7				Jour JE 23 9 345	77	- . REVW GROUP-SPEC,PARAMS.TABLES	
	Fast				Jour JE 23 9 345	77	- . REVW GROUP-SPEC,PARAMS.TABLES	
Delayd Neuts	Maxwl		MNZ	Expt	Jour NIM 144 253	77	Franz+ SPECTR. I-137 DELAYED NS.	
Delayd Neuts	Maxwl		SWR	Theo	Jour JRC 36 591	77	Rudstam. DEL-N SPEC CALC,FINE STRUCT	
				Expt	Jour NIM 139 239	Dec 76	- + SURVEY OF OSIRIS PROGRAMME	
Frag Neuts	Fast		ORL	Expt	Jour PR 74 1645	Dec 48	Debenedetti+ ANGDISTR N-N COINC.	

92 Uranium 235

Quantity	Energy (ev) Min	Max	Lab	Type	Documentation Ref Vol Page	Date	Author, Comments	Data
Frag Neuts	Maxwl		CCP	Expt Jour	AE 8 15	Jan 60	Apalin+.YIELD FOR DIFF FRAGMENTS GVN	
				Jour	SJA 8 10	Apr 61	TRANSLATN.* JNE AB17 25 1/63	
				Jour	KE 3 633	Jul 60	.TRANSLATN	
Frag Neuts	None		LAS	Revw Jour	PR 127 880	Aug 62	Terrell.ANALYSIS OF TOF+RADIOCHEM	
Frag Neuts	Maxwl		COP	Theo Jour	NP 46 129	Jul 63	Vandenbosch. EFF OF FRAG SHELL STRUC	
Frag Neuts	Maxwl		KUR	Expt Jour	ZET 46 1197	Apr 64	Apalin+,NU VS FRAG MASS CURVE	
				Rept	AEC-TR-6254	Apr 64	TRANSLATN.*+ AEC-TR-6285 /64	
Frag Neuts	Maxwl		KUR	Expt Rept	IAE-819	65	Apalin+ GRPHS NEUT NO NU(FRAG-MASS)	
Frag Neuts	Maxwl		CRC	Expt Conf	65Salzburg 2 39	Mar 65	Milton+,PPR.45,TBLS AND GRAPHS	
Frag Neuts	Maxwl		KUR	Expt Conf	65Salzburg 1 587	Mar 65	Apalin+,SYMMETRIC FISS,GRPHS,CFD XPT	
				Jour	YF 1 639	Apr 65	SEE ALSO *NP 71 553 9/65	
				Jour	SNP 1 457	Oct 65	. ENGL OF YF 1 639	
Frag Neuts	None		LAS	Revw Conf	65Salzburg 2 3	Mar 65	Terrell.PPR.43,XPTL WORK CFD TH,GRPH	
Frag Neuts	None		MIT	Theo Conf	65Salzburg 2 73	Mar 65	Gordon+,PPR.48,MONTE CARLO CALC CFD	
Frag Neuts	Maxwl		CIS	Theo Jour	NP 84 595	Sep 66	Erba+ STATMOD CFD EXPT,NU VS A(FRAG)	
Frag Neuts	Pile		IOW	Expt Conf	67Vienna 103	Apr 67	Day+,NEUT DELAY,A-SEPARATOR + GE-LI	
Frag Neuts	Maxwl		ALD	Expt Jour	PR 164 1520	Dec 67	Maslin+VERSUS FRAG MASS+TOT.K.E.	
				Rept	AWRE-O-43/67	Jun 67	- + NS ASSOCIATED WITH FRAGS	
				Conf	65Salzburg 2 481	Mar 65	- + SUPERSEDED	
Frag Neuts	Maxwl		ITK	Theo Conf	68Madras 1 302	Feb 68	Mukherji+ CALC NU VS HEAVY MASS,GRPH	
Frag Neuts	2.0+6	6.0+6	CCP	Expt Jour	YF 8 286	Aug 68	Dyachenko+TBL NU(6NEUT-ES,H+L FRAGS)	
				Jour	SNP 8 165	Feb 69	TRANSLATN.*	
Frag Neuts			IOW	Expt Jour	PR 177 1805	Jan 69	Talbert+ DELAYD NEUTS VS. FRAG MASS	
Frag Neuts	Maxwl		FEI	Theo Jour	YF 9 357	Feb 69	Ignatyuk.CALC DEFORM-E(A)OKS XPTL NU	
				Jour	SNP 9 208	Aug 69	TRANSLATN.*	
Frag Neuts	Maxwl		EDG	Revw Conf	69Vienna 83	Jul 69	Feather.PPR201.REVW,CENTRAL+FRAG NU	
Frag Neuts		+3	KFI	Theo Conf	69Vienna 927	Jul 69	Kluge.PPR9. CALCULATED NU VS FRAG-A	
	Maxwl			Jour	PL/B 27 65	Jun 68	- + E+NU US FRAG MASS STATIS.CAL	
Frag Neuts	Maxwl		KUR	Expt Conf	69Vienna 957	Jul 69	Blinov+PPR144. COINC NEUTS OF 2FRAGS	
Frag Neuts	Maxwl		KUR	Expt Conf	69Vienna 958	Jul 69	Blinov+PPR145. NU VS(FRAG-TOT-KIN-E)	
Frag Neuts	Maxwl		MCM	Theo Conf	69Vienna 845	Jul 69	Thind+PPR50. FRAG-EXCIT-E CFD NU(A)	
				Jour	CJP 46 1137	May 68	Gorman+ CALCULATD NEUT YLDS CFD EXPT	
Frag Neuts	Maxwl		WAS	Expt Conf	69Vienna 813	Jul 69	Wahl+PPR116.TERRELS METHOD,NU(A),TBL	
				Rept	COO-1162-35	69	.EQUIVALENT	
Frag Neuts	Maxwl		FTI	Expt Jour	YF 10 923	Nov 69	Blinov+ NU OF HEAVY+LIGHT FRAGMENTS	
				Jour	SNP 10 533	May 70	TRANSLATN.*	
Frag Neuts	Maxwl		MNZ	Theo Jour	ZN/A 24 2000	Dec 69	Denschlag+MODIFIED MOD CALC,CFD EXPT	
Frag Neuts	Maxwl		MOL	Comp Conf	70Helsinki 2 535	Jun 70	Fabry+39. TABLE OF DATA SETS	
Frag Neuts	Maxwl		RI	Expt Jour	YF 12 41	Jul 70	Blinov+ N-ANGDIST VS FRAG-E, GRAPH	
					-		= ENGLISH $SNP 12 22 1/71$	
Frag Neuts	Maxwl		COL	Expt Jour	PR/C 2 1554	Oct 70	Melkonian+,NEUT YLD VS FRAG MASS,KE	
Frag Neuts	Maxwl		AUA	Expt Rept	AAEC/TM-581	Mar 71	Boldeman+ NU VERSUS KINE+MASS GRAPHS	
					-		SEE ALSO AAEC/PR33-P PAGE P7 /70	
Frag Neuts	Pile		AUA	Expt Jour	AUJ 24 821	Dec 71	Boldeman+ NU VS A,K-E,GRAPHS,PRELIM	
	None			Conf	69Vienna 929	Jul 69	Bolgman.PPR34. NU(FRAG A,FRAG Z)	
Frag Neuts	None		RI	Expt Prog	YFI-12 102	72	Korostylev+ ABST,TBL NUBAR(HEAVY-A)	
				Prog	INDC(CCP)-30	Sep 72	.PAGE 88,ENGLISH OF YFI-12 102	
Frag Neuts	Maxwl		TRM	Expt Jour	PR/C 5 1410	Apr 72	Iyer+ NU VS FRAG CHARGE+MASS GIVEN	
Frag Neuts	7.0+5	6.0+6	KUR	Expt Jour	YF 16 1161	Dec 72	Savin+ NUBAR VS EN,TOF.GRAPH	
				Jour	SNP 16 638	Jun 73	. ENGL OF YF 16 1161	
Frag Neuts	Maxwl		SAC	Revw Conf	73Rochester 2 117	Aug 73	Nifenecker+ NU VS FRAG-A,KIN-E,GRPHS	
Frag Neuts	Maxwl		SOR	Revw Conf	IAEA-169 2 33	74	Amiel.PRECURSOR DELAYED-N SPECS,GRPH	
Frag Neuts	Maxwl		AUA	Expt Prog	AAEC/PR-40P 28	Jul 74	Boldeman+ NU(FRGM-MASS),TBD	
Frag Neuts	2.5-2		ORE	Theo Abst	ANS 22 673	Nov 75	Liaw.FRAG N YLD,EMISSION PROB CALC.	
Frag Neuts	2.0+6	1.5+7	TRM	Theo Jour	PR/C 14 181	Jul 76	Sharma+2E.ORDER-DISORDER MDL.CFD EXP	
Frag Neuts	5.5+5		TUE	Expt Conf	76Lowell 1406	Jul 76	Muller+NUMBER PROMPT N FN FRAG.NDG.	
Frag Neuts	Maxwl		SAH	Theo Conf	76Ahmedabd 2 124	Dec 76	Majumdar. RGM-MODL.NU(A)CFD OTHS.FIG	
Spect Fiss n	Maxwl		ANL	Expt Jour	PR 87 1034	Sep 52	Hill. 0.4-7MEV NEUTS, MAX .75MEV	
Spect Fiss n	Maxwl		LAS	Expt Jour	PR 87 1032	Sep 52	Bonner+ CLOUD CHAMBER .05-7MEV NEUTS	
				Rept	AECD-3250	Oct 51	Nereson.PHOTOPLATES,0.4-7MEV NEUTS	
Spect Fiss n	Maxwl		LAS	Expt Jour	PR 87 1037	Sep 52	Watt+PROT RECOIL COUNT 3.3-17MEV NS	
Spect Fiss n	Maxwl		CRC	Expt Jour	PR 88 536	Nov 52	Fraser+ANGULAR DIST CURVES CFD THEOR	
Spect Fiss n	Maxwl		LAS	Expt Jour	PR 89 1288	Mar 53	Nicodemus+ IONIZATION CHAMBER 1-4MEV	
Spect Fiss n	Maxwl		LAS	Expt Rept	TID-10073	May 54	Frye+.NEUT SPEC FROM 0.3-12MEV.	
Spect Fiss n	Pile		LAS	Revw Conf	55Geneva 2 193	Aug 55	Leachman.P592,CURVE,EXPT DESCRIBED	
Spect Fiss n	Maxwl		LAS	Expt Conf	55Geneva 4 97	Aug 55	Rosen.P582,CURVE,THEORET FIT	
Spect Fiss n	Maxwl		LAS	Expt Abst	BAP 1 95	Feb 56	Grundl+ NP237+U238 FISS CHAMBERS	

92 Uranium 235

Quantity	Energy (ev) Min	Max	Lab	Type	Documentation Ref Vol Page	Author, Comments Date	Data
Spect Fiss n	5.0+3	8.0+4	LAS	Expt	Jour PR 103 662	Aug 56 Cranberg+,TOF TO 3MEV	
	Maxwl				Jour PR 103 662	Aug 56 - +,FOTOPL TO 12MEV CFD TH	
Spect Fiss n	5.0+5	1.0+6	LAS	Expt	Jour PR 104 731	Nov 56 Allen+,ANGULAR DISTRIBUTION ISOTROP	
Spect Fiss n	None		GEN	Eval	Rept DC- 56-1-75	Dec 56 Silverstein.PROMPT AND PROMPT+DELAYD	
Spect Fiss n	Maxwl		LAS	Theo	Jour PR 105 1511	Mar 57 Leachman+,CALCTD CURVE CFD CF252	
Spect Fiss n	Maxwl	1.0+7	CCP	Theo	Jour AE 3 15	Jul 57 Bat+KUDRIN.EVAP THEOR.E SPECTR CALC	
					Jour JNE 8 74	Nov 58 TRANSLATN.*	
					Jour SJA 3 735	57 TRANSLATN.*	
Spect Fiss n	Maxwl		CCP	Expt	Jour ZET 33 1069	Oct 57 Kovalev.THRESHOLD – DETECTORS	
	None			Theo	Jour JET 8 545	Mar 59 .TRANSLATN.*	
	Maxwl				Jour AE 5 649	Dec 58 Kovalev+ THEORY COMPARED WITH EXPT	
	None				Jour ZET 35 787	Sep 58 - . NEW TH OKS XPT	
	Maxwl			Expt	Jour JET 6 825	Apr 58 TRANSLATN.*	
				Theo	Jour SJA 5 1588	58 .TRANSLATN.*	
				Expt	-	FRENCH CEA–TR–R–725	
Spect Fiss n	5.0+4	7.0+5	CCP	Expt	Jour ZET 34 501	Feb 58 CLOUD CHAMB,AGREES WITH WATT, T=1MEV	
					Jour JET 7 345	Aug 58 TRANSLATN.*	
Spect Fiss n	1.4+7		CCP	Expt	Jour AE 4 337	Apr 58 Zamiatnin+ FISS+EVAP SPECTR FIT DATA	
					Jour JNE 9 194	Jun 59 TRANSLATN.*	
					Jour SJA 4 443	58 TRANSLATN.*	
Spect Fiss n	Maxwl		ANL	Expt	Conf 58Geneva 15 392	Sep 58 Smith+.PPR690,CURVE	
Spect Fiss n	Maxwl		LAS	Eval	Jour PR 113 527	Jan 59 Terrell.TH CFD C EXPT,STAT ANALYSIS	
Spect Fiss n	Maxwl	3.3+6	CCP	Expt	Jour ZET 37 1822	Dec 59 TR DET,TEMP CHGE,DT/DE=.008+ - .004	
					Jour JET 10 1286	Jun 60 TRANSLATN.*	
Spect Fiss n	1.4+7		CCP	Expt	Jour ZET 38 671	Mar 60 Vasil'Ev. TOF,0.4 – 5MEV,GRAPHS,TABLES	
					Jour SJA 9 990	Oct 61 .TRANSLATN.*	
					Jour AE 9 449	Dec 60 Vasilev+ TOF AT 0 45 90DEG TO FRAGTS	
					Jour JET 11 483	Sep 60 TRANSLATN.*	
Spect Fiss n	Pile		CCP	Expt	Jour ZET 38 1657	Jun 60 NEUT SPECT AT 5 AS,CFD EVAP MODEL	
					Jour JET 11 1195	Dec 60 TRANSLATN.*	
Spect Fiss n	Maxwl		RIC	Expt	Jour NP 23 116	Feb 61 Bonner.MOD SPH SP. T=1.332+ - 0.030MEV	
Spect Fiss n	Maxwl		TRM	Expt	Conf 61Bombay 170	Feb 61 Ramanna+.ENERGY+ANGLE OF PROMPT NS	
Spect Fiss n	Maxwl		TRM	Expt	Jour NP 25 136	May 61 Ramanna+.ANGCORR PROMPT N+FISS FRAGM	
Spect Fiss n	Maxwl		MOL	Expt	Jour NP 30 232	Feb 62 Beets+.RECOIL PS IN ILFORD L4.	
Spect Fiss n	Maxwl		CCP	Expt	Jour ZET 42 1017	Apr 62 ENERGY AND ANGULAR DISTR. MEASURED	
					Jour JET 15 704	Oct 62 TRANSLATN.*	
Spect Fiss n	1.6+6	2.0+6	BET	Eval	Rept WAPD-BT-25	May 62 Shure.SPECT	
Spect Fiss n	1.0-2	1.0+7	KFK	Eval	Rept KFK-120 2	Dec 62 Schmidt.GRAPHS AND TABULATED DATA	+
	Maxwl				Data KEDAK-3	Oct 75 219 DATA SETS	
Spect Fiss n	Maxwl		KJL	Expt	Jour NP 45 72	Jul 63 Skarsvag+.ENERGY,ANGDIST.PROMPT NEUT	+
Spect Fiss n	Maxwl		TRM	Expt	Jour PR 131 283	Jul 63 Kapoor+ NEUTS COINC C LT+HEAVY FRAGS	
Spect Fiss n	1.0+3	1.5+7	UK	Eval	Rept AWRE–O–82/63	Dec 63 Parker.(ALD).UKNDL – DFN 155	+
	1.0-4	1.5+7			Data UKNDL–DFN 159B	Mar 73 1 RANGES	
Spect Fiss n	Maxwl		ORL	Eval	Rept ORNL–TM–795	Feb 64 Halperin+ FISS SPEC .01–25MEV TABLE	
Spect Fiss n	Maxwl		CCP	ExTh	Jour ZET 46 1139	Mar 64 Ang.,ENERGY OF FISSION NEUTRONS	
					Jour JET 19 771	Sep 64 TRANSLATN.*	
Spect Fiss n	None		WES	Eval	Rept WANL–TME–1028	Nov 64 Drawbaugh+.CURVE	
Spect Fiss n	Maxwl		CCP	Expt	Jour AE 18 108	Feb 65 Blinov+SPEC+ANGDIST REL FRAGS CFD TH	
				ExTh	Jour YF 4 1179	Dec 66 - .TOF,CRVS GVN	
				Expt	Jour JNE 20 381	May 66 TRANSLATN.*	
					Jour EAF 18 2 34	Feb 65 TRANSLATN.*	
					Jour SJA 18 140	Feb 65 TRANSLATN.*	
Spect Fiss n	Maxwl		ISL	Theo	Rept IA–1007	Feb 65 Nebenzahl.CALCULATION OKS EXPERIMENT	
Spect Fiss n	None		CAD	Eval	Conf 65IAEA 349	Mar 65 Benezech+MODERTD WATT–SPEC,XPTL GRPH	
Spect Fiss n	Maxwl		IIT	Comp	Conf 65IAEA 251	Mar 65 Barrall+ 3 FISS FORMULA CFD,GRPH	
Spect Fiss n	4.0+4	1.5+6	FOA	Expt	Jour AF 29 313	Apr 65 Conde+ 2ES.FISS CH.+PSC.MAXWELL FIT	+
					Conf 65Salzburg 93	Mar 65 - + EQU TO AF 29 313	
	4.0+4	1.5+6			Data EXFOR20575.	Aug 76 26PTS.AVG.K.E.	
Spect Fiss n	Maxwl		HAR	Eval	Jour NP 71 228	Sep 65 Barnard+ CORRELATED WITH NU BAR	
	1.0+5			Expt	Jour NP 71 228	Sep 65 - + MAXWELLIAN T=1.30+ - .02	
Spect Fiss n	Maxwl		NIR	Expt	Jour YF 3 465	Mar 66 Nefedov+.N–SPECTRA AT 2ANGLS,GRAPHS	
					Jour SNP 3 325	Sep 66 TRANSLATN.*	
Spect Fiss n	Maxwl		NIR	Expt	Jour AE 20 342	Apr 66 Nefedov+ TERNARY+DOUBLE FISS–SPECTRA	
Spect Fiss n	-		TRM	Theo	Jour NUK 8 408	Jul 66 Iyer+CALC CFD PR 88 536 DATA.NU=2.53	
Spect Fiss n	Maxwl		NRD	Theo	Jour PR/B 139 56	Jul 65 Ferguson+MODEL FOR FISS YLDS,	
					Jour PR 150 1018	Oct 66 - + NEUT PROB EMISS T.	
Spect Fiss n	Maxwl		CCP	Expt	-	ENGL SNP5 523 (0/67)	
					Jour SNP 5 523	Oct 67 . ENGL OF YF 5 737	

92 Uranium 235

Quantity	Energy (ev) Min	Max	Lab	Type	Documentation Ref Vol Page	Date	Author, Comments	Data
Spect Fiss n	6.0+6	2.0+7	MHG	Expt	Abst ANS 10 555	Nov 67	King+ RECOIL SPEC REACT LEAKAGE SPEC	
Spect Fiss n	Maxwl		LAS	Expt	Jour NSE 31 191	Feb 68	Grundl+8 ACT DET CFD .8-16MEV RANGE	
					Abst DA 25 6704	May 65	- . REL U233,PU239.	
					Rept LAMS-2883	May 63	- +ACT DETECTOR 0.6-16MEV NEUTS	
Spect Fiss n	1.4+7		FEI	Expt	Jour IZV 32 653	Apr 68	Salnikov+ FISSN+OTHER NEUT SPECS,CRV	
					Jour BAS 32 600	69	.ENGLISH TRANSL OF IZV 32 653 4/68	
Spect Fiss n	Pile		CCP	Expt	Jour DOK 180 836	Jun 68	Nasyrov+ N-SPEC 0.6TO24.MEV CFD TH	
					Jour SPD 13 6 559	Dec 68	TRANSLATN.*	
Spect Fiss n	1.0+4	1.0+7	HEB	Theo	Priv NISSIMOV	69	Nissimov+MICROSC SIG CHECK BY N-SPEC	
Spect Fiss n	Pile		NIL	Expt	Prog INDC(PAK)-1 2	May 69	. TOF,E-SPEC OF PROMPT,TO BE DONE	
Spect Fiss n	Maxwl		IBJ	Expt	Conf 69Vienna 115	Jul 69	Blocki+PPR68.ANGDIST GRPH,TERN FISSN	
Spect Fiss n	Maxwl		KFI	Theo	Jour PL/B 30 311	Oct 69	Kluge+	
		+3			Conf 69Vienna 927	Jul 69	- .PPR9. CALC NEUTRON E+ANG SPECS	
	Maxwl				Conf JINR-D3893 96	May 68	- + NU(A)+AVG E,STATMOD CFD EXPT	
					Jour KFI 16 129	Apr 68	- +.AVERG N-ENERGIES CFD EXPT	
				ExTh	Jour KFI 14 359	Dec 66	- .GRAPH E-DSTRB AT 5AS CFD TH	
Spect Fiss n	-		SCU	Theo	Rept ICD-7 SUPPL 1	70	Saveliev.ANAL OF N-SPEC CALC,CURVES	
					Rept INDC(CCP)-18	Dec 71	. ENGL OF ICD-7 SUPPL 1	
Spect Fiss n	Pile		BNW	Revw	Rept STI/DOC/10-107	May 70	Dahl+ WATT,GRUNDL,CRANBERG SPECS CFD	
Spect Fiss n	Maxwl		NIR	Expt	Jour AE 29 95	Aug 70	Kroshkin+ AVG FISSN NEUT E +SPEC CRV	
					Jour SJA 29 790	Aug 70	. ENGL OF AE 29 95	
Spect Fiss n	Maxwl		KFI	Theo	Rept KFKI-71-35	71	Jeki+ CALC E+ANGDIST.CF LIT.GRPH	
				Expt	Conf 70Helsinki 2 87	Jun 70	- +PPR4. NEUT SPEC GRAPH CFD TH	
Spect Fiss n		5.0+6	FEI	Theo	Rept FEI-242	May 71	Prokhorova+ AVG KE(NEUT-E),GRAPH	
Spect Fiss n	3.5+4	4.0+5	ANL	Expt	Jour NSE 44 439	Jun 71	Smith. 2INCIDENT NEUT ES,REL MEAST	
	4.0+5	1.6+6			Prog ANL-7910 18	Jan 72	- . CURVES	
	1.0+5	4.5+5			Prog INDC-6 18	Jun 70	- + MAXWELLIAN E GIVEN, TB CONT'D	
Spect Fiss n	None		CRC	Revw	Rept STI/DOC/10-127	Jun 71	Boyd.PG7.REVIEW ,FISS NEUTS,TBL,GRPH	
Spect Fiss n	Maxwl		MHG	Expt	Abst DA/B 31 7332	Jun 71	Sherwood.SPECT FROM 6-20MEV.	
Spect Fiss n	None		UJV	Revw	Rept STI/DOC/10-127	Jun 71	Kadlec.PG55.E PROPERTY+EMISSION TIME	
Spect Fiss n	Maxwl	1.4+7	ANL	Revw	Conf 71Vienna 3	Aug 71	Smith. MEAN-E OF NEUTS,EXPTS CFD,TBL	
Spect Fiss n	1.4+7		FR	Expt	Prog EANDC(E)140U	Aug 71	Bertin+	
Spect Fiss n	Maxwl	1.4+7	IAE	Revw	Conf 71Vienna 19	Aug 71	Koster.MEAN-E OF NS,DIFFTL EXPTS,TBL	
Spect Fiss n	None		KFK	Revw	Conf 71Vienna 129	Aug 71	Kiefhaber+ DATA FILES SPECS CFD,TBLS	
Spect Fiss n	Maxwl		MOL	Expt	Conf 71Vienna 97	Aug 71	Fabry.SIG EXPTS CFD PU239 FISS-SPEC	
				Revw	Conf 70Helsinki 2 535	Jun 70	- +39. SPEC GRAPHS GIVEN	
Spect Fiss n	Maxwl		TEH	Expt	Prog INDC(SEC)-18	Aug 71	PG87.FISS-SPEC,THRESH-DET,TBD	
Spect Fiss n	Maxwl		WIN	Expt	Conf 71Vienna 33	Aug 71	Campbell+ MEAN-E+SPEC-SHAPE CFD,TBLS	
Spect Fiss n	9.5+5		AE	Expt	Rept AE-429	Sep 71	Almen+. .95-9 MEV. GRAPH. TEMP DEDCD	
Spect Fiss n	None		KFI	Theo	Rept KFKI-71-55	Oct 71	Kluge.PARS OF APPROX CFD EXPT.TBL	
	Maxwl				Conf 71Vienna 149	Aug 71	- .TABLE MAXW TEMP,MODELS CFD	
Spect Fiss n	1.0+5	1.0+7	KFK	Theo	Rept KFK-1271 3	Nov 71	Kiefhaber+(P.122-1) CALC 3 DATA SETS	
Spect Fiss n	7.0-1	5.0+4	ORL	Expt	Prog ORNL-4743 85	Dec 71	Dabbs+. CURVE	
Spect Fiss n	1.8+6		LAS	Expt	Prog USNDC-3 118	72	Auchampaugh+. VDG. CURVE	
Spect Fiss n	Maxwl		KFK	Expt	Jour JNE 26 165	Apr 72	Werle+ PROT RECOIL,HE003 SPECT.AV EN	+
					Jour NIM 99 295	Mar 72	- .FISSION SPECTR ONLY GRAPH	
					Conf 71Vienna 65	Aug 71	- + P-RECOIL CFD HE-DET,TBL,GRAPH	
	2.5-2				Data EXFOR20616.	Jun 76	85PTS.AVG.K.E.	
Spect Fiss n	4.0+5		GEL	Expt	Jour JPRC 33 33	Aug 72	Knitter+ WATT, MAXWELL DIST ANAL	+
					Jour NSE 50 108	Feb 73	Islam+ AVG PROMPT NEUT E = 2.06MEV.	
	4.0+5				Data EXFOR20385.	Oct 74	92PTS.AVG.K.E.	
Spect Fiss n	1.5+6	2.3+6	GEL	Expt	Jour ZP 257 108	Dec 72	Knitter+ TOF,ANG DIST,MEAN FISS ES	+
					Conf 71Vienna 41	Aug 71	- + TOF,ANGDIST,TBL AVG E	
	1.5+6	2.3+6			Data EXFOR20394.	Oct 74	59PTS.AVG.K.E.	
Spect Fiss n	Maxwl		KJL	Theo	Rept KR-148	Jan 73	Skarsvag+ TBL. SPECT PROMPT NS.	
Spect Fiss n	None		LON	Eval	Jour JNE 27 591	Aug 73	Wood.WATT SPECTRA RE-FITTD TO DATA.	
Spect Fiss n	+5		BET	Expt	Rept WAPD-TM-1129	Dec 73	Green+. 0.8-10 MEV NEUTRONS.CURVES.	
Spect Fiss n	1.0+5	9.5+6	BIR	Revw	Jour RPP 37 951	74	Beynon+ COMPAR N-SPEC+MEAN MAXWELL-E	
Spect Fiss n	1.5+5	1.5+6	LAS	Expt	Prog USNDC-11 155	Jun 74	Evans+ TBL,GRPHS.	
Spect Fiss n	1.3+6	2.3+6	RAM	Expt	Conf 74Dacca 33	Nov 74	Islam. E-SPEC AT 1.5MEV.AVG E AT 5ES	
Spect Fiss n	1.0+5		FEI	Expt	Jour AE 38 108	Feb 75	Aleksandrova+ N-SPEC,GRAPH	+
					Jour SJA 38 140	Aug 75	. ENGL OF AE 38 108	
	1.0+5				Data EXFOR40358.	May 77	N/SPEC(1.5-14MEV),65 PNTS(ARB UNIT)	
Spect Fiss n	Maxwl		HED	Eval	Conf 75Wash. 189	Mar 75	Mcelroy. GRPH.SAND-3	
Spect Fiss n	2.5-2		IAE	Eval	Conf 75Wash. 286	Mar 75	Lemmel. 3RD IAEA-EVAL BY LSQ FIT	
				Revw	Jour REA 7 43	Dec 69	Hanna+ N-SPECTRUM IN NU-BAR EXPTS	
Spect Fiss n	1.0+5	1.0+7	KFK	Expt	Rept KFK-2200 97	Apr 75	Bluhm+ EXPT METHODS DISCUSSED	
					Rept JUEL-1178 97	Apr 75	- + SAME AS KFK-2000	

92 Uranium 235

Quantity	Energy (ev) Min	Max	Lab	Type	Documentation Ref Vol Page	Date	Author, Comments	Data
Spect Fiss n	Maxwl		SEO	Theo Jour	KNS 7 119	Jun 75	Seung Gy Ro+ 1 - PARAM - FORM,EQUAT+GRPH	
Spect Fiss n	Fast		ANL	Eval Abst	ANS 22 671	Nov 75	Saphier+ 6 GPS DELAYED NEUT SPECT	
Spect Fiss n	4.0+4	1.4+7	FEI	Comp Rept	YK - 22 9	76	Seregina+ AVG E+MAXW T.VS NEUT - E,TBL	
	Maxwl			Rept	YK - 22 9	76	- + AVG E+MAXW T.VS NEUT - E,TBL	
Spect Fiss n	Maxwl		NBS	Eval Prog	ERDA - NDC - 3 159	May 76	Grundl+UPDATE 75 WASH CONF EVAL.	
				Conf	75Wash. 250	Mar 75	- +EVL.MEAS,E AV=1.97+ -.014 MEV	
Spect Fiss n	5.2+5		HAR	Expt Prog	NEANDC(E)172 8	Aug 76	Adams+ TOF SPECTRE FISSION	
				Prog	UKNDC(75)P71	Jul 75	- + TOF SPEC FISS N GRPH	
				Conf	75Kiev 5 153	May 75	- + N - SPEC(1 - 18MEV),GRPH+FORMULA	
Spect Fiss γ	Maxwl		HAR	Expt Rept	NRDC - 58	Feb 55	. ROUGH EXPT CF GAMBLE BUT MORE GS.	
Spect Fiss γ	Maxwl		ANL	Expt Rept	ANL - 5609 39	Nov 56	Huddleston+CS CURVSCFD GS P102MEV	
Spect Fiss γ	Maxwl		CCP	Expt Jour	ZET 32 256	Feb 57	ULT 250 KEV,MOSTLY FROM FF	
				Jour	JET 5 220	Sep 57	TRANSLATN.*	
Spect Fiss γ	Maxwl		CCP	Expt Jour	ZET 32 263	Feb 57	101 TO 590 KEV GS,8ES,PROBABLY FF	
				Jour	JET 5 184	Sep 57	TRANSLATN.*	
Spect Fiss γ	2.8+6	1.4+7	CCP	Expt Jour	ZET 34 331	Feb 58	PROMPT G SPECT,NO N ENERGY DEPEND	
				Jour	JET 7 231	Aug 58	TRANSLATN.*	
Spect Fiss γ	Maxwl		ORL	Expt Conf	58Geneva 15 366	Sep 58	Maienschein+.PPR670,CURVE,COMPTON	
Spect Fiss γ	Maxwl		ORL	Revw Conf	60Vienna 273	Oct 60	Peelle+.CURVE,EXPT DESCRIBED	
Spect Fiss γ	Pile		KFI	Expt Conf	61Wien 3 205	Oct 61	Szabo+ GAM - E VS TIME,CURVES	
Spect Fiss γ	Maxwl		CCP	Expt Jour	ZET 43 1644	Nov 62	Blinov. ANG ANISOTROPY OF GS,GRAPH	
				Jour	JET 16 1159	May 63	TRANSLATN.*	
Spect Fiss γ	Maxwl		MUN	Expt Jour	ZP 172 143	Jan 63	Hohmann.X - RAY - SPECT.	
Spect Fiss γ	Maxwl		MUN	Expt Jour	ADP 10 252	Mar 63	Rau.CURVES GIVEN	
Spect Fiss γ	Maxwl		LAS	Expt Jour	PR/B 133 714	Feb 64	Hoffman.GAM - FRAG ANGULAR CORRELATNS	
Spect Fiss γ	Maxwl		TRM	Expt Jour	PR/B 133 598	Feb 64	Kapoor+ GAM ANG DIST,LIGHT FRAGS	
Spect Fiss γ	Maxwl		FTI	Expt Jour	ZET 47 2064	Nov 64	G YLDS FOR 9AS,ANISOTROPY=(11+ - 1)PC	
				Jour	JET 20 1387	Jun 65	TRANSLATN.*	
Spect Fiss γ	1.2+1		GA	Expt Jour	NIM 31 125	Dec 64	Haddad+ LIQUID SCINTILL,FISS CHAMBER	
Spect Fiss γ	Maxwl		JUL	Expt Rept	JUEL - 331 - NP	65	Maier - Leibnitz+FRAGM AVG E+NMBR OF G	
				Conf	65Salzburg 2 143	Mar 65	- +	
Spect Fiss γ	Maxwl		JUL	Revw Rept	JUEL - 405 - NP	65	Maier - Leibnitz+FISS - G CORR.GAM.SPECT	
				Conf	65Salzburg 2 143	Mar 65	- +	
Spect Fiss γ	Maxwl		FTI	Expt Jour	AE 18 64	Jan 65	Petrov. ANG CORREL GS - FISFRAGMENTS	
				Jour	JNE 20 91	Jan 66	TRANSLATN.*	
				Jour	EAF 18 1 107	Jan 65	TRANSLATN.*	
				Jour	SJA 18 72	Jan 65	TRANSLATN.*	
Spect Fiss γ	+0	+3	CAI	Theo Jour	NP 62 667	Feb 65	Stavinsky+(N,GF)PROB ABOUT=(N,GAMMA)	
Spect Fiss γ	Maxwl		FTI	Expt Jour	YF 1 476	Mar 65	Petrov.GRAPH SPEC ANGL ANISOTROPY	
				Jour	SNP 1 338	Sep 65	TRANSLATN.*	
Spect Fiss γ	Maxwl		FTI	Expt Jour	AE 18 223	Mar 65	Valski+MOST GAMMAS WITHIN 0.5NANOSEC	
				Jour	EAF 18 3 37	65	. FRENCH TRANSL OF AE 18 223 3/65	
				Jour	SJA 18 279	65	.ENGLISH TRANSL OF AE 18 223 3/65	
				Jour	JNE 20 227	65	.ENGLISH TRANSL OF AE 18 223 3/65	
Spect Fiss γ	Maxwl		HAR	Expt Conf	65Salzburg 2 233	Mar 65	Tomlinson.P.62,G SPEC OF SB 128TO130	
Spect Fiss γ	Maxwl		KFI	Expt Conf	65Salzburg 2 163	Mar 65	Graff+,P.55,ANGULAR DISTRIBUTION	
				Jour	PL 3 343	Feb 63	Desi+ ANGULAR DISTRIBUTION	
Spect Fiss γ	Maxwl		ORL	Expt Conf	65Salzburg 2 143	Mar 65	Maier - Leibnitz+,P.54,GS VS FRAG.MASS	
Spect Fiss γ	Maxwl		FEI	Expt Prog	INDSWG - 126 35	66	Popeko.TABLE OF E - GAMMA AND INTENSTY	
Spect Fiss γ	Maxwl		CCP	Expt Jour	AE 20 342	Apr 66	Nefedov+TERNARY FISS CFD USUAL FISS	
Spect Fiss γ	Maxwl		NRD	Theo Jour	PR/B 139 56	Jul 65	Ferguson+ MODEL FOR FISS YLDS.	
				Jour	PR 150 1018	Oct 66	- +	
Spect Fiss γ	Maxwl		UI	Expt Jour	PR 157 1083	May 67	Wehring+ K XRAYS 12 - 20KEV COINC FISS	
				Jour	PR 145 963	May 66	.TIME + E SPECT X - RAYS TO 50KEV/FRAG	
				Jour	APL 7 161	Sep 65	.SUPERSEDED	
Spect Fiss γ	Maxwl		KFI	Expt Jour	KFI 15 333	Jun 67	Kluge+.ANGULAR DISTR OF FISS - GAMMAS	
Spect Fiss γ	Maxwl		PTN	Theo Jour	PR 159 980	Jul 67	Thomas+ CALC SUM GAM E AGREES EXPT	
Spect Fiss γ	Maxwl		CCP	Expt Jour	ZEP 6 898	Nov 67	Ivanov+,ANIS VS FRAG MASS AND KE	
Spect Fiss γ	None		LRL	Expt Jour	AF 36 287	Nov 67	John+. GAMMAS FROM FISSION SOURCE	
	Maxwl			Jour	PL/B 24 336	Apr 67	- + FISS PRODUCT X - RAY INTENSITIE	
Spect Fiss γ	Maxwl		FTI	Expt Conf	68Riga	Jan 68	Valskij+ ABST,G ANIS VS FRAG A AND E	
Spect Fiss γ	Maxwl		NIR	Expt Rept	NIIAR - P - 5	Oct 68	Ivanov+ ANISOTROPY OF GAMMAS, GRPH	
Spect Fiss γ	Pile		AUS	Expt Prog	EANDC(OR)86L	Jan 69	Sgarumpold+	
Spect Fiss γ	Maxwl		TRM	Expt Jour	PR 177 1776	Jan 69	Kapoor+ NAI - DET,K - X RAY SPECTRA,GRPH	
Spect Fiss γ	8.8+0		GEL	Expt Jour	NP/A 134 535	Sep 69	Weigmann+ LINAC,GE(LI) 297 - 1278HEVGS	+
				Conf	69Studsvik 687	Aug 69	- +GAM E+INTENS TBL,BELOW 1MEV	
	8.8+0			Data	EXFOR20135.004	Mar 73	19PTS.	
Spect Fiss γ	5.0+0	2.4+1	RPI	Expt Prog	RPI - 328 - 171 31	Sep 69	Reed+,LINAC+TOF,SPEC FOR P.79EV RES	

92 Uranium 235

Quantity	Energy (ev) Min	Max	Lab	Type	Documentation Ref Vol Page	Date	Author, Comments	Data
Spect Fiss γ	Maxwl		AE	Expt	Rept AE – 374	Oct 69	Higbie. .1 – .7 PS. INT(T). INT,E VS A	
Spect Fiss γ	Maxwl		CUA	Theo	Abst DA/B 30 2222	Nov 69	Rogers.	
Spect Fiss γ	None		ITK	Theo	Prog BARC – 474 54	70	Mukherji+ CALC TOTAL GAM – E OKS EXPT	
Spect Fiss γ	Maxwl		SCU	Theo	Rept ICD – 7 SUPPL 1	70	Saveliev.CALC SPEC CFD EXPT,GRAPH	
					Rept INDC(CCP) – 18	Dec 71	. ENGL OF ICD – 7 SUPPL 1	
Spect Fiss γ	Maxwl		TRM	Expt	Prog BARC – 501 19	70	Kataria+ KX – RAY COINC FRAG KIN – E.NDG	
Spect Fiss γ	1.4+7		KFI	Expt	Jour KFI 18 13	Feb 70	Jeki+ GAM – ANISOTROPY – COEFFICIENT GVN	
					Conf 69Vienna 561	Jul 69	– +PPR10. GAM – ANGDIST/FRAG – MOTION	
Spect Fiss γ	Maxwl		SAH	Theo	Jour PL/B 33 263	Oct 70	Sarkar+ ESYLDS AS FN FRAG MASS	
Spect Fiss γ	Maxwl		ORL	Expt	Jour PR/C 3 373	Jan 71	Peelle+,ABSOL GAM SPEC 0.01 – 10MEV	
					Jour NSE 40 485	Jun 70	.SUPERSEDED	
					Rept ORNL – 4457	Apr 70	.SUPERSEDED	
Spect Fiss γ	Pile		SRC	Expt	Jour JNE 25 1	Jan 71	Scobie+ BETA EN RELESE RATE REL U233	
Spect Fiss γ	Maxwl		JUL	Expt	Jour ZN/A 26 512	Mar 71	Labus+ YLDS+ANISOTROP VS G – EN,FRMASS	
					Prog EANDC(E)127U	Apr 70	– +,ANISO+YLD OF PROMPT G	
					Rept JUEL – 643 – FN	Feb 70	.YLD+ANISOTR AS FN OF FRAG MASS	
					Conf 69Vienna 545	Jul 69	Armbruster+PPR23.G ANISOT VS FP MASS	
Spect Fiss γ	Maxwl		AE	Expt	Rept AE – 417	Apr 71	Albinsson+.PRMPT GS VS FRGM AND EKIN	
Spect Fiss γ	None		COL	Expt	Prog NCSAC – 38 66	May 71	Derengowski+.ANAL TBC,NO DATA GIVEN	
Spect Fiss γ	None		CRC	Revw	Rept STI/DOC/10 – 127	Jun 71	Boyd.PG13.REVIEW,FISS GAMS ,TBL,GRPH	
Spect Fiss γ	Maxwl	3.5+1	DUB	Expt	Jour PL/B 35 507	Jul 71	Panteleev+G YIELD GIVES SIG(N,GF)	
Spect Fiss γ	2.5 – 2		SRC	Theo	Jour JNE 25 339	Aug 71	Scobie+ VAR.BETA EN REL RATE WTH TME	
Spect Fiss γ	Maxwl		LIN	Expt	Conf 72Kiev 1 190	Jan 72	Val'Skij+ ABST,NDG.G – POL+ANG ANISOTR	
Spect Fiss γ	– 1	+2	NYU	Expt	Abst DA/B 32 4793	Feb 72	Graves. EPITHERMAL NEUTS.	
Spect Fiss γ	1.0+0	1.0+2	LRL	Expt	Jour PRL 28 617	Mar 72	Browne+.GAMS PRECEDING ISOMERIC FISS	
Spect Fiss γ	Maxwl		ORL	Expt	Jour PR/C 6 1023	Sep 72	Pleasonton+.AVG NUMBER+E VS.FRAG A,E	
					Conf 73Rochestr 2 494	Aug 73	– + ABS, AVE GAM – E, NDG	
Spect Fiss γ	Maxwl		KFK	Expt	Priv WIETKAMP	73	Weitkamp. SPECTRA.PROMPT+DELAYED	
					Rept KFK – 1214	Jul 70	Matussek+ G – SPEC,GRPHS	
Spect Fiss γ	Maxwl		ATI	Expt	Jour NP/A 206 374	May 73	Schindler+ GE – LI,300 – 1300KEV.CFD CF	
Spect Fiss γ	Maxwl		SAC	Expt	Prog EANDC(E) – 157U2	May 73	Albinsson+	
Spect Fiss γ	Maxwl	3.7+1	BNL	Expt	Jour PR/C 8 781	Aug 73	Graves+. GE(LI).PROMPT+DELAYED FISSN	
Spect Fiss γ	Maxwl		ORL	Expt	Conf 73Rochestr 2 494	Aug 73	Pleasonton+ ABST,BELOW 5 NSECS,NDG	
					Prog USNDC – 7 170	Jun 73	– +. NO DATA GIVEN	
					Prog ORNL – 4844 109	Apr 73	– +. PROMPT GAMS. CURVES	
Spect Fiss γ	Maxwl		SAC	Revw	Conf 73Rochestr 2 117	Aug 73	Nifenecker+ G – YLD+AVG – E(FRAG),GRAPHS	
	2.0+0	4.5+1		Expt	Conf 73Rochestr 2 201	Aug 73	Frehaut+ MEAN EN OF PROMPT GAMS,GRAPH	
Spect Fiss γ	Maxwl		IRT	Expt	Jour PR/C 10 853	Aug 74	Sund+ TBL, GRPHS.	
					Jour PR/C 7 1173	Mar 73	Verbinski+ GAMS 0 – 10 NS AFTER FISS	
					Rept AD – 748643	Apr 72	Sund+ GE(LI) DET. ISOM GAMMAS	
	None				Conf 69Vienna 929	Jul 69	Verbinsky.PPR33. MEAN GAMM E+YLD GVN	
Spect Fiss γ	2.0+3		KFK	Expt	Prog NEANDC(E)161U	Aug 74	Matussek+ NP FR2 REAC.NDG. SC FILT.TBC	
Spect Fiss γ	Maxwl		SRC	Expt	Jour ANE 1 573	Nov 74	Alam+ BETA ENERGY REL AT SHORT TIME	
Spect Fiss γ	None		BRC	Revw	Conf 75Wash. 202	Mar 75	Michaudon. FISSION REVIEW.TH+EXPTS.	
Spect Fiss γ	Maxwl		LAS	Theo	Conf 75Wash. 193	Mar 75	Stamatelatos+GRPHS G SPECT,CINDER	
Spect Fiss γ	Maxwl		LIN	Expt	Conf 75Kiev 6 116	May 75	Popeko+ KX – RAY SPEC,GELI.GRAPH	
Spect Fiss γ	Maxwl		LIN	Expt	Jour YF 22 462	Sep 75	Teterev+ G – SPEC CFD U,PU,CF – FIS.GRPH	
					Conf 75Kiev 6 121	Jun 75	– + G – SPEC,YLD FISS GAMMAS,GRAPHS	
					Jour SNP 22 238	Sep 75	. ENGL OF YF 22 462	
Spect Fiss γ	2.0+0	5.8+1	BRC	Expt	Jour ASL 26 25	76	Trochon+ (N,GF) – INVESTIG,RESULTS GVN	
	2.0+0	7.5+1			Conf 73Munich 1 606	Aug 73	Frehaut+ CORRELATION TO NUBAR.NDG.	
Spect Fiss γ	Maxwl		IJE	Eval	Rept INDC(CCP) – 78	Jan 76	Konshin+ ALSO GRAPHS OF FITS,IN ENGL	
Spect Fiss γ	2.5 – 2		LAS	Eval	Prog LA – 6560 6	Nov 76	Foster+ TIME DEP SPECTRA, NDG	
Spect Fiss γ	2.0+0	2.1+1	DUB	Expt	Jour CZJB 26 1334	Dec 76	Dlouhy+ KX – RAY.(N,GF),G – SPC CALC,FIG	
Fiss Prod γ	Pile		CLI	Expt	Jour PR 71 573	May 47	Bernstein+ PERIODS,YIELDS.G – N IN D2O	
					Abst PR 71 140	Jan 47	.SUPERSEDED.(ABST. C5)	
Fiss Prod γ	Maxwl		LAS	Expt	Jour PR 83 990	Sep 51	Brolley+NO GS OR BS OBS BELOW .43SEC	
					Rept LA – 1188	Jan 51	.SUPERSEDED	
Fiss Prod γ	Pile		IPS	Expt	Jour AF 9 137	Jan 55	Thulin. KR AND XE ISOT. GAM E+INT	
					Jour AF 5 191	Aug 52	Bergstroem.DECAY OF KR AND XE ISTPS	
Fiss Prod γ	Slow		HAR	Expt	Jour BJA 6 444	Dec 55	Peirson+2CRYST.GAM RAY SPECTROMETER	
					Jour NKA 2 57	57	– + TRANSLATION.	
Fiss Prod γ	Pile		CIS	Expt	Jour EN 3 32	Feb 56	Germagnoli+	
Fiss Prod γ	Pile		CCP	Expt	Jour AE 2 278	Mar 57	Leipunsky.ABSORPTION,DECAY 1.5 – 17SEC	
					Jour JNE 6 170	Dec 57	TRANSLATN.*	
					Jour SJA 2 337	57	TRANSLATN.*	
Fiss Prod γ	Maxwl		ORL	Expt	Abst BAP 2 197	Apr 57	Love+ .28 – 5MEV GAMS 1.2 – 1500SEC	

92 Uranium 235

Quantity	Energy (ev) Min	Max	Lab	Type	Documentation Ref Vol Page	Date	Author, Comments	Data
Fiss Prod γ	Pile		CCP Expt	Jour	AE 3 334	Oct 57	Sakharov+.GAM POWER 1-1000HR AFTER F	
				Jour	SJA 3 1161	57	TRANSLATN.*	
Fiss Prod γ	Pile		GDT Theo	Rept	NARF-58-37T	Aug 58	Scoles.CALCULATED GAM SPEC TBLS+CRVS	
Fiss Prod γ	Maxwl		LAS Expt	Conf	58Geneva 15 331	Sep 58	Leachman.PPR665,CURVE	
Fiss Prod γ	None		DOD Theo	Rept	AFSWP-524	Mar 59	Dolan.GAMMA SPEC VS. TIME TBLS+CURVS	
Fiss Prod γ	None		NBS Expt	Rept	HP 1 427	Mar 59	Nelms+. BETA+GAM SPECT. VS. TIME	
Fiss Prod γ	Pile		MTR Expt	Jour	PR 115 185	Jul 59	Schuman+,BA141,141 LA141,142 G SPECT	
Fiss Prod γ	Maxwl		CCP Expt	Jour	AE 7 168	Aug 59	Petrov.FPG POWER 0.6S-11H AFTER FISS	
				Jour	SJA 7 675	Feb 61	TRANSLATN.*	
				Jour	JNEA 12 129	Jun 60	TRANSLATN.*	
Fiss Prod γ	Maxwl		NRD Expt	Rept	USNRDL-TR-359	Aug 59	Mackin+,SCINT,PHOTON DECAY RATES	
Fiss Prod γ	Maxwl		HAR Eval	Rept	AERE-R-3033	Sep 59	Macbean. GRAPH DECAY POWER VS. TIME	
				Rept	AERE-M-494	Sep 59	- .	
Fiss Prod γ	Maxwl		MIT Expt	Prog	MIT-905-26	Sep 59	Canty+,REL INTENSITY OF K-ALFA LINES	
Fiss Prod γ	Maxwl	1.4+7	FOA Expt	Jour	AF 16 293	Feb 60	Bjoernstedt.G-SPEC 0-5MEV.1H-100YR	
Fiss Prod γ	Maxwl		NRD Expt	Rept	USNRDL-TR-400	Feb 60	Zigman+,GAMMA SPECT+TOTAL ENERGY	
Fiss Prod γ	Pile		IPS Expt	Jour	AF 17 521	Jun 60	Alvaeger. E,HL FOR M4 IN XE135M	
				Jour	AF 12 319	Sep 57	- +. DECAY OF TE133M FROM FPRD	
Fiss Prod γ	Maxwl		ORL Expt	Conf	60Vienna 273	Oct 60	Peelle+.TABLE,EXPT DESCRIBED	
Fiss Prod γ	Maxwl		GEA Eval	Rept	TID-11552	Nov 60	Smith.GAMMA E RELEASE RATE VS. TIME	
				Rept	XDC-60-1-157	Dec 59	-.GAMMA SPEC+POWER VS. TIME	
				Rept	DC-59-10-135	Sep 59	Capo.SPECTRA VS. TIME AFTER SHUTDOWN	
Fiss Prod γ	Pile		IPS Expt	Jour	AF 20 209	Oct 61	Erman+. XE133 DECAY.G E+INT.BETA SPC	
Fiss Prod γ	Pile		KFI Expt	Conf	61Wien 3 205	Oct 61	Szabo+ GAM-E VS TIME,CURVES	
Fiss Prod γ	Maxwl		ORL Expt	Conf	61Wien 3 3	Oct 61	Maienschein.GRPH GAM-E(T AFTER FISS)	
				Conf	58Geneva 15 366	Sep 58	- +.PPR670,TBL OF GAMMA-ES	
Fiss Prod γ	Pile		LAS Expt	Jour	JIN 24 1301	62	Dropesky+ GS FROM SN-SB ISOBAR-PAIRS	
Fiss Prod γ	Maxwl		IPS Expt	Jour	AF 21 35	May 62	Uhler+.HL,GAM SPECS FOR SN,SB ISOTPS	
Fiss Prod γ	Maxwl		RED Eval	Rept	AD-415052	Jul 63	Perkins. CURVS BETA+GAMMA DECAY RATE	
Fiss Prod γ	Maxwl		TRM Expt	Jour	PR/B 133 598	Feb 64	Kapoor+ GAM ANG DIST OF FRAGS,GRAPHS	
Fiss Prod γ	Maxwl		MUN Expt	Jour	ZP 178 226	Mar 64	Hovestadt+ SR94.G=1.4MEV,BETA TO 2.1	
				Jour	ZP 176 226	Oct 63	Kienle+ BETAS+GAMMAS FROM TC 103-5	
Fiss Prod γ	Fiss		LAS Expt	Jour	PR/B 134 796	May 64	Fisher.GDIVA NS,GS TO6MEV,T=.2 TO45S	
Fiss Prod γ	+6		LAS Theo	Jour	PR/B 134 817	May 64	Griffin.FPROD SYSTMTCS FOR G SPECTRA	
	None			Rept	LA-2811	Dec 62	- . BETA,GAMMA DECAY CALC	
Fiss Prod γ	Maxwl		AUA Theo	Rept	AAEC/TM-252	Jun 64	Frost.FRAG BETA-ACTIVITY(TIME),GRPHS	
Fiss Prod γ	Pile		BEP Comp	Jour	KE 7 604	Aug 64	Albrecht.TOT ACTIVITY TABLES	
	Maxwl			Eval Jour	KE 6 390	Jan 63	- .TABLE,MANY REFS	
Fiss Prod γ	Maxwl		KFI Expt	Jour	KFI 13 177	Jun 65	Graff.ANGULAR DSTRB OF FISGAMMAS,TBL	
Fiss Prod γ	Pile		BET Expt	Jour	NSE 22 386	Jul 65	Klein+CD RATIO CFD FISSN XSECT	
Fiss Prod γ	Maxwl		FTI Expt	Jour	AE 19 186	Aug 65	Popeko+ YIELD OF DEL G IN 10-70 NSEC	+
				Jour	EAF 19 2 121	65	. FRENCH TRANSL OF AE 19 186 8/65	
				Jour	JNE 20 811	65	.ENGLISH TRANSL OF AE 19 186 8/65	
				Jour	SJA 19 1082	65	.ENGLISH TRANSL OF AE 19 186 8/65	
Fiss Prod γ	Maxwl		FOA Theo	Jour	AF 29 359	Dec 65	Loew+.VS TIME 2H-5DAYS.100KEV-3MEV	
	Maxwl	+6	Expt	Jour	AF 29 359	Dec 65	- +.VS TIME 2H-7DAYS.NAI. GRAPHS	
	Maxwl			Theo Jour	AF 13 85	Feb 58	- + FISS PROD ACTIVITY VS T. CURV	
Fiss Prod γ	Maxwl	1.4+7	NRD Theo	Rept	USNRDL-TR-1009	Dec 65	Turner+FISS SPEC NEUTS,GROSS F PROD	
Fiss Prod γ	Pile		BUC Expt	Rept	IFA-NR-24	Jan 66	Cojocaru+,GS BR-88 AND 86+87,TABLES	+
	Pile			Data	EXFOR30225.	Dec 72	GAMMA SPECTRA OF BR-86,87 AND BR-88	
Fiss Prod γ	Maxwl		NRD Expt	Rept	USNRDL-TR-934	Jan 66	Yamamoto.G-RAY SPEC FROM CS-137	
Fiss Prod γ	Pile		SGA Expt	Jour	AKE 11 167	Apr 66	Buba+ BURN-UP DET,NUCL FUEL,MTR-ELEM	
				Rept	SGAE-PH-18	65	- + EQUIVALENT.	
Fiss Prod γ	None		GA Expt	Jour	PR 146 824	Jun 66	Sund+.N SPECT,GS 50-700MUSEC,ABSOL.	
Fiss Prod γ	Maxwl		UI Expt	Jour	APL 7 161	Sep 65	Bridwell+.K X-RAYS AT FEW NANOSECOND	
				Abst	DA 26 7383	Jun 66	.THESIS ABS	
Fiss Prod γ	Maxwl		MIT Expt	Rept	MIT-905-68	Jul 66	Gordon+,LI-GE DET,1,5,9 D AFTER IRR	
Fiss Prod γ	Pile		UKW Expt	Conf	66Berkeley 323	Sep 66	Mossop+ FISS CH,ELECTRODES DISSOLVED	
Fiss Prod γ	Maxwl		GA Expt	Rept	GA-7348	Oct 66	Walton+ NAI DET,DELAYED GS,ES+YLDS	
	None			Rept	GA-6445	May 65	- . DELAYED GAMMAS	
Fiss Prod γ	Maxwl		CCP Expt	Jour	IZV 30 2040	Dec 66	Popeko+ DELAYD G SPEC+YIELD VS A-NO	
				Jour	BAS 30 2025	66	. ENGL OF IZV 30 2040	
Fiss Prod γ	Pile		IOW Expt	Jour	BAP 11 915	Dec 66	Tucker+TALBERT.GS FROM BR,KR,I,XE	
Fiss Prod γ	Maxwl		OKL Expt	Abst	DA/B 27 2074	Dec 66	Boggs. 16SPECT .5S-2H POST F,HI RSLN	
Fiss Prod γ	Maxwl		UI Expt	Jour	NSE 26 435	Dec 66	Kutcher+ SPEC FP BETAS VS DECAY TIME	
				Abst	DA/B 27 920	Sep 66	.SEE ALSO	
Fiss Prod γ	Maxwl		FTI Expt	Jour	YF 5 734	Apr 67	Valskij+ G ANISOTR ON RATIO FRAG MAS	+
				Jour	SNP 5 521	Oct 67	. ENGL OF YF 5 734	

92 Uranium 235

Quantity	Energy (ev) Min Max	Lab	Type	Documentation Ref Vol Page	Date	Author, Comments	Data
Fiss Prod γ	Maxwl	KJL Expt	Jour	NP/A 96 385	Apr 67	Skarsvag.GAMMA - FRAGMENT ANG CORREL.	
Fiss Prod γ	Maxwl	CCP Expt	Jour	YF 5 1192	Jun 67	Eismont+.CURV OF K - RADIATION	
			Jour	SNP 5 852	Dec 67	TRANSLATN.*	
Fiss Prod γ	Maxwl	JAP Expt	Jour	NST 4 372	Jul 67	OI+ GE - LI. G SPECT AT SHORT PERIOD	
			Jour	NST 3 200	May 66	Takayanagi+ GE - LI. G SPECT GIVEN	
Fiss Prod γ	+6	NRD Expt	Jour	NSE 29 432	Sep 67	Bunney+ GAM SPEC 15MIN - 72H AFTER IRR	
Fiss Prod γ	Maxwl	KJL Expt	Jour	AF 36 211	Nov 67	Hoffman+. SPECTRA FOR CE - 145,146,147	
Fiss Prod γ	-2	FTI Expt	Prog	YFI - 6 84	68	Val'Skij+ TABLES, TO BE PUBL IN YF	
			Rept	INDC - 260E	69	. ENGL OF YFI - 6 84	
Fiss Prod γ	2.5 - 2	RI Expt	Prog	YFI - 6 100	68	Davydov+. SUBMITTED TO YF	
			Rept	INDC - 260E	69	. ENGL OF YFI - 6 100	
Fiss Prod γ	Maxwl	FTI Expt	Conf	68Riga	Jan 68	Popeko+ ABST,70 - 700 KEV,30 - 120 NSDEL	
Fiss Prod γ	Maxwl	SAC Expt	Jour	JPRC 29 1 154	Jan 68	Nifenecker+ PRELIMINARY RESULTS	
			Conf	69Vienna 951	Jul 69	- +PPR79.X - RAY EXPT,YLD(Z,A)	
Fiss Prod γ	None	COR Expt	Abst	DA/B 28 3728	Mar 68	Osias.COMPUTERISED EVAL COMPLEX SPEC	
Fiss Prod γ	Maxwl	AAA Comp	Jour	JNE 22 231	Apr 68	DE TOURREIL.FPG POWER 1S - 3D AFTER F	
Fiss Prod γ	Maxwl	HAR Expt	Rept	AERE - R - 5741	Apr 68	Bullock. G - SPECTS OF AG - 112,CS - 138.	
Fiss Prod γ	Maxwl	IPS Expt	Jour	AF 37 1	Jun 68	Holm.ISOL.E + INT XE137 DECAY GS.LEVLS	
	0.0+0 1.0+0		Jour	AF 34 433	Nov 67	- . TABLE+GRAPH OF RB - 87 SPECTRUM	
			Jour	AF 34 477	Nov 67	- +. TBL+GRPH. XE139 FROM FISSION	
	Maxwl		Jour	AF 34 413	Nov 67	Borg+.CS140,XE140,KR91,RB91 HL.	
	Pile		Jour	AF 15 387	May 59	Holm+.E+INT OF I133,134 DECAY GAMMAS	
			Jour	AF 13 177	Mar 58	Ryde+.E+INT FOR GAMMAS IN LA142 DEC.	
Fiss Prod γ	Maxwl	CCP Expt	Jour	YF 8 50	Jul 68	Ivanov+ANISOT(FRAG - E,MASS RAT),GRPHS	
			Jour	SNP 8 29	Jan 69	TRANSLATN.*	
Fiss Prod γ	Maxwl	IPS Expt	Jour	AF 37 203	Aug 68	Berg+.E+INT GS FR TE134 AND I134 DEC	
			Jour	AF 37 213	Aug 68	- +.E+INT GS FR DEC OF TE133 ISOM	
Fiss Prod γ	Maxwl	AE Expt	Rept	AE - 374	69	Higbie. PRELIMINARY DATA	
Fiss Prod γ	Pile	UJV Expt	Rept	UJV - 2164	69	Kristak+ BURN - UP,FISS - PROD'S GAM E+HL	
Fiss Prod γ	Maxwl	TRM Expt	Jour	PR 177 1776	Jan 69	Kapoor+ K - X RAY YLD OF FRAGS,GRAPHS	
	Pile		Jour	PR/C 4 2165	Dec 71	- +.SI(LI) DET. K X - RAY SPECTRA	
Fiss Prod γ	+6	GA Expt	Jour	PR 178 1894	Feb 69	Walton+ LINAC,NAI DET,T=2 - 80 MUSEC	
Fiss Prod γ	Maxwl	ALD Expt	Jour	JNE 23 73	Mar 69	Mcnair+ BETA POWER 10S - 6D AFTER FISS	
Fiss Prod γ	Pile	CCP Expt	Jour	AE 26 380	Apr 69	Voinov+ LONG LIVING GAM - SPECS GVN	
			Jour	EAF 26 4 87	Apr 69	TRANSLATN.*	
Fiss Prod γ	Maxwl	FTI Expt	Prog	YFI - 7 30	Apr 69	Popeko+ GAM YLD+E+HL VS FRAG A,TABLE	
			Rept	INDC(CCP) - 7U33	Feb 70	TRANSLATN.*	
Fiss Prod γ	Maxwl	IPS Expt	Jour	AF 39 7	May 69	Fransson.CONV RTIOS XE133M.NEW G FND	
Fiss Prod γ	Maxwl	HAR Expt	Conf	69Vienna 637	Jul 69	Large+PPR59. E - GAM=MEV,HLS=MIN TO H	
Fiss Prod γ	Maxwl	HFA Expt	Conf	69Vienna 947	Jul 69	Notea+PPR36. GAM SPECS FOR CHAIN YLD	
Fiss Prod γ	Maxwl	KFK Expt	Rept	KFK - 1013	Jul 69	Horsch+ SPEC,39 GS ASSIGNED TO FRAG	
			Conf	69Vienna 527	Jul 69	- +PPR44. E VS A,SHORT HLS	
Fiss Prod γ	Maxwl	LRL Expt	Conf	69Vienna 535	Jul 69	John+DISCUSSN.GAM E+HL+YLD VS FRAG A	
			Rept	UCRL - 70298	Feb 67	- +,K X - RAY SYSTEMATICS TBP PRL	
			Rept	UCRL - 70045	Aug 66	- + CRYST SPEC INTENSITIES+TIME	
Fiss Prod γ	Maxwl	TRM Expt	Conf	69Vienna 741	Jul 69	Dange+PPR97.GE - LI SPEC VS COOLING - T	
			Rept	BARC/I - 79 46	70	. SAME SPECTRA	
Fiss Prod γ	2.5 - 2	FTI Expt	Conf	69Montreal 680	Aug 69	Kaminker+ISOMERIC G - SPEC FROM FRAGS	
Fiss Prod γ	-	UJV Expt	Rept	UJV - 2241	Aug 69	Krtil+ CHEM EXTRACTN 137 - CS,GAM - SPEC	
Fiss Prod γ	Pile	UPP Expt	Conf	69Studsvik 141	Aug 69	Baecklin+ GAM+ELECTR SPECS VS CAPTUR	
Fiss Prod γ	Maxwl	THA Theo	Jour	ATP 15 340	Oct 69	Dreisvogt. GS SPEC CALC CFD EXPT	
Fiss Prod γ	Maxwl	LAS Expt	Jour	PR 187 1506	Nov 69	Berick+,SCINT,SPECTRA VS. TIME	
			Conf	69Vienna 647	Jul 69	East+PPR109. DELAYED GAMSPEC,+REVW	
Fiss Prod γ	Maxwl	MIT Expt	Jour	CJP 47 2371	Nov 69	Nakahara+,GE(LI),GROSS FFRAG,VS.TIME	
Fiss Prod γ	-	WIN Eval	Jour	JNE 23 517	Nov 69	JAMES MEAN E 7.2+ - 1.3MEV/FISS	
Fiss Prod γ	2.5 - 2	IAE Revw	Jour	REA 7 4 3	Dec 69	Hanna+ DELAYD GAMMAS IN NU - BAR EXPTS	
Fiss Prod γ	5.0+6 1.5+7	LOK Expt	Prog	AD - 698558	Dec 69	Imhof+,VDG,GE(LI),CURVS	
Fiss Prod γ	Maxwl	UI Expt	Jour	PR 188 1909	Dec 69	Bohn+,K X - RAY SPEC VS.FRAG MASS,E	
			Abst	DA/B 29 2464	Jan 69	- .SPEC.YLDS AS FN FRAG.MASS AND	
			Jour	APL 12 199	Mar 68	.SUPERSEDED	
Fiss Prod γ	Pile	AE Expt	Rept	AE - 381	Jan 70	Malmskog+.E+INT SR91 GS AFTR RB DCAY	
Fiss Prod γ	Maxwl	NRD Expt	Jour	NSE 39 81	Jan 70	Bunney+,GAM SPEC 15MIN - 72H AFTER IRR	
Fiss Prod γ	1.4+7	KFI Expt	Jour	KFI 18 13	Feb 70	Jeki+ GAM - ANISOTROPY - COEFFICIENT GVN	
			Conf	69Vienna 561	Jul 69	- +PPR10. GAM - ANGDIST/FRAG - MOTION	
Fiss Prod γ	Maxwl	FOA Expt	Rept	FOA4 - 4420 28	Apr 70	De Geer. GE(LI) DETECTOR.	
Fiss Prod γ	Pile	AE Expt	Rept	AE - 391	May 70	Berg+. E+INT I134 GS. HL FOR 3 LVLS	
			Rept	AE - 394	May 70	- +. E+INT LA141 GS. LVLS, HLS	
Fiss Prod γ	Pile	TRM Expt	Jour	NP/A 154 458	Oct 70	Kataria+ SI(LI).SPECTR TO 1MUSEC.	

92 Uranium 235

Quantity	Energy (ev) Min Max	Lab	Type	Documentation Ref Vol Page	Date	Author, Comments	Data
Fiss Prod γ	Pile	FRS ExTh	Jour	HPA 43 693	Nov 70	Winiger+ SCINT SPECT	
Fiss Prod γ	Maxwl	FTI Expt	Jour	YF 12 913	Nov 70	Valskij+ ANG-ANISOTR OF FRAG'S GAMMA	
			Jour	SNP 12 497	May 71	TRANSLATN.*	
Fiss Prod γ	Maxwl 1.5+7	LOK Expt	Prog	NCSAC-33 123	Dec 70	Imhof+,(GE(LI) DET,NO DATA GIVEN	
Fiss Prod γ	Maxwl	SAH Theo	Conf	70Madurai 2 619	Dec 70	Sarkar+ NUMBER+E OF GAMS VS A,GRAPHS	
Fiss Prod γ	-	SRC Expt	Jour	JNE 24 493	Dec 70	Macmahon+ EN FROM B-RAD	
Fiss Prod γ	Pile	GRE Expt	Jour	JRC 7 309	71	Blachot+ GE-LI.G-SPEC GRPH,G-ES TABL	
Fiss Prod γ	Pile	HLT Expt	Jour	ZP 242 107	Mar 71	Lundan.DECAY OF I-ISOM TO XE	
			Conf	69Vienna 936	Jul 69	- +PPR41. GAM SPECS+HLS OF BR+I	
Fiss Prod γ	Pile	KFK Expt	Rept	KFK-EXT-4 33	Mar 71	Wolff. GE-LI SPEC FOR 6 DECAY TIMES	
Fiss Prod γ	Maxwl	TRM Expt	Rept	STI/DOC/10-125	Apr 71	Ramanna.PG41.X-RAY YLD VS A+E,T VS Z	
Fiss Prod γ	None	UJV Revw	Rept	STI/DOC/10-127	Jun 71	Kadlec.PG56.TOTAL E RELEASE VS TIME	
Fiss Prod γ	None	FAR Expt	Jour	JNE 25 285	Jul 71	Costa+ BETA,GAMMA ACT,TH CFD EXPT.	
Fiss Prod γ	Maxwl	AE Expt	Jour	PS 3 113	Aug 71	Albinsson. HL+INT 3 G-GRPS 7.5-60PS	
			Prog	EANDC(OR)99L33	Aug 70	- . (CTH) SPEC VS TIME + MASS	
			Rept	AE-398	Jun 70	- + YLD VS FRAG MASS .01-1 NS	
			Conf	69Vienna 930	Jul 69	- +PPR40.GAM YLD(MASS,TIME,E)	
Fiss Prod γ	Maxwl	FTI Expt	Jour	YF 14 507	Sep 71	Valsky+ SCINT,POLRZ OF FRAG-GS,GRPHS	
			Jour	SNP 14 284	Mar 72	* ENGL OF YF 14 507	
Fiss Prod γ	1.9+6	LOK Expt	Prog	NCSAC-42 142	Nov 71	Imhof+. 4MIN TO 24HR. ANAL TBC. NDG	
Fiss Prod γ	Maxwl	ANL Expt	Jour	NP/A 177 337	Dec 71	Reisdorf+SIMULT MEAS K.E. ANG G-SPEC	
Fiss Prod γ	None	RI Expt	Prog	YFI-12 102	72	Korostylev+ ABST,VS FRAG MASS,NDG	
			Prog	INDC(CCP)-30	Sep 72	.PAGE 88,ENGLISH OF YFI-12 102	
Fiss Prod γ	Maxwl	UI Expt	Abst	DA/B 33 376	Jul 72	Lerche. K X-RAY YLDS VS. TIME	
Fiss Prod γ	Maxwl	JUL Expt	Rept	JUEL-879N	Aug 72	Grueter. G+X RAYS,SPEC,ISOMERS	
			Jour	PL/B 33 474	Dec 70	Gruter+ MUS ISOM G EMITTERS IDENTIFD	
			Jour	NP/A 141 289	Jan 71	Eidens+ DECAY STUDY SHORT LIVED F.P.	
Fiss Prod γ	-2 +0	SAC ExTh	Jour	JPRC 33 32	Aug 72	Albinson.	
Fiss Prod γ	Maxwl	BEP Theo	Jour	KE 15 311	Sep 72	Krueger. SPEC+TOT E-EMISS VS DECAY-T	
Fiss Prod γ	Maxwl	KFK Expt	Priv	WIETKAMP	73	Weitkamp. DELAYED SPECTS OF F PRODS	
			Rept	KFK-1214	Jul 70	Matussek+ G-SPEC OF FPROD, GRPHS	
		TRM Theo	Jour	BARC-706 149	73	Iyer+ COMPUTER-PROGR FOR G-SPEC, NDG	
Fiss Prod γ	Pile	CRC Eval	Conf	73Paris 1 459	Mar 73	Walker.SPECS 5-20H AFTER IRRADIATION	
Fiss Prod γ	Pile	KFK Expt	Rept	KFK-1770	Apr 73	Khan+ ES OF GAM+CONVERSION ELECTRONS	
Fiss Prod γ	Maxwl	IAK Expt	Jour	NP/A 205 488	May 73	Khan+ GAMMAS+CONV ELECTRONS.TBL VS A	
Fiss Prod γ	Maxwl	ITK Theo	Jour	AUJ 26 279	Jun 73	Mukherji+ MEAN-E VS FRAG-MASS,GRAPH	
	None		Prog	BARC-474 54	70	- + CALC GAM-E/FRAG CFD EXPT	
Fiss Prod γ	Pile	JUL Expt	Rept	JUEL-977RE 81	Jul 73	Rehm.G-SPEC OF FISS-GASES,0-2400KEV	
Fiss Prod γ	Maxwl	BNL Expt	Jour	PR/C 8 781	Aug 73	Graves+GE(LI),DELAYED FISS GAMMAS	
			Conf	70Helsinki 1 377	Jun 70	Chrien.42. DELAYED GAMMA SPEC GIVEN	
			Rept	IAEA-124 303	Feb 70	- .G-SPEC(4.2-4.5MEV)CA MS DELAY	
Fiss Prod γ	Maxwl	MIT Theo	Conf	73Rochestr 2 482	Aug 73	Yarman.ABST,CALC F-PROD GAM DECAY	
Fiss Prod γ	None	MIP Expt	Jour	EN 12 691	Dec 73	Brasca+	
Fiss Prod γ	Maxwl +6	CAD Revw	Conf	IAEA-169 2 115	74	Lott.AFTERHEAT,EVALS+EXPTS CFD,TBLS	
Fiss Prod γ	Pile	GRE Expt	Jour	RCA 21 8	74	Schussler+ SR-93, LVL-SCH OF Y-93	
Fiss Prod γ	Pile	MIT Expt	Jour	RCA 21 1	74	Erten+ SB-130,LVL-SCH OF TE-130	
Fiss Prod γ	Maxwl	CCP Expt	Jour	AE 36 66	Jan 74	Jurova+ GE-LI,CFD U238,GRAPH	
			Jour	SJA 36 75	Jul 74	. ENGLISH OF AE 36	
Fiss Prod γ	Maxwl	MNZExpt	Jour	ZP 266 397	Feb 74	Grimm+.29 G-ES,DECAY-SCH GIVEN,SR 95	
			Jour	ZP 259 67	Mar 73	- + DECAY OF SR-94	
	Pile		Jour	ZP 257 424	Dec 72	Herzog+ G-SPEC + DECAY-SCH OF SR-93	
Fiss Prod γ	Fast	BEP Theo	Jour	KE 17 109	Apr 74	Pulz+ TOT G-EMISSION VS DECAY-TIME	
Fiss Prod γ	Maxwl	AE Expt	Jour	NP/A 241 237	Apr 75	Kawase+MASS SEP.AG-119 DECAY SPEC	
			Jour	NP/A 224 13	May 74	Mcdonald+MASS SEP.CD-119G,M DECAYS	
			Conf	73Munich 227	Aug 73	Fogelberg+PRELIM REPT.AG-119 DECAY	
Fiss Prod γ	Maxwl	SAH Theo	Jour	PL/B 56 325	May 75	Datta.ENERGY PARTITION IN FISSION.	
Fiss Prod γ	Maxwl	BRK Expt	Jour	NP/A 250 1	Sep 75	NUH+ G-RAYSPECT OF BR85 FP,TBL E+INT	
	Pile		Jour	PL/B 53 435	Jan 75	NUH+ G-RAY FROM FP I137	
Fiss Prod γ	Pile	JUL Expt	Jour	ZP/A 275 289	Dec 75	Khan+ CONVERSION ELECTRONS OF MO+ZR	
Fiss Prod γ	Maxwl	GHT Eval	Jour	NIM 134 299	76	Thierens+ FOR MASS YLD DETERM TBL	
Fiss Prod γ	Maxwl	AE Expt	Jour	ZP 276 381	Feb 76	Fogelberg+ A=121,123,125 ISOBARS BAM	
Fiss Prod γ	Fast	KAL Eval	Conf	76Bombay 550	Mar 76	Murthy+ E/FIS.SEC VS COOL TIME.GRAPH	
Fiss Prod γ	Maxwl	KTO Expt	Jour	NST 13 141	Mar 76	Kiso+.GAMMA SPECTRA OF MO-101,102	
Fiss Prod γ	Maxwl	GRE Expt	Conf	76Corsica 503	May 76	Monnard+ CS,BA,LA-144 SPECTRA.	
Fiss Prod γ	Maxwl Fiss	ORL Expt	Prog	ERDA-NDC-3 190	May 76	Dickens+SPEC MEAS.TOT YLDS.CFD ENDF	
Fiss Prod γ	Pile	MNZExpt	Prog	NEANDC(E)172 5	Jul 76	Ahrens+P.59. A=96-112,ES,HL	
Fiss Prod γ	Maxwl	AE Expt	Jour	NP/A 267 317	Aug 76	Fogelberg+MASS SEP.AG-117 DECAY SPEC	

92 Uranium 235

Quantity	Energy (ev) Min	Max	Lab	Type	Documentation Ref Vol Page	Date	Author, Comments	Data
Fiss Prod γ	Maxwl		MNZ Expt	Jour	PL/B 65 231	Nov 76	Kratz+ SPECTS OF 6 MASSES.CFD DEL NS	
				Jour	NP/A 250 13	Sep 75	− + RADIOACTIVITY OF AS80−86 FP	
Fiss Prod γ	Maxwl		SWR Expt	Jour	NIM 139 239	Dec 76	Rudstam+ SURVEY OF OSIRIS PROGRAMME	
Fiss Prod γ	Pile		MNZ Expt	Jour	RCA 23 2 98	77	Skarnemark+ PR147,148,149,150	
Fiss Prod β	Maxwl		MUN Expt	Jour	ZP 178 226	Mar 64	Hovestadt+ SR−94. BETA TO 2−1.	
				Jour	ZP 176 226	Oct 63	Kienle+ TC−103−105. BETAS.	
				Jour	ZP 170 274	Nov 62	Armbruster+ BETAS/FISS+E(BETA)CFD TH	
Fiss Prod β	Maxwl		AAA Expt	Jour	JNE 22 231	Apr 68	De Tourrell.FPB POWER 15−3D AFTER F	
Fiss Prod β	Fast		KAL Eval	Conf	76Bombay 550	Mar 76	Murthy+ BETA+GAM−E RELEAS(TIME).GRPH	
Fiss Prod β	Maxwl		GRE Expt	Conf	76Corsica 503	May 76	Monnard+ CS,BA,LA−144 SPECTRA.	
Fiss Prod β	Maxwl		MNZ Expt	Conf	76Corsica 304	May 76	Kratz+ BETAS FROM DEL N PRECURSORS.	
Fiss Prod β	Maxwl Fiss		ORL Expt	Prog	ERDA−NDC−3 190	May 76	Dickens+SPEC MEAS.TOT YLDS.CFD ENDF	
Fiss Prod β	Maxwl		JUL Expt	Rept	JUEL−1376	Dec 76	Sadler. ZR96,98 GAM IN Y B−DECAY	
				Jour	NP/A 252 365	Nov 75	− + Y−96 BETA DECAY. ZR−96 LVLS	
Fiss Yield	Maxwl		COL Expt	Jour	PR 59 52	Jan 41	Anderson+ FISS PC FOR RADIOACTSERIES	
Fiss Yield	None		USA Comp	Jour	RMP 18 513	46	Siegel. FISSION YIELDS FOR MANY FRAG	
Fiss Yield	Maxwl		CRC Expt	Jour	NAT 158 163	Aug 46	Grummitt+.GRAPH OF RADIOCHEM DATA	
Fiss Yield	None		LAS Expt	Jour	PR 71 327	Mar 47	Farwell+ FREQUENLY,MAX RANGE ALPHAS.	
Fiss Yield	Maxwl		PCF Expt	Jour	JPR 8 165	Jul 47	Tsien San Tsiang+ STUDY OF FRAGS	
				Jour	JPR 8 200	Jul 47	− +	
				Jour	PR 71 382	Mar 47	− + EVIDENCE TERNARY F	
Fiss Yield	Maxwl		ANL Expt	Jour	PR 75 1339	May 49	Marshall.EMULSION,TERNARY= 1/230	
Fiss Yield	Maxwl		COP Expt	Jour	PR 76 279	Jul 49	Koch+ MASS−SPECT,REL YLDS KR85,87,88	
Fiss Yield	None		KAP Theo	Jour	PR 76 136	Jul 49	Kingdon. (A−Z)/Z PLOT CFD CHG DIST.	
Fiss Yield	−		PCF Revw	Jour	PR 76 870	Sep 49	Chastel+ REFS TO FRENCH WORK,3−4FISS	
Fiss Yield	Pile		CHI Expt	Jour	PR 79 271	50	Inghram+MASS.SPECT.CURVE A=140TO160	
Fiss Yield	Pile		MIT Expt	Abst	PR 77 755	Mar 50	Coryell+YIELDS OF 95,97ZR CHEN.SEPAR	
Fiss Yield	Maxwl		MCM Expt	Jour	PR 78 129	Apr 50	Mcnamara+MASS SPECT HL+YIELD OF133XE	
Fiss Yield	Maxwl		ANL Expt	Jour	PR 78 624	Jun 50	Steinberg+ ZR93,EXISTENCE+APPROX H−L	
Fiss Yield	Maxwl		LAS Expt	Jour	PR 78 533	Jun 50	Rosen+ SYMMETRIC 3−FISS.3COINC IONCH	
Fiss Yield	Pile		ANL Expt	Jour	PR 79 271	Jul 50	Hess+ MASS SPEC MASS RANGE 143−160	
Fiss Yield	Maxwl		YAM Theo	Jour	PR 79 740	Aug 50	YASAKI CONCENTRIC−SPH MOD FOR ASSYM	
Fiss Yield	Pile		CRC Expt	Jour	PR 80 181	Oct 50	Allen+ E SPECT,FAST ALPHAS+FISSFRAGS	
Fiss Yield	Maxwl		CRC Expt	Rept	CRC−470	Mar 51	Grummitt+,RADIOCHEM,YLDS 21FRAGS	
Fiss Yield	Pile		CRC Expt	Jour	PR 82 392	May 51	Allen+ NON TERNARY,SHORT−RANGE DISTR	
				Jour	PR 76 181	Jul 49	.SUPERSEDED	
Fiss Yield	None		ANL Expt	Rept	ANL−4680 50	Aug 51	Steinberg+ZR+MO ISOTOPES YLDS.M.SPEC	
Fiss Yield	Maxwl		ANL Expt	Rept	ANL−4927	52	Engelkemeir+ YIELD SB127,I131,BA140	
Fiss Yield	Maxwl		LAS Expt	Jour	PR 85 570	Feb 52	Wahl+RELATIONSHIP+YLD FOR A=115CHAIN	
Fiss Yield	Maxwl		ANL Expt	Rept	ANL−4927	Nov 52	Seiler+ 9MASSES A=109 TO 156	
Fiss Yield	Maxwl		CRC Expt	Jour	CJC 31 242	53	Brown+ INDEP YIELD OF XE135.	
Fiss Yield	Pile		ANL Expt	Jour	PR 89 194	Jan 53	Stehney+ RADIOCHEM BR87 YLD=3.1PC	
Fiss Yield	Pile		CRC Expt	Jour	CJC 31 120	Feb 53	Bartholomew+YLD OF 131I/YLD OF 140BA	
Fiss Yield	Maxwl		LAS Expt	Jour	PR 89 570	Feb 53	Sugarman.YLD OF77GE,AS,73GE,AS.	
Fiss Yield	Pile		HAR Expt	Rept	AERE−C/R−1180	May 53	Hardwick. RU−106,RU−103 REL YLDS	
Fiss Yield	Maxwl		MCM Expt	Jour	CJP 31 419	May 53	Wiles+ MASS SPEC. SR88,90+RB+CS133−7	+
Fiss Yield	Maxwl		HAR Expt	Jour	PM 44 900	Aug 53	Cuninghame.YIELD AS78 AS79 REL BA140	
Fiss Yield	Maxwl		BNL Expt	Jour	PR 91 1458	Sep 53	Katcoff+ XE133 YLD=6.62+−0.15PC	
				Rept	BNL−1652	53	− + ABSOL RADIOCHEM KR85+XE133	
Fiss Yield	Fiss		LAS Expt	Abst	PR 92 1091	Nov 53	Terrell+YIELD OF 99MO (THR)OKS OTHRS	
Fiss Yield	Maxwl		ANL Expt	Jour	PR 92 1473	Dec 53	Reed+ SR89+91 ZR97 MO99 BA139+140	
Fiss Yield	Maxwl		NOR Expt	Jour	ZEC 58 623	Oct 54	Wiles.PRIMARY FISS YIELD FINE STRUCT	
Fiss Yield	Maxwl		NRD Expt	Jour	PR 96 102	Oct 54	Freiling+ GD159 AND TB161 YIELDS	
Fiss Yield	Maxwl		OSL Theo	Jour	ZEC 58 620	Oct 54	Pappas.PREDICTED FINE STRUCT OKS XPT	
Fiss Yield	Maxwl		CRC Expt	Jour	CJC 32 1017	Nov 54	Yaffe+ (6.32+−0.24)PC BA140 NSA9 467	
Fiss Yield	Maxwl		MIT Expt	Jour	PR 96 696	Nov 54	Wiles+ FINE STRUCT FOR MASS 99−106	
Fiss Yield	Pile		HAR Theo	Rept	AERE−C/R−1715	55	Lock. CUM YIELDS 3,6,9,12 MONTHS	
Fiss Yield	Maxwl		MCM Expt	Jour	CJC 33 830	May 55	Melaika+ MASS SPEC ND+SM REL YLDS	
Fiss Yield	Maxwl		ANL Expt	Jour	PR 98 1327	Jun 55	Reed.SR−90,Y−91 YLD REL SR−89,MO−99	
				Rept	ANL−5306	Mar 54	.SUPERSEDED	
Fiss Yield			ANL Eval	Conf	55Geneva 7 3	Aug 55	Steinberg+ P614.EXPTL+BEST YLD,TABLE	
Fiss Yield	Maxwl 1.4+7		LAS Expt	Jour	PR 99 730	Aug 55	Wahl+2ES I ISOTOPE REL+INDEP YLDS	
				Rept	AECD−3657	Oct 54	.SUPERSEDED	
Fiss Yield	1.0+4	3.0+6	MTR Expt	Conf	55Geneva 7 19	Aug 55	Pappas+.P881,YIELD FOR SOME FRGMNTS	
Fiss Yield	Maxwl		MCM Expt	Jour	CJP 33 541	Sep 55	Wanless+ MASS−SPECT,XE+KR REL YIELDS	
Fiss Yield	Maxwl		MCM Expt	Jour	CJP 33 640	Nov 55	Petruska+ MSPEC CS133 135 137 YLDS	
Fiss Yield	Maxwl		MCM Expt	Jour	CJP 33 693	Nov 55	Petruska+ 28 ABSOL YLDS 2−3PC ERROR	
Fiss Yield	Maxwl		KAP Expt	Jour	NUC 13 12 30	Dec 55	Robb+PC POISONS.BURNUP CURVS	

92 Uranium 235

Quantity	Energy (ev) Min	Max	Lab	Type	Documentation Ref Vol Page	Date	Author, Comments	Data
Fiss Yield	Pile		CIS	Expt	Jour EN 3 32	Feb 56	Germagnoli+CHAIN SEQ A95TO144 CFD	
Fiss Yield	Maxwl		LAS	Expt	Rept LA- 1997	Feb 56	Ford+ +FISS SPEC NEUTS MASS YIELDS	
					Rept AECD-3551	Aug 53	- + LA141 INDEP YLD IN 141 CHAIN	
Fiss Yield	Maxwl		CRC	Expt	Jour CJC 34 201	Mar 56	Bartholomew+4PI CS138 REL BA140	
Fiss Yield	Maxwl		MCM	Expt	Jour CJC 34 233	Mar 56	Blades+ KR86/XE134 XE/KR RATIOS	
Fiss Yield	Maxwl		MCM	Expt	Jour PR 103 323	Jul 56	Kennett+YLDS I128 130 BR80 82	
Fiss Yield	Maxwl		ORL	Expt	Jour NSE 1 216	Jul 56	Robinson+,CURVES MANY PRODUCTS	
Fiss Yield	Fiss		ANL	Expt	Jour JIN 4 239	57	Kafalas+.YLD CS137.ASSUMED 32.6 YR	
Fiss Yield	Maxwl		CRC	Expt	Jour JIN 5 93	57	Grummitt+INDEPEND.YLD OF LA140Y90,91	
Fiss Yield	None		NRD	Expt	Jour NUC 15 2 81	Feb 57	Bunney+ DY166 HO166 TBP	
Fiss Yield	Pile		UK	Expt	Abst PA 60 3685	Apr 57	Mclusky.XEPOIS ANALOGCOMPTH.PROCIEE	
Fiss Yield	None		LAS	Expt	Jour PR 106 1359	Jun 57	Keepin.6 NEUTRON DELAY TIME GROUPS	
Fiss Yield	Pile		CCP	Expt	Jour AE 3 11	Jul 57	Gorshkov+.LA PR PM REL ND146,MASS SP	+
					Jour JNE 8 69	Nov 58	TRANSLATN.*	
					Jour SJA 3 729	57	TRANSLATN.*	
Fiss Yield	Maxwl	+0	LAS	Expt	Jour PR 107 325	Jul 57	Bayhurst+ THR/RES FISS CFD	
	Maxwl				Rept TID-5787	57	- +ALSO FISS SPEC,SR90 YIELDS	
Fiss Yield	1.0+6		ANL	Expt	Jour NSE 2 567	Sep 57	Dillon+,A=74 TO 157 YIELDS TABLE	
Fiss Yield	Pile		BNL	Expt	Conf 57Paris 1 50	Sep 57	Stang.TUCKER+ IODINE YIELD AND DECAY	
Fiss Yield	Maxwl		CRC	Expt	Jour CJC 35 980	Sep 57	Bartholomew+ REL TO BA140	
Fiss Yield	Maxwl				Jour PR 108 94	Oct 57	Stein.TOF MASS AND ENERGY DISTRIBUT	
Fiss Yield	+0	+2	ANL	Expt	Prog WASH-745	Nov 57	Rolnd+MDIST THR EPI 8DRES GB LA	
Fiss Yield	None		COL	Expt	Prog WASH-745	Nov 57	RAE+MDIST BY L1 NS TBDQ	
Fiss Yield	1.1+0	9.5+0	ANL	Expt	Jour PR 108 1522	Dec 57	Ringo+,AG111 CD115 SB127YLD REL SR89	
Fiss Yield	Maxwl		WAS	Expt	Jour JIN 6 263	58	Wahl. CUMUL YIELD KR,XE ISOTOPES.	
Fiss Yield	4.0-2	8.7+0	HAN	Expt	Rept HW- 54591 13	Apr 58	Seppi.TERNARY FISSION	
Fiss Yield	1.5+7		CCP	Expt	Jour AE 5 130	Aug 58	Protopopov+ 10 RADCHEM YLDS REL MO99	
					Jour JNEA 10 80	Jul 59	TRANSLATN.*	
					Jour SJA 5 885	58	TRANSLATN.*	
Fiss Yield	Maxwl		CCP	Expt	Conf 58Geneva 15 446	Sep 58	Anikina+.PPR2040,TBL OF MASSYIELDS	
Fiss Yield	+6		LAS	Revw	Conf 58Geneva 15 544	Sep 58	Hemmendinger.PPR663,CURVE,MANY REFS	
Fiss Yield	Fiss		NRD	Expt	Conf 58Geneva 15 449	Sep 58	Bunney+ YLDS REL MO99,REL U235 THR	
Fiss Yield	None		LAS	Expt	Prog WASH-1006	Oct 58	Simmons. AD MANYNEUTES TBD	
Fiss Yield	Pile		LAS	Expt	Prog WASH-1006	Oct 58	Jurney. SMALLTD5 DCAYSCH TBD	
Fiss Yield	None		LAS	Expt	Jour JIN 10 1	59	Wahl.CD113M HL,YLD CD113M/YLD CD115M	
Fiss Yield	Maxwl		LRL	Expt	Rept UCRL-8926	59	Chu. YLD OF 140,142CE+143ND TO 155EU	
Fiss Yield	-3	+7	TRM	Revw	Conf 59Calcutta 152	Feb 59	Ramanna. REVIEW YLD(5),5 E-RANGES	
Fiss Yield	None		NRD	Theo	Jour NSE 5 156	Mar 59	Bolles+,F PROD YLD AND ACTIVITS CALC	
					Rept USNRDL-456	Aug 56	.SUPERSEDED	
Fiss Yield	Pile		HAN	Expt	Rept HW- 60431	May 59	Merckx. KR+XE YIELDS TABULATED	
Fiss Yield	Fast		RI	Expt	Jour AE 6 577	May 59	BAK+ RADCHEM,RU103+106 YLD REL MO99	
					Jour KE 3 95	Jan 60	. ENGL OF AE 6 577	
					Jour SJA 6 429	Dec 59	. ENGL OF AE 6 577	
Fiss Yield	Maxwl		LAS	Expt	Jour JIN 10 183	Jul 59	Knight+	
Fiss Yield	Maxwl		OSL	Expt	Jour JIN 11 173	Sep 59	Kjelberg+,INDEP YLD OF 78AS	
Fiss Yield	Pile		RI	ExTh	Conf 59Tashkent 1 222	Sep 59	Krizhanskij.GRAPH YLD OF MANY NUCLEI	
					Rept AEC-TR-6398	64	.VOL 1,P288.ENGL OF 59TASHKE 1 222	
Fiss Yield	Maxwl		HAR	Theo	Rept NRDC-1024	Oct 59	Pattenden. FISS PROD POISONING DATA.	
Fiss Yield	Maxwl	1.7+7	LAS	Expt	Prog WASH-1026 34	Oct 59	Armstrong. WORK TO BE DONE	
Fiss Yield	-1	+1	HAR	Expt	Rept AERE-M-559	Nov 59	Wraight. SPINS OF FISSN.RESONANCES	
Fiss Yield	Fiss	1.4+7	CCP	Expt	Rept AEC-TR-4682	60	Bonyushkin+.ABSOL RADIOCHEM YLDS GVN	
Fiss Yield	Pile		LAS	Expt	Jour JIN 12 206	60	Sattizahn+ YLD OF SHORT LIVED BR-84	
Fiss Yield	Pile		ORL	Expt	Jour JIN 12 223	60	Marinsky+ YLD OF GA-74	
Fiss Yield	Pile		WAS	Expt	Jour JIN 12 201	60	Wolfsberg+ YLD OF XE-142	
Fiss Yield	1.4+7		HAR	Comp	Rept AERE-R-3209	Jan 60	CROALL COMP OF INDP YLDS(NSA 14 1397	
	Maxwl				Rept AERE-R-3209	Jan 60	Croall.COMP OF INDP YLDS(NSA 14 1397	
Fiss Yield	Maxwl	1.4+7	LRL	Expt	Jour PR 117 186	Jan 60	Stevenson+GIVES YIELD OF MO99	
Fiss Yield	Maxwl		MCG	Expt	Jour CJC 38 464	Mar 60	Santry+ BA140 YLD 6.36+-0.12PC	
Fiss Yield	-2		RI	Expt	Jour ZET 38 998	Mar 60	Dmitriev.TRIPLE FISSION PROBABILITY	
					Jour JET 11 718	Sep 60	TRANSLATN.*	
Fiss Yield	Maxwl		CRC	Revw	Conf 60Kingston 862	Aug 60	Hanna.CURVE,THEORET DISCUSSIONS	
Fiss Yield	Maxwl		HAR	Expt	Rept AERE-R-3524	Oct 60	Melkonian.MASSDIST(INC 3-FISS)SI DET	
Fiss Yield	Fast		BNL	Eval	Jour NUC 18 11 201	Nov 60	Katcoff.RECOMMENDED YLD-SET,TBL	
					Jour NUC 16 4 78	Apr 58	.SUPERSEDED	
Fiss Yield	Maxwl		BNL	Eval	Jour NUC 18 11 201	Nov 60	Katcoff.RECOMMENDED YLD-SET,TBL,GRPH	
					Jour NUC 16 4 78	Apr 58	.SUPERSEDED	
Fiss Yield	1.4+7		BNL	Eval	Jour NUC 18 11 201	Nov 60	Katcoff.RECOMMENDED YLD-SET,TBL,GRPH	
					Jour NUC 16 4 78	Apr 58	.SUPERSEDED	

92 Uranium 235

Quantity	Energy (ev) Min Max	Lab	Type	Documentation Ref Vol Page	Date	Author, Comments	Data
Fiss Yield	Maxwl	CRC	Expt	Jour CJC 38 2147	Nov 60	Baerg+ CS134M,136 INDEPENDENT YLDS	
Fiss Yield	Fiss 1.5+7	CCP	Expt	Book NEJTRONFIZ 224	61	Bonjushkin+ RADIOCHEM YLDS,TBL,GRPHS	+
				Book SPN 164	61	+AEC-TR-4682,ENGL OF NEJTRONFIZ 224	
Fiss Yield	None	GA	Revw	Rept GA-2307	61	Fischer+TABLES OF YLD FOR A=81TO159	
Fiss Yield	Fiss	RI	Expt	Book NEJTRONFIZ 217	61	Petrzhak+ RADCHEM YLDS 6NUC,TBL+GRPH	
				Rept AEC-TR-4696	61	.ENGL OF NEJTRONFIZ 217	
Fiss Yield	1.5+7	CCP	Expt	Jour AE 10 13	Jan 61	Bonjuskin+.ABS YIELD OF FRGMNTS,GRPH	
				Jour SJA 10 10	Nov 61	TRANSLATN.*GERMAN KE4 553 7/61	
Fiss Yield	Maxwl	CRC	Expt	Jour CJP 39 315	Feb 61	ROY. FISS YLD MG28,NI66,BE7	
Fiss Yield	None	BNL	Theo	Jour NSE 9 495	Apr 61	Levine.XE135 FROM EQUAL Z DISPL.RULE	
Fiss Yield	Pile	MTR	Expt	Prog IDO-16710 29	Apr 61	Schuman+PM1481SOMERS N CAPT RATES	
Fiss Yield	Maxwl	DKE	Theo	Jour PR 122 1224	May 61	Newson.MASS DIST ASYMMETRIC+SYMMETR	
Fiss Yield	Maxwl	HAR	Expt	Jour PPS 77 1097	May 61	Gooding.YIELD CURVE VERSUS TOTAL KE	
Fiss Yield	2.8-1 6.1+1	LAS	Expt	Jour PR 122 1286	May 61	Cowan+SYMMETRY AT RESONANCES	
				Jour PR 130 2380	Jun 63	- + SEE ALSO	
	8.8+0 4.0+1			Rept PNE-114F	Feb 63	.SUPERSEDED	
Fiss Yield	Maxwl	SYR	Theo	Jour PR 122 1543	May 61	Fong.STATISTICAL THEORY CFD DATA	
Fiss Yield	Maxwl	TRM	Expt	Jour NP 25 136	May 61	Ramanna+.ANGCORR PROMPT N+FISS FRAGM	
Fiss Yield	2.0+6 1.0+7	LRL	Expt	Jour PR 124 544	Oct 61	Levy+ 6 ES,YLDS REL MO99,REL U235THR	
Fiss Yield	Pile	CRC	Expt	Jour JIN 20 6	Nov 61	Grummitt+MILTON.DIRECT YLD CS136	
Fiss Yield	None	LAS	Expt	Prog WASH-1034 23	Dec 61	Thorpe. AVG NU=2.43PM0.02	
Fiss Yield	Fiss	GA	Eval	Jour NSE 12 115	Jan 62	Garrison+.(Z,A).WEIGHTD AVRAGE OTHRS	
Fiss Yield	2.5-2	ANL	Expt	Jour JIN 24 337	Feb 62	Sloth+ TRITIUM YLD PER FISSION	
Fiss Yield	Maxwl	HAR	Expt	Jour JIN 24 221	Mar 62	Croall+RADIOCHEM.SE81,SE83 BA140 YLD	
	Pile			Jour JIN 16 358	Feb 61	- . DIRECT YLD NB96	
Fiss Yield	Maxwl 1.0+6	LAS	Expt	Jour PR 126 1508	May 62	Nobles. YIELD OF LONG RANGE FFRGM	
Fiss Yield	Maxwl	WAS	Expt	Jour PR 126 1112	May 62	Wahl+, FRAC CUM + INDEP YIELD GIVEN	
Fiss Yield	7.0-1 1.0+1	ANL	Expt	Jour ANS 5 20	Jun 62	Glendenin+ RADIOCH. DECREASE IN SYMM	
Fiss Yield	5.0+6	CCP	Expt	Jour AE 12 461	Jun 62	Okolovich+AV.E FRAGM F/TH	
				Jour SJA 12 491	Jun 62	- +	
				Jour EAF 12 6 1	Jun 62	- +	
Fiss Yield	Maxwl	CCP	Expt	Jour AE 12 461	Jun 62	Okolovich+RATIO AV E FRAGM F/TH0.999	
				Jour AE 13 64	Jul 62	- +RATIO AE E FRAGM F/TH0.989	
				Jour SJA 13 652	Jul 62	. ENGLISH TRANSLATION.	
				Jour EAF 12 6 1	Jun 62	. FRENCH TRANSLATION	
				Jour SJA 12 491	Jun 62	Okolovich+ENGLISH TRANSLATION.	
Fiss Yield		MCM	Expt	Jour NP 34 367	Jun 62	Farrar+ALL A131-155,EXTRAPOL 117-159	+
Fiss Yield	1.5+7	CCP	Expt	Jour AE 13 64	Jul 62	Okolovich+AV.E FRAGM F/TH	
				Jour EAF 13 1 100	62	- +	
				Jour SJA 13 652	62	- +	
Fiss Yield	Maxwl	MCM	Expt	Jour CJP 40 1017	Aug 62	Farrar+ MASS-SPEC,LIGHT A-PEAK YLDS	
Fiss Yield	Maxwl	MCM	Theo	Jour CJP 40 943	Aug 62	Farrar+STRUCTURE IN MASS YLD CURVE	
Fiss Yield	None	MTR	Expt	Rept AERE-M-1078 12	Aug 62	Burgus.	
	2.0-3 5.0-1			Rept IDO-16797	Jul 62	- .RADIOCHEM ASYM/SYM YLD RATIOS	
Fiss Yield	Maxwl	NRD	Expt	Rept AERE-M-1078 14	Aug 62	Strom.YIELDS TO Z=50	
Fiss Yield	Pile	UPP	Expt	Jour AF 22 349	Sep 62	Andersson+. YIELD OF SB129,TE129M	
Fiss Yield	1.4+7	LRL	Expt	Jour PR 128 700	Oct 62	Hicks+ YIELD REL MO99 REL THR	
Fiss Yield	Maxwl	MUN	Expt	Jour ZP 170 62	Oct 62	FROEHNER TE+I135YIELDS REL T134 YLD	
Fiss Yield	1.5+7	CCP	Expt	Jour AE 13 474	Nov 62	Kovalenko+KINETIC E OF FRAG.	
				Jour EAF 13 5 74	62	- +	
				Jour SJA 13 1092	62	- +	
Fiss Yield	Maxwl	CCP	Expt	Jour AE 13 474	Nov 62	Kovalenko+KINETIC E OF FRAGMENTS,2ES	
				Jour SJA 13 1092	Nov 62	. ENGLISH	
				Jour EAF 13 5 74	Nov 62	. FRENCH	
Fiss Yield	Maxwl	CCP	Expt	Rept AEC-TR-6183	63	Andreev+,TBL FISS YLD,H3,H5,HE3,4,6	
Fiss Yield	Maxwl	MNZ	Expt	Rept NP-13996	63	Lange.THESIS. SB124+126 INDEPEN YLDS	
Fiss Yield	Maxwl	ROS	Expt	Jour KE 6 225	Jan 63	Muenze+.GRAPH,RADIOCHEMICAL METHOD	
				Jour KE 5 472	Jan 62	- .YIELD FOR NI66,MULTIPLE FISS	
				Jour KE 5 564	Jan 62	- .YIELD FOR CU67 IN TERNRY FISS	
Fiss Yield	Maxwl 1.4+7	NRD	Eval	Rept USNRDL-TR-633	Mar 63	Weaver+2ES+FISS SPECT.EST OF YLDS	
Fiss Yield	Maxwl	ORL	Expt	Jour PR 130 1466	May 63	Troutner+ZR99-NB99-MO00 YIELDS	
				Rept ORNL-3425 76	63	.SUPERSEDED	
				Jour PRL 9 427	Nov 62	.SUPERSEDED	
Fiss Yield	Pile	UPP	Expt	Jour JIN 25 615	Jun 63	Hagebo. 127SB 129SB.CHEMICAL METHOD	
Fiss Yield	Maxwl	WAS	Expt	Jour PR 131 830	Jul 63	Wahl+ SN121 INDEPENDENT YIELD	

92 Uranium 235

Quantity	Energy (ev) Min	Max	Lab	Type	Documentation Ref Vol Page	Author, Comments Date	Data
Fiss Yield	2.0−3	5.0−1	MTR	Expt Jour	PR 131 1746	Aug 63 Faler+ RADIOCHEM METHOD MASS YLD CRV	
	2.5−2	5.0−1		Jour	ANS 5 22	Jun 62 − + PEAK/VALLEY RATIO VERSUS E(N)	
	2.0−3	5.0−1		Prog	IDO−16781 19	62 .SUPERSEDED	
				Prog	IDO−16805 12	62 .SUPERSEDED	
				Rept	IDO−16760 16	Oct 61 .SUPERSEDED	
Fiss Yield	Maxwl		NRD	Expt Jour	AC 35 1712	Oct 63 Greendale+ YLD HL 131SN 132SN 133SN	
Fiss Yield	Maxwl		ORL	Expt Prog	ORNL−3488	Oct 63 Ferguson+,INDEP YLD OF SB127,CURVES	
Fiss Yield	Maxwl		PSU	Expt Jour	PR 132 371	Oct 63 Cooperman+ COINC WITH PROMPT GAMMAS	
				Abst	DA 24 3379	Feb 64 .	
Fiss Yield	1.0+0	5.7+1	COL	Expt Abst	ANS 6 262	Nov 63 Melkonian+ 1 DEP OF FISS E P ALPHAS	
Fiss Yield	2.5−2		JNE	Expt Rept	JEN−131 DF/I42	64 Domingo. PROB OF TERNARY FISSION	
Fiss Yield	Maxwl		KUR	Expt Rept	IAE−709	64 Apalin+.ENERGY OF FISSIONFRAGMENTS	
Fiss Yield	Maxwl		KUR	Expt Rept	IAE−710	64 Apalin+.GRAPH,DSTRB OF FFRGM+FPRODS	
Fiss Yield	6.0−2	1.0+1	KUR	Expt Jour	AE 16 3	Jan 64 Mostovaya+ PROB.OF TERNARY FISSION	
				Jour	SJA 16 1	Jan 64 . ENGL OF AE 16 3	
Fiss Yield	Maxwl		YOK	Expt Jour	NIM 25 265	Jan 64 Tsukada.RATIO CIRCUIT. MASS DISTRIB.	
Fiss Yield	2.5−2		BNL	Theo Jour	PR/B 133 976	Feb 64 Thomas+CF FRAG YIELD VS EN RELEASE	
Fiss Yield	Maxwl		CCP	Expt Jour	ZET 46 1178	Apr 64 H3 BUT NO H5 FOUND	
				Jour	JET 19 797	Oct 64 TRANSLATN.*	
Fiss Yield	Maxwl		KUR	Expt Jour	ZET 46 1197	Apr 64 Apalin+,FRAG MASS DIST+EXCIT E+KIN−E	
				Rept	AEC−TR−6254	Apr 64 TRANSLATN.*+AEC−TR−6285 4/64	
Fiss Yield	Maxwl		CRC	Expt Conf	64Geneva 7 430	May 64 Fraser+ MILTON DOUBLE VEL. MEAST.	
Fiss Yield	Maxwl		MIS	Expt Jour	PR/B 134 1027	Jun 64 Troutner+ FRACT INDEP +CUM YLD SB127	
Fiss Yield	Maxwl		MUN	ExTh Jour	NP 54 586	Jun 64 Armbruster+MEAN PRIMARY CHARGE DETER	
Fiss Yield	Maxwl		MCM	Expt Prog	EANDC(CAN)−21	Jul 64 Pleva+ INDEP. YLDS BR82,I126,BR80	
Fiss Yield	Pile		NYB	Expt Jour	JIN 26 1129	Jul 64 Tercho.YIELD OF MO104	
Fiss Yield	Fast		ANL	Expt Prog	ANL−6900 337	Aug 64 Meyer+ TC99 YLD REL CS137,RADIOCHEM	
Fiss Yield	Maxwl		CER	Theo Jour	NP 58 177	Sep 64 Faissner+ASSYMETRIC,CLUSTER MODEL	
				Jour	PL 2 212	Oct 62 − + SUPERSEDED	
Fiss Yield	Maxwl		BKB	Expt Jour	IBK 15 217	Oct 64 Juric+ LARGE MASS TER FIS,P=1/4000	
Fiss Yield	Maxwl	+6	CIS	Expt Rept	CISE−171R	65 Faccinni+. BA140 REL+ABSOL YLDS	
	Maxwl Fiss		TRM	Comp Rept	AEET−209	65 Rangajaran+ YLDS+PRODUC,TABL	
	1.4+7			Rept	AEET−209	65 Rangarajan+ YLDS+PRODUCTN RATIO,TBLS	
Fiss Yield	−3	+7	TRM	Revw Rept	AEET−235	65 Methasiri.TERNRY FISS EXPTS,TBL,GRPH	
Fiss Yield	Maxwl	7.2+5	FEI	Expt Jour	YF 2 92	Jan 65 D'Jachenko+ YIELD OF 20 MASSNUMBERS	+
				Conf	65Salzburg 1 601	Mar 65 .CONTINUATION OF YF 2 92 1/65	
				Jour	SNP 2 65	Jan 66 .ENGLISH TRANSL OF YF 2 92 1/65	
	2.5−2	7.2+5		Prog	INDSWG−120E 4	65 .ENGLISH TRANSL OF YFI−1 5 /65	
Fiss Yield	Maxwl		ISL	Expt Prog	IA−1021 25	Jan 65 Gozez.ALFA ASSOCIATED FISS TBD	
Fiss Yield	Maxwl		YOK	Expt Jour	JPJ 20 176	Jan 65 Kobayashi+OBTAINED BEFORE N.EMISSION	
Fiss Yield	3.0−3	3.0−1	BNL	Expt Jour	PR/B 137 519	Feb 65 Schroder+RATIO BINRY−TERN CONST VS E	
Fiss Yield	7.0+5	1.5+5	LAS	ExTh Jour	PR/B 137 814	Feb 65 Leachman+ REL ANG DIST CFD OPTMDL	
Fiss Yield	1.4+7		LAS	Expt Jour	PR/B 137 929	Feb 65 Wolfsberg. K,XE ISOTOPE YLDS	
Fiss Yield	Maxwl		NRD	Expt Jour	JIN 27 273	Feb 65 Bunney+.RADCHEM YIELDS A=91,143−161	+
				Rept	USNRDL−TR−679	Sep 63 − + RAD CHEM MEAS MASS YLDS.	
Fiss Yield	4.0+6		TRM	Expt Conf	65Calcutta 33	Feb 65 .SUPERSEDED	
				Jour	PR/B 137 511	Feb 65 Kapoor+ FRAGS VS KE,MASS ASYMM VS A	
Fiss Yield	1.0−1	5.0+1	DUB	Expt Conf	65Salzburg 2 439	Mar 65 Kvitek+,P.87,TOF,TERNARY FISS,GRPH	
				Jour	YF 2 4 677	Oct 65 − .TOF,TERNARY FISSION, GRAPH	
				Rept	JINR−P−2025	65 .SEE ALSO	
				Jour	SNP 2 485	Apr 66 .ENGL TRANSL OF YF 2	
				Rept	ANL−TRANS−194	65 . ENGL OF 65SALZBU 2 439	
Fiss Yield	Maxwl		KUR	Expt Conf	65Salzburg 1 587	Mar 65 Apalin+,P.92,GRPH MASS DIST,FISS SYM	
					−	ENGL ANL−TR−205 /64,SNP 1 457 0/65	
				Jour	SNP 1 457	Oct 65 . ENGL OF YF 1 639	
Fiss Yield	−2	1.8+6	LAS	ExTh Conf	65Salzburg 1 333	Mar 65 Ford+,P.24,GRPHS AND DISCUSSION	
	4.7+6	1.8+7		Jour	PR/B 137 826	Feb 65 − + YLDS CFD STATSTCL TH	
Fiss Yield	5.0−3	2.0−1	MOL	Expt Conf	65Salzburg 429	Mar 65 Deruytter.NEVE.BIN/TER RATIO	
				Conf	64Paris 192	Jul 64 − .B/T RATIO+TERNR/SPECTR	
Fiss Yield	2.5−2	1.0+0	MTR	Expt Rept	IDO−17073	Mar 65 Miller+.REL TERN−TO−BIN FISS YIELD	
Fiss Yield	Maxwl		PTN	Expt Conf	65Salzburg 1 467	Mar 65 Thomas+ MASS YIELD CURVES	
Fiss Yield	Maxwl		SAC	Expt Rept	CEA−R−2408	Dec 63 Chartache.	
				Conf	65Salzburg 1 561	Mar 65 − . FOR MASS DISTRIBUTION.	
				Rept	EANDC(E)57U	Feb 65 − . ABST. PROMPT NEUTRONS.	
Fiss Yield	Maxwl		WAS	Revw Conf	65Salzburg 1 317	Mar 65 Wahl.P.22,GRPHS TH CFD EXPTS	
Fiss Yield	Maxwl		MIT	Expt Jour	PR/B 138 353	Apr 65 Sarantites+ YIELDS TE131, TE133	
Fiss Yield	Pile		SGA	Expt Jour	NUK 7 169	Apr 65 Balcarczyk+. CS,RU YIELDS REL BA140	+

92 Uranium 235

Quantity	Energy (ev) Min	Max	Lab	Type	Documentation Ref Vol Page	Date	Author, Comments	Data
Fiss Yield	Maxwl		KUR Expt	Jour	YF 1 816	May 65	Apalin+,TOTAL KIN−E VS MASS RATIO	
				Jour	NP 71 546	Sep 65	SEE ALSO *IAE−709 /64	
				Jour	SNP 1 457	Oct 65	. ENGL OF YF 1 639	
Fiss Yield	Maxwl		ANL Eval	Abst	ANS 8 12	Jun 65	Marsh+ TRITIUM YIELD STUDY	
Fiss Yield	Maxwl		CRC Expt	Jour	CJP 43 1036	Jun 65	Okazaki+I135,BA140 YIELDS	
Fiss Yield	Thrsh Up		TRM Theo	Jour	NP 67 529	Jun 65	Ramanna+FISSION AS MARKOV PROCESS	
	None			Jour	PL 10 321	Jun 64	− . DIST BY TH OF RANDOM FLIGHT	
Fiss Yield	Maxwl		BNL Expt	Jour	JIN 27 1447	Jul 65	Katcoff.KR85G YIELD .273PC	
Fiss Yield	Maxwl		NRD Expt	Jour	PR/B 139 304	Jul 65	Weiss. YLD +GENETICS MASS 121	
Fiss Yield	Maxwl		YOK Expt	Prog	INDSWG−90 32	Jul 65	Kobayashi.FISFRGM E−SPCTR,GRAPHS	
Fiss Yield	Pile		LRL Expt	Jour	PR/B 139 1264	Sep 65	Stevenson+ IONS IN FISS	
Fiss Yield	1.5+7		LRL Expt	Jour	PR/B 139 1505	Sep 65	Nethaway+YIELD Y92,NB96,CS136	
Fiss Yield	Maxwl		NRD Expt	Jour	JIN 27 1917	Sep 65	Weiss.IN121M YIELD .0032PC	
				Jour	PR/B 139 304	Jul 65	− + YLD+GENETICS MASS 121	
				Conf	65Salzburg 1 423	Mar 65	− +,P.29, YIELD OF MASS 121	
				Rept	USNRDL−TR−816	Feb 65	− +CD121,SN121YLDS	
Fiss Yield	Maxwl		OSL Expt	Jour	CJC 43 2493	Sep 65	Strom+ INDEPENDENT YIELDS SB−124,126	
Fiss Yield	Maxwl		GEV Expt	Rept	GEAP−5060	Nov 65	Rider+ND AND CS ISOTOPES YIELDS	
				Rept	GEAP−4716	Sep 64	− +MASS.SPECTRO.YIELDS OF ND ISOT	
Fiss Yield	Maxwl		NRD Expt	Rept	USNRDL−TR−935	Nov 65	Strom+ YLDS OF 3ADJACENT MASS CHAINS	
Fiss Yield	Maxwl		ORL Expt	Rept	ORNL−TM−1333	Dec 65	Niece.ZR95 YIELD, CHG DISP MASS 95	
Fiss Yield	None		ORL Theo	Rept	ORNL−P−2848	66	Schmitt.CALCTD FISS MODES TBP AF	
Fiss Yield	Maxwl		CRC Expt	Jour	CJP 44 237	Jan 66	Okazaki+ DIRECT YIELD OF XE135	
				Jour	CJP 49 498	Feb 71	.CORRECTED DATA	
	None			Prog	EANDC(CAN)−23	Apr 65	Bigham+DIRECT YIELD OF XE135	
Fiss Yield	Maxwl		ORL Expt	Jour	PR 141 1146	Jan 66	Schmitt+PRE−NEUT YLDS CFD AFTER NS	
Fiss Yield	Maxwl		BNL Expt	Jour	PR 142 716	Feb 66	Stoener+ UPPER LIM AR YIELD	
Fiss Yield	Pile		JAE Expt	Rept	JAERI−1103	Feb 66	Umezawa.PM148 CHEM SEPA,INDEPT YIELD	
Fiss Yield	Maxwl		MUN Expt	Prog	EANDC(E)66U	Feb 66	Ewald+ TBC.MASS 130−139	
Fiss Yield	Maxwl		LEB Expt	Jour	YF 3 468	Mar 66	Belovitskij.NUMBER OF ELECTRONS	
				Jour	SNP 3 340	Sep 66	TRANSLATN.*	
Fiss Yield	Maxwl		MCM Expt	Prog	EANDC(CAN)−28	Mar 66	Tomlinson+ YLDS OF BR−87,−88,−89	
Fiss Yield	Maxwl		ORL Expt	Jour	JIN 28 763	Mar 66	Aras+ YLDS SB	
				Prog	MIT−905−21	Dec 65	− +,REL YLDS OF SB124,125,126, CF	
	Pile			Jour	NP 69 337	Jul 65	− + KE DEFICIT AT SYMMETRIC FISS	
Fiss Yield	Maxwl		LAS Expt	Jour	PR 145 911	May 66	Daniels+ CUM YLD EU156 THRU 159	
Fiss Yield	None		MTR Expt	Rept	IDO−14676	May 66	Maeck+ RU101,102,104,106 YIELDS	
Fiss Yield	Maxwl		WAS Expt	Jour	PR 146 926	Jun 66	Norris+ DIRECT YIELD Y92,93,94,95	
				Abst	DA 25 569	Jul 64	.ABSTRACT	
Fiss Yield	Maxwl		WAS Expt	Jour	PR 146 931	Jun 66	Wahl+ INDEPENDENT YIELDS RB92,RB93	
				Conf	65Salzburg 317	Mar 65	.SUPRSEDED	
Fiss Yield	Maxwl		AE Expt	Jour	NAT 211 618	Aug 66	Anderson+.INDEP YLD CS134	
Fiss Yield	Maxwl	1.4+7	CIS Theo	Jour	NP 84 595	Sep 66	Erba+ STATMOD CFD EXPT,2ES,TBLS,CURV	
Fiss Yield	Maxwl		KAP Expt	Jour	JIN 28 1787	Sep 66	Mchugh.86RB,132CS,134CS,136CS YIELDS	
				Rept	KAPL−3113	Sep 65	− . RB86CS132 134 136 YLD M−SPEC	
Fiss Yield	Maxwl		SRL Expt	Jour	JIN 28 1763	Sep 66	Ondrejcin.137CS−YIELD+CAL FLUX FACT.	
Fiss Yield	Maxwl		NRD Theo	Jour	PR 150 1018	Oct 66	Ferguson+ EXTENDS PR 139 B56NEW DATA	
Fiss Yield	Maxwl		ANL Expt	Prog	ANL−7225 232	Nov 66	Meyer+ ABS YLDS FOR TC99,CS133,CS137	
				Rept	ANL−6900 338	Jun 64	.SUPERSEDED	
Fiss Yield	Maxwl		WAL Comp	Rept	WANL−TME−574	Nov 66	Trammell+ INDEP+CUMUL YLD LIBRARY	
Fiss Yield	Maxwl		SOR Expt	Prog	IA−1128 63	Dec 66	Yashida+ IODINE INDEPENDT YLDS GIVEN	
Fiss Yield	Maxwl		SRC Expt	Jour	PL 23 583	Dec 66	Marshall+YIELD OF ALPHAS,TRITONS	
Fiss Yield	Maxwl		COL Expt	Rept	TID−23889	67	Derengowski.PRE,POST NEUTRON EMISSN	
				Prog	NYO−GEN72−132	Jan 67	.SUPERSEDED	
Fiss Yield	Maxwl		ISL Expt	Prog	IA−1168 67	Jan 67	CHUL LEE+ YLD VALUES OF BR,SR,Y,MO	
Fiss Yield	Maxwl		WWA Expt	Jour	PL/B 24 87	Jan 67	Chwaszczewska+ REL INTENS LIGHT PART	
				Rept	INP−1033	Feb 69	− + P,T REL HE−YLD,TRIPAR	
				Rept	INR−765/IA/PL	Oct 66	Sowinski+ SIMILAR TEXT,SAME DATA	
Fiss Yield	6.0+4	2.0+6	COL Expt	Conf	67Kanpur 327	Feb 67	Mehta. SYMMETRY IN P−WAVE FISS	
Fiss Yield	−		FEI Expt	Conf	67Kharkov	Feb 67	Vorob'Eva+. TBP IN IZV	
Fiss Yield	None		HNS Theo	Rept	HNS−1229−77	Feb 67	Castagnola. ALSO FISS SPEC 28FRAGS	
Fiss Yield	Maxwl		LAS Expt	Jour	PR 156 1277	Apr 67	Stein+ SI DETECT,CURVE YIELDS,ENERGY	
Fiss Yield	Maxwl		MUN Expt	Conf	67Juelich 24	Apr 67	Zicha+ MO102−5 REL MO99,CFD SN+CALC	
Fiss Yield	Maxwl		MIS Expt	Abst	DA/B 27 3897	May 67	Runnalls.FRACTION YLD BA143−4,CE147	
				Rept	ORNL−3994 8	Sep 66	Runnals+RADIOCHEM.RATIO BA/CE143,144	
Fiss Yield	Maxwl		NRD Expt	Jour	JIN 28 2067	May 67	Weiss+. PD115 YIELD	
				Rept	USNRDL−TR−943	Nov 65	.SUPERSEDED	
Fiss Yield	Maxwl		SAC Expt	Jour	NP/A 99 41	Jun 67	Signarbieux+ SYMMETRIC YIELDS AGREE	

92 Uranium 235

Quantity	Energy (ev) Min Max	Lab	Type	Documentation Ref Vol Page	Author, Comments Date	Data
Fiss Yield	Maxwl	WWA	Expt Jour	PL/B 25 213	Aug 67 Dakowski+ REL INTENS OF P,D,T,HE4+6	
			Rept	INP-702/PS	Jun 70 - + SEMICOND RESULTS,CFD THEO	
Fiss Yield	Maxwl	FLA	Expt Jour	PR 161 1266	Sep 67 Muga+ NO ALPHAS FROM BINARY FISSION	
			Jour	PRL 18 404	Mar 67 .SUPERSEDED	
			Jour	PRL 11 129	Aug 63 Muga.EVIDENCE FOR FISS TO 3 HVY FRAG	
Fiss Yield	2.9+6	IFJ	Expt Jour	APP 32 485	Sep 67 Benisz+ TERNARY FISS,MASS-YLDS,GRPHS	
			Rept	INP-529	Mar 67 EQUIVALENT*	
Fiss Yield	Pile	ISP	Expt Jour	JIN 29 1189	Sep 67 Bresesti+ RADCHEM,GE-LI,YLD OF 6NUCL	
Fiss Yield	Maxwl	MUN	Expt Jour	RCA 7 105	Sep 67 Wunderlich.IODINE FRACT INDEP YLDS	
Fiss Yield	Maxwl	WAS	Expt Jour	JIN 29 2133	Sep 67 Brown+ RADIOCHEM.INDEP.YLD. SN123TO8	
Fiss Yield	Maxwl	ITE	Expt Prog	YFI-5 25	Oct 67 Andreev+ TBL YIELD OF 9 LIGHT FRGMTS	
			Rept	INDC-232E	67 . ENGL OF YFI-5 25	
Fiss Yield	Maxwl	YOK	Expt Conf	67Tokai 115	Oct 67 Hosoe+XPTL GRPH YLD(A),CFD OTHER,TBP	
Fiss Yield	1.4+7	CCP	Expt Jour	YF 6 919	Nov 67 Krisjuk+,ZR97 YIELD	
Fiss Yield	Maxwl	CCP	Expt Jour	YF 6 930	Nov 67 Adamov+,YLD OF P,T,A AT TERNARY FISS	
Fiss Yield	1.4+7	CCP	Expt Jour	YF 6 930	Nov 67 Adamov+,YLD OF P,T,A AT TERNARY FISS	
Fiss Yield	Maxwl	JLU	Revw Jour	AF 36 311	Nov 67 Ewald.DESCRIBES GARCHING MASSPECWORK	
Fiss Yield	Maxwl	WUR	Expt Jour	RCA 8 112	Nov 67 Von Gunten+ YLDS OF MO-99 + BA-139	
Fiss Yield	-	CCP	Expt	-	(FRENCH EAF 23 100,ENGL SJA 23 1336)	
			Jour	SJA 23 1336	Dec 67 . ENGL OF AE 23 559	
Fiss Yield	Maxwl 1.3+6	FEI	Expt Jour	YF 6 1167	Dec 67 Djachenko+ FRAG YIELD CFD THR,GRAPH	
	6.0+6		ExTh	YF 10 61	Jul 69 D'Jachenko+ STATMOD+LVL DENS ANAL	
	Maxwl 1.3+6		Expt	SNP 6 848	Jun 68 *	
			Prog	INDC-E-187 4	67 .ENGLISH TRANSL OF YFI-4 5 5/67	
Fiss Yield	-2	FTI	Expt Prog	YFI-6 88	68 Vorob'Ev+ TABLES YIELD MASS 2-12	
			Rept	INDC-260E	69 . ENGL OF YFI-6 88	
Fiss Yield	2.5-2	RI	Expt Prog	YFI-6 96	68 Solov'Ev+. GRAPH, FISSION ALFAS	
			Rept	INDC-260E	69 . ENGL OF YFI-6 96	
Fiss Yield	Maxwl	TRM	Expt Rept	BARC-363	68 Kapoor+ YIELD(A) GRAPH, K-X-RAY EXPT	
	-		Conf	67Kanpur § N114	Feb 67 Patwardhan.METHOD FOR YLD VS MASS	
Fiss Yield	1.6+7	FEI	Expt Jour	YF 7 36	Jan 68 D'Jachenko+ EXPT U235,CALC U236-COMP	+
			Prog	YFI-5 7	Oct 67 - + CURVE MASS AND E SPECTRA	
			Jour	SNP 7 1 27	Jul 68 .TRANSLATION OF YF 7 36	
			Rept	INDC-232E	67 . ENGL OF YFI-5 7	
	1.6+7		Data	EXFOR40234.002	Dec 74 .EN=15.5 MEV, 39 DATA LINES GVN	
Fiss Yield	Maxwl	FTI	Expt Conf	68Riga	Jan 68 Vorob'Ev+ABST,LIGHT NUCLEIS YIELD	
Fiss Yield	Maxwl +6	HAR	Eval Rept	AERE-R-5086	Jan 68 Croall.TBL YLDS(FAST TO FISS)REL THR	
	Fast		Rept	AERE-R-5086	Jan 68 - .RECOMMENDED CUMULAT YLDS,TBL	
	Maxwl		Rept	AERE-R-5086	Jan 68 - .RECOMMENDED CUMULAT YLDS,TBL	
Fiss Yield	Maxwl	ITE	ExTh Conf	68Riga	Jan 68 Andreev+ ABST,LI,BE,B,C,N,O,F YIELDS	
Fiss Yield	Maxwl	ITE	ExTh Conf	68Riga	Jan 68 Andreev+ ABST,LI,BE,B,C,N,O,F E-DIST	
Fiss Yield	None	MHG	Expt Abst	DA/B 28 2759	Jan 68 Tsoukatos.REL.FRACT.YLDS I ISOTOPES	
Fiss Yield	Maxwl	MIS	Expt Rept	TID-24500	Jan 68 Roche.AG112 INDEP YLD+ PD115 CUM YLD	
			Abst	DA/B 29 927	Sep 68 - .	
Fiss Yield	Maxwl	SAL	Expt Jour	EN 15 272	Apr 68 Ciufollotti.BA-140 YLD,BA-STANDARD	
Fiss Yield	Maxwl	THD	Expt Jour	RCA 9 27	May 68 Bachmann.YIELD FOR PM148	
Fiss Yield	Maxwl 3.0+6	TRM	Expt Jour	NP/A 112 241	May 68 Nadkarni. LONG RANGE ALPHA, BIN/TERN	+
	Maxwl		Conf	70Madurai 2 73	Dec 70 - +LONG-RANGE-PART-PROBAB GIVN	
	Maxwl 3.0+6		Conf	67Kanpur 318	Feb 67 - .	
			Rept	AEET-267 2	Aug 66 - .	
	Maxwl 3.0+6		Data	EXFOR30093.	Mar 71 BIN/TER VS ANG, TER SIG AT 3MEV	
Fiss Yield	Maxwl	BOL	Comp Rept	CEC(68)-6	Jun 68 Cenacci.YLDS,DECAY CHAINS,FPROD DATA	
			Rept	RT/FI-68 4	68 .EQUIVALENT	
Fiss Yield	Maxwl	MTR	Expt Rept	NSE 42 191	Nov 70 Lisman+,YLDS STABLE+LONG-LIVED FRAGS	
			Rept	IN- 1277	Jun 68 - + SUMMARIZES RESULTS	
	Fast		Rept	IN- 1277	Jun 68 - + SUMMARIZES RESULTS	
Fiss Yield	Maxwl	ITE	Expt Jour	YF 8 38	Jul 68 Andreev+ TERN-F,LONG-RANGE Z=2 TO 9	
			Jour	SNP 8 22	Jan 69 TRANSLATN.*	
Fiss Yield	Maxwl	NRD	Expt Jour	PR 172 1262	Aug 68 Wish+RADIOCHEM GA77 FRACT CHAIN YLD	
			Rept	USNRDL-TR-68	Feb 67 .SUPERSEDED	
Fiss Yield	Maxwl	NRD	Expt Jour	PR 172 1269	Aug 68 Weiss+ RADIOCHEM PD117 CHAIN YIELD	
			Rept	USNRDL-TR-68	Feb 67 .SUPERSEDED	
Fiss Yield	Maxwl	CCP	Expt Jour	YF 8 454	Sep 68 Solov'Eva. LONG-R-ALPHA,KE-SPECS,CVS	
			Jour	SNP 8 264	Mar 69 TRANSLATN.*	
Fiss Yield	Pile	HLT	Expt Jour	AAF 6 288	Sep 68 Lundan+ I-136 ISOMERIC YLD RATIO	
			Rept	INIS-MF-179	Sep 71 - + I-136 YLD.	

92 Uranium 235

Quantity	Energy (ev) Min	Max	Lab	Type	Documentation Ref Vol Page	Date	Author, Comments	Data
Fiss Yield	Maxwl		KFI	Expt	Jour YF 8 443	Sep 68	Nagy+ DOUB/TER GVN,L-R ALFAS	
					Jour SNP 8 257	Mar 69	.ENGLISH OF YF 8,443	
	-2	1.4+7			Jour KFI 15 85	Apr 67	Nagy+ TERN,ALFA PROBABILITY,TBL	
Fiss Yield	Maxwl		NRD	Expt	Jour PR 173 1159	Sep 68	Delucchi+ SB134 CUMUL YLD=.32+-.04PC	
Fiss Yield	Maxwl		WWA	Expt	Rept INR-952/IAIIPL	Sep 68	Blocki+ REL YLD OF BE LI NUCLEI	
Fiss Yield	6.0-3	2.0+1	DUB	Expt	Rept JINR-P3-4110	Oct 68	Bochvarov+ RELATIVE YLD,EKIN,CRV+TBL	
					Conf 69Vienna 465	Jul 69	- +PPR73. RELATIV YLD+FRAG EK	
					Prog YFI-7 58	69	.ABSTRACT	
					Prog INDC(CCP)-7U	Feb 70	.ENGL TRANSL OF YFI-7	
Fiss Yield	Maxwl		KYU	Theo	Jour JPJ 25 933	Oct 68	Katase.TERNARY.3 POINT CHARGE MODEL	
Fiss Yield	Maxwl		TAT	Expt	Conf 68Bombay 2 110	Dec 68	Iyengar+ LEXAN DETECTOR, YIELD(MASS)	
Fiss Yield	Maxwl	6.0+6	ANL	Expt	Jour PR 177 1817	Jan 69	Meadows+ 4ES MASS-ENERGY DISTRIBUTNS	
	Maxwl				Prog ANL-7450	Apr 68	.CALCULATED TRITIUM YIELDS	
Fiss Yield	Maxwl		CCP	Expt	Jour IZV 33 159	Jan 69	Solov'Ev+ BIN+TERN CFD,FRAG K-X-RAYS	
					Jour BAS 33 145	69	TRANSLATN.*NO 1	
Fiss Yield	Maxwl		WWA	Expt	Jour APP 35 187	Jan 69	Chwaszczewska+ LOW EN ALPHA SPECTRUM	
Fiss Yield	Pile		CCP	Theo	Conf 69Erevan	Feb 69	Zalite+.ABST,TERN FISS,E SPECTRA	
Fiss Yield	Maxwl	+7	FEI	Theo	Jour YF 9 357	Feb 69	Ignatyuk. YLD GRPHS,TH-MODLS CPD XPT	
					Jour SNP 9 208	Aug 69	TRANSLATN.*	
	2.5-2			Expt	Prog YFI-6 40	68	Ignatjuk. CURVE. TO BE PUBL IN YF	
	Maxwl			Theo	Prog YFI-4 3	May 67	- +.,CURVES GIVEN	
	2.5-2			Expt	Rept INDC-260E	69	. ENGL OF YFI-6 40	
	Maxwl			Theo	Rept INDC-187E	67	. ENGL OF YFI-4 3	
Fiss Yield	Maxwl		MIS	Expt	Jour RCA 11 51	Mar 69	Hastings+,FRACT CUMUL YLD OF MO ISOT	
					Abst DA/B 28 1844	Nov 67	- .NO DIRECT YLD TC103,105,106	
					Rept ORNL-3994 11	Sep 66	- +RADIOCHEM.MO/RU103 MO/RH105	
Fiss Yield	Maxwl		ORL	Expt	Jour PR 179 1188	Mar 69	Ferguson+ BA143,144 FRACT CUMUL YLDS	
					Rept ORNL-3994 8	Sep 66	.SUPERSEDED	
Fiss Yield	Maxwl		ORL	Expt	Jour RCA 11 51	Mar 69	Ferguson+ MO103 105 106 FRACTNL YLDS	
					Rept ORNL-3994 11	Sep 66	.SUPERSEDED	
Fiss Yield	Maxwl		IBJ	Expt	Jour NP/A 127 495	Apr 69	Blocki+ LI,BE YLDS FROM SPEC	+
					Rept INR-952/IAIIPL	Sep 68	- + REL YLD OF BE,LI NUCLEI	
	Maxwl				Data EXFOR30317.003	Jan 75	RELATIVE YIELDS OF LI AND BE	
Fiss Yield	2.5+6	1.4+7	KFI	Expt	Jour SNP 8 257	May 69	.ENGLISH OF YF 8,443	
					Jour YF 8 443	Sep 68	Nagy+ 2 ES.DOUB/TER GVN,ALFS	
Fiss Yield	1.5+7		LRL	Expt	Jour PR 182 1251	Jun 69	Nethaway+ MASS YLD DIST=GAUSSIAN	
Fiss Yield	Maxwl		CCP	Expt	Jour AE 27 31	Jul 69	Vorob'Ev+ YLD OF LIGHT NUCLEI,TBLS	+
					Jour SJA 27 713	Jul 69	. ENGL OF AE 27 31	
	2.5-2				Data EXFOR40243.	May 75	.SECONDRY FISS-FRAG YIELD,3 SUBENTR.	
Fiss Yield	Maxwl		EDG	Revw	Conf 69Vienna 83	Jul 69	Feather.PPR201. SURVEY,TERNARY-YIELD	
Fiss Yield		6.0+5	FEI	Expt	Conf 69Vienna 955	Jul 69	D'Jachenko+PPR137. KIN-E,Z,YIELD,NU	
Fiss Yield		+3	FTI	Expt	Conf 69Vienna 900	Jul 69	Adamov+PPR146.LONG RANGE PARTICL YLD	
	Maxwl	1.4+7			Jour YF 9 732	Apr 69	- + PROTON,T,D AND ALFA YLD GIVN	
					Jour SNP 9 424	Oct 69	. ENGL OF YF 9 732	
Fiss Yield	8.8+0	2.1+1	GEL	Expt	Conf 69Vienna 898	Jul 69	Deruytter+ LINAC,TOF,BIN/TERN	+
	8.8+0	2.1+1			Data EXFOR20127.002	Mar 73	4PTS.TER/BIN	
Fiss Yield	Maxwl		HFA	Expt	Conf 69Vienna 947	Jul 69	Notea+PPR36. CHAIN YLDS VS TIME,GELI	
Fiss Yield	Maxwl		IBJ	Expt	Conf 69Vienna 115	Jul 69	Blocki+PPR68.TBL,TERN LIGHT FRAG YLD	
Fiss Yield	Maxwl		ISL	Expt	Prog IA-1190 99	Jul 69	Yellin+ ISOM/GROUND-STATE 135XE YLD	
Fiss Yield	Maxwl		ISL	Expt	Prog IA-1190 101	Jul 69	Isak+ Y-90 INDEPEND YLD,UPPER LIMIT	
Fiss Yield	Maxwl		MCM	Theo	Conf 69Vienna 845	Jul 69	Thind+PPR50. YLD(Z,A)+NU(A)+EXCIT E	
	None				Jour CJP 47 275	Feb 69	- +,CALCTD CUMULATIVE YIELDS,CURV	
Fiss Yield	Maxwl		ORL	Expt	Conf 69Vienna 67	Jul 69	Schmitt.PPR122. YLD GRPH,COMP OF PR	
Fiss Yield	Maxwl		OSL	Revw	Conf 69Vienna 669	Jul 69	Pappas+PPR206. INITIAL+FINAL YLD(A)	
Fiss Yield	Maxwl		PAR	Expt	Conf 69Vienna 955	Jul 69	Chaumont+PPR141.YLD OF ALKALI FRAGS	
Fiss Yield	Maxwl	1.4+7	SAC	Comp	Rept CEA-N-1180	Jul 69	Bessis+ ENERGY VARIATION +CAPT IN FR	
Fiss Yield	Maxwl		SOR	Expt	Conf 69Vienna 948	Jul 69	Amiel+ PPR38.ABST.BR,KR,I,XE IND YLD	
					Prog IA-1190 98	Jul 69	- + 94KR+143XE YLD,ISOTOP-SEPERTR	
Fiss Yield	Maxwl		SOR	Expt	Prog IA-1190 100	Jul 69	Feldstein+ SB-ISOT-YLDS,CHEMICAL	
Fiss Yield	Maxwl		TRM	Theo	Conf 69Vienna 41	Jul 69	Ramamurthy+PPR15. CALC GRPH.CFD EXPT	
					Conf JINR-D3893 97	May 68	Ramanna+ CALC YLD(FRAG) GRPH CFD XPT	
					Conf 68Madras 1 298	Feb 68	- + CALC MASS-YLD CFD EXPT,GRPH	
					Jour PL 21 437	Jun 66	- + MASS DIST ON STOCHASTIC MDL	
Fiss Yield	Maxwl		TUE	Theo	Conf 69Bochum 175	Jul 69	Goennenwein+ CALCULATD YIELD GRAPH	
Fiss Yield	Maxwl		WAS	Expt	Conf 69Vienna 813	Jul 69	Wahl+PPR116.TOT FISSN+FRACT YLDS,TBL	
					Jour JRC 7 309	71	Blachot+ TABLE OF RESULTS GIVEN	
					Rept COO-1162-35	69	.EQUIVALENT	

92 Uranium 235

Quantity	Energy (ev) Min Max	Lab	Type	Documentation Ref Vol Page	Author, Comments Date	Data
Fiss Yield	Maxwl	WUU	Theo	Conf 69Vienna 33	Jul 69 Hasse.PPR28. GRPH,SHELL-TH CFD EXPT	
				Jour NP/A 128 609	May 69 - . CHARGED LIQUID DROP MODEL.	
Fiss Yield	Maxwl	CCP	Expt	Jour YF 10 721	Oct 69 Adamov+ LONG RANGE ALPHA KE SPECS	
				Jour SNP 10 4 416	Apr 70 TRANSLATN.*	
Fiss Yield	Pile	JAE	Expt	Jour NST 6 551	Oct 69 Morozumi+.FISS RATE FROM FISS YIELDS	
Fiss Yield	Maxwl	WAS	Expt	Jour JIN 31 2993	Oct 69 Erdal+,CUMULATIVE YLD OF SN + SB	
				Prog COO-1162-32	Dec 67 - + SN123+SN125 CUMULATIVE YIELDS	
Fiss Yield	Maxwl	WAS	Expt	Jour JIN 31 3005	Oct 69 Erdal+,FISS YLD OF SN ISOTOPES	
Fiss Yield	Maxwl	CUA	Theo	Abst DA/B 30 2222	Nov 69 Rogers.	
Fiss Yield	2.5-2 6.0+5	FEI	Expt	Rept YFI-8 7	Dec 69 Djachenko+	+
	Maxwl			Conf 69Vienna 923	Jul 69 Vorob'Eva+PPR133. FRAG YLD+E(NEUT-E)	
	2.5-2 1.6+7			Jour YF 8 286	Aug 68 D'Jachenko+ GRPHS YLD(A,15 NEUT-ES)	
				Jour SNP 8 165	Feb 69 .TRANSLATION OF YF 8 286	
	2.5-2 1.6+7			Data EXFOR40235.	Jul 75 .40DATA OF FISS-FRAG-YLD AT 14ES GVN	
	2.5-2 6.0+5			Data EXFOR40017.	Nov 73 .7 SUBENT FOR 7 ES,EACH 40 LINES	
Fiss Yield	Maxwl	MNZ	ExTh	Jour ZN/A 24 2000	Dec 69 Denschlag+MODIFIED MOD CALC,CFD EXPT	
			Expt	Jour JIN 31 1873	Jul 69 - .INDEP YIELD OF 135I	
Fiss Yield	Maxwl	NRD	Expt	Jour PR 188 1893	Dec 69 Weiss+,AG 117,118 PD118 CHAIN YIELDS	
				Conf 69Vienna 953	Jul 69 - +PPR115. PD118+CD118 YIELD GIVN	
Fiss Yield	Pile	ROS	Expt	Jour KE 12 380	Dec 69 Muenze+FISS YLD OF DY166,TERNARY FIS	
Fiss Yield	Maxwl	FEI	Eval	Prog YFI-11 19	70 Maksyutenko.ABST,PRECURSOR YLDS,NDG	
				Prog INDC(CCP)-31	Dec 72 .ENGLISH OF YFI-11 19 PAGE 18,	
Fiss Yield	1.0+1 2.0+7	MIL	Theo	Jour APPA 38 537	70 Facchini+ N-INDUCED FISS YLD DIAGRAM	
Fiss Yield	Maxwl	OSA	Expt	Jour RRL 3 1	70 Ohyoshi+ CHROMATOGR. 5INDEP YLDS GVN	
Fiss Yield	Maxwl	MIS	Expt	Jour PR/C 1 312	Jan 70 Niece+ FRACT INDEPEND YLD OF ZR-95	
				Abst DA/B 27 1249	Oct 66 - .INDEP.YIELD ZR95 .0040+-.0006	
Fiss Yield	1.0-3 1.0+2	CCP	Revw	Jour IZV 34 438	Feb 70 Soloveva.ALF-EMISSN PROBABILITY,GRPH	
				Jour BAS 34 378	Jan 71 .ENGL TRANSL OF IZV 34 438	
Fiss Yield	6.0+6 3.7+7	CCP	Revw	Jour IZV 34 438	Feb 70 Soloveva.ALF-EMISSN PROBABILITY,GRPH	
				Jour BAS 34 378	Jan 71 .ENGL TRANSL OF IZV 34 438	
Fiss Yield	Maxwl 1.5+7	FTI	Expt	Jour YF 11 290	Feb 70 Artemev+YLD(A,AVG KINE),THR+FAST CFD	
				Jour SNP 11 162	Aug 70 TRANSLATN.*NO 2	
Fiss Yield	Maxwl +6	ANL	Theo	Rept ANL-7678	Mar 70 Burris+,PROMPT+DELAYED MANY FRAGS	
Fiss Yield	Maxwl	BOR	Expt	Jour NP/A 145 657	Apr 70 Asghar+MULTIPARAM ANAL BIN-,TERNARY	
				Conf 69Vienna 896	Jul 69 Carles+PPR82. YLD(A),BIN+TERNARY CFD	
	None		Theo	Conf 69Vienna 894	Jul 69 Doan+PPR81.ALFA EMISSION CFD SCHMITT	
	Maxwl			Jour NP/A 96 588	Apr 67 - +ALPHA YIELD CALCULATED	
Fiss Yield	Maxwl	NRD	Expt	Jour PR/C 1 1491	Apr 70 Delucchi+,I131 132 133 135 TE135 YLD	
				Rept USNRDL-TR-69	Dec 68 .SUPERSEDED	
Fiss Yield	6.0-2 8.5-2	BKB	Expt	Conf 70Barcelna 2 481	Jul 70 Juric+ TERNARY FISS BY NUCL EMULS	
Fiss Yield	Maxwl	MCM	Expt	Jour CJP 48 1708	Jul 70 Tracy+,BR80,82 I128,130 INDEPEN YLDS	
Fiss Yield	2.0+1 1.0+4	LAS	Expt	Jour PR/C 2 615	Aug 70 Cowan+CD115/MO99 NFY MEAS.MANY RES.	
Fiss Yield	Maxwl	SOR	Expt	Prog IA-1218 93	Aug 70 Braun+ BR+I ISOTOPES YIELD,TABLE	
				Prog IA-1190 104	Jul 69 - + YIELD OF DEL-N-PRECURSOR=BR+I	
Fiss Yield	Maxwl	WAS	Expt	Jour JIN 32 2501	Aug 70 Lin+ FRACT CUMULATIVE YLD OF SN-132	
Fiss Yield	Maxwl	COL	Expt	Jour PR/C 2 1554	Oct 70 Melkonian+,PRE- +POST-NEUT MASS DIST	
Fiss Yield	None	BOR	Theo	Jour JPR 31 919	Nov 70 Doan+TERNARY FISSION	
Fiss Yield	1.4+7	KFK	Comp	Rept KFK-EXT-6 2	Nov 70 Hofmann. CUMULATIVE YLD A=71-161	
	Fiss			Rept KFK-EXT-6 2	Nov 70 - . CUMULATIVE YLD A=71-161	
Fiss Yield	Pile	MNZ	Expt	Jour JIN 32 3149	Nov 70 Fahland+ YLD OF SB124G,126G,TB160	
Fiss Yield	Maxwl 1.4+7	ANL	Eval	Rept ANL-7749	Dec 70 Flynn+ ALSO FISS SPEC NEUTS TBL+CURV	
Fiss Yield	Maxwl	CNA	Theo	Jour PR/C 2 2403	Dec 70 Talat Erben+ ISOTOPIC MASS DISPERSN	
				Rept NP-12309	62 Talat-Erban.CALCULATED CURV YLD VS.Z	
Fiss Yield	Maxwl 1.5+7	LOK	Expt	Jour NCSAC-33 123	Dec 70 Imhof+,11 ES,NO DATA GIVEN	
Fiss Yield	Fast	HAR	Expt	Conf 71Canterby 147	71 Crouch. MASS-SPEC RB,CS,ND.TBL.	
Fiss Yield	Pile	FTI	Expt	Jour IZV 35 2	Jan 71 Artjukh+ HE-4,6,8,10 YLDS+CALC,GRPHS	
				Jour BAS 35 3	Jan 71 *ENGL OF IZV 35 2	
Fiss Yield	Maxwl	MIS	Expt	Jour JIN 33 1	Jan 71 Harbour+ NB99M YLD	
				Abst DA/B 30 1578	Oct 69 - . FCY, HL NB099	
Fiss Yield	Maxwl	MCM	Expt	Jour PR/C 3 849	Feb 71 Kugler+,TERNARY FISS,NE+AR ISOT YLDS	
Fiss Yield	Pile	JUL	Expt	Jour ZN/A 26 512	Mar 71 Labus+ MASS YLD	
Fiss Yield	Maxwl	LAS	Expt	Jour JIN 33 587	Mar 71 Wolfsberg+ XE145 YLD	
Fiss Yield	Pile	MTR	Expt	Jour JIN 33 643	Mar 71 Lisman+ YLD OF KR-85	
Fiss Yield	Maxwl	CRC	Expt	Jour CJP 49 785	Apr 71 Hawkings+ XE135 INDEP/I135 CUMUL YLD	
Fiss Yield	Maxwl	KEN	Expt	Jour RCA 16 2 103	Apr 71 Birgul+ CUM YLDS AT MASS CHAIN 129	
Fiss Yield	Maxwl	MIT	Expt	Abst BAP 16 516	Apr 71 Coryell+. LA CE PR CHAIN YLDS	
Fiss Yield	Maxwl	ORL	Expt	Jour RCA 16 2 66	Apr 71 Roche+ INDEP YLD OF 112AG	
Fiss Yield	1.5+7	FEI	Expt	Conf 71Kiev	May 71 Sergachev+.FRAG YLD,KE OF FRAG,GRPHS	

92 Uranium 235

Quantity	Energy (ev) Min	Max	Lab	Type	Documentation Ref Vol Page	Date	Author, Comments	Data
Fiss Yield	2.5−2		NIR	Expt	Conf 71Kiev 2 78	May 71	Korostylev+	+
	2.5−2			Data	EXFOR40293.002	May 75	.PRIMARY FF YIELD,RELAT DATA,26LINES	
Fiss Yield	+0	6.0+6	FEI	Theo	Jour YF 13 1170	Jun 71	Prokhorova+ SYMMETRIC YLD VS NE,GRPH	
					Jour SNP 13 673	Dec 71	. ENGL OF YF 13 1170	
Fiss Yield	Maxwl		USA	Expt	Abst DA/B 31 7330	Jun 71	Mclaughlin. CUMUL BY G−RAY SPEC	
Fiss Yield	Maxwl		CCP	Theo	Jour AE 31 23	Jul 71	Antsyshkin+ YLD SHIFT AT HIGH FLUXES	
					Jour SJA 31 712	Feb 72	* ENGL OF AE 31 23	
Fiss Yield	Pile		MCM	Expt	Prog INDC(CAN)−9 6	Jul 71	Weller+ YIELD OF SN−ISOTOPES,TB CONT	
Fiss Yield	Maxwl		MIS	Expt	Jour JIN 33 1543	Jul 71	Eichor+ FRACT INDEP YLD OF BA139,140	
Fiss Yield	None		TEH	Expt	Prog INDC(SEC)−18	Aug 71	PG87.EXPT TBD,NDG	
Fiss Yield	Fast		DOU	Revw	Conf 71Canterby 45	Sep 71	Sinclair+DOUNREAY DATA CFD OTHER.TBL	
				Expt	Jour RCA 12 173	Dec 69	Davies.MASS−SPEC,SR90,CS137,ND YLDS	
Fiss Yield	Maxwl		GA	Eval	Rept GA−12071	Sep 71	Mathews+. RECOMMENDED VALUES	
Fiss Yield	Maxwl		WAS	Expt	Jour JIN 33 9 2763	Sep 71	Erdal+ MODES OF FORM OF SN FISS PROD	
Fiss Yield	1.7+5	6.3+5	ANL	Expt	Abst ANS 14 809	Oct 71	Dudey. 6ES.TRITIUM/ALPHA RELATV YLDS	
Fiss Yield	Maxwl		ANL	Expt	Jour NP/A 177 337	Dec 71	Reisdorf+SIMULT MEAS K.E. ANG G−SPEC	
					Conf 69Vienna 781	Jul 69	.PRELIMIN	
Fiss Yield	Maxwl		ANL	Expt	Prog ANL−7850 103	Dec 71	Fluss+CURVE OF TRITIUM YLDS SHOWN.	
	Maxwl	5.4+5			Prog ANL−7824 11	Aug 71	− +.PRELIM YLDS OF TRITIUM GIVEN	
Fiss Yield	Pile		AUA	Expt	Jour AUJ 24 821	Dec 71	Boldeman+ PROMT MASS DIST,GRAPH	
	Maxwl				Rept AAEC/TM−581	Mar 71	− + YIELD(A) GRAPH,NU−EXPERMNT	
Fiss Yield	6.0+5	3.0+6	FEI	Expt	Jour YF 14 1129	Dec 71	Djachenko+ SYMM+ASYM YLD VS N−E,GRPH	
					Jour SNP 14 629	Jun 72	*ENGL OF YF 14 1129	
					Prog INDC(CCP)−31	Dec 72	.PAGE 13.ENGLISH OF YFI−11 14 /70	
Fiss Yield	Maxwl		TRM	Expt	Prog BARC−633 57	72	Kapoor+ FOUR−FRAGMENT FISSION ,GRPH	
Fiss Yield	Maxwl		GEV	Eval	Rept NEDO−12154	Jan 72	Meek+.TABULATD RECOMMENDED YIELDS	
					Rept APED−5398	Oct 68	− + ALSO FISS SPECTRUM, TABLES	
					Rept GEAP−5356	Sep 67	Rider+ TABULATED CHAIN YLDS 90MASSES	
Fiss Yield	Pile		BOS	Expt	Conf 72Bombay 2 53	Feb 72	RAO+ NATURAL U,PILE−N YLDS,SEE U,TBL	
Fiss Yield	Maxwl		MCM	Expt	Jour PR/C 5 551	Feb 72	Kugler+.T HE3 HE4 REL AND ABSOL YLDS	
Fiss Yield	Maxwl		NYU	Expt	Jour PR/C 5 549	Feb 72	Ruddy+. LONG−RANGE FRAGMENTS	
Fiss Yield	None		AUA	Expt	Prog AAEC/PR−36P 4	Mar 72	Rose. REL 140−YIELDS.NDG,TBC.	
Fiss Yield	+1	+6	MOL	Expt	Prog INDC(SEC)−26	May 72	Vanassche.YLDS AT RES,GE−LI,PROPOSED	
Fiss Yield	Maxwl		WAS	Expt	Jour JIN 34 5 1479	May 72	LIN+ CUM YLD OF SN ISOTOPES	
Fiss Yield	2.5+5	7.7+5	ANL	Expt	Abst ANS 15 483	Jun 72	Dudey+. TRITIUM YLDS FOR 10 NEUT ES.	
Fiss Yield	Fast		KFK	Expt	Prog KFK−1272 1	Jun 72	Scholtyssek. P121−14,GAM−ES + YIELDS	
	Pile				Prog KFK−1272 1	Jun 72	− . P121−14,GAM−ES + YIELDS	
Fiss Yield	Maxwl		WAU	Expt	Abst DA/B 32 6899	Jun 72	Mcfarland. SB128 129 130 SN130 YLDS	
Fiss Yield	1.4+7		GRE	Expt	Jour NP/A 189 556	Jul 72	Bocquet+ON−LINE ISOT SEPAR.INDEP,CUM	
Fiss Yield	6.4+0	3.2+1	GEL	Expt	Jour NP/A 194 657	Oct 72	Wagemans+ TER/BIN RATIO VS J STUDIED	+
	6.4+0	4.0+1			Jour JPRC 33 18	Aug 72	− + TERNARY/BIN FISS RATIO	
	8.8+0	5.6+1			Conf 70Helsinki 1 449	Jun 70	Poortmans+ PPR20. NO YLD−J CORRELTN.	
	6.4+0	3.2+1			Data EXFOR20381.	Oct 74	18PTS.TER/BIN.	
Fiss Yield	Maxwl		MNZ	ExTh	Jour JPRC 33 31	Aug 72	Franz+ SHORT LIVED FP YIELDS	
Fiss Yield	Maxwl		SOR	Expt	Jour PR/C 6 618	Aug 72	Ehrenberg+. KR87−94 XE137−143 YLDS	
					Prog IA−1262 77	Dec 72	− + KR+XE INDEPENDT YLDS,GRPH	
Fiss Yield	Maxwl		WAS	Expt	Jour JIN 34 8 2413	Aug 72	Wahl+ CUM YLD OF 83SEC 136I	
Fiss Yield	Pile		JUL	Expt	Jour KT 14 484	Oct 72	Stechemesser.FISS GAS ANAL,NDG	
Fiss Yield	Maxwl		MOL	Expt	Jour NP/A 194 140	Oct 72	Del Marmol+ A FROM 78 TO 84	
					Prog INDC(BLG)−1G	Apr 70	DEL MARMOL+ YIELD OF BR88+I137, NDG	
					Priv DELMARMOL	Apr 68	Del Marmol.FRACT.CUM.YLD.AS83,84(JIN	
Fiss Yield	Maxwl		GER	Expt	Jour RCA 18 4 202	Dec 72	Debertin.REL YLDS OF SEV NUCL	
Fiss Yield	Maxwl		HEB	Prog	Prog IA−1262 80	Dec 72	Venezia. I−ISOTOPES INDEP YIELDS,GRAPH	
Fiss Yield	1.4+7		MNZ	Expt	Jour NP/A 198 228	Dec 72	Alexander. XE133,5 INDP YLDS+ISOMRAT	
Fiss Yield	1.4+7		MNZ	Expt	Jour NP/A 198 228	Dec 72	Alexander. XE133,5 INDP YLDS+ISOMRAT	
Fiss Yield	Maxwl		BUC	Revw	Rept IFA−RN−50	73	Cristu.MASS−+CHARGE−+E−DISTR REVIEW	
	Fast				Rept IFA−RN−50	73	− .MASS−+CHARGE−+E−DISTR REVIEW	
Fiss Yield	Maxwl	1.5+7	LRL	Comp	Rept UCRL−51458	73	Nethaway+.ALSO FISS SPEC. 111 FRAGS.	
Fiss Yield	Pile		TRM	Expt	Rept BARC−690 137	73	Bhargava+ RADIOCHEM,CFD OTHS,TBL+GRP	
	Maxwl				Rept BARC−584	71	Jain+ FLUX REL CO,RADIOCHEM MO99 YLD	
Fiss Yield	Fast		ANL	Expt	Prog ANL−7979 7	Mar 73	Larson. YLDS OF 10 FRAGMENTS GIVEN.	
					Abst ANS 15 483	Jun 72	− +.ZPR−3 MEAST.YLDS 7 FRAGS GVN	
					Prog ANL−7850 108	Dec 71	.YLDS 7FRAGS VS.ZPR−3 POSITION	
Fiss Yield	Maxwl		GRE	Eval	Conf 73Paris 1 477	Mar 73	Devillers+ YLD+DECAY DATA LIBRRY,NDG	
					Rept CEA−N−1526	Mar 72	.YIELDS+GAM TRANSITIONS,TABLES	

92 Uranium 235

Quantity	Energy (ev) Min Max	Lab	Type	Documentation Ref Vol Page	Date	Author, Comments	Data
Fiss Yield	Fast	GRE	Eval	Conf 73Paris 1 477	Mar 73	Devillers+ YLD+DECAY DATA LIBRARY.ND	
				Rept CEA−N−1526	Mar 72	− + YLDS+GAM TRANSITIONS.TBLS	
				Rept CEA−N−1423	Mar 71	− + SUPERSEDED BY CEA−N−1526	
				Rept CEA−N−1269	Apr 70	− + SUPERSEDED BY CEA−N−1526	
Fiss Yield	Maxwl	ANL	Expt	Jour NP/A 205 348	Apr 73	Reisdorf+ MASS DIST AT GIVEN E. CURV	
Fiss Yield	Maxwl	CRC	Eval	Rept AECL−3037 2	Apr 73	Walker.ALL DETAILS,CHAIN YIELDS,TBLS	
				Conf 73Paris 1 459	Mar 73	.SOME REL+ABSOL YLDS,TBLS,GRPH	
				Conf 70Helsinki 1 685	Jun 70	.SUPERSEDED	
				Conf 66Paris 1 521	Oct 66	.SUPERSEDED	
				Rept AECL−2497	66	.SUPERSEDED	
				Rept AECL−2111	Nov 64	Walker. PSUEDO FPY	
				Rept CRRP−913	Mar 60	.SUPERSEDED	
				Rept CRRP−760	Oct 58	Hurst+ CALC YIELDS	
Fiss Yield	Maxwl	IAK	Expt	Jour NP/A 205 488	May 73	Khan+ NDG, USED IN ANAL OF GAMMAS+CE	
Fiss Yield	1.0+6 1.4+7	IIT	Expt	Abst BAP 18 768	May 73	Mandler+. 20 MASS CHAIN YLDS. NDG	
Fiss Yield	Maxwl	BKB	Expt	Jour FIZS 6 8	Jun 73	Antanasijevic+ ABST.A GREATER 16 DET	
Fiss Yield	Maxwl	IBJ	Expt	Jour NP/A 208 381	Jun 73	Piasecki+ POLAR ALF EMIS PROBABILITY	+
	Maxwl			Data EXFOR30319.003	Jan 76	1 PNT,SIG(POLAR ALFAS)	
Fiss Yield	1.8+7 2.1+7	KAZ	Expt	Jour YF 17 1143	Jun 73	Pavlov+ HEAVY MASS YLD REL U235,GRPH	
				Jour SNP 17 595	Dec 73	.ENGLISH OF YF 17 1143	
Fiss Yield	Maxwl	BLA	Theo	Conf 73Munich 1 589	Aug 73	Slavov+ 2CENTR SHELMDL,HVY/LGHT MASS	
Fiss Yield	Fiss	BNW	Expt	Conf 73Rochestr 2 498	Aug 73	Kaye+ ABST,GE(LI),SHORT HL XE,KR,NDG	
Fiss Yield	Maxwl	LIN	Expt	Conf 73Munich 1 716	Aug 73	Vorobjov+ Z=1−8 MASS−SPC,ODD−EVN,NDG	
Fiss Yield	Maxwl	MNZ	Expt	Conf 73Rochestr 2 95	Aug 73	Kratz+ INDEP YLDS AS,SE,A=83−88,TBLS	+
	Pile			Jour JIN 35 1407	May 73	− +	
				Jour JIN 32 3713	Dec 70	− +HERRMANN YLD OF SE87,88+AS87	
	Pile			Data EXFOR20521.003	Apr 76	4PTS.	
Fiss Yield	Maxwl	MNZ	Theo	Conf 73Munich 1 590	Aug 73	Lichtner+ 2CENTR SHELMDL,MASS−CURVE	
Fiss Yield	Pile	UJV	Expt	Jour CZJB 23 8 809	Aug 73	Bischof+ ALF−SPEC FROM TERN FISS,TBL	+
	Pile			Data EXFOR30270.	Jul 74	.ALFA SPEC FOR THERMAL AND RESON NS	
Fiss Yield	Pile	TRM	ExTh	Prog INDC(SEC)−35	Sep 73	Kapoor+ P82.2 LIGHT CHARGD PLES,NDG	
Fiss Yield	Maxwl	MCM	Expt	Prog INDC(CAN)−13	Oct 73	Mathews+ SN+CD YLDS,CONTINUING,NDG	
				Prog INDC(CAN)−9 6	Jul 71	Lum−Hee+ YIELD(A=110 TO 126) GRAPH	
Fiss Yield	Pile	NIR	Expt	Jour YF 18 710	Oct 73	Zakharova+ KE OF FRAG,NEUT−SPEC,GRPH	
				Jour SNP 18 364	Apr 74	. ENGLISH OF YF 18,710.	
Fiss Yield	Maxwl	CAN	Expt	Jour RRL 15 335	Nov 73	Parsons+ INDEP YLD 131−134,GE−LI.TBL	
Fiss Yield	Maxwl	ITE	Expt	Jour YF 18 976	Nov 73	Andreev+ TER,ALF E−SPEC,GRPH	
				Jour SNP 18 503	May 74	. ENGLISH OF YF 18, 976.	
Fiss Yield	Maxwl Pile	CRC	Revw	Conf IAEA−169 1 285	74	Walker.STATUS CHAIN+INDEP YLDS,TBLS	
				Rept AECL−4704	73	.SAME AS 73 BOLOGNA	
Fiss Yield	Maxwl	FAR	Expt	Conf IAEA−169 3 59	74	Robin+ ND148,STABL ND−ISOT/ND148,TBL	
Fiss Yield	Fast	FAR	Expt	Conf IAEA−169 3 59	74	Robin+ ND148 AND STABLE ND YLDS.TBL	
Fiss Yield	Maxwl 8.0+5	HAR	Revw	Conf IAEA−169 1 353	74	Cuninghame.SURVEY TRITIUM YLDS,TBL	
	Fast			Conf IAEA−169 1 353	74	− .FAST+N−E DEPEND,TBLS,GRPH	
	Maxwl 8.0+5			Rept AERE−R−7548	Sep 73	.SAME AS 73BOLOGNA	
	Fast			Rept AERE−R−7548	Sep 73	.SAME AS 73BOLOGNA,EVALUATIONS CFD	
Fiss Yield	Maxwl	SOR	Revw	Conf IAEA−169 2 33	74	Amiel.DELAYED−N PRECURSOR YLDS,TBL	
Fiss Yield	Pile	KFK	Expt	Rept KFK−1888	Jan 74	Hawa+ CUMULATIVE FISS YLD OF KR88	
Fiss Yield	Maxwl	IBJ	Theo	Jour APPB 5 247	Apr 74	Piasecki+ P,D,T,HE−YLDS,CALC,GRAPHS	
Fiss Yield	Pile	TRM	Expt	Jour PR/C 9 1506	Apr 74	Rao+. SEARCH FOR LOW−YIELD FRAGS.	
Fiss Yield	Maxwl	WAS	Expt	Jour JIN 36 6 1201	Jun 74	Malcolm+ FRACT INDEP YLD SB−ISOTOPS	
Fiss Yield	Pile	WAS	Expt	Jour JIN 36 1201	Jun 74	Fowler+ YLDS OF SB−SN A=128−130	
				Jour JIN 36 1191	Jun 74	− + FRAG YLD OF SN131,HL 128−133	
				Prog COO−1162−46 3	72	Wahl+ SN131,SB132,SB133 YIELDS	
				Prog COO−1162−46 2	72	+ SB128,129,130 YIELDS	
Fiss Yield	Maxwl	ANL	Expt	Jour NSE 54 263	Jul 74	Larson+	
				Conf 73Rochestr 2 19	Aug 73	Unik+ PROMPT YLDS,MASS DISTRIB,GRPHS	
				Prog ANL−7979 7	Mar 73	Larson. YLDS OF 10 FRAGMENTS GIVEN.	
Fiss Yield	Fiss	AUA	Eval	Prog AAEC/PR−40P 75	Jul 74	Musgrove. GAUSS−FIT TO CUM YLD,CURVS	
	Maxwl 1.4+7			Prog AAEC/PR−40P 75	Jul 74	− . GAUSS−FIT TO CUM YLD,CURVS	
			Theo	Conf IAEA−169 2 163	74	− + GAUSS FIT MASS YLDS,GRAPH	
Fiss Yield	Maxwl	AUA	Expt	Prog AAEC/PR−40P 28	Jul 74	Boldeman+ MASS−DISTRIBUTION,TBD	
Fiss Yield	1.3+5 1.7+6	HAR	Expt	Jour JIN 36 1453	Jul 74	Cuninghame+ FISS YLDS MO,AG,ND,SM	+
	1.3+5 1.7+6			Data EXFOR20769.002	May 78	30PTS.	
Fiss Yield	1.4+7	MIF	Theo	Jour IVU 17 7 7	Jul 74	Koldobskij+ CUM YLDS(4ISOT)CFD EXPTS	
Fiss Yield		EMY	Theo	Jour PR/C 10 1122	Sep 74	Fong.CALC MASS DISTR VIA STAT TH	
				Conf 73Rochestr 2 43	Aug 73	− .DYNAMIC+STATIST TH CFD EXP,GRP	
Fiss Yield	Maxwl	MCM	Expt	Prog INDC(CAN)−14	Sep 74	Shima+ REL CUMUL PD−ISOT.MASS−SPECTR	

92 Uranium 235

Quantity	Energy (ev) Min	Energy (ev) Max	Lab	Type	Documentation Ref Vol Page	Date	Author, Comments	Data
Fiss Yield	Maxwl		NBS	Expt Rept	HEDL-TME-74-45	Nov 74	Gilliam+ILRR PROG.CUMUL.YLD CFD ENDF	
Fiss Yield	2.2+6		TRM	Expt Prog	INDC(SEC)-42	Dec 74	Ajitanand+ IONIZ CHAMBER,NDG	
Fiss Yield	Pile		TRM	Theo Prog	INDC(SEC)-42	Dec 74	Marathe+ EXPLAN OF BUMPS IN LOW-YLD	
Fiss Yield	1.4+7		FR	ExTh Rept	FRNC-TH-575	75	Cavallini. MASS DIST STUDY	
Fiss Yield	Pile			THD Expt Jour	ZP/A 274 203	75	Clerc+ FISS FRAG 80-A-107	
Fiss Yield	Maxwl			TRM Expt Prog	BARC-821 187	75	Marathe+ A=66,67,170-172.GRAPH	
Fiss Yield	+6	+7	TUE	Expt Rept	ORO-4856-26	75	Holubarsch+ P.591,ABSTRACT.	
Fiss Yield	Maxwl		HAR	Eval Rept	AERE-R-7785	Feb 75	Crouch.CHAIN+INDEPENDENT YLDS TBL	
	Pile			Rept	AERE-R-7680	May 74	- . FRACTIONAL INDEPENDENT YLD	
	Fast	1.4+7		Rept	AERE-R-7394	May 73	- .CHAIN YLDS RECOMMENDED TBL	
Fiss Yield	Fast		ITU	Expt Prog	NEANDC(E)162U	Feb 75	Cottone+ SB-125,XE,CS,ND VOL.5.P.42.	
Fiss Yield	Fiss		LRL	Theo Rept	UCRL-51759	Feb 75	Delucchi.KR-85,XE-131,133,135.YLD(T)	
Fiss Yield	1.5+7		LRL	Theo Rept	UCRL-51759	Feb 75	Delucchi.KR-85,XE-131,133,135.YLD(T)	
Fiss Yield	Maxwl		PAH	Theo Jour	PL/B 55 144	Feb 75	Hooshyar+ISOMERIC FISS,TH CFD EXPTAL	
Fiss Yield	Maxwl		BNW	Expt Conf	75Wash. 401	Mar 75	Reeder+ TBL IND,CUM YLDS RB,CS,BR	
				Conf	73Rochestr 2 498	Aug 73	- + ABST,INDEP YLD,ONLINE MS,NDG	
Fiss Yield	Fiss		SOR	Eval Jour	PR/C 11 845	Mar 75	Amiel+ TBLS,GRPHS.ODD-EVEN EFFECT.	
Fiss Yield	Maxwl			THD Theo Jour	PR/C 11 782	Mar 75	Carjan+ ALPHA EMISS PROB IN FISS	
Fiss Yield	Maxwl		ANL	Expt Jour	JIN 37 869	Apr 75	Flynn+ CHEM.INDEP RB84,86,CS136.TBLS	+
	Maxwl			Data	EXFOR10517.003	Apr 78	. 3PTS.INDEPENDENT FISS YLDS.	
Fiss Yield	Maxwl		GRE	Expt Jour	PRL 34 1034	Apr 75	Siegert+IND YLD,NUC CHARGE.A=92-100	
Fiss Yield	Maxwl	9.9-2	WAI	Expt Jour	CJP 53 775	Apr 75	De-Laeter+ CD YLD REL CD-116	
Fiss Yield	Maxwl		IBJ	Expt Jour	IAEA-R-1126	May 75	Piasecki+ TERN,MASSDIST(POLAR).GRPHS	
Fiss Yield	Maxwl		RI	Expt Conf	75Kiev 6 97	Jun 75	Kondurov+ YLD ALPHA-PART,GRAPH,TBL	
Fiss Yield	Fast		DOU	Expt Prog	UKNDC(75)P71	Jul 75	Davies+IRRAD.MASS SPEC MEAS DFR PFR	
Fiss Yield	Fast		HAR	Expt Prog	UKNDC(75)P71	Jul 75	Crouch+ IRRADIATION DFR	
Fiss Yield	Maxwl Pile		GRE	Expt Prog	NEANDC(E)162U	Aug 75	Blachot+ 16 YIELDS TBL	
Fiss Yield	Maxwl		SOR	Expt Jour	IA-1308 107	Sep 75	Amiel+ ODD-EVN-Z,TBL INDEP ELEM-YLDS	
				Eval Jour	PR/C 11 845	Mar 75	- + TBLS,GRPHS.ODD-EVEN EFFECT.	
				Conf	73Rochestr 2 65	Aug 73	- + INDEP+CUMUL YLDS,GRAPHS,TABLS	
Fiss Yield	Pile		MOL	Expt Jour	ZP/A 275 149	Nov 75	Wagemans+ YIELD OF LONGE-RANGE A	
Fiss Yield	Maxwl		ORU	Theo Abst	ANS 22 672	Nov 75	Liaw+ SR,XE YIELDS CALC.GRPH	
Fiss Yield	Maxwl		GRE	Expt Jour	NP/A 255 461	Dec 75	Brissot+ YIELDS OF RARE GAS ISOTOPES	
Fiss Yield	Maxwl		IBJ	Expt Jour	NP/A 255 387	Dec 75	Piasecki+ FULL PAPER,DISCUSS,RESULTS	
	Pile			Prog	INDC(SEC)-42	Dec 74	- + POLAR T,D,P,HE6 E-SPC,GRPH	
	Maxwl			ExTh Conf	73Rochestr 2 383	Aug 73	- + POLAR P,D,T,A YLD+CALC,FIG	
Fiss Yield	Pile		MOL	Expt Jour	ZP/A 275 359	Dec 75	Fettweis+YLD,DECAY SCH OF RU-ISOTOP	
Fiss Yield	Fast		WUR	Expt Jour	NSE 58 414	Dec 75	Rajagopalan+ PROTEUS SPECT.27 MASSES	
				Prog	INDC(SEC)-43	Dec 74	- + CHEM+G-SPC.REL 140,TBL	
Fiss Yield	Maxwl		GHT	Expt Jour	NIM 134 299	76	Thierens+ REL MASS YLD TBL	
Fiss Yield	Maxwl		MNZ	Expt Prog	MAINZ-1975	76	Meixler+ STEARAT METHOD CUM.YIELD	+
	2.5-2			Data	EXFOR20711.002	Feb 77	2PTS.	
Fiss Yield	Maxwl		SOR	Expt Jour	IA-1338 97	76	Shmid+ RB,CS,BA-ISOT,CFD SYSTEM.FIGS	
Fiss Yield	Maxwl		TRM	Expt Jour	PRM 6 2 64	76	Choudhury+ REL MASS-YLD(BIN,LRA).FIG	
Fiss Yield	Maxwl		HAR	Eval Rept	AERE-R-8152	Jan 76	Crouch. ADJUSTED FISSION YIELD,TABLE	
	Fast			Rept	AERE-R-8152	Jan 76	- . ADJUSTED FISSION YIELD,TABLE	
	Maxwl			Conf	73Paris 1 393	Mar 73	- .EXPTL DATA+EVAL CHAIN YLD,TBL	
				Rept	AERE-R-7209	Jan 73	- .88 CHAIN YLDS RECOMMENDED TBL	
				Theo Rept	AERE-R-6056	Mar 69	- .CALC FRACT INDEPEND YLDS,TBLS	
Fiss Yield	+6	+7	RAM	Expt Prog	INDC(SEC)-50	Jan 76	Islam+ P7,VERY BRIEF.FRG(NEUT-E),TBD	
Fiss Yield	Maxwl		UBE	Expt Jour	JIN 38 205	Feb 76	Gaeggeler+ PM150,RADIOCHEM.MANY TBLS	
				Diss	GAEGGELER	Dec 73	- . COMPLETE EXPT DESCRIPTION	
				Conf	73Rochester 2 475	Aug 73	- + ABST,PM150 INDEP YLD GIVN	
Fiss Yield	2.5-2		EMY	Theo Jour	PR/C 13 1259	Mar 76	Fong.ASYMM FISS VIA DYNAMICAL TH.CFD	
Fiss Yield	Pile		GRE	Expt Rept	IKDA-7616	May 76	Schmidt+MASS DISTR,LIGHT FISFRAG	
Fiss Yield	Maxwl		UJV	Expt Jour	NP/A 262 301	May 76	Wilhelm+ SIG POLAR ALF GVN,SEE ASL25	+
				Jour	ASL 25 199	75	Bayer+ INTEGSIG FOR POLAR ALFAS GIVN	
	Maxwl			Data	EXFOR30279.004	Nov 74	SIG FOR POLAR ALFA, 1 POINT	
Fiss Yield	2.0+6	1.4+7	AUA	Theo Jour	AUJ 29 125	Jun 76	Cook+ 2ES.GAUSSFIT PARAMS VS E.TBLS	
	Maxwl			Jour	AUJ 29 125	Jun 76	- + GAUSSFIT.FOR E-DEPEND OF PARA	
	Maxwl	1.4+7		Rept	AAEC/E-386	Mar 76	- + 3-GAUSS FIT,SAME 3ES AS AUJ 2	
Fiss Yield	Maxwl		PAH	ExTh Conf	76Lowell 725	Jul 76	Hooshyar+STATMDL APLD TO EXPT.DATA	
	1.6+7	2.2+7		Conf	76Lowell 725	Jul 76	- + 2ES.STATMDL CFD XPT	
Fiss Yield	2.0+6	1.5+7	TRM	Theo Jour	PR/C 14 181	Jul 76	Sharma+2E.ORDER-DISORDER MDL.CFD EXP	
Fiss Yield	2.5-2	1.8+6	TRM	Expt Conf	76Lowell 1409	Jul 76	Nadkarni+ ALF YLD,E-SPEC DEP.TBL,FIG	
	7.5+5	1.8+6			Prog BARC-878 47	76	- + REL THERM.LRA EMISSN,TABLE	
	2.4-2	1.7+6			Conf 75Calcutta 2 131	Dec 75	- +YIELD,ESPECTRA ALFAS,TABLE	
Fiss Yield	5.5+5		TUE	Expt Conf	76Lowell 1406	Jul 76	Muller+FRAG MASSES DETERMINED.NDG	

92 Uranium 235

Quantity	Energy (ev) Min	Max	Lab	Type	Documentation Ref Vol Page	Author, Comments Date	Data
Fiss Yield	Fast		HAR Expt	Rept	AERE-R-6862	May 72 Cuninghame+ 14 ABSOL YLDS.DFR SPEC	+
				Prog	NEANDC(E)172 8	Aug 76 - + FAST REACTOR SPECTRA	
				Prog	UKNDC(75)P71	Jul 75 - + YLDS VS REACTOR N SPEC.	
				Prog	NEANDC(UK)160	Jul 74 - + YLDS DIFF ZEBRA SPEC.TBD	
	1.0+6			Data	EXFOR20768.002	May 78 19PTS.	
Fiss Yield	Maxwl		ILL Expt	Jour	PL/B 63 275	Aug 76 Wohlfarth+MASS DIST,LIGHT PRODS.TBL.	
				Conf	76Corsica 509	May 76 Clerc+ (LOHENGRIN) YLDS LIGHT FRAGS	
Fiss Yield	Maxwl		LIN Theo	Jour	YF 24 270	Aug 76 Val'Skii+ A=1TO20 YLD,4PARAM FORMULA	
				Jour	SNP 24 140	Aug 76 . ENGLISH OF YF 24 270	
Fiss Yield	Fast		GA Expt	Abst	ANS 24 458	Nov 76 Buzzelli+TRITIUM FAST FISS YLD.TBL	
Fiss Yield	Maxwl		SOR Expt	Jour	JIN 38 2133	Dec 76 Lavi+ YLD-RATIO I134M/I132M GIVN,CFD	+
	Maxwl			Data	EXFOR30365.002	Dec 76 ISOM.YIELD RATIO OF I-132M,I-134M.	
Fiss Yield	Maxwl		SWR Expt	Jour	NIM 139 239	Dec 76 Rudstam+ SURVEY OF OSIRIS PROGRAMME	
Fiss Yield	Maxwl		BRC Expt		NEANDC(E)172 4	77 Amoudry+ ABSTRACT ONLY,COIN METHOD	
Fiss Yield	1.0+4	3.0+5	GEL Expt	Prog	BLG-520	77 Wagemans+ TBC.NDG.	
Fiss Yield	Fiss		GRE Expt	Rept	CEA-N-1979	77 Ferrieu+ ABSTRACT,TABLE GIVEN	
Fiss Yield	Maxwl		GRE Expt	Prog	CEA-N-2015	77 Asghar+TABLE OF MEAN PARAMETERS	
Fiss Yield	Maxwl		GRE Expt	Prog	CEA-N-2015	77 Bocquet+ISOM.RATIO FOR FORMATION FP	
Fiss Yield	1.0+6	2.5+7	LIN Expt	Conf	77Kiev	77 Grachev+ ANG+E CORREL OF ALPHA-PART	
	Maxwl			Conf	75Kiev	May 75 Vorob'Ev+ EN AND ANG CORRELATION	
Fiss Yield	1.4+7		TIL Expt	Rept	YK- 27 42	77 Petrzhak+ YLD XE-131,132,134,136,TBL	
Frag Spectra	None		COL Theo	Jour	PR 58 696	Oct 40 Lamb+STOPPING CALC FOR Z=42.50 FRAGS	
Frag Spectra	None		CRC Expt	Jour	PR 70 974	Dec 46 Demers. DISTRIB. OF RANGES. EMULS.	
Frag Spectra	None		LAS Expt	Abst	PR 71 141	Jan 47 Richards+ RANGE DISTRIB IN EMULSION.	
Frag Spectra	None		ANL Theo	Jour	PR 72 431	Sep 47 Dempster. K.E. OF PAIRS CALCULATED.	
Frag Spectra	None		LAS Expt	Jour	PR 72 926	Nov 47 Fowler+'SLOW','FAST'D-BE NS.E-DISTRB	
Frag Spectra	Maxwl		CRC Expt	Jour	PR 75 990	Mar 49 Brunton+ E-DIST VS MASS. CFD U233+PU	
				Jour	PR 76 1798	Dec 49 - + CHG DIST	
Frag Spectra	9.0+7		BRK Expt	Jour	PR 76 1112	Oct 49 Jungerman+ PROMPT NS TAKE SURPLUS E	
Frag Spectra	-		COP Expt	Jour	PR 76 988	Oct 49 Boggild+ CLOUDCH,E BY PO(A)+N14(NP)	
Frag Spectra	Maxwl		CRC Expt	Jour	CJR 28 190	Mar 50 Brunton+. ENERGY DISTRIBUTION	
Frag Spectra	Maxwl	1.4+7	LAS Expt	Rept	AECU-929	Mar 50 Friedland. E-DIST AT 2 ENERGIES	
Frag Spectra	None		CRC Expt	Jour	PR 80 181	Oct 50 Allen+ ALFA RANGE-ENERGY DISTRIBUTNS	
Frag Spectra	None		LAS Expt	Jour	PR 87 444	Aug 52 Leachman+ TOF VELOCITY DIST CURVES	
Frag Spectra	Maxwl		ANL Expt	Jour	PR 87 1049	Sep 52 Hill+ALFA+PROTON RANGE DISTRIBUTIONS	
Frag Spectra	Maxwl	1.4+7	LAS Expt	Jour	PR 94 640	May 54 Brolley+ 2ES ANG DIST+ 0DEG/90DEG	
Frag Spectra	Maxwl	1.4+7	LAS Expt	Jour	PR 95 126	Jul 54 Wahl+2ES FRAG ENERGY DIST IONIZ CHMB	
Frag Spectra	Maxwl		LAS Expt	Jour	PR 96 1366	Dec 54 Leachman+ VELOCTY DIST OF SLOWD FRAG	
Frag Spectra	Maxwl		LAS Expt	Jour	CJP 33 357	Jul 55 Leachman+ AVG KE=167.1+-1.6MEV CALOR	
Frag Spectra	Pile		LAS Revw	Conf	55Geneva 2 193	Aug 55 Leachman.P592,FISSFRGMNT-ENERGY	
Frag Spectra	2.5-2		CCP Expt	Rept	AEC-TR-2386	Mar 56 Varfolomeev+. FRAG ANGULAR DISTR	
Frag Spectra	Maxwl		ORL Expt	Jour	PR 104 1046	Nov 56 Cohen+,ENERGY DISTR FOR A=91 AND 97	
				Jour	PHY 22 1187	Nov 56 .SUPERSEDED	
Frag Spectra	Maxwl		ANL Expt	Abst	BAP 2 70	Feb 57 Trail+ FRAG+GAMMA ANGULAR CORRELATN	
Frag Spectra	Maxwl		LRL Expt	Jour	PR 107 1642	Sep 57 Gunn+,AVG FFRAG KE 166+-2MEV	
Frag Spectra	Maxwl		LAS Expt	Jour	PR 108 94	Oct 57 Stein+TOF MASS AND ENERGY DISTRIBUT	
Frag Spectra	Pile		ORL Expt	Jour	PR 108 370	Oct 57 Fulmer+,CS PHS E DISTR PROMPT ALFAS	
Frag Spectra	1.5+7		RI ExTh	Jour	ZET 34 250	Jan 58 Protopopov.DEGREE OF ANISOTROPY	
				Jour	JET 7 173	Jul 58 TRANSLATN.*	
Frag Spectra	Maxwl		CCP Expt	Jour	AE 4 547	Jun 58 Kovrigin+.CFS U238 SP F,IONIZN METHD	
				Jour	SJA 4 721	58 TRANSLATN.*	
Frag Spectra	+6		LAS Revw	Conf	58Geneva 15 344	Sep 58 Hemmendinger.PPR663,CURVE,REL ANGLE	
Frag Spectra		2.0+7	TRM Revw	Conf	59Calcutta 152	Feb 59 Ramanna. REVIEW,GRPH ANGDIST(NEUT-E)	
Frag Spectra	Maxwl		CCP Expt	Jour	AE 7 372	Oct 59 Mostovoi+. TERNARY FISS, FRAG E DISTR	
				Jour	SJA 7 851	Mar 61 TRANSLATN.*	
				Jour	JNEA 13 84	Oct 60 TRANSLATN.*	
Frag Spectra	6.0+6	2.0+7	CRC Expt	Jour	CJP 37 1418	Dec 59 Baerg+. FRAG ANG DIST ISOTROPIC	
Frag Spectra	1.4+7		LRL Expt	Jour	PR 117 186	Jan 60 Stevenson. AV KINETIC E = 174+-4 MEV	
Frag Spectra	None		SPN Expt	Jour	ARS 56 19	Feb 60 .A PART.SPECT,E AND ANG DISTRIBUTION	
Frag Spectra	Maxwl		SPN Expt	Jour	ARS 56 39	Feb 60 .MAX LIMIT LIGHT PART SPECT	
Frag Spectra	None		CCP Theo	Jour	ZET 38 955	Mar 60 Geilikman. EXCIT E VS FRAG RATIO,CRV	
				Jour	JET 11 688	Sep 60 TRANSLATN.*	
				Jour	AE 6 298	Mar 59 SEE ALSO *= SJA 6 184 N/60	
Frag Spectra	Maxwl		CCP Revw	Jour	UFN 71 471	Jul 60 Perfilov+.GRAPH,FRGMNT+ALFA E-DISTRB	
				Jour	SPU 3 542	Jan 61 . ENGL TRANSL OF UFN 71 471	
Frag Spectra	Pile		RI Expt	Jour	ZET 39 556	Sep 60 Dmitriev.E-SPCTR FROM TRIPLE FISSION	
				Jour	JET 12 390	Mar 61 TRANSLATN.*	
Frag Spectra	Maxwl		HAR Expt	Rept	AERE-R-3524	Oct 60 Melkonian.SI DETECTORS.	

92 Uranium 235

Quantity	Energy (ev) Min	Max	Lab	Type	Documentation Ref Vol Page	Date	Author, Comments	Data
Frag Spectra	5.2 – 5	2.3+7	LAS Expt	Jour	PR 120 198	Oct 60	Simmons+ FRAGMENT ANGULAR DIST 28ES	
Frag Spectra	Maxwl		MUNRevw	Conf	60Vienna 63	Oct 60	Maierleibnitz.CURVE,EXPT DESCRIBED	
Frag Spectra	1.4+7		LAS Expt	Jour	NP 19 366	Nov 60	Leachman+.ZR97,BA139 FORE/AFT RATIO	
Frag Spectra	Maxwl		LRL Expt	Jour	PR 120 874	Nov 60	Alexander.FROM RADIOCHEM+RANGE-E	
Frag Spectra	Maxwl		TRM Expt	Conf	61Bombay 170	Feb 61	Ramanna+.ENERGY+ANGLE OF FRGMNT	
Frag Spectra	Maxwl		ROS Expt	Jour	KE 5 158	Jan 62	Muenze.LONGRANGE ALFAS,TERNARY FISS	
				Jour	KE 5 488	Jan 62	– .LONGRANGE ALFAS,TERNARY FISS	
Frag Spectra	Maxwl		TRM Expt	Conf	62Madras 79	Feb 62	Kapoor+.GRPH,ANG CORREL FRGMNT+GAMMA	
Frag Spectra	+6		LAS Theo	Jour	AP 18 274	May 62	Leachman+ CALC ANISOTROPY CFD EXPTS	
Frag Spectra	Maxwl		LAS Expt	Jour	PR 126 1508	May 62	Nobles. E SPEC OF LONG RANGE FFRGM	
Frag Spectra	Maxwl		CRC Expt	Jour	CJP 40 1626	Nov 62	Milton+FRASER DOUBLE VEL MEASUREMNTS	
Frag Spectra	Maxwl		COP Theo	Jour	NP 46 129	Jul 63	Vandenbosch. EFF OF FRAG SHELL STRUC	
Frag Spectra	7.0+6	2.0+7	CCP Expt	Jour	ZET 45 8	Aug 63	D'Jachenko.MEAN KINETIC FRG-E AT 3ES	
				Jour	JET 18 6	Jan 64	TRANSLATN.*	
Frag Spectra	Maxwl		ITE Expt	Rept	ITE –	Oct 63	Perfilov+TERNARY FISS.ALPHA SPEC,GRP	
Frag Spectra	Maxwl		PSU Expt	Jour	PR 132 371	Oct 63	Cooperman+ COINC WITH PROMPT GAMMAS	
Frag Spectra	Maxwl		CCP ExTh	Jour	AE 15 419	Nov 63	Okolovich+ AV EK REL U238. THEORY	
				Jour	JNE 18 533	Sep 64	TRANSLATN.*	
				Jour	SJA 15 1177	Nov 63	TRANSLATN.*	
Frag Spectra	–		CCP Revw	Rept	INDSWG–64 266	64	Maksjutenko.FRGMTS EMITNG DELAYED NS	
	8.0+4	1.3+6	CCP Expt	Rept	ANL-TR–179	64	Bondarenko+,ANG DIST FRAGS,GRPH	
Frag Spectra	Maxwl		GER Expt	Rept	SGAE–PH–10	64	Schneeberger+. FRAG KE DISTR MEASD	
Frag Spectra	2.5 – 2		JNE Expt	Rept	JEN–131 DF/I42	64	Domingo. TERN FIS,ALPHA E+ANG DIST	
Frag Spectra	1.5+7	2.0+7	CCP Expt	Jour	AE 16 521	Jun 64	Okolovich+MEAN KINETIC E.OF FRAGMENT	
				Jour	SJA 16 644	64	. ENGL OF AE 16 521	
Frag Spectra	Maxwl		ISL Expt	Rept	IA–1082 55	65	Gozez+.NDG,SEE ALSO IA–1021 P25	
Frag Spectra	–3	+6	TRM Revw	Rept	AEET–235	65	Methasiri.ALF E+ANG DIST,GRPH,CFD TH	
Frag Spectra	Maxwl	7.2+5	FEI Expt	Jour	YF 2 92	Jan 65	D'Jachenko.KE VS MASS.THR CFD FAST	+
	6.0+6			ExTh Jour	YF 10 61	Jul 69	– + FRAG TOT E,STATMOD ANAL	
	Maxwl			Expt Jour	SNP 6 848	Jun 68	. *	
				Jour	YF 6 1167	Dec 67	Djachenko+ FRAG K-E REL THR,TBL,GRPH	
				Prog	INDC–E–187 4	67	.ENGLISH TRANSL OF YFI–4 5 5/67	
	Maxwl	7.2+5		Conf	65Salzburg 1 601	Mar 65	.CONTINUATION OF YF 2 92 1/65	
				Prog	YFI–1 5	65	.ABSTRACT	
				Jour	SNP 2 65	Jan 66	.ENGLISH TRANSL OF YF 2 92 1/65	
	2.5 – 2	7.2+5		Prog	INDSWG–120E 4	65	.ENGLISH TRANSL OF YFI–1 5 /65	
	8.0+4	2.5+6		Data	EXFOR40158.007	Mar 73	REL E-KIN OF FRGMNTS AT 11 ES	
Frag Spectra	4.0+6		TRM Expt	Jour	PR/B 137 511	Feb 65	Kapoor+ ANG+ENERGY+A DISTRIBUTN,CRVS	
				Conf	65Calcutta 33	Feb 65	SUPERSEDED*	
				ExTh Conf	65Calcutta 27	Feb 65	Nadkarni. ANGDIST GRAPHS,THEO+EXPT	
				Expt Conf	64Chandgrh 120	Feb 64	Kapoor+ GRAPH,ANISOTROPY,E–DISTRIB	
Frag Spectra	Maxwl		TRM Theo	Conf	65Salzburg 20	Feb 65	Ramanna+ DEFORM–E(FRAG A),MARKOV–TH	
Frag Spectra	8.8+0	4.0+1	COL Expt	Conf	65Salzburg 355	Mar 65	Melkonian+ KIN E AND MASS DISTR	
Frag Spectra	Maxwl		CRC Revw	Conf	65Salzburg 451	Mar 65	Fraser.DISCUSSION OF VARIOUS XPTS	
Frag Spectra	Maxwl		EDG Theo	Conf	65Salzburg 2 387	Mar 65	Feather.ALPHA EMISSION IN FISSION	
Frag Spectra	Maxwl		KUR Expt	Conf	65Salzburg 1 587	Mar 65	Apalin+,EXCIT ENERGY+KIN–E,GRPHS	
				Jour	YF 1 639	Apr 65	SEE ALSO *NP 71 553 9/65	
				Jour	SNP 1 457	Oct 65	. ENGL OF YF 1 639	
Frag Spectra	None		MIT Theo	Conf	65Salzburg 73	Mar 65	Gordon.ARAS.MONTE CARLO CALC CFD XPT	
Frag Spectra	Pile		MUNExpt	Conf	65Salzburg 505	Mar 65	Ewald.REVW OF XPTS MASS–SPCTMTR MUN	
Frag Spectra	–2		ORL Theo	Conf	65Salzburg 39	Mar 65	Dabbs.ANISOTROPY OF ALFAS CALCULATED	
Frag Spectra	None		ORL Theo	Conf	65Salzburg 1 369	Mar 65	Halpern. ALPHA EMISSION IN FISSION	
Frag Spectra	Maxwl		PTN Expt	Conf	65Salzburg 1 467	Mar 65	Thomas+ SINGLE FRAG E–SPECTRA	
Frag Spectra	3.0+6		TRM Expt	Conf	65Salzburg 397	Mar 65	.ALPHA EMISSION IN FISSION	
				Conf	65Calcutta 27	Feb 65	Hattangadi+ LONG–R–ALFA,E–SPEC GRPHS	
				Prog	AEET–214 27	65	– + ALF E–SPEC+ANGDIST GIVEN	
Frag Spectra	Maxwl		KUR Expt	Jour	YF 1 816	May 65	Apalin+,FRAG K.E +ENERGY BALANCE	
				Jour	NP 71 546	Sep 65	SEE ALSO * IAE–709 /64	
				Jour	SNP 1 457	Oct 65	. ENGL OF YF 1 639	
Frag Spectra	Maxwl		TRM Expt	Prog	AEET–228 5	Aug 65	Murthy. FRAG A+EKIN DISTRIBUTN, NDG	
Frag Spectra	None		AGNExTh	Jour	NSE 23 8	Sep 65	Kahn+ EN MONTE CARLO ANLYS	
Frag Spectra	Maxwl	7.0+6	FEI Expt	Rept	FEI–24	Nov 65	Vorobeva+ E–KIN VS MASS.THR,5,6,7–MEV	
				Rept	LA–TR–66–36	66	.ENGLISH TRANSL OF FEI–24	
Frag Spectra	Maxwl		ORL Expt	Jour	PR 141 1146	Jan 66	Schmitt+ MASS. ENERGY DIST.	
				Jour	NIM 29 205	Oct 64	– + N(E1E2) ARRAY.	
				Conf	63ANL 441	Oct 63	.SUPERSEDED	

92 Uranium 235

Quantity	Energy (ev) Min	Energy (ev) Max	Lab	Type	Documentation Ref Vol Page	Date	Author, Comments	Data
Frag Spectra	Maxwl		MIT	Expt	Rept TID – 23365	Aug 66	Nakahara.FRAG RANGES + KE DEFICITS	
					Jour CJP 47 2371	Nov 69	– +,RANGES IN ALUMINUM	
					Rept MIT – 905 – 21	Dec 65	.SUPERSEDED	
Frag Spectra	Maxwl	1.4+7	CIS	Theo	Jour NP 84 595	Sep 66	Erba+ STATMOD CFD EXPT,FRAG E VS A	
Frag Spectra		2.0+6	CCP	Comp	Jour ICD – 3 26	Oct 66	Bolshov+.GRAPHS CFD TH,MANY REFS	
					Rept INDC – 152E	67	. ENGL OF ICD – 3 26	
Frag Spectra	Maxwl		NRD	Theo	Jour PR 150 1018	Oct 66	Ferguseon+EXTENDS PR139 B56	
Frag Spectra	8.0+4	6.1+6	FEI	Expt	Jour YF 4 993	Nov 66	Nesterov+ ANG DISTRB OF FRAGMENTS	+
					Rept FEI – 33	65	.FRAG ANGDIST(E),GRAPH,TABLE	
					Jour SNP 4 713	May 67	.ENGLISH TRANSL OF YF 4 933 11/66	
					Rept LA – TR – 66 – 41	66	.ENGLISH TRANSL OF FEI – 33 /65	
Frag Spectra	Maxwl		CCP	Expt	Jour IZV 30 2040	Dec 66	Popeko+ E – SPEC FRAGS,DELAYD – G EMITTG	
					Jour BAS 30 2025	66	. ENGL OF IZV 30 2040	
Frag Spectra	Maxwl		ISL	Expt	Rept IA – 1128	Dec 66	Katase+.NDG,SPECTRM OF ALFAS	
Frag Spectra	Maxwl		SRC	Expt	Jour PL 23 583	Dec 66	Marshall+E SPECTRA ALPHAS,TRITONS	
Frag Spectra	Maxwl		COL	Expt	Rept TID – 23889	67	Derengowski.MASS DIST FROM E+TOF	
Frag Spectra	Maxwl		SOR	Expt	Prog IA – 1168 12	Jan 67	Gazit+ GRPHS YLD VS KIN – E,BIN+TERN	
Frag Spectra	3.7+5	2.1+6	TRM	Expt	Conf 67Kanpur 325	Feb 67	Nadkarni+,FISS FRAG KE DIST,NU CALC	+
	Maxwl				Prog AEET – 267 4	Aug 66	– . AVG FRAG – EKIN	
		2.0+6			Prog AEET – 267 4	Aug 66	– . AVG FRAG – EKIN,21ES	
	3.7+5	2.1+6			Data EXFOR30022.002	Jun 70	AVG – KE MINUS AVG – KE(THR) AT 21 ES.	
Frag Spectra	Maxwl		ALD	Expt	Jour NP/A 94 537	Mar 67	Andritsopoulos+ TOF,SOLID STATE DET.	
					Conf 65Salzburg 1 481	Mar 65	– + SUPERSEDED	
Frag Spectra	Maxwl		FLA	Expt	Jour PRL 18 404	Mar 67	Muga+2. E SPEC IN TERNARY FISSION	
					Conf 65Salzburg 1 409	Mar 65	– + TERNARY FISSION	
Frag Spectra	Maxwl		LAS	Expt	Jour PR 156 1277	Apr 67	Stein+ FRAG ENERGIES VS MASS,+ TOTAL	
Frag Spectra	Maxwl		MCM	Expt	Jour NIM 49 220	Apr 67	Oakey+ELECTROSTATIC GUIDE,TGT TO DET	
Frag Spectra	Maxwl		FEI	Theo	Prog YFI – 4 3	May 67	Ignatjuk+.,CURVES GIVEN	
	None				Jour YF 7 1043	May 68	– . E – KIN(FRAG – A),SHELLMODEL	
	Maxwl				Rept INDC – 187E	67	. ENGL OF YFI – 4 3	
Frag Spectra	2.0 – 2	1.1+1	MTR	Expt	Jour PR 157 1055	May 67	Moore+ YLD HIGH KE FRAG VS NEUT E	
					Rept IN – 1033	Nov 66	– +SEE FOR MORE EXPT DETAILS	
					Conf 65Salzburg 1 87	Mar 65	.SUPERSEDED	
Frag Spectra	Maxwl		SAC	Expt	Jour NP/A 99 41	Jun 67	Signarbieux+FISS PRODUCT KINETIC E	
	None				Conf 69Vienna 951	Jul 69	Nifenecker+ PPR79.YLD(Z,A),X – RAY – XPT	
	Maxwl				Prog EANDC(E)115U	Mar 69	– .ANG – E CORR IN TERN FISS	
					Prog EANDC(E)89U172	Feb 68	– +SEARCH LIGHT FRAGM	
					Conf CEA – R – 3309	Mar 67	Ribrag.DEDUCE FISS YIELD FROM E DIST	
					Rept CEA – R – 2408	Dec 63	Chartache. SEE ALSO	
Frag Spectra	Pile		WWA	Expt	Rept INR – 817/IA/PL	Aug 67	Sowinski+ LONG RANGE ALPHA+ TERN FIS	
Frag Spectra	Maxwl		WWA	Expt	Jour PL/B 25 213	Aug 67	Dakowski+ P,D,T,HE4,HE6 SPEC,CURVES	
					Rept INP – 702/PS	Jun 70	– + SEMICOND RESULTS CFD THEO	
					Jour APP 34 173	Jul 68	Chwaszczewska+ ALF – SPEC ONLY	
					Rept INR – 822/IA/PL	Aug 68	.SAME TEXT,MORE CURVES	
Frag Spectra	2.9+6		IFJ	Expt	Jour APP 32 485	Sep 67	Benisz+ TERNARY TOT K – E,E – A CORREL	
					Rept INP – 529	Mar 67	EQUIVALENT*	
Frag Spectra		1.4+6	FEI	Expt	Jour YF 6 1162	Dec 67	Bolshov+ AVG FRAG KIN – E(NEUT – E)GRAPH	
	1.0+5	2.0+6			Rept FEI – 49	66	Bol'Shov+.MEAN FISS FRAG – E VS NEUT – E	
	Maxwl	1.3+6			Jour SNP 6 844	Jun 68	Bolshov+ TRANSLATION	
	1.0+5	2.0+6			Rept LA – TR – 68 – 19	68	. ENGL OF FEI – 49	
Frag Spectra	Maxwl		KFK	Comp	Rept KFK – 693	Dec 67	Muenzel+ RANGE DIST OF FISS FRAG	
Frag Spectra	Pile		PR	Expt	Jour JIN 29 2831	Dec 67	Almodovar+	
Frag Spectra	2.9 – 1	1.9+1	BLA	Theo	Jour CRB 21 199	68	Bochvarov+ AVG EKIN VARIAT WITH RES	
Frag Spectra	– 2		FTI	Expt	Prog YFI – 6 84	68	Val'Skij+ TABLES, TO BE PUBL IN YF	
					Rept INDC – 260E	69	. ENGL OF YFI – 6 84	
Frag Spectra	Maxwl		GEL	Expt	Conf IAEA – 107 237	68	Spaepen. FRAG – E – SPEC VS FOIL – THCKNSS	
					Conf 67Brussels	May 67	– . PPR13. EQU TO IAEA – 107.	
Frag Spectra	2.5 – 2		RI	Expt	Prog YFI – 6 98	68	Solov'Ev+. GRAPH, E – SPEC OF FRAGMNTS	
					Rept INDC – 260E	69	. ENGL OF YFI – 6 98	
Frag Spectra	1.6+7		FEI	Expt	Jour YF 7 36	Jan 68	D'Jachenko+ E – SPEC,U236 – CMPOUND CALC	+
					Prog YFI – 5 7	Oct 67	– + CURVE MASS AND E SPECTRA	
	2.0 – 2	1.6+7			Rept ICD – 4 346	67	– +.ENERGY,MASS FRGM DST TBL	
	1.6+7				Jour SNP 7 1 27	Jul 68	.TRANSLATION OF YF 7 36	
					Rept INDC – 232E	67	. ENGL OF YFI – 5 7	
	1.6+7				Data EXFOR40234.003	Dec 74	.EN = 15.5 MEV, 38 DATA LINES GIVEN	
Frag Spectra	Maxwl		FTI	Expt	Conf 68Riga	Jan 68	Vorob'Ev+ ABST,E DIST,LIGHT NUCLEI	
Frag Spectra	Maxwl		RI	ExTh	Conf 68Riga	Jan 68	Blinov+ ABST,ANG ANIS VS FRAG KIN E	
Frag Spectra	Maxwl		RI	ExTh	Conf 68Riga	Jan 68	Aleksandrov+ ABST,E DIST OF FISS FR	

92 Uranium 235

Quantity	Energy (ev) Min	Energy (ev) Max	Lab	Type	Documentation Ref Vol Page	Date	Author, Comments	Data
Frag Spectra	Maxwl		KFI	Theo	Jour KFI 16 45	Feb 68	Kluge+.GRAPHS,MYERS-SWIATECKI FORML	
Frag Spectra	Maxwl		KFI	Theo	Jour KFI 16 129	Apr 68	Kluge+.TEMPS OF FRGMNTS,STATISTL MDL	
Frag Spectra	Maxwl		TRM	Expt	Jour NP/A 112 241	May 68	Nadkarni. TERNARY FRAG ANISOTR,TABLE	+
	3.0+6				Jour NP/A 112 241	May 68	- . ANISOTROPY FOR BINARY+TERN	
	Maxwl				Conf 67Kanpur 334	Feb 67	Hattangadi.E SPECT OF LONG RANGE A	
	3.0+6				Conf 67Kanpur 318	Feb 67	.	
					Conf 66Bombay 38	Feb 66	Nadkarni. GRPH,ANGDIS BIN+TER FISS	
	Maxwl	3.0+6			Data EXFOR30093.	Mar 71	ANG + E DISTRIBUTION OF FRAGMENTS	
Frag Spectra	Maxwl		EDG	Theo	Jour PR 170 1118	Jun 68	Feather. MEAN E DIFFER BINARY-TERNRY	
Frag Spectra	Fiss		IBJ	Expt	Jour APP 34 173	Jul 68	Chwaszczewska+ UPPER LMT OF SIG GVN	
Frag Spectra	Maxwl		ITE	Expt	Jour YF 8 38	Jul 68	Andreev+ LONG-RANGE Z=2 TO 6,E-SPECS	
					Jour SNP 8 22	Jan 69	TRANSLATN.*	
Frag Spectra	1.6+7		FEI	Expt	Jour YF 8 286	Aug 68	D'Jachenko+ CVS RELATNG FRAG+NEUTE,A	+
					Jour SNP 8 165	Feb 69	.TRANSLATION OF YF 8 286	
	2.5-2	1.6+7			Data EXFOR40235.	Jul 75	.AV KIN-E AND KIN-E OF FISS-FRAG GVN	
Frag Spectra	Maxwl		FTI	Expt	Jour YF 8 297	Aug 68	Valsky+CVS RELATG G-ANISOTR,FRAG E+A	
					Jour SNP 8 187	Feb 69	TRANSLATN.*	
					Rept YFI-3 19	Sep 66	Val'Skij+ FRG-MASSRATIO CFD G-ANISOT	
					Rept INDC-140E 20	67	. ENGL OF YFI-3 19	
Frag Spectra	6.0-3	2.0+1	DUB	Expt	Rept JINR-P3-4110	Oct 68	Bochvarov+ RELATIVE YLD,EKIN,CRV+TBL	
					Conf 69Vienna 465	Jul 69	- +PPR73. RELATIV YLD+FRAG EK	
					Prog YFI-7 58	69	.ABSTRACT	
					Prog INDC(CCP)-7U	Feb 70	.ENGL TRANSL OF YFI-7	
Frag Spectra	-		IBJ	Theo	Jour NP/A 122 417	Dec 68	Blocki+.E DISTR H TO O16,TERNRY FISS	
	Maxwl			Expt	Conf JINR-D3893 89	May 68	- +ABSTRACT,LIGHT PARTICL E-SPEC	
Frag Spectra	Maxwl	1.5+6	TRM	Expt	Conf 68Bombay 2 133	Dec 68	Nadkarni+ FRAG ANGDIST(E) GRAPHS,VDG	
Frag Spectra	Maxwl	6.0+6	ANL	Expt	Jour PR 177 1817	Jan 69	Meadows+ 4ES MASS-ENERGY DISTRIBUTNS	
Frag Spectra	Maxwl		IBJ	Expt	Jour APP 35 187	Jan 69	Chwaszczewska+ GRAPH,ALF 6 TO17.5MEV	+
	Maxwl				Data EXFOR30272.003	Aug 74	E SPEC OF FISS A,TELESC COUNT	
Frag Spectra	1.5+7		RI	Expt	Jour YF 9 19	Jan 69	Artem'Ev+ GRPHS RELATG TOT EKIN + A	
					Jour YF 5 527	Mar 67	- + GRPH KIN-E OF FRAGMENTS	
					Conf 67Kharkov 216	Feb 67	- +.CFD YFI-3 (3) PAGE18	
					Jour SNP 5 373	Sep 67	. ENGL OF YF 5 527	
Frag Spectra	Maxwl		RI	Expt	Jour IZV 33 116	Jan 69	Solov'Ev+ FRAG E+RANGE IN AIR + MICA	
					Jour IZV 32 106	69	TRANSLATN.*NO 1	
Frag Spectra	Maxwl	+7	FEI	Theo	Jour YF 9 357	Feb 69	Ignatyuk.AVG FRAG-E(A,EXCT-E)CFD XPT	
					Jour SNP 9 208	Aug 69	TRANSLATN.*	
Frag Spectra	None		AUA	ExTh	Prog AAEC/PR-31P 9	Apr 69	Musgrove. ABSTR,SIMPLE MODEL TBD	
Frag Spectra	3.0+6		FEI	Expt	Prog YFI-7 14	Apr 69	Vorobeva+ ANGDIST(FRAG-A) TABLE+GRPH	
					Rept INDC(CCP)-7U16	Feb 70	TRANSLATN.*	
	Maxwl				Jour YF 10 491	Sep 69	Voboreva+ANGDIST CRV,KINE AVG+SPREAD	
					Jour SNP 10 282	Mar 70	. ENGL OF YF 10 491	
Frag Spectra	Maxwl		FTI	Expt	Jour IZV 33 741	Apr 69	Baranov+ FINE STRUCTUR SPEC(KINE,A)	
					Jour BAS 33 682	70	TRANSLATN.*NO 4	
Frag Spectra	Maxwl		IBJ	Expt	Jour NP/A 127 495	Apr 69	Blocki+ LI,BE E-SPEC OKS OTH	+
					Rept INR-952/IAIIPL	Sep 68	- + E-SPEC,REL YLD LI,BE.GRAPH	
	Maxwl				Data EXFOR30317.002	Jan 75	ENERGY SPECT OF LI AND BE	
Frag Spectra	Maxwl		RI	Theo	Prog YFI-7 33	Apr 69	Rubchenya. SIZE OF DIP IN FRAG-E(A)	
					Rept INDC(CCP)-7U36	Feb 70	TRANSLATN.*	
					Jour YF 9 1192	Jun 69	Rubchenja. SHELLMOD.FRAG KIN-E,CURVS	
					Jour SNP 9 697	Dec 69	. ENGL OF YF 9 1192	
Frag Spectra		+3	RI	Expt	Prog YFI-7 36	Apr 69	Adamov+ KIN-E IN BIN+TERN FISSN CFD	
					Rept INDC(CCP)-7U39	Feb 70	TRANSLATN.*	
Frag Spectra	Pile		NIL	Expt	Prog INDC(PAK)-1 2	May 69	. TOF,E-DISTR OF FRAGS,TO BE DONE	
Frag Spectra	Maxwl		CCP	Expt	Jour AE 27 31	Jul 69	Vorob'Ev+ LIGHT NUCLEI,E-SPECS,GRPHS	
					Jour SJA 27 713	Jul 69	. ENGL OF AE 27 31	
Frag Spectra	+3	+7	CIS	Theo	Conf 69Vienna 887	Jul 69	Facchini+PPR19. STATMOD CFD EXPTS	
Frag Spectra		2.0+6	COP	Revw	Conf 69Vienna 155	Jul 69	Strutinsky+PPR203. GRPH ANGANISTR(E)	
Frag Spectra	-		COP	Theo	Conf 69Vienna 213	Jul 69	Damgaard+PPR62.FRAG ANISOTR,SHELL-TH	
Frag Spectra			EDG	Revw	Conf 69Vienna 83	Jul 69	Feather.PPR201. REVW,LIGHT-PART-SPEC	
Frag Spectra	Maxwl	1.6+7	FEI	Expt	Conf 69Vienna 923	Jul 69	Vorob'Eva+PPR133. FRAG YLD+E(NEUT-E)	
Frag Spectra	Maxwl		FLA	Expt	Conf 69Vienna 107	Jul 69	Muga+PPR99. BINARY+TERN+PU E-KIN CFD	
Frag Spectra		+3	FTI	Expt	Conf 69Vienna 900	Jul 69	Adamov+PPR146. ALFA+TRIT+PROTON SPEC	
Frag Spectra	Maxwl		IBJ	Expt	Conf 69Vienna 115	Jul 69	Blocki+PPR68. ALPHA-ANGDIST-GRPH GVN	
Frag Spectra	None		IBJ	Theo	Conf 69Vienna 894	Jul 69	Blocki+PPR66. LIGHT PART E+ANG SPEC	
Frag Spectra	None		JAE	Expt	Conf 69Vienna 942	Jul 69	Ishimori+PPR6.FRAG RANGE-DISTR IN AL	
Frag Spectra	2.5+6	1.4+7	KFI	Expt	Conf 69Vienna 890	Jul 69	Kovacs+PPR8.ANGDIST OF TERNARY FISSN	
					Jour KFI 16 325	Oct 68	- +ANG-ANISOTROPY,TERNARY-FISS	

92 Uranium 235

Quantity	Energy (ev) Min	Max	Lab	Type	Documentation Ref Vol Page	Date	Author, Comments	Data
Frag Spectra	Maxwl		KUR	Expt	Conf 69Vienna 957	Jul 69	Blinov+ PPR144. EXCITATION – E OF FRAGS	
Frag Spectra	Maxwl		ORL	ExTh	Conf 69Vienna 67	Jul 69	Schmitt.PPR122.GRPH,(EKIN+ – RMS) VS A	
Frag Spectra	Maxwl		OSL	Revw	Conf 69Vienna 669	Jul 69	Pappas+ PPR206. YLD(A,KE),E – BALANCE	
Frag Spectra	1.1+0	3.5+1	SAC	Expt	Conf 69Vienna 913	Jul 69	Signarbieux+ PPR77.DISTS AT 11RESON	
Frag Spectra	Maxwl		WUU	Theo	Conf 69Vienna 33	Jul 69	Hasse.PPR28. AVG E – KIN(A),TH CFD XPT	
					Jour NP/A 128 609	May 69	– . CHARGED LIQUID DROP.E SPECTR.	
Frag Spectra	Maxwl		FTI	Expt	Jour YF 10 721	Oct 69	Adamov+ ALFA+FRAG KIN–E SPEC GRAPHS	
					Conf 69Vienna 901	Jul 69	– +PPR151. ALFA VS FRAGS KINET–E	
	Maxwl	1.4+7			Jour YF 9 732	Apr 69	– + AVG ALFA,T,P ENERGY + – SPREAD	
					Jour SNP 9 424	Oct 69	. ENGL OF YF 9 732	
Frag Spectra		+3	FTI	Expt	Jour YF 10 713	Oct 69	Arifov+ ANG+KE SPECS AT SYMMET FISSN	
					Jour SNP 10 4 412	Apr 70	TRANSLATN.*	
Frag Spectra	Maxwl		FTI	Expt	Jour YF 10 1149	Dec 69	Baranov+ YIELD VS KIN–E, FINE STRUCT	
					Jour SNP 10 654	Jun 70	TRANSLATN.*	
Frag Spectra	Maxwl		RI	Expt	Prog YFI – 9 20	Dec 69	Baranov+ YLD FINE STRUCT VS KINE	
					Rept INDC(CCP) – 9U25	Dec 70	TRANSLATN.*	
Frag Spectra	Maxwl		SAH	Theo	Prog BARC – 474 31	70	Sarkar+ EXCIT+KIN E OKS EXPT,TBP PR	
	0.0+0	1.0+0			Conf 69Roorke 2 217	Dec 69	– + E BALANCE OKS EXPTS, GRAPHS	
	None				Conf 68Bombay 2 122	Dec 68	RATNA SARKAR+ EXCIT+KIN E(A),GRAPHS	
Frag Spectra	Maxwl		TRM	Expt	Rept BARC – 456	70	Chaudhry. FRAG E – SPEC,SURFACE – B – DET	
Frag Spectra	1.0+5	3.2+6	TRM	Expt	Prog BARC – 501 22	70	Nadkarni+ ANGULAR ANISOTR,20 ES.GRPH	
	1.0+5	3.1+6			Conf 69Vienna 909	Jul 69	Nadkarmi+ PPR43. FRAG E SPECS,3ANGS	
Frag Spectra	Maxwl		AUA	Theo	Rept AAEC/TM – 528	Jan 70	Musgrove. FIT TO EXPTL E – KIN,FONG – TH	
Frag Spectra		+3	BUC	Expt	Jour RRP 15 225	Feb 70	Haseganu+ EMULSION,H+L FRAGM TRACKS	
Frag Spectra		6.0+5	FEI	Revw	Jour PL/B 31 122	Feb 70	Dyachenko+KINETIC ENS VS MASS AND EN	
				Expt	Conf 69Vienna 955	Jul 69	D'Jachenko+ PPR137. KIN – E,Z,YIELD,NU	
Frag Spectra	Maxwl	1.5+7	FTI	Expt	Jour YF 11 290	Feb 70	Artemev+ YLD(A,AVG KINE),THR+FAST CFD	
					Jour SNP 11 162	Aug 70	TRANSLATN.*NO 2	
					Prog YFI – 8 18	Dec 69	Artem'Ev+ FRAG YLD(FRAG KINE,2 N – ES)	
					Prog INDC(CCP) – 8 24	Dec 70	. ENGL OF YFI – 8 18	
Frag Spectra	2.0+5	9.0+5	TRM	Expt	Jour NP/A 144 1	Mar 70	Ajitanand+ AVERAGE E.SOLID STATE DET	
Frag Spectra	Maxwl		BOR	Expt	Jour NP/A 145 657	Apr 70	Asghar+ MULTIPARAM ANAL BIN – ,TERNARY	
					Conf 69Vienna 896	Jul 69	Carles+PPR82.(ALFA – PROBAB)VS(FRAG – A)	
					Conf 69Vienna 119	Jul 69	– +PPR80.GRPHS=ALPHA(ANG,E,MASS)	
				Theo	Jour CR 267 981	Oct 68	Doan+ BI+TERN.FISS;MOD OF 3ALIGN.SPER	
Frag Spectra	Maxwl		SAC	Expt	Prog EANDC(E)127U	Apr 70	Dabbs+,ANISOTR EMISS OF FRAG FROM	
Frag Spectra	Maxwl		COL	Expt	Jour NCSAC – 31 52	May 70	Derengowski+,NO DATA GIVN IN PR	
Frag Spectra	1.5+5	1.7+6	DUB	ExTh	Rept JINR – P3 – 5081	May 70	Dermendshiev+ KIN E SPEC VS THICKNES	+
				Expt	Rept JINR – P3 – 4873	Dec 69	Dermendzhiev+ AVG FRAG KIN–E REL THR	
					Conf 69Vienna 934	Jul 69	– +PPR161.HEAVY FRAG KIN – E	
	1.5+5	1.7+6			Data EXFOR40011.	Jun 70	14 DATA POINTS+4 PRELIMINARY VALUES	
Frag Spectra		7.0+5	IRE	Expt	Jour ZEP 11 489	May 70	Smirenkin+ ANG ANISOTR(NEUT – E),GRPHS	
					Jour JEL 11 333	May 70	TRANSLATN.*NO10	
Frag Spectra	+0	4.0+1	MOL	Expt	Conf 70Helsinki 1 449	Jun 70	Poortmans+20. FRAGANGDIST CFD SPINS	
Frag Spectra	3.0 – 1	1.8+2	ORL	Expt	Prog ORNL – 4513 86	Jun 70	Dabbs+,ALIGNED TARG,FRAG ANG ANISOTR	
				ExTh	Conf 69Vienna 321	Jul 69	– +PPR123. 0.61DEGK,ORIENTED FISS	
Frag Spectra	None		POL	Expt	Prog INDC – 6 10	Jun 70	Sujkowski+ ANGDIST OF ALFAS, TB PUBL	
Frag Spectra	Maxwl	6.0+6	FEI	Theo	Jour AE 29 130	Aug 70	Vorobeva+ AVG KIN – E(NEUT – E) CFD NU	+
	None			Expt	Jour YF 19 954	May 74	Vorob'Eva+ AVG FRAG KE(NEUT – E),GRAPH	
	+0	6.0+6		Theo	Jour YF 13 1170	Jun 71	Prokhorova+ AVG KE(N – E)CFD EXPT,GRPH	
	2.5 – 2	6.0+6			Conf 70Helsinki 2 177	Jun 70	.SAME AS AE 29 130 8/70	
	None			Expt	Jour SNP 19 489	Nov 74	. ENGLISH OF YF 19 954	
	+0	6.0+6		Theo	Jour YF 13 673	Dec 71	. ENGL OF YF 13 1170	
	Maxwl	6.0+6			Jour SJA 29 835	Aug 70	.ENGLISH TRANSL OF AE 29 130 8/70	
	2.5 – 2	3.5+6		Expt	Data EXFOR40281.003	May 75	.AVER KIN – E OF FF AT 32 ES GVN	
Frag Spectra	1.4+7		KFI	Expt	Jour NP/A 153 652	Sep 70	Kovacs+ ANISOTROPY OF TERNARY F FRAG	+
					Jour AHP 29 239	Jul 70	– + ANGDIST,BIN+TERNRY FISSN CFD	
	1.4+7				Data EXFOR30326.002	Mar 76	ALPHA ACCOMP TERN FISS,90/0DEG,1PNT	
	Maxwl	3.6+6	FEI	Expt	Rept INDC(CCP) – 8U9	Dec 69	TRANSLATN.*	+
	2.5 – 2	6.0+5			Rept YFI – 8 7	Dec 69	Djachenko+ SPEC(FRAG E,FRAG A),TABLE	
	2.5 – 2	6.0+5			Data EXFOR40017.	Nov 73	.7 SUBENT FOR 7 ES,EACH 40 LINES	
Frag Spectra	Pile		TRM	Theo	Conf 70Madurai 2 79	Dec 70	Prakash+ KIN – E CFD SHELL – STRUCT, CRV	
Frag Spectra	Maxwl	1.0+6	AUA	Expt	Prog AAEC/PR – 35P 10		71 Boldeman+ FRAG ANGDIST AT 6ANGLS,NDG	
Frag Spectra	6.0 – 8	2.0+1	BLA	Expt	Jour IFI 20 87		71 Bochvarov+ COOP DUBNA, E – KIN VARIATN	
Frag Spectra	Maxwl		KFI	Theo	Rept KFKI – 71 – 35		71 Jeki+ CALC E+ANGDST OF F – AS§7 – 1 S	
Frag Spectra	Maxwl		KTO	Theo	Jour JPJ 30 927	Apr 71	Okamoto+.CALC BY STATMDL.FIGS GIVN	

92 Uranium 235

Quantity	Energy (ev) Min	Max	Lab	Type	Documentation Ref Vol Page	Date	Author, Comments	Data
Frag Spectra	2.0−1	2.0+3	HAR	Expt	Jour NP/A 167 225	May 71	Pattenden+ FRAG ANG DIST ALIGNED NUC	
					Rept RCN−142	Jun 71	Kuiken. DISTR OF FRAG.ALIGNED U.	
					Prog AERE−PR/NP17	Dec 70	Pattenden+ A2 FOR 55 RES.GRPH	
					Conf 69Vienna 910	Jul 69	− . SUPERSEDED.	
					Conf 69Vienna 330	Jul 69	− . EXPT WITH RCN.	
Frag Spectra	2.5−2		NIR	Expt	Conf 71Kiev 2 78	May 71	Korostylev+	+
	2.5−2				Data EXFOR40293.003	May 75	.FF SPECT,30 DATA LINES	
Frag Spectra	None		CRC	Revw	Rept STI/DOC/10−127	Jun 71	Boyd.PG16.AVG RANGES OF FRAGS,TBL	
Frag Spectra	Maxwl		CAI	Expt	Jour IPA 9 470	Jul 71	Elmekkwi+ ANISOTROPY OF GMA YIELD	
Frag Spectra	Maxwl		SOR	Expt	Jour PR/C 4 223	Jul 70	Gazit+.ALPHA ANGULAR+ENERGY DISTR	
				Theo	Prog IA−1238 19	Dec 70	− + LRA,TRAJ CALC.GRPH E−,ANG−DIS	
Frag Spectra	2.0−1	1.9+1	DUB	Expt	Rept JINR−P3−6026	Sep 71	Wilhelm+ TERN.FISS.ALPHA SPEC,GRPH	
Frag Spectra	Maxwl		ANL	Expt	Jour NP/A 177 337	Dec 71	Reisdorf+SIMULT MEAS K.E. ANG G−SPEC	
					Conf 69Vienna 781	Jul 69	.SUPERSEDED	
Frag Spectra	3.3+5	4.1+5	ANL	Expt	Prog ANL−7850 103	Dec 71	Fluss+T SPEC 330KEV,ALFA SPEC 410KEV	
Frag Spectra	Pile		AUA	Expt	Jour AUJ 24 821	Dec 71	Boldeman+ MEAN K−E VS A,GRPH,PRELIM	
	Maxwl				Rept AAEC/TM−581	Mar 71	− + MEAN TOT KINE VS A GRAPH	
Frag Spectra	6.0+5	3.0+6	FEI	Expt	Jour YF 14 1129	Dec 71	Djachenko+ AVG FRAG KE REL THR,GRPHS	+
					Jour SNP 14 629	Jun 72	*ENGL OF YF 14 1129	
					Prog INDC(CCP)−31	Dec 72	.PAGE 13.ENGLISH OF YFI−11 14 /70	
	1.2+5	6.0+6			Data EXFOR40283.	Jun 75	.AVER KIN−E OF FF GVN	
Frag Spectra	5.5+4	7.4+5	FEI	Expt	Rept INDC(CCP)−15	Dec 71	. *P24,ENG OF YFI−10	
					Prog YFI−10 22	May 71	Smirenkin+ ANG ANISOTROPY,TBL,GRAPH	
	+0	8.1+5			Prog YFI−11 16	70	− + ABST,ANISOTROPY(N−E),GRPH	
					Prog INDC(CCP)−31	Dec 72	.PAGE 15,ENGLISH OF YFI−11 16	
Frag Spectra	1.6+7		TRM	Expt	Prog BARC−628 94	72	Iyer+ ANGULAR ANISOTROPY OF FRAG,TBL	+
	Maxwl	1.6+7			Conf 70Madurai 2 57	Dec 70	− + ANGDISTR,GRAPH+TABLE,TRACK−DE	
	1.6+7				Data EXFOR30235.	Jul 73	COS.COEF.OF ANG.DIST. OF FIS.FRAGM.	
Frag Spectra	Maxwl		CCP	Expt	Jour YF 15 209	Feb 72	Bogdanov+ A−RECOIL(TERNARY),TBL,GRPH	
					Jour SNP 15 473	Oct 72	*CORRECT ENGL, YF 15 209	
					Jour SNP 15 119	Aug 72	*ERROR,ENGL OF YF 15 209	
Frag Spectra	Maxwl		MCM	Expt	Jour PR/C 5 551	Feb 72	Kugler+.T+HE4 E DIST.TERNARY FISSION	
Frag Spectra	Maxwl		TRM	Expt	Jour NP/A 196 209	Nov 72	Nadkarni+ ALPHA E DIST AT 90,46,27 D	
					Conf 72Bombay 2 45	Feb 72	− + E,ANG DISTRBN OF ALFA,GRPH	
					Prog BARC−633 58	72	− + ENERGY SPEC OF ALPHAS,GRPH	
					Rept BARC−362	68	. ALFA ENERGY−ANGLE CORRELATIONS	
Frag Spectra	Maxwl		CUA	Theo	Abst DA/B 32 5980	Apr 72	Lee. CALC OF TOT FRAG KE DISTRIBUTS	
Frag Spectra	Maxwl		NBS	Expt	Rept USNDC−1 122	May 72	Schroder. FRAG/ALPHA KE CORRELATNS	
Frag Spectra	6.0+0	3.4+1	SAC	Expt	Prog EANDC(E)150U	May 72	Barreau+,ALPHA PART IN TERNARY FISS	
Frag Spectra	Pile		KUR	Expt	Jour YF 16 649	Oct 72	Zakharova+ MASS+E DIST OF FRAGS,GRPH	
					Rept IAE−2069	Feb 71	− .KE OF PAIRS VS MASS RATIO	
					Jour SNP 16 364	Apr 73	. ENGL OF YF 16 649	
Frag Spectra	8.6−2	9.1−2	BKB	Expt	Jour FIZ 4 245	Dec 72	Antanasijevic+ RATIO BINARY/TERN,TBL	
Frag Spectra	−2		BLA	Expt	Jour IFI 24 170	73	Kashukeev+ E/MASS/ANGLE−CORRELATION	
Frag Spectra	Fast		BUC	Revw	Rept IFA−RN−50	73	Cristu. MASS−+CHARGE−+E−DISTR REVIEW	
	Maxwl				Rept IFA−RN−50	73	− . MASS−+CHARGE−+E−DISTR REVIEW	
Frag Spectra	Maxwl		IBJ	Expt	Jour NP/A 208 381	73	Piasecki+ ALF E+ANG−SPEC,POLAR EMIS	+
					Rept INR−1429	72	− + THESIS.POLAR ALFA−EMISSION	
					Prog INR−1318 27	Apr 71	− + FISSN ALFS,GRPH E VS ANGLE	
					Rept INR−1318 27	Apr 71	− + FISSN ALFS,GRPH E VS ANG	
					Jour PL/B 33 568	Dec 70	− + E−ANGDIST FISSION ALPHAS	
	Maxwl				Data EXFOR30319.002	Jan 76	ENERGY−ANG.DISTR.OF A, 352 PTS.	
Frag Spectra	+0	+4	GEL	Expt	Prog EANDC(E)157U I	Mar 73	Deruytter+ TOT KIN ENERGY OF FRAGM	
Frag Spectra	Maxwl		ISP	ExTh	Conf 73Paris 1 559	Mar 73	Rustichelli.FISSPROD RANGES,TBL,GRPH	
				Expt	Conf 69Vienna 963	Jul 69	Aiello+PPR154. FRAG RANGE IN METALS	
Frag Spectra	Maxwl		ANL	Expt	Jour NP/A 205 348	Apr 73	Reisdorf+ MASS DIST AT GIVEN E. CURV	
					Conf 73Rochestr 2 19	Aug 73	Unik+ TOTAL KIN−E OF FRAGS,GRPH	
Frag Spectra	Maxwl		IAK	Expt	Jour NP/A 205 488	May 73	Khan+ NDG, USED IN ANAL OF GAMMAS+CE	
Frag Spectra	Maxwl		PAV	Expt	Rept STI/DOC/10−144	May 73	Pinelly+ LIGHT FRAG SPEC,NDG,TBP NC	
					Prog EANDC(E)140U	Aug 71	Cambiaghi+, ENERGY DISTRIB.FOR HE6	
Frag Spectra	None		FEI	Theo	Prog YFI−16 6	Jun 73	Stavinskij+ SHORT NOTE, NO DATA	
					Rept FEI−316	May 72	Stavinskii+ LIQU.DROP MODEL,GRAPH	
Frag Spectra	Maxwl		ITK	Theo	Jour AUJ 26 279	Jun 73	Mukherji+ CALC KE VS FRAG−MASS,GRAPH	
	None				Conf 69Roorke 2 226	Dec 69	− + TOT−KINE(A) CRV,LIQID−DROP	
Frag Spectra	1.8+7	2.1+7	KAZ	Expt	Jour YF 17 1143	Jun 73	Pavlov+ KIN−E OF HEAVY FRAGS,GRAPH	
					Jour SNP 17 595	Dec 73	.ENGLISH OF YF 17 1143	
Frag Spectra	None		EMY	Theo	Conf 73Rochestr 2 43	Aug 73	Fong.E−RELEASE VS FRAG−A RATIO,GRAPH	
Frag Spectra	None		GRE	Expt	Conf 73Rochestr 2 387	Aug 73	Ashgar.DISCUSSN.E−SPEC OF ALFAS,GRPH	

92 Uranium 235

Quantity	Energy (ev) Min	Energy (ev) Max	Lab	Type	Documentation Ref Vol Page	Date	Author, Comments	Data
Frag Spectra	Maxwl		LIN	Expt Conf	73Munich 1 716	Aug 73	Vorobjov+ Z=1...8 E-SPECTRUM,NDG	
Frag Spectra	Maxwl		AUA	Revw Conf	IAEA-169 2 163	74	Musgrove+ AVG FRAG MASS,GRAPH	
Frag Spectra	Maxwl		IBJ	Theo Jour	APPB 5 247	Apr 74	Piasecki+ P,D,T,HE-EVAPORATION,GRPHS	
Frag Spectra	Maxwl		UJV	Expt Jour	CZJB 24 743	Jul 74	Bayer+ SI-DET,E-SPEC OF ALFAS,GRAPH	+
	Maxwl			Data	EXFOR30278.	Nov 74	SPECTRUM OF FISSION-ALPHAS,141 PTS	
Frag Spectra	Maxwl	1.2+1	GRN	Revw Conf	74Petten 619	Sep 74	Postma+ANISOTROPY OF FISSION FRAGM.	
Frag Spectra	Maxwl	2.2+6	TRM	Expt Conf	74Bombay 2 97	Dec 74	Ajitanand+ GRID-ION CHAMBER,NDG	
Frag Spectra	3.0+4	1.9+6	WUC	Expt Conf	74Bombay 2 93	Dec 74	Walsh+ ANGDIST+E-SPEC OF FRAGMENTS	
Frag Spectra	0.0+0	1.1+6	AUA	ExTh Prog	AAEC/PR-41P 32	75	Boldeman+ AVG TOT E CALC+COMPIL,GRPH	
Frag Spectra	Maxwl		TRM	ExTh Prog	BARC-843 50	75	Kataria. QUAT.CORREL 2LIGHT PART,FIG	
Frag Spectra	+6	+7	TUE	Expt Rept	ORO-4856-26	75	Holubarsch+ P.591.ABSTR.EKIN-DISTRIB	
Frag Spectra	Maxwl		PAH	Theo Jour	PL/B 55 144	Feb 75	Hooshyar+ISOMERIC FISS,TH CFD EXPTAL	
Frag Spectra	4.0-1	1.0+3	COL	Expt Conf	75Wash. 580	Mar 75	Felvinci+E OF ONE FISS FRAG MEAS.	
Frag Spectra	2.0+5	9.0+5	AUA	Expt Jour	AEA 18 2 2	Apr 75	Walsh. AVG E-KIN(E-NEUT),GRAPH	
		2.0+6		Prog	INDC-291	May 69	.AVG.TOTAL E-KIN(NEUT-E),CFD OTHER	
		1.0+6		Prog	AAEC/PR-31P 7	Apr 69	Boldeman.AVG E-KIN(NEUT-E)=KONST,N47	
	+3	1.8+6	AUA	Expt Conf	75Kiev 5 191	May 75	Bertram+ W(0)/W(90) CFD OTHERS,GRAPH	
	2.0+4	1.9+6		Jour	AEA 18 2 2	Apr 75	Walsh. W(0DEG)/W(90DEG) VS E-N,GRAP	
	3.0+4	1.9+6		Conf	74Bombay 2 92	Dec 74	- + W(0)/W(90)VS E,ANALYSIS.GRPHS	
	6.0+4	2.0+6		Prog	AAEC/PR-40P 28	Jul 74	Boldeman+ W(0)/W(90) CFD OTHRS,GRPH	
Frag Spectra	2.5-2	2.9-1	BLA	Expt Conf	75Kiev 5 137	May 75	Dermendzhiev+ AVG FRAG KE AT 2ES GVN	
Frag Spectra	Maxwl		MNZ	Expt Jour	ZP/A 273 77	May 75	Kaffrell+ G-RAY-SPEC,DECAY OF TC-105	
Frag Spectra	1.0+4	1.5+5	FEI	Expt Jour	YF 22 692	Oct 75	Gonin+ ANG ANIZOTR OF FRAGS,ANALTBL	
				Conf	75Kiev 6 92	May 75	- + ANG ANIZOTR,GRAPH,COMPARED	
	Maxwl	1.0+4		Jour	ZEP 20 503	Oct 74	- + ORIENT+NONORIENT U,FRG-ANISOT	
	5.0+4	1.5+5		Jour	ZEP 20 503	Oct 74	- + ORIENTED U,FRG-ANISOTR AT 3ES	
	1.0+4	1.5+5		Jour	SNP 22 358	Oct 75	. ENGL OF YF 22,692	
	5.0+4	1.5+5		Jour	JEL 20 229	Oct 74	. ENGLISH OF ZEP 20 503	
	Maxwl	1.0+4		Jour	JEL 20 229	Oct 74	. ENGLISH OF ZEP 20 503	
Frag Spectra	Maxwl		GHT	Expt Prog	INDC(SEC)-51	Dec 75	Jacobs+ P20.MASS-KE CORREL.AVG E GVN	
Frag Spectra	Maxwl		IBJ	Expt Jour	NP/A 255 387	Dec 75	Piasecki+P,D,T,ALF EMISSION MEASURED	
				ExTh Conf	73Rochestr 2 383	Aug 73	- + POLAR P,D,T-SPECS CFD THEO	
Frag Spectra	Maxwl		ISP	Theo Jour	IAEA-190 2 379	76	Matthes. AVG FRG-E(MASS)CFD XPT,GRPH	
Frag Spectra	Maxwl		TRM	Expt Prog	BARC-878 49	76	Choudhury+ ANG CORREL LRA-FRAGS,GRPH	
				Jour	PRM 6 2 64	76	- + LRA.MASS+E-CORREL,TBL+FIG	
				Conf	75Calcutta 2 128	Dec 75	- + ALFA ANG CORRELATIONGRAPH	
				Prog	BARC-843 53	75	- + E-CORREL OF FRGM+LRA,FIGS	
				Conf	74Bombay 2 140	Dec 74	Nadkarni+ LRA-E VS MASS+E OF FRG.FIG	
Frag Spectra	7.5+5	1.8+6	TRM	Expt Conf	BARC-878 47	76	Nadkarni+ REL THERM.LRA E-SPEC,GRPHS	
Frag Spectra	1.9+5	7.3+5	BRC	Expt Prog	CEA-N-1875 81	Apr 76	Abou Yehia+ KINETIC AND MASS DIST	
Frag Spectra	Fiss		ORL	Theo Jour	PR/C 13 2385	Jun 76	Davies+DEP ON VISCOSITY CALC.CFD EXP	
Frag Spectra	5.7+6	8.8+6	UPP	Expt Conf	76ANL 128	Jun 76	Nordborg+ANG DISTR.GRPHS.TBP.BY SELF	
	5.0+6	1.0+7		Conf	75Gothenbg	Jun 75	- +ABSTR,SCT CHAMBER,MACROFOL	
Frag Spectra	None		DKE	Theo Jour	76Lowell 1403	Jul 76	Newson.EXCIT E,3-50MEV.FINE STRUC.ND	
Frag Spectra	None		GER	Theo Conf	76Lowell 1468	Jul 76	Kolb.ANAL Z114 BIN,TER FRAGMENTATION	
Frag Spectra	2.0+6	1.5+7	TRM	Theo Jour	PR/C 14 181	Jul 76	Sharma+2E.ORDER-DISORDER MDL.CFD EXP	
Frag Spectra	5.5+5		TUE	Expt Conf	76Lowell 1406	Jul 76	Muller+DBL TOF.FRAG UEL,E MEAS.NDG	
Frag Spectra	Maxwl		SAH	Theo Conf	76Ahmedabd 2 124	Dec 76	Majumdar. RGM-MODL.KE,FISS-E(A).GRPH	
	None			Jour	PL/B 56 325	May 75	Datta.E PARTITION IN FIS,RGM-PES	
Frag Spectra	Maxwl		GRE	Expt Prog	CEA-N-2015	77	Asghar+TABLE OF MEAN PARAMETERS	
Frag Charge	None		KAP	Theo Jour	PR 76 136	Jul 49	Kingdon+(A-Z)/Z PLOT CFD CHG DIST	
Frag Charge	None		CRC	Theo Jour	PR 76 1798	Dec 49	Brunton.EQUAL CHAIN LENGTH HYPOTHESE	
Frag Charge	Maxwl		ANL	Eval Conf	55Geneva 7 3	Aug 55	Steinberg+ P614.CHARGE DISPERSN,GRPH	
Frag Charge	None		MTR	Expt Conf	55Geneva 7 19	Aug 55	Pappas+.P881,CHARGE DISTRIBTN CURVE	
Frag Charge	Maxwl		WAS	Expt Jour	JIN 6 263	58	Wahl. MOST PROB CHARGE VERSUS MASS.	
Frag Charge	Pile		ORL	Expt Jour	NP 6 547	Apr 58	Cohen+. WIDTH OF CH DIST A=91,97,133	
Frag Charge	Maxwl		MUN	revw Conf	60Vienna 63	Oct 60	Maierleibnitz.CURVE,EXPT DESCRIBED	
Frag Charge	None		BNL	Theo Jour	NSE 9 495	Apr 61	Levine.MOST PROB Z.FROM =CHG DISPL.	
Frag Charge	Maxwl		WAS	Expt Jour	PR 131 830	Jul 63	Wahl+ CHARGE LESS THAN 50 FOR A=121	
Frag Charge	Maxwl		MIS	Expt Jour	PR/B 134 1027	Jun 64	Troutner+ MOST PROB CHARGE A=127	
Frag Charge	None		JUL	ExTh Conf	65Salzburg 103	Mar 65	Armbruster.CHG-DSTRB CALCLTD,CFD XPT	
Frag Charge	None		MIT	Theo Conf	65Salzburg 73	Mar 65	Gordon.ARAS.MONTE CARLO CALC CFD XPT	
Frag Charge	1.4+7		WAS	Revw Conf	65Salzburg 317	Mar 65	Wahl.GRAPHS TH CFD XPTS	
Frag Charge	Maxwl		NRD	Expt Jour	PR 144 984	Apr 66	Storm+YLD VS Z CHAINS A=131,132,133	
Frag Charge	Maxwl		WAS	Revw Jour	PR 146 926	Jun 66	Norris + CHARGE DISPERSION,10MASS NOS	
Frag Charge	Maxwl		THA	Theo Jour	ZN/A 21 1021	Jul 66	Faissner. CURVES, CFD EXPT	
Frag Charge	Maxwl		ANL	Theo Jour	PR 157 1038	May 67	Wing+ FONG TH + NEW MASSES, OKS EXPT	

92 Uranium 235

Quantity	Energy (ev) Min	Max	Lab	Type	Documentation Ref Vol Page	Date	Author, Comments	Data
Frag Charge	Maxwl		MUN	Expt Jour	NP/A 100 465	Jul 67	Konecny+ FOR MASSES 137,138,139	
				Conf	65Salzburg 1 401	Mar 65	- +.MASSES 132,4,6,7.GRPHS,TBLS	
Frag Charge	2.5-2		IFJ	Expt Jour	APP 32 673	Oct 67	Benisz+ FISSION INTO 4 PARTS	
Frag Charge	Maxwl		MUN	Expt Jour	ZP 209 77	Dec 67	Reisdorf.CURV OF MEAN PRIMARY CHARGE	
				Jour	PL/B 24 501	May 67	- + MEAN PRIMARY CHG.LIGHT FRG	
Frag Charge	Maxwl		ITK	Theo Conf	68Madras 1 308	Feb 68	Mukherji.CALC CHARGE DISPERSION,GRPH	
Frag Charge	Maxwl		KFI	Theo Jour	KFI 16 45	Feb 68	Kluge+.GRAPHS,MYERS-SWIATECKI FORML	
Frag Charge	Maxwl		NRD	Expt Jour	PR 172 1269	Aug 68	Weiss+ MOST PROBABLE CHG 117 CHAIN	
Frag Charge	Maxwl	1.4+7	GEP	Comp Rept	APED-5398	Oct 68	Meek+ ALSO FISS SPECTRUM,TABLES	
Frag Charge	Maxwl		TRM	Expt Conf	68Bombay 2 116	Dec 68	Kapoor+ FRAG CHARGE YLD(Z),X RAY XPT	
	-			Revw	68Madras 1 62	Feb 68	- .PPR19.X-RAY+CHEM EXPTS CFD	
Frag Charge	Maxwl		CCP	Expt Jour	IZV 33 159	Jan 69	Solov'Ev+ K-X-RAYS IN BIN+ALFA FISSN	
				Jour	BAS 33 145		69 TRANSLATN.*NO 1	
Frag Charge	Maxwl		HAR	Theo Rept	AERE-R-6056	Mar 69	Crouch.CALC CHARGE DISPERSION,ZP,TBL	
Frag Charge	Maxwl		ORL	Expt Jour	PR 179 1188	Mar 69	Ferguson+ A=143,144 CHARGE DISTRIBUT	
				Prog	ORNL-3994 8	Sep 66	- +,MASS 143,144 CHG DIST PROB	
Frag Charge	Maxwl	1.4+7	RAM	Revw Jour	NSPA 5 43	Apr 69	Khan. REVIEW,CHARGE DISTRIBUTN GRPHS	
Frag Charge	Maxwl		SOR	Theo Jour	PR 182 1331	Jun 69	Notea.EMPIRICAL FUNCTION DERIVED	
Frag Charge	Maxwl		AUA	Expt Conf	69Vienna 929	Jul 69	Bolgman.PPR34. PRELIMINARY RESULTS	
Frag Charge		6.0+5	FEI	Expt Conf	69Vienna 955	Jul 69	D'Jachenko+PPR137. KIN-E,Z,YIELD,NU	
Frag Charge	Maxwl		NRD	Expt Conf	69Vienna 953	Jul 69	Weiss+PPR115. PD118+CD118 YIELD GIVN	
Frag Charge	Maxwl		OSL	Revw Conf	69Vienna 669	Jul 69	Pappas+PPR206.CHARGE DIST GRPHS,REVW	
Frag Charge	Maxwl		SOR	Expt Conf	69Vienna 948	Jul 69	Amiel+PPR38.ABST.FROM INDEP YLD,NDG	
Frag Charge	Maxwl		TRM	Theo Conf	69Vienna 41	Jul 69	Ramamurthy+PPR15. CALC GRPH CFD EXPT	
				Conf	JINR-D3893 97	May 68	Ramanna+ DISTRIBUTN GRPH CFD EXPT	
				Conf	68Madras 1 298	Feb 68	- + CHARGEDISTRIB CFD EXPT,GRPH	
Frag Charge	Maxwl		TUE	Theo Conf	69Bochum 175	Jul 69	Goennenwein+ AVG CHARGE VS A GRAPHS	
Frag Charge	Maxwl		WAS	Expt Conf	69Vienna 813	Jul 69	Wahl+PPR116.CHARGE DISPERSN PLOTS,ZP	
				Rept	COO-1162-35	69	- .	
Frag Charge	Maxwl		FEI	Theo Jour	SNP 9 208	Aug 69	.TRANSLATN.*	
				Jour	YF 9 357	Feb 69	Ignatyuk.GRPHS CHARG(FRAG-A) CFD XPT	
				Prog	YFI-3 12	Sep 66	Ignatjvk. GRAPH	
Frag Charge	Maxwl		CUA	Expt Abst	DA/B 30 2222	Nov 69	Rogers.	
Frag Charge	Maxwl		JUL	Expt Jour	NP/A 139 289	Dec 69	Sistemich+.PRIMARY CHG.B-DECAY.M SEP	
				Conf	69Vienna 943	Jul 69	- +PPR24.AVG CHARGE+-VARIANCE	
				Prog	EANDC(E)115U	Mar 69	- +, MASS DEP	
Frag Charge	Maxwl		UI	Expt Jour	PR 188 1909	Dec 69	Bohn+,MOST PROB CHG DIST FROM K XRAY	
				Jour	APL 12 199	Mar 68	.SUPERSEDED	
Frag Charge			FEI	Eval Prog	YFI-11 19	70	Maksyutenko.ABST,BR,RB+I DISPERS,NDG	
				Prog	INDC(CCP)-31	Dec 72	.PAGE 18,ENGLISH OF YFI-11 19	
Frag Charge	Maxwl		MUN	Expt Jour	ZP 231 59	Jan 70	Konecny+ MEAN NUCLEAR CHARGE GIVEN.	
Frag Charge	Maxwl		ORL	Expt Jour	PR/C 1 312	Jan 70	Ferguson+,MASS-95 CHARGE DISPERSION	
Frag Charge	Maxwl		SAC	Expt Prog	EANDC(E)127U	Apr 70	Signarbieux+CHG DIST.KIN E AND MASS.	
	None			Conf	69Vienna 951	Jul 69	Nifenecker+PPR79. YLD(Z,A),X-RAY-XPT	
	Maxwl			Conf	67Bordeaux	Mar 67	- +MASS+CHARGE DISTRIBUTION	
				Rept	EANDC(E)66U	Feb 66	Audias+	
Frag Charge	Maxwl		CNA	Theo Jour	PR/C 2 2403	Dec 70	Talat Erben+ IA VS. Z CURVES	
				Jour	PR/B 134 972	Jun 64	Talat+ N,CHARGE DIST IN FISS PRODS.	
				ExTh Rept	CNAEM-12	63	- + TBL AVERAGE CHARGE/NUCLEON	
				Theo Rept	NP-12309	62	Talat-Erban.CALCULATED CURV YLD VS.Z	
Frag Charge	Maxwl		ANL	Expt Abst	BAP 16 98	Jan 71	Unik.K X-RAY METHOD. NO DATA GIVEN	
Frag Charge	+6	+7	JAE	Revw Jour	NP/A 160 65	Jan 71	Umezawa+ SYSTEMATICS VS FRAG MASS	
Frag Charge	Maxwl		JAE	Revw Jour	NP/A 160 65	Jan 71	Umezawa+ SYSTEMATICS VS FRAG MASS	
Frag Charge	Maxwl		KTO	Theo Jour	JPJ 30 927	Apr 71	Okamoto+.CALC BY STATMDL.FIGS GIVN	
Frag Charge	Maxwl		ANL	Expt Jour	NP/A 177 337	Dec 71	Reisdorf+SIMULT MEAS K.E. ANG G-SPEC	
				Conf	69Vienna 781	Jul 69	.SUPERSEDED	
Frag Charge	Maxwl		MIS	Eval Jour	JIN 33 12 4327	Dec 71	Troutner.	
Frag Charge	Maxwl		MNZ	Expt Jour	JIN 34 6 1785	Jun 72	Naeumann+ CHARGE DISTR MASS CHAIN132	
Frag Charge	Pile		JLU	Expt Jour	NP/A 196 401	Nov 72	Gunther+ EMULS A=131 TO 140	
	Maxwl			Prog	EANDC(E)115U	Mar 69	Konecny+,FINE STRUCT IN FRAG CHARGE	
				Jour	ZN/A 22 1808	Nov 67	Gunther+ MASSES 132-134 AS FN OF KE	
				Jour	AF 36 319	Nov 67	Konecny+. CHARGE+E DIST,A=134,8,9GVN	
Frag Charge	Fast		BUC	Revw Rept	IFA-RN-50	73	Cristu.MASS-+CHARGE-+E-DISTR REVIEW	
	Maxwl			Rept	IFA-RN-50	73	- .MASS-+CHARGE-+E-DISTR REVIEW	
Frag Charge	Maxwl		TRM	Theo Rept	BARC-706 143	73	Iyer+ YIELD(Z)+(N),NUBAR(Z,N),CURVES	
				Rept	BARC-690 142	73	Manohar+ 2 HARD CORES,DISTR(A)CFD XP	
Frag Charge	Maxwl		FEI	Theo Jour	YF 17 481	Mar 73	Maksyutenko.ZP(A) CFD EXPTS,GRPH,TBL	
				Jour	SNP 17 246	Sep 73	.ENGLISH OF YF 17 481	

92 Uranium 235

Quantity	Energy (ev) Min Max	Lab	Type	Documentation Ref Vol Page	Author, Comments Date	Data
Frag Charge	Maxwl	ANL Theo	Jour	NP/A 205 348	Apr 73 Reisdorf+ CORRELATION WITH MASS DIST	
Frag Charge	Maxwl	MNZ Expt	Conf	73Rochestr 2 111	Aug 73 Denschlag.DISTR CHANGED BY N−EMISSN	
			Conf	73Rochestr 2 95	Aug 73 Kratz+ ZP FROM FRACTNL YLDS,TBL,GRPH	
			ExTh Jour	ZN/A 24 2000	Dec 69 Denschlag+MODIFIED MOD CALC,CFD EXPT	
			Expt Conf	69Vienna 945	Jul 69 − +PPR26. CHARGE DISPERSION	
Frag Charge	Maxwl	AUA Revw	Conf	IAEA−169 2 163	74 Musgrove+ CHARGE DISPERSN PARS,GRPHS	
Frag Charge	Maxwl	JAP Eval	Conf	IAEA−169 3 215	74 Zukeran. ZP(A),GAUSS−WID,CFD,GRPH+TB	
Frag Charge	Maxwl	LRL Comp	Rept	UCRL−51640	Jul 74 Nethaway. TBL.	
Frag Charge	1.8+6	LRL Comp	Rept	UCRL−51640	Jul 74 Nethaway. TBL.	
Frag Charge	Maxwl	MIF Theo	Jour	IVU 17 7 7	Jul 74 Koldobskij+ A=93,CALC Z−DIST,CFD XPT	
Frag Charge	Pile	CAN Expt	Jour	JIN 36 10 2392	Oct 74 Parsons+CHARGE DISTRIBTN A=131−134	
Frag Charge	Maxwl	ILL Expt	Jour	PL/B 53 45	Nov 74 Siegert+ LOHENGRIN,ISOBARCHAIN 90−91	
Frag Charge	Maxwl	SOR Eval	Jour	PR/C 11 845	Mar 75 Amiel+ FRACT IND,ODD−EVN EFF.TBL+GRF	
			Conf	73Rochestr 2 65	Aug 73 − + DISPERSN,ZP,ODD−EVEN,GRPH,TBL	
Frag Charge	Maxwl	ANL Expt	Jour	JIN 37 869	Apr 75 Flynn+ FRAC INDEP RB84,86,CS136.CURV	+
	Maxwl		Data	EXFOR10517.006	Apr 78 . 3PTS.CHARGE DISTRB DATA	
Frag Charge	Maxwl	FLA Expt	Jour	PR/C 11 1287	Apr 75 Muga+ STRUCTURE IN NUCLEAR CHARGE	
Frag Charge	Maxwl	HEB Expt	Rept	INIS−MF−1689	May 75 Venezia. IN HEBREW.A=136−139,GRAPHS	
Frag Charge	Fiss	LAS Expt	Jour	JIN 37 1125	May 75 Wolfsberg+ FRACT CUM KR−,XE−ISOT YLD	
Frag Charge	Pile	THD Expt	Prog	GSI−J−1−75 18	Nov 75 Clerc+ CHARGE DISTRIBUTION FOR A=102	
			Jour	ZP/A 274 203	75 − + FISS FRAG 80−A−107	
Frag Charge	Maxwl	GHT Expt	Prog	INDC(SEC)−51	Dec 75 Jacobs+ P19. ZP TOBE DETERMINED. NDG	
Frag Charge	Maxwl	ISP Theo	Conf	IAEA−190 2 379	76 Matthes. P(Z),A=84−95,131−144.CFD XP	
Frag Charge	Maxwl	UBE Expt	Jour	JIN 38 205	Feb 76 Gaeggeler+ ZP(A=150),GRPH Z−SYSTEMAT	
			Diss	GAEGGELER	Dec 73 − . COMPLETE EXPT DESCRIPTION	
			Conf	73Rochestr 2 475	Aug 73 − + ABST,ZP FOR A=150 GIVEN	
Frag Charge	Pile	GRE Expt	Jour	ZP 277 1 71	Apr 76 Ristori+ A=91,93,94,95,137,139 CHAIN	
Frag Charge	Pile	GRE Expt	Rept	IKDA−7616	May 76 Schmidt+CHARGE−DISTR,LIGHT FISFRAG	
Frag Charge	Maxwl	ILL Expt	Conf	76Corsica 509	May 76 Clerc+ (LOHENGRIN) YLDS LIGHT FRAGS	
Frag Charge	Maxwl	ILL Expt	Conf	76Corsica 517	May 76 Wollnik+ (JLU) MASSES 79−103. ZA	
Frag Charge	2.5−2	OKL Theo	Abst	ANS 23 495	Jun 76 Liaw+CHG DISTR CORR TO FRAG EXCIT.	
Frag Charge	None	GRE Expt	Conf	76Lowell 65	Jul 76 Mossbauer. GRPH PROTON + NEUTRON YLD	
Frag Charge	2.5−2	JLU Expt	Jour	PR/C 14 1864	Nov 76 Siegert+RECOIL SEPARATORS.GRPHS,TBLS	
Frag Charge	Pile	GER Expt	Jour	RCA 24 1 8	77 Kreiner. CHARGE DIST A=99,100,101	
Reson Params	2.0+0	COL Expt	Rept	CU−123	Jan 54 Havens+ SEEN IN FISS ALPHA 6D2PM2DO.	
Reson Params	−.8+0	KJL Expt	Jour	JNE 1 3	Aug 54 Popovic. B−W ESTIMATE OF −VE RES.EN	
Reson Params	2.9−1 1.1+0	SAC Expt	Jour	JNE 1 306	Jun 55 Auclair+.RES E 0.29 1.13EV	
Reson Params	1.0−2 1.0+2	CCP Expt	Conf	55Moscow 87	Jul 55 Nikitin+.SIMULTAN ABS AND FISS,TABLE	+
			Rept	AEC−TR−2435 81	56 . ENGL TRANSL OF 55MOSCOW 87	
Reson Params	Maxwl	BKB Theo	Conf	55Geneva 2 164	Aug 55 Popovic.FISSION−WIDTH,LIFETIME U236	
Reson Params	−1 3.5+1	BNL Eval	Conf	55Geneva 4 199	Aug 55 Sailor.TABLE,TOTAL+FISS PARAMS,P586	
Reson Params	3.0−1 3.4+1	HAR Revw	Conf	55Geneva 4 210	Aug 55 Lynn+.TABLE,TOTAL WIDTH+ RES−E,P423	+
Reson Params	5.0−3 3.4+1	HAR Expt	Jour	JNE 2 128	Dec 55 Price.9 RES.ENERGIES GIVEN	+
Reson Params	8.8+0 1.9+1	KAP Expt	Jour	PR 104 479	56 Yeater+	
			Prog	KAPL−1565	May 56 − +,SIG(ZERO)*WF FOR 4 RESON	
	8.8+0 1.9+1		Data	EXFOR12414.002	Jun 76 . 4 RES,FIS−PCS	
Reson Params	Maxwl 5.0+1	HAR	Rept	TID−5298C	Feb 56 . ANALYSIS 60 LEVELS.NDG.	
Reson Params	9.3+0 6.1+1	MTR Expt	Jour	PR 103 971	Aug 56 Simpson+ AREA ANALYSIS, 41 RESONANCS	+
	9.3+0 6.1+1		Data	EXFOR12412.002	Jun 76 . 41RES E0,WN0,WF	
Reson Params	None	LAS Theo	Jour	PR 104 483	Oct 56 Porter+ ANAL FLUCT WF	
Reson Params	2.9−1 3.5+1	BNL Expt	Jour	PR 103 1342	Sep 56 Pilcher+ FC 47ES WN WT WF WG STRN FN	+
	3.5+1		Jour	PHY 22 994	Nov 56 Hughes.HISTOGRAM,CUMULATIVE WN VS E	
	2.9−1 3.5+1		Data	EXFOR12413.	Jun 76 . 47 RES. E0,WT,WN,WG,WF.	
Reson Params	−	CCP Theo	Jour	NP 2 575	Jan 57 Gurevich+. DISTR OF D. 'REPULSION'EF	
Reson Params	5.0+1 1.3+3	HAR ExTh	Rept	AERE−NP/R−2076	Jan 57 Egelstaff. SIG(F) FLUCT. AVG WN. P−T	
Reson Params	2.9−1 1.9+1	CCP Expt	Jour	AE 2 129	Feb 57 Sokolovsky+.TABLE 15 RES E, WT,WF,WG	
			Jour	JNE 5 389	Nov 57 TRANSLATN.*	
			Jour	SJA 2 147	57 TRANSLATN.*	
Reson Params	3.6+0 3.5+1	CCP Expt	Jour	AE 2 129	Feb 57 Sokolovsky+.TABLE 41 E RES,GWN,12 WT	+
			Jour	JNE 5 389	Nov 57 TRANSLATN.*	
			Jour	SJA 2 147	57 TRANSLATN.*	
Reson Params	2.9−1 9.0+0	COL Expt	Jour	NSE 3 435	Apr 58 Melkonian+.WT WG WF STF AREA ANALYS	+
			Rept	CU−163	Jun 57 .SUPERSEDED	
	2.9−1 9.0+0		Data	EXFOR12403.	Jun 76 . 8 RES E0,WT,WN,WN0,WG,WF,PCS	
Reson Params	2.8−1 1.9+1	BNL Revw	Conf	58Geneva 16 8	Sep 58 Hughes.PPR2483,PARAMS FOR 17ES GVN	
Reson Params	5.9+0 8.4+1	CCP Comp	Conf	58Geneva 15 309	Sep 58 Vladimirsky+.PPR2221,PARAMS FOR 86ES	
Reson Params	2.8−1 +2	COL Revw	Conf	58Geneva 15 99	Sep 58 Havens+.PPR655,MANY REFS	

92 Uranium 235

Quantity	Energy (ev) Min	Max	Lab	Type	Documentation Ref Vol Page	Date	Author, Comments	Data
Reson Params	−.1+1	8.8+0	BNL	Expt	Jour PR 112 191	Oct 58	Shore. ES,WF,WG,J,WT,MULTILV	+
					Conf 58Geneva 648	Sep 58	.SUPERDEDED	
					Jour PRL 1 193	Aug 58	.SUPERSEDED.	
					Conf ORNL−2309	Jun 57	.SUPERSEDED	
	−.1+1			ExTh	Conf AERE−NP/R−2076	Jan 57	Sailor. WN0=3, WF=185, WT=200 MV	
	−.1+1	8.8+0		Expt	Data EXFOR12418.002	Jun 76	. 7 RES. E0,WT,WG,WF.	
Reson Params	−.1+0	3.2+0	CRC	Theo	Jour PR 112 203	Oct 58	Vogt.MULTILVL TH CFD EXP DATA	
	−.1−2	4.8+0			Jour PR 118 724	May 60	− . MULTILEVEL FIT TO BNL 325 DAT	
	−.1+0	3.2+0			Rept CRT−665	Mar 58	.SUPERSEDED	
Reson Params	6.1+0	2.4+1	HAR	Expt	Rept NRDC−117	59	= 1 DATA INDEX LINES	+
Reson Params	6.0+0	5.0+1	COL	Expt	Jour PR 116 1538	Dec 59	Havens+ TRNS VEL SPEC DEDUCED WN,WF	+
Reson Params	None		BRK	Revw	Conf 60Kingston 659	Aug 60	Harvey.CURVE,FISS WIDTH DISTRBUTION	
Reson Params	1.1+0	9.4+0	HAR	Expt	Conf 61RPI 109	May 61	Brooks. 10RES	
Reson Params	−.1+1	3.0+0	CCP	Expt	Jour AE 12 408	May 62	Gordeev.MULTILVL FIT,CF VOGT	
					Jour EAF 12 5 59	62	. FRENCH	
					Jour SJA 12 433	62	. ENGLISH	
Reson Params	5.5+0	3.3+1	LRL	Expt	Jour PR 130 1482	May 63	Bowman+	+
	5.0+0	4.0+1			Rept UCRL−6926	Jan 63	− + 49 RES, CFD OTHER SOURCES	
	4.8+0	3.9+1			Data EXFOR12429.	Jun 76	. 35RES WF,FIS − PCS,7RES,E0	
Reson Params	−.2+1	2.0+1	ITE	Expt	Jour AE 16 110	Feb 64	Ignat'Ev+ GAM − F,GAM − GAM,TBL,2METHODS	+
					Jour AE 16 211	Mar 64	.CONTINUATION FROM AE 16 110=PAPER 2	
					Rept ITE−153	Apr 64	.SIMILAR TO AE 16 211 (PAPER2)	
					Rept ITE−147	63	.SIMILAR TO AE 16 110 (PAPER1)	
					Jour JNAB 18 719	Dec 64	. ENGLISH OF AE 16 110. (PAPER1)	
					Jour JNAB 18 523	Sep 64	. ENGLISH OF AE 16 211 (PAPER2)	
					Jour SJA 16 251	Mar 64	. ENGLISH OF AE 16 211 (PAPER2)	
					Jour EAF 16 3 31	Mar 64	. FRENCH OF AE 16 211 (PAPER2)	
					Jour SJA 16 121	Feb 64	. ENGLISH OF AE 16 110. (PAPER1)	
					Jour EAF 16 2 19	Feb 64	. FRENCH OF AE 16 110 (PAPER1)	
					Rept INDSWG−8E	64	. ENGLISH OF ITE−153	
	−.2+0	2.0+1			Jour EAF 16 3 31	64	. FRENCH TRANSL OF AE 16 211 3/64	
					Rept INDSWG−8E	63	.ENGLISH TRANSL OF ITE−153	
					Rept INDSWG−7E	63	.ENGLISH TRANSL OF ITE−147 /63	
	−.2+0	7.1+0			Data EXFOR40157.	Mar 73	.TOT − WID,FIS − WID AT 12 RES,CAPT − WID	
Reson Params	−.2+2	7.1+0	CCP	Theo	Jour AE 16 211	Mar 64	Kirpichnikov+ INTERFERENCE+RES ANAL	
					Jour SJA 16 251	Mar 64	TRANSLATN.*NO 3	
Reson Params	1.0+0	1.5+2	SAC	Expt	Jour NP 69 545	Jul 65	Michaudon+ ALSO TERNARY FIS VALS.	+
					Rept CEA−R−2552	May 64	− + BREIT − WIGNER 1 − LEVEL FIT	
					Jour NP 69 573	Jul 65	− + SEE ALSO	
					Conf 64Paris 2 1120	Jul 64	− + TER FISSION IN RES.	
					Conf 64Paris 2 712	Jul 64	− + RESONANCE ANAL	
					Jour JPR 22 712	Oct 61	− + SUPERSEDED.	
					Conf 61Vienna 55	Aug 61	− + SUPERSEDED.	
					Jour JPR 21 429	May 60	− + SUPERSEDED.	
	4.0+0	2.0+3			Rept CEA−R−1093	Jan 59	− +TOF WT WF	
Reson Params	3.1+0	2.3+1	DUB	Expt	Conf JINR−1845 128	Jun 64	VAN SHI − DI+. SCINT,TBL 15RES,GRAPHS	
Reson Params		+7	FEI	Theo	Jour AE 17 479	Dec 64	Usachev+ FISS CHANNL THRESH ESTIMATD	
Reson Params	−.1+1	6.1+1	CJD	Comp	Rept INDSWG−101 25	65	.TBL OF 60 RES FROM VARIOUS SOURCES	
Reson Params	+0	+3	CAI	Expt	Jour NP 62 667	Feb 65	Stavinsky+(N,GF)PROB ABOUT=(N,GAMMA)	
Reson Params	2.0+0	5.0+1	DUB	Expt	Conf 65Salzburg 1 287	Mar 65	VAN SHI − DI+,76RES BY AREA ANALYS,TBL	
					Rept JINR−P−2024	65	Van Shi Di+ AREA ANAL	
					Rept BNL−TR−16	Jul 65	− + ENGL OF 65SALZ.	
Reson Params	1.8+1	1.0+2	COL	Expt	Conf 65Antwerp § 95	Jul 65	Rainwater+. TABLE OF RES. ENERGIES	+
	1.8+1	3.0+2			Data EXFOR11516.002	Jun 76	. 269 RES,E0	
Reson Params	2.0+0	7.2+1	DUB	Expt	Jour AE 19 43	Jul 65	VAN SHI − DI+ 55RES,TOF.GRAPH+TABLE	+
					Jour JNE 20 602	Jul 66	Van Shi Di+ ENGL OF AE 19 43	
					Jour EAF 19 1 63	Jul 65	− + FRENCH OF AE 19 43.	
					Jour SJA 19 907	Jul 65	− + ENGL OF AE 19 43	
Reson Params	2.0+0	4.9+1	WAL	Eval	Rept WANL−TME−1228	Aug 65	Gibson+.RESOLVED+STATISTICAL RES	
					Rept WANL−TME−1028	Nov 64	Drawbaugh+.WN WABS WF WG 62LVLS. D	
Reson Params	−		CAI	Theo	Rept UARAEE−20	66	Shaker+ AVG FISSN WIDTH, PORTER − THOM	
Reson Params	−.1+1	1.5+2	KFK	Eval	Conf 66S.Diego 2 223	Feb 66	Schmidt. EVAL OF WG,WF,WN.	
	1.3+4	7.8+5			Rept KFK−120 1	Feb 66	− .25E0 I,PARITIES,K	
	−.1+1	1.5+2			Rept KFK−120 1	Nov 65	− . 217LVLS. WG,WF,WN.	
Reson Params	8.0−1	1.7+2	KUR	Expt	Rept ICD−3 10	Oct 66	Mostovaja+.GRAPH FISS WIDTH	
					Rept INDC−152E 10	67	. ENGL OF ICD−3 10	
Reson Params	8.8+0	1.2+1	MOL	Expt	Conf 66Paris 2 211	Oct 66	Poortmans+.P/79.WN/WT,G,J FOR 2ES	+
					Conf 66Wash. 755	Mar 66	− +DETAILS ON ANALYSIS METHOD	

92 Uranium 235

Quantity	Energy (ev) Min	Energy (ev) Max	Lab	Type	Documentation Ref Vol Page	Author, Comments Date	Data
Reson Params	1.7−1	3.7+1	AI	Eval	Rept NAA−SR−11980 5	May 67 Hennies.WN WG WF +AVG PARS TO 10KEV	
Reson Params	2.9−1	2.1+0	AUA	Theo	Jour AUJ 20 253	Jun 67 Cook+ TABLE ASYMMETRY PARAMETERS	
Reson Params	−		CCP	Eval	Jour AE 23 6	Jul 67 Kirpitchnikov.FISS−,N−WIDTH,STRNTH−F	
					Jour SJA 23 669	Jul 67 TRANSLATN.*	
Reson Params		1.0+6	AUA	Theo	Jour AUJ 20 477	Oct 67 Cook. TBL OF AVG LVL SPACING D,L=0,1	
Reson Params	1.0+2	5.0+5	JAP	Theo	Jour NST 5 86	Feb 68 KIKUCHI P AN.WF CALCULATION	
Reson Params	7.5−2	2.0+0	BNL	Expt	Jour PR 167 1121	Mar 68 Schermer+ POL NEUT+NUCL J DISCUSSED	+
Reson Params	6.0+0	1.5+1	GEL	Expt	Jour JNE 22 211	Apr 68 Cao+.LINAC TOF SHAPE ANAL WF	+
					Conf 68Wash. 481	Mar 68 CAO+ TOF.FN+FFRAG DET.NDG. PPR D3	
	6.4+0	3.0+3			Data EXFOR20129.	Mar 73 267PTS.NF AREA,WF,AVG.WF,SIG*WF,WG	
	7.4+0	1.5+1			Data EXFOR20140.	Mar 73 4PTS.NF AREA.	
Reson Params	−		SUK	Theo	Conf 68Bombay 2 170	Dec 68 Narayana. CALCULTD QUADRUPOLE MOMENT	
Reson Params	Pile		TRM	Expt	Rept BARC−421	69 Mahalingam+CRITICL−XPT CFD DATA−SETS	
Reson Params	5.0+1	4.0+3	KUR	Theo	Jour SNP 8 122	Jan 69 . ENGL OF YF 8 214	
	+0	+2			Jour SNP 7 582	Nov 68 . ENGL OF YF 7 967	
	5.0+1	4.0+3			Jour YF 8 214	Jul 68 Vorotnikov. WF,WG,WN DISCUSSD,GRPHS	
	+0	+2			Jour YF 7 967	May 68 − + GRAPH WF−DISTRIBUTION	
	−1	3.0+1		Expt	Jour YF 6 765	Oct 67 − . F,N−WID CORREL MASS−DIST	
					Jour SNP 6 555	Apr 68 . ENGL OF YF 6 765	
Reson Params	−		FEI	Theo	Rept FEI−157	Feb 69 Ignatjuk+ 2HUMPED−BARR−CALCUL,WN/WF	
Reson Params	1.7+1	7.1+1	LAS	Expt	Jour NP/A 126 471	Mar 69 Cramer.WN0,WF,WG,J,PI.MULTLVL FIT NF	+
					Rept LA−3917	Apr 68 .SUPERSEDED	
	1.7+1	7.1+1			Data EXFOR12425.002	Jun 76 . 80 RES,E0,J,WN0,WF1,WF2.	
Reson Params	−		FEI	Theo	Prog YFI−7 17	Apr 69 Lukyanov+ FISSN−WIDTH,PORT−THOM ANAL	
					Rept INDC(CCP)−7U20	Feb 70 TRANSLATN.*	
Reson Params	+3	+7	CIS	Theo	Conf 69Vienna 887	Jul 69 Facchini+PPR19. STATMOD,WF VS NEUT−E	
Reson Params	5.0+1	3.0+3	DUB	Theo	Conf 69Vienna 934	Jul 69 Ryabov+PPR160. EGELSTAFF−ANAL,FISSN	
Reson Params	−		HAR	Revw	Conf 69Vienna 249	Jul 69 Lynn. TBL STRUTINSKY PARS,FISS+CAPT	
Reson Params	None		LAS	Expt	Conf 69Vienna 183	Jul 69 Bolsterli+PPR100.HIGH J LVL IN FISSN	
Reson Params	6.4+0	3.9+1	GEL	Expt	Jour NP/A 134 535	Sep 69 Weigmann+ SPIN 18E0 FROM 642KEVGLINE	+
					Conf 69Studsvik 687	Aug 69 − + RESON SPIN TBL,CFD OTHER	
	6.4+0	4.0+1			Data EXFOR20135.	Mar 73 20PTS.AVG.WF,J.	
Reson Params		+1	LRL	Expt	Prog WASH−1136 93	Sep 69 Bowman+,J FROM N,G.ANAL TBC,NO DATA	
Reson Params	None		CAI	Theo	Jour YF 10 790	Oct 69 Luk'Yanov+ PORTER THOMAS CHANNL ANAL	
					Jour SNP 10 4 456	Apr 70 TRANSLATN.*	
Reson Params	−.2+2	6.2+0	CCP	Revw	Rept ICD−6 7	70 Lukyanov.T−,G−,F−WIDS OF 11 RES,TBLS	
Reson Params	None		TRM	Theo	Prog BARC−471 5	70 Sood+ CORREL ANAL,D CLASS II VAL GVN	
	2.0+1	1.0+6			Conf 69Roorke 2 198	Dec 69 − + AVG LEVL SPACING D,2−HUMPED−T	
Reson Params	3.0−1	2.0+3	DUB	Theo	Jour CRB 23 141	Feb 70 Bochvarov+ STAT+CORR ANAL,D,WN,WF	
Reson Params	2.9−1	5.0+1	DUB	Expt	Rept JINR−P3−4992	Apr 70 Rjabov+ TOT+N+G+F−WIDS,78 RES,D,TBL	+
					Jour SNP 13 255	Sep 71 * ENGL OF YF 13 457	
					Jour YF 13 457	Mar 71 *SOME DATA+AVG WIDS,GRPH	
					Prog YFI−11 27	70 Rjabov+ ABST,SAME TBL AS JINR−4992	
					Prog INDC(CCP)−31	Dec 72 .P26, ENGL.OF YFI−11 27	
	2.9−1	5.0+1			Data EXFOR40070.	Aug 70 TOT+N+GAM+FISS−WIDTHS 78 RESON +D	
Reson Params	1.5+2	1.0+5	TOK	Theo	Jour NST 7 157	Apr 70 Kikuchi+.CHANNEL TH,SPIN DEPENDNT WF	
					Jour NST 5 86	Feb 68 − + SUPERSEDED.	
Reson Params	6.1+1	3.0+2	WAL	Eval	Rept WANL−TME−2705	May 70 Drawbaugh+,WF WC WN FOR MANY RESON	
	2.8+0	6.2+1			Rept WANL−TME−1586	Mar 67 Gibson+2G*WN WF WG TRIPLE−FIT PARAMS	
Reson Params	8.7+0	5.6+1	GEL	Expt	Conf 70Helsinki 1 449	Jun 70 Poortmans+PPR70 GWN,WT,J 11E0	+
					Conf 69Vienna 911	Jul 69 − + SUPERSEDED.	
	8.8+0	5.7+1			Data EXFOR20145.	Mar 73 54PTS.AVG.WF,WT,J,2G*WN,2G*WN/WT.	
Reson Params		6.2−2	GEL	Expt	Conf 70Helsinki 1 117	Jun 70 Deruytter+ BR2 CHOPPER	+
		6.2−2			Data EXFOR20143.003	Mar 73 1PNT.NF AREA.	
Reson Params		7.0+3	SDC	Theo	Conf 70Helsinki 2 799	Jun 70 Garrison.DISCUSSN. RESONANCE ANAL	
Reson Params		5.0+1	UI	Theo	Conf 70Helsinki 2 777	Jun 70 Adler+50. MULTILEVEL PARS GIVEN	
Reson Params	1.9+1	6.1+1	LAS	Expt	Jour PR/C 2 615	Aug 70 Cowan+MANY RES ES.J ASSIGNMENTS.	+
	1.9+1	6.1+1			Data EXFOR10067.002	Jun 71 30 PTS.J VALUES.	
Reson Params	−.2−2	6.1+1	ORL	Theo	Prog ORNL−4705 16	71 Desaussure+ MULTILEVEL ANALYSIS	
Reson Params	None		DUB	Theo	Jour YF 13 240	Feb 71 Malecki+G−WID,THEO CFD EXPT.TBL,GRPH	
					Jour SNP 13 133	Aug 71 − + ENGL OF YF 13 240.	
Reson Params	2.0+1	1.0+5	LAS	Expt	Jour NSE 43 281	Mar 71 Lemley+FISS AREA INTEGS.CFD OTHERS	+
	2.0+1	1.0+5			Data EXFOR10120.003	Mar 76 26PTS.FISSION AREAS	
Reson Params	8.8+0	1.9+1	MTR	Expt	Jour NP/A 164 34	Mar 71 Simpson+ POOR RESOL DATA,LINAC,CRVS	
	8.8+0	1.9+1			Data EXFOR10132.003	Jan 73 4PTS,J	
Reson Params	1.0−1	4.9+1	SAC	Eval	Conf 71Knoxvill 410	Mar 71 Krebs+.WT G*WN WG WF TABULATED	
	3.1+1	4.1+1			Conf 70Helsinki 1 571	Jun 70 Ribon.108.EVALUATION PROBLEMS,TABLE	
	+0	5.0+1		Theo	Conf 70Helsinki 2 789	Jun 70 Krebs+65.NEW LSQ RESONANCE ANALYSIS	

92 Uranium 235

Quantity	Energy (ev) Min	Max	Lab	Type	Documentation Ref Vol Page	Date	Author, Comments	Data
Reson Params	6.2 – 1	5.0+4	SRL	Theo Conf	71Knoxvill 714	Mar 71	Mccrosson. STAT CALCULATN AVG PARAMS	
Reson Params	7.0 – 1	2.1+1	GEL	Expt Jour	JNE 25 263	Jun 71	Deruyter+	+
				Rept	EANDC(E) – 129AL	Jun 70	– +	
	7.0 – 1	2.1+1		Data	EXFOR20131.	Mar 73	9PTS.NF AREA.	
	7.0 – 1	2.1+1		Data	EXFOR20128.	Mar 73	9PTS.NF AREA.	
Reson Params	2.9 – 1	1.5+2	CCP	Revw Jour	AE 31 595	Dec 71	Sukhoruchkin.N+G+F+T – WIDS,J CFD,TBLS	
				Jour	SJA 31 1380	Jun 72	*ENGL OF AE 31 595	
Reson Params	6.4+0	3.2+1	GEL	Expt Jour	NP/A 194 657	Oct 72	Wagemans+ RES FISSION ENERGIES.	+
	6.4+0	3.2+1		Data	EXFOR20381.004	Oct 74	12PTS.E0.	
Reson Params	–.1+0	8.8+1	MTR	Eval Rept	ANCR – 1044	Dec 71	Smith+. J WT WN WG WF FOR ENDF/B3	
	–.1+1	8.7+1		Prog	ANCR – 1088 21	Oct 72	– +J,WT,WN,WG,ENDF3B.TBL	
Reson Params	1.1+0	4.5+1	COL	Expt Abst	ANS 15 944	Nov 72	Felvinci+.WT SIG0*WF GIVEN FOR 70RES	+
	1.1+0	4.5+1		Data	EXFOR10322.002	Nov 76	70RES E.WT AND PEAK CS TIMES WF.	
Reson Params	None		AUA	Theo Prog	AAEC/PR – 38P 15	Mar 73	Bertram+ ADLER – ADLER RES PARAMS, NDG	
Reson Params	1.5+0	5.8+1	GEL	Expt Jour	NP/A 203 145	Mar 73	Corvi+ J FOR 14 RES,PROPERTIES VS J	+
	2.9 – 1	5.6+1		Data	EXFOR20382.	Oct 74	16PTS.AVG.WF.J.	
Reson Params	–.2 – 2	6.1+1	ORL	Expt Jour	PR/C 7 2018	May 73	De Saussure+MULTILVL ANAL.TBL PARS	+
	–.1+0	1.0+2		Conf	70Helsinki 2 757	Jun 70	Desaussure. MULTILEVEL RES PAR	
		5.0+3		Conf	69Vienna 283	Jul 69	Perez+ FISS SIG ANAL,AVG D CFD OTHER	
	–.2+1	1.0+2		Data	EXFOR10079.	Dec 78	. 143 ADLER PARS,91.REICH – MOORE PARS	
Reson Params	9.3+0	1.5+2	SAC	Expt Jour	NSE 51 130	Jun 73	Blons+ REVIEW FISS XSECT MEAS SACLAY	+
	3.0 – 1	1.5+2		Conf	73Kiev 2 239	May 73	– . AVERAGE F – WIDTH + NU – BAR GIVN	
	9.3+0	1.5+2		Conf	71Knoxvill 829	Mar 71	– + 2G.WN,WT,WF,S.WF,WG.SHAPE AN	
				Jour	AE 29 395	Nov 70	Derrien+.ABST FRANC SOV SEM DUBNA/70	
				Jour	SJA 29 1156	Nov 70	– + TRANSLATION OF AE	
	0.0+0	1.5+2		Data	EXFOR20483.	Nov 75	186PTS.AVG.WF,2G*WN.	
Reson Params	2.0+0	3.2+1	BNL	Expt Jour	PR/C 8 781	Aug 73	Graves+. J PI FOR 6 RESON FROM CAPT	+
	2.9 – 1	3.2+1		Abst	DA/B 32 4793	Feb 72	– . EPITHERMAL NEUTS.WF J PI	
	2.0+0	3.2+1		Data	EXFOR10344.002	Oct 74	6PTS.J FOR 6 RES ES	
Reson Params	4.0 – 1	2.5+4	WIN	Eval Prog	EANDC(UK) 151	Aug 73	James+ GENEX EVALUATION	
Reson Params	2.9 – 1	2.6+1	RPI	Expt Prog	COO – 3058 – 39 9	Sep 73	Reed+. J GIVEN FOR 21 RESONANCES.	
	1.1 – 2	3.0+1		Conf	73Rochestr 2 503	Aug 73	– + ABST,SPIN FROM NUBAR,NDG	
	6.4+0	2.4+1		Conf	69Vienna 477	Jul 69	Weinstein+PPR113.SPIN,13RESON,NU – XPT	
Reson Params	1.1+0	5.9+1	LAS	Expt Jour	PRL 31 1077	Oct 73	Keyworth+. J FOR 65 RESON.CFD OTHERS	+
	1.1+0	5.9+1		Data	EXFOR10371.002	Jun 74	. 65 PTS. J VALUES	
Reson Params	8.8+0	3.9+1	GEL	Expt Rept	RCN – 203 100	Dec 73	Theobald+ N MULTIPL IN FISS RES	
Reson Params	2.2 – 1	6.0+1	KTO	Eval Jour	NST 10 709	Dec 73	Otani+.SINGLE – AND MULTI – LVL ANAL.	
	–.1+1	8.8+0	BUC	Theo Rept	INIS – MF – 1592	74	Mihailescu. THESIS.CALC WIDTHS,TABLS	
Reson Params	2.0+0	1.5+2	CCP	Theo Rept	YK – 16 121	74	Gorbachev+ G+F+N+TOT – WIDTHS, TBL	
Reson Params	1.0+4	4.0+4	ORL	Expt Abst	ANS 17 495	74	James+2 INTERMED STRUCT STAT TESTS	
Reson Params	2.9 – 1	1.4+1	BNL	Expt Jour	NP/A 218 84	Jan 74	Reddingius+ TJ,18E0 POLARIZ.MEAS.	+
	2.9 – 1	1.4+1		Data	EXFOR10390.002	Jun 74	15 PTS	
Reson Params	2.9 – 1	1.0+2	AUA	Theo Jour	AUJ 27 1	Feb 74	Rose+ ADLER RESPARS STATISTICS,TBLS	
Reson Params	6.5+6		DUB	Theo Conf	74Petten 175	Sep 74	Malov+ DOBS,SEMI – MICROSCOPIC CALC.	
Reson Params	2.9 – 1	6.1+2	GRN	Revw Conf	74Petten 619	Sep 74	Postma+SPINS REVIEW	
Reson Params	1.1+0	5.9+1	LAS	Expt Rept	INDC – 15 75	Oct 74	Hansen+ SPINS CFD OTHERS,TABLE	
Reson Params	2.7 – 1	1.4+1	RCN	Expt Prog	INDC(SEC) – 43	Dec 74	Reddingius+ POL N+U235,SPINS TABLE	
	2.8 – 1	1.4+1		Prog	NEANDC(E) – 161U	Aug 74	– +	
				Rept	NEANDC – 203 358	Dec 73	– + J	
Reson Params	1.0+2	1.0+5	IFB	Eval Rept	YK – 20/1 126	75	Antsipov+ EVAL OF XPTAL DATA.TABLES	
Reson Params	+0		DUB	Theo Jour	YF 21 40	Jan 75	Voronov+ MEAN D,WITH ROTAT.CFD EXPT	
				Jour	SNP 21 20	Jul 75	. ENGLISH OF YF 21,40	
Reson Params	None		COL	Theo Abst	BAP 20 149	Feb 75	Cacuci+LVL DENSITY CALC CFD EXPT.	
Reson Params	1.4+1	3.0+2	OSA	Theo Conf	JAERI – M – 5984	Feb 75	Kitazoe+TBL RES PARS.R MATRX+HIERACH	
	1.5+2	2.5+2		Eval Jour	AKE 20 13	Sep 72	– + 21 RESON FROM TOT SIG	
Reson Params	1.0+0	3.9+1	COL	Expt Conf	75Wash. 580	Mar 75	Felvinci+ LOW LYING RES.SPINS	
Reson Params	2.8 – 1	2.8+1	AUA	Theo Jour	AUJ 28 491	Oct 75	Cook+ AVG F – WIDS FOR 3 CHANNELS GIVN	
Reson Params	–.1+1	1.5+2	KFK	Eval Prog	NEANDC(E)172 5	Jul 76	Goel+P.18.KEDAK 3 REVISED DATA	+
	–.1+2	1.5+2		Data	KEDAK – 3	Oct 75	197 DATA SETS	
Reson Params	1.0+2	2.5+4	KAL	Theo Conf	75Calcutta 2 35	Dec 75	Ganesan. MEAN FISS WIDTH COMPUTED	
Reson Params	2.0+0	2.1+1	DUB	Expt Rept	JINR – P3 – 9613	Apr 76	Dlouhy+ (N,GF),X – RAYS.GF – WID ESTIMAT	
Reson Params	7.8+0	2.0+3	BRC	Revw Conf	76Lowell 641	Jul 76	Michaudon.PROPERTIES OF FIS RESON.	
Reson Params	Maxwl		KUK	Theo Conf	76Ahmedabd 2 1	Dec 76	Sharma+AVG S – WAVE REDUCED N – WID ANAL	
Strnth Fnctn		– 1	3.5+1	BNL Eval Conf	55Geneva 4 199	Aug 55	Sailor.VAL GVN,THEORET DISCUSS,P586	
Strnth Fnctn		5.0+1	MTR	Expt Jour	ND 103 971	Aug 56	Simpson+,STF=1.0+ – 0.2 TRNS	+
	9.3+0	1.8+1		Data	EXFOR12412.	Jun 76	. 2 PTS. STF,D	
Strnth Fnctn		3.5+1	BNL	Expt Jour	PR 103 1342	Sep 56	Pilcher+ FC STF=0.9+ – 0.2	+
	2.9 – 1	3.5+1		Data	EXFOR12413.005	Jun 76	. 1 PT.	

92 Uranium 235

Quantity	Energy (ev) Min	Energy (ev) Max	Lab	Type	Documentation Ref Vol Page	Date	Author, Comments	Data
Strnth Fnctn	-.2+1	3.5+1	BNL	Revw Jour	PHY 22 994	Nov 56	Hughes.0.9+ - 0.2 CUMUL WN VS E	
	2.0+2	6.0+3		Jour	PHY 22 994	Nov 56	- .1.3+ -.0.2TRANSMIS.V TOF SLOPE	
Strnth Fnctn		4.0+3	COL	Expt Jour	NSE 3 435	Apr 58	Melkonian+.S WAVE.FROM AREA ANALYSIS	+
				Rept	CU - 163	Jun 57	.SUPERSEDED	
	1.0+2	4.0+3		Data	EXFOR12403.007	Jun 76	. 1 PT.	
Strnth Fnctn	2.0+1	1.0+3	MTR	Expt Abst	BAP 3 176	May 58	Simpson+ FAST CHOPPER STF=0.90+ - 0.1	
Strnth Fnctn	5.9+0	8.4+1	CCP	Expt Conf	58Geneva 15 309	Sep 58	Vladimirsky+.PPR2221,VAL GVN	
Strnth Fnctn	2.8-1	+2	COL	Expt Conf	58Geneva 15 99	Sep 58	Havens+.PPR655,VAL GVN,MANY REFS	
Strnth Fnctn	+3		BNL	Expt Jour	PRL 1 461	Dec 58	Hughes. FC, 1.05+ - 0.15	
Strnth Fnctn	None		DKE	Theo Jour	NP 24 169	Apr 61	Seth. J - DEPENDENCE OF S - WAVE STRFUNC	
Strnth Fnctn	None		WAL	Eval Rept	WANL - TME - 1028	Nov 64	Drawbaugh+.XPT CFD WIGNER DISTRIBUTN	
Strnth Fnctn	3.0+2	3.0+4	DUB	Expt Conf	65Antwerp § 184	Jul 65	Ryabov+,SO=.91+ -.03,S1=2.8+ -.4,TOF	
				Rept	BNL - TR - 20	Aug 65	TRANSLATN.* DUB - P - 2068 /65	
Strnth Fnctn	-		SAC	Expt Jour	NP 69 545	Jul 65	Michaudon+ S0=.915+ -.05 X10-4	+
Strnth Fnctn	5.0+1	1.0+4	KFK	Eval Conf	66S.Diego 2 223	Feb 66	Schmidt.DEDUCED FROM EXP DATA	
Strnth Fnctn	+3	+4	COL	Expt Prog	WASH - 1068 35	Mar 66	Garg+,TRNS,ANALYSIS TBC,NDG	
Strnth Fnctn	1.0+2	1.0+7	HAR	Expt Conf	66Paris 1 165	Oct 66	Uttley+ PPR36.TABLE,CURVES S+P+DWAVE	+
	1.0+3	1.0+5		Conf	64Paris 2 700	Jul 64	- .	
	1.0+2	7.0+4		ExTh Rept	AERE - M - 1272	Dec 63	- .AVR TRNS..S,P WAVE,ALPHA TH	
Strnth Fnctn	3.0-1	2.0+3	DUB	Theo Jour	CRB 23 141	Feb 70	Bochvarov+ STAT+CORR ANAL,TBL,SO VAL	
Strnth Fnctn	2.9-1	5.0+1	DUB	Expt Rept	JINR - P3 - 4992	Apr 70	Rjabov+ MAXIMUM LIKELIHOOD VALUE S0	+
				Jour	SNP 13 255	Sep 71	*ENGL OF YF 13 457	
				Jour	YF 13 457	Mar 71	Rjabov+ S - 0 GIVEN	
	2.9-1	5.0+1		Data	EXFOR40070.027	Aug 70	S - WAVE STRENGTH FUNCTION S0	
Strnth Fnctn		1.0+5	GA	Theo Jour	NP/A 159 305	Dec 70	Garrison. S,P - WAVE.TO FIT AVG NG,NF	
Strnth Fnctn		3.0+4	DUB	Expt Jour	YF 13 1039	May 71	Ryabov+ TOF,FITTED S0+S1 VALUES GIVN	+
				Jour	SNP 13 596	Nov 71	. ENGL OF YF 13 1039	
	1.0+2	3.0+4		Data	EXFOR40123.002	Sep 72	STRENGTH - FUNCTION, S AND P - WAVE	
Strnth Fnctn	None		AUA	Eval Rept	AAEC/E - 277	Mar 73	Musgrove.TBLS EXPTL DATA+BEST VALUES	
Strnth Fnctn	2.8-1	2.8+1	AUA	Theo Jour	AUJ 28 491	Oct 75	Cook+ AVG STRENGTH FOR 3CHANNELS GVN	
Lvl Density	-		COP	Theo Jour	NP 6 62	Mar 58	Ericson. LVL DENSITY FORM CFD EXP	
Lvl Density		2.0+7	IFJ	Theo Jour	PL 6 342	Oct 63	Lewandowski. TEMP(E),CURV.SUPERCOND	
Lvl Density	+6		MIL	Theo Jour	EN 15 1 54	Jan 68	Facchini+. LDL PARS FROM LOW EN RES	
Lvl Density	1.4+7		FEI	Expt Jour	IZV 32 653	Apr 68	Salnikov+ A+TEMP GVN,LE COUTEUR EXPT	+
				Prog	YFI - 4 21	May 67	.DENSITY+NUCLEAR TEMP.TABLE	
				Jour	BAS 32 600	69	.ENGLISH TRANSL OF IZV 32 653 4/68	
				Prog	INDC - E - 187 29	67	.ENGLISH TRANSL OF YFI - 4	
	1.4+7			Data	EXFOR40332.	Feb 76	TEMP(.007),LVL DENS PARAM(.008)	
Lvl Density		2.5+1	KUR	Theo Jour	YF 9 303	Feb 69	Vorotnikov.LVL DEN(EXCIT - E),TBL GRPH	
				Jour	SNP 9 179	Aug 69	TRANSLATN.*	
Lvl Density	-		COP	Theo Conf	69Vienna 213	Jul 69	Damgaard+ PPR62.FISS,TEMPRTR SHELL - TH	
Lvl Density	None		LAS	Theo Conf	69Vienna 183	Jul 69	Bolsterli+ PPR100.SINGL NEUT - DEN,FISS	
Lvl Density	2.5+5	4.0+6	BUC	ExTh Jour	RRP 16 473	Apr 71	Boca+ CONST - TEMP - TH IN ISOM/IND - FISS	
Lvl Density	1.5+6	2.3+6	GEL	Expt Jour	ZP 257 108	Dec 72	Knitter+ N TEMP FROM INELASTIC SPECT	+
	1.5+6	2.3+6		Data	EXFOR20394.010	Oct 74	3PTS.NUCL.T.	
Lvl Density	None		MUN	Theo Jour	NP/A 217 269	Dec 73	Dilg+ A,DELTA. BACK SHIFTED FERMIGAS	
Lvl Density	None		COP	Theo Jour	NP/A 222 493	Apr 74	Dossing+COLL ROTAT.SPAC. ACCUR ESTIM	
Lvl Density	None		ROC	Theo Jour	NP/A 223 589	May 74	Huizenga+ PPR CFD MICROSC TH AX SYMM	
Lvl Density	+6		DUB	Theo Rept	JINR - E4 - 9236	Nov 75	Komov+ AVG LVL - SPAC,SEMIMICRO CFD XP	
Lvl Density	Maxwl		KTO	Expt Jour	NP/A 263 141	May 76	Imanishi+PRIMARY J AND SP CUT - OFF F.	
(γ,n)	None		LRL	Expt Prog	ERDA - NDC - 2 75	May 75	Alvarez+TBC.NDG.	
Photo - Fissn	2.3+7		HAR	Expt Jour	PR 76 142	Jul 49	Titterton+ EMULSION,TERNARY=CA.1/400	
Photo - Fissn	5.0+6	8.5+6	UI	Expt Jour	PR 77 329	Feb 50	Koch+ FISS COUNTS PER ROENTGN / E(G)	
Photo - Fissn		2.2+7	LAS	Expt Jour	PR 81 342	Feb 51	Mcelhinney+ SIGMA REL TO GF(U238)	
Photo - Fissn	1.2+7	2.0+7	ANL	Expt Jour	PR 95 1009	Aug 54	Huizenga+ 3ES RELATIVE FISS YIELDS	
Photo - Fissn	6.0+6	2.0+7	CRC	Expt Jour	CJP 37 1418	Dec 59	Baerg+. FRAG ANG DIST ISOTROPIC	
Photo - Fissn	7.0+6		ANL	Expt Jour	NP 34 439	Jun 62	Huizenga+ 6.91+7.12MEV GAMMAS.	
Photo - Fissn	9.0+6	1.9+7	LRL	Expt Abst	BAP 8 370	Apr 63	Auchampaugh+. 170MB AT 13 MEV	
Photo - Fissn	None		CCP	Expt Jour	ZET 44 1950	Jun 63	FISSN TR FROM(D,PF)AND(GF)JET17 1312	
Photo - Fissn	6.0+6	1.1+7	LRL	Expt Jour	NIM 24 213	Sep 63	Bowman+. SPARK CHAMBER. ARBITR.UNITS	
Photo - Fissn	1.5+7		CCP	Expt Jour	AE 20 268	Mar 66	Nikotin+.DELAYED NEUT YIELD,6 GROUPS	
				Jour	SJA 20 300	Mar 66	. ENGL OF AE 20 268	
Photo - Fissn	1.0+7	2.5+7	CCP	Expt Jour	AE 20 514	Jun 66	Kondratko+ PEAK/VALLEY YLD VS MAX EG	
	8.0+6	2.5+7		Jour	AE 23 559	Dec 67	Kondrat'Ko+.GRAPH+TABLE,FRGMNT DISTR	
	1.0+7	2.5+7		Jour	JNE 21 537	Jun 67	TRANSLATN.*	
				Jour	EAF 20 6 88	Jun 66	TRANSLATN.*	
				Jour	SJA 20 594	Jun 66	TRANSLATN.*	
	8.0+6	2.5+7		Jour	SJA 23 1336	Dec 67	. ENGL OF AE 23 559	

92 Uranium 235

Quantity	Energy (ev) Min	Max	Lab	Type	Documentation Ref Vol Page	Date	Author, Comments	Data
Photo–Fissn	None		GA	Expt	Jour PR 146 824	Jun 66	Sund+LINAC,GS ABOVE .5MEV TO 1SEC	
Photo–Fissn	1.5+7		MNZ	Theo	Jour AF 36 453	Nov 67	Patzelt+.FROM DERIVED N–EMISS PROB.	
Photo–Fissn		1.2+7	RI	Expt	Jour YF 9 949	May 69	Petrzhak+ GRPHS,FRAG KE,MASS DISTRIB	
		2.5+7			Jour YF 7 970	May 68	– + A – YLDS,NU,EKIN(FRGM).GRPHS	
		1.2+7			Jour SNP 9 556	Sep 69	. ENGL OF YF 9 949.	
		2.5+7			Jour SNP 7 584	Nov 68	. ENGL OF YF 7 970.	
Photo–Fissn	2.5+7		OSL	Revw	Conf 69Vienna 669	Jul 69	Pappas+PPR206. YLD(FRAG A,FRAG KE)	
Photo–Fissn	8.0+6	1.0+7	GA	Expt	Jour NSE 39 163	Feb 70	Kull+,2ES,DELAYED NEUT YLDS VS. TIME	
Photo–Fissn	5.0+6	8.3+6	CRC	Expt	Jour NP/A 179 333	Jan 72	Khan+.VARIABLE E MONOCHROMATOR.	
Photo–Fissn		1.5+7	IAE	Eval	Jour REA 10 637	Dec 72	Manero+ DELAYED NEUTRON YIELD,TBL	
Photo–Fissn	6.7+6	8.9+6	LAS	Expt	Jour NSE 56 179	Feb 75	Caldwell+ TBL,GRPH NU PROMPT+DELAYED	
	8.0+6	1.2+7			Conf 73Rochester 1 431	Aug 73	– + PROMPT+DELAYED–N YLDS,TBLS	
					Conf 73Pacif.Gr 1 651	Mar 73	– + PROMPT,DELAY NS,GN/GF,TBL	
					Rept LA–UR–73–968	73	+.PROMPT AND DELAYD NEUT YLD	
Photo–Fissn		6.0+6	GA	Expt	Conf 73Rochestr 2 501	Aug 73	Gozani. ABST,DEL+PROMPT–N YLD/FISYLD	
	4.5+6	1.5+7			Rept GULF–RT–10538	Feb 71	Bramblett+ CURVS SIG,PROMPT,DELAY NU	
Photo–Fissn	1.4+7		CCP	Expt	Jour AE 35 214	Sep 73	Kondrat'Ko+ YLD OF FRAGS,GRAPH	
					Jour SJA 35 866	Mar 74	.ENGLISH OF AE 35 214,SYMMETRIC FISS	
Photo–Fissn	5.0+6	8.0+6	IOW	Expt	Jour NP/A 212 221	Sep 73	Anderl+COMPTON GS. CFD FISS CHANNEL	
					Abst DA/B 33 4952	Apr 73	– .PROMINENT STRUCTURE SEEN	
					Jour NIM 102 101	Jul 72	– + EXP METHOD	
Photo–Fissn	6.0+6	1.2+7	CCP	Expt	Jour AE 36 404	May 74	Ivanov+ INTEG YLD/INTG U238–YLD,GRPH	
	5.0+6	1.2+7			Jour ZEP 17 610	Jun 73	– + SIGMA+ANISOTROPY,GRAPHS	
	6.0+6	1.2+7			Jour SJA 36 515	Nov 74	. ENGLISH OF AE 36 404	
	5.0+6	1.2+7			Jour JEL 17 429	Jun 73	.ENGLISH TRANSL OF ZEP 17 610 JUN/72	
Photo–Fissn	6.0+6	1.5+7	RI	Expt	Rept YFI–18 41	Aug 74	Ivanov+ YLD(E–GAMMA) AND ANGDISTR	
	5.0+6	1.2+7			Rept INDC(CCP)–49	Feb 75	– + ENGL OF YFI–18 41.GRAPHS	
Photo–Fissn		2.5+7	GHT	Expt	Prog INIS–MF–1933	75	Jacobs+ MASS+KIN–E DISTR.AVG E+M GVN	
Photo–Fissn	+7		BLA	Expt	Conf 75Kiev 6 146	Jun 75	Dragnev+ SIG(E–GAMMA),GRAPHS	
	6.4+6	9.0+6			Prog INDC(SEC)–42	Dec 74	– + ABST.8CAPT–GAMS,TBL SIG(E)	
Photo–Fissn		2.5+7	GHT	Expt	Prog INDC(SEC)–51	Dec 75	Jacobs+ P21.BIN/TER,LRA E–SPEC.NDG	
Photo–Fissn		1.7+7	IJI	Expt	Rept KIYAI–76–40	76	Aleksandrov+ DELAY NS,GROUPS INT+HL	
Photo–Fissn	8.0+6	1.6+7	BUC	Expt	Prog INDC(SEC)–50	Jan 76	Galatanu+ DELAY GAMS VS INCOM E,TABL	
Photo–Fissn	6.1+6	7.0+6	ANL	Expt	Rept ANL–5853	Jun 76	Clarke. 2GAMMA ES IONIZATION CHAMBER	
Photo–Fissn	4.8+6	7.0+6	IFP	Expt	Jour NIM 136 373	Jul 76	Zhuchko+ BREMSTRLNG.GRPH SIG GIVEN	
Photo–Fissn	5.0+6	7.0+6	FEI	Expt	Rept YK–21 65	Oct 76	Ostapenko+ YLD(E),GRAPH	
Photo–Fissn	1.5+7	2.0+7	TIL	Expt	Rept YFI–22 28	Dec 76	Petrzhak+ YLD XE–131,132,134,136	
		2.0+7			Rept YFI–22 128	Dec 76	– + BREMSSTR.REL XE–YLDS,TABLE	
	5.0+6	1.2+7			Rept YK–22 83	76	Ivanov+ SIG U235/238 VS EGAM,TBL+FIG	
Photo–Fissn	1.5+7	2.0+7	TIL	Expt	Rept YK–27 42	77	Petrzhak+ 15+20MEV BREMS.XE–YLDS,TBL	

92 Uranium 236

Quantity	Energy (ev) Min	Max	Lab	Type	Documentation Ref Vol Page	Date	Author, Comments	Data
Evaluation	5.0+5	1.5+7	LRL	Eval	Rept UCRL–5351	Nov 58	Howerton. CURVES.	
Evaluation	4.1–1	1.0+7	GA	Eval	Rept GA–2451	Aug 61	Joanou+.68GRP ABS,NF,NU,TRNSF(EL,IN)	
Evaluation	2.5–2	1.0+7	GEN	Eval	Rept APEX–704	Nov 61	Cooper+. CONTENT OF C–FINE TAPES	
Evaluation	1.0–3	1.0+7	AI	Eval	Rept NAA–SR–M–8904	Aug 63	Alter+.SAME AS MO+NF NU N2N.RES GAP	
Evaluation	2.5–2	1.1+7	FEI	Eval	Book ABAGJAN	64	26 GROUP CONST,TOT,FISS,NU,CAPT,SCAT	
Evaluation		+2	BNL	Eval	Rept BNL–982	Aug 66	Pearlstein. TOT,FISS,NG(THR),RIF,RIG	
Evaluation	2.5–2		TRM	Eval	Rept AEET–257	Aug 66	Singh.NG RIG(BNL325 SUPPL NO.2)	
Evaluation	5.0+2	3.7+6	TRM	Eval	Rept AEET–257	Aug 66	Singh.16GROUPS SIN DIN NF NU NG	
Evaluation	1.0+3	1.4+7	UK	Eval	Rept AHSB(S)R–124	May 67	Hart.(RLY).UK–DFN 336.UPDATES NSE 26	
	1.0+3	1.5+7			Rept AWRE–O–30/64	Jul 64	Parker.(ALD).UKNDL–DFN 173	
Evaluation	None		GA	Eval	Rept GA–8135	Sep 67	Drake+NG,SEL,TOT,RES,SNE,NF,SIN,N2N	
Evaluation	2.5–2	1.0+7	KFK	Eval	Rept KFK–1186	Jul 70	Hinkelmann.RES,STF,N2N,NF,NU,NG,R.I.	
					Conf 70Helsinki 2 721	Jun 70	– + ALL QUANTITIES.	
Evaluation	3.0+3	1.0+6	BRC	Theo	Rept CEA–R–4631	74	Thomet.	
Total	4.1+0	9.5+0	ORL	Expt	Prog ORNL–1477 13	Dec 52	Pawlicki+	+
	4.1+0	9.5+0			Data EXFOR12473.002	Jun 76	. 18 PTS.	
Total	Pile		ORL	Expt	Prog WASH–191	Jun 56	Halperin+ 34B FROM LOG IRRAD.	
Total	2.8+0	7.0+2	ORL	Expt	Jour PR 109 471	Jan 58	Harvey+.FAST CHOP,TRANSM,RESOL.3–2EV	+
	2.8+0	7.0+2			Data EXFOR12339.010	Jun 76	. 240 PTS. SIGMA.	
Total	1.0–2	2.0+1	HAR	Expt	Jour JNE 6 181	Apr 58	Mccallum.FC CURVE, 18.7+ – 1.7B AT THR	+
Total	2.0–1	1.0+7	B+W	Eval	Rept BAW–158	Jun 61	Roach+ AVERAGED SIG 40 GROUPS	
Total	1.0+3	1.5+7	UK	Eval	Rept AWRE–O–30/64	Jul 64	Parker.(ALD).UKNDL–DFN 173	+
	1.0–5	1.5+7			Data UKNDL–DFN 954A	Mar 73	305 PNTS	

92 Uranium 236

Quantity	Energy (ev) Min	Energy (ev) Max	Lab	Type	Documentation Ref Vol Page	Date	Author, Comments	Data
Total	5.0+6	1.6+7	LAS	Theo	Rept LA-3538	Sep 66	Agee+ OPTICAL MODEL CALCULATION	
Total	1.0-2	1.0+3	MTR	Expt	Prog WASH-1127 60	Apr 69	Harlan.FAST CHOPPER.RESON PARAMS GVN	
Total	5.0+0	4.2+2	GEL	Expt	Jour NP/A 181 639	Feb 72	Theobald+ LINAC.TOF.RES ANAL.	+
	5.0+0	4.2+2			Data EXFOR20501.	Mar 76	0PTS.SEE RESONANCE PARAMETERS.	
Total	3.0+1	1.8+3	MOL	Expt	Conf 75Wash. 729	Mar 75	Mewissen+TBL,RES PAR	
					Conf NEANDC(E)-163U	75	- + LINAC TOF WN WG GIVEN	
					Rept RCN-203 279	Dec 73	- + AVG WG,D,S0	
Total	-3	1.9+0	THS	Theo	Rept IKE-6 89 55	Jun 75	Keinert. DATA LIBRARY	
Total	3.7+1	4.1+3	GEL	Expt	Jour NP/A 257 333	Feb 76	Carraro+ LINAC,TOF,TRANS,GRPH	+
	4.0+1	4.1+3			Conf 72Budapest 200	Aug 72	- + TOF,NAI,U3O8 POWDER, NDG	
	3.7+1	4.1+3			Data EXFOR20699.	Jun 77	0PTS. SEE RESONANCE PARAMETERS	
Elastic	Maxwl		HAR	Expt	Jour JNE 6 181	Apr 58	Mccallum. 10.6+ - 0.4B EST BY RES PAR	+
Elastic	1.0+3	1.5+7	UK	Eval	Rept AWRE-O-30/64	Jul 64	Parker.(ALD).UKNDL-DFN 173	+
	1.0-5	1.5+7			Data UKNDL-DFN 954A	Mar 73	305 PNTS	
Elastic	5.0+6	1.6+7	LAS	Theo	Rept LA-3538	Sep 66	Agee+ OPTMDL+H-F FOR COMP.	
Elastic	3.0+1	1.8+3	MOL	Expt	Conf 75Wash. 729	Mar 75	Mewissen+MEAS REL PB SCAT=11.28B	
					Conf NEANDC(E)163U	75	- +LINAC.TOF.WN.WG GIVEN	
					Rept RCN-203 279	Dec 73	- + AVG WG,D,S0	
Diff Elastic	1.0+3	1.5+7	UK	Eval	Rept AWRE-O-30/64	Jul 64	Parker.(ALD).UKNDL-DFN 173	
	1.0-5	1.5+7			Data UKNDL-DFN 954A	Mar 73	17 PNTS,C.M.	
Diff Elastic	5.0+6	1.6+7	LAS	Theo	Rept LA-3538	Sep 66	Agee+ OPTMDL+H-F FOR COMP.	
Diff Elastic	5.0+6	1.6+7	LAS	Theo	Rept LA-3788	67	Beery+.OPTMOD CALC POLARIZ ANG DISTR	
Polarization	5.0+6	1.6+7	LAS	Theo	Rept LA-3788	67	Beery+.OPTMOD CALC COS(THETA) DISTR	
Tot Inelastc	Thrsh	1.5+7	UK	Eval	Rept AWRE-O-30/64	Jul 64	Parker.(ALD).UKNDL-DFN 173	+
	4.6+4	1.5+7			Data UKNDL-DFN 954A	Mar 73	68 PNTS	
Tot Inelastc	6.7+4	3.7+6	TRM	Eval	Rept AEET-257	Aug 66	Singh. 9GROUPS CALC FROM AWREO30/64	
Diff Inelast	Thrsh	1.5+7	UK	Eval	Rept AWRE-O-30/64	Jul 64	Parker.(ALD).UKNDL-DFN 173	+
	4.6+4	2.0+6			Data UKNDL-DFN 954A	Mar 73	1ST-6TH LVL,ANGDIST	
	9.0+5	1.5+7			Data UKNDL-DFN 954A	Mar 73	.TO CONTINUUM.47 PTS.E DIST.ANGDIST.	
Diff Inelast	1.1+5	3.7+6	TRM	Eval	Rept AEET-257	Aug 66	Singh. 8GROUPS J-J+K MATRIX K=0TO9	
Diff Inelast	1.4+7		LRL	Theo	Rept UCRL-50181	Feb 67	Lutz+.CALC ANG DIST FOR FIRST 2+ LVL	
Diff Inelast	3.0+3	1.0+6	BRC	Eval	Rept CEA-R-4631	Nov 74	Thomet. STAT MDL ANAL TBLS GRPHS	
Scattering	1.0+3	1.5+7	UK	Eval	Rept AWRE-O-30/64	Jul 64	Parker.(ALD).UKNDL-DFN 173	
Nonelastic	1.0+3	1.5+7	UK	Eval	Rept AWRE-O-30/64	Jul 64	Parker.(ALD).UKNDL-DFN 173	
Absorption	Cold		ANL	Revw	Conf 55Geneva 5 125	Aug 55	Spinrad+.P835	
Absorption	Fast		ANL	Revw	Conf 55Geneva 5 125	Aug 55	Spinrad+.P835	
Absorption	Maxwl		HAR	Expt	Jour JNE 6 181	Apr 58	Mccallum. 8.1+ - 2B FROM SIGT-EST SIGS	+
Absorption	2.5-2	1.0+7	AI	Eval	Rept NAA-SR-M-3013	Aug 58	Kistler. 32-GROUP SIGS TABULATED	
Absorption	2.0-1	1.0+7	B+W	Eval	Rept BAW-158	Jun 61	Roach+ AVERAGED SIG 40 GROUPS	
Absorption	5.0-3	2.5+0	GA	Eval	Rept GA-2113	Jun 61	Wikner+.TABLE+CURVE.100 E POINTS	
Absorption	Pile		SRL	Expt	Conf 68Wash. 1271	Mar 68	Hennelly+ ABOUT 12B	
Absorption	6.2-1	1.0+7	SRL	Theo	Conf 71Knoxvill 714	Mar 71	Mccrosson. SPECTRUM-AVERAGED SIG	
Absorption	1.0-3	2.0+0	JUL	Expt	Rept JUEL-746-RG 49	Apr 71	Bonka.KUGEL-THERMOS-LIBR,T=300K,CURV	
Absorption	None		MUN	Theo	Diss GRYNTAKIS	Mar 76	Gryntakis.,CALC.OF WESTCOTTS G-FUNCT	
					Jour RCA 22 128	Mar 75	- +,EQUIVALENT TO THESIS	
Res Int Abs	None		BNL	Expt	Abst BAP 1 187	Apr 56	Pilcher+ TRANS,310B INCLUDING 1/V	
Res Int Abs	5.0-1		SGA	Comp	Conf 73Paris 1 233	Mar 73	Eder+ REDUCED RES INTEG CAPTURE,TBL	
					Rept SGAE-PH-141	Feb 73	.SAME AS 73PARIS,NO DETAILS,TBP	
(n,γ)	Maxwl		ANL	Expt	Prog ANL-4490 5	Jun 50	Fields. THERMAL.	+
	Maxwl				Data EXFOR12463.002	Jun 76	. 1 PT. SIGMA.	
(n,γ)	Maxwl		ANL	Expt	Prog ANL-4490 9	Jun 50	Diamond. THERMAL	+
	Maxwl				Data EXFOR12464.002	Jun 76	. 1 PT. SIGMA.	
(n,γ)	Maxwl		ORL	Expt	Rept ORNL-CF-51-12	Dec 51	Pomerance.	+
	Maxwl				Data EXFOR12353.003	Jun 76	. 1 PT. SIGMA.	
(n,γ)	Maxwl		ANL	Expt	Prog ANL-4873 9	Apr 52	Huizenga. THERMAL.	+
	Maxwl				Data EXFOR12465.002	Jun 76	. 1 PT. SIGMA.	
(n,γ)	Pile		SAC	Expt	Conf 55Geneva 4 235	Aug 55	Auclair+.VAL GVN,BETA-ACTIVITY,P354	+
					Jour JPR 17 564	Jul 56	Charon+REPEAT.24+ - 7B,CF 9+ - 2B IN USA	
					Jour CR 241 392	Jul 55	Auclair+ ACTIVATION.	
(n,γ)	Pile		CCP	Expt	Jour AE 1 5 130	Nov 56	Efimov+ SIGMA GVN,RFT REACT REFLECTR	
					Jour JNE 5 158	Jul 57	- + TRANSLATION	
					Jour SJA 1 5 811	56	- + TRANSLATION	
(n,γ)	Maxwl		ORL	Expt	Jour NSE 3 395	Apr 58	Halperin+	+
					Conf 58Geneva 16 64	Sep 58	- +	
	Maxwl				Data EXFOR12447.002	Jun 76	. 1 PT. SIGMA.	
	Maxwl				Data EXFOR12447.002	Jun 76	. 1 PT, SIG	
(n,γ)	Maxwl		CRC	Expt	Jour JNE 7 81	Aug 58	Cabell+ SUB-CD,5.5+ - .3B REL CO 36.5B	+
	Maxwl				Data EXFOR12449.003	Jun 76	. 1 PT. SIGMA.	

92   Uranium   236

Quantity	Energy (ev) Min	Max	Lab	Type	Documentation Ref Vol Page	Date	Author, Comments	Data
(n,γ)	Maxwl		CRC	Expt	Conf 58Geneva 16 54	Sep 58	Eastwood+.PPR203,SIGMA GVN,ACTIVATIN	
(n,γ)	Pile		ORL	Eval	Jour NSE 6 100	Aug 59	Stoughton+,BEST VALUE .025EV=6+−2B	
					Conf 58Geneva 16 54	Sep 58	Halperin+ VAL CFD, MANY REFS.	
(n,γ)	Maxwl		CRC	Eval	Rept AECL−1054	Mar 60	Walker+ (CRRP−913)	
(n,γ)	2.0+5	5.0+6	ANL	Revw	Conf 61Vienna 1 29	Aug 61	Smith.PPR76,CURVE,ACTIVATION METHOD	
(n,γ)	3.0+5	4.0+6	ALD	Expt	Jour PPS 78 801	Nov 61	Barry+. ACTIVATION.14ES TABLE+CURVE	+
(n,γ)	3.0+5	1.7+6	ANL	Expt	Jour JNAB 15 200	Dec 61	Stupegia+ SIG AT 8ES REL U235F,CFD	+
	3.0+5	1.7+6			Data EXFOR12450.002	Jun 76	. 8 PTS. SIGMA.	
(n,γ)	1.0+3	1.5+7	UK	Eval	Rept AWRE−O−30/64	Jul 64	Parker.(ALD).UKNDL−DFN 173	+
	1.0−5	1.5+7			Data UKNDL−DFN 954A	Mar 73	305 PNTS	
(n,γ)	5.0+2	3.7+6	TRM	Eval	Rept AEET−257	Aug 66	Singh.16GROUPS PPS78 801 AWREO30/64	
(n,γ)	2.0+4	+6	GSF	Theo	Jour AF 36 509	Nov 67	Truran+.STAT MODEL. TWO MASS FORMLS	
(n,γ)	Maxwl		RI	Revw	Jour AE 23 561	Dec 67	BAK+ OTHER SIG VAL GIVEN,TABLE	
					Jour SJA 23 1340	Dec 67	. ENGL OF AE 23 561	
(n,γ)	Maxwl		AUA	Theo	Jour NSE 31 234	Feb 68	Cook+ STATISTICAL CALC CFD EXPT	
(n,γ)	3.0+4	1.0+6	ANL	Expt	Prog WASH−1093 3	Apr 68	Lister+ GE−LI DET NDG	
(n,γ)	Maxwl		SRL	Expt	Jour NSE 32 265	May 68	Baumann+ ACT 6.0+−0.5B BY CD RATIO	
	Maxwl				Data EXFOR12466.003	Jun 76	. 1 PT. SIGMA.	
(n,γ)	Maxwl		MTR	Expt	Rept IN−1296	May 69	Schuman+ THERMAL.	+
	Maxwl				Data EXFOR11687.009	Jun 76	. 1 PT. SIGMA.	
(n,γ)	None		LAS	Expt	Prog WASH−1136 110	Sep 69	Silbert+,PHYSICS−8 SHOT,ANAL TBC	
(n,γ)	1.0−2	2.0+4	GGA	Expt	Jour NP/A 141 577	Feb 70	Carlson+CAPT,SELF INDIC.GRPH.	+
	1.0−2	2.0+4			Data EXFOR10695.	Aug 78	. 60 PTS.1PT THERMAL CS FROM EXTRAPL	
(n,γ)	2.5−2		KFK	Eval	Rept KFK−1186	Jul 70	Hinkelmann. RECOMMENDED 5.6 B	
	2.5−2	1.0+7			Rept KFK−1186	Jul 70	− .5−GROUP SIG,THR+FAST SPEC	
(n,γ)	1.0−2	1.0+7	ORL	Revw	Jour REA 8 473	Sep 70	Kasten. REVIEW,SIG(NEUT−E) GRAPH	
(n,γ)	Maxwl		HAR	Expt	Rept AERE−R−6761	Mar 71	Cabell+ SIG=8.47+−4.0 BY MASS SPEC	+
	Pile				Data EXFOR20449.	Jan 76	2PTS.SIGMA.	
(n,γ)	Maxwl	Fiss	SGA	Comp	Conf 73Paris 1 233	Mar 73	Eder+ DATA FROM EXPTS+EVALS,TABLE	
					Rept SGAE−PH−141	Feb 73	.SAME AS 73PARIS,NO DETAILS	
(n,γ)	1.0+3	1.0+6	BRC	Revw	Conf 75Wash. 202	Mar 75	Michaudon.CALC CFD MEAS	
	3.0+3	1.0+6		Eval	Jour JAERI−M−5984	Feb 75	Thomet.STATMOD.2 HUMP BARRIER.GRPH	
					Rept CEA−R−4631	Nov 74	− . STAT MDL ANAL TBLS GRPHS	
(n,γ)	3.0+1	1.8+3	MOL	Expt	Conf 75Wash. 729	Mar 75	Mewissen+MEAS.REL 10B(N,AG)	
					Conf NEANDC(E)−163U	75	− + LINAC TOF WN WG GIVEN	
					Rept RCN−203 279	Dec 73	− + AVG WG,D,S0	
(n,γ)	Maxwl		MTR	Expt	Prog IDO−16827 18	Jan 63	Berreth+ THER CS GIVEN	+
	Maxwl				Data EXFOR12635.004	Jun 76	. 1 PT, SIGMA.	
Res Int Capt	5.0−1		CRC	Expt	Jour JNE 7 81	Aug 58	Cabell+ EPI−CD,257+−22B REL CO 48.6B	+
	5.0−1				Data EXFOR12449.004	Jun 76	. 1PT. RI.	
Res Int Capt	5.0−1		ORL	Expt	Conf 58Geneva 16 64	Sep 58	Halperin+.PPR1072,VAL CFD MANY REFS	+
	5.0−1				Data EXFOR12447.003	Jun 76	. 1 PT.	
Res Int Capt	5.0−1	1.0+6	ORL	Eval	Jour NSE 6 100	Aug 59	Stoughton+ BEST VALUE 400+−100B	
					Conf 58Geneva 1072	Sep 58	.SUPERSEDED	
Res Int Capt	None		CRC	Eval	Rept AECL−2111	Nov 64	Walker. REDUCED RESONNANCE INTEGRAL.	
Res Int Capt	5.0−1		SRL	Expt	Jour NSE 32 265	May 68	Baumann+ ACT 2METHODS CFD 417,419B	+
					Conf 68Wash. 1271	Mar 68	Hennelly+ ABOUT 400+−40B	
	5.0−1				Data EXFOR12466.002	Jun 76	. 1 PT.	
Res Int Capt	5.0−1		MTR	Expt	Rept IN−1296	May 69	Schuman+. PILE ACT. 381+−30B. 1/V	+
	5.0−1				Data EXFOR11687.010	Jun 76	. 1 PT. RI	
Res Int Capt	5.4−1		GA	Expt	Jour NP/A 141 577	Jan 70	Carlson+ CALCULATED FROM RES PARAMS.	
Res Int Capt	5.0−1		GGA	Expt	Jour NP/A 141 577	Feb 70	Carlson+CALC FROM RESPARS,S0,S1.	+
	5.0−1				Data EXFOR10695.008	Aug 78	. 1PT.RIG=350+−25B.	
Res Int Capt	4.7−1	1.0+7	KFK	Eval	Rept KFK−1186	Jul 70	Hinkelmann. INFIN DILUTION RES INTEG	
Res Int Capt	5.0−1		MTR	Expt	Prog WASH−1041 37	Oct 62	Berreth+SIGMA GVN,VERY THIN SAMPLE	+
	5.0−1				Data EXFOR12635.007	Jun 76	. 1 PT, RI	
Spect (n,γ)	Maxwl		LAS	Expt	Prog WASH−1127 147	Apr 69	Shera+ TO BE COMPLETED,NO DATA GIVEN	
(n,2n)	Thrsh	1.5+7	UK	Eval	Rept AWRE−O−30/64	Jul 64	Parker.(ALD).UKNDL−DFN 173	
	7.0+6	1.5+7			Data UKNDL−DFN 954A	Mar 73	.21 PTS.E DIST.ANG DIST,LAB.	
(n,2n)	1.3+7	1.5+7	BNL	Theo	Jour NSE 23 238	Nov 65	Pearlstein.3ES.STAT MDL CALC.TBL CS.	
(n,2n)	Fiss		BNL	Theo	Jour NSE 23 238	Nov 65	Pearlstein.STATMDL CALC.SPEC AVG.TBL	
(n,2n)	8.0+5	1.0+7	KFK	Eval	Rept KFK−1186	Jul 70	Hinkelmann.AVG SIG FOR THR+FAST SPEC	
(n,2n)	2.0+6	1.5+7	BRC	Eval	Prog NEANDC(E)162U	Aug 75	Michaudon+.	
					Conf JAERI−M−5984	Feb 75	Jary.P 76.STATMOD/OPTMOD. CURVES.	
					Rept CEA−R−4647	Jan 75	− . EVAL,STAT MDL, 15 VALS	
(n,xn) x>2	Thrsh	1.5+7	ALD	Eval	Rept AWRE−O−30/64	Jul 64	Parker.N3N. UKAEA DFN−173 LIBRARY.	
(n,xn) x>2	Fiss		BNL	Theo	Jour NSE 23 238	Nov 65	Pearlstein.SPEC AVG STATMDL CALC N3N	
(n,xn) x>2	1.2+7	1.5+7	UK	Eval	Data UKNDL−DFN 954A	Mar 73	.6 PTS. E DIST.ANG DIST,LAB. N3N.	

92 Uranium 236

Quantity	Energy (ev) Min	Energy (ev) Max	Lab	Type	Documentation Ref Vol Page	Author, Comments Date	Data
(n,xn) x>2	2.0+6	1.5+7	BRC	Eval Prog	NEANDC(E)162 4	Aug 75 Michaudon+	
				Conf	JAERI−M−5984	Feb 75 Jary.P 76.STATMOD/OPTMOD. CURVES.N3N	
				Rept	CEA−R−4647	Jan 75 − . EVAL,STAT MDL, 15 VALS	
Fission	1.5+7		LAS	Expt Rept	LAMS−938	Jun 50 Nyer+ FISS CHAMBER RELATIVE TO U238	+
	1.5+7			Data	EXFOR12306.005	Jun 76 . 1 PT. SIGMA	
Fission	Pile		LAS	Expt Rept	LA−1250	May 51 Jurney. FAST REACTOR SPEC AVG SIG.	
Fission	6.9+5	1.4+7	LAS	Expt Rept	LA−1258	May 51 Nyer+ FISS CHAMB	+
	6.9+5	1.4+7		Data	EXFOR12472.002	Jun 76 . 6 PTS. SIGMA	
Fission	2.5+6	1.4+7	LAS	Expt Rept	LA−1681	Jun 54 Wahl.	+
	2.5+6	1.4+7		Data	EXFOR12437.003	Jun 76 . 2 PTS. SIGMA.	
Fission	Cold		ANL	Revw Conf	55Geneva 5 125	Aug 55 Spinrad+.P835	
Fission	Fast		ANL	Revw Conf	55Geneva 5 125	Aug 55 Spinrad+.P835	
Fission	6.9+5	4.0+6	ORL	Expt Jour	PR 104 1654	Dec 56 Lamphere.CURVE REL U235	+
	Thrsh	4.0+6		Jour	PR 100 763	Nov 55 − +,DIPS MAY BE DUE TO RES	
	3.1+5	4.1+6		Data	EXFOR12338.	Jun 76 . 160 PTS. SIGMA.	
Fission	6.0+5	7.0+6	LAS	Revw Rept	LA−2122	Jun 57 Henkel.CURV,REPLACES LA−1714	
Fission	Maxwl		ORL	Comp Conf	58Geneva 16 64	Sep 58 Halperin+.PPR1072,VAL GVN,MANY REFS	
Fission	5.5+0		HAN	Expt Rept	HW−67219	Oct 60 Leonard+LESS THAN 1B	
Fission	5.1+5	1.0+7	B+W	Eval Rept	BAW−158	Jun 61 Roach+ AVERAGED SIG 10 GROUPS	
Fission	6.0+5	4.0+6	ANL	Revw Conf	61Vienna 1 29	Aug 61 Smith.P76,CURVE,MANY REFS GVN	
Fission	Fiss		AI	Expt Conf	62Harwell 2 385	Dec 62 Strominger. SIG IN VARIOUS CORES,TBL	
Fission	4.0+4	5.0+5	ALD	Expt Conf	65Salzburg 1 219	Mar 65 White+ 6 ENERGIES.TBL.REL TO U235.	
Fission	−2	+2	HAR	ExTh Conf	65Salzburg 187	Mar 65 RAE.REVIEW,SOME CALCULATIONS CFD XPT	
Fission	2.4+4		ALD	Expt Jour	JNE 19 423	Jun 65 Perkin+.CALIB SB−BE SRCE. BELOW 4MB	+
	2.4+4			Data	EXFOR20584.005	Jul 76 1PNT.SIGMA.	
Fission	None		BRK	Revw Jour	NP 81 1	Jun 66 Myers+ TABLE2 FISS BARRIER	
Fission	5.0+5	3.7+6	TRM	Eval Rept	AEET−257	Aug 66 Singh. 5GROUPS PR104 1654,LA2122DATA	
Fission	1.0+3	1.4+7	UK	Eval Rept	AHSB(S)R−124	May 67 Hart.(RLY).UK−DFN 336.UPDATES NSE 26	+
	Thrsh	1.5+7		Rept	AWRE−O−30/64	Jul 64 Parker.(ALD).UKNDL−DFN 173	
	6.0+5	1.5+7		Data	UKNDL−DFN 954A	Mar 73 54 PNTS	
Fission	Pile		WIN	Expt Rept	AEEW−R−526	Jun 67 Stevenson+.FISS RATIO TO U235.ZEBRA	+
Fission	1.0+6	1.4+7	ALD	Expt Jour	JNE 21 671	Aug 67 White+ 4ES REL U235. CFD OTHER DATA	+
Fission	6.0+5	1.2+6	WAU	Theo Jour	NP/A 101 460	Sep 67 Vandenbosch. CHANNEL ANALYSIS	
	8.4+5			Conf	66Gatlinbg § 7.3	Sep 66 − .H−F ANAL SIG+ANG DISTR	
Fission	Maxwl		RI	Revw Jour	AE 23 561	Dec 67 BAK+ OTHER SIG VAL GIVEN,TABLE	
				Jour	SJA 23 1340	Dec 67 . ENGL OF AE 23 561	
Fission	1.0+6	5.0+6	LAS	Expt Conf	68Wash. 627	Mar 68 Stein+ VDG TOF TBL+CURV U236/U235	+
				Rept	LA−DC−9205	67 .SUPERSEDED	
				Conf	66Paris 1 419	Oct 66 .SUPERSEDED	
	1.0+6	5.0+6		Data	EXFOR12452.002	Jun 76 . 16 PTS. SIGMA.	
Fission	4.5+6	1.0+7	ANL	Eval Jour	NSE 32 35	Apr 68 Davey. RE−EVALUATION OF DATA.	
	1.0+3	1.0+7		Jour	NSE 26 149	Oct 66 − . EVALUATION.	
Fission	Spont		COP	Revw Conf	69Vienna 155	Jul 69 Strutinsky+PPR203. HL GVN,'SHELL−TH'	
Fission	−		HAR	Revw Conf	69Vienna 249	Jul 69 Lynn. REVW=STRUTINSKY TH + EXPTS,TBL	
	None			Rept	AERE−R−5891	Sep 68 − .STRUCTURE IN FISS.DISCUSSED.ND	
Fission	None		LAS	Expt Conf	69Vienna 918	Jul 69 Britt+PPR101.(D,P FISSN)CFD(N,FISSN)	
Fission	4.0+5	9.0+5	ROC	ExTh Conf	69Vienna 403	Jul 69 Huizenga+PPR118. SIG(6ES)CHANNL ANAL	
					70 Kapil. 6 GROUP SIG,2 N−SPECS,TABLES		
Fission	4.0+5	1.0+7	TRM	Eval Rept	BARC/I−96	Apr 70 Cramer+,NUCL SHOT,TOF,TABLES+CURVES	+
Fission	3.5+1	2.9+6	LAS	Expt Rept	LA−4420	Jul 71 2061PTS.	
	3.5+1	2.9+6		Data	EXFOR10058.002		
Fission	2.5−2	1.0+7	KFK	Eval Rept	KFK−1186	Jul 70 Hinkelmann.5−GROUP SIG,THR+FAST SPEC	
	2.5−2			Rept	KFK−1186	Jul 70 − . RECOMMENDED 0 B	
Fission	Spont		SUN	Expt Prog	INDC(SAF)−4 14	71 Pilcher+ REL U235(N,F) AT 30KEV+HL	
Fission	Spont		DUB	Expt Jour	JINR−P7−5497	Jan 71 Belov+ U235(N,G)U236,ISOM FISSN HL	
Fission		5.0+6	FEI	Theo Jour	YF 13 1170	Jun 71 Prokhorova+ SIG(NEUT−E),GRAPH	
Fission	3.0+0	1.0+3	GEL	Expt Jour	NP/A 181 639	Feb 72 Theobald+ LINAC TOF NDG	+
	0.0+0	1.0+0		Revw Jour	AKE 18 229	Nov 71 − + SUB−BARRIER FISS EXPTS,TH	
	3.0+0	1.0+3		Expt Data	EXFOR20501.	Mar 76 0PTS. SEE RESONANCE PARAMETERS	
Fission	Spont		MRY	Theo Jour	PL/B 38 495	Apr 72 Hooshyar+ TOTAL DELAY HALF LIFE CALC	
				Prog	ORO−4028−28	71 Jackson+. SPON FISSION HALF−LIFE GVN	
Fission	5.0+5	2.6+6	ORL	Expt Jour	PL/B 38 501	Apr 72 Rosler+ TOF EXPT FLUX BY TWO METHODS	+
	4.9+5	9.5+6		Data	EXFOR10262.002	Apr 76 1484PTS.SIGMA	
Fission	0.0+0	1.0+0	GEL	ExTh Jour	NP/A 187 305	Jun 72 Weigmann+ FIS BAR PARAMS	
Fission	2.5−2		JUL	Theo Jour	ZP 257 389	Dec 72 Mcminn. 6.08 E−3 BARNS	
Fission	Spont		NEU	Theo Jour	HPA 45 567	Dec 72 Hooshyar+ HL GROUNDST AND FISS ISOM.	
Fission	Fiss		SGA	Eval Conf	73Paris 1 233	Mar 73 Eder+ FISS SPEC REL U238(N,F),TBLS	
				Rept	SGAE−PH−141	Feb 73 .SAME AS 73PARIS,NO DETAILS,TBP	
Fission	None		FRK	Theo Jour	NP/A 207 225	Jun 73 Albrecht. 2CENTRE SHELLMOD,DEF−E MAP	

92 Uranium 236

Quantity	Energy (ev) Min	Max	Lab	Type	Documentation Ref Vol Page	Date	Author, Comments	Data
Fission	None		ORL Theo	Jour	PR/C 10 1529	Oct 74	Kolb+ ASYMM.FISS.K-MATRIX CALC.	
	Spont			Prog	ORNL-4937 219	May 74	- +ASYM.FISS.K-MATRIX.MODEL.GRPHS	
Fission	2.0+6	1.5+7	BRC Eval	Conf	JAERI-M-5984	Feb 75	Jary.P 76.STATMOD/OPTMOD. CURVES.	
Fission	1.0+3	1.0+6	BRC Revw	Conf	75Wash. 202	Mar 75	Michaudon.CALC CFD MEAS	
	3.0+3	1.0+6	Eval	Conf	JAERI-M-5984	Feb 75	Thomet.STATMOD.2 HUMP BARRIER.GRPH	
				Rept	CEA-R-4631	Nov 74	- . STAT MDL ANAL TBLS GRPHS	
Fission	3.0+6	5.0+6	LAS Theo	Conf	75Wash. 129	Mar 75	Moore.GRPH R MATR STAT CALC CFD EXP	
Fission	3.5+1	1.4+7	JAE Revw	Conf	IAEA-186 3 1	76	Igarasi. REVW AVAIL DATA,GRPH+BIBLIO	
	1.0+3	5.5+6		Rept	JAERI-M-6315	Nov 75	- +GRPHS.4 DATA SETS COMPARED.	
Fission	Maxwl		MOL Theo	Jour	NP/A 259 423	Mar 76	Wagemans+ CALC FOR DOUBLE HUMP + IH0	
Res Int Fiss	4.7-1	1.0+7	KFK Eval	Rept	KFK-1186	Jul 70	Hinkelmann. INFIN DILUTION RES INTEG	
Res Int Fiss	5.0-1	+6	COR Expt	Jour	NSE 46 31	Oct 71	Draper.INTEGRAL SIG TIMES E.4 SPECTR	
	+0	+1		Abst	DA/B 31 1466	Sep 70	.EXPT FOR 4 SPEC,GOOD CFD CALC	
Eta	Cold		ANL Revw	Conf	55Geneva 5 125	Aug 55	Spinrad+.P835	
Eta	Fast		ANL Revw	Conf	55Geneva 5 125	Aug 55	Spinrad+.P835	
Eta	1.0+3	1.5+7	UK Eval	Rept	AWRE-O-30/64	Jul 64	Parker.(ALD).UKNDL-DFN 173	
Nu	Thrsh	1.5+7	UK Eval	Rept	AWRE-O-30/64	Jul 64	Parker.(ALD).UKNDL-DFN 173	+
	6.0+5	1.5+7		Data	UKNDL-DFN 954A	Mar 73	ANGDIST OF FISS NEUT, 2 PNTS,LAB.	
	6.0+5	1.5+7		Data	UKNDL-DFN 954A	Mar 73	19 PNTS	
Nu	5.0+5	3.7+6	TRM Eval	Rept	AEET-257	Aug 66	Singh. 5GROUPS CALC FROM AWREO30/64	
Nu	-		BOR Theo	Jour	CR 267 1350	Dec 68	Doan+ BASED ON MODEL OF 3 ALIGN.SPERE	
Nu	4.7+4	8.0+5	KFK Eval	Rept	KFK-1186	Jul 70	Hinkelmann.AVG VALUE OF MEAN NUMBER	
	8.0+5	1.0+7		Rept	KFK-1186	Jul 70	- .MEAN NUMBER, TABLE, GRPH	
Nu	7.7+5	6.7+6	FOA Expt	Priv	CONDE	Feb 71	Conde+ DATA TBP IN JNE	+
				Jour	JNE 25 331	71	- + CFD OTHERS,LIN FIT,GRAPH+TABL	
				Conf	73Kiev 4 130	May 73	- . SUMMARY OF NUBAR(EN),NO VALUE	
	7.7+5	6.7+6		Data	EXFOR20037.002	Sep 71	. 21PTS.PROMPT.	
Nu	Spont		FOA Expt	Priv	CONDE	Feb 71	Conde+ DATA TBP IN JNE	+
				Jour	JNE 25 331	71	- + FRAG-N COINCS.	
				Conf	73Kiev 4 130	May 73	- + NUBAR GIVN,CFD NUBAR(E)U235	
	Spont			Data	EXFOR20037.003	Sep 71	. 1PNT.PROMPT.	
Nu		5.0+6	FEI Theo	Jour	YF 13 1170	Jun 71	Prokhorova+ NUBAR(NEUT-E),GRAPH	
Nu	+0	1.5+7	IAE Eval	Jour	REA 10 637	Dec 72	Manero+ SURVEY,TBLS+GRPHS,RECOMM VAL	
	Spont			Jour	REA 10 637	Dec 72	- + EXTENSIVE SURVEY,TBL,AVG VAL	
Nu	Spont		AUA Eval	Rept	AAEC/E-304	Mar 74	Musgrove. META. BIN NUBAR ESTIM GIVN	
Nu	5.0+6	1.7+7	LRL Expt	Prog	UCID-16514 6	Jun 74	Alvarez+	
Nu	Spont		HED Eval	Abst	ANS 22 673	Nov 75	Johnson. TBL,GRPH NU FROM SPON FISS	
Nu	0.0+0	1.5+7	BRC Eval	Rept	CEA-R-4791	Oct 76	Bois+NUBAR VS EN,CALC CFD EXP,TABLES	
Delayd Neuts	1.1+7	1.7+7	LRL Expt	Prog	UCID-16514 6	Jun 74	Alvarez+	
Spect Fiss n	Thrsh	1.5+7	UK Eval	Rept	AWRE-O-30/64	Jul 64	Parker.(ALD).UKNDL-DFN 173	+
	6.0+5	1.5+7		Data	UKNDL-DFN 954A	Mar 73	1 RANGES	
Spect Fiss n	3.0-1	1.0+3	GEL Expt	Jour	NP/A 181 639	Feb 72	Theobald+LINAC.B SLAB.LIKE E(-0.89)	
Spect Fiss n	1.5+6	2.3+6	GEL Expt	Prog	EANDC(E)150U	May 72	Knitter+,VDG TOF ENERGY SPECTRUM	
Fiss Prod γ			WIN Theo	Jour	JNE 25 513	Oct 71	James.MEAN EN OF DELAYD GAMS,BETAS.	
Fiss Yield	Spont		CRC Theo	Jour	CJP 35 195	Feb 57	Hay+ TABLE CALCTD FISS PROD MASS+E	
Fiss Yield	6.0+5	9.0+6	LAS Expt	Prog	WASH-1026 33	Oct 59	Simmons. ANG DISTR OF FRAGMENTS	
Fiss Yield	9.0+6	1.5+7	LAS ExTh	Jour	PR/B 137 81	Feb 65	Leachman+ RLTV ANG DIST FISS-FRAG.	
Fiss Yield	-		TRM Theo	Conf	65Calcutta 20	Feb 65	. FISS AS MARKOV PROCESS,MASS DISTR	
Fiss Yield	Maxwl		FLA Expt	Rept	ORO-2843-10	Dec 66	Muga+,TERNARY MASS YLD CURVS TBP PR	
Fiss Yield	-		FEI Theo	Prog	YFI-4 14	May 67	Ignatjuk.CURVES GIVEN	
	2.5-2		Expt	Rept	INDC-260E	69	.ENGL.OF YFI-6 40	
				Prog	YFI-6 40	68	Ignatjuk. CURVE. TO BE PUBL IN YF	
	-		Theo	Rept	INDC-187E		. ENGL OF YFI-4 14	
Fiss Yield	None		IBJ Theo	Rept	INR-932/IAIIPL	Aug 68	Blocki+ TERN,LIGHT PART E-SPEC	
Fiss Yield	None		KFK Theo	Conf	69Vienna 25	Jul 69	Dickmann+PPR45. MASS-RATIO VAL GVN	
Fiss Yield	None		BAS Theo	Jour	PL/B 34 264	Mar 71	Pauli+ FRAG MASS RATIO AS STRUTINSKY	
Fiss Yield		5.0+6	FEI Theo	Jour	YF 13 1170	Jun 71	Prokhorova+ YIELD(NEUT-E),GRAPH	
Fiss Yield	Spont		ORL Expt	Jour	NP/A 172 33	Aug 71	Ferguson+ISOMER.M+E DISTR OKS DIRECT	
				Jour	PL/B 31 526	Apr 70	- .	
				Jour	PR 141 1146	Jan 66	- .	
Fiss Yield	-		JUL Theo	Jour	PL/B 37 483	Dec 71	Slavov+ ASYMMETRY BY 2-CENTRE SHELL	
Fiss Yield	Spont		MUU Theo	Jour	PL/B 37 467	Dec 71	Schultheis+ SEMI-EMPIRIC SHELL CORRC	
Fiss Yield	Spont		MRY Theo	Jour	PL/B 38 495	Apr 72	Hooshyar+ SPON AND ISOMERIC YIELDS	
Fiss Yield	1.5+7		LRL Expt	Jour	PR/C 6 1821	Nov 72	Nethaway+. 30 YLDS A=66-172	
Fiss Yield	None		MNZ Theo	Jour	ZP/A 272 397	Apr 75	Lichtner+ CALC FISS-MASS-YLD-DISTR.	
Fiss Yield	Pile		GRE Expt	Prog	NEANDC(E)162U	Aug 75	Blachot+ 21 YIELDS	
Fiss Yield	1.5+7		AUA Theo	Rept	AAEC/E-386	Mar 76	Cook+ 3-GAUSS FIT,PARAMS GIVEN	
Fiss Yield	2.5-2	1.4+7	LAS Expt	Prog	ERDA-NDC-3 94	May 76	Ford+NFY COMPILATION.SEE LA-6129.NDG	

92 Uranium 236

Quantity	Energy (ev) Min	Max	Lab	Type	Documentation Ref Vol Page	Date	Author, Comments	Data
Fiss Yield	Spont		PAH	ExTh Conf	76Lowell 725	Jul 76	Hooshyar+STATMDL APLD TO EXPT.DATA	
				Theo Jour	PL/B 55 144	Feb 75	- + TH VALUES CFD TO EXPTAL	
Fiss Yield	2.0+6	1.4+7	LAS	Eval Abst	ANS 24 462	Nov 76	Madland+PAIR EFFECT ON FISS PROD YLD	
	1.0+6	1.4+7		Rept	LA – 6430	Jul 76	- +PAIR EFFECT ON INDEP YLD.TBL	
Fiss Yield	Fiss		GRE	Expt Rept	CEA – N – 1979	77	Ferrieu+ ABSTRACT,TABLE GIVEN	
Fiss Yield	Spont		TRM	Theo Rept	INIS – MF – 3797	77	Chakraborthy+ O – D – MOD.ISOTOP YLD,FIG	
Frag Spectra			CRC	Theo Jour	CJP 35 195	Feb 57	Hay+ TABLE CALCTD ENERGY RELEASES	
Frag Spectra	6.0+6	2.0+7	CRC	Expt Jour	CJP 37 1418	Dec 59	Baerg+. FRAG ANG DIST ANISOTROPIC	
Frag Spectra	Spont		CCP	Theo Jour	ZET 38 955	Mar 60	Geilikman. EXCIT E VS FRAG RATIO,CRV	
	None			Jour	SNP 7 1 155	Jul 68	.TRANSLATN.*	
				Jour	YF 7 215	Jan 68	Gejlikman+ FRAG – DEFORMATN – E,SHELL – TH	
	Spont			Jour	JET 11 688	Sep 60	TRANSLATN.*	
				Jour	AE 6 298	Mar 59	SEE ALSO *= SJA 6 184 N/60	
Frag Spectra	6.0–5	9.2+6	LAS	Expt Jour	PR 120 198	Oct 60	Simmons+ FRAGMENT ANGULAR DIST 20ES	
Frag Spectra	4.0+5	1.6+6	ORL	ExTh Conf	65Salzburg 63	Mar 65	Lamphere.ANISTRPY OF FRGS,TH CFD XPT	
Frag Spectra	Maxwl		FLA	Expt Rept	ORO – 2843 – 10	Dec 66	Muga+ TERNARY FRAG KE DISTR TBP PR	
Frag Spectra	None		MIT	Theo Rept	MIT – 905 – 81	Dec 66	Gordon+,PREDICT RB86+CS136 KE DEFICT	
Frag Spectra	–		FEI	Theo Prog	YFI – 4 14	May 67	Ignatjuk.CURVES GIVEN	
				Rept	INDC – 187E	67	. ENGL OF YFI – 4 14	
Frag Spectra	5.0+5	1.2+6	WAU	Theo Jour	NP/A 101 460	Sep 67	Vandenbosch. CHANNEL ANALYSIS	
Frag Spectra	4.0+5	1.1+6	ROC	Expt Prog	NYO – 3938 – 3 29	Jun 70	Huizenga+,FRAG ANG DIST AT 7ES,CURVS	+
				ExTh Conf	69Vienna 403	Jul 69	- +PPR118. DIST(E,ANG)GRPH +TH	
	4.0+5	1.1+6		Expt Data	EXFOR10199.002	Jun 74	112PTS,FRG DSIGMA AT 7 ES	
Frag Spectra	Spont		ORL	Expt Jour	NP/A 172 33	Aug 71	Ferguson+ISOMER.E DIST+CORR OK DIRCT	
				Jour	PL/B 31 526	Apr 70	- .	
				Jour	PR 141 1146	Jan 66	- .	
Frag Spectra	Spont		MRY	Theo Jour	PL/B 38 495	Apr 72	Hooshyar+ KINETIC – E FN OF HEAVY MASS	
Frag Spectra	Spont		AUA	Eval Rept	AAEC/E – 304	Mar 74	Musgrove. META. BIN+TER,MEAN FRGM – E	
Frag Spectra	Spont		MUU	Theo Jour	NKA 19 645	Sep 74	Schultheis+ DEFORM – E VS FRAGM – MASS	
				Jour	NCL 6 169	Feb 73	- + E – KIN(MASS) CALC,CFD XPT	
Frag Spectra	Spont		PAH	Theo Jour	PL/B 55 144	Feb 75	Hooshyar+ TH VALUES CFD TO EXPTAL	
Frag Spectra	5.0+5	1.1+6	BRC	Eval Conf	75Kiev 1 252	May 75	Thomet. ANGDIS REL 90DEG,6ES.EVAL	
Frag Spectra	5.0+5	1.0+7	FOA	Expt Conf	75Gothenbg	Jun 75	Nordborg+ ABST,SCT CHAMBER,MACROFOL	
Frag Spectra	Spont		FTI	Theo Jour	YF 23 1175	Jun 76	Geilikman+ KE FRG – MASS CALC.	
				Jour	SNP 23 624	Jun 76	. ENGL OF YF 23 1175	
Frag Charge	1.8+6	1.5+7	LRL	Comp Rept	UCRL – 51640	Jul 74	Nethaway. TBL.	
Frag Charge	Spont		FRK	Expt Jour	PRL 35 353	Jul 75	Gupta+ GRPHS CFD EXP YIELDS	
Frag Charge	Spont		TRM	Theo Rept	INIS – MF – 3797	77	Chakraborthy+ O – D – MOD.ZP – Z(UCD),GRPH	
Reson Params		1.4+2	BNL	Expt Abst	BAP 1 187	Apr 56	Pilcher+ TRANS,WN+D,ASSUMED WG	
Reson Params	1.0+0		BNL	Revw Jour	PHY 22 994	Nov 56	Hughes.LVL SPACING DIST,+TH+U234,238	
Reson Params	5.5+0	3.8+2	ORL	Expt Jour	PR 109 471	Jan 58	Harvey+.WN FROM DIP AREA.ASSUMED WG.	+
	5.5+0	3.8+2		Data	EXFOR12339.	Jun 76	. 13 RES. E0, WN, WN0	
Reson Params	–.8+1	5.5+0	HAR	Expt Jour	JNE 6 181	Apr 58	Mccallum. 5.5EV RES WT WN,NEG ER EST	+
Reson Params		1.0+6	AUA	Theo Jour	AUJ 20 477	Oct 67	Cook. TBL OF AVG LVL SPACING D,L=0,1	
Reson Params	5.5+0		SRL	Expt Jour	NSE 32 265	May 68	Baumann. WN, WG.	+
	5.5+0			Data	EXFOR12466.004	Jun 76	. 1 RES. WN, WG.	
Reson Params	+5	+6	CCP	Theo Jour	YF 7 1228	Jun 68	Vorotnikov.D,EXPT CFD DEGEN – FERM – GAS	
				Jour	SNP 7 732	Dec 68	TRANSLATN.*	
Reson Params	5.5+0	3.8+2	MTR	Expt Prog	WASH – 1127 60	Apr 69	Harlan.WN GIVN FOR 13ES FROM TOT SIG	
Reson Params	–		HAR	Revw Conf	69Vienna 249	Jul 69	Lynn. PARS IN STRUTNSKY TH+EXPTS,TBL	
Reson Params	4.0+5	9.0+5	ROC	Theo Conf	69Vienna 403	Jul 69	Huizenga+PPR118.CHANNL ANAL,FISS XPT	
Reson Params	–.1+2	1.0+3	GA	Expt Jour	NP/A 141 577	Jan 70	Carlson+ WN,WG. NG+SELF – IND.E0 431UP	
				Rept	GA – 9057	Oct 68	.SUPERSEDED*	
Reson Params	–.1+2	4.2+2	GGA	Expt Jour	NP/A 141 577	Feb 70	Carlson+CAPT,SELF INDIC.E0,WN,WG,D.	+
	–.1+2	4.2+2		Data	EXFOR10695.	Aug 78	. 29 RES.E0,WG,WN,D GVN	
Reson Params	1.0+3	4.6+4	KFK	Eval Rept	KFK – 1186	Jul 70	Hinkelmann. AVG.WG,WF,WN,LVL SPACING	
Reson Params	None		DUB	Theo Jour	YF 13 240	Feb 71	Malecki+G – WID,THEO CFD EXPT.TBL,GRPH	
				Jour	SNP 13 133	Aug 71	- + ENGL OF YF 13 240.	
Reson Params	6.2–1	5.0+4	SRL	Theo Conf	71Knoxvill 714	Mar 71	Mccrosson. STAT CALCULATN AVG PARAMS	
Reson Params	5.4+0	4.2+2	GEL	Expt Jour	NP/A 181 639	Feb 72	Theobald+ WF FROM AREA ANAL.	+
	5.0+0	4.2+2		Data	EXFOR20501.	Mar 76	17PTS.WF,AVG.WF.	
Reson Params	–.8+1	3.8+2	CCP	Theo Rept	YK – 16 121	74	Gorbachev+ TOT+N+G – WIDTHS, TBL	
Reson Params	0.0+0	1.0+3	BOL	Expt Conf	JINR – D3 – 7991	Apr 74	Coceva.P266.NG,65 RES,63 L=0 OKS TH	
Reson Params	2.5–2		COL	Expt Conf	75Wash. 335	Mar 75	Felvinci+MOD ERICSON CALC CFD EXPT.	

92 Uranium 236

Quantity	Energy (ev) Min	Max	Lab	Type	Documentation Ref Vol Page	Date	Author, Comments	Data
Reson Params	3.4+1	1.8+3	MOL	Expt	Conf 75Wash. 729	Mar 75	Mewissen+TBL,EO,WN,WN0,WG	+
					Conf NEANDC(E)-163U	75	- + LINAC TOF WN WG GIVEN	
	3.0+1	1.8+3			Rept RCN-203 279	Dec 73	- + AVG WG,D,S0	
	3.4+1	1.8+3			Conf 73Petten § 73E1	May 73	- + LINAC TOF. ENRICHED U236	
	3.4+1	1.8+3			Data EXFOR20399.	Oct 74	263PTS.E0,WG,AVG WG,WN,AVG.WN0.	
Reson Params	4.4+1	4.1+3	GEL	Expt	Jour NP/A 257 333	Feb 76	Carraro+EN,N-WID FOR 189 RES	+
					Conf NEANDC(E)-163U	Jan 75	- +EN,N-WID FOR 190 RES,TBL	
	1.4+2	1.7+2			Conf 72Budapest 200	Aug 72	- + AREA ANALYSIS,N-WID,39RES	
	4.4+1	4.1+3			Data EXFOR20699.002	Jun 77	187PTS.E0,G*WN.	
Reson Params	5.5+0		HAN	Expt	Abst BAP 6 8	Feb 61	Leonard+ ABST. A8 LASSS THAN 1B.	+
	5.5+0				Data EXFOR12256.006	Jun 76	. 1 PT. FISS-PCS	
Reson Params	Maxwl		KUK	Theo	Conf 76Ahmedabd 2 1	Dec 76	Sharma+AVG S-WAVE REDUCED N-WID ANAL	
Strnth Fnctn		1.4+2	BNL	Expt	Abst BAP 1 187	Apr 56	Pilcher+ TRANS,STF=1.3	
Strnth Fnctn	+3		BNL	Expt	Jour PRL 1 461	Dec 58	Hughes. FC 1.3+-0.3	
Strnth Fnctn	None		DKE	Theo	Jour NP 24 169	Apr 61	Seth. J-DEPENDENCE OF S-WAVE STRFUNC	
Strnth Fnctn	2.6+6	4.1+6	AI	Theo	Rept NAA-SR-M-12538	Oct 67	Gigas.OPTMDL CALC AVG S0,S1,S2	
Strnth Fnctn	0.0+0	2.0+4	GGA	Expt	Jour NP/A 141 577	Feb 70	Carlson+CAPT,SELF INDIC.S0,S1 GVN.	+
	0.0+0	2.0+4			Data EXFOR10695.006	Aug 78	. 2PT.S0=(1.02+.4-.2)-4 S1=(2.3+-.6)	
Strnth Fnctn	1.0+3	4.6+4	KFK	Eval	Rept KFK-1186	Jul 70	Hinkelmann. S0=1.3 SI=2.	
Strnth Fnctn	None		AUA	Eval	Rept AAEC/E-277	Mar 73	Musgrove.TBLS EXPTL DATA+BEST VALUES	
Strnth Fnctn	3.0+1	1.8+3	MOL	Expt	Conf 75Wash. 729	Mar 75	Mewissen+S0=(1.05+-0.14)E-4	+
					Conf NEANDC(E)-163U	75	- + S0=1.05+-0.15	
					Conf 73Petten § 73E1	May 73	- + LINAC.TOF.ENRICHED U236.	
	3.0+1	1.8+3			Data EXFOR20399.007	Oct 74	2PTS.L=0	
Strnth Fnctn	4.4+1	4.1+3	GEL	Expt	Jour NP/A 257 333	Feb 76	Carraro+S0=1.0+-0.1 FROM RES PARAM	+
	0.0+0	4.1+3			Data EXFOR20699.003	Jun 77	1PNT.	
Lvl Density	-		COP	Theo	Jour NP 6 62	Mar 58	Ericson. LVL DENSITY FORM CFD EXP	
Lvl Density	+6		MIL	Theo	Jour EN 15 1 54	Jan 68	Facchini+ LDL PARS FROM LOW EN RES	
Lvl Density	-3	+0	IFU	Theo	Jour UFZ 13 700	Apr 68	Pisanko+ LEVEL SPACING CALC,TBL	
					Jour UPJ 13 498	Oct 68	TRANSLATN.*	
Lvl Density		1.4+2	KUR	Theo	Jour YF 9 303	Feb 69	Vorotnikov.LVL DEN(EXCIT-E),TBL GRPH	
					Jour SNP 9 179	Aug 69	TRANSLATN.*	
Lvl Density	3.4+1	1.8+3	GEL	Expt	Conf 73Petten § 73E1	May 73	Mewissen+ LINAC TOF. ENRICHED U236	+
	3.4+1	1.2+3			Data EXFOR20399.008	Oct 74	1PNT.MEANLVLSP0.	
Lvl Density	3.4+1	1.8+3	MOL	Expt	Conf 73Petten § 73E1	May 73	Mewissen+ LINAC(CBNM).TOF. RES ANAL	+
	3.4+1	1.2+3			Data EXFOR20399.008	Oct 74	1PNT.MEAN LVL SPACING. L=0	
Lvl Density	None		MUN	Theo	Jour NP/A 217 269	Dec 73	Dilg+ A,DELTA. BACK SHIFTED FERMIGAS	
Lvl Density	None		ROC	Theo	Jour NP/A 223 589	May 74	Huizenga+ EXP CFD MICROSC TH AX SYMM	
Lvl Density	+6		DUB	Theo	Rept JINR-E4-9236	Nov 75	Komov+ AVG LVL-SPAC,SEMIMICRO CFD XP	
	None				Jour NP/A 224 396	May 74	Malov+ 1/2 MICROSC.MODEL. DEFORM NUC	
Lvl Density	5.4+0	1.6+3	GEL	Expt	Jour NP/A 257 333	Feb 76	Carraro+OBS LVL SPACING=16.2+-0.8EV	
(γ,n)	None		LRL	Expt	Prog ERDA-NDC-2 75	May 75	Alvarez+TBC.NDG.	
Photo-Fissn	1.2+7	2.0+7	ANL	Expt	Jour PR 95 1009	Aug 54	Huizenga+ 3ES RELATIVE FISS YIELDS	
Photo-Fissn	6.1+6	7.0+6	ANL	Expt	Diss ANL-5853	Jul 58	Clarke.2 GAMMA ES IONIZATION CHAMBER	
Photo-Fissn	6.0+6	2.0+7	CRC	Expt	Jour CJP 37 1418	Dec 59	Baerg+. FRAG ANG DIST ANISOTROPIC	
Photo-Fissn	7.0+6		ANL	Expt	Jour NP 34 439	Jun 62	Huizenga+ 6.91+7.12MEV GAMMAS.	
Photo-Fissn	5.2+6	6.8+6	ROC	Expt	Prog NYO-3938-3	Jun 70	Huizinga+. FRAG ANG DISTR AT 3ES CRV	
Photo-Fissn	5.0+6	8.0+6	IOW	Expt	Jour NP/A 206 593	May 73	Yester+ COMPTON GS,SIG FROM YLD,TBL	
					Abst DA/B 4955	Apr 73	- . STRUCTURE SEEN. NO DATA GVN	
					Rept IS-T-544	Nov 72	Anderl. STRUCTURE SEEN. SIG MEASD.	
Photo-Fissn	None		AI	Eval	Jour NSE 56 37	Jan 75	Tuttle.TBL RVW MEAS.REC VAL DELAY N	
Photo-Fissn	6.7+6	8.9+6	LAS	Expt	Jour NSE 56 179	Feb 75	Caldwell+ TBL,GRPH NU PROMPT+DELAYED	
Photo-Fissn	5.5+6	1.8+7	LRL	Expt	Abst BAP 20 582	Apr 75	Alvarez+(G,F+G,NF). NUBAR MEAS.	
Photo-Fissn	5.2+6	6.4+6	LND	Expt	Jour NP/A 271 1	Oct 76	ALM+ANG DIST+YLD OF FRAGS.2 HUMP ANL	

92 Uranium 237

Quantity	Energy (ev) Min	Max	Lab	Type	Documentation Ref Vol Page	Date	Author, Comments	Data
Evaluation	2.5-2	1.0+7	KFK	Eval	Rept KFK-1186	Jul 70	Hinkelmann.RES,STF,N2N,NF,NU,NG,R.I.	
					Conf 70Helsinki 2 721	Jun 70	- + ALL QUANTITIES.	
Total	5.0+6	1.6+7	LAS	Theo	Rept LA-3538	Sep 66	Agee+ OPTICAL MODEL CALCULATION	
Total	1.0+4	7.0+5	SOR	Eval	Data VIEN-V0005.002	Sep 76	OPTMDL+STAT TH CALC.,ABACUS-NEAREX	+
Elastic	5.0+6	1.6+7	LAS	Theo	Rept LA-3538	Sep 66	Agee+ OPTMDL+H-F FOR COMP	
Elastic	1.0+4	7.0+5	SOR	Eval	Data VIEN-V0005.003	Sep 76	OPTMDL+STAT TH CALC.,ABACUS-NEAREX	+
Diff Elastic	5.0+6	1.6+7	LAS	Theo	Rept LA-3538	Sep 66	Agee+ OPTMDL+H-F FOR COMP.	
Diff Elastic	5.0+6	1.6+7	LAS	Theo	Rept LA-3788	67	Beery+.OPTMOD CALC POLARIZ ANG DISTR	
Polarization	5.0+6	1.6+7	LAS	Theo	Rept LA-3788	67	Beery+.OPTMOD CALC COS(THETA) DISTR	

92 Uranium 237

Quantity	Energy (ev) Min	Max	Lab	Type	Documentation Ref Vol Page	Date	Author, Comments	Data
Tot Inelastc	1.0+4	7.0+5	SOR	Eval	Data VIEN-V0005.006	Sep 76	OPTMDL+STAT TH CALC.,ABACUS-NEARREX	+
Diff Inelast	1.0+4	7.0+5	SOR	Eval	Data VIEN-V0005.007	Sep 76	OPTMDL+STAT TH CALC.,ABACUS-NEARREX	+
Absorption	Pile		SRL	Expt	Jour NSE 31 149	Jan 68	Cornman+ 370+-124B BY NP237 FORMATN	+
					Conf 68Wash. 1271	Mar 68	Hennelly+ 372B	
	Pile				Data EXFOR12455.002	Jun 76	. 1 PT. SIGMA.	
(n,γ)	Pile		ORL	Expt	Prog ORNL-3994 1	Sep 66	Halperin+,SIG=APPROX. 100B	
(n,γ)	2.0+4	+6	GSF	Theo	Jour AF 36 509	Nov 67	Truran+.STAT MODEL. TWO MASS FORMLS	
(n,γ)	2.5-2		KFK	Eval	Rept KFK-1186	Jul 70	Hinkelmann. RECOMMENDED 480 B	
	2.5-2	1.0+7			Rept KFK-1186	Jul 70	- .5-GROUP SIG,THR+FAST SPEC	
(n,γ)	Pile		SGA	Comp	Conf 73Paris 1 233	Mar 73	Eder+ DATA FROM EXPTS+EVALS, TABLE	
					Rept SGAE-PH-141	Feb 73	.SAME AS 73PARIS. NO DETAILS.	
(n,γ)	1.0+4	7.0+5	SOR	Eval	Data VIEN-V0005.004	Sep 76	OPTMDL+STAT TH CALC.,ABACUS-NEARREX	+
Res Int Capt	5.0-1		ORL	Expt	Prog ORNL-4306 1	Sep 68	Halperin+ PRELIMINARY VALUE GIVEN	
Res Int Capt	4.7-1	1.0+7	KFK	Eval	Rept KFK-1186	Jul 70	Hinkelmann. INFIN DILUTION RES INTEG	
(n,2n)	8.0+5	1.0+7	KFK	Eval	Rept KFK-1186	Jul 70	Hinkelmann.AVG SIG FOR THR+FAST SPEC	
(n,2n)	2.0+6	1.5+7	BRC	Eval	Conf JAERI-M-5984	Feb 75	Jary.P 76.STATMOD/OPTMOD. CURVES.	
					Rept CEA-R-4647	Jan 75	- . EVAL,STAT MDL, 15 VALS	
(n,xn) x>2	2.0+6	1.5+7	BRC	Eval	Conf JAERI-M-5984	Feb 75	Jary.P 76.STATMOD/OPTMOD. CURVES.N3N	
					Rept CEA-R-4647	Jan 75	- . EVAL,STAT MDL, 15 VALS	
Fission	1.0+2	1.0+7	LAS	Expt	Rept LA-1669 43	Jan 55	Yarnell+ AVG SIG=0.71B+-10PC	
Fission	Maxwl	Fiss	LAS	Expt	Rept LA-1669 8	Jan 55	Cowan+ 2ENERGIES SIG VALUES GIVEN	+
	Maxwl				Data EXFOR12500.002	Jun 76	. 1 PT. SIGMA.	
Fission	None		BRK	Revw	Jour NP 81 1	Jun 66	Myers+ TABLE 2 FISS BARRIER.	
Fission	Pile		FEI	Expt	Jour AE 23 396	Nov 67	Lejpunskij.RATIO REL U235(N,F),PILE	
					Jour EAF 23 5 21	Nov 67	. FRENCH TRANSL OF AE 23 396 11/67	
					Jour SJA 23 1150	Nov 67	.ENGLISH TRANSL OF AE 23 396 11/67	
Fission	Pile		SRL	Expt	Conf 68Wash. 1271	Mar 68	Hennelly+ 2B	
Fission	Maxwl	Pile	LAS	Expt	Prog WASH-1124 110	Nov 68	Barr+2PILE SPECTRA+THR VALUES GIVEN	
Fission	Maxwl		CCP	Comp	Jour AE 26 436	May 69	Romanov. UPPER SIG LIMIT ESTIMATED	
					Jour SJA 26 498	69	. ENGL OF AE 26 436.	
					Jour EAF 26 48	69	. FRENCH OF AE 26 436.	
Fission	2.5-2		KFK	Eval	Rept KFK-1186	Jul 70	Hinkelmann. RECOMMENDED 2 B	
	2.5-2	1.0+7			Rept KFK-1186	Jul 70	- .5-GROUP SIG,THR+FAST SPEC	
Fission	5.0+5	2.3+6	LAS	Theo	Jour NSE 41 177	Aug 70	Cramer+,SIG FROM(T,P+FISS)+H-F CALC	
Fission	-		GEL	Revw	Jour AKE 18 229	Nov 71	Theobald+ SUB-BARRIER FISS EXPTS,TH	
Fission	-		GEL	ExTh	Jour NP/A 187 305	Jun 72	Weigmann+ F.B.PARAMS FROM DATA ANAL.	
Fission	Maxwl	Fiss	SGA	Eval	Conf 73Paris 1 233	Mar 73	Eder+ FISS SPEC REL U238(N,F),TBLS	
					Rept SGAE-PH-141	Feb 73	.SAME AS 73PARIS,NO DETAILS,TBP	
Fission	4.3+1	2.0+6	LAS	Expt	Jour PR/C 9 717	Feb 74	Mcnally+ NUCL SHOT,GAP 1KEV-0.1MEV	+
	4.4+1	1.8+6			Rept LA-4420	Apr 70	- + TABULATION OF DATA	
	4.3+1	1.8+6			Data EXFOR10059.002	Jul 71	1116PTS.	
Fission	3.0+6	5.0+6	LAS	Theo	Conf 75Wash. 129	Mar 75	Moore.GRPH R MATR STAT CALC CFD EXP	
Fission	2.0+6	2.0+7	BRC	Eval	Conf 75Kiev 1 239	May 75	Jary. STATMOD CALC,VALUES GIVEN	
	2.0+6	1.5+7			Conf JAERI-M-5984	Feb 75	- .P 76.STATMOD/OPTMOD. CURVES.	
Fission	1.0+4	7.0+5	SOR	Eval	Data VIEN-V0005.005	Sep 76	OPTMDL+STAT TH CALC.,ABACUS-NEARREX	+
Res Int Fiss	4.7-1	1.0+7	KFK	Eval	Rept KFK-1186	Jul 70	Hinkelmann. INFIN DILUTION RES INTEG	
Alpha	1.0+4	2.0+4	LAS	Theo	Jour PR 158 1127	Jun 67	Bell. PREDICT 10-20KEV BY SYSTEMATCS	
Nu		1.4+7	LAS	Theo	Rept LA-1863	Dec 54	Leachman.AVG NU+NEUT EMISSION PROBAB	
Nu	8.0+5	1.0+7	KFK	Eval	Rept KFK-1186	Jul 70	Hinkelmann.MEAN NUMBER, TABLE, GRPH	
	4.7+4	8.0+5			Rept KFK-1186	Jul 70	- .AVG VALUE OF MEAN NUMBER	
Nu	Maxwl		IAE	Eval	Jour REA 10 637	Dec 72	Manero+ CALC,SYSTEMATICS,TBL	
Nu	Spont		HED	Eval	Abst ANS 22 673	Nov 75	Johnson. TBL,GRPH.NU FROM SPON FISS	
Fiss Yield	2.5-2	1.4+7	LAS	Eval	Rept LA-6430	Jul 76	Madland+PAIR EFFECT ON INDEP YLD.TBL	
Frag Charge	Maxwl		CNA	Theo	Jour PR/B 134 972	Jun 64	Talat+ N,CHARGE DIST IN FISS PRODS.	
				ExTh	Rept CNAEM-12	63	- + TBL AVERAGE CHARGE/NUCLEON	
Reson Params		+7	CCP	Theo	Jour AE 17 479	Dec 64	Usachev+ FISS CHANNEL THRESHOLDS EST	
					Jour JNE 19 987	Dec 65	TRANSLATN.*	
		+8			Jour SJA 17 1242	Dec 64	TRANSLATN.*	
Reson Params	1.0+3	4.6+4	KFK	Eval	Rept KFK-1186	Jul 70	Hinkelmann. AVG.WG,WF LVL SPACING	
Reson Params	4.3+1	2.2+2	LAS	Expt	Jour PR/C 9 717	Feb 74	Mcnally+RES AREAS,LVL SPACING AVG WF	
Strnth Fnctn	1.0+3	4.6+4	KFK	Eval	Rept KFK-1186	Jul 70	Hinkelmann. SO=1.0 SI=2.	
Strnth Fnctn	None		AUA	Eval	Rept AAEC/E-277	Mar 73	Musgrove.TBLS EXPTL DATA+BEST VALUES	
Lvl Density	+6		MIL	Theo	Jour EN 15 1 54	Jan 68	Facchini+ LDL PARS FROM LOW EN RES	
Lvl Density	None		MUN	Theo	Jour NP/A 217 269	Dec 73	Dilg+ A,DELTA. BACK SHIFTED FERMIGAS	
Lvl Density	None		COP	Theo	Jour NP/A 222 493	Apr 74	Dossing+COLL ROTAT.SPAC. ACCUR ESTIM	
Lvl Density	None		ROC	Theo	Jour NP/A 223 589	May 74	Huizenga+ EXP CFD MICROSC TH AX SYMM	
Lvl Density	6.0+6	1.1+7	ANL	Eval	Rept ANL-75-34	Jun 75	Davey+N2NEVAL.CONSTANT T,LVL DEN FIT	

92 Uranium 237

Quantity	Energy (ev) Min	Max	Lab	Type	Documentation Ref Vol Page	Date	Author, Comments	Data
Lvl Density	+6	None	DUB	Theo	Rept JINR - E4 - 9236	Nov 75	Komov+ AVG LVL - SPAC,SEMIMICRO CFD XP	
					Jour NP/A 224 396	May 74	Malov+ 1/2 MICROSC.MODEL. DEFORM NUC	

92 Uranium 238

Quantity	Energy (ev) Min	Max	Lab	Type	Documentation Ref Vol Page	Date	Author, Comments	Data
Evaluation	2.5 - 2	4.2 + 2	LAS	Eval	Rept LA - 2144	Jun 58	Devaney+.TOT,SCT,NG.FNCT TARGET TEMP	
Evaluation	6.0 - 2	1.0 + 7	LAS	Eval	Jour NSE 4 166	Aug 58	Kiehn.TOT,FISS,NG,NU,TRANSF.10GROUPS	
Evaluation	2.5 - 2	1.4 + 7	PCT	Eval	Rept NP - 8216	Oct 58	Lamarsh+ ALL DATA	
Evaluation	5.0 + 5	1.5 + 7	LRL	Eval	Rept UCRL - 5351	Nov 58	Howerton. CURVES.	
Evaluation	5.0 + 2	1.0 + 7	ANL	Eval	Book FRC	60	Yiftah+ 16 E GROUPS FAST REACT DATA.	
Evaluation	4.1 - 1	1.0 + 7	GA	Eval	Rept GA - 2451	Aug 61	Joanou+ 68 GROUP DATA FOR GAM I	
Evaluation	2.5 - 2	1.0 + 7	GEN	Eval	Rept APEX - 704	Nov 61	Cooper+. CONTENT OF C - FINE TAPES	
Evaluation	1.0 - 3	1.0 + 7	AI	Eval	Rept NAA - SR - M - 8904	Aug 63	Alter+.SAME AS MO +NF NU N2N.RES GAP	
	9.5 + 3	1.4 + 7			Rept NAA - SR - TDR6545	Jun 61	- .TOT,SEL,SIN.MTECARLO DEL,DIN	
	1.0 + 0	1.0 + 7			Rept NAA - SR - TDR5861	Nov 60	- .TABULATED TOT,SEL,SIN.MTECARLO	
Evaluation	1.0 - 3	5.6 + 0	UK	Eval	Rept AEEW - M - 414	Dec 63	Sumner.TOT,SCT,NG XPT + BRT - WGNER CALC	
	1.0 - 3	1.5 + 7			Rept AWRE - O - 28/60	Mar 61	Buckingham.(ALD).EVAL FOR UKNDL	
Evaluation	2.5 - 2	1.1 + 7	FEI	Eval	Book ABAGJAN	64	26 GROUP CONST,TOT,FISS,NU,CAPT,SCAT	
Evaluation	1.0 + 3	1.5 + 7	ALD	Eval	Rept AWRE - O - 79/63	Jan 64	Parker.BEST XPT,TH DATA DEC1961	
Evaluation	3.7 - 2	1.8 + 7	UNC	Eval	Rept UNC - 5099	Dec 64	Troubetzkoy+	
Evaluation	1.0 - 3	1.5 + 7	GA	Eval	Rept GA - 6087	Apr 65	Joanou+. COMPLETE SET OF XSECTIONS.	
Evaluation	- 3	1.5 + 7	B + W	Eval	Rept BAW - 316	May 67	Wittkopf+.,TOT,NF,SEL,SIN,DEL,N2N,N3N	
Evaluation	1.0 + 3	1.4 + 7	UK	Eval	Rept AHSB(S)R - 124	May 67	Hart.(RLY).UK - DFN 338.UPDATES NSE 26	
	1.0 - 3	1.5 + 7			Rept AEEW - R - 351	Feb 64	Barrington+(WIN).UKNDL LOW EN REVISN	
Evaluation	1.0 + 4	1.0 + 7	HEB	Eval	Conf 67Karlsrhe 1 255	Nov 67	Rakavy+.FISSION,CAPTURE ETC,LEAST - SQ	
	6.1 + 6	1.4 + 7			Conf 66Paris 2 309	Oct 66	Pazy+ (N,F),(N,G),ELAS,INEL,NU	
Evaluation	1.0 - 3	1.0 + 7	KFK	Eval	Rept KFK - 750	Jan 68	Schmidt.TOT,SEL,N2N,DEL,NG,NF,SIN.	
	1.0 - 2	1.0 + 7			Rept KFK - 120 1	Feb 66	- .CURVS + TBLS SIG TOT,ELAS,N2N	
					Rept KFK - 120 2	Dec 62	- .CURV + TBLS SIG TOT,ELAS,(N2N)	
Evaluation	Fast		KFK	Eval	Rept KFK - 770	Apr 68	Huschke+ 26 EGROUPS FAST REACT SPEC	
Evaluation	1.0 + 3	1.4 + 7	LAS	Eval	Rept LA - 3527	Aug 68	Hunter+ TOT NG NF SIN SEL N2N N3N NU	
Evaluation	1.0 + 4	1.0 + 7	CAD	Eval	Rept EANDC(E)120L	Mar 69	Barre+RAVIER EVAL OF INTEGRAL MEAS	
	1.0 + 4	1.5 + 7			Rept EDF - HX - 1/1375	Feb 68	Vastel.PART OF DFN 401 IN UK LIBRARY	
Evaluation		2.0 + 7	TRM	Eval	Conf 69Roorke 2 106	Dec 69	Garg+INDIAN EVALUATN ACTIVITIES, NDG	
Evaluation	1.0 + 4	1.5 + 7	BNL	Eval	Conf 70Helsinki 2 825	Jun 70	Prince.91. ALL QUANTITIES TO ENDF/B	
Evaluation	1.0 + 3	1.4 + 7	FEI	Eval	Conf INDC(CCP) - 11	Mar 71	Abagyan+ SIGMA,RESPARS,S0,S1 GIVEN	
Evaluation	2.0 + 5	1.5 + 7	WEW	Eval	Rept WARD - 4181 - 1	Mar 71	Pitterle. CURVES. EVAL FOR ENDF/B	
	1.0 - 5	1.5 + 7			Conf 70Helsinki 2 687	Jun 70	- .83. EVALUATION,ENDF/B FILE	
Evaluation	1.0 - 3	1.5 + 7	FEI	Eval	Conf 73Kiev 1 239	May 73	Abagjan+ 14 REACT,RES + SIG - INEL GRPHS	+
					Rept INDC(CCP) - 44	Jun 74	.P37. ENGLISH OF 73KIEV 1 239	
	1.0 - 3	1.5 + 7			Data SOKRATOR - 2001	76	TOT,EL,INEL,N2N,N3N,NF,NUBAR,RESPAR	
Evaluation	Maxwl	+ 6	KFK	Eval	Jour NSE 54 300	Jul 74	Bluhm+	
Evaluation		+ 6	CCP	Eval	Rept YK - 22 90	76	Naumov+.NF,TOT,INEL,N - YLDS.GRAPHS	
Total	2.0 + 2	1.2 + 3	KAP	Expt	Priv YEATER	Oct 56	Yeater.	+
	2.0 + 2	1.2 + 3			Data EXFOR12469.002	Jun 76	. 144 PTS. SIGMA.	
Total	3.0 + 0	5.0 + 2	AMS	Expt	Jour PHY 22 1131	Nov 56	Radkevich+ABSTRACT,FAST CHOPPER. NDG	
Total	1.0 + 3		BNL	Revw	Jour PHY 22 994	Nov 56	Hughes.1KEV RES FOR THICK TGT CORR.	
	2.0 + 1	8.0 + 1			Jour PHY 22 994	Nov 56	- .CURVE	
Total	4.5 + 0	1.0 + 4	CCP	Expt	Jour AE 1 5 55	Nov 56	Radkevich+.TRANSM. CS CURVE 20 - 260EV	+
					Jour JNE 5 92	Jul 57	TRANSLATN.*	
					Jour SJA 1 5 727	56	TRANSLATN.*	
Total	-		HAR	Theo	Jour PHY 22 1132	Nov 56	Lynn.ABSTRACT,INTERF.METH,SLOW N.	
Total	5.0 + 0	3.0 + 2	ANL	Expt	Jour PR 105 661	Jan 57	Bollinger+,CP5 FC CURV ABS TRNS	+
					Abst PR 98 223	Apr 55	.SUPERSEDED.	
	1.1 + 0	3.9 + 2			Data EXFOR12457.013	Jun 76	. 402 PTS. SIGMA.	
Total	5.8 + 2	6.1 + 7	KAP	Eval	Rept KAPL - 1756 1	Jun 57	Baraff.TBL D25LETHARGYSTEPS	
Total	2.0 + 1	8.0 + 1	DKE	Theo	Jour RMP 30 442	Apr 58	Seth.NUCLEAR RADII STUDY.	
Total	2.2 + 1	8.0 + 1	BNL	Expt	Jour PR 110 692	May 58	Seth+.ABSOLUTE CURVE. FAST CHOPPER.	+
Total	7.1 + 6	1.4 + 7	LRL	Expt	Jour PR 110 927	May 58	Bratenahl+ SC TRNS, 5 ES.	+
					Conf 58Geneva 14 109	Sep 58	- +.P1881,TBL,CURV,CFD OPTMDL	
	7.1 + 6	1.4 + 7			Data EXFOR11155.033	Jun 76	. 5 PTS. SIGMA.	
Total		1.0 + 7	LAS	Theo	Jour LA 110 1080	Jun 58	Chase+,ROTATIONAL - OPTICAL MDL TH CRV	
Total	4.0 + 2	2.0 + 3	BRK	Revw	Conf 60Kingston 659	Aug 60	Harvey.CURVE,THEORET DISCUSSION	
Total	4.0 + 2	2.0 + 3	ORL	Expt	Conf 60Kingston 757	Aug 60	Firk.CURVE,TRSMISSION METHOD	
Total	8.2 - 4	8.2 - 2	COL	Revw	Conf 60Vienna 203	Oct 60	Safford+.TABLE AT 25ES,EXPT DSCRIBED	

92 Uranium 238

Quantity	Energy (ev) Min	Max	Lab	Type	Documentation Ref Vol Page	Date	Author, Comments	Data
Total	1.7+7	2.9+7	LRL	Expt	Jour PR 120 521	Oct 60	Peterson+ TRANS 4ES CURV CFD OPTMDL	+
				Conf	58Geneva 14 109	Sep 58	Bratenahl+ TBL,CURV,CFD OPTMDL.	
	1.7+7	2.9+7		Data	EXFOR11108.042	Jun 76	. 4 PTS. SIGMA.	
Total	2.0−1	1.0+7	B+W	Eval	Rept BAW−158	Jun 61	Roach+ AVERAGED SIG 40 GROUPS	
Total	6.7+0		SAC	Expt	Jour JPR 24 176	Mar 63	Le Pipec+ TEMPERATURE EFFECTS.	
					Jour CR 255 2086	Oct 62	Michaudon+TOF RES AT 4,77,300 DEGK	
Total	4.0+2	2.0+3	HAR	Expt	Jour NP 41 614	Mar 63	Firk+.TRANSMISSION DATA FROM 30EV	+
Total	4.5+1	1.8+7	UNC	Eval	Rept TID−21294	Mar 63	GOLDSTEIN TABLE.FOR SHIELDING CALCUL	
Total	1.0−3	5.6+0	WIN	Eval	Rept AEEW−M−414	Dec 63	Sumner.TABLE,CURVE.BR−WIGN.BRAGG SCT	
Total	1.0+3	1.5+7	UK	Eval	Rept AWRE−O−79/63	Jan 64	Parker.(ALD).UKNDL−DFN 156	
Total	1.0−3	1.8+3	UK	Eval	Rept AEEW−R−351	Feb 64	Barrington+(WIN).UKNDL LOW EN REVISN	
Total	5.0+1	3.9+3	COL	Expt	Jour PR/B 134 985	Jun 64	Garg+ TOF,CURVES,TRANS.	+
	3.2+1	4.1+3		Data	EXFOR12278.005	Jun 76	. 7311 PTS. SIGMA.	
Total	4.7+0	1.0+4	FEI	Expt	Conf JINR−1845 108	Jun 64	Nikolaev+ TABLE,SIG OF E−GROUPS,TOF	
Total	9.8+5		SHE	Theo	Jour NP 54 417	Jun 64	Maddison.OPTMOD FIT TO TOWLE GILBOY	
Total	2.0+5	2.0+6	BNL	Expt	Jour PR/B 135 895	Aug 64	Auerbach+OPTMDL CFD XPT,TBL BNL818	
Total	5.0+4	1.5+7	BOL	Theo	Jour NC 33 1145	Aug 64	Baldoni+ROTAT.OPTMOD ANALYS.XPT OTHR	
	2.0+6	1.0+7			Rept EANDC(E)89 85	Jan 68	Zuffi.FROM ADIAB COUPLED−CH SCT CALC	
					Conf 67Tokyo § 8.88	Sep 67	− . CURVES.CFD EXPT	
Total	1.0+4	1.5+7	FEI	Theo	Jour AE 17 304	Oct 64	Marchuk+ OPTMOD,GRPH SIG(E) CFD XPTS	
	4.0+4	1.6+7			Jour AE 13 371	Oct 62	Kolesov+ SPH OPTMOD CFD 1959 DATA	
	1.0+4	1.5+7			Jour JNE 20 77	Jan 66	. ENGL OF AE 17 304	
					Jour EAF 17 4 103	Oct 64	. FRENCH OF AE 17 304	
					Jour SJA 17 1038	Oct 64	. ENGL OF AE 17 304	
	4.0+4	1.6+7			Jour SJA 13 980	Jun 63	. ENGL OF AE 13 371	
					Jour JNE 5 92	Oct 62	. ENGL OF AE 13 371	
Total	2.0+6	7.0+6	ALD	Expt	Jour NP 65 236	Mar 65	Batchelor+ TRANS CFD SUM OF PARTIALS	+
Total	1.0+0	1.0+2	ANL	Expt	Prog WASH−1056 9	Mar 65	Bollinger+ P RES WITH THICK SMPL.TBC	
Total	5.0+3	2.0+5	COL	Expt	Prog WASH−1056 20	Mar 65	Havens.VEL S,NDG ANALYSIS TBC	
Total	2.5+6	1.5+7	BNW	Expt	Jour NIM 36 1	Sep 65	.EXPT DETAILS	+
	2.3+6	1.5+7			Data EXFOR10047.	Aug 73	488PTS.	
Total	1.0+3	1.0+7	KFK	Eval	Rept KFK−120 1	Feb 66	Schmidt.OTHERS'XPTS+CURV.TABL TO3MEV	
	1.0−2	1.0+7			Rept KFK−120 2	Dec 62	− .GRAPHS AND TABULATED DATA	
Total		1.0+3	ORL	Eval	Rept ORNL−TM−1448	Jun 66	Webster+.862ES TABLE+PLOT 300 DEG K	
Total	2.0+6	1.6+7	LAS	Theo	Rept LA−3538	Sep 66	Agee+ OPTICAL MODEL CALCULATION	
Total	6.5+3	9.5+5	HAR	Expt	Conf 66Paris 1 165	Oct 66	Uttley. = 1 DATA INDEX LINES	+
Total	7.5+3	3.0+4	KFK	Expt	Rept INDC−156 8	Oct 66	Miessner+RES−SHIELDED TRANSPORT SIG	
					Conf 66Paris 1 502	Oct 66	− +PPR8.ABST.	
Total	4.6+0	2.1+3	FEI	Theo	Rept ICD−4 392	67	Abagjan+.AVERAGE GROUP DATA+SELFSHIL	
Total	3.0+6		SAC	Expt	Diss CEA−3124R	67	Thibault.D−D NS.ASSOC PARTICLE METHD	
Total	1.0+4	1.5+7	AI	Eval	Rept NAA−SR−M−12314	Mar 67	Dunford.NONSPHERICAL OPTMDL ANALYSIS	
Total		1.5+6	CCP	Theo	Jour YF 8 704	Oct 68	Ermagambetov+OPTMOD−PARS,GRPHS,REVW	
					Jour SNP 8 409	Apr 69	TRANSLATN.*	
Total	None		TRM	Theo	Prog BARC−418 1	69	Garg.TEMP DEPENDENT SIG CALC.NDG	
Total	1.0+5	1.2+7	CAD	Eval	Rept EANDC(E)120L	Mar 69	Barre+RAVIER EVAL OF INTEGRAL MEAS	
	1.0+4	1.5+7			Rept EDF−HX−1/1375	Feb 68	Vastel.PART OF DFN 401 IN UK LIBRARY	
Total	6.0+0	3.0+2	HAR	Expt	Prog AERE−PR/NP16	Aug 69	Moxon+ TOF LINAC DEPLETED SAMPLE	
Total	5.7+9		MHG	Expt	Rept UNIV−MI−3028−3	Nov 69	Parker+TBLS,DATA GVN,OPT MDL FIT.	+
					Jour PL/B 31 250	Feb 70	− +GRPHS,RESULTS,CFD OTHERS.	
	5.7+9				Data EXFOR10043.013	Aug 71	. 1 PT. CS=3620+−60.	
Total	7.5+4	1.5+7	FEI	Theo	Prog YFI−9 3	Dec 69	Anikin+ OPTMOD PARAMETERS GIVN,TBL	
					Rept INDC(CCP)−9U5	Dec 70	TRANSLATN.*	
					Jour AE 28 420	May 70	Anikin+ BEST FIT OPTMOD PARAMS GIVEN	
					Jour EAF 28 5 56	May 70	. FRENCH OF AE 28 420	
Total	1.0+5	1.5+6	THS	Theo	Rept BNL−TR−318	Dec 69	Buehler+ HF+MOL DAUER CFD XPT,GRAPH	
Total	1.0+5	1.2+6	ANL	Revw	Conf 70Helsinki 2 3	Jun 70	Poenitz.111. SIG(E) GRAPH, REVIEW	
Total	1.0+3	1.0+5	FEI	Expt	Conf 70Helsinki 1 559	Jun 70	Van'Kov+85. TRANSMISSN,TEMP INFLUENC	
Total	5.0+4	1.5+7	JAE	Eval	Conf 70Helsinki 2 869	Jun 70	Igarasi+27. SIG(E) GRAPH,ANAL OF XPT	
Total	+3		JAE	Theo	Jour NST 7 592	Nov 70	Takano+.NUMBER OF RES TO GET AVG SIG	
Total	1.0+0	1.0+2	AUA	Theo	Jour AUJ 23 823	Dec 70	Clayton. R−MATRIX ANALYSIS,SIG−GRAPH	
Total	1.0+5	1.0+7	ANL	ExTh	Prog ANL−7710 9	Jan 71	Barnard+. BEST FIT CURV EXP+TH SHOWN	+
	1.0+5	1.5+6		Expt	Data EXFOR10009.	Nov 70	. 528 PTS. SIGMA.	
Total	6.0+1	1.4+3	GEL	Expt	Conf 70Helsinki 1 403	Jun 70	Carraro+17. SIG EXPT, RESON ANALYSIS	+
	6.0+1	1.4+4			Conf 71Knoxvill 701	Mar 71	.RESON PARAMS ONLY,NO SIG	
	6.5+1	1.4+4			Data EXFOR20115.	Jul 72	10617PTS.	
Total	1.0+5	1.0+7	TRM	Eval	Prog INDC(IND)−12 2	Jul 71	Garg.FIT TO EXPTL DATA+THEO CALC,NDG	
Total	1.8+6	5.0+6	ANL	Expt	Prog ANL−8010 408	Jun 72	Whalen+ TOF. GRAPH.	

92 Uranium 238

Quantity	Energy (ev) Min	Max	Lab	Type	Documentation Ref Vol Page	Date	Author, Comments	Data
Total	1.0+1	1.0+4	COL	Expt	Jour PR/C 5 1854	Nov 72	Rahn+ TRANS.	
	1.0+1	9.2+3			Prog NYO-73-340 3	Dec 70	- +.TRANS.CURVES.	
Total	1.3+7	1.5+7	DEB	Eval	Rept IAEA-153 173	73	Boedy+ MOST PROBABLE VAL OF SIG,TBL	
Total	1.0+4	1.0+5	RPI	Expt	Prog COO-3058-34 7	Mar 73	Byoun+SELF INDIC ANAL.RES PARS DRVD	+
					Conf 72Kiamesha 1	Sep 72	- +TRNS,SELF INDIC.3T.GRPH,TBLS	
	1.5+2	1.0+5			Data EXFOR10577.	Nov 76	.417PT.CS=LOG(TRNS,VAL/SAMPL THICK)	
Total	8.0+5	3.0+7	RPI	Expt	Jour NSE 50 243	Mar 73	Hayes+.LINAC.CFD ENDF/B-3 DATA.TOF	+
	7.0+5	3.0+7			Data EXFOR10279.002	Aug 72	. 747 PTS. SIGMA.	
Total	5.0+3	8.0+4	FEI	Expt	Conf 73Kiev 2 199	May 73	Kononov+ TOF,SIG(NEUT-E),GRAPH	+
	5.5+3	8.2+4			Data EXFOR40328.002	Nov 76	.SIG AT 32 EN GVN	
Total		1.0+7	FEI	Expt	Conf 73Kiev 2 213	May 73	Van'Kov+ TOF,SIG(NEUT-E),GRAPH,CFD	
Total	2.0+6	8.0+6	TOH	Expt	Prog EANDC(J)30L 66	Sep 73	Baba+.LINAC,120M TOF.NDG	
Total	1.0+5	6.0+6	BRC	Expt	Rept CEA-R-4524	Nov 73	Cabe+,VDG,5-50KEV EN.RESOL. TABLE	+
					Conf 70Helsinki 2 31	Jun 70	- +68. SIG(E) GRAPH,TRANSMISSN,VD	
	1.1+5	6.0+6			Data EXFOR20480.	Feb 76	431PTS.	
Total	1.0+6	2.0+7	AUW	Theo	Prog BARC-770 36	74	Satyanarayana+ STRONG ABSORP MDL,NDG	
Total	Fast		HAR	Expt	Prog AERE-PR/NP21	Mar 74	Sowerby+AV TRANS VS TEMP.DOPPLER.	
Total	1.7+6	1.4+7	NIL	Expt	Jour NIM 115 345	Mar 74	Mubarakmand+ TBL,GRPH	+
	1.7+6	1.4+7			Data EXFOR30305.004	Jul 75	12 PTS	
Total	4.8+5	1.5+7	NBS	Expt	Jour NSE 54 322	Jul 74	Schwartz+DATA CFD RPI,ENDF/B-III.	+
					Rept NBS-MONO-138	Jan 74	- +LINAC,TOF,GRPHS.	
	5.0+5	1.5+7			Data EXFOR10280.006	Dec 73	. 1706 PTS. SIGMA.	
Total	None		SAC	Theo	Jour JPR 35 4	Sep 74	Lagrange+OPTMDL FOR EVEN ISO.DEFORMT	
Total	1.0+3	2.0+6	JAE	Theo	Conf JAERI-M-5984	Feb 75	Igarasi+OPT/STAT MDL.TBL+CURVE	
Total	2.5+5	1.5+7	JAE	Theo	Conf JAERI-M-5984	Feb 75	Tanaka.OPTMDL/COUPLD CH.GRPH CFD EXP	
Total	5.0+4	2.0+7	BRC	Eval	Conf 75Kiev 1 216	May 75	Jary+ EXPTAL POINTS+EVAL CURVE GIVEN	
	1.0+4	2.0+7			Conf JAERI-M-5984	Feb 75	Lagrange.COUPLD CHANL MDL.GRPH.	
Total	-3	1.9+0	THS	Theo	Rept IKE-6 89 56	Jun 75	Keinert. DATA LIBRARY	
Total	1.0+4		BRC	Theo	Jour ASL 26 32	76	Lagrange. OPTMOD-CURVES+PARS CFD EXP	
	1.0+6	2.0+7			Conf JAERI-M-5984	Feb 75	- .EFF OF DEFORMATION.GRPHS	
Total	1.0+4	5.0+6	LRL	Theo	Prog ERDA-NDC-3 68	May 76	Gardner+ STAT MDL CALC.CFD ENDF.NDG	
Total	2.0+3		IJI	Expt	Conf 77Kiev 2 223	77	Gnidak+.SIG,THIN,THICK SAMPLE	
	2.0+3				Data EXFOR40562.005	Dec 77	E-RESOL=.3KEV. 1 PNT	
Elastic	2.5-2		ANL	Expt	Prog ANL-4680 5	Sep 51	Hibdon+	+
	2.5-2				Data EXFOR11434.008	Jun 76	. 1 PT. SIGMA.	
Elastic	5.0+5	1.0+6	LAS	Expt	Jour NSE 2 787	Nov 57	Allen.2ES SIG=7.3 AND 5.4B	+
					Jour PR 104 731	Nov 56	.SUPERSEDED	
	5.0+5	1.0+6			Data EXFOR12207.010	Jun 76	. 2 PTS. SIGMA.	
Elastic	5.0+5	6.0+6	CUW	Theo	Rept CWR-4028	Jun 58	Mandeville+. TABLE 0.50-MEV STEPS	
Elastic	5.0-1	1.0+7	BET	Eval	Rept WAPD-BT-17 51	Feb 60	Amster. 54 GROUP	
Elastic	4.5+1	1.8+7	UNC	Eval	Rept TID-21294	Mar 63	GOLDSTEIN TABLE.FOR SHIELDING CALCUL	
Elastic	Maxwl		HAR	Expt	Jour PRSA 274 122	Jun 63	Willis.COH NEUT DIFFRACTION BY UO2	
Elastic	1.0+3	1.5+7	UK	Eval	Rept AWRE-O-79/63	Jan 64	Parker.(ALD).UKNDL-DFN 156	
Elastic	1.0-3	1.8+3	UK	Eval	Rept AEEW-R-351	Feb 64	Barrington+(WIN).UKNDL LOW EN REVISN	
Elastic		2.5+2	LRL	Expt	Abst BAP 10 12	Jan 65	Bowman+ NDG	
Elastic	2.0+6	7.0+6	ALD	Expt	Jour NP 65 236	Mar 65	Batchelor+ BY INT OF DIFF CROSS SECT	+
Elastic	5.0+4	1.0+7	KFK	Eval	Rept KFK-120 1	Feb 66	Schmidt.OTHERS'XPTS+CURVE	
	1.0-2	1.0+7			Rept KFK-120 2	Dec 62	- .GRAPHS AND TABULATED DATA	
Elastic	7.5+4	5.5+5	HAR	Expt	Jour NP 80 46	May 66	Barnard+ BY OPTMDL FIT TO DEL6+INT	
Elastic	2.5-2	1.0+3	ORL	Eval	Rept ORNL-TM-1448	Jun 66	Webster+.TABLE 862 E POINTS 300DEG K	
Elastic	5.0+0	1.0+3	HAR	Expt	Jour NP 85 305	Sep 66	Asghar+ TOF LI GLASS SCINTILLATORS	
Elastic	2.0+6	1.6+7	LAS	Theo	Rept LA-3538	Sep 66	Agee+ OPTMDL MODEL+H-F FOR COMP.	
Elastic	6.1+6	1.4+7	HEB	Expt	Jour 66Paris 2 309	Oct 66	Pazy+ CORR-FACTORS BY INTEG EXPT,TBL	
Elastic	4.6+0	2.1+6	FEI	Theo	Rept ICD-4 392	67	Abagjan+.AVERAGE GROUP DATA+SELFSHIL	
Elastic	4.8+5	4.0+6	TRM	Eval	Rept BARC-279	May 67	Garg+ CALC FROM TOTSCAT-INEL SIG.TBL	
Elastic	1.5+6		IFU	Expt	Prog YFI-5 42	Oct 67	Korzh+ TBL OPTMDL PARAMS + TOTELAST	
					Rept INDC-232E	67	. ENGL OF YFI-5 42	
Elastic	1.5+6		IFU	Comp	Jour YF 7 277	Feb 68	Korzh+ OPTMOD PARS-FIT TO EXPTL-SIG	
					Jour SNP 7 2 190	Aug 68	TRANSLATN.*	
Elastic	2.0+5	9.0+6	CAD	Eval	Rept EANDC(E)120L	Mar 69	Barre+RAVIER EVAL OF INTEGRAL MEAS	
	1.0+4	1.5+7			Rept EDF-HX-1/1375	Feb 68	Vastel.PART OF DFN 401 IN UK LIBRARY	
Elastic	7.5+4	1.5+7	FEI	Theo	Prog YFI-9 3	Dec 69	Anikin+ OPTMOD PARAMETERS GIVN,TBL	
					Rept INDC(CCP)-9U5	Dec 70	TRANSLATN.*	
Elastic	5.0+4	1.5+7	JAE	Eval	Conf 70Helsinki 2 869	Jun 70	Igarasi+27. SIG(E) GRAPH,ANAL OF XPT	
Elastic	1.0+0	1.0+2	AUA	Theo	Jour AUJ 23 823	Dec 70	Clayton. MULTILEVEL ANALYSIS	
Elastic	1.0+5	1.5+6	ANL	Expt	Prog ANL-7710 9	Jan 71	Barnard+. BEST FIT CURV EXP+TH SHOWN	
Elastic	1.5+6	5.5+6	GEL	Expt	Jour ZP 244 358	Jun 71	Knitter+,TOF,CURVES + TBL GIVEN	+
	1.5+6	5.5+6			Data EXFOR20137.	Mar 73	7PTS.SOME N'.	

92 Uranium 238

Quantity	Energy (ev) Min	Max	Lab	Type	Documentation Ref Vol Page	Date	Author, Comments	Data
Elastic	1.0+5	1.0+7	TRM	Eval	Prog INDC(IND)-12 2	Jul 71	Garg.FIT TO EXPTL DATA+THEO CALC,NDG	
Elastic	1.5+1	1.0+3	MOL	Expt	Prog INDC(SEC)-43	Dec 74	Weigmann+ C6F6-DET,NDG.IN PROGRESS	
Elastic	5.0+4	2.0+7	ANL	Eval	Conf JAERI-M-5984	Feb 75	Guenther+P269.GRPH EXP+EVAL DATA.	
Elastic	1.0+3	2.0+6	JAE	Theo	Conf JAERI-M-5984	Feb 75	Igarasi+OPT/STAT MDL.TBL+CURVE	
Elastic	4.3+6	4.9+6	ORL	Expt	Rept ORNL-4804	Jun 73	Kinney+ ANGLE INTEG SIGMAS	+
					Conf 75Wash. 883	Mar 75	- +26NUCLIDES ELAS,INEL CS RVW.	
	4.3+6	4.9+6			Data EXFOR10286.004	Jun 74	. 2 PTS. SIGMA	
Elastic	5.0+4	1.0+7	KFK	Expt	Rept KFK-2200 97	Apr 75	Bluhm+ EXPT METHODS DISCUSSED	
					Rept JUEL-1178 97	Apr 75	- + SAME AS KFK-2000.	
Elastic	5.0+4	1.5+7	CCP	Eval	Data SOKRATOR-1041	76	51 PTS	+
Elastic	1.0-3	1.5+7	FEI	Eval	Data SOKRATOR-2001	76	93 PTS	+
Elastic	1.0+4	5.0+6	LRL	Theo	Prog ERDA-NDC-3 68	May 76	Gardner+ STAT MDL CALC.CFD ENDF.NDG	
Diff Elastic	5.0+5	1.0+6	LAS	Revw	Conf 55Geneva 2 18	Aug 55	Walt.P588, CURVE FOR 2 N-ES,DISCUSSN	
Diff Elastic	7.0+6		LRL	Theo	Rept UCRL-4927	Jul 57	Bjorklund+ OPTMDL CALC 6-PARAM FIT	
Diff Elastic	5.0+5	1.0+6	LAS	Expt	Jour NSE 2 787	Nov 57	Allen+2ES THETA=25-130DEG MON DECR.	+
					Jour PR 104 731	Nov 56	- +	
	5.0+5	1.0+6			Data EXFOR12207.011	Jun 76	. 18 PTS. DSIGMA.	
Diff Elastic	2.5+6		LAS	Theo	Jour PR 110 1080	Jun 58	Chase+,ROTATIONAL-OPTICAL MDL TH CRV	
Diff Elastic	9.8+5		LAS	Expt	Rept LA-2177	Jun 59	Cranberg. ALSO 1MEV TOF CURVES	+
	9.8+5				Data EXFOR12373.002	Jun 76	. 15 PTS. DSIGMA.	
Diff Elastic	5.0-1	1.0+7	BET	Eval	Rept WAPD-BT-17 51	Feb 60	Amster. 54 GROUP	
	1.5+7		CCP		Jour AE 11 395	Oct 61	RING CFD BJ-F AND COON, OK	
					Jour SJA 11 1041	61	. ENGL TRANSL OF AE 11 395	
Diff Elastic	2.8+7		LVN	Expt	Jour JPR 22 652	Oct 61	Deconninck+.AT 5DEG. .87PC ERROR	+
Diff Elastic		1.0+7	LAS	Theo	Conf 63Houston 268	Feb 63	DAY. CORRECTN TO BEYSTER TRANSM COEF	
Diff Elastic	8.6+1	1.8+7	UNC	Eval	Rept TID-21294	Mar 63	Goldstein. TABLE,LEGENDRE EXP.TO P8	
Diff Elastic	3.5+5	7.0+6	AI	Eval	Rept NAA-SR-M-9025	Sep 63	Alter+.MT CARLO LEAST SQ ANAL BNL400	
Diff Elastic	1.0+3	1.5+7	UK	Eval	Rept AWRE-O-79/63	Jan 64	Parker.(ALD).UKNDL-DFN 156	
Diff Elastic	1.0-3	1.8+3	UK	Eval	Rept AEEW-R-351	Feb 64	Barrington+(WIN).UKNDL LOW EN REVISN	
Diff Elastic	5.5+5		IFU	Theo	Jour UFZ 9 251	Mar 64	Ol'Khovskij. TH GRAPH CFD PR109 2063	
					Jour IZV 29 319	Feb 65	.	
					Jour BAS 29 322	Feb 64	.ENGLISH TRANSL OF IZV 29 319 2/65	
Diff Elastic	9.8+5		SHE	Theo	Jour NP 54 417	Jun 64	Maddison.OPTMOD FIT TO TOWLE GILBOY	
Diff Elastic	3.5+5	1.3+6	BNL	Theo	Jour PR/B 135 895	Aug 64	Auerbach+OPTMDL CALC CFD XPT.TBL	
Diff Elastic	6.5+5	2.5+7	BOL	Expt	Jour NC 33 1145	Aug 64	Baldoni+.0.65 TO 25.2MEV OKS XPT	
Diff Elastic	4.5+6		FEI	Expt	Prog INDSWG-120 9	65	Anikin. A=2.5-24DEG, NDG	
Diff Elastic	2.0+6	7.0+6	ALD	Expt	Jour NP 65 236	Mar 65	Batchelor+ CFD OPTMDL CALCS	
Diff Elastic	7.5+4	5.5+5	OXF	Theo	Conf 65Antwerp § 40	Jul 65	Wilmore.OPT.MOD.PARAMETERS	
Diff Elastic	9.5+4		FOA	Expt	Jour NP 71 511	Sep 65	Stromberg+REL PB208 AT 105DEG	+
	9.5+4				Data EXFOR20060.002	Sep 71	1PNT.D/DA.	
Diff Elastic	+0	1.6+7	KFK	Eval	Rept KFK-120 1	Feb 66	Schmidt.OTHERS'XPTS+CURVE.MU ONLY	+
	1.0+4	1.4+7			Data KEDAK-3	Oct 75	42 ENERGIES.	
Diff Elastic	7.5+4	5.5+5	HAR	Expt	Rept NP 80 46	May 66	Barnard+90DEG EXCIT FN OKS SMITH ANL	
				ExTh	Rept INDC-156	67	Wilmore+ ANGDISTS AT 5ENS CFD OPTMOD	
					Conf 66Paris 1 443	Oct 66	- + ABST. EXPT CFD OPTMOD CALCS	
				Expt	Conf 65Antwerp 504	Jul 65	Barnard+ PARTIAL CROSS SECTS.	
Diff Elastic	2.0+6	1.6+7	LAS	Theo	Rept LA-3538	Sep 66	Agee+ OPTMDL MODEL+H-F FOR COMP	
Diff Elastic	5.0+6	1.6+7	LAS	Theo	Rept LA-3788	67	Beery+.OPTMOD CALC POLARIZ AND DISTR	
Diff Elastic	4.2+5	7.7+5	JAE	Theo	Rept JAERI-1126 1	Jan 67	Kawai+IGARASI.OPT MDL CAL C ELIESE-2	
Diff Elastic	1.5+7		AI	Eval	Rept NAA-SR-M-12314	Mar 67	Dunford.NONSPH OPTMDL ANAL ANG DISTR	
Diff Elastic	5.0+4	1.4+7	AI	Eval	Rept NAA-SR-11980	Apr 67	Campbell+ LEG COEFS TBL+CURVS C-MSYS	
Diff Elastic	4.8+5	2.5+6	TRM	Eval	Rept BARC-279	May 67	Garg+ OPTMOD FIT TO EXPTL DATA.TBL	
Diff Elastic	1.0+4	1.5+7	EDF	Eval	Rept EDF-HX-1/1375	Feb 68	Vastel.PART OF DFN 401 IN UK LIBRARY	
					Rept EDF-HX-1/1346	Jun 67	- .COMPARISON OF EVALUATIONS	
Diff Elastic	1.5+6		IFU	Comp	Jour YF 7 277	Feb 68	Korzh+ GRPH SIG(ANG),OPTMOD PARS-FIT	
					Jour SNP 7 2 190	Aug 68	TRANSLATN.*	
Diff Elastic	5.0+4	1.5+7	FEI	ExTh	Conf 68Dubna § 9	Jun 68	Nikolaev+ EVALUATED LEGENDRE COEFF	+
Diff Elastic	2.5+6	1.4+7	THS	Theo	Jour ZN/A 24 52	Jan 69	Buehler. OPTMDL TH CFD EXPT	
					Conf 68Wash. 933	Mar 68	- .ALSO 7MEV OPTMDL CALCS.CURVS	
					Rept BMWF-FBK67-90	Dec 67	Buhler+OPTMO DEF OPTICAL POTENTIAL	
					Diss BUEHLER	Jul 67	Buehler+ (THESIS)	
					Rept BNL-TR-318	Dec 69	. ENGLISH OF BMWF-FBK67-90	
Diff Elastic	1.6+5	5.5+5	AUA	Theo	Rept AAEC/TM-545	Jul 70	Bertram. SIG(ANG) GRAPHS AT 3 N-ES	
Diff Elastic	1.5+6	5.5+6	GEL	Expt	Jour ZP 244 358	Mar 71	Knitter+ VDG.TOF.REL TO H(N,N).	+
	1.5+6	5.5+6			Data EXFOR20137.	Mar 73	119PTS.SOME N'.	
Diff Elastic	1.4+7		KFI	Theo	Jour PL/B 35 477	Jul 71	Palla. OPTMOD,SMALL ANGLE SCATT CALC	
Diff Elastic	1.0+5	1.0+7	TRM	Eval	Prog INDC(IND)-12 2	Jul 71	Garg.ANGDIST FIT FOR OPTMOD PARS,NDG	

92 Uranium 238

Quantity	Energy (ev) Min	Max	Lab	Type	Documentation Ref Vol Page	Date	Author, Comments	Data
Diff Elastic	1.4+7		BRC	Expt	Prog EANDC(E)140U	Aug 71	Migeon+	+
					Prog EANDC(E)127U	Apr 70	Cadeau+	
	1.4+7	1.4+7			Rept CEA-R-3503	Jul 68	Voignier. = 1 DATA INDEX LINES	
Diff Elastic	5.0+5	1.5+7	FEI	Theo	Jour YF 14 269	Aug 71	Anikin+ ANGDIST FIT,0-20DEG,GRPH,TBL	
					Rept FEI-243	Mar 71	+ SIG(ANG),GRAPHS,ANALYSIS	
	7.5+4	1.5+7			Jour AE 28 420	May 70	+ BEST FIT OPTMOD PARAMS GIVEN	
	5.0+5	1.5+7			Jour SNP 14 152	Feb 72	. ENGLISH OF YF 14 269	
	7.5+4	1.5+7			Jour EAF 28 5 56	May 70	. FRENCH OF AE 28 420	
					Rept BNL-TR-366	70	. ENGL OF AE 28 420	
Diff Elastic	0.0+0	1.5+7	FEI	Eval	Book NIKOLAEV 187	72	.LEG COEFFS+ANG DISTRIBUTS,GRAPH	
Diff Elastic	1.4+7		KFI	Expt	Jour MFF 20 335	72	Adam. THESIS,HUNGAR. XPT CFD TH,GRPH	
					Jour AHP 25 261	Dec 68	− + EXPTL SIG(ANG)=INELAST+OPTMOP	
	1.5+7				Jour PL 22 475	Sep 66	− + XPT RELATING TO FORWARD ANOMA	
Diff Elastic	1.4+7		LRL	Expt	Abst DA/B 33 4954	Apr 73	Kammerdiener.TOF.20−160DEG.NO DATA.	
					Rept UCRL-51232	Jul 72	− . RING GEOM.ANG DISTR	
			FEI	Eval	Conf 73Kiev 1 239	May 73	Abagjan+ FROM'NIKOLAEV'(BOOK),NDG	
					Rept INDC(CCP)-44	Jun 74	.P37. ENGLISH OF 73KIEV 1 239	
Diff Elastic	6.0+5		FEI	Theo	Rept YK-13 59	74	Ignatjuk+ OPTMOD,DIFF CODES CFD,GRPH	
Diff Elastic	4.6+3	6.5+6	FEI	Theo	Rept INDC(CCP)-39	Jul 74	.P1. ENGLISH OF YK-8/2 3	
					Rept YK-8/2 3	Sep 72	Bazazjants+ ANISOTR GROUP-PARAMS,TBL	
Diff Elastic	None		AUW	Theo	Prog BARC-831 34	75	Satyanarayana+ STRONG ABSORP MDL,NDG	
Diff Elastic	1.5+7		BRC	Eval	Conf JAERI-M-5984	Feb 75	Lagrange.COUPLD CHANL MDL.12 GRPHS.	
Diff Elastic	4.3+6	4.9+6	ORL	Expt	Rept ORNL-4804	Jun 73	Kinney+. 3ES. OKS OTHER EXPTS	+
					Conf 75Wash. 883	Mar 75	− +26NUCLIDES ELAS,INEL CS RVW.	
	4.3+6	4.9+6			Data EXFOR10286.002	Jun 74	. 39 PTS. DSIGMA AT 2 ENERGIES.	
Diff Elastic		3.0+6	ANL	Expt	Prog ERDA-NDC-2 18	May 75	Guenther+GRPH.	
	2.5+6	4.0+6		ExTh	Rept JAERI-M-5984	Feb 75	− +P269.GRPHS ANGDISTS CFD FIT	
Diff Elastic	2.0+6	1.5+7	BRC	Eval	Conf 75Kiev 1 216	May 75	Jary+ ANGDIST AT 11ES,EVAL CURV GIVN	
Diff Elastic	7.0+6	1.4+7	BRL	Expt	Jour PRL 35 1419	Nov 75	Bucher+ GRPHS CFD OPT MDL+OTHER EXPT	+
					Conf 75Wash. 946	Mar 75	.SUPERSEDED	
	7.0+6	1.4+7			Data EXFOR10510.003	Jul 75	.4ES.4ANGS.16 DATA PTS.	
Diff Elastic	5.0+4	1.5+7	CCP	Eval	Data SOKRATOR-1041	76	51 PTS	+
Diff Elastic	1.0-3	1.5+7	FEI	Eval	Data SOKRATOR-2001	76	51 PTS	+
Diff Elastic	1.0+4	5.0+6	LRL	Theo	Prog ERDA-NDC-3 68	May 76	Gardner+ STAT MDL CALC.CFD ENDF.NDG	
Diff Elastic	6.0+5	2.2+6	ORE	Expt	Abst DA/B 37 307	Jul 76	YU.3 SMALL ANGS.CFD OPTMDL CALC.	+
	6.0+5	2.3+6			Data EXFOR10570.002	Jun 76	. 54 PTS. SMALL ANGLE CS DATA.	
Diff Elastic	1.0+4	1.0+5	FEI	Eval	Conf 77Kiev	77	Nikolaev+ GRAPH	
Polarization	5.0+6	1.6+7	LAS	Theo	Rept LA-3788	67	Beery+.OPTMOD CALC COS(THETA) DISTR	
Potntal Scat	1.0+6		BNL	Revw	Jour PHY 22 994	Nov 56	Hughes.10.7B OK WITH TRANSMISS CURV	
Potntal Scat	5.0+0	3.0+2	ANL	Expt	Jour PR 105 661	Jan 57	Bollinger+,CP5 FC 10.48B	
Potntal Scat	−		UK	Expt	Rept NRDC-138 26	Jan 63	.11.0+−0.3B FOR E APPROACHING ZERO.	
Potntal Scat		6.5+6	DKE	ExTh	Jour PL 13 70	Nov 64	Seth+0,1PHASE FRM SIG TOT AV 3-650KV	
Potntal Scat	4.8+5	2.5+6	TRM	Eval	Rept BARC-279	May 67	Garg+ TOT-EL AND COMPOUND-EL SIG TBL	
Potntal Scat	2.5+6		THS	Theo	Rept BNL-TR-318	Dec 69	Buehler+ DEFORMD OPT POT,ANGDIS CURV	
Potntal Scat	1.0+3	1.0+6	GA	Expt	Conf 71Knoxvill 252	Mar 71	Fricke+. SIG=11.0B	
Potntal Scat	+0	1.0+5	FEI	Expt	Rept INDC(CCP)-16	Jul 71	Vankov+PG49.EXTRAPOL ZERO,FITTED.TBL	
Potntal Scat	1.0+4		BRC	Eval	Conf JAERI-M-5984	Feb 75	Lagrange.COUPLD CHANL MDL.TBL SIG	
Tot Inelastc	1.4+7		LAS	Expt	Rept LA-2111	Apr 57	Rosen.	+
	1.4+7				Data EXFOR12372.003	Jun 76	. 1 PT. SIGMA.	
Tot Inelastc	5.0+5		HAR	Theo	Jour PPSA 70 557	Aug 57	Lane+.THEORY AGREES WITH EXPER.DATA	
Tot Inelastc	2.5+6	6.0+6	CUW	Theo	Rept CWR-4028	Jun 58	Mandeville+.TBLS SIGS+NEUT E DISTS	
		6.0+6	LAS	Theo	Jour PR 110 1080	Jun 58	Chase+. ROTATIONAL-OPTICAL MDL TH CRV	
Tot Inelastc	4.0+5	2.0+6	TRM	Revw	Conf 59Calcutta 152	Feb 59	Ramanna. FISS-SIG CFD INEL NEUT-LVLS	
Tot Inelastc	5.0-1	1.0+7	BET	Eval	Rept WAPD-BT-17 51	Feb 60	Amster. 54 GROUP	
Tot Inelastc	Fiss		KUR	Revw	Conf 60Vienna 159	Oct 60	Bondarenko+.TABLE,EXPT DESCRIBED	
Tot Inelastc	1.4+5	1.0+7	B+W	Eval	Rept BAW-158	Jun 61	Roach+ AVERAGED SIG 14 GROUPS	
Tot Inelastc	Thrsh	1.0+6	KFK	Theo	Jour NSE 10 142	Jun 61	Dresner.CALCULATION USING HAUSER-FES	
Tot Inelastc	5.0+4	2.0+6	ANL	Expt	Conf 61Vienna 1 171	Aug 61	Moldauer+.PPR35,CURVE BY NEW CALCLTN	
Tot Inelastc		1.0+7	KFK	Revw	Conf 61Vienna 1 3	Aug 61	Schmidt.P4,CURVE, MANY REFERENCES	
Tot Inelastc	1.4+7	1.4+7	ALD	Expt	Jour JNE 16 261	62	White. = 1 DATA INDEX LINES	+
Tot Inelastc	Pile		AI	Expt	Abst ANS 5 69	Jun 62	Campise.PARTIAL RESULTS FROM SPHTRNS	
Tot Inelastc	Thrsh	1.0+7	ALD	Expt	Prog EANDC(UK)18L	Jan 63	Batchelor+FERGUSON NDG TBD.ALSO HAR	
Tot Inelastc	3.5+4	1.8+7	UNC	Eval	Rept TID-21294	Mar 63	GOLDSTEIN TABLE.FOR SHIELDING CALCUL	
Tot Inelastc	4.0+5	1.9+7	CJD	Comp	Rept INDSWG-64 251	64	. TBL SIG(E) FROM MANY REFERENCES	
Tot Inelastc	Thrsh	1.5+7	UK	Eval	Rept AWRE-O-79/63	Jan 64	Parker.(ALD).UKNDL-DFN 156	
Tot Inelastc	5.0+4	1.5+7	BOL	Theo	Jour NC 33 1145	Aug 64	Baldoni+ROTAT.OPTMOD ANALYS.XPT OTHR	
Tot Inelastc	2.0+6	7.0+6	ALD	Expt	Jour NP 65 236	Mar 65	Batchelor+ BY INT OVER ENERGY	+

92 Uranium 238

Quantity	Energy (ev) Min	Max	Lab	Type	Documentation Ref Vol Page	Date	Author, Comments	Data
Tot Inelastc	+6		BNL	Theo	Conf 65Antwerp 25	Jul 65	Auerbach+NDG COMPLEX POTENTIAL MODL	
	5.0+4	1.3+6			Jour PR/B 135 895	Aug 64	- +OPTMDL CALC CFD XPT,TBL	
Tot Inelastc	4.5+4	1.6+7	KFK	Eval	Rept KFK-120 1	Feb 66	Schmidt.OTHERS'XPTS+CURV.TABL TO2MEV	
	4.7+4	1.0+7			Rept KFK-120 2	Dec 62	- .GRAPHS AND TABULATED DATA	
Tot Inelastc	6.1+6	1.4+7	HEB	Eval	Conf 66Paris 2 309	Oct 66	Pazy+ CORR-FACTORS BY INTEG EXPT,TBL	
Tot Inelastc	4.0+5	3.0+6	AI	Eval	Rept NAA-SR-M-12314	Mar 67	Dunford.NONSPH OPTMDL 149KEV LVL EXC	
	6.0+6	1.5+7		Theo	Conf 66Paris 1 429	Oct 66	- . NONSPHERCL OPTMDL, CURV.	
Tot Inelastc	Fiss		ANL	Expt	Jour NSE 28 111	Apr 67	Davey+ SPECTRUM WEIGHTED SIG	
Tot Inelastc	4.8+5	4.0+6	TRM	Eval	Rept BARC-279	May 67	Garg+ STATMOD FIT TO LVL-PARS.TBL	
Tot Inelastc	1.0+5	1.1+6	CCP	Theo	Jour YF 8 704	Oct 68	Ermagambetov+OPTMOD-PARS,GRPHS,REVW	
					Jour SNP 8 409	Apr 69	TRANSLATN.*	
Tot Inelastc	1.0+5	3.0+6	CAD	Eval	Rept EANDC(E)120L	Mar 69	Barre+RAVIER EVAL OF INTEGRAL MEAS	
	1.0+4	1.5+7			Rept EDF-HX-1/1375	Feb 68	Vastel.PART OF DFN IN UK LIBRARY	
Tot Inelastc	1.0+5	7.0+6	AUA	Theo	Prog AAEC/PR-31P 9	Apr 69	Bertram. H-F CALCULTN CFD XPTS,N47	
Tot Inelastc	1.0+1	1.0+7	AE	Theo	Conf 70Helsinki 2 459	Jun 70	Haeggblom.DISCUSSN. GRAPH,CFD INTGRL	
Tot Inelastc	1.0+5	+7	GEB	Revw	Conf 70Helsinki 1 17	Jun 70	Greebler+102. UNCERTAINTY+REACT CALC	
Tot Inelastc	5.0+4	1.5+7	JAE	Eval	Conf 70Helsinki 2 869	Jun 70	Igarasi+27. SIG(E) GRAPH,ANAL OF XPT	
Tot Inelastc	None		FEI	Theo	Jour AE 29 395	Nov 70	Popov.ABST FRANC-SOV SEM DUBNA 6/70	
					Jour SJA 29 1159	Nov 70	. ENGL OF AE 29 395	
Tot Inelastc	+6	+7	DUB	Expt	Rept JINR-P3-5528	Jan 71	Gangrskij+ GND+ISOM FISSN STATE SIGS	
Tot Inelastc	1.0+5	1.0+7	TRM	Eval	Prog INDC(IND)-12 2	Jul 71	Garg.FIT TO EXPTL DATA+THEO CALC,NDG	
Tot Inelastc	+4	2.5+6	BOL	Theo	Conf INDC(SEC)-31	Jan 73	Benzi+ P25.MODIFIED SIG CFD,GRAPH	
Tot Inelastc	Fast		SAC	Expt	Conf INDC(SEC)-31	Jan 73	Corcuera+P93. ADJUSTED TO FIT N-SPEC	
Tot Inelastc	1.5+6	2.3+6	GEL	Expt	Jour ZP 244 358	Mar 71	Knitter+ TOF,CURVES+TABLE GIVEN	+
	1.5+6	2.3+6			Data EXFOR20137.	Mar 73	7PTS.SIG.	
Tot Inelastc	1.0+4	1.0+7	KFK	Expt	Jour ATW 18 175	Apr 73	Blumm+ INVESTIGAT. BY N-SPEC-MEAS.	
Tot Inelastc	5.0+4	6.4+6	FEI	Eval	Conf 73Kiev 1 239	May 73	Abagjan+ EVALUATION CFD OTHERS,GRAPH	
					Rept INDC(CCP)-44	Jun 74	.P37. ENGLISH OF 73KIEV 1 239	
Tot Inelastc	5.0+4	6.0+6	KFK	Eval	Rept KFK-1798	May 73	Bluhm. INTEG EXPTS,RECOMMENDED CURVE	
Tot Inelastc	4.5+4	4.0+6	HED	Theo	Abst BAP 20 150	Feb 75	Schmittroth.STDY.OF.CALC.MDLS.75WASH	
Tot Inelastc	1.0+3	2.0+6	JAE	Theo	Conf JAERI-M-5984	Feb 75	Igarasi+ OPT/STAT MDL.TBL+CURVE	
Tot Inelastc	5.0+4	2.0+6	BRC	Theo	Conf IAEA-190 251	76	Delaroche+ COUPL-CHAN+HF CFD XPT,FIG	
Tot Inelastc	1.0+4	5.0+6	LRL	Theo	Prog ERDA-NDC-3 68	May 76	Gardner+ STAT MDL CALC.CFD ENDF.NDG	
Diff Inelast	2.4+6		LAS	Expt	Jour PR 103 343	Jul 56	Cranberg+,TOF CURVE 90DEG	+
	2.4+6				Data EXFOR11396.026	Jun 76	. 1 PT. DSIGMA.	
Diff Inelast	1.4+7		LAS	Expt	Rept LA-2111	57	Rosen+	+
	1.4+7				Data EXFOR12372.005	Jun 76	. 9 PTS. DSIGMA.	
Diff Inelast	2.5+6	3.5+6	CCP	Expt	Jour AE 3 211	Sep 57	Fetisov.INEL SPECTRA AT 2 ENERGIES	
					Jour JNE 8 156	Nov 58	TRANSLATN.*	
					Jour SJA 3 995	57	TRANSLATN.*	
Diff Inelast	1.5+5	5.0+5	LAS	Expt	Jour NSE 2 787	Nov 57	Allen.3ES INCL.25MEV .44 .48 .67B	+
					Jour PR 105 1796	Mar 57	.SUPERSEDED	
	1.5+5	5.0+5			Data EXFOR12458.	Jun 76	. 8 PTS. SIGMA.	
Diff Inelast	1.4+7		CCP	Expt	Jour AE 4 337	Apr 58	Zamiatnin+ FISS+EVAP SPECTR FIT DATA	
					Jour JNE 9 194	Jun 59	TRANSLATN.*	
					Jour SJA 4 443	58	TRANSLATN.*	
Diff Inelast	5.5+5		LAS	Theo	Jour PR 110 1080	Jun 58	Chase+,ROTATIONAL-OPTICAL MDL TH CRV	
Diff Inelast	1.3+6	1.6+6	ALD	Expt	Jour PPS 73 193	Feb 59	Batchelor+ TOF, AGREES WITH CRANBERG	
Diff Inelast	5.0+5	2.0+6	LAS	Expt	Jour PR 109 2063	Mar 58	Cranberg+,TOF SC ABS CRVS	+
	5.5+5	2.0+6			Rept LA-2177	Jun 59	- .TOF PULSED BEAM METHOD CURV	
					Conf 57Col.Univ § 4C1	Sep 57	- + TOF. 3 ES, 1 MEV.	
	5.0+5	2.0+6			Data EXFOR12378.	Jun 76	. 21 PTS. DSIGMA.	
	5.0+5	2.0+6			Data EXFOR12378.	Jun 76	. 3 PTS. SIGMA.	
Diff Inelast	4.0+6	7.0+6	LAS	Expt	Prog WASH-1028 26	Apr 60	Thomson+ TBA	
Diff Inelast	2.5+6	3.5+6	CCP		Jour NSA 14 1408	Jun 60	USSR-ABSTRACT NO 11130-TEMP GIVEN	
Diff Inelast	2.5+5	2.0+6	BNL	Eval	Conf 61Vienna 1 435	Aug 61	Chernick+.TABLE FOR EXCITATN OF LVLS	
Diff Inelast	Thrsh	1.2+6	CCP	Theo	Jour AE 13 371	Oct 62	Kolesov+ OPTMOD H-F CALC CFD DATA	
					Jour SJA 13 980	Jun 63	TRANSLATN.*	
					Jour EAF 13 4 92	Oct 62	TRANSLATN.*	
Diff Inelast	1.4+7		BAS	Expt	Jour PL 5 202	Jul 63	Huber+ INELASTIC SPECT MEASURED.NDG.	
					Jour HPA 35 733	Dec 62	Poppelbaum+T=0.36MEV MAY INC FISS NS	
					Jour HPA 34 815	Dec 61	Huber+ NUCLEAR TEMP.IS 0.36+-0.02MEV	
Diff Inelast	1.0+5	1.6+6	ANL	Expt	Jour NP 47 633	Sep 63	Smith.SIG 6LVLS.45KEV SYM ABOUT 90DG	+
	5.6+5				Conf 63Houston 92	Feb 63	- . GRAPH TIME-SPECTRA 30-145DEGS	
	5.0+4	1.5+6			Conf 61Vienna 1 29	Aug 61	- .P76,CURVE,MANY REFS GVN	
	3.5+5	1.5+6			Data EXFOR12382.	Jun 76	. 58 PTS. SIGMA.	
Diff Inelast	Thrsh	1.5+7	UK	Eval	Rept AWRE-O-79/63	Jan 64	Parker.(ALD).UKNDL-DFN 156	

92 Uranium 238

Quantity	Energy (ev) Min	Max	Lab	Type	Documentation Ref Vol Page	Date	Author, Comments	Data
Diff Inelast	5.5+5		IFU	Theo	Jour UFZ 9 251	Mar 64	Ol'Khovskij. TH GRAPH CFD PR109 2063	
					Jour IZV 29 319	Feb 65	.	
					Jour BAS 29 322	Feb 66	.ENGLISH TRANSL OF IZV 29 319 2/65	
Diff Inelast	5.6+5		BNL	Theo	Jour PR/B 135 895	Aug 64	Auerbach+OPTMDL CAL CFD XPT,ANL 2LVL	
Diff Inelast	5.5+5	1.5+7	BOL	Expt	Jour NC 33 1145	Aug 64	Baldini+2+ 2.5,4,7,14,15.2MEV OK XPT	
Diff Inelast	1.0+5	7.5+5	HAR	Expt	Conf 64Geneva § 167	Sep 64	RAE.	
Diff Inelast	2.0+6	7.0+6	ALD	Expt	Jour NP 65 236	Mar 65	Batchelor+ SPECTRA ANALYSED SOME AD	
Diff Inelast	1.0+5	9.0+5	OXF	Theo	Conf 65Antwerp § 40	Jul 65	Wilmore.OPT.MOD.PARAMETERS	
Diff Inelast	9.5+4		FOA	Expt	Jour NP 71 511	Sep 65	Stromberg+TO 2+ LEVEL,AT 105DEG,60MB	+
	9.5+4				Data EXFOR20060.003	Sep 71	1PNT. PARTIAL SIG TO 2+LVL	
Diff Inelast	4.5+4	2.0+6	KFK	Eval	Rept KFK – 120 1	Feb 66	Schmidt.TABLES+CURVES.TO 24 LEVELS	
	4.7+4	1.0+6			Rept KFK – 120 2	Dec 62	– .IN ES. 5XCIT – LVLS	
Diff Inelast	+5	+6	ANL	Theo	Conf 66Wash. 613	Mar 66	Moldauer.CALC OF N – GAM – N PROCESS	
Diff Inelast	4.0+4	1.5+7	AI	Theo	Conf 66Paris 1 429	Oct 66	Dunford. NONSPHERCL OPTMDL,CURV	
Diff Inelast	1.0+5	1.6+6	FEI	Comp	Rept ICD – 4 57	67	Sluchevskaja.SELECTIV COMPIL,TBL+CRV	
Diff Inelast	7.5+4	1.6+6	HAR	Expt	Jour NP 80 46	May 66	Barnard+90DEG EXCIT FN,LVLS TO 1.5MV	
					Jour IZV 31 74	Jan 67	Ferguson+.CURVES+TABLES,CFD H – F TH	
					Conf 65Antwerp § 504	Jul 65	.ABSTRACT ,	
					Jour BAS 31 80	Jan 67	. ENGLISH TRANSLATION OF 1ZV 31	
Diff Inelast	1.4+7		LRL	Theo	Rept UCRL – 50181	Feb 67	Lutz+.CALC ANG DIST FOR FIRST 2+ LVL	
Diff Inelast	4.8+5	2.5+6	TRM	Eval	Rept BARC – 279	May 67	Garg+ STATMOD FIT TO LVL – PARS.TBL	
Diff Inelast	1.4+7		FEI	Expt	Prog YFI – 6 16	68	Sal'Nikov+. TABLE, 5 ANGLES	
					Prog YFI – 7 3	Apr 69	.E+ANG SPECTRA OF N'.NO DATA GIVEN	
					Prog INDC(CCP) – 7 3	Jan 70	.ENGLISH TRANSL OF YFI – 7 3 4/69	
					Prog INDC(CCP) – 003	Mar 69	.ENGLISH TRANSL OF YFI – 6 16 /68	
Diff Inelast	8.5+5	1.5+6	SUN	Expt	Prog INDC – 282 3	68	Mcmurray+ REL EXCIT – SIG FOR LVL ANAL	
Diff Inelast	1.0+4	1.5+7	EDF	Eval	Rept EDF – HX – 1/1375	Feb 68	Vastel.PART OF DFN 401 IN UK LIBRARY	
Diff Inelast	5.0+4	1.5+6	THS	Theo	Jour ZN/A 23 955	Jul 68	Schmidt. H – F TH FOR INELAST SCAT SIG	
	Thrsh	1.5+6			Jour JNE 22 187	Mar 68	– + OPTMODEL H – F ANALYSIS	
Diff Inelast	2.5+6	1.4+7	THS	Theo	Jour ZN/A 24 52	Jan 69	Buehler. OPTMDL TH CFD EXPT	
					Conf 68Wash. 933	Mar 68	– .DIRECT SIGS TO 2+ 4+ STATES	
					Rept BMWF – FBK67 – 90	Dec 67	Buhler+DIRECT SIGM BY COUPL CHANNELS	
					Diss BUEHLER	Jul 67	Buehler+ (THESIS)	
					Rept BNL – TR – 318	Dec 69	. ENGLISH OF BMWF – FBK67 – 90	
Diff Inelast	1.4+3	1.5+6	ANL	Revw	Conf 70Helsinki 2 3	Jun 70	Poenitz.111. SIG(N,N') GRAPHS+TABLE	
Diff Inelast		1.0+6	HAR	Revw	Conf 70Helsinki 1 93	Jun 70	Lynn.105. SIG(E)GRAPHS FOR SOME LVLS	
Diff Inelast	5.0+4	1.5+7	JAE	Eval	Conf 70Helsinki 2 869	Jun 70	Igarasi+27. SIG(E) GRAPH,ANAL OF XPT	
Diff Inelast	1.0+5	1.4+6	PEL	Expt	Conf 70Helsinki 2 103	Jun 70	Barnard+PPR5. SIG(N,N',ANG) GRAPHS	+
	1.2+5	1.3+6			Data EXFOR30030.	Aug 70	SCAT AT 90 DEG,4 LVLS,ANGDIS+LEG – FIT	
Diff Inelast		1.7+6	AUA	Theo	Rept AAEC/TM – 545	Jul 70	Bertram. SIG(E) GRAPHS FOR SOME LVLS	
Diff Inelast	5.0+4	2.0+6	CCP	Theo	Jour AE 29 48	Jul 70	Vorotnikov. SIG(E)CURVS,OPTMOD+EXPTS	
					Jour SJA 29 735	Jul 70	TRANSLATN.*	
Diff Inelast	1.5+6	2.3+6	GEL	Expt	Jour ZP 244 358	Mar 71	Knitter+,VDG TOF	+
	1.5+6	2.3+6			Data EXFOR20137.	Mar 73	119PTS.	
Diff Inelast	1.4+7		VNV	Expt	Conf 71Knoxvill 196	Mar 71	Voignier+ SIG VS.E(PRIME) 90DEG CRV	+
					Rept CEA – R – 4132	Feb 71	Bertrand+EP=.1,5MEV THETA=30,135DG	
					Rept CEA – R – 3503	Jul 68	Voignier. = 1 DATA INDEX LINES	
Diff Inelast	9.2+6		FEI	Expt	Conf 71Kiev	May 71	Zhuravlev+.TOF,SPEC OF SECOND NS	
Diff Inelast	Thrsh	7.6+6	CCP	Expt	Jour AE 31 156	Aug 71	Gangrsky+ SIG FOR SPON – FISS ISOM,TBL	
					Jour SJA 31 874	Mar 72	*ENGL OF AE 31 156	
Diff Inelast	+6		KFI	Expt	Jour MFF 21 555	73	Nagy. THESIS,HUNG. TO FISS ISO,GRND	
	+4	2.0+6	BOL	Theo	Conf INDC(SEC) – 31	Jan 73	Benzi+ P25.MODIFIED SIG 2LVLS,GRPH	
	1.0+6	7.0+6	SAC	Expt	Conf INDC(SEC) – 31	Jan 73	L'Heriteau+ P79. SIG(E,E'),TEMP – LAW	
	1.4+7		LRL	Expt	Abst DA/B 33 4954	Apr 73	Kammerdiener.TOF.20 – 160DEG.NO DATA.	
					Rept UCRL – 51232	Jul 72	– . RING GEOM.ANG DISTR	
Diff Inelast	None		FEI	Eval	Conf 73Kiev 1 239	May 73	Abagjan+ ASSUMED ISOTROPIC, NDG	
					Rept INDC(CCP) – 44	Jun 74	.P37. ENGLISH OF 73KIEV 1 239	
Diff Inelast	6.0+5		FEI	Theo	Rept YK – 13 59	74	Ignatjuk+ OPTMOD,TO 2+,CODES CFD.FIG	
	5.0+4	1.2+6			Jour AE 17 304	Oct 64	Marchuk+ H – F THEO CFD XPTAL DATA	
					Jour SJA 17 1038	65	. ENGL OF AE 17 304	
					Jour JNE 20 77	65	. ENGL OF AE 17 304	
Diff Inelast	None		AUW	Theo	Prog BARC – 831 34	75	Satyanarayana+ STRONG ABSORP MDL,NDG	
Diff Inelast	6.4+6	8.6+6	ORL	Expt	Rept ORNL – 4804	Jun 73	Kinney+.SIGS TO LVLS UP TO 0.309MEV	+
					Conf 75Wash. 883	Mar 75	– +26NUCLIDES ELAS,INEL CS RVW.	
	6.4+6	8.6+6			Data EXFOR10286.	Jun 74	. 11034 PTS. DBL DIFF SIGMA.	
Diff Inelast	2.0+5	1.9+6	BRC	Eval	Conf 75Kiev 1 216	May 75	Jary+ SIG TO 13LVLS,EVAL CFD ENDF – B4	
Diff Inelast	3.0+6		DUB	Expt	Conf 75Kiev 5 245	May 75	Gangrskij+ SIG TO SPONFIS ISO.TABLE	

92 Uranium 238

Quantity	Energy (ev) Min	Max	Lab	Type	Documentation Ref Vol Page	Author, Comments Date	Data
Diff Inelast	1.0+5	3.0+6	ANL Expt	Rept	ANL – NDM – 16	Sep 75 Guenther+TBL,GRPH.CFD CALC.ENDF VALS	+
	3.0+5	3.0+6		Conf	75Wash. 862	Mar 75 – + GND ST ROT BANDS EXCIT,NDG	
	5.0+4	1.0+7	ExTh	Conf	JAERI – M – 5984	Feb 75 – +P269.GRPH SEVERAL EVALS.	
	1.5+5	3.0+6	Expt	Data	EXFOR10560.002	Nov 76 .69PTS.4 DATA SETS.DIFF.DBL DIFF GVN	
Diff Inelast	1.4+7		FEI Expt	Rept	FEI – 671	76 Baryba+ (N,N')+(N,2N)+(N,3N) N – SPEC	
Diff Inelast	1.0+5	5.0+6	LRL Theo	Prog	ERDA – NDC – 3 68	May 76 Gardner+ STAT MDL CALC.CFD ENDF.NDG	
Diff Inelast	4.0+6	1.4+7	FEI Theo	Rept	YK – 21 58	Oct 76 Kornilov+ NEUT SPEC FROM U – 238	
Diff Inelast	+5	+7	HAR Theo	Rept	AERE – R – 8529	Dec 76 Lynn. CALC N – GAMMA – N REACTION.	
		3.0+6		Prog	NEANDC(UK)160	Jul 74 – . SIG FOR N – GAM – N PROCESS GRPH	
Diff Inelast	2.0+6	1.6+7	TRM Theo	Conf	76Ahmedabd 2 116	Dec 76 Chatterjee+ DELAY/PROMPT FISS.GRAPH	
Diff Inelast	+7		FEI Eval	Conf	77Kiev	77 Bychkov+ SIG(NEUT – E),GRAPH	
Diff Inelast	6.0+6	3.0+7	IJE Expt	Conf	77Kiev	77 Krasin+ CALCUL.+,N,N'F,GRAPH	
Thermal Scat	6.7+0	1.9+2	CAI Theo	Jour	AKE 22 102	Oct 73 Saad+ INTERMEDIATE RESON – INTEG CALC	
	6.7+0	6.0+2		Jour	AKE 22 51	Sep 73 – + INTERMEDIATE RESON – INTEG CALC	
Scattering	5.0+5		ALD Expt	Jour	JNAB 16 261	May 62 White.TRANSPORT 5.2+ – .8B BROAD E GRP	
Scattering	1.0–3	5.6+0	WIN Expt	Rept	AEEW – M – 414	Dec 63 Sumner.TABLE,CURVE.BR – WIGN.BRAGG SCT	
Scattering	1.0+3	1.5+7	UK Eval	Rept	AWRE – O – 79/63	Jan 64 Parker.(ALD).UKNDL – DFN 156	
Scattering	4.8+5	4.0+6	TRM Eval	Rept	BARC – 279	May 67 Garg+ OPTMOD FIT TO EXPTL DATA.TBL	
Scattering	6.0+5	5.0+6	CAD Eval	Rept	EANDC(E)120L	Mar 69 Barre+RAVIER EVAL OF INTEGRAL MEAS	
Scattering	2.5+6	1.4+7	THS Theo	Rept	BNL – TR – 318	Dec 69 Buehler+ DWBA+COUPL CHANNL,TBL+CURVS	
Scattering	1.6+6		ANL Revw	Conf	70Helsinki 2 3	Jun 70 Poenitz.111. REVIEW, VALUE GIVEN	
Scattering	7.5+3	1.2+7	FEI Eval	Prog	INDC – 6 42	Jun 70 Anikin+ OPTMOD ANAL OF SCAT – EXPT,NDG	
Scattering	5.5+3		AI Theo	Conf	BNL – 50387 79	Apr 73 Levitt. SIMILAR NSE 49,LESS DETAILED	
				Jour	NSE 49 450	72 – . MTE – CRLO,PROBABILTY TBLS.TBL	
Scattering	4.0+6	7.5+6	BRC Theo	Conf	IAEA – 190 251	76 Delaroche+ AT 2ES,COUPL – CHANNEL,GRPH	
	+7			Jour	ASL 26 32	76 Lagrange. OPTMOD – CURVS+PARAMS CFD XP	
	4.0+6	1.7+6					
Nonelastic	3.6+5	1.7+6	LAS Expt	Priv	ENNIS	Sep 52 Ennis.	+
	3.6+5	1.7+6		Data	EXFOR12472.002	Jun 76 . 25 PTS. SIGMA.	
Nonelastic	1.4+7		LAS Expt	Rept	LA – 1532	Apr 53 Graves+ NOT INCL DEST SIG	
Nonelastic	4.0+6	4.5+6	LAS Expt	Rept	LA – 1939	Aug 55 Bethe+ ALSO FISS SPEC NEUTS SPH TRNS	+
	4.0+6	4.5+6		Data	EXFOR12397.005	Jun 76 . 2 PTS. SIGMA.	
Nonelastic	2.0+5	3.0+6	LAS Revw	Conf	55Geneva 2 18	Aug 55 Walt.P588, CURVE,DISCUS OF RESULTS	
Nonelastic	1.0+5	5.0+5	LAS Expt	Rept	PR 105 1796	Mar 57 Allen.	+
	1.0+5	5.0+5		Data	EXFOR12458.005	Jun 76 . 3 PTS. SIGMA.	
Nonelastic	1.4+7		LAS Expt	Rept	LA – 2111	Apr 57 Rosen+	+
	1.4+7			Data	EXFOR12372.004	Jun 76 . 1 PT. SIGMA.	
Nonelastic	3.9+5	6.1+7	KAP Eval	Rept	KAPL – 1756 1	Jun 57 Baraff.TBL D25LETHARGYSTEPS	
Nonelastic	1.5+5	1.0+6	LAS Expt	Jour	NSE 2 787	Nov 57 Allen.4ES ABS+LVL EFFECTS SAVE 1MEV	
				Jour	PR 104 731	Nov 56 .SUPERSEDED R105 1796	
	1.5+5	1.0+6		Data	EXFOR12207.009	Jun 76 . 2 PTS. SIGMA.	
Nonelastic	1.4+7		CCP Expt	Jour	AE 3 542	Dec 57 Vasilev+.SECONDARY SPECTRUM BY TOF	
				Jour	JNE 9 43	Jun 59 TRANSLATN.*	
				Jour	SJA 3 1430	57 TRANSLATN.*	
Nonelastic	1.3+7	1.8+7	CCP Expt	Jour	AE 11 397	Oct 61 SPH,4ES, 2.79PM.1 2.66PM.06B	+
				Jour	SJA 11 1043	61 . ENGL TRANSL OF AE 11 397	
Nonelastic	8.1+6	1.4+7	LRL Expt	Jour	PR 130 1471	May 63 Macgregor+ SPH TRANS ALSO 11.9MEV	+
	8.1+6	1.4+7		Data	EXFOR11120.005	Jun 76 . 3 PTS. SIGMA.	
Nonelastic	1.0+3	1.5+7	UK Eval	Rept	AWRE – O – 79/63	Jan 64 Parker.(ALD).UKNDL – DFN 156	
Nonelastic	3.0+6	7.0+6	ALD Expt	Jour	NP 65 236	Mar 65 Batchelor+ EXPT+OTHER DATA,DEDUCED.	
Nonelastic	8.1+6	1.8+7	CCP Expt	Jour	AE 19 456	Nov 65 Degtjarev.SPHERE TRANSM, 3.10B 2.71B	+
Nonelastic	None		CCP Theo	Conf	68Riga	Jan 68 Gordeev+ ABST,EXCITATION FN CALCUL	
Nonelastic	1.0+5	5.0+6	CAD Eval	Rept	EANDC(E)120L	Mar 69 Barre+RAVIER EVAL OF INTEGRAL MEAS	
	1.0+1	1.5+7		Eval	EDF – HX – 1/1375	Feb 68 Vastel.PART OF DFN 401 IN UK LIBRARY	
Nonelastic	7.0+5	3.0+6	HAR Theo	Prog	AERE – PR/NP21	Mar 74 Lynn.GRPH SIG.IMPORTANCE FOR REACT.	
Nonelastic	1.4+7		ANL Eval	Rept	ANL – 75 – 34	Jun 75 Davey+CORRC APPLIED TO N2N CS.TBLS.	
Absorption	Maxwl		HAR Expt	Jour	JNE 1 92	Aug 54 Egelstaff. 2.8+ – .1B FROM LOW E TRNSM	+
Absorption	Maxwl		HAR Expt	Jour	JNE 1 319	Jun 55 Small. LOCAL PILE OSC REL MNSO4	
Absorption	1.0+1	1.0+7	HAR Expt	Conf	64Geneva § 167	Sep 64 RAE+	
Absorption	2.5–2		BEP Revw	Jour	KE 8 625	Jan 65 Wenzel.VAL GVN,MANY REFERENCES	
Absorption	2.4+4		FEI Expt	Jour	AE 19 3	Jul 65 Belanova+ 2 METHODS,ABSOL EXPT,TABLE	+
				Jour	JNE 20 411	66 .ENGLISH TRANSL OF AE 19 3 7/65	
				Jour	SJA 19 858	65 .ENGLISH TRANSL OF AE 19 3 7/65	
				Jour	EAF 19 1 11	65 . FRENCH TRANSL OF AE 19 3 7/65	
	2.4+4			Data	EXFOR40072.019	Jul 71 SIGMA AT 24 KEV AS PUBLISHED	
Absorption	2.4+4		FEI Expt	Jour	AE 20 431	May 66 Koroleva+ ABSOL EXPT,TBL CFD OTHERS	+
				Jour	SJA 20 493	Nov 66 .ENGLISH TRANSL OF AE 20 431 5/66	
	2.4+4			Data	EXFOR40074.006	Jul 71 SIGMA AS PUBLISHED,GAMMAS DETECTED	
Absorption	Pile		ROS Theo	Rept	ZFK – 201	Apr 70 Adam. EFFECTIVE SIG CALC	

92 Uranium 238

Quantity	Energy (ev) Min	Energy (ev) Max	Lab	Type	Documentation Ref Vol Page	Date	Author, Comments	Data
Absorption	1.0−3	2.0+0	JUL Theo	Rept	JUEL−746−RG 49	Apr 71	Bonka.KUGEL−THERMOS−LIBR,T=300K,CURV	
Absorption	1.0−3	1.5+7	KFK Eval	Data	KEDAK−3	Oct 75	4395 DATA SETS	+
Absorption	None		MUN Theo	Diss	GRYNTAKIS	Mar 76	Gryntakis.,CALC.OF WESTCOTTS G−FUNCT	
				Jour	RCA 22 128	Mar 75	− +,EQUIVALENT TO THESIS	
Res Int Abs	+0		HAR Expt	Conf	55Geneva 5 102	Aug 55	Crocker.VAL GVN,ACTIVATION M,PPR427	
Res Int Abs	6.6+0		FEI Theo	Jour	AE 4 520	Jun 58	Marchuk+ HOMOGEN MEDIA,+DOPPLER BROD	
				Jour	JNE 9 267	Jun 59	. ENGL OF AE 4 520	
				Jour	SJA 4 683	58	. ENGL OF AE 4 520	
Res Int Abs	−		ANK Theo	Jour	JNE 8 215	Jan 59	Erginsoy.CALC FROM RES PAR,L=0−3.	
Res Int Abs	Pile		AE Expt	Conf	59Vienna 109	Sep 59	Plomberg+ GRPHS,TEMPERATURE−INFLUENC	
Res Int Abs	Pile		HAR Eval	Conf	59Vienna 74	Sep 59	Bolton.BEST FIT FORMLA TO OTHER XPTS	
Res Int Abs	5.0−1		HAR Expt	Jour	JNE 12 32	May 60	Tattersall+. ABOVE 1/V. OSC. CF CALC	+
			ExTh	Rept	AERE−R−2887	Aug 59	−. PILE OSC.REL BORON	
	6.7−1			Expt Data	EXFOR20638.069	Jul 76	1PNT.	
Res Int Abs	+0	1.0+6	ROS Theo	Jour	KE 3 963	Oct 60	Lehmann+.VAL GVN CFD EXPT	
Res Int Abs	−		WIN Expt	Jour	JNAB 16 335	Jul 61	Moore+.CD TUBED OSC. RANGE OF S/M	
				Rept	AEEW−R−57	Aug 61	− + EQU TO JNE(A+B)16 335	
Res Int Abs	6.7+0		WUR Theo	Rept	EANDC(OR)20	Feb 63	Vernon. SENSITIVITY TO RES PARS.	
Res Int Abs	4.0−1		AUA Eval	Rept	AAEC/TM−270	Oct 64	Doherty.TBL.EFFECT OF SPEC,RESPARAMS	
Res Int Abs	None		ISP Expt	Conf	66S.Diego 2 421	Feb 66	Amyot+ RI OF RODS S/M=.095 TO .290	
Res Int Abs	4.0−1		AUA Theo	Rept	AAEC/E−168	Dec 66	Keane+ INF DILUTE+EFFECTIVE,DOPPLER	
	Pile			Eval Rept	AAEC/E−150	Apr 66	−. COMPARISON WITH GYMEA CODE	
	4.0−1			Theo Rept	AAEC/E−147	Mar 66	−. COMPARISON WITH GYMEA CODE	
				Rept	AAEC/E−166	66	Kletzmayr. LUBRA CODE USED	
				−			BIBLIOGRAPHY OF CODES AAEC/TM−343 9/	
Res Int Abs	6.7+0		TIT Expt	Jour	NST 4 40	Jan 67	Kadotani+.CALC C XTL BINDING EFFECT	
Res Int Abs	Pile		UJV Theo	Rept	UJV−2224	69	Stepanek. 6 GROUP CONSTANTS	
Res Int Abs	5.5−1		RCN Revw	Conf	73Paris 2 271	Mar 73	Zijp.ACT,RECOMM FROM LITERATURE,TBL	
Res Int Abs	5.0−1		SGA Comp	Conf	73Paris 1 233	Mar 73	Eder+ REDUCED RES INTEG CAPTURE,TBL	
				Rept	SGAE−PH−141	Feb 73	.SAME AS 73PARIS,NO DETAILS,TBP	
Res Int Abs	5.0−1		GHT Expt	Jour	JRC 20 695	74	Van Der Linden+ BY (N,G).CFD OTH,TBL	+
	5.5−1			Conf	73Paris 2 241	Mar 73	− + ACT,REL THR+GOLD,TBL	
	5.5−1			Data	EXFOR20645.064	Jul 76	1PNT.CAPTURE.	
Res Int Abs	5.0−1		KFI Eval	Rept	KFKI−74−45	Jul 74	Gado.CAPT,PART+TOT FROM RES−PARS,TBL	
				Theo Rept	KFKI−73−49	Sep 73	− + ABSORPT,CODE CALC CFD EVAL,TB	
Res Int Abs	5.0+0	2.5+2	TRM Theo	Jour	AKE 25 265	75	Menon+ T−DEPENDENT RES−INTEGRALS	
(n,γ)		5.0−1	COL Expt	Jour	PR 55 1106	Jun 39	Anderson+ U239 BETAS.CHECK VS MN(NG)	
(n,γ)	None		COL Expt	Rept	PR 58 475	Aug 40	Booth+. DEPLETED TGT,RESON CAPT SHOWN	
(n,γ)	Pile		ANL Expt	Prog	CP−2376	44	Seren.	
(n,γ)	Pile		MON Expt	Rept	MC−70	44	Grumitt+	+
	Pile			Data	EXFOR12040.004	Jun 76	. 1 PT, SIGMA	
(n,γ)	Pile		ANL Expt	Prog	CP−2079	Aug 44	Anderson.	
	Pile			Data	EXFOR12445.002	Jun 76	. 1 PT, SIGMA	
(n,γ)	4.0+5	3.0+6	CAV Expt	Rept	BR−574	45	Broda. = 1 DATA INDEX LINES	
(n,γ)	5.0+3	5.9+6	LAS Expt	Rept	LA−467	Jan 46	Linenberger+	+
	5.0+3	5.9+6		Data	EXFOR11945.013	Jun 76	. 14 PTS. SIGMA	
(n,γ)	Maxwl		LAS Expt	Rept	LA−467	Jan 46	Linenberger+	+
	Maxwl			Data	EXFOR11945.012	Jun 76	. 1 PT. SIGMA.	
(n,γ)	None		PTN Theo	Jour	PR 69 366	Apr 46	Turner.1940 LETTER.USE OF U238 IN U.	
(n,γ)	1.1+1		COL Expt	Jour	PR 80 499	Nov 50	Anderson+ SELF ABSORPTION.	
(n,γ)	Maxwl		ORL Expt	Rept	ORNL−CF−51−12	Dec 51	Pomerance.	+
	Maxwl			Data	EXFOR12353.004	Jun 76	. 1 PT.	
(n,γ)	Pile		ANL Expt	Prog	ANL−5032 7	May 53	Harris.	+
	Pile			Data	EXFOR12470.002	Jun 76	. 1 PT. SIGMA	
(n,γ)	2.5−2		HAR Expt	Jour	JNE 1 234	55	Crocker. ACTIVATION. THERMAL VAL.	+
	Maxwl			Rept	AERE−RP/R−1511	Oct 54	−. ACT CS REL AU−197 GIVEN	
(n,γ)	2.5−2		HAR Expt	Jour	JNE 1 319	55	Small. = 1 DATA INDEX LINES	+
(n,γ)	Cold		ANL Revw	Conf	55Geneva 5 125	Aug 55	Spinrad+.VAL GVN,DISCUSSN,P835	
(n,γ)	1.0+4	3.0+6	ANL Revw	Conf	55Geneva 5 347	Aug 55	Okrent+.P609,GRAPH,NO EXPT DETAILS	
(n,γ)	Maxwl		BNL Expt	Conf	55Geneva 4 147	Aug 55	Palevsky+	+
	Maxwl			Data	EXFOR12446.002	Jun 76	. 1 PT. SIGMA	
(n,γ)	2.5−2	2.5−2	HAR Expt	Rept	NRDC−84 9	Dec 55	Cocking. = 1 DATA INDEX LINES	+
(n,γ)	Maxwl	6.0+6	ORL Theo	Jour	NSE 1 103	May 56	Dresner.SEVERAL METHODS CFD BNL−325	
(n,γ)	Fast		HAR Expt	Rept	AERE−R/R−2151	57	Absalom+ ZEPHYR+TH ENVELOPE.	
(n,γ)	1.0+4	6.0+5	KAP Theo	Rept	NSE 2 334	May 57	Storm+,CALC .56 .14B CFD BNL325 NG	
(n,γ)	2.6+2	6.5+2	COL Expt	Rept	ORNL−2309	Jun 57	Rainwater+TOF NEVIS NOTABS 16EPKS RD	

92 Uranium 238

Quantity	Energy (ev) Min	Max	Lab	Type	Documentation Ref Vol Page	Date	Author, Comments	Data
(n,γ)	2.4+4		ORL	Expt Jour	PR 107 504	Jul 57	Macklin+.SB-BE NS,610+ -61MB	+
				Conf	58Geneva 671	Sep 58	.SUPERSEDED	
	2.4+4			Data	EXFOR11399.052	Jun 76	. 1 PT, SIGMA	
(n,γ)	1.0+4	1.0+6	HAR	Theo Jour	PPSA 70 557	Aug 57	Lane+.THEORY AGREES WITH EXPER.DATA	
(n,γ)	Maxwl		ORL	Expt Jour	NSE 3 395	Apr 58	Halperin+	+
				Conf	58Geneva 16 64	Sep 58	- +.PPR1072,VAL GVN,MANY REFS	
	Maxwl			Data	EXFOR12453.003	Jun 76	. 1 PT.	
(n,γ)	1.0+4	4.0+6	BNL	Comp Conf	58Geneva 16 8	Sep 58	Hughes.PPR2483,CURVE,MANY REFS	
(n,γ)	Pile		KUR	Expt Conf	58Geneva 12 3	Sep 58	Leipunskij+.PPR2038,VAL AU197/PU239	
(n,γ)	2.0+5	4.0+6	KUR	Expt Conf	58Geneva 15 50	Sep 58	Leipunskij+.PPR2219,TBL AT 3ES	+
(n,γ)	1.4+7		ALD	Expt Jour	PPS 72 505	Oct 58	Perkin+ACT ANAL.3.3MB+ -15PC, B-W TH	+
(n,γ)	3.6+5	1.5+6	ANL	Expt Prog	WASH - 1013 2	Nov 58	Bollinger+ACT TBC HIGHER THAN BNL325	
(n,γ)	2.9+5	8.4+5	HAR	Expt Jour	JNE 8 197	Jan 59	Hanna+.ACTIVN.ERRATA JNE 9 310 (1959	+
				Rept	AERE-NP/R-2076	Jan 57	- + *CFD LANE TH	
(n,γ)	2.0+5		ORL	Expt Jour	PR 114 1619	Jun 59	Lyon+.ABS GAMMA COUNT 120+ -17MB ACT	+
	2.0+5			Data	EXFOR11407.034	Jun 76	. 1 PT. SIGMA	
(n,γ)	Pile		ORL	Eval Jour	NSE 6 100	Aug 59	Stoughton+,BEST VALUE .025EV=2.72B	
(n,γ)	Fiss		ALD	Eval Rept	AWRE-O-02/60	Apr 60	Hinves+AWRE EVAL DATA CFD XPT.	
(n,γ)	2.5+3	2.2+5	DKE	Expt Jour	AP 10 455	Aug 60	Bilpuch.GRPH SIG(E),S-P-WAVE COMPONT	+
	2.5+3	2.2+5		Data	EXFOR11187.006	Jun 76	. 15 PTS. SIGMA	
(n,γ)	Fiss		KUR	Revw Conf	60Vienna 159	Oct 60	Bondarenko+.TABLE FOR 1E ,EXPT DSCRB	
(n,γ)	1.8+5	1.0+6	LAS	Expt Jour	PR 120 556	Oct 60	Diven.SC-T.	+
				Conf	58Geneva 15 60	58	.SUPERSEDED	
	1.8+5	1.0+6		Data	EXFOR11616.030	Jun 76	. 7 PTS, SIGMA	
(n,γ)	3.0+4	6.5+4	ORL	Expt Jour	PR 122 182	Apr 61	Gibbons+	+
				Jour	PR 129 2695	Mar 63	Macklin+ LIQ SCINT,473 AND 302MB	
	3.0+4	6.5+4		Data	EXFOR11329.073	Jun 76	. 2 PTS. SIGMA	
(n,γ)	5.0-3	2.5+0	GA	Eval Rept	GA-2113	Jun 61	Wikner+.TABLE+CURVE.100 E POINTS	
(n,γ)	2.0+2	6.5+6	ORL	Expt Conf	61Vienna 1 95	Aug 61	Neiler.PPR73,TABLE FOR SOME ES,GRAPH	
(n,γ)	Pile		CRC	Eval Rept	CRRP-960	Jan 62	Westcott. EFF SIG, TBL 2-1300DEG C	
(n,γ)	5.0+4	1.2+6	CCP	Theo Jour	AE 13 371	Oct 62	Kolesov+ OPTMOD H-F CALC CFD DATA	
				Jour	SJA 13 980	Jun 63	TRANSLATN.*	
				Jour	EAF 13 4 92	Oct 62	TRANSLATN.*	
(n,γ)	6.0+3	2.0+5	FOA	Theo Jour	AF 23 417	Mar 63	Bergqvist.CALC L=0,1,2,3 CONTRIBTNS	
(n,γ)	3.0+4	6.4+4	ORL	Expt Rept	EANDC-33 64	Sep 63	Weston+SCINT TANK REL U235+IN,2ES	+
	3.0+4	6.4+4		Data	EXFOR12456.002	Jun 76	. 4 PTS. SIGMA AND RATIO TO U235.	
(n,γ)	5.0+3	2.0+5	FEI	Expt Jour	AE 15 414	Nov 63	Tolstikov+ ACTIV,CFD B10(N,A) CURVE	
				Jour	SJA 15 1170	63	. ENGL OF AE 15 414	
(n,γ)	1.0-3	5.6+0	WIN	Eval Jour	AEEW-M-414	Dec 63	Sumner.TABLE,CURVE.BR-WIGN.BRAGG SCT	
(n,γ)	1.0+3	1.5+7	UK	Eval Rept	AWRE-O-79/63	Jan 64	Parker.(ALD).UKNDL-DFN 156	
(n,γ)	1.0-3	1.8+3	UK	Eval Rept	AEEW-R-351	Feb 64	Barrington+(WIN).UKNDL LOW EN REVISN	
(n,γ)	1.0+4	5.8+4	ORL	Expt Priv	GIBBONS	Mar 64	Gibbons.	+
	1.0+4	5.8+4		Data	EXFOR12229.002	Jun 76	. 126 PTS, SIGMA	
(n,γ)	Pile		CCP	Expt Jour	AE 17 113	Aug 64	Bondarenko+VAL GVN REL TO U-235(N,F)	
				Jour	SJA 17 821	Aug 64	TRANSLATN.*	
(n,γ)	1.2+5	7.6+6	ALD	Expt Jour	JNE 18 481	Sep 64	Barry+. + -5PC.NP239 ACT REL H SCAT	+
(n,γ)	Pile		CCP	Expt Jour	AE 17 294	Oct 64	Batyrbekov+VAL GVN REL TO PU239(N,F)	+
				Jour	SJA 17 1025	Oct 64	TRANSLATN.*	
(n,γ)	1.0+3	1.0+6	FEI	Theo Jour	AE 17 304	Oct 64	Marchuk+ HAUSER-FESHBACH CFD DATA	
				Jour	SJA 17 1038	Oct 64	. ENGL OF AE 17 304	
(n,γ)	+5	+7	RLY	Revw Conf	64Vienna 56	Dec 64	Kronberger.FAST REACTOR,1-GROUP SIGS	
(n,γ)	5.0+3	9.0+4	ORL	Theo Jour	RMP 37 166	Jan 65	Macklin+.CALC FOR KT=5TO90KEV	
(n,γ)	2.0+6	7.0+6	ALD	Expt Jour	NP 65 236	Mar 65	Batchelor. = 1 DATA INDEX LINES	+
(n,γ)	Fiss		IIT	Comp Conf	65IAEA 251	Mar 65	Barrall+CALC AVG SIGS OF 3FISS-SPECS	
(n,γ)	Maxwl	+2	FEI	Expt Jour	AE 19 292	Sep 65	Stavisskij+ REL TO PU-239(N,F)	
				Jour	SJA 19 1210	Sep 65	. ENGL OF AE 19 292	
(n,γ)	2.0+4		LAS	ExTh Jour	PR/B 139 1207	Sep 65	Bell. STATISTCL TH CALC CF WEAPONXPT	
(n,γ)	4.0+3	1.5+4	TRM	Comp Rept	AEET-272	66	SHANKAR SINGH+ GROUP SIGS,TEMPERATUR	
(n,γ)	Fiss		ANL	Eval Jour	NSE 24 26	Jan 66	Davey. RATIO TO 235 FISSION	
(n,γ)	1.0+3	1.5+7	KFK	Eval Jour	KFK-120 1	Feb 66	Schmidt.OTHERS'XPTS+CURVE	
	1.0-2	1.0+7		Rept	KFK-120 2	Dec 62	- .GRAPHS AND TABULATED DATA.	
	1.0+3	1.0+7		Revw Conf	61Vienna 1 3	Aug 61	- .P4,CURVE, MANY REFERENCES	
(n,γ)	1.0+4	3.0+6	WIN	Theo Jour	JNAB 20 146	Feb 66	Beynon.EFFECT OF STATISTIC CORRECTNS	
(n,γ)	2.5-2		BNW	Theo Conf	66Wash. 75	Mar 66	Liikala+, TBLS OF LITER. VALUES	
(n,γ)	Maxwl		CNA	Expt Prog	EANDC(OR)50L	Mar 66	Ertek+.TBC.EPI-CD/SUB-CD CAPT RATIO	
(n,γ)	3.7+1	2.0+3	LAS	Expt Conf	66Wash. 766	Mar 66	Glass.BOMB SOURCE NS(=LADC-7613)	
(n,γ)		1.0+3	ORL	Eval Rept	ORNL-TM-1448	Jun 66	Webster+. PLOT 300 DEG K	

92 Uranium 238

Quantity	Energy (ev) Min	Energy (ev) Max	Lab	Type	Documentation Ref Vol Page	Date	Author, Comments	Data
(n,γ)	5.0+0	1.0+3	HAR	Expt	Jour NP 85 305	Sep 66	Asghar+ TOF MOXON–RAE DETECTOR	+
	6.0+3	9.7+4		Priv	MOXON1	Apr 64	Moxon. = 1 DATA INDEX LINES	
(n,γ)	None		ANL	Expt	Conf 66Vienna 613	Oct 66	Armani.CAPTURE RATE TH OF EXP,NODATA	
					Conf 63Amsterdm 227	Sep 63	– . THEORY OF E	
(n,γ)	6.1+6	1.4+7	HEB	Eval	Conf 66Paris 2 309	Oct 66	Pazy+ CORR–FACTORS BY INTEG EXPT,TBL	
(n,γ)	7.5+3	3.0+4	KFK	Expt	Conf 66Paris 1 502	Oct 66	Miessner+ ABST.RES–SHLD SIG.	
					Jour NSE 26 573	Dec 66	– + TECHNICAL NOTE. TBL	
					Rept KFK–451	Oct 66	– + EFF SIG. REPRINT OF 66PAR.	
					Rept INDC–156 8	Oct 66	– + EQU TO NSE 26 573	
					Rept KFK–540	Aug 66	– + EFF CAPT+TRANSPORT SIG.2ES	
					Jour NUK 8 428	66	– + NEUT DECAY IN U.	
(n,γ)	2.4+4		ALD	Expt	Jour JNE 20 921	Nov 66	Perkin+ DOPPLER EFF TO 770 DEG K.	
(n,γ)	4.6+0	2.1+3	FEI	Theo	Rept ICD–4 392	67	Abagjan+.AVERAGE GROUP DATA+SELFSHIL	
(n,γ)	1.0+4	1.5+7	AI	Eval	Rept NAA–SR–M–12314	Mar 67	Dunford.NONSPHERICAL OPTMDL ANALYSIS	
(n,γ)	1.0+3	1.5+7	LAS	Eval	Prog WASH–1074 79	Apr 67	Diven. NDG SEE EANDC(US)–96U	
(n,γ)	Pile		AE	Expt	Jour NUK 10 141	Sep 67	Tiren. RATIO U238 CAPT/U235 FISS SIG	
(n,γ)	Pile		FEI	Expt	Jour AE 23 396	Nov 67	Lejpunskij.RATIO REL U235(N,F),PILE	
					Jour EAF 23 5 21	Nov 67	. FRENCH TRANSL OF AE 23 396 11/67	
					Jour SJA 23 1150	Nov 67	.ENGLISH TRANSL OF AE 23 396 11/67	
(n,γ)	2.0+4	+6	GSF	Theo	Jour AF 36 509	Nov 67	Truran+.STAT MODEL. TWO MASS FORMLS	
(n,γ)	2.0+2	3.5+4	KFK	Expt	Conf 67Karlsrhe 1 77	Nov 67	Seufert+,HOT–TO–COLD CAPTURE RATIO	
(n,γ)	4.5+4	1.5+6	THS	Expt	Rept BMWF–FBK67–90	Dec 67	Schmidt+SIGM CALC WITH LEVEL DENSITY	
(n,γ)	Maxwl		AUA	Theo	Jour NSE 31 234	Feb 68	Cook+ STATISTICAL CALC CFD EXPT	
(n,γ)	Fiss		MOL	Expt	Conf 68Wash. 2 1263	Mar 68	Fabry+ ACT 85+–8MB	+
	Fiss			Data	EXFOR20264.007	May 74	1PNT.SIGMA.	
(n,γ)	2.5+4	5.0+5	KFK	Expt	Jour NSE 33 24	Jul 68	Menlove+ ACT. TABLE,GRAPH.+NEW ABSOL	+
				Conf	67Karlsrhe 1 67	Nov 67	Beckurts+,ABSOLUTE AT 30KEV,GRAPH	
				Rept	KFK–635	Oct 67	Poenitz+ GRPH.ABS VALUE AT 30KEV	
	2.4+4	5.0+5		Data	EXFOR20362.002	Sep 74	9PTS.SIGMA.	
(n,γ)	–		IEA	Comp	Rept IEA–INF–10 6	Aug 68	Atalla. TABLES OF HL,SIG AND GAMM–E	
(n,γ)	Pile		CCP	Expt	Jour AE 25 292	Oct 68	Golubev+ EXPTL+CALC MEAN SIG VAL GVN	
					Jour EAF 25 4 37	Oct 68	TRANSLATN.*	
(n,γ)	Pile		CCP	Expt	Jour AE 25 297	Oct 68	Abagian+ DOPPLER–EFFECT,REACTOR–TH	
					Jour EAF 25 4 45	Oct 68	TRANSLATN.*	
(n,γ)	4.0+3	8.0+4	WEW	Theo	Jour NSE 34 181	Nov 68	Dyos.STATISTICAL CALC TOTAL+PART NG	
(n,γ)	2.0–3	2.1+1	BNL	Expt	Jour NP/A 121 630	Dec 68	Price+ RATIO PARTIAL/TOTAL N,G,4E(G)	
					Jour PL/B 25 195	Aug 67	.SUPERSEDED	
(n,γ)	Pile		CCP	Theo	Jour AE 25 466	Dec 68	Usynin. OTHER MEAN SIG GIVEN.	
					Jour EAF 25 6 6	Dec 68	TRANSLATN.*	
(n,γ)	3.0+1	1.2+4	TRM	Expt	Rept BARC–421	69	Mahalingam+CRITICL–XPT CFD DATA–SETS	
(n,γ)	4.7+0	2.2+3	THS	Theo	Jour AKE 14 30	Jan 69	Knapp+ F–GAMMA FACTORS ABN GROUPS	
(n,γ)	2.3+4		ANL	Theo	Jour NSE 35 295	Feb 69	Miller+.RES CORREC FOR BELANOVA DATA	
(n,γ)	1.0+4	1.5+7	FEI	Expt	Prog YFI–7 16	Apr 69	Tolstikov. RECOMMENDED SIG(E), TABLE	
	1.0+3	1.0+5		Eval	Rept YK–20/2 61	75	– + STATMOD,SIG(E).TABL+GRAPH	
	1.0+4	1.5+7		Expt	Rept INDC(CCP)–7U19	Feb 70	TRANSLATN.*	
(n,γ)	2.0+3		MTR	Expt	Prog WASH–1127 72	Apr 69	Schuman+ FILTERED BEAM,RELATVE CURVS	
(n,γ)	Maxwl		CRC	Expt	Jour CJP 47 1317	Jun 69	Bigham+	+
	Maxwl			Prog	EANDC(CAN)–34	Jan 68	.SUPERSEDED	
				Data	EXFOR12444.	Jun 76	2 PTS. SIGMA AND RATIO TO U235.	
(n,γ)	Fast		KFK	Expt	Conf 69London § 1.9	Jun 69	Kiefhaber+ INTEGRL XPT CFD MICRO SIG	
(n,γ)	None		LAS	Expt	Prog WASH–1136 110	Sep 69	Silbert+,PHYSICS–8 SHOT,ANAL TBC	
(n,γ)	–		NPL	Expt	Jour JNE 23 705	Dec 69	Hunt+ SIG=2.69+–.03B,REL.AU.HL U239.	
(n,γ)	1.0+5	1.3+6	THS	Theo	Rept BNL–TR–318	Dec 69	Buehler+ MOLDAUER CALC OKS XPT,GRAPH	
(n,γ)	2.0+3	1.0+7	IFB	Eval	Jour VBF 1970 3 42	70	Konshin. SIG(NEUT–E),TABLES	
(n,γ)	1.0+3	5.5+6	KFK	Revw	Jour AKE 15 26	70	Schmidt. REVW ON EXPTS, GRPH	
	1.0+3	1.0+7			Rept KFK–966	Apr 69	– . GRPH. EXPTS CFD EVALS.	
(n,γ)	1.0+3	1.0+7	TRM	Eval	Rept BARC/I–96	70	Kapil.14 GROUP SIG,2 N–SPECS,TABLES	
(n,γ)	2.0+3	1.5+7	ANL	Eval	Jour NSE 39 337	Mar 70	Davey.EVAL OF ALL AVAILABLE DATA	
(n,γ)	+2	+5	JAE	Theo	Jour NSE 40 25	Apr 70	Ishiguro+,STATISTICAL CALCULATN,CURV	
(n,γ)	1.0+4	1.0+6	LRL	Theo	Prog NCSAC–31 108	May 70	Gardner+,OPTMDL CALCULATION,CURVE	
(n,γ)	1.0+1	1.0+7	AE	Theo	Conf 70Helsinki 2 459	Jun 70	Haeggblom.DISCUSSN. GRAPH,CFD INTGRL	
(n,γ)	1.3+5	1.4+6	ANL	Expt	Jour NSE 40 383	Jun 70	Poenitz.CS RATIOS U235NF AND PU239NF	+
	1.3+5	1.4+6		Data	EXFOR10086.	Feb 72	.21PTS.CS RATIOS WITH U235NF.PU239NF	
(n,γ)	1.0+4	6.0+7	ANL	Revw	Conf 70Helsinki 2 119	Jun 70	Davey.112.STATUS OF DATA, GRAPH GIVN	
(n,γ)	1.0+4	1.0+7	CAD	Expt	Conf 70Helsinki 2 465	Jun 70	Barre+73. MICROSC CFD INTEGRAL DATA	
	1.0+3	1.0+7		Eval	Conf 69London 115	Jun 69	– +INTEGRL XPT CORRECTS MICROSIG	
					Rept EANDC(E)120L	Mar 69	– +RAVIER EVAL OF INTEGRAL MEAS	

92 Uranium 238

Quantity	Energy (ev) Min	Max	Lab	Type	Documentation Ref Vol Page	Date	Author, Comments	Data
(n,γ)	5.0+0	3.0+4	FEI	Expt Conf	70Helsinki 2 51	Jun 70	Stavisskij+78. SIG(E)GRPH,PB-SL-DOWN	
	4.5+0	3.1+4		Rept	ICD-6 32	70	Bergman+ REL AU,3 SAMPLES,RAW DATA	
	1.0-1	4.0+4		Jour	SJA 31 814	Mar 72	. ENGL OF AE 31 107	
(n,γ)	2.4+4	1.5+5	FEI	Expt Conf	70Helsinki 2 57	Jun 70	Panitkin+77. SIG(E) GRAPH,VDG,GE-LI	
(n,γ)	1.0+0	1.5+7	FEI	Eval Conf	70Helsinki 2 667	Jun 70	Abagyan+ 80.EVALUAT SIG(E)+26 GROUPS	
				Rept	KFK-TR-382	Jun 71	. GERMAN OF 7OHELSINKI 2 667	
(n,γ)	5.0+1	1.0+3	GEL	Expt Conf	70Helsinki 1 413	Jun 70	Rohr+18. SIG EXPT, RESONANCE-ANALYS	
(n,γ)	+2	+7	HAR	Revw Conf	70Helsinki 1 267	Jun 70	James.107. ACCURACY CFD REACTOR COST	
(n,γ)	1.0+3	1.0+6	HAR	Revw Conf	70Helsinki 1 93	Jun 70	Lynn.105. SIG(E)GRAPHS FOR SOME LVLS	
(n,γ)		3.5+2	HAR	Expt Conf	70Helsinki 1 373	Jun 70	Thomas+36. SIG(N,G) BY LOW-E-GAMMAS	
(n,γ)	2.2+6		HAR	Expt Jour	NP/A 148 337	Jun 70	Elwyn+ STUDY OF SHORT-LIVED ISOMERS.	
(n,γ)	1.0+4	1.0+7	LAS	Eval Conf	70Helsinki 2 517	Jun 70	Best+92. SIG(E) REVISED,INTEGRL TEST	
(n,γ)	4.5+0	3.1+4	LEB	Expt Conf	70Helsinki 2 51	Jun 70	Bergman+	+
	4.5+0	3.1+4		Data	EXFOR40059.	Mar 71	REVISED SIGMA, TABLES WITH 3 SAMPLES	
(n,γ)	1.0-5	1.5+7	WEW	Eval Conf	70Helsinki 2 687	Jun 70	Pitterle.83. EVALUATION,ENDF/B FILE	
(n,γ)	+6	+7	WIN	Revw Conf	70Helsinki 2 391	Jun 70	Campbell.116. MICROSCOPIC VS INTEGRL	
(n,γ)	1.0-2	1.0+7	ORL	Revw Jour	REA 8 473	Sep 70	Kasten. REVIEW,SIG(NEUT-E) GRAPH	
(n,γ)	1.0+4	1.0+6	ANL	Revw Conf	70ANL 320	Oct 70	Poenitz. REVIEW ABSOL MEASTS,CURVE	
	1.0+4	2.0+6		Conf	70Helsinki 2 3	Jun 70	- .111. REVIEW, GRAPHS + TABLE	
(n,γ)	+5	+7	KFK	Revw Rept	KFK-1303	Oct 70	Boehme+ MICROSC CFD INTEGRL DATA	
				Conf	70Helsinki 2 427	Jun 70	- + SAME AS KFK-1303	
(n,γ)	+3		JAE	Theo Jour	NST 7 592	Nov 70	Takano+.NUMBER OF RES TO GET AVG SIG	
(n,γ)	+2	+3	COL	Expt Prog	NYO-73-340 18	Dec 70	Arbo+.MOXON-RAE DET.CURV COUNTS/CHAN	
(n,γ)	1.0+5		HAR	Expt Prog	AERE-PR/NP17	Dec 70	Coates+ LARGE LIQ SCIN. TBC	
(n,γ)	1.0-2	1.0+2	HAR	Expt Prog	AERE-PR/NP17	Dec 70	Moxon+ TOF LINAC ANAL TBC	+
	5.0+2	1.0+5		Rept	AERE-R-6074	Jun 69	- .LINAC TOF TBL AVG SIG GRAPH	
	3.0+4			Rept	AERE-R-6074	Jun 69	- .BEST VALUE AT 30KEV OBTAINED	
	1.0+3	1.0+5		Rept	NP-17644	Jul 68	- .THESIS.MOXON-RAE DET.AVG SIG	
	1.0+3	1.0+5		Data	EXFOR20465.002	Jan 76	18PTS.SIGMA.	
(n,γ)	4.0+5		WWA	Expt Jour	APPB 2 489	71	Brzosko+ PARTIAL,TOTAL SIG CFD THEO	+
				Rept	INR-1318 28	Apr 71	*SHORT REPORT,DATA GIV	
				Jour	CJP 47 2849	Dec 69	*TH.CALCULATIONS OF SIG	
	4.0+5			Data	EXFOR30159.	Apr 72	PARTIAL,TOTAL SIGMAS GIVEN	
(n,γ)	2.5-2	1.5+7	FEI	Eval Rept	INDC(CCP)-11	Mar 71	Abagyan+ EVALUATED SIGMA,1.KEV-15MEV	
(n,γ)	1.0+3	1.0+6	GA	Expt Conf	71Knoxvill 252	Mar 71	Fricke+,ABSOL AVG SIG,CURVE	+
				Rept	N-70-41999	Jun 70	Friesenhahn+ TOF ABSOL SIG(E) MEASD	
				ExTh	70Helsinki 2 265	Jun 70	Fricke+ TOF	
	1.0+3	7.5+5		Expt Data	EXFOR10049.008	Jul 71	. 93 PTS, SIGMA	
(n,γ)	1.0+3	1.0+7	IAE	Eval Conf	71Knoxvill 393	Mar 71	Byer+ PRELIM RESULTS OF NEW EVAL	
	2.0+3	1.0+7		Rept	INDC(NDS)-18	Mar 70	Konshin.STATUS OF DATA,RENORM VALUES	
				Comp Rept	INDC(NDS)-14	Oct 69	- .COMPIL OF EXP AND EVAL DATA	
(n,γ)	Pile		MTR	Expt Conf	71Knoxvill 79	Mar 71	Scoville.RATIO TO AU197 NG,U235 NF	
(n,γ)	2.4+4	1.1+6	FEI	Expt Conf	71Kiev	May 71	Stavissky+.ACT,GRPH SIG(NEUT-E),TBL	
(n,γ)	1.0+3	1.0+7	FEI	Eval Conf	FEI-259	May 71	Abramov+ REEVAL OF DATA,SIG(N-E),TBL	
(n,γ)	1.0+6		FEI	Expt Conf	71Kiev 1 325	May 71	Ivanov+ SIGMA GIVEN	+
	1.0+6			Data	EXFOR40153.002	Apr 74	.1 DATA LINE	
(n,γ)	1.0-1	4.0+4	FEI	Expt Jour	AE 31 107	Aug 71	Stavisskij+ REL AU-197,AG.GRPH CFD	
(n,γ)	1.4+7		LAS	Expt Jour	PL/B 36 557	Oct 71	Drake+ SPECTRUM SUMMED CFD PB208 NG	+
	1.4+7			Data	EXFOR10193.007	Jun 72	. 1 PT. SIGMA	
(n,γ)	+1	+4	CCP	Revw Jour	AE 31 595	Dec 71	Sukhoruchkin.DISCREPANCIES OF EXPTS	
				Jour	SJA 31 1380	Jun 72	*ENGL OF AE 31 595	
(n,γ)	1.0+4	1.0+6	FEI	Theo Rept	FEI-293	Jan 72	Dovbenko+ STAT-TH,CALC CFD EXPT,GRPH	
(n,γ)	Pile		FAR	Expt Prog	EANDC(E)150U	May 72	Vidal.INTEGR CROSS SECTION RATIOS	
(n,γ)	1.0+2	1.0+6	LRL	Expt Prog	USNDC-1 94	May 72	Czirr+. TO BE COMPLETED. NO DATA GVN	
(n,γ)	1.4+7		GRE	Theo Jour	NP/A 189 334	Jul 72	Boisson+.DIR,COLLECT.CURV. DEFORMNUC	
(n,γ)	1.2+6	4.0+6	FEI	Expt Jour	AE 33 782	Sep 72	Panitkin+ SIG(NEUT-E),GRAPH+TABLE	+
				Jour	SJA 33 893	Mar 73	. ENGLISH OF AE 33 782	
	1.2+6	4.0+6		Data	EXFOR40121.002	Sep 72	SIGMA AT 11 ES	
(n,γ)	2.4+4		RPI	Expt Conf	72Kiamesha 2 1107	Sep 72	Block+ .FE-FILTERED BEAM.RELATV MEAST	+
	2.4+4			Data	EXFOR10594.003	Aug 76	. 1 PT. REL TO AU. CS=.47B	
(n,γ)	2.0+2	3.5+4	FEI	Expt Prog	YFI-13 6	Oct 72	Chelnokov+ ABSTRACT,TBL SIGMA VS N-E	+
	1.2+6	4.0+6		Prog	INDC(CCP)-32	Apr 73	.PAGE 15.ENGLISH OF YFI-13 13	
	2.0+2	3.5+4		Prog	INDC(CCP)-32	Apr 73	.PAGE 8.ENGLISH OF YFI-13 6	
	2.0+2	3.5+4				Jun 72	SIG AT 26ES,ABSOL+REL U235NF PU239NF	
(n,γ)	Fast		DUB	Expt Rept	JINR-P12-6810	Nov 72	Ngo Quoc Buu+ ACT ANALYS, CD-RATIOS	
(n,γ)	None		AUA	Expt Prog	AAEC/PR-38P 11	Mar 73	Allen+ IN PROGRESS,NDG	
(n,γ)	7.2+6	1.3+7	ORE	Expt Conf	73Pacif.Gr 2 951	Mar 73	Mcdaniels+ TO GND,1ST ST,GRPH SIG(E)	
(n,γ)	2.5-2		RCN	Revw Conf	73Paris 2 271	Mar 73	Zijp.RECOMMENDED FROM LITERATURE,TBL	

92 Uranium 238

Quantity	Energy (ev) Min	Max	Lab	Type	Documentation Ref Vol Page	Date	Author, Comments	Data
(n,γ)	Maxwl	Fiss	SGA	Comp	Conf 73Paris 1 233	Mar 73	Eder+ DATA FROM EXPTS+EVALS,TABLE	
				Rept	SGAE-PH-141	Feb 73	.SAME AS 73PARIS,NO DETAILS	
(n,γ)	5.5+3		AI	Theo	Conf BNL-50387 79	Apr 73	Levitt. SIMILAR NSE 49,LESS DETAILED	
				Jour	NSE 49 450	72	- . MTE-CRLO,PROBABILTY TBLS.TBL	
(n,γ)	5.0+6	2.0+7	FEI	Expt	Jour AE 33 825	Oct 72	Panitkin+ SIG(NEUT-E),GRAPH,TBL	+
				Jour	SJA 33 945	Apr 73	.ENGL OF AE 33 825	
	5.0+6	2.0+7		Data	EXFOR40177.002	Nov 73	.SIGMA AT 7 ES GIVEN	
(n,γ)	1.0+4	1.0+7	KFK	Expt	Jour ATW 18 175	Apr 73	Blumm+ INVESTIGAT. BY N-SPEC-MEAS.	
(n,γ)	5.0+3	8.0+4	CCP	Expt	Conf 73Kiev 2 199	May 73	Kononov+ TOF,SIG(NEUT-E),GRAPH	
(n,γ)	1.0+4	5.0+6	KFK	Eval	Rept KFK-1798	May 73	Bluhm. INTEG EXPTS,RECOMMENDED CURVE	
(n,γ)	+7		CCP	Expt	Jour AE 35 47	Aug 73	Jurova+ SIGNG U-238/SIGNF U-235,TBL	
(n,γ)	1.5+5	6.3+5	NPL	Expt	Jour JNE 27 519	Aug 73	Ryves+ ACT.METHOD.REL LONG COUNTER	
(n,γ)	5.0+0	1.0+5	ORL	Expt	Jour NSE 51 385	Aug 73	Desaussure+ LINAC,TOF.AVG CAPT CS.	+
	5.0+1	1.0+5		Conf	NEANDC(E)163	Jan 75	- . NEW MEAS.SEE NSE51,P385.	
	1.0+3	1.0+6		Rept	CONF-740903-7	Sep 74	- + CURVS. OTH,ENDF CFD.	
	5.0+0	1.0+5		Rept	ORNL-TM-4059	Feb 73	- + MEAS CAPT,PROBABILTY TBL	
	1.0+2	1.2+3		Prog	ORNL-4800	May 72	Silver+. AVERAGED SIGS. TABLE	
	5.0+0	1.0+5		Conf	71Knoxvill 728	Mar 71	.SUPERSEDED	
	1.0+2	1.0+5		Data	EXFOR10101.	Mar 76	. 27PTS. AVG AND RAW DATA AVAILABLE	
(n,γ)	2.0+2	7.0+6	FEI	Eval	Rept YK-13 3	74	Davletshin+ REL U235(N,F),SIG(E) TBL	
	2.0+2	8.0+6		Conf	73Kiev 1 252	May 73	- + RATIO TO U235(N,F),CURVE	
(n,γ)	1.0+1	4.7+2	KFK	Theo	Rept KFK-1890	Feb 74	Broeders-Siep.RES SHIELD ON EFF SIG	
(n,γ)	7.0+5	3.0+6	HAR	Theo	Prog AERE-PR/NP21	Mar 74	Lynn.COMPARED WITH N,GN' CROSS SECT	
(n,γ)	1.4+7		LAS	Expt	Prog USNDC-11 151	Jun 74	Arthur+ ANG DISTR GAMMAS, NDG.	+
(n,γ)	1.0+2	2.0+7	HAR	Eval	Jour ANE 1 409	Jul 74	Sowerby+ LSQ WITH F9 F5 ABOVE .1MEV	
	1.0+3	2.0+7		Rept	AERE-R-7273	Feb 73	- +LINKED EVAL U235 PU239 TBL	
	1.0+2	2.0+7		Rept	AERE-M-2497	Feb 72	- +LINKED EVAL U235 SIGF TBL	
				Conf	70Helsinki 2 703	Jun 70	- + PPR34. EVAL WITH FISS SIG	
(n,γ)	Fast		IFB	Expt	Jour AE 37 337	Oct 74	Bychkov+ ABST,SIG REL U235(N,F) GIVN	
				Jour	SJA 37 1073	Apr 75	. ENGLISH OF AE 37 337	
(n,γ)	2.0+4	5.5+5	KFK	Expt	Conf NEANDC(E)-163U	Jan 75	Spencer+VDG,PRELIM,REL U235 NF,GRPHS	
	2.0+4	1.4+5		Conf	KFK-1274 2	Oct 74	Beer+ PP121. REL U-235 FISS SIG	
(n,γ)	1.0+3	2.0+6	JAE	Theo	Conf JAERI-M-5984	Feb 75	Igarasi+OPT/STAT MDL.TBL+CURVE	
(n,γ)	+4	+7	MOL	Expt	Abst BAP 20 145	Feb 75	Pinter+75WASH INTEGRAL MEAS MOL SPEC	
(n,γ)	None		UCN	Theo	Abst BAP 20 151	Feb 75	Mcknight+EFFECTS OF UNCERT.NDG.	
(n,γ)	2.5-2	1.5+1	BNL	Eval	Prog BNL-50451 147	Mar 75	Chrien.2EXPT TBD.U238 NG DISCREPANCY	
(n,γ)	6.6+0	6.7+1	BNL	Revw	Prog BNL-50451 255	Mar 75	Bhat+WN,WG,WT.TBL.PARS EFFECT ON NG	
(n,γ)	1.0+1	1.6+3	GEL	Expt	Conf 75Wash. 732	Mar 75	Corvi+ NAI DET.LINAC.GRAPH.	
(n,γ)	5.0+4	5.0+6	LAS	Theo	Conf 75Wash. 129	Mar 75	Moore.GRPH R MATR STAT CALC CFD ENDF	
(n,γ)	1.0+4	1.4+5	ORL	Expt	Prog BNL-NCS-5041	Mar 75	Perez+SUMMARY OF CS DATA ABOVE RES.	
	1.0+4	5.6+5		Prog	BNL-5041 103	Mar 75	- +REVW.TBLS,GRPHS.CFD ENDF,OTH.	
	5.0+3	1.0+5		Conf	75Wash. 623	Mar 75	- + STAT MODEL TESTS	
(n,γ)	2.0+4	5.5+5	ORL	Expt	Conf 75Wash. 620	Mar 75	Spencer+TBL.SHAPE REL 235U NF +AU TBL	
(n,γ)	6.7+0	2.6+3	WIN	Revw	Prog BNL-50451 45	Mar 75	Askew+RVW U238 RES PARS.TBLS	
(n,γ)	1.0+3	5.0+6	BRC	Eval	Conf 75Kiev 1 216	May 75	Jary+ POINTS+EVAL CURV,CFD ENDF/B-4	
(n,γ)	+3	+4	FEI	Expt	Conf 75Kiev 3 200	May 75	Van'Kov+ TOF,HE3-COUNT.SOME SIGS GVN	+
	2.1+2	1.0+5		Data	EXFOR30460.	Dec 78	SUPERSEDES 75KIEV 3,200.SEE ZFK-341	
(n,γ)	5.9+5	1.0+6	FEI	Expt	Conf 75Kiev 4 109	May 75	Davletshin+ ACT,GE-LI,TBL	
	5.9+5	1.0+6		Data	EXFOR40403.002	Oct 76	SIGMA AT 4 ES	
(n,γ)	2.4+4		BNL	Expt	Conf AERE-R-8082	Jul 75	Rimawi+ABSTR,IRON FILTER TECHN,NDG	+
				Conf	75Wash. 920	Mar 75	- + CS=475+-36MB.CFD OTHER EXPT	
	2.4+4			Data	EXFOR10434.003	Mar 75	. 1 PT, SIGMA	
(n,γ)	3.0+4		FEI	Expt	Jour AE 39 17	Jul 75	Panitkin+ ACTIV,GELI.ABSOLUT,CFD.TBL	
				Jour	SJA 39 591	Jan 76	. ENGLISH OF AE 39 17	
(n,γ)	1.6+4	2.0+7	FEI	Comp	Jour AE 39 17	Jul 75	Panitkin+ OWN MEASMNTS NORMALZD,TBL	+
				Jour	SJA 39 591	Jan 76	. ENGLISH OF AE 39 17	
	2.4+4	2.0+7		Expt	Data EXFOR40431.002	Feb 77	CS AT 42 ES	
(n,γ)	1.4+7		LND	Expt	Conf AERE-R-8082	Jul 75	Magnusson+ TBD WITH IMPROV ACT TECHN	
				Conf	75Gothenbg	Jun 75	- +ABSTR,IMPROV ACT TECHN TBD	
(n,γ)	2.0+4	3.5+6	ANL	Expt	Jour NSE 57 300	Aug 75	Poenitz.238U/197AU RATIO DET	+
	2.0+4	5.0+5		Conf	75Wash. 901	Mar 75	- . GRAPH	
	2.0+4	3.5+6		Data	EXFOR10421.	Apr 75	. 54PTS.SIGMA AND RATIO 197AU NG	
(n,γ)	1.0+3	1.0+5	JAE	Eval	Prog JAERI-M-6320	Nov 75	Takano+GRPH EVAL CFD EXP DATA.	
(n,γ)	5.0+4	1.0+5	LAS	Eval	Prog LA-6164-PR 2	Dec 75	Stewart.NDG.DISCREPANCY IN NG CS.	
(n,γ)	1.2+5	2.7+6	LRL	Expt	Jour NSE 59 381	Apr 76	Lindner+REL U235NF.TBL,CRVS.CFD ENDF	+
	1.2+5	2.7+6		Data	EXFOR10221.	Aug 75	. 23 PTS, SIGMA	
(n,γ)	None		ANL	Eval	Prog ERDA-NDC-3 28	May 76	Poenitz.EVAL OF U238 NG CS UNDERWAY.	
(n,γ)	1.0+4	5.0+6	LRL	Theo	Prog ERDA-NDC-3 68	May 76	Gardner+ STAT MDL CALC.CFD ENDF.NDG	

92 Uranium 238

Quantity	Energy (ev) Min	Max	Lab	Type	Documentation Ref Vol Page	Date	Author, Comments	Data
(n,γ)	2.4+4	1.8+5	RPI Expt	Prog	ERDA–NDC–3 266	May 76	Quan.REL B10.6ES.GRPH.TBL.CFD ENDF.	+
	1.5+2	1.0+5		Data	EXFOR10577.	Nov 76	417PT.CS=−LOG(SELF−INDIC RATIO/SAMP)	
(n,γ)		1.0+3	KUK Eval	Conf	76Lowell 1280	Jul 76	Malik+VARIOUS CAPT DATA CFD AND ANAL	
(n,γ)	8.0+4	1.6+6	HAR Expt	Prog	NEANDC(E)172 8	Aug 76	Pearstein+ ACTIVATION METHOD,GRAPH	
	5.0+4	1.6+6		Prog	AERE−PR/NP23	Mar 76	Pearstein+GRPH CFD EVAL(SOWERBY)TBP	
	8.0+4	1.6+6		Abst	75Harwell 41	Mar 75	− +ABST.IBIS,ACTIV. NDG	
				Prog	EANDC(UK) 151	Aug 73	− + ACT REL 235,LONG COUNTER	
(n,γ)	+7		FEI Theo	Rept	YK− 21 3	Oct 76	Blokhin+ SIG(NEUT−E),GRAPH	
(n,γ)	1.0+4	6.0+5	CAD Expt	Rept	CEA−R−4788	Nov 76	Le Rigoleur+ VDG,TOF,WEIGHTING METH	+
	1.5+4	5.3+5		Conf	75Wash. 953	Mar 75	− + GRPH CFD EVALS	
	1.5+4	5.3+5		Data	EXFOR20572.015	Feb 76	25PTS.SIGMA.	
(n,γ)	Pile		FEI Expt	Rept	YK− 24 48	77	Andrijakhina+ AVG SIG AT DIFF POSITS	
Res Int Capt	3.4−1		COL Expt	Jour	PR 80 499	Nov 50	Anderson.	+
	3.4−1			Data	EXFOR12467.002	Jun 76	. 1 PT.	
Res Int Capt	5.0+0	+6	BNL Expt	Jour	PR 99 10	Jul 55	Harvey+.FC TRANSM. 276+−12B	
Res Int Capt	None		ORL Theo	Jour	NSE 1 68	Mar 56	Dresner.EFF RIA CALCTD FROM RES PARS	
Res Int Capt	5.0−1		ORL Expt	Jour	JNE 2 243	Jun 56	Macklin+. 281+−20B REL.AU. CFD TH232	
				Conf	55Geneva 5 96	Aug 55	− +.P833 ,EXPT CFD THEORY,TABLE	
	5.0−1			Data	EXFOR12261.003	Jun 76	. 1 PT.	
Res Int Capt	None		CRC Expt	Rept	TNCC(CAN)−3	Oct 56	Butler. TO BE DONE	
Res Int Capt	6.7+0		ANL Expt	Jour	PR 105 661	Jan 57	Bollinger+,CP5 FC 279+−20B	
Res Int Capt	None		AI Theo	Jour	NSE 4 649	Nov 58	Chernick+,ABS INT CALC FROM RES PARS	
Res Int Capt	5.0−1	1.0+6	ORL Eval	Jour	NSE 6 100	Aug 59	Stoughton+ BEST VALUE 280+−15B	
	3.0−1	+6		Conf	58Geneva 16 64	Sep 58	Halperin+.PPR1072,VAL CFD MANY REFS	
Res Int Capt	Pile		CRC Revw	Conf	59Vienna 101	Sep 59	Critoph+ REVIEW,EXPERIMENTAL METHODS	
Res Int Capt	5.0−1		GA Expt	Rept	GA−3069	Sep 62	Sampson.	+
Res Int Capt	5.0−1		BET ExTh	Jour	NSE 14 358	Dec 62	Hardy+	+
				Conf	62Wien 211	May 62	Klein+,FUEL ROD EFF RES INT,ACT+CALC	
	5.0−1			Expt Data	EXFOR12454.002	Jun 76	. 1 PT.	
Res Int Capt	5.5−1		SRL Expt	Abst	ANS 7 27	Jun 64	Baumann+CD FOIL.REL AU.NO 1.V. 280B	+
				Rept	DP−817	Jan 63	− .	
	5.5−1			Data	EXFOR12442.002	Jun 76	. 1 PT.	
Res Int Capt	4.0−1	1.8+7	IIT Comp	Conf	65IAEA 251	Mar 65	Barrall+ RECOMENDED VAL,LITER−SURVEY	
Res Int Capt	None		WES Eval	Rept	WANL−TME−1228	Aug 65	Gibson+.INFINITE DILUTION GIVEN	
Res Int Capt	5.0−1		AE Revw	Conf	66S.Diego 2 161	Feb 66	Hellstrand.REVW MEAS AND CALC R.INT.	
Res Int Capt	6.8−1	1.0+7	BNWTheo	Conf	66Wash. 75	Mar 66	Liikala+,3−ENERGY−GROUP CALCTNS,TBL	
Res Int Capt		1.0+3	ORL Eval	Rept	ORNL−TM−1448	Jun 66	Webster+.CALCULATED FROM NG	
Res Int Capt	−		KFK Expt	Conf	67Karlsrhe 1 77	Nov 67	Seufert+,STATISTICAL ENERGY REGION	
Res Int Capt	3.9+3	1.5+4	WEWTheo	Jour	NSE 34 181	Nov 68	Dyos.STATISTICAL CALC 1.224+−0.029B	
Res Int Capt	5.0−1		KJL Expt	Jour	JIN 34 2699	Sep 72	Steinnes. ACT. AU MONITOR	+
	5.0−1			Data	EXFOR20188.031	May 74	1PNT.	
Res Int Capt	5.0−1		STF Expt	Abst	DA/B 34 6026	Jun 74	Underhill. I=269.4+−5.2BARNS.	+
	5.0−1			Data	EXFOR10448.003	Nov 74	1PT	
Res Int Capt	6.6+0	6.7+1	BNL Revw	Prog	BNL−50451 255	Mar 75	Bhat+CHANGING WG EFFECT ON RIG.TBL	
Res Int Capt	1.0+2	6.8+2	ORL Eval	Jour	NSE 61 496	Dec 76	Desaussure+ ENDFB4 CALC VS MLBW.TBL.	
				Rept	ORNL−TM−5256	Dec 75	Olsen+SLBW CALC VS RM WITH LADDERS	
Spect (n,γ)	Pile		ANL Expt	Jour	NSE 1 193	Jul 56	Kaufmann+ EBR,ACT RATIO REL U235,TH	
Spect (n,γ)	Maxwl		LRL Expt	Abst	BAP 1 389	Dec 56	Kenney+ CRYST SPEC 3 GAMMAS SEEN	
Spect (n,γ)	2.5+4		ORL Expt	Conf	58Geneva 15 68	Sep 58	Macklin.PPR671,SIGMA+G−ENERGY GVN	
Spect (n,γ)	+0	+2	KAP Expt	Prog	WASH−1006	Oct 58	Yeater. TOF CS RES XPT TBD	
Spect (n,γ)	Maxwl		CRC Expt	Jour	CJP 37 377	Mar 59	Campion+ CRYST SPEC 10 GAMMAS RESLVD	
Spect (n,γ)	6.7+0	3.7+1	YAL Expt	Jour	NP 14 693	Jan 60	Draper+REL GAMMA WIDTHS,3RES.CRYSPEC	
Spect (n,γ)	Maxwl		BNL Expt	Prog	WASH−1028 12	Apr 60	Zimmerman+. PARTIAL RADIATION WIDTHS	
Spect (n,γ)	1.0+4	3.0+5	FOA Expt	Jour	AF 23 417	Mar 63	Bergqvist.TOF SPECTRUM OKS STATMODEL	
Spect (n,γ)	Maxwl		FRK Expt	Rept	IKF−8	Jul 63	Fiebiger. DECAY SCHEME OF U 239	
Spect (n,γ)	Maxwl		ANL Expt	Prog	WASH−1044 5	Aug 63	Smith+ BENT XTAL NDG TBD.	
Spect (n,γ)	6.7+0	2.4+2	ANL Expt	Jour	PR/B 134 931	Jun 64	Jackson. 4 TRANS. 12 RES X−BNL	
				Conf	63ANL 333	Oct 63	.SUPERSEDED	
Spect (n,γ)	Maxwl		RIS Expt	Jour	ZP 184 143	Apr 65	Maier+ 61 GS FROM 31 TO 780 KEV.	
Spect (n,γ)	6.7+1	2.4+2	SAC Expt	Diss	CEA−2810R	Jun 65	Huynh.DET=2 NAI(TL)COAXIAL CRYSTALS	
Spect (n,γ)	+1	+2	ANL Expt	Prog	WASH−1064 9	Oct 65	Jackson+ GE−LI DET. HI E TBC,NDG	
Spect (n,γ)	2.7+4	4.0+4	ORL ExTh	Jour	NP 74 15	Dec 65	Bergqvist+OKS STAT THEORY CALC	
				Expt Prog	ORNL−3778 44	May 65	Harvey.FC+LI−GE DET,MANY UNREP LINES	
				Rept	ORNL−P−1343	65	Bergqvist.SC,CFD THEORY+JACKSON	
Spect (n,γ)	2.5−2		LAS Expt	Jour	PR 151 1011	Nov 66	Jurney+.GE(LI) DET.	+
Spect (n,γ)	2.0−3	1.2+2	BNL Expt	Jour	NP/A 121 630	Dec 68	Price+ EVIDENCE FOR DIR.CAPT.WG(E(G)	
	3.5−2	3.7+1		Conf	69Studsvik 627	Aug 69	Chrien. GAM−LINES GRPHS,THR+RES NEUT	
	2.0−3	1.2+2		Jour	PL/B 25 195	Aug 67	.SUPERSEDED	

92 Uranium 238

Quantity	Energy (ev) Min	Energy (ev) Max	Lab	Type	Documentation Ref Vol Page	Date	Author, Comments	Data
Spect (n,γ)	Maxwl		LAS	Expt Prog	WASH – 1127 147	Apr 69	Shera+ TO BE DONE MOSTLY 1/2+ EXCIT	
Spect (n,γ)	None		ORL	Theo Jour	NSE 36 220	May 69	Yost+ CALCULAT BY GAMMA CASCADE MDL	
Spect (n,γ)	3.5 – 1	8.7+0	BNL	Revw Rept	IAEA – 124 303	Feb 70	Chrien.INT OF GS(CA 4MEV)VS N – E,GRPH	
Spect (n,γ)	+0	+2	COL	Expt Prog	NCSAC – 33 59	Dec 70	Derengowski+,GE DET,1 – 8MEV GAMS,NDG	
Spect (n,γ)	5.6+0	1.0+5	GA	Expt Prog	NCSAC – 33 82	Dec 70	John+.GE(LI) – NAI(TL) SPEC.CURVES.	
Spect (n,γ)	6.0+0	3.5+2	HAR	Expt Prog	AERE – PR/NP17	Dec 70	Murray+NO CORR PARTIAL WG REDUCED WN	
		3.5+2		Conf	70Helsinki 1 373	Jun 70	Thomas+36. SPEC(NEUT – E,GAM – E),HALF – L	
	6.0+0	3.5+2		Prog	AERE – PR/NP16	Aug 69	– + TBL PARTIAL WG 15 RES	
Spect (n,γ)	6.8+0		HAR	Expt Prog	AERE – PR/NP17	Dec 70	Coates+ MULTIPLICITY OF GS MEASURED	
Spect (n,γ)	Maxwl		ORL	Expt Rept	ORNL – 4691	Aug 71	Booth+. GAMMA SPEC ABOVE 1 MEV.CURVS	
				Abst	ANS 12 929	Nov 69	– +. GAMMA SPECT ABOVE 1MEV GIVEN	
Spect (n,γ)	4.0+5		WWA	Expt Jour	APPB 2 489	Aug 71	Brzosko+ GAMMA – EN = 3 TO 7 MEV,GRAPH	
Spect (n,γ)	6.7+0	6.0+2	BNL	Expt Jour	PR/C 4 900	Sep 71	Chrien+. CAPT SPEC FROM 28RESON	
Spect (n,γ)	1.4+7		LAS	Expt Jour	PL/B 36 557	Oct 71	Drake+ SPECTRUM CFD HO AND PB208	
Spect (n,γ)		1.1+6	ORL	Theo Jour	NSE 47 8	Jan 72	Booth+. DUCAL CODE CALCULATN.CFD XPT	
Spect (n,γ)	Maxwl		LAS	Expt Prog	USNDC – 1 118	May 72	Jurney+. ANAL TBC. NO DATA GIVEN	
Spect (n,γ)	2.4+4		RPI	Expt Prog	COO – 3058 – 20 16	Jun 72	Block+. CURVE PULSE – HEIGHT SPECTRA	
Spect (n,γ)	Pile		ANL	Expt Jour	PR/C 6 1322	Oct 72	Bollinger+. GAMMA SPECT.3.3 – 4.8MEV	
				Prog	ANL – 7848 6	Mar 71	– +.SPEC SHOWN.VERY PURE U238	
				Conf	69Studsvik 601	Aug 69	Smither+ NO DATA GVN,TB CFD STATMOD	
Spect (n,γ)	–2	1.0+6	AUA	Expt Prog	AAEC/PR – 38P 11	Mar 73	Allen+ SHORT NOTE. DEPLETED.NA – I,NDG	
Spect (n,γ)	Maxwl	1.0+2	BNL	Theo Jour	NSE 51 296	Jul 73	Takahashi.STAT MODEL CALC.8 NEUT ES	
Spect (n,γ)	2.4+4		BNL	Expt Prog	USNDC – 9 52	Dec 73	Rimawi+. CURV OF COUNTS/CHANNEL.	
Spect (n,γ)	None		NBS	Expt Prog	USNDC – 11 169	Jun 74	Bowman+ G TRANS IN 2ND WELL U239,TBD	+
Spect (n,γ)	7.2+2	1.2+3	GEL	Expt Conf	74Petten 673	Sep 74	Weigmann+ NO ANOMAL GROSS SHAPE	
Spect (n,γ)	Maxwl		KFK	Expt Conf	74Petten 749	Sep 74	Weitkamp+ NONDESTR FUEL ASSAY APPL.	
Spect (n,γ)	None		GEL	Expt Prog	NEANDC(E)162 3	Feb 75	Rohr+LINAC TOF IN RES WITH ENHA.FISS	
Spect (n,γ)	2.5 – 2	1.0+6	KYU	Theo Prog	NEANDC(J)44L	Aug 76	Ohsawa+.STATISTICAL MDL CALC. ND7	
Spect (n,γ)	Maxwl		RCN	Expt Rept	INIS – MF – 3352	Oct 76	Kopecky+ ABSTRACT	
Inelastic γ	None		LAS	Expt Prog	WASH – 1048 53	Jun 64	Day.PULSED BEAM TOF,TBC	
Inelastic γ	1.1+6	2.1+6	TNC	Expt Prog	WASH – 1068 194	Mar 66	Morgan+ SIG. AT 1.09,1.7,2.1 MEV	
Inelastic γ	1.0+6		TNC	Expt Prog	NCSAC – 31 214	May 70	Nellis+,TO BE COMPLETED,NO DATA GIVN	
Inelastic γ	1.5+6		ANL	Expt Conf	70Helsinki 2 3	Jun 70	Poenitz.111. GAM SPEC GRAPH, GE(LI)	
Inelastic γ	Fast		CCP	Expt Jour	AE 29 338	Nov 70	Barkov+ AVG SIG FOR GAM PROD.TBLS	
				Jour	SJA 29 1080	Nov 70	TRANSLATN.*	
Inelastic γ	Fiss		FEI	Expt Jour	AE 29 338	Nov 70	Bakov+	+
	Fiss			Data	EXFOR40131.014	Jan 73	PRODUCTION OF 3 GAMMA – LINES	
Inelastic γ	Pile		FEI	Expt Prog	YFI – 12 14	72	Bakov+ AVG SIG OF GAM YLD,ABST,NDG	
				Prog	INDC(CCP) – 30	Dec 72	.PG 11,ENGLISH OF YFI – 12 14	
Inelastic γ	–		SUN	Expt Jour	ZP 253 289	Aug 72	Mcmurray+ LVL SCHEME OF U – 238	
	None			Prog	INDC(SEC) – 28	Sep 72	– + STUDY OF LEVELS ,TBL	
	7.0+2	1.9+3		Conf	72Budapest 10	Aug 72	– + LVLS, G – ES,BRANCH.RAT,TBL	
Inelastic γ	Maxwl		LAS	Eval Conf	75Wash. 149	Mar 75	Young. MEAS CFD ENDF – 4	
Inelastic γ	1.5+5	1.5+6	KUR	Expt Conf	75Leningrd 159	Jan 75	Demidov+ ABST,GE – LI,ES + INTENSIT,TBL	+
	1.0+6			Data	EXFOR40318.002	Oct 75	.GAM/100N AT 81 ES GVN	
Nonelastic γ	1.4+7		CCP	Expt Jour	AE 8 361	Apr 60	Veretennikov+ GAMMA SPEC 0.5 – 2.5MEV	
				Jour	JNAB 16 121	Feb 62	TRANSLATN.*	
				Jour	SJA 8 311	Jun 61	TRANSLATN.*	
Nonelastic γ	+5	2.0+6	ANL	Expt Conf	61Vienna 1 29	Aug 61	Smith.PPR76,CURVE CFD REFS	
Nonelastic γ		1.0+7	GEN	Eval Rept	GEMP – 360	Aug 65	Edwards.15 – GROUP GAMMA PRODUCTN SIGS	
Nonelastic γ	1.5+7		LRL	Theo Jour	NSE 32 178	May 68	Howerton+ 11.4B CALC,CFD EXPT 10.7B	
Nonelastic γ	1.4+7		SAC	Expt Rept	CEA – R – 4132	Feb 71	Bertrand. 30 TO 130 DEGREES	
Nonelastic γ	1.0 – 5	2.0+7	LAS	Eval Rept	LA – 4918	Jul 72	Stewart+. GAMMA PRODUCTION SIGS	
Nonelastic γ		2.0+7	LRL	Theo Abst	BAP 18 625	Apr 73	Gardner+.SIG+SPEC.NO DATA GIVEN.	
Nonelastic γ	2.0+6	2.0+7	BNL	Theo Jour	NSE 51 296	Jul 73	Takahashi.CALC GAM SPECT.12 NEUT ES	
Nonelastic γ	1.4+7		KUR	Expt Conf	75Kiev 4 133	May 75	Bezotosnyj+ NA – I.SIG(.5 – 8.0 MEV) GVN	
(n,2n)	1.4+7	1.4+7	HAR	Expt Rept	AERE – NP/R – 2033	56	= 1 DATA INDEX LINES	+
(n,2n)	1.4+7		LAS	Expt Rept	LA – 2111	57	Rosen+	+
	1.4+7			Data	EXFOR12372.005	Jun 76	. 9 PTS. DSIGMA.	
(n,2n)	Fiss		KAP	Expt Rept	KAPL – 1779	May 57	Schuman+. SIG = 4.7MB ACTIVATION.	
(n,2n)	Fiss		CCP	Expt Jour	AE 4 87	Jan 58	Sherman. 17 + – 3MB,ACT IN FAST REACTOR	
				Jour	JNE 9 113	Jun 59	TRANSLATN.*	
				Jour	SJA 4 113	58	TRANSLATN.*	
(n,2n)	6.0+6	2.0+7	BNL	Comp Conf	58Geneva 16 8	Sep 58	Hughes.PPR2483,CURVE,MANY REFS	
(n,2n)	Pile		KUR	Expt Conf	58Geneva 12 3	Sep 58	Leipunskij+.PPR2038,VAL GVN	
(n,2n)	1.5+7		CCP	Expt Jour	AE 5 456	Oct 58	Antropov+. ACT, 2EXPTS FROM 1952+1957	+
				Jour	JNEA 10 184	59	TRANSLATN.*	
				Jour	SJA 5 1352	58	TRANSLATN.*	

92 Uranium 238

Quantity	Energy (ev) Min	Max	Lab	Type	Documentation Ref Vol Page	Date	Author, Comments	Data
(n,2n)	6.0+6	1.6+7	LAS	Expt Jour	PR 112 259	Oct 58	Knight+,D−D T−D NS,RADIOCHEM	+
	6.0+6	1.6+7		Data	EXFOR12459.	Jun 76	. 17 PTS. SIGMA.	
(n,2n)	Fiss		GES	Revw Jour	NUC 17 1 54	Jan 59	Rochlin.47 ISOTOPES.ACT.RVS.TBL	
(n,2n)	5.0−1	1.0+7	BET	Eval Rept	WAPD−BT−17 51	Feb 60	Amster. 54 GROUP	
(n,2n)	Fiss		ALD	Eval Rept	AWRE−O−02/60	Apr 60	Hinves+AWRE EVAL DATA CFD XPT.	
(n,2n)	1.5+7		ALD	Expt Jour	JNAB 14 69	May 61	Perkin+ ABSOLUTE ACTIVN 0.69+−0.04B	+
(n,2n)	Thrsh	1.6+7	ANL	Theo Jour	NP 25 511	Jun 61	Vandenbosh+EVAPORATION TH CFD DATA	
(n,2n)	Thrsh	Up	LAS	Theo Jour	PR 123 859	Aug 61	Barr. THEOR FIT SIG(E,EP) DATA.	
(n,2n)	Fiss		TRM	Theo Conf	63Bombay 232	Feb 63	Singh.VAL COMPUTD BY SEMIEMP FORMULA	
(n,2n)	Thrsh	1.5+7	UK	Eval Rept	AWRE−O−79/63	Jan 64	Parker.(ALD).UKNDL−DFN 156	
(n,2n)	7.0+6	7.0+6	ALD	Expt Jour	NP 65 236	Mar 65	Batchelor. = 1 DATA INDEX LINES	+
(n,2n)	1.4+7		HAM	Comp Jour	NP 65 257	Mar 65	Bormann. 1EXPT VALS.CFD SHELL EFFECT	
(n,2n)	Fiss		IIT	Comp Conf	65IAEA 251	Mar 65	Barrall+CALC AVG SIGS OF 3FISS−SPECS	
(n,2n)	1.3+7	1.5+7	BNL	Theo Jour	NSE 23 238	Nov 65	Pearlstein.3ES.STAT MDL CALC.TBL CS.	
(n,2n)	Fiss		BNL	Theo Jour	NSE 23 238	Nov 65	Pearlstein.STATMDL CALC.SPEC AVG.TBL	
(n,2n)	6.0+6	1.5+7	AI	Theo Conf	66Paris 1 429	Oct 66	Dunford. NONSPHERCL OPTMDL,CURV.	
(n,2n)	1.0+4	1.5+7	EDF	Eval Rept	EDF−HX−1/1375	Feb 68	Vastel.PART OF DFN 401 IN UK LIBRARY	
(n,2n)	3.2+6	8.0+6	ALD	Expt Prog	AWRE−CNRPR/10	Apr 68	Mather+	
(n,2n)	Thrsh	Up	JAP	Expt Jour	NST 5 265	Jun 68	Sakanoue+,EFFECTIVE−SIG=2.8B	
(n,2n)	1.4+7		FEI	Expt Prog	YFI−7 3	Apr 69	Salnikov+ SPECTRUM OF 2ND NEUT, NDG	
				Rept	INDC(CCP)−7 3	69	. ENGL OF YFI−7 3	
(n,2n)	1.4+7		ALD	Expt Rept	AWRE−O−47/69	Aug 69	Mather+PAIN LARGE LIQUID SCINT	+
	1.4+7			Data	EXFOR20794.013	Oct 78	1PNT.SIGMA.	
(n,2n)	1.5+7		DEB	Comp Jour	REA 7 4 93	Dec 69	Csikai+ SIG+HL COMPILTN,N−ACTIV−ANAL	
(n,2n)	6.0+6	1.1+7	AUA	Theo Rept	AAEC/TM−542	May 70	Bertram. CALC SIG(E) CFD EXPT,GRAPHS	
	6.0+6	1.6+7		Rept	AAEC/TM−522	Nov 69	− . CALC SIG(E)GRAPHS CFD EXPTS	
(n,2n)	1.4+7	1.5+7	JYV	Eval Rept	JU−RR−3/1970	Jun 70	Leppaemaeki+ TABLE OF EVAL AVG SIG	
(n,2n)	1.5+7		DUB	Expt Jour	AE 31 156	Aug 71	Gangrskij+ UPPER LIMIT FOR SPON−ISOM	
	+6	+7		Rept	JINR−P3−5528	Jan 71	− + GND+ISOM FISSN STATE SIGS	
	1.5+7			Jour	SJA 31 874	Mar 72	. ENGL OF AE 31 156	
(n,2n)	7.0+6	1.2+7	ALD	Expt Rept	AWRE−O−72/72	Nov 72	Mather+ LARGE LIQ SCINTILLATOR.	+
	7.0+6	1.2+7		Data	EXFOR20795.012	Oct 78	3PTS.SIGMA.	
(n,2n)	1.5+7		DUB	Expt Jour	IJP 47 232	73	Belov+ SIG TO SPONFIS GIVN,FRAGM−DET	
				Rept	JINR−E15−6807	Nov 72	− + SPON FISS ISOMER PRODUCTN,TBL	
(n,2n)	1.5+7		KFI	Expt Jour	MFF 21 555	73	Nagy. THESIS,HUNG. TO FISS ISO,GRND	
(n,2n)	Thrsh	1.6+7	BNW	Revw Conf	73Paris 1 39	Mar 73	Wolkenhauer+ N2N+N3N FROM ENDF,GRAPH	
(n,2n)	1.5+7		DEB	Eval Rept	REA 11 1 153	Mar 73	Boedy. COMPILATION+RECOMM.VALUE,TBL	
				Rept	IAEA−153 173	73	− . RECOMM. VALUE ONLY	
(n,2n)	None		IJE	Eval Conf	73Kiev 1 209	May 73	Konshin+ MODEL DEVELOPD,OKS EXPT,NDG	
(n,2n)	1.5+7		JAE	Expt Jour	JPJ 35 936	Sep 73	Takekoshi+.SEARCH FOR FISSION−ISOMER	
(n,2n)	1.4+7	1.5+7	LRL	Expt Jour	PR/C 8 1938	Nov 73	Landrum+. SIG MEASD REL TO AL27(NA).	+
				Rept	UCRL−74262	Oct 72	.SUPERSEDED	
	1.4+7	1.5+7		Data	EXFOR10376.002	Apr 74	. 7 PTS 13.7 MEV TO 14.94MEV	
(n,2n)	None		CJD	Theo Rept	INDC(CCP)−44	Jun 74	.P1. ENGLISH OF 73KIEV 1 209	
(n,2n)	6.5+6	2.0+7	BRC	Eval Conf	75Kiev 1 216	May 75	Jary+ EVAL CFD XPTS,TABLE+CURVE	
	2.0+6	1.5+7		Conf	JAERI−M−5984	Feb 75	− .P 76.STATMOD/OPTMOD. CURVES.	
				Rept	CEA−R−4647	Jan 75	− . EVAL,STAT MDL, 15 VALS	
(n,2n)	1.3+7	1.8+7	HAM	Expt Conf	75Wash. 819	Mar 75	Ackermann+ACT.GRPH CFD STAT THEORY	+
	1.3+7	1.8+7		Data	EXFOR20499.002	Mar 76	10PTS.SIGMA.	
(n,2n)	6.0+6	1.1+7	ANL	Eval Rept	ANL−75−34	Jun 75	Davey+CONSTANT T MDL,LVL DEN MDL FIT	
(n,2n)	1.4+7		FEI	Expt Rept	FEI−671	76	Baryba+ (N,N')+(N,2N)+(N,3N) N−SPEC	
(n,2n)		5.0+6	LRL	Theo Abst	BAP 21 655	Apr 76	Gardner+U237 PROD STUDY.CFD EXPT.NDG	
(n,2n)	7.9+6	1.5+7	BRC	Expt Jour	NIM 135 511	Jun 76	Frehaut.GD LOADED SCIN.EXPT DETAILS.	+
				Conf	75Kiev 4 303	May 75	− + LIQSCIN.SIG(E),CFD.GRPH+TBL	
				Conf	75Wash. 855	Mar 75	− + TBL.GRPH.REL 238U(N,F)	
	Thrsh	1.5+7		Rept	CEA−R−4627	74	− +	
	6.0+6	1.5+7		Conf	70Helsinki 2 109	Jun 70	− +66. 2 NEUT−ES VS TIME SPECS	
	7.9+6	1.5+7		Data	EXFOR20416.021	Jul 75	15PTS.SIGMA.	
(n,2n)	1.4+7		LRL	Expt Jour	AE 40 491	Jun 76	Browne+ SIG TO SPONFIS ISO.NOT FOUND	
				Jour	SJA 40 587	Dec 76	− + ENGL OF AE 40 491	
(n,2n)	Fast		KTO	Expt Jour	NST 13 531	Oct 76	Kobayashi+.ACT.SIG=15.7+−0.80 MB	+
	1.5+6			Rept	NEANDC(J)42L31	76	− +	
	1.5+6			Data	EXFOR20693.015	Nov 76	1PNT.SIGMA.	
(n,2n)	+7		FEI	Eval Conf	77Kiev	77	Bychkov+ SIG(NEUT−E),GRAPH	
(n,2n)	+6		IJE	Expt Conf	77Kiev	77	Krasin+ CALCUL,+N2NF,GRAPH	
(n,xn) x>2	1.2+7	1.8+7	LAS	Expt Prog	WASH−1006	Oct 58	Henkel.EXPT CFD CALC.N3N CS CURV.	
(n,xn) x>2	1.4+7		ALD	Expt Jour	JNE 14 100	61	Allen. N3N. 1 DATA INDEX LINE.	
(n,xn) x>2	1.3+7	1.9+7	ALD	Expt Jour	JNE 16 261	May 62	White+ N,3N.CFD STAT MDL. 0.89B,14MV	

92 Uranium 238

Quantity	Energy (ev) Min	Max	Lab	Type	Documentation Ref Vol Page	Date	Author, Comments	Data
(n,xn) x>2	Thrsh	1.5+7	ALD	Eval Rept	AWRE-O-79/63	Jan 64	Parker. EVAL FOR UKNDL-DFN 156.(N3N)	
(n,xn) x>2	Fiss		BNL	Theo Jour	NSE 23 238	Nov 65	Pearlstein.SPEC AVG STATMDL CALC N3N	
(n,xn) x>2	1.2+7	1.5+7	AI	Theo Conf	66Paris 1 429	Oct 66	Dunford+N3N.GRPH.NONSPHERICAL OPTMDL	
(n,xn) x>2	1.0+4	1.5+7	EDF	Eval Rept	EDF-HX-1/1375	Feb 68	Vastel.PART OF DFN 401 IN UK LIBRARY	
(n,xn) x>2	1.4+7		ALD	Expt Rept	AWRE-O-47/69	Aug 69	Mather+ N3N. LARGE LIQUID SCIN.	+
	1.4+7			Data	EXFOR20794.014	Oct 78	1PNT.SIGMA.	
(n,xn) x>2	7.0+6	1.2+7	ALD	Expt Rept	AWRE-O-72/72	Nov 72	Mather+ N,3N. REL U-238(N,F)	+
	7.0+6	1.2+7		Data	EXFOR20795.013	Oct 78	1PNT.SIGMA.	
(n,xn) x>2	2.0+6	2.0+7	BRC	Eval Conf	75Kiev 1 239	May 75	Jary. (N,3N) STATMOD CALC,VALUES GVN	
	2.0+6	1.5+7		Conf	JAERI-M-5984	Feb 75	- .P 76.STATMOD/OPTMOD. CURVES.N3	
				Rept	CEA-R-4647	Jan 75	- . EVAL,STAT MDL, 15 VALS.	
(n,xn) x>2	1.4+7		FEI	Expt Rept	FEI-671	76	Baryba+ (N,N')+(N,3N) N-SPEC	
(n,xn) x>2	1.2+7	1.5+7	BRC	Expt Jour	NIM 135 511	Jun 76	Frehaut.N3N.GD LOADD SCIN.EXP DTLS.	+
				Conf	75Kiev 4 303	May 75	- + (N,3N).LIQSCIN,SIG(E)TABLE	
				ExTh Conf	75Kiev 1 216	May 75	Jary+ EVAL CFD EXPTS,TABLE+CURVE	
				Expt Conf	75Wash. 855	Mar 75	Frehaut+ TBL.GRPH.REL 238U(N,F)	
				Conf	70Helsinki 2 109	Jun 70	+66. SIG TBD,LIQUID SCINT	
	1.2+7	1.5+7		Data	EXFOR20416.022	Jul 75	7PTS.SIGMA.	
(n,xn) x>2	+6		IJE	Theo Conf	77Kiev	77	Krasin+ N3N,CALCUL,+N,3NF,GRAPH	
n Emission	1.8+7	1.9+7	ALD	Expt Jour	JNAB 16 261	May 62	White.(N,4N)EST 0.5+-.6B,0.15+-.6B	
n Emission	1.4+7		FEI	Expt Jour	IZV 32 653	Apr 68	Salnikov+ E SPECS OF SECONDARY NEUTS	+
				Rept	FEI-441	73	- + DOUBLEDIFFSIG,TBL+GRAPHS	
				Jour	BAS 32 600	69	.ENGLISH TRANSL OF IZV 32 653 4/68	
	1.4+7			Data	EXFOR40332.002	Feb 76	DOUBLE-DIFF CS AT 92DEG, 61 PNTS	
n Emission	Thrsh	1.4+7	CCP	Eval Rept	ICD-6 212	70	Popov+ TABLE OF RECOMMENDED COEFS	
n Emission	1.4+7		LRL	Expt Prog	ERDA-NDC-2 76	May 75	Wong.PLSD.SPHER.MEASMT.TBL.GRPH.	
(n,p)	1.4+7		SAH	Comp Jour	NP 60 273	Nov 64	Chatterjee.MEAN OF EXPT CFD SHELLMOD	
(n,p)	1.5+7		MNZ	Expt Jour	RCA 11 168	Jun 69	Trautmann+,ACTIV METHOD	
(n,p)	6.0+5	3.0+7	KFK	Expt Rept	KFK-1495	Mar 71	Cierjacks+ TOF SPEC OF SCAT EVENTS	
(n,np)	1.5+7		MNZ	Expt Jour	RCA 11 168	Jun 69	Trautmann+,ACTIV METHOD	
(n,t)	2.0+6	7.0+6	ALD	Expt Jour	NP 65 236	Mar 65	Batchelor. = 1 DATA INDEX LINES	+
(n,t)	1.5+7		JUL	Comp Conf	72Budapest 50	Aug 72	Qaim. (N-Z)/A SYSTEMATICS ,GRPH	
(n,α)	1.4+7		ALD	Expt Jour	PPS 73 215	Feb 59	Coleman+. ACTIVATION	+
(n,α)	1.4+7		CIS	Theo Jour	NP 51 460	Feb 64	Facchini+STATMOD SIG XPT/CALC=14K	
(n,α)	Maxwl		PR	Expt Jour	ZP 177 451	Feb 64	Almodovar+ SEMICOND DET	
(n,α)	1.0-3	1.8+3	UK	Eval Rept	AEEW-R-351	Feb 64	Barrington+(WIN).UKNDL LOW EN REVISN	
(n,α)	1.5+7		MNZ	Expt Jour	RCA 11 168	Jun 69	Trautmann+,ACTIV METHOD	
(n,α)	1.5+7		DEB	Comp Jour	REA 7 4 93	Dec 69	Csikai+ SIG+HL COMPILTN,N-ACTIV-ANAL	
(n,α)	1.4+7	1.5+7	JYV	Eval Rept	JU-RR-3/1970	Jun 70	Leppaemaeki+ TABLE OF EVAL AVG SIG	
(n,α)	Maxwl		ILL	Expt Prog	BLG-515	76	Asghar+ VALUE GIVEN.ABST.	
(n,α)	Maxwl		GRE	Expt Jour	NP/A 259 429	Mar 76	Asghar+ ALPHAS DET. SIG=1.3+-0.6MUB.	+
	2.5-2			Data	EXFOR20588.002	Aug 76	1PNT.SIGMA.	
(n,nα)	1.5+7		KFI	Expt Jour	PL 22 475	Sep 66	Adam+ DIRECT (N,AN) CS SMALL	
	1.4+7			Jour	AHP 20 227	Mar 66	- . SIG LESS THAN 0.5 MB	
Fission	Maxwl		MIN	Expt Jour	PR 57 546	Mar 40	Nier+ MASS SPECTR SEPARION OF ISOT.	
				Jour	PR 57 748	Apr 40	.CONTINUED	
Fission	Maxwl		GES	Expt Jour	PR 57 749	Apr 40	Kingdon+ FISSION RATE	
Fission	+6		MIN	Expt Jour	PR 57 748	Apr 40	Nier+ EVIDENCE FOR FAST N FISS ONLY	
				Jour	PR 57 546	Mar 40	.CONTINUED	
Fission	+6	+7	COP	Theo Jour	PR 58 864	Nov 40	Bohr. PROB INC ABOV 10MV BY N ESCAPE	
Fission	3.4+6	5.9+6	LAS	Expt Rept	LA-520	Mar 46	Williams.	+
	3.4+6	5.9+6		Data	EXFOR12312.004	Jun 76	. 3 PTS. SIGMA	
Fission	1.4+7		LAS	Expt Rept	LAMS-774	Sep 48	Phillips+	+
	1.4+7			Data	EXFOR12495.002	Jun 76	. 1 PT.	
Fission	1.4+7		LAS	Expt Rept	LA-719	Dec 48	Nyer.	
	1.4+7			Data	EXFOR12514.002	Jun 76	. 1 PT. SIGMA	
Fission	3.0+4	1.4+6	WES	Expt Jour	PR 75 785	Mar 49	Shoupp+ EXCIT FN FOR FISS THRESHOLD	
Fission	Spont		NIH	Expt Jour	PR 76 702	Sep 49	Yagoda+ EMULSION,T1/2 FOR SPON FISS	
Fission	2.5+6		LAS	Expt Rept	LA-1571	Jul 53	Jarvis+	+
Fission	Fast		KJL	Expt Jour	NUC 13 2 67	Feb 55	Raisic.D27 PM D03B AVG OVER SPECTRUM	+
	Fiss			Data	EXFOR20076.	Sep 71	2PTS.	
Fission	1.0+4	3.0+6	ANL	Revw Conf	55Geneva 5 347	Aug 55	Okrent+.P609,GRAPH,NO EXPT DETAILS	
Fission	Pile		HAR	Revw Conf	55Geneva 5 331	Aug 55	Holmes+.P404,RATIO PU239/U 238 GVN	
Fission	1.4+7		HAR	Expt Rept	AERE-NP/R-1996	Jun 56	Uttley+.BACK TO BACK FISS CHAMBER	+
Fission	Pile		ANL	Expt Jour	NSE 1 193	Jul 56	Kaufmann+,EBR,CURVS REL U235,CFD TH	
Fission	1.0+6	4.0+6	SAC	Expt Abst	PHY 22 1187	Nov 56	Ballini+ NDG. VDG SOURCE	+

92 Uranium 238

Quantity	Energy (ev) Min	Max	Lab	Type	Documentation Ref Vol Page	Date	Author, Comments	Data
Fission	4.2+5	3.0+6	ORL	Expt	Jour PR 104 1654	Dec 56	Lamphere.CURVE	+
	4.2+5	4.3+6		Prog	ORNL-1926 11	55	- .	
	4.2+5	4.3+6		Data	EXFOR12338.005	Jun 76	. 147 PTS. SIGMA	
	4.2+5	3.0+6		Data	EXFOR12338.	Jun 76	. 90 PTS. SIGMA+RATIO U235	
Fission	Fast		HAR	Expt	Rept AERE-R/R-2151	57	Absalom+ ZEPHYR+TH ENVELOPE.	
					Jour BJAS 5 32	56	Shepherd+.ZEPHYR REACTOR	
Fission	Fiss		LAS	Expt	Jour JNE 4 38	Jan 57	Leachman+ (756+ -8MB)/(U235 THR NU)	+
	Fiss			Data	EXFOR12448.002	Jun 76	. 1 PT.	
Fission	1.0+6	6.1+7	KAP	Eval	Rept KAPL-1756 1	Jun 57	Baraff.TBL D25LETHARGYSTEPS	
Fission	8.0+5	7.0+6	LAS	Expt	Rept LA-2122	Jun 57	Henkel.CURV,REPLACES LA-1714	
Fission	3.0+4	3.0+6	HAR	Expt	Jour PPSA 70 573	Aug 57	Allen+.SIGF TO +-3PERCENT,AND RATIOS	+
Fission	1.1+6	3.9+6	LAS	Expt	Conf 57Col.Univ § 3B76	Sep 57	Northrop+ EXCIT CURV FROM D,P STRIPP	
Fission	1.4+6	3.7+6	ORL	Expt	Abst BAP 3 37	Jan 58	Schmitt+	+
	1.4+6	3.7+6		Data	EXFOR11541.002	Jun 76	. 48 PTS. SIGMA	
Fission	5.0+5	2.0+7	BNL	Comp	Conf 58Geneva 16 8	Sep 58	Hughes.PPR2483,CURVE,MANY REFS	
Fission	3.0+6	1.1+7	KUR	Expt	Conf 58Geneva 16 136	Sep 58	Kalinin+.PPR2149,CURVE,CYCLOTRON	+
Fission	1.0+6	1.0+7	LAS	Revw	Conf 58Geneva 15 344	Sep 58	Hemmendinger.PPR663,CURVE,MANY REFS	
Fission	1.4+7		SAC	Expt	Conf 58Geneva 16 106	Sep 58	Billaud+.PPR1186,VAL GVN,C-W	
Fission	Thrsh	Up	LAS	Expt	Prog WASH-1006	Oct 58	Stokes. SLOPE AS U233 238 DPXPRT	
Fission	1.5+7		CCP	Expt	Jour AE 5 657	Dec 58	Flerov+ (1952 WORK) 1.13+-0.05 BARN	+
					Jour JNEA 11 173	Feb 60	TRANSLATN.*	
					Jour SJA 5 1600		58 TRANSLATN.*	
Fission	1.5+7		CCP	Expt	Jour AE 5 659	Dec 58	Berezin+ 14.6MEV U235/U238=2.03+-.09	
					Jour JNEA 11 175	Feb 60	TRANSLATN.*	
					Jour SJA 5 1604		58 TRANSLATN.*	
Fission	1.7+6	4.1+6	ORL	Expt	Jour PR 115 1707	59	Murray+	+
	1.7+6	4.1+6		Data	EXFOR11105.004	Jun 76	. 11 PTS. SIGMA	
Fission	4.0+5	2.0+6	TRM	Revw	Conf 59Calcutta 152	Feb 59	Ramanna. SIG(E) CFD INEL-NEUT-LVLS	
Fission	2.5+6		CCP	Expt	Jour AE 8 137	Feb 60	Soloveva. TERNARY FISSION 1 IN 600	
					Jour JNAB 15 62	Sep 61	TRANSLATN.*	
					Jour SJA 8 124	May 61	TRANSLATN.*	
Fission	Pile		HAR	Expt	Rept AERE-R-3205	Feb 60	Carter+ FISSION RATIO TO U 235.	
					Rept AERE-M-723	Aug 60	+ RELATIVE U-235.	
Fission	Fiss		ALD	Eval	Rept AWRE-O-02/60	Apr 60	Hinves+AWRE EVAL DATA CFD XPT.	
Fission	+5	+7	GEA	Revw	Conf 60S-Vienna 383	Jun 60	Moteff+ THRS-SIG-TBL FOR DOSIMETRY	
Fission	6.7+0		HAN	Expt	Rept HW-67219	Oct 60	Leonard+UPPER LIMIT ON FISSION	
Fission	Fiss		KUR	Revw	Conf 60Vienna 159	Oct 60	Bondarenko+.TABLE,EXPT DESCRIBED	
Fission	1.0+7	2.1+7	CCP	Expt	Jour AE 9 399	Nov 60	Pankratov+.TOF,FISS CH,NORM AT 14MEV	+
Fission	1.4+7	1.5+7	KYU	Expt	Priv KATASE	61	C-W.PPL.S AT 3 ES	+
	1.4+7	1.5+7		Data	EXFOR20299.003	Jun 74	3PTS.SIGMA.	
Fission	1.5+7		ORL	Expt	Jour PR 121 827	Feb 61	Schmitt+	+
	1.5+7			Data	EXFOR11530.003	Jun 76	. 1 PT. SIGMA	
Fission	1.3+7	1.9+7	ALD	Expt	Jour JNAB 14 85	May 61	Adams+.TABLE+CURVE.REL SIGMA NP	+
Fission	7.1+5	1.0+7	B+W	Eval	Rept BAW-158	Jun 61	Roach+ AVERAGED SIG 9 GROUPS	
Fission	Maxwl		KUR	Expt	Conf 61Vienna 3 315	Aug 61	Leipunskij+ SIG GIVN,TABLE	
	Pile			Conf	58Geneva 12 3	Sep 58	- +.PPR2038,VAL U238/PU239	
	Maxwl			Rept	ANL-TR-9	62	. ENGL TRANSL OF 61VIENNA 3 315	
Fission	1.4+7		TAT	Expt	Conf 62Madras 71	Feb 62	Ramanna+.GRAPHS,BINARY+TERNARY FISS	
Fission	Fiss		AI	Expt	Conf 62Harwell 2 385	Dec 62	Strominger. SIG IN VARIOUS CORES,TBL	
Fission	1.3+6	+7	ANL	Expt	Conf 62Harwell 2 275	Dec 62	Rossin+ GROUP SIGS IN FIS-SPEC,TABLE	
Fission	Fiss		EGG	Eval	Conf 62Harwell 2 487	Dec 62	Humpherys. GRPH EFF-SIG,RECOMM VALUE	
Fission	Fiss		GDT	Revw	Conf 62Harwell 1 153	Dec 62	Romanko+FISS AVG. VAL GVN.	
Fission	1.0+6	1.0+7	ISP	Revw	Conf 62Harwell 1 27	Dec 62	Bresesti+ SIG(E) GRAPH,THRESHOLD-DET	
Fission	3.0+6	3.6+7	CCP	ExTh	Jour AE 14 177	Feb 63	Pancratov+.TOF SC CURVE GIVEN	+
					Jour SJA 14 167		63 . ENGL OF AE 14 177	
Fission	1.4+7		CIS	Expt	Jour NP 43 124	May 63	Mangalajo+ XSECT APPROX CONST,1.3B	
Fission	Thrsh	1.5+7	UK	Eval	Rept AWRE-O-79/63	Jan 64	Parker.(ALD).UKNDL-DFN 156	
Fission	2.5+6	1.4+7	CCP	Expt	Jour AE 16 144	Feb 64	Drapchinskii+ REL TERNARY FIS RATIOS	
					Jour JNAB 19 69	Jan 65	TRANSLATN.*	
					Jour SJA 16 164	Feb 64	TRANSLATN.*	
Fission	1.4+7		THU	Expt	Jour NSF 3 3 1	Feb 64	LIEN-SHENG CHUANG+ EXPTL SIGMA GIVEN	
Fission	Pile		CCP	Expt	Jour AE 17 113	Aug 64	Bondarenko+VAL GVN REL TO U-235(N,F)	+
					Jour SJA 17 821	Aug 64	TRANSLATN.*	
Fission	Pile		CCP	Expt	Jour AE 17 294	Oct 64	Batyrbekov+VAL GVN REL TO PU239(N,F)	+
					Jour SJA 17 1025	Oct 64	TRANSLATN.*	
Fission	+5	+7	RLY	Revw	Conf 64Vienna 56	Dec 64	Kronberger.FAST REACTOR,1-GROUP SIGS	
Fission	2.0+6	2.0+6	ALD	Expt	Jour NP 65 236	Mar 65	Batchelor+	+
Fission	1.7+6	4.6+6	CAT	Expt	Jour NP 63 641	Mar 65	Emma+ MIN AT 3.3MEV 0.42B PH PLATES	+

92 Uranium 238

Quantity	Energy (ev) Min	Max	Lab	Type	Documentation Ref Vol Page	Date	Author, Comments	Data
Fission	Fiss		IIT	Comp	Conf 65IAEA 251	Mar 65	Barrall+ CALC SIGS,3 SPECS,CFD EXPT	
Fission	Fiss		LAS	Expt	Abst DA 25 6704	May 65	Grundl. U235 SPEC., REL U235	
Fission	1.4+7		FTI	Expt	Jour SPD 10 617	66	.ENGLISH OF DOK 163 71	
					Jour DOK 163 71	Jul 65	Komar+ (NF)(N,NF)(N,2NF)SIGMA GIVEN	
Fission	4.0+5	1.0+7	KFK	Eval	Rept KFK-120 1	Feb 66	Schmidt.OTHERS' XPTS+CURVE	
	6.0+5	1.0+7			Rept KFK-120 2	Dec 62	- .GRAPHS AND TABULATED DATA.	
Fission	Spont		JAE	Expt	Rept JAERI-1102 95	Mar 66	Ishimori.TD5=35 E20 MIN PM 20TO30PC	
Fission	None		BRK	Revw	Jour NP 81 1	Jun 66	Myers+ TABLE 2 FISS BARRIER	
Fission	1.5+7		KFI	Expt	Jour PL 22 475	Sep 66	Adam+ DIRECT (N,FN) CS SMALL	
Fission	None		ANL	Expt	Conf 66Vienna 613	Oct 66	Armani.FISSION RATE,TH OF EXP,NODATA	
					Conf 63Amsterdm 227	Sep 63	.SEE ALSO	
Fission	6.1+6	1.4+7	HEB	Eval	Conf 66Paris 2 309	Oct 66	Pazy+ CORR-FACTORS BY INTEG EXPT,TBL	
Fission	None		KAP	Eval	Conf 66Paris 2 267	Oct 66	Francis+ NDG,XPT FIT TO OPTMDL	
	Thrsh	1.5+7			Rept KAPL/CSNL-4 66	Jun 66	Lubitz+ FISS AV 265 MB	
Fission	1.0+5	1.5+7	AI	Eval	Rept NAA-SR-M-12314	Mar 67	Dunford.NONSPHERICAL OPTMDL ANALYSIS	
					Conf 66Paris 1 429	Oct 66	- . NONSPHERCL OPTMDL, CURV.	
Fission	1.0+6	2.3+7	LAS	Expt	Prog WASH-1074 75	Apr 67	Hansen+ REVISED 1956 SIGS	+
					Prog WASH-1074 135	Nov 66	- + REVISED 1956 SIGS TBP	
	1.0+6	1.0+7			Rept LA-2114	Feb 57	Henkel+ ABSOL CURV REVIEWS ALL DATA	
	1.0+6	2.3+7			Data EXFOR12316.007	Jun 76	. 44 PTS. SIGMA.	
Fission	1.0+3	1.5+7	LAS	Eval	Prog WASH-1074 79	Apr 67	Diven. NDG SEE EANDC(US)-96U	
	1.0+3	1.4+7	RLY	Eval	Rept AHSB(S)R-124	May 67	HART UPDATES NSE26 149. UKAEA DFN338	
	1.0+3	1.4+7	UK	Eval	Rept AHSB(S)R-124	May 67	Hart.(RLY).UK - DFN 338.UPDATES NSE 26	
	1.0-3	1.8+3			Rept AEEW-R-351	Feb 64	Barrington+(WIN).UKNDL LOW EN REVISN	
Fission	1.3+7	1.8+7	NRD	Expt	Jour HP 13 654	Jun 67	Rago+	+
	1.3+7	1.8+7			Data EXFOR12284.002	Jun 76	. 16 PTS. SIGMA	
Fission	Pile		WIN	Expt	Rept AEEW-R-526	Jun 67	Stevenson+.FISS RATIO TO U235.ZEBRA	+
Fission	1.0+6	1.4+7	ALD	Expt	Jour JNE 21 671	Aug 67	White+ 3ES REL U235. CFD OTHER DATA	
Fission	1.2+6	1.4+7	LAS	Expt	Jour NSE 30 39	Oct 67	Grundl+DETECTOR EXCITATION MEASTS	+
	1.1+6	1.7+6			Data EXFOR10416.004	Dec 74	. 2 PTS. SIGMA	
Fission	Pile		FEI	Expt	Jour AE 23 396	Nov 67	Lejpunskij.RATIO REL U235(N,F),PILE	
					Jour EAF 23 5 21	Nov 67	. FRENCH TRANSL OF AE 23 396 11/67	
					Jour SJA 23 1150	Nov 67	.ENGLISH TRANSL OF AE 23 396 11/67	
Fission		1.4+7	SOR	Revw	Conf IAEA-107 57	68	Ben-David.GRPH THRS-SIG(NEUT-E) GVN	
	1.0+6	2.1+7	FEI	Expt	Jour YF 7 274	Feb 68	Maksjutenko+ GRPH=SIG+DELAYED NEUTS	
					Jour SNP 7 189	Aug 68	. ENGL OF YF 7 274	
Fission	1.0+6	5.0+6	LAS	Expt	Conf 68Wash. 627	Mar 68	Stein+ VDG TOF TBL+CURV U238/U235	+
					Rept LA-DC-9205	67	.EQUIVALENT	
					Conf 66Paris 1 419	Oct 66	.SUPERSEDED	
	1.0+6	5.0+6			Data EXFOR12452.003	Jun 76	. 14 PTS. SIGMA	
Fission	Fiss		MOL	Expt	Conf 68Wash. 2 1263	Mar 68	Fabry+ 353+ -30MB	+
	Fiss				Data EXFOR20264.008	May 74	1PNT.SIGMA.	
Fission	5.0+5	1.0+7	ANL	Eval	Jour NSE 32 35	Apr 68	Davey. RE-EVALUATION OF DATA	
	1.0+3	1.0+7			Jour NSE 26 149	Oct 66	- . EVALUATION	
	6.0-1	1.0+7			Conf 66Wash. 796	Mar 66	- .CURVE EVALUATED DATA	
Fission	Fiss		BNW	Theo	Rept BNWL-SA-1794	Apr 68	Mcelroy. SAND 2 CALCULATN.	
Fission	Pile		CCP	Expt	Jour AE 25 292	Oct 68	Golubev+ EXPTL+CALC MEAN SIG VAL GVN	
					Jour EAF 25 4 37	Oct 68	TRANSLATN.*	
Fission	Spont		CCP	Expt	Jour AE 25 428	Nov 68	Shukoljukov+.SPON FISS LIFETIME	
Fission	Pile		CCP	Theo	Jour AE 25 466	Dec 68	Usynin.AVG SUM SIG(N,G)+SIG(N,F) GVN	
					Jour SJA 25 1290	Dec 68	TRANSLATN.*	
Fission	-		TPI	Theo	Jour YF 9 102	Jan 69	Korostov+ CV,SHELL CORR,LIQU-DROP-E	
					Jour SNP 9 62	Jul 69	TRANSLATN.*	
Fission	1.3+7	1.5+7	WWA	Expt	Rept INR-970	Feb 69	Turkiewicz. FLUCT IN EXCIT FUNCT	
					Rept INR-830	Dec 67	- .CURVE,SCINT,EXPT DESCRBD	
Fission	1.5+6	1.3+7	CAD	Eval	Rept EANDC(E)120L	Mar 69	Barre+RAVIER EVAL OF INTEGRAL MEAS	
	1.0+4	1.5+7			Rept EDF-HX-1/1375	Feb 68	Vastel.PART OF DFN 401 IN UK LIBRARY	
Fission	1.5+7		STF	Expt	Rept AFWL-TR-68-134	Mar 69	Barrall.	+
	1.5+7				Data EXFOR10022.025	Nov 72	. 1 PT. SIGMA.	
Fission	Fast		JAE	Expt	Conf 69London § 1.7	Jun 69	Kuroi+ RATIO U235,EVALS CFD INT EXPT	
Fission	Spont		COP	Revw	Conf 69Vienna 155	Jul 69	Strutinsky+PPR203. HL GVN,'SHELL-TH'	
				Theo	Conf 68DUBSY 431	Jul 68	- +,INTERM. STATES IN FISS.	
Fission	Spont		FR	Expt	Conf 69Vienna 952	Jul 69	Monnin+PPR83. SPON FISSN HALF-LIFE	
Fission	None		LAS	Expt	Conf 69Vienna 918	Jul 69	Britt+PPR101.(D,P FISSN)CFD(N,FISSN)	
Fission	4.0+5	1.0+7	TRM	Eval	Rept BARC/I-96	70	Kapil. 6 GROUP SIG,2 N-SPECS,TABLES	
Fission	1.4+7		KFI	Expt	Prog INDC(HUN)-1G	Mar 70	Nagy+ HLS+SIG,SPON-FISSN-ISOMER U238	
Fission	1.0+4	2.0+7	BNW	Eval	Rept BNWL-1312	May 70	Simons+ TABLE+CURVE	
Fission	+6	+7	HAR	Revw	Rept STI/DOC/10-107	May 70	Wright. PAGE37,THRESHOLD DETECT DATA	

92 Uranium 238

Quantity	Energy (ev) Min	Max	Lab	Type	Documentation Ref Vol Page	Date	Author, Comments	Data
Fission	Fiss		ISP	Expt	Jour NSE 40 331	May 70	Bresesti+ EXCITATION CURVE.AVG SIGMA	+
	Fiss				Data EXFOR20734.011	Apr 77	1PNT.SIGMA.	
Fission	+5	+7	ANL	Revw	Conf 70Helsinki 2 119	Jun 70	Davey.112.STATUS OF DATA ABOVE RESON	
Fission	+6	+7	GEB	Revw	Conf 70Helsinki 1 17	Jun 70	Greebler+102. UNCERTAINTY+REACT CALC	
Fission	+5	+7	HAR	Revw	Conf 70Helsinki 1 267	Jun 70	James.107. ACCURACY CFD REACTOR COST	
Fission	Spont		SWT	Expt	Jour HPA 43 593	Nov 70	Hahn. HL SPON FISS, ROTAT CHAMBER	
Fission	Spont		MRY	Theo	Prog ORO-4028-28	71	Jackson+. SPON FISSION HALF-LIFE GVN	
Fission	+6	+7	DUB	Expt	Rept JINR-P3-5528	Jan 71	Gangrskij+U238(N,N' + 2N)ISOM FISSN	
Fission	2.5+6		RI	Expt	Jour AE 30 55	Jan 71	Kuks+ ABSOL EXPT,A-COUNTING,SIG GIVN	+
					Rept INDC(CCP)-15	Dec 71	*P45,ENG OF YFI-10	
					Jour SJA 30 64	Aug 71	*ENGL OF AE 30 55	
					Rept YFI-10 41	May 71	*	
	2.5+6				Data EXFOR40081.001	Nov 71	(N,FISSION) CROSS-SECTION	
Fission	Thrsh		CCP	Expt	Conf 71Moscow	Feb 71	Vorotnikov+.ABST,SIG(NEUT-E)	
Fission	Pile		MTR	Expt	Conf 71Knoxvill 79	Mar 71	Scoville.RATIO TO U235 NF	
Fission	Fiss		IAE	Eval	Conf KNS 3 77	Jun 71	Bak+ RECOMMENDED AVG SIG CFD OTHERS	
	1.0+5	2.0+7			Jour KNS 3 77	Jun 71	BAK+ FIT TO EXPTS,POINT SIG TBL+GRPH	
Fission	Pile		ORL	Expt	Abst ANS 14 381	Jun 71	Jenkins+. EFFECTIVE SIG=189MB	
Fission	1.0+4	1.0+5	LAS	Expt	Jour PR/C 4 220	Jul 71	Silbert+.NUCL SHOT. AVG SIG MEASURED	+
	1.0+4	1.0+5			Data EXFOR10290.003	Jan 73	. 2 PTS. SIGMA.	
Fission	Fiss		ANL	Revw	Conf 71Vienna 3	Aug 71	Smith. EXPTL AVG SIGS CFD CALC, TBL	
Fission	Fiss		WIN	Revw	Conf 71Vienna 33	Aug 71	Campbell+ REVIEW OF EXPTL SIGMA,TBL	
	Fast				Conf 70Helsinki 2 391	Jun 70	- .116. MICROSCOPIC VS INTEGRL	
Fission	Fiss		AMS	Expt	Jour JNE 25 457	Sep 71	Pauw+ CF252 SPEC,SIG=310+-25MB	
Fission	Fiss		IAE	Revw	Rept INDC(NDS)-47	72	Vlasov+ REVIEW DATA STATUS ,TBL+GRPH	
Fission	1.7+6	3.3+6	MOS	Expt	Jour NP/A 180 241	Jan 72	Melikov+ REACT TIME BY SHADOW EFFECT	
	3.0+6				Jour YF 12 50	Jul 70	- + TIME OF FISSION PROCESS GVN	
					Jour SNP 12 27	Jan 71	- + ENGLISH OF YF 12 50	
Fission	1.0+3	1.0+6	HAR	Eval	Prog AERE-PR/NP18	Mar 72	Gayther+LINAC TOF NU*SIGF GRPH TBC	
Fission	1.4+7		BAS	Expt	Prog EANDC(OR)116L	Jun 72	Noelpp+LIFETIME OF COMPOUNDNUCLEUS	
					Abst HPA 45 55	Jun 72	- + LIFETIME OF COMPOUNDNUCLEUS	
					Priv SWISS PH 5	Oct 71	- + BLOCKING EFF,ANGDIST IN UO2	
Fission	-		GEL	ExTh	Jour NP/A 187 305	Jun 72	Weigmann+ F.B.PARAMS FROM DATA ANAL.	
Fission	2.0+6	3.0+6	ANL	Expt	Jour JNE 26 483	Sep 72	Poenitz+ REL U235.TOF,GAS SCINT.	+
	2.0+6	3.0+6			Data EXFOR10232.	May 73	. 6PTS,RATIOS TO U235 NF	
Fission	1.0+6	5.0+6	ANL	Expt	Jour NSE 49 310	Nov 72	Meadows. RATIO TO U235 SIG MEASD	+
	9.0+5	5.3+6			Data EXFOR10237.	Jan 73	. 22PTS,RATIO TO U-235 NF	
Fission	2.5-2		JUL	Theo	Jour ZP 257 389	Dec 72	Mcminn. 3.21 E-4 BARNS	
Fission	Thrsh	1.6+7	BNW	Revw	Conf 73Paris 1 39	Mar 73	Wolkenhauer+ FROM ENDF/B FILE,GRAPH	
Fission	Fiss		SGA	Eval	Conf 73Paris 1 233	Mar 73	Eder+ FISS SPEC REL U238(N,F),TBLS	
					Rept SGAE-PH-141	Feb 73	.SAME AS 73PARIS,NO DETAILS,TBP	
Fission	2.0+6	3.0+6	CCP	Eval	Conf 73Kiev 1 227	May 73	Borisov+ SIG(NEUT-E),TBL,CFD OTHERS	
Fission	1.5+6		CCP	Expt	Conf 73Kiev 4 13	May 73	Alkhazov+ SIG GVN	
Fission	Fiss		CCP	Expt	Conf 73Kiev 4 21	May 73	Adamov+ SIG=288+-7MB AT CF-252SPON	+
	1.0+6				Data EXFOR40296.003	May 73	.DATA GVN	
Fission	Fiss		FEI	Eval	Conf 73Kiev 1 239	May 73	Abagjan+ AVG FIS-SIG CFD INTEGR XPTS	
					Rept INDC(CCP)-44	Jun 74	.P37. ENGLISH OF 73KIEV 1 239	
Fission	1.5+7		RI	Expt	Conf 73Kiev 4 13	May 73	Alkhazov+ DATA GIVEN	+
	1.5+7				Data EXFOR40256.002	Apr 75	.N-FISS CS AT 14.8 MEV GVN	
Fission	None		FRK	Theo	Jour NP/A 207 225	Jun 73	Albrecht. 2CENTRE SHELLMOD,DEF-E MAP	
Fission	7.2+2	3.5+4	RPI	Expt	Jour PRL 31 247	Jul 73	Block+. SUBTHRESHOLD FISSION SEEN	+
	1.0+4	1.0+5			Data EXFOR10569.	Jun 76	2 NF AVG CS+DATA UNOBTAINABLE.	
Fission	+7		CCP	Expt	Jour AE 35 47	Aug 73	Jurova+ SIGNF-U-238/SIGNF U-235,TBL	
Fission	Thrsh	2.0+7	RCN	Comp	Rept RCN-196	Oct 73	Zijp+COMPIL.EVAL.CS.FAST N.METROLGY	
	Fiss			Revw	Conf 73Paris 2 271	Mar 73	- .RECOMM INTEG CFD DIFF CALC,TBL	
Fission	5.0+5	2.5+6	TUE	Expt	Jour PL/B 48 25	Jan 74	Mueller+CFD SHAPE ISOM FISS,U+PU,NDG	
Fission	2.0+3	4.0+4	ORL	Expt	Conf JINR-D-37991	Apr 74	Harvey. PG157, SUBTHR FISS,GRPH+CURV	
Fission	1.0+2	2.0+7	HAR	Eval	Prog ANE 1 409	Jul 74	Sowerby+ LSQ WITH P9 U5 ABOVE .1MEV	
	6.0+6	2.0+7			Rept AERE-R-7273	Feb 73	- +LINKED EVAL U235 PU239 TBL	
					Rept AERE-M-2497	Feb 72	- +LINKED EVAL U235 PU239 TBL	
					Conf 70Helsinki 2 703	Jun 70	- + PPR34. EVAL WITH CAPT SIG	
Fission	1.0+3	3.0+7	ORL	Revw	Rept CONF-740903-7	Sep 74	De Saussure+OTH CFD.MEAS REL U 235.	
Fission	1.0+6	2.0+7	AUW	Theo	Prog INDC(SEC)-42	Dec 74	Satyanarayana+ ABS-MDL,CFD XPT,NDG	
Fission	5.0+5	1.8+7	IFL	Eval	Book LAPENAS	75	Lapenas. FULL DOCUM OF EVAL,TABLES	+
	Fiss				Book LAPENAS	75	- . EVAL DATA AVGD,VALUE GIVEN	
	5.0+5	1.8+7			Data VIEN-V0002.005	Nov 75	SIGMA AT 172 ENERGIES	
	Fiss				Data VIEN-V0003.005	Nov 75	WATT-SPECTRUM, 1 POINT	
Fission	Fiss		PTB	Eval	Rept PTB-FMRB-60	Feb 75	Alberts. CF252-SPC,EVAL DATA AVG,TBL	

92 Uranium 238

Quantity	Energy (ev) Min	Max	Lab	Type	Documentation Ref Vol Page	Author, Comments Date	Data
Fission	6.0+5	2.2+7	HAR Expt	Conf	75Wash. 568	Mar 75 Coates+U238/U235 FISS CS RATIO	+
	6.3+5	2.2+7		Conf	75Kiev 6 41	May 75 - + U238/U235 SIG(E).CFD,GRAPHS	
	6.3+5	2.2+7		Data	EXFOR20414.002	Dec 78 224PTS.SIGMA.	
Fission	Fiss		HED Expt	Conf	75Wash. 189	Mar 75 Mcelroy.235U THERM FISS SPECT AVG CS	
Fission	3.0+6	5.0+6	LAS Theo	Conf	75Wash. 129	Mar 75 Moore.GRPH R MATR STAT CALC CFD EXP	
Fission	9.0+5	2.0+7	NBS Revw	Conf	75Wash. 293	Mar 75 Carlson. GRPH CS CFD U235,NP237	
Fission	1.7+3	3.6+3	AAU Expt	Jour	NP/A 241 317	Apr 75 Andersen+ 3 ENS.T1/2 OF 239PU DEDUCD	
Fission	1.0+6	3.0+6	ANL Expt	Priv	MEADOWS	Apr 75 Meadows. U238/U235 RATIO	+
	1.0+6	3.0+6		Data	EXFOR10504.002	May 75 . 30 PTS. RATIO TO U235	
Fission	2.0+6	2.0+7	BRC Eval	Conf	75Kiev 1 239	May 75 Jary. STATMOD CALC,VALUES GIVEN	
Fission	1.0+6	2.0+7	BRC Eval	Conf	75Kiev 1 216	May 75 Jary+ EVAL CFD XPTS,TABLE+CURVE	
Fission	1.5+5	1.6+6	KUR Expt	Rept	YFI−20 9	May 75 Vorotnikov+ SIG(NEUT−E),TBL	+
	5.5+5	1.5+6		Conf	71Kiev	May 71 - +.SIG(NEUT−E),GRAPH	
	1.5+5	1.6+6		Rept	INDC(CCP)−66	Feb 76 .P 6. ENGL OF YFI−20 9	
	5.5+5	1.5+6		Prog	INDC(CCP)−30	Dec 72 .PG 19,ENGLISH OF YFI−12 22	
	1.6+5	1.5+6		Data	EXFOR40325.002	Oct 75 .SIG AT 71 EN GVN	
	5.5+5	1.5+6		Data	EXFOR40110.002	Nov 72 SIGMA AT 19 ES	
Fission	Spont		PSU Expt	Abst	ANS 22 676	Nov 75 LEE+(NU)(NF CS) AVG.CF252 SPEC.CFD.	
Fission	1.1+6	2.0+7	CRC Eval	Jour	NSE 58 377	Dec 75 Cross+ ANALYTICAL FIT TO DATA	
Fission	1.0+6	6.0+6	LAS Eval	Prog	LA−6164−PR 2	Dec 75 Stewart.NDG.DISCREPANCY IN NF CS.	
Fission	Fiss		MOL Expt	Prog	INDC(SEC)−51	Dec 75 Fabry.P85.AVG(U35−SPEC),CFD ENDF,TBL	
				Conf	75Wash. 254	Mar 75 - +INTEG CS.MOL STANDARD N FIELD	
Fission	0.0+0	1.0+7	CAI Theo	Jour	AKE 27 1 47	76 El Nadi+ QUASI−MOLECULAR MODEL	
Fission	Fast		FEI Expt	Rept	YK−23 127	76 Bychkov+ SIG U38/35,FAST−THERM ASSEM	
Fission	+3		GEL Expt	Prog	NEANDC(E)172 3	Feb 76 Migneco+LINAC TOF SUB−BARR FISS	
	6.5+2	1.3+3		Conf	75Wash. 597	Mar 75 Wartena+RES DATA.TOF.GRPH	
Fission	1.0+4	5.0+6	LRL Theo	Prog	ERDA−NDC−3 68	May 76 Gardner+ STAT MDL CALC.CFD ENDF.NDG	
Fission	5.3+6	1.0+7	ANL Expt	Jour	NSE 58 255	Oct 75 Meadows.TBL,GRPH 238/235U NF RATIO	+
	1.0+5	1.0+7		Conf	76ANL 73	Jun 76 - .U238/U235 RATIO.GRPH.CFD OTH	
	5.3+6	1.0+7		Data	EXFOR10506.002	Mar 76 . 20PTS.U238NF/U238NF CS RATIO	
Fission	1.0+6	3.0+7	ANL Eval	Conf	76ANL 156	Jun 76 Poenitz+U238/U235 EVAL.GRPH,TBL.CFD	
Fission	6.0+5	3.0+7	ANL Revw	Conf	76ANL	Jun 76 Poenitz+SUPPLEMENT TO CONF.DATA FILE	
Fission	1.2+6	2.0+7	KFK Expt	Conf	76ANL 246	Jun 76 Levgers+REL H SCT.NORM.TBL,GRPH.CFD	
Fission	7.0+6	1.4+7	LRL Expt	Prog	WASH−1006	Oct 58 Goldberg+ PRC SC CFD LA PRELIM	+
	7.0+6	1.4+7		Data	EXFOR12468.002	Jun 76 . 5 PTS. SIGMA	
Fission	1.5+6	2.0+7	BRC Revw	Conf	76Lowell 641	Jul 76 Michaudon.RVW OF FISSION PROCESSES	
Fission	7.0+5	2.0+7	GEL,Revw	Conf	76Lowell 1110	Jul 76 Liskien. STATUS AS STANDARD.	
Fission	Fast		LON Expt	Prog	NEANDC(E)172 8	Aug 76 Hannan+ REACTOR SPECT,RATIO TO U5NF	
Fission	2.8+6	1.8+7	TUD Expt	Prog	ZFK−315 172	Aug 76 Arlt+ SIG AT 4ES,1−2PERC PRECIS.TBD	
Fission	Fast		KTO Expt	Jour	NST 13 531	Oct 76 Kobayashi+.ACT.SIG=294+−15 MB	+
	1.5+6			Rept	NEANDC(J)42L31	76 - +	
	1.5+6			Data	EXFOR20693.016	Nov 76 1PNT.SIGMA.	
Fission	2.0+6	1.6+7	TRM Theo	Conf	76Ahmedabd 2 116	Dec 76 Chatterjee+ DELAY/PROMPT FISS.GRAPH	
Res Int Fiss	5.0−1	+6	COR Expt	Jour	NSE 46 31	Oct 71 Draper.INTEGRAL SIG TIMES E.4 SPECTR	
	+0	+1		Abst	DA/B 31 1466	Sep 70 - .EXPT FOR 4 SPEC,GOOD CFD CALC	
Alpha	Fast		CCP Expt	Jour	AE 20 60	Jan 66 Yurova+ 0.42+−.03 IN BR−1 FAST REACT	+
				Jour	JNE 21 106	Jan 67 TRANSLATN.*	
				Jour	EAF 20 1 90	Jan 66 TRANSLATN.*	
				Jour	SJA 20 75	Jan 66 TRANSLATN.*	
Alpha	0.0+0	6.0+6	FEI Eval	Prog	YFI−11 13	70 Vorobyeva+ ABST,TBL VALUE FOR 1.5MEV	
				Prog	INDC(CCP)−31	Dec 72 .PAGE 12,ENGLISH OF YFI−11 13	
Alpha	Pile		ANL Expt	Jour	NSE 45 87	Jul 71 Bretscher+.FAST SPEC.INTEG MEAST	
Alpha	Pile		ANL Expt	Jour	NSE 53 9	Jan 74 Dudey+. INTEGRAL MEASTS IN EBR−2.	
				Rept	ANL−7791	Jul 71 Heinrich+. INTEGRAL MEAST IN EBR−2	
Alpha	Fast		HAR Expt	Prog	UKNDC(75)P71	Jul 75 Crouch+ IRRADIATION DFR IN PROGRESS	
Eta	1.4+7		CCP Expt	Jour	AE 5 653	Dec 58 Flerov+ (1954) 3.71+−.20 SPHERE TRNS	+
				Jour	JNEA 11 169	Feb 60 TRANSLATN.*	
				Jour	SJA 5 1593	58 TRANSLATN.*	
Eta	1.4+7	1.4+7	ALD Expt	Jour	JNE 14 100	61 Allen. = 1 DATA INDEX LINES	+
Eta	1.2+7	1.9+7	ALD Expt	Jour	JNAB 16 261	May 62 White. SPHERE METHOD.TABLE, 3.1−4.1	+
Eta	1.0+3	1.5+7	UK Eval	Rept	AWRE−O−79/63	Jan 64 Parker.(ALD).UKNDL−DFN 156	
Eta	+5	+7	RLY Revw	Conf	64Vienna 56	Dec 64 Kronberger. VAL TABLE OF ETA+NU+SIGS	
Eta	1.0+6		LAS Expt	Rept	TID−22431	65 Barton+	
Eta	2.5−2	1.0+6	BEP Revw	Jour	KE 8 625	Jan 65 Wenzel. VAL FOR 3ES GVN,MANY REFS	
Eta	2.0+6	7.0+6	ALD Expt	Jour	NP 65 236	Mar 65 Batchelor+ CONSISTENT VALUES GIVEN	+
Eta	1.0+4	1.5+7	EDF Eval	Rept	EDF−HX−1/1375	Feb 68 Vastel.PART OF DFN 401 IN UK LIBRARY	
Eta	Thrsh	1.6+7	BNW Revw	Conf	73Paris 1 39	Mar 73 Wolkenhauer+ CALC FROM SIGS,GRAPH	
Nu	Spont		LAS Expt	Jour	PR 86 21	Apr 52 Segre.FROM U DATA+238 SPON DECAY CST	

92 Uranium 238

Quantity	Energy (ev) Min	Max	Lab	Type	Documentation Ref Vol Page	Date	Author, Comments	Data
Nu	2.0+6	1.4+7	LAS	Theo Rept	LA- 1863	Dec 54	Leachman.NEUT EMISSION PROBABILITY	
Nu	4.5+6		LAS	Expt Rept	LA- 1939	Aug 55	Bethe+ ALSO FISS SPEC NEUTS SPH TRNS	+
	4.5+6			Data	EXFOR12397.004	Jun 76	. 1 PT.	
Nu	1.4+7		HAR	Expt Jour	JIN 5 1	57	Cuninghame.NU=4+ -0.5	
Nu	1.5+6		LAS	Expt Priv	DIVEN	57	Diven.	+
	1.5+6			Data	EXFOR12436.003	Jun 76	. 1 PT.	
Nu	1.5+6		LAS	Expt Jour	PR 108 783	Nov 57	Terrell.	+
Nu	Fiss		CCP	Expt Jour	AE 4 187	Feb 58	Kuzminov+ REL U235 NU THR,PROMPT NS	
				Jour	JNE 9 153	Jun 59	TRANSLATN.*	
				Jour	SJA 4 250	58	TRANSLATN.*	
Nu	6.0-2	1.0+7	LAS	Eval Jour	NSE 4 166	Aug 58	Kiehn.10GROUPS FOR SN CALCULATIONS	
	-2	1.5+7	CCP	Expt Conf	58Geneva 15 353	Sep 58	Bondarenko+.PPR2187,CURVE CFD REFS	
Nu	Pile		LAS	Expt Conf	58Geneva 15 331	Sep 58	Leachman.PPR665,VAL REL TO U235 GVN	
Nu	Fiss	1.4+7	TRM	Expt Conf	58Geneva 15 364	Sep 58	Nargundkar+.PPR1632,2VALS GVN CFD TH	
Nu	1.4+7		CCP	Expt Jour	AE 5 653	Dec 58	Flerov+ (1954) 4.13+ -.24 SPHERE TRNS	
				Jour	JNEA 11 169	Feb 60	TRANSLATN.*	
				Jour	SJA 5 1593	58	TRANSLATN.*	
Nu	1.4+7		CCP	Expt Jour	AE 5 654	Dec 58	Flerov+ 4.45+ -.35, DOUBLE COINC RATE	+
				Jour	JNEA 11 171	Feb 60	TRANSLATN.*	
				Jour	SJA 5 1596	58	TRANSLATN.*	
Nu	1.4+6		ANL	Expt Jour	PR 115 1242	59	Smith+	+
	1.4+6			Data	EXFOR12276.002	Jun 76	. 1 PT.	
Nu	2.3+6	1.6+7	CCP	Expt Rept	AEC-TR-3944	59	Kuz'Minov.3ES.AVG NU VS. E	
Nu	Spont		CCP	Expt Jour	ZET 37 406	Aug 59	Kuz'Minov.DECAY-CONST,HL,NU=2.1+ -.1	
				Jour	JET 10 290	Feb 60	TRANSLATN.*	
Nu	Spont		CCP	Theo Jour	AE 8 49	Jan 60	Gerling.VAL CALCD FROM HALFLIFE	
				Jour	SJA 8 41	Jan 61	TRANSLATN.*GERMAN KE3 774 8/60	
Nu	1.4+7		CCP	Expt Jour	ZET 38 671	Mar 60	Vasil'Ev. 4.28+ -0.30,CFD OTHER XPTS	+
				Jour	JET 11 483	Sep 60	TRANSLATN.*	
Nu	Fiss	1.4+7	CCP	Theo Jour	AE 8 409	May 60	Zysin+.VAL CALCD FROM FRGMNT-DISTRBS	
				Jour	SJA 8 343	Jun 61	TRANSLATN.*JNE AB17 41 1/61	
				Jour	KE 4 40	Jan 61	.TRANSLATN	
Nu	Fiss		BNL	Expt Jour	JNEA 12 101	Jun 60	Sher+. NU PROMPT REL U235 THR NF	
				Prog	BNL-694 3	Oct 61	- . NU=2.79,4.75	
Nu	1.5+6	4.0+6	CRC	Revw Rept	EANDC(CAN)-5	Jun 60	Hanna.(CRP-936) CORR.TO 3.2 MEV	
Nu	1.4+7		SAC	Expt Jour	JPR 21 617	Aug 60	Leroy.REL U235 THR,SPON+FISS SP=1MEV	+
				Conf	58Geneva 16 106	Sep 58	Billaud+.PPR1186,VAL GVN, C-W	
				Jour	JPR 19 66	Jan 58	- + REL U-235.	
Nu	2.3+6	3.8+6	FEI	Expt Book	NEJTRONFIZ 241	61	Kuz'Minov. 2ES,GRPH+TBL.BF3-COUNTER	
Nu	1.4+7		CCP	Expt Jour	AE 10 68	Jan 61	Flerov+.VAL GVN,GRAPHIT-PRISMA DTCTR	
				Jour	SJA 10 65	Nov 61	TRANSLATN.*JNE17 423 N/63	
				Jour	KE 4 574	Jul 61	.TRANSLATN	
Nu	Spont		RI	Revw Jour	UFN 73 655	Apr 61	Petrzhak+ TABLE,MANY REFS,DISCUSSION	
				Jour	SPU 4 305	Sep 61	. ENGL OF UFN 73 655	
Nu		1.5+7	ANL	Revw Conf	61Vienna 1 29	Aug 61	Smith.PPR76,CURVE MANY REFS	
Nu	1.4+7		ALD	Expt Jour	JNAB 15 102	Oct 61	Moat+,REL CF252 SPONT FIS,SCINT TANK	+
Nu	3.6+6	1.5+7	FOA	Expt Jour	NSE 11 397	Dec 61	Conde. 2ES. N-FRAG COINC. REL CF-252	+
				Jour	AF 29 33	Apr 65	- . NEW CORRECTIONS TO OLD VALS.	
				Conf	65Salzburg 2 57	Mar 65	- + DIFF CORRECTIONS.	
	3.6+6	1.5+7		Data	EXFOR20072.003	Sep 71	2PTS.PROMPT.	
Nu	Fiss		REH	Theo Rept	IA- 757	Jul 62	Sieger+ CALC FRM CHAIN-Y,CFD OTH.TBL	
Nu	Spont		FOA	Expt Jour	NSE 15 213	Feb 63	Conde+ LIQ SC. REL CF-252	+
Nu	Fast		FOA	Comp Rept	NP- 16440	Mar 63	Asplund-Nilsson. REVIEW TABLE.	
Nu	Spont		FOA	Comp Rept	NP- 16440	Mar 63	Asplund-Nilsson. REVIEW TABLE.	
Nu	1.4+7		THU	Expt Jour	CHP 1 9	Apr 63	Chuang+ VAL GVN.VDG,MANGANESE BATH	
Nu	Thrsh	1.5+7	UK	Eval Rept	AWRE-O-79/63	Jan 64	Parker.(ALD).UKNDL-DFN 156	
Nu	Thrsh	1.5+7	LRL	Expt Jour	JNAB 18 125	Mar 64	Schuster+ E DEPENDNCE THEOR,CFD EXPT	
Nu	3.5+6	6.5+6	ANL	Expt Prog	WASH-1048 12	Jun 64	Meadows+ PROMPT NU(E) REL TO CF252.	
Nu	1.5+6	1.5+7	FOA	Expt Jour	NSE 20 527	Dec 64	Asplund-Nilsson+ POSSIBLE STEP 6MEV	+
				Conf	73Kiev 4 130	May 73	Conde. SUMMARY OF NUBAR. NDG.	
				Rept	FOA4-A4368 411	Apr 64	Asplund-Nilsson+ SAME AS EANDC(OR)31	
	1.5+6	1.5+7		Data	EXFOR20075.002	Sep 71	9PTS. PROMPT	
Nu	+5	+7	RLY	Revw Conf	64Vienna 56	Dec 64	Kronberger. VAL TABLE OF ETA+NU+SIGS	
Nu	1.4+6	4.0+6	ALD	Expt Jour	NP 66 149	Apr 65	Mather+ PROMPT SC-T LEAST SQ FIT	+
Nu	2.1+6	4.9+6	HAR	Expt Jour	NP 71 228	Sep 65	Barnard+ AVG VALS FOR 2 INC ENEGIES	+
Nu	5.0+6	7.0+6	FEI	Expt Conf	66Paris 2 85	Oct 66	PPR110,D'JACHENKO+. NU GVN AT 2ES	
Nu	6.1+6	1.4+7	HEB	Eval Conf	66Paris 2 309	Oct 66	Pazy+ CORR-FACTORS BY INTEG EXPT,TBL	
Nu	1.0+3	1.5+7	LAS	Eval Prog	WASH-1074 79	Apr 67	Diven. NDG SEE EANDC(US)-96U	

92 Uranium 238

Quantity	Energy (ev) Min	Max	Lab	Type	Documentation Ref Vol Page	Author, Comments Date	Data
Nu	Fast		WAP	Theo	Jour NUK 10 177	Oct 67 Murley+ FAST FISS FACTOR IN U FUELROD	
Nu	Thrsh	1.5+7	AI	Eval	Jour JNE 22 79	Feb 68 Fillmore.DATA TBL,GRAPH.LEAST SQ FIT	
Nu	1.0+6	1.5+7	CAD	Eval	Rept EANDC(E)120L	Mar 69 Barre+ RAVIER EVAL OF INTEGRAL MEAS	
	1.0+4	1.5+7			Rept EDF-HX-1/1375	Feb 68 Vastel.PART OF DFN 401 IN UK LIBRARY	
		2.0+6	AUA	Expt	Prog AAEC/PR-31P 7	Apr 69 Boldeman. ABSTR,NU BAR(NEUT-E),NDG	
Nu	+6	+7	AE	Eval	Conf 70Helsinki 2 93	Jun 70 Almen+57. NU VERSUS TEMPERATURE PLOT	
Nu	+6	+7	GEB	Revw	Conf 70Helsinki 1 17	Jun 70 Greebler+102. UNCERTAINTY+REACT CALC	
Nu	Maxwl	1.5+7	HAR	Revw	Conf 70Helsinki 2 195	Jun 70 Colvin.PPR99. REPORT ON DATA STATUS	
Nu	1.5+6	6.0+6	FEI	Theo	Jour AE 29 130	Aug 70 Vorobeva+ RECOMMENDED NU(E) GRAPH	
					Conf 70Helsinki 2 177	Jun 70 .SAME AS AE 29 130 8/70	
	0.0+0	6.0+6		Eval	Prog YFI-11 13	70 Vorobyeva+ ABST,TBL VALUE FOR 1.5MEV	
					Prog INDC(CCP)-31	Dec 72 .PAGE 12,ENGLISH OF YFI-11 13	
	1.5+6	6.0+6		Theo	Jour SJA 29 835	Aug 70 .ENGLISH TRANSL OF AE 29 130 8/70	
Nu		1.5+7	ANL	Eval	Jour NSE 44 345	Jun 71 Davey. PROMPT NEUTS PER FISSION	
					Conf 70Helsinki 2 119	Jun 70 .SUPERSEDED.(P/112)	
Nu	4.5+5	1.5+7	ALD	Eval	Rept AWRE-O-44/71	Jul 71 Mather+ USE PRE-1971 DATA,3 ST LINES	
Nu	1.3+6		KUR	Expt	Jour AE 32 408	May 72 Savin+ TOF,NU-BAR AT 46ES, TBL+GRAPH	+
	1.3+6	7.0+6			Prog YFI-12 16	72 - + TOF,NUBAR(N-E),TBL,ABST	
	1.3+6	5.9+6			Conf 71Kiev	May 71 - + TABLE NU-BAR VS NEUT-E	
					Rept FEI-12 16	71 - +	
	1.3+6	7.0+6			Prog INDC(CCP)-30	Dec 72 .PG 13,ENGLISH OF YFI-12 16	
	1.3+6	5.9+6			Jour SJA 32 474	May 72 .ENGL TRANSL OF AE 32 408	
	1.3+6	5.9+6			Data EXFOR40138.002	Mar 73 .46 DATA LINES	
	Spont		IAE	Eval	Jour REA 10 637	Dec 72 Manero+ EXTENSIVE SURVEY,TBL,AVG VAL	
	1.4+6	1.5+7			Jour REA 10 637	Dec 72 - + SURVEY,TBLS+GRPHS,RECOMM VAL	
Nu	Maxwl		BUC	Revw	Rept IFA-RN-50	73 Cristu. NU(FRAGM-E,MASS.COMP-EXCIT	
	Fast				Rept IFA-RN-50	73 - . NU(FRAGM-E,MASS.COMP-EXCIT	
	1.4+6	1.5+7	BRC	Expt	Conf EANDC(E)154 67	Mar 73 Frehaut+ TOF.TAND.VDG.	+
					Conf 69Vienna 931	Jul 69 Soleilhac+ PPR93.NU(NEUT-E)OKS OTHER	
					Jour JNE 23 257	May 69 - +TOF.REF.IS CF252 SPON.FIS	
	1.4+6	1.5+7			Data EXFOR20490.002	Mar 76 29PTS.PROMPT.	
Nu	Spont		FOA	Expt	Jour JNE 25 331	Aug 71 Conde+.ALSO SPONT.FISS.HL REL U236	+
					Conf 73Kiev 4 130	May 73 - . NUBAR GIVN,CFD U238(G,F)	
					Priv CONDE	71 - + DATA FOR COMPILATION.TBP JNE	
	Spont				Data EXFOR20037.004	Sep 71 1PNT.PROMPT.	
	Spont				Data EXFOR20073.002	Sep 71 1PNT.PROMPT.	
Nu	5.0+6	1.7+7	LRL	Expt	Prog UCID-16514 6	Jun 74 Alvarez+	
Nu	0.0+0	6.0+6	FEI	Expt	Rept YK-15 3	Aug 74 Vorob'Eva+ NUBAR(NEUT-E),GRAPH,TBL	
Nu	4.0+5	1.5+7	TOH	Theo	Conf 75Wash. 342	Mar 75 Yamamoto+ STAT MODEL CALC CFD EXPT.	
Nu	1.4+6	4.0+6	FEI	Comp	Conf 75Kiev 5 170	May 75 Prokhorova+ NU(EN),EVAL ACCURACS.TBL	
	0.0+0	5.0+6		Eval	Rept YK-20/1 104	75 - + NUBAR(NEUT-E),GRAPH,TBL	
	5.0+4	5.0+6			Rept INDC(CCP)-91	Jun 76 . ENGL OF YK-20 104(TBLS+GRPHS GIVN)	
Nu	1.0+6	1.5+7	HED	Theo	Abst ANS 21 518	Jun 75 Schenter+TBL CALC FROM ENDF FP FILE	
Nu	+6		FEI	Expt	Jour AE 39 199	Sep 75 Nurpeisov+ NUBAR(NEUT-E),TBL,GRAPH	
	1.0+6	5.0+6			Conf 75Kiev 5 175	May 75 - + NUBAR(E),GRPH.CFD LINEAR	
					Jour SJA 39 807	Mar 76 . ENGLISH OF AE 39 199	
Nu	Spont		HED	Eval	Abst ANS 22 673	Nov 75 Johnson. TBL,GRPH.NU FROM SPON FISS	
Nu	1.6+6		ANL	Expt	Conf 61Vienna 1 125	Aug 61 Butler+.PPR36,VAL REL TO U235	+
	1.6+6				Data EXFOR12462.002	Jun 76 . 1 PT.	
Nu	0.0+0	1.5+7	BRC	Eval	Rept CEA-R-4791	Oct 76 Bois+NUBAR VS EN,CALC CFD EXP,TABLES	
Delayd Neuts	+7		WES	Expt	Jour PR 79 3	Jul 50 Sun+ DELAYED NEUTRON YIELDS CFD OTHR	
Delayd Neuts	Fiss		LAS	Expt	Jour NUC 13 10 49	Oct 55 Paxton+	
Delayd Neuts	Fiss		ANL	Expt	Jour NSE 1 174	May 56 Brunson+,EBR NUD=2.23+-.25 REL U235	
Delayd Neuts	Pile		HAR	Revw	Jour NPW 1 114	Jul 56 Cox. YIELD+HALF LIFES OF DEL-NEUTS	
Delayd Neuts	Fast		HAR	Expt	Jour JNE 4 141	Jun 57 Rose+ ZEPHYR. 5 GROUPS.TBL YLD+FRACT	+
Delayd Neuts	Fiss		LAS	Expt	Jour PR 107 1044	Aug 57 Keepin+,0.0412+-0.0017 N/FISS 6GRPS	
	Fast				Rept LA-1970	Oct 55 - . NEUT YLDS+SPECTR,CURVS+TABLS	
					Conf 55Geneva 4 162	Aug 55 - +.P/831. PRELIMINARY.	
Delayd Neuts	None		LAS	Theo	Jour JNE 7 13	Aug 58 Keepin.THEOR DEL NEUT PRECURSRS,YLDS	
					Jour SJA 4 339	Mar 58 .SEE ALSO	
					Jour AE 4 250	Mar 58 .SEE ALSO	
Delayd Neuts	2.4+6	1.5+7	FEI	Expt	Jour ZET 35 815	Sep 58 Maksjutenko. YLD OF 5GROUPS AT 3ES	+
					Jour AE 7 474	Nov 59 .YIELD AT 3ES REL U235 THERMAL NU	
					Jour JET 8 565	Mar 59 TRANSLATN.*	
					Jour SJA 7 943	Mar 61 .ENGLISH TRANSL OF AE 7 474 11/59	
					Jour JNE 12 141	Jun 60 .SECTION A.ENGL OF AE 7 474 11/59	
Delayd Neuts	Maxwl		OSL	Expt	Conf 58Geneva 15 373	Sep 58 Pappas+.PPR583,TBL CFD THEORIE	
Delayd Neuts	None		LAS	Expt	Abst BAP 4 31	Jan 59 Fisher. SCINT	

92 Uranium 238

Quantity	Energy (ev) Min	Max	Lab	Type	Documentation Ref Vol Page	Date	Author, Comments	Data
Delayd Neuts		2.3+6	ANL Revw	Conf	61Vienna 1 457	Aug 61	Meneghetti.MULTIGROUP DSTRBS,TABLE	
Delayd Neuts	2.0+6		LAS Revw	Jour	NUC 20 8 150	Aug 62	Keepin+	
Delayd Neuts	1.1+6	2.4+6	ANL Expt	Prog	WASH – 1041 4	Oct 62	COX.YIELD INCREASES NEAR THRESHOLD	
Delayd Neuts	2.3+6	1.5+7	FEI Expt	Rept	ICD – 3 75	66	Maksjutenko. TBL OF REL YIELD.TBP YF	+
				Conf	66Paris 2 45	Oct 66	.SAME DATA,REPORT SIMILAR TO ICD – 3	
				Jour	AE 19 46	Jul 65	.MORE DATA AND INFORMATION	
				Conf	65Salzburg 2 215	Mar 65	.MORE DATA AND INFORMATION	
				Prog	ICD – 1 266	64	.MORE DATA AND INFORMATION	
				Rept	INDC – E – 152	67	.ENGLISH TRANSL OF ICD – 3 75 1966	
				Jour	JNE 20 607	Jul 66	.ENGLISH TRANSL OF AE 19 46 7/65	
				Jour	EAF 19 1 70	Jul 65	. FRENCH TRANSL OF AE 19 46 7/65	
				Jour	SJA 19 910	Jul 65	.ENGLISH TRANSL OF AE 19 46 7/65	
				Prog	INDSWG – 64E 24	64	.ENGLISH TRANSL OF ICD – 1 266 /64	
Delayd Neuts	3.0+6	1.5+7	DEB Expt	Jour	AE 20 153	Feb 66	Butzko.HL – GROUPS(15MEV),YLD 3VS15MEV	+
				Jour	JNE 21 302	Apr 66	*ENGL OF AE 20 153	
				Jour	SJA 20 187	Feb 66	*ENGL OF AE 20 153	
				Jour	EAF 20 2 81	66	. FRENCH OF AE 20 153	
	3.0+6			Data	EXFOR30111.003	Jan 72	.RATIO OF TOT – YLD 14.7/3.MEV	
	1.5+7			Data	EXFOR30111.002	Jan 72	REL YLD FOR 5 HALF – LIVES(FROM AE TBL	
Delayd Neuts		+7	HFA Revw	Conf	67Vienna 23	Apr 67	Yiftah+ TBL OF YLD+HL,REACTR DYNAMIC	
Delayd Neuts	1.4+7		MNZExpt	Conf	67Vienna 147	Apr 67	Herrmann+,ABS NEUT YLD REL U235(THR)	
Delayd Neuts	Fiss	1.4+7	SOR Expt	Conf	67Vienna 115	Apr 67	Amiel+ DEL – N PRECURSORS,TBL=XPT+COMP	
				Rept	IA – 1190 95	Jul 69	– + NEW INFORMATION	
Delayd Neuts	Fiss		MNZTheo	Jour	AF 36 453	Nov 67	Patzelt+.FROM DERIVED N – EMISS PROB.	
Delayd Neuts	1.4+7		MNZExpt	Jour	AF 36 453	Nov 67	Patzelt+. HALOGEN – NON HALOGEN ACTVTY	
Delayd Neuts	5.0+6	2.1+7	FEI Expt	Jour	YF 7 274	Feb 68	Maksjutenko+FRACTIONL YLD(HL,NEUT – E)	+
	1.5+7	2.1+7		Conf	67Vienna 203	Apr 67	Maksiutenko.REL YLDS,CFD U235 +U238	
	5.0+6	2.1+7		Jour	SNP 7 189	Aug 68	.TRANSLATION	
	1.8+7	2.1+7		Data	EXFOR40169.	May 74	.7 SUBENT FOR 7 ES,EACH 5 DATA LINES	
Delayd Neuts	5.5+6	6.9+6	FEI Expt	Rept	FEI – 145	Nov 68	Maksjutenko+ TBL OF PRECURSORS+HLS	+
	5.0+6	8.0+6		Conf	67Vienna 191	Apr 67	.REL YIELDS FOR 5 GROUPS	
	5.0+6	7.8+6		Conf	66Paris 2 45	Oct 66	.PPR102.TABLE HALFLIFE OF 5 GROUPS	
	5.5+6	6.9+6		Rept	LA – TR – 69 – 3	Dec 69	. ENGLISH OF FEI – 145	
Delayd Neuts	1.4+7		CCP Comp	Jour	YF 7 670	Mar 69	Krisyuk+ DEL NEUT YLD FROM BR+I ISOT	
				Jour	SNP 9 3 387	Sep 69	TRANSLATN.*	
Delayd Neuts	Fiss		HAR Expt	Rept	AERE – M – 2199	Apr 69	Tomlinson+ ESTIMATE YLD AL 1 MIN+	
Delayd Neuts	3.1+6	1.5+7	LAS Expt	Jour	NSE 36 202	May 69	Masters+ 2ES RELATIVE+ABSOL MEASTS	+
				Jour	ANS 11 179	Jun 68	.SUPERSEDED	
				Rept	LA – DC – 9403	65	.SUPERSEDED	
	3.0+6	1.4+7		Data	EXFOR12288.	Jun 76	. 2 PTS.	
Delayd Neuts	1.4+7		SOR Expt	Prog	IA – 1190 95	Jul 69	Notea.TOTAL+RELAT YIELD FOR 5 GROUPS	+
	1.4+7			Data	EXFOR30238.	May 73	.TOTL DELAYED NEUT YLD FOR 5 GROUPS.	
Delayd Neuts	9.0+5	2.4+6	ANL Expt	Prog	ANL – 7610 45	Jan 70	COX+. CURV DELAYED NEUTRON YIELD	
	Thrsh	2.4+6		Prog	ANL – 7410 27	Jan 69	COX+,YLD,PERIOD CURVES	
Delayd Neuts	1.4+7		KOS Expt	Prog	INDC(HUN) – 1G	Apr 70	.PROG REPORT.NEUT – SPEC,PREL EXPT TBD	
Delayd Neuts	Fast	1.4+7	HAR Theo	Rept	AERE – R – 6596	Nov 70	Tomlinson. CALC DEL – N GROUP YLDS.TBL	
Delayd Neuts		1.5+7	KEN Expt	Jour	RCA 15 109	Apr 71	Brown+ YIELDS+HALFLIVES,FOUR GROUPS.	
	1.5+7		MNZExpt	Jour	RCA 17 1 61	Feb 72	Benedict+ REL TO THR FISS OF 235U	
Delayd Neuts	1.7+6	6.9+6	LAS Expt	Jour	NSE 53 80	Jan 73	Evans+REVISED NUD DATA.TBLS.	+
	1.6+6	6.5+6		Jour	NSE 47 311	Mar 72	Krick+SPRSDD.DATA REVISED	
	1.7+6	6.9+6		Data	EXFOR10117.	Jul 74	. 14 PTS.	
Delayd Neuts	1.0+5	1.5+7	IAE Eval	Jour	REA 10 637	Dec 72	Manero+ SURVEY,AVERAGE YLD,TBL+GRPHS	
Delayd Neuts	1.4+7		KFK Expt	Jour	JNE 26 585	Dec 72	Fieg.EN SPECT,AS FN TIME AFTER FISS	
				Prog	KFK – 1272 1	Jun 72	– .P121 – 6,MEAN ES OF 5 GROUPS	
				Rept	KFK – EXT – 4 31	May 71	– . SPEC EXPT, 5 – GROUP SPECS CALC	
Delayd Neuts	Fast		BUC Revw	Rept	IFA – RN – 50	73	Cristu. NUD(FRAGM – MASS),H – L,E – SPEC	
	Maxwl			Rept	IFA – RN – 50	73	– . NUD(FRAGM – MASS),H – L,E – SPEC	
Delayd Neuts	Fast		HFA Expt	Jour	NSE 51 52	May 73	Shalev+ HE – 3 DET. NEUT ENERGY DISTR	
Delayd Neuts	Fast		ALD Expt	Prog	EANDC(UK) 151	Aug 73	Mctaggart.0.0472+ – 0.0025 N/F TBC	
Delayd Neuts	1.5+5	1.5+7	BIR Revw	Jour	RPP 37 951	74	Beynon+ COMPAR TOT DELAYED N – YLD(E)	
Delayd Neuts	1.0+5	1.5+7	LAS Expt	Conf	IAEA – 169 377	74	Evans. TBL YLD,GROSS E – SPEC GRAPH	
	Thrsh	1.5+7		Conf	69Vienna 647	Jul 69	East+PPR109. YLD TABLE,REVW,SAFGUARD	
Delayd Neuts	Fiss	1.5+7	SOR Revw	Conf	IAEA – 169 2 33	74	Amiel.ALL YLDS,DEL – N SPECS,TBL,GRPHS	
Delayd Neuts	1.0+5	4.0+6	ANL Expt	Abst	BAP 19 597	Apr 74	COX. 4ES. ABSOL YLD MEASD.NO DATA.	
Delayd Neuts	2.0+6		ANL Eval	Rept	ANL – NDM – 5	Apr 74	COX. REL YLD, HL, GRPH	
Delayd Neuts	1.1+7	1.7+7	LRL Expt	Prog	UCID – 16514 6	Jun 74	Alvarez+	

92 Uranium 238

Quantity	Energy (ev) Min	Max	Lab	Type	Documentation Ref Vol Page	Date	Author, Comments	Data
Delayd Neuts	1.5+6	1.5+7	HAR	Eval	Prog NEANDC(UK)160	Jul 74	Story+ (WIN) EVAL IN UKNDL	+
				Rept	AERE-R-6993	Feb 72	Tomlinson.TOTAL+GROUP YLDS SPEC TBL	
	1.4+7			Revw	Conf 71Canterby 239	71	- .EXP CFD CALCULATIONS.TABLE	
	Fast	1.5+7		Eval	Data UKNDL-DFN-935	74	GRP YLDS.SPECTRA.	
Delayd Neuts	9.0+5	1.5+7	AI	Eval	Jour NSE 56 37	Jan 75	Tuttle.TBL.GRPH.RVW MEAS.CFD REC VAL	
	2.5-2				Prog AI-AEC-13025	May 72	Springer+ VALUE=0.0438+-0.0013	
Delayd Neuts	1.0+6	1.5+7	HED	Theo	Abst ANS 21 518	Jun 75	Schenter+TBL CALC FROM ENDF FP FILE	
Delayd Neuts	3.9+6	7.1+6	FEI	Expt	Jour YF 22 251	Aug 75	Maksyutenko+ TOT+10GROUP-YLDS(E),TBL	+
					Rept YFI-20 4	May 75	- + 10GROUPS,REL YLD(E),TBL	
	3.9+6	5.1+6			Prog YFI-13 5	Oct 72	- + ABST,REL YIELDS,TBL	
					Rept YK- 9 41	72	Maksjutenko+ REL YIELD(E)+HL(E),TBL	
	3.9+6	7.1+6			Rept INDC(CCP)-66	Feb 76	.P 2. ENGL OF YFI-20 4	
				ExTh	Jour SNP 22 129	Aug 75	. ENGL OF YF 22 251	
	3.9+6	5.1+6		Expt	Rept INDC(CCP)-42	Aug 74	.P7 ENGLISH OF YK-9	
					Prog INDC(CCP)-32	Apr 73	.PAGE 6.ENGLISH OF YFI-13 5	
	3.9+6	5.1+6			Data EXFOR40067.002	May 75	.5GROUP-YLDS(E) GVN	
Delayd Neuts	2.5+6	5.0+6	ANL	Expt	Rept ANL-NDM-18	Jan 76	Meadows.NUD VS E GRPH.PU241/U238 AVG	
Delayd Neuts	1.4+7		NRL	Expt	Abst BAP 5 33	Jan 60	Mcgarry+.DELAYED FRACTION=.066+-.017	+
	1.4+7				Data EXFOR12435.003	Jun 76	. 1 PT.	
Delayd Neuts	None		ALD	Expt	Prog NEANDC(E)172 8	Aug 76	Besant+ DELAYED N YIELD	
Delayd Neuts	Fast	1.5+7	CSR	Revw	Jour JE 23 9 345	77	Tinka. REVW GROUP-SPEC,PARAMS.TABLES	
Frag Neuts	1.4+7		TOR	Expt	Conf 69Vienna 939	Jul 69	Sharma+PPR142. RADIOCHEM YLD(FRAG-A)	
Frag Neuts	1.5+7		KEN	Expt	Jour RCA 16 2 104	Apr 71	Birgul+ PROMPT NEUT YLDS	
Frag Neuts	1.5+7		KYU	Expt	Jour NST 13 678	Nov 76	Yamamoto+.CFD C TERREL CURVE IN FIG	
Spect Fiss n	1.0+6	1.0+7	CCP	Theo	Jour AE 3 15	Jul 57	Bat+KUDRIN.EVAP THEOR.ANG DIST CALC	
					Jour JNE 8 74	Nov 58	TRANSLATN.*	
					Jour SJA 3 735	57	TRANSLATN.*	
Spect Fiss n	1.4+7		CCP	Expt	Jour AE 4 337	Apr 58	Zamiatnin+ FISS+EVAP SPECTR FIT DATA	
					Jour JNE 9 194	Jun 59	TRANSLATN.*	
					Jour SJA 4 443	58	TRANSLATN.*	
Spect Fiss n	3.0+6		CCP	Theo	Jour AE 5 649	Dec 58	Kovalev+ THEORY COMPARED WITH EXPT	
					Jour JNEA 11 166	Feb 60	TRANSLATN.*	
					Jour SJA 5 1588	58	TRANSLATN.*	
Spect Fiss n	1.4+7		CCP	Expt	Jour ZET 38 671	Mar 60	Vasil'Ev. TOF,0.4-5MEV,GRAPHS,TABLES	
					Jour JET 11 483	Sep 60	TRANSLATN.*	
Spect Fiss n	1.0-2	1.0+7	KFK	Eval	Rept KFK-120 2	Dec 62	Schmidt.SAME DATA AS U235	+
	Maxwl				Data KEDAK-3	Oct 75	206 DATA SETS	
Spect Fiss n	Thrsh	1.5+7	UK	Eval	Rept AWRE-O-79/63	Jan 64	Parker.(ALD).UKNDL-DFN 156	
Spect Fiss n	3.0+6	7.0+6	ALD	Expt	Jour NP 65 236	Mar 65	Batchelor+ DEDUCED FROM SNE3 SPEC	
Spect Fiss n	1.4+7		SAC	Expt	Conf 65Antwerp § 171	Jul 65	Didier+TOF LIQ SC.MEAS.AT 83DEGR.	
Spect Fiss n	2.1+6	5.0+6	HAR	Expt	Jour NP 71 228	Sep 65	Barnard+ CORRELATED WITH NU BAR	
Spect Fiss n	1.0+4	1.5+7	EDF	Eval	Rept EDF-HX-1/1574	Feb 68	Vastel.PART OF DFN 401 IN UK LIBRARY	
Spect Fiss n	1.4+7		FEI	Expt	Jour IZV 32 653	Apr 68	Salnikov+ FISSN+OTHER NEUT SPECS,CRV	
					Jour BAS 32 600	69	.ENGLISH TRANSL OF IZV 32 653 4/68	
Spect Fiss n	6.1+6		HKU	Expt	Jour CHP 6 25	Apr 68	Chuang.GRPH,(EVAP+F)SPEC-EXPTAL SPEC	
Spect Fiss n	1.4+6	1.4+7	ANL	Revw	Conf 71Vienna 3	Aug 71	Smith. MEAN-E OF NEUTS,EXPTS CFD,TBL	
Spect Fiss n	1.5+6	2.3+6	GEL	Expt	Jour ZP 244 358	Mar 71	Knitter+,VDG TOF AV E + ANGDIST	+
					Conf 71Vienna 41	Aug 71	- + TOF,ESPEC+ANGDIST,TBL AVG E	
	1.5+6	2.3+6			Data EXFOR20137.	Mar 73	11PTS.AVG.K.E,D/DA.	
Spect Fiss n	None		KFK	Revw	Conf 71Vienna 129	Aug 71	Kiefhaber+ DATA FILES SPECS CFD,TBLS	
Spect Fiss n	1.4+6	2.0+6	AE	Expt	Rept AE-429	Sep 71	Almen+. 2 ES. 1.35-10 MEV.GRPHS.TEMP	
					Prog EANDC(OR)99 31	Aug 70	- +. TEMP GVN OKS PREV RESULTS	
	1.3+6	2.0+6			Conf 70Helsinki 2 93	Jun 70	- +57. SPECTRA AT 2ES AND 3 ANGLS	
Spect Fiss n	4.0+6	7.0+6	VNV	Expt	Prog EANDC(E)150U	May 72	Bertin.	
	1.4+7				Conf 71Knoxvill 286	Mar 71	- +,TOF+FISS CHAMBER,.2-12MEV NS	
					Conf 67Bordeaux	Mar 67	Bertrand+30-150DEG,0.8-12MEV. FP JPR	
Spect Fiss n	1.3+6	2.2+7	LAS	Expt	Prog USNDC-7 127	Jun 73	Auchampaugh+. 7ES. NO DATA GIVEN.TBP	
Spect Fiss n	1.9+6	2.3+6	RAM	Expt	Conf 74Dacca 33	Nov 74	Islam. AVG FISS-N-EN VS E,2PTS.TABLE	
Spect Fiss n	2.1+6		AE	Expt	Conf 75Wash. 572	Mar 75	Johansson+ ANG DIST PROMPT NEUTRONS	
					Conf 73Kiev 3 87	May 73	Holmqvist. N-SPEC REL U-235, GRAPH	
Spect Fiss n	1.4+7		LRL	Expt	Conf 75Wash. 704	Mar 75	Wong+ GRPHS EMISSION SPECTRA	
Spect Fiss n	Fast		ANL	Eval	Abst ANS 22 671	Nov 75	Saphier+ 6 GPS DELAYED NEUT SPECT	
Spect Fiss γ	2.8+6	1.5+7	RI	Expt	Jour ZET 36 954	Mar 59	Protopopov. GRAPH AT 2ES CFD U235	
					Jour JET 9 674	Sep 59	TRANSLATN.*	
Spect Fiss γ	1.4+7		KFI	Expt	Jour KFI 18 13	Feb 70	Jeki+ GAM-ANISOTROPY-COEFFICIENT GVN	
Spect Fiss γ	8.0+6	2.0+7	CSE	Expt	Abst DA/B 30 4322	Mar 70	Sobel.SPEC FROM SPONT. FISS.	
Spect Fiss γ	Spont		CSE	Expt	Jour PR/C 7 1564	Apr 73	Crouch+.LIQ SCINT.UNDERGROUND MEAST	
Spect Fiss γ	Fast		LAS	Theo	Conf 75Wash. 193	Mar 75	Stamatelatos+GRPHS G SPECT,CINDER	

92 Uranium 238

Quantity	Energy (ev) Min	Max	Lab	Type	Documentation Ref Vol Page	Date	Author, Comments	Data
Spect Fiss γ	Maxwl		LIN	Expt Conf	75Kiev 6 121	Jun 75	Teterev+ G−SPEC,YLD GAMMAS,GRAPHS	
Spect Fiss γ	6.0+2	9.0+2	LRL	Expt Conf	76Lowell 1402	Jul 76	Browne.2.9MEV/2.9TO4.8MEV G RATIO	
Fiss Prod γ	1.0+6	4.0+6	LAS	Expt Prog	WASH−1006	Oct 58	Leachman. SC 4ES CONST PM6PC	
Fiss Prod γ	1.4+7		DOD	Theo Rept	DASA−526	May 59	Dolan. CALC SPEC VARIOUS TIMES.	
Fiss Prod γ	Fiss	1.4+7	FOA	Theo Jour	AF 16 293	Feb 60	Bjoernerstedt.G−SPEC 0−5MEV.1H−100YR	
Fiss Prod γ	Pile		SAC	Rept	CEA−1202	Jun 60	. CEA. TO 500KEV GS. NSA 14 1542.	
Fiss Prod γ	Maxwl		ORL	Comp Conf	61Wien 3 3	Oct 61	Maienschein.GRPH GAM−E(T AFTER FISS)	
Fiss Prod γ	None		LAS	Theo Rept	LA−2811	Dec 62	Griffin. BETA+GAMMA DECAY CALCULATNS	
Fiss Prod γ	None		GA	Expt Jour	PR/B 134 824	May 64	Walton+ LIHAC.G−FISSN.SPECT	
				Rept	GA−6445	May 65	−.DELAYD G(S) FROM PHOTO FISS	
Fiss Prod γ	Fast		LAS	Expt Jour	PR/B 134 796	May 64	Fisher.GDIVA NS,GS TO6MEV,T=.2 TO45S	
Fiss Prod γ	5.9+6	6.6+6	LND	Expt Jour	NP 64 420	Mar 65	Kivikas+CD117+BA139 FIT TO TH YIELD	
Fiss Prod γ	Fiss		NRD	Theo Rept	USNRDL−TR−1009	Dec 65	Turner.GROSS F PROD GAMMA SPEC CALCT	
Fiss Prod γ	1.4+7		SOR	Comp Conf	67Vienna 115	Apr 67	Amiel+ GRAPH SPEC,FOR DEL−NEUTS−EXPT	
Fiss Prod γ	+6		NRD	Expt Jour	NSE 29 432	Sep 67	Bunney+ GAM SPEC 15MIN−72H AFTER IRR	
Fiss Prod γ	1.0+6	2.0+7	SOR	Revw Conf	IAEA−107 57	68	Ben−David.NEW THRS−REACT TBD,GE−DET	
Fiss Prod γ	Pile		CCP	Expt Conf	69Erevan	Feb 69	Popeko+.ABST,GE−LI,ISOM LVLS IMIS	
Fiss Prod γ	Maxwl		LAS	Revw Conf	69Vienna 647	Jul 69	East+PPR109.DELAYD GAM FOR SAFEGUARD	
Fiss Prod γ	−		WIN	Eval Jour	JNE 23 517	Nov 69	JAMES MEAN E 9.2+−2.0MEV/FISS	
Fiss Prod γ	5.0+6	1.5+7	LOK	Expt Prog	AD−698558	Dec 69	Imhof+,VDG,GE(LI),CURVS	
Fiss Prod γ	1.4+7		KFI	Expt Jour	KFI 18 13	Feb 70	Jeki+ GAM−ANISOTROPY−COEFFICIENT GVN	
Fiss Prod γ	Maxwl	+1	BNL	Expt Prog	NCSAC−33 27	Dec 70	Sailor+,DELAYED GAM YLDS TO BE MEASD	
Fiss Prod γ	1.9+6		LOK	Expt Prog	NCSAC−42 142	Nov 71	Imhof+. 4MIN TO 24HR. ANAL TBC. NDG	
Fiss Prod γ	Fast		CEG	Eval Rept	RD/B/M−2669	Jun 73	Tobias. BETA GAMMA DECAY SCH ALL FP	
Fiss Prod γ	Maxwl	+6	BNL	Theo Jour	NSE 51 296	Jul 73	Takahashi.CALC GAM SPECT.12 NEUT ES	
Fiss Prod γ	Pile		CCP	Expt Jour	AE 36 66	Jan 74	Jurova+ GE−LI,CFD U235,GRAPH	
				Jour	SJA 36 75	Jul 74	. ENGLISH OF AE 36	
Fiss Prod γ	Fast		BEP	Theo Jour	KE 17 109	Apr 74	Pulz+ SPEC+ TOT−EMISSION VS DECAY−T	
Fiss Prod γ	Fast		KAL	Eval Conf	76Bombay 550	Mar 76	Murthy+ E/FIS.SEC VS COOL TIME.GRAPH	
Fiss Yield	Spont		MCM	Expt Jour	PR 80 471	Nov 50	Macnamara+ YIELD OF XE,KR ISOTOPES.	
Fiss Yield	2.5+6		CBR	Expt Jour	PR 83 673	Aug 51	Titterton.EMISS OF LONG RANGE FRAGM.	
Fiss Yield	Pile		ANL	Expt Rept	ANL−4927	Nov 52	Seiler+ FAST PILE 12YLDS A=77 TO 156	
Fiss Yield	Spont		CHI	Expt Jour	PR 92 907	Nov 53	Wetherill.YIELD KR83−86 XE129−136	
Fiss Yield	Fiss		ANL	Expt Jour	PR 94 969	May 54	Keller+ YLDS 15 FRAGS RADIOCHEM,CFD	
Fiss Yield	Fast		ANL	Revw Conf	55Geneva 7 3	Aug 55	Steinberg+ P614.EXPTL YLD TBL+GRPH	
Fiss Yield	Fast		MCM	Expt Jour	CJP 33 541	Sep 55	Wanless+ MASS−SPEC,XE+KR REL YIELDS	
Fiss Yield	Fast		LAS	Expt Rept	LADC−1997	56	Ford+ YLDS OF 89SR,RH,PD,AG,TO 144CE	
Fiss Yield	Spont		ARK	Expt Jour	JCP 25 603	Sep 56	Kuroda+HALF−LIFE BY I ISOTOPE YLDS	
Fiss Yield	Spont		ARK	Expt Jour	JIN 5 12	57	Ashizawa+SHORT−LIVD ZA.NAT+DEPLETD U	
Fiss Yield	Fiss		LAS	Expt Rept	TID−5787	57	Bayhurst. 2 ES, SR90 YIELDS	
Fiss Yield	−		CCP	Expt Jour	AE 2 275	Mar 57	.SR90 Y90	
Fiss Yield	7.3+6		CCP	Theo Jour	AE 2 508	Jun 57	Strutinsky.ANG DN,STATIST TH CFD EXP	
				Jour	JNE 7 239	Sep 58	TRANSLATN.*	
				Jour	SJA 2 621	57	TRANSLATN.*	
Fiss Yield	Spont		ARK	Expt Jour	JIN 5 153	58	Parker+MO99/U238 IN U SOLUTN. YDL MO	
Fiss Yield	1.4+7		HAR	Expt Jour	JIN 5 1	58	Cunningham.14AS,CURV CF U235NF,238GF	
				Rept	AERE−C/R−1646	55	Cunninghame.	
Fiss Yield	1.5+7		CCP	Expt Jour	AE 5 130	Aug 58	Protopopov+ 12 RADCHEM YLDS REL MO99	
				Jour	JNEA 10 80	Jul 59	TRANSLATN.*	
				Jour	SJA 5 885	58	TRANSLATN.*	
Fiss Yield	Fiss		NRD	Expt Conf	58Geneva 15 449	Sep 58	Bunney+ YLDS REL MO99,REL U235 THR	
	8.0+6			Conf	58Geneva 15 449	Sep 58	− + YLDS REL MO99,REL U235 THR	
Fiss Yield	+6	+7	TRM	Revw Conf	59Calcutta 152	Feb 59	Ramanna. REVIEW YLD(A),3 E−RANGES	
Fiss Yield	1.4+7		DOD	Theo Rept	DASA−525	May 59	Dolan. CALC YLDS+ACT MANY NUCLIDES	
Fiss Yield	6.0+5	9.0+6	LAS	Expt Prog	WASH−1026 33	Oct 59	Simmons. ANG DISTR OF FRAGMENTS	
Fiss Yield	Spont		ARK	Expt Jour	JIN 12 12	Dec 59	Heydegger+ RADIOCHEM, BA140 YIELD	
Fiss Yield	Fiss	1.4+7	CCP	Expt Rept	AEC−TR−4682	60	Bonyushkin+.ABSOL RADIOCHEM YLDS GVN	
Fiss Yield	1.4+7		LRL	Expt Jour	PR 117 186	Jan 60	Stevenson. YIELD OF MO99	
Fiss Yield	Spont		MCM	Expt Jour	CJP 38 1	Jan 60	Young+ XE+KR ISOTOPE ABSOL YLDS	
Fiss Yield	1.4+7		BNL	Eval Jour	NUC 18 11 201	Nov 60	Katcoff.RECOMMENDED YLD−SET,TBL	
				Jour	NUC 16 4 78	Apr 58	.SUPERSEDED	
Fiss Yield	Fiss	1.5+7	CCP	Expt Book	NEJTRONFIZ 224	61	Bonjushkin+ RADIOCHEM YLDS,TBL,GRPHS	+
				Book	SPN 164	61	+AEC−TR−4682,ENGL OF NEJTRONFIZ 224	
Fiss Yield	1.4+7	1.5+7	KYU	Expt Priv	KATASE	61	Katase. AD OF FF BY PPL.TBL+FIGS	
Fiss Yield	Spont		RI	Revw Jour	UFN 73 655	Apr 61	Petrzhak+ CURVE,MANY REFS,DISCUSSION	
	Fiss			Expt Book	NEJTRONFIZ 217	61	− + RADCHEM YLDS 6NUC,TBL+GRPH	
				Rept	AEC−TR−4696	61	.ENGL OF NEJTRONFIZ 217	
	Spont			Revw Jour	SPU 4 305	Sep 61	. ENGL OF UFN 73 655	

92 Uranium 238

Quantity	Energy (ev) Min	Max	Lab	Type	Documentation Ref Vol Page	Author, Comments Date	Data
Fiss Yield	2.8+6		DKE	Theo Jour	PR 122 1224	May 61 Newson.MASS DIST ASYMMETRIC+SYMMETR	
Fiss Yield	2.0+6	1.0+7	LRL	Expt Jour	PR 124 544	Oct 61 Levy+ 6 ES,YLDS REL MO99,REL U235THR	
Fiss Yield	3.0+6		RI	Expt Jour	ZET 41 1003	Oct 61 Baranov.GRAPH YLD VS MASSRATIO AT2AS	
				Jour	JET 14 713	Apr 62 TRANSLATN.*	
Fiss Yield	3.0+6	1.5+7	CCP	Jour	AE 12 150	Feb 62 KINETIC ENERGY OF FRAGMENTS	
				Jour	SJA 12 162	Feb 62 . ENGL OF AE 12 150	
Fiss Yield	1.5+7		ARK	Expt Jour	PR 126 627	Apr 62 Broom. ABS YIELD BETA COUNT A=89-140	
				Rept	ORO-435	61 .SEE ALSO	
Fiss Yield	1.4+7		CCP	Expt Jour	RAK 4 711	Dec 62 PARTIAL YLDS OF A=138 ISOBARS	
				Jour	SRA 4 631	Dec 62 TRANSLATN.*	
Fiss Yield	Fiss		LAS	Expt Rept	LADC-5821	63 Bennett.MASS YIELD DISTRIBUT CURVES	
Fiss Yield	Spont		TRM	Expt Conf	63Bombay 229	Feb 63 Rao.TABLE FOR FRGMNT SR,ZR,CS,BA GVN	
Fiss Yield	Maxwl		NRD	Eval Rept	USNRDL-TR-633	Mar 63 Weaver+ 2ES+FISS SPECT.	
Fiss Yield	1.5+7		ARK	Expt Jour	JIN 26 401	Mar 64 Menon+YIELD MASS 141 143 144 147	+
Fiss Yield	1.5+7		DUR	Expt Jour	RCA 3 76	Oct 64 James+ .2MEV RESOL.FINE STRUCT 133-5	
Fiss Yield	Fiss		CRC	Eval Rept	AECL-2111	Nov 64 Walker. SUPPLEMENTS AECL-1537 (1962)	
	Fiss	1.4+7		Rept	AECL-1537	Jun 62 .SUPERSEDED	
Fiss Yield	Maxwl	+6	CIS	Expt Rept	CISE-171R	65 Faccinni+. BA140 REL+ABSOL YLDS	
Fiss Yield	1.4+7		FTI	Expt Prog	INDSWG-120 31	65 Komar.MASS+ANGLE-DSTRB DISCUSSED,NDG	
Fiss Yield	Fiss	1.4+7	TRM	Comp Rept	AEET-209	65 Rangarajan. YLDS+PRODUCT,TBL	
Fiss Yield	1.4+7		TRM	Comp Rept	AEET-209	65 Rangarajan+ YLDS+PRODUCTN RATIO,TBLS	
Fiss Yield	-3	+7	TRM	Revw Rept	AEET-235	65 Methasiri.TERNRY FISS EXPTS,GRAPH	
Fiss Yield	1.4+7		CCP	Expt Jour	RAK 7 96	Jan 65 BR86,87,88,89-90 I136,137,138 YIELDS	
				Jour	SRA 7 94	Feb 65 . ENGL OF RAK 7 96	
Fiss Yield	5.0+6	1.5+7	LAS	ExTh Jour	PR/B 137 817	Feb 65 Leachman+ ANG DIST, CF OPTMDL TH	
Fiss Yield	Fiss		TRM	Expt Conf	65Calcutta 54	Feb 65 Mathews. FINE STRUCTURE IN MASS-DIST	
Fiss Yield	Spont		ARK	Expt Jour	JIN 27 3 503	Mar 65 RAO+YIELD OF ZR95, ZR97, MO99	
Fiss Yield	4.7+6	1.8+7	LAS	ExTh Jour	PR/B 137 826	Feb 65 Ford+YLDS FOR4-5 NUCLEI.	
	+5	1.8+7		Conf	65Salzburg 333	Mar 65 - .GRAPHS,DISCUSSION	
Fiss Yield	Fiss		MCM	Expt Rept	EANDC(CAN)-23	Apr 65 Tomlinson+ ABS CUM YLDS, MASS SPECT	
Fiss Yield	1.4+7		MNZ	Expt Rept	NP-16155	66 Grau.KR91 92 93 94,XE139 140 141 142	
Fiss Yield	1.5+6	1.4+7	LEB	Expt Jour	YF 3 468	Mar 66 Belovitskij.NUMBER OF ELECTRONS	
				Jour	SNP 3 340	Sep 66 TRANSLATN.*	
				Conf	64Paris 2 1149	Jul 64 SEE ALSO *	
Fiss Yield	Spont		ARK	Expt Jour	PR 147 884	Jul 66 Rao+,DPLTD U,TE132 YLD,MASS-YLD CURV	
Fiss Yield	1.5+6	1.8+7	KUR	Expt Conf	66Paris 2 88	Oct 66 Borisova+ ABSTRACT ONLY	+
				Rept	INDC-156	66 . FULL PAPER	
Fiss Yield	1.5+7		ARK	Expt Jour	PR 151 960	Nov 66 Ganapathy+YLD5.3H 1SOM MO103=.056PC	
Fiss Yield	Spont		ARK	Expt Prog	ORO-3235-21	Jan 67 Borden+,PRELIM KR88 89,XE138 139 YLD	
Fiss Yield	Spont		ARK	Expt Prog	ORO-3235-21	Jan 67 Sabu+,RU103 BA140 YLDS NDG TBC	
Fiss Yield	Fiss	1.4+7	HNS	Theo Rept	HNS-1229-77	Feb 67 Castagnola.ALSO THERMONUCLEAR 28FRAG	
Fiss Yield	Spont		KLN	Expt Jour	JIN 29 863	Mar 67 RAO. YLD OF ZR-97	
Fiss Yield	Fiss		LAS	Expt Jour	PR 156 1277	Apr 67 Stein+ SI DETECT,CURVE YIELDS,ENERGY	
Fiss Yield	1.5+7		ARK	Expt Jour	JIN 28 3071	May 67 Ganapathy+ MO YIELD	
Fiss Yield	2.5+6	7.0+6	FEI	Expt Prog	YFI-4 14	May 67 Senchenko+.CURVES GVN AT 2ES,TBP YF	
	2.0+6	7.0+6		Jour	YF 6 708	Oct 67 - + YLD CURVS AT 3ES COMPARED	
	2.5+6	7.0+6		Jour	SNP 6 516	Apr 68 . ENGL OF YF 6 708	
				Rept	INDC-187E	67 . ENGL OF YFI-4 14	
Fiss Yield	1.5+6	1.8+7	CCP	Expt Jour	YF 6 454	Sep 67 Borisova+ YLDS REL MO99 VS N-E,TBL	
Fiss Yield	-		JAE	Expt Jour	RCA 7 95	Sep 67 Ishimori+SPONTANEOUS FISSION	
Fiss Yield	1.5+7		TUE	Expt Jour	ZP 207 209	Oct 67 Pfeiffer+,CURVE OF MASS-DISTRIBUTION	
	1.4+7			ExTh Jour	ZP 181 281	Oct 64 Goennenwein.SEMICND,GRPH YLD VS MASS	
Fiss Yield	1.0+6	2.0+7	SOR	Conf	IAEA-107 57	68 Ben-David.NEW THRS-REACT TBD,GE-DET	
Fiss Yield	Fiss		HAR	Eval Rept	AERE-R-5086	Jan 68 CROALL TBL SELF-CONSISTENT SET YLDS	
	Fast			Rept	AERE-R-5086	Jan 68 Croall.RECOMMENDED CUMULAT YLDS,TBL	
	Pile			Comp Rept	AERE-R-3209	Jan 60 - .COMP OF INDEPENDENT YIELDS	
Fiss Yield	1.4+7		RI	ExTh Conf	68Riga	Jan 68 Adamov+ ABST,A-PARTICLES,TRITON YLD	
Fiss Yield	1.4+7		RI	ExTh Conf	68Riga	Jan 68 Adamov+ ABST,LONG-RANGE PARTICLES YL	
Fiss Yield	-		CCP	Theo Jour	YF 7 832	Apr 68 Shigin. YLD CONFIRMS LVL-DEN-CALC	
				Jour	SNP 7 4 506	Oct 68 TRANSLATN.*	
Fiss Yield	Fiss		SAL	Expt Jour	EN 15 272	Apr 68 Ciufollotti.BA-140 YLD REL U-235 THR	
Fiss Yield	1.4+7		MCM	Expt Jour	CJC 46 1663	May 68 Gorman+,REL+ABSOL YLDS MASS SP+GE-LI	
Fiss Yield	2.5+6	1.4+7	KFI	Expt Jour	YF 8 443	Sep 68 Nagy+DOUB/TERN FISS GVN,LONG-R-ALPHA	
				Jour	SNP 8 257	Mar 69 TRANSLATN.*	
	-2	1.4+7		Jour	KFI 15 85	Apr 67 Nagy+ TERN,ALFA PROBABILITY,TBL	
Fiss Yield	1.4+7		TAT	Expt Prog	BARC-401 18	69 Iyengar+ FRAG-A-DISTR CFD PHOTO-FISS	
				Conf	68Bombay 2 110	Dec 68 - + LEXAN DETECTOR, YIELD(MASS)	

92 Uranium 238

Quantity	Energy (ev) Min	Max	Lab	Type	Documentation Ref Vol Page	Author, Comments Date	Data
Fiss Yield	Maxwl		ANL	Expt	Jour PR 177 1817	Jan 69 Meadows+ 2ES MASS-ENERGY DISTRIBUTNS	
					Prog ANL-7450	Apr 68 .CALCULATED TRITIUM YIELDS	
Fiss Yield	2.9+6		IFJ	Expt	Jour APP 35 67	Jan 69 Benisz.TERNARY TOT K-E,E-MASS CORREL	
					Jour APP 32 485	Sep 67 *EXPTL DETAILS+CALCS	
					Rept INP-547	Jun 67 *	
Fiss Yield	-		TPI	Theo	Jour YF 9 102	Jan 69 Korostova+SHELL INFL,HEAV+L+SYM FRAG	
					Jour SNP 9 62	Jul 69 TRANSLATN.*	
Fiss Yield	Maxwl	+7	FEI	Theo	Jour YF 9 357	Feb 69 Ignatyuk. GRPH YLD SYM/ASYM CFD EXPT	
					Jour SNP 9 208	Aug 69 TRANSLATN.*	
Fiss Yield	Fiss		LRL	ExTh	Jour NP/A 124 130	Feb 69 Ingley.NUC EXPLOSION EXPTS.A=242-257	
Fiss Yield	None		MCM	Theo	Jour CJP 47 275	Feb 69 Thind+,CALCTD CUMULATIVE YIELDS,CURV	
Fiss Yield	1.5+7		ARK	Expt	Jour JIN 31 591	Mar 69 Rao+,INDEP YLD OF 124,126SB+136CS	
Fiss Yield	Fast		HAR	Theo	Rept AERE-R-6056	Mar 69 Crouch.CALC FRACT INDEPEND YLDS,TBLS	
Fiss Yield	1.5+7		LRL	Expt	Jour PR 182 1251	Jun 69 Nethaway+ MASS YLD DIST=GAUSSIAN	
Fiss Yield	+3	+5	BRC	Expt	Conf 69Vienna 952	Jul 69 Communeau+PPR94.YLD(A),GAM+BETA EXPT	
Fiss Yield	-		EDG	Revw	Conf 69Vienna 83	Jul 69 Feather.PPR201. SURVEY,TERNARY FISSN	
Fiss Yield	Maxwl	1.6+7	FEI	Expt	Conf 69Vienna 923	Jul 69 Vorob'Eva+PPR133. FRAG YLD+E(NEUT-E)	
Fiss Yield	Spont		FR	Expt	Conf 69Vienna 952	Jul 69 Monnin+PPR83. SPON FISSN HALF-LIFE	
Fiss Yield	1.4+7		FTI	Expt	Conf 69Vienna 900	Jul 69 Adamov+PPR146.LONG-RANGE-YLD VAL GVN	
					Jour YF 9 732	Apr 69 - + PROTON,T,D AND ALFA YLD GIVN	
					Jour SNP 9 424	Oct 69 . ENGL OF YF 9 732	
Fiss Yield	+5	+7	OSL	Revw	Conf 69Vienna 669	Jul 69 Pappas+PPR206.REVW,INITIAL MASS DIST	
Fiss Yield	Maxwl	1.4+7	SAC	Comp	Rept CEA-N-1180	Jul 69 Bessis+ CAPT FOR FIS FRAG + 'NU'	
Fiss Yield	1.3+6	6.9+6	FEI	Expt	Jour SNP 9 175	Aug 69 .TRANSLATN.*	
					Jour YF 9 296	Feb 69 Vorobeva+ GRPHS YLD(FRAG-A,6NEUT-ES)	
	1.4+6	6.9+6			Rept LA-TR-21	68 - + 6ES,FRAG MASS DIST CFD TH	
	-				Conf 67Kharkov	Feb 67 Vorob'Eva+. TBP IN IZV	
Fiss Yield	1.5+7		RI	Expt	Rept ICD-6 266	70 Petrzhak+ MASS-SPEC XE YLDS,TBL,GRPH	
	1.4+7				Conf 77Kiev	77 - + YLD XE-131,132,134,136,TBL	
	1.5+7				Prog YFI-11 50	70 - + ABST,MASS-SPEC,XE YLDS,NDG	
					Prog INDC(CCP)-31	Dec 72 .PAGE 49,ENGLISH OF YFI-11 50	
Fiss Yield	2.8+6	1.4+7	SAH	Theo	Rept BARC-474 35	70 Sarkar+ CALCULATD(RGM) YLD OKS EXPTS	
	2.8+6	7.0+7			Conf 69Roorke 2 222	Dec 69 - . CALCULAT YIELD GRAPHS AT 6ES	
Fiss Yield	7.0+6	2.4+7	CCP	Revw	Jour IZV 34 438	Feb 70 Soloveva.ALF-EMISSN PROBABILITY,GRPH	
					Jour BAS 34 378	Jan 71 *ENGL OF BAS 34 438	
Fiss Yield	None		BLA	Expt	Prog INDC(BUL)-1G	Apr 70 Kashukeev+ PRELIMIN EXPT,NDG	
Fiss Yield	None		ARK	Expt	Prog ORO-3235-10	Jul 70 RAO+,ISOMERIC YLD RATIO CD115M/G GVN	
Fiss Yield	2.5+6	1.4+7	CCP	ExTh	Jour YF 12 471	Sep 70 Bogdanov+ TERN FISSN,EXPT+THEORY CFD	
					Jour SNP 12 257	Mar 71 TRANSLATN.*	
Fiss Yield	Fiss		KFK	Comp	Rept KFK-EXT-6 2	Nov 70 Hofmann. CUMULATIVE YLD A=72-163	
Fiss Yield	1.4+7		KFK	Comp	Rept KFK-EXT-6 2	Nov 70 Hofmann. CUMULATIVE YLD A=72-163	
Fiss Yield	8.0+6	1.4+7	ANL	Eval	Rept ANL-7749	Dec 70 Flynn+ ALSO FISS SPEC NEUTS TBL+CURV	
Fiss Yield	Pile		MIS	Expt	Jour JIN 33 1	Jan 71 Harbour+ NB099M YLD	
	Maxwl				Abst DA/B 30 1578	Oct 69 - . FCY, HL NB099	
Fiss Yield	Pile		ISP	Expt	Jour JNE 25 85	Feb 71 Dierckx+ LA140 YLD REL U235 THR FISS	
Fiss Yield	1.5+7		ARK	Expt	Jour JIN 33 651	Mar 71 Swindle+ YLD FOR 5 MASS CH. A=73-81	
	2.9+6	1.5+7			Abst DA/B 32 5093	Mar 72 - . RADIOCHEM MASS YLDS FOR 2ES	
	2.9+6				Prog ORO-3235-14	Jul 70 -,A=73-81,141-156YLDS,TBC,NDG	
Fiss Yield	Spont		ARK	Expt	Jour JIN 33 876	Mar 71 Swindle+ YLD OF RU-ISOTOPES	
Fiss Yield	6.0+5	3.0+7	KFK	Expt	Rept KFK-1495	Mar 71 Cierjacks+ TOF SPEC OF FISS EVENTS	
Fiss Yield	3.0+6	1.5+7	KEN	Expt	Jour RCA 16 2 103	Apr 71 Birgul+ CUM YLDS AT MASS CHAIN 129	
	3.0+6				Jour RCA 13 3 167	May 70 Lyle+ MASS 91-145 CUMULATIVE YIELDS	
	3.0+6	1.5+7			Jour RCA 12 43	Jul 69 - +,FINE STRUCT YLD MASS 131-135	
Fiss Yield	-		TPI	Theo	Jour PL/B 35 125	May 71 Adeev+ ENERGY SURFACES AS STRUTINSKY	
Fiss Yield	1.4+7		CCP	Theo	Jour AE 31 23	Jul 71 Antsyshkin+ YLD SHIFT AT HIGH FLUXES	
					Jour SJA 31 712	Feb 72 * ENGL OF AE 31 23	
Fiss Yield	Pile		MCM	Expt	Prog INDC(CAN)-9 6	Jul 71 Weller+ YIELD OF SN-ISOTOPES,TB CONT	
Fiss Yield	Spont		ORL	Expt	Jour NP/A 172 33	Aug 71 Ferguson+ISOMER.M+E DISTR OKS DIRECT	
					Jour PR 141 1146	Jan 66 .SEE ALSO	
Fiss Yield	Fast		GA	Eval	Rept GA-12071	Sep 71 Mathews+. RECOMMENDED VALUES	
Fiss Yield	Fiss	1.4+7	GEV	Eval	Rept NEDO-12154	Jan 72 Meek+.TABULATD RECOMMENDED YIELDS	
	Fiss				Rept APED-5398	Oct 68 - + TABLES. REVISED.	
Fiss Yield	1.4+7		TOR	Expt	Jour CJC 48 641	Feb 70 Gevaert+,RADIOCHEM YLDS 10 FRAGMENTS	
					Abst DA/B 32 3838	Jan 72 - . RADIOCHEM. A=99-125 YLDS	
					Conf 69Vienna 939	Jul 69 Sharma+PPR142. RADIOCHEMICAL YLD(A)	
Fiss Yield	None		AUA	Expt	Prog AAEC/PR-36P 4	Mar 72 Rose. REL 140-YIELDS.NDG,TBC.	
Fiss Yield	Spont		CLA	Theo	Jour NP/A 184 417	Apr 72 Tsang+.ASSYM FROM FERMIGAS+WKB CALC.	

92 Uranium 238

Quantity	Energy (ev) Min	Max	Lab	Type	Documentation Ref Vol Page	Date	Author, Comments	Data
Fiss Yield	1.4+7		GRE Expt	Jour	NP/A 189 556	Jul 72	Bocquet+ON–LINE ISOT SEPAR.INDEP,CUM	
				Conf	71Canterby 13	Sep 71	.GE(LI) G–SPECTRA ANAL.CUMUL YLD,TBL	
Fiss Yield	Fast		MCM Expt	Jour	CJP 50 3100	Dec 72	Mathews+.CUMULATIVE YLDS HEAVY FRGS	
Fiss Yield	1.4+7		MNZ Expt	Jour	NP/A 198 228	Dec 72	Alexander. XE133,5 INDP YLDS+ISOMRAT	
Fiss Yield	1.4+7		MNZ Expt	Jour	NP/A 198 228	Dec 72	Alexander. XE133,5 INDP YLDS+ISOMRAT	
Fiss Yield	Fast		BUC Revw	Rept	IFA–RN–50	73	Cristu.MASS–+CHARGE–+E–DISTR REVIEW	
	Maxwl			Rept	IFA–RN–50	73	– .MASS–+CHARGE–+E–DISTR REVIEW	
Fiss Yield	Maxwl	1.5+7	LRL Comp	Rept	UCRL–51458	73	Nethaway+.ALSO FISS SPEC. 111 FRAGS.	
Fiss Yield	Pile		TRM Expt	Prog	BARC–690 137	73	Bhargava+ CD–WRAP,RADIOCHEM,TBL+GRPH	
Fiss Yield	Fast		GRE Eval	Conf	73Paris 1 477	Mar 73	Devillers+ YLD+DECAY DATA LIBRRY,NDG	
				Rept	CEA–N–1526	Mar 72	.YIELDS+GAM TRANSITIONS,TABLES	
Fiss Yield	1.0+6	1.4+7	IIT Expt	Abst	BAP 18 768	May 73	Mandler+. 20 MASS CHAIN YLDS. NDG	
Fiss Yield	Fast		KFK Expt	Rept	KFK–1273 1	Jun 73	Scholtyssek. G–EXPT,ABS YIELDS	
Fiss Yield	Spont		SAH Expt	Jour	JIN 35 1793	Jun 73	Purkayastha+ YLD OF I133, MO99	
				Prog	INIS–MF–292 37	71	Purkayasta+ MO–99+I–133 YLDS GIVEN	
Fiss Yield	Fiss	1.5+7	BNW Expt	Conf	73Rochestr 2 498	Aug 73	Kaye+ ABST,GE(LI),SHORT HL XE,KR,NDG	
Fiss Yield	1.5+7		ARK Expt	Jour	JIN 34 8 2405	Aug 72	RAO. ISOM YLD RATIO 115CD	
				Abst	DA/B 34 1934	Nov 73	RAO.CUMULATIVE CD115 ISOMER YLDS	
Fiss Yield	2.2+7	2.6+7	ARK Expt	Jour	NSE 52 466	Dec 73	Swindle+.FRAG MASS DISTR.PHOTOFISSN.	
Fiss Yield	Fast		FAR Expt	Conf	IAEA–169 3 59	74	Robin+ ND148,STABL ND–ISOT/ND148,TBL	
Fiss Yield	Fast	1.4+7	HAR Revw	Rept	IAEA–169 1 353	74	Cuninghame.FAST+N–E DEPEND,TBLS,GRPH	
				Rept	AERE–R–7548	Sep 73	.SAME AS 73BOLOGNA,EVALUATIONS CFD	
Fiss Yield	Fast		IAE Revw	Conf	IAEA–169 3 245	74	Lammer. XPTS+EVALUATNS DISCUSSD,TBLS	
Fiss Yield	1.4+7		KOS Eval	Conf	IAEA–169 3 281	74	Daroczy+ CUM+CHAIN YLDS RECOMMND,TBL	
	1.4+7	1.5+7		Comp Rept	YK–15 25	Aug 73	– + FISS PRODUCT YIELDS,TABLES	
Fiss Yield	Pile		CCP Expt	Jour	AE 36 66	Jan 74	Jurova+ G–SPECTROSC,REL U235	
	+0	+7		Conf	73Kiev 3 315	May 73	– + GE–LI,YLD OF FISS PRODUCTS	
	Pile			Jour	SJA 36 75	Jul 74	. ENGLISH OF AE 36	
Fiss Yield	Pile		TRM Expt	Jour	PR/C 9 1506	Apr 74	Rao+. SEARCH FOR LOW–YIELD FRAGS.	
Fiss Yield	Fast		ANL Expt	Jour	NSE 54 263	Jul 74	Larson+ YLDS 7 FRAGS GVN.	
Fiss Yield	Fast		HAR Expt	Rept	AERE–R–6862	May 72	Cuninghame+10 ABSOL YLDS DFR SPEC	+
				Prog	NEANDC(UK)160	Jul 74	– + YLDS DIFF ZEBRA SPEC TBD	
	1.0+6			Data	EXFOR20768.003	May 78	11PTS.	
Fiss Yield	1.4+7		MIF Theo	Jour	IVU 17 7 7	Jul 74	Koldobskij+ CUM YLDS(2ISOT)CFD EXPTS	
Fiss Yield	1.4+7		GRE Expt	Prog	NEANDC(E)161U	Aug 74	Dasilva+ YIELD FOR RARE GASES	
				Rept	CEA–N–1784	74	– + 9 FP YIELDS,WOLSBERG MTH	
Fiss Yield	Fiss		LAS Expt	Jour	PR/C 10 1872	Nov 74	Balestrini+ RB+CS.ODD–EVEN.Z=20PCT.	
				Rept	INIS–MF–1412	Aug 73	– + P359.MASS–SPEC,INDEP YLD	
				Rept	LA–UR–73–838	73	– +.CS138–146 REL+ABSOL YLDS	
Fiss Yield	1.4+7		FR ExTh	Rept	FRNC–TH–574	75	Cavallini. MASS DIST STUDY	
Fiss Yield	1.4+7		GRE Expt	Rept	FRNC–TH–584	75	Feu Alvim. THESIS.13 CHAIN–YLDS,TBL	
Fiss Yield	Pile		TRM Expt	Prog	BARC–821 187	75	Marathe A=66,67,170–172.GRAPH	
Fiss Yield	+6	+7	TUE Expt	Prog	ORO–4856–26	75	Holubarsch+ P.591,ABSTRACT.	
Fiss Yield	1.5+7		LRL Theo	Rept	UCRL–51759	Feb 75	Delucchi.KR–85,XE–131,133,135.YLD(T)	
	Fiss			Rept	UCRL–51759	Feb 75	– .KR–85,XE–131,133,135.YLD(T)	
Fiss Yield	–1		WAI Expt	Jour	CJP 53 775	Apr 75	De–Laeter+ CD YLD REL CD–116	
Fiss Yield	Fast		DOU Expt	Prog	UKNDC(75)P71	Jul 75	Davies+ IRRADIATION ISOTOPES PFR	
Fiss Yield	4.0+6	2.0+7	FEI ExTh	Prog	YF 22 251	Aug 75	Maksyutenko+ FWHM(BR–ISO)VS E,TBL+GR	
				Jour	SNP 22 129	Aug 75	. ENGL OF YF 22 251	
Fiss Yield	Fiss		GRE Expt	Prog	NEANDC(E)162U	Aug 75	Blachot+ 21 YIELDS	
	1.0+6	3.0+6		Prog	NEANDC(E)161U	Aug 74	– + MASS DISTRIBUTION	
	1.4+7			Jour	JIN 36 3 495	Mar 74	– + FISS PROD ACTIV MEAS	
	3.0+6	1.5+7	ARK Expt	Abst	DA/B 36 2799	Dec 75	Adams.2ES.RADIOCHEM.YLDS CFD LIT VAL	
	1.5+7			Jour	JIN 37 419	Feb 75	– + RADIOCHEM,46CHAIN–YLDS,TBL+GR	
Fiss Yield	Fast		HAR Eval	Rept	AERE–R–8152	Jan 76	Crouch. ADJUSTED FISSION YIELD,TABLE	
			Expt	Prog	UKNDC(75)P71	Jul 75	– + IRRADIATION DFR IN PROGRESS	
	Fast	1.4+7	Eval	Rept	AERE–R–7785	Feb 75	.CHAIN+INDEPENDENT YLDS TBL	
	Pile			Rept	AERE–R–7680	May 74	. FRACTIONAL INDEPENDENT YLD	
	Fast			Rept	AERE–R–7394	May 73	.CHAIN YLDS RECOMMENDED TBL	
Fiss Yield	1.4+7		IEN Expt	Prog	INDC(SEC)–50	Jan 76	Bellido+ P35,ABST.REL YLDS(GELI),NDG	
Fiss Yield	1.4+7		WUR Expt	Jour	JIN 38 351	Feb 76	Rajagopalan+ SHORT.32 CUM YLDS,TABLE	
				Prog	INDC(SEC)–43	Dec 74	– + G–ANAL.REL 140,TBL.TBC	
				Prog	NEANDC(OR)–140	Jun 74	– G–SPEC.19CUM A–YLDS,TBL	
Fiss Yield	2.5–2	1.4+7	LAS Expt	Prog	ERDA–NDC–3 94	May 76	Ford+NFY COMPILATION.SEE LA–6129.NDG	
Fiss Yield	2.0+6	1.4+7	AUA Theo	Jour	AUJ 29 125	Jun 76	Cook+ 2ES.GAUSSFIT PARAMS VS E.TBLS	
				Rept	AAEC/E–386	Mar 76	– + 3–GAUSS FIT,PARAMS AT 2ES GIV	
	Maxwl			Rept	AAEC/E–386	Mar 76	– + 3–GAUSS FIT,PARAMS GIVEN	
Fiss Yield	2.0+6	1.4+7	LAS Eval	Rept	LA–6430	Jul 76	Madland+PAIR EFFECT ON INDEP YLD.TBL	

92 Uranium 238

Quantity	Energy (ev) Min	Max	Lab	Type	Documentation Ref Vol Page	Date	Author, Comments	Data
Fiss Yield	Fast		GA	Expt Abst	ANS 24 458	Nov 76	Buzzelli+TRITIUM FAST FISS YLD.TBL	
Fiss Yield	Fiss		GRE	Expt Rept	CEA-N-1979	77	Ferrieu+ ABSTRACT,TABLE GIVEN	
Fiss Yield	1.4+7		TIL	Expt Rept	YK- 27 42	77	Petrzhak+ YLD XE-131,132,134,136,TBL	
Frag Spectra	4.5+7	9.0+7	BRK	Expt Jour	PR 76 1112	Oct 49	Jungerman+ PROMPT NS TAKE SURPLUS E	
Frag Spectra	1.4+7		LAS	Expt Jour	PR 94 640	May 54	Brolley+ ANG DIST+0 DEG/90 DEG RATIO	
Frag Spectra	Maxwl	1.4+7	LAS	Expt Jour	PR 95 126	Jul 54	Wahl. ALSO 2.5MEV FRAG ENERGY DIST	
Frag Spectra	4.0+6	1.7+7	CCP	Expt Rept	AEC-TR-2386	Mar 56	Varfolomeev+. 4ES. FRAG ANG DISTR	
Frag Spectra	1.3+6	2.0+7	LAS	Expt Jour	PR 103 1292	Sep 56	Henkel+,FRAG ANG ANISOTROPY 0/90 CRV	
Frag Spectra	1.4+7		CCP	Expt Jour	AE 4 194	Feb 58	Protopopov+ 0/180DEG SYM FOR LT FRAG	
				Jour	JNE 9 164	Jun 58	TRANSLATN.*	
				Jour	SJA 4 265	58	TRANSLATN.*	
Frag Spectra	Spont		CCP	Expt Jour	AE 4 547	Jun 58	Kovrigin+.CFS U235 THR F,IONIZ METHD	
				Jour	SJA 4 721	58	TRANSLATN.*	
Frag Spectra		2.0+7	TRM	Revw Conf	59Calcutta 152	Feb 59	Ramanna. REVIEW,GRPH ANGDIST(NEUT-E)	
Frag Spectra	1.5+7		RI	Expt Jour	ZET 36 1608	May 59	Protopopov.DEGREE OF ANISOTROPY	
				Jour	JET 9 1143	Nov 59	TRANSLATN.*	
	1.4+7			Jour	AE 6 644	Jun 59	Protopopov+ ANG DISTR VS FRAGM MASS	
				Jour	SJA 6 471	Dec 59	. ENGL OF AE 6 644	
Frag Spectra	+6	+7	LAS	Theo Jour	PR 116 107	Oct 59	Griffin.ANISOTROPY OF FRAGS BOHR TH	
Frag Spectra	6.0+6	2.0+7	CRC	Expt Jour	CJP 37 1418	Dec 59	Baerg+. FRAG ANG DIST ANISOTROPIC	
Frag Spectra	1.4+7		LRL	Expt Jour	PR 117 186	Jan 60	Stevenson. AV KINETIC E = 175+-2 MEV	
Frag Spectra	1.2+6	8.5+6	LAS	Expt Jour	PR 120 198	Oct 60	Simmons+ FRAGMENT ANGULAR DIST 15ES	
Frag Spectra	1.4+7	1.5+7	KYU	Expt Priv	KATASE	61	Katase. AD OF FF BY PPL.TBL+ FIGS	
Frag Spectra	1.4+7		RI	Expt Jour	ZET 41 11	Jul 61	Perfilov.TERNARY FISS,ALFA-SPCT,GRPH	
				Jour	JET 14 7	Jan 62	TRANSLATN.*	
Frag Spectra	3.0+6		RI	Expt Jour	ZET 41 1003	Oct 61	Baranov.ANG ANISOTROPY VS MASS RATIO	
				Jour	JET 14 713	Apr 62	TRANSLATN.*	
Frag Spectra	1.2+6	1.7+6	LAS	Expt Jour	NP 33 70	May 62	Manley.EMULSION.ANGDIST VS FRAG A+E	
Frag Spectra	1.5+7		CCP	Expt Jour	ZET 42 1475	Jun 62	Adamov.GRPH E-SPC FOR DIFF MASSRTIOS	
				Jour	JET 15 1024	Dec 62	TRANSLATN.*	
Frag Spectra	Fiss		LAS	Expt Rept	LADC-5821	63	Bennett.FRAG KE DISTRIBUTION CURVES	
Frag Spectra	1.4+7		TAT	Expt Jour	PR 129 1350	Feb 63	Ramanna. E+ANG DIST OF LONG-RANGE-A	
Frag Spectra	1.4+7		CCP	Expt Jour	AE 15 191	Sep 63	Bochagov+.KINETIC E OF FISSION FRAGM	
				Jour	SJA 15 891	Sep 63	. ENGL OF AE 15 191	
Frag Spectra	2.0+6		CCP	ExTh Jour	AE 15 419	Nov 63	Okolovich+ AV EK REL PHOTOFISS.THEOR	
				Jour	JNE 18 533	Sep 64	TRANSLATN.*	
				Jour	SJA 15 1177	Nov 63	TRANSLATN.*	
Frag Spectra	-		CCP	Revw Rept	INDSWG-64 266	64	Maksjutenko.FRGMTS EMITNG DELAYED NS	
Frag Spectra	1.5+7		CCP	Expt Jour	AE 16 521	Jun 64	Okolovich+MEAN KIN.E.OF FRAG.1.93MEV	
				Jour	SJA 16 644	64	. ENGL OF AE 16 521	
Frag Spectra	1.4+7		FTI	Expt Prog	INDSWG-120 31	65	Komar.MASS+ANGLE-DSTRB DISCUSSED,NDG	
Frag Spectra	1.4+7		TRM	Revw Rept	AEET-235	65	Methasiri.ALF ANGULAR CORREL CFD TH	
Frag Spectra	8.0+5	2.0+6	ORL	ExTh Conf	65Salzburg 63	Mar 65	Lamphere.ANISTRPY OF FRGS,TH CFD XPT	
Frag Spectra	1.4+7		TAM	Expt Jour	PR 150 1027	Oct 66	Desai+ KE 8FRAG NUCLEI MEASD BY RNGE	
Frag Spectra	1.4+7		BOR	Expt Conf	67Bordeaux	Mar 67	Carles+EMULSION,TRIPART FISS. FP JPR	
				Jour	CR 262 4 296	Jan 66	- + ANGDIST ALPHAS AND FRAGS.	
Frag Spectra	1.5+7		DEB	Expt Jour	JNE 21 375	Apr 67	Csikai+ GLASS DET,ANG DIST,RELVE CRV	+
	1.5+7			Data	EXFOR30068.002	Nov 70	ANG DIST FISS FRAGM,NORM S(NF)=1.228	
Frag Spectra	Fiss		LAS	Expt Jour	PR 156 1277	Apr 67	Stein+ FRAG ENERGIES VS MASS,+ TOTAL	
Frag Spectra	2.5+6	7.0+6	FEI	Expt Prog	YFI-4 14	May 67	Senchenko+.CURVES GVN AT 2ES,TBP YF	
	2.0+6	7.0+6		Jour	YF 6 708	Oct 67	- + AVG EKIN VS MASS,AT 3 ES	
				Rept	FEI-65	66	Sentchenko+.FISS FRAG YLD+KIN E DIST	
				Jour	SNP 6 516	Apr 68	. ENGL OF YF 6 708	
	2.5+6	7.0+6		Rept	INDC-187E	67	. ENGL OF YFI-4 14	
Frag Spectra	+6		FEI	Expt Prog	YFI-6 42	68	Smirenkin+ ANISOTROPY, CURVE,	
				Rept	INDC-260E	69	. ENGL OF YFI-6 42	
Frag Spectra	2.0+6	1.5+7	KAZ	Expt Jour	YF 7 39	Jan 68	Kuvatov+ EXPTL+OTHER AVG FRAGM-E GVN	
				Jour	SNP 7 1 29	Jul 68	TRANSLATN.*	
Frag Spectra	1.4+7		RI	ExTh Conf	68Riga	Jan 68	Adamov+ ABST,E-DIST OF A-PART,TRITON	
Frag Spectra	4.5+6	6.5+6	IFP	ExTh Jour	YF 7 521	Mar 68	Kurchatov+SYM+ASYM YLD(G-E),PHOTO-FS	
				Jour	SNP 7 3 326	Sep 68	TRANSLATN.*	
Frag Spectra	+5	+7	CCP	Theo Jour	YF 8 704	Oct 68	Ermagambetov+OPTMOD-REVW,CRV,ANGDIST	
				Jour	SNP 8 409	Apr 69	TRANSLATN.*	
Frag Spectra	5.0+5	5.0+6	CCP	Expt Jour	ZEP 8 545	Nov 68	Shpak+ ANG-ANISOTR COEF,PRELIMINARY	
				Jour	JEL 8 332	Nov 68	TRANSLATN.*	
Frag Spectra	1.5+6	5.6+6	ANL	Expt Jour	PR 177 1817	Jan 69	Meadows+ 2ES MASS-ENERGY DISTRIBUTNS	

92 Uranium 238

Quantity	Energy (ev) Min	Max	Lab	Type	Documentation Ref Vol Page	Date	Author, Comments	Data
Frag Spectra	2.9+6		IFJ	Expt	Jour APP 35 67	Jan 69	Benisz.TERNARY FISS,MASS YLDS,GRAPHS	
					Jour APP 32 485	Sep 67	*EXPTL DETAILS+CALCS	
					Rept INP-547	Jun 67	*	
Frag Spectra	1.3+6	5.3+6	FEI	Expt	Jour YF 9 296	Feb 69	Vorobeva+CVS,AVG E-KIN(FRAG-A,6N-ES)	
					Jour SNP 9 175	Aug 69	TRANSLATN.*	
	1.4+6	6.9+6			Rept LA-TR-21	68	Vorobeva+6ES,FRAG KE DIST CFD TH	
Frag Spectra	None		COL	Expt	Prog WASH-1127 38	Apr 69	Felvinci+ FRAG KE DISTRIBUTION,TBC	
Frag Spectra	1.6+6		FEI	Expt	Prog YFI-7 14	Apr 69	Vorobeva+ ANGDIST(FRAG-A) TABLE+GRPH	
					Rept INDC(CCP)-7U16	Feb 70	TRANSLATN.*	
					Jour YF 10 491	Sep 69	Voboreva+ANGDIST CRV,KINE AVG+SPREAD	
					Jour SNP 10 282	Mar 70	. ENGL OF YF 10 491	
Frag Spectra	Maxwl	1.6+7	FEI	Expt	Conf 69Vienna 923	Jul 69	Vorob'Eva+PPR133. FRAG YLD+E(NEUT-E)	
Frag Spectra	1.4+7		FTI	Expt	Conf 69Vienna 900	Jul 69	Adamov+PPR146. ALFA+TRITIUM SPECTRUM	
					Jour YF 9 732	Apr 69	- + AVG ALFA,T,P ENERGY + -SPREAD	
					Jour SNP 9 424	Oct 69	. ENGL OF YF 9 732	
Frag Spectra	+5	+7	ORL	ExTh	Conf 69Vienna 67	Jul 69	Schmitt.PPR122.GRPH,(EKIN+-RMS) VS A	
Frag Spectra	None		TUE	Theo	Conf 69Bochum 175	Jul 69	Goennenwein+ ANGDIST VS A,CLUSTER-TH	
	4.6+6			Expt	Jour ZN/A 22 1133	Jul 67	- + ANGDIST IN SOL-STAT DET	
	1.4+7			ExTh	Jour ZP 181 281	Oct 64	- .E-DSTRB CFD FISS-MODELS	
Frag Spectra	+5	+7	SAH	Theo	Prog BARC-474 31	70	Sarkar+ EXCIT+KIN E OKS EXPT,TBP PR	
	None				Conf 68Bombay 2 122	Dec 68	RATNA SARKAR+ EXCIT+KIN E(A),GRAPHS	
Frag Spectra	None		BLA	Expt	Prog INDC(BUL)-1G	Apr 70	Kashukeev+ PRELIMIN EXPT,NDG	
Frag Spectra	Thrsh	+6	FEI	Expt	Jour AHP 29 357	Aug 70	Androsenko+ ANGDIST CFD 2-HUMPD-BARR	
	8.0+5	2.2+6		ExTh	Conf 69Vienna 419	Jul 69	- +PPR134. XPTL ANGDIST + TH	
	8.0+5	3.4+6		Expt	Jour ZEP 8 181	Aug 68	- + ANGDIST VS NEUTRON E	
Frag Spectra	1.5+6	6.0+6	FEI	Theo	Jour AE 29 130	Aug 70	Vorobeva+ AVG KIN-E(NEUT-E) CFD NU	+
	None			Expt	Jour YF 19 954	May 74	Vorob'Eva+ AVG FRAG KE(NEUT-E),GRAPH	
					Jour SNP 19 489	Nov 74	. ENGLISH OF YF 19 954	
	1.5+6	6.0+6		Theo	Jour SJA 29 835	Aug 70	.ENGLISH TRANSL OF AE 29 130 8/70	
	1.3+6	3.4+6		Expt	Data EXFOR40281.004	May 75	.AVER KIN-E OF FF AT 12 ES GVN	
Frag Spectra	1.4+7		KFI	Expt	Jour NP/A 153 652	Sep 70	Kovacs+ ANISOTROPY OF TERNARY F FRAG	+
					Jour AHP 29 239	Jul 70	- + ANGDIST,BIN+TERNRY FISSN CFD	
					Conf 69Vienna 890	Jul 69	- +PPR8.ANGDIST OF TERNARY FISSN	
					Jour KFI 16 325	Oct 68	- +ANG-ANISOTROPY,TERNARY-FISS	
	1.4+7				Data EXFOR30326.003	Mar 76	ALPHA ACCOMP TERN FISS,90/0DEG,1PNT	
Frag Spectra	1.2+6	2.7+6	CAT	ExTh	Jour NCL 4 17 808	Oct 70	Lonigro+ FRAGMENT ANGDIST,THEOR ANAL	+
				Expt	Jour NP/A 151 182	Aug 70	Lo Nigro+ ANGDISTR+ANISOTR 9ES.	
	1.7+6	5.2+6			Jour NP 63 641	Mar 65	Emma+ FRAG ANISOT. NUCL EMULSION.	
Frag Spectra	1.2+7	1.8+7	CAT	Expt	Jour NP/A 157 449	Nov 70	Emma+ D-T NS.GLASS DET.ANG DIST.	+
					Jour NCL 3 542	70	- + METHOD	
Frag Spectra	Pile		TRM	Theo	Conf 70Madurai 2 79	Dec 70	Prakash+ KIN-E CFD SHELL-STRUCT, CRV	
Frag Spectra	1.4+7		CCP	Theo	Jour IZV 35 169	Jan 71	Bochagov+ ANALYS,DROP MODL,FRAG KINE	
					Jour BAS 35 152	Jan 71	*ENGL OF IZV 35 169	
Frag Spectra	-		CCP	Expt	Conf 71Moscow	Feb 71	Vorotnikov+.ABSTANG RESOL=12 DEG	
Frag Spectra	7.0+5	4.0+6	FEI	Expt	Prog YFI-10 25	May 71	Androsenko+ ABST+TABLES OF ANGDIST	
					Rept INDC(CCP)-15	Dec 71	*P27,ENG OF YFI-10	
Frag Spectra	5.5+5	1.5+6	KUR	Expt	Conf 71Kiev	May 71	Vorotnikov+.GIVEN GRAPH	
Frag Spectra	Maxwl	+7	CRC	Theo	Prog INDC(CAN)-9 4	Jul 71	Walker. THR+FAST FISSN,ENERGY-BALANC	
Frag Spectra	Spont		ORL	Expt	Jour NP/A 172 33	Aug 71	Ferguson+ISOMER.E DIST+CORR OK DIRCT	
					Jour PR 141 1146	Jan 66	.SEE ALSO	
Frag Spectra	1.4+7		KOS	Expt	Jour NP/A 173 571	Oct 71	Barutcugil+ TRACK DET.SIG(THETAFRAG)	+
	1.4+7				Data EXFOR30117.003	Feb 71	ANG DISTRB OF FISFRAGMNTS AT 21ANGLS	
Frag Spectra	6.0+5		KUR	Expt	Prog YFI-12 22	72	Vorotnikov+ ANGDIST OF FRAG,TBL,ABST	+
					Prog INDC(CCP)-30	Dec 72	.PG 19,ENGLISH OF YFI-12 22	
	6.0+5	1.5+6			Data EXFOR40110.	Nov 72	ANG DSTRB OF FRGMNTS, 3ANGLS, 18EN	
Frag Spectra	1.6+7		TRM	Expt	Prog BARC-628 94	72	Iyer+ ANGULAR ANISOTROPY OF FRAG,TBL	+
	1.4+7	1.6+7			Conf 70Madurai 2 57	Dec 70	- + ANGDISTR,GRAPH+TABLE,TRACK-DE	
	1.6+7				Data EXFOR30235.	Jul 73	COS.COEF.OF ANG.DIST. OF FIS.FRAGM.	
Frag Spectra	1.5+6	1.8+7	CAT	Expt	Jour NCL 3 147	Jan 72	Arena+ AVG E FISS FRAG FN EXCIT E	+
	1.5+6	1.8+7			Data EXFOR20752.002	Jan 78	3PTS.AVG.K-E.	
Frag Spectra	2.5+6	1.9+7	CCP	Expt	Jour YF 15 209	Feb 72	Bogdanov+ A-RECOIL(TERNARY),TBL,GRPH	
					Jour SNP 15 119	Aug 72	*ERROR,ENGL OF YF 15 209	
Frag Spectra	Fast		BUC	Revw	Rept IFA-RN-50	73	Cristu. MASS-+CHARGE-+E-DISTR REVIEW	
	Maxwl				Rept IFA-RN-50	73	. MASS-+CHARGE-+E-DISTR REVIEW	
Frag Spectra	1.5+6	5.3+6	FEI	Expt	Rept YK-12 1 3	Jan 73	Sergachev+ DATA TABLES AND CURVES	+
	1.5+6	5.3+6			Data EXFOR40210.	Jun 74	.SPECTR OF FISFRAG AT 2EN,AVER KIN-E	
Frag Spectra	+6	+7	TUE	Expt	Rept ORO-4856-26	75	Holubarsch+ P.591,ABSTR.EKIN-DISTRIB	
Frag Spectra	Fiss		KOS	Expt	Conf 75Karlsrhe 29	Apr 75	Csikai. CF52-NS.SSTR,W(0)/W(ANG)CURV	

92 Uranium 238

Quantity	Energy (ev) Min	Max	Lab	Type	Documentation Ref Vol Page	Date	Author, Comments	Data
Frag Spectra	5.0+6	1.0+7	FOA Expt	Conf	76ANL 128	Jun 76	Nordborg+(UPP).ANGDIST.GRPHS.TBP.	
				Conf	75Gothenbg	Jun 75	- +(UPP).ABST.SCT CH.MACROFOL	
Frag Spectra	4.7+6		RAM Expt	Jour	NSPB 9 17	Oct 76	Kasim+ ANGDIST GRAPH (NUCL EMULSION)	+
	4.7+6			Data	EXFOR30428.002	Feb 78	ANG.DIST.AT 9ANGLS.	
Frag Charge	1.4+7		CCP Expt	Jour	RAK 4 711	Dec 62	CHARGE DISTR BETWEEN A=138 ISOBARS	
Frag Charge	Maxwl		CNA Theo	Jour	PR/B 134 972	Jun 64	Talat+ N,CHARGE DIST IN FISS PRODS.	
				ExTh Rept	CNAEM-12	63	- + TBL AVERAGE CHARGE/NUCLEON	
Frag Charge	1.4+7		WAS Revw	Conf	65Salzburg 317	Mar 65	Wahl.GRAPHS TH CFD XPTS	
Frag Charge	5.5+6	6.9+6	FEI Expt	Rept	FEI-145	68	Maksyutenko+ P(Z=35)VS A,BY DELAY NS	
				Rept	LA-TR-69-3	Dec 69	. ENGLISH OF FEI-145	
Frag Charge	Fiss		GEV Comp	Rept	APED-5398	Oct 68	Meek+ TABLES. REVISED.	
Frag Charge	Fast		HAR Theo	Rept	AERE-R-6056	Mar 69	Crouch.CALC CHARGE DISPERSION,ZP,TBL	
Frag Charge	1.4+7		RAM Revw	Jour	NSPA 5 43	Apr 69	Khan. REVIEW,CHARGE DISTRIBUTN EXPTS	
Frag Charge	1.4+7		OSL Revw	Conf	69Vienna 669	Jul 69	Pappas+PPR206. REVW OF EXPTS+METHODS	
Frag Charge	Maxwl		BUC Revw	Rept	IFA-RN-50	73	Cristu.MASS-+CHARGE-+E-DISTR REVIEW	
	Fast			Rept	IFA-RN-50	73	- .MASS-+CHARGE-+E-DISTR REVIEW	
Frag Charge	1.8+6		LRL Comp	Rept	UCRL-51640	Jul 74	Nethaway. TBL.	
Frag Charge	Fiss		LAS Expt	Jour	JIN 37 1125	May 75	Wolfsberg+ FRACT CUM KR-,XE-ISOT YLD	
Frag Charge	1.4+7		GRE Expt	Rept	CEA-R-4862	77	Feualvim.EFFECT OF CHARGE PARITY	
				Rept	FRNC-TH-584	75	Feu Alvim. THESIS.ZP,FWHM.GRPHS+TBLS	
Reson Params	1.1+1		COL Expt	Jour	PR 80 499	Nov 50	Anderson+ B ABSORPTION+ RES ACT. WT.	
Reson Params	7.0+0		ANL Expt	Prog	ANL-4680 5	Sep 51	Hibdon.	+
	7.0+0			Data	EXFOR11434.	Jun 76	. 1 RES. WT,WN,WG,WT**2/PCS,PCS.	
Reson Params	1.0+3	4.0+5	RIC Expt	Jour	KAPL-793	Aug 52	Rich. THQ WG,WN,D DEDUCED FROM XPT.	
Reson Params	6.7+0	3.7+1	BNL ExTh	Jour	JNE 1 237	Jun 55	Hughes. WT WN ANALYSES FOR 3 RES	
Reson Params	6.7+0	4.2+2	BNL Expt	Jour	PR 99 10	Jul 55	Harvey+.FC TRANSM. 18 RES. AREA ANAL	+
	6.7+0	4.2+2		Data	EXFOR11912.043	Jun 76	. 18 RES. E0,WT,WN,WN0,WG.	
Reson Params	6.7+0	2.1+2	HAR Revw	Conf	55Geneva 4 210	Aug 55	Lynn+.TABLE,TOTAL-,N-,GAMMA-W, P423	+
Reson Params	6.7+0	3.7+1	BNL Expt	Jour	PR 101 1328	Feb 56	Levin+,ALSO 21EV WG=30+-10MV	+
	6.7+0	3.7+1		Data	EXFOR12274.004	Jun 76	. 3 RES. E0,WT,WN,WG,PCS.	
Reson Params	2.1+1	2.0+2	MTR Expt	Jour	PR 103 1778	Sep 56	Fluharty+ TRNS+FC 8RES ES WN WG	+
	2.1+1	2.0+2		Data	EXFOR11946.	Jun 76	. 8 RES. WN,WN0,WG,WT**2,PCS.	
Reson Params	1.0+0		AMS Expt	Jour	PHY 22 1131	Nov 56	Radkevich+ GAMMA N,G.DIST NOT EXPONTL	
Reson Params	6.7+0	4.1+2	CCP Expt	Jour	AE 1 5 55	Nov 56	Radkevich+. 20 RES, WG, WN. D PLOT	
				Jour	JNE 5 92	Jul 57	TRANSLATN.*	
				Jour	SJA 1 5 727	56	TRANSLATN.*	
Reson Params	-		HAR Theo	Jour	PHY 22 1132	Nov 56	Lynn.ABSTRACT,INTERF.METH.SLOW N,WT	
Reson Params	6.7+0	2.4+2	ANL Expt	Jour	PR 105 661	Jan 57	Bollinger+,CP5 FC 14ES ALL PARAMS	+
				Rept	ANL-5420	May 56	.SUPERSEDED	
				Abst	PR 98 223	Apr 55	.SUPERSEDED	
	6.7+0	2.4+2		Data	EXFOR12457.	Jun 76	. 13 RES. WT,WN,WN0,WG,PCS.	
Reson Params	-		CCP Theo	Jour	NP 2 575	Jan 57	Gurevich+. DISTR OF D. 'REPULSION'EF	
Reson Params	6.0+3	3.0+5	DKE Expt	Rept	ORNL-2309	Jun 57	Newson. ABS CURV WGOV D PVALUE 2XS.	
Reson Params	1.0+2	1.0+3	COL Expt	Jour	PR 118 687	May 60	Rosen+ PARAMS FOR 55 RES.	+
				Rept	CU-174	Mar 58	.SUPERSEDED	
	1.0+2	1.0+3		Data	EXFOR12460.002	Jun 76	. 48 RES. E0,WT,WN,WN0,WG.	
Reson Params	2.4+2	6.2+2	BRK Revw	Conf	60Kingston 659	Aug 60	Harvey.TABLE,GAMMA+N-WIDTH	
Reson Params	6.7+0		ANL Expt	Jour	PR 127 461	Jul 62	Jackson+ E,WT,WN, FROM SIG TOT	+
	6.7+0			Data	EXFOR11373.003	Jun 76	. 1 RES. WT,WN.	
Reson Params	6.7+0	1.8+3	HAR Expt	Jour	NP 41 614	Mar 63	Firk+100RESONANCE FROM TRANSMIS.DATA	+
				Rept	AERE-NP/GEN 15	Aug 60	- + 100RES.P-T WIDTH WIGNER SPACE	
Reson Params	-.2+2	1.1+3	UK Eval	Rept	AEEW-R-351	Feb 64	Barrington+(WIN).UKNDL LOW EN REVISN	
Reson Params	6,7+0	2.4+2	ANL Expt	Jour	PR/B 134 931	Jun 64	Jackson. PARTIAL WG 4TRANS,FLUCTNS	
Reson Params	5.0+0	2.0+3	BRK Expt	Jour	NIM 28 205	Jun 64	Firk.DATA IN LINAC EXPT REVIEW	
Reson Params	7.0+1	3.9+3	COL Expt	Jour	PR/B 134 985	Jun 64	Garg+ MANY LEVELS,WN ONLY.	
Reson Params	6.6+0	3.9+3	CJD Comp	Rept	INDSWG-101 25	65	. TBL 230RES FROM VARIOUS SOURCES	
Reson Params		2.5+2	LRL Expt	Abst	BAP 10 12	Jan 65	Bowman+ NDG.	
Reson Params	6.7+0	1.9+3	WES Eval	Rept	WANL-TME-1228	Aug 65	Gibson+.RESOLVED+STATISTICAL RES	
Reson Params	4.5+4	1.5+6	KFK Eval	Rept	KFK-120 1	Feb 66	Schmidt.25EO I,PARITIES	
	4.4+0	3.9+3		Conf	66S.Diego 2 223	Feb 66	- . SEE KFK-120	
				Rept	KFK-120 1	Nov 65	- .240 E0.L,J,WN,WG.STAT RS S,P	
Reson Params	6.7+0	3.2+3	SAC Expt	Conf	66Paris 1 193	Oct 66	Barros+ PPR63.CURVES.EXP/TH.	
	6.7+0	2.6+2		Jour	JPR 22 722	Oct 61	Corge+TOF NAI(TL) WG PARTIAL 13PARAM	
Reson Params		1.0+6	AUA Theo	Jour	AUJ 20 477	Oct 67	Cook. TBL OF AVG LVL SPACING D,L=0,1	
Reson Params	8.1+5	4.1+2	NIL Theo	Rept	PINST-RT-1	68	Bhatti+WN,WG,E GVN,8RESON,R LATTICE	
Reson Params	8.5+5	1.5+6	SUN Expt	Prog	INDC-282 3	68	Mcmurray+ LVL ANAL,WORK TB CONTINUED	

92 Uranium 238

Quantity	Energy (ev) Min	Max	Lab	Type	Documentation Ref Vol Page	Date	Author, Comments	Data
Reson Params	3.0+1	2.0+3	LAS	Expt	Conf 68Wash. 573	Mar 68	Glass+ TOF BOMB 62S,200P LVLS,PARAMS	+
					Rept LA-DC-9181	67	.SUPERSEDED	
	4.5+1	2.1+3			Data EXFOR12471.003	Jun 76	. 226 RES. E0,WN,WN0,WG.	
Reson Params	+5	+6	CCP	Theo	Jour YF 7 1228	Jun 68	Vorotnikov.D,EXPT CFD DEGEN-FERM-GAS	
					Jour SNP 7 732	Dec 68	TRANSLATN.*	
Reson Params	4.4+0	1.7+2	ANL	Expt	Jour PR 171 1293	Jul 68	Bollinger+ TRANS 16 P-WAVE RES SEEN	+
					Conf 65Antwerp 96	Jul 65	.SUPERSEDED	
	4.4+0	1.7+2			Data EXFOR12461.002	Jun 76	. 16 RES. WN.	
Reson Params	Pile		TRM	Expt	Rept BARC-421	69	Mahalingam+CRITICL-XPT CFD DATA-SETS	
Reson Params	6.7+0		KFK	Expt	Prog EANDC(E)115U	Mar 69	Albold. TEMP DEP OF LINE SHAPE	
					Prog EANDC(E)89U	Jan 68	Schweiss+ DOPPLER BROADENING,FN OF T	
Reson Params	6.0+0	3.0+2	HAR	Expt	Prog AERE-PR/NP16	Aug 69	Moxon+ TBD FROM SIGT + SIGG DATA	+
	1.0+3	1.0+5			Rept NP-17644	Jul 68	-.THESIS. AVG D,WG,AND WG/D	
	6.6+0	8.2+2			Jour NP 85 305	Sep 66	Asghar+ GN+GG FOR 27 RESONANCES	
	3.6+1	6.7+2			Jour NIM 28 205	Jun 64	Firk.(MOXON).TBL WG,WN IN LINAC REV	
Reson Params	6.7+0		DUB	Expt	Rept JINR-P3-4992	Apr 70	Rjabov+ TOT+N+G-WID FOR 6.68EV GIVEN	+
					Prog YFI-11 27	70	- + ABST,SAME TBL AS JINR-4992	
					Prog INDC(CCP)-31	Dec 72	.PAGE 26,ENGLISH OF YFI-11 27	
	6.7+0				Data EXFOR40070.	Aug 70	TOT-WIDTH,N-WIDTH,GAM-WIDTH,6.68EV	
Reson Params	1.0+3	1.0+5	FEI	Expt	Conf 70Helsinki 1 559	Jun 70	Van'Kov+85. RES PARS AND TEMPERATURE	
Reson Params	6.6+1	1.1+3	GEL	Expt	Conf 70Helsinki 1 413	Jun 70	Rohr+18. NEUT+GAMMA WIDTH OF 28RESON	+
	6.6+1	1.1+3			Data EXFOR20144.	Mar 73	57PTS.WG,AVG WG,WN.	
Reson Params	+2	2.0+3	HAR	Comp	Conf 70Helsinki 1 267	Jun 70	James.107. GAM-WIDTH VS E GRAPH	
Reson Params		1.0+6	HAR	Revw	Conf 70Helsinki 1 93	Jun 70	Lynn.105. GAM-WIDTH(NEUT-E) GRAPHS	
Reson Params		3.5+2	HAR	Expt	Conf 70Helsinki 1 373	Jun 70	Thomas+36. ISOMERIC LEVEL AT 134.KEV	
Reson Params	4.5+4	1.5+6	JAE	Eval	Conf 70Helsinki 2 869	Jun 70	Igarasi+27. TBL OF RES-E,SPIN,PARITY	
Reson Params	-		DUB	Revw	Rept JINR-E4-5469	Nov 70	Soloviev. U-239,SINGL PARTICL STATES	
Reson Params	None		DUB	Expt	Jour AE 29 395	Nov 70	Pikel'Ner+ ABST FRANC-SOV SEM DUBNA	
					Jour SJA 29 1156	Nov 70	TRANSLATN.*	
Reson Params	1.0+0	1.0+2	AUA	Theo	Jour AUJ 23 823	Dec 70	Clayton.MULTILEVEL ANALYS,ELAST SCAT	
Reson Params	None		DUB	Theo	Jour YF 13 240	Feb 71	Malecki+G-WID,THEO CFD EXPT.TBL,GRPH	
					Jour SNP 13 133	Aug 71	- + ENGL OF YF 13 240.	
Reson Params	2.5-2	1.5+7	FEI	Eval	Rept INDC(CCP)-11	Mar 71	Abagyan+ AVG NEUT+GAM WIDTHS,D-DISTR	
Reson Params	1.0+3	1.0+6	GA	Expt	Conf 71Knoxvill 252	Mar 71	Fricke+,AVG WG AND D GIVEN	
Reson Params	7.6+2	3.6+3	GEL	Expt	Conf 71Knoxvill 701	Mar 71	Carraro+.WN+AVG D GIVEN	+
	6.0+1	5.7+3			Conf 70Helsinki 1 403	Jun 70	- +17. NEUTRON-W AND D,TBL+GRPH	
	7.6+2	3.6+3			Data EXFOR20505.	Mar 76	295PTS.71KNOX DATA	
	6.6+1	5.8+3			Data EXFOR20115.	Jul 72	508PTS.E0,WN,WN0,AVG.WN0.	
Reson Params	5.0+2		SAC	Eval	Conf 71Knoxvill 438	Mar 71	Ribon+.DISCREPANCIES AMONG WN DATA	
Reson Params	6.2-1	5.0+4	SRL	Theo	Conf 71Knoxvill 714	Mar 71	Mccrosson. STAT CALCULATN AVG PARAMS	
Reson Params	4.6+2	1.2+4	FEI	Expt	Rept INDC(CCP)-16	Jul 71	Vankov+PG49.D,AVG N+G-WID FITTED.TBL	
Reson Params	6.7+0	6.0+2	BNL	Expt	Jour PR/C 4 900	Sep 71	Chrien+.PARTIAL WG DIST,RESON CAPTUR	
					Jour PR/C 4 2294	Dec 71	.CORRECTION.	
					Conf 68DUBSY 342	Jul 68	.SUPERSEDED	
Reson Params	+1	+4	CCP	Revw	Jour AE 31 595	Dec 71	Sukhoruchkin.G+N-WIDS,DATA CFD,GRPH	
					Jour SJA 31 1380	Jun 72	*ENGL OF AE 31 595	
Reson Params	6.6+1	1.2+3	DUB	Expt	Jour AE 32 49	Jan 72	Maleckij+ TRANS,G-WID,N-WID,TBL,GRPH	+
					Rept JINR-P3-5609	Mar 71	Malecki+ NEUT+G WIDTH AT 38RES,TABLE	
					Jour SJA 32 45	Jul 72	. ENGL OF AE 32 49	
	6.6+1	1.2+3			Data EXFOR40068.	Jun 71	N-WIDTH AND G-WIDTH AT 50 RESONANCES	
Reson Params	+3	+5	AUA	Expt	Prog AAEC/PR-36P 11	Mar 72	Allen+ ORELA.DATA TO BE ANALYZED,NDG	
Reson Params	1.5+0	3.0+1	COL	Eval	Prog COO-2176-1 7	Jun 72	Felvinci+. SINGLE+MULTILVL FITS	
Reson Params	1.0+4	1.0+5	RPI	Expt	Prog COO-3058-34	Mar 73	Byoun+D,WG,WG0.TBL.CFD.SELF INDIC.	
	1.5+4	1.0+5			Conf 72Kiamesha 1	Sep 72	- +WG,WG0,D DRVD FROM BEST FIT.	
	1.0+4	1.0+5			Data EXFOR10577.	Nov 76	. 20 PTS. WG,WN0,J,L,D, GVN.	
Reson Params	6.6+0	4.6+3	COL	Expt	Jour PR/C 5 1854	Nov 72	Rahn+.WN WG G*WN.L=0,1.ALSO P-T DIST	+
					Conf 71Albany 205	Aug 71	Camarada+WG GVN.TBP PR.	
					Conf 71Knoxvill 658	Mar 71	.SUPERSEDED	
	6.6+0	5.0+3			Prog NYO-73-340 3	Dec 70	Rahn+.WT,G*WN,WG DISTR. MANY RESON	
	6.6+0	4.6+3			Data EXFOR10274.011	Feb 75	. 5 PTS.	
	6.6+0	4.6+3			Data EXFOR10274.	Feb 75	. 211 RES,RED N-WID	
Reson Params	4.4+0	1.0+5	FEI	Eval	Conf 73Kiev 1 239	May 73	Abagjan+ N-WIDS,AVG+GROUP PARAM,GRPH	
					Rept INDC(CCP)-44	Jun 74	.P37. ENGLISH OF 73KIEV 1 239	
Reson Params	6.6+0	3.5+3	COL	Expt	Jour NSE 51 119	Jun 73	Wynchank+. E0 ONLY FOR 25 RESONANCES	
Reson Params	7.2+2	1.2+3	RPI	Expt	Jour PRL 31 247	Jul 73	Block+. WF TABULATED FOR 2 RESONANCS	+
	7.2+2	1.2+3			Data EXFOR10569.	Jun 76	. 2 RES ES,WF,FISS AREAS.	
Reson Params	5.2+2	6.0+2	ORL	Expt	Jour NSE 51 385	Aug 73	Desaussure+ WN,WG CALC. CFD OTHERS.	+
	5.2+2	6.0+2			Data EXFOR10101.004	Mar 76	. 11 PTS.E0,WN,WG.	

92 Uranium 238

Quantity	Energy (ev) Min	Max	Lab	Type	Documentation Ref Vol Page	Date	Author, Comments	Data
Reson Params	4.0-1	2.5+4	WIN	Eval Prog	EANDC(UK) 151	Aug 73	James+ GENEX EVALUATION	
Reson Params	1.0+3	6.0+3	ORL	Revw Rept	CONF-740903-7	Sep 74	Desaussure+ NG CS FRM RES PARS, NDG	
Reson Params		1.0+4	HAR	Expt Conf	NEANDC(E)163U	Jan 75	Sowerby.COMMENT ON UNRESOL RES PARAM	
Reson Params	4.4+0	4.6+3	HAR	Expt Conf	NEANDC(E)-163U	Jan 75	Moxon. TABLE OF RECOMMENDED VALUES	
Reson Params	2.0+2	1.0+5	FEI	Expt Rept	INDC(CCP)-49	Feb 75	Vankov+ ENGLISH OF YFI-18 11	
Reson Params	6.6+0	6.7+1	BNL	Revw Prog	BNL-50451 263	Mar 75	Bhat+WN,WG,WT.TBL.PARS EFFECT ON NG	
Reson Params	None		COL	Expt Conf	75Wash. 335	Mar 75	Felvinci+MOD ERICSON CALC CFD EXPT	
Reson Params	6.6+2	1.3+3	GEL	Expt Conf	75Wash. 597	Mar 75	Wartena+ TOF.TBL EO,WF	+
	6.6+2	1.3+3		Data	EXFOR20760.002	Jan 78	18PTS.WF.	
Reson Params	6.4+1	1.5+3	GEL	Expt Conf	75Wash. 733	Mar 75	Corvi+ TBL EO,GWN,P-WAVE ASSIGN.	+
	6.3+1	1.5+3		Data	EXFOR20430.	Mar 75	59PTS.AVG.G*WN1,MEAN LVLSP,G*WN1.	
Reson Params	2.1+1	4.7+3	JAE	Expt Conf	75Wash. 738	Mar 75	Nakajima+ TBL EO,WNO CFD EXPT	
	2.1+1	4.7+3		Data	EXFOR20431.002	Jul 75	176PTS.WN0.	
Reson Params	1.5+3	2.7+3	SAC	Eval Prog	BNL-50451 156	Mar 75	Derrien+COMMENTS ON WN EVAL.TBL.CFD	
	1.5+3	1.8+3		Conf	NEANDC(E)163U	Jan 75	- +SHAPE ANAL OF VARIOUS DATA	
Reson Params	6.7+0	2.6+3	WIN	Revw Prog	BNL-50451 45	Mar 75	Askew+RVW U238 RES PARS.TBLS	
Reson Params	None		COL	Eval Prog	ERDA-NDC-2 59	May 75	Melkonian+CORRELATION OF EL/WID.	
Reson Params	+0	+6	SAC	ExTh Prog	NEANDC(E)162U	Aug 75	Blons+ INTERMEDIATE STRUC ANAL	
Reson Params	6.0+0	7.2+0	ORL	Expt Prog	ORNL-5101 1	Jan 76	Desaussure+ CAPT WID OF 6.67EV LVL.	
Reson Params	1.4+3	2.7+3	GEL	Expt Prog	NEANDC(E)172 3	Feb 76	Boeckhoff+LINAC TOF RES ENERGIES	
Reson Params	6.7+1	1.0+1	HAN	Expt Abst	BAP 6 8	Feb 61	Leonard+ ABST A8	+
	6.7+1	1.0+1		Data	EXFOR12286.008	Jun 76	. 2 RES, PCS-FISS	
Reson Params	6.0+2	9.0+2	LRL	Expt Conf	76Lowell 1402	Jul 76	Browne.EVIDENCE 2ND WELL G DECAY.	
Reson Params	+7		FEI	Theo Rept	YK- 21 3	Oct 76	Blokhin+ D,WG,WG/D,TBL	
Reson Params	Maxwl		KUK	Theo Conf	76Ahmedabd 2 1	Dec 76	Sharma+AVG S-WAVE REDUCED N-WID ANAL	
Strnth Fnctn	1.7+1	5.2+1	MTR	Expt Jour	PR 103 1778	Sep 56	Fluharty+ TRNS+FC STF=1.55+-0.50	+
	2.1+1	2.0+2		Data	EXFOR11946.	Jun 76	. 2 PTS. S0,D.	
Strnth Fnctn	3.0+0	5.0+2	AMS	Expt Jour	PHY 22 1131	Nov 56	Radkevich+ABSTRACT,NDG	
Strnth Fnctn	1.0+0		BNL	Revw Jour	PHY 22 994	Nov 56	Hughes.DISTRIBUTN OF LEVEL SPACINGS	
Strnth Fnctn	6.7+0	2.9+2	CCP	Expt Jour	AE 1 5 55	Nov 56	Radkevich+. S0=1.5+-0.18	+
				Jour	JNE 5 92	Jul 57	TRANSLATN.*	
				Jour	SJA 1 5 727		56 TRANSLATN.*	
Strnth Fnctn	6.7+0	2.4+2	ANL	Expt Jour	PR 105 661	Jan 57	Bollinger+,CP5 FC 1.43+-0.4	+
	6.7+0	2.4+2		Data	EXFOR12457.	Jun 76	. 2 PTS. STF,D.	
Strnth Fnctn	0.0+0	1.0+7	LAS	Theo Jour	PR 110 1080	Jun 58	Chase+,ROTATIONAL-OPTICAL MDL TH CRV	
Strnth Fnctn	+3		BNL	Expt Jour	PRL 1 461	Dec 58	Hughes. FC 1.15+-0.15	
Strnth Fnctn	6.7+0	1.0+3	COL	Expt Jour	PR 118 687	May 60	Rainwater+ 0.95+-0.15.	
Strnth Fnctn	1.0+3	4.0+5	DKE	Eval Jour	AP 10 455	Aug 60	Bilpuch+ CALC FROM CAPT SIG L=1.	+
	1.0+3	4.0+5		Expt Data	EXFOR11187.009	Jun 76	. 1 PT. STF.	
Strnth Fnctn	4.0+2	2.0+3	ORL	Expt Conf	60Kingston 757	Aug 60	Firk.CURVE,TRSMISSION METHOD	
Strnth Fnctn	None		DKE	Theo Jour	NP 24 169	Apr 61	Seth. J-DEPENDENCE OF S-WAVE STRFUNC	
Strnth Fnctn	3.0+3	5.0+4	HAR	Theo Jour	PPS 82 903	Dec 63	Lynn.S1=2.5+-.4 ,MULTILVL ANAL TRNSM	
Strnth Fnctn	6.7+0	1.8+3	HAR	Expt Jour	NP 41 614	Mar 63	Firk+ 0.000100+-0.000014	+
				Jour	NIM 28 205	Jun 64	- .DATA IN LINAC EXPT REVIEW	
	6.0+0	1.8+3		Rept	TNCC(UK)-44	Aug 59	- + 70 RES.THICK SAMPLE METHOD.	
Strnth Fnctn		2.0+3	COL	Expt Jour	PL 12 240	Oct 64	Garg. LVL SPACING DIST TH232+U238	+
	+1	+3		Jour	PR/B 134 985	Jun 64	- + S0 ONLY	
Strnth Fnctn	3.0+3	6.5+6	DKE	ExTh Jour	PL 13 70	Nov 64	Seth+,S,P,D STF FRM SIG TOT 3-650KEV	
	5.0+3	1.5+5		Expt Conf	64Paris 2 916	Jul 64	- + S0,S1,S2 R PRIME/R.	
	3.0+3	6.5+6		Data	EXFOR11665.035	Jun 76	. 3 PTS. STF.	
Strnth Fnctn	+3		KFK	Eval Conf	66S.Diego 2 223	Feb 66	Schmidt.DEDUCED FROM EXP DATA	
Strnth Fnctn	1.0+2	1.0+7	HAR	Expt Conf	66Paris 1 165	Oct 66	Uttley+ PPR36.TABLE,CURVES,S+P+DWAVE	+
	1.0+3	1.0+5		Conf	64Paris 2 700	Jul 64	-	
Strnth Fnctn	3.0+1	2.1+3	LAS	Expt Conf	68Wash. 573	Mar 68	Glass+ TOF BOMB 1.8+-0.3	
	3.0+1	2.1+3		Data	EXFOR12471.	Jun 76	. 3 PTS. S0,D,AVE WN0.	
Strnth Fnctn	4.4+0	1.7+2	ANL	Expt Jour	PR 171 1293	Jul 68	Bollinger+ TRANS PWAVE 2.14+2.0-1.0	
				Conf	65Antwerp § 96	Jul 65	.SUPERSEDED	
Strnth Fnctn	1.0+3	1.0+5	HAR	Expt Rept	NP-17644	Jul 68	Moxon.THESIS.MOXON-RAE DET.S+P+DWAVE	+
	0.0+0	1.0+0			NP 85 305	Sep 66	Asghar+ S WAVE .70+-.15 10-4	
Strnth Fnctn	+5	+7	CCP	Theo Jour	YF 8 704	Oct 68	Ermagambetov+OPTMOD-REVW,TBL S0+S1	
				Jour	SNP 8 409	Apr 69	TRANSLATN.*	
Strnth Fnctn		2.0+3	ANL	Theo Prog	WASH-1136 12	Sep 69	Monahan+,LVL SPACING DISTR,OKS EXPT	
Strnth Fnctn	2.5-2	1.5+7	FEI	Eval Rept	INDC(CCP)-11	Mar 71	Abagyan+ EVALUATED S0+S1 VALUES GIVN	
Strnth Fnctn	1.0+3	1.0+6	GA	Expt Conf	71Knoxvill 252	Mar 71	Fricke+, S0 AND S1 GIVEN	
Strnth Fnctn		5.8+3	GEL	Expt Conf	71Knoxvill 701	Mar 71	Carraro+.SO=1.00+-0.13	+
	6.0+1	5.7+3		Conf	70Helsinki 1 403	Jun 70	- +17. S0 VALUE DETERMINED	
	0.0+0	5.8+3		Data	EXFOR20505.	Mar 76	12PTS.L=0.	
	6.0+1	2.0+3		Data	EXFOR20115.010	Jul 72	1PNT.L=0.	

92 Uranium 238

Quantity	Energy (ev) Min	Max	Lab	Type	Documentation Ref Vol Page	Date	Author, Comments	Data
Strnth Fnctn	3.7+1	2.4+2	LAS Expt	Jour	PR/C 4 220	Jul 71	Silbert+.NUCL SHOT. AVG WF FOR 8RES	+
	3.7+1	2.4+2		Data	EXFOR10290.002	Jan 73	. 1 PT. AVG.WF.	
Strnth Fnctn	+1	+4	CCP Revw	Jour	AE 31 595	Dec 71	Sukhoruchkin.EXPTL DATA CFD+GIVEN	
				Jour	SJA 31 1380	Jun 72	*ENGL OF AE 31 595	
Strnth Fnctn	1.0+4	1.0+5	RPI Expt	Prog	COO−3058−34	Mar 73	Byoun+S0,S1.TBLS.	+
				Conf	72Kiamesha 1	Sep 72	− +LEAST SQ METHOD.S0,S1 TBLS.	
	1.0+3	1.0+5		Data	EXFOR10577.	Nov 76	10 PTS.S AND P WAVE.	
Strnth Fnctn	6.6+0	4.6+3	COL Expt	Jour	PR/C 5 1854	Nov 72	Rahn+. S0=1.08+−0.10,S1=1.4 APPROX	
	+1	+3		Rept	EANDC(US)−179	72	.SUPERSEDED	
	6.6+0	4.6+3		Conf	71Albany 205	Aug 71	Camarada+S0 GVN	
	6.6+0	5.0+3		Prog	NYO−73−340 3	Dec 70	Rahn+.S0=1.02+−0.10	
Strnth Fnctn	None		AUA Eval	Rept	AAEC/E−277	Mar 73	Musgrove.TBLS EXPTL DATA+BEST VALUES	
Strnth Fnctn	+3	+4	BET Theo	Jour	NSE 52 461	Dec 73	Goldsmith.OPTMOD CALC. S1 GIVN.	
Strnth Fnctn	1.0+4		BRC Eval	Conf	JAERI−M−5984	Feb 75	Lagrange.COUPLD CHANL MDL.TBL S0,S1	
Strnth Fnctn	2.0+2	1.0+5	FEI Expt	Rept	INDC(CCP)−49	Feb 75	Vankov+ ENGLISH OF YFI−18 11	
Strnth Fnctn	None		COL Expt	Conf	75Wash. 780	Mar 75	Hacken+ TBL AVG WG,STF,NUMBER GWN,WG	
Strnth Fnctn	1.0+1	1.6+3	GEL Expt	Conf	75Wash. 733	Mar 75	Corvi+ S0,S1,DO	+
	6.3+1	1.5+3		Data	EXFOR20430.	Mar 75	2PTS.L=0,L=1.	
Strnth Fnctn	2.0+1	1.8+3	MOL Expt	Prog	INDC(SEC)−51	Dec 75	Poortmans+P67.ABST,BY SCAT+CAPT,NDG	
Strnth Fnctn	1.0+3	3.0+4	KAL Eval	Conf	76Bombay 559	Mar 76	Ganesan+ S1−SET ADJUSTD TO SIG.TABLE	
Lvl Density	−		COP Theo	Jour	NP 6 62	Mar 58	Ericson. LVL DENSITY FORM CFD EXP	
Lvl Density	6.0+6		DKE Expt	Rept	AD−299005	62	Seth+,NUCL TEMP+FERMI LVL DENS COEFF	
Lvl Density	1.4+7		BAS Expt	Jour	PL 5 202	Jul 63	Huber+TBL OF NUC TEMP AND LVL DENSTY	
				Jour	HPA 35 733	Dec 62	Poppelbaum+ NUCLEAR TEMP=0.36MEV	
				Jour	HPA 34 815	Dec 61	Huber+ NUCLEAR TEMP=0.36MEV.	
Lvl Density	2.5+6		ISL Theo	Conf	64Geneva § 511	May 64	Szwarcbaum+.T FROM 3 FORMLS CFD EXPS	
Lvl Density	−		VNV Expt	Conf	67Bordeaux	Mar 67	Bertrand+FROM FISS+EVAP N SP. FP JPR	
Lvl Density	−		CCP Theo	Jour	YF 7 832	Apr 68	Shigin.GRPH LVL DEN(FISS−FRAG−A),YLD	
				Jour	SNP 7 4 506	Oct 68	TRANSLATN.*	
Lvl Density	1.4+7		FEI Expt	Jour	IZV 32 653	Apr 68	Salnikov+ A+TEMP GVN,LE COUTEUR EXPT	+
				Prog	YFI−4 21	May 67	.DENSITY+NUCLEAR TEMP.TABLE	
				Jour	BAS 32 600	69	.ENGLISH TRANSL OF IZV 32 653 4/68	
				Prog	INDC−E−187 29	67	.ENGLISH TRANSL OF YFI−4	
	1.4+7			Data	EXFOR40332.	Feb 76	TEMP(.009),LVL DENS PARAM(.010)	
Lvl Density		5.0+2	KUR Theo	Jour	YF 9 303	Feb 69	Vorotnikov.LVL DEN(EXCIT−E),TBL GRPH	
				Jour	SNP 9 179	Aug 69	TRANSLATN.*	
Lvl Density	1.4+7		BAS Expt	Jour	HPA 42 225	Apr 69	Boschung+.NUCL TEMP TOF CFD TH+EXP	
Lvl Density	0.0+0	2.0+3	GEL Expt	Conf	70Helsinki 1 403	Jun 70	Carraro+.	+
		2.0+3		Data	EXFOR20115.011	Jul 72	1PNT.SP.CUT(0).	
Lvl Density	−		KTO Expt	Jour	NST 8 173	Mar 71	Kimura+.(G,FN+N),NUC TEMP IN FIG+TBL	
Lvl Density	9.2+6		FEI Expt	Conf	71Kiev	May 71	Zhuravlev+.TOF,TEMP AND LVL DEN,TBL	
Lvl Density	2.5+5	4.0+6	SAC Theo	Conf	INDC(SEC)−31	Jan 73	L'Heriteau+ P79. TEMPERAT−LAW, CURVE	
Lvl Density	None		COP Theo	Jour	JP/A 222 493	Apr 74	Dossing+COLL ROTAT.SPAC. ACCUR ESTIM	
Lvl Density	3.5+3	5.8+3	JAE ExTh	Jour	JPJ 37 581	Sep 74	Ideno.LVL SPACING CORRELATIONS.TBL.	
				Rept	JAERI−M−5490	Nov 73	.LEVEL SPACING CORRELATIONS.TBL	
Lvl Density	1.0+1	1.6+3	GEL Expt	Conf	75Wash. 733	Mar 75	Corvi+ DO = 22.4 +− 1.0 EV	
Lvl Density	+0		DUB Theo	Conf	75Kiev 3 23	May 75	Voronov. LVL SPACING OF U 239.TABLE	
Lvl Density	+6		DUB Theo	Rept	JINR−E4−9236	Nov 75	Komov+ AVG LVL−SPAC,SEMIMICRO CFD XP	
Lvl Density	None			Jour	NP/A 224 396	May 74	Malov+ 1/2 MICROSC.MODEL. DEFORM NUC	
Lvl Density	None		FEI Theo	Rept	FEI−636	Dec 75	Nikolaev+ PARITY DEPENDNC,FROM P−RES	
(γ,n)	8.0+6	2.0+7	ANL Expt	Conf	55Geneva 2 208	Aug 55	Huizenga.P836,CURVE,ALSO FISS−YIELD	
(γ,n)	+7		BSP Revw	Conf	55Geneva 2 169	Aug 55	Souza−Santos+.P897,THRESHOLD VAL GVN	
(γ,n)	6.0+6	9.0+6	REH Expt	Jour	NP 61 17	Jan 65	Lindner.RATIO TO GF WN/WF CONST VS E	
(γ,n)	6.0+6	2.0+7	RIO ExTh	Jour	NDF 15 319	Nov 69	Carvalho+ PHOT−REACTN SIG GRPHS,REVW	
(γ,n)	6.0+6	7.5+6	CRC Expt	Prog	AECL−4205	Mar 72	Knowles. SIGMA NEAR PHOTOFISSION	
	5.0+6	8.0+6		Prog	AECL−4147 49	Dec 71	Guidicini+. TO BE COMPLETED. NDG	
(γ,n)	8.0+6	1.8+7	SAC Expt	Prog	NEANDC(E)161U	Aug 74	Bergere+ ALSO (G,2N)	
(γ,n)	None		LRL Expt	Prog	ERDA−NDC−2 75	May 75	Alvarez+TBC.NDG.	
(γ,n)	6.0+6	8.0+6	DUB Theo	Jour	JEL 23 75	Jan 76	Voronov+ RAD STRNGTH−F CFD XPTS.GRPH	
Photo−Fissn	4.8+6	6.8+6	UI Expt	Jour	PR 77 329	Feb 50	Koch FISS COUNTS PER ROENTGN / E(G)	
Photo−Fissn		2.2+7	LAS Expt	Jour	PR 81 344	Feb 51	Ogle+ EXCITATION CURVE.SIG MAX 15MEV	
Photo−Fissn	8.0+6	2.2+7	UI Expt	Jour	PR 89 1042	Mar 53	Duffield+ BETATRON EXCITATION CURVE	
Photo−Fissn	1.2+7	2.0+7	ANL Expt	Jour	PR 95 1009	Aug 54	Huizenga+ 3ES RELATIVE FISS YIELDS	
Photo−Fissn	9.0+6	1.6+7	MIT Expt	Jour	PR 95 1550	Sep 54	Richter+ LINAC FISS YIELDS CURVS	
Photo−Fissn	1.3+7		NOR Expt	Jour	ZEC 58 623	Oct 54	Wiles.PRIMARY FISS YIELD FINE STRUCT	
Photo−Fissn	1.3+7		MIT Expt	Jour	PR 96 696	Nov 54	Wiles+ FINE STRUCT FOR MASS 99−106	
Photo−Fissn	5.0+6	2.5+7	LEB Expt	Conf	55Moscow 306	Jul 55	Lazareva. N−YILD IN FOTOFIS,CURV+TBL	
				Rept	AEC−TR−2435	56	. P 217. ENGL TRANSL OF 55MOSCOW 306	

92 Uranium 238

Quantity	Energy (ev) Min	Max	Lab	Type	Documentation Ref Vol Page	Author, Comments Date	Data
Photo – Fissn	6.0+6	1.9+7	ANL	Expt	Jour PR 104 425	Oct 56 Gindler+,RADIOCHEM BETATRON EXC FNCT	
Photo – Fissn	4.5+6	1.0+7	UI	Expt	Jour PR 105 1277	Feb 57 Schmitt+,ACTVTN FN SYM/ASYM FISS	
Photo – Fissn	6.1+6	7.0+6	ANL	Expt	Diss ANL–5853	Jul 58 Clarke. 2 GAMMA ES, ION CHAMBER	
Photo – Fissn		1.2+7	CCP	Expt	Jour ZET 36 315	Jan 59 FRAGMENT ENERGY SPECT,E MAX 12.5MEV	
					Jour JET 9 217	Jul 59 TRANSLATN.*	
Photo – Fissn	6.0+6	2.0+7	CRC	Expt	Jour CJP 37 1418	Dec 59 Baerg+. FRAG ANG DIST ANISOTROPIC	
Photo – Fissn	8.0+6	4.8+7	CCP	Theo	Jour AE 8 409	May 60 Zysin+.NU CALCD FROM FRGMNT–DISTRIBS	
					Jour SJA 8 343	Jun 61 TRANSLATN.*JNE AB17 41 1/61	
					Jour KE 4 40	Jan 61 .TRANSLATN	
Photo – Fissn	7.0+6		FEI	Expt	Jour AE 8 457	May 60 Prokhorova+ REL U235,F19(P,ALF)O16.	
					Jour KE 4 74	Jan 61 . GERMAN OF AE 8 457	
					Jour SJA 8 390	May 60 . ENGL OF AE 8 457	
Photo – Fissn	None		GA	Expt	Rept GA– 2010	Feb 61 Walton.DELAYED GAMMA INTENSITIES	
Photo – Fissn	6.9+6	2.0+7	RIO	Expt	Jour NC 19 1131	Mar 61 DE CARVALHO+,ANG.DIST.,EMULSIONS SEE ALSO NCS 19 24 1961,DESCRIPTIO	+
Photo – Fissn	1.2+7	2.0+7	USP	Expt	Jour PR 126 1098	May 62 Moscati+.DELAYED NEUT YLD.TBL+CURVES	
	2.2+7				Jour PR 126 1098	May 62 – +. DELAYED NEUT YLDS	
Photo – Fissn	7.0+6		ANL	Expt	Jour NP 34 439	Jun 62 Huizenga+ 6.91+7.12MEV GAMS+MO99PROD	
Photo – Fissn	1.7+7	5.0+7	FTI	Expt	Jour ZET 43 1611	Nov 62 Bochagov.E–DSTRB OF FOTOFISS–FRGMTS	
					Jour JET 16 1135	May 63 TRANSLATN.*	
Photo – Fissn		1.4+7	RI	Expt	Jour AE 15 308	Oct 63 Petrzhak+ YIELD(MASS)+REL YIELDS.	
Photo – Fissn	+6	+7	FEI	Theo	Rept INDSWG–72	65 Soldatov+.FISS BY QUADRUPOLE ABSORPT	
Photo – Fissn	6.1+6	9.0+6	ETH	Expt	Conf 65Salzburg 343	Mar 65 Cavacho+ANG.DISTR.FRAGM.TABLES.GRAPH	
Photo – Fissn	1.0+7	1.5+7	CCP	Expt	Jour AE 19 185	Aug 65 Nikotin+NEUTRON YIELD VS.DELAY OF GP	
					Jour JNE 20 711	Aug 66 TRANSLATN.*	
					Jour EAF 19 2 119	Aug 65 TRANSLATN.*	
					Jour SJA 19 1080	Aug 65 TRANSLATN.*	
Photo – Fissn	5.2+6	9.3+6	IFP	Expt	Jour ZET 49 476	Aug 65 Bocharova+ FRAGMENT–ANGDIST GRAPHS	
					Jour JET 22 335	Feb 66 TRANSLATN.*	
Photo – Fissn	6.1+6		LND	Expt	Jour NP 70 209	Aug 65 Albertsson+FRAG.ANGULAR DISTRIBUTION	
Photo – Fissn	7.0+6		FOA	Expt	Jour AF 29 301	Dec 65 Holmberg+.PROMPT NU.F19+P GAM.LIQ SC	
					Conf 65Salzburg 2 57	Mar 65 – + PROMPT VAL.SEE AF 29 301	
Photo – Fissn	1.5+7		CCP	Expt	Jour AE 20 268	Mar 66 Nikotin+.DELAYED NEUT YIELD,6 GROUPS	
					Jour SJA 20 300	Mar 66 . ENGL OF AE 20 268	
Photo – Fissn	None		GA	Expt	Jour PR 146 824	Jun 66 Sund+ LINAC SOURCE	
Photo – Fissn	4.5+6	6.5+6	KUR	Expt	Rept IAE–1448	67 Kurchatov+ ASYM CUM YLD(E),GRPHS+TBL	
Photo – Fissn	5.4+6	6.5+6	IFP	ExTh	Jour ZEP 6 495	Jul 67 Kapica+.,CD115 YIELD VS E,CURVE	
Photo – Fissn	5.1+6	9.7+6	WIS	Expt	Abst DA/B 28 719	Aug 67 Oblock.(NG) SOURCES USED	
Photo – Fissn	1.5+7		MNZ	Theo	Jour AF 36 453	Nov 67 Patzelt+.FROM DERIVED N–EMISS PROB.	
Photo – Fissn	5.0+6	8.0+6	FEI	Expt	Jour PL/B 26 4 218	Jan 68 Rabotnov+ANGDIST FISS FRAG AT THRES	
					Prog YFI–4 12	May 67 .CURVES GIVEN	
	5.0+6	9.0+6		ExTh	Conf 67Kharkov 216	Feb 67 .ANG DISTRIB,CHANNEL EFFECTS	
	5.2+6	9.2+6		Expt	Conf 65Salzburg 1 135	Mar 65 .ANG DISTRIB,FOTO FISS FRAGMENTS	
					Conf 65Salzburg 1 135	Mar 65 Rabotnov+ ANG DIST FOTO FISS FRAGMTS	
	5.0+6	9.0+6			Jour PL 14 217	Feb 65 Soldatov+ ANGLE DIST.OF FRAGS.	
	5.2+6	9.3+6			Prog INDSWG–120 4	65 – .A–DSTR FOTOFFRGM, TBP, NDG	
	5.0+6	8.0+6			Prog INDC–E–187	67 .ENGLISH TRANSL OF YFI–4 12 5/67	
	5.2+6	9.2+6			Rept ANL–TRANS–245	65 . ENGL TRANSL OF 65SALZBU 1 135	
					Rept ANL–TRANS–245	65 .ENGLISH TRANSL OF 65SALZBG	
Photo – Fissn	5.6+6	2.1+7	CCP	Expt	Jour YF 7 264	Feb 68 Zhagrov+OTHER YLD(G–E),THRESH,CFD RA	
					Jour SNP 7 2 183	Aug 68 .ENGL TRANSL	
Photo – Fissn	4.5+6	6.5+6	IFP	ExTh	Jour YF 7 521	Mar 68 Kurchatov+ SYM+ASYM YLD,DISAGREES TH	
					Jour SNP 7 3 326	Sep 68 TRANSLATN.*	
Photo – Fissn	4.0+6	6.0+6	KUR	Theo	Rept IAE–1734	Nov 68 Vorotnikov+ ASYM+ANISOTROPY GRPH	
Photo – Fissn	1.7+7		TAT	Expt	Prog BARC–401 18	69 Iyengar+ FRAG–A–DISTR CFD NEUT–FISS	
	1.8+7				Conf 68Bombay 2 110	Dec 68 – + PHOTO–EMULSION,YLD(MASS)	
Photo – Fissn		8.0+6	IFP	ExTh	Jour ZEP 9 128	Jan 69 Kapitza+SIG ANGDIST CV,2–HUMP–BARIER	
					Jour JEL 9 2 73	Jan 69 .ENGLISH TRANSL OF ZEP 9 128 1/69	
					Rept ANL–TRANS–639	69 .ENGLISH TRANSL OF ZEP 9 128	
Photo – Fissn	1.0+9		CCP	Conf	69Erevan	Feb 69 Bochagov+.ABST,FRAG MASS,E DIST	
Photo – Fissn	5.0+7	9.0+7	FEI	ExTh	Prog YFI–7 21	Apr 69 Rabotnov+ SIG+YLD+ANGDIST VS E GRPHS	
					Rept INDC(CCP)–7U24	Feb 70 TRANSLATN.*	
Photo – Fissn	5.4+6	8.9+6	ROM	Expt	Jour NP/A 127 687	Apr 69 Manfredini+ (MES).AT 12 E(G).TH RAT	+
					Jour NP/A 123 664	Jan 69 – +SIGMA 12ES,ANGDISTR FRAG.	
					Jour NC/B 44 1 218	Jul 66 De Carvalho+ SIGMA GIVEN.	
					Jour NC 29 463	Jul 63 – + ANG DISTR OF FRAGMENTS.	
Photo – Fissn	4.0+6	6.5+6	KUR	Theo	Jour YF 9 1197	Jun 69 Vorotnikov. GRPHS,SIG+YLD CFD EXPT	
					Jour SNP 9 6 700	Dec 69 TRANSLATN.*	

92 Uranium 238

Quantity	Energy (ev) Min	Max	Lab	Type	Documentation Ref Vol Page	Date	Author, Comments	Data
Photo – Fissn	5.0+6	8.0+6	FEI	ExTh	Conf 69Vienna 419	Jul 69	Androsenko+PPR134. XPTL ANGDIST + TH	
Photo – Fissn	Thrsh	+7	IFP	Expt	Conf 69Vienna 925	Jul 69	Kapica+PPR135.SIG+ANGDIST,STRUTINSKY	
Photo – Fissn	1.1+7	2.0+7	RIO	ExTh	Jour NDF 15 319	Nov 69	Carvalho+ PHOT – REACTN SIG GRPHS,REVW	
Photo – Fissn	8.0+6	1.0+7	GA	Expt	Jour NSE 39 163	Feb 70	Kull+,2ES,DELAYED NEUT YLDS VS. TIME	
Photo – Fissn	2.5+7		TOR	Expt	Jour CJC 48 652	Feb 70	Gevaert+,RADIOCHEM YLDS 9 FRAGMENTS	
					Abst DA/B 32 3838	Jan 72	– . FRAG YLDS A=99–125	
		3.3+7			Conf 69Vienna 939	Jul 69	Sharma+PPR142. YIELD+NU VS FRAG MASS	
Photo – Fissn	2.8+7		DEB	Expt	Jour AHP 28 169	Mar 70	Medveczky+ TBL=TERN+BINARY FISSN CFD	
		2.8+7			Conf 69Vienna 897	Jul 69	– +PPR95.SYMMETRIC TERN FISSN	
Photo – Fissn	+6	+7	FEI	Expt	Jour YF 11 508	Mar 70	Rabotnov+ ANGDIST+YLD+SIG,GRPHS+TBLS	
					Jour SNP 11 285	Sep 70	.TRANSLATN.*0,NO 3	
Photo – Fissn	4.7+6	8.0+6	IOW	Expt	Abst DA/B 31 3632	Dec 70	Hall.YLD.COMPTON SCATT.MONOCHROMATOR	
Photo – Fissn	2.0+8	9.0+8	LND	Expt	Jour NP/A 158 433	Dec 70	Methasiri.GLASS DET.RESON AT 350MEV	
Photo – Fissn	1.0+7	1.8+7	OHO	Theo	Jour NP/A 161 191	Jan 71	Updegraff+ C.S SYM FISS.HYDRODN MODL	
Photo – Fissn	None		BLA	Expt	Prog INDC(SEC)–18	Aug 71	Kashukeev+ PG21.FRAG MEAN–E DIST,TBL	
Photo – Fissn	5.0+6	7.0+6	BUC	Expt	Prog INDC(SEC)–18	Aug 71	Catana+ PG 159.SIG(G–E),GRPH	
Photo – Fissn		5.3+7	CLE	Expt	Jour NP/A 173 465	Oct 71	Tamain+ DELAYED FRAG HALF LIVES	
					Conf 69Vienna 915	Jul 69	– +PPR84.FRAGMENT ANGDISTRIBUTN	
Photo – Fissn	4.6+6	7.5+6	IFP	Expt	Jour ZET 61 1284	Oct 71	Ignatyuk+ SIG,FRAG ANGDIST,TBL,GRPHS	
					Jour JET 34 684	Apr 72	*ENGL OF ZET 61 1284	
Photo – Fissn	1.5+7	2.5+7	RI	Expt	Jour YF 14 950	Nov 71	Petrzhak+ MASS–SPEC XE YLDS,TBL,GRPH	
					Jour SNP 14 532	May 72	. ENGL OF YF 14 950	
Photo – Fissn	5.6+6	9.0+6	TAM	Expt	Jour NP/A 175 501	Nov 71	Dowdy+ ANGDISTR OF FRAGMENTS.	
	5.0+6	9.0+6			Abst DA/B 31 1315	Sep 70	– .FRAGMENT ANGDIST	
Photo – Fissn	5.0+6	9.0+6	CRC	Expt	Jour NP/A 179 333	Jan 72	Knowles+ (N,G)–SOURCE,GRPH ABSOL SIG	
					Rept AECL–3912 64	Mar 71	.PROGRESS REPORT,NDG	
					Jour IZV 34 1627	Aug 70	.SAME EXPT+RESULTS,GRPH	
					Jour BAS 34 1445	Aug 71	.ENGL OF IZV 34 1627	
Photo – Fissn	5.6+6	9.0+6	MIS	Expt	Abst DA/B 33 374	Jul 72	Domaschko. 7ES. ABSOL SIG VALUES GUN	
Photo – Fissn	1.0+8	7.6+8	LND	Expt	Jour NP/A 193 555	Oct 72	Schroeder. GELI. YIELDS GIVEN.	
	3.0+8	6.0+9			Rept INIS–MF–427	Jun 72	– .PPR23.3,ABST,MASS YLDSGRPH	
	3.0+8	1.1+9			Jour NP/A 143 449	Mar 70	Schroder+ MASS–YIELD DIST. TH MODEL.	
		1.5+7	IAE	Eval	Jour REA 10 637	Dec 72	Manero+ DELAYED NEUTRON YIELD,TBL	
Photo – Fissn	6.5+6	8.9+6	LAS	Expt	Jour NSE 56 179	Feb 75	Caldwell+ TBL,GRPH NU PROMPT+DELAYED	
	8.0+6	1.2+7			Conf 73Rochestr 1 431	Aug 73	– + PROMPT+DELAYED–N YLDS,TBLS	
					Conf 73Pacif.Gr 1 651	Mar 73	– + PROMPT,DELAY NS,GN/GF,TBL	
					Rept LA–UR–73–968	73	– +.PROMPT AND DELAYD NEUT YLD	
Photo – Fissn	8.0+6	1.8+7	SAC	Expt	Jour NP/A 199 45	Jan 73	Veyssiere+ MONOCHROMAT.NEW ANAL TECH	
Photo – Fissn	5.0+6	8.3+6	SOR	Revw	Conf 73Pacif.Gr 1 277	Mar 73	Arad+ SIG+FRGM–ANGDIST,GRPHS+DISCUSS	
		6.0+6	IRT	Expt	Conf 73Rochestr 2 501	Aug 73	Gozani. ABST,DEL+PROMPT–N YLD/FISYLD	
	5.3+6	8.0+6			Conf 73Pacif.Gr 1 649	Mar 73	– + PROMPT,DELAY N–YLDS,GRAPHS	
	4.5+6	1.5+7			Rept GULF–RT–10538	Feb 71	Bramblett+ CURVS SIG,PROMPT,DELAY NU	
Photo – Fissn	5.0+6	8.0+6	IOW	Expt	Jour NP/A 212 221	Sep 73	Anderl+COMPTON GS. CFD FISS CHANNEL	
					Abst DA/B 33 4952	Apr 73	– .PROMINENT STRUCTURE SEEN	
					Rept IS–T–544	Nov 72	– . SIG MEASD. 0.1–MEV STEPS	
					Jour NIM 102 101	Jul 72	– + EXP METHOD + PRELIM CURVE.	
Photo – Fissn	None		CAN	Expt	Jour RRL 15 335	Nov 73	Parsons+ YIELDS BY GAM–SPECTROSC,NDG	
Photo – Fissn	4.5+6	6.5+6	LND	Expt	Jour NP/A 215 461	Nov 73	ALM+SUBBARRIER. AG,CD,BA YIELDS.	
	4.6+6	6.5+6		ExTh	Conf 73Rochestr 1 55	Aug 73	ALM+ SYMMETRIC+ASYM YLDS+SIG,GRAPHS	
	4.5+6	6.5+6		Expt	Conf 73Pacif.Gr 1 645	Mar 73	ALM+ SYM,ASYM FIS–YLDS CFD OTHS,GRPH	
					Rept INIS–MF–427	Jun 72	ALM+ PPR23.4,ABST,REL MASS YLDS,NDG	
Photo – Fissn	2.2+7	2.6+7	ARK	Expt	Jour NSE 52 466	Dec 73	Swindle+.FRAG MASS DISTR. RADIOCHEM.	
Photo – Fissn	5.4+6	9.0+6	IEA	Expt	Rept IEA–324	Jan 74	Mafra+ 12 CAPT–GAMS.TBL,CFD OTH GRPH	
Photo – Fissn	1.3+6		CCP	Expt	Jour AE 36 403	May 74	Ivanov+ ABST.SIG FOR CO60–GAM GIVEN	
					Jour SJA 36 514	Nov 74	. ENGLISH OF AE 36 403	
Photo – Fissn	6.0+6	1.2+7	BUC	Expt	Prog INDC(SEC)–42	Dec 74	Baciu+ ABST.TBL DELAYED/PROMPT NUBAR	
Photo – Fissn	5.4+6		IEA	Expt	Rept IEA–366	Dec 74	Kuniyoshi+ AVG FRGM ANGDIST,TBL+GRPH	
Photo – Fissn	5.0+6	1.2+7	TIL	Expt	Rept YK–19 42	75	Ivanov+ YLD OF FRAGS,GRAPH,CFD,TBL	
					Prog INDC(CCP)–65	Dec 74	.P10.ENGL ABSTR OF YK–19	
Photo – Fissn	+6		OHO	Theo	Abst DA/B 35 4100	Feb 75	Bhandari.SUBTR CALC.DOUBL–HUMPED POT	
Photo – Fissn		6.0+7	TOH	Expt	Conf 75Wash. 611	Mar 75	Iwasaki+TBL,GRPHS,DELAYED N–SPECT.	
Photo – Fissn	+7		BLA	Expt	Conf 75Kiev 6 146	Jun 75	Dragnev+ SIG(E–GAMMA),GRAPHS	
	6.4+6	9.0+6			Prog INDC(SEC)–42	Dec 74	– + ABST.8CAPT–GAMS,TBL SIG(E)	
Photo – Fissn	5.0+6	8.0+6	UI	Theo	Jour PRL 35 501	Aug 75	Dickey+ GRPHS GF,GN,GF+GN.TBL PARAM	
					Abst DA/B 36 297	Jul 75	– .G,F CS.NS,G DETECTED.STRUCT	
					Prog A–WAU–75 177	Jun 75	– . TBL,GRPH FISSION BARRIER PAR	
Photo – Fissn	2.8+6	5.8+6	NBS	Expt	Jour PR/C 12 863	Sep 75	Bowman+ TBL,GRPHS.SHELF IN CS	
Photo – Fissn		2.5+7	GHT	Expt	Prog INDC(SEC)–51	Dec 75	Jacobs+ MASS–YLDS,FIG.ZP,NDG.AVG K–E	

92 Uranium 238

Quantity	Energy (ev) Min	Max	Lab	Type	Documentation Ref Vol Page	Date	Author, Comments	Data
Photo – Fissn		1.7+7	IJI	Expt Rept	KIYAI – 76 – 40	76	Aleksandrov+ DELAY NS,GROUPS INT+HL	
Photo – Fissn	1.2+7	3.0+7	USP	Expt Prog	INDC(SEC) – 50	Jan 76	Miyao+ P32.VERY BRIEF.DELAY NEUT.NDG	
Photo – Fissn	None		CRC	Expt Abst	BAP 21 776	May 76	Pich+MONOCHROMATIC PHOTONS.NDG	
Photo – Fissn	Thrsh		USP	Revw Jour	NSE 60 19	May 76	Bhandari+GF,(G,N),CS.ANG DISTR FRAGS	
Photo – Fissn	9.0+6		ARK	Expt Jour	JIN 38 1109	Jun 76	James+ BREMS. 21CHAIN – YLDS,TBL+GRAPH	
				Abst	DA/B 36 2800	Dec 75	– +21 MASS CHAINS.RADIO – CHEM TECH	
Photo – Fissn	3.8+6	5.3+6	IFP	Expt Jour	ZEP 24 309	Sep 76	Zhuchko+ YIELD, ANGDIST OF FRAGS	
				Jour	JEL 24 277	Sep 76	– + ENGLISH OF ZEP 24 309	
Photo – Fissn	5.0+6	7.0+6	FEI	Expt Rept	YK – 21 65	Oct 76	Ostapenko+ YLD(E),GRAPH	
Photo – Fissn		5.8+8	CAN	Expt Jour	ZP/A 279 331	Nov 76	Kiely+ SIG,FRAG MASSES+ES,FISSILITY	
Photo – Fissn	1.5+7	2.5+7	TIL	Expt Rept	YK – 27 42	77	Petrzhak+ 15+20MEV BREMS.XE – YLDS,TBL	

92 Uranium 239

Quantity	Energy (ev) Min	Max	Lab	Type	Documentation Ref Vol Page	Date	Author, Comments	Data
Total	1.0+5	1.2+6	BRC	Expt Prog	EANDC(E)127U	Apr 70	Adam+,VDG	
Total	1.0+1	2.5+6	LRL	Theo Prog	ERDA – NDC – 2 72	May 75	Gardner.ABST.NDG.STAT.MDL.CALC.	
				Rept	UCID – 16679	Apr 75	– +STAT MDL CALC.TBLS,GRPHS.	
Elastic	1.0+1	2.5+6	LRL	Theo Rept	UCID – 16679	Apr 75	Gardner+STAT MDL CALC.TBLS,GRPHS.	
Tot Inelastc	1.0+1	2.5+6	LRL	Theo Rept	UCID – 16679	Apr 75	Gardner+STAT MDL CALC.TBLS,GRPHS.	
(n,γ)	Maxwl		ORL	Revw Conf	55Geneva 7 258	Aug 55	Halperin+.P732,VAL GVN,EXPT DESCRIBD	
(n,γ)	2.0+4		LAS	ExTh Jour	PR/B 139 1207	Sep 65	Bell.STATISTCL TH CALC CF WEAPON XPT	
(n,γ)	2.0+4	+6	GSF	Theo Jour	AF 36 509	Nov 67	Truran+.STAT MODEL. TWO MASS FORMLS	
(n,γ)	1.0+1	2.5+6	LRL	Theo Rept	UCID – 16679	Apr 75	Gardner+STAT MDL CALC.TBLS,GRPHS.	
Spect (n,γ)	Maxwl		ANL	Expt Prog	USNDC – 1 18	May 72	Thomas+. ABSOL GAMMA INTENSITY MEASD	
(n,2n)	Thrsh	1.5+7	BRC	Expt Rept	CEA – R – 4627	Nov 74	Frehaut+ LARGE LIQ SCINT METH13 VAL	
(n,2n)	2.0+6	1.5+7	BRC	Eval Prog	NEANDC(E)162U	Aug 75	Michaudon+	
				Rept	CEA – R – 4647	Jan 75	Jary. EVAL,STAT MDL, 15 VALS	
(n,xn) x>2	2.0+6	1.5+7	BRC	Eval Prog	NEANDC(E)162 4	Aug 75	Michaudon+	
				Rept	CEA – R – 4647	Jan 75	Jary. EVAL,STAT MDL, 15 VALS	
Fission	Maxwl		LRL	Expt Prog	WASH – 190	Feb 56	Crane+ 15PM3B	
Fission	Maxwl		ANL	Expt Jour	NSE 2 33	Feb 57	Fields+,MTR SIG UPPER LIMIT=20B	
Fission	Pile		FEI	Expt Jour	AE 23 396	Nov 67	Lejpunskij.RATIO REL U235(N,F),PILE	
				Jour	EAF 23 5 21	Nov 67	. FRENCH TRANSL OF AE 23 396 11/67	
				Jour	SJA 23 1150	Nov 67	.ENGLISH TRANSL OF AE 23 396 11/67	
Fission	–		HAR	Theo Conf	68DUBSY 463	Jul 68	Lynn.REVIEW,STRUCT EFFECTS IN FISS.	
Fission	5.0+5	2.3+6	LAS	Expt Jour	NSE 41 177	Aug 70	Cramer+,SIG FROM(T,P+FISS)+H – F CALC	
Fission	–		GEL	ExTh Jour	NP/A 187 305	Jun 72	Weigmann+ F.B.PARAMS FROM DATA ANAL.	
Fission	Spont		TPI	Theo Jour	YF 16 919	Nov 72	Adeev+ FISS BARRIER CFD EVEN,GRAPH	
				Jour	SNP 16 507	May 73	.ENGLISH OF YF 16 919	
Fission	3.0+6	5.0+6	LAS	Theo Conf	75Wash. 129	Mar 75	Moore.GRPH R MATR STAT CALC CFD EXP	
Fission	1.0+1	2.5+6	LRL	Theo Rept	UCID – 16679	Apr 75	Gardner+STAT MDL CALC.TBLS,GRPHS.	
Fission	Thrsh	1.5+7	BRC	Eval Rept	CEA – N – 1798 107	Jun 75	Jary+ STAT MDL CALC	
Nu	Spont		HED	Eval Abst	ANS 22 673	Nov 75	Johnson. TBL,GRPH.NU FROM SPON FISS	
Fiss Yield	Pile		CRC	Expt Jour	PR 80 181	Oct 50	Allen+ E SPECT,FAST ALPHAS+FISSFRAGS	
Fiss Yield	1.5+7		CCP	Expt Jour	AE 10 13	Jan 61	Bonjuskin+.ABS YIELD OF FRGMNTS,GRPH	
				Jour	SJA 10 10	Nov 61	TRANSLATN.*GERMAN KE4 553 7/61	
Frag Spectra		2.0+6	COP	Revw Conf	69Vienna 155	Jul 69	Strutinsky+PPR203. GRPH ANGANISTR(E)	
Reson Params	1.0+6	8.1+6	DUB	Theo Conf	72Budapest 256	Aug 72	Malov+ DENSITY OF 1/2+ STATES ,TBL	
Reson Params	None		FEI	Eval Rept	YK – 20 253	75	Tolstikov+ RES PARMS,NG,D	
Lvl Density	+6		MIL	Theo Jour	EN 15 1 54	Jan 68	Facchini+ LDL PARS FROM LOW EN RES	
Lvl Density	None		MUN	Theo Jour	NP/A 217 269	Dec 73	Dilg+ A,DELTA. BACK SHIFTED FERMIGAS	
Lvl Density	None		COP	Theo Jour	NP/A 222 493	Apr 74	Dossing+COLL ROTAT.SPAC. ACCUR ESTIM	
Lvl Density	None		DUB	Theo Jour	NP/A 224 396	May 74	Malov+ 1/2 MICROSC.MODEL. DEFORM NUC	
Lvl Density	None		ROC	Theo Jour	NP/A 223 589	May 74	Huizenga+ EXP CFD MICROSC TH AX SYMM	

92 Uranium 240

Quantity	Energy (ev) Min	Max	Lab	Type	Documentation Ref Vol Page	Date	Author, Comments	Data
(n,γ)	2.0+4		LAS	ExTh Jour	PR/B 139 1207	Sep 65	Bell.STATISTCL TH CALC CF WEAPON XPT	
(n,γ)	2.0+4	+6	GSF	Theo Jour	AF 36 509	Nov 67	Truran+.STAT MODEL. TWO MASS FORMLS	
Fission	2.5 – 2		JUL	Theo Jour	ZP 257 389	Dec 72	Mcminn. 6.49 E – 5 BARNS	

92 Uranium 241

Quantity	Energy (ev) Min	Max	Lab	Type	Documentation Ref Vol Page	Date	Author, Comments	Data
(n,γ)	2.0+4		LAS	ExTh Jour	PR/B 139 1207	Sep 65	Bell.STATISTCL TH CALC CF WEAPON XPT	
(n,γ)	2.0+4	+6	GSF	Theo Jour	AF 36 509	Nov 67	Truran+.STAT MODEL. TWO MASS FORMLS	

92 Uranium 242

Quantity	Energy (ev) Min	Max	Lab	Type	Documentation Ref Vol Page	Date	Author, Comments	Data
(n,γ)	2.0+4		LAS	ExTh Jour	PR/B 139 1207	Sep 65	Bell.STATISTCL TH CALC CF WEAPON XPT	
(n,γ)	2.0+4	+6	GSF	Theo Jour	AF 36 509	Nov 67	Truran+.STAT MODEL. TWO MASS FORMLS	
(n,γ)	2.0+4		LRL	ExTh Jour	NP/A 124 130	Feb 69	Ingley.FROM U238 FISS YIELD HEAVY EL	

92 Uranium 243

Quantity	Energy (ev) Min	Max	Lab	Type	Documentation Ref Vol Page	Date	Author, Comments	Data
(n,γ)	2.0+4		LAS	ExTh Jour	PR/B 139 1207	Sep 65	Bell.STATISTCL TH CALC CF WEAPON XPT	
(n,γ)	2.0+4	+6	GSF	Theo Jour	AF 36 509	Nov 67	Truran+.STAT MODEL. TWO MASS FORMLS	
(n,γ)	2.0+4		LRL	ExTh Jour	NP/A 124 130	Feb 69	Ingley.FROM U238 FISS YIELD HEAVY EL	

92 Uranium 244

Quantity	Energy (ev) Min	Max	Lab	Type	Documentation Ref Vol Page	Date	Author, Comments	Data
(n,γ)	2.0+4		LAS	ExTh Jour	PR/B 139 1207	Sep 65	Bell.STATISTCL TH CALC CF WEAPON XPT	
(n,γ)	2.0+4	+6	GSF	Theo Jour	AF 36 509	Nov 67	Truran+.STAT MODEL. TWO MASS FORMLS	
(n,γ)	2.0+4		LRL	ExTh Jour	NP/A 124 130	Feb 69	Ingley.FROM U238 FISS YIELD HEAVY EL	

92 Uranium 245

Quantity	Energy (ev) Min	Max	Lab	Type	Documentation Ref Vol Page	Date	Author, Comments	Data
(n,γ)	2.0+4		LAS	ExTh Jour	PR/B 139 1207	Sep 65	Bell.STATISTCL TH CALC CF WEAPON XPT	
(n,γ)	2.0+4	+6	GSF	Theo Jour	AF 36 509	Nov 67	Truran+.STAT MODEL. TWO MASS FORMLS	
(n,γ)	2.0+4		LRL	ExTh Jour	NP/A 124 130	Feb 69	Ingley.FROM U238 FISS YIELD HEAVY EL	

92 Uranium 246

Quantity	Energy (ev) Min	Max	Lab	Type	Documentation Ref Vol Page	Date	Author, Comments	Data
(n,γ)	2.0+4		LAS	ExTh Jour	PR/B 139 1207	Sep 65	Bell.STATISTCL TH CALC CF WEAPON XPT	
(n,γ)	2.0+4	+6	GSF	Theo Jour	AF 36 509	Nov 67	Truran+.STAT MODEL. TWO MASS FORMLS	
(n,γ)	2.0+4		LRL	ExTh Jour	NP/A 124 130	Feb 69	Ingley.FROM U238 FISS YIELD HEAVY EL	

92 Uranium 247

Quantity	Energy (ev) Min	Max	Lab	Type	Documentation Ref Vol Page	Date	Author, Comments	Data
(n,γ)	2.0+4		LAS	ExTh Jour	PR/B 139 1207	Sep 65	Bell.STATISTCL TH CALC CF WEAPON XPT	
(n,γ)	2.0+4	+6	GSF	Theo Jour	AF 36 509	Nov 67	Truran+.STAT MODEL. TWO MASS FORMLS	
(n,γ)	2.0+4		LRL	ExTh Jour	NP/A 124 130	Feb 69	Ingley.FROM U238 FISS YIELD HEAVY EL	

92 Uranium 248

Quantity	Energy (ev) Min	Max	Lab	Type	Documentation Ref Vol Page	Date	Author, Comments	Data
(n,γ)	2.0+4		LAS	ExTh Jour	PR/B 139 1207	Sep 65	Bell.STATISTCL TH CALC CF WEAPON XPT	
(n,γ)	2.0+4	+6	GSF	Theo Jour	AF 36 509	Nov 67	Truran+.STAT MODEL. TWO MASS FORMLS	
(n,γ)	2.0+4		LRL	ExTh Jour	NP/A 124 130	Feb 69	Ingley.FROM U238 FISS YIELD HEAVY EL	

92 Uranium 249

Quantity	Energy (ev) Min	Max	Lab	Type	Documentation Ref Vol Page	Date	Author, Comments	Data
(n,γ)	2.0+4		LAS	ExTh Jour	PR/B 139 1207	Sep 65	Bell.STATISTCL TH CALC CF WEAPON XPT	
(n,γ)	2.0+4	+6	GSF	Theo Jour	AF 36 509	Nov 67	Truran+.STAT MODEL. TWO MASS FORMLS	
(n,γ)	2.0+4		LRL	ExTh Jour	NP/A 124 130	Feb 69	Ingley.FROM U238 FISS YIELD HEAVY EL	
Alpha	2.0+4		LRL	ExTh Jour	NP/A 124 130	Feb 69	Ingley.FROM U238 FISS YIELD HEAVY EL	

92 Uranium 245

Quantity	Energy (ev) Min	Max	Lab	Type	Documentation Ref Vol Page	Date	Author, Comments	Data
(n,γ)	2.0+4		LAS	ExTh Jour	PR/B 139 1207	Sep 65	Bell.STATISTCL TH CALC CF WEAPON XPT	
(n,γ)	2.0+4	+6	GSF	Theo Jour	AF 36 509	Nov 67	Truran+.STAT MODEL. TWO MASS FORMLS	
(n,γ)	2.0+4		LRL	ExTh Jour	NP/A 124 130	Feb 69	Ingley.FROM U238 FISS YIELD HEAVY EL	

92 Uranium 246

Quantity	Energy (ev) Min	Max	Lab	Type	Documentation Ref Vol Page	Date	Author, Comments	Data
(n,γ)	2.0+4		LAS	ExTh Jour	PR/B 139 1207	Sep 65	Bell.STATISTCL TH CALC CF WEAPON XPT	
(n,γ)	2.0+4	+6	GSF	Theo Jour	AF 36 509	Nov 67	Truran+.STAT MODEL. TWO MASS FORMLS	
(n,γ)	2.0+4		LRL	ExTh Jour	NP/A 124 130	Feb 69	Ingley.FROM U238 FISS YIELD HEAVY EL	

92 Uranium 247

Quantity	Energy (ev) Min	Max	Lab	Type	Documentation Ref Vol Page	Date	Author, Comments	Data
(n,γ)	2.0+4		LAS	ExTh Jour	PR/B 139 1207	Sep 65	Bell.STATISTCL TH CALC CF WEAPON XPT	
(n,γ)	2.0+4	+6	GSF	Theo Jour	AF 36 509	Nov 67	Truran+.STAT MODEL. TWO MASS FORMLS	
(n,γ)	2.0+4		LRL	ExTh Jour	NP/A 124 130	Feb 69	Ingley.FROM U238 FISS YIELD HEAVY EL	

92 Uranium 248

Quantity	Energy (ev) Min	Max	Lab	Type	Documentation Ref Vol Page	Date	Author, Comments	Data
(n,γ)	2.0+4		LAS	ExTh Jour	PR/B 139 1207	Sep 65	Bell.STATISTCL TH CALC CF WEAPON XPT	
(n,γ)	2.0+4	+6	GSF	Theo Jour	AF 36 509	Nov 67	Truran+.STAT MODEL. TWO MASS FORMLS	
(n,γ)	2.0+4		LRL	ExTh Jour	NP/A 124 130	Feb 69	Ingley.FROM U238 FISS YIELD HEAVY EL	

92 Uranium 249

Quantity	Energy (ev) Min	Max	Lab	Type	Documentation Ref Vol Page	Date	Author, Comments	Data
(n,γ)	2.0+4		LAS	ExTh Jour	PR/B 139 1207	Sep 65	Bell.STATISTCL TH CALC CF WEAPON XPT	
(n,γ)	2.0+4	+6	GSF	Theo Jour	AF 36 509	Nov 67	Truran+.STAT MODEL. TWO MASS FORMLS	
(n,γ)	2.0+4		LRL	ExTh Jour	NP/A 124 130	Feb 69	Ingley.FROM U238 FISS YIELD HEAVY EL	
Alpha	2.0+4		LRL	ExTh Jour	NP/A 124 130	Feb 69	Ingley.FROM U238 FISS YIELD HEAVY EL	

92 Uranium 250

Quantity	Energy (ev) Min	Max	Lab	Type	Documentation Ref Vol Page	Date	Author, Comments	Data
(n,γ)	2.0+4		LAS	ExTh Jour	PR/B 139 1207	Sep 65	Bell.STATISTCL TH CALC CF WEAPON XPT	
(n,γ)	2.0+4	+6	GSF	Theo Jour	AF 36 509	Nov 67	Truran+.STAT MODEL. TWO MASS FORMLS	

92 Uranium 251

Quantity	Energy (ev) Min	Max	Lab	Type	Documentation Ref Vol Page	Date	Author, Comments	Data
(n,γ)	2.0+4		LAS	ExTh Jour	PR/B 139 1207	Sep 65	Bell.STATISTCL TH CALC CF WEAPON XPT	
(n,γ)	2.0+4	+6	GSF	Theo Jour	AF 36 509	Nov 67	Truran+.STAT MODEL. TWO MASS FORMLS	
Alpha	2.0+4		LRL	ExTh Jour	NP/A 124 130	Feb 69	Ingley.FROM U238 FISS YIELD HEAVY EL	

92 Uranium 252

Quantity	Energy (ev) Min	Max	Lab	Type	Documentation Ref Vol Page	Date	Author, Comments	Data
(n,γ)	2.0+4		LAS	ExTh Jour	PR/B 139 1207	Sep 65	Bell.STATISTCL TH CALC CF WEAPON XPT	
(n,γ)	2.0+4	+6	GSF	Theo Jour	AF 36 509	Nov 67	Truran+.STAT MODEL. TWO MASS FORMLS	

92 Uranium 253

Quantity	Energy (ev) Min	Max	Lab	Type	Documentation Ref Vol Page	Date	Author, Comments	Data
(n,γ)	2.0+4		LAS	ExTh Jour	PR/B 139 1207	Sep 65	Bell.STATISTCL TH CALC CF WEAPON XPT	
(n,γ)	2.0+4	+6	GSF	Theo Jour	AF 36 509	Nov 67	Truran+.STAT MODEL. TWO MASS FORMLS	

92 Uranium 254

Quantity	Energy (ev) Min Max	Lab	Type	Documentation Ref Vol Page	Author, Comments Date	Data
(n,γ)	2.0+4	LAS	ExTh Jour	PR/B 139 1207	Sep 65 Bell.STATISTCL TH CALC CF WEAPON XPT	
(n,γ)	2.0+4 +6	GSF	Theo Jour	AF 36 509	Nov 67 Truran+.STAT MODEL. TWO MASS FORMLS	

92 Uranium 255

Quantity	Energy (ev) Min Max	Lab	Type	Documentation Ref Vol Page	Author, Comments Date	Data
(n,γ)	2.0+4	LAS	ExTh Jour	PR/B 139 1207	Sep 65 Bell.STATISTCL TH CALC CF WEAPON XPT	
(n,γ)	2.0+4 +6	GSF	Theo Jour	AF 36 509	Nov 67 Truran+.STAT MODEL. TWO MASS FORMLS	

92 Uranium 256

Quantity	Energy (ev) Min Max	Lab	Type	Documentation Ref Vol Page	Author, Comments Date	Data
(n,γ)	2.0+4	LAS	ExTh Jour	PR/B 139 1207	Sep 65 Bell.STATISTCL TH CALC CF WEAPON XPT	
(n,γ)	2.0+4 +6	GSF	Theo Jour	AF 36 509	Nov 67 Truran+.STAT MODEL. TWO MASS FORMLS	

92 Uranium 257

Quantity	Energy (ev) Min Max	Lab	Type	Documentation Ref Vol Page	Author, Comments Date	Data
(n,γ)	2.0+4	LAS	ExTh Jour	PR/B 139 1207	Sep 65 Bell.STATISTCL TH CALC CF WEAPON XPT	
(n,γ)	2.0+4 +6	GSF	Theo Jour	AF 36 509	Nov 67 Truran+.STAT MODEL. TWO MASS FORMLS	

92 Uranium 258

Quantity	Energy (ev) Min Max	Lab	Type	Documentation Ref Vol Page	Author, Comments Date	Data
(n,γ)	2.0+4 +6	GSF	Theo Jour	AF 36 509	Nov 67 Truran+.STAT MODEL. TWO MASS FORMLS	

92 Uranium 259

Quantity	Energy (ev) Min Max	Lab	Type	Documentation Ref Vol Page	Author, Comments Date	Data
(n,γ)	2.0+4 +6	GSF	Theo Jour	AF 36 509	Nov 67 Truran+.STAT MODEL. TWO MASS FORMLS	

92 Uranium 260

Quantity	Energy (ev) Min Max	Lab	Type	Documentation Ref Vol Page	Author, Comments Date	Data
(n,γ)	2.0+4 +6	GSF	Theo Jour	AF 36 509	Nov 67 Truran+.STAT MODEL. TWO MASS FORMLS	

92 Uranium 261

Quantity	Energy (ev) Min Max	Lab	Type	Documentation Ref Vol Page	Author, Comments Date	Data
(n,γ)	2.0+4 +6	GSF	Theo Jour	AF 36 509	Nov 67 Truran+.STAT MODEL. TWO MASS FORMLS	

92 Uranium 262

Quantity	Energy (ev) Min Max	Lab	Type	Documentation Ref Vol Page	Author, Comments Date	Data
(n,γ)	2.0+4 +6	GSF	Theo Jour	AF 36 509	Nov 67 Truran+.STAT MODEL. TWO MASS FORMLS	

92 Uranium 263

Quantity	Energy (ev) Min Max	Lab	Type	Documentation Ref Vol Page	Author, Comments Date	Data
(n,γ)	2.0+4 +6	GSF	Theo Jour	AF 36 509	Nov 67 Truran+.STAT MODEL. TWO MASS FORMLS	

92 Uranium 264

Quantity	Energy (ev) Min Max	Lab	Type	Documentation Ref Vol Page	Author, Comments Date	Data
(n,γ)	2.0+4 +6	GSF	Theo Jour	AF 36 509	Nov 67 Truran+.STAT MODEL. TWO MASS FORMLS	

93 Neptunium

Quantity	Energy (ev) Min	Max	Lab	Type	Documentation Ref Vol Page	Date	Author, Comments	Data
Thermal Scat	1.0−4	1.0+3	MUN	Revw Jour	EEN 80 1	77	Koester. SCAT LENGTH	

93 Neptunium 231

Quantity	Energy (ev) Min	Max	Lab	Type	Documentation Ref Vol Page	Date	Author, Comments	Data
Fission	2.5−2		JUL	Theo Jour	ZP 257 389	Dec 72	Mcminn. 1.02 E+2 BARNS	

93 Neptunium 232

Quantity	Energy (ev) Min	Max	Lab	Type	Documentation Ref Vol Page	Date	Author, Comments	Data
Fission	+5	3.0+6	LAS	Theo Conf	75Wash. 218	Mar 75	Wilhelmy+ CALC USING U233(HE3,TF)	

93 Neptunium 233

Quantity	Energy (ev) Min	Max	Lab	Type	Documentation Ref Vol Page	Date	Author, Comments	Data
Fission	2.5−2		JUL	Theo Jour	ZP 257 389	Dec 72	Mcminn. 5.57 E+0 BARNS	
Fission	+5	3.9+6	LAS	Theo Conf	75Wash. 218	Mar 75	Wilhelmy+ CALC USING U234(HE3,TF)	
Fiss Yield	8.5+6		BOR	Theo Jour	JPR 31 919	Nov 70	Doan+TERNARY FISSION	
Fiss Yield	1.3+7		BOR	Theo Jour	JPR 31 919	Nov 70	Doan+TERNARY FISSION	

93 Neptunium 234

Quantity	Energy (ev) Min	Max	Lab	Type	Documentation Ref Vol Page	Date	Author, Comments	Data
(n,γ)	2.0+4	+6	GSF	Theo Jour	AF 36 509	Nov 67	Truran+.STAT MODEL. TWO MASS FORMLS	
(n,p)	Maxwl		IFU	Theo Rept	ICD−4 20	67	Dadakina+ PENETR COEFF CALC,TABLE	
Fission	+5	6.2+6	LAS	Theo Conf	75Wash. 218	Mar 75	Wilhelmy+ CALC USING U235(HE3,TF)	
Alpha	1.0+4	2.0+4	LAS	Theo Jour	PR 158 1127	Jun 67	Bell. PREDICT 10−20KEV BY SYSTEMATCS	

93 Neptunium 235

Quantity	Energy (ev) Min	Max	Lab	Type	Documentation Ref Vol Page	Date	Author, Comments	Data
(n,γ)	2.0+4	+6	GSF	Theo Jour	AF 36 509	Nov 67	Truran+.STAT MODEL. TWO MASS FORMLS	
(n,γ)	Maxwl		LRL	Expt Rept	UCRL−51263	Aug 72	Landrum+ ACT, REL NP237	+
	Maxwl			Data	EXFOR10294.002	Dec 72	1PT,SIGMA	
(n,p)	Maxwl		IFU	Theo Rept	ICD−4 20	67	Dadakina+ PENETR COEFF CALC,TABLE	
Fission	2.5−2		JUL	Theo Jour	ZP 257 389	Dec 72	Mcminn. 5.14 E−1 BARNS	
Fission	+5	6.6+6	LAS	Theo Conf	75Wash. 218	Mar 75	Wilhelmy+ CALC USING U235(HE3,DF)	

93 Neptunium 236

Quantity	Energy (ev) Min	Max	Lab	Type	Documentation Ref Vol Page	Date	Author, Comments	Data
(n,γ)	2.0+4	+6	GSF	Theo Jour	AF 36 509	Nov 67	Truran+.STAT MODEL. TWO MASS FORMLS	
(n,p)	Maxwl		IFU	Theo Rept	ICD−4 20	67	Dadakina+ PENETR COEFF CALC,TABLE	
Fission	Pile		ANL	Expt Jour	PR 97 88	Jan 55	Studier.	+
	Pile			Data	EXFOR12486.002	Jun 76	. 1 PT.	
Fission	Maxwl		ANL	Expt Prog	ANL−6600 12	61	Jaffey.	+
	Maxwl			Data	EXFOR12251.005	Jun 76	. 1 PT.	
Fission	Maxwl		TRM	Revw Conf	66Bombay 1	Feb 66	Ramanna.VALS CFD TH,SIG,BINDING,DEF.	
Fission	None		BRK	Revw Jour	NP 81 1	Jun 66	Meyers+ TABLE 2, FISSION BARRIER.	
Fission	+5	4.3+6	LAS	Theo Conf	75Wash. 218	Mar 75	Wilhelmy+ CALC USING U237(HE3,TF)	
Alpha	1.0+4	2.0+4	LAS	Theo Jour	PR 158 1127	Jun 67	Bell. PREDICT 10−20KEV BY SYSTEMATCS	
Nu	Maxwl		ANL	Expt Prog	ANL−6600 124	61	Jaffey. THESIS.	+
	Maxwl			Data	EXFOR12251.004	Jun 76	. 1 PT.	
Nu	Spont		HED	Eval Abst	ANS 22 673	Nov 75	Johnson. TBL,GRPH.NU FROM SPON FISS	

93 Neptunium 237

Quantity	Energy (ev) Min	Max	Lab	Type	Documentation Ref Vol Page	Date	Author, Comments	Data
Evaluation		1.5+7	MTR	Eval Rept	IN− 1182	May 69	Smith+ ENDF/B EVALUATION	

93 Neptunium 237

Quantity	Energy (ev) Min	Max	Lab	Type	Documentation Ref Vol Page	Author, Comments Date	Data
Evaluation	2.5−2	1.0+7	KFK	Eval	Rept KFK−1186	Jul 70 Hinkelmann.RES,STF,N2N,NF,NU,NG,R.I.	
					Conf 70Helsinki 2 721	Jun 70 − + ALL QUANTITIES.	
Evaluation	1.0−5	2.5+7	SRL	Eval	Rept EPRI−NP−161	Dec 75 Benjamin+ENDF4B.REVISIONS	
Total	8.0−3	1.0+1	CCP	Expt	Conf 55Geneva 4 216	Aug 55 Adamchuk+.GRAPH,TRANSMISSN, PPR645	+
Total	2.0−2	2.8+0	MTR	Expt	Jour PR 107 525	Jul 57 Smith+ CRYSTLSPECT.	+
	2.0−2	2.9+0			Data EXFOR12487.004	Jun 76 . 252 PTS. SIGMA.	
Total	2.0−1	3.6+1	ORL	Expt	Abst BAP 3 364	Nov 58 Slaughter+ TOF FAST CHOPPER 32EOS	
Total	2.7+0	1.2+4	CCP	Expt	Jour AE 6 569	May 59 Adamchuk+.GRAPH,FAST CH,HIGH RESOLTN	+
					Jour SJA 6 420	Dec 60 TRANSLATN.* JNE A13 72 0/60	
					Jour KE 3 282	Mar 60 .TRANSLATN	
Total	2.4+1	1.0+2	ORL	Expt	Conf 61Saclay 23	Jul 61 Harvey.TOF MEASUREMENTS,SIG(E)GRPH	+
	2.0−1	1.0+2			Conf 61RPI 64	May 61 − . CURVE	
	+0	+3			Conf 60Vienna 535	Oct 60 Block+.NDG,EXPT DESCRIBED	
	2.2−1	4.1+1			Data EXFOR12478.002	Jun 76 . 744 PTS.	
Total	None		COL	Expt	Prog NCSAC−33 41	Dec 70 Camarda+,TRANSMISSION,NO DATA GIVEN	
Total	6.3−1	4.0+3	SAC	Expt	Diss FRNC−TH−341	Oct 72 Paya. FINAL DATA GIVEN.	+
					Conf 69Vienna 307	Jul 69 − + STUDY OF INTERMED STRUCT.MEAS	
					Rept INDC−156	67 − . FULL PAPER OF 66PARIS	
					Conf 66Paris 2 128	Oct 66 − + FIRST MEASUREMENT	
	6.3−1	4.0+3			Data EXFOR20447.002	Oct 75 13789PTS.	
Total	1.0+0	1.0+2	LAS	Expt	Jour PR/C 8 2352	Dec 73 Keyworth+TRNS.NO CS DATA GVN.I TBL.	
					Conf 73Rochestr 1 85	Aug 73 .SUPERSEDED	
Total	−3	1.9+0	THS	Theo	Rept IKE−6 89 65	Jun 75 Keinert. DATA LIBRARY	
Total	1.0−2	3.5+1	MTR	Expt	Abst BAP 4 270	Apr 59 Cline+. 1.52 LVLS/EV TO 32EV.	+
	3.0+0	3.6+1			Data EXFOR12477.006	Jun 76 . 393 PTS.	
Elastic	1.0−3	1.0+7	KAP	Revw	Abst ANS 7 84	Jun 64 Goldman+	
Elastic	2.5+1	1.0+5	LAS	Expt	Prog WASH−1136 114	Sep 69 Hoffman+,PHYSICS−8 SHOT,ANAL TBC	+
	2.0+1	2.5+5			Data EXFOR10366.004	Apr 76 . 2080 PTS.	
Diff Elastic	Maxwl		ANL	Expt	Jour PCS 28 1651	Sep 67 Heaton+ COH SCAT AMP	+
	Maxwl				Data EXFOR10131.002	May 73 . 1 PT. COH SCAT AMP.	
Scattering	2.0+1	2.0+6	LAS	Expt	Abst BAP 21 655	Apr 76 Semon+TOF.RES ANAL.REPORT TBP.NDG.	
Absorption	Maxwl		HAR	Expt	Rept AERE−R/R−2516	Mar 58 Jowitt+. PILE OSC.REL BORON.293DEGK.	
Absorption	2.5−2		HAR	Expt	Jour JNEA 12 32	May 60 Tattersall+ PILE OSCILLATOR.	+
	2.5−2				Data EXFOR20638.070	Jul 76 1PNT.SIGMA.	
Absorption	None		MUN	Theo	Diss GRYNTAKIS	Mar 76 Gryntakis.,CALC.OF WESTCOTTS G−FUNCT	
					Jour RCA 22 128	Mar 75 − +,EQUIVALENT TO THESIS	
Res Int Abs	2.7+0	1.2+4	CCP	Expt	Jour AE 6 569	May 59 Adamchuk+.VAL GVN,FAST CH,HIGH RSLTN	
					Jour SJA 6 420	Dec 60 TRANSLATN.* JNE A13 72 0/60	
					Jour KE 3 282	Mar 60 .TRANSLATN	
Res Int Abs	5.0−1		HAR	Expt	Jour JNE 12 32	May 60 Tattersall+ ABOVE 1/V,OSCIL,REL B+AU	+
					Rept AERE−R−2887	Aug 59 − . PILE OSC.REL BORON	
					Conf 58Geneva 16 34	Sep 58 Rose+ SUPERSEDED	
	6.7−1				Data EXFOR20638.071	Jul 76 1PNT.	
Res Int Abs	Pile		KFK	Expt	Prog KFK−1456 51	Aug 71 Eberle+ 805 B	
Res Int Abs	5.0−1		SGA	Comp	Conf 73Paris 1 233	Mar 73 Eder+ REDUCED RES INTEG CAPTURE,TBL	
					Rept SGAE−PH−141	Feb 73 .SAME AS 73PARIS,NO DETAILS,TBP	
Res Int Abs	1.0−1		KFK	Theo	Rept KFK−1917	Feb 74 Klunker.INFIN DILUTION+EFF RESINTEG	
(n,γ)	Maxwl		HAR	Expt	Jour JIN 2 205	Apr 56 Brown+ CD DIFFERENCE METH,THR+EPICD N	
					Rept AERE−C/R−1799	Dec 55 − + SIG GVN,APPRECIABLE RES ACT	
(n,γ)	Maxwl		MTR	Expt	Jour PR 107 525	Jul 57 Smith+,CS+TRNS,170+−22B	+
					Rept IDO−16225	May 55 − + SIGMA GIVEN	
	Maxwl				Data EXFOR12487.005	Jun 76 . 1 PT.	
(n,γ)	Maxwl		CRC	Eval	Rept AECL−1054	Mar 60 Walker+ (CRRP−913).	
(n,γ)	Pile		CRC	Eval	Rept CRRP−960	Nov 60 Westcott. EFF SIG TBL 20−1300 DEG C.	
					Rept CRRP−862	Aug 59 .SUPERSEDED.	
					Rept CRRP−787	Sep 58 .SUPERSEDED.	
					Rept CRRP−680	Jan 57 .SUPERSEDED.	
(n,γ)	1.0−3	1.0+7	KAP	Revw	Abst ANS 7 84	Jun 64 Goldman+	
					Rept CONF−446−10	May 64 − + FULL REPORT.	
(n,γ)	Maxwl	Pile	BNL	Eval	Prog BNL−982 22	Aug 66 Pearlstein. 151B, 161B, FROM RES PAR	
(n,γ)	1.5+5	1.5+6	ANL	Expt	Jour NSE 29 218	Aug 67 Stupegia+ ACT CRYST SPEC 8ES TABLE	+
	1.0+4	2.0+6			Conf 66Paris 1 520	Oct 66 − + CURV. CFD STATIST MDL.	
	1.5+5	1.5+6			Data EXFOR12483.002	Jun 76 . 8 PTS.	
(n,γ)	2.0+4		CCP	Theo	Jour AE 23 319	Oct 67 Zagrafov+ CURV(N,G)VS MASS,A=237−275	
					Jour EAF 23 4 62	Oct 67 . FRENCH OF AE 23 319	
(n,γ)	2.0+4	+6	GSF	Theo	Jour AF 36 509	Nov 67 Truran+.STAT MODEL. TWO MASS FORMLS	
(n,γ)	Maxwl		RI	Revw	Jour AE 23 561	Dec 67 BAK+ OTHER SIG VAL GIVEN,TABLE	
					Jour SJA 23 1340	Dec 67 . ENGL OF AE 23 561	

93 Neptunium 237

Quantity	Energy (ev) Min	Max	Lab	Type	Documentation Ref Vol Page	Date	Author, Comments	Data
(n,γ)	Maxwl		AUA	Theo Jour	NSE 31 234	Feb 68	Cook+ STATISTICAL CALC CFD EXPT	
(n,γ)	Pile		SRL	Expt Conf	68Wash. 1271	Mar 68	Hennelly+ 152B	
(n,γ)	Maxwl		MTR	Expt Prog	IN- 1218 40	Dec 68	Schuman. ACTIVATION. SIG GIVEN	
(n,γ)	1.0+4	1.0+6	KUR	Theo Jour	YF 9 538	Mar 69	Vorotnikov.SIG L=0,1,2,3 - FISS ANAL	
				Jour	SNP 9 308	Sep 69	TRANSLATN.*	
(n,γ)	None		COL	Expt Prog	NCSAC-31 50	May 70	Arbo+,NEVIS,MOXON - RAE DET,TO BE DONE	
(n,γ)	Pile		BNL	Expt Rept	BNL-50242	Jun 70	Hellstrand+,PILE OSC IN 2 SPECT	
(n,γ)	2.5-2	1.0+7	KFK	Eval Rept	KFK-1186	Jul 70	Hinkelmann.5-GROUP SIG,THR+FAST SPEC	
	2.5-2			Rept	KFK-1186	Jul 70	- . RECOMMENDED 170 B	
(n,γ)	6.2-1	1.0+7	SRL	Theo Conf	71Knoxvill 714	Mar 71	Mccrosson. SPECTRUM - AVERAGED SIG	
(n,γ)	1.0+6		FEI	Expt Conf	71Kiev 1 325	May 71	Ivanov+ RATIO NP237(NG)/U238(NG) GVN	+
	1.0+6			Data	EXFOR40153.004	Apr 74	.1 DATA LINE	
(n,γ)	Pile		KFK	Expt Prog	KFK-1456 51	Aug 71	Eberle+ 184 B	
(n,γ)	Maxwl	Fiss	SGA	Comp Conf	73Paris 1 233	Mar 73	Eder+ DATA FROM EXPTS+EVALS,TABLE	
				Rept	SGAE-PH-141	Feb 73	.SAME AS 73PARIS,NO DETAILS	
(n,γ)	None		ORL	Expt Conf	75Wash. 229	Oct 75	Weston+NDG.TBD	
(n,γ)	1.0+5	3.0+6	JAE	Revw Conf	IAEA-186 3 1	76	Igarasi. REVW AVAIL DATA,GRPH+BIBLIO	
				Rept	JAERI-M-6315	Nov 75	- +GRPH. 2 DATA SETS COMPARED.	
(n,γ)	2.5-1	1.0+5	LAS	Expt Prog	NCSAC-31 148	May 70	Hoffman+,NUCL SHOT,ANAL TO BE DONE	+
	2.0+1	2.5+5		Data	EXFOR10366.003	Apr 76	. 1930 PTS. SIGMA.	
(n,γ)	2.0+1	2.0+6	LAS	Expt Abst	BAP 21 655	Apr 76	Semon+TOF.RES ANAL.REPORT TBP.NDG.	
(n,γ)	1.2+5	2.7+6	LRL	Expt Jour	NSE 59 381	Apr 76	Linder+REL U235NF.TBL,GRPHS.CFD ENDF	+
	1.2+5	2.7+6		Data	EXFOR10221.	Aug 75	. 23 PTS. SIGMA.	
Res Int Capt	None		CRC	Eval Rept	AECL-1054	Mar 60	Walker+ REDUCED RESONANCE INTEGRAL.	
Res Int Capt	5.5-1		BNL	Eval Prog	BNL-982 22	Aug 66	Pearlstein. 500B CALC, RECOMMENDED	
Res Int Capt	Pile		SRL	Expt Conf	68Wash. 1271	Mar 68	Hennelly+ 850B	
Res Int Capt	5.0-1		MTR	Expt Rept	IN- 1296	May 69	Schuman+. PILE ACT. 807+ -40B. 1/V	+
				Rept	IN- 1195	May 68	Scoville+	
	5.0-1			Data	EXFOR11820.022	Jun 76	. 1 PT.	
Res Int Capt	Pile		BNL	Expt Rept	BNL-50242	Jun 70	Hellstrand+,PILE OSC IN 2 SPECT	
Res Int Capt	4.7-1	1.0+7	KFK	Eval Rept	KFK-1186	Jul 70	Hinkelmann. INFIN DILUTION RES INTEG	
Spect (n,γ)	3.0+1	5.0+1	GEL	Expt Prog	EANDC(E)127U	Apr 70	Rohr+,LINAC TOF	
				Jour	PL/B 30 624	Dec 69	Weigmann+COUPLING IN SUB-THRES.FISS.	
Spect (n,γ)	None		COL	Expt Prog	NCSAC-38 60	May 71	Felvinci+. GAMMA MULTIPOL,ANAL TBC	
Spect (n,γ)	None		BNL	Expt Abst	BAP 16 841	Aug 71	Kane. RESON CAPT. 12GAMMA ES GIVEN	
Spect (n,γ)	4.0+1	1.2+2	GEL	Expt Conf	74Petten 673	Sep 74	Weigmann+ NO ANOMAL GROSS SHAPE	
Spect (n,γ)	None		GEL	Expt Prog	NEANDC(E)162 3	Feb 75	Rohr+LINAC TOF IN RES WITH ENHA.FISS	
Spect (n,γ)	Maxwl		FRS	Expt Abst	HPA 49 2 192	May 76	Ionescu+ LVL SCHEME NP238 Q VALUE	
(n,2n)	1.5+7		ALD	Expt Jour	JNAB 14 69	May 61	Perkin+ ABSOLUTE ACTIVN 0.39+ -0.07B	+
(n,2n)	1.4+7		HAM	Comp Jour	NP 65 257	Mar 65	Bormann. 1EXPT VALS.CFD SHELL EFFECT	
(n,2n)	1.3+7	1.5+7	BNL	Theo Jour	NSE 23 238	Nov 65	Pearlstein.3ES.STAT MDL CALC.TBL CS.	
(n,2n)	Fiss		BNL	Theo Jour	NSE 23 238	Nov 65	Pearlstein.STATMDL CALC.SPEC AVG.TBL	
(n,2n)	Pile		ORL	Expt Prog	ORNL-4306 1	May 68	Halperin+,PRELIMINARY VALUE GIVEN	
(n,2n)	8.0+5	1.0+7	KFK	Eval Rept	KFK-1186	Jul 70	Hinkelmann.AVG SIG FOR THR+FAST SPEC	
(n,2n)	1.5+7		JAE	Expt Jour	JPJ 35 936	Sep 73	Takekoshi+.SEARCH FOR FISSION-ISOMER	
				Jour	JPJ 30 284	Jan 71	- + SEE ALSO	
(n,2n)	1.0+6		FEI	Expt Conf	71Kiev 1 325	May 71	Ivanov+ RATIO NP237(N2N)/NP237(NG)	+
	1.0+6			Data	EXFOR40153.008	Apr 74	.1 DATA LINE	
(n,2n)	1.5+7		DUB	Expt Jour	IJP 47 232	73	Belov+ SIG TO SPONFIS GIVN,FRAGM - DET	
				Rept	JINR-E15-6807	Nov 72	- + SPON FISS ISOMER PRODUCTN,TBL	
(n,2n)	1.5+7		KFI	Expt Jour	MFF 21 555	73	Nagy. THESIS,HUNG. TO FISS ISO,GRND	
(n,2n)	1.4+7	1.5+7	LRL	Expt Jour	PR/C 8 1938	Nov 73	Landrum+. SIG MEASD REL TO AL27(NA).	+
	1.4+7	1.5+7		Data	EXFOR10376.	Jun 74	. 10 PTS. DET M-ST + GND-ST.	
(n,2n)	6.8+6		SRL	Expt Jour	NSE 55 24	Sep 74	Paulson+AV OVER U235 FISS SPECT.	+
	6.8+6			Data	EXFOR10549.002	Feb 76	. 1 PT. CS=(63+ -6)MB.	
(n,2n)	1.4+7		LRL	Expt Jour	JIN 37 633	Mar 75	Myers+ THRMONUCL TEST.ISOM RATIO GVN	+
	1.4+7			Data	EXFOR10408.002	Apr 75	. 1 PT. ISOMER RATIO.	
(n,2n)	9.6+6	1.4+7	KTO	Expt Prog	NEANDC(J)42L20	Sep 75	Nishi+.VDG,C-W.ACTIVATION.SIGS GIVEN	+
	9.6+6	1.4+7		Data	EXFOR20692.002	Nov 76	2PTS.SIGMA.	
(n,2n)	1.5+7		MUN	Expt Jour	PR/C 12 1507	Nov 75	Lindeke+ CS=247+ -22 MB.	+
	1.5+7			Data	EXFOR20672.002	Oct 76	1PNT.SIGMA.	
(n,2n)	1.4+7	1.5+7	JAE	Revw Conf	IAEA-186 3 1	76	Igarasi. REVW AVAIL DATA,GRPH+BIBLIO	
(n,xn) x>2	Fiss		BNL	Theo Jour	NSE 23 238	Nov 65	Pearlstein.SPEC AVG STATMDL CALC N3N	
(n,p)	1.4+7		ALD	Expt Jour	PPS 73 215	Feb 59	Coleman+. ACT. CFD DIRECT INTERACTN	+
(n,p)	1.5+7		SAH	Comp Jour	NUC 23 8 112	Aug 65	Chatterjee. TABLE WITH REFS.	
	1.4+7			Jour	NP 60 273	Nov 64	- .MEAN OF EXPT CFD SHELLMOD	
(n,p)	Maxwl		IFU	Theo Rept	ICD-4 20	67	Dadakina+ PENETR COEFF CALC,TABLE	
(n,p)	1.4+7	1.5+7	JYV	Eval Rept	JU-RR-3/1970	Jun 70	Leppaemaeki+ TABLE OF EVAL AVG SIG	

93 Neptunium 237

Quantity	Energy (ev) Min	Max	Lab	Type	Documentation Ref Vol Page	Date	Author, Comments	Data
(n,α)	Fiss		GDT	Revw Conf	62Harwell 1 153	Dec 62	Romanko+ FISSN AVERAGE VALUE GIVEN	
(n,α)	Maxwl		ILL	Expt Prog	BLG-520	77	Wagemans+ PRELIM.ABST.NDG.	
Fission	2.5+5	3.0+6	LAS	Expt Jour	PR 72 88	Jul 47	Klema. P-LI7,D-D NS. KEL U235.	+
	2.5+5	3.0+6		Data	EXFOR12492.002	Jun 76	. 16 PTS.	
Fission	Pile		HAR	Revw Conf	55Geneva 5 331	Aug 55	Holmes+.P404,RATIO PU239/NP237 GVN	
Fission	2.5+5	3.0+6	PTN	Expt Conf	55Geneva 2 155	Aug 55	Wheeler.P593,CURVE,THEORET DISCUSSN	
Fission	Fast		HAR	Expt Rept	AERE-R/R-2151	57	Absalom+ ZEPHYR+TH ENVELOPE.	
Fission	2.0+5	7.5+6	LAS	Revw Rept	LA-2122	Jun 57	Henkel.CURV,REPLACES LA-1714	
Fission	1.5+7		CCP	Expt Jour	AE 4 190	Feb 58	Protopopov+ 2.4+-0.2B, T(DN)HE COUNT	+
				Jour	JNE 9 157	Jun 59	TRANSLATN.*	
				Jour	SJA 4 256	58	TRANSLATN.*	
Fission	Maxwl		CRC	Expt Conf	58Geneva 16 54	Sep 58	Eastwood+ PPR203 LESS THAN 1MB	+
	Maxwl			Data	EXFOR12011.003	Jun 76	. 1 PT.	
Fission	Pile		KUR	Expt Conf	58Geneva 12 3	Sep 58	Leipunskij+.PPR2038,VAL NP237/PU239	
Fission	3.0+6	8.0+6	KUR	Expt Conf	58Geneva 16 136	Sep 58	Kalinin+.PPR2149,CURVE,CYCLOTRON	+
Fission	1.0+4	1.0+7	LAS	Revw Conf	58Geneva 15 344	Sep 58	Hemmendinger.PPR663,CURVE,MANY REFS	
Fission	+0	+2	MTR	Expt Prog	WASH-1006 28	Oct 58	Burgus+ NDG	
Fission	1.2+6	8.0+6	ORL	Expt Jour	PR 115 1707	59	Murray+	+
	1.2+6	8.0+6		Data	EXFOR11105.	Jun 76	. 24 PTS.	
Fission	1.2+4	1.5+6	KUR	Expt Conf	59Tashkent 1 57	Sep 59	Gokhberg.VDG,RSLN 2-20KEV, GRAPH	+
				Rept	AEC-TR-6398	64	.VOL 1,P59 .ENGL OF 59TASHKE 1 57	
Fission	9.0+5	8.0+6	ORL	Expt Conf	PR 116 1575	Dec 59	Schmitt+ REL TO T(P,N) AND U238	+
	9.1+5	7.4+6		Data	EXFOR12488.	Jun 76	. 121 PTS.	
Fission	1.2+4	1.5+6	CCP	Jour	SPD 4 1074	Mar 60	SF AND FISS ANISOTROPY	
Fission	+5	+7	GEA	Revw Conf	60S-Vienna 383	Jun 60	Moteff+ THRS-SIG-TBL FOR DOSIMETRY	
Fission	9.7+6	2.2+7	CCP	Expt Jour	AE 9 399	Nov 60	Pankratov+ TOF,FISS CH,NORM AT 14MEV	+
				Jour	JNAB 16 494	Oct 62	TRANSLATN.*	
	9.8+6	2.2+7		Jour	SJA 9 939	Sep 61	TRANSLATN.*	
Fission	Spont		DUB	Expt Jour	ZET 40 1296	May 61	Druin. HL OF SPONTANEOUS FISSION	
				Jour	JET 13 913	Nov 61	TRANSLATN.*	
Fission	2.0+5	1.0+7	ANL	Revw Conf	61Vienna 1 29	Aug 61	Smith.P76,CURVE,MANY REFS GVN	
Fission	Fiss		AI	Eval Conf	62Harwell 2 385	Dec 62	Strominger. SIG IN VARIOUS CORES,TBL	
Fission	Fiss		EGG	Eval Conf	62Harwell 2 487	Dec 62	Humpherys. GRPH EFF-SIG,RECOMM VALUE	
Fission	3.0+5	1.0+7	ISP	Revw Conf	62Harwell 1 27	Dec 62	Bresesti+ SIG(E) GRAPH,THRESHOLD-DET	
Fission	2.7+6	2.7+7	CCP	ExTh Jour	AE 14 177	Feb 63	Pancratov+.TOF SC CURVE GIVEN	+
				Jour	SJA 14 167	63	. ENGL OF AE 14 177	
Fission	4.0+5	4.0+6	KUR	Expt Rept	IAE-833	65	Borisova.SIG OF SYMMETR AND ASSYM F	
				Rept	AEC-TR-6728	66	. ENGL OF IAE-833	
Fission	4.0+4	5.0+5	ALD	Expt Conf	65Salzburg 1 219	Mar 65	White+ 6 ENERGIES.TBL.REL TO U235.	
Fission	Fiss		IIT	Comp Conf	65IAEA 251	Mar 65	Barrall+ CALC SIGS,3 SPECS,CFD EXPTS	
Fission	2.4+4		ALD	Expt Jour	JNE 19 423	Jun 65	Perkin+.CALIB SB-BE SRCE. 11+-2MB	+
	2.4+4			Data	EXFOR20584.006	Jul 76	1PNT.SIGMA.	
Fission	4.0+5	4.2+6	CCP	Expt Jour	YF 2 243	Aug 65	SYMMETR-FISS THRESHOLD MEASD,CFD TH	
				Jour	SNP 2 173	Feb 66	TRANSLATN.*	
Fission	None		BRK	Revw Jour	NP 81 1	Jun 66	Myers+ TABLE 2. FISSION BARRIER.	
Fission	None		KAP	Eval Conf	66Paris 2 267	Oct 66	Francis+ NDG. XPT FIT TO OPTMDL.	
	Fiss			Rept	KAPL/CSNL-4 66	Jun 66	Lubitz. EVAL CS. FISS AV 1.2 2	
Fission	Pile		WIN	Expt Rept	AEEW-R-526	Jun 67	Stevenson+.FISS RATIO TO U235.ZEBRA	
Fission	1.0+6	1.4+7	ALD	Expt Jour	JNE 21 671	Aug 67	White+ 4ES REL U235. CFD OTHER DATA	+
Fission	1.1+6	8.1+6	LAS	Expt Jour	NSE 30 39	Oct 67	Grundl+ DETECTOR EXCITATION MEASTS.	+
				Abst	DA 25 6704	May 65	- . U235 SPEC., REL U235	
	1.1+6	8.1+6		Data	EXFOR10416.003	Dec 74	. 17 PTS. SIGMA.	
Fission	Maxwl		RI	Revw Jour	AE 23 561	Dec 67	BAK+ OTHER SIG VAL GIVEN,TABLE	
				Jour	SJA 23 1340	Dec 67	. ENGL OF AE 23 561	
Fission		1.4+7	SOR	Revw Conf	IAEA-107 57	68	Ben-David.GRPH THRS-SIG(NEUT-E) GVN	
Fission	1.0+6	5.0+6	LAS	Expt Conf	68Wash. 627	Mar 68	Stein+ VDG TOF TBL+CURV NP237/U235	+
				Rept	LA-DC-9205	67	.EQUIVALENT	
				Conf	66Paris 1 419	Oct 66	.SUPERSEDED	
				Conf	66Wash. 623	Mar 66	Stein.REL SIG,TOF(=LADC-7617)	
	1.0+6	4.5+6		Data	EXFOR12452.004	Jun 76	. 12 PTS.	
Fission	9.1+3	1.0+7	ANL	Eval Jour	NSE 32 35	Apr 68	Davey+ RE-EVALUATION OF DATA.	
	1.0+3	1.0+7		Jour	NSE 26 149	Oct 66	- + EVALUATION.	
Fission	Fiss		BNW	Theo Rept	BNWL-SA-1794	Apr 68	Mcelroy. SAND 2 CALCULATION.	
Fission	Fiss		CCP	Expt Jour	DOK 180 836	Jun 68	Nasyrov+(AVG+EFFECTIV)THRESH-SIG-TBL	
				Jour	SPD 13 6 559	Dec 68	TRANSLATN.*	
Fission	1.2+7	1.8+7	NRD	Expt Jour	HP 14 595	Jun 68	Rago+ TRACK COUNTING REL U238(NF)	+
Fission	4.0+1	1.0+3	CCP	Theo Jour	YF 9 535	Mar 69	Gejlikman. SIG MAXIMA+QUASISTAT LVLS	
				Jour	SNP 9 306	Sep 69	TRANSLATN.*	

93 Neptunium 237

Quantity	Energy (ev) Min	Max	Lab	Type	Documentation Ref Vol Page	Date	Author, Comments	Data
Fission	1.0+4	1.0+6	KUR	Theo	Jour YF 9 538	Mar 69	Vorotnikov. FISS ANAL,S+P COMPOUND	
					Jour SNP 9 308	Sep 69	TRANSLATN.*	
Fission	1.0+4	1.0+6	KUR	Theo	Jour YF 9 538	Mar 69	Vorotnikov.WF FOR S- AND P-NS,CURVS	
Fission	Fast		JAE	Expt	Conf 69London § 1.7	Jun 69	Kuroi+ RATIO U235,EVALS CFD INT EXPT	
Fission	Spont		COP	Revw	Conf 69Vienna 155	Jul 69	Strutinsky+PPR203. HL GVN,'SHELL-TH'	
Fission	-		FEI	Theo	Conf 69Vienna 337	Jul 69	Gaj+PPR132. 2HUMPD-BARR-CALC,TBL+CRV	
Fission	-2	+3	DUB	Expt	Prog YFI-9 24	Dec 69	Gavrilov+ SIG EXPT,INTERM STR,NDG	
					Rept INDC(CCP)-9U31	Dec 70	TRANSLATN.*	
	Fiss				Jour AE 28 362	Apr 70	Gavrilov+ AVG SIG,SUBBARRIER FISSION	
	1.0-2	1.0+3			Jour AE 28 362	Apr 70	- + SIG(E) GRAPH,RESON-ANALYS	
	1.0-2	6.0+2			Rept JINR-P3-4449	May 69	- + TOF,GRPH SIG VS NEUTRON-E	
	1.0-2	1.0+3			Rept EAF 28 4 117	Apr 70	FRENCH OF AE 28 362	
Fission	1.4+7		TRM	Expt	Conf 69Roorke 2 289	Dec 69	Iyer+ SIGMA RELATIVE TO U238	+
	1.4+7				Data EXFOR30035.005	Dec 72	ONE VALUE	
Fission	1.0+3	1.0+7	TRM	Eval	Rept BARC/I-96	70	Kapil.14 GROUP SIG,2 N-SPECS,TABLES	
Fission	1.0-4	1.8+7	BNW	Eval	Rept BNWL-1312	May 70	Simons+ EVALUATION.	
Fission	2.5-2	1.0+7	KFK	Eval	Rept KFK-1186	Jul 70	Hinkelmann.5-GROUP SIG,THR+FAST SPEC	
	2.5-2				Rept KFK-1186	Jul 70	- . RECOMMENDED 0 B	
Fission	3.2+1	2.8+6	LAS	Expt	Jour NP/A 156 609	Nov 70	Brown+ BOMB EXPT.FL CALB LI(NA)U(NF)	+
					Rept LA-4372	Jan 70	- +POMMARD EVENT,TOF,TBL,CURVS.	
	3.2+1	2.8+6			Data EXFOR10060.002	Nov 71	. 2496 PTS. SIGMA.	
Fission	1.0+1	5.0+2	SAC	Expt	Diss FRNC-TH-341	Oct 72	Paya.	
					Rept CEA-N-1339	Nov 70	- + FISSION ISOMER STUDY.	
				ExTh	Conf 69Vienna 307	Jul 69	+SIG GRPH,TOF,INTERMEDIAT ANAL	
				Expt	Jour JPRC 29 1 159	Jan 68	- +67BORDEAUX ONLY 1/5 OF SIGTOT	
					Rept INDC-156	67	- + FULL TEXT OF 66PARIS.	
Fission	+0	+1	COL	Expt	Prog NCSAC-33 59	Dec 70	Felvinci+,RESON AT 39.07EV,ANAL TBC	
Fission	3.2+5	2.5+6	TRM	Expt	Conf 70Madurai 2 67	Dec 70	Iyengar+ SIGMA EXPT TB CONT'D, NDG	
Fission	Fiss		IAE	Eval	Jour KNS 3 77	Jun 71	Bak+ RECOMMENDED AVG SIG CFD OTHERS	
	1.0+5	1.9+7			Jour KNS 3 77	Jun 71	BAK+ FIT TO EXPTS,POINT SIG TBL+GRPH	
Fission	Fiss		AMS	Expt	Jour JNE 25 457	Sep 71	Pauw+ CF252 SPEC,SIG=1260+- 60MB	
Fission	1.0+1	5.0+2	HAR	Revw	Rept AERE-R-2505	Dec 71	Lynn.GRPH. 2-HUMP STRUCTURE IN FISS	
	None				Conf 69Vienna 249	Jul 69	- . TBL=2 HUMPED FISS BARR PARAMS	
		1.0+2		Expt	Conf 68JINR 115	Jul 68	RAE.INTERMED.STRUCT.EFFECTS IN FISS.	
	1.0+1	5.0+2		Revw	Conf 68DUBSY 463	Jul 68	Lynn.REVIEW,STRUCT EFFECTS IN FISS.	
	-2	+2			Conf 65Salzburg 187	Mar 65	RAE.REVIEW,SOME CALCULATIONS CFD XPT	
Fission	Fiss		IAE	Revw	Rept INDC(NDS)-47	72	Vlasov+ REVIEW DATA STATUS ,TBL+GRPH	
	2.0+1	6.0+1	GEL	Expt	Jour ZP 248 355	Sep 71	Kolar+,LINAC TOF SUBTR FISS	+
					Jour NP/A 187 305	Jun 72	Weigmann+FIS.BAR.PARAMS	
	2.0+1	5.2+1			Data EXFOR20138.002	Mar 73	1171PTS.	
Fission	3.5+6	4.9+6	KTO	Expt	Prog EANDC(J)26L39	Aug 72	Kobayashi+.CFD C OTHER DATA IN FIG	+
	Fast				Prog EANDC(J)26L39	Aug 72	- +.CFD C OTHER DATA IN TABLE	
					Prog EANDC(J)22L26	Aug 71	Kimura+.AVG SIGMA=1.33+-0.11 BARN	
					Conf 71Vienna 113	Aug 71	- + ACTIVATION,TBL CFD OTHERS	
	Fast				Data EXFOR20300.	Jun 74	9PTS.SIGMA.	
Fission	2.0+1	7.0+6	LAS	Expt	Jour NSE 48 412	Aug 72	Jiacoletti+.NUCL SHOT.TOF.CURVS+TABL	+
					Rept LA-4763	Sep 71	- + TBLS. FULL DATA.	
	2.0+5	7.7+6			Data EXFOR10182.002	Aug 75	. 1021 PTS. SIGMA.	
Fission	Spont		TPI	Theo	Jour YF 16 919	Nov 72	Adeev+ FISS BARRIER CFD EVEN,NUCLEI	
					Jour SNP 16 507	May 73	.ENGLISH OF YF 16 919	
Fission	Maxwl	Fiss	SGA	Eval	Conf 73Paris 1 233	Mar 73	Eder+ FISS SPEC REL U238(N,F),TBLS	
					Rept SGAE-PH-141	Feb 73	.SAME AS 73PARIS,NO DETAILS,TBP	
Fission	1.0+6	1.8+7	CCP	Eval	Conf 73Kiev 1 227	May 73	Borisov+ SIG(NEUT-E),TBL,CFD OTHERS	
Fission	+6		AUA	Eval	Prog INDC(SEC)-35	Sep 73	.SHORT NOTE,NO DATA GIVEN	
Fission	Thrsh	2.0+7	RCN	Comp	Rept RCN-196	Oct 73	Zijp+COMPIL.EVAL.CS.FAST N.METROLGY	
	Fiss			Revw	Conf 73Paris 2 271	Mar 73	- .RECOMM INTEG CFD DIFF CALC,TBL	
Fission	1.0+0	1.0+3	LAS	Expt	Jour PR/C 8 2352	Dec 73	Keyworth+.POL BEAM+TARG.INTERM STRCT	
	2.5+1	5.5+1			Conf JINR-D-37991	Apr 74	Harvey.P157.POL N+TARG,RES-SPINS DET	
	1.0+0	1.0+3			Conf 73Rochestr 1 85	Aug 73	.SUPERSEDED	
Fission	1.0+5	1.2+6	CCP	Eval	Rept YK-13 159	74	Vasiljev+ EFFSIG(E),20SPECS.TBL,GRPH	
Fission	None		LAS	Eval	Prog LA-5570-PR	Apr 74	Foster+ ABSTRACT	
Fission	Fiss		TEX	Expt	Rept UMO-74-24,841	May 74	Chromik. THESIS.CF252-NEUTRONS	
Fission	Fiss		IFL	Eval	Book LAPENAS	75	Lapenas. EVAL DATA AVGD,VALUE GIVEN	+
	1.0+5	1.8+7			Book LAPENAS	75	. FULL DOCUM OF EVAL,TABLES	
	Fiss				Data VIEN-V0003.002	Nov 75	WATT-SPECTRUM, 1 POINT	
	1.0+5	1.8+7			Data VIEN-V0002.002	Nov 75	SIGMA AT 175 ENERGIES	
Fission	Fiss		PTB	Eval	Rept PTB-FMRB-60	Feb 75	Alberts. CF252-SPC,EVAL DATA AVG,TBL	
Fission	Fiss		HED	Expt	Conf 75Wash. 189	Mar 75	Mcelroy.235U THERM FISS SPECT AVG CS	

93 Neptunium 237

Quantity	Energy (ev) Min	Max	Lab	Type	Documentation Ref Vol Page	Date	Author, Comments	Data
Fission	+5	7.7+6	LAS	Theo Conf	75Wash. 218	Mar 75	Wilhelmy+CALC USING U238(HE3,TF)	
Fission	1.0+5	2.0+7	NBS	Revw Conf	75Wash. 293	Mar 75	Carlson. GRPH CS CFD U235,U238	
Fission	1.0+5	2.5+7	CRC	Eval Jour	NSE 58 377	Dec 75	Cross+ ANALYTICAL FIT TO DATA	
Fission	Fiss		MOL	Expt Prog	INDC(SEC)-51	Dec 75	Fabry.P85.AVG(U35 - SPEC),CFD ENDF,TBL	
				Conf	75Wash. 254	Mar 75	- +INTEG CS REL U238NF= 4.35+-.13	
Fission	4.0+4	1.8+7	JAE	Revw Conf	IAEA-186 3 1	76	Igarasi. REVW AVAIL DATA,GRPH+BIBLIO	
	4.0+4	1.5+7		Rept	JAERI-M-6315	Nov 75	- +GRPH. 8 DATA SETS COMPARED.	
Fission	Maxwl		MOL	Theo Jour	NP/A 259 423	Mar 76	Wagemans+ CALC FOR DOUBLE HUMP + IH0	
Fission	None		MUN	Theo Diss	GRYNTAKIS	Mar 76	Gryntakis.,CALC.OF WESTCOTTS G-FUNCT	
				Jour	RCA 22 128	Mar 75	- +,EQUIVALENT TO THESIS	
Fission	2.0+1	5.0+5	LAS	Expt Abst	BAP 16 1181	Oct 71	Hoffman+. TOF. SOME DATA	+
	2.0+1	2.5+5		Data	EXFOR10366.002	Apr 76	. 1930 PTS. SIGMA.	
Fission	2.0+1	2.0+6	LAS	Expt Abst	BAP 21 655	Apr 76	Semon+TOF.RES ANAL.REPORT TBP.NDG	
Fission	4.1-2	5.3+0	HAN	Expt Prog	HW-59126 3	Jan 59	Leonard+ FILTERED BEAM RELATIVE B	+
	4.1-2	5.3+0		Data	EXFOR12476.002	Jun 76	. 100 PTS.	
Fission		5.0+2	BRC	Revw Conf	76Lowell 641	Jul 76	Michaudon.STRUCTURE EFFECTS.GRPH.	
	2.5+1	5.5+1		Conf	75Wash. 202	Mar 75	- .RVW EXP SUBTR FISS DATA	
Fission	3.0+0	5.0+1	YAL	ExTh Conf	76Lowell 389	Jul 76	Firk. SPIN.DETERMIN.OF RES.	
Fission	Fast		LON	Expt Prog	NEANDC(E)172 8	Aug 76	Hannan+ REACTOR SPECT,RATIO TO U5NF	
Fission	3.0+0	3.5+4	SAC	Expt Jour	NSE 61 477	Dec 76	Plattard+ TOF.LINAC.GRPHS.	+
				Diss	FRNC-TH-??	Nov 73	Platard.AREA FOR CLASS 2 STATES	
				Conf	73Rochestr 2 486	Aug 73	Plattard+.ABST,HIGH RESOL EXPT,NDG	
	+0	5.0+3		Conf	73Munich 1 603	Aug 73	- + CLASS II - STUDY,FEW DETAILS	
	3.0+0	3.5+4		Conf	73Kiev 2 254	May 73	- + LINAC,TOF,GAS SCINT. CURVE	
	2.7+0	3.5+4		Data	EXFOR20448.002	Oct 75	3923PTS.SIGMA.	
Fission	1.0+5	2.0+6	SAC	Expt Jour	NSE 61 477	Dec 76	Plattard+ TOF,LINAC,GRPHS.FIS BARR	+
				Prog	CEA-N-1861 92	Apr 76	Blons. LINAC,TOF,INT STR,FIS BAR STD	
				Abst	ANS 22 665	Nov 75	Plattard+ GRPH,TBL.CFD ENDF+EXPTS.	
				Conf	75Kiev 6 34	May 75	- + HIGH RESOL.SIG(E).TBL.GRPH	
	1.0+5	2.0+6		Data	EXFOR20423.002	Aug 75	1592PTS.SIGMA.	
Res Int Fiss	-4	+7	BNW	Eval Rept	BNWL-1312	May 70	Simons+ RI=6.12 B.	
Res Int Fiss	4.7-1	1.0+7	KFK	Eval Rept	KFK-1186	Jul 70	Hinkelmann. INFIN DILUTION RES INTEG	
Res Int Fiss	5.0-1	+6	COR	Expt Jour	NSE 46 31	Oct 71	Draper.INTEGRAL SIG TIMES E.4 SPECTR	
	+0	+1		Abst	DA/B 31 1466	Sep 70	- .EXPT FOR 4 SPEC,CFD CALC	
Res Int Fiss	5.0-1		SGA	Comp Conf	73Paris 1 233	Mar 73	Eder+ REDUCED RES INTEGRAL,TABLE	
				Rept	SGAE-PH-141	Feb 73	.SAME AS 73PARIS,NO DETAILS,TBP	
Res Int Fiss	1.0+0	3.5+3	SAC	Eval Jour	NSE 61 477	Dec 76	Plattard+ 100EV INTERVALS.TBL.CFD.	
Alpha	Fast		ITU	Expt Prog	NEANDC(E)162U	Feb 75	Cottone+ SB-125,XE,CS,ND VOL.5.P.42.	
Nu	Fiss		CCP	Expt Jour	AE 4 187	Feb 58	Kuzminov+ REL U235 NU THR,PROMPT NS	
				Jour	JNE 9 153	Jun 59	TRANSLATN.*	
				Jour	SJA 4 250	58	TRANSLATN.*	
Nu	Pile		LAS	Expt Conf	58Geneva 15 331	Sep 58	Leachman.PPR665,VAL REL TO U235 GVN	
Nu	Fiss		CCP	Expt Jour	AE 10 371	Apr 61	Lebedev+.VAL GVN,REL TO U235	
				Jour	SJA 10 357	Jan 62	TRANSLATN.* JNE17 577 D/63	
				Jour	KE 4 985	Dec 61	. GERMAN OF AE 10 371	
Nu	4.2+5	1.3+6	CCP	Expt Jour	YF 7 1185	Jun 68	Kozlov+ LINEAR NU(NEUT-E) CV EXPECTD	
				Jour	SNP 7 707	Dec 68	TRANSLATN.*	
Nu	2.5-2	1.0+7	KFK	Eval Rept	KFK-1186	Jul 70	Hinkelmann.MEAN NUMBER VS E	
	4.7+4	8.0+5		Rept	KFK-1186	Jul 70	- .AVG VALUE OF MEAN NUMBER	
Nu	5.0+6	1.7+7	LRL	Expt Prog	UCID-16514 6	Jun 74	Alvarez+	
Nu	Spont		HED	Eval Abst	ANS 22 673	Nov 75	Johnson. TBL,GRPH.NU FROM SPON FISS	
Delayd Neuts	4.0+5	5.1+6	FEI	Expt Rept	INDC(CCP)-51	75	Maksjutenko+ 10H-L GROUPS,YLD(E) TBL	+
	4.0+5	1.2+6			Jour YF 19 748	Apr 74	- + REL GROUP - YLDS,TBL+GRPH	
					Jour SNP 19 380	Oct 74	. ENGLISH OF YF 19 748	
	4.0+5	1.2+6		Data	EXFOR40303.	Feb 76	.DATA AT 9 ES GVN	
Fiss Prod γ	1.0+6	2.0+7	SOR	Revw Conf	IAEA-107 57	68	Ben-David.NEW THRS-REACT TBD,GE-DET	
Fiss Prod γ	-		WIN	Theo Jour	JNE 25 513	Oct 71	James.MEAN EN OF DELAYD GAMS,BETAS.	
Fiss Yield	Fiss		LAS	Expt Rept	LA-1997	Feb 56	Ford+ DEGRADED SPEC 11MASS YIELDS	
Fiss Yield	1.5+7		ALD	Expt Jour	JIN 14 8		60 Coleman+ MASS YLD CURVE GIVEN	
Fiss Yield	9.0+6	1.5+7	LAS	ExTh Jour	PR/B 137 814	Feb 65	Leachman+ RLTV ANGDIST FISS-FRAG.	
Fiss Yield	1.2+7	2.4+7	LAS	ExTh Prog	WASH-1056 4	Mar 65	Blumbrg.FISSION ANISOTROPY,NDG	
Fiss Yield	Fiss		TRM	Expt Conf	65Salzburg 439	Mar 65	Iyer.YLD OF VARIOUS ISOTOPS,TBL,GRPH	
Fiss Yield	4.0+5	4.2+6	CCP	Expt Jour	YF 2 243	Aug 65	YLDS OF MO99,AG111,CD115,BA140	
					Jour SNP 2 173	Feb 66	TRANSLATN.*	
Fiss Yield	Fiss		LAS	Expt Jour	PR 156 1277	Apr 67	Stein+ SI DETECT,CURVE YIELDS,ENERGY	
Fiss Yield	1.0+6	2.0+7	SOR	Revw Conf	IAEA-107 57	68	Ben-David.NEW THRS-REACT TBD,GE-DET	
Fiss Yield	1.4+7		RI	ExTh Conf	68Riga	Jan 68	Adamov+ ABST,LONG-RANGE PARTICLES YL	
Fiss Yield	1.4+7		RI	ExTh Conf	68Riga	Jan 68	Adamov+ ABST,A-PARTICLES,TRITON YLD	

93 Neptunium 237

Quantity	Energy (ev) Min	Max	Lab	Type	Documentation Ref Vol Page	Date	Author, Comments	Data
Fiss Yield	Pile		TRM	Expt	Jour JIN 30 2305	Sep 68	Namboodini+ YLD OF 20 NUCLIDE	
Fiss Yield	Maxwl	1.6+7	FEI	Expt	Conf 69Vienna 923	Jul 69	Vorob'Eva+PPR133. FRAG YLD+E(NEUT−E)	
Fiss Yield	1.4+7		FTI	Expt	Conf 69Vienna 900	Jul 69	Adamov+PPR146.LONG−RANGE−YLD VAL GVN	
					Jour YF 9 732	Apr 69	− + PROTON,T,D AND ALFA YLD GIVN	
					Jour SNP 9 424	Oct 69	. ENGL OF YF 9 732	
Fiss Yield	+5	+7	OSL	Revw	Conf 69Vienna 669	Jul 69	Pappas+PPR206.REVW,INITIAL MASS DIST	
Fiss Yield	Fast		MCM	Expt	Prog EANDC(CAN)−40	Sep 69	Thode+ MASS−SPEC,REL CUM KR+XE GIVEN	
Fiss Yield	Pile		PAV	Expt	Jour JIN 31 3739	Dec 69	Stella+ FISS YLD OF 17 MASS BETWEEN	
Fiss Yield	7.0+5	5.4+6	FEI	Expt	Jour YF 11 297	Feb 70	Kuzminov+ YIELD(FRAG−A)GRPHS AT 8 ES	+
					Jour SNP 11 166	Aug 70	TRANSLATN.*NO 2	
	8.0+5	2.2+6			Data EXFOR40172.	Nov 73	.5 SUBENT FOR 5 ES,EACH 41 LINES	
Fiss Yield	None		TRM	Expt	Prog INIS−MF−334 64	72	.RADIOCHEM+GAM−SPEC,SHORT NOTE,NDG	
Fiss Yield	Pile		RI	Expt	Jour YF 15 860	May 72	Petrzhak+ TBL REL XE YLDS,EPI−CD	
					Jour SNP 15 482	Nov 72	. ENGL OF YF 15 860	
Fiss Yield	Fast	1.4+7	HAR	Eval	Rept AERE−R−7394	May 73	Crouch.CHAIN YLDS RECOMMENDED TBL	
	Pile				Conf 73Paris 1 393	Mar 73	− .EXPTL DATA+EVAL CHAIN YLD,TBL	
					Rept AERE−R−7209	Jan 73	− .23 CHAIN YLDS RECOMMENDED TBL	
Fiss Yield	Maxwl		MCM	Expt	Jour JIN 35 8 2639	Aug 73	Tracy+ CUMUL KR + XE YIELDS	
Fiss Yield	Fast	1.4+7	HAR	Revw	Conf IAEA−169 1 353	74	Cuninghame.FAST+N−E DEPEND,TBLS,GRPH	
					Rept AERE−R−7548	Sep 73	.SAME AS 73BOLOGNA,EVALUATIONS CFD	
Fiss Yield	Fast		ITU	Expt	Prog NEANDC(E)162U	Feb 75	Cottone+ SB−125,XE,CS,ND VOL.5.P.42.	
Fiss Yield	1.4+7		AMS	Expt	Diss POLAK	76	Polak. SYSTEMATICS OF YLDS.(P,FISS)	
Fiss Yield	2.0+6		AUA	Theo	Rept AAEC/E−386	Mar 76	Cook+ 3−GAUSS FIT,PARAMS GIVEN	
Fiss Yield	2.5−2	1.4+7	LAS	Expt	Prog ERDA−NDC−3 94	May 76	Ford+NFY COMPILATION.SEE LA−6129.NDG	
Fiss Yield	Maxwl		GRE	Expt	Prog CEA−N−2015	77	Asghar+TABLE OF MEAN PARAMETERS	
Fiss Yield	1.4+7		RI	Expt	Conf 77Kiev	77	Petrzhak+ YLD XE−131,132,134,136,TBL	
Frag Spectra	1.4+7		LAS	Expt	Jour PR 94 640	May 54	Brolley+ 0 DEG/90 DEG INTENSIT RATIO	
Frag Spectra	3.5+5	1.5+6	KUR	Expt	Conf 59Tashkent 1 57	Sep 59	Gokhberg.VDG,GRPH FISS−ANISTRPY VS E	
					Book NEJTRONFIZ 211	61	Otroshchenko. GRPH FISSION−ANISOTROP	
					Rept AEC−TR−6398	64	.VOL 1,P59 .ENGL OF 59TASHKE 1 57	
					Book SPN 155	61	. ENGL TRANSL OF NEJTRONFIZ 211	
Frag Spectra	6.0+6	2.0+7	CRC	Expt	Jour CJP 37 1418	Dec 59	Baerg+. FRAG ANG DIST ISOTROPIC	
Frag Spectra	1.0+6	8.8+6	LAS	Expt	Jour PR 120 198	Oct 60	Simmons+ FRAGMENT ANGULAR DIST 20ES	
Frag Spectra	1.4+7		LAS	Expt	Jour NP 19 366	Nov 60	Leachman+.ZR97,BA139 FORE/AFT RATIO	
Frag Spectra	Fiss		LAS	Expt	Jour PR 156 1277	Apr 67	Stein+ FRAG ENERGIES VS MASS,+ TOTAL	
Frag Spectra	1.4+7		RI	ExTh	Conf 68Riga	Jan 68	Adamov+ ABST,E−DIST OF A−PART,TRITON	
Frag Spectra	4.2+5	1.3+6	CCP	Expt	Jour YF 7 1185	Jun 68	Kozlov+ GRPH,MEAN FRAG−KIN−E(NEUT−E)	
					Jour SNP 7 707	Dec 68	TRANSLATN.*	
Frag Spectra		7.0+6	FEI	ExTh	Conf 69Vienna 419	Jul 69	Androsenko+PPR134. XPTL ANGDIST + TH	
Frag Spectra	Maxwl	1.6+7	FEI	Expt	Conf 69Vienna 923	Jul 69	Vorob'Eva+PPR133. FRAG YLD+E(NEUT−E)	
Frag Spectra	1.4+7		FTI	Expt	Conf 69Vienna 900	Jul 69	Adamov+PPR146. ALFA+TRITIUM SPECTRUM	
					Jour YF 9 732	Apr 69	− + AVG ALFA,T,P ENERGY + −SPREAD	
					Jour SNP 9 424	Oct 69	. ENGL OF YF 9 732	
Frag Spectra	+5	+7	ORL	ExTh	Conf 69Vienna 67	Jul 69	Schmitt.PPR122.GRPH,(EKIN+−RMS) VS A	
Frag Spectra	7.0+5	5.4+6	FEI	Expt	Jour YF 11 297	Feb 70	Kuzminov+ AVG KINE + KINE(A) GRAPHS	
	8.0+5	2.2+6			Data EXFOR40172.	Nov 73	.5 SUBENT FOR 5 ES,EACH 41 LINES	
	7.0+5	5.4+6			Jour SNP 11 166	Aug 70	TRANSLATN.*NO 2	
Frag Spectra	3.0+5	7.2+6	FEI	Expt	Jour YF 12 35	Jul 70	Shpak+ ANGDIST+ANISOTROPY,GRPH+TBL	+
					Jour SNP 12 19	Jan 71	*	
	5.0+5	5.0+6			Jour ZEP 8 545	Nov 68	Shpak+ ANG ANISOTR COEF,PRELIMINARY	
					Jour JEL 8 332	Nov 68	. ENGL OF ZEP 8 545	
	3.0+5	7.2+6			Data EXFOR40015.002	Aug 70	ANGULAR ANISOTROPY AT 55 N−ENERGIES	
Frag Spectra	Thrsh	+6	FEI	Expt	Jour AHP 29 357	Aug 70	Androsenko+ ANGDIST CFD 2−HUMPD−BARR	
Frag Spectra	Pile		TRM	Theo	Conf 70Madurai 2 79	Dec 70	Prakash+ KIN−E CFD SHELL−STRUCT, CRV	
Frag Spectra	1.6+7		TRM	Expt	Prog BARC−628 94	72	Iyer+ ANGULAR ANISOTROPY OF FRAG,TBL	+
	1.4+7	1.6+7			Conf 70Madurai 2 57	Dec 70	− + ANGDISTR,GRAPH+TABLE,TRACK−DE	
	1.6+7				Data EXFOR30235.	Jul 73	COS.COEF.OF ANG.DIST. OF FIS.FRAGM.	
Frag Spectra	4.0−1	2.0+3	HAR	Expt	Jour NP/A 196 389	Nov 72	Kuiken+ ANGDIST ALIGNED NUC	
					Prog EANDC(E)140U	Aug 71	Pattenden+ ORIENTED TGTS.	
					Rept RCN−142	Jun 71	Kuiken+ ANG DIST OF FRAGS.ALIGNED U.	
	4.0−2	2.0+3			Conf 69Vienna 910	Jul 69	Pattenden.PPR57. ANGDISTRIBUTION,TBD	
	3.1+1	8.7+2		ExTh	Conf 69Vienna 330	Jul 69	− .DISSCUSSN.ANGDIST,PREL TBL	
Frag Spectra	4.0−1	2.0+3	LEI	Expt	Jour NP/A 196 389	Nov 72	Kuiken+ ALIGND NUC A−DIST.2HUMP ANAL	
Frag Spectra	7.0+5	5.4+6	FEI	Expt	Rept YK−12 1 3	Jan 73	Sergachev+ DATA TABLES AND CURVES	+
	7.0+5	5.4+6			Data EXFOR40210.	Jun 74	.SPECTR OF FISFRAG AT 2EN,AVER KIN−E	

93 Neptunium 237

Quantity	Energy (ev) Min	Max	Lab	Type	Documentation Ref Vol Page	Author, Comments Date	Data
Frag Spectra	Pile		TRM	Expt Jour	PR/C 11 1251	Apr 75 Dange+ TBL,GRPHS FRAG ENERGY DIST	+
				Conf	73Bangalor 2 5	Dec 73 Manohar+TOTAL KINETIC E DISTRB GRAPH	
				Prog	BARC-628 80	72 Dange+ KINET.EN.DISTRIBUTION,TBL	
	Pile			Data	EXFOR30307.002	Aug 75 11 PTS, FRAG.KINETIC ENERGY,2 DATA.	
Frag Spectra	Maxwl		GRE	Expt Prog	CEA-N-2015	77 Asghar+TABLE OF MEAN PARAMETERS	
Frag Charge	1.8+6	1.5+7	LRL Comp	Rept	UCRL-51640	Jul 74 Nethaway. TBL AT 2 ES	
Frag Charge	4.0+5	5.1+6	FEI	Expt Rept	INDC(CCP)-51	75 Maksjutenko+ ZP(E)BY DELAY-N-YLD,TBL	
Reson Params	4.9-1	1.5+0	MTR	Expt Jour	PR 107 525	Jul 57 Smith.	+
				Abst	PR 99 611	Jul 55 - + B6 TRANSM 2ND E AT 1D34 3 ES.	
	4.9-1	1.5+0		Data	EXFOR12487.	Jun 76 . 12 RES. E0,WT,PCS,W0,W.	
Reson Params	4.9-1	3.5+1	MTR	Expt Abst	BAP 4 270	59 Cline+ ABSTR. SA3.	+
	4.9-1	3.5+1		Data	EXFOR12477.	Jun 76 . 44 RES. E0,WT,WN,PCS,WT**2/PCS.	
Reson Params	3.9+0	1.9+1	CCP	Expt Jour	AE 6 569	May 59 Adamchuk+.TABLE OF RES-ENERGS,FC	+
				Jour	SJA 6 420	Dec 60 TRANSLATN.* JNE A13 72 0/60	
				Jour	KE 3 282	Mar 60 .GERMAN	
Reson Params		1.0+6	AUA	Theo Jour	AUJ 20 477	Oct 67 Cook. TBL OF AVG LVL SPACING D,L=0,1	
Reson Params	4.9-1	1.1+2	SAC	Expt Diss	FRNC-TH-341	Oct 72 Paya+ FINAL VALUES FOR COMPILATION.	+
				Jour	AE 29 395	Nov 70 Michaudon.ABST FRANC-SOV SEM DUBNA	
				ExTh Conf	69Vienna 307	Jul 69 Paya+INTERMEDIATE STRUCTURE ANALYS.	
				Expt Jour	PRL 20 1373	Jun 68 Fubini+	
				Jour	JPRC 29 1 159	Jan 68 Paya+67BORDEAUX FROM SIG TOTAL+FISS	
				Conf	66Paris 2 128	Oct 66 - + PPR69.ABST.WT,2G.WN,WG. SHAPE	
				Jour	SJA 29 1156	Nov 70 Michaudon+ TRANSLATION OF AE	
	4.9-1	2.4+2		Data	EXFOR20447.003	Oct 75 248PTS.WT.	
Reson Params		1.0+6	KUR	Theo Jour	YF 9 538	Mar 69 Vorotnikov.RES-PARS-LVS IN FISS-ANAL	
				Jour	SNP 9 308	Sep 69 TRANSLATN.*	
Reson Params	-		CCP	Theo Jour	ZEP 9 510	May 69 Ermagambetov+WF ANAL OF OTHER EXPT	
				Jour	JEL 9 9 309	May 69 TRANSLATN.*	
Reson Params	+0	+5	COP	Revw Conf	69Vienna 155	Jul 69 Strutinsky+ PPR203.INTERMED WF STRUCT	
Reson Params	None		HAR	Revw Conf	69Vienna 249	Jul 69 Lynn. TBL STRUTINSKY PARS,FISS+CAPT	
	2.5+1	4.6+1		Rept	AERE-R-5891	Sep 68 - . TBL STRONG FISS RESPARS	
		1.0+2		Expt Conf	68JINR 115	Jul 68 RAE.INTERMED.STRUCT.EFFECTS IN FISS.	
	-			Theo Conf	68DUBSY 463	Jul 68 Lynn.REVIEW,STRUCT EFFECTS IN FISS.	
Reson Params	4.9-1	7.5+0	DUB	Expt Prog	YFI-9 24	Dec 69 Gavrilov+ GAM FISSN+GAM N GIVEN,TBL	+
				Rept	INDC(CCP)-9U31	Dec 70 TRANSLATN.*	
				Jour	AE 28 362	Apr 70 Gavrilov+ TABLE OF FISSN+NEUT WIDTHS	
				Jour	EAF 28 4 117	70 .FRENCH OF AE 28 362	
				Jour	SJA 28 464	70 .ENGL OF AE 28 362	
	4.9-1	7.5+0		Data	EXFOR40018.	Apr 74 .2 SUBENT,DATA FOR 7 RES-EN GVN	
Reson Params	+2		FEI	Theo Rept	INDC(CCP)-7U22	Feb 70 .TRANSLATN.*	
	+2	+6		Jour	YFI 10 542	Sep 69 GAI+ FISSN WIDTH TBL,DISTRIBUTN CRVS	
	+2			Prog	YFI-7 19	Apr 69 GAI+ FISSN-WIDTH-DISTR,CRV CFD EXPT	
	-			Rept	FEI-158	Feb 69 Gaj+ FISSN WIDTH,2HUMPED-BARR-CALCUL	
	+2	+6		Jour	SNP 10 311	Mar 70 . ENGL OF YF 10 542	
Reson Params	1.0+3	4.6+4	KFK	Eval Rept	KFK-1186	Jul 70 Hinkelmann. AVG WG,WF LVL SPACING	
Reson Params	None		COL	Expt Prog	NCSAC-33 41	Dec 70 Camarda+,TRANSMISSION,NO DATA GIVEN	
Reson Params	3.9+1		COL	Expt Prog	NCSAC-33 59	Dec 70 Felvinci+,PRELIM WF GVN,ANAL TBC	
Reson Params	8.0+0	7.0+1	GEL	Expt Conf	71Knoxvill 667	Mar 71 Poortmans+ LINAC. TBL RES PARS.	
		7.0+1		Prog	EANDC(E)150U	May 72 - +,LINAC TOF	
Reson Params	6.2-1	5.0+4	SRL	Theo Conf	71Knoxvill 714	Mar 71 Mccrosson. STAT CALCULATN AVG PARAMS	
Reson Params	+0		CCP	Theo Jour	AE 31 18	Jul 71 Vorotnikov.S+P-NEUT FISS-WIDS DERIVD	
				Jour	SJA 31 706	Feb 72 * ENGL OF AE 31 18 7/71	
Reson Params	8.0+0	6.0+1	GEL	Expt Prog	EANDC(E)140U	Aug 71 Rohr+ AREA ANAL. FROM CAPT.TBL GIVEN	
Reson Params	2.0+1	5.0+1	GEL	Expt Jour	NP/A 187 305	Jun 72 Weigmann+ FIS BARRIER PARAMETERS.	+
				Jour	ZP 248 355	Sep 71 Kolar+ SUBTHRESHOLD FISS RES PARS	
	2.0+1	5.0+1		Data	EXFOR20138.003	Mar 73 28PTS.WF.	
Reson Params	3.9+0	1.6+2	SAC	Expt Diss	FRNC-TH-??	Nov 73 Platard.AREA FOR CLASS 2 STATES	+
	3.8+0	1.6+2		Jour	NSE 61 477	Dec 76 Plattard+ WT,WF,WG,2G*WN.TBL.	
	3.9+0	1.6+2		Conf	73Munich 1 603	Aug 73 - + CLASS II SPINS,FEW DETAILS	
				Conf	73Kiev 2 254	May 73 - + CLASS II,I=3 STATIST,GRAPH	
				Theo Jour	JPRC 33 21	Aug 72 - + INTERMEDIATE STRUCT ANAL	
	3.9+0	1.6+2		Expt Data	EXFOR20448.003	Oct 75 191PTS.WF.	
Reson Params		+2	GEL	Theo Rept	RCN-203 172	Dec 73 Werz+ ESTIMATION OF WF CLASS-2 RES	
Reson Params	1.5+0	8.8+2	LAS	Expt Jour	PR/C 8 2352	Dec 73 Keyworth+.J FOR 109RES FROM NF+TRANS	+
				Conf	73Rochestr 1 85	Aug 73 .SUPERSEDED	
	1.5+0	8.8+2		Data	EXFOR10532.	Mar 76 . 121 PTS. I FROM TRNS AND FISS MEAS	
Reson Params	2.5+1	5.5+1	GRN	Revw Conf	74Petten 619	Sep 74 Postma+SPINS,SUBTHR. FISSION	

93 Neptunium 237

Quantity	Energy (ev) Min	Max	Lab	Type	Documentation Ref Vol Page	Author, Comments Date	Data
Reson Params	4.9−1	1.5+0	HAN Expt	Abst	BAP 4 31	Jan 59 Leonard+ 3RES IN FISS,SMALL WF VS TH	+
	3.1−1	1.3+0		Data	EXFOR12476.005	Jun 76 . 3 RES. E0.	
	4.9−1	1.5+0		Data	EXFOR12482.002	Jun 76 . 3 RES, NF/PCS	
Reson Params	4.9−1	3.5+1	ORL Expt	Abst	BAP 3 364	Nov 58 Slaughter+ TOF FAST CHOP 32EOS WG D	+
	4.9−1	3.5+1		Data	EXFOR12485.002	Jun 76 . 33 RES. WN.	
Reson Params	4.8−1	1.0+2	ORL Expt	Abst	BAP 6 70	Feb 61 Slaughter+	+
	4.8−1	1.0+2		Data	EXFOR12478.004	Jun 76 . 75 RES. WN0.	
Reson Params		1.3+2	BRC Revw	Conf	76Lowell 641	Jul 76 Michaudon.STRUCTURE EFFECTS.GRPH.	
Reson Params	3.0+0	5.0+1	YAL ExTh	Conf	76Lowell 389	Jul 76 Firk. DETER.OF SPINS.USING POL.	
Reson Params	Maxwl		KUK Theo	Conf	76Ahmedabd 2 1	Dec 76 Sharma+AVG S−WAVE REDUCED N−WID ANAL	
Strnth Fnctn	6.0−1		MTR Expt	Jour	PR 107 525	Jul 57 Smith.	+
Strnth Fnctn	1.0+2	1.2+4	CCP Expt	Jour	AE 6 569	May 59 Adamchuk+.VAL GVN DERIVD FROM TRSMIS	+
				Jour	SJA 6 420	Dec 60 TRANSLATN.* JNE A13 72 0/60	
				Jour	KE 3 282	Mar 60 .TRANSLATN	
Strnth Fnctn	1.0+0	2.0+3	SAC Expt	Prog	EANDC(E)76U162	Jan 67 Michaudon+ S−WAVE.	
Strnth Fnctn	1.0+3	4.6+4	KFK Eval	Rept	KFK−1186	Jul 70 Hinkelmann. SO=1.0 SI=2.	
Strnth Fnctn	None		AUA Eval	Rept	AAEC/E−277	Mar 73 Musgrove.TBLS EXPTL DATA+BEST VALUES	
Strnth Fnctn	4.9−1	3.5+1	ORL Expt	Abst	BAP 3 364	Nov 58 Slaughter+ TOF FAST CHOP 1.1+−0.2	+
	4.9−1	3.5+1		Data	EXFOR12485.003	Jun 76 . 3 PTS. STF,D.	
Strnth Fnctn	4.9−1	1.0+2	ORL Expt	Abst	BAP 6 70	Feb 61 Slaughter+ ABST. X8.	+
	4.9−1	1.0+2		Data	EXFOR12478.	Jun 76 . 2 PTS. STF,D.	
Lvl Density	−		COP Theo	Jour	NP 6 62	Mar 58 Ericson. LVL DENSITY FORM CFD EXP	
Lvl Density		1.4+1	KUR Theo	Jour	YF 9 303	Feb 69 Vorotnikov.LVL DEN(EXCIT−E),TBL GRPH	
				Jour	SNP 9 179	Aug 69 TRANSLATN.*	
Lvl Density	+0		DUB Theo	Conf	75Kiev 3 23	May 75 Voronov. LVL SPACING OF NP238.TABLE	
Lvl Density	+6		DUB Theo	Rept	JINR−E4−9236	Nov 75 Komov+ AVG LVL−SPAC,SEMIMICRO CFD XP	
				Rept	JINR−P4−8102	Jul 74 Malov+ SEMI−MICROSC CALC OKS XPT,TBL	
	None			Rept	UCRL−TR−10845	Apr 75 . ENGL OF JINR−P4−8102	
(γ,n)	None		SRL Expt	Abst	ANS 14 807	Oct 71 Ahlfeld+.AL CAPTURE GAMS. SIG GIVEN	
(γ,n)	5.0+6	1.7+7	LRL Expt	Prog	UCID−16514 6	Jun 74 Alvarez+	
(γ,n)	9.0+6	1.6+7	SAC Expt	Prog	NEANDC(E)161U	Aug 74 Bergere+ ALSO (G,2N)	
Photo−Fissn	1.2+7	2.0+7	ANL Expt	Jour	PR 95 1009	Aug 54 Huizenga+ 3ES RELATIVE FISS YIELDS	
Photo−Fissn	6.1+6	7.0+6	ANL Expt	Rept	ANL−5853	Jul 58 Clarke+ 2 GAMMA ES. ION CHAMBER.	
Photo−Fissn	6.0+6	2.0+7	CRC Expt	Jour	CJP 37 1418	Dec 59 Baerg+. FRAG ANG DIST ISOTROPIC	
Photo−Fissn	7.0+6		ANL Expt	Jour	NP 34 439	Jun 62 Huizenga+ 6.91+7.12MEV GAMMAS.	
Photo−Fissn	9.0+6	1.6+7	SAC Expt	Jour	NP/A 199 45	Jan 73 Veyssiere+ MONOCHROMAT.NEW ANAL TECH	
Photo−Fissn	1.4+7		CCP Expt	Jour	AE 35 214	Sep 73 Kondrat'Ko+ SYMMETRIC FRAG YLDS,GRPH	
	1.0+7	2.4+7		Jour	AE 35 211	Sep 73 − + FRAG YLDS,6 ES,TBL,GRAPH	
				Jour	AE 34 52	Jan 73 − + FISS PRODUCT YLDS,TBL	
	1.4+7			Jour	SJA 35 866	Mar 74 .ENGLISH OF AE 35 214	
	1.0+7	2.4+7		Jour	SJA 35 862	Mar 74 .ENGLISH OF AE 35 211	
				Jour	SJA 34 69	Jul 73 .ENGLISH OF AE 34 52	
Photo−Fissn	4.0+6	1.3+7	CCP Expt	Jour	AE 36 404	May 74 Ivanov+ INTEG YLD/INTG U238−YLD,GRPH	
				Jour	SJA 36 515	Nov 74 . ENGLISH OF AE 36 404	
Photo−Fissn	9.0+6	1.6+7	SAC Expt	Prog	NEANDC(E)161U	Aug 74 Bergere+	
Photo−Fissn	5.0+6	1.2+7	TIL Expt	Rept	YK−19 42	75 Ivanov+ YLD OF FRAGS,GRAPH,CFD,TBL	
				Rept	INDC(CCP)−65	Dec 74 .P10.ENGL ABSTR OF YK−19	
Photo−Fissn	7.7+6	9.9+6	LAS Expt	Jour	NSE 56 179	Feb 75 Caldwell+ TBL,GRPH NU PROMPT+DELAYED	
Photo−Fissn	3.8+6	5.5+6	IFP Expt	Jour	ZEP 22 225	Aug 75 Zhuchko+ SIG(E),GRPH.DOUBL−HUMP MODL	
				Jour	JEL 22 118	Aug 75 . ENGL OF ZEP 22 225	
Photo−Fissn		1.7+7	IJI Expt	Rept	KIYAI−76−40	76 Aleksandrov+ DELAY NS,GROUPS INT+HL	
Photo−Fissn	4.8+6	1.5+7	TIL Expt	Rept	YK−22 83	76 Ivanov+ SIG NP37/U38 VS EGAM,TBL+FIG	
Photo−Fissn	1.5+7	2.0+7	TIL Expt	Rept	YK−27 42	77 Petrzhak+ 15+20MEV BREMS.XE−YLDS,TBL	

93 Neptunium 238

Quantity	Energy (ev) Min	Max	Lab	Type	Documentation Ref Vol Page	Author, Comments Date	Data
Evaluation	2.5−2	1.0+7	KFK Eval	Rept	KFK−1186	Jul 70 Hinkelmann.RES,STF,N2N,NF,NU,NG,R.I.	
				Conf	70Helsinki 2 721	Jun 70 − + ALL QUANTITIES.	
Evaluation	1.0−5	2.0+7	SRL Eval	Rept	EPRI−NP−161	Dec 75 Benjamin+ENDF4B.GENPAR MDL REVISIONS	
Absorption	Pile		SRL Expt	Conf	68Wash. 1271	Mar 68 Hennelly+ 1620+−100B	
Res Int Abs	Pile		SRL Expt	Conf	68Wash. 1271	Mar 68 Hennelly+ 1500+−500B LOW−FLUX	
Res Int Abs	5.0−1		SGA Comp	Conf	73Paris 1 233	Mar 73 Eder+ REDUCED RES INTEG CAPTURE,TBL	
				Rept	SGAE−PH−141	Feb 73 .SAME AS 73PARIS,NO DETAILS,TBP	
(n,γ)	2.0+4		LAS ExTh	Jour	PR/B 139 1207	Sep 65 Bell.STATISTCL TH CALC CF WEAPON XPT	
(n,γ)	2.0+4	+6	GSF Theo	Jour	AF 36 509	Nov 67 Truran+.STAT MODEL. TWO MASS FORMLS	

93 Neptunium 238

Quantity	Energy (ev) Min	Max	Lab	Type	Documentation Ref Vol Page	Date	Author, Comments	Data
(n,γ)	2.5−2	1.0+7	KFK	Eval Rept	KFK−1186	Jul 70	Hinkelmann.5−GROUP SIG,THR+FAST SPEC	
	2.5−2			Rept	KFK−1186	Jul 70	− . RECOMMENDED 43 B	
(n,γ)	Pile		KFK	Eval Prog	KFK−1544 61	Jan 72	Eberle+FOR 2−GROUP SIG,FITTED TO EXP	
(n,γ)	Maxwl	Fiss	SGA	Comp Conf	73Paris 1 233	Mar 73	Eder+ DATA FROM EXPTS+EVALS,TABLE	
				Rept	SGAE−PH−141	Feb 73	.SAME AS 73PARIS,NO DETAILS	
Res Int Capt	4.7−1	1.0+7	KFK	Eval Rept	KFK−1186	Jul 70	Hinkelmann. INFIN DILUTION RES INTEG	
Res Int Capt	Pile		KFK	Eval Prog	KFK−1544 61	Jan 72	Eberle+600B	
(n,2n)	8.0+5	1.0+7	KFK	Eval Rept	KFK−1186	Jul 70	Hinkelmann.AVG SIG FOR THR+FAST SPEC	
(n,p)	Maxwl		IFU	Theo Rept	ICD−4 20	67	Dadakina+ PENETR COEFF CALC,TABLE	
Fission	Maxwl		CRC	Eval Rept	AECL−1054	Mar 60	Walker+ (CRRP−913).	
Fission	Spont		DUB	Theo Jour	JINR−E−2515	Dec 65	Malov+ SPON FISSN ISOMER, LIFE−TIME	
Fission	Maxwl		TRM	Revw Conf	66Bombay 1	Feb 66	Ramanna.VALS CFD TH,SIG,BINDING,DEF.	
Fission	Maxwl		RI	Revw Jour	AE 23 561	Dec 67	BAK+ OTHER SIG VAL GIVEN,TABLE	
				Jour	SJA 23 1340	Dec 67	. ENGL OF AE 23 561	
Fission	Pile		SRL	Expt Conf	68Wash. § H10	Mar 68	Hennelly+ 1520+−100B HIGH−FLUX	+
Fission	Maxwl		SRL	Expt Abst	ANS 12 284	Jun 69	Spencer.	
	Maxwl			Data	EXFOR12475.002	Jun 76	. 1 PT.	
Fission	2.5−2	1.0+7	KFK	Eval Rept	KFK−1186	Jul 70	Hinkelmann.5−GROUP SIG,THR+FAST SPEC	
	2.5−2			Rept	KFK−1186	Jul 70	− . RECOMMENDED2200 B	
Fission	−		GEL	Revw Jour	AKE 18 229	Nov 71	Theobald+ SUB−BARRIER FISS EXPTS,TH	
Fission	Pile		KFK	Eval Prog	KFK−1544 61	Jan 72	Eberle+FOR 2−GROUP SIG,FITTED TO EXP	
Fission	−		GEL	ExTh Jour	NP/A 187 305	Jun 72	Weigmann+ F.B.PARAMS FROM DATA ANAL.	
Fission	Maxwl	Fiss	SGA	Eval Conf	73Paris 1 233	Mar 73	Eder+ FISS SPEC REL U238(N,F),TBLS	
				Rept	SGAE−PH−141	Feb 73	.SAME AS 73PARIS,NO DETAILS,TBP	
Fission	+5	5.2+6	LAS	Theo Conf	75Wash. 218	Mar 75	Wilhelmy+ CALC USING U238(HE3,DF)	+
Res Int Fiss	5.0−1		SRL	Expt Abst	ANS 12 284	Jun 69	Spencer.	+
	5.0−1			Data	EXFOR12475.003	Jun 76	. 1 PT.	
Res Int Fiss	4.7−1	1.0+7	KFK	Eval Rept	KFK−1186	Jul 70	Hinkelmann. INFIN DILUTION RES INTEG	
Res Int Fiss	Pile		KFK	Eval Prog	KFK−1544 61	Jan 72	Eberle+880B	
Res Int Fiss	5.0−1		SGA	Comp Conf	73Paris 1 233	Mar 73	Eder+ REDUCED RES INTEGRAL,TABLE	
				Rept	SGAE−PH−141	Feb 73	.SAME AS 73PARIS,NO DETAILS,TBP	
Alpha	1.0+4	2.0+4	LAS	Theo Jour	PR 158 1127	Jun 67	Bell. PREDICT 10−20KEV BY SYSTEMATCS	
Nu	2.5−2		KFK	Eval Rept	KFK−1186	Jul 70	Hinkelmann.MEAN VALUE	
	2.5−2	1.0+7		Rept	KFK−1186	Jul 70	− .MEAN NUMBER VS E	
Nu	Spont		HED	Eval Abst	ANS 22 673	Nov 75	Johnson. TBL,GRPH.NU FROM SPON FISS	
Fiss Yield	−3	+7	TRM	Revw Rept	AEET−235	65	Methasiri.TERNRY FISS EXPTS,GRAPH	
Fiss Yield	1.1+7	2.1+7	CCP	Revw Jour	IZV 34 438	Feb 70	Soloveva.ALF−EMISSN PROBABILITY,GRPH	
				Jour	BAS 34 378	Jan 71	.ENGL TRANSL OF IZV 34 438	
Fiss Yield	Maxwl		MCM	Expt Jour	CJP 48 1708	Jul 70	Tracy+,BR80,82 I128,130 INDEPEN YLDS	
Fiss Yield	Pile		RI	Expt Jour	YF 15 860	May 72	Petrzhak+ TBL REL XE YLDS,MAINLY THR	
				Jour	SNP 15 482	Nov 72	. ENGL OF YF 15 860	
Fiss Yield	Maxwl		MCM	Expt Jour	JIN 35 8 2639	Aug 73	Tracy+ CUMUL KR + XE YIELDS	
Reson Params	1.0+3	4.6+4	KFK	Eval Rept	KFK−1186	Jul 70	Hinkelmann. AVG.WG,WF,WN,LVL SPACING	
Strnth Fnctn	1.0+3	4.6+4	KFK	Eval Rept	KFK−1186	Jul 70	Hinkelmann. S0=1.3 S1=2.	
Strnth Fnctn	None		AUA	Eval Rept	AAEC/E−277	Mar 73	Musgrove.TBLS EXPTL DATA+BEST VALUES	
Lvl Density	+6		MIL	Theo Jour	EN 15 1 54	Jan 68	Facchini+ LDL PARS FROM LOW EN RES	
Lvl Density	None		MUN	Theo Jour	NP/A 217 269	Dec 73	Dilg+ A,DELTA. BACK SHIFTED FERMIGAS	
Lvl Density	None		COP	Theo Jour	NP/A 222 493	Apr 74	Dossing+COLL ROTAT.SPAC. ACCUR ESTIM	
Lvl Density	None		ROC	Theo Jour	NP/A 223 589	May 74	Huizenga+ EXP CFD MICROSC TH AX SYMM	

93 Neptunium 239

Quantity	Energy (ev) Min	Max	Lab	Type	Documentation Ref Vol Page	Date	Author, Comments	Data
Evaluation	4.1−1	1.0+7	GA	Eval Rept	GA−2451	Aug 61	Joanou+.68GRP ABS,NF,NU,TRNSF(EL,IN)	
Tot Inelastc	3.0+4	1.0+7	KYU	Eval Jour	NST 10 583	Sep 73	Ohta+.RESULTS IN FIG.	
Absorption	Pile		CRC	Expt Rept	TNCC(CAN)−3	Oct 56	.TBD	
(n,γ)	Pile		BNW	Expt Abst	BAP 1 62	Jan 56	Lefevre+ ACT 7MIN+1HR ISOMERS SIGS	
(n,γ)	Pile		ORL	Expt Jour	NSE 1 108	May 56	Halperin+,EFF S=80+−15B THR+EPITHR	
				Conf	55Geneva 7 258	Aug 55	− +.P732,VAL GVN,EXPT DESCRIBD	
(n,γ)	Pile		KAP	Expt Jour	NSE 5 264	Apr 59	Kinderman+. ACT. ISOMERIC SIGS	
(n,γ)	Pile		ORL	Eval Jour	NSE 6 100	Aug 59	Stoughton+,BEST VALUE .025EV=45+−15B	
(n,γ)	5.0−3	2.5+0	GA	Eval Rept	GA−2113	Jun 61	Wikner+.TABLE 100 E POINTS	
(n,γ)	2.0+4		LAS	ExTh Jour	PR/B 139 1207	Sep 65	Bell.STATISTCL TH CALC CF WEAPON XPT	
(n,γ)	2.0+4		CCP	Theo Jour	AE 23 319	Oct 67	Zagrafov+ CURV(N,G)VS MASS,A=237−275	
				Jour	EAF 23 4 62	Oct 67	. FRENCH OF AE 23 319	
(n,γ)	2.0+4	+6	GSF	Theo Jour	AF 36 509	Nov 67	Truran+.STAT MODEL. TWO MASS FORMLS	
(n,γ)	1.0−2	+7	ORL	Revw Jour	REA 8 473	Sep 70	Kasten. REVIEW,SIG(NEUT−E) GRAPH	

93 Neptunium 239

Quantity	Energy (ev) Min	Max	Lab	Type	Documentation Ref Vol Page	Date	Author, Comments	Data
(n,γ)	Maxwl		SGA	Comp Conf	73Paris 1 233	Mar 73	Eder+ DATA FROM EXPTS+EVALS,TABLE	
				Rept	SGAE-PH-141	Feb 73	.SAME AS 73PARIS,NO DETAILS	
(n,p)	Maxwl		IFU	Theo Rept	ICD-4 20	67	Dadakina+ PENETR COEFF CALC,TABLE	
Fission	+5	+7	ORL	Revw Jour	REA 8 473	Sep 70	Kasten. REVIEW,SIG(NEUT-E) GRAPH	
Fission	-		GEL	ExTh Jour	NP/A 187 305	Jun 72	Weigmann+ F.B.PARAMS FROM DATA ANAL.	
Fission	2.5-2		JUL	Theo Jour	ZP 257 389	Dec 72	Mcminn. 4.33 E-3 BARNS	
Nu	Spont		HED	Eval Abst	ANS 22 673	Nov 75	Johnson. TBL,GRPH.NU FROM SPON FISS	

93 Neptunium 240

Quantity	Energy (ev) Min	Max	Lab	Type	Documentation Ref Vol Page	Date	Author, Comments	Data
(n,γ)	2.0+4		LAS	ExTh Jour	PR/B 139 1207	Sep 65	Bell.STATISTCL TH CALC CF WEAPON XPT	
(n,γ)	2.0+4	+6	GSF	Theo Jour	AF 36 509	Nov 67	Truran+.STAT MODEL. TWO MASS FORMLS	
Fission	Spont		DUB	Theo Rept	JINR-E-2515	Dec 65	Malov+ SPON FISSN ISOMER, LIFE-TIME	
Fission	Maxwl		CCP	Comp Jour	AE 26 436.	May 69	Romanov. UPPER SIG LIMIT ESTIMATED	
				Jour	SJA 26 498	69	. ENGL OF AE 26 436.	
				Jour	EAF 26 48	69	. FRENCH OF AE 26 436.	
Fission	-		GEL	ExTh Jour	NP/A 187 305	Jun 72	Weigmann+ F.B.PARAMS FROM DATA ANAL.	
Alpha	1.0+4	2.0+4	LAS	Theo Jour	PR 158 1127	Jun 67	Bell. PREDICT 10-20KEV BY SYSTEMATCS	

93 Neptunium 241

Quantity	Energy (ev) Min	Max	Lab	Type	Documentation Ref Vol Page	Date	Author, Comments	Data
(n,γ)	2.0+4		LAS	ExTh Jour	PR/B 139 1207	Sep 65	Bell.STATISTCL TH CALC CF WEAPON XPT	
(n,γ)	2.0+4	+6	GSF	Theo Jour	AF 36 509	Nov 67	Truran+.STAT MODEL. TWO MASS FORMLS	
Fission	2.5-2		JUL	Theo Jour	ZP 257 389	Dec 72	Mcminn. 3.28 E-4 BARNS	

93 Neptunium 242

Quantity	Energy (ev) Min	Max	Lab	Type	Documentation Ref Vol Page	Date	Author, Comments	Data
(n,γ)	2.0+4		LAS	ExTh Jour	PR/B 139 1207	Sep 65	Bell.STATISTCL TH CALC CF WEAPON XPT	
(n,γ)	2.0+4	+6	GSF	Theo Jour	AF 36 509	Nov 67	Truran+.STAT MODEL. TWO MASS FORMLS	
Fission	Spont		DUB	Theo Rept	JINR-E-2515	Dec 65	Malov+ SPON FISSN ISOMER, LIFE-TIME	
Alpha	1.0+4	2.0+4	LAS	Theo Jour	PR 158 1127	Jun 67	Bell. PREDICT 10-20KEV BY SYSTEMATCS	

93 Neptunium 243

Quantity	Energy (ev) Min	Max	Lab	Type	Documentation Ref Vol Page	Date	Author, Comments	Data
(n,γ)	2.0+4		LAS	ExTh Jour	PR/B 139 1207	Sep 65	Bell.STATISTCL TH CALC CF WEAPON XPT	
(n,γ)	2.0+4	+6	GSF	Theo Jour	AF 36 509	Nov 67	Truran+.STAT MODEL. TWO MASS FORMLS	
Fission	2.5-2		JUL	Theo Jour	ZP 257 389	Dec 72	Mcminn. 7.66 E-5 BARNS	

93 Neptunium 244

Quantity	Energy (ev) Min	Max	Lab	Type	Documentation Ref Vol Page	Date	Author, Comments	Data
(n,γ)	2.0+4		LAS	ExTh Jour	PR/B 139 1207	Sep 65	Bell.STATISTCL TH CALC CF WEAPON XPT	
(n,γ)	2.0+4	+6	GSF	Theo Jour	AF 36 509	Nov 67	Truran+.STAT MODEL. TWO MASS FORMLS	
Fission	Spont		DUB	Theo Rept	JINR-E-2515	Dec 65	Malov+ SPON FISSN ISOMER, LIFE-TIME	

93 Neptunium 245

Quantity	Energy (ev) Min	Max	Lab	Type	Documentation Ref Vol Page	Date	Author, Comments	Data
(n,γ)	2.0+4	+6	GSF	Theo Jour	AF 36 509	Nov 67	Truran+.STAT MODEL. TWO MASS FORMLS	

93 Neptunium 246

Quantity	Energy (ev) Min	Max	Lab	Type	Documentation Ref Vol Page	Date	Author, Comments	Data
(n,γ)	2.0+4		LAS	ExTh Jour	PR/B 139 1207	Sep 65	Bell.STATISTCL TH CALC CF WEAPON XPT	
(n,γ)	2.0+4	+6	GSF	Theo Jour	AF 36 509	Nov 67	Truran+.STAT MODEL. TWO MASS FORMLS	

93 Neptunium 247

Quantity	Energy (ev) Min	Max	Lab	Type	Documentation Ref Vol Page	Date	Author, Comments	Data
(n,γ)	2.0+4		LAS	ExTh Jour	PR/B 139 1207	Sep 65	Bell.STATISTCL TH CALC CF WEAPON XPT	
(n,γ)	2.0+4	+6	GSF	Theo Jour	AF 36 509	Nov 67	Truran+.STAT MODEL. TWO MASS FORMLS	

93 Neptunium 248

Quantity	Energy (ev) Min	Max	Lab	Type	Documentation Ref Vol Page	Date	Author, Comments	Data
(n,γ)	2.0+4		LAS	ExTh Jour	PR/B 139 1207	Sep 65	Bell.STATISTCL TH CALC CF WEAPON XPT	
(n,γ)	2.0+4	+6	GSF	Theo Jour	AF 36 509	Nov 67	Truran+.STAT MODEL. TWO MASS FORMLS	

93 Neptunium 249

Quantity	Energy (ev) Min	Max	Lab	Type	Documentation Ref Vol Page	Date	Author, Comments	Data
(n,γ)	2.0+4		LAS	ExTh Jour	PR/B 139 1207	Sep 65	Bell.STATISTCL TH CALC CF WEAPON XPT	
(n,γ)	2.0+4	+6	GSF	Theo Jour	AF 36 509	Nov 67	Truran+.STAT MODEL. TWO MASS FORMLS	

93 Neptunium 250

Quantity	Energy (ev) Min	Max	Lab	Type	Documentation Ref Vol Page	Date	Author, Comments	Data
(n,γ)	2.0+4		LAS	ExTh Jour	PR/B 139 1207	Sep 65	Bell.STATISTCL TH CALC CF WEAPON XPT	
(n,γ)	2.0+4	+6	GSF	Theo Jour	AF 36 509	Nov 67	Truran+.STAT MODEL. TWO MASS FORMLS	

93 Neptunium 251

Quantity	Energy (ev) Min	Max	Lab	Type	Documentation Ref Vol Page	Date	Author, Comments	Data
(n,γ)	2.0+4		LAS	ExTh Jour	PR/B 139 1207	Sep 65	Bell.STATISTCL TH CALC CF WEAPON XPT	
(n,γ)	2.0+4	+6	GSF	Theo Jour	AF 36 509	Nov 67	Truran+.STAT MODEL. TWO MASS FORMLS	

93 Neptunium 252

Quantity	Energy (ev) Min	Max	Lab	Type	Documentation Ref Vol Page	Date	Author, Comments	Data
(n,γ)	2.0+4		LAS	ExTh Jour	PR/B 139 1207	Sep 65	Bell.STATISTCL TH CALC CF WEAPON XPT	
(n,γ)	2.0+4	+6	GSF	Theo Jour	AF 36 509	Nov 67	Truran+.STAT MODEL. TWO MASS FORMLS	

93 Neptunium 253

Quantity	Energy (ev) Min	Max	Lab	Type	Documentation Ref Vol Page	Date	Author, Comments	Data
(n,γ)	2.0+4		LAS	ExTh Jour	PR/B 139 1207	Sep 65	Bell.STATISTCL TH CALC CF WEAPON XPT	
(n,γ)	2.0+4	+6	GSF	Theo Jour	AF 36 509	Nov 67	Truran+.STAT MODEL. TWO MASS FORMLS	

93 Neptunium 254

Quantity	Energy (ev) Min	Max	Lab	Type	Documentation Ref Vol Page	Date	Author, Comments	Data
(n,γ)	2.0+4		LAS	ExTh Jour	PR/B 139 1207	Sep 65	Bell.STATISTCL TH CALC CF WEAPON XPT	
(n,γ)	2.0+4	+6	GSF	Theo Jour	AF 36 509	Nov 67	Truran+.STAT MODEL. TWO MASS FORMLS	

93 Neptunium 255

Quantity	Energy (ev) Min	Max	Lab	Type	Documentation Ref Vol Page	Date	Author, Comments	Data
(n,γ)	2.0+4		LAS	ExTh Jour	PR/B 139 1207	Sep 65	Bell.STATISTCL TH CALC CF WEAPON XPT	
(n,γ)	2.0+4	+6	GSF	Theo Jour	AF 36 509	Nov 67	Truran+.STAT MODEL. TWO MASS FORMLS	

93 Neptunium 256

Quantity	Energy (ev) Min	Max	Lab	Type	Documentation Ref Vol Page	Date	Author, Comments	Data
(n,γ)	2.0+4		LAS	ExTh Jour	PR/B 139 1207	Sep 65	Bell.STATISTCL TH CALC CF WEAPON XPT	
(n,γ)	2.0+4	+6	GSF	Theo Jour	AF 36 509	Nov 67	Truran+.STAT MODEL. TWO MASS FORMLS	

93 Neptunium 257

Quantity	Energy (ev) Min Max	Lab	Type	Documentation Ref Vol Page	Date	Author, Comments	Data
(n,γ)	2.0+4	LAS	ExTh Jour	PR/B 139 1207	Sep 65	Bell.STATISTCL TH CALC CF WEAPON XPT	
(n,γ)	2.0+4 +6	GSF	Theo Jour	AF 36 509	Nov 67	Truran+.STAT MODEL. TWO MASS FORMLS	

93 Neptunium 258

Quantity	Energy (ev) Min Max	Lab	Type	Documentation Ref Vol Page	Date	Author, Comments	Data
(n,γ)	2.0+4 +6	GSF	Theo Jour	AF 36 509	Nov 67	Truran+.STAT MODEL. TWO MASS FORMLS	

93 Neptunium 259

Quantity	Energy (ev) Min Max	Lab	Type	Documentation Ref Vol Page	Date	Author, Comments	Data
(n,γ)	2.0+4 +6	GSF	Theo Jour	AF 36 509	Nov 67	Truran+.STAT MODEL. TWO MASS FORMLS	

93 Neptunium 260

Quantity	Energy (ev) Min Max	Lab	Type	Documentation Ref Vol Page	Date	Author, Comments	Data
(n,γ)	2.0+4 +6	GSF	Theo Jour	AF 36 509	Nov 67	Truran+.STAT MODEL. TWO MASS FORMLS	

93 Neptunium 261

Quantity	Energy (ev) Min Max	Lab	Type	Documentation Ref Vol Page	Date	Author, Comments	Data
(n,γ)	2.0+4 +6	GSF	Theo Jour	AF 36 509	Nov 67	Truran+.STAT MODEL. TWO MASS FORMLS	

93 Neptunium 262

Quantity	Energy (ev) Min Max	Lab	Type	Documentation Ref Vol Page	Date	Author, Comments	Data
(n,γ)	2.0+4 +6	GSF	Theo Jour	AF 36 509	Nov 67	Truran+.STAT MODEL. TWO MASS FORMLS	

93 Neptunium 263

Quantity	Energy (ev) Min Max	Lab	Type	Documentation Ref Vol Page	Date	Author, Comments	Data
(n,γ)	2.0+4 +6	GSF	Theo Jour	AF 36 509	Nov 67	Truran+.STAT MODEL. TWO MASS FORMLS	

93 Neptunium 264

Quantity	Energy (ev) Min Max	Lab	Type	Documentation Ref Vol Page	Date	Author, Comments	Data
(n,γ)	2.0+4 +6	GSF	Theo Jour	AF 36 509	Nov 67	Truran+.STAT MODEL. TWO MASS FORMLS	

94 Plutonium

Quantity	Energy (ev) Min	Max	Lab	Type	Documentation Ref Vol Page	Date	Author, Comments	Data
Total	2.5+5	1.5+7	JAE	Theo Conf	JAERI – M – 5984	Feb 75	Tanaka.OPTMDL/COUPLD CH.GRPH CFD EXP	

94 Plutonium 233

Quantity	Energy (ev) Min	Max	Lab	Type	Documentation Ref Vol Page	Date	Author, Comments	Data
Lvl Density	Maxwl		KTO	Expt Jour	NP/A 263 141	May 76	Imanishi+ PRIMARY J AND SP CUT-OFF F.	

94 Plutonium 234

Quantity	Energy (ev) Min	Max	Lab	Type	Documentation Ref Vol Page	Date	Author, Comments	Data
Fission	Spont		DUB	Theo Rept	JINR – P – 2265	Jul 65	Mekhedov. FISS+ALPH HLS ESTIMATED	
Fission	Spont		CCP	Comp Jour	AE 26 436	May 69	Romanov. HALF-LIFE VAL ESTIMATD,GRPH	
				Jour	EAF 26 48	69	. FRENCH OF AE 26 436.	
				Jour	SJA 26 498	69	. ENGL OF AE 26 436.	
Fission	2.5 – 2		JUL	Theo Jour	ZP 257 389	Dec 72	Mcminn. 3.97 E+2 BARNS	
Spect Fiss γ	Fast		NMX	Expt Abst	DA/B 31 3444	Dec 70	Moore.DELAYED SPEC. CFD U235	
Lvl Density	– 3	+0	IFU	Theo Jour	UFZ 13 700	Apr 68	Pisanko+ LEVEL SPACING CALC,TBL	
				Jour	UPJ 13 498	Oct 68	TRANSLATN.*	

94 Plutonium 235

Quantity	Energy (ev) Min	Max	Lab	Type	Documentation Ref Vol Page	Date	Author, Comments	Data
Fission	Maxwl		CCP	Comp Jour	AE 26 436	May 69	Romanov. UPPER SIG LIMIT ESTIMATED	
				Jour	EAF 26 48	69	. FRENCH OF AE 26 436.	
				Jour	SJA 26 498	69	. ENGL OF AE 26 436.	
Fission	–		HEI	Expt Conf	69Vienna 449	Jul 69	Metag+ PPR29. HE-INDUCED ISOM FISS HL	
Fission	–		GEL	ExTh Jour	NP/A 187 305	Jun 72	Weigmann+ F.B.PARAMS FROM DATA ANAL.	
Nu	Maxwl		IAE	Eval Jour	REA 10 637	Dec 72	Manero+ CALC,SYSTEMATICS,TBL	

94 Plutonium 236

Quantity	Energy (ev) Min	Max	Lab	Type	Documentation Ref Vol Page	Date	Author, Comments	Data
Evaluation	2.5 – 2	1.0+7	KFK	Eval Rept	KFK – 1186	Jul 70	Hinkelmann.RES,STF,N2N,NF,NU,NG,R.I.	
				Conf	70Helsinki 2 721	Jun 70	– + ALL QUANTITIES.	
Evaluation	1.0 – 5	2.0+7	SRL	Eval Rept	EPRI – NP – 161	Dec 75	Benjamin+ ENDF4B.GENPAR MDL REVISIONS	
(n,γ)	2.5 – 2	1.0+7	KFK	Eval Rept	KFK – 1186	Jul 70	Hinkelmann.5-GROUP SIG,THR+FAST SPEC	
	2.5 – 2			Rept	KFK – 1186	Jul 70	– . RECOMMENDED 33 B	
Res Int Capt	4.7 – 1	1.0+7	KFK	Eval Rept	KFK – 1186	Jul 70	Hinkelmann. INFIN DILUTION RES INTEG	
(n,2n)	8.0 – 5	1.0+7	KFK	Eval Rept	KFK – 1186	Jul 70	Hinkelmann.AVG SIG FOR THR+FAST SPEC	
(n,p)	Maxwl		IFU	Theo Rept	ICD – 4 20	67	Dadakina+ PENETR COEFF CALC,TABLE	
Fission	Spont		LRL	Expt Rept	UCRL – 1772	Apr 52	Ghiorso+,FISSION RATE AND HALF-LIFE	
Fission	Maxwl		ANL	Expt Jour	PR 115 1271	Sep 59	Gindler+,170+ – 35B REL PU239 793B	
				Jour	PRL 2 188	Feb 59	.SUPERSEDED	
Fission	Maxwl		LRL	Expt Prog	WASH – 1033 28	Aug 61	Hulet+ 162B	
Fission	Spont		BRK	Revw Jour	NP 81 1	Jun 66	Myers.TBL CALC FISS BARRIERS.	
Fission	Spont		COP	Revw Conf	69Vienna 155	Jul 69	Strutinsky+ PPR203. HL GVN,'SHELL-TH'	
Fission	Spont		WAU	Expt Conf	69Vienna 439	Jul 69	Vandenbosch+ PPR110. ISOM FISS HL GVN	
Fission	2.5 – 2	1.0+7	KFK	Eval Rept	KFK – 1186	Jul 70	Hinkelmann.5-GROUP SIG,THR+FAST SPEC	
	2.5 – 2			Rept	KFK – 1186	Jul 70	– . RECOMMENDED 162 B	
Fission	Spont		MRY	Theo Prog	ORO – 4028 – 28	71	Jackson+. SPON FISSION HALF-LIFE GVN	
Fission	–		GEL	ExTh Jour	NP/A 187 305	Jun 72	Weigmann+ F.B.PARAMS FROM DATA ANAL.	
Res Int Fiss	4.7 – 1	1.0+7	KFK	Eval Rept	KFK – 1186	Jul 70	Hinkelmann. INFIN DILUTION RES INTEG	
Nu	Spont		BRK	Expt Jour	PR 101 1016	Feb 56	Hicks+,SPONT FIS,REL PU240,PROBABIL.	
Nu	Spont		LRL	Expt Jour	PR 101 1804	Mar 56	Crane+,LII – CRYST+FIS.COUNT.COINC.	
Nu	Spont		RI	Revw Jour	UFN 73 655	Apr 61	Petrzhak+ TABLE,MANY REFS,DISCUSSION	
				Jour	SPU 4 305	Sep 61	. ENGL OF UFN 73 655	
Nu	2.5 – 2		KFK	Eval Rept	KFK – 1186	Jul 70	Hinkelmann.MEAN VALUE	
	2.5 – 2	1.0+7		Rept	KFK – 1186	Jul 70	– . VS E,CALC FROM SYSTEMAT	
Nu	Spont		IAE	Eval Jour	REA 10 637	Dec 72	Manero+ EXTENSIVE SURVEY,TBL,AVG VAL	
Nu	Spont		DUB	Comp Jour	YF 18 724	Oct 73	Dakovsky+ NUBAR VS FISNUCLEUS,TBL+GRP	
				Eval Rept	JINR – P15 – 7119	Jun 73	Dakowski+ NUBAR+P(NU)-DISTR,TBL,GRPH	
				Comp Jour	SNP 18 371	Apr 74	. ENGLISH OF YF 18, 724.	
Nu	Spont		HED	Eval Abst	ANS 22 673	Nov 75	Johnson. TBL,GRPH.NU FROM SPON FISS	

94 Plutonium 236

Quantity	Energy (ev) Min	Max	Lab	Type	Documentation Ref Vol Page	Date	Author, Comments	Data
Frag Spectra	Spont		DUB Expt	Rept	JINR – P7 – 6466	May 72	Gangrsky+ ANG.DIST.FISS.FRAGM.,TBL	
				Rept	ANL – TRANS – 936	73	. ENGLISH OF JINR – P7 – 6466	
Reson Params	1.0+3	4.6+4	KFK Eval	Rept	KFK – 1186	Jul 70	Hinkelmann. AVG.WG,WF,WN,LVL SPACING	
Strnth Fnctn	1.0+3	4.6+4	KFK Eval	Rept	KFK – 1186	Jul 70	Hinkelmann. SO=1.0 SI=2.	
Strnth Fnctn	None		AUA Eval	Rept	AAEC/E – 277	Mar 73	Musgrove.TBLS EXPTL DATA + BEST VALUES	

94 Plutonium 237

Quantity	Energy (ev) Min	Max	Lab	Type	Documentation Ref Vol Page	Date	Author, Comments	Data
(n,p)	Maxwl		IFU Theo	Rept	ICD – 4 20	67	Dadakina+ PENETR COEFF CALC,TABLE	
Fission	Maxwl		ANL Expt	Jour	PR 115 1271	Sep 59	Gindler+,2500+ – 500B REL PU239 793B	
				Jour	PRL 2 188	Feb 59	.SUPERSEDED	
Fission	Maxwl		LRL Expt	Prog	WASH – 1033 28	Aug 61	Hulet+ 2200B	
Fission	Maxwl		TRM Revw	Conf	66Bombay 1	Feb 66	Ramanna.VALS CFD TH,SIG,BINDING,DEF.	
Fission	Spont		HEI Expt	Conf	69Vienna 449	Jul 69	Metag+PPR29. HE – INDUCED ISOM FISS HL	
Fission	Spont		WAU Expt	Conf	69Vienna 439	Jul 69	Vandenbosch+PPR110. ISOM FISS HL GVN	
Fission	–		GEL ExTh	Jour	NP/A 187 305	Jun 72	Weigmann+ F.B.PARAMS FROM DATA ANAL.	
Fission	Spont		TPI Theo	Jour	YF 16 919	Nov 72	Adeev+ FISS BARRIER CFD EVEN,NUCLEI	
				Jour	SNP 16 507	May 73	.ENGLISH OF YF 16 919	
Nu	Maxwl		IAE Eval	Jour	REA 10 637	Dec 72	Manero+ CALC,SYSTEMATICS,TBL	
Nu	Spont		HED Eval	Abst	ANS 22 673	Nov 75	Johnson. TBL,GRPH.NU FROM SPON FISS	
Fiss Yield	Spont		ORL Expt	Jour	NP/A 172 33	Aug 71	Ferguson+ISOMER.M+E DISTR OKS DIRECT	
				Jour	PR 141 1146	Jan 66	.SEE ALSO	
Frag Spectra	Spont		ORL Expt	Jour	NP/A 172 33	Aug 71	Ferguson+ISOMER.E DIST+CORR OK DIRCT	
				Jour	PR 141 1146	Jan 66	.SEE ALSO	
Frag Spectra	Spont		DUB Expt	Rept	JINR – P7 – 6466	May 72	Gangrsky+ ANG.DIST.FISS.FRAGM.,TBL	
				Rept	ANL – TRANS – 936	73	. ENGLISH OF JINR – P7 – 6466	

94 Plutonium 238

Quantity	Energy (ev) Min	Max	Lab	Type	Documentation Ref Vol Page	Date	Author, Comments	Data
Evaluation	2.5-2	1.4+7	GEN Eval	Rept	GEMP – 411	Feb 66	Prince.TOT ABS SEL DEL NG NF N2N SIN	
Evaluation	1.0-3	1.0+7	AI Eval	Rept	NAA – SR – 12271	May 67	Dunford+ RE – EVALUATION OF DATA	
				Rept	AI – 65 – 190	Nov 65	.SUPERSEDED	
Evaluation	–		CCP Eval	Jour	AE 23 6	Jul 67	Kirpitchnikov.RESON PARAMS,MANY REFS	
				Jour	SJA 23 669	Jul 67	TRANSLATN.*	
Evaluation	2.5-2	1.0+7	KFK Eval	Rept	KFK – 1186	Jul 70	Hinkelmann.RES,STF,N2N,NF,NU,NG,R.I.	+
				Conf	70Helsinki 2 721	Jun 70	– + ALL QUANTITIES.	
	1.0-3	1.5+7		Data	KEDAK – 3	Oct 75	DATA FILES FOR 15 QUANTITIES	
Evaluation	2.3-2	1.0+7	FEI Eval	Conf	73Kiev 1 246	May 73	Abagjan+ GROUP – SIGS + REFERNCES TBLS	
				Rept	INDC(CCP) – 44	Jun 74	.P45. ENGLISH OF 73KIEV 1 246	
Evaluation	None		SOR Eval	Prog	IA – 1308 46	75	Caner+ NEW EVAL STARTED,NDG	
Evaluation	1.0-3	1.5+7	SOR Eval	Jour	NSE 59 46	Jan 76	Caner+RESPARS,NG,NF,NU AVG.CFD ENDF4	
	-3	1.5+7		Rept	IA – 1301	Jul 74	– + ALL SIGS,RESPARS,TABLS+GRAPHS	
Total	2.0+1	1.0+6	LAS Expt	Prog	WASH – 1071 123	Nov 66	Divin+TOF PERSIMMON 1967 TBD	
Total	8.0-3	6.5+3	MTR Expt	Jour	NSE 30 355	Dec 67	Young+ FC+TRNS CURVS 16RES ANALYZED	+
	8.2-3	6.5+3		Data	EXFOR12484.008	Jun 76	. 785 PTS.	
Total	2.0+5	5.5+6	BOL Theo	Conf	70Helsinki 2 863	Jun 70	Benzi+22. SIG(E) GRPH,OPTMOD CFD XPT	
Total	1.0-4	1.5+7	UK Eval	Data	UKNDL – DFN 274A	Mar 73	44 PNTS	+
Total	2.5-2		IKE Eval	Rept	IKE – 6 – 80	Apr 74	Mattes+ ENDF/B,UKNDL,KEDAK CFD	
Total	1.0-3	1.0+0	REH Eval	Rept	IA – 1301	Jul 74	Caner+ OPTMDL,CFD ENDF/B+XPT,CURVES	
	Maxwl			Rept	IA – 1301	Jul 74	– + TBL XPTL SIGS + RECOMM VALUE	
	5.0+2	1.5+7		Rept	IA – 1301	Jul 74	– + OPTMDL,CFD ENDF/B+XPT,CRV+TBL	
Total	-3	1.9+0	THS Theo	Rept	IKE – 6 89 57	Jun 75	Keinert. DATA LIBRARY	
Total	1.0-3	1.5+7	KFK Eval	Data	KEDAK – 3	Oct 75	2176 DATA SETS	+
Elastic	1.0-4	1.5+7	UK Eval	Data	UKNDL – DFN 274A	Mar 73	44 PNTS	+
Elastic	2.5-2		IKE Eval	Rept	IKE – 6 – 80	Apr 74	Mattes+ ENDF/B,UKNDL,KEDAK CFD	
Elastic	5.0+2	1.5+7	REH Eval	Rept	IA – 1301	Jul 74	Caner+ OPTMDL,CFD ENDF/B,CURVS+TABLE	
	Maxwl			Rept	IA – 1301	Jul 74	– + OPTMDL CALC WITH PU241 – PARAMS	
Elastic	1.0-3	1.5+7	KFK Eval	Data	KEDAK – 3	Oct 75	2100 DATA SETS	+
Diff Elastic	1.0+4	1.5+7	AI Eval	Rept	NAA – SR – 11980	Apr 67	Campbell+ LEG COEFS TABLE C – M SYSTEM	
	1.0+4	1.0+7		Conf	66Wash. 335	Mar 66	Davis.TBL LEG COEF,ANG DISTR CURVES	
Diff Elastic	1.9+5	5.5+6	BOL Theo	Conf	70Helsinki 2 863	Jun 70	Benzi+22. SIG(E,ANG) GRAPH, OPTMOD	
Diff Elastic	1.0-4	1.5+7	UK Eval	Data	UKNDL – DFN 274A	Mar 73	26 PNTS,C.M.	+
Diff Elastic	5.0+4	1.5+7	REH Eval	Rept	IA – 1301	Jul 74	Caner+ OPTMDL,3 ENERGIES,CURVS+TABLE	
Diff Elastic	4.6+2	1.5+7	KFK Eval	Data	KEDAK – 3	Oct 75	126 ENERGIES	+

94 Plutonium 238

Quantity	Energy (ev) Min	Max	Lab	Type	Documentation Ref Vol Page	Date	Author, Comments	Data
Tot Inelastc	4.0+4	1.5+7	REH	Eval Rept	IA - 1301	Jul 74	Caner+ OPTMDL,CFD ENDF/B,CURVS+TABLE	
Tot Inelastc	5.0+4	1.5+7	KFK	Eval Data	KEDAK-3	Oct 75	75 DATA SETS + 19 EXCT LVLS	+
Diff Inelast	3.8+5		BOL	Theo Conf	70Helsinki 2 863	Jun 70	Benzi+22. CALCULTED DIRECT SIG(ANG)	
Diff Inelast	1.4+7		LRL	Expt Rept	UCRL - 51232	Jul 72	Kammerdiener. RING GEOM.ANG DISTR	
Diff Inelast	5.0+5	1.5+7	UK	Eval Data	UKNDL - DFN 274A	Mar 73	.TO CONTINUUM.26 PTS.E DIST.ANGDIST.	
Diff Inelast	4.4+4	1.7+6	REH	Eval Rept	IA - 1301	Jul 74	Caner+ OPTMDL,TO 7LEVELS,TABLS,CURVS	
Diff Inelast	3.0+3	1.0+6	BRC	Eval Rept	CEA - R - 4631	Nov 74	Thomet. STAT MDL ANAL TBLS GRPHS	
Nonelastic	1.0-4		UK	Eval Data	UKNDL - DFN 274A	Mar 73	44 PNTS	+
Nonelastic	4.6+2	1.5+7	REH	Eval Rept	IA - 1301	Jul 74	Caner+ INTEGRAL SIGMA, TABLE	
Nonelastic	1.0-3	1.5+7	KFK	Eval Data	KEDAK-3	Oct 75	2223 DATA SETS	+
Absorption	Maxwl		MTR	Expt Jour	NSE 30 355	Dec 67	Young+ EFFECTIVE SIG=532+15-25B	+
	Maxwl			Data	EXFOR12484.003	Jun 76	. 1 PT.	
Absorption	4.6+2	1.5+7	REH	Eval Rept	IA - 1301	Jul 74	Caner+ TABLE	
Absorption	1.0-3	1.5+7	KFK	Eval Data	KEDAK-3	Oct 75	2222 DATA SETS	+
Absorption	+2	+7	FEI	Eval Rept	YK - 23 40	76	Abagjan+ 26 - AND 21 GROUP SIGS,TBLS	
Res Int Abs	5.0-1		SGA	Comp Conf	73Paris 1 233	Mar 73	Eder+ INCLUDING 1/V PART,CAPTURE,TBL	
				Rept	SGAE - PH - 141	Feb 73	.SAME AS 73PARIS,NO DETAILS,TBP	
Res Int Abs	2.9+0	5.0+2	FEI	Eval Conf	73Kiev 1 246	May 73	Abagjan+RI(N,G)=165B FROM RES - PARAMS	
				Rept	INDC(CCP)-44	Jun 74	.P45. ENGLISH OF 73KIEV 1 246	
(n,γ)	Pile		ANL	Expt Prog	ANL - 4215 1	Oct 48	Bruehlman.	+
	Pile			Data	EXFOR12493.003	Jun 76	. 1 PT. SIG	
(n,γ)	Maxwl	Pile	CRC	Expt Jour	CJP 35 147	Feb 57	Butler+403B.ALSO PILE N SIG.REL CO59	+
	Maxwl	Pile		Data	EXFOR12481.	Jun 76	. 2 PTS, SIG	
(n,γ)	None		KAP	Comp Rept	KAPL - 1781	Jul 57	Schuman. SIGMA GIVEN	
(n,γ)	Maxwl		LRL	Expt Jour	PR 107 1294	Sep 57	Hulet+. 520+-40B REL CO.PU239 GROWTH	+
	Maxwl			Data	EXFOR12497.003	Jun 76	. 1 PT.	
(n,γ)	Maxwl		CRC	Eval Rept	AECL - 1054	Mar 60	Walker. (CRRP - 913)	
(n,γ)	+1	+5	LAS	Expt Prog	WASH - 1064 94	Oct 65	Divin+ CYCLAMEN 1966, NDG	
(n,γ)	Maxwl	Pile	BNL	Eval Rept	BNL - 982 22	Aug 66	Pearlstein. 500B, 434B, FROM RES PAR	
(n,γ)	Maxwl		MTR	Expt Jour	NSE 30 355	Dec 67	Young+	+
	Maxwl			Data	EXFOR12484.002	Jun 76	. 1 PT.	
(n,γ)	Maxwl		RI	Revw Jour	AE 23 561	Dec 67	BAK+ OTHER SIG VAL GIVEN,TABLE	
				Jour	SJA 23 1340	Dec 67	. ENGL OF AE 23 561	
(n,γ)	Pile		SRL	Expt Conf	68Wash. 1271	Mar 68	Hennelly+ 382B	
(n,γ)	2.5-2		KFK	Eval Rept	KFK - 1186	Jul 70	Hinkelmann. RECOMMENDED 547 B	
	2.5-2	1.0+7		Rept	KFK - 1186	Jul 70	- .5 - GROUP SIG,THR+FAST SPEC	
(n,γ)	6.2-1	1.0+7	SRL	Theo Conf	71Knoxvill 714	Mar 71	Mccrosson. SPECTRUM - AVERAGED SIG	
(n,γ)	Pile		KFK	Expt Prog	KFK - 1544 61	Jan 72	Eberle+FOR 2 - GROUP SIG,FITTED TO EXP	
(n,γ)	Pile		JUL	Expt Jour	JIN 34 8 2427	Aug 72	Ihle+ REACTOR CROSS SECTION	
(n,γ)	Maxwl	Fiss	SGA	Comp Conf	73Paris 1 233	Mar 73	Eder+ DATA FROM EXPTS+EVALS,TABLE	
				Rept	SGAE - PH - 141	Feb 73	.SAME AS 73PARIS,NO DETAILS	
(n,γ)	1.0-4	3.0+6	UK	Eval Data	UKNDL - DFN 274A	Mar 73	27 PNTS	+
(n,γ)	2.3-2	1.0+7	FEI	Eval Conf	73Kiev 1 246	May 73	Abagjan+ REFERENCES,GROUP - SIGS TABLE	
	2.3-2			Conf	73Kiev 1 246	May 73	- + SIG=545B FROM RES - PARAMS	
	2.3-2	1.0+7		Rept	INDC(CCP)-44	Jun 74	.P45. ENGLISH OF 73KIEV 1 246	
	2.3-2			Rept	INDC(CCP)-44	Jun 74	.P45. ENGLISH OF 73KIEV 1 246	
(n,γ)	1.8+1	2.0+5	LAS	Expt Jour	NSE 52 187	Oct 73	Silbert+ TABULATED DATA IN LA - 5024	+
				Rept	LA - 5024	Aug 72	- . NUCLEAR SHOT. TABLES	
	1.8+1	2.0+5		Data	EXFOR10291.002	Feb 73	. 3505 PTS, SIG	
(n,γ)	2.5-2		IKE	Eval Rept	IKE - 6 - 80	Apr 74	Mattes+ ENDF/B,UKNDL,KEDAK CFD	
(n,γ)	5.0+2	1.5+7	REH	Eval Rept	IA - 1301	Jul 74	Caner+ OPTMDL,CFD ENDF/B+XPT,CRV+TBL	
	Maxwl			Rept	IA - 1301	Jul 74	- + TBL XPTL SIGS+RECOMM VALUE	
(n,γ)	3.0+3	1.0+6	BRC	Eval Conf	JAERI - M - 5984	Feb 75	Thomet.STATMOD.2 HUMP BARRIER.GRPH	
(n,γ)	1.0+3	1.0+6	BRC	Revw Conf	75Wash. 202	Mar 75	Michaudon.CALC CFD MEAS	
	3.0+3	1.0+6		Eval Rept	CEA - R - 4631	Nov 74	Thomet. STAT MDL ANAL TBLS GRPHS	
(n,γ)	1.0-3	1.5+7	KFK	Eval Data	KEDAK-3	Oct 75	2236 DATA SETS	+
(n,γ)	1.0+2	1.4+7	CCP	Eval Data	SOKRATOR - 1044	76	34 PTS	+
Res Int Capt	5.0-1		CRC	Expt Jour	CJP 35 147	Feb 57	Butler+ NRX 3260B REL CO59+U238	+
	5.0-1			Data	EXFOR12481.	Jun 76	. 2 PTS.	
Res Int Capt	5.5-1		BNL	Eval Rept	BNL - 982 22	Aug 66	Pearlstein. 150B CALC, RECOMMENDED	
Res Int Capt	5.0-1		MTR	Expt Jour	NSE 30 355	Dec 67	Young+ RIA=164+-15B	
Res Int Capt	5.0-1		SRL	Expt Conf	68Wash. 1271	Mar 68	Hennelly+ 169B	
Res Int Capt	4.7-1	1.0+7	KFK	Eval Rept	KFK - 1186	Jul 70	Hinkelmann. INFIN DILUTION RES INTEG	
Res Int Capt	Pile		KFK	Expt Prog	KFK - 1544 61	Jan 72	Eberle+164B	
Spect (n,γ)	Maxwl		KFK	Expt Conf	74Petten 655	Sep 74	Matussek+DECAY SCHEME,Q PU - 239	
				Prog	NEANDC(E) - 161U	Aug 74	- +	
				Priv	WIETKAMP	73	Weitkamp. SPECTRA FOR COMPILATION	
Spect (n,γ)	Maxwl		KFK	Expt Conf	74Petten 749	Sep 74	Weitkamp+ NONDESTR FUEL ASSAY APPL	

94 Plutonium 238

Quantity	Energy (ev) Min	Max	Lab	Type	Documentation Ref Vol Page	Date	Author, Comments	Data
(n,2n)	8.0+5	1.0+7	KFK	Eval Rept	KFK-1186	Jul 70	Hinkelmann.AVG SIG FOR THR+FAST SPEC	
(n,2n)	6.0+6	1.5+7	UK	Eval Data	UKNDL-DFN 274A	Mar 73	.14 PTS.E DIST.ANG DIST,LAB.	
(n,2n)	5.0+6	1.5+7	REH	Eval Rept	IA-1301	Jul 74	Caner+ STATMDL,CFD ENDF/B,CURVS+TABL	
(n,2n)	7.0+6	1.5+7	KFK	Eval Data	KEDAK-3	Oct 75	15 DATA SETS	+
(n,xn) x>2	1.3+7	1.5+7	UK	Eval Data	UKNDL-DFN 274A	Mar 73	.2 PTS. E DIST.ANG DIST,LAB. N3N.	
(n,xn) x>2	1.3+7	1.5+7	REH	Eval Rept	IA-1301	Jul 74	Caner+ N,3N.STATMOD CFD ENDF,TBL+CRV	
(n,xn) x>2	1.3+7	1.5+7	KFK	Eval Data	KEDAK-3	Oct 75	6 DATA SETS N3N.	+
n Emission	1.7+6		LAS	Expt Priv	STUBBINS	Sep 65	Stubbins.	+
	1.7+6			Data	EXFOR12491.002	Jun 76	. 1 PT.	
Fission	Maxwl		CRC	Expt Jour	PR 81 893	Mar 51	Hanna+.ABOUT 20B.NO DETAILS GIVEN	+
	Maxwl			Data	EXFOR12496.002	Jun 76	. 1 PT.	
Fission	Maxwl		LRL	Expt Jour	PR 107 1294	Sep 57	Hulet+. 18.4+-0.9B REL SIGF PU239	+
	Maxwl			Data	EXFOR12497.002	Jun 76	. 1 PT.	
Fission	Maxwl		CRC	Expt Conf	58Geneva 16 54	Sep 58	Eastwood+ 17.1+-0.4B REL U235 575B	+
				Rept	KAPL-1781	Jul 57	Butler+ 16.5+-0.5 BARNS	
	Maxwl			Data	EXFOR12011.004	Jun 76	. 1 PT.	
Fission	Spont		DUB	Expt Jour	ZET 40 1296	May 61	Druin. HL OF SPONTANEOUS FISSION	
				Jour	JET 13 913	Nov 61	TRANSLATN.*	
Fission	+0	+2	MTR	Expt Rept	EANDC(US)-28	Sep 62	Young+NDG,TBD,MTR	
Fission	4.0+5	1.4+6	ANL	Expt Conf	CONF-46-37	Apr 63	Butler+VDG,MAX AT 1 MEV	+
	1.4+5	1.7+6		Data	EXFOR12480.002	Jun 76	. 78 PTS.	
Fission	5.0+4	1.4+6	KUR	Expt Rept	IAE-817	65	Dubrovina+,GRAPH SIG VS E	
				Rept	ANL-TRANS-242	65	. ENGL OF IAE-817	
Fission		1.0+2	HAR	Expt Conf	65Salzburg 1 235	Mar 65	James.6 RES.TBL.GF LIMIT.PURITY ERR.	
Fission	2.4-2	4.2+2	KUR	Expt Rept	YFI-2 16	66	Gerasimov.	+
	2.4-2	4.2+2		Data	EXFOR40270.	Mar 75	.3 SUBENT,242 DATA LINES	
Fission	5.0+4	1.4+6	ITE	Expt Jour	YF 3 479	Mar 66	Vorotnikov+.GRAPH SIG(E)	+
				Jour	SNP 3 348	Sep 66	TRANSLATN.*	
Fission	1.0+5	1.5+6	KUR	Expt Jour	YF 3 479	Mar 66	.	+
	5.0+4	1.4+6		Conf	65Salzburg 157	Mar 65	Vorotnikov.GRAPH	
	1.0+5	1.5+6		Data	EXFOR40077.002	Aug 71	SIGMA AT 23 ENERGIES	
Fission	Spont		BRK	Revw Jour	NP 81 1	Jun 66	Myers.TBL CALC FISS BARRIERS.	
Fission	Maxwl		BNL	Eval Rept	BNL-982 22	Aug 66	Pearlstein. 17.5B FROM RESON PARAMS	
Fission	5.0+4	1.4+6	CCP	Expt Jour	SNP 3 348	Sep 66	.ENGLISH TRANSLATION OF YF 3,348	+
				Jour	YF 3 479	Mar 66	Vorotnikov+ GRAPH SIG(E)	
	5.0+4	1.4+6		Data	EXFOR40077.002	Aug 71	SIGMA AT 30 ENERGIES	
Fission	2.4-2	4.2+2	KUR	Expt Conf	66Paris 2 129	Oct 66	PPR112,GERASIMOV.CURVS,SIG.253EV GVN	+
				Jour	YF 4 5 985	Nov 66	Gerasimov. TOF,CURVE GIVEN	
	2.4-2	4.2+2		Data	EXFOR40085.006	Dec 73	.SIGMA FOR 236 ES GIVEN	
Fission	2.0+0	4.0+6	LRL	Expt Jour	PR 154 1111	Feb 67	Stubbins+SIG TO300EV +POOR HI E DATA	+
				Conf	66Paris 2 149	Oct 66	Bowman+	
	2.0+0	3.0+2		Data	EXFOR12489.004	Jun 76	. 253 PTS, SIG	
Fission	1.5+7		KUR	Expt Jour	YF 5 966	May 67	Fomushkin+ SIG GIVEN,FISS ANISOTROPY	
				Jour	SNP 5 689	Nov 67	. ENGL OF YF 5 966	
Fission	None		WAU	Theo Jour	NP/A 101 460	Sep 67	Vandenbosch.	
Fission	1.0+6	1.5+7	LAS	Expt Jour	PR 162 1070	Oct 67	Barton+	+
	1.0+6	1.5+7		Data	EXFOR12490.002	Jun 76	. 4 PTS.	
Fission	Maxwl		RI	Revw Jour	AE 23 561	Dec 67	BAK+ OTHER SIG VAL GIVEN,TABLE	
				Jour	SJA 23 1340	Dec 67	. ENGL OF AE 23 561	
Fission	Pile		SRL	Expt Conf	68Wash. 1271	Mar 68	Hennelly+ 12B	
Fission	+0	+2	CCP	Theo Jour	YF 7 967	May 68	Vorotnikov+(N,GAM F)-PROCESS DISCUSD	
				Jour	SNP 7 582	Nov 68	TRANSLATN.*	
Fission	1.0+5	1.6+6	CCP	Theo Jour	YF 8 704	Oct 68	Ermagambetov+OPTMOD-PARS,GRPHS,REVW	
				Jour	SNP 8 409	Apr 69	TRANSLATN.*	
Fission	2.4-2	1.7+7	FEI	Expt Jour	AE 25 527	Dec 68	Ermagambetov+SIG(E) REL U235,U238	+
				Jour	SJA 25 1364	69	.ENGLISH OF AE 25 527	
				Jour	EAF 25 115	69	.FRENCH OF AE 25 527	
	5.0+5	1.7+7		Data	EXFOR40253.002	Apr 75	.N-FISS CS AT 19 ES GVN	
Fission	-		KUR	Theo Jour	YF 9 538	Mar 69	Vorotnikov. FISS-ANAL CFD 241AM(N,F)	
				Jour	SNP 9 308	Sep 69	TRANSLATN.*	
Fission	4.4+5	3.6+6	KUR	Expt Prog	YFI-7 25	Apr 69	Fomushkim+ TABLE OF REL SIG AT 14 ES	+
				Rept	INDC(CCP)-7U28	Feb 70	TRANSLATN.*	
	4.4+5	3.6+6		Data	EXFOR40012.008	Aug 70	SIGMA AT 14 ENERGIES	
Fission	1.0+3	1.0+6	CCP	Expt Jour	ZEP 9 510	May 69	Ermagambetov+SIG,OPTMOD,WF DISCUSSED	
				Jour	JEL 9 9 309	May 69	TRANSLATN.*	
Fission	-		BER	Theo Conf	69Vienna 197	Jul 69	Krappe+PPR96. 1+2 FISSN BARRIER TBL	
Fission	Spont		COP	Revw Conf	69Vienna 155	Jul 69	Strutinsky+PPR203. HL GVN,'SHELL-TH'	
Fission	-		FEI	Theo Conf	69Vienna 337	Jul 69	Gaj+PPR132. 2HUMPD-BARR-CALC,TBL	

94 Plutonium 238

Quantity	Energy (ev) Min	Max	Lab	Type	Documentation Ref Vol Page	Date	Author, Comments	Data
Fission	Spont		HEI	Expt	Conf 69Vienna 449	Jul 69	Metag+ PPR29. HE – INDUCED ISOM FISS HL	
Fission	Spont		WAU	Expt	Conf 69Vienna 439	Jul 69	Vandenbosch+ PPR110. ISOM FISS HL GVN	
Fission	4.4+5	3.6+6	KUR	Expt	Jour YF 10 917	Nov 69	Fomushkin+ SIG(E)REL U235.TBL+GRAPH	
					Jour SNP 10 529	May 70	. ENGL. OF YF 10917	
Fission	3.2+1	2.6+6	LAS	Expt	Rept LA – 4420	Apr 70	Drake+, NUCL SHOT,TOF,TABLES+CURVES	+
	3.2+1	2.6+6			Data EXFOR10061.002	Jan 75	2613PTS.	
Fission	Pile		ROS	Theo	Rept ZFK – 201	Apr 70	Adam. EFFECTIVE SIG CALC	
Fission	1.0–4	1.8+7	BNW	Eval	Rept BNWL – 1312	May 70	Simons+.	
Fission	+5	+6	FEI	Theo	Jour YF 11 992	May 70	Soldatov+ ANALYSIS,CFD PU – 239(GAM,F)	
					Jour SNP 11 552	Nov 70	. ENGL OF YF 11 992	
Fission	2.5–2		KFK	Eval	Rept KFK – 1186	Jul 70	Hinkelmann. RECOMMENDED 16 B	
	2.5–2	1.0+7			Rept KFK – 1186	Jul 70	– .5 – GROUP SIG,THR+FAST SPEC	
Fission	2.4+3	2.4+6	FEI	Expt	Jour AE 29 422	Dec 70	Ermagambetov+ REL U235,31ES,TBL,GRPH	+
					Jour SJA 29 1190	Dec 70	*ENGL OF AE 29 422	
					Jour ZEP 9 9 510	Sep 69	Ermagambetov+ GRAPHS ARE GVN	
	2.4+3	2.4+6			Data EXFOR40079.002	Oct 71	.SIGMA AT 31 ES GVN	
Fission	Spont		MRY	Theo	Prog ORO – 4028 – 28	71	Jackson+. SPON FISSION HALF – LIFE GVN	
Fission	1.0+2	1.0+6	CCP	Theo	Jour AE 31 18	Jul 71	Vorotnikov.CALC SIG(N – E)+EXPTS,GRPH	
					Jour SJA 31 706	Feb 72	* ENGL OF AE 31 18 7/71	
Fission	1.0+3	1.5+7	LRL	Expt	Prog NCSAC – 42 130	Nov 71	Bowman+. TO BE DONE	
Fission	Pile		KFK	Eval	Prog KFK – 1544 61	Jan 72	Eberle+FOR 2 – GROUP SIG,FITTED TO EXP	
Fission	1.7+1	1.0+6	ALD	Expt	Rept AWRE O – 13/72	Mar 72	Moat.PERSIMMON BOMB SHOT,TOF,TABLES	
					Rept INDC(USA) – 44	72	. EXPT DETAILS.GRAPHS.	
Fission	1.3+7	1.5+7	FEI	Expt	Jour ZEP 15 323	Mar 72	Shpak+	+
					Jour JEL 15 228	Mar 72	. ENGL OF ZEP 15 323	
	1.3+7	1.5+7			Data EXFOR40111.003	Aug 72	SIGMA REL TH232(N,F) AT 10 ES	
Fission	–		GEL	ExTh	Jour NP/A 187 305	Jun 72	Weigmann+ F.B.PARAMS FROM DATA ANAL.	
Fission	Pile		JUL	Expt	Jour JIN 34 8 2427	Aug 72	Ihle+ REACTOR CROSS SECTION	
Fission	Maxwl	Fiss	SGA	Eval	Conf 73Paris 1 233	Mar 73	Eder+ FISS SPEC REL U238(N,F),TBLS	
					Rept SGAE – PH – 141	Feb 73	.SAME AS 73PARIS,NO DETAILS,TBP	
Fission	1.0–4	1.5+7	UK	Eval	Data UKNDL – DFN 274A	Mar 73	44 PNTS	+
Fission	1.8+1	3.0+6	LAS	Expt	Jour NSE 52 176	Oct 73	Silbert+.NUCL SHOT.FULL DATA=LA – 4674	+
					Rept LA – 4674	May 71	– . PERSIMMON EVENT,TABLES	
	1.8+1	3.0+6			Data EXFOR10032.	May 73	. 6759 PTS, SIG	
Fission	2.5–2		IKE	Eval	Rept IKE – 6 – 80	Apr 74	Mattes+ ENDF/B,UKNDL,KEDAK CFD	
Fission	5.0+2	1.5+7	REH	Eval	Rept IA – 1301	Jul 74	Caner+ OPTMDL,CFD ENDF/B+XPT,CRV+TBL	
	Maxwl				Rept IA – 1301	Jul 74	– + TBL XPTL SIGS+RECOMM VALUE	
	1.0–3	1.0+0			Rept IA – 1301	Jul 74	– + OPTMDL,CFD ENDF/B+XPT,CURVES	
Fission	1.0+3	1.0+6	BRC	Revw	Conf 75Wash. 202	Mar 75	Michaudon.CALC CFD MEAS	
	3.0+3	1.0+6		Eval	Conf JAERI – M – 5984	Feb 75	Thomet.STATMOD.2 HUMP BARRIER.GRPH	
					Rept CEA – R – 4631	Nov 74	– . STAT MDL ANAL TBLS GRPHS	
Fission	3.0+6	5.0+6	LAS	Theo	Conf 75Wash. 129	Mar 75	Moore.GRPH R MATR STAT CALC CFD EXP	
Fission	1.0–3	1.5+7	KFK	Eval	Data KEDAK – 3	Oct 75	2195 DATA SETS	+
Fission	1.0+3	1.4+7	CCP	Eval	Data SOKRATOR – 1044	76	46 PTS	+
Fission	+2	+7	FEI	Eval	Rept YK – 23 40	76	Abagjan+ 26 – AND 21 GROUP SIGS,TBLS	+
	2.3–2	1.0+7			Conf 73Kiev 1 246	May 73	– + REFERENCES,GROUP – SIGS TABLE	
					Rept INDC(CCP) – 44	Jun 74	.P45. ENGLISH OF 73KIEV 1 246	
	1.3+7	1.5+7		Expt	Data EXFOR40111.003	Aug 72	SIGMA REL TH232NF AT 10 ES	
Fission	2.0+0	1.7+7	JAE	Revw	Conf IAEA – 186 3 1	76	Igarasi. REVW AVAIL DATA,GRPH+BIBLIO	
	2.0+3	1.5+7			Rept JAERI – M – 6315	Nov 75	– +GRPHS.9 DATA SETS COMPARED.	
Res Int Fiss	6.0–1		CRC	Expt	Conf 58Geneva 16 54	Sep 58	Eastwood+ PPR203,25+ – 5B	
Res Int Fiss	5.5–1		BNL	Eval	Rept BNL – 982 22	Aug 66	Pearlstein. 25B CALC, RECOMMENDED	
Res Int Fiss	7.7+1	3.0+2	LAS	Expt	Prog WASH – 1127 124	Apr 69	Drake+ POMMARD EVENT,PRELIM VALUES	
Res Int Fiss	4.7–1	1.0+7	KFK	Eval	Rept KFK – 1186	Jul 70	Hinkelmann. INFIN DILUTION RES INTEG	
Res Int Fiss	Pile		KFK	Eval	Prog KFK – 1544 61	Jan 72	Eberle+ 24B	
Res Int Fiss	5.0–1		SGA	Comp	Conf 73Paris 1 233	Mar 73	Eder+ REDUCED RES INTEGRAL,TABLE	
					Rept SGAE – PH – 141	Feb 73	.SAME AS 73PARIS,NO DETAILS,TBP	
Res Int Fiss	2.9+0	5.0+2	FEI	Eval	Conf 73Kiev 1 246	May 73	Abagjan+ RI(N,F)=23B FROM RES – PARAMS	
					Rept INDC(CCP) – 44	Jun 74	.P45. ENGLISH OF 73KIEV 1 246	
Res Int Fiss	3.0+1	3.0+6	LAS	Expt	Jour NSE 52 176	Oct 73	Silbert+.NUCL SHOT.10 INTERVALS	
Alpha		+7	FEI	Expt	Rept FEI – 246	Mar 71	Voropaev+ GVN ALPHA,TBL,CALC CFD EXP	
Alpha	4.6+2	1.5+7	REH	Eval	Rept IA – 1301	Jul 74	Caner+ TABLE	
Alpha	1.0–3	1.5+7	KFK	Eval	Data KEDAK – 3	Oct 75	1091 DATA SETS	+
Eta	4.6+2	1.5+7	REH	Eval	Rept IA – 1301	Jul 74	Caner+ TABLE	
Eta	1.0–3	1.5+7	KFK	Eval	Data KEDAK – 3	Oct 75	992 DATA SETS	+
Nu	Spont		BRK	Expt	Jour PR 101 1016	Feb 56	Hicks+,SPONT FIS,REL PU240,PROBABIL.	
Nu	Spont		LRL	Expt	Jour PR 101 1804	Mar 56	Crane+,LII – CRYST+FIS.COUNT.COINC.	

94 Plutonium 238

Quantity	Energy (ev) Min	Max	Lab	Type	Documentation Ref Vol Page	Author, Comments Date	Data
Nu	Spont		RI	Revw	Jour UFN 73 655	Apr 61 Petrzhak+ TABLE,MANY REFS,DISCUSSION	
					Jour SPU 4 305	Sep 61 . ENGL OF UFN 73 655	
Nu	Maxwl		ANL	Expt	Jour NP/A 145 1	Apr 70 Jaffey+ REL TO U,PU STANDARDS.	+
					Rept ANL – 7625	Nov 69 – +COMPLETE DATA GVN.	
	Maxwl				Data EXFOR10125.003	May 72 1PT.PROMPT N YLD=2.895+ – .027	
Nu	Maxwl	1.5+7	HAR	Revw	Conf 70Helsinki 2 195	Jun 70 Colvin.PPR99. REPORT ON DATA STATUS	
Nu	2.5 – 2	1.0+7	KFK	Eval	Rept KFK – 1186	Jul 70 Hinkelmann. VS E,CALC FROM SYSTEMAT	
	2.5 – 2				Rept KFK – 1186	Jul 70 – .MEAN VALUE	
Nu	Maxwl		NIR	Expt	Jour AE 29 95	Aug 70 Kroshkin+ NU BAR + – 3.0 PERCENT GIVN	+
					Jour SJA 29 790	Aug 70 . ENGL OF AE 29 95	
	2.5 – 2				Data EXFOR40064.007	Sep 73 .1 DATA LINE	
Nu	1.0+3	1.5+7	LRL	Expt	Prog NCSAC – 42 130	Nov 71 Bowman+. TO BE DONE	
Nu	Spont		IAE	Eval	Jour REA 10 637	Dec 72 Manero+ EXTENSIVE SURVEY,TBL,AVG VAL	
	Maxwl				Jour REA 10 637	Dec 72 – + EXTENSIVE SURVEY,TBL,AVG VAL	
Nu	None		MND	Theo	Abst BAP 18 1403	73 Wolfe+. NU VS. E FORMULA GIVEN.	
Nu	1.0 – 4	1.5+7	UK	Eval	Data UKNDL – DFN 274A	Mar 73 .19 PTS.ANG DIST OF FISS NEUTS,LAB.	
Nu	Spont		DUB	Comp	Jour YF 18 724	Oct 73 Dakovsky+NUBAR VS FISNUCLEUS,TBL+GRP	
				Eval	Rept JINR – P15 – 7119	Jun 73 Dakowski+ NUBAR+P(NU) – DISTR,TBL,GRPH	
				Comp	Jour SNP 18 371	Apr 74 . ENGLISH OF YF 18, 724.	
Nu	2.5 – 2		IKE	Eval	Rept IKE – 6 – 80	Apr 74 Mattes+ ENDF/B,UKNDL,KEDAK CFD	
Nu	4.6+2	1.5+7	REH	Eval	Rept IA – 1301	Jul 74 Caner+ LINEAR NUBAR(E) FIT. TABLE	
Nu	1.0 – 3	1.5+7	KFK	Eval	Data KEDAK – 3	Oct 75 2 DATA SETS	+
Nu	Spont		HED	Eval	Abst ANS 22 673	Nov 75 Johnson. TBL,GRPH.NU FROM SPON FISS	
Spect Fiss n	Spont		CCP	Theo	Jour AE 5 649	Dec 58 Kovalev+ THEORY COMPARED WITH EXPT	
					Jour JNEA 11 166	Feb 60 TRANSLATN.*	
					Jour SJA 5 1588	58 TRANSLATN.*	
Spect Fiss n	Maxwl	3.3+6	CCP	Expt	Jour ZET 37 1822	Dec 59 TR DET,TEMP CHGE,DT/DE=.01+ – .004	
					Jour JET 10 1286	Jun 60 TRANSLATN.*	
Spect Fiss n	Maxwl		NIR	Expt	Jour AE 29 95	Aug 70 Kroshkin+ AVG FISSN NEUT E +SPEC CRV	+
					Jour SJA 29 790	Aug 70 . ENGL OF AE 29 95	
	2.5 – 2				Data EXFOR40064.013	Sep 73 .1 DATA LINE	
Spect Fiss n	Maxwl		ANL	Revw	Conf 71Vienna 3	Aug 71 Smith. MEAN – E OF NEUTS,EXPTS CFD,TBL	
Spect Fiss n	8.0+5	1.1+6	CCP	Expt	Jour IZV 36 215	Jan 72 Nikolaev+.AVG KE OF FRAGMENTS	
Spect Fiss n	1.0 – 4	1.5+7	UK	Eval	Data UKNDL – DFN 274A	Mar 73 1 RANGES	+
Spect Fiss n	Maxwl		KFK	Eval	Data KEDAK – 3	Oct 75 2 DATA SETS.CRANBERG PARAMS	+
Spect Fiss γ	+0	+2	CCP	Theo	Jour YF 7 967	May 68 Vorotnikov+(N,GAM F) – PROCESS DISCUSD	
					Jour SNP 7 582	Nov 68 TRANSLATN.*	
Spect Fiss γ	Maxwl		KFK	Expt	Prog NEANDC(E) – 161U	Aug 74 Matussek+	
					Priv WIETKAMP	73 Weitkamp. SPECTRA.PROMPT+DELAYED	
Spect Fiss γ	Maxwl		LIN	Expt	Jour YF 22 462	Sep 75 Teterev+ G – SPEC CFD U,PU,CF – FIS.GRPH	
					Jour SNP 22 238	Sep 75 . ENGL OF YF 22 462	
Fiss Prod γ	–		WIN	Theo	Jour JNE 25 513	Oct 71 James.MEAN EN OF DELAYD GAMS,BETAS.	
Fiss Prod γ	Maxwl		KFK	Expt	Priv WIETKAMP	73 Weitkamp. DELAYED SPECTS OF F PRODS	
Fiss Yield	8.0+5	1.7+7	FEI	Expt	Rept FEI – 204	70 D'Jachenko+ REL U235(N,F)THERM,CURVS	
Fiss Yield		1.5+7	FEI	Expt	Conf 71Kiev	May 71 Sergachev+.FRAG YLD,KE OF FRAG,GRPHS	
Fiss Yield	2.0+6	1.4+7	LAS	Eval	Abst ANS 24 462	Nov 76 Madland+PAIR EFFECT ON FISS PROD YLD	
	2.5 – 2	1.4+7			Rept LA – 6430	Jul 76 – +PAIR EFFECT ON INDEP YLD.TBL	
Frag Spectra	Spont		CCP	Expt	Conf 55Moscow 226	Jul 55 Goldin+.ALFA SPECTRUM.EXPT FROM 1953	
					Rept AEC – TR – 2435	56 . P 167.ENGL TRANSL OF 55MOSCOW 226	
Frag Spectra	Spont		ITE	Expt	Rept ITE –	Oct 63 Perfilov+TERNARY FISS.ALPHA SPEC,GRP	
Frag Spectra	5.0+4	1.4+6	KUR	Expt	Rept IAE – 817	65 Dubrovina+,ANG DIST FRAGMENTS,GRAPH	
					Rept ANL – TRANS – 242	65 . ENGL OF IAE – 817	
Frag Spectra	Spont		TRM	Revw	Rept AEET – 235	65 Methasiri.ALF E – SPEC,CFD PU,U	
Frag Spectra	1.0+5	1.5+6	ITE	Expt	Jour YF 3 479	Mar 66 Vorotnikov+.GRAPH ANISOTROPY VS E	+
					Jour SNP 3 348	Sep 66 TRANSLATN.*	
Frag Spectra	1.0+5	1.5+6	KUR	Expt	Jour YF 3 479	Mar 66 .	+
	1.0+5	1.2+6			Conf 65Salzburg 157	Mar 65 Vorotnikov.A – DSTRB,GRAPHS	
	1.0+5	1.5+6			Data EXFOR40077.	Aug 71 ANG DSTRB OF FRGMNTS, 3ANGLS, 23EN	
Frag Spectra	1.5+7		KUR	Expt	Jour YF 5 966	May 67 Fomushkin+ ANGDIST OF FRAGMENTS	
					Jour SNP 5 689	Nov 67 . ENGL OF YF 5 966	
Frag Spectra	6.0+4	7.2+6	FEI	Expt	Prog YFI – 7 11	Apr 69 Shpak+ ANGDIST(E) GRAPH, TBP IN YF	
					Rept INDC(CCP) – 7U9	Feb 70 TRANSLATN.*	
	5.0+5	5.0+6			Jour ZEP 8 545	Nov 68 Shpak+ ANG ANISOTR COEF,GRAPH	
					Jour JEL 8 332	Nov 68 . ENGL OF ZEP 8 545	
Frag Spectra	4.4+5	3.6+6	KUR	Expt	Prog YFI – 7 25	Apr 69 Fomushkim+ LEGCOEF OF FRAG – ANGDISTR	+
					Rept INDC(CCP) – 7U28	Feb 70 TRANSLATN.*	
	4.4+5	3.6+6			Data EXFOR40012.	Aug 70 LEG – COEFFS, ANG DSTRB OF FRAGMNTS	

94 Plutonium 238

Quantity	Energy (ev) Min	Max	Lab	Type	Documentation Ref Vol Page	Date	Author, Comments	Data
Frag Spectra	6.0+4	7.2+6	FEI	Expt	Jour YF 9 940	May 69	Shpak+ FRAG-ANGDISTR-GRPHS,2HUMP-BAR	+
					Jour SNP 9 5 551	Sep 69	TRANSLATN.*	
	6.0+4	7.2+6			Data EXFOR40233.002	Sep 74	.DATA AT 62 ES GIVEN	
Frag Spectra	4.4+5	3.6+6	KUR	Expt	Jour YF 10 917	Nov 69	Fomushkin+ ANGDIST(E) LEG-COEF,GRAPH	
					Jour SNP 10 529	May 70	. ENGL OF YF 10 917	
Frag Spectra	8.0+5	1.7+7	FEI	Expt	Rept FEI-204	70	D'Jachenko+ REL U235(THERM,E-SPEC	
Frag Spectra	+5	+6	FEI	Theo	Jour YF 11 992	May 70	Soldatov+ ANGDIST CFD PU-239(GAM,F)	
					Jour SNP 11 552	Nov 70	. ENGL OF YF 11 992	
Frag Spectra	Thrsh	+6	FEI	Expt	Jour AHP 29 357	Aug 70	Androsenko+ ANGDIST CFD 2-HUMPD-BARR	
		7.0+6		ExTh	Conf 69Vienna 419	Jul 69	- +PPR134. XPTL ANGDIST + TH	
Frag Spectra	Spont		CCP	Expt	Jour IZV 35 180	Jan 71	Nikolaev.AVG FRAG KIN-E,GRAPHS	+
					Jour BAS 35 163	Jan 71	*ENGL OF IZV 35 180	
	Spont				Data EXFOR40160.002	May 73	.AVERAGE KIN-E OF SPONTAN FRAGMENTS	
Frag Spectra	Spont		RI	Expt	Prog YFI-12 96	72	Nikolaev.ABST,AVG KIN-E,NDG	
	Pile	1.1+6			Prog YFI-12 96	72	- .ABST,AVG KIN-E,NDG	
	Spont				Prog INDC(CCP)-30	Sep 72	.PAGE 84,ENGLISH OF YFI-12 96	
	Pile	1.1+6			Prog INDC(CCP)-30	Sep 72	.PAGE 84,ENGLISH OF YFI-12 96	
Frag Spectra	8.0+5	1.1+6	CCP	Expt	Jour IZV 36 215	Jan 72	Nikolaev+.AVG DISTR OF FISS FRAGS	+
					Conf 71Moscow	Feb 71	- +.ABST,AVG FRAG KE AT 18ANG	
	Spont				Data EXFOR40159.002	May 73	AVERAGE E-KIN OF SPONTAN FRAGMENTS	
	7.6+5	1.1+6			Data EXFOR40159.	May 73	ANG DSTRB + AV E-KIN OF FRAGMENTS	
Frag Spectra	1.3+7	1.5+7	FEI	Expt	Prog YFI-13 4	Oct 72	Shpak+ ANG ANISOTR OF FRAGMTS,TBL	+
					Jour ZEP 15 323	Mar 72	- + ANGULAR ANISOTR AT 11ES,GRAPH	
					Prog INDC(CCP)-32	Apr 73	.PAGE 4.ENGLISH OF YFI-13 4	
					Jour JEL 15 228	Mar 72	. ENGL OF ZEP 15 323	
	1.3+7	1.5+7			Data EXFOR40111.	Aug 72	ANG DSTRB OF FRGMNTS AT 11ES,COS-FIT	
Frag Spectra	7.0+5	3.5+6	FEI	Expt	Conf 73Kiev 3 270	May 73	Vorob'Yeva+	+
	8.0+5				Data EXFOR40284.002	May 75	.AVER KIN-E OF FF GVN	
Reson Params	-.5-1	1.9+1	HAR	Expt	Conf 65Salzburg 235	Mar 65	James.LIMITS OF WF AT 4 RES	
Reson Params	5.0+4	1.5+6	CCP	ExTh	Jour YF 3 479	Mar 66	Vorontnikov+.GRAPH FISS-WIDTH VS E	
					Jour SNP 3 348	Sep 66	TRANSLATN.*	
Reson Params	2.9+0	8.3+1	KUR	Expt	Conf 66Paris 2 129	Oct 66	PPR112,GERASIMOV.PARAMS FOR 5 RES	+
					Jour YF 4 5 985	Nov 66	Gerasimov. TOF,TABLE 5 RESONANCES	
	2.9+0	8.3+1			Data EXFOR40085.002	Dec 73	.DATA IN B*EV FOR 5 RES-EN GIVEN	
Reson Params	2.9+0	2.8+2	LRL	Expt	Jour PR 154 1111	Feb 67	Stubbins+ LINAC. WNWF/W FOR 16 RESON	+
					Jour PRL 18 15	Jan 67	.SUPERSEDED	
	2.9+0	2.8+2			Data EXFOR12489.002	Jun 76	. 16 RES,WT,WN0,WF	
Reson Params	4.5+6	7.0+6	CCP	ExTh	Jour YF 5 728	May 67	Vorotnikov.GRAPH N+GAMMA FISSWIDTH	
					Jour SNP 5 728	Nov 67	TRANSLATN.*	
Reson Params	-		CCP	Eval	Jour AE 23 6	Jul 67	Kirpitchnikov.FISS-,N-WIDTH,STRNTH-F	
					Jour SJA 23 669	Jul 67	TRANSLATN.*	
Reson Params	-.1+2	1.9+2	MTR	Expt	Jour NSE 30 355	Dec 67	Young+ FC+TRNS B-W ANAL 16RES WG WN	+
	-.1+1	2.2+2			Prog IN-1083 34	May 67	- . TABLE WN WG FOR 21 RESON	
	-.1+2	1.9+2			Data EXFOR12484.	Jun 76	. 16 RES,WN0,WG, 3 RES,E0,WT,WN	
Reson Params	+0	+2	CCP	Theo	Jour YF 7 967	May 68	Vorotnikov+ GRPH,DISTRIBUTION OF WF	
					Jour SNP 7 582	Nov 68	TRANSLATN.*	
Reson Params	+5	+6	CCP	Theo	Jour YF 7 1228	Jun 68	Vorotnikov.LARGE WN,D,QUASISTABLE-TH	
					Jour SNP 7 732	Dec 68	TRANSLATN.*	
Reson Params	-		CCP	ExTh	Jour ZEP 9 510	May 69	Ermagambetov+ DISCREPANCY AVG+RES WF	
					Jour JEL 9 9 309	May 69	TRANSLATN.*	
Reson Params	+2	+6	FEI	Theo	Jour YF 10 542	Sep 69	Gai+ TABLE OF RESON+FAST FISSN WIDTH	
					Jour SNP 10 311	Mar 70	. ENGL OF YF 10 542	
Reson Params	1.0+3	4.6+4	KFK	Eval	Rept KFK-1186	Jul 70	Hinkelmann. AVG.WG,WF,WN,LVL SPACING	+
	-.4+0	5.0+2			Data KEDAK-3	Oct 75	52 DATA SETS	
Reson Params	+0		CCP	Theo	Jour AE 31 18	Jul 71	Vorotnikov.S+P-NEUT FISS-WIDS DERIVD	
					Jour SJA 31 706	Feb 72	* ENGL OF AE 31 18 7/71	
Reson Params	2.9+0	5.0+2	FEI	Eval	Conf 73Kiev 1 246	May 73	Abagjan+ REFERENCES GIVEN, NDG	
					Rept INDC(CCP)-44	Jun 74	.P45. ENGLISH OF 73KIEV 1 246	
Reson Params	1.9+1	5.0+2	LAS	Expt	Jour NSE 52 187	Oct 73	Silbert+.NUCL SHOT.WN WF AREA 49RES	+
	1.9+1	4.7+2			Data EXFOR10032.	Nov 75	49PTS WN*WF/WT.	
	1.9+1	5.0+2			Data EXFOR10291.003	Feb 73	. 49 RES, E0,WN,WF	
Reson Params	-.1+2	5.0+2	REH	Eval	Rept IA-1301	Jul 74	Caner+ TBL G+F+N-WIDS,AVG PARS,LVLS	
Reson Params	1.0+2	1.4+7	CCP	Eval	Data SOKRATOR-1044		76 53 RES PARAMS	+
Reson Params	Maxwl		KUK	Theo	Conf 76Ahmedabd 2 1	Dec 76	Sharma+AVG S-WAVE REDUCED N-WID ANAL	
Strnth Fnctn	8.0-3	5.0+3	MTR	Expt	Jour NSE 30 355	Dec 67	Young+ S-WAVE STF=1.10+-0.20	+
		6.0+2			Data EXFOR12484.004	Jun 76	. 1 PT.	
Strnth Fnctn	1.0+3	4.6+4	KFK	Eval	Rept KFK-1186	Jul 70	Hinkelmann. SO=1.1 SI=2.	
Strnth Fnctn	6.2-1	5.0+4	SRL	Theo	Conf 71Knoxvill 714	Mar 71	Mccrosson. STAT CALCULATN AVG PARAMS	

94 Plutonium 238

Quantity	Energy (ev) Min	Max	Lab	Type	Documentation Ref Vol Page	Date	Author, Comments	Data
Strnth Fnctn	None		AUA	Eval	Rept AAEC/E – 277	Mar 73	Musgrove.TBLS EXPTL DATA+BEST VALUES	
Strnth Fnctn	1.9+1	5.0+2	LAS	Expt	Jour NSE 52 187	Oct 73	Silbert+.NUCL SHOT. SO GIVEN	+
	1.9+1	5.0+2		Data	EXFOR10291.004	Feb 73	SILBERT+ 1PT = 1.27+ –0.25	
Strnth Fnctn	+0	+3	REH	Eval	Rept IA – 1301	Jul 74	Caner+ S+P–WAVE	
Lvl Density	–3	+0	IFU	Theo	Jour UFZ 13 700	Apr 68	Pisanko+ LEVEL SPACING CALC,TBL	
					Jour UPJ 13 498	Oct 68	TRANSLATN.*	
Lvl Density		1.3+2	KUR	Theo	Jour YF 9 303	Feb 69	Vorotnikov.LVL DEN(EXCIT – E),TBL GRPH	
					Jour SNP 9 179	Aug 69	TRANSLATN.*	
Lvl Density	+6		DUB	Theo	Rept JINR – E4 – 9236	Nov 75	Komov+ AVG LVL – SPAC,SEMIMICRO CFD XP	
Photo – Fissn		8.0+6	IFP	ExTh	Jour ZEP 9 128	Jan 69	Kapitza+SIG ANGDIST CV,2 – HUMP – BARIER	
					Jour JEL 9 2 73	Jan 69	TRANSLATN.*	
Photo – Fissn	5.0+7	9.0+7	FEI	ExTh	Prog YFI–7 21	Apr 69	Rabotnov+ SIG+YLD+ANGDIST VS E GRPHS	
	+6	+7		Expt	Jour SNP 11 285	Sep 70	.TRANSLATN.*0,NO 3	
					Jour YF 11 508	Mar 70	Rabotnov+ ANGDIST+YLD+SIG,GRPHS+TBLS	
	5.0+7	9.0+7		ExTh	Rept INDC(CCP) – 7U24	Feb 70	TRANSLATN.*	
Photo – Fissn	5.0+6	8.0+6	FEI	ExTh	Conf 69Vienna 419	Jul 69	Androsenko+PPR134. XPTL ANGDIST + TH	
Photo – Fissn	Thrsh	+7	IFP	Expt	Conf 69Vienna 925	Jul 69	Kapica+PPR135.SIG+ANGDIST,STRUTINSKY	
Photo – Fissn	7.5+6	1.2+7	UCN	Expt	Jour NSE 45 47	Jul 71	Shapiro+.BETATRON.2 ANALYSIS METHODS	
					Abst DA/B 29 2579	Jan 69	.THESIS ABST	

94 Plutonium 239

Quantity	Energy (ev) Min	Max	Lab	Type	Documentation Ref Vol Page	Date	Author, Comments	Data
Evaluation	2.5–2	4.3–1	LAS	Eval	Rept LA – 2127	Jul 57	Devaney+.NG NF SCT TOT TABLES+GRAPHS	
Evaluation	6.0–2	1.0+7	LAS	Eval	Jour NSE 4 166	Aug 58	Kiehn.TOT,FISS,NG,NU,TRANSF.10GROUPS	
Evaluation	5.0+5	1.5+7	LRL	Eval	Rept UCRL – 5351	Nov 58	Howerton. CURVES.	
Evaluation	5.0+2		ANL	Eval	Book FRC	60	Yftah+.16E GROUPS.FAST REACT DATA	
Evaluation	4.1–1	1.0+7	GA	Eval	Rept GA – 2451	Aug 61	Joanou+.68GRP ABS.EL,IN TRANSF.NF.NU	
Evaluation	2.5–2	1.0+7	GEN	Eval	Rept APEX – 704	Nov 61	Cooper+. CONTENT OF C – FINE TAPES	
Evaluation	1.0–3	1.0+7	AI	Eval	Rept NAA – SR – M – 8904	Aug 63	Alter+.SAME AS MO +NF NU N2N.RES GAP	
Evaluation	2.5–2	1.1+7	FEI	Eval	Book ABAGJAN	64	.ENGLISH TRANSL SUPERSEDES ORIGINAL.	
Evaluation	3.7–2	1.8+7	UNC	Eval	Rept UNC – 5099	Dec 64	Troubetzkoy+	
Evaluation	2.5–2		BNL	Eval	Rept BNL – 918	Mar 65	Sher+. SIGS,FISSN DATA LEAST SQ ANAL	
					Rept BNL – 722	62	.SUPERSEDED	
Evaluation	1.0–3	1.5+7	GA	Eval	Rept GA – 6576	Jul 65	Drake. EVAL FROM VAR SOURCES	
Evaluation	4.7+0	1.0+4	INA	Eval	Conf 66Paris 2 333	Oct 66	Hennies.PPR5.RES INT CAPT+FISS,ALPHA	
					Rept NAA – SR – 11980 5	May 67	– . RECOMMENDED DATA.REVISED.	
Evaluation	1.0–3	1.5+7	GEB	Eval	Rept GEAP – 5272	Dec 66	Greebler+	
Evaluation	1.0–4	1.5+7	UK	Eval	Rept AHSB(S)R – 125	May 67	Hart.(RLY).UK – DFN 184 REVD TO DFN329	
	1.0+3	1.4+7			Rept AHSB(S)R – 124	May 67	– .(RLY).UK – DFN 339.UPDATES NSE 2	
	1.0+3	1.5+7			Rept AWRE – O – 79/64	Jan 65	Douglas.(ALD).UKNDL – DFN 184	
	2.0–3	1.4+7			Rept AEEW – R – 351	Feb 64	Barrington+(WIN).UKNDL LOW EN REVISN	
	2.5–2	1.5+7			Rept AWRE – O – 28/60	Mar 61	Buckingham.(ALD).EVAL FOR UKNDL	
Evaluation	–		CCP	Eval	Jour AE 23 6	Jul 67	Kirpitchnikov.RESON PARAMS,MANY REFS	
					Jour SJA 23 669	Jul 67	TRANSLATN.*	
Evaluation	1.0+4	1.0+7	HEB	Eval	Conf 67Karlsrhe 1 255	Nov 67	Rakavy+,FISSION,CAPTURE ETC,LEAST–SQ	
Evaluation	1.0–3	1.0+7	KFK	Eval	Rept KFK – 750	Jan 68	Schmidt.CURVES,TBLS ALL QUANTITIES	
	–.1+1	3.0+2			Rept KFK – 120 1	Feb 66	– .64RES.WG,WF,WN,STAT.	
	1.0–2	1.0+7			Rept KFK – 120 1	Feb 66	– .CURVS+TBLS SIG TOT,ELAS,N2N,	
	–.1+1	3.0+2			Conf 66S.Diego 2 223	Feb 66	– . SEE KFK – 120	
	1.0–2	1.0+7			Rept KFK – 120 2	Dec 62	– .CURVS+TBLS SIG TOT,ELAS,N2N,	
Evaluation	Fast		KFK	Eval	Rept KFK – 770	Apr 68	Huschke+ 26 EGROUPS FAST REACT SPEC	
Evaluation	1.0+3	1.4+7	LAS	Eval	Rept LA – 3528	Jul 68	Hunter+ TOT NF SEL NG SIN N2N N3N NU	
Evaluation	1.0+3	1.0+7	CAD	Eval	Rept EANDC(E)120L	Mar 69	Barre+RAVIER EVAL OF INTEGRAL MEAS	
Evaluation		2.0+7	TRM	Eval	Conf 69Roorke 2 106	Dec 69	Garg+INDIAN EVALUATN ACTIVITIES, NDG	
Evaluation	3.0+2	3.0+4	GEB	Eval	Rept GEAP – 13591	Apr 70	Hitchcock+,ENDF/B WF,ALFA,STF,TOT,NF	
Evaluation	1.0–3	1.0+7	KFK	Eval	Rept KFK – 1340	Feb 71	Hinkelmann+TBLS OF ALL QUANTITIES.	
		1.0+7			Prog EANDC(E)140U	Aug 71	– +, FISSION,NU,ALPHA	
Evaluation	1.0+4	2.0+7	BNL	Eval	Rept BNL – 50388	Apr 73	Prince+. REVISIONS TO ENDF/B FILE	
	None				Conf 71Knoxvill 418	Mar 71	– +. TOT,NF,DEL,SCT,SEL,DIN,CRVS	
	1.0+4	1.5+7			Conf 70Helsinki 2 825	Jun 70	– .91. ALL QUANTITIES TO ENDF/B	
Evaluation	7.8+3	2.0+7	LAS	Eval	Rept LA – 5172	Jun 73	Hunter+. CURVES+TABLES. RECOMMD SIGS	
Evaluation	1.0–3	1.5+7	IJE	Eval	Jour YK – 16 329	74	Konshin+ ABS,FISS,ALF,ETA,NUBAR,TABL	+
	1.0–5	1.5+7			Data SOKRATOR – 2021	76	TOT,EL,INEL,N2N,N3N,NF,NG,NU,RESPAR	
Evaluation	1.0+2	2.0+7	HAR	Eval	Jour ANE 1 409	Jul 74	Sowerby+ LINKED EVAL WITH U235,238	
					Rept AERE – R – 7273	Feb 73	– + SAME AS ANE 1 409	
					Conf 70Helsinki 2 703	Jun 70	– +34. SIMULTAN F+GAM EVALUATN	

94 Plutonium 239

Quantity	Energy (ev) Min	Energy (ev) Max	Lab	Type	Documentation Ref Vol Page	Date	Author, Comments	Data
Evaluation	7.8+0	6.6+2	SAC	Eval	Conf NEANDC(E)163U	Jan 75	Derrien. SEE CEA-N-1484	
	Maxwl	1.5+7			Rept CEA-N-1484	Nov 71	Ribon+SAME AS EANDC(E)138AL	
Evaluation	Maxwl		IAE	Eval	Conf 75Wash. 286	Mar 75	Lemmel. 3RD IAEA-EVAL, BY LSQ FIT	
Total	Pile		LAS	Expt	Rept LA- 266	Apr 45	Anderson+	+
	Pile				Data EXFOR12519.	Jun 76	. 1 PT. SIGMA.	
Total	2.9-3	7.4-1	COL	Expt	Rept CUD- 92	May 51	Havens.	+
	2.9-3	7.4-1			Data EXFOR12517.	Jun 76	. 59 PTS. SIGMA.	
Total	1.4+7		LAS	Expt	Rept LA- 1446	Jul 52	Coon+	+
	1.4+7				Data EXFOR12524.002	Jun 76	. 1 PT. SIGMA.	
Total	7.0+0	5.8+3	ANL	Expt	Prog ANL- 4983 4	Nov 52	Bollinger+	+
	7.0+0	5.8+3			Data EXFOR12346.003	Jun 76	. 138 PTS. SIGMA.	
	4.1+4	2.1+7	LAS	Expt	Rept LA- 1493	Nov 52	Henkel.TRANS GAP75KEV-17MEV CURVE	+
	4.1+4	2.1+7			Data EXFOR12396.005	Jun 76	. 59 PTS. SIGMA.	
Total	1.2+3	1.6+5	ANL	Expt	Prog ANL- 5175 7	Feb 54	Hibdon+	+
	1.2+3	1.6+5			Data EXFOR11002.006	Jun 76	. 35 PTS. SIGMA.	
Total	1.5+5	2.2+6	HAR	Expt	Rept AERE-NP/R-1643	May 55	Meads. NEUTRONS FROM LI7(PN)+T(PN)	
Total	3.0-2	1.5+0	CCP	Expt	Conf 55Moscow 294	Jul 55	Abov. BENT QUARTZ CRYSTAL. CURVE	
					Rept AEC-TR-2435	56	.PAGE 209. ENGL TRANSL OF 55MOSCOW	
Total	1.2-2	5.5-1	KUR	Expt	Conf 55Moscow 15	Jul 55	Gerasimov+ EARLY RUSSIAN EXPT,CURVE	
					Rept AEC-TR-2435 1	56	. ENGL TRANSL OF 55MOSCOW 15	
Total	1.0-2	1.0+2	CCP	Expt	Conf 55Geneva 4 224	Aug 55	Nikitin+.GRAPH,CYCLOTRON,TRANSM,P646	+
Total	5.0-3	+5	HAN	Revw	Conf 55Geneva 4 193	Aug 55	Leonard+.CURVE,SUM OF SEV EXPTS,P589	
Total		1.0+2	SAC	Expt	Conf 55Geneva 4 235	Aug 55	Auclair+.GRAPH,VAL2200M+25KEV,P354	
Total	1.0-2	5.5-1	CCP		Rept AEC-TR-2435PT1	56	.USSR CURVE PAGE 10	
Total	5.0+0	5.0+1	HAR		Jour BJAS 5 1	56	Cockcroft+SCIENTI.PROBL.IN NUCLEAR E	
Total	1.6-3	5.0+0	HAR	Expt	Jour JNE 2 187	Mar 56	Pattenden.ERRATUM IN JNE 2 300 (6/56	+
					Jour JNE 2 300	Jun 56	- . SIG=1015+ -30B AT 0.025EV	
Total	2.0-2	5.0-1	HAN	Expt	Rept HW- 44525 47	Jul 56	Leonard+	+
	2.5-2	5.0-1			Data EXFOR12518.002	Jun 76	. 22 PTS. SIGMA.	
Total	9.5+0	5.0+2	CCP	Expt	Jour AE 2 129	Feb 57	Sokolovsky+.FAST CHOP,TRANSMIS CURVE	+
	9.6+0	5.0+2			Jour JNE 5 389	Nov 57	TRANSLATN.*	
	9.5+0	5.0+2			Jour SJA 2 147	57	TRANSLATN.*	
Total	5.8+2	6.1+7	KAP	Eval	Rept KAPL-1756 1	Jun 57	Baraff.TBL D25LETHARGYSTEPS	
Total	7.0+6	1.4+7	LRL	Expt	Jour PR 110 927	May 58	Bratenahl+ SC TRNS 5ES	+
					Conf 58Geneva 14 109	Apr 58	- + TBL,CURV,CFD OPTMDL	
	7.0+6	1.4+7			Data EXFOR11155.035	Jun 76	. 5 PTS. SIGMA.	
Total	4.0+2	2.0+3	HAR	Theo	Jour PPS 71 910	Jun 58	Egelstaff.FLUCTUATIONS CFD THEORY	+
	2.3-1	5.1+4		Expt	Jour JNE 6 303	May 58	- .CURVES FROM FC TRANSM	
Total	1.0-2	7.0+1	ANL	Expt	Conf 58Geneva 15 127	Sep 58	Bollinger+.PPR687,CURVE,EXPT DESCRBD	+
	5.0+0	7.0+1			Rept AERE-NP/R-2076	Jul 56	- . FIG 1D3	
	1.4-2	7.6+1			Data EXFOR12502.	Jun 76	. 768 PTS. SIGMA.	
Total	+0	+1	CCP	Revw	Conf 58Geneva 15 309	Sep 58	Vladimirsky+.PPR2221,NDG,REFS	
Total	1.7+7	2.9+7	LRL	Expt	Jour PR 120 521	Oct 60	Peterson+	+
					Conf 58Geneva 14 109	Sep 58	Bratenahl+.P1881,TBL,CURV,CFD OPTMDL	
	1.7+7	2.9+7			Data EXFOR11108.041	Jun 76	. 4 PTS. SIGMA,RATIO TO U235	
Total	Maxwl		HAN	Eval	Conf 61RPI 3	May 61	Leonard+	
		1.0+0			Rept TNCC(US)- 58	Aug 59	- +	
Total	2.0-1	1.0+7	B+W	Eval	Rept BAW- 158	Jun 61	Roach+ AVERAGED SIG 40 GROUPS	
Total	2.9-3	1.0-1	COL	Expt	Jour NSE 11 65	Sep 61	Safford+,VALUES AT 17ES	+
	2.9-3	1.0-1			Data EXFOR12507.002	Jun 76	. 17 PTS. SIGMA.	
Total	5.0-3	1.0-1	BNL	Revw	Rept BNL- 722	Jun 62	Sher+ REVIEW CURVE GIVEN	
Total	2.0-2	2.0+1	ITE	Expt	Jour AE 16 110	Feb 64	Ignat'Ev+. SIGTOT+ETA EXPT, NDG	
					Rept ITE- 147	63	.SIMILAR TO AE 16 110 2/64	
					Jour SJA 16 121	64	.ENGLISH TRANSL OF AE 16 110 2/64	
					Jour EAF 16 2 19	64	. FRENCH TRANSL OF AE 16 110 2/64	
					Jour JNE 18 719	64	.ENGLISH TRANSL OF AE 16 110 2/64	
					Rept INDSWG- 7E	63	.ENGLISH TRANSL OF ITE-147 /63	
Total	7.0+0	1.0+2	CCP	Expt	Rept INDSWG- 69	Nov 64	.TOF.2ONS/M RSLN,NDG.	
Total	Maxwl		CRC	Expt	Jour CJP 42 2384	Dec 64	Craig+	+
	Maxwl				Data EXFOR12528.017	Jun 76	. 1 PT. SIGMA.	
Total	1.0-2	1.0+6	RLY	Revw	Conf 64Vienna 56	Dec 64	Kronberger.GRPH SIG(E),PU-ISOT,U-235	
Total	7.0+0	5.5+2	ITE	Expt	Jour EON 2 77	Feb 65	Ignatev+KIRPICHNIKOV ANALYSED FOR RP	
Total	4.0+1	4.9+2	HAR	Expt	Conf 65Antwerp 535	Jul 65	Uttley+ GRAPH, 2.6NANOSEC/M RESOL	+
	1.0+3	1.0+5			Priv UTTLEY	Nov 64	- .GRPH AVG SIG,S,P WAVE STF	
	4.0+1	4.9+2			Rept EANDC(UK)40L	Jun 64	- + CURVES	
Total	7.9+0	8.6+1	LRL	Expt	Jour PRL 15 761	Nov 65	Sauter.	+
Total	1.0-3	1.0+7	AI	Eval	Conf 66Wash. 270	Mar 66	Lemke.AIDA ANAL OF AWRE+AI DATA FILE	
Total	1.0-2	1.0+0	MTR	Eval	Conf 66Wash. 840	Mar 66	Moore+,MULTILEVEL ANAL CURVE CFD XPT	

94 Plutonium 239

Quantity	Energy (ev) Min	Max	Lab	Type	Documentation Ref Vol Page	Author, Comments Date	Data
Total	5.0+6	1.6+7	LAS	Theo Rept	LA – 3538	Sep 66 Agee+ OPTICAL MODEL CALCULATION.	
Total	1.0+1	3.0+4	HAR	Expt Conf	66Paris 2 117	Oct 66 Patrick+ PPR30,GRAPHS,LINAC,LIQSCINT	+
	1.0+1	1.0+3		Rept	AERE – M – 1709	Sep 66 Brooks+ LINAC.TOF. NDG.	
Total	5.4+0	4.0+3	SAC	Expt Diss	FRNC – TH – 487	Nov 73 Derrien.SINGLE+MULTI LVLS ANALYSIS	+
	5.4+0	1.6+2		Conf	70Helsinki 1 481	Jun 70 – .61.SIG(E) GRAPH,PULSD LINAC	
	5.0+2	6.6+2		ExTh Conf	69Vienna 307	Jul 69 Paya+TOT+FISS SIG,TOF EXPT,ANALYSIS	
	3.0–1	4.4+2		Expt Conf	66Paris 2 195	Oct 66 Derrien+ PPR70 EXPT+ANALYSIS,BUT NDG	
	5.4+0	4.0+3		Data	EXFOR20445.002	Oct 75 17685PTS.	
Total	1.0–4	1.5+7	UK	Eval Rept	AHSB(S)R – 125	May 67 Hart.(RLY).UK – DFN 184 REVD TO DFN329	+
	2.0–3	6.0+0		Rept	AEEW – R – 351	Feb 64 Barrington+(WIN).UKNDL LOW EN REVISN	
	1.0–4	1.5+7		Data	UKNDL – DFN 161A	Mar 73 1530 PNTS	
Total	1.0+6	1.0+7	TRM	Theo Rept	67Karlsrhe 1 95	Nov 67 Garg+ OPTMOD CALC,CFD EXPT,TBL+GRPH	
Total	8.0+1	1.1+2	SAC	Eval Prog	ORNL – 4280 11	Oct 68 Derrien.MULTILVL ANAL+LEAST SQUARES	
Total	5.0+1	3.0+4	HAR	Expt Prog	AERE – PR/NP16	Aug 69 James+ WEAK COPR OBSERVED 460 EV	
	5.0+1	1.0+4		ExTh Conf	69Vienna 391	Jul 69 – +PPR52. TOT+FISSN CORRELTN ANAL	
Total	2.0+3		MTR	Expt Prog	WASH – 1136 59	Sep 69 Simpson+,TRANS,SIG VS.SAMPLE THICKNS	
Total	None		RPI	Expt Jour	NP/A 138 556	Nov 69 King+WT CALC FROM TRANS DATA.NDG	
Total	1.1–3	6.6–1	BNL	Expt Jour	REA 7 4 3	Dec 69 Zimmerman+	+
	1.1–3	6.6–1		Data	EXFOR12520.	Jun 76 . 174 PTS. SIGMA.	
Total	–1	+1	DUB	Expt Rept	JINR – P3 – 4992	Apr 70 Rjabov+ PULSD REACTOR,TOF,LIQ SCINT	
Total	+3		JAE	Theo Jour	NST 7 592	Nov 70 Takano+.NUMBER OF RES TO GET AVG SIG	
Total	–1	+3	SAC	Theo Rept	CEA – N – 1522	71 Barreau+ INTERMEDIATE STRV RESEARCH	
Total	2.5+6	1.5+7	BNW	Expt Jour	PR/C 3 576	Feb 71 Foster+.TRANS CURVS CFD OTHERS+THEOR	+
				Jour	NIM 36 1	Sep 65 .EXPT DETAILS	
	2.3+6	1.5+7		Data	EXFOR10047.100	Aug 73 243PTS.	
Total	1.0–3	1.0+7	KFK	Eval Rept	KFK – 1340	Feb 71 Hinkelmann+TABLE OF EVALUATED DATA	
				Rept	KFK – 750	Jan 68 Schmidt. CURVES.	
				Rept	KFK – 120 1	Feb 66 – . THEMAL + GRAPH,TBL.	
				Rept	KFK – 120 2	Dec 65 – . REISSUED.	
	1.0–2	1.0+7		Rept	KFK – 120 2	Dec 62 – .GRAPHS AND TABULATED DATA	
	1.0+3	1.0+7		Rept	KFK – 120 3	Dec 62 – . SUPERSEDED.	
Total	1.0+5	1.5+7	TRM	Eval Prog	INDC(IND) – 12 2	Jul 71 Garg.FIT TO EXPTL DATA+THEO CALC,NDG	
Total	1.3+7	1.5+7	DEB	Eval Jour	AHP 30 115	Oct 71 Angeli+ AVG SIG,CFD CALC.TBLS.GRAPH	
Total	7.0+0	2.0+1	KUR	Expt Rept	IAE – 2168	Nov 71 Biryukov+ DOPPLER EFFECT STUDY,GRAPH	
Total	1.0+0	3.0+2	MTR	Eval Prog	NCSAC – 42 4	Nov 71 Simpson+. FOR ENDF/B 3. NO DATA GIVN	
Total	1.0+4	1.0+6	SAC	Expt Prog	EANDC(E)150U	May 72 Cauvin+ANALYSIS FOR S AND P WAVE	
Total	1.5+6	4.0+6	ANL	Expt Prog	USNDC – 3 13	Oct 72 Guenther+. NO DATA GIVEN	
Total	–3	1.0+1	IKE	Theo Rept	IKE – 6 – 61/2	Jan 73 Keinert.DATA LIBRARY	
Total	0.0+0	1.5+7	UK	Eval Data	UKNDL – DFN 404B	Mar 73 . 2826 POINTS. RIBON+, SACLAY	+
Total	6.5+5	1.5+6	ANL	Expt Jour	JNE 27 317	May 73 Smith+ TRANS.CFD OPTMOD,STATMOD	+
	6.5+5	1.5+6		Data	EXFOR10212.002	Jan 73 393PTS,SIGMA	
Total		1.0+5	FEI	Expt Conf	73Kiev 2 213	May 73 Van'Kov+ TOF,SIG,TBL	
Total	5.0+5	3.0+7	RPI	Expt Prog	COO – 3058 – 39 33	Sep 73 Nadolny+TRNS.CFD FOSTER,GLASLOW.NDG.	
	5.0+5	3.1+7		Data	EXFOR10589.002	Nov 76 . 719 PTS. SIGMA.	
Total	1.0+5	6.0+6	BRC	Expt Rept	CEA – R – 4524	Nov 73 Cabe+, VDG,5 – 50KEV EN.RESOL.	+
				Conf	70Helsinki 2 31	Jun 70 – +68. SIG(E) GRAPH,TRANSMISSN,VD	
	1.6+5	6.0+6		Data	EXFOR20480.	Feb 76 148PTS.	
Total	1.0+6	2.0+7	AUW	Theo Prog	BARC – 770 36	74 Satyanarayana+ STRONG ABSORP MDL,NDG	
Total	3.0+2	3.0+4	IFB	Eval Prog	VBF 1974 3 17	74 Antsipov+ FROM EVAL RES – DATA,CFD XPT	
				Rept	INDC(CCP) – 62	Feb 75 . ENGLISH OF VBF 1974 3 17	
Total	2.5–2		IKE	Eval Rept	IKE – 6 – 80	Apr 74 Mattes+ ENDF/B,UKNDL,KEDAK CFD	
Total	–2	1.5+7	CJD	Eval Rept	INDC(CCP) – 44	Jun 74 .P1. ENGLISH OF 73KIEV 1 209	
Total	5.0+5	1.5+7	NBS	Expt Jour	NSE 54 322	Jul 74 Schwartz+CFD RPI,ENDF/B – III.	
				Rept	NBS – MONO – 138	Jan 74 – +LINAC,TOF,GRPHS.	
	5.0+5	1.5+7		Data	EXFOR10280.007	Dec 73 . 1680 PTS. SIGMA.	
Total	2.5+5	1.5+7	JAE	Theo Conf	JAERI – M – 5984	Feb 75 Tanaka.OPTMDL/COUPLD CH.GRPH CFD EXP	
Total	2.5–2		IAE	Eval Conf	75Wash. 286	Mar 75 Lemmel. TBL LSQ ANAL.CFD OTHER EVAL.	
Total	–3	1.9+0	THS	Theo Rept	IKE – 6 89 58	Jun 75 Keinert. DATA LIBRARY	
Total	5.0–1	1.2+2	MTR	Expt Rept	IDO – 16373 39	Jul 57 Simpson.CS MEAS FOR RES PARS.NDG	+
	5.5+0	1.2+2		Data	EXFOR12503.002	Jun 76 . 735 PTS. SIGMA.	
Elastic	5.0+0	5.0+0	HAR	Expt Jour	JNE 2 187	56 Pattenden. = 1 DATA INDEX LINES	
Elastic	5.0+5	1.0+6	LAS	Expt Jour	NSE 2 787	Nov 57 Allen.2ES SIG=6.1 AND 4.1B	+
				Jour	PR 104 731	Nov 56 .SUPERSEDED	
	5.0+5	1.0+6		Data	EXFOR12207.014	Jun 76 . 2 PTS. SIGMA.	
Elastic	5.5+5	2.0+6	LAS	Expt Rept	LA – 2177	Jun 59 Cranberg.	+
	5.5+5	2.0+6		Data	EXFOR12373.012	Jun 76 . 3 PTS. SIGMA.	
Elastic	Maxwl		HAN	Eval Conf	61RPI 3	May 61 Leonard.	

94 Plutonium 239

Quantity	Energy (ev) Min	Max	Lab	Type	Documentation Ref Vol Page	Date	Author, Comments	Data
Elastic	4.2−2		LAS	Expt	Jour ACR 15 351	62	Roof+NUCL COH SCAT AMPL, REL NI	+
	4.2−2			Data	EXFOR11435.005	Jun 76	. 1 PT. COH AMP.	
Elastic	5.0+5	2.0+6	AGN	Eval	Rept TID−21629	Dec 64	Perkins+ 4 ES. FRM BNL−400,UCRL5573.	
Elastic	1.0−3	1.0+7	AI	Eval	Conf 66Wash. 270	Mar 66	Lemke.AIDA ANAL OF AWRE+AI DATA FILE	
Elastic	5.0+6	1.6+7	LAS	Theo	Rept LA− 3538	Sep 66	Agee+ OPTMDL.MODEL+H−F FOR COMP.	
Elastic	1.5+1	3.0+2	HAR	Expt	Jour NP/A 98 33	May 67	Ashgar.TOF.SPIN ASSGNS OF 50RES.	
Elastic	1.0−4	1.5+7	UK	Eval	Rept AHSB(S)R−125	May 67	Hart.(RLY).UK − DFN 184 REVD TO DFN329	+
	2.0−3	6.0+0			Rept AEEW−R−351	Feb 64	Barrington+(WIN).UKNDL LOW EN REVISN	
	1.0−4	1.5+7			Data UKNDL−DFN 161A	Mar 73	1530 PNTS	
Elastic	1.9+5	3.8+5	DGE	Expt	Jour ZP 228 286	Oct 69	Coppola+,CFD WITH OPTMOD CALCULATION	
Elastic	1.9+5	3.8+5	GEL	Expt	Jour ZP 228 286	Jul 69	Knitter+ VDG.TOF. INTEG DIFF.	+
	1.9+5	3.8+5			Data EXFOR20136.002	Mar 73	5PTS.SOME N'.	
Elastic	4.2+1	1.2+2	RPI	Expt	Jour NP/A 138 556	Nov 69	King+ELAS SCT YIELDS MEAS NOT CS.	
		1.4+3			Abst DA/B 30 3819	Feb 70	− +SUPERSEDED.	
Elastic	2.0+3		MTR	Expt	Prog NCSAC−31 75	May 70	Smith+,ANAL TO BE COMPLETED,NO DATA	
Elastic	1.0−3	1.0+7	KFK	Eval	Rept KFK−1340	Feb 71	Hinkelmann+TABLE OF EVALUATED DATA	+
					Rept KFK−750	Jan 68	Schmidt. CURVES	
					Rept KFK−120 2	Dec 65	− . REISSUED	
	2.5−2				Rept KFK−120 1	Nov 65	− .+EVAL REVIEW.	
	1.0−2	1.0+7			Rept KFK−120 2	Dec 62	− .GRAPHS AND TABULATED DATA.	
	1.0−3	1.5+7			Data KEDAK−3	Oct 75	5547 DATA SETS	
Elastic	2.0+0	4.5+2	MTR	Expt	Jour NP/A 164 34	Mar 71	Simpson+ POOR RESOL DATA,LINAC,CRVS	+
	2.0+0	4.5+2			Data EXFOR10132.006	Jan 73	0PTS,SIGMA	
Elastic	1.0+5	1.0+7	TRM	Eval	Prog INDC(IND)−12 2	Jul 71	Garg.FIT TO EXPTL DATA+THEO CALC,NDG	
Elastic	1.0−2	2.5−2	MOL	Expt	Prog EANDC(E)140U	Aug 71	Ceulemans+ UNSUCCESSFUL.NDG.	
Elastic	8.2+2		AI	Theo	Jour NSE 49 450	72	Levitt. MTE − CRLO,PROBABILTY TBLS.TBL	
Elastic	1.0+5	1.5+7	SOR	Eval	Rept IAEA−153 141	73	Ilberg+ EVALUATD DATA FILES CFD,GRPH	
Elastic	0.0+0	1.5+7	UK	Eval	Data UKNDL−DFN 404B	Mar 73	Ribon+ (SACLAY). 2826 POINTS	+
Elastic	3.0+5	1.5+6	ANL	Expt	Jour JNE 27 217	May 73	Smith+ FROM ANGULAR DIST FIT	+
					Prog ANL−7210 7	Dec 66	− .VDG,TOF,SIG VS N−E,GRAPH	
	3.0+5	1.5+6			Data EXFOR10212.003	Jan 73	. 135 PTS. SIGMA.	
Elastic	2.5−2		IKE	Eval	Rept IKE−6−80	Apr 74	Mattes+ ENDF/B,UKNDL,KEDAK CFD	
Elastic	1.0+0	1.0+2	BOL	Theo	Conf NEANDC(E)−163U	Jan 75	Menapace+MULTLVL EFFECT,GRAPHS	
Elastic	2.5−2		IAE	Eval	Conf 75Wash. 286	Mar 75	Lemmel. TBL LSQ ANAL.CFD OTHER EVAL.	
Elastic	1.0+5	1.5+7	CCP	Eval	Data SOKRATOR−1042	76	99 PTS	+
Elastic	1.0−5	1.5+7	IJE	Eval	Data SOKRATOR−2021	76	429 PTS	+
Elastic	6.0+0	6.6+6	SAC	Expt	Diss TROCHON	77	Trochon. RES SCAT AREA.FOR SPIN.	
	1.6+1	6.6+2			Conf 70Helsinki 1 495	Jun 70	− +62.SIG(E),GRAPH AT 15RESON	
					Conf 69Vienna 912	Jul 69	− +PPR76. SIG(E) EXPT,LINAC+TOF	
Diff Elastic	2.0+6		KUR	Expt	Jour ZET 33 294	Jul 57	Aleksandrov.HE4 − CHAMBR,4−25DEG,GRAPH	
					Jour JET 6 228	Jan 58	.ENGL TRANSL	
Diff Elastic	7.0+6		LRL	Theo	Rept UCRL−4927	Jul 57	Bjorklund+ OPTMDL CALC 6−PARAM FIT	
Diff Elastic	5.0+5	1.0+6	LAS	Expt	Rept NSE 2 787	Nov 57	Allen.2ES THETA=25−130DEG MON DECR	+
					Jour PR 104 731	Nov 56	.SUPERSEDED	
					Conf 55Geneva 2 18	Aug 55	Walt.P588, CURVE FOR 2 N−ES,DISCUSSN	
	5.0+5	1.0+6			Data EXFOR12207.015	Jun 76	. 18 PTS. DSIGMA.	
Diff Elastic	5.5+5	2.0+6	LAS	Expt	Rept LA− 2177	Jun 59	Cranberg. ALSO 1 MEV TOF CURVES.	+
	5.5+5	2.0+6			Data EXFOR12373.	Jun 76	. 46 PTS. DSIGMA.	
Diff Elastic	5.5+5	2.0+6	ANL	Revw	Conf 61Vienna 1 29	Aug 61	Smith.TABLE,GRAPH OF ANGL DISTRB 1E	
Diff Elastic	5.0+5	2.0+6	AI	Eval	Rept NAA−SR−M−9026	Sep 63	Alter+.MT CARLO LEAST SQ ANAL BNL400	
Diff Elastic	2.0−3	6.0+0	UK	Eval	Rept AEEW−R−351	Feb 64	Barrington+(WIN).UKNDL LOW EN REVISN	+
	1.0−4	1.5+7			Data UKNDL−DFN 161A	Mar 73	17 PNTS,C.M.	
Diff Elastic	5.0+5	2.0+6	AGN	Eval	Rept TID−21629	Dec 64	Perkins+ 4 ES.LEGNDR COEF.	
Diff Elastic	5.0+6	1.6+7	LAS	Theo	Rept LA− 3538	Sep 66	Agee+ OPTMDL MODEL+H−F FOR COMP.	
Diff Elastic	5.0+6	1.6+7	LAS	Theo	Rept LA− 3788	67	Beery+.OPTMOD CALC POLARIZ ANG DISTR	
Diff Elastic	5.0+5	2.0+6	AI	Eval	Rept NAA−SR−11980	Apr 67	Campbell+ LEG COEFS TABLE C−M SYSTEM	
Diff Elastic	1.5+5	1.6+6	HAR	Expt	Rept AERE−R−5972	Mar 69	Cavanagh+ GRAPH CFD OPTMDL TABLE	+
Diff Elastic	1.9+5	3.8+5	GEL	Expt	Jour ZP 228 286	Jul 69	Knitter+,VDG TOF	+
	1.9+5	3.8+5			Data EXFOR20136.	Mar 73	25PTS.LEG.FIT+N'.	
Diff Elastic	2.0+6	4.0+6	ALD	Expt	Rept AWRE−O−55/69	Aug 69	Batchelor+TOF TBL CFD OTHERS	+
	2.0+6	4.0+6			Data EXFOR20036.	Sep 71	27PTS.D/DA.	
Diff Elastic	1.9+5	3.8+5	DGE	Expt	Jour ZP 228 286	Oct 69	Coppola+,CURVE,TBL OF LEG COEF GIVEN	
Diff Elastic	1.5+5	4.0+6	CCP	Comp	Rept ICD−6 50	70	Bazazjanc+ ANGDIST EXPTS,GRPH AT12ES	
Diff Elastic	1.5+5	5.5+6	GEL	Expt	Jour ZP 232 286	Feb 70	Coppola+ DIFFSIG AT 7 INCIDENT N−ES	+
	1.5+6	5.5+6			Data EXFOR20392.002	Oct 74	74PTS.D/DA	
Diff Elastic	1.0+6	6.0+6	CCP	Revw	Jour AE 28 310	Apr 70	Lebedeva+ ANOMALOUS SIG(ANG),GRAPHS	
					Jour EAF 28 4 35	70	.FRENCH TRANSL OF AE 28	
					Jour SJA 28 398	70	.ENGLISH TRANSL OF AE 28	

94 Plutonium 239

Quantity	Energy (ev) Min	Max	Lab	Type	Documentation Ref Vol Page	Author, Comments Date	Data
Diff Elastic	1.0+5	1.0+7	TRM Eval	Prog	INDC(IND)-12 2	Jul 71 Garg.ANGDIST FIT FOR OPTMOD PARS,NDG	
Diff Elastic	0.0+0	1.5+7	FEI Eval	Book	NIKOLAEV 197	72 .LEG COEFFS+ANG DISTRIBUTS,GRAPH	
Diff Elastic	1.5+6	4.0+6	ANL Expt	Prog	USNDC-3 13	Oct 72 Guenther+. NO DATA GIVEN	
Diff Elastic	-3	1.0+1	IKE Theo	Rept	IKE-6-61/2	Jan 73 Keinert.DATA LIBRARY	
Diff Elastic	0.0+0	1.5+7	UK Eval	Data	UKNDL-DFN 404B	Mar 73 Ribon+ (SACLAY). 17POINTS, C.M.	+
Diff Elastic	1.4+7		LRL Expt	Abst	DA/B 33 4954	Apr 73 Kammerdiener.TOF.20-160DEG.NO DATA.	
				Rept	UCRL-51232	Jul 72 - . RING GEOM.ANG DISTR	
Diff Elastic	3.0+5	1.5+6	ANL Expt	Jour	JNE 27 217	May 73 Smith+ LEG COEFF FIT, 25-155DEG.	+
	3.0+5	1.5+6		Data	EXFOR10212.004	Jan 73 . 5 COEFF AT 136 ES.	
Diff Elastic	None		IJE Eval	Conf	73Kiev 1 209	May 73 Konshin+ LEGENDR-COEFF(ANGDIS),NDG.	
Diff Elastic	None		CJD Eval	Rept	INDC(CCP)-44	Jun 74 .P1. ENGLISH OF 73KIEV 1 209	
Diff Elastic	4.6+3	6.5+6	FEI Theo	Rept	INDC(CCP)-39	Jul 74 .P1. ENGLISH OF YK-8/2 3	
				Rept	YK- 8/2 3	Sep 72 Bazajants+ ANISOTR GROUP-PARAMS,TBL	
Diff Elastic	None		AUW Theo	Prog	BARC-831 34	75 Satyanarayana+ STRONG ABSORP MDL,NDG	
Diff Elastic	5.5+5	5.5+6	JAE Theo	Conf	JAERI-M-5984	Feb 75 Tanaka.OPTMDL/COUPLD CH.9 ENS CFD EX	
Diff Elastic	1.0+4	1.5+7	KFK Eval	Data	KEDAK-3	Oct 75 43 ENERGIES	+
Diff Elastic	1.0+5	1.5+7	CCP Eval	Data	SOKRATOR-1042	76 99 PTS	+
Diff Elastic	1.0-5	1.5+7	IJE Eval	Data	SOKRATOR-2021	76 693 PTS	+
Polarization	5.0+6	1.6+7	LAS Theo	Rept	LA- 3788	67 Beery+.OPTMOD CALC COS(THETA) DISTR	
Potntal Scat	6.0+0		COL Expt	Rept	CUD-92	May 51 Havens+	+
	6.0+0			Data	EXFOR12517.003	Jun 76 . 1 PT.	
Potntal Scat	5.0+2	5.0+4	HAR Expt	Jour	JNE 6 303	May 58 Egelstaff. 11+ -2B FROM AV SIGT ANAL	
Potntal Scat	1.0+3	1.0+5	HAR Expt	Priv	UTTLEY	Nov 64 Uttley. AVERAGE TRANS MEASUREMENT	
	4.0+2	1.5+4		Rept	EANDC(UK)40L	Jun 64 - .MEAN 10.3BARNS FROM AVGE TRNS	
Potntal Scat	1.0+6	1.0+7	TRM Theo	Conf	67Karlsrhe 1 95	Nov 67 Garg+ OPTMOD CALC,TBL	
Potntal Scat	2.5-2		IAE Revw	Jour	REA 7 4 3	Dec 69 Hanna+WESTCOTT+ DISCUSSION	
Tot Inelastc	6.7+4	6.1+7	KAP Expt	Rept	KAPL-1756 1	Jun 57 Baraff.TBL D25LETHARGYSTEPS	
Tot Inelastc	Fiss		KUR Revw	Conf	60Vienna 159	Oct 60 Bondarenko+.TABLE,EXPT DESCRIBED	
Tot Inelastc	Fiss	9.0+5	CCP Expt	Book	NEJTRONFIZ 287	61 Andreev.THRESH DET.SIG FOR SPEC+.9MV	+
				Book	SPN 211	61 . ENGL TRANSL OF NEJTRONFIZ 287	
Tot Inelastc	1.4+5	1.0+7	B+W Eval	Rept	BAW-158	Jun 61 Roach+ AVERAGED SIG 14 GROUPS	
Tot Inelastc	1.0+4	1.0+6	ANL Eval	Conf	61Vienna 1 171	Aug 61 Moldauer+.PPR35,CURVE BY NEW CALCLTN	
Tot Inelastc	Thrsh	1.5+7	UK Eval	Rept	AWRE-O-79/64	Jan 65 Douglas.(ALD).UKNDL-DFN 184	
Tot Inelastc	8.0+3	1.0+7	AI Eval	Conf	66Wash. 270	Mar 66 Lemke.AIDA ANAL OF AWRE+AI DATA FILE	
Tot Inelastc	2.0+6	4.0+6	ALD Expt	Rept	AWRE-O-55/69	Aug 69 Batchelor+TOF TBL CFD OTHERS	+
	2.0+6	4.0+6		Data	EXFOR20036.	Sep 71 43PTS.D/DE,SIG.	
Tot Inelastc	1.0+4	1.0+7	LAS Eval	Conf	70Helsinki 2 517	Jun 70 Best+ 92.SIG(E) REVISED.INTEGRL TEST	
Tot Inelastc	1.0-3	1.0+7	KFK Eval	Rept	KFK-1340	Feb 71 Hinkelmann+TABLE OF EVALUATED DATA	+
	8.5+6	1.0+7		Rept	KFK-750	Jan 68 Schmidt. CURVES.	
				Rept	KFK-120 2	Dec 65 - . REISSUED.	
	8.5+3	1.0+7		Rept	KFK-120 2	Dec 62 - .GRAPHS AND TABULATED DATA.	
	8.5+3	1.5+7		Data	KEDAK-3	Oct 75 110 DATA SETS + 7 EXCT LVLS	
Tot Inelastc	1.0+5	1.0+7	TRM Eval	Prog	INDC(IND)-12 2	Jul 71 Garg.FIT TO EXPTL DATA+THEO CALC,NDG	
Tot Inelastc	1.0+4	5.0+5	AUA Theo	Prog	AAEC/PR-38P 15	Mar 73 Bertram. CHANNEL THEORY, NDG	
Tot Inelastc	8.0+3	8.5+5	IJE Eval	Conf	73Kiev 1 209	May 73 Konshin+ STATMOD,CFD EXPTS,NDG.	
Tot Inelastc	8.0+3	8.5+5	CJD Eval	Rept	INDC(CCP)-44	Jun 74 .P1. ENGLISH OF 73KIEV 1 209	
Diff Inelast	1.4+7		CCP Expt	Jour	AE 4 337	Apr 58 Zamiatnin+ FISS+EVAP SPECTR FIT DATA	
				Jour	JNE 9 194	Jun 59 TRANSLATN.*	
				Jour	SJA 4 443	58 TRANSLATN.*	
Diff Inelast	5.5+5	2.0+6	LAS Expt	Rept	LA- 2177	Jun 59 Cranberg.TOF PULSED BEAM METHOD CURV	+
	5.5+5	2.0+6		Data	EXFOR12373.	Jun 76 . 46 PTS. DSIGMA.	
	5.5+5	2.0+6		Data	EXFOR12373.012	Jun 76 . 3 PTS. SIGMA.	
Diff Inelast	4.0+6	7.0+6	LAS Expt	Prog	WASH-1028 26	Apr 60 Thomson+ TBA	
Diff Inelast	5.0+5		CCP	Jour	AE 13 321	Oct 62 HF CALCULATION CFD DATA	
				Jour	SJA 13 931	62 . ENGL OF AE 13 321	
Diff Inelast	8.5+3	5.5+5	KFK Eval	Rept	KFK-120 2	Dec 62 Schmidt.KIN.ES.7 XCIT-LVLS	
Diff Inelast	Thrsh	1.5+7	UK Eval	Rept	AHSB(S)R-125	May 67 Hart.(RLY).UK-DFN 184 REVD TO DFN329	+
	8.5+3	4.0+6		Data	UKNDL-DFN 161A	Mar 73 1ST- 9TH LVL,ANGDIST	
	4.5+5	1.5+7		Data	UKNDL-DFN 161A	Mar 73 .TO CONTINUUM.89 PTS.E DIST.ANGDIST.	
Diff Inelast	1.0+4	1.0+7	HEB Theo	Priv	NISSIMOV	69 Nissimov+MICROSC SIG CHECK BY N-SPEC	
Diff Inelast	1.5+5	1.6+6	HAR Expt	Rept	AERE-R-5972	Mar 69 Cavanagh+ TBL 90 DEG DIFFSIG CFD H-F	+
Diff Inelast	1.9+6	5.5+6	GEL Expt	Jour	ZP 232 286	Feb 70 Coppola+,E-SPEC AT 3 INCIDENT N-ES	
Diff Inelast	+5	1.5+7	ANL Revw	Conf	70Helsinki 2 3	Jun 70 Poenitz.111. SIG(E) GRAPH, 4 LEVELS	
Diff Inelast	2.0+6	5.5+6	BOL Expt	Rept	70Helsinki 2 863	Jun 70 Benzi+,FIT NON-SPHERIC POT COUPL CHA	
Diff Inelast	1.4+7		VNV Expt	Conf	71Knoxvill 196	Mar 71 Voignier+,SIG VS. E(PRIME) 90DEG CRV	
Diff Inelast	1.5+6	4.0+6	ANL Expt	Prog	USNDC-3 13	Oct 72 Guenther+. NO DATA GIVEN	
Diff Inelast	6.0+5	1.5+7	UK Eval	Data	UKNDL-DFN 404B	Mar 73 .TO CONTINUUM.66 PTS.E DIST.ANGDIST.	+
	8.5+3	8.0+5		Data	UKNDL-DFN 404B	Mar 73 1ST- 10TH LVL,ANGDIST	

94 Plutonium 239

Quantity	Energy (ev) Min	Max	Lab	Type	Documentation Ref Vol Page	Date	Author, Comments	Data
Diff Inelast	1.4+7		LRL Expt	Abst	DA/B 33 4954	Apr 73	Kammerdiener.TOF.20 – 160DEG.NO DATA.	
Diff Inelast	None		AUW Theo	Prog	BARC – 831 34	75	Satyanarayana+ STRONG ABSORP MDL,NDG	
Diff Inelast	1.0+5	4.0+6	CCP Theo	Conf	75Kiev	May 75	Antsipov+ SIG,FISS,LVLWIDTHS,STATMDL	
Diff Inelast	1.5+7		DUB Expt	Conf	75Kiev 5 245	May 75	Gangrskij+ SIG TO SPONFIS ISO.TABLE	
				Jour	IJP 47 232	73	Belov+ SIG TO SPONFIS GIVN,FRAGM – DET	
				Rept	JINR – E15 – 6807	Nov 72	– + SPONFIS ISOMER PRODUCTN,TBL	
Diff Inelast	1.4+7		FEI Expt	Rept	YK – 23 14	76	Devkin+ TOF,SECOND N – SPEC,TBL,GRAPHS	
Thermal Scat	2.5-2	2.0-1	ANL Theo	Jour	ACR 20 587	Apr 66	Atoji. E DEPENDENCE OF RE AND IM.	
Thermal Scat	1.0+4	1.0+7	HEB Theo	Priv	NISSIMOV	69	Nissimov+MICROSC SIG CHECK BY N – SPEC	
Scattering	1.0+3	1.5+7	UK Eval	Rept	AWRE – O – 79/64	Jan 65	Douglas.(ALD).UKNDL – DFN 184	
Scattering	1.4+1	3.0+2	HAR Expt	Jour	NP/A 98 33	May 67	Ashgar.TOF.SPIN ASSIGNEMENT OF 50RES	
				Rept	EANDC(UK)70	Jan 67	. TOF. SUPPLEMENT.	
Scattering	1.4+1	1.0+6	LAS Expt	Conf	70Helsinki 1 543	Jun 70	Farrell+ 46.SIG(E) CRV.EXPLOSN SRCE.	+
	None			Data	EXFOR10326.	Dec 74	. DATA UNAVAILABLE.	
Scattering	1.0-3	2.0+0	JUL Theo	Rept	JUEL – 746 – RG 50	Apr 71	Bonka.KUGEL – THERMOS – LIBR,T=300K,CURV	
				Rept	JUEL – 746 – RG 59	Apr 71	.KUGEL – THERMOS – LIBR,T=300,1500K	
Scattering	-3	1.0+1	IKE Theo	Rept	IKE – 6 – 61/2	Jan 73	Keinert.DATA LIBRARY	
Nonelastic	1.4+7		LAS Expt	Rept	LA – 1532	Apr 53	Graves+ NOT INCL DEST SIG	
Nonelastic	4.0+6	4.5+6	LAS Expt	Rept	LA – 1939	Aug 55	Bethe+ ALSO FISS SPEC NEUTS SPH TRNS	+
	4.0+6	4.5+6		Data	EXFOR12397.007	Jun 76	. 2 PTS, 2 DETECTORS	
Nonelastic	2.5+5	1.0+6	LAS Expt	Jour	NSE 2 787	Nov 57	Allen.3ES INCL.5MEV ABS+LVL EFFECTS	+
	5.0+5	1.0+6		Jour	PR 104 731	Nov 56	– . SUPERSEDED.	
	2.5+5	1.0+6		Data	EXFOR12402.003	Jun 76	. 4 PTS.	
Nonelastic	1.7+7		CCP Expt	Jour	AE 11 397	Oct 61	SPH, 2.87 PM.1 B	+
				Jour	SJA 11 1043	61	. ENGL TRANSL OF AE 11 397	
Nonelastic	8.1+6	1.4+7	LRL Expt	Jour	PR 130 1471	May 63	Macgregor+ SPH TRANS ALSO 11.9MEV	+
	8.1+6	1.4+7		Data	EXFOR11120.006	Jun 76	. 3 PTS.	
Nonelastic	1.3+7	1.8+7	CCP Expt	Jour	AE 19 456	Nov 65	Degtjarev.SPHERE TRANSM AT 3ES,TABLE	+
Nonelastic	1.0-4	1.5+7	UK Eval	Rept	AHSB(S)R – 125	May 67	Hart.(RLY).UK – DFN 184 REVD TO DFN329	+
	1.0-4	1.5+7		Data	UKNDL – DFN 161A	Mar 73	1530 PNTS	
Nonelastic	2.0+6	4.0+6	ALD Expt	Rept	AWRE – O – 55/69	Aug 69	Batchelor+ TOF. TBL CFD OTHER DATA.	+
	2.0+6	4.0+6		Data	EXFOR20036.	Sep 71	60PTS.D/DE.	
Nonelastic	2.0+3		MTR Expt	Prog	WASH – 1136 61	Sep 69	Simpson+,VALUE GIVEN	
Nonelastic	1.0-3	1.0+7	KFK Eval	Rept	KFK – 1340	Feb 71	Hinkelmann+TABLE OF EVALUATED DATA	+
				Rept	KFK – 750	Jan 68	Schmidt. CURVES.	
				Rept	KFK – 120 2	Dec 65	– . REISSUED	
	1.0+3	1.0+7		Rept	KFK – 120 2	Dec 62	– .GRAPHS AND TABULATED DATA.	
	1.0-3	1.5+7		Data	KEDAK – 3	Oct 75	8465 DATA SETS	
Absorption	1.0-2	5.0+1	LAS Expt	Rept	LA – 266	Apr 45	Anderson+,2 RESONANCES SEEN	+
	1.0-2	3.0+0		Rept	LA – 91	Jun 44	– + TRANS 1057B AT 0.025EV	
	2.5-2			Data	EXFOR12519.003	Jun 76	. 1 PT. SIGMA.	
Absorption	1.0-2	1.0+2	CCP Expt	Conf	55Moscow 87	Jul 55	Nikitin+.SIMULTAN ABS AND FISS,CURVE	
				Rept	AEC – TR – 2435 81	56	. ENGL TRANSL OF 55MOSCOW 87	
Absorption	Cold		ANL Revw	Conf	55Geneva 5 125	Aug 55	Spinrad+.P835	
Absorption	Fast		ANL Revw	Conf	55Geneva 5 125	Aug 55	Spinrad+.P835	
Absorption	2.5-2		IAE Revw	Conf	55Geneva 4 287	Aug 55	Worldvalue+ERROR GVN (2200M/SEC)	
				Eval Jour	NAT 176 619	Oct 55	.SEE ALSO *	
				Revw Jour	JET 2 271	55	.SAME ARTICLE,RUSSIAN ZET 29 1455	
Absorption	2.5-2		FR Eval	Jour	CR 241 669	Sep 55	Perrin.QUOTES WORLD SIGMA =1032+ – 15B	
Absorption	Maxwl		HAR Revw	Jour	NAT 176 619	Oct 55	Gaunt+1032+ – 15B WORLD AVG VALUES	
Absorption	Maxwl		KAP Expt	Rept	KAPL – 1464	Dec 55	Mcmillan+ FROM TTRSP53T 1V71133B	
Absorption	4.4+3	4.9+4	ORL Expt	Jour	PR 102 797	May 56	Macklin+,SPH TRNS FALLS TO FLAT 2.2B	+
				Rept	ORNL – 2022	Feb 56	.SUPERSEDED	
	4.4+3	4.9+4		Data	EXFOR12334.005	Jun 76	. 6 PTS. SIGMA.	
Absorption	2.5-2	6.5-2	ORL Expt	Prog	ORNL – 56 41	Jun 56	Harvey.AVERAGED OVER MAXWELLIAN,4ES	
Absorption	Maxwl		ANL Expt	Jour	NSE 1 204	Jul 56	Jaffey.1145B FROM ORNL ANL DATA	
Absorption	2.5-2		BNL Eval	Rept	BNL – 325	Jan 57	Hughes+ WORLD CONSIST,VAL. 1025+ – 13	
Absorption	7.0+0	3.0+1	CCP Expt	Jour	AE 2 247	Mar 57	Kirpichnikov+.GRAPH,FROM SIGTOT – 10B	
				Jour	JNE 6 163	Dec 57	TRANSLATN.*	
				Jour	SJA 2 299	57	TRANSLATN.*	
Absorption	2.0-2	2.4-1	CUW Theo	Rept	CWR – 400 – 1	Sep 57	Roberts.MAXWELL – BOLTZMANN AVGD SIGS.	
Absorption	Maxwl		HAR Eval	Rept	AERE – NP/R – 2140	Dec 57	Egelstaff+ CONSISTENT VALUES 2200M/S	
				Comp Rept	AERE – NP/R – 2104	Mar 57	– .EXPT METHODS FOR HAR VALUE	
Absorption	2.4+4	8.8+5	CCP Expt	Jour	AE 4 185	Feb 58	Andreev.ALSO AT 240KEV,SPHERE METHOD	+
				Jour	JNE 9 151	Jun 59	TRANSLATN.*	
				Jour	SJA 4 247	58	TRANSLATN.*	
Absorption	Maxwl		BNL Comp	Conf	58Geneva 16 8	Sep 58	Hughes.PPR2483,VAL V=2200M/SEC GVN	
Absorption	Maxwl		CRC Expt	Jour	NUC 16 10 108	Oct 58	Westcott. NRX ABSOL CURVE 20 – 760 DEG	

94 Plutonium 239

Quantity	Energy (ev) Min	Max	Lab	Type	Documentation Ref Vol Page	Date	Author, Comments	Data
Absorption	Pile		ORL	Eval	Jour NSE 6 100	Aug 59	Stoughton+,BEST VALUE .025EV=1030B	
Absorption	2.5-2		AE	Comp	Rept AE- 11	Apr 60	Story+,DISCUSSION+TABULATN OF MEASTS	
Absorption	Maxwl		HAN	Eval	Conf 61RPI 3	May 61	Leonard.	
		1.0+0			Rept TNCC(US)-58	Aug 59	-.	
Absorption	5.0-3	2.5+0	GA	Eval	Rept GA- 2113	Jun 61	Wikner+.TABLE+CURVE.100 E POINTS	
Absorption	Maxwl		CRC	Expt	Conf 61Saclay 57	Jul 61	Westcott. 2200METRE/SEC SIG GIVEN	
Absorption	2.9-3	1.0-1	COL	Expt	Jour NSE 11 65	Sep 61	Safford+ TOT MEASRD,ABS DEDUCD,TABLE	+
	2.9-3	1.0-1			Data EXFOR12507.003	Jun 76	. 16 PTS. SIGMA.	
Absorption	5.0-3	1.0-1	BNL	Revw	Rept BNL- 722	Jun 62	Sher+ REVIEW CURVE GIVEN	
Absorption	Maxwl		CRC	Revw	Rept EANDC(CAN)- 15	Nov 62	Hanna+ COMPARES MANY VALUES.	
Absorption	Pile		CJD	Eval	Rept INDSWG-64 285	64	Galanin. TBL EFF SIG FOR MANY SPECTR	
Absorption	2.5-2		BEP	Expt	Jour KE 8 625	Jan 65	Wenzel.VAL GVN,MANY REFERENCES	
Absorption	1.0+3	1.5+7	UK	Eval	Rept AWRE-O-79/64	Jan 65	Douglas.(ALD).UKNDL-DFN 184	
Absorption	7.0+0	5.5+2	ITE	Expt	Jour EON 2 77	Feb 65	Ignatev+KIRPICHNIKOV ANALYSED FOR RP	
Absorption	2.4+4		FEI	Expt	Jour AE 19 41	Jul 65	Vankov.STAVISSKY 12.75+-.16B	+
					Jour JNE 20 600	Jul 66	TRANSLATN.*	
					Jour SJA 19 903	Jul 65	TRANSLATN.*	
					Jour EAF 19 1 61	Jul 65	TRANSLATN.*	
Absorption	2.5-2		BNW	Theo	Conf 66Wash. 75	Mar 66	Liikala+, TBLS OF LITER. VALUES	
Absorption	2.4+4		FEI	Expt	Conf 66Paris 1 455	Oct 66	PPR96,BELANOVA+.VAL GVN,SB- BE SOURCE	
Absorption	2.0-2	5.0-1	MTR	Eval	Conf 66Paris 2 50	Oct 66	Smith+ TBL+CURV.LEASTSQUARE FIT	
	1.0-2	5.0-1			Conf 66Wash. 985	Mar 66	Fluharty+,COEF OF SIG EXPANSN CALCTD	
Absorption	Maxwl		ITE	Theo	Conf ICD-4 385	67	Birzgal+.AVERAGING OVER MAXWELL SPEC	
Absorption	Maxwl	2.5-2	HAR	Expt	Rept AERE-R-5874	Aug 68	Cabell. RE-ASSESSED.T=116C.TBL	+
	Maxwl				Jour JIN 28 2467	May 67	-+. IRR. IN MAXWELLIAN SPECTRUM	
					Rept AERE-R-5166	Apr 66	-. 1012PM40 MAXWELLIAN N SPEC	
Absorption	Maxwl		IFB	Theo	Prog YFI-7 45	Apr 69	Naumov+ CODES FOR EFFECTIV-SIG,TABLE	
					Rept INDC(CCP)-7U48	Feb 70	TRANSLATN.*	
Absorption	Fast		JAE	Expt	Conf 69London § 1.7	Jun 69	Kuroi+ EVALS CFD INTEGRAL EXPERIMENT	
Absorption	2.5-2		CRC	Expt	Prog EANDC(CAN)- 40	Sep 69	Lounsbury+ REL ABS-SIG U, SIG GIVEN	
Absorption	Pile		ROS	Theo	Rept ZFK- 201	Apr 70	Adam. EFFECTIVE SIG CALC	
Absorption	1.0+2	3.0+4	HAR	Expt	Conf 70Helsinki 1 315	Jun 70	Schomberg+33. SIG TABLE FOR 22RANGES	+
	1.0+2	3.0+4			Data EXFOR20476.006	Jan 76	21PTS.SIGMA.	
Absorption	1.0-3	1.0+7	KFK	Eval	Rept KFK- 1340	Feb 71	Hinkelmann+TABLE OF EVALUATED DATA	+
					Rept KFK- 750	Jan 68	Schmidt. EVAL SUPERSEDED	
					Rept KFK- 120 2	Dec 65	-. EVAL SUPERSEDED	
		2.5+0			Rept KFK- 120 1	Nov 65	-.+EVAL REVIEW.CURVE TO .76 EV	
	1.0-3	1.5+7			Rept KEDAK- 3	Oct 75	8453 DATA SETS	
Absorption	2.5-2		ANL	Eval	Conf 71Knoxvill 560	Mar 71	DE VOLPI. ADJUSTED VALUE GIVEN	
Absorption	6.2-1	1.0+7	SRL	Theo	Conf 71Knoxvill 714	Mar 71	Mccrosson. SPECTRUM-AVERAGED SIG	
Absorption	1.0-3	2.0+0	JUL	Theo	Rept JUEL-746-RG 59	Apr 71	Bonka.KUGEL-THERMOS-LIBR,T=300,1500K	
					Rept JUEL-746-RG 49	Apr 71	-.KUGEL-THERMOS-LIBR,T=300K,CURV	
Absorption	2.0-2	3.0+4	ORL	Expt	Jour NSE 45 25	Jul 71	Gwin+IONIZ CH,METAL FOIL CFD ENDF/B.	
					Jour NSE 40 306	May 70	+CS SPRSDD BY JNSE 45 PAGE 25.	
Absorption	2.5-2		IFB	Eval	Rept YK- 9 34	72	Morogovsky. COMPUTR RE-EVAL,DATA GVN	
					Rept INDC(CCP)-42	Aug 74	.P1.ENGLISH OF YK-9	
Absorption	1.0-3	1.0+0	IJE	Eval	Conf 73Kiev 1 209	May 73	Konshin+ REFERENCES,ACCURACY,NDG	
Absorption	2.5-2	2.0+4	ORL	Expt	Prog USNDC-7 179	Jun 73	Weston+. NO DATA GIVEN	
Absorption	1.0-3	1.0+0	CJD	Eval	Rept INDC(CCP)-44	Jun 74	.P1. ENGLISH OF 73KIEV 1 209	
Absorption	None		MUN	Theo	Diss GRYNTAKIS	Mar 76	Gryntakis.,CALC.OF WESTCOTTS G-FUNCT	
					Jour RCA 22 128	Mar 75	-+,EQUIVALENT TO THESIS	
Res Int Abs	-		CCP	Expt	Abst AE 1 3 27	Jun 56	DOROFEEV QUOTED, 460+-23B EPI-CD	
					Jour JNE 4 86	Jan 57	TRANSLATN.*	
					Jour SJA 1 3 311		56 TRANSLATN.*	
Res Int Abs	1.5-1	1.0+6	ORL	Eval	Jour NSE 6 100	Aug 59	Stoughton+,BEST VALUE 3500+-500B	
Res Int Abs	4.4-1		ANL	Theo	Abst ANS 6 39	Jun 63	Persiani+RNEGCRESRCONTRIB.INFNITLDIL	
Res Int Abs	5.0-1	1.0+7	BNW	Theo	Conf 66Wash. 75	Mar 66	Liikala+, TBLS OF RES.INTEGRALS	
Res Int Abs	Pile		UJV	Theo	Rept UJV- 2224		69 Stepanek. 6 GROUP CONSTANTS	
Res Int Abs	6.3-1		CAS	Expt	Jour NSE 40 51		70 Gibello+,EVAL. RES. INT. = 490 B	
Res Int Abs	Maxwl	1.0+5	IAE	Revw	Rept INDC(NDS)-47		72 Vlasov+ REVIEW DATA STATUS ,TBL+GRPH	
Res Int Abs	5.0-1		IAE	Revw	Rept IAEA- 143 897	Apr 72	Lemmel.CAPT,EVALUTS+RECENT EXPTS,TBL	
Res Int Abs	5.0-1		SGA	Comp	Conf 73Paris 1 233	Mar 73	Eder+ INCLUDING 1/V PART,CAPTURE,TBL	
					Rept SGAE-PH-141	Feb 73	.SAME AS 73PARIS,NO DETAILS,TBP	
Res Int Abs	5.0-1		KFI	Eval	Rept KFKI- 74- 45	Jul 74	Gado.CAPT,PART+TOT FROM RES-PARS,TBL	
(n,γ)	Maxwl		ANL	Expt	Rept PR 78 472	May 50	Chamberlain+(QUOTED)FIRST EVIDENCE	
(n,γ)	Cold		ANL	Revw	Conf 55Geneva 5 125	Aug 55	Spinrad+ PAPER 835	
(n,γ)	Fast		ANL	Revw	Conf 55Geneva 5 125	Aug 55	Spinrad+	
(n,γ)	Fast		HAR		Jour BJAS 5 32		56 Hepherd+ZEPHYR REACTOR	

94 Plutonium 239

Quantity	Energy (ev) Min	Energy (ev) Max	Lab	Type	Documentation Ref Vol Page	Date	Author, Comments	Data
(n,γ)	Maxwl		MCM	Expt	Jour CJP 34 193	Mar 56	Fleming+ MASS-SPEC,XE131-136 REL YLD	
(n,γ)	Pile		ORL	Expt	Jour NSE 1 108	May 56	Halperin+,EFF S=400+-40B THR+EPITHR	
					Conf 55Geneva 7 258	Aug 55	- +.P732,VAL GVN,EXPT DESCRIBD	
(n,γ)	Maxwl		ANL	Expt	Jour NSE 1 204	Jul 56	Jaffey.340B FROM ORNL ANL DATA	
(n,γ)	None		KAP	Comp	Rept KAPL-1781	Jul 57	Schuman. SIGMA GIVEN	
(n,γ)	Pile		CRC	Expt	Conf 58Geneva 16 83	Sep 58	Craig+ PPR205	+
	Pile				Data EXFOR12355.008	Jun 76	. 1 PT. SIGMA.	
(n,γ)	4.0+5		LAS	Expt	Conf 58Geneva 15 60	Sep 58	Diven.PPR667,RATIO CAPTURE/FISSION	
(n,γ)	Maxwl		CRC	Expt	Jour NUC 16 10 108	Oct 58	Westcott. NRX ABSOL CURVE 20-760DEGC	
(n,γ)	Maxwl		MCM	Expt	Jour CJP 37 926	Aug 59	Fickel+ MASS-SPEC CS TO SM YLDS,TBLS	
					Jour CJP 39 1391	Sep 61	.CORRECTION TO CJP,37,926	
					Conf 58Geneva 15 459	Sep 58	.SEE ALSO.	
(n,γ)	Pile		ORL	Eval	Jour NSE 6 100	Aug 59	Stoughton+,BEST VALUE .025EV=280B	
					Conf 58Geneva 16 64	Sep 58	Halperin+.PPR1072,VAL GVN,MANY REFS	
(n,γ)	Maxwl		HAN	Eval	Conf 61RPI 3	May 61	Leonard.	
(n,γ)	5.0-3	2.5+0	GA	Eval	Rept GA-2113	Jun 61	Wikner+.NFISSION,ALPHA GIVEN 100 ES	
(n,γ)	1.0+3	3.7+6	HFA	Eval	Rept IA-642	Jul 61	Yiftah. 16-GROUP SIGS	
(n,γ)	Pile		CRC	Eval	Rept CRRP-1191	Jan 62	Westcott. EFF SIG	
(n,γ)	3.0+4	1.0+6	LAS	Expt	Jour NSE 12 169	Feb 62	Hopkins+. CALCULATED FROM ALPHA(XPT)	+
	3.0+4	1.0+6			Data EXFOR12331.006	Jun 76	. 9 PTS. SIGMA.	
(n,γ)	Maxwl		ITE	Expt	Jour AE 16 110	Feb 64	Ignatjev+ FROM TOT,FISS,SCAT-XSECTS	
					Jour JNE 18 719	Dec 64	. ENGL OF AE 16 110	
					Jour EAF 16 2 1	Feb 64	. FRENCH OF AE 16 110	
					Jour SJA 16 121	64	. ENGL OF AE 16 110	
(n,γ)	7.0+0	5.0+2	ITE	Expt	Conf JINR-1845 133	Jun 64	Ignatev+ SIG(E) GRAPH,TOF	
(n,γ)	7.0+0	5.5+2	CCP	Expt	Rept INDSWG-69	Nov 64	.TOF.SC-T,CORR FOR FISSION GS. CURVE	
(n,γ)	2.6-2		CEA	Revw	Conf 64Vienna 19	Dec 64	Vendryes+ VALUE TBL,OTHER COMPILATNS	
	Maxwl		RLY	Revw	Conf 64Vienna 120	Dec 64	Raievski. TBL,AVG SIG OF 20+400DEG C	
(n,γ)	+5	+7	RLY	Revw	Conf 64Vienna 56	Dec 64	Kronberger.FAST REACTOR,1-GROUP SIGS	
	Maxwl		RLY	Revw	Conf 64Vienna 56	Dec 64	Kronberger.ADV-G-COOLD-R,1-GROUP-SIG	
(n,γ)	+0	+6	ANL	Revw	Abst ANS 8 217	Jun 65	Cote. REVIEW TALK NDG	
	Maxwl	+2	FEI	Expt	Jour SJA 19 1210	Sep 65	. ENGL OF AE 19 292	
(n,γ)	3.0+1	4.0+3	TRM	Comp	Rept AEET-272	66	SHANKAR SINGH+ GROUP SIGS,TEMPERATUR	
(n,γ)	1.0-3	1.0+7	AI	Eval	Conf 66Wash. 270	Mar 66	Lemke.AIDA ANAL OF AWRE+AI DATA FILE	
(n,γ)	2.5-2		BNW	Theo	Conf 66Wash. 75	Mar 66	Liikala+, TBLS OF LITER. VALUES	
(n,γ)	4.7+0	1.0+4	INA	Eval	Conf 66Paris 2 333	Oct 66	Hennies.PPR5.TBL RECOM DATA CFD OTHR	
					Rept NAA-SR-11980 5	May 67	- . RECOMMENDED DATA.REVISED.	
(n,γ)	2.0+1	1.0+6	LAS	Expt	Prog WASH-1071 124	Nov 66	Diven+ TBD.BOMB NS. 30M FLT PATH.	
(n,γ)	1.0+3	1.5+7	LAS	Eval	Prog WASH-1074 79	Apr 67	Diven+ NDG SEE EANDC(US)-96U.	
(n,γ)	6.0+0	3.0+2	DUB	Expt	Jour YF 5 925	May 67	Ryabov+.CURVE OF FISS-EVENTS ONLY	
					Jour SNP 5 657	Nov 67	TRANSLATN.*	
(n,γ)	1.0-4	1.5+7	UK	Eval	Rept AHSB(S)R-125	May 67	Hart.(RLY).UK-DFN 184 REVD TO DFN329	+
	1.0+3	1.5+7			Rept AWRE-O-79/64	Jan 65	Douglas.(ALD).UKNDL-DFN 184	
	2.0-3	6.0+0			Rept AEEW-R-351	Feb 64	Barrington+(WIN).UKNDL LOW EN REVISN	
	1.0-4	1.5+7			Data UKNDL-DFN 161A	Mar 73	1530 PNTS	
(n,γ)	1.0+2	2.5+2	ALD	Eval	Jour NIM 62 29	Jan 68	Horsley+ EVALUATION	
(n,γ)	Maxwl		AUA	Theo	Jour NSE 31 234	Feb 68	Cook+ STATISTICAL CALC CFD EXPT	
	Maxwl	2.5-2	HAR	Expt	Rept AERE-R-5874	Aug 68	Cabell. RE-ASSESSED.T=116C.TBL	+
	Maxwl				Jour JIN 28 2467	May 67	- +. IRR. IN MAXWELLIAN SPECTRUM	
(n,γ)	Pile		CCP	Theo	Jour AE 25 466	Dec 68	Usynin. OTHER MEAN SIG GVN	
					Jour SJA 25 1290	Dec 68	TRANSLATN.*	
(n,γ)	Fast		KFK	Expt	Conf 69London § 1.9	Jun 69	Kiefhaber+ INTEGRL XPT CFD MICRO SIG	
(n,γ)	1.0+3	1.0+7	TRM	Eval	Rept BARC/I-96	70	Kapil.14 GROUP SIG,2 N-SPECS,TABLES	
(n,γ)	1.5+4	1.9+6	ORL	Eval	Rept ORNL-TM-2797	Jan 70	Greene+,TABLE EVALUATED SIGS	
(n,γ)	9.9+1	9.8+3	ITE	Expt	Conf 70Helsinki 1 339	May 70	Beljaev+	+
	9.9+1	9.8+3			Data EXFOR40087.006	Nov 73	.SIGMA AT 96 ES GIVEN	
(n,γ)	+5	+7	ANL	Revw	Conf 70Helsinki 2 119	Jun 70	Davey.112.STATUS OF DATA ABOVE RESON	
(n,γ)	+1	+7	CAD	Theo	Conf 70Helsinki 2 465	Jun 70	Barre+73. MICROSC CFD INTEGRAL DATA	
(n,γ)	2.0+2	+6	GEB	Revw	Conf 70Helsinki 1 17	Jun 70	Greebler+102. UNCERTAINTY+REACT CALC	
(n,γ)	1.0+2	3.0+4	HAR	Expt	Conf 70Helsinki 1 315	Jun 70	Schomberg+33. SIG TABLE FOR 22RANGES	+
	1.0+2	3.0+4			Data EXFOR20476.002	Jan 76	21PTS.SIGMA.	
(n,γ)	1.0+4	1.0+7	LAS	Eval	Conf 70Helsinki 2 517	Jun 70	Best+ 92.SIG(E) REVSD,INTEGRL TEST.	
(n,γ)	1.4+1	1.0+6	LAS	Expt	Conf 70Helsinki 1 543	Jun 70	Farrell+46.SIG(E)CRV.EXPPLOSN SOURCE	
	None				Data EXFOR10326.	Dec 74	0 PTS.DATA UNAVAILABLE	
(n,γ)		7.0+3	SDC	Theo	Conf 70Helsinki 2 799	Jun 70	Garrison.DISCUSSN. RESONANCE ANAL	
(n,γ)	+3		JAE	Theo	Jour NST 7 592	Nov 70	Takano+.NUMBER OF RES TO GET AVG SIG	
(n,γ)	1.0+2	1.0+5	GA	Theo	Jour NP/A 159 305	Dec 70	Garrison.AVERAGE C.S.=NO RES INTERF	

94 Plutonium 239

Quantity	Energy (ev) Min	Max	Lab	Type	Documentation Ref Vol Page	Date	Author, Comments	Data
(n,γ)	1.0−3	1.0+7	KFK	Eval	Rept KFK−1340	Feb 71	Hinkelmann+TABLE OF EVALUATED DATA	
	1.0−3	1.5+7			Conf 75Wash. 1 313	Mar 75	Goel+ NEW EVALUATION.	
	1.0−3	1.0+7			Rept KFK−750	Jan 68	Schmidt. EVAL SUPERSEDED	
					Rept KFK−120 2	Dec 65	− . EVAL SUPERSEDED	
	1.0−2	2.5+0			Rept KFK−120 1	Nov 65	− .+EVAL REVIEW.TABLE 18ES	
	1.0−2	1.0+7			Rept KFK−120 2	Dec 62	− .GRAPHS AND TABULATED DATA.	
(n,γ)	2.5−2		ANL	Eval	Conf 71Knoxvill 560	Mar 71	DE VOLPI. ADJUSTED VALUE GIVEN	
(n,γ)	None		DUB	Expt	Jour YF 13 457	Mar 71	Ryabov+ TOF,SELF−INDICATION METH,NDG	
	−1	+1			Rept JINR−P3−4992	Apr 70	Rjabov+ PULSD REACTOR,TOF,LIQ SCINT	
	None				Jour SNP 13 255	Sep 71	. ENGL OF YF 13 457	
(n,γ)	2.0−2	3.0+4	ORL	Expt	Jour NSE 45 25	Jul 71	Gwin+.RPI LINAC.SIMULTANEOUS NF,NG	+
					Rept ORNL−4707	Jul 71	.DATA	
					Jour NSE 40 306	May 70	Gwin+CS SPRSDD BY JNSE 45 PAGE 25.	
	1.9−2	2.0+3			Data EXFOR10035.	Nov 72	3639 PTS.	
(n,γ)	1.0+0	3.0+2	MTR	Eval	Prog NCSAC−42 4	Nov 71	Simpson+. FOR ENDF/B 3. NO DATA GIVN	
(n,γ)	Pile		FEI	Expt	Rept FEI−295	Jan 72	Vankov+ INTEG SIG REL STANDARDS GIVN	
(n,γ)	Pile		KFK	Expt	Rept KFK−1453	Mar 72	Eberle+ 2−GROUP SIGS,FITTED TO EXPT	
(n,γ)	Pile		FAR	Expt	Prog EANDC(E)150U	May 72	Vidal.INTEGR CROSS SECTION RATIOS	
(n,γ)	Pile		JUL	Expt	Jour JIN 34 8 2427	Aug 72	Ihle+ REACTOR CROSS SECTION	
(n,γ)	2.0+2	1.2+4	FEI	Expt	Prog YFI−13 6	Oct 72	Chelnokov+ ABSTRACT,TBL SIGMA VS N−E	+
					Prog INDC(CCP)−32	Apr 73	.PAGE 8.ENGLISH OF YFI−13 6	
	2.0+2	6.0+3			Data EXFOR40105.016	Jun 72	SIGMA AT 22 ENERGIES	
(n,γ)	Maxwl		LIN	Expt	Jour YF 16 667	Oct 72	Val'Skii+ SIG TO SPON FISS ISOMER	
					Jour SNP 16 374	Apr 73	.ENGLISH OF YF 16 667	
(n,γ)	1.0+5	1.0+7	SOR	Eval	Rept IAEA−153 141	73	Ilberg+ EVALUATD DATA FILES CFD,GRPH	
(n,γ)	1.0+4	5.0+5	AUA	Theo	Prog AAEC/PR−38P 15	Mar 73	Bertram. CHANNEL THEORY, NDG	
(n,γ)	0.0+0	1.5+7	UK	Eval	Data UKNDL−DFN 404B	Mar 73	2826 PNTS	+
(n,γ)	8.2+2		AI	Theo	Rept BNL−50387 79	Apr 73	Levitt. SIMILAR NSE 49,LESS DETAILED	
					Jour NSE 49 450	72	− . MTE−CRLO,PROBABILTY TBLS.TBL	
(n,γ)	1.0+2	1.0+4	KUR	Expt	Conf 73Kiev 4 49	May 73	Bolotskij+	+
	1.0+2	1.0+4			Data EXFOR40259.004	Feb 75	CS PU239,NG/CS PU239,FISS AT18ES GVN	
(n,γ)	1.0+1	4.7+2	KFK	Theo	Rept KFK−1890	Feb 74	Broeders−Siep.RES SHIELD ON EFF SIG	
(n,γ)	2.5−2		IKE	Eval	Rept IKE−6−80	Apr 74	Mattes+ ENDF/B,UKNDL,KEDAK CFD	
(n,γ)	1.0+3	1.0+6	ORL	Revw	Rept CONF−740903−7	Sep 74	De Saussure+IN TERMS OF ALF.	
(n,γ)	6.0+2	8.0+3	KAL	Eval	Conf 74Bombay 2 89	Dec 74	Ganesan. BEST GROUP−VALUS BY WF−EVAL	
(n,γ)	1.0+4	8.0+4	FEI	Expt	Jour AE 38 82	Feb 75	Kononov+ TOF,AVG SIG(NEUT−E),TBL	+
					Rept YK−15 12	Aug 74	− + TOF,VDG,AVGED SIG,TBL	
					Jour SJA 38 105	Aug 75	ENGL OF AE 38 82	
	1.0+4	8.0+4			Data EXFOR40412.007	Jan 77	SIG FOR 7 E−RANGES	
(n,γ)	None		MUN	Theo	Diss GRYNTAKIS	Mar 76	Gryntakis.,CALC.OF WESTCOTTS G−FUNCT	
					Jour RCA 22 128	Mar 75	− +,EQUIVALENT TO THESIS	
(n,γ)	1.0+2	1.0+6	FEI	Eval	Rept YK−25 23	77	Kononov+ EVAL SIG VS AVG E,TBLS+FIGS	
(n,γ)	Pile		FEI	Expt	Rept YK−24 48	77	Andrijakhina+ AVG SIG AT DIFF POSITS	
Res Int Capt	5.0−1	+6	CRC	Expt	Rept CRC−633	Mar 56	Cornish+ NRX RESON INTGRL=656+−26B	
Res Int Capt	1.0+0	+2	ANL	Expt	Conf 58Geneva 15 127	Sep 58	Bollinger+.PPR687,VALS FOR 3E−RANGES	
Res Int Capt	1.5−1	1.0+6	ORL	Eval	Jour NSE 6 100	Aug 59	Stoughton+ BEST VALUE 1500+−300B	
	3.0−1	+6			Conf 58Geneva 16 64	Sep 58	Halperin+.PPR1072,VAL CFD MANY REFS	
Res Int Capt	4.7+0	1.0+4	INA	Eval	Conf 66Paris 2 333	Oct 66	Hennies.PPR5.TBL RECOM DATA CFD OTHR	
					Jour NAA−SR−11980 5	May 67	− . RECOMMENDED DATA.REVISED.	
Res Int Capt		2.0+4	DUB	Expt	Prog YFI−5 61	Oct 67	Rjabov+ TABLES	
					Rept INDC−232E	67	. ENGL OF YFI−5 61	
Res Int Capt	2.9+2	3.0+3	WEW	Theo	Jour NSE 34 181	Nov 68	Dyos. STATISTICAL CALC 10.36+−0.80B	
Res Int Capt	None		TRM	Eval	Prog BARC−418 1	69	Singh+ CALC FROM RES PARS.NDG.TBP	
Res Int Capt	1.0+2	3.0+2	ANL	Expt	Jour NSE 35 297	Feb 69	Pennington+ 1−LVL+MULTILVL CALC CFD	
Res Int Capt	3.0+0		KAP	Expt	Jour NSE 44 180	May 71	Eiland+ CD−RH FILTER 167+−7B	+
	3.0+0				Data EXFOR10143.014	Aug 73	. 1PT.	
Res Int Capt	Pile		KFK	Eval	Rept KFK−1453	Mar 72	Eberle+ 195B	
Spect (n,γ)	Maxwl		HAR		Rept NRDC−58	Feb 55	.ROUGH EXPT MORE LOW E GS THAN FIS	
Spect (n,γ)	Pile		ANL	Expt	Jour NSE 1 193	Jul 56	Kaufmann+ EBR,ACT RATIO REL U235,TH	
Spect (n,γ)	3.0+5		TNC	Expt	Prog WASH−1136 189	Sep 69	Nellis+. NO DATA GIVEN	
Spect (n,γ)	Maxwl		UPP	Expt	Prog EANDC(OR)99 19	Aug 70	Baecklin+. CONVERSION ELECTRON SPEC	
Spect (n,γ)	Maxwl		LAS	Expt	Prog NCSAC−33 152	Dec 70	Jurney.PRELIM GAM ES 4.4−6.8MEV GIVN	
Spect (n,γ)	7.8+0	1.2+1	BNL	Expt	Conf 71Knoxvill 792	Mar 71	Chrien+. SPECT OF 2RESON,4 PKS	
	Maxwl				Conf 70Helsinki 1 377	Jun 70	− .42. GAM SPECS,7.8+11.9EV RES	
	3.0−1	4.2+1			Rept IAEA−124 303	Feb 70	− .ALSO 7.8EV,GAMSPECS,RES SPINS	

94 Plutonium 239

Quantity	Energy (ev) Min	Max	Lab	Type	Documentation Ref Vol Page	Date	Author, Comments	Data
Spect (n,γ)	2.0+3		KFK	Expt	Conf 72Budapest 88	Aug 72	Matussek+ AVR.E1+M1 RAD.WIDTHS ,TBL	+
	Maxwl				Conf 74Petten 749	Sep 74	Weitkamp+ NONDESTR FUEL ASSAY APPL	
					Priv WIETKAMP	73	- . SPECTRA FOR COMPILATION	
	2.0+3				Prog KFK-1618 38	Sep 72	- . ES + ABSOL INT OF 6 GAM	
	Maxwl				Conf 72Budapest 86	Aug 72	Matussek+ LEVEL SCHEME OF PU240,GRPH	
	Pile				Rept KFK-1214	Jul 70	- + GRPHS+TBL, LVL SCH PU-240	
	2.0+3				Data EXFOR20373.002	Sep 74	21PTS.	
Inelastic γ	4.0+6	7.7+6	LAS	Expt	Jour NSE 40 294	May 70	Drake+,TOF,NAI(TL) DET,DIFFNTL SIGS	+
					Conf 66Paris 1 419	Oct 66	.SUPERSEDED	
					Conf 66Wash. 735	Mar 66	.SUPERSEDED	
	4.0+6	7.5+6			Data EXFOR10025.020	Jul 74	51 PTS. DSIGMA.	
Inelastic γ	None		TNC	Expt	Prog NCSAC-31 214	May 70	Nellis+,TO BE COMPLETED,NO DATA GIVN	
Nonelastic γ	1.5+7		LRL	Theo	Jour NSE 32 178	May 68	Howerton+ 13.2B CALC,CFD EXPT 17.2B	
Nonelastic γ	2.5-2		IFB	Eval	Rept YK-9 34	72	Morogovsky. SIG G-PROD EVAL,DATA GVN	
					Rept INDC(CCP)-42	Aug 74	.P1.ENGLISH OF YK-9	
Nonelastic γ	1.1+6	2.0+7	LAS	Eval	Rept LA-4901	Jul 72	Hunter+. CURVES+TABLE	
Nonelastic γ	1.0+6	2.0+6	LAS	Expt	Rept LA-5048	Dec 72	Drake. GAM SPEC AND PRODUCTION SIGS	+
					Jour NSE 55 427	Dec 72	- . TOF,CFD EXPERIMENTS	
	1.0+6	2.0+6			Data EXFOR10460.003	Jan 75	28PTS,DSIGMA AT 2 ENERGIES	
Nonelastic γ	1.4+7		KUR	Expt	Conf 75Kiev 4 133	May 75	Bezotosnyj+ NA-I.SIG(.5-8.0 MEV) GVN	
(n,2n)	Fiss		ALD	Eval	Rept AWRE-O-02/60	Apr 60	Hinves+AWRE EVAL DATA CFD XPT.	
(n,2n)	1.3+7	1.5+7	BNL	Theo	Jour NSE 23 238	Nov 65	Pearlstein.3ES.STAT MDL CALC.TBL CS.	
(n,2n)	Fiss		BNL	Theo	Jour NSE 23 238	Nov 65	Pearlstein.STATMDL CALC.SPEC AVG.TBL	
(n,2n)	5.8+6	1.0+7	AI	Eval	Conf 66Wash. 270	Mar 66	Lemke.AIDA ANAL OF AWRE+AI DATA FILE	
(n,2n)	Thrsh	1.5+7	UK	Eval	Rept AHSB(S)R-125	May 67	Hart.(RLY).UK-DFN 184 REVD TO DFN329	
	5.8+6	1.5+7			Data UKNDL-DFN 161A	Mar 73	.31 PTS.E DIST,ANG DIST,LAB.	
(n,2n)	3.2+6	8.0+6	ALD	Prog	AWRE-CNRPR/10	Apr 68	Mather+.	
(n,2n)	5.8+6	1.0+7	KFK	Eval	Rept KFK-1340	Feb 71	Hinkelmann+TABLE OF EVALUATED DATA	
					Rept KFK-750	Jan 68	Schmidt. CURVES.	
					Rept KFK-120 2	Dec 65	- . REISSUED.	
					Rept KFK-120 2	Dec 62	- .GRAPHS AND TABULATED DATA	
(n,2n)	6.5+6	1.3+7	ALD	Expt	Rept AWRE-O-72/72	Nov 72	Mather+ LARGE LIQ SCINTILLATOR.	+
	6.5+6	1.3+7			Data EXFOR20795.	Oct 78	5PTS.SIGMA.	
(n,2n)	1.5+7		KFI	Expt	Jour MFF 21 555	73	Nagy. THESIS,HUNG. TO FISS ISO,GRND	
(n,2n)	5.8+6	1.5+7	UK	Eval	Data UKNDL-DFN 404B	Mar 73	.34 PTS.E DIST,ANG DIST,LAB.	
(n,2n)	6.0+6	1.5+7	IFB	Theo	Jour VBF 1974 3 23	74	Sukhovitskij+ STATMDL CALC,GRPH+TBL	
					Rept INDC(CCP)-63	Feb 75	. ENGLISH OF VBF 1974 3 23	
(n,2n)	2.0+6	2.0+7	BRC	Eval	Conf 75Kiev 1 239	May 75	Jary. STATMOD CALC,VALUES GIVEN	
(n,2n)	1.5+7		DUB	Expt	Conf 75Kiev 5 245	May 75	Gangrskij+ SIG TO SPONFIS ISO.TABLE	
					Jour AE 31 156	Aug 71	- + UPPER LIMIT FOR SPON-ISOM	
	+6	+7			Rept JINR-P3-5528	Jan 71	- + GND+ISOM FISSN STATE SIGS	
	1.5+7				Jour SJA 31 874	Mar 72	. ENGL OF AE 31 156	
(n,2n)	Thrsh	1.5+7	BRC	Expt	Rept CEA-N-1798 34	Jun 75	Frehaut+ LARGE LIQ SCINT METH	
(n,xn) x>2	Thrsh	1.5+7	ALD	Eval	Rept AWRE-O-79/64	Jan 65	Douglas. N3N. UKAEA DFN-184 LIBRARY.	
(n,xn) x>2	Thrsh	1.5+7	UK	Eval	Rept AHSB(S)R-125	May 67	Hart.(RLY).UK-DFN 184 REVD TO DFN329	
	1.3+7	1.5+7			Data UKNDL-DFN 161A	Mar 73	.8 PTS. E DIST,ANG DIST,LAB. N3N.	
	1.3+7	1.5+7			Data UKNDL-DFN 404B	Mar 73	.7 PTS. E DIST,ANG DIST,LAB. N3N.	
(n,xn) x>2	6.0+6	1.3+7	ALD	Expt	Rept AWRE-O-72/72	Nov 72	Mather+ N3N.REL TO FISS SIG U-238.	+
	1.3+7				Data EXFOR20795.016	Oct 78	1PNT.SIGMA.	
(n,xn) x>2	1.3+7	1.5+7	IFB	Theo	Jour VBF 1974 3 23	74	Sukhovitskij+ (N,3N).STATMOD,TBL+FIG	
					Rept INDC(CCP)-63	Feb 75	. ENGLISH OF VBF 1974 3 23	
(n,xn) x>2	2.0+6	2.0+7	BRC	Eval	Conf 75Kiev 1 239	May 75	Jary. (N,3N) STATMOD,VALUES GVN	
(n,xn) x>2	Thrsh	1.5+7	BRC	Expt	Rept CEA-N-1798 34	Jun 75	Frehaut+ LARGE LIQ SCINT METH	
n Emission	1.4+7		SAC	Expt	Rept CEA-R-3936	Aug 70	Bertrand+ EMITTED NS.ASSOC PART METH	+
	1.4+7				Data EXFOR20578.	Jul 76	133PTS.D/DA.DE.	
(n,p)	1.4+7		ALD	Expt	Jour PPS 73 215	Feb 59	Coleman+. ACT. CFD DIRECT INTERACTN	+
(n,p)	2.0-3	6.0+0	UK	Eval	Rept AEEW-R-351	Feb 64	Barrington+(WIN).UKNDL LOW EN REVISN	
(n,p)	1.5+7		SAH	Comp	Jour NUC 23 8 112	Aug 65	Chatterjee. TABLE WITH REFS.	
	1.4+7				Jour NP 60 273	Nov 64	- . MEAN OF EXPT CFD SHELLMOD	
(n,p)	Maxwl		IFU	Theo	Rept ICD-4 20	67	Dadakina+ PENETR COEFF CALC,TABLE	
(n,p)	1.4+7	1.5+7	JYV	Eval	Rept JU-RR-3/1970	Jun 70	Leppaemaeki+ TABLE OF EVAL AVG SIG	
(n,p)	1.0-3	1.0+7	KFK	Eval	Rept KFK-1340	Feb 71	Hinkelmann+TABLE OF EVALUATED DATA	
(n,α)	Pile		IBJ	Expt	Jour PL 6 321	Oct 63	Sowinsky+ ALF-SPEC, NDG	
(n,α)	2.0-3	6.0+0	UK	Eval	Rept AEEW-R-351	Feb 64	Barrington+(WIN).UKNDL LOW EN REVISN	
(n,α)	Maxwl		LEB	Expt	Conf 65Antwerp § 176	Jul 65	Andreev+ CFD TH NDG	
					Jour YF 1 252	Feb 65	- . IONIZ-CHAMBER,SIG= 2 MILLIB	
					Jour SNP 1 177	Aug 65	. ENGL OF YF 1 252	
(n,α)	1.0-3	1.0+7	KFK	Eval	Rept KFK-1340	Feb 71	Hinkelmann+TABLE OF EVALUATED DATA	

94 Plutonium 239

Quantity	Energy (ev) Min	Max	Lab	Type	Documentation Ref Vol Page	Author, Comments Date	Data
Fission	8.0+4	1.5+6	LAS	Expt	Rept LA- 28	Oct 43 Taschek.RELATIVE TO U235 NF,CURVE	
Fission	5.2-1	4.8+2	LAS	Expt	Rept LA- 266	Apr 45 Anderson+,3 RESONANCES SEEN	+
	5.2-1	4.8+2			Data EXFOR12519.006	Jun 76 . 38 PTS. SIGMA.	
Fission	3.4+6	5.9+6	LAS	Expt	Rept LA- 520	Mar 46 Williams+	+
	3.4+6	5.9+6			Data EXFOR12312.005	Jun 76 . 3 PTS. SIGMA.	
Fission	Spont		BRK	Expt	Jour PR 69 367	Apr 46 Kennedy+1941LETTER.SEARCH SPON FISS.	
Fission	1.4+7		LAS	Expt	Rept LAMS-938	Jun 50 Nyer+ FISS CHAMBER RELATIVE TO U238	+
	1.4+7				Data EXFOR12306.006	Jun 76 . 1 PT. SIGMA.	
Fission	1.1-2	5.4-1	CRC	Expt	Rept CRGP-458	Jan 51 Tunnicliffe.	+
	1.1-2	5.4-1			Data EXFOR12515.	Jun 76 . 80 PTS. SIGMA.	
Fission	Maxwl	Pile	SAC	Expt	Jour CR 235 159	Jul 52 Cohen+ PILE, REL U. OKS BACK-TO-BACK	
	Maxwl				Jour JPR 15 101	Feb 54 Leveque+ DESCRIPTION OF CR ARTICLES	
	Maxwl	Pile			Jour CR 234 2355	Jun 52 Cohen+ THERMAL VAL GIVEN.	
Fission	Maxwl		ANL	Expt	Prog ANL-5411 10	53 Sellers+	+
	Maxwl				Data EXFOR12352.	Jun 76 . 2 PTS. SIGMA + RATIO U235.	
Fission	2.5+6	1.4+7	LAS	Expt	Rept LA- 1681	Jun 54 Wahl+	+
	2.5+6	1.4+7			Data EXFOR12437.004	Jun 76 . 2 PTS. SIGMA + RATIO TO U235.	
Fission	8.0-3	2.5+1	SAC	Expt	Jour CR 239 1128	Nov 54 Galula+ TOF,ABSOL+RATIO U235,GRAPHS	
Fission	1.0-2	4.0+0	SAC	Expt	Jour JNE 1 306	Jun 55 Auclair+ GRAPH REL BORON,CONTINUATN	+
					Conf 55Geneva 4 235	Aug 55 - + PPR354.	
					Jour JPRS 16 50	Jul 55 - + OKS TOF EXPT	
					Jour CR 240 2306	Jun 55 - +.(U233/PU239).RATIO.FISS CH	
	1.0-2	4.0+0			Jour CR 239 1034	Oct 54 - + CRYSTSPEC.	
Fission	1.0-2	1.0+2	CCP	Expt	Conf 55Moscow 87	Jul 55 Nikitin+.SIMULTAN ABS AND FISS,CURVE	
					Rept AEC-TR-2435 81	56 . ENGL TRANSL OF 55MOSCOW 87	
Fission	Cold		ANL	Revw	Conf 55Geneva 5 125	Aug 55 Spinrad+.P835	
Fission	1.0+4	3.0+6	ANL	Revw	Conf 55Geneva 5 347	Aug 55 Okrent+.P609,GRAPH,NO EXPT DETAILS	
Fission	Fast		ANL	Revw	Conf 55Geneva 5 125	Aug 55 Spinrad+.P835	
Fission	1.0-2	1.0+3	CCP	Expt	Conf 55Geneva 4 216	Aug 55 Adamchuk+.GRAPH,SLOW CHOPPER, PPR645	+
Fission	5.0-3	5.0+2	HAN	Expt	Conf 55Geneva 4 193	Aug 55 Leonard+.CURVE,SUM OF SEV EXPTS,P589	+
	5.0-3	2.5+0			Data EXFOR12522.004	Jun 76 . 143 PTS. SIGMA.	
Fission	2.5-2		IAE	Revw	Conf 55Geneva 4 287	Aug 55 Worldvalue+ERROR GVN (2200M/SEC)	
				Eval	Jour NAT 176 619	Oct 55 .SEE ALSO *	
				Revw	Jour JET 2 271	55 .SAME ARTICLE,RUSSIAN ZET 29 1455	
Fission	+3	2.0+6	SAC	Expt	Conf 55Geneva 4 245	Aug 55 Szteinsznaider+.GRAPH+TBL REL U238	
					Jour NKA 1 2 95	Sep 65 - +	
Fission	2.5-2		FR	Eval	Jour CR 241 669	Sep 55 Perrin.QUOTES WORLD SIGMA =729+ - 15B	
Fission	Maxwl		HAR	Revw	Jour NAT 176 619	Oct 55 Gaunt+729+ - 15B WORLD AVG VALUES	
Fission	Maxwl		KAP	Expt	Rept KAPL-1464	Dec 55 Mcmillan+,SIG=742B REL U235	
Fission	5.0-3	4.0-1	CCP	Expt	-	ENGL TRANSL AEC-TR-2435 PAGE 1	
					Rept AEC-TR-2435 1	56 . ENGL OF 55MOSCOW 15	
Fission	5.0-3	3.0-1	CCP		Rept AEC-TR-2435PT1	56 .USSR CURVE PAGE 9	
Fission	+0	+2	BNL	Prog	WASH-190 9	Feb 56 Hughes+ FAST CHOPPER. TBD	
Fission	6.8-3	6.9+2	HAR	Expt	Jour JNE 2 177	Mar 56 Richmond+.TABULAR DATA IN NRDC 81	+
					Rept NRDC-81	56 - + TABLE.	
Fission	1.4+7		HAR	Expt	Rept AERE-NP/R- 1996	Jun 56 Uttley+.BACK TO BACK FISS CHAMBER	+
Fission	2.5-2	6.5-2	ORL	Expt	Prog ORNL-56 41	Jun 56 Harvey.AVERAGED OVER MAXWELLIAN,4ES	
Fission	Pile		ANL	Expt	Jour NSE 1 193	Jul 56 Kaufmann+,EBR,CURVS REL U235,CFD TH	
Fission	Maxwl		ANL	Expt	Jour NSE 1 204	Jul 56 Jaffey.805B FROM ORNL ANL DATA	
					Rept ANL-5397	Mar 55 - +	
	Maxwl				Data EXFOR12521.	Jun 76 . 2 PTS. SIGMA + RATIO U235	
Fission	7.0+5	3.4+6	SAC	Expt	Jour JPR 17 565	Jul 56 Netter+VDG. 1.6 - 1.9B,MAX2.15 AT2.2MV	+
	1.0+6	4.0+6			Abst PHY 22 1187	Nov 56 Ballini+.VDG SOURCE	
	7.0+5	3.4+6			Jour NP 1 530	Jun 56 Netter+ COMMENT IN SEMINAR REPORT.	
Fission	5.0+0	6.0+1	HAR	Expt	Jour JNE 3 33	Aug 56 Farley.TOF,FROM ETA,ASSUMES CONST NU	
Fission	Maxwl	2.5-2	HAR	Expt	Rept AERE-NP/R- 2104	57 Cockroft. REL U. BEPO. ABST.	
	Maxwl	Pile			Rept AERE-N/R- 890	Mar 52 - . CFD NATURAL URANIUM	
Fission	Fast		HAR	Expt	Rept AERE-R/R- 2151	57 Absalom+ ZEPHYR+TH ENVELOPE.	
					Jour BJAS 5 32	56 Shepherd+ZEPHYR REACTOR	
Fission	2.5-2		BNL	Eval	Rept BNL-325	Jan 57 Hughes+ WRLD CONSIST, VAL. 738+ - 9B	
Fission	3.0+3	5.0+6	CCP	Expt	Jour AE 2 10	Jan 57 Dorofeev+.REL+ABS DATA, 5 GN SOURCES	+
					Jour JNE 5 217	Nov 57 TRANSLATN.*	
					Jour SJA 2 9	57 TRANSLATN.*	
Fission	5.0+4	1.4+6	LAS	Expt	Rept LA- 2114	Feb 57 Henkel+ ABSOL CURV REVIEWS ALL DATA	+
	5.0+4	1.4+6			Data EXFOR12321.003	Jun 76 . 1 PT. SIGMA.	
Fission	7.0+0	2.5+2	CCP	Expt	Jour AE 2 247	Mar 57 Kirpichnikov+.GRAPHS.PULSD CYCLOTRON	
					Jour JNE 6 163	Dec 57 TRANSLATN.*	
					Jour SJA 2 299	57 TRANSLATN.*	

94 Plutonium 239

Quantity	Energy (ev) Min	Max	Lab	Type	Documentation Ref Vol Page	Date	Author, Comments	Data
Fission	2.0−2	1.0+0	HAN	Expt Prog	HW− 48893 98	Mar 57	Leonard.	+
	2.5−2	1.0+0		Data	EXFOR12434.	Jun 76	. 2 PTS. SIGMA.	
Fission	5.8+2	6.1+7	KAP	Eval Rept	KAPL− 1756 1	Jun 57	Baraff.TBL D25LETHARGYSTEPS	
Fission	9.0+4	4.5+6	LAS	Revw Rept	LA− 2122	Jun 57	Henkel.CURV,REPLACES LA−1714	
Fission	None		KAP	Comp Rept	KAPL−1781	Jul 57	Schuman. SIGMA GIVEN	
Fission	3.0+4	3.0+6	HAR	Expt Jour	PPSA 70 573	Aug 57	Allen+.SIGF TO +−3PERCENT,AND RATIOS	+
Fission	2.0−2	2.4−1	CUW	Theo Jour	CWR− 400 − 1	Sep 57	Roberts.MAXWELL − BOLTZMANN AVGD SIGS.	
Fission	2.5−3	4.7−3	HAN	Expt Prog	HW− 55879 3	Apr 58	Seppi+.CRYSTSPEC,SIG REL .1EV,TABLE	+
	2.5−3	4.7−3		Data	EXFOR11791.005	Jun 76	. 10 PTS. SIGMA.	
Fission	6.8−3	5.0+3	HAR	Theo Jour	JNE 7 35	Aug 58	EGELSTAFF CORRELATION ANAL,W+SPACING	
	Maxwl			Eval Rept	AERE− NP/R − 2140	Dec 57	Egelstaff+ CONSISTENT VALUES 2200M/S	
Fission	2.4−2	3.5+4	ANL	Expt Conf	58Geneva 15 127	Sep 58	Bollinger+. FC. FISS,ETA MEAS DATA	↵
	6.0+0	7.0+1		Conf	ORNL− 2309	Jun 57	− +FC ABSCURVSP DETAIL 9−13EV	
	5.0+0	7.0+1		Rept	AERE− NP/R − 2076	Jul 56	− . FIG 1D4	
	2.4−2	3.5+4		Data	EXFOR12502.	Jun 76	. 635 PTS. SIGMA.	
Fission	1.0−3	1.0+0	BNL	Comp Conf	58Geneva 16 8	Sep 58	Hughes.PPR2483,CURVE,MANY REFS	
Fission	3.0+4	8.0+6	KUR	Expt Conf	58Geneva 16 136	Sep 58	Kalinin+.PPR2149,CURVE,CYCLOTRON	+
Fission	1.0+4	1.0+7	LAS	Revw Conf	58Geneva 15 344	Sep 58	Hemmendinger.PPR663,CURVE,MANY REFS	
Fission	4.0+5		LAS	Expt Conf	58Geneva 15 60	Sep 58	Diven.PPR667,RATIO CAPTURE/FISSION	
Fission	−2	−1	SAC	Expt Conf	58Geneva 16 106	Sep 58	Billaud+.PPR1186,CURVE,CRYSTALSPECTR	
Fission	Maxwl		CRC	Expt Jour	NUC 16 10 108	Oct 58	Westcott.NRX ABSOL CURVE 20−760DEGC	
Fission	Thrsh	Up	LAS	Expt Prog	WASH−1006	Oct 58	Stoke. S SLOPE AS U233 235 DPXPT	
Fission	Maxwl	Pile	HAR	Expt Rept	AERE− R − 2998	Jul 59	Raffle.SIG AT 0.025EV=704+−20B	+
	1.0−2	1.0+3		Conf	55Geneva 4 187	Aug 55	− +.CURV+VAL 2200M/SEC,PPR422	
	Pile	2.5−2		Rept	NRDC−51	Oct 54	− .BEPO CORE+THR COL+TOF 2200M/S	
Fission	Pile		ORL	Eval Jour	NSE 6 100	Aug 59	Stoughton+,BEST VALUE .025EV=750B	
Fission	Maxwl		CRC	Expt Jour	NSE 6 379	Nov 59	Bigham.DEPEND ON MOD TEMP 0 TO 100C	+
				Jour	NSE 59 50	Jan 76	− +CS OF 1958 WORK.REVISED	
				Prog	EANDC(CAN)−15	Nov 62	Hanna. COMPARES MANY VALUES	
				Conf	58Geneva 16 125	Sep 58	Bigham+,P.204,RATIO U235/PU239	
				Rept	AERE− NP/R − 2076	Jan 57	Hanna. RATIO TO U235 =1.428+−1.7PC	
	Maxwl			Data	EXFOR12356.	Jun 76	. 3 PTS. RATIO TO 233, 235, 241	
Fission	2.5−2		AE	Comp Rept	AE − 11	Apr 60	Story+,DISCUSSION+TABULATN OF MEASTS	
Fission	Fiss		ALD	Eval Rept	AWRE− O − 02/60	Apr 60	Hinves+AWRE EVAL DATA CFD XPT.	
Fission	Fiss		KUR	Revw Conf	60Vienna 159	Oct 60	Bondarenko+.TABLE,EXPT DESCRIBED	
Fission	Maxwl		CCP	Expt Jour	AE 10 372	Apr 61	Mostovaya.TERN FISS PROBABL REL U235	
				Jour	SJA 10 359	Jan 62	TRANSLATN.* JNE AB 17 424 N/63	
				Jour	KE 4 986	Dec 61	. GERMAN OF AE 10 372	
Fission	1.3+7	1.9+7	ALD	Expt Jour	JNAB 14 85	May 61	Adams+.TABLE+CURVE.RELATIVE TO U238	+
Fission	Maxwl		HAN	Eval Conf	61RPI 3	May 61	Leonard.	
		1.0+0		Rept	TNCC(US)−58	Aug 59	− .	
Fission	2.0−1	1.0+7	B+W	Eval Rept	BAW− 158	Jun 61	Roach+ AVERAGED SIG 40 GROUPS	
Fission	5.0−3	2.5+0	GA	Eval Rept	GA− 2113	Jun 61	Wikner+.TABLE+CURVE.100 E POINTS	
Fission	Maxwl		CRC	Expt Conf	61Saclay 57	Jul 61	Westcott. 2200METRE/SEC SIG GIVEN	
Fission	Maxwl		KUR	Expt Conf	61Vienna 3 315	Aug 61	Leipunskij+ SIG GIVN,TABLE	
	Pile			Conf	58Geneva 12 3	Sep 58	− +.PPR2038,VAL GVN	
	Maxwl			Rept	ANL− TR−9	62	. ENGL TRANSL OF 61VIENNA 3 315	
Fission	None		LRL	Expt Rept	UCRL− 3827	62	English.RA − BE SOURCE PARAF MODERATOR	
Fission	Pile		CRC	Eval Rept	CRRP−1191	Jan 62	Westcott. EFF SIGMA.	
Fission	Fiss		AI	Eval Conf	62Harwell 2 385	Dec 62	Strominger. SIG IN VARIOUS CORES,TBL	
Fission	5.0−2	7.0−1	CCP	Expt Jour	ZET 43 1998	Dec 62	Prob.TRIPLE FISS.INDEPENDENT OF E	
Fission	Fiss		EGG	Eval Conf	62Harwell 2 487	Dec 62	Humpherys. GRPH EFF − SIG,RECOMM VALUE	
Fission	−2	3.0+7	KFI	Revw Jour	MFF 11 325	Jan 63	Szabo.REVIEW,GRAPHS TABLES MANY REFS	
Fission	Pile		CJD	Eval Jour	INDSWG− 64 285	64	Galanin. TBL EFF SIG FOR MANY SPECTR	
Fission	Maxwl		KUR	Theo Rept	IAE− 562 3	64	Geylikman+,NO RESULT GIVEN	
				Rept	ANL− TR− 68	64	TRANSLATN.*	
Fission	Maxwl		CRC	Expt Rept	CRRP−1183	Feb 64	Bigham.	+
	Maxwl			Data	EXFOR12230.010	Jun 76	. 1 PT. SIGMA.	
Fission	3.1+0	9.9+1	ITE	Expt Jour	AE 16 110	Feb 64	Ignat'Ev+,PLSD CYCL,TOF,GRAPHS+TBLS	+
				Conf	JINR− 1845 133	Jun 64	.	
				Jour	AE 16 211	Mar 64	.CONTINUATION OF AE 16 110 RES ANALY	
				Jour	SJA 16 251	Mar 64	.ENGLISH TRANSL OF AE 16 211 3/64	
				Jour	SJA 16 121	Feb 64	.ENGLISH TRANSL OF AE 16 121 2/64	
				Jour	EAF 16 2 19	64	. FRENCH TRANSL OF AE 16 121 2/64	
				Jour	EAF 16 3 31	64	. FRENCH TRANSL OF AE 16 211 3/64	
	3.2+0	3.0+1		Data	EXFOR40156.006	Mar 73	.SIGMA AT 19 ES GIVEN	
Fission	1.0+1	1.9+1	CCP	Theo Jour	AE 16 211	Mar 64	Kirpichnikov+ SIG(E) GRAPHS,RES − ANAL	
				Jour	SJA 16 251	Mar 64	TRANSLATN.*NO 3	

94 Plutonium 239

Quantity	Energy (ev) Min	Energy (ev) Max	Lab	Type	Documentation Ref Vol Page	Documentation Date	Author, Comments	Data
Fission	1.5+3	1.3+6	KUR	Expt	Jour DOK 157 561	Jul 64	Dubrovina+,CURVE SIG VS E,OKS OTHERS	+
					Jour SPD 9 579	Jan 65	TRANSLATN.*ANL−TR−176 7/64	
Fission	Pile		CCP	Expt	Jour AE 17 113	Aug 64	Bondarenko+VAL GVN REL TO U−235(N,F)	+
					Jour SJA 17 821	Aug 64	TRANSLATN.*	
Fission	2.6−2		CEA	Revw	Conf 64Vienna 19	Dec 64	Vendryes+ VALUE TBL,OTHER COMPILATNS	
Fission	Maxwl		RLY	Revw	Conf 64Vienna 120	Dec 64	Raievski. TBL,AVG SIG OF 20+400DEG C	
Fission	+5	+7	RLY	Revw	Conf 64Vienna 56	Dec 64	Kronberger.FAST REACTOR,1−GROUP SIGS	
Fission	Maxwl		RLY	Revw	Conf 64Vienna 56	Dec 64	Kronberger.ADV−G−COOLD−R,1−GROUP−SIG	
Fission	2.5−2		BEP	Revw	Jour KE 8 625	Jan 65	Wenzel.VAL GVN,MANY REFERENCES	
Fission	+0	+3	CAI	Theo	Jour NP 62 667	Feb 65	Stavinsky+(N,GF)PROB ABOUT=(N,GAMMA)	
Fission	7.0+0	5.5+2	ITE	Expt	Jour EON 2 77	Feb 65	Ignatev+KIRPICHNIKOV ANALYSED FOR RP	
Fission	4.0+4	5.0+5	ALD	Expt	Conf 65Salzburg 1 219	Mar 65	White+ 6 ENERGIES.TBL. PU239/U235.	
Fission	−2	+2	HAR	ExTh	Conf 65Salzburg 187	Mar 65	RAE.REVIEW,SOME CALCULATIONS CFD XPT	
Fission	Fiss		IIT	Comp	Conf 65IAEA 251	Mar 65	Barrall+CALC AVG SIGS OF 3FISS−SPECS	
Fission	2.5−2	2.8−1	ISP	Expt	Conf 65Salzburg 255	Mar 65	Fraysse.ISPRA,CS,TABLE SIG AT 4 ES	+
Fission	−2		LAS	Theo	Conf 65Salzburg 23	Mar 65	Griffin.TRANSITION STATE NUCL	
Fission	Maxwl		CAD	Expt	Conf CEA−R−2775	Apr 65	Fraysse+REL BORON ABS XSCT+U235	
	3.0−2	2.7−1			Jour JPR 24 899	Nov 63	− +NDG,CALCULATIONS TO BE DONE	
Fission	+0	+6	ANL	Revw	Abst ANS 8 217	Jun 65	Cote. REVIEW TALK NDG.	
Fission	+0	+1	HAR	Theo	Jour PL 18 31	Aug 65	LYNN SLOW (N,GAMMA F) REACTION CALCD	
Fission	1.0+3	1.0+4	LAS	Revw	Jour PT 18 8 17	Aug 65	Diven. SRVEY BMB MTHD,PRELIM ABS CRV	
Fission	Maxwl	+2	FEI	Expt	Jour AE 19 292	Sep 65	Stavisskij+ (N,G)−SIGS REL PU239(NF)	
Fission	3.0+1	4.0+3	TRM	Comp	Rept AEET−272	66	SHANKAR SINGH+ GROUP SIGS,TEMPERATUR	
Fission	1.3+7	1.6+7	IBJ	Expt	Rept INR−688/I/PH	Feb 66	Czyzewski. SIG REL U238,MICA DET,TBL	+
	1.3+7	1.6+7			Data EXFOR30084.002	Sep 74	SIG AT 5 ES.	
Fission	Maxwl		TRM	Revw	Conf 66Bombay 1	Feb 66	Ramanna.VALS CFD TH,SIG,BINDING,DEF.	
Fission	1.0−3	1.0+7	AI	Eval	Conf 66Wash. 270	Mar 66	Lemke.AIDA ANAL OF AWRE+AI DATA FILE	
Fission	2.5−2		BNW	Theo	Conf 66Wash. 75	Mar 66	Liikala+, TBLS OF LITER. VALUES	
Fission	1.0+1	1.0+7	LAS	Expt	Conf 66Paris 2 219	Oct 66	Hemmendinger.DETONATION TOF	+
	2.0+1	2.0+6			Conf 66Wash. 979	Mar 66	Shunk+ BOMB NEUTS TOF(=LADC−7620)	
	2.0+1	1.2+2			Conf 65Antwerp	Jul 65	Diven. ABOMB. CURVE GIVEN. TBC.	
	2.0+1	3.0+4			Data EXFOR12523.002	Jun 76	2867 PTS. SIGMA.	
Fission	1.0−2	5.0−1	MTR	Theo	Conf 66Wash. 985	Mar 66	Fluharty+,COEF OF SIG EXPANSN CALCTD	
Fission	None		BRK	Revw	Jour NP 81 1	Jun 66	Myers+ TABLE2 FISS BARRIER	
Fission	1.6+0	1.0+1	HAR	Expt	Priv BROOKS3	Aug 66	Brooks. = 1 DATA INDEX LINES	+
Fission	1.6−2	5.5−1	ALD	Expt	Conf 66Paris 2 29	Oct 66	White+ TBL.DISCRETE ENS + MAXW SIGS.	+
Fission	6.7+5	1.0+7	ANL	Eval	Jour NSE 32 35	Apr 68	Davey. RE−EVALUATIONNNNN OF DATA.	
	1.0+3	1.0+7			Jour NSE 26 149	Oct 66	− . EVALUATION	
					Conf 66Wash. 796	Oct 66	.SUPERSEDED	
Fission	4.7+0	1.0+4	INA	Eval	Conf 66Paris 2 333	Oct 66	Hennies. PPR5.TBL RECOM DATA CF OTHR	
Fission	5.0+3	1.5+5	KFK	Expt	Conf 66Paris 1 295	Oct 66	Gilboy+VDG,REL TO U235,GRPHS.PPR7	+
					Rept KFK−450	Oct 66	− + REPRINT OF 66PARIS.	
	2.0−2	5.0−1	MTR	Eval	Conf 66Paris 2 50	Oct 66	Smith+ TBL+CURV.LEASTSQUARE FIT	
	1.0−2	1.0+0			Conf 66Wash. 840	Mar 66	Moore+,MULTILEVEL ANAL CURVE CFD XPT	
Fission	2.4+4		ALD	Expt	Jour JNE 19 423	Jun 65	Perkin+.CALIB SB−BE SRCE. 1.66+−.07B	+
					Jour JNE 20 921	Nov 66	− + DOPPLER EFF TO 770 DEG K.	
	2.4+4				Data EXFOR20584.007	Jul 76	1PNT.SIGMA.	
Fission	Maxwl		ORL	Expt	Prog ORNL−2081 102	Nov 66	Pratt+	+
	Maxwl				Data EXFOR12509.	Jun 76	2 PTS. SIGMA AND RATIO U235	
Fission	Maxwl		ITE	Theo	Rept ICD−4 385	67	Birzgal+.AVERAGING OVER MAXWELL SPEC	
Fission	7.6−4	4.0−3	BUC	Expt	Jour RRP 12 43	Jan 67	Grama+ SLOW CHOPPER,TOF,CURVE,NODATA	+
	7.6−4	4.0−3			Data EXFOR30019.	Oct 70	DATA FROM PRIV COM BALLY	
Fission	Maxwl		MOL	Expt	Conf 67Brussels 85	Mar 67	Debrue+ SIGMA EFF, RATIO PU239/U235	
Fission	1.0+5	1.5+7	LAS	Expt	Prog WASH−1074 79	Apr 67	Diven. NDG SEE EANDC(US)−96U	
Fission	2.2+0	1.0+4	LRL	Expt	Jour NSE 28 62	Apr 67	Czirr+ GROUP CS FOR BULK PU239.	
Fission	6.0+0	3.0+2	DUB	Expt	Jour YF 5 925	May 67	Ryabov+.CURVE OF FISS−EVENTS ONLY	+
					Jour SNP 5 657	Nov 67	TRANSLATN.*	
	5.5+0	1.0+5			Prog YFI−5 61	Oct 67	Rjabov+ CURVES	
					Rept INDC−E−232	67	.ENGL TRANSLATION	
	5.5+0	2.4+4			Rept JINR−P−2713	May 66	Rjabov.PLSD REACTR.GRPH COUNTS/CHANL	
	0.0+0	2.1+2			Data EXFOR40104.009	Jun 72	RATIO AV FIS/AV ABS AT 5 ES	
Fission	1.0−4	1.5+7	UK	Eval	Rept AHSB(S)R−125	May 67	Hart.(RLY).UK−DFN 184 REVD TO DFN329	+
	1.0+3	1.4+7			Rept AHSB(S)R−124	May 67	− .(RLY).UK−DFN 339.UPDATES NSE 2	
	2.0−3	6.0+0			Rept AEEW−R−351	Feb 64	Barrington+(WIN).UKNDL LOW EN REVISN	
	1.0−4	1.5+7			Data UKNDL−DFN 161A	Mar 73	1530 PNTS	
Fission	Pile		WIN	Expt	Rept AEEW−R−526	Jun 67	Stevenson+.FISS RATIO TO U235.ZEBRA	+
Fission	1.0+6	1.4+7	ALD	Expt	Jour JNE 21 671	Aug 67	White+ 4ES REL U235. CFD OTHER DATA	+
Fission	4.0+1	2.5+5	AI	Theo	Rept NAA−SR−12515	Oct 67	Otter+CHANNEL FISSION CALC OKS EXPT	

94 Plutonium 239

Quantity	Energy (ev) Min	Max	Lab	Type	Documentation Ref Vol Page	Date	Author, Comments	Data
Fission	3.0+6	1.5+7	LAS	Expt Jour	PR 162 1070	Oct 67	Barton+	+
	3.0+6	1.5+7		Data	EXFOR12490.003	Jun 76	. 2 PTS. SIGMA.	
Fission	1.0+4		ALD	Revw Conf	IAEA-107 41	68	Batchelor.EXPTS DISCUSSD+TBD,TBL	
				Conf	67Brussels	May 67	- + PPR3.	
Fission	1.4+1	9.0+1	LAS	Eval Jour	PR 165 1371	Jan 68	Farrell. REICH-MOORE FIT TO DATA.	
Fission	3.0+5	2.5+6	FEI	Expt Jour	AE 24 185	Feb 68	Nesterov+ SIG PU239/U235 RATIO	+
				Rept	YFI-5 40	67	- + RATIO	
	3.5+5	2.6+6		Rept	ICD-4 339	67	Smirnkin+.MEAS OF RATIO SIG PU9/U5	
	3.0+5	2.5+6		Rept	INDSWG-64 260	64	. TABULATED DATA	
				Jour	AE 13 366	Oct 62	Smirnkin+ E-STEPS 30KEV.CFD OTHERS	
				Jour	SJA 24 101	68	. ENGL OF AE 24 185	
				Rept	INDC-232E	67	. ENGL OF YFI-5 40	
				Jour	EAF 13 4 82	Oct 62	. FRENCH OF AE 13 366	
	9.9+5	2.5+6		Data	EXFOR40309.002	Oct 75	SIG PU-239/U-235 FOR 3 EN GIVEN	
	3.3+5	2.5+6		Data	EXFOR40027.	Oct 72	RATIO PU-239/U-235, 4 EN, VDG, REAC.	
Fission	Maxwl		ALD	Expt Jour	JNE 22 477	Aug 68	Keith+ REL.TO CAPT XSEC CO59	
Fission	4.0+1	1.5+2	ANL	Theo Prog	WASH-1124 5	Nov 68	Hill+ KAPUR-PEIERLS FIT PETREL DATA	
Fission	Pile		CCP	Theo Jour	AE 25 466	Dec 68	Usynin.AVG SUM SIG(N,G)+SIG(N,F) GVN	
				Jour	EAF 25 6 6	Dec 68	TRANSLATN.*	
Fission	Pile		CCP	Theo Jour	AE 25 466	Dec 68	Usynin.AVG SUM SIG(N,G)+SIG(N,F) GVN	
				Jour	SJA 25 1290	Dec 68	TRANSLATN.*	
Fission	Pile		TRM	Expt Rept	BARC-421	69	Mahalingam+CRITICL-XPT CFD DATA-SETS	
Fission	Pile		AUA	ExTh Rept	AAEC/TM-496	Apr 69	Cripps.MARKS.FISS-RATIO CFD SIG-SETS	
Fission	1.0+1	2.0+4	HAR	Comp Rept	AERE-M-2157	Jun 69	James+ TBL AVG SIGF DATA FROM SCISRS	
	1.0+3	1.0+5		Eval Rept	AERE-M-2065	Oct 68	- + L SQ FIT PU239 U235 AND RATIO	
Fission	Fast		JAE	Expt Conf	69London § 1.7	Jun 69	Kuroi+ RATIO U235,EVALS CFD INT EXPT	
Fission	Fast		KFK	Expt Conf	69London § 1.9	Jun 69	Kiefhaber+ INTEGRL XPT CFD MICRO SIG	
Fission	Spont		COP	Revw Conf	69Vienna 155	Jul 69	Strutinsky+PPR203. HL GVN,'SHELL-TH'	
				Theo Conf	68DUBSY 431	Jul 68	- +,INTERM. STATES IN FISS.	
Fission	-		COP	Expt Conf	69Vienna 351	Jul 69	Back+PPR74.(D,P FISSN)-REACTN,GRPHS	
Fission	None		CRC	Expt Conf	69Vienna 363	Jul 69	Specht+PPR128. (D,P FISSION)-REACTN	
Fission	5.0+1	3.0+3	DUB	Theo Conf	69Vienna 934	Jul 69	Ryabov+PPR160. EGELSTAFF-CORR-ANALYS	
Fission	-		HAR	Revw Conf	69Vienna 249	Jul 69	Lynn. REVW=STRUTINSKY TH+EXPTS,TBL	
Fission	Spont		HEI	Expt Conf	69Vienna 449	Jul 69	Metag+PPR29. HE-INDUCED ISOM FISS HL	
Fission		5.0+3	ORL	Theo Conf	69Vienna 283	Jul 69	Perez+ SIG(E) CALC,INTERMED-STRUCTUR	
Fission	Spont		WAU	Expt Conf	69Vienna 439	Jul 69	Vandenbosch+PPR110. ISOM FISS HL GVN	
Fission	1.0-1	1.0+1	BUC	Theo Jour	RRP 14 841	Aug 69	Cristu+ CALC SIG CFD OTH EXPTS,GRAPH	
	1.0-4	1.0+2		Rept	IFA-NR-27	69	- + MULTILVL CFD XPTS,PROGRM GVN	
Fission	2.0-2	2.0-1	MTR	Expt Prog	WASH-1136 74	Sep 69	Simpson+,CORRELATION CHOPPER,NO DATA	
Fission	8.2+5	5.4+6	KUR	Expt Prog	YFI-8 12	Dec 69	Savin+ SIG REL U235 AT 35 N-ES,TABLE	+
				Rept	INDC(CCP)-8 16	Dec 70	*ENGL OF YFI-8 12	
	8.2+5	5.4+6		Data	EXFOR40020.002	Aug 70	RATIO TO U-235 AT 35 ENERGIES	
Fission	1.4+7		TRM	Expt Conf	69Roorke 2 289	Dec 69	Iyer+ SIGMA RELATIVE TO U238	+
	1.4+7			Data	EXFOR30035.006	Dec 72	ONE VALUE	
Fission	1.0+3	5.0+5	KFK	Revw Jour	AKE 15 26	70	Schmidt. REVW ON EXPTS,GRPHS,CFD TH	
	1.0+3	1.0+6		Rept	KFK-966	Apr 69	- . GRPH. EXPTS CFD EVALS.	
Fission	1.0+3	1.0+7	TRM	Eval Rept	BARC/I-96	70	Kapil.14 GROUP SIG,2 N-SPECS,TABLES	
Fission	1.5+5	1.5+7	ORL	Eval Rept	ORNL-TM-2797	Jan 70	Greene+ ,TABLE EVALUATED SIGS	
Fission	2.4+2	2.4+4	ANL	Expt Jour	NSE 39 361	Mar 70	Lehto.FISS CS RATIO TO U235.TBL GVN.	+
	2.4+2	2.4+4		Data	EXFOR10084.002	Jul 71	26PTS.FISS CS RATIO TO U235.	
Fission	None		ORL	Theo Jour	PL/B 31 413	Mar 70	Desaussure+AUTO-CORR INTERMED SUBTHR	
Fission	Pile		FTI	Expt Jour	AE 28 359	Apr 70	BAK+.CD FILTERS USED,U235-RATIO,TABL	+
				Jour	EAF 28 4 112	Apr 70	. FRENCH OF AE 28 359	
				Jour	SJA 28 460	Apr 70	.ENGLISH OF AE 28 359	
	Pile			Data	EXFOR40349.007	Dec 77	SIG(N,F)PU-239/SIG(N,F)U-235, 1 PNT	
Fission	+2	+5	JAE	Theo Jour	NSE 40 25	Apr 70	Ishiguro+,STATISTICAL CALCULATN,CURV	
Fission	1.5+2	1.0+5	TOK	Theo Jour	NST 7 157	Apr 70	Kikuchi+.CALC USING SPIN DEPENDNT WF	
Fission	4.0+1	1.0+2	ANL	Eval Jour	NSE 40 342	May 70	Lambropoulos.ANALYSIS OF SACLAY DATA	
Fission	1.0-4	1.8+7	BNW	Eval Rept	BNWL-1312	May 70	Simons+.	
Fission	9.9+1	9.8+3	ITE	Expt Conf	70Helsinki 1 339	May 70	Beljaev+	+
	9.9+1	9.8+3		Data	EXFOR40087.007	Nov 73	.SIGMA AT 96 ES GIVEN	
Fission	1.3+5	1.4+6	ANL	Expt Jour	NSE 40 385	Jun 70	Poenitz.CS RATIOS U238NG AND U235NF	+
	1.5+5	1.4+6		Data	EXFOR10086.	Feb 72	16PTS.CS RATIOS WITH U238NG,U235NF.	
Fission	+5	+7	ANL	Revw Conf	70Helsinki 2 119	Jun 70	Davey.112.STATUS OF DATA ABOVE RESON	
Fission	1.0+3	1.0+7	ANL	Revw Conf	70Helsinki 2 3	Jun 70	Poenitz.111. SIG(E) GRAPHS REL U-235	
Fission	2.0+5	1.4+6	BRC	Expt Conf	70Helsinki 2 145	Jun 70	Soleilhac+67. SIG(E) RELATIVE U235	+
	2.1+5	1.4+6		Data	EXFOR20568.003	Mar 76	40PTS.SIGMA.	

94 Plutonium 239

Quantity	Energy (ev) Min	Max	Lab	Type	Documentation Ref Vol Page	Date	Author, Comments	Data
Fission	+1	+7	CAD Theo	Conf	70Helsinki 2 465	Jun 70	Barre+73. MICROSC CFD INTEGRAL DATA	
	1.0+4	1.0+7	Eval	Conf	69London 115	Jun 69	− +INTEGRL XPT CORRECTS MICROSIG	
	1.0+3	5.0+6		Rept	EANDC(E)120L	Mar 69	− +RAVIER EVAL OF INTEGRAL MEAS	
Fission	Maxwl	2.6−2	CRC Expt	Conf	70Helsinki 1 287	Jun 70	Lounsbury+PPR2. VALUE GVN,THRML FLUX	+
	Maxwl			Data	EXFOR10013.	Sep 72	2PTS.CS RATIO/U233,U235 GVN.	
Fission	1.0+2	3.0+4	DUB Expt	Rept	JINR−P3−5112	Jun 70	Kononov+ E−GROUPS AVGD SIG,TBLS+GRPH	
				Rept	INDC(CCP)−15	Dec 71	*PG 38.ENGL OF YFI−10	
				Rept	YFI−10 35	May 71	*	
				Conf	70Helsinki 1 345	Jun 70	. *SAME DATA TBL 4	
Fission	1.0+2	+6	GEB Revw	Conf	70Helsinki 1 17	Jun 70	Greebler+102. UNCERTAINTY+REACT CALC	
Fission	1.0−2	3.0+1	GEL Revw	Conf	70Helsinki 1 127	Jun 70	Deruytter.106.INTEGRAL SIG CFD OTHER	
				Conf	70Helsinki 1 151	Jun 70	− + SEE ALSO PPR1	
Fission	1.0+1	2.0+4	HAR Expt	Conf	70Helsinki 1 267	Jun 70	James.107. SIG AT 25RANGES,CFD OTHER	+
	1.0+3	2.5+4		Conf	66ANL 16	Oct 66	− .TOF CFD OTHER EXPTS TABLES	
	1.0+1	1.7+1		Prog	AERE−PR/NP10	Sep 66	− .MULTI−LEVEL ANALYSIS TBL PARAM	
	1.0+0	3.0+4		Prog	AERE−PR/NP9	Apr 66	− .TOF TABLE OF AVERAGE SIG FISS	
	5.0+1	1.0+2		Conf	65Salzburg 235	Mar 65	− .GRAPH, 4EV TO 35KEV TBP	
	1.0+3	1.5+4		Prog	AERE−PR/NP6 3	Apr 64	− . = 1 DATA INDEX LINES	
	1.0+3	1.6+5		Rept	EANDC−33U14	64	− .M 10KEV OKS ANL.P 35KV BACKG Q	
Fission	1.0+2	3.0+4	HAR Expt	Conf	70Helsinki 1 315	Jun 70	Schomberg+33. SIG TABLE FOR 22RANGES	+
	1.0+2	3.0+4		Data	EXFOR20476.	Jan 76	26PTS.SIGMA.	
Fission	2.2+6		HAR Expt	Jour	NP/A 148 337	Jun 70	Elwyn+ STUDY OF SHORT−LIVED ISOMERS	
				Prog	AERE−PR/NP17	Dec 70	− + SPON FISS ISOMS HL 29−4−5 NS	
Fission	5.0+3	1.0+6	KFK Expt	Jour	NSE 40 375	Jun 70	Kaeppeler+ TOF. RELATIVE TO U−235.	+
				Rept	KFK−1240	Jun 70	− + SIG RATIO /U235, TOF EXPT	
	5.2+3	1.0+6		Data	EXFOR20363.003	Sep 74	48PTS.SIGMA.	
Fission	1.0+4	1.0+7	LAS Eval	Conf	70Helsinki 2 517	Jun 70	Best+ 92.SIG(E) REVISED,INTEGRL TEST	
Fission	1.4+1	1.0+6	LAS Expt	Conf	70Helsinki 1 543	Jun 70	Farrell+46.SIG(E) CRV,EXPLOSN SOURCE	
	None			Data	EXFOR10326.	Dec 74	0 PTS.DATA UNAVAILABLE	
Fission		7.0+3	SDC Theo	Conf	70Helsinki 2 799	Jun 70	Garrison.DISCUSSN. RESONANCE ANAL	
Fission	2.5−2		BUC Expt	Rept	IFA−NR−33	Jul 70	Petrascu+ SIGMA REL B10 BRANCHRATIO	+
	2.5−2			Data	EXFOR30089.	Aug 72	SIGMA WITH REVISED REFERENCE−VALUES	
Fission	2.0+6	7.0+6	TRM Theo	Jour	NP/A 151 532	Aug 70	Sood+ CORREL ANAL OF INTERM STRUCTUR	
	None			Prog	BARC−471 5	70	− + CORREL ANAL,D CLASS II VAL GV	
	+0			ExTh Jour	PL/B 30 523	Dec 69	− +CORREL.ANAL CLASS 2LVLS.	
Fission	7.0+5	5.0+6	CCP Expt	Jour	AE 29 218	Sep 70	Sabin+ SIGMA(E) REL U−235 RATIO,GRPH	
				Jour	SJA 29 938	Sep 70	TRANSLATN.*	
Fission	3.5+4	9.7+5	CAD Expt	Conf	70ANL 257	Oct 70	Szabo+ ABSOL. CFD OTHERS.	
Fission	+5	+7	KFK Revw	Rept	KFK−1303	Oct 70	Boehme+ MICROSC CFD INTEGRL DATA	
				Conf	70Helsinki 2 427	Jun 70	− + SAME AS KFK−1303	
Fission	5.0+1	3.0+4	HAR ExTh	Jour	PL/B 28 258	Dec 68	Patrick+CORRELATION ANAL	+
	1.0+2	3.0+4		Expt Prog	AERE−PR/NP14	Oct 68	− + TOF LINAC TBL AVG VALUES	
				Priv	PATRICK(.)	Apr 68	− . LINAC.TOF.AV VALUES GIVEN.	
	1.0+1	3.0+4		Conf	66Paris 2 117	Oct 66	− + GRAPHS,LINAC,LIQSCINT	
	1.0+2	3.0+4		Data	EXFOR20002.	Nov 70	5332PTS.	
Fission	+3		JAE Theo	Jour	NST 7 592	Nov 70	Takano+.NUMBER OF RES TO GET AVG SIG	
Fission	1.0+2	1.0+5	GA Theo	Jour	NP/A 159 305	Dec 70	Garrison.AVERAGE C.S. = NO RES INTERF	
Fission	3.2+5	2.5+6	TRM Expt	Conf	70Madurai 2 67	Dec 70	Iyengar+ SIGMA EXPT TB CONT'D, NDG	
Fission	−1	+2	SAC Theo	Rept	CEA−N−1522	71	Barreau+ INTERMEDIATE STRC RESEARCH	
Fission	+6	+7	DUB Expt	Rept	JINR−P3−5528	Jan 71	Gangrskij+ PU239(N,2N)ISOM FISSN SIG	
Fission	1.0−3	1.0+7	KFK Eval	Rept	KFK−1340	Feb 71	Hinkelmann+TABLE OF EVALUATED DATA	
				Rept	KFK−750	Jan 68	Schmidt. CURVES	
	1.0+3	1.0+7		Rept	KFK−120 1	Feb 66	− .OTHERS'XPTS+CURVE	
	1.0−3	1.0+7		Rept	KFK−120 2	Dec 65	− . REISSUED.	
		2.5+0		Rept	KFK−120 1	Nov 65	− .+EVAL REVIEW.CURVE TO .76 EV	
	1.0−2	1.0+7		Rept	KFK−120 2	Dec 62	− .GRAPHS AND TABULATED DATA	
	1.0+3	1.0+7		Rept	KFK−120 3	Dec 62	.SUPERSEDED*10KEV UP	
Fission	2.5−2		ANL Eval	Conf	71Knoxvill 560	Mar 71	Devolpi. ADJUSTED VALUE GIVEN	
Fission	1.1+4	2.0+5	CAD Expt	Conf	71Knoxvill 573	Mar 71	Szabo+ TOF,IONIZAT CHAMB.15ES,CURVE	+
				Rept	CEA−R−4804	Dec 76	− + SAME AS 71KNOX.	
	1.1+4	2.0+5		Data	EXFOR20569.003	Mar 76	15PTS.SIGMA.	
Fission	None		DUB Expt	Jour	YF 13 457	Mar 71	Ryabov+ TOF,SELF−INDICATION METH,NDG	
				Jour	SNP 13 255	Sep 71	. ENGL OF YF 13 457	

94 Plutonium 239

Quantity	Energy (ev) Min	Max	Lab	Type	Documentation Ref Vol Page	Date	Author, Comments	Data
Fission	1.0+2	3.0+4	DUB	Expt	Jour AE 30 362	Apr 71	Kurov+ TOF,FISS – CHAMBR.AVG SIG,TABLE	
	5.5+0	2.0+4		Rept	JINR – P3 – 5113	Jun 70	Rjabov+ E – GROUPS AVGD SIG,TBLS+GRPH	
	-1	+1		Rept	JINR – P3 – 4992	Apr 70	– + PULSD REACTOR,TOF,LIQ SCINT	
	5.5+0	2.0+4		Prog	YFI – 11 35	70	Kurov+ ABST,SAME TBL AS JINR – 5113	
				Prog	INDC(CCP) – 31	Dec 72	.PAGE 34,ENGLISH OF YFI – 11 35	
	1.0+2	3.0+4		Jour	SJA 30 446	Nov 71	. ENGL OF AE 30 362	
Fission	1.0-3	2.0+0	JUL	Theo	Rept JUEL – 746 – RG 59	Apr 71	Bonka.KUGEL – THERMOS – LIBR,T=300,1500K	
				Rept	JUEL – 746 – RG 50	Apr 71	– .KUGEL – THERMOS – LIBR,T=300K,CURV	
Fission	1.0+2	8.0+3	ANL	Eval	Rept ANL – 7814	May 71	Kikuchi.ANAL PETREL DATA INTERM STRC	
Fission	1.1-1	4.4+4	FEI	Expt	Prog YFI – 10 4	May 71	Samsonov+ 83 ES,ABS+REL U235,TBL,TBP	
				Rept	INDC(CCP) – 15	Dec 71	*ENGL OF YFI – 10 4	
	1.0-1	4.0+4		Jour	AE 31 103	Aug 71	Samsonov+ REL B10(N,A)+ REL THR.GRPH	
				Jour	SJA 31 809	Mar 72	. ENGL OF AE 31 103	
Fission		1.0+2	FEI	Theo	Conf 71Kiev	May 71	Luk'Janov.ANAL FISS SIG,LVL PARS,TBL	
Fission	2.8+2	2.0+3	JAP	Theo	Jour NST 8 349	Jun 71	Ohnishi+ CAL USING AVG RES PARAMS	
					Jour NST 6 715	Dec 69	– +.CAL USING AVG RES PARAMS	
Fission	5.0+1	1.0+4	HAR	ExTh	Jour NP/A 170 309	Jul 71	James.DISTRIB FREE STATIST ANAL	
					Prog AERE – PR/NP17	Dec 70	– + TEST SHOWS INTERMEDT IN SIG F	
					Conf 69Vienna 391	Jul 69	– +PPR52. TOT+FISSN CORRELTN ANAL	
					Prog AERE – PR/NP14	Oct 68	– + FLUCTUATION ANAL MEDT SEEN	
Fission	2.0-2	3.0+4	ORL	Expt	Jour NSE 45 25	Jul 71	Gwin+.RPI LINAC.SIMULTANEOUS NF,NG	+
					Rept ORNL – 4707	Jul 71	.DATA	
					Jour NSE 40 306	May 70	Gwin+CS SPRSDD BY JNSE 45 PAGE 25.	
	1.9-2	2.0+3			Data EXFOR10035.	Nov 72	3639 PTS.	
Fission	Fiss		AMS	Expt	Jour JNE 25 457	Sep 71	Pauw+ CF252 SPEC,SIG=1800+ – 60MB	
Fission	3.0+4	+5	ORL	Expt	Rept ORNL – 4705 21	Oct 71	Peelle+. TO BE DONE	
Fission	–		GEL	Revw	Jour AKE 18 229	Nov 71	Theobald+ SUB – BARRIER FISS EXPTS,TH	
Fission	1.0+0	3.0+2	MTR	Eval	Prog NCSAC – 42 4	Nov 71	Simpson+. FOR ENDF/B 3. NO DATA GIVN	
Fission	+1	2.2+3	DUB	Theo	Rept JINR – P3 – 6239	72	Mateeva+ TH ANALYS OF EXPT DATA,GRPH	
					Rept KFK – TR – 406	Jun 72	.GERMAN OF JINR – P3 – 6239	
Fission	Maxwl	1.0+5	IAE	Revw	Rept INDC(NDS) – 47	72	Vlasov+ REVIEW DATA STATUS ,TBL+GRPH	
Fission	2.5-2		IFB	Eval	Rept YK – 9 34	72	Morogovsky. COMPUTR RE – EVAL,DATA GVN	
					Rept INDC(CCP) – 42	Aug 74	.P1.ENGLISH OF YK – 9	
Fission	3.0+4	5.4+6	ANL	Expt	Jour NSE 47 228	Feb 72	Poenitz. RATIO TO U235.GAP 30 – 500KEV	+
	3.0+4	5.5+6			Data EXFOR10253.002	Sep 72	. 27PTS,RATIO TO U235 NF	
Fission	Pile		KFK	Eval	Rept KFK – 1453	Mar 72	Eberle+ 2 – GROUP SIGS,FITTED TO EXPT	
Fission	Pile		FAR	Eval	Prog EANDC(E)150U	May 72	Vidal.INTEGRAL CROSS SECTION TO U235	
Fission	5.0+1	2.0+3	GEL	Expt	Prog EANDC(E)150U	May 72	Theobald+,LINAC TOF DOUBLE/TRI COINC	
					Prog EANDC(E)140U	Aug 71	Migneco+, DOUBLE+TRIPEL COINC.COUNTS	
					Priv THEOBALD+,	Apr 71	Theobald+,FISS NEUT 2+3 COINCID	
Fission	–		GEL	ExTh	Jour NP/A 187 305	Jun 72	Weigmann+ F.B.PARAMS FROM DATA ANAL.	
Fission	Pile		JUL	Expt	Jour JIN 34 8 2427	Aug 72	Ihle+ REACTOR CROSS SECTION	
Fission	3.9+1	3.0+4	SAC	Expt	Jour NSE 51 130	Jun 73	Blons.HIGH RESOL.LINAC.CURVES	+
	1.0+1	3.0+4			Conf 70Helsinki 1 513	Jun 70	– +63. SIG(E) GRAPH+TBL 29 RANGES	
	7.0+0	6.6+2			Diss FRNC – TH – 487	Nov 73	Derrien.SINGLE+MULTI LVLS ANALYSIS	
	5.0+0	3.0+4			Conf 73Kiev 2 239	May 73	Blons. CFD OTHERS, NDG.	
	+1	6.6+2		ExTh	Jour JPRC 33 22	Aug 72	– + INTERMEDIATE STRUCT ANAL	
	4.0+1	3.0+4		Expt	Jour AE 29 395	Nov 70	Michaudon.ABST FRANC – SOV SEM DUBNA	
	5.7+0	1.6+2			Conf 70Helsinki 1 481	Jun 70	Derrien.61.SIG(E) GRAPH,PULSD LINAC	
	0.0+0	6.6+2		ExTh	Conf 69Vienna 307	Jul 69	Paya+SIG GRPH,TOF,STRUTINSKY ANALYS	
	4.5+2	3.5+4		Expt	Conf 69Vienna 915	Jul 69	Blons+PPR91. SIG(E) EXPT,LINAC	
	5.0+2	4.0+3			Rept KFK – 966	Apr 69	– . DATA GRPH IN REVIEW.	
					Conf 68DUBSY 483	Jul 68	Paya+SHORT CONTRIBTN,GRPH SIG(E)	
	2.0+0	6.6+3			Conf 66Paris 2 195	Oct 66	Derrien+ PPR70.EXPT+ANALYSIS,BUT NDG	
					Jour CR 262 79	Jan 66	Blons. SUPERSEDED.	
					Conf 65Salzburg 1 205	Mar 65	– . SUPERSEDED.	
					Jour CR 259 3498	Nov 64	– . SUPERSEDED.	
	4.0+1	3.0+4			Jour SJA 29 1156	Nov 70	Michaudon. TRANSL OF AE 29	
	3.8+0	3.0+4			Data EXFOR20001.002	Oct 75	7295PTS.SIGMA.	
Fission	2.0+2	3.5+4	FEI	Expt	Prog YFI – 13 6	Oct 72	Chelnokov+ ABSTRACT,TBL SIGMA VS N – E	+
					Prog INDC(CCP) – 32	Apr 73	.PAGE 8.ENGLISH OF YFI – 13 6	
	2.0+2	3.5+4			Data EXFOR40105.	Jun 72	SIG AT 26ES, ABS+REL U235NF U238NG	
Fission	1.0+3	1.0+7	IAE	Eval	Rept REA 10 529	Dec 72	Byer. SIMULT EVAL PU239+RATIO TO U235	
Fission	1.0+5	1.0+7	SOR	Eval	Rept IAEA – 153 141	73	Ilberg+ EVALUATD DATA FILES CFD,GRPH	
Fission	1.0+2	2.0+7	HAR	Eval	Jour ANE 1 409	Jul 74	Sowerby+ LSQ WITH U5 U8 ABOVE .1MEV	
					Rept AERE – R – 7273	Feb 73	– +LINKED EVAL U235 U238 TBL	
					Rept AERE – M – 2497	Feb 72	– +LINKED EVAL U235 U238 TBL	
					Conf 70Helsinki 2 703	Jun 70	– + PPR34.	

94 Plutonium 239

Quantity	Energy (ev) Min	Max	Lab	Type	Documentation Ref Vol Page	Date	Author, Comments	Data
Fission	1.0+4	5.0+5	AUA	Theo Prog	AAEC/PR-38P 15	Mar 73	Bertram. CHANNEL THEORY CFD EXPT,NDG	
Fission	Fiss		RCN	Revw Conf	73Paris 2 271	Mar 73	Zijp.RECOMM INTEG CFD DIFF CALC,TBLS	
	2.5-2			Conf	73Paris 2 271	Mar 73	- .RECOMMENDED,FROM LITERATURE,TB	
Fission	Fiss		SGA	Eval Conf	73Paris 1 233	Mar 73	Eder+ FISS SPEC REL U238(N,F),TBLS	
				Rept	SGAE-PH-141	Feb 73	.SAME AS 73PARIS,NO DETAILS,TBP	
Fission	0.0+0	1.5+7	UK	Eval Data	UKNDL-DFN 404B	Mar 73	2826 PNTS	+
Fission	Maxwl		LRL	Expt Jour	JIN 35 1063	Apr 73	Wild+ THR COL,T = 40 DEGS C.	+
	Maxwl			Data	EXFOR10341.004	Jun 74	1 PT	
Fission	2.0-2	3.0+1	GEL	Expt Jour	JNE 26 293	Jun 72	Deruytter. NORM 2200 M,CALC FISS INT	+
				Conf	73Kiev 4 26	May 73	- . SEE JNE 26. GRAPH	
	2.0-2	2.0+2		Data	EXFOR20132.002	Mar 73	560PTS	
Fission	2.5+2	9.5+3	KUR	Expt Conf	73Kiev 4 49	May 73	Bolotskij+	+
	2.5+2	9.5+3		Data	EXFOR40259.003	Feb 75	.CS PU239,FISS/CS U235,FISS AT 17 ES	
Fission	+6		AUA	Expt Prog	INDC(SEC)-35	Sep 73	.SHORT NOTE,NO DATA GIVEN	
Fission	Maxwl		LIN	Expt Jour	YF 18 492	Sep 73	Val'Skii+ SPONFIS - ISOM/INST FIS,TBL	
				Jour	SNP 18 253	Apr 74	.ENGLISH OF YF 18 492	
Fission	None		DUB	Expt Jour	FDP 22 199	74	Gangrsky+ FIS - BARRIER,GRPH EMAX+EMIN	
	Spont			Rept	JINR-E15-7362	Jul 73	- + ISOMER HALFLIFE,TABLE,GRPH	
Fission	3.0+2	3.0+4	IFB	Eval Jour	VBF 1974 3 17	74	Antsipov+ FROM EVAL RES - DATA,CFD XPT	
				Rept	INDC(CCP)-62	Feb 75	. ENGLISH OF VBF 1974 3 17	
Fission	5.0+5	7.0+6	FEI	Expt Jour	YF 19 50	Jan 74	Fursov+	+
	5.0+5	7.0+6		Data	EXFOR40201.002	Mar 74	.RATIO CF246(NF)/PU239(NF) FOR 13 ES	
Fission	5.0+5	2.5+6	TUE	Expt Jour	PL/B 48 25	Jan 74	Mueller+ SHAPE ISOM RATIO TO PROMPT	
Fission	1.0+1	4.7+2	KFK	Theo Rept	KFK-1890	Feb 74	Broeders - Siep.RES SHIELD ON EFF SIG	
Fission	2.5-2		IKE	Eval Rept	IKE-6-80	Apr 74	Mattes+ ENDF/B,UKNDL,KEDAK CFD	
Fission	5.0-3	1.0-1	GEL	Expt Jour	ANE 1 311	May 74	Deruytter+ SLOW CHOP,THR VALUE	+
	2.5-2			Conf	73Rochestr 2 51	Aug 73	- + REL PROMPT FRAG YLDS,GRPH	
				Conf	73Kiev 4 26	May 73	- . SIG=741.9+ -3.4 B	
	2.0-3	1.0-1		Conf	70Helsinki 1 117	Jun 70	- +100. SIGMA AT 2200 M/SEC	
				Rept	EANDC(E)131AL	70	- + MEASUREMENT+NORMALISATION	
	2.5-2			Data	EXFOR20143.004	Mar 73	1PNT.	
Fission	Fiss		TEX	Expt Rept	UMO-74-24,841	May 74	Chromik. THESIS.CF252 - NEUTRONS	
Fission	1.0-3	1.0+0	CJD	Eval Rept	INDC(CCP)-44	Jun 74	.P1. ENGLISH OF 73KIEV 1 209	
	1.0+3	1.5+7		Rept	INDC(CCP)-44	Jun 74	.P1. ENGLISH OF 73KIEV 1 209	
Fission	Maxwl		IRT	Expt Jour	PR/C 10 853	Aug 74	Sund+ ISOM G SPECT TBL, GRPHS.	
Fission	1.0+3	1.0+7	ORL	Revw Rept	CONF-740903-7	Sep 74	De Saussure+CURVS,OTH,ENDF CFD.	
Fission	1.0+1	1.7+2	ORL	Expt Jour	PR/C 10 1402	Oct 74	Weston+ TBLS.GRPHS.	
	2.5-2	3.0+4		Abst	ANS 15 480	Jun 72	- +DATA TO BE ANALYZED.	
Fission	1.0+6	2.0+7	AUW	Theo Prog	INDC(SEC)-42	Dec 74	Satyanarayana+ ABS - MDL,CFD XPT,NDG	
Fission	6.0+2	8.0+3	KAL	Eval Conf	74Bombay 2 89	Dec 74	Ganesan. BEST GROUP - VALUS BY WF - EVAL	
Fission	1.0+0	1.0+2	BOL	Theo Conf	NEANDC(E)-163U	Jan 75	Menapace+MULTLVL EFFECT,GRAPHS	
Fission	1.5+3	2.0+3	FEI	Expt Conf	AE 38 43	Jan 75	Dvukhsherstnov+ SIGPU - 239/SIGU - 235	+
	2.0+3			Jour	SJA 38 49	Jul 75	. ENGLISH OF AE 38,43	
	1.5+3	2.0+3		Data	EXFOR40321.002	Feb 76	.RATIO PU239 TO U235 GVN	
Fission	1.0-2	3.0+1	MOL	Expt Conf	NEANDC(E)-163U	Jan 75	Wagemans+GRAPH,TBL,CFD OTHER RESULTS	
	8.0-3	3.0+1		Jour	ANE 2 1 25	Jan 75	- + 2 EXPTS MERGED.G TEMP DEP	
Fission	None		MUU	ExTh Jour	NP/A 256 220	Jan 75	Glassel+ DOUBLE HUMPED BARR VIA DPF	
Fission	1.0+4	8.0+4	FEI	Expt Jour	AE 38 82	Feb 75	Kononov+ TOF,AVGSIG(NEUT - E),TBL	+
				Rept	YK-15 12	Aug 74	. TOF,VDG.AVGD SIG, TABLE	
				Jour	SJA 38 105	Aug 75	.ENGLISH OF AE 38 82 2/75	
	1.0+4	8.0+4		Data	EXFOR40412.	Jan 77	SIG FOR 7 E - RANGES+ U-235 RATIO	
Fission	Fiss		NBS	Expt Jour	NT 25 237	Feb 75	Grundl+ RATIO TO U235 IN CFRMF	+
	Fiss			Data	EXFOR10479.004	Apr 75	1PT,RATIO TO U235	
Fission	None		UCN	Theo Abst	BAP 20 151	Feb 75	Mcknight+EFFECTS OF UNCERT.NDG.	
Fission	1.0+3	1.0+6	HAR	Expt Conf	75Kiev 6 49	May 75	Gayther+ SIG(E),TABLE.CFD OTHS,GRAPH	+
				Conf	75Wash. 564	Mar 75	- .TBLS,GRPHS.CFD EVAL SIG	
	1.0+3	1.0+6		Data	EXFOR20428.	Jul 75	360PTS.SIGMA.	
Fission		+6	HAR	Expt Prog	AERE-PR/NP22	Mar 75	Coates+TOF.GAS SCIN DET.REL U235.TBD	
Fission	Fiss		HED	Eval Conf	75Wash. 189	Mar 75	Mcelroy.235U THERM FISS SPECT AVG CS	
Fission	3.0+6	5.0+6	LAS	Theo Conf	75Wash. 129	Mar 75	Moore.GRPH R MATR STAT CALC CFD EXP	
Fission	1.1+1	2.6+1	BLA	Expt Conf	75Kiev 6 87	May 75	Toshkov+ SIG(E) CFD CALC.GRAPH	
Fission	2.0+6	2.0+7	BRC	Eval Conf	75Kiev 1 239	May 75	Jary. STATMOD CALC,VALUES GIVEN	
Fission	2.5-2	2.4+4	FEI	Expt Conf	75Kiev 6 67	May 75	Zhuravlev+ SIG AT 3ES.TABLE	
Fission	2.0+3	3.0+4	LEB	Expt Conf	75Kiev 6 61	May 75	Bergman+ SDS. AVG SIG(6E - RANGES).TBL	
Fission	2.5-2		NIR	Expt Conf	75Kiev 6 71	May 75	Gavrilov+ REL AU197,CO59(NG).SIG GVN	
Fission	5.0+4	6.0+6	SAC	Expt Conf	75Kiev 6 24	May 75	Blons+ GAS SCIN,STRUCT OBSERVD.	
Fission	7.0+0	6.0+1	BRC	Expt Rept	CEA-N-1798 67	Jun 75	Simon+ (N,GF)) REAC ANAL	
				ExTh Conf	75Kiev 5 323	May 75	Trochon+ (N,GF).G SPEC VS - E.GRAPH	

94 Plutonium 239

Quantity	Energy (ev) Min	Energy (ev) Max	Lab	Type	Documentation Ref Vol Page	Date	Author, Comments	Data
Fission	2.0+2	3.0+4	FEI	Expt	Jour AE 39 291	Oct 75	Bergman+ AVGSIG(NEUT-E),TBL	+
					Jour SJA 39 916	Apr 76	. ENGL OF AE 39 291	
	2.0+2	3.0+4		Data	EXFOR40435.003	Nov 76	AVG SIG FOR 21 E-RANGES	
Fission	2.5-2		NIR	Expt	Jour AE 39 285	Oct 75	Zhuravlev+ SIG GIVEN,BY CD-DIFFERENC	+
					Rept YK- 19 3	May 75	- + CD-DIFFERENCE, SIG GIVEN	
					Jour SJA 39 907	Apr 76	. ENGL OF AE 39 285	
	2.5-2				Data EXFOR40339.002	Mar 76	1 PNT	
Fission	1.0+6	6.0+6	LAS	Eval	Prog LA- 6164-PR 2	Dec 75	Stewart.NDG.DISCREPANCY IN NF CS.	
Fission	2.5-2		MAG	Eval	Rept EPRI-NP-163	Dec 75	Beer+MONTECARLO ANAL 70HELSINKI P287	
Fission	Fiss		MOL	Expt	Prog INDC(SEC)-51	Dec 75	Fabry.P85.AVG(U35-SPEC),CFD ENDF,TBL	
					Conf 75Wash. 254	Mar 75	- +INTEG CS REL U238NF= 5.93+-.13	
Fission	0.0+0	1.0+7	CAI	Theo	Jour AKE 27 1 47	76	El Nadi+ QUASI-MOLECULAR MODEL	
Fission	2.0+3	1.4+5	FEI	Expt	Rept YK- 22 3	76	Zhuravlev+ SIG FOR 4 ES,TABLE	
Fission	None		MUN	Theo	Diss GRYNTAKIS	Mar 76	Gryntakis.,CALC.OF WESTCOTTS G-FUNCT	
					Jour RCA 22 128	Mar 75	- +,EQUIVALENT TO THESIS	
Fission	1.0+1	7.0+4	LRL	Expt	Prog ERDA-NDC-3 66	May 76	Czirr+.TOF.CS REL LI6.ANAL TBD.NDG	
Fission	1.0+5	6.0+6	ANL	Eval	Conf 76ANL 156	Jun 76	Poenitz+ U238/U235 EVAL.GRPH,TBL.CFD	
					Conf 76ANL 156	Jun 76	- +PU239/U235EVAL.GRPH,CFD.	
Fission	1.0+4	2.0+7	ANL	Revw	Conf 76ANL	Jun 76	Poenitz+SUPPLEMENT TO CONF.DATA FILE	
Fission	2.0+6	1.0+7	LAS	Expt	Abst BAP 2 196	Apr 57	Smith+,REL U238,DBL ION CHAMB,+ -5PC	+
	2.0+6	2.0+7			Data EXFOR12316.009	Jun 76	. 26 PTS. SIGMA.	
Fission	1.5+6	5.0+6	NYB	Expt	Jour PL/B 62 280	Jun 76	Goldstone+VIBRATIONL RES IDENTIFD.	
Fission	2.0+2	1.5+3	BRC	Revw	Conf 76Lowell 641	Jul 76	Michaudon.RVW FISSION PROCESSES	
	None				Conf 75Wash. 202	Mar 75	. FISSION REVIEW.TH+EXPTS.	
Fission	Maxwl		PAH	ExTh	Conf 76Lowell 725	Jul 76	Hooshyar+STATMDL APLD TO EXPT.DATA	
	7.0+6	1.6+7			Conf 76Lowell 725	Jul 76	- + 2ES.STATMD CFD XPT	
Fission	Fast		LON	Expt	Prog NEANDC(E)172 8	Aug 76	Hannan+ REACTOR SPECT,RATIO TO U5NF	
Fission	2.8+6	1.8+7	TUD	Expt	Prog ZFK-315 172	Aug 76	Arlt+ SIG AT 4ES,1-2PERC PRECIS.TBD	
Fission	1.0+6	2.6+6	CAD	Expt	Conf 73Kiev 3 27	May 73	Szabo+ SUMMARY,CFD OTHERS.GRAPH+TABL	+
	8.0+5	2.6+6			Rept CEA-R-4804	Dec 76	- +73KIEV MODIFIED	
	3.5+4	9.7+5			Rept CEA-R-4804	Dec 76	- +SAME AS 70ANL	
	2.5+4	1.0+6			Jour AE 29 395	Nov 70	Leroi.ABST FRANC-SOV SEM DUBNA 6/70	
					Jour SJA 29 1156	Nov 70	.	
	8.0+5	2.6+6			Data EXFOR20570.003	Mar 76	20PTS.SIGMA.	
Fission	1.0+4	5.5+6	CAD	Expt	Conf 76ANL 208	Jun 76	Szabo+NEW+REVISED VALS.GRPH.TBLS.CFD	+
	2.3+6	5.5+6			Rept CEA-R-4804	Dec 76	- + NEW MEASUREMENT,GRAPHS,TABLES	
	2.3+6	5.5+6			Data EXFOR20618.003	Jun 76	13PTS.SIGMA.	
Fission	3.0-1	2.0+2	BRC	Expt	Diss TROCHON	77	Trochon.N GAMMA F PROCESSUS IN RES	
Fission	+7		RI	Expt	Conf 77Kiev	77	Adamov+ SIG=1861+-30 MB	
Res Int Fiss	None		ORL	Revw	Conf 55Geneva 5 96	Aug 55	Macklin+.P833 ,EXPT CFD THEORY,TABLE	
Res Int Fiss	8.0-1	7.0+2	HAR	Expt	Jour JNE 2 177	Mar 56	Richmond+.SF/E AVERAGED FOR 6 E GRPS	
Res Int Fiss	1.0+0	5.0+1	ANL	Expt	Conf 58Geneva 15 127	Sep 58	Bollinger+.PPR687,VAL GVN	
Res Int Fiss	1.5-1	1.0+6	ORL	Eval	Jour NSE 6 100	Aug 59	Stoughton+,BEST VALUE 2000+-200B	
Res Int Fiss	5.0-1		BET	Expt	Jour NSE 9 341	Mar 61	Hardy+ 327+-22B REL AU 1535B	+
	5.0-1				Data EXFOR12405.003	Jun 76	. 1 PT. RI	
Res Int Fiss	4.4-1		ANL	Theo	Abst ANS 6 39	Jun 63	Persiani+RNEGCRESRCONTRIB.INFNITLDIL	
Res Int Fiss	5.3-1		WIN	Expt	Rept AEEW-R-217	Aug 63	Hardiman+.CD RATIOS.E-CD VALUES CALC	
Res Int Fiss	4.5-1		CRC	Expt	Rept CRRP-1183	Feb 64	Bigham. NRX REL IN,B,LI,AU 324+-9B	+
	4.5-1				Data EXFOR12230.	Jun 76	. 2 PTS. RATIO	
Res Int Fiss	5.0-1	1.0+6	AE	Expt	Rept AE-181	Apr 65	Hellstrand.CD+B FILTERS USED	+
	5.0-1				Prog EANDC(OR)33L	Jun 64	- + ABST.VALUE GIVEN 319+-12	
	5.0-1	1.0+6			Data EXFOR20018.003	Sep 71	1PNT.	
Res Int Fiss	5.0-1		KAP	Comp	Conf 66S.Diego 2 299	Feb 66	Feiner+.COMPIL PREV RESULTS+RECOMMND	
Res Int Fiss	5.0-1	1.0+7	BNW	Theo	Conf 66Wash. 75	Mar 66	Liikala+, TBLS OF RES.INTEGRALS	
Res Int Fiss	4.7+0	1.0+4	INA	Eval	Conf 66Paris 2 333	Oct 66	Hennies.PPR5.TBL RECOM DATA CFD OTHR	
					Rept NAA-SR-11980 5	May 67	- . RECOMMENDED DATA.REVISED	
Res Int Fiss	5.0-1		JAE	Expt	Jour NST 4 43	Jan 67	Yasuno.CD-RATIO,366PM26B.REL TO AU	+
	5.0-1				Data EXFOR20310.002	Jun 74	1PNT.	
			2.0+4	DUB Expt	Prog YFI-5 61	Oct 67	Rjabov+ TABLES	
					Rept INDC-232E	67	. ENGL OF YFI-5 61	
Res Int Fiss	2.9+2	3.0+3	WEW	Theo	Jour NSE 34 181	Nov 68	Dyos.STATISTICAL CALC 17,81+-1,1.41B	
Res Int Fiss	Pile		UJV	Theo	Rept UJV-2224	69	Stepanek. 6 GROUP CONSTANTS	
Res Int Fiss	1.0+1	2.0+4	HAR	Comp	Rept AERE-M-2157	Jan 69	James+ TBL RES INTEG SCISRS DATA	
Res Int Fiss	1.0+2	3.0+2	ANL	Theo	Jour NSE 35 297	Feb 69	Pennington+ 1-LVL+MULTILVL CALC CFD	
Res Int Fiss	6.3-1		CAS	Eval	Jour NSE 40 51	70	Gibello+,EVAL. RES. INT. = 289 B	

94 Plutonium 239

Quantity	Energy (ev) Min	Max	Lab	Type	Documentation Ref Vol Page	Date	Author, Comments	Data
Res Int Fiss	Maxwl		FTI	Expt	Jour AE 28 359	Apr 70	BAK+.INTEGRAL VALUE GIVEN,CFD OTHER	+
					Jour SJA 28 460	Apr 70	.ENGLISH OF AE 28 359	
					Jour EAF 28 4 112	Apr 70	. FRENCH OF AE 28 359	
	Maxwl				Data EXFOR40349.003	Dec 77	CD – DIFF,REL U235. 1 DATAPNT	
Res Int Fiss		+7	RI	Expt	Jour AE 28 359	Apr 70	BAK+ INTEGRAL VALUE GIVEN,CFD OTHER	
	5.0 – 1				Prog YFI – 8 17	Dec 69	BAK+ CD – RATIO,REL U – 235,VALUES GIVEN	
					Prep INDC(CCP) – 8	Dec 70	. P.22. ENGL OF YFI – 8 17	
		+7			Jour EAF 28 4 112	Apr 70	. FRENCH OF AE 28 359	
Res Int Fiss	– 4	+7	BNW	Eval	Rept BNWL – 1312	May 70	Simons+MCELROY,RI=345.6B	
Res Int Fiss	5.0 – 1		RI	Expt	Rept INDC(CCP) – 8	Dec 70	. P22.ENGL OF YFI – 8 17	
Res Int Fiss	3.0+0		KAP	Expt	Jour NSE 44 180	May 71	Eiland+ CD – RH FILTER 231+ – 14B	+
	3.0+0				Data EXFOR10143.015	Aug 73	1PNT.	
Res Int Fiss	5.0 – 1	+6	COR	Expt	Jour NSE 46 31	Oct 71	Draper.INTEGRAL SIG TIMES E.4 SPECTR	
	+0	+1			Abst DA/B 31 1466	Sep 70	– .EXPT FOR 4 SPEC,CFD CALC	
Res Int Fiss	Pile		KFK	Eval	Rept KFK – 1453	Mar 72	Eberle+ 324B	
Res Int Fiss	5.0 – 1		IAE	Revw	Rept IAEA – 143 897	Apr 72	Lemmel.FISS,EVALUTS+RECENT EXPTS,TBL	
Res Int Fiss	9.0+0	3.0+1	GEL	Expt	Jour JNE 26 293	Jun 72	DERUYTTER FISS,RES INTGLS,IN 6 – 30EV.	+
	9.0+0	3.0+1			Data EXFOR20132.003	Mar 73	6PTS.	
Res Int Fiss	2.0+1	1.2+2	NIL	Theo	Rept PINST – 73 1	Feb 73	Bhatti+ IN PUO2,CRYSTAL – BINDING EFF	
Res Int Fiss	5.5 – 1		RCN	Revw	Conf 73Paris 2 271	Mar 73	Zijp.RECOMMENDED,FROM LITERATURE,TBL	
Res Int Fiss	5.0 – 1		SGA	Comp	Conf 73Paris 1 233	Mar 73	Eder+ INCLUDING 1/V PART OF SIG,TBL	
					Rept SGAE – PH – 141	Feb 73	.SAME AS 73PARIS,NO DETAILS,TBP	
Res Int Fiss	5.0 – 1		KFI	Eval	Rept KFKI – 74 – 45	Jul 74	Gado.PARTIAL+TOTAL FROM RES – PARS,TBL	
Res Int Fiss	5.0 – 1		NIR	Expt	Jour AE 39 285	Oct 75	Zhuravlev+ RI GIVEN,BY CD – DIFFERENCE	+
					Rept YK – 19 3	May 75	– + CD – DIFFERENCE,RES – INT GVN	
					Jour SJA 39 907	Apr 76	. ENGL OF AE 39 285	
	5.0 – 1				Data EXFOR40337.002	Mar 76	1 PNT	
Alpha	2.5 – 2	1.0+0	LAS	Expt	Rept LA – 266	Apr 45	Anderson+,VARIATION UNCERTAIN	
Alpha	1.0 – 2	1.0+6	NDA	ExTh	Rept NDA – MEMO – 15 1	Jul 52	Weisskopf.EXPT+THEOR PREDICTIONS	
Alpha	Pile		ANL	Revw	Conf 55Geneva 3 198	Aug 55	Zinn.P814,VAL GVN,DISCUSS OF RESULTS	
Alpha	Pile		ANL	Expt	Conf 55Geneva 4 105	Aug 55	Inghram+.P596,VAL GVN,MASS – SPECTRM	
Alpha	1.0 – 2	1.0 – 1	BNL	Revw	Conf 55Geneva 4 311	Aug 55	Palevsky.GRAPH,EXPT DESCRIBED,P587	
Alpha	Pile	1.5+6	KAP	Expt	Conf 55Geneva 4 315	Aug 55	Kanne+.TABLE FOR SEVERAL ES,PPR595	+
	Pile				Data EXFOR12421.003	Jun 76	. 1 PT.	
Alpha	Maxwl	5.0+5	ORL	Revw	Conf 55Geneva 3 19	Aug 55	Weinberg.P862,VAL FOR 6ES GVN,REFS	
Alpha	1.5 – 2	5.0 – 1	CCP		Rept AEC – TR – 2435PT1	56	.USSR CURVE OF 1OVER1PLUSALPHA P11	
Alpha	+0	+2	BNL	Expt	Prog WASH – 190 9	Feb 56	Hughes+ FAST CHOPPER. TBD	
Alpha	4.5 – 1		CRC	Expt	Rept CRC – 633	Mar 56	Cornish+ NRX ALFA=0.60	
	Pile				Rept CRC – 633	Mar 56	– + NRX ALFA=0.43+ – 0.020	
	6.0+0	1.0+2			Rept CRC – 633	Mar 56	– + NRX ALFA=0.48+ – 0.037	
Alpha	2.0 – 2	8.0 – 1	ANL	Expt	Rept AERE – NP/R – 2076	Jul 56	Bollinger.CURVE AGREES WITH S	
	7.8+0	2.2+1			Rept AERE – NP/R – 2076	Jul 56	– .ONLY NEAR RES CFD S	
Alpha	1.8 – 2	7.0 – 1	BNL	Expt	Jour JNE 3 177	Oct 56	Palevsky+ CALC FROM ETA,IF NU CONST	
Alpha	2.5 – 2		BNL	Eval	Rept BNL – 325	Jan 57	Hughes+ WORLD CONSIST. VAL. .39+ – .03	
Alpha	4.6+2	1.0+7	KAP	Eval	Rept KAPL – 1756 1	Jun 57	Baraff.CURV REV PCALC ASU NU 2D90	
Alpha	Pile		ANL	Expt	Jour NSE 2 657	Sep 57	Kafalas+,3PTS EBR – I CURVS NO E	
Alpha	Maxwl		HAR	Eval	Rept AERE – NP/R – 2140	Dec 57	Egelstaff+ CONSISTENT VALUES 2200M/S	
				Comp	Rept AERE – NP/R – 2104	Mar 57	– .EXPT METHODS FOR HAR VALUE	
				Revw	Conf 55Geneva 4 307	Aug 55	– +.VAL GVN,EXPT DESCRBD,P425	
Alpha	1.1 – 3		HAR	Expt	Jour JNE 6 285	May 58	Cocking.FILTER NEUTS,ALFA=.300+ – .040	+
Alpha	1.0 – 3	1.0+0	BNL	Comp	Conf 58Geneva 16 8	Sep 58	Hughes.PPR2483,CURVE,MANY REFS	
Alpha	1.0+2	1.0+6	KAP	Expt	Jour NSE 4 745	Dec 58	Sampson+,CURVE GIVEN	
Alpha	Maxwl	2.8+1	CCP	Revw	Jour AE 7 429	Nov 59	Kirpichnikov+ CURVE OF COMPILED DATA	
					Jour SJA 7 898	Mar 61	TRANSLATN.*	
Alpha	2.5 – 2		AE	Comp	Rept AE – 11	Apr 60	Story+,DISCUSSION+TABULATN OF MEASTS	
Alpha			HAN	Eval	Conf 61RPI 3	May 61	Leonard.	
Alpha	5.0 – 3	2.5+0	GA	Eval	Rept GA – 2113	Jun 61	Wikner+.TABLE 100 E POINTS	
Alpha	Maxwl		CRC	Expt	Conf 61Saclay 57	Jul 61	Westcott. 2200METRE/SEC SIG GIVEN	
Alpha	+4	1.0+6	ANL	Eval	Conf 61Vienna 1 29	Aug 61	Smith.P76,CURVE,MANY REFS GVN	
Alpha	2.5 – 2	1.0+6	ROS	Revw	Jour KE 5 701	Jan 62	Falkenberg.VAL GVN,REFERENCES	
Alpha	3.0+4	1.0+6	LAS	Expt	Jour NSE 12 169	Feb 62	Hopkins+ TABLE+CURVE CFD OTHER EXPTS	+
					Conf 61Vienna 1 111	Aug 61	.SUPERSEDED	
					Conf 61Saclay 407	Jul 61	.SUPERSEDED	
	3.0+4	1.0+6			Data EXFOR12331.007	Jun 76	. 9 PTS.	
Alpha	Maxwl		CRC	Revw	Rept EANDC(CAN) – 15	Nov 62	Hanna. COMPARES VALUES	
Alpha	Fast		CCP	Expt	Jour AE 16 497	Jun 64	Ivanov+ VARIATION ON AXIS BR5 REACTR	
					Jour JNE 19 451	Jun 65	TRANSLATN.*	
					Jour SJA 16 615	Jun 64	TRANSLATN.*	

94 Plutonium 239

Quantity	Energy (ev) Min	Energy (ev) Max	Lab	Type	Documentation Ref Vol Page	Date	Author, Comments	Data
Alpha	2.6−2		CEA	Revw Conf	64Vienna 19	Dec 64	Vendryes+ VALUE TBL,OTHER COMPILATNS	
Alpha	Fast		ANL	Expt Jour	NSE 21 179	Feb 65	Hoffman+ CFD. WITH DIVEN, ANL.	
Alpha	1.0−1	5.0+1	RPI	Expt Prog	WASH−1064 158	Oct 65	Weston+,LINAC,TBD	
Alpha	2.5−2		BNW	Theo Conf	66Wash. 75	Mar 66	Liikala+, TBLS OF LITER. VALUES	
Alpha	3.0−1	1.1+1	HAR	Expt Rept	AERE−M−1709	Sep 66	Brooks+ TOF.LINAC. GRPH.	
	3.5−1	1.0+1		Data	EXFOR20623.009	Dec 76	7PTS.	
Alpha	Maxwl		CRC	Expt Conf	66Paris 2 17	Oct 66	Durham+ XPT DESCRIBED, MASSPECTRM.	+
	Maxwl			Data	EXFOR12428.008	Jun 76	. 1 PT.	
Alpha	2.0+4	6.0+5	ORL	Expt Conf	66ANL 22	Oct 66	Lottin+ PULSED NEUTS+SCINT +−10PC	
				Rept	ORNL−P−2599	Dec 66	.FULL PAPER.	
Alpha	1.7+4	6.0+6	ORL	Expt Conf	66Paris 2 233	Oct 66	Desaussure+PPR48.TBL,SIMULT CAPT+FIS	+
	1.8+4	6.0+6		Data	EXFOR12409.	Jun 76	. 41 PTS.	
Alpha	1.0+4	2.0+4	LAS	Theo Jour	PR 158 1127	Jun 67	Bell. PREDICT 10−20KEV BY SYSTEMATCS	
Alpha	4.0+1	2.5+5	AI	Theo Rept	NAA−SR−12515	Oct 67	Otter. CHANNEL FISSION CALC OKS EXPT	
Alpha	5.5+0	6.0+4	DUB	Expt Prog	YFI−5 61	Oct 67	Rjabov+ CURVES	
				Rept	INDC−232E	67	. ENGL OF YFI−5 61	
Alpha	Pile		BNW	Expt Jour	NSE 30 222	Nov 67	Reardon+ PRTR,AVG ALFA=0.426+−0.019	
Alpha	2.0+2	3.0+4	HAR	Expt Rept	EANDC(UK)96	68	Patrick+ TOF.LINAC.	+
	2.0+2	3.0+4		Data	EXFOR20002.007	Nov 70	20PTS.	
Alpha	Maxwl	+3	RPI	Expt Prog	WASH−1093 113	Apr 68	Weinstein+ LINAC ANAL TBC NDG	
Alpha	1.0+2	1.2+4	FEI	Theo Conf	68Dubna § 2	Jun 68	Abagyan+.MEAN W FLUCTUATION EFFECT	
	1.0+2	3.0+4		Rept	BNL−TR−367	Sep 70	. ENGLISH OF 68DUBNA	
Alpha	1.0+0	1.0+6	WIN	Eval Rept	JAERI−1162	Jun 68	Durston.KATSURAGI(JAE)	
Alpha	Maxwl	2.5−2	HAR	Expt Rept	AERE−R−5874	Aug 68	Cabell. RE−ASSESSED.T=116C.TBL	+
	Maxwl			Jour	JIN 28 2467	May 67	− +. IRR. IN MAXWELLIAN SPECTRUM	
	2.5−2			Conf	66Paris 2 3	Oct 66	− . = 1 DATA INDEX LINES	
	Maxwl			Rept	AERE−R−4173	Sep 63	− +ADDENDUM.	
				Jour	JIN 25 607	Jun 63	− +PLUTO REACTOR	
Alpha	Fast		AE	Expt Abst	AF 37 326	Sep 68	Andersson+. DIFFERENT FR0 SPEC. NDG	
Alpha	1.0+2	3.0+4	HAR	Expt Conf	70Helsinki 1 315	Jun 70	Schomberg+33. EXPTL+EVALUATED DATA	+
				Prog	AERE−PR/NP15	May 69	− + GRAPH DET MODIFIED TBD	
				Prog	AERE−PR/NP14	Oct 68	Patrick+ TOF LINAC TBL AVG VALUES	
	1.0+2	3.0+4		Data	EXFOR20476.005	Jan 76	22PTS.	
Alpha	1.0−2	3.0+4	GA	Expt Prog	WASH−1124 46	Nov 68	Friesenhahn+ TOF+SCINT NO DATA GIVEN	
Alpha	1.0+2	3.0+4	TRM	Expt Rept	BARC−421	69	Mahalingam+ 0−POWER TEST OF NEW VALS	
	1.0+2	1.0+5		Revw Conf	68Bombay 2 321	Dec 68	Garg. SURVEY OF ALFA(E)+−ERROR DATA	
Alpha	1.0+2	3.0+2	ANL	Expt Jour	NSE 35 297	Feb 69	Pennington+ 1−LVL+MULTILVL CALC CFD	
Alpha	5.0+2	1.0+5	SAC	Eval Prog	EANDC(E)115U	Mar 69	Ribon+, EVALUATION	
Alpha	1.0+2	1.0+5	CCP	Revw Jour	AE 27 363	Oct 69	Kazachovskij. 3 DATA SETS CFD,TABLE	
				Jour	SJA 27 1138	Oct 69	.TRANSLATN.*NO 4	
Alpha	1.0+2	1.0+5	ITK	Theo Conf	69Roorke 2 204	Dec 69	Sengupta+ ALFA VS E,STAT RESON ANAL	
Alpha	1.0+2	3.0+4	DUB	Expt Priv	RYABOV	70	ACCURACY ANALYSIS,REVW+RECOM VALUES	
Alpha	0.0+0	6.0+6	FEI	Eval Prog	YFI−11 13	70	Vorobyeva+ ABST,TBL VALUE FOR MAXW	
				Prog	INDC(CCP)−31	Dec 72	.PAGE 12,ENGLISH OF YFI−11 13	
Alpha	1.0+2	1.0+6	KFK	Revw Jour	AKE 15 26	70	Schmidt. REVW ON EXPTS,GRPHS,CFD TH	
				Rept	KFK−966	Apr 69	− . GRPH EXPT DATA+ EVALS.	
Alpha	1.0+2	1.0+5	CCP	Revw Jour	AE 28 38	Jan 70	Sukhoruchkin. REVIEW,ALFA(E) GRAPHS	
				Jour	EAF 28 1 49	Jan 70	. FRENCH OF AE 28 38	
Alpha	1.5+4	1.0+6	ORL	Eval Rept	ORNL−TM−2797	Jan 70	Greene+,CURVE EVALUATED ALFA	
Alpha	Pile		ANL	Expt Jour	NSE 39 368	Mar 70	Redman+,LOW−FLUX METH,0.516+−0.040	
Alpha	Pile		ANL	Expt Jour	NSE 40 132	Apr 70	Till+,NULL−REACTIVITY METHOD	
Alpha	+2	+5	JAE	Theo Jour	NSE 40 25	Apr 70	Ishiguro+,STATISTICAL CALCULATN,CURV	
Alpha	1.5+2	1.0+5	TOK	Theo Jour	NST 7 157	Apr 70	Kikuchi+.CALC USING SPIN DEPENDNT WF	
				Jour	NST 5 86	Feb 68	− + SUPERSEDED.	
Alpha	+5	+7	ANL	Revw Conf	70Helsinki 2 119	Jun 70	Davey.112.STATUS OF DATA ABOVE RESON	
Alpha	1.0+2	1.0+7	CAD	Eval Conf	70Helsinki 2 465	Jun 70	Barre+73 MICROSC CFD INTEGRAL DATA	
				Conf	69London § 1.15	Jun 69	− + INTEGRL XPT CORRECTS MICROSIG	
				Rept	EANDC(E)120L	Mar 69	+RAVIER EVAL INTEGRAL MEAS	
				Rept	CEA−N−989	Sep 68	− + ADJUSTD TO INTEGR XPTS.TBL+GR	
Alpha	2.5−2		CRC	Expt Conf	70Helsinki 1 287	Jun 70	Lounsbury+THR FLUX VAL AT 2200 M/S.−	+
	2.5−2			Data	EXFOR10013.004	Sep 72	1PT.VAL AT 2200M/S.	
Alpha	1.0+2	3.0+4	DUB	Expt Rept	JINR−P3−5112	Jun 70	Kononov+ E−GROUPS AVGD ALF,TBLS+GRPH	+
				Rept	INDC(CCP)−15	Dec 71	*PG 38.ENGL OF YFI−10	
				Rept	YFI−10 35	May 71	*	
				Conf	70Helsinki 1 345	Jun 70	*SAME DATA TBL 6+GRAPH	

94 Plutonium 239

Quantity	Energy (ev) Min	Max	Lab	Type	Documentation Ref Vol Page	Date	Author, Comments	Data
Alpha	1.0+2	2.0+4	DUB	Expt	Rept JINR-P3-5113	Jun 70	Rjabov+ E-GROUPS AVGD ALF,TBLS+GRPH	+
	1.0+2	3.0+4			Jour AE 30 362	Apr 71	Kurov+ TOF. AVG ALF(A),TABLE,GRAPH	
	1.0+2	2.0+4			Jour AE 30 258	Mar 71	- + TOF,SCINT,AVG ALFA.TABL+GRAPH	
					Conf 70Helsinki 1 345	Jun 70	. *SAME DATA TBL1+3,GRPH	
					Prog YFI-11 35	70	Kurov+ ABST,SAME TBL AS JINR-5113	
					Jour EAF 24 81	Apr 68	*	
					Jour AE 24 351	Apr 68	*SUPERSEDED BY JINR-5113	
					Jour SJA 24 435	Apr 68	* ENGL OF AE 24 351	
					Prog INDC(CCP)-31	Dec 72	.PAGE 34,ENGLISH OF YFI-11 35	
	1.0+2	3.0+4			Jour SJA 30 446	Nov 71	. ENGL OF AE 30 362	
	1.0+2	2.0+4			Jour SJA 30 315	Oct 71	. ENGL OF AE 30 258	
	1.0+2	3.0+4			Data EXFOR40025.	Aug 70	ALFA AT 19 ES,JINR,2 TOF RESOLUTIONS	
	1.0+2	2.0+4			Data EXFOR40024.003	Aug 70	ALFA AT 19 ES,JINR-P3-5113 TABLE III	
Alpha	Pile		FAR	Expt	Conf 70Helsinki 2 487	Jun 70	Bouchard+96. 2 TYPES OF INTEGRL XPTS	
				Diss	DARROUZET	Mar 70	Darrouzet.ERMINE	
Alpha	+2	+7	HAR	Revw	Conf 70Helsinki 1 267	Jun 70	James.107. ACCURACY CFD REACTOR COST	
Alpha	1.5+2	9.5+5	ITE	Revw	Conf 70Helsinki 1 307	Jun 70	Sukhoruchkin.127.TABLE OF DATA SETS	
Alpha	Maxwl	1.0+4	ITE	Expt	Conf 70Helsinki 1 339	Jun 70	Beljaev+89. TABLE OF ALPHA(E) GIVEN	+
					Rept ITE-780	70	Belyaev+ TOF,2 METHODS,MANY ES,TBLS	
					Rept YFI-9 18	Dec 69	.	
	7.8+0	1.0+4			Data EXFOR40087.	Nov 73	.5 SUBENTRIES	
Alpha	1.0+2	1.0+4	LAS	Expt	Conf 70Helsinki 1 543	Jun 70	Farrell+46. ALFA VS E. GRAPH+TABLE.	+
	1.0+2	2.0+4			Data EXFOR10326.002	Dec 74	20 PTS	
Alpha	1.0+2	6.5+2	SAC	Expt	Conf 70Helsinki 1 495	Jun 70	Trochon+62. TABLE OF ALFA AT 6RANGES	
Alpha	+6	+7	WIN	Revw	Conf 70Helsinki 2 391	Jun 70	Campbell.116. MICROSCOPIC VS INTEGRL	
Alpha	2.9-1	3.0+4	LRL	Expt	Jour NSE 41 56	Jul 70	Czirr+,LINAC,RESOLVD+UNRESOLVD RESON	+
	1.0+2	3.0+4			Conf 70Helsinki 1 331	Jun 70	- +47. TABLE OF ALFA(E), LINAC	
	1.0+2	3.0+4			Data EXFOR12424.005	Jun 76	. 20 PTS.	
Alpha	1.0+2	5.0+4	IAE	Revw	Conf INDC(NDS)-25L	Aug 70	Konshin+ RECOMMENDATIONS OF PANEL	
Alpha	+5	+7	KFK	Revw	Rept KFK-1303	Oct 70	Boehme+ MICROSC CFD INTEGRL DATA	
					Conf 70Helsinki 2 427	Jun 70	.EQUIVALENT*	
Alpha	Pile		BNL	Expt	Rept ANS 13 754	Nov 70	Takahashi+.HFBR INTEGRAL MEAST.TABLE	
Alpha	None		KUR	Expt	Jour AE 29 395	Nov 70	Muradjan+ ABST FRANC-SOV SEM DUBNA	+
	1.0+2	3.0+3			Conf 71Kiev 1 309	May 71	- + ALFA(E) GIVEN	
	None				Jour SJA 29 1156	Nov 70	TRANSLATN.*	
	1.0+2	3.0+3			Data EXFOR40373.002	Dec 77	AVG ALFA(E),9 PNTS.	
Alpha	2.0+4	5.0+5	SAC	Expt	Rept CEA-N-1368	Nov 70	Lottin. WITH OAKRIDGE VGF	
	2.0+4	6.0+5			Prog EANDC(E)89U	Jan 68	Michaudon+AT ORNL 5MEV VDG	
Alpha	2.0-2	1.0+5	TRM	Revw	Conf 70Madurai 2 635	Dec 70	Rastogi+ REVIEW OF EXPTL STATUS, TBL	
Alpha	1.0-3	1.0+7	KFK	Eval	Rept KFK-1340	Feb 71	Hinkelmann+TABLE OF EVALUATED DATA	
	1.0+2	1.0+5			Rept KFK-1340	Feb 71	- +EXPT DATA,EVALUATED CURVE	
	1.0-3	1.0+7			Rept KFK-750	Jan 68	Schmidt. CURVES	
	1.0-2	2.5+0			Conf 66S.Diego 2 223	Feb 66	- . SEE KFK-120	
	1.0-3	1.0+7			Rept KFK-120 2	Dec 65	- . REISSUED	
	1.0-2	2.5+0			Rept KFK-120 1	Nov 65	- .+EVAL REVIEW.TABLE 18ES	
	1.0-2	1.0+7			Rept KFK-120 2	Dec 62	- .GRAPHS AND TABULATED DATA	
	1.0-2	2.5+0			Conf 61Vienna 1 3	Aug 61	- . P4. SUPERSEDED	
Alpha	2.5-2		ANL	Eval	Jour 71Knoxvill 560	Mar 71	DE VOLPI. ADJUSTED VALUE GIVEN	
Alpha	Pile		KAP	Expt	Jour NSE 44 180	May 71	Eiland+ CD-RH FILTER 0.723+ - 0.044	
Alpha	Pile		ANL	Expt	Jour NSE 45 37	Jul 71	Kato+.FAST REACTOR SPEC. INTEG MEAST	
					Jour ANS 13 88	Jul 70	.SUPERSEDED	
Alpha	Pile		ANL	Expt	Jour NSE 45 87	Jul 71	Bretscher+.FAST SPEC.INTEG MEAST	
					Abst ANS 13 89	Jul 70	- +,REACTIVITY - REACTION RATE	
	2.0-2	3.0+4	ORL	Expt	Jour NSE 45 25	Jul 71	Gwin+IONIZ CH,METAL FOIL CFD ENDF/B.	
	2.0-2	2.0+3			Rept ORNL-4707	Jul 71	- +CAPTURE AND FISSION DATA.	
	2.0-2	3.0+4			Jour NSE 40 306	May 70	- +CS SPRSDD BY JNSE 45 PAGE 25.	
Alpha	2.5-2	3.0+4	CCP	Revw	Jour AE 31 245	Sep 71	Sukhoruchkin.DIRECT EXPTS,TBLS,GRPHS	
					Jour SJA 31 977	Apr 72	* ENGL OF AE 31 245	
Alpha	2.5-2		HAR	Revw	Conf 71Canterby 65	Sep 71	Fudge+.FOR BURN-UP.TABLE AVAIL DATA.	
Alpha	Pile		ANL	Expt	Rept ANL-7795	Dec 71	Iskenderian+.BARE+CD-COVERED SAMPLES	
					Abst ANS 14 371	Jun 71	- . CFD OTHERS	
Alpha	1.0+2	6.5+2	CCP	Revw	Jour AE 31 595	Dec 71	Sukhoruchkin.FROM RESPARS CFD EXPTS	
					Jour SJA 31 1380	Jun 72	*ENGL OF AE 31 595	
Alpha	2.0+2	1.3+4	FEI	Expt	Jour YF 14 1123	Dec 71	Bergman+ REL THR,TBL,GRPH CFD OTHERS	+
					Jour SNP 14 625	Jun 72	*ENGL OF YF 14 1123	
					Rept INDC(CCP)-22	Apr 72	*ENGL OF YF 14 1123	
	2.0+2	1.3+4			Data EXFOR40103.002	Dec 73	.25 DATA LINES	

94 Plutonium 239

Quantity	Energy (ev) Min	Max	Lab	Type	Documentation Ref Vol Page	Date	Author, Comments	Data
Alpha	9.4+3	1.0+6	CCP	Expt	Rept YK- 9 37	72	Kononov+ ALFA(E),LIQ SCIN DET,TBL	
					Rept INDC(CCP)-42	Aug 74	.P3.ENGLISH OF YK-9	
Alpha	2.5-2		IFB	Eval	Rept YK- 9 34	72	Morogovsky. COMPUTR RE-EVAL,DATA GVN	
					Rept INDC(CCP)-42	Aug 74	.P1.ENGLISH OF YK-9	
Alpha	1.0+4	1.0+6	FEI	Expt	Jour AE 32 85	Jan 72	Kononov+ TOF,SCIN-TANK,GRPH CFD OTHR	+
	1.0+4	8.0+4			Jour AE 38 82	Feb 75	- + TOF,ALF(NEUT-E),TBL	
					Rept YK- 15 12	Aug 74	- . TOF,VDG.AVGD ALFA,TABLE	
	1.0+4	1.0+6			Jour SJA 32 95	Jul 72	*	
	9.4+4	1.0+5			Prog YFI-12 8	72	Kononov+ TOF, ALFA(NEUT-E), TABLE	
	9.4+3	1.0+6			Rept FEI-274	Oct 71	- + ABSOLUTE,VDG ,SC-TANK,TABLE	
	1.0+4	8.0+4			Jour SJA 38 105	Aug 75	. ENGL OF AE 38 82	
	9.4+3	1.0+6			Data EXFOR40412.005	Jan 77	ALFA AT 52 ENERGIES	
Alpha	1.0+2	1.5+7	HAR	Eval	Prog AERE-PR/NP18	Mar 72	Sowerby+ EVAL GRPH ERROR 12PC <30KEV	
Alpha	2.0+2	1.2+4	FEI	Expt	Prog YFI-13 6	Oct 72	Chelnokov+ ABSTRACT, TBL ALFA(N-E)	+
					Prog INDC(CCP)-32 8	Apr 73	.ENGL TRANSL OF YFI-13 6	
	2.0+2	6.0+3			Data EXFOR40105.015	Jun 72	ALFA AT 22 ENERGIES	
Alpha	Pile		FEI	Expt	Prog YFI-13 3	Oct 72	Dvukhsherstnov+ ABST,INTEG EXPT,TBL	
					Prog INDC(CCP)-32	Apr 73	.PAGE 3.ENGLISH OF YFI-13 3	
Alpha	1.0+2	1.0+6	IAE	Eval	Jour REA 10 453	Dec 72	Sowerby+ EXTENSIVE SURVEY,TBLS+GRPHS	
Alpha	1.0+4	1.0+6	SOR	Revw	Prog IA- 1282 37	73	Yiftah+ ENDF CFD USSR EXPT,DISCUSSN	
Alpha	1.0+2	3.0+4	DUB	Expt	Conf 73Kiev 4 49	May 73	Bolotsky+ TOF,ALPHA(NEUT-E),AVGE,TBL	
Alpha	3.0+3	2.0+5	KUR	Expt	Conf 73Kiev 4 42	May 73	Vorotnikov+ COINC,ALPHA(NEUT-E),TABLE	+
					Rept INDC(CCP)-44	Jun 74	P27. ENGLISH OF 73KIEV 4 42	
	3.0+3	2.5+5			Data EXFOR40343.002	Feb 76	ALPHA FOR 20 EN-RANGES	
Alpha	2.5-2	2.0+5	ORL	Expt	Prog USNDC-7 179	Jun 73	Weston+. NO DATA GIVEN	
Alpha	9.0+3	6.0+4	KFK	Expt	Jour NSE 48 324	Jul 72	Bandl+ VDG.TOF.TBL AND GRAPH.	+
	8.0+3	6.0+4			Rept KFK-1457	Sep 71	- + SUPERSEDED	
					Conf 71Knoxvill 273	Mar 71	- + SUPERSEDED	
	9.0+3	6.0+4			Data EXFOR20158.003	Oct 73	21PTS.	
Alpha	6.5+3	7.0+4	BIR	Revw	Jour RPP 37 951	74	Beynon+ GRPH COMPAR RECENT MEASURMTS	
Alpha	2.0+2	3.0+4	IFB	Eval	Jour VBF 1974 3 17	74	Antsipov+ FROM EVAL RES-DATA,CFD XPT	
					Rept INDC(CCP)-62	Feb 75	. ENGLISH OF VBF 1974 3 17	
Alpha	Pile		ANL	Expt	Jour NSE 53 9	Jan 74	Dudey+. INTEGRAL MEASTS IN EBR-2.	
					Rept ANL-7791	Jul 71	Heinrich+. INTEGRAL MEAST IN EBR-2	
Alpha	1.0+2	1.5+7	CJD	Eval	Rept INDC(CCP)-44	Jun 74	.P1. ENGLISH OF 73KIEV 1 209	
	1.0-3	1.0+0			Rept INDC(CCP)-44	Jun 74	.P1. ENGLISH OF 73KIEV 1 209	
Alpha	Maxwl		FEI	Expt	Rept YFI-18 3	Aug 74	Dvukhsherstnov+ VAL GVN IN TBL	+
	2.0+3	3.0+4			Jour AE 37 131	Aug 74	- + ALPHA GVN IN TBL	
	2.0+3	2.4+4			Jour AE 33 577	Jul 72	- + ALFA GIVN,CFD OTHERS	
	2.4+4				Rept FEI-285	Jan 72	Dvuhsherstnov+ FE-FILTER,SCINT,VALUE	
	1.0+2	6.0+4			Prog YFI-12 5	72	Bergman+ TOF,AVGED ALFA(NEUT-E),TBL	
	2.0+3	2.4+4			Prog YFI-12 7	72	Dvukhsherstnov+ TABLE ALFA(NEUT-E)	
	2.0+3				Conf 71Kiev	May 71	- +.ALPHA=1.35+-0.09	
	2.0+3	1.4+5			Rept INDC(CCP)-49	Feb 75	- + ENGLISH OF YFI-18 3	
	2.0+4	3.0+4			Jour SJA 37 828	Feb 75	. ENGLISH OF AE 37 131	
	2.0+3	2.4+4			Jour SJA 33 666	Jan 73	.ENGL TRANSL OF AE 33 577	
	2.0+3	1.4+5			Data EXFOR40092.	Feb 75	.4SUBENT EACH 1 LINE,3ES	
Alpha	1.0+2	1.0+6	ORL	Revw	Rept CONF-740903-7	Sep 74	De Saussure+TBL.OTH CFD.	
Alpha	6.0+2	8.0+3	KAL	Eval	Conf 74Bombay 2 89	Dec 74	Ganesan. BEST GROUP-VALUS BY WF-EVAL	
Alpha	Fast		ITU	Expt	Prog NEANDC(E)162U	Feb 75	Cottone+ SB-125,XE,CS,ND VOL.5.P.42.	
Alpha	2.0+2	3.0+4	LEB	Expt	Conf 75Kiev 6 61	May 75	Bergman+ SDS. ALFABAR(6E-RANGES).TBL	
Alpha	Fast		HAR	Expt	Prog UKNDC(75)P71	Jul 75	Crouch+ IRRADIATION PFR	
Alpha	1.0+2	1.0+4	FEI	Expt	Jour AE 39 291	Oct 75	Bergman+ ALF AVG(NEUT-E),TBL,GRAPH	+
					Jour SJA 39 916	Apr 76	. ENGL OF AE 39 291	
	2.0+2	3.0+4			Data EXFOR40435.002	Nov 76	ALPHA FOR 21 E-RANGES	
Alpha	1.0+3	2.0+4	JAE	Eval	Prog JAERI-M-6320	Nov 75	Takano+GRPH EVAL CFD EXP DATA.	
Alpha	2.5-2		MAG	Eval	Rept EPRI-NP-163	Dec 75	Beer+MONTECARLO ANAL 70HELSINKI P287	
					Abst ANS 23 509	Jun 76	- +MONTCARLO ANAL CRC DATA.TBL.CF	
Alpha	2.0-2	2.0+5	ORL	Expt	Jour NSE 59 79	Feb 76	Gwin+GRPHS,TBLS.CFD OTH	+
	1.0+2	2.0+5			Conf 75Wash. 627	Mar 75	- + CFD 2 EXPT.AVG DIFF 6PCT	
	5.0+1	2.0+5			Data EXFOR10267.	Nov 75	175 PTS.	
Eta	Pile		LAS	Expt	Rept LA- 102	44	Snyder+	+
	Pile				Data EXFOR12395.004	Jun 76	. 1 PT.	
Eta	Maxwl		ANL	Revw	Conf 55Geneva 3 198	Aug 55	Zinn.VAL 2200M/SEC GVN,	
Eta	Cold		ANL	Revw	Conf 55Geneva 5 125	Aug 55	Spinrad+.P835	
Eta	Fast		ANL	Revw	Conf 55Geneva 5 125	Aug 55	Spinrad+.P835	
Eta	Maxwl		CCP	Expt	Conf 55Geneva 4 295	Aug 55	Spivak+.VAL GVN,EXPT DESCRIBED,P657	+
Eta	Maxwl		CCP	Expt	Conf 55Geneva 4 301	Aug 55	Alichanov+.VAL GVN,EXPT DESCRBD,P658	

94 Plutonium 239

Quantity	Energy (ev) Min	Max	Lab	Type	Documentation Ref Vol Page	Date	Author, Comments	Data
Eta	Maxwl		ORL Revw	Conf	55Geneva 3 19	Aug 55	Weinberg.P862,VAL GVN,REFS GVN	
Eta	Pile		HAR Theo	Rept	AERE – R/R – 1225	Nov 55	. 2.18+ – .01 MDCE 2.22ASS.FOR SAFETY	
Eta	Maxwl		KAP Expt	Rept	KAPL – 1464	Dec 55	Mcmillan+,ETA=1.93+ – 0.02 REL U235	
Eta	Maxwl	1.3+2	CCP Expt	Jour	AE 1 3 13	Jun 56	Spivak+.AVERAGES IN 5 BROAD SPECTRA	
				Jour	JNE 4 70	Jan 57	TRANSLATN.*	
				Jour	SJA 1 3 295		56 TRANSLATN.*	
Eta	3.0+4	9.0+5	CCP Expt	Jour	AE 1 3 21	Jun 56	Spivak+.DATA AT 4 ENERGIES	+
				Jour	JNE 4 79	Jan 57	TRANSLATN.*	
				Jour	SJA 1 3 303		56 TRANSLATN.*	
Eta	Pile		ANL Expt	Jour	NSE 1 204	Jul 56	Jaffey.2.02 FROM ORNL ANL DATA	
Eta	Pile		ANL Expt	Jour	NSE 1 204	Jul 56	Jaffey. EFFECTIVE ETA VERSUS TIME.	
Eta	2.5–2	5.0–1	HAN Expt	Prog	HW – 44525 47	Jul 56	Leonard.	+
	2.5–2	5.0–1		Data	EXFOR12518.004	Jun 76	. 30 PTS.	
Eta	3.8–2	6.0+1	HAR Expt	Jour	JNE 3 33	Aug 56	Farley.TOF,GRAPH REL TO THERMAL ETA	+
Eta	1.8–2	7.0–1	BNL Expt	Jour	JNE 3 177	Oct 56	Palevsky+ SC+FC GRAPH,28 DATA POINTS	+
	1.0–2	1.0–1		Conf	55Geneva 4 311	Aug 55	– .GRAPH,EXPT DESCRIBED,P587	
	1.7–2	6.8–1		Data	EXFOR12322.004	Jun 76	. 28 PTS.	
Eta	2.5–2		BNL Eval	Rept	BNL – 325	Jan 57	Hughes+ WORLD CONSIST, VAL. 2.09+ – .0	
Eta	3.0–2	5.0–1	HAR Theo	Rept	AERE – NP/R – 2076	Jan 57	Leonard. AGREES WITH S NOT RES PARAM	
Eta	6.0+0	7.0+1	HAR Expt	Rept	AERE – NP/R – 2076	Jan 57	Sanders. RATIO TO THR LIN AC	
Eta	7.0+0	3.0+1	CCP Expt	Jour	AE 2 247	Mar 57	Kirpichnikov+.TABLE 10 RES,REL THR	+
				Jour	JNE 6 163	Dec 57	TRANSLATN.*	
				Jour	SJA 2 299		57 TRANSLATN.*	
Eta	Pile		ANL Expt	Jour	NSE 2 657	Sep 57	Kafalas+,CURVS HOR VERT DISTR EBR – I	
Eta	Maxwl		HAR Eval	Rept	AERE – NP/R – 2140	Dec 57	Egelstaff+ CONSISTENT VALUES 2200M/S	
			Expt	Rept	AERE – NP/R – 2104	57	Richmond. REL U – 235. ABST. DATA.	
				Conf	55Geneva 4 351	56	– . SUPERSEDED.	
				Rept	AERE – R/M – 63	Aug 55	– . CFD U235	
				Revw Conf	55Geneva 4 307	Aug 55	Egelstaff+.VAL GVN,EXPT DESCRBD,P425	
Eta	2.4+4	8.8+5	CCP Expt	Jour	AE 4 185	Feb 58	Andreev.ALSO AT 240KEV,SPHERE METHOD	+
				Jour	JNE 9 151	Jun 59	TRANSLATN.*	
				Jour	SJA 4 247		58 TRANSLATN.*	
Eta	7.0–3	3.6–1	HAR Expt	Jour	JNE 6 212	Apr 58	Skarsgard+.CS CURVE REL 2.02 AT THR	+
Eta	Maxwl		KAP Expt	Jour	NSE 3 758	Jun 58	Gaerttner+,1.927+ – .024 SUBCADMIUM TH	+
				Rept	KAPL – 1468	Feb 56	.SUPERSEDED	
	Maxwl			Data	EXFOR12327.003	Jun 76	. 1 PT.	
Eta	1.0–2	2.8+1	ANL Expt	Conf	58Geneva 15 127	Sep 58	Bollinger+.PPR687,CURVE,OF ETA/NU	+
	7.8+0	2.2+1		Conf	ORNL – 2309	Jun 57	.RATIOTONU 5RESCURVS	
	1.7–2	2.3+1		Data	EXFOR12502.007	Jun 76	. 118 PTS.	
Eta	Maxwl		BNL Comp	Conf	58Geneva 16 8	Sep 58	Hughes.PPR2483,VAL V=2200M/SEC GVN	
Eta	+0	+1	CCP Revw	Conf	58Geneva 15 309	Sep 58	Vladimirsky+.PPR2221,NDG,REFS	
Eta	Maxwl		ANL Expt	Jour	NSE 5 225	Apr 59	Muehlhause+ OSC. 2.04+ – 0.04	+
	Maxwl			Data	EXFOR12361.004	Jun 76	. 1 PT.	
Eta	2.5–2		AE Comp	Rept	AE – 11	Apr 60	Story+,DISCUSSION+TABULATN OF MEASTS	
Eta	7.0+0	3.0+1	CCP	Jour	NSA 14 1408	Jun 60	USSR – ABSTRACT NO 11129	
Eta	Maxwl		HAR Expt	Rept	TNCC(UK) – 77	Aug 60	Cabell+ PILE OSC.REL.U235	
				Conf	58Geneva 16 34	Sep 58	Rose+.PPR14,VAL REL TO U235,PILEOSCL	
				Rept	AERE – R/R – 2457	Feb 58	– + RATIO TO U235. PILE OSC METHO	
Eta	7.8+0	2.2+1	MTR Revw	Conf	60Vienna 93	Oct 60	Evans+ CURVE,MANY REFS,FAST CH	
Eta	1.4+7		CCP Expt	Jour	AE 10 68	Jan 61	Flerov+.VAL GVN,GRAPHIT – PRISMA DTCTR	
				Jour	SJA 10 65	Nov 61	TRANSLATN.*JNE17 423 N/63	
				Jour	KE 4 574	Jul 61	.TRANSLATN	
			HAN Eval	Conf	61RPI 3	May 61	Leonard.	
Eta	5.0–3	2.5+0	GA Eval	Rept	GA – 2113	Jun 61	Wikner+.TABLE 100 E POINTS	
Eta	Maxwl		CRC Expt	Conf	61Saclay 57	Jul 61	Westcott. 2200METRE/SEC SIG GIVEN	
Eta	Pile		CRC Eval	Rept	CRRP – 1191	Jan 62	Westcott. EFF SIG.	
Eta	2.5–2	1.0+6	ROS Revw	Jour	KE 5 701	Jan 62	Falkenberg.VAL GVN,REFERENCES	
Eta	Maxwl		ORL Expt	Jour	NSE 12 359	Mar 62	Gwin+,FLUX TRAP ASSEMBLY ETA=2.032	+
				Jour	NSE 44 266	May 71	Magnuson.RE – ANAL GWIN – MAGNUSON DATA	
				Data	EXFOR10207.	Dec 71	2PTS.	
Eta	Maxwl		ORL Expt	Jour	NSE 14 101	Sep 62	Macklin+.MN BATH ETA=2.143+ – 0.014	+
	Maxwl			Data	EXFOR12508.	Jun 76	. 2 PTS. ETA + RATIO U235	
Eta	Maxwl		CRC Revw	Rept	EANDC(CAN) – 15	Nov 62	Hanna. COMPARES MANY VALUES	
Eta	Pile		CJD Eval	Rept	INDSWG – 64 285	64	Galanin. TBL EFF ETA FOR MANY SPECTR	

94 Plutonium 239

Quantity	Energy (ev) Min	Max	Lab	Type	Documentation Ref Vol Page	Date	Author, Comments	Data
Eta	2.0−2	2.0+1	ITE	Expt	Jour AE 16 110	Feb 64	Ignat'Ev+. SIGTOT+ETA EXPT, NDG	
					Rept ITE−147	63	.SIMILAR TO AE 16 110 2/64	
					Jour JNE 18 719	64	.ENGLISH TRANSL OF AE 16 121 2/64	
					Jour EAF 16 2 19	64	. FRENCH TRANSL OF AE 16 121 2/64	
					Rept INDSWG−7E	63	.ENGLISH TRANSL OF ITE−147 /63	
Eta	Maxwl		WIN	Expt	Jour JNAB 18 105	Mar 64	Carter+ ETA RATIO U235/PU239 = 1.02	
					Rept AEEW−R−201	Jan 63	− + RATIO TO U−235.	
Eta	7.0+0	2.1+2	CCP	Expt	Rept INDSWG−69	Nov 64	.TOF.AVG IN 4E−GRPS FROM RES+AVG SIG	
Eta	2.6−2		CEA	Revw	Conf 64Vienna 19	Dec 64	Vendryes+ VALUE TBL,OTHER COMPILATNS	
Eta	2.6−2		RLY	Revw	Conf 64Vienna 120	Dec 64	Raievski. RATIO REL U235 +−ERROR GVN	
Eta	+5	+7	RLY	Revw	Conf 64Vienna 56	Dec 64	Kronberger. VAL TABLE OF ETA+NU+SIGS	
Eta	Maxwl		RLY	Revw	Conf 64Vienna 56	Dec 64	Kronberger. AGR−REACTOR,TBL,NU+SIGS	
Eta	2.5−2	1.0+6	BEP	Revw	Jour KE 8 625	Jan 65	Wenzel. VAL FOR 3ES GVN,MANY REFS	
Eta	7.0+0	2.1+0	ITE	Expt	Jour EON 2 77	Feb 65	Ignatev+KIRPICHNIKOV RATIO AVF TO AB	
Eta	2.4+4		FEI	Expt	Jour AE 19 41	Jul 65	Vankov.STAVISSKY 12.15+−.06	+
					Jour JNE 20 600	Jul 66	TRANSLATN.*	
					Jour SJA 19 903	Jul 65	TRANSLATN.*	
					Jour EAF 19 1 61	Jul 65	TRANSLATN.*	
Eta	2.5−2	5.7−2	MTR	Expt	Rept IDO−17083	Feb 66	Smith+,MONOCHROM NEUTS.MNSO4 BATH	+
	None				Prog ERDA−NDC−2 7	May 75	− .REANAL.DATA.ETA=2.110+−0.008	
				ExTh	Conf 66Wash. 919	Mar 66	− +,MN BATH+MTR REL MEASTS,CFD TH	
	2.5−2	5.7−2		Expt	Rept IDO−16977 23	59	.SUPERSEDED	
	2.5−2	5.7−2			Data EXFOR12318.	Jun 76	. 2 PTS.	
Eta	2.5−2		BNW	Theo	Conf 66Wash. 75	Mar 66	Liikala+, TBLS OF LITER. VALUES	
Eta	1.0−2	1.0+0	MTR	Eval	Conf 66Wash. 840	Mar 66	Moore+,MULTILEVEL ANAL CURVE CFD XPT	
Eta	3.5−2	1.1+1	HAR	Expt	Rept AERE−M−1709	Sep 66	Brooks+LINAC.TOF	+
					Conf 66S.Diego 2 193	Feb 66	− .LINAC	
	3.0−1	1.1+1			Data EXFOR20623.	Dec 76	10PTS.ETA/NU BAR.	
Eta	2.0−2	5.0−1	MTR	Eval	Conf 66Paris 2 50	Oct 66	Smith. TBLCURV.LEAST SQUARE FIT	
Eta	Maxwl		MTR	Expt	Rept IN−1060	Feb 67	Fast+. THR+.025EV VALUES REL U235GVN	+
	Maxwl				Data EXFOR12505.	Feb 76	. 2 PTS ETA + RATIO TO U235	
Eta	2.5−2		WIN	Expt	Conf 67Brussels 28	Mar 67	Kinchin. ETA(0) DEDUCD FROM INT EXP	
Eta	1.0+2	3.0+4	HAR	Expt	Rept EANDC(UK)96	68	Patrick. TOF.LINAC.	+
	1.0+2	3.0+4			Data EXFOR20002.006	Nov 70	5302PTS.	
	2.0+3		MTR	Expt	Abst ANS 13 300	Jul 70	Smith+,MANGANESE BATH	
Eta	1.0−2	1.0+7	ORL	Revw	Jour REA 8 473	Sep 70	Kasten. REVIEW,ETA(E)+AVG ETA,GRAPHS	
Eta	−		UFP	Expt	Rept CCEN−17	Dec 70	CLEMENTE REL TO U235,FISSION CHAMB.	
					Conf 70Helsinki 1 295	Jun 70	.SEE ALSO *	
Eta	1.0−2	1.0+7	KFK	Eval	Rept KFK−1340	Feb 71	Hinkelmann+TABLE OF EVALUATED DATA	+
					Rept KFK−750	Jan 68	Schmidt. CURVES	
					Rept KFK−120 2	Dec 65	− . REISSUED	
	1.0−2	2.5+0			Rept KFK−120 1	Nov 65	− .+EVAL REVIEW.TABLE 18ES	
	1.0−2	1.0+7			Rept KFK−120 2	Dec 62	− .GRAPHS AND TABULATED DATA	
	1.0−3	1.5+7			Data KEDAK−3	Oct 75	6134 DATA SETS	
Eta	2.5−2		ANL	Eval	Conf 71Knoxvill 560	Mar 71	DE VOLPI. ADJUSTED VALUE GIVEN	
Eta	2.5−2		IFB	Eval	Rept YK−9 34	72	Morogovsky. COMPUTR RE−EVAL,DATA GVN	
					Rept INDC(CCP)−42	Aug 74	.P1.ENGLISH OF YK−9	
Eta	1.0−3	1.0+0	IJE	Eval	Conf 73Kiev 1 209	May 73	Konshin+ REFERENCES,ACCURACY,NDG	
Eta	1.0−3	1.0+0	CJD	Eval	Rept INDC(CCP)−44	Jun 74	.P1. ENGLISH OF 73KIEV 1 209	
Eta	1.0−2	5.0−1	HAR	Expt	Prog AERE−PR/NP23	Mar 76	Moxon+EN DEPENDENCE.TBD	
Nu	Pile		LAS	Expt	Rept LA−104	44	Dewire+	+
	Pile				Data EXFOR12504.002	Jun 76	. 1 PT.	
Nu	Pile		LAS	Expt	Rept LA−102	Jun 44	Snyder+	+
	Pile				Data EXFOR12395.003	Jun 76	. 1 PT.	
Nu	2.0+6	1.4+7	LAS	Theo	Rept LA−1863	Dec 54	Leachman.AVG NU+NEUT EMISSION PROBAB	
Nu	Maxwl		CCP	Expt	Conf 55Moscow 156	Jul 55	Kalashnikova+.RATIOS+ABSOLUTE VALUES	+
					Rept AEC−TR−2435	56	. P 123. ENGL TRANSL OF 55MOSCOW 156	
Nu	2.0−1	1.0+2	CCP	Expt	Conf 55Moscow 369	Jul 55	Erozolimsky+. TABLE NU−EFF REL THR	
					Rept AEC−TR−2435	56	. P 255. ENGL TRANSL OF 55MOSCOW 369	
Nu	Pile		ANL	Revw	Conf 55Geneva 3 198	Aug 55	Zinn.P814,VAL GVN,DISCUSS OF RESULTS	
Nu	2.5−2	1.3+2	CCP	Expt	Conf 55Geneva 5 172	Aug 55	Spivak+.VAL GVN CFD REF,PPR659	
Nu	Maxwl		HAR	Revw	Conf 55Geneva 4 307	Aug 55	Egelstaff+.VAL GVN,EXPT DESCRBD,P425	
Nu	4.0+6	4.5+6	LAS	Expt	Rept LA−1939	Aug 55	Bethe+ ALSO FISS SPEC NEUTS SPH TRNS	+
	4.0+6	4.5+6			Data EXFOR12397.006	Jun 76	. 2 PTS.	
Nu	None		ORL	Revw	Conf 55Geneva 3 19	Aug 55	Weinberg.P862,VAL GVN,REFS GVN	
Nu	Maxwl		KAP	Expt	Rept KAPL−1464	Dec 55	Mcmillan+,NU=3.07+−0.073 REL U235	+
	Maxwl				Data EXFOR12357.	Jun 76	. 2 PTS. NU + RATIO TO U235	
Nu	Maxwl		CCP		Rept AEC−TR−2435PT1	56	.USSR 3D0 PM 4PERCENT PAGE 131	

94 Plutonium 239

Quantity	Energy (ev) Min	Energy (ev) Max	Lab	Type	Documentation Ref Vol Page	Author, Comments Date	Data
Nu	Fast		HAR		Jour BJAS 5 32	56 Shepherd+ZEPHYR REACTOR	
Nu	8.0+4		LAS	Expt	Jour PR 101 1012	Feb 56 Diven+,LIQ SCINT,+PROB EMISS	+
					Conf 55Geneva 2 193	Aug 55 Leachman.P592,CURVE,EXPT DESCRIBED	
	8.0+4				Data EXFOR12337.004	Jun 76 . 1 PT.	
Nu	2.5−2	1.0+0	HAN	Expt	Rept HW− 43441 58	May 56 Leonard+	
Nu	Maxwl	5.0−1	CCP	Expt	Jour AE 1 3 11	Jun 56 Kalashnikova+.NU CONSTANT +−2PERCENT	
					Jour JNE 4 67	Jan 57 TRANSLATN.*	
					Jour SJA 1 3 291	56 TRANSLATN.*	
Nu	Pile		ANL	Expt	Jour NSE 1 204	Jul 56 Jaffey.2.88 FROM ORNL ANL DATA	
Nu	5.0+0	6.0+1	HAR	Expt	Jour JNE 3 33	Aug 56 Farley.EVIDENCE NU CONST +−15PERCENT	
Nu	Maxwl	3.0−1	BNL	Expt	Jour JNE 3 177	Oct 56 Palevsky+ NU(THR)/(RES)=1.015+−0.025	
Nu	5.0+5	1.0+6	LAS	Expt	Jour PR 104 731	Nov 56 Allen+,1.3+−0.2 RATIO TO U235 AVG	+
	5.0+5	1.0+6			Data EXFOR12207.012	Jun 76 . 2 PTS.	
Nu	Maxwl	Fiss	SAC	Expt	Abst PHY 22 1187	Nov 56 Auclair+RATIO AT HIGH TO THR=1,065	
	1.0−1	8.1+0			Jour JPR 17 563	Jul 56 − + BE CRYSTAL	
	Maxwl				Jour CR 241 1935	Dec 55 − +NACC,RELATIVE MEASURES	
Nu	2.5−2		BNL	Eval	Rept BNL−325	Jan 57 Hughes+WORLD CONSIST. VAL. 2.91+−.04	
Nu	Maxwl	Fiss	CCP	Expt	Jour AE 2 18	Jan 57 Kalashnikova+.FAST/THR=1.109+−0.01	+
Nu	Maxwl	9.0+5	CCH	Expt	Rept NP−TR−440	Sep 57 Saunders. NDG NSA 14 2213 9/60	
Nu	+0	+6	LAS	Revw	Jour PR 108 783	Nov 57 Terrell.SUMMARY CURVE NU VS. E	
Nu	Maxwl		HAR	Eval	Rept AERE−NP/R−2140	Dec 57 Egelstaff+ CONSISTENT VALUES 2200M/S	+
				Comp	Rept AERE−NP/R−2104	Mar 57 − .EXPT METHODS FOR HAR VALUE	
	2.5−2	3.0−1		Expt	Jour JNE 3 70	Aug 56 Sanders+ NU(RES)/(THR)=0.995+−.008	
	Maxwl				Jour JNE 2 247	Jun 56 − .PROMPT NEUTS. REL+ABS VALUES	
	2.5−2	3.0−1			Rept NRDC−88	Feb 56 Harwell.CONSTANT	
	Maxwl				Rept AERE−RP/R−1655	May 55 Sanders.CFD PU240 SPON FISSN.	
					Rept AERE−RP/R−1627	Mar 55 − . MAXW AVG.	
Nu	2.5−2		SAC	Expt	Jour CEA−R−652	58 Jacob. = 2 DATA INDEX LINES	+
Nu	4.0+6	1.5+7	FEI	Expt	Jour AE 4 188	Feb 58 Smirenkin+ REL NU THERM,PROMPT NEUTS	
					Jour JNE 9 155	Jun 59 . ENGL OF AE 4 188	
					Jour SJA 4 253	58 . ENGL OF AE 4 188	
Nu	1.0−2	2.3+1	ANL	Expt	Conf 58Geneva 15 127	Sep 58 Bollinger+.PPR687,CURVE ETA/NU	+
	1.7−2	2.3+1			Rept AERE−NP/R−2076	Jul 56 − .FLAT RPTD WASH56MTG	
	1.7−2	2.3+1			Data EXFOR12502.007	Jun 76 . 118 PTS.	
Nu	Maxwl		BNL	Comp	Conf 58Geneva 16 8	Sep 58 Hughes.PPR2483,VAL V=2200M/SEC GVN	
Nu	−2	1.5+7	CCP	Expt	Conf 58Geneva 15 353	Sep 58 Bondarenko+.PPR2187,CURVE CFD REFS	
Nu	Pile		LAS	Expt	Conf 58Geneva 15 331	Sep 58 Leachman.PPR665,VAL REL TO U235 GVN	
Nu	+6		LAS	Revw	Conf 58Geneva 15 344	Sep 58 Hemmendinger.PPR663,CURVE,MANY REFS	
Nu	Maxwl		ORL	Expt	Jour NSE 5 49	Jan 59 Desaussure+,NU=1.23+−0.01REL TO U235	+
	Maxwl				Data EXFOR12328.003	Jun 76 . 1 PT.	
Nu	Maxwl		ANL	Expt	Jour JNEA 11 21	Nov 59 Jaffey+ NU.SIGF REL U233 U235 PU241	
					Conf ORNL−2309	Jun 57 .LIQ SCINT FOR FAST NS NUCONST	
Nu	2.5−2		AE	Comp	Rept AE− 11	Apr 60 Story+,DISCUSSION+TABULATN OF MEASTS	
	Maxwl		CCP	Theo	Jour AE 8 409	May 60 Zysin+.VAL CALCD FROM FRGMNT−DISTRBS	
					Jour SJA 8 343	Jun 61 TRANSLATN.*JNE AB17 41 1/61	
					Jour KE 4 40	Jan 61 .TRANSLATN	
Nu	1.4+7		SAC	Expt	Jour JPR 21 617	Aug 60 Leroy. 4.75+−0.4 REL TO U235 THERMAL	+
Nu	1.4+7		CCP	Expt	Jour AE 10 68	Jan 61 Flerov+.VAL GVN,GRAPHIT−PRISMA DTCTR	+
					Jour SJA 10 65	Nov 61 TRANSLATN.*JNE17 423 N/63	
					Jour KE 4 574	Jul 61 .TRANSLATN	
Nu	Maxwl		HAN	Eval	Conf 61RPI 3	May 61 Leonard.	
Nu	Maxwl		CRC	Expt	Conf 61Saclay 57	Jul 61 Westcott. 2200METRE/SEC SIG GIVEN	
Nu		1.5+7	ANL	Revw	Conf 61Vienna 1 29	Aug 61 Smith.PPR76,CURVE MANY REFS	
Nu	2.5−2	1.0+6	ROS	Revw	Conf KE 5 701	Jan 62 Falkenberg.VAL GVN,REFERENCES	
Nu	Maxwl		ISL	Theo	Rept IA− 757	Jul 62 CALCULTD FROM CHAIN−YIELDS'2.94+−.12	
Nu	Maxwl		CRC	Comp	Rept EANDC(CAN)−15	Nov 62 Hanna. COMPARES MANY VALUES.	
Nu	Maxwl		CCP	Expt	Jour ZET 43 2053	Dec 62 .AVG.NU=2.89.COMP. WITH THEORY	
					Jour JET 16 1451	Jun 63 .TRANSLATN.	
Nu	Maxwl		UK		Rept NRDC−138 7	Jan 63 2.955PM.038	
Nu	Maxwl	1.5+7	FOA	Comp	Rept NP−16440	Mar 63 ASPLUND−NILSSON. REVIEW. TABLE.	
Nu	2.5−2	1.4+7	LAS	Expt	Jour NP 48 433	Oct 63 Hopkins+,SCINT TANK,RELAT TO CF252	+
					Conf 61Vienna 1 149	Aug 61 .SUPERSEDED	
	2.5−2	1.4+7			Data EXFOR12326.	Jun 76 . 7 PTS.	
Nu	−.6+5	1.5+7	LRL	Expt	Jour JNAB 18 125	Mar 64 Schuster+ E DEPENDNCE THEOR,CFD EXPT	
Nu	2.6−2		CEA	Revw	Conf 64Vienna 19	Dec 64 Vendryes+ VALUE TBL,OTHER COMPILATNS	
Nu	+5	+7	RLY	Revw	Conf 64Vienna 56	Dec 64 Kronberger. VAL TABLE OF ETA+NU+SIGS	
Nu	Maxwl		RLY	Revw	Conf 64Vienna 56	Dec 64 Kronberger. AGR−REACTOR,TBL,ETA+SIGS	

94 Plutonium 239

Quantity	Energy (ev) Min	Max	Lab	Type	Documentation Ref Vol Page	Date	Author, Comments	Data
Nu	Maxwl		HAR	Expt	Conf 65Salzburg 2 25	Mar 65	Colvin+ PPR44.BORONPILE.RATIO/U−235	+
					Prog AERE−PR/NP8 9	Feb 65	− +TBL.NU=2.819+−0.026.ABS.	
					Conf 58Geneva 16 121	Sep 58	− + PPR 52	
Nu	None		LAS	Revw	Conf 65Salzburg 3	Mar 65	Terrell.XPTL WORK CFD THEORY.GRAPHS	
Nu	Maxwl	4.0+6	ALD	Expt	Jour NP 66 149	Apr 65	Mather+ PROMPT SC−T LEAST SQ FIT	+
Nu	2.5−2		HAR	Expt	Jour NP 71 228	Sep 65	Barnard+ AVG VAL FROM 6 EXPS=2.83	+
Nu	Maxwl		KUR	Expt	Jour NP 71 553	Sep 65	Apalin+NU VERSUS FRAGMENT MASS	
Nu		1.5+7	KFK	Eval	Rept KFK−120 1	Feb 66	Schmidt.OTHERS'XPTS+CURVE	
	2.5−2				Rept KFK−120 1	Nov 65	− .+EVAL REVIEW.	
	1.0+3	1.0+7			Rept KFK−120 2	Dec 62	− .PROMPT AND DELAYED NS	
Nu	1.0−2	1.0+7	AI	Eval	Conf 66Wash. 270	Mar 66	Lemke.AIDA ANAL OF AWRE+AI DATA FILE	
Nu	3.0−1	1.1+1	HAR	Expt	Rept AERE−M−1709	Sep 66	Brooks+ LINAC.TOF. RATIO ETA/NU.	+
	3.0−1	1.1+1			Data EXFOR20623.	Dec 76	10PTS.ETA/NU BAR.	
Nu	1.0+3	1.5+7	LAS	Eval	Prog WASH−1074 79	Apr 67	Diven. NDG SEE EANDC(US)−96U	
Nu	1.0−4	1.5+7	UK	Eval	Rept AHSB(S)R−125	May 67	Hart.(RLY).UK−DFN 184 REVD TO DFN329	
	1.0−4	1.5+7			Data UKNDL−DFN 161A	Mar 73	.23 PTS.ANG DIST OF FISS NEUTS,LAB.	
Nu	4.2+6	1.5+7	FOA	Expt	Jour JNE 22 53	Jan 68	Conde+ NU PROMPT AT 5 ENS REL CF−252	+
					Conf 73Kiev 4 130	May 73	− . SUMMARY OF NUBAR. NDG.	
					Rept FOA4−C4318 22	Oct 67	− + EQUIVALENT.	
	4.2+6	1.5+7			Data EXFOR20052.002	Sep 71	5PTS.PROMPT	
Nu	Maxwl	1.5+7	AI	Eval	Jour JNE 22 79	Feb 68	Fillmore.DATA TBL,GRAPH.LEAST SQ FIT	
Nu	2.0+1	1.0+2	RPI	Expt	Conf PRL 22 195	Feb 69	Weinstein+ LINAC+TOF NU BAR VS. E	
	None				Abst DA/B 30 3823	Feb 70	− . LINAC.VAR WITH NEUT ENERG	
	1.0−2	1.0+2			Conf 69Vienna 477	Jul 69	− +PPR113. NU(NEUT−E) GRPH	
Nu	1.4+6	1.5+7	BRC	Expt	Jour JNE 23 257	May 69	Soleilhac+ TOF.REL CF−252 SPON	+
					Conf EANDC(E)154 67	Mar 73	Frehaut+ TOF.TAND.VDG.	
					Conf 69Vienna 931	Jul 69	Soleilhac+ PPR93.NU(E) AGREES OTHERS	
	1.4+6	1.5+7			Data EXFOR20490.003	Mar 76	29PTS.PROMPT.	
Nu	Maxwl		CUA	Theo	Abst DA/B 30 2222	Nov 69	Rogers.	
Nu	None		KFK	Revw	Jour AKE 15 26	70	Schmidt. REPORT ON RESON RANGE EXPT	
	Maxwl	5.5+7	AE	Comp	Conf 70Helsinki 2 93	Jun 70	Almen+57. COMPILATN AND NU−TEMP−PLOT	
Nu		6.0+6	FEI	Theo	Conf 70Helsinki 2 177	Jun 70	Vorobeva+88. NU(E) GRAPH CALCULATED	
Nu		1.6+6	FEI	Expt	Conf 70Helsinki 2 167	Jun 70	Nesterov+,NU−BAR AT 9 EN,REL CF252	+
	0.0+0	6.0+6		Eval	Prog YFI−11 13	70	Vorobyeva+ ABST,TBL VALUE FOR MAXW	
					Prog INDC(CCP)−31	Dec 72	.PAGE 12,ENGLISH OF YFI−11 13	
	2.5−2	1.5+6		Expt	Data EXFOR40033.003	Aug 70	NU−BAR AT 9 ES REL CF252	
Nu	+2	+7	GEB	Revw	Conf 70Helsinki 1 17	Jun 70	Greebler+102. UNCERTAINTY+REACT CALC	
Nu	+2	+7	HAR	Expt	Conf 70Helsinki 1 267	Jun 70	James.107. ACCURACY CFD REACTOR COST	
Nu	Maxwl	1.5+7	HAR	Revw	Conf 70Helsinki 2 195	Jun 70	Colvin.PPR99. REPORT ON DATA STATUS	
	2.5−2	1.5+7		Eval	Conf 69Vienna 930	Jul 69	− .PPR55. RECOMMENDATION+REVIEW	
Nu	6.0+5	5.0+6	SCU	Expt	Conf 70Helsinki 2 157	Jun 70	Savin+40. NU(E) GRAPH, RELATIV CF252	+
	8.9+5	4.7+6			Data EXFOR40058.003	Mar 71	PROMPT NU−BAR AT 41 ENERGIES	
Nu	4.0+4	1.2+6	ALD	Expt	Rept AWRE−O−42/70	Aug 70	Mather+.11 E BANDS,1PC,NO STRUCTURE	+
	4.0+4	1.2+6			Data EXFOR20453.	Jan 76	20PTS.PROMPT.	
Nu	2.5−2		IAE	Revw	Conf INDC(NDS)−25L	Aug 70	Konshin+ 2200M/SEC STATUS AND RECOMM	
Nu	3.0+5	1.4+6	BRC	Expt	Conf 70Helsinki 2 145	Jun 70	Soleilhac+ 67.NU(E) GRAPH + TABLE	+
					Jour AE 29 395	Nov 70	− +ABST FRANC−SOV SEM DUBNA	
					Prog EANDC(E)127U	Apr 70	Frehaut+,VDG TOF	
					Jour SJA 29 1156	Nov 70	Soleilhac+ENGLISH TRANSLATION	
	2.1+5	1.4+6			Data EXFOR20568.004	Mar 76	40PTS.PROMPT.	
Nu	None		FEI	Eval	Jour AE 29 395	Nov 70	Smirenkin.ABST FRANC−SOV SEM DUBNA	
					Jour SJA 29 1156	Nov 70	. ENGL OF AE 29 395	
Nu	Maxwl	1.5+7	ALD	Eval	Rept AWRE−O−86/70	Dec 70	Mather+ USE DATA PRE−7/70,4 ST LINES	
Nu	8.0+4		TOK	Theo	Jour NST 7 635	Dec 70	Hara.CAL CFD C DIVEN EXP	
Nu	2.5−2		ANL	Eval	Conf 71Knoxvill 560	Mar 71	Devolpi.ADJUSTED VALUE GIVEN	
Nu	8.9+5	4.7+6	KUR	Expt	Prog YFI−10 32	May 71	Savin+ TOF,LIQUID SCINT,NU VS EN,TBL	
					Rept INDC(CCP)−15	Dec 71	*P34,ENG OF YFI−10	
					Jour PTE 14 6 27	Dec 69	*TECHNIQUE DESCRIBD	
					Jour IET 14 1388	Dec 69	*ENG OF PTE 14 6 27	
Nu		1.5+7	ANL	Eval	Jour NSE 44 345	Jun 71	Davey. PROMPT NEUTS PER FISSION	
					Conf 70Helsinki 2 119	Jun 70	.SUPERSEDED.(P/112)	
Nu	Maxwl	5.0+6	AUA	Eval	Jour JNE 25 321	Aug 71	Walsh+ 2 LINE FIT,SLOPES GIVEN,GRAPH	
					Prog INDC(AUL)−8 2	May 70	.2 LINE SLOPES GIVN,PARTLY SUPERSEDD	

94 Plutonium 239

Quantity	Energy (ev) Min	Energy (ev) Max	Lab	Type	Documentation Ref Vol Page	Author, Comments Date	Data
Nu	7.9+0	8.6+1	DUB	Expt Jour	YF 14 927	Nov 71 Ryabov+ SPIN DEPENDENCE OF NU,GRAPH	
				Rept	JINR − P3 − 5297	Oct 70 Rjabov+ SAME AS YF 14 927	
	7.8+0	8.6+1		Rept	JINR − P3 − 5119	Jun 70 − + NU EXPT DESCRIBED,AVG NU GVN	
				Conf	JINR − D3893 88	May 68 Ryabov+ TWO NU(NEUT − E) DATA SETS GVN	
	7.9+0	8.6+1		Jour	SNP 14 519	May 72 Rjabov+ ENGL OF YF 14 927	
				Rept	BNL − TR − 401	72 .ENGLISH TRANS	
Nu	2.5−2		IFB	Eval Rept	YK − 9 34	72 Morogovsky. EVAL+RECOMM VALUE,CF OTH	
				Rept	INDC(CCP) − 42	Aug 74 .P1.ENGLISH OF YK − 9	
Nu	Maxwl	1.6+6	FEI	Expt Jour	AE 32 83	Jan 72 Kolosov+ FROM FRAG A − KE − BALANCE,GRPH	+
	0.0+0	1.6+6		Eval Prog	YFI − 11 13	70 − +°ABST,ANALYSIS OF EXPTS,NDG	
				Prog	INDC(CCP) − 31	Dec 72 PAGE 11,ENGLISH OF YFI − 11 13	
	Maxwl	1.6+6		Expt Jour	SJA 32 92	Jul 72 . ENGL OF AE 32 83	
	8.0+4	1.6+6		Data	EXFOR40130.004	Sep 72 NU − BAR AT 16 ES REL THERMAL	
Nu	Maxwl		CUA	Theo Abst	DA/B 32 5980	Apr 72 Lee. CALC OF AVG PROMPT NU	
Nu	2.5−2	1.6+6	FEI	Expt Jour	AE 33 901	Nov 72 Volodin+ NU VS EN CFD OTHERS,TBL,GRF	+
				Jour	SJA 33 1045	May 73 .ENGLISH OF AE 33 901 NOV/72	
	2.5−2	1.6+6		Data	EXFOR40148.	Jun 73 .4 SUBENTRIES	
Nu	1.2−2	2.0+2	IAE	Eval Jour	REA 10 637	Dec 72 Manero+ SURVEY NUBAR(SPIN),TBL+GRAPH	
Nu	2.5−2		IAE	Eval Jour	REA 10 637	Dec 72 Manero+ SURVEY,TBLS+GRPHS,RECOMM VAL	
Nu	Fast		BUC	Revw Rept	IFA − RN − 50	73 Cristu. NU(FRAGM − E,MASS.COMP − EXCIT)	
	Maxwl			Rept	IFA − RN − 50	73 − . NU(FRAGM − E,MASS.COMP − EXCIT)	
Nu	0.0+0	1.5+7	UK	Eval Data	UKNDL − DFN 404B	Mar 73 .5 PTS. ANG DIST OF FISS NEUTS,LAB.	
Nu	−2	1.5+7	IJE	Eval Conf	73Kiev 1 209	May 73 Konshin+ NUBAR. ACCURACY,NDG	
Nu	1.0−2	4.0+1	ITE	Expt Conf	73Kiev 4 70	May 73 Bolotsky+ NUBAR(NEUTR − E),TBL,CFD	
Nu	1.0−2	4.0+1	KUR	Expt Conf	73Kiev 4 70	May 73 Bolotsky+ NUBAR(NEUT − E),TBL,CFD	+
	1.0−2	4.0+1		Data	EXFOR40265.002	Feb 75 DATA AT 6 E − RANGES GIVEN	
Nu	Fast		FOA	Expt Conf	70Helsinki 2 139	Jun 70 Conde+59 PILE AVG NU AND NU(E) GIVEN	+
				Jour	JNE 27 395	Jun 73 Widen+ IN 3 SPECT, CFD WITH TH SPEC	
				Conf	73Kiev 4 130	May 73 Conde+ LINEAR NUBAR(E),NO VALUES GVN	
				Prog	EANDC(OR)99 30	Aug 70 − +. IN FR0. 6.7 PC BELOW THRMVAL	
	Fast			Data	EXFOR20113.	Sep 71 2PTS.PROMPT. 2 SPEC AVG VALUES.	
Nu	2.5−2		ANL	Expt Conf	73Rochestr 2 19	Aug 73 Unik+NU TOTAL VS MASS 13 NUCLIDES.	
Nu	7.8+0	4.0+2	BRC	Expt Conf	73Munich 1 606	Aug 73 Frehaut+ CORREL TO E − GAM STUDY,GRAPH	
Nu	1.0−2	1.0+2	RPI	Expt Conf	73Rochestr 2 502	Aug 73 Hockenbury+ ABST,NUBAR(N − E),CFD,NDG	
Nu	7.8+0	4.0+2	SAC	Expt Conf	73Rochestr 2 201	Aug 73 Frehaut+ NU(E) FOR RESON NEUTS,GRAPH	
				Conf	73Kiev 3 145	May 73 .SEE 73ROCHESTR.	
Nu	1.3+6	1.5+7	DUB	Comp Jour	YF 18 724	Oct 73 Dakovsky+ DISPERSION VS NUBAR, GRAPH	
				Jour	SNP 18 371	Apr 74 . ENGLISH OF YF 18 724	
Nu	2.6−1	2.0+2	SAC	Expt Jour	NP/A 216 395	Dec 73 Ryabov+LINAC.NU FLUCT,G − MLTPLCTY/NU	+
	1.0+1	3.0+2			Jour JPR 34 131	Feb 73 Trochon+VARIATION WITH RESONANCES	
	1.5+1	1.1+2			Jour PL/B 42 334	Dec 72 Shackleton+ NU FLUCTUATIONS+N,GAMM E	
	2.6−1	2.0+2			Jour PL/B 42 344	Dec 72 Shackleton+SAME NU,EG VS RES PLOT	
	1.0+1	3.0+1		ExTh Jour	JPRC 33 25	Aug 72 Trochon+ 60 MEV LINAC TOF GRPHS	
	2.6−1	2.0+2			Jour JPRC 33 24	Aug 72 Shackleton+ PROMPT N AND G YIELDS	
	1.0+1	3.0+2		Expt Prog	EANDC(E)150U	May 72 Trochon+,VARIATION OF MULTIPLICITY	
	7.8+0	4.0+2		Data	EXFOR20503.002	Mar 76 44PTS.PROMPT.	
Nu	0.0+0	5.0+6	BIR	Revw Jour	RPP 37 951	74 Beynon+ COMPAR NUBAR − MEASURMNTS,GRPH	
Nu	2.5−2		IKE	Eval Rept	IKE − 6 − 80	Apr 74 Mattes+ ENDF/B,UKNDL,KEDAK CFD	
Nu	2.0+5	2.0+6	AUA	Expt Jour	ANE 1 353	Jun 74 Walsh+ LIQ SCIN.EVAL DATA TO 5 MEV.	+
	2.0+5	1.9+6			Jour JNE 25 321	Aug 71 − + GRPH WITH PRELIM DATA AT 8 ES	
	Maxwl	2.3+6			Prog AAEC/PR − 33P 6	70 Boldeman+ NU − BAR VS NEUT − E GRAPH	
	1.1+5	1.9+6			Data EXFOR30006.004	Jan 73 DATA AT 8 ES FROM PRIV COMM NOV 1972	
Nu	−2	1.5+7	CJD	Eval Rept	INDC(CCP) − 44	Jun 74 .P1. ENGLISH OF 73KIEV 1 209	
Nu	5.0+7	1.7+7	LRL	Expt Prog	UCID − 16514 6	Jun 74 Alvarez+	
Nu	2.0+5	1.3+6	KFK	Expt Prog	NEANDC(E) − 161U	Aug 74 Bandl+ PLANNED	
				Prog	EANDC(E)157U I	Mar 73 − + ENERGY DEPEND	
Nu	Maxwl		SAC	Expt Prog	NEANDC(E)161U	Aug 74 Girard+	
Nu	1.0+1	1.7+2	ORL	Expt Jour	PR/C 10 1402	Oct 74 Weston+ GRPHS.TBL.	+
				Rept	ORNL − TM − 3331	Apr 71 − . TABULATED DATA	
	1.4+1	2.0+2		Conf	71Knoxvill 861	Mar 71 − .	
	1.0+1	1.7+2		Data	EXFOR10162.002	Sep 75 46PTS,NU	
Nu	Maxwl		AUA	Expt Jour	AEA 18 2 2	Apr 75 Walsh. REVW OF WORK,RESULTS GIVEN	+
				Rept	AAEC/E − 172	Mar 67 .EXPTL DETAILS,DATA SUPERSEDED	
	Maxwl			Data	EXFOR30046.004	Jan 73 .FINAL VALUE FROM PRIV COMM NOV 1972	
Nu	4.1+6		BRC	Expt Jour	JPRL 36 80	Apr 75 Lachkar+ VDG,DATA AND GRAPH GIVEN	
Nu	1.4+6	4.0+6	FEI	Comp Conf	75Kiev 5 170	May 75 Prokhorova+ NU(EN),EVAL ACCURACS.TBL	
	0.0+0	5.0+6		Eval Rept	YK − 20/1 104	75 − + NUBAR(NEUT − E),GRAPH,TBL	
	5.0+4	5.0+6		Rept	INDC(CCP) − 91	Jun 76 . ENGL OF YK − 20 104(TBLS+GRPHS GIVN)	

94 Plutonium 239

Quantity	Energy (ev) Min	Energy (ev) Max	Lab	Type	Documentation Ref Vol Page	Date	Author, Comments	Data
Nu	1.1+6	2.1+6	KUR	Expt Conf	75Kiev 5 86	May 75	Khokhlov+ NUBAR(EN),DISPERS(EN).TABL	
Nu	1.0+6	2.0+6	HED	Theo Abst	ANS 21 518	Jun 75	Schenter+ TBL CALC FROM ENDF FP FILE	
	2.5-2			Abst	ANS 21 518	Jun 75	- + TBL CALC FROM ENDF FP FILE	
Nu	+6	5.0+6	FEI	Expt Jour	AE 39 199	Sep 75	Nurpeisov+ NUBAR(NEUT-E),TBL,GRAPH	
	1.0+5	5.0+6		Conf	75Kiev 5 175	May 75	- + NUBAR(E),GRPH.	
	1.0+6	5.0+6		Jour	SJA 39 807	Mar 76	. ENGLISH OF AE 39 199	
Nu	Spont		HED	Eval Abst	ANS 22 673	Nov 75	Johnson. TBL,GRPH.NU FROM SPON FISS	
Nu		6.6+2	BRC	Revw Conf	76Lowell 641	Jul 76	Michaudon.COMP THEO.WITH EXP.DATA	
	1.0+0	1.8+2		Conf	75Wash. 202	Mar 75	- . GRPH NUBAR VS E FOR J=1+	
Nu	0.0+0	1.5+7	BRC	Eval Rept	CEA-R-4791	Oct 76	Bois+NUBAR VS EN,CALC CFD EXP,TABLES	
Nu	Maxwl		NIR	Expt Conf	77Kiev	77	Basova+ NU(NEUT-E),GRAPH	
				Conf	75Kiev 5 160	May 75	- + NU(FRAG-MASS,AVG EKIN).GRPH	
Delayd Neuts	None		LAS	Expt Jour	PR 71 560	Apr 47	Wilson. YIELD VERSUS TIME. REL U235	
				Rept	LA- 76	May 44	- +,RELATIVE TO U235	
Delayd Neuts	Pile		CHI	Expt Jour	PR 72 570	Oct 47	Redman+ 4 PERIODS, RELATIVE INTENSTY	
Delayd Neuts	Pile		LAS	Expt Jour	PR 72 567	Oct 47	Dehoffman+ DECAY CURVE, 4 PERIODS.	
Delayd Neuts	Fiss		LAS	Expt Jour	NUC 13 10 49	Oct 55	Paxton+	
Delayd Neuts	Maxwl	Fiss	ANL	Expt Jour	NSE 1 174	May 56	Brunson+ EBR NUD=.360 .405+-11PC	
				Rept	ANL-5480	Aug 55	.SUPERSEDED	
Delayd Neuts	Pile		HAR	Revw Jour	NPW 1 114	Jul 56	Cox. YIELD+HALF LIFES OF DEL-NEUTS	
Delayd Neuts	Fast		HAR	Expt Jour	JNE 4 141	Jun 57	Rose+ ZEPHYR. 5 GROUPS.TBL YLD+FRACT	+
Delayd Neuts	Maxwl	Fiss	LAS	Expt Jour	PR 107 1044	Aug 57	Keepin+,0.0063+- 0.0003 N/FISS 6GRPS	
				Jour	JNE 6 1	Dec 57	- +. SAME DATA AS PR(8/57)	
				Rept	LA- 1970	Oct 55	- . NEUT YLDS+SPECTR,CURVS+TABLS	
				Conf	55Geneva 4 162	Aug 55	- +.P/831. PRELIMINARY.	
Delayd Neuts	None		LAS	Theo Jour	JNE 7 13	Aug 58	Keepin.THEOR DEL NEUT PRECURSRS,YLDS	
				Jour	AE 4 250	Mar 58	.SEE ALSO	
				Jour	SJA 4 339		58 .SEE ALSO	
Delayd Neuts	Maxwl		OSL	Expt Conf	58Geneva 15 373	Sep 58	Pappas+.PPR583,TBL CFD THEORIE	
Delayd Neuts	Maxwl		ANL	Expt Conf	61Vienna 1 125	Aug 61	Butler+.P36,6 GROUPS,YIELD+PERIODS	
Delayd Neuts	Maxwl		LAS	Expt Conf	61Vienna 1 149	Aug 61	Diven+.PPR56,TABLE REL TO CF252	
Delayd Neuts	1.5+7		RI	Expt Jour	AE 11 539	Dec 61	Shpakov+ T(D,N)SOURCE,BORON COUNTERS	+
				Jour	SJA 11 1190	May 62	TRANSLATN.*	
Delayd Neuts	Maxwl		LAS	Revw Jour	NUC 20 8 150	Aug 62	Keepin.	
Delayd Neuts	3.8+6	1.5+7	RI	Expt Jour	AE 15 157	Aug 63	Petrzhak+ 6 GROUPS GIVEN	
				Jour	SJA 15 849	Aug 63	. ENGL OF AE 15 157	
Delayd Neuts	3.8+6	1.5+7	FEI	Expt Rept	ICD-1 266	64	Maksjutenko. YIELD AT 2ES, TBL,CURVS	+
				Rept	INDSWG-64E 24	64	. ENGL OF ICD-1 266	
Delayd Neuts	5.0+6	8.0+6	FEI	Expt Conf	67Vienna 191	Apr 67	Maksjutenko.REL YLDS FOR 5GROUPS	
Delayd Neuts		+7	HFA	Revw Conf	67Vienna 23	Apr 67	Yiftah+ TBL OF YLD+HL,REACTR DYNAMIC	
Delayd Neuts	Maxwl		SOR	Comp Conf	67Vienna 115	Apr 67	Amiel+ DEL-N PRECURSRS,TBL=CALC+COMP	
				Rept	IA- 1190 95	Jul 69	NEW INFOR.*	
Delayd Neuts	Maxwl		MNZ	Theo Jour	AF 36 453	Nov 67	Patzelt+.FROM DERIVED N-EMISS PROB.	
Delayd Neuts	Maxwl		VIP	Expt Rept	TID-25643	Nov 68	Huizinga.DELAYED NEUT GROUPS.H2O,D2O	
Delayd Neuts	Fiss		HAR	Expt Rept	AERE-M-2199	Apr 69	Tomlinson+ ESTIMATE YLD AL 1 MIN+	
Delayd Neuts	3.1+6	1.5+7	LAS	Expt Jour	NSE 36 202	May 69	Masters+ 2ES RELATIVE+ABSOL MEASTS	+
				Conf	69Vienna 647	Jul 69	East+PPR109.SAFEGUARD PROBL,XPT+REVW	
	3.1+6	1.5+7		Data	EXFOR12288.	Jun 76	. 2 PTS.	
Delayd Neuts	Maxwl		MNZ	Expt Conf	69Vienna 591	Jul 69	Schuessler+PPR22. I-137 PRECURS EXPT	
Delayd Neuts	Maxwl	+7	SOR	Revw Conf	69Vienna 569	Jul 69	Amiel.PPR205. REVW,EXPTS+TH,TABLES	
Delayd Neuts	2.5-2		SOR	Expt Prog	IA- 1190 95	Jul 69	Notea.RELATIVE TO U235,CFD OTHERS	+
	2.5-2			Data	EXFOR30238.003	May 73	.TOTL DELAYED NEUT YLD FOR 5 GROUPS.	
Delayd Neuts	Maxwl		HAR	Theo Rept	AERE-R-6596	Nov 70	Tomlinson. CALC DEL-N GROUP YLDS.TBL	
Delayd Neuts	Maxwl		BNL	Expt Jour	NSE 44 173	May 71	Conant+ DELAYED NEUT FRACTION	+
	Maxwl			Data	EXFOR10144.003	Mar 72	1PT	
Delayd Neuts	1.8+7	2.1+7	FEI	Expt Prog	YFI-10 27	May 71	Maksjutenko+ ABST,YLDS REL BR87,TBL	
				Rept	INDC(CCP)-15	Dec 71	*P29,ENG OF YFI-10	
				Jour	YF 13 293	Feb 71	Maksjutenko+ 11GROUPS REL YLD.TABLE	
				Jour	SNP 13 163	Aug 71	. ENGL OF YF 13 293	
Delayd Neuts	2.5-2	1.5+7	IAE	Eval Jour	REA 10 637	Dec 72	Manero+ SURVEY,AVERAGE YIELD,TBLS	
Delayd Neuts	1.4+7		KFK	Expt Jour	JNE 26 585	Dec 72	Fieg.EN SPECT,AS FN TIME AFTER FISS	
				Rept	KFK-EXT-4 31	May 71	- . SPEC EXPT, 4-GROUP SPECS CALC	
Delayd Neuts	Fast		BUC	Revw Rept	IFA-RN-50	73	Cristu. NUD(FRAGM-MASS),H-L,E-SPEC	
	Maxwl			Rept	IFA-RN-50	73	- . NUD(FRAGM-MASS),H-L,E-SPEC	
Delayd Neuts		5.0+6	FEI	Expt Jour	YFK 12 15	Jan 73	Balakshev+	+
		5.0+6		Data	EXFOR40209.	May 74	.3 SUBENT EACH 4 DATA LINES	
Delayd Neuts	Maxwl		HFA	Expt Jour	NSE 51 52	May 73	Shalev+ HE-3 DET. NEUT ENERGY DISTR	
Delayd Neuts	Fast		ALD	Expt Prog	EANDC(UK) 151	Aug 73	Mctaggart.TBD	

94 Plutonium 239

Quantity	Energy (ev) Min	Max	Lab	Type	Documentation Ref Vol Page	Date	Author, Comments	Data
Delayd Neuts	Maxwl		FEI	Theo	Conf IAEA-169 3 105	74	Maksjutenko+ CALC PROBAB(H-L),GRAPHS	
					Jour YF 17 1149	Jun 73	Tarasko+ TRANSFORM OF HL-GROUPS,GRPH	
					Rept FEI-369	72	- + SAME AS YF 17 1149	
					Jour SNP 17 598	Dec 73	.ENGL OF YF 17 1149	
					Rept KFK-TR-437	73	. GERMAN OF FEI-370	
Delayd Neuts	5.0+4	1.8+6	LAS	Expt	Jour NSE 53 80	Jan 74	Evans+REVISED NUD DATA TBLS.	+
	1.0+5	1.5+7			Conf IAEA-169 377	74	- . TBL YLD,AT 3 ES+FAST FISSION	
	1.0+5	1.8+6			Jour NSE 47 311	Mar 72	Krick+SPRSDD.DATA REVISED	
	5.0+4	1.8+6			Data EXFOR10117.008	Jul 74	18PTS	
Delayd Neuts	Maxwl	1.5+7	SOR	Revw	Conf IAEA-169 2 33	74	Amiel.ALL YLDS,DEL-N SPECS,TBL,GRPHS	
Delayd Neuts	1.0+6	4.0+6	ANL	Expt	Abst BAP 19 597	Apr 74	COX. 4ES. ABSOL YLD MEASD.NO DATA.	
Delayd Neuts	Maxwl	1.5+7	ANL	Eval	Rept ANL-NDM-5	Apr 74	COX. REL YLD, HL, GRPH	
Delayd Neuts	Maxwl		HAR	Eval	Prog NEANDC(UK)160	Jul 74	Story+ (WIN) EVAL OF TOMLNSN REVISD	
					Rept AERE-R-6993	Feb 72	Tomlinson.TOTAL+GROUP YLDS SPEC TBL	
	2.5-2			Revw	Conf 71Canterby 239	71	- .EXP CFD CALCULATIONS.TABLE	
Delayd Neuts	2.5-2	1.5+7	AI	Eval	Jour NSE 56 37	Jan 75	Tuttle.TBL.GRPH.RVW MEAS.CFD REC VAL	
	2.5-2				Prog AI-AEC-13025	May 72	Springer+ VALUE=0.00658+-0.00011	
Delayd Neuts	2.5-2		IAE	Eval	Conf 75Wash. 286	Mar 75	Lemmel. TBL LSQ ANAL.CFD OTHER EVAL.	
Delayd Neuts	2.5-2		HED	Theo	Abst ANS 21 518	Jun 75	Schenter+ TBL CALC FROM ENDF FP FILE	
Delayd Neuts	1.0+6	2.0+6	HED	Theo	Abst ANS 21 518	Jun 75	Schenter+ TBL CALC FROM ENDF FP FILE	
Delayd Neuts	+6		FEI	Expt	Rept YK-23 110	76	Maksjutenko+ YLD DELAYED NEUTS,GRAPH	
Delayd Neuts	Maxwl		FEI	Expt	Rept INDC(CCP)-66	Feb 76	.P 1. ENGL OF YFI-20 3	
Delayd Neuts	Fast		CSR	Revw	Jour JE 23 9 345	77	Tinka. REVW GROUP-SPEC,PARAMS.TABLES	
	Maxwl				Jour JE 23 9 345	77	- . REVW GROUP-SPEC,PARAMS.TABLES	
Delayd Neuts	Maxwl		SWR	Theo	Jour JRC 36 591	77	Rudstam. DEL-N SPEC CALC,FINE STRUCT	
Frag Neuts	None		LAS	Revw	Jour PR 127 880	Aug 62	Terrell.ANALYSIS OF TOF+RADIOCHEM	
Frag Neuts	Maxwl		KUR	Expt	Rept IAE-819	65	Apalin+ GRPHS NEUT NO NU(FRAG-MASS)	
Frag Neuts	Maxwl		KUR	Expt	Conf 65Salzburg 1 587	Mar 65	Apalin+,SYMMETRIC FISS,GRPHS,CFD XPT	
					Jour YF 1 639	Apr 65	SEE ALSO *NP 71 553 9/65	
					Jour SNP 1 457	Oct 65	. ENGL OF YF 1 639	
Frag Neuts	None		LAS	Revw	Conf 65Salzburg 3	Mar 65	Terrell.XPTL WORK CFD THEORY.GRAPHS	
Frag Neuts	Maxwl		CRC	Expt	Jour ARN 16 379	Apr 66	Fraser+ GRAPH NEUTRON YIELD	
					Conf 65Salzburg 2 39	Mar 65	Milton+ TABLE NEUTRON YIELD + TEMP	
Frag Neuts	Maxwl		ITK	Theo	Conf 68Madras 1 302	Feb 68	Mukherji+ CALC NU VS HEAVY MASS,GRPH	
Frag Neuts	Maxwl		MCM	Theo	Conf 69Vienna 845	Jul 69	Thind+PPR50. FRAG-EXCIT-E CFD NU(A)	
Frag Neuts	Maxwl		KFI	Theo	Jour PL/B 30 311	Oct 69	Kluge+	
Frag Neuts	Maxwl		AUA	Expt	Prog AAEC/PR-40P 28	Jul 74	Boldeman+ NU(FRGM-MASS),TBD	
Frag Neuts	Maxwl		NIR	Expt	Conf 75Kiev 5 160	May 75	Basova+ NU(FRAG-MASS,AVG EKIN).GRPH	
Frag Neuts	Maxwl		NIR	Expt	Rept YK-27 38	77	Basova+ TOF,NUBAR(FRAGMASS),GRAPHS	
Spect Fiss n	Maxwl		LAS	Expt	Rept LA-1078	Mar 50	Carlson+ NUCLEAR EMULSION 0.4-7MEV	
Spect Fiss n	Maxwl		CRC	Expt	Jour PR 88 536	Nov 52	Fraser+ANGULAR DIST CURVES CFD THEOR	
Spect Fiss n	Maxwl		LAS	Expt	Jour PR 88 823	Nov 52	Nereson+ FOTOPLATE 0.5-8MEV NEUTS	
Spect Fiss n	5.0+5	1.0+6	LAS	Expt	Jour PR 104 731	Nov 56	Allen+,ANGULAR DISTR ISOTROPIC	
Spect Fiss n	Maxwl		CCP	Expt	Jour ZET 33 1069	Oct 57	Kovalev.HARDER THAN U235,THRESHLDDET	
					Jour JET 6 825	Apr 58	TRANSLATN.*	
					-		FRENCH CEA-TR-R-725	
Spect Fiss n	5.0+4	7.0+5	CCP	Expt	Jour ZET 34 501	Feb 58	CLOUD CHAMB,AGREES WITH WATT, T=1MEV	
					Jour JET 7 345	Aug 58	TRANSLATN.*	
Spect Fiss n	1.4+7		CCP	Expt	Jour AE 4 337	Apr 58	Zamiatnin+ FISS+EVAP SPECTR FIT DATA	
					Jour JNE 9 194	Jun 59	TRANSLATN.*	
					Jour SJA 4 443	58	TRANSLATN.*	
Spect Fiss n	Maxwl	3.0+6	CCP	Theo	Jour AE 5 649	Dec 58	Kovalev+ THEORY COMPARED WITH EXPT	
					Jour JNEA 11 166	Feb 60	TRANSLATN.*	
					Jour SJA 5 1588	58	TRANSLATN.*	
Spect Fiss n	Maxwl		LAS	Eval	Jour PR 113 527	Jan 59	Terrell.TH CFD C EXPT,STAT ANALYSIS	
Spect Fiss n	Fiss		KUR	Revw	Conf 60Vienna 159	Oct 60	Bondarenko+.NDG,MEASRMNT REL TO U235	
Spect Fiss n	Maxwl		RIC	Expt	Jour NP 23 116	Feb 61	Bonner.MOD SPH SP. T=1.385+-0.030MEV	
Spect Fiss n	Maxwl		ORL	Eval	Rept ORNL-TM-795	Feb 64	Halperin+ FISS SPEC .01-25MEV TABLE	
Spect Fiss n	4.0+4		FOA	Expt	Jour AF 29 313	Apr 65	Conde+ FISS CH.+PLSTSC.MAXWELL TEMP.	+
					Conf 65Salzburg 93	Mar 65	- + EQU TO AF 29 313	
	4.0+4				Data EXFOR20575.	Aug 76	14PTS.AVG.K.E.	
Spect Fiss n	1.4+7		SAC	Expt	Conf 65Antwerp § 171	Jul 65	Didier+TOF LIQ SC.AT 83 AND 53DEGR	
Spect Fiss n	Maxwl	1.4+7	HAR	Eval	Jour NP 71 228	Sep 65	Barnard+ CORRELATED WITH NU BAR	
Spect Fiss n	2.5-2		RI	Expt	Prog YFI-6 94		Belov+. SPECTRUM TEMPERATURE, TABLE	
					Rept INDC-260E	69	. ENGL OF YFI-6 94	
Spect Fiss n	Maxwl		RI	ExTh	Conf 68Riga	Jan 68	Belov+ ABST,SPECTRUM OF NEUTRONS	

94 Plutonium 239

Quantity	Energy (ev) Min	Max	Lab	Type	Documentation Ref Vol Page	Date	Author, Comments	Data
Spect Fiss n	Maxwl		LAS	Expt	Jour NSE 31 191	Feb 68	Grundl+8 ACT DET CFD.8 - 16MEV RANGE	
					Abst DA 25 6704	May 65	- . REL U233,U235.	
					Rept LAMS - 2883	May 63	- +ACT DETECTOR 0.6 - 16MEV NEUTS.	
					Rept TNCC(US) - 8	May 56	- + TR DETECT 16PC LESS 25	
Spect Fiss n	Maxwl		RI	Expt	Prog YFI - 6 94	Oct 68	Belov+ TABLE N(E) AND MAXWELL - TEMP	+
					Rept INDC - E - 260 94	Feb 69	.TRANSLATN.* TO BE PUBL IN YF	
	Maxwl				Data EXFOR40137.004	Mar 73	SPECT OF FIS - NEUTS .3 - 7.MEV	
Spect Fiss n	1.0+4	1.0+7	HEB	Theo	Priv NISSIMOV	69	Nissimov+MICROSC SIG CHECK BY N - SPEC	
Spect Fiss n	1.5+5	1.5+6	HAR	Expt	Rept AERE - R - 5972	Mar 69	Cavanagh+ MEAN N E CONSTANT + - 2PC	
Spect Fiss n	Maxwl		FTI	Expt	Jour YF 9 727	Apr 69	Belov+ EXPTL NEUT - SPEC GRPH+AVG EKIN	
					Jour SNP 9 421	Oct 69	TRANSLATN.*NO4	
Spect Fiss n	Maxwl		KFI	Theo	Jour PL/B 30 311	Oct 69	Kluge+	
Spect Fiss n	1.0 - 3	1.0+7	KFK	Eval	Rept KFK - 1340	Feb 71	Hinkelmann+TABLE OF EVALUATED DATA	+
					Rept KFK - 750	Jan 68	Schmidt. EVAL SUPERSEDED	
					Rept KFK - 120 2	Dec 65	- . SUPERSEDED	
	1.0 - 2	1.0+7			Rept KFK - 120 2	Dec 62	- .GRAPHS AND TABULATED	
	Maxwl				Data KEDAK - 3	Oct 75	175 DATA SETS + CRANBERG PARAMS	
Spect Fiss n	3.5+4	4.0+5	ANL	Expt	Jour NSE 44 439	Jun 71	Smith. 2INCIDENT NEUT ES,REL MEAST	
Spect Fiss n	Maxwl	1.4+7	ANL	Revw	Conf 71Vienna 3	Aug 71	Smith. MEAN - E OF NEUTS,EXPTS CFD,TBL	
Spect Fiss n	1.5+6	5.5+6	GEL	Expt	Jour ZP 232 286	Feb 70	Coppola+,E - SPEC GIVEN,TBL OF MEAN - ES	+
					Conf 71Vienna 41	Aug 71	Knitter+ TOF,E - SPEC,7 N - ES,TBL AVG E	
	1.5+6	5.5+6			Data EXFOR20392.003	Oct 74	7PTS.AVG.K.E.	
Spect Fiss n	Maxwl	5.5+6	IAE	Revw	Conf 71Vienna 19	Aug 71	Koster.MEAN - E OF NS,DIFFTL EXPTS,TBL	
Spect Fiss n	Maxwl		MOL	Expt	Conf 71Vienna 97	Aug 71	Fabry.SIG EXPTS CFD U - 235 FISS - SPEC	
Spect Fiss n	Maxwl		WIN	Revw	Conf 71Vienna 33	Aug 71	Campbell+ MEAN - E+SPEC - SHAPE CFD,TBLS	
Spect Fiss n	Maxwl		KFK	Theo	Rept KFK - 1271 3	Nov 71	Kiefhaber+(P.122 - 1) CALC 3 DATA SETS	
				Revw	Conf 71Vienna 129	Aug 71	- + DATA FILES SPECS CFD,TBLS	
Spect Fiss n	3.0+5	8.0+6	ANL	Expt	Prog ANL - 7910 18	Jan 72	Smith. RATIO TO U 235. CURVE	
Spect Fiss n	Maxwl		KFK	Expt	Jour JNE 26 165	Apr 72	Werle+ PROT RECOIL,HE003 SPECT.AV EN	+
					Jour NIM 99 295	Mar 72	- .FISSION SPECTR ONLY GRAPH	
					Conf 71Vienna 65	Aug 71	- + P - RECOIL CFD HE - DET,TBL,GRAPH	
	2.5 - 2				Data EXFOR20616.	Jun 76	85PTS.AVG.K.E.	
Spect Fiss n	1.8+6		LAS	Expt	Prog USNDC - 3 118	Oct 72	Auchampaugh+. VDG. CURVE	
Spect Fiss n	1.0 - 4	1.5+7	UK	Eval	Data UKNDL - DFN 161A	Mar 73	5 RANGES	+
Spect Fiss n	0.0+0	1.5+7	UK	Eval	Data UKNDL - DFN 404B	Mar 73	3 RANGES	+
Spect Fiss n	1.0+4	5.8+4	CAD	Expt	Conf 73Kiev 3 47	May 73	Abramson+GRPH.T=1.37MEV.	
Spect Fiss n	1.0+5	5.0+5	HAR	Expt	Prog EANDC(UK) 151	Aug 73	Adams+ ROSE DATA BEING FINALISED	
Spect Fiss n	1.0+5	9.5+6	BIR	Revw	Jour RPP 37 951	74	Beynon+ COMPAR N - SPEC+MEAN MAXWELL - E	
Spect Fiss n	1.5+6	5.5+6	RAM	Expt	Conf 74Dacca 33	Nov 74	Islam. AVG FISS - N - EN VS E,7PTS.TABLE	
	2.1+5		GEL	Expt	Jour AKE 26 2 76	75	Knitter. E - SPEC 0.25 - 15 MEV	+
	2.1+5				Data EXFOR20576.	Jun 76	184PTS.AVG.K.E.	
Spect Fiss n	1.0+5		FEI	Expt	Jour AE 38 108	Feb 75	Aleksandrova+ N - SPEC,GRAPH	+
					Jour SJA 38 140	Aug 75	. ENGL OF AE 38 108	
	1.0+5				Data EXFOR40358.	May 77	N - SPEC(1.5 - 11MEV),54 PNTS(ARB UNIT)	
Spect Fiss n	1.0+5	2.1+6	AE	Expt	Conf 75Wash. 572	Mar 75	Johansson+ SHAPE FIT TO WATT DISTR.	
Spect Fiss n	2.5 - 2		IAE	Eval	Conf 75Wash. 286	Mar 75	Lemmel. 3RD IAEA - EVAL, BY LSQ FIT	
				Revw	Jour REA 7 4 3	Dec 69	Hanna+ N - SPECTRUM IN NU - BAR EXPTS	
Spect Fiss n	1.0+5	1.0+7	KFK	Expt	Rept KFK - 2200 97	Apr 75	Bluhm+ EXPT METHODS DISCUSSED	
					Rept JUEL - 1178 97	Apr 75	- + SAME AS KFK - 2200	
Spect Fiss n	Fast		ANL	Eval	Abst ANS 22 671	Nov 75	Saphier+ 6 GPS DELAYED NEUT SPECT	
Spect Fiss n	1.0+5	2.0+5	GEB	Eval	Abst ANS 24 452	Nov 76	Kujawski+WATT SPEC VS MAXW,CFD.	
Spect Fiss γ	Maxwl		HAR		Rept NRDC - 58	Feb 55	.ROUGH EXPT BUT VERY CLOSE TO U235	
Spect Fiss γ	Maxwl		LAS	ExTh	Jour PR/B 133 714	Feb 64	Hoffman. G - FRAG ANG CORR FITS.	
Spect Fiss γ	Maxwl		FTI	Expt	Jour ZET 47 2064	Nov 64	G YLDS FOR 9AS,ANISOTROPY=(16+ - 1)PC	
					Jour JET 20 1387	Jun 65	TRANSLATN.*	
Spect Fiss γ	Maxwl		JUL	Revw	Rept JUEL - 405 - NP	65	Maier - Leibnitz+ANG CORR GAM - FISSFRAG	
					Conf 65Salzburg 2 113	Mar 65	- +	
Spect Fiss γ	Maxwl		FTI	Expt	Jour AE 18 64	Jan 65	Petrov. ANG CORREL GS - FISFRAGMENTS	
					Jour JNE 20 91	Jan 65	TRANSLATN.*	
					Jour EAF 18 1 107	Jan 65	TRANSLATN.*	
					Jour SJA 18 72	Jan 65	TRANSLATN.*	
Spect Fiss γ	+0	+3	CAI	Theo	Jour NP 62 667	Feb 65	Stavinsky+(N,GF)PROB ABOUT=(N,GAMMA)	
Spect Fiss γ	Maxwl		UI	Expt	Abst DA 26 7383	Jun 66	Bridwell.X - RAYS AT FEW NANOSECS	
					Jour PR 145 963	May 66	- + X - RAYS TO 50KEV/FRAG.	
Spect Fiss γ	Maxwl		CUA	Theo	Jour DA/B 30 2222	Nov 69	Rogers.	
Spect Fiss γ	None		ITK	Theo	Prog BARC - 474 54	70	Mukherji+ CALC TOTAL GAM - E OKS EXPT	
Spect Fiss γ	4.5+5	9.0+5	SAC	Expt	Prog EANDC(E)127U	Apr 70	Lottin+,GE(LI) DET	

94 Plutonium 239

Quantity	Energy (ev) Min	Energy (ev) Max	Lab	Type	Documentation Ref Vol Page	Author, Comments Date	Data
Spect Fiss γ	Maxwl		KFK	Expt	Priv WIETKAMP	73 Weitkamp. SPECTRA.PROMPT+DELAYED	
	Pile				Rept KFK-1214	Jul 70 Matussek+ G-SPEC,GRPHS	
Spect Fiss γ	2.5-2		SRC	Theo	Jour JNE 25 339	Aug 71 Scobie+ VAR.BETA EN REL RATE WTH TME	
Spect Fiss γ	Maxwl		GA	Expt	Jour PR/C 7 1173	Mar 73 Verbinski+ GAMS 0-10 NS AFTER FISS	
	None				Conf 69Vienna 929	Jul 69 Verbinsky.PPR33. MEAN GAMM E+YLD GVN	
Spect Fiss γ	Maxwl		ATI	Expt	Jour NP/A 206 374	May 73 Schindler+ GE-LI,300-1300KEV.CFD CF	
Spect Fiss γ	2.6-1	2.0+2	SAC	Expt	Conf 73Kiev 2 232	May 73 Trochon+ (N,GF) EVIDENCE,GF-WID CALC	
Spect Fiss γ	7.8+0	4.0+2	SAC	Expt	Conf 73Rochestr 2 201	Aug 73 Frehaut+MEAN EN OF PROMPT GAMS,GRAPH	
					Conf 73Kiev 3 145	May 73 .SEE 73ROCHESTR.	
Spect Fiss γ	2.6-1	2.0+2	SAC	Expt	Jour NP/A 216 395	Dec 73 Ryabov+LINAC. IN CORREL WITH NU FLUC	
					Jour PL/B 42 344	Dec 72 Shackelton+ SAME NU,EG VS RES PLOT	
Spect Fiss γ	1.0+1	1.7+2	ORL	Expt	Jour PR/C 10 1402	Oct 74 Weston+ TBL.	
Spect Fiss γ	None		BRC	Revw	Conf 75Wash. 202	Mar 75 Michaudon. FISSION REVIEW.TH+EXPTS.	
Spect Fiss γ	2.5-2		LAS	Theo	Conf 75Wash. 193	May 75 Stamatelatos+GRPHS.G SPECT.CINDER	
Spect Fiss γ	Maxwl		LIN	Expt	Jour YF 22 462	Sep 75 Teterev+ G-SPEC CFD U,PU,CF-FIS.GRPH	
					Conf 75Kiev 6 121	Jun 75 - + G-SPEC,YLD GAMMAS,GRAPHS	
					Jour SNP 22 238	Sep 75 . ENGL OF YF 22 462	
Spect Fiss γ	1.5+1	1.1+2	BRC	Expt	Jour ASL 26 25	76 Trochon+ (N,GF)-INVESTIG,TBLS+CURVES	
	7.0+0	6.0+1		ExTh	Conf 75Kiev 5 323	May 75 - + (N,GF).G-SPEC VS EXC-E.GRPH	
	7.8+0	4.0+2		Expt	Conf 73Munich 1 606	Aug 73 Frehaut+ CORREL TO NUBAR STUDY.GRAPH	
Fiss Prod γ	Pile		CCP	Expt	Jour AE 2 278	Mar 57 Leipunsky.DECAY CURVE 1.5 TO 8 SEC	
					Jour JNE 6 170	Dec 57 TRANSLATN.*	
					Jour SJA 2 337	57 TRANSLATN.*	
Fiss Prod γ	Maxwl		LAS	Expt	Conf 58Geneva 15 331	Sep 58 Leachman.PPR665,CURVE,THEORET DISCUS	
Fiss Prod γ	Maxwl		CCP	Expt	Jour AE 7 168	Aug 59 Petrov.FPG POWER 0.6S-11H AFTER FISS	
					Jour SJA 7 675	Feb 61 TRANSLATN.*	
					Jour JNEA 12 129	Jun 60 TRANSLATN.*	
Fiss Prod γ	Fiss	1.4+7	FOA	Theo	Jour AF 16 293	Feb 60 Bjoernerstedt.G-SPEC 0-5MEV.1H-100YR	
Fiss Prod γ	Maxwl		NRD	Expt	Rept USNRDL-TR-528	Sep 61 Strom+ 1SEC-22HOURS AFTER FISSION	
Fiss Prod γ	None		LAS	Theo	Rept LA-2811	Dec 62 Griffin.BETA+GAMMA DECAY CALCULATNS	
Fiss Prod γ	Fiss		LAS	Expt	Jour PR/B 134 796	May 64 Fisher.GDIVA NS,GS TO6MEV,T=.2 TO45S	
Fiss Prod γ	Maxwl		AUA	Theo	Rept AAEC/TM-252	Jun 64 Frost.FRAG BETA-ACTIVITY(TIME),GRPHS	
Fiss Prod γ	Maxwl		FOA	Expt	Rept AF 29 359	Dec 65 Loew+.VS TIME 2H-7DAYS.NAI. GRAPHS	
Fiss Prod γ	Fiss		NRD	Theo	Rept USNRDL-TR-1009	Dec 65 Turner. GROSS F PROD G SPEC CALCT.	
Fiss Prod γ	Maxwl		GA	Expt	Jour PR 146 824	Jun 66 Sund+LINAC GS 50-700MICROS,ABS	
					Rept GA-7348	Oct 66 Walton+ NAI DET,DELAYED GS,ES+YLDS	
	None				Rept GA-6912	Jan 66 .SUPERSEDED.	
					Rept GA-6445	May 65 Walton. DELAYED GAMMAS	
	Maxwl				Rept GA-6051	Jan 65 Sund. GAMMA SPECT ABOVE 500 KEV.	
Fiss Prod γ	Pile		UKW	Expt	Conf 66Berkeley 323	Sep 66 Mossop+ FISS CH,ELECTRODES DISSOLVED	
Fiss Prod γ	Maxwl		AAA	Comp	Jour JNE 22 231	Apr 68 DE TOURREIL.FPG POWER 1S-3D AFTER F	
Fiss Prod γ	Pile		UJV	Expt	Rept UJV-2164	69 Kristak+BURN-UP,FISS-PROD'S GAM E+HL	
Fiss Prod γ	+6		GA	Expt	Jour PR 178 1894	Feb 69 Walton+ LINAC,NAI DET,T=2-80 MUSEC	
Fiss Prod γ	Maxwl		HFA	Expt	Conf 69Vienna 947	Jul 69 Notea+PPR36. GAM SPECS FOR CHAIN YLD	
Fiss Prod γ	Maxwl		TRM	Expt	Conf 69Vienna 741	Jul 69 Dange+PPR97.GE-LI SPEC VS COOLING-T	
Fiss Prod γ	Maxwl		LAS	Expt	Jour PR 187 1506	Nov 69 Berick+,SCINT,SPECTRA VS. TIME	
					Conf 69Vienna 647	Jul 69 East+PPR109. DELAYED G-SPEC,SAFGUARD	
Fiss Prod γ			WIN	Eval	Jour JNE 23 517	Nov 69 JAMES MEAN E 6.3+-1.4MEV/FISS	
Fiss Prod γ	-		ALD	Expt	Jour JNE 23 697	Dec 69 Mcnair+ BETA DECAY ENERGY	
Fiss Prod γ	2.5-2		IAE	Revw	Jour REA 7 4 3	Dec 69 Hanna+ DELAYD GAMMAS IN NU-BAR EXPTS	
Fiss Prod γ	Maxwl	5.0+1	BNL	Expt	Conf 70Helsinki 1 377	Jun 70 Chrien.42. DELAYED GAMMA SPEC GIVEN	
Fiss Prod γ	Pile		LAS	Expt	Abst DA/B 31 3444	Dec 70 Moore. DELAYD SPEC.CFD U235.GSPECT.	
					Rept LA-4257	Sep 69 - .GE(LI),SPECTRA SHORT-LIVED GS	
Fiss Prod γ	Pile		KFK	Expt	Rept KFK-EXT-4 33	Mar 71 Wolff. GE-LI SPEC FOR 6 DECAY TIMES	
Fiss Prod γ	Maxwl		LOK	Expt	Prog NCSAC-42 142	Nov 71 Imhof+. 4MIN TO 24HR. ANAL TBC. NDG	
Fiss Prod γ	Maxwl		ANL	Expt	Jour NP/A 177 337	Dec 71 Reisdorf+SIMULT MEAS K.E. ANG G-SPEC	
					Conf 69Vienna 781	Jul 69 - + PRELIMINARY.	
Fiss Prod γ	Maxwl		ORU	Expt	Prog RLO-2227-T7-8	Mar 72 Loveland. PROMPT-GAM ANG CORRELATNS	
Fiss Prod γ	Maxwl		ORU	Expt	Prog RLO-2227-T7-8	Mar 72 Button+. PROMPT-GAMMA MULTIPLICITY	
Fiss Prod γ	Maxwl		BEP	Theo	Jour KE 15 311	Sep 72 Krueger. TOT E-EMISS VS DECAY-T,SPEC	
Fiss Prod γ	Maxwl		KFK	Expt	Priv WIETKAMP	73 Weitkamp. DELAYED SPECTS OF F PRODS	
	Pile				Rept KFK-1214	Jul 70 Matussek+ G-SPEC OF FPROD, GRPHS	
Fiss Prod γ	Maxwl		TRM	Theo	Rept BARC-706 149	73 Iyer+ COMPUTER-PROGR FOR G-SPEC, NDG	
Fiss Prod γ	Maxwl		ITK	Theo	Jour AUJ 26 279	Jun 73 Mukherji+ MEAN-E VS FRAG-MASS,GRAPH	
	None				Prog BARC-474 54	70 - + CALC GAM-E/FRAG CFD EXPT	
Fiss Prod γ	Maxwl		ORL	Expt	Jour NP/A 213 413	Oct 73 Pleasonton. AVE NB,EG/CORR FRAG M,E	
					Conf 73Rochester 2 494	Aug 73 - + ABST,AVG GAM-E(FRAG),NDG	
Fiss Prod γ	Maxwl	+6	CAD	Revw	Conf IAEA-169 2 115	74 Lott.AFTERHEAT,EVALS+EXPTS CFD,TBLS	

94 Plutonium 239

Quantity	Energy (ev) Min	Max	Lab	Type	Documentation Ref Vol Page	Date	Author, Comments	Data
Fiss Prod γ	Fast		BEP	Theo Jour	KE 17 109	Apr 74	Pulz+ TOT G-EMISSION VS DECAY-TIME	
Fiss Prod γ	Maxwl		CAI	Expt Jour	NP/A 224 468	May 74	Kandil+ GS PER 10E6 FISS 90-180DEG L	+
	2.5-2			Data	EXFOR30411.	Oct 77	PROMPT GAMS(2E-GROUPS),5ANGS.10 PTS	
Fiss Prod γ	Maxwl		GA	Expt Jour	PR/C 10 853	Aug 74	Sund+ TBL, GRAPHS	
				Rept	AD-748643	Apr 72	- +. GE(LI) DET. ISOMERIC GAMMAS	
Fiss Prod γ	Fast		KAL	Eval Conf	76Bombay 550	Mar 76	Murthy+ E/FIS.SEC VS COOL TIME.GRAPH	
Fiss Prod γ	Pile		MNZ	Expt Prog	NEANDC(E)172 5	Jul 76	Ahrens+P.59. A=96-112,ES,HL	
Fiss Prod β	Maxwl		AAA	Expt Jour	JNE 22 231	Apr 68	De Tourrell.FPB POWER 15-3D AFTER F	
Fiss Prod β	Fast		KAL	Eval Conf	76Bombay 550	Mar 76	Murthy+ E/FIS.SEC VS COOL TIME.GRAPH	
Fiss Yield	None		LAS	Expt Jour	PR 71 327	Mar 47	Farwell+ FREQUENLY,MAX RANGE ALPHAS.	
Fiss Yield	Maxwl		CRC	Expt Jour	PR 76 848	Sep 49	Brunton+ COINC-FRAGMENTS(CFD CHEMIC)	
Fiss Yield	Maxwl		BNL	Expt Rept	BNL-1652	53	Katcoff+ ABSOL RADIOCHEM YLD KR85	
Fiss Yield	Maxwl		ANL	Revw Conf	55Geneva 7 3	Aug 55	Steinberg+ P614.EXPTL YLD TBL+GRPH	
Fiss Yield	1.0+4	3.0+6	MTR	Expt Conf	55Geneva 7 19	Aug 55	Pappas+.P881,YIELD FOR SOME FRGMNTS	
Fiss Yield	Maxwl		MCM	Expt Jour	CJC 34 227	Mar 56	Wiles+ REL YLDS CS CE ND SM XE ISOT	
Fiss Yield	Maxwl		MCM	Expt Jour	CJC 34 193	Mar 56	Fleming+. XE ISOTOPE RELATIVE YLDS	
Fiss Yield	Maxwl		MCM	Expt Jour	PR 103 323	Jul 56	Kennett+ NRX YLDS I128,130,BR80,82.	
Fiss Yield	Fiss		ANL	Expt Jour	JIN 4 239	57	Kafalas+.YLD CS137.ASSUMED 32.6 YR	
Fiss Yield	Pile		CCP	Expt Jour	AE 2 276	Mar 57	Krizhansky+REL ISOT YLDS CS CE ND SM	+
				Jour	JNE 6 260	Apr 58	TRANSLATN.*	
				Jour	SJA 2 334	57	TRANSLATN.*	
Fiss Yield	2.0+6		ANL	Expt Jour	NSE 2 567	Sep 57	Dillon+,A=74 TO 157 YIELDS TABLE	
Fiss Yield	Maxwl		LAS	Expt Jour	PR 108 94	Oct 57	Stein+ TOF. MASS AND ENERGY DISTRIB.	
				Rept	TID-5787	57	Bayhurst+ SR90 YLD=2.12+-0.09 PC.	
				Rept	LA-1997	Feb 56	Ford+ 2ES RELATIVE YLDS+MO99 ABS YLD	
Fiss Yield	Pile		CCP	Expt Jour	AE 4 77	Jan 58	Krizhanskii+ SR88 SR90 REL ND143,MS	+
				Jour	JNEA 10 163	Sep 59	TRANSLATN.*	
				Jour	SJA 4 95	58	TRANSLATN.*	
				Conf	58Geneva 2040	58	.SEE ALSO *	
Fiss Yield	1.5+7		CCP	Expt Jour	AE 5 130	Aug 58	Protopopov+ 6 RADCHEM YLDS REL MO99	
				Jour	JNEA 10 80	Jul 59	TRANSLATN.*	
				Jour	SJA 5 885	58	TRANSLATN.*	
Fiss Yield	Maxwl		CCP	Expt Conf	58Geneva 15 446	Sep 58	Anikina+.PPR2040,TBL OF MASSYIELDS	
Fiss Yield	Pile		HAR	Expt Conf	58Geneva 15 464	Sep 58	Crouch+.PPR7,RARE EARTH YIELDS,TBL	
Fiss Yield	Maxwl		MCM	Expt Conf	58Geneva 15 436	Sep 58	Fritze+PPR187.MASS-SPEC,KR YLD+XE/KR	
Fiss Yield	Pile		NRD	Expt Rept	USNRDL-TR-268	Oct 58	Bunney+ RADCHM RARE EARTH YIELDS	
				Conf	58Geneva 15 444	Sep 58	.SEE ALSO	
Fiss Yield	Maxwl		CRC	Expt Jour	CJC 37 660	Apr 59	Bartholomew+ BA139,140 LA141 SR89,91	
Fiss Yield	Pile		HAN	Expt Rept	HW-60431	May 59	Merckx. KR+XE YIELDS TABULATED.	
Fiss Yield	Fast		RI	Expt Jour	AE 6 577	May 59	BAK+ RADCHEM,RU103+106 YLD REL MO99	
				Jour	KE 3 95	Jan 60	. ENGL OF AE 6 577	
				Jour	SJA 6 429	Dec 59	. ENGL OF AE 6 577	
Fiss Yield	Maxwl		MCM	Expt Jour	CJP 37 916	Aug 59	Fickel+ CUM YLDS RB,SR,Y,ZR,MO,RU	
Fiss Yield	Pile		RI	ExTh Conf	59Tashkent 1 222	Sep 59	Krizhanskij.TBL+GRPH YLD OF MANY NCL	
				Rept	AEC-TR-6398	60	. ENGL OF 59TASHKENT	
Fiss Yield	-1	+1	HAR	Expt Rept	AERE-M-559	Nov 59	Wraight. SPINS OF FISSN.RESONANCES	
	Maxwl			Rept	AERE-M-536	Sep 59	- + FISSN.RATE FOR BA140 YIELD	
Fiss Yield	Maxwl		CRC	Eval Rept	AECL-1054	Mar 60	Walker.(CRRP-913)	
Fiss Yield	-2		RI	Expt Jour	ZET 38 998	Mar 60	Dmitriev.TRIPLE FISSION PROBABILITY	
				Jour	JET 11 718	Sep 60	TRANSLATN.*	
Fiss Yield	6.0-2	3.6-1	MTR	Expt Jour	PR 119 2017	Sep 60	Regier. MO/CD,MO/SN .3EV CFD THR	
Fiss Yield	Fast		BNL	Eval Jour	NUC 18 11 201	Nov 60	Katcoff.RECOMMENDED YLD-SET,TBL	
				Jour	NUC 16 4 78	Apr 58	.SUPERSEDED	
Fiss Yield			BNL	Eval Jour	NUC 18 11 201	Nov 60	Katcoff.RECOMMENDED YLD-SET,TBL,GRPH	
				Jour	NUC 16 4 78	Apr 58	.SUPERSEDED	
Fiss Yield	Maxwl		GA	Revw Rept	GA-2307	61	Fischer+TABLES OF YLD FOR A=81TO159	
Fiss Yield	Fiss	1.5+7	CCP	Expt Jour	AE 10 13	Jan 61	Bonjuskin+.ABS YIELD OF FRGMNTS,GRPH	
				Jour	SJA 10 10	Nov 61	TRANSLATN.*GERMAN KE4 553 7/61	
Fiss Yield	None		BNL	Theo Jour	NSE 9 495	Apr 61	Levine.XE135 FROM EQUAL Z DISPL.RULE	
Fiss Yield	Spont		RI	Revw Jour	UFN 73 655	Apr 61	Petrzhak+ CURVE,MANY REFS,DISCUSSION	
	Fiss			Expt Book	NEJTRONFIZ 217	61	- + RADCHEM YLDS 6NUC,TBL+GRPH	
				Rept	AEC-TR-4696	61	.ENGL OF NEJTRONFIZ 217	
	None			Revw	SPU 4 305	Sep 61	. ENGL OF UFN 73 655	
Fiss Yield	Maxwl		DKE	Theo Jour	PR 122 1224	May 61	Newson.MASS DIST ASYMMETRIC+SYMMETR	
Fiss Yield	2.0+5	3.0+6	CCP		AE 10 620	Jun 61	ANISOTROPY OF FISS FRAGM	
				Jour	SJA 10 613	Mar 62	TRANSLATN.*	
Fiss Yield	Pile		CRC	Expt Jour	JIN 20 6	Nov 61	Grummitt+MILTON.DIRECT YLD CS136	
Fiss Yield	Fiss		GA	Eval Jour	NSE 12 115	Jan 62	Garrison+.(Z,A).WEIGHTD AVRAGE OTHRS	

94 Plutonium 239

Quantity	Energy (ev) Min Max	Lab	Type	Documentation Ref Vol Page	Author, Comments Date	Data
Fiss Yield	Maxwl 1.0+6	LAS Expt	Jour	PR 126 1508	May 62 Nobles. YIELD OF LONG RANGE FFRGM	
Fiss Yield	Maxwl	WAS Expt	Jour	PR 126 1112	May 62 Wahl+.FRACT INDEPENDENT YIELD GIVEN	
Fiss Yield	6.0-2 3.6-1	MTR Expt	Rept	IDO-16797	Jul 62 Burgus. RADIOCHM ASYM/SYM YLD RATIOS	
Fiss Yield	Maxwl	HAN Expt	Rept	HW-7760 1	Jan 63 Kirby.RADIOCHEMICAL 89SR TO 149PM	
Fiss Yield	Maxwl 1.4+7	NRD Eval	Rept	USNRDL-TR-633	Mar 63 Weaver+ 2ES+FISPECT.EST UNMEASD YLD.	
Fiss Yield	Maxwl	KUR Expt	Rept	IAE-710	64 Apalin+.GRAPH,DSTRB OF FFRGM+FPRODS	
Fiss Yield	Pile	ORL Expt	Jour	PR/B 133 1500	Mar 64 Walter. SI DETECTOR.OKS PREV TOF XPT	
			Conf	63ANL 441	Oct 63 .SUPERSEDED	
Fiss Yield	-2 -1	WWA Expt	Jour	NKA 9 511	Jul 64 Aleksandrowicz+ BRIEF.TERN FISS,NDG	
Fiss Yield	Maxwl	CAI Theo	Jour	NP 58 601	Sep 64 Abdelmalek+DISTRIB OF MASS RATIOS	
Fiss Yield	Maxwl	CER Theo	Jour	NP 58 177	Sep 64 Faissner+ASSYMETRIC,CLUSTER MODEL	
Fiss Yield	Maxwl	GEV Expt	Rept	GEAP-4716	Sep 64 Rider+MASS.SPECTRO.YIELDS OF ND ISOT	
Fiss Yield	Pile	HAR Expt	Rept	AERE-R-4723	Sep 64 Croall.CFD THERML,EPI CD FISS.	+
	Maxwl		Jour	JIN 25 1213	Oct 63 - .RADCHEM YLDS SE81,83 BR83,84	
	Pile		Rept	AERE-R-4148	Aug 62 - +/SE81+SE83 ISOMER YIELD	
	Maxwl		Rept	AERE-R-3879	Nov 61 - .LIMIT ON YIELD OF RH 1067	
	Pile		Jour	JIN 16 358	Feb 61 - . DIRECT YLD NB96	
	Maxwl		Comp Rept	AERE-R-3209	Jan 60 - .COMP OF INDP YLDS(NSA 14 1397	
Fiss Yield	2.5-2 1.4+7	TRM Comp	Rept	AEET-209	65 Rangarajan+ YLDS+PRODUCTN RATIO,TBLS	
Fiss Yield	-3 +7	TRM Revw	Rept	AEET-235	65 Methasiri.TERNRY FISS EXPTS,GRAPH	
Fiss Yield	Maxwl	MCG Expt	Jour	CJC 43 249	Jan 65 Marsden+ ABS YIELD RADCHEM+SME IND YL	+
Fiss Yield	9.5+6 1.2+7	LAS ExTh	Jour	PR/B 137 814	Feb 65 Leachman+ RLTV ANG DIST FISS.	
Fiss Yield	Maxwl	LAS Expt	Jour	PR/B 137 929	Feb 65 Wolfsberg+ K,XE ISOTOPE YLDS.	
Fiss Yield	Maxwl	BNL Expt	Conf	65Salzburg 1 467	Mar 65 Thomas+ MASS YIELD CURVES	
			Jour	PR/B 133 976	Feb 64 - +FRAG E MASS FORMULA	
Fiss Yield	Maxwl	KUR Expt	Conf	65Salzburg 1 587	Mar 65 Apalin+,GRPH MASS DIST,SYMMETR FISS	
			Jour	YF 1 639	Apr 65 SEE ALSO *NP 71 553 9/65	
			Jour	SNP 1 457	Oct 65 . ENGL OF YF 1 639	
Fiss Yield	1.2+7 2.4+7	LAS ExTh	Prog	WASH-1056 4	Mar 65 Blumberg. FISSION ANISOTROPY. NDG.	
Fiss Yield	2.0+2 6.0+2	LAS Expt	Conf	65Salzburg 347	Mar 65 Cowan.TOF WHEEL-METHOD,SYMMETRIC YLD	
			Rept	LA-DC-6639	63 - . TOF. SYMM IN RES REGION.CURVS	
Fiss Yield	Maxwl	CCP Expt	Rept	ANL-TR-205	Jun 65 TRANSL FROM RUSSIAN,CRVS,CFD OTHERS	
Fiss Yield	Maxwl	CRC Expt	Jour	CJP 43 1036	Jun 65 Okazaki+ I135 BA140 REL U235 FISS.	
			Rept	EANDC(CAN)-23	Apr 65 .SEE ALSO PAGE4	
			Conf	64Geneva 7 430	May 64 Fraser+MILTON DOUBLE VEL. MEAST.	
Fiss Yield	Maxwl	BNL Expt	Jour	JIN 27 1447	Jul 65 Katcoff.KR85G YIELD .099PC	
Fiss Yield	2.0-2 1.0+1	MTR Expt	Rept	IDO-17105	Nov 65 Miller+	
Fiss Yield	+6	LAS Theo	Rept	LA-3383	Dec 65 Anderson.INDEP+CUMUL YLDS VS Z AND A	
Fiss Yield	None	ORL Theo	Rept	ORNL-P-2848	66 Schmitt.CALCTD FISS MODES TBP AF	
Fiss Yield	Maxwl	CRC Expt	Jour	CJP 44 237	Jan 66 Okazaki+ XE135 DRCT YLD.	
			Jour	CJP 49 498	Feb 71 .CORRECTS CJP 44 237	
	None		Prog	EANDC(CAN)-23	Apr 65 Bigham+DIRECT YIELD OF XE135	
Fiss Yield	6.0+0 1.0+2	COL Expt	Conf	66Bombay 33	Feb 66 Mehta+.GRPH TERN FISS-YIELD, E-ALFAS	
Fiss Yield	Maxwl	MCM Expt	Jour	RCA 5 57	Mar 66 Fritze.ZN72 THR/EPICD YLD	
Fiss Yield	1.5+1 3.0+2	LAS Expt	Jour	PR 144 979	Apr 66 Cowan+,BOMB SOURCE,VAR SYMMETRY VS E	
Fiss Yield	Maxwl	TRM Theo	Jour	PL 21 437	Jun 66 Ramanna+ MASS DIST ON STOCHASTIC MDL	
	Thrsh Up		Jour	NP 67 529	Jun 65 - +FISSION AS MARKOV PROCESS	
	Maxwl		Conf	65Calcutta 20	Feb 65 - + YIELD(A) GRPH,MARKOV-PROCES	
Fiss Yield	3.0+4 1.5+7	HAR Expt	Jour	NP 84 49	Aug 66 Cuninghame+ PEAK TO V1LL5Y R1T9W§	
Fiss Yield	Maxwl	ORL Expt	Jour	PR 149 894	Sep 66 Neiler+ PRE-NEUT EMISSION YLDS.	
Fiss Yield	Maxwl 1.4+7	HNS Theo	Rept	HNS-1229-77	Feb 67 Castagnola. ALSO FISS SPEC 28FRAGS	
Fiss Yield	Maxwl	FLA Expt	Jour	PRL 18 404	Mar 67 Muga+ HEAVY TERNARY FISSION.	
			Conf	69Vienna 107	Jul 69 - +PPR99. TERNARY YLD(A) GRPHS GV	
			Rept	ORO-2843-9	Dec 66 .SUPERSEDED	
Fiss Yield	Fiss	LRL Comp	Rept	UCRL-50243 2	Mar 67 Fleming.CURVS FPROD DECAY CHAINS	
Fiss Yield	Maxwl	BOR Theo	Jour	NP/A 96 588	Apr 67 Doan+ ALPHA YIELD CALCULATED	
Fiss Yield	Maxwl	LAS Expt	Jour	PR 156 1277	Apr 67 Stein+ SI DETECT,CURVE YIELDS,ENERGY	
	-2	ITE Expt	Prog	YFI-6 81	68 Andreev+ TABLE YIELD MASS= 3-6	
			Rept	INDC-260E	69 . ENGL OF YFI-6 81	
Fiss Yield	Maxwl	HAR Eval	Rept	AERE-R-5086	Jan 68 Croall.RECOMMENDED CUMULAT YLDS,TBL	
Fiss Yield	Maxwl	MTR Expt	Jour	NSE 31 241	Feb 68 Nisle+ I135 YLD=1.006+-.067 REL U235	
			Jour	NSE 25 93	May 66 - . I135YIELD REL TO U235 1.204	
Fiss Yield	Maxwl	BOL Comp	Rept	CEC(68)-6	Jun 68 Cenacci.YLDS,DECAY CHAINS,FPROD DATA	
			Rept	RT/FI-68 4	68 .EQUIVALENT	
Fiss Yield	Maxwl	CCP Expt	Jour	YF 8 454	Sep 68 Solov'Eva. LONG-R-ALPHA, KE-SPECS,CVS	
			Jour	SNP 8 264	Mar 69 TRANSLATN.*	
Fiss Yield	Maxwl	ITE Expt	Jour	YF 9 23	Jan 69 Andreev+ TERN-FISS,HE+LI+BE+B+C YLD	
			Jour	SNP 9 14	Jul 69 TRANSLATN.*	

94 Plutonium 239

Quantity	Energy (ev) Min	Max	Lab	Type	Documentation Ref Vol Page	Date	Author, Comments	Data
Fiss Yield	Maxwl		SAC	Expt Prog	EANDC(E)115U	Mar 69	Nifenecker. SYMM FISS	
Fiss Yield	+3	+5	BRC	Expt Conf	69Vienna 952	Jul 69	Communeau+PPR94.YLD(A),GAM+BETA EXPT	
Fiss Yield	Maxwl		EDG	Revw Conf	69Vienna 83	Jul 69	Feather.PPR201. SURVEY,TERNARY−YIELD	
Fiss Yield	Maxwl		HFA	Expt Conf	69Vienna 947	Jul 69	Notea+PPR36. CHAIN YLDS VS TIME,GELI	
Fiss Yield	Maxwl		MCM	Theo Conf	69Vienna 845	Jul 69	Thind+PPR50. YLD(Z,A)+NU(A)+EXCIT E	
Fiss Yield	Maxwl		ORL	Expt Conf	69Vienna 67	Jul 69	Schmitt.PPR122. YLD GRPH,COMP OF PR	
Fiss Yield	Maxwl		OSL	Revw Conf	69Vienna 669	Jul 69	Pappas+PPR206. INITIAL+FINAL YLD(A)	
Fiss Yield	Maxwl	1.4+7	SAC	Comp Rept	CEA−N−1180	Jul 69	Bessis+ CAPT FOR FIS FRAG + 'NU'	
Fiss Yield	Maxwl		TRM	Expt Conf	69Vienna 741	Jul 69	Dange+PPR97.GE−LI,REL U235/MO99,TBL	
Fiss Yield	Maxwl		TUE	Revw Conf	69Bochum 175	Jul 69	Goennenwein+ CLUSTER MODEL,YLD GRAPH	
Fiss Yield	Maxwl		CUA	Theo Abst	DA/B 30 2222	Nov 69	Rogers.	
Fiss Yield	Pile		MCM	Expt Jour	RCA 12 4 179	Dec 69	Tong+ 72ZN YIELD IN EPI−SM FISS	
Fiss Yield	Maxwl		TRM	Expt Rept	BARC/I−62	70	Jain+ GELI.REL MO99,10 ISOTOPS,TBL	
Fiss Yield	Maxwl	+6	ANL	Theo Rept	ANL−7678	Mar 70	Burris+,PROMPT+DELAYED MANY FRAGS	
Fiss Yield	None		BLA	Expt Prog	INDC(BUL)−1G	Apr 70	Kashukeev+ PRELIMIN EXPT,NDG	
Fiss Yield		6.0+6	FEI	Theo Conf	70Helsinki 2 177	Jun 70	Vorobeva+88. E−BALANCE TO CALC NU(E)	
Fiss Yield	Maxwl		IBJ	Expt Rept	INP−702/PS	Jun 70	Dakowski+ SEMICOND DET RESLTS CFD TH	+
				Conf	69Vienna 893	Jul 69	Krogulski+PPR65.LIGHT PART,E+YLD TBL	
				Jour	NP/A 128 219	Apr 69	− + REL YLDS P,D,T,HE−4,5,6	
	Maxwl			Data	EXFOR30320.004	Jan 76	6 PTS,REL YLDS P,D,T,HE4,6,8	
Fiss Yield	Maxwl		MNZ	Expt Jour	JIN 32 1767	Jun 70	Qaim+ INDEP YLD OF 133,134,135I	
Fiss Yield	Pile		RI	Expt Jour	AE 31 99	Aug 71	Sorokina+ MICA,ABSOL+REL CE−144,TBLS	
				Jour	RAK 12 492	Jun 70	− + RADCHEM,8YLDS REL 144,TBLS	
				Jour	RAK 12 487	Jun 70	Skovorodkin+ 12 YLDS REL CE−144,TBLS	
				Jour	SJA 31 804	Mar 72	.ENGL OF AE 31 99	
Fiss Yield	Pile		ANL	Expt Abst	ANS 13 90	Jul 70	Armani+,BA140 MO99 YLD,ZPR−3 ASSEMBL	
				Conf	70Barcelna 2 495	Jul 70	− + YIELD OF MO−99 AND BA−140	
Fiss Yield	Maxwl		MCM	Expt Jour	CJP 48 1708	Jul 70	Tracy+,BR80,82 I128,130 INDEPEN YLDS	
Fiss Yield	Pile		ANL	Expt Jour	NP/A 151 65	Aug 70	Horrocks+ TRITIUM FISS YIELD(PRELIM)	
Fiss Yield	Fiss		LRL	Theo Rept	UCRL−50656	Oct 70	Barg.KR+XE DELAYD RELEASE TIME CURVS	
Fiss Yield	Fiss		KFK	Comp Rept	KFK−EXT−6 2	Nov 70	Hofmann. CUMULATIVE YLD A=72−163	
Fiss Yield	1.0+7		KFK	Comp Rept	KFK−EXT−6 2	Nov 70	Hofmann. CUMULATIVE YLD A=72−163	
Fiss Yield	1.4+7		KFK	Comp Rept	KFK−EXT−6 2	Nov 70	Hofmann. CUMULATIVE YLD A=72−163	
Fiss Yield	2.5−2		KFK	Comp Rept	KFK−EXT−6 2	Nov 70	Hofmann. CUMULATIVE YLD A=72−163	
Fiss Yield	Maxwl	Pile	MTR	Expt Jour	NSE 42 191	Nov 70	Lisman+,YLDS STABLE+LONG−LIVED FRAGS	
	Maxwl			Rept	IN−1277	Jun 68	− + SUMMARIZES RESULTS	
	Fast			Rept	IN−1277	Jun 68	− + SUMMARIZES RESULTS	
Fiss Yield	Fast		LAS	Expt Abst	DA/B 31 3444	Dec 70	Moore. SHORT−LIVED FPRODS.	
Fiss Yield	Maxwl	1.5+7	LOK	Expt Prog	NCSAC−33 123	Dec 70	Imhof+,11 ES,NO DATA GIVEN	
Fiss Yield	Fast		ANL	Expt Prog	ANL−7750 82	71	Flynn+ YLD REL BA140.	
Fiss Yield	2.5−2	4.5+6	FEI	Expt Jour	YF 13 3 484	71	Akimov+	+
	0.0+0	5.5+6		Prog	YFI−11 15	70	− + ABST,FRAG YIELD VS N−E,NDG	
				Prog	INDC(CCP)−31	Dec 72	.PAGE 14,ENGLISH OF YFI−11 15	
	2.5−2	4.5+6		Data	EXFOR40144.	Apr 73	.5 SUBENT EACH 41 DATA LINES,5 ES	
Fiss Yield	Pile		MTR	Expt Jour	JIN 33 643	Mar 71	Lisman+ YLD OF KR−85	
Fiss Yield	Maxwl		CRC	Expt Jour	CJP 49 785	Apr 71	Hawkings+ XE135 INDEP/I135 CUMUL YLD	
Fiss Yield		1.5+7	FEI	Expt Conf	71Kiev	May 71	Sergachev+.FRAG YLD,KE OF FRAG,GRPHS	
Fiss Yield	None		COL	Expt Jour	PR/C 4 267	Jul 71	Toraskar+.SM AND BE FILTERED NEUTS	
Fiss Yield	Fast		DOU	Revw Conf	71Canterby 45	Sep 71	Sinclair+DOUNREAY DATA CFD OTHER.TBL	
				Expt Jour	RCA 12 173	Dec 69	Davies.MASS−SPEC,SR90,CS137,ND YLDS	
Fiss Yield			GA	Eval Rept	GA−12071	Sep 71	Mathews+. RECOMMENDED VALUES	
Fiss Yield	5.5+6	1.5+7	FEI	Expt Jour	YF 14 935	Nov 71	Surin+ FRAG YIELD,2 ES CFD THR,GRAPH	+
				Jour	SNP 14 523	May 72	* ENGL OF YF 14 935	
				Prog	YFI−11 14	70	Surin+ ABST,YIELD OF FRAGS,NDG	
				Prog	INDC(CCP)−31	Dec 72	.ENGLISH OF YFI−11 14,PAGE 13	
	2.5−2	1.5+7		Data	EXFOR40112.	Nov 73	.3SUBENTRIES FOR 3EN,EACH 42DATALINE	
Fiss Yield	Maxwl		ANL	Expt Jour	NP/A 177 337	Dec 71	Reisdorf+SIMULT MEAS K.E. ANG G−SPEC	
				Conf	69Vienna 781	Jul 69	− + PRELIMINARY.	
Fiss Yield	Maxwl	3.0−1	NIL	Prog	IAEA−147 41	72	Alam+ PROMPT MASS DIST,THR+RES,GRAPH	
Fiss Yield	Maxwl		GEV	Eval Rept	NEDO−12154	Jan 72	Meek+.TABULATD RECOMMENDED YIELDS	
				Rept	APED−5398	Oct 68	− + TABLES	
				Rept	GEAP−5356	Sep 67	Rider+ TABULATED CHAIN YLDS 95MASSES	
Fiss Yield	Maxwl		IAE	Revw Rept	IAEA−143 897	Apr 72	Lemmel.YDLS FROM RECENT EVALUATN,TBL	
Fiss Yield	Pile		RI	Expt Jour	AE 33 709	Aug 72	Petrzhak+ XE−131,132,134,136 YLD,TBL	
Fiss Yield	Pile		NBS	Expt Jour	NP/A 195 257	Nov 72	Schroeder. B/T RATIO SUBTH,THR,RES	
Fiss Yield	1.4+7		MNZ	Expt Jour	NP/A 198 228	Dec 72	Alexander. XE133,5 INDP YLDS+ISOMRAT	
Fiss Yield	1.4+7		MNZ	Expt Jour	NP/A 198 228	Dec 72	Alexander. XE133,5 INDP YLDS+ISOMRAT	

94 Plutonium 239

Quantity	Energy (ev) Min Max	Lab	Type	Documentation Ref Vol Page	Date	Author, Comments	Data
Fiss Yield	Fast	BUC	Revw Rept	IFA – RN – 50	73	Cristu.MASS – +CHARGE – +E – DISTR REVIEW	
	Maxwl		Rept	IFA – RN – 50	73	– .MASS – +CHARGE – +E – DISTR REVIEW	
	Maxwl 1.5+7	LRL	Comp Rept	UCRL – 51458	73	Nethaway+.ALSO FISS SPEC. 111 FRAGS.	
Fiss Yield	Maxwl	GEL	Expt Prog	EANDC(E) – 157U	Mar 73	Deruytter+ MASS DISTR CFD PU240 SPON	
			Prog	EANDC(E) – 89U	Feb 68	– + CFD FRAG SPEC SPON 240PU	
Fiss Yield	Fast	GRE	Eval Conf	73Paris 1 477	Mar 73	Devillers+ YLD+DECAY DATA LIBRRY,NDG	
			Rept	CEA – N – 1526	Mar 72	.YIELDS+GAM TRANSITIONS,TABLES	
Fiss Yield	Fast	GRE	Eval Conf	73Paris 1 477	Mar 73	Devillers+ YLD+DECAY DATA LIBRARY.ND	
			Rept	CEA – N – 1526	Mar 72	– + YLDS+GAM TRANSITIONS.TBLS	
			Rept	CEA – N – 1423	Mar 71	– + SUPERSEDED BY CEA – N – 1526	
			Rept	CEA – N – 1269	Apr 70	– + SUPERSEDED BY CEA – N – 1526	
Fiss Yield	Maxwl	SGA	Eval Conf	73Paris 1 505	Mar 73	Lammer+ EVAL DISCUSSN,TBL ALL A YLDS	
Fiss Yield	Maxwl	CRC	Eval Rept	AECL – 3037 2	Apr 73	Walker.ALL DETAILS,CHAIN YIELDS,TBLS	
			Conf	73Paris 1 459	Mar 73	– .EVAL PROCEDURE,SELECTED TBLS	
			Conf	66Paris 1 521	Oct 66	– .EARLIER EVAL,SUPERSEDED	
			Rept	AECL – 2497	66	.SAME AS 66PARIS 1 521,SUPERSEDED	
			Rept	AECL – 2111	Nov 64	Walker.PSUEDO FPY	
			Rept	CRRP – 913	Mar 60	– .SUPERSEDED	
			Rept	CRRP – 760	Oct 58	Hurst+ SUPERSEDED	
Fiss Yield	Fast	KFK	Expt Rept	KFK – 1273 1 121	Jun 73	Scholtyssek. G – EXPT,ABS YLDS	
Fiss Yield	Maxwl 1.5+7	BNW	Expt Conf	73Rochestr 2 498	Aug 73	Kaye+ ABST, +FISS,SHORT HL XE,KR,NDG	
Fiss Yield	Pile	MCM	Expt Jour	JIN 35 3079	Sep 73	Tong+ YLD RATIO, EPI – CD AND EPI – SM	
Fiss Yield	Maxwl	MCM	Expt Prog	INDC(CAN) – 13	Oct 73	Mathews+ SN+CD YLDS,CONTINUING,NDG	
Fiss Yield	2.0 – 2 3.0 – 1	GEL	Expt Rept	RCN – 203 147	Dec 73	Wagemans+ TERN/BIN RATIO.	+
	2.0 – 2 5.0+1		Jour	NP/A 212 556	Oct 73	– + LINAC. TOF. TABLES.	
			Conf	73Rochestr 2 417	Aug 73	Deruytter+ BIN/TERN YLD(RES),TBL,FIG	
	2.0 – 2 5.0+1		Data	EXFOR20384.	Oct 74	55PTS.TER/BIN.	
Fiss Yield	3.0 – 1	MOL	Expt Rept	RCN – 203 95	Dec 73	Van Assche+ MASS DISTR	
			Conf	73Rochestr 2 492	Aug 73	Vandenput+ ABST,MASS YLDS REL TH,NDG	
Fiss Yield	Maxwl	MOL	Expt Rept	RCN – 203 135	Dec 73	Wegener Penning+ GRPH	
Fiss Yield	Maxwl	TRM	Expt Jour	RCA 19 2 90	Dec 73	Jain+ MO99 – YLD	
			Rept	BARC – 584	71	– + RADCHEM MO99 YLD ABSOL+RELU23	
Fiss Yield	Maxwl	AUA	Theo Conf	IAEA – 169 2 163	74	Musgrove+ GAUSS FIT MASS YLDS,GRAPH	
Fiss Yield	Maxwl Pile	CRC	Revw Conf	IAEA – 169 1 285	74	Walker.STATUS CHAIN+INDEP YLDS,TBLS	
			Rept	AECL – 4704	73	.SAME AS 73BOLOGNA,EVALS CFD,DICUSSN	
Fiss Yield	Maxwl	FAR	Expt Conf	IAEA – 169 3 59	74	Robin+ ND148,STABL ND – ISOT/ND148,TBL	
Fiss Yield	Fast	FAR	Expt Conf	IAEA – 169 3 59	74	Robin+ ND148 AND STABLE ND YLDS.TBL	
Fiss Yield	Maxwl	HAR	Revw Conf	IAEA – 169 1 353	74	Cuninghame.SURVEY TRITIUM YLDS,TBL	
	Fast		Conf	IAEA – 169 1 353	74	– .FAST+N – E DEPEND,TBLS,GRPH	
			Rept	AERE – R – 7548	Sep 73	.SAME AS 73BOLOGNA,EVALUATIONS CFD	
	Maxwl		Rept	AERE – R – 7548	Sep 73	.SAME AS 73BOLOGNA	
Fiss Yield	Pile	UBE	Expt Jour	RCA 21 200	74	Egger+ ABS YIELD OF MO 99	
Fiss Yield	Pile	KFK	Expt Jour	KFK – 1888	Jan 74	Hawa+ CUMULATIVE FISS YLD OF KR88	
Fiss Yield	Pile	ANL	Expt Jour	NSE 54 263	Jul 74	Larsen+	
			Conf	73Rochestr 2 19	Aug 73	Unik+ PROMPT YLDS,MASS DISTRIB,GRPHS	
Fiss Yield	Maxwl	AUA	Expt Prog	AAEC/PR – 40P 28	Jul 74	Boldeman+ MASS – DISTRIBUTION,TBD	
Fiss Yield	Maxwl 1.4+7	MIF	Theo Jour	IVU 17 7 7	Jul 74	Koldobskij+ CUM YLDS(4ISOT)CFD EXPTS	
Fiss Yield	Pile	LIN	Expt Jour	YF 20 461	Sep 74	Vorob'Ev+ Z=2,...,8 YIELDS,TOF.TBL	
			Conf	73Munich 1 716	Aug 73	Vorobjov+ Z=1 – 8 MASS – SPEC,GRAPHS	
	Pile		Jour	SNP 20 248	Mar 75	. ENGL OF YF 20 461	
Fiss Yield	4.5+5	LRL	Expt Abst	ANS 19 397	Oct 74	Jensen+ TBL.27CC.GELI.NORM.PILE.MEAS	
	Pile		Abst	ANS 19 397	Oct 74	– + TBL.27CC.GELI.NORM.97ZR.MEEK	
Fiss Yield	Fast	ITU	Expt Prog	NEANDC(E)162U	Feb 75	Cottone+ SB – 125,XE,CS,ND VOL.5.P.42.	
Fiss Yield	Fiss	LRL	Theo Jour	UCRL – 51759	Feb 75	Delucchi.KR – 85,XE – 131,133,135.YLD(T)	
	1.5+7		Rept	UCRL – 51759	Feb 75	– .KR – 85,XE – 131,133,135.YLD(T)	
Fiss Yield	Maxwl	PAH	Theo Jour	PL/B 55 144	Feb 75	Hooshyar+ISOMERIC FISS,TH CFD EXPTAL	
Fiss Yield	Maxwl	ANL	Expt Jour	JIN 37 869	Apr 75	Flynn+ CHEM.INDEP RB84,86,CS136.TBLS	
Fiss Yield	Maxwl	RI	Expt Conf	75Kiev 6 97	Jun 75	Kondurov+ YLD ALPHA – PART,GRAPH,TBL	
Fiss Yield	Fast	DOU	Expt Prog	UKNDC(75)P71	Jul 75	Davies+ IRRAD.MASS.SPEC MEAS DFR PFR	
Fiss Yield	Fast	HAR	Expt Prog	UKNDC(75)P71	Jul 75	Crouch+ IRRADIATION PFR	
Fiss Yield	Maxwl	LAS	Expt Jour	PR/C 12 413	Aug 75	Balestrini+ RB,CS INDEP YIELDS	
Fiss Yield	Pile	MOL	Expt Jour	ZP/A 275 149	Nov 75	Wagemans+ YIELD OF LONGE – RANGE A	
Fiss Yield	Fast	WUR	Expt Jour	NSE 58 414	Dec 75	Rajagopalan+ PROTEUS SPECT.21 MASSES	
			Prog	INDC(SEC) – 43	Dec 74	– + CHEM+G – SPC.REL 140,TBL	

94 Plutonium 239

Quantity	Energy (ev) Min	Energy (ev) Max	Lab	Type	Documentation Ref Vol Page	Date	Author, Comments	Data
Fiss Yield	Maxwl		HAR	Eval Rept	AERE-R-8152	Jan 76	Crouch. ADJUSTED FISSION YIELD,TABLE	
	Fast			Rept	AERE-R-8152	Jan 76	- . ADJUSTED FISSION YIELD,TABLE	
	Maxwl	Fiss		Rept	AERE-R-7785	Feb 75	- .CHAIN+INDEPENDENT YLDS TBL	
	Pile			Rept	AERE-R-7680	May 74	- . FRACTIONAL INDEPENDENT YLD	
	Fast			Rept	AERE-R-7394	May 73	- .CHAIN YLDS RECOMMENDED TBL	
	Maxwl			Conf	73Paris 1 393	Mar 73	- .EXPTL DATA+EVAL CHAIN YLD,TBL	
				Rept	AERE-R-7209	Jan 73	- .95 CHAIN YLDS RECOMMENDED TBL	
				Theo Rept	AERE-R-6056	Mar 69	- .CALC FRACT INDEPEND YLDS,TBLS	
				Rept	AERE-R-5488	May 67	- . SUPERSEDED	
				Rept	AERE-R-5250	Apr 66	- . SUPERSEDED	
Fiss Yield	Maxwl		UBE	Expt Jour	JIN 38 205	Feb 76	Gaeggeler+ PM150,RADIOCHEM.MANY TBLS	
				Diss	GAEGGELER	Dec 73	- . COMPLETE EXPT DESCRIPTION	
				Conf	73Rochestr 2 475	Aug 73	- + ABST,PM150 INDEP YLD GIVN	
Fiss Yield	2.5-2	1.4+7	LAS	Expt Prog	ERDA-NDC-3 94	May 76	Ford+NFY COMPILATION.SEE LA-6129.NDG	
Fiss Yield	Maxwl		AUA	Theo Jour	AUJ 29 125	Jun 76	Cook+ GAUSSFIT.FOR E-DEPEND OF PARAM	
	2.0+6	1.4+7		Jour	AUJ 29 125	Jun 76	- + 2ES.GAUSSFIT PARAMS VS E.TBLS	
	Maxwl	2.0+6		Rept	AAEC/E-386	Mar 76	- + 3-GAUSS FIT,PARAMS AT 2ES GIV	
Fiss Yield	7.0+6	1.6+7	PAH	ExTh Conf	76Lowell 725	Jul 76	Hooshyar+ 2ES.STATMD CFD XPT	
	Maxwl			Conf	76Lowell 725	Jul 76	- +STATMDL APLD TO EXPT.DATA	
Fiss Yield	Maxwl		UI	Expt Conf	76Lowell 1404	Jul 76	Diiorio+FISS FRAG MASS YLD.NDG.TBD	
Fiss Yield	Maxwl		LIN	Theo Jour	YF 24 270	Aug 76	Val'Skii+ A=1TO20 YLD,4PARAM FORMULA	
				Jour	SNP 24 140	Aug 76	. ENGLISH OF YF 24 270	
Fiss Yield	Fast		GGA	Expt Abst	ANS 24 458	Nov 76	Buzzelli+TRITIUM FISS YLD.NDG. TBD.	
Fiss Yield	2.0+6	1.4+7	LAS	Eval Abst	ANS 24 462	Nov 76	Madland+PAIR EFFECT ON FISS PROD YLD	
	2.5-2	1.4+7		Rept	LA-6430	Jul 76	- +PAIR EFFECT ON INDEP YLD.TBL	
Fiss Yield	Fiss		BRC	Expt	NEANDC(E)172 4	77	Adam+ ABSTRACT ONLY	
Fiss Yield	1.4+7		TIL	Expt Rept	YK-27 42	77	Petrzhak+ YLD XE-131,132,134,136,TBL	
Frag Spectra	Maxwl		CRC	Expt Jour	PR 76 848	Sep 49	Brunton+ E SPECT FOR DIFFT MASS DIST	
Frag Spectra	None		CRC	Expt Jour	PR 80 181	Oct 50	Allen+ ALFA RANGE-ENERGY DISTRIBUTNS	
Frag Spectra	None		LAS	Expt Jour	PR 87 444	Aug 52	Leachman+ TOF VELOCITY DIST CURVES	
Frag Spectra	Maxwl	1.4+7	LAS	Expt Jour	PR 95 126	Jul 54	Wahl+ 2 ES.IONCHMBR. FRAG E DIST.	
Frag Spectra	Maxwl		LAS	Expt Jour	PR 96 1366	Dec 54	Leachman+ VELOCTY DIST OF SLOWD FRAG	
Frag Spectra	Spont		CCP	Expt Conf	55Moscow 226	Jul 55	Goldin+.ALFA SPECTRUM.EXPT FROM 1953	
				Rept	AEC-TR-2435	56	. P 167.ENGL TRANSL OF 55MOSCOW 226	
Frag Spectra	Maxwl		LAS	Expt Jour	PR 108 94	Oct 57	Stein. TOF. MASS,ENERGY DISTRIB.	
Frag Spectra	1.5+7		RI	ExTh Jour	ZET 34 250	Jan 58	Protopopov.DEGREE OF ANISOTROPY	
				Jour	JET 7 173	Jul 58	TRANSLATN.*	
Frag Spectra	+6		LAS	Revw Conf	58Geneva 15 344	Sep 58	Hemmendinger.PPR663,CURVE REL ANGLE	
Frag Spectra	+6	+7	LAS	Theo Jour	PR 116 107	59	Griffin.ANISOTROPY OF FRAGS.BOHR TH	
Frag Spectra	6.8+5	1.5+7	LAS	Expt Jour	PR 116 102	Oct 59	Blumberg+,ANISOTROPY OF FRAGMENTS	
Frag Spectra	6.0+6	2.0+7	CRC	Expt Jour	CJP 37 1418	Dec 59	Baerg+. FRAG ANG DIST ISOTROPIC	
Frag Spectra	None		CCP	Theo Jour	ZET 38 955	Mar 60	Geilikman. EXCIT E VS FRAG RATIO,CRV	
				Jour	JET 11 688	Sep 60	TRANSLATN.*	
				Jour	AE 6 298	Mar 59	SEE ALSO *= SJA 6 184 N/60	
Frag Spectra	5.0-5	7.5+6	LAS	Expt Jour	PR 120 198	Oct 60	Simmons+ FRAGMENT ANGULAR DIST 14ES	
Frag Spectra	Maxwl		LRL	Expt Jour	PR 120 874	Nov 60	Alexander.FROM RADIOCHEM+RANGE-E	
Frag Spectra	+6		LAS	Theo Jour	AP 18 274	May 62	Leachman+ CALC ANISOTROPY CFD EXPTS	
Frag Spectra	Maxwl		CRC	Expt Jour	CJP 40 1626	Nov 62	Milton+ DOUBLE VEL.MEASUREMENTS.	
Frag Spectra	Maxwl		ITE	Expt Rept	ITE-	Oct 63	Perfilov+TERNARY FISS.ALPHA SPEC,GRP	
Frag Spectra	-		CCP	Revw Rept	INDSWG-64 266	64	Maksjutenko.FRGMTS EMITNG DELAYED NS	
Frag Spectra	8.0+4	1.3+6	CCP	Expt Rept	ANL-TR-179	64	Bondarenko+,ANG DIST FRAGS,GRPH	
Frag Spectra	1.5+7		CCP	Expt Jour	AE 16 521	Jun 64	Okolovich+MEAN FRAG ENERGY 3.46MEV	
				Jour	SJA 16 644	64	. ENGL OF AE 16 521	
Frag Spectra	-2	+2	FTI	Expt Prog	INDSWG-120 32	65	Borukhovich.E-KIN OF SYMTR FRGMS,NDG	
Frag Spectra	Maxwl		TRM	Revw Rept	AEET-235	65	Methasiri.ALF E-SPEC CFD U-235,TBL	
Frag Spectra	Maxwl		TRM	Theo Conf	65Calcutta 20	Feb 65	Ramanna+ DEFORM-E(FRAG A), MARKOV-TH	
Frag Spectra	Maxwl		CRC	Revw Conf	65Salzburg 451	Mar 65	Fraser.DISCUSSION OF VARIOUS XPTS	
Frag Spectra	5.4+6	7.9+6	FEI	Expt Conf	65Salzburg 1 135	Mar 65	Rabotnov+,ANG DIST FOTO FISS FRAGMTS	
				Rept	FEI-12	65	.ANG ANISOTROPY OF FISS-PROD	
				Rept	LA-TR-66-46	66	.ENGLISH TRANSL OF FEI-12 /65	
Frag Spectra	Maxwl		PTN	Expt Conf	65Salzburg 1 467	Mar 65	Thomas+ SINGLE FRAG E-SPECTRA	
Frag Spectra	Maxwl		KFK	Expt Rept	KFK-401	Feb 66	Rohde.RANGE DIST IN AU+AL,E CALC	
Frag Spectra	Maxwl	-1	FTI	Expt Jour	YF 3 476	Mar 66	Borukhovich+. GRAPH ENERGY-DISTRIB	
				Jour	SNP 3 346	Sep 66	TRANSLATN.*	
Frag Spectra	Maxwl		ORL	Expt Jour	PR 149 894	Sep 66	Neiler+MASS ENERGY DIST	

94 Plutonium 239

Quantity	Energy (ev) Min	Energy (ev) Max	Lab	Type	Documentation Ref Vol Page	Date	Author, Comments	Data
Frag Spectra	8.0+4	1.5+6	FEI	Expt	Jour YF 4 993	Nov 66	Nesterov+ ANG DISTRB OF FRAGMENTS	+
					Rept FEI – 33	65	.FRAG ANGDIST(E),GRAPH,TABLE	
					Jour SNP 4 713	May 67	.ENGLISH TRANSL OF YF 4 933 11/66	
	8.0+4	6.1+6			Rept LA – TR – 66 – 41	66	.ENGLISH TRANSL OF FEI – 33 /65	
Frag Spectra	Maxwl		TRM	Expt	Conf 67Kanpur 334	Feb 67	Hattangadi.E SPECT OF LONG RANGE A	
Frag Spectra	Maxwl		FLA	Expt	Jour PRL 18 404	Mar 67	Muga+ E SPEC IN TERNARY FISSION.	
					Conf 69Vienna 107	Jul 69	– +PPR99. TERNARY E – KIN SPECS GVN	
					Rept ORO – 2843 – 9	Dec 66	.SUPERSEDED	
Frag Spectra	Maxwl		LAS	Expt	Jour PR 156 1277	Apr 67	Stein+ FRAG ENERGIES VS MASS,+ TOTAL	
Frag Spectra	None		FEI	ExTh	Prog YFI – 4 17	May 67	Smirenkin+.,TBP YF	
					Rept INDC – 187E	67	. ENGL OF YFI – 4 17	
Frag Spectra	1.0+6	5.0+6	FEI	Theo	Prog YFI – 4 7	May 67	Nesterov+ ANG ANISOTROPY OF FRAGMNTS	
					Prog INDC – 187E 8	68	. ENGL TRANSL OF YFI – 4 7	
Frag Spectra	Maxwl	3.0 – 1	FTI	Expt	Prog YFI – 4 43	May 67	Borukhovich+.TABLE KINETIC E OF FRGM	
					Rept INDC – 187E 55	67	. ENGL OF YFI – 4 43	
Frag Spectra	2.0 – 2	5.0 – 1	MTR	Expt	Jour PR 157 1055	May 67	Moore+ YLD HIGH KE FRAG VS NEUT E	
					Rept IN – 1033	Nov 66	.SEE ALSO	
Frag Spectra	Maxwl		KFK	Comp	Rept KFK – 693	Dec 67	Muenzel+ RANGE DIST OF FISS FRAG	
				Expt	Rept KFK – 498	Aug 66	Hollstein+.RANGE DIST IN AL	
					Rept KFK – 496	Jul 66	– + FRAGMENT RANGES	
					Jour RCA 5 195	66	– + FRAGMENT RANGES	
					Jour RCA 6 9	66	– + FRAGMENT RANGES	
					Conf 65Salzburg 573	Mar 65	Muenzel.RANGE OF SOME FPROD IN AL	
					Rept KFK – 306	Feb 65	Hollstein+ FISS FRAG RANGES. (GER)	
					Rept UCRL – TR – 1253	65	– . ENGLISH OF KFK – 306	
Frag Spectra	Maxwl		ITE	Expt	Rept ITE – 609	68	Andreev+ SPECTRA OF LIGHT IONS	
Frag Spectra	Maxwl		KFK	Expt	Jour RCA 9 187	68	Ishimori+E OF FP,TBL,TOTAL ENERGY	
Frag Spectra	1.5+5	1.5+6	ANL	Expt	Jour PR 174 1539	Oct 68	Huizenga+ 13ES ANG DIST 6ANGS	
					Rept NYO – 3938 – 1	Jun 68	.SUPERSEDED	
					Conf 68Wash. 603	Mar 68	.SUPERSEDED	
Frag Spectra	Maxwl		ITE	Expt	Jour YF 9 23	Jan 69	Andreev+LONG – RANG HE+LI+BE+B+C SPECS	
					Jour SNP 9 14	Jul 69	TRANSLATN.*	
Frag Spectra	+1	+4	LAS	Expt	Prog WASH – 1127 130	Apr 69	Harlow+ PLANNED FOR PHYSICS 8.	
Frag Spectra		2.0+6	COP	Revw	Conf 69Vienna 155	Jul 69	Strutinsky+PPR203. GRPH ANGANISTR(E)	
Frag Spectra	Maxwl		ORL	ExTh	Conf 69Vienna 67	Jul 69	Schmitt.PPR122.GRPH,(EKIN+ – RMS) VS A	
Frag Spectra	2.5 – 2		HEI	Theo	Conf 69Montreal 652	Aug 69	Norenberg+CALC ROTATIONAL STATES.NDG	
Frag Spectra	Maxwl		YAL	Theo	Jour NP/A 136 465	Oct 69	Rasmussen+DISTR ROT ANG MOMENT.A=108	
Frag Spectra	None		SAH	Theo	Conf 69Roorke 2 217	Dec 69	Sarkar+ E BALANCE OKS EXPTS, GRAPHS	
					Prog BARC – 401 21	69	– + FRAGS EXCIT+KIN E OKS EXPTS	
					Conf 68Bombay 2 122	Dec 68	RATNA SARKAR+ EXCIT+KIN E(A),GRAPHS	
Frag Spectra	Maxwl		SAH	Theo	Prog BARC – 474 31	70	Sarkar+ EXCIT+KIN E OKS EXPT,TBP PR	
Frag Spectra	None		BLA	Expt	Prog INDC(BUL) – 1G	Apr 70	Kashukeev+ PRELIMIN EXPT,NDG	
Frag Spectra		7.0+5	IRE	Expt	Jour ZEP 11 489	May 70	Smirnkin+ ANG ANISOTR(NEUT – E),GRPHS	
					Jour JEL 11 333	May 70	TRANSLATN.*NO10	
Frag Spectra		6.0+6	FEI	Theo	Conf 70Helsinki 2 177	Jun 70	Vorobeva+88. E – BALANCE TO CALC NU(E)	
Frag Spectra	Maxwl		IBJ	Expt	Rept INP – 702/PS	Jun 70	Dakowski+ SEMICOND DET RESLTS CFD TH	+
					Rept INR – 1142/II/PL	Nov 69	Krogulski. LIGHT PART E – SPC CFD THEO	
					Conf 69Vienna 893	Jul 69	– +PPR65.LIGHT PART E – SPC,TBL	
	Pile				Jour NP/A 128 219	Apr 69	– + E SPEC OF P,D,T,HE4,6,8	
	Maxwl				Data EXFOR30320.	Jan 76	231PTS,E SPEC OF P,D,T AND HE4,6,8	
Frag Spectra	1.8+5	1.5+6	FEI	Expt	Jour YF 12 260	Aug 70	Androsenko+ ANGANISOTROPY VS E,TABLE	
					Jour SNP 12 142	Feb 71	TRANSLATN.*	
Frag Spectra	Maxwl	1.6+7	TRM	Expt	Conf 70Madurai 2 57	Dec 70	Iyer+ ANGDISTR,GRAPH+TABLE,TRACK – DET	+
	1.6+7				Data EXFOR30235.	Jul 73	COS.COEF.OF ANG.DIST. OF FIS.FRAGM.	
Frag Spectra	5.0+4	5.3+6	FEI	Expt	Jour YF 13 3 484	71	Akimov+	+
	0.0+0	5.5+6			Prog YFI – 11 15	70	– + ABST,FRAG KIN – E VS N – E,NDG	
					Prog INDC(CCP) – 31	Dec 72	.PAGE 14,ENGLISH OF YFI – 11 15	
	5.0+4	5.3+6			Data EXFOR40144.007	Apr 73	.AVERAGE KIN – EN OF FISS – FRAG,35 LINS	
Frag Spectra	8.0+5	1.1+6	CCP	Expt	Conf 71Moscow	Feb 71	Nikolaev+.ABST,AVG FRAG KE AT 18ANG	
Frag Spectra	Maxwl		ORU	Expt	Prog RLO – 2277 – 1	Mar 71	Loveland+.FRAG – PROMPT GAM ANG CORREL	
Frag Spectra	1.5+4	7.4+5	FEI	Expt	Prog YFI – 10 22	May 71	Smirenkin+ ANG ANISOTROPY,TBL,GRAPH	
					Rept INDC(CCP) – 15	Dec 71	*P24,ENG OF YFI – 10	
	+0	8.0+5			Prog YFI – 11 16	70	Smirenkin+ ABST,ANISOTROPY(N – E),GRPH	
					Prog INDC(CCP) – 31	Dec 72	.PAGE 15,ENGLISH OF YFI – 11 16	
Frag Spectra	1.5+4	7.2+6	FEI	Expt	Jour YF 13 950	May 71	Shpak+ ANG – ANISOTROPY(N – E),TBL,GRPHS	+
					Jour SNP 13 547	Nov 71	. ENGL OF YF 13 950	
	1.5+4	7.2+6			Data EXFOR40124.	Sep 72	ANG DSTRB OF FRGMNTS AT 67ES,COS – FIT	
Frag Spectra	9.9+1	2.2+3	DUB	Theo	Rept JINR – P3 – 6239	Jun 71	Mateeva+ INTERMED.STRUCTURE OF SIG	

94 Plutonium 239

Quantity	Energy (ev) Min	Max	Lab	Type	Documentation Ref Vol Page	Date	Author, Comments	Data
Frag Spectra	+0	+7	TOK Theo	Jour	PTP 45 1808	Jun 71	Ohta.MOMENT OF INERTIA FROM FISS TH	
Frag Spectra	None		COL Expt	Jour	PR/C 4 267	Jul 71	Toraskar+.SM+BE FILTER,KE DISTRIBUTN	
Frag Spectra	5.5+6	1.5+7	FEI Expt	Jour	YF 14 935	Nov 71	Surin+ FRAG KIN−E,2 ES CFD THR,GRAPH	+
				Jour	SNP 14 523	May 72	* ENGL OF YF 14 935	
	2.5−2	1.5+7		Data	EXFOR40112.	Nov 73	.KIN−E AND AVERAGE KIN−E,4SUBENT	
Frag Spectra	Maxwl		ANL Expt	Jour	NP/A 177 337	Dec 71	Reisdorf+SIMULT MEAS K.E. ANG G−SPEC	
				Conf	69Vienna 781	Jul 69	− + PRELIMINARY.	
Frag Spectra	Maxwl	3.0−1	NIL Expt	Prog	IAEA−147 41	72	Alam+ AVG KIN−E+WIDTH OF DISTRIB,TBL	
Frag Spectra	1.6+7		TRM Expt	Prog	BARC−628 94	72	Iyer+ ANGULAR ANISOTROPY OF FRAG,TBL	
Frag Spectra	2.5−2	1.6+6	FEI Expt	Jour	AE 32 83	Jan 72	Kolosov+	+
	Maxwl	1.6+6		Jour	AE 32 83	Jan 72	− + FRAG AVG KIN−E REL THR,GRPH	
				Jour	SJA 32 92	Jul 72	. ENGL OF AE 32 83	
	2.5−2	1.6+6		Data	EXFOR40130.002	Sep 72	AVERAGE E−KIN OF FRGMNTS AT 17 ES	
Frag Spectra	8.0+5	1.1+6	RI Expt	Jour	IZV 36 215	Jan 72	Nikolaev+ AVG FRAGM−E DISTRIBUTION	
	Pile	1.1+6		Prog	YFI−12 96	72	− .ABST,AVG KIN−E,NDG	
				Prog	INDC(CCP)−30	Sep 72	.PAGE 84,ENGLISH OF YFI−12 96	
Frag Spectra	Maxwl		CUA Theo	Abst	DA/B 32 5980	Apr 72	Lee. CALC OF TOT FRAG KE DISTRIBUTS	
Frag Spectra	Maxwl		TRM Expt	Jour	JIN 34 9 2685	Sep 72	Prakash+ KIN ENERGY DISTR	
	Pile			Conf	70Madurai 2 79	Dec 70	− + KIN−E VS MASS RATIO, GRAPHS	
	Maxwl			Conf	69Chandigr 1 182	Sep 69	Dange+ FRAG RANGE IN AL,KIN E,TABLES	
				Conf	69Vienna 741	Jul 69	− +PPR97.RANGES IN AL+KIN−E,TBL	
				Prog	BARC−401	69	SATYA PRAKASH+,RANGE−ENERGYCORR,ABST	
Frag Spectra	Pile		NBS Expt	Jour	NP/A 195 257	Nov 72	Schroeder. ALPHA SPECTRUM	
Frag Spectra	Maxwl		BUC Revw	Rept	IFA−RN−50	73	Cristu. MASS−+CHARGE−+E−DISTR REVIEW	
	Fast			Rept	IFA−RN−50	73	− . MASS−+CHARGE−+E−DISTR REVIEW	
Frag Spectra	Maxwl		ISP Theo	Conf	73Paris 1 559	Mar 73	Rustichelli.FISSPROD RANGES,TBL,GRPH	
Frag Spectra	2.5−2		FEI Expt	Conf	73Kiev 3 270	May 73	Vorob'Yeva+	+
	2.5−2			Data	EXFOR40284.003	May 75	.AVER KIN−E OF FF GVN	
Frag Spectra	Maxwl		ITK Theo	Jour	AUJ 26 279	Jun 73	Mukherji+ CALC KE VS FRAG−MASS,GRAPH	
	None			Conf	69Roorke 2 226	Dec 69	− + TOT−KINE(A) CRV,LIQID−DROP	
Frag Spectra	Maxwl		PAV Expt	Jour	NP/A 208 196	Jun 73	Fossati+ HE4+HE6 E+ANG DISTS,CURVES.	
				Jour	NCL 10 93	Jun 74	Brera+ANG DIST OF HE3,AVG E,GRPH,TBL	
				Conf	69Vienna 891	Jul 69	− +PPR16.EMISSN OF LIGHT PART	
				Jour	NC/B 51 1 235	Sep 67	Bollini+HE ISOTOPES ENERGY SPECT	
Frag Spectra	Maxwl		ANL Expt	Conf	73Rochestr 2 19	Aug 73	Unik+ TOTAL KIN−E OF FRAGS,GRPH	
Frag Spectra	Maxwl		GEL Expt	Conf	73Rochestr 2 51	Aug 73	Deruytter+ FRAG KIN−E+AVG,TBL,GRAPH	
				Prog	EANDC(E)89U154	Feb 68	− +.CFD FRAG SPEC SPON 240PU	
				Conf	64Paris § EC191	Jul 64	− + SUM−KINETIC E DISTR.	
Frag Spectra	3.0−1		MOL Expt	Conf	73Rochestr 2 492	Aug 73	Vandenput+ ABST,TOTAL KE REL TH GIVN	
Frag Spectra	Maxwl		MUU Revw	Conf	73Rochestr 2 61	Aug 73	Specht.AVG KIN−E VS EXCIT−E CFD,GRPH	
Frag Spectra	None		FEI Theo	Conf	ZFK−271 7	Nov 73	Ignatjuk+ TH FOR ANGDIST OF FRAGMNTS	
Frag Spectra	Maxwl		MOL Expt	Rept	RCN−203 135	Dec 73	Wegener Penning+ GRPH	
Frag Spectra	Maxwl		AUA Revw	Conf	IAEA−169 2 163	74	Musgrove+ AVG FRAG MASS,GRAPH	
Frag Spectra	Pile		LIN Expt	Jour	YF 20 461	Sep 74	Vorob'Ev+ LIGHT FRG E−SPEC,TBL+GRAPH	
	Maxwl			Conf	73Munich 1 716	Aug 73	Vorobjov+ Z=1...8 E−SPECTRUM,NDG	
	Pile			Jour	SNP 20 248	Mar 75	. ENGL OF YF 20 461	
Frag Spectra	Maxwl		PAH Theo	Jour	PL/B 55 144	Feb 75	Hooshyar+ISOMERIC FISS,TH CFD EXPTAL	
Frag Spectra	9.5+6		BRC Expt	Jour	JPRL 36 80	Apr 75	Lachkar+ VDG,DATA AND GRAPH GIVEN	
Frag Spectra	Pile		TRM Theo	Jour	PR/C 11 1251	Apr 75	Dange+ FRGM−EKIN FORMUL CFD OTHS,FIG	
Frag Spectra	+7		FEI Theo	Conf	75Kiev	May 75	Ermagambetov+ ANGANIZOTR,ANALYS,GRPH	
Frag Spectra	Maxwl		MNZ Expt	Jour	ZP/A 273 77	May 75	Kaffrell+ G−RAY−SPEC,DECAY OF TC−105	
Frag Spectra	Maxwl		ANL Expt	Abst	BAP 20 1155	Sep 75	Roche+ AV TOT KE = (D,PF) REACTION	
Frag Spectra	None		DKE Theo	Conf	76Lowell 1403	Jul 76	Newson.EXCIT E,3−50MEV.FINE STRUC.ND	
Frag Charge	Maxwl		ANL Eval	Conf	55Geneva 7 3	Aug 55	Steinberg+ P614.CHARGE DISPERSN,GRPH	
Frag Charge	None		MTR Expt	Conf	55Geneva 7 19	Aug 55	Pappas+ P881,CHARGE DISTRIBTN CURVE	
Frag Charge	None		BNL Theo	Jour	NSE 9 495	Apr 61	Levine.MOST PROB Z.FROM =CHG DISPL.	
Frag Charge	Maxwl		CNA Theo	Jour	PR/B 134 972	Jun 64	Talat+ N,CHARGE DIST IN FISS PRODS.	
				ExTh Rept	CNAEM−12	63	− + TBL AVERAGE CHARGE/NUCLEON	
Frag Charge	Maxwl		FEI Theo	Prog	YFI−3 12	Sep 66	Ignatjvk. GRAPH	
Frag Charge	Fast		FAR Theo	Rept	BNWL−TR−18	May 67	Mechali+ ISOT 130−136,TBL,NO DETAILS	
Frag Charge	Maxwl		GEV Comp	Rept	APED−5398	Oct 68	Meek+ TABLES	
Frag Charge	Maxwl		HAR Theo	Rept	AERE−R−6056	Mar 69	Crouch.CALC CHARGE DISPERSION,ZP,TBL	
				Rept	AERE−R−5488	May 67	− + SUPERSEDED	
				Rept	AERE−R−5250	Apr 66	− + SUPERSEDED	
Frag Charge	Maxwl		RAM Revw	Jour	NSPA 5 43	Apr 69	Khan. REVIEW,CHARGE DISTRIBUTN EXPTS	
Frag Charge	Maxwl		SOR Theo	Jour	PR 182 1331	Jun 69	Notea.EMPIRICAL FUNCTION DERIVED	
Frag Charge	Maxwl		ANL Expt	Conf	69Vienna 781	Jul 69	Glendenin+PPR114.CHARGE DIST,K X−RAY	
Frag Charge	Maxwl		MCM Theo	Conf	69Vienna 845	Jul 69	Thind+PPR50. YLD(Z,A)+NU(A)+EXCIT E	

Plutonium 239

Quantity	Energy (ev) Min	Max	Lab	Type	Documentation Ref Vol Page	Date	Author, Comments	Data
Frag Charge	Maxwl		MNZ	Expt	Conf 69Vienna 945	Jul 69	Denschlag+PPR26. CHARGE DISPERSION	
Frag Charge	Maxwl		TRM	Expt	Conf 69Vienna 741	Jul 69	Dange+PPR97. YLD OF 17ISOTOPS,GE(LI)	
Frag Charge	Maxwl		CUA	Theo	Abst DA/B 30 2222	Nov 69	Rogers.	
Frag Charge	Maxwl		JAE	Revw	Jour NP/A 160 65	Jan 71	Umezawa+ SYSTEMATICS VS FRAG MASS	
Frag Charge	Maxwl		ANL	Expt	Jour NP/A 177 337	Dec 71	Reisdorf+SIMULT MEAS K.E. ANG G-SPEC	
					Conf 69Vienna 781	Jul 69	- + PRELIMINARY.	
Frag Charge	Fast		BUC	Revw	Rept IFA-RN-50	73	Cristu.MASS-+CHARGE-+E-DISTR REVIEW	
	Maxwl				Rept IFA-RN-50	73	- .MASS-+CHARGE-+E-DISTR REVIEW	
Frag Charge	Maxwl		AUA	Revw	Conf IAEA-169 2 163	74	Musgrove+ CHARGE DISPERSN PARS,GRPHS	
Frag Charge	Maxwl		LRL	Comp	Rept UCRL-51640	Jul 74	Nethaway. TBL.	
Frag Charge	1.8+6	1.5+7	LRL	Comp	Rept UCRL-51640	Jul 74	Nethaway. TBL.	
Frag Charge	Maxwl		ANL	Expt	Jour JIN 37 869	Apr 75	Flynn+ FRAC INDEP RB84,86,CS136.CURV	+
	Maxwl				Data EXFOR10517.007	Apr 78	. 3PTS.CHARGE DISTRB DATA	
Frag Charge	Maxwl		UBE	Expt	Jour JIN 38 205	Feb 76	Gaeggeler+ ZP(A=150),GRPH Z-SYSTEMAT	
					Diss GAEGGELER	Dec 73	- . COMPLETE EXPT DESCRIPTION	
					Conf 73Rochestr 2 475	Aug 73	- + ABST,ZP FOR A=150 GIVEN	
Frag Charge	Pile		GER	Expt	Jour RCA 24 1 8	77	Kreiner. CHARGE DIST A=99,100,101	
Reson Params	3.0-1		LAS	Expt	Rept LA-266	Apr 45	Anderson.	+
	3.0-1				Data EXFOR12519.004	Jun 76	. 1 RES. E0,WT,PCS	
Reson Params	-.2+0	2.6+1	COL	Expt	Rept CUD-92	May 51	Havens.	+
	-.2+0	2.6+1			Data EXFOR12517.	Jun 76	. 8 RES. WT,PCS,WT**2/PCS.	
Reson Params	2.9-1		BNL	Expt	Priv PALEVSKY	55	Palevsky.	+
	2.9-1				Data EXFOR12520.004	Jun 76	. 1 RES. WT,WF.	
Reson Params	3.0-1		SAC	Expt	Jour JNE 1 306	Jun 55	Auclair+ E,W(TOTAL)EXPT FROM SIGFISS	
					Jour CR 239 1128	Nov 54	Galula+ FISSION WIDTH	
					Jour CR 239 1034	Oct 54	Vendryes+ RES PARAMS.TBL.	
Reson Params	1.0-2	1.0+2	CCP	Expt	Conf 55Moscow 87	Jul 55	Nikitin+.SIMULTAN ABS AND FISS,TABLE	+
					-		ENGL TRANSL AEC-TR-2435 PAGE 81	
Reson Params	3.0-1		CCP	Expt	Conf 55Moscow 294	Jul 55	Abov. BENT QUARTZ CRYSTAL. TABLE	
					Rept AEC-TR-2435	56	. PAGE 209.ENGL OF 55MOSCOW 294	
Reson Params	3.0-1		HAN	Expt	Conf 55Geneva 4 193	Aug 55	Leonard+.TABLE,TOTAL WIDTH, PPR589	+
	3.0-1				Data EXFOR12522.002	Jun 76	. 1 RES. E0,WT,NF/PCS,WT**2/PCS.	
Reson Params	3.0-1	3.3+1	HAR	Expt	Conf 55Geneva 4 187	Aug 55	Raffle+.RESON-ES,TOT+FISS-WIDTH,P422	
Reson Params	3.0-1	1.1+1	CCP		Rept AEC-TR-2435PT1	56	.USSR ALSO 8D07EV PAGE 85	
Reson Params	3.0-1		CCP		Rept AEC-TR-2435PT1	56	.USSR PAGES211 AND 213	
Reson Params	5.0+0	1.0+2	HAR		Jour BJAS 5 1	56	Cockcroft+SCIENTI.PROBL.IN NUCLEAR E	
Reson Params	1.8+1	1.8+1	HAR	Expt	Rept NRDC-81 1	56	Lynn. = 8 DATA INDEX LINES	+
Reson Params	-.5-2	2.7+1	HAR	Expt	Jour JNE 2 177	Mar 56	Richmond+.8 RES.ENERGIES GIVEN	+
Reson Params	1.0-2	3.0-1	HAR	Expt	Jour JNE 2 187	Mar 56	Pattenden.ER GWN WT	+
Reson Params		4.9+1	HAR	Expt	Jour JNE 3 33	Aug 56	Farley.ETA USED ESTIMATE WF OF 25RES	+
Reson Params	7.8+0		HAR	ExTh	Rept AERE-NP/R-2076	Jan 57	Egelstaff.P22. 2LVLS ASSUMD.OK S,ETA	
Reson Params	7.8+0		UK		Rept A-8 21	Jan 57	.REVIEW WGD043 WFD023 WND002EV	
Reson Params	7.8+0	8.6+1	CCP	Expt	Jour AE 2 129	Feb 57	Sokolovsky+.TABLE 26 E RES,GWN,14 WT	+
					Jour JNE 5 389	Nov 57	TRANSLATN.*	
					Jour SJA 2 147	57	TRANSLATN.*	
Reson Params	3.0-1	2.6+1	CCP	Expt	Jour AE 2 247	Mar 57	Kirpichnikov+.TABLE 10 ER,ETA,WIDTHS	+
					Jour JNE 6 163	Dec 57	TRANSLATN.*	
					Jour SJA 2 299	57	TRANSLATN.*	
Reson Params	5.0-1	1.2+2	MTR	Expt	Prog IDO-16373 39	Jul 57	Simpson.NDG.	
Reson Params	2.0-2	3.0-1	HAR	Expt	Jour JNE 6 212	Apr 58	Skarsgard+.SHAPE FIT TO ETA DATA	
Reson Params	3.0-1	4.2+1	HAR	Expt	Jour JNE 6 303	May 58	Egelstaff+,FC TRANSMISSION,WT+WN,TBL	+
Reson Params	-.1+0	5.3+1	ANL	Expt	Conf 58Geneva 15 127	Sep 58	Bollinger+.PPR687,PARAMS FOR 20LVLS	+
	1.0-2	2.8+1			Conf ORNL-2309	Jun 57	Block+ EDITORS.WG D04 WF D08EVAVG.	
	3.0-1	4.1+1			Rept AERE-NP/R-2076	Jul 56	Bollinger. 14LEVELS AS HGX0456	
	-.1+0	5.3+1			Data EXFOR12502.	Jun 76	. 20 RES,E0,WT,WN,WG,WF,WF**2,PCS.	
Reson Params	2.9-1	5.3+1	BNL	Revw	Conf 58Geneva 16 8	Sep 58	Hughes.PPR2483,PARAMS FOR 16ES GVN	
Reson Params	7.8+0	2.6+1	CCP	Expt	Conf 58Geneva 15 309	Sep 58	Vladimirsky+.PPR2221,PARAMS FOR 9 ES	
Reson Params	-.1+0	1.5+1	CRC	ExTh	Jour PR 118 724	May 60	Vogt. MULTILEVEL FIT TO BNL 325 DATA	+
Reson Params	7.8+0	4.5+1	HAR	ExTh	Jour NP 30 269	Feb 62	Fraser+. SPIN OF 8 RESONANCES	+
Reson Params	3.0-1	2.3+1	ITE	Theo	Jour ZET 45 875	Oct 63	Ignat'Ev+ SPINDEPEND OF LEVELDENSITY	
					Jour JET 18 602	Mar 64	TRANSLATN.*	

94 Plutonium 239

Quantity	Energy (ev) Min	Energy (ev) Max	Lab	Type	Documentation Ref Vol Page	Date	Author, Comments	Data
Reson Params	7.8+0	9.6+1	ITE	Expt	Jour AE 16 110	Feb 64	Ignat'Ev+ PLSD CYCL,3PARAMS AT 23RES	+
					Rept ICD-1 40	Aug 64	.MORE PARAMETERS	
					Jour AE 16 211	Mar 64	.CONTINUATION OF AE 16 110 2/64	
					Rept ANL-TRANS-168	Apr 67	.PAGE 40.ENGLISH OF ICD-1 40 8/64	
					Rept INDSWG-69E	Nov 64	.ENGLISH TRANSL OF ITE-282 9/64	
					Rept ITE-282	Sep 64	.TABLE GAM-F/GAM-A AT 21RESONANCES	
					Jour SJA 16 251	Mar 64	.ENGLISH TRANSL OF AE 16 211 3/64	
					Jour EAF 16 2 19	64	. FRENCH TRANSL OF AE 16 121 2/64	
					Jour EAF 16 3 31	64	. FRENCH TRANSL OF AE 16 211 3/64	
					Jour SJA 16 121	64	.ENGLISH TRANSL OF AE 16 121 2/64	
Reson Params		2.3+1	ITE	Theo	Jour AE 16 211	Mar 64	Kirpichnikov+ INTERFERENCE+RES ANAL	+
	7.8+0	2.3+1		Expt	Jour AE 16 211	Mar 64	- +	
		2.3+1		Theo	Jour SJA 16 251	Mar 64	. ENGL OF AE 16 211	
	7.8+0	2.3+1		Expt	Data EXFOR40157.005	Mar 73	TOT-WIDTH AT 8 RES	
Reson Params		+7	CCP	Theo	Jour AE 17 479	Dec 64	Usachev+ FISS CHANNEL THRESHOLDS EST	
		+8			Jour JNE 19 987	Dec 65	TRANSLATN.*	
		+7			Jour SJA 17 1242	Dec 64	TRANSLATN.*	
Reson Params	None		CEA	Revw	Conf 64Vienna 19	Dec 64	Vendryes+D,WG,WN GVN,OTHER COMPILTNS	
Reson Params	-.1+1	9.6+1	CJD	Comp	Rept INDSWG-101 25	65	.TBL OF 27 RES FROM VARIOUS SOURCES	
Reson Params	+0	+3	CAI	Theo	Jour NP 62 667	Feb 65	Stavinsky+(N,GF)PROB ABOUT=(N,GAMMA)	
Reson Params	7.8+0	9.1+1	ITE	Expt	Jour EON 2 77	Feb 65	Ignat'Ev+. SIMULTAN CAPT+NU+TRANSM	+
Reson Params	1.0+2	3.0+2	HAR	ExTh	Conf 65Antwerp 535	Jul 65	Uttley+ PPR98.SINGLE LVL ANALYSIS.	+
Reson Params	-.1+1	3.0+2	KFK	Eval	Rept KFK-120 1	Nov 65	Schmidt.123RES.S-WAVE,STATS.	
					Conf 66S.Diego 2 223	Feb 66	- . SEE KFK-120.	
Reson Params	7.9+0	8.6+1	LRL	Expt	Jour PRL 15 761	Nov 65	Sauter+ 12 ARE J=1,3.	+
	7.9+0	7.5+1			Abst DA/B 28 307	Jul 67	- .J FOR 15RES,FROM SIGSCAT	
	7.9+0	8.6+1			Data EXFOR12512.012	Jun 76	. 14 RES. J,WT,WN**2.	
Reson Params	-		CAI	Theo	Rept UARAEE-20	66	Shaker+ AVG FISSN WIDTH, PORTER-THOM	
Reson Params	1.8+1	8.2+1	LAS	Expt	Jour PR 144 979	Apr 66	Cowan+,J FOR 20RES FROM YLD VAR VS E	+
	1.8+1	8.2+1			Data EXFOR12517.002	Jun 76	. 17 RES. J.	
Reson Params	7.8+0	1.0+5	GEB	Eval	Rept GEAP-5272	Dec 66	Greebler+.L=0.J WT WN WG WF+AVERAGE	
Reson Params	3.0-1	3.0+2	AI	Eval	Rept NAA-SR-11980 5	May 67	Hennies.WN WG WF +AVG PARS TO 10KEV	
Reson Params	3.0-1	2.1+2	DUB	Expt	Jour YF 5 925	May 67	Ryabov+.TABLE,N-,GAMMA-,FISS-W,SPIN	
					Jour SNP 5 657	Nov 67	TRANSLATN.*	
Reson Params	1.5+1	3.0+2	HAR	Expt	Jour NP/A 98 33	May 67	Asghar+ SPIN OF 50 RES GIVEN	
Reson Params	-		CCP	Eval	Jour AE 23 6	Jul 67	Kirpitchnikov.FISS-,N-WIDTH,STRNTH-F	
					Jour SJA 23 669	Jul 67	TRANSLATN.*	
Reson Params		1.0+6	AUA	Theo	Jour AUJ 20 477	Oct 67	Cook. TBL OF AVG LVL SPACING D,L=0,1	
Reson Params	-		FEI	Theo	Prog YFI-6 37	68	Duk'Janov+. STRUCTURE OF SIG-FIS(E)	
					Prog INDC(CCP)-3	69	.ABSTRACT.ENGLISH TRANSL OF YFI-6	
Reson Params	1.4+1	8.6+1	LAS	ExTh	Jour PR 165 1371	Jan 68	Farrell. REICH-MOORE FT TO FISS SIG.	+
	1.4+1	8.6+1		Expt	Data EXFOR12516.002	Jun 76	. 47 RES. E0,J,WN,WF.	
Reson Params	1.0+2	5.0+5	JAP	Theo	Jour NST 5 86	Feb 68	KIKUCHI P AN.WF CALCULATION	
Reson Params	-.3+0	3.5+1	UI	Eval	Conf 68Wash. 967	Mar 68	Adler+ MULTILVL ANALYSIS TBS	
Reson Params	+0	+2	CCP	Theo	Jour YF 7 967	May 68	Vorotnikov+ GRPH,DISTRIBUTION OF WF	
					Jour SNP 7 582	Nov 68	TRANSLATN.*	
Reson Params		4.0+3	TRM	Expt	Rept BARC-421	69	Mahalingam+CRITICL-XPT CFD DATA-SETS	
Reson Params	-		FEI	Theo	Rept FEI-157	Feb 69	Ignatjuk+ 2HUMPED-BARR-CALCUL,WN/WF	
Reson Params	2.2+1	8.1+1	RPI	Expt	Jour PRL 22 195	Feb 69	Weinstein+ LINAC+TOF J FOR 11 RESON	+
	2.2+1	1.2+2			Rept EANDC(US)-118	Feb 69	Block+ J FOR 14RESON NU+SCAT MEASTS	
	2.2+1	8.1+1			Data EXFOR12513.002	Jun 76	. 11 RES. J.	
Reson Params	-.2+0	3.0-1	COL	Expt	Prog WASH-1127 38	Apr 69	Toraskar+ J FOR NEG,.3EV LVLS DEDUCD	
Reson Params	2.0+1	5.5+1	FEI	Theo	Prog YFI-7 18	Apr 69	Lukyanov+ FISSN,MULTILEVEL-ANAL, NDG	
					Rept INDC(CCP)-7U21	Feb 70	TRANSLATN.*	
Reson Params	5.0+1	3.0+3	DUB	Theo	Conf 69Vienna 934	Jul 69	Ryabov+PPR160. EGELSTAFF-ANAL,FISSN	
Reson Params	-		HAR	Revw	Conf 69Vienna 249	Jul 69	Lynn. PARS IN STRUTNSKY TH+EXPTS,TBL	
Reson Params	3.0-1	9.0+1	RPI	Expt	Conf 69Vienna 477	Jul 69	Weinstein+PPR113.SPIN,20RESON,NU-XPT	
Reson Params	-.1+1	1.6+1	BUC	Theo	Jour RRP 14 841	Aug 69	Cristu+ RES-PARS USED IN SIG-CALCUL	
Reson Params	4.0+1	1.0+2	ANL	Theo	Prog WASH-1136 12	Sep 69	Lambropoulos.ANALYSIS OF SACLAY DATA	
Reson Params	-.1+1	8.6+1	CCP	Revw	Rept ICD-6 7		70 Lukyanov.D,J,N+F-WIDS OF 52 RES,TBLS	
Reson Params	+2	+5	ITK	Theo	Prog BARC-474 53		70 Sengupta+ STATISTICL ANAL OF DATA	
	1.0+2	1.0+5			Conf 69Roorke 2 204	Dec 69	- + STATIST RES ANALYSIS, ALFA	
Reson Params	None		TRM	Theo	Prog BARC-501 28		70 Sood+ CLASS II LVL SPACING,FISS	
					Prog BARC-471 5		70 - + CORREL ANAL,D CLASS II VAL GV	
	2.0+1	1.0+6			Conf 69Roorke 2 198	Dec 69	- + AVG LEVL SPACING D,2-HUMPED-T	
Reson Params	4.2+1	1.2+2	RPI	Expt	Abst DA/B 30 3819	Feb 70	King.SUPERSEDED.	+
	4.2+1	1.2+2			Data EXFOR10040.	Jul 71	. 24 RES. E0,WN,WT,J.	

94 Plutonium 239

Quantity	Energy (ev) Min	Max	Lab	Type	Documentation Ref Vol Page	Date	Author, Comments	Data
Reson Params	3.0−1	8.6+1	DUB	Expt	Rept JINR−P3−4992	Apr 70	Rjabov+ TOT+N+G+F−WIDS,32 RES,D,TBL	+
					Jour SNP 13 255	Sep 71	*ENGL OF YF 13 457	
					Jour YF 13 457	Mar 71	Rjabov+ AVG WIDTHS, LVL SPACING	
	2.9−1	8.7+1			Prog YFI−11 27	70	− + ABST,SAME TBL AS JINR−4992	
					Prog INDC(CCP)−31	Dec 72	.PAGE 26,ENGLISH OF YFI−11 27	
	7.8+0	8.6+1			Data EXFOR40104.	Jun 72	N−WID AT 48RES, FIS−WID AT 31RES, D	
	3.0−1	8.6+1			Data EXFOR40070.	Aug 70	TOT+N+GAM+FISS−WIDTHS 32 RESON +D	
Reson Params	1.5+2	1.0+5	TOK	Theo	Jour NST 7 157	Apr 70	Kikuchi+.CHANNEL TH,SPIN DEPENDNT WF	
					Jour NST 5 86	Feb 68	− + SUPERSEDED.	
Reson Params	3.0−1	4.2+0	BNL	Expt	Conf 70Helsinki 1 377	Jun 70	Chrien.42. SPINS + GAMMA WIDTHS	
Reson Params	0.0+0	6.0−2	GEL	Expt	Conf 70Helsinki 1 117	Jun 70	Deruytter+.	+
		6.0−2			Data EXFOR20143.005	Mar 73	1PNT.NF AREA.	
Reson Params		6.6+2	HAR	Revw	Conf 70Helsinki 1 267	Jun 70	James.107. AVG FISSN WIDTHS, 2 SPINS	
	7.8+1	8.8+1		Theo	Jour JNE 22 263	Apr 68	− .MULTILEVEL FIT TO DERRIEN DATA	
	5.6+1	8.6+1		Expt	Conf 65Salzburg 235	Mar 65	− .TABLE OF 10 RES,E AND WT ONLY	
Reson Params	1.6+1	6.6+2	SAC	Expt	Conf 70Helsinki 1 495	Jun 70	Trochon+ PPR62.WN,WF,SPINS.	
	1.6+1	3.0+2			Conf 69Vienna 912	Jul 69	− + PPR76 RES−SPIN DETERMINATN.	
Reson Params		7.0+3	SDC	Theo	Conf 70Helsinki 2 799	Jun 70	Garrison.DISCUSSN. RESONANCE ANAL	
Reson Params	3.0+2	2.0+4	GEB	Eval	Jour NSE 41 143	Jul 70	Evatt+,AVG WN WF D FROM EXPTL DATA	
Reson Params	1.9+1	5.9+1	LAS	Expt	Jour PR/C 2 615	Aug 70	Cowan+.	+
Reson Params	None		DUB	Theo	Jour YF 13 240	Feb 71	Malecki+G−WID,THEO CFD EXPT.TBL,GRPH	
					Jour SNP 13 133	Aug 71	− + ENGL OF YF 13 240.	
Reson Params	7.8+0	1.2+2	MTR	Expt	Jour NP/A 164 34	Mar 71	Simpson+ J FROM POOR RESOL MEAS	+
	7.8+0	1.2+2			Data EXFOR10132.002	Jan 73	. 23 RES. J.	
Reson Params	6.2−1	5.0+4	SRL	Theo	Conf 71Knoxvill 714	Mar 71	Mccrosson. STAT CALCULATN AVG PARAMS	
Reson Params	8.3+1	7.5+3	ANL	Eval	Rept ANL−7814	May 71	Kikuchi.INTERMEDIATE RESON PARAMS	
Reson Params	−.2−2	1.0+2	ORL	Expt	Jour NSE 45 25	Jul 71	Gwin+PARS DRVD IN MULTILVL ANAL,NDG.	+
	−.2+0	1.0+2			Rept ORNL−4707	Jul 71	− +PARS DRVD IN MULTILVL ANAL,TBL	
	−.2−2	1.0+2			Data EXFOR10035.010	Nov 75	. 48 RES. WF,WG.	
Reson Params	5.7+1	1.0+2	SAC	Eval	Rept EANDC(E)138AL	Nov 71	Ribon+ EVALUATION	
					Conf 70Helsinki 1 571	Jun 70	− .108. EVALUATION PROBLEMS,TABLE	
Reson Params	5.7+1	1.0+2	CCP	Revw	Jour AE 31 595	Dec 71	Sukhoruchkin.N+G+F+T−WIDS,J CFD,TBLS	
					Jour SJA 31 1380	Jun 72	*ENGL OF AE 31 595	
Reson Params	1.0+2	3.0+4	HAR	Eval	Prog AERE−PR/NP18	Mar 72	Sowerby+ AVG VALUES TO FIT SIGF+SIGG	
Reson Params	9.0+0	3.0+1	GEL	Expt	Jour JNE 26 293	Jun 72	Deruytter+ AREA ANALYSIS.	+
	9.0+0	3.0+1			Data EXFOR20132.004	Mar 73	6PTS. NF AREA.	
Reson Params	7.8+0	4.8+1	DUB	Expt	Jour IZV 37 82	Jan 73	Zen Chan Bom+ FIS,GAM−YILD I=0,1.TBL	
					Jour BAS 37 1 72	Jan 73	.ENGLISH OF IZV 37 82	
Reson Params	7.6+0	8.1+0	NIL	Theo	Rept PINST−73 1	Feb 73	Bhatti+ IN PUO2,CRYSTAL−BINDING EFF	
	+0	+2	SAC	Expt	Conf 73Rochestr 2 485	Aug 73	Shackleton+ ABST,WIDTH(N,G−FIS) GIVN	
Reson Params	4.0−1	2.5+4	WIN	Eval	Prog EANDC(UK) 151	Aug 73	James+ GENEX EVALUATION	
Reson Params	2.0−2	5.0+1	MOL	Expt	Jour NP/A 212 556	Oct 73	Wagemans+ J DEP B/T. 52E0 FISSION.	+
	3.0−1	5.0+1			Conf 73Rochestr 2 417	Aug 73	Deruytter+ SPINS FROM B/T RATIOS.TBL	
	3.0−1	5.0+1			Data EXFOR20384.004	Oct 74	12PTS.E0.	
Reson Params	7.8+0	6.6+2	SAC	Expt	Diss FRNC−TH−487	Nov 73	Derrien. SINGLE+MULTI LVL ANALYSIS.	+
	4.4+1	2.8+2			Rept CEA−N−1638	Mar 73	− + RES PAR ANALYSIS.	
	7.8+0	6.6+2			Data EXFOR20445.	Oct 75	342PTS.AVG WG,WT(R−M),WN(R−M),ETC.	
Reson Params		4.0−1	GEL	Expt	Rept RCN−203 100	Dec 73	Theobald+ N MULTIPL IN FISS RES GRPH	
Reson Params	3.0+2	3.0+4	IFB	Eval	Jour VBF 1974 3 17	74	Antsipov+ S−WAVE,AVG WN(E),WF(E).TBL	
					Prog INDC(CCP)−62	Feb 75	. ENGLISH OF VBF 1974 3 17	
Reson Params	1.0−3	5.0+2	CJD	Theo	Rept INDC(CCP)−44	Jun 74	.P1. ENGLISH OF 73KIEV 1 209	
	6.0+2	2.5+4			Rept INDC(CCP)−44	Jun 74	.P1. ENGLISH OF 73KIEV 1 209	
Reson Params	2.1+2	1.9+3	BLA	Theo	Prog INDC(SEC)−42	Dec 74	Yaneva. ANALYS OF XPTL (N,F)SIGS,TBL	
Reson Params	1.0+0	1.0+2	BOL	Theo	Rept NEANDC(E)−163U	Jan 75	Menapace+MULTLVL+DOPPLER EFFECT,TBL	
Reson Params	2.0+4	2.0+7	LAS	Theo	Abst BAP 20 140	Feb 75	Moore. R MATRIX STAT CALC 75WASH	
Reson Params	1.1+1	2.6+1	BLA	Expt	Conf 75Kiev 6 87	May 75	Toshkov+ N,FIS−WIDS OF 7RES.TABLE	
Reson Params		6.6+2	BRC	Revw	Conf 76Lowell 641	Jul 76	Michaudon.PROPERTIES OF FIS RESON.	
Reson Params	Maxwl		KUK	Theo	Conf 76Ahmedabd 2 1	Dec 76	Sharma+AVG S−WAVE REDUCED N−WID ANAL	

94 Plutonium 239

Quantity	Energy (ev) Min	Energy (ev) Max	Lab	Type	Documentation Ref Vol Page	Date	Author, Comments	Data
Reson Params	7.8+0	6.6+2	SAC	Expt	Jour NSE 51 130	Jun 73	Blons. 1LVL SHAPE ANAL,WF,S.WF,WFAVG	+
					Conf 70Helsinki 1 513	Jun 70	− +63. TABLE OF NEUT+FISSN WIDTH	
	6.0+0	6.6+2		Diss	TROCHON	77	Trochon. SPIN DETERMINATION	
	3.0−1	6.6+2			Conf 73Kiev 2 239	May 73	Blons. AVERAGE F−WIDTH + NU−BAR GIVN	
	None				Jour AE 29 395	Nov 70	Derrien.ABST FRANC−SOV SEM DUBNA /70	
					Jour SJA 29 1156	Nov 70	Translatn.	
	3.0−1	1.6+2		ExTh	Conf 70Helsinki 1 481	Jun 70	Derrien.61.SINGLE+MULTILEVEL ANAL	
	7.8+0	6.6+2			Conf 69Vienna 307	Jul 69	Paya+ INTERMEDIATE STRUCTURE ANALYS	
				Expt	Conf 69Vienna 915	Jul 69	Blons+PPR91.RESONANCE ANALYSIS	
					Jour CR 267 901	Oct 68	− . SUPERSEDED.	
	3.0−1	4.4+2			Conf 66Paris 2 195	Oct 66	Derrien+ PPR70.PARAMS FOR 180 RESONS	
					Jour CR 262 1 79	Jan 66	Blons+ D,WN,WF. SUPERSEDED.	
					Conf 65Salzburg 1 205	Mar 65	− + COMPARED WITH OTHERS.	
	0.0+0	6.6+2			Data EXFOR20001.	Oct 75	264PTS.AVG.WF,SIG*WF.	
Strnth Fnctn	+0	+5	HAR	Expt	Jour JNE 6 303	May 58	Egelstaff. 1.05+ − 0.2, 1.3+ − 0.2	+
Strnth Fnctn		5.3+1	ANL	Expt	Conf 58Geneva 15 127	Sep 58	Bollinger+.PPR687,VAL GVN	+
					Conf ORNL−2309	Jun 57	− +	
		5.3+1			Data EXFOR12502.017	Jun 76	. 1 PT. STF,D,AVE WF.	
Strnth Fnctn	+3		BNL	Expt	Jour PRL 1 461	Dec 58	Hughes. FC. 1.2+ − 0.4.	
Strnth Fnctn	None		CEA	Revw	Conf 64Vienna 19	Dec 64	Vendryes+ VAL TBL,OTHER COMPILATIONS	
Strnth Fnctn	4.0+2	1.0+5	HAR	Expt	Prog AERE−PR/NP9	Feb 66	Uttley. VALUE GIVEN. BRIEF REPT.	
	1.0+3	1.0+5		Priv	UTTLEY	Nov 64	− .GRPH AVG SIG,S,P WAVE STF	
					Conf 64Paris 2 700	Jul 64	− .	
	4.0+2	1.0+5			Rept EANDC(UK)40L	Jun 64	− .S,P WAVE. TOF TRANSMISSN EXPT	
Strnth Fnctn	1.0+2	5.0+3	KFK	Eval	Conf 66S.Diego 2 223	Feb 66	Schmidt.DEDUCED FROM EXP DATA	
Strnth Fnctn	3.0−1	2.1+2	DUB	Expt	Jour YF 5 925	May 67	Ryabov+.VAL+ERROR GVN,PULSED REACTOR	+
					Jour SNP 5 657	Nov 67	TRANSLATN.*	
	0.0+0	2.1+2			Rept JINR−P−2713	May 66	Ryabov+	
	0.0+0	2.1+2			Data EXFOR40104.008	Jun 72	STRENGTH−FUNCTION, S−WAVE	
Strnth Fnctn	0.0+0	5.0+2	LAS	Expt	Rept LA−4108	May 69	Silbert. AVERAGE D	
Strnth Fnctn		5.0+3	ORL	Theo	Conf 69Vienna 283	Jul 69	Perez+ FISS SIG ANAL,AVG D CFD OTHER	
Strnth Fnctn	−		DUB	Revw	Jour YF 11 111	Jan 70	Malecki+ VALUES FOR TWO SPIN STATES	
					Jour SNP 11 61	Jul 70	− + ENGL OF YF 11 61.	
	3.0−1	8.6+1	DUB	Expt	Rept JINR−P3−4992	Apr 70	Rjabov+ MAXIMUM LIKELIHOOD VALUE S0	+
					Jour SNP 13 255	Sep 71	*ENGL OF YF 13 457	
					Jour YF 13 457	Mar 71	Rjabov+ S−0 GIVEN	
	3.0−1	8.6+1			Data EXFOR40070.026	Aug 70	S−WAVE STRENGTH FUNCTION S0	
Strnth Fnctn	3.0+2	3.0+4	GEB	Eval	Rept GEAP−13591	Apr 70	Hitchcock+,CURV ENDF/B S−WAVE STF	
Strnth Fnctn		1.0+5	GA	Theo	Jour NP/A 159 305	Dec 70	Garrison. S,P−WAVE.TO FIT AVG NG,NF	
Strnth Fnctn		3.0+4	DUB	Expt	Jour YF 13 1039	May 71	Ryabov+ TOF,FITTED S0+S1 VALUES GIVN	+
	3.0+2	3.0+4		Theo	Conf 69Erevan	Feb 69	Rjabov+ ABST,S0,S1 CALCULATION	
		3.0+4		Expt	Jour SNP 13 596	Nov 71	. ENGL OF YF 13 1039	
	1.0+2	3.0+4			Data EXFOR40123.003	Sep 72	STRENGTH−FUNCTION, S AND P−WAVE	
Strnth Fnctn	1.0+4	1.0+6	SAC	Expt	Rept CEA−N−1522	Oct 72	Cauvin+ S0,S1 FROM TOTAL SIG.	
Strnth Fnctn	None		AUA	Eval	Rept AAEC/E−277	Mar 73	Musgrove.TBLS EXPTL DATA+BEST VALUES	
Strnth Fnctn	7.0+0	6.6+2	SAC	Expt	Diss FRNC−TH−487	Nov 73	Derrien.OVER 254RES.S0(0+),S0(1+)GIV	+
					Conf 70Helsinki 1 495	Jun 70	Trochon+62.S0(0+),S0(1+)VALUES GIVEN	
	7.0+0	4.4+2			Conf 66Paris 2 195	Oct 66	Derrien+ P/70. OVER 180 RES.	
	7.0+0	6.6+2			Data EXFOR20445.	Nov 75	3PTS.L=0.	
Strnth Fnctn	3.0+2	3.0+4	IFB	Eval	Jour VBF 1974 3 17	74	Antsipov+ AVG S0(E)TBL,FROM SIG−DATA	
					Rept INDC(CCP)−62	Feb 75	. ENGLISH OF VBF 1974 3 17	
Lvl Density	−		COP	Theo	Jour NP 6 62	Mar 58	Ericson. LVL DENSITY FORM CFD EXP	
Lvl Density		4.0+2	HAR	Expt	Rept EANDC(UK)40L	Jun 64	Uttley. SPACING VS E ONLY.CFD WTG D.	
Lvl Density	+6		MIL	Theo	Jour EN 15 1 54	Jan 68	Facchini+ LDL PARS FROM LOW EN RES	
Lvl Density		7.0+1	KUR	Theo	Jour YF 9 303	Feb 69	Vorotnikov.LVL DEN(EXCIT−E),TBL GRPH	
	None				Jour IZV 36 175	Jan 72	− + LEVLDENS(EXCIT−E),GRAPH	
		7.0+1			Jour SNP 9 179	Aug 69	TRANSLATN.*	
	None				Jour BAS 36 165	73	. ENGL OF IZV 36 175	
Lvl Density	1.9+6	5.5+6	GEL	Expt	Jour ZP 232 286	Nov 70	Coppola+ N TEMP. INEL+FISS N SPECTRA	+
	1.9+6	5.5+6			Data EXFOR20392.004	Oct 74	6PTS.NUCL.T.	
Lvl Density	None		IBJ	Revw	Jour PF 23 561	Sep 72	Jastrzebski. SPONTAN FISSION ISOMERS	
Lvl Density	7.0+6	1.6+7	DUB	ExTh	Rept JINR−E15−7362	Jul 73	Gangrsky+ PARS FROM (G,N),(G,G),GRPH	
Lvl Density	None		MUN	Theo	Jour NP/A 217 269	Dec 73	Dilg+ A,DELTA. BACK SHIFTED FERMIGAS	
Lvl Density	None		COP	Theo	Jour NP/A 222 493	Apr 74	Dossing+COLL ROTAT.SPAC. ACCUR ESTIM	
Lvl Density	None		ROC	Theo	Jour NP/A 223 589	May 74	Huizenga+ EXP CFD MICROSC TH AX SYMM	
Lvl Density	0.0+0	3.0+2	SAC	ExTh	Jour NP/A 242 45	Apr 75	Jain+ SPACING CORRELATIONS	
				Theo	Conf 72Budapest 180	Aug 72	− + HIGHER ORDER SPACING DIST,GRP	
Lvl Density	+6		DUB	Theo	Rept JINR−E4−9236	Nov 75	Komov+ AVG LVL−SPAC,SEMIMICRO CFD XP	

94 Plutonium 239

Quantity	Energy (ev) Min	Energy (ev) Max	Lab	Type	Documentation Ref Vol Page	Date	Author, Comments	Data
(γ,n)	5.0+6	1.7+7	LRL	Expt Prog	UCID - 16514 6	Jun 74	Alvarez+	
(γ,n)	5.0+6	2.0+7	CCP	Expt Rept	YK - 23 117	76	Antropov+ SIG(E - GAMMA),GRAPH	
Photo - Fissn	4.9+6	7.2+6	UI	Expt Jour	PR 77 329	Feb 50	Koch+ FISS COUNTS PER ROENTGN / E(G)	
Photo - Fissn		2.2+7	LAS	Expt Jour	PR 81 342	Feb 51	Mcelhinney+ SIGMA REL TO GF(U238)	
Photo - Fissn	1.2+7	2.0+7	ANL	Expt Jour	PR 95 1009	Aug 54	Huizenga+ 3ES RELATIVE FISS YIELDS	
Photo - Fissn	6.0+6	2.0+7	CRC	Expt Jour	CJP 37 1418	Dec 59	Baerg+ . FRAG ANG DIST ISOTROPIC	
Photo - Fissn	None		CCP	Expt Jour	ZET 44 1950	Jun 63	FISSN TR FROM(D,PF)AND(GF)JET17 1312	
Photo - Fissn	5.2+6	9.3+6	FEI	Expt Prog	INDSWG - 120 4	65	Soldatov.A - DSTR FOTOFFRGM, TBP, NDG	
Photo - Fissn	1.5+7		CCP	Expt Jour	AE 20 268	Mar 66	Nikotin+ .DELAYED NEUT YIELD,6 GROUPS	
				Jour	SJA 20 300	Mar 66	. ENGL OF AE 20 268	
Photo - Fissn	None		GA	Expt Jour	PR 146 824	Jun 66	Sund+LINAC,GS ABOVE .5MEV TO .02S	
Photo - Fissn	None		WAU	Theo Jour	NP/A 101 460	Sep 67	Vandenbosch. ANISOTROPY ANALYZED	
Photo - Fissn	1.5+7		MNZ	Theo Jour	AF 36 453	Nov 67	Patzelt+ .FROM DERIVED N - EMISS PROB.	
Photo - Fissn	5.0+6	8.0+6	FEI	Expt Jour	PL/B 26 4 218	Jan 68	Rabotnov+ANGDIST FISS FRAG AT THRES	
				Prog	YFI - 4 12	May 67	.CURVES GIVEN	
	5.4+6	7.9+6		Conf	65Salzburg 1 135	Mar 65	.ANG DISTRIB FOTO FISS FRAGMENTS	
				Rept	FEI - 12	65	.ANG ANISOTROPY OF FISS - PROD	
	5.0+6	8.0+6		Prog	INDC - E - 187	67	.ENGLISH TRANSL OF YFI - 4 12 5/67	
	5.4+6	7.9+6		Rept	LA - TR - 66 - 46	66	.ENGLISH TRANSL OF FEI - 12 /65	
				Rept	ANL - TRANS - 245	65	.ENGLISH TRANSL OF 65SALZBG	
Photo - Fissn	None		GA	Expt Prog	WASH - 1127 53	Apr 69	Rundquist+ GE(LI),FRAG GAM SPECT,NDG	
Photo - Fissn	2.8+7		DEB	Expt Jour	AHP 28 169	Mar 70	Medveczky+ TBL=TERN+BINARY FISSN CFD	
		2.8+7		Conf	69Vienna 897	Jul 69	- +PPR95.SYMMETRIC TERN FISSN	
Photo - Fissn	5.0+6	7.0+6	FEI	Expt Jour	YF 11 992	May 70	Soldatov+ SIG(G - E),ANISOTROPY,GRAPHS	
				Rept	INDC(CCP) - 15	Dec 71	*P26,ENG OF YFI - 10	
				Jour	SNP 11 552	Nov 70	*ENGL OF YF 11 992	
Photo - Fissn	7.5+6	1.2+7	UCN	Expt Jour	NSE 45 47	Jul 71	Shapiro+ .BETATRON.2 ANALYSIS METHODS	
				Abst	DA/B 29 2579	Jan 69	.	
Photo - Fissn	None		BLA	Expt Prog	INDC(SEC) - 18	Aug 71	Kashukeev+ PG21.FRAG MEAN - E DIST,TBL	
Photo - Fissn		5.3+7	CLE	Expt Jour	NP/A 173 465	Oct 71	Tamain+ DELAYED FRAG HALF LIVES	
Photo - Fissn	5.5+6	6.0+6	UCN	Expt Abst	BAP 18 626	Apr 72	Stubbins. TOF.LINAC. NEUT SPECTRUM	
Photo - Fissn		1.5+7	IAE	Eval Jour	REA 10 637	Dec 72	Manero+ DELAYED NEUTRON YIELD,TBL	
Photo - Fissn	5.5+6	6.0+6	ANL	Expt Jour	USNDC - 7 19	Jun 73	Stubbins. TOF. 2ES.LINAC.NEUT SPECT	
Photo - Fissn	5.0+6	1.0+7	GA	Expt Conf	73Rochestr 2 501	Aug 73	Gozani. ABST,DEL + PROMPT - N YLD/FISYLD	
Photo - Fissn	6.0+6	1.9+7	DUB	Expt Jour	FDP 22 199	74	Gangrsky+ GRPH (G,F)SIG VS E - GAM	
	1.0+7	1.5+7		Jour	YF 16 271	Aug 72	Gangriski'+ FISS/SPONT FISS ISOMER	
				Jour	SNP 16 151	Feb 73	. ENGLISH OF YF 16 271 8/72	
Photo - Fissn	6.0+6	1.2+7	CCP	Expt Jour	AE 36 404	May 74	Ivanov+ INTEG YLD/INTG U238 - YLD,GRPH	
				Jour	SJA 36 515	Nov 74	. ENGLISH OF AE 36 404	
Photo - Fissn	5.0+6	1.7+7	LRL	Expt Prog	UCID - 16514 6	Jun 74	Alvarez+	
Photo - Fissn	5.0+6	1.2+7	TIL	Expt Rept	YK - 19 42	75	Ivanov+ YLD OF FRAGS,GRAPH,CFD,TBL	
				Rept	INDC(CCP) - 65	Dec 74	.P10.ENGL ABSTR OF YK - 19	
Photo - Fissn	7.7+6	9.7+6	LAS	Expt Jour	NSE 56 179	Feb 75	Caldwell+ TBL,GRPH NU PROMPT+DELAYED	
	1.0+7	1.2+7		Conf	73Rochestr 1 431	Aug 73	- + PROMPT+DELAYED - N YLDS,TBLS	
				Conf	73Pacif.Gr 1 651	Mar 73	- + PROMPT,DELAY NS,GN/GF,TBL	
	8.0+6	1.2+7		Rept	LA - UR - 73 - 968	73	- +.PROMPT AND DELAYD NEUT YLD	
Photo - Fissn	+7		BLA	Expt Conf	75Kiev 6 146	Jun 75	Dragnev+ SIG(E - GAMMA),GRAPHS	
	6.4+6	7.9+6		Prog	INDC(SEC) - 42	Dec 74	- + ABST.7CAPT - GAMS,TBL SIG(E)	
Photo - Fissn		1.7+7	IJI	Expt Rept	KIYAI - 76 - 40	76	Aleksandrov+ DELAY NS,GROUPS INT+HL	
Photo - Fissn	5.0+6	1.2+7	TIL	Expt Rept	YK - 22 83	76	Ivanov+ SIG PU39/238 VS EGAM,TBL+FIG	
Photo - Fissn	1.0+6	2.4+7	RI	Expt Jour	AE 40 72	Jan 76	Kondratko+ REL CD,AG - YLD VS EMAX.TBL	
				Jour	SJA 40 83	Jul 76	. ENGL OF AE 40,72.	
Photo - Fissn	5.0+6	7.0+6	FEI	Expt Rept	YK - 21 65	Oct 76	Ostapenko+ YLD(E),GRAPH	
Photo - Fissn	1.5+7	2.0+7	TIL	Expt Rept	YK - 27 42	77	Petrzhak+ 15+20MEV BREMS.XE - YLDS,TBL	

94 Plutonium 240

Quantity	Energy (ev) Min	Energy (ev) Max	Lab	Type	Documentation Ref Vol Page	Date	Author, Comments	Data
Evaluation	6.0-2	1.0+7	LAS	Eval Jour	NSE 4 166	Aug 58	Kiehn.TOT,FISS,NG,NU,TRANSF.10GROUPS	
Evaluation	5.0+2	1.0+7	ANL	Eval Book	FRC	60	Yftah+ .16E GROUPS.FAST REACT DATA	
Evaluation	Maxwl	1.0+7	GEL	Eval Rept	EANDC(E)17U	Aug 60	PROSDOCIMI	
Evaluation	4.1-1	1.0+7	GA	Eval Rept	GA - 2451	Aug 61	Joanou+ .68GRP ABS.EL,IN TRANSF.NF.NU	
Evaluation	1.0-3	1.0+7	AI	Eval Rept	NAA - SR - M - 8904	Aug 63	Alter+ .SAME AS MO +NF NU N2N.RES GAP	
Evaluation	2.5-2	1.1+7	FEI	Eval Book	ABAGJAN	64	26 GROUP CONST,TOT,FISS,NU,CAPT,SCAT	
Evaluation	3.7-2	1.8+7	UNC	Eval Rept	UNC - 5099	Dec 64	Troubetzkoy+	
Evaluation	1.0-3	1.5+7	GA	Eval Rept	GA - 6576	Jul 65	Drake. EVAL FROM VAR SOURCES	

94 Plutonium 240

Quantity	Energy (ev) Min	Energy (ev) Max	Lab	Type	Documentation Ref Vol Page	Date	Author, Comments	Data
Evaluation	1.0+3	1.4+7	UK	Eval	Rept AHSB(S)R – 124	Feb 66	Hart.(RLY).UK – DFN 340.UPDATES NSE 26	
	1.0+3	1.5+7			Rept AWRE – O – 91/64	Jan 65	Douglas+(ALD).UKNDL – DFN 201	
	1.0-3	1.4+7			Rept AEEW – R – 351	Feb 64	Barrington+(WIN).UKNDL LOW EN REVISN	
	2.5-2	1.5+7			Rept AWRE – O – 28/60	Mar 61	Buckingham.(ALD).EVAL FOR UKNDL	
Evaluation	1.0-3	1.5+7	APD	Eval	Rept APDA – 218	Jun 68	Pitterle+ EVAL FOR ENDF/B CURVES	
Evaluation	1.0+3	1.4+7	LAS	Eval	Rept LA – 3528	Jul 68	Hunter+ TOT NF SEL NG SIN N2N N3N NU	
Evaluation		2.0+7	TRM	Eval	Conf 69Roorke 2 106	Dec 69	Garg+ INDIAN EVALUATN ACTIVITIES, NDG	
Evaluation	Maxwl	1.5+7	SAC	Eval	Rept CEA – N – 1273	Mar 70	L'Heriteau.SAME EANDC(E)126AL	
					Rept EANDC(E)126AL	Mar 70	– + COMPLETE EVALUATION.	
Evaluation	1.0+4	1.5+7	BNL	Eval	Conf 70Helsinki 2 825	Jun 70	Prince.91. ALL QUANTITIES TO ENDF/B	
Evaluation	1.0-3	1.5+7	SOR	Eval	Rept IA – 1243	May 72	Caner+ ALL QUANTITIES FOR KEDAK,TBLS	
	1.0-3	1.5+7			Data KEDAK – 3	Oct 75	DATA FILES FOR 15 QUANTITIES.	
Evaluation	2.5-2		SOR	Eval	Rept IA – 1243	May 72	Caner+ TOT,FISS,CAPT,SCAT SIGMA,TBLS	
	Maxwl				Data KEDAK – 3	Oct 75	THERMAL VALUE.	
Evaluation	4.0+4	2.0+7	LAS	Eval	Rept LA – 5172	Jun 73	Hunter+	
Evaluation	Maxwl	3.0+4	GEL	Eval	Conf NEANDC(E) – 163U	Jan 75	Weigmann+ N – WID+S – WID+F – WID+AVG VALUE	
Evaluation	1.0+3	1.0+5	CCP	Eval	Conf 75Kiev	May 75	Antsipov+ TOT SIG,CAPT,FISS,INELAST	
Total	8.2-1	1.4+0	BNL	Expt	Priv ZIMMERMAN	Oct 56	Zimmerman.	+
	8.2-1	1.4+0			Data EXFOR11787.003	Jun 76	. 52 PTS.	
Total	5.0-1	1.2+2	MTR	Expt	Prog IDO – 16373 39	Jul 57	Simpson.CS MEAS FOR RES PARS.NDG	+
	5.0-1	5.0+3			Abst BAP 2 219	Apr 57	– + FAST CHOPR NEW RESON NDG	
	3.4-2	4.3+1			Data EXFOR12526.002	Jun 76	. 240 PTS.	
Total	4.0-2	4.0+1	HAR	Expt	Jour JNE 6 303	May 58	Egelstaff.FC CURVE .04EV+3 RES PEAKS	+
Total	+0	+1	CCP	Revw	Conf 58Geneva 15 309	Sep 58	Vladimirsky+.PPR2221,NDG,REFS	
Total	1.0-2	1.0+1	HAR	Expt	Jour JNEA 11 14	Nov 59	Pattenden+ CRYST SPEC,CURV,.025VALUE	+
					Rept AERE – NP/GEN 9	Mar 59	– + METHOD.	
					Conf 58Geneva 16 44	Sep 58	– + PPR11.	
Total	2.0-2	1.5-1	ORL	Expt	Jour NSE 8 112	Aug 60	Block+,FC SIG(.0253EV)=290+ – 8B TABLE	+
					Conf 60Vienna 535	Oct 60	– +.VAL(2200M/SEC) GVN,EXPT DESCR	
	2.0-2	1.5-1			Data EXFOR12024.011	Jun 76	. 40 PTS.	
Total	2.0-1	1.0+7	B+W	Eval	Rept BAW – 158	Jun 61	Roach+ AVERAGED SIG 40 GROUPS	
Total	2.5-2	1.2+2	LAS	Expt	Rept LA – 2574	Aug 61	Devaney+.TABLES.T-.025TO.2EV.MAXWELN	
Total	1.0-3	1.0+6	RLY	Revw	Conf 64Vienna 56	Dec 64	Kronberger.GRPH SIG(E),PU – ISOT,U – 235	
Total	1.0+3	1.5+7	UK	Eval	Rept AWRE – O – 91/64	Jan 65	Douglas.ALD.UKNDL – DFN 201.SUPERSEDED	+
	1.0-3	2.5+1			Rept AEEW – R – 351	Feb 64	Barrington+(WIN).UKNDL LOW EN REVISN	
	1.0-4	1.5+7			Data UKNDL – DFN 77B	Mar 73	243 PNTS	
Total	5.0+6	1.6+7	LAS	Theo	Rept LA – 3538	Sep 66	Agee+ OPTICAL MODEL CALCULATION	
Total	2.0+1	9.5+2	HAR	Expt	Conf 66Paris 2 145	Oct 66	Asghar+ GRAPHS 200 – 600 EV,LINAC	
Total	2.0+1	5.7+3	GEL	Expt	Jour JNE 22 299	May 68	Kolar+.LINAC TOF+AREA ANAL SEE RES	+
					Conf 68Wash. 1 519	Mar 68	– + FINAL RESULTS.NDG	
	2.0+1	5.0+3			Conf 66Paris 2 135	Oct 66	Boeckhoff+.LINAC TOF.TRANSM .8TO5KEV	
	0.0+0	0.0+0			Data EXFOR20139.002	Mar 73	. 0PTS. SEE 20117.	
	2.0+1	5.7+3			Data EXFOR20117.	Jul 72	39295PTS.	
Total	5.0+0	2.9+1	COP	Revw	Conf 69Vienna 155	Jul 69	Strutinsky+PPR203. SIG(E),CFD FISSN	
Total	2.5-2	1.0+7	SAC	Eval	Rept CEA – N – 1273	Mar 70	L'Heriteau+ SEE EANDC(E)126AL.	
Total	2.5-2	1.0+7	SAC	Eval	Rept EANDC(E)126AL	Mar 70	L'Heriteau+ COMPLETE EVALUATION.	
Total	1.0-2	3.0-1	MTR	Expt	Prog NCSAC – 33 89	Dec 70	Kroger+,FAST CHOPPER,ANAL TBC,NDG	
Total	9.0-1	1.2+0	KUR	Expt	Rept IAE – 2168	Nov 71	Biryukov+ DOPPLER EFFECT STUDY,GRAPH	
Total	1.0+5	1.5+6	ANL	Expt	Jour NSE 47 19	Jan 72	Smith+. 25 – KEV STEPS. TRANSMISSION	+
					Rept IAEA – 153 447	73	– + EXPTS CFD EVALUATIONS ,GRAPH	
	1.2+5	1.5+6			Data EXFOR10179.002	Nov 71	55PTS,SIGMA	
Total	1.0+3	1.5+7	SOR	Eval	Rept IA – 1243	May 72	Caner+ EVALUATION FOR KEDAK,TBL	
	1.0-3	1.5+7			Data KEDAK – 3	Oct 75	2417 DATA SETS (KFK FILE)	
Total		1.0+3	HAR	Expt	Prog AERE – PR/NP19	Sep 72	Moxon+ TOF LINAC TO GET RESON PARAMS	
Total	3.0+1	5.0+2	RPI	Expt	Jour NSE 49 153	Oct 72	Hockenbury+. TRANS. NO DATA GIVEN	
	2.0+1	3.0+4			Conf 72Budapest 224	Aug 72	– + TOTAL SIG,TOF,LINAC,NDG	
Total	-3	1.0+1	IKE	Theo	Rept IKE – 6 – 61/2	Jan 73	Keinert.DATA LIBRARY	
Total	0.0+0	1.5+7	UK	Eval	Data UKNDL – DFN 402B	Mar 73	1424 PNTS	+
Total	2.5-2		IKE	Eval	Rept IKE – 6 – 80	Apr 74	Mattes+ ENDF/B,UKNDL,KEDAK CFD	
Total	-3	1.9+0	THS	Theo	Rept IKE – 6 89 59	Jun 75	Keinert. DATA LIBRARY	
Total	2.0+4	5.5+5	KFK	Expt	Prog KFK – 2223 23	Dec 75	Kaeppeler+ EXPTAL SET – UP	
Total	1.0+3	1.4+5	IFB	Eval	Rept INDC(CCP) – 77	Jan 76	Antsipov+ CALC SIG(E) CFD EXPTS,GRPH	
Elastic	1.0+3	1.5+7	UK	Eval	Rept AWRE – O – 91/64	Jan 65	Douglas.ALD.UKNDL – DFN 201.SUPERSEDED	+
	1.0-3	2.5+1			Rept AEEW – R – 351	Feb 64	Barrington+(WIN).UKNDL LOW EN REVISN	
	1.0-4	1.5+7			Data UKNDL – DFN 77B	Mar 73	243 PNTS	
Elastic	5.0+6	1.6+7	LAS	Theo	Rept LA – 3538	Sep 66	Agee+ OPTMDL MODEL+H – F FOR COMP	
Elastic	1.8+1	3.0+3	GEL	Expt	Conf 68Wash. 1 513	Mar 68	CAO+. LINAC. TOF SCAT YLD	+
	1.9+1	3.0+3			Data EXFOR20142.	Mar 73	7136PTS.SCT.YLD.	

94 Plutonium 240

Quantity	Energy (ev) Min	Max	Lab	Type	Documentation Ref Vol Page	Date	Author, Comments	Data
Elastic	2.5−2		RPI	Expt	Jour JNM 34 281	70	Green+SCT AMPLITUDE FROM DIFFRACT.	+
	2.5−2				Data EXFOR10126.002	Oct 72	1PT.COHERENT SCT AMPLITUDE=3.8−13 CM	
Elastic	2.5−2		ANL	Expt	Jour ACRB 27 2284	Nov 71	Lander+ COH SCAT AMP	+
	2.5−2				Data EXFOR10282.002	May 73	. 1 PT. COH. AMP.	
Elastic	1.0+5	1.5+6	ANL	Expt	Jour NSE 47 19	Jan 72	Smith+ CURV, FROM DEL	
					Rept IAEA−153 447	73	− + EXPTS CFD EVALUATIONS ,GRAPH	
					Prog ANL−7910 5	Jan 72	− +. CURV. CFD ENDF	
	3.0+5	1.5+6			Data EXFOR10179.003	Nov 71	30PTS,SIGMA	
Elastic	1.0+3	1.5+7	SOR	Eval	Rept IA−1243	May 72	Caner+ EVALUATION FOR KEDAK,TBL	
	1.0+3	8.0+5			Rept KFK−1340	Feb 71	Hinkelmann+ KEDAK MODIFICATIONS.	
	1.0−3	1.5+7			Data KEDAK−3	Oct 75	2392 DATA SETS (KFK FILE)	
Elastic	1.0+5	1.0+7	SOR	Eval	Rept IAEA−153 141	73	Ilberg+ EVALUATD DATA FILES CFD,GRPH	
					Rept TNSD−R−424	Jan 72	Yiftah+ COMPAR.OF EVALUATIONS, GRAPH	
Elastic	0.0+0	1.5+7	UK	Eval	Data UKNDL−DFN 402B	Mar 73	1424 PNTS	+
Elastic	2.5−2		IKE	Eval	Rept IKE−6−80	Apr 74	Mattes+ ENDF/B,UKNDL,KEDAK CFD	
Diff Elastic	1.0+3	1.5+7	UK	Eval	Rept AWRE−O−91/64	Jan 65	Douglas.ALD.UKNDL−DFN 201.SUPERSEDED	+
	1.0−3	2.5+1			Rept AEEW−R−351	Feb 64	Barrington+(WIN).UKNDL LOW EN REVISN	
	1.0−4	1.5+7			Data UKNDL−DFN 77B	Mar 73	17 PNTS,C.M.	
Diff Elastic	5.0+6	1.6+7	LAS	Theo	Rept LA−3538	Sep 66	Agee+OPTMDL MODEL+H−F FOR COMP	
Diff Elastic	5.0+6	1.6+7	LAS	Theo	Rept LA−3788	67	Beery+.OPTMOD CALC POLARIZ ANG DISTR	
Diff Elastic	+3		ISL	Theo	Prog IA−1218 14	Aug 70	Kaner.CODE FOR COMPOUND − SIG CALC,NDG	
Diff Elastic	3.0+5	1.5+6	ANL	Expt	Rept NSE 47 19	Jan 72	Smith+. ANGULAR DISTRIBUTNS SHOWN	+
					Rept IAEA−153 447	73	− + EXPTS CFD EVALUATIONS ,GRAPH	
	3.0+5	1.5+6			Data EXFOR10179.	Nov 71	5LEG COEF AT 30 ENERGIES	
Diff Elastic	−3	1.0+1	IKE	Theo	Rept IKE−6−61/2	Jan 73	Keinert.DATA LIBRARY	
Diff Elastic	0.0+0	1.5+7	UK	Eval	Data UKNDL−DFN 402B	Mar 73	45 PNTS,C.M.	+
Diff Elastic	1.0−3	1.5+7	SOR	Eval	Prog INDC(SEC)−42	Dec 74	Caner+ EVALUATION,NDG.	
	1.0−3	1.5+7			Data KEDAK−3	Oct 75	70 DATA SETS (KFK FILE)	
Polarization	5.0+6	1.6+7	LAS	Theo	Rept LA−3788	67	Beery+.OPTMOD CALC COS(THETA) DISTR	
Potntal Scat	1.1+0	5.7+3	SOR	Eval	Rept IA−1243	May 72	Caner+ RECOMMENDED VALUE GIVEN	
Tot Inelastc	Thrsh	1.5+7	UK	Eval	Rept AWRE−O−91/64	Jan 65	Douglas+(ALD).UKNDL−DFN 201	
Tot Inelastc	4.0+4	1.0+7	SAC	Eval	Rept CEA−N−1273	Mar 70	L'Heriteau+ SEE EANDC(E)126AL.	
Tot Inelastc	4.0+4	1.0+7	SAC	Eval	Rept EANDC(E)126AL	Mar 70	L'Heriteau+ COMPLETE EVALUATION.	
Tot Inelastc	1.0+3	1.5+7	SOR	Eval	Rept IA−1243	May 72	Caner+ EVALUATION FOR KEDAK,TBL	
	1.0−3	1.5+7			Data KEDAK−3	Oct 75	59 DATA SETS (KFK FILE)	
Diff Inelast	Thrsh	1.5+7	UK	Eval	Rept AWRE−O−91/64	Jan 65	Douglas.ALD.UKNDL−DFN 201.SUPERSEDED	+
	6.0+5	1.5+7			Data UKNDL−DFN 77B	Mar 73	TO CONTINUUM,ANGDIST, 3 RNGS,LAB.	
	6.0+5	1.5+7			Data UKNDL−DFN 77B	Mar 73	.TO CONTINUUM.89 PTS.E DIST.ANGDIST.	
	4.8+4	2.0+6			Data UKNDL−DFN 77B	Mar 73	1ST−3RD LVL,ANGDIST	
Diff Inelast	1.4+7		LRL	Theo	Rept UCRL−50181	Feb 67	Lutz+.CALC ANG DIST FOR FIRST 2+ LVL	
Diff Inelast	3.0+5	1.5+6	ANL	Expt	Jour NSE 47 19	Jan 72	Smith+. CURVS FOR EXCITATN OF 5 LVLS	+
					Rept IAEA−153 447	73	− + EXPTS CFD EVALUATIONS ,GRAPH	
	+5	1.5+6			Conf 70Helsinki 2 3	Jun 70	Poenitz.111. SIG(E) GRAPH, 2 LEVELS	
	3.5+5	1.5+6			Data EXFOR10179.	Nov 71	60PTS,SIGMA,5LEVELS	
Diff Inelast	9.1+5	1.5+7	UK	Eval	Data UKNDL−DFN 402B	Mar 73	TO CONTINUUM, 37 PNTS	+
	9.1+5	1.5+7			Data UKNDL−DFN 402B	Mar 73	TO CONTINUUM,ANGDIST, 1 RNGS,LAB.	
	4.6+4	1.1+6			Data UKNDL−DFN 402B	Mar 73	1ST−5TH LVL,ANGDIST	
	4.6+4	1.1+6			Data UKNDL−DFN 402B	Mar 73	1ST−5TH LVL	
	9.1+5	1.5+7			Data UKNDL−DFN 402B	Mar 73	TO CONTINUUM, E DIST, 5 RANGES	
Diff Inelast	3.0+3	1.0+6	BRC	Eval	Rept CEA−R−4631	Nov 74	Thomet. STAT MDL ANAL TBLS GRPHS	
Scattering	1.0+3	1.5+7	UK	Eval	Rept AWRE−O−91/64	Jan 65	Douglas+(ALD).UKNDL−DFN 201	
Scattering	2.0+1	9.5+2	HAR	Expt	Conf 66Paris 2 145	Oct 66	Ashgar+ PPR31.LINAC.GRPHS 80−160EV	
					Rept INDC−156	67	− +	
Scattering	1.0−3	2.0+0	JUL	Theo	Rept JUEL−746−RG 80	Apr 71	Bonka.KUGEL−THERMOS−LIBR,T=300,1500K	
	2.5−3	1.9+1			Rept JUEL−746−RG 13	Apr 71	− . AVG SIG CALC	
Scattering	−3	1.0+1	IKE	Theo	Rept IKE−6−61/2	Jan 73	Keinert.DATA LIBRARY	
Scattering	2.5−2		IFB	Eval	Rept INDC(CCP)−76	Jan 76	Antsipov+ CALC FROM RESPARS,SIG GIVN	
Nonelastic	1.0+3	1.5+7	UK	Eval	Rept AWRE−O−91/64	Jan 65	Douglas.ALD.UKNDL−DFN 201.SUPERSEDED	+
	1.0−4	1.5+7			Data UKNDL−DFN 77B	Mar 73	243 PNTS	
Nonelastic	1.0−3	1.5+7	SOR	Eval	Rept IA−1243	May 72	Caner+ EVALUATION FOR KEDAK−3.	
	1.0−3	1.5+7			Data KEDAK−3	Oct 75	123 DATA SETS (KFK FILE)	
Absorption	Fast		ANL	Revw	Conf 55Geneva 5 125	Aug 55	Spinrad+.P835	
Absorption	Maxwl		HAR	Expt	Jour BJAS 5 1	56	Cockcroft+SCIENTI.PROBL.IN NUCLEA.E	
Absorption	Maxwl		CCP	Expt	Jour AE 2 240	Mar 57	Krupchinsky.PILE OSC 460+−45B	
					Jour JNE 6 155	Dec 57	TRANSLATN.*	
					Jour SJA 2 291	57	TRANSLATN.*	
Absorption	1.1−3	4.0−2	HAR	Expt	Jour JNE 6 303	May 58	Egelstaff+,.0253VALUE(3METHODS)GIVEN	+
	Maxwl				Rept AERE−NP/R−2076	Jan 57	− . SIG=350+−100B	

94 Plutonium 240

Quantity	Energy (ev) Min	Max	Lab	Type	Documentation Ref Vol Page	Author, Comments Date	Data
Absorption	2.0 – 1	1.0 + 7	B+W	Eval	Rept BAW – 158	Jun 61 Roach + AVERAGED SIG 40 GROUPS	
Absorption	5.0 – 3	2.5 + 0	GA Eval	Rept	GA – 2113	Jun 61 Wikner+ .TABLE+CURVE.100 E POINTS	
Absorption	2.5 – 2		HAR	Expt	Jour JNEA 12 32	May 60 Tattersall+ PILE OSCILLATOR.	+
	Maxwl				Rept AEEW – R – 115	Mar 62 – .PILE OSC REL HARWELL B	
					Rept AERE – R/R – 2516	Mar 58 Jowitt+ PILE OSC.REL BORON.293DEGK.	
	2.5 – 2				Data EXFOR20638.072	Jul 76 1PNT.SIGMA.	
Absorption	Pile		CJD	Eval	Rept INDSWG – 64 285	64 Galanin. TBL EFF SIG FOR MANY SPECTR	
Absorption	Pile		TRM	Expt	Conf 64Vienna 26	Dec 64 Paranjpe+ SIG FIT TO RECYCLE EXPTS	
Absorption	1.0 + 3	1.5 + 7	UK Eval	Rept	AWRE – O – 91/64	Jan 65 Douglas+(ALD).UKNDL – DFN 201	
Absorption	Maxwl		HAR	Expt	Jour JIN 28 2467	May 67 Cabell+. IRR. IN MAXWELLIAN SPECTRUM	
Absorption	3.8 + 1	8.2 + 2	GEL	Expt	Jour JNE 22 317	May 68 Weigmann+ HIGH RSLN TOF REL B10(N,AG	+
	3.8 + 1	8.2 + 2			Data EXFOR20130.	Mar 73 0PTS. SEE RES PARAMS	
Absorption	2.5 – 3	1.9 + 1	JUL Theo	Rept	JUEL – 746 – RG 13	Apr 71 Bonka. AVG SIG CALC	
Absorption	1.0 – 3	2.0 + 0	JUL Theo	Rept	JUEL – 746 – RG 49	Apr 71 Bonka.KUGEL – THERMOS – LIBR,T=300K,CURV	
					Rept JUEL – 746 – RG 80	Apr 71 – .KUGEL – THERMOS – LIBR,T=300,1500K	
Absorption	8.0 – 2		ANL	Expt	Rept ACRB 27 2284	Nov 71 Lander+ MEAS 205B	+
	8.0 – 2				Data EXFOR10282.003	May 73 1PT,SIGMA	
Absorption	1.0 – 3	1.5 + 7	SOR Eval	Rept	IA – 1243	May 72 Caner+ EVALUATION FOR KEDAK – 3	
	1.0 – 3	1.5 + 7			Data KEDAK – 3	Oct 75 138 DATA SETS (KFK FILE)	
Res Int Abs	5.0 – 1	1.0 + 6	CCP	Expt	Conf 55Geneva 5 172	Aug 55 Spivak+.VAL GVN CFD REF,PPR659	
Res Int Abs	–		CCP	Expt	Jour AE 1 3 27	Jun 56 Erozolimsky+. 9000+3000B REL PU239	
					Jour JNE 4 86	Jan 57 TRANSLATN.*	
					Jour SJA 1 3 311	56 TRANSLATN.*	
Res Int Abs	2.0 – 1		CCP	Expt	Jour AE 2 240	Mar 57 Krupchinsky.PILE OSC 10000+ – 2800B	+
					Jour JNE 6 155	Dec 57 TRANSLATN.*	
					Jour SJA 2 291	57 TRANSLATN.*	
Res Int Abs	Maxwl		CCP	Expt	Conf 58Geneva 15 309	Sep 58 Vladimirsky+.PPR2221,VAL GVN	
Res Int Abs	5.0 – 1		HAR	Expt	Jour JNE 12 32	May 60 Tattersall+ ABOVE 1/V,OSCIL,REL B+AU	+
					Rept AEEW – R – 115	Mar 62 – .PILE OSC REL AU	
					Rept AERE – R – 2887	Aug 59 – . PILE OSC.REL BORON	
	6.7 – 1				Data EXFOR20638.073	Jul 76 1PNT.	
Res Int Abs	Pile		AUA Theo	Rept	AAEC/E – 168	Dec 66 Keane+ EFFECTIV INTEGRL,TEMP+DOPPLER	
					Rept AAEC/E – 164	Oct 66 Kletzmayr. LUBRA CODE USED	
					Rept AAEC/TM – 343	Sep 66 .BIBLIOGRAPHY OF CODES	
				Eval	Rept AAEC/E – 150	Apr 66 Keane. COMPARISON WITH GYMEA CODE	
				Theo	Rept AAEC/E – 147	Mar 66 – . COMPARISON WITH GYMEA CODE	
Res Int Abs	–		AUA Theo	Rept	AAEC/TM – 362	Dec 66 Cook+ TWO RESONANCE CALCULATNS CFD	
					Rept AAEC/TM – 343	Sep 66 .BIBLIOGRAPHY OF CODES	
					–	SEE AAEC/E – 119,E – 126 AND E – 163	
Res Int Abs	Pile		UJV Theo	Rept	UJV – 2224	69 Stepanek. 5 GROUP CONSTANTS	
Res Int Abs	5.0 – 1		IAE Revw	Rept	IAEA – 143 897	Apr 72 Lemmel.CAPT,EVALUTS+RECENT EXPTS,TBL	
Res Int Abs	5.0 – 1		SGA Comp	Conf	73Paris 1 233	Mar 73 Eder+ REDUCED RES INTEG CAPTURE,TBL	
					Rept SGAE – PH – 141	Feb 73 .SAME AS 73PARIS,NO DETAILS,TBP	
(n,γ)	Maxwl		BRK	Expt	Jour PR 78 472	May 50 Ghiorso+ AM241 PROD,PU239DOUBLE CAPT	
(n,γ)	Cold		ANL Revw	Conf	55Geneva 5 125	Aug 55 Spinrad+.P835	
(n,γ)	Fast		ANL Revw	Conf	55Geneva 5 125	Aug 55 Spinrad+.P835	
(n,γ)	Pile		ANL	Expt	Jour NSE 1 62	Mar 56 Fields+,SIG=530+ – 50B	+
					Conf 55Geneva 7 261	Aug 55 Bentley+.P809,VAL GVN,CHEMICAL METHD	
	Pile				Data EXFOR12535.003	Jun 76 . 1 PT, SIG	
(n,γ)	Pile		CRC	Expt	Rept CRC – 633	Mar 56 Cornish+ NRX SIG=250+ – 35B	+
					Rept TNCC(CAN) – 4	Mar 56 .SUPERSEDED	
	Pile				Data EXFOR12367.003	Jun 76 . 1 PT.	
(n,γ)	Maxwl		ANL	Expt	Jour NSE 1 204	Jul 56 Jaffey.530B FROM ORNL ANL DATA	
(n,γ)	Maxwl		HAR	Expt	Jour NPW 1 200	Sep 56 Cockcroft. SIGMA EXPTL ESTIMATED	
(n,γ)	None		KAP Comp	Rept	KAPL – 1781	Jul 57 Schuman. SIGMA GIVEN	
(n,γ)	Pile		ORL Eval	Jour	NSE 2 481	Jul 57 Halperin+ CALC 1200B FROM XPTL DATA	
(n,γ)	Pile		CRC	Expt	Conf 58Geneva 16 83	Sep 58 Craig+ PPR205	+
	Pile				Data EXFOR12355.009	Jun 76 . 1 PT.	
(n,γ)	Maxwl		HAN Eval	Jour	NSE 5 32	Jan 59 Leonard+,275+ – 20B CALCTD FROM RESPAR	
(n,γ)	2.5 – 2		ORL	Expt	Jour JIN 9 1	Jan 59 Halperin+ PILE OSC,285+ – 15B AT.025EV	
(n,γ)	Pile		ORL	Expt	Jour NSE 6 100	Aug 59 Stoughton+,BEST VALUE .025EV=280B	
					Conf 58Geneva 16 64	Sep 58 Halperin+.PPR1072,VAL GVN,MANY REFS	
(n,γ)	Pile		CRC	Expt	Jour CJP 38 57	Jan 60 Walker+ NRX 270+ – 17B MEAN VALUE	
(n,γ)	Pile		ORL	Expt	Jour NSE 8 112	Aug 60 Block+,FC 288+ – 8B SIG(TOT) – SIG(SCT)	+
	Maxwl				Data EXFOR12024.010	Jun 76 . 1 PT.	
(n,γ)	2.5 – 2	1.2 + 2	LAS Eval	Rept	LA – 2574	Aug 61 Devaney+.TABLES.T-.025TO.2EV.MAXWELN	
(n,γ)	Pile		CRC Eval	Rept	CRRP – 960	Jan 62 Westcott. EFF SIG,TBL 20 – 13000DEG C	
(n,γ)	+5	+7	RLY Revw	Conf	64Vienna 56	Dec 64 Kronberger.FAST REACTOR,1 – GROUP SIGS	

94 Plutonium 240

Quantity	Energy (ev) Min	Energy (ev) Max	Lab	Type	Documentation Ref Vol Page	Date	Author, Comments	Data
(n,γ)	1.0+3	1.5+7	UK	Eval Rept	AWRE-O-91/64	Jan 65	Douglas+(ALD).UKNDL-DFN 201	+
	1.0-3	2.5+1		Rept	AEEW-R-351	Feb 64	Barrington+(WIN).UKNDL LOW EN REVISN	
	1.0-4	1.5+7		Data	UKNDL-DFN 77B	Mar 73	243 PNTS	
(n,γ)	2.5-2		BNW	Theo Conf	66Wash. 75	Mar 66	Liikala+, TBLS OF LITER. VALUES	
(n,γ)	2.0+1	1.0+6	LAS	Expt Conf	66Wash. 903	Mar 66	Byers.BOMB SOURCE NS(=LADC-7623)	
	2.0+1	2.0+2		Rept	LA-7864		66 Brown+ GRPH.PETRAL DATA	
(n,γ)	Maxwl	Pile	BNL	Eval Rept	BNL-982 22	Aug 66	Pearlstein. 246B, 235B, FROM RES PAR	
(n,γ)	2.0+1	9.5+2	HAR	Expt Conf	66Paris 2 145	Oct 66	Asghar+ GRAPHS 200-600 EV,LINAC	
				Rept	INDC-156	67	- + FULL PAPER OF 66PARIS.	
(n,γ)	1.0+3	1.5+7	LAS	Eval Prog	EANDC(US)-96	Feb 67	Diven+ NDG	
(n,γ)	Pile		CRC	ExTh Conf	67Wien 15	Apr 67	Ward. SIGMA DEDUCED FRM ISOTOP RATIO	
	Maxwl		HAR	Expt Jour	JIN 28 2467	May 67	Cabell+. IRR. IN MAXWELLIAN SPECTRUM	+
	Maxwl	2.5-2		Rept	AERE-R-5874	Aug 68	-. RE-ASSESSED.T=116C.TBL	
	Maxwl			Rept	AERE-R-5166	Apr 66	- + SUPERSEDED.	
(n,γ)	1.0+3	4.0+4	WEW	Theo Jour	NSE 34 181	Nov 68	Dyos.STATISTICAL CALC TOTAL+PART NG	
(n,γ)	Pile		CCP	Theo Jour	AE 25 466	Dec 68	Usynin. OTHER MEAN SIG GVN	
				Jour	EAF 25 6 6	Dec 68	.TRANSLATN	
				Jour	SJA 25 1290	Dec 68	TRANSLATN.*	
(n,γ)		5.7+3	TRM	Comp Prog	BARC-423 6	69	Garg. SELF-SHIELD SIG,TEMP-INFL, NDG	
(n,γ)	1.0+3	7.0+6	KFK	Revw Jour	AKE 15 26	70	Schmidt. REVW ON EXPTS, GRPH	
	1.0+3	1.0+7		Rept	KFK-966	Apr 69	-. EVALS COMPARED.	
(n,γ)	2.5-2	6.0+6	SAC	Eval Rept	CEA-N-1273	Mar 70	L'Heriteau+ SEE EANDC(E)126AL.	
(n,γ)	2.5-2	6.0+6	SAC	Eval Rept	EANDC(E)126AL	Mar 70	L'Heriteau+ COMPLETE EVALUATION.	
(n,γ)	+2	+5	JAE	Theo Jour	NSE 40 25	Apr 70	Ishiguro+,STATISTICAL CALCULATN,CURV	
(n,γ)	+5	+7	ANL	Revw Conf	70Helsinki 2 119	Jun 70	Davey.112.STATUS OF DATA ABOVE RESON	
(n,γ)	+1	+7	CAD	Theo Conf	70Helsinki 2 465	Jun 70	Barre+73. MICROSC CFD INTEGRAL DATA	
(n,γ)	2.5-2		CRC	Expt Conf	70Helsinki 1 287	Jun 70	Lounsbury+PPR2. VALUE GVN,THRML FLUX	+
	2.5-2			Data	EXFOR10013.008	Sep 72	1PT.CS AT 2200M/S.	
(n,γ)	1.0+2	+6	GEV	Revw Conf	70Helsinki 1 17	Jun 70	Greebler+102. UNCERTAINTY+REACT CALC	
(n,γ)	+2	+7	HAR	Revw Conf	70Helsinki 1 267	Jun 70	James.107. ACCURACY CFD REACTOR COST	
(n,γ)	1.0-2	1.0+7	ORL	Revw Jour	REA 8 473	Sep 70	Kasten. REVIEW,SIG(NEUT-E) GRAPH	
	Maxwl	Fiss	ORL	Expt Rept	ORNL-4581 36	Sep 70	Bemis+ UPPER LIMIT ISOMER PROD	
(n,γ)	6.2-1	1.0+7	SRL	Theo Conf	71Knoxvill 714	Mar 71	Mccrosson. SPECTRUM-AVERAGED SIG	
(n,γ)	Pile		KFK	Eval Rept	KFK-1453	Mar 72	Eberle+ 2-GROUP SIGS,FITTED TO EXPT	
(n,γ)	Maxwl		IAE	Revw Rept	IAEA-143 897	Apr 72	Lemmel.EVALUATIONS+RECENT EXPTS,TBL	
	2.5-2			Rept	IAEA-143 897	Apr 72	- .EVALUATIONS+RECENT EXPTS,TBL	
	1.0-2	3.0+0		Rept	IAEA-143 897	Apr 72	- .GRAPH OF EVALUATED SIGMA	
(n,γ)	Pile		FAR	Expt Prog	EANDC(E)150U	May 72	Vidal.INTEGR CROSS SECTION RATIOS	
(n,γ)	1.0+3	1.5+7	SOR	Eval Rept	IA-1243	May 72	Caner+ EVALUATION FOR KEDAK,TBL	
	1.0+3	8.0+5		Rept	KFK-1340	Feb 71	Hinkelmann+ (KFK) REVISIONS TO KEDAK	
				Conf	67Karlsrhe 1 123	Nov 67	Yiftah+ EVAL SUPERSEDED.	
(n,γ)	Pile		JUL	Expt Jour	JIN 34 8 2427	Aug 72	Ihle+ REACTOR CROSS SECTION	
(n,γ)	6.0-1	2.0+2	HAR	Expt Prog	AERE-PR/NP19	Sep 72	Moxon+ TOF LINAC TO GET RESON PARAMS	
(n,γ)	2.0+1	3.0+4	RPI	Expt Jour	NSE 49 153	Oct 72	Hockenbury+HI,LOW BIAS,LINAC.CURVS.	+
				Conf	72Budapest 224	Aug 72	.SUPERSEDED	
	2.0+1	1.0+3		Conf	71Knoxvill 721	Aug 71	.SUPERSEDED.	
	6.0+3	2.8+4		Data	EXFOR10127.004	Feb 76	11PTS.AVG CAPT CS.	
(n,γ)	1.0+5	1.0+7	SOR	Eval Rept	IAEA-153 141	73	Ilberg+ EVALUATD DATA FILES CFD,GRPH	
				Rept	TNSD-R-424	Jan 72	Yiftah+ COMPAR.OF EVALUATIONS, GRAPH	
(n,γ)	Maxwl		SGA	Comp Conf	73Paris 1 233	Mar 73	Eder+ DATA FROM EXPTS+EVALS,TABLE	
				Rept	SGAE-PH-141	Feb 73	.SAME AS 73PARIS,NO DETAILS	
(n,γ)	0.0+0	1.5+7	UK	Eval Data	UKNDL-DFN 402B	Mar 73	1424 PNTS	+
(n,γ)	2.5-2		IKE	Eval Rept	IKE-6-80	Apr 74	Mattes+ ENDF/B,UKNDL,KEDAK CFD	
(n,γ)	6.0+3	3.0+4	GEL	Eval Conf	NEANDC(E)-163U	Jan 75	Weigmann+DYOS TYPE CALCULATION,GRAPH	
	2.5-2			Conf	NEANDC(E)-163U	Jan 75	- + 286B FROM 1.056 RES	
(n,γ)	1.0+3	1.0+6	BRC	Revw Conf	75Wash. 202	Mar 75	Michaudon.CALC CFD MEAS	
	3.0+3	1.0+6		Eval Conf	JAERI-M-5984	Feb 75	Thomet.STATMOD.2 HUMP BARRIER.GRPH	
				Rept	CEA-R-4631	Nov 74	- . STAT MDL ANAL TBLS GRPHS	
(n,γ)	2.5-2		IFB	Eval Rept	INDC(CCP)-76	Jan 76	Antsipov+ CALC FROM RESPARS,SIG GVN	
(n,γ)	Pile		FEI	Expt Rept	YK-24 48	77	Andrijakhina+ AVG SIG AT DIFF POSITS	
Res Int Capt	5.0-1		CRC	Expt Rept	CRC-633	Mar 56	Cornish+ NRX RESON INTGRL=8700+-800B	+
	5.0-1			Data	EXFOR12367.002	Jun 76	. 1 PT	
Res Int Capt	None		HAN	Eval Jour	NSE 5 32	Jan 59	Leonard+,ABS INTEGRAL=8700+-800B	
Res Int Capt	5.0-1		ORL	Eval Jour	NSE 6 100	Aug 59	Stoughton+ BEST VALUE 9000+-1500B	
				Conf	58Geneva 16 64	Sep 58	Halperin+.PPR1072,VAL CFD MANY REFS	
Res Int Capt	5.0-1		CRC	Expt Jour	CJP 38 57	Jan 60	Walker+ NRX 8780+-550B REL AU	+
	5.0-1			Data	EXFOR11525.004	Jun 76	. 1 PT.	
Res Int Capt	5.5-1		HAN	Expt Jour	NSE 17 144	63	Nichols.,CD-RATIO, 8607 B, INCL 1/V	

94 Plutonium 240

Quantity	Energy (ev) Min	Max	Lab	Type	Documentation Ref Vol Page	Author, Comments Date	Data
Res Int Capt	5.5−1		IIT Expt	Abst	ANS 6 258	Nov 63 Klopp. EFFCTV RES INT VS ATOMDENSITY	
Res Int Capt	5.0−1	1.0+7	BNW Theo	Conf	66Wash. 75	Mar 66 Liikala+, TBLS OF RES.INTEGRALS	
Res Int Capt	5.5−1		BNL Eval	Rept	BNL−982 22	Aug 66 Pearlstein. 8000B CALC, RECOMMENDED	
Res Int Capt	6.8+2	1.5+4	WEW Theo	Jour	NSE 34 181	Nov 68 Dyos. STATISTICAL CALC 6.131+ −0.378B	
Res Int Capt		1.5+7	SAC Eval	Rept	EANDC(E)126AL	Mar 70 Ribon+L'HERITEAU. SAME REF CEA−N1273	
Res Int Capt	Pile		KFK Eval	Rept	KFK−1453	Mar 72 Eberle+ 8453B	
Spect (n,γ)	1.1+0		BNL Expt	Conf	70Helsinki 1 377	Jun 70 Chrien.42. TABLE OF GAM E+INTENSITY	
Spect (n,γ)	1.0+0		HAR Expt	Prog	AERE−PR/NP17	Dec 70 Coates+ MULTIPLICITY+TOTAL FS ENERGY	
Spect (n,γ)	Maxwl		ANL Expt	Jour	PR/C 6 1374	Oct 72 Braid+. PU241 LVL ONLY GIVEN	
Spect (n,γ)	Maxwl		LAS Expt	Prog	USNDC−3 124	Oct 72 Jurney. CURVES	
Spect (n,γ)		2.0+3	HAR Expt	Conf	74Petten 668	Sep 74 Thomas+ RES CAPT.,Q−VALUE	
		1.0+2		Prog	EANDC(UK) 151	Aug 73 − + GS STRENGTH CORR GRPHS	
Spect (n,γ)	Maxwl		KFK Expt	Conf	74Petten 749	Sep 74 Weitkamp+ NONDESTR FUEL ASSAY APPL	
				Conf	74Petten 655	Sep 74 Matussek+DECAY SCHEME,Q PU−241	
(n,2n)	Thrsh	1.5+7	UK Eval	Rept	AWRE−O−91/64	Jan 65 Douglas+(ALD).UKNDL−DFN 201	+
	6.5+6	1.5+7		Data	UKNDL−DFN 77B	Mar 73 26 PNTS	
	6.5+6	1.5+7		Data	UKNDL−DFN 77B	Mar 73 ENERGY DISTRIBUTION , 8 RANGES	
	6.5+6	1.5+7		Data	UKNDL−DFN 77B	Mar 73 ANGULAR DISTRIBUTION, 1 RNGS,LAB.	
(n,2n)	6.0+6	1.6+7	SAC Eval	Rept	CEA−N−1273	Mar 70 L'Heriteau+ SEE EANDC(E)126AL.	
(n,2n)	6.0+6	1.6+7	SAC Eval	Rept	EANDC(E)126AL	Mar 70 L'Heriteau+ COMPLETE EVALUATION.	
(n,2n)	1.0−3	1.5+7	SOR Eval	Rept	IA−1243	May 72 Caner+ EVALUATION FOR KEDAK−3.	
	1.0−3	1.5+7		Data	KEDAK−3	Oct 75 12 DATA SETS (KFK FILE)	
(n,2n)	1.5+7		DUB Expt	Jour	IJP 47 232	73 Belov+ SIG TO SPONFIS GIVN,FRAGM−DET	
				Rept	JINR−E15−6807	Nov 72 − + SPON FISS ISOMER PRODUCTN,TBL	
(n,2n)	1.5+7		KFI Expt	Jour	MFF 21 555	73 Nagy. THESIS,HUNG. TO FISS ISO,GRND	
(n,2n)	6.7+6	1.5+7	UK Eval	Data	UKNDL−DFN 402B	Mar 73 ANGULAR DISTRIBUTION, 1 RNGS,LAB.	+
	7.0+6	1.5+7		Data	UKNDL−DFN 402B	Mar 73 12 PNTS	
	6.7+6	1.5+7		Data	UKNDL−DFN 402B	Mar 73 ENERGY DISTRIBUTION , 8 RANGES	
(n,xn) x>2	Thrsh	1.5+7	ALD Eval	Rept	AWRE−O−91/64	Jan 65 Douglas.DFN 201 DATA UK LIBRARY	
(n,xn) x>2	1.2+7	1.6+7	FR Eval	Rept	EANDC(E)126AL	Mar 70 L'Heriteau+	
(n,xn) x>2	1.2+7	1.6+7	SAC Eval	Rept	CEA−N−1273	Mar 70 L'Heriteau+ SEE EANDC(E)126AL.	
(n,xn) x>2	1.2+7	1.6+7	SAC Eval	Rept	EANDC(E)126AL	Mar 70 L'Heriteau+ COMPLETE EVALUATION.N3N	
	1.0−3	1.5+7	SOR Eval	Rept	IA−1243	May 72 Caner+ EVALUATION FOR KEDAK−3.	
	1.0−3	1.5+7		Data	KEDAK−3	Oct 75 5 DATA SETS (KFK FILE) (N,3N)	
(n,xn) x>2	1.2+7	1.5+7	UK Eval	Data	UKNDL−DFN 77B	Mar 73 ANGULAR DISTRIBUTION, 1 RNGS,LAB.	+
	1.3+7	1.5+7		Data	UKNDL−DFN 402B	Mar 73 ENERGY DISTRIBUTION , 1 RANGES	
	1.3+7	1.5+7		Data	UKNDL−DFN 402B	Mar 73 ANGULAR DISTRIBUTION, 1 RNGS,LAB.	
	1.2+7	1.5+7		Data	UKNDL−DFN 77B	Mar 73 7 PNTS	
	1.3+7	1.5+7		Data	UKNDL−DFN 402B	Mar 73 3 PNTS	
	1.2+7	1.5+7		Data	UKNDL−DFN 77B	Mar 73 ENERGY DISTRIBUTION , 1 RANGES	
(n,α)	1.0−3	2.5+1	UK Eval	Rept	AEEW−R−351	Feb 64 Barrington+(WIN).UKNDL LOW EN REVISN	
(n,nα)		1.0+2	HAR Expt	Prog	AERE−PR/NP15	May 69 Pattenden+ MAX WALPHA FOR RES	
Fission	Pile		LAS Expt	Rept	LA−1201	Nov 50 Jurney+ FAST REACTOR SPEC AVG SIG	
Fission	Spont		HAN Expt	Rept	HW−27660	Apr 53 Kinderman.FISS RATE GIVEN	
Fission	Pile		HAR Revw	Conf	55Geneva 5 331	Aug 55 Holmes+.P404,RATIO PU239/PU240 GVN	
Fission	Maxwl		LRL Expt	Jour	PR 102 1621	Jun 56 Hulet+,MTR 4.4+ −5B	
Fission	Fast		HAR Expt	Rept	AERE−R/R−2151	57 Absalom+ ZEPHYR+TH ENVELOPE.	
Fission	3.0+3	5.0+6	CCP Expt	Jour	AE 2 10	Jan 57 Dorofeev+.REL+ABS DATA, 5 GN SOURCES	+
				Jour	JNE 5 217	Nov 57 TRANSLATN.*	
				Jour	SJA 2 9	57 TRANSLATN.*	
Fission	2.7+5	8.1+6	LAS Expt	Rept	AECD−4256	Mar 57 Henkel+ IONIZATION CHAMBER REL U235	+
	2.7+5	8.1+6		Data	EXFOR12549.002	Jun 76 . 21 PTS.	
Fission	7.5−2	1.3+0	HAN Expt	Prog	ORNL−2309	Jun 57 Leonard.ZERO TO D8EV 35BAT1EVRES	+
	7.5−2	1.2+0		Rept	AERE−NP/R−2076	Jan 57 − .NONE AT THR RES AT 1DO	
	7.5−2	1.1+0		Rept	TNCC−3	Aug 56 − + 11.5+ −3MB AT 1.05 EV	
	3.0−1	1.3+0		Data	EXFOR12525.002	Jun 76 . 67 PTS.	
Fission	Pile		HAR Expt	Rept	AERE−R/M−167	Mar 58 Sanders. ZEPHYR REACTOR CORE	
Fission	1.5+6	1.5+7	CCP Expt	Jour	ZET 35 532	Aug 58 ION CHAMB,REL TO PU239,PLATEAU 2.6B	
				Jour	JET 8 367	Feb 59 TRANSLATN.*	
Fission	Maxwl		CRC Expt	Conf	58Geneva 16 54	Sep 58 Eastwood+ PPR203,SIGMA GIVEN	+
				Jour	CJP 36 503	Apr 58 Bigham. −.8+ −.7B,CORRECTS LRL 4.4B	
				Rept	KAPL−1781	Jul 57 Butler+LESS THAN 0.1 BARN	
	Maxwl			Data	EXFOR12011.006	Jun 76 . 1 PT.	
Fission	Pile		KUR Expt	Conf	58Geneva 12 3	Sep 58 Leipunskij+.PPR2038,VAL PU240/PU239	
Fission	Maxwl		MTR Expt	Prog	WASH−1006 28	Oct 58 Simpson. TBD	
Fission	1.0+5	4.0+6	CCP Expt	Rept	AEC−TR−3945	59 Nesterov+,MIN .07B,1.6B AT 1−4 MEV	
Fission	2.5+6	1.5+7	CCP Expt	Jour	AE 8 139	Feb 60 Kazarinova+ 1.6+ −0.3B, 2.4+ −0.3B	+
				Jour	SJA 8 125	May 61 TRANSLATN.*	

94 Plutonium 240

Quantity	Energy (ev) Min	Max	Lab	Type	Documentation Ref Vol Page	Author, Comments Date	Data
Fission	7.5−2	2.0+1	HAN	Expt Prog	HW− 67219 4	Oct 60 Leonard+	
Fission	1.4+5	1.0+7	B+W	Eval Rept	BAW− 158	Jun 61 Roach+ AVERAGED SIG 14 GROUPS	
Fission	2.0+5	8.0+6	ANL	Revw Conf	61Vienna 1 29	Aug 61 Smith.P76,CURVE,MANY REFS GVN	
Fission	4.0+4	1.0+7	KFK	Revw Conf	61Vienna 1 3	Aug 61 Schmidt.P4,CURVE, MANY REFERENCES	
Fission	2.5−2	2.0+0	LAS	Eval Rept	LA− 2574	Aug 61 Devaney+.TABLES.T−.025TO.2EV.MAXWELN	
Fission	Spont		ALD	Expt Jour	PR 126 264	Apr 62 Watt+,SPON FISSION HALF−LIFE MEASD	
				Rept	AWRE−NR/P−4 60	Dec 60 − + HALF LIFE.	
Fission	4.0+4	3.8+6	FEI	Expt Rept	INDSWG−64 260	64 . TABLE GIVEN,AE 9 16 GRAPH ONLY	+
				Jour	AE 9 16	Jul 60 Nesterov+	
				Jour	SJA 9 511	Jul 61 . ENGLISH OF AE 9 16	
				Jour	KE 4 137	Feb 61 . GERMAN OF AE 9 16	
	4.0+4	3.8+6		Data	EXFOR40021.002	Aug 70 SIGMA AT 73 ENERGIES	
Fission	2.0+1	1.2+2	HAR	Expt Rept	EANDC(UK)41L	Jun 64 Brooks+ LIMIT TO WF,8RES THRESH CALC	
Fission	6.1+4	4.8+5	ALD	Expt Jour	JNE 18 561	Oct 64 Ruddick. = 1 DATA INDEX LINES	+
Fission	+5	+7	RLY	Revw Conf	64Vienna 56	Dec 64 Kronberger.FAST REACTOR,1−GROUP SIGS	
Fission	3.0+4	2.0+6	HAR	Expt Rept	65Salzburg 1 281	Mar 65 Devroey+PPR19.REL U235,CFD THEO,GRPH	
Fission	2.4+4		ALD	Expt Jour	JNE 19 423	Jun 65 Perkin+.CALIB SB− BE SRCE. 106+−18MB	
	2.4+4			Data	EXFOR20584.008	Jul 76 1PNT.SIGMA.	
Fission	1.0+3	1.4+7	UK	Eval Rept	AHSB(S)R−124	Feb 66 Hart.(RLY).UK−DFN 340.UPDATES NSE 26	+
	1.0+3	1.5+7		Rept	AWRE−O−91/64	Jan 65 Douglas+(ALD).UKNDL−DFN 201	
	1.0−3	2.5+1		Rept	AEEW−R−351	Feb 64 Barrington+(WIN).UKNDL LOW EN REVISN	
	1.0−1	1.5+7		Data	UKNDL−DFN 77B	Mar 73 243 PNTS	
Fission	2.0+1	2.0+6	LAS	Expt Conf	66Wash. 903	Mar 66 Byers+ BOMB TOF(=LADC−7623)	+
	2.0+1	1.0+6		Rept	LA−3586 8	Dec 66 Diven.TOF BOMB NS FROM PETREL JUNE65	
	1.0+1	1.0+7		Conf	66Paris 2 219	Oct 66 Hemmendinger.DETONATION TOF	
	2.0+1	2.0+2		Rept	LA− 7864	66 Brown+ GRPH.PETRAL DATA	
	2.0+1	9.8+5		Data	EXFOR12552.002	Jun 76 . 2374 PTS.	
Fission	None		BRK	Revw Jour	NP 81 1	Jun 66 Myers+ TABLE2 FISS BARRIER	
Fission	Maxwl	Pile	BNL	Eval Rept	BNL−982 22	Aug 66 Pearlstein. 60MB, 50MB, FROM RES PAR	
Fission	5.0+3	1.5+5	KFK	Expt Conf	66Paris 1 295	Oct 66 Gilboy+VDG,REL TO U235,GRPHS.PPR7	+
				Rept	KFK−450	Oct 66 − + REPRINT OF 66PARIS.	
				Rept	EANDC(E)66U	Feb 67 − +2 METHODS.CORRCT VALS AT CCDN	
Fission	Pile		ORL	Expt Rept	ORNL−P−2081	Nov 66 Pratt.	+
	Pile			Data	EXFOR12509.005	Jun 76 . 1 PT, SIG	
Fission	1.0+3	1.5+7	LAS	Eval Prog	EANDC(US)−96	Feb 67 Diven+ NDG	
Fission	Pile		WIN	Expt Rept	AEEW−R−526	Jun 67 Stevenson+.FISS RATIO TO U235.ZEBRA	+
Fission	1.0+6	1.4+7	ALD	Expt Jour	JNE 21 671	Aug 67 White+ 4ES REL U235. CFD OTHER DATA	+
Fission	Spont		ALD	Expt Jour	JNE 21 749	Oct 67 Fieldhouse+ BY N YLD STANDARD SOURCE	
Fission	9.1+3	1.0+7	ANL	Eval Jour	NSE 32 35	Apr 68 Davy. RE−EVALUATION OF DATA	
	1.0+3	1.0+7		Jour	NSE 26 149	Oct 66 − .	
Fission	1.0+4	4.0+6	CCP	Theo Jour	YF 8 704	Oct 68 Ermagambetov+OPTMOD−PARS,GRPHS,REVW	
				Jour	SNP 8 409	Apr 69 TRANSLATN.*	
Fission	+5	+6	LAS	Expt Prog	WASH−1124 110	Nov 68 Smith+ TO BE PUBLISHED IN NSE NDG	
Fission	Pile		CCP	Theo Jour	AE 25 466	Dec 68 Usynin.AVG SUM SIG(N,G)+SIG(N,F) GVN	
				Jour	EAF 25 6 6	Dec 68 .TRANSLATN	
				Jour	SJA 25 1290	Dec 68 TRANSLATN.*	
Fission		9.5+2	TRM	Comp Prog	BARC−423 6	69 Garg. SELF−SHIELD SIG,TEMP−INFL, NDG	
Fission	7.5+2	2.8+3	CCP	Theo Jour	YF 9 535	Mar 69 Gejlikman. SIG MAXIMA+QUASISTAT LVLS	
				Jour	SNP 9 306	Sep 69 TRANSLATN.*	
Fission	Spont		COP	Revw Conf	69Vienna 155	Jul 69 Strutinsky+PPR203. HL GVN,'SHELL−TH'	
	5.0+0	2.9+1		Conf	69Vienna 155	Jul 69 − +PPR203. RESON SIG(E) GRPH	
Fission	−		FEI	Theo Conf	69Vienna 337	Jul 69 Gaj+PPR132. 2HUMPD−BARR−CALC,TBL+CRV	
Fission	Spont		HEI	Theo Conf	69Vienna 449	Jul 69 Metag+PPR29. HE−INDUCED ISOM FISS HL	
Fission	None		LAS	Expt Conf	69Vienna 918	Jul 69 Britt+PPR101.(D,P FISSN)CFD(N,FISSN)	
Fission	Spont		WAU	Expt Conf	69Vienna 439	Jul 69 Vandenbosch+PPR110. ISOM FISS HL GVN	
Fission	2.0+3		IPS	Theo Jour	NP/A 137 241	Nov 69 Jaegare.ANAL 2−BLE HUMPED BARRIER NF	
Fission	5.2+5	3.7+6	KUR	Expt Prog	YFI−8 12	Dec 69 Savin+ SIG REL U235 AT 26 N−ES,TABLE	+
				Rept	INDC(CCP)−8 16	Dec 70 *ENGL OF YFI−8 12	
	5.2+5	3.7+6		Data	EXFOR40020.003	Aug 70 RATIO TO U−235 AT 26 ENERGIES	
Fission	1.0+3	1.0+7	KFK	Revw Jour	AKE 15 26	70 Schmidt. REVW ON EXPTS, GRPH	
				Rept	KFK−966	Apr 69 − . EVALS COMPARED.	
Fission	1.0+3	1.0+7	TRM	Eval Rept	BARC/I−96	70 Kapil.14 GROUP SIG,2 N−SPECS,TABLES	
Fission	2.5−2	1.0+7	SAC	Eval Rept	CEA−N−1273	Mar 70 L'Heriteau+ SEE EANDC(E)126AL.	
Fission	2.5−2	1.0+7	SAC	Eval Rept	EANDC(E)126AL	Mar 70 L'Heriteau+ COMPLETE EVALUATION.	
Fission	+3	+5	JAE	Theo Jour	NSE 40 25	Apr 70 Ishiguro+,STATISTICAL CALCULATN,CURV	
Fission	Spont		MOL	Expt Prog	INDC(BLG)−1G	Apr 70 Deruytter+ CONFERED TO PU−239 FISSN	
Fission	+5	+7	ANL	Revw Conf	70Helsinki 2 119	Jun 70 Davey.112.STATUS OF DATA ABOVE RESON	
Fission	+1	+7	CAD	Theo Conf	70Helsinki 2 465	Jun 70 Barre+73. MICROSC CFD INTEGRAL DATA	

94 Plutonium 240

Quantity	Energy (ev) Min	Max	Lab	Type	Documentation Ref Vol Page	Date	Author, Comments	Data
Fission	1.0+3	+6	GEV	Revw Conf	70Helsinki 1 17	Jun 70	Greebler+102. UNCERTAINTY+REACT CALC	
Fission	+2	+7	HAR	Revw Conf	70Helsinki 1 267	Jun 70	James.107. ACCURACY CFD REACTOR COST	
Fission	5.0-3	2.0+1	HAR	Revw Prog	INDC-6 23	Jun 70	Rae.HANNA+ ISOMERIC PU-241 DISCUSSED	
	0.0+0	1.0+0		Conf	69Vienna 249	Jul 69	Lynn. REVW=STRUTINSKY TH + EXPTS,TBL	
	5.0+2	3.0+4		Expt Conf	68JINR 115	Jul 68	RAE.INTERMED.STRUCT.EFFECTS IN FISS.	
				Jour	ZP 214 7	Jul 68	Weigmann+ SEE ALSO.	
	Maxwl	+6		Revw Conf	65Salzburg 1 187	Mar 65	RAE.PPR12.SUBTHRESHOLD FISS DISCUSSD	
Fission	1.0+3	1.0+6	FEI	Comp Jour	YF 12 260	Aug 70	Androsenko+ SIG(E) GRAPHS,DISCUSSION	+
				Jour	SNP 12 142	Feb 71	TRANSLATN.*	
	1.9+5	1.5+6		Expt Data	EXFOR40084.	Dec 72	ANGDIST OF FRAGS,COS-COEFF	
Fission	+3		ISL	Theo Prog	IA-1218 14	Aug 70	Kaner. CODE FOR SIG CALCULATION, NDG	
	2.0+6	7.0+6	TRM	Theo Jour	NP/A 151 532	Aug 70	Sood+ CORREL ANAL OF INTERM STRUCTUR	
	2.0+1	2.0+6		Jour	PL/B 30 523	Dec 69	- + CORREL ANAL,D CLASS II VAL GV	
Fission	7.0+5	5.0+6	CCP	Expt Jour	AE 29 218	Sep 70	Sabin+ SIGMA(E) REL U-235 RATIO,GRPH	
				Jour	SJA 29 938	Sep 70	TRANSLATN.*	
Fission	Spont		MRY	Theo Prog	ORO-4028-28	71	Jackson+. SPON FISSION HALF-LIFE GVN	
Fission	5.0-1	+6	COR	Expt Jour	NSE 46 31	Oct 71	Draper.INTEGRAL SIG TIMES E.4 SPECTR	
Fission	-		GEL	Revw Jour	AKE 18 229	Nov 71	Theobald+ SUB-BARRIER FISS EXPTS,TH	
Fission	2.5-2		IAE	Revw Rept	IAEA-143 897	Apr 72	Lemmel.EVALUATIONS+RECENT EXPTS,TBL	
Fission	Spont		MRY	Theo Jour	PL/B 38 495	Apr 72	Hooshyar+ TOTAL DELAY HALF LIFE CALC	
Fission	Pile		FAR	Expt Prog	EANDC(E)150U	May 72	Vidal.INTEGRAL CROSS SECTION TO U235	
Fission	Thrsh		LIE	Theo Jour	NP/A 186 561	May 72	Cugnon. DOORWAY PARAM SUBTHRESH FIT	
Fission	2.0+2	8.0+3	GEL	Expt Jour	NP/A 142 603	May 68	Migneco+ STRUCTURE OBSERVED	+
				ExTh Jour	NP/A 187 305	Jun 72	Weigmann+ F.B.PARAMS FROM DATA ANAL.	
		+5		Jour	ZP 214 7	Jul 68	- .SUBTHRS STRUCT INTERPRETED	
	2.0+2	8.0+3		Expt Conf	68Wash. 1 527	Mar 68	Migneco+LINAC TOF SUB TR FISS GROUPS	
	2.0+2	8.0+3		Data	EXFOR20005.002	Nov 70	3290PTS.	
Fission	Spont		DUB	Expt Jour	YF 16 271	Aug 72	Gangriski'+ SPONT FISS ISOMER (G,N)	
				Jour	SNP 16 151	Feb 73	. ENGLISH OF YF 16 271 8/72	
Fission	+2	1.0+6	HAR	Expt Prog	AERE-PR/NP19	Sep 72	Belcher+ TOF CYCLOTRON GRPH	
Fission	Spont		LIN	Expt Jour	YF 16 667	Oct 72	Val'Skii+ SPONFISS ISOMER,REL SIG+HL	
				Jour	SNP 16 374	Apr 73	.ENGLISH OF YF 16 667	
Fission	2.0+1	3.0+4	RPI	Expt Jour	NSE 49 153	Oct 72	Hockenbury+HI,LOW BIAS,LINAC.CURVS.	
				Conf	72Budapest 224	Aug 72	.SUPERSEDED	
	2.0+1	1.0+3		Conf	71Knoxvill 721	Aug 71	.SUPERSEDED.	
Fission	2.5-2		JUL	Theo Jour	ZP 257 389	Dec 72	Mcminn. 3.21 E-1 BARNS	
Fission	Spont		NEU	Theo Jour	HPA 45 567	Dec 72	Hooshyar+ HL GROUNDST AND FISS ISOM.	
Fission	1.0+5	1.0+7	SOR	Eval Rept	IAEA-153 141	73	Ilberg+ EVALUATD DATA FILES CFD,GRPH	
	1.0+5	1.5+7		Rept	IA-1243	May 72	Caner+ EVALUATION FOR KEDAK,TBL	
	1.0+5	1.0+7		Rept	TNSD-R-424	Jan 72	Yiftah+ COMPAR.OF EVALUATIONS, GRAPH	
	1.0-3	1.5+7		Data	KEDAK-3	Oct 75	2445 DATA SETS (KFK FILE)	
Fission	Maxwl	Fiss	SGA	Eval Conf	73Paris 1 233	Mar 73	Eder+ FISS SPEC REL U238(N,F),TBLS	
				Rept	SGAE-PH-141	Feb 73	.SAME AS 73PARIS,NO DETAILS,TBP	
Fission	0.0+0	1.5+7	UK	Eval Data	UKNDL-DFN 402B	Mar 73	1424 PNTS	+
Fission	None		FRK	Theo Jour	NP/A 207 225	Jun 73	Albrecht. 2CENTRE SHELLMOD,DEF-E MAP	
Fission	Spont		GEL	Expt Conf	73Rochestr 2 51	Aug 73	Deruytter+ REL PROMPT FRAG YLDS,GRPH	
Fission	None		DUB	Revw Jour	FDP 22 199	74	Gangrsky+ FIS-BARRIER,GRPH EMAX+EMIN	
Fission	Spont		MRY	Theo Rept	ORO-4317-36	Feb 74	Mustafa+ ANG MOM DEPEN.TBL,GRPH.	
Fission	2.5-2		IKE	Eval Rept	IKE-6-80	Apr 74	Mattes+ ENDF/B,UKNDL,KEDAK CFD	
Fission	1.3+3	2.1+3	ORL	Revw Conf	JINR-D-37991	Apr 74	Harvey.P157.ORELA,SUBTHRESH-FIS,PLOT	
Fission	1.9+6	1.5+7	BRC	Expt Rept	CEA-R-4626	Nov 74	Frehaut. REL U-235.	+
	1.9+6	1.5+7		Data	EXFOR20488.002	Mar 76	22PTS.SIGMA.	
Fission	1.0+1	1.0+4	CCP	Theo Jour	YF 21 14	Jan 75	Marshalkin+ TWO-BUMP BARRIER	
Fission	Maxwl	3.0+4	GEL	Eval Conf	NEANDC(E)-163U	Jan 75	Weigmann+F-WID BACKGROUND=0.23MEV	
Fission	3.0+6	5.0+6	LAS	Theo Conf	75Wash. 129	Mar 75	Moore.GRPH R MATR STAT CALC CFD EXPT	
Fission	3.0+3	1.0+6	BRC	Eval Conf	75Kiev 1 252	May 75	Thomet. STATMOD EVAL,CURVE CFD XPTS	
				Conf	JAERI-M-5984	Feb 75	- .STATMOD.2 HUMP BARRIER.GRPH	
				Rept	CEA-R-4631	Nov 74	- . STAT MDL ANAL TBLS GRPHS	
Fission	None		BRC	Expt Rept	CEA-N-1798 70	Jun 75	Lachkar+ DYN EFFECTS AT LOW ENER	
Fission	None		ORL	Expt Rept	75Wash. 229	Oct 75	Weston+TOF.NDG	
Fission	5.0+2	1.0+4	ORL	Expt Jour	PR/C 12 1850	Dec 75	Auchampaugh+ TBLS,GRPHS.SUBTR FISS	+
	6.1+2	2.9+3		Conf	75Wash. 560	Mar 75	- +SUBTR FISS.GRPH.RES PAR	
	5.0+2	1.0+4		Data	EXFOR10564.003	Apr 76	DATA NOT OBTAINED FROM AUTHORS.	
Fission	2.0+1	1.5+7	JAE	Revw Conf	IAEA-186 3 1	76	Igarasi. REVW AVAIL DATA,GRPH+BIBLIO	
	1.0+3	1.5+7		Rept	JAERI-M-6315	Nov 75	+GRPHS.MANY DATA SETS CFD.	
Fission	1.0+3	1.4+5	IFB	Eval Rept	INDC(CCP)-77	Jan 76	Antsipov+ CALC SIG(E) CFD EXPTS,GRPH	
Fission	Maxwl		MOL	Theo Jour	NP/A 259 423	Mar 76	Wagemans+ CALC FOR DOUBLE HUMP + IH0	

94 Plutonium 240

Quantity	Energy (ev) Min	Max	Lab	Type	Documentation Ref Vol Page	Date	Author, Comments	Data
Fission	1.0−1	1.8+0	COL	Expt	Rept CUD−92	May 51	Havens+	+
	1.0−1	1.8+0			Data EXFOR12517.007	Jun 76	. 40 PTS.	
Fission	None		BRC	Revw	Conf 76Lowell 641	Jul 76	Michaudon.DYNAMICAL EFFECTS OF NF	
	1.0+3	1.0+6			Conf 75Wash. 202	Mar 75	− .CALC CFD MEAS	
Res Int Fiss	None		CRC	Expt	Conf 58Geneva 16 54	Sep 58	Eastwood+ RESINT/THERMALSIGMA CA 100	
Res Int Fiss	6.8+2	1.5+4	WEW	Theo	Jour NSE 34 181	Nov 68	Dyos. STATISTICAL CALC 0.265+ − 0.013B	
Res Int Fiss	+0	+1	COR	Expt	Abst DA/B 31 1466	Sep 70	Draper.EXPT FOR 4 SPEC,CFD CALC	
Res Int Fiss	5.0−1		IAE	Revw	Rept IAEA − 143 897	Apr 72	Lemmel.FISS,EVALUTS+RECENT EXPTS,TBL	
Alpha	+5	+7	ANL	Revw	Conf 70Helsinki 2 119	Jun 70	Davey.112.STATUS OF DATA ABOVE RESON	
Alpha	1.0−3	1.5+7	SOR	Eval	Rept IA − 1243	May 72	Caner+ EVALUATION FOR KEDAK−3	
	1.0−3	1.5+7			Data KEDAK−3	Oct 75	186 DATA SETS (KFK FILE)	
Alpha	Pile		ANL	Expt	Rept NSE 53 9	Jan 74	Dudey+. INTEGRAL MEASTS IN EBR−2.	
					Rept ANL−7791	Jul 71	Heinrich+. INTEGRAL MEAST IN EBR−2	
Alpha	Fast		ITU	Expt	Prog NEANDC(E)162U	Feb 75	Cottone+ SB − 125,XE,CS,ND VOL.5.P.42.	
Eta	+5	+7	RLY	Revw	Conf 64Vienna 56	Dec 64	Kronberger. VAL TABLE OF ETA+NU+SIGS	
Eta	1.0+3	1.5+7	UK	Eval	Rept AWRE−O−91/64	Jan 65	Douglas+(ALD).UKNDL−DFN 201	
Eta	1.0−3	1.5+7	SOR	Eval	Rept IA − 1243	May 72	Caner+ EVALUATION FOR KEDAK−3	
	1.0−3	1.5+7			Data KEDAK−3	Oct 75	78 DATA SETS (KFK FILE)	
Nu	Spont		HAR	Expt	Rept AERE−N/R−831	Dec 51	Barclay+ FISSN CHAMBER N/FISSN COINC	
Nu	Spont		LAS	Expt	Jour PR 100 190	Oct 55	Hammel+,PROB DISTR FOR PROMPT NS	
					Conf 55Geneva 2 193	Aug 55	Leachman.P592,CURVE,EXPT DESCRIBED	
Nu	Spont		CCP		Rept AEC−TR−2435PT1	56	.USSR 2D2 PM 4PERCENT PAGE 131	
Nu	Spont		LAS	Expt	Jour PR 101 1012	Feb 56	Diven+,LIQ SCINT,+PROB EMISS	+
	Spont				Data EXFOR12337.005	Jun 76	. 1 PT.	
Nu	Spont		LRL	Expt	Jour PR 101 1804	Mar 56	Crane+,LII − CRYST+FIS.COUNT.COINC.	
Nu	Spont		UK		Rept A− 8 21	Jan 57	.REVIEW CURVVE C AID INDUCED FDATA	
Nu	Pile		HAR	Expt	Rept AERE−R/M−167	Mar 58	Sanders. ZEPHYR REACTOR CORE	
Nu	Fast		LAS	Expt	Conf 58Geneva 15 331	Sep 58	Leachman.PPR665,VAL REL TO U235 GVN	
Nu	+6		LAS	Revw	Conf 58Geneva 15 344	Sep 58	Hemmendinger.PPR663,CURVE,MANY REFS	
Nu	3.6+6	1.5+7	CCP	Expt	Rept AEC−TR−4710	60	Kuzminov.NU PROMPT REL PU239 THR NF	+
Nu	3.6+6	1.5+7	FEI	Expt	Book NEJTRONFIZ 246	61	Kuz'Minov. 2ES,REL PU239 NU THERMAL	
Nu	Pile		LAS	Expt	Rept LAMS−2489	Apr 61	Barton.	+
	Pile				Data EXFOR12533.002	Jun 76	. 1 PT.	
Nu		1.5+7	ANL	Revw	Conf 61Vienna 1 29	Aug 61	Smith.PPR76,CURVE MANY REFS	
Nu	Spont		ALD	Expt	Jour JNAB 15 102	Oct 61	Moat+,REL CF252 SPONT FIS,SCINT TANK	+
Nu	Spont		REH	Theo	Rept IA− 757	Jul 62	Sieger+ CALC FRM CHAIN−Y,CFD OTH.TBL	
Nu	−		KUR	Expt	Jour NP 41 92	Feb 63	Apalin+	
Nu	Spont		FOA	Comp	Rept NP− 16440	Mar 63	ASPLUND − NILSSON. REVIEW. TABLE.	
Nu	Spont		LAS	Expt	Jour NP 48 433	Oct 63	Hopkins+,SCINT TANK,RELAT TO CF252	+
					Conf 61Vienna 1 149	Aug 61	.SUPERSEDED	
Nu	+5	+7	RLY	Revw	Conf 64Vienna 56	Dec 64	Kronberger. VAL TABLE OF ETA+NU+SIGS	
Nu	1.0+3	1.5+7	UK	Eval	Rept AWRE−O−91/64	Jan 65	Douglas+(ALD).UKNDL−DFN 201	+
	1.0−4	1.5+7			Data UKNDL−DFN 77B	Mar 73	19 PNTS	
	1.0−4	1.5+7			Data UKNDL−DFN 77B	Mar 73	ANGDIST OF FISS NEUT, 1 RNGS,LAB.	
Nu	Spont		HAR	Expt	Conf 65Salzburg 2 25	Mar 65	Colvin+PPR44.BORONPILE.RATIO/U − 235	+
					Prog AERE−PR/NP8 9	Feb 65	− +TBL.NU=2.127+ − 0.013.ABS.	
					Conf 58Geneva 16 121	Sep 58	− + PPR 52.SUPERSEDED.	
Nu	Spont		SAC	Expt	Prog EANDC(E)66U	Feb 66	Baron+ TBC	
Nu	1.0+5	1.6+6	HAR	Expt	Jour JNAB 20 191	Mar 66	Devroey+.NU PROMPT AT 3 ES REL U235	+
Nu	4.0+6	1.4+6	BRC	Expt	Conf 66Paris 2 57	Oct 66	Baron+PPR77,VALUE GIVEN,P(NU)	
Nu	1.0+3	1.5+7	LAS	Eval	Rept EANDC(US)−96	Feb 67	Divin.	
Nu	Thrsh	1.5+7	AI	Eval	Jour JNE 22 79	Feb 68	Fillmore.DATA TBL,GRAPH.LEAST SQ FIT	
Nu	Spont		AUA	Expt	Jour JNE 22 63	Feb 68	Boldeman.PROMPT NU+DISTBN,REL CF252	+
					Conf 73Kiev 4 114	May 73	− . DATA REVISED,TABLE	
	Spont				Data EXFOR30367.003	Jan 77	NU−BAR PROMPT,REPLACES EXF30047.002	
	Spont				Data EXFOR30047.002	Nov 70	NUBAR+ EMISSION PARAMETERS	
Nu	1.0+5	1.5+7	SAC	Eval	Rept EANDC(E)126AL	Mar 70	L'Heriteau+	
	Fiss				Prog EANDC(E)127U	Apr 70	RIBON	
Nu	Spont		AE	Comp	Conf 70Helsinki 2 93	Jun 70	Almen+57. COMPILATN AND NU−TEMP−PLOT	
Nu	+1	+7	CAD	Theo	Conf 70Helsinki 2 465	Jun 70	Barre+73. MICROSC CFD INTEGRAL DATA	
Nu	Maxwl	1.5+7	HAR	Revw	Conf 70Helsinki 2 195	Jun 70	Colvin.PPR99. REPORT ON DATA STATUS	
	−3	1.4+7		Eval	Conf 69Vienna 930	Jul 69	− .PPR55. RECOMMENDATION+REVIEW	
Nu	6.0+5	5.0+6	SCU	Expt	Conf 70Helsinki 2 157	Jun 70	Savin+40. NU(E) GRAPH, RELATIV CF252	+
	1.0+6	4.0+6			Data EXFOR40058.002	Mar 71	PROMPT NU−BAR AT 24 ENERGIES	
Nu	Spont		FEI	Expt	Jour AE 30 250	Mar 71	Prokhorova+ COINC,REL CF252,NU GIVEN	
					Jour SJA 30 307	Oct 71	*ENGL OF AE 30 250	

94 Plutonium 240

Quantity	Energy (ev) Min	Max	Lab	Type	Documentation Ref Vol Page	Date	Author, Comments	Data
Nu	1.1+6	3.9+6	KUR	Expt	Prog YFI-10 32	May 71	Savin+ TOF,LIQUID SCINT,NU VS EN,TBL	
					Rept INDC(CCP)-15	Dec 71	*P34,ENG OF YFI-10	
					Jour PTE 14 6 27	Dec 69	*TECHNIQUE DESCRIBD	
					Jour IET 14 1388	Dec 69	*ENG OF PTE 14 6 27	
Nu		1.5+7	ANL	Eval	Jour NSE 44 345	Jun 71	Davey. PROMPT NEUTS PER FISSION	
					Conf 70Helsinki 2 119	Jun 70	.SUPERSEDED.(P/112)	
Nu	1.0+3	1.5+7	LRL	Expt	Prog NCSAC-42 130	Nov 71	Bowman+. TO BE DONE	
Nu	2.5-2		IAE	Revw	Rept IAEA-143 897	Apr 72	Lemmel.EVALUATIONS+RECENT EXPTS,TBL	
Nu	1.0-3	1.5+7	SOR	Eval	Rept IA- 1243	May 72	Caner+ EVALUATION FOR KEDAK-3	
	1.0-3	1.5+7			Data KEDAK-3	Oct 75	2 DATA SETS (KFK FILE)	
Nu	+0		IAE	Eval	Jour REA 10 637	Dec 72	Manero+ SURVEY,TBLS+GRPHS,RECOMM VAL	
	Spont				Jour REA 10 637	Dec 72	- + EXTENSIVE SURVEY,TBL,AVG VAL	
	0.0+0	1.5+7	UK	Eval	Data UKNDL-DFN 402B	Mar 73	ANGDIST OF FISS NEUT, 1 RNGS,LAB.	+
	0.0+0	1.5+7			Data UKNDL-DFN 402B	Mar 73	95 PNTS	
Nu	Spont		FOA	Expt	Jour NSE 15 213	Feb 63	Conde+,LIQ SC,NU=2.15+-.03 REL CF252	+
					Conf 73Kiev 4 130	May 73	- . NO VALUE.CFD NUBAR(E)PU-239	
	Spont				Data EXFOR20073.003	Sep 71	1PNT.PROMPT.	
Nu	Spont		DUB	Comp	Jour YF 18 724	Oct 73	Dakovsky+NUBAR VS FISNUCLEUS,TBL+GRP	
				Eval	Rept JINR-P15-7119	Jun 73	Dakowski+ NUBAR+P(NU)-DISTR,TBL,GRPH	
				Comp	Jour SNP 18 371	Apr 74	. ENGLISH OF YF 18, 724.	
Nu	1.5+6	1.5+7	BRC	Expt	Rept CEA-R-4626	74	Fremaut+ VDG TANDEM	+
					Conf 73Kiev 3 153	May 73	Frehaut+ NUBAR(E) TBL,CFD OTHS GRAPH	
					Conf 73Kiev 3 165	May 73	- + LIQ SCIN BKD ANALYSIS.	
	1.9+6	1.5+7			Data EXFOR20488.003	Mar 76	22PTS.PROMPT.	
Nu	2.5-2		IKE	Eval	Rept IKE-6-80	Apr 74	Mattes+ ENDF/B,UKNDL,KEDAK CFD	
Nu	0.0+0	6.0+6	FEI	Expt	Rept YK- 15 3	Aug 74	Vorob'Eva+ NUBAR(NEUT-E),GRAPH,TBL	
Nu	Spont		SAC	Expt	Prog NEANDC(E)161U	Aug 74	Girard+	
Nu	Spont		KFK	Expt	Prog KFK-1980 2 44	Oct 74	Boehnel. NEUTRON COINC EXPTS	
Nu	4.1+6	9.5+6	BRC	Expt	Jour JPRL 36 79	Apr 75	Lachkar+ (D,PF).NUBAR VS EXC-E,GRAPH	
Nu	Spont		HED	Eval	Abst ANS 22 673	Nov 75	Johnson. TBL,GRPH.NU FROM SPON FISS	
Nu	Maxwl		IFB	Eval	Rept INDC(CCP)-76	Jan 76	Antsipov+ EVAL NUBAR REL CF252 GIVEN	
Nu	0.0+0	1.5+7	BRC	Eval	Rept CEA-R-4791	Oct 76	Bois+ NUBAR VS EN,CALC CFD EXP,TABLES	
Delayd Neuts	Fiss		LAS	Expt	Jour PR 107 1044	Aug 57	Keepin+,0.0088+-0.0006 N/FISS 6GRPS	
					Jour JNE 6 1	Dec 57	- +. SAME DATA AS PR(8/57)	
					Conf 55Geneva 4 162	Aug 55	- +.P/831. PRELIMINARY.	
Delayd Neuts	None		LAS	Theo	Jour JNE 7 13	Aug 58	Keepin.THEOR DEL NEUT PRECURSRS,YLDS	
					Jour AE 4 250	Mar 58	.SEE ALSO	
					Jour SJA 4 339	58	.SEE ALSO	
Delayd Neuts	Maxwl		ANL	Expt	Conf 61Vienna 1 125	Aug 61	Butler+.P36,6 GROUPS,YIELD+PERIODS	
Delayd Neuts	6.3+6		LAS	Expt	Conf 61Vienna 1 149	Aug 61	Diven+.PPR56,TABLE REL TO CF252	
Delayd Neuts	2.0+6		LAS	Revw	Jour NUC 20 8 150	Aug 62	Keepin+	
Delayd Neuts		+7	HFA	Revw	Jour 67Vienna 23	Apr 67	Yiftah+ TBL OF YLD+HL,REACTR DYNAMIC	
Delayd Neuts	Fiss		MNZ	Theo	Jour AF 36 453	Nov 67	Patzelt+.FROM DERIVED N-EMISS PROB.	
Delayd Neuts	1.5+7		LAS	Expt	Conf 69Vienna 647	Jul 69	East+PPR109. YLD TABLE,SAFEGUARD	
Delayd Neuts	6.6+5	3.1+6	HAR	Eval	Rept AERE-R-6993	Feb 72	TOMLINSON TOTAL+GROUP YLDS TBL	
Delayd Neuts	2.5-2		AI	Eval	Prog AI-AEC-13025	May 72	Springer+ VALUE=0.0092+-0.0010	
Delayd Neuts	1.0+5	1.5+7	IAE	Eval	Jour REA 10 637	Dec 72	Manero+ SURVEY,AVERAGE YLD,TBL+GRPHS	
Delayd Neuts	Fiss		SOR	Revw	Conf IAEA-169 2 33	74	Amiel.TOTAL+GROUP YIELDS,TABLES	
Delayd Neuts	2.0+6	1.5+7	ANL	Eval	Rept ANL-NDM-5	Apr 74	COX. REL YLD, HL, GRPH	
Delayd Neuts	2.1+6	1.5+7	AI	Eval	Jour NSE 56 37	Jan 75	Tuttle.TBL.GRPH.RVW MEAS.CFD REC VAL	
Spect Fiss n	Spont		CCP	Theo	Jour AE 5 649	Dec 58	Kovalev+ THEORY COMPARED WITH EXPT	
					Jour JNEA 11 166	Feb 60	TRANSLATN.*	
					Jour SJA 5 1588	58	TRANSLATN.*	
Spect Fiss n	Spont		RIC	Expt	Jour NP 23 116	Feb 61	Bonner.MOD SPH SP. T=1.189+-0.030MEV	
Spect Fiss n	Spont		FOA	Expt	Conf 62Harwell 2 351	Dec 62	Brunfelter+ PLAST SCIN,GRPH CFD MAXW	
Spect Fiss n	1.0+3	1.5+7	UK	Eval	Rept AWRE-O-91/64	Jan 65	Douglas+(ALD).UKNDL-DFN 201	+
	1.0-4	1.5+7			Data UKNDL-DFN 77B	Mar 73	5 RANGES	
Spect Fiss n	Spont		HAR	Eval	Jour NP 71 228	Sep 65	Barnard+ CORRELATED WITH NU BAR	
Spect Fiss n	Spont		ALD	ExTh	Jour JNE 20 549	Jun 66	Fieldhouse+ REVISED HAR PU240 SOUR35	
				Theo	Conf 62Harwell 2 565	Dec 62	- + 24PERCNT 240,GRPH N-SPEC	
Spect Fiss n	Spont		IAE	Revw	Jour REA 7 4 3	Dec 69	Hanna+ N-SPECTRUM IN NU-BAR EXPTS	
Spect Fiss n	Spont		ANL	Revw	Conf 71Vienna 3	Aug 71	Smith.MEAN-E OF NS,ALSO REL U235,TBL	
Spect Fiss n	Maxwl		SOR	Eval	Rept IA- 1243	May 72	Caner+ EVALUATION FOR KEDAK-3	
	1.0-3	1.5+7			Data KEDAK-3	Oct 75	2 DATA SETS (KFK FILE)	
Spect Fiss n	0.0+0	1.5+7	UK	Eval	Data UKNDL-DFN 402B	Mar 73	5 RANGES	+
Spect Fiss n	Spont		CCP	Expt	Jour AE 36 282	Apr 74	Aleksandrova+ NEUT-SPEC OF FISS,GRPH	
					Jour SJA 36 355	Oct 74	. ENGLISH OF AE 36 282	
Spect Fiss γ	Maxwl	2.0+3	KFK	Expt	Prog EANDC(E)157U 1	Mar 73	Ottmar+ FR2 REAC.+SC FILT FOR 2KEV	

94 Plutonium 240

Quantity	Energy (ev) Min	Max	Lab	Type	Documentation Ref Vol Page	Date	Author, Comments	Data
Fiss Prod γ	–		WIN	Theo Jour	JNE 25 513	Oct 71	James.MEAN EN OF DELAYD GAMS,BETAS.	
Fiss Prod β	Maxwl		TRM	Expt Jour	JNE 24 171	Jul 70	Iyer+ BETA ACT.SHORT TIME AFTER FISS	
Fiss Yield	2.0+5	3.0+6	CCP	Jour	AE 10 620	Jun 61	ANISOTROPY OF FISS FRAGM	
				Jour	SJA 10 613	Mar 62	TRANSLATN.*	
Fiss Yield	Spont		ALD	Expt Jour	JIN 24 1485	62	Laider+ TABLE YIELD MASS=89 - 147	
Fiss Yield	Spont		LAS	Expt Jour	PR 126 1508	May 62	Nobles. YIELD OF LONG RANGE FFRGM	
Fiss Yield	6.5+5	8.0+6	LAS	Expt Jour	PR/B 137 809	Feb 65	Simmons+RELATIVE ANG DIST FISS FRAG	
Fiss Yield	–		TRM	Theo Conf	65Calcutta 20	Feb 65	. FISS AS MARKOV PROCESS,MASS DIST	
Fiss Yield	None		BAS	Theo Jour	PL/B 34 264	Mar 71	Pauli+ FRAG MASS RATIO AS STRUTINSKY	
	Spont			Abst	HPA 43 741	Dec 70	Brack+ ASYM FISS FRAGMENTS	
Fiss Yield	Spont		COL	Expt Jour	PR/C 4 1391	Oct 71	Toraskar+.FRAG MASS+KE CFD PU239	
Fiss Yield	Spont		CLA	Theo Jour	NP/A 184 417	Apr 72	Tsang+.ASSYM FROM FERMIGAS+WKB CALC.	
Fiss Yield	Spont		MRY	Theo Jour	PL/B 38 495	Apr 72	Hooshyar+ SPON AND ISOMERIC YIELDS	
Fiss Yield	Spont		GEL	Expt Prog	EANDC(E)157U I	Mar 73	Deruytter+ MASS DISTR CFD PU239 THR	
Fiss Yield	None		COP	Theo Jour	NP/A 210 282	Aug 73	Jensen+ MASS DISTN VS EXCITATION E.	
Fiss Yield	Fast		AUA	Theo Conf	IAEA - 169 2 163	74	Musgrove+ GAUSS FIT MASS YLDS,GRAPH	
Fiss Yield	Fast		FAR	Expt Conf	IAEA - 169 3 59	74	Robin+ ND148,STABL ND - ISOT/ND148,TBL	
Fiss Yield	Pile		HAR	Eval Rept	AERE - R - 7680	Mar 74	Crouch. FRACTIONAL INDEPENDANT YLD.	
Fiss Yield	Spont		MUU	Expt Jour	NP/A 221 414	Mar 74	Weber+U238(A,2N) - .ISOM FISS. M YIELD	
Fiss Yield	Fast		ITU	Expt Prog	NEANDC(E)162U	Feb 75	Cottone+ SB - 125,XE,CS,ND VOL.5.P.42.	
Fiss Yield	Fast		DOU	Expt Prog	UKNDC(75)P71	Jul 75	Davies+IRRAD.MASS SPEC MEAS DFR PFR	
Fiss Yield	Fast		HAR	Eval Rept	AERE - R - 8152	Jan 76	Crouch. ADJUSTED FISSION YIELD,TABLE	
				Rept	AERE - R - 7785	Feb 75	- .CHAIN+INDEPENDENT YLDS TBL	
				Theo Rept	AERE - R - 6056	Mar 69	- .CALC FRACT INDEPND YLDS,TBLS	
Fiss Yield	7.0+5	5.0+6	FEI	Expt Jour	YF 23 269	Feb 76	Djachenko+.GRAPH,FRAG DISTR	
				Jour	SNP 23 141	Feb 76	. ENGL OF YF 23 269	
Fiss Yield	2.0+6	1.4+7	AUA	Theo Rept	AAEC/E - 386	Mar 76	Cook+ 3 - GAUSS FIT,MASS - YLDS AT 2ES	
	Maxwl			Rept	AAEC/E - 386	Mar 76	- + 3 - GAUSS FIT,TBL OF MASS - YIELD	
Fiss Yield	Spont		AUA	Theo Jour	AUJ 29 125	Jun 76	Cook+ GAUSSFIT.FOR E - DEPEND OF PARAM	
				Rept	AAEC/E - 386	Mar 76	- + 3 - GAUSS FIT,PARAMS GIVEN	
Fiss Yield	Spont		PAH	ExTh Conf	76Lowell 725	Jul 76	Hooshyar+STATMDL APLD TO EXPT.DATA	
				Theo Jour	PL/B 55 144	Feb 75	- + TH VALUES CFD TO EXPTAL	
Fiss Yield	2.0+6	1.4+7	LAS	Eval Abst	ANS 24 462	Nov 76	Madland+PAIR EFFECT ON FISS PROD YLD	
	5.0+5	1.4+7		Rept	LA - 6430	Jul 76	- +PAIR EFFECT ON INDEP YLD.TBL	
Fiss Yield	Spont		TRM	Theo Rept	INIS - MF - 3797	77	Chakraborthy+ O - D - MOD.ISOTOP YLD,FIG	
Frag Spectra	Spont		CCP	Expt Conf	55Moscow 226	Jul 55	Goldin+.ALFA SPECTRUM.EXPT FROM 1953	
				Rept	AEC - TR - 2435	56	. P 167.ENGL TRANSL OF 55MOSCOW 226	
Frag Spectra	Maxwl		ANL	Conf	58Geneva 15 392	Sep 58	Smith+.PPR690,ENERGY OF FRAGMENTS	
Frag Spectra	6.0+2	2.0+7	CRC	Expt Jour	CJP 37 1418	Dec 59	Baerg+. FRAG ANG DIST ANISOTROPIC	
Frag Spectra	Spont		CCP	Theo Jour	ZET 38 955	Mar 60	Geilikman. EXCIT E VS FRAG RATIO,CRV	
				Jour	JET 11 688	Sep 60	TRANSLATN.*	
				Jour	AE 6 298	Mar 59	SEE ALSO *= SJA 6 184 N/60	
Frag Spectra	Spont		ITE	Expt Rept	ITE -	Oct 63	Perfilov+TERNARY FISS.ALPHA SPEC,GRP	
Frag Spectra	Spont		TRM	Revw Rept	AEET - 235	65	Methasiri.ALF E - SPEC,CFD PU,U	
Frag Spectra	3.0+5	1.6+6	ORL	ExTh Conf	65Salzburg 63	Mar 65	Lamphere.ANISTRPY OF FRGS,TH CFD XPT	
				Expt Rept	ORNL - P - 1082	64	.FISS CHAMB,ANG ANISOTROPY,CRVS	
Frag Spectra	1.8+5	1.5+6	FEI	Expt Jour	YF 12 260	Aug 70	Androsenko+ ANGANISOTROPY TABLE+GRPH	
				Jour	SNP 12 142	Feb 71	TRANSLATN.*	
	Thrsh	+6		Jour	AHP 29 357	Aug 70	Androsenko+ ANGDIST CFD 2 - HUMPD - BARR	
	2.0+5	2.0+6		ExTh Conf	69Vienna 419	Jul 69	- +PPR134. XPTL ANGDIST + TH	
Frag Spectra	Spont		COL	Expt Jour	PR/C 4 1391	Oct 71	Toraskar+.FRAG MASS+KE CFD PU239	
Frag Spectra	Spont		MRY	Theo Jour	PL/B 38 495	Apr 72	Hooshyar+ KINETIC - E FN OF HEAVY MASS	
Frag Spectra	Spont		GEL	Expt Conf	73Rochestr 2 51	Aug 73	Deruytter+ FRAG KIN - E+AVG,TBL,GRAPH	
Frag Spectra	Spont		MUU	Revw Conf	73Rochestr 2 61	Aug 73	Specht.AVG KIN - E VS EXCIT - E CFD,GRPH	
Frag Spectra	Spont		MUU	Expt Jour	NP/A 221 414	Mar 74	Weber+U238(A,2N) - .ISOM FISS KE VS M	
Frag Spectra	1.3+6		FEI	Expt Jour	YF 19 5 954	May 74	Vorobyeva+	+
	7.0+5	3.5+6		Conf	73Kiev 3 270	May 73	Vorob'Yeva+	
	1.3+6			Data	EXFOR40281.006	May 75	.AVER KIN - E OF FF AT 1.3MEV N - E GVN	
	1.3+6			Data	EXFOR40284.004	May 75	.AVER KIN - E OF FF GVN	
Frag Spectra	Spont		PAH	Theo Jour	PL/B 55 144	Feb 75	Hooshyar+ TH VALUES CFD TO EXPTAL	
Frag Spectra	4.1+6	9.5+6	BRC	Expt Jour	JPRL 36 79	Apr 75	Lachkar+ (D,PF).AVG FRGM - E VS EXC - E	
Frag Spectra	3.0+3	1.0+6	BRC	Eval Conf	75Kiev 1 252	May 75	Thomet. W(0)/W(90),EVAL CURV CFD XPT	
Frag Spectra	7.0+5	5.0+6	FEI	Expt Jour	YF 23 269	Feb 76	Djachenko+.GRAPH,KE OF FRAGS	
				Jour	SNP 23 141	Feb 76	. ENGL OF YF 23 269	
Frag Spectra			FTI	Theo Jour	YF 23 1175	Jun 76	Geilikman+ KE FRG - MASS CALC.	
				Jour	SNP 23 624	Jun 76	. ENGL OF YF 23 1175	
Frag Spectra	Spont		RI	Expt Rept	YK - 24 19	77	Basova+ SPEC OF AVG FRAGM - E,GRAPH	
Frag Charge	Fast		HAR	Theo Rept	AERE - R - 6056	Mar 69	Crouch.CALC CHARGE DISPERSION,ZP,TBL	

94 Plutonium 240

Quantity	Energy (ev) Min	Max	Lab	Type	Documentation Ref Vol Page	Date	Author, Comments	Data
Frag Charge	Spont		LRL	Comp Rept	UCRL – 51640	Jul 74	Nethaway. TBL.	
Frag Charge	1.5+7		LRL	Comp Rept	UCRL – 51640	Jul 74	Nethaway. TBL.	
Frag Charge	Spont		TRM	Theo Rept	INIS – MF – 3797	77	Chakraborthy+ O – D – MOD.ZP – Z(UCD),GRPH	
Reson Params	1.1+0		COL	Expt Rept	CUD – 92	May 51	Havens.	+
	1.1+0			Data	EXFOR12517.	Jun 76	. 1 RES, WT,PCS,WT**2/PCS	
Reson Params	1.1+0		CCP	Expt Conf	55Moscow 294	Jul 55	Abov. BENT QUARTZ CRYSTAL. TABLE	+
				Rept	AEC – TR – 2435	56	. PAGE 209.ENGL OF 55MOSCOW 294	
Reson Params	1.1+0		CCP	Rept	AEC – TR – 2435PT1	56	.USSR PAGE 212	
Reson Params	1.1+0		HAR	Expt Rept	NRDC – 86	Feb 56	Raffle+ RES EN AND TOTAL – W GIVEN	+
				Rept	NRDC – 84 9	Dec 55	Cocking+ WT AND ENERGY.	
				Conf	55Geneva 4 187	Aug 55	Raffle+.RESON – E+SIGMA0+TOT – W,PPR422	
Reson Params	1.1+0		BNL	Expt Priv	ZIMMERMAN	Oct 56	Zimmerman.	+
	1.1+0			Data	EXFOR11787.	Jun 76	. 1 RES, WT,WN,WT**2/PCS	
Reson Params	1.0+0	1.2+2	MTR	Expt Prog	IDO – 16373 39	Jul 57	Simpson.WN,WN0.TBL.11 RES ES	+
	1.1+0	1.2+2		Data	EXFOR12526.003	Jun 76	. 11 RES, E0,WN,WN0	
Reson Params	1.1+0	3.8+1	HAR	Expt Jour	JNE 6 303	May 58	Egelstaff+,FC TRANSMISSION,WT+WN TBL	+
	2.0+1			Rept	AERE – NP/R – 2076	Jan 57	- .WN 20PC LESS THAN ANL	
Reson Params	1.1+0		CRC	Eval Conf	58Geneva 16 70	Sep 58	Westcott+.PPR202, VAL CFD MANY REFS	
				Rept	AERE – NP/R – 2076	Jan 57	- .TO FIT CRC633 THR ABS	
Reson Params	1.1+0		HAN	Expt Jour	NSE 5 32	Jan 59	Leonard.	+
				Conf	55Geneva 4 193	Aug 55	- +.TABLE,TOTAL WIDTH, PPR589	
	1.1+0			Data	EXFOR12536.	Jun 76	. 1 RES, E0,WT,WG,PCS	
Reson Params	1.1+0	3.8+1	ANL	Expt Jour	PR 114 505	Apr 59	Cote+ TOF TRNS WN WG WT FIRST 3 RES	+
				Jour	PRL 2 136	Feb 59	.SUPERSEDED	
				Conf	58Geneva 16 77	Sep 58	.SUPERSEDED	
	2.0+1	3.8+1		Rept	AERE – NP/R – 2076	Jul 56	Bollinger.WT 2RES AS HEX 0456	
	1.1+1	3.8+1		Data	EXFOR12539.	Jun 76	. 3 RES, E0,WT,WN,WG,PCS	
Reson Params	1.0-2	1.0+1	HAR	Expt Jour	JNEA 11 14	Nov 59	Pattenden+ 1.0575EV,WG29.6 WN2.47MV	+
				Jour	JNE 2 187	Mar 56	- + EARLY XPT SUPERSEDED.	
Reson Params	1.0+0	2.0+1	HAN	Expt Prog	HW – 67219 4	Oct 60	Leonard+	
Reson Params	1.1+0	1.0+2	UK	Eval Rept	AEEW – R – 351	Feb 64	Barrington+(WIN).UKNDL LOW EN REVISN	
Reson Params	1.1+0	1.2+2	CJD	Comp Rept	INDSWG – 101 25	65	. TBL 11 RES FROM VARIOUS SOURCES	
Reson Params	2.0+1	1.0+3	LAS	Expt Conf	66Wash. 2 903	Mar 66	Byers+	+
	2.0+1	1.0+3		Data	EXFOR12552.	Jun 76	. 1RES,E0,WT,WN,WG, 52 RES,E0	
Reson Params		1.0+6	AUA	Theo Jour	AUJ 20 477	Oct 67	Cook. TBL OF AVG LVL SPACING D,L=0,1	
Reson Params	2.0+1	2.9+2	GEL	Expt Conf	68Wash. 1 513	Mar 68	CAO+.AERA ANAL OF SCAT YLD WN	+
	2.0+1	2.9+2		Data	EXFOR20142.	Mar 73	28PTS.SCT.AREA,WN.	
Reson Params	2.0+1	5.7+2	GEL	Expt Jour	JNE 22 299	May 68	Kolar+.AREA ANAL E WN STATPROPERTIES	+
	3.8+1	6.7+2		Conf	NEANDC(E) – 163U	Jan 75	Weigmann+REANALYSIS OF PART OF JNE22	
	2.0+1	5.7+3		Conf	68Wash. 1 519	Mar 68	Kolar+ FINAL RESULTS.TBL.	
	2.0+1	5.0+3		Conf	66Paris 2 135	Oct 66	Boeckhoff+158E0.SHAPE ANAL.E 800EVUP	
	2.0+1	5.1+3		Data	EXFOR20139.	Mar 73	. 213PTS.E0,WN,WN0,WT. 66PARIS.	
	2.0+1	5.7+3		Data	EXFOR20117.	Jul 72	527PTS.E0,WN,WN0.	
Reson Params	7.5+2	3.4+3	GEL	Expt Jour	NP/A 112 603	May 68	Migneco+ WF FROM 1 LVL AREA ANALYSIS	+
	2.0+2	3.3+2		Conf	68Wash. § D8	Mar 68	- +THEOBALD.AERA ANAL WF INTERP	
	7.5+2	3.4+3		Data	EXFOR20005.	Nov 70	34PTS.WF,G*WN*WF/WT.	
Reson Params	+5	+6	CCP	Theo Jour	YF 7 1228	Jun 68	Vorotnikov.D,EXPT CFD DEGEN – FERM – GAS	
				Jour	SNP 7 732	Dec 68	TRANSLATN.*	
Reson Params	-		CCP	Theo Jour	ZEP 9 510	May 69	Ermagambetov+WF ANAL OF OTHER EXPT	
				Jour	JEL 9 9 309	May 69	TRANSLATN.*	
Reson Params	+0	+1	COP	Revw Conf	69Vienna 155	Jul 69	Strutinsky+PPR203.INTERMED WF STRUCT	
Reson Params	-		HAR	Revw Conf	69Vienna 249	Jul 69	Lynn. PARS IN STRUTNSKY TH+EXPTS,TBL	
	7.5+2	2.1+3		Rept	AERE – R – 5891	Sep 68	- . TBL STRONG FISS RESPARS	
Reson Params	+2	+6	FEI	Theo Jour	YF 10 542	Sep 69	Gai+ FISSN WIDTH TBL,DISTR GRAPH	
	None			Rept	FEI – 158	Feb 69	GAJ+ FISSN WIDTH,2HUMPED – BARR – CALCUL	
	+2	+6		Jour	SNP 10 311	Mar 70	. ENGL OF YF 10 542	
Reson Params	2.0+1	1.0+6	TRM	Theo Conf	69Roorke 2 198	Dec 69	Sood+ AVG LEVL SPACING D,2 – HUMPED – TH	
	2.0+1	2.0+2		Jour	PL/B 30 523	Dec 69	- + CORREL ANAL,D CLASS II VAL GV	
Reson Params	1.4+3	2.0+3	SAC	Eval Conf	70Helsinki 1 571	Jun 70	Ribon.108. EVALUATION PROBLEMS,TABLE	
		3.0+2		Rept	EANDC(E)126AL	Mar 70	- +L'HERITEAU.SAME REF CEA – N1273	
Reson Params	1.1+0		TRM	Expt Conf	70Helsinki 1 553	Jun 70	Ramakrishna+,TRANSM,WT+WN+SIGMA MAX	+
	1.0+0			Data	EXFOR30039.	Mar 71	SIGMA(0),TOTWIDTH,N – WIDTH	
Reson Params	None		DUB	Theo Jour	YF 13 240	Feb 71	Malecki+G – WID,THEO CFD EXPT.TBL,GRPH	
				Jour	SNP 13 133	Aug 71	- + ENGL OF YF 13 240.	
Reson Params	6.2-1	5.0+4	SRL	Theo Conf	71Knoxvill 714	Mar 71	Mccrosson. STAT CALCULATN AVG PARAMS	
Reson Params	1.0+2	1.0+4	CCP	Theo Jour	AE 31 18	Jul 71	Vorotnikov.REDUCD N – WID(NEUT – E),GRPH	
				Jour	SJA 31 706	Feb 72	* ENGL OF AE 31 18 7/71	

94 Plutonium 240

Quantity	Energy (ev) Min	Max	Lab	Type	Documentation Ref Vol Page	Author, Comments Date	Data
Reson Params	1.0+0	+3	CCP Revw	Jour	AE 31 595	Dec 71 Sukhoruchkin.TOT+N+G-WIDS CFD,TABLE	
				Jour	SJA 31 1380	Jun 72 *ENGL OF AE 31 595	
Reson Params	1.1+0	5.7+3	SOR Eval	Rept	IA- 1243	May 72 Caner+ ALL WIDTHS+E,265 RES,D,TABLES	
Reson Params		1.0+2	HAR Expt	Prog	AERE-PR/NP19	Sep 72 Moxon+ MEAN WG APPROX 30MILLIVOLTS	+
	0.0+0	1.0+0		Prog	AERE-PR/NP12	Aug 67 Asghar+ LINAC FURTHER DATA OBTAINED	
	2.0+1	9.5+2		Conf	66Paris 2 145	Oct 66 - + PPR31.WN+WG FOR 17RES,LINAC	
Reson Params	2.0+1	5.0+2	RPI Expt	Jour	NSE 49 153	Oct 72 Hockenbury+. WN WG FOR 35 RESONANCES	+
				Conf	72Budapest 224	Aug 72 - + GAM-WID,N-WID,35RES,TBL	
				Conf	71Knoxvill 721	Mar 71 .SUPERSEDED.	
	2.0+1	2.0+3		Data	EXFOR10127.	Feb 76 109PTS.WN,WG,TOT WIDTHS.	
Reson Params	3.8+1	6.7+2	GEL Expt	Jour	JNE 26 643	Dec 72 Weigmann+N,G,TOT RE-ANAL OF 1968DATA	+
	3.8+1	8.2+2		Jour	JNE 22 317	May 68 - + 46 RES FROM SIGT+NG AREAS	
				Conf	68Wash. 1 533	Mar 68 - + ENERGIES+G-WIDTHS	
	3.8+1	6.7+2		Data	EXFOR20133.	Mar 73 94PTS.WG,AVG WG,WN,WG*WN/WT.	
	3.8+1	8.2+2		Data	EXFOR20130.	Mar 73 50PTS.WF,WG,AVG WG,WN.	
Reson Params	4.0-1	2.5+4	WIN Eval	Prog	EANDC(UK) 151	Aug 73 James+ GENEX EVAL WG=26.9 MILLIVOLT	
Reson Params	1.0+0	5.7+3	GEL Eval	Conf	NEANDC(E)-163U	Jan 75 Weigmann+TABLE OF RECOMMENDED VALUES	
Reson Params	None		GEL Eval	Conf	NEANDC(E)162 3	Feb 75 Poortmans+SPEC.MEET.SACLAY MAY 74	
Reson Params	2.5-2		COL Expt	Conf	75Wash. 335	Mar 75 Felvinci+MOD ERICSON CALC CFD EXPT.	
Reson Params	6.1+2	2.9+3	ORL Expt	Jour	PR/C 12 1850	Dec 75 Auchampaugh+ SUBTR FISS,TBL WF,WNO	+
				Conf	75Wash. 560	Mar 75 - +SUBTR FISS.TBL WF,WNO,EO	
	6.1+2	2.9+3		Data	EXFOR10564.002	Apr 76 82PTS NF/WID.	
Reson Params	2.0+6	9.0+6	BOL Theo	Conf	IAEA-190 2 453	76 Benzi. N/G-WID VS E,SEMIEMPIR,TBL+GR	
Reson Params	2.5-2	1.0+3	IFB Eval	Rept	INDC(CCP)-76	Jan 76 Antsipov+ AVG LVL-SPAC,G-,F-WID GIVN	
Reson Params	1.0+2	2.4+4	BNL Expt	Prog	ERDA-NDC-3 51	May 76 Block+WG DET REL TO AU197 WID.NDG	
Reson Params	1.1+0	2.0+1	HAN Expt	Abst	BAP 1 248	Jun 56 Leonard+	+
	1.1+0	2.0+1		Data	EXFOR12525.003	Jun 76 . 2 RES, NF/PCS	
Reson Params	Maxwl		KUK Theo	Conf	76Ahmedabd 2 1	Dec 76 Sharma+AVG S-WAVE REDUCED N-WID ANAL	
Strnth Fnctn	-		HAR Expt	Prog	AERE-PR/NP11	Apr 67 Asghar+ S0 =0.93PM0.14 *10-4 TBC	+
Strnth Fnctn	2.6+6	4.1+6	AI Theo	Rept	NAA-SR-M-1253	Oct 67 Gigas.OPTMDL CALC AVG S0,S1,S2	
Strnth Fnctn	2.0+1	1.5+3	GEL Expt	Jour	JNE 22 299	May 68 Kolar+ S0=1.05+-.16 FROM RESOLVD RES	+
				Conf	68Wash. 1 519	Mar 68 - + FINAL VALUE GIVEN.	
	2.0+1	1.5+3		Data	EXFOR20117.007	Jul 72 1PNT.L=0.	
Strnth Fnctn	1.1+0	5.7+3	SOR Eval	Rept	IA- 1243	May 72 Caner+ S+P-WAVE STRENGTH FUNCTS,TBL	
Strnth Fnctn	2.0+1	5.0+2	RPI Expt	Jour	NSE 49 153	Oct 72 Hockenbury+. S0 AND S1 GIVEN	+
				Conf	72Budapest 224	Aug 72 .SUPERSEDED.	
	2.0+1	2.0+3		Data	EXFOR10127.006	Feb 76 2PTS	
Strnth Fnctn	None		AUA Eval	Rept	AAEC/E-277	Mar 73 Musgrove.TBLS EXPTL DATA+BEST VALUES	
Strnth Fnctn	6.0+3	3.0+4	GEL Eval	Conf	NEANDC(E)-163U	Jan 75 Weigmann+S1=2.2+-0.2 FROM UNRESOLVED	
	1.0+0	5.7+3		Conf	NEANDC(E)-163U	Jan 75 - +S0=1.04+-0.14 FROM RES PARS	
Strnth Fnctn	1.0+3	1.4+5	IFB Eval	Rept	INDC(CCP)-77	Jan 76 Antsipov+ S1 GIVN,BY FIT OF CALC SIG	
Strnth Fnctn	1.1+0	9.7+1	MTR Expt	Abst	BAP 2 219	Apr 57 Simpson+ FAST CHOPR 2.3+-0.7	+
	0.0+0	1.2+2		Data	EXFOR12526.	Jun 76 . 2 PTS, S0,D	
Lvl Density	-		COP Theo	Jour	NP 6 62	Mar 58 Ericson. LVL DENSITY FORM CFD EXP	
Lvl Density	+6		MIL Theo	Jour	EN 15 1 54	Jan 68 Facchini+ LDL PARS FROM LOW EN RES	
Lvl Density	-3	+0	IFU Theo	Jour	UFZ 13 700	Apr 68 Pisanko+ LEVEL SPACING CALC,TBL	
				Jour	UPJ 13 498	Oct 68 TRANSLATN.*	
Lvl Density	0.0+0	1.5+3	GEL Expt	Jour	JNE 22 299	May 68 Kolar+ FROM RESOLVED RESONANCES.	+
		1.5+3		Data	EXFOR20117.008	Jul 72 1PNT.SP.CUT(0).	
Lvl Density		1.8+2	KUR Theo	Jour	YF 9 303	Feb 69 Vorotnikov.LVL DEN(EXCIT-E),TBL GRPH	
				Jour	SNP 9 179	Aug 69 TRANSLATN.*	
Lvl Density		6.0+7	ROC Theo	Jour	NP/A 187 225	Jun 72 Williams+ A,COMBIN+STATIST+SHELLCORR	
Lvl Density	None		MUN Theo	Jour	NP/A 217 269	Dec 73 Dilg+ A,DELTA. BACK SHIFTED FERMIGAS	
Lvl Density	None		COP Theo	Jour	NP/A 222 493	Apr 74 Dossing+COLL ROTAT.SPAC. ACCUR ESTIM	
Lvl Density	None		ROC Theo	Jour	NP/A 223 589	May 74 Huizenga+ EXP CFD MICROSC TH AX SYMM	
Lvl Density	1.0+0	5.7+3	GEL Eval	Conf	NEANDC(E)-163U	Jan 75 Weigmann+SPACING IN INTERMD STRUCT	
Lvl Density	0.0+0	3.0+2	SAC ExTh	Jour	NP/A 242 45	Apr 75 Jain+ SPACING CORRELATIONS	
Lvl Density	+6		DUB Theo	Rept	JINR-E4-9236	Nov 75 Komov+ AVG LVL-SPAC,SEMIMICRO CFD XP	
Lvl Density	1.0+3	1.4+5	IFB Expt	Rept	INDC(CCP)-77	Jan 76 Antsipov+ CALC FROM AVG LVL-SPACING	
(γ,n)	7.0+6	1.6+7	DUB Expt	Rept	JINR-E15-7362	Jul 73 Gangrsky+ SPON FISS ISOMER,TBL,GRAPH	
	1.0+7	1.5+7	ExTh	Rept	JINR-P15-6145	Jan 72 - + EXCIT.FU. SPO.FISS PU239	
Photo-Fissn	6.0+6	2.0+7	CRC Expt	Jour	CJP 37 1418	Dec 59 Baerg+. FRAG ANG DIST ANISOTROPIC	
Photo-Fissn	5.2+6	9.3+6	FEI Expt	Prog	INDSWG-120 4	65 Soldatov.A-DSTR FOTOFFRGM, TBP, NDG	

94 Plutonium 240

Quantity	Energy (ev) Min	Max	Lab	Type	Documentation Ref Vol Page	Date	Author, Comments	Data
Photo-Fissn	5.0+6	8.0+6	FEI	Expt Jour	PL/B 26 4 218	Jan 68	Rabotnov+ ANGDIST FISS FRAG AT THRES	
				Prog	YFI-4 12	May 67	.CURVES GIVEN	
	5.0+6	9.0+6		ExTh Conf	67Kharkov 216	Feb 67	.ANG DISTRIB,CHANNEL EFFCTS	
	5.4+6	7.9+6		Expt Conf	65Salzburg 1 135	Mar 65	.ANG DISTRIB FOTO FISS FRAGMENTS	
	5.0+6	8.0+6		Prog	INDC-E-187	67	.ENGLISH TRANSL OF YFI-4 12 5/67	
	5.4+6	7.9+6		Rept	ANL-TRANS-245	65	.ENGLISH TRANSL OF 65SALZBG	
Photo-Fissn		8.0+6	IFP	ExTh Jour	ZEP 9 128	Jan 69	Kapitza+ SIG ANGDIST CV,2-HUMP-BARIER	
				Jour	JEL 9 2 73	Jan 69	.ENGLISH TRANSL OF ZEP 9 128 1/69	
				Rept	ANL-TRANS-639	69	.ENGLISH TRANSL OF ZEP 9 128 1/69	
Photo-Fissn	5.0+6	8.0+6	FEI	ExTh Conf	69Vienna 419	Jul 69	Androsenko+ PPR134. XPTL ANGDIST + TH	
Photo-Fissn	Thrsh	5.2+6	IFP	Expt Conf	69Vienna 925	Jul 69	Kapica+ PPR135.SIG+ANGDIST,STRUTINSKY	
Photo-Fissn	+6	+7	FEI	Expt Jour	YF 11 508	Mar 70	Rabotnov+ ANGDIST+YLD+SIG,GRPHS+TBLS	
				Jour	SNP 11 285	Sep 70	.TRANSLATN.*0,NO 3	
	5.0+7	9.0+7		ExTh Rept	INDC(CCP)-7U24	Feb 70	.TRANSLATN.*	
				Prog	YFI-7 21	Apr 69	Rabotnov+ SIG+YLD+ANGDIST VS E GRPHS	
Photo-Fissn	Thrsh		USP	Revw Jour	NSE 60 19	May 76	Bhandari+ GF,(G,N),CS.ANG DISTR FRAGS	

94 Plutonium 241

Quantity	Energy (ev) Min	Max	Lab	Type	Documentation Ref Vol Page	Date	Author, Comments	Data
Evaluation	5.0+2	1.0+7	ANL	Eval Book	FRC	60	Yftah+ .16E GROUPS.FAST REACT DATA	
Evaluation	Maxwl	1.0+7	GEL	Eval Rept	EANDC(E)17U	Aug 60	PROSDOCIMI	
Evaluation	4.1-1	1.0+7	GA	Eval Rept	GA-2451	Aug 61	Joanou+ .68GRP ABS.EL,IN TRANSF.NF.NU	
Evaluation	1.0-3	1.0+7	AI	Eval Rept	NAA-SR-M-8904	Aug 63	Alter+	
Evaluation	1.0-3	1.5+7	GA	Eval Rept	GA-6576	Jul 65	Drake. EVAL FROM VAR SOURCES	
Evaluation	1.0+3	1.4+7	UK	Eval Rept	AHSB(S)R-124	Feb 66	Hart.(RLY).UK-DFN 341.UPDATES NSE 26	
	1.0+3	1.5+7		Rept	AWRE-O-101/64	Feb 65	Douglas+(ALD).UKNDL-DFN 203	
	2.5-2	1.5+7		Rept	AWRE-O-28/60	Mar 61	Buckingham.(ALD).EVAL FOR UKNDL	
Evaluation	1.0+3	1.5+7	SOR	Eval Rept	IA-1094	Jun 66	Segev.GRAPHS EVALUATED CROSS-SECTNS	
Evaluation	5.0-1	1.0+4	INA	Eval Conf	66Paris 2 333	Oct 66	Hennies.PPR5.RES INT FISS+CAPT,ALPHA	
				Rept	NAA-SR-11980 5	May 67	- . RECOMMENDED DATA.REVISED.	
Evaluation	1.0-4	1.0+3	WIN	Eval Rept	AEEW-M-714	Dec 66	Doherty.DESCRIPTION OF DFN40 UKAEA.	
Evaluation	-		CCP	Eval Jour	AE 23 6	Jul 67	Kirpichnikov.RESON PARAMS,MANY REFS	
				Jour	SJA 23 669	Jul 67	TRANSLATN.*	
Evaluation		2.0+7	TRM	Eval Conf	69Roorke 2 106	Dec 69	Garg+ INDIAN EVALUATN ACTIVITIES, NDG	
Evaluation	1.0+4	1.5+7	BNL	Eval Conf	70Helsinki 2 825	Jun 70	Prince.91. ALL QUANTITIES TO ENDF/B	
Evaluation	Maxwl		IAE	Eval Conf	75Wash. 286	Mar 75	Lemmel. 3RD IAEA-EVAL, BY LSQ FIT	
				Jour	REA 7 4 3	Dec 69	Hanna+ SUPERSEDED	
Total	1.0-2	5.0+1	BNL	Expt Abst	BAP 3 176	May 58	Schwartz+ FC, ANAL TBC	+
	1.0-2	5.4-1		Data	EXFOR12527.002	Jun 76	. 45 PTS.	
Total	2.0+0	7.5+0	HAR	Expt Jour	JNE 6 303	May 58	Egelstaff.FC TRANS NDG,ONLY RES PAR	
Total	2.0-1	1.0+7	B+W	Eval Rept	BAW-158	Jun 61	Roach+ AVERAGED SIG 40 GROUPS	
Total	1.0-2	1.2+1	MTR	Eval Conf	66Wash. 840	Mar 66	Moore+,MULTILEVEL ANAL CURVE CFD XPT	
	2.0-2	1.1+1		Rept	IDO-16954	Dec 63	Simpson+ DOPPLER BROADENING 5 TEMPS	
	2.0-2	1.2+1		Jour	PR 123 559	Jul 61	- + MULTILVL FIT TO DATA CURVES	
Total	2.0-2	2.0+3	MTR	Expt Jour	NSE 11 111	Sep 61	Simpson+.GRAPH,PUO2 SAMPLES,FAST CH	+
	1.6-2	2.0+1		Rept	IDO-16679	Aug 61	.DATA TABLES	
	2.0-2	2.0+3		Conf	60Vienna 93	60	Simpson+	
	1.6-2	2.0+1		Data	EXFOR12537.002	Jun 76	. 1456 PTS.	
Total		2.0+3	UK		Rept	NRDC-138 21	Jan 63	LOW RESOLUTION NDG	
Total	3.0+0	5.0+3	HAR	Expt Conf	63ANL 369	Oct 63	Pattenden+ LINAC+TOF CURVES	+
				Priv	PATTENDEN	Nov 64	- + RES ANAL. 33 RES PARS	
Total	2.5-2	1.0+3	CRC	Expt Jour	CJP 42 2384	Dec 64	Craig+CURV.(NO DATA FROM0.75TO13.8EV	+
				Rept	AECL-1948	Mar 64	.SEE ALSO	
	2.5-2	7.5+5		Data	EXFOR12528.	Jun 76	. 4339 PTS.	
Total	1.0+3	1.5+7	UK	Eval Rept	AWRE-O-101/64	Feb 65	Douglas+(ALD).UKNDL-DFN 203	+
	1.0-4	1.5+7		Data	UKNDL-DFN 60A	Mar 73	802 PNTS	
Total	5.0+1	1.5+7	SOR	Eval Rept	IA-1094 FIG.1	Jun 66	Segev.GRAPH AVERAGED EVAL.CROSS-SCTN	
Total	2.0+0	5.0+1	MTR	Eval Prog	IN-1407 57	Jun 70	Smith+. CURVES,ENDF/B EVALUATION	
Total	-1	+2	SAC	Theo Rept	CEA-N-1522	71	Barreau+ INTERMEDIATE STRC RESEARCH	
Total	6.8-1	7.3+2	GEL	Expt Conf	71Knoxvill 823	Mar 71	Kolar+ LINAC.TOF.	+
	7.0-1	7.0+2		Conf	71Knoxvill 707	Mar 71	- +.TRANS,CURV UP TO 100EV SHOWN	
	6.8-1	7.3+2		Data	EXFOR20116.	Jul 72	6996PTS.	
Total	5.0+1	1.0+5	JAE	Eval Jour	NST 8 656	Nov 71	Takano.FIG GIVEN	
Total	-3	1.0+1	IKE	Theo Rept	IKE-6-61/2	Jan 73	Keinert.DATA LIBRARY	
Total	0.0+0	1.5+7	UK	Eval Data	UKNDL-DFN 403B	Mar 73	646 PNTS	+

94 Plutonium 241

Quantity	Energy (ev) Min	Max	Lab	Type	Documentation Ref Vol Page	Date	Author, Comments	Data
Total	1.0+0	1.0+2	SAC Expt	Jour	NSE 51 130	Jun 73	Blons. REVIEW OF SACLAY DATA	
	1.0+1	1.0+2		Jour	JPR 37 6 659	Jun 76	− + LINAC,REICH − MOORE ANALYSIS	
	1.0+0	1.0+2		Prog	EANDC(E)157U 2	May 73	− + SHAPE ANALYSIS	
Total	2.5−2		IKE Eval	Rept	IKE−6−80	Apr 74	Mattes+ ENDF/B,UKNDL,KEDAK CFD	
Total	1.0+0	3.0+3	ORL Expt	Prog	ORNL−4937 179	May 74	Harvey+NDG.	
	5.0−1	8.0+6		Prog	USNDC−7 168	Jun 73	Simpson+.LINAC. TBC. NO DATA.	
Total	5.1−4	1.0−1	MTR Expt	Prog	WASH−1136 43	Sep 69	Smith+,CRYST SPEC,TRANS,TABLE+CURVE	+
	8.5−3	3.6+0		Data	EXFOR10406.	Jul 74	374PTS,SIGMA	
Total	2.5−2		IAE Eval	Conf	75Wash. 286	Mar 75	Lemmel. TBL LSQ ANAL CFD OTHER EVAL.	
Total	−3	1.9+0	THS Theo	Rept	IKE−6 89 60	Jun 75	Keinert. DATA LIBRARY	
Elastic	2.0−2	1.1+1	MTR Expt	Rept	IDO−16954	Dec 63	Simpson+ DOPPLER BROADENING 5 TEMPS	
Elastic	1.0+3	1.5+7	UK Eval	Rept	AWRE−O−101/64	Feb 65	Douglas+(ALD).UKNDL−DFN 203	+
	1.0−4	1.5+7		Data	UKNDL−DFN 60A	Mar 73	802 PNTS	
Elastic	2.0+0	3.2+1	LRL Expt	Jour	PR 174 1413	Oct 68	Sauter+ LINAC+SCINT REICH−MOORE FIT	+
				Conf	68Wash. 541	Mar 68	.SUPERSEDED	
	3.0+0	3.2+1		Jour	NIM 55 141	Sep 67	Sauter+ TOF SEVERAL RES	
	2.0+0	3.2+1		Abst	DA/B 28 307	Jul 67	.THESIS ABS	
				Prog	UCRL−50001 2	Sep 66	Sauter+. CURVE.	
	3.0+0	3.3+1		Data	EXFOR12344.004	Jun 76	. 299 PTS.	
Elastic	1.0+5	1.0+7	SOR Eval	Rept	IAEA−153 141	73	Ilberg+ EVALUATD DATA FILES CFD,GRPH	
Elastic	0.0+0	1.5+7	UK Eval	Data	UKNDL−DFN 403B	Mar 73	646 PNTS	+
Elastic	2.5−2		IKE Eval	Rept	IKE−6−80	Apr 74	Mattes+ ENDF/B,UKNDL,KEDAK CFD	
Elastic	2.5−2		IAE Eval	Conf	75Wash. 286	Mar 75	Lemmel. TBL LSQ ANAL CFD OTHER EVAL.	
Diff Elastic	1.0+3	1.5+7	UK Eval	Rept	AWRE−O−101/64	Feb 65	Douglas+(ALD).UKNDL−DFN 203	+
	1.0−4	1.5+7		Data	UKNDL−DFN 60A	Mar 73	17 PNTS,C.M.	
Diff Elastic	1.0+4	1.5+7	SOR Eval	Rept	IA−1094 FIG12	Jun 66	Segev.GRAPH AVERAGE COSINE(LAB)	
Diff Elastic	+3		ISL Theo	Prog	IA−1218 14	Aug 70	Kaner.CODE FOR COMPOUND−SIG CALC,NDG	
Diff Elastic	−3	1.0+1	IKE Theo	Rept	IKE−6−61/2	Jan 73	Keinert.DATA LIBRARY	
Diff Elastic	0.0+0	1.5+7	UK Eval	Data	UKNDL−DFN 403B	Mar 73	45 PNTS,C.M.	+
Diff Elastic	1.0−3	1.5+7	SOR Eval	Rept	IA−1276	May 73	Caner+ EVALUATION FOR KEDAK	
	1.0−3	1.5+7		Data	KEDAK−3	Oct 77	7 DATA SETS	
Potntal Scat	2.5−2		IAE Revw	Jour	REA 7 4 3	Dec 69	Hanna+WESTCOTT+ DISCUSSION	
Tot Inelastc	Thrsh	1.5+7	UK Eval	Rept	AWRE−O−101/64	Feb 65	Douglas+(ALD).UKNDL−DFN 203	
Tot Inelastc	1.0+4	1.5+7	SOR Eval	Rept	IA−1094 10	Jun 66	Segev.GRAPH EVALUATED CROSS−SECTION	
Tot Inelastc	1.0+4	5.0+5	AUA Theo	Prog	AAEC/PR−38P 15	Mar 73	Bertram. CHANNEL THEORY, NDG	
Tot Inelastc	5.0+4	1.5+7	SOR Eval	Rept	IA−1276	May 73	Caner+ EVALUATION FOR KEDAK	
	5.0+4	1.5+7		Data	KEDAK−3	Oct 77	53 DATA SETS+ 20 EXCT LVLS	
Diff Inelast	Thrsh	1.5+7	UK Eval	Rept	AWRE−O−101/64	Feb 65	Douglas+(ALD).UKNDL−DFN 203	+
	4.5+4	1.5+7		Data	UKNDL−DFN 60A	Mar 73	TO CONTINUUM, 70 PNTS	
	4.5+4	1.5+7		Data	UKNDL−DFN 60A	Mar 73	TO CONTINUUM, E DIST, 4 RANGES	
	4.5+4	1.5+7		Data	UKNDL−DFN 60A	Mar 73	TO CONTINUUM,ANGDIST, 3 RNGS,LAB.	
Diff Inelast	None		ANL Expt	Jour	PL 18 149	Aug 65	Braid+ IMPT INFO ON ENERGY LEVELS	
Diff Inelast	3.0+5	1.5+7	UK Eval	Data	UKNDL−DFN 403B	Mar 73	TO CONTINUUM, 48 PNTS	+
	3.3+4	5.0+5		Data	UKNDL−DFN 403B	Mar 73	1ST− 4TH LVL	
	3.0+4	5.0+5		Data	UKNDL−DFN 403B	Mar 73	1ST− 4TH LVL,ANGDIST	
	3.0+5	1.5+7		Data	UKNDL−DFN 403B	Mar 73	TO CONTINUUM,ANGDIST, 1 RNGS,LAB.	
	3.0+5	1.5+7		Data	UKNDL−DFN 403B	Mar 73	TO CONTINUUM, E DIST, 4 RANGES	
Scattering	1.0+3	1.5+7	UK Eval	Rept	AWRE−O−101/64	Feb 65	Douglas+(ALD).UKNDL−DFN 203	
Scattering	1.0−3	2.0+0	JUL Theo	Rept	JUEL−746−RG 50	Apr 71	Bonka.KUGEL−THERMOS−LIBR,T=300K,CURV	
Scattering	−3	1.0+1	IKE Theo	Rept	IKE−6−61/2	Jan 73	Keinert.DATA LIBRARY	
Nonelastic	1.0+3	1.5+7	UK Eval	Rept	AWRE−O−101/64	Feb 65	Douglas+(ALD).UKNDL−DFN 203	+
	1.0−4	1.5+7		Data	UKNDL−DFN 60A	Mar 73	802 PNTS	
Nonelastic	1.0+3	1.5+7	SOR Eval	Rept	IA−1094 8	Jun 66	Segev.GRAPH SIG OF SEVERAL PROCESSES	
Absorption	Cold		ANL Revw	Conf	55Geneva 5 125	Aug 55	Spinrad+.P835	
Absorption	Fast		ANL Revw	Conf	55Geneva 5 125	Aug 55	Spinrad+.P835	
Absorption	2.5−2		HAR Expt	Rept	NRDC−84 9	Dec 55	Cocking. = 1 DATA INDEX LINES	+
Absorption	Maxwl		KAP Expt	Rept	KAPL−1464	Dec 55	Mcmillan+SUBCD AVG IN TTR 1057B	
Absorption	Pile		ANL Expt	Jour	NSE 1 62	Mar 56	Fields+1450+ − 250B	+
				Conf	55Geneva 7 261	Aug 55	Bentley+.P809,VAL GVN,CHEMICAL METHD	
	Pile			Data	EXFOR12535.	Jun 76	. 2 PTS, FOR 2 SPECTRA	
Absorption	Maxwl		ANL Expt	Jour	NSE 1 204	Jul 56	Jaffey.1450B FROM ORNL ANL DATA	
Absorption	Maxwl		CRC Expt	Conf	58Geneva 1 683	Sep 58	Craig.	+
	Maxwl			Data	EXFOR12355.010	Jun 76	. 1 PT.	
Absorption	Maxwl		CRC Expt	Jour	NUC 16 10 108	Oct 58	Westcott+ NRX,ABSOL CURV 20−760DEG C	
Absorption	Pile		ORL Eval	Jour	NSE 6 100	Aug 59	Stoughton+,BEST VALUE .025EV=1400B	
Absorption	Pile		CRC Eval	Rept	CRRP−960	Nov 60	Westcott.G,S FACTORS,EFFECTIVE SIGMA	
Absorption	2.0−1	1.0+7	B+W Eval	Rept	BAW−158	Jun 61	Roach+ AVERAGED SIG 40 GROUPS	
Absorption	5.0−3	2.5+0	GA Eval	Rept	GA−2113	Jun 61	Wikner+.TABLE+CURVE.100 E POINTS	

94 Plutonium 241

Quantity	Energy (ev) Min	Max	Lab	Type	Documentation Ref Vol Page	Date	Author, Comments	Data
Absorption	Pile		CJD	Eval Rept	INDSWG – 64 285	64	Galanin. TBL EFF SIG FOR MANY SPECTR	
Absorption	2.5 – 2		BEP	Revw Jour	KE 8 625	Jan 65	Wenzel.VAL GVN,MANY REFERENCES	
Absorption	1.0+3	1.5+7	UK	Eval Rept	AWRE – O – 101/64	Feb 65	Douglas +(ALD).UKNDL – DFN 203	
Absorption	2.0 – 2	5.0 – 1	MTR	Eval Conf	66Paris 2 50	Oct 66	Smith.TBL+CURVE,LEAST SQUARE FIT	
	1.0 – 2	5.0 – 1		Conf	66Wash. 985	Mar 66	Fluharty+,COEF OF SIG EXPANSN CALCTD	
Absorption	Maxwl		ITE	Theo Rept	ICD – 4 385	67	Birzgal+.AVERAGING OVER MAXWELL SPEC	
Absorption	Maxwl		HAR	Expt Jour	JIN 28 2467	May 67	Cabell+. IRR. IN MAXWELLIAN SPECTRUM	+
	Maxwl	2.5 – 2		Rept	AERE – R – 5874	Aug 68	– . RE – ASSESSED.T=116C.TBL	
Absorption	6.2 – 1	1.0+7	SRL	Theo Conf	71Knoxvill 714	Mar 71	Mccrosson. SPECTRUM – AVERAGED SIG	
Absorption	1.0 – 3	2.0+0	JUL	Theo Rept	JUEL – 746 – RG 49	Apr 71	Bonka.KUGEL – THERMOS – LIBR,T=300K,CURV	
Absorption	2.5 – 2		IFB	Eval Rept	YK – 9 34	72	Morogovsky. COMPUTR RE – EVAL,DATA GVN	
				Rept	INDC(CCP) – 42	Aug 74	.P1.ENGLISH OF YK – 9	
Absorption	1.0 – 3	1.5+7	SOR	Eval Prog	INDC(SEC) – 42	Dec 74	Caner+ DERIVED FROM EVAL DATA,NDG	
Absorption	None		MUN	Theo Diss	GRYNTAKIS	Mar 76	Gryntakis.,CALC.OF WESTCOTTS G – FUNCT	
				Jour	RCA 22 128	Mar 75	– +,EQUIVALENT TO THESIS	
Res Int Abs	1.5 – 1	1.0+6	ORL	Eval Jour	NSE 6 100	Aug 59	Stoughton+,BEST VALUE 2800+ – 500B	
Res Int Abs	Pile		UJV	Theo Jour	UJV – 2224	69	Stepanek. 3 GROUP CONSTANTS	
Res Int Abs	5.0 – 1		IAE	Revw Rept	IAEA – 143 897	Apr 72	Lemmel.CAPT,EVALUTS+RECENT EXPTS,TBL	
Res Int Abs	5.0 – 1		SGA	Comp Conf	73Paris 1 233	Mar 73	Eder+ INCLUDING 1/V PART,CAPTURE,TBL	
				Rept	SGAE – PH – 141	Feb 73	.SAME AS 73PARIS,NO DETAILS,TBP	
(n,γ)	Fast		ANL	Revw Conf	55Geneva 5 125	Aug 55	Spinrad+.P835	
(n,γ)	Pile		ANL	Expt Jour	NSE 1 62	Mar 56	Fields+1450+390+ – 80B	+
				Conf	55Geneva 7 261	Aug 55	Bentley+.P809,VAL GVN,CHEMICAL METHD	
	Pile			Data	EXFOR12535.007	Jun 76	. 1 PT.	
(n,γ)	Maxwl		HAR	Expt Jour	NPW 1 200	Sep 56	Cockcroft. SIGMA EXPTL ESTIMATED	
				Jour	BJAS 5 1	56	– +SCIENTI.PROBL.IN NUCLEA.E	
(n,γ)	None		KAP	Comp Rept	KAPL – 1781	Jul 57	Schuman. SIGMA GIVEN	
(n,γ)	Maxwl		CCP	Expt Conf	58Geneva 15 446	Sep 58	Anikina+.PPR2040,VAL GVN	
(n,γ)	Pile		CRC	Expt Conf	58Geneva 16 83	Sep 58	Craig+ PPR205	+
	Pile			Data	EXFOR12548.003	Jun 76	. 1 PT.	
(n,γ)	Pile		ORL	Eval Jour	NSE 6 100	Aug 59	Stoughton+,BEST VALUE .025EV=375B	
(n,γ)	Pile		CRC	Expt Rept	CRRP – 960	Nov 60	Westcott.G,S FACTORS,EFFECTIVE SIGMA	
(n,γ)	2.0 – 2	1.1+1	MTR	Eval Rept	IDO – 16954	Dec 63	Simpson+ DOPPLER BROADENING 5 TEMPS	
(n,γ)	Maxwl		MCM	Expt Jour	CJP 42 2063	Nov 64	Farrar+ MASS – SPEC+INTERPOL,A=120 – 164	
(n,γ)	+5	+7	RLY	Revw Conf	64Vienna 56	Dec 64	Kronberger.FAST REACTOR,1 – GROUP SIGS	
(n,γ)	Maxwl		RLY	Revw Conf	64Vienna 56	Dec 64	Kronberger.ADV – G – COOLD – R,1 – GROUP – SIG	
(n,γ)	1.0+3	1.5+7	UK	Eval Rept	AWRE – O – 101/64	Feb 65	Douglas+(ALD).UKNDL – DFN 203	+
	1.0 – 4	8.2+6		Data	UKNDL – DFN 60A	Mar 73	790 PNTS	
(n,γ)	1.0+3	1.5+7	SOR	Eval Rept	IA – 1094 10	Jun 66	Segev.GRAPHS EVALUATED CROSS – SECTION	
(n,γ)	Maxwl	Pile	BNL	Eval Rept	BNL – 982 22	Aug 66	Pearlstein. 345B, 390B, FROM RES PAR	
(n,γ)	5.0 – 1	1.0+4	INA	Eval Conf	66Paris 2 333	Oct 66	Hennies.PPR5.TBL RECOM DATA CFD OTHR	
				Rept	NAA – SR – 11980 5	May 67	– . RECOMMENDED DATA.REVISED.	
(n,γ)	2.5 – 2		CRC	ExTh Conf	67Wien 15	Apr 67	Ward. SIGMA DEDUCED FRM ISOTOP RATIO	
(n,γ)	Maxwl		AUA	Theo Jour	NSE 31 234	Feb 68	Cook+ STATISTICAL CALC CFD EXPT	
(n,γ)	2.0+3		MTR	Expt Prog	WASH – 1093 61	Apr 68	Simpson+ TBD	
(n,γ)	Maxwl	2.5 – 2	HAR	Expt Rept	AERE – R – 5874	Aug 68	Cabell. RE – ASSESSED.T=116C.TBL	+
	Maxwl			Jour	JIN 28 2467	May 67	– +. IRR. IN MAXWELLIAN SPECTRUM	
(n,γ)	Pile		CCP	Theo Rept	AE 25 466	Dec 68	Usynin. OTHER MEAN SIG GVN	
				Jour	SJA 25 1290	Dec 68	TRANSLATN.*	
				Jour	EAF 25 6 6	Dec 68	.TRANSLATN	
(n,γ)		6.2+1	TRM	Comp Prog	BARC – 423 6	69	Garg. SELF – SHIELD SIG,TEMP – INFL, NDG	
(n,γ)	+5	+7	ANL	Revw Conf	70Helsinki 2 119	Jun 70	Davey.112.STATUS OF DATA ABOVE RESON	
(n,γ)	+1	+7	CAD	Revw Conf	70Helsinki 2 465	Jun 70	Barre+73. MICROSC CFD INTEGRAL DATA	
(n,γ)	+2	+6	GEV	Revw Conf	70Helsinki 1 17	Jun 70	Greebler+102. UNCERTAINTY+REACT CALC	
(n,γ)	5.0+1	1.0+5	JAE	Eval Jour	NST 8 656	Nov 71	Takano.FIG GIVEN	
(n,γ)	Pile		KFK	Eval Rept	KFK – 1453	Mar 72	Eberle+ 2 – GROUP SIGS,FITTED TO EXPT	
(n,γ)	Pile		FAR	Expt Prog	EANDC(E)150U	May 72	Vidal.INTEGR CROSS SECTION RATIOS	
(n,γ)	Pile		JUL	Expt Jour	JIN 34 8 2427	Aug 72	Ihle+ REACTOR CROSS SECTION	
(n,γ)	1.0+5	1.0+7	SOR	Eval Rept	IAEA – 153 141	73	Ilberg+ EVALUATD DATA FILES CFD,GRPH	
(n,γ)	1.0+4	5.0+5	AUA	Theo Prog	AAEC/PR – 38P 11	Mar 73	Bertram. CHANNEL THEORY, NDG	
(n,γ)	0.0+0	1.5+7	UK	Eval Data	UKNDL – DFN 403B	Mar 73	646 PNTS	+
(n,γ)	2.5 – 2		IKE	Eval Rept	IKE – 6 – 80	Apr 74	Mattes+ ENDF/B,UKNDL,KEDAK CFD	
(n,γ)	None		MUN	Theo Diss	GRYNTAKIS	Mar 76	Gryntakis.,CALC.OF WESTCOTTS G – FUNCT	
				Jour	RCA 22 128	75	– +,EQUIVALENT TO THESIS	
(n,γ)	Pile		FEI	Expt Rept	YK – 24 48	77	Andrijakhina+ AVG SIG AT DIFF POSITS	
Res Int Capt	1.5 – 1	1.0+6	ORL	Eval Jour	NSE 6 100	Aug 59	Stoughton+ BEST VALUE 1000+ – 300B	
Res Int Capt	5.5 – 1		BNL	Eval Rept	BNL – 982 22	Aug 66	Pearlstein. 260B CALC, RECOMMENDED	

94 Plutonium 241

Quantity	Energy (ev) Min	Max	Lab	Type	Documentation Ref Vol Page	Author, Comments Date	Data
Res Int Capt	5.0−1	1.0+4	INA Eval	Conf	66Paris 2 333	Oct 66 Hennies.PPR5.TBL RECOM DATA CFD OTHR	
				Rept	NAA−SR−11980 5	May 67 − . RECOMMENDED DATA.REVISED.	
Res Int Capt	3.0+0		KAP Expt	Jour	NSE 44 180	May 71 Eiland+ CD−RH FILTER 162+ −8B	+
	3.0+0			Data	EXFOR10143.017	Aug 73 . 1PT.	
Res Int Capt	Pile		KFK Eval	Rept	KFK−1453	Mar 74 Eberle+ 166B	
Spect (n,γ)	Maxwl		KFK Expt	Conf	74Petten 749	Sep 74 Weitkamp+ NONDESTR FUEL ASSAY APPL	
				Priv	WIETKAMP	73 − . SPECTRA FOR COMPILATION	
				Prog	KFK−1618 38	Sep 72 − . ES + ABSOL INT OF 11 GAM	
				Conf	72Budapest 89	Aug 72 Matussek+ LEVEL SCHEME OF PU242,GRPH	
Nonelastic γ	2.5−2		IFB Eval	Rept	YK− 9 34	72 Morogovsky. SIG G−PROD EVAL,DATA GVN	
				Rept	INDC(CCP)−42	Aug 74 .P1.ENGLISH OF YK−9	
(n,2n)	Thrsh	1.5+7	UK Eval	Rept	AWRE−O−101/64	Feb 65 Douglas+(ALD).UKNDL−DFN 203	+
	5.5+6	1.5+7		Data	UKNDL−DFN 60A	Mar 73 19 PNTS	
	5.5+6	1.5+7		Data	UKNDL−DFN 60A	Mar 73 ANGULAR DISTRIBUTION, 1 RNGS,LAB.	
	5.5+6	1.5+7		Data	UKNDL−DFN 60A	Mar 73 ENERGY DISTRIBUTION , 8 RANGES	
(n,2n)	5.5+6	1.5+7	SOR Eval	Rept	IA− 1094 FIG.8	Jun 66 Segev.GRAPH EVALUATED CROSS−SECTION	
(n,2n)	Fiss		BNL Eval	Rept	BNL−982 22	Aug 66 Pearlstein. 10MB CALCULATED	
(n,2n)	5.0+6	1.5+7	UK Eval	Data	UKNDL−DFN 403B	Mar 73 ANGULAR DISTRIBUTION, 1 RNGS,LAB.	+
	5.6+6	1.5+7		Data	UKNDL−DFN 403B	Mar 73 19 PNTS	
	5.0+6	1.5+7		Data	UKNDL−DFN 403B	Mar 73 ENERGY DISTRIBUTION , 8 RANGES	
(n,2n)	6.1+6	1.5+7	SOR Eval	Rept	IA− 1276	May 73 Caner+ EVALUATION FOR KEDAK.	
	6.1+6	1.5+7		Data	KEDAK−3	Oct 77 1200 DATA SETS	
(n,2n)	1.5+7		DUB Expt	Conf	75Kiev 5 245	May 75 Gangrskij+ SIG TO SPONFIS ISO.TABLE	
(n,xn) x>2	Thrsh	1.5+7	ALD Eval	Rept	AWRE−O−101/64	Feb 65 Douglas.DFN 203 DATA UK LIBRARY	
(n,xn) x>2	1.2+7	1.5+7	SOR Eval	Rept	IA− 1094 FIG.8	Jun 66 Segev.(N3N),GRAPH EVALUATED SIGMA	
(n,xn) x>2	1.2+7	1.5+7	UK Eval	Data	UKNDL−DFN 60A	Mar 73 ANGULAR DISTRIBUTION, 1 RNGS,LAB.	+
	1.2+7	1.5+7		Data	UKNDL−DFN 60A	Mar 73 9 PNTS	
	1.2+7	1.5+7		Data	UKNDL−DFN 403B	Mar 73 ENERGY DISTRIBUTION , 1 RANGES	
	1.2+7	1.5+7		Data	UKNDL−DFN 403B	Mar 73 9 PNTS	
	1.2+7	1.5+7		Data	UKNDL−DFN 60A	Mar 73 ENERGY DISTRIBUTION , 1 RANGES	
	1.2+7	1.5+7		Data	UKNDL−DFN 403B	Mar 73 ANGULAR DISTRIBUTION, 1 RNGS,LAB.	
(n,xn) x>2	1.2+7	1.5+7	SOR Eval	Rept	IA− 1276	May 73 Caner+ EVALUATION FOR KEDAK.	
	1.2+7	1.5+7		Data	KEDAK−3	Oct 77 16 DATA SETS	
(n,p)	Maxwl		IFU Theo	Rept	ICD−4 20	67 Dadakina+ PENETR COEFF CALC,TABLE	
Fission	Fast		LAS Expt	Rept	LA− 1201	Nov 50 Jurney. FAST REACTOR SPEC AVG SIG	
Fission	Cold		ANL Revw	Conf	55Geneva 5 125	Aug 55 Spinrad+.P835	
Fission	Fast		ANL Revw	Conf	55Geneva 5 125	Aug 55 Spinrad+.P835	
Fission	1.1−2	7.4+2	KUR Expt	Conf	55Geneva 4 216	Aug 55 Adamchuk+ GRAPH,FC,TABLES IN NRDC99	+
Fission	2.5−2		HAR Expt	Rept	NRDC−84 9	Dec 55 Cocking. = 1 DATA INDEX LINES	+
Fission	Maxwl		KAP Expt	Rept	KAPL−1464	Dec 55 Mcmillan+,SIG=858B,LARGE Q,REL U235	
Fission	Pile		ANL Expt	Jour	NSE 1 62	Mar 56 Fields+,SIG=1060+ −210B	+
				Conf	55Geneva 7 261	Aug 55 Bentley+.P809,VAL GVN,CHEMICAL METHD	
	Pile			Data	EXFOR12535.006	Jun 76 . 1 PT.	
Fission	6.2−3	7.5+0	HAR Expt	Jour	JNE 2 177	Mar 56 Richmond+.TABULAR DATA IN NRDC 81	+
Fission	Maxwl		ANL Expt	Jour	NSE 1 204	Jul 56 Jaffey.1100B FROM ORNL ANL DATA	+
				Rept	ANL−5397	Mar 55 − + 1100+ −30B IF PU239 IS 1/V	
	Maxwl			Data	EXFOR12521.	Jun 76 . 2 PTS, RATIO, MAXW AND .025 EV	
Fission	Maxwl		HAR Expt	Rept	NPW 1 200	Sep 56 Cockcroft. SIGMA EXPTL ESTIMATED	
				Jour	BJAS 5 1	56 − +SCIENTI.PROBL.IN NUCLEA.E	
Fission	None		KAP Comp	Rept	KAPL−1781	Jul 57 Schuman. SIGMA GIVEN	
Fission	2.5−2	1.0−1	HAN Expt	Prog	HW− 53492 25	Nov 57 Seppi+.CRYSTSPEC,19.2 PC PU241,CURVS	+
				Prog	HW− 48893 98	Mar 57 Leonard.	
	2.5−2	2.5+4		Data	EXFOR12434.	Jun 76 . 3 PTS	
Fission	2.5−3	4.7−3	HAN Expt	Prog	HW− 55879 3	Apr 58 Seppi+.CRYSTSPEC,SIG REL .1EV,TABLE	+
	2.5−3	4.7−3		Data	EXFOR11791.006	Jun 76 . 10 PTS.	
Fission	Maxwl		CRC Expt	Conf	58Geneva 16 125	Sep 58 Bigham+,P.204,RATIO PU241/PU239	+
				Jour	NSE 59 50	Jan 76 − +CS OF 1958 WORK.REVISED	
				Rept	AERE−NP/R−2076	Jan 57 Hanna. RATIO TO U235 =1.28 + −2.2PC	
	Maxwl			Data	EXFOR12356.012	Jun 76 . 1 PT, RATIO TO PU239	
Fission	Maxwl		CRC Expt	Jour	NUC 16 10 108	Oct 58 Westcott.NRX ABSOL CURVE 20−760DEGC	
Fission	6.1−3	9.4−2	HAR Expt	Rept	AERE−R−2998	Jul 59 Raffle.CF NSA14 PAGE 880	+
	1.0−2	1.0+1		Conf	55Geneva 4 187	Aug 55 − +.CURV+VAL 2200M/SEC,PPR422	
	Pile	2.5−2		Rept	NRDC−51	Oct 54 − .BEPO CORE+THR COL+TOF 2200M/S	
Fission	Pile		ORL Eval	Jour	NSE 6 100	Aug 59 Stoughton+,BEST VALUE .025EV=1025B	
Fission	1.0−1	2.3+1	HAN Expt	Prog	HW− 62727 19	Oct 59 Leonard+.CRYSTSPEC,96.6PC PU241,CURV	+
	2.5−2	8.8−1		Data	EXFOR12551.	Jun 76 . 54 PTS.	
Fission	2.5+6	1.5+7	CCP Expt	Jour	AE 8 139	Feb 60 Kazarinova+ 1.2+ −0.2B, 2.05+ −0.1B	+
				Jour	SJA 8 125	May 61 TRANSLATN.*	

94 Plutonium 241

Quantity	Energy (ev) Min	Max	Lab	Type	Documentation Ref Vol Page	Date	Author, Comments	Data
Fission	Pile		CRC	Eval	Rept CRRP - 960	Nov 60	Westcott.G,S FACTORS,EFFECTIVE SIGMA	
Fission	Maxwl		CCP	Expt	Jour AE 10 372	Apr 61	Mostovaya.TERN FISS PROBABL REL U235	
					Jour SJA 10 359	Jan 62	TRANSLATN.* JNE AB 17 424 N/63	
					Jour KE 4 986	Dec 61	. GERMAN OF AE 10 372	
Fission	2.0 - 1	1.0 + 7	B+W	Eval	Rept BAW - 158	Jun 61	Roach+ AVERAGED SIG 40 GROUPS	
Fission	5.0 - 3	2.5 + 0	GA	Eval	Rept GA - 2113	Jun 61	Wikner+.TABLE+CURVE.100 E POINTS	
Fission	2.0 + 5	1.0 + 7	ANL	Revw	Jour 61Vienna 1 29	Aug 61	Smith.P76,CURVE,MANY REFS GVN	
Fission	2.0 + 4	1.8 + 6	ANL	Expt	Jour PR 124 1129	Nov 61	Butler+ GAS SC, REL U235	+
					Conf 61Vienna 1 125	Aug 61	.SUPERSEDED	
	2.1 + 4	1.8 + 6			Data EXFOR12543.002	Jun 76	. 90 PTS.	
Fission	1.2 + 5	2.1 + 7	LAS	Expt	Jour PR 125 1329	Feb 62	Smith.TABLE OF SIG AT 34ES. SIG+ - 6PC	+
	1.2 + 5	2.1 + 7			Data EXFOR12544.002	Jun 76	. 33 PTS, SIG AND RATIO	
Fission	8.8 - 3	1.0 + 4	UK		Rept NRDC - 138 10	Jan 63	G D JAMES CURVE	
Fission	2.0 - 2	1.1 + 1	MTR	Eval	Rept IDO - 16954	Dec 63	Simpson+ DOPPLER BROADENING 5 TEMPS	
Fission	Pile		CJD	Eval	Rept INDSWG - 64 285	64	Galanin. TBL EFF SIG FOR MANY SPECTR	
Fission	Maxwl		CRC	Expt	Rept CRRP - 1183	Feb 64	Bigham.	+
	Maxwl				Data EXFOR12230.011	Jun 76	. 1 PT.	
Fission	2.0 - 2	1.0 + 2	MTR	Expt	Jour PR/B 133 390	Jan 64	Watanabe+ FC	+
					Rept IDO - 16995	Jun 64	.FULL INFORMATION TBLS,GRPHS ETC.	
	2.4 - 2	2.9 + 3			Data EXFOR12529.	Jun 76	. 817 PTS.	
Fission	2.0 + 0	1.0 + 2	RPI	Expt	Jour PR/B 135 945	Aug 64	Moore+.GRAPHS,50MEV PULSD LINAC,TOF	+
					Rept IDO - 16976	Apr 64	.TABLE	
	2.2 + 0	1.0 + 2			Data EXFOR12545.	Jun 76	. 1018PTS.	
Fission	+5	+7	RLY	Revw	Conf 64Vienna 56	Dec 64	Kronberger.FAST REACTOR,1 - GROUP SIGS	
Fission	Maxwl		RLY	Revw	Conf 64Vienna 56	Dec 64	Kronberger.ADV - G - COOLD - R,1 - GROUP - SIG	
Fission	2.5 - 2		BEP	Revw	Jour KE 8 625	Jan 65	Wenzel.VAL GVN,MANY REFERENCES	
Fission	4.0 + 4	5.0 + 5	ALD	Expt	Conf 65Salzburg 1 219	Mar 65	White+ 6 ENERGIES.TBL.REL TO U235.	
Fission	Spont		HAR	Expt	Rept AERE - R - 4865	Apr 65	Cabell+ RE - NORM VAL 13.04+ - 0.28Y	
					Jour JNE 2 264	56	Rose+T(1/2) REL AM241=12.95+ - 0.28Y	
Fission	2.4 + 4		ALD	Expt	Jour JNE 19 423	Jun 65	Perkin+.CALIB SB - BE SRCE. 2.83+ - .21B	+
	2.4 + 4				Data EXFOR20584.009	Jul 76	1PNT.SIGMA.	
Fission	+0	+1	HAR	Theo	Jour PL 18 31	Aug 65	LYNN SLOW (N,GAMMA F) REACTION CALCD	
Fission	1.0 + 3	1.0 + 4	LAS	Revw	Jour PT 18 8 17	Aug 65	Divin.SURVEY BOMB MTHD,PRELIM ABS CU	
Fission	1.0 + 3	1.4 + 7	UK	Eval	Rept AHSB(S)R - 124	Feb 66	Hart.(RLY).UK - DFN 341.UPDATES NS	+
	1.0 + 3	1.5 + 7			Rept AWRE - O - 101/64	Feb 65	Douglas+(ALD).UKNDL - DFN 203	
	1.0 - 4	1.5 + 7			Data UKNDL - DFN 60A	Mar 73	802 PNTS	
Fission	2.0 + 1	2.0 + 6	LAS	Expt	Conf 66Wash. 2 910	Mar 66	Simpson+ ANAL TO 200EV BOMB NEUTRONS	+
	1.0 + 1	1.0 + 7			Conf 66Paris 2 219	Oct 66	Hemmendinger.DETONATION TOF	
	2.0 + 1	9.8 + 5			Data EXFOR12553.002	Jun 76	. 2554 PTS.	
Fission	1.0 - 2	3.2 + 1	MTR	Eval	Conf 66Wash. 840	Mar 66	Moore+,MULTILEVEL ANAL CURVE CFD XPT	
Fission	1.0 - 2	5.0 - 1	MTR	Expt	Rept IN - 1012	Jun 66	Watanabe.MTR FC CURVES CFD OTHERS	+
	6.3 - 3	5.0 - 1			Data EXFOR12530.002	Jun 76	. 256 PTS.	
Fission	1.0 + 3	1.5 + 7	SOR	Eval	Rept IA - 1094 8	Jun 66	Segev.GRAPHS EVALUATED CROSS - SECTION	
Fission	Maxwl	Pile	BNL	Eval	Rept BNL - 982 22	Aug 66	Pearlstein. 950B, 1030B FROM RES PAR	
Fission	2.0 - 2	5.0 - 1	MTR	Expt	Conf 66Paris 2 50	Oct 66	Smith+TBL+CURV,LEASTSQUARE FIT	
	1.0 - 2	5.0 - 1			Conf 66Wash. 985	Mar 66	Fluharty+,COEF OF SIG EXPANSN CALCTD	
Fission	Maxwl		ITE	Theo	Rept ICD - 4 385	67	Birzgal+.AVERAGING OVER MAXWELL SPEC	
Fission	Pile		WIN	Expt	Rept AEEW - R - 526	Jun 67	Stevenson+.FISS RATIO TO U235.ZEBRA	+
Fission	1.0 + 6	1.4 + 7	ALD	Expt	Jour JNE 21 671	Aug 67	White+ 4ES REL U235. CFD OTHER DATA	+
Fission	2.0 + 0	3.2 + 1	LRL	Expt	Conf 68Wash. 541	Mar 68	Sauter+ LINAC SCINT CURVE	
Fission	4.5 + 6	1.0 + 7	ANL	Eval	Jour NSE 32 35	Apr 68	Davey. RE - EVALUATION OF DATA	
	1.0 + 3	1.0 + 7			Jour NSE 26 149	Oct 66	- . EVALUATION	
Fission	2.0 + 3		MTR	Expt	Prog WASH - 1093 61	Apr 68	Simpson+ VALUE GIVN CFD OTHERS TBC	
Fission	Pile		CCP	Theo	Jour AE 25 466	Dec 68	Usynin.AVG SUM SIG(N,G)+SIG(N,F) GVN	
					Jour EAF 25 6 6	Dec 68	.TRANSLATN	
					Jour SJA 25 1290	Dec 68	TRANSLATN.*	
Fission		9.5 + 2	TRM	Comp Prog	BARC - 423 6	69	Garg. SELF - SHIELD SIG,TEMP - INFL, NDG	
Fission	1.0 + 1	2.0 + 4	HAR	Comp Rept	AERE - M - 2157	Jun 69	James+ TBL AVG SIGF DATA FROM SCISRS	
Fission	-		COP	Expt	Jour 69Vienna 351	Jul 69	Back+PPR74.(D,P FISSN) - REACTN,GRPHS	
Fission	-		HAR	Revw	Conf 69Vienna 249	Jul 69	Lynn. TBL=2HUMPED FISS - BARRIER PARS	
Fission	1.0 + 3	1.0 + 7	TRM	Eval	Rept BARC/I - 96	70	Kapil.14 GROUP SIG,2 N - SPECS,TABLES	
Fission	Pile		FTI	Expt	Jour AE 28 359	Apr 70	BAK+.CD FILTERS USED,U235 - RATIO,TABL	+
					Jour EAF 28 4 112	Apr 70	. FRENCH OF AE 28 359	
					Jour SJA 28 460	Apr 70	.ENGLISH OF AE 28 359	
	Pile				Data EXFOR40349.008	Dec 77	SIG(N,F)PU - 241/SIG(N,F)U - 235, 1 PNT	
Fission	1.5 + 2	1.0 + 5	TOK	Theo	Jour NST 7 157	Apr 70	Kikuchi+.CALC USING SPIN DEPENDNT WF	
Fission	+5	+7	ANL	Eval	Conf 70Helsinki 2 119	Jun 70	Davey.112.STATUS OF DATA ABOVE RESON	
Fission	+1	+7	CAD	Theo	Conf 70Helsinki 2 465	Jun 70	Barre+73. MICROSC CFD INTEGRAL DATA	

94 Plutonium 241

Quantity	Energy (ev) Min	Max	Lab	Type	Documentation Ref Vol Page	Date	Author, Comments	Data
Fission	1.0+0	2.0+3	GEL Expt	Conf	70Helsinki 1 437	Jun 70	Migneco+95. SIG(E) GRAPHS + TABLE	+
	2.7+0	4.0+3		Data	EXFOR20009.	Nov 70	10441PTS.	
Fission	+2	+6	GEV Revw	Conf	70Helsinki 1 17	Jun 70	Greebler+102. UNCERTAINTY+REACT CALC	
Fission	Spont		HAR Revw	Prog	INDC–6 23	Jun 70	Rae.HANNA+ ISOMERIC PU–241 DISCUSSED	
Fission	2.0+0	5.0+1	MTR Eval	Prog	IN– 1407 57	Jun 70	Smith+. CURVES,ENDF/B EVALUATION	
Fission	+3		ISL Theo	Prog	IA– 1218 14	Aug 70	Kaner. CODE FOR SIG CALCULATION, NDG	
Fission	5.0+5	2.3+6	LAS Theo	Jour	NSE 41 177	Aug 70	Cramer+,SIG FROM(T,P+FISS)+H–F CALC	
Fission	2.0+6	7.0+6	TRM Theo	Jour	NP/A 151 532	Aug 70	Sood+ CORREL ANAL OF INTERM STRUCTUR	
	–			Prog	BARC–471 5	70	– + CORREL ANAL,D CLASS II VAL GV	
Fission	–1	+2	SAC Theo	Rept	CEA–N–1522	71	Barreau+ INTERMEDIATE STRC RESEARCH	
Fission	1.2+1	1.0+2	GEL Expt	Conf	71Knoxvill 823	Mar 71	Kolar+ CURVE.LINAC. RES ANALYSIS.	+
	1.2+1	1.0+2		Data	EXFOR20116.	Jun 72	0PTS. SEE RESONANCE ANALYSIS	
Fission	5.0–2	2.0+1	HAR Expt	Rept	AERE–R–6676	Mar 71	JAMES SIGF SAME FOR OLD AND NEW 241	+
	2.0+1	2.0+3		Conf	70Helsinki 1 267	Jun 70	James.107. SIG AT 16RANGES,CFD OTHER	
	1.0+3	2.5+4		Conf	66ANL 16	Oct 66	– .TOF CFD OTHER EXPTS TABLES	
	1.0–2	3.0+3		Jour	NP 65 353	Mar 65	– .TOF BELOW 11EV OKS SIMPSON PAR	
				Conf	65Salzburg 1 235	Mar 65	– . TOF.	
				Rept	AERE–R–4597	May 64	– . TOF.TBL.	
				Conf	61Saclay 115	Sep 61	– . SUPERSEDED	
Fission	3.5+0	3.0+4	SAC Expt	Jour	NSE 51 130	Jun 73	Blons. HIGH RESOL. LINAC. CURVES	+
				Conf	71Knoxvill 836	Mar 71	– + LINAC TOF	
				Jour	JPR 37 6 659	Jun 76	– + LINAC,REICH–MOORE ANALYSIS	
				Conf	73Kiev 2 239	May 73	– . CFD OTHERS, NDG.	
				Jour	AE 29 395	Nov 70	Michaudon.ABST FRANC–SOV SEM DUBNA	
				Conf	70Helsinki 1 469	Jun 70	Blons+ SUPERSEDED.	
				Jour	SJA 29 1156	Nov 70	Michaudon. ENG OF AE 29	
	3.5+0	3.0+4		Data	EXFOR20484.002	Jun 72	7714PTS.SIGMA.	
Fission	1.0–3	2.0+0	JUL Theo	Rept	JUEL–746–RG 50	Apr 71	Bonka.KUGEL–THERMOS–LIBR,T=300K,CURV	
Fission	1.0+2	6.0+3	ANL Eval	Rept	ANL–7815	May 71	Kikuchi.ANAL PETREL DATA INTERM STRC	
Fission	–		GEL Revw	Jour	AKE 18 229	Nov 71	Theobald+ SUB–BARRIER FISS EXPTS,TH	
Fission	5.0+1	1.0+5	JAE Eval	Jour	NST 8 656	Nov 71	Takano.FIG GIVEN	
Fission	2.5–2		IFB Eval	Rept	YK– 9 34	72	Morogovsky. COMPUTR RE–EVAL,DATA GVN	
				Rept	INDC(CCP)–42	Aug 74	.P1.ENGLISH OF YK–9	
Fission	Pile		KFK Eval	Rept	KFK–1453	Mar 72	Eberle+ 2–GROUP SIGS,FITTED TO EXPT	
Fission	Pile		FAR Expt	Prog	EANDC(E)150U	May 72	Vidal.INTEGRAL CROSS SECTION TO U235	
Fission	–		GEL ExTh	Jour	NP/A 187 305	Jun 72	Weigmann+ F.B.PARAMS FROM DATA ANAL.	
Fission	Pile		JUL Expt	Jour	JIN 34 8 2427	Aug 72	Ihle+ REACTOR CROSS SECTION	
Fission	Spont		TPI Theo	Jour	YF 16 919	Nov 72	Adeev+ FISS BARRIER CFD EVEN,GRAPH	
				Jour	SNP 16 507	May 73	.ENGLISH OF YF 16 919	
Fission	1.0+5	1.0+7	SOR Eval	Rept	IAEA–153 141	73	Ilberg+ EVALUATD DATA FILES CFD,GRPH	
Fission	1.0+4	5.0+5	AUA Theo	Prog	AAEC/PR–38P 15	Mar 73	Bertram. CHANNEL THEORY CFD XPT, NDG	
Fission	Fiss		SGA Eval	Conf	73Paris 1 233	Mar 73	Eder+ FISS SPEC REL U238(N,F),TBLS	
				Rept	SGAE–PH–141	Feb 73	.SAME AS 73PARIS,NO DETAILS,TBP	
Fission	0.0+0	1.5+7	UK Eval	Data	UKNDL–DFN 403B	Mar 73	646 PNTS	+
Fission	1.4+4	1.1+6	KFK Expt	Jour	NSE 51 124	Jun 73	Kappeler+. 43ES.REL TO U235 NF.	+
	1.4+4	1.1+6		Data	EXFOR20364.002	Sep 74	43PTS.SIGMA.	
Fission	Spont		DUB Expt	Jour	FDP 22 199	74	Gangrsky+ FIS–BARRIER,GRPH EMAX+EMIN	
				Rept	JINR–E15–7362	Jul 73	– + ISOMER HALFLIFE,TABLE,GRPH	
				Rept	JINR–E15–5071	May 70	– + PU242(GAM,N)PU241–M–FISSN	
Fission	2.5–2		IKE Eval	Rept	IKE–6–80	Apr 74	Mattes+ ENDF/B,UKNDL,KEDAK CFD	
Fission	Spont		HAR Expt	Rept	AERE–R–7906	Dec 74	Wilkins.MASS SP.T(1/2)=15.02+–.1 YRS	
Fission	None		UCN Theo	Abst	BAP 20 151	Feb 75	Mcknight+EFFECTS OF UNCERT.NDG.	
Fission	3.0+6	5.0+6	LAS Theo	Conf	75Wash. 129	Mar 75	Moore.GRPH R MATR STAT CALC CFD EXP	
Fission	1.0+3	1.4+7	JAE Revw	Conf	IAEA–186 3 1	76	Igarasi. REVW AVAIL DATA,GRPH+BIBLIO	
	1.0+3	1.5+7		Rept	JAERI–M–6315	Nov 75	– +GRPHS.7 DATA SETS COMPARED.	
Fission	None		MUN Theo	Diss	GRYNTAKIS	Mar 76	Gryntakis.,CALC.OF WESTCOTTS G–FUNCT	
				Jour	RCA 22 128	Mar 75	– +,EQUIVALENT TO THESIS	
Fission	1.0–2	5.0+1	GEL Expt	Jour	NSE 60 44	May 76	Wagemans+ LINAC.NORM TO 2200M/S.GRPH	+
				Jour	ANE 2 541	Aug 75	– + FOR WESTCOTT G FACT.	
	1.9–2	4.4+1		Conf	75Wash. 603	Mar 75	– + LINAC.TOF. REL B–10	
	1.9–2	4.4+1		Data	EXFOR20429.	Jul 75	341PTS.SIGMA.	
Fission	Maxwl		GEL Expt	Jour	NSE 60 44	May 76	Wagemans+ WESTCOTT FACTOR 20.4C GIVN	
				Jour	ANE 2 541	Aug 75	– + DERIVATION OF W FACTOR.	
Fission	3.0+0	3.0+1	GEL Expt	Jour	NSE 60 44	May 76	Wagemans+ LINAC.NORM TO B–10.GRAPH	+
	3.0+0	3.0+1		Data	EXFOR20807.004	Oct 78	806PTS.SIGMA.	
Fission	1.0–2	3.0+4	LRL Expt	Conf	76ANL 47	Jun 76	Behrens+CFD THR E NF CS RATIOS.TBL.	

94 Plutonium 241

Quantity	Energy (ev) Min	Max	Lab	Type	Documentation Ref Vol Page	Date	Author, Comments	Data
Fission	1.2+6	2.6+6	CAD	Expt Rept	CEA-R-4804	Dec 76	Szabo+73KIEV MODIFIED	+
	1.0+4	2.6+6		Conf	73Kiev 3 27	May 73	- + SUMMARY,CFD OTHERS.GRAPH+TABL	
	1.2+6	2.6+6		Data	EXFOR20570.004	Mar 76	6PTS.SIGMA.	
Fission	3.5+4	9.7+5	CAD	Expt Rept	CEA-R-4804	Dec 76	Szabo+ 70ANL RENORMALISED.FACTOR .99	
				Conf	70ANL 257	Oct 70	- + ABSOL. +-3PC. CFD OTHERS.	
Res Int Fiss	1.5-1	1.0+6	ORL	Eval Jour	NSE 6 100	Aug 59	Stoughton+,BEST VALUE 1800+-300B	
Res Int Fiss	5.0-1		BET	Expt Jour	NSE 9 341	Mar 61	Hardy+ 557+-33B REL AU 1535B	+
	5.0-1			Data	EXFOR12405.005	Jun 76	. 1 PT.	
Res Int Fiss	Pile		CRC	Expt Rept	CRRP-1183	Feb 64	Bigham+ NRX, REL B,LI,AU, 541+-14B	+
	Pile			Data	EXFOR12230.008	Jun 76	. 1 PT.	
Res Int Fiss	5.0-1		KAP	Comp Conf	66S.Diego 2 299	Feb 66	Feiner+.COMPIL PREV RESULTS+RECOMMND	
Res Int Fiss	5.5-1		BNL	Eval Rept	BNL-982 22	Aug 66	Pearlstein. 545B RECOMMENDED	
Res Int Fiss	5.0-1	1.0+4	INA	Eval Conf	66Paris 2 333	Oct 66	Hennies.PPR5.TBL RECOM DATA CFD OTHR	
				Rept	NAA-SR-11980 5	May 67	- . RECOMMENDED DATA.REVISED.	
Res Int Fiss	Pile		UJV	Theo Rept	UJV-2224	69	Stepanek. 3 GROUP CONSTANTS	
Res Int Fiss	1.0+1	2.0+4	HAR	Comp Rept	AERE-M-2157	Jan 69	James+ TBL RES INTEG SCISRS DATA	
Res Int Fiss	Pile		RI	Expt Prog	YFI-8 17	Dec 69	BAK+ REL EXPT TO U-235,VALUES GIVEN	
				Rept	INDC(CCP)-8U22	Dec 70	TRANSLATN.*	
		+7		Jour	AE 28 359	Apr 70	BAK+ INTEGRAL VALUE GIVEN,CFD OTHER	
				Jour	EAF 28 4 112	Apr 70	. FRENCH OF AE 28 359	
Res Int Fiss	Maxwl		FTI	Expt Jour	AE 28 359	Apr 70	BAK+.INTEGRAL VALUE GIVEN,CFD OTHER	+
				Jour	SJA 28 460	Apr 70	.ENGLISH OF AE 28 359	
				Jour	EAF 28 4 112	Apr 70	. FRENCH OF AE 28 359	
	Maxwl			Data	EXFOR40349.004	Dec 77	CD-DIFF,REL U235. 1 DATAPNT	
Res Int Fiss	1.0+0	2.0+3	GEL	Expt Conf	70Helsinki 1 437	Jun 70	Migneco+95. 28 RANGES,TBL CFD OTHER	+
	2.0+1	2.0+3		Data	EXFOR20009.005	Nov 70	19PTS.	
Res Int Fiss	3.0+0		KAP	Expt Jour	NSE 44 180	May 71	Eiland+ CD-RH FILTER 569+-37B	+
	3.0+0			Data	EXFOR10143.018	Aug 73	1PNT.	
Res Int Fiss	5.0-1		COR	Expt Jour	NSE 46 31	Oct 71	Draper.INTEGRAL SIG TIMES E.4 SPECTR	
				Abst	DA/B 31 1466	Sep 70	- .EXPT FOR 4 SPEC,CFD CALC	
Res Int Fiss	Pile		KFK	Eval Rept	KFK-1453	Mar 72	Eberle+ 541B	
Res Int Fiss	5.0-1		IAE	Revw Rept	IAEA-143 897	Apr 72	Lemmel.FISS,EVALUTS+RECENT EXPTS,TBL	
Res Int Fiss	5.0-1		SGA	Comp Conf	73Paris 1 233	Mar 73	Eder+ INCLUDING 1/V PART OF SIG,TBL	
				Rept	SGAE-PH-141	Feb 73	.SAME AS 73PARIS,NO DETAILS,TBP	
Res Int Fiss	3.0+0	5.2+1	GEL	Expt Jour	NSE 60 44	May 76	Wagemans+ TBL INTEGRALS.13 E RANGES	
Alpha	Maxwl		HAR	Revw Conf	55Geneva 4 307	Aug 55	Egelstaff+.VAL GVN,EXPT DESCRBD,P425	
Alpha	2.5-2		HAR	Expt Rept	NRDC-84 9	Dec 55	Cocking. = 1 DATA INDEX LINES	+
Alpha	4.3+0	8.6+0	HAN	Eval Rept	HW-62727 19	Oct 59	Leonard+CALC FROM HAN-FISS,BNL325TOT	
Alpha	Maxwl		HAR	Expt Jour	JIN 28 2467	May 67	Cabell+. IRR. IN MAXWELLIAN SPECTRUM	+
	Maxwl	2.5-2		Rept	AERE-R-5874	Aug 68	- . RE-ASSESSED.T=116C.TBL	
	Maxwl			Conf	66Paris 2 3	Oct 66	- + SUPERSEDED	
				Rept	AERE-R-5166	Apr 66	- + SUPERSEDED	
	Maxwl	2.5-2		Rept	AERE-R-4865	Apr 65	- + MASS SPEC. PLUTO. TBL.	
Alpha	1.0+4	2.0+4	LAS	Theo Jour	PR 158 1127	Jun 67	Bell. PREDICT 10-20KEV BY SYSTEMATCS	
Alpha	1.5+2	1.0+5	TOK	Theo Jour	NST 7 157	Apr 70	Kikuchi+.CALC USING SPIN DEPENDNT WF	
Alpha	+5	+7	ANL	Revw Conf	70Helsinki 2 119	Jun 70	Davey.112.STATUS OF DATA ABOVE RESON	
Alpha	2.5-2		HAR	Revw Conf	71Canterby 65	Sep 71	Fudge+FOR BURN-UP.TABLE AVAIL DATA.	
Alpha	Pile		ANL	Expt Rept	ANL-7795	Dec 71	Iskenderian+.BARE+CD-COVERED SAMPLES	
				Abst	ANS 14 371	Jun 71	- . CFD OTHERS	
Alpha	2.5-2		IFB	Eval Rept	YK-9 34	72	Morogovsky. COMPUTR RE-EVAL,DATA GVN	
				Rept	INDC(CCP)-42	Aug 74	.P1.ENGLISH OF YK-9	
Alpha	1.0-4	6.1+5	UK	Eval Data	UKNDL-DFN 60A	Mar 73	760 PNTS	+
Alpha	1.0-3	1.5+7	SOR	Eval Rept	IA-1276	May 73	Caner+ EVALUATION FOR KEDAK.	
	1.0-3	1.5+7		Data	KEDAK-3	Oct 77	1007 DATA SETS	
Alpha	Fast		ITU	Expt Prog	NEANDC(E)162U	Feb 75	Cottone+ SB-125,XE,CS,ND VOL.5.P.42.	
Eta	Cold		ANL	Revw Conf	55Geneva 5 125	Aug 55	Spinrad+.P835	
Eta	Fast		ANL	Revw Conf	55Geneva 5 125	Aug 55	Spinrad+.P835	
Eta	Maxwl		HAR	Revw Conf	55Geneva 4 307	Aug 55	Egelstaff+.VAL GVN,EXPT DESCRBD,P425	
Eta	2.5-2		HAR	Expt Rept	NRDC-84 9	Dec 55	Cocking. = 1 DATA INDEX LINES	+
Eta	Maxwl		KAP	Expt Rept	KAPL-1464	Dec 55	Mcmillan+,SUBCD AVG,2.228+-0.046	
Eta	Pile		ANL	Expt Jour	NSE 1 204	Jul 56	Jaffey.2.2 FROM ORNL ANL DATA	
Eta	Maxwl		KAP	Expt Jour	NSE 3 758	Jun 58	Gaerttner+,2.213+-.07 SUBCADMIUM TH	+
				Rept	KAPL-1468	Feb 56	.SUPERSEDED	
	Maxwl			Data	EXFOR12327.005	Jun 76	. 1 PT, SIG	
Eta	1.0-2	5.0-1	HAN	Eval Rept	HW-62727 19	Oct 59	Leonard+CALC FROM HAN-FISS,BNL325TOT	
Eta	Pile		CJD	Eval Rept	INDSWG-64 285	64	Galanin. TBL EFF ETA FOR MANY SPECTR	
Eta	+5	+7	RLY	Revw Conf	64Vienna 56	Dec 64	Kronberger. VAL TABLE OF ETA+NU+SIGS	
Eta	Maxwl		RLY	Revw Conf	64Vienna 56	Dec 64	Kronberger. AGR-REACTOR,TBL,NU+SIGS	

94 Plutonium 241

Quantity	Energy (ev) Min	Max	Lab	Type	Documentation Ref Vol Page	Author, Comments Date	Data
Eta	2.5-2	1.0+6	BEP	Revw Jour	KE 8 625	Jan 65 Wenzel. VAL FOR 3ES GVN,MANY REFS	
Eta	1.0+3	1.5+7	UK	Eval Rept	AWRE-O-101/64	Feb 65 Douglas+(ALD).UKNDL-DFN 203	
Eta	2.0-2	5.0-1	MTR	Eval Conf	66Paris 2 50	Oct 66 Smith.TBL+CURV,LEASTSQUARE FIT	
Eta	Maxwl		MTR	Expt Rept	IN- 1060	Aug 67 Fast+,THR+.025EV VALUES REL TO U235	+
	Maxwl			Data	EXFOR12505.	Jun 76 . 2 PTS, MAXW AND .025 EV	
Eta	2.5-2	6.0-2	MTR	Expt Conf	68Wash. 589	Mar 68 Smith+ 2ES CRYST SPEC MN BATH ABSOL	+
	None			Prog	ERDA-NDC-2 7	May 75 - .REANAL.DATA.ETA=2.165+-0.010	
	2.5-2	6.0-2		Data	EXFOR12554.002	Jun 76 .2 PTS.	
Eta	6.0-2	2.6-1	MTR	Expt Prog	IN- 1407 39	Jun 70 Smith+. 3ES,MN BATH,TABLE+CURVE	
Eta	1.0-2	1.0+7	ORL	Revw Jour	REA 8 473	Sep 70 Kasten. REVIEW,ETA(E)+AVG ETA,GRAPHS	
Eta	2.5-2		IFB	Eval Rept	YK- 9 34	72 Morogovsky. COMPUTR RE-EVAL,DATA GVN	
				Rept	INDC(CCP)-42	Aug 74 .P1.ENGLISH OF YK-9	
Eta	1.0-3	1.5+7	SOR	Eval Rept	IA- 1276	May 73 Caner+ EVALUATION FOR KEDAK.	
	1.0-3	1.5+7		Data	KEDAK-3	Oct 77 653 DATA SETS	
Nu	Maxwl		CCP	Expt Conf	55Moscow 156	Jul 55 Kalashnikova+.RATIOS+ABSOLUTE VALUES	+
				Rept	AEC-TR-2435	56 . P 123. ENGL TRANSL OF 55MOSCOW 156	
Nu	2.5-2		HAR	Expt Rept	NRDC-84 9	Dec 55 Cocking. = 1 DATA INDEX LINES	+
Nu	Maxwl		KAP	Expt Rept	KAPL-1464	Dec 55 Mcmillan+,NU=3.21+-0.11 REL TO U235	+
	Maxwl			Data	EXFOR12357.006	Jun 76 . 1 PT.	
Nu	Maxwl		CCP	Rept	AEC-TR-2435PT1	56 .USSR NU241 TO NU239 IS 1D04PMD01	
Nu	Maxwl		HAR	Expt Jour	JNE 2 247	Jun 56 Sanders.PROMPT NEUTS.REL+ABS VALUES	+
	2.5-2			Conf	55Geneva	Aug 55 Egelstaff+VAL GVN,EXPT DESCRIBD,P425	
Nu	Pile		ORL	Expt Prog	WASH-191	Jun 56 Pratt+ 3.25+1.12 BASED ON U235	
Nu	Pile		ANL	Expt Jour	NSE 1 204	Jul 56 Jaffey.2.91 FROM ORNL ANL DATA	
				Conf	55Geneva 7 261	Aug 55 Bentley+.P809,VAL GVN,CHEMICAL METHD	
				Rept	ANL-5396	Mar 55 Jaffey+ 2.91+-.10 IF SIGF=1100+-30B	
Nu	Maxwl		ORL	Expt Jour	NSE 5 49	Jan 59 Desaussure+,NU=1.295+-0.02 REL U235	+
	Maxwl			Data	EXFOR12328.004	Jun 76 . 1 PT.	
Nu	Maxwl		ANL	Expt Jour	JNEA 11 21	Nov 59 Jaffey+ NU.SIGF REL U233 U235 PU239	+
	Maxwl			Data	EXFOR12532.002	Jun 76 . 1 PT.	
Nu		1.5+7	ANL	Revw Conf	61Vienna 1 29	Aug 61 Smith.PPR76,CURVE MANY REFS	
Nu	Maxwl		ANL	Expt Jour	PR 123 2140	Sep 61 Smith.	+
	Maxwl			Data	EXFOR12542.002	Jun 76 . 1 PT.	
Nu	Maxwl		UK	Rept	NRDC-138 7	Jan 63 3.167PM.078	
Nu	Maxwl		FOA	Comp Rept	NP- 16440	Mar 63 ASPLUND-NILSSON. REVIEW. TABLE.	
Nu	+5	+7	RLY	Revw Conf	64Vienna 56	Dec 64 Kronberger. VAL TABLE OF ETA+NU+SIGS	
Nu	Maxwl		RLY	Revw Conf	64Vienna 56	Dec 64 Kronberger. AGR=REACTOR,TBL,ETA+SIGS	
Nu	1.0-4	1.5+7	UK	Eval Rept	AWRE-O-101/64	Feb 65 Douglas+(ALD).UKNDL-DFN 203	+
	1.0-4	1.5+7		Data	UKNDL-DFN 60A	Mar 73 ANGDIST OF FISS NEUT, 1 RNGS,LAB.	
	1.0-4	1.5+7		Data	UKNDL-DFN 60A	Mar 73 23 PNTS	
Nu	Maxwl		HAR	Expt Conf	65Salzburg 2 25	Mar 65 Colvin+PPR44.BORONPILE.RATIO/U-235	+
				Prog	AERE-PR/NP8 9	Feb 65 - +TBL.NU=2.886+-0.032.ABS.	
				Conf	58Geneva 16 121	Sep 58 - + PPR 52. SUPERSEDED	
Nu	None		LAS	Revw Conf	65Salzburg 3	Mar 65 Terrell.XPTL WORK CFD THEORY.GRAPHS	
Nu		1.5+7	SOR	Eval Rept	IA- 1094 FIG14	Jun 66 Segev.GRAPH.LINEAR FIT,VALUES GIVEN	
Nu	5.2+5	1.5+7	FOA	Expt Jour	JNE 22 53	Jan 68 Conde+ NU PROMPT AT 5ES REL CF252	+
				Conf	73Kiev 4 130	May 73 - . SUMMARY OF NUBAR(EN),NO VALUE	
				Rept	FOA4-C4318 22	Jan 67 - + EQU TO JNE 22 53.	
				Conf	66Paris 2 51	Oct 66 - +(P/19).SUPERSEDED	
				Rept	EANDC(OR)52L	Mar 66 - + TBL.GRPH. 5ENS REL CF-252	
	5.2+5	1.5+7		Data	EXFOR20052.003	Sep 71 5PTS.PROMPT.	
Nu	Maxwl	1.5+7	AI	Eval Jour	JNE 22 79	Feb 68 Fillmore.DATA TBL,GRAPH.LEAST SQ FIT	
Nu	Maxwl		ANL	Expt Jour	NP/A 145 1	Apr 70 Jaffey+ REL TO U,PU STANDARDS.	+
				Rept	ANL-7625	Nov 69 - +COMPLETE DATA GVN.	
	Maxwl			Data	EXFOR10125.002	May 72 1PT.PROMPT N YLD=2.874+-.015	
Nu	Fiss		SAC	Eval Prog	EANDC(E)127U	Apr 70 RIBON	
Nu	Maxwl		AE	Comp Conf	70Helsinki 2 93	Jun 70 Almen+57. COMPILATN AND NU-TEMP-PLOT	
Nu	+1	+7	CAD	Theo Conf	70Helsinki 2 465	Jun 70 Barre+73. MICROSC CFD INTEGRAL DATA	
Nu	Maxwl	+7	HAR	Revw Conf	70Helsinki 2 195	Jun 70 Colvin.PPR99. REPORT ON DATA STATUS	
	-3	1.4+7		Eval Conf	69Vienna 930	Jul 69 - .PPR55. RECOMMENDATION+REVIEW	
Nu		1.5+7	ANL	Eval Jour	NSE 44 345	Jun 71 Davey. PROMPT NEUTS PER FISSION	
				Conf	70Helsinki 2 119	Jun 70 .SUPERSEDED.(P/112)	
Nu	1.0+3	1.5+7	LRL	Expt Prog	NCSAC-42 130	Nov 71 Bowman+. TO BE DONE	
Nu	2.5-2		IFB	Eval Rept	YK- 9 34	72 Morogovsky. EVAL+RECOMM VALUE,CF OTH	
				Rept	INDC(CCP)-42	Aug 74 .P1.ENGLISH OF YK-9	
Nu	Maxwl		CUA	Theo Abst	DA/B 32 5980	Apr 72 Lee. CALC OF AVG PROMPT NU	
Nu	2.5-2		IAE	Eval Jour	REA 10 637	Dec 72 Manero+ SURVEY,TBLS+GRPHS,RECOMM VAL	
Nu	1.0-3	1.5+7	UK	Eval Data	UKNDL-DFN 403B	Mar 73 164 PNTS	+

94 Plutonium 241

Quantity	Energy (ev) Min	Max	Lab	Type	Documentation Ref Vol Page	Date	Author, Comments	Data
Nu	0.0+0	1.5+7	UK	Eval	Data UKNDL-DFN 403B	Mar 73	ANGDIST OF FISS NEUT, 1 RNGS,LAB.	+
Nu	1.0-3	1.5+7	SOR	Eval	Rept IA- 1276	May 73	Caner+ EVALUATION FOR KEDAK.	
	1.0-3	1.5+7			Data KEDAK-3	Oct 77	2 DATA SETS	
Nu	1.5+6	1.5+7	BRC	Expt	Rept CEA-R-4626	74	Frehaut+ VDG TANDEM	+
	1.9+6	1.5+7			Data EXFOR20488.004	Mar 76	23PTS.PROMPT.	
Nu	2.8+5	5.0+6	CCP	Expt	Jour AE 36 321	Apr 74	D'Jachenko+ NUBAR(NEUT-E),GRAPH,TBL	
Nu	2.8+5	5.0+6	FEI	Expt	Jour AE 36 321	Apr 74	Djachenko+ NUBAR(NEUT-E),GRAPH+TABLE	+
					Rept FEI-411 3	73	D'Jachenko+	
					Jour SJA 36 406	Oct 74	. ENGL OF AE 36 321	
	2.8+5	5.0+6			Data EXFOR40204.003	May 74	DATA AT 15 ES GIVEN	
Nu	2.5-2		IKE	Eval	Rept IKE-6-80	Apr 74	Mattes+ ENDF/B,UKNDL,KEDAK CFD	
Nu	0.0+0	6.0+0	FEI	Expt	Rept YK- 15 3	Aug 74	Vorob'Eva+ NUBAR(NEUT-E),GRAPH,TBL	+
	2.8+5	5.0+6			Data EXFOR40204.003	May 74	.DATA AT 15 ES GIVEN	
Nu	2.5-2		HED	Theo	Abst ANS 21 518	Jun 75	Schenter+ TBL CALC FROM ENDF FP FILE	
Nu	Spont		HED	Eval	Abst ANS 22 673	Nov 75	Johnson. TBL,GRPH.NU FROM SPON FISS	
Nu	4.3+0	9.1+1	BRC	Expt	Conf 75Kiev 5 337	May 75	Simon+ NUBAR VS RES-ENERGY.TBL+GRAPH	+
				ExTh	Diss SIMON	Dec 75	- . (N,GAM/FIS) ANAL	
	4.3+0	9.1+1		Expt	Data EXFOR20425.002	Jul 75	64PTS.PROMPT.	
Nu	0.0+0	1.5+7	BRC	Eval	Rept CEA-R-4791	Oct 76	Bois+NUBAR VS EN,CALC CFD EXP,TABLES	
Delayd Neuts	Maxwl		ANL	Expt	Jour PR 123 1735	Sep 61	COX+ TOT YIELD .0154	
					Conf 61Vienna 1 125	Aug 61	Butler+,6 GROUPS,YIELD+PERIODS,TOTAL	
Delayd Neuts	Maxwl		LAS	Revw	Jour NUC 20 8 150	Aug 62	Keepin+	
Delayd Neuts		+7	HFA	Revw	Conf 67Vienna 23	Apr 67	Yiftah+ TBL OF YLD+HL,REACTR DYNAMIC	
Delayd Neuts	Maxwl		MNZ	Theo	Jour AF 36 453	Nov 67	Patzelt+.FROM DERIVED N-EMISS PROB.	
Delayd Neuts	1.5+7		LAS	Expt	Conf 69Vienna 647	Jul 69	East+PPR109. YLD TABLE,SAFEGUARD	
	1.4+7	1.5+7			Prog LA- 4320	Jun 69	.YLD/NEUT GIVN 2ES.CFD MASTERS+.	
Delayd Neuts	Maxwl	3.1+6	HAR	Eval	Rept AERE-R-6993	Feb 72	TOMLINSON TOTAL+GROUP YLDS TBL	
Delayd Neuts	2.5-2	1.5+7	IAE	Eval	Jour REA 10 637	Dec 72	Manero+ SURVEY,AVERAGE YLD,TBL+GRPHS	
Delayd Neuts	Maxwl		SOR	Revw	Conf IAEA-169 2 33	74	Amiel.TOTAL+GROUP YIELDS,TABLES	
Delayd Neuts	Maxwl	1.5+7	ANL	Eval	Rept ANL-NDM-5	Apr 74	COX. REL YLD, HL, GRPH	
Delayd Neuts	2.5-2	1.5+7	AI	Eval	Jour NSE 56 37	Jan 75	Tuttle.TBL.GRPH.RVW MEAS.CFD REC VAL	
	2.5-2				Prog AI-AEC-13025	May 72	Springer+ VALUE=0.0165+-0.0016	
Delayd Neuts	2.5-2		IAE	Eval	Conf 75Wash. 286	Mar 75	Lemmel. TBL LSQ ANAL CFD OTHER EVAL.	
Delayd Neuts	2.5-2		HED	Theo	Abst ANS 21 518	Jun 75	Schenter+ TBL CALC FROM ENDF FP FILE	
Delayd Neuts	1.5+5	5.0+6	ANL	Expt	Rept ANL-NDM-18	Jan 76	Meadows.NUD VS E GRPH.PU241/U238 AVG	
Delayd Neuts	Maxwl		CSR	Revw	Jour JE 23 9 345	77	Tinka. REVW GROUP-SPEC,PARAMS.TABLES	
Spect Fiss n	Maxwl		ANL	Expt	Jour PR 123 2140	Sep 61	Smith+ TOF, MAXW T=1.335MEV	
					Conf 61Vienna 1 125	Aug 61	Butler+.PPR36,GRAPH,LEAST SQUARE FIT	
					Conf 58Geneva 15 392	Sep 58	.SUPERSEDED	
Spect Fiss n	1.0+3	1.5+7	UK	Eval	Rept AWRE-O-101/64	Feb 65	Douglas+(ALD).UKNDL-DFN 203	+
	1.0-4	1.5+7			Data UKNDL-DFN 60A	Mar 73	5 RANGES	
Spect Fiss n	Maxwl		HAR	Eval	Jour NP 71 228	Sep 65	Barnard+ CORRELATED WITH NU BAR	
Spect Fiss n	Maxwl		ANL	Revw	Conf 71Vienna 3	Aug 71	Smith. MEAN-E OF NEUTS,EXPTS CFD,TBL	
Spect Fiss n	0.0+0	1.5+7	UK	Eval	Data UKNDL-DFN 403B	Mar 73	5 RANGES	+
Spect Fiss n	Maxwl		SOR	Eval	Rept IA- 1276	May 73	Caner+ EVALUATION FOR KEDAK.	
Spect Fiss n	2.5-2		IAE	Eval	Conf 75Wash. 286	Mar 75	Lemmel. 3RD IAEA-EVAL, BY LSQ FIT	
Spect Fiss n	Fast		ANL	Eval	Abst ANS 22 671	Nov 75	Saphier+ 6 GPS DELAYED NEUT SPECT	
Spect Fiss γ	-		CCP	Expt	Jour IZV 29 163	Jan 65	Baranov+.GRAPH SPEC. ENGL BAS29 161	
Spect Fiss γ	2.5-2		SRC	Theo	Jour JNE 25 339	Aug 71	Scobie+ BETA EN REL RATE,CFD EXPT.	
Spect Fiss γ	Maxwl		KFK	Expt	Priv WIETKAMP	73	Weitkamp. SPECTRA.PROMPT+DELAYED	
Spect Fiss γ	2.5-2	1.4+7	LAS	Theo	Prog LA- 6018-PR 25	Jul 75	Stamatelatos+FPG SPEC CALC.	
Spect Fiss γ	4.3+0	9.1+1	BRC	ExTh	Diss SIMON	Dec 75	Simon. (N,GAM/FIS) ANAL	
				Expt	Conf 75Kiev 5 337	May 75	- + EGAM VS RES-EN.(N,GF).TBL+FIG	
Fiss Prod γ	Maxwl		LAS	Expt	Conf 69Vienna 647	Jul 69	East+PPR109. FPG SPEC,SAFGUARD	
Fiss Prod γ	-		WIN	Eval	Jour JNE 23 517	Nov 69	JAMES MEAN E 7.8+-1.6MEV/FISS	
Fiss Prod γ	2.5-2		IAE	Revw	Jour REA 7 4 3	Dec 69	Hanna+ DELAYD GAMMAS IN NU-BAR EXPTS	
Fiss Prod γ	Maxwl		KFK	Expt	Priv WIETKAMP	73	Weitkamp. DELAYED SPECTS OF F PRODS	
Fiss Yield	Maxwl		ANL	Expt	Jour PR 106 779	May 57	Smith+,MASS-ENERGY DISTR CFD XPT+TH	
Fiss Yield	2.0-1		MTR	Expt	Jour PR 119 2017	Sep 60	Regier.MO/CD,MO/SN P .2EV CFD THR	
Fiss Yield	Maxwl	1.0+6	LAS	Expt	Rept PR 126 1508	May 62	Nobles. YIELD OF LONG RANGE FFRGM	
Fiss Yield	Maxwl		HAN	Expt	Rept HW- 7760 1	Jan 63	Kirby.RADIOCHEMICAL	
Fiss Yield	Pile		ORL	Expt	Jour PR/B 133 1500	Mar 64	Walter. SI DETECT.CF PU239,PEAKSHIFT	
					Conf 63ANL 441	Oct 63	.SUPERSEDED	
Fiss Yield	-3	+7	TRM	Revw	Rept AEET-235	65	Methasiri.TERNRY FISS EXPTS,GRAPH	
Fiss Yield	6.5+5	8.2+6	LAS	Expt	Jour PR/B 137 809	Feb 65	Simmons+REL ANG DIST FISS FRAG	
Fiss Yield	None		CRC	Expt	Prog EANDC(CAN)-23	Apr 65	Bigham+DIRECT YIELD OF XE135	
Fiss Yield	Maxwl		CRC	Expt	Jour CJP 43 1036	Jun 65	Okazaki+ RELU235FISS CF CUMUL YLDS	
					Rept EANDC(CAN)-23	Apr 65	.SEE ALSO	

94 Plutonium 241

Quantity	Energy (ev) Min	Energy (ev) Max	Lab	Type	Documentation Ref Vol Page	Date	Author, Comments	Data
Fiss Yield	None		ORL	Theo Rept	ORNL – P – 2848	66	Schmitt.CALCTD FISS MODES TBP AF	
Fiss Yield	Maxwl		CRC	Expt Jour	CJP 44 237	Jan 66	Okazaki+ DRCT YLD CUMYLD	
				Jour	CJP 49 498	Feb 71	.REVISED	
Fiss Yield	None		LAS	Expt Jour	PR 145 911	May 66	Daniels+.CUMUL.YLD IN 28MEV HE4 – U238	
Fiss Yield	Maxwl		ORL	Expt Jour	PR 149 894	Sep 66	Neiler+PRE – NEUT EMISSYLD CFD POST – NE	
Fiss Yield	Maxwl		FLA	Expt Jour	PRL 18 404	Mar 67	Muga+2. HEAVY TERNARY FISSION	
				Conf	69Vienna 107	Jul 69	– +PPR99. TERNARY YLD(A) GRPHS GV	
				Rept	ORO – 2843 – 9	Dec 66	.SUPERSEDED	
Fiss Yield	Maxwl		BOR	Theo Jour	NP/A 96 588	Apr 67	Doan+ ALPHA YIELD CALCULATED	
Fiss Yield	Maxwl		HAR	Eval Rept	AERE – R – 5086	Jan 68	Croall.RECOMMENDED CUMULAT YLDS,TBL	
Fiss Yield	Maxwl		MTR	Expt Jour	NSE 31 241	Feb 68	Nisle+ I135 YLD=1.221+ – .089 REL U235	
				Rept	IN – 1096	Sep 67	.SUPERSEDED	
				Rept	IN – 1048 56	Sep 66	.SUPERSEDED	
Fiss Yield	Maxwl		ANL	Eval Prog	ANL – 7450	Apr 68	.CALCULATED TRITIUM YIELDS	
Fiss Yield	Maxwl		CCP	Expt Jour	YF 8 454	Sep 68	Solov'Eva. LONG – R – ALPHA,KE – SPECS,CVS	
				Jour	SNP 8 264	Mar 69	TRANSLATN.*	
Fiss Yield	Maxwl		HAR	Theo Rept	AERE – R – 6056	Mar 69	Crouch. CALC FRACT INDEP YLDS. TBL	
				Rept	AERE – R – 5488	May 67	– .SUPERSEDED	
				Rept	AERE – R – 5250	Apr 66	– .SUPERSEDED	
Fiss Yield	Maxwl		ORL	Expt Conf	69Vienna 67	Jul 69	Schmitt.PPR122. YLD GRPH,COMP OF PR	
Fiss Yield	Maxwl		OSL	Revw Conf	69Vienna 669	Jul 69	Pappas+PPR206. INITIAL+FINAL YLD(A)	
Fiss Yield	Maxwl		SAC	Comp Rept	CEA – N – 1180	Jul 69	Bessis+ CAPT FOR FIS FRAG + 'NU'	
Fiss Yield	Pile		HAR	Expt Rept	AERE – R – 6154	Aug 69	Croall+ YLD 14 NUCLEI REL PU239	
Fiss Yield	6.0+6	3.7+7	CCP	Revw Jour	IZV 34 438	Feb 70	Soloveva.ALF – EMISSN PROBABILITY,GRPH	
				Jour	BAS 34 378	Jan 71	.ENGL TRANSL OF IZV 34 438	
Fiss Yield	2.5 – 2		KFK	Comp Rept	KFK – EXT – 6 2	Nov 70	Hofmann. CUMULATIVE YLD A=72 – 163	
Fiss Yield	Maxwl		MTR	Expt Jour	NSE 42 191	Nov 70	Lisman+,YLDS STABLE+LONG – LIVED FRAGS	
	None			Rept	IN – 1215	Aug 68	– + MASS – SPEC	
	Maxwl			Rept	IN – 1277	Jun 68	– + SUMMARIZES RESULTS	
Fiss Yield	Maxwl		ANL	Eval Rept	ANL – 7749	Dec 70	Flynn+ TOTAL CHAIN YLDS GIVEN	
Fiss Yield	Pile		MTR	Expt Jour	JIN 33 643	Mar 71	Lisman+ YLD OF KR – 85	
Fiss Yield	Maxwl		CRC	Expt Jour	CJP 49 785	Apr 71	Hawkings+ XE135 INDEP/I135 CUMUL YLD	
Fiss Yield	Maxwl		GA	Eval Rept	GA – 12071	Sep 71	Mathews+. RECOMMENDED VALUES	
Fiss Yield	Maxwl		GEP	Eval Rept	NEDO – 12154	Jan 72	Meek+.TABULATD RECOMMENDED YIELDS	
				Rept	APED – 5398A	Oct 68	– +,TABLES	
				Rept	APED – 5398	Mar 68	– + TABLES	
				Rept	GEAP – 5356	Sep 67	Rider+ TABULATED CHAIN YLDS 85MASSES	
Fiss Yield	Maxwl		IAE	Revw Rept	IAEA – 143 897	Apr 72	Lemmel.YDLS FROM RECENT EVALUATN,TBL	
Fiss Yield	+1	+6	MOL	Expt Prog	INDC(SEC) – 26	May 72	Deruytter+ TERN/BINAR,EXPLOS,PROPOSD	
Fiss Yield	Maxwl		TRM	Expt Rept	BARC – 690 134	73	Chitambar+ REL,G+MASS – SPEC+CHEM,TBL.	
Fiss Yield	Maxwl		CRC	Eval Rept	AECL – 3037 2	Apr 73	Walker.ALL DETAILS,CHAIN YIELDS,TBLS	
				Conf	73Paris 1 459	Mar 73	– .EVAL PROCEDURE,SELECTED TBLS	
				Conf	66Paris 1 521	Oct 66	– .EARLIER EVAL,SUPERSEDED	
				Rept	AECL – 2111	Nov 64	– . PSUEDO FPY	
				Rept	CRRP – 913	Mar 60	– .SUPERSEDED	
				Rept	CRRP – 760	Oct 58	Hurst+ CALC YIELDS	
Fiss Yield	2.5 – 2		FEI	Expt Conf	73Kiev 3 270	May 73	Vorob'Yeva+	+
	2.5 – 2			Data	EXFOR40284.008	May 75	.PRIMARY FF YIELD GVN	
Fiss Yield	1.0+6	3.5+6	FEI	Expt Conf	73Kiev 3 270	May 73	Vorob'Eva+ FRAGM MASS – DISTR,GRAPH	+
	7.0+5	3.5+6		Data	EXFOR40284.009	May 75	.PRIMARY FF YIELD AT 2.74MEV N – E GVN	
Fiss Yield	Maxwl		CRC	Revw Conf	73Bologna § 11A	Nov 73	Walker.STATUS CHAIN+INDEP YLDS,TBLS	
				Rept	AECL – 3037	Apr 73	– .CUMUL YLDS MANY FRAGS.TABLES.	
				Rept	AECL – 4704	73	.SAME AS 73BOLOGNA,EVALS CFD,DICUSSN	
Fiss Yield	Maxwl		AUA	Theo Conf	IAEA – 169 2 163	74	Musgrove+ GAUSS FIT MASS YLDS,GRAPH	
Fiss Yield	Fast		FAR	Expt Conf	IAEA – 169 3 59	74	Robin+ ND148,STABL ISOT/ND148,TBL	
				Prog	EANDC(E) – 157U2	May 73	Vidal. YIELD FOR ND – ISOTOPES	
Fiss Yield	2.5 – 2	5.0+6	FEI	Expt Jour	YF 19 6 1216		74 Vorobjeva+	+
				Jour	SNP 19 621	Dec 74	. ENGL OF YF 19,1216	
	2.5 – 2	5.0+6		Data	EXFOR40282.	Aug 74	41 DATA LINES AT 6 ES GIVEN	
Fiss Yield	Pile		RI	Expt Jour	AE 35 409	Dec 73	Skovorodkin+ MORE YLDS,ABS+REL PU239	+
				Jour	AE 31 99	Aug 71	Sorokina+ MICA,ABSOL+REL CE – 144,TBLS	
				Jour	RAK 12 492	Jun 70	– + RADCHEM,8 YLDS REL 144,TBL	
				Jour	RAK 12 487	Jun 70	Skovorodkin+ 12 YLDS,REL CE – 144,TBL	
				Jour	SJA 35 1109	Jun 74	.ENGL OF AE 35 804	
				Jour	SJA 31 804	Mar 72	.ENGL OF AE 31 99	
	2.5 – 2			Data	EXFOR40389.004	Feb 77	.CUMUL FISS PROD YIELDS GVN	

94 Plutonium 241

Quantity	Energy (ev) Min	Energy (ev) Max	Lab	Type	Documentation Ref Vol Page	Date	Author, Comments	Data
Fiss Yield	Maxwl		FEI	Expt	Rept YFI – 17 3	Aug 74	Djachenko+ MASS – YIELD(M = 121 – 162),TBL	
					Jour YF 17 696	Apr 73	D'Jachenko+ MASS – YLD+YLD(KIN – E),GRPH	
					Rept INDC(CCP) – 48	Feb 75	. ENGLISH OF YFI – 17 3	
					Jour SNP 17 362	Oct 73	.ENGLISH OF YF 17 696	
Fiss Yield	1.0 – 2	5.0+1	GEL	Expt	Jour NP/A 234 285	Dec 74	Wagemans+ TERN/BIN FIS,CURV+TBL.	+
	1.8 – 2	5.0+1			Data EXFOR20585.002	Jul 76	44PTS.TER/BIN.	
Fiss Yield	Fast		ITU	Expt	Prog NEANDC(E)162U	Feb 75	Cottone+ SB – 125,XE,CS,ND VOL.5.P.42.	
Fiss Yield	Fast		DOU	Expt	Prog UKNDC(75)P71	Jul 75	Davies+ IRRADIATION ISOTOPES PFR	
Fiss Yield	Maxwl		HAR	Eval	Rept AERE – R – 8152	Jan 76	Crouch. ADJUSTED FISSION YIELD,TABLE	
	Fast				Rept AERE – R – 8152	Jan 76	– . ADJUSTED FISSION YIELD,TABLE	
	Maxwl Fiss				Rept AERE – R – 7785	Feb 75	– .CHAIN+INDEPENDENT YLDS TBL	
	Pile				Rept AERE – R – 7680	May 74	– . FRACTIONAL INDEPENDENT YLD	
	1.4+7				Rept AERE – R – 7394	May 73	– .CHAIN YLDS RECOMMENDED TBL	
	Maxwl				Conf 73Paris 1 393	Mar 73	– .EXPTL DATA+EVAL CHAIN YLD,TBL	
					Rept AERE – R – 7209	Jan 73	– .85 CHAIN YLDS RECOMMENDED TBL	
Fiss Yield	Maxwl		AUA	Theo	Rept AAEC/E – 386	Mar 76	Cook+ 3 – GAUSS FIT,PARAMS GIVEN	
Fiss Yield	2.0+6	1.4+7	LAS	Eval	Abst ANS 24 462	Nov 76	Madland+PAIR EFFECT ON FISS PROD YLD	
	2.5 – 2	1.4+7			Rept LA – 6430	Jul 76	– +PAIR EFFECT ON INDEP YLD.TBL	
Frag Spectra	Maxwl		FEI	Expt	Prog INDSWG – 126 36	66	Borukhovich.GRAPH E – KIN VS FRGM – MASS	
Frag Spectra	Maxwl		FTI	Expt	Jour YF 4 791	Sep 66	Borukhovich+.CURVE. (=ENGL SNP 4 563	
Frag Spectra	Maxwl		ORL	Expt	Jour PR 149 894	Sep 66	Neiler+MASS.EN DIST AND THEIR CORREL	
Frag Spectra	Maxwl		FLA	Expt	Jour PRL 18 404	Mar 67	Muga+2. E SPEC IN TERNARY FISSION	
					Conf 69Vienna 107	Jul 69	– +PPR99. TERNARY E – KIN SPECS GVN	
					Rept ORO – 2843 – 9	Dec 66	.SUPERSEDED	
Frag Spectra	Maxwl		FTI	Expt	Prog YFI – 4 44	May 67	Borukhovich+.TBL KINETIC E OF FRGMNT	
					Rept INDC – 187E 57	67	. ENGL OF YFI – 4 44	
Frag Spectra	– 2		RI	Expt	Prog YFI – 6 93	68	Solov'Eva. SPECTRUM OF ALFAS	
					Rept INDC – 260E	69	. ENGL OF YFI – 6 93	
Frag Spectra	Maxwl		RI	Expt	Conf 68Riga	Jan 68	Solov'Eva.ABST, E – SPECTRUM OF ALFAS	
Frag Spectra	2.5 – 2		FTI	Expt	Jour IZV 32 693	Apr 68	Baranov+ TOTAL E – KIN OF FRAGMNTS GVN	+
					Jour BAS 32 639	69	.TRANSLATION OF IZV 32 693	
	2.5 – 2				Data EXFOR40320.003	Oct 75	.ONE LINE DATA LINE	
Frag Spectra		2.0+6	COP	Revw	Conf 69Vienna 155	Jul 69	Strutinsky+PPR203. GRPH ANGANISTR(E)	
Frag Spectra	Maxwl		ORL	ExTh	Conf 69Vienna 67	Jul 69	Schmitt.PPR122.GRPH,(EKIN+ – RMS) VS A	
Frag Spectra	None		TRM	Theo	Prog BARC – 501 19	70	Ramamurthy+ ANGDIST WITH EXITATION – E	
Frag Spectra	Pile		TRM	Theo	Conf 70Madurai 2 79	Dec 70	Prakash+ KIN – E CFD SHELL – STRUCT, CRV	
Frag Spectra	Maxwl		CUA	Theo	Abst DA/B 32 5980	Apr 72	Lee. CALC OF TOT FRAG KE DISTRIBUTS	
Frag Spectra	2.8+5	5.0+6	FEI	Expt	Jour YF 17 696	Apr 73	Djachenko+ FRAG KIN – E+AVG,TBL,GRAPH	+
					Rept FEI – 411 3	73	D'Jachenko+	
					Jour SNP 17 362	Oct 73	. ENGLISH OF YF 17,696	
	2.8+5	5.0+6			Data EXFOR40204.002	May 74	DATA AT 15 ES GIVEN	
Frag Spectra	Maxwl		FEI	Expt	Rept YFI – 17 3	Aug 74	Djachenko+ TBL YLD(E – KIN)+E – KIN(MASS	
					Rept INDC(CCP) – 48	Feb 75	. ENGL OF YFI – 17 3	
Frag Spectra	None		DKE	Theo	Conf 76Lowell 1403	Jul 76	Newson.EXCIT E,3 – 50MEV.FINE STRUC.ND	
Frag Charge	Maxwl		GEP	Comp	Rept APED – 5398	Oct 68	Meek+ TABLES	
Frag Charge	Maxwl		HAR	Theo	Rept AERE – R – 6056	Mar 69	Crouch.CALC CHARGE DISPERSION,ZP,TBL	
					Rept AERE – R – 5488	May 67	– + SUPERSEDED	
					Rept AERE – R – 5250	Apr 66	– + SUPERSEDED	
Frag Charge	Maxwl		LRL	Comp	Rept UCRL – 51640	Jul 74	Nethaway. TBL.	
Frag Charge	1.8+6	1.4+7	LRL	Comp	Rept UCRL – 51640	Jul 74	Nethaway. TBL.	
Reson Params	2.6 – 1		HAR	Expt	Conf 55Geneva 4 187	Aug 55	Raffle+.RESON – E+SIGMA0+TOT – W,PPR422	+
Reson Params	2.6 – 1	4.5+0	HAR	Expt	Jour JNE 2 177	Mar 56	Richmond+.2 RES.ENERGIES GIVEN	+
Reson Params	2.5 – 1	8.7+0	BNL	Expt	Abst BAP 3 176	May 58	Schwartz. FAST CHOPPER,WT WG WF	+
	2.5 – 1	8.7+0			Data EXFOR12527.	Jun 76	7 RES, E0,WT,WN,WG,WF,WT**2	
Reson Params	4.3+0	6.8+0	HAR	Expt	Jour JNE 6 303	May 58	Egelstaff+,WN FOR 4.3EV,3 E – RES,TBL	+
	2.7+0	4.3+0			Rept AERE – NP/R – 2076	Jan 57	– . 2 RES S0 MAY BE PU242	
Reson Params	4.3+0	1.5+1	HAN	Expt	Rept HW – 62727 19	Oct 59	Leonard+.AREA ANALYS OF 6RES FROM NF	+
	4.3+0	1.5+1			Data EXFOR12551.002	Jun 76	. 6 RES, E0,WF**2	
Reson Params	– .2+0	1.0+1	MTR	Expt	Jour PR 123 559	61	Simpson.	+
	– .2+0	1.0+1			Data EXFOR12541.002	Jun 76	.9 RES, E0,WN,WF1,WF2	
Reson Params	4.3+0	3.5+1	RPI	Expt	Jour PR/B 135 945	Aug 64	Moore+LINAC MULLVL PAR WN,WF IF WG40	+
	4.3+0	3.5+1			Data EXFOR12545.004	Jun 76	. 21 RES, E0,WN,WF1,WF2	
Reson Params	1.3+1	5.0+1	HAR	Expt	Priv PATTENDEN	Nov 64	Pattenden+ WT,WN 33 RES FROM TRANSM	+
					Prog AERE – PR/NP6 10	Apr 64	– + G*GAMMA N,25RES.AREA ANAL	
					Conf 63ANL 369	Oct 63	– + LINAC.TOF. CURVES FOR RES	
Reson Params		+7	CCP	Theo	Jour AE 17 479	Dec 64	Usachev+ FISS CHANNEL THRESHOLDS EST	
		+8			Jour JNE 19 987	Dec 65	TRANSLATN.*	
		+7			Jour SJA 17 1242	Dec 64	TRANSLATN.*	

94 Plutonium 241

Quantity	Energy (ev) Min	Max	Lab	Type	Documentation Ref Vol Page	Author, Comments Date	Data
Reson Params	1.2+1	3.1+1	CRC	Expt	Jour CJP 42 2384	Dec 64 Craig+ 1LVL BW FIT SEE ALSO AECL1948	+
	1.5+1	3.1+1			Data EXFOR12528.018	Jun 76 . 12 RES, E0,WT,WN,PCS	
Reson Params	-.2+0	3.5+1	CJD	Comp Rept	INDSWG-101 25	65 .TBL OF 23 RES FROM VARIOUS SOURCES	
Reson Params	1.1+1	1.7+1	HAR	ExTh Jour	NP 65 353	Mar 65 JAMES TOF MULTILEVEL ANALYSIS+AV PAR	+
					Conf 65Salzburg 235	Mar 65 James. TOF DATA.MULTILEVEL ANALYSIS.	
	1.0-2	1.7+1		Expt	Rept AERE-R-4597	May 64 - .TOF XPT.MULTILEVEL ANAL	
	4.3+0	1.8+1			Conf 61Saclay	Jul 61 - .WF.TABLE 14 RESONANCES.	
Reson Params	1.5+1	6.2+1	LAS	Expt	Conf 66Wash. 2 910	Mar 66 Simpson.	+
	1.5+1	5.5+1			Rept IDO-17174	Apr 66 - +.50 E0,WN0,WF MULTILEVEL FIT	
	1.5+1	6.2+1			Data EXFOR12553.003	Jun 76 . 56 RES, E0,WN,WF1,WF2	
Reson Params	1.0+0	1.3+2	MTR	Theo	Conf 66Wash. 840	Mar 66 Moore+,TBL CALCTD PARS FOR 50 ES	
Reson Params	2.6-1	3.5+1	AI	Eval	Rept NAA-SR-11980 5	May 67 Hennies.WN WG WF +AVG PARS TO 10KEV	
Reson Params	-		CCP	Eval	Jour AE 23 6	Jul 67 Kirpitchnikov.FISS-,N-WIDTH,STRNTH-F	
					Jour SJA 23 669	Jul 67 TRANSLATN.*	
Reson Params		1.0+6	AUA	Theo	Jour AUJ 20 477	Oct 67 Cook. TBL OF AVG LVL SPACING D,L=0,1	
Reson Params	4.3+0	3.1+1	LRL	Expt	Jour PR 174 1413	Oct 68 Sauter+ LINAC 20 RESON ES+PARAMS	+
					Conf 68Wash. 541	Mar 68 .SUPERSEDED	
	4.3+0	3.1+1			Data EXFOR12344.006	Jun 76 . 20 RES, E0,J,WN,WG,WF	
Reson Params	-		HAR	Revw	Conf 69Vienna 249	Jul 69 Lynn. TBL STRUTINSKY PARS,FISS+CAPT	
Reson Params	4.3+0	3.1+1	CCP	Revw	Rept ICD-6 7	70 Lukyanov.J,G+N+F-WIDS OF 20 RES,TBLS	
Reson Params	None		TRM	Theo	Prog BARC-471 5	70 Sood+ CORREL ANAL,D CLASS II VAL GVN	
	2.0+1	1.0+6			Conf 69Roorke 2 198	Dec 69 - + AVG LEVL SPACING D,2-HUMPED-T	
Reson Params	1.5+2	1.0+5	TOK	Theo	Jour NST 7 157	Apr 70 Kikuchi+.CHANNEL TH,SPIN DEPENDNT WF	
Reson Params	-.2+0	5.9+1	MTR	Eval	Prog IN-1407 57	Jun 70 Smith+. J WT WN WG WF ENDF/B EVALUAT	
Reson Params	1.0+0	1.6+2	SAC	Expt	Jour AE 29 395	Nov 70 Derrien.ABST FRANC-SOV SEM DUBNA /70	+
					Jour JPR 37 659	Jun 76 Blons+ SHAPE ANAL + MULTILVL ANAL	
	4.3+0	1.6+2			Jour NSE 51 130	Jun 73 - + REVIEW FISS XSECT MEAS SACLAY	
	3.0-1	1.6+2			Conf 73Kiev 2 239	May 73 - . AVERAGE F-WIDTH + NU-BAR GIVN	
	1.0+0	1.0+2			Conf 73Kiev 2 263	May 73 - + MULTILVL,LSQ. N+F-WIDS,GR+TBL	
					Conf 72Kiev	72 - + MULTILEVEL ANALYSIS.	
	1.0+0	6.3+1			Conf 70Helsinki 1 469	Jun 70 - +60.SINGLE+MULTILEVEL ANALYSIS	
	1.0+0	1.6+2			Jour SJA 29 1156	Nov 70 - + TRANSLATION	
	0.0+0	1.0+2			Data EXFOR20680.	Sep 77 102PTS.E0,WF,AVG WF,SIG*WF,WT,- - - -	
Reson Params	None		DUB	Theo	Jour YF 13 240	Feb 71 Malecki+G-WID,THEO CFD EXPT.TBL,GRPH	
					Jour SNP 13 133	Aug 71 - + ENGL OF YF 13 240.	
Reson Params	1.2+1	1.0+2	GEL	Expt	Conf 71Knoxvill 823	Mar 71 Kolar+. WT WG WF 2G*WN TABULATED	+
	7.0-1	7.0+2			Conf 71Knoxvill 707	Mar 71 - +.AVG D AND AVG 2G*WN GIVEN	
	1.3+1	1.0+2			Data EXFOR20116.	Jul 72 354PTS.WF,AVG.WF,WG,AVG WG,WT,- -	
Reson Params	6.2-1	5.0+4	SRL	Theo	Conf 71Knoxvill 714	Mar 71 Mccrosson. STAT CALCULATN AVG PARAMS	
Reson Params	2.5+2	5.9+3	ANL	Eval	Rept ANL-7815	May 71 Kikuchi.INTERMEDIATE RESON PARAMS	
Reson Params	4.3+0	9.1+1	BRC	Expt	Conf 75Kiev 5 337	May 75 Simon+ J(PI),GF,NU,E-GAM VS EN.TABLE	
Reson Params	4.3+0	1.6+2	SAC	Expt	Jour JPR 37 659	Jun 76 Blons+ SHAPE ANALYSIS RESULTS.	+
					Conf 71Knoxvill 836	Mar 71 - + WF,WT,2G.WN,S.WF,WF,WG. SHAPE	
	0.0+0	1.6+2			Data EXFOR20484.	Nov 75 121PTS.AVG.WF,WT,MEANVLSP0.	
Reson Params	Maxwl		KUK	Theo	Conf 76Ahmedabd 2 1	Dec 76 Sharma+AVG S-WAVE REDUCED N-WID ANAL	
Reson Params	1.0+2	1.0+5	IFB	Expt	Rept YK-25 32	77 Ancipov+ AVG PARS(E),FRM RESOLVD RES	
Strnth Fnctn	2.0-2	2.0+3	MTR	Expt	Jour NSE 11 111	Sep 61 Simpson+.GRAPH,PUO2 SAMPLES,FAST CH	+
					Rept IDO-16679	Aug 61 .SEE ALSO	
		1.0+4			Data EXFOR12537.004	Jun 76 . 1 PT.	
Strnth Fnctn	6.0+0	6.0+0	HAR	Expt	Prog AERE-PR/NP6 3	Apr 64 James. = 1 DATA INDEX LINES	+
Strnth Fnctn	1.5+1		CRC	Expt	Jour CJP 42 2384	Dec 64 Craig.	+
	1.2+1	3.2+1			Data EXFOR12528.007	Jun 76 . 1 PT.	
Strnth Fnctn	7.0-1	7.0+2	GEL	Expt	Conf 71Knoxvill 707	Mar 71 Kolar+.SO=2.49+-0.7	+
	1.3+1	5.0+1			Conf 71Knoxvill 823	Mar 71 - + FROM TOT.LINAC.TOF.	
	1.3+1	5.0+1			Data EXFOR20116.017	Jul 72 1PNT.L=0.	
Strnth Fnctn		1.6+2	SAC	Expt	Conf 71Knoxvill 836	Mar 71 Blons+ SINGLE LVL, L=0	+
					Jour NSE 51 130	Jun 73 - + REVIEW FISS XSECT MEAS SACLAY	
	0.0+0	1.6+2			Data EXFOR20484.005	Nov 75 1PNT.L=0.	
Strnth Fnctn	None		AUA	Eval	Rept AAEC/E-277	Mar 73 Musgrove.TBLS EXPTL DATA+BEST VALUES	
Strnth Fnctn	4.3+0	1.6+2	SAC	Expt	Jour JPR 37 659	Jun 76 Blons+ FROM MULTILEVEL ANALYSIS.	+
	0.0+0	1.0+2			Data EXFOR20680.007	Sep 77 3PTS.L=0.	
Lvl Density	-		COP	Theo	Jour NP 6 62	Mar 58 Ericson. LVL DENSITY FORM CFD EXP	
Lvl Density	+6		MIL	Theo	Jour EN 15 1 54	Jan 68 Facchini+ LDL PARS FROM LOW EN RES	
Lvl Density		3.0+1	KUR	Theo	Jour YF 9 303	Feb 69 Vorotnikov.LVL DEN(EXCIT-E),TBL GRPH	
					Jour SNP 9 179	Aug 69 TRANSLATN.*	
Lvl Density	1.3+1	5.0+1	GEL	Expt	Conf 71Knoxvill 823	Mar 71 Kolar+ FROM RESOLVED RESONANCES.	+
	1.3+1	5.0+1			Data EXFOR20116.018	Jul 72 1PNT.SP.CUT.	
Lvl Density	7.0+6	1.6+7	DUB	ExTh	Rept JINR-E15-7362	Jul 73 Gangrsky+ PARS FROM (G,N),(G,G),GRPH	

94 Plutonium 241

Quantity	Energy (ev) Min	Max	Lab	Type	Documentation Ref Vol Page	Date	Author, Comments	Data
Lvl Density	None		MUN	Theo Jour	NP/A 217 269	Dec 73	Dilg+ A,DELTA. BACK SHIFTED FERMIGAS	
Lvl Density	None		COP	Theo Jour	NP/A 222 493	Apr 74	Dossing+COLL ROTAT.SPAC. ACCUR ESTIM	
Lvl Density	None		ROC	Theo Jour	NP/A 223 589	May 74	Huizenga+ EXP CFD MICROSC TH AX SYMM	
Lvl Density	+6		DUB	Theo Rept	JINR – E4 – 9236	Nov 75	Komov+ AVG LVL – SPAC,SEMIMICRO CFD XP	

94 Plutonium 242

Quantity	Energy (ev) Min	Max	Lab	Type	Documentation Ref Vol Page	Date	Author, Comments	Data
Evaluation	5.0+2	1.0+7	ANL	Eval Book	FRC	60	Yftah+.16E GROUPS.FAST REACT DATA	
Evaluation	Maxwl	1.0+7	GEL	Eval Rept	EANDC(E)17U	Aug 60	PROSDOCIMI	
Evaluation	4.1−1	1.0+7	GA	Eval Rept	GA− 2451	Aug 61	Joanou+.68GRP ABS.EL,IN TRANSF.NF.NU	
Evaluation	2.5−2	1.1+7	FEI	Eval Book	ABAGJAN	64	26 GROUP CONST,TOT,FISS,NU,CAPT,SCAT	
Evaluation	1.0−3	1.5+7	GA	Eval Rept	GA− 6576	Jul 65	Drake. EVAL FROM VAR SOURCES	
Evaluation	1.0+3	1.5+7	SOR	Eval Rept	IA− 1094	Jun 66	Segev.GRAPHS EVALUATED CROSS – SECTNS	
Evaluation	1.0−3	1.0+7	AI	Eval Rept	NAA−SR−12271	May 67	Dunford+ TOT RES SEL SIN NF NG+ CRVS	
Evaluation	1.0−3	1.5+7	SOR	Eval Rept	IA− 1275	Feb 73	Caner+ COMPLETE KEDAK EVAL,TBLS,FIGS	
	1.0−3	1.5+7		Data	KEDAK−3	Oct 75	DATA FILES FOR 13 QUANTITIES	
Evaluation	1.0−5	2.0+7	SRL	Eval Rept	EPRI−NP−161	Dec 75	Benjamin+ENDF4B.DIFF DATA REVISIONS	
Total	2.0+0	7.5+0	HAR	Expt Jour	JNE 6 303	May 58	Egelstaff.FC TRANS NDG,ONLY RES PAR	
Total	2.3+0	5.5+1	ANL	Expt Jour	PR 114 505	Oct 59	Cote+	+
				Conf	58Geneva 16 77	Sep 58	− +.PPR685,NDG,TOF	
	2.3+0	5.5+1		Data	EXFOR12539.006	Jun 76	. 50 PTS.	
Total	1.0−2	1.0+6	RLY	Revw Conf	64Vienna 56	Dec 64	Kronberger.GRPH SIG(E),PU – ISOT,U – 235	
Total	2.0−2	4.0+2	LRL	Expt Jour	PR 146 840	Jun 66	Auchampaugh+.LINAC.TOF.	+
				Rept	UCRL−12379	65	.SUPERSEDED	
	2.5−2	3.9+2		Data	EXFOR12546.	Jun 76	. 183 PTS.	
Total	5.0+1	1.5+7	SOR	Eval Rept	IA− 1094 FIG.1	Jun 66	Segev.GRAPH AVERAGED EVAL.CROSS – SCTN	
Total	1.5−3	8.1+3	MTR	Expt Jour	NSE 40 389	Jun 70	Young+ FAST CHOPPER.TRANS.OXIDE SAMPL	+
	1.5−3	8.0+3		Rept	IN− 1132	Jun 68	− +TRNS AND CS DATA TBL	
	1.3−3	7.7+3		Data	EXFOR10123.	Mar 76	1017PTS.	
Total	1.5−3	1.0+0	MTR	Expt Jour	NSE 43 341	Mar 71	Young+,METAL SAMPLES,CFD OTHERS,CURV	+
	1.3−3	2.0+0		Data	EXFOR10133.002	Nov 72	79PTS.	
Total	−3	1.0+1	IKE	Theo Rept	IKE−6−61/2	Jan 73	Keinert.DATA LIBRARY	
Total	2.5−2	1.5+7	SOR	Eval Rept	IA− 1275	Feb 73	Caner+ RECOMMENDED SIG(E),TBLS,GRPHS	
	1.0−3	1.5+7		Data	KEDAK−3	Oct 75	1696 DATA SETS	
Total	5.0−1	5.0+3	ORL	Expt Prog	ORNL−4844 90	Apr 73	Harvey+. ORELA. TOF. NO DATA GIVEN	+
	1.5+1	3.0+4		Data	EXFOR10617.003	Aug 76	DATA UNOBTAINABLE FROM AUTHORS.	
Total	6.0+2	3.8+3	LAS	Expt Jour	PR/C 7 2085	May 73	Auchampaugh+LINAC.RES PARS DRVD.	+
	6.0+2	3.8+3		Data	EXFOR10616.004	Aug 76	DATA UNOBTAINABLE FROM AUTHORS	
Total	2.7+0	1.3+3	GEL	Expt Jour	NP/A 207 342	Jun 73	Poortmans+ LINAC.HE3.AREA RES ANAL.	+
	2.7+0	1.3+3		Data	EXFOR20383.	Oct 74	0PTS. SEE RESONANCE PARAMETERS.	
Total	2.5−2		IKE	Eval Rept	IKE−6−80	Apr 74	Mattes+ ENDF/B,UKNDL,KEDAK CFD	
Total	−3	1.9+0	THS	Theo Rept	IKE−6 89 61	Jun 75	Keinert. DATA LIBRARY	
Total	1.0−3	1.5+7	KFK	Eval Data	KEDAK−3	Oct 75	1696 DATA SETS	+
Elastic	2.5−2		ANL	Expt Jour	ACRB 27 2284	Nov 71	Lander+ COH SCAT AMP	+
	2.5−2			Data	EXFOR10282.004	May 73	. 1 PT, COH AMP	
Elastic	1.0+5	1.0+7	SOR	Eval Rept	IAEA−153 141	73	Ilberg+ EVALUATD DATA FILES CFD,GRPH	
Elastic	2.0+2	1.5+7	SOR	Eval Rept	IA− 1275	Feb 73	Caner+ RECOMMENDED SIG(E),TBLS,GRPHS	
	1.0−3	1.5+7		Data	KEDAK−3	Oct 75	1656 DATA SETS	
Elastic	2.7+0	1.3+3	GEL	Expt Jour	NP/A 207 342	Jun 73	Poortmans+ LINAC.HE3.REL PB.RES GIVN	+
				Rept	RCN−203 113	Dec 73	− + RES PARAMETERS ONLY.	
	2.7+0	1.3+3		Data	EXFOR20383.	Oct 74	0PTS. SEE RESONANCE PARAMETERS.	
Elastic	2.5−2		IKE	Eval Rept	IKE−6−80	Apr 74	Mattes+ ENDF/B,UKNDL,KEDAK CFD	
Diff Elastic	1.0+4	1.5+7	SOR	Eval Rept	IA− 1094 FIG12	Jun 66	Segev.GRAPH AVERAGE COSINE(LAB)	
Diff Elastic	1.0+4	1.5+7	AI	Eval Rept	NAA−SR−11980	Apr 67	Campbell+ LEG COEFS TABLE C – M SYSTEM	
Diff Elastic	+3		ISL	Theo Prog	IA− 1218 14	Aug 70	Kaner.CODE FOR COMPOUND – SIG CALC,NDG	
Diff Elastic	−3	1.0+1	IKE	Theo Rept	IKE−6−61/2	Jan 73	Keinert.DATA LIBRARY	
Diff Elastic	2.0+2	1.5+7	SOR	Eval Rept	IA− 1275	Feb 73	Caner+ ALSO TRANSPORT,COSINE,TBLS	
	2.0+2	1.5+7		Data	KEDAK−3	Oct 75	74 ENERGIES	
Tot Inelastc	4.0+4	1.5+7	SOR	Eval Rept	IA− 1094 FIG11	Jun 66	Segev.GRAPH.PARTLY SAME AS PU240	
Tot Inelastc	1.0+7	1.2+7	SOR	Eval Rept	IA− 1152	Dec 67	Yftah+ RECOMMEND SIG(E),GRAPH+TABLE	
	5.0+4	1.5+7		Data	KEDAK−3	Oct 75	55 DATA SETS+ 17 EXCT LVLS	
Tot Inelastc	5.0+4	1.5+6	SOR	Eval Rept	IA− 1175 −	Feb 73	Caner+ RECOMMENDED SIG(E),TBLS,GRPHS	
Diff Inelast	1.4+7		LRL	Theo Rept	UCRL−50181	Feb 67	Lutz+.CALC ANG DIST FOR FIRST 2+ LVL	
Diff Inelast	Thrsh	7.6+6	DUB	Expt Jour	AE 31 156	Aug 71	Gangrskij+ SIG FOR SPON – FISS ISO,TBL	
	+6	+7		Rept	JINR−P3−5528	Jan 71	− + GND+ISOM FISS STATE SIGS	
	Thrsh	7.6+6		Jour	SJA 31 874	Mar 72	. ENGL OF AE 31 156	

94 Plutonium 242

Quantity	Energy (ev) Min	Max	Lab	Type	Documentation Ref Vol Page	Date	Author, Comments	Data
Diff Inelast	+6		KFI	Expt Jour	MFF 21 555	73	Nagy. THESIS,HUNG. TO FISS ISO,GRND	
Diff Inelast	5.0+4	1.5+6	SOR	Eval Rept	IA - 1275	Feb 73	Caner+ SIG(E) TO 10 LEVELS,TBL,GRPHS	
Scattering	2.5-2		SOR	Eval Conf	67Karlsrhe 1 123	Nov 67	Yiftah+,RECOMMENDED VALUE GIVEN	
Scattering	-3	1.0+1	IKE	Theo Rept	IKE - 6 - 61/2	Jan 73	Keinert.DATA LIBRARY	
Nonelastic	1.0+3	1.5+7	SOR	Eval Rept	IA - 1094 3	Jun 66	Segev.SAME AS PU240 RECOMMENDED	
Nonelastic	2.0+2	1.5+7	SOR	Eval Rept	IA - 1275	Feb 73	Caner+ RECOMMENDED SIG(E),TBLS,GRPHS	
	1.0-3	1.5+7		Data	KEDAK - 3	Oct 75	1738 DATA SETS	
Absorption	Maxwl		CRC	Expt Jour	CJP 35 147	Feb 57	Butler.	+
	Maxwl			Data	EXFOR12481.007	Jun 76	. 1 PT.	
Absorption	5.0-3	2.5+0	GA	Eval Rept	GA - 2113	Jun 61	Wikner+.TABLE 100 E POINTS	
Absorption	Pile		SRL	Expt Conf	68Wash. 2 1279	Mar 68	Folger.	+
	Pile			Data	EXFOR12534.002	Jun 76	. 1 PT.	
Absorption	2.5-2		MTR	Expt Jour	NSE 40 389	Jun 70	Young+ASSUME A POT SCT R.OXIDE SAMPL	
Absorption	2.5-2		MTR	Expt Jour	NSE 43 341	Mar 71	Young+METAL SAMPL MEAS CFD OXIDE VAL	
Absorption	6.2-1	1.0+7	SRL	Theo Conf	71Knoxvill 714	Mar 71	Mccrosson. SPECTRUM - AVERAGED SIG	
Absorption	1.0-3	2.0+0	JUL	Theo Rept	JUEL - 746 - RG 49	Apr 71	Bonka.KUGEL - THERMOS - LIBR,T=300K,CURV	
Absorption	Pile		SRL	Expt Abst	ANS 14 344	Jun 71	Rusche. VALUE GIVEN	
Absorption	8.0-2		ANL	Expt Jour	ACRB 27 2284	Nov 71	Lander+ MEAS 15B	+
	8.0-2			Data	EXFOR10282.005	May 73	1PT,SIGMA	
Absorption	2.0+2	1.5+7	SOR	Eval Rept	IA - 1275	Feb 73	Caner+ RECOMMENDED SIG(E),TBLS,GRPHS	
	1.0-3	1.5+7		Data	KEDAK - 3	Oct 75	1736 DATA SETS	
Res Int Abs	+0		ANL	Expt Conf	58Geneva 16 77	Sep 58	Cote+.PPR685,VAL GVN,EXPT DESCRIBED	+
Res Int Abs	9.2-1		SRL	Expt Conf	68Wash. 21 279	Mar 68	Folger.	+
	9.2-1			Data	EXFOR12534.003	Jun 76	. 1 PT.	
Res Int Abs	5.0-1		MTR	Expt Jour	NSE 40 389	Jun 70	Young+FROM RES PARS AND LVL SPACING.	+
	5.0-1			Data	EXFOR10123.004	Mar 76	1PT.RIA =1100+ - 70B.	
Res Int Abs	None		SRL	Expt Abst	ANS 14 344	Jun 71	Rusche. VALUE GIVEN	
Res Int Abs	5.0-1		IAE	Revw Rept	IAEA - 143 897	Apr 72	Lemmel.CAPT,EVALUTS+RECENT EXPTS,TBL	
(n,γ)	Pile		ANL	Expt Jour	PR 83 1267	Sep 51	Sullivan+ 50PERCENT UNCERTAINTY.	
(n,γ)	2.5+4		ANL	Expt Jour	PR 93 1433	Mar 54	Studier.	+
	2.5+4			Data	EXFOR12538.002	Jun 76	. 1 PT.	
(n,γ)	Pile		ANL	Expt Jour	NSE 1 62	Mar 56	Fields+1450+30+ - 10B	
				Conf	55Geneva 7 261	Aug 55	Bentley+.P809,VAL GVN,CHEMICAL METHD	
	Pile			Data	EXFOR12535.008	Jun 76	. 1 PT.	
(n,γ)	Maxwl		ANL	Expt Jour	NSE 1 204	Jul 56	Jaffey.30B FROM ORNL ANL DATA	
(n,γ)	Maxwl	Pile	CRC	Expt Jour	CJP 35 147	Feb 57	Butler+ 55+ - 15B AS DESTRUCTION SIG	+
	Maxwl	Pile		Data	EXFOR12481.	Jun 76	. 2 PTS	
(n,γ)	None		KAP	Comp Rept	KAPL - 1781	Jul 57	Schuman. SIGMA GIVEN	
(n,γ)	Maxwl		ANL	Expt Conf	58Geneva 16 77	Sep 58	Cote+.PPR685,VAL GVN,1/V ASSUMED	
(n,γ)	Pile		ORL	Eval Jour	NSE 6 100	Aug 59	Stoughton+,BEST VALUE .025EV=25+ - 10B	
(n,γ)	Maxwl		CRC	Eval Rept	AECL - 1054	Mar 60	Walker. (CRRP - 913)	
(n,γ)	Pile		CRC	Eval Rept	CRRP - 960	Jan 62	Wescott. EFF SIG, TBL 20 - 760DEG C	
(n,γ)	Maxwl		ORL	Expt Prog	ORNL - 3679	Sep 64	Halperin+,LITR IRRADIATION	
(n,γ)	+5	+7	RLY	Revw Conf	64Vienna 56	Dec 64	Kronberger.FAST REACTOR,1 - GROUP SIGS	
(n,γ)	1.0+3	1.5+7	SOR	Eval Rept	IA - 1094 3	Jun 66	Segev.SAME AS PU240 RECOMMENDED	
(n,γ)	Maxwl	Pile	BNL	Eval Rept	BNL - 982 22	Aug 66	Pearlstein. 15.7B,14.3B FROM RES PAR	
(n,γ)	Maxwl		SRL	Expt Rept	DP - MS - 66 - 69	Oct 66	ICE.	+
	Maxwl			Data	EXFOR12550.002	Jun 76	. 2 PTS, MAXW AND 25 - 2	
(n,γ)	Maxwl		BNL	Theo Abst	ANS 10 228	Jun 67	Prince. CALC SIG = 30B	
(n,γ)	2.0+4		LRL	Expt Jour	AF 36 509	Nov 67	Ingley+ QUOTED BY TRURAN	
(n,γ)	Pile		CCP	Revw Jour	AE 24 247	Mar 68	Bak+ OTHER SIG VAL GVN,TBL	
				Jour	SJA 24 300	Mar 68	TRANSLATN.*	
(n,γ)	2.5-2		SRL	Expt Conf	68Wash. 1279	Mar 68	Folger+ ACT 20B	+
				Rept	DP - MS - 67 - 112	Mar 68	.SAME	
(n,γ)	Pile		CCP	Theo Jour	AE 25 466	Dec 68	Usynin. OTHER MEAN SIG GVN	
				Jour	SJA 25 1290	Dec 68	TRANSLATN.*	
(n,γ)		3.9+2	TRM	Comp Prog	BARC - 423 6	69	Garg. SELF - SHIELD SIG,TEMP - INFL, NDG	
(n,γ)	None		LAS	Expt Prog	WASH - 1136 110	Sep 69	Silbert+,PHYSICS - 8 SHOT,ANAL TBC	
(n,γ)	Maxwl		CRC	Expt Jour	CJP 48 716	Mar 70	Durham+,BY MEAST OF AM243 PRODUCTION	+
	Maxwl			Data	EXFOR10171.002	Jun 72	1PNT.SIGMA.	
(n,γ)	+1	+7	CAD	Theo Conf	70Helsinki 2 465	Jun 70	Barre+73. MICROSC CFD INTEGRAL DATA	
(n,γ)	1.0-2	1.0+7	ORL	Revw Jour	REA 8 473	Sep 70	Kasten. REVIEW,SIG(NEUT - E) GRAPH	
(n,γ)	Pile		KFK	Eval Rept	KFK - 1453	Mar 72	Eberle+ 2 - GROUP SIGS,FITTED TO EXPT	
(n,γ)	Maxwl		IAE	Revw Rept	IAEA - 143 897	Apr 72	Lemmel.EVALUATIONS+RECENT EXPTS,TBL	
	2.5-2			Rept	IAEA - 143 897	Apr 72	- .EVALUATIONS+RECENT EXPTS,TBL	
	1.0-2	3.0+0		Rept	IAEA - 143 897	Apr 72	- .GRAPH OF EVALUATED SIGMA	
(n,γ)	Pile		JUL	Expt Jour	JIN 34 8 2427	Aug 72	Ihle+ REACTOR CROSS SECTION	
(n,γ)	Pile		HEI	Expt Jour	RCA 19 188	73	Baumgartner+ SIG=39 B OBTAINED	

94 Plutonium 242

Quantity	Energy (ev) Min	Max	Lab	Type	Documentation Ref Vol Page	Date	Author, Comments	Data
(n,γ)	2.5−2	1.5+7	SOR Eval	Rept	IA− 1275	Feb 73	Caner+ RECOMMENDED SIG(E),TBLS,GRPHS	
	1.0+5	1.0+7		Rept	IAEA− 153 141	73	Ilberg+ EVALUATD DATA FILES CFD,GRPH	
	1.0−3	1.5+7		Data	KEDAK− 3	Oct 75	1745 DATA SETS	
(n,γ)	2.7+0	1.3+3	GEL Expt	Jour	NP/A 207 342	Jun 73	Poortmans+ LINAC.60M.MR.AREA RES ANL	+
				Rept	RCN− 203 113	Dec 73	− + RES PARAMETERS ONLY.	
	2.7+0	1.3+3		Data	EXFOR20383.	Oct 74	0PTS. SEE RESONANCE PARAMETERS.	
(n,γ)	2.0+0	1.3+3	MOL Expt	Jour	NP/A 207 342	Jun 73	Poortmans+ LINAC,MOXON−RAE DET. NDG	
(n,γ)	2.5−2		IKE Eval	Rept	IKE− 6−80	Apr 74	Mattes+ ENDF/B,UKNDL,KEDAK CFD	
(n,γ)	2.0+2	7.0+4	RPI Expt	Conf	75Wash. 584	Mar 75	Hockenbury+ TABLE,GRAPH	+
	6.3+3	8.7+4		Data	EXFOR10436.002	Oct 74	251PTS,SIGMA	
(n,γ)	2.5−2		SRL Eval	Conf	75Wash. 224	Mar 75	Benjamin+ TBL BEST FIT TRANSPU PROD.	
(n,γ)	None		ORL Expt	Conf	75Wash. 229	Oct 75	Weston+NDG.TBD	
Res Int Capt	5.0−1		CRC Expt	Jour	CJP 35 147	Feb 57	Butler+ NRX 1275B REL CO59+U238	+
	5.0−1			Data	EXFOR12481.011	Jun 76	. 1 PT.RI	
Res Int Capt	1.5−1	1.0+6	ORL Eval	Jour	NSE 6 100	Aug 59	Stoughton+ BEST VALUE 130+ −30B	
Res Int Capt	None		CRC Expt	Rept	AECL−1054	Mar 60	Walker. REDUCED RI	
Res Int Capt	Maxwl		ORL Expt	Prog	ORNL−3679	Sep 64	Halperin+,LITR IRRADIATION	
Res Int Capt	5.5−1		BNL Eval	Rept	BNL−982 22	Aug 66	Pearlstein. 1150B CALC, RECOMMENDED	
Res Int Capt	Maxwl		BNL Theo	Abst	ANS 10 228	Jun 67	Prince. CALC RI=1150B	
Res Int Capt	5.0−1		SRL Expt	Conf	68Wash. 1279	Mar 68	Folger+ ACT 1180B	
				Rept	DP−MS−67−112	Mar 68	.SAME	
Res Int Capt	Pile		KFK Eval	Rept	KFK−1453	Mar 72	Eberle+ 1180B	
Res Int Capt	6.3−1		SRL Eval	Conf	75Wash. 224	Mar 75	Benjamin+ TBL BEST FIT TRANSPU PROD.	
(n,2n)	6.0+6	1.5+7	SOR Eval	Rept	IA− 1094 FIG.3	Jun 66	Segev.SAME AS PU240 RECOMMENDED	
(n,2n)	6.2+6	+6	ORL Expt	Prog	ORNL−4581 36	Sep 70	Bemis+ UPPER LIMIT TO ISOMER PROD	
(n,2n)	1.5+7		DUB Expt	Jour	IJP 47 232	73	Belov+ SIG TO SPONFIS GIVN,FRAGM−DET	
				Rept	JINR−E15−6807	Nov 72	− + SPON FISS ISOMER PRODUCTN,TBL	
(n,2n)	1.5+7		KFI Expt	Jour	MFF 21 555	73	Nagy. THESIS,HUNG. TO FISS ISO,GRND	
(n,2n)	6.3+6	1.5+7	SOR Eval	Rept	IA− 1275	Feb 73	Caner+ ALSO N3N,SIG(E),TABLES+GRAPHS	
	6.7+6	1.5+7		Data	KEDAK−3	Oct 75	12 DATA SETS	
(n,2n)	1.4+7		LRL Expt	Jour	AE 40 491	Jun 76	Browne+ SIG TO SPONFIS ISO.NOT FOUND	
				Jour	SJA 40 587	Dec 76	. ENGL OF AE 40 491	
(n,xn) x>2	1.2+7	1.5+7	SOR Eval	Rept	IA− 1094 FIG.3	Jun 66	Segev.(N3N),GRAPH EVALUATED SIGMA	
(n,xn) x>2	1.0−3	1.5+7	SOR Eval	Prog	INDC(SEC)−42	Dec 74	Caner+ N,3N. EVALUATION,NDG	
	1.2+7	1.5+7		Data	KEDAK−3	Oct 75	5 DATA SETS (N,3N)	
Fission	Spont		ANL Expt	Jour	PR 103 340	Jul 56	Mech+,ALFAS/FISSION + SPON FISS HL	
Fission	Maxwl		CRC Expt	Conf	58Geneva 16 54	Sep 58	Eastwood+ PPR203,ZERO+ −0.2B	
				Rept	KAPL−1781	Jul 57	Butler+ LESS THAN 0.3 BARN	
	Maxwl			Data	EXFOR12011.005	Jun 76	. 1 PT.	
Fission	1.0+5	1.7+6	ANL Expt	Jour	PR 117 1305	Mar 60	Butler+	+
	3.0+4	1.7+6		Conf	61Vienna 1 125	Aug 61	− +.PPR36,GRAPH,HIGH PRECISION	
	1.4+5	1.7+6		Data	EXFOR12540.002	Jun 76	. 65 PTS.	
Fission	2.7+0		HAN Expt	Rept	HW− 67219	Oct 60	Leonard+LESS THAN 41B	
Fission	Spont		DUB Expt	Jour	ZET 40 1296	May 61	Druin. HL OF SPONTANEOUS FISSION	
				Jour	JET 13 913	Nov 61	TRANSLATN.*	
Fission	3.0+6	6.0+6	ANL Expt	Rept	EANDC(US)−28	Sep 62	.NDG TBD ANL	
Fission	+5	+7	RLY Revw	Conf	64Vienna 56	Dec 64	Kronberger.FAST REACTOR,1−GROUP SIGS	
Fission	Spont		BRK Revw	Jour	NP 81 1	Jun 66	Myers.TBL CALC FISS BARRIERS	
Fission	1.0+5	1.5+7	SOR Eval	Rept	IA− 1094 FIG11	Jun 66	Segev.GRAPH.ABOVE 1.7MEV EQU PU240	
Fission	1.0+3	1.0+7	ANL Eval	Jour	NSE 26 149	Oct 66	Davey. EVALUATION	
Fission	1.5+7		KUR Expt	Jour	YF 5 966	May 67	Fomushkin+ SIG GIVEN,FISSANISOTROPY	
				Jour	SNP 5 689	Nov 67	. ENGL OF YF 5 966	
Fission	Maxwl		BNL Theo	Abst	ANS 10 228	Jun 67	Prince. SIG=.035B	
Fission	Pile		WIN Expt	Rept	AEEW−R−526	Jun 67	Stevenson+.FISS RATIO TO U235.ZEBRA	+
Fission	Pile		CCP Theo	Jour	AE 25 466	Dec 68	Usynin.AVG SUM SIG(N,G)+SIG(N,F) GVN	
				Jour	SJA 25 1290	Dec 68	TRANSLATN.*	
Fission		9.5+2	TRM Comp	Prog	BARC−423 6	69	Garg. SELF−SHIELD SIG,TEMP−INFL, NDG	
Fission	1.6+1	3.5+4	HAR Expt	Jour	NP/A 123 24	Jan 69	James. TOF. SPON FISS SUBTRACTED.	+
				Rept	AERE−R−5924	Oct 68	− .SUB THRS MEDT OBSERVED WF 2RES	
Fission	−		TPI Theo	Jour	YF 9 102	Jan 69	Korostova+ CV,SHELL CORR,LIQU−DROP−E	
				Jour	SNP 9 62	Jul 69	TRANSLATN.*	
Fission	4.4+5	3.6+6	KUR Expt	Prog	YFI−7 25	Apr 69	Fomushkim+ TABLE OF REL SIG AT 14 ES	+
				Rept	INDC(CCP)−7U28	Feb 70	TRANSLATN.*	
	4.4+5	3.6+6		Data	EXFOR40012.009	Aug 70	SIGMA AT 14 ENERGIES	
Fission	Spont		COP Revw	Conf	69Vienna 155	Jul 69	Strutinsky+PPR203. HL GVN,'SHELL−TH'	
	−			Theo Conf	68DUBSY 431	Jul 68	− +,INTERM. STATES IN FISS.	
Fission	−		FEI Theo	Conf	69Vienna 337	Jul 69	Gaj+PPR132. 2HUMPD−BARR−CALC,TBL	
Fission	−		HAR Revw	Conf	69Vienna 249	Jul 69	Lynn. REVW=STRUTINSKY TH + EXPTS,TBL	

94 Plutonium 242

Quantity	Energy (ev) Min	Energy (ev) Max	Lab	Type	Documentation Ref Vol Page	Date	Author, Comments	Data
Fission	None		LAS	Expt Conf	69Vienna 918	Jul 69	Britt+PPR101.(D,P FISSN)CFD(N,FISSN)	
Fission	4.4+5	3.6+6	KUR	Expt Jour	YF 10 917	Nov 69	Fomushkin+ SIG(E) REL U235.TBL+GRAPH	
				Jour	SNP 10 529	May 70	. ENGL OF YF 10 917	
Fission	1.0+4	4.0+6	TRM	Eval Rept	BARC/I−96	70	Kapil. 9 GROUP SIG,2 N−SPECS,TABLES	
Fission	+1	+7	CAD	Theo Conf	70Helsinki 2 465	Jun 70	Barre+73. MICROSC CFD INTEGRAL DATA	
Fission	+3		ISL	Theo Prog	IA−1218 14	Aug 70	Kaner. CODE FOR SIG CALCULATION, NDG	
Fission	Spont		MRY	Theo Prog	ORO−4028−28	71	Jackson+. SPON FISSION HALF−LIFE GVN	
Fission	+6	+7	DUB	Expt Rept	JINR−P3−5528	Jan 71	Gangrskij+ PU242(N,N')ISOM FISSN SIG	
Fission	5.0+1	3.0+6	LAS	Expt Jour	NP/A 163 577	Mar 71	Bergen+ NUCL EXPLOSION, 5−100KEV GAP	+
	5.1+1	3.0+6		Rept	LA−4420	Apr 70	− +, NUCL SHOT,TOF,TABLES+CURVES	
	5.1+1	3.0+6		Data	EXFOR10062.002	Apr 71	1647PTS,SIGMA.	
Fission	2.0+1	1.0+7	LAS	Expt Jour	NP/A 171 31	Aug 71	Auchampaugh+ BOMB.REL LI6(NT),U235NF	+
	2.0+2	9.6+6		Data	EXFOR10266.	Sep 72	.6601PTS,SIGMA.	
Fission	0.0+0	1.0+0	GEL	Revw Jour	AKE 18 229	Nov 71	Theobald+ SUB−BARRIER FISS EXPTS,TH	
Fission	2.5−2		IAE	Revw Rept	IAEA−143 897	Apr 72	Lemmel.EVALUATIONS+RECENT EXPTS,TBL	
Fission	Pile		FAR	Expt Prog	EANDC(E)150U	May 72	Vidal.INTEGRAL CROSS SECTION TO U235	
Fission	−		GEL	ExTh Jour	NP/A 187 305	Jun 72	Weigmann+ F.B.PARAMS FROM DATA ANAL.	
Fission	Pile		JUL	Expt Jour	JIN 34 8 2427	Aug 72	Ihle+ REACTOR CROSS SECTION	
Fission	3.0+3	6.0+4	RPI	Expt Prog	USNDC−3 155	Oct 72	Hockenbury+. TO BE COMPLETED. NDG	
Fission	2.0+2	1.5+7	SOR	Eval Rept	IA−1275	Feb 73	Caner+ RECOMMENDED SIG(E),TBLS,GRPHS	
	1.0+5	1.0+7		Rept	IAEA−153 141	73	Ilberg+ EVALUATD DATA FILES CFD,GRPH	
	1.0−3	1.5+7		Data	KEDAK−3	Oct 75	1179 DATA SETS	
Fission	None		FRK	Theo Jour	NP/A 207 225	Jun 73	Albrecht. 2CENTRE SHELLMOD,DEF−E MAP	
Fission	2.5−2	1.0+5	LRL	Expt Prog	USNDC−9 82	Dec 73	Behrens+REL B10.NDG.TBD	
Fission	None		DUB	Revw Jour	FDP 22 199	74	Gangrsky+ FIS−BARRIER,GRPH EMAX+EMIN	
Fission	2.5−2		IKE	Eval Rept	IKE−6−80	Apr 74	Mattes+ ENDF/B,UKNDL,KEDAK CFD	
Fission	3.0+6	5.0+6	LAS	Expt Conf	75Wash. 129	Mar 75	Moore.GRPH R MATR STAT CALC CFD EXP	
Fission	2.5−2		SRL	Eval Conf	75Wash. 224	Mar 75	Benjamin+ TBL BEST FIT TRANSPU PROD.	
Fission	2.0+1	1.0+7	JAE	Revw Conf	IAEA−186 3 1	76	Igarasi. REVW AVAIL DATA,GRPH+BIBLIO	
	1.0+3	1.5+7		Rept	JAERI−M−6315	Nov 75	− +GRPHS.4 DATA SETS COMPARED.	
Res Int Fiss	Maxwl		BNL	Theo Abst	ANS 10 228	Jun 67	Prince. CALC RI=0.6B	
Res Int Fiss	5.0−1		IAE	Revw Rept	IAEA−143 897	Apr 72	Lemmel.FISS,EVALUTS+RECENT EXPTS,TBL	
Res Int Fiss	6.3−1		SRL	Eval Conf	75Wash. 224	Mar 75	Benjamin+ TBL BEST FIT TRANSPU PROD.	
Alpha	Fiss		LRL	ExTh Jour	NP/A 124 130	Feb 69	Ingley.FROM PU242FISS YIELD HEAVY EL	
Alpha	2.0+2	1.5+7	SOR	Eval Rept	IA−1275	Feb 73	Caner+ RECOMMENDED ALF(E),TBLS,GRPHS	
Alpha	Pile		ANL	Expt Jour	NSE 53 9	Jan 74	Dudey+. INTEGRAL MEASTS IN EBR−2.	
				Rept	ANL−7791	Jul 71	Heinrich+. INTEGRAL MEAST IN EBR−2	
Eta	+5	+7	RLY	Revw Conf	64Vienna 56	Dec 64	Kronberger. VAL TABLE OF ETA+NU+SIGS	
Eta	2.0+2	1.5+7	SOR	Eval Rept	IA−1275	Feb 73	Caner+ RECOMMENDED ETA(E),TBLS,GRPHS	
Nu	Spont		BRK	Expt Jour	PR 101 1016	Feb 56	Hicks+,SPONT FIS,REL PU240,PROBABIL.	
Nu	Spont		LRL	Expt Jour	PR 101 1804	Mar 56	Crane+,LII−CRYST+FIS.COUNT.COINC.	
Nu	Spont		RI	Revw Jour	UFN 73 655	Apr 61	Petrzhak+ TABLE,MANY REFS,DISCUSSION	
				Jour	SPU 4 305	Sep 61	. ENGL OF UFN 73 655	
Nu	Spont		FOA	Comp Rept	NP−16440	Mar 63	ASPLUND−NILSSON. REVIEW. TABLE.	
Nu	+5	+7	RLY	Revw Conf	64Vienna 56	Dec 64	Kronberger. VAL TABLE OF ETA+NU+SIGS	
Nu		1.5+7	SOR	Eval Rept	IA−1094 FIG13	Jun 66	Segev.SAME AS PU240 RECOMMENDED	
Nu	Spont		AUA	Expt Jour	JNE 22 63	Feb 68	Boldeman.PROMPT NU+DISTBN,REL CF252	+
				Conf	73Kiev 4 114	May 73	− . DATA REVISED,TABLE	
	Spont			Data	EXFOR30367.004	Jan 77	NU−BAR PROMPT,REPLACES EXF30047.003	
	Spont			Data	EXFOR30047.003	Nov 70	NUBAR+ EMISSION PARAMETERS	
Nu	Spont		FEI	Expt Jour	AE 25 530	Dec 68	Prokhorova+ VAL GVN REL CM−244	+
				Rept	BNL−TR−266	Apr 69	.ENGLISH OF AE 25 530	
				Jour	EAF 25 6 122	Dec 68	.TRANSLATION INTO FRENCH	
	Spont			Data	EXFOR40242.002	Jul 75	.1 DATA LINE	
Nu	Spont		AE	Expt Conf	70Helsinki 2 93	Jun 70	Almen+57. COMPILATN AND NU−TEMP−PLOT	
Nu	+1	+7	CAD	Theo Conf	70Helsinki 2 465	Jun 70	Barre+73. MICROSC CFD INTEGRAL DATA	
Nu	2.5−2		IAE	Revw Rept	IAEA−143 897	Apr 72	Lemmel.EVALUATIONS+RECENT EXPTS,TBL	
Nu	Spont		IAE	Eval Jour	REA 10 637	Dec 72	Manero+ EXTENSIVE SURVEY,TBL,AVG VAL	
Nu	2.0+2	1.5+7	SOR	Eval Rept	IA−1275	Feb 73	Caner+ RECOMMENDED NU(E),TBLS,GRPHS	
	1.0−3	1.5+7		Data	KEDAK−3	Oct 75	2 DATA SETS	
Nu	Spont		DUB	Eval Rept	JINR−P15−7119	Jun 73	Dakowski+ NUBAR+P(NU)−DISTR,TBL,GRPH	
Nu	2.5−2		IKE	Eval Rept	IKE−6−80	Apr 74	Mattes+ ENDF/B,UKNDL,KEDAK CFD	
Nu	Spont		HED	Eval Abst	ANS 22 673	Nov 75	Johnson. TBL,GRPH.NU FROM SPON FISS	
Delayd Neuts	1.5+7		LAS	Expt Abst	ANS 13 760	Nov 70	East+.NEUT ABUNDANCES+HALF−LIVES.	
Delayd Neuts	1.0+5	5.0+6	IAE	Eval Jour	REA 10 637	Dec 72	Manero+ SURVEY,AVERAGE YLD,TBL+GRPHS	
Delayd Neuts	6.4+5	1.3+6	LAS	Expt Jour	NSE 53 80	Jan 73	Evans+REVISED NUD DATA.TBLS.	+
	7.0+5	1.3+6		Jour	NSE 47 311	Mar 72	Krick+SPRSDD.DATA REVISED.	
	6.4+5	1.3+6		Data	EXFOR10117.009	Jul 74	4PTS.	

94 Plutonium 242

Quantity	Energy (ev) Min	Max	Lab	Type	Documentation Ref Vol Page	Date	Author, Comments	Data
Delayd Neuts	1.0+5	1.5+7	LAS	Revw Conf	IAEA – 169 3 377	74	Evans. TBL YLD,AT 3 ES+FAST FISSION	
Delayd Neuts	1.0+6	1.8+7	SOR	Revw Conf	IAEA – 169 2 33	74	Amiel.TOT(N – E)+GROUP(FISS) – YLDS,TBLS	
Delayd Neuts	7.5+5	3.1+6	HAR	Eval Prog	NEANDC(UK)160	Jul 74	Story+ (WIN) EVAL OF TOMLNSN REVISD	
				Rept	AERE – R – 6993	Feb 72	TOMLINSON TOTAL+GROUP YLDS TBL	
Delayd Neuts	7.0+5	1.3+6	AI	Eval Jour	NSE 56 37	Jan 75	Tuttle.TBL.GRPH.RVW MEAS.CFD REC VAL	
	2.5 – 2			Prog	AI – AEC – 13025	May 72	Springer+ VALUE=0.0155+ – 0.0050	
Spect Fiss n	Spont		CCP	Theo Jour	AE 5 649	Dec 58	Kovalev+ THEORY COMPARED WITH EXPT	
				Jour	JNEA 11 166	Feb 60	TRANSLATN.*	
				Jour	SJA 5 1588	58	TRANSLATN.*	
Spect Fiss n	Spont		RI	Expt Prog	YFI – 6 94	Oct 68	Belov+ TABLE N(E) AND MAXWELL – TEMP	+
				Rept	INDC – E – 260 94	Feb 69	.TRANSLATN.* TO BE PUBL IN YF	
	Spont			Data	EXFOR40137.003	Mar 73	SPECT OF FIS – NEUTS .3 – 5.MEV	
Spect Fiss n	Spont		FTI	Expt Jour	YF 9 727	Apr 69	Belov+ EXPTL NEUT – SPEC GRPH+AVG EKIN	
				Jour	SNP 9 421	Oct 69	TRANSLATN.*NO4	
Spect Fiss n	Spont		ANL	Revw Conf	71Vienna 3	Aug 71	Smith. MEAN – E OF NEUTS,EXPTS CFD,TBL	
Spect Fiss n	Maxwl		SOR	Eval Data	KEDAK – 3	Oct 75	2 DATA SETS.CRANBERG PARAMS	
Spect Fiss γ	None		LRL	Eval Prog	USNDC – 1 94	May 72	Browne+. GAMS BEFORE ISOM FISS. NDG	
Fiss Prod γ			WIN	Theo Jour	JNE 25 513	Oct 71	JAMES MEAN ENGS DEL G – RAYS,BETA RAYS	
Fiss Yield	Spont		ANL	Expt Jour	PR 106 779	May 57	Smith+,MASS – ENERGY DISTR CFD XPT+TH	
Fiss Yield	Spont		LAS	Expt Jour	PR 126 1508	May 62	Nobles. YIELD OF LONG RANGE FFRGM	
Fiss Yield	6.5+5	8.0+6	LAS	Expt Jour	PR/B 137 809	Feb 65	Simmons+REL ANG DIST FISS FRAG	
Fiss Yield	Spont		ARK	Expt Abst	DA/B 29 319	Jul 68	Ganapathy.RADIOCHEM,I131 132 133 135	
				Prog	ORO – 3235 – 7	Jan 67	– .I131 132 133 134YLD TBP PR	
				Rept	ORO – 3235 – 11	Jan 67	– +,MASS YLD DISTR A=131 – 135	
Fiss Yield	Spont		MUU	Theo Jour	PL/B 37 467	Dec 71	Schultheis+ SEMI – EMPIRIC SHELL CORRC	
Fiss Yield	None		TRM	Expt Prog	INIS – MF – 334 64	72	.RADIOCHEM+GAM – SPEC,SHORT NOTE,NDG	
Fiss Yield	Spont		FEI	Expt Conf	73Kiev 3 270	May 73	Vorob'Eva+ FRAGM – MASS DISTR,GRAPH	+
	1.0+6	3.5+6		Conf	73Kiev 3 270	May 73	– + FRAGM MASS – DISTR,GRAPH	
	7.0+5	3.5+6		Data	EXFOR40284.	May 75	.PRIMARY FISS – FRAG YIELD AT 3N – E GVN	
Fiss Yield	Spont		FEI	Expt Rept	YFI – 17 3	Aug 74	Djachenko+ YLD(FRAG MASS),TBL	
				Jour	YF 17 696	Apr 73	D'Jachenko+ MASS – YLD+YLD(KIN – E),GRPH	
				Rept	INDC(CCP) – 48	Feb 75	. ENGLISH OF YFI – 17 3	
				Jour	SNP 17 362	Oct 73	.ENGLISH OF YF 17 696	
Fiss Yield	7.0+5	5.0+6	FEI	Expt Jour	YF 23 269	Feb 76	Djachenko+.GRAPH,FRAG DISTR	
				Jour	SNP 23 141	Feb 76	. ENGL OF YF 23 269	
Fiss Yield	2.0+6	1.4+7	LAS	Eval Abst	ANS 24 462	Nov 76	Madland+PAIR EFFECT ON FISS PROD YLD	
	5.0+5	1.4+7		Rept	LA – 6430	Jul 76	– +PAIR EFFECT ON INDEP YLD.TBL	
Frag Spectra	Maxwl		ANL	Expt Conf	58Geneva 15 392	Sep 58	Smith+.PPR690,ENERGY OF FRAGMENTS	
Frag Spectra	1.5+7		KUR	Expt Jour	YF 5 966	May 67	Fomushkin+ ANGDIST OF FRAGMENTS	
				Jour	SNP 5 689	Nov 67	. ENGL OF YF 5 966	
Frag Spectra	4.4+5	3.6+6	KUR	Expt Prog	YFI – 7 25	Apr 69	Fomushkim+ LEGCOEF OF FRAG – ANGDISTR	+
				Rept	INDC(CCP) – 7U28	Feb 70	TRANSLATN.*	
	4.4+5	3.6+6		Data	EXFOR40012.	Aug 70	LEG – COEFFS, ANG DSTRB OF FRAGMNTS	
Frag Spectra	6.0+5	2.0+6	FEI	ExTh Conf	69Vienna 419	Jul 69	Androsenko+PPR134. XPTL ANGDIST + TH	
Frag Spectra	4.4+5	3.6+6	KUR	Expt Jour	YF 10 917	Nov 69	Fomushkin+ ANGDIST(E) LEG – COEF,GRAPH	
				Jour	SNP 10 529	May 70	. ENGL OF YF 10 917	
Frag Spectra	5.0+5	1.2+6	ROC	Expt Jour	NP/A 144 502	Apr 70	Otozai+ ANGDISTR CFD SING PART+STATM	
				Prog	NYO – 3938 – 3	Jun 70	Huizinga+.FRAG ANG DISTR AT 5ES.CRVS	
Frag Spectra	Thrsh	+6	FEI	Expt Jour	AHP 29 357	Aug 70	Androsenko+ ANGDIST CFD 2 – HUMPD – BARR	
Frag Spectra	None		TRM	Expt Prog	INIS – MF – 334 64	72	.RANGES+KIN – E DISTR,SHORT NOTE,NDG	
Frag Spectra	1.0+6	3.5+6	FEI	Expt Conf	73Kiev 3 270	May 73	Vorob'Eva+ AVG FRAGM – E AT 2N – ES,GRPH	+
	7.0+5	3.5+6		Data	EXFOR40284.	May 75	.KIN – E AND AVER KIN – E OF FF GVN	
Frag Spectra	Spont		FEI	Expt Rept	YFI – 17 3	Aug 74	Djachenko+ TBL YLD(E – KIN)+E – KIN(MASS	+
	None			Jour	YF 19 954	May 74	Vorob'Eva+ AVG FRAG KE(NEUT – E),GRAPH	
	Spont			Jour	YF 17 696	Apr 73	D'Jachenko+ FRAG KIN – E+AVG,TBL,GRAPH	
				Rept	INDC(CCP) – 48	Feb 75	. ENGLISH OF YFI – 17 3	
	None			Jour	SNP 19 489	Nov 74	. ENGLISH OF YF 19 954	
	Spont			Jour	SNP 17 362	Oct 73	.ENGLISH OF YF 17 696	
	5.5+5	3.4+6		Data	EXFOR40281.008	May 75	.AVER KIN – E OF FF AT 14 ES	
Reson Params	2.7+0		HAR	Expt Jour	JNE 6 303	May 58	Egelstaff+,FC,WN FOR 2.67 EV RES,TBL	+
	2.7+0	4.3+0		Rept	AERE – NP/R – 2076	Jan 57	– . 2 RES S0 MAY BE PU241	
Reson Params	2.6+0	5.4+1	ANL	Expt Jour	PR 114 505	Apr 59	Cote+ TOF TRNS WN WG WT 2 RESONANCES	+
				Jour	PRL 2 136	Feb 59	.SUPERSEDED	
				Conf	58Geneva 16 77	Sep 58	.SUPERSEDED	
	2.7+0	5.4+1		Data	EXFOR12539.004	Jun 76	. 2 RES, E0,WT,WN,WG,PCS	
Reson Params	2.7+0		HAN	Expt Abst	BAP 6 8	61	Leonard.	+
				Rept	HW – 67219	Oct 60	– +	
	2.7+0			Data	EXFOR12286.007	Jun 76	. 1 PT. NF/PCS.	

94 Plutonium 242

Quantity	Energy (ev) Min	Energy (ev) Max	Lab	Type	Documentation Ref Vol Page	Author, Comments Date	Data
Reson Params	1.4+1	8.3+2	HAR	Expt Conf	65Antwerp 533	Jul 65 Pattenden. AREA ANALYSIS. WGN 17 RES	+
Reson Params	2.6+0	3.9+2	LRL	Expt Jour	PR 146 840	Jun 66 Auchapaugh+LINAC TOF.14RES	+
				Rept	UCRL-12379	Oct 65 .SUPERSEDED	
	2.6+0	3.9+2		Data	EXFOR12546.	Jun 76 . 14 RES, WT,WN	
Reson Params		1.0+6	AUA	Theo Jour	AUJ 20 477	Oct 67 Cook. TBL OF AVG LVL SPACING D,L=0,1	
Reson Params	7.7+2	3.0+4	HAR	Expt Jour	NP/A 123 24	Jan 69 James. WF,WN,FROM FISS+TRANSM(OTHRS)	+
	7.6+2	2.9+4		Rept	AERE-R-5924	Oct 68 - .WF 2 RES	
Reson Params	-		HAR	Revw Conf	69Vienna 249	Jul 69 Lynn. PARS IN STRUTNSKY TH+EXPTS,TBL	
Reson Params	+2	+6	FEI	Theo Jour	YF 10 542	Sep 69 Gai+ TABLE OF RESON+FAST FISSN WIDTH	
	None			Rept	FEI-158	Feb 69 GAJ+ FISSN WIDTH,2HUMPED-BARR-CALCUL	
	+2	+6		Jour	SNP 10 311	Mar 70 . ENGL OF YF 10 542	
Reson Params	2.7+1	1.5+2	MTR	Expt Jour	NSE 40 389	Jun 70 Young+WG,WN FROM SHAPE FIT,AREA ANAL	+
	-.2-1	1.5+2		Rept	IN- 1132	Jun 68 - +WG,WN DRVD FROM TRNS.	
	2.7+1	1.5+2		Data	EXFOR10123.	Mar 76 10PTS.WG.REDUCED WN.	
Reson Params	None		DUB	Theo Jour	YF 13 240	Feb 71 Malecki+G-WID,THEO CFD EXPT.TBL,GRPH	
				Jour	SNP 13 133	Aug 71 - ENGL OF YF 13 240.	
Reson Params	5.3+1	7.9+2	LAS	Expt Jour	NP/A 163 577	Mar 71 Bergen+ NUCL EXPLOSION,F-WID	+
	5.3+1	7.9+2		Data	EXFOR10062.	Apr 71 23RES,PCS*F-WID 16RES,F-WID.	
Reson Params	6.2-1	5.0+4	SRL	Theo Conf	71Knoxvill 714	Mar 71 Mccrosson. STAT CALCULATN AVG PARAMS	
Reson Params	+0		CCP	Theo Jour	AE 31 18	Jul 71 Vorotnikov.S+P-NEUT FISS-WIDS DERIVD	
				Jour	SJA 31 706	Feb 72 * ENGL OF AE 31 18 7/71	
		3.9+2	MTR	Eval Prog	NCSAC-42 3	Nov 71 Young+. FOR ENDF/B 3. NO DATA GIVEN	
Reson Params	2.7+0	4.9+2	SOR	Eval Rept	IA- 1275	Feb 73 Caner+ N-,FIS-,GAM-WIDS,RES-E,TABLES	
	2.6+0	4.9+2		Data	KEDAK-3	Oct 75 37 DATA SETS	
Reson Params	2.7+0	4.9+2	ORL	Expt Prog	ORNL-4844 90	Apr 73 Harvey+. WN FOR 35 RESON GIVEN	+
	2.3+1	4.9+2		Data	EXFOR10617.002	Aug 76 34RES ES.WNRED,WG GVN.	
Reson Params	6.0+2	3.8+3	LAS	Expt Jour	PR/C 7 2085	May 73 Auchampaugh+. PARAMS FOR 71 RESON	+
	6.0+2	3.8+3		Data	EXFOR10616.002	Dec 78 . 79 PTS.WF,WN GVN FOR 79 RES.	
Reson Params	2.7+0	1.3+3	GEL	Expt Jour	NP/A 207 342	Jun 73 Poortmans+TBL OF ES,NW,GW	+
				Rept	RCN-203 113	Dec 73 - + WG,WN,S0,AVG WG.	
				Conf	72Budapest 56	Aug 72 - + AVG G-WID,AVG LVL SPACING	
	2.7+0	1.3+3		Data	EXFOR20383.	Oct 74 99PTS.WG,AVG WG,WN,AVG WN0.	
Reson Params	7.6+2	1.8+3	LRL	Expt Conf	73Rochestr 2 493	Aug 73 Browne+ ABST,G-WID TO ISOM,UPP LIMIT	
Reson Params		+3	GEL	Theo Rept	RCN-203 172	Dec 73 Werz+ ESTIMATION OF WF CLASS-2 RES	
Reson Params	2.1+2	3.8+2	RPI	Expt Conf	75Wash. 584	Mar 75 Hockenbury+ TABL EO,WN	
Strnth Fnctn	0.0+0	5.4+1	ANL	Expt Jour	PR 114 505	Oct 59 Cote.	+
	2.7+0	5.4+1		Conf	58Geneva 16 77	Sep 58 - +.PPR685,VAL GVN	
	0.0+0	5.4+1		Data	EXFOR12539.003	Jun 76 . 1 PT.	
Strnth Fnctn		3.1+2	HAR	ExTh Conf	65Antwerp 533	Jul 65 Pattenden. PPR93.FROM RES ANAL.	+
Strnth Fnctn	2.0-2	4.0+2	LRL	Expt Jour	PR 146 840	Jun 66 Auchampaug+LINAC TOF,L=0 FR 14RES	+
				Rept	UCRL-12379	Oct 65 .SUPERSEDED	
	2.6+0	3.9+2		Data	EXFOR12546.007	Jun 76 . 1 PT.	
	2.6+6	4.1+6	AI	Theo Rept	NAA-SR-12538	Oct 67 Gigas.OPTMDL CALC AVG SO,S1,S2	
Strnth Fnctn	0.0+0	1.8+2	MTR	Expt Jour	NSE 40 389	Jun 70 Young+TRNS.ANAL OVER 8 RES ES.S0 GVN	+
	0.0+0	8.0+3		Rept	IN- 1132	Jun 68 - +VALS FOUND UP TO 8KEV.	
	0.0+0	1.8+2		Data	EXFOR10123.003	Mar 76 . 2 PTS.S0=.99+-.44,D=16.5EV	
Strnth Fnctn	2.7+0		SOR	Eval Rept	IA- 1275	Feb 73 Caner+ RECOMMENDED VALUE + D,TABLE	
Strnth Fnctn	None		AUA	Eval Rept	AAEC/E-277	Mar 73 Musgrove.TBLS EXPTL DATA+BEST VALUES	
Strnth Fnctn	2.7+0	1.0+3	GEL	Expt Jour	NP/A 207 342	Jun 73 Poortmans+ S WAVE.	+
	2.7+0	1.3+3		Conf	72Budapest 56	Aug 72 - + S-WAVE STRENGTH FUNCTION	
	2.7+0	1.0+3		Data	EXFOR20383.006	Oct 74 1PNT.L=0.	
Strnth Fnctn	2.3-2		RPI	Expt Conf	75Wash. 584	Mar 75 Hockenbury+S0=1.16E-04.	
Lvl Density	+6		MIL	Expt Jour	EN 15 1 54	Jan 68 Facchini+ LDL PARS FROM LOW EN RES	
Lvl Density	-3	+0	IFU	Theo Jour	UFZ 13 700	Apr 68 Pisanko+ LEVEL SPACING CALC,TBL	
				Jour	UPJ 13 498	Oct 68 TRANSLATN.*	
Lvl Density		6.0+7	ROC	Theo Jour	NP/A 187 225	Jun 72 Williams+ A,COMBIN+STATIST+SHELLCORR	
Lvl Density	2.7+0	1.0+3	GEL	Expt Jour	NP/A 207 342	Jun 73 Poortmans+ S WAVE.	+
	2.7+0	1.0+3		Data	EXFOR20383.007	Oct 74 1PNT.MEANLVLSP0.	
Lvl Density	None		COP	Theo Jour	NP/A 222 493	Apr 74 Dossing+COLL ROTAT.SPAC. ACCUR ESTIM	
Lvl Density	None		ROC	Theo Jour	NP/A 223 589	May 74 Huizenga+ EXP CFD MICROSC TH AX SYMM	
Lvl Density	+6		DUB	Theo Rept	JINR-E4-9236	Nov 75 Komov+ AVG LVL-SPAC,SEMIMICRO CFD XP	
(γ,n)	7.0+6	1.6+7	DUB	Expt Rept	JINR-E15-7362	Jul 73 Gangrsky+ SPON FISS ISOMER,TBL,GRAPH	
	8.0+6	1.3+7		Rept	JINR-E15-5071	May 70 - + PU242(GAM,N)PU241-M-FISSN	
Photo-Fissn	5.0+6	8.0+6	FEI	Expt Jour	PL/B 26 4 218	Jan 68 Rabotnov+ANGDISTR FISS FRAG AT THRES	
				Prog	YFI-4 12	May 67 .CURVES GIVEN	
	5.0+6	9.0+6		ExTh Conf	67Kharkov 216	Feb 67 .ANG DISTRIB,CHANNEL EFFCTS	
	5.0+6	8.0+6		Expt Prog	INDC-E-187	67 .ENGLISH TRANSL OF YFI-4 12 5/67	

94 Plutonium 242

Quantity	Energy (ev) Min	Max	Lab	Type	Documentation Ref Vol Page	Date	Author, Comments	Data
Photo – Fissn		8.0+6	IFP	ExTh	Jour ZEP 9 128	Jan 69	Kapitza+ SIG ANGDIST CV,2 – HUMP – BARIER	
					Jour JEL 9 2 73	Jan 69	.ENGLISH TRANSL OF ZEP 9 128 1/69	
					Rept ANL – TRANS – 639	69	.ENGLISH TRANSL OF ZEP 9 128 1/69	
Photo – Fissn	5.0+7	9.0+7	FEI	ExTh	Prog YFI – 7 21	Apr 69	Rabotnov+ SIG+YLD+ANGDIST VS E GRPHS	
	+6	+7		Expt	Jour SNP 11 285	Sep 70	.TRANSLATN.*0,NO 3	
					Jour YF 11 508	Mar 70	Rabotnov+ ANGDIST+YLD+SIG,GRPHS+TBLS	
	5.0+7	9.0+7		ExTh	Rept INDC(CCP) – 7U24	Feb 70	TRANSLATN.*	
Photo – Fissn	5.0+6	8.0+6	FEI	ExTh	Conf 69Vienna 419	Jul 69	Androsenko+ PPR134. XPTL ANGDIST + TH	
Photo – Fissn	Thrsh	+7	IFP	Expt	Conf 69Vienna 925	Jul 69	Kapica+ PPR135.SIG+ANGDIST,STRUTINSKY	
Photo – Fissn	8.0+6	1.3+7	IFP	Expt	Jour PL/B 32 182	Jun 70	Gangsky+ PROMPT+DEL FRAGYLD IN PU241	
Photo – Fissn	6.0+6	1.3+7	DUB	Expt	Jour FDP 22 199	74	Gangrsky+ GRPH (G,F)SIG VS E – GAM	
	8.0+6	1.3+7			Rept JINR – E15 – 5071	May 70	– PU242(GAM,N)PU241 – M – FISSN	

94 Plutonium 243

Quantity	Energy (ev) Min	Max	Lab	Type	Documentation Ref Vol Page	Date	Author, Comments	Data
Evaluation	1.0 – 5	2.0+7	SRL	Eval	Rept EPRI – NP – 161	Dec 75	Benjamin+ENDF4B.GENPAR MDL REVISIONS	
Diff Inelast	None		ANL	Expt	Jour PL 18 149	Aug 65	Braid+ IMPT INFO ON ENERGY LEVELS	
(n,γ)	2.5+4		ANL	Expt	Jour PR 93 1433	Mar 54	Studier.	+
	2.5+4				Data EXFOR12538.003	Jun 76	. 1 PT.	
(n,γ)	Pile		ANL	Expt	Jour NSE 1 62	Mar 56	Fields+1450+170+ – 90B	+
					Conf 55Geneva 7 261	Aug 55	Bentley+.P809,VAL GVN,CHEMICAL METHD	
	Pile				Data EXFOR12535.009	Jun 76	. 1 PT.	
(n,γ)	None		KAP	Comp	Rept KAPL – 1781	Jul 57	Schuman. SIGMA GIVEN	
(n,γ)	Pile		CCP	Revw	Jour AE 24 247	Mar 68	Bak+ OTHER SIG VAL GVN,TBL	
					Jour SJA 24 300	Mar 68	TRANSLATN.*	
(n,γ)	Fiss		LRL	ExTh	Jour NP/A 124 130	Feb 69	Ingley.FROM PU242FISS YIELD HEAVY EL	
				Expt	Jour AF 36 509	Nov 67	Truran+ QUOTES INGLEY	
(n,γ)	Pile		KFK	Eval	Rept KFK – 1453	Mar 72	Eberle+ 2 – GROUP SIGS,FITTED TO EXPT	
(n,γ)	2.5 – 2		SRL	Eval	Conf 75Wash. 224	Mar 75	Benjamin+ TBL BEST FIT TRANSPU PROD.	
(n,γ)	Pile		SRL	Expt	Rept DP – MS – 66 – 69	Oct 66	ICE.	+
	Pile				Data EXFOR12550.003	Jun 76	. 1 PT.	
Res Int Capt	6.3 – 1		SRL	Eval	Conf 75Wash. 224	Mar 75	Benjamin+ TBL BEST FIT TRANSPU PROD.	
Fission	Maxwl		LRL	Expt	Rept EANDC(US) – 28	Sep 62	Hulet+ NDG, TBD	
Fission	1.0+4		LAS	Expt	Jour PR 158 1127	Jun 67	Bell. ESTIMATED FROM TWEED EVENT,TH	
Fission	Pile		CCP	Revw	Jour AE 24 247	Mar 68	Bak+ OTHER SIG VAL GVN,TBL	
					Jour SJA 24 300	Mar 68	TRANSLATN.*	
Fission	Maxwl		ANL	Expt	Jour JIN 30 2553	Oct 68	Diamond+,ION CHAMB IN THR COLUMN	+
	Maxwl				Data EXFOR12531.002	Jun 76	. 1 PT.	
Fission	Spont		COP	Revw	Conf 69Vienna 155	Jul 69	Strutinsky+PPR203. HL GVN,'SHELL – TH'	
Fission	5.0+5	2.0+6	LAS	Theo	Jour NSE 41 177	Aug 70	Cramer+,SIG FROM(T,P+FISS)+H – F CALC	
Fission	Pile		KFK	Eval	Rept KFK – 1453	Mar 72	Eberle+ 2 – GROUP SIGS,FITTED TO EXPT	
Fission	–		GEL	ExTh	Jour NP/A 187 305	Jun 72	Weigmann+ F.B.PARAMS FROM DATA ANAL.	
	0.0+0	1.0+0		Revw	Jour AKE 18 229	Nov 71	Theobald+ SUB – BARRIER FISS EXPTS,TH	
Fission	None		DUB	Expt	Jour FDP 22 199	74	Gangrsky+ FIS – BARRIER,GRPH EMAX+EMIN	
Fission	3.0+6	5.0+6	LAS	Theo	Conf 75Wash. 129	Mar 75	Moore.GRPH R MATR STAT CALC CFD EXP	
Fission	2.5 – 2		SRL	Eval	Conf 75Wash. 224	Mar 75	Benjamin+ TBL BEST FIT TRANSPU PROD.	
Res Int Fiss	6.3 – 1		SRL	Eval	Conf 75Wash. 224	Mar 75	Benjamin+ TBL BEST FIT TRANSPU PROD.	
Alpha	1.0+4	2.0+4	LAS	Theo	Jour PR 158 1127	Jun 67	Bell. PREDICT 10 – 20KEV BY SYSTEMATCS	
Alpha	Fiss		LRL	ExTh	Jour NP/A 124 130	Feb 69	Ingley.FROM PU242FISS YIELD HEAVY EL	
Nu	Maxwl		IAE	Eval	Jour REA 10 637	Dec 72	Manero+ CALC,SYSTEMATICS,TBL	
Nu	Spont		HED	Eval	Abst ANS 22 673	Nov 75	Johnson. TBL,GRPH.NU FROM SPON FISS	
Frag Spectra		2.0+6	COP	Revw	Conf 69Vienna 155	Jul 69	Strutinsky+PPR203. GRPH ANGANISTR(E)	
Lvl Density	None		COP	Theo	Jour NP/A 222 493	Apr 74	Dossing+COLL ROTAT.SPAC. ACCUR ESTIM	
Lvl Density	None		ROC	Theo	Jour NP/A 223 589	May 74	Huizenga+ EXP CFD MICROSC TH AX SYMM	

94 Plutonium 244

Quantity	Energy (ev) Min	Max	Lab	Type	Documentation Ref Vol Page	Date	Author, Comments	Data
Evaluation	1.0 – 5	2.0+7	SRL	Eval	Rept EPRI – NP – 161	Dec 75	Benjamin+ENDF4B.GENPAR MDL.REVISIONS	
(n,γ)	Pile		ANL	Expt	Jour NSE 1 62	Mar 56	Fields+1450+1.5+ – 0.3B	+
					Jour JIN 1 262	Oct 55	– + PRODUCTN OF PU245 AND AM245	
					Conf 55Geneva 7 261	Aug 55	Bentley+.P809,VAL GVN,CHEMICAL METHD	
	Pile				Data EXFOR12535.011	Jun 76	. 1 PT.	
(n,γ)	Pile		CRC	Expt	Jour PR 103 634	Aug 56	Butler+,NRX SIG=2.1+ – 0.3B CFD OTHERS	
(n,γ)	None		KAP	Comp	Rept KAPL – 1781	Jul 57	Schuman. SIGMA GIVEN	

94 Plutonium 244

Quantity	Energy (ev) Min	Max	Lab	Type	Documentation Ref Vol Page	Author, Comments Date	Data
(n,γ)	Fiss		LRL	Expt Jour	AF 36 509	Nov 67 Truran+ QUOTES INGLEY	
(n,γ)	None		LAS	Expt Prog	WASH-1136 110	Sep 69 Silbert+,PHYSICS-8 SHOT,ANAL TBC	
(n,γ)	2.5-2		ORL	Expt Prog	ORNL-4706 55	Sep 71 Druschel+. VALUE GIVEN	
(n,γ)	Maxwl	5.0-1	MTR	Expt Prog	WASH-1136 51	Sep 69 Schuman.VALUE GIVN,THR AVG CD CUTOFF	+
	Maxwl			Data	EXFOR12510.002	Jun 76 . 1 PT.	
Res Int Capt	5.0-1		ORL	Expt Prog	ORNL-4706 55	Sep 71 Druschel+. VALUE GIVEN	
Res Int Capt	5.0-1		MTR	Expt Prog	WASH-1136 51	Sep 69 Schuman.VALUE GIVN,THR AVG CD CUTOFF	+
	5.0-1			Data	EXFOR12510.003	Jun 76 . 1 PT.	
(n,2n)	1.4+7		LRL	Expt Jour	AE 40 491	Jun 76 Browne+ SIG TO SPONFIS ISO.NOT FOUND	
				Jour	SJA 40 587	Dec 76 . ENGL OF AE 40 491	
Fission	Spont		BRK	Revw Jour	NP 81 1	Jun 66 Myers.TBL CALC FISS BARRIERS.	
Fission	Spont		COP	Revw Conf	69Vienna 155	Jul 69 Strutinsky+PPR203. HL GVN,'SHELL-TH'	
Fission	Spont		MRY	Theo Prog	ORO-4028-28	71 Jackson+. SPON FISSION HALF-LIFE GVN	
Fission	2.0+1	1.0+7	LAS	Expt Jour	NP/A 171 31	Aug 71 Auchampaugh+ BOMB.REL LI6(NT),U235NF	+
	2.0+1	9.7+6		Data	EXFOR10266.	Sep 72 8003PTS.SIGMA.	
Fission	-		GEL	ExTh Jour	NP/A 187 305	Jun 72 Weigmann+ F.B.PARAMS FROM DATA ANAL.	
Fission	2.5-2		JUL	Theo Jour	ZP 257 389	Dec 72 Mcminn. 2.77 E-3 BARNS	
Fission	3.0+6	5.0+6	LAS	Theo Conf	75Wash. 129	Mar 75 Moore.GRPH R MATR STAT CALC CFD EXP	
Fission	5.2+5	2.5+6	KUR	Expt Rept	YFI-22 11	Dec 76 Fomushkin+ SIG(NEUT-E),TBL	+
	5.2+5	2.5+6		Data	EXFOR40407.002	Jan 77 .SIG AT 9 EN GVN	
Nu	Spont		LAS	Expt Jour	NSE 43 54	Jan 71 Orth.SEPARATE COUNT OF NS+SPON FISS	+
	Spont			Data	EXFOR10115.002	Jul 71 1PT.AVG NU=2.30+-.19 REL CF 252.	
Nu	Spont		IAE	Eval Jour	REA 10 637	Dec 72 Manero+ EXTENSIVE SURVEY,TBL,AVG VAL	
Nu	Spont		HED	Eval Abst	ANS 22 673	Nov 75 Johnson. TBL,GRPH.NU FROM SPON FISS	
Fiss Yield	2.5-2	1.4+7	LAS	Eval Rept	LA-6430	Jul 76 Madland+PAIR EFFECT ON INDEP YLD.TBL	
Reson Params	1.2+3	1.8+4	LAS	Expt Prog	NCSAC-33 132	Dec 70 Bergen+,NUCL SHOT,TBL SUM FISSN AREA	

94 Plutonium 245

Quantity	Energy (ev) Min	Max	Lab	Type	Documentation Ref Vol Page	Author, Comments Date	Data
(n,γ)	Pile		ANL	Expt Jour	NSE 1 62	Mar 56 Fields+ 1450+260+-145B	+
				Conf	55Geneva 7 261	Aug 55 Bentley+.P809,VAL GVN,CHEMICAL METHD	
	Pile			Data	EXFOR12535.010	Jun 76 . 1 PT.	
(n,γ)	None		KAP	Comp Rept	KAPL-1781	Jul 57 Schuman. SIGMA GIVEN	
(n,γ)	Fiss		LRL	ExTh Jour	NP/A 124 130	Feb 69 Ingley.FROM PU242FISS YIELD HEAVY EL	
				Expt Jour	AF 36 509	Nov 67 Truran+ QUOTES INGLEY	
(n,γ)	Maxwl		ORL	Expt Prog	ORNL-4706 55	Sep 71 Druschel+. VALUE GIVEN	
Res Int Capt	5.0-1		ORL	Expt Prog	ORNL-4706 55	Sep 71 Druschel+. VALUE GIVEN	
Fission	1.0+4		LAS	Expt Jour	PR 158 1127	Jun 67 Bell. ESTIMATED FROM TWEED EVENT,TH	
Fission	-		GEL	ExTh Jour	NP/A 187 305	Jun 72 Weigmann+ F.B.PARAMS FROM DATA ANAL.	
Fission	None		DUB	Expt Jour	FDP 22 199	74 Gangrsky+ FIS-BARRIER,GRPH EMAX+EMIN	
Alpha	1.0+4	2.0+4	LAS	Theo Jour	PR 158 1127	Jun 67 Bell. PREDICT 10-20KEV BY SYSTEMATCS	
Alpha	Fiss		LRL	ExTh Jour	NP/A 124 130	Feb 69 Ingley.FROM PU242FISS YIELD HEAVY EL	

94 Plutonium 246

Quantity	Energy (ev) Min	Max	Lab	Type	Documentation Ref Vol Page	Author, Comments Date	Data
(n,γ)	Fiss		LRL	Expt Jour	AF 36 509	Nov 67 Truran+ QUOTES INGLEY	
Fission	2.5-2		JUL	Theo Jour	ZP 257 389	Dec 72 Mcminn. 8.48 E-5 BARNS	

94 Plutonium 247

Quantity	Energy (ev) Min	Max	Lab	Type	Documentation Ref Vol Page	Author, Comments Date	Data
(n,γ)	Fiss		LRL	ExTh Jour	NP/A 124 130	Feb 69 Ingley.FROM PU242FISS YIELD HEAVY EL	
				Expt Jour	AF 36 509	Nov 67 Truran+ QUOTES INGLEY	
Fission	1.0+4		LAS	Expt Jour	PR 158 1127	Jun 67 Bell. ESTIMATED FROM TWEED EVENT,TH	
Alpha	1.0+4	2.0+4	LAS	Theo Jour	PR 158 1127	Jun 67 Bell. PREDICT 10-20KEV BY SYSTEMATCS	
Alpha	Fiss		LRL	ExTh Jour	NP/A 124 130	Feb 69 Ingley.FROM PU242FISS YIELD HEAVY EL	

94 Plutonium 248

Quantity	Energy (ev) Min	Max	Lab	Type	Documentation Ref Vol Page	Author, Comments Date	Data
(n,γ)	Fiss		LRL	Expt Jour	AF 36 509	Nov 67 Truran+ QUOTES INGLEY	

94 Plutonium 248

Quantity	Energy (ev) Min Max	Lab	Type	Documentation Ref Vol Page	Date	Author, Comments	Data
Fiss Yield	–	TPI	Theo Jour	YF 9 102	Jan 69	Korostova+SHELL INFL,HEAV+L+SYM FRAG	
			Jour	SNP 9 62	Jul 69	TRANSLATN.*	

94 Plutonium 249

Quantity	Energy (ev) Min Max	Lab	Type	Documentation Ref Vol Page	Date	Author, Comments	Data
(n,γ)	Fiss	LRL	ExTh Jour	NP/A 124 130	Feb 69	Ingley.FROM PU242FISS YIELD HEAVY EL	
Fission	1.0+4	LAS	Expt Jour	PR 158 1127	Jun 67	Bell. ESTIMATED FROM TWEED EVENT,TH	
Alpha	1.0+4 2.0+4	LAS	Theo Jour	PR 158 1127	Jun 67	Bell. PREDICT 10-20KEV BY SYSTEMATCS	
Alpha	Fiss	LRL	ExTh Jour	NP/A 124 130	Feb 69	Ingley.FROM PU242FISS YIELD HEAVY EL	

94 Plutonium 251

Quantity	Energy (ev) Min Max	Lab	Type	Documentation Ref Vol Page	Date	Author, Comments	Data
(n,γ)	Fiss	LRL	ExTh Jour	NP/A 124 130	Feb 69	Ingley.FROM PU242FISS YIELD HEAVY EL	
Fission	1.0+4	LAS	Expt Jour	PR 158 1127	Jun 67	Bell. ESTIMATED FROM TWEED EVENT,TH	
Alpha	Fiss	LRL	ExTh Jour	NP/A 124 130	Feb 69	Ingley.FROM PU242FISS YIELD HEAVY EL	

94 Plutonium 253

Quantity	Energy (ev) Min Max	Lab	Type	Documentation Ref Vol Page	Date	Author, Comments	Data
(n,γ)	Fiss	LRL	ExTh Jour	NP/A 124 130	Feb 69	Ingley.FROM PU242FISS YIELD HEAVY EL	
Fission	1.0+4	LAS	Expt Jour	PR 158 1127	Jun 67	Bell. ESTIMATED FROM TWEED EVENT,TH	
Alpha	Fiss	LRL	ExTh Jour	NP/A 124 130	Feb 69	Ingley.FROM PU242FISS YIELD HEAVY EL	

95 Americium 237

Quantity	Energy (ev) Min Max	Lab	Type	Documentation Ref Vol Page	Author, Comments Date	Data
Fission	Spont	COP	Expt Conf	69Vienna 461	Jul 69 Sletten.DISCUSSN. ISOM FISSN HL GVN	
Fission	-	GEL	ExTh Jour	NP/A 187 305	Jun 72 Weigmann+ F.B.PARAMS FROM DATA ANAL.	
Fission	2.5-2	JUL	Theo Jour	ZP 257 389	Dec 72 Mcminn. 2.55 E+2 BARNS	

95 Americium 238

Quantity	Energy (ev) Min Max	Lab	Type	Documentation Ref Vol Page	Author, Comments Date	Data
Fission	Spont	DUB	Theo Rept	JINR-E-2515	Dec 65 Malov+ SPON FISSN ISOMER, LIFE-TIME	
Fission	Maxwl	CCP	Comp Jour	AE 26 436	May 69 Romanov. UPPER SIG LIMIT ESTIMATED	
			Jour	EAF 26 48	69 . FRENCH OF AE 26 436.	
			Jour	SJA 26 498	69 . ENGL OF AE 26 436.	
Fission	Spont	COP	Revw Conf	69Vienna 155	Jul 69 Strutinsky+PPR203. ISOM-HL,SHELL-TH	
Fission	Spont	HAR	Revw Conf	69Vienna 249	Jul 69 Lynn. TBL=2HUMPED FISS-BARRIER PARS	
Fission	-	GEL	ExTh Jour	NP/A 187 305	Jun 72 Weigmann+ F.B.PARAMS FROM DATA ANAL.	
Fission	Spont	TPI	Theo Jour	YF 16 919	Nov 72 Adeev+ FISS BARRIER CFD EVEN,NUCLEI	
			Jour	SNP 16 507	May 73 .ENGLISH OF YF 16 919	

95 Americium 239

Quantity	Energy (ev) Min Max	Lab	Type	Documentation Ref Vol Page	Author, Comments Date	Data
Fission	Spont	COP	Expt Conf	69Vienna 461	Jul 69 Sletten.DISCUSSN. ISOM FISSN HL GVN	
Fission	Spont	HAR	Revw Conf	69Vienna 249	Jul 69 Lynn. TBL=2HUMPED FISS-BARRIER PARS	
Fission	-	HEI	Expt Conf	69Vienna 449	Jul 69 Metag+PPR29. HE-INDUCED ISOM FISS HL	
Fission	-	GEL	ExTh Jour	NP/A 187 305	Jun 72 Weigmann+ F.B.PARAMS FROM DATA ANAL.	
Fission	2.5-2	JUL	Theo Jour	ZP 257 389	Dec 72 Mcminn. 2.90 E+1 BARNS	
Fiss Yield	Spont	ORL	Expt Jour	NP/A 172 33	Aug 71 Ferguson+ISOMER.M+E DISTR OKS DIRECT	
			Jour	PL/B 31 526	Apr 70 .PRELIMIN	
			Jour	PR 141 1146	Jan 66 .SEE ALSO	
Frag Spectra	Spont	ORL	Expt Jour	NP/A 172 33	Aug 71 Ferguson+ISOMER.E DIST+CORR OK DIRCT	
			Jour	PL/B 31 526	Apr 70 .PRELIMIN	
			Jour	PR 141 1146	Jan 66 .SEE ALSO	

95 Americium 240

Quantity	Energy (ev) Min Max	Lab	Type	Documentation Ref Vol Page	Author, Comments Date	Data
(n,2n)	1.5+7	DUB	Expt Conf	75Kiev 5 245	May 75 Gangrskij+ SIG TO SPONFIS ISO.TABLE	
Fission	Spont	DUB	Theo Rept	JINR-E-2515	Dec 65 Malov+ SPON FISSN ISOMER, LIFE-TIME	
Fission	None	BRK	Revw Jour	NP 81 1	Jun 66 Myers+ TABLE 2, FISS BARRIER	
Fission	Spont	COP	Expt Jour	YF 8 459	Sep 68 Bjornholm+PROD OF FISSILE-ISOM-STATE	
				SNP 8 267	Mar 69 - + ENGLISH TRANSLATION	
Fission	Maxwl	CCP	Comp Jour	AE 26 436	May 69 Romanov. UPPER SIG LIMIT ESTIMATED	
			Jour	EAF 26 48	69 . FRENCH OF AE 26 436.	
			Jour	SJA 26 498	69 . ENGL OF AE 26 436.	
Fission	Spont	COP	Revw Conf	69Vienna 155	Jul 69 Strutinsky+PPR203. ISOM-HL,SHELL-TH	
Fission	Spont	COP	Expt Conf	69Vienna 461	Jul 69 Sletten.DISCUSSN. ISOM FISSN HL GVN	
Fission	Spont	HAR	Revw Conf	69Vienna 249	Jul 69 Lynn. TBL=2HUMPED FISS-BARRIER PARS	
Fission	Spont	IFP	Expt Jour	YF 11 54	Jan 70 Gangrskij+AM241(G,N)AM240 ISOM FISSN	
			Jour	SNP 11 30	Jul 70 . ENGL OF YF 11 54	
Fission	-	GEL	ExTh Jour	NP/A 187 305	Jun 72 Weigmann+ F.B.PARAMS FROM DATA ANAL.	
Fission	Spont	DUB	Expt Jour	FDP 22 199	74 Gangrsky+ FIS-BARRIER,GRPH EMAX+EMIN	
			Rept	JINR-E15-7362	Jul 73 - + ISOMER HALFLIFE,TABLE,GRPH	
Nu	Spont	HED	Eval Abst	ANS 22 673	Nov 75 Johnson. TBL,GRPH.NU FROM SPON FISS	
Lvl Density	7.0+6 1.6+7	DUB	ExTh Rept	JINR-E15-7362	Jul 73 Gangrsky+ PARS FROM (G,N),(G,G),GRPH	

95 Americium 241

Quantity	Energy (ev) Min Max	Lab	Type	Documentation Ref Vol Page	Author, Comments Date	Data
Evaluation	-	CCP	Eval Jour	AE 23 6	Jul 67 Kirpitchnikov.RESON PARAMS,MANY REFS	
			Jour	SJA 23 669	Jul 67 TRANSLATN.*	
Evaluation	2.5-2 1.0+7	KFK	Eval Rept	KFK-1186	Jul 70 Hinkelmann.RES,STF,N2N,NF,NU,NG,R.I.	
			Conf	70Helsinki 2 721	Jun 70 - + SEE KFK-1186.	
Evaluation	None	SAC	Eval Prog	EANDC(E)-157U2	May 73 Ribon.	
	Fiss		Prog	EANDC(E)127U	Apr 70 - .	

95 Americium 241

Quantity	Energy (ev) Min	Max	Lab	Type	Documentation Ref Vol Page	Date	Author, Comments	Data
Evaluation	None		SOR	Eval	Prog IA – 1308 46	75	Caner+ NEW EVAL STARTED,NDG	
Evaluation	1.0 – 5	2.0+7	SRL	Eval	Rept EPRI – NP – 161	Dec 75	Benjamin+ENDF4B.BRANCH RATIO REVISED	
Total	5.0 – 3	1.0+2	CCP	Expt	Conf 55Geneva 4 216	Aug 55	Adamchuk+.GRAPH,TRANSMISSN, PPR645	+
Total	2.4 – 1	4.2+1	ORL	Expt	Conf 61RPI 64	May 61	Harvey+ CURVE	+
	+0	+3			Conf 60Vienna 535	Oct 60	Block+.NDG,EXPT DESCRIBED	
	2.5 – 1	4.2+1			Data EXFOR12478.003	Jun 76	. 454 PTS.	
Total	2.5 – 2		HAR	Eval	Prog AERE – PR/NP20 9	Mar 73	Sowerby+TBL RECOMMNDD SIGS.	
Total	8.0 – 1	1.0+3	SAC	Expt	Conf 75Wash. 637	Mar 75	Derrien+SHAPE ANALYSIS TO 150 EV	+
	7.8 – 1	1.1+3			Data EXFOR20415.003	Jul 75	13840PTS.	
Total	– 3	1.9+0	THS	Theo	Rept IKE – 6 89 65	Jun 75	Keinert. DATA LIBRARY	
Tot Inelastc		2.0+7	HAR	Theo	Prog NEANDC(E)172 8	Aug 76	Lynn.EVALUATION AND CALCULD XSECTS	
Diff Inelast	1.5+7		DUB	Expt	Conf 75Kiev 5 245	May 75	Gangrskij+ SIG TO SPONFIS ISO.TABLE	
					Jour IJP 47 232	73	Belov+ SIG TO SPONFIS GIVN,FRAGM – DET	
					Rept JINR – E15 – 6807	Nov 72	– + SPONFIS ISOMER PRODUCTN,TBL	
Absorption	Pile		CRC	Expt	Jour PR 81 486	Feb 51	Hanna+. FROM MEA= 1 DATA INDEX LINE	+
	Pile				Data EXFOR12582.003	Jun 76	. 1 PT.	
Absorption	Maxwl		ORL	Expt	Prog ORNL – 1879 5	55	Pomerance.	+
	Maxwl				Data EXFOR11885.009	Jun 76	. 1 PT.	
Absorption	Maxwl		LRL	Expt	Jour JNE 8 224	Oct 59	Hoff.	+
	Maxwl				Data EXFOR12578.004	Jun 76	. 1 PT.	
Absorption	6.2 – 1	1.0+7	SRL	Theo	Conf 71Knoxvill 714	Mar 71	Mccrosson. SPECTRUM – AVERAGED SIG	
Absorption	2.5 – 2		HAR	Eval	Prog AERE – PR/NP20 9	Mar 73	Sowerby+TBL RECOMMNDD SIGS.	
Absorption	None		MUN	Theo	Diss GRYNTAKIS	Mar 76	Gryntakis.,CALC.OF WESTCOTTS G – FUNCT	
					Jour RCA 22 128	Mar 75	– +,EQUIVALENT TO THESIS	
Res Int Abs	None		RI	Expt	Jour AE 23 316	Oct 67	BAK+ VAL GVN,CALC – METHOD DESCRIBED	+
					Jour SJA 23 1059	Oct 67	BAK+ TRANSL OF AE 23 316 IN ENGLISH	
					Jour EAF 23 4 56	Oct 67	BAK+ TRANSL OF AE 23 316 IN FRENCH	
	4.0 – 1				Data EXFOR40062.	Apr 71	.RES – INT CAPTURE,TO GROUND+METASTABL	
Res Int Abs	1.0 – 1		KFK	Theo	Rept KFK – 1917	Feb 74	Klunker.INFIN DILUTION+EFF RESINTEG	
Res Int Abs	0.0+0	+7	FEI	Expt	Rept YK – 22 53	76	Ivanov+ DATA GVN IN TBL	
Res Int Abs	3.7 – 1	3.5+5	ORL	Expt	Jour NSE 61 356	Nov 76	Weston+CALC VAL=152G+ – 92B.CFD.	
(n,γ)	Pile		ANL	Expt	Rept CS – 3471 4	46	Seaborg.	+
	Pile				Data EXFOR12576.	Jun 76	. 2 PTS, SIG FOR GND + META	
(n,γ)	Pile		BRK	Expt	Abst PR 79 530	Aug 50	Street.	+
	Pile				Data EXFOR12581.002	Jun 76	. 1 PT.	
(n,γ)	Pile		CRC	Expt	Jour PR 81 486	Feb 51	Hanna+. FROM MEAS OF CM242 PRODUCTN	+
	Pile				Data EXFOR12582.002	Jun 76	. 1 PT.	
(n,γ)	Pile		BRK	Expt	Jour PR 85 135	Jan 52	Street.	+
					Rept AECD – 3268	Mar 51	– +,SIG=APPROX.50B	
	Pile				Data EXFOR12583.	Jun 76	. 2 PTS, SIG FOR GND + META	
(n,γ)	None		KAP	Comp	Rept KAPL – 1781	Jul 57	Schuman. SIGMA GIVEN	
(n,γ)	Pile		LRL	Expt	Jour JNE 8 224	Jan 59	Hoff+ SIGMA (N,G) (N,G)M GIVEN	+
	Pile				Data EXFOR12578.	Jun 76	. 2 PTS, SIG FOR GND + META	
(n,γ)	Pile		CRC	Eval	Rept CRRP – 960	Jan 62	Westcott.EFF SIG TABLE 20 – 1300DEG C	
(n,γ)	Maxwl		LRL	Expt	Jour PL 19 226	Oct 65	White+ NO 13 MS SPON F AM242 MADE	+
	Maxwl				Data EXFOR12566.002	Jun 76	. 1 PT.	
(n,γ)	Maxwl		DUB	Expt	Jour YF 3 455	Mar 66	Markov+.SIGMA AND ISOMERIC RATIO	+
					Rept JINR – P – 2347	Sep 65	– + AM241(N,G)AM242 SPON FISSN	
					Jour SNP 3 325	Sep 66	– + ENGL OF YF 3 455.	
(n,γ)	Maxwl	Pile	BNL	Eval	Rept BNL – 982 22	Aug 66	Pearlstein. 622B, 800B, FROM RES PAR	
(n,γ)	Maxwl		RI	Expt	Rept ICD – 4 337	67	Bak+ SIG LEADING TO AM242M =70+ – 5 B	
(n,γ)	Maxwl		RI	Expt	Rept ICD – 4 337	67	Bak+ SIGMA(N,G)=670+ – 60B AT THR EN	
(n,γ)	Pile		MOL	Expt	Prog EANDC(E)76U102	Jan 67	Wagemans+ ACT. TO METASTABLE FISSION	+
	Pile				Data EXFOR20181.002	May 74	1PNT.SIGMA.	
(n,γ)	Pile		RI	Expt	Prog YFI – 5 49	Oct 67	Bak+ VALUE GIVEN	+
	Maxwl				Jour AE 23 316	Oct 67	BAK+ VAL AM241(N,G)AM242+AM242M GVN	
	Pile				Rept INDC – 232E	Jan 69	. ENGL OF YFI – 5 49	
	Maxwl				Jour SJA 23 1059	Oct 67	BAK+ TRANSL OF AE 23 316 IN ENGLISH	
					Jour EAF 23 4 56	Oct 67	BAK+ TRANSL OF AE 23 316 IN FRENCH	
	Pile				Data EXFOR40062.	Apr 71	AV SIG BELOW CD – LIMIT,TO GND+METSTBL	
(n,γ)	Maxwl		AUA	Theo	Jour NSE 31 234	Feb 68	Cook+ STATISTICAL CALC CFD EXPT	
(n,γ)	Pile		CCP	Revw	Jour AE 24 247	Mar 68	Bak+ OTHER SIG VAL GVN,TBL	
					Jour SJA 24 300	Mar 68	TRANSLATN.*	
(n,γ)		1.5+7	LEB	Theo	Jour YF 8 326	Aug 68	Baldin+ 'SHAPE – ISOMERISM' CFD EXPT	
					Jour SNP 8 187	Feb 69	TRANSLATN.*	
(n,γ)	2.0+6	3.0+6	DUB	Expt	Rept JINR – P6 – 4307	Feb 69	Gangrskij. SIG TO SPONFIS ISOM,GRAPH	
(n,γ)	+4	+6	KUR	Theo	Jour YF 9 538	Mar 69	Vorotnikov. SIG TBD FOR FISS ANAL	
					Jour SNP 9 308	Sep 69	TRANSLATN.*	

95 Americium 241

Quantity	Energy (ev) Min	Energy (ev) Max	Lab	Type	Documentation Ref Vol Page	Date	Author, Comments	Data
(n,γ)		5.0+7	DUB	Expt	Jour IZV 33 695	Apr 69	Jungclaussen+ SIG(E)GRPHS,ISOM-FISSN	
					Jour BAS 33 641	Apr 69	. ENGL OF IZV 33 695	
(n,γ)	Maxwl		DUB	Expt	Jour YF 10 65	Jul 69	Gangrskij+ AM241(N,G)AM242 SPON FISS	
					Jour SNP 10 38	Jan 70	. ENGL OF YF 10 65	
(n,γ)	3.0+6		IPS	Theo	Jour NP/A 137 241	Nov 69	Jaegare.ANAL 2-HUMP BARR.FISS.ISOM R	
(n,γ)	Maxwl	Fiss	FEI	Expt	Jour YFI-9 4	Dec 69	Dovbenko+ THR VALUE+ISOM RATIOS GVN	
					Rept INDC(CCP)-9U7	Dec 70	TRANSLATN.*	
(n,γ)	Pile		CCP	Expt	Rept ICD-6 42	70	Dobchenko+ A-ACT,SIG AM-242M+G GIVEN	
					Rept LA-TR-71-74	Sep 71	. ENGLISH OF ICD-6 42	
(n,γ)	Pile		BNL	Expt	Rept BNL-50242	Jun 70	Hellstrand+,PILE OSC IN 2 SPECT	
(n,γ)	2.0-1	2.0+1	DUB	Expt	Jour NP/A 148 492	Jun 70	Dalhsuren+ SIGMA FOR ISOMER PRODUCTN	
(n,γ)		7.0+6	BUC	Expt	Jour SCF 22 795	Jul 70	Vilcov. (N,GAM)AM242 SPON-F-SIG(E)	+
	3.0+5	6.8+6			Priv VILCOV	70	- . PUBL DATA SUPSEDD BY PRIVCOM	
					Jour NP/A 134 541	Sep 69	Flerov+ TO SPONFIS ISO,SUPERSEDED	
	3.0+5	6.8+6			Data EXFOR30021.	Aug 70	DATA AT 9 ES, PRIV COM N.VILCOV	
(n,γ)	2.5-2		KFK	Eval	Rept KFK-1186	Jul 70	Hinkelmann. RECOMMENDED 582 B	
	2.5-2	1.0+7			Rept KFK-1186	Jul 70	- .5-GROUP SIG,THR+FAST SPEC	
(n,γ)	1.0+6		FEI	Expt	Conf 71Kiev 1 325	May 71	Ivanov+ RATIO AM241(NG)/U238(NG) GVN	+
	1.0+6				Data EXFOR40153.005	Apr 74	.1 DATA LINE	
(n,γ)	Fiss		KUR	Expt	Jour SJA 30 452	Nov 71	.ENGL OF AE 30 4 369	+
					Jour AE 30 369	Apr 71	Ivanova+ AM-242 BETAS,SCINT,SIG GIVN	
	Fiss				Data EXFOR40190.002	Jan 74	.1 DATA LINE	
(n,γ)	Pile		KFK	Eval	Prog KFK-1544 61	Jan 72	Eberle+FOR 2-GROUP SIG,FITTED TO EXP	
(n,γ)	Pile		JUL	Expt	Jour JIN 34 8 2427	Aug 72	Ihle+ REACTOR CROSS SECTION	
(n,γ)	2.5-2	1.0+6	KFI	Expt	Jour MFF 21 555	73	Nagy. THESIS,HUNG. TO FISS ISO,GRND	
(n,γ)	1.0+2	1.0+7	UK	Eval	Prog AERE-PR/NP20	Mar 73	Sowerby.(HAR).UKNDL CREATD.DFN-1001	
(n,γ)	2.5-2		SRL	Expt	Jour NSE 50 364	Apr 73	Harbour+ EQUIVALENT 1/V CS TO M+G ST	+
	2.5-2				Data EXFOR10317.	Jun 74	2 PTS FOR ISOMER + GND STATE	
(n,γ)	Fast		HAR	Expt	Prog EANDC(UK) 151	Aug 73	Wiltshire+ SIG TO CM-242	
					Rept AERE-R-7363	Jul 73	- +SIG TO CM 242 OBTAINED	
(n,γ)	2.5-2	1.0+7	HAR	Eval	Prog EANDC(UK) 151	Aug 73	Sowerby+ USES LYNN CALC SIG	
	2.5-2				Prog AERE-PR/NP20 9	Mar 73	- +TBL RECOMMNDD SIGS.PC TO MS.	
(n,γ)	3.0+5	8.0+5	LAS	Expt	Jour NIM 128 607	75	Forman+ NUC EXPL. GS PROD,GRPH	
(n,γ)	2.0+5	1.3+6	KUR	Expt	Conf 75Kiev 5 241	May 75	Vorotnikov+ SIG(SPONFIS ISO/FIS)GRPH	
(n,γ)	Fast		DOU	Expt	Prog UKNDC(75)P71	Jul 75	Davies+ IRRADIATION PFR	
(n,γ)	Maxwl		LIN	Expt	Jour YF 22 701	Oct 75	Val'Skij+ SIG TO SPONFIS ISO,VAL GVN	
					Conf 75Kiev 5 236	May 75	- + SIG(SPONFIS ISO/FISS) GIVN	
					Jour SJA 39 363	Oct 75	. ENGL OF YF 22,701	
(n,γ)	2.5-2	3.5+5	ORL	Expt	Conf 75Wash. 229	Oct 75	Weston+NDG.DATA ANAL TBD.	
(n,γ)	0.0+0	+7	FEI	Expt	Rept YK-22 53	76	Ivanov+ SIG,TBL,ISOMER RATIO	
(n,γ)	2.5-2		ITE	Expt	Conf IAEA-186 2 121	76	Kalebin. TOF,SIG CFD INTEG XPTS,TABL	
(n,γ)	None		MUN	Theo	Diss GRYNTAKIS	Mar 76	Gryntakis.,CALC.OF WESTCOTTS G-FUNCT	
					Jour RCA 22 128	Mar 75	- +,EQUIVALENT TO THESIS	
(n,γ)	Maxwl		MTR	Expt	Jour WASH-1053 76	64	Deal+ TO GND STATE	+
	Maxwl				Data EXFOR12573.002	Jun 76	. 1 PT.	
(n,γ)		4.0+6	HAR	Theo	Prog NEANDC(E)172 8	Aug 76	Lynn.EVALUATION AND CALCULD XSECTS	
(n,γ)	Fast		WIN	Expt	Prog NEANDC(E)172 8	Aug 76	Sweet. AVERAGE FAST REACTOR	
					Prog UKNDC(75)P71	Jul 75	Glover+REAC SPEC AV. CM-242 PROD.	
Res Int Capt	5.5-1		BNL	Eval	Rept BNL-982 22	Aug 66	Pearlstein. 1600B CALC, RECOMMENDED	
Res Int Capt	Maxwl		RI	Expt	Rept ICD-4 337	67	Bak+ RES INTEGR CAPT=2100+-200BARNS	
Res Int Capt	Maxwl		RI	Expt	Rept ICD-4 337	67	Bak+ RIG LEADING TO AM242M=300+-30B	
Res Int Capt	5.0-1		MTR	Expt	Rept IN-1296	May 69	Schuman+. PILE ACT. INCLUDING 1/V	
Res Int Capt	None		BNL	Expt	Rept BNL-50242	Jun 70	Hellstrand+,PILE OSC IN 2 SPECT	
Res Int Capt	4.7-1	1.0+7	KFK	Eval	Rept KFK-1186	Jul 70	Hinkelmann. INFIN DILUTION RES INTEG	
Res Int Capt	Pile		KFK	Eval	Prog KFK-1544 61	Jan 72	Eberle+1440B/250B	
Res Int Capt	Fast		HAR	Eval	Prog AERE-PR/NP20 9	Mar 73	Sowerby.FRACTION TO AM242M	
	5.0-1				Prog AERE-PR/NP20 9	Mar 73	- .FRACTION TO AM242M	
Res Int Capt	3.7-1		SRL	Expt	Jour NSE 50 364	Apr 73	Harbour+.208+-18B TO M,1330B TO GND	+
	3.7-1				Data EXFOR10317.	Jun 74	2 PTS FOR ISOMER + GND STATE	
Res Int Capt	5.0-1		MTR	Expt	Prog WASH-1053 76	Oct 64	Deal+ TO AM242 GND STATE,SIGMA GVN	+
	5.0-1				Data EXFOR12573.003	Jun 76	. 1 PT.	
Spect (n,γ)		+3	RI	Expt	Prog YFI-7 34	Apr 69	Alexanrov+ HALF-LIFE OF AM242,TBP AE	
					Rept INDC(CCP)-7U37	Feb 70	TRANSLATN.*	
Spect (n,γ)	Pile		FRS	Expt	Prog INDC(SEC)-43	Dec 74	Gasser+ PAIRSPEC,ES+INTS,LVL SCH,NDG	
(n,2n)	8.0+5	1.0+7	KFK	Eval	Rept KFK-1186	Jul 70	Hinkelmann.AVG SIG FOR THR+FAST SPEC	
(n,2n)	8.0+5	1.0+7	KFK	Eval	Rept KFK-1186	Jul 70	Hinkelmann.CALC FROM PEARLSTEIN SYST	
(n,2n)	1.5+7		DUB	Expt	Jour IJP 47 232	73	Belov+ SIG TO SPONFIS GIVN,FRAGM-DET	
					Rept JINR-E15-6807	Nov 72	- + SPON FISS ISOMER PRODUCTN,TBL	

95 Americium 241

Quantity	Energy (ev) Min	Max	Lab	Type	Documentation Ref Vol Page	Date	Author, Comments	Data
(n,2n)		2.0+7	HAR	Theo Prog	NEANDC(E)172 8	Aug 76	Lynn.EVALUATION AND CALCULD XSECTS	
(n,xn) x>2		2.0+7	HAR	Theo Prog	NEANDC(E)172 8	Aug 76	Lynn.EVALUATION AND CALCULD XSECTS	
(n,p)	Maxwl		IFU	Theo Rept	ICD-4 20	67	Dadakina+ PENETR COEFF CALC,TABLE	
(n,α)	1.4+7	1.5+7	JYV	Eval Rept	JU-RR-3/1970	Jun 70	Leppaemaeki+ TABLE OF EVAL AVG SIG	
Fission	Maxwl		LRL	Expt Rept	AECD-3075	Dec 50	Cunningham+,SIG=3.0+-0.2B	
Fission	Pile		CRC	Expt Jour	PR 81 893	Mar 51	Hanna+. 3.0 BARNS.NO DETAILS GIVEN	+
	Pile			Data	EXFOR12496.003	Jun 76	. 1 PT.	
Fission	Maxwl		BRK	Expt Jour	PR 82 558	May 51	Cunningham+ REL PU239	
Fission	5.0+5	7.0+6	LAS	Expt Abst	PR 99 616	Jul 55	Nobles+LA EXCITATION CURVES	+
	4.9+5	7.3+6		Data	EXFOR12569.002	Jun 76	. 13 PTS.	
Fission	None		KAP	Comp Rept	KAPL-1781	Jul 57	Schuman. SIGMA GIVEN	
Fission	Maxwl		LRL	Expt Jour	PR 107 1294	Sep 57	Hulet+. 3.13+-0.15B REL SIGF PU239	+
	Maxwl			Data	EXFOR12497.004	Jun 76	. 1 PT.	
Fission	1.5+7		CCP	Expt Jour	AE 6 67	Jan 59	Protopopov+ 2.35+-.15B,T(DN)HE COUNT	
				Jour	SJA 6 36	Aug 60	TRANSLATN.*	
				Jour	JNEA 11 191	Feb 60	TRANSLATN.*	
Fission	3.1-2	5.3+0	HAN	Expt Prog	HW-59126 3	Jan 59	Leonard+ FILTERED BEAM RELATIVE B	+
	3.1-2	5.3+0		Data	EXFOR12476.004	Jun 76	. 110 PTS.	
Fission	2.5+6	1.5+7	CCP	Expt Jour	AE 8 139	Feb 60	Kazarinova+ 1.95+-0.2B, 2.95+-0.15B	
				Jour	SJA 8 125	May 61	TRANSLATN.*	
Fission	Spont		DUB	Expt Jour	ZET 40 1261	May 61	Druin.HL OF SPONTANEOUS FISSION	
				Jour	JET 13 889	Nov 61	TRANSLATN.*	
Fission	2.0+5	1.0+7	ANL	Revw Conf	61Vienna 1 29	Aug 61	Smith.P76,CURVE,MANY REFS GVN	
Fission	3.2-2	8.0+1	LRL	Expt Jour	PR/B 137 326	Jan 65	Bowman+ LINAC CRV NORM TO .025EV	+
	3.2-2	5.2+3		Data	EXFOR12571.007	Jun 76	. 483 PTS.	
Fission	2.9+0	8.3+1	KUR	Expt Prog	INDSWG-126 16	66	Gerasimov. GRAPH SIG(E)	
Fission	2.3-2	5.0+1	KUR	Expt Rept	YFI-2 16	66	Gerasimov.	+
	2.3-2	5.0+1		Data	EXFOR40270.	Mar 75	.FISS+(F-WID)/(T-WID),588+13 LINES	
Fission	None		BRK	Revw Jour	NP 81 1	Jun 66	Myers+ TABLE2 FISS BARRIER	
Fission	Maxwl	Pile	BNL	Eval Rept	BNL-982 22	Aug 66	Pearlstein. 2.91B,3.49B FROM RES PAR	
Fission	Maxwl		KYU	Expt Priv	HYAKUTAKE	Aug 66	Hyakutake.SSD,PRELIMINARY REP.	+
	Maxwl			Data	EXFOR20274.002	Jun 74	1PNT.SIGMA.	
Fission	2.0+1	1.0+6	LAS	Expt Jour	NP/A 96 605	Apr 67	Seeger+ FROM PETREL EXPLOSION	+
				Rept	LA-3586 8	Dec 66	Diven.TOF BOMB NS FROM PETREL JUNE65	
	2.0+1	2.0+6		Conf	66Paris 2 219	Oct 66	Hemmendinger+.BOMB TOF.CURVS 20-60EV	
	2.0+1	5.2+4		Data	EXFOR12558.002	Jun 76	. 2342 PTS.	
Fission	1.0+6	1.0+7	LRL	Expt Conf	66Paris 2 149	Oct 66	Bowman+CURV 1-10MEV, SPARKCHMB	
Fission	2.3-2	5.0+1	KUR	Expt Jour	YF 4 5 985	Nov 66	Gerasimov. TOF,CURVE GIVEN	+
	2.0-2	5.0+1		Conf	66Paris 2 129	Oct 66	PPR112,GERASIMOV.CURVS,SIG.253EV GVN	
	2.3-2	5.0+1		Data	EXFOR40085.005	Dec 73	.SIGMA FOR 592 ES GIVEN	
Fission	Maxwl		RI	Expt Rept	ICD-4 337	67	Bak+ SIG FISSION =3.15+-0.1BARNS	
Fission	1.5+7		KUR	Expt Jour	YF 5 966	May 67	Fomushkin+ SIG GIVEN,FISS ANISOTROPY	
Fission	Pile		RI	Expt Prog	YFI-5 49	Oct 67	Bak+ VALUE GIVEN	
	Maxwl			Jour	AE 23 316	Oct 67	BAK+ VAL GVN,MANY REFERENCES	
	Pile			Rept	INDC-232E	Jan 69	. ENGL OF YFI-5 49	
	Maxwl			Jour	EAF 23 4 56	Oct 67	BAK+ TRANSL OF AE 23 316 IN FRENCH	
				Jour	SJA 23 1059	Oct 67	BAK+ TRANSL OF AE 23 316 IN ENGLISH	
Fission	Pile		CCP	Revw Jour	AE 24 247	Mar 68	Bak+ OTHER SIG VAL GVN,TBL	
				Jour	SJA 24 300	Mar 68	TRANSLATN.*	
Fission	1.0+3	1.0+4	HAR	Expt Jour	NP/A 96 605	Apr 67	RAE. INTERMEDIATE STRUCTURE.	
				Conf	68JINR 115	Jul 68	Rae.INTERMED.STRUCT.EFFECTS IN FISS.	
	-2	+2		ExTh Conf	65Salzburg 187	Mar 65	RAE.REVIEW,SOME CALCULATIONS CFD XPT	
Fission	1.0+4	1.0+6	KUR	Theo Jour	YF 9 538	Mar 69	Vorotnikov. OTHER SIG GRPH,FISS-ANAL	
				Jour	SNP 9 308	Sep 69	TRANSLATN.*	
Fission	1.0+4	1.0+6	KUR	Expt Jour	YF 9 538	Mar 69	Vorotnikov.WF FOR S- AND P-NS,CURVS	
Fission		5.0+7	DUB	Expt Jour	IZV 33 695	Apr 69	Jungclaussen+ SIG(E)GRPHS,ISOM-FISSN	
				Jour	BAS 33 641	Apr 69	. ENGL OF IZV 33 695	
Fission	4.4+5	3.6+6	KUR	Expt Prog	YFI-7 25	Apr 69	Fomushkim+ TABLE OF REL SIG AT 14 ES	+
				Rept	INDC(CCP)-7U28	Feb 70	TRANSLATN.*	
	4.4+5	3.6+6		Data	EXFOR40012.010	Aug 70	SIGMA AT 14 ENERGIES	
Fission	Pile		CCP	Expt Jour	AE 27 41	Jul 69	Aleksandrov+ FISS-HALF-LIFE OF AM242	
				Jour	SJA 27 724	70	. ENGL OF AE 27 41	
Fission	Spont		COP	Revw Conf	69Vienna 155	Jul 69	Strutinsky+PPR203. HL GVN,'SHELL-TH'	
Fission	Maxwl		DUB	Expt Jour	YF 10 65	Jul 69	Gangrskij+ AM241(N,G)AM242 SPON FISS	
				Jour	SNP 10 38	Jan 70	. ENGL OF YF 10 65	
Fission	-		FEI	Theo Conf	69Vienna 337	Jul 69	Gaj+PPR132. 2HUMPD-BARR-CALC,TBL	
Fission	1.0+0	3.0+3	GEL	Expt Conf	69Vienna 926	Jul 69	Migneco+PPR140. SUB-THRESH-STRUCTURE	

95 Americium 241

Quantity	Energy (ev) Min	Energy (ev) Max	Lab	Type	Documentation Ref Vol Page	Date	Author, Comments	Data
Fission	Spont		HAR	Revw	Conf 69Vienna 249	Jul 69	Lynn. REVW=STRUTINSKY TH + EXPTS,TBL	
	None				Rept AERE−R−5891	Sep 68	− .STRUCTURE IN FISS.DISCUSSED.ND	
Fission	4.4+5	3.6+6	KUR	Expt	Jour YF 10 917	Nov 69	Fomushkin+ SIG(E) REL U235.TBL+GRAPH	
					Jour SNP 10 529	May 70	. ENGL OF YF 10 917	
Fission	8.0+3	3.3+6	FEI	Expt	Prog YFI−8 4	Dec 69	Shpak+ REL PU239(N,F),GLASS−DET,TBL	+
					Rept INDC(CCP)−8 6	Dec 70	*ENGL OF YFI−8 4	
	1.0+3	4.0+6			Jour ZEP 10 276	Sep 69	Shpak+ GRPH SIG(NEUT−E),FISS−ANALYS	
					Jour JEL 10 175	Sep 69	. ENGL OF ZEP 10 276	
	8.0+3	3.3+6			Data EXFOR40010.	Jun 70	SIG AT 43 ENERGIES FROM PUBLICATION	
Fission	1.4+7		TRM	Expt	Conf 69Roorke 2 289	Dec 69	Iyer+ SIGMA RELATIVE TO U238	+
	1.4+7				Data EXFOR30035.007	Dec 72	ONE VALUE	
Fission	Pile		FTI	Expt	Jour AE 28 359	Apr 70	BAK+.CD FILTERS USED,U235−RATIO,TABL	+
					Jour EAF 28 4 112	Apr 70	. FRENCH OF AE 28 359	
					Jour SJA 28 460	Apr 70	.ENGLISH OF AE 28 359	
	Pile				Data EXFOR40349.009	Dec 77	SIG(N,F)AM−241/SIG(N,F)U−235, 1 PNT	
Fission	4.9+1	3.0+6	LAS	Expt	Rept LA−4420 138	Apr 70	Seeger.	+
Fission	2.0−1	2.0+1	DUB	Expt	Jour NP/A 148 492	Jun 70	Dalhsuren+ SIGMA FOR ISOMER PRODUCTN	
Fission		7.0+6	BUC	Expt	Jour SCF 22 795	Jul 70	Vilcov. (N,GAM)AM242 SPON−F−SIG(E)	
Fission	2.5−2	1.0+7	KFK	Eval	Rept KFK−1186	Jul 70	Hinkelmann.5−GROUP SIG,THR+FAST SPEC	
	2.5−2				Rept KFK−1186	Jul 70	− . RECOMMENDED 3 B	
	1.0+4	1.0+7			Rept KFK−1186	Jul 70	− .RECOMMENDED SHAPE OF SIG	
Fission	Spont		SWT	Expt	Jour HPA 43 593	Nov 70	Hahn. HL SPON FISS, ROTAT CHAMBER	
Fission	3.2+5	2.5+6	TRM	Expt	Conf 70Madurai 2 67	Dec 70	Iyengar+ EXPTL SIG(E) GRPH CFD OTHER	
Fission	5.0+5	1.6+6	DUB	Expt	Jour AHP 30 3 293	71	Nad'+ SPONT FISS ISOMER/ FISS ,GRPH	
		1.6+7			Rept JINR−P7−5162	Jul 70	− +SIG(E)PROMPT CFD SPON FISSN 24	
Fission	Thrsh	1.6+7	CCP	Expt	Conf 71Moscow	Feb 71	Belov+.ABST,SIG(NEUT−E),TWO−HUMPBARR	
Fission	5.0−1	+6	COR	Expt	Jour NSE 46 31	Oct 71	Draper.INTEGRAL SIG TIMES E.4 SPECTR	
Fission	Pile		KFK	Eval	Prog KFK−1544 61	Jan 72	Eberle.+FOR 2−GROUP SIG,FITTED TO EXP	
Fission	Pile		FAR	Eval	Prog EANDC(E)150U	May 72	Vidal.INTEGRAL CROSS SECTION TO U235	
Fission	0.0+0	1.0+0	GEL	ExTh	Jour NP/A 187 305	Jun 72	Weigmann+ FIS BAR PARAMETERS	
Fission	Pile		JUL	Expt	Jour JIN 34 8 2427	Aug 72	Ihle+ REACTOR CROSS SECTION	
Fission	−2	4.0+6	BUC	Revw	Rept IFA−CRD−54	73	Poenaru. REVIEW FOR SPONFIS−ISOMER.	
	+5	+7			Conf 69Vienna 908	Jul 69	Vilkov.PPR18. SPON FISS ISOMER,AM242	
Fission	1.0+2	1.0+7	UK	Eval	Prog AERE−PR/NP20	Mar 73	Sowerby.(HAR).UKNDL CREATD.DFN−1001	
Fission	2.5−2	1.0+7	HAR	Eval	Prog EANDC(UK) 151	Aug 73	Sowerby+ FOR UKNDL DFN 1001	
	2.5−2				Prog AERE−PR/NP20 9	Mar 73	− +TBL RECOMMNDD SIGS.	
Fission	Fiss		TEX	Expt	Rept UMO−74−24,841	74	Chromik. THESIS.CF252−NEUTRONS	
Fission	1.0+0	1.0+4	GEL	Expt	Prog NEANDC(E)161U	Aug 74	Weigmann+ SPARK CHAMBER	
	+0	+3			Prog EANDC(E)157U I	Mar 73	Theobald+ SUBTHRESH FISS IN PROGR	
Fission	8.0+5	6.0+6	LAS	Expt	Jour NIM 128 607	75	Forman+ NUC EXPL. GS PROD,GRPH	
Fission	+5	6.7+6	LAS	Theo	Conf 75Wash. 218	Mar 75	Wilhelmy+ CALC USING PU242(HE3,TF)	
Fission	2.0+5	1.3+6	KUR	Expt	Conf 75Kiev 5 241	May 75	Vorotnikov+ SPONFIS AND FIS−SIG.GRPH	
Fission	Maxwl		LIN	Expt	Conf 75Kiev 5 236	May 75	Val'Skij+ SIG(SPONFIS ISO/FISS) GIVN	
Fission	Maxwl		FEI	Expt	Jour AE 39 285	Oct 75	Zhuravlev+ SIG GIVEN,BY CD−DIFFERENC	
					Jour SJA 39 907	Apr 76	. ENGL OF AE 39 285	
Fission	2.5−2	3.5+5	ORL	Expt	Conf 75Wash. 229	Oct 75	Weston+NDG.DATA ANAL TBD.	
Fission	1.0+3	1.0+7	JAE	Eval	Conf IAEA−190 2 181	76	Igarasi. STATMOD.18PARAM−FIT,CURVES	
Fission	2.0+1	1.5+7	JAE	Revw	Conf IAEA−186 3 1	76	Igarasi. REVW AVAIL DATA,GRPH+BIBLIO	
	1.0+3	1.5+7			Rept JAERI−M−6315	Nov 75	− +GRPHS.9 DATA SETS COMPARED.	
Fission	5.0+5	2.5+6	TRM	Expt	Prog BARC−872 106	76	Iyer+ ABST.REL U235.SIG(E) TABLE	
Fission	None		MUN	Theo	Diss GRYNTAKIS	Mar 76	Gryntakis.,CALC.OF WESTCOTTS G−FUNCT	
					Jour RCA 22 128	Mar 75	− +,EQUIVALENT TO THESIS	
Fission	8.0−1	1.5+2	SAC	Expt	Conf 75Wash. 637	Mar 75	Derrien+TBL.EO,WF	+
	1.0+1	1.5+2			ExTh Prog CEA−N−1861 93	Apr 76	Lucas+ FISSION WIDTH ANAL	
	4.7+0	5.0+1			Expt Rept FRNC−TH−648	76	− .SAME AS IPNO−TH−75−187	
					ExTh Rept IPNO−TH−75−187	75	− . AL,TOF METH, BOWMAN NORM	
	1.0+0	4.0+1			Expt Data EXFOR20415.002	Jul 75	2156PTS.SIGMA.	
Fission		2.0+7	HAR	Theo	Prog NEANDC(E)172 8	Aug 76	Lynn.EVALUATION AND CALCULD XSECTS	
Fission	None		RCN	Revw	Rept ECN−2	Sep 76	Zijp+ INTERCOMP. INTEGRAL SIG SAND−2	
Res Int Fiss	5.5−1		BNL	Eval	Rept BNL−982 22	Aug 66	Pearlstein. 8.5B CALC, RECOMMENDED	
Res Int Fiss	Maxwl		RI		Rept ICD−4 337	67	Bak+ RES INT FISS=21+−2BARNS AT THR	
Res Int Fiss	Pile		RI	Expt	Prog YFI−5 49	Oct 67	Bak+ VALUE GIVEN	
	None				Jour AE 23 316	Oct 67	BAK+ VAL GVN,CALC−METHOD DESCRIBED	
	Pile				Rept INDC−232E	Jan 69	. ENGL OF YFI−5 49	
	None				Jour EAF 23 4 56	Oct 67	BAK+ TRANSL OF AE 23 316 IN FRENCH	
					Jour SJA 23 1059	Oct 67	BAK+ TRANSL OF AE 23 316 IN ENGLISH	

95 Americium 241

Quantity	Energy (ev) Min	Max	Lab	Type	Documentation Ref Vol Page	Date	Author, Comments	Data
Res Int Fiss	Pile		RI Expt	Prog	YFI-8 17	Dec 69	Bak+ REL EXPT TO U-235,VALUES GIVEN	
				Rept	INDC(CCP)-8U22	Dec 70	TRANSLATN.*	
		+7		Jour	AE 28 359	Apr 70	BAK+ INTEGRAL VALUE GIVEN,CFD OTHER	
				Jour	EAF 28 4 112	Apr 70	. FRENCH OF AE 28 359	
Res Int Fiss	Maxwl		FTI Expt	Jour	AE 28 359	Apr 70	BAK+ .INTEGRAL VALUE GIVEN,CFD OTHER	+
				Jour	SJA 28 460	Apr 70	.ENGLISH OF AE 28 359	
				Jour	EAF 28 4 112	Apr 70	. FRENCH OF AE 28 359	
	Maxwl			Data	EXFOR40349.005	Dec 77	CD - DIFF,REL U235. 1 DATAPNT	
Res Int Fiss	4.7-1	1.0+7	KFK Eval	Rept	KFK-1186	Jul 70	Hinkelmann. INFIN DILUTION RES INTEG	
Res Int Fiss	+0	+1	COR Expt	Abst	DA/B 31 1466	Sep 70	Draper.EXPT FOR 4 SPEC,CFD CALC	
Res Int Fiss	5.0-1		FEI Expt	Jour	AE 39 285	Oct 75	Zhuravlev+ RI GIVEN,BY CD-DIFFERENC	
				Jour	SJA 39 907	Apr 76	. ENGL OF AE 39 285	
Nu	Pile		HAR Expt	Jour	JIN 4 1	57	Cuninghame.NU BAR IS 3+-0.5	
Nu	Maxwl		CCP Expt	Jour	AE 5 176	Aug 58	Lebedev+ PROMPT RATIO TO U235 NU THR	+
				Jour	JNEA 10 90	Jul 59	TRANSLATN.*	
				Jour	SJA 5 1019	58	TRANSLATN.*	
Nu	Pile		CCP Theo	Jour	AE 8 409	May 60	Zysin+.VAL CALCD FROM FRGMNT-DISTRBS	
				Jour	SJA 8 343	Jun 61	TRANSLATN.*JNE AB17 41 1/61	
				Jour	KE 4 40	Jan 61	.TRANSLATN	
Nu	Maxwl		ANL Expt	Jour	NP/A 145 1	Apr 70	Jaffey+ REL TO U,PU,CF STANDARDS.	+
				Rept	ANL-7625	Nov 69	- +COMPLETE DATA GVN.	
	Maxwl			Data	EXFOR10125.004	May 72	1PT.PROMPT N YLD=3.219+-.038	
Nu	2.5-2		KFK Eval	Rept	KFK-1186	Jul 70	Hinkelmann.MEAN VALUE	
	2.5-2	1.0+7		Rept	KFK-1186	Jul 70	- .MEAN NUMBER VS E	
Nu	Maxwl		IAE Eval	Jour	REA 10 637	Dec 72	Manero+ EXTENSIVE SURVEY,TBL,AVG VAL	
Nu	Spont		HED Eval	Abst	ANS 22 673	Nov 75	Johnson. TBL,GRPH.NU FROM SPON FISS	
Spect Fiss n	Maxwl		CCP Theo	Jour	AE 5 649	Dec 58	Kovalev+ THEORY COMPARED WITH EXPT	
				Jour	JNEA 11 166	Feb 60	TRANSLATN.*	
				Jour	SJA 5 1588	58	TRANSLATN.*	
Fiss Yield	Pile		HAR Expt	Jour	JIN 4 1	57	Cuninghame.YLD A89TO136CURV CFDPU239	
Fiss Yield	Pile		HAR Comp	Rept	AERE-R-3209	Jan 60	CROALL COMP OF INDP YLDS(NSA 14 1397	
Fiss Yield	Maxwl		ORL Expt	Jour	NSE 23 115	Oct 65	Rickard. MASS-FISSION-YIELD	
Fiss Yield	Maxwl		CCP Expt	Jour	YF 8 454	Sep 68	Solov'Eva. LONG-R-ALPHA,KE-SPECS,CVS	
				Jour	SNP 8 264	Mar 69	TRANSLATN.*	
Fiss Yield	Pile		CCP Expt	Jour	YF 8 454	Sep 68	Solovyeva.TRIPLE FISS ALFA-SPEC,GRPH	
Fiss Yield	Maxwl		KTO Expt	Jour	JIN 33 10 3239	Oct 71	Nakahara+ MASS YLD OF 23 MASS CHAINS	
Fiss Yield	None		TRM Expt	Prog	INIS-MF-334 64	72	.RADIOCHEM+GAM-SPEC,SHORT NOTE,NDG	
Fiss Yield	Pile		MUN Expt	Jour	RCA 17 1 18	Feb 72	Weinlaender+ MASS YLDS OF 35 MASSES	
	Maxwl			Conf	69Vienna 951	Jul 69	- .PPR72. YLD(A),GELI-EXPT	
Fiss Yield	Pile		HAR Eval	Conf	73Paris 1 393	Mar 73	Crouch.EXPTL DATA+EVAL CHAIN YLD,TBL	
				Rept	AERE-R-7209	Jan 73	.27 CHAIN YLDS RECOMMENDED TBL	
Fiss Yield	Maxwl		KSU Expt	Conf	73Munich 1 608	Aug 73	Fontenla+ MASSDIST CFD AM-242M,GRAPH	
Fiss Yield	Maxwl		MCM Expt	Jour	JIN 35 2639	Aug 73	Tracy+ CUMUL KR+XE YIELDS	
				Prog	EANDC(CAN)-32	Jan 67	Thode+ YLDS OF STABLE KR+XE ISOTOPES	
Fiss Yield	Pile		RI Expt	Jour	AE 35 409	Dec 73	Skovorodkin+ MICA-DET,ABSOL+REL,TBLS	+
				Jour	SJA 35 1109	Jun 74	.ENGLISH OF AE 35 409	
	2.5-2			Data	EXFOR40389.	Feb 77	.CUMUL FISS PROD YIELDS GVN	
Fiss Yield	Maxwl		AUA Theo	Rept	AAEC/E-386	Mar 76	Cook+ 3-GAUSS FIT,PARAMS GIVEN	
Frag Spectra	Spont		CCP Expt	Conf	55Moscow 226	Jul 55	Goldin+.ALFA SPECTRUM.EXPT FROM 1954	
				Rept	AEC-TR-2435	56	. PAGE 167. ENGL OF 55MOSCOW 226	
Frag Spectra	1.5+7		RI Expt	Jour	ZET 36 920	Mar 59	Protopopov. DEGREE OF ANISOTROPY	
				Jour	JET 9 650	Sep 59	TRANSLATN.*	
Frag Spectra	6.0+6	2.0+7	CRC Expt	Jour	CJP 37 1418	Dec 59	Baerg+. FRAG ANG DIST ISOTROPIC	
Frag Spectra	5.0+4	1.4+6	KUR Expt	Rept	IAE-817	65	Dubrovina+,ANG DIST FRAGMENTS,GRAPH	
				Rept	ANL-TRANS-242	65	. ENGL OF IAE-817	
Frag Spectra	1.0+5	5.0+6	KUR Expt	Conf	65Salzburg 157	Mar 65	Vorotnikov.A-DSTRB,E=.1TO1.2, 4,5MEV	
Frag Spectra	6.0+2	5.0+3	CCP Expt	Jour	DOK 169 314	Jul 66	Veinberg.ANGULAR DISTRIB OF FRAG	
				Jour	SPD 11 591	Jan 67	TRANSLATN.*	
Frag Spectra	6.0+5	1.4+6	CCP Expt	Jour	DOK 169 314	Jul 66	Vorotnikov+ FISSION ANISOTROPY	
Frag Spectra	-		KYU Expt	Priv	HYAKUTAKE	Aug 66	Hyakutake.SSD,PRELIMINARY REP.	
Frag Spectra	1.5+7		KUR Expt	Jour	YF 5 966	May 67	Fomushkin+ ANGDIST OF FRAGMENTS	
				Jour	SNP 5 689	Nov 67	. ENGL OF YF 5 966	
Frag Spectra	-2		RI Expt	Prog	YFI-6 93	68	Solov'Eva. SPECTRUM OF ALFAS	
				Rept	INDC-260E	69	. ENGL OF YFI-6 93	
Frag Spectra	2.5-2		FTI Expt	Jour	IZV 32 693	Apr 68	Baranov+ TOTAL E-KIN OF FRAGMNTS GVN	+
				Jour	BAS 32 639	69	.TRANSLATION OF IZV 32 693	
	2.5-2			Data	EXFOR40320.002	Oct 75	.ONE DATA LINE	

95   Americium   241

Quantity	Energy (ev) Min	Energy (ev) Max	Lab	Type	Documentation Ref Vol Page	Date	Author, Comments	Data
Frag Spectra	4.4+5	3.6+6	KUR	Expt	Prog YFI - 7 25	Apr 69	Fomushkim+ LEGCOEF OF FRAG - ANGDISTR	+
					Rept INDC(CCP) - 7U28	Feb 70	TRANSLATN.*	
	4.4+5	3.6+6			Data EXFOR40012.006	Aug 70	LEG - COEFFS, ANG DSTRB OF FRAGMNTS	
Frag Spectra	4.4+5	3.6+6	KUR	Expt	Jour YF 10 917	Nov 69	Fomushkin+ ANGDIST(E) LEG - COEF,GRAPH	
					Jour SNP 10 529	May 70	. ENGL OF YF 10 917	
Frag Spectra	3.0+5	7.2+6	FEI	Expt	Jour YF 12 35	Jul 70	Shpak+ ANGDIST+ANISOTROPY,GRPH+TBL	+
					Jour SNP 12 19	Jan 71	*	
					Rept INDC(CCP) - 7U11	Feb 70	.TRANSLATN.*	
					Prog YFI - 7 13	Apr 69	Shpak+ ANGDIST(E) GRAPH,TO BE PUBL.	
					Jour ZEP 9 196	Feb 69	- + ANG ANISOTR,GLASS - DET,GRAPH	
					Jour JEL 9 114	Feb 69	. ENGLISH OF ZEP 9 169	
	3.0+5	7.2+6			Data EXFOR40015.003	Aug 70	ANGULAR ANISOTROPY AT 53 N - ENERGIES	
Frag Spectra	Thrsh	+6	FEI	Expt	Jour AHP 29 357	Aug 70	Androsenko+ ANGDIST CFD 2 - HUMPD - BARR	
	7.0+6			ExTh	Conf 69Vienna 419	Jul 69	- +PPR134. XPTL ANGDIST + TH	
Frag Spectra	1.4+7	1.6+7	TRM	Expt	Conf 70Madurai 2 57	Dec 70	Iyer+ ANGDISTR,GRAPH+TABLE,TRACK - DET	+
	1.6+7				Data EXFOR30235.	Jul 73	COS.COEF.OF ANG.DIST. OF FIS.FRAGM.	
Frag Spectra	Pile		TRM	Expt	Jour RCA 18 1 35	Dec 72	Prakash+ KIN ENERG DISTR	
					Conf 70Madurai 2 79	Dec 70	- + KIN - E VS MASS RATIO, GRAPHS	
					Conf 67Tokai 49	Oct 67	Shankar. PRELIMIN,E - KIN CFD 235U,NDG	
Frag Spectra	Maxwl		KSU	Expt	Conf 73Munich 1 608	Aug 73	Fontenla+ E KIN - SPEC CFD AM242M,GRPH	
Frag Spectra	Pile		KTO	Expt	Jour JIN 36 5 965	May 74	Fujiwara+ FRAG RANG + 28MASS CHAIN	
Frag Spectra	Pile		LIN	Expt	Jour YF 20 461	Sep 74	Vorob'Ev+ LIGHT FRG E - SPEC,TBL+GRAPH	
					Jour SNP 20 248	Mar 75	. ENGL OF YF 20 461	
Reson Params	None		BNL	Expt	Prog WASH - 1006 5	Oct 58	Hughes+ 6RES,NDG	
	3.1 - 1	1.7+1	ORL	Expt	Prog ORNL - 2718	59	Block+	+
	3.1 - 1	1.7+1			Data EXFOR12565.002	Jun 76	. 22 RES, E0,WN0,WG	
Reson Params	3.1 - 1	1.3+0	HAN	Expt	Abst BAP 4 31	Jan 59	Leonard+ 3RES IN FISS, WF OKS THEORY	
Reson Params	3.0 - 1	4.3+1	ORL	Expt	Prog ORNL - 3085 42	61	Slaughter+	+
	3.0 - 1	4.3+1			Data EXFOR12478.	Jun 76	. 53 RES, WN0	
Reson Params	1.9+0	2.3+0	HAR	Expt	Prog AERE - PR/NP6 10	Apr 64	Pattenden.WN OF 2 RES	
Reson Params	3.1 - 1	1.5+1	CJD	Comp	Rept INDSWG - 101 25	65	. TBL 15 RES FROM VARIOUS SOURCES	
Reson Params	3.1 - 1	1.5+1	LRL	Expt	Jour PR/B 137 326	Jan 65	Bowman+WF 15RESFROM SIG FISS.W/ORNL	+
	- .6+0	6.2+0			Data EXFOR12571.	Jun 76	. 22RES, WT, WF,1RES, WN0, WF	
Reson Params	3.0 - 1	1.5+1	KUR	Expt	Prog INDSWG - 126 16	66	Gerasimov. TABLE OF 15 RES	
Reson Params	3.1 - 1	1.5+1	KUR	Expt	Jour YF 4 5 985	Nov 66	Gerasimov. TOF,TABLE 15 RESONANCES	+
	3.0 - 1	1.5+1			Conf 66Paris 2 129	Oct 66	PPR112,GERASIMOV.PARAMS FOR 13RES	
	3.1 - 1	1.5+1			Data EXFOR40085.003	Dec 73	.DATA IN MILLI - EV FOR 15 RES - EN GVN	
	3.1 - 1	1.5+1			Data EXFOR40085.004	Dec 73	.(NF/WID)/(TOT/WID)AT 15 RES - EN GVN	
Reson Params	-		CCP	Eval	Jour AE 23 6	Jul 67	Kirpitchnikov.FISS. ,N - WIDTH,STRNTH - F	
					Jour SJA 23 669	Jul 67	TRANSLATN.*	
Reson Params		1.0+6	AUA	Theo	Jour AUJ 20 477	Oct 67	Cook. TBL OF AVG LVL SPACING D,L=0,1	
Reson Params	-		FEI	Theo	Rept FEI - 157	Feb 69	Ignatjuk+ 2HUMPED - BARR - CALCUL,WN/WF	
Reson Params	-		FEI	Theo	Rept FEI - 158	Feb 69	Gaj+ FISSN WIDTH,2HUMPED - BARR - CALCUL	
Reson Params		1.0+6	KUR	Theo	Jour YF 9 538	Mar 69	Vorotnikov. W - FISS GRPH IN FISS - ANAL	
					Jour SNP 9 308	Sep 69	TRANSLATN.*	
Reson Params	None		HAR	Revw	Conf 69Vienna 249	Jul 69	Lynn. PARS IN STRUTINSKY TH +EXPT.	
	-			Theo	Conf 68DUBSY 463	Jul 68	- .REVIEW,STRUCT EFFECTS IN FISS.	
Reson Params	+2	+6	FEI	Theo	Jour YF 10 542	Sep 69	Gai+ TABLE OF RESON+FAST FISSN WIDTH	
					Jour SNP 10 311	Mar 70	. ENGL OF YF 10 542	
Reson Params	+4		FEI	Expt	Jour ZEP 10 276	Sep 69	Shpak+ RESPARS FOR FISSION - ANALYSIS	
					Jour JEL 10 175	Sep 69	. ENGL OF ZEP 10 276	
Reson Params	1.0+3	4.6+4	KFK	Eval	Rept KFK - 1186	Jul 70	Hinkelmann. AVG.WG,WF LVL SPACING	
Reson Params	None		DUB	Theo	Jour YF 13 240	Feb 71	Malecki+G - WID,THEO CFD EXPT.TBL,GRPH	
					Jour SNP 13 133	Aug 71	- + ENGL OF YF 13 240.	
Reson Params	6.2 - 1	5.0+4	SRL	Theo	Conf 71Knoxvill 714	Mar 71	Mccrosson. STAT CALCULATN AVG PARAMS	
Reson Params	+0		CCP	Theo	Conf AE 31 18	Jul 71	Vorotnikov.S+P - NEUT FISS - WIDS DERIVD	
					Jour SJA 31 706	Feb 72	* ENGL OF AE 31 18 7/71	
Reson Params	- .4+0	2.6+1	ITE	Expt	Conf IAEA - 186 2 121	76	Kalebin. 39ES,GAM,GAM - N CFD OTHS,TBL	
Reson Params	3.1 - 1	1.5+2	SAC	Expt	Conf 75Wash. 637	Mar 75	Derrien+TBL.EO,2GWN,WG	+
	4.7+0	5.0+1			Rept FRNC - TH - 648	76	Lucas.SAME AS IPNO - TH - 75 - 187	
	1.3+0	1.5+2			Conf IAEA - 186 2 149	76	- + N - ,G - WIDS.UPTO 50EV F - WID.TBL	
	3.0 - 1	1.5+2			Prog NEANDC(E)162U	Aug 75	Derrien+ TBLS,WN,WG,WF,189 RES ANAL	
	4.7+0	5.0+1		ExTh	Rept IPNO - TH - 75 - 187	75	Lucas. AL,TOF METH,N ANF F WIDTHS	
	2.0+1	1.5+2		Expt	Conf 73Kiev 2 246	May 73	Derrien+ LINAC. N - WIDS TBL,AVG G - WID	
	0.0+0	5.0+1			Data EXFOR20415.	Jul 75	228PTS.WF,AVG.WF,AVG WG,MEAN LVLSP	
Reson Params	- .2+0	4.9+1	ORL	Expt	Jour NSE 61 356	Nov 76	Weston+2G*WN,WG.TBL.CFD	+
	- .2+0	4.9+1			Data EXFOR10767.003	Sep 78	. 66 RES ES.E0,WN*2G,WG GVN.	

PAGE 1804

95 Americium 241

Quantity	Energy (ev) Min	Max	Lab	Type	Documentation Ref Vol Page	Date	Author, Comments	Data
Strnth Fnctn	5.4+0	4.3+1	ORL	Expt Prog	ORNL-3085 42	61	Slaughter+	+
	5.4+0	4.3+1		Data	EXFOR12478.008	Jun 76	2 PTS, S0,D	
Strnth Fnctn	1.0+3	4.6+4	KFK	Eval Rept	KFK-1186	Jul 70	Hinkelmann. S0=1.0 SI=2.	
Strnth Fnctn	None		AUA	Eval Rept	AAEC/E-277	Mar 73	Musgrove.TBLS EXPTL DATA+BEST VALUES	
Strnth Fnctn		1.5+2	SAC	Expt Conf	75Wash. 637	Mar 75	Derrien+S0=0.94E-04.	+
	2.0+1	1.5+2		Conf	73Kiev 2 246	May 73	- + S-WAVE, D-DISTR+STRFCT GIVN	
	0.0+0	1.5+2		Data	EXFOR20415.008	Jul 75	2PTS.	
Strnth Fnctn	4.0-2	3.0+1	NIR	Expt Conf	75Kiev 3 214	May 75	Belanova+ BY TOTSIG.S0 GIVEN	
Strnth Fnctn	-.4+0	2.6+1	ITE	Expt Conf	IAEA-186 2 121	76	Kalebin. FROM 39RES.S=.76+-.18(10-4)	
Strnth Fnctn		1.7+1	ORL	Expt Prog	ORNL-2718 28	59	Block+	+
		1.7+1		Data	EXFOR12565.003	Jun 76	2 PTS, S0, D	
Lvl Density		1.1+1	KUR	Theo Jour	YF 9 303	Feb 69	Vorotnikov.LVL DEN(EXCIT-E),TBL GRPH	
				Jour	SNP 9 179	Aug 69	TRANSLATN.*	
Lvl Density	None		IBJ	Revw Jour	PF 23 561	Sep 72	Jastrzebski. SPONTAN FISSION ISOMERS	
Lvl Density	7.0+6	1.6+7	DUB	ExTh Rept	JINR-E15-7362	Jul 73	Gangrskij+ PARS FROM (G,N),(G,G),GRPH	
Lvl Density	+6		DUB	Theo Rept	JINR-E4-9236	Nov 75	Komov+ AVG LVL-SPAC,SEMIMICRO CFD XP	
(γ,n)	1.0+7	1.4+7	IFP	Expt Jour	YF 11 54	Jan 70	Gangrskij+AM241(G,N)AM240 ISOM FISSN	
				Jour	SNP 11 30	Jul 70	. ENGL OF YF 11 54	
(γ,n)	7.0+6	1.6+7	DUB	Expt Rept	JINR-E15-7362	Jul 73	Gangrsky+ SPON FISS ISOMER,TBL,GRAPH	
Photo-Fissn	6.0+6	2.0+7	CRC	Expt Jour	CJP 37 1418	Dec 59	Baerg+. FRAG ANG DIST ISOTROPIC	
Photo-Fissn	1.0+7	1.4+7	IFP	Expt Jour	YF 11 54	Jan 70	Gangrsky+AM241(G,N)AM240 ISOM FISSN	
				Jour	SNP 11 30	Jul 70	. ENGL OF YF 11 54	
Photo-Fissn	6.0+6	1.9+7	DUB	Expt Jour	FDP 22 199	74	Gangrsky+ GRPH (G,F)SIG VS E-GAM	

95 Americium 242

Quantity	Energy (ev) Min	Max	Lab	Type	Documentation Ref Vol Page	Date	Author, Comments	Data
Evaluation	1.0-5	2.0+7	SRL	Eval Rept	EPRI-NP-161	Dec 75	Benjamin+ENDF4B.GENPAR MDL.REVISIONS	
Total	None		KAP	Comp Rept	KAPL-1781	Jul 57	Schuman. SIGMA GIVEN	
Total	None		MTR	Expt Prog	WASH-1056 94	Mar 65	Schuman.AM242M BEING PREPARED,TBC	
Tot Inelastc	Maxwl		CCP	Expt Jour	YF 9 1328	Jun 69	Romanov. UPPER SIG AM242M(N,N')LIMIT	
				Jour	SNP 9 774	Dec 69	.TRANSLATN.*9,NO6	
Tot Inelastc		2.0+7	HAR	Theo Prog	NEANDC(E)172 8	Aug 76	Lynn.EVALUATION AND CALCULD XSECTS	
Absorption	Pile		CRC	Expt Jour	PR 81 893	Mar 51	Hanna+. 8000+-800B FOR 100YR ISOMER	+
	Pile			Data	EXFOR12496.005	Jun 76	1 PT, META TARGET	
Absorption	Pile		BRK	Expt Jour	PR 85 135	Jan 52	Street.	+
	Pile			Data	EXFOR12583.006	Jun 76	1 PT, META TARGET	
Res Int Abs	5.0-1		MTR	Expt Rept	IN-1296	May 69	Schuman+. PILE ACT. 152-YR ISOMER	
(n,γ)	Pile		BRK	Expt Jour	PR 79 530	Aug 50	Street.	+
	Pile			Data	EXFOR12581.003	Jun 76	1 PT, META TARGET	
(n,γ)	Pile		BRK	Expt Jour	PR 85 135	Jan 52	Street.	+
				Rept	AECD-3268	Mar 51	.SUPERSEDED.	
	Pile			Data	EXFOR12583.007	Jun 76	1 PT, META TARGET	
(n,γ)			CCP	Revw Jour	AE 24 247	Mar 68	Bak+ OTHER SIG VAL GVN,TBL	
				Jour	SJA 24 300	Mar 68	TRANSLATN.*	
(n,γ)	Pile		KFK	Eval Prog	KFK-1544 61	Jan 72	Eberle+FOR 2-GROUP SIG,FITTED TO EXP	
(n,γ)	Pile		JUL	Expt Jour	JIN 34 8 2427	Aug 72	Ihle+ REACTOR CROSS SECTION	
(n,γ)	1.0+2	1.0+7	UK	Eval Prog	AERE-PR/NP20	Mar 73	Sowerby.(HAR).UKNDL CREATD.DFN-1002	
(n,γ)	2.5-2	1.0+7	HAR	Eval Prog	EANDC(UK) 151	Aug 73	Sowerby+ USES LYNN CALC SIG	
	2.5-2			Prog	AERE-PR/NP20 9	Mar 73	- +TBL RECOMMNDD SIGS.MS ONLY	
(n,γ)	3.0+6		DUB	Expt Conf	75Kiev 5 245	May 75	Gangrskij+ SIG TO SPONFIS ISO.TABLE	
(n,γ)	1.5-3	4.7+6	SAC	Eval Rept	CEA-N-1821	Sep 75	Tellier. EXP+STAT MDL ANAL,CURVES	
(n,γ)	None		ORL	Expt Prog	ORNL-5101 11	Jan 76	Weston.AM242 MSTATE.NDG.TBD.	
(n,γ)		4.0+6	HAR	Theo Prog	NEANDC(E)172 8	Aug 76	Lynn.EVALUATION AND CALCULD XSECTS	
Res Int Capt	Pile		KFK	Eval Prog	KFK-1544 61	Jan 72	Eberle+1100B	
(n,2n)	1.5+7		DUB	Expt Conf	75Kiev 5 245	May 75	Gangrskij+ SIG TO SPONFIS ISO.TABLE	
(n,2n)		2.0+7	HAR	Theo Prog	NEANDC(E)172 8	Aug 76	Lynn.EVALUATION AND CALCULD XSECTS	
(n,xn) x>2		2.0+7	HAR	Theo Prog	NEANDC(E)172 8	Aug 76	Lynn.EVALUATION AND CALCULD XSECTS	
(n,p)	Maxwl		IFU	Theo Rept	ICD-4 20	67	Dadakina+ PENETR COEFF CALC,TABLE	
Fission	Maxwl		CRC	Expt Jour	PR 81 893	Mar 51	Hanna+. 500/G BARNS.TEXT DEFINES G	+
	Maxwl			Data	EXFOR12496.	Jun 76	2 PTS, GND+META TARGET	
Fission	Pile		BRK	Expt Jour	PR 85 135	Jan 52	Street.	+
				Rept	AECD-3268	Mar 51	- +,SIG=ABOUT 6000B,AM242M=2000B	
	Pile			Data	EXFOR12583.008	Jun 76	1 PT, SIG	
Fission	Maxwl		BRK	Expt Jour	PR 94 735	May 54	Higgins+ AM242M NF SIG=2950B	+
	Maxwl			Data	EXFOR12584.002	Jun 76	1 PT, META TARGET	
Fission	None		KAP	Comp Rept	KAPL-1781	Jul 57	Schuman. SIG AM242(NF)AND AM242M(NF)	

95 Americium 242

Quantity	Energy (ev) Min	Max	Lab	Type	Documentation Ref Vol Page	Author, Comments Date	Data
Fission	Maxwl		LRL	Expt	Jour PR 107 1294	Sep 57 Hulet+. 6390+ –500B FOR 100YR ISOMER	+
	Maxwl				Data EXFOR12497.005	Jun 76 . 1 PT.	
Fission	Spont		DUB	Theo	Rept JINR–E–2515	Dec 65 Malov+ SPON FISSN ISOMER, LIFE–TIME	
				Expt	Rept JINR–P–2347	Sep 65 Markov+ AM241(N,G)AM242 SPON FISSN	
Fission	Maxwl		LAS	Expt	Jour JNAB 20 588	Jul 66 Wolfsberg+ 152YR ISOMER,7200+ –300B	+
	Maxwl				Data EXFOR12563.002	Jun 76 . 1 PT, META TARGET	
Fission	Maxwl		RI	Expt	Rept ICD–4 337	67 Bak+ SIG FISSION =2100+ –200 B AT THR	
Fission	Spont		LRL	Expt	Jour PR 155 1309	Mar 67 Caldwell+HALF LIFE OF AM–242M	
Fission	2.0+1	9.3+5	LAS	Expt	Jour NP/A 96 605	Apr 67 Hemmendinger.	+
	2.0+1	2.0+6			Conf 66Paris 2 219	Oct 66 – +.BOMB TOF.CURVES	
	2.0+1	1.0+6			Rept LA–3586 8	Dec 66 Diven.TOF BOMB NS FROM PETREL JUNE65	
	2.0+1	9.3+5			Data EXFOR12558.003	Jun 76 . 1860 PTS.	
Fission	Pile		RI	Expt	Prog YFI–5 49	Oct 67 Bak+ VALUE GIVEN	+
	Maxwl				Jour AE 23 316	Oct 67 BAK+ VAL GVN,MANY REFERENCES	
	Pile				Rept INDC–232E	Jan 69 . ENGL OF YFI–5 49	
	Maxwl				Jour EAF 23 4 56	Oct 67 BAK+ TRANSL OF AE 23 316 IN FRENCH	
					Jour SJA 23 1059	Oct 67 BAK+ TRANSL OF AE 23 316 IN ENGLISH	
	Pile				Data EXFOR40062.004	Apr 71 AV SIG BELOW CD–LIMIT	
Fission	2.0–2	6.0+6	LRL	Expt	Jour PR 166 1219	Feb 68 Bowman+ LINAC+TOF AM242M CURVES	+
					Conf 66Paris 2 149	Oct 66 .SUPERSEDED	
	2.0–2	5.7+6			Data EXFOR12572.007	Jun 76 . 1091 PTS.	
Fission	Pile		CCP	Revw	Jour AE 24 247	Mar 68 Bak+ OTHER SIG VAL GVN,TBL	
					Jour SJA 24 300	Mar 68 TRANSLATN.*	
Fission	4.1–1	3.7+6	LRL	Eval	Jour NSE 32 131	Apr 68 Perkins+ AVGD DATA 68GRPS META STATE	
Fission	Spont		COP	Expt	Jour YF 8 459	Sep 68 Bjornholm+PROD OF FISSILE–ISOM–STATE	
					Jour SNP 8 267	Mar 69 – + ENGLISH TRANSLATION	
Fission	Spont		CCP	Expt	Jour AE 27 41	Jul 69 Aleksandrov+ FISSN HALF LIFE GIVEN	
					Jour SJA 27 724	70 . ENGL OF AE 27 41	
Fission	Spont		COP	Revw	Conf 69Vienna 155	Jul 69 Strutinsky+PPR203. ISOM–HL,SHELL–TH	
Fission	Spont		DUB	Expt	Jour YF 10 65	Jul 69 Gangrskij+ AM241(N,G)AM242 SPON FISS	
					Jour FDP 22 199	74 Gangrsky+ FIS–BARRIER,GRPH EMAX+EMIN	
					Rept JINR–E15–7362	Jul 73 – + ISOMER HALFLIFE,TABLE,GRPH	
					Jour SNP 10 38	Jan 70 . ENGL OF YF 10 65	
Fission	–		HAR	Revw	Conf 69Vienna 249	Jul 69 Lynn. REVW=STRUTINSKY TH + EXPTS,TBL	
	0.0+0	1.0+0		Theo	Conf 68DUBSY 463	Jul 68 – .REVIEW,STRUCT EFFECTS IN FISS.	
Fission	Spont		IFP	Expt	Jour YF 11 54	Jan 70 Gangrskij+AM243(G,N)AM242 ISOM FISSN	
					Jour SNP 11 30	Jul 70 . ENGL OF YF 11 54	
Fission	2.0+6	7.0+6	TRM	Theo	Jour NP/A 151 532	Aug 70 Sood+ CORREL ANAL OF INTERM STRUCTUR	
	None			Expt	Prog BARC–501 21	70 – + CLASS II LVL SPACING DETMD.ND	
	–			Theo	Prog BARC–471 5	70 – + CORREL ANAL,D CLASS II VAL GV	
Fission	Spont		DUB	Expt	Jour AHP 30 3 293	71 Nad'+ SPONT FISS ISOMER/ FISS ,GRPH	
					Rept JINR–P7–5162	Jul 70 + FISS ISOMER REL AM241(NF),GRP	
Fission	5.0–1		COR	Expt	Jour NSE 46 31	Oct 71 Draper.INTEGRAL SIG TIMES E.4 SPECTR	
Fission	0.0+0	1.0+0	GEL	Revw	Jour AKE 18 229	Nov 71 Theobald+ SUB–BARRIER FISS EXPTS,TH	
Fission	1.0–2	1.4+7	LRL	Expt	Prog NCSAC–42 135	Nov 71 Browne+. TO BE DONE. AM242M	
Fission	Pile		KFK	Eval	Prog KFK–1544 61	Jan 72 Eberle+FOR 2–GROUP SIG,FITTED TO EXP	
Fission	–		GEL	ExTh	Jour NP/A 187 305	Jun 72 Weigmann+ F.B.PARAMS FROM DATA ANAL.	
Fission	Pile		JUL	Expt	Jour JIN 34 8 2427	Aug 72 Ihle+ REACTOR CROSS SECTION	
Fission	Spont		TPI	Theo	Jour YF 16 919	Nov 72 Adeev+ FISS BARRIER CFD EVEN,GRAPH	
					Jour SNP 16 507	May 73 .ENGLISH OF YF 16 919	
Fission	1.0+2	1.0+7	UK	Eval	Prog AERE–PR/NP20	Mar 73 Sowerby.(HAR).UKNDL CREATD.DFN–1002	
	2.5–2	1.0+7	HAR	Eval	Prog EANDC(UK) 151	Aug 73 Sowerby+ FOR UKNDL DFN 1002	
	2.5–2				Prog AERE–PR/NP20 9	Mar 73 – +TBL RECOMMNDD SIGS.MS+GS.	
Fission	Maxwl		USP	Expt	Conf 73Munich 1 588	Aug 73 Fontenla+ PROMPT+ISOM PEAK/VALLY,TBL	
Fission	+5	4.6+6	LAS	Theo	Conf 75Wash. 218	Mar 75 Wilhelmy+242M CALC.PU242(HE3,DF)	
Fission	1.5–3	4.7+6	SAC	Eval	Rept CEA–N–1821	Sep 75 Tellier. EXP+STAT MDL ANAL,CURVES	
Fission	Maxwl		FEI	Expt	Jour AE 39 285	Oct 75 Zhuravlev+ AM–242M.SIG GVN,CD–DIFFER	
					Jour SJA 39 907	Apr 76 . ENGL OF AE 39 285	
Fission	1.0+3	6.0+6	JAE	Revw	Conf IAEA–186 3 1	76 Igarasi. REVW AVAIL DATA,GRPH+BIBLIO	
	1.0+3	7.0+6			Rept JAERI–M–6315	Nov 75 – +GRPH. 2 DATA SETS COMPARED.	
Fission		2.0+7	HAR	Theo	Prog NEANDC(E)172 8	Aug 76 Lynn.EVALUATION AND CALCULD XSECTS	
Res Int Fiss	Maxwl		RI	Expt	Rept ICD–4 337	67 Bak+ RES INT FISS=300 BARNS AT THR	
Res Int Fiss	Pile		RI	Expt	Prog YFI–5 49	Oct 67 Bak+ UPPER LIMIT OF SIGMA GIVEN	
	None				Jour AE 23 316	Oct 67 BAK+ VAL GVN,CALC–METHOD DESCRIBED	
	Pile				Rept INDC–232E	Jan 69 . ENGL OF YFI–5 49	
	None				Jour EAF 23 4 56	Oct 67 BAK+ TRANSL OF AE 23 316 IN FRENCH	
					Jour SJA 23 1059	Oct 67 BAK+ TRANSL OF AE 23 316 IN ENGLISH	

95 Americium 242

Quantity	Energy (ev) Min	Max	Lab	Type	Documentation Ref Vol Page	Author, Comments Date	Data
Res Int Fiss	5.0−1		LRL	Expt	Jour PR 166 1219	Feb 68 Bowman.	+
	5.0−1			Data	EXFOR12572.008	Jun 76 . 1 PT.	
Res Int Fiss	5.0−1	3.7+6	LRL	Eval	Jour NSE 32 131	Apr 68 Perkins+ META STATE 1570+ − 110B	
Res Int Fiss	+0	+1	COR	Expt	Abst DA/B 31 1466	Sep 70 Draper.EXPT FOR 4 SPEC,FOR AM242M	
Res Int Fiss	Pile		KFK	Eval	Prog KFK−1544 61	Jan 72 Eberle+5500B	
Res Int Fiss	5.0−1		FEI	Expt	Jour AE 39 285	Oct 75 Zhuravlev+ AM−242M.RI GVN,CD−DIFFER	
					Jour SJA 39 907	Apr 76 . ENGL OF AE 39 285	
Alpha	1.0+4	2.0+4	LAS	Theo	Jour PR 158 1127	Jun 67 Bell. PREDICT 10−20KEV BY SYSTEMATCS	
Nu	Maxwl		LRL	Expt	Jour PR 152 1046	Dec 66 Fultz+ ISOM STATE,3.24+ − .12REL CF252	+
					Conf 66Paris 2 149	Oct 66 .SUPERSEDED	
	Maxwl				Data EXFOR12345.004	Jun 76 . 1 PT. META TARGET	
Nu	2.5−2		ANL	Expt	Jour NP/A 145 1	Apr 70 Jaffey+REL TO U,PU,CF STNDRD.METAST.	+
					Rept ANL−7625	Nov 69 − +COMPLETE DATA GVN.	
	2.5−2				Data EXFOR10125.005	May 72 1PT.PROMPT N YLD=3.264+ − .024.	
Nu	Maxwl	1.5+7	HAR	Revw	Conf 70Helsinki 2 195	Jun 70 Colvin.PPR99. REPORT ON DATA STATUS	
Nu	Maxwl		NIR	Expt	Jour AE 29 95	Aug 70 Kroshkin+ NU BAR +− 3.0 PERCENT GIVN	+
					Jour SJA 29 790	Aug 70 . ENGL OF AE 29 95	
	2.5−2				Data EXFOR40064.002	Sep 73 .1 DATA LINE	
Nu	Maxwl		IAE	Eval	Jour REA 10 637	Dec 72 Manero+ EXTENSIVE SURVEY,TBL,AVG VAL	
Nu	Spont		HED	Eval	Abst ANS 22 673	Nov 75 Johnson. TBL,GRPH.NU FROM SPON FISS	
Spect Fiss n	Maxwl		NIR	Expt	Jour AE 29 95	Aug 70 Kroshkin+ AVG FISSN NEUT E +SPEC CRV	+
					Jour SJA 29 790	Aug 70 . ENGL OF AE 29 95	
	2.5−2				Data EXFOR40064.008	Sep 73 .1 DATA LINE	
Spect Fiss n	Maxwl		ANL	Revw	Conf 71Vienna 3	Aug 71 Smith. MEAN−E OF NEUTS,EXPTS CFD,TBL	
Fiss Yield	Maxwl		MUN	Expt	Conf 69Vienna 951	Jul 69 Weinlaender.PPR72. META AM242,YLD(A)	
Fiss Yield	Maxwl		LAS	Expt	Conf PR/C 3 1333	Mar 71 Ford+,META,35CHAIN YLDS,XE+KR CUMULT	
Fiss Yield	Maxwl		HAR	Eval	Conf 73Paris 1 393	Mar 73 Crouch.EXPTL DATA+EVAL CHAIN YLD,TBL	
					Rept AERE−R−7209	Jan 73 − .35 CHAIN YLDS RECOMMENDED TBL	
Fiss Yield	0.0+0	3.0+7	CCP	Expt	Conf 73Kiev 3 298	May 73 Vorob'Ev+ TERN,YLD OF 13NUCLEI,SPEC	
Fiss Yield	Maxwl		LIN	Expt	Conf 73Munich 1 716	Aug 73 Vorobjov+ META. Z=1−8 MASS−SPEC,NDG	
Fiss Yield	Maxwl		MCM	Expt	Jour JIN 35 8 2639	Aug 74 Tracy+ CUMUL KR + XE YIELDS	
					Prog EANDC(CAN)−32	Jan 67 Thode+ YLDS OF STABLE KR+XE ISOTOPES	
Fiss Yield	Maxwl		USP	Expt	Conf 73Munich 1 588	Aug 73 Fontenla+ PROMPT+ISOM AVG FRGM−MASS	
Fiss Yield	1.5−3	4.7+6	SAC	Eval	Rept CEA−N−1821	Sep 75 Tellier. EXP+STAT MDL ANAL,CURVES	
Fiss Yield	Maxwl		AUA	Theo	Rept AAEC/E−386	Mar 76 Cook+ 3−GAUSS FIT,PARAMS GIVEN	
Fiss Yield	+7		RI	Expt	Conf 77Kiev	77 Kondurov+ YLD ALPHA−PART,GRAPH	
Frag Spectra	Spont		LAS	Expt	Jour NP/A 108 689	Feb 68 Erkkila+.FISS OF AM242M.RECOIL METH	
Frag Spectra		2.0+6	COP	Revw	Conf 69Vienna 155	Jul 69 Strutinsky+PPR203. GRPH ANGANISTR(E)	
Frag Spectra	Maxwl		LIN	Expt	Conf 73Munich 1 716	Aug 73 Vorobjov+ META. Z=1...8 E−SPEC,NDG	
Frag Spectra	Maxwl		USP	Expt	Conf 73Munich 1 588	Aug 73 Fontenla+ PROMPT+ISOM AVG FRGM−E,TBL	
Frag Charge	Maxwl		LRL	Comp	Rept UCRL−51640	Jul 74 Nethaway. TBL.	
Reson Params	1.7−1	3.2+0	LRL	Expt	Jour PR 166 1219	Feb 68 Bowman+ AM242M WT WN WF D FROM NF 6E	+
	1.7−1	3.2+0			Data EXFOR12572.	Jun 76 . 6 RES, WT, WN, WN0, WF, PCS	
Reson Params	None		TRM	Theo	Prog BARC−471 5	70 Sood+ CORREL ANAL,D CLASS II VAL GVN	
	2.0+1	1.0+6			Conf 69Roorke 2 198	Dec 69 − + AVG LEVL SPACING D,2−HUMPED−T	
Strnth Fnctn	1.7−1	3.2+0	LRL	Expt	Jour PR 166 1219	Feb 68 Bowman+ TOF STF=1.8+ − 1.1	
Strnth Fnctn	None		AUA	Eval	Rept AAEC/E−277	Mar 73 Musgrove.TBLS EXPTL DATA+BEST VALUES	
Lvl Density	+6		MIL	Theo	Jour EN 15 1 54	Jan 68 Facchini+ LDL PARS FROM LOW EN RES	
Lvl Density		6.0+0	KUR	Theo	Jour YF 9 303	Feb 69 Vorotnikov.LVL DEN(EXCIT−E),TBL GRPH	
					Jour SNP 9 179	Aug 69 TRANSLATN.*	
Lvl Density	7.0+6	1.6+7	DUB	ExTh	Rept JINR−E15−7362	Jul 73 Gangrsky+ PARS FROM (G,N),(G,G),GRPH	
Lvl Density	None		COP	Theo	Jour NP/A 222 493	Apr 74 Dossing+COLL ROTAT.SPAC. ACCUR ESTIM	
Lvl Density	None		ROC	Theo	Jour NP/A 223 589	May 74 Huizenga+ EXP CFD MICROSC TH AX SYMM	
Lvl Density	+6		DUB	Theo	Rept JINR−E4−9236	Nov 75 Komov+ AVG LVL−SPAC,SEMIMICRO CFD XP	

95 Americium 243

Quantity	Energy (ev) Min	Max	Lab	Type	Documentation Ref Vol Page	Author, Comments Date	Data
Evaluation	2.3−2	1.0+7	FEI	Eval	Conf 73Kiev 1 246	May 73 Abagjan+ GROUP−SIGS + REFERNCES TBLS	
					Rept INDC(CCP)−44	Jun 74 .P45. ENGLISH OF 73KIEV 1 246	
Evaluation	1.0−5	2.0+7	SRL	Eval	Rept EPRI−NP−161	Dec 75 Benjamin+ENDF4B.REVISIONS	
Total	1.4−3	1.5+1	ANL	Expt	Jour PR 114 505	Oct 59 Cote+	+
	1.0−3	+1			Conf 58Geneva 16 77	Sep 58 − +.PPR685,CURVE,SIGMA(V=2200M/SE	
	1.0+0	2.0+1			Conf 57Col.Univ 117	Sep 57 − +. CURVES	
	1.4−3	1.5+1			Data EXFOR12539.	Jun 76 . 201 PTS.	
Total		6.0+1	MTR	Theo	Prog NCSAC−31 69	May 70 Simpson+,B−W FIT TO RESON,T=320DEGK	

95 Americium 243

Quantity	Energy (ev) Min	Energy (ev) Max	Lab	Type	Documentation Ref Vol Page	Date	Author, Comments	Data
Total	1.0−2	2.6+1	MTR	Expt Prog	IN− 1407 66	Jun 70	Berreth+. TRANSMISSION,CURVES	+
	1.0−2	2.6+1		Data	EXFOR10272.	Nov 72	923PTS,SIGMA	
Total	5.0−1	1.0+3	MTR	Expt Jour	NSE 55 273	Nov 74	Simpson+ ORELA.TRANS.GRAPHS	+
	8.0−3	2.6+1		Data	EXFOR10204.	Oct 74	8282PTS,SIGMA	
Total	4.2−1	1.5+2	ITE	Expt Conf	75Kiev	May 75	Kalebin+	
Elastic	Maxwl		ANL	Expt Conf	58Geneva 16 77	Sep 58	Cote+.PPR685,VAL GVN,EXPT DESCRIBED	
Tot Inelastc		2.0+7	HAR	Theo Prog	NEANDC(E)172 8	Aug 76	Lynn.EVALUATION AND CALCULD XSECTS	
Diff Inelast	Thrsh	7.6+6	CCP	Expt Jour	AE 31 156	Aug 71	Gangrsky+ SIG FOR SPON−FISS ISOM,TBL	
				Jour	SJA 31 874	Mar 72	*ENGL OF AE 31 156	
Diff Inelast	Thrsh	7.6+6	DUB	Expt Jour	AE 31 156	Aug 71	Gangrskij+ SIG FOR SPONFIS ISO,TABLE	
	+6	+7		Rept	JINR−P3−5528	Jan 71	− + GROUND+ISO FISS STATE SIG	
	Thrsh	7.6+6		Jour	SJA 31 874	Mar 72	. ENGL OF AE 31 156	
Diff Inelast	1.5+7		DUB	Expt Jour	IJP 47 232	73	Belov+ SIG TO SPONFIS GIVN,FRAGM−DET	
				Rept	JINR−E15−6807	Nov 72	− + SPONFIS ISOMER PRODUCTN,TBL	
Diff Inelast	+6		KFI	Expt Jour	MFF 21 555	73	Nagy. THESIS,HUNG. TO FISS ISO,GRND	
Diff Inelast	3.0+6	1.5+7	DUB	Expt Conf	75Kiev 5 245	May 75	Gangrskij+ SIG TO SPONFIS ISO.TABLE	
Absorption	Maxwl		ANL	Expt Jour	NSE 1 204	Jul 56	Jaffey.115B FROM ORNL ANL DATA	
Absorption	2.5−2		SRL	Expt Conf	68Wash. 1285	Mar 68	Smith+ SIG=86.6B PILE IRRADIATION	+
				Rept	DP−MS−67−111	Feb 68	.SAME	
	2.5−2			Data	EXFOR12580.002	Jun 76	. 1 PT.	
Absorption	6.2−1	1.0+7	SRL	Theo Conf	71Knoxvill 714	Mar 71	Mccrosson. SPECTRUM−AVERAGED SIG	
Absorption	2.5−2		SRL	Expt Abst	ANS 14 344	Jun 71	Rusche. VALUE GIVEN	
Absorption	+2	+7	FEI	Eval Rept	YK− 23 40	76	Abagjan+ 26−AND 21 GROUP SIGS,TBLS	
Absorption	None		MUN	Theo Diss	GRYNTAKIS	Mar 76	Gryntakis.,CALC.OF WESTCOTTS G−FUNCT	
				Jour	RCA 22 128	Mar 75	− +,EQUIVALENT TO THESIS	
Res Int Abs	+0		ANL	Expt Conf	58Geneva 16 77	Sep 58	Cote+.PPR685,VAL GVN,EXPT DESCRIBED	+
Res Int Abs	Pile		RI	Expt Jour	AE 23 316	Oct 67	BAK+ VAL GVN,CALC−METHOD DESCRIBED	+
				Rept	INDC−E−232	68	.TRANSLATION IN ENGL	
				Prog	YFI−5 49	Oct 67	BAK+ VALUE GIVEN	
				Jour	EAF 23 4 56	Oct 67	BAK+ TRANSL OF AE 23 316 IN FRENCH	
				Jour	SJA 23 1059	Oct 67	BAK+ TRANSL OF AE 23 316 IN ENGLISH	
	4.0−1			Data	EXFOR40062.008	Apr 71	.RES−INT CAPTURE	
Res Int Abs	None		SRL	Expt Abst	ANS 14 344	Jun 71	Rusche. VALUE GIVEN	
Res Int Abs	Pile		KFK	Expt Prog	KFK−1456 51	Aug 71	Eberle+1930 B	
Res Int Abs	4.0−1	2.5+2	FEI	Eval Conf	73Kiev 1 246	May 73	Abagjan+ RI(N,G)=1800B FROM RES−PARS	
				Rept	INDC(CCP)−44	Jun 74	.P45. ENGLISH OF 73KIEV 1 246	
(n,γ)	Pile		BRK	Expt Jour	PR 79 530	Aug 50	Street.	+
	Pile			Data	EXFOR12581.004	Jun 76	. 1 PT.	
(n,γ)	Pile		ANL	Expt Jour	PR 94 974	May 54	Stevens+ ACT+MASS SPECTR 115+−20B	+
	Pile			Data	EXFOR12585.002	Jun 76	. 1 PT.	
(n,γ)	Pile		BRK	Expt Jour	PR 95 581	Jul 54	Harvey+. AM244 YLD 140+−50 B IN MTR	+
	Pile			Data	EXFOR12567.002	Jun 76	. 1 PT.	
(n,γ)	Maxwl		ANL	Expt Jour	NSE 1 204	Jul 56	Jaffey.115B FROM ORNL ANL DATA	
				Conf	55Geneva 7 261	Aug 55	Bentley+.P809,VAL GVN,CHEMICAL METHD	
(n,γ)	Maxwl		CRC	Expt Jour	CJP 35 147	Feb 57	Butler+73.6B ALSO PILE N SIG REL CO	+
				Rept	CRC−628	Jan 56	.SUPERSEDED	
	Maxwl			Data	EXFOR12481.012	Jun 76	. 1 PT, SIG	
(n,γ)	None		KAP	Comp Rept	KAPL−1781	Jul 57	Schuman. SIGMA GIVEN	
(n,γ)	Maxwl		ANL	Expt Conf	58Geneva 16 77	Sep 58	Cote+.PPR685,VAL GVN,EXPT DESCRIBED	
(n,γ)	Pile		CRC	Eval Rept	CRRP−960	Jan 62	Westcott.EFF SIG TABLE 20−760 DEG C	
(n,γ)	Pile		ANL	Expt Jour	JIN 26 219	Feb 64	Vandenbosch+ CS (N,G)M/(N,G) GVN	+
	Pile			Data	EXFOR12561.002	Jun 76	. 1 PT, ISOMER RATIO	
(n,γ)	Maxwl		CRC	Eval Rept	AECL−1054	Mar 66	Walker. (CRRP−913)	
(n,γ)	Maxwl	Pile	BNL	Eval Rept	BNL−982 22	Aug 66	Pearlstein. 142B, 127B, FROM RES PAR	
(n,γ)	Maxwl		RI	Expt Rept	ICD−4 337	67	Bak+ SIG (N,G)=73+−6 BARNS AT THR EN	
(n,γ)	Maxwl		BNL	Theo Abst	ANS 10 228	Jun 67	Prince. CALCULATED SIG=180B	
(n,γ)	Pile		RI	Expt Prog	YFI−5 49	Oct 67	Bak+ VALUE GIVEN	+
	Maxwl			Jour	AE 23 316	Oct 67	BAK+ VAL GVN,MANY REFERENCES	
	Pile			Rept	INDC−232E	Jan 69	. ENGL OF YFI−5 49	
	Maxwl			Jour	EAF 23 4 56	Oct 67	BAK+ TRANSL OF AE 23 316 IN FRENCH	
	Pile			Jour	SJA 23 1059	Oct 67	BAK+ TRANSL OF AE 23 316 IN ENGLISH	
				Data	EXFOR40062.005	Apr 71	AV SIG BELOW CD−LIMIT	
(n,γ)	Maxwl		MTR	Expt Prog	IN− 1126	Dec 67	Schuman.	+
	Maxwl			Data	EXFOR12577.002	Jun 76	. 1 PT.	
(n,γ)	Maxwl		AUA	Theo Jour	NSE 31 234	Feb 68	Cook+ STATISTICAL CALC CFD EXPT	
(n,γ)	Pile		CCP	Revw Jour	AE 24 247	Mar 68	Bak+ OTHER SIG VAL GVN,TBL	
				Jour	SJA 24 300	Mar 68	TRANSLATN.*	

95 Americium 243

Quantity	Energy (ev) Min	Energy (ev) Max	Lab	Type	Documentation Ref Vol Page	Date	Author, Comments	Data
(n,γ)	Maxwl		SRL	Expt	Conf 68Wash. 1279	Mar 68	Folger+ ACT	+
				Rept	DP−MS−67−112	Mar 68	.SAME	
	Maxwl			Data	EXFOR12534.004	Jun 76	. 1 PT.	
(n,γ)	4.0+5	3.0+6	CCP	Expt	Conf 69Erevan	Feb 69	Vilkov+.ABST,ISOM FIN STATE,EXCIT FN	
(n,γ)	3.0+5	4.0+6	BUC	Expt	Jour NP/A 134 541	Sep 69	Boca+,SIGMA TO SPON FISS ISOM AM−244	+
					Jour NP/A 102 443	Oct 67	*	
	3.0+5	4.0+6			Data EXFOR30034.	Aug 70	SIG TO AM244MF + RATIOS/(N,F),13 ENS	
(n,γ)	None		LAS	Expt	Prog WASH−1136 110	Sep 69	Silbert+,PHYSICS−8 SHOT,ANAL TBC	
(n,γ)		6.0+1	MTR	Theo	Prog NCSAC−31 69	May 70	Simpson+,B−W FIT TO RESON,T=320DEGK	
(n,γ)	2.0−1	2.0+1	DUB	Expt	Jour NP/A 148 492	Jun 70	Dalhsuren+ SIGMA FOR ISOMER PRODUCTN	
(n,γ)	1.0+6		FEI	Expt	Conf 71Kiev 1 325	May 71	Ivanov+ RATIO AM243(NG)/U238(NG) GVN	+
	1.0+6				Data EXFOR40153.006	Apr 74	.1 DATA LINE	
(n,γ)	Pile		KFK	Eval	Rept KFK−1453	Mar 72	Eberle+ 2−GROUP SIGS,FITTED TO EXPT	
				Expt	Prog KFK−1456 51	Aug 71	− + 77 B	
(n,γ)	Pile		JUL	Expt	Jour JIN 34 8 2427	Aug 72	Ihle+ REACTOR CROSS SECTION	
(n,γ)	2.5−2	1.0+6	KFI	Expt	Jour MFF 21 555	73	Nagy. THESIS,HUNG. TO FISS ISO,GRND	
(n,γ)	1.0+2	1.0+7	UK	Eval	Prog AERE−PR/NP20	Mar 73	Sowerby.(HAR).UKNDL CREATD.DFN−1003	
(n,γ)	2.3−2		FEI	Eval	Conf 73Kiev 1 246	May 73	Abagjan+ SIG=75B FROM RES−PARAMETERS	
	2.3−2	1.0+7			Conf 73Kiev 1 246	May 73	− + FROM (N,G)AM−244M,SIG−TABLE	
	2.3−2				Rept INDC(CCP)−44	Jun 74	.P45. ENGLISH OF 73KIEV 1 246	
	2.3−2	1.0+7			Rept INDC(CCP)−44	Jun 74	.P45. ENGLISH OF 73KIEV 1 246	
(n,γ)	1.0+3	1.0+7	HAR	Eval	Prog EANDC(UK) 151	Aug 73	Sowerby+ USES LYNN CALC SIG	
(n,γ)	2.5−2		SRL	Eval	Conf 75Wash. 224	Mar 75	Benjamin+ TBL BEST FIT TRANSPU PROD.	
(n,γ)	Fast		DOU	Expt	Prog UKNDC(75)P71	Jul 75	Davies+ IRRADIATION PFR	
(n,γ)	Fast		WIN	Expt	Prog UKNDC(75)P71	Jul 75	Sweet.REACTOR SPEC AVERAGE	
(n,γ)	None		ORL	Expt	Conf 75Wash. 229	Oct 75	Weston+NDG.TBD	
(n,γ)	4.0+1	1.4+7	CCP	Eval	Data SOKRATOR−1045	76	44 PTS	+
(n,γ)	Maxwl		SRL	Expt	Rept DP−MS−66−69	Oct 66	ICE+	+
	Maxwl				Data EXFOR12550.	Jun 76	. 3 PTS. TOT, GND, META	
(n,γ)		4.0+6	HAR	Theo	Prog NEANDC(E)172 8	Aug 76	Lynn.EVALUATION AND CALCULD XSECTS	
Res Int Capt	5.0−1		CRC	Expt	Jour CJP 35 147	Feb 57	Butler+ NRX 2290B REL CO59+U238	+
	5.0−1				Data EXFOR12481.	Jun 76	. 2 PTS, FOR GND + META	
Res Int Capt	5.5−1		CRC	Eval	Rept AECL−1054	Mar 60	Walker. REDUCED RI	
Res Int Capt	5.5−1		BNL	Eval	Rept BNL−982 22	Aug 66	Pearlstein. 1400B CALC, RECOMMENDED	
Res Int Capt	Maxwl		RI	Expt	Rept ICD−4 337	67	Bak+ RES INT CAPT=2300+−200 BARNS	
Res Int Capt	Maxwl		BNL	Theo	Abst ANS 10 228	Jun 67	Prince.CALCULATED RES INTGRL=1400B	
Res Int Capt	8.3−1		SRL	Expt	Conf 68Wash. 1279	Mar 68	Folger+ ACT 2250B	+
					Rept DP−MS−67−112	Mar 68	.SAME	
	8.3−1				Data EXFOR12534.005	Jun 76	. 1 PT.	
Res Int Capt	5.0−1		MTR	Expt	Rept IN−1296	May 69	Schuman+. PILE ACT. INCLUDING 1/V	+
					Prog IN−1126	Dec 67	−	
	5.0−1				Data EXFOR12577.	Jun 76	. 2 PTS, FOR GND + META	
Res Int Capt	Pile		KFK	Eval	Rept KFK−1453	Mar 72	Eberle+ 2250B	
Res Int Capt	5.0−1	1.0+3	MTR	Expt	Jour NSE 55 273	Nov 74	Simpson+ CALC FROM RES PAR.	+
	6.2−1	1.0+3			Rept ANCR−1060	Mar 72	− + CALC FROM RES PAR.	
	5.0−1	1.0+3			Data EXFOR10204.	Oct 74	6VALUES,DIFF RES PAR,DIFF CUTOFF	
Res Int Capt	6.3−1		SRL	Eval	Conf 75Wash. 224	Mar 75	Benjamin+ TBL BEST FIT TRANSPU PROD.	
(n,2n)	1.4+7		DUB	Expt	Jour NP 63 173	Mar 65	Linev+0.15MB TOSPON FISS ISOMER	+
(n,2n)	8.0+6	1.4+7	BUC	Expt	Jour NP/A 97 444	Apr 67	Flerov+ SIG TO SPON−FISS AM242M GIVN	+
	8.0+6	1.5+7			Jour SCF 22 795	Jul 70	Vilcov. AM242,SPON FISS SIG(E) GRAPH	
	8.0+6	1.4+7			Rept IFA−CRD−32	67	.EQU TO NP/A 97.GRPH	
	8.0+6	1.4+7			Data EXFOR30209.002	Nov 72	SIG AT 11 ES	
(n,2n)	1.4+7		DUB	Revw	Jour YF 7 83	Jan 68	Jungclaussen. OTHER ISOM−SIG−RATIO	
					Jour SNP 7 1 60	Jul 68	TRANSLATN.*	
(n,2n)	1.4+7	1.5+7	JYV	Eval	Rept JU−RR−3/1970	Jun 70	Leppaemaeki+ TABLE OF EVAL AVG SIG	
(n,2n)	1.4+7		KFI	Comp	Jour JRC 7 365	Jun 71	Nagy+ SIGMA, MAX GAMMA−E, HALF−LIFE	
(n,2n)	1.5+7		DUB	Expt	Jour AE 31 156	Aug 71	Gangrskij+ SIG TO SPON−FIS ISOM.TABL	
	+6	+7			Rept JINR−P3−5528	Jan 71	− + GND+ISOM FISSN STATE SIGS	
	1.5+7				Jour SJA 31 874	Mar 72	. ENGL OF AE 31 156	
(n,2n)	1.5+7		DUB	Expt	Jour IJP 47 232	73	Belov+ SIG TO SPONFIS GIVN,FRAGM−DET	
					Rept JINR−E15−6807	Nov 72	− + SPON FISS ISOMER PRODUCTN,TBL	
(n,2n)	1.5+7		KFI	Expt	Jour MFF 21 555	73	Nagy. THESIS,HUNG. TO FISS ISO,GRND	
(n,2n)		2.0+7	HAR	Theo	Prog NEANDC(E)172 8	Aug 76	Lynn.EVALUATION AND CALCULD XSECTS	
(n,xn) x>2		2.0+7	HAR	Theo	Prog NEANDC(E)172 8	Aug 76	Lynn.EVALUATION AND CALCULD XSECTS	
(n,p)	Maxwl		IFU	Theo	Rept ICD−4 20	67	Dadakina+ PENETR COEFF CALC,TABLE	
Fission	Pile		BRK	Expt	Jour PR 85 135	Jan 52	Street+	+
	Pile				Data EXFOR12483.008	Jun 76	. 1 PT, SIG	
Fission	None		KAP	Comp	Rept KAPL−1781	Jul 57	Schuman. UPPER LIMIT SIG GVN	

95 Americium 243

Quantity	Energy (ev) Min	Energy (ev) Max	Lab	Type	Documentation Ref Vol Page	Author, Comments Date	Data
Fission	Maxwl		LRL	Expt	Jour PR 107 1294	Sep 57 Hulet+. LESS THAN 72 MB	+
	Maxwl				Data EXFOR12497.006	Jun 76 . 1 PT.	
Fission	2.0+5	1.0+7	ANL	Revw	Conf 61Vienna 1 29	Aug 61 Smith.P76,CURVE,MANY REFS GVN	
Fission	2.0+4	1.8+6	ANL	Expt	Jour PR 124 1129	Nov 61 Butler+ GAS SC, REL U−235	+
					Conf 61Vienna 1 125	Aug 61 .SUPERSEDED	
	3.0+5	1.7+6			Data EXFOR12543.003	Jun 76 . 65 PTS.	
Fission	Spont		RI	Expt	Prog INDSWG−120 35	65 Aleksandrov.T=3.3 X 10EXP13 YEARS	
Fission	+1	+5	LAS	Expt	Prog WASH−1064 94	Oct 65 Diven+CYCLAMEN 1966, NDG.	
Fission	1.5+7		KUR	Expt	Jour YF 5 966	May 67 Fomushkin+ SIG GIVEN,FISS ANISOTROPY	
Fission	Maxwl		BNL	Theo	Abst ANS 10 228	Jun 67 Prince.CALCULATED SIG=.45B	
Fission	2.0+1	1.0+6	LAS	Expt	Prog WASH−1079 98	Oct 67 Diven+PSANGAREE 1968, TBD	
Fission	3.0+5	4.0+6	BUC	Expt	Jour NP/A 134 541	Sep 69 Boca+,RATIO SIG(N,G)MS/SIG(N,F),CRV	+
	+5	+7		Revw	Conf 69Vienna 908	Jul 69 Vilkov.PPR18. SPON FISS ISOMER,AM244	
Fission	4.9+1	3.0+6	LAS	Expt	Rept LA−4420	Apr 70 Seeger. NUCL SHOT,TOF,TABLES+CURVES	+
	4.9+1	3.0+6			Data EXFOR10063.002	Jan 75 . 2199 PTS.	
Fission	2.0−1	2.0+1	DUB	Expt	Jour NP/A 148 492	Jun 70 Dalhsuren+ SIGMA FOR ISOMER PRODUCTN	
Fission	8.0+6	1.5+7	BUC	Expt	Jour SCF 22 795	Jul 70 Vilcov. (N,2N)SPON−F−ISOM SIG(E) CRV	
Fission	5.0+5	1.6+7	DUB	Expt	Jour AHP 30 3 293	71 Nad'+ SPONT FISS ISOMER/ FISS ,GRPH	
		1.6+7			Rept JINR−P7−5162	Jul 70 − +SIG(E)PROMPT CFD SPON FISSN 24	
Fission	Thrsh	1.6+7	CCP	Expt	Conf 71Moscow	Feb 71 Belov+.ABST,SIG(NEUT−E),TWO−HUMPBARR	
Fission	5.0−1	+6	COR	Expt	Jour NSE 46 31	Oct 71 Draper.INTEGRAL SIG TIMES E.4 SPECTR	
Fission	−		GEL	ExTh	Jour NP/A 187 305	Jun 72 Weigmann+ F.B.PARAMS FROM DATA ANAL.	
Fission	Spont		TPI	Theo	Jour YF 16 919	Nov 72 Adeev+ FISS BARRIER CFD EVEN,NUCLEI	
					Jour SNP 16 507	May 73 .ENGLISH OF YF 16 919	
Fission	−2	4.0+6	BUC	Revw	Rept IFA−CRD−54	73 Poenaru. REVIEW FOR SPONFIS−ISOMER.	
Fission	1.0+2	1.0+7	UK	Eval	Prog AERE−PR/NP20	Mar 73 Sowerby.(HAR).UKNDL CREATD.DFN−1003	
Fission	2.3−2	1.0+7	FEI	Eval	Conf 73Kiev 1 246	May 73 Abagjan+ REFERENCES,GROUP−SIGS TABLE	
					Rept INDC(CCP)−44	Jun 74 .P45. ENGLISH OF 73KIEV 1 246	
Fission	1.0+3	1.0+7	HAR	Eval	Prog EANDC(UK) 151	Aug 73 Sowerby+ FOR UKNDL DFN 1003	
Fission	Spont		DUB	Expt	Jour FDP 22 199	74 Gangrsky+ FIS−BARRIER,GRPH EMAX+EMIN	
					Rept JINR−E15−7362	Jul 73 − + ISOMER HALFLIFE,TABLE,GRPH	
	+6	+7			Rept JINR−P3−5528	Jan 71 Gangrskij+AM243(N,N' + 2N)ISOM FISSN	
Fission	Fiss		TEX	Expt	Rept UMO−74−24,841	74 Chromik. THESIS.CF252−NEUTRONS	
Fission	2.5−2		SRL	Eval	Conf 75Wash. 224	Mar 75 Benjamin+ TBL BEST FIT TRANSPU PROD.	
Fission	Maxwl		FEI	Expt	Jour AE 39 285	Oct 75 Zhuravlev+ SIG GIVEN,BY CD−DIFFERENC	
					Jour SJA 39 907	Apr 76 . ENGL OF AE 39 285	
Fission	4.0+1	1.4+7	CCP	Eval	Data SOKRATOR−1045	76 23 PTS	+
Fission	+2	+7	FEI	Eval	Rept YK−23 40	76 Abagjan+ 26−AND 21 GROUP SIGS,TBLS	
Fission	5.0+1	1.5+7	JAE	Revw	Conf IAEA−186 3 1	76 Igarasi. REVW AVAIL DATA,GRPH+BIBLIO	
	1.0+3	4.0+6			Rept JAERI−M−6315	Nov 75 − +GRPH. 4 DATA SETS COMPARED.	
Fission	3.0+5	5.0+6	SAC	Expt	Conf IAEA−186 2 159	76 Blons+. ABST.REL U235,IN PROGRESS,NDG	
Fission		2.0+7	HAR	Theo	Prog NEANDC(E)172 8	Aug 76 Lynn.EVALUATION AND CALCULD XSECTS	
Res Int Fiss	Maxwl		BNL	Theo	Abst ANS 10 228	Jun 67 Prince.CALCULATED RES INTGRL=1.5B	
Res Int Fiss	+0	+1	COR	Expt	Abst DA/B 31 1466	Sep 70 Draper.EXPT FOR 4 SPEC,CFD CALC	
Res Int Fiss	6.3−1		SRL	Eval	Conf 75Wash. 224	Mar 75 Benjamin+ TBL BEST FIT TRANSPU PROD.	
Res Int Fiss	5.0−1		FEI	Expt	Jour AE 39 285	Oct 75 Zhuravlev+ RI GIVEN,BY CD−DIFFERENC	
					Jour SJA 39 907	Apr 76 . ENGL OF AE 39 285	
Nu	Spont		HED	Eval	Abst ANS 22 673	Nov 75 Johnson. TBL,GRPH.NU FROM SPON FISS	
Frag Spectra	1.5+7		KUR	Expt	Jour YF 5 966	May 67 Fomushkin+ ANGDIST OF FRAGMENTS	
					Jour SNP 5 689	Nov 67 . ENGL OF YF 5 966	
Reson Params	9.8−1	1.5+1	ANL	Expt	Jour PR 114 505	Apr 59 Cote+ TOF TRNS WN WG WT 11RESONANCES	+
					Jour PRL 2 136	Feb 59 .SUPERSEDED	
					Conf 58Geneva 16 77	Sep 58 .SUPERSEDED	
	9.8−1	1.5+1			Data EXFOR12539.	Jun 76 . 12 RES, E0,WT,WN,WG,PCS	
Reson Params		1.0+6	AUA	Theo	Jour AUJ 20 477	Oct 67 Cook. TBL OF AVG LVL SPACING D,L=0,1	
Reson Params	3.0+1	4.7+1	MTR	Expt	Prog WASH−1093 63	Apr 68 Berreth+ WN(ZERO) FOR 19 RESON ES	
Reson Params	−.2+0	2.5+1	MTR	Expt	Prog IN−1407 66	Jun 70 Berreth+. TRANS,WN+WG GIVN 36RESON	+
	−.2+0	2.5+1			Data EXFOR10272.	Nov 72 42PTS.E0,WG,WN0.	
Reson Params	6.2−1	5.0+4	SRL	Theo	Conf 71Knoxvill 714	Mar 71 Mccrosson. STAT CALCULATN AVG PARAMS	
Reson Params	4.0−1	2.5+2	FEI	Eval	Conf 73Kiev 1 246	May 73 Abagjan+ REFERENCES GIVEN, NDG	
					Rept INDC(CCP)−44	Jun 74 .P45. ENGLISH OF 73KIEV 1 246	
Reson Params	−.4−1	2.5+2	MTR	Expt	Jour NSE 55 273	Nov 74 Simpson+ 218RES.	+
					Prog USNDC−11 193	Jun 74 .SUPERSEDED	
					Rept ANCR−1060	Mar 72 Simpson+. ORELA TRANS. WG,2G*WN,D	
	−.4−1	2.5+2			Data EXFOR10204.	Oct 74 220RES,RED N−WID,SOME G−WID	
Reson Params	4.0+1	1.4+7	CCP	Eval	Data SOKRATOR−1045	76 82 RES PARAMS	+
Reson Params	4.2−1	3.4+1	ITE	Expt	Conf IAEA−186 2 121	76 Kalebin. 48ES,GAM,GAM−N CFD OTHS,TBL	

95 Americium 243

Quantity	Energy (ev) Min	Max	Lab	Type	Documentation Ref Vol Page	Author, Comments Date	Data
Strnth Fnctn	0.0+0	1.5+1	ANL Expt	Jour	PR 114 505	Oct 59 Cote+	+
		1.5+1		Conf	58Geneva 16 77	Sep 58 - +.PPR685,VAL GVN,EXPT DESCRIBED	
	0.0+0	1.5+1		Data	EXFOR12539.010	Jun 76 . 1 PT.	
Strnth Fnctn	None		AUA Eval	Rept	AAEC/E – 277	Mar 73 Musgrove.TBLS EXPTL DATA+BEST VALUES	
Strnth Fnctn	4.2 – 1	2.5+2	ORL Expt	Jour	NSE 55 273	Nov 74 Simpson+ S0=0.000096+ – 0.000010	
				Rept	ANCR – 1060	Mar 72 – +. ORELA TRANS. S0=0.96+ – 0.10	
Strnth Fnctn	4.0 – 1	4.0+1	NIR Expt	Conf	75Kiev 3 219	May 75 Belanova+ BY TOTSIG.S0 GIVEN	
Strnth Fnctn	4.2 – 1	3.4+1	ITE Expt	Conf	IAEA – 186 2 121	76 Kalebin. FROM 48RES.S=.89+ – 921(10 – 4)	
Lvl Density		4.0+0	KUR Theo	Jour	YF 9 303	Feb 69 Vorotnikov.LVL DEN(EXCIT – E),TBL GRPH	
				Jour	SNP 9 179	Aug 69 TRANSLATN.*	
Lvl Density	7.0+6	1.6+7	DUB ExTh	Rept	JINR – E15 – 7362	Jul 73 Gangrsky+ PARS FROM (G,N),(G,G),GRPH	
Lvl Density	None		MUN Theo	Jour	NP/A 217 269	Dec 73 Dilg+ A,DELTA. BACK SHIFTED FERMIGAS	
Lvl Density	None		ROC Theo	Jour	NP/A 223 589	May 74 Huizenga+ EXP CFD MICROSC TH AX SYMM	
Lvl Density		+6	DUB Theo	Rept	JINR – E4 – 9236	Nov 75 Komov+ AVG LVL – SPAC,SEMIMICRO CFD XP	
(γ,n)	1.0+7	1.4+7	IFP Expt	Jour	YF 11 54	Jan 70 Gangrskij+AM243(G,N)AM242 ISOM FISSN	
				Jour	SNP 11 30	Jul 70 . ENGL OF YF 11 54	
(γ,n)	7.0+6	1.6+7	DUB Expt	Rept	JINR – E15 – 7362	Jul 73 Gangrsky+ SPON FISS ISOMER,TBL,GRAPH	
Photo – Fissn	1.0+7	1.4+7	IFP Expt	Jour	YF 11 54	Jan 70 Gangrskij+AM243(G,N)AM242 ISOM FISSN	
				Jour	SNP 11 30	Jul 70 . ENGL OF YF 11 54	
Photo – Fissn	6.0+6	1.3+7	DUB Expt	Jour	FDP 22 199	74 Gangrsky+ GRPH (G,F)SIG VS E – GAM	

95 Americium 244

Quantity	Energy (ev) Min	Max	Lab	Type	Documentation Ref Vol Page	Author, Comments Date	Data
(n,γ)	3.0+6		DUB Expt	Conf	75Kiev 5 245	May 75 Gangrskij+ SIG TO SPONFIS ISO.TABLE	
Fission	Maxwl		LRL Expt	Prog	WASH – 1033 28	Aug 61 Hulet+ 1440 B	
Fission	Maxwl		ANL Expt	Jour	JIN 23 187	Apr 62 Vandenbosch+. REL TO U233	+
	Maxwl			Data	EXFOR12560.002	Jun 76 . 1 PT.	
Fission	Spont		DUB Theo	Rept	JINR – E – 2515	Dec 65 Malov+ SPON FISSN ISOMER, LIFE – TIME	
Fission	Spont		COP Expt	Jour	YF 8 459	Sep 68 Bjornholm+ ISOM,DECAY+HL CFD OTHER'S	
				Jour	SNP 8 267	Mar 69 – + ENGLISH TRANSLATION	
Fission	Spont		COP Expt	Conf	69Vienna 461	Jul 69 Sletten.DISCUSSN. ISOM FISSN HL GVN	
Fission	Spont		DUB Expt	Jour	AHP 30 3 293	71 Nad'+ SPONT FISS ISOMER/ FISS ,GRPH	
				Rept	JINR – P7 – 5162	Jul 70 – + FISS ISOMER REL AM243(NF),GRP	
Fission	0.0+0	1.0+0	GEL Revw	Jour	AKE 18 229	Nov 71 Theobald+ SUB – BARRIER FISS EXPTS,TH	
Fission	Pile		KFK Eval	Rept	KFK – 1453	Mar 72 Eberle+ 2 – GROUP SIGS,FITTED TO EXPT	
Fission	–		GEL ExTh	Jour	NP/A 187 305	Jun 72 Weigmann+ F.B.PARAMS FROM DATA ANAL.	
Alpha	1.0+4	2.0+4	LAS Theo	Jour	PR 158 1127	Jun 67 Bell. PREDICT 10 – 20KEV BY SYSTEMATCS	
Nu	Spont		HED Eval	Abst	ANS 22 673	Nov 75 Johnson. TBL,GRPH.NU FROM SPON FISS	
Lvl Density		+6	MIL Theo	Jour	EN 15 1 54	Jan 68 Facchini+ LDL PARS FROM LOW EN RES	
Lvl Density	None		COP Theo	Jour	NP/A 222 493	Apr 74 Dossing+COLL ROTAT.SPAC. ACCUR ESTIM	
Lvl Density	None		ROC Theo	Jour	NP/A 223 589	May 74 Huizenga+ EXP CFD MICROSC TH AX SYMM	

95 Americium 245

Quantity	Energy (ev) Min	Max	Lab	Type	Documentation Ref Vol Page	Author, Comments Date	Data
Fission	2.5 – 2		JUL Theo	Jour	ZP 257 389	Dec 72 Mcminn. 1.43 E – 2 BARNS	
Frag Charge	Maxwl		OSL Revw	Conf	69Vienna 669	Jul 69 Pappas+PPR206. REVW OF EXPTS+METHODS	

95 Americium 246

Quantity	Energy (ev) Min	Max	Lab	Type	Documentation Ref Vol Page	Author, Comments Date	Data
Fission	Spont		DUB Theo	Rept	JINR – E – 2515	Dec 65 Malov+ SPON FISSN ISOMER, LIFE – TIME	
Alpha	1.0+4	2.0+4	LAS Theo	Jour	PR 158 1127	Jun 67 Bell. PREDICT 10 – 20KEV BY SYSTEMATCS	

95 Americium 247

Quantity	Energy (ev) Min	Max	Lab	Type	Documentation Ref Vol Page	Author, Comments Date	Data
Fission	2.5 – 2		JUL Theo	Jour	ZP 257 389	Dec 72 Mcminn. 1.35 E – 3 BARNS	

95 Americium 248

Quantity	Energy (ev) Min	Max	Lab	Type	Documentation Ref Vol Page	Date	Author, Comments	Data
Alpha	1.0+4	2.0+4	LAS	Theo Jour	PR 158 1127	Jun 67	Bell. PREDICT 10-20KEV BY SYSTEMATCS	

95 Americium 250

Quantity	Energy (ev) Min	Max	Lab	Type	Documentation Ref Vol Page	Date	Author, Comments	Data
Alpha	1.0+4	2.0+4	LAS	Theo Jour	PR 158 1127	Jun 67	Bell. PREDICT 10-20KEV BY SYSTEMATCS	

96 Curium

Quantity	Energy (ev) Min	Max	Lab	Type	Documentation Ref Vol Page	Date	Author, Comments	Data
Fission	Spont		KTO	Theo Jour	PL/B 47 227	Nov 73	Ohnishi. SPON FISS VS STELLAR TEMP	

96 Curium 238

Quantity	Energy (ev) Min	Max	Lab	Type	Documentation Ref Vol Page	Date	Author, Comments	Data
Fission	Spont		DUB	Theo Rept	JINR-P-2265	Jul 65	Mekhedov. FISS+ALPH HLS ESTIMATED	
Fission	Spont		CCP	Comp Jour	AE 26 436	May 69	Romanov. HALF-LIFE VAL ESTIMATD,GRPH	
				Jour	EAF 26 48	69	. FRENCH OF AE 26 436.	
				Jour	SJA 26 498	69	. ENGL OF AE 26 436.	

96 Curium 240

Quantity	Energy (ev) Min	Max	Lab	Type	Documentation Ref Vol Page	Date	Author, Comments	Data
(n,p)	Maxwl		IFU	Theo Rept	ICD-4 20	67	Dadakina+ PENETR COEFF CALC,TABLE	
Fission	Spont		LRL	Expt Rept	UCRL-1772	Apr 52	Ghiorso+ FISSION RATE AND HALF-LIFE.	
Fission	Spont		BRK	Revw Jour	NP 81 1	Jun 66	Myers.TBL CALC FISS BARRIERS.	
Fission	Spont		COP	Revw Conf	69Vienna 155	Jul 69	Strutinsky+PPR203. HL GVN,'SHELL-TH'	
Fission	Spont		MRY	Theo Prog	ORO-4028-28	71	Jackson+ SPON FISSION HALF-LIFE GVN.	
Fission	2.5-2		JUL	Theo Jour	ZP 257 389	Dec 72	Mcminn. 2.15 E +3 BARNS	
Fission	Spont		COP	Expt Jour	PL/B 60 153	Jan 76	Sletten+ PICO-SEC FISSION ISOMER	
Nu	Spont		HED	Eval Abst	ANS 22 673	Nov 75	Johnson. TBL,GRPH.NU FROM SPON FISS	
Lvl Density	-3	+0	IFU	Theo Jour	UFZ 13 700	Apr 68	Pisanko+ LEVEL SPACING CALC,TBL	
				Jour	UPJ 13 498	Oct 68	TRANSLATN.*	

96 Curium 241

Quantity	Energy (ev) Min	Max	Lab	Type	Documentation Ref Vol Page	Date	Author, Comments	Data
(n,p)	Maxwl		IFU	Theo Rept	ICD-4 20	67	Dadakina+ PENETR COEFF CALC,TABLE	
Fission	Spont		COP	Expt Conf	69Vienna 461	Jul 69	Sletten.DISCUSSN. ISOM FISSN HL GVN	
Fission	-		HEI	Expt Conf	69Vienna 449	Jul 69	Metag+PPR29. HE-INDUCED ISOM FISS HL	
Fission	-		GEL	ExTh Jour	NP/A 187 305	Jun 72	Weigmann+ F.B.PARAMS FROM DATA ANAL.	
Nu	Maxwl		IAE	Eval Jour	REA 10 637	Dec 72	Manero+ CALC,SYSTEMATICS,TBL	
Nu	Spont		HED	Eval Abst	ANS 22 673	Nov 75	Johnson. TBL,GRPH.NU FROM SPON FISS	
Frag Spectra	None		CCP	Theo Jour	ZET 38 955	Mar 60	Geilikman. EXCIT E VS FRAG RATIO,CRV	
				Jour	JET 11 688	Sep 60	TRANSLATN.*	
				Jour	AE 6 298	Mar 59	SEE ALSO *= SJA 6 184 N/60	
Frag Charge	Maxwl		CNA	Theo Jour	PR/B 134 972	Jun 64	Talat+ N,CHARGE DIST IN FISS PRODS.	
				ExTh Rept	CNAEM-12	63	- + TBL AVERAGE CHARGE/NUCLEON	

96 Curium 242

Quantity	Energy (ev) Min	Max	Lab	Type	Documentation Ref Vol Page	Date	Author, Comments	Data
Evaluation	1.0-5	2.0+7	SRL	Eval Rept	EPRI-NP-161	Dec 75	Benjamin+ENDF4B.GENPAR MDL.REVISIONS	
(n,γ)	None		KAP	Comp Rept	KAPL-1781	Jul 57	Schuman. SIGMA GIVEN	
(n,γ)	Pile		CCP	Revw Jour	AE 24 247	Mar 68	Bak+ OTHER SIG VAL GVN,TBL	
				Jour	SJA 24 300	Mar 68	TRANSLATN.*	
(n,γ)	2.5-2	1.0+7	KFK	Eval Rept	KFK-1186	Jul 70	Hinkelmann.5-GROUP SIG,THR+FAST SPEC	
	2.5-2			Rept	KFK-1186	Jul 70	- . RECOMMENDED 20 B	
(n,γ)	Pile		KFK	Eval Prog	KFK-1544 61	Jan 72	Eberle+FOR 2-GROUP SIG,FITTED TO EXP	
(n,γ)	Pile		JUL	Expt Jour	JIN 34 8 2427	Aug 72	Ihle+ REACTOR CROSS SECTION	
(n,γ)	1.0+2	1.0+7	UK	Eval Prog	AERE-PR/NP20	Mar 73	Sowerby.(HAR).UKNDL CREATD.DFN-1004	
(n,γ)	1.0+3	1.0+7	HAR	Eval Prog	EANDC(UK) 151	Aug 73	Sowerby+ USES LYNN CALC SIG	
Res Int Capt	5.0-1		MTR	Expt Rept	IN-1296	May 69	Schuman+ PILE ACT, 150+ -40B, 1/V.	
Res Int Capt	4.7-1	1.0+7	KFK	Eval Rept	KFK-1186	Jul 70	Hinkelmann. INFIN DILUTION RES INTEG	
Res Int Capt	Pile		KFK	Eval Prog	KFK-1544 61	Jan 72	Eberle+150B	
(n,2n)	8.0+5	1.0+7	KFK	Eval Rept	KFK-1186	Jul 70	Hinkelmann.AVG SIG FOR THR+FAST SPEC	
(n,p)	Maxwl		IFU	Theo Rept	ICD-4 20	67	Dadakina+ PENETR COEFF CALC,TABLE	
Fission	Maxwl		CRC	Expt Jour	PR 81 893	Mar 51	Hanna+ NOT ABOVE 5B,NO DETAILS GIVEN	+
	Maxwl			Data	EXFOR12496.008	Jun 76	. 1 PT. SIGMA.	
Fission	None		KAP	Comp Rept	KAPL-1781	Jul 57	Schuman. UPPER LIMIT SIG GVN	
Fission	Spont		KUR	Theo Rept	IAE-562 3	64	Geylikman+,TRIPLE FISS,E DIST CFDEXP	
				Rept	ANL-TR-68	64	TRANSLATN.*	
Fission	Spont		BRK	Revw Jour	NP 81 1	Jun 66	Myers.TBL CALC FISS BARRIERS.	

96 Curium 242

Quantity	Energy (ev) Min	Max	Lab	Type	Documentation Ref Vol Page	Date	Author, Comments	Data
Fission	None		ANL	Expt Conf	66Vienna 621	Oct 66	Armani+ SPON FISS HALF-LIFE,VAL GVN.	
Fission	1.5+7		KUR	Expt Jour	YF 5 966	May 67	Fomushkin+ SIG GIVEN,FISS ANISOTROPY	
Fission	Pile		CCP	Revw Jour	AE 24 247	Mar 68	Bak+ OTHER SIG VAL GVN,TBL	
				Jour	SJA 24 300	Mar 68	TRANSLATN.*	
Fission	Spont		COP	Revw Conf	69Vienna 155	Jul 69	Strutinsky+PPR203. HL GVN,'SHELL-TH'	
Fission	2.5-2		KFK	Eval Rept	KFK-1186	Jul 70	Hinkelmann. RECOMMENDED 0.8 B	
	2.5-2	1.0+7		Rept	KFK-1186	Jul 70	- .5-GROUP SIG,THR+FAST SPEC	
Fission	Spont		MRY	Theo Prog	ORO-4028-28	71	Jackson+. SPON FISSION HALF-LIFE GVN	
Fission	Pile		KFK	Eval Rept	KFK-1544 61	Jan 72	Eberle+FOR 2-GROUP SIG,FITTED TO EXP	
Fission	-		GEL	ExTh Jour	NP/A 187 305	Jun 72	Weigmann+ F.B.PARAMS FROM DATA ANAL.	
Fission	Pile		JUL	Expt Jour	JIN 34 8 2427	Aug 72	Ihle+ REACTOR CROSS SECTION	
Fission	2.5-2		JUL	Theo Jour	ZP 257 389	Dec 72	Mcminn. 7.19 E +1 BARNS	
Fission	1.0+2	1.0+7	UK	Eval Prog	AERE-PR/NP20	Mar 73	Sowerby.(HAR).UKNDL CREATD.DFN-1004	
Fission	1.0+3	2.5+3	HAR	Eval Prog	EANDC(UK) 151	Aug 73	Sowerby+ LYNN CALC SIG DFN 1004	
Fission	Spont		COP	Expt Jour	PL/B 60 153	Jan 76	Sletten+ PICO-SEC FISSION ISOMER	
Res Int Fiss	4.7-1	1.0+7	KFK	Eval Rept	KFK-1186	Jul 70	Hinkelmann. INFIN DILUTION RES INTEG	
Res Int Fiss	Pile		KFK	Eval Prog	KFK-1544 61	Jan 72	Eberle+ 0B	
Nu	Spont		HAR	Expt Jour	PPSA 66 447	May 53	Barclay+.COINC METHOD, 3.0+-0.5 N/F	
Nu	Spont		LAS	Revw Conf	55Geneva 2 193	Aug 55	Leachman.P592,CURVE,EXPT DESCRIBED	
Nu	Spont		BRK	Expt Jour	PR 101 1016	Feb 56	Hicks+,SPONT FIS,REL PU240,PROBABIL.	
Nu	Spont		LRL	Expt Jour	PR 101 1804	Mar 56	Crane+ LII-CRYST+FIS.COUNT.COINC.	
Nu	Spont		REH	Theo Rept	IA-757	Jul 62	Sieger+ CALC FRM CHAIN-Y,CFD OTH.TBL	
Nu	Spont		FOA	Comp Rept	NP-16440	Mar 63	ASPLUND-NILSSON. REVIEW. TABLE.	
Nu	2.5-2	1.0+7	KFK	Eval Rept	KFK-1186	Jul 70	Hinkelmann.MEAN NUMBER VS E	
	2.5-2			Rept	KFK-1186	Jul 70	- .MEAN VALUE	
Nu	5.0-1	4.7+1	KFK	Eval Rept	KFK-1186	Jul 70	Hinkelmann. AVG VALUE OF MEAN NUMBER	
Nu	Spont		IAE	Eval Jour	REA 10 637	Dec 72	Manero+ EXTENSIVE SURVEY,TBL,AVG VAL	
Nu	Spont		DUB	Comp Jour	YF 18 724	Oct 73	Dakovsky+NUBAR VS FISNUCLEUS,TBL+GRP	
				Eval Rept	JINR-P15-7119	Jun 73	Dakowski+ NUBAR+P(NU)-DISTR,TBL,GRPH	
				Comp Jour	SNP 18 371	Apr 74	. ENGLISH OF YF 18, 724.	
Nu	Spont		HED	Eval Abst	ANS 22 673	Nov 75	Johnson. TBL,GRPH.NU FROM SPON FISS	
Fiss Yield	Spont		ANL	Expt Jour	PR 95 431	Jul 54	Steinberg+ RADIOCHEM YLDS SR91-BA140	
				Conf	55Geneva 7 3	Aug 55	- + RADIOCHEM A=91-140 YLDS.	
				Rept	AECD-3520	May 53	- + RADIOCHEM A=91-140 YLDS	
Fiss Yield	Spont		HAR	Comp Rept	AERE-R-3209	Jan 60	CROALL.COMP OF INDEPENDENT YIELDS	
Fiss Yield	Spont		RI	Revw Jour	UFN 73 655	Apr 61	Petrzhak+ CURVE,MANY REFS,DISCUSSION	
				Jour	SPU 4 305	Sep 61	. ENGL OF UFN 73 655	
Fiss Yield	Spont		LAS	Expt Jour	PR 126 1508	May 62	Nobles. YIELD OF LONG RANGE FFRGM	
Fiss Yield	Spont		CCP	Expt Jour	YF 11 501	Mar 70	Alkhazov+ AVG HEAVY+L MASS VAL+DISTR	
				Jour	SNP 11 281	Sep 70	.TRANSLATN.*0,NO 3	
Fiss Yield	Spont		CLA	Theo Jour	NP/A 184 417	Apr 72	Tsang+.ASSYM FROM FERMIGAS+WKB CALC.	
Fiss Yield	Maxwl		JUL	Theo Rept	JUEL-844-KP	Apr 72	Slavov. DEFORM-E+FRAG MASS YLD CALC	
	-			Jour	PL/B 37 483	Dec 71	- + ASYMMETRY BY 2-CENTRE SHELL	
Fiss Yield	Spont		BLA	Theo Conf	73Munich 1 589	Aug 73	Slavov+ 2CENTR SHELMDL,HVY/LGHT MASS	
Fiss Yield	Spont		AUA	Theo Rept	AAEC/E-386	Mar 76	Cook+ 3-GAUSS FIT,PARAMS GIVEN	
Fiss Yield	2.5-2	1.4+7	LAS	Eval Rept	LA-6430	Jul 76	Madland+PAIR EFFECT ON INDEP YLD.TBL	
Frag Spectra	Spont		CRC	Expt Jour	PR 81 466	Feb 51	Hanna+ MOST PROB E HEAVY,LIGHT FRAG.	
Frag Spectra	Maxwl		ANL	Expt Conf	58Geneva 15 392	Sep 58	Smith+ PPR690,ENERGY OG FRAGMENTS.	
Frag Spectra	Spont		CCP	Theo Jour	ZET 38 955	Mar 60	Geilikman. EXCIT E VS FRAG RATIO,CRV	
				Jour	JET 11 688	Sep 60	TRANSLATN.*	
					AE 6 298	Mar 59	SEE ALSO * = SJA 6 184 N/60	
Frag Spectra	1.5+7		KUR	Expt Jour	YF 5 966	May 67	Fomushkin+ TBLS+CURVES GIVEN	
				Jour	SNP 5 689	Nov 67	. ENGL OF YF 5 966	
Frag Spectra	Spont		CCP	Expt Jour	YF 11 501	Mar 70	Alkhazov+ FRAG KE+A DISTRIBUTNS,CRVS	
				Jour	SNP 11 281	Sep 70	.TRANSLATN.*0,NO 3	
Frag Spectra	Spont		FTI	Theo Jour	YF 23 1175	Jun 76	Geilikman+ KE FRG-MASS CALC.	
				Jour	SNP 23 624	Jun 76	. ENGL OF YF 23 1175	
Frag Charge	Spont		ANL	Eval Conf	55Geneva 7 3	Aug 55	Steinberg+ P614.CHARGE DISPERSN,GRPH	
Frag Charge	Spont		JAE	Revw Jour	NP/A 160 65	Jan 71	Umezawa+ SYSTEMATICS VS FRAG MASS	
Frag Charge	Spont		LRL	Comp Rept	UCRL-51640	Jul 74	Nethaway. TBL.	
Reson Params	1.0+3	4.6+4	KFK	Eval Rept	KFK-1186	Jul 70	Hinkelmann. AVG.WG,WF,WN,LVL SPACING	
Strnth Fnctn	1.0+3	4.6+4	KFK	Eval Rept	KFK-1186	Jul 70	Hinkelmann. SO=0.76 SI=2.	
Strnth Fnctn	None		AUA	Eval Rept	AAEC/E-277	Mar 73	Musgrove.TBLS EXPTL DATA+BEST VALUES	
Lvl Density	-3	+0	IFU	Theo Jour	UFZ 13 700	Apr 68	Pisanko+ LEVEL SPACING CALC,TBL	
				Jour	UPJ 13 498	Oct 68	TRANSLATN.*	

96 Curium 243

Quantity	Energy (ev) Min	Max	Lab	Type	Documentation Ref Vol Page	Author, Comments Date	Data
Evaluation	2.5−2	1.0+7	KFK	Eval	Rept KFK−1186	Jul 70 Hinkelmann.RES,STF,N2N,NF,NU,NG,R.I.	
					Conf 70Helsinki 2 721	Jun 70 − + SEE KFK−1186.	
Total		3.0+1	MTR	Theo	Prog NCSAC−38 81	May 71 Berreth+ CALC FROM RES PAR, CURVE	
Res Int Abs	4.0−1		MTR	Expt	Jour NSE 49 145	Oct 72 Berreth+. TRANS. RI=2345+ −470B	+
	4.0−1				Data EXFOR10271.009	Nov 74 . 1 PT, RI	
(n,γ)	None		KAP	Comp	Rept KAPL−1781	Jul 57 Schuman. SIGMA GIVEN	
(n,γ)	Pile		CCP	Revw	Jour AE 24 247	Mar 68 Bak+ OTHER SIG VAL GVN,TBL	
					Jour SJA 24 300	Mar 68 TRANSLATN.*	
(n,γ)	None		LAS	Expt	Prog WASH−1136 110	Sep 69 Silbert+ PHYSICS−8 SHOT, ANAL TBC.	
(n,γ)	1.0+0	1.0+1	MTR	Theo	Prog IN−1317 17	Jan 70 Berreth+ CALCTD FROM RESON PARS,CURV	
(n,γ)	Pile		KFK	Eval	Prog KFK−1544 61	Jan 72 Eberle+FOR 2−GROUP SIG,FITTED TO EXP	
(n,γ)	Pile		JUL	Expt	Jour JIN 34 8 2427	Aug 72 Ihle+ REACTOR CROSS SECTION	
(n,γ)	1.0+2	1.0+7	UK	Eval	Prog AERE−PR/NP20	Mar 73 Sowerby.(HAR).UKNDL CREATD.DFN−1005	
(n,γ)	1.0+3	1.0+7	HAR	Eval	Prog EANDC(UK) 151	Aug 73 Sowerby+ USES LYNN CALC SIG	
Res Int Capt	Pile		KFK	Eval	Prog KFK−1544 61	Jan 72 Eberle+200B	
(n,p)	Maxwl		IFU	Theo	Rept ICD−4 20	67 Dadakina+ PENETR COEFF CALC,TABLE	
Fission	None		KAP	Comp	Rept KAPL−1781	Jul 57 Schuman. SIGMA GIVEN	
Fission	Maxwl		LRL	Expt	Jour PR 107 1294	Sep 57 Hulet+ 690+ −50B REL SIGF PU239.	+
	Maxwl				Data EXFOR12497.007	Jun 76 . 1 PT SIGMA	
Fission	Pile		CCP	Revw	Jour AE 24 247	Mar 68 Bak+ OTHER SIG VAL GVN,TBL	
					Jour SJA 24 300	Mar 68 TRANSLATN.*	
Fission	Spont		COP	Expt	Conf 69Vienna 461	Jul 69 Sletten.DISCUSSN. ISOM FISSN HL GVN	
Fission	1.0+0	1.0+1	MTR	Expt	Prog IN−1317 17	Jan 70 Berreth+,CALCTD FROM RESON PARS,CURV	
Fission	1.1+5	2.9+6	LAS	Expt	Prog LA−4420 101	Apr 70 Fullwood+,NUCL SHOT,TOF,TABLES+CURVS	+
	1.0+5	2.9+6			Data EXFOR10064.002	Jul 72 . 134 PTS, SIGMA.	
Fission	1.0−2	1.4+7	LRL	Expt	Prog NCSAC−42 135	Nov 71 Browne+. TO BE DONE.	
Fission	Pile		KFK	Eval	Prog KFK−1544 61	Jan 72 Eberle+FOR 2−GROUP SIG,FITTED TO EXP	
Fission	−		GEL	ExTh	Jour NP/A 187 305	Jun 72 Weigmann+ F.B.PARAMS FROM DATA ANAL.	
Fission	Pile		JUL	Expt	Jour JIN 34 8 2427	Aug 72 Ihle+ REACTOR CROSS SECTION	
Fission	1.0+2	1.0+7	UK	Eval	Prog AERE−PR/NP20	Mar 73 Sowerby.(HAR).UKNDL CREATD.DFN−1005	
Fission	1.0+3	1.0+7	HAR	Eval	Prog EANDC(UK) 151	Aug 73 Sowerby+ LYNN CALC SIG DFN 1005	
Fission	1.5+1	3.0+6	LAS	Expt	Rept LA−6239	Mar 76 Silbert.TOF.UNDERGROUND EXPLO.TBL	+
	1.5+1	3.3+6			Data EXFOR10679.002	Nov 77 . 2972PTS.CS NORM TO AREA OF 2 RES.	
Res Int Fiss	Pile		KFK	Eval	Prog KFK−1544 61	Jan 72 Eberle+1860B	
Alpha	1.0+4	2.0+4	LAS	Theo	Jour PR 158 1127	Jun 67 Bell. SYSTEMATCS TH FOR 10−20KEV ALF	
Nu	Maxwl		ANL	Expt	Jour NP/A 145 1	Apr 70 Jaffey+ REL TO U,PU,CF STANDARDS.	+
					Rept ANL−7625	Nov 69 − +COMPLETE DATA GVN.	
	Maxwl				Data EXFOR10125.007	May 72 . 1 PT.PROMPT N YLD=3.43+ − .047	
Nu	Maxwl		IAE	Eval	Jour REA 10 637	Dec 72 Manero+ EXTENSIVE SURVEY,TBL,AVG VAL	
Nu	2.5−2		NIR	Expt	Conf 73Kiev 4 57	May 73 Zhuravlev+	+
	2.5−2				Data EXFOR40297.009	May 75 .DATA GVN	
Nu	Spont		HED	Eval	Abst ANS 22 673	Nov 75 Johnson. TBL,GRPH.NU FROM SPON FISS	
Spect Fiss n	2.5−2		NIR	Expt	Conf 73Kiev 4 57	May 73 Zhuravlev+	+
	2.5−2				Data EXFOR40297.003	May 75 .DATA GVN	
Frag Spectra	Spont		DUB	Expt	Rept JINR−P7−6466	May 72 Gangrskij+ FRGM−ANISOTROPY,TBL	
					Rept ANL−TRANS−936	73 . ENGLISH OF JINR−P7−6466	
Reson Params	1.5+0	2.6+1	MTR	Expt	Jour NSE 49 145	Oct 72 Berreth+. TRANS. WN WF FOR 15 RESON	+
	1.5+0	2.6+1			Data EXFOR10271.	Nov 74 . 19RES.RED N−WID,F−WID.	
Reson Params	6.7+6		DUB	Theo	Conf 74Petten 175	Sep 74 Malov+ DOBS,SEMI−MICROSCOPIC CALC.	
Reson Params	+0		DUB	Theo	Jour YF 21 40	Jan 75 Voronov+ MEAN D,WITH ROTAT.CFD EXPT	
					Jour SNP 21 20	Jul 75 . ENGLISH OF YF 21,40	
Reson Params	1.5+0	8.0+1	LAS	Expt	Prog ERDA−NDC−3 95	May 76 Silbert.WF=225MEV,D=.85+ −.09EV.TBC	
Reson Params	Maxwl		KUK	Theo	Conf 76Ahmedabd 2 1	Dec 76 Sharma+AVG S−WAVE REDUCED N−WID ANAL	
Strnth Fnctn	None		AUA	Eval	Rept AAEC/E−277	Mar 73 Musgrove.TBLS EXPTL DATA+BEST VALUES	
Strnth Fnctn	1.5+0	8.0+1	LAS	Expt	Prog ERDA−NDC−3 95	May 76 Silbert.S0=(1.04+ −.30)−4.ANAL TBC.	

96 Curium 244

Quantity	Energy (ev) Min	Max	Lab	Type	Documentation Ref Vol Page	Author, Comments Date	Data
Evaluation	2.5−2	1.4+7	GEN	Eval	Rept GEMP−411	Feb 66 Prince.TOT ABS SEL DEL NG NF N2N SIN	
Evaluation		+2	BNL	Eval	Rept BNL−982 22	Aug 66 Pearlstein. TOT,FISS,NG(THR),RIF,RIG	
Evaluation	1.0−3	1.0+7	AI	Eval	Rept NAA−SR−12271	May 67 Dunford+ RE−EVALUATION OF DATA	
					Rept AI−65−190	Nov 65 .SUPERSEDED	
Evaluation	2.3−2	1.0+7	FEI	Eval	Conf 73Kiev 1 246	May 73 Abagjan+ GROUP−SIGS + REFERNCES TBLS	
					Rept INDC(CCP)−44	Jun 74 .P45. ENGLISH OF 73KIEV 1 246	

96 Curium 244

Quantity	Energy (ev) Min	Energy (ev) Max	Lab	Type	Documentation Ref Vol Page	Date	Author, Comments	Data
Total	1.0−2	9.0+2	ANL	Expt	Jour PR/B 134 1281	Jun 64	Cote.FC. NDG 21RES,SOME ANALYSED	+
	4.3+0	7.8+2			Data EXFOR12570.002	Jun 76	.328 PTS SIGMA.	
Total		3.0+1	MTR	Theo	Prog NCSAC−38 81	May 71	Berreth+ CALC FROM RES PAR, CURVE	
Total	Maxwl	5.0+2	MTR	Eval	Prog NCSAC−4 4	Nov 71	Berreth+ FOR ENDF/B 3. NO DATA GIVN	
Total	1.0−2	1.0+3	MTR	Expt	Prog ANCR−1088 39	Oct 72	Simpson+	
Total	1.0−2	2.0+2	MTR	Expt	Jour NSE 49 145	Oct 72	Berreth+ TRANS. SIG=23+−3B.	+
	2.5−2				Data EXFOR10271.011	Nov 74	.1PT.SIGMA.	
Total	1.0+0	3.0+2	CCP	Expt	Conf 73Kiev 2 137	May 73	Belanova+ TOF,GRAPH	
Diff Elastic	1.0+4	1.5+7	AI	Eval	Rept NAA−SR−11980	Apr 67	Campbell+ LEG COEFS TABLE C−M SYSTEM	
Absorption	Maxwl		CRC	Eval	Rept AECL−1054	Mar 60	Walker.(CRP−913)	
Absorption	Pile		SRL	Expt	Conf 68Wash. 1285	Mar 68	Smith+ SIG=14.5B PILE IRRADIATION	+
	Pile				Data EXFOR12580.003	Jun 76	.1PT SIGMA	
Absorption	Pile		SRL	Expt	Conf 68Wash. 1279	Mar 68	Folger+ ACT	+
					Rept DP−MS−67−112	Mar 68	−+ FOIL MEASUREMENTS.	
	Pile				Data EXFOR12534.006	Jun 76	.1 PT. SIGMA	
Absorption	6.2−1	1.0+7	SRL	Theo	Conf 71Knoxvill 714	Mar 71	Mccrosson. SPECTRUM−AVERAGED SIG	
Absorption	Pile		SRL	Expt	Abst ANS 14 344	Jun 71	Rusche. VALUE GIVEN	
Absorption	+2	+7	FEI	Eval	Rept YK−23 40	76	Abagjan+ 26− AND 21−GROUP SIGS,TBLS	
Res Int Abs	8.3−1		SRL	Expt	Conf 68Wash. 1279	Mar 68	Folger+ ACT 700B	+
					Rept DP−MS−67−112	Mar 68	−+ FOIL MEASUREMENTS.	
	8.3−1				Data EXFOR12534.007	Jun 76	.1 PT. RI	
Res Int Abs	None		SRL	Expt	Abst ANS 14 344	Jun 71	Rusche. VALUE GIVEN	
Res Int Abs	4.0−1		MTR	Expt	Jour NSE 49 145	Oct 72	Berreth+. TRANS. RI=605+−40B	+
	4.0−1				Data EXFOR10271.008	Nov 74	.1PT. SIGMA	
Res Int Abs	−.1+1	5.2+2	MTR	Eval	Prog USNDC−3 4	Oct 72	Simpson+.RECOMMENDED VALUE GIVEN	
Res Int Abs	7.8+0	9.7+2	FEI	Eval	Conf 73Kiev 1 246	May 73	Abagjan+ RI(N,G)=635B FROM RES−PARS	
					Rept INDC(CCP)−44	Jun 74	.P45. ENGLISH OF 73KIEV 1 246	
(n,γ)	Pile		ANL	Expt	Jour PR 94 974	May 54	Stevens+ ACT+MASS SPECTR 25+−10B	+
(n,γ)	Pile				Data EXFOR12585.003	Jun 76	.1PT. SIGMA	
(n,γ)	Maxwl		ANL	Expt	Jour NSE 1 204	Jul 56	Jaffey.20B FROM ORNL ANL DATA	
					Conf 55Geneva 7 261	Aug 55	Bentley+.P809,VAL GVN,CHEMICAL METHD	
(n,γ)	None		KAP	Comp	Rept KAPL−1781	Jul 57	Schuman. SIGMA GIVEN	
(n,γ)	Pile		SRL	Expt	Rept DP−MS−66−69	Oct 66	ICE. HIGHLY THERMAL SPECTRUM.	+
	Pile				Data EXFOR12550.007	Jun 76	. 1 PT. SIGMA.	
(n,γ)	Maxwl		BNL	Theo	Abst ANS 10 228	Jun 67	Prince. CALCULATED SIG=10B.	
(n,γ)	Pile		CCP	Revw	Jour AE 24 247	Mar 68	Bak+ OTHER SIG VAL GVN,TBL	
					Jour SJA 24 300	Mar 68	TRANSLATN.*	
(n,γ)	2.0+1	1.0+4	LAS	Expt	Jour PR/C 3 1656	Apr 71	Moore+ NUCLEAR SHOT, CURVES.	+
					Rept LA−4566	Apr 71	Baybarz+ POINT DATA	
					Conf 70Helsinki 1 527	Jun 70	.SUPERSEDED	
	2.0+1	1.0+4			Data EXFOR10121.032	Nov 74	.3791 PTS, SIGMA.	
(n,γ)	Maxwl	5.0+2	MTR	Eval	Prog NCSAC−42 4	Nov 71	Berreth+. FOR ENDF/B 3. NO DATA GIVN	
(n,γ)	Pile		KFK	Eval	Rept KFK−1453	Mar 72	Eberle+ 2−GROUP SIGS,FITTED TO EXPT	
(n,γ)	Pile		JUL	Expt	Jour JIN 34 8 2427	Aug 72	Ihle+ REACTOR CROSS SECTION	
(n,γ)	1.0+2	1.0+7	UK	Eval	Prog AERE−PR/NP20	Mar 73	Sowerby.(HAR).UKNDL CREATD.DFN−1007	
(n,γ)	2.3−2	1.0+7	FEI	Eval	Conf 73Kiev 1 246	May 73	Abagjan+ H−F CALC GROUP−SIGS,TABLE	
	2.3−2				Conf 73Kiev 1 246	May 73	−+ SIG=12.6B FROM RES−PARAMS	
	2.3−2	1.0+7			Rept INDC(CCP)−44	Jun 74	.P45. ENGLISH OF 73KIEV 1 246	
	2.3−2				Rept INDC(CCP)−44	Jun 74	.P45. ENGLISH OF 73KIEV 1 246	
(n,γ)	1.0+3	1.0+7	HAR	Eval	Prog EANDC(UK) 151	Aug 73	Sowerby+ USES LYNN CALC SIG	
(n,γ)	Pile		SRL	Eval	Conf 75Wash. 224	Mar 75	Benjamin+ TBL BEST FIT TRANSPU PROD.	
(n,γ)	4.0+2	1.4+7	CCP	Eval	Data SOKRATOR−1046	76	68 PTS	+
Res Int Capt	Maxwl		BNL	Theo	Abst ANS 10 228	Jun 67	Prince. CALCULATED RES INTGRL=650B.	
Res Int Capt	5.0−1		MTR	Expt	Rept IN−1296	May 69	Schuman+. PILE ACT. 650+−50B. 1/V	
Res Int Capt	Pile		KFK	Eval	Rept KFK−1453	Mar 72	Eberle+ 650B	
Res Int Capt	−.1+1	5.2+2	MTR	Eval	Prog USNDC−3 4	Oct 72	Simpson+.RECOMMENDED VALUE GIVEN	
Res Int Capt	6.3−1		SRL	Eval	Conf 75Wash. 224	Mar 75	Benjamin+ TBL BEST FIT TRANSPU PROD.	
Res Int Capt	5.0−1		ITE	Expt	Conf IAEA−186 2 121	76	Kalebin. CALC FROM RESPARS,CFD.TABLE	
Fission	Spont		LRL	Expt	Rept UCRL−1772	Apr 52	Ghiorso+ FISSION RATE AND HALF−LIFE.	
Fission	Spont		BRK	Revw	Jour NP 81 1	Jun 66	Myers.TBL CALC FISS BARRIERS.	
Fission	None		ANL	Expt	Conf 66Vienna 621	Oct 66	Armani+,SPON FISS HALF−LIFE,VAL GVN	
Fission	1.5+7		KUR	Expt	Jour YF 5 966	May 67	Fomushkin+ SIG GIVEN,FISS ANISOTROPY	
Fission	Maxwl		BNL	Theo	Abst ANS 10 228	Jun 67	Prince. CALCULATED SIG=2.7B.	
Fission	2.0+1	2.0+6	LAS	Expt	Conf 68Wash. 567	Mar 68	Fullwood+ BOMB SOURCE TOF 55+−16DEG	+
	2.3+1	1.4+3			Data EXFOR12564.002	Jun 76	. 43 PTS. SIGMA.	
Fission	1.0+6	1.5+7	LAS	Expt	Conf 68Wash. 597	Mar 68	Koontz+ SI CRYST DET 4ES REL U235	
					Rept LA−DC−9188	67	.EQUIVALENT	
	1.0+6	1.5+7			Data EXFOR12579.002	Jun 76	. 4 PTS. SIGMA.	

96 Curium 244

Quantity	Energy (ev) Min	Max	Lab	Type	Documentation Ref Vol Page	Author, Comments Date	Data
Fission	–		TPI	Theo	Jour YF 9 102	Jan 69 Korostova+ SHELL-TH OKS HLS CM+CF+FM	
					Jour SNP 9 62	Jul 69 TRANSLATN.*	
Fission	Spont		COP	Revw	Conf 69Vienna 155	Jul 69 Strutinsky+PPR203. HL GVN,'SHELL-TH'	
Fission	–		HEI	Expt	Conf 69Vienna 449	Jul 69 Metag+PPR29. HE-INDUCED ISOM FISS HL	
Fission	Maxwl		NIR	Expt	Jour AE 29 95	Aug 70 Kroshkin+ THERMAL SIGMA+ - ERROR GIVEN	
					Jour SJA 29 790	Aug 70 TRANSLATN.*	
Fission	Spont		MRY	Theo	Prog ORO-4028-28	71 Jackson+ SPON FISSION HALF-LIFE GVN	
Fission	2.0+1	2.8+6	LAS	Expt	Jour PR/C 3 1656	Apr 71 Moore+ NUCLEAR SHOT. CURVES.	+
					Rept LA- 4566	Apr 71 Baybarz+ POINT DATA	
	2.0+1	3.0+6			Conf 70Helsinki 1 527	Jun 70 .SUPERSEDED	
	2.0+1	2.8+6			Data EXFOR10121.027	Nov 74 . 4311 PTS, SIGMA.	
Fission	Pile		SRL	Expt	Jour JIN 33 1553	Jul 71 Thompson+ CD CUT-OFF	
Fission	Spont		MND	Expt	Rept MLM-1845	Oct 71 Hastings+ HALF-LIFE GIVEN.	
Fission	Maxwl	5.0+2	MTR	Eval	Prog NCSAC-42 4	Nov 71 Berreth+ FOR ENDF/B 3, NO DATA GIVN.	
Fission	Maxwl		SRL	Expt	Jour NSE 47 203	Feb 72 Benjamin+FISS CHS,FISS TRACK MEAS.	+
					Conf 71Knoxvill 843	Mar 71 .SUPERSEDED.	
	Maxwl				Data EXFOR10128.002	Feb 73 . 1 PT.CS=1.1+-.5B,REL U235.	
Fission	Pile		KFK	Eval	Rept KFK-1453	Mar 72 Eberle+ 2-GROUP SIGS,FITTED TO EXPT	
Fission	–		GEL	ExTh	Jour NP/A 187 305	Jun 72 Weigmann+ F.B.PARAMS FROM DATA ANAL.	
Fission	Pile		JUL	Expt	Jour JIN 34 8 2427	Aug 72 Ihle+ REACTOR CROSS SECTION	
Fission	6.0+0	5.0+2	MTR	Expt	Prog USNDC-3 4	Oct 72 Simpson+ TRANS. NO DATA GIVEN	
Fission	Spont		NEU	Theo	Jour HPA 45 567	Dec 72 Hooshyar+ HL GROUNDST AND FISS ISOM.	
Fission	+0	+7	KUR	Expt	Jour YF 17 24	Jan 73 Fomushkin+ SIG GIVEN,TABLE	+
					Jour SNP 17 12	Jul 73 . ENGL OF YF 17 24	
	1.0+7				Data EXFOR40150.002	May 74 .NF SIG SPECT AVER AND RATIO TO U235	
Fission	1.0+2	1.0+7	UK	Eval	Prog AERE-PR/NP20	Mar 73 Sowerby.(HAR).UKNDL CREATD.DFN-1007	
Fission	2.3-2	1.0+7	FEI	Eval	Conf 73Kiev 1 246	May 73 Abagjan+ REFERENCES,GROUP-SIGS TABLE	
	2.3-2				Conf 73Kiev 1 246	May 73 - + SIG=1.1B FROM RES-PARAMS	
	2.3-2	1.0+7			Rept INDC(CCP)-44	Jun 74 .P45. ENGLISH OF 73KIEV 1 246	
	2.3-2				Rept INDC(CCP)-44	Jun 74 .P45. ENGLISH OF 73KIEV 1 246	
Fission	None		FRK	Theo	Jour NP/A 207 225	Jun 73 Albrecht. 2CENTRE SHELLMOD,DEF-E MAP	
Fission	1.0+3	1.0+7	HAR	Eval	Prog EANDC(UK) 151	Aug 73 Sowerby+ FOR UKNDL DFN 1007	
Fission	Pile		SRL	Eval	Conf 75Wash. 224	Mar 75 Benjamin+ TBL BEST FIT TRANSPU PROD.	
Fission	2.5-2		NIR	Expt	Jour AE 39 285	Oct 75 Zhuravlev+ SIG GIVEN,BY CD-DIFFERENC	+
					Rept YK- 19 3	May 75 - + CD-DIFFERENCE, SIG GIVEN	
					Jour SJA 39 907	Apr 76 . ENGL OF AE 39 285	
	2.5-2				Data EXFOR40339.003	Mar 76 1 PNT	
Fission	4.0+2	1.4+7	CCP	Eval	Data SOKRATOR-1046	76 68 PTS	+
Fission	2.0+1	1.5+7	JAE	Revw	Conf IAEA-186 3 1	76 Igarasi. REVW AVAIL DATA,GRPH+BIBLIO	
	1.0+3	1.5+7			Rept JAERI-M-6315	Nov 75 - +GRPH. 4 DATA SETS COMPARED.	
Res Int Fiss	Maxwl		BNL	Theo	Abst ANS 10 228	Jun 67 Prince. CALCULATED RES INTGRL=72B.	
Res Int Fiss	5.0-1		SRL	Expt	Jour JIN 33 1553	Jul 71 Thompson+ CD CUT-OFF	
Res Int Fiss	-.1+1	5.2+2	MTR	Eval	Prog USNDC-3 4	Nov 71 Simpson+ RECOMMENDED VALUE GIVEN.	
Res Int Fiss	6.3-1		SRL	Expt	Jour NSE 47 203	Feb 72 Benjamin+CD COVER.MASS SPEC.	+
					Conf 71Knoxvill 843	Mar 71 .SUPERSEDED.	
	6.3-1				Data EXFOR10128.003	Feb 73 . 1 PT.RIF=772+ -40B REL U235.	
Res Int Fiss	Pile		KFK	Eval	Rept KFK-1453	Mar 72 Eberle+ 30B	
Res Int Fiss	7.8+0	9.7+2	FEI	Eval	Conf 73Kiev 1 246	May 73 Abagjan+ RI(N,F)=18B FROM RES-PARAMS	
					Rept INDC(CCP)-44	Jun 74 .P45.ENGLISH OF 73KIEV 1 246	
Res Int Fiss	6.3-1		SRL	Eval	Conf 75Wash. 224	Mar 75 Benjamin+ TBL BEST FIT TRANSPU PROD.	
Res Int Fiss	5.0-1		NIR	Expt	Jour AE 39 285	Oct 75 Zhuravlev+ RI GIVEN,BY CD-DIFFERENCE	+
					Rept YK- 19 3	May 75 - + CD-DIFFERENCE,RES-INT GVN	
					Jour SJA 39 907	Apr 76 . ENGL OF AE 39 285	
	5.0-1				Data EXFOR40337.003	Mar 76 1 PNT	
Alpha	1.0+2	5.0+3	LAS	Expt	Prog NCSAC-33 136	Dec 70 Moore+,NUCL SHOT,CURVE,TBP	
Nu	Spont		LRL	Expt	Jour PR 99 183	Jul 55 Higgins+ MN-TANK,REL TO P0-BE SOURCE	
Nu	Spont		LAS	Revw	Conf 55Geneva 2 193	Aug 55 Leachman.P592,CURVE,EXPT DESCRIBED	
Nu	Spont		BRK	Expt	Jour PR 101 1016	Feb 56 Hicks+,SPONT FIS,REL PU240,PROBABIL.	
					Abst PR 99 616	Jul 55 Pyle+,SCINT TANK,RATIO TO CF252,PROB	
					Jour PR 98 1521	Jun 55 Hicks+ PRELIM VALUE.	
Nu	Spont		LAS	Expt	Jour PR 101 1012	Feb 56 Diven+ LIQ SCINT,+PROB EMISS.	+
	Spont				Data EXFOR12337.006	Jun 76 . 1 PT.	
Nu	Spont		LRL	Expt	Jour PR 101 1804	Mar 56 Crane+ LII CRYST+FIS COUNT,REL RABE.	
Nu	Spont		FOA	Comp	Rept NP- 16440	Mar 63 ASPLUND-NILSSON. REVIEW. TABLE.	

96 Curium 244

Quantity	Energy (ev) Min Max	Lab	Type	Documentation Ref Vol Page	Date	Author, Comments	Data
Nu	Spont	FEI	Expt	Jour AE 17 28	Jul 64	Bolshov+ .2.71 + − 0.04,FISSION CHAMBER	+
				Jour JNE 19 457	65	.ENGLISH TRANSL OF AE 17 28 1964	
				Jour EAF 17 1 47	Jul 64	. FRENCH TRANSL OF AE 17 28 1964	
				Jour SJA 17 715	64	.ENGLISH TRANSL OF AE 17 28 7/64	
	Spont			Data EXFOR40219.	Jun 74	.SPONT FISS TOT NU+AVER KIN−E OF FF	
Nu	Spont	CCP	Expt	Jour YF 5 42	Jan 67	Adamov+.VAL GVN REL TO ALPHA−ENERGY	
				Jour SNP 5 30	Jul 67	. ENGL OF YF 5 42	
Nu	Spont	FEI	Expt	Prog YFI−6 38	68	Prokhorova+. VALUE GIVEN. TBP AE	+
				Jour AE 33 767	Sep 72	− + NUBAR TBL,CFD OTHERS	
				Jour SJA 30 307	Oct 71	. *ENGL OF AE 30 250	
				Jour AE 30 250	Mar 71	Prokhorova+ COINC,REL CF252,NU GIVEN	
				Rept INDC−260E	69	. ENGL OF YFI−6 38	
	Spont			Data EXFOR40140.002	Mar 73	NU−BAR REL CF252	
Nu	Maxwl	ANL	Expt	Jour NP/A 145 1	Apr 70	Jaffey+ REL TO U,PU,CF STANDARDS.	+
				Rept ANL−7625	Nov 69	− +COMPLETE DATA GVN.	
	Maxwl			Data EXFOR10125.006	May 72	.1 PT.PROMPT N YLD=2.692+−.024.	
Nu	Spont	AE	Expt	Conf 70Helsinki 2 93	Jun 70	Almen+57. COMPILATN AND NU−TEMP−PLOT	
Nu	Spont	HAR	Revw	Conf 70Helsinki 2 195	Jun 70	Colvin.PPR99. REPORT ON DATA STATUS	
Nu	Spont	NIR	Expt	Jour AE 29 95	Aug 70	Kroshkin+ NU BAR +− 3.0 PERCENT GIVN	+
				Jour SJA 29 790	Aug 70	. ENGL OF AE 29 95	
	Spont			Data EXFOR40064.003	Sep 73	.1 DATA LINE	
Nu	Spont	RI	Expt	Prog YFI−12 91	72	Alkhazov+ ABST,RECALIBRATED VAL GIVN	
				Prog INDC(CCP)−30	Sep 72	.PAGE 79,ENGLISH OF YFI−12 91	
Nu	Spont	IAE	Eval	Jour REA 10 637	Dec 72	Manero+ EXTENSIVE SURVEY,TBL,AVG VAL	
Nu	Spont	AUA	Expt	Conf 73Kiev 4 114	May 73	Boldeman. NUBAR+P(NU),DATA WITHDRAWN	
Nu	2.5−2	NIR	Expt	Conf 73Kiev 4 57	May 73	Zhuravlev+	+
	2.5−2			Data EXFOR40297.008	May 75	.DATA GVN	
Nu	Spont	DUB	Expt	Jour YF 18 724	Oct 73	Dakovsky+ P(NU),NUBAR,DISPERSION.TBL	+
				Rept JINR−P15−7119	Jun 73	Dakowski+ REL CM246,NUBAR+P(NU),TBL	
				Jour SNP 18 371	Apr 74	. ENGLISH OF YF 18,724.	
	Spont			Data EXFOR40203.002	Mar 74	.1 DATA LINE	
Nu	Spont	DUB	Comp	Jour YF 18 724	Oct 73	Dakovsky+NUBAR VS FISNUCLEUS,TBL+GRP	
				Jour SNP 18 371	Apr 74	. ENGLISH OF YF 18, 724.	
Nu	Spont	NIR	Expt	Rept YFI−18 45	Aug 74	Golushko+ NUBAR GVN IN TBL,CFD	+
				Jour AE 34 135	Feb 73	− + REL CF252,TBL,CFD OTHER	
				Rept INDC(CCP)−49	Feb 75	− + (REL CF252).ENGL OF YFI−18	
				Jour SJA 34 178	Aug 73	. ENGL OF AE 34 135	
	Spont			Data EXFOR40260.002	Feb 75	1 DATA LINE, CFD VALUES GIVEN	
Nu	Spont	HED	Eval	Abst ANS 22 673	Nov 75	Johnson. TBL,GRPH.NU FROM SPON FISS	
Nu	Spont	KUR	Expt	Rept YK−23 3	76	Khokhlov+ NUBAR,TABLES	
				Conf 75Kiev 5 86	May 75	− + NUBAR,CFD OTH WORKS.TABLE	
Frag Neuts	Spont	RI	Expt	Jour YF 15 22	Jan 72	Alkhazov+ NU VS FRAG MASS+EKIN,GRPHS	
				Prog YFI−12 91	72	− + ABST,NUBAR(KIN−E,MASS),TBL	
				Prog INDC(CCP)−30	Sep 72	.PAGE 79,ENGLISH OF YFI−12 91	
				Jour SNP 15 12	Jul 72	. ENGL OF YF 15 22	
Spect Fiss n	Spont	LRL	Expt	Jour PR 98 1327	Jun 55	Hicks+ NEUT NUMBER DISTR	
Spect Fiss n	Spont	CCP	Theo	Jour AE 5 649	Dec 58	Kovalev+ THEORY COMPARED WITH EXPT	
				Jour JNEA 11 166	Feb 60	TRANSLATN.*	
				Jour SJA 5 1588	58	TRANSLATN.*	
Spect Fiss n	Spont	SRL	Expt	Rept DP−949	Jul 65	Richard.HE3 DET.SPEC.5−6MEV,.75MEVMX	
Spect Fiss n	Spont	RI	Expt	Prog YFI−6 94	Oct 68	Belov+ TABLE N(E) AND MAXWELL−TEMP	+
				Rept INDC−E−260 94	Feb 69	.TRANSLATN.* TO BE PUBL IN YF	
	Spont			Data EXFOR40137.002	Mar 73	SPECT OF FIS−NEUTS .3−6.2MEV	
Spect Fiss n	Spont	FTI	Expt	Jour YF 9 727	Apr 69	Belov+ EXPTL NEUT−SPEC GRPH+AVG EKIN	
				Jour SNP 9 421	Oct 69	TRANSLATN.*NO4	
Spect Fiss n	Spont	NIR	Expt	Jour AE 29 95	Aug 70	Kroshkin+ AVG FISSN NEUT E +SPEC CRV	+
				Jour SJA 29 790	Aug 70	. ENGL OF AE 29 95	
	Spont			Data EXFOR40064.009	Sep 73	.1 DATA LINE	
Spect Fiss n	Maxwl	ANL	Revw	Conf 71Vienna 3	Aug 71	Smith. MEAN−E OF NEUTS,EXPTS CFD,TBL	
Spect Fiss n	2.5−2	NIR	Expt	Conf 73Kiev 4 57	May 73	Zhuravlev+	+
	2.5−2			Data EXFOR40297.002	May 75	.DATA GVN	
Spect Fiss n	Spont	CCP	Expt	Jour AE 36 282	Apr 74	Aleksandrova+ NEUT−SPEC OF FISS,GRPH	
				Jour SJA 36 355	Oct 74	. ENGLISH OF AE 36 282	
Spect Fiss γ	Spont	CCP	Expt	Jour YF 5 42	Jan 67	Adamov+.GRAPH,GAMMA+N IN TERNRY FISS	
				Jour SNP 5 30	Jul 67	. ENGL OF YF 5 42	
Fiss Prod γ	Spont	FTI	Expt	Jour YF 5 923	Apr 67	Adamov+ TERN.NO OF GAMS VS ALF−E.FIG	
				Jour SNP 5 655	Oct 67	. ENGL OF YF 5 923	
Fiss Yield	Spont	LAS	Expt	Jour PR 126 1508	May 62	Nobles. YIELD OF LONG RANGE FFRGM	

96 Curium 244

Quantity	Energy (ev) Min	Max	Lab	Type	Documentation Ref Vol Page	Date	Author, Comments	Data
Fiss Yield	Spont		FTI	Expt	Conf 69Vienna 900	Jul 69	Adamov+PPR146.LONG RANGE PARTICL YLD	
					Jour YF 9 732	Apr 69	- + PROTON,T,D AND ALFA YLD GIVN	
					Jour SNP 9 424	Oct 69	. ENGL OF YF 9 732	
Fiss Yield	None		BAS	Theo	Jour PL/B 34 264	Mar 71	Pauli+ FRAG MASS RATIO AS STRUTINSKY	
Fiss Yield	Spont		CCP	Expt	Jour YF 13 1162	Jun 71	Barashkov+ FRAG MASS+KE DISTR,CURVS	
					Jour SNP 13 668	Dec 71	.ENGL TRANSL	
Fiss Yield	None		TRM	Expt	Prog INIS - MF - 334 64	72	.RADIOCHEM+GAM - SPEC,SHORT NOTE,NDG	
Fiss Yield	Spont		CCP	Expt	Jour YF 15 22	Jan 72	Alkhazov+ REL FRAGMENT YIELD,GRAPHS	
					Jour SNP 15 12	Jul 72	* ENGL OF YF 15 22	
					Conf 69Vienna 961	Jul 69	*ABST ONLY,NO DATA	
Fiss Yield	Spont		CLA	Theo	Jour NP/A 184 417	Apr 72	Tsang+ ASSYM FROM FERMIGAS+WKB CALC.	
Fiss Yield	Spont		ANL	Expt	Jour PR/C 6 2211	Dec 72	Flynn+ RADIOCHEM+MASS SPECTROMETER.	
Fiss Yield	Maxwl		TRM	Expt	Conf 75Calcutta 2 141	Dec 75	Ramaswamy+MASS YIELD,RADIO CHEMICAL	
Fiss Yield	Spont		AUA	Theo	Rept AAEC/E - 386	Mar 76	Cook+ 3 - GAUSS FIT,PARAMS GIVEN	
Fiss Yield	2.5 - 2	1.4+7	LAS	Eval	Rept LA - 6430	Jul 76	Madland+ PAIR EFFECT ON INDEP YLD.TBL	
Frag Spectra	Spont		ANL	Expt	Conf 58Geneva 15 392	Sep 58	Smith+ PPR690,ENERGY OF FRAGMENTS.	
Frag Spectra	Spont		CCP	Expt	Jour AE 15 249	Sep 63	Malkin+.KINETIC E OF FISSION FRAGM	
					Jour SJA 15 955	64	. ENGL OF AE 15 249	
Frag Spectra	Spont		CCP	Expt	Jour ZET 46 2244	Jun 64	Perfilov.ALFA - SPCT IN TERN SPON FISS	
					Jour JET 19 1514	Dec 64	TRANSLATN.*	
Frag Spectra	Spont		FEI	Expt	Jour AE 17 28	Jul 64	Bolshov+KINETIC DISTR OF FRAGMENTS	+
					Jour JNE 19 457	65	.ENGLISH TRANSL OF AE 17 28 1964	
					Jour EAF 17 1 47	Jul 64	. FRENCH TRANSL OF AE 17 28 1964	
Frag Spectra	Spont		FTI	Expt	Jour YF 5 923	Apr 67	Adamov+ TERN.ALF E - SPEC VS GAM - E.FIG	
					Jour SNP 5 655	Oct 67	. ENGL OF YF 5 923	
Frag Spectra	1.5+7		KUR	Expt	Jour YF 5 966	May 67	Fomushkin+ TBLS+CURVES GIVEN	
					Jour SNP 5 689	Nov 67	. ENGL OF YF 5 966	
Frag Spectra	Spont		FTI	Expt	Conf 69Vienna 900	Jul 69	Adamov+PPR146. ALFA+TRIT+PROTON SPEC	
					Jour YF 9 732	Apr 69	- + AVG ALFA,T,P ENERGY + - SPREAD	
					Jour SNP 9 424	Oct 69	. ENGL OF YF 9 732	
Frag Spectra	Spont		RI	Expt	Prog YFI - 9 19	Dec 69	Alkhasov+ FRAG KIN E MEASURD,NDG	
					Jour YF 15 22	Jan 72	Alkhazov+ KIN - E DISTR OF FRAGS,GRPHS	
					Rept INDC(CCP) - 9U24	Dec 70	TRANSLATN.*	
					Jour SNP 15 12	Jul 72	. ENGL OF YF 15 22	
Frag Spectra	Spont		CCP	Expt	Jour AE 28 73	Jan 70	Gorshkov+ SI - GLASS - DET,E - KIN - DISTR	
					Jour SJA 28 88	Jan 70	TRANSLATN.*NO 1	
					Jour EAF 28 105	Jan 70	TRANSLATN.* NO 1	
Frag Spectra	Spont		CCP	Expt	Jour YF 13 1162	Jun 71	Barashkov+ TOF,KE DISTRIB,TBL,GRPHS	
					Jour SNP 13 668	Dec 71	. ENGL OF YF 13 1162	
Frag Spectra	None		TRM	Expt	Prog INIS - MF - 334 64	72	.RANGES+KIN - E DISTR,SHORT NOTE,NDG	
Frag Charge	Spont		ANL	Expt	Jour PR/C 6 2211	Dec 72	Flynn+ RADIOCHEM+MASS SPECTROMETER.	
Frag Charge	Spont		LRL	Comp	Rept UCRL - 51640	Jul 74	Nethaway. TBL.	
Reson Params	7.7+0	7.7+2	ANL	Expt	Jour PR/C 134 1281	Jun 64	Cote.FC.21RES,WN FOR15,WG FOR3=37MV	+
	7.7+0	7.7+2			Data EXFOR12570.	Jun 76	. 21 RES E0,WN,WG,WT, AND TOT PCS.	
Reson Params	+5	+6	CCP	Theo	Jour YF 7 1228	Jun 68	Vorotnikov.D,EXPT CFD DEGEN - FERM - GAS	
					Jour SNP 7 732	Dec 68	TRANSLATN.*	
Reson Params	None		DUB	Theo	Jour YF 13 240	Feb 71	Malecki+G - WID,THEO CFD EXPT.TBL,GRPH	
					Jour SNP 13 133	Aug 71	- + ENGL OF YF 13 240.	
Reson Params	6.2 - 1	5.0+4	SRL	Expt	Conf 71Knoxvill 714	Mar 71	Mccrosson. STAT CALCULATN AVG PARAMS	
Reson Params	2.3+1	9.7+2	LAS	Expt	Jour PR/C 3 1656	Apr 71	Moore+.NUCL SHOT.PARAMS FOR 65 RESON	+
	2.3+1	2.7+2			Conf 70Helsinki 1 527	Jun 70	.SUPERSEDED	
	2.3+1	9.7+2			Data EXFOR10121.	Nov 74	. 197 PTS. WN,WG,WF,	
Reson Params	+0		CCP	Theo	Jour AE 31 18	Jul 71	Vorotnikov.S+P - NEUT FISS - WIDS DERIVD	
					Jour SJA 31 706	Feb 72	* ENGL OF AE 31 18 7/71	
Reson Params	-.1+0	5.2+2	MTR	Expt	Prog ANCR - 1088 39	72	Simpson+.WN WG WF FOR 36 RESON	
Reson Params	7.7+0	8.5+1	MTR	Expt	Jour NSE 49 145	Oct 72	Berreth+. TRANS. WN FOR 7 RESON	+
	7.7+0	8.5+1			Data EXFOR10271.004	Nov 74	. 7 RES,WG AND WN0.	
Reson Params	7.8+0	9.7+2	FEI	Eval	Conf 73Kiev 1 246	May 73	Abagjan+ REFERENCES GIVEN, NDG	
					Rept INDC(CCP) - 44	Jun 74	.P45.ENGLISH OF 73KIEV 1 246	
Reson Params	4.0+2	1.4+7	CCP	Eval	Data SOKRATOR - 1046	76	68 RES PARAMS	+
Strnth Fnctn	0.0+0	2.7+2	ANL	Expt	Jour PR/B 134 1281	Jun 64	Cote.FC.S=.76+.35, -.17, L=0 ONLY	+
	0.0+0	2.7+2			Data EXFOR12570.005	Jun 76	. 2 PTS, STF, D	
Strnth Fnctn	2.6+6	4.1+6	AI	Theo	Rept NAA - SR - M - 12538	Oct 67	Gigas.OPTMDL CALC AVG S0,S1,S2	
Strnth Fnctn	2.3+1	9.7+2	LAS	Expt	Jour PR/C 3 1656	Apr 71	Moore+DRVD FROM RESOLVED RESONS.	+
	2.3+1	9.7+2			Data EXFOR10121.	Jun 76	. 2 PTS, SO, D	
Strnth Fnctn	None		AUA	Eval	Rept AAEC/E - 277	Mar 73	Musgrove.TBLS EXPTL DATA+BEST VALUES	
Strnth Fnctn	7.7+0	1.0+2	ITE	Expt	Conf 75Kiev	May 75	Kalebin+	

96 Curium 244

Quantity	Energy (ev) Min	Max	Lab	Type	Documentation Ref Vol Page	Date	Author, Comments	Data
Lvl Density	−3	+0	IFU	Theo Jour	UFZ 13 700	Apr 68	Pisanko+ LEVEL SPACING CALC,TBL	
				Jour	UPJ 13 498	Oct 68	TRANSLATN.*	
Lvl Density		1.0+2	KUR	Theo Jour	YF 9 303	Feb 69	Vorotnikov.LVL DEN(EXCIT−E),TBL GRPH	
				Jour	SNP 9 179	Aug 69	TRANSLATN.*	
Lvl Density	None		IBJ	Revw Jour	PF 23 561	Sep 72	Jastrzebski. SPONTAN FISSION ISOMERS	
Lvl Density	+6		DUB	Theo Rept	JINR−E4−9236	Nov 75	Komov+ AVG LVL−SPAC,SEMIMICRO CFD XP	

96 Curium 245

Quantity	Energy (ev) Min	Max	Lab	Type	Documentation Ref Vol Page	Date	Author, Comments	Data
Evaluation	1.0−5	2.0+7	SRL	Eval Rept	EPRI−NP−161	Dec 75	Benjamin+ENDF4B.REVISIONS.	
Total	1.0+0	1.0+1	MTR	Theo Prog	IN−1317 17	Jan 70	Berreth+,CALCTD FROM RESON PARS,CURV	
Total	1.0−2	1.0+0	MTR	Expt Jour	NSE 49 145	Oct 72	Berreth+. TRANS. SIG=2900+−450B	+
	2.5−2			Data	EXFOR10271.012	Nov 74	.1 PT. SIGMA	
Total	None		NIR	Expt Conf	76Lowell 1255	Jul 76	Belanova+TRNS.RES PARS DRVD.NDG	
Absorption	Pile		SRL	Expt Conf	68Wash. 1285	Mar 68	Smith+ SIG=2210B THERMALIZED SPEC	+
				Rept	DP−MS−68−111	Feb 68	− + SRL IRRADIATION.	
	Pile			Data	EXFOR12580.004	Jun 76	.1 PT. SIGMA.	
Absorption	Pile		SRL	Expt Abst	ANS 14 344	Jun 71	Rusche. VALUE GIVEN	
Res Int Abs	8.3−1		SRL	Expt Conf	68Wash. 1279	Mar 68	Folger+ ACT 260B	+
				Rept	DP−MS−67−112	Jun 76	− + FOIL MEASUREMENTS.	
	8.3−1			Data	EXFOR12534.008	Jun 76	.1 PT. RI	
Res Int Abs	5.0−1		MTR	Expt Rept	IN−1296	May 69	Schuman+. PILE ACT. 680+−300B. 1/V	
Res Int Abs	None		SRL	Expt Abst	ANS 14 344	Jun 71	Rusche. VALUE GIVEN	
Res Int Abs	4.0−1		MTR	Expt Jour	NSE 49 145	Oct 72	Berreth+. TRANS. RI=897+−180B	+
	4.0−1			Data	EXFOR10271.010	Nov 74	.1 PT. SIGMA.	
(n,γ)	Pile		ANL	Expt Jour	PR 94 974	May 54	Stevens+ ACT+MASS SPECTR 200+−100B	+
	Pile			Data	EXFOR12585.004	Jun 76	.1 PT. SIGMA.	
(n,γ)	Maxwl		ANL	Expt Jour	NSE 1 204	Jul 56	Jaffey.200B FROM ORNL ANL DATA	
				Conf	55Geneva 7 261	Aug 55	Bentley+.P809,VAL GVN,CHEMICAL METHD	
(n,γ)	None		KAP	Comp Rept	KAPL−1781	Jul 57	Schuman. SIGMA GIVEN	
(n,γ)	Maxwl		SRL	Expt Rept	DP−MS−66−69	Oct 66	ICE. HIGHLY THERMAL SPECTRUM.	
	Maxwl			Data	EXFOR12550.009	Jun 76	.1 PT. SIGMA.	
(n,γ)	Maxwl		BNL	Theo Abst	ANS 10 228	Jun 67	Prince. CALCULATED SIG=3358.	
(n,γ)	Maxwl		ORL	Expt Prog	ORNL−4437 20	Sep 69	Halperin+. THR+0.025EV SIGS GIVEN	+
	Maxwl			Data	EXFOR10164.002	Nov 72	. 1 PT. SIGMA.	
(n,γ)	1.0+0	1.0+1	MTR	Theo Prog	IN−1317 17	Jan 70	Berreth+,CALCTD FROM RESON PARS,CURV	
(n,γ)	Pile		KFK	Eval Rept	KFK−1453	Mar 72	Eberle+ 2−GROUP SIGS,FITTED TO EXPT	
(n,γ)	1.0+2	1.0+7	UK	Eval Prog	AERE−PR/NP20	Mar 73	Sowerby.(HAR).UKNDL CREATD.DFN−1006	
(n,γ)	1.0+3	1.0+7	HAR	Eval Prog	EANDC(UK) 151	Aug 73	Sowerby+ USES LYNN CALC SIG	
(n,γ)	2.5−2		SRL	Eval Conf	75Wash. 224	Mar 75	Benjamin+ TBL BEST FIT TRANSPU PROD.	
(n,γ)	None		ORL	Expt Prog	ORNL−5101 11	Jan 76	Weston.NDG.TBD	
Res Int Capt	Maxwl		BNL	Theo Abst	ANS 10 228	Jun 67	Prince. CALCULATED RES INTGRL=133B.	
Res Int Capt	5.4−1		ORL	Expt Prog	ORNL−4437 20	Sep 69	Halperin+. CD RATIO+MASS SPECTR	+
	5.4−1			Data	EXFOR10164.003	Nov 72	. 1 PT. RI.	
Res Int Capt	Pile		KFK	Eval Rept	KFK−1453	Mar 72	Eberle+ 100B	
Res Int Capt	6.3−1		SRL	Eval Conf	75Wash. 224	Mar 75	Benjamin+ TBL BEST FIT TRANSPU PROD.	
Fission	Pile		BRK	Expt Priv	SEABORG	Jun 55	Seaborg. (TO J.R.HUIZENGA)ACTIVATION	
	Pile			Data	EXFOR12557.002	Jun 76	.1 PT. SIGMA.	
Fission	Maxwl		ANL	Expt Jour	NSE 1 204	Jul 56	Jaffey.1800B FROM ORNL ANL DATA	+
				Conf	55Geneva 7 261	Aug 55	Bentley+.P809,VAL GVN,CHEMICAL METHD	
Fission	None		KAP	Comp Rept	KAPL−1781	Jul 57	Schuman. SIGMA GIVEN	
Fission	Maxwl		LRL	Expt Jour	PR 107 1294	Sep 57	Hulet+. 1880+−150B REL SIGF PU239	
	Maxwl			Data	EXFOR12497.008	Jun 76	.1 PT. SIGMA	
Fission	Pile		SRL	Expt Rept	DP−MS−66−69	Oct 66	ICE. HIGHLY THERMAL SPECTRUM.	+
	Pile			Data	EXFOR12550.008	Jun 76	.1 PT. SIGMA.	
Fission	Maxwl		BNL	Theo Abst	ANS 10 228	Jun 67	Prince. CALC SIG=1900B	
Fission	Pile		SRL	Expt Conf	68Wash. § H12	Mar 68	Smith+ SIG=1880B THERMALIZED SPEC	+
				Rept	DP−MS−67−111	Feb 68	− + SRL IRRADIATION.	
	Pile			Data	EXFOR12580.005	Jun 76	.1 PT. SIGMA	
Fission	Maxwl		ANL	Expt Jour	JIN 30 2553	Oct 68	Diamond+,ION CHAMB IN THR COLUMN	+
	Maxwl			Data	EXFOR12531.003	Jun 76	.1 PT. SIGMA	
Fission	−		BER	Theo Conf	69Vienna 197	Jul 69	Krappe+ PPR96. 1+2 FISSN BARRIER TBL	
Fission	Spont		HEI	Expt Conf	69Vienna 449	Jul 69	Metag+ PPR29. HE−INDUCED ISOM FISS HL	
Fission	1.0+0	1.0+1	MTR	Theo Prog	IN−1317 17	Jan 70	Berreth+,CALCTD FROM RESON PARS,CURV	
Fission	2.5−2		ORL	Expt Prog	ORNL−4581 37	Sep 70	Halperin+. FISSION TRACK COUNTING	+
	2.5−2			Data	EXFOR10165.002	Jan 73	.1 PT. SIGMA	

96 Curium 245

Quantity	Energy (ev) Min	Max	Lab	Type	Documentation Ref Vol Page	Author, Comments Date	Data
Fission	1.0+6	1.5+7	LAS	Expt Prog	NCSAC-33 148	Dec 70 Barton+,TO BE DONE	
Fission	2.0+1	2.8+6	LAS	Expt Jour	PR/C 3 1656	Apr 71 Moore+. NUCLEAR SHOT. CURVES	+
				Rept	LA- 4566	Apr 71 Baybarz+ POINT DATA	
				Conf	70Helsinki 1 527	Jun 70 .SUPERSEDED	
	2.0+1	2.8+6		Data	EXFOR10121.028	Nov 74 . 4301 PTS. SIGMA.	
Fission	Spont		MTR	Expt Prog	NCSAC-38 81	May 71 Simpson+. TO BE DONE	
Fission	Pile		SRL	Expt Jour	JIN 33 1553	Jul 71 Thompson+ CD CUT-OFF	
				Abst	ANS 14 344	Jun 71 Rusche. VALUE GIVEN	
Fission	Maxwl		SRL	Expt Jour	NSE 47 203	Feb 72 Benjamin+FISS CHS,FISS TRACK MEAS.	+
				Conf	71Knoxvill 843	Mar 71 .SUPERSEDED	
	Maxwl			Data	EXFOR10128.004	Feb 73 1PT.CS=2018+-37B.REL U235	
Fission	Pile		KFK	Eval Rept	KFK-1453	Mar 72 Eberle+ 2-GROUP SIGS,FITTED TO EXPT	
Fission	-		GEL	ExTh Jour	NP/A 187 305	Jun 72 Weigmann+ F.B.PARAMS FROM DATA ANAL.	
Fission	+0	+7	KUR	Expt Jour	YF 17 24	Jan 73 Fomushkin+ SIG GIVEN,TABLE	+
				Jour	SNP 17 12	Jul 73 . ENGL OF YF 17 24	
	1.0+7			Data	EXFOR40150.003	May 74 .NF SIG SPECT AVER AND RATIO TO U235	
Fission	1.0+3	1.0+7	UK	Eval Prog	AERE-PR/NP20	Mar 73 Sowerby.(HAR).UKNDL CREATD.DFN-1006	
Fission	1.0+3	1.0+7	HAR	Eval Prog	EANDC(UK) 151	Aug 73 Sowerby+ FOR UKNDL DFN 1006	
Fission	Pile		SRL	Eval Conf	75Wash. 224	Mar 75 Benjamin+ TBL BEST FIT TRANSPU PROD.	
Fission	2.5-2		NIR	Expt Jour	AE 39 285	Oct 75 Zhuravlev+ SIG GIVEN,BY CD-DIFFERENC	+
				Rept	YK- 19 3	May 75 - + CD-DIFFERENCE, SIG GIVEN	
				Jour	SJA 39 907	Apr 76 . ENGL OF AE 39 285	
	2.5-2			Data	EXFOR40339.004	Mar 76 1 PNT	
Fission	1.0+3	3.0+6	JAE	Revw Rept	JAERI-M-6315	Nov 75 Igarasi+GRPH. DATA OF MOORE 1971.	
Res Int Fiss	Maxwl		BNL	Theo Abst	ANS 10 228	Jun 67 Prince. CALCULATED RES INTGRL=345B.	
Res Int Fiss	5.4-1		ORL	Expt Prog	ORNL-4581 37	Sep 70 Halperin+. FISSION TRACK COUNTING	+
	5.4-1			Data	EXFOR10165.003	Jan 73 . 1 PT. RI	
Res Int Fiss	5.0-1		SRL	Expt Jour	JIN 33 1553	Jul 71 Thompson+ CD CUT-OFF	
Res Int Fiss	6.3-1		SRL	Expt Jour	NSE 47 203	Feb 72 Benjamin+CD COVER.MASS SPEC.	+
				Conf	71Knoxvill 843	Mar 71 .SUPERSEDED	
	6.3-1			Data	EXFOR10128.005	Feb 73 . 1 PT. RIF=772+-40B, REL U235.	
Res Int Fiss	Pile		KFK	Eval Rept	KFK-1453	Mar 72 Eberle+ 580B	
Res Int Fiss	6.3-1		SRL	Eval Conf	75Wash. 224	Mar 75 Benjamin+ TBL BEST FIT TRANSPU PROD.	
Res Int Fiss	5.0-1		NIR	Expt Jour	AE 39 285	Oct 75 Zhuravlev+ RI GIVEN,BY CD-DIFFERENCE	+
				Rept	YK- 19 3	May 75 - + CD-DIFFERENCE,RES-INT GVN	
				Jour	SJA 39 907	Apr 76 . ENGL OF AE 39 285	
	5.0-1			Data	EXFOR40337.004	Mar 76 1 PNT	
Alpha	1.0+4	2.0+4	LAS	Theo Jour	PR 158 1127	Jun 67 Bell. SYSTEMATCS TH FOR 10-20KEV ALF	
Eta	Pile		ANL	Expt Jour	NSE 1 204	Jul 56 Jaffey.2.7 FROM ORNL ANL DATA	
Nu	Pile		ANL	Expt Jour	NSE 1 204	Jul 56 Jaffey.3.0 EST FROM ORNL ANL DATA	
Nu	Maxwl		ANL	Expt Jour	NP/A 145 1	Apr 70 Jaffey+ REL TO U,PU,STANDARDS.	+
				Rept	ANL-7625	Nov 69 - +COMPLETE DATA GVN.	
	Maxwl					May 72 . 1 PT. PROMPT N YLD=3.832+=.034.	
Nu	Maxwl	1.5+7	HAR	Revw Conf	70Helsinki 2 195	Jun 70 Colvin.PPR99. REPORT ON DATA STATUS	
Nu	Maxwl		NIR	Expt Jour	AE 29 95	Aug 70 Kroshkin+ NU BAR +- 3.0 PERCENT GIVN	+
				Jour	SJA 29 790	Aug 70 . ENGL OF AE 29 95	
	2.5-2			Data	EXFOR40064.004	Sep 73 .1 DATA LINE	
Nu	Maxwl		CUA	Theo Abst	DA/B 32 5980	Apr 72 Lee. CALC OF AVG PROMPT NU	
Nu	Maxwl		IAE	Eval Jour	REA 10 637	Dec 72 Manero+ EXTENSIVE SURVEY,TBL,AVG VAL	
Nu	2.5-2		NIR	Expt Conf	73Kiev 4 57	May 73 Zhuravlev+	+
	2.5-2			Data	EXFOR40297.011	May 75 .DATA GVN	
Nu	Maxwl		ANL	Revw Conf	73Rochestr 2 19	Aug 73 Unik+NU TOTAL VS MASS 13 NUCLIDES.	
Nu	Maxwl		AUA	Revw Conf	IAEA-169 2 163	74 Musgrove+ TOTAL NU-BAR,GRAPH	
Nu	Spont		HED	Eval Abst	ANS 22 673	Nov 75 Johnson. TBL,GRPH.NU FROM SPON FISS	
Spect Fiss n	Maxwl		NIR	Expt Jour	AE 29 95	Aug 70 Kroshkin+ AVG FISSN NEUT E +SPEC CRV	+
				Jour	SJA 29 790	Aug 70 . ENGL OF AE 29 95	
	2.5-2			Data	EXFOR40064.010	Sep 73 .1 DATA LINE	
Spect Fiss n	Maxwl		ANL	Revw Conf	71Vienna 3	Aug 71 Smith. MEAN-E OF NEUTS,EXPTS CFD,TBL	
Spect Fiss n	2.5-2		NIR	Expt Conf	73Kiev 4 57	May 73 Zhuravlev+	+
	2.5-2			Data	EXFOR40297.005	May 75 .DATA GVN	
Fiss Yield	Maxwl		ANL	Expt Jour	PR 161 1192	Sep 67 VON GUNTEN+ YIELD VS MASS CURVE	
Fiss Yield	Maxwl		SRL	Expt Jour	PR/C 4 505	Aug 71 Troutner+.TE132,134 FRACT CUMUL YLDS	
Fiss Yield	Maxwl		SRL	Expt Jour	JIN 34 7 2109	Jul 72 Harbour+ YLD OF 21 MASS CHAINS	
Fiss Yield	Maxwl		HAR	Eval Conf	73Paris 1 393	Mar 73 Crouch.EXPTL DATA+EVAL CHAIN YLD,TBL	
				Rept	AERE-R-7209	Jan 73 - .34 CHAIN YLDS RECOMMENDED TBL	
Fiss Yield	Maxwl		ANL	Expt Conf	73Rochestr 2 19	Aug 73 Unik+ PROMPT YLDS,MASS DISTRIB,GRPHS	
Fiss Yield	Maxwl		AUA	Revw Conf	IAEA-169 2 163	74 Musgrove+ PROMPT,EVEN-Z POSITN,GRAPH	

96 Curium 245

Quantity	Energy (ev) Min	Max	Lab	Type	Documentation Ref Vol Page	Date	Author, Comments	Data
Fiss Yield	Maxwl		SRL	Expt Jour	PR/C 10 769	Aug 74	Harbour+ XE135 YIELD,TBL,GRPH.	
				Rept	DP− MS−73−29	73	− +. XE135 FRACTNL INDEPEND YLD	
Fiss Yield	Maxwl		TRM	Expt	BARC−900 87	76	Ramaswamy+ 17MASS YLDS,CFD.TBL+GRPH	+
	Pile			Prog	BARC−872 104	76	Ramaswami+ ASYM MASS−YLDS CFD,TABLE	
	Maxwl			Prog	BARC−872 104	76	− + PRELIM.RESULTS	
	Maxwl			Data	EXFOR30437.002	Apr 78	CHN YLDS FOR 17 A−VALUES	
Frag Spectra	Maxwl		CUA	Theo Abst	DA/B 32 5980	Apr 72	Lee. CALC OF TOT FRAG KE DISTRIBUTS	
Frag Spectra	Maxwl		ANL	Expt Conf	73Rochestr 2 19	Aug 73	Unik+ TOTAL KIN−E OF FRAGS,GRPH,TBL	
Frag Spectra	Maxwl		AUA	Revw Conf	IAEA−169 2 163	74	Musgrove+ AVG FRAG MASS,GRAPH	
Frag Charge	Maxwl		ANL	Expt Jour	PR 161 1192	Sep 67	VON GUNTEN+ MOST PROB CHARGE 2PRODS	
Frag Charge	Maxwl		OSL	Revw Conf	69Vienna 669	Jul 69	Pappas+PPR206. REVW OF EXPTS+METHODS	
Frag Charge	Maxwl		LRL	Comp Rept	UCRL−51640	Jul 74	Nethaway. TBL.	
Reson Params	1.0−2	9.0+2	ANL	Expt Jour	PR/B 134 1281	Jun 64	Cote.FC.NO RES SEEN WITH 1.6PC CM245	
Reson Params	6.2−1	5.0+4	SRL	Theo Conf	71Knoxvill 714	Mar 71	Mccrosson. STAT CALCULATN AVG PARAMS	
Reson Params	2.1+1	6.0+1	LAS	Expt Jour	PR/C 3 1656	Apr 71	Moore+.NUCL SHOT.PARAMS FOR 26 RESON	+
				Conf	70Helsinki 1 527	Jun 70	.SUPERSEDED.	
	2.1+1	6.0+1		Data	EXFOR10121.	Nov 74	. 28 PTS. WN,WG,WF.	
Reson Params	2.0+0	2.9+1	MTR	Expt Jour	NSE 49 145	Oct 72	Berreth+. TRANS. WN WF FOR 10 RESON	+
	2.0+0	2.9+1		Data	EXFOR10271.	Nov 74	. 10 RES, WF AND WN0.	
Reson Params	9.8−1	1.6+1	ORL	Expt Conf	75Wash. 81	Mar 75	Dabbs+ TBL E0,REL HEIGHTS	
Strnth Fnctn	2.1+1	6.0+1	LAS	Expt Jour	PR/C 3 1656	Apr 71	Moore+DRVD FROM RESOLVED RESONS.	+
	2.1+1	6.0+1		Data	EXFOR10121.	Nov 74	. 2 PTS. SO, D	
Strnth Fnctn	None		AUA	Eval Rept	AAEC/E−277	Mar 73	Musgrove.TBLS EXPTL DATA+BEST VALUES	
Strnth Fnctn	1.9+0	1.0+2	ITE	Expt Conf	75Kiev	May 75	Kalebin+	
Strnth Fnctn	None		NIR	Expt Conf	76Lowell 1255	Jul 76	Belanova+TRNS.STF CALC.NDG.	
Lvl Density	+6		MIL	Theo Jour	EN 15 1 54	Jan 68	Facchini+ LDL PARS FROM LOW EN RES	
Lvl Density	None		MUN	Theo Jour	NP/A 217 269	Dec 73	Dilg+ A,DELTA. BACK SHIFTED FERMIGAS	
Lvl Density	None		COP	Theo Jour	NP/A 222 493	Apr 74	Dossing+COLL ROTAT.SPAC. ACCUR ESTIM	
Lvl Density	None		ROC	Theo Jour	NP/A 223 589	May 74	Huizenga+ EXP CFD MICROSC TH AX SYMM	
Lvl Density	+6		DUB	Theo Rept	JINR−E4−9236	Nov 75	Komov+ AVG LVL−SPAC,SEMIMICRO CFD XP	

96 Curium 246

Quantity	Energy (ev) Min	Max	Lab	Type	Documentation Ref Vol Page	Date	Author, Comments	Data
Total	1.0−2	9.0+2	ANL	Expt Jour	PR/B 134 1281	Jun 64	Cote.FC. NDG 3RES,SOME ANALYSED	
Total		3.0+1	MTR	Theo Prog	NCSAC−38 81	May 71	Berreth+ CALC FROM RES PAR, CURVE	
Total	5.0−1	3.0+3	ORL	Expt Jour	NSE 55 440	Nov 74	Benjamin+ ORELA,TOF, IMPURITY CM−248	
Total	None		NIR	Expt Conf	76Lowell 1255	Jul 76	Belanova+TRNS.RES PARS DRVD.NDG	
Absorption	Maxwl		SRL	Expt Conf	68Wash. 1279	Mar 68	Folger+ ACTIVATION.	+
				Rept	DP−MS−67−112	Mar 68	− + FOIL MEASUREMENTS.	
	Maxwl			Data	EXFOR12534.009	Jun 76	. 1 PT. SIGMA.	
Absorption	Pile		SRL	Expt Abst	ANS 14 344	Jun 71	Rusche. VALUE GIVEN	
Res Int Abs	8.3−1		SRL	Expt Conf	68Wash. 1279	Mar 68	Folger+ ACT 260B	+
				Rept	DP−MS−67−112	Mar 68	− + FOIL MEASUREMENTS.	
	8.3−1			Data	EXFOR12534.010	Jun 76	. 1 PT. RI.	
Res Int Abs	None		SRL	Expt Abst	ANS 14 344	Jun 71	Rusche. VALUE GIVEN	
(n,γ)	Pile		ANL	Expt Jour	PR 94 974	May 54	Stevens+ ACT+MASS SPECTR 15+−10B	+
	Pile			Data	EXFOR12585.005	Jun 76	. 1 PT. SIGMA	
(n,γ)	Pile		ANL	Revw Conf	55Geneva 7 261	Aug 55	Bentley+.P809,VAL GVN,CHEMICAL METHD	
(n,γ)	None		KAP	Comp Rept	KAPL−1781	Jul 57	Schuman. SIGMA GIVEN	
(n,γ)	Maxwl		BNL	Theo Abst	ANS 10 228	Jun 67	Prince. CALCULATED SIG=15B.	
(n,γ)	Maxwl		ORL	Expt Prog	ORNL−4437 20	Sep 69	Halperin+. THR+0.025EV SIGS GIVEN	+
	Maxwl			Data	EXFOR10164.004	Nov 72	. 1 PT. SIGMA	
(n,γ)	Maxwl		CCP	Comp Jour	AE 28 388	May 70	Bol'Shov+ OTHER'S SIG VALUE GIVEN	
				Jour	EAF 28 5 9	70	. FRENCH OF AE 28 388.	
(n,γ)	8.0+1	3.8+2	LAS	Expt Jour	PR/C 3 1656	Apr 71	Moore+. NUCLEAR SHOT. CURVES	+
				Rept	LA−4566	Apr 71	Baybarz+ POINT DATA	
				Conf	70Helsinki 1 527	Jun 70	.SUPERSEDED	
	8.0+1	3.8+2		Data	EXFOR10121.033	Nov 74	. 157 PTS. SIGMA.	
(n,γ)	Pile		KFK	Eval Prog	KFK−1544 61	Jan 72	Eberle+FOR 2−GROUP SIG,FITTED TO EXP	
(n,γ)	2.5−2		ORL	Expt Abst	BAP 19 599	Apr 74	Harvey+.ORELA.RESON CONTRIB TO SIG	
(n,γ)	Pile		SRL	Eval Conf	75Wash. 224	Mar 75	Benjamin+ TBL BEST FIT TRANSPU PROD.	
Res Int Capt	Maxwl		BNL	Theo Abst	ANS 10 228	Jun 67	Prince. CALCULATED RES INTGRL=2800B.	
Res Int Capt	5.0−1		MTR	Expt Jour	IN−1296	May 69	Schuman+. PILE ACT. 110+−40B. 1/V	
Res Int Capt	5.4−1		ORL	Expt Prog	ORNL−4437 20	Sep 69	Halperin+. CD RATIO+MASS SPECTR	+
	5.4−1			Data	EXFOR10164.005	Nov 72	. 1 PT. RI.	
Res Int Capt	Pile		KFK	Eval Prog	KFK−1544 61	Jan 72	Eberle+121B	

96 Curium 246

Quantity	Energy (ev) Min	Max	Lab	Type	Documentation Ref Vol Page	Date	Author, Comments	Data
Res Int Capt	5.0-1	3.0+3	ORL	Expt	Abst BAP 19 599	Apr 74	Harvey+.ORELA. RI=94B.	
Res Int Capt	6.3-1		SRL	Eval	Conf 75Wash. 224	Mar 75	Benjamin+ TBL BEST FIT TRANSPU PROD.	
Res Int Capt	5.0-1		ITE	Expt	Conf IAEA-186 2 121	76	Kalebin. CALC FROM RESPARS,CFD.TABLE	
Fission	Spont		BRK	Revw	Jour NP 81 1	Jun 66	Myers.TBL CALC FISS BARRIERS.	
Fission	Maxwl		BNL	Theo	Abst ANS 10 228	Jun 67	Prince. CALCULATED SIG=.23B.	
Fission	-		BER	Theo	Conf 69Vienna 197	Jul 69	Krappe+PPR96. 1+2 FISSN BARRIER TBL	
Fission	Spont		COP	Revw	Conf 69Vienna 155	Jul 69	Strutinsky+PPR203. HL GVN,'SHELL-TH'	
Fission	1.0+6	1.5+7	LAS	Expt	Prog NCSAC-33 148	Dec 70	Barton+,TO BE DONE	
Fission	Spont		MRY	Theo	Prog ORO-4028-28	71	Jackson+. SPON FISSION HALF-LIFE GVN	
Fission	2.0+1	2.8+6	LAS	Expt	Jour PR/C 3 1656	Apr 71	Moore+. NUCLEAR SHOT. CURVES	+
					Rept LA-4566	Apr 71	Baybarz+ POINT DATA	
					Conf 70Helsinki 1 527	Jun 70	.SUPERSEDED	
	2.0+1	2.8+6			Data EXFOR10121.029	Nov 74	. 2797 PTS. SIGMA.	
Fission	Pile		SRL	Expt	Jour JIN 33 1553	Jul 71	Thompson+ CD CUT-OFF	
Fission	Maxwl		SRL	Expt	Jour NSE 47 203	Feb 72	Benjamin+FISS CHS,FISS TRACK MEAS.	+
					Conf 71Knoxvill 843	Mar 71	.SUPERSEDED	
	Maxwl				Data EXFOR10128.006	Feb 73	. 1 PT.CS=.17+-.10B,REL U235.	
Fission	Pile		KFK	Eval	Rept KFK-1453	Mar 72	Eberle+ 2-GROUP SIGS,FITTED TO EXPT	
Fission	-		GEL	ExTh	Jour NP/A 187 305	Jun 72	Weigmann+ F.B.PARAMS FROM DATA ANAL.	
Fission	+0	+7	KUR	Expt	Jour YF 17 24	Jan 73	Fomushkin+ SIG GIVEN,TABLE	+
					Jour SNP 17 12	Jul 73	. ENGL OF YF 17 24	
	1.0+7				Data EXFOR40150.004	May 74	.NF SIG SPECT AVER AND RATIO TO U235	
Fission	Pile		SRL	Eval	Conf 75Wash. 224	Mar 75	Benjamin+ TBL BEST FIT TRANSPU PROD.	
Fission	2.5-2		NIR	Expt	Jour AE 39 285	Oct 75	Zhuravlev+ SIG GIVEN,BY CD-DIFFERENC	+
					Rept YK-19 3	May 75	- + CD-DIFFERENCE, SIG GIVEN	
					Jour SJA 39 907	Apr 76	. ENGL OF AE 39 285	
	2.5-2				Data EXFOR40339.005	Mar 76	1 PNT	
Res Int Fiss	Maxwl		BNL	Theo	Abst ANS 10 228	Jun 67	Prince. CALCULATED RES INTGRL=18B.	
Res Int Fiss	5.0-1		SRL	Expt	Jour JIN 33 1553	Jul 71	Thompson+ CD CUT-OFF	
Res Int Fiss	6.3-1		SRL	Expt	Jour NSE 47 203	Feb 72	Benjamin+CD COVER.MASS SPEC.	+
					Conf 71Knoxvill 843	Mar 71	.SUPERSEDED.	
	6.3-1				Data EXFOR10128.007	Feb 73	. 1 PT. RIF=10.0+-.4B REL U235.	
Res Int Fiss	Pile		KFK	Eval	Rept KFK-1453	Mar 72	Eberle+ 121B	
Res Int Fiss	6.3-1		SRL	Eval	Conf 75Wash. 224	Mar 75	Benjamin+ TBL BEST FIT TRANSPU PROD.	
Res Int Fiss	5.0-1		NIR	Expt	Jour AE 39 285	Oct 75	Zhuravlev+ RI GIVEN,BY CD-DIFFERENCE	+
					Rept YK-19 3	May 75	- + CD-DIFFERENCE,RES-INT GVN	
					Jour SJA 39 907	Apr 76	. ENGL OF AE 39 285	
	5.0-1				Data EXFOR40337.005	Mar 76	1 PNT	
Nu	Spont		SRL	Expt	Jour PR/C 2 763	Aug 70	Thompson.AVG NU=3.20+-0.22 REL CF252	+
	Spont				Data EXFOR10358.002	Jul 74	. 1 PT.	
Nu	Spont		FEI	Expt	Jour AE 33 767	Sep 72	Prokhorova+ NUBAR TBL,CFD OTHERS	+
					Jour SJA 33 875	Mar 73	. ENGL OF AE 33 767	
	Spont				Data EXFOR40140.003	Mar 73	NU-BAR REL CF252	
Nu	Spont		IAE	Eval	Jour REA 10 637	Dec 72	Manero+ EXTENSIVE SURVEY,TBL,AVG VAL	
Nu	Spont		CCP	Expt	Jour AE 34 135	Feb 73	Golushko+ REL TO CF252,TBL,CFD OTHER	
					Jour SJA 34 178	Aug 73	.ENGLISH OF AE 34 135	
Nu	Spont		ORL	Expt	Jour NSE 50 169	Feb 73	Stoughton+.NU=2.86+-0.06 REL CF252	+
	Spont				Data EXFOR10605.002	Nov 76	. 1 PT.	
Nu	2.5-2		NIR	Expt	Conf 73Kiev 4 57	May 73	Zhuravlev+	+
	2.5-2				Data EXFOR40297.010	May 75	.DATA GVN	
Nu	Spont		DUB	Expt	Jour YF 18 724	Oct 73	Dakovsky+ REL CM244,NUBAR+P(NU),TBL	+
					Rept JINR-P15-7119	Jun 73	Dakowski+ REL CM244,NUBAR+P(NU),TBL	
					Jour SNP 18 371	Apr 74	. ENGLISH OF YF 18,724.	
	Spont				Data EXFOR40203.003	Mar 74	.1 DATA LINE	
Nu	Spont		DUB	Comp	Jour YF 18 724	Oct 73	Dakovsky+NUBAR VS FISNUCLEUS,TBL+GRP	
					Jour SNP 18 371	Apr 74	. ENGLISH OF YF 18, 724.	
Nu	Spont		NIR	Expt	Rept YFI-18 45	Aug 74	Golushko+ NUBAR GVN IN TBL,CFD	+
					Jour AE 34 135	Feb 73	- + REL CF252,TBL,CFD OTHER	
					Rept INDC(CCP)-49	Feb 75	- + (REL CF252).ENGL OF YFI-18	
					Jour SJA 34 178	Aug 73	. ENGL OF AE 34 135	
	Spont				Data EXFOR40260.003	Feb 75	1 DATA LINE, CFD VALUES GIVEN	
Nu	Spont		HED	Eval	Abst ANS 22 673	Nov 75	Johnson. TBL,GRPH.NU FROM SPON FISS	
Nu	Spont		KUR	Expt	Rept YK-23 3	76	Khokhlov+ NUBAR,TABLES	
					Conf 75Kiev 5 86	May 75	- + NUBAR,CFD OTH WORKS.TABLE	+
Spect Fiss n	2.5-2		NIR	Expt	Conf 73Kiev 4 57	May 73	Zhuravlev+	
	2.5-2				Data EXFOR40297.004	May 75	.DATA GVN	
Fiss Yield	Spont		ORL	Expt	Jour PR/C 8 1018	Sep 73	Pleasonton+. FRAG MASS DISTRIBUTIONS	
					Prog USNDC-9 150	Dec 73	- +. FRAG MASS DIST MEASD.	

96 Curium 246

Quantity	Energy (ev) Min	Max	Lab	Type	Documentation Ref Vol Page	Date	Author, Comments	Data
Fiss Yield	Spont		ANL Expt	Prog	USNDC-9 30	Dec 73	Unik+. CURVE OF FRAG MASS DIST GIVEN	
				Conf	73Rochestr 2 19	Aug 73	- + PROMPT YLDS,MASS DISTRIB,GRPH	
Fiss Yield	Spont		AUA Revw	Conf	IAEA-169 2 163	74	Musgrove+ PROMPT,EVEN-Z POSITN,GRAPH	
Fiss Yield	Spont		AUA Theo	Rept	AAEC/E-386	Mar 76	Cook+ 3-GAUSS FIT,PARAMS GIVEN	
Fiss Yield	Spont		TRM Theo	Rept	INIS-MF-3797	77	Chakraborthy+ O-D-MOD.ISOTOP YLD,FIG	
Frag Spectra	Spont		ANL Expt	Conf	73Rochestr 2 19	Aug 73	Unik+ TOTAL KIN-E OF FRAGS,GRPH,TBL	
Frag Spectra	Spont		ORL Expt	Jour	PR/C 8 1018	Sep 73	Pleasonton+. FRAG MASS+KE DISTRIBUTS	
				Prog	USNDC-9 150	Dec 73	- +. MASS+KE DISTR MEASD.	
				Prog	USNDC-7 166	Jun 73	.SUPERSEDED	
				Prog	ORNL-4844 107	Apr 73	Pleasonton+SUPERSEDED	
Frag Spectra	Spont		AUA Revw	Conf	IAEA-169 2 163	74	Musgrove+ AVG FRAG MASS,GRAPH	
Reson Params	4.3+0	8.5+1	ANL Expt	Jour	PR/B 134 1281	Jun 64	Cote.FC.3RES SURE,2Q.WNFOR 3,WG=35MV	+
	4.3+0	8.5+1		Data	EXFOR12570.006	Jun 76	. 5 RES E0,WG,WN,WT, AND TOT PCS.	
Reson Params	None		DUB Theo	Jour	YF 13 240	Feb 71	Malecki+G-WID,THEO CFD EXPT.TBL,GRPH	
				Jour	SNP 13 133	Aug 71	- + ENGL OF YF 13 240.	
Reson Params	6.2-1	5.0+4	SRL Theo	Conf	71Knoxvill 714	Mar 71	Mccrosson. STAT CALCULATN AVG PARAMS	
Reson Params	8.4+1	3.8+2	LAS Expt	Jour	PR/C 3 1656	Apr 71	Moore+.NUCL SHOT.PARAMS FOR 9 RESON	+
				Conf	70Helsinki 1 527	Jun 70	.SUPERSEDED	
	8.4+1	3.8+2		Data	EXFOR10121.	Nov 74	. 30 PTS. WN,WG,WF	
Reson Params	4.3+0	1.5+1	MTR Expt	Jour	NSE 49 145	Oct 72	Berreth+. TRANS. WN WG FOR 2 RESON	+
	4.3+0	1.5+1		Data	EXFOR10271.007	Nov 74	. 2 RES. WN0.	
Reson Params	4.3+0	1.6+2	ORL Expt	Jour	NSE 55 440	Nov 74	Benjamin+ ORELA,TOF, IMPURITY CM-248	+
	4.3+0	1.6+2		Data	EXFOR10461.	Aug 75	. 5 RES. WN0,1 RES,WG	
Strnth Fnctn		8.5+1	ANL Expt	Jour	PR/B 134 1281	Jun 64	Cote.FC.S=.5+.57,-.16, L=0 ONLY	+
		8.5+1		Data	EXFOR12570.007	Jun 76	. 1 PT. STF.	
Strnth Fnctn	2.6+6	4.1+6	AI Theo	Rept	NAA-SR-M-12538	Oct 67	Gigas.OPTMDL CALC AVG S0,S1,S2	
Strnth Fnctn	8.4+1	3.8+2	LAS Expt	Jour	PR/C 3 1656	Apr 71	Moore+DRVD FROM RESOLVED RESONS.	+
	8.4+1	3.8+2		Data	EXFOR10121.	Nov 74	. 2 PTS, SO, D	
Strnth Fnctn	4.3+0	1.0+2	ITE Expt	Conf	75Kiev	May 75	Kalebin+	
Strnth Fnctn	None		NIR Expt	Conf	76Lowell 1255	Jul 76	Belanova+TRNS.STF CALC.NDG	
Lvl Density	None		MUN Theo	Jour	NP/A 217 269	Dec 73	Dilg+ A,DELTA. BACK SHIFTED FERMIGAS	
Lvl Density	None		COP Theo	Jour	NP/A 222 493	Apr 74	Dossing+COLL ROTAT.SPAC. ACCUR ESTIM	
Lvl Density	None		ROC Theo	Jour	NP/A 223 589	May 74	Huizenga+ EXP CFD MICROSC TH AX SYMM	
Lvl Density	+6		DUB Theo	Rept	JINR-E4-9236	Nov 75	Komov+ AVG LVL-SPAC,SEMIMICRO CFD XP	

96 Curium 247

Quantity	Energy (ev) Min	Max	Lab	Type	Documentation Ref Vol Page	Date	Author, Comments	Data
Evaluation	1.0-5	2.0+7	SRL Eval	Rept	EPRI-NP-161	Dec 75	Benjamin+ENDF4B.REVISIONS.	
Absorption	Pile		SRL Expt	Conf	68Wash. 1285	Mar 68	Smith+ SIG=457B THERMALIZED SPEC	+
				Rept	DP-MS-67-111	Feb 68	- + SRL IRRADIATION.	
	Pile			Data	EXFOR12580.006	Jun 76	. 1 PT. SIGMA.	
Absorption	Pile		SRL Expt	Abst	ANS 14 344	Jun 71	Rusche. VALUE GIVEN	
Res Int Abs	None		SRL Expt	Abst	ANS 14 344	Jun 71	Rusche. VALUE GIVEN	
(n,γ)	Pile		BRK Expt	Priv	SEABORG	Jun 55	Seaborg+ (TO J.R.HUIZENGA)ACTIVATION	+
	Pile			Data	EXFOR12554.004	Jun 76	. 1 PT. SIGMA.	
(n,γ)	Pile		ANL Revw	Conf	55Geneva 7 261	Aug 55	Bentley+.P809,VAL GVN,CHEMICAL METHD	
(n,γ)	None		KAP Comp	Rept	KAPL-1781	Jul 57	Schuman. SIGMA GIVEN	
(n,γ)	Maxwl		SRL Expt	Rept	DP-MS-66-69	Oct 66	ICE. HIGHLY THERMAL SPECTRUM.	+
	Maxwl			Data	EXFOR12550.011	Jun 76	. 1 PT. SIGMA.	
(n,γ)	Maxwl		BNL Theo	Abst	ANS 10 228	Jun 67	Prince. CALCULATED SIG=180B.	
(n,γ)	Maxwl		CCP Comp	Jour	AE 28 388	May 70	Bol'Shov+ OTHER'S SIG VALUE GIVEN	
				Jour	EAF 28 5 9	70	. FRENCH OF AE 28 388.	
(n,γ)	Pile		KFK Eval	Prog	KFK-1544 61	Jan 72	Eberle+FOR 2-GROUP SIG,FITTED TO EXP	
(n,γ)	Pile		SRL Eval	Conf	75Wash. 224	Mar 75	Benjamin+ TBL BEST FIT TRANSPU PROD.	
(n,γ)	None		ORL Expt	Prog	ORNL-5101 11	Jan 76	Weston.NDG.TBD	
Res Int Capt	Maxwl		BNL Theo	Abst	ANS 10 228	Jun 67	Prince. CALCULATED RES INTGRL=200B.	
Res Int Capt	Pile		KFK Eval	Prog	KFK-1544 61	Jan 72	Eberle+ 800B	
Res Int Capt	6.3-1		SRL Eval	Conf	75Wash. 224	Mar 75	Benjamin+ TBL BEST FIT TRANSPU PROD.	
Fission	Maxwl		SRL Expt	Rept	DP-MS-66-69	Oct 66	ICE. HIGHLY THERMAL SPECTRUM.	+
	Maxwl			Data	EXFOR12550.010	Jun 76	. 1 PT. SIGMA.	
Fission	Maxwl		BNL Theo	Abst	ANS 10 228	Jun 67	Prince. CALCULATED SIG=1026B.	
Fission	Pile		SRL Expt	Conf	68Wash. 1285	Mar 68	Smith+ SIG=409B THERMALIZED SPEC	+
				Rept	DP-MS-67-111	Feb 68	- + SRL IRRADIATION.	
	Pile			Data	EXFOR12580.007	Jun 76	. 1 PT. SIGMA	
Fission	Maxwl		ANL Expt	Jour	JIN 30 2553	Oct 68	Diamond+,ION CHAMB IN THR COLUMN	+
	Maxwl			Data	EXFOR12531.004	Jun 76	. 1 PT. SIGMA.	

96 Curium 247

Quantity	Energy (ev) Min	Max	Lab	Type	Documentation Ref Vol Page	Author, Comments Date	Data
Fission	Maxwl		CCP	Comp	Jour AE 28 388	May 70 Bol'Shov+ OTHER'S SIG VALUE GIVEN	
					Jour EAF 28 5 9	70 . FRENCH OF AE 28 388.	
Fission	Maxwl		ORL	Expt	Prog ORNL-4581 37	Sep 70 Halperin+. FISSION TRACK COUNTING	+
	Maxwl				Data EXFOR10165.004	Jan 73 . 1 PT. SIGMA	
Fission	2.0+1	1.9+6	LAS	Expt	Jour PR/C 3 1656	Apr 71 Moore+. NUCLEAR SHOT. CURVES	+
					Rept LA-4566	Apr 71 Baybarz+ POINT DATA	
					Conf 70Helsinki 1 527	Jun 70 .SUPERSEDED	
	2.0+1	1.9+6			Data EXFOR10121.030	Nov 74 .4296 PTS.SIGMA.	
Fission	Pile		SRL	Expt	Jour JIN 33 1553	Jul 71 Thompson+ CD CUT-OFF	
Fission	1.0-2	1.4+7	LRL	Expt	Prog NCSAC-42 135	Nov 71 Browne+. TO BE DONE.	
Fission	Pile		KFK	Eval	Prog KFK-1544 61	Jan 72 Eberle+FOR 2-GROUP SIG,FITTED TO EXP	
Fission	Maxwl		SRL	Expt	Jour NSE 47 203	Feb 72 Benjamin+FISS CHS,FISS TRACK MEAS.	+
					Conf 71Knoxvill 843	Mar 71 .SUPERSEDED	
	Maxwl				Data EXFOR10128.008	Feb 73 . 1 PT.CS=82+-5B.REL U235.	
Fission	-		GEL	ExTh	Jour NP/A 187 305	Jun 72 Weigmann+ F.B.PARAMS FROM DATA ANAL.	
Fission	+0	+7	KUR	Expt	Jour YF 17 24	Jan 73 Fomushkin+ SIG GIVEN,TABLE	+
					Jour SNP 17 12	Jul 73 . ENGL OF YF 17 24	
	1.0+7				Data EXFOR40150.005	May 74 .NF SIG SPECT AVER AND RATIO TO U235	
Fission	Pile		SRL	Eval	Conf 75Wash. 224	Mar 75 Benjamin+ TBL BEST FIT TRANSPU PROD.	
Fission	2.5-2		NIR	Expt	Jour AE 39 285	Oct 75 Zhuravlev+ SIG GIVEN,BY CD-DIFFERENC	+
					Rept YK-19 3	May 75 - + CD-DIFFERENCE, SIG GIVEN	
					Jour SJA 39 907	Apr 76 . ENGL OF AE 39 285	
	2.5-2				Data EXFOR40339.006	Mar 76 1 PNT	
Res Int Fiss	Maxwl		BNL	Theo	Abst ANS 10 228	Jun 67 Prince. CALCULATED RES INTGRL=492B.	
Res Int Fiss	5.4-1		ORL	Expt	Prog ORNL-4581 37	Sep 70 Halperin+. FISSION TRACK COUNTING	+
	5.4-1				Data EXFOR10165.005	Jan 73 . 1 PT. RI.	
Res Int Fiss	5.0-1		SRL	Expt	Jour JIN 33 1553	Jul 71 Thompson+ CD CUT-OFF	
Res Int Fiss	Pile		KFK	Eval	Prog KFK-1544 61	Jan 72 Eberle+ 1060B	
Res Int Fiss	6.3-1		SRL	Expt	Jour NSE 47 203	Feb 72 Benjamin+CD COVER.MASS SPEC.	+
					Conf 71Knoxvill 843	Mar 71 .SUPERSEDED.	
	6.3-1				Data EXFOR10128.009	Feb 73 . 1 PT.RIF=778+-50B, REL U235.	
Res Int Fiss	6.3-1		SRL	Eval	Conf 75Wash. 224	Mar 75 Benjamin+ TBL BEST FIT TRANSPU PROD.	
Res Int Fiss	5.0-1		NIR	Expt	Jour AE 39 285	Oct 75 Zhuravlev+ RI GIVEN,BY CD-DIFFERENCE	+
					Rept YK-19 3	May 75 - +CD-DIFFERENCE,RES-INT GVN	
					Jour SJA 39 907	Apr 76 . ENGL OF AE 39 285	
	5.0-1				Data EXFOR40337.006	Mar 76 1 PNT	
Alpha	1.0+4	2.0+4	LAS	Theo	Jour PR 158 1127	Jun 67 Bell. SYSTEMATCS TH FOR 10-20KEV ALF	
Nu	Maxwl		IAE	Eval	Jour REA 10 637	Dec 72 Manero+ CALC,SYSTEMATICS,TBL	
Nu	2.5-2		NIR	Expt	Conf 73Kiev 4 57	May 73 Zhuravlev+	+
	2.5-2				Data EXFOR40297.013	May 75 .DATA GVN	
Spect Fiss n	2.5-2		NIR	Expt	Conf 73Kiev 4 57	May 73 Zhuravlev+	+
	2.5-2				Data EXFOR40297.007	May 75 .DATA GVN	
Reson Params	6.2-1		SRL	Expt	Conf 71Knoxvill 714	Mar 71 Mccrosson. STAT CALCULATN AVG PARAMS	
Reson Params	2.1+1	5.0+4	LAS	Expt	Jour PR/C 3 1656	Apr 71 Moore+.NUCL SHOT.PARAMS FOR 29 RESON	+
					Conf 70Helsinki 1 527	Jun 70 .SUPERSEDED	
	2.1+1	6.0+1			Data EXFOR10121.	Nov 74 . 31 PTS.WN,WG,WF,	
Reson Params	2.1+1	6.0+1	ORL	Theo	Jour NSE 52 412	Nov 73 De Saussure+.1-LVL PARS FROM MULTLVL	
Strnth Fnctn	2.1+1	6.0+1	LAS	Expt	Jour PR/C 3 1656	Apr 71 Moore+.DRVD FROM RESOLVED RESONS.	+
	2.1+1	6.0+1			Data EXFOR10121.	Nov 74 . 2 PTS, S0, D	
Lvl Density	None		MUN	Theo	Jour NP/A 217 269	Dec 73 Dilg+ A,DELTA. BACK SHIFTED FERMIGAS	
Lvl Density	None		COP	Theo	Jour NP/A 222 493	Apr 74 Dossing+COLL ROTAT.SPAC. ACCUR ESTIM	
Lvl Density	None		ROC	Theo	Jour NP/A 223 589	May 74 Huizenga+ EXP CFD MICROSC TH AX SYMM	
Lvl Density	+6		DUB	Theo	Rept JINR-E4-9236	Nov 75 Komov+ AVG LVL-SPAC,SEMIMICRO CFD XP	

96 Curium 248

Quantity	Energy (ev) Min	Max	Lab	Type	Documentation Ref Vol Page	Author, Comments Date	Data
Total	5.0-1	3.0+3	ORL	Expt	Jour NSE 55 440	Nov 74 Benjamin+ ORELA,TOF	
Total	None		NIR	Expt	Conf 76Lowell 1255	Jul 76 Belanova+TRNS.RES PARS DRVD.NDG	
Absorption	Pile		SRL	Expt	Conf 68Wash. 1285	Mar 68 Smith+ AVG SIG=5.4B THERMALIZED SPEC	+
					Rept DP-MS-67-111	Feb 68 - + SRL IRRADIATION.	
	Pile				Data EXFOR12580.008	Jun 76 . 1 PT. SIGMA.	
Absorption	Pile		SRL	Expt	Abst ANS 14 344	Jun 71 Rusche. VALUE GIVEN	
Res Int Abs	None		SRL	Expt	Abst ANS 14 344	Jun 71 Rusche. VALUE GIVEN	
(n,γ)	Pile		BRK	Expt	Priv SEABORG	Jun 55 Seaborg.(TO J.R.HUIZENGA)ACTIVATION	+
	Pile				Data EXFOR12557.003	Jun 76 . 1 PT. SIGMA.	
(n,γ)	Pile		ANL	Revw	Conf 55Geneva 7 261	Aug 55 Bentley+.P809,VAL GVN,CHEMICAL METHD	

96 Curium 248

Quantity	Energy (ev) Min	Energy (ev) Max	Lab	Type	Documentation Ref Vol Page	Date	Author, Comments	Data
(n,γ)	Pile		CRC	Expt Jour	JIN 6 261	Jun 58	Eastwood+ MTR IRRADIATION ABOUT 6B.	
(n,γ)	Maxwl		ORL	Expt Prog	ORNL-3832 1	Sep 65	Halperin+. VALUE GIVEN.	
(n,γ)	Maxwl		BNL	Theo Abst	ANS 10 228	Jun 67	Prince. CALCULATED SIG=6B.	
(n,γ)	Maxwl		CCP	Comp Jour	AE 28 388	May 70	Bol'Shov+ OTHER'S SIG VALUE GIVEN	
				Jour	EAF 28 5 9	70	. FRENCH OF AE 28 388.	
(n,γ)	2.5+1	1.0+2	LAS	Expt Jour	PR/C 3 1656	Apr 71	Moore+. NUCLEAR SHOT. CURVES	+
				Rept	LA- 4566	Apr 71	Baybarz+ POINT DATA	
	2.5+1	1.0+2		Data	EXFOR10121.034	Nov 74	. 119 PTS. SIGMA	
(n,γ)	Pile		KFK	Eval Prog	KFK-1544 61	Jan 72	Eberle+FOR 2-GROUP SIG,FITTED TO EXP	
(n,γ)	Maxwl		ORL	Expt Prog	ORNL-4891 23	Sep 73	Druschel+. VALUE GIVEN.	
(n,γ)	2.5-2		ORL	Expt Abst	BAP 19 599	Apr 74	Harvey+.ORELA.RESON CONTRIB TO SIG	
(n,γ)	Pile		SRL	Eval Conf	75Wash. 224	Mar 75	Benjamin+ TBL BEST FIT TRANSPU PROD.	
Res Int Capt	5.0-1		ORL	Expt Prog	ORNL-3832 1	Sep 65	Halperin+. VALUE GIVEN.	
Res Int Capt	Maxwl		BNL	Theo Abst	ANS 10 228	Jun 67	Prince. CALCULATED RES INTGRL=600B.	
Res Int Capt	Pile		KFK	Eval Prog	KFK-1544 61	Jan 72	Eberle+275B	
Res Int Capt	5.0-1		ORL	Expt Prog	ORNL-4891 23	Sep 73	Druschel+. VALUE GIVEN.	
Res Int Capt	5.0-1	3.0+3	ORL	Expt Abst	BAP 19 599	Apr 74	Harvey+.ORELA. RI=262B.	
Res Int Capt	6.3-1		SRL	Eval Conf	75Wash. 224	Mar 75	Benjamin+ TBL BEST FIT TRANSPU PROD.	
Res Int Capt	5.0-1		ITE	Expt Conf	IAEA-186 2 121	76	Kalebin. CALC FROM RESPARS,CFD.TABLE	
Fission	Spont		BRK	Revw Jour	NP 81 1	Jun 66	Myers.TBL CALC FISS BARRIERS.	
Fission	Maxwl		BNL	Theo Abst	ANS 10 228	Jun 67	Prince. CALCULATED SIG=.0045B.	
Fission	Spont		COP	Revw Conf	69Vienna 155	Jul 69	Strutinsky+PPR203. HL GVN,'SHELL-TH'	
Fission	1.0+6	1.5+7	LAS	Expt Prog	NCSAC-33 148	Dec 70	Barton+,TO BE COMPLETED,NO DATA GIVN	
Fission	Spont		MRY	Theo Prog	ORO-4028-28	71	Jackson+. SPON FISSION HALF-LIFE GVN	
Fission	2.0+1	2.8+6	LAS	Expt Jour	PR/C 3 1656	Apr 71	Moore+. NUCLEAR SHOT. CURVES	+
				Rept	LA- 4566	Apr 71	Baybarz+ POINT DATA	
				Conf	70Helsinki 1 527	Jun 70	.SUPERSEDED	
	2.0+1	2.8+6		Data	EXFOR10121.031	Nov 74	.2795 PTS. SIGMA	
Fission	Pile		SRL	Expt Jour	JIN 33 1553	Jul 71	Thompson+ CD CUT-OFF	
Fission	Maxwl		SRL	Expt Jour	NSE 47 203	Feb 72	Benjamin+FISS CHS,FISS TRACK MEAS.	+
				Conf	71Knoxvill 843	Mar 71	.SUPERSEDED	
	Maxwl			Data	EXFOR10128.010	Feb 73	. 1 PT.CS=.34+-.7B, REL U235.	
Fission	+0	+7	KUR	Expt Jour	YF 17 24	Jan 73	Fomushkin+ SIG GIVEN,TABLE	+
				Jour	SNP 17 12	Jul 73	. ENGL OF YF 17 24	
	1.0+7			Data	EXFOR40150.006	May 74	.NF SIG SPECT AVER AND RATIO TO U235	
Fission	Pile		SRL	Eval Conf	75Wash. 224	Mar 75	Benjamin+ TBL BEST FIT TRANSPU PROD.	
Fission	2.5-2		NIR	Expt Jour	AE 39 285	Oct 75	Zhuravlev+ SIG GIVEN,BY CD-DIFFERENC	+
				Rept	YK- 19 3	May 75	- + CD-DIFFERENCE, SIG GIVEN	
				Jour	SJA 39 907	Apr 76	. ENGL OF AE 39 285	
	2.5-2			Data	EXFOR40339.007	Mar 76	1 PNT	
Res Int Fiss	Maxwl		BNL	Theo Abst	ANS 10 228	Jun 67	Prince. CALCULATED RES INTGRL=0.2B.	
Res Int Fiss	5.0-1		SRL	Expt Jour	JIN 33 1553	Jul 71	Thompson+ CD CUT-OFF	
	None			Abst	ANS 14 344	Jun 71	Rusche. VALUE GIVEN	
Res Int Fiss	6.3-1		SRL	Expt Jour	NSE 47 203	Feb 72	Benjamin+CD COVER.MASS SPEC.	+
				Conf	71Knoxvill 843	Mar 71	.SUPERSEDED.	
	6.3-1			Data	EXFOR10128.011	Feb 73	. 1 PT. RIF=13.2+-.8 REL U235.	
Res Int Fiss	6.3-1		SRL	Eval Conf	75Wash. 224	Mar 75	Benjamin+ TBL BEST FIT TRANSPU PROD.	
Res Int Fiss	5.0-1		NIR	Expt Jour	AE 39 285	Oct 75	Zhuravlev+ RI GIVEN,BY CD-DIFFERENCE	+
				Rept	YK- 19 3	May 75	. + CD-DIFFERENCE,RES-INT GVN	
				Jour	SJA 39 907	Apr 76	. ENGL OF AE 39 285	
	5.0-1			Data	EXFOR40337.007	Mar 76	1 PNT	
Nu	Spont		LAS	Expt Jour	NSE 43 54	Jan 71	Orth.SEPARATE COUNT OF NS+ SPON FISS	+
	Spont			Data	EXFOR10115.003	Jul 71	. 1 PT. AVG NU=3.11+-.09 REL CF252.	
Nu	Spont		FEI	Expt Jour	AE 33 767	Sep 72	Prokhorova+ NUBAR TBL,CFD OTHERS	+
				Jour	SJA 33 875	Mar 73	. ENGL OF AE 33 767	
	Spont			Data	EXFOR40140.004	Mar 73	NU-BAR REL CF252	
Nu	Spont		IAE	Eval Jour	REA 10 637	Dec 72	Manero+ EXTENSIVE SURVEY,TBL,AVG VAL	
Nu	Spont		CCP	Expt Jour	AE 34 135	Feb 73	Golushko+ REL TO CF252,TBL,CFD OTHER	
				Jour	SJA 34 178	Aug 73	.ENGLISH OF AE 34 135	
Nu	Spont		ORL	Expt Jour	NSE 50 169	Feb 73	Stoughton+.NU=3.14+-0.06 REL CF252	+
	Spont			Data	EXFOR10605.003	Nov 76	. 1 PT.	
Nu	Spont		AUA	Expt Conf	73Kiev 4 114	May 73	Boldeman. NUBAR+P(NU) REL CF252.TABL	+
	Spont			Data	EXFOR30367.002	Jan 77	NU-BAR PROMPT.	
Nu	2.5-2		NIR	Expt Conf	73Kiev 4 57	May 73	Zhuravlev+	+
	2.5-2			Data	EXFOR40297.012	May 75	.DATA GVN	

96 Curium 248

Quantity	Energy (ev) Min	Max	Lab	Type	Documentation Ref Vol Page	Author, Comments Date	Data
Nu	Spont		NIR	Expt	Rept YFI-18 45	Aug 74 Golushko+ NUBAR GVN IN TBL,CFD	+
					Jour AE 34 135	Feb 73 - + REL CF252,TBL,CFD OTHER	
					Rept INDC(CCP)-49	Feb 75 - + (REL CF252).ENGL OF YFI-18	
					Jour SJA 34 178	Aug 73 . ENGL OF AE 34 135	
	Spont				Data EXFOR40260.004	Feb 75 1 DATA LINE, CFD VALUES GIVEN	
Nu	Spont		KUR	Expt	Rept YK- 23 3	76 Khokhlov+ NUBAR,TABLES	
					Conf 75Kiev 5 86	May 75 - + NUBAR,CFD OTH WORKS.TABLE	
Spect Fiss n	2.5-2		NIR	Expt	Conf 73Kiev 4 57	May 73 Zhuravlev+	+
	2.5-2				Data EXFOR40297.006	May 75 .DATA GVN	
Fiss Prod γ	Spont		NIL	Expt	Prog INDC(SEC)-50	Jan 76 . ABST. CORREL TO FRGM-E,TBD,NDG	
Fiss Yield	Spont		LRL	Expt	Jour PR 131 2617	Sep 63 Brandt+ MASS DISTRIBUTION REL CF252	
Fiss Yield	Spont		OSL	Revw	Conf 69Vienna 669	Jul 69 Pappas+ PPR206.REVW,INITIAL MASS DIST	
Fiss Yield	Spont		ANL	Expt	Conf 73Rochestr 2 19	Aug 73 Unik+ PROMPT YLDS,MASS DISTRIB,GRPHS	
Fiss Yield	Spont		AUA	Revw	Conf IAEA-169 2 163	74 Musgrove+ PROMPT,EVEN-Z POSITN,GRAPH	
Fiss Yield	Spont		NIL	Expt	Prog INDC(SEC)-50	Jan 76 . ABST. CORREL TO FRG-GAMS,TBD,NDG	
Fiss Yield	Spont		AUA	Theo	Rept AAEC/E-386	Mar 76 Cook+ 3-GAUSS FIT,PARAMS GIVEN	
Frag Spectra	Spont		LRL	Expt	Jour PR 131 2617	Sep 63 Brandt+ E DIST REL CF252 CURVES	
Frag Spectra	Spont		ANL	Expt	Conf 73Rochestr 2 19	Aug 73 Unik+ TOTAL KIN-E OF FRAGS,GRPH	
Frag Spectra	Spont		AUA	Revw	Conf IAEA-169 2 163	74 Musgrove+ AVG FRAG MASS,GRAPH	
Frag Spectra	Spont		NIL	Expt	Prog INDC(SEC)-42	Dec 74 . CORREL E-KIN,E-GAM OF FRGMS.TBD	
Reson Params	6.2-1	5.0+4	SRL	Theo	Conf 71Knoxvill 714	Mar 71 Mccrosson. STAT CALCULATN AVG PARAMS	
Reson Params	2.7+1	4.2+2	LAS	Expt	Jour PR/C 3 1656	Apr 71 Moore+.NUCL SHOT.PARAMS FOR 8 RESON	+
					Conf 70Helsinki 1 527	Jun 70 .SUPERSEDED	
	2.7+1	4.2+2			Data EXFOR10121.	Nov 74 . 19 PTS. WG,WF,	
Reson Params	7.2+0	3.0+3	ORL	Expt	Jour NSE 55 440	Nov 74 Benjamin+ ORELA,TOF	+
	7.2+0	3.0+3			Data EXFOR10461.	Aug 75 . 47 RES,WN0,3 RES WG.	
Strnth Fnctn	2.7+1	4.2+2	LAS	Expt	Jour PR/C 3 1656	Apr 71 Moore+DRVD FROM RESOLVED RESONS.	+
	2.7+1	4.2+2			Data EXFOR10121.026	Nov 74 . 1 PT. D	
Strnth Fnctn	5.0-1	3.0+3	ORL	Expt	Jour NSE 55 440	Nov 74 Benjamin+ S0=1.2+-.2	
Strnth Fnctn	7.3+0	1.0+2	ITE	Expt	Conf 75Kiev	May 75 Kalebin+	
Strnth Fnctn	None		NIR	Expt	Conf 76Lowell 1255	Jul 76 Belanova+TRNS.STF CALC.NDG.	
Lvl Density	None		COP	Theo	Jour NP/A 222 493	Apr 74 Dossing+COLL ROTAT.SPAC. ACCUR ESTIM	
Lvl Density	+6		DUB	Theo	Rept JINR-E4-9236	Nov 75 Komov+ AVG LVL-SPAC,SEMIMICRO CFD XP	

96 Curium 249

Quantity	Energy (ev) Min	Max	Lab	Type	Documentation Ref Vol Page	Author, Comments Date	Data
(n,γ)	Pile		ANL	Expt	Rept ANL-7330	May 67 Diamond+ HI-FLUX PILE ACT,EST S=1.6B	+
	Pile				Data EXFOR12555.002	Jun 76 . 1 PT. SIGMA	
(n,γ)	Maxwl		CCP	Theo	Jour AE 28 388	May 70 Bol'Shov+ SIGMA VALUE ESTIMATED, TBL	
					Jour EAF 28 5 9	70 . FRENCH OF AE 28 388.	
(n,γ)	Pile		KFK	Eval	Prog KFK-1544 61	Jan 72 Eberle+FOR 2-GROUP SIG,FITTED TO EXP	
Fission	Maxwl		CCP	Theo	Jour AE 28 388	May 70 Bol'Shov+ SIGMA VALUE ESTIMATED, TBL	
					Jour EAF 28 5 9	70 . FRENCH OF AE 28 388.	
Fission	Pile		KFK	Eval	Prog KFK-1544 61	Jan 72 Eberle+FOR 2-GROUP SIG,FITTED TO EXP	
Alpha	1.0+4	2.0+4	LAS	Theo	Jour PR 158 1127	Jun 67 Bell. SYSTEMATCS TH FOR 10-20KEV ALF	
Nu	Maxwl		IAE	Eval	Jour REA 10 637	Dec 72 Manero+ CALC,SYSTEMATICS,TBL	
Fiss Yield	2.5-2	1.4+7	LAS	Eval	Rept LA-6430	Jul 76 Madland+PAIR EFFECT ON INDEP YLD.TBL	
Lvl Density	None		MUN	Theo	Jour NP/A 217 269	Dec 73 Dilg+ A,DELTA. BACK SHIFTED FERMIGAS	
Lvl Density	None		COP	Theo	Jour NP/A 222 493	Apr 74 Dossing+COLL ROTAT.SPAC. ACCUR ESTIM	
Lvl Density	None		ROC	Theo	Jour NP/A 223 589	May 74 Huizenga+ EXP CFD MICROSC TH AX SYMM	

96 Curium 250

Quantity	Energy (ev) Min	Max	Lab	Type	Documentation Ref Vol Page	Author, Comments Date	Data
(n,γ)	Maxwl		SRL	Expt	Rept DP-MS-66-69	Oct 66 ICE. HIGHLY THERMAL SPECTRUM.	+
	Maxwl				Data EXFOR12550.012	Jun 76 . 1 PT. SIGMA.	
(n,γ)	Maxwl		CCP	Theo	Jour AE 28 388	May 70 Bol'Shov+ SIGMA VALUE ESTIMATED, TBL	
					Jour EAF 28 5 9	70 . FRENCH OF AE 28 388.	
Fission	Spont		DUB	Theo	Rept JINR-P-2265	Jul 65 Mekhedov. FISS+ALPH HLS ESTIMATED	
Fission	Spont		COP	Revw	Conf 69Vienna 155	Jul 69 Strutinsky+PPR203. HL GVN,'SHELL-TH'	
Fission	Spont		MRY	Theo	Prog ORO-4028-28	71 Jackson+. SPON FISSION HALF-LIFE GVN	
Fission	2.5-2		JUL	Theo	Jour ZP 257 389	Dec 72 Mcminn. 2.88 E -3 BARNS	
Nu	Spont		LAS	Expt	Jour NSE 43 54	Jan 71 Orth+SEPARATE COUNT OF NS+ SPON FISS	+
	Spont				Data EXFOR10115.004	Jul 71 . 1 PT. AVG NU=3.31+-.08 REL CF 252.	
Nu	Spont		IAE	Eval	Jour REA 10 637	Dec 72 Manero+ EXTENSIVE SURVEY,TBL,AVG VAL	

96 Curium 250

Quantity	Energy (ev) Min Max	Lab	Type	Documentation Ref Vol Page	Author, Comments Date	Data
Fiss Prod γ	Spont	ANL	Expt Jour	PR 107 1087	Aug 57 Huizenga+,HALFLIFE,LEAST−SQRSFIT	
Fiss Yield	Spont	LAS	Expt Jour	PR/C 7 276	Jan 73 Hoffman+. MASS−YLD CURV FROM FRG KE	
Fiss Yield	Spont	NEU	Theo Jour	HPA 46 724	Jul 73 Hooshyar+ MASS A.CHARGE DISTR, HL	
Frag Spectra	Spont	LAS	Expt Jour	PR/C 7 276	Jan 73 Hoffman+.KEDISTR. SI DETECTOR	

96 Curium 251

Quantity	Energy (ev) Min Max	Lab	Type	Documentation Ref Vol Page	Author, Comments Date	Data
(n,γ)	Maxwl	SRL	Expt Rept	DP−MS−66−69	Oct 66 ICE. HIGHLY THERMAL SPECTRUM.	+
	Maxwl		Data	EXFOR12550.014	Jun 76 . 1 PT. SIGMA.	
(n,γ)	Maxwl	CCP	Theo Jour	AE 28 388	May 70 Bol'Shov+ SIGMA VALUE ESTIMATED, TBL	
			Jour	EAF 28 5 9	70 . FRENCH OF AE 28 388.	
Fission	Maxwl	SRL	Expt Rept	DP−MS−66−69	Oct 66 ICE. HIGHLY THERMAL SPECTRUM.	+
	Maxwl		Data	EXFOR12550.013	Jun 76 . 1 PT. SIGMA.	
Fission	Maxwl	CCP	Theo Jour	AE 28 388	May 70 Bol'Shov+ SIGMA VALUE ESTIMATED, TBL	
			Jour	EAF 28 5 9	70 . FRENCH OF AE 28 388.	
Alpha	1.0+4 2.0+4	LAS	Theo Jour	PR 158 1127	Jun 67 Bell. SYSTEMATCS TH FOR 10−20KEV ALF	

96 Curium 252

Quantity	Energy (ev) Min Max	Lab	Type	Documentation Ref Vol Page	Author, Comments Date	Data
(n,γ)	Maxwl	CCP	Theo Jour	AE 28 388	May 70 Bol'Shov+ SIGMA VALUE ESTIMATED, TBL	
			Jour	EAF 28 5 9	70 . FRENCH OF AE 28 388.	
Nu	Spont	KUR	Eval Rept	IAE−2738	75 Zakharova. NUBAR=4.3+−0.5	

96 Curium 254

Quantity	Energy (ev) Min Max	Lab	Type	Documentation Ref Vol Page	Author, Comments Date	Data
Eta	Spont	EDG	Revw Conf	69Vienna 83	Jul 69 Feather.PPR201.BINARY+TERN FISSN CFD	
Nu	Spont	EDG	Revw Conf	69Vienna 83	Jul 69 Feather.PPR201.BINARY+TERN FISSN CFD	

97 Berkelium 240

Quantity	Energy (ev) Min Max	Lab	Type	Documentation Ref Vol Page	Date	Author, Comments	Data
Fission	Spont	DUB	Theo Rept	JINR-E-2515	Dec 65	Malov+ SPON FISSN ISOMER, LIFE-TIME	

97 Berkelium 242

Quantity	Energy (ev) Min Max	Lab	Type	Documentation Ref Vol Page	Date	Author, Comments	Data
Fission	Spont	DUB	Theo Rept	JINR-E-2515	Dec 65	Malov+ SPON FISSN ISOMER, LIFE-TIME	

97 Berkelium 243

Quantity	Energy (ev) Min Max	Lab	Type	Documentation Ref Vol Page	Date	Author, Comments	Data
Fission	Spont	HEI	Expt Conf	69Vienna 449	Jul 69	Metag+PPR29. HE-INDUCED ISOM FISS HL	
Fission	2.5-2	JUL	Theo Jour	ZP 257 389	Dec 72	Mcminn. 6.78 E +2 BARNS	

97 Berkelium 244

Quantity	Energy (ev) Min Max	Lab	Type	Documentation Ref Vol Page	Date	Author, Comments	Data
Fission	Spont	DUB	Theo Rept	JINR-E-2515	Dec 65	Malov+ SPON FISSN ISOMER, LIFE-TIME	
Fission	Spont	HEI	Expt Conf	69Vienna 449	Jul 69	Metag+PPR29. HE-INDUCED ISOM FISS HL	
Fission	-	GEL	ExTh Jour	NP/A 187 305	Jun 72	Weigmann+ F.B.PARAMS FROM DATA ANAL.	

97 Berkelium 245

Quantity	Energy (ev) Min Max	Lab	Type	Documentation Ref Vol Page	Date	Author, Comments	Data
(n,p)	Maxwl	IFU	Theo Rept	ICD-4 20	67	Dadakina+ PENETR COEFF CALC,TABLE	
Fission	-	GEL	ExTh Jour	NP/A 187 305	Jun 72	Weigmann+ F.B.PARAMS FROM DATA ANAL.	
Fission	Spont	TPI	Theo Jour	YF 16 919	Nov 72	Adeev+ FISS BARRIER CFD EVEN,GRAPH	
			Jour	SNP 16 507	May 73	.ENGLISH OF YF 16 919	
Fission	2.5-2	JUL	Theo Jour	ZP 257 389	Dec 72	Mcminn. 2.31 E +2 BARNS	

97 Berkelium 246

Quantity	Energy (ev) Min Max	Lab	Type	Documentation Ref Vol Page	Date	Author, Comments	Data
(n,p)	Maxwl	IFU	Theo Rept	ICD-4 20	67	Dadakina+ PENETR COEFF CALC,TABLE	
Fission	Spont	DUB	Theo Rept	JINR-E-2515	Dec 65	Malov+ SPON FISSN ISOMER, LIFE-TIME	
Fission	Maxwl	CCP	Comp Jour	AE 26 436	May 69	Romanov. UPPER SIG LIMIT ESTIMATED	
			Jour	SJA 26 498	69	. ENGL OF AE 26 436.	
			Jour	EAF 26 48	69	. FRENCH OF AE 26 436.	
Fission	-	GEL	ExTh Jour	NP/A 187 305	Jun 72	Weigmann+ F.B.PARAMS FROM DATA ANAL.	

97 Berkelium 247

Quantity	Energy (ev) Min Max	Lab	Type	Documentation Ref Vol Page	Date	Author, Comments	Data
(n,p)	Maxwl	IFU	Theo Rept	ICD-4 20	67	Dadakina+ PENETR COEFF CALC,TABLE	
Fission	2.5-2	JUL	Theo Jour	ZP 257 389	Dec 72	Mcminn. 1.63 E +1 BARNS	

97 Berkelium 248

Quantity	Energy (ev) Min Max	Lab	Type	Documentation Ref Vol Page	Date	Author, Comments	Data
Nu	Maxwl	IAE	Eval Jour	REA 10 637	Dec 72	Manero+ CALC,SYSTEMATICS,TBL	

97 Berkelium 249

Quantity	Energy (ev) Min Max	Lab	Type	Documentation Ref Vol Page	Date	Author, Comments	Data
Evaluation	1.0-5 2.0+7	SRL	Eval Rept	EPRI-NP-161	Dec 75	Benjamin+ENDF4B.GENPAR MDL.REVISIONS	
Absorption	Pile	LRL	Expt Jour	PR 95 581	Jul 54	Harvey+ MTR MEASUREMENTS.	+
	Pile		Data	EXFOR12567.003	Jun 76	. 1 PT. SIGMA.	
Absorption	Pile	SRL	Expt Conf	68Wash. 1279	Mar 68	Folger+ ACTIVATION.	+
			Rept	DP-MS-67-112	Mar 68	- + FOIL MEASUREMENTS.	
	Pile		Data	EXFOR12534.011	Jun 76	. 1 PT. SIGMA.	

97 Berkelium 249

Quantity	Energy (ev) Min	Max	Lab	Type	Documentation Ref Vol Page	Author, Comments Date	Data
Absorption	Pile		SRL	Expt Abst	ANS 14 344	Jun 71 Rusche. VALUE GIVEN	
Absorption	None		ORL	Expt Prog	ERDA-NDC-3 198	May 76 Harvey+ABS CS DRVD FROM TOT MEAS.NDG	
Res Int Abs	5.5-1		SRL	Expt Conf	68Wash. 1279	Mar 68 Folger+ ACT 1240B	+
				Rept	DP-MS-67-112	Mar 68 - + FOIL MEASUREMENTS.	
	5.5-1			Data	EXFOR12534.012	Jun 76 . 1 PT. RI.	
Res Int Abs	None		SRL	Expt Abst	ANS 14 344	Jun 71 Rusche. VALUE GIVEN	
(n,γ)	Pile		ANL	Expt Jour	PR 96 1576	Dec 54 Magnusson+.CF250 ALPHA COUNTED. MTR	+
				Conf	55Geneva 7 261	Aug 55 Bentley+.P809,VAL GVN,CHEMICAL METHD	
	Pile			Data	EXFOR12568.002	Jun 76 . 1 PT. SIGMA.	
(n,γ)	None		KAP	Comp Rept	KAPL-1781	Jul 57 Schuman. SIGMA GIVEN	
(n,γ)	Maxwl		SRL	Expt Rept	DP-MS-66-69	Oct 66 ICE. HIGHLY THERMAL SPECTRUM.	+
	Maxwl			Data	EXFOR12550.015	Jun 76 . 1 PT. SIGMA.	
(n,γ)	Maxwl		BNL	Theo Abst	ANS 10 228	Jun 67 Prince. CALCULATED SIGMA=500 B.	
(n,γ)	None		LAS	Expt Prog	WASH-1136 110	Sep 69 Silbert+,PHYSICS-8 SHOT,ANAL TBC	
(n,γ)	Maxwl		CCP	Comp Jour	AE 28 388	May 70 Bol'Shov+ OTHER'S SIG VALUE GIVEN	
				Jour	EAF 28 5 9	70 . FRENCH OF AE 28 388.	
(n,γ)	Pile		KFK	Eval Prog	KFK-1544 61	Jan 72 Eberle+FOR 2-GROUP SIG,FITTED TO EXP	
(n,γ)	Maxwl		SRL	Eval Conf	75Wash. 224	Mar 75 Benjamin+ TBL BEST FIT TRANSPU PROD.	
Res Int Capt	Maxwl		BNL	Theo Abst	ANS 10 228	Jun 67 Prince. CALCULATED RI=1850 B.	
Res Int Capt	Pile		KFK	Eval Prog	KFK-1544 61	Jan 72 Eberle+1240B	
Res Int Capt	6.3-1		SRL	Eval Conf	75Wash. 224	Mar 75 Benjamin+ TBL BEST FIT TRANSPU PROD.	
Fission	Spont		BRK	Revw Jour	NP 81 1	Jun 66 Myers.TBL CALC FISS BARRIERS.	
Fission	Maxwl		BNL	Theo Abst	ANS 10 228	Jun 67 Prince. CALCULATED SIGMA=2.8 B.	
Fission	Spont		KUR	Expt Jour	YF 10 726	Oct 69 Vorotnikov+ SPON FISS HALF-LIVE GVN	
				Jour	SNP 10 4 419	Apr 70 TRANSLATN.*	
Fission	2.0+5	5.0+6	KUR	Expt Jour	YF 10 726	Oct 69 Vorotnikov+ SIG(E),THRESH+PLATEAU	+
	6.0+5	4.6+6		Jour	NP/A 150 56	Jul 70 - +. GLASS DETECTOR	
	2.0+5	5.0+6		Jour	SNP 10 4 419	Apr 70 TRANSLATN.*	
	6.5+5	4.6+6		Prog	YFI-11 3	70 Vorotnikov+ ABST,SIG AT 23 ES,TBL	
				Prog	INDC(CCP)-31	Dec 72 .PAGE 1,ENGLISH OF YFI-11 3	
	6.5+5	5.0+6		Data	EXFOR40252.002	Apr 75 .N-FISS CS AT 23 ES GVN	
Fission	Pile		SRL	Expt Abst	ANS 14 344	Jun 71 Rusche. VALUE GIVEN	
Fission	1.5+6	1.5+7	KUR	Expt Jour	YF 14 73	Jul 71 Fomushkin+ +FAST+3MEV,REL U235,TABLE	
				Jour	SNP 14 42	Jan 72 . ENGL OF YF 14 73	
Fission	1.0-2	1.4+7	LRL	Expt Prog	NCSAC-42 135	Nov 71 Browne+ INDICATED WORK TBD.	
Fission	Pile		SRL	Eval Conf	75Wash. 224	Mar 75 Benjamin+ TBL BEST FIT TRANSPU PROD.	
Fission	2.5-2		NIR	Expt Conf	75Kiev 6 71	May 75 Gavrilov+ REL AU197,CO59(NG).SIG GVN	
Fission	6.0+5	1.5+7	JAE	Revw Conf	IAEA-186 3 1	76 Igarasi. REVW AVAIL DATA,GRPH+BIBLIO	
	2.0+5	1.5+7		Rept	JAERI-M-6315	Nov 75 - +GRPH. 3 DATA SETS COMPARED	
Res Int Fiss	Maxwl		BNL	Theo Abst	ANS 10 228	Jun 67 Prince. CALCULATED RI=5 B.	
Res Int Fiss	6.3-1		SRL	Eval Conf	75Wash. 224	Mar 75 Benjamin+ TBL BEST FIT TRANSPU PROD.	
Nu	Spont		CCP	Expt Jour	AE 33 788	Sep 72 Kosjakov+ NUBAR(A), GRAPH	+
				Jour	SJA 33 903	Mar 73 .ENGLISH OF AE 33 788	
	Spont			Data	EXFOR40126.002	Dec 72 SPONTANEOUS PROMPT NU-BAR	
Nu	Spont		IAE	Eval Jour	REA 10 637	Dec 72 Manero+ EXTENSIVE SURVEY,TBL,AVG VAL	
Frag Spectra	2.0+5	5.0+6	KUR	Expt Jour	YF 10 726	Oct 69 Vorotnikov+ FRAG ANGDISTR TBD	
				Jour	SNP 10 4 419	Apr 70 TRANSLATN.*	
Frag Spectra	8.1+5	4.6+6	KUR	Expt Prog	YFI-11 3	70 Vorotnikov+ ABST,ANGDIST OF FRAG,TBL	
	8.1+5			Prog	INDC(CCP)-31	Dec 72 .PAGE 1,ENGLISH OF YFI-11 3	
Frag Spectra	6.0+5	4.6+6	KUR	Expt Jour	NP/A 150 56	Jul 70 Vorotnikov+. GLASS DETECTOR.ANGDISTR	
Frag Spectra	1.5+6	1.5+7	KUR	Expt Jour	YF 14 73	Jul 71 Fomushkin+ ALSO 3MEV,ANISOTROPY,TABL	
				Jour	SNP 14 42	Jan 72 . ENGL OF YF 14 73	
Reson Params	6.2-1	5.0+4	SRL	Theo Conf	71Knoxvill 714	Mar 71 Mccrosson. STAT CALCULATN AVG PARAMS	
Strnth Fnctn	5.0-1	6.2+1	ORL	Expt Rept	DP-MS-77-44	77 Benjamin+TRNS.STF ANAL TBD.	

97 Berkelium 250

Quantity	Energy (ev) Min	Max	Lab	Type	Documentation Ref Vol Page	Author, Comments Date	Data
(n,γ)	Maxwl		CCP	Comp Jour	AE 28 388	May 70 Bol'Shov+ OTHER'S SIG VALUE GIVEN	
				Jour	EAF 28 5 9	70 . FRENCH OF AE 28 388.	
(n,γ)	Pile		KFK	Eval Prog	KFK-1544 61	Jan 72 Eberle+FOR 2-GROUP SIG,FITTED TO EXP	
Fission	Maxwl		ANL	Expt Jour	JIN 30 2553	Oct 68 Diamond+,ION CHAMB IN THR COLUMN	+
	Maxwl			Data	EXFOR12531.005	Jun 76 . 1 PT. SIGMA.	
Fission	Maxwl		CCP	Comp Jour	AE 28 388	May 70 Bol'Shov+ OTHER'S SIG VALUE GIVEN	
				Jour	EAF 28 5 9	70 . FRENCH OF AE 28 388.	
Fission	Pile		KFK	Eval Prog	KFK-1544 61	Jan 72 Eberle+FOR 2-GROUP SIG,FITTED TO EXP	
Alpha	1.0+4	2.0+4	LAS	Theo Jour	PR 158 1127	Jun 67 Bell. SYSTEMATCS TH FOR 10-20KEV ALF	

97 Berkelium 251

Quantity	Energy (ev) Min Max	Lab	Type	Documentation Ref Vol Page	Author, Comments Date	Data
(n,γ)	Maxwl	CCP	Theo Jour	AE 28 388	May 70 Bol'Shov+ SIGMA VALUE ESTIMATED, TBL	
			Jour	EAF 28 5 9	70 . FRENCH OF AE 28 388.	
Fission	2.5 – 2	JUL	Theo Jour	ZP 257 389	Dec 72 Mcminn. 5.23 E –2 BARNS	

97 Berkelium 252

Quantity	Energy (ev) Min Max	Lab	Type	Documentation Ref Vol Page	Author, Comments Date	Data
(n,γ)	Maxwl	CCP	Theo Jour	AE 28 388	May 70 Bol'Shov+ SIGMA VALUE ESTIMATED, TBL	
			Jour	EAF 28 5 9	70 . FRENCH OF AE 28 388.	
Fission	Maxwl	CCP	Theo Jour	AE 28 388	May 70 Bol'Shov+ SIGMA VALUE ESTIMATED, TBL	
			Jour	EAF 28 5 9	70 . FRENCH OF AE 28 388.	
Alpha	1.0+4 2.0+4	LAS	Theo Jour	PR 158 1127	Jun 67 Bell. SYSTEMATCS TH FOR 10–20KEV ALF	

98 Californium

Quantity	Energy (ev) Min Max	Lab	Type	Documentation Ref Vol Page	Author, Comments Date	Data
Frag Spectra	Spont	REH	Expt Jour	PRL 36 1072	May 76 Wolf+ KE FRAGS.TE134 MAGNETIC MOMENT	

98 Californium 245

Quantity	Energy (ev) Min Max	Lab	Type	Documentation Ref Vol Page	Author, Comments Date	Data
Nu	Maxwl	IAE	Eval Jour	REA 10 637	Dec 72 Manero+ CALC,SYSTEMATICS,TBL	
Fiss Yield	Spont	AUA	Theo Rept	AAEC/E – 386	Mar 76 Cook+ 3 – GAUSS FIT,PARAMS GIVEN	

98 Californium 246

Quantity	Energy (ev) Min Max	Lab	Type	Documentation Ref Vol Page	Author, Comments Date	Data
Fission	Spont	LRL	Expt Rept	UCRL – 2005	Nov 52 Hulet+ ,FISSION RATE+ HALF – LIFE	
Fission	Spont	BRK	Revw Jour	NP 81 1	Jun 66 Myers.TBL CALC FISS BARRIERS.	
Fission	Spont	COP	Revw Conf	69Vienna 155	Jul 69 Strutinsky+ PPR203. HL GVN,'SHELL – TH'	
Fission	Spont	MRY	Prog	ORO – 4028 – 28	71 Jackson+. SPON FISSION HALF – LIFE GVN	
Fission	Spont	NEU	Theo Jour	HPA 45 567	Dec 72 Hooshyar+ HL GROUNDST AND FISS ISOM.	
Nu	Spont	IAE	Eval Jour	REA 10 637	Dec 72 Manero+ EXTENSIVE SURVEY,TBL,AVG VAL	
Nu	Spont	DUB	Expt Jour	YF 17 692	Apr 73 Dakovsky+ REL NUBAR,P(NU),TBL,GRAPHS	+
			Rept	JINR – P15 – 6730	Sep 72 Dakowski+ MEASURED NU – BAR REL CM244	
			Jour	SNP 17 360	Oct 73 .ENGLISH OF YF 17 692	
	Spont		Data	EXFOR40188.002	Nov 73 .1 DATA LINE	
Nu	Spont	DUB	Comp Jour	YF 18 724	Oct 73 Dakovsky+NUBAR VS FISNUCLEUS,TBL+GRP	
			Eval Rept	JINR – P15 – 7119	Jun 73 Dakowski+ NUBAR+P(NU) – DISTR,TBL,GRPH	
			Comp Jour	SNP 18 371	Apr 74 . ENGLISH OF YF 18, 724.	
Fiss Yield	None	KFK	Theo Conf	69Vienna 25	Jul 69 Dickmann+PPR45. MASS – RATIO VAL GVN	
Frag Spectra	Spont	ANL	Expt Jour	PR 131 1203	Aug 63 Friedman+ FRAG MOST PROBABLE ENERGY	

98 Californium 248

Quantity	Energy (ev) Min Max	Lab	Type	Documentation Ref Vol Page	Author, Comments Date	Data
Fission	Spont	BRK	Revw Jour	NP 81 1	Jun 66 Myers.TBL CALC FISS BARRIERS.	
Fission	Spont	MRY	Theo Prog	ORO – 4028 – 28	71 Jackson+. SPON FISSION HALF – LIFE GVN	
Fission	2.5 – 2	JUL	Theo Jour	ZP 257 389	Dec 72 Mcminn. 7.30 E +2 BARNS	
Fission	None	FRK	Theo Jour	NP/A 207 225	Jun 73 Albrecht. 2CENTRE SHELLMOD,DEF – E MAP	
Nu	Maxwl	IAE	Eval Jour	REA 10 637	Dec 72 Manero+ CALC,SYSTEMATICS,TBL	
Fiss Yield	None	BAS	Theo Jour	PL/B 34 264	Mar 71 Pauli+ FRAG MASS RATIO AS STRUTINSKY	
Frag Spectra	Spont	ANL	Expt Jour	PR 131 1203	Aug 63 Friedman+ FRAG MOST PROBABLE ENERGY	

98 Californium 249

Quantity	Energy (ev) Min Max	Lab	Type	Documentation Ref Vol Page	Author, Comments Date	Data
Evaluation	1.0 – 5 2.0+7	SRL	Eval Rept	EPRI – NP – 161	Dec 75 Benjamin+ ENDFB4.REVISIONS	
Absorption	Pile	BRK	Expt Jour	PR 95 581	Jul 54 Harvey+	+
	Pile		Data	EXFOR12567.004	Jun 76 . 1 PT. SIGMA	
Absorption	Maxwl	SRL	Expt Abst	ANS 14 344	Jun 71 Rusche. VALUE GIVEN	
Absorption	2.5 – 2	ORL	Expt Prog	ERDA – NDC – 3 201	May 76 Harvey+NDG.THR VAL TBD.	
Res Int Abs	None	SRL	Expt Abst	ANS 14 344	Jun 71 Rusche. VALUE GIVEN	
(n,γ)	Pile	BRK	Expt Jour	PR 95 581	Jul 54 Harvey+.MEASURED CF250 YIELD. MTR	+
	Pile		Data	EXFOR12567.005	Jun 76 . 1 PT. SIGMA	
(n,γ)	Pile	ANL	Revw Conf	55Geneva 7 261	Aug 55 Bentley+.P809,VAL GVN,CHEMICAL METHD	
(n,γ)	None	KAP	Comp Rept	KAPL – 1781	Jul 57 Schuman. SIGMA GIVEN	
(n,γ)	None	LAS	Expt Prog	WASH – 1136 110	Sep 69 Silbert+,PHYSICS – 8 SHOT,ANAL TBC	
(n,γ)	Maxwl	CCP	Comp Jour	AE 28 388	May 70 Bol'Shov+ OTHER'S SIG VALUE GIVEN	
			Jour	EAF 28 5 9	70 . FRENCH OF AE 28 388.	
(n,γ)	Maxwl	ORL	Expt Prog	ORNL – 4706 47	Sep 71 Halperin+AVG VAL.MASS SPEC ANAL.	+
	Maxwl		Data	EXFOR10119.002	Mar 76 . 1 PT. NG CS =478+ – 25.	
(n,γ)	Pile	KFK	Eval Prog	KFK – 1544 61	Jan 72 Eberle+FOR 2 – GROUP SIG,FITTED TO EXP	
(n,γ)	Maxwl	SRL	Eval Conf	75Wash. 224	Mar 75 Benjamin+ TBL BEST FIT TRANSPU PROD.	
Res Int Capt	5.0 – 1	ORL	Expt Prog	ORNL – 4706 47	Sep 71 Halperin+MASS SPEC ANAL.CD COVER.	+
	5.0 – 1		Data	EXFOR10119.003	Mar 76 . 1 PT. RIG =765+ – 35B	
Res Int Capt	Pile	KFK	Eval Prog	KFK – 1544 61	Jan 72 Eberle+1030B	
Res Int Capt	6.3 – 1	SRL	Eval Conf	75Wash. 224	Mar 75 Benjamin+ TBL BEST FIT TRANSPU PROD.	
(n,p)	Maxwl	IFU	Theo Rept	ICD – 4 20	67 Dadakina+ PENETR COEFF CALC,TABLE	

98 Californium 249

Quantity	Energy (ev) Min	Max	Lab	Type	Documentation Ref Vol Page	Date	Author, Comments	Data
Fission	Pile		BRK	Expt	Jour PR 95 581	Jul 54	Harvey+	+
	Pile			Data	EXFOR 12567.006	Jun 76	. 1 PT, SIGMA	
Fission	Pile		ANL	Revw Conf	55Geneva 7 261	Aug 55	Bentley+.P809,VAL GVN,CHEMICAL METHD	
Fission	None		KAP	Comp Rept	KAPL–1781	Jul 57	Schuman. SIGMA GIVEN	
Fission	Maxwl		ANL	Expt Jour	JIN 27 33	Jan 65	Metta+ SIG=1735+–70B REL U233=526B	+
	Maxwl			Data	EXFOR 12562.002	Jun 76	. 1 PT. SIGMA	
Fission	Spont		COP	Revw Conf	69Vienna 155	Jul 69	Strutinsky+PPR203. HL GVN,'SHELL–TH'	
Fission	Spont		KUR	Expt Jour	YF 10 726	Oct 69	Vorotnikov+ SPON FISS HL ESTIMATED	
				Jour	SNP 10 4 419	Apr 70	TRANSLATN.*	
Fission	4.0+5	6.0+6	KUR	Expt Jour	YF 10 726	Oct 69	Vorotnikov+ SIG VALUE+–ERROR GVN	
				Jour	SNP 10 4 419	Apr 70	TRANSLATN.*	
Fission	Maxwl		CCP	Comp Jour	AE 28 388	May 70	Bol'Shov+ SIGMA VALUE ESTIMATED, TBL	
				Jour	EAF 28 5 9	70	. FRENCH OF AE 28 388.	
Fission	Maxwl		ORL	Expt Prog	ORNL–4581 37	Sep 70	Halperin+. FISSION TRACK COUNTING	+
	Maxwl			Data	EXFOR 10165.006	Jan 73	. 1 PT. SIGMA	
Fission	1.0+6	1.5+7	LAS	Expt Prog	NCSAC 3 148	Dec 70	Barton+,TO BE DONE	
Fission	Maxwl		SRL	Expt Abst	ANS 14 344	Jun 71	Rusche. VALUE GIVEN	
Fission	2.5–3	1.5+7	KUR	Expt Jour	YF 14 73	Jul 71	Fomushkin+ ALSO FAST,REL U235,TABLE	
				Jour	SNP 14 42	Jan 72	. ENGL OF YF 14 73	
Fission	1.0–2	1.4+7	LRL	Expt Prog	NCSAC–42 135	Nov 71	Browne+. TO BE DONE.	
Fission	Pile		KFK	Eval Prog	KFK–1544 61	Jan 72	Eberle+FOR 2–GROUP SIG,FITTED TO EXP	
Fission	1.6+5	1.6+6	KUR	Expt Jour	YF 15 29	Jan 72	Vorodnikov+ GLASS–DET,SIG 16 ES,GRPH	
				Jour	SNP 15 20	Jul 72	*	
Fission	Maxwl		SRL	Expt Jour	NSE 47 203	Feb 72	Benjamin+FISS CHS,FISS TRACK MEAS.	+
				Conf	71Knoxvill 843	Mar 71	.SUPERSEDED.	
	Maxwl			Data	EXFOR 10128.012	Feb 73	. 1PT.CS=1660+–50B.REL U 235	
Fission	5.0+5	5.0+6	FEI	Expt Jour	SJA 32 205	Aug 72	.ENGL OF AE 32 178	+
	Maxwl			Jour	SJA 32 205	Aug 72	.ENGL OF AE 32 178	
	5.0+5	5.0+6			Jour AE 32 178	Feb 72	Fursov+ SIGMA REL PU239 AT 7 ES,TBL	
	Maxwl			Jour	AE 32 178	Feb 72	– + IONIZ CHAMBER,REL PU239,TBL	
	2.5–2			Data	EXFOR 40102.002	Dec 73	.1 DATA LINE	
	5.0+5	5.0+6		Data	EXFOR 40102.003	Dec 73	.7 DATA LINES	
Fission	1.6+5	1.6+6	KUR	Expt Prog	YFI–13 7	Oct 72	Vorotnikov+ ABSTRACT ONLY,TBL	
				Theo Prog	INDC(CCP)–32	Apr 73	.PAGE 21.ENGLISH OF YFI–13 17	
Fission	1.3+1	2.9+6	LAS	Expt Jour	NSE 51 376	Aug 73	Silbert+ TOF,NUCLEAR EXPL. CURVES.	+
				Rept	LA–5042	Sep 72	– +.NUCL SHOT.TABULATD VALUES	
	1.3+1	2.9+6		Data	EXFOR 10292.002	Aug 73	. 5170 PTS. SIGMA.	
Fission	5.0+5	7.0+6	FEI	Expt Jour	YF 19 50	Jan 74	Fursov+ TOF,SIG(E)REL PU239,GRPH+TBL	+
				Jour	SNP 19 25	Jul 74	. ENGLISH OF YF 19 50	
	5.0+5	7.0+6		Data	EXFOR 40201.	Mar 74	.ABSOL AND REL TO PU239(NF) FOR 13ES	
Fission	3.0–1	2.0+1	HAR	Expt Prog	AERE–PR/NP21	Mar 74	James+ORELA.11 RES FOUND.	
Fission	3.5–1	7.0+1	ORL	Expt Prog	ORNL–4937 181	May 74	Dabbs+GRPH.OF FISS.CS.	+
	3.0–1	2.0+1		Conf	73Rochestr 2 505	Aug 73	– + ABST,SIG REL U235 FIS–SIG,NDG	
	3.0–1	2.0+1		Data	EXFOR 10349.004	May 75	. 0 PTS. DATA UNAVAILABLE.	
Fission	Maxwl		SRL	Eval Conf	75Wash. 224	Mar 75	Benjamin+ TBL BEST FIT TRANSPU PROD.	
Fission	2.5+5	5.2+6	KUR	Expt Jour	SNP 22 236	Sep 75	. ENGL OF YF 22 459	+
				Jour	YF 22 459	Sep 75	Fomushkin+ TRACK DET.SIG(E),GRPH+TBL	
	2.5+5	5.1+6		Rept	INDC(CCP)–65	Dec 74	.P6. ABST.TBL SIG(E),ENGL OF YFI–19	
	2.5+5	5.2+6		Data	EXFOR 40352.002	Feb 77	.SIG AT 27 EN GVN	
Fission	Maxwl		FEI	Expt Jour	AE 39 285	Oct 75	Zhuravlev+ SIG GIVEN,BY CD–DIFFERENC	
				Jour	SJA 39 907	Apr 76	. ENGL OF AE 39 285	
Fission	2.0+5	7.0+6	CCP	Eval Rept	YK–22 77	76	Zherebcov+ SIG(NEUT–E),TBL	
Fission	1.3+1	1.5+7	JAE	Revw Conf	IAEA–186 3 1	76	Igarasi. REVW AVAIL DATA,GRPH+BIBLIO	
	1.0+3	7.0+6		Rept	JAERI–M–6315	Nov 75	– +GRPH. 5 DATA SETS COMPARED	
Res Int Fiss	5.4–1		ORL	Expt Prog	ORNL–4581 37	Sep 70	Halperin+. FISSION TRACK COUNTING	+
	5.4–1			Data	EXFOR 10165.007	Jan 73	. 1 PT.	
Res Int Fiss	None		SRL	Expt Abst	ANS 14 344	Jun 71	Rusche. VALUE GIVEN	
Res Int Fiss	Pile		KFK	Eval Prog	KFK–1544 61	Jan 72	Eberle+2940B	
Res Int Fiss	6.3–1		SRL	Expt Jour	NSE 47 203	Feb 72	Benjamin+CD COVER.MASS SPEC.	+
				Conf	71Knoxvill 843	Mar 71	.SUPERSEDED	
	6.3–1			Data	EXFOR 10128.013	Feb 73	. 1PT.CS=2114+–70B.REL U 235.	
Res Int Fiss	3.0–1	2.0+1	HAR	Expt Prog	AERE–PR/NP21	Mar 74	James+ORELA.75PERCENT FROM 0.71EV R	
Res Int Fiss	5.5–1	2.0+6	ORL	Expt Prog	ORNL–4976 36	Oct 74	Bemis+RI=1630B.LARGE RES AT 0.708EV	
Res Int Fiss	6.3–1		SRL	Eval Conf	75Wash. 224	Mar 75	Benjamin+ TBL BEST FIT TRANSPU PROD.	
Res Int Fiss	5.0–1		FEI	Expt Jour	AE 39 285	Oct 75	Zhuravlev+ SIG GIVEN,BY CD–DIFFERENC	
				Jour	SJA 39 907	Apr 76	. ENGL OF AE 39 285	
Alpha	1.0+4	2.0+4	LAS	Theo Jour	PR 158 1127	Jun 67	Bell. SYSTEMATCS TH FOR 10–20KEV ALF	

98 Californium 249

Quantity	Energy (ev) Min Max	Lab	Type	Documentation Ref Vol Page	Date	Author, Comments	Data
Alpha	Maxwl	ORL Expt	Prog	ORNL-4706 47	Sep 71	Halperin+ THR AND EPI THR VAL CALC.	+
	Maxwl		Data	EXFOR10119.009	Dec 77	. 1PT.ALF=.29	
Nu	Maxwl 1.5+7	HAR Revw	Conf	70Helsinki 2 195	Jun 70	Colvin.PPR99. REPORT ON DATA STATUS	
Nu	Maxwl	NIR Expt	Conf	70Helsinki 2 183	Jun 70	Zamjatnin+90. NUBAR REL U-235	
Nu	Maxwl	NIR Expt	Conf	70Helsinki § 90	Jun 70	Zamjatnin+.NUBAR REL U-235,TBL	
Nu	Pile	KUR Expt	Jour	YF 14 943	Nov 71	Kurchatov+ NUBAR FROM MASS YLD CURVE	
			Jour	SNP 14 528	May 72	*ENGL OF YF 14 943	
Nu	Spont	FEI Expt	Jour	YF 15 29	Jan 72	Volodin+ NU-BAR,ROUGH VALUE GIVEN	
			Jour	SNP 15 17	Jul 72	*	
Nu	Maxwl	FEI Expt	Jour	YF 15 29	Jan 72	Volodin+ NU-BAR REL CF-252 GIVEN	+
	Pile		Prog	YFI-12 12	72	- + ABSTRACT,NUBAR GIVEN	
			Prog	INDC(CCP)-30	Dec 72	.PG10,ENGLISH OF YFI-12 12	
	Maxwl		Jour	SNP 15 17	Jul 72	.ENGLISH OF YF 15 29	
	2.5-2		Data	EXFOR40125.002	Dec 72	PROMPT NUBAR REL CF-252	
Nu	Spont	IAE Eval	Jour	REA 10 637	Dec 72	Manero+ EXTENSIVE SURVEY,TBL,AVG VAL	
	Maxwl		Jour	REA 10 637	Dec 72	- + EXTENSIVE SURVEY,TBL,AVG VAL	
Nu	Maxwl	ANL Expt	Conf	73Rochestr 2 19	Aug 73	Unik+ NU TOTAL VS MASS 13 NUCLIDES.	
Nu	Maxwl	AUA Revw	Conf	IAEA-169 2 163	74	Musgrove+ TOTAL NU-BAR,GRAPH	
Spect Fiss n	Maxwl	NIR Expt	Conf	70Helsinki 2 183	Jun 70	Zamjatnin+90. NU(E) GRAPH,TEMPERATUR	
Spect Fiss n	Maxwl	NIR Expt	Conf	70Helsinki § 90	Jun 70	Zamjatnin+.SPECTR-TEMP REL U-235	
Spect Fiss n	Maxwl	ANL Revw	Conf	71Vienna 3	Aug 71	Smith. MEAN-E OF NEUTS,EXPTS CFD,TBL	
Spect Fiss n	Pile	FEI Expt	Prog	YFI-12 12	72	Volodin+ ABST,AVG FRAG KIN-E GIVEN	
			Prog	INDC(CCP)-30	Dec 72	.PG10,ENGLISH OF YFI-12 12	
Fiss Prod γ	Pile	MNZExpt	Prog	NEANDC(E)172 5	Jul 76	Ahrens+P.59. A=96-112,ES,HL	
Fiss Yield	Maxwl	WURExpt	Prog	EANDC(OR)93L	Jun 70	Flynn+ MASS AND CHARGE DISTR TBL	
			Rept	EIR-175	69	- +	
			Jour	HCA 52 00	69	- + MASS YIELDS.	
Fiss Yield	Maxwl	SRL Expt	Jour	PR/C 4 505	Aug 71	Troutner+.TE132,134 FRACT CUMUL YLDS	
Fiss Yield	Pile	KUR Expt	Jour	YF 14 943	Nov 71	Kurchatov+ YLDS 35 RADNUCL,TBL,GRAPH	+
			Jour	SNP 14 528	May 72	*ENGL OF YF 14 943	
	2.5-2		Data	EXFOR40145.002	Apr 73	CUMULATIVE F-PROD YIELD	
Fiss Yield	Maxwl	SRL Expt	Jour	JIN 34 3 801	Mar 72	Troutner+ FRACT INDEP YLD OF 140LA	
Fiss Yield	Maxwl	SRL Expt	Jour	JIN 35 1 11	Jan 73	Troutner+ FRACT INDEP YLD111MPD112AG	
Fiss Yield	Maxwl	HAR Eval	Conf	73Paris 1 393	Mar 73	Crouch.EXPTL DATA+EVAL CHAIN YLD,TBL	
			Rept	AERE-R-7209	Jan 73	- .24 CHAIN YLDS RECOMMENDED TBL	
Fiss Yield	Maxwl	ANL Expt	Conf	73Rochestr 2 19	Aug 73	Unik+ PROMPT YLDS,MASS DISTRIB,GRPHS	
Fiss Yield	Maxwl	AUA Revw	Conf	IAEA-169 2 163	74	Musgrove+ PROMPT,EVEN-Z POSITN,GRAPH	
Fiss Yield	Maxwl	SRL Expt	Jour	PR/C 10 769	Aug 74	Harbour+ XE135 YIELD,TBL,GRPH.	
			Rept	DP-MS-73-29	73	- +. XE135 FRACTNL INDEPEND YLD	
Fiss Yield	Maxwl	MIS Expt	Jour	JIN 36 3880	Dec 74	Eichor+ IND YLD OF CS-138	
			Abst	DA/B 34 1034	Sep 73	- .CS138 FRACT CHAIN YLD GIVEN.	
Fiss Yield	Spont	MNZExpt	Prog	MAINZ-1975	76	Meixler+ STEARAT METHOD CUM.YIELD	+
	2.5-2		Data	EXFOR20711.003	Feb 77	6PTS.	
Fiss Yield	Maxwl	AUA Theo	Rept	AAEC/E-386	Mar 76	Cook+ 3-GAUSS FIT,PARAMS GIVEN	
Frag Spectra	1.5+7	KUR Expt	Jour	YF 14 73	Jul 71	Fomushkin+ FRGMS ANG ANISOTROPY,TABL	
			Jour	SNP 14 42	Jan 72	. ENGL OF YF 14 73	
Frag Spectra	Maxwl	FEI Expt	Jour	YF 15 29	Jan 72	Volodin+ KE DIST+AVG REL CF252,GRPHS	+
			Jour	SNP 15 17	Jul 72	*	
	2.5-2		Data	EXFOR40125.003	Dec 72	AVERAGE E-KIN OF FRAGMENTS	
Frag Spectra	5.0+5 5.0+6	FEI Expt	Jour	SJA 32 205	Aug 72	.ENGL OF AE 32 178	+
			Jour	AE 32 178	Feb 72	Fursov+ ANGULAR ANISOTROPY,7ES,TBL	
			Prog	YFI-12 3	72	.FRAG ANG ANISOTR 0/90 DEG,TBL	
	5.0+5 5.0+6		Data	EXFOR40102.004	Dec 73	.7 DATA LINES	
Frag Spectra	1.6+5 5.0+6	KUR Expt	Jour	YF 16 664	Oct 72	Vorotnikov+ ANG DISTR OF FRAG,GRAPH	+
			Prog	YFI- 14 7	72	- + ANG DISTR OF FRAGS,TBL	
			Jour	SNP 16 372	Apr 73	.ENGLISH OF YF 16 664	
	1.6+5 5.0+6		Data	EXFOR40166.002	Nov 73	.9 DATA LINES	
Frag Spectra	Maxwl	ANL Expt	Conf	73Rochestr 2 19	Aug 73	Unik+ TOTAL KIN-E OF FRAGS,GRPH,TBL	
Frag Spectra	Maxwl	AUA Revw	Conf	IAEA-169 2 163	74	Musgrove+ AVG FRAG MASS,GRAPH	
Frag Spectra	5.0+5 7.0+6	FEI Expt	Jour	YF 19 50	Jan 74	Fursov+ ANG ANISOTR 0/90,GRAPH+TABLE	+
			Jour	SNP 19 25	Jul 74	. ENGLISH OF YF 19 50	
	5.0+5 7.0+6		Data	EXFOR40201.004	Mar 74	.DATA FOR 13 ES GIVEN	
Frag Spectra	+7	FEI Theo	Conf	75Kiev	May 75	Ermagambetov+ ANGANIZOTR,ANALYS,GRPH	
Frag Charge	Maxwl	WURExpt	Prog	EANDC(OR)93L	Jun 70	Flynn+	
			Jour	HCA 52 00	69	- + CHARGE DISTRIBUTION.	
			Rept	EIR-175	69	- +	
Frag Charge	Pile	KUR Expt	Jour	YF 14 943	Nov 71	Kurchatov+ MOST PROBL CHRG,A=82,136	
			Jour	SNP 14 528	May 72	*ENGL OF YF 14 943	

98 Californium 249

Quantity	Energy (ev) Min	Max	Lab	Type	Documentation Ref Vol Page	Author, Comments Date	Data
Frag Charge	Maxwl		MIS	Expt Abst	DA/B 34 1034	Sep 73 Eichor.MOST PROBABLE CHARGE DISTRBTN	
Frag Charge	Maxwl		LRL	Comp Rept	UCRL – 51640	Jul 74 Nethaway. TBL.	
Frag Charge	Maxwl		UBE	Expt Jour	JIN 38 205	Feb 76 Gaeggeler+ ZP(A=150),GRPH Z – SYSTEMAT	
				Diss	GAEGGELER	Dec 73 – . COMPLETE EXPT DESCRIPTION	
Reson Params	–		FEI	Theo Rept	FEI – 157	Feb 69 Ignatjuk+ 2HUMPED – BARR – CALCUL,WN/WF	
Reson Params	6.2–1	5.0+4	SRL	Theo Conf	71Knoxvill 714	Mar 71 Mccrosson. STAT CALCULATN AVG PARAMS	
Reson Params	1.6+1	6.9+1	LAS	Expt Jour	NSE 51 376	Aug 73 Silbert.TOF.NUCLEAR EXPL.WN WF AVG D	+
	1.6+1	6.9+1		Data	EXFOR10292.	Aug 73 . 43RES,RED N – WID,F – WID,AVE D	
Reson Params	3.0–1	2.0+1	HAR	Expt Prog	AERE – PR/NP21	Mar 74 James+ORELA.11 RES FROM NF.WT OF.7EV	
Reson Params	7.1–1	1.7+1	ORL	Expt Prog	ORNL – 4937 181	May 74 Dabbs+TBL.OF RES.BELOW 20 EV.	+
	3.0–1	2.0+1		Conf	73Rochestr 2 505	Aug 73 – ABST,RES – E,TOT – WID,REL U235	
	7.1–1	1.7+1		Data	EXFOR10349.002	May 75 . 11 PTS.	
Strnth Fnctn	1.5+1	7.0+1	LAS	Expt Jour	NSE 51 376	Aug 73 Silbert.TOF.NUCLEAR EXPL.S0=1.S+ – 0.3	+
	1.5+1	7.0+1		Data	EXFOR10292.005	Aug 73 . 1 PT.	

98 Californium 250

Quantity	Energy (ev) Min	Max	Lab	Type	Documentation Ref Vol Page	Author, Comments Date	Data
Evaluation	1.0–5	2.0+7	SRL	Eval Rept	EPRI – NP – 161	Dec 75 Benjamin+ENDF4B.GENPAR MDL.REVISIONS	
Absorption	Maxwl		SRL	Expt Conf	68Wash. 1285	Mar 68 Smith+ SIG=1090B DEDUCED SIGMA	+
				Rept	DP – MS – 67 – 111	68 – +	
	Maxwl			Data	EXFOR12580.009	Jun 76 . 1 PT, SIGMA	
Absorption	Maxwl		SRL	Expt Conf	68Wash. 1279	Mar 68 Folger+ ACT	+
				Rept	DP – MS – 67 – 112	Mar 68 – +	
	Maxwl			Data	EXFOR12534.013	Jun 76 . 1 PT, SIGMA	
Absorption	Maxwl		SRL	Expt Abst	ANS 14 344	Jun 71 Rusche. VALUE GIVEN	
Res Int Abs	9.2–1		SRL	Expt Conf	68Wash. 1279	Mar 68 Folger+ ACT 5300B	+
				Rept	DP – MS – 67 – 112	Mar 68 – +	
	9.2–1			Data	EXFOR12534.017	Jun 76 . 1 PT.	
Res Int Abs	None		SRL	Expt Abst	ANS 14 344	Jun 71 Rusche. VALUE GIVEN	
(n,γ)	Pile		ANL	Expt Jour	PR 96 1576	Dec 54 Magnusson+.MASS SPECTRM.AROUND 1500B	+
				Conf	55Geneva 7 261	Aug 55 Bentley+.P809,VAL GVN,CHEMICAL METHD	
	Pile			Data	EXFOR12568.003	Jun 76 . 1 PT, SIGMA	
(n,γ)	None		KAP	Comp Rept	KAPL – 1781	Jul 57 Schuman. SIGMA GIVEN	
(n,γ)	Spont		ANL	Expt Rept	ANL – 6252	Feb 61 Vandenbosch+.	
(n,γ)	Maxwl		BNL	Theo Abst	ANS 10 228	Jun 67 Prince. CALCULATED SIG=1500B	
(n,γ)	Maxwl		CCP	Comp Jour	AE 28 388	May 70 Bol'Shov+ OTHER'S SIG VALUE GIVEN	
				Jour	EAF 28 5 9	70 . FRENCH OF AE 28 388.	
(n,γ)	Maxwl		ORL	Expt Prog	ORNL – 4706 47	Sep 71 Halperin+MASS SPEC ANAL.AVG CS.	+
	Maxwl			Data	EXFOR10119.004	Mar 76 . 1 PT.NG CS=2030+ – 200B.	
(n,γ)	Pile		KFK	Eval Prog	KFK – 1544 61	Jan 72 Eberle+FOR 2 – GROUP SIG,FITTED TO EXP	
(n,γ)	Maxwl		SRL	Eval Conf	75Wash. 224	Mar 75 Benjamin+ TBL BEST FIT TRANSPU PROD.	
Res Int Capt	Maxwl		BNL	Theo Abst	ANS 10 228	Jun 67 Prince. CALCULATED RES INTGRL=940B	
Res Int Capt	5.0–1		ORL	Expt Prog	ORNL – 4706 47	Sep 71 Halperin+MASS SPEC ANAL. CD COVER.	+
	5.0–1			Data	EXFOR10119.005	Mar 76 . 1PT.RIG=11,600+ – 500B.	
Res Int Capt	Pile		KFK	Eval Prog	KFK – 1544 61	Jan 72 Eberle+5300B	
Res Int Capt	6.3–1		SRL	Eval Conf	75Wash. 224	Mar 75 Benjamin+ TBL BEST FIT TRANSPU PROD.	
Fission	Maxwl		ANL	Expt Priv	METTA	64 Metta+	+
	Maxwl			Data	EXFOR12562.003	Jun 76 . 1 PT. SIGMA	
Fission	Spont		BRK	Revw Jour	NP 81 1	Jun 66 Myers.TBL CALC FISS BARRIERS.	
Fission	Maxwl		BNL	Theo Abst	ANS 10 228	Jun 67 Prince. CALCULATED SIG=335B.	
Fission	Spont		COP	Comp Conf	69Vienna 155	Jul 69 Strutinsky+PPR203. HL GVN,'SHELL – TH'	
	–			Theo Conf	68DUBSY 431	Jul 68 – +,INTERM. STATES IN FISS.	
Fission	Spont		MRY	Theo Prog	ORO – 4028 – 28	71 Jackson+. SPON FISSION HALF – LIFE GVN	
Fission	2.5–2		SRL	Eval Conf	75Wash. 224	Mar 75 Benjamin+ TBL BEST FIT TRANSPU PROD.	
Res Int Fiss	Maxwl		BNL	Theo Abst	ANS 10 228	Jun 67 Prince. CALCULATED RES INTGRL=85B	
Res Int Fiss	6.3–1		SRL	Eval Conf	75Wash. 224	Mar 75 Benjamin+ TBL BEST FIT TRANSPU PROD.	
Nu	Spont		LAS	Expt Jour	NSE 43 54	Jan 71 Orth.SEPARATE COUNT OF NS +SPON FISS	+
	Spont			Data	EXFOR10115.005	Jul 71 . 1PT.AVG NU=3,53+ – .09 REL CF 252.	
Nu	Spont		DUB	Comp Rept	JINR – P15 – 6730	Sep 72 Dakowski+ MASS DEPEN.OF NU – BAR IN CF	
Nu	Spont		IAE	Eval Jour	REA 10 637	Dec 72 Manero+ EXTENSIVE SURVEY,TBL,AVG VAL	
Nu	Spont		LAS	Expt Prog	ERDA – NDC – 3 93	May 76 Veeser+LIQ SCINT.NU MEAS.NDG	
Fiss Yield	Spont		OSL	Revw Conf	69Vienna 669	Jul 69 Pappas+.PPR206.REVW,INITIAL MASS DIST	
Fiss Yield	Spont		LAS	Expt Jour	PR/C 7 276	Jan 73 Hoffman+.MASS – YLD CURV FROM FRAG KE	
Fiss Yield	Spont		ANL	Expt Conf	73Rochestr 2 19	Aug 73 Unik+ PROMPT YLDS,MASS DISTRIB,GRPHS	
Fiss Yield	Spont		AUA	Revw Conf	IAEA – 169 2 163	74 Musgrove+ PROMPT,EVEN – Z POSITN,GRAPH	

98 Californium 250

Quantity	Energy (ev) Min	Max	Lab	Type	Documentation Ref Vol Page	Date	Author, Comments	Data
Fiss Yield	Spont		MNZ	Expt	Prog MAINZ-1975		76 Meixler+ STEARAT METHOD CUM.YIELD	+
	0.0+0				Data EXFOR20711.004	Feb 77	2PTS.	
Fiss Yield	Spont		AUA	Theo	Rept AAEC/E-386	Mar 76	Cook+ 3-GAUSS FIT,PARAMS GIVEN	
Frag Spectra	Spont		LAS	Expt	Jour PR/C 7 276	Jan 73	Hoffman+.KE DISTR. SI DETECTOR	
Frag Spectra	Spont		ANL	Expt	Conf 73Rochestr 2 19	Aug 73	Unik+ TOTAL KIN-E OF FRAGS,GRPH,TBL	
Frag Spectra	Spont		AUA	Revw	Conf IAEA-169 2 163	74	Musgrove+ AVG FRAG MASS,GRAPH	
Reson Params	6.2-1	5.0+4	SRL	Theo	Conf 71Knoxvill 714	Mar 71	Mccrosson. STAT CALCULATN AVG PARAMS	

98 Californium 251

Quantity	Energy (ev) Min	Max	Lab	Type	Documentation Ref Vol Page	Date	Author, Comments	Data
Evaluation	1.0-5	2.0+7	SRL	Eval	Rept EPRI-NP-161	Dec 75	Benjamin+ENDF4B.GENPAR MDL.REVISIONS	
Total	None		KAP	Comp	Rept KAPL-1781	Jul 57	Schuman. SIGMA GIVEN	
Absorption	Maxwl		SRL	Expt	Conf 68Wash. 1285	Mar 68	Smith+ SIG=4970B THERMALIZED SPEC	+
					Rept DP-MS-67-111	Mar 68	- +	
	Maxwl				Data EXFOR12580.010	Jun 76	. 1 PT, SIGMA	
Absorption	Maxwl		SRL	Expt	Conf 68Wash. 1279	Mar 68	Folger+ ACT	+
					Rept DP-MS-67-112	Mar 68	- +	
	Maxwl				Data EXFOR12534.014	Jun 76	. 1 PT, SIGMA	
Absorption	Maxwl		SRL	Expt	Abst ANS 14 344	Jun 71	Rusche. VALUE GIVEN	
Absorption	Pile		ORL	Expt	Prog ORNL-4706 47	Sep 71	Halperin+MASS SPEC.ITERATIVE CALC.	
	Pile				Data EXFOR10119.008	Dec 77	. 1PT. EFFECTIVE ABS CS=6900B.	
Absorption	2.5-2		ORL	Expt	Prog ORNL-4706 51	Sep 71	Bemis+EFFECTIVE VALS GVN.	
Res Int Abs	9.2-1		SRL	Expt	Conf 68Wash. 1279	Mar 68	Folger+ ACT 980B	+
					Rept DP-MS-67-112	Mar 68	- +	
	9.2-1				Data EXFOR12534.018	Jun 76	. 1 PT.	
Res Int Abs	None		SRL	Expt	Abst ANS 14 344	Jun 71	Rusche. VALUE GIVEN	
Res Int Abs	5.0-1		ORL	Expt	Prog ORNL-4706 51	Sep 71	Bemis+CD FILTER.RIA=7000B.	
(n,γ)	Pile		ANL	Expt	Jour PR 96 1576	Dec 54	Magnusson+.MASS SPECTRM.AROUND 3000B	+
					Conf 55Geneva 7 261	Aug 55	Bentley+.P809,VAL GVN,CHEMICAL METHD	
	Pile				Data EXFOR12568.004	Jun 76	. 1 PT, SIGMA	
(n,γ)	Spont		ANL	Expt	Rept ANL-6252	Feb 61	Vandenbosch+.	
(n,γ)	Maxwl		BNL	Theo	Abst ANS 10 228	Jun 67	Prince. CALCULATED SIG=1100B	
(n,γ)	Maxwl		CCP	Comp	Jour AE 28 388	May 70	Bol'Shov+ OTHER'S SIG VALUE GIVEN	
					Jour EAF 28 5 9	70	. FRENCH OF AE 28 388.	
(n,γ)	2.5-2		ORL	Expt	Prog ORNL-4706 51	Sep 71	Bemis+VALS GVN.DEP ON ABS CS GVN.TBL	
(n,γ)	Maxwl		ORL	Expt	Prog ORNL-4706 47	Sep 71	Halperin+MASS SPEC ANAL.AVG CS.	+
	Maxwl				Data EXFOR10119.006	Mar 76	1PT.NG CS=2850+ - 150.	
(n,γ)	Pile		KFK	Eval	Prog KFK-1544 61	Jan 72	Eberle+FOR 2-GROUP SIG,FITTED TO EXP	
(n,γ)	Maxwl		SRL	Eval	Conf 75Wash. 224	Mar 75	Benjamin+ TBL BEST FIT TRANSPU PROD.	
Res Int Capt	Maxwl		BNL	Theo	Abst ANS 10 228	Jun 67	Prince. CALCULATED RES INTGRL=172B	
Res Int Capt	5.0-1		ORL	Expt	Prog ORNL-4706 47	Sep 71	Halperin+MASS SPEC ANAL.CD COVER.	+
	5.0-1				Data EXFOR10119.007	Mar 76	. 1 PT. RIG CS=1600+ - 30B.	
Res Int Capt	Pile		KFK	Eval	Prog KFK-1544 61	Jan 72	Eberle+ 730B	
Res Int Capt	6.3-1		SRL	Eval	Conf 75Wash. 224	Mar 75	Benjamin+ TBL BEST FIT TRANSPU PROD.	
Fission	Maxwl		ANL	Expt	Jour JIN 27 33	Jan 65	Metta+ SIG=3000+ -260B REL PU239=803B	+
	Maxwl				Data EXFOR12562.004	Jun 76	. 1 PT. SIGMA	
Fission	Maxwl		BNL	Theo	Abst ANS 10 228	Jun 67	Prince. CALCULATED SIG=3000B	
Fission	Maxwl		SRL	Expt	Conf 68Wash. 1285	Mar 68	Smith+SIG=3550B PAPER H12.THERM SPEC	+
					Rept DP-MS-67-111	Feb 68	- +	
	Maxwl				Data EXFOR12580.011	Jun 76	. 1 PT, SIGMA	
Fission	Maxwl		CCP	Comp	Jour AE 28 388	May 70	Bol'Shov+ SIGMA VALUE ESTIMATED, TBL	
					Jour EAF 28 5 9	70	. FRENCH OF AE 28 388.	
Fission	Maxwl		SRL	Expt	Abst ANS 14 344	Jun 71	Rusche. VALUE GIVEN	
Fission	Maxwl		ORL	Expt	Prog ORNL-4706 51	Sep 71	Bemis+NF EFFECTIVE=(ABS-NG)EFFECTIVE	
Fission	Pile		KFK	Eval	Prog KFK-1544 61	Jan 72	Eberle+FOR 2-GROUP SIG,FITTED TO EXP	
Fission	Maxwl		LRL	Expt	Jour PR/C 9 399	Jan 74	Ragaini. SIG=4800+ -250B.	+
					Conf 73Rochestr 2 47	Aug 73	- + ABSTRACT,SIGMA GIVEN	
	Maxwl				Data EXFOR10393.002	Jun 74	. 1 PT.	
Fission	Maxwl		SRL	Eval	Conf 75Wash. 224	Mar 75	Benjamin+ TBL BEST FIT TRANSPU PROD.	
Fission	Maxwl		ANL	Expt	Jour PR/C 11 1676	May 75	Flynn+MASS DISTR.REL CO59.THR CS GVN	+
	2.5-2				Data EXFOR10516.008	Apr 78	. 1PT.CS=5300+ -530B	
Res Int Fiss	Maxwl		BNL	Theo	Abst ANS 10 228	Jun 67	Prince. CALCULATED RES INTGRL=445B	
Res Int Fiss	None		SRL	Expt	Abst ANS 14 344	Jun 71	Rusche. VALUE GIVEN	
Res Int Fiss	Pile		KFK	Eval	Prog KFK-1544 61	Jan 72	Eberle+1370B	
Res Int Fiss	6.3-1		SRL	Eval	Conf 75Wash. 224	Mar 75	Benjamin+ TBL BEST FIT TRANSPU PROD.	
Alpha	1.0+4	2.0+4	LAS	Theo	Jour PR 158 1127	Jun 67	Bell. SYSTEMATCS TH FOR 10-20KEV ALF	

98 Californium 251

Quantity	Energy (ev) Min	Max	Lab	Type	Documentation Ref Vol Page	Date	Author, Comments	Data
Alpha	2.5–2		ORL	Expt Prog	ORNL–4706 51	Sep 71	Bemis+TBL.=(NG/NF)EFFECTIVE	
Nu	Maxwl		IAE	Eval Jour	REA 10 637	Dec 72	Manero+ CALC,SYSTEMATICS,TBL	
Nu	Maxwl		AUA	Revw Conf	IAEA–169 2 163	74	Musgrove+ TOTAL NU–BAR,GRAPH	
Nu	2.5–2		ANL	Expt Jour	PR/C 11 1676	May 75	Flynn+MASS DISTR.TBL.THR NU GVN.	+
	2.5–2			Data	EXFOR10516.006	Apr 78	. 1PT.NU=4.1+–.5	
Fiss Yield	–		CCP	Theo Jour	YF 7 832	Apr 68	Shigin.GRPH TH–YLD(FRAG–A,EXCIT–E)	
				Jour	SNP 7 4 506	Oct 68	TRANSLATN.*	
Fiss Yield	Maxwl		LRL	Expt Jour	PR/C 9 399	Jan 74	Ragaini. FRAG MASS DISTRIBUTS. CURVS	
				ExTh Conf	73Rochestr 2 47	Aug 73	– + ABST,MASS YLD FROM KE,NDG	
Fiss Yield	Maxwl		ANL	Expt Jour	PR/C 11 1676	May 75	Flynn+ TBL,GRPH 915S TO 156 SM	+
				Conf	73Rochestr 2 19	Aug 73	Unik+PRELIM.MASS DISTRB 16 NUCLIDES	
	2.5–2			Data	EXFOR10516.002	Apr 78	. 26PTS.MASS YLDS.4PT MASS CHAIN YLD	
Fiss Yield	Maxwl		AUA	Theo Rept	AAEC/E–386	Mar 76	Cook+ 3–GAUSS FIT,PARAMS GIVEN	
Frag Spectra	None		CCP	Theo Jour	AE 6 298	Mar 59	Geilikman. FRAG POT+KIN+EXCIT E,TABL	
				Jour	SJA 6 184	Nov 60	TRANSLATN.*	
Frag Spectra	Maxwl		LRL	Expt Jour	PR/C 9 399	Jan 74	Ragaini. FRAG KE+MASS DISTR. CURVES.	
				Conf	73Rochestr 2 47	Aug 73	– + ABSTRACT,MEAN FRAG–KE GIVEN	
Reson Params	6.2–1	5.0+4	SRL	Theo Conf	71Knoxvill 714	Mar 71	Mccrosson. STAT CALCULATN AVG PARAMS	
Lvl Density	–		CCP	Theo Jour	YF 7 832	Apr 68	Shigin.GRPH LVL DEN(FISS–FRAG–A),YLD	
				Jour	SNP 7 4 506	Oct 68	TRANSLATN.*	

98 Californium 252

Quantity	Energy (ev) Min	Max	Lab	Type	Documentation Ref Vol Page	Date	Author, Comments	Data
Evaluation	Spont	1.5+7	BNL	Comp Rept	BNL–50168	Apr 69	Prince.REVIEW ALL SIGS,FISS DATA ETC	
Evaluation	1.0–5	2.0+7	SRL	Eval Rept	EPRI–NP–161	Dec 75	Benjamin+ENDF4B.GENPAR MDL.REVISIONS	
Absorption	Maxwl		SRL	Expt Conf	68Wash. 1279	Mar 68	Folger+ ACT	+
				Rept	DP–MS–67–112	Mar 68	– +	
	Maxwl			Data	EXFOR12534.015	Jun 76	. 1 PT, SIGMA	
Absorption	Maxwl		SRL	Expt Abst	ANS 14 344	Jun 71	Rusche. VALUE GIVEN	
Absorption	Pile		CCP	Expt Jour	AE 32 493	Jun 72	Anufriev+ SIG GIVEN,CFD OTHER EXPTS	
				Jour	SJA 32 584	Dec 72	– + ENGLISH OF AE 32 493	
Res Int Abs	5.0–1		SRL	Expt Conf	68Wash. 1279	Mar 68	Folger+ ACT 42B	+
				Rept	DP–MS–67–112	Mar 68	– +	
	5.0–1			Data	EXFOR12534.019	Jun 76	. 1 PT. SIGMA	
Res Int Abs	Pile		BNL	Expt Prog	WASH–1093 16	Apr 68	Gordon+ UPPER LIMIT GIVEN EPI–THR	
Res Int Abs	Pile		KFK	Expt Rept	KFK–1338	Apr 71	Eberle+ 40 B,CF–253+ES–253 YLDS CALC	
Res Int Abs	None		SRL	Expt Abst	ANS 14 344	Jun 71	Rusche. VALUE GIVEN	
(n,γ)	Pile		BRK	Expt Jour	PR 95 581	Jul 54	Harvey+.MEASURED E253 YIELD.MTR. 30B	+
	Pile			Data	EXFOR12567.007	Jun 76	. 1 PT, SIGMA	
(n,γ)	Pile		ANL	Expt Jour	PR 96 1576	Dec 54	Magnusson+. 25 B FROM CF250 YLD. MTR	
				Conf	55Geneva 7 261	Aug 55	Bentley+.P809,VAL GVN,CHEMICAL METHD	
	Pile			Data	EXFOR12568.005	Jun 76	. 1 PT, SIGMA	
(n,γ)	None		KAP	Comp Rept	KAPL–1781	Jul 57	Schuman. SIGMA GVN	
(n,γ)	Maxwl		ORL	Expt Jour	NSE 37 228	Aug 69	Halperin+. ACT.20.4+–2B AT 0.025EV	+
	Maxwl			Data	EXFOR10018.002	Sep 73	. 1PT=20.4+–2 AT2299M/S	
(n,γ)	None		LAS	Expt Prog	WASH–1136 110	Sep 69	Silbert+,PHYSICS–8 SHOT,ANAL TBC	
(n,γ)	Maxwl		CCP	Comp Jour	AE 28 388	May 70	Bol'Shov+ OTHER'S SIG VALUE GIVEN	
				Jour	EAF 28 5 9	70	. FRENCH OF AE 28 388.	
(n,γ)	Pile		KFK	Eval Prog	KFK–1544 61	Jan 72	Eberle+FOR 2–GROUP SIG,FITTED TO EXP	
				Expt Rept	KFK–1338	Apr 71	– + 20 B,CF–253+ES–253 YLDS CALC	
(n,γ)	Pile		NIR	Expt Jour	AE 36 286	Apr 74	Anufriev+ EFFECT SIG,FROM ABSORPTION	
				Jour	SJA 36 359	Oct 74	. ENGLISH OF AE 36 286	
(n,γ)	Maxwl		SRL	Eval Conf	75Wash. 224	Mar 75	Benjamin+ TBL BEST FIT TRANSPU PROD.	
Res Int Capt	5.4–1		ORL	Expt Jour	NSE 37 228	Aug 69	Halperin+.	+
	5.4–1			Data	EXFOR10018.003	Sep 73	. 1PT. RES INTEG=43.5+–3.	
Res Int Capt	5.0–1		ORL	Expt Prog	ORNL–4706 51	Sep 71	Bemis+CD FILTER.RIG=1620+–100B.	
Res Int Capt	Pile		KFK	Expt Rept	KFK–1544 61	Jan 72	Eberle+42B	
Res Int Capt	6.3–1		SRL	Eval Conf	75Wash. 224	Mar 75	Benjamin+ TBL BEST FIT TRANSPU PROD.	
(n,2n)	Spont		CCP	Expt Jour	YF 15 1121	Jun 72	Ivanov.ANG ANISOTROPY IN TERNARY,TBL	
				Jour	SNP 15 620	Dec 72	– . ENGLISH OF YF 15 1121	
Fission	Spont		KUR	Theo Rept	IAE–562 3	64	Geylikman+,TRIPLE FISS,E DIST CFDEXP	
				Rept	ANL–TR–68	64	TRANSLATN.*	
Fission	Spont		BRK	Revw Jour	NP 81 1	Jun 66	Myers.TBL CALC FISS BARRIERS.	
Fission	Spont		JAE	Theo Prog	EANDC(J)7L17	Jan 67	E.TAKEKOSHI,FITTING FORM FOR PR NEUT	
Fission	Spont		TRM	Expt Conf	67Kanpur § N63	Feb 67	Hattangadi.E DISTR OF ALPHA PARTICLS	
Fission	Spont		PUR	Expt Prog	COO–1716–6	Jan 69	Cobble.RADIOCHEM,TERN/BIN UPPR LIMIT	

98 Californium 252

Quantity	Energy (ev) Min	Max	Lab	Type	Documentation Ref Vol Page	Date	Author, Comments	Data
Fission	–		TPI	Theo	Jour YF 9 102	Jan 69	Korostova+ SHELL-TH OKS HLS CM+CF+FM	
					Jour SNP 9 62	Jul 69	TRANSLATN.*	
Fission	Spont		COP	Revw	Conf 69Vienna 155	Jul 69	Strutinsky+PPR203. HL GVN,'SHELL-TH'	
Fission	Spont		RI	Expt	Jour AE 28 361	Apr 70	Aleksandrov+ SPON FISS+ALF HLS GIVEN	
					Rept INDC(CCP)-15	Dec 71	*P46,ENG OF YFI-10	
					Rept YFI-10 41	May 71	*	
					Jour SJA 28 462	Apr 70	*ENGL OF AE 28 361	
					Jour EAF 28 4 115	Apr 70	*FRENCH OF AE 28	
Fission	Spont		MRY	Theo	Prog ORO-4028-28	71	Jackson+. SPON FISSION HALF-LIFE GVN	
Fission	2.0+1	5.0+6	LAS	Expt	Jour PR/C 4 273	Jul 71	Moore+.NUCL SHOT.MUCH STRUCTURE SEEN	+
					Conf 70Helsinki 1 527	Jun 70	.SUPERSEDED	
	2.4+1	4.7+6			Data EXFOR10323.002	Dec 73	. 1396 PTS.	
Fission	Maxwl		ORL	Expt	Prog ORNL-4706 53	Sep 71	Halperin+. VALUE GIVEN.	+
	Maxwl				Data EXFOR10222.002	Nov 72	. 1 PT. SIGMA	
Fission	Spont		MND	Expt	Rept MLM-1845	Oct 71	Hastings+. HALF-LIFE GIVEN	
Fission	Pile		KFK	Eval	Prog KFK-1544 61	Jan 72	Eberle+FOR 2-GROUP SIG,FITTED TO EXP	
Fission	None		FRK	Theo	Jour NP/A 207 225	Jun 73	Albrecht. 2CENTRE SHELLMOD,DEF-E MAP	
Fission	Spont		LRL	Expt	Jour PR/C 10 795	Aug 74	Dietrich+ G SPECT 8-20MEV, GRPHS.	
Fission	Maxwl		SRL	Eval	Conf 75Wash. 224	Mar 75	Benjamin+ TBL BEST FIT TRANSPU PROD.	
Fission	Spont		TUE	Theo	Jour PL/B 57 7	Jun 75	Schultheis+ INTERNAL EXCIT ENERGY	
Fission	Spont		PAV	Theo	Jour NP/A 249 185	Sep 75	Fossati+DIST ALPHA PARTICLE,TER FISS	
Fission	1.0+3	5.0+6	JAE	Revw	Rept JAERI-M-6315	Nov 75	Igarasi+GRPH. DATA OF MOORE 1971.	
Res Int Fiss	None		SRL	Expt	Abst ANS 14 344	Jun 71	Rusche. VALUE GIVEN	
Res Int Fiss	5.4-2		ORL	Expt	Prog ORNL-4706 53	Sep 71	Halperin+. VALUE GIVEN.	+
	5.4-2				Data EXFOR10222.003	Nov 72	. 1 PT. SIGMA	
Res Int Fiss	Pile		KFK	Eval	Prog KFK-1544 61	Jan 72	Eberle+12B	
Res Int Fiss	6.3-1		SRL	Eval	Conf 75Wash. 224	Mar 75	Benjamin+ TBL BEST FIT TRANSPU PROD.	
Eta	Spont		INL	Expt	Conf 75Wash. 262	Mar 75	Smith.MN-BATH.CFD MONTE CARLO CALC	
Nu	Spont		ANL	Expt	Jour JIN 1 45	Mar 55	Glendenin+,RADIOCHEM,AVG NU=5+-1	
Nu	Spont		BRK	Expt	Jour PR 105 1507	Mar 57	Hicks+,CURVS CORRELAT WITH FRAG KE	
					Jour PR 101 1016	Feb 56	- +,SPONT FIS,REL PU240,PROBABIL.	
					Jour PR 98 1521	Jun 55	.SEE ALSO PRELIM VALUE	
					Jour PR 97 564	Jan 55	.SEE ALSO MULTIPLICITIES	
Nu	Spont		LRL	ExTh Expt	Jour PR 101 1804	Mar 56	Crane+,LII CRYST+FIS COUNT,REL RABE	+
					Jour PR 97 727	Mar 55	- .	
					Jour PR 97 242	Jan 55	- +.MN BATH,REL TO MOCK FIS SOURC	
Nu	Spont		LAS	Expt	Jour PR 101 1012	Feb 56	Diven+,LIQ SCINT,+PROB EMISS 0.8 NS	+
					Rept TNCC(US)-7	May 56	.CO4116 AVG PLUS FLUCT	
					Conf 55Geneva 2 193	Aug 55	Leachman.P592,CURVE,EXPT DESCRIBED	
	Spont				Data EXFOR12337.007	Jun 76	. 1 PT.	
Nu	Spont		LAS	Theo	Jour PR 105 1511	Mar 57	Leachman+,CURVE	
Nu	Spont		LAS	Expt	Jour PR 110 476	Apr 58	Stein+ NU=3.86+-0.07	
Nu	Spont		LAS	Expt	Rept AECD-4261	Apr 58	Wahl.	+
	Spont				Data EXFOR12587.002	Jun 76	. 1 PT.	
Nu	Spont		LRL	Expt	Conf 58Geneva 15 212	Sep 58	Bowman+,NU AND MULTIPLICITIES.	+
					Rept UCRL-5038	Jul 59	.SEE ALSO,SAME RESULTS.	
Nu	Spont		LAS	Expt	Jour PR 114 581	Apr 59	Whetstone.NU=3.86+-.07	
					Prog WASH-1048 54	Jun 64	Terrell. RE-EVAL WHETSTONE PR114,581	
Nu	Spont		CCP	Theo	Jour AE 8 409	May 60	Zysin+.VAL CALCD FROM FRGMNT-DISTRBS	
					Jour SJA 8 343	Jun 61	TRANSLATN.*JNE AB17 41 1/61	
					Jour KE 4 40	Jan 61	.TRANSLATN	
Nu	Spont		RI	Revw	Jour UFN 73 655	Apr 61	Petrzhak+ CURV,NU REL FRGM-MASSRATIO	
					Jour SPU 4 305	Sep 61	. ENGL OF UFN 73 655	
Nu	Spont		ALD	Expt	Jour JNAB 15 102	Oct 61	Moat+.REL STANDARD N SOURCE	+
					Jour JNAB 20 549	Jul 66	Fieldhouse+REVISN HAR PU240 N STRNGTH	
Nu	–		CCP	Theo	Jour ZET 42 180	Jan 62	Blinov.GRAPH NUCL-SHELL-TH CFD XPTS	
					Jour JET 15 130	Jul 62	TRANSLATN.*	
Nu	Spont		ANL	Expt	Jour PR 126 197	Apr 62	Meadows+,PROMPT+TOTAL NU,REL NU-U235	+
	Spont				Data EXFOR12419.002	Jun 76	. 6 PTS.	
Nu	Spont		REH	Theo	Rept IA- 757	Jul 62	Sieger+ CALC FRM CHAIN-Y,CFD OTH.TBL	
Nu	Spont		ANL	Revw	Conf 62Harwell 2 581	Dec 62	Fields+ PROMPT NUBAR MEASMENTS,TABLE	
Nu	Spont		FOA	Comp	Rept NP-16440	Mar 63	ASPLUND-NILSSON. REVIEW. TABLE.	
Nu	Spont		FOA	Expt	Jour NSE 16 124	May 63	Asplund-Nilsson+. LIQUID SCINT.	+
					Conf 73Kiev 4 130	May 73	Conde. SHORT DESCRIPT.VALUE GIVN.TBC	
					Conf 61Vienna 155	Aug 61	- . PPR75. SUPERSEDED.	
	Spont				Data EXFOR20074.002	Sep 71	1PNT.PROMPT.	

98 Californium 252

Quantity	Energy (ev) Min	Max	Lab	Type	Documentation Ref Vol Page	Date	Author, Comments	Data
Nu	Spont		LAS	Expt	Jour NP 48 433	Oct 63	Hopkins+,SCINT TANK,ABSOL	+
					Conf 61Vienna 1 149	Aug 61	.SEE ALSO	
	Spont				Data EXFOR12326.007	Jun 76	. 1 PT.	
Nu	Spont		YAM	Theo	Jour JPJ 18 1697	Nov 63	Honda.CALC E FISSFRAGS VS A.TBCFD NU	
Nu	Spont		BAR	Theo	Jour NP 53 113	Apr 64	Lang.STATMOD ANALYS.BOWMAN EXPERIMT.	
Nu	Spont		ISL	Expt	Rept IA- 1082 55	65	Nardi+.NDG,SEE ALSO IA - 1021 P27	
Nu	Spont		HAR	Expt	Conf 65Salzburg 2 25	Mar 65	Colvin+PPR44.BORONPILE.ABSOL+RATIOS	+
					Conf 66Paris 1 307	Oct 66	- .	
					Prog AERE-PR/NP8 9	Feb 65	- +TBL.NU=3.713+ - 0.015.ABS.	
Nu	None		LAS	Revw	Conf 65Salzburg 3	Mar 65	Terrell.XPTL WORK CFD THEORY.GRAPHS	
Nu	Spont		CCP	Theo	Rept ICD-3 34	Oct 66	Zommer+.GRAPH REL FRGMNT LVL DENSITY	
					Rept INDC-152E 34	67	. ENGL OF ICD-3 34	
Nu	Spont		SAC	Expt	Conf 66Paris 2 57	Oct 66	Baron+ (PPR77) VALUE GIVEN, P(NU)	
Nu	Spont		LRL	Expt	Prog WASH-1071 87	Nov 66	Fultz+. CFD OTHERS	
Nu	Spont		AI	Eval	Jour JNE 22 79	Feb 68	Fillmore.REVIEWS DATA TO OCT 1966	
Nu	Spont		ALD	Expt	Jour JNE 22 73	Feb 68	White+ MN-BATH,ABS FISS RATE + N YLD	+
Nu	Spont		SOR	Expt	Jour PRL 20 1248	May 68	Nardi+ CURV NU VS. FRAG MASS	
Nu	Spont		ORL	Expt	Prog WASH-1124 142	Nov 68	Schmitt. OKS OTHERS, NDG	
Nu	-		BOR	Theo	Jour CR 267 1350	Dec 68	Doan+BASED ON MODEL OF 3 ALIGN.SPERE	
Nu	Spont		EDG	Revw	Conf 69Vienna 83	Jul 69	Feather.PPR201. SURVEW,TERNARY NU	
Nu	Spont		IBJ	Expt	Conf 69Vienna 892	Jul 69	Piekarz+PPR64. NU VAL GVN,TERN-FISSN	+
	Spont				Data EXFOR30318.002	Jan 76	7 PTS, ANG DISTRIBUTION.	
Nu	Spont		KFK	Revw	Jour AKE 15 26	70	Schmidt. REVW ON EXPTS, GRPH	
					Rept KFK-966	Apr 69	- . EXPTS COMPARED.	
Nu	Spont		NPL	Expt	Priv AXTON	Feb 70	Axton+,EXPERIMENT RESTARTED	+
					Prog NEANDC(UK)160	Jul 74	- + EVAL MN BATH CORRECTIONS TBC	
					Prog EANDC(UK) 151	Aug 73	- .VALUE 3.725 N/F TBC	
					Jour JNE 23 457	Aug 69	- + ABSOL FIS COUNT METHOD.	
Nu	Spont		CCP	Expt	Jour YF 11 1001	May 70	Adamov+ NU(ALFA-ENERGY),TERN-FISSION	
					Jour SNP 11 557	Nov 70	. ENGL OF YF 11 1001	
Nu	Spont		AE	Expt	Conf 70Helsinki 2 93	Jun 70	Almen+57. COMPILATN AND NU-TEMP-PLOT	
Nu	Spont		ANL	Revw	Conf 70Helsinki 2 119	Jun 70	Davey.112.TABLE OF NU VALUES	
Nu	Spont		HAR	Revw	Conf 70Helsinki 2 195	Jun 70	Colvin.PPR99. REPORT ON DATA STATUS	
				Eval	Conf 69Vienna 930	Jul 69	- .PPR55. RECOMMENDATION+REVIEW	
Nu	Spont		IAE	Revw	Conf INDC(NDS)-25L	Aug 70	Konshin+ STANDARD STATUS,PANEL RECOM	
Nu	Spont		NIR	Expt	Jour AE 29 95	Aug 70	Kroshkin+ NU BAR + - 3.0 PERCENT GIVN	+
					Jour SJA 29 790	Aug 70	. ENGL OF AE 29 95	
					Data EXFOR40064.005	Sep 73	.1 DATA LINE	
Nu	Spont		NIR	Expt	Conf 71Vienna 89	Aug 71	Nefedov+ TOF,PLASTIC SCIN,E-SPEC	
Nu	Spont		KFI	Theo	Jour PL/B 37 217	Nov 71	Kluge. TOTAL ENERGY AND ANGDIST CALC	
Nu	Spont		RI	Eval	Prog YFI-12 89	72	Petrzhak+ ABST,EXPTS CFD+MEAN,TBL	
					Prog INDC(CCP)-30	Sep 72	.PAGE 78,ENGLISH OF YFI-12 89	
Nu	Spont		ANL	Expt	Jour JNE 26 75	Feb 72	DE VOLPI+ YIELD=3.729+ - 0.015	+
					Jour PR/C 1 683	Feb 70	.SUPERSEDED	
					Abst DA/B 27 4510	Jun 67	.SUPERSEDED	
					Conf 66Paris 1 297	Oct 66	.SUPERSEDED	
					Conf 66Vienna 693	Oct 66	.SUPERSEDED	
	Spont				Data EXFOR10166.003	Nov 74	. 1 PT.	
Nu	Spont		SAC	Expt	Jour NP/A 189 285	Jul 72	Nifenecker+ LIQ SCINT. VS A,EK.NDG	
					Prog EANDC(E)150U	May 72	- +,DEPEND ON FRAG CHARGE	
					Prog EANDC(E)150U	May 72	Poitou+,TERNARY FISS	
					Prog EANDC(E)140U	Aug 71	Signarbieux+,CORREL.WITH MASS+ENERGY	
Nu	Spont		DUB	Comp	Rept JINR-P15-6730	Sep 72	Dakowski+ MASS DEPEN.OF NU-BAR IN CF	
Nu	Spont		FOA	Revw	Conf 72Vienna 277	Nov 72	Conde. CRITICAL NUBAR - REEVAL.TBL.	
					Conf IAEA-107 87	68	- . EQU TO 67BRUSSE.	
					Conf 67Brussels	May 67	- . EXPTS DISCUSSED.GRPHS.TBLS.	
Nu	Spont		IAE	Eval	Jour REA 10 637	Dec 72	Manero+ EXTENSIVE SURVEY,TBL,AVG VAL	
Nu	Spont		KJL	Theo	Rept KR- 148	Jan 73	Skarsvaag.TBL EN ANGDIST PRMPT NEUTS	
Nu	Spont		SAC	Expt	Jour PR/C 7 373	Jan 73	Mehta+ NU DIST,BINARY+ LRA FISSION.	
Nu	Spont		ORL	Expt	Jour NSE 50 169	Feb 73	Stoughton+DET CALIB FOR CM NU MEAS.	
Nu	Spont		AUA	Expt	Prog AAEC/PR-38P 10	Mar 73	Boldeman.NUBAR=3.725+ - 0.014,LIQ SCIN	
Nu	Spont		RI	Expt	Conf 73Kiev 4 171	May 73	Blinov+ ANG CORREL FOR FISS NS	
Nu	Spont		LBL	Theo	Rept LBL-1950	Jul 73	Nifenecker+.NU VARIATN WITH FRAG KE	
Nu	Spont		ANL	Expt	Conf 73Rochestr 2 19	Aug 73	Unik+NU TOTAL VS MASS 13 NUCLIDES.	
Nu	Spont		NPL	Eval	Prog EANDC(UK) 151	Aug 73	Axton.FOR IAEA 2200M/S EVAL TBL	
					Conf 72Vienna 261	Nov 72	- . TBL RE-EVAL NUBAR OF 11XPTS	

98 Californium 252

Quantity	Energy (ev) Min Max	Lab	Type	Documentation Ref Vol Page	Author, Comments Date	Data
Nu	Spont	DUB	Comp Jour	YF 18 724	Oct 73 Dakovsky+ NUBAR VS FISNUCLEUS,TBL+GRP	
			Eval Rept	JINR - P15 - 7119	Jun 73 Dakowski+ NUBAR+P(NU) - DISTR,TBL,GRPH	
			Comp Jour	SNP 18 371	Apr 74 . ENGLISH OF YF 18, 724.	
Nu	Spont	AUA	Revw Conf	IAEA - 169 2 163	74 Musgrove+ TOTAL NU - BAR,GRAPH	
Nu	Spont	SAC	Expt Rept	CEA - N - 1700	74 Girard+ PROMPT NU VS PROMPT G ENERGY	
Nu	Spont	REH	Expt Jour	PR/C 9 632	Feb 74 Gavron+.VARIATION WITH FRAG MASS,KE	
			Jour	PRL 27 1761	Dec 71 - + ERRATUM TO PRL 27 1148	
			Jour	PRL 27 1148	71 - +.VARIATION WITH FRAG MASS,KE	
Nu	Spont	AUA	Revw Rept	AAEC/E - 304	Mar 74 Musgrove. NUBAR(ALFA - EKIN) CFD,GRAPH	
			Eval Rept	AAEC/E - 304	Mar 74 - . ESTIMATE OF BIN NUBAR GIVN	
Nu	Spont	AUA	Expt Jour	NSE 55 188	Oct 74 Boldeman. PROMPT NEUTRON YIELD	+
			Prog	AAEC/PR - 39P 36	Jan 74 .SMALL CORRECTIONS.NEW FINAL VALUE.	
			Prog	INDC(SEC) - 35	Sep 73 Boldeman+ SHORT NOTE,ERR ANALYS,DATA	
			Conf	73Kiev 4 83	May 73 . FULL PAPER.DETAILED ERROR - ANALYSIS	
			Conf	72Vienna 291	Nov 72 Boldeman. LIQ SCIN,NUBAR CFD OTHERS	
			Rept	AAEC/E - 172	Mar 67 - + DETAILS,NUBAR SUPERSEDED	
	Spont		Data	EXFOR30046.006	Jan 73 .FINAL VALUE FROM PRIV COMM NOV 1972	
Nu	Spont	KUR	Expt Conf	75Kiev 5 86	May 75 Vasil'Ev+ NU(FRAG - A,E).GRAPHS+TABLE	
Nu	Spont +7	RI	Expt Conf	75Kiev 5 166	May 75 Aleksandrov+ IMPROVD VAL=3.747+-.036	+
			Conf	73Kiev 4 76	May 73 - + 3METHDS.NU=3.770+-.045	
	Spont		Data	EXFOR40264.002	Jan 75 1 DATA LINE	
Nu	Spont	SUN	Expt Jour	PRL 35 1563	Dec 75 Pringle+ ANGULAR CORRELATIONS,GRAPH	
Nu	Spont	RI	Expt Rept	INDC(CCP) - 66	Feb 76 .P15. ENGL OF YFI - 20 21	
Nu	Spont	LAS	Expt Prog	ERDA - NDC - 3 93	May 76 Veeser+LIQ SCINT.NU MEAS.NDG	
Nu	None	GER	Theo Conf	76Lowell 1468	Jul 76 Kolb.ANAL Z114 BIN,TER FRAGMENTATION	
Nu	+6	KUR	Theo Conf	77Kiev	77 Vasil'Ev+ TOF,TBL	
Nu	Spont	NIR	Expt Conf	77Kiev	77 Basova+ NU(NEUT - E),GRAPH	
			Conf	75Kiev 5 160	May 75 - + NU(FRAG - MASS,AVG EKIN).GRP	
Delayd Neuts	Spont	ANL	Expt Jour	PR 112 960	Nov 58 Cox+,DELAYED NS IN 3 PERIODS	
			Conf	58Geneva 690	Sep 58 .SUPERSEDED*	
Delayd Neuts	Spont	LAS	Expt Conf	61Vienna 1 149	Aug 61 Diven+.PPR56,TABLE REL TO U235	
Delayd Neuts	Spont	LAS	Expt Prog	WASH - 1068 119	Mar 66 Stein+,ANAL TBC,NDG	
Delayd Neuts	Spont	SOR	Comp Conf	67Vienna 115	Apr 67 Amiel+ DEL - N PRECURSRS,TBL=CALC+COMP	
			Revw Conf	69Vienna 569	Jul 69 - .PPR205. REVW,EXPTS+TH,TABLES	
Delayd Neuts	Spont	ORL	Expt Jour	NP/A 168 250	Jun 71 Chulick+ TOF SPEC 2SEC GROUP.11PEAKS	
			ExTh Jour	RCA 16 1 8	Feb 71 - + ANALYSIS OF DELAY NEUT YLDS	
Delayd Neuts	Spont	IAE	Eval Jour	REA 10 637	Dec 72 Manero+ RECOMMENDED NEUTRON YIELD	
Delayd Neuts	Spont	BUC	Revw Rept	IFA - RN - 50	73 Cristu. NUD(FRAGM - MASS),H - L,E - SPEC	
Delayd Neuts	Spont	RI	Expt Conf	73Kiev 4 155	May 73 Nefedov+ NEUT - SPEC,TOT YIELD.GRAPH	
			Prog	YFI - 12 104	72 - + ABST,TBLS GROUP YLDS+E - SPEC	
			Prog	INDC(CCP) - 30	Sep 72 .PAGE 90,ENGLISH OF YFI - 12 104	
Delayd Neuts	Spont	FEI	Expt Jour	YF 19 1212	Jun 74 Djachenko+ SEARCH,NO DELAY NS FOUND	
			Rept	KFKI - 73 - 45	Sep 73 Dyachenko+ NO RETARDED NS OBSERVED	
			Jour	SNP 19 619	Dec 74 . ENGLISH OF YF 19 1212	
Delayd Neuts	Spont	IAE	Eval Conf	75Wash. 286	Mar 75 Lemmel. 3RD IAEA - EVAL BY LSQ FIT	
Frag Neuts	Spont	CCP	Revw Jour	AE 8 15	Jan 60 Apalin+.YIELD FOR DIFF FRAGMENTS GVN	
			Jour	SJA 8 10	Apr 61 TRANSLATN.* JNE AB17 25 1/63	
			Jour	KE 3 633	Jul 60 .TRANSLATN	
Frag Neuts	Spont	CRC	Revw Conf	60Kingston 862	Aug 60 Hanna.CURVE,THEORET DISCUSSIONS	
Frag Neuts	Spont	LRL	Expt Jour	PR 126 2120	Jun 62 Bowman+,NEUT E,A DSTR REL FFRGM	
			Conf	58Geneva 15 212	Sep 58 .SUPERSEDED	
Frag Neuts	Spont	LAS	Expt Jour	PR 127 880	Aug 62 Terrell.ANALYSIS OF TOF+RADIOCHEM	
Frag Neuts	Spont	COP	Theo Jour	NP 46 129	Jul 63 Vandenbosch. EFF OF FRAG SHELL STRUC	
Frag Neuts	-	ROM	Theo Jour	NCS 3 4 1268	65 STATISTICAL MODEL CALC.	
Frag Neuts	None	LAS	Revw Conf	65Salzburg 3	Mar 65 Terrell.XPTL WORK CFD THEORY.GRAPHS	
Frag Neuts	Spont	ORL	Expt Abst	BAP 11 334	Apr 66 Schmitt+TOF. PULSE - HT	
Frag Neuts	Spont	CIS	Theo Jour	NP 84 595	Sep 66 Erba+ STATISTICAL MODEL CFD XPT	
Frag Neuts	Spont	BOR	Theo Conf	69Vienna 894	Jul 69 Doan+PPR81.TERNARY NU(FRAG A)OKS XPT	
Frag Neuts	Spont	IBJ	Expt Conf	69Vienna 892	Jul 69 Piekarz+PPR64. BIN+TERNARY FISSN CFD	
Frag Neuts	Spont	KFI	Theo Conf	69Vienna 927	Jul 69 Kluge.PPR9. CALCULATED NU VS FRAG - A	
			Jour	PL/B 27 65	Jun 68 - + E+NU VS FRAG MASS STATIS.CAL	
Frag Neuts	Spont	KUR	Theo Jour	YF 10 321	Aug 69 Pick - Pichak. HEAVY+LIGHT N - SPECS,TBL	
			Jour	SNP 10 185	Feb 70 . ENGL OF YF 10 321	
Frag Neuts	Spont	SCU	Theo Rept	ICD - 7 SUPPL 1	70 Saveliev.CALC N - SPECS OF FRAGS,GRPHS	
			Rept	INDC(CCP) - 18	Dec 71 . ENGL OF ICD - 7 SUPPL 1	
Frag Neuts	Spont	RI	Expt Prog	YFI - 12 100	72 Blinov+ ABST,N - ANISOTR(FRAG - MASS)TBL	
			Prog	INDC(CCP) - 30	Sep 72 .PAGE 87,ENGLISH OF YFI - 12 100	

98 Californium 252

Quantity	Energy (ev) Min	Energy (ev) Max	Lab	Type	Documentation Ref Vol Page	Date	Author, Comments	Data
Frag Neuts	Spont		RI	Expt	Prog YFI-12 101	72	Adamov+ ABST,NUBAR(ALF-E,ANG),RESULT	
					Prog INDC(CCP)-30	Sep 72	.PAGE 88,ENGLISH OF YFI-12 101	
Frag Neuts	Spont		CCP	Expt	Jour YF 16 1155	Dec 72	Blinov+ NU VS TOT E OF FISFRAG,GRAPH	
					Jour SNP 16 634	Jun 73	. ENGLISH TRANSLATION OF YF 16 1155	
Frag Neuts	Spont		LAS	Expt	Conf 73Rochestr 2 191	Aug 73	Balagna+ NU VS FRAG KIN-E,GRAPHS	
Frag Neuts	Spont		LBL	Expt	Conf 73Rochestr 2 435	Aug 73	Nifenecker.NU VS CHARGE+MASS,GRAPHS	
Frag Neuts	Spont		SAC	Expt	Conf 73Rochestr 2 179	Aug 73	Signarbieux+ NU(A,KE),COMPLEMNT FRAG	
				Revw	Conf 73Rochestr 2 117	Aug 73	Nifenecker+ NU VS FRAG-A,KIN-E,GRPHS	
				ExTh	Jour JPRC 33 28	Aug 72	Poitou+ N YIELD VS FRAG CHARGE	
				Theo	Jour JPRC 33 25	Aug 72	Signarbieux+ PROMPT N FROM FISFRAG	
				Expt	Jour NP/A 189 285	Jul 72	Nifenecker+LIQ SCINT.E VS A,VS KE	
					Prog EANDC(E)127U	Apr 70	Signarbieux+	
					Jour NP/A 141 674	Feb 70	SEE ALSO *	
	Spont				Conf 69Vienna 491	Jul 69	Nifenecker+PPR78.NU(FRAG Z,KE)GRPHS	
	-				Jour NP/A 131 261	Jun 69	- + AVERAGE NU VERSUS FRAG Z	
Frag Neuts	Spont		TUE	Expt	Conf 73Rochestr 2 483	Aug 73	Hipp+ ABST,NU(FRAG),NDG,NU(KE) GIVEN	
Frag Neuts	Spont		AUA	Revw	Jour IAEA-169 2 163	74	Musgrove+ NU-BAR VS FRAG MASS,GRAPH	
Frag Neuts	Spont		GRE	Expt	Jour JRC 26 107	75	Blachot+ CALC NU(A) FRM FIS-YLD,GRPH	
Frag Neuts	Spont		KUR	Expt	Conf 75Kiev 5 86	May 75	Vasil'Ev+ NU(FRAG-MASS,E).GRPHS+TABL	+
					Jour YF 16 6 1161	Jun 72	Savin+ GRAPHS	
	Spont				Data EXFOR40262.002	Oct 75	.SPON-FISS,PROMPT NU-BAR	
Frag Neuts	Spont		NIR	Expt	Conf 75Kiev 5 160	May 75	Basova+ NU(FRAG-MASS,AVG EKIN).GRPH	
Frag Neuts	Spont		KFI	Expt	Prog INDC(SEC)-50	Jan 76	Jeki+ P66,ABST.ANG+E-DIST(FRGM),NDG	
Frag Neuts	Spont		LAS	Theo	Jour PR/C 13 2562	Jun 76	Gavron+ANG DISTR STATMDL CALC.CURV	
Frag Neuts	Spont		AUA	Expt	Prog AAEC/PR-42P 26	Sep 76	Walsh+ BRIEF.NU(A),EVN-ODD EFF.GRAPH	
Frag Neuts	Spont		NIR	Expt	Rept YK-27 38	77	Basova+ TOF,NUBAR(FRAGMASS),GRAPHS	
Spect Fiss n	Spont		LRL	Expt	Jour PR 98 1327	Jun 55	Hicks+ NEUT NUMBER DISTR	
Spect Fiss n	Spont		IPS	Expt	Jour AF 10 357	Mar 56	Hjalmar+. PROTON RECOIL IN EMULSION	
					Jour PR 100 1542	Dec 55	Hjalmer+,FOTOPLATE CURVE	
Spect Fiss n	Spont		LAS	Theo	Jour PR 105 1511	Mar 57	Leachman+,CURVES CFD U235 THR	
Spect Fiss n	Spont		ANL	Expt	Jour PR 108 411	Oct 57	Smith+,TOF+P RECOIL FOTOPL.2-7MEV NS	
					Conf 58Geneva 15 392	Sep 58	- +.PPR690,CURVE	
Spect Fiss n	Spont		BRK	Expt	Conf 58Geneva 15 212	Sep 58	Bowman+.PPR652,CURVE,EXPT DESCRIBED	
Spect Fiss n	-		CCP	Theo	Jour ZET 35 787	Sep 58	Kovalev. NEW TH OKS XPT	
					Jour JET 8 545	Mar 59	TRANSLATN.*	
	Spont				Jour AE 5 649	Dec 58	Kovalev+ THEORY COMPARED WITH EXPT	
					Jour SJA 5 1588	58	.TRANSLATN.*	
Spect Fiss n	Spont		ANL	Expt	Abst BAP 4 31	Jan 59	Smith+ EMISS LT/HVY 1025 SPECTSAME	
Spect Fiss n	Maxwl		LAS	Eval	Jour PR 113 527	Jan 59	Terrell.TH CFD C EXPT,STAT ANALYSIS	
Spect Fiss n	Spont		YAL	Expt	Abst BAP 5 33	Jan 60	Anderson+. RECOIL+CRYST SPEC,NO DATA	
Spect Fiss n	Spont		RIC	Expt	Jour NP 23 116	Feb 61	Bonner.MOD SPH SP. T=1.367+-0.030MEV	
Spect Fiss n	Spont		LRL	Expt	Jour PR 126 2120	Jun 62	Bowman+,MOST NEUTS EVAP FROM FFRGM	
Spect Fiss n	Spont		ANL	Revw	Conf 62Harwell 2 581	Dec 62	Fields+ E-SPEC MEASUREMENTS, GRAPH	
Spect Fiss n	Spont		LRL	Expt	Jour PR 129 2133	Mar 63	Bowman+,TOF,E SPECTRA+ANGULAR DIST	
Spect Fiss n	Spont		ORL	Eval	Rept ORNL-TM-795	Feb 64	Halperin+ FISS SPEC .01-25MEV TABLE	
Spect Fiss n	Spont		BAR	Theo	Jour NP 53 113	Apr 64	Lang.STATMOD ANALYS.BOWMAN EXPERIMT.	
Spect Fiss n	Spont		FOA	Expt	Jour AF 29 313	Apr 65	Conde+ FISS CH.+LI6-GLASS+PSC. TEMP.	+
					Conf 65Salzburg 2 93	Mar 65	- + PPR49.	
	0.0+0				Data EXFOR20575.	Aug 76	12PTS.AVG.K.E.	
Spect Fiss n	Spont		CCP	Theo	Jour AE 19 59	Jul 65	SAVELEV SPEC SAME FOR LT+HVY FRAGS	
					Jour JNE 20 608	Jul 66	TRANSLATN.*	
					Jour EAF 19 1 91	Jul 65	TRANSLATN.*	
					Jour SJA 19 928	Jul 65	TRANSLATN.*	
Spect Fiss n			HAR	Eval	Jour NP 71 228	Sep 65	Barnard+ CORRELATED WITH NU BAR	
Spect Fiss n	Spont		CCP	Theo	Rept ICD-3 34	Oct 66	Zommer+.GRAPH,MANY REFS	
					Jour AE 23 327	Oct 67	- +.CALCD CURV CFD EXPT	
					Jour EAF 23 4 73	Oct 67	. FRENCH OF AE 23 327	
					Rept INDC-152E 34	67	. ENGL OF ICD-3 34	
Spect Fiss n	Spont		ANL	Expt	Jour PR 157 1076	May 67	Meadows.TOF.ABSOL GRAPH 3KEV-15MEV.	+
	Spont				Data EXFOR10612.	Nov 76	.98PTS.6RUNS.AVG KE SPEC=2.34MEV	
Spect Fiss n	Spont		JUL	Expt	Rept JUEL-522-RG	Apr 68	Cloth+ HE-3 SPECT EXPT	
Spect Fiss n	Spont		NIR	Expt	Rept NIIAR-52	69	Nefedov. CRYS-SPEC+TOF,TOT+90DEG,GRF	
Spect Fiss n	Spont		CCP	Theo	Jour IZV 33 163	Jan 69	Zommer. AVG NEUT-E VS FRAG A+E,TABLS	
					Jour IZV 32 148		69 TRANSLATN.*NO 1	
Spect Fiss n	Spont		CCP	Expt	Jour AE 26 384	Apr 69	Moshkin+ SOME EXPTL NEUT-E-SPECS GVN	
					Jour SJA 26 439	Apr 69	.ENGLISH	
Spect Fiss n	Spont		EDG	Revw	Conf 69Vienna 83	Jul 69	Feather.PPR201. REVW,TERNARY NU-SPEC	
Spect Fiss n	Spont		IBJ	Expt	Conf 69Vienna 115	Jul 69	Blocki+PPR68.ANGDIST GRPH,TERN FISSN	

98 Californium 252

Quantity	Energy (ev) Min Max	Lab	Type	Documentation Ref Vol Page	Author, Comments Date	Data
Spect Fiss n	Spont	KUR	Theo	Jour YF 10 321	Aug 69 Pick – Pichak. NEUT(ANG,E) FUNCTN+PARS	
				Jour SNP 10 185	Feb 70 . ENGL OF YF 10 321	
Spect Fiss n	Spont	CCP	Theo	Jour AE 27 568	Dec 69 PIK PICHAK. NEUT+FRAG EXCIT E SPECS	
				Jour EAF 27 110	Dec 69 TRANSLATN.*NO6	
Spect Fiss n	Spont	SCU	Theo	Rept ICD – 7 SUPPL 1	70 Saveliev.ANAL OF N – SPEC CALC,CURVES	
				Rept INDC(CCP) – 18	Dec 71 . ENGL OF ICD – 7 SUPPL 1	
Spect Fiss n	Spont	CER	Expt	Jour NP/A 146 273	May 70 Piekarz+ ANGDISTR YIELDS FOR BI – TERN	
Spect Fiss n	Spont	BRC	Expt	Conf 70Helsinki 2 109	Jun 70 Frehaut+66. NEUTRONS VS TIME GRAPHS	
Spect Fiss n	Spont	NIR	Expt	Jour AE 29 95	Aug 70 Kroshkin+ AVG FISSN NEUT E +SPEC CRV	+
				Jour SJA 29 790	Aug 70 . ENGL OF AE 29 95	
	Spont			Data EXFOR40064.011	Sep 73 .1 DATA LINE	
Spect Fiss n	Spont	KFI	Theo	Rept KFKI – 71 – 35	71 Jeki+ CALC E+ANGDIST.CF LIT.GRPH	
				Jour PL/B 30 311	Oct 69 Kluge+	
				Conf 69Vienna 927	Jul 69 - .PPR9. CALC NEUTRON E+ANG SPECS	
				Conf JINR – D3893 96	May 68 - + NU(A)+AVG E,STATMOD CF 0 – T	
				Jour KFI 16 129	Apr 68 - +.AVERG N – ENERGIES CFD EXPT	
Spect Fiss n	Spont	CCP	Expt	Conf 71Moscow	Feb 71 Blinov+.ABST,ANISTR EMIT NS(FRAG KE)	
Spect Fiss n	Spont	CCP	Expt	Conf 71Moscow	Feb 71 Bochagov+.ABST,TOF,TERN FISS,N – SPEC	
Spect Fiss n	Spont	KFI	Eval	Rept KFKI – 71 – 9	Mar 71 Jeki+ REVW OF FIS – SPEC, RECOM TEMP	
Spect Fiss n	Spont	ANL	Revw	Conf 71Vienna 3	Aug 71 Smith. MEAN – E OF NEUTS,EXPTS CFD,TBL	
Spect Fiss n	Spont	IAE	Revw	Conf 71Vienna 19	Aug 71 Koster.MEAN – E OF NS,DIFFTL EXPTS,TBL	
Spect Fiss n	Spont	AMS	Expt	Jour JNE 25 457	Sep 71 Pauw+ THRESH REACTIONS METHOD	
Spect Fiss n	Spont	KFI	Expt	Rept KFKI – 71 – 63	Nov 71 Jeki+ TOF,N – SPCTR 0.002 TO 1MEV,TBL	+
				Jour MFF 24 281	76 - . FULL PAPER,IN HUNGARIAN	
				Jour AE 33 784	Sep 72 .SHORTER PAPER, GRAPH, NDG	
				Conf 71Vienna 81	Aug 71 .SIMILAR TO KFKI,TABLE+GRAPH,	
				Jour SJA 33 896	Mar 73 .ENGLISH OF AE 33 784	
	Spont			Data EXFOR30099.	Jun 72 88 DATA LINES	
Spect Fiss n	Spont	KFI	Theo	Jour PL/B 37 217	Nov 71 Kluge.CALCS SPECT, DOUBTS SCISSION N	
				Rept KFKI – 71 – 55	Oct 71 - .PARS OF APPROX CFD EXPT.GRAPHS	
				Conf 71Vienna 149	Aug 71 - .CALC SPECS,TBL MAXW – T,MODL CFD	
Spect Fiss n	Spont	NIR	Expt	Jour YF 14 1134	Dec 71 Averchenkov+ TOF,PROMPT G – COINC,GRPH	
				Rept YFI – 17 46	Aug 74 - + TOF,NEUT – SPEC,VAL GVN	
				Conf 73Kiev 4 143	May 73 - + TOF,NEUT – SPEC,GRAPH	
				Rept INDC(CCP) – 48	Feb 75 .P46. ENGL OF YFI – 17 46	
				Jour SNP 14 632	Jun 72 . ENGL OF YF 14 1134	
Spect Fiss n	Spont	FEI	Expt	Conf 72Vienna 321	Nov 72 Kuzminov.(RUSS).LIQ SCIN,1 – 7MEV,GRPH	
Spect Fiss n	Spont	CCP	Expt	Jour YF 16 1155	Dec 72 Blinov+ N – SPECT VS TOT E OF FF,GRAPH	
				Jour SNP 16 634	Jun 73 . ENGLISH TRANSLATION OF YF 16 1155	
Spect Fiss n	Spont	BET	Expt	Jour NSE 50 257	Mar 73 Green+TOF,.5 – 13MEV.MAXW T,MEAN E GVN	+
				Jour NSE 37 232	Aug 69 - .TRANS.MAXW SPEC ASSUMED.CFD	
				Rept WAPD – TM – 830	Mar 69 .SEE ALSO MAXW T=1.39+ – .04MEV	
	Spont			Data EXFOR10614.	Nov 76 . 2101PTS.LOG(N(E)/SQRT(E)FOR 6 RUNS	
Spect Fiss n	Spont	SAC	Expt	Prog EANDC(E) – 157U2	May 73 Babinet+ DEPENDING ON FRAGM.CHARGE	
				Prog EANDC(E) – 157U2	May 73 Girard+ SPECTRUM FOR INDIVID.FRAGM.	
Spect Fiss n	Spont	HAR	Expt	Prog EANDC(UK) 151	Aug 73 Adams+ ROSE DATA BEING FINALISED	
Spect Fiss n	Spont	GEL	Expt	Jour AKE 22 84	Oct 73 Knitter+ TOF,0.15 – 15MEV MAXWELL – DIST	+
				Conf 73Kiev 4 177	May 73 - + SAME AS AKE 22 84	
	Spont			Data EXFOR20401.	Apr 75 184PTS.AVG.K.E.	
Spect Fiss n	Spont	LIN	Expt	Jour SNP 17 366	Oct 73 .ENGLISH OF YF 17 703	
				Jour YF 18 720	Oct 73 Graevsky+ TERNARY FISS,N – SPEC,GRAPHS	
				Jour YF 17 703	Apr 73 - + TERNARY FIS – N,ANGDIST,GRPH	
				Jour ZEP 15 572	May 72 Graevskii+ TERNARY SPEC+MEAN – E,GRAPH	
				Jour JEL 15 407	May 72 .ENGLISH OF ZEP 15 572	
				Jour SNP 18 720	Oct 73 . ENGLISH OF YF 18 720	
Spect Fiss n	Spont	NIR	Expt	Jour YF 18 1145	Dec 73 Zakharova+ E AND MASS SPEC OF FRAGS	+
	Spont			Data EXFOR40232.	Nov 74 .PRIM FIS – FRAG YLD+AVER KIN – E OF FF	
Spect Fiss n	Spont	NIR	Expt	Rept INDC(CCP) – 60	74 Nefedov+ N – SPEC(0.01 – 10MEV),GRAPH	
				Conf 73Kiev 4 163	May 73 - + DEVIATION FR MAXW=DELAYD NS	
				Conf 71Vienna 89	Aug 71 - + TOF,PLASTIC SCIN,N – SPEC	
Spect Fiss n	Spont	FEI	Expt	Jour AE 36 282	Apr 74 Aleksandrova+ NEUT – SPEC OF FISS,GRPH	+
				Jour SJA 36 355	Oct 74 . ENGLISH OF AE 36 282	
	Spont			Data EXFOR40250.002	Dec 74 29 ES GIVEN	
Spect Fiss n	Spont	MIS	Expt	Abst ANS 19 480	Oct 74 Meyer+ GRPHS.P – RECOIL.50KEV – 8MEV	
Spect Fiss n	Spont	TEX	Eval	Abst ANS 19 395	Oct 74 Etzion+ SAND 2 CALC.GRPH	
Spect Fiss n	Spont	LRL	Theo	Jour PR/C 10 2545	Dec 74 Browne+ GRPH.HF.CALC.CFD.EXPT	
Spect Fiss n	Spont	EDG	Expt	Abst 75Harwell 54	Mar 75 Scobie+ SEARCH FOR STRUC IN SPECTRUM	

98 Californium 252

Quantity	Energy (ev) Min	Max	Lab	Type	Documentation Ref Vol Page	Date	Author, Comments	Data
Spect Fiss n	Spont		IAE Eval	Conf	75Wash. 286	Mar 75	Lemmel. 3RD IAEA-EVAL, BY LSQ FIT	
			Revw	Jour	REA 7 4 3	Dec 69	Hanna+ N-SPECTRUM IN NU-BAR EXPTS	
Spect Fiss n	Spont		UI Expt	Conf	75Wash. 62	Mar 75	Johnson+ GRPH.FITS MAXW T=1.43MEV	
Spect Fiss n	Spont		KFK Expt	Jour	JNE 26 165	Apr 72	Werle+ PROT RECOIL,HE003 SPECT.AV EN	+
			Revw	Conf	75Karlsrhe 3	Apr 75	-. SPEC,MEAN E.VALS GIVN+DISCUSD	
			Expt	Jour	NIM 99 295	Mar 72	- + FISSION SPECTR ONLY.GRAPH.	
				Conf	71Vienna 65	Aug 71	- + P-RECOIL CFD HE-DET,TBL,GRAPH	
	Spont			Data	EXFOR20616.	Jun 76	82PTS.AVG.K.E.	
Spect Fiss n	1.0+5	1.0+7	KFK Expt	Rept	KFK-2200 97	Apr 75	Bluhm+ EXPT METHODS DISCUSSED	
				Rept	JUEL-1178 97	Apr 75	- + SAME AS KFK-2200	
Spect Fiss n	Spont		TRM Expt	Conf	75Karlsrhe 21	Apr 75	Iyer+ P-REC.SPEC(1-11MEV)+MEAN E GVN	
Spect Fiss n	Spont		FEI Expt	Conf	75Kiev 5 109	May 75	Kotel'Nikova+ SPEC=MAXW,T=1.46MV.FIG	
				Rept	FEI-575	75	Kotelnikova+ .5-7MEV,TOF.GRAPH SPEC	
				Rept	INDC(CCP)-81	May 76	. ENGLISH OF FEI-575	
Spect Fiss n	Spont		KUR Expt	Conf	75Kiev 5 86	May 75	Vasil'Ev+ NSPEC(FRAG-A,E).AVG E,TBL	
Spect Fiss n	8.0+4	1.0+6	BRC Expt	Rept	CEA-N-1798 58	Jun 75	Bertin. SPECT ANAL	
Spect Fiss n	Spont		SUN Expt	Jour	PRL 35 1563	Dec 75	Pringle+ ANGULAR CORRELATIONS,GRAPH	
Spect Fiss n	Spont		ANL Expt	Rept	ANL-NDM-19	Mar 76	Guenther+TOF..5 TO 13 MEV SPEC.GRPH.	
Spect Fiss n	Spont		NBS Eval	Prog	ERDA-NDC-3 159	May 76	Grundl+UPDATE 75 WASH CONF EVAL.	
				Conf	75Wash. 250	Mar 75	- +EVL.MEAS,E AV=2.13+-.027 MEV	
Spect Fiss n	Spont		GEL Revw	Conf	76Lowell 1110	Jul 76	Liskien+N STANDARDS STATUS.GRPH.	
Spect Fiss γ	Spont		LAS Theo	Jour	PR 105 1511	Mar 57	Leachman+,AVERAGE G ENERGY=4.0MEV	
Spect Fiss γ	Spont		CRC Expt	Jour	PR 111 877	Aug 58	Milton+,TOF PHS CS I INDEP OF TOT KE	
				Conf	ORNL-2309	Jun 57	.SUPERSEDED	
Spect Fiss γ	Spont		ANL Expt	Jour	PR 104 699	Nov 56	Smith+,10.3GS PER F AVG TOT E 8.2MEV	
				Conf	58Geneva 15 392	Sep 58	- +.PPR690,CURVE	
Spect Fiss γ	Spont		BRK Expt	Conf	58Geneva 15 212	Sep 58	Bowmann+.PPR652,CURVE,EXPT DESCRIBED	
Spect Fiss γ	Spont		BRK Expt	Jour	NP 60 378	Dec 64	Johansson. HALF YIELD VERSUS A	
Spect Fiss γ	Maxwl		JUL Revw	Rept	JUEL-405-NP	65	Maier-Leibnitz+ AVG E+NUMBER OF GAM	
				Conf	65Salzburg 2 113	Mar 65	- +	
Spect Fiss γ	Spont		KJL Expt	Jour	NP 62 103	Feb 65	Skarsvag+ANG.CORREL.WITH FRAGMENTS	
Spect Fiss γ	Spont		LRL Expt	Jour	PRL 14 183	Feb 65	Watson+,300-600KEV GS EACH FRAGMENT	
Spect Fiss γ	Spont		BRK Expt	Jour	NP 64 147	Mar 65	Johansson. SPEC MEAS 0-300NS	
Spect Fiss γ	Spont		CRC Expt	Prog	AECL-2595	Sep 65	Skarsvag+ NO DATA,ALSO AECL2610,2612	
Spect Fiss γ	Spont		PTN Expt	Jour	PR 148 1206	Aug 66	Atneosen+ K-XRAYS VS TIME AFTER FISS	
				Conf	65Salzburg 385	Mar 65	- +	
Spect Fiss γ	Spont		CCP Theo	Rept	ICD-3 34	Oct 66	Zommer+.GRAPH,MANY REFS	
				Jour	AE 23 327	Oct 67	- +.CALCD CURV CFD EXPT	
				Jour	EAF 23 4 73	Oct 67	. FRENCH OF AE 23 327	
				Rept	INDC-152E 34	67	. ENGL OF ICD-3 34	
Spect Fiss γ	-		TRM Expt	Conf	67Kanpur 340	Feb 67	Kapoor.SPONTA FISS ANISOTRO.16+-.01	
Spect Fiss γ	Spont		NBS Expt	Prog	WASH-1079 119	Oct 67	Schroder. TERNARY FISS NDG ANAL TBC	
Spect Fiss γ	Spont		SGA Expt	Jour	APA 27 40	Nov 68	Axmann+ 100-300KEV GE-LI	
				Rept	SGAE-PH-59	67	- + GE-LI 0.1-0.3MEV GAMMAS	
Spect Fiss γ	Spont		AUS Expt	Prog	EANDC(OR)86L	Jan 69	Sgarumpold+	
Spect Fiss γ	-		CCP Expt	Conf	69Erevan	Feb 69	Aleksandrov+.ABST,SPEC ANALYS,SI-DET	
Spect Fiss γ	Spont		SGA Expt	Conf	69Vienna 519	Jul 69	Rumpold+PPR21. PRMPT E-GAM VS FRAG-A	
Spect Fiss γ	Spont		FTI Expt	Jour	YF 10 240	Aug 69	Valskij+ ANGDIST(GAM-E)+YLD GRAPHS	
				Jour	SNP 10 137	Feb 70	. ENGL OF YF 10 240	
Spect Fiss γ	Spont		TRM Expt	Jour	NP/A 133 625	Aug 69	Ajitanand.NAI(TL).BINARY CFD TERNARY	
				Prog	BARC-501 27	70	- .PROMPT YLD BINARY/TERNARY	
				Conf	68Madras 305	Feb 68	DATA *PAPER N42	
Spect Fiss γ	Spont		AUA Expt	Prog	AAEC/PR-33P 7	70	Ajitanand+ TABLES OF GAMMA YLD+E+HL	
Spect Fiss γ	Spont		ITK Theo	Prog	BARC-474 54	70	Mukherji+ CALC TOTAL GAM-E OKS EXPT	
Spect Fiss γ	Spont		SCU Theo	Rept	ICD-7 SUPPL 1	70	Saveliev.CALC SPEC CFD EXPT,GRAPH	
				Rept	INDC(CCP)-18	Dec 71	. ENGL OF ICD-7 SUPPL 1	
Spect Fiss γ	Spont		CCP Expt	Jour	YF 11 1001	May 70	Adamov+ GAMM QUANTA IN TERNARY FISSN	
				Jour	SNP 11 557	Nov 70	. ENGL OF YF 11 1001	
Spect Fiss γ	Spont		SAH Theo	Jour	PL/B 33 263	Oct 70	Sarkar+ ESYLDS AS FN FRAG MASS	
Spect Fiss γ	Spont		AUA Expt	Prog	AAEC/PR-34P	Apr 71	Boldeman+ KX-RAY-FRAG YLD+SPEC.NDG	
Spect Fiss γ	Spont		ORU Expt	Prog	RLO-2227-T7-8	Mar 72	Loveland. PROMPT-GAM ANG CORRELTS	
Spect Fiss γ	Spont		TRM Expt	Rept	BARC-694 62	73	Choudhury+ NUMBR DISTRBTN OF GS,GRAF	
Spect Fiss γ	Spont		GA Expt	Jour	PR/C 7 1173	Mar 73	Verbinski+ GAMS 0-10 NS AFTER FISS	
				Conf	69Vienna 929	Jul 69	Verbinsky.PPR33. MEAN GAMM E+YLD GVN	
Spect Fiss γ	Spont		IRV Expt	Jour	PR/C 7 1579	Apr 73	Brooks+.FRAG MASS/GAMMA E CORRELATN	
Spect Fiss γ	Spont		KFI Expt	Conf	73Rochestr 2 249	Aug 73	Lajtai+ ANG ANISOTROPY OF GAMS,GRPHS	
Spect Fiss γ	Spont		LBL Expt	Conf	73Rochestr 2 435	Aug 73	Nifenecker.K-XRAY YLD PER FRAG,GRAPH	
Spect Fiss γ	Spont		MRY Expt	Conf	73Rochestr 2 221	Aug 73	Clark+ PRIMARY FRAG GAMS,TBLS,GRAPHS	

98 Californium 252

Quantity	Energy (ev) Min Max	Lab	Type	Documentation Ref Vol Page	Date	Author, Comments	Data
Spect Fiss γ	Spont	ORL	Expt Conf	73Rochestr 2 494	Aug 73	Pleasonton+ ABST,BELOW 5 NSECS,NDG	
Spect Fiss γ	Spont	SAC	Revw Conf	73Rochestr 2 117	Aug 73	Nifenecker+ G-YLD+AVG-E(FRAG),GRAPHS	
			Expt Jour	PR/C 7 373	Jan 73	Mehta+ TOT GAM EN,BINARY+LRA FISSION	
Spect Fiss γ	Spont	SOR	Expt Jour	PR/C 8 2293	Dec 73	Nardi+.TOT GAM E VS.FRAG MASS+KE	
Spect Fiss γ	Spont	IRT	Expt Jour	PR/C 10 853	Aug 74	Sund+ TBL, GRPHS.	
			Conf	73Rochestr 2 499	Aug 73	Gozani. ABST,CORREL GSPEC-MULTIPLCTY	
Spect Fiss γ	Spont	LRL	Expt Jour	PR/C 10 795	Aug 74	Dietrich+ 8-20MEV G,GRPHS.	
Spect Fiss γ	Spont	CCP	Expt Jour	YF 22 462	Sep 75	Teterev+ G-SPEC,GRAPH	
Fiss Prod γ	Spont	LRL	Expt Prog	UCRL-11828 95	Jan 65	Bowman+. K X-RAY SPECT. SI(LI) DET.	
Fiss Prod γ	Spont	ANL	ExTh Jour	PL 15 153	Mar 65	Glendenin+ K X-RAY SPEC CFD CALC	
Fiss Prod γ	Spont	RUT	Expt Abst	DA/B 28 1085	Sep 67	Dolce. DELAYED X-RAYS TO FEW NANOSEC	
Fiss Prod γ	Spont	LRL	Expt Jour	PR 162 1169	Oct 67	Watson+ SI(LI) DET K X-RAY YIELDS	
			Rept	UCRL-17518	May 67	.SUPERSEDED	
			Rept	UCRL-17289	Jan 67	Watson+ GAM+CONV ELECTR SPEC TBP ND	
			Conf	65Salzburg 125	Mar 65	.SUPERSEDED	
Fiss Prod γ	Spont	TRM	Expt Jour	PR 166 1190	Feb 68	Kapoor+ SI(LI) DET K X-RAY YLDS+SPEC	
			Jour	PR/C 4 2165	Dec 71	- +.SI(LI) DET. K X-RAY SPECTRA	
			Rept	BARC-557 46	71	.ABST	
			Conf	70Madurai 2 349	Dec 70	Kapoor+ KX-RAYS OF FRAGMENTS,GRAPHS	
			Prog	BARC-501 24	70	Nadkarni+ KX-RAYS COINC FRAGS.GRPHS	
			Conf	69Roorke 2 134	Dec 69	- + K-XRAY-SPECS,HEAVY+L FRAGS	
			Revw Conf	68Madras 1 62	Feb 68	Kapoor.PPRI9.GAM+X-RAY EXPTS,GRAPHS	
			Expt Rept	BARC-363	68	SUPERSEDED*	
Fiss Prod γ	Spont	PTN	Expt Jour	PR 167 1091	Mar 68	Alvager+GE(LI) MASS 137-142 SPECTRA	
Fiss Prod γ	Spont	LRL	Expt Jour	PR 179 1109	Mar 69	Watson.SI(LI)DET.K X-RAY INTENSITY	
Fiss Prod γ	Spont	FTI	Expt Prog	YFI-7 32	Apr 69	Alexandrov+ GAM-ANGDIST(FRAG E), TBL	
			Rept	INDC(CCP)-7U35	Feb 70	TRANSLATN.*	
Fiss Prod γ	Spont	PTN	Expt Jour	PR 180 1177	Apr 69	Thomas+ K X-RAY LIFETIMES+YIELDS	
Fiss Prod γ	Spont	SGA	Expt Jour	69Vienna 519	Jul 69	Rumpold+PPR21. GAM-E VS A,SHORT HLS	
Fiss Prod γ	Spont	FTI	Expt Jour	YF 10 240	Aug 69	Valskij+ ANGDIST+YLD(FRAG KINE)GRPHS	
			Jour	SNP 10 137	Feb 70	. ENGL OF YF 10 240	
Fiss Prod γ	Spont	UI	Expt Jour	PR 188 1948	Dec 69	Long+,K XRAY YLD VS.TIME,MASS 1-56NS	
Fiss Prod γ	Spont	LRL	Expt Jour	NP/A 141 449	Jan 70	Watson+ MASS SORTED BETA,G SPECTRA.	
Fiss Prod γ	Spont	ASU	Expt Jour	PR/C 1 631	Feb 70	Rueseggr+,LA CE PR GAMS+K X RAYS	
Fiss Prod γ	Spont	LRL	Expt Jour	PR/C 1 1866	May 70	Watson+,K X-RAY DIST VS. A,Z	
Fiss Prod γ	Spont	LRL	Expt Jour	PR/C 2 1451	Oct 70	John+,GE(LI) DET,144 GAMS VS.T,FRAG	
			Jour	PL/B 30 340	Oct 69	- +REL G INT VS A PROMPT+DEL	
			Conf	69Vienna 535	Jul 69	- +DISCUSSN. DELAYED GAM VS FRAG	
Fiss Prod γ	Spont	SAH	Theo Conf	70Madurai 2 619	Dec 70	Sarkar+ NUMBER+E OF GAMS VS A,GRAPHS	
Fiss Prod γ	Spont	TRM	Expt Conf	70Madurai 2 339	Dec 70	Ajitanand. GAMMA E,HALF-L,INT TABLE	
Fiss Prod γ	Spont	ASU	Expt Jour	PR/C 3 877	Feb 71	Roy+,BA AND CS K X RAYS+GAMMAS	
Fiss Prod γ	Spont	ORU	Expt Prog	RLO-2277-1	Mar 71	Loveland+.FRAG-PROMPT GAM ANG CORREL	
			Prog	RLO-2060-8	Mar 70	- +,FRAG GAMMA ANG CORRELTS	
			TRM Expt Rept	STI/DOC/10-125	Apr 71	Ramanna.PG41.X-RAY SPEC OF FRAGS CFD	
Fiss Prod γ	Spont	UI	Expt Jour	PR/C 3 2464	Jun 71	Shapiro+. CONVERSION ELECTRONS+X RAY	
Fiss Prod γ	Spont	TEX	Expt Jour	PR/C 4 1927	Nov 71	Hopkins+.LOW-E GAMMA+K X-RAY TRANSIT	
			Prog	AD-739731	Mar 72	Richard+. X RAYS FROM FISSION	
			Rept	AD-731288	Oct 71	.SUPERSEDED	
		TEX	Expt Jour	PR/C 4 1948	Nov 71	ST.-LAURENT+.INTERNAL-CONVERSN CASCA	
			Abst	DA/B 33 4445	Mar 73	St-Laurent. SI(LI)+GE(LI) DET.X-RAY	
Fiss Prod γ	Spont	ANL	Expt Jour	NP/A 177 337	Dec 71	Reisdorf+SIMULT MEAS K.E. ANG G-SPEC	
			Conf	69Vienna 781	Jul 69	.PRELIMINARY	
Fiss Prod γ	Spont	TEX	Expt Jour	PR/C 5 1015	Mar 72	Hopkins+. GE(LI) DET.0.15-1MEV GAMS	
Fiss Prod γ	Spont	CCP	Expt Jour	ZEP 15 652	Jun 72	Aleksandrov+ FISS PROD X-RAYS,GRAPH	
			Jour	JEL 15 462	Jun 72	*ENGL OF ZEP 15 652	
Fiss Prod γ	Spont	LRL	Expt Jour	PR/C 5 2041	Jun 72	Wilhelmy+. GAMMA ANGULAR DISTRIBUTN	
			Rept	UCRL-18978	Aug 69	- .X+GAMMA YLDS+EN5,THESIS	
Fiss Prod γ	Spont	SAC	Expt Jour	NP/A 189 285	Jul 72	Nifenecker+ LIQ SCINT. E VS KE,A,NU	
		AUA	Revw Conf	72Vienna 291	Nov 72	Conde. TBL ES+YLDS,H-L=0.16-80MICROS	
			Expt Jour	NP/A 164 300	Mar 71	Ajitanand.GE(LI).HL11LINES .3-5MUSEC	
Fiss Prod γ	Spont	ANL	Expt Prog	ANL-7996 13	Feb 73	Talbert+. TABLE ISOMERIC GAMMAS.	
			Abst	DA 33 1725	Oct 72	- . ISOMERIC DECAY OF FRAGMENTS	
Fiss Prod γ	Spont	ITK	Theo Jour	AUJ 26 279	Jun 73	Mukherji+ MEAN-E VS FRAG-MASS,GRAPH	
			Prog	BARC-474 54	70	- + CALC GAM-E/FRAG CFD EXPT	
		TEX	Expt Jour	PR/C 8 380	Jul 73	Hopkins+. GE(LI) DET. GAMMA COINCIDN	
			Abst	DA/B 33 4443	Mar 73	- . GE(LI). GAMMA COINCIDENCES	
Fiss Prod γ	Spont	LBL	Expt Conf	73Rochestr 2 211	Aug 73	Jared+ GAM-E OF NSEC FISPRODUCTS,TBL	
Fiss Prod γ	Spont	MRY	Expt Conf	73Rochestr 2 221	Aug 73	Clark+ PRIMARY FRAG GAMS,TBLS,GRAPHS	

98 Californium 252

Quantity	Energy (ev) Min	Max	Lab	Type	Documentation Ref Vol Page	Date	Author, Comments	Data
Fiss Prod γ	Spont		ORL	Expt Conf	73Rochestr 2 494	Aug 73	Pleasonton+ ABST,AVG GAM−E(FRAG),NDG	
Fiss Prod γ	Spont		RI	Expt Jour	YF 18 270	Aug 73	Donichkin+ K−XRAYS(FRAG−Z),SPECTRA	
				Conf	73Kiev 3 291	May 73	− + CORREL TO Z ODD OR EVEN	
				Jour	SNP 18 138	Feb 74	.ENGLISH OF YF 18 270	
Fiss Prod γ	Spont		SAC	Revw Conf	73Rochestr 2 117	Aug 73	Nifenecker+ G+XRAY(FRAG CHARGE),GRPH	
				ExTh Jour	JPRC 33 29	Aug 72	− + EVN−ODD EFFCT IN DEEXCT	
Fiss Prod γ	Spont		UI	Expt Jour	NSE 53 47	Jan 74	Knief+. ABSOL MEAST BETA SPECTRA.	
Fiss Prod γ	Spont		KJL	Expt Jour	NP/A 253 274	Nov 75	Skarsvag. TIME DIST FOR SHORT TIMES	
				Jour	NP/A 153 82	Sep 70	− .TIME DISTR .1−120NS 100EVUP	
				Conf	69Vienna 927	Jul 69	− . PPR2.YLDS+H−LIVES > 100KEV	
Fiss Prod γ	Spont		GHT	Eval Jour	NIM 134 299	76	Thierens+ FOR MASS YLD DETERM TBL	
Fiss Prod γ	Spont		KFI	Expt Prog	INDC(SEC)−50	Jan 76	Jeki+ P67,ABST.GAS−PRESSUR EFFEC,NDG	
Fiss Prod γ	Spont		NIL	Expt Prog	INDC(SEC)−50	Jan 76	. ABST. CORREL TO FRGM−E,IN PROG,NDG	
Fiss Prod γ	Spont		ASU	Expt Jour	NSE 61 366	Nov 76	Bolig+TERNARY FRAG K X−RAYS ANAL.	
Fiss Yield	Spont		ANL	Expt Jour	JIN 1 45	Mar 55	Glendenin+,RADIOCHEM,YLDS 15 FRAGS	
Fiss Yield	Spont		ANL	Expt Jour	PR 102 813	May 56	Smith+,DOUBLE IONIZ CH,MASS DISTR	
				Jour	JIN 1 45	Mar 55	.SUPERSEDED	
Fiss Yield	Spont		LAS	Expt Abst	BAP 1 281	Jun 56	Yarnell+ TOF MASS+KE DISTS	
Fiss Yield	Spont		HAR	Expt Jour	JIN 6 181	58	Cuninghame.YIELD OF ZR,MO,PR,ND,SM.	
Fiss Yield	Spont		CRC	Expt Jour	PR 111 877	Aug 58	Milton+,TOF PHS CS 182MEV AT 4/3 MAX	
				Conf	ORNL−2309	Jun 57	.SUPERSEDED	
Fiss Yield	Spont		BRK	Expt Conf	58Geneva 15 212	Sep 58	Bowmann+.PPR652,CURVE,EXPT DESCRIBED	
Fiss Yield	Spont		ANL	Expt Jour	PR 112 960	Nov 58	Cox+,CHARGE−MASS CURVE	
Fiss Yield	Spont		LRL	Expt Jour	PR 119 1685	Sep 60	Nervik.FINDS 36NUCLIDES BY RADIOCHEM	
Fiss Yield	Spont		LRL	Expt Jour	PR 121 270	Jan 61	Muga. MASS−ENERGY DISTR NUCL EMUL	
Fiss Yield	Spont		RI	Revw Jour	UFN 73 655	Apr 61	Petrzhak+ CURVE,MANY REFS,DISCUSSION	
				Jour	SPU 4 305	Sep 61	. ENGL OF UFN 73 655	
Fiss Yield	Spont		SYR	Theo Jour	PR 122 1543	May 61	Fong. STAT TH CFD DATA	
Fiss Yield	Spont		LAS	Expt Jour	PR 126 1508	May 62	Nobles. YIELD OF LONG RANGE FFRGM	
Fiss Yield	Spont		WAS	Expt Jour	PR 126 1112	May 62	Wahl+ FRACTIONAL CUMUL+INDEPEND YLDS	
Fiss Yield	Spont		LAS	Expt Jour	PR 131 1232	Aug 63	Whetstone+ TOF FRAGMENT MASS DIST	
Fiss Yield	Spont		LAS	Expt Jour	NIM 24 13	Aug 63	Britt+ E−SPEC VS TOF SHOWS PROMPT NS	
Fiss Yield	Spont		ORL	Expt Rept	ORNL−3692	64	Kiker.POST−NEUT MASS YLDS.TABL+CURVS	
Fiss Yield	Spont		ANL	Expt Jour	PR/B 134 1219	Jun 64	Horrocks.YLD, BY SC−T,=.000221+−2PC	
Fiss Yield	Spont		CER	Theo Jour	NP 58 177	Sep 64	Faissner+ASSYMETRIC,CLUSTER MODEL	
Fiss Yield	Spont		TRM	Revw Rept	AEET−235	65	Methasiri.TERNRY FISS EXPTS,TBL,GRPH	
Fiss Yield	Maxwl		ISL	Expt Prog	IA−1021 25	Jan 65	Gozez.E−ALFA,ANGL,MASSRATIO CORRELTD	
Fiss Yield	Spont		ORL	Expt Jour	PR/B 137 837	Feb 65	Schmitt+E−VEL FISS−FRAG DIST	
				Jour	RSI 35 1116	Sep 64	.FRAGMENT PULSE−HEIGHT SPECTRUM	
Fiss Yield	Spont		WAS	Revw Conf	65Salzburg 317	Mar 65	Wahl.GRAPHS TH CFD XPTS	
Fiss Yield	Maxwl		ANL	Eval Abst	ANS 8 12	Jun 65	Marsh+TRITIUM YIELD STUDY	
Fiss Yield	Spont		ORL	Theo Rept	ORNL−P−2848	66	Schmitt.CALCTD FISS MODES TBP AF	
Fiss Yield	Spont		ORL	Expt Jour	PR 141 1146	Jan 66	Schmitt+ EMISS YLDS CFD, NS	
Fiss Yield	Spont		LAS	Expt Jour	PR 144 1060	Apr 66	Thomas+,1LIGHT FRAG/289+−16 FISS,CFD	
Fiss Yield	Spont		TRM	Theo Jour	PL 21 437	Jun 66	Ramanna+ MASS DIST ON STOCHASTIC MDL	
				Jour	NP 67 529	Jun 65	− +FISSION AS MARKOV PROCESS	
				Conf	65Calcutta 20	Feb 65	.SUPERSEDED	
Fiss Yield	Spont		CIS	Theo Jour	NP 84 595	Sep 66	Erba+ STATISTICAL MODEL CFD XPT	
Fiss Yield	Spont		NEG	Theo Prog	IA−1168 11	Jan 67	Boneh+ LIGHT PART YLD+SPEC CFD EXPTS	
Fiss Yield	Spont		LAS	Expt Jour	PR 154 1174	Feb 67	Whetstone+ YLD 10 FRAGS,H TO BE	
				Jour	PRL 15 298	Aug 65	.SUPERSEDED	
Fiss Yield	Spont		LRL	Expt Jour	PR 154 1193	Feb 67	Cosper+.YLD 15 FRAGS H,HE,LI,BE NUCL	
Fiss Yield	Spont		FLA	Expt Jour	PRL 18 404	Mar 67	Muga+2. HEAVY TERNARY FISSION	
				Rept	ORO−2843−9	Dec 66	.SUPERSEDED	
Fiss Yield	Spont		LAS	Expt Jour	PR 156 1277	Apr 67	Stein+ SI DETECT,CURVE YIELDS,ENERGY	
Fiss Yield	−		FEI	Theo Prog	YFI−4 14	May 67	Ignatjuk.CURVES GIVEN	
	Spont			Jour	YF 7 1043	May 68	− . SHELL TH OKS FRAG MASS RAT	
	−			Rept	INDC−187E	67	. ENGL OF YFI−4 14	
Fiss Yield	Spont		HAR	Comp Rept	AERE−R−5086	Jan 68	Croall.REL YLDS OF LIGHT PARTICLES	
Fiss Yield	None		KUR	Theo Conf	68Riga	Jan 68	Shigin.ABST,MASS DIST,EXC E 6+21 MEV	
Fiss Yield	Spont		YAL	Theo Jour	PRL 20 870	Mar 68	Kelson. QUANTUM THEORY OF FISSION	
Fiss Yield	Spont		PTN	Expt Jour	PR 169 993	May 68	Thomas+ LONG−RANGE FRAGS YLD VS RANG	
Fiss Yield	Spont		PTN	Expt Jour	PR 172 1272	Aug 68	Raisbuck+ YIELDS OF LIGHT FRAGS	
Fiss Yield	Spont		CCP	Expt Jour	YF 8 454	Sep 68	Solov'Eva. LONG−R−ALPHA,KE−SPECS,CVS	
				Jour	SNP 8 264	Mar 69	TRANSLATN.*	
Fiss Yield	Pile		CCP	Expt Jour	YF 8 454	Sep 68	Solovyeva.TRIPLE FISS ALFA−SPEC,GRPH	
Fiss Yield	Maxwl		KYU	Theo Jour	JPJ 25 933	Oct 68	Katase.TERNARY.3 POINT CHARGE MODEL	
Fiss Yield	Spont		LRL	Theo Rept	UCRL−18632	Feb 69	Watson+,CALCTD YLDS Z=36 TO 62	

98 Californium 252

Quantity	Energy (ev) Min Max	Lab	Type	Documentation Ref Vol Page	Author, Comments Date	Data
Fiss Yield	Spont	MIS Expt	Jour	PR 179 1166	Mar 69 Srinivasan+ XE+KR ISOTOPIC REL YLDS	
Fiss Yield	Spont	EDG Revw	Conf	69Vienna 83	Jul 69 Feather.PPR201. SURVEY,TERNARY - YIELD	
Fiss Yield	Spont	IBJ Expt	Conf	69Vienna 115	Jul 69 Blocki+PPR68.TBL,TERN LIGHT FRAG YLD	
Fiss Yield	Spont	ORL Expt	Conf	69Vienna 67	Jul 69 Schmitt.PPR122. YLD GRPH,COMP OF PR	
Fiss Yield	Spont	OSL Revw	Conf	69Vienna 669	Jul 69 Pappas+PPR206. INITIAL+FINAL YLD(A)	
Fiss Yield	-	TRM Theo	Conf	69Vienna 41	Jul 69 Ramamurthy+PPR15. CALCTD GRPH YLD(A)	
Fiss Yield	Spont	TUE Revw	Conf	69Bochum 175	Jul 69 Goennenwein+ CLUSTER MODEL,YLD GRAPH	
Fiss Yield	Spont	MCM Expt	Prog	EANDC(CAN)-40	Sep 69 Clarke+ MASS-SPC+GE-LI.XE GVN,KR TBC	
Fiss Yield	Spont	ANL Expt	Jour	JIN 31 3357	Nov 69 Von Gunten+ YLDS BR82,RB86,CS136	
Fiss Yield	Spont	ORL Expt	Jour	PR/C 1 1044	Mar 70 Troutner+,AG112 I134 CS138 IND YLDS	
			Prog	ORNL-4306 34	May 68 - .I134 INDEPENDENT YLD GIVEN	
Fiss Yield	Spont	SOR Expt	Jour	PR/C 1 2101	Jun 70 Gazit+,YLDS Z=3-8 FRAGMENTS	
Fiss Yield	Spont	CCP Theo	Jour	YF 12 471	Sep 70 Bogdanov+ TERN FISSN,EXPT+THEORY CFD	
			Jour	SNP 12 257	Mar 71 TRANSLATN.*	
Fiss Yield	Spont	ORL Expt	Jour	JIN 33 1	Jan 71 Harbour+TROUTNER NB99M YLD	
			Abst	DA/B 30 1578	Oct 69 - + FCY,HL NP99. CUM.A=99-147.	
Fiss Yield	None	BAS Theo	Jour	PL/B 34 264	Mar 71 Pauli+ FRAG MASS RATIO AS STRUTINSKY	
Fiss Yield	Spont	AUA Theo	Rept	AAEC/TM-595	Jun 71 Musgrove.CALC H,HE YLDS REL ALF-YLD	
Fiss Yield	Spont	CCP Expt	Jour	YF 13 1162	Jun 71 Barashkov+ TOF,PRIMARY MASS YLD,GRPH	
			Jour	SNP 13 668	Dec 71 . ENGL OF YF 13 1162	
Fiss Yield	Spont	MIS Expt	Jour	JIN 33 8 2271	Aug 71 Troutner+ FRACT CUM YLD 131SB+131MTE	
Fiss Yield	Spont	LRL Expt	Jour	PR/C 4 1913	Nov 71 Cheifetz+.MASS DISTR, NEW METHOD	
			Jour	PRL 25 1122	Oct 70 .SUPERSEDED	
			Prog	UCRL-20426 153	70 Wilhelmy+. TABLES+CURVES	
Fiss Yield	Spont	ANL Expt	Jour	NP/A 177 337	Dec 71 Reisdorf+SIMULT MEAS K.E. ANG G-SPEC	
			Conf	69Vienna 781	Jul 69 .PRELIMINARY.	
Fiss Yield	Spont	RI Expt	Prog	YFI-14 12	72 Skovorodkin+ YLD OF 39 FRAGS,TBL	
Fiss Yield	Spont	ORU Expt	Prog	RLO-2227-T7-8	Mar 72 Loveland. NO SHORT-RANGE ALPHAS SEEN	
Fiss Yield	Spont	CLA Theo	Jour	NP/A 184 417	Apr 72 Tsang+.ASSYM FROM FERMIGAS+WKB CALC.	
Fiss Yield	Spont	ANL Expt	Jour	PR/C 7 353	Jan 73 Fluss+. MASS-YLD CURV FOR LRA FISSN	
Fiss Yield	Spont	SAC Expt	Jour	PR/C 7 373	Jan 73 Mehta+ MASS DISTN,BINARY+LRA FISSION	
			Jour	NP/A 189 285	Jul 72 Nifenecker+ LIQ SCINT. E VS KE,A,NDG	
Fiss Yield	Spont	IRV Expt	Jour	PR/C 7 1579	Apr 73 Brooks+.FRAG MASS/GAMMA E CORRELATN	
Fiss Yield	Spont	RI Expt	Conf	73Kiev 3 277	May 73 Adamov+ LIGHT PART YIELD,GRAPHS	+
			Jour	AE 34 365	May 73 Skovorodkin+ YLD OF FRAGS,TBL,GRAPH	
			Jour	SJA 34 449	May 73 .ENGLISH OF AE 34 5 365	
	Maxwl		Jour	IZV 37 118	Jan 73 Adamov+ TERN,N-ANGDIST,TABLE	
	Spont		Conf	73Kiev 3 306	May 73 - + YLD OF H-4,HE-5,HE-6,GRAPHS	
	Maxwl		Jour	BAS 37 103	Jan 73 . ENGL OF IZV 37 118	
	Spont		Data	EXFOR40205.	Apr 74 .6 SUBENTRIES	
Fiss Yield	Spont	NEU Theo	Jour	HPA 46 720	Jul 73 Hooshyar+ MASS A.CHARGE DISTR, HL	
Fiss Yield	Spont	LBL Expt	Conf	73Rochestr 2 435	Aug 73 Nifenecker.ALF YLD VS FRAG(Z,A),GRPH	
Fiss Yield	Spont	MIS Expt	Abst	DA/B 34 1034	Sep 73 Eichor.CS138 FRACT CHAIN YLD GIVEN.	
Fiss Yield	Spont	AUA Revw	Conf	IAEA-169 2 163	74 Musgrove+ PROMPT,EVEN-Z POSITN,GRAPH	
Fiss Yield	Spont	HAR Revw	Conf	IAEA-169 1 353	74 Cuninghame.TERNARY H TO BE YLDS,TBL	
			Rept	AERE-R-7548	Sep 73 .SAME AS 73BOLOGNA	
Fiss Yield	Spont	ASU Expt	Abst	DA/B 34 5616	May 74 Mirell.E SPEC+YLD Z=1,2.SOME DATA	
Fiss Yield	Spont	LBL Expt	Prog	LBL-2366 45	May 74 Kataria+SUPERSEDED	
Fiss Yield	+7	RI Expt	Conf	YFI-17 35	Aug 74 Adamov+ YLD P,T (3 ANGLS)REL ALF,TBL	
	Spont		Rept	INDC(CCP)-48	Feb 75 .P 36. ENGLISH OF YFI-17 35	
Fiss Yield	Spont	BOL Expt	Jour	NC/A 23 85	Sep 74 Bertin+FINE STRUCTURE IN MASS YIELD	
Fiss Yield	Spont	TRM Theo	Conf	74Bombay 2 137	Dec 74 Kataria. QUATERN FISSN,ALFA-ENERGY	
Fiss Yield	Spont	ANL Expt	Jour	JIN 37 881	Apr 75 Flynn+ RADIOCHEM,CFD OTH.RECOMM VALS	
			Conf	73Rochestr 2 19	Aug 73 Unik+DBL E EXPT.TBL.MASS DISTR CURVS	
			Conf	75Kiev 5 82	May 75 Donichkin+ BY XRAYS.CUMYLD 10NUC.TBL	
Fiss Yield	Spont	TRM Expt	Jour	NP/A 246 505	Jul 75 Ajitanand+ TER,AVG FRAG-MASS FOR 8Z.	+
			Rept	BARC-768 63	74 - + BIN,TER.MASSDIS 8ELEM GVN	
	Spont		Data	EXFOR30418.003	Oct 77 8 PTS. TERNARY YIELD FOR EVEN-Z.	
Fiss Yield	Spont	GRE Expt	Prog	NEANDC(E)162U	Aug 75 Blachot+ 28 YIELDS	
			Jour	JRC 26 107	75 - + GELI,CUM ISOT+CHAIN-YLD,TBL	
			Prog	NEANDC(E)161U	Aug 74 - + MASS DISTRIBUTION	
Fiss Yield	Spont	ANK Expt	Jour	JIN 37 2247	Nov 75 Gokturk+ FOR A=105-108,RADIOCHEM,TBL	
Fiss Yield	Spont	GHT Expt	Jour	NIM 134 299	76 Thierens+ REL MASS YLD TBL	
Fiss Yield	Spont	NIL Expt	Prog	INDC(SEC)-50	Jan 76 . ABST. CORREL TO FRG-GAMS,TBD,NDG	
Fiss Yield	Spont	REH Expt	Prog	INDC(SEC)-50	Jan 76 Gavron+ ABST.PROTONS/LRA GIVEN	
Fiss Yield	Spont	BON Expt	Jour	PL/B 60 445	Feb 76 David+MASS YLD DIST AS FUNC OF TOT E	
Fiss Yield	Spont	AUA Theo	Rept	AAEC/E-386	Mar 76 Cook+ 3-GAUSS FIT,PARAMS GIVEN	

98 Californium 252

Quantity	Energy (ev) Min Max	Lab	Type	Documentation Ref Vol Page	Date	Author, Comments	Data
Fiss Yield	Spont	THD	Theo	Jour JPR 37 1279	Nov 76	Carjan+ ORIGIN OF ALPHA IN FISSION	
				Jour PR/C 11 782	Mar 75	- + ALPHA EMISS PROB IN FISS	
Fiss Yield	Spont	UI	Expt	Abst ANS 24 460	Nov 76	Lipinski+ GRPH. DET FROM X RAY YLDS.	
				Conf 76Lowell 1416	Jul 76	- + ELEMENT YLDS MEAS.CFD.NDG	
Fiss Yield	Spont	BRC	Expt	NEANDC(E)172 4	77	Amoudry+ ABSTRACT ONLY,COIN METHOD	
Fiss Yield	Spont	TRM	Theo	Rept INIS-MF-3797	77	Chakraborthy+ O-D-MOD.ISOTOP YLD,FIG	
Frag Spectra	Spont	LRL	Expt	Jour PR 105 1507	Mar 57	Hicks+,FRAG KE CORREL WITH NU AVG	
Frag Spectra	Spont	LAS	Expt	Jour PR 110 476	Apr 58	Stein+ TOF ENERGY DISTRIB	
Frag Spectra	Spont	ANL	Expt	Jour PR 102 813	May 56	Smith+,DOUBLE IONIZATION CH,FRAG ES	
				Conf 58Geneva 15 392	Sep 58	- +.PPR690,ENERGY OF FRAGMENTS	
Frag Spectra	Spont	BRK	Expt	Conf 58Geneva 15 212	Sep 58	Bowmann+.PPR652,CURVE,EXPT DESCRIBED	
Frag Spectra	Spont	CCP	Theo	Jour AE 6 298	Mar 59	Geilikman. FRAG POT+KIN+EXCIT E,TABL	
				Jour SJA 6 184	Nov 60	TRANSLATN.*	
Frag Spectra	Spont	YAL	Expt	Jour PR 121 230	Jan 61	Watson.TRITON+ALPHA ENERGY SPECTRA	
Frag Spectra	Spont	LRL	Expt	Jour JIN 21 15	Dec 61	Marsh+,ENERGY-RANGE CORRELAT 19FRAGS	
Frag Spectra	Spont	LAS	Expt	Jour PR 126 1508	May 62	Nobles.	
Frag Spectra	Spont	COP	Theo	Jour NP 46 129	Jul 63	Vandenbosch. EFF OF FRAG SHELL STRUC	
Frag Spectra	Spont	LAS	Expt	Jour NIM 24 13	Jul 63	Britt+AVR TOT K.E VERSUS M,E RATIOS	
Frag Spectra	Spont	LAS	Expt	Jour PR 131 1232	Aug 63	Whetstone. TOF FRAG VELOCITY+KE DIST	
Frag Spectra	Spont	CRC	Expt	Jour CJP 41 2080	Dec 63	Fraser+ DOUBLE VEL MEASUREMENTS.	
Frag Spectra	Spont	ORL	Expt	Rept ORNL-3692	64	Kiker.TOF.FRAG MASS,VELOCITY,KE DIST	
Frag Spectra	Spont	ORL	Expt	Jour IRE 11 232	Jun 64	.SI DET.PULSE HEIGHT SPECTGRA	
Frag Spectra	Spont	TRM	Revw	Rept AEET-235	65	Methasiri.ALF E-SPEC+ANGDIST REVWD	
Frag Spectra	Spont	TRM	Theo	Conf 65Calcutta 20	Feb 65	Ramanna+ DEFORM-E(FRAG A), MARKOV-TH	
Frag Spectra	Spont	CRC	Revw	Conf 65Salzburg 451	Mar 65	Fraser.REVW OF XPTS AND RESULTS,TBL	
Frag Spectra	Spont	EDG	Theo	Conf 65Salzburg 2 387	Mar 65	Feather.ALPHA EMISSION IN FISSION	
Frag Spectra	None	ORL	Theo	Conf 65Salzburg 1 369	Mar 65	Halpern. ALPHA EMISSION IN FISSION	
Frag Spectra	Spont	ORL	Expt	Jour PR 141 1146	Jan 66	Schmitt+MASS.ENERGY DIST CORR	
Frag Spectra	Spont	CIS	Theo	Jour NP 84 595	Sep 66	Erba+ STATISTICAL MODEL CFD XPT	
Frag Spectra	Spont	CCP	Theo	Rept ICD-3 34	Oct 66	Zommer+.NDG,FONGS THEORY	
				Jour AE 23 327	Oct 67	- +.LVL-DENSITY REL FRGMNTMASS	
				Jour EAF 23 4 73	Oct 67	. FRENCH OF AE 23 327	
				Rept INDC-152E 34	67	. ENGL OF ICD-3 34	
Frag Spectra	Spont	BRK	Expt	Jour NP/A 90 145	Jan 67	Kleinheinz+ E SPEC OF CONV ELECTRONS	
Frag Spectra	Spont	LAS	Expt	Jour PR 154 1174	Feb 67	Whetstone+ E SPECT 6LIGHT FRAGMENTS	
				Jour PRL 15 298	Aug 65	.SUPERSEDED	
Frag Spectra	Spont	LRL	Expt	Jour PR 154 1193	Feb 67	Cosper+.AVG E,WIDTH 8FRAGS H TO BE	
				Prog UCRL-17299 170	Jan 67	- +. SPECTRA OF Z=1-4 PARTICLES	
Frag Spectra	-	TRM	Expt	Conf 67Kanpur 334	Feb 67	Hattangadi.SPONTANE FISS,E SPECT A	
Frag Spectra	Spont	FLA	Expt	Jour PRL 18 404	Mar 67	Muga+2. E SPEC IN TERNARY FISSION	
				Rept ORO-2843-9	Dec 66	.SUPERSEDED	
				Conf 65Salzburg 409	Mar 65	.SUPERSEDD	
Frag Spectra	Spont	LAS	Expt	Jour PR 156 1277	Apr 67	Stein+ FRAG ENERGIES VS MASS,+TOTAL	
				Conf 65Salzburg 491	Mar 65	.SUPERSEDED	
Frag Spectra	Spont	LRL	Expt	Jour PR 156 1283	Apr 67	Fraenkel+ENERGY-ANG DISTRIBTN ALPHAS	
				Jour PRL 13 438	Oct 64	.SUPERSEDED	
Frag Spectra	Spont	NEG	Theo	Jour PR 156 1305	Apr 67	Boneh+ PART OF RESULTS GIVEN	
				Prog IA-1168 11	Jan 67	- + LIGHT PART YLD+SPEC CFD EXPTS	
Frag Spectra	Spont	BRK	Expt	Abst DA/B 27 4078	May 67	Watson.CONV ELECTRON SPEC,FEW NANSEC	
Frag Spectra	-	FEI	Theo	Prog YFI-4 14	May 67	Ignatjuk.CURVES GIVEN	
	Spont			Jour YF 7 1043	May 68	- . E-KIN(FRAG-A),SHELLMODEL	
	None			Jour YF 7 1043	May 68	- + E-KIN(FRAG-A),SHELLMODEL	
				Jour SNP 7 626	Nov 68	. ENGL OF YF 7 1043	
	-			Rept INDC-187E	67	. ENGL OF YFI-4 14	
Frag Spectra	6.0+6 2.1+7	KUR	Theo	Rept IAE-1389	Jun 67	Shigin.STAT FISS MDL,FRAG MASS DISTR	
Frag Spectra	Spont	KFK	Comp	Rept KFK-693	Dec 67	Muenzel+ RANGE DIST OF FISS FRAG	
Frag Spectra	Spont	KFI	Theo	Jour KFI 16 45	Feb 68	Kluge+.GRAPHS,MYERS-SWIATECKI FORML	
Frag Spectra	Spont	LAS	Expt	Jour NP/A 108 689	Feb 68	Erkkila+.FRAGMT ES NORM TO KNOWN ES.	
Frag Spectra	Spont	KFI	Theo	Jour KFI 16 129	Apr 68	Kluge+.TEMPS OF FRGMNTS,STATISTL MDL	
Frag Spectra	Spont	MUR	Theo	Rept ORO-3638-2	May 68	Bucy.	
Frag Spectra	Spont	PTN	Expt	Jour PR 169 993	May 68	Thomas+ LONG-RANGE FRAGS YLD VS RANG	
Frag Spectra	Spont	PTN	Expt	Jour PR 172 1272	Aug 68	Raisbuck+ LIGHT FRAG E+ANG DIST	
Frag Spectra	Maxwl	BOR	Theo	Jour CR 267 981	Oct 68	Doan+BI+TERN.FISS;MOD OF 3ALIGN.SPER	
Frag Spectra	Spont	CCP	Theo	Jour IZV 33 163	Jan 69	Zommer. FRAG EXCIT E + N EMISSN,TBLS	
				Jour IZV 32 148		69 TRANSLATN.*NO 1	
Frag Spectra	Maxwl	RI	Revw	Jour IZV 33 116	Jan 69	Solov'Ev+ FRAG E+RANGE IN AIR + MICA	
	Spont		Expt	Prog YFI-16 12	Jun 73	- + FRAG KIN EN DISTR NO DATA	
	Maxwl		Revw	Jour IZV 32 106		69 TRANSLATN.*NO 1	

98 Californium 252

Quantity	Energy (ev) Min	Max	Lab	Type	Documentation Ref Vol Page	Date	Author, Comments	Data
Frag Spectra	Spont		RI	Theo	Prog YFI-7 33	Apr 69	Rubchenya. SIZE OF DIP IN FRAG-E(A)	
					Rept INDC(CCP)-7U36	Feb 70	TRANSLATN.*	
					Jour YF 9 1192	Jun 69	Rubchenja. SHELLMOD.FRAG KIN-E,CURVS	
					Jour SNP 9 697	Dec 69	. ENGL OF YF 9 1192	
Frag Spectra	Spont		ANK	Expt	Conf 69Vienna 950	Jul 69	Aras+ PPR49. FRAGMENT RANGE+ES IN AL	
Frag Spectra	Spont		EDG	Revw	Conf 69Vienna 83	Jul 69	Feather.PPR201. SURVEY,TERNARY-SPECS	
Frag Spectra	Spont		GIT	Theo	Conf 69Vienna 133	Jul 69	Fong.PPR108.GRPHS,ALPHA-SPEC CFD XPT	
Frag Spectra	Spont		IBJ	Expt	Conf 69Vienna 115	Jul 69	Blocki+ PPR68. ALPHA-ANGDIST-GRPH GVN	
Frag Spectra	Spont		IBJ	Expt	Conf 69Vienna 892	Jul 69	Piekarz+ PPR64. TOT EKIN,TERN+BINARY	
Frag Spectra	Spont		ORL	Theo	Conf 69Vienna 67	Jul 69	Schmitt.PPR122.GRPH,(EKIN+ - RMS) VS A	
Frag Spectra	Spont		SOR	Theo	Conf 69Vienna 143	Jul 69	Nardi+ PPR11.FIT TO LIGHT-PARTICL XPT	
Frag Spectra	Spont		SAH	Theo	Conf 69Roorke 2 217	Dec 69	Sarkar+ E BALANCE OKS EXPTS, GRAPHS	
					Jour PL/B 30 313	Oct 69	- +CALC EXCIT+KE PROMPT FRAGS	
Frag Spectra	Spont		RI	Expt	Prog YFI-11 48	70	Adamov+ ABST,FRAG KE+A-ANGDIST GIVEN	
					Prog INDC(CCP)-31	Dec 72	.PAGE 47,ENGLISH OF YFI-11 48	
Frag Spectra	Spont		CCP	Expt	Jour YF 11 1001	May 70	Adamov+ TERN FISSN,ALFA ENERGY+WIDTH	
					Jour YF 13 939	May 71	- + FRAG+ALF-KE,ALF ANGDIST,GRPH	
					Jour SNP 13 540	Nov 71	. ENGL OF YF 13 939	
					Jour SNP 11 557	Nov 70	. ENGL OF YF 11 1001	
Frag Spectra	Spont		SOR	Expt	Jour PR/C 1 2101	Jun 70	Gazit+,ENERGY SPECT Z=3-8 FRAGMENTS	
Frag Spectra	Spont		KUR	Expt	Rept IAE-2036	Sep 70	Zakharova.KE OF PAIRS VS MASS RATIO	
Frag Spectra	Spont		CCP	Expt	Jour YF 13 1162	Jun 71	Barashkov+ TOF,KE DISTRIB,TBL,GRPHS	
					Jour SNP 13 668	Dec 71	. ENGL OF YF 13 1162	
Frag Spectra	Spont		ANL	Expt	Jour NP/A 177 337	Dec 71	Reisdorf+SIMULT MEAS K.E. ANG G-SPEC	
					Conf 69Vienna 781	Jul 69	.PRELIMINARY.	
Frag Spectra	Spont		ORL	Expt	Jour NIM 100 467	72	Adair+ CF252 OVERCOATED WITH C+AU	
Frag Spectra		+7	RI	Expt	Prog YFI-14 11	72	Blinov+ TOF,GRAPH	
Frag Spectra	Spont		LRL	Expt	Jour PR/C 5 2041	Jun 72	Wilhelmy+. FRAGMEN MOMENTUM DISTR	
					Prog UCRL-20426 161	70	.SUPERSEDED	
Frag Spectra	Spont		PTN	Expt	Jour PR/C 5 2064	Jun 72	Rajagopalan+. ALPHA ANGULAR DIST	
					Abst DA/B 32 6899	Jun 72	.THESIS ABST	
Frag Spectra	Spont		SOR	Expt	Jour PRL 29 805	Sep 72	Gavron+. HE5 EMISSION.PARTICLE SPECT	
Frag Spectra	Spont		AUA	Theo	Jour AUJ 25 499	Oct 72	Musgrove.TERNARY FISS ALPHA,T,P.	
					Rept AAEC/TM-595	Jun 71	- .CALC H,HE E-SPECS CFD EXPTS	
					Jour AUJ 24 129	Apr 71	- . ANG+E SPEC GRAPHS OF ALFA	
Frag Spectra	Spont		ANK	Expt	Jour RCA 18 4 198	Dec 72	Birguel+ KIN ENERG FROM RECOIL RANGE	
Frag Spectra	Spont		ANL	Expt	Jour PR/C 7 353	Jan 73	Fluss+. ALFA KE AND ANGULAR DISTR.	
Frag Spectra	Spont		PAV	Expt	Prog STI/DOC/10-144	May 73	Pinelly+ LIGHT FRAG SPEC,NDG,TBP NC	
					Prog EANDC(E)140U	Aug 71	Cavallari+, ENERGY DISTRIBUTION	
Frag Spectra	Spont		SAC	Expt	Prog EANDC(E)-157U2	May 73	Babinet+CORRELATION OF EXC.ENERGY	
					Jour PR/C 7 373	Jan 73	Mehta+ KIN E DIST,BINARY+LRA FISSION	
					Jour NP/A 189 285	Jul 72	Nifenecker+ LIQ SCINT. E VS A,EK.NDG	
					Conf 69Vienna 491	Jul 69	- +PPR78.NU(FRAG Z KE)GRAPHS	
Frag Spectra	Spont		GA	Expt	Prog USNDC-7 95	Jun 73	Gozani.GAM MULTIPLIC/SPEC CRLN.CURV	
Frag Spectra	Spont		ITK	Theo	Jour AUJ 26 279	Jun 73	Mukherji+ CALC KE VS FRAG-MASS,GRAPH	
					Conf 69Roorke 2 226	Dec 69	- + TOT-KINE(A) CRV,LIQID-DROP	
Frag Spectra	Spont		LBL	Theo	Rept LBL-1950	Jul 73	Nifenecker+.NU VARIATN WITH FRAG KE	
Frag Spectra	Spont		ANL	Expt	Conf 73Rochestr 2 19	Aug 73	Unik+ TOTAL KIN-E OF FRAGS,GRPH	
Frag Spectra	Spont		KYU	Expt	Conf 73Rochestr 2 405	Aug 73	Tsuji+ E-+ANGDIST OF ALFS,TBLS,GRPHS	
Frag Spectra	Spont		LBL	Expt	Conf 73Rochestr 2 389	Aug 73	Kataria+ 2 LIGHT PARTICLES,TBL,GRPHS	
Frag Spectra	Spont		TUE	Expt	Conf 73Rochestr 2 483	Aug 73	Hipp+ ABST,FRAG KIN-E,MEAN KE GIVEN	
Frag Spectra	Spont		RI	Expt	Jour NP/A 213 520	Oct 73	Solovjev+.K X-RAY STUDY EVEN/ODD Z.	
Frag Spectra	Spont		MRY	Expt	Prog MNC-4028-12	Nov 73	.TBL+CURV RANGE VS. MASS.	
Frag Spectra	Spont		AUA	Revw	Conf IAEA-169 2 163	74	Musgrove+ AVG FRAG MASS,GRAPH	
Frag Spectra	Spont		ORU	Expt	Jour PR/C 9 395	Jan 74	Loveland.COUNTER TELESC.ALFA SPECTRA	
Frag Spectra	Spont		RI	Expt	Jour PL/B 48 311	Feb 74	Adamov+ ANG+E DIST OF P,T,ALPHA	
Frag Spectra	Spont		AUA	Eval	Rept AAEC/E-304	Mar 74	Musgrove. BIN+TER,MEAN FRGM-EKIN GVN	
Frag Spectra	Spont		ASU	Expt	Abst DA/B 34 5616	May 74	Mirell.E SPEC+YLD Z=1,2.SOME DATA	
Frag Spectra	Spont		REH	Expt	Jour PR/C 10 338	Jul 74	Gavron+ P-YLD(E)+GAUSS-FIT,GRAPH	
Frag Spectra	Spont		RI	Expt	Jour YF 20 266	Aug 74	Baranov+ ENERGY SPEC OF FRAGS,GRAPHS	
					Conf 73Kiev 3 277	May 73	- + FINE STRUCT OF E-DIST,GRAPH	
					Jour SNP 20 141	Feb 75	. ENGLISH OF YF 20 266	
Frag Spectra	Spont		RI	Expt	Rept YFI-17 35	Aug 74	Adamov+ YLD P,T (3ANGLS)REL ALF,TBL	
					Rept INDC(CCP)-48	Feb 75	.P 36. ENGLISH OF YFI-17 35	
Frag Spectra	Spont		BOL	Expt	Jour NC/A 23 85	Sep 74	Bertin+ E DISTRIBUTION,GRAPH	
					Conf 73Rochestr 2 505	Aug 73	- + (UBO).ABST. K-E OF FRAG.AVG.	
Frag Spectra	Spont		NIL	Expt	Prog INDC(SEC)-42	Dec 74	. CORREL E-KIN,E-GAM OF FRGMS.TBC	
Frag Spectra	Spont		BOR	ExTh	Rept CEN(BG)-75 19	75	Benfoughal. FINE STRUCTURE ANAL	

98 Californium 252

Quantity	Energy (ev) Min Max	Lab	Type	Documentation Ref Vol Page	Date	Author, Comments	Data
Frag Spectra	Spont	GHT	Expt Prog	INIS – MF – 1933	75	Jacobs+ TERN,HIGH – E ALFSPEC,NDG	
Frag Spectra	Spont	TRM	ExTh Prog	BARC – 843 50	75	Kataria. QUAT.CORREL 2LIGHT PART,FIG	
			Theo Conf	74Bombay 2 137	Dec 74	– . QUAT,2ALFS.E,ANG CORREL.FIG	
Frag Spectra	Spont	ASU	Expt Abst	DA/B 35 3508	Jan 75	Bolig.E SPECT H,HE IN TERNARY FISS	
			Rept	UMO – 75 – 1663	74	– . FULL TEXT OF THESIS	
Frag Spectra	Spont	THD	Expt Jour	RCA 23 3 161	76	Klonk+ RANGES+KIN.EN OF 9 FISSPROD	
Frag Spectra	Spont Maxwl	TRM	Expt Jour Conf	BARC – 878 45 75Calcutta 2 124	76 Dec 75	Kataria+ LRA E – DIST.AVG ALF – E(Z),FIG – + E SPECT ALFAS,TERNARY,GRAPH	
Frag Spectra	Spont	REH	Expt Jour	PRL 36 1072	May 76	Wolf+ KE FRAGS.TE – 134 MAGNETIC MOMNT	
Frag Spectra	Spont	FTI	Theo Jour	YF 23 1175	Jun 76	Geilikman+ KE FRG – MASS CALC.	
			Jour	SNP 23 624	Jun 76	. ENGL OF YF 23 1175	
Frag Spectra	Spont	GEL	Expt Conf	76ANL 415	Jun 76	Budtz Jorgensen+TWIN IONIZ CH.GRPHS.	
Frag Spectra	Spont	ORL	Theo Jour	PR/C 13 2385	Jun 76	Davies+DEP ON VISCOSITY CALC.CFD EXP	
Frag Spectra	Spont	DKE	Theo Conf	76Lowell 1403	Jul 76	Newson.EXCIT E,3 – 50MEV.FINE STRUC.ND	
Frag Spectra	None	GER	Theo Conf	76Lowell 1468	Jul 76	Kolb.ANAL Z114 BIN,TER FRAGMENTATION	
Frag Charge	Maxwl Spont	CNA	Theo Jour ExTh Rept	PR/B 134 972 CNAEM – 12	Jun 64 63	Talat+ N,CHARGE DIST IN FISS PRODS. – + TBL AVERAGE CHARGE/NUCLEON	
Frag Charge	None	JUL	Theo Conf	65Salzburg 103	Mar 65	Armbruster.CHG – DSTRB CALCLTD,GRAPHS	
Frag Charge	Spont	ANL	Expt Jour Conf	PR/B 140 1301 65Salzburg 369	Dec 65 Mar 65	Glendenin+CHG VS FRAG MASS BY XRAY .SUPERSEDED	
Frag Charge	Spont	LRL	Expt Jour Prog	PR/B 140 1310 UCRL – 11828 95	Dec 65 Jan 65	Bowman+ FRAG K X – RAY – +. MOST PROBABLE Z VS.A.CURVE	
Frag Charge	Spont	ORL	Expt Abst	BAP 11 334	Apr 66	Schmitt+FRAG EN COIN WITH K X – RAYS	
Frag Charge	Spont	ANL	Theo Jour	PR 157 1038	May 67	Wing+ FONG TH + NEW MASSES, OKS EXPT	
Frag Charge	Spont	RUT	Expt Abst	DA/B 28 1085	Sep 67	Dolce.AV CHG VS FRAG MASS BY K X – RAY	
Frag Charge	Spont	KFI	Theo Jour	KFI 16 45	Feb 68	Kluge+.GRAPHS,MYERS – SWIATECKI FORML	
Frag Charge	Spont	TRM	Revw Conf	68Madras 1 62	Feb 68	Kapoor.PPRI9.X – RAY+CHEM EXPTS CFD	
Frag Charge	–	CCP	Theo Jour Jour	YF 7 1043 SNP 7 626	May 68 Nov 68	Ignatyuk. CHARGE(FRAG – A),SHELL – TH TRANSLATN.*	
Frag Charge	Spont	SOR	Theo Jour	PR 182 1331	Jun 69	Notea.EMPIRICAL FUNCTION DERIVED	
Frag Charge	Spont	MNZ	Expt Conf	69Vienna 945	Jul 69	Denschlag+PPR26. CHARGE DISPERSION	
Frag Charge	Spont	OSL	Revw Conf	69Vienna 669	Jul 69	Pappas+PPR206. REVW OF EXPTS+METHODS	
Frag Charge	Spont	SAC	Expt Conf	69Vienna 491	Jul 69	Nifenecker+PPR78. NU(FRAG Z,KE)GRPHS	
Frag Charge	Spont	ANL	Expt Jour	JIN 31 3357	Nov 69	Von Gunten+ CHARGE DISTRIBUTION	
Frag Charge	Spont	ORL	Expt Jour	PR/C 1 1044	Mar 70	Troutner+,ZP FOR AG112 I134 CS138	
Frag Charge	Spont	LRL	Expt Jour Prog	PR/C 1 1866 UCRL – 19530 165	May 70 Jan 70	Watson+,FRAG CHG FROM K X – RAY YLDS – +,TBL MOST PROBABLE CHARGE	
Frag Charge	Spont	ANL	Expt Abst	BAP 16 98	Jan 71	Unik.K X – RAY METHOD. NO DATA GIVEN	
Frag Charge	Spont	JAE	Revw Jour	NP/A 160 65	Jan 71	Umezawa+ SYSTEMATICS VS FRAG MASS	
Frag Charge	Spont	LRL	Expt Jour Prog	PR/C 4 1913 UCRL – 20426 153	Nov 71 70	Cheifetz+.CHARGE DISTR, NEW METHOD Wilhelmy+. TABLES+CURVES	
Frag Charge	Spont	ANL	Expt Jour Conf	NP/A 177 337 69Vienna 781	Dec 71 Jul 69	Reisdorf+SIMULT MEAS K.E. ANG G – SPEC .PRELIMINARY.	
Frag Charge	Spont	FLA	Expt Abst	BAP 18 626	Apr 73	Clem+. UNUSUAL CHARGE DISTR.NO DATA	
Frag Charge	Spont	RI	Expt Conf Conf	73Kiev 3 291 73Kiev 3 283	May 73 May 73	Donichkin+ ODD – EVEN EFFECTS ON Z – YLD – + ZP CORREL TO MASS+E – KIN	
Frag Charge	Spont	LBL	Expt Conf	73Rochestr 2 435	Aug 73	Nifenecker.YLD VS CHARGE,TBL,GRAPH	
Frag Charge	Spont	MIS	Expt Abst	DA/B 34 1034	Sep 73	Eichor.MOST PROBABLE CHARGE DISTRBTN	
Frag Charge	Spont	AUA	Revw Conf	IAEA – 169 2 163	74	Musgrove+ CHARGE DISPERSN PARS,GRPHS	
Frag Charge	Spont	TRM	Expt Rept	BARC – 768 63	74	Ajitanand+ YIELD(Z),BIN CFD TER,GRPH	
Frag Charge	Spont	LRL	Comp Rept	UCRL – 51640	Jul 74	Nethaway. TBL.	
Frag Charge	Spont	GHT	Expt Prog	INDC(SEC) – 51	Dec 75	Jacobs+ P19. ZP(134,135),NDG.	
Frag Charge	Spont	TPI	Theo Jour Jour	YF 23 30 SNP 23 15	Jan 76 Jan 76	Adeev+ STRUTIN.(ZP – UCD) VS FRGM.CURV . ENGL OF YF 23 30	
Frag Charge	Spont	TRM	Theo Rept	INIS – MF – 3797	77	Chakraborthy+ O – D – MOD.ZP – Z(UCD),GRPH	
Reson Params	Spont	CCP	Theo Rept Rept	ICD – 3 34 INDC – 152E 34	Oct 66 67	Zommer+.TABLE,MANY REFS . ENGL OF ICD – 3 34	
Reson Params	6.2 – 1 5.0+4	SRL	Theo Conf	71Knoxvill 714	Mar 71	Mccrosson. STAT CALCULATN AVG PARAMS	
Reson Params	2.5+1 9.8+2 2.5+1 5.8+2	LAS	Expt Jour Conf Data	PR/C 4 273 70Helsinki 1 527 EXFOR10323.003	Jul 71 Jun 70 Dec 73	Moore+.NUCL SHOT. PARAMS FOR 35RESON .SUPERSEDED . 35 RES,E0	+
Lvl Density	–	CCP	Theo Jour	YF 4 1255	Dec 66	Zommer+SAVEL'EV,SPONT FISS,TBL GVN	
Lvl Density	+6	DUB	Theo Rept	JINR – E4 – 9236	Nov 75	Komov+ AVG LVL – SPAC,SEMIMICRO CFD XP	

98 Californium 253

Quantity	Energy (ev) Min Max	Lab Type	Documentation Ref Vol Page	Date	Author, Comments	Data
Evaluation	1.0−5 2.0+7	SRL Eval	Rept EPRI−NP−161	Dec 75	Benjamin+ ENDF4B.GENPAR MDL.REVISIONS	
Absorption	Maxwl	SRL Expt	Conf 68Wash. 1285	Mar 68	Smith+ AVG SIG=165B THERMALIZED SPEC	+
			Rept DP−MS−67−111	Feb 68	−.	
	Maxwl		Data EXFOR12580.012	Jun 76	. 1 PT.	
Absorption	Maxwl	SRL Expt	Abst ANS 14 344	Jun 71	Rusche. VALUE GIVEN	
Absorption	Pile	CCP Expt	Jour AE 32 493	Jun 72	Anufriev+ SIG GIVEN,CFD OTHER EXPTS	
			Jour SJA 32 584	Dec 72	− + ENGLISH OF AE 32 493	
Res Int Abs	None	SRL Expt	Abst ANS 14 344	Jun 71	Rusche. VALUE GIVEN	
(n,γ)	Maxwl	BNL Theo	Abst ANS 10 228	Jun 67	Prince. CALCULATED SIG=40B	
(n,γ)	Maxwl	CCP Comp	Jour AE 28 388	May 70	Bol'Shov+ OTHER'S SIG VALUE GIVEN	
			Jour EAF 28 5 9	70	. FRENCH OF AE 28 388.	
(n,γ)	5.4−1	ORL Expt	Jour NSE 41 146	Jul 70	Bemis+EFFECTIVE CS BASED ON THR FLUX	+
	5.4−1		Data EXFOR10129.002	Mar 76	. 1PT.EFFECTIVE NG CS=17.6+−1.8B	
(n,γ)	Pile	KFK Eval	Prog KFK−1544 61	Jan 72	Eberle+FOR 2−GROUP SIG,FITTED TO EXP	
(n,γ)	Pile	NIR Expt	Jour AE 36 286	Apr 74	Anufriev+ EFFECT SIG,FROM ABSORPTION	
			Jour AE 32 493	Jun 72	− + ESTIMATED FROM CF−254	
			Jour SJA 36 359	Oct 74	. ENGLISH OF AE 36 286	
			Jour SJA 32 584	Dec 72	. ENGL OF AE 32 493	
(n,γ)	Maxwl	SRL Eval	Conf 75Wash. 224	Mar 75	Benjamin+ TBL BEST FIT TRANSPU PROD.	
Res Int Capt	Maxwl	BNL Theo	Abst ANS 10 228	Jun 67	Prince. CALCULATED RES INTGRL=540B	
Res Int Capt	6.3−1	SRL Eval	Conf 75Wash. 224	Mar 75	Benjamin+ TBL BEST FIT TRANSPU PROD.	
Fission	Maxwl	BNL Theo	Abst ANS 10 228	Jun 67	Prince. CALCULATED SIG=33B	
Fission	Maxwl	CCP Comp	Jour AE 26 436	May 69	Romanov. UPPER SIG LIMIT ESTIMATED	
			Jour EAF 26 48	69	. FRENCH OF AE 26 436.	
			Jour SJA 26 498	69	. ENGL OF AE 26 436.	
Fission	Pile	ORL Expt	Jour NSE 41 146	Jul 70	Bemis+FROM CHANGE IN A DECAY RATE.	+
	Pile		Data EXFOR10129.003	Mar 76	. 1PT. ABS CS=NF CS=2550+−400B.	
Fission	Maxwl	SRL Expt	Abst ANS 14 344	Jun 71	Rusche. VALUE GIVEN	
Fission	Pile	KFK Eval	Prog KFK−1544 61	Jan 72	Eberle+FOR 2−GROUP SIG,FITTED TO EXP	
Fission	Maxwl	LRL Expt	Jour JIN 35 4 1063	Apr 73	Wild+MICA FISS FRAGM TRACK REC	+
	Maxwl		Data EXFOR10341.003	Jun 74	. 1 PT.	
Fission	Pile	NIR Expt	Jour AE 36 286	Apr 74	Anufriev+ EFFECT SIG,FROM ABSORPTION	
			Jour SJA 36 359	Oct 74	. ENGLISH OF AE 36 286	
Fission	Maxwl	SRL Eval	Conf 75Wash. 224	Mar 75	Benjamin+ TBL BEST FIT TRANSPU PROD.	
Res Int Fiss	Maxwl	BNL Theo	Abst ANS 10 228	Jun 67	Prince. CALCULATED RES INTGRL=198B	
Res Int Fiss	None	SRL Expt	Abst ANS 14 344	Jun 71	Rusche. VALUE GIVEN	
Res Int Fiss	6.3−1	SRL Eval	Conf 75Wash. 224	Mar 75	Benjamin+ TBL BEST FIT TRANSPU PROD.	
Alpha	1.0+4 2.0+4	LAS Expt	Jour PR 158 1127	Jun 67	Bell. SYSTEMATCS TH FOR 10−20KEV ALF	
Nu	Maxwl	IAE Eval	Jour REA 10 637	Dec 72	Manero+ CALC,SYSTEMATICS,TBL	
Fiss Yield	2.5−2	PAH Theo	Abst BAP 21 655	Apr 76	Hooshyar+PC MASS YLD SPEC CALC.NDG	
Frag Spectra	2.5−2	PAH Theo	Abst BAP 21 655	Apr 76	Hooshyar+KE SPEC CALC.CFD EXPT.NDG	
Frag Charge	2.5−2	PAH Theo	Abst BAP 21 655	Apr 76	Hooshyar+PC CHARG YLD SPEC CALC.NDG	
Reson Params	6.2−1 5.0+4	SRL Theo	Conf 71Knoxvill 714	Mar 71	Mccrosson. STAT CALCULATN AVG PARAMS	
Lvl Density	None	COP Theo	Jour NP/A 222 493	Apr 74	Dossing+COLL ROTAT.SPAC. ACCUR ESTIM	

98 Californium 254

Quantity	Energy (ev) Min Max	Lab Type	Documentation Ref Vol Page	Date	Author, Comments	Data
Absorption	Maxwl	SRL Expt	Abst ANS 14 344	Jun 71	Rusche. VALUE GIVEN	
Absorption	Pile	NIR Expt	Jour AE 36 286	Apr 74	Anufriev+ EFFECT SIG,=(N,G)+(N,F)	
			Jour SJA 36 359	Oct 74	. ENGLISH OF AE 36 286	
Res Int Abs	None	SRL Expt	Abst ANS 14 344	Jun 71	Rusche. VALUE GIVEN	
(n,γ)	Pile	BRK Expt	Jour PR 95 581	Jul 54	Harvey+ UPPER LIMIT 2B. MTR	+
	Pile		Data EXFOR12567.008	Jun 76	. 1 PT. SIGMA	
(n,γ)	Pile	ANL Revw	Conf 55Geneva 7 261	Aug 55	Bentley+.P809,VAL GVN,CHEMICAL METHD	
(n,γ)	None	KAP Comp	Rept KAPL−1781	Jul 57	Schuman. UPPER LIMIT SIG (N,G) GVN	
(n,γ)	Maxwl	BNL Theo	Abst ANS 10 228	Jun 67	Prince. CALCULATED SIG=2B	
(n,γ)	Maxwl	CCP Comp	Jour AE 28 388	May 70	Bol'Shov+ OTHER'S SIG VALUE GIVEN	
			Jour EAF 28 5 9	70	. FRENCH OF AE 28 388.	
Res Int Capt	Maxwl	BNL Theo	Abst ANS 10 228	Jun 67	Prince. CALCULATED RES INTGRL=1650B	
Fission	Spont	DUB Theo	Rept JINR−P−2265	Jul 65	Mekhedov. FISS+ALPH HLS ESTIMATED	
Fission	Maxwl	BNL Theo	Abst ANS 10 228	Jun 67	Prince. CALCULATED SIG=0.086B	
Fission	Spont	COP Revw	Conf 69Vienna 155	Jul 69	Strutinsky+PPR203. HL GVN,'SHELL−TH'	
Fission	Spont	MRYTheo	Prog ORO−4028−28	71	Jackson+. SPON FISSION HALF−LIFE GVN	
Res Int Fiss	Maxwl	BNL Theo	Abst ANS 10 228	Jun 67	Prince. CALCULATED RES INTGRL=28B	

98 Californium 254

Quantity	Energy (ev) Min	Max	Lab	Type	Documentation Ref Vol Page	Date	Author, Comments	Data
Nu	Spont		LAS	Expt Jour	NSE 43 54	Jan 71	Orth.SEPARATE COUNT OF NS+ SPON FISS	+
	Spont			Data	EXFOR10115.006	Jul 71	1PT.AVG NU=3.93+ −.05 REL CF 252	
Nu	Spont		DUB	Comp Rept	JINR − P15 − 6730	Sep 72	Dakowski+ MASS DEPEN.OF NU − BAR IN CF	
Nu	Spont		IAE	Eval Jour	REA 10 637	Dec 72	Manero+ EXTENSIVE SURVEY,TBL,AVG VAL	
Fiss Prod γ	Spont		ANL	Expt Jour	PR 107 1087	Aug 57	Huizenga+,HALFLIFE,LEAST − SQRSFIT	
Fiss Yield	Spont		LRL	Expt Jour	PR 131 2617	Sep 63	Brandt+ MASS DISTRIBUTION REL CF252	
Fiss Yield	Spont		OSL	Revw Conf	69Vienna 669	Jul 69	Pappas+PPR206.REVW,INITIAL MASS DIST	
Fiss Yield	Spont		NEU	Theo Jour	HPA 46 724	Jul 73	Hooshyar+ MASS A.CHARGE DISTR, HL	
Fiss Yield	Spont		ANL	Expt Conf	73Rochestr 2 19	Aug 73	Unik+ PROMPT YLDS,MASS DISTRIB,GRPHS	
Fiss Yield	Spont		AUA	Revw Conf	IAEA − 169 2 163	74	Musgrove+ PROMPT,EVEN − Z POSITN,GRAPH	
Fiss Yield	Spont		LAS	Expt Rept	LA − UR − 77 − 2901	77	Hoffman+ MASS − YIELD CFD OTHER,CURVE	
Frag Spectra	Spont		ANL	Expt Jour	PR 131 1203	Aug 63	Friedman+ FRAG MOST PROBABLE ENERGY	
Frag Spectra	Spont		LRL	Expt Jour	PR 131 2617	Sep 63	Brandt+ E DIST REL CF252 CURVES	
Frag Spectra	Spont		ANL	Expt Conf	73Rochestr 2 19	Aug 73	Unik+ TOTAL KIN − E OF FRAGS,GRPH	
Frag Spectra	Spont		AUA	Revw Conf	IAEA − 169 2 163	74	Musgrove+ AVG FRAG MASS,GRAPH	
Frag Spectra	Spont		LAS	Expt Rept	LA − UR − 77 − 2901	77	Hoffman+ TOT KE VS MASS,PRELIM.CURVE	
Frag Charge	Spont		LRL	Comp Rept	UCRL − 51640	Jul 74	Nethaway. TBL.	
Reson Params	6.2 − 1	5.0+4	SRL	Theo Conf	71Knoxvill 714	Mar 71	Mccrosson. STAT CALCULATN AVG PARAMS	

99 Einsteinium 244

Quantity	Energy (ev) Min Max	Lab	Type	Documentation Ref Vol Page	Date	Author, Comments	Data
Fission	Spont	DUB	Theo Rept	JINR-E-2515	Dec 65	Malov+ SPON FISSN ISOMER, LIFE-TIME	

99 Einsteinium 248

Quantity	Energy (ev) Min Max	Lab	Type	Documentation Ref Vol Page	Date	Author, Comments	Data
Fission	Spont	DUB	Theo Rept	JINR-E-2515	Dec 65	Malov+ SPON FISSN ISOMER, LIFE-TIME	

99 Einsteinium 251

Quantity	Energy (ev) Min Max	Lab	Type	Documentation Ref Vol Page	Date	Author, Comments	Data
(n,p)	Maxwl	CCP	Theo Rept	ICD-4 20	67	Dadakina+ PENETRATION COEF CALC,TABLE	
Fission	2.5-2	JUL	Theo Jour	ZP 257 389	Dec 72	Mcminn. 1.01 E +2 BARNS	

99 Einsteinium 252

Quantity	Energy (ev) Min Max	Lab	Type	Documentation Ref Vol Page	Date	Author, Comments	Data
(n,p)	Maxwl	CCP	Theo Rept	ICD-4 20	67	Dadakina+ PENETRATION COEF CALC,TABLE	
Alpha	1.0+4 2.0+4	LAS	Theo Jour	PR 158 1127	Jun 67	Bell. SYSTEMATCS TH FOR 10-20KEV ALF	
Fiss Yield	None	BAS	Theo Jour	PL/B 34 264	Mar 71	Pauli+ FRAG MASS RATIO AS STRUTINSKY	

99 Einsteinium 253

Quantity	Energy (ev) Min Max	Lab	Type	Documentation Ref Vol Page	Date	Author, Comments	Data
Evaluation	1.0-5 2.0+7	SRL	Eval Rept	EPRI-NP-161	Dec 75	Benjamin+ ENDF4B.GENPAR MDL.REVISIONS	
Absorption	Maxwl	SRL	Expt Conf	68Wash. 2 1279	Mar 68	Folger+. ACTIVATION	+
			Rept	DP-MS-67-112	Mar 68	.SAME	
	Maxwl		Data	EXFOR12534.016	Jun 76	. 1 PT, SIG	
(n,γ)	Pile	BRK	Expt Jour	PR 95 581	Jul 54	Harvey+.MEASURED FM254 YLD.IRRAD CF	+
	Pile		Data	EXFOR12567.009	Jun 76	. 1 PT, SIG	
(n,γ)	Pile	KAP	Expt Jour	PR 102 203	Apr 56	Jones+	+
	Pile		Data	EXFOR12586.002	Jun 76	. 1 PT, SIG	
(n,γ)	Pile	KAP	Expt Rept	KAPL-1781	Jul 57	Schuman. SIG (N,G)M GVN	
(n,γ)	Pile	ANL	Expt Jour	NP/A 96 440	Apr 67	Fields+ 13B TO ES254 338B TO ES254M	+
	Pile		Data	EXFOR12574.	Jun 76	. 2 PTS, SIG TO GND AND META	
(n,γ)	None	LAS	Expt Prog	WASH-1136 110	Sep 69	Silbert+,PHYSICS-8 SHOT,ANAL TBC	
(n,γ)	Maxwl	SRL	Expt Jour	JIN 35 6 1821	Jun 73	Harbour+	+
	Maxwl		Data	EXFOR10363.	Jan 75	2 PTS M-ST,GND-ST	
(n,γ)	Pile	NIR	Expt Jour	AE 36 286	Apr 74	Anufriev+ EFFECT SIG,TO GND+META GVN	
			Jour	SJA 36 359	Oct 74	. ENGLISH OF AE 36 286	
(n,γ)	Maxwl	SRL	Eval Conf	75Wash. 224	Mar 75	Benjamin+ TBL BEST FIT TRANSPU PROD.	
Res Int Capt	5.5-1	SRL	Expt Conf	68Wash. 2 1279	Mar 68	Folger+ ACT 3600B	+
			Rept	DP-MS-67-112	Mar 68	.SAME	
	5.5-1		Data	EXFOR12534.020	Jun 76	. 1 PT, RI	
Res Int Capt	4.1-1	SRL	Expt Jour	JIN 35 6 1821	Jun 73	Harbour+ REL TO 59CO	+
	4.1-1		Data	EXFOR10363.	Jan 75	2 PTS M-ST,GND-ST	
Res Int Capt	6.3-1	SRL	Eval Conf	75Wash. 224	Mar 75	Benjamin+ TBL BEST FIT TRANSPU PROD.	
(n,p)	Maxwl	CCP	Theo Rept	ICD-4 20	67	Dadakina+ PENETRATION COEF CALC,TABLE	
Fission	Spont	BRK	Revw Jour	NP 81 1	Jun 66	Myers.TBL CALC FISS BARRIERS.	
Fission	1.5+1 2.0+6	LAS	Expt Prog	USNDC-3 115	Oct 72	Silbert. NUCL SHOT. NO DATA GIVEN	
Fission	2.5-2	JUL	Theo Jour	ZP 257 389	Dec 72	Mcminn. 8.68 E +0 BARNS	
Fission	Maxwl	SRL	Eval Conf	75Wash. 224	Mar 75	Benjamin+ TBL BEST FIT TRANSPU PROD.	
Res Int Fiss	6.3-1	SRL	Eval Conf	75Wash. 224	Mar 75	Benjamin+ TBL BEST FIT TRANSPU PROD.	
Nu	Spont	AUA	Revw Conf	IAEA-169 2 163	74	Musgrove+ TOTAL NU-BAR,GRAPH	
Nu	Spont	ANL	Expt Jour	JIN 38 661	Apr 76	Flynn+ NUBAR GIVN,FRM MEAS ISOT-YLDS	
			Conf	73Rochestr 2 19	Aug 73	Unik+ PRELIM.TBL 13 NUCLIDES	
Fiss Yield	Spont	LRL	Expt Jour	PR 131 2617	Sep 63	Brandt+ MASS DISTRIBUTION REL CF252	
Fiss Yield	Spont	AUA	Theo Rept	AAEC/E-386	Mar 76	Cook+ 3-GAUSS FIT,PARAMS GIVEN	
Fiss Yield	Spont	ANL	Expt Jour	JIN 38 661	Apr 76	Flynn+RADIO-CHEM.MASS DISTR.TBL,CURV	
			Conf	73Rochestr 2 19	Aug 73	Unik+ PRELIM.MASS DISTRB 16 NUCLIDES	
Frag Spectra	Spont	LRL	Expt Jour	PR 131 2617	Sep 63	Brandt+ E DIST REL CF252 CURVES	

99 Einsteinium 254

Quantity	Energy (ev) Min	Max	Lab	Type	Documentation Ref Vol Page	Date	Author, Comments	Data
Total	Pile		KAP	Expt Jour	JIN 6 1	Apr 58	Schuman. KAPL-1781,TOT DESTRUCT CS	
Absorption	Pile		NIR	Expt Jour	AE 36 286	Apr 74	Anufriev+(GND,META).EFFECT SIG GIVN	
				Jour	SJA 36 359	Oct 74	. ENGLISH OF AE 36 286	
(n,γ)	Pile		BRK	Expt Jour	PR 95 581	Jul 54	Harvey+.UPPER LIMIT 15 B. MTR	+
	Pile			Data	EXFOR12567.010	Jun 76	. 1 PT, SIG	
(n,γ)	Pile		KAP	Expt Jour	JIN 6 1	Apr 58	Schuman. KAPL-1781,ULT OF ACT CS GVN	
	None			Rept	KAPL-1781	Jul 57	- . UPPER LIMIT SIG ES254M(N,G)	
Fission	Spont		BRK	Revw Jour	NP 81 1	Jun 66	Myers.TBL CALC FISS BARRIERS.	
Fission	Maxwl		ANL	Expt Prog	WASH-1124 8	Nov 68	.SUPERSEDED	+
				Jour	JIN 30 2553	Oct 68	Diamond+,ION CHAMB IN THR COLUMN	
				Prog	WASH-1093 12	Apr 68	.SUPERSEDED	
	Maxwl			Data	EXFOR12531.006	Jun 76	. 1 PT, SIG	
Fission	Maxwl		SRL	Expt Jour	JIN 34 2 449	Feb 72	Macmurdo+ SIG=2830+ -130B	+
	Maxwl			Data	EXFOR10281.003	Nov 73	1PT,SIGMA	
Res Int Fiss	6.3-1		SRL	Expt Jour	JIN 34 2 449	Feb 72	Macmurdo+ I=2200+ -90B	+
	6.3-1			Data	EXFOR10281.002	Nov 73	1PT	
Alpha	1.0+4	2.0+4	LAS	Theo Jour	PR 158 1127	Jun 67	Bell. SYSTEMATCS TH FOR 10-20KEV ALF	
Nu	Maxwl		AUA	Revw Conf	IAEA-169 2 163	74	Musgrove+ TOTAL NU-BAR,GRAPH	
Nu	Maxwl		ANL	Expt Jour	JIN 38 661	Apr 76	Flynn+ NUBAR GIVN,FRM MEAS ISOT-YLDS	
				Conf	73Rochestr 2 19	Aug 73	Unik+PRELIM.TBL 13 NUCLIDES	
Fiss Yield	Maxwl		AUA	Revw Conf	IAEA-169 2 163	74	Musgrove+ PROMPT,EVEN-Z POSITN,GRAPH	
Fiss Yield	Maxwl		AUA	Theo Rept	AAEC/E-386	Mar 76	Cook+ 3-GAUSS FIT,PARAMS GIVEN	
Fiss Yield	Maxwl		ANL	Expt Jour	JIN 38 661	Apr 76	Flynn+RADIO-CHEM.MASS DISTR.TBL.CURV	
				Conf	73Rochestr 2 19	Aug 73	Unik+PRELIM.PHYSICAL+RADIOCHEM EXPT	
Frag Spectra	Maxwl		ANL	Expt Conf	73Rochestr 2 19	Aug 73	Unik+ TOTAL KIN-E OF FRAGS,GRPH	
Frag Spectra	Maxwl		AUA	Revw Conf	IAEA-169 2 163	74	Musgrove+ AVG FRAG MASS,GRAPH	

99 Einsteinium 255

Quantity	Energy (ev) Min	Max	Lab	Type	Documentation Ref Vol Page	Date	Author, Comments	Data
(n,γ)	None		KAP	Comp Rept	KAPL-1781	Jul 57	Schuman. SIGMA (N,G) GIVEN	
Fission	2.5-2		JUL	Theo Jour	ZP 257 389	Dec 72	Mcminn. 1.50 E +0 BARNS	
Alpha	1.0+4	2.0+4	LAS	Theo Jour	PR 158 1127	Jun 67	Bell. SYSTEMATCS TH FOR 10-20KEV ALF	

99 Einsteinium 256

Quantity	Energy (ev) Min	Max	Lab	Type	Documentation Ref Vol Page	Date	Author, Comments	Data
Fission	Maxwl		CCP	Comp Jour	AE 26 436	May 69	Romanov. UPPER SIG LIMIT ESTIMAT54	
				Rept	BNL-TR-286	69	. ENGLISH OF AE 26 436	
				Jour	EAF 26 48	69	. FRENCH TRANS	
				Jour	SJA 26 498	69	. ENGLISH TRANSLATION	

100 Fermium 244

Quantity	Energy (ev) Min Max	Lab Type	Documentation Ref Vol Page	Author, Comments Date	Data
Fission	Spont	DUB Revw Jour	REA 8 255	Jun 70 Flerov+ REVIEW,TBL OF HALF-LIVES	
Fission	Spont	MRY Theo Prog	ORO-4028-28	71 Jackson+. SPON FISSION HALF-LIFE GVN	
Nu	Spont	KUR Eval Rept	IAE-2738	75 Zakharova. NUBAR=3.0+-0.5	

100 Fermium 246

Quantity	Energy (ev) Min Max	Lab Type	Documentation Ref Vol Page	Author, Comments Date	Data
Fission	Spont	DUB Expt Rept	JINR-P7-4817	Dec 69 Druin+ EXPTL HALF-LIVE GIVN	
Fission	Spont	DUB Revw Jour	REA 8 255	Jun 70 Flerov+ REVIEW,TBL OF HALF-LIVES	
Fission	Spont	MRY Theo Prog	ORO-4028-28	71 Jackson+. SPON FISSION HALF-LIFE GVN	
Nu	Spont	KUR Eval Rept	IAE-2738	75 Zakharova. NUBAR=3.3+-0.5	

100 Fermium 248

Quantity	Energy (ev) Min Max	Lab Type	Documentation Ref Vol Page	Author, Comments Date	Data
Fission	Spont	CCP Comp Jour	AE 26 436	May 69 Romanov. HALF-LIFE VAL ESTIMATD,GRPH	
		Jour	EAF 26 48	69 . FRENCH OF AE 26 436.	
		Jour	SJA 26 498	69 . ENGL OF AE 26 436.	
Fission	Spont	DUB Expt Rept	JINR-P7-4817	Dec 69 Druin+ EXPTL HALF-LIVE GIVN	
Fission	Spont	MRY Theo Prog	ORO-4028-28	71 Jackson+. SPON FISSION HALF-LIFE GVN	

100 Fermium 250

Quantity	Energy (ev) Min Max	Lab Type	Documentation Ref Vol Page	Author, Comments Date	Data
Fission	Spont	DUB Theo Rept	JINR-P-2265	Jul 65 Mekhedov. FISS+ALPH HLS ESTIMATED	
Fission	Spont	CCP Comp Jour	AE 26 436	May 69 Romanov. HALF-LIFE VAL ESTIMATD,GRPH	
		Jour	EAF 26 48	69 . FRENCH OF AE 26 436.	
		Jour	SJA 26 498	69 . ENGL OF AE 26 436.	
Fission	Spont	DUB Expt Rept	JINR-P7-4817	Dec 69 Druin+ EXPTL HALF-LIVE GIVN	
Fission	Spont	DUB Revw Jour	REA 8 255	Jun 70 Flerov+ REVIEW,TBL OF HALF-LIVES	
Fission	Spont	MRY Theo Prog	ORO-4028-28	71 Jackson+. SPON FISSION HALF-LIFE GVN	

100 Fermium 252

Quantity	Energy (ev) Min Max	Lab Type	Documentation Ref Vol Page	Author, Comments Date	Data
Fission	Spont	COP Revw Conf	69Vienna 155	Jul 69 Strutinsky+PPR203. HL GVN,'SHELL-TH'	
Fission	Spont	DUB Revw Jour	REA 8 255	Jun 70 Flerov+ REVIEW,TBL OF HALF-LIVES	
Fission	Spont	MRY Theo Prog	ORO-4028-28	71 Jackson+. SPON FISSION HALF-LIFE GVN	
Fission	None	FRK Theo Jour	NP/A 207 225	Jun 73 Albrecht. 2CENTRE SHELLMOD,DEF-E MAP	
Frag Charge	Spont	MRY Theo Jour	PR/C 11 1059	Mar 75 Nustafa.CALC SHELL CORR TO MASS DIST	

100 Fermium 253

Quantity	Energy (ev) Min Max	Lab Type	Documentation Ref Vol Page	Author, Comments Date	Data
(n,p)	Maxwl	CCP Theo Rept	ICD-4 20	67 Dadakina+PENETRATION COEF CALC,TABLE	
Nu	Maxwl	IAE Eval Jour	REA 10 637	Dec 72 Manero+ CALC,SYSTEMATICS,TBL	
Fiss Yield	2.5-2	PAH Theo Abst	BAP 21 655	Apr 76 Hooshyar+PC MASS YLD SPEC CALC.NDG	
Frag Spectra	2.5-2	PAH Theo Abst	BAP 21 655	Apr 76 Hooshyar+KE SPEC CALC.CFD EXPT.NDG	
Frag Charge	2.5-2	PAH Theo Abst	BAP 21 655	Apr 76 Hooshyar+PC CHARG YLD SPEC CALC.NDG	

100 Fermium 254

Quantity	Energy (ev) Min Max	Lab Type	Documentation Ref Vol Page	Author, Comments Date	Data
Absorption	Pile	NIR Expt Jour	AE 36 286	Apr 74 Anufriev+(EFFECT SIG,=(N,G)+(N,F)	
		Jour	SJA 36 359	Oct 74 . ENGLISH OF AE 36 286	
Fission	Spont	BRK Revw Jour	NP 81 1	Jun 66 Myers.TBL CALC FISS BARRIERS.	
Fission	–	TPI Theo Jour	YF 9 102	Jan 69 Korostova+ SHELL-TH OKS HLS CM+CF+FM	
		Jour	SNP 9 62	Jul 69 TRANSLATN.*	
Fission	Spont	COP Revw Conf	69Vienna 155	Jul 69 Strutinsky+PPR203. HL GVN,'SHELL-TH'	
Fission	Spont	MRY Theo Prog	ORO-4028-28	71 Jackson+. SPON FISSION HALF-LIFE GVN	
Fission	2.5-2	JUL Theo Jour	ZP 257 389	Dec 72 Mcminn. 2.88 E +3 BARNS	

100 Fermium 254

Quantity	Energy (ev) Min	Max	Lab	Type	Documentation Ref Vol Page	Date	Author, Comments	Data
Alpha	1.0+4	2.0+4	LAS	Theo Jour	PR 158 1127	Jun 67	Bell. SYSTEMATCS TH FOR 10-20KEV ALF	
Nu	Spont		LRL	Expt Jour	PR 102 766	May 56	Choppin+,AVERAGE NU=4.05+-0.19,SC-T	
Nu	Spont		FOA	Comp Rept	NP- 16440	Mar 63	ASPLUND-NILSSON. REVIEW. TABLE.	
Nu	Spont		IAE	Eval Jour	REA 10 637	Dec 72	Manero+ EXTENSIVE SURVEY,TBL,AVG VAL	
Nu	Spont		ANL	Expt Conf	73Rochestr 2 19	Aug 73	Unik+NU TOTAL VS MASS 13 NUCLIDES.	
Nu	Spont		DUB	Comp Jour	YF 18 724	Oct 73	Dakovsky+NUBAR VS FISNUCLEUS,TBL+GRP	
				Eval Rept	JINR-P15-7119	Jun 73	Dakowski+ NUBAR+P(NU)-DISTR,TBL,GRPH	
				Comp Jour	SNP 18 371	Apr 74	. ENGLISH OF YF 18, 724.	
Nu	Spont		AUA	Revw Conf	IAEA-169 2 163	74	Musgrove+ TOTAL NU-BAR,GRAPH	
Fiss Yield	Spont		LRL	Expt Jour	PR 131 2617	Sep 63	Brandt+ MASS DISTRIBUTION REL CF252	
Fiss Yield	–		TPI	Theo Jour	YF 9 102	Jan 69	Korostova+SHELL INFL,HEAV+L+SYM FRAG	
				Jour	SNP 9 62	Jul 69	TRANSLATN.*	
Fiss Yield	Spont		OSL	Revw Conf	69Vienna 669	Jul 69	Pappas+PPR206.REVW,INITIAL MASS DIST	
Fiss Yield	None		TRM	Theo Conf	72Bombay 2 201	Feb 72	Ramamurthy+ DISTRIBTN OF MASSES,GRPH	
	Spont			Prog	BARC-633 64	72	- . FRAG MASS DISTRIB ,GRPH	
Fiss Yield	Maxwl		JUL	Theo Rept	JUEL-844-KP	Apr 72	Slavov. DEFORM-E+FRAG MASS YLD CALC	
	–			Jour	PL/B 37 483	Dec 71	- + ASYMMETRY BY 2-CENTRE SHELL	
Fiss Yield	Spont		SRL	Expt Jour	PR/C 8 1488	73	Harbour+. RELATIVE YLDS 20 CHAINS.	
Fiss Yield	Spont		ANL	Expt Conf	73Rochestr 2 19	Aug 73	Unik+RADIOCHEM +PHYS MEAS.CURVS,TBLS	
Fiss Yield	Spont		BLA	Theo Conf	73Munich 1 589	Aug 73	Slavov+ 2CENTR SHELMDL,HVY/LGHT MASS	
Fiss Yield	Spont		AUA	Theo Rept	AAEC/E-386	Mar 76	Cook+ 3-GAUSS FIT,PARAMS GIVEN	
Frag Spectra	Spont		ANL	Expt Conf	58Geneva 15 392	Sep 58	Smith+.PPR690,ENERGY OF FRAGMENTS	
Frag Spectra	Spont		LRL	Expt Jour	PR 131 2617	Sep 63	Brandt+ E DIST REL CF252 CURVES	
Frag Spectra	Spont		ANL	Expt Prog	USNDC-9 36	Dec 73	Flynn+. RADIOCHEM. MASS DIST. CURVE	
Frag Charge	Spont		SRL	Expt Jour	PR/C 8 1488	73	Harbour+. RELATIVE YLDS 20 CHAINS.	
Frag Charge	Spont		LRL	Comp Rept	UCRL-51640	Jul 74	Nethaway. TBL.	
Reson Params	4.0+6	7.0+7	DUB	Theo Rept	JINR-P7-6619	Jul 72	Barashenkov+ GAMMA-N/GAMMA-F ,GRPH	
				Rept	KFK-TR-423	73	. GERMAN OF JINR-P7-6619	

100 Fermium 255

Quantity	Energy (ev) Min	Max	Lab	Type	Documentation Ref Vol Page	Date	Author, Comments	Data
(n,γ)	Pile		LRL	Expt Prog	WASH-1071 83	Nov 66	Hulet.SIG MEASD BY FM256 FORMATION	
Fission	Spont		COP	Revw Conf	69Vienna 155	Jul 69	Strutinsky+PPR203. HL GVN,'SHELL-TH'	
Fission	Maxwl		LRL	Expt Jour	PR/C 9 399	Jan 74	Ragaini+. SIG=3400+-170B.	+
				Conf	73Rochestr 2 47	Aug 73	- + ABSTRACT,SIGMA GIVEN	
	Maxwl			Data	EXFOR10393.003	Jun 74	1 PT	
Fission	Maxwl		ANL	Expt Jour	PR/C 11 1676	May 75	Flynn+MASS DISTR.REL CO59.THR CS GVN	+
	2.5-2			Data	EXFOR10516.009	Apr 78	. 1PT.CS=3200+-320B	
Alpha	1.0+4	2.0+4	LAS	Theo Jour	PR 158 1127	Jun 67	Bell. SYSTEMATCS TH FOR 10-20KEV ALF	
Nu	Maxwl		AUA	Revw Conf	IAEA-169 2 163	74	Musgrove+ TOTAL NU-BAR,GRAPH	
Nu	2.5-2		ANL	Expt Jour	PR/C 11 1676	May 75	Flynn+MASS DISTR.TBL.THR NU GVN.	+
	Maxwl			Conf	73Rochestr 2 19	Aug 73	Unik+NU TOTAL VS MASS 13 NUCLIDES.	
	2.5-2			Data	EXFOR10516.007	Apr 78	. 1PT.NU=4.0+-.5	
Fiss Yield	Maxwl		LRL	Expt Jour	PR/C 9 399	Jan 74	Ragaini. FRAG MASS DISTRIBUTS. CURVS	
				ExTh Conf	73Rochestr 2 47	Aug 73	- + ABST,MASS YLD FROM KE,NDG	
Fiss Yield	Maxwl		ANL	Expt Jour	PR/C 11 1676	May 75	Flynn+ TBL,GRPH 93Y TO 157EV	+
				Conf	73Rochestr 2 19	Aug 73	Unik+PRELIM.MASS DISTR 16 NUCLIDES	
	2.5-2			Data	EXFOR10516.003	Apr 78	. 22PTS.MASS YLDS.4PT MASS CHAIN YLD	
Fiss Yield	Maxwl		AUA	Theo Rept	AAEC/E-386	Mar 76	Cook+ 3GAUSS- FIT,PARAMS GIVEN	
Fiss Yield	2.5-2		PAH	Theo Abst	BAP 21 655	Apr 76	Hooshyar+PC MASS YLD SPEC CALC.NDG	
Frag Spectra	Maxwl		LRL	Expt Jour	PR/C 9 399	Jan 74	Ragaini. FRAG KE+MASS DISTR. CURVES.	
				Conf	73Rochestr 2 47	Aug 73	- + ABSTRACT,MEAN FRAG-KE GIVEN	
Frag Spectra	2.5-2		PAH	Theo Abst	BAP 21 655	Apr 76	Hooshyar+KE SPEC CALC.CFD EXPT.NDG	
Frag Charge	2.5-2		PAH	Theo Abst	BAP 21 655	Apr 76	Hooshyar+PC CHARG YLD SPEC CALC.NDG	

100 Fermium 256

Quantity	Energy (ev) Min	Max	Lab	Type	Documentation Ref Vol Page	Date	Author, Comments	Data
Fission	Spont		COP	Revw Conf	69Vienna 155	Jul 69	Strutinsky+PPR203. HL GVN,'SHELL-TH'	
Fission	Spont		MRY	Theo Prog	ORO-4028-28	71	Jackson+. SPON FISSION HALF-LIFE GVN	
Alpha	1.0+4	2.0+4	LAS	Theo Jour	PR 158 1127	Jun 67	Bell. SYSTEMATCS TH FOR 10-20KEV ALF	

100 Fermium 256

Quantity	Energy (ev) Min	Max	Lab	Type	Documentation Ref Vol Page	Date	Author, Comments	Data
Nu	Spont		DUB	Expt Rept	KFK – TR – 413	Oct 72	. ENGLISH OF JINR – P15 – 6218	+
				Rept	JINR – P15 – 6218	Jun 72	Dakowski +	
				Rept	JINR – P15 – 6518	72	Dakovskii + REL CM244,NUBAR,T1/2.TBL	
				Rept	KFK – TR – 413	Jul 73	. GERMAN OF JINR – P15 – 6518	
	Spont			Data	EXFOR40141.002	Mar 73	SPONTAN PROMPT NU – BAR REL TO CF252	
Nu	Maxwl		IAE	Eval Jour	REA 10 637	Dec 72	Manero + CALC,SYSTEMATICS,TBL	
Nu	Spont		ANL	Expt Jour	PR/C 5 1725	May 72	Flynn +. AVERAGE NU = 3 + – 1	
				Conf	73Rochestr 2 19	Aug 73	Unik + NU TOTAL VS MASS 13 NUCLIDES.	
Nu	Spont		DUB	Comp Jour	YF 18 724	Oct 73	Dakovsky + NUBAR VS FISNUCLEUS,TBL + GRP	
				Eval Rept	JINR – P15 – 7119	Jun 73	Dakowski + NUBAR + P(NU) – DISTR,TBL,GRPH	
				Comp Jour	SNP 18 371	Apr 74	. ENGLISH OF YF 18, 724.	
Nu	Spont		LAS	Expt Prog	ERDA – NDC – 3 93	May 76	Veeser + LIQ SCINT.NU MEAS.NDG	
Frag Neuts	Spont		DUB	Expt Jour	YF 16 1167	Nov 72	Dakovskii + NU REL NU(CM244),TBL,GRAF	
				Jour	SNP 16 641	Jun 73	. ENGLISH TRANSLATION OF YF 16 1167	
Fiss Yield	Spont		CLA	Theo Jour	NP/A 184 417	Apr 72	Tsang +.ASSYM FROM FERMIGAS + WKB CALC.	
Fiss Yield	Spont		ANL	Expt Jour	PR/C 5 1725	May 72	Flynn +.RADIOCHEM.YLDS 28 MASS CHAINS	
				Conf	73Rochestr 2 19	Aug 73	Unik + RADIOCHEM + PHYS MEAS.CURVS.TBLS	
Fiss Yield	Spont		AUA	Revw Conf	IAEA – 169 2 163	74	Musgrove + PROMPT,EVEN – Z POSITN,GRAPH	
Fiss Yield	Spont		AUA	Theo Rept	AAEC/E – 386	Mar 76	Cook + 3 – GAUSS FIT,PARAMS GIVEN	
Fiss Yield	Spont		TRM	Theo Rept	INIS – MF – 3797	77	Chakraborthy + O – D – MOD.ISOTOP YLD,FIG	
Frag Spectra	Spont		ANL	Expt Conf	73Rochestr 2 19	Aug 73	Unik + TOTAL KIN – E OF FRAGS,GRPH	
Frag Spectra	Spont		AUA	Revw Conf	IAEA – 169 2 163	74	Musgrove + AVG FRAG MASS,GRAPH	
Frag Spectra	Spont		LAS	Expt Rept	LA – UR – 77 – 2901	77	Hoffman + TOT KE DIST,VERY ROUGH.CURV	
Frag Charge	Spont		MRY	Theo Jour	PR/C 11 1059	Mar 75	Nustafa.CALC SHELL CORR TO MASS DIST	

100 Fermium 257

Quantity	Energy (ev) Min	Max	Lab	Type	Documentation Ref Vol Page	Date	Author, Comments	Data
Absorption	Pile		ORL	Expt Prog	ORNL – 4581 43	Sep 70	Bemis + MEAS BURN – OUT REL CM244	+
	Pile			Data	EXFOR10650.	Nov 77	.2PT.PILE = 6100 + – 600B.MAXW = 5600B	
Res Int Abs	5.0 – 1		ORL	Expt Prog	ORNL – 4581 43	Sep 70	Bemis + UPPER LIMIT	+
	5.0 – 1			Data	EXFOR10650.003	Nov 77	.1PT.RIA = 5000B.	
(n,γ)	Pile		ORL	ExTh Prog	ORNL – 4581 43	Sep 70	Bemis + EST FROM BURN – OUT + CORRLTN	
Fission	Spont		COP	Revw Conf	69Vienna 155	Jul 69	Strutinsky + PPR203. HL GVN,'SHELL – TH'	
Fission	Spont		DUB	Revw Jour	REA 8 255	Jun 70	Flerov + REVIEW,TBL OF HALF – LIVES	
Fission	Maxwl		LRL	Expt Prog	UCID – 15749	Nov 70	Hulet + (N,F) + (N,G)TO SPONFIS,PRELIM	
Fission	Spont		TPI	Theo Jour	YF 16 919	Nov 72	Adeev + FISS BARRIER CFD EVEN,GRAPH	
				Jour	SNP 16 507	May 73	.ENGLISH OF YF 16 919	
Fission	Maxwl		LRL	Expt Jour	JIN 35 4 1063	Apr 73	Wild + MICA FISS FRAGM TRACK REC	+
	Maxwl			Data	EXFOR10341.002	Jul 74	1 PT	
Fission	Maxwl		EMY	Eval Jour	PR/C 9 2448	Jun 74	Fong. SYMMETRIC FISSION	
Nu	Spont		BRK	Expt Jour	PR/C 3 2017	May 71	Cheifetz + REL CF252	+
	Spont			Data	EXFOR10140.002	Jul 71	1PNT,PROMPT	
Nu	Spont		IAE	Eval Jour	REA 10 637	Dec 72	Manero + EXTENSIVE SURVEY,TBL,AVG VAL	
Nu	Spont		LAS	Expt Conf	73Rochestr 2 191	Aug 73	Balagna + P(NU) + NUBAR REL CF252,TBL	+
	Spont			Data	EXFOR10300.002	Jul 74	1PT	
Nu	Spont		DUB	Comp Jour	YF 18 724	Oct 73	Dakovsky + NUBAR VS FISNUCLEUS,TBL + GRP	
				Eval Rept	JINR – P15 – 7119	Jun 73	Dakowski + NUBAR + P(NU) – DISTR,TBL,GRPH	
				Comp Jour	SNP 18 371	Apr 74	. ENGLISH OF YF 18, 724.	
Nu	Spont		LAS	Expt Prog	ERDA – NDC – 3 93	May 76	Veeser + LIQ SCINT.TBD	
Nu	None		GER	Theo Conf	76Lowell 1468	Jul 76	Kolb.ANAL Z114 BIN,TER FRAGMENTATION	
Frag Neuts	Spont		LAS	Expt Conf	73Rochestr 2 191	Aug 73	Balagna + NU VS FRAG KIN – E,GRAPHS	
Fiss Yield	Spont		LAS	Expt Jour	PRL 26 145	Jan 71	Balagna +,SI DET,MASS YLD SYMMETRIC	
Fiss Yield	Spont	Maxwl	LRL	Expt Jour	PRL 27 45	Jul 71	John +. MASS DISTR CURVES SHOWN	
Fiss Yield	Spont		ANL	Expt Jour	PR/C 12 1478	Nov 75	Flynn + MASSES 112,127,132,140 DET	
Fiss Yield	Spont		AUA	Theo Rept	AAEC/E – 386	Mar 76	Cook + 3 – GAUSS FIT,PARAMS GIVEN	
	Maxwl			Rept	AAEC/E – 386	Mar 76	– + 3 – GAUSS FIT,PARAMS GIVEN	
Fiss Yield	2.5 – 2		PAH	Theo Abst	BAP 21 655	Apr 76	Hooshyar + PC MASS YLD SPEC CALC.NDG	
Fiss Yield	Spont		TRM	Theo Rept	INIS – MF – 3797	77	Chakraborthy + O – D – MOD.ISOTOP YLD,FIG	
Frag Spectra	Spont		LAS	Expt Jour	PRL 26 145	Jan 71	Balagna +,SI DET,KE DISTRIBUTION	
Frag Spectra	Spont	Maxwl	LRL	Expt Jour	PRL 27 45	Jul 71	John +. SYMMETRIC AND ASYMMETRIC FISS	
Frag Spectra	2.5 – 2		PAH	Theo Abst	BAP 21 655	Apr 76	Hooshyar + KE SPEC CALC.CFD EXPT.NDG	
Frag Spectra	None		GER	Theo Conf	76Lowell 1468	Jul 76	Kolb.ANAL Z114 BIN,TER FRAGMENTATION	
Frag Charge	2.5 – 2		PAH	Theo Abst	BAP 21 655	Apr 76	Hooshyar + PC CHARG YLD SPEC CALC.NDG	

100 Fermium 258

Quantity	Energy (ev) Min	Max	Lab	Type	Documentation Ref Vol Page	Date	Author, Comments	Data
Fission	Spont		DUB	Theo Rept	JINR–P–2265	Jul 65	Mekhedov. FISS+ALPH HLS ESTIMATED	
Fission	Spont		CCP	Comp Jour	AE 26 436	May 69	Romanov. HALF–LIFE VAL ESTIMATD,GRPH	
				Jour	SJA 26 498	69	. ENGL OF AE 26 436.	
				Jour	EAF 26 48	69	. FRENCH OF AE 26 436.	
Fission	Spont		DUB	Revw Jour	REA 8 255	Jun 70	Flerov+ REVIEW,TBL OF HALF–LIVES	
Fission	Spont		MRY	Theo Prog	ORO–4028–28	71	Jackson+. SPON FISSION HALF–LIFE GVN	
Fission	Spont		LRL	Expt Jour	PRL 26 523	Mar 71	Hulet+,HALF–LIFE(SPON FISS) MEASD	
				Prog	UCRL–20426 33	70	.SUPERSEDED	
Fiss Yield	None		TRM	Theo Conf	72Bombay 2 201	Feb 72	Ramamurthy+ DISTRIBTN OF MASSES,GRPH	
	Spont			Prog	BARC–633 64	72	– . FRAG MASS DISTRIB ,GRPH	
Fiss Yield	Spont		NEU	Theo Jour	HPA 46 724	Jul 73	Hooshyar+ MASS A.CHARGE DISTR, HL	
Fiss Yield	Spont		LAS	Expt Rept	LA–UR–77–2901	77	Hoffman+ ES255(N,A).PRELIM MASS–CURV	
Frag Spectra	Spont		LAS	Expt Rept	LA–UR–77–2901	77	Hoffman+ TOT KE DIST,PRELIM.CURVE	
Frag Charge	Spont		MRY	Theo Jour	PR/C 11 1059	Mar 75	Nustafa.CALC SHELL CORR TO MASS DIST	

100 Fermium 259

Quantity	Energy (ev) Min	Max	Lab	Type	Documentation Ref Vol Page	Date	Author, Comments	Data
Fission	Spont		LAS	Expt Jour	AF 36 533	Nov 67	Hoffman.POSSIBLE HL RANGE DEDUCED	
				Conf	JINR–D–73548	Oct 66	Cowan.SPON–FISS–HL,LIMITS ESTIMATED	
Nu	None		GER	Theo Conf	76Lowell 1468	Jul 76	Kolb.ANAL Z114 BIN,TER FRAGMENTATION	
Frag Spectra	None		GER	Theo Conf	76Lowell 1468	Jul 76	Kolb.ANAL Z114 BIN,TER FRAGMENTATION	

100 Fermium 264

Quantity	Energy (ev) Min	Max	Lab	Type	Documentation Ref Vol Page	Date	Author, Comments	Data
Frag Charge	Spont		MRY	Theo Jour	PR/C 11 1059	Mar 75	Nustafa.CALC SHELL CORR TO MASS DIST	

101   Mendelevium   256

Quantity	Energy (ev) Min Max	Lab	Type	Documentation Ref Vol Page	Author, Comments Date	Data
Fission	None	BER	Theo Conf	69Vienna 197	Jul 69 Krappf+ 1+2 FISSION BARRIER TABLE.	

101   Mendelevium   257

Quantity	Energy (ev) Min Max	Lab	Type	Documentation Ref Vol Page	Author, Comments Date	Data
Fission	2.5 – 2	JUL	Theo Jour	ZP 257 389	Dec 72 Mcminn.	2.60 E +3 BARNS

102 Nobelium 252

Quantity	Energy (ev) Min Max	Lab	Type	Documentation Ref Vol Page	Date	Author, Comments	Data
Nu	Spont	DUB	Expt Jour Rept	PL/B 52 321 JINR – P15 – 8095	Oct 74 Jul 74	Lazarev+ MULT DISTR,MEASURED AVG NU – + P(NU)+NUBAR REL CM 244,GRPH	
Nu	Spont	KUR	Eval Rept	IAE – 2738	75	Zakharova. NUBAR=3.7+ – 0.5	

102 Nobelium 254

Quantity	Energy (ev) Min Max	Lab	Type	Documentation Ref Vol Page	Date	Author, Comments	Data
Fission	Spont	CCP	Expt Jour Jour	AE 22 494 SJA 22 611	Jun 67 Jun 67	Flerov+.HALF LIVES+ALFA – ENERGIES GVN TRANSLATN.*	

102 Nobelium 256

Quantity	Energy (ev) Min Max	Lab	Type	Documentation Ref Vol Page	Date	Author, Comments	Data
Fission	Spont	COP	Revw Conf	69Vienna 155	Jul 69	Strutinsky+PPR203. HL GVN,'SHELL – TH'	
Fiss Yield	None	BAS	Theo Jour	PL/B 34 264	Mar 71	Pauli+ FRAG MASS RATIO AS STRUTINSKY	

102 Nobelium 258

Quantity	Energy (ev) Min Max	Lab	Type	Documentation Ref Vol Page	Date	Author, Comments	Data
Fission	Spont	CCP	Comp Jour Jour Jour	AE 26 436 SJA 26 498 EAF 26 48	May 69 69 69	Romanov. HALF – LIFE VAL ESTIMATD,GRPH . ENGL OF AE 26 436. . FRENCH OF AE 26 436.	
Fission	2.5 – 2	JUL	Theo Jour	ZP 257 389	Dec 72	Mcminn. 1.92 E +3 BARNS	

102 Nobelium 259

Quantity	Energy (ev) Min Max	Lab	Type	Documentation Ref Vol Page	Date	Author, Comments	Data
Fission	Spont	LAS	Expt Conf	JINR – D – 73548	Oct 66	Cowan.SPON – FISS – HL,LIMITS ESTIMATED	

102 Nobelium 260

Quantity	Energy (ev) Min Max	Lab	Type	Documentation Ref Vol Page	Date	Author, Comments	Data
Fission	Spont	CCP	Comp Jour Jour Jour	AE 26 436 EAF 26 48 SJA 26 498	May 69 69 69	Romanov. HALF – LIFE VAL ESTIMATD,GRPH . FRENCH OF AE 26 436. . ENGL OF AE 26 436.	
Fission	2.5 – 2	JUL	Theo Jour	ZP 257 389	Dec 72	Mcminn. 2.47 E +3 BARNS	

102 Nobelium 262

Quantity	Energy (ev) Min Max	Lab	Type	Documentation Ref Vol Page	Date	Author, Comments	Data
Fission	Spont	CCP	Comp Jour Jour Jour	AE 26 436 SJA 26 498 EAF 26 48	May 69 69 69	Romanov. HALF – LIFE VAL ESTIMATD,GRPH . ENGL OF AE 26 436. . FRENCH OF AE 26 436.	

102 Nobelium 263

Quantity	Energy (ev) Min Max	Lab	Type	Documentation Ref Vol Page	Date	Author, Comments	Data
Fission	2.5 – 2	JUL	Theo Jour	ZP 257 389	Dec 72	Mcminn. 1.53 E +0 BARNS	

103 Lawrencium 257

Quantity	Energy (ev) Min Max	Lab	Type	Documentation Ref Vol Page	Date	Author, Comments	Data
Fission	Spont	DUB	Expt Jour	AE 30 73	Jan 71	Boganesyan. SPON HALF – LIFE,LOWER LIM	
			Jour	SJA 30 86	Aug 71	.ENGLISH	

103 Lawrencium 261

Quantity	Energy (ev) Min Max	Lab	Type	Documentation Ref Vol Page	Date	Author, Comments	Data
Fission	2.5 – 2	JUL	Theo Jour	ZP 257 389	Dec 72	Mcminn. 1.23 E +3 BARNS	

104 Kurchatovium 255

Quantity	Energy (ev) Min Max	Lab	Type	Documentation Ref Vol Page	Author, Comments Date	Data
Nu	Spont	KUR Eval	Rept	IAE-2738	75 Zakharova. NUBAR=4.1+ -0.5	

104 Kurchatovium 260

Quantity	Energy (ev) Min Max	Lab	Type	Documentation Ref Vol Page	Author, Comments Date	Data
Fission	Spont	CCP Comp	Jour	AE 26 436	May 69 Romanov. ESTIMATED HALF-LIFE, GRAPH.	
			Jour	SJA 26 498	May 69 .ENGLISH	
			Jour	EAF 26 48	May 69 .FRENCH	
Fission	Spont	COP Revw	Conf	69Vienna 155	Jul 69 Strutinsky+ PPR203.HL GVN,'SHELL-TH'	
Nu	Spont	KUR Eval	Rept	IAE-2738	75 Zakharova. NUBAR=1.7+ -0.5	
Fiss Yield	Spont	TRM Theo	Rept	INIS-MF-3797	77 Chakraborthy+ O-D-MOD.ISOTOP YLD,FIG	

104 Kurchatovium 262

Quantity	Energy (ev) Min Max	Lab	Type	Documentation Ref Vol Page	Author, Comments Date	Data
Nu	Spont	KUR Eval	Rept	IAE-2738	75 Zakharova. NUBAR=1.5+ -0.5	

104 Kurchatovium 264

Quantity	Energy (ev) Min Max	Lab	Type	Documentation Ref Vol Page	Author, Comments Date	Data
Fission	2.5-2	JUL Theo	Jour	ZP 257 389	Dec 72 Mcminn. 8.26 E +2 BARNS	

104 Kurchatovium 266

Quantity	Energy (ev) Min Max	Lab	Type	Documentation Ref Vol Page	Author, Comments Date	Data
Fission	2.5-2	JUL Theo	Jour	ZP 257 389	Dec 72 Mcminn. 1.92 E +3 BARNS	

Many

Quantity	Energy (ev) Min	Max	Lab	Type	Documentation Ref Vol Page	Date	Author, Comments	Data
Evaluation	None		KFK	Eval Rept	KFK - 772	May 68	Scmidt+ METHODS OF EVALUATION	
Evaluation	None		KFK	Eval Rept	KFK - 791	Jul 68	Schmidt+ HISTORY OF COMPIL.+ EVALUAT	
Evaluation	None		AI	Eval Conf	70Helsinki 2 643	Jun 70	Alter+120. USE OF COMPUTER GRAPHICS	
Evaluation	None		INL	Eval Prog	USNDC-11 1	Jun 74	Reich+ 199 NUCLDS,DECAYS + NF TBLS	
Evaluation	None		JAE	Eval Jour	NST 12 663	Nov 75	Kuroi+.SIG ADJUST BY INTEGRAL EXPT	
Total	None		PTN	Theo Jour	PR 49 519	Apr 36	Breit+ TH OF DAMPING APPLIED.	
Total	None		PAR	Expt Jour	JPR 9 123	Mar 38	Baschwitz.RA - BE,STUDY RADIO - PRODUCTS	
Total	5.0-1	1.0+0	COR	Theo Jour	PR 57 1125	Jun 40	Bethe.GENERAL.CONTINUUM TH CPD NUCL.	
Total	Maxwl		COL	Expt Jour	PR 60 702	Nov 41	Carroll. SIG(PROTON) IN C(N)H(2N+2).	
Total	1.0+5	1.5+6	MIT	Theo Jour	PR 76 1550	Dec 49	Feshbach+ SIG VS R+E(NUCLEON IN NUC)	
Total	-2	+8	BNL	Comp Jour	RMP 22 249	Jul 50	Adair.SIGS OF ELEMENTS.MANY CURVES	
				Jour	RMP 19 259		47 Goldsmith+.SIGS OF ELEMENTS.MANY CRV	
Total	1.0+5	3.0+6	WIS	Expt Jour	PR 86 431	May 52	Barschall. AREA VERSUS E AND A.	
Total	4.4+6		WES	Theo Rept	AECU-3387	55	Emmerich.CURVS SIG VS. R.6CALCULATN	
Total	None		ZAG	Rept	PMPA-10 47	55	. SLOW NEUTS	
Total	-		CER	Theo Jour	PM 46 376	Apr 55	Jankovic.CURVS FM OF R S WAVE NEUTS	
Total		3.0+6	FR	Revw Jour	CDP 59 5	Jul 55	Meyer.FESHBACH THEOR CFD EXPT.RESULT	
Total	+6	+7	MIT	Revw Conf	55Geneva 2 23	Aug 55	Weisskopf+.P830,REVIEW OF THEORIES	
Total	-1	+0	BNL	Comp Jour	PR 100 1414	Dec 55	Landon. SUMMRY BEST RECENT DATA WG.	
Total	2.5+6	4.3+6	CCP	Theo Jour	ZET 30 551	Mar 56	TH CFD PIC P714,CURVES	
				Jour	JET 3 484	Nov 56	TRANSLATN.*	
Total	1.0+3		HAR	ExTh Jour	PHY 22 1133	Nov 56	Gayther+ABSTRACT,A96TO209 TRANSM.NDG	
	+3	+5		Revw Jour	NAT 175 1029	Jun 55	- + REVIEWED BY ALLEN+EGELSTAF	
Total	1.0+6		CCP	Theo Jour	ZET 32 1143	May 57	CFD XPT CURVES A30-90	
				Jour	JET 5 932	Dec 57	TRANSLATN.*	
Total	1.4+7		LRL	Theo Jour	PR 109 1295	Feb 58	Bjorklund+,OPTMDL FIT XPT CRV A1/3	
Total	4.1+6		LRL	Theo Jour	RMP 30 414	Apr 58	Fernbach.TH CURVE AND EXPTL PTS	
Total		+3	HAR	Theo Jour	PPS 71 910	Jun 58	Egelstaff.SIG FLUCTUATION THEORY	
Total	1.4+7		CCP	Theo Jour	ZET 35 750	Sep 58	Luk'Ianov. OPTMODL OKS XPTS, GRAPHS	
				Jour	JET 8 521	Mar 59	TRANSLATN.*	
Total	5.0+2	1.0+7	ANL	Theo Book	FRC	60	Yiftah+ CALC METH FAST REACT.	
Total	None		SAC	ExTh Jour	JPR 21 759	Oct 60	Corge+ ASSUMPTION ABOUT RES.PAR.EVAL	
Total	3.0+8	5.0+9	LON	Theo Jour	NP 23 681	Mar 61	Elton. SEMI - CLASSICAL FORMULA.	
Total	3.5+5	1.4+6	ANL	Theo Jour	PR 124 826	Nov 61	Sokoloff. HARM OSC POT SIG VS A.3 ES	
Total	1.4+7		TNC	Comp Rept	EANDC(US)-58	Jun 63	Mathur+ SIG,Q VALUE,PRODCT H-L+DECAY	
Total	2.0+5	1.0+6	ANL	Theo Jour	NP 47 65	Aug 63	Moldauer.SIG VS A CFD OPTMODEL	
Total	-		AUA	Comp Rept	AAEC/E-119	Apr 64	Doherty. NUCLEAR DATA CARD LIBRARY	
				Rept	AAEC/E-164	Oct 66	.LUBRA-0 CODE TO CREATE SIGMA	
				Rept	AAEC/E-114	Dec 63	.MULGA CODE,GROUP AVERAGE SIGMA	
Total	Maxwl	1.0+4	BNL	Revw Jour	AP 30 269	Nov 64	Garrison. WN,LVL SPACING DIST.	
Total	-4	+0	CAI	Comp Rept	UARAEE-12	65	OSAMA H. SALLAM+ SIG(E)GRPHS COMPILD	
Total	1.0+6	2.4+7	LAS	Theo Prog	WASH-1056 40	Mar 65	Rosen.AVG OPTMDL PAR CALCT,CFD EXPT	
Total	3.0+5	8.0+5	IFU	ExTh Jour	AE 20 8	Jan 66	Korzh+ TABLE SIG AT 4 ES	
Total	2.5+5	1.6+6	LAS	Theo Rept	LA-3538	Sep 66	Agee+OPTMDL CALC LI6-PU240	
Total	-		FEI	Theo Rept	ICD-4 327	67	Popov+ ALGOL-PROGR FOR OPTIC MOD CAL	
Total	1.5+7		CCP	Theo Jour	YF 5 1008	May 67	Inopin.ADIABAT APPROXM BLACK NUCL TH	
				Jour	SNP 5 719	Nov 67	TRANSLATN.*	
Total	None		WIS	Theo Jour	AP 43 91	Jun 67	Mcvoy. GIANT RES PEAKS.OPTMDL CALCS.	
Total	+0	+7	SOR	Theo Conf	67Ann Arbr 1 323	Jul 67	Finkelstein.PPR8.TEMPRTR+SCAT KERNEL	
Total	+0	+5	LAS	Revw Jour	AF 36 47	Nov 67	Brown+. BOMB.NDG.GRPH OF PETREL SPEC	
Total	4.0+6		IFU	Theo Jour	UFZ 13 51	Jan 68	Kashuba+ SIG(A=1TO230),EXPT+OPTMOD	
				Jour	UPJ 13 33	Jul 68	TRANSLATN.*	
Total	6.0+6	1.5+7	OHO	Theo Jour	NC/B 53 2 363	Feb 68	Cassola+ OPTMDL CALC CFD EXPT.	
Total		9.0+0	CCP	Expt Conf	69Erevan	Feb 69	Vertebnij+.ABST,SCAT LENGTH IN OPTMD	
Total	1.5+4	6.0+5	DKE	Expt Diss	PINEO	70	.3 COMPDS,20 NUCLIDES.AVG CS.TBLS.	
Total	None		ANL	Revw Conf	70Helsinki 2 3	Jun 70	Poenitz. RECENT EXPTL DATA HEAVY NUC	
Total	-1	+5	BOL	Revw Conf	70Helsinki 2 379	Jun 70	Benzi.115. A BELOW 220, DATA STATUS	
Total	None		COL	Expt Prog	INDC-6 13	Jun 70	Havens+ NEVIS CYCLOTRON,TB PUBLISHED	
Total	+3	+4	DUB	Theo Jour	YF 11 1152	Jun 70	Samosvat. SIG(A=40-240),OPTMOD ANAL	
				Jour	SNP 11 639	Dec 70	. ENGL OF YF 11 1152.	
Total	4.1+6	1.5+7	MUA	Theo Conf	70Madurai 2 15	Dec 70	Saharia+ PLATEU-SIG,GLAUBER-TH,GRPHS	
Total	1.0+5	1.4+7	RAM	Expt Rept	AECD/EP-21	Jan 71	Ullah+ OPTMODL,SIG VS NUCL RADIUS,TBL	
Total	4.0+6	2.0+7	ORL	Theo Prog	ORNL-4743 15	Dec 71	Wong+.NUCL COLLECTIVITY EFFECTS.NDG	
Total	None		JAE	Eval Prog	EANDC(J)26L30	Aug 72	Kawai+.OPT-MDL CALC. IN FIGS	

Many

Quantity	Energy (ev) Min	Max	Lab	Type	Documentation Ref Vol Page	Date	Author, Comments	Data
Total	None		KOS	Theo Conf	73Paris 2 35	Mar 73	Csikai.MODEL CALC VS A CFD EXPT,GRPH	
	1.4+7			Rept	IAEA-153 189	73	Angeli+ INTERPRETATN OF TRENDS,GRAPH	
				Comp Rept	IAEA-153 155	73	Csikai+ EXPTL DATA COMPARED,GRAPH	
	5.0+5	4.2+7		Theo Jour	NP/A 170 577	Jul 71	Angeli+ ANALYTICAL FIT FOR A OVER27	
	1.4+7			Jour	NP/A 158 389	Dec 70	- + PHYSICAL INTERPR FORM. VS A	
				Conf	70Helsinki 2 243	Jun 70	Csikai+ DISCUSSN.SIG(A)GRAPH,OPTMOD	
Total	2.5+5	1.5+7	JAE	Eval Prog	EANDC(J)30L 10	Sep 73	Tanaka.COUPLED-CHANNEL AND OPTMDL	
Total	None		JAE	Theo Jour	NST 12 67	Feb 75	Igarasi.SIG CAL METHOD C COMPETITION	
Total	1.5+7	2.5+9	HSL	Eval Rept	HASL-293	Apr 75	Sanna.MASSES 12 TO 64 FIT TO 25.5GEV	
				Abst	ANS 18 362	Jun 74	- . A=12-64 EVL DATA OVER 15 MEV	
Total	1.0-4	6.0-2	NDC	Theo Conf	AKE 27 2 144	76	Schett. EMPIRICAL FN OF T+E DEDUCED	
Total	2.7+3		MUN	Expt Conf	71Albany 327	Aug 76	Dilg+TRNS.AVG CS GVN.31 ELEMENT GRPH	
Elastic	None		OSA	Theo Jour	JPJO 18 157	36	Yukawa+.SIG FORM DERIVED	
Elastic	5.0+5	7.0+6	HRV	Theo Jour	PR 50 560	Sep 36	Fay. POLARIZATION EFFECTS NEGLECTED.	
Elastic	5.0-1	1.0+0	COR	Theo Jour	PR 57 1125	Jun 40	Bethe.GENERAL.CONTINUUM TH CPD NUCL.	
Elastic	None		AUS	Theo Jour	APA 5 240	Dec 51	Bergmann.SCAT N-NUCLEUS	
Elastic	-		AML	Theo Jour	NP 18 245	Aug 60	Swan. NEW APPROX CFD BORN APPROXMNS	
Elastic	-		AUA	Comp Rept	AAEC/E-119	Apr 64	Doherty. NUCLEAR DATA CARD LIBRARY	
				Rept	AAEC/E-114	Dec 63	.MULGA CODE,GROUP AVERAGE SIGMA	
Elastic	Pile		CRC	Revw Conf	64Wien 17	Jul 64	Boyd+ EFFECTIVE SIG IN AECL-1003.	
Elastic	Maxwl		CAI	Comp Rept	UARAEE-12	65	OSAMA H. SALLAM+ COMPILED SIGMA TABL	
Elastic	3.0+5	8.0+5	IFU	ExTh Jour	AE 20 8	Jan 66	Korzh+ TABLE SIG AT 4 ES	
Elastic	2.5+5	1.6+6	LAS	Theo Rept	LA-3538	Sep 66	Agee+OPTMDL CALC LI6-PU240,CE+SE	
		2.0+7	SAH	Theo Conf	67Kanpur § N9	Feb 67	Mukherjee.OPTICAL WELL SCAT ANALYSIS	
Elastic	1.0+6		BUC	Theo Conf	67Tokyo § 8.135	Sep 67	Hulubei+ OPTMOD CFD P-B CALCS,43NUCS	
Elastic	1.5+6		IFU	Comp Jour	YF 7 277	Feb 68	Korzh+ SIG(20 TO 240=A),EXPT+OPTMOD	
				Jour	SNP 7 2 190	Aug 68	TRANSLATN.*	
Elastic	6.0+6	1.5+7	OHO	Theo Jour	NC/B 53 2 363	Feb 68	Cassola+ OPTMDL PARS FROM EXPTS.	
Elastic	None		CSD	Theo Abst	DA/B 28 3838	Mar 68	Payne. 2NUCLEON+1HOLE STATES STUDIED	
Elastic	-3		IFU	Revw Jour	UFZ 13 599	Apr 68	Kolotyi+A=40TO200,POT+ELAST SCAT CFD	
				Jour	UPJ 13 420	Oct 68	TRANSLATN.*	
Elastic	None		IFU	Theo Jour	UFZ 13 1415	Sep 68	Kolomiets+CFD (N,G)+(N,N'G) CHANNELS	
				Jour	UPJ 13 1011	Mar 69	TRANSLATN.*	
Elastic	None		IFU	Theo Jour	UFZ 13 1415	Sep 68	Kolomiets+.ALLOWANCE OF RAD CHANNELS	
Elastic	+5	+6	AUA	Theo Prog	AAEC/PR-31P 9	Apr 69	Bertram. A ABOVE 25,COMPOST PROGRAM	
Elastic	1.0+6		BHU	Theo Conf	69Roorke 2 122	Dec 69	Sharma+ COMPOUND SIG(A=40-230) GRAPH	
Elastic		2.0+6	BHU	Theo Prog	BARC-474 47	70	Sharma+ OPTMOD PARS FIT TO XPTL DATA	
Elastic	1.0+6	5.0+7	WWA	Revw Jour	PF 21 69	Jan 70	Cwiok.DOORWAY STATES TH N EL SCT SIG	
Elastic	Maxwl		CCP	Theo Jour	ZET 58 1086	Mar 70	Baryshevskii+ MAGNTC SCAT AT LOW ANG	
				Jour	ZET 56 1273	Apr 69	.SEE ALSO	
				Jour	JET 31 583	Sep 70	.ENGL TRANS OF ZET 58	
				Jour	JET 29 685	69	.ENGL TRANS OF ZET 56	
Elastic	-1	+5	BOL	Revw Conf	70Helsinki 2 379	Jun 70	Benzi.115. A BELOW 220, DATA STATUS	
Elastic		1.5+6	CCP	Eval Prog	INDC-6 42	Jun 70	Abramov+ STATUS OF SOVIET EVALUATION	
Elastic	-		REH	Theo Jour	PL/B 36 269	Sep 71	Vager. TIME REVERSAL INVARIANT H-F	
Elastic	+6		USA	Theo Abst	DA/B 32 2340	Oct 71	Skerry. TH OF HIGH EN NUCLEAR SCAT.	
Elastic	1.5+6	6.1+6	IJI	Expt Prog	YFI-12 81	72	Pasechnik+ OPTMDL CALC FOR 48<A<137	
	1.0-2	3.0-1		Prog	INDC(CCP)-30	Sep 72	.PAGE 71,ENGLISH OF YFI-12 81	
Elastic	+4	+6	AE	Theo Rept	INIS-MF-427	Jun 72	Holmqvist+ PPR15.2,ABST,NEW MODL,NDG	
Elastic	Maxwl		USA	Expt Jour	ACR 428 357	Jul 72	Bacon. COH SCAT AMPL FOR MANY ISOTOP	
Elastic	1.4+7		KOS	Theo Conf	73Paris 2 35	Mar 73	Csikai.MODEL CALC VS A CFD EXPT,GRPH	
Elastic	1.0+6		KUK	Theo Jour	IPA 11 388	Jun 73	Kulkarni+ COMPOUND-EL SIG VS A,GRAPH	
Elastic	None		JAE	Theo Jour	NST 12 67	Feb 75	Igarasi.SIG CAL METHOD C COMPETITION	
Elastic	None		STR	Theo Jour	ZP/A 273 195	Jun 75	Richert+ DIRECT INTERACT.PROCESS-TH.	
Elastic	2.5-2	2.0+2	LIE	Theo Jour	NP/A 263 61	May 76	Cugnon.SYSTEMATIC SCAT LNGTH,VAL CAP	
Elastic	7.6+6	1.4+7	KTY	Revw Conf	76Lowell 171	Jul 76	Mcellistrem.SMALL-ANG.SCAT.	
Diff Elastic	Cold		USC	Theo Jour	PR 76 1117	Oct 49	Halpern+ NEUTRON DIFF IN SMALL ANGLE	
Diff Elastic	-		UPP	Theo Jour	AF 8 521	Dec 54	Sjoelander+. POLARIZATION FORMULAS	
Diff Elastic	4.4+6		WES	Rept	AECU-3387	55	Emmerich.CURVS SIG VS. R.60-150DEG	
Diff Elastic	1.0+6		LAS	Revw Conf	55Geneva 2 18	Aug 55	Walt.P588,CURV,DISCUS OF RESULTS	
Diff Elastic	+6	+7	MIT	Revw Conf	55Geneva 2 23	Aug 55	Weisskopf+.P830,REVIEW OF THEORIES	
Diff Elastic	1.0+3	1.0+6	ORL	Expt Jour	PHY 22 1136	Nov 56	Fowler.ABSTRACT 3METH.9ISO=LI6TONE20	
Diff Elastic	1.0+5	5.0+5	CCP	Theo Jour	ZET 32 1143	May 57	CFD XPT CURVES A84-100	
				Jour	JET 5 932	Dec 57	TRANSLATN.*	
Diff Elastic	+8		UPP	Theo Jour	NP 6 161	Mar 58	Koehler.APPROX FORML.FORWARD SCATT.	
Diff Elastic	1.4+7		CCP	Theo Jour	ZET 35 750	Sep 58	Luk'Ianov. OPTMDL OKS XPTS, GRAPHS	
				Jour	JET 8 521	Mar 59	TRANSLATN.*	

Many

Quantity	Energy (ev) Min	Max	Lab	Type	Documentation Ref Vol Page	Date	Author, Comments	Data
Diff Elastic	None		ORL	Theo Jour	NP 18 110	Aug 60	Satchler. SYMMETRY PROPERTIES OF DWB	
Diff Elastic	-		NSW	Theo Jour	NP 18 654	Sep 60	Lyness.PHASESHFT CALC.POSSIBL APPLIC	
Diff Elastic	-		AML	Theo Jour	NP 27 620	Oct 61	Swan.DISTORTED WAVE EXPANS.APPL TO H	
Diff Elastic	1.4+7		CCP	Theo Jour	ZET 41 1634	Nov 61	STUDY OF POTENTIAL OF OPTMDL	
				Jour	JET 14 1164	May 62	TRANSLATN.*	
Diff Elastic	3.8+5	2.1+6	ORL	Theo Jour	NP 32 353	May 62	Perey+ POLARIZN EXPTS CFD OPTMDL.	
Diff Elastic	-		NZW	Theo Jour	ZP 171 226	Nov 62	Hooton. RESON POLARIZN,CU AS EXAMPLE	
Diff Elastic	2.0+7	1.8+8	UPP	Theo Jour	AF 24 1	Jun 63	Eriksson+.OPT MDL CFD SEMICLASS APPR	
Diff Elastic	2.0+5	1.0+6	ANL	Theo Jour	NP 47 65	Aug 63	Moldauer.SIG VS A CFD OPTMODEL	
Diff Elastic	-		AUA	Comp Rept	AAEC/E – 119	Apr 64	Doherty. NUCLEAR DATA CARD LIBRARY	
							MULGA – CODE,GROUP AVG SIG,AAEC/E – 114	
Diff Elastic	1.0+8	1.0+9	SAF	Theo Jour	AP 27 135	Apr 64	.OPTMD.STRONG ABSORPTION.POLARIZTION	
Diff Elastic	Maxwl	1.0+7	KAP	Theo Rept	KAPL – 3020	Jun 64	Goldman+ OPTMDL COMPUTER PROGRAM.	
Diff Elastic	1.0+5	2.5+7	DUB	ExTh Rept	JINR – P – 2426	65	Lehar+,SOURCES OF POLRZ NS,TBLS	
				Rept	ANL – TR – 342	65	TRANSLATN.*	
Diff Elastic	1.3+5	2.0+7	PUR	Theo Abst	DA 25 4771	Feb 65	Gerardo. CALCS TO FILL EXPTL GAPS.	
Diff Elastic	1.0+6	2.4+7	LAS	Theo Prog	WASH – 1056 40	Mar 65	Rosen.AVG OPTMDL PAR CALCT,CFD EXPT	
Diff Elastic	3.0+5	8.0+5	IFU	ExTh Jour	AE 20 8	Jan 66	Korzh+ CURVES GIVEN AT 4 ES	
Diff Elastic	8.3+5		ANL	Theo Jour	PR 142 758	Feb 66	Elwyn+ CALC LO A SCAT OPTMDL.	
Diff Elastic	3.4+6		FEI	ExTh Jour	YF 3 439	Mar 66	Otstavnov+.POLARIZATION OF NS VS Z,A	
				Jour	SNP 3 316	Sep 66	TRANSLATN.*	
Diff Elastic	None		MIT	Theo Rept	MIT – 2098 242	Jun 66	Stamp.OPTICAL POTENT+SPIN – SPIN TERM	
Diff Elastic	Cold		MHG	ExTh Abst	DA/B 27 508	Aug 66	Werner.MOSAIC XTAL,SECONDRY EXTINCTN	
Diff Elastic	2.5+5	1.6+7	LAS	Theo Rept	LA – 3538	Sep 66	Agee+OPTMDL CALC LI6 – PU240,CURVES	
Diff Elastic	3.0+5	1.5+6	ANL	Expt Conf	66Paris 1 399	Oct 66	Smith+ A=8 – 239,EXPT CFD CALC.	
				ExTh Conf	65Antwerp 36	Jul 65	- + TOF.CFD OPTMDL AND H – F.NDG	
Diff Elastic	1.5+6		CBR	ExTh Jour	AJS 29 119	Oct 66	Nurzynski.OPTMDL CFD XPT.CONTD PG119	
				Jour	AJS 29 93	Oct 66	- .OPTMDL CFD XPT.CONTD PG119	
Diff Elastic	1.0+6	1.6+7	LAS	Theo Rept	LA – 3788	67	Beery+.OPTMOD CALC POLARIZ ANG DISTR	
Diff Elastic	+6	+8	UPP	Theo Jour	AF 33 387	Jun 67	Rinander+ALGOL60 OPTMDL PROGR LIST	
				Jour	AF 33 377	Jun 67	- +ALGOL60 OPTMDL PROGR LIST	
Diff Elastic	-		SAF	Theo Jour	NP/A 106 660	Dec 67	Hahne.CLOSED FORMULA. 0 – SPIN TARGET.	
Diff Elastic	2.5+6	9.6+7	CCP	Theo Jour	YF 7 283	Feb 68	Averyanov+.OPTMOD CALCULATION	
Diff Elastic	Cold		HAR	Theo Jour	JP/C 1 88	Feb 68	Marshall.INCOH SC BY MIXED MAGNETICS	
Diff Elastic	None		FEI	Eval Conf	68Dubna § 11	Jun 68	Popov+.EXP DATA INTERPOLATION METHOD	
	-			Theo Rept	ICD – 4 327	67	- + ALGOL – PROGR FOR OPTIC MOD CAL	
Diff Elastic	+7		IFU	Theo Jour	UFZ 13 1693	Oct 68	Konstantinov+ EV – EV – NUCLEI,PHONON – TH	
				Jour	UPJ 13 1203	Apr 69	TRANSLATN.*	
Diff Elastic	None		BAT	Theo Jour	PR 177 1706	Jan 69	Hogan+ OPTMDL CALC WITH MAGN INTERCT	
Diff Elastic	3.0+5	1.4+7	IFU	Theo Conf	69Erevan	Feb 69	Kashuba+ ABSTR.OPTMOD PARS VS N,Z,E	
Diff Elastic	+6	+8	UMX	Theo Jour	NP/A 125 425	Feb 69	Cocho+'CROSSED PARTIAL WAVE EXPANSN'	
Diff Elastic	-		SUL	Theo Jour	NP/A 134 209	Sep 69	Gubkin. OPTMDL.OKS EXPT LARGE ANGLES	
Diff Elastic	+6	+7	AUA	Theo Rept	AAEC/TM – 524	Nov 69	Bertram. COMPOST=OPTMOD CALC PROGRAM	
Diff Elastic	None		DAC	Expt Prog	AECD/MISC2 14	Dec 69	Hussain+ EXPTL SET UP+COMP PROGR,TBD	
Diff Elastic		2.0+6	BHU	Theo Prog	BARC – 474 47	70	Sharma+ OPTMOD PARS FIT TO XPTL DATA	
Diff Elastic	3.0+5	1.5+6	KUR	Theo Prog	YFI – 11 5	70	Averjanov+ ABST,CALC A=23TO238,NDG	
				Prog	INDC(CCP) – 31	Dec 72	.PAGE 3,ENGLISH OF YFI – 11 5	
Diff Elastic	+5	+7	CCP	Revw Jour	AE 28 310	Apr 70	Lebedeva+ ANOMALOUS SIG(ANG) GRAPHS	
				Jour	EAF 28 4 35	Apr 70	. FRENCH OF AE 28 310	
Diff Elastic	None		BNL	Eval Rept	BNL – 400	Jun 70	Garber+.3RD EDITION.ANGULAR DISTR	
Diff Elastic		1.2+6	CCP	Eval Prog	INDC – 6 42	Jun 70	Abramov+ STATUS OF SOVIET EVALUATION	
Diff Elastic	None		TUD	Theo Jour	KE 13 324	Oct 70	Hoehn+ SCATTER VOLUME CORRC METHOD	
				Jour	KE 13 283	Sep 70	- + SCATTER VOLUME CORRC METHOD	
				Jour	KE 13 263	Sep 70	- + SCATTER VOLUME CORRC METHOD	
Diff Elastic	-		JAE	Comp Prog	EANDC(J)22L23	Aug 71	Igarasi+.O,NA,CR,FE,NI,U,PU,NDG	
Diff Elastic	1.5+6	6.1+6	IJI	Expt Prog	YFI – 12 81	72	Pasechnik+ OPTMOD CALC FOR 48<A<137	
	1.0 – 2	3.0 – 1		Prog	INDC(CCP) – 30	Sep 72	.PAGE 71,ENGLISH OF YFI – 12 81	
Diff Elastic	+4	+6	AE	Theo Rept	INIS – MF – 427	Jun 72	Holmqvist+ PPR15.2,ABST,NEW MODL,NDG	
	2.5+6	8.0+6		ExTh Rept	AE – 430	Sep 71	- + TBLS + GEN OPTMOD FITS	
				Theo Jour	PL/B 27 411	Sep 68	- + OPTMOD,N – RADIUS CFD P – RAD	
	6.0+6	8.0+6		ExTh Jour	PL/B 26 10 620	Apr 68	- + SYMMETRY TERM IN OPTMOD	
	-			Theo Jour	AF 34 481	Nov 67	- + MULTI – SCAT+ATTN BY M – CRLO	
Diff Elastic	None		JAE	Eval Prog	EANDC(J)26L30	Aug 72	Kawai+.OPT – MDL CALC. NDG	
Diff Elastic	None		KUK	Theo Jour	IPA 11 388	Jun 73	Kulkarni+ ROLE OF OPTMOD PARS,GRAPH	
Diff Elastic	1.5+6	8.0+6	JAE	Eval Prog	EANDC(J)30L 10	Sep 73	Tanaka.COUPLED – CHANNEL AND OPTMDL	
Diff Elastic	None		JUL	Theo Jour	ZP 270 337	Nov 74	Dederichs+.SMALL ANG SCAT IN CRYSTAL	
Polarization	+6		HRV	Theo Jour	PR 73 407	Feb 48	Schwinger.POLARIZ IN COULOMB FIELD.	

Many

Quantity	Energy (ev) Min	Max	Lab	Type	Documentation Ref Vol Page	Date	Author, Comments	Data
Polarization	None		NYU	Theo	Jour PR 74 1285	Nov 48	Borowitz+ DEPOLARIZATION OF THERM NS	
Polarization	None		ORL	Theo	Jour PR 75 213	Jan 49	Rose. 2 PAPERS,EXPTS SUGGESTED.	
Polarization	+8		UPP	Theo	Jour NP 1 433	May 56	Koehler.FORMULA.L−S SPH POTENTIAL.	
					Jour NP 9 49	Nov 58	−. APPROX FORM FOR INELASTIC.	
					Jour NP 6 161	Mar 58	−.APPROX FORML.FORWARD SCATT.	
					Jour NC 2 911	55	−. EQU TO NP 1 433.	
Polarization	+8		UPP	Theo	Jour NP 3 213	Apr 57	Maris.FORMULA. COLLECTIVE POTENTIAL	
Polarization	+7	+9	UFT	Theo	Jour NP 9 412	Jan 59	Sitenko.DIFFRACT L.S POT.STRIPPED NS	
Polarization	None		LAS	Theo	Jour NP 15 72	Feb 60	Rodberg.POL AS FUNCTION OF ANGDISTR	
Polarization	2.1+6		LAS	Expt	Conf 60Basel 311	Jul 60	Cranberg.22 NUCLEI.50,90,125DEG.GRPH	
Polarization	−		MAN	Theo	Jour NP 18 353	Sep 60	Goldfarb+ FORMULA.DIRECT INEL SCATT.	
Polarization	None		OSU	Theo	Jour NP 22 498	Feb 61	Margolis.LOW E S RES SPIN 0 NUCL.NDG	
Polarization	Maxwl		CCP	Theo	Jour ZET 49 925	Sep 65	Mamaladze+ SUPERCONDUCTOR 2ND KIND	
					Jour JET 22 643	Mar 66	TRANSLATN.*	
Polarization	−3	−1	IFB	Theo	Jour ZET 51 1587	Nov 66	Baryshevskij. COHERENT SCAT+POLARZTN	
					Jour JET 24 1068	May 67	TRANSLATN.*	
Polarization	1.0+6	1.6+7	LAS	Expt	Rept LA− 3788	67	Beery+.OPTMOD CALC COS(THETA) DISTR	
Polarization	Maxwl		UJV	Expt	Jour CZJB 19 278	Jun 68	Michalec+"ABSORPTION"IN FERROMAGNT	
Polarization	−2		KGU	Theo	Jour UFZ 13 1553	Sep 68	NGUYEN VAN TRONG.SEMICOND,SPIN−WAVES	
					Jour UPJ 13 1106	Mar 69	TRANSLATN.*	
Polarization	None		BAT	Theo	Jour PR 177 1706	Jan 69	Hogan+ OPTMDL CALC WITH MAGN INTERCT	
Polarization	+6	+8	UMX	Theo	Jour NP/A 125 425	Feb 69	Cocho+'CROSSED PARTIAL WAVE EXPANSN'	
Polarization	−		SUL	Theo	Jour NP/A 134 209	Sep 69	Gubkin. OPTMDL.OKS EXPT LARGE ANGLES	
Polarization	Maxwl		CCP	Theo	Jour ZET 58 1086	Mar 70	Baryshevskij+ MAGNTC SCAT AT LOW ANG	
					Jour JET 31 583	Sep 70	TRANSLATN.* SEE ALSO	
					Jour ZET 56 1273	Apr 69	.	
					Jour JET 29 685	Oct 69	. ENGL TRANSL OF ZET 56 1273	
Polarization	Maxwl		DUB	Theo	Rept JINR−P3−5554	Feb 71	Shapiro. PARAMAGN,POL NEUT DIFFRACTN	
Polarization	4.0+6		IJI	Theo	Jour YF 13 1026	May 71	Pasechnik+ POLRZ(ANG) FROM DIFFSIG	
					Jour SNP 13 589	Nov 71	. ENGL OF YF 13 1026	
Polarization	Maxwl		RCN	Expt	Prog INDC(NED)−2G	May 71	Reddingius+ POLARZD NUCLEI+N, (N,G)	
Polarization	1.5+6	6.1+6	IJI	Expt	Prog YFI−12 81	72	Pasechnik+. POLARIZATION FOR 48<A<137	
	1.0−2	3.0−1			Prog INDC(CCP)−30	Sep 72	.PAGE 71,ENGLISH OF YFI−12 81	
Polarization	−		UJV	Expt	Jour CZJB 22 38	Jan 72	Honzatko+ EFFECT OF THICK TARGET	
Potntal Scat	None		HRV	Theo	Jour PR 92 941	Nov 53	Selove. RES EFFECTS+SPIN DEPENDNCE.	
Potntal Scat	1.0+5	1.0+8	MIT	Revw	Conf 55Geneva 2 23	Aug 55	Weisskopf+.P830,REVIEW OF THEORIES	
Potntal Scat	+4		HAR	Expt	Jour PPSA 70 51	Jan 57	Gayther+ FROM AVG SIGTOT,A=95 TO 209	
	1.0+3			ExTh	Jour PHY 22 1133	Nov 56	− +ABSTRACT,A96TO209 EXP CFD TH	
Potntal Scat	None		BNL	Theo	Jour NP 50 157	Jan 64	Jain.OPTMOD.R PRIME VERSUS A	
Potntal Scat	None		PEN	Theo	Jour JPJ 19 1518	Sep 64	Wada.FORMAL TH OF SCAT.DISC OPT.POT.	
Potntal Scat	−		HAR	Revw	Conf 66Trieste 831	Dec 66	Rae.EXPTL SCAT LENGTHS CFD THS,GRAPH	
Potntal Scat	−3		IFU	Revw	Jour UFZ 13 599	Apr 68	Kolotyi+A=40TO200,POT+ELAST SCAT CFD	
					Jour UPJ 13 420	Oct 68	TRANSLATN.*	
Potntal Scat	+7		IFU	Theo	Jour UFZ 13 1693	Oct 68	Konstantinov+ EV−EV−NUCLEI,PHONON−TH	
					Jour UPJ 13 1203	Apr 69	TRANSLATN.*	
Potntal Scat	None		TOK	Theo	Jour PTP 40 796	Oct 68	Ishidzu.S−WAVE SCAT WITH W−S POTENT	
Potntal Scat	None		DAC	Theo	Jour NSPB 5 7	Oct 69	Sumrabuddin+ OPTMOD,WELL DEPTH VS A	
Potntal Scat	3.0+3	6.5+5	DKE	Expt	Diss PINEO 0	73	.3 COMPDS,20 NUCLIDES.GRPHS,TBLS.CFD	
Tot Inelastc			MIT	Theo	Jour PR 87 366	Jul 52	Hauser+FESHBACH.STAT MDL CALCULATION	
Tot Inelastc	None		MIT	Revw	Conf 55Geneva 2 23	Aug 55	Weisskopf+.P830,REVIEW OF THEORIES	
Tot Inelastc	2.0+5	1.5+6	OXF	Theo	Jour PPSA 68 994	Nov 55	Brink.SURFACE COUPLING CFD COMPNUCL	
Tot Inelastc	Thrsh	Up	CCP	Theo	Jour ZET 30 141	Jan 56	BM NO COMPD NCLS ROT XCITS VALUES	
					Jour JET 3 98	Aug 56	TRANSLATN.*	
Tot Inelastc	2.5+6	4.3+6	CCP	Theo	Jour ZET 30 551	Mar 56	TH CFD PIC P714,CURVES	
					Jour JET 3 484	Nov 56	TRANSLATN.*	
Tot Inelastc	None		BNL	Theo	Jour PR 104 1533	Dec 56	Lamarsh+,DIRECT INT DISTORT WAVE TH	
Tot Inelastc	2.5+6		CCP		Jour JET 31 907	57	26 NUCLIDES (PA 60 4741 5/57)	
Tot Inelastc	7.0+6	1.4+7	LRL	Theo	Rept UCRL−50181	Feb 57	Lutz+,CALC SIG FOR NUCLEI NE TO PU	
Tot Inelastc	2.0+6	1.4+7	IFU	Expt	Conf 58Geneva 15 18	Sep 58	Pasechnik+.PPR2030,MAGIC NUCLEI	
Tot Inelastc	1.4+7		MIL	Comp	Jour NC 22 1237	Dec 61	Erba+COMPAR.WITH STAT.MODEL.	
Tot Inelastc	−		AUA	Comp	Rept AAEC/E−119	Apr 64	Doherty. NUCLEAR DATA CARD LIBRARY	
					Rept AAEC/E−114	Dec 63	.MULGA CODE,GROUP AVERAGE SIGMA	
Tot Inelastc	None		ANL	Theo	Jour PR/B 135 642	Aug 64	Moldauer. FLUCT EFFECTS OVERLAP LVLS	
					Conf 64Paris 2 681	Jul 64	−.LOW E FLUCTS.OKS EXPT.NDG	
Tot Inelastc	Maxwl		CCP	Theo	Jour ZET 49 1504	Nov 65	Kagan+ INELASTIC CFD CRYSTAL SCAT	
					Jour JET 22 1032	May 66	TRANSLATN.*	
Tot Inelastc	8.0+5	4.1+6	IFU	ExTh	Jour AE 20 8	Jan 66	Korzh+ TABLE GIVEN.SIG AT 5 ES	

Many

Quantity	Energy (ev) Min	Max	Lab	Type	Documentation Ref Vol Page	Date	Author, Comments	Data
Tot Inelastc	1.0+6		BUC	Theo Conf	67Tokyo § 8.135	Sep 67	Hulubei+ OPTMOD CFD P-B CALCS,43NUCS	
Tot Inelastc	None		IFU	Theo Jour	UFZ 13 1415	Sep 68	Kolomiets+CFD (N,N)+(N,G) CHANNELS	
				Jour	UPJ 13 1011	Mar 69	TRANSLATN.*	
Tot Inelastc	None		IFU	Theo Jour	UFZ 13 1415	Sep 68	Kolomiets+.ALLOWANCE OF RAD CHANNELS	
Tot Inelastc	+7		IFU	Theo Jour	UFZ 13 1693	Oct 68	Konstantinov+ EV-EV-NUCLEI,PHONON-TH	
					UPJ 13 1203	Apr 69	TRANSLATN.*	
Tot Inelastc	+6	+7	AUA	Theo Jour	AUJ 22 135	Apr 69	Bertram. QUASI-COMPOUND-TH,SCAT AMPL	
	+5	+6		Prog	AAEC/PR-31P 9	Apr 69	- . A ABOVE 25,COMPOST PROGRAM	
	+6	+7		Rept	AAEC/TM-474	Aug 68	- .QUASI-COMPOUND NUCLEUS-TH	
Tot Inelastc	-		FEI	Theo Jour	YF 9 775	Apr 69	Rabotnov. INEL+FISSN,RESON ANALYSIS	
				Jour	SNP 9 451	Oct 69	TRANSLATN.*NO4	
Tot Inelastc	+6	+7	AUA	Theo Rept	AAEC/TM-524	Nov 69	Bertram. COMPOST=OPTMOD CALC PROGRAM	
Tot Inelastc	-		AUA	Theo Prog	AAEC/PR-33P 11	70	Bertram. GAMMAS AND SIGMA CALC, NDG	
Tot Inelastc		2.0+6	BHU	Theo Prog	BARC-474 47	70	Sharma+ OPTMOD PARS FIT TO XPTL DATA	
Tot Inelastc	-1	+5	BOL	Revw Conf	70Helsinki 2 379	Jun 70	Benzi.115. A BELOW 220, DATA STATUS	
Tot Inelastc	-		FEI	Theo Conf	70Helsinki 2 885	Jun 70	Ignatjuk+76. SUPERFLUID-MODL OKS XPT	
Tot Inelastc	None		FEI	Eval Prog	INDC-6 42	Jun 70	Abramov+ STATUS OF SOVIET EVALUATION	
Tot Inelastc	None		GLS	Expt Prog	INDC-6 11	Jun 70	Rae+ POSSIBLE FUTURE EXPERIMENTS,NDG	
Tot Inelastc	+7		IBJ	Theo Prog	INR-1318 14	Apr 71	Decowski+ PARTICLE+G EMISSN,NDG,TBL	
Tot Inelastc	1.4+7		TUD	Theo Prog	ZFK-223 21	Sep 71	Seeliger+ CALC SIG(Z)+A-DEPEND,GRAPH	
Tot Inelastc	None		JAE	Eval Prog	EANDC(J)26L30	Aug 72	Kawai+.SIMPLE MDL.RESULT IN FIGS	
Tot Inelastc		2.0+7	BNL	Theo Jour	JNE 27 81	Feb 73	Pearlstein.STATMOD CALN.FISS-SP AV	
Tot Inelastc	1.4+7		KOS	Revw Jour	ASL 25 88	75	Csikai. SIG(N-Z).FROM 9 ISOTOPS,GRPH	
Tot Inelastc	None		JAE	Theo Jour	NST 12 67	Feb 75	Igarasi.SIG CAL METHOD C COMPETITION	
Tot Inelastc	1.4+7		JUL	Revw Conf	75Wash. 664	Mar 75	Qaim. GRAPH SYSTEMATICS	
Tot Inelastc	2.0+6	4.5+6	AE	Expt Conf	75Gothenbg	Jun 75	Ramstrom.ABSTR,SYSTEMATIC A=27-209	
Tot Inelastc	None		STR	Theo Jour	ZP/A 273 195	Jun 75	Richert+ DIRECT INTERACT.PROCESS-TH.	
Tot Inelastc	7.0+6	1.4+7	FEI	Theo Rept	YK-21 49		76 Pljaskin+ MODLPARAMS FROM N-SPEC.FIG	
Tot Inelastc	None		TUD	Theo Jour	IAEA-190 2 263		76 Hermsdorf+ PREEQ-SIG(MASS),OPTMD.FIG	
Tot Inelastc	7.0+6	8.0+6	BRC	Theo Conf	76Lowell 365	Jul 76	Frehaut.SYST.NT.CASCADE REACTIONS.	
Diff Inelast	None		MIT	Theo Jour	PR 87 366	Jul 52	Hauser+ STAT MDL CALCULATION.	
Diff Inelast	2.0+5	1.5+6	OXF	Theo Jour	PPSA 68 994	Nov 55	Brink.SURFACE COUPLING CFD COMPNUCL	
Diff Inelast	Thrsh	Up	CCP	Theo Jour	ZET 30 141	Jan 56	BM NO COMPD NCLS ROT XCITS VALUES	
				Jour	JET 3 98	Aug 56	TRANSLATN.*	
Diff Inelast	Fast		KAP	Theo Jour	PHY 22 1163	Nov 56	Francis.ABSTRACT. CALCS CFD H-F	
Diff Inelast	None		BNL	Theo Jour	PR 104 1633	Dec 56	Lamarsh+,DIRECT INT DISTORT WAVE TH	
Diff Inelast	7.0+6	1.4+7	LRL	Theo Rept	UCRL-50181	Feb 57	Lutz+,CALC ANG DISTR NUCLEI NE TO PU	
Diff Inelast	1.4+7		CCP	Expt Jour	AE 3 540	Dec 57	Zamyatnin+. 16 TEMPS, CFD OTHERS	
				Jour	JNE 9 41	Jun 59	TRANSLATN.*	
				Jour	SJA 3 1427		57 TRANSLATN.*	
Diff Inelast	1.4+7		BRU	Theo Jour	JPR 21 382	May 60	Demeur.TH ANG DIST.DIRECT INELAST.N	
Diff Inelast	-		MAN	Theo Jour	NP 18 353	Sep 60	Goldfarb+. DIRECT REACTION THEORY	
Diff Inelast	Maxwl		IND	Theo Jour	PIA 27 216		61 MAGNETIC INELASTIC SCATTERING	
Diff Inelast	Fast		CBR	Expt Jour	NP 26 434	Aug 61	Lang.COMPILATION OF LEVEL DENS PARAM	
Diff Inelast	1.4+7		ROM	Expt Jour	NCS 370	Sep 63	Giannini+CURV A VS AT WT FROM 20-204	
Diff Inelast	-		AUA	Comp Rept	AAEC/E-119	Apr 64	Doherty. NUCLEAR DATA CARD LIBRARY	
				Rept	AAEC/E-114	Dec 63	.MULGA CODE,GROUP AVERAGE SIGMA	
Diff Inelast	None		ANL	Conf	64Paris 2 681	Jul 64	Moldauer.LOW E FLUCTS.OKS EXPT.NDG	
Diff Inelast	-		OSL	Theo Rept	ORNL-TM-930	Aug 64	Smith.COMPUTR PROG FOR ANG DISTR H-F	
Diff Inelast	1.0+6	1.0+7	KAP	Theo Jour	AP 29 232	Sep 64	Francis+ EFF INTRCTN NUC SURFACE.	
Diff Inelast	3.0+5	1.5+6	ANL	Expt Conf	66Paris 1 399	Oct 66	Smith+ A=8-239,EXPT CFD CALC.	
				ExTh Conf	65Antwerp 36	Jul 65	- + TOF.CFD OPTMDL AND H-F.NDG.	
Diff Inelast	-		FEI	Theo Rept	ICD-4 216		67 Nikolaev+LEG COEF EXPANS COMP PROGR	
Diff Inelast	+0	+7	SOR	Theo Conf	67Ann Arbr 1 323	Jul 67	Finkelstein.PPR8.TEMPRTR+SCAT KERNEL	
Diff Inelast	-		SAF	Theo Jour	NP/A 106 660	Dec 67	Hahne.CLOSED FORMULA. 0-SPIN TARGET	
Diff Inelast	None		FEI	Eval Conf	68Dubna § 11	Jun 68	Popov+.EXP DATA INTERPOLATION METHOD	
Diff Inelast	-		AUA	Theo Rept	AAEC/TM-478	Sep 68	Bertram.QUASI-COMP-NUCL-TH USED	
Diff Inelast	+7		IFU	Theo Jour	UFZ 13 1693	Oct 68	Konstantinov+ EV-EV-NUCLEI,PHONON-TH	
					UPJ 13 1203	Apr 69	TRANSLATN.*	
Diff Inelast	3.0+5	1.5+6	KUR	Theo Prog	YFI-11 5		70 Averjanov+ ABST,CALC A=23TO238,NDG	
				Prog	INDC(CCP)-31	Dec 72	.PAGE 3,ENGLISH OF YFI-11 5	
Diff Inelast	None		BNL	Eval Rept	BNL-400	Jun 70	Garber+.3RD EDITION ANGULAR DISTR	
Diff Inelast	+6	+7	KFI	Comp Rept	KFKI-70-18	Jul 70	Nagy+ MAP+TBL OF GAM HLS+NTENSTS S	
Diff Inelast	None		TUD	Theo Jour	KE 13 324	Oct 70	Hoehn+ SCATTER VOLUME CORRC METHOD	
				Jour	KE 13 283	Sep 70	- + SCATTER VOLUME CORRC METHOD	
				Jour	KE 13 263	Aug 70	- + SCATTER VOLUME CORRC METHOD	
Diff Inelast	None		FEI	Theo Conf	71Kiev	May 71	Ignatjuk+.DEP LVLDEN ON N-EVAPORSPEC	

Many

Quantity	Energy (ev) Min	Max	Lab	Type	Documentation Ref Vol Page	Date	Author, Comments	Data
Diff Inelast	–		JAE	Comp Prog	EANDC(J)22L23	Aug 71	Igarasi+.O,NA,CR,FE,NI,U,PU,NDG	
Diff Inelast	1.4+7		TUD Theo	Rept	ZFK – 243 22	Sep 72	Hermsdorf+PRE – EQU STATES,LVL – WIDS(A)	
Diff Inelast	None		TUD Theo	Jour	KE 15 384	Dec 72	Giera+ STATMOD TH FOR INEL SCAT SPEC	
Diff Inelast		1.2+8	KFK Theo	Rept	KFK – 1730	May 73	Roehm+ EXCIT FNS FOR P – NUMBER=13TO92	
Diff Inelast	1.4+7		TUD Theo	Jour	KE 16 252	Aug 73	Hermsdorf+ SIG+SPEC PARAMETRISATION	
				Expt Jour	KE 14 115	Apr 71	Giera+ SIG+SPEC CALC FROM TOF EXPT	
Diff Inelast	1.5+7		TUD Theo	Prog	ZFK – 283 4	Aug 74	Meister+ PRECOMPND TRANSITION – RATES	
				Conf	73Munich 1 514	Aug 73	Hermsdorf+ SEE ZFK – 262 30	
	1.4+7			Expt Prog	ZFK – 243 28	Sep 72	– + SPIN CUTOFF PARAM,GRAPHS	
Diff Inelast	7.0+6	1.4+7	FEI Revw	Rept	YFI – 22 9	Dec 76	Pljaskin+ ANALYS OF NS – SPEC	
Thermal Scat	None		PTN Theo	Jour	PR 49 229	Feb 36	Condon+ E DISTRIB AFTER N COLL.	
Thermal Scat	None		CHI Theo	Jour	PR 71 294	Mar 47	Goldberger+ REFR,REFL,SCATT IN CRYST	
Thermal Scat	None		ANL Theo	Jour	PR 72 907	Nov 47	Finkelstein.EINST POLYCRST.+EJECT CS	
Thermal Scat	None		CHI Theo	Jour	PR 74 335	Aug 48	Sternheimer.RESONANCE NS IN CRYSTALS	
Thermal Scat	None		LAS Theo	Jour	PR 83 289	Jul 51	Goldstein.COH SCATT B – E,F – D FLUIDS.	
Thermal Scat	Pile		BNL Expt	Jour	PR 83 863	Aug 51	Weiss+ STUDY ON MONOCHROMATC CRYSTLS	
Thermal Scat	0.0+0	1.0+0	UPP Theo	Jour	AF 3 209	Aug 51	Holte. SPACE – E DISTR OF SLOWD DWN NS	
	–			Jour	AF 2 523	Feb 51	– . SPACE – E DISTR IN INF HOM MODR	
Thermal Scat	None		MHG Theo	Jour	PR 83 1226	Sep 51	Slotnick.MAGNETIC DIFFRACTION PATTRN	
Thermal Scat	5.0 – 1	5.0+0	MRY Theo	Jour	PR 88 466	Nov 52	Gurney. POLYCRYSTALLINE MEDIA.	
Thermal Scat	Slow		UPP Theo	Jour	AF 6 113	Feb 53	Froeman.SPIN,TEMP,ISOT EFFCTS SNGLCR	
	None			Jour	AF 4 183	Aug 52	Waller+.DIFFR AND HEAT VIBR.SNGLCRYS	
				Jour	AF 4 191	Aug 52	Froeman+ PART II	
	Slow			Jour	AF 5 53	Aug 52	– .EL,INEL SCAT FROM POLYCRYSTL	
Thermal Scat	Maxwl		ORL Theo	Jour	PR 92 1387	Dec 53	Trammel. TRIVAL.RARE EARTH MAG.SCAT.	
Thermal Scat	– 3		BIR Theo	Jour	PPSA 67 85	Jan 54	MARSHALL MAG SCAT FROM FERROMAG XTL	
Thermal Scat	None		PTN Theo	Jour	PR 93 1207	Mar 54	Placzek+ CRYST INEL SCAT E+ANG DIST	
				Jour	PR 93 895	Feb 54	– + INCOHER SCAT BY POLYCRYSTLS	
Thermal Scat	Maxwl		IBJ Theo	Jour	APP 14 173	May 55	Kolos+ HINDERED ROTATION OF PROTONS	
				Jour	BPP 2 423	Sep 54	– + HINDERED ROTATION CFD,METHOD	
				Jour	BPP 2 63	Feb 54	– + HINDERED ROTATION IN N – SCATT	
				Jour	APP 13 67	Jan 54	– + HINDERED ROTATION OF PROTONS	
Thermal Scat	Cold		SAC ExTh	Jour	JPRS 16 35	Jul 55	Herpin+REFLEXION FROM MONOCRYSTALS	
Thermal Scat	–		TAT Theo	Jour	PRSA 231 293	Sep 55	Kothari+.COH INCOH MULTI PHONON THEO	
Thermal Scat	1.0+0	1.0+7	UPP Theo	Jour	AF 10 129	Jan 56	Olsson. TIME – E DISTR. FREE STAT ATMS	
Thermal Scat	Maxwl		LEB Theo	Jour	ZET 31 696	Oct 56	Kazarnovskii.RELATION TO SPECIF HEAT	
				Jour	JET 4 600	May 57	TRANSLATN.*	
Thermal Scat	None		KAP Theo	Jour	PR 106 290	Apr 57	Nelkin+,MOLECULAR SCATTERING THEORY	
Thermal Scat	Maxwl		BNL Theo	Jour	PR 110 999	Jun 58	Vineyard.SCAT THEORY OF LIQUIDS	
Thermal Scat	Slow		UPP Theo	Jour	AF 14 315	Oct 58	Sjoelander.MULTIPHON PROC.CRYSTLSCAT	
		+0		Jour	AF 13 199	Mar 58	– . 2 – PHONON DIFF XSECTION	
	Slow			Jour	AF 7 375	Mar 54	– .ISOTR.ANISO CRSTL.BRAGGLM	
Thermal Scat	Maxwl		AE Eval	Jour	AF 15 147	Apr 59	Sjoestrand.CORR TO DIFFSN COOL COEFF	
Thermal Scat	–		UPP Theo	Jour	AF 16 1	Sep 59	Eriksson.SLOWING – DOWN.TIME – E DISTR.	
Thermal Scat	–		IBJ Revw	Rept	INR – 134/I – B	Jan 60	Oconnor+ PARASIT BRAGG SCATTERING	
Thermal Scat	None		ANL Theo	Jour	AF 16 385	Feb 60	Singwi.GENRL THRY OF DIFFSN COOLING	
Thermal Scat	None		BNL Revw	Rept	IS/P – 7	Jul 60	Egelstaff. SCATTERING LAW REVIEW.	
Thermal Scat	None		BNL Theo	Jour	AP 11 338	Nov 60	Corngold. CHEMICAL BINDING EFFECTS.	
Thermal Scat			HAR Theo	Rept	AERE – R – 3847	Jul 61	Mclatchie+ TABLES OF CALC. S VALUES	
Thermal Scat	Cold		KRK Revw	Jour	PF 12 465	Jul 61	JANIK NS VS AUTODIFFUSION IN LIQUIDS	
Thermal Scat		+0	KJL Theo	Jour	PNV 1 127	62	Loevseth.LIGHT MONONUCL DIAT MOLECLS	
Thermal Scat	None		MHG Theo	Rept	TID – 18429	62	Summerfield+ G(R,T) FROM EXPTL DATA	
Thermal Scat	None		MHG Theo	Rept	TID – 18424	62	Plummer+ SCATTERING BY BOUND PROTON	
Thermal Scat	None		HAR Theo	Jour	NSE 12 260	Jan 62	Egelstaff+EVALN.METHODS FOR S.	
				Rept	AERE – R – 3803	Aug 61	.SUPERSEDED*	
	–			Revw Rept	AERE – R – 3623	Jun 60	EGELSTAFF SCATTERING THEORY REVW.	
	0.0+0	1.0+0	Theo	Rept	AERE – NP/GEN 13	Jan 60	Egelstaff+TABLES NOM+ENERGY TRANSFR	
Thermal Scat	Maxwl		BNL Theo	Conf	62BNL 1 238	Apr 62	Purohit+ SCAT IN DOPPLER APPROXIMATN	
Thermal Scat	Cold		TRM Theo	Jour	NSE 13 40	May 62	Sharma+,INELASTIC SCAT BY POLYXTLS	
Thermal Scat	None		MHG Theo	Rept	TID – 18587	Jun 62	YIP. SCAT BY POLAR LIQUIDS.	
				Conf	62BNL 1 289	Apr 62	YIP+ DIFF SIGS BY HINDERD ROTATR MDL	
Thermal Scat	None		MTR Comp	Rept	IDO – 16699(REV)	Jul 62	Brugger. COMPILED S(A,B) CURVES.	
Thermal Scat	None		ANL Theo	Conf	62Chalk R. 1 215	Sep 62	Singh+ FREQUENCY SPECT OF LIQUIDS.	
Thermal Scat	–		JUL Theo	Conf	62Chalk R. 1 37	Sep 62	Hahn.ANHARMONIC EFFECTS ON N SCAT	
Thermal Scat	–		UTR Theo	Conf	62Chalk R. 1 15	Sep 62	Kokeddee.PHONON+ELECTRON EXCIT,NSCAT	
Thermal Scat	Cold		KRK Revw	Jour	PF 14 167	Mar 63	JANIK NS SCT MOLECULES TH CFD EXPT	
Thermal Scat	None		LRL Theo	Rept	UCRL – 7267	Mar 63	Stuart. DEBYE MDL OF CRYST SCAT.	

Many

Quantity	Energy (ev) Min	Max	Lab	Type	Documentation Ref Vol Page	Date	Author, Comments	Data
Thermal Scat	−2	−1	MTR	Theo Jour	NSE 15 429	Apr 63	Mcmurry. APPROX MTHDS.SEMIRIGID MOLE	
	−1	+0		Rept	IDO − 16749	Apr 62	− . CALC OF DIFF SCAT SIGS.	
	None			Conf	62BNL 1 144	Apr 62	− . EVAL OF CALCULATION METHODS	
	Maxwl			Rept	IDO − 16592	Mar 60	− . NEUT SCAT BY GASEOUS MOLEC.	
Thermal Scat	Cold		WWA	Revw Jour	PF 14 627	Nov 63	Buras. NEUTRONOGRAPHY IN WARSAW	
Thermal Scat	+0		BNL	Theo Jour	PR/A 133 1366	Feb 64	Blume. SPIN − ORBIT,SCAT POLARZD NS.	
Thermal Scat	Cold		KFI	Theo Rept	KFKI − 64 − 3	Mar 64	Kosaly+ TH OF N − SCAT BY MOLECULES	
Thermal Scat	None		MTR	Theo Rept	IDO − 16956	Apr 64	Mcmurry+ MOLECULAR AGGREGATE MODEL	
Thermal Scat	−		AE	Theo Rept	AE − 148	Jun 64	Hakansson.CALC 4 ANG MOMNTS F MONATG	
Thermal Scat	−		LEB	Theo Jour	ZET 47 139	Jul 64	CORRLTN FNCTS+DIFF SIGS CALCULATED	
				Jour	JET 20 94	Jan 65	TRANSLATN.*	
Thermal Scat	None		WES	Theo Jour	PR/A 135 1071	Aug 64	Maradudin. SCAT FNCT ANHARMONIC XTLS	
Thermal Scat	Maxwl		CCP	Theo Jour	ZET 47 1544	Oct 64	SCAT BY DISORDERED CRYSTALS	
				Jour	JET 20 1041	Apr 65	TRANSLATN.*	
Thermal Scat	Maxwl		CCP	Theo Jour	ZET 47 1997	Nov 64	ANHARMONIC EFFECTS ON INEL SCAT SIG	
				Jour	JET 20 1340	May 65	TRANSLATN.*	
Thermal Scat	−3	−1	KRK	Theo Jour	NKA 9 839	Nov 64	Wanic.NEUTRON MAGNON SCATT SURFACE	
Thermal Scat	Slow		CTH	Theo Conf	64Bombay 1 61	Dec 64	Sjoelander+. MODFS BORN − VON KARAMAN	
Thermal Scat	Pile		KRK	Revw Jour	PF 16 104	Jan 65	REVIEW ON MAGNON SPECTRA 39 REFS	
Thermal Scat	None		MHG	Theo Jour	PR/B 137 271	Jan 65	Rosenbaum+ SEMI − CLASSICAL SCAT KERNL	
				Conf	62BNL 1 276	Apr 62	− + CLASSICAL+QUASICLASSIC TH	
Thermal Scat	5.0−1	+6	CCP	Theo Jour	AE 18 118	Feb 65	Turchin+ SOME ASYMPTOTIC RELATIONS	
	5.0−1	+7		Jour	JNE 20 313	Apr 66	TRANSLATN.*	
				Jour	EAF 18 2 55	Feb 65	TRANSLATN.*	
	5.0−1	+6		Jour	SJA 18 146	Feb 65	TRANSLATN.*	
Thermal Scat	Maxwl		IND	Theo Conf	65Calcutta 297	Feb 65	Aggarwal+ FREQUENCY DISTR,NEW THEORY	
Thermal Scat	Maxwl		COL	Theo Jour	JCP 42 1863	Mar 65	Steele+ FLUIDS OF NONSPHERICAL MOLES	
Thermal Scat	−		KFK	Theo Jour	ZN/A 20 380	Mar 65	SCAT BY FREE MOLECULES,CFD XPT	
Thermal Scat	Cold		ORL	Revw Jour	JAP 36 1078	Mar 65	Koehler. N DIFFR BY RARE EARTHS	
Thermal Scat	Maxwl		CCP	Theo Jour	ZET 48 1448	May 65	SMALL − ANGLE SCAT BY FERROMAGNETS	
				Jour	JET 21 969	Nov 65	TRANSLATN.*	
Thermal Scat	−3	−1	KRK	Theo Rept	INP − 409/PS	May 65	Fulinski.NONEQUIL.SYSTEMS,APP 29163	
				Jour	APP 26 19	Jul 64	− .CONTINUED APP VOLS 27 + 29	
Thermal Scat	Maxwl		CCP	Theo Jour	AE 19 67	Jul 65	Mayorov.ASYMPTOTIC FORM OF SCAT.LAW	
				Jour	SJA 19 940	65	. ENGL OF AE 19 67	
Thermal Scat	Maxwl		RPI	Theo Abst	DA 26 295	Jul 65	Dahlberg.TEMP DEPENDNCE 3CAT KERNELS	
Thermal Scat	Maxwl		CCP	Theo Jour	ZET 49 925	Sep 65	Mamaladze+ SUPERCONDUCTOR 2ND KIND	
				Jour	JET 22 643	Mar 66	TRANSLATN.*	
Thermal Scat	Maxwl		CCP	Theo Jour	ZET 49 1504	Nov 65	Kagan+ CRYSTAL,DYNAMICAL THEORY	
				Jour	JET 22 1032	May 66	TRANSLATN.*	
Thermal Scat	Maxwl		CCP	Theo Jour	AE 19 428	Nov 65	Turchin.TSL CALC BY TIME INTEGRATION	
Thermal Scat	Pile		KRK	Revw Jour	PF 16 667	Nov 65	.REVIEW ON INEL NEUTR.SCATT IN 3RYST	
				Rept	INP − 368	Nov 64	JANIK REV.MOLEC.DYNAMICS,89 REFS	
Thermal Scat	1.0−3	9.0−1	JAE	Theo Rept	JAERI − 1095	Dec 65	.JNDC.CAL THR SCAT KERNEL,MANY MODEL	
Thermal Scat	Maxwl		HAR	Theo Rept	AERE − R − 4535	Mar 66	Stringfellow.SCT BY FERROM SPINWAVES	
Thermal Scat	None		ICP	Theo Jour	ZET 50 726	Mar 66	Ivanov. MOLECULES,QUASI + ELASTIC SCAT	
Thermal Scat	Cold		CRC	Theo Prog	AECL − 2611	Jun 66	Sears.SCAT TH OF POLYATOMIC LIQUIDS	
Thermal Scat	+0	+3	IFU	Theo Jour	UFZ 11 581	Jun 66	SCATTERING N BY LINEAR MOLECULES	
Thermal Scat	None		MTR	Theo Prog	IDO − 17191 28	Jun 66	Mcmurry. CALC OF INTERFERENCE TERMS.	
Thermal Scat	Maxwl		CCP	Theo Jour	UFN 90 47	Aug 66	Ivanov+SAJASOV 40 PAGES THEORY	
Thermal Scat	0.0+0	1.0+0	AE	Expt Rept	AE − 259	Nov 66	Purohit.DISC QUASI − EL SCAT HYDROGLIQ	
	−			Theo Conf	65Karlsrhe 1 289	May 65	− +.CRIT DISC OF THRMLZN PARAMS	
	None				Rept	AE − 154	Sep 64	− . DISC 3 SETS OF INTEG PARAMS	
Thermal Scat	−		ISS	Theo Jour	JPJ 21 2178	Nov 66	Oguchi+TH OF CRITICAL MAGNE SCATT S	
Thermal Scat	−		UPP	Theo Jour	AF 31 537	Nov 66	Goodman+.DER VAN HOVE − GLAUBER FORMLA	
Thermal Scat	None		ANL	Theo Prog	ANL − 7210 342	Dec 66	COX. MULTIPLE SCAT CORR. CURVES.	
Thermal Scat	Cold		DUB	Theo Rept	JINR − P4 − 3158	67	Baryshevsky+.N AND TARGET POLARIZED	
Thermal Scat	Maxwl		CCP	Theo Jour	ZET 52 557	Feb 67	Brovman+ METALS,PHONONS + ELECTRONS	
				Jour	JET 25 365	Aug 67	TRANSLATN.*	
Thermal Scat	None		MTR	Theo Rept	IN − 1045	Feb 67	Plummer. MULTIPLE SCATTERING THEORY.	
Thermal Scat	−		HAR	Revw Jour	AIP 16 147	Apr 67	Egelstaff.NEUT X − RAY SCT LIQUID METL	
Thermal Scat	None		BNL	Revw Conf	67Ann Arbr 1 125	Jul 67	Michael+ PPR49.PULSD+WAVE TECHNIQ CFD	
Thermal Scat	−3	+0	BNW	Theo Conf	67Ann Arbr 1 271	Jul 67	Gibbs+ PPR51.SIG(E,E'),SIG(E) CALC	
	None			Rept	BNWL − SA − 1085	Jul 67	− − LEG MOMENTS BY S(A,B) INTEGR	
Thermal Scat	−3	+1	GA	Theo Jour	NSE 30 199	Nov 67	Slaggie. MULTISCAT CORRCT DBL DIFF.	
				Conf	67Ann Arbr 1 311	Jul 67	.PPR53.MULTIPLE − SCAT − CORRECTN	
				Rept	GA − 8052	Jul 67	.SAME.	

Many

Quantity	Energy (ev) Min	Max	Lab	Type	Documentation Ref Vol Page	Date	Author, Comments	Data
Thermal Scat	None		GA	Theo Conf	67Ann Arbr 1 333	Jul 67	Koppel+PPR54. SOLIDS,NEW SCAT KERNEL	
	5.0−3	1.0+1		Rept	GA− 6281	Apr 65	Young.REVIEW THERMAL SCATTER.KERNELS	
Thermal Scat	−3	+1	KFK Revw	Conf	67Ann Arbr 1 235	Jul 67	Glaeser.PPR104.SCAT−LAW IN MODERATOR	
Thermal Scat	None		MHG	Theo Conf	67Ann Arbr 1 283	Jul 67	Summerfield+PPR65.QUASICL MOLEC SCAT	
Thermal Scat	None		RPI	Theo Conf	67Ann Arbr 1 183	Jul 67	Daitch+PPR58.PULSD−N,THERMALZN−MODEL	
Thermal Scat	+0	+7	SOR	Theo Conf	67Ann Arbr 1 323	Jul 67	Finkelstein.PPR8.TEMPRTR+SCAT KERNEL	
Thermal Scat	−1	+0	UNC	Theo Conf	67Ann Arbr 1 537	Jul 67	Bollacasa+PPR74.ON 'UPSCAT' REACT−TH	
Thermal Scat	Maxwl		WAL	Theo Rept	WANL−TME−1640	Jul 67	Johnston.SCAT LAW FOR POLYCRYSTALS	
Thermal Scat	−		BIR	Theo Jour	PPS 91 917	Aug 67	Oconnor.DYNAM THEOR NEUT−PHONON SCAT	
Thermal Scat	−		OXF	Theo Jour	PPS 91 903	Aug 67	Elliott+ GROUP THEOR SELECTION RULES	
Thermal Scat	Cold		AE	Theo Jour	AF 34 121	Oct 67	Hoegberg.ANHRM CRYST.GREEN FN METHOD	
	−			Rept	AE− 274	Apr 67	− +.CALC 3+4TH ORDEF ANHRMCRYS	
Thermal Scat	−		HAR	Theo Jour	PPS 92 390	Oct 67	Collins+ PARAMAG SCAT,APPROX METHODS	
Thermal Scat	Cold		KRK Revw	Rept	INP−570/PS 11	Dec 67	Szytula.MAGN CRYSTAL STRUCTURE	
Thermal Scat	Cold		KRK Revw	Rept	INP−570/PS 17	Dec 67	Maniawski.MAGNETICS STUD BY POLAR NS	
Thermal Scat	Maxwl		MHG	Theo Jour	JCP 47 4923	Dec 67	Zweifel+ SCATTERING BY A QUANTUM GAS	
Thermal Scat	Cold		WWA Revw	Rept	INP−570/PS 23	Dec 67	Blinowski.MAGNETIZ FLUCTUAT STUD NS	
Thermal Scat	Cold		KUR	Theo Conf	68Riga	Jan 68	Baz+ ABST,CORRECTED FERMI ESTIMATION	
Thermal Scat	Cold		OSA	Theo Prog	EANDC(J)8L64	Jan 68	Sekiya+. TH OF MULTIPLE SCATTERING	
				Jour	PTP 39 37	Jan 68	Sunakawa+.MULT−SCAT FORMULA IMPROVED	
				Jour	PTP 37 1051	Jun 67	− .TH OF N SCAT+CORRLTN FNCTNS	
Thermal Scat	+0		BNL	Theo Jour	PR 166 554	Feb 68	Schermer+ NUCLEAR POLARIZATN EFFECTS	
Thermal Scat	Maxwl		IFU	Theo Jour	UFZ 13 294	Feb 68	Koval'Chuk.DISORDERED−SOLID,1−PHONON	
				Jour	UPJ 13 204	Aug 68	TRANSLATN.*	
Thermal Scat	Cold		MUN	Theo Jour	ZP 210 434	Mar 68	Mehringer. CFD WITH EXPERIMT	
Thermal Scat	Maxwl		UFT	Theo Jour	UFZ 13 492	Mar 68	Akhiezer+ SCAT IN MAGN−ORDERED CRYST	
				Jour	UPJ 13 344	Sep 68	TRANSLATN.*	
Thermal Scat	−		DLH	Theo Jour	PR 168 752	Apr 68	Kothari+ S(AB) CALC N−DIMENS LATTICE	
Thermal Scat	Cold		KRK Revw	Rept	INP−600/PS	Apr 68	Janik.MOLEC DYNAMICS,SCATT +HYDRBOND	
Thermal Scat	Cold		KTH Revw	Conf	68Copenhgn 1 397	May 68	Larsson.PPR220.MONATMC,MOLECLR LIQDS	
	+0			Conf	64Bombay 2 3	Dec 64	− .SCAT FROM LIQUIDS	
Thermal Scat	None		STF	ExTh Abst	DA/B 28 4602	May 68	Feinstein. HI−DEN.TERM FLUID SCATLAW	
Thermal Scat	None		CRC	Theo Jour	CJP 46 1499	Jun 68	Woods. CRYST FLD EFFECTS INEL SCAT.	
Thermal Scat	Maxwl		HAR	Expt Jour	JP/C 1 784	Jun 68	North+ STRUCTURE FACTOR LIQID METALS	
Thermal Scat	Maxwl		OSA	Theo Priv	SEKIYA	Jun 68	Sekiya+ N SCT.ASUMMETRIC TOP MOLECLE	
	Cold			Prog	EANDC(J)8L60	Jan 68	− +.SCATT TH OF ROTATING MOLECUL	
Thermal Scat	−		LON	Theo Jour	BJAS 2 957	Aug 68	Williams.SYNTHETIC SCATT.KERNEL	
Thermal Scat	None		CRC	Theo Rept	AECL−3189	Sep 68	Cowley+ LIQUID SCAT CALC TOF MEASTS	
Thermal Scat	−2		KGU	Theo Jour	UFZ 13 1553	Sep 68	NGUYEN VAN TRONG.SEMICOND,SPIN−WAVES	
				Jour	UPJ 13 1106	Mar 69	TRANSLATN.*	
Thermal Scat	−2		IFU	Theo Jour	UFZ 13 1682	Oct 68	Dzyub. MAGN SCAT ON IMPURE FERROMAGN	
				Jour	UPJ 13 1196	Apr 69	TRANSLATN.*	
Thermal Scat	Maxwl		JAP	Theo Jour	JPJ 25 1001	Oct 68	Yamada+ INELAST SCAT BY SPIN WAVE	
Thermal Scat	Maxwl		NAG	Theo Jour	JPJ 25 1001	Oct 68	Yamada+CALCUL.BASED ON SPIN WAVES	
Thermal Scat		+6	UPP	Theo Jour	AF 37 569	Oct 68	Waller.TIME−E DISTR SLWD DWN NS.THRY	
	−			Conf	64Bombay 1 225	Dec 64	− .ANHARM AND IMPURITY EFFECTS	
Thermal Scat	Maxwl		GIT	Theo Jour	JP/C 1 1563	Dec 68	Kwon+ SCATT.FROM PARAMAGNETS	
	None			Jour	PR 167 458	Mar 68	− + PARAMAG SCAT HEISENBERG SYSTE	
Thermal Scat	Maxwl	−3	KRK	Theo Jour	APP 34 1037	Dec 68	Fulinski+ NEUT−SCAT BY REAL GAS	
Thermal Scat	None		TEX	Theo Jour	PR 176 784	Dec 68	Wette+ POLYCRYSTALS INEL SIG CALCTD	
Thermal Scat	−3	+0	TRM Revw	Conf	68Bombay 1 177	Dec 68	SATYA MURTY+ MAGNETISM,EXCH−INTEGRAL	
Thermal Scat	−3	+0	TRM Revw	Conf	68Bombay 1 215	Dec 68	Chidambaram.NON LINEAR H−BOND,SURVEY	
Thermal Scat	−3	−1	UMX Revw	Diss	MEXICO	69	Lonngi. SCATTERING ON LIQUIDS,REVIEW	
Thermal Scat	−3	−1	UMX Revw	Diss	MEXICO	69	Ayala. MOLECULAR DYNAMICS IN LIQUIDS	
Thermal Scat	−		HAR	Theo Jour	JP/C 2 470	Mar 69	Lovesey Scat.OF NTNS.BY MAGNTIC IONS	
Thermal Scat	−		HAR	Theo Jour	JP/C 2 539	Mar 69	Marshall+ SPIN WAVE SCAT.IN FERROMAG	
Thermal Scat	−		HAR	Theo Jour	JP/C 2 556	Mar 69	Hubbard+ SIG(INEL,COH) BY NEW LIQ.TH	
Thermal Scat	None		ANL	Theo Jour	NSE 37 368	Sep 69	Agrawal+ MOLECULAR LIQUIDS	
Thermal Scat	−4		WWA	Theo Jour	APP 36 697	Oct 69	Kocinski+ CRITL SCAT NS IN FERROMAGN	
	Maxwl			Jour	APP 35 61	Jan 69	− +CRITICAL SCAT ANTIFERROMAGN	
	Cold			Jour	APP 33 13	Jan 68	− . TH CRIT FERRO,ANTIFERROMAG	
Thermal Scat	−3	+0	KRK Revw	Jour	NKA 14 1193	Dec 69	Janik.POLISH REVIEW ON NEUTS+SOLIDS	
				Jour	AE 27 533	Dec 69	SEE ALSO *SHORTENED	
				Jour	EAF 27 55		69 . FRENCH OF AE 27 533	
Thermal Scat	None		MHG	Theo Jour	PR 188 1445	Dec 69	Summerfield+,SYMMETRY RELATIONS	
Thermal Scat	None		SRL	Theo Rept	DP− 1224	Jan 70	Clifford.DIFFUSIVE LAW FOR LIQUIDS	

Many

Quantity	Energy (ev) Min	Max	Lab	Type	Documentation Ref Vol Page	Date	Author, Comments	Data
Thermal Scat	-3	-1	CCP	Theo Jour	ZEP 11 235	Feb 70	Kagan. NEUTRON LIFETIME IN MATTER	
				Jour	JEL 11 147	Feb 70	TRANSLATN.*	
Thermal Scat	Maxwl		CCP	Theo Jour	ZET 58 1086	Mar 70	Baryshevskij+ MAGNTC SCAT AT LOW ANG	
				Jour	ZET 56 1273	Apr 69	.SEE ALSO	
				Jour	JET 31 583	Sep 70	.ENGL TRANS OF ZET 58	
	-2			Jour	JET 29 685	69	.ENGL TRANS OF ZET 56	
Thermal Scat	Maxwl		MHG	Theo Jour	JPJ 28 644	Mar 70	Summerfield+ INCOH N SCATT AND NMR.	
Thermal Scat	Maxwl		OSU	Theo Abst	DA/B 30 4755	Apr 70	Markworth. MAGNTIC SCAT.BY SOLIDS.	
Thermal Scat	Maxwl		BUC	Theo Jour	RRP 15 669	Jun 70	Caprini – Gologan. THERMALIZATN MODEL	
				Jour	RRP 15 533	May 70	Caprini+ SOLUTN OF THERMALIZN EQUATN	
				Jour	RRP 15 141	Feb 70	- + ON A THERMALIZATION MODEL	
Thermal Scat	-		ISL	Expt Prog	IA- 1218 58	Aug 70	Shaked. MAGNETIC STRUCTURE+REFLECTNS	
Thermal Scat	-3	+0	DUB	Theo Rept	JINR – E4 – 5348	Oct 70	Priezzhev. CLASS.LIQUIDS,ZERO SOUND	
	-			Rept	JINR – P4 – 4741	Oct 69	- . LIQUID,1 PARTICL EXCITATN	
Thermal Scat	Cold		AUS	Theo Jour	APPA 39 83	Jan 71	Weil. N SCT SIG ON NUC IN ELMAGFIELD	
	-			Jour	ZP 233 178	Mar 70	- .SCAT IN LEIBFRIED – BRENIG MODEL	
Thermal Scat	0.0+0	1.0+0	IAE	Theo Jour	RRP 16 19	Jan 71	Weil. VAN HOVE THEORY+SUNAKAWA DISTR	
	-3	+0		Jour	CZJB 20 950	Aug 70	- . ON NEUT SCAT IN DEBYE LATTICE	
Thermal Scat	-3	-1	IBJ	Theo Rept	INR – 1260	Jan 71	Arkuszewski+ SCATLAW CODE,DIFFSIG(E)	
	None			Prog	INR – 1300	71	- + POLYCRYST,CODE EL – SCAT	
	Maxwl			Prog	INR – 1197/I/PL	May 70	- .PROGRAM = MINIGASKET,ABSTR	
Thermal Scat	Maxwl		DUB	Theo Rept	JINR – P3 – 5554	Feb 71	Shapiro. PARAMAGN,POL NEUT DIFFRACTN	
Thermal Scat	-3	-1	DUB	Expt Rept	JINR – E3 – 5612	Mar 71	Dobrzynski. MAGNONS+PULSED NEUTRONS	
Thermal Scat	Maxwl		USA	Expt Abst	DA/B 31 6541	May 71	Livingston. TOF.FREQS IN ORG.SUBSTS.	
Thermal Scat	Maxwl		OSA	Theo Jour	NST 8 406	Jul 71	Nishigori+ MEAN SQUARE DISPLACEMENT	
				Jour	PTP 43 1423	Jun 70	- .SHORT – COLLISION – TIME APPR	
	Cold			Jour	PTP 41 619	Mar 69	- +.FORMAL TH C RECOIL EFFECT	
Thermal Scat	Maxwl		TOK	Expt Jour	JPJ 31 301	Jul 71	Yamaoka+ MAGN STRUCT BY N – DIFF.NDG	
Thermal Scat	Maxwl		OSA	Theo Jour	PTP 46 1666	Dec 71	Hama+.N SCAT SIG BY SPHERICAL ROTORS	
Thermal Scat	Pile		JUL	Revw Jour	EEN 64	72	SPRINGER. LIQUID+SOLID SCAT,TH+EXPT	
Thermal Scat	Cold		IFJ	Revw Jour	PF 23 114	Mar 72	Wanic.INEL N SCT+DIFF IN MAGNETICS	
Thermal Scat	Cold		UJK	Theo Jour	APPA 41 549	May 72	Rosciszewski. CRYST.QUASI – EL SIGS	
Thermal Scat	None		AE	Expt Rept	INIS – MF – 427	Jun 72	Rolandson.PPR20.6,ALKALI MALIDES,NDG	
Thermal Scat	Maxwl		BNW	Theo Rept	BNWL – 1675	Jun 72	Gibbs+.CODE FOR CALC SCAT KERNELS	
Thermal Scat	Pile		JUL	Comp Rept	JUEL – 875 – RX	Aug 72	Scharenberg. DATA ON FILTERMATERIALS	
Thermal Scat	Cold		MUN	Theo Jour	ZP 254 169	Aug 72	Steyerl.EFFECT OF SURFACE ROUGHNESS	
Thermal Scat	Cold		WWA	Revw Jour	PF 23 475	Sep 72	Kocinski+ INEL SCAT NEAR CRIT POINT	
Thermal Scat	Maxwl		GRE	Expt Jour	ZP 255 146	Oct 72	Mezei.POLARIZED THR N – TECHNIQUE	
Thermal Scat	Maxwl		JAE	Theo Jour	NST 9 743	Dec 72	NAKAHARA.INTERPOLATION,TEMP.INTRVAL	
Thermal Scat	None		BUC	Theo Rept	RRP 18 997	73	Rapeanu+ SCAT – LAW SOLID+LIQUID,GRPHS	
Thermal Scat	None		OSA	Theo Jour	AKE 20 249	Jan 73	Sekiya+GG – KERNELS FOR ELAS+INEL SCAT	
Thermal Scat	Cold		DLH	Theo Jour	PL/A 46 471	Feb 74	Sarma+CALC SCAT FROM MOLECULAR SOLID	
				Jour	PL/A 45 481	Nov 73	- +CALC SCAT INCOHERENT LATTICE	
				Jour	PL/A 44 519	Aug 73	- +CALCULATION SCATT IN CRYSTAL	
Thermal Scat	Maxwl	2.5-2	KTO	Theo Jour	JPJ 36 406	Feb 74	Tani.PHONON IN ANHARMONIC,MAG CRYST	
	Maxwl			Jour	JPJ 29 594	Sep 70	- .NEUT SCATT BY LATTICE VIBRATIO	
Thermal Scat	None		JUL	Theo Jour	ZP 271 289	Dec 74	Breuer.PHONON – SPEC FROM COH – SCAT	
Thermal Scat	None		JAE	Revw Rept	JAERI – M – 6857	Dec 76	Sakamoto+.BIBLIOGRAPHY 5TH EDITION	
	-			Rept	JAERI – 4043 3	Nov 71	- +.BIBLIOGRAPHY FOR NEUT SCAT	
	None			Rept	JAERI – 4043 2	Jul 69	- +.BIBLIOGRAPHY FOR NEUT SCAT	
				Rept	JAERI – 4043	Mar 68	Iijima+ VERY IMPORTANT BIBLIOGRAPHY	
Thermal Scat	1.0-4	1.0+3	MUN	Revw Jour	EEN 80 1	77	Koester. SCAT LENGTH,FREE+INCOH SIG	
Scattering	None		HRV	Theo Jour	PR 48 367	Aug 35	Vanvleck. SYSTEMATIX XOK MAJORANA.	
Scattering	None		PTN	Theo Jour	PR 49 519	Apr 36	Breit+ TH OF DAMPING APPLIED.	
Scattering	None		ROC	Theo Jour	PR 57 472	Mar 40	Weisskopf+ GENERAL FORMULA,A OVER 50	
Scattering	5.0-1	1.0+0	COR	Theo Jour	PR 57 1125	Jun 40	Bethe.GENERAL.CONTINUUM TH CPD NUCL.	
Scattering	None		AMH	Theo Jour	PR 69 369	Apr 46	Grahame.1942LETTER.LOCAL EXCIT HYP.	
Scattering	9.0+7		CHI	Theo Jour	PR 74 1269	Nov 48	Goldberger. STATIST MODEL.ANG,E DIST	
Scattering	9.0+7		BRK	Theo Jour	PR 75 1352	May 49	Fernbach+ FITS OPAQUE SPH,R = 1.37A1/3	
Scattering	None		PTN	Theo Jour	PR 86 377	May 52	Placzek+SCATT BY SYST HEAVY NUCLEI	
				Jour	PR 82 392	May 51	- +SHORT – WAVE INTERF HEAVY NUCL	
Scattering	None		AUS	Theo Jour	APA 6 30	Sep 52	Sexl.EFF.RANGE SCAT TH N – NUCLEUS	
	Fast			Jour	APA 2 368	Feb 49	Urban.TH OF SCAT OF NUCLEONS	
				Jour	APA 1 177	Nov 47	Sexl.TH OF SCAT N – NUCLEUS	
Scattering	Maxwl		CAV	Theo Jour	PM 45 751	Jul 54	Scott.DISTRIBN OF COH SCAT LENGTHS	
				Jour	PM 45 1322	Dec 54	- . A MEDIUM INTERACTION MODEL.	
Scattering	1.0-1	1.4+7	GLS	Theo Jour	PM 46 795	Jul 55	Morrison+.THEOR.CFD FPW STRENGTH FNS	

Many

Quantity	Energy (ev) Min	Max	Lab	Type	Documentation Ref Vol Page	Date	Author, Comments	Data
Scattering	None		IBJ	Revw Jour	APP 15 249	56	Dabrowski. CFD PICKUP THEORY	
Scattering	-		UFT	Theo Jour	ZET 30 210	Jan 56	Inopin.SEMITRANSPARENT NONSPHRCL NCL	
				Jour	JET 3 134	Aug 56	TRANSLATN.*	
Scattering	-		CCP	Theo Jour	ZET 30 786	Apr 56	Drozdov.SCT OF FAST NS BY NONSPH NCL	
				Jour	ZET 28 734	55	-	
							SEE ALSO ZET 28 734,736 =JET 1 588,5	
	None			Jour	JET 1 588	54	. ENGL OF ZET 28 734	
Scattering	None		COL	Theo Jour	PR 106 105	Apr 57	Margolis+,A=90-240 SPHEROID POT,CRVS	
Scattering	+7	+9	UFT	Theo Jour	NP 9 412	Jan 59	Sitenko.DIFFRACT L.S POT.STRIPPED NS	
Scattering	+6		RIC	Theo Jour	NP 20 648	Nov 60	Tombrello+ A 2-BODY CLUSTER MODEL.	
Scattering	None		BET	Theo Abst	ANS 6 8	Jun 63	Gelbard.T MATRIX CLOSED FORM EXPRES.	
Scattering	None		ANL	Theo Conf	63Manchstr § 3.12	Sep 63	Moldauer.ABSORPTIVE POT SHAPE LOW ES	
Scattering	None		ANL	Theo Prog	WASH-1048 1	Jun 64	Monahan. POL OF SCATT NS AT AS 20DEG	
Scattering		+5	CCP	Theo Jour	AE 19 183	Aug 65	Ivanov+ RES SCT,MOLEC DOPPLER EFFECT	
		+6		Jour	JNE 20 708	Aug 66	TRANSLATN.*	
				Jour	EAF 19 2 115	Aug 65	TRANSLATN.*	
		+5		Jour	SJA 19 1077	Aug 65	TRANSLATN.*	
Scattering	Maxwl		CCP	Theo Jour	AE 19 428	Nov 65	Turchin.INTEGRATED VANHOFE-FORMULA	
				Jour	SJA 19 1387	65	. ENGL OF AE 19 428	
Scattering	Maxwl		CCP	Theo Jour	ZET 49 1504	Nov 65	Kagan+ CRYSTAL,DYNAMICAL THEORY	
				Jour	JET 22 1032	May 66	TRANSLATN.*	
Scattering	-		AUA	Comp Rept	AAEC/E-147	Mar 66	Pollard+ GYMEA=REACTOR DATA LIBRARY	
				Rept	AAEC/TM-343	Sep 66	.BIBLIOGRAPHY OF CODES	
				Rept	AAEC/E-150	Apr 66	.DESCRIPTION GYMEA PROGRAM	
				Rept	AAEC/E-119	Apr 64	.NUCLEAR DATA CARD LIBRARY	
				Rept	AAEC/E-114	Dec 63	.MULGA CODE,GROUP AVERAGE CALCULATN	
Scattering	None		NBS	Theo Conf	66Paris 1 339	Oct 66	Goldman. OPTMDL CALCULATIONS.	
Scattering	-		ITK	Theo Conf	67Kanpur § N7	Feb 67	Narasimham.OPTMODEL /SEPAR POTENTIAL	
Scattering	1.0+5	4.6+6	SAH	Theo Conf	67Kanpur § N8	Feb 67	Mukherjee.REGGE TYPE ANALYS SCAT AMP	
Scattering	1.0+5	1.0+7	TRM	Theo Conf	67Kanpur § N77	Feb 67	Garg.OPTMOD + STATMOD + H-F THEORY	
Scattering	5.0+7		KRK	Theo Rept	INP-534/PL	Mar 67	Czyz +LESNIAK DIFF TH HIGH EN,REHOVO	
Scattering	None		WIS	Theo Abst	DA/B 28 3437	Feb 68	Romo. UNIFIED THEOR BOUND+RES STATES	
Scattering	None		HEI	Theo Jour	NP/A 111 392	Apr 68	Dietrich+.S-MATRIX FROM SHELL MODEL	
Scattering	5.0+5	2.1+8	OSU	Theo Abst	DA/B 29 1802	Nov 68	Hogan. ELECTRMAG.SCAT.IN OPTMDL CALC	
Scattering	Pile		TRM	Revw Prog	BARC-423 7	69	Garg. REACTOR DATA REVW,DISCREPANCY	
Scattering	2.0+5	9.0+6	JAE	Comp Prog	EANDC(J)13L22	Aug 69	Igarasi+. TRANSMIS-COEF FOR A=20TO79	
Scattering	None		BNL	Eval Rept	BNL-400	Jun 70	Garber+.3RD EDITION ANGULAR DISTR.	
Scattering	1.4+7		BOS	Theo Conf	75Calcutta 2 34	Dec 75	Chatterjee+ OPTCL MODL PARAMETERS	
Scattering	None		GER	Theo Jour	ZP/A 279 4 349	Dec 76	Meyer+ S-WAVE RES, SQARE WELL POT	
Nonelastic	1.0+5	1.5+6	MIT	Theo Jour	PR 76 1550	Dec 49	Feshbach+ SIG VS R+E(NUCLEON IN NUC)	
Nonelastic	4.4+6		WES	Theo Rept	AECU-3387	55	Emmerich.CURVS SIG VS. R.6CALCULATN	
Nonelastic	1.0+6	4.0+6	LAS	Revw Conf	55Geneva 2 18	Aug 55	Walt. CURVE FOR 2 N-ES,DISCUSSION.	
Nonelastic	+6	+7	MIT	Revw Conf	55Geneva 2 23	Aug 55	Weisskopf+.P830,REVIEW OF THEORIES	
Nonelastic	Fiss		LAS	Theo Jour	JNE 4 147	Feb 57	Bethe+.SPHERE TRNSMISS THEORY,PART 4	
				Jour	JNE 4 3	Jan 57	- +.SPHERE TRNSMISS THEORY,PART 3	
				Jour	JNE 3 273	Nov 56	- +.SPHERE TRNSMISS THEORY,PART 2	
				Jour	JNE 3 207	Oct 56	- +.SPHERE TRNSMISS THEORY,PART 1	
Nonelastic	1.4+7		LRL	Theo Jour	PR 109 1295	Feb 58	Bjorklund+,OPTMDL FIT XPT CRV A1/3	
Nonelastic	4.1+6		LRL	Expt Jour	RMP 30 414	Apr 58	Fernbach.TH CURVE AND EXPTL PTS	
Nonelastic	3.5+6		JAE	Theo Rept	JAERI-1008	Jul 60	Harada+ COMPOUND-FORM SIG BY OPTMOD	
Nonelastic	-		MOS	Theo Jour	NP 40 117	Jan 63	Blokhintsev+. DIR REACT GRAPHS	
Nonelastic	None		KRK	Revw Jour	PF 15 385	Jul 64	REVIEW ON WORK IN KRAKOW,100REFS	
Nonelastic	1.5+7		LAS	Theo Prog	WASH-1056 40	Mar 65	Rosen.CRV S VS A1/3 CLCTD FROM OPTMD	
Nonelastic	1.3+7	1.5+7	BNL	Theo Jour	NSE 23 258	Nov 65	Pearlstein. STATISTICAL MODEL.	
Nonelastic	None		BNL	Eval Rept	BNL-400	Jun 70	Garber+.3RD EDITION.ANGULAR DISTR	
Nonelastic	-1	+5	BOL	Revw Conf	70Helsinki 2 379	Jun 70	Benzi.115. A BELOW 220, DATA STATUS	
Nonelastic	1.4+7		KOS	Theo Conf	73Kiev 3 71	May 73	Angeli+ SHORT. GRAPH OF SIG(A)-XPTAL	
				Conf	73Paris 2 35	Mar 73	Csikai.MODEL CALC VS A CFD EXPT,GRPH	
Nonelastic	1.4+7		TUD	Theo Conf	ZFK-271 63	Nov 73	Seeliger+ N-EMISSION VS A,TH CFD XPT	
				Jour	KE 16 252	Aug 73	Hermsdorf+ MODL CALC,SIG VS A GRAPH	
Nonelastic	8.0+6	3.5+7	ANL	Eval Rept	ANL-75-34	Jun 75	Davey+CORRC APPLIED TO N2N CS. TBLS	
Nonelastic	1.4+7		BOS	Theo Conf	76Ahmedabd 2 8	Dec 76	PAL+ OPTMOD.CALC SIG(A) CFD EXP.GRPH	
Absorption	None		OSA	Theo Jour	JPJO 18 157	36	Yukawa+.SIG FORM DERIVED	
Absorption	Maxwl		MTR	Eval Rept	IDO-16163	Apr 54	Evans.CONTOUR CURVS	
Absorption	2.5+6	4.3+6	CCP	Theo Jour	ZET 30 551	Mar 56	TH CFD PIC P714,CURVES	
				Jour	JET 3 484	Nov 56	TRANSLATN.*	

Many

Quantity	Energy (ev) Min	Max	Lab	Type	Documentation Ref Vol Page	Date	Author, Comments	Data
Absorption	Maxwl		SAC	Comp Rept	CEA – N – 238	Mar 57	Pontis.	
				Rept	CEA – N – 190	56	– .	
				Rept	CEA – N – 104	56	– .	
Absorption	–		HAR	Revw Rept	AERE – C/R – 2833	Jan 59	Cornish.CHEMICAL METHODS DISCUSSED	
Absorption	3.0+7	6.0+7	MIN	Theo Jour	NP 20 590	Nov 60	Kikuchi. SIG(DIRECT PROCESS REACT).	
Absorption	3.0+8	5.0+9	LON	Theo Jour	NP 23 681	Mar 61	Elton. SEMI – CLASSICAL FORMULA.	
Absorption	None		ANL	Theo Conf	63Manchstr § 3.12	Sep 63	Moldauer.ABSORPTIVE POT SHAPE.LOW ES	
Absorption	Maxwl		NRL	Eval Rept	NRL – 6124	May 64	Podgor+ REGULARITIES SHOWN.	
Absorption	1.0+5	2.5+7	FRK	Theo Jour	ZP 180 362	Sep 64	Meldner+GRPH ABS(E),TRANSCOEF,OPTMOD	
Absorption	Maxwl		CAI	Comp Rept	UARAEE – 12	65	OSAMA H. SALLAM+ COMPILED SIGMA TABL	
Absorption	Maxwl		JUL	Revw Rept	JUEL – 354 – RG	Dec 65	Stippel. FOR Z=89 TO 98	
Absorption	–		AUA	Comp Rept	AAEC/E – 147	Mar 66	Pollard= GYMEA=REACTOR DATA LIBRARY	
				Rept	AAEC/E – 164	Oct 66	.LUBRA – 4 – CODE,GROUP AVERAGE SIGMA	
				Rept	AAEC/TM – 343	Sep 66	.BIBLIOGRAPHY OF CODES	
				Rept	AAEC/E – 163	Sep 66	.GUNYA CODE,COMPILATION+CALCULATION	
				Rept	AAEC/TM – 250	May 64	.GUNYA CODE,GROUP+AVG SIGMA CALCULTN	
				Rept	AAEC/E – 114	Apr 64	.MULGA CODE,GROUP AVERAGE CALCULATN	
				Rept	AAEC/E – 119	Apr 64	.NUCLEAR DATA CARD LIBRARY	
				–			GYMEA PROGRAM DESCRIPTION SEE AAEC/E	
Absorption	1.0+5	2.5+7	FR	Expt Prog	EANDC(E)73	Jul 66	Lindner. ABS VS A (P – B) OPTMOD	
Absorption	1.0 – 1	2.5+7	FRK	Theo Rept	IKF – 17	Jul 66	Lindner. P – B CALC ABS4 FOR A=20TO240	
Absorption	2.0 – 1	5.0+5	BFR	Theo Jour	KE 11 292	Dec 68	Fritzsch.EFFECTIV – SIG,THIN 1/V SAMPL	
Absorption	Maxwl	+7	AUA	Theo Rept	AAEC/TM – 520	Nov 69	Ferguson. GUNYA+GYMEA,SIG – GENERATION	
Absorption	None		MUN	Theo Diss	GRYNTAKIS	Mar 76	Gryntakis.,CALC.OF WESTCOTTS G – FUNCT	
				Jour	RCA 22 128	Mar 75	– +,EQUIVALENT TO THESIS	
Res Int Abs		+5	ANL	Expt Jour	PR 79 11	Jul 50	Harris+ EPI – CD NS,BW SINGLE RES ANAL	
Res Int Abs	–		AUA	Theo Rept	AAEC/E – 126	Aug 64	Pollard. PEAS=CODE FOR EFFECT INTEGR	
Res Int Abs	–		JUL	Revw Rept	JUEL – 354 – RG	Dec 65	Stippel. FOR Z=89 TO 98	
Res Int Abs	None		AUA	Theo Jour	AUJ 20 253	Jun 67	Cook.INTFNCE+ASYM RES EFFECT ON XSCN	
Res Int Abs	5.5 – 1		MUN	Expt Diss	GRYNTAKIS	Mar 76	Gryntakis.ACT MEASUR.OF RES.INTEGRAL	
(n,γ)	–		PAR	Expt Jour	JPR 4 21	Jan 33	Curie+PROOF OF NEUTRON EXISTENCE	
(n,γ)	None		PAR	Expt Jour	CR 199 1404	Dec 34	WENLI YEH. ABOUT A SHELL STRUCTURE	
(n,γ)	Maxwl		PAR	Theo Jour	CR 200 1749	May 35	Perrin.	
	None			Jour	JPR 6 194	May 35	– +CAPTURE THEORY	
	Maxwl			Jour	CR 200 450	Feb 35	– +STUDY NG VERSUS Z,A	
(n,γ)	None		PTN	Theo Jour	PR 49 519	Apr 36	Breit+ TH OF DAMPING APPLIED.	
(n,γ)	None		HRV	Expt Jour	PR 51 592	Apr 37	Furry. THROUGH ACTIVATN AQUEOUS SOL.	
				Jour	PR 50 381	Aug 36	.SUPERSEDED	
(n,γ)	None		ROC	Theo Jour	PR 57 472	Mar 40	Weisskopf+ GENERAL FORMULA,A OVER 50	
(n,γ)	5.0 – 1	1.0+0	COR	Theo Jour	PR 57 1125	Jun 40	Bethe.GENERAL.CONTINUUM TH CPD NUCL.	
(n,γ)	Maxwl		ORL	Comp Rept	AECD – 2138	Feb 48	Way+ EARLY COMPILATION	
(n,γ)	+6		JHU	Theo Jour	PR 73 803	Apr 48	Alpher+ CREATION. ABUN/A.	
(n,γ)	Fiss		ANL	Expt Jour	PR 75 1781	Jun 49	Hughes+ SIG VS A,SMOOTH TO A=100	
(n,γ)	Fiss		ANL	Revw Jour	PR 78 632	Jun 50	Hughes+ SHELL EFFECT AT N=50,82,126	
(n,γ)	Fast		OXF	Revw Jour	NAT 175 1029	Jun 55	Beghian. REVIEWED BY ALLEN+EGELSTAF	
(n,γ)	None		BER	Theo Jour	PHY 22 1164	Nov 56	Beck.ABSTRACT.OPTMOD CFD(P,GAMMA)EXP	
(n,γ)	1.0+6		CCP	Theo Jour	ZET 32 1143	May 57	CFD XPT CURVES A30 – 90	
				Jour	JET 5 932	Dec 57	TRANSLATN.*	
(n,γ)	+6		NDA	Theo Rept	NDA – 2093 – 7	May 58	Kalos. STATISTICAL THEORY.	
(n,γ)	1.5+5	2.0+5	KUR	Expt Conf	58Geneva 15 50	Sep 58	Leipunskij+.PPR2219,N – CAPTURE	
(n,γ)	1.5+7		ALD	Expt Jour	PPS 72 505	Oct 58	Perkin+ ACT 30 NUCL,STAT MDL TOO LOW	
(n,γ)	1.0+8	2.0+8	MUU	Theo Jour	NP 9 140	Nov 58	Beck.COMPLEX SQ POT.MEDIUM NUCL.	
(n,γ)	None		LRL	Theo Rept	UCRL – 5419	Feb 59	Ashby+. CALCULATD Q – VALUES TABULATED	
(n,γ)	None		ANL	Theo Jour	PR 120 1305	Nov 60	Huizenga+ ISOMER RATIOS CFD G,N+EXPT	
(n,γ)	3.0+4		CAL	Theo Jour	AP 12 331	Mar 61	Clayton+ NEUTRON CAPTURE.	
(n,γ)	2.4+4	2.0+5	STR	Theo Jour	CR 254 1258	Feb 62	Timores+CFD EXPERIMENTAL RESULTS	
(n,γ)	1.0+3	1.0+6	CCP	Comp Jour	AE 14 185	Feb 63	Belanova+.SEARCH FOR SYSTEMATICS	
				Jour	JNE 18 225	Apr 64	– +. ENGLISH	
				Jour	EAF 14 2 5	64	– +. FRANCAIS	
				Jour	SJA 14 175	64	– +. ENGLISH	
(n,γ)	3.0+4		LEB	Expt Conf	JINR – 1845 100	Jun 64	Konks+ PB – SPECTR,SIG(A,ODDZ) – GRAPH	
(n,γ)	3.0+4		LEB	Expt Conf	JINR – 1845 104	Jun 64	Kapchigashev+ PB – SPECTR,SIG(A) – GRAPH	
(n,γ)	+3	+5	FEI	Theo Conf	64Paris 2 755	Jul 64	Zakharova+ MEAN RADIAT.WITH VS A	
(n,γ)	+3	+5	FEI	ExTh Conf	64Paris 2 757	Jul 64	Kazanski+ EVIDENCES FOR DIRECT CAPT.	
(n,γ)	None		KRK	Revw Jour	PF 15 385	Jul 64	REVIEW ON WORK IN KRAKOW, 100REFS	
(n,γ)		1.0+4	LEB	Theo Conf	64Paris 2 751	Jul 64	Fenin+ FOR EVEN – EVEN N.FROM SCAT.NDG	

Many

Quantity	Energy (ev) Min	Max	Lab	Type	Documentation Ref Vol Page	Date	Author, Comments	Data
(n,γ)	-		DUB	Theo	Jour ZET 47 777	Aug 64	RELATION BETWEEN SIG AND SCAT LENGTH	
					Jour JET 20 519	Feb 65	TRANSLATN.*	
(n,γ)	Maxwl		ANL	Comp	Jour NP 60 241	Nov 64	Bishop+EXP AND TH ISOMER RATIO 39NUC	
(n,γ)	2.5-2		BET	Theo	Abst ANS 7 242	Nov 64	Harris+ PROB OF LARGE NG SIG.	
(n,γ)	Maxwl	1.0+4	BNL	Revw	Jour AP 30 269	Nov 64	Garrison. NEG LEVEL CONTRIBUTION.	
(n,γ)	Maxwl		CAI	Comp	Rept UARAEE-12	65	OSAMA H. SALLAM+ COMPILED SIGMA TABL	
(n,γ)	5.0+3	1.0+5	ORL	Revw	Rept ORNL-P-1226	65	Macklin. 13REFS,SYSTEMATICS	
(n,γ)	1.0+3	1.0+5	CCP	Theo	Jour AE 18 114	Feb 65	Dovbenko+ STATIST MOD CURVE CFD DATA	
					Jour JNE 20 675	Aug 66	TRANSLATN.*	
					Jour EAF 18 2 44	Feb 65	TRANSLATN.*	
					Jour SJA 18 140	Feb 65	TRANSLATN.*	
(n,γ)	2.5+4		BOL	Theo	Jour JNAB 19 364	May 65	Benzi+. ODD-EVEN SYSTEMATICS	
(n,γ)	+6	+7	BOL	Theo	Jour NC 38 216	Jul 65	Benzi+ STATISTICAL MODEL,N=40 TO 90	
(n,γ)	-		AUA	Comp	Rept AAEC/E-147	Mar 66	Pollard+ GYMEA=REACTOR DATA LIBRARY	
					Rept AAEC/E-164	Oct 66	.LUBRA-0-CODE,SIGMA CALCULATION	
					Rept AAEC/TM-343	Sep 66	.BIBLIOGRAPHY OF CODES	
					Rept AAEC/E-163	Sep 66	.GUNYA CODE,COMPILATION+CALCULATION	
					Rept AAEC/TM-250	May 64	.GUNYA CODE,GROUP+AVG SIGMA CALCULTN	
					Rept AAEC/E-119	Apr 64	.NUCLEAR DATA CARD LIBRARY	
					Rept AAEC/E-114	Apr 64	.MULGA CODE,GROUP AVERAGE CALCULATN	
					-		GYMEA PROGRAM DESCRIPTION SEE AAEC/E	
(n,γ)	None		IIT	Theo	Conf 66Wash. 315	Mar 66	Klopp.PREDICTION OF THR+EPI-THR SIGS	
(n,γ)	1.4+7		SC	Comp	Rept SC-RR-66-229	Jun 66	Kenna+. SIG AND Q-VALUE TABULATED.	
(n,γ)	2.5+4		BHU	Expt	Conf 67Kanpur § N66	Feb 67	Tiwari.ACTIVATION.REL AU(NG)	
(n,γ)	Maxwl	+6	HUN	Comp	Jour MFF 15 3	Feb 67	Kiss.MANY REFERENCES,TABLES+CURVES	
(n,γ)	2.4+4		MUA	ExTh	Conf 67Kanpur § N107	Feb 67	Chaubey.ISOMER SIGMA RATIOS CFD CALC	
(n,γ)	+3		TRM	ExTh	Conf 67Kanpur § N74	Feb 67	Chandramoleswar.PB SPECTR.XPT CFD TH	
(n,γ)	None		UI	Eval	Rept COO-1546-5	Mar 67	Adler.COMPUTER PROG FOR MULTLVL ANAL	
(n,γ)	Maxwl		AUA	Theo	Rept AAEC/TM-391	Jun 67	Cook.TABLE,MONTECARLO METH,REFS GVN	
(n,γ)	2.0+6	1.5+7	LOK	Theo	Jour JNE 21 577	Jul 67	Grench.COMPNUC METHODS IN MEV RANGE	
(n,γ)	2.0+4		CCP	Theo	Jour AE 23 319	Oct 67	Zagrafov+.SUPERHEAVY ISOTOPS OF U,NP	
					Jour EAF 23 4 62	Oct 67	. FRENCH OF AE 23 319	
(n,γ)	+3	+6	GSF	Theo	Jour AF 36 509	Nov 67	Truran+.STAT FORMLS FAST N MULT CAPT	
(n,γ)	+0	+5	LAS	Revw	Jour AF 36 47	Nov 67	Brown+. BOMB.NDG.GRPH OF PETREL SPEC	
(n,γ)	Maxwl		CCP	Revw	Jour IZV 32 111	Jan 68	Demidov+ REVIEW ON WG SYSTEMATC,CRVS	
					Jour BAS 32 108	Jan 68	TRANSLATN.*NO 1	
(n,γ)	Maxwl		LEB	Theo	Conf 68Riga	Jan 68	Popov.ABST	
(n,γ)	Maxwl		AUA	Theo	Jour NSE 31 234	Feb 68	Cook+ STAT CALC 87NUCLIDES CFD EXPT	
(n,γ)	None		RPI	Theo	Jour NP/A 113 689	Jun 68	Sperber+.ISOM RATIOS 34NUCL CFD REFS	
					Conf 67Tokyo § 8.104	Sep 67	.NDG	
(n,γ)	None		IFU	Theo	Jour UFZ 13 1415	Sep 68	Kolomiets+CFD (N,N)+(N,N'G) CHANNELS	
					Jour UPJ 13 1011	Mar 69	TRANSLATN.*	
(n,γ)	Maxwl	+6	ANL	Theo	Abst BAP 13 1389	Nov 68	Poenitz. RATIOS OF OCCUPATN PROB,NDG	
(n,γ)	Maxwl		AUA	Theo	Jour JNE 22 657	Nov 68	MUSGROVE MEAN AND VAR OF SIG CALC.	
(n,γ)	+7		LEB	Theo	Jour IZV 32 2051	Dec 68	Popov. ON COLLECTIVE DOORWAY-STATE	
					Jour BAS 32 1885	Dec 69	. ENGL OF IZV 32 2051	
(n,γ)	2.4+4		MUA	Theo	Conf 68Bombay 2 82	Dec 68	Chaubey+ SIG(NEUT-NUMBER)GRPHS,S+P	
(n,γ)	1.0+2	1.0+5	TRM	Revw	Prog BARC-423 7	69	Garg. REACTOR DATA REVW,DISCREPANCY	
(n,γ)	1.0+7	2.0+7	BOL	Theo	Jour NP/A 127 503	Apr 69	Longo+ DIRECT+COLL.NEAR-MAGIC A=40UP	
(n,γ)	1.0+3	7.0+5	GA	Theo	Jour PL/B 29 393	Jun 69	Fricke+G STRENTH FN AS FN EXCIT E	
(n,γ)	Maxwl		ROS	Revw	Conf 69Studsvik 527	Aug 69	Gersch+ CAPT-REVW=CHANNL+POT+DOORWAY	
				Theo	Rept ZFK-187	Jul 69	- +CAPT MECHANISM INVESTIGATION	
					Jour FDP 17 313	69	GERSCH CHANNEL CAPT IN RES REGION	
(n,γ)	None		RPI	Theo	Jour PR 184 1201	Aug 69	Sperber.STATISTICAL CALC OF EXC FNCT	
(n,γ)	Maxwl	+7	AUA	Theo	Rept AAEC/TM-520	Nov 69	Ferguson. GUNYA+GYMEA,SIG-GENERATION	
(n,γ)	2.0+5		MUA	Theo	Conf 69Roorke 2 129	Dec 69	Chaubey+ BEST FIT TO SIG,D AND G-WID	
(n,γ)	+3	+5	AUA	Theo	Prog AAEC/PR-33P 10	70	Cook. RESONANCE STATISTICS, NO DATA	
(n,γ)	-		AUA	Theo	Prog AAEC/PR-33P 11	70	Bertram. ISOM SIG CALCULATION, NDG	
(n,γ)	2.0+4		MUA	ExTh	Prog BARC-474 44	70	Chaubey+ STAT CALC OKS EARLIER EXPT	
(n,γ)	-3	-1	CCP	Theo	Jour ZEP 11 235	Feb 70	Kagan. NEUTRON LIFETIME IN MATTER	
					Jour JEL 11 147	Feb 70	TRANSLATN.*	
(n,γ)	-1	+5	BOL	Revw	Conf 70Helsinki 2 379	Jun 70	Benzi.115. A BELOW 220, DATA STATUS	
(n,γ)	+3	+7	FEI	Revw	Conf 70Helsinki 2 245	Jun 70	Abramov.114. A BELOW 220,DATA STATUS	
(n,γ)	None		GLS	Expt	Prog INDC-6 11	Jun 70	Rae+ POSSIBLE FUTURE EXPERIMENTS,NDG	
(n,γ)	3.0+4		ORL	Comp	Prog ORNL-4513 33	Jun 70	Allen+,MAXWELLIAN AVGD SIGS,NDG,TBP	
(n,γ)	-		DUB	Theo	Jour YF 12 82	Jul 70	Gabrakov+ MAGNETIC DIPOL RESON,(N,G)	
					Jour SNP 12 44	Jan 71	. ENGL OF YF 12 82	

Many

Quantity	Energy (ev) Min	Max	Lab	Type	Documentation Ref Vol Page	Date	Author, Comments	Data
(n,γ)	Maxwl	+7	KFI	Comp Rept	KFKI – 70 – 18	Jul 70	Nagy+ MAP+TBL OF GAM HLS+INTENS,SIGS	
(n,γ)	+3	+5	AE	Expt Prog	EANDC(OR)99 14	Aug 70	Beshai+. VDG.MODIF M – R DET.IN PREPTN	
(n,γ)	None		LRL	Comp Rept	UCRL – 50400 9	Sep 70	Howerton.TABULATION OF THRESHOLDS	
(n,γ)	None		SAH	Theo Prog	INIS – MF – 292	71	Mukherjee+ PG127.BRIEF,CALC SIG,NDG	
(n,γ)	None		AUA	Theo Prog	INDC(SEC) – 18	Aug 71	Cook.PG10.NEW MULTILVL – TH,SHORT NOTE	
(n,γ)	1.3+5		MUA	Theo Prog	BARC – 553 19	Aug 71	Alam+ RATIO D/G – WID,STATMOD,ABST,NDG	
				Conf	70Madurai 2 34	Dec 70	. SAME ABSTRACT ONLY	
(n,γ)	+7		CCP	Theo Conf	72Kiev	Jan 72	Dovbenko+ ABST	
(n,γ)	–		OSA	Theo Jour	PTP 47 1428	Apr 72	Matsuoka+.(N – Z) DEPENDENCE OF SIG	
(n,γ)	2.5 – 2		UJV	Theo Jour	PL/B 38 499	Apr 72	Honzatko+ INTERFERENCE IN POLRZ EXPT	
(n,γ)	1.4+7		NJS	Revw Conf	72Budapest 252	Aug 72	Cvelbar+ A – DEPENDENCE,EXPTS CFD,GRPH	
(n,γ)	Pile		ROS	ExTh Prog	ZFK – 243 93	Sep 72	Mohsen+ NG – SYSTEMAT. FOR RARE EARTHS	
				Theo Prog	ZFK – 243 151	Sep 72	– + INPUT – CHAN ANAL,EVEN – NUCLEI	
				Prog	ZFK – 243 148	Sep 72	– + INPUT – CHAN ANAL,A = 165 – 187	
(n,γ)	1.0+6	1.4+7	DEB	Comp Rept	IAEA – 153 155	73	Csikai+ EXPTL DATA COMPARED ,GRPH	
				Jour	REA 7 4 93	Dec 69	– +SIG(N,Z),1+3+14MEV,ACTIV – ANAL	
(n,γ)	None		LRL	Theo Abst	BAP 18 625	Apr 73	Gardner+. MODEL CALCULATIONS.NO DATA	
(n,γ)		1.1+7	RCN	Theo Rept	RCN – 191	Jun 73	Lautenbach.FISPROD GROUP CONST TBL	
(n,γ)	2.5 – 2	1.5+7	LRL	Comp Jour	ND/A 11 621	Jul 73	Alley+. MANY CURVES	
	+6	+7		Rept	UCRL – 50484	Aug 72	– +. EXTENSIVE COMPILATION.CURVES	
(n,γ)	None		WAU	Revw Conf	73Rochestr 1 251	Aug 73	Vandenbosh.SIG ISOM/GND SYSEMATICS	
(n,γ)	+3	+6	AML	Theo Jour	ZP 265 55	Oct 73	Barrett.OPTMOD – CALC FOR A = 40 – 70	
(n,γ)	1.0+5	4.0+6	HED	Theo Rept	HEDL – TME – 73 – 19	Nov 73	Schmittroth. STATISTICAL CALC.CURVS.	
(n,γ)	None		HAR	Theo Jour	PL/B 50 204	May 74	Lane. VALENCE MOD,CORR WITH E1 DECAY	
	0.0+0	1.0+0		Jour	PL/B 31 344	Mar 70	– .NOW – STATIST.EFF.IN RES CAPT.	
	Maxwl	+5		Revw Conf	69Studsvik 513	Aug 69	– . REVIEW OF CAPTURE THEORY	
	+0	+3		Theo Jour	NP 17 563	Jul 60	– +DIRECT+RES CAPT,MAY INTERFERE.	
	+6	+7		Jour	NP 11 646	Jun 59	– +CONTRIBUTION OF DIRECT CAPTURE	
	+0	+3		Rept	AERE – R – 2891	May 59	.SEE ALSO *	
(n,γ)	1.4+7	1.5+7	LND	Revw Jour	NKA 19 411	May 74	Bergqvist.ERRORS OF METHODS CFD,GRPH	
(n,γ)	None		DEB	Theo Jour	PL/B 50 316	Jun 74	Gyarmati+ E1 STRENGTH DECOUPL FR GDR	
(n,γ)	1.4+7	1.5+7	LND	ExTh Conf	74Petten 199	Sep 74	Bergqvist+SYSTEMATICS 14 – 15 MEV DATA	+
(n,γ)		+6	HAR	Theo Rept	AERE – R – 7468	Nov 74	Lynn.SYSTEMATICS N REACTION ACTINDES	
(n,γ)	Maxwl		RCN	Expt Prog	INDC(SEC) – 43	Dec 74	Kopecky+ CORREL TO (D,P) VS A,GRAPHS	
	– 3	+3		Eval Conf	73Munich 1 523	Aug 73	– + CORREL TO (D,P),A = 24 – 80,GRF	
(n,γ)	Maxwl		AUA	Comp Prog	AAEC/PR – 41P 38	75	Allen+ KT = 30KEV AVG.GRPHS ODD+EVEN Z	
(n,γ)	None		JAE	Theo Jour	NST 12 67	Feb 75	Igarasi.SIG CAL METHOD C COMPETITIO	
(n,γ)	1.4+7		JUL	Revw Conf	75Wash. 664	Mar 75	Qaim. GRAPH SYSTEMATICS	
(n,γ)	1.0 – 3	1.5+7	RCN	Eval Rept	RCN – 239 11	Nov 75	Gruppelaar. SUPERSEDED.	
		1.1+7		Theo Rept	RCN – 192	Jun 73	Dragt+ FISPROD ERROR ANALYSIS	
(n,γ)	None		KFK	Theo Prog	KFK – 2223 64	Dec 75	Dickmann. 2 – CENTRE OSCILL MOD CALC	
(n,γ)	Maxwl		MUN	ExTh Diss	GRYNTAKIS	Mar 76	Gryntakis.,ACT.MEAS.,CALC OF G – FUNCT	
	None				RCA 22 128	Mar 75	– +,CALC WESTCOTTS G – FUNCTION	
(n,γ)	2.5 – 2	5.0+2	LIE	Theo Jour	NP/A 263 61	May 76	Cugnon.SYSTEMATICS OF VALENCE CAPT.	
(n,γ)	Fast		WIN	Expt Prog	NEANDC(E)172 8	Aug 76	Taylor.ACTIVATION AVERAGE FAST REACT	
(n,γ)	+3	1.0+7	CAL	Theo Abst	DA/B 37 1310	Sep 76	Holmes.GLOBL STATMDL CALC.NE THRU BI	
(n,γ)	Fast		RCN	Expt Rept	ECN – 10	Oct 76	Veenema+ STEK REACTIVITY WORTHS TBL.	
(n,γ)	1.0 – 3	1.0+7	RCN	Revw Rept	ECN – 12	Nov 76	Gruppelaar+ INTERCOMP. F.P.EVAL.	
(n,γ)	None		DUB	Theo Rept	JINR – P4 – 10953	77	Baznat+ INTEG E1 – RES SIGS,CFD XP.FIG	
Res Int Capt	–		AUA	Theo Rept	AAEC/E – 163	Sep 66	Cook. RESON PARS FIT TO EXPTL VALUE	
				Rept	AAEC/TM – 343	Sep 66	.BIBLIOGRAPHY OF CODES	
				Rept	AAEC/E – 147	Mar 66	.GUNYA+GYMEA CODE,SEE AAEC/E – 150	
Res Int Capt	–		AUA	Theo Rept	AAEC/E – 164	Oct 66	Kletzmayr. CALC OF INF DILUTE INTEGR	
				Rept	AAEC/TM – 343	Sep 66	.BIBLIOGRAPHY OF CODES	
Res Int Capt	+0	+2	AUA	Theo Jour	AUJ 20 253	Jun 67	Cook+ TBL RES ASYMMETRY PARAMETERS	
Spect (n,γ)	Pile		ANL	Expt Jour	PR 79 277	Jul 50	Muehlhause. GAMMAS/CAPT VS Z,A.	
Spect (n,γ)	None		ORL	Theo Jour	PR 83 683	Aug 51	Biedenharn+ POLRZ OF GS FOR POLR2 NS	
Spect (n,γ)	Pile		KRK	Revw Jour	PF 4 298	Jul 53	STRZALKOWSKI REV EXPTL METHODS GAMMA	
Spect (n,γ)	Maxwl		CRC	Expt Jour	CJP 31 1025	Nov 53	Kinsey+ PAIR SPECT.ODD Z.	
				Jour	CJP 31 1051	Nov 53	.SEE ALSO	
				Jour	PR 89 375	Jan 53	.SEE ALSO	
				Jour	CJP 31 49	53	.SEE ALSO	
				Jour	PR 85 1012	Mar 52	.SEE ALSO	
				Jour	PR 83 519	Aug 51	.SEE ALSO	
				Jour	PR 82 380	May 51	.SEE ALSO	
				Jour	PR 79 218	Jul 50	.SEE ALSO	
				Jour	PR 78 481	May 50	.SEE ALSO	

Many

Quantity	Energy (ev) Min	Max	Lab	Type	Documentation Ref Vol Page	Date	Author, Comments	Data
Spect (n,γ)	Maxwl		CCP	ExTh Jour	AE 3 91	Aug 57	Groshev+.ODD-ODD NUCLIDES,A BELOW 61	
Spect (n,γ)	2.0+8		MUU	Theo Jour	NP 9 140	Nov 58	Beck.COMPLEX SQ POT.MEDIUM NUCL.	
Spect (n,γ)	Maxwl		CCP	ExTh Jour	ZET 38 588	Feb 60	Groshev.THEORIES AND REVIEW OF XPTS	
				Jour	JET 11 20 430	Aug 60	TRANSLATN.*	
Spect (n,γ)	Maxwl		CCP	ExTh Jour	ZET 38 598	Feb 60	Groshev.THEORIES AND REVIEW OF XPTS	
				Jour	JET 11 20 430	Aug 60	TRANSLATN.*	
Spect (n,γ)	Maxwl		CCP	Theo Jour	NP 16 657	Jun 60	Strutinski+ CONTINUOUS SPECTRA CALC.	
Spect (n,γ)	Maxwl		CCP	ExTh Jour	NP 16 645	Jun 60	Groshev+EXPT SPECTRA CFD THEORY	
Spect (n,γ)	+0	+3	HAR	Theo Jour	NP 17 586	Jul 60	Lane+.DIRECT+RES CAPTURE CFD DATA	
Spect (n,γ)	Maxwl		ORL	Comp Rept	ORNL-2904	Jan 61	Troubetzkoy+ TBLS+CURVS MANY ELEMENT	
Spect (n,γ)	Maxwl		CRC	Revw Jour	ARN 11 259	Oct 61	Bartholomew.	
Spect (n,γ)	–		FOA	Theo Jour	NP 53 397	Apr 64	Starfelt.MI GIANT RES AT 2ND STF PK	
Spect (n,γ)	–		ISP	Comp Rept	EUR-2408E	65	Girardi+.IDENTIFCTN CHART F ACT ANAL	
Spect (n,γ)	None		NRD	Comp Rept	USNRDL-TR-888	Aug 65	Crocker+ GAMMAS FROM ACTIVATION.	
Spect (n,γ)	Maxwl		IIT	Comp Rept	IITRI-1193-53	Oct 65	Greenwood+ EXTENSIVE TBLS+CRVS.	
Spect (n,γ)	Maxwl		GA	Expt Rept	GA-6209	Dec 65	Yule.GAM-RAY THR NEUT INDUCED ACTIVT	
Spect (n,γ)	Maxwl		CRC	Comp Jour	ND/A 3 367	Dec 67	Bartholomew+,UP TO Z=46	
Spect (n,γ)	None		ITE	Expt Conf	68Riga	Jan 68	Beljaev+ ABST,A FROM 100 TO 130	
Spect (n,γ)	None		ROS	Revw Rept	ZFK-136	Jan 68	Gersch.CFD DIRECT+COMPOUND CONTRIBUT	
				Rept	ANL-TRANS-811	Mar 70	. ENGLISH OF ZFK-136	
Spect (n,γ)	+3		AUA	Expt Rept	AAEC/TM-462	Jul 68	Allen. KEV CAPTURE,DESCRIPTN OF EXPT	
Spect (n,γ)	None		ORL	Theo Jour	NSE 36 220	May 69	Yost+ CALC BY GAMMA CASCADE MODEL	
				Jour	NSE 32 62	Apr 68	– . CALCULATION METHOD.	
				Rept	ORNL-TM-1867	Jun 67	– . CALCULATN METHOD LIGHT NUCLEI	
Spect (n,γ)	Maxwl	+3	BNL	Revw Conf	69Studsvik 627	Aug 69	Chrien. REVIEW,'RES-N-CAPT GAM-RAYS'	
Spect (n,γ)	Maxwl	+5	CRC	Revw Conf	69Studsvik 553	Aug 69	Bartholomew. ON '5.5MEV GAM ANOMALY'	
Spect (n,γ)	Pile		MUN	Revw Conf	69Studsvik 127	Aug 69	Egidy.CONV-ELECTR-SPECTROMTRS,REVIEW	
Spect (n,γ)	Maxwl		MUN	Theo Conf	69Studsvik 541	Aug 69	Egidy. STATMOD CALC OF GAMMA-SPEC	
Spect (n,γ)	Maxwl		IID	Revw Conf	69Roorke 2 109	Dec 69	Tripathi. HIGH RESOLUTION EXPTS, NDG	
Spect (n,γ)	+3	+5	AUA	Expt Prog	AAEC/PR-33P 8	70	Bird+ AVERAGE GAMMA VS RES-PARS, NDG	
Spect (n,γ)	Maxwl		AUA	Expt Prog	AAEC/PR-33P 8	70	Hille. ANGULAR CORRELATION EXP3§ ED7	
Spect (n,γ)	–		AUA	Theo Prog	AAEC/PR-33P 11	70	Bertram. GAM SPEC CALCULATED,NO DATA	
Spect (n,γ)	1.0+6	5.0+7	WWA	Revw Jour	PF 21 97	Jan 70	Brzosko.G SPEC FROM N CAPT IN NUCLEI	
Spect (n,γ)	Maxwl		MRY	Comp Jour	NIM 80 149	Mar 70	Duffey. CAPTURE GAM ANALYSIS TABLES.	
Spect (n,γ)	Maxwl	+7	KFI	Comp Rept	KFKI-70-18	Jul 70	Nagy+ MAP+TBL OF GAM HLS+INTENS,SIGS	
Spect (n,γ)	Maxwl		WAL	Eval Rept	WANL-TME-2713	Jul 70	Fody.CAPT YLD TABLES FOR 26 ELEMENTS	
Spect (n,γ)	+3	+6	AUA	Revw Rept	AAEC/TM-565	Sep 70	Allen.EXPTS AND TECHNIQUES REVWD.TBL	
				–			FULL TEXT OF PAPER AT 70CHICAGO (APS	
Spect (n,γ)	Maxwl		MRY	Comp Jour	NIM 93 425	Jan 71	Senftle+ TABLEFOR ELEMENTAL ANALYSIS	
Spect (n,γ)	Maxwl		GA	Expt Conf	71Knoxvill 816	Mar 71	Orphan+.CONTINUUM GAM YLDS 75ELEMNTS	
Spect (n,γ)	Maxwl		ANL	Theo Jour	PR/C 3 2071	May 71	Bollinger. STATISTICAL THEORY	
				Conf	68DUBSY 317	Jul 68	– .ANAL.RAD. TRANSITIONS.	
Spect (n,γ)	Maxwl		RCN	Expt Prog	INDC(NED)-2G	May 71	Reddingius+ GAMMA-SPECS,N+NUCL POLZD	
Spect (n,γ)	Maxwl		ROS	Revw Jour	ZFK-231	Mar 72	Rudolph.ANAL OF N-CAPT FOR A=20-65	
Spect (n,γ)	Pile		IEA	Expt Prog	IEA-INF-22 3	Aug 72	Goldemberg.E SPECT,RARE EARTHS,TBD	
Spect (n,γ)	5.0+3	3.0+5	AUA	Comp Jour	ND/A 11 433	May 73	Bird+. EXTENSIVE COMPILATION	
				Prog	AAEC/PR33 8	70	.SUPERSEDED	
Spect (n,γ)	None		JUL	Comp Rept	JUEL-1003	Sep 73	Erdtmann+ G-RAY ENERGIES	
Spect (n,γ)	None		INL	Eval Prog	USNDC-11 3	Jun 74	Heath. NG SPECT LIBRARY 300 NUCLDS	
Spect (n,γ)	None		JUL	Comp Rept	JUEL-1087	Jul 74	Meixner. G-RAY ENERGIES	
				Rept	JUEL-812-RX	Dec 71	– .G-ES,REL INT,HL,SAT ACTIVITY	
Spect (n,γ)	None		BNL	Revw Conf	74Petten 53	Sep 74	Mughabghab+NON STAT. EFFECTS	
Spect (n,γ)	2.4+4		BNL	Expt Conf	AERE-R-8082	Jul 75	Rimawi+ ABSTR,G-RAY FROM P-WAVE N	
Spect (n,γ)	Pile		KIG	Comp Rept	GKSS-77/E/47	77	Greim+ G-DETECTION LIMITS N-ACT ANAL	
Spect (n,γ)	1.4+7		KIG	Comp Rept	GKSS-77/E/50	77	Fanger+ DATA FOR ACT ANAL MN-MODULES	
Inelastic γ	–		MAN	Theo Jour	NP 18 353	Sep 60	Goldfarb+. DIRECT REACTION THEORY	
Inelastic γ	+8		OXF	Theo Jour	NP 27 431	Oct 61	Clegg+CALC NUCL-GAM CORR+SPIN INTERC	
Inelastic γ	1.0+5	1.5+7	LRL	Comp Rept	UCRL-14007 1	Aug 65	Chazan.TABULATED FROM MANY REFERENCS	
Inelastic γ	+3	+6	ETH	Theo Jour	RMP 38 143	Jan 66	.THEOR CALC OF GAM-RAY ANGL DISTR	
Inelastic γ	–		AUA	Theo Prog	AAEC/PR-33P 11	70	Bertram. GAMMAS AND SIGMA CALC, NDG	
Inelastic γ	3.0+6		KOS	Expt Prog	INDC(HUN)-1G	Apr 70	.PROG REPORT. EXPT GAM E+YIELD TBD	
Inelastic γ	+6	+8	KFI	Comp Rept	KFKI-70-18	Jul 70	Nagy+ MAP+TBL OF GAM HLS+INTENS,SIGS	
Inelastic γ	+7		IBJ	Theo Prog	INR-1318 14	Apr 71	Decowski+ PARTICLE+G EMISSN,NDG,TBL	
Nonelastic γ	–		OXF	Theo Jour	PPSA 68 1037	Nov 55	Satchler.ANGDIST DIRECT VS COMPMODEL	
Nonelastic γ	5.0+6	1.5+7	LRL	Theo Jour	NSE 32 178	May 68	Howerton+ CFD EXPTS AVG DEVIAT 18PC	
				Rept	UCRL-50185	Jan 67	.SUPERSEDED	
Nonelastic γ		2.0+7	LRL	Theo Abst	BAP 18 625	Apr 72	Gardner+ SIG+SPEC. NO DATA GIVEN.	

Many

Quantity	Energy (ev) Min	Max	Lab	Type	Documentation Ref Vol Page	Date	Author, Comments	Data
Nonelastic γ	1.4+7		LRL	Expt Prog	USNDC-7 114	Jun 73	Multhauf+. TO BE DONE. GE(LI)+NAI.	
(n,2n)	None		ROC	Theo Jour	PR 57 472	Mar 40	Weisskopf+ GENERAL FORMULA,A OVER 50	
(n,2n)	None		JHU	Theo Jour	NP 5 669	Mar 58	Berlin+. PHASE SPACE DISTR FORMULAS	
(n,2n)	1.4+7		CIS	Expt Jour	NC 16 1109	Jun 60	Facchini+STAT.TH CFD OK DATA Z=10-40	
(n,2n)	1.5+7		MUA	Expt Jour	NP 28 560	Dec 61	Khurana+VALUES CFD STATiSTICJ3 - MFDN3	
	1.4+7			ExTh Conf	61Bombay 21	Feb 61	- +.GRAPH,SIGMA REL MASS	
(n,2n)	None		VNS	Theo Jour	JPR 23 78	Feb 62	Xuan Chuan+ DISTR FUNCT,3 - PART EMISS	
(n,2n)	Thrsh	Up	RED	Theo Rept	NP- 11667	Apr 62	Alford.DERIVAT.OF APPROX EXPRESS XS	
	1.4+7	1.5+7	HAM	Comp Rept	EUR - 122E	63	Neuert+	
(n,2n)	1.4+7		TNC	Comp Rept	EANDC(US) - 58	Jun 63	Mathur+ SIG,Q VALUE,PRODCT H - L+DECAY	
	1.4+7		HAM	Theo Jour	NP 65 257	Mar 65	Bormann.COMPILED XSECTS CFD SHELLMOD	
	1.4+7		NAP	Theo Conf	65Antwerp 544	Jun 65	Cuzzocrea+SHELL EFFECT STUDY	
				Rept	INFN/BE - 65 - 3	Apr 65	- + SHELL EFFECT	
(n,2n)	1.4+7		IRK	Theo Conf	65Antwerp 545	Jul 65	Hille+ PPR117.ABST.(N - Z)SYSTEMATICS	
				Jour	APA 23 37	May 66	Breunlich+ EXPT/TH+(N - Z)SYSTEMATICS	
	1.4+7	1.5+7		Jour	OAWS 174 11	65	Hille+ XPT/TH COMPARISONS.	
(n,2n)	Fiss		BNL	Theo Jour	NSE 23 238	Nov 65	Pearlstein+ STATISTICAL MODEL.	
				Rept	BNL - 11505	66	- + FISS SPEC AVG TBP ND.	
(n,2n)	1.3+7	1.5+7	BNL	Theo Jour	NSE 23 238	Nov 65	Pearlstein.3ES.STAT MDL CALC.TBL CS.	
(n,2n)	-		DEB	ExTh Jour	PL 20 52	Jan 66	Csikai+ AT EN=THRESH+3MEV,SYSTEMATCS	
(n,2n)		2.0+7	HAM	Comp Jour	ND/A 1 103	Feb 66	Jessen+ GRAPHS XCIT CURVS,XPTS TO665	
(n,2n)	-		AUA	Comp Rept	AAEC/E - 147	Mar 66	Pollard+ GYMEA=REACTOR DATA LIBRARY	
				Rept	AAEC/TM - 343	Sep 66	.BIBLIOGRAPHY OF CODES	
				Rept	AAEC/E - 163	Sep 66	.GUNYA CODE,COMPILATION+CALCULATION	
				Rept	AAEC/E - 150	Apr 66	.DESCRIPTION GYMEA PROGRAM	
				Rept	AAEC/TM - 250	May 64	.GUNYA CODE FOR SIGMA COMPILATION	
				Rept	AAEC/E - 119	Apr 64	.NUCLEAR DATA CARD LIBRARY	
				Rept	AAEC/E - 114	Dec 63	.MULGA CODE,GROUP AVERAGE CALCULATN	
(n,2n)	None		IIT	Theo Conf	66Wash. 315	Mar 66	Klopp.STAT MDL+FERMI LVL DENS,CFDXPT	
(n,2n)	1.5+7		LRL	Theo Conf	66Wash. 713	Mar 66	Gardner.STATISTICAL MODEL CALCS	
(n,2n)	1.4+7		SC	Comp Rept	SC - RR - 66 - 229	Jun 66	Kenna+. SIG AND Q - VALUE TABULATED.	
(n,2n)	+7		BOS	Expt Conf	67Kanpur § N69	Feb 67	Chatterjee.ABSOL MEAS.CFD THEORY	
(n,2n)	Thrsh	2.0+7	GEL	Comp Rept	EUR - 119E VOL.2	Apr 67	Liskien+PAULSEN.ALL DATA EXCIT FUNCT	
				ExTh Rept	EUR - 2456E	Jul 65	- + XCT FNS NEAR Z=28.EXP+ST TH	
(n,2n)	+6	2.0+7	WWA	Revw Rept	INR - 830/I/PL	Dec 67	Turkiewicz. ERICSON FLUCT EXCIT	
	1.0+6	2.0+7		Rept	INR - 776/I/PL	Mar 67	Wilhelmi. EXPTS,SIGS,ISOM,SPECS	
(n,2n)	None		FEI	Theo Conf	68Riga	Jan 68	Shubin.ABST,E DIST OF NEUTRONS	
	1.4+7			Rept	FEI - 93	Jul 67	- .N - SPEC CALC FROM STAT TH	
(n,2n)	+7		SAH	Theo Conf	68Bombay 2 105	Dec 68	Chatterjee+ SIGMA SYSTEMATIC,GRAPHS	
(n,2n)	1.4+7	1.5+7	IRK	Comp Jour	OAWS 177 467	69	Hille.	
	1.4+7			Revw Jour	NP/A 107 49	Jan 68	- .(N - Z)/A DEPENDANCE OBSERVED.	
(n,2n)	3.0+6	7.0+6	SAH	Theo Prog	BARC - 401 21	69	Chatterjee+ SIG(NEUT - EXCESS) CFD XPT	
(n,2n)	None		RPI	Theo Abst	BAP 14 54	Jan 69	Liggett+ CALCULATN OF ISOMER RATIOS	
(n,2n)	3.0+6	7.0+6	SAH	Comp Jour	NP/A 125 593	Feb 69	Chatterjee+ 3 TRENDS DISCUSSED.	
(n,2n)	+5	+6	AUA	Theo Prog	AAEC/PR - 31P 9	Apr 69	Bertram. STATMOD,H - F TH,TB CONTINU54	
(n,2n)	Maxwl	+7	AUA	Theo Rept	AAEC/TM - 520	Nov 69	Ferguson. GUNYA+GYMEA,SIG - GENERATION	
(n,2n)	1.5+7		DEB	Comp Jour	REA 7 4 93	Dec 69	Csikai+ SIG+HL COMP FOR N - ACTIV - ANAL	
(n,2n)	+7		KFI	Comp Jour	AHP 26 335	Dec 69	Adam+ EXPTL SIG CFD FN((N - Z)/A),GRPH	
				Rept	KFKI - 71 - 8	Feb 71	Jeki. FITTED FORMULA TO EXPTL SIGS	
				-			=KFI 16 NO5 PAGE 331 0/68 IN HUNGAR	
(n,2n)	None		TEX	Theo Rept	ORO - 3992 - 47	70	Recami+. CALC OF AMPLITUDES,HEAVY NU	
(n,2n)	None		SAH	Theo Jour	NP/A 143 277	Mar 70	Chatterjee.FREE FERMIGS;6MEV RESDEXC	
	+5	+7		Prog	BARC - 474 27	70	- + RGM = RENORM.F - GAS MODEL	
	+6	+7		Conf	69Roorke 2 209	Dec 69	- . SIG(N,Z) AT 6MEV EXCIT - E	
(n,2n)	-1	+5	BOL	Revw Conf	70Helsinki 2 379	Jun 70	Benzi.115. A BELOW 220, DATA STATUS	
(n,2n)	+5	+6	KFK	Revw Conf	70Helsinki 2 219	Jun 70	Cierjacks.113. SIG(N - Z),6.MEV EXC - E	
(n,2n)	Maxwl	+7	KFI	Comp Rept	KFKI - 70 - 18	Jul 70	Nagy+ MAP+TBL OF GAM HLS+INTENS,SIGS	
(n,2n)	1.4+7		TUP	Theo Jour	NP/A 152 387	Aug 70	Guidetti+ THEOR CFD EXPT MEDIUM A	
(n,2n)	None		LRL	Comp Rept	UCRL - 50400 9	Sep 70	Howerton.TABULATION OF THRESHOLDS	
				Rept	UCRL - 14000	May 64	.SUPERSEDED	
(n,2n)	None		SAH	Theo Prog	INIS - MF - 292	71	Mukherjee+ PG127.BRIEF,CALC SIG,NDG	
(n,2n)	+7		IBJ	Theo Prog	INR - 1318 14	Apr 71	Decowski+ PARTICLE+G EMISSN,NDG,TBL	
(n,2n)	1.4+7		GIT	Expt Abst	DA/B 31 6488	May 71	LU. MIXD POWDR.EMP.FIT AS FN Z,A.	
(n,2n)	1.0+7	2.0+7	KGU	Theo Conf	72Kiev 2 18	Jan 72	Ezhov+ ABST,NDG.INVESTIG OF N - SPECS	
	1.5+7		MUA	ExTh Prog	INDC(SEC) - 28	Sep 72	Gupta+. SHELL EFFECTS IN SIG ,NDG	
				Theo Prog	BARC - 614 37	72	. SIG - XPT/SIG - CALC VS Z,44 ISOT.NDG	
(n,2n)		2.0+7	BNL	Theo Jour	JNE 27 81	Feb 73	Pearlstein.STATMOD CALN.FISS - SP AV	

Many

Quantity	Energy (ev) Min	Max	Lab	Type	Documentation Ref Vol Page	Date	Author, Comments	Data
(n,2n)	1.5+7		DEB	Eval Jour	REA 11 1	Mar 73	Boedy+ SIG FOR ELEMENTS,GRAPH EXPTS	
				Conf	73Paris 2 38	Mar 73	Csikai.SAME GRAPHS AS REA 11 1	
	1.4+7			Comp Rept	IAEA-153 155	73	- + EXPTL DATA COMPARED ,GRPH	
(n,2n)	+7		KFK	Expt Rept	KFK-1783 87	Apr 73	Muenzel+ MAX-SIG AS FN OF Z	
(n,2n)	2.5-2	1.5+7	LRL	Comp Jour	ND/A 11 621	Jul 73	Alley+. MANY CURVES	
	+6	+7		Rept	UCRL-50484	Aug 72	- +. EXTENSIVE COMPILATION.CURVES	
(n,2n)	1.5+7		TAT	Theo Conf	73Bangalor 2 216	Dec 73	Kondaiah+SIG USING PEARLSTEIN EQUATN	
(n,2n)	1.4+7	1.5+7	RBZ	Revw Jour	ASL 25 158	75	Cindro. REVW OF SYSTMATCS,FOR STRUCT	
(n,2n)	1.4+7		RBZ	Theo Jour	PL/B 56 143	Apr 75	Holub+ NONSTATIST PREEGUIL EFFECT	
	1.5+7			Revw Jour	ASL 25 180	75	- . SIG(N-Z,EXC-E),GRAPH	
(n,2n)	8.0+6	3.5+7	ANL	Eval Rept	ANL-75-34	Jun 75	Davey+CONSTANT T MDL,LVL DEN MDL FIT	
(n,2n)	1.4+7		KUK	Theo Jour	JPJ 39 1147	Nov 75	Mohindra+.SHELL EFFECT ON SIG. FIGS	
				Theo Conf	74Bombay 2 112	Dec 74	Wadhwa+ SHELL EFFECT SYSTEMATICS	
(n,2n)	+7		BRC	Revw Jour	PL/B 60 442	Feb 76	Cindro+ XPTS REFUTE CSIKAI-SYSTEMATI	
(n,2n)	Fast		WIN	Expt Prog	NEANDC(E)172 8	Aug 76	Taylor.ACTIVATION AVERAGE FAST REACT	
(n,2n)	1.4+7	1.5+7	PAT	Revw Jour	CS 45 785	Nov 76	Garg+ POST 1974DATA,SIG VS A,Z.GRPHS	
				Conf	72Chandigr 2 123	Dec 72	- +EMPIRICAL BEHAVIOUR OF SIG VS	
(n,2n)	1.5+7		BOS	Eval Conf	76Ahmedabd 2 12	Dec 76	Nath+ CORREL((N-Z)/A,THR-E,SIG).GRPH	
(n,2n)	1.5+7		IBJ	Theo Jour	ASL 27 186	77	Rurarz+ A=107-143,ISO RATIO CFD EXPT	
(n,2n)	1.4+7		KIG	Comp Rept	GKSS-77/E/50	77	Fanger+ DATA FOR ACT ANAL MN-MO4ULES	
(n,xn) x>2	0.0+0	1.0+0	AUA	Comp Rept	AAEC/E-119	Apr 64	Doherty.(N,3N)SIGS,CARD LIBRARY	
				Rept	AAEC/E-114	Dec 63	. (N,3N).MULGA CODE,AVG GROUP SIGMA	
(n,xn) x>2	Fiss		BNL	Theo Jour	NSE 23 238	Nov 65	Pearlstein.SPEC MATMDL CALC N3N	
				Rept	BNL-11505	66	- .N3N TBL CALC CS.TBP.NDG.	
(n,xn) x>2	+7		GEL	ExTh Rept	EANDC(E)101AL	May 67	Liskien. STATISTICAL MODEL CFD EXPT	
(n,xn) x>2	-1	+5	BOL	Revw Conf	70Helsinki 2 379	Jun 70	Benzi.115. A BELOW 220, DATA STATUS	
(n,xn) x>2	0.0+0	1.0+0	LRL	Comp Rept	UCRL-50400 9	Sep 70	Howerton.TABULATION OF THRESHOLDS	
(n,xn) x>2		2.0+7	BNL	Theo Jour	JNE 27 81	Feb 73	Pearlstein.N3N.STATMDL CALC.FISS.SP.	
(n,xn) x>2	2.5-2	1.5+7	LRL	Comp Jour	ND/A 11 621	Jul 73	Alley+N3N.MEAS+SEMIEMPIRICAL CURVS.	
n Emission	None		HEB	Theo Jour	NP 40 293	Jan 63	Nebenzahl+ EVAPOR SPEC DEP ON N NUMB	
n Emission	None		IFJ	Revw Jour	PF 15 385	Jul 64	.REVIEW ON WORK IN KRAKOW,100 REFS	
n Emission	Thrsh	Up	CCP	Theo Rept	ICD-4 286	67	Kormushkin+EFFECT THRESH METHOD ANAL	
n Emission	1.4+7	1.5+7	TAT	Theo Prog	INDC(SEC)-42	Dec 74	Kondaiah+ REL NON-ELAS,VS(N-Z)/A,NDG	
(n,p)	None		OSA	Theo Jour	JPJO 18 157	36	Yukawa+.SIG FORM DERIVED	
(n,p)	None		ROC	Theo Jour	PR 57 472	Mar 40	Weisskopf+ GENERAL FORMULA,A OVER 50	
(n,p)	None		AUS	Theo Jour	APA 6 329	Jan 53	Sexl.DIFF.EQUATION OF N-P SCAT	
	Maxwl			Jour	APA 5 89	Nov 51	Katscher.N-P INTERACTION	
	None			Jour	APA 4 62	Jul 50	Bergmann.DIFF EQUAT FOR N-P SCAT	
(n,p)	None		COR	Theo Jour	PR 92 350	Oct 53	Austern+ CALC OF PROTON ANG DISTS	
(n,p)	-		BRU	Theo Jour	JPR 16 73	Jan 55	Demeur.ANGDIST	
(n,p)	None		IBJ	Revw Jour	APP 15 249	56	Dabrowski. CFD PICKUP THEORY	
(n,p)	1.4+7		CIS	Theo Jour	NC 5 502	Feb 57	Colli+10ELEM MGTOZR CFD PPPRIME CURV	
(n,p)	None		POL	Theo Jour	APP 16 93	Mar 57	Sawicki.DIRECT INT,N POLARIZ+DIF SIG	
(n,p)	1.5+7		GLS	Theo Jour	PM 2 473	Apr 57	Brown+ (N,PG) COMPNUC+DIRECT CFD XPT	
(n,p)	Maxwl		IAP	Expt Jour	PR 106 272	Apr 57	Butler.DIRECT PROCESS CFD PICKUP TH	
(n,p)	None		WWA	Revw Jour	PF 8 327	May 57	Sawicki. NUCLEON POLARIZ THEORY	
(n,p)	None		POL	Theo Jour	APP 17 21	Jan 58	Sawicki+ ,COLL MODEL+DIFF SIG CORREC	
(n,p)	None		KAP	Theo Abst	BAP 3 365	Nov 58	Francis+ CALC E DEPEND NEAR THRESHLD	
(n,p)	None		LRL	Theo Rept	UCRL-5419	Feb 59	Ashby+.CALCULATD Q VALUES TABULATED	
(n,p)	1.4+7		CIS	Expt Jour	NC 16 1109	Jun 60	Facchini+STAT TH CFD,OK DATA Z=10-40	
(n,p)	1.4+7		MUA	ExTh Conf	61Bombay 21	Feb 61	Khurana+.GRAPH,SIGMA REL MASS	
(n,p)	1.4+7		HAR	Expt Jour	NP 24 274	Apr 61	Allan.40NUCLEI,CFD STATISTICAL MODEL	
(n,p)	4.0+6	1.6+7	MIL	Comp Jour	NC 22 1237	Dec 61	Erba+COMPAR.WITH STAT.MODEL.	
(n,p)	1.4+7		ARK	Comp Jour	NP 29 373	Jan 62	Gardner.THEOR.CROSSECTION EQUATION	
(n,p)	1.4+7		FRK	Theo Jour	ZP 171 379	Dec 62	Lindner.STATMOD,CF CJP 31 267,TH+XPT	
(n,p)	1.4+7	1.5+7	HAM	Comp Rept	EUR-122E	63	Neuert+	
(n,p)	1.4+7		TNC	Comp Rept	EANDC(US)-58	Jun 63	Mathur+ SIG,Q VALUE,PRODCT H-L+DECAY	
(n,p)	1.4+7		CCP	Comp Jour	ZET 45 305	Aug 63	Compilation.GIVES EXC.SIMPLE EQ.	
				Jour	JET 18 213	Mar 64	TRANSLATN.*	
(n,p)	1.4+7		SAC	Comp Jour	NP 47 157	Aug 63	Jeronymo+ LARGE DIFFERENCES IN MEAS.	
(n,p)	None		NIN	Expt Conf	63Manchstr § 3.08	Sep 63	Batty+ INV.N E SPECT 0DEG.30+50MEV PS	
(n,p)	1.4+7		SAC	Theo Jour	NC 32 1092	May 64	Theory.EXP.COMPARED.OPTICAL MODER	
(n,p)	Pile		CRC	Revw Conf	64Wien 17	Jul 64	Boyd+ EFFECTIVE SIG IN AECL-1003.	
(n,p)	1.0+6	1.0+7	KAP	Theo Jour	AP 29 232	Sep 64	Francis+ EFF INTRCTN NUC SURFACE.	
(n,p)	+7		SAH	Revw Conf	65Calcutta 132	Feb 65	Chatterjee. SIGMA SYSTEMATIC+REVIEW	

Many

Quantity	Energy (ev) Min	Max	Lab	Type	Documentation Ref Vol Page	Author, Comments Date	Data
(n,p)	1.4+7		NAP	Theo Conf	65Antwerp 544	Jun 65 Cuzzocrea+SHELL EFFECT STUDY	
				Rept	INFN/BE-67-10	Jul 67 - + SHELL EFFECT	
				Rept	INFN/BE-65-1	Feb 65 - + SHELL EFFECT	
(n,p)	1.4+7		SAH	Theo Conf	65Antwerp § 113	Jul 65 Chatterjee. SHELL EFF. AND STAT.MOD	
(n,p)	1.2+7	1.8+7	SAH	Comp Jour	NUC 23 8 112	Aug 65 Chatterjee. TABLE WITH REFS.	
(n,p)		2.0+7	HAM	Comp Jour	ND/A 1 103	Feb 66 Jessen+ GRAPHS XCIT CURVS,XPTS TO665	
(n,p)	1.4+7		IIT	Revw Abst	BAP 11 202	Feb 66 Gardner+ EXISTENCE OF SHELL EFFECTS.	
(n,p)	-		AUA	Comp Rept	AAEC/E-147	Mar 66 Pollard+ GYMEA=REACTOR DATA LIBRARY	
				Rept	AAEC/TM-343	Sep 66 .BIBLIOGRAPHY OF CODES	
				Rept	AAEC/E-114	Apr 64 .MULGA CODE,GROUP AVERAGE CALCULATN	
				Rept	AAEC/E-119	Apr 64 .NUCLEAR DATA CARD LIBRARY GYMEA PROGRAM DESCRIPTION SEE AAEC/E	
(n,p)	None		IIT	Theo Conf	66Wash. 315	Mar 66 Klopp.STAT MDL+FERMI LVL DENS,CFDXPT	
(n,p)	1.4+7		SC	Comp Rept	SC-RR-66-229	Jun 66 Kenna+. SIG AND Q-VALUE TABULATED.	
(n,p)	Fiss	1.4+7	FEI	Comp Rept	ICD-4 234	67 Abagian+CHRGD PARTCL REACT Q+SIG,TBL	
(n,p)	Maxwl		IFU	Theo Rept	ICD-4 20	67 Dadakina+ PENETR COEFF CALC,TABLE	
(n,p)	1.4+7		BOS	Comp Conf	67Kanpur § N70	Feb 67 Mitra.LOW Z.XPTL VALUES CFD TH	
(n,p)	Thrsh	2.0+7	GEL	Comp Rept	EUR-119E VOL.2	Apr 67 Liskien+PAULSEN.ALL DATA EXCIT FUNCT	
(n,p)	1.4+7		IIT	Theo Jour	NP/A 96 121	Apr 67 Gardner+ CALC CFD LEVKOVSKII+XPT	
(n,p)	+6	2.0+7	WWA	Revw Rept	INR-830/I/PL	Dec 67 TURKIEWICZ ERICSON.FLUCTUATIONS XCIT	
	1.0+6	2.0+7		Rept	INR-776/I/PL	Mar 67 Wilhelmi. EXPTS,SIGS,ISOM,SPECS	
(n,p)	-		SAF	Theo Jour	NP/A 107 129	Jan 68 Frahn.QUASI ELASTIC CLOSED FORMALISM	
(n,p)	None		TOR	Theo Abst	DA/B 28 3189	Feb 68 Hsiang. RELATES ISOTPC SIG(NP) DATA	
(n,p)	-		BUC	Theo Jour	RRP 13 749	Sep 68 CALBOREANU DISTORTED WAVE,SHELL TH	
(n,p)	1.4+7		PUC	Theo Conf	68Bombay 2 92	Dec 68 Cheema+ NUCL TEMP(Z),CALC FROM N-P	
				Conf	68Madras 241	Feb 68 .	
(n,p)	1.4+7	1.5+7	IRK	Comp Jour	OAWS 177 467	69 Hille.	
(n,p)	1.5+7		MUA	Expt Prog	BARC-474 44	70 Prasad+ A=6 TO 167,ACT-EXPT,CFD OTHR	
(n,p)	+5	+7	SAH	Theo Prog	BARC-474 27	70 Chatterjee+ RGM = RENORM.F-GAS MODEL	
(n,p)	Maxwl	+6	AE	Theo Conf	70Helsinki 2 881	Jun 70 Eriksson.52. SIGMA TB CALCULATD, NDG	
(n,p)	None		HAR	Expt Prog	INDC-6 11	Jun 70 Rae+ NO OSCILLATIONS IN SIG(E), NDG	
(n,p)	Maxwl	+7	KFI	Comp Rept	KFKI-70-18	Jul 70 Nagy+ MAP+TBL OF GAM HLS+INTENS,SIGS	
(n,p)	None		LRL	Comp Rept	UCRL-50400 9	Sep 70 Howerton.TABULATION OF THRESHOLDS	
				Rept	UCRL-14000	May 64 .SUPERSEDED	
(n,p)	1.4+7	1.5+7	MNZ	Comp Jour	ZN/A 25 1977	Dec 70 Qaim. P-SHELL EFFECTS SEARCH IN SIG	
(n,p)	1.4+7		OTU	Theo Jour	NP/A 164 526	Mar 71 Pai+ SHELL/PAIR-INDEP STATMD.A=32-98	
(n,p)	1.4+7		NAP	Comp Jour	NC/A 4 2 251	Jul 71 Cuzzocrea+ EXP CFD STATMOD	
(n,p)	1.4+7		JYV	Eval Jour	ZN/A 27 1015	Jun 72 Holmberg+ SIG FN OF Z+N,SHELL EFFECT	
(n,p)	1.4+7		SF	Eval Jour	ZN/A 27 1015	Jun 72 HOLMBERG SIG FN OF Z+N,SHELL EFFECTS	
(n,p)	1.4+6	1.5+6	ATI	Expt Jour	ZP 253 335	Aug 72 Eder+,PHENOMEN.(A,N,Z)-FORMULA GIVEN	
(n,p)	1.0+7	2.0+7	CIS	Theo Jour	PR/C 6 1398	Oct 72 Braga-Marcazzan+. PRE-EQUILIBR MODEL	
(n,p)	1.4+7		DEB	Comp Rept	IAEA-153 155	73 Csikai+ EXPTL DATA COMPARED ,GRPH	
	1.5+7			Jour	REA 7 4 93	Dec 69 - + SIG+HL COMP FOR N-ACTIV-ANAL	
(n,p)		2.0+7	BNL	Theo Jour	JNE 27 81	Feb 73 Pearlstein.STATMOD CALN.FISS-SP AV	
(n,p)	+7		KFK	Expt Rept	KFK-1783 87	Apr 73 Muenzel+ MAX-SIG AS FN OF Z	
(n,p)	2.5-2	1.5+7	LRL	Comp Jour	ND/A 11 621	Jul 73 Alley+. MANY CURVES	
	+6	+7		Rept	UCRL-50484	Aug 72 - +. EXTENSIVE COMPILATION.CURVES	
(n,p)	1.4+7		TUD	Theo Rept	ZFK-261 77	Aug 73 Seeliger. A GREATR 100,SIG TH/SIG XP	
(n,p)	None		CAL	Theo Abst	BAP 20 1487	Dec 75 Holmes+ SEMI-EMPIRICAL STAT MODEL	
(n,p)	5.9+6	5.6+7	RBZ	Revw Conf	76Lowell 272	Jul 76 Slaus.REVIEW OF REAC.SYSTEMATICS	
(n,p)	Fast		WIN	Expt Prog	NEANDC(E)172 8	Aug 76 Taylor.ACTIVATION AVERAGE FAST REACT	
(n,p)	1.4+7		SAH	Theo Conf	76Ahmedabd 2 19	Dec 76 Ganguly. BRIEF.EXCITONMOD.SIG(A),FIG	
(n,p)	Pile		KIG	Comp Rept	GKSS-77/E/47	77 Greim+ G-DETECTION LIMITS N-ACT ANAL	
(n,p)	1.4+7		KIG	Comp Rept	GKSS-77/E/50	77 Fanger+ DATA FOR ACT ANAL MN-MO4UL5S	
(n,PN*)	1.5+7		GLS	Theo Jour	PM 2 473	Apr 57 Brown+ (N,PN*) COMPNUC+DIRECT CFD XPT	
(n,p)	None		JHU	Theo Jour	PR 108 1512	Dec 57 Hart+,SIG ENERGY DEP NEAR THRESHOLD	
(n,p)	1.4+7		CIS	Expt Jour	NC 16 1109	Jun 60 Facchini+STAT TH CFD,OF DATA Z=10-40	
(n,p)	1.4+7		HAR	Expt Jour	NP 24 274	Apr 61 Allan.13NUCLEI,CFD STATISTIC1L-MFDN3	
(n,np)	1.4+7	1.5+7	HAM	Comp Rept	EUR-122E	63 Neuert+	
(n,np)		2.0+7	HAM	Comp Jour	ND/A 1 103	Feb 66 Jessen+ GRAPHS XCIT CURVS,XPTS TO665	
				Rept	NP-15018	Jan 65 - +.GRAPHS XCITATION CURVES	
(n,np)	None		LRL	Comp Rept	UCRL-50400 9	Sep 70 Howerton.TABULATION OF THRESHOLDS	
				Rept	UCRL-14000	May 64 .SUPERSEDED	
(n,np)		2.0+7	BNL	Theo Jour	JNE 27 81	Feb 73 Pearlstein.STATMOD CALN.FISS-SP AV	
(n,np)	2.5-2	1.5+7	LRL	Comp Jour	ND/A 11 621	Jul 73 Alley+. MANY CURVES	
	+6	+7		Rept	UCRL-50484	Aug 72 - +. EXTENSIVE COMPILATION.CURVES	
(n,d)	1.0+8		COR	Theo Jour	PR 80 171	Oct 50 Heidmann. FERMI MDL CORR FOR PICKUP	

Many

Quantity	Energy (ev) Min	Max	Lab	Type	Documentation Ref Vol Page	Author, Comments Date	Data
(n,d)	None		IBJ	Revw Jour	APP 15 249	56 Dabrowski. CFD PICKUP THEORY	
(n,d)	None		LRL	Theo Rept	UCRL-5419	Feb 59 Ashby+.CALCULATD Q VALUES TABULATED	
(n,d)	1.4+7	1.5+7	HAM	Comp Rept	EUR-122E	63 Neuert+	
(n,d)	-		AUA	Comp Rept	AAEC/E-119	Apr 64 Doherty. NUCLEAR DATA CARD LIBRARY	
				Rept	AAEC/E-114	Apr 64 .MULGA CODE,GROUP AVERAGE CALCULATN	
(n,d)	1.2+7	1.8+7	SAH	Comp Jour	NUC 23 8 112	Aug 65 Chatterjee. TABLE WITH REFS.	
(n,d)	Fiss	1.4+7	FEI	Comp Rept	ICD-4 234	67 Abagian+CHRGD PARTCL REACT Q+SIG,TBL	
(n,d)	None		LRL	Comp Rept	UCRL-50400 9	Sep 70 Howerton.TABULATION OF THRESHOLDS	
				Rept	UCRL-14000	May 64 .SUPERSEDED	
(n,d)		2.0+7	BNL	Theo Jour	JNE 27 81	Feb 73 Pearlstein.STATMOD CALN.FISS-SP AV	
(n,d)	None		RBZ	Revw Conf	76Lowell 272	Jul 76 Slaus.REVIEW OF REAC.SYSTEMATICS	
(n,nd)	None		LRL	Comp Rept	UCRL-50400 9	Sep 70 Howerton.TABULATION OF THRESHOLDS	
				Rept	UCRL-14000	May 64 .SUPERSEDED	
(n,nd)		2.0+7	BNL	Theo Jour	JNE 27 81	Feb 73 Pearlstein.STATMOD CALN.FISS-SP AV	
(n,t)	None		LRL	Theo Rept	UCRL-5419	Feb 59 Ashby+.CALCULATD Q VALUES TABULATED	
(n,t)	1.4+7	1.5+7	HAM	Comp Rept	EUR-122E	63 Neuert+	
(n,t)	-		AUA	Comp Rept	AAEC/E-119	Apr 64 Doherty. NUCLEAR DATA CARD LIBRARY	
				Rept	AAEC/E-114	Apr 64 .MULGA CODE,GROUP AVERAGE CALCULATN	
(n,t)	1.2+7	1.8+7	SAH	Comp Jour	NUC 23 8 112	Aug 65 Chatterjee. TABLE WITH REFS.	
(n,t)		2.0+7	HAM	Comp Jour	ND/A 1 103	Feb 66 Jessen+ GRAPHS XCIT CURVS,XPTS TO665	
(n,t)	Fiss	1.4+7	FEI	Comp Rept	ICD-4 234	67 Abagian+CHRGD PARTCL REACT Q+SIG,TBL	
(n,t)	None		LRL	Comp Rept	UCRL-50400 9	Sep 70 Howerton.TABULATION OF THRESHOLDS	
				Rept	UCRL-14000	May 64 .SUPERSEDED	
(n,t)	+6	+7	LRL	Comp Rept	UCRL-50484	Aug 72 Alley+. EXTENSIVE COMPILATION.CURVES	
(n,t)		2.0+7	BNL	Theo Jour	JNE 27 81	Feb 73 Pearlstein.STATMOD CALN.FISS-SP AV	
(n,t)	1.4+7		KOS	Revw Jour	ASL 25 88	75 Csikai. SIG(Z),((N-Z)/A).CFD TH,GRPH	
	None			Conf	73Paris 2 38	Mar 73 - .SURVEY OF SIG VS ELEMENT,GRPH	
(n,t)	1.4+7	1.5+7	JUL	Eval Prog	NEANDC(E)172 5	Jul 76 Qaim+P.42. Z=23-92,GRAPH	
	1.4+7			Revw Conf	75Wash. 664	Mar 75 - . GRAPH SYSTEMATICS	
(n,t)	2.7+6	1.4+7	RBZ	Revw Conf	76Lowell 272	Jul 76 Slaus.REVIEW OF REAC.SYSTEMATICS	
(n,nt)		2.0+7	HAM	Comp Jour	ND/A 1 103	Feb 66 Jessen+ GRAPHS XCIT CURVS,XPTS TO665	
(n,nt)	None		LRL	Comp Rept	UCRL-50400 9	Sep 70 Howerton.TABULATION OF THRESHOLDS	
				Rept	UCRL-14000	May 64 .SUPERSEDED	
(n,nt)		2.0+7	BNL	Theo Jour	JNE 27 81	Feb 73 Pearlstein.STATMOD CALN.FISS-SP AV	
(n,He3)	None		LRL	Theo Rept	UCRL-5419	Feb 59 Ashby+.CALCULATD Q VALUES TABULATED	
(n,He3)	1.4+7	1.5+7	HAM	Comp Rept	EUR-122E	63 Neuert+	
(n,He3)	Fiss	1.4+7	FEI	Comp Rept	ICD-4 234	67 Abagian+CHRGD PARTCL REACT Q+SIG,TBL	
(n,He3)	None		CCP	Theo Jour	YF 12 302	Aug 70 Kadmenskij+ INVERSE,STRIPPING REACTN	
				Jour	SNP 12 160	Feb 71 . ENGL OF YF 12 302	
(n,He3)	None		LRL	Comp Rept	UCRL-50400 9	Sep 70 Howerton.TABULATION OF THRESHOLDS	
				Rept	UCRL-14000	May 64 .SUPERSEDED	
(n,He3)		2.0+7	BNL	Theo Jour	JNE 27 81	Feb 73 Pearlstein.STATMOD CALN.FISS-SP AVG	
(n,He3)	1.4+7		JUL	Revw Conf	75Wash. 664	Mar 75 Qaim. GRAPH SYSTEMATICS	
(n,α)	None		IBJ	Revw Jour	APP 15 249	56 Dabrowski. CFD PICKUP THEORY	
(n,α)	None		LRL	Theo Rept	UCRL-5419	Feb 59 Ashby+.CALCULATD Q VALUES TABULATED	
(n,α)	1.4+7		MUA	ExTh Conf	61Bombay 21	Feb 61 Khurana+.GRAPH,SIGMA REL MASS	
(n,α)	1.4+7		FRK	Theo Jour	ZP 171 379	Dec 62 Lindner.STATMOD,CF CJP 31 267,TH+XPT	
(n,α)	1.4+7	1.5+7	HAM	Comp Rept	EUR-122E	63 Neuert+	
(n,α)	1.4+7		TNC	Comp Rept	EANDC(US)-58	Jun 63 Mathur+ SIG,Q VALUE,PRODCT H-L+DECAY	
(n,α)	1.4+7		CCP	Comp Jour	ZET 45 305	Aug 63 Compilation.GIVES EXC.SIMPLE EQ.	
				Jour	JET 18 213	Mar 64 TRANSLATN.*	
(n,α)	1.4+7		SAC	Comp Jour	NP 47 157	Aug 63 Jeronymo+LARGE DIFFERENCES IN MEAS.	
				Theo Jour	NC 32 1092	May 64 .THEORY.EXP.COMPARED.OPTICAL MODEL	
(n,α)	1.4+7		SAH	Comp Jour	NP 49 686	Dec 63 Chatterjee. SIG(Z = 0 TO 90) GRAPHS	
	1.4+7	1.5+7		Jour	NP 47 511	Sep 63 - .EXPERIMENTAL RESULTS	
	1.4+7			Eval Conf	63Bombay 166	Feb 63 - .TRENDS IN N-ALFA,GRAPH	
(n,α)	1.4+7		CIS	Theo Jour	NP 51 460	Feb 64 Facchini+FORMULA FOR STATMOD CALCUL.	
				Jour	PL 3 361	Feb 63 - + SUPERSEDED.	
(n,α)	-		CIS	Eval Jour	EN 11 324	Jun 64 MOSTLY 14 MEV,STATISTICAL MODEL ANAL	
(n,α)	Pile		CRC	Revw Conf	64Wien 17	Jul 64 Boyd+ EFFECTIVE SIG IN AECL-1003.	
(n,α)	1.0+7	2.4+7	FRK	Theo Jour	PL 11 333	Aug 64 Rubbino+ COMPOUND,STATMDL	
				Conf	65Antwerp 548	Jul 65 - + ABST. PPR124.	
(n,α)	1.4+7		IIT	Revw Jour	NP 60 49	Nov 64 Gardner+ Z IN RANGE 6,TO 30	
				Conf	64Paris 2 675	Jul 64 - +	
(n,α)	+7		SAH	Revw Conf	65Calcutta 132	Feb 65 Chatterjee. SIGMA SYSTEMATIC+REVIEW	
	1.4+7	1.5+7		Jour	NUC 22 8 108	Aug 64 - .	

Many

Quantity	Energy (ev) Min	Max	Lab	Type	Documentation Ref Vol Page	Author, Comments Date	Data
(n,α)	1.4+7		NAP	Theo Conf	65Antwerp 544	Jun 65 Cuzzocrea+ SHELL EFFECT STUDY	
				Rept	INFN/BE – 67 – 11	Sep 67 – + SHELL EFFECT	
				Rept	INFN/BE – 65 – 1	Feb 65 – + SHELL EFFECT	
(n,α)	1.4+7		SAH	Theo Conf	65Antwerp § 113	Jul 65 Chatterjee. SHELL EFF. AND STAT.MOD	
(n,α)		2.0+7	HAM	Comp Jour	ND/A 1 103	Feb 66 Jessen+ GRAPHS XCIT CURVS,XPTS TO665	
				Rept	NP – 15018	Jan 65 – +.GRAPHS XCITATION CURVES	
(n,α)	–		AUA	Comp Rept	AAEC/E – 147	Mar 66 Pollard+ GYMEA=REACTOR DATA LIBRARY	
				Rept	AAEC/TM – 343	Sep 66 .BIBLIOGRAPHY OF CODES	
				Rept	AAEC/E – 114	Apr 64 .MULGA CODE,GROUP AVERAGE CALCULATN	
				Rept	AAEC/E – 119	Apr 64 .NUCLEAR DATA CARD LIBRARY	
				–		GYMEA PROGRAM DESCRIPTION SEE AAEC/E	
(n,α)	None		IIT	Theo Conf	66Wash. 315	Mar 66 Klopp.STAT MDL+FERMI LVL DENS,CFDXPT	
(n,α)	1.4+7		SC	Comp Rept	SC – RR – 66 – 229	Jun 66 Kenna+. SIG AND Q – VALUE TABULATED.	
(n,α)	Fiss	1.4+7	FEI	Comp Rept	ICD – 4 234	67 Abagian+CHRGD PARTCL REACT Q+SIG,TBL	
(n,α)	Thrsh	2.0+7	GEL	Comp Rept	EUR – 119E VOL.2	Apr 67 Liskien+ PAULSEN.ALL DATA EXCIT FUNCT	
(n,α)	1.4+7		IIT	ExTh Abst	DA/B 27 4267	Jun 67 YU. EXPT DATA CFD STATIST MODEL.	
(n,α)	1.4+7	1.5+7	IRK	Comp Jour	OAWS 177 465	69 Hille.	
(n,α)	1.0+7	5.0+7	WWA	Revw Jour	INR – 970	Feb 69 Turkiewicz. EXCIT FUNC FLUCT CFD TH	
	+6	2.0+7		Rept	INR – 830/I/PL	Dec 67 – . ERICSON FLUCTUATNS EXCIT	
	1.0+6	2.0+7		Rept	INR – 776/I/PL	Mar 67 Wilhelmi. EXPTS,SIGS,ISOM,SPECS	
(n,α)	1.5+7		DEB	Comp Jour	REA 7 4 93	Dec 69 Csikai+ SIG+HL COMP FOR N – ACTIV – ANAL	
(n,α)	+5	+7	SAH	Theo Prog	BARC – 474 27	70 Chatterjee+ RGM = RENORM.F – GAS MODEL	
(n,α)	Maxwl	+6	AE	Theo Conf	70Helsinki 2 881	Jun 70 Eriksson.52. SIGMA TB CALCULATD, NDG	
(n,α)	Maxwl	+7	KFI	Comp Rept	KFKI – 70 – 18	Jul 70 Nagy+ MAP+TBL OF GAM HLS+INTENS,SIGS	
(n,α)	None		LRL	Comp Rept	UCRL – 50400 9	Sep 70 Howerton.TABULATION OF THRESHOLDS	
				Rept	UCRL – 14000	May 64 .SUPERSEDED	
(n,α)	1.4+7	1.5+7	MNZ	Comp Jour	ZN/A 25 1977	Dec 70 Qaim. P – SHELL EFFECTS SEARCH IN SIG	
(n,α)	1.4+7		NAP	Comp Jour	NC/A 4 2 251	Jul 71 Cuzzocrea+ EXP CFD STATMOD	
(n,α)	1.4+7	1.5+7	IND	Theo Jour	IPA 10 197	Mar 72 Choudhury+ DEPEND ON (N – Z),CFD XPTS	
(n,α)	1.4+7		JYV	Eval Jour	ZN/A 27 1015	Jun 72 Holmberg+ SIG FN OF Z+N,SHELL EFFECT	
(n,α)	1.4+7		SF	Eval Jour	ZN/A 27 1015	Jun 72 HOLMBERG SIG FN OF Z+N,SHELL EFFECTS	
(n,α)		2.0+7	BNL	Theo Jour	JNE 27 81	Feb 73 Pearlstein.STATMOD CALN.FISS – SP AV	
(n,α)			KFK	Expt Rept	KFK – 1783 87	Apr 73 Muenzel+ MAX – SIG AS FN OF Z	
(n,α)	2.5 – 2	1.5+7	LRL	Comp Jour	ND/A 11 621	Jul 73 Alley+. MANY CURVES	
	+6	+7		Rept	UCRL – 50484	Aug 72 – +. EXTENSIVE COMPILATION.CURVES	
(n,α)	None		CIS	Theo Jour	NP/A 210 297	Aug 73 Milazzo – Colli+ PRE – EQUILM EM,CFD XPT	
	1.4+7	2.0+7		Jour	PL/B 38 155	Feb 72 Colli – Milazzo+ A – SPECT+EXCIT FN CALC	
(n,α)	None		CAL	Theo Abst	BAP 20 150	Feb 75 Mann+ CALC.RATES.FOR N,A MASS 45 – 65.	
(n,α)	None		CAL	Theo Abst	BAP 20 1487	Dec 75 Holmes+ SEMI – EMPIRICAL STAT MODEL	
(n,α)	1.4+7		TOR	Theo Jour	ANE 3 129	Feb 76 PAI.CALN SHELL INDEP PARAMS.CFD EXP	
(n,α)	Fast		WIN	Expt Prog	NEANDC(E)172 8	Aug 76 Taylor.ACTIVATION AVERAGE FAST REACT	
(n,α)	Pile		KIG	Comp Rept	GKSS – 77/E/47	77 Greim+ G – DETECTION LIMITS N – ACT ANAL	
(n,α)	1.4+7		KIG	Comp Rept	GKSS – 77/E/50	77 Fanger+ DATA FOR ACT ANAL MN – MODULES	
(n,nα)	1.4+7	1.5+7	HAM	Comp Rept	EUR – 122E	63 Neuert+.	
(n,nα)	–		AUA	Comp Rept	AAEC/E – 119	Apr 64 Doherty. NUCLEAR DATA CARD LIBRARY	
				Rept	AAEC/E – 114	Apr 64 .MULGA CODE,GROUP AVERAGE CALCULATN	
(n,nα)		2.0+7	HAM	Comp Jour	ND/A 1 103	Feb 66 Jessen+ GRAPHS XCIT CURVS,XPTS T065	
(n,nα)	None		LRL	Comp Rept	UCRL – 50400 9	Sep 70 Howerton.TABULATION OF THRESHOLDS	
				Rept	UCRL – 14000	May 64 .SUPERSEDED	
(n,nα)	+6	+7	LRL	Comp Rept	UCRL – 50484	Aug 72 Alley+. EXTENSIVE COMPILATION.CURVES	
(n,nα)		2.0+7	BNL	Theo Jour	JNE 27 81	Feb 73 Pearlstein.STATMOD CALN.FISS – SP AV	
(n,nα)	1.4+7		JUL	Expt Jour	JRC 30 35	May 76 Qaim+ FOR FUSION.GRPH SIG VS (N – Z)/A	
				Jour	AK 18 335	76 – +SYSTEMATICS VS (N – Z)/A.FUS REA	
Fission	–		COP	Theo Jour	PR 56 426	Sep 39 Bohr+WHEELER LIQUID DROP MODEL	
Fission	None		CHI	Theo Jour	PR 72 914	Nov 47 Frankel+ ENIAC CALC ON LIQUID DROP M	
Fission	–		YAM	Theo Jour	PR 80 754	Nov 50 Yasaki+ SYM – ASSYM FISS RATIO VS E.	
Fission	Thrsh		UPP	Theo Abst	AF 11 133	Nov 56 Swiatecki.EMPIRICAL THRES.55KTH CONF	
	Spont			Abst	AF 11 133	Nov 56 – .HL SYSTEMATICS. 55KTH CONF	
Fission	Spont		EDG	Theo Jour	PREA 66 20	Aug 62 Feather.SYSTEMATICS SPON FISS RATES	
Fission	Spont	9.9+6	EDG	Theo Jour	PREA 66 192	Jun 64 Feather.MODELS LONG RANGE ALFA EMISS	
Fission	Maxwl	1.0+4	BNL	Revw Jour	AP 30 269	Nov 64 Garrison. WF DIST.	
Fission	None		GEL	Comp Rept	EUR – 2508E	65 Demine. BIBLIOGRAPHY OF TRANS – PU	
Fission	None		GSF	Theo Jour	CJP 43 1723	Oct 65 Cameron+ FISS THRESHLD SYSTEMATICS.	
Fission	1.0+5	1.4+6	KUR	Theo Rept	IAE – 1179	66 Vorotnikov. WF VS EXCIT E,CURVS	
Fission	Spont		DUB	Revw Rept	JINR – P – 2539	Jan 66 Flerov+ SPON FISSN LIFETIMES, GRAPHS	

Many

Quantity	Energy (ev) Min	Max	Lab	Type	Documentation Ref Vol Page	Date	Author, Comments	Data
Fission			AUA	Comp Rept	AAEC/E-147	Mar 66	Pollard+ GYMEA=REACTOR DATA LIBRARY	
				Rept	AAEC/E-164	Oct 66	.LUBRA-4-CODE,GROUP AVERAGE SIGMA	
				Rept	AAEC/E-164	Oct 66	.LUBRA-0-CODE,SIGMA CALCULATION	
				Rept	AAEC/TM-343	Sep 66	.BIBLIOGRAPHY OF CODES	
				Rept	AAEC/TM-250	May 64	.GUNYA CODE,GROUP+AVG SIGMA CALCULTN	
				Rept	AAEC/E-119	Apr 64	.NUCLEAR DATA CARD LIBRARY	
				Rept	AAEC/E-114	Apr 64	.MULGA CODE,GROUP AVERAGE CALCULATN	
				-			GUNYA CODE,COMPILTN+CALCULTN,AAEC/E-	
				-			GYMEA PROGRAM DESCRIPTION SEE AAEC/E	
Fission	-		COP	Theo Jour	NP 81 61	Jun 66	Nix+FISSILITY VERSUS Z(SQUARED)/A	
Fission	Spont		ANL	Theo Jour	NP 82 65	Jul 66	Viola+ T 1/2+BARRIERS Z=88-108	
Fission	-		TRM	Theo Conf	67Kanpur § N59	Feb 67	Ramanna.STOCHASTIC THEORY	
Fission	Spont		LRL	Eval Jour	PR 155 1309	Mar 67	Caldwell+FIT TO H-LIFE VS Z(SQ)/A	
Fission	None		UI	Eval Rept	COO-1546-5	Mar 67	Adler.COMPUTER PROG FOR MULTLVL ANAL	
Fission	+0	+5	LAS	Revw Jour	AF 36 47	Nov 67	Brown+. BOMB.NDG.GRPH OF PETREL SPEC	
Fission	None		LRL	Revw Jour	AF 36 267	Nov 67	Thompson.SHORT REVW RECENT BRK WORK	
Fission	5.0+4	1.5+6	KUR	Theo Conf	68Riga	Jan 68	Vorotnikov.ABST,IRREGULAR AT THRESH	
Fission	None		TPI	Theo Conf	68Riga	Jan 68	Korostova+ ABST,SHELL-EFFECTS	
Fission	-		CCP	Theo Jour	YF 7 1051	May 68	Stavinskij+ LIQUID-DROP-MODL,SYMM-F	
				Jour	SNP 7 631	Nov 68	TRANSLATN.*	
Fission	+5	+6	CCP	Theo Jour	YF 7 1228	Jun 68	Vorotnikov. QUASISTABLE-STATE-TH	
				Jour	SNP 7 732	Dec 68	TRANSLATN.*	
Fission	1.0+5	1.0+6	CCP	Theo Jour	YF 7 1128	Jun 68	Vorotnikov.EFFECT QUASISTABLE STATES	
Fission	-		DUB	Expt Conf	68DUBSY 449	Jul 68	Polikanov.REVIEW SPONT FISS ISOTOP	
Fission	-		DUB	ExTh Conf	68DUBSY 489	Jul 68	Oganesyan.FISS AT HIGH EXCIT ENERGY	
Fission	Spont		LEB	Theo Jour	YF 8 326	Aug 68	Baldin+ 'SHAPE-ISOMERISM' IN TRANS-U	
				Jour	SNP 8 187	Feb 69	TRANSLATN.*	
Fission	+5	+7	CCP	Theo Jour	YF 8 704	Oct 68	Ermagambetov+OPTMD,CHANNEL ANAL,REVW	
				Jour	SNP 8 409	Apr 69	TRANSLATN.*	
Fission	1.0+2	1.0+5	TRM	Revw Prog	BARC-423 7	69	Garg. REACTOR DATA REVW,DISCREPANCY	
Fission	-		TPI	Theo Jour	YF 9 102	Jan 69	Korostova+ SHELL CORR TO LIQU-DROP-E	
				Jour	SNP 9 62	Jul 69	TRANSLATN.*	
Fission	None		CCP	Theo Conf	69Erevan	Feb 69	Gejlikman+.ABST,ORIGIN TWO-HUMP BARR	
Fission	None		CCP	Theo Conf	69Erevan	Feb 69	Ignatuk+.ABST,TWO-HUMP BARRIER CALC	
Fission	-		CCP	Theo Jour	YF 9 535	Mar 69	Gejlikman. SIG MAXIMA+QUASISTAT LVLS	
				Jour	SNP 9 306	Sep 69	TRANSLATN.*	
Fission	Pile		CCP	Theo Jour	YF 9 535	Mar 69	Gejlikman.EFF OF QUASI-STATIONARY ST	
Fission	None		CCP	Theo Jour	YF 9 894	Apr 69	Geilikman. SHELLS AT LARGE DEFORMATN	
				Jour	SNP 9 521	Oct 69	TRANSLATN.*NO4	
Fission	Fiss		CCP	Theo Jour	PL/B 29 159	Apr 69	Ignatyuk+ODD-EVEN EFFECTS AT BARRIER	
Fission	-		FEI	Theo Prog	YFI-7 9	Apr 69	Ignatyuk+BARRIER+WIDTH CRVS,STRUT-TH	
				Rept	INDC(CCP)-7U7	Feb 70	TRANSLATN.*	
Fission	-		FEI	Theo Prog	YFI-7 15	Apr 69	Stavinskij+ LIQUID-DROP-MODEL,TBP YF	
				Rept	INDC(CCP)-7U18	Feb 70	TRANSLATN.*	
	None			Jour	SNP 9 454	Oct 69	.TRANSLATN.*NO4	
				Jour	YF 9 779	Apr 69	Stavinskij+ EFFECTIV MASS,DROP MODEL	
Fission	-		FEI	Theo Jour	YF 9 775	Apr 69	Rabotnov. INEL+FISSN,RESON ANALYSIS	
				Jour	SNP 9 451	Oct 69	TRANSLATN.*NO4	
Fission	Spont		FTI	Revw Jour	DOK 185 1025	Apr 69	Berlovich+ 'DELAYED FISS',N-Z-RANGE	
				Jour	SPD 14 4 349	Oct 69	TRANSLATN.*	
Fission	Maxwl		CCP	Comp Jour	AE 26 436	May 69	Romanov.TBLS,SIG(N-Z,BINDNG-BARRIER)	
				Jour	EAF 26 48	69	. FRENCH OF AE 26 436.	
				Jour	SJA 26 498	69	. ENGL OF AE 26 436.	
Fission	Fiss		CCP	Theo Jour	PL/B 29 209	May 69	Ignatyuk+TWO HUMP BARRIER CLASS APP.	
Fission	-		COP	Revw Conf	69Vienna 155	Jul 69	Strutinsky+PPR203."SHELL-EFFECTS"	
	None			Theo Jour	NP/A 122 1	Dec 68	- + SHELLS IN DEFORMD NUCLEI	
Fission	Spont		JAE	Theo Conf	69Vienna 902	Jul 69	Takekoshi. §4. HALFILE FORMULA	
Fission	Maxwl	+7	AUA	Theo Rept	AAEC/TM-520	Nov 69	Ferguson. GUNYA+GYMEA,SIG-GENERATION	
Fission	3.0+6		KFK	Eval Rept	KFK-1186	Jul 70	Hinkelmann. FN OF(Z/A) FOR A=226-240	
Fission	None		MUA	Theo Conf	70Madurai 2 263	Dec 70	Ramamurty+ SUPERHEAVY NUCL,FISS PARS	
Fission	-		GEL	Revw Jour	AKE 18 229	71	Theobald+,REVIEW SUB-THRESH FISSION	
Fission	-		TOK	Theo Jour	PTP 45 70	Jan 71	Ohta.GENERAL THEORY OF FISSION	
Fission	Maxwl		SAC	Theo Jour	JNE 25 273	Jul 71	Koenig+ EFFECT OF LVL INTERFERENCE.	
Fission	None		AUA	Theo Prog	INDC(SEC)-18	Aug 71	Cook.PG10.NEW MULTILVL-TH,SHORT NOTE	
Fission	Spont		BAS	Theo Abst	HPA 44 604	Aug 71	Ledergerber+ WF FISSHL SHELLCORRECT	
Fission	Thrsh		BAS	ExTh Jour	NP/A 175 545	Nov 71	Pauli+ ISOSPIN DEP. FISSILITY PARAM.	

Many

Quantity	Energy (ev) Min	Max	Lab	Type	Documentation Ref Vol Page	Date	Author, Comments	Data
Fission	–		CCP	Revw Jour	AE 31 595	Dec 71	Sukhoruchkin.SUBTHRESHOLD CFD TH,NDG	
				Jour	SJA 31 1380	Jun 72	*ENGL OF AE 31 595	
Fission	Spont		FRK	Theo Jour	NP/A 177 174	Dec 71	Fraser+ SUPERHEAVY.INCDNCE ON BARRIER	
Fission	None		WAU	Theo Jour	PL/B 37 335	Dec 71	Mosel+ FISS BARRIERS CALC A=180-212	
Fission	Spont		BRK	Theo Jour	NP/A 180 337	Jan 72	Moretto.STABILITY Z=108-126 SHELLMDL	
Fission	None		LND	Theo Jour	NP/A 192 529	Sep 72	Moeller.FISSBARR PARMS,ASYM,Z=84-120	
				Jour	PL/B 34 349	Mar 71	Gustafsson+ FISS BARRIER ASYMMETRY	
Fission	Spont		BHU	Theo Conf	72Chandigr 2 209	Dec 72	Sood+ SHORT NOTE.HL CFD FISSILTY,NDG	
Fission	2.5-2		JUL	Theo Jour	ZP 257 389	Dec 72	Mcminn.CALC FOR 223<=A<=302	
Fission	None		PUC	Theo Conf	72Chandigr 2 203	Dec 72	Gupta+ GOVERNOR MDL FOR FISSION	
Fission	–2	1.4+7	BUC	Revw Rept	IFA–CRD–54	73	Poenaru. RANGE OF SIGS TO FIS–ISOM.	
Fission	None		FRK	Theo Jour	NP/A 207 225	Jun 73	Albrecht. 2–CENTRE SHELLMOD,ACTINIDS	
Fission	None		MGW	Theo Jour	NP/A 208 514	Jul 73	Leboeuf+ DOUBLE HUMP BARRIER PENETR.	
Fission	None		BRK	ExTh Jour	NP/A 217 221	Dec 73	Randrup+ FISS H.L. PREDIC. Z=92TO106	
Fission	None		COP	Theo Jour	NP/A 224 116	May 74	Hofmann.COLL HAMILTONIAN.ANAL AMPLIT	
Fission	None		COP	Theo Jour	NP/A 228 323	Aug 74	Back. STRENGTH FN, 2–HUMP BARRIERMOD	
Fission		+6	HAR	Rept	AERE–R–7468	Nov 74	Lynn.SYSTEMATICS N REACTION ACTINDES	
				Eval Prog	EANDC(UK) 151	Aug 73	– .EVAL FISSION BARRIERS AND SIG	
	None			Theo Jour	JP/A 6 542	Apr 73	– . FISSION BARRIER.	
	0.0+0	1.0+0		Conf	68DUBSY 463	Jul 68	– .REVIEW,STRUCT EFFECTS IN FISS.	
	Maxwl	+6		Comp Conf	66Paris 2 89	Oct 66	– .THEORETCL INTERPRETATION	
	+0	+3		Theo Jour	PRL 13 412	Sep 64	– .SHAPE OF SIMULATD MLTILVL RES	
Fission	–1	+8	MUN	Revw Jour	ACH 87 77	75	Aumann.REVW ON NUCLEAR FISSION	
Fission	Spont		BAS	Theo Rept	EIR–218	Jul 75	Goetz+ CALC FISS.BARRIERS	
				Jour	PL/B 39 436	May 72	– + CALC FISSION BARRIERS	
Fission	None		LND	Theo Jour	ZP/A 275 11	Nov 75	Schroeder+ FISSION BARRIER CALC	
Fission	None		AUW	Theo Conf	75Calcutta 2 40	Dec 75	Ramamurthy+ SHELL MODL FOR FISSION.	
Fission	Maxwl		MUN	ExTh Diss	GRYNTAKIS	Mar 76	Gryntakis.,ACT.MEAS.,CALC OF G–FUNCT	
	None			Theo Jour	RCA 22 128	Mar 75	– +,CALC WESTCOTTS G–FUNCTION	
Fission	None		TUE	Theo Jour	ZP/A 278 1 15	Jul 76	Goennenwein+A=210-258,CLUSTER–CORREL	
	Maxwl			Jour	PL/B 61 430	Apr 76	Gonnenwein+ASSYMETRIC FISS NEAR RD.	
Res Int Fiss	–		AUA	Theo Rept	AAEC/E–164	Oct 66	Kletzmayr. CALC OF INF DILUTE INTEGR	
				Rept	AAEC/TM–343	Sep 66	.BIBLIOGRAPHY OF CODES	
Res Int Fiss	5.0-1		MUN	Expt Diss	GRYNTAKIS	Mar 76	Gryntakis.,MEAS OF RESON INTEGRALS	
Alpha	1.4+7		CLC	Theo Jour	PR 134 374	Apr 64	SHELL EFFECTS CONTINUM THEORY CF XPT	
Alpha	+3		FEI	Theo Conf	68Dubna § 2	Jun 68	Abagyan+.MEAN W FLUCTUATION EFFECT	
Eta	–		AUA	Theo Rept	AAEC/E–164	Oct 66	Kletzmayr. COMP+CALC GROUP AVG VALUE	
				Rept	AAEC/TM–343	Sep 66	.BIBLIOGRAPHY OF CODES	
Nu	Maxwl		HAR	Theo Rept	AERE–R–3452	Jul 55	Story POSS.RELATION NU TO EXN.OR Z,A	
Nu	None		LAS	Revw Jour	PR 108 783	Nov 57	Terrell.TH GAUSSIAN DISTR CFD XPT	
Nu	–		CCP	ExTh Jour	ZET 34 503	Feb 58	Kuz'Minov.GRAPH NU VS Z–A,TH CFD XPT	
				Jour	JET 7 346	Aug 58	TRANSLATN.*	
Nu	None		CCP	Eval Conf	58Geneva 15 353	Sep 58	Bondarenko+.NU REL TO A,Z–NUMBER	
Nu	–		TRM	Revw Conf	59Calcutta 152	Feb 59	RAMANNA REVIEW–ARTICLE ON FISSION	
Nu	Fiss		ANL	Eval Book	FRC	60	Yiftah+ EFFECTIVE NU CALC FROM NU,NF	
Nu	0.0+0		CCP	Comp Jour	AE 14 530	Jun 63	Gordeeva.EMPIRICAL FORMULA	
				Jour	SJA 14 562	63	. ENGL OF AE 14 530	
Nu	–		JAP	Theo Jour	JPJ 18 1697	Nov 63	.NDG.XCIT ES OF FF AT SCISSION CALCD	
Nu	Thrsh	1.5+7	LRL	Expt Jour	JNAB 18 125	Mar 64	Schuster+ E DEPENDNCE THEORY	
Nu	0.0+0		CCP	Theo Jour	AE 16 300	Apr 64	Babkin.LIQUID DROP MDL CALC CFD DATA	
				Jour	SJA 16 366	64	. ENGL OF AE 16 300	
Nu	Spont		CCP	ExTh Jour	AE 17 28	Jul 64	Bolshov+ DEPENDENCE ON MASS NUMBER A	
				Jour	JNE 19 457	Jun 65	TRANSLATN.*	
				Jour	EAF 17 1 47	Jul 64	TRANSLATN.*	
				Jour	SJA 17 715	Jul 64	TRANSLATN.*	
Nu	–		AUA	Comp Rept	AAEC/E–147	Mar 66	Pollard+ GYMEA=REACTOR DATA LIBRARY	
				Rept	AAEC/E–164	Oct 66	.LUBRA–4–CODE,GROUP AVERAGE SIGMA	
				Rept	AAEC/TM–343	Sep 66	.BIBLIOGRAPHY OF CODES	
				Rept	AAEC/TM–250	May 64	.GUNYA–CODE FOR(FISSN.NU) CALCULTN GYMEA PROGRAM DESCRIPTION SEE AAEC/E	
Nu	–		FTI	Expt Jour	YF 9 727	Apr 69	Belov+ AVG NEUT–E(NU)COMPILD+DISCUSD	
				Jour	SNP 9 421	Oct 69	TRANSLATN.*NO4	
Nu	None		NEG	Theo Conf	69Vienna 891	Jul 69	Boneh+ NECK POTENT–E,N–EMISSION	
Nu	–		CCP	Eval Prog	INDC–6 42	Jun 70	Abramov+ STATUS OF SOVIET EVALUATION	
Nu	None		MUA	Theo Conf	70Madurai 2 263	Dec 70	Ramamurty+ SUPERHEAVY NUCL,CALC NU	
Nu	None		BNL	Theo Jour	JNE 25 599	Dec 71	TU+ CORR NU WITH COULOMB EN,ETC.	

Many

Quantity	Energy (ev) Min	Max	Lab	Type	Documentation Ref Vol Page	Date	Author, Comments	Data
Nu	–		FEI	Expt Jour	YF 15 29	Jan 72	Volodin+ HEAVY Z–A–SYSTEMATICS,GRPH	
				Jour	SNP 15 17	Jul 72	*	
Nu	None		ORL	Theo Jour	NP/A 186 1	May 72	Schmitt+ K.E.STATIC SCISS.A=220TO310	
Nu	Spont		DUB	Comp Jour	YF 18 724	Oct 73	Dakovsky+SPONFIS–NUBAR(Z,A),TBL+GRPH	
				Eval Rept	JINR–P15–7119	Jun 73	Dakowski+ Z–A SYSTEMATICS NU–DISTRIB	
				Jour	YF 17 692	Apr 73	Dakovsky+ NUBAR VS A,CF ISOTOPS,GRPH	
				Comp Jour	SNP 18 371	Apr 74	. ENGLISH OF YF 18, 724.	
				Eval Jour	SNP 17 360	Oct 73	.ENGLISH OF YF 17 692	
Nu	Maxwl		AUA	Revw Conf	IAEA–169 2 163	74	Musgrove+ NU–BAR VS MASS–NR,GRAPH	
Delayd Neuts	–		COP	Theo Jour	PR 56 426	Sep 39	Bohr+WHEELER LIQUID DROP MODEL	
Delayd Neuts	–		SAH	Theo Jour	NAT 162 853	Nov 48	Das.ELECTRON REACT MECHANISM PROPOSD	
Delayd Neuts	None		LAS	Theo Jour	JNE 7 13	Aug 58	Keepin.THEOR DEL NEUT PRECURSRS,YLDS	
				Jour	AE 4 250	Mar 58	.SEE ALSO	
				Jour	SJA 4 339	58	.SEE ALSO	
Delayd Neuts	–		CCP	Revw Rept	INDSWG–64 266	64	Maksjutenko.REVIEW ON DELAYED NS	
Delayd Neuts	–		CCP	Theo Jour	AE 16 146	Feb 64	Krisiuk.DEL N YLD FROM BR I ISOTOPES	
				Jour	JNE 18 662	Nov 64	TRANSLATN.*	
				Jour	SJA 16 168	Feb 64	TRANSLATN.*	
Delayd Neuts	–		MNZ	Expt Conf	65Salzburg 2 197	Mar 65	Hermann+EXPTS CFD THEORY	
Delayd Neuts	None		SOR	Revw Conf	65Salzburg 171	Mar 65	Amiel. EXPTS CFD THEORY.TABLES,GRPHS	
Delayd Neuts	–		OSL	Revw Conf	67Vienna 35	Apr 67	Jahnsen+ THEORY+PRECURSOR SYSTEMATIC	
Delayd Neuts	0.0+0	1.0+0	OSL	Revw Conf	69Vienna 937	Jul 69	Pappas+PPR51. SEMITHEORY CFD EXPTS	
				Revw Jour	AF 36 445	Nov 67	– +. STATUS 1966. SYSTEMATICS	
	0.0+0	1.0+0		Theo Jour	NP 21 353	Dec 60	– + TH REVIEW,PRECURS SYSTEMATCS	
Delayd Neuts	–		PAR	Theo Conf	69Vienna 621	Jul 69	Gauvin+PPR85. CALC DEL–NEUT–SPECS	
Delayd Neuts	Fiss		SOR	Revw Jour	PL/B 31 59	Jan 70	Amiel+SEMI–EMP CALC EMISS PROBS.	
Delayd Neuts	–		ISL	Expt Prog	IA–1218 58	Aug 70	Shaked. MAGNETIC STRUCTURE+REFLECTNS	
Delayd Neuts	–		TOH	Theo Prog	EANDC(J)22L40	Aug 71	Nakaya+.SEMI–EMPIRICAL EQ OF N–EMIT	
Delayd Neuts	Maxwl		FEI	Theo Jour	YF 17 481	Mar 73	Maksjutenko+ YLD DELAY–NS(N–ES),GRPH	
	+0	+7		Jour	SNP 17 246	Sep 73	.ENGLISH OF YF 17 481	
Frag Neuts	None		CCP	Theo Conf	68Riga	Jan 68	Sommer.ABST,N EMISSION MECHANISM	
Frag Neuts	–		CCP	Theo Jour	YF 7 1043	May 68	Ignatyuk.SHELL–TH,INCREASE VS SYMM–F	
				Jour	SNP 7 626	Nov 68	TRANSLATN.*	
Frag Neuts	Maxwl		MCM	Theo Jour	CJP 46 1137	May 68	Gorman+ NEUT YLD VS. FRAG MASS	
Frag Neuts	–		FTI	Expt Jour	YF 9 727	Apr 69	Belov+ AVG NEUT–E(NU)COMPILD+DISCUSD	
				Jour	SNP 9 421	Oct 69	TRANSLATN.*NO4	
Frag Neuts	Spont	1.4+7	AUA	Revw Conf	IAEA–169 2 163	74	Musgrove+ FINESTRUCTURE DISCUSSD,NDG	
Spect Fiss n		1.0+7	CCP	Theo Jour	AE 3 15	Jul 57	Bat+KUDRIN.EVAP THEOR.E+ANG DISTRIBN	
				Jour	JNE 8 74	Nov 58	TRANSLATN.*	
				Jour	SJA 3 735	57	TRANSLATN.*	
Spect Fiss n		+7	ANL	Eval Book	FRC	60	Yiftah+ ASSUMED SAME ALL FISSNUCL,ES	
Spect Fiss n	–		AUA	Comp Rept	AAEC/E–119	Apr 64	Doherty. NUCLEAR DATA CARD LIBRARY	
Spect Fiss n	–		ISL	Theo Rept	IA–1007	Feb 65	Nebenzahl.GENERAL FORMULAE,U235 CALC	
Spect Fiss n	2.0+7	+6	CCP	Theo Jour	AE 19 113	Aug 65	Eismont.N EMISSION DURING FRAG ACCLN	
	2.0+7	+7		Jour	JNE 20 875	Oct 66	TRANSLATN.*	
				Jour	EAF 19 2 8	Aug 65	TRANSLATN.*	
	2.0+7	+6		Jour	SJA 19 1000	Aug 65	TRANSLATN.*	
Spect Fiss n	None		CCP	Theo Conf	69Erevan	Feb 69	Gamalja+.ABST,EFF SINGLE–PART EXCIT	
Spect Fiss n	+7		CCP	Revw Prog	INDC–6 19	Jun 70	Abramov. FISSN SPECTRA DISCUSSED	
Spect Fiss n	Maxwl	1.4+7	MOL	Theo Conf	71Vienna 161	Aug 71	De Leeuw+ NEW APPROACH,MEAN–E,GRAPHS	
Spect Fiss n	None		TRM	Theo Conf	72Bombay 2 37	Feb 72	Ajitanand+ N–E,ANGDIST CALC	
Spect Fiss γ	–		MUN	Revw Conf	65Salzburg 113	Mar 65	Maier–Leibnitz.EXTNSIV DISC.GRAPHS	
Spect Fiss γ	None		CCP	Theo Conf	69Erevan	Feb 69	Gamalja+.ABST,EFF SINGLE–PART EXCIT	
Spect Fiss γ	3.1+4		SAC	Expt Prog	CEA–N–1522	72	.ANNUAL PROGR.REP,121INF TO INF180	
Fiss Prod γ	None		ORL	Expt Jour	PR 73 1318	Jun 48	WAY+ DECAY RATE OF FISS PROD.	
Fiss Prod γ	+6		LAS	Theo Jour	PR/B 134 817	May 64	Griffin.FPROD SYSTMTCS FOR G SPECTRA	
	None			Rept	LA–2811	Dec 62	– . BETA+GAMMA DECAY CALCULATNS	
Fiss Prod γ	None		NRD	Eval Rept	USNRDL–TR–878	Jun 65	Jones+ TAB DATA FPG(S),G(S) AND ENG.	
Fiss Prod γ	–		JAE	Comp Rept	JAERI–1124	Dec 66	Kamemoto.G–SPECT.COMPILATION	
Fiss Prod γ	–		KFK	Expt Jour	RCA 6 9	May 67	Irr. IN FR2 RANGES OF FISSION PROD.	
Fiss Prod γ	None		CCP	Theo Conf	68Riga	Jan 68	Sommer.ABST,TOT E OF FRAG G–EMISSION	
Fiss Prod γ	Pile		CCP	Expt Jour	AE 25 524	Dec 68	Miller+ FISS–PROD IN COOLANT,GE–DET	
				Jour	EAF 25 6 110	Dec 68	TRANSLATN.*	
Fiss Prod γ	Pile		CCP	Expt Jour	AE 25 524	Dec 68	Miller+ FISS–PROD IN COOLANT,GE–DET	
				Jour	SJA 25 1359	69	. ENGL OF AE 25 524	
Fiss Prod γ			EDG	Theo Jour	PR/C 1 747	Feb 70	Feather. YIELD EVEN–Z GS TERN > BIN	

Many

Quantity	Energy (ev) Min	Max	Lab	Type	Documentation Ref Vol Page	Date	Author, Comments	Data
Fiss Prod γ	None		FAR	Comp Rept	CEA – N – 1423	Mar 71	Barre + NUCLEAR DATA OF FISSION PRODCT	
				Expt Rept	CEA – N – 1269	70	– +SEE ALSO	
Fiss Prod γ	None		CEG	Eval Prog	NEANDC(UK)160	Jul 74	Tobias. BETA GAMMA DECAY SCH ALL FP	
Fiss Yield	None		GEN	Theo Jour	PR 72 1265	Dec 47	Gast.UNCERTAINTY PPL INTERPRETATION.	
				Jour	PR 73 529	Mar 48	.ERRATUM.	
Fiss Yield	None		CHI	Theo Jour	PR 76 1226	Oct 49	Mayer+ ORIGIN OF UNIV,FISS IN N – FLUID	
Fiss Yield	–		CCP	Theo Jour	ZET 30 599	Mar 56	Ryzhanov.ASYM FISS,TH CFD XPTS,GRPHS	
				Jour	JET 3 632	Nov 56	TRANSLATN.*	
Fiss Yield	None		UPP	Theo Abst	AF 11 133	Nov 56	Swiatecki.ASYMM.EMPIRICAL.55KTH CONF	
Fiss Yield	2.0+6	2.0+7	CCP	Theo Jour	AE 2 508	Jun 57	Strutinsky.STATIST THEOR FRAG ANG DN	
				Jour	JNE 7 239	Sep 58	TRANSLATN.*	
				Jour	SJA 2 621	57	TRANSLATN.*	
Fiss Yield	–		TRM	Revw Conf	59Calcutta 152	Feb 59	RAMANNA REVIEW – ARTICLE ON FISSION	
Fiss Yield	–		JAE	Revw Rept	JAERI – 6013	Aug 63	Shiba+.CHARACTERISTICS OF FIS – PRODUC	
Fiss Yield	None		LAS	Theo Rept	LA – 3169	Sep 64	Wolfsberg.TABLES.EST OF FRACT YIELDS	
Fiss Yield	–		TRM	Revw Rept	AEET – 235	65	Methasiri.RATIO BINARY/TERNARY CFD	
Fiss Yield	None		LAS	Theo Jour	PR/B 137 807	Feb 65	Gibbs+ S – O IN OPTMDL XOKS FRAG ANIST	
Fiss Yield	None		BRK	Theo Jour	NP 71 1	Sep 65	NIX+ LIQUID DROP THEORY.	
				Abst	DA 25 4209	Jan 65	NIX. LIQUID – DROP FISS.TH.USED.	
Fiss Yield	–		CCP	Theo Jour	RAK 7 692	Nov 65	Krisyuk+,PARTICULAR+TOTAL YLDS CALC	
				Jour	SRA 7 690	Nov 65	TRANSLATN.*	
Fiss Yield	–		DUB	Theo Jour	AE 20 151	Feb 66	KARAMYAN HEAVY ION DIFF METHOD	
				Jour	JNE 21 301	Mar 67	TRANSLATN.*	
				Jour	EAF 20 2 78	Feb 66	TRANSLATN.*	
				Jour	SJA 20 185	Feb 66	TRANSLATN.*	
Fiss Yield	–		PAK	Revw Jour	NSP 2 33	Apr 66	Rahman.MASS DISTRB REVIEW, GRAPHS	
Fiss Yield	–		YAM	Theo Jour	JPJ 21 813	Apr 66	Honda.FIS MODL C CORE.CFD C FRAG YLD	
Fiss Yield	–		AUA	Theo Rept	AAEC/E – 163	Sep 66	Cook. COMPIL+CALC OF FISS – FRAG YIELD	
				Rept	AAEC/TM – 343	Sep 66	.BIBLIOGRAPHY OF CODES	
Fiss Yield	Maxwl		AE	Expt Jour	JIN 28 2111	May 67	HAMMAR FORMATION OF N13 F17 F18	
Fiss Yield	1.5+7		ARK	Expt Jour	JIN 28 2071	May 67	Canapathy+. MASS DISTR. TH232 FISS.	
Fiss Yield	Maxwl		JUL	Expt Jour	AF 36 310	Nov 67	Armbruster+.DESCR OF MASS SEPART.NDG	
				Jour	AF 36 293	Nov 67	– +.DESCR OF MASS SEPART.NDG	
Fiss Yield	Maxwl		CCP	Theo Conf	68Riga	Jan 68	Nadykto.ABST,FISSION FRAG ASYMMETRY	
Fiss Yield	None		TEX	Theo Conf	JINR – D – 3893	May 68	Mcintyre+ THEORY ON FRAG DIVISION	
Fiss Yield	Maxwl	1.4+7	CIS	Theo Jour	PL/B 28 534	Feb 69	Facchini+ REPULSIVE NUC – NUC FORCES	
Fiss Yield	Maxwl	1.4+7	CCP	Expt Jour	YF 9 732	Apr 69	Adamov+ TERN FISSN VS Z/A,XPT+COMPIL	
				Jour	SNP 9 424	Oct 69	TRANSLATN.*NO4	
Fiss Yield	Fiss		COP	Theo Jour	PL/B 29 143	Apr 69	Wong+PENETRATION OF DOUBLE BARRIER	
Fiss Yield	Fiss		COP	Theo Jour	PL/B 29 177	Apr 69	Pedersen+RESON NEAR – BARRIER FISS	
Fiss Yield	Fiss		FTI	Theo Jour	PL/B 29 155	Apr 69	Berlovich+DELAYED FISS AFTER N CAPT	
Fiss Yield	–		EDG	Revw Conf	69Vienna 83	Jul 69	Feather.PPR201. SURVEY,TERNARY FISSN	
Fiss Yield	None		HEI	Theo Conf	69Vienna 51	Jul 69	Noerenberg.PPR30.'UNIFIED'THEORY GVN	
Fiss Yield	None		MRY	Revw Conf	69Vienna 3	Jul 69	Griffin.PPR200.TH + REVIEW OF FISSION	
Fiss Yield	–		OSL	Revw Conf	69Vienna 669	Jul 69	Pappas+PPR206. HEAVY+LIGHT SYSTEMATC	
Fiss Yield	–		TUE	Theo Conf	69Bochum 175	Jul 69	Goennenwein+ CLUSTER – LIQU – DROP – MODEL	
Fiss Yield	–		WUR	Revw Conf	69Vienna 731	Jul 69	Flynn+PPR1. YLD – PEAK – GRPH,+TH227 XPT	
Fiss Yield	None		NEG	Theo Rept	NRCN – 252	Oct 69	Boneh+ LIGHT FRAG EMISSION,TBL,GRAPH	
Fiss Yield	None		WUR	Revw Rept	EIR – 170	Nov 69	Von Guten. MASS DISTR.	
Fiss Yield	–		SAH	Theo Prog	BARC – 474 35	70	Sarkar+ A = 185 TO 260,PROGRAM+TH TBP	
Fiss Yield	None		CCP	Revw Jour	IZV 34 438	Feb 70	Soloveva.Z – A SYSTEMATICS OF ALF,GRPH	
				Jour	BAS 34 378	Jan 71	.ENGL TRANSL OF IZV 34 438	
Fiss Yield	–		DUB	Theo Rept	JINR – P4 – 5581	Jan 71	Pashkevich. MASS – ASSYMETRY CFD EXPTS	
	None			Rept	ANL – TRANS – 878	70	. ENGLISH OF JINR – P4 – 5581	
Fiss Yield	None		BAS	Theo Jour	PL/B 34 264	Mar 71	Pauli+ FRAG MASS RATIO AS STRUTINSKY	
Fiss Yield	None		CIS	Theo Jour	PL/B 34 572	Apr 71	Facchini+ TERNARY FISS SUDDEN MODEL	
Fiss Yield	None		TEN	Theo Jour	PL/B 34 587	Apr 71	Nosel+FRAG SHELL MODEL FOR ASYM FISS	
Fiss Yield	None		TOK	Theo Jour	PTP 45 1493	May 71	Ohta.PHASE TRANSITION IN FISSION	
	–			Jour	PTP 44 389	Aug 70	– .ADIABATIC THEORY	
Fiss Yield	–		JAP	Theo Jour	PTP 45 1999	Jun 71	Lin.FISS – EVAPORATION CASCADE	
Fiss Yield	–		LND	Theo Jour	PL/B 38 269	Mar 72	Larsson+ ENERGY SURFACES CALCULATED	
Fiss Yield	Spont	1.4+7	AUA	Revw Conf	IAEA – 169 2 163	74	Musgrove+ CALC YLD METHODS DISCUSSED	
Fiss Yield	None		MNZ	Theo Jour	PL/B 49 312	Apr 74	Reinhard+ 2 – CENTRE SHELLMOD,ASS FISS	
Fiss Yield	None		ITK	Theo Conf	74Bombay 2 144	Dec 74	Krishnarajulu+ ANTICORREL LRA FISS	
	Maxwl			Conf	73Bangalor 2 17	Dec 73	– +TERNARY ALPHA – ANG GRAF	
Fiss Yield	None		TRM	Theo Prog	INDC(SEC) – 42	Dec 74	Choudhury+ TERN,ALF – TRAJECT CALC,NDG	
Fiss Yield	None		AUA	Eval Prog	AAEC/PR – 41P 64	75	Cook+ MASS – YLD,3 ASYM GAUSS FIT.NDG	

Many

Quantity	Energy (ev) Min	Max	Lab	Type	Documentation Ref Vol Page	Date	Author, Comments	Data
Fiss Yield	None		TRM	Revw Prog	BARC – 821 180	75	Ramaswami+ A(LIGHT)/A(HEAV)VS A(COMP	
Fiss Yield	Maxwl		HAR	Eval Rept	AERE – R – 7785	Feb 75	Crouch.CHAIN+INDEPENDENT YLDS TBL	
	None			Prog	NEANDC(UK)160	Jul 74	– . OBJECTIVE EVAL UPDATES R7394	
	Fast			Rept	AERE – R – 7394	May 73	– . CHAIN YLDS. TBL	
Fiss Yield	None		MNZ	Theo Jour	ZP/A 272 397	Apr 75	Lichtner+ CALC FISS – MASS – YLD – DISTR.	
Fiss Yield	Maxwl		JAE	Theo Jour	PTP 55 115	Jan 76	Iwamoto+.TWO – CENTER SHELL MODEL	
Fiss Yield	Maxwl		KTO	Theo Jour	PTP 55 1812	Jun 76	Kuratsuji.GENERAL TH OF ASYMMETRIC – F	
Fiss Yield	2.5 – 2	1.4+7	LAS	Eval Rept	LA – 6595 – MS	Nov 76	Madland+ACTINIDE ISOM NFY DIST.ENDF5	
Frag Spectra	+7		CCP	Theo Jour	ZET 30 606	Mar 56	Strutinskii. ANG DSTRB OF FRGMTS	
				Jour	JET 3 638	Nov 56	TRANSLATN.*	
Frag Spectra	None		LAS	Theo Jour	PR 103 1296	Sep 56	Wilets+,FRAG ANG DIST BOHR TH CFDXPT	
Frag Spectra	–		TRM	Revw Conf	59Calcutta 152	Feb 59	RAMANNA REVIEW – ARTICLE ON FISSION	
Frag Spectra	1.6+6		ATI	Theo Jour	NP 18 346	Aug 60	Hittmair. ANG DISTR FORM.CFD TH – DATA	
Frag Spectra	+6	+7	CCP	Theo Jour	ZET 39 781	Sep 60	Strutinskij.TH ANG DSTRB OF FFRGMTS	
				Jour	JET 12 546	Mar 61	TRANSLATN.*	
Frag Spectra	+6		LAS	Theo Jour	AP 18 274	May 62	Leachman+ SPIN – DEPEND FISS ANISOTROP	
Frag Spectra	–		CCP	Theo Jour	AE 15 419	Nov 63	Okolovich+ SYSTEMATICS AV KINETIC E	
				Jour	JNE 18 533	Sep 64	TRANSLATN.*	
				Jour	SJA 15 1177	Nov 63	TRANSLATN.*	
Frag Spectra	–		KUR	Theo Rept	IAE – 735 1	64	STRUTINSKII,DROP MOD,ANG DIST FISS	
				Rept	ANL – TR – 157	64	TRANSLATN.*	
Frag Spectra	Thrsh	Up	CCP	ExTh Rept	AE 17 28	Jul 64	Bolshov+ SYSTEMATICS,LIQUID – DROP MOD	
				Jour	JNE 19 457	Jun 65	TRANSLATN.*	
				Jour	SJA 17 715	Jul 65	TRANSLATN.*	
				Jour	EAF 17 1 47	Jul 64	TRANSLATN.*	
Frag Spectra	None		FEI	Theo Prog	INDSWG – 120 5	65	Bol'Shov.ANG CORREL PROMPT NS/FFRGMS	
Frag Spectra	–		TRM	Revw Rept	AEET – 235	65	Methasiri.ALF E+ANG DIST,GRPH,CFD TH	
Frag Spectra	–		CAI	Theo Jour	NP 62 145	Feb 65	Stavinsky+FOR 6 FRAG.CONFIGURATIONS	
Frag Spectra	None		CRC	Revw Conf	65Salzburg 451	Mar 65	Fraser.GRPH FRGM – E VS Z/A,AND OTHER	
Frag Spectra	None		BRK	Theo Jour	NP 71 1	Sep 65	Nix+LIQUID DROP THEORY	
Frag Spectra	None		FEI	Theo Rept	FEI – 66	66	Nesterov+.QUANT MECH CALC ANG ANISOT	
Frag Spectra	None		FEI	Theo Rept	FEI – 67	66	Smirenkin+.ANGDIST VS E CFD OTHER TH	
Frag Spectra	Thrsh	Up	FEI	Theo Rept	FEI – 73	Sep 66	Rabotnov+ANGDIST FISSFRAG FOTOFISS	
Frag Spectra	–		ITK	Expt Conf	67Kanpur § N112	Feb 67	Khare.METHOD TO STUDY ANG+E DISTRIB	
Frag Spectra	–		FEI	Theo Rept	FEI – 76	Mar 67	Ignatiuk+STAT FISS THEORY,CFD EXPTS	
Frag Spectra	None		FEI	Theo Rept	FEI – 104	Sep 67	Ignatiuk.FISSFRAG DEFORM AND FISSION	
Frag Spectra	None		TPI	Theo Jour	IVU 9 34	Sep 67	Cherdancev+.COULOMB ENERGY CALC	
Frag Spectra	+6		CCP	Theo Jour	YF 6 1111	Nov 67	Gejlikman.FRAG KE VS EXCIT FISS NUCL	
Frag Spectra	–		FRK	Theo Jour	NP/A 106 117	Dec 67	Hasse+. EFFECTIVE MASSES.LIQUID DROP	
Frag Spectra	–		CCP	Theo Jour	YF 7 215	Jan 68	Gejlikman+ FRAG – DEFORMATN – E,SHELL – TH	
				Jour	SNP 7 1 155	Jul 68	TRANSLATN.*	
Frag Spectra	5.0+4	1.5+6	KUR	Theo Conf	68Riga	Jan 68	Vorotnikov.ABST,ANGDIST NEAR THRESH	
Frag Spectra	1.0+5	1.0+6	CCP	Theo Jour	YF 7 1128	Jun 68	Vorotnikov.EFFECT QUASISTABLE STATES	
Frag Spectra	None		CCP	Theo Conf	69Erevan	Feb 69	Gamalja+.ABST, EFF SINGLE – PART EXCIT	
Frag Spectra	None		HEI	Theo Conf	69Vienna 51	Jul 69	Noerenberg.PPR30.FRAG EXCIT+KIN E,TH	
Frag Spectra	–		KFK	Revw Conf	69Vienna 949	Jul 69	Muenzel+ PPR46. FRAG RANGE IN SOLIDS	
Frag Spectra	None		MRY	Revw Conf	69Vienna 3	Jul 69	Griffin.PPR200.TH+REVIEW OF FISSION	
Frag Spectra	None		NEG	Theo Rept	NRCN – 252	Oct 69	Boneh+ LIGHT FRAGS,CALC KIN – E,TBL	
				Conf	69Vienna 891	Jul 69	– + NECK POTENT – E,LIGHT FRAGM – E	
Frag Spectra	+3	+7	TRM	Theo Prog	BARC – 471 4	70	Ramamurthy+ ANGDIST CFD STRUTINSKY	
	–			Conf	69Roorke 2 191	Dec 69	– + ANISOTROPY,STRUTINSKY – TH	
Frag Spectra	–		CLC	Theo Jour	PR/C 1 619	Feb 70	Sarkar+,CALC OF E DISTR OKS EXPT	
Frag Spectra	None		IBJ	Theo Jour	NP/A 144 617	Apr 70	Krogulski+ A,E DISTR.CLASSIC 3 – BODY.	
	–			Rept	INR – 1138/IA,II	Nov 69	– + E+DIFF SIG PART TERN FIS	
				FEI Theo Jour	YF 12 746	Oct 70	Smirenkin+ J – INFLUENCE ON ANGDIST	
				Jour	SNP 12 403	Apr 71	TRANSLATN.*	
Frag Spectra	None		MUA	Theo Conf	70Madurai 2 263	Dec 70	Ramamurty+ SUPERHEAVY NUCL,E – RELEASE	
Frag Spectra	None		CCP	Theo Conf	71Moscow	Feb 71	Bochagov+.ABST,PARAMS OF FISS MODL	
Frag Spectra	None		TPI	Theo Jour	IVU 14 157	Mar 71	Kurochkin+.LIQUID DROP MODL,MASS PAR	
Frag Spectra	None		BNL	Theo Jour	JNE 25 599	Dec 71	TU+ CORR PROB K.E. WITH COULOMB EN.	
Frag Spectra	–		FEI	Expt Jour	YF 15 29	Jan 72	Volodin+ AVG KE,Z – A – SYSTEMATICS,GRPH	
				Jour	SNP 15 17	Jul 72	*	
Frag Spectra	None		ORL	Theo Jour	NP/A 186 1	May 72	Schmitt+ K.E.STATIC SCISS.A=220TO310	
Frag Spectra	Maxwl		AUA	Revw Conf	IAEA – 169 2 163	74	Musgrove+ AVG FRAG MASS VS A,GRAPH	
Frag Spectra	None		FSU	Theo Jour	NP/A 222 252	Apr 74	Holub+ Z – VIBR+SHELL EFF STRUTINSKY	
Frag Spectra	None		ITK	Theo Prog	INDC(SEC) – 42	Dec 74	Krishnarajulu+ ALFA – TRAJECT CALC,NDG	
Frag Spectra	None		TRM	Revw Prog	BARC – 821 180	75	Ramaswami+ TOT AVG EKIN VS COMP – NUCL	

Many

Quantity	Energy (ev) Min	Max	Lab	Type	Documentation Ref Vol Page	Date	Author, Comments	Data
Frag Spectra	Maxwl		ITK	Theo Conf	75Calcutta 2 134	Dec 75	Krishnarajulu+ SCISSION DEFORMATION	
Frag Spectra	Fiss		ORL	Theo Jour	PR/C 13 2385	Jun 76	Davies+DEP ON VISCOSITY CALC.CFD EXP	
Frag Spectra	None		TRM	Theo Conf	76Ahmedabd 2 127	Dec 76	Prakash+SCISSN CONFIG ENTROPY METHOD	
Frag Spectra	Spont		LAS	Eval Rept	LA−UR−77−2901	77	Hoffman+ TOT KE SYSTEM,CM TO NO.CURV	
Frag Charge	None		TEN	Theo Jour	PR 72 7	Jul 47	Present. DIVISION OF NUCLEAR CHARGE.	
Frag Charge	−		FAR	Theo Rept	CEA−33	May 49	Gueron.POSS Z−DEPEND OF A−CHAINS.	
Frag Charge	None		MIT	Theo Jour	CJC 39 646	Mar 61	Coryell+ CORRELN Z COMPOSN EXCIT.	
Frag Charge	Maxwl		ITK	Theo Jour	NP/A 129 297	May 69	Mukherji. SAME MOST PROB N/Z OKS XPT	
Frag Charge	−		OSL	Revw Conf	69Vienna 669	Jul 69	Pappas+PPR206. REVW OF EXPTS+METHODS	
Frag Charge	−		JUL	Theo Jour	NP/A 140 385	Jan 70	Armbruster.QUASI STATIC SCISSN.CALCS	
Frag Charge	+0	+7	FEI	Theo Jour	YF 17 481	Mar 73	Maksyutenko.FORMULA ZP(FRAG,Z,A,N−E)	
				Jour	SNP 17 246	Sep 73	.ENGLISH OF YF 17 481	
Frag Charge	None		NIL	Theo Jour	JPJ 34 845	Apr 73	Ghani+.CALCULATED RESULT IN FIG	
Frag Charge	None		FSU	Theo Jour	NP/A 212 387	Sep 73	Holub+ CHARGE VIBR 2−SPH DROP.	
Frag Charge	Spont	1.4+7	AUA	Revw Conf	IAEA−169 2 163	74	Musgrove+ EMPIRICAL MODELS DISCUSSED	
Frag Charge	None		FSU	Theo Jour	NP/A 222 252	Apr 74	Holub+ Z−VIBR+SHELL EFF STRUTINSKY	
Frag Charge	1.5+7		LRL	Comp Rept	UCRL−51640	Jul 74	Nethaway.FISS.FRAG.CHG.HEAVY ELMNTS.	
	Maxwl			Rept	UCRL−51640	Jul 74	− .FISS.FRAG.CHG.HEAVY ELMNTS.	
	1.8+6			Rept	UCRL−51640	Jul 74	− .FISS.FRAG.CHG.HEAVY ELMNTS.	
	Spont			Rept	UCRL−51640	Jul 74	− .FISS.FRAG.CHG.HEAVY ELMNTS.	
Reson Params	None		HRV	Expt Jour	PR 51 592	Apr 37	Furry. THROUGH ACTIVATN AQUEOUS SOL.	
Reson Params	None			Jour	PR 50 381	Aug 36	.SUPERSEDED	
Reson Params	−		WIS	Theo Jour	PR 58 1068	Dec 40	Breit+ DECAY CH COMPETITION IN RES.	
Reson Params	−		CAV	Expt Jour	PR 94 741	May 54	HUGHES STATISTICAL FACTORS IN WG	
Reson Params	None		BNL	ExTh Jour	JNE 1 237	Jun 55	Hughes.AREA ANAL.NO SCAT INTERFERNCE	
Reson Params	−1	+0	BNL	Comp Jour	PR 100 1414	Dec 55	Landon. SUMMRY BEST RECNT DATA WG.	
Reson Params	−		CCP	Theo Jour	ZET 29 880	Dec 55	STATISTICAL TH OF FISSION WIDTH	
				Jour	JET 2 746	Jul 56	TRANSLATN.*	
Reson Params	3.0−2	3.0+3	BNL	Comp Jour	PR 101 1328	Feb 56	Levin+,RADIAT WIDTHS FOR 33ELEMENTS	
Reson Params	+1	+6	CCP	Theo Jour	ZET 31 335	Aug 56	Nosov.E−DEPENDENCE OF FISSION WIDTH	
				Jour	JET 4 251	Mar 57	TRANSLATN.*	
Reson Params	None		LAS	Theo Jour	PR 104 483	Oct 56	Porter+ ANAL FLUCT WF.	
Reson Params	1.0+0		BNL	Revw Jour	PHY 22 994	Nov 56	Hughes.WN 3DIST CURVES CFD WITH EXPT	
Reson Params	None		ITE	Theo Abst	PHY 22 1189	Nov 56	Nossoff.WF AS EXPON.FISSION ENERGY	
Reson Params	−		CCP	Theo Jour	NP 2 575	Jan 57	Gurevich+. DISTR OF D. 'REPULSION'EF	
Reson Params	None		CRC	Theo Jour	CJP 35 666	May 57	Cameron+ WG CALC BY NEWTONS EQN CRV.	
Reson Params	1.0+2	1.0+6	KAP	Theo Jour	NSE 2 334	May 57	Storm+,CALC A83 TO 157 D WG WN DISTR	
Reson Params	+0	+2	BNL	Revw Conf	57Col.Univ 9	Sep 57	Hughes+ DIST SPACINGS / SPIN NUCLEI	
Reson Params	3.0+6		ANL	Theo Jour	PR 109 484	Jan 58	Huizenga.CORREL OF N EMISS−NF COMPET	
Reson Params		+3	HAR	Theo Jour	PPS 71 910	Jun 58	Egelstaff.SIG FLUCTUATION THEORY	
Reson Params	3.0+6		ANL	Revw Conf	58Geneva 15 285	Sep 58	Vandenbosch+.PPR688,TBL,HEAVY ELEMNT	
Reson Params	4.0+6	1.9+7	HAR	Theo Conf	58Geneva 15 38	Sep 58	Lane+.PPR4, N−WIDTH REL TO N−NUMBER	
Reson Params	None		CRC	Expt Jour	PR 115 182	Jul 59	Egelstaff. R+ AND R−DIST,FROM DATA.	
Reson Params	None		HAR	Theo Rept	AERE−R−3353 5	May 60	Lynn.AREA FN.TABLES FOR RESON.TRANS.	
Reson Params	−			ExTh Jour	JNE 4 418	Apr 57	− +RAE.ANALYSIS OF RESONANCE DATA	
Reson Params	−		SAC	Theo Jour	NP 18 395	Sep 60	Metha+.LVL−SPACING DISTR.RNDM MATRIX	
	None			Jour	NP 18 420	Sep 60	Mehta+.LVL−SPACING DISTR.RNDM MATRIX	
Reson Params	None		NRL	ExTh Rept	NRL−5592	Feb 61	Saenz+ CALC OF J FROM MULTISCAT	
Reson Params	None		NBS	Theo Jour	PR 123 1293	Aug 61	Trees. REPULSION OF LEVELS.	
Reson Params	Slow		MIL	Comp Jour	NC 22 1237	Dec 61	Erba+COMPAR.WITH STAT.MODEL.	
Reson Params	None		NDA	Comp Rept	NYO−3078	Aug 63	Feld.TABLE,PARAMS FOR MANY NUCLIDES	
Reson Params	−		AUA	Comp Rept	AAEC/E−119	Apr 64	Doherty. NUCLEAR DATA CARD LIBRARY	
Reson Params	−		DUB	Comp Conf	JINR−1845 81	Jun 64	Sharapov+ WG(NEUTS=30 TO 62) GRAPH	
Reson Params	1.0+3	1.0+5	FEI	Theo Conf	JINR−1845 78	Jun 64	Zakharova+ WG VS A,GRAPHS,CFD EXPT	
Reson Params		1.0+4	LEB	Theo Conf	64Paris 2 751	Jul 64	Fenin+ WG EVEN−EVEN N.FROM SCAT.NDG	
Reson Params	−		UTR	Expt Conf	64Paris 2 382	Jul 64	Vanderleun.WG FOR A=20−40	
Reson Params	None		ANL	Theo Jour	PR/B 136 947	Nov 64	Moldauer.MONTE−CARLO CALC R−MTX PROP	
Reson Params		1.0+4	BNL	Revw Jour	AP 30 269	Nov 64	Garrison. SRVEY EXPT,TH LVL PAR DIST	
Reson Params	None		BNL	Theo Jour	AP 30 269	Nov 64	Garrison.STATISTICAL ANALYSIS	
Reson Params	1.0+3	1.0+5	CCP	Theo Jour	AE 18 114	Feb 65	Dovbenko+ WG, AVERAGE RES SPACING	
				Jour	JNE 20 675	Aug 66	TRANSLATN.*	
				Jour	SJA 18 140	Feb 65	TRANSLATN.*	
				Jour	EAF 18 2 44	Feb 65	TRANSLATN.*	
Reson Params	None		BNL	Eval Abst	BAP 10 513	Apr 65	Farrell+ A=40−62.OKS PORTER−THOMAS	
Reson Params	None		LRL	Revw Rept	UCRL−16348	Aug 65	Sikkeland. FORMULA+SYSTEMATICS WN/WF	
Reson Params	−		DUB	Comp Jour	NP 72 298	Oct 65	Iliescu+ RAD WIDTHS MN TO AG	
Reson Params	1.0+4	2.0+6	FEI	ExTh Rept	FEI−43	66	Kononov.STRG FUNC FROM RAD CAPT ANAL	

Many

Quantity	Energy (ev) Min	Energy (ev) Max	Lab	Type	Documentation Ref Vol Page	Date	Author, Comments	Data
Reson Params	–		MIL	Theo Rept	INFN/BE – 66 – 3	Feb 66	Gadioli+ LEVEL WIDTHS CFD STATISTMOD	
Reson Params	–		AUA	Comp Rept	AAEC/E – 147	Mar 66	Pollard+ GYMEA = REACTOR DATA LIBRARY	
				Rept	AAEC/E – 164	Oct 66	.GUNYA CODES COMPILATION+CALCULATION	
				Rept	AAEC/E – 163	Sep 66	.LUBRA CODE FOR GROUP+AVG SIGMA	
				Rept	AAEC/TM – 343	Sep 66	.BIBLIOGRAPHY OF CODES	
				Rept	AAEC/E – 150	Apr 66	.DESCRIPTION GYMEA PROGRAM	
				Rept	AAEC/TM – 250	May 64	.GUNYA CODE FOR SIGMA CALCULATION	
				Rept	AAEC/E – 119	Apr 64	.NUCLEAR DATA CARD LIBRARY	
	None			Eval Rept	AAEC/E – 114	Dec 63	.NUCLEAR DATA CARD LIBRARY	
Reson Params	None		GA	Theo Conf	66Wash. 55	Mar 66	Frohner+,ACCURACY OF PARAM MEASTS	
Reson Params	–		DUB	Theo Rept	JINR – P – 2863	Aug 66	Balashov+NUCL.WIDTH,CFD EXPT	
Reson Params	+2		FEI	Theo Rept	FEI – 56	Aug 66	Gai+ CORREL RESPARS FISSIL NUCL,GRPH	
Reson Params	–		BOL	Eval Conf	66Paris 1 537	Oct 66	Benzi.AVERAGE WG VERSUS N NUMBER	
Reson Params	–		BOL	Theo Conf	66Trieste 243	Dec 66	Benzi.CALC GAM – WID VS N – NUMBER,GRAPH	
Reson Params	–		HAR	Revw Conf	66Trieste 831	Dec 66	Rae.GAM – WIDTH VS MASS – NR,GRAPH	
Reson Params	+0	+3	FEI	Theo Rept	ICD – 4 420	67	Nikolaev+PROGR CALC SUB – GROUP CONST	
Reson Params	None		AUA	Theo Jour	AUJ 20 67	Feb 67	COOK MULTILVL FISS INTFNCE+DOPP BRDN	
Reson Params	None		FEI	Theo Rept	FEI – 78	Apr 67	Luk'Ianov.SIGMA MULTILVL ANALYSIS	
Reson Params	Thrsh	Up	CCP	Theo Jour	YF 5 1021	May 67	Vorotnikov.G AND N FISS,CURVES GVN	
				Rept	ICD – 4 366	67	.SUPERSEDED	
Reson Params	None		AUL	Theo Jour	NST 4 313	Jun 67	Wilkins.DISCUSSION ON MISSED RES	
	–			Jour	NST 4 37	Jan 67	– .DISCUSSION ON MISSED RES	
Reson Params	+0	+3	ITE	Theo Jour	AE 23 6	Jul 67	Kirpichnikov. TBL,CURVES,FISSION	
				Jour	SJA 23 669	Jul 67	TRANSLATN.*	
Reson Params	None		FEI	Theo Jour	YF 6 1313	Dec 67	GAJ+ SPIN,RES PARS CORRELTN ANAL,NDG	
				Jour	SNP 6 952	Jun 68	.TRANSLATION	
Reson Params	Maxwl		CCP	Revw Jour	IZV 32 111	Jan 68	Demidov+ REVIEW ON WG SYSTEMATC,CRVS	
				Jour	BAS 32 108	Jan 68	TRANSLATN.*NO 1	
Reson Params	–		CCP	Theo Jour	YF 7 541	Mar 68	Kuklin.GRPH WG(80 TO 200=A),OKS EXPT	
				Jour	SNP 7 3 337	Sep 68	TRANSLATN.*	
Reson Params		2.0+3	SAC	Expt Jour	NP/A 132 129	Jul 69	Julien+AVRG WG,D VERSUS J,A=26 – 201	
				ExTh Conf	JINR – D3893 118	May 68	Morgenstern+AVG D+WG(A=35 – 100)GRPHS	
				Expt Conf	68Wash. 867	Mar 68	– + PPR E27.	
				Conf	68Wash. 867	Mar 68	– .CURVES D AND WG VS. A	
				Conf	66Paris 1 559	Oct 66	Huynh+ ABST.NDG. SEE INDC – 156	
Reson Params	+6		DUB	Theo Priv	FURMAN	Jun 68	Furman+.N RES DENSITY+DEFORM,STATMOD	
Reson Params	Maxwl		ANL	Theo Conf	68DUBSY 317	Jul 68	Bollinger.AVERAGE VALUES REDUC. W – M1	
Reson Params	None		AUA	Theo Rept	AAEC/TM – 463	Jul 68	Musgrove.METHOD TO FIND MISSED LVLS	
Reson Params	–		DUB	Expt Conf	68DUBSY 349	Jul 68	Pikelner.RARE EARTH,AVERAG LVL SPAC	
Reson Params		+4	DUB	Expt Conf	68DUBSY 349	Jul 68	Pikelner.GE AN SE ISOTOP,WG,S0 VS A	
Reson Params	None		CCP	Theo Jour	ZEP 8 158	Aug 68	Shapiro.GIANT RESONANCES STRUCTURE	
Reson Params	None		IFU	Theo Jour	UFZ 13 1415	Sep 68	Kolomiets+WN OF (N,N)(N,G)(N,N'G),TH	
				Jour	UPJ 13 1011	Mar 69	TRANSLATN.*	
Reson Params	None		CCP	Theo Jour	AE 25 435	Nov 68	Lukianov+ FORMULA SIG(E,RES – PARS)GVN	
				Jour	EAF 25 5 122	Nov 68	TRANSLATN.*	
Reson Params		+3	AUA	Theo Jour	AUJ 21 779	Dec 68	Musgrove. ON UNRESOLVED RESONANCES	
Reson Params	+7		LEB	Theo Jour	IZV 32 2051	Dec 68	Popov. A=70+190,WG TBL,DOORWAY – STATE	
				Jour	BAS 32 1885	Dec 69	. ENGL OF IZV 32 2051	
Reson Params		2.0+5	TRM	Revw Prog	BARC – 423 7	69	Garg. REACTOR DATA REVW,MISSING XPTS	
Reson Params	None		SDC	Theo Jour	NP/A 124 577	Feb 69	Freeman+ DISTRIB.INTERFERING RES.	
Reson Params	–		CCP	Theo Jour	YF 9 535	Mar 69	Gejlikman.WF+SIG,QUASISTATONARY LVLS	
				Jour	SNP 9 306	Sep 69	TRANSLATN.*	
Reson Params	–		AUA	Comp Prog	AAEC/PR – 31P 8	Apr 69	Cook. LIGHT+FISSILE NUCLEI,TB CONTn4	
Reson Params	None		BNL	Theo Prog	WASH – 1127 21	Apr 69	Chrien+STATISTICAL THEORY OF WG DIST	
Reson Params	–		FEI	Theo Prog	YFI – 7 9	Apr 69	Ignatyuk+EVEN+ODD WN+WF CRV,STRUT – TH	
				Rept	INDC(CCP) – 7U7	Feb 70	TRANSLATN.*	
Reson Params			FEI	Theo Jour	YF 9 775	Apr 69	Rabotnov. WIDTH FLUCTUATN+SIG ANALYS	
				Jour	SNP 9 451	Oct 69	TRANSLATN.*NO4	
Reson Params	–		BUC	Theo Jour	SCF 21 660	Jun 69	Aldeda+ REVIEW OF WN WG DISTRIBUTION	
Reson Params	+3	+5	AUA	Expt Conf	69Studsvik 587	Aug 69	Bird+ A=40 – 70,P+D CAPTURE,TB CONTIND	
Reson Params	None		BNL	Theo Jour	PR 181 1422	May 69	Beer. WIDTH CORRELATIONS+DISTRIBUTNS	
	Maxwl			Revw Conf	69Studsvik 627	Aug 69	Chrien. REVIEW,'RES – N – CAPT GAM – RAYS'	
Reson Params	None		ANL	Theo Prog	WASH – 1136 12	Sep 69	Monahan+,METHOD FOR LVL SPACING DIST	
Reson Params		+4	ITE	Theo Jour	YF 10 496	Sep 69	Sukhoruchkin. WN+D STATMOD ANAL,GRPH	
					–		SEE ALSO ABSTRACT IN 68RIGA	
				Jour	SNP 10 285	Mar 70	. ENGL OF YF 10 496	
Reson Params	Maxwl	+7	AUA	Theo Rept	AAEC/TM – 520	Nov 69	Ferguson. GUNYA+GYMEA,RES – PARS CALC	

Many

Quantity	Energy (ev) Min	Energy (ev) Max	Lab	Type	Documentation Ref Vol Page	Date	Author, Comments	Data
Reson Params	2.0+5		MUA	Theo Conf	69Roorke 2 129	Dec 69	Chaubey+ CAPT – SIG,G – WIDTH AND D FIT	
Reson Params	–		AUA	Theo Prog	AAEC/PR – 33P 10	70	Cook. FISSILE NUCLIDES,MULTILVL ANAL	
Reson Params	–		AUA	Theo Prog	AAEC/PR – 33P 10	70	Cook. RESONANCE STATISTICS, NO DATA	
Reson Params	–		DUB	Comp Rept	JINR – P3 – 4929	Feb 70	Maletskij+ GAM – GAM EMPIRICAL FORMULA	
Reson Params	–		AUA	Theo Jour	AUJ 23 117	Apr 70	Musgrove. MEAN D+ – ERROR ANALYS,SPIN	
				Rept	AAEC/TM – 515	Jul 69	*	
Reson Params	–		DUB	Theo Rept	JINR – E4 – 5135	May 70	Soloviev.ALFA+G WIDTH CFD WAVEFUNCTN	
Reson Params		1.0+3	DUB	Theo Conf	70Helsinki 1 669	Jun 70	Popov+125. SYSTEMATIC OF ALPHA – WIDTH	
Reson Params	–		FEI	Theo Conf	70Helsinki 2 909	Jun 70	Zakharova+82. GAM – W(A = 60 – 200) GRPHS	
Reson Params	5.0+2	2.0+3	KUR	Revw Conf	70Helsinki 1 603	Jun 70	Muradyan+ EXP CFD TH, LVL SCH CORR	
Reson Params	–		DUB	Theo Jour	YF 12 82	Jul 70	Gabrakov+ MAGNETIC DIPOL RESON,(N,G)	
				Jour	SNP 12 44	Jan 71	. ENGL OF YF 12 82	
Reson Params	None		REH	Theo Prog	IA – 1218 12	Aug 70	GUR+ FISSILE NUCLEI,UNRESOLVD,ENDF/B	
Reson Params		3.0+5	CCP	Revw Jour	AE 29 187	Sep 70	Sukhoruchkin. Z BELOW 30,RESON ES	
				Jour	SJA 29 896	Sep 70	TRANSLATN.*	
Reson Params	–		DUB	Theo Jour	JINR – P2 – 5328	Sep 70	Lyuboshits. MULTICHANL SCAT+RES ANAL	
Reson Params	–		REH	Theo Rept	IA – 1208	Sep 70	Gur+ CALC FLUCTUATN FACTOR,TBL,GRPHS	
Reson Params	–		FEI	Theo Jour	YF 12 746	Oct 70	Smirenkin+ FISSN ANGDIST VERSUS J	
				Jour	SNP 12 403	Apr 71	TRANSLATN.*	
Reson Params	–		AUA	Theo Rept	AAEC/E – 211	Nov 70	Musgrove. GAMMA – WIDTH VS Z, BEST FIT	
Reson Params	–		DUB	Revw Jour	JINR – E4 – 5469	Nov 70	Soloviev. SINGLE PART.ENERGY VS A	
Reson Params	None		TRM	Theo Conf	70Madurai 2 279	Dec 70	Ramamurty+ SUPERHEAVY NUCL,N+F – WIDS	
Reson Params	+0	+7	CJD	Eval Rept	YK – 7	71	Zakharova+ SURVEY+SYSTEMATICS,GW,TBL	
				Rept	INDC(CCP) – 27	Nov 72	.ENGLISH TRANSLATION OF YK – 7 /71	
Reson Params	–		JAE	Theo Jour	JPJ 30 620	Mar 71	Ideno+.CORRELATION ANAL OF RES – SPACE	
	0.0+0	2.0+4		Jour	JPJ 37 581	Sep 74	– .CORRELATION IN LEVEL SPACING	
	None			Expt Prog	EANDC(J)19L15	Aug 70	– +.CORRELATION ANAL OF RES – SPACE	
Reson Params	None		FEI	Theo Conf	71Kiev	May 71	Jadrovsky+.3 METH OF NUC WIDTHS CALC	
Reson Params	None		FEI	Theo Conf	71Kiev	May 71	Ignatjuk+.AVG WG,SUPERFLUID – MDL,GRPH	
Reson Params	+0		CCP	Theo Jour	AE 31 18	Jul 71	Vorotnikov.RATIO S/P F – WIDS VS Z2/A	
				Jour	SJA 31 706	Feb 72	* ENGL OF AE 31 18 7/71	
Reson Params	1.3+5		MUA	Theo Prog	BARC – 553 19	Aug 71	Alam+ STATIST THEO,SIG CALC,ABST,NDG	
				Conf	70Madurai 2 34	Dec 70	. SAME ABSTRACT ONLY	
Reson Params	2.5+4		AUW	Expt Conf	72Chandigr 2 119	Dec 72	Rama Rao+ S+P – WVE (N,G) VS A, NDG	
Reson Params	None		HED	Eval Rept	HEDL – TME – 73 – 30	Jan 73	Schmittroth.AVG D L=0 RESON 85NUCLEI	
Reson Params	None		DUB	Theo Jour	YF 17 293	Feb 73	Alfimenkov+ P – RES STUDY BY POLRZD NS	
				Jour	SNP 17 149	Aug 73	.ENGLISH OF YF 17 293	
Reson Params		+7	BER	Theo Jour	ZP 258 301	Mar 73	LIU. APPLICATION OF RES SCAT TH	
Reson Params	1.5+7		TUD	Theo Conf	73Munich 1 514	Aug 73	Hermsdorf+ PRE – EQU WIDS FROM INEL NS	
Reson Params	+7	+8	IJI	Theo Jour	PL/B 47 121	Oct 73	Strutinsky. FISS WIDTH VS BARRIER FM	
Reson Params	2.1+1	6.0+1	ORL	Theo Jour	NSE 52 412	Nov 73	Desaussure+ .1 – LVL PARS FROM MULTLVL	
Reson Params		+3	GEL	Eval Rept	RCN – 203 194	Dec 73	Weigmann+ SYSTEMATICS OF AVG WG	
Reson Params	None		DUB	Theo Rept	YFI – 17 25	Aug 74	Solovjev. WN,WG	
				Jour	PL/B 36 199	Sep 71	Soloviev.CORR PARTIAL RADIATIVE W	
				Rept	JINR – E4 – 5711	Apr 71	– .RESONANCE STRUCTURE STUDY	
	–			Rept	JINR – P4 – 5583	Feb 71	– .CORRELATN OF NEUT+GAM WIDTH	
Reson Params	None		ITE	Theo Conf	75Kiev 4 90	May 75	Beljaev+ NONSTATIST EFF IN LVL SPACI	
Reson Params	None		JAP	Theo Jour	PTP 54 1378	Nov 75	Izumo.THEORY ON CORRELATED LEVELS	
Reson Params	+0	+4	BUC	Revw Jour	RRP 21 619	Jun 76	Aldea+ AVG RED N – WIDS VS N,Z,A.GRPHS	
	None			Expt Jour	SCF 24 165	Feb 72	Mateiciuc.RED N – WID VS N – NUMBER,GRPH	
	–			Revw Rept	IFA – NR – 39	71	Aldea+ REDUCED N – WID+D VS Z,A,GRAPHS	
Reson Params	+0	+3	JUL	Theo Conf	JINR – D – 9920	Jun 76	Schult. P176. G – AND N – WIDS CORRELTD	
Reson Params	None		KUK	Theo Conf	76Lowell 1428	Jul 76	Sharma+WN ANAL.DEG OF FREEDOM CALC.	
Reson Params	+0	+5	AUA	Comp Prog	AAEC/PR – 42P 26	Sep 76	Bird+ AVG S,P G – WIDS(A) SYSTEMAT.FIG	
Strnth Fnctn	None		BNL	Comp Jour	PR 96 113	Oct 54	Carter+ AG107 TO TH232 CF EXPT+THEOR	
Strnth Fnctn	–		CAV	Theo Jour	PM 45 1322	Dec 54	Scott.A MEDIUM INTERACTION MODEL	
Strnth Fnctn	–		CER	Theo Jour	PM 46 376	Apr 55	Jankovic.CURVS FM OF R S WAVE NEUTS	
Strnth Fnctn	–		MIT	Revw Conf	55Geneva 2 23	Aug 55	Weisskopf+.P830,REVIEW OF THEORIES	
Strnth Fnctn	1.0+0		BNL	Revw Jour	PHY 22 994	Nov 56	Hughes.INDIV.RES AND AVGED VALUS CFD	
Strnth Fnctn	+4		HAR	Expt Jour	PPSA 70 51	Jan 57	Gayther+ FROM AVG SIGTOT,A = 95 TO 239	
	1.0+3			ExTh Jour	PHY 22 1133	Nov 56	– +ABSTRACT,A96TO209EXPT CFD TH	
Strnth Fnctn	None		COL	Theo Jour	PR 106 105	Apr 57	Margolis+,A = 90 – 240 SPHEROID POT,CRVS	
Strnth Fnctn	None		PUR	Theo Jour	NP 3 255	Apr 57	Peaslee. EFFECT OF APPRX OF DIF EDGE	
Strnth Fnctn	–		SAC	Theo Jour	NP 3 137	Apr 57	Bloch. RELATION TO COMPLEX POTENTIAL	
Strnth Fnctn	–		CCP	Theo Jour	ZET 32 1143	May 57	CFD XPT CURVES	
				Jour	JET 5 932	Dec 57	TRANSLATN.*	
Strnth Fnctn	1.0+2	1.0+6	KAP	Theo Jour	NSE 2 334	May 57	Storm+,CALC A83 TO 157	

Many

Quantity	Energy (ev) Min	Max	Lab	Type	Documentation Ref Vol Page	Author, Comments Date	Data
Strnth Fnctn	–		CCP	Theo Jour	NP 6 295	Mar 58 Vladimirsky+.OPT MDL FOR PROLATE NUC	
Strnth Fnctn	None		DKE	Expt Jour	RMP 30 442	Apr 58 Seth.VARIOUS TH CURVES WITH EXPTS	
				Conf	TID – 7547	Sep 57 .CURVS. L=0 A35 – 80,L=1 A80 – 110.	
Strnth Fnctn	+1	+6	BNL	Comp Conf	58Geneva 16 8	Sep 58 Hughes.PPR2483,CURVE,MANY REFS	
Strnth Fnctn	–		HAR	Theo Jour	PRL 2 424	May 59 Lane+,THEOR CURVS STRNTH FNCT VS. A	
Strnth Fnctn	None		GA	Theo Rept	GA – 920	Jul 59 Bell.LEAST – SQ FIT TO RESON DATA	
Strnth Fnctn		+3	ANL	Revw Jour	NP 14 120	Dec 59 Leblanc+VARIATION FOR A=40 – 90 CFD TH	
Strnth Fnctn	None		FSU	Theo Jour	NP 15 337	Feb 60 Khanna+SURFACE ABS OPTMOD CFD DATA	
Strnth Fnctn	None		BRK	Revw Conf	60Kingston 659	Aug 60 Harvey.CURVE,THEORET DISCUSSION	
Strnth Fnctn	None		DKE	Eval Jour	AP 10 477	Aug 60 Weston+ L=0 FROM LITERATURE,L=1 FITS	
Strnth Fnctn	1.0+5	4.0+6	ANL	Theo Rept	ANL – 6323	Mar 61 Moldauer.OPTMDL CALCS TBLS+CURVS	
Strnth Fnctn	None		DKE	Theo Jour	NP 24 169	Apr 61 Seth. J – DEPENDENCE OF S – WAVE STRFUNC	
Strnth Fnctn	–		CCP	Theo Jour	ZET 41 959	Sep 61 Elagin.OPTMDL,GRAPH STF VS A	
				Jour	JET 14 682	Mar 62 TRANSLATN.*	
Strnth Fnctn	None		WAD	Theo Jour	NP 28 578	Dec 61 Krueger+ OPTMDL CALC CFD EXPERIMENTS	
Strnth Fnctn	+3	+4	DKE	Expt Rept	TID – 16059	62 Furr.CURVES AVG STF VS. A	
Strnth Fnctn	None		GA	Eval Jour	NSE 12 115	Jan 62 Garrison+.S WAVE. CURVE VERSUS A	
Strnth Fnctn	None		ORL	Theo Jour	NP 32 353	May 62 Perey+ S – WAVE A=35 – 238 CFD OPTMDL.	
Strnth Fnctn	None		MIT	Theo Rept	TID – 16603	Sep 62 Block+. STF VS. A. CURV.SHELL MODEL	
Strnth Fnctn	–		SAF	Theo Jour	AP 19 428	Sep 62 . CALCULATED P – WAVE STRENGTH FUNCTN	
Strnth Fnctn	–		STL	Theo Jour	NP 38 686	Nov 62 Fiedeldey+.EXPT CFD THEORY,A=40 – 180	
Strnth Fnctn	None		ORL	Theo Conf	63Houston 193	Feb 63 Gibbons. S(1) VS A, SPH, COLLECT MDL	
Strnth Fnctn	2.0+5	1.0+6	ANL	Theo Jour	NP 47 65	Aug 63 Moldauer.SIG VS A CFD OPTMODEL	
Strnth Fnctn	2.8+5	8.5+5	ANL	Theo Jour	PR/B 133 80	Jan 64 Elwyn+ 2 PEAKS NEAR A100 L1.	
Strnth Fnctn	None		BNL	Theo Jour	NP 50 157	Jan 64 Jain.OPTMOD.S+P WAVE STRENTH FN VS A	
Strnth Fnctn	1.0+3	6.0+6	BNL	Theo Jour	PR/B 134 1	Apr 64 Jain. OPTMDL CALC TOT VS STRNTHFN.	
Strnth Fnctn	–		CHF	Theo Jour	CHP 2 32	Apr 64 JENN – LIN HWANG+ S – PEAKS VS A,CFD TH	
Strnth Fnctn	+2	+4	KUR	ExTh Conf	JINR – 1845 45	Jun 64 Adamchuk+ OPTMODL,TH CFD XPTS,GRAPH	
Strnth Fnctn	4.0+6	5.0+6	JAE	Expt Jour	PL 11 141	Jul 64 Tsukada+ FROM FLUCT, COMPD FORM SIG	
Strnth Fnctn	None		ANL	ExTh Jour	PL 11 331	Aug 64 Vonach+ A=190 TO 210 CFD OPTMDL.	
Strnth Fnctn	3.0+4	6.5+5	DKE	ExTh Jour	PL 13 70	Nov 64 Seth+ TBL S – ,P – ,D – WAVE VALUES.	
Strnth Fnctn	None		BNL	Theo Rept	BNL – 8711	Dec 64 Chrien. COMPUTER PROGRAM FOR S0 ANAL	
Strnth Fnctn	1.0+3	1.0+5	ORL	Eval Jour	RMP 37 166	Jan 65 Macklin+ UNRESV PARAM FRM VAR SRCES.	
Strnth Fnctn	None		KUR	Theo Rept	IAE – 902	Jun 65 Muradyan+THEOR METHOD CFD OPTMOD	
Strnth Fnctn	–		MUA	Theo Jour	NP 76 475	Feb 66 Khan.ODD+EVEN A CFD REL I/I IN OPTMD	
	None			Jour	NP 67 413	May 65 – . S – WAVE STR – FUNC SURFACE FITTE	
Strnth Fnctn	None		DKE	Expt Conf	66Wash. 562	Mar 66 Newson.MED WT NUCLEI,P – S WAVE STF	
Strnth Fnctn		7.0+5	ALD	Eval Jour	ND/A 2 243	Sep 66 HORSLEY TOT,DEL,NG EVL	
Strnth Fnctn	None		FEI	Theo Rept	YFI – 3 10	Sep 66 Kononov. FROM (N,G) ANALYSIS	
				Rept	INDC – 140E 12	67 . ENGL TRANSL OF YFI – 3 10	
Strnth Fnctn	None		MCM	Theo Jour	NP 85 641	Sep 66 Slavinkas+ ESTIMATION FROM XPT DATA	
Strnth Fnctn		7.0+5	NWU	Comp Jour	ND/A 2 299	Sep 66 Seth. EXPT COMPIL+EVAL F TO CM,L=0.	
Strnth Fnctn	+0	1.8+4	ITE	Eval Conf	66Paris 1 159	Oct 66 PPP105,SUKHORUCHKIN.REVIEW+ANALYSIS	
Strnth Fnctn	–		HAR	Revw Conf	66Trieste 831	Dec 66 Rae.EXPTL S,P VS A CFD THEO,GRPHS	
Strnth Fnctn	–		JAE	Theo Rept	JAERI – 1126 1	Jan 67 Kawai+IGARASI.OPT MDL CAL C ELIESE – 2	
Strnth Fnctn	–		SAF	Eval Jour	AP 42 262	Apr 67 Engelbrecht+ OPTMDL CALCS CFD EXPTS	
Strnth Fnctn	+6		AUA	Theo Rept	AAEC/TM – 392	Jun 67 Cook+.S,P – WAVE STRNTHFUNC,VAL GIVEN	
Strnth Fnctn	1.0+1		IAC	Theo Jour	IJP 41 816	Nov 67 Ganguly.STRGH FUNCTN,A=40=200CFD EXP	
	None			Jour	IJP 40 623	Nov 66 – . S – WAVE STRNGTH FUNC,OPTMOD	
Strnth Fnctn	5.5+2	4.9+4	CCP	Expt Jour	AE 24 173	Feb 68 Maletski+ GRPH S0(A=40TO100),GE ISOT	
				Jour	SJA 24 207	Feb 68 TRANSLATN.*	
Strnth Fnctn	–		DUB	Expt Jour	YF 7 225	Feb 68 Karzhavina+SO(130 TO 200 =A),GRPH	
				Jour	SNP 7 2 161	Aug 68 – + ENGL OF YF 7 225.	
Strnth Fnctn	–		DUB	Comp Jour	YF 7 493	Mar 68 Konks+ S1(A=60 – 240) GRAPH,COMPIL+XPT	
				Jour	SNP 7 310	Sep 68 – + ENGL OF YF 7 493.	
Strnth Fnctn	Maxwl		CCP	ExTh Jour	YF 7 937	May 68 Groshev+S – PEAK – WIDTH,A=208,5MEV GAM	
				Jour	SNP 7 563	Nov 68 TRANSLATN.*	
Strnth Fnctn	None		AUA	Theo Rept	AAEC/TM – 463	Jul 68 Musgrove.METHOD TO FIND MISSED LVLS	
Strnth Fnctn	None		WIS	Theo Jour	NP/A 115 504	Jul 68 Goebel+ S – WAVE,SCATTLNGTH APPROX.	
Strnth Fnctn		1.0+6	SAC	Expt Rept	CEA – R – 3609	Sep 68 Morgenstern.RADIUS FOR A=51 TO 209	+
	1.0+0	9.9+5		ExTh Conf	JINR – D3893 118	May 68 – +S1,S0(A=35 TO 200)GRAPH	
		9.9+5		Expt Conf	68Wash. 867	Mar 68 – + PPR E27	
				Conf	66Paris 1 183	Oct 66 – + PPR65.ABST.NDG.INDC – 156	
				Conf	65Antwerp 531	Jul 65 – + PPR87.ABST.NDG.	
Strnth Fnctn		+3	AUA	Theo Jour	AUJ 21 779	Dec 68 Musgrove. ON UNRESOLVED RESON, S0	
Strnth Fnctn		6.0+6	CCP	Expt Conf	69Erevan	Feb 69 Sukhoruchkin.ABST,NONSTAT LVL DISTR	

Many

Quantity	Energy (ev) Min	Max	Lab	Type	Documentation Ref Vol Page	Author, Comments Date	Data
Strnth Fnctn	None		AI	Theo	Jour NP/A 127 465	Apr 69 Gigas. 2 – EVN ROTOR A=220 – 262,4 MDLS.	
					Jour NP/A 112 527	May 68 .EARLY RESULTS.	
					Rept AI – 12652A	68 Gigas. TABLE.	
Strnth Fnctn	None		DUB	Theo	Rept JINR – P3 – 4484	Jun 69 Malecki+ ANALYT EXPRESS BY STATMODL	
	–			Expt	Conf 68DUBSY 349	Jul 68 Pikelner.RARE EARTH,ANALYSIS OPT MOD	
Strnth Fnctn	None		CRC	Revw	Jour 69Studsvik 553	Aug 69 Bartholomew. ON '5.5MEV GAM ANOMALY'	
Strnth Fnctn	–		DUB	Theo	Rept JINR – P4 – 4511	Oct 69 Fenin. S0 VERSUS A GRAPHS, OPTMODEL	
Strnth Fnctn	+3	+5	AUA	Theo	Prog AAEC/PR – 33P 10	70 Cook. RESONANCE STATISTICS, NO DATA	
Strnth Fnctn	+3	+4	DUB	Theo	Jour YF 11 1152	Jun 70 Samosvat. S0(A=40 – 240),OPTMOD ANAL	
					Jour SNP 11 639	Dec 70 – . ENGL OF YF 11 1152.	
Strnth Fnctn	5.0+2	2.0+3	KUR	Revw	Conf 70Helsinki 1 603	Jun 70 Muradyan+ EXP CFD TH, LVL SCH CORR	
Strnth Fnctn	None		AUA	Revw	Rept AAEC/TM – 565	Sep 70 Allen.CALC P,D – WAVE CFD EXPTS.GRPHS	
					–	FULL TEXT OF PAPER AT 70CHICAGO (APS	
Strnth Fnctn	–		CCP	Revw	Jour AE 29 187	Sep 70 Sukhoruchkin. S0 VERSUS A GRAPHS	
					Jour SJA 29 896	Sep 70 TRANSLATN.*	
Strnth Fnctn	–		AUA	Theo	Rept AAEC/E – 211	Nov 70 Musgrove. S0,S1 AND S2 VERSUS A, TBL	
Strnth Fnctn	–		DUB	Revw	Rept JINR – E4 – 5469	Nov 70 Soloviev. STRENGTH FUNCTION VERSUS A	
Strnth Fnctn	None		KFK	Expt	Rept KFK – EXT – 4 28	Nov 70 Chou. COMP OF EXPT+CALC SI,A=80 – 165	
Strnth Fnctn	–		MIF	Theo	Jour ZEP 13 646	Jun 71 Zaretskii+ CALC S – WAVE,A=20 – 242.GRPH	
					Jour JEL 13 460	Jun 71 . ENGL OF ZEP 13 646	
Strnth Fnctn	2.4+4		MUA	Theo	Prog BARC – 553 19	Aug 71 Chaubey+ ABST ONLY,S1 CALC,NDG	
					Conf 70Madurai 2 34	Dec 70 . SAME ABSTRACT ONLY	
Strnth Fnctn	2.5+4		AUW	Theo	Prog BARC – 614 40	72 RAMA RAO+ P – WAVE VS A CFD THEORIES	
Strnth Fnctn	None		BUC	Expt	Jour SCF 24 165	Feb 72 Mateiciuc.S – WAVE STRENGTH VS A,GRAPH	
	–			Revw	Rept IFA – NR – 39	71 Aldea+ S – WAVE EXPTL+THEO VS A,GRAPH	
Strnth Fnctn	None		RPI	Theo	Conf 72Budapest 136	Aug 72 Turinsky+ P – WAVE STRENGTH – FUNCT,GRPH	
Strnth Fnctn	None		AUA	Eval	Rept AAEC/E – 277	Mar 73 Musgrove. S,P – WVE STRNGF,F TO CM,TBL	
Strnth Fnctn		+6	KUR	Theo	Conf 73Kiev 2 39	May 73 Adamchuk+ S – AND P – NEUTS,OPTMOD,GRAPH	
Strnth Fnctn	1.0+0		KFK	Revw	Conf JINR – D3 – 7991	Apr 74 Cierjacks.P196.L=1,CALC FROM XPTS	
					Conf JINR – D3 – 7991	Apr 74 – .P196.P – WAVE,XPT+TH SUMMARY	
Strnth Fnctn	None		DUB	Theo	Rept YFI – 17 25	Aug 74 Solovjev. S – AND P – NEUTS,CALC,CFD XPT	
Strnth Fnctn	+1	+4	KUK	Expt	Jour 74Bombay 2 111	Dec 74 Sharma+ REDUCD WIDTHS,STATIST ANALYS	
Strnth Fnctn	None		SAC	Theo	Jour JPC 36 335	75 Jain.OPTMDL,SURFACE ABSORTION EFFECT	
Strnth Fnctn		+5	KFK	Theo	Conf JAERI – M – 5984	Feb 75 Newstead.P230.TBL.CURVES VS A.S0,S1	
	None				Conf 72Budapest 142	Aug 72 – + A – DEPEND SN,TE,XE,BA,GRAPH	
Strnth Fnctn	None		OSA	Theo	Conf JAERI – M – 5984	Feb 75 Kitazoe+OPT MDL. GRPH VS MASS NO.	
Strnth Fnctn	3.0+4	3.0+5	RPI	Theo	Conf JAERI – M – 5984	Feb 75 Sierra+SYSTEMATICS OF STRENGTH FN.	
Strnth Fnctn	None		CBE	Revw	Conf 75Wash. 806	Mar 75 Newstead.FLUCTUATIONS IN STF.	
Strnth Fnctn	None		KAP	Theo	Conf 75Wash. 338	Mar 75 Kirouac.CALC FLUCTUATIONS CFD EXP	
Strnth Fnctn	2.5 – 2	5.0+2	LIE	Theo	Jour NP/A 263 61	May 76 Cugnon.SYSTEMATICS OF VALENCE CAPT.	
Strnth Fnctn	Thrsh		LIE	Theo	Jour NP/A 263 47	May 76 Cugnon.L=C ST – FUNCT NEAR THRESHOLD	
Strnth Fnctn	2.7+3		MUN	Expt	Conf 71Albany 327	Aug 76 Dilg+TRNS.S0 STF GVN.31 ELEMENT GRPH	
Lvl Density	–		MIN	Theo	Jour PR 82 243	Apr 51 Critchfield+EMPRCL FORML LIGHT NUCL	
Lvl Density	8.0+6		BNL	Expt	Jour PR 91 1423	Sep 53 Hughes+.LEVEL SPACING VERSUS A.	
Lvl Density	None		CAL	Theo	Jour PR 93 1094	Mar 54 Bloch.STATISTICAL MODEL	
Lvl Density	1.0+6	2.0+8	LVP	Theo	Jour PPSA 67 586	Jul 54 Lang+ FERMI GAS MODEL,CFD EXPT	
Lvl Density	None		MIT	Revw	Conf 55Geneva 2 23	Aug 55 Weisskopf+.P830,REVIEW OF THEORIES	
Lvl Density	2.0+6	8.0+6	GLS	Theo	Jour PM 2 473	Apr 57 Brown+ REACTN DATA CF LANG – LECOUTEUR	
Lvl Density	–		COP	Theo	Jour NP 6 62	Mar 58 Ericson. LVL DENSITY FOR DEFORMD NUC	
Lvl Density		+3	HAR	Theo	Jour PPS 71 910	Jun 58 Egelstaff.SIG FLUCTUATION THEORY	
Lvl Density	0.0+0	1.0+0	CAI	Theo	Jour NP 9 22	Nov 58 El – Nadi+EMPIRICAL CURVE.OKS FERMIGAS	
	None				Conf 58Geneva 14 54	Sep 58 Elnadi+.PPR1481,CURVES	
Lvl Density	–		CBR	Theo	Jour NP 13 32	Oct 59 LE COUTEUR+REVIEW +TH CURV T VS XCIT	
Lvl Density	–		SAC	Theo	Jour NP 13 594	Nov 59 Ballian.DENS.BY GRAND PARTITION FUNC	
Lvl Density	+6	+7	JAP	Theo	Conf 62Padua 312	Sep 62 IZUMO //PARTIAL HEATING//HYPOTHESIS	
Lvl Density	None		BNL	Theo	Jour NP 40 167	Jan 63 Porter.NEXTNEAREST LVL DIST+RELAT.TH	
Lvl Density	–		OSA	Theo	Jour PTP 29 397	Mar 63 Sano+SUPERCONDUCT TH CFD C FERMI GAS	
					Conf 62Padua 325	62 – + ALSO P330.	
Lvl Density	None	9.9+3	CBR	Theo	Jour NP 42 353	Apr 63 Lang.PAIR CORREL.MODELS CFD FERMIGAS	
Lvl Density	–		FEI	ExTh	Jour ZET 45 316	Aug 63 Malyshev.FERMIGAS PARAMETERS,CURVES	+
					Rept JINR – 1845 30	Oct 64 .PROCEEDINGS OF 64DUBNA	
					Conf 64Paris 2 759	Jul 64 SEE ALSO *	
					Jour JET 18 221	Jan 64 .ENGLISH TRANSL OF ZET 45 316 8/63	
Lvl Density	–		CIS	Eval	Jour NP 51 449	Feb 64 Saettamenichella+SMALL A.13 – 50NEUTRS	
Lvl Density	–		CIS	Eval	Jour NP 51 460	Feb 64 Facchini+DENSITY VS NEUT NO,10 – 160	
					Jour PL 3 361	Feb 63 – + SUPERSEDED.	
Lvl Density	–		BRD	Eval	Jour NP 52 630	Apr 64 Aspinall+SPECTROGRAPH+N RES DATA CFD	

Many

Quantity	Energy (ev) Min	Max	Lab	Type	Documentation Ref Vol Page	Date	Author, Comments	Data
Lvl Density	None		IOW	Theo Abst	DA 24 4748	May 64	Leff. STAT TH FOR LVL SPACING DIST.	
Lvl Density	2.0+7	4.0+7	PRT	Theo Jour	NP 53 558	May 64	Thomas.ANGULAR MOMENTUM DEPENDENCE	
Lvl Density	-		PRT	Theo Jour	NP 53 577	May 64	Thomas.N EMISS AT HIGH ANG.MOMENTUM	
Lvl Density	2.0+7	4.0+7	WAS	Eval Jour	NP 54 65	May 64	Hurwitz+ A/17 TO A/21 IN 40-120 RANGE	
Lvl Density		+7	HEI	Theo Jour	PL 10 331	Jun 64	Weidenmuller.DOUBT ON EXP RHO WITH E	
Lvl Density	1.0+6	8.0+6	LRL	ExTh Jour	NP 57 515	Aug 64	Wong+ A=A/8 BY (PN),V51-RH103.	
Lvl Density	+6	+7	CAI	Theo Jour	NP 58 601	Sep 64	Abdelmacek+PARAM A CFD FISS YIELD	
Lvl Density	None		ANL	Theo Jour	PR/B 136 923	Nov 64	Wing+ NEW SEMI-EMPRCAL MASS EQ.	
Lvl Density	None		ANL	Theo Jour	NP 60 70	Nov 64	Vonach+SUPERCOND TH+SIMPLE FERMI GAS	
Lvl Density	None		DKE	ExTh Jour	NP 60 17	Nov 64	Buccino+VALUES LITTLE A ETC	
Lvl Density	-		MEX	Theo Jour	NP 61 177	Jan 65	Canuto+ODD-EVEN EFFECT+SUPERFLUID MD	
Lvl Density	1.4+7		HAM	Theo Jour	NP 65 257	Mar 65	Bormann.IN RELATION TO SIGMA(N,2N)	
Lvl Density	-		COL	Theo Jour	CJP 43 1248	Jul 65	Gilbert+ NUCLEI WITH Z LESS THAN 30.	
Lvl Density	None		COL	Theo Jour	CJP 43 1446	Aug 65	Gilbert+ COMPOSITE FORMULA.	
Lvl Density		5.0+4	FEI	Eval Rept	FEI-36	66	Kapchigashev+.45NUCLEI,FROM(N,GAMMA)	+
				Jour	YF 4 686	Sep 66	.SHORT VERSION OF FEI 36.TABLE	
				Prog	YFI-3 3	Sep 66	.ABSTRACT.TABLE LDL+NUCL.EXCIT.E	
				Jour	SNP 4 486	67	.ENGLISH TRANSL OF YF 4 686 9/66.	
				Prog	INDC-E-140 3	66	.ENGLISH TRANSL OF YFI-3	
Lvl Density	+3	+6	UI	Revw Jour	RMP 38 41	Jan 66	Perdrisat. SURVEY OF NUCL LVLS,E-1.	
Lvl Density	None		CSD	Theo Jour	NP 77 477	Mar 66	Thompson+CURVE OF ENERGY GAP VS A	
				Jour	PL 14 147	Jan 65	- + ENERGY GAP CALC FOR P.	
Lvl Density	-		HAM	Expt Jour	ZN/A 21 988	Sep 66	Bormann+.SPIN CUTOFF PARAM VERSUS A	
Lvl Density	None		FEI	Theo Conf	66Paris 1 163	Oct 66	PPP106,SHUBIN+.TBL+CURVS,REVIEW	
				Rept	INDC-156	66	. FULL PAPER INCLUDED	
Lvl Density	None		WIS	Expt Jour	NP 88 689	Nov 66	Borchers+(P,N)SPEC GIVE LDL ANORMAL	
Lvl Density	-		BOL	Theo Conf	66Trieste 243	Dec 66	Benzi.LVL-DENS PAR VS N-NUMBER,GRAPH	
Lvl Density	1.4+7		CCP	Theo Jour	YF 4 1154	Dec 66	Sal'Nikov.SPECTRUM OF NEUTRONS GVN	
Lvl Density	-		HAR	Revw Conf	66Trieste 831	Dec 66	Rae.CORRECTED LVL-DENSITY VS A,GRAPH	
Lvl Density	-		FEI	Theo Rept	ICD-4 304	67	Shubin.LVL DENS PARAM A CALCUL,TBL.	
Lvl Density	None		PTN	Theo Jour	NP/A 92 1	Feb 67	Williams+ ANGULAR MOMENTUM EFFECTS	
Lvl Density	None		ANL	Theo Jour	NP/A 98 614	Jun 67	Huizenga+ SPACING DISTRIBUTION	
Lvl Density	-		ANL	Theo Prog	ANL-7384	Sep 67	Rosenzweig+ TIME-REVERSAL EFFECTS	
Lvl Density	-		JAE	Expt Conf	67Tokyo § 8.127	Sep 67	Maruyama+ A OR TEMP FROM INEL SCAT	
Lvl Density	-		AUA	Theo Jour	AUJ 20 477	Oct 67	Cook+ TBL OF CORRECTNS TO GILBERT+CA	
Lvl Density	-		CCP	Theo Jour	YF 6 921	Nov 67	Smirenkin+,FERMI-GAS MDL,PAIR CORR	
Lvl Density	None		FEI	Theo Conf	68Riga	Jan 68	Ignatjuk+ ABST,EFFECT OF PAIR CORR	
Lvl Density	None		FEI	Theo Conf	68Riga	Jan 68	Ignatjuk+ ABST,FERMI-PARTICLES MODEL	
Lvl Density	+6		MIL	Theo Jour	EN 15 54	Jan 68	Facchini+LDL PARS FROM LOW ENERG.RES	
Lvl Density	-		CIS	Eval Jour	PL/B 26 5 278	Feb 68	Facchini+LVL DENS PAR AT 8MEV CFD 20	
Lvl Density	-		CCP	Theo Jour	YF 7 541	Mar 68	Kuklin.GRPH LVL DENS(50 TO 210=A)	
				Jour	SNP 7 3 337	Sep 68	TRANSLATN.*	
Lvl Density	-		ITE	Theo Conf	68Wash. § F2	Mar 68	Sukhoruchkin.STATIST LVL DIST CURVES	
Lvl Density	-		MIL	Theo Jour	PR 167 1016	Mar 68	Gadioli+ A LESS THAN 71 CALC PARAMS	
				Jour	NP/A 128 339	Apr 69	- +	
Lvl Density	-3	+0	IFU	Theo Jour	UFZ 13 700	Apr 68	Pisanko+ LEVEL SPACING CALC,TBL	
				Jour	UPJ 13 498	Oct 68	TRANSLATN.*	
Lvl Density	-		ALD	Expt Jour	NP/A 112 337	May 68	Owens+.DENSITIES VERSUS A.TO1MEVEXCT	
Lvl Density	-		CCP	Theo Jour	YF 7 1193	Jun 68	Shubin.1-PART-LVL-DEN(A=36TO153,N-Z)	
				Jour	SNP 7 712	Dec 68	TRANSLATN.*	
Lvl Density	+0	+2	DUB	Theo Rept	JINR-P3-3925	Jun 68	Furman+ LVL-DENS-PARAM VS A,N-NUMBER	
Lvl Density	None		FEI	Theo Conf	68Dubna § 4	Jun 68	Shubin+.STATMOD LVL DENS CALC,TBL	
Lvl Density	1.4+7		PUC	Theo Conf	68Bombay 2 92	Dec 68	Cheema+ NUCL TEMP(ATOMIC NUMBER)CRVS	
Lvl Density	-		TPI	Theo Jour	YF 9 102	Jan 69	Korostova+FISSIONABL NUCL,SHELL INFL	
				Jour	SNP 9 62	Jul 69	TRANSLATN.*	
Lvl Density	None		CCP	Theo Conf	69Erevan	Feb 69	Ignatuk+.ABST,SHELL EFF IN STATMOD	
Lvl Density	None		CCP	Theo Conf	69Erevan	Feb 69	Furman+.ABST,NUCL DEF EFF IN STATMOD	
Lvl Density		+2	KUR	Theo Jour	YF 9 303	Feb 69	Vorotnikov.HEAVY NUCL,LVL DEN(EXC-E)	
				Jour	SNP 9 179	Aug 69	TRANSLATN.*	
Lvl Density	+6		FEI	Theo Prog	YFI-7 5	Apr 69	Ignatyuk+ ANGULAR MOMENT VS A,GRAPHS	
				Rept	INDC(CCP)-7U6	Feb 70	TRANSLATN.*	
Lvl Density	-		COP	Revw Conf	69Vienna 155	Jul 69	Strutinsky+PPR203. SINGLE PART,SHELL	
Lvl Density	Maxwl		MUN	Theo Conf	69Studsvik 541	Aug 69	Egidy. FORMULA GVN FOR GAM-SPEC-CALC	
Lvl Density	-		MIL	Theo Jour	NP/A 138 321	Nov 69	Gadioli+.SHELL EFFECT NEAR PB208.	
Lvl Density	-		SAH	Theo Conf	69Roorke 2 214	Dec 69	Ghosh+ A-PARAM(A=50 TO 200) GRAPH	
Lvl Density	-		FEI	Theo Rept	FEI-219	70	Ignatjuk+ CORRECTN TO WEISSKOPF-FORM	

Many

Quantity	Energy (ev) Min	Max	Lab	Type	Documentation Ref Vol Page	Date	Author, Comments	Data
Lvl Density	None		FEI	Theo Prog	YFI – 11 6	70	Ignatjuk+ ABST,EXCITED STATES,NDG	
				Prog	INDC(CCP) – 31	Dec 72	.PAGE 4,ENGLISH OF YFI – 11 6	
Lvl Density	+5	+7	SAH	Theo Prog	BARC – 474 27	70	Chatterjee+ RGM = RENORM.F – GAS MODEL	
Lvl Density	–		SCU	Theo Rept	ICD – 7 SUPPL 1	70	Saveliev.LVLDENS – PAR VS A(NOT Z),TBL	
				Rept	INDC(CCP) – 18	Dec 71	. ENGL OF ICD – 7 SUPPL 1	
Lvl Density	–		BUC	Expt Jour	NP/A 140 23	Jan 70	Magda+ CALC LVLDEN – PAR(MASS)CFD EXPT	
Lvl Density	+5	+7	AUA	Theo Rept	AAEC/TM – 536	Apr 70	Bertram. MASS = 65 – 160,PARAM A FORMULA	
Lvl Density	0.0+0	1.0+0	AE	Theo Prog	EANDC(OR)99 28	Aug 70	Eriksson.LVL DENS FR CNT BCS – SHELLM	
	Maxwl	+6		Conf	70Helsinki 2 881	Jun 70	– .52. SHELL – TH,N – P,N – A CALCUL	
Lvl Density	None		FEI	Theo Jour	YF 11 1213	Jun 70	Ignatyuk+ SPIN DEPENDENCE OF DENSITY	
				Jour	SNP 11 674	Dec 70	. ENGL OF YF 11 1213	
Lvl Density	–		FEI	Theo Conf	70Helsinki 2 885	Jun 70	Ignatjuk+76. SUPERFLUID CFD FERMI – TH	
Lvl Density	–		FEI	Theo Conf	70Helsinki 2 909	Jun 70	Zakharova+82. FERMI GAS MODEL,GAM – W	
Lvl Density	–		AUA	Theo Rept	AAEC/E – 211	Nov 70	Musgrove. BEST FIT OF A – PARAM TO XPT	
Lvl Density	None		JAE	Theo Jour	NP/A 159 625	Dec 70	Baba.NEW LVL DENS FORM. PARAM VS A,E	
	–			Comp Rept	JAERI – 1183	Aug 69	– +.TBLS+FIGS OF PARAMS,Z=9 TO 96	
Lvl Density	None		MUA	Theo Conf	70Madurai 2 263	Dec 70	Ramamurty+ SUPERHEAVY NUCL,NUCL TEMP	
Lvl Density	–		TRM	Theo Rept	BARC – 557 45	71	Ramamurthy+ EFFECTS ON LVL – DENS PAR	
				Conf	70Madurai 2 271	70	. FORMULAE GIVEN	
Lvl Density	None		KUR	Theo Jour	YF 13 17	Jan 71	Medvedev.DEFORMD NUC,MOMENT OF INERT	
Lvl Density	None		ROS	Theo Jour	YF 13 60	Jan 71	Frauendorf+.SPEC OF EVEN – EVEN DEFNUC	
Lvl Density	1.4+7		OTU	Theo Jour	NP/A 164 526	Mar 71	Pai+ SHELL/PAIR – INDEP STATMD.A = 32 – 98	
				Prog	INDC(CAN) – 9 5	Jul 71	PAI+ ABSTRACT,STATMOD+SHELL,SEE NP/A	
Lvl Density	1.4+7		TUD	ExTh Jour	ZFK – 223 25	Sep 71	Giera+ GRPH TH LVL – DENS – PAR/A VS Z,N	
Lvl Density	–		SAC	Theo Jour	NP/A 184 507	Apr 72	Gervois.STATIST MECH CALC IN A SHELL	
Lvl Density	None		HED	Eval Rept	HEDL – TME – 73 – 30	Jan 73	Schmittroth.A PARAMETER 85 NUCLEI.	
Lvl Density	None		FEI	Theo Jour	YF 17 502	Mar 73	Ignatjuk.SPIN DEPENDENCE OF DENSITY	
				Jour	SNP 17 258	Sep 73	.ENGLISH OF YF 17 502	
Lvl Density	None		ROS	Revw Conf	ZFK – 271 1	Feb 74	Muenchow.LVL – DENSITY – PAR VS A,GRAPH	
Lvl Density	None		ROC	Theo Jour	NP/A 223 577	May 74	Huizenga+ EXP CFD MICROSC TH SPH NUC	
Lvl Density	None		ROC	Theo Jour	NP/A 223 589	May 74	Huizenga+ EXP CFD MICROSC TH AX SYMM	
Lvl Density	+7		FEI	Theo Jour	YF 21 485	Mar 75	Ignatjuk+ LVL DENS PARAM(MASS),GRPHS	
	None			Rept	YFI – 18 11	Aug 74	– + SUPERFLUID MODL CALCULATN	
	+0	+7		Jour	YF 18 989	Nov 73	– + SUPERLIQUID MODEL,TBL,GRPH	
	+7			Jour	SNP 21 255	Sep 75	. ENGLISH OF YF 21 485	
	+0	+7		Jour	SNP 18 510	May 74	.ENGLISH OF YF 18, 989.	
Lvl Density	+7		TPI	Theo Jour	YF 21 491	Mar 75	Adeev+ STRUTINSKI,LVL DENS,A,TBL+FIG	
				Jour	SNP 21 258	Sep 75	. ENGLISH OF YF 21 491	
Lvl Density	None		IJI	Theo Jour	UFZ 20 684	Apr 75	Pshenichny+.LDL FOR A=130 – 200,GRPH	
	+0	+4		Rept	KIYAI – 74 – 17	74	Pshenichnij. A=130 – 200,OKS XPTS,GRPH	
Lvl Density	8.0+6	3.5+7	ANL	Eval Rept	ANL – 75 – 34	Jun 75	Davey+N2NEVAL.CONSTANT T,LVL DEN FIT	
Lvl Density	None		FEI	Revw Rept	YK – 21 3	76	Blokhin+ GRPH LVLDENS VS A,A=145 – 250	
				Theo Conf	75Kiev	May 75	– + SHELL STRUCTURE	
Lvl Density	None		TUD	Theo Conf	IAEA – 190 2 263	76	Hermsdorf+ LVL – DENS(MASS),CFD XP.FIG	
	1.4+7			Prog	ZFK – 283 5	Aug 74	Meister+ FROM INEL N – SPC,PREEQU,GRPH	
				Conf	ZFK – 271 85	Feb 74	– + LVL – DENS – PAR(A),TH+EXP,GRPH	
				Jour	KE 16 252	Aug 73	Hermsdorf+ FIT LVLDENS PAR VS A,GRPH	
Lvl Density	0.0+0	0.0+0	JAE	Theo Jour	PTP 55 721	Mar 76	Baba.DEGENERATE SINGLE PARTICLE MDL	
Lvl Density	None		TRM	Theo Conf	76Ahmedabd 2 4	Dec 76	Kataria+ CALC/EXP LVL SPAC VS A.GRPH	
Lvl Density	+6		FEI	Theo Conf	77Kiev	77	Shubin.THERMODYN FNS+ LD	
(γ,n)	None		NCA	Theo Jour	PR 74 1538	Nov 48	Bowers. DISCUSS EXPTS CFD SATIST TH.	
(γ,n)	–		FR	Theo Jour	CR 237 556	Sep 53	Mercier+. POTENTIAL MODEL.	
(γ,n)	None		LRL	Theo Rept	UCRL – 5419	Feb 59	Ashby+.CALCULATD Q VALUES TABULATED	
(γ,n)	2.4+6		AML	Revw Jour	NCS 2 243	64	Spicer.METHOD+ERROR IN XSECT EXPTS	
(γ,n)	2.4+6		BOL	Revw Jour	NCS 2 196	64	Sawicki.REVW OF NEUT.POLARIZN.EXPTS	
(γ,n)	7.0+6	1.1+7	HEI	Theo Jour	ZP 179 256	May 64	Heiss. DIR INT TH+VALS CALC A=50 – 200	
(γ,n)	None		KRK	Revw Jour	PF 15 385	Jul 64	REVIEW ON WORK IN KRAKOW,100REFS	
(γ,n)		7.0+8	IAE	Revw Jour	REA 3 3 3	Dec 65	Shevchenko.GIANT RES TBL,338REFERENC	
(γ,n)	4.0+6	3.8+7	LRL	Comp Rept	UCRL – 75694	Jun 74	Berman.COMP.NG.CROSS – SECTS.GRPHS.	
Photo – Fissn	–		COP	Theo Jour	PR 56 426	Sep 39	Bohr+WHEELER LIQUID DROP MODEL	
Photo – Fissn	5.0+6		TOR	Expt Abst	DA/B 29 3041	Feb 69	Hussain. Z=28 – 50.YLD,ANGDST FAST NS.	

Fprod

Quantity	Energy (ev) Min	Max	Lab	Type	Documentation Ref Vol Page	Date	Author, Comments	Data
Evaluation	2.5−2	1.0+7	ORL	Eval Rept	ORNL−2869	Mar 60	Nephew.32GROUPS.12PSEUDOELMTS.3FUELS	
Evaluation	2.8−3	1.0+6	GA	Eval Jour	NSE 12 115	Jan 62	Garrison+.NG.RES STF RIG FOR Z,A	
Evaluation	2.0+5	2.0+6	CAD	Eval	NEANDC(E)172 4	77	Fort.ABSTRACT ONLY	
Total	Maxwl		ORL	Expt Abst	BAP 4 34	Jan 59	Block+TOF FC TBP	
Total	1.0+0	1.0+3	KIL	ExTh Conf	70Helsinki 1 679	Jun 70	Jung+ PRELIMINARY RESULTS	
				Theo Jour	AKE 15 189	70	− +GRPH,16700 RESON OF 195 FISPRO	
Total	4.6+0	2.3+1	KIL	Expt Jour	AKE 17 144	Mar 71	Jung+ TRANS TOF SPECT EXPT	
	1.0+0	3.0+1		Conf	70Helsinki 1 679	Jun 70	− + PRELIMINARY RESULTS	
Total	1.0+0	2.4+2	KIL	Expt Conf	75Wash. 744	Mar 75	Priesmeyer+ GRAPH	
	1.0+0	2.0+2		Abst	BAP 20 166	Feb 75	− +NDG.75WASH.	
Potntal Scat	−		AUA	Theo Rept	AAEC/E−163	Sep 66	Cook. COMPILATN+CALC PROGRAM=GUNYA 1	
				Rept	AAEC/TM−343	Sep 66	.BIBLIOGRAPHY OF CODES	
Tot Inelastc	4.1−1	1.0+7	GA	Eval Rept	GA−2451	Aug 61	Joanou+.68GROUP CS MATRIX FOR GAM−I	
Tot Inelastc	Fast		RCN	Eval Rept	ECN−11	Nov 76	Heijboer+ LUMPED F.P.MIXTURES	
Absorption	Cold		ANL	Revw Conf	55Geneva 5 125	Aug 55	Spinrad+.P835	
Absorption	Fast		ANL	Revw Conf	55Geneva 5 125	Aug 55	Spinrad+.P835	
Absorption	1.0+2	1.0+6	KAP	Theo Jour	NSE 2 334	May 57	Storm+,STAT CALC A=83−157 5 E GRPS	
Absorption	Maxwl		HAR	Comp Rept	AERE−NP/R−2651	Jul 58	Pattenden+	
Absorption	Maxwl		BNL	Revw Conf	58Geneva 16 8	Sep 58	Hughes.PPR2483,VAL V=2200M/SEC GVN	
Absorption	2.5+4		ORL	Expt Conf	58Geneva 15 68	Sep 58	Macklin.PPR671,U235 FISSPR CFD REFS	
Absorption	−2		KAP	Theo Rept	KAPL−M−ECH−3	Oct 59	Hansen+ REVISED CALC.TH+EPI	
Absorption	Maxwl		ORL	Eval Rept	ORNL−2869	Mar 60	Nephew.10GROUPS 69−2704DEG F 12FPROD	
Absorption	2.5−2	1.0+7	ORL	Eval Rept	ORNL−2869	Mar 60	Nephew.32GROUPS.12PSEUDOELMTS.3FUELS	
Absorption	4.1−1	1.0+7	GA	Eval Rept	GA−2451	Aug 61	Joanou+.68GROUP DATA FOR GAM−I	
Absorption	3.6+0	1.0+6	GA	Eval Jour	NSE 12 115	Jan 62	Garrison+ 54 GROUPS.	
Absorption	−3	+6	TRM	Revw Rept	AEET−234	65	SHANKAR SINGH.GROSS SIG CALC,STATUS	
Absorption	Maxwl		CRC	Expt Rept	AECL−2510	Nov 65	Okazaki+,U233+U235+PU239 GROSS FPROD	
Absorption	Maxwl		JUL	Revw Rept	JUEL−354−RG	Dec 65	Stippel.THR SIG + RESON INTEG	
Absorption	Maxwl		CRC	Eval Conf	66Paris 1 521	Oct 66	Walker. TBL, COMPUTER CALC.	
Absorption	Pile		KAP	Theo Abst	ANS 9 481	Nov 66	Hansen+ TABLES HARD AND SOFT SPEC	
Absorption	Fast		AE	Expt Conf	70Helsinki 2 603	Jun 70	Andersson. MOCK UP FPRODS. PILE OSC.	
				Conf	69London 1 4	69	− . PRELIMINARY	
Absorption	Pile		CRC	Eval Conf	73Paris 1 459	Mar 73	Walker.FISS PRODUCT ABS IN PU+U,TBL	
				Conf	70Helsinki 1 703	Jun 70	.SEE ALSO. PAPER 58.	
				Conf	70Helsinki 1 685	Jun 70	Walker.PPR3.(U33,35,PU39)EXPT+CALCUL	
Absorption	Maxwl		IAE	Revw Rept	IAEA−143 897	Apr 72	Lemmel.EFFECTIVE ABS FROM U,PU,TBL	
Absorption	Maxwl		RCN	Revw Conf	IAEA−169 2 53	74	Bustraan.EXPTS PSEUDO−FP TBLS,GRPHS	
	Fiss			Conf	IAEA−169 2 53	74	− .EXPTS PSEUDO−FP TBLS,GRPHS	
Res Int Abs	Maxwl		HAR	Comp Rept	AERE−NP/R−2651	Jul 58	Pattenden+	
Res Int Abs	1.0+0	1.0+2	FEI	Comp Conf	58Geneva 16 141	Sep 58	Gordeev+.PPR2223,TBL U235 FISS−FRAGM	
Res Int Abs	1.0+0	1.0+2	ORL	Eval Rept	ORNL−2869	Mar 60	Nephew.RIA(E−UP)4FPRODS U233,5,PU239	
Res Int Abs	+3	+5	BOL	Theo Conf	61Vienna 1 179	Aug 61	Benzi+.PPR11,CAPT TABLE CFD EXPERIME	
Res Int Abs	1.3−1		CRC	Expt Rept	AECL−2510	Nov 65	Okazaki+,U233+U235+PU239 GROSS FPROD	
Res Int Abs	None		CRC	Revw Conf	66Paris 1 521	Oct 66	Walker. U233,U235,PU239 FPROD.	
				Rept	AECL−2497	66	.SAME	
Res Int Abs	Pile		KAP	Theo Abst	ANS 9 481	Nov 66	Hansen+ TABLES HARD AND SOFT SPEC	
Res Int Abs	Maxwl	Pile	CRC	ExTh Conf	70Helsinki 1 685	Jun 70	Walker.PPR3.(U33,35,PU39)EXPT+CALCUL	
				Conf	70Helsinki 1 703	Jun 70	.SEE ALSO PAPER 58.	
(n,γ)	Cold		ANL	Revw Conf	55Geneva 5 125	Aug 55	Spinrad+.P835	
(n,γ)	Fast		ANL	Revw Conf	55Geneva 5 125	Aug 55	Spinrad+.P835	
(n,γ)	1.0+2	1.0+6	CIS	Theo Jour	JNE 4 319	Mar 57	Businaro+.CONTINUUM TH,CFD KAPL CALC	
(n,γ)	Pile		CRC	Expt Conf	58Geneva 16 83	Sep 58	Craig+ PPR205,CURVE	
(n,γ)	Pile		HAR	Expt Conf	58Geneva 15 464	Sep 58	Crouch+.PPR7,RARE EARTH YIELDS,TBL	
(n,γ)	5.0−3	2.5+0	GA	Eval Rept	GA−2113	Jun 61	Wikner+.U233,U235,PU239.NONSATURATN	
(n,γ)	+3	+5	BOL	Theo Conf	61Vienna 1 179	Aug 61	Benzi+.PPR11,TABLE CFD EXPERIMENT	
(n,γ)	2.8−3	1.0+6	GA	Eval Jour	NSE 12 115	Jan 62	Garrison+.55GROUPS.NONSAT233 235 239	
(n,γ)	−		AUA	Theo Rept	AAEC/E−163	Sep 66	Cook. COMPILATN+CALC PROGRAM=GUNYA 1	
				Rept	AAEC/TM−343	Sep 66	.BIBLIOGRAPHY OF CODES	
(n,γ)	1.0+3	1.0+7	BOL	Theo Conf	66Paris 1 537	Oct 66	Benzi+ TBL,STATIST MDL CALC	
(n,γ)	Pile		CRC	Revw Conf	66Paris 1 521	Oct 66	Walker. U,U233,U235,PU239 FISSPROD.	
				Rept	AECL−2497	66	.SAME	
(n,γ)	Maxwl	1.4+7	SAC	Comp Rept	CEA−N−1180	Jul 69	Bessis+ YLD+CAPTURE+'NU',U+PU ISOTS.	
(n,γ)	+2	+6	GEB	Revw Conf	70Helsinki 1 17	Jun 70	Greebler+102. UNCERTAINTY+REACT CALC	
(n,γ)	+2	+7	HAR	Revw Conf	70Helsinki 1 267	Jun 70	James.107. ACCURACY CFD REACTOR COST	
(n,γ)	Maxwl	Fiss	SAC	Revw Conf	IAEA−169 1 235	74	Ribon.+30KEV,ACCURACY PSEUDO−FP,TBL	
(n,γ)	Fast		RCN	ExTh Rept	RCN−205	Jan 74	Gruppelaar+INTEGRAL EXP,LUMPED GR.CS	
				Expt Prog	EANDC(E)150U	May 72	Bustraan+ FISS PROD CAPTURE.	

Fprod

Quantity	Energy (ev) Min	Max	Lab	Type	Documentation Ref Vol Page	Date	Author, Comments	Data
(n,γ)	1.0+3	1.0+7	FEI	Eval Rept	INDC(CCP)-39	Jul 74	.P102. ENGLISH OF YK-8/2 97	
				Rept	YK- 8/2 97	Sep 72	Abagjan+ U-233,235,PU-239 SIG(E),TBL	
(n,γ)	Fast		RCN	Eval Rept	ECN-11	Nov 76	Heijboer+ LUMPED F.P.MIXTURES	
Res Int Capt	4.0-1		GA	Eval Jour	NSE 12 115	Jan 62	Garrison+.RAPID/SLOW/NON-SATURATING	
Delayd Neuts	Pile		GRE	Expt Jour	JIN 37 2229	Nov 75	Asghar+MEASURD PN VAL FOR KR,RB,XE	
Fiss Prod γ	None		MHG	Expt Abst	DA/B 28 2760	Jan 68	Wakat. PM152 ND152 HL ES REL INT GS.	
Fiss Prod γ	None		JUL	Comp Rept	JUEL-813-RX	Dec 71	Meixner.G - ES,REL INT,HL,CHAIN YLD	
Fiss Prod γ	Pile		JAE	Expt Jour	NST 10 560	Sep 73	Tsuruta.FROM U235,PU239.TIME-DEPEND.	
Fiss Prod γ	None		UK	Theo Jour	JNE 27 725	Oct 73	Tobias. CALC MEAN BETA,G,DECAY ENS.	
Fiss Prod γ	None		ILL	Expt Jour	ZP/A 273 283	75	Bailleul+ FP FROM 235UO2 TARGET	
Reson Params	+0	+2	FEI	Comp Conf	58Geneva 16 141	Sep 58	Gordeev+.PPR2223,PARAMS OF U235FRAGM	
Reson Params	-		AUA	Theo Rept	AAEC/E-163	Sep 66	Cook. COMPILATN+CALC PROGRAM=GUNYA 1 BIBLIOGRAPHY OF CODES AAEC/TM-343 9/	
Reson Params	None		AUA	Theo Conf	66Paris 1 549	Oct 66	PPR78,COOK.TBL,STATISTICAL CALC	
Reson Params	1.0+0	1.0+3	KIL	ExTh Conf	70Helsinki 1 679	Jun 70	Jung+ PRELIMINARY RESULTS	
				Theo Jour	AKE 17 189	70	- +GRPH.16700 RES OF 195 FIS PROD	
Reson Params	Pile		JUL	Expt Jour	ZN/A 26 512	Mar 71	Labus+ U-235 FISSFRAG PRIMARY SPINS	
Reson Params	3.6+0	1.9+2	KIL	Expt Conf	75Wash. 744	Mar 75	Priesmeyer+ TABLE	
	None			Abst	BAP 20 166	Feb 75	- +NDG.75WASH.	
Strnth Fnctn	+0	+6	FEI	Comp Conf	58Geneva 16 141	Sep 58	Gordeev+.PPR2223,CURVE	
Strnth Fnctn	+3	+5	BOL	Theo Conf	61Vienna 1 179	Aug 61	Benzi+.PPR11,TABLE CFD EXPERIMENT	
Strnth Fnctn	None		GA	Eval Jour	NSE 12 115	Jan 62	Garrison+ AVERAGE WG,D,STF(S,P).	
Lvl Density	-		CCP	Theo Jour	AE 23 327	Oct 67	Zommer+.FRAGMENTS OF CF252	
(γ,n)	Fiss		ISL	Expt Rept	IA- 1082 167	65	Jose+.U235 FPROD IN D2O,COMPUT CALC	

1 Hydrogen BNZ

Quantity	Energy (ev) Min	Max	Lab	Type	Documentation Ref Vol Page	Date	Author, Comments	Data
Total	2.0−4	3.6−2	MUN	Expt Jour	ZP 163 218	May 61	Heincoth. CURVES AT VARIOUS TEMPS.	
	7.8−3			Revw Conf	60Vienna 63	Oct 60	Maierleibnitz.CURVE REL TO TEMPRTR	
Total	1.0−3	1.0−1	ITY	Expt Conf	62Chalk R. 1 285	Sep 62	Boffi+,SIG PER H2 ATOM,300DEGK	
Total	7.8−4	3.6−2	IFJ	Revw Rept	INP−255	Apr 63	Janik+ TOTSIG VS T CFD H2O,GRPH 2ES	
Total	1.0−3	1.0−1	KFI	Expt Conf	64Geneva § 651	May 64	PAL+ REACTOR NEUTRONS,MECH SELECTOR	
Total	7.0−4	1.0−1	CAS	Expt Jour	PHY 32 119	Jan 66	Antonini+TOF SOLID + LIQUID SAMPLES	
				Jour	PHY 30 1647	Aug 64	SUPERSEDED*	
Total	−3	+1	GA	Revw Rept	GA− 7952	Apr 67	Beyster+ COMPARISON OF TH+EXPT CURV	
Total	1.0−3	1.0+0	GA	Theo Conf	67Ann Arbr 1 437	Jul 67	Sprevak+PPR76. TH SIG(E)CV CFD OTHR	
Total	1.0−3	1.0+1	GA	ExTh Conf	67Ann Arbr 1 509	Jul 67	Neill+PPR55.XPTL SIG(E)OKS MOLEC−TH	
Total	1.0−3	1.0+0	ISP	Theo Conf	67Ann Arbr 1 467	Jul 67	Ardente+PPR40.SIGBOUND/FREE CFD XPT	
Total	1.0−3	1.0+0	MTR	Theo Conf	67Ann Arbr 1 457	Jul 67	Marsden+PPR71. TH SIG(E) CV OKS XPT	
Total	2.0−4	3.0−3	AMU	Expt Conf	71Knoxvill 695	Mar 71	Sefidvash.BENZENE, BOUND H SIG	
Total	4.0−3	2.3−2	KIG	Expt Jour	AKE 17 121	Mar 71	Suszkin. H−SIG IN BENZENE	
				Conf	67Juelich 236	Apr 67	− + SIG(P) IN SOLN VS E.	
Elastic	1.0−3		MUN	Expt Jour	ZAP 14 738	Dec 62	Maier−Leibniz.COH.SCAT.LGTH.REFRAKT	+
Thermal Scat	Cold		MTR	Expt Jour	NSE 5 99	Feb 59	Brugger+,THETA=90DEG BENZENE CURVE	
Thermal Scat	Cold		CCP	Expt Conf	62BNL 1 66	Apr 62	Zemlyanov+ 20DEGC INELAST NEUT SPEC	
Thermal Scat	None		GA	Theo Conf	62BNL 1 69	Apr 62	Boffi+ CALC OF SCAT KERN+MOL VIBR	
Thermal Scat	−		CCP	Expt Conf	62Chalk R. 1 297	Sep 62	Zemljanov+,TOF,N SPECT INEL SCAT	
Thermal Scat	−		ITY	Expt Conf	62Chalk R. 1 285	Sep 62	Boffi+,SCAT LAW AT 300DEGK,GASEOUS	
Thermal Scat		5.3−3	KUR	Expt Jour	AE 14 257	Mar 63	Zemiyanov+ LIQUID,SCAT−N−SPEC,GRAPH	
				Jour	SJA 14 252	Jan 64	TRANSLATN.*NO 3	
Thermal Scat	6.0−3	1.8−1	KRK	Expt Jour	NKA 8 581	Sep 63	Maniawski+.TOT+DIFF SIG CFD K−N TH	
Thermal Scat	1.4−2	2.3−3	IFJ	Expt Jour	APP 25 845	Jun 64	Janik+ DIMETHOXYAZOXYBENZ.GRAPH SIG	
Thermal Scat	2.5−2	5.9−2	KFK	ExTh Rept	KFK−264	Dec 64	Glaeser+.T=20DEG.C	
	1.8−2	8.0−2		Expt Jour	NSE 20 236	Oct 64	− + ROT XTL SPECT+TOF.HARM CALC	
Thermal Scat	3.0−2	5.0−1	CCP	Expt Jour	AE 18 277	Mar 65	Anisov+E−EXCHANGE PER COLLISION	
				Jour	JNE 20 333	Apr 66	TRANSLATN.*	
				Jour	SJA 18 350	Mar 65	TRANSLATN.*	
				Jour	EAF 18 3 109	Mar 65	TRANSLATN.*	
Thermal Scat	Maxwl		KFK	ExTh Rept	KFK−305	May 65	Kallfelz+BENZENE.N SPEC	
Thermal Scat	2.2−2	1.0−1	MUN	ExTh Jour	NUK 7 286	Jul 65	Hofmeyr.4ES.ANGDIST.MU,DIFF C VS T	
				Rept	JUEL−160−NP	May 64	Hofmeyer+ SUPERSEDED.	
				Conf	64Geneva § 763	May 64	− + SUPERSEDED.	
Thermal Scat	−2	+0	COL	Expt Prog	NYO−GEN−72−132	Jan 67	Leung+ HEXAMETHYL BENZENE VS.T NDG	
Thermal Scat	None		GA	Revw Rept	GA− 7952	Apr 67	Beyster+ STATUS OF SCATTERING TH	
Thermal Scat		5.0−3	BIR	Expt Conf	67Ann Arbr 1 477	Jul 67	Ross+PPR1.XPTL+TH SIG−CVS CFD OTHER	
Thermal Scat	Maxwl		BOL	Expt Conf	67Ann Arbr 1 617	Jul 67	Cupini+PPR29.SCAT KERN,NEUT−DIFFUSN	
Thermal Scat	2.0−3	1.0+1	GA	ExTh Prog	GA− 8085	Jul 67	Beyster+ EXPTL POINTS CFD SPREVAK	
	−3	+0		Conf	67Ann Arbr 1 509	Jul 67	Neill+PPR55.INTGRL−XPT OKS MOLEC−TH	
	2.0−3	1.0+1		Expt Rept	GA− 8050	Jun 67	− + CURVE CFD SPREVAK MODEL	
Thermal Scat	1.4−2	1.1+0	GA	Expt Prog	GA− 8085	Jul 67	Beyster+ CURVS 7ES 40−160DEG	
	−3	1.0+1		Conf	67Ann Arbr 1 493	Jul 66	− +PPR75.GRPHS,XPTL SIG OKS TH	
Thermal Scat	−3	−1	GA	Theo Conf	67Ann Arbr 1 437	Jul 67	Sprevak+PPR76.SIG CALCUL OKS EXPT	
				Rept	GA− 7674	Mar 67	− +. CURVES+TABLES.	
Thermal Scat	−3	+0	ISP	Theo Conf	67Ann Arbr 1 467	Jul 67	Ardente+PPR40.REACTOR PARS/MOLEC−TH	
Thermal Scat	1.0−3	1.0+0	MTR	Theo Conf	67Ann Arbr 1 457	Jul 67	Marsden+PPR71. SIG+DIFFUSN CFD XPTS	
Thermal Scat	5.0−3		AE	Expt Conf	68Copenhgn 1 475	May 68	Holmryd+TOLUOL,.10TS 243−333K TBC	
				Conf	68Copenhgn 1 475	May 68	− +.C6H6 293−333K.DIFFCOEF.TBC	
Thermal Scat	5.2−3	5.0−1	BIR	Expt Conf	68Copenhgn 2 299	May 68	Beg+PPR117.DOWN−SCAT−EXPT,CRV GVN	
Thermal Scat	Maxwl		GA	Theo Jour	NUK 11 233	Sep 68	Sprevak+ CFD EXP TOT+ANG SCAT SIG	
Thermal Scat	None		MTR	Theo Rept	IN− 1269	Mar 69	Marsden. NORMAL FREQNCY+S(A,B)CALCD.	
Thermal Scat	1.0−3	4.0−1	HLT	Theo Jour	JNE 23 306	May 69	Sefidvash. CALC−SIG(E) CFD EXPT	
Thermal Scat	Maxwl		PIC	Theo Jour	JCP 53 3417	Nov 70	Logan+BENZENE(SOLID),T=77−270DEGK	
Thermal Scat	None		BUC	Theo Jour	SCF 23 699	71	Trepadus.GAUSS APPROX.CRVS CFD EXPT	
	4.2−3			Expt Jour	JCP 46 3273	Aug 67	Tarina.INEL SCAT SPECTRA AT 6 TEMP	
	4.2−3			Data	EXFOR30228.	Dec 72	/INEL SCAT SPECTRA AT 6 TEMP.	
Thermal Scat	Maxwl		OSA	Theo Prog	EANDC(J)26L56	Aug 72	Sekiya+.TBP IN TECH.REPOT OSAKA U.	
Thermal Scat	8.0−3		BUC	Expt Jour	RRP 19 731	Jul 74	Trepadus. LIQUID.TH CFD XPT,GRAPH.	
Thermal Scat	Cold		MUN	Expt Jour	ZP/A 272 189	Feb 75	Koester+COH.SCT.AMP.BENZENE+CLORO−B	
				Jour	PRL 27 956	Oct 71	− +BENZENE SCAT AMPL.REFLEC	
Scattering	3.0−2	5.0−1	CCP	Expt Jour	AE 18 277	Mar 65	Anisov+TOF GRAPH SIG(E) FROM TRANS	
				Jour	JNE 20 333	Apr 66	TRANSLATN.*	
				Jour	EAF 18 3 109	Mar 65	TRANSLATN.*	
				Jour	SJA 18 350	Mar 65	TRANSLATN.*	

1 Hydrogen BNZ

Quantity	Energy (ev) Min	Max	Lab	Type	Documentation Ref Vol Page	Date	Author, Comments	Data
Absorption	3.0+6	1.5+7	FEI	Expt	Book NEJTRONFIZ 278	61	Kukhtevich+ SIGMA AT 2ES	
					Book SPN 205	61	.ENGL TRANSL OF NEJTRONFIZ 278	

1 Hydrogen CXX

Quantity	Energy (ev) Min	Max	Lab	Type	Documentation Ref Vol Page	Date	Author, Comments	Data
Total	Maxwl		COL	Expt	Jour PR 60 702	Nov 41	Carroll.C4H10,48.7B PER PROTON(H2O)	
Total	Maxwl		COL	Expt	Jour PR 60 702	Nov 41	Carroll.C3H8,46.9B PER PROTON(H2O)	
Total	Maxwl		COL	Expt	Jour PR 60 702	Nov 41	Carroll.ETHANE,46.4B PER PROTON H2O	
Total	Maxwl		COL	Expt	Jour PR 60 702	Nov 41	Carroll. 52.8B/P. NORMAL C32 – H66.	
Total	8.1−1	1.0+2	COR	Expt	Jour PR 74 364	Aug 48	Jones.C6H12,TOF TRANSM.ALSO SIG/H	
Total	3.0−3	1.0+0	COL	Expt	Jour PR 76 12	Dec 49	Melkonian. H IN ETHANE. GRPH. CFD.	
Total	3.0−3	1.0+0	COL	Expt	Jour PR 76 12	Dec 49	Melkonian. H IN PROPANE. GRPH. CFD.	
Total	3.0−3	1.0+0	COL	Expt	Jour PR 76 12	Dec 49	Melkonian. H IN N − BUTANE, GAS,LIQ.	
Total	3.0−3	1.0+0	COL	Expt	Jour PR 76 12	Dec 49	Melkonian. H IN CETANE. GRPH. CFD.	
Total	3.0−3	1.0+0	COL	Expt	Jour PR 76 12	Dec 49	Melkonian. H IN ETHYLENE. GRPH. CFD.	
Total	3.0−3	1.0+0	COL	Expt	Jour PR 76 12	Dec 49	Melkonian. H IN 1,3 BUTADIENE. CFD.	
Total	9.5+7		BRK	Expt	Jour PR 77 606	Mar 50	Dejuren+ BI FISS CH.MELAMINE=C3H6N6	
Total	9.6+7		BRK	Expt	Jour PR 77 606	Mar 50	Dejuren+PENTANE,BYFISSION CH.	
Total	1.4+7		LAS	Expt	Rept LA − 1279	Jul 51	Meyer+FORMIC ACID,TRANS,5.84+ − .10B	
Total	2.0−4	3.6−2	MUN	Expt	Jour ZP 163 218	May 61	Heinloth.CH2O2,CURV FOR VARIOUS TEMP	
	7.8−3			Revw	Conf 60Vienna 63	Oct 60	Maierleibnitz.CH2O2,CURV REL TO TEMP	
Total	7.8−4	3.6−2	IFJ	Revw	Rept INP − 255	Apr 63	Janik+ HCOOH,TOT VS T CFD H2O,GRAPH	
Total	1.2−2	1.0−1	IBJ	Expt	Jour NKA 10 201	Jul 65	Borowski+ CH3OH.TOTSIG/PROT VS EN	
Total	Cold		YUG	Expt	Jour PL 19 15	Sep 65	ATA+ETHER,FOR GAS+LIQ.PHASES VS TEMP	
Total	2.5−2	2.5−2	ATI	Expt	Jour AKE 12 159	Mar 66	Lasinger+ POLYSTYRENE.THR,BE − ,BI − FLT	+
	Pile				Data EXFOR20028.	Sep 71	9PTS.	
Total	3.7−2	2.9−1	KIL	Expt	Conf 67Juelich 232	Apr 67	MATUSSEK SIG(P)IN C12H22O11 CRYSTAL	
Total	8.0−4		BUC	Expt	Conf 68Copenhgn 1 501	May 68	Tarina.C6H12,PPR59,GRPHS SIG(TEMP)	
Total	Cold		WAS	Expt	Abst DA/B 29 2466	Jan 69	Lindstrom. 7 ALKANOIC ACIDS. TRANS.	
Total	4.0−3	2.3−2	KIG	Expt	Jour AKE 17 121	Mar 71	Suszkin. H − SIG IN DIOXANE	
	3.7−3	3.3−2			Jour AKE 17 121	Mar 71	− . H − SIG IN METHANOL − BENZENE	
	4.0−3	2.3−2			Jour AKE 17 121	Mar 71	− . H − SIG IN METHANOL	
	3.7−3	3.3−2			Jour AKE 17 121	Mar 71	− . H − SIG IN ACETIC ACID − DIOXN	
	4.0−3	2.3−2			Jour AKE 17 121	Mar 71	− . H − SIG IN ACETIC ACID	
	3.7−3	3.3−2			Jour AKE 17 121	Mar 71	− . H − SIG IN DIOXANE − BENZENE	
	3.7−3	1.6−2			Jour AKE 17 121	Mar 71	− . H − SIG IN ACETIC ACID − H2O	
	3.7−3	3.3−2			Jour AKE 17 121	Mar 71	− . H − SIG IN ACETIC ACID − BENZ	
	2.9−3	2.3−2			Conf 67Juelich 236	Apr 67	− . H − SIG IN METHANOL − H2O	
	2.3−3	5.7−2			Jour AKE 11 433	Jun 66	− . H − SIG IN DIOXANE − H2O	
	2.4−2	5.8−1			Rept EANDC(E)66U 52	Feb 66	− . WATER − DIOXANE SOLN.CURVE	
Total	1.0+5	6.5+5	DKE	Expt	Abst DA/B 31 6821	May 71	Pineo.RUBBER,2EN RANGE AVGS CFD OPTM	
Total	1.3−3	6.7−3	BUC	Expt	Jour SCF 23 865	Aug 71	Rapeanu+ CH3OH,C2H5OH,C2H4(OH)2,/H	
Total	3.0+7	1.4+8	LAU	Expt	Priv SWISS PH S	Oct 71	Jenefsky+ ABSOL EFF OF NE − 102, − 223	
Total	7.1−3	2.1+1	CAB	Expt	Jour NSE 49 392	Nov 72	CASTRO MADERO+ SIGMA TOTAL OF MYLAR	+
	7.1−3	2.1+1			Data EXFOR30223.002	Dec 72	/TOTAL CROSS SECTION AT 141 EN	
Elastic	1.0−3		MUN	Expt	Jour ZAP 14 738	Dec 62	Maier − Leibniz.ETHYL,COH SCAT LENGTH	
Diff Inelast	1.6+7	3.3+8	KUR	Expt	Rept IAE − 404	Mar 63	Mostovoj+C15H16 SIG(E,E',THETA)GRPH	
Diff Inelast	−3	+0	ISP	Expt	Jour NIM 35 203	Aug 65	Strub.HEXAMINE,LI6I(EU)+BF3 DETS	
Thermal Scat	Maxwl		BRK	Expt	Jour PR 50 575	Sep 36	Libby+C7H16,TEMPER.EQUILIBRUM HYP.	
Thermal Scat	7.0−3	2.5−2	KRK	Expt	Jour BPP 1 45	Jan 53	Janik+.CH3OH,RA+BE SOURCE,B DET.SIG	
	6.9−3	2.4−2			Jour APP 13 167	Jul 54	. CONTINUATION	
	7.0−3	2.5−2			Jour BPP 2 225	May 54	. CONTINUATION	
					Jour APP 12 45	Jun 53	*	
Thermal Scat	7.0−3	2.5−2	KRK	Expt	Jour BPP 1 45	Jan 53	Janik+CH3I,RA+BE SOURCE,BORON DET	
Thermal Scat	Maxwl		IBJ	ExTh	Jour APP 14 173	May 55	Kolos+ CH3OH,INFL HIND ROT ON MOLEC	
Thermal Scat	5.7−4	3.3−3	COL	Expt	Prog CU − 174 21	Mar 58	Gould+ POLYETH,CH2 POLYMERS. GRPH.	
Thermal Scat	3.0−2	2.5−1	KRK	Expt	Jour APP 17 483	Nov 58	Janik+.P − AZOXYANISOL(POLARIZD − N+NOT	
Thermal Scat	1.0−3	5.0−1	KRK	ExTh	Jour APP 17 489	Nov 58	Janik+.ETHYLENE,KRIEGER − NELKIN TH	
Thermal Scat	3.0−2	2.5−1	WWA	Expt	Rept INR − 48/II,I − B	Dec 58	Janik+.P − AZOXYANISOL(POLAR+NOT)+TH	
Thermal Scat	Cold		MTR	Expt	Jour NSE 5 99	Feb 59	Brugger+AMYL ALCOHOL,THETA=90DEG	
Thermal Scat	Cold		MTR	Expt	Jour NSE 5 99	Feb 59	Brugger+ETHYL ALCOHOL THETA=90DEG	
Thermal Scat	Maxwl		AE	Eval	Jour AF 15 147	Apr 59	Sjoestrand.CH2 − DIFFSN COOL COEFF	
Thermal Scat	1.0−2	1.0−1	MTR	Expt	Rept PR 125 933	Feb 62	Strong.C3H8,GAS AT ROOM TEMP S(A,B)	
Thermal Scat	5.9−2		BUC	Expt	Conf 62Chalk R. 1 451	Sep 62	Bally+ ETHYLENE,ANGDIST OKS K − N − TH	+
	5.9−2				Data EXFOR30163.003	Apr 72	/DIST AT 5 − 90 DEGREES,C2H6 AT 4PRESS	

1 Hydrogen CXX

Quantity	Energy (ev) Min	Max	Lab	Type	Documentation Ref Vol Page	Date	Author, Comments	Data
Thermal Scat	5.0−3		HAR	Expt	Conf 62Chalk R. 1 413	Sep 62	Saunderson+AMYL ALCOHOL,E TRANSFER	
					Conf 62Chalk R. 1 413	Sep 62	− +ETHYL E TRANSFER SPECTRUM	
					Conf 62Chalk R. 1 413	Sep 62	− +CH3OH,E TRANSF.SPEC 21DC	
Thermal Scat	2.5−2	1.0−1	MTR	Expt	Prog WASH−1041 38	Oct 62	Brugger+C4H10,3ES NO DATA GIVEN	
Thermal Scat	Cold		MTR	Expt	Prog WASH−1041 39	Oct 62	Strong. ETHANE. NDG. 90 DEG SCAT.	
Thermal Scat	Cold		MTR	Expt	Prog WASH−1041 39	Oct 62	Strong. C4H10. NDG. 90 DEG SCAT.	
Thermal Scat	−4	−1	IFJ	Revw	Rept INP−255	Apr 63	Janik+ C2H4,EXPTS CFD K−N THEO,GRPH	
Thermal Scat	3.0−3	1.0+1	IFJ	Revw	Rept INP−255	Apr 63	Janik+ GAS+LIQUID SIG/H,GRPH N−BUTAN	
Thermal Scat	2.5−2	1.0−1	MTR	Theo	Jour NSE 15 438	Apr 63	Mcmurry+C3H8,SIG VS SCAT N E CFD TH	
	1.0−2	1.0−1			Conf 62BNL 1 172	Apr 62	− +C3H8,CALCTD DIFF SIGS CURVE	
Thermal Scat	Cold		BNL	Expt	Prog WASH−1048 15	Jun 64	Otnes+ CH3I.NDG.NSPC CFD SACHS−TELL.	
Thermal Scat	5.0−2	1.6−1	BNW	Expt	Prog WASH−1053 36	Oct 64	Kottwitz+POLYSTYRENE TBC NDG	
Thermal Scat	Pile		KRK	Revw	Rept INP−368	Nov 64	Janik.CH3**,REV.MOL.DYNAMC,BOMBAY64	
Thermal Scat	2.2−2	7.3−2	BUC	Expt	Conf 64Bombay 2 421	Dec 64	Bally+ETHYLENE,SCAT LAW CFD TH	+
	2.5−2	7.2−2			Data EXFOR30227.	Dec 72	/DSIG/DE*DOMEGA AT 4 ANGLES, 2 ES.	
Thermal Scat		+0	KTH	Revw	Conf 64Bombay 2 3	Dec 64	Larsson.OLEIC,LIQUID DYNAMC.N SCAT	
	5.0−3			Expt	Jour PHY 30 1561	64	− +OLEIC,T=−19TO170DEG C TH	
Thermal Scat		+0	KTH	Revw	Conf 64Bombay 2 3	Dec 64	Larsson.GLYCERIN,LIQUID DYNAM,N SCA	
	5.0−3			Expt	Jour PHY 30 1561	64	− +GLYCERIN,T=−7TO180 DEG C.TH	
Thermal Scat	3.0−2	5.0−1	CCP	Expt	Jour AE 18 277	Mar 65	Anisov+CH3COONA E−EXCHANGE/COLLI.	
					Jour JNE 20 333	Apr 66	TRANSLATN.*	
					Jour SJA 18 350	Mar 65	TRANSLATN.*	
					Jour EAF 18 3 109	Mar 65	TRANSLATN.*	
Thermal Scat	3.0−2	5.0−1	CCP	Expt	Jour AE 18 277	Mar 65	Anisov+C6H5CH3 E−EXCHANGE PER COLL.	
					Jour JNE 20 333	Apr 66	TRANSLATN.*	
					Jour SJA 18 350	Mar 65	TRANSLATN.*	
					Jour EAF 18 3 109	Mar 65	TRANSLATN.*	
Thermal Scat	Cold		MTR	ExTh	Prog WASH−1056 97	Mar 65	Mcmurry.ETHANE,SCAT VS MOL ORIENT.	
Thermal Scat	Cold		MTR	ExTh	Prog WASH−1056 97	Mar 65	Mcmurry.C4H10,MOL ORIENT AVG.	
Thermal Scat	−		AE	Theo	Conf 65Karlsrhe 1 273	May 65	Purohit.CH2− T/T(GAS) VS TEFF/T	
Thermal Scat	None		MTR	Theo	Prog BNL−940 149	Sep 65	Griffing. GLYCEROL.LANGEVIN EQ.FIT.	
Thermal Scat	Cold		YUG	Expt	Jour PL 19 15	Sep 65	ATA+ETHER,NEAR CRITIC.T,ROOM T	
Thermal Scat	2.0−2	1.1−1	MHG	Expt	Jour JCP 43 4134	Dec 65	Straker.ETHANE,GAS+LIQUID,22−90DEG	
Thermal Scat	2.5−2	7.0−2	BUC	ExTh	Jour RRP 11 265	Mar 66	Ripeanu.C5H12,XPTS+DISCUS OF SCTLAW	
Thermal Scat	Maxwl		COL	Expt	Prog WASH−1068 42	Mar 66	Leung+,SILASTIC POLYMERS,NDG	
Thermal Scat	Maxwl		COL	Expt	Prog WASH−1068 42	Mar 66	Leung+NATURAL RUBBER,NDG	
Thermal Scat	Maxwl		COL	Expt	Prog WASH−1068 42	Mar 66	Leung+METHYL LUCITE,NDG	
Thermal Scat	Maxwl		COL	Expt	Prog WASH−1068 42	Mar 66	Leung+ ETHYLENE−PROPYLENE COPOLYMER.	
Thermal Scat	Maxwl		COL	Expt	Prog WASH−1068 42	Mar 66	Leung+ POLYPROPYLENE,POLYETHYLENE.	
Thermal Scat	Maxwl		COL	Expt	Prog WASH−1068 42	Mar 66	Leung+ D−CAMPHOR,C2H2 BR2. TRNS. NDG	
Thermal Scat	Maxwl		COL	Expt	Prog WASH−1068 42	Mar 66	Leung+ ETHYLENE DIBROMIDE. NDG.	
Thermal Scat	None		COL	Expt	Prog WASH−1071 43	Nov 66	Leung+ DURENE.CFD TH CALC. NDG.	
Thermal Scat	Cold		KTH	Expt	Jour PR 151 126	Nov 66	Larsson+NPROPYL ALCHL QUASIELASTIC	
Thermal Scat	Cold		KTH	Expt	Jour PR 151 126	Nov 66	Larsson+PENTANE,QUASIELSTIC CFD TH	
Thermal Scat	5.0−3	1.3−1	DUB	Expt	Rept JINR−E3−3057	Dec 66	Janik+CH3I,SCAT NEUT VS E(N) GRAPHS	
Thermal Scat	−2	+0	COL	Expt	Prog NYO−GEN72−132	Jan 67	Leung+ TETRAMETHYL SILANE,TBD, NDG	
Thermal Scat	−2	+1	COL	Expt	Prog NYO−GEN72−132	Jan 67	Leung+NEOPENTANE,NDG,TBD,CFD TH	
Thermal Scat	−2	+0	COL	Expt	Prog NYO−GEN72−132	Jan 67	Leung+DURENE,TEMP DEPEND NDG	
Thermal Scat	1.0−1		MTR	Expt	Jour JCP 47 421	Feb 67	Strong.+ ETHANE, 2 ANGS. GRPH.	
Thermal Scat	Cold		ANL	Expt	Jour JCP 46 2285	Mar 67	Rush. SOL+LIQ METHYLCHLOROFORM.	
Thermal Scat	Cold		ANL	Expt	Jour JCP 46 2285	Mar 67	Rush.ETHANE,TOF SPECTRA SOL+LIQ	
Thermal Scat	Cold		ANL	Expt	Jour JCP 46 2285	Mar 67	Rush.NEOPENTANE,TOF SPECT SOLID+LIQ	
Thermal Scat	Cold		ISP	Expt	Jour PL/A 25 435	Sep 67	VERDAN 85DEGK TOF CFD K−N	
Thermal Scat	Cold		ISP	Expt	Jour PL/A 25 435	Sep 67	Verdan.ETHYLENE,85DEGK TOF CFD K−N	
Thermal Scat	5.0−3		AE	Expt	Jour NIM 56 305	Nov 67	Skold+ C(CH3)4,1NELSCAT VS PRESSURE	
Thermal Scat	Cold		TRM	Revw	Conf 68Madras 2 144	Feb 68	Dasannacharya.GLYCEROL,N−EXPTS REVW	
Thermal Scat	−2		BUC	Expt	Jour RRP 13 287	Mar 68	Rapeanu+PENTANOL,NDG,CFD VAN HOVE	
	Maxwl				Jour PL/A 26 72	Dec 67	− +QUASIELAS ANGDIST.C5H11OH	
Thermal Scat	1.0−1	1.0−1	KRK	Expt	Jour APP 33 419	Mar 68	Janik+CH2I2,CRYST AT 160,+23DEGC	
Thermal Scat	Cold		KRK	Revw	Rept INP−600/PS	Apr 68	Janik+METHYL−IODIDE NS SCATT SOLID	
	1.0−2	1.0−1		Expt	Jour APP 33 419	Mar 68	− +METHYL−IODIDE SOLID,GRPH+TBL	
Thermal Scat		5.2−3	BUC	Expt	Conf 68Copenhgn 1 501	May 68	Tarina.C6H12,PPR59,TOF,15DEG,LIQ+SOL	
Thermal Scat	1.8−1	2.6−1	GA	Expt	Conf 68Copenhgn 2 175	May 68	Whittemore.POLY−L−GLUTAM−ACID(PPR76)	
Thermal Scat	9.0−4	1.5−1	IEA	Expt	Conf 68Copenhgn 2 197	May 68	Herdade.7 CH3 COMPOUND,TOT+SCAT SIG	+
	9.1−4	1.5−1			Jour NIM 63 13	68	.TOF DESCRIPTION	
	9.0−4	1.5−1			Rept IEA−152 97	Oct 67	* PORTUGUESE,GRAPHS	
					Rept IEA−136	Feb 67	* TOF SPEC DESCRIPTION	
	9.0−4	1.5−1			Data EXFOR30226.	Dec 72	/METHYL IN 8COMPOUNDS, TOTAL+SCAT	

1 Hydrogen CXX

Quantity	Energy (ev) Min	Max	Lab	Type	Documentation Ref Vol Page	Date	Author, Comments	Data
Thermal Scat	3.7−3		KTH Revw	Conf	68Copenhgn 1 397	May 68	Larsson.C5H12,PPR200,HINDRD ROT148K	
	2.9−3	5.0−3	Expt	Conf	68Copenhgn 1 581	May 68	Dahlborg+C5H12,INV FLTR.133 − 295K	
		+0	Revw	Conf	64Bombay 2 3	Dec 64	Larsson.C5H12,LIQUID DYNAM.,N SCAT	
	5.0−3		Expt	Jour	PHY 30 1561	64	− +C5H12,T= − 35TO20DEG C.TH	
Thermal Scat	2.9−3	5.0−3	KTH Expt	Conf	68Copenhgn 1 581	May 68	Dahlborg+AMYL−,INV.FLTR 198 − 353K	
Thermal Scat	Maxwl		ROS Expt	Jour	KE 11 132	May 68	Albert+ SIG OF H IN PLASTIC MIRAMID	
Thermal Scat	Maxwl		MHGTheo	Abst	DA/B 29 1381	Oct 68	Lynch. SCATT. BY HIGH POLYMERS.	
Thermal Scat	Maxwl		JUL Theo	Rept	JUEL − 588 − FN	Apr 69	Axmann+TOF SPEC IN C10H16,CFD EXT	
Thermal Scat	Cold		COL Expt	Prog	WASH − 1136 31	Sep 69	Markisz+ DIMETHYLACETYLENE. NDG.	
Thermal Scat	Cold		COL Expt	Prog	WASH − 1136 31	Sep 69	Markisz+ETHANE,ANAL TO BE COMPLETED	
Thermal Scat	4.8−3		TRM Expt	Conf	69Roorke 3 201	Dec 69	Deniz+ETHYL ETHER+GLYCOL,E − SPECS	
Thermal Scat	−3	−2	BUC Expt	Jour	SCF 22 29	Jan 70	Rapeanu.PENTAN(OL),SIG CRVS,THESIS	
	−3	−1		Jour	RRP 15 121	Jan 70	Iliescu+ C5H12,ALCOHOLS,GLYC.SIG/H	
Thermal Scat	−3	−1	BUC Expt	Jour	SCF 22 29	Jan 70	Rapeanu.H+DEUTERPTD GLYCERIN,GRPHS	
	5.2−3			Jour	RRP 13 913	Oct 68	− . C3H5(OD)3.FREQ − SPECS,3TEMPS	
Thermal Scat	5.0−2		MTR Expt	Prog	IN − 1317 166	Jan 70	Pugmire+ ISOBUTANE, CURVS.	
	7.0−2		MTR Expt	Prog	IN − 1317 170	Jan 70	Pugmire+ NEOPENTANE, CURVES.	
	5.1−2			Jour	PRL 20 984	Apr 68	Grant+ NEOPENTANE, LIBRATION SEEN.	
Thermal Scat	1.0−1		MTR Expt	Prog	IN − 1317 162	Jan 70	Pugmire+ SOLID,LIQ,GAS CURV.PROPANE.	
Thermal Scat	1.7−4	8.2−3	BUC Expt	Jour	RRP 15 213	Feb 70	Todireanu+ ETHYLENE,C2H4.SIG(LAMBDA)	
Thermal Scat	Cold		MTR Expt	Jour	JCP 52 2277	Mar 70	Strong+,ETHYL CHLORIDE,CURVES	
	5.0−2			Prog	IN − 1317 162	Jan 70	Pugmire+ ETHYL CHLORIDE, CURVES.	
	None			Conf	69Wien 199	Dec 69	Strong+ ETHYL − CHLORIDE,SOLID,DIFSIG	
Thermal Scat		5.3−3	NJS Expt	Rept	NIJS − R − 582	Apr 70	Blinc+ LIQUID CRYSTAL,DIFFUSN − COEFF	
Thermal Scat	−3	−1	BUC Expt	Jour	RRP 15 783	Jul 70	Diaconescu+CYCLOHEXANE,SPEC − GRAPHS	
	−3	−2		Prog	INDC(RUM) − 1G	Apr 70	− +CYCLOHEXANE,TBP IN RRP	
Thermal Scat	−3	−1	BUC Expt	Jour	RRP 15 783	Jul 70	Diaconescu+METHYLIC ALCOHOL,GRAPHS	
Thermal Scat	−3	−1	ISL Expt	Prog	IA − 1218 51	Aug 70	Pelah+TRIGLYCINE SULFATE,FERROELEC.	
Thermal Scat	None		IFJ Expt	Rept	INP − 724/PL	Sep 70	Luty+,ACENAPHTENE,IBR DUBNA,CFD TH	
Thermal Scat	Cold		DEL Expt	Jour	PL/A 33 87	Oct 70	.C6H10H,LIQUID,QUASI ELAS SCAT	
	5.0−3			Rept	BNL − 940 138	Sep 65	De Graaf. CYCLOMEXANE.165 − 330DEG K.	
Thermal Scat	5.0−8	5.0−6	MUNExpt	Jour	ZP 238 221	Oct 70	BIR.GLYCERIN.QUASI − EL.LINE BROADENG	
Thermal Scat	−3	+0	KFI Expt	Jour	PL/A 33 338	Nov 70	Bata+ETHER,INEL SCAT ON COEXIS.CURV	
Thermal Scat	Maxwl		USA Expt	Abst	DA/B 31 6541	May 71	Livingston.C3H8,TOR FREQS IN SOL.L.G	
Thermal Scat	Maxwl		OSA Theo	Jour	NST 8 319	Jun 71	Nishigori+.HCL.PHOTON TYPE EXPANSN.	
Thermal Scat	Cold		MUNExpt	Jour	PRL 27 956	Oct 71	Koester+XYLENE SCAT AMPL.REFLEC	
				Jour	ZP/A 272 189	Feb 75	− +COH.SCT.AMP.M+P XYLENE,TOLNE	
				Jour	ZP 198 187	Dec 66	− + SUPERSEDED.	
Thermal Scat	8.0−3		KJL Expt	Jour	PL/A 33 335	Feb 72	Othes+AZOXI.293 − 423DEGK DIFFU.CONST	
Thermal Scat	1.3−3	6.7−3	BUC Theo	Jour	SCF 24 775	Jul 72	Padureanu.CH3OH,MULTIPL − SCAT EFFECT	
			Expt	Jour	SCF 23 865	Aug 71	Rapeanu+ CH3OH,C2H5OH,C2H4(OH)2,/H	
	5.4−3	8.0−3		Prog	INDC(SEC) − 18	Aug 71	− +P147.CH3OH,C2H5OH,C2H4(OH)2	
Thermal Scat	5.0−3	1.0−1	IEA Expt	Jour	JNE 26 379	Jul 72	Rodrigues + ETHANOL ETC.SIG/H,GRAPHS	+
	8.0−4	1.0−1		Data	EXFOR30230.	Jan 73	/FOR METHANOL,ETHANOL,PROPANOL,	
	8.0−4	1.0−1		Data	EXFOR30230.	Jan 73	/ISOPROPANOL,ETHANEDIOL,PROPANETRIOL	
	8.0−4	1.0−1		Data	EXFOR30230.	Jan 73	/SCATTERING CROSS SECTION PER H − ATOM	
Thermal Scat	Cold		BUC Expt	Jour	RRP 18 195	73	Rapeanu+ CH3,CH2,OH GROUPS,FREQUENCY	
Thermal Scat	8.4−3		BUC Expt	Jour	RRP 18 313	73	Trepadus+ MOLECULAR MOTION IN PHENOL	
Thermal Scat	Maxwl		NBS Expt	Jour	JCP 58 5193	Jun 73	Barnes.TOF.N − NONADECANE.291 301DEGK.	
Thermal Scat	Cold		BUC Expt	Prog	INDC(SEC) − 35	Sep 73	Todireanu+ P177.TOLUENE,BRIEF,NDG	
Thermal Scat	Pile		IEA Expt	Prog	INDC(SEC) − 35	Sep 73	Amaral+ P46.CYCLOHEXANE ETC,TOF,NDG	
Thermal Scat	4.9−3		TRM Expt	Rept	BARC − 768 118	74	Deniz+(HBPA).EN − SPECS(MAGN − FILD)GRPH	
Thermal Scat	1.5−3	5.1−3	IEA Expt	Rept	IEA − 328	Mar 74	Amaral+(CH3)3 − COH.0 − 40DEGC,TOTSIG	
Thermal Scat	2.2−3	6.7−3	IEA Expt	Rept	IEA − 342	May 74	Fulfaro+ (DNA).TOTSIG+SIG/H(EN),GRPH	
Scattering	3.0−2	5.0−1	CCP Expt	Jour	AE 18 277	Mar 65	Anisov+CH3COONA TOF GRAPH SIG(E)	
				Jour	JNE 20 333	Apr 66	TRANSLATN.*	
				Jour	SJA 18 350	Mar 65	TRANSLATN.*	
				Jour	EAF 18 3 109	Mar 65	TRANSLATN.*	
Scattering	3.0−2	5.0−1	CCP Expt	Jour	AE 18 277	Mar 65	Anisov+C6H5CH3 TOF GRAPH SIG(E)	
				Jour	JNE 20 333	Apr 66	TRANSLATN.*	
				Jour	SJA 18 350	Mar 65	TRANSLATN.*	
				Jour	EAF 18 3 109	Mar 65	TRANSLATN.*	
Absorption	8.0+5	1.0+7	FAR Theo	Conf	58Geneva 13 31	Sep 58	Bourgeois+ CRV,(CH)2.N,(CH)N,REMOV S	
Absorption	−2		KFI Expt	Conf	65Karlsrhe 1 165	May 65	PAL+.XYLENE.PULSED N XPTS.SIG.V GVN	
	1.0−3	1.0−1		Conf	64Geneva § 651	May 64	PAL+ VARIOS ORGAN COMPS,MECH SELECTR	

1 Hydrogen MTH

Quantity	Energy (ev) Min	Max	Lab	Type	Documentation Ref Vol Page	Date	Author, Comments	Data
Total	Maxwl		COL	Expt Jour	PR 60 702	Nov 41	Carroll. 45.4 B PER PROTON (WATER).	
Total	5.7-3	1.0-1	KRK	Expt Conf	62Chalk R. 1 405	Sep 62	Janik+,TOT SIG PER P CFD K-N TH	
Total	8.0-4	2.0-1	GA	Expt Jour	NSE 18 182	Feb 64	Whittemore. TOF.2 TEMP. CURV CFD TH.	
Diff Elastic	Cold		SGA	ExTh Rept	SGAE-PH-65	May 68	Eder.MET-A,FP IAEA 68COPENH	
Diff Elastic	Cold		TRM	Theo Abst	JP/C 4 2725	Dec 71	Rao+ CAL MULT SCATT IN METHANE(LIQ)	
Thermal Scat	Maxwl		GWU	Theo Jour	PR 60 18	Jul 41	Sachs+ MASS TENSOR METHOD.	
Thermal Scat	1.5-2	5.0-1	GWU	Theo Jour	PR 60 18	Jul 41	Sachs+ MASS TENSOR METHOD.	
Thermal Scat	7.0-2		CRC	Expt Jour	PR 83 1100	Sep 51	Alcock+SCATT INTENSITY VS ANGLE	
Thermal Scat	7.3-2		HRV	Theo Jour	PR 101 129	Jan 56	Zemach+,GAS DIFFR TH CFD EXPT	
Thermal Scat	5.7-4	3.3-3	COL	Expt Prog	CU-174 21	Mar 58	Gould+ CHEM BINDING EFFECT.GRPH.	
Thermal Scat	2.5-2	1.0-1	MTR	Expt Conf	60Wien 277	Oct 60	Brugger+ ANGDIST CFD THRSCATLAW	
				Conf	60Vienna 93	Oct 60	.SEE ALSO	
Thermal Scat	1.0-2	1.0-1	MTR	Expt Jour	PR 124 460	Oct 61	Randolph+. E(THETA) DIST CFD THEORY	
Thermal Scat	1.5-2	2.5-2	MTR	Theo Jour	PR 124 1489	Dec 61	Griffing.ROTAT LVLS OF GAS.CFD EXPT	
Thermal Scat	Cold		MTR	Expt Prog	WASH-1041 39	62	Strong. 90 DEG SCT. NDG.	
Thermal Scat	Pile		MOL	Expt Prog	EANDC(E)23L	Feb 62	Stiller+,LIQUID CH4	
Thermal Scat	1.5-2	7.1-2	MTR	Theo Jour	PR 127 1179	Aug 62	Griffing. DIFF INELAST OKS XPT	
Thermal Scat	-3	-1	IFJ	Revw Rept	INP-255	Apr 63	Janik+ LIQU+GAS,EXPTS CFD K-N,GRPHS	
	5.8-3	1.1-1		Expt Rept	INP-215	Oct 62	Rogalska.LIQUID,SIG/H CFD K-N,GRAPH	
Thermal Scat	1.5-2	3.1-1	MTR	Theo Jour	NSE 15 438	Apr 63	Mcmurry+ CALC CFD EXPT.	
				Conf	62Chalk R. 1 435	Sep 62	.SUPERSEDED	
	-2	-1		Conf	62BNL 1 172	Apr 62	Mcmurry+ CALCTD DIFF SIGS CURVES	
		3.1-1		Rept	IDO-16692	Aug 61	- + KRIEGER - NELKIN THEORY EVAL	
Thermal Scat	5.2-3	2.4-2	JUL	Expt Jour	PSS 5 511	64	Dorner+ FREQ SPECT IN SOLID METHANE	
				Rept	JUEL-429-NP	64	- + REPRINT OF PSS 5 511	
	4.2-3	2.0-2		Jour	ZP 166 393	Feb 62	Stiller+ E-DIST OF N SCAT IN LIQD	
Thermal Scat	9.0-3	1.2-1	GA	Expt Jour	NSE 18 182	Feb 64	Whittemore. FC,LINAC. CURV. CFD TH.	
Thermal Scat	None		HAR	Expt Abst	BAP 9 421	Apr 64	Brugger+CH4,(DC4),NDG	
Thermal Scat	-2		WWA	Expt Jour	NKA 9 511	Jul 64	Aleksandrowicz+ BRIEF.THERM VIBR,NDG	
Thermal Scat	2.2-2	7.2-2	BUC	Expt Conf	64Bombay 2 421	Dec 64	Bally+DIFF SIG CFD TH,SIG(LAMBDA)	+
	2.6-2			Jour	RRP 9 507	Sep 64	- . GAS,XPTL+TH SIG(E,E') GRPH	
	2.5-2			Data	EXFOR30227.	Dec 72	/DSIG/DE'*DOMEGA AT 2 ANGLES	
Thermal Scat	Cold		BNL	Expt Abst	BAP 10 42	Jan 65	Otnes. SOLID,LIQ,GAS. NDG.	
Thermal Scat	2.5-2	1.0-1	MTR	Expt Jour	JCP 42 275	Jan 65	Harker+ SOLID,LIQ,GAS. CFD.	
Thermal Scat	1.5-3	4.5-3	KRK	ExTh Jour	APP 27 581	Apr 65	.ROTATION DYNAMICS SOLID+L9Q MOCETM3	
	Pile			Revw Rept	INP-368	Nov 64	JANIK REV.SOL.+LIQ.METH.,BOMBAY 64	
Thermal Scat	-3	-2	BNL	Theo Jour	PR/A 138 692	May 65	Michael. SPIN CORREL. SMALL EFFECT.	
Thermal Scat	4.9-3	7.0-2	MTR	Theo Jour	JCP 43 3328	Nov 65	Griffing. LANGEVIN EQ. CFD EXPT.	
Thermal Scat	3.0-1		GA	Expt Prog	GA-6583	Dec 65	Whittemore.THETA=150DEG CFD MCMURRY	
Thermal Scat	Maxwl		MTR	Expt Prog	WASH-1068 171	Mar 66	Harker.THETA=48DEG,T=5-22DEG K,CRVS	
Thermal Scat	-		KFI	Theo Jour	PHY 32 1571	Sep 66	Kosaly+ TH FOR ROTL FREEDOM X 86DEG	
Thermal Scat	2.5-2		TRM	Theo Jour	PR 149 1	Sep 66	Sinh+ NUC SPIN CORREL, LARGE LO TMP	
Thermal Scat	5.0-3		TRM	Theo Jour	PPS 89 379	Oct 66	Venkataraman+. CH4 GAS. CFD EXPT	
Thermal Scat	-2	+0	COL	Expt Prog	NYO-GEN72-132	Jan 67	Leung+ LIQD+SOLID METHANE, TBC, NDG	
Thermal Scat	Cold		CRC	Theo Jour	CJP 45 237	Feb 67	Sears. 98DEGK THETA=30-90DEG CFD XPT	
Thermal Scat	None		MIT	Theo Jour	JCP 46 1999	Mar 67	Agrawal+ T=99DEGK CURVS DIFF SIG	
Thermal Scat	4.9-3		TRM	Expt Jour	PR 156 196	Apr 67	Venkataraman+,LIQUID 98DEG K,CFD TH	
Thermal Scat	Cold		ISP	Expt Jour	PL/A 25 435	Sep 67	VERDAN 85DEGK TOF CFD K-N	
Thermal Scat	4.6-3		HAR	Expt Jour	PPS 92 912	Dec 67	Webb.EXPT AT 20DEGC COMPARED THEORY	
	5.0-3			Conf	62Chalk R. 1 457	Sep 62	- .DIFF SIG 20-90DEG AT 21DEGC	
Thermal Scat	Cold		TRM	Revw Conf	68Madras 2 144	Feb 68	Dasannacharya.LIQUID,E+ANGDIST,GRPH	
Thermal Scat	Cold		KRK	Revw Rept	INP-600/PS	Apr 68	Janik Gas+SOLID,LIQ CFD GRIFFIN	
Thermal Scat	3.0-3	1.0-1	KRK	Expt Rept	INP-608/PS	May 68	Bajorek+ CURVES DOUBLE DIFF AT 2ANG	
Thermal Scat	Maxwl		KRK	ExTh Rept	INP-608	May 68	Bajorek+.NDG,GASEOUS+SOLID METHANE	
Thermal Scat	4.9-3		KTH	Revw Conf	68Copenhgn 1 397	May 68	Larsson.PPR200.SIG(E'),6ANGS,LIQUID	
Thermal Scat	Maxwl		UJK	Theo Jour	PL/A 27 9	May 68	Fulinski+ SCAT BY GAS+INTERMOL FORCE	
Thermal Scat	Maxwl		ANL	Theo Jour	JCP 49 2443	Sep 68	Skold. QUASI-ELAST SCAT BY SOLID CH4	
Thermal Scat	5.0-3	1.0-1	DUB	Expt Jour	PHY 41 397	Mar 69	Bajorek+ DOUBLE DIFFSIG 80 DEGK	
Thermal Scat	None		ANL	Theo Jour	NSE 37 368	Sep 69	Agrawal+INCOHERENT SIG CALC,OKS XPT	
Thermal Scat	-3	-2	HLT	Expt Prog	INDC(FIN)-2G	70	Palmgren+ TRIPLE POINT, NO DATA GVN	
Thermal Scat	-3		UJK	Theo Jour	PHY 48 126	70	Fulinski+ T=120K.MOLEC INTERACT CALC	
	Cold			Rept	INP-677/PL	Sep 69	- + SCT FUNCT FOR MOLEC INTER	
	-3	-2		Jour	APP 34 1047	Dec 68	- + SIG-GRPH,CFD OTHER TH+EXPT	
Thermal Scat	Cold		KFK	Expt Rept	KFK-1489	Jan 72	Kapulla. DOUBLE DIFF SCAT SIG EXPT	
Thermal Scat	-3		TRM	ExTh Conf	72Bombay 2 619	Feb 72	RAO+ INEL SIG CFD THEO,CURVE GIVEN	
	Cold			Theo Prog	BARC-557 89	71	. LIQUID, MULTIPLE SCAT, NDG.	
				Jour	CJP 45 3185	Sep 67	Rao+ 98DEGK THETA=30-90DEGK CFD EXP	

1 Hydrogen MTH

Quantity	Energy (ev) Min	Max	Lab	Type	Documentation Ref Vol Page	Author, Comments Date	Data
Thermal Scat	5.0−3		MOLExTh Conf		72Grenoble 489	Mar 72 Hautecler+ SCAT SIG, TOF, GRPH	
Thermal Scat	4.0−3	2.2−2	Expt Conf		62Chalk R. 1 423	Sep 62 − +,MOLECULAR MOTIONS,LIQUID	
Thermal Scat	Maxwl		OSA Theo Jour		PTP 50 1142	Oct 73 Hama+METHANE GAS,ZEMACH GLAUBER APRX	
Thermal Scat	4.9−3	7.0−2	NSU Theo Jour		KNS 5 265	Dec 73 Hyun Chung+ LIQ.DOUBLDIF CFD XP,GRPH	
Thermal Scat	2.4−3		SAC Expt Jour		PL/A 54 285	Sep 75 Kahn. SOLID CH4 AT T=4.2K	

1 Hydrogen PFN

Quantity	Energy (ev) Min	Max	Lab	Type	Documentation Ref Vol Page	Author, Comments Date	Data
Total	Maxwl		COL Expt Jour		PR 60 702	Nov 41 Carroll. 54.8 B PER PROTON (WATER).	
Total	2.5+6		UI Expt Jour		PR 69 405	May 46 Manley+TIME DISTRIB SCT NS.14CM SCT	
Thermal Scat	None		COL Expt Jour		PR 49 103	Jan 36 Fink+VELOC DISTR 90,300DEGK,RA−BE N	+
Thermal Scat	Maxwl		BRK Expt Jour		PR 50 575	Sep 36 Libby+ TEMPERATURE EQUILIBRUM HYPOT	+
Thermal Scat	Maxwl		BRK Expt Jour		PR 50 577	Sep 36 Libby+ EFFECT OF CHEMICAL BOND.	
Thermal Scat	Maxwl		COL Expt Jour		PR 50 571	Sep 36 Amaldi+ ALBEDO. INVALID HYPOTHESIS.	
Thermal Scat	5.7−4	3.3−3	COL Expt Prog		CU− 174 21	Mar 58 Gould+ CHEM BINDING EFFECT. GRPH.	
Thermal Scat	Cold		MTR Expt Jour		NSE 5 99	Feb 59 Brugger+,THETA=90DEG PARAFFIN CURVE	
Thermal Scat	1.0−2	1.0+0	RPI Expt Conf		67Ann Arbr 2 61	Jul 67 Cerbone+PPR62.PLYTH−SCATKERN,N−SPEC	
(n,γ)	Maxwl		COL Expt Jour		PR 50 738	Oct 36 Fink. RATE OF ABSORPTION ONLY	
(n,γ)	Maxwl		ORL Expt Jour		PR 73 956	May 48 Bernstein. PER CUBIC CM.	

1 Hydrogen PHL

Quantity	Energy (ev) Min	Max	Lab	Type	Documentation Ref Vol Page	Author, Comments Date	Data
Total	2.5−2		MTR Expt Jour		PR 126 29	Apr 62 Brugger. CS FOR TERPHENYLS MEAS.	
Total	7.0−4	1.0−1	CAS Expt Jour		PHY 32 119	Jan 66 Antonini+TOF SOLID + LIQUID SAMPLES	
				Rept	EANDC(E)57U79	Feb 65 MENTIONED *	
				Jour	PHY 30 1647	Aug 64 SUPERSEDED*	
Total	2.0−3	4.0−1	KIL Expt Conf		67Juelich 226	Apr 67 SCHLESR PROTONS IN C12H10,22+95DEGC	
Total	1.0−3	1.0+0	ISP Theo Conf		67Ann Arbr 1 467	Jul 67 Ardente+PPR40.SIGBOUND/FREE CFD XPT	
Total	2.0−3	3.0−3	AMUExpt Conf		71Knoxvill 695	Mar 71 Sefidvash. DI−,TERPHENYL.BOUND H−SIG	
Total	8.9−3	1.5+0	SHI Expt Jour		INER − 210	Dec 76 Chi−Fong Ai. (HB−40) TOF.TBL,GRAPH	
Thermal Scat	Cold		CCP Expt Conf		62BNL 1 66	Apr 62 Zemlyanov+ 20DEGC DIPHENYL INEL SPC	
Thermal Scat	None		GA Theo Conf		62BNL 1 69	Apr 62 Boffi+ DIPHENYL,TERPHENYL CALC.	
Thermal Scat	1.0−2	1.0−1	MTR Expt Jour		PR 126 29	Apr 62 Brugger. SOLID,LIQ TERPHENYL. CURVS.	
Thermal Scat	−		CCP Expt Conf		62Chalk R. 1 297	Sep 62 Zemljanov+,TOF,N SPECT INEL SCAT	
Thermal Scat		5.3−3	KUR Expt Jour		AE 14 247	Mar 63 Zemiyanov+ POLYCRYST,SCAT NEUT SPEC	
				Jour	SJA 14 252	Jan 64 TRANSLATN.*NO 3	
Thermal Scat	5.0−3	5.0−1	CCP Expt Conf		64Geneva § 367	May 64 Mostovoy+ MONOISOPROPYLDIPH.,C15H16	
Thermal Scat	1.9−2	8.0−2	KFK Expt Jour		NUK 7 64	Feb 65 Glaeser. BENSOL, DIPHENYL, DIPHYL	
				Jour	NSE 20 236	Oct 64 − . SEE ALSO.	
				Conf	62Chalk R. 1 307	Sep 62 − .SCAT LAW 21DEGC,CURVES	
Thermal Scat	2.2−2	1.0−1	MUNExTh Jour		NUK 7 286	Jul 65 Hofmeyr.4ES.ANGDIST+CALCS.O−M−P−TER	
				Conf	64Geneva § 763	May 64 Hofmeyer+ SUPERSEDED	
				Rept	JUEL−160−NP	May 64 − + SUPERSEDED	
Thermal Scat	Maxwl		OSA Theo Prog		EANDC(J)7L27	Jan 67 Sekiya.FREQ DISTR CFD XPT	
Thermal Scat	5.0−3	6.0−2	LON Eval Jour		BJA 18 205	Feb 67 LIQ SANTOWAX−R FIT DATA OF BRUGGER	
Thermal Scat	−3	+0	GA ExTh Conf		67Ann Arbr 1 509	Jul 67 Neill+PPR55.INTGRL−XPT OKS MOLEC−TH	
Thermal Scat	−3	+0	ISP Theo Conf		67Ann Arbr 1 467	Jul 67 Ardente+PPR40.REACTOR PARS/MOLEC−TH	
Thermal Scat	2.0−3	1.0+0	GA Theo Prog		GA− 8449	Jan 68 Beyster+ DIPHENYL EXPTL+THEOR CURVE	
	None			Prog	GA− 8085	Jul 67 − + DIPHENYL CALC OF MOL VIBR	
Thermal Scat	2.0−3	1.0+0	GA Theo Jour		NSE 35 80	Jan 69 Sprevak+ S(A,B) AT 80DEGC CALCULTD	
Thermal Scat	Maxwl		HLT ExTh Jour		JNE 23 225	Apr 69 Sefidvash+ DIPHENYL ,DIFFUSNPARAMS	+
Thermal Scat	−		LON Theo Jour		JNE 23 225	Apr 69 Sefidvash+ DIF.LENGTH CFD MODEL CAL	
Thermal Scat	1.0−3	4.0−1	HLT Theo Jour		JNE 23 306	May 69 Sefidvash. CALC−SIG(E) CFD EXPT	
Thermal Scat	Maxwl		CSR Expt Jour		CZJB 19 911	Jul 69 Bayer+PULSD−N−TECHN,DIFFUS−PARS GVN	
Thermal Scat	Maxwl		JAE Theo Rept		JAERI−1181 68	Sep 69 Iijima+.CALC OF SCAT SIG	
Thermal Scat	−3	+0	HLT Expt Rept		INDC(FIN)−1G	Apr 70 Palmgren+ SUBTHERMAL CROSS−SECTION	
Thermal Scat	Cold		MUNExpt Jour		PRL 27 956	Oct 71 Koester+DIPHNLMETH.SCAT AMPL.REFLEC	
				Jour	ZP/A 272 189	Feb 75 − +COH.SCT.AMP.DIPHENYLMETHANE	
				Jour	ZP 198 187	Dec 66 − +SUPERSEDED.	
Absorption	−2		KFI Expt Conf		65Karlsrhe 1 165	May 65 PAL.PULSED NEUTRON XPTS, SIG.V GVN	
	1.0−3	1.0−1		Conf	64Geneva § 651	May 64 PAL+ REACTOR NEUTRONS,MECH SELECTOR	
(n,γ)	Maxwl		CSR Expt Jour		CZJB 19 911	Jul 69 Bayer+PULSED−N−TECHN,AVG NACR−SIG	

1 Hydrogen PLE

Quantity	Energy (ev) Min	Max	Lab	Type	Documentation Ref Vol Page	Date	Author, Comments	Data
Total	1.4+7		LAS	Expt Rept	LA- 1279	Jul 51	Meyer+,TRANS,T-D NEUTS,2.64+ -0.03B	
Total	1.3+6		MIT	Expt Jour	PR 95 1252	Sep 54	Storrs+ TRANSMISSION 9.542+ -.035B	
Total	1.0-3	1.0+0	KAP	ExTh Conf	62Chalk R. 1 389	Sep 62	Goldman+,TOT SIG VS N ENERGY CFD TH	
Total	2.0-3	1.0+0	GA	Theo Conf	65Karlsrhe 1 385	May 65	Young.SCATT KERNEL,GRPH TH CFD XPT.	
				Rept	GA- 5600	Sep 64	Koppel+SCAT KERNEL CFD XPT SIGMA	
Total	0.0+0	1.0+0	COL	Expt Prog	WASH-1064 28	Oct 65	Leung+ SILASTIC POLYMER.NDG.TBP JCP.	
Total	2.0+6	1.7+7	CSE	Expt Prog	WASH-1064 24	Oct 65	Galloway+ NDG. OKS OTHER EXPTS.	
Total	3.0-3	7.0+1	KAP	ExTh Jour	NSE 23 192	Oct 65	Armstrong. TOF.MEAS TOT CFD SCT CALC	
Total	2.5-2	2.5-2	ATI	Expt Jour	AKE 12 159	Mar 66	Lasinger+ THR BE-,BI-FILT. 4,80,290K	+
	Pile			Data	EXFOR20028.	Sep 71	9PTS.	
Total	-3	+0	GA	Revw Rept	GA- 7952	Apr 67	Beyster+ STATUS OF THEORY+EXPT CURV	
Total	8.2-4	1.4-1	IEA	Expt Prog	INDC(BZL)-2 22	May 69	Herdade+ SCAT-SIG(E)/H-ATOM	+
	8.2-4	1.3-1		Rept	IEA-310	Sep 73	- + TOF+CRYSTAL-SPEC,TBL+GRAPH.	
				Prog	INDC-6 15	Jun 70	Santos+ LIEAR FITTED PARAMS GIVEN	
	8.2-4	1.3-1		Data	EXFOR30229.	Jan 73	SIG TOT AT 147 ENERGIES	
Total	-3	1.0+1	IKE	Theo Rept	IKE-6-61/1	Jan 73	Keinert.DATA LIBRARY	
Total	5.5+6	9.6+6	THS	Expt Diss	HEUER	Apr 74	Heuer. TRANSMISSION	+
	5.5+6	9.6+6		Data	EXFOR20560.002	Mar 76	27PTS.	
Diff Elastic	-3	1.0+1	IKE	Theo Rept	IKE-6-61/1	Jan 73	Keinert.DATA LIBRARY	
Diff Inelast	4.0+6		ALD	Expt Jour	NIM 30 77	Nov 64	Parker+TOF SPECT AT 50DEG.THIN SMPL	
Thermal Scat	5.7-4	3.3-3	COL	Expt Prog	CU- 174 21	Mar 58	Gould+ CS VS WAVELENGTH.	
Thermal Scat	Maxwl		AE	Expt Jour	AF 15 471	May 59	Sjoestrand+.DIFFUSN PARAMS.PLSD NS	
Thermal Scat	Cold		CCP	Expt Conf	62BNL 1 66	Apr 62	Zemlyanov+ 20DEGC INELAST NEUT SPEC	
Thermal Scat	-		CCP	Expt Conf	62Chalk R. 1 297	Sep 62	Zemljanov+,TOF,N SPECT INEL SCAT	
Thermal Scat	1.0-3	1.0+1	KAP	Theo Conf	62Chalk R. 1 389	Sep 62	Goldman+ SCAT LAW AT 21 DEG C.	
				Conf	62BNL 1 100	Apr 62	- + CALC OF NEUTRON SPECTRA	
	None			Rept	TID-16691	62	- + INELASTIC SCATTERING CALC	
Thermal Scat		5.3-3	KUR	Expt Jour	AE 14 257	Mar 63	Zemiyanov+ RADIATION DAMAGE,N'-SPEC	
				Jour	SJA 14 252	Jan 64	TRANSLATN.*NO 3	
Thermal Scat	9.0-2	3.4-1	GA	Expt Prog	GA- 5554 45	Sep 64	Whittemore. XPT CFD CALC. GRPHS.	
	9.2-3	8.9-2		Prog	GA- 3409 47	Nov 62	- . CURVS,CFD TH.PRELIM.	
Thermal Scat	1.0-3	1.0+0	GA	Theo Prog	GA- 6096 29	Jan 65	Beyster. CALCD CS, ANG DISTR.	
Thermal Scat	1.0-3	1.0+0	GA	Theo Jour	NSE 21 268	Feb 65	Koppel+ SCT KERNEL TO CALC SPEC.	
				Conf	66S.Diego 1 27	Feb 66	- . COMPARED WITH THEO OF SCTLAW	
				Conf	65Karlsrhe 1 385	May 65	Young. SCATT KERNEL, TH CFD XPT.	
Thermal Scat	2.5-2	1.5-1	MHG	Expt Abst	DA 25 7333	Jun 65	Donovan. INL SCT.PHON FREQS,TBL,3TMP	
	3.0-2			Jour	JCP 42 4299	Jun 65	Myers+ PHONON FREQ SPEC CFD CURVES.	
Thermal Scat	Maxwl		MHG	Theo Jour	JCP 43 1079	Aug 65	Summerfield. CS FORMULA DERVD.	
Thermal Scat	3.0-3	7.0+1	KAP	ExTh Jour	NSE 23 192	Oct 65	Armstrong. TOF.MEAS TOT CFD SCT CALC	
Thermal Scat	None		MTR	Expt Prog	WASH-1064 153	Oct 65	Moore+ SHEET VS DRAWN FIBER. NDG.	
Thermal Scat	1.5-2	3.2-1	IFU	Expt Prog	INDSWG-126 24	66	Ivanickij. 5 AS, 7 ES, TBL. TBP AE	
Thermal Scat	1.5-2	3.2-1	IFU	Expt Jour	AE 20 30	Jan 66	Ivanitski+.SCAT SPECT,S(ALPHA,BETA)	+
				Jour	SJA 20 36	Jan 66	. ENGL OF AE 20 30	
Thermal Scat	Maxwl		COL	Expt Prog	WASH-1068 42	Mar 66	Leung+,HIGH- AND LOW-DENSITY,NDG	
Thermal Scat	1.6-1	5.0-1	GA	ExTh Jour	NSE 24 394	Apr 66	Whittemore.MODEL COMPARISONS	
				Rept	GA- 6583	Dec 65	.SUPERSEDED.	
	1.7-1	5.0-1		Rept	GA- 6456	Jun 65	.SAME AS NSE 24,394.	
Thermal Scat	Maxwl		PCT	Expt Jour	JCP 45 757	Jul 66	Trevino. TOF, PLYTH 293DEG K, CURVE	
Thermal Scat	3.0-2	1.1+0	RPI	Expt Jour	NIM 42 197	Jul 66	Pan+ELECTR.LINAC FILTR.DIFFER.METHD	
Thermal Scat	8.3-1	1.8+0	RPI	ExTh Jour	NSE 25 300	Jul 66	Kirouac+ 3 ES. LINAC. MDL PARS.	
	1.0-1	1.8+0		Expt Abst	DA/B 27 266	Jul 66	- .TOF,LINAC+FC.CFD EINSTN MOD	
	1.5-1	1.8+0		Conf	66Wash. 122	Mar 66	- +,25 60 90DEG,9ES,CURVES	
Thermal Scat	Maxwl		MHG	Expt Abst	DA/B 27 586	Aug 66	Myers. STRETCH-ORIENTED.100 DEG K.	
	3.0-2			Jour	JCP 44 184	Jan 66	- + STRETCH-ORIENTED. GRAPH.	
Thermal Scat	1.2-2	1.7+0	GA	Expt Prog	WASH-1071 63	Nov 66	Borgonovi.(CH2-)CURVES FOR7ENERGIES	
Thermal Scat	5.0-3		UCS	Expt Jour	JCP 45 3787	Nov 66	Safford+ N SPECT CFD CALC	
Thermal Scat	None		MHG	ExTh Abst	BAP 12 409	Mar 67	Summerfield+ NORMAL,DEUTERATED PLY.	
Thermal Scat	None		GA	Revw Rept	GA- 7952	Apr 67	Beyster+ STATUS OF THEORY+EXPT	
Thermal Scat	3.3-1	1.0+1	RPI	Expt Prog	WASH-1074 103	Apr 67	Bischoff+ 3ES DIFF SIG CURVES 2ES	
	1.6-1	4.9-1		Prog	WASH-1071 184	Nov 66	- + CURVES FOR 0.486 EV.	
Thermal Scat	-3	1.0+1	GA	Expt Conf	67Ann Arbr 1 493	Jul 67	Beyster+ PPR75.GRPHS,XPTL SIG CFD TH	
Thermal Scat	None		MTR	Theo Conf	67Ann Arbr 1 643	Jul 67	Griffing.PPR72.SCAT KERN+DECAY CONS	
Thermal Scat	-		OSA	Theo Jour	JCP 47 337	Jul 67	Kitagawa+ CALC OF INELAS SCAT SIG	
Thermal Scat	1.0-2	1.0+0	RPI	Expt Conf	67Ann Arbr 2 61	Jul 67	Cerbone+PPR62.SCAT-KERNS CFD N-SPEC	
Thermal Scat	-		THS	Expt Jour	AKE 12 279	Jul 67	Keinert+NELKIN MDL THR SPECTRUM	
Thermal Scat	-1	+0	UNC	Theo Conf	67Ann Arbr 1 537	Jul 67	Bollacasa+PPR74.'UPSCAT' REACTOR-TH	
Thermal Scat	Cold		MHG	ExTh Jour	JCP 48 912	Jan 68	Lynch+ MEAS DEL 55-90DEG	

1 Hydrogen   PLE

Quantity	Energy (ev) Min	Max	Lab	Type	Documentation Ref Vol Page	Date	Author, Comments	Data
Thermal Scat	2.3+1		RPI	Expt Prog	WASH – 1093 126	Apr 68	Moore+ DIFF INEL SIGS 6ANGS CURVES	
	1.0 – 1	1.0+0		Rept	RPI – 328 – 102	67	– + DOUBLE DIFF INEL SCAT SIGS	
Thermal Scat	3.0 – 2	8.0 – 2	MTR	Expt Rept	IN – 1151	May 68	Myers. 3ES,TEMP=4.2,77,300DEGK. TBLS	
Thermal Scat	None		GA	Theo Jour	NUK 12 87	Jan 69	Sprevak+ SCAT SIG+SPECT CFD EXPT.	
Thermal Scat	8.2 – 4	1.4 – 1	IEA	Expt Prog	INDC(BZL) – 2 22	May 69	Herdade+ SCAT – SIG(E)/H – ATOM	+
	8.2 – 4	1.3 – 1		Rept	IEA – 310	Sep 73	– + SCT – SIG/H – ATOM FROM TOT – SIG	
	8.2 – 4	1.3 – 1		Data	EXFOR30229.	Jan 73	SIG SCAT PER H – ATOM AT 147 ENERGIES	
Thermal Scat	1.5 – 2	9.0 – 2	IFU	Expt Jour	UFZ 14 1525	Sep 69	Ivanickij+.TOF,SCAT SPEC,3 NEUT ES	
Thermal Scat	Maxwl		KAP	Theo Rept	KAPL – P – 3860	Nov 69	Kirouac+,IMPROVED CALCTN,OKS EXPT	
Thermal Scat	7.5 – 3		JAE	Expt Rept	JAERI – 1197 109	Aug 70	Doi+.TOF SPECTRUM OF N INEL SCATT.	
Thermal Scat	Fiss		JUL	Expt Rept	JUEL – 1046	Feb 74	Fils.N – TRANSPORT IN HYDROGEN MATTER	
Thermal Scat	1.0+6	1.5+7	UI	Expt Conf	75Wash. 169	Mar 75	Johnson+GRPH,LEAKAGE N/252CF SOURC N	
Thermal Scat	– 3	1.9+0	THS	Theo Rept	IKE – 6 89 20	Jun 75	Keinert. DATA LIBRARY	
Scattering	– 3	1.0+1	IKE	Theo Rept	IKE – 6 – 61/1	Jan 73	Keinert.DATA LIBRARY	

1 Hydrogen   WTR

Quantity	Energy (ev) Min	Max	Lab	Type	Documentation Ref Vol Page	Date	Author, Comments	Data
Evaluation	9.3 – 3	1.0+7	GEN	Eval Rept	APEX – 467	Jun 58	Tralli+.ABS SCT XI,MU(SCT),XSEC/P	
	Maxwl			Rept	APEX – 467	Jun 58	– + SCT,ABS 68 – 3000DEGF+XS/P,TSL	
Evaluation	Pile		HAR	Eval Rept	AERE – R – 3931	Jan 62	EGELSTAFF SCATTERING LAW AT24DEG C	
Evaluation	3.6 – 2	2.6 – 1	HAR	Eval Rept	AERE – R – 4484	Jan 64	Haywood.SCATTERING LAW 22,150 DEG C	
Evaluation	6.0 – 4	5.0 – 1	UK	Eval Rept	AEEW – R – 351	Feb 64	Barrington+(WIN).UKNDL FILE.	
Evaluation	1.0 – 3	1.5+7	KFK	Eval Data	KEDAK – 3	Oct 75	H BOUND IN H2O.	+
Total	Maxwl		COL	Expt Jour	PR 60 702	Nov 41	Carroll. 44.6 B PER PROTON (WATER).	
Total	Cold		CHI	Expt Jour	PR 70 815	Dec 46	Anderson+ C – FILTERED NS TO 18DEG K.	
Total	3.5+5	6.0+6	MIN	Expt Jour	PR 70 805	Dec 46	Nuckolls+ TRNS. TBL, GRAPHS.	+
	3.5+5	6.0+6		Data	EXFOR11142.003	Jun 76	. 15 PTS. SIGMA.	
Total	3.0 – 3	1.0+2	COR	Expt Jour	PR 74 364	Aug 48	Jones.TOF.TRANSM.ALSO SIGMA PER H.	
Total	3.3 – 3	5.2+0	COL	Expt Jour	PR 76 1750	Dec 49	Melkonian. H IN H2O. GRPH. CFD.	+
	3.3 – 3	5.3+0		Data	EXFOR11150.003	Jun 76	. 40 PTS. SIGMA.	
Total	9.5+7		BRK	Expt Jour	PR 77 606	Mar 50	Dejuren+ BI FISSION CH.	
	9.5+7			Data	EXFOR11174.004	Jun 76	. 1 PT. SIGMA.	
Total	1.4+7		LAS	Expt Rept	LA – 1279	Jul 51	Meyer+,TRANS,T – D NEUTS,2.97+ – 0.03B	
Total	6.4 – 3	9.0 – 3	BNL	Expt Priv	SMITH	53	Smith.	+
	6.4 – 3	9.0 – 3		Data	EXFOR11172.002	Jun 76	. 29 PTS. SIGMA.	
Total	1.7 – 3	2.5 – 2	FAR	Expt Rept	CEA – 162	Jan 53	Ertaud+.GRPHT FILTER. TRNSM.3ES	
Total	1.1+8	1.7+8	UPP	Expt Rept	PM 46 295	Mar 55	Alphonce+TRANSMISSION	
Total	1.4+7		LEB	Expt Jour	AE 5 71	57	Katsarov+TRANSMISSION,2940+ – 8MB	
				Jour	SJA 5 53	58	. *	
Total	1.3 – 3	1.8+1	GA	Expt Priv	WALTON	60	Walton. SIGMA.	+
	1.3 – 3	1.8+1		Data	EXFOR11173.002	Jun 76	. 111 PTS. SIGMA.	
Total	6.0 – 4		TAT	Theo Jour	JNEA 11 89	Feb 60	RIGID ASYM ROTOR 230 – 290 BARNS	
Total	2.0 – 4	3.6 – 2	MUN	Expt Jour	ZP 163 218	May 61	Heinloth.CURV.FOR VARIOUS TEMPS	+
				Conf	60Wien 323	Oct 60	SEE ALSO *	
	7.8 – 3			Revw Conf	60Vienna 63	Oct 60	Maierleibnitz.CURVE REL TO TEMPRTR	
Total	1.2 – 2	5.2 – 1	MUN	ExTh Jour	NUK 3 110	Jul 61	Mech.MONOCHROMETER.SOL,LIQ,GAS PHSE	
Total	1.0 – 3	1.0+0	KAP	ExTh Conf	62Chalk R. 1 389	Sep 62	Goldman+,TOT SIG VS N ENERGY CFD TH	
Total	4.4 – 3	8.0 – 2	KRK	Expt Conf	62Chalk R. 1 405	Sep 62	Janik+,TOT SIG PER P CFD K – N TH	
Total	1.8 – 4	3.6 – 2	IFJ	Revw Rept	INP – 255	Apr 63	Janik+ TOTSIG OF MOLECULE VS T,GRPH	
Total	4.2 – 1	1.7+3	MTR	Expt Jour	NIM 30 293	64	Simpson.	+
	4.2 – 1	1.7+3		Data	EXFOR11020.002	Jun 76	. 68 PTS. SIGMA.	
Total	6.0 – 4	5.0 – 1	UK	Eval Rept	AEEW – R – 351	Feb 64	Barrington+(WIN).UKNDL FILE.	
Total	3.0 – 4	2.0 – 1	GA	Expt Prog	GA – 4434	Sep 64	Whittemore.LINAC FC,LIQD ORTHO – PARA	
Total	1.4+0		ORL	Expt Jour	NP 61 381	Jan 65	Rayburn+ IN RES. TRNS.CS=46.1+ – 0.2 B	+
	1.4+0			Data	EXFOR11026.002	Jun 76	. 1 PT. SIGMA.	
Total	3.0 – 3	1.0+0	GA	Theo Conf	65Karlsrhe 1 385	May 65	Young.SCATT KERNEL,GRPH TH CFD XPT.	
Total	1.0 – 4	1.0+3	UK	Eval Rept	AWRE – O – 23/65	Jul 65	Horsley.(ALD).UKNDL – DFN 212.	
Total	1.0 – 3	1.0+0	GA	Theo Rept	GA – 7581	Mar 66	Beyster.CALCULATED CURVE CFD EXPT	
				Conf	66S.Diego 1 151	Feb 66	– + COMPARED WITH SCATT LAW	
Total	1.0 – 2	1.5+1	GA	Expt Rept	GA – 7581	Dec 66	Russell.TOF TRANS CURVS CFD THEORY	+
	3.5 – 3	1.6+1		Data	EXFOR11162.	Jun 76	. 134 PTS. SIGMA. 1 PT. BAS.	
Total	– 3	+1	GA	Revw Rept	GA – 7952	Apr 67	Beyster+ COMPARISON OF TH+EXPT CURV	
Total	1.0 – 3	1.0+1	HAR	Conf	67Ann Arbr 1 361	Jul 67	Haywood+PPR19.550DEG – K,GRPHS SIG(E)	
Total	2.0 – 3	1.2 – 1	IST	Theo Conf	67Ann Arbr 2 131	Jul 67	Goddard+PPR4.SCAT – MODL – CALC CFD XPT	
Total	– 5	+0	KFK	Theo Conf	67Ann Arbr 2 411	Jul 67	Reichardt.PPR15. GRPH SIG(E,TEMPTR)	

1 Hydrogen WTR

Quantity	Energy (ev) Min	Max	Lab	Type	Documentation Ref Vol Page	Date	Author, Comments	Data
Total	1.0−2	1.0+1	ATH	Expt	Rept EANDC(OR)63	Aug 67	Dritsa+ CHOPPER,CRYST − SPEC,GRPH 2TS	+
					Rept IAEA − 124 57	Feb 70	SEE ALSO *SIG AT 2TS,GRPH	
					Rept EANDC(OR)58	Jan 66	SEE ALSO *,ABST,CFD SIG(H)	
	1.0−2	1.5+1			Data EXFOR20176.	May 74	486PTS.	
	1.0−2	9.4+0			Data EXFOR20038.	Sep 71	984PTS.	
Total	2.5−3	1.0+1	GA	Expt	Jour NSE 33 265	Aug 68	Neill+ LINAC+TOF CFD THEORY CURVES	
Total	2.0−3	1.0+0	FRK	Expt	Rept IKF − 22	Nov 68	Daubert+ TOF EXPT AT FEW TEMP + ICE	
Total	8.2−4	1.4−1	IEA	Expt	Prog INDC(BZL) − 2 22	May 69	Herdade+ SIGMA TOT	+
	8.2−4	1.3−1			Rept IEA − 310	Sep 73	− + TOF,GRAPH CFD OTHERS,TABLE.	
	8.2−4	1.3−1			Data EXFOR30229.	Jan 73	SIG TOT AT 147 ENERGIES	
Total	5.0+5	1.7+7	CCP	Expt	Jour AE 27 141	Aug 69	Kukhtevich+ TRANSMISSN+RES SHIELDNG	
					Jour SJA 27 76	Aug 69	.TRANSLATN.SEE ALSO P 852	
Total	2.0−3	5.0−2	GRC	Expt	Prog EANDC(OR)87L	Sep 69	Dritsa+	
Total	4.0−3	2.3−2	KIG	Expt	Jour AKE 17 121	Mar 71	Suszkin. H − SIG IN H2O	
Total	1.3−2	1.0+0	IFU	Expt	Prog YFI − 12 79	Jun 71	Vertebny+	+
	1.3−2	1.0+0			Data EXFOR40109.006	Dec 72	SIGMA AT 28 ES	
Total	1.0−2	1.0+0	IJI	Expt	Prog YFI − 12 74	72	Vertebny+ ABSTRACT,TBL SIG(N − E)	
	1.0−2	3.0−1			Prog INDC(CCP) − 30	Sep 72	.PAGE 64,ENGLISH OF YFI − 12 74	
Total	−3	1.0+1	IKE	Theo	Rept IKE − 6 − 61/1	Jan 73	Keinert.DATA LIBRARY	
Total	Fiss		KFI	Theo	Rept KFKI − 74 − 63	Aug 74	Palfalvi+ MTE − CARLO N − SPEC(10,40 CM)	
Total	1.0−3	1.5+7	KFK	Eval	Data KEDAK − 3	Oct 75	H BOUND IN H2O. 55 DATA SETS	+
Elastic	Maxwl		TAT	Theo	Jour JNEA 11 89	Feb 60	RIGID ASYM ROTOR 10 − 23 BARNS	
Elastic	2.5−4	3.0−3	MUN	Expt	Jour ZP 164 111	Jul 61	Springer+ SIGMA VS E AT 4DEG	
Elastic	1.0−3		MUN	Expt	Jour ZAP 14 738	Dec 62	Maier − Leibniz.COH.SCAT.LGTH.REFRAKT	
Elastic	6.0−4	5.0−1	UK	Eval	Rept AEEW − R − 351	Feb 64	Barrington+(WIN).UKNDL FILE.	
Elastic	1.0−4	1.0+3	UK	Eval	Rept AWRE − O − 23/65	Jul 65	Horsley.(ALD).UKNDL − DFN 212.	
Elastic	1.0−3	1.5+7	KFK	Eval	Data KEDAK − 3	Oct 75	H BOUND IN H2O. 54 DATA SETS	+
Diff Elastic	3.9−2	7.8−2	MUN	Expt	Jour ZP 163 424	Jun 61	Reinsch. CURVES FOR 3 TEMPERATURES	
					Jour ZN/A 16 112	Jan 61	− +AT SEVERAL TARGET TEMPERAT.	
	3.6−2				Revw Conf 60Vienna 63	Oct 60	Maierleibnitz.CURVE ANGLE,ICE + H2O	
Diff Elastic	6.0−4	5.0−1	UK	Eval	Rept AEEW − R − 351	Feb 64	Barrington+(WIN).UKNDL FILE.	
Diff Elastic	−3	1.0+1	IKE	Theo	Rept IKE − 6 − 61/1	Jan 73	Keinert.DATA LIBRARY	
Diff Elastic	5.0+4	1.5+7	KFK	Eval	Data KEDAK − 3	Oct 75	H BOUND IN H2O. 19 ENERGIES	+
Diff Inelast	1.0+6	1.4+7	ANL	Expt	Prog WASH − 745 6	Nov 57	Casson+ TOF. PRELIM MEAS. NDG.	
Diff Inelast	1.6+7	3.3+8	KUR	Expt	Rept IAE − 404	Mar 63	Mostovoj+ SIG INEL(E,E',THETA)GRPHS	
Thermal Scat	Maxwl		MHG	Expt	Jour PR 50 570	Sep 36	Zahn+ RATIO ABS/SCATT.PRELIMINARY.	
Thermal Scat	Maxwl		GWU	Theo	Jour PR 60 18	Jul 41	Sachs+ MASS TENSOR METHOD.	
Thermal Scat	1.5−2	5.0−1	GWU	Theo	Jour PR 60 18	Jul 41	Sachs+ MASS TENSOR METHOD.	
Thermal Scat	Maxwl		FOA	Expt	Jour AF 2 47	Jun 50	Larsson. DIFFUSION LENGTH.2ND MOMNT	
Thermal Scat	Maxwl		KRK	ExTh	Jour APP 12 45	Jun 53	Janik.SIG CFD SACHS − TELLER THEORY	
Thermal Scat	2.0+5	2.0+6	UPP	Theo	Jour AF 8 165	Oct 54	Holte.SPACE − E DISTR(AROUND 1EV) βBL	
	2.5+6				Jour AF 3 209	Aug 51	− .SPACE − E DISTR OF SLOWD DWN NS	
Thermal Scat	Maxwl		AE	Expt	Jour PR 96 1245	Dec 54	VON DARDEL+.DIFFSN PRMS.COOLINGCOEF	
					Jour AF 7 357	Mar 54	Von Dardel. EFF N TEMP VS TIME	
Thermal Scat	−1		SAC	Expt	Conf 55Geneva 5 77	Aug 55	Jacrot+SPECTRUM OF SCATTRD NS,P357	
Thermal Scat	−1	+0	LEB	ExTh	Jour ZET 31 717	Oct 56	Goldanskii.SUGGESTS TOF − XPT	
					Jour JET 4 604	May 57	TRANSLATN.*	
Thermal Scat	5.7−4	3.3−3	COL	Expt	Prog CU − 174 21	Mar 58	Gould+ CHEM BINDING EFFECT.GRPH.	
Thermal Scat	−2	4.0−1	BNL	Expt	Conf 58Geneva 16 297	Sep 58	Mcreynolds+.PPR1540,CURV CFD THEORY	
Thermal Scat	Cold		MTR	Expt	Jour NSE 5 99	Feb 59	Brugger+,THETA=90DEG CURVE	
Thermal Scat	Maxwl		AE	Eval	Jour AF 15 147	Apr 59	Sjoestrand.CORR TO DIFFSN COOL COEF	
Thermal Scat	2.0−2	1.0−1	KRK	ExTh	Jour APP 18 255	May 59	Wanic.SIG CFD KRIEGER − NELKEN TH	
	1.0−2	5.0−1			Jour NKA 4 241	May 59	Janik.SIG+THERMLIZ CFD KOLOS+K − N − TH	
Thermal Scat	1.0−2	1.0+0	GA	Theo	Jour PR 119 741	Jul 60	Nelkin. THEORY CFD EXPT.	
Thermal Scat	3.0−3	1.0−1	BNL	Expt	Jour PR 119 872	Aug 60	Hughes+ MEAS AT VARIOUS TEMPS.	
Thermal Scat	5.0−4	1.0−1	GA	Expt	Conf 60Wien 511	Oct 60	Whittemore+ CURVE, REL LOW TEMPS.	
	Maxwl				Rept GA − 1690	Sep 60	Mcreynolds+LINAC,TOF SPEC 4 − 295DEGK	
Thermal Scat	2.5−4	3.0−3	MUN	Expt	Jour ZP 164 111	61	Springer+ TRANS,4DEG K.INCOHERNT SIG	
Thermal Scat	5.0−3		KRK	Expt	Jour PF 12 473	Aug 61	SPEC OF NS AT ANGL=90DEG,TEMP=22CGR	
Thermal Scat	1.0−1	2.5−1	HAN	Expt	Prog WASH − 1034 16	Dec 61	Smith+H2O,E=.1,.15,.25EV,AT ROOM T	
Thermal Scat	3.5−2	1.5−1	HAR	Comp	Rept AERE − R − 3931	Jan 62	EGELSTAFF TABLES FOR 24 DEGC	
Thermal Scat	3.6−2	7.8−2	MUN	Expt	Prog EANDC(E)23L	Feb 62	Heinloth+,SCAT XSECT BETW − 150+200C	
Thermal Scat	3.6−2	2.5−1	CRC	Expt	Conf 62BNL 1 26	Apr 62	Haywood+ 20 150DEGC S(A,B)+P(BETA)	
	3.5−2	1.4−1			Conf 60Wien 309	Jul 60	Egelstaff+20+150DEGC	
Thermal Scat	1.3−3	1.2+0	GEV	Theo	Rept GEAP − 3944	May 62	Kerr. CALC SCAT KERNLS,4 TEMPS,TBLS.	
Thermal Scat	−		CCP	Expt	Conf 62Chalk R. 1 383	Sep 62	Bajorik+,QUASI − EL SCAT,RESOL .5PC	

1 Hydrogen WTR

Quantity	Energy (ev) Min	Energy (ev) Max	Lab	Type	Documentation Ref Vol Page	Date	Author, Comments	Data
Thermal Scat	None		CRC	Expt	Conf 62Chalk R. 1 343	Sep 62	Egelstaff+ SCAT LAW, FREQUENCY SPEC.	
	-2	-1			Rept AERE-R-4019	Apr 62	- . 293 DEGK.SCT LAW. GRPH.	
	4.0-2	1.0-1			Rept AERE-R-4041	Apr 62	- . 293+423 DEGK. RVW SCT LAW	
Thermal Scat	5.0-3		CRC	Revw	Conf 62Chalk R. 1 189	Sep 62	Brockhouse+,E DIST+SCAT FN,2TEMP	
					Jour JPJ 17 370	62	.SEE ALSO	
Thermal Scat	1.5-1	4.0-1	GEN	Expt	Conf 62Chalk R. 1 359	Sep 62	Kottwitz+,SCAT LAW 22DEGC,4-72DEG	
Thermal Scat	1.0-3	1.0+0	KAP	Theo	Conf 62Chalk R. 1 389	Sep 62	Goldman+ DIFF SIG IN ANG+E CFD TH.	
	None				Rept TID-16691	62	- + INELASTIC SCATTERING CALC	
Thermal Scat	1.0-1	2.5-1	HAN	Expt	Rept HW- 75147	Oct 62	Kottwitz+H2O,3ES QUASI ELASTIC,22DEG	
					Rept HW-SA-2542	Aug 62	.SUPERSEDED	
Thermal Scat	Cold		ANL	Theo	Rept TID-17871	Nov 62	Singwi. QUASI-ELASTIC SCAT CURVE.	
					Conf 62Chalk R. 1 215	Sep 62	- + FREQ SPECT AT 300DEG K.	
	3.0-3	4.0-2			Jour PR 119 863	Aug 60	- + 2 MDLS. CURVS. CFD EXPT.	
Thermal Scat	1.5-1	4.0-1	HAN	Expt	Rept HW- 75526	Nov 62	Kottwitz+H2O,T=22DEC EGELSTAFF SCAT	
					Rept HW-SA-2541	Aug 62	.SUPERSEDED	
Thermal Scat	5.5-2		MHG	ExTh	Abst BAP 8 41	Jan 63	King+. CF DIFFERENT MODELS	
Thermal Scat	-1		CCP	Theo	Jour ZET 44 573	Feb 63	Ivanov.TH LARGE E-TRNSFR,TBL 2TEMPS	
					Jour JET 17 390	Aug 63	TRANSLATN.*	
Thermal Scat	3.6-2	2.6-1	ANL	Eval	Rept RPC-9	Mar 63	Greenspan+ REVISES RPCC NEWSLETTER 3	
					Rept RPC-3	Mar 62	- +. AT 293,423 DEG K	
Thermal Scat	Maxwl		ISL	Theo	Rept IA- 875	Oct 63	Pelah+.NDG,ANOMALIE OF LIQUID H2O	
					Rept IA- 1082 65	65	.CONTINUATION,NDG	
Thermal Scat	None		MTR	Theo	Prog IDO-16977 34	Dec 64	Mcmurry.NELKIN FIT TO HAYWOOD DATA	
Thermal Scat	-2		CCP	Comp	Rept INDSWG-64 8	64	Mostovoj.P(BETA),SMALL GRAPH ONLY	
Thermal Scat	5.0-3		KTH	Expt	Jour PHY 30 1561	64	Larsson+. T=-3 TO 92DEG C.TH DISCUS	
	Cold				Rept EANDC(OR)59L	Dec 66	Dahlborg+.LIQUID-VAPOR TRANSITION.	
		+0		Revw	Conf 64Bombay 2 3	Dec 64	Larsson. LIQUID DYNAMICS AND N SCAT	
	5.0-3			Expt	Conf 62Chalk R. 1 317	Sep 62	- + SUPERSEDED.	
Thermal Scat	5.0-3	5.0-1	AE	Expt	Rept AE- 133	Jan 64	Skoeld+.298K.INEL SPEC 2 AS. GRAPHS	
	0.0+0	1.0+0			Jour NIM 56 305	Nov 67	Skold+ INEL SCAT VS PRESSURE.GRAPHS	
	5.0-3				Jour NIM 27 61	Apr 64	Skoeld+ INELASTIC SCT.ROOM TEMP.	
Thermal Scat	5.0-3	5.0-1	CCP	Expt	Conf 64Geneva § 367	May 64	Mostovoy+. TEMP.=23,90 DEGR.	
Thermal Scat	1.0-3	4.0+0	GA	Rept	GA- 5373	Jun 64	Beyster+ ANGDIST. GRPH CFD TH.	
Thermal Scat	None		HAN	Expt	Prog WASH-1048 47	Jun 64	Kottwitz.H2O,TEMP=95CELS NDG TBC	
	-3	+0			Prog WASH-1053 36	Oct 64	- +H2O,IN PROG TO IMPROVE DATA	
Thermal Scat	2.0-3	1.0-1	BUC	Expt	Jour RRP 9 737	Aug 64	Teutsch+ N-SPEC AT 88DEG,25CENTIGRAD	
	4.9-3				Rept IFA-FN-24	64	- +,TOF,SCT N SPECS,GRAPHS,THS	
Thermal Scat	1.0-3	1.0+1	GA	Theo	Jour NSE 19 412	Aug 64	Koppel+ ANISOTROPIC SCT KERNEL. CFD.	
	2.0-3	1.0+0			Rept GA- 4850	Dec 63	- . SCT KERNEL CFD XPT, MDL.	
					Abst ANS 6 293	Nov 63	- . ANISOTROPIC MDL. CURV. CFD.	
Thermal Scat	-		CTH	Expt	Jour AF 27 215	Sep 64	Grosshoeg.SLOW-DWN TIME TO .5,.3 EV	
Thermal Scat	Pile		IFJ	Revw	Rept INP-368	Nov 64	Janik. REVIEW MOLECULAR DYNAMICS	
	3.0-3	5.0-1			Rept INP-255	Apr 63	- + LIQUID,N-SPEC+FREQUENCY-DIST	
Thermal Scat	3.0-4	8.0-2	KFK	Theo	Jour ZN/A 20 380	Mar 65	Zech.IMPROVES VOLKIN TH. CF EXP,K-N	
Thermal Scat	1.0-3	1.0+0	GA	Theo	Conf 65Karlsrhe 1 385	May 65	Young.SCATT KERNEL, TH CFD XPT.	
Thermal Scat	6.0-3	2.0+0	GA	Expt	Conf 65Karlsrhe 1 407	May 65	Beyster+ TOF. ANGDIST. GRPHS. CFD TH	
					Rept GA- 6295	Mar 65	.IDENTICAL TO 65KRLSRH, P407.	
Thermal Scat	2.2-2	1.0-1	MUN	ExTh	Jour NUK 7 265	Jul 65	Lemmel.4ES.ANGDIST.MU,DIFF C VS T	
Thermal Scat	None		MTR	Theo	Rept BNL-940 149	Sep 65	Griffing. LANGEVIN EQUATION FIT	
Thermal Scat	1.5-1	3.0-1	BNW	Expt	Prog WASH-1064 16	Oct 65	Harling.H2O,24 DEGC,BETA TO 12 NDG.	
Thermal Scat	7.8-4		CCP	Theo	Jour AE 19 428	Nov 65	Turchin.SIG(E,E*) FOR ICE AND WATER	
					Jour JNE 20 1019	Dec 66	TRANSLATN.*	
					Jour SJA 19 1387	Nov 65	TRANSLATN.*	
					Jour EAF 19 5 25	Nov 65	TRANSLATN.*	
Thermal Scat	1.0-3	9.0-1	JAE	Theo	Rept JAERI-1095	Dec 65	Egelst-Schof+NELKIN TH,CFD EXPT	
Thermal Scat	None		KAP	Theo	Rept KAPL-P-3179	66	Kirouac.SCAT MODELS CFD WITH EXPT	
					Abst ANS 9 495	Nov 66	.SUPERSEDED	
Thermal Scat	Maxwl		KUR	Theo	Rept IAE-1109	66	Fedulov.CALC N SPEC.NEW MOD CFD EXP	
Thermal Scat	1.5-1	1.8-0	RPI	Expt	Rept KAPL-M-6536	Jan 66	Kirouac+ LINAC TOF 302DEGK 3ANGS	
	8.3-1	1.8+0			Jour NSE 25 300	Jul 66	- + 3 ES. LINAC. GRAPHS.	
	1.5-1	1.8+0			Conf 66Wash. 91	Mar 66	- . SEE ALSO FOR CURVES.	
Thermal Scat	Maxwl		CCP	Expt	Jour AE 20 164	Feb 66	Antonov+.DIFFUSION PARAMS VERSUS T	
					Jour JNE 21 307	Mar 67	TRANSLATN.*	
					Jour SJA 20 205	Feb 66	TRANSLATN.*	
					Jour EAF 20 2 103	Feb 66	TRANSLATN.*	
Thermal Scat	1.0-3	1.0+0	GA	ExTh	Conf 66S.Diego 1 27	Feb 66	Koppel. COMPARED WITH THEO OF SCTLAW	

1 Hydrogen WTR

Quantity	Energy (ev) Min	Max	Lab	Type	Documentation Ref Vol Page	Date	Author, Comments	Data
Thermal Scat		2.0+6	AE	Expt	Jour AF 31 255	Mar 66	Moeller.TIME,SPACE DISTR AT 1.46 EV	
					Rept AE - 208	Dec 65	- . SLOWING - DOWN T DIST IN H2O	
					Conf 65Karlsrhe 1 155	May 65	- .SLOWDWN SPEC VS TIME.LQ.ICE	
		+6			Jour AF 27 501	May 65	- +H2O,SL - DWN,THRMLZN TIME PLSD	
		2.0+6			Rept AE - 125	Nov 63	- +.SLOWING - DOWN,THRMLZN TIME	
Thermal Scat	-2		BUC	ExTh	Jour SCF 18 463	Apr 66	Ripeanu.SOME XPTS,DISCUSN OF SCTLAW	
Thermal Scat	2.0+0		GA	ExTh	Rept GA - 7091	Apr 66	Beyster.NDG DATA AVAIL ON ENDF TAPE	
Thermal Scat	4.4-6	6.0-6	ISL	Theo	Jour PL 21 248	May 66	Pelah+IMRY SOREQ QUASIELASTIC SCAT	
Thermal Scat	0.0+0	1.0+0	AE	Theo	Rept AE - 228	Jun 66	Purohit.INT PRMS OF GEN FREQCY SPEC	
					Rept AE - 226	Apr 66	- .TIME - DEP SPEC.SVRL DET,MDLS	
					Conf 65Karlsrhe 1 273	May 65	- .CD,SM,GD RATES.GAS,BOUND P	
					Conf 65Karlsrhe 1 289	May 65	- +.M2 PARM DED FR EXPS CFD TH	
					Rept AE - 154	Sep 64	- .INTGR PRMS.MDLS CFD INT EXP	
Thermal Scat		1.0-1	MTR	Theo	Jour NSE 25 248	Jul 66	Mcmurry. ROOM TEMP. SCAT LAW	
Thermal Scat	Maxwl		MTR	Theo	Rept IN - 1019	Aug 66	Mcmurry.MCMURRY - RUSSELL TH CFD EXPT	
Thermal Scat	Maxwl		CCP	Theo	Jour ZET 51 1120	Nov 66	Ivanov. FINE STRUCTURE OF QASIELAST	
					Jour JET 24 749	Apr 67	TRANSLATN.*	
Thermal Scat	Maxwl		JAE	Theo	Prog EANDC(J)7L21	Jan 67	Gotoh.TH OF SCAT LAW CFD XPT	
Thermal Scat	-		RR	Eval	Jour JNE 21 56	Jan 67	Harper.EGLSTF NELKN MODELS CFD EXPT	
Thermal Scat	-3	-1	CRC	Expt	Rept AERE - R - 5408	Feb 67	Page+ PRELIMINARY TABLES.	+
					Prog EANDC(CAN) - 38	Dec 68	.SUPERSEDED. (PAGE 2).	
					Prog EANDC(CAN) - 34	Jan 68	.SUPERSEDED. (PAGE 5).	
					Prog EANDC(CAN) - 28	Mar 66	.SUPERSEDED. (PAGE 3).	
					Prog EANDC(CAN) - 21	Jul 64	.SUPERSEDED. (PAGE 1).	
					Prog EANDC(CAN) - 17	Mar 63	.SUPERSEDED. (PAGE 1).	
					Prog EANDC(CAN) - 16	Jan 63	.SUPERSEDED. (PAGE 3).	
Thermal Scat	6.0-3	1.8-1	GA	Revw	Rept GA - 7952	Apr 67	Beyster+ STATUS OF TH+EXPT,CURVES	
	6.5-2	8.5-1			Conf 66Wash. 91	Mar 66	- + CALC CURVE CFD EXPT.	
	2.0-2	1.0+0			Conf 66S.Diego 1 151	Feb 66	- + COMPARED WITH SCATT LAW	
Thermal Scat	1.5-1	6.3-1	RPI	Expt	Prog WASH - 1074 103	Apr 67	Bischoff+ 5ES DIFF SIG CURVES 2ES	
Thermal Scat	5.0-3	1.0+2	GA	ExTh	Jour NSE 28 259	May 67	Young+ POISONED H2O. HAYWARD MOD.	
Thermal Scat	None		BNW	Comp	Rept BNWL - 436	Jun 67	Harling. 268,299DEGK S(A,B)+DIFF SIG	
Thermal Scat	-3	+0	BAT	Expt	Conf 67Ann Arbr 1 271	Jul 67	Gibbs+PPR51.TBLS SIG(E,E')	
Thermal Scat	2.0-3	7.0-1	BET	Expt	Conf 67Ann Arbr 2 209	Jul 67	Volpe.PPR93.TEST=N - SPEC/SCAT - MODELS	
Thermal Scat		5.0-3	BIR	Expt	Conf 67Ann Arbr 1 477	Jul 67	Ross+PPR1.XPTL+TH SIG - CVS CFD OTHER	
Thermal Scat	Maxwl		BNL	Theo	Conf 67Ann Arbr 1 571	Jul 67	Dorning.PPR50.SCAT KERN+DECAY CONST	
Thermal Scat	None		CRC	Theo	Conf 67Ann Arbr 1 261	Jul 67	Jarvis.PPR23. CVS,GENERALZD FR - DIST	
Thermal Scat	None		GA	Theo	Prog GA - 8085	Jul 67	Beyster+ S(A,B) CALC AT RM TEMP NDG	
Thermal Scat	-2	+0	GA	Theo	Jour NSE 30 199	Nov 67	Slaggie. MULTISCAT CORRECTION.	
	5.2-3	3.9-2			Rept GA - 8052	Jul 67	.SUPERSEDED.	
					Conf 67Ann Arbr 1 311	Jul 67	Slaggie.PPR53.GRPHS,MULT - SCAT - CORRC	
Thermal Scat	Maxwl		GIT	Theo	Conf 67Ann Arbr 1 555	Jul 67	Kallfelz+PPR69.APPLICTN SCAT - KERNLS	
Thermal Scat	-3	+1	HAR	Theo	Conf 67Ann Arbr 1 361	Jul 67	Haywood+PPR19.550DEG - K,CFD EXPT	
	0.0+0	1.0+0			Jour JNE 21 249	Mar 67	- .PHONON SPEC.FROM EXP DATA.	
	3.6-2	2.6-1		Eval	Rept AERE - R - 4484	Jan 64	- .AT 22,150 DEG C	
Thermal Scat	Maxwl		IEA	Expt	Conf 67Ann Arbr 2 395	Jul 67	Paiano+PPR28.DIFFUS - PARS,PULSD - NEUT	
					Rept IEA - 147	Aug 67	SEE ALSO *	
Thermal Scat	Maxwl		IST	Expt	Conf 67Ann Arbr 2 131	Jul 67	Goddard+PPR4.XPTL TEST OF SCAT - MODL	
Thermal Scat	1.4-1		KFK	Expt	Conf 67Ann Arbr 2 411	Jul 67	Reichardt.PPR15.21DEG K,THERMALIZTN	
	Maxwl			ExTh	Rept KFK - 305	May 65	Kallfelz+H2O,ICE N - SPEC(TIME,ANG)	
Thermal Scat	1.5-1	6.3-1	RPI	Expt	Conf 67Ann Arbr 1 389	Jul 67	Kirouac+PPR64.2DIFF - SIG - GRPH,CFD TH	
					Rept KAPL - P - 3338	67	.SUPERSEDED.	
Thermal Scat	-1	+0	UNC	Theo	Conf 67Ann Arbr 1 537	Jul 67	Bollacasa+ PPR74. UPSCAT REACTOR TH.	
Thermal Scat	1.0-1	3.8-1	BNW	Expt	Rept BNWL - 345	Aug 67	Smith. CRYSPEC. 95 DEG C.CURVS+TBLS.	
Thermal Scat	2.0-4	1.0-1	THS	Expt	Rept NUK 10 129	Sep 67	Pucher+ NELKIN MOD WITH CORRECTIONS	
				Diss	PUCHER	Jul 67	- + (THESIS)	
Thermal Scat	Maxwl		DUB	Expt	Jour ZET 54 29	Jan 68	Samosvat+ DOUBLE DIFF SIG GRAPHS	
					Jour JET 27 15	Jul 68	TRANSLATN.*	
Thermal Scat	6.0-3	1.0+1	GA	Expt	Jour NSE 31 254	Feb 68	Beyster. CFD SEVRL MDLS. CURVS+TBLS.	+
	6.0-3	1.0+1			Data EXFOR11029.002	Jun 76	. 1044 PTS. SIGMA.	
Thermal Scat	None		ORL	Expt	Abst BAP 13 469	Mar 68	Moon+. POLARIZATION,INCOHER SCAT	
Thermal Scat	Cold		KRK	Revw	Rept INP - 600/PS	Apr 68	Janik Ns Scatt Water + ICE, H - BONDS	
Thermal Scat	5.0-3		KRK	Expt	Rept INP - 601/PS	Apr 68	Bajorek+,ICE,H2O GROUP DYNAMICS,IBR	
Thermal Scat	Cold		MIT	Expt	Jour JCP 48 3367	Apr 68	Yip+ HEXAGONAL ICE 150DEGK TOF SPEC	
Thermal Scat	5.2-3	5.0-1	BIR	Expt	Conf 68Copenhgn 2 299	May 68	Beg+PPR117.DOWN - SCAT - EXPT,CRV GVN	
Thermal Scat	Maxwl		CTH	Expt	Rept NUK 11 159	Jun 68	Elkert. N DIFFUSION PARAMS	
Thermal Scat	Maxwl		KIG	Theo	Jour AKE 13 177	Jun 68	Lahann+ THR NEUT SPECT CALC	
Thermal Scat	5.6-2	1.0-1	HAR	Expt	Rept AERE - R - 5832	Jul 68	Page.H2O - D2O MIXT,2ES,300DEGK,S(AB)	

1 Hydrogen WTR

Quantity	Energy (ev) Min	Max	Lab	Type	Documentation Ref Vol Page	Date	Author, Comments	Data
Thermal Scat	Maxwl		AE	Expt Jour	NSE 33 218	Aug 68	Larsson+.DECAY PURE+CD,B POIS H2O	
	0.0+0	1.0+0		ExTh Rept	AE- 223	Mar 66	- +.DEC CNST.PURE,CD - POIS.CFTH	
	Cold			Expt Rept	AE- 47	Dec 60	- +.E+INEL N.SVRL AS.20-90DEGC	
Thermal Scat	5.0-2		MTR	Expt Jour	NSE 33 187	Aug 68	Brugger. S(A,B)+ANGDIST INEL SCAT.	
				Rept	IN- 1141	May 68	.SUPERSEDED	
Thermal Scat	Maxwl		ISP	Theo Jour	NUK 11 251	Sep 68	Ardente+ NELKIN MDL WITH CORRC	
	Cold			Jour	PR 148 124	Aug 66	- + CF TH MODEL C EXP SCAT LAW	
Thermal Scat	1.8-2	7.0-2	KFK	Expt Jour	NSE 20 236	Oct 64	Glaeser+ TEMP 230-270DEG.SCAT LAW	
	Maxwl			Revw Jour	NUK 11 282	Oct 68	- . SCAT CALC CFD EXPT	
				Expt Rept	KFK- 602	Jul 67	- .EXPT CFD TH OF THR SCAT	
	-3	+1		Revw Conf	67Ann Arbr 1 235	Jul 67	- .PPR104.SCAT-LAW IN MODERATR	
	1.8-2	7.0-2			Rept KFK- 264	Dec 64	- + SAME AS NSE 20 236	
Thermal Scat	Maxwl		JAE	Theo Jour	NST 5 635	Dec 68	Nakahara.ICE,COMPARED WITH EXPT	
Thermal Scat	-3		TRM	Expt Conf	68Bombay 3 217	Dec 68	Thaper+ DYNAMICS OF CRYSTAL-WATER	
				Conf	68Madras 265	Feb 68	. SIMILAR 68BOMBAY 3 217.ALSO P.529.	
Thermal Scat	Maxwl		CAI	Theo Rept	UARAEE- 80	69	Fouad+ SCATTERNG KERNELS,GRAPHS+TBL	
Thermal Scat	-3	-1	UMX	Revw Diss	MEXICO	69	Lonngi. REVIEW,MANY REFERENCES	
Thermal Scat	2.0-2	3.5+2	AUA	Expt Rept	AAEC/TM- 497	Apr 69	Dalton.LATTICE,N-SPEC OKS DATA-SETS	
Thermal Scat	Maxwl		JUL	Theo Rept	JUEL- 587-FN	Apr 69	Reichelt+ SCAT SIG CALC, CFD EXPT	
Thermal Scat	Maxwl		GA	Revw Rept	NP- 17997	May 69	Borgonovi+ REVIEW OF SCAT LAW MEAST	
Thermal Scat	8.2-4	1.4-1	IEA	Expt Prog	INDC(BZL)- 2 22	May 69	Herdade+ SCAT-SIG(E)/H-ATOM	+
	8.2-4	1.3-1		Rept	IEA- 310	Sep 73	- + SCT-SIG/H-ATOM FROM TOT-SIG	
	8.2-4	1.3-1		Data	EXFOR30229.	Jan 73	SIG SCAT PER H-ATOM AT 147 ENERGIES	
Thermal Scat	1.5-1	6.2-1	BAT	Expt Jour	JCP 50 5279	Jun 69	Harling.268+299DEGK,S(A,B)+DIFF SIG	
				Conf	68Copenhgn 1 507	May 68	.SUPERSEDED	
				Rept	BNWL- 400 55	Apr 67	.SUPERSEDED	
Thermal Scat	Maxwl		CSR	Expt Jour	CZJB 19 911	Jul 69	Bayer+PULSD-N-TECHN,DIFFUS-PARS GVN	
Thermal Scat	Maxwl		KFI	Expt Jour	NUK 12 237	Aug 69	Kosaly+ SCAT SIG + THR SPEC CALC	
Thermal Scat	Maxwl		JAE	Theo Rept	JAERI- 1181 17	Sep 69	Otake+.CALC OF SCAT SIG	
Thermal Scat	Maxwl		JAE	Theo Rept	JAERI- 1181 23	Sep 69	Kadotani.CALC FOR 100DEGC VAPOUR	
Thermal Scat	Maxwl		THS	Revw Jour	AKE 14 97	Oct 69	Emendoerfer. VARIOUS SCAT MODELS	
Thermal Scat	1.0-3	9.6-1	BUC	Theo Rept	IFA- DNBR- 2	70	Stefan+ SCAT CODE,KOPPEL-YOUNG TH	
Thermal Scat	-3	-2	HLT	Expt Prog	INDC(FIN)- 2G	70	Palmgren+ TOTAL SIGMA EXPT,NO DATA	
Thermal Scat	-3	-1	BUC	Revw Jour	SCF 22 365	Apr 70	Purica.THESIS,TBLS,NEUT THERMALIZTN	
Thermal Scat	Maxwl		CCP	Expt Jour	AE 28 356	Apr 70	Vasil'Ev+DIFFUSN-COEF IN MOVING H2O	
				Jour	EAF 28 4 105	70	. FRENCH OF AE 28 356	
Thermal Scat	Maxwl	Fiss	WIN	Eval Conf	70Helsinki 1 721	Jun 70	Story.110.EVALUATN PROBLEMS,TBL CRV	
Thermal Scat	5.0-3	1.7-1	CCP	Expt Jour	AE 29 91	Aug 70	Goshchitskij+ SCAT LENGTH(E) GRAPH	
				Jour	SJA 29 786	Aug 70	TRANSLATN.*	
Thermal Scat	Maxwl		KTO	Expt Prog	EANDC(J)19L45	Aug 70	Fujita+.N-PSPECTR C GD,CD,B POISONS	
Thermal Scat	5.2-3		KTH	Expt Jour	ATP 16 324	Oct 70	Burgmann.ICE,INEL SCAT SPEC,2ANG,4T	
Thermal Scat	None		BNL	Theo Jour	NSE 45 126	Aug 71	Takahashi+. CURVES,CALCULATN CFD TH	
Thermal Scat	4.0-2	6.3-1	RPI	Expt Jour	NSE 46 223	Nov 71	Esch+.LINAC. TEMPERATURE DEPENDENCE	
				Rept	KAPL- 3908	Sep 71	.DATA	
				Abst	DA/B 32 1137	Aug 71	Esch+ S(A,B),27,170,270 DEG C.	
				Rept	RPI- 328- 210	69	- +,LINAC,27 170 270DEGC	
Thermal Scat	Maxwl		THS	Theo Jour	AKE 18 219	Nov 71	Royl. CADILHAC SCAT KERNEL	
Thermal Scat	-2		CCP	Expt Conf	72Kiev 2 24	Jan 72	Gordeev+ ABST,NDG.AT 3TEMPS,5ANGLES	
Thermal Scat	Cold		AMU	Expt Conf	72Budapest 4	Aug 72	Sefidvash. SATUR.+SUPERHT.VAPOR,GRPH	
Thermal Scat	Maxwl		JAE	Theo Jour	NST 9 743	Dec 72	Nakahara.CALC SCATT SIG FOR 150DEGC	
Thermal Scat	Cold		MUN	Expt Jour	ZN/A 29 1284	Jun 74	Nistler. COH SCAT AMP. TOT REFLECT.	+
	1.5-4	4.2-3		Data	EXFOR20601.004	Jun 76	1PNT.COH.SC.AMP.	
Thermal Scat	+0		WIN	Eval Prog	NEANDC(UK)160	Jul 74	Butland. NEW DATA AT 7 TEMPS	
Thermal Scat	Cold		HLT	Expt Jour	AKE 25 285	75	Sefidvash.SCAT FROM VAPOR MOLECULES	
Thermal Scat	2.5-3	2.6-2	FEI	Expt Conf	75Kiev 2 71	May 75	Novikov+ DOUBLDIFSIG(T=300-600K).FIG	
Thermal Scat	-3	1.9+0	THS	Theo Rept	IKE- 6 89 9	Jun 75	Keinert. DATA LIBRARY	
Scattering	Maxwl		ETH	Expt Jour	HPA 20 105	Apr 47	Rossel. SIG H2O 77 TO 292 DEGK	
Scattering	1.0-3	9.6-1	BUC	Theo Rept	IFA- DNBR- 2	70	Stefan+ SCAT CODE,KOPPEL-YOUNG TH	
Scattering	-3	1.0+1	IKE	Theo Rept	IKE- 6- 61/1	Jan 73	Keinert.DATA LIBRARY	
Nonelastic	1.0-3	1.5+7	KFK	Eval Data	KEDAK- 3	Oct 75	H BOUND IN H2O. 100 DATA SETS	+
Absorption	Maxwl		MHG	Expt Jour	PR 50 570	Sep 36	Zahn+ RATIO ABS/SCATT.PRELIMINARY.	
Absorption	8.0+5	1.0+7	FAR	Theo Conf	58Geneva 13 31	Sep 58	Bourgeois+ PPR1190,CURVE,REMOVAL SIG	
Absorption	4.0+6	1.5+7	FEI	Expt Book	NEJTRONFIZ 263	61	Broder+ REMOVAL CS, GRAPH CFD	
				Book	SPN 194	61	.ENGL TRANSL OF NEJTRONFIZ 263	
Absorption	6.0-4	5.0-1	UK	Eval Rept	AEEW- R- 351	Feb 64	Barrington+(WIN).UKNDL FILE.	
Absorption	-2		AI	Expt Conf	65Karlsrhe 1 323	May 65	Dejuren.PLSD N XPT, SIG.V GVN	
Absorption	Maxwl		VIP	Expt Abst	DA/B 27 1248	Oct 66	Mcclure.AVERAGE SIGS AT 1,-19DEG.C.	
Absorption	Thrsh	+7	BUC	Expt Rept	IFA- FR- 77	69	Grancea+ REMOVAL CS GVN,THRESH-DETEC	

1 Hydrogen WTR

Quantity	Energy (ev) Min	Max	Lab	Type	Documentation Ref Vol Page	Author, Comments Date	Data
Absorption	Maxwl		IFB Theo	Prog	YFI – 7 45	Apr 69 Naumov+ CODES FOR EFFECTIV – SIG,TBL	
				Rept	INDC(CCP) – 7U48	Feb 70 TRANSLATN.*	
Absorption	1.0 – 3	1.5+7	KFK Eval	Data	KEDAK – 3	Oct 75 H BOUND IN H2O. 100 DATA SETS	+
(n,γ)	Maxwl		COL Expt	Jour	PR 50 738	Oct 36 Fink. RATE OF ABSORPTION ONLY	
(n,γ)	Maxwl		CSR Expt	Jour	CZJB 19 911	Jul 69 Bayer+PULSED – N – TECHN,AVG NACR – SIG	
(n,γ)	1.0 – 3	1.5+7	KFK Eval	Data	KEDAK – 3	Oct 75 H BOUND IN H2O. 100 DATA SETS	+
Spect (n,γ)	2.0+6	2.0+7	IRT Expt	Abst	BAP 20 141	Feb 75 Harris+TOF,EN.SPC.,75WASH,NDG.	
Spect (n,γ)	1.4+7		NED Expt	Jour	RCA 24 4 227	77 Mijnheer. AVERAGE – EN OF GAM – RAYS	
Nonelastic γ	1.4+7		ALD Expt	Jour	PPS 75 855	Jun 60 Deuchars+ SCINT SP WITH TOF DISCRIM	
Nonelastic γ	1.0+6	2.0+7	ORL Expt	Rept	ORNL – TM – 5018	Aug 75 Morgan.SECONDRY G SPEC.H2O GRPH.TBL	
n Emission	1.0+6	2.0+7	ORL Expt	Rept	ORNL – TM – 5018	Aug 75 Morgan.SECONDRY N SPEC.H2O GRPH.TBL	

1 Hydrogen CMP

Quantity	Energy (ev) Min	Max	Lab	Type	Documentation Ref Vol Page	Author, Comments Date	Data
Total	6.0 – 3	2.0 – 1	KRK Expt	Jour	APP 22 517	Dec 62 Tubbs+ GAS CFD KRIEGER – NELKIN. CURV	
	5.0 – 3	2.0 – 1		Conf	62Chalk R. 1 405	Sep 62 Janik+,TOT SIG PER P CFD K – N TH	
Total	1.0 – 1	7.0 – 1	KIL Expt	Jour	AKE 12 385	Dec 67 Schmidt.TIHX,GRPH,VS OF H – COWC.CF TH	
	1.0 – 1	7.3 – 1		Conf	67Juelich 229	Apr 67 – .TIHX,(X = .58 – 1.92) SIG(PROTN)	
Total	1.0 – 1	7.0 – 1	KIL Expt	Jour	AKE 17 113	Mar 71 Brand+VHX,(X = 0.6/0.39).HYDROGEN SIG	
Total	2.0 – 3	1.6+0	TOR Expt	Jour	NSE 57 12	May 75 Robitaille+ HB – 40 TERPHENYL CFD C6H6	
Diff Elastic	4.2 – 3		JUL Expt	Rept	JUEL – 1158	Feb 75 Bauer. H+D SOLVED IN NB	
Thermal Scat	2.0 – 3	1.0 – 1	KRK ExTh	Jour	APP 18 255	May 59 Wanic.SIG CFD KRIEGER – NELKEN TH	
Thermal Scat	1.0 – 2	2.5+0	MTR Theo	Conf	62BNL 1 172	Apr 62 Mcmurry+ HYDROXYL MOLECULE TH CURVS	
Thermal Scat	5.0 – 3		BNL Expt	Abst	BAP 7 500	Aug 62 Boutin+H – F,(TA3)	
Thermal Scat	5.8 – 3	1.9 – 1	IFJ Expt	Rept	INP – 213	Oct 62 Rzany+ LIQUID H2S,CFD GAS+K – N,GRPHS	
	– 3	– 1		Rept	INP – 160	Jul 62 Tubbs+ GASEOUS H2S,EL CFD K – N,GRAPH	
	3.0 – 2	1.1 – 1		Jour	APP 18 255	59 Wanic.H2S,TRANS,REL AG,CFD K – N,GRPH	
Thermal Scat	– 2		WWA Expt	Jour	NKA 9 511	Jul 64 Aleksandrowicz+ BRIEF.THERM VIBR,NDG	
Thermal Scat	1.0 – 3	5.0 – 3	KRK ExTh	Rept	INP – 360	Oct 64 Janik+H3OCLO4,HINDERED ROTATION	
Thermal Scat	Maxwl		IFJ Revw	Rept	INP – 368	Nov 64 Janik. HF – SOLID,REVIEW AT 64BOMBAY	
	– 2	– 1		Rept	INP – 255	Apr 63 – + HYDRIDES,CFD FERMI – TH,GRAPHS	
Thermal Scat	Maxwl		KRK Revw	Rept	INP – 368	Nov 64 Janik.HF – SOLID,REVIEW AT 64BOMBAY	
Thermal Scat	Pile		KRK Revw	Rept	INP – 368	Nov 64 Janik+H3OCLO4,REV.MOL:DYNAM,GABOMBAY	
Thermal Scat	2.5 – 2	1.0 – 1	MTR Expt	Jour	JCP 42 1568	Mar 65 Brugger+ PHASED CHOP. 3 ES.	
Thermal Scat	– 2		IFU Expt	Prog	INDSWG – 126 21	66 Vertebnyj.ZR – T2, FEW REMARKS, NDG	
Thermal Scat	5.5 – 2		CRC Expt	Prog	EANDC(CAN) – 28	Mar 66 Thorson+ HB – 40,TEMP = 27 DEG C. NDG.	
Thermal Scat	5.0 – 3	1.3 – 1	DUB Expt	Rept	JINR – E3 – 3058	Dec 66 Janik+HNO3,SCAT NEUT VS E(N),GRAPHS	
Thermal Scat	1.0 – 2		MSU Theo	Conf	67Ann Arbr 1 283	Jul 67 Summerfield+HF,PPR65.TH – SIG(E,E')	
Thermal Scat	1.0 – 2	1.0 – 1	KRK Expt	Jour	APP 33 419	Mar 68 Janik+H3O.NO3 SOLID,GRAPHS+TABLE	
Thermal Scat	5.0 – 3		KRK Expt	Rept	INP – 601/PS	Apr 68 Bajorek+ NISO4.7H2O,NISO4.6H2OHBOND	
Thermal Scat	– 3		KRK Revw	Rept	INP – 600/PS	Apr 68 Janik.H3O.NO3,HYDRONIUM VIBRATIONS	
Thermal Scat	Cold		NBS Expt	Jour	JCP 48 3795	Apr 68 Rush+VHX, X = 7VALUES,5TEMPS TOF SPECT	
Thermal Scat	–		DUB Theo	Rept	JINR – E4 – 6171	Dec 71 Stamenkovic.TH,SCAT OF H IN FERROEL	
	None			Rept	JINR – E4 – 6172	Dec 71 – .TH,SCAT OF H IN FERROEL	
Thermal Scat	Cold		ISP Expt	Jour	PL/A 43 279	Mar 73 Gissler+QUASIELAST SCT IN NB,GRAPH	

1 Hydrogen DXX

Quantity	Energy (ev) Min	Max	Lab	Type	Documentation Ref Vol Page	Author, Comments Date	Data
Total	5.0 – 2	4.0 – 1	KIL Expt	Jour	AKE 12 385	Dec 67 Schmidt.TIDX,GRPH,CFD TH.	
	6.0 – 2	3.8 – 1		Conf	67Juelich 229	Apr 67 – .TID1.15,CRYST SP,SIG(D)	
Total	5.0 – 2	4.0 – 1	KIL Expt	Jour	AKE 17 113	Mar 71 Brand.VDX(X = 0.61),DEUTERON SIGMA	
Thermal Scat	2.0 – 2	5.0 – 2	TRM Expt	Conf	62Madras 355	Feb 62 Iyengar. ND4CL. N – SPECTRUM REL TEMP	
Thermal Scat	–		CTH Expt	Jour	AF 24 543	Sep 63 Nilsson+C7H16,PLSD NS,18 – 80C,D – COOL	
Thermal Scat	2.5 – 2	1.0 – 1	MTR ExTh	Jour	PR/A 136 988	Nov 64 Griffing.CD4,T = 100K, SCAT LAW CF TH	
Thermal Scat	None		MTR Theo	Prog	IDO – 17191 28	Jun 66 Mcmurry.CD4 INTERFERENCE TERM CALC	
Thermal Scat	5.0 – 2	7.0 – 2	MTR Expt	Jour	PR 148 163	Aug 66 West+CD4,SCAT LAW CF TH MOLCL VIBS	
Thermal Scat	5.0 – 3		TRM ExTh	Jour	PR 161 133	Sep 67 Rao+CD4,LIQUID 95DEGK,TOF , CF TH	
	4.9 – 3			Rept	BARC – 286	67 RAO+CD4(LIQUID)CFD CH4,MDL DRVD GRPH	
Thermal Scat	Cold		MHG ExTh	Jour	JCP 48 912	Jan 68 Lynch+(CD2)N SIN MEAS	
Thermal Scat	2.9 – 3		KTH Revw	Conf	68Copenhgn 1 397	May 68 Larsson.CD3OH,PPR200,290K,20,90DEG	
						May 68 – .CH3OD,PPR200,290K,20,90DEG	
Thermal Scat	None		MHG Theo	Conf	68Copenhgn 2 205	May 68 Carpenter.CD4,PPR88,CFD OTHER+EXPT	
Thermal Scat	Pile	2.5 – 2	ISP Expt	Rept	EUR – 4455 D	Apr 70 Seiffert.DEUTERIUM H%RI	
Thermal Scat	1.0 – 3	1.0 – 1	ISP Expt	Jour	ZN/A 25 967	Jun 70 Seiffert+TOT SCAT,LIQUID HD	

1 Hydrogen DXX

Quantity	Energy (ev) Min	Max	Lab	Type	Documentation Ref Vol Page	Author, Comments Date	Data
Thermal Scat	Maxwl		TOH Expt	Prog	EANDC(J)19 L62	Aug 70 Kimura+TAD,TOF,POWDER DIFFR NDG	
Thermal Scat	Cold		JUL Expt	Rept	JUEL – 738 – FF	Feb 71 Press.CD4,COH SCAT ON SOLID CD4	
Thermal Scat	Maxwl		TOK Expt	Jour	JPJ 35 842	Sep 73 Niimura+SOLID DCL,N – DIFFR,MOL.LIBRTN	

1 Hydrogen D2O

Quantity	Energy (ev) Min	Max	Lab	Type	Documentation Ref Vol Page	Author, Comments Date	Data
Evaluation	Pile		HAR Eval	Rept	AERE – R – 3931	Jan 62 EGELSTAFF SCATTERING LAW AT24DEG C	
Evaluation	5.0–4	9.0+0	UK Eval	Rept	AEEW – R – 351	Feb 64 Barrington+(WIN).UKNDL FILE.	
Total	4.9–3	8.0+0	COL Expt	Jour	PR 57 976	Jun 40 Beyer+HDO,INTERFER.EFFECT H2O+D2O	+
	4.9–3	8.0+0		Data	EXFOR11145.002	Jun 76 . 46 PTS. SIGMA.	
Total	Cold		COL Expt	Jour	PR 60 702	Nov 41 Carroll. SIG=5.73+ – 0.14 B.	
Total	Cold		CHI Expt	Jour	PR 70 815	Dec 46 Anderson+ C–FILTERED NS TO 18DEG K.	
Total	3.5+5	6.0+6	MIN Expt	Jour	PR 70 805	Dec 46 Nuckolls+ TRNS. TBL. GRAPH.	+
	3.5+5	6.0+6		Data	EXFOR11142.004	Jun 76 . 15 PTS. SIGMA.	
Total	5.0+0	1.7+3	COL Expt	Jour	PR 73 733	Jan 48 Rainwater+ GRPH. BINDING EFFECT.	
Total	9.5+7		BRK Expt	Jour	PR 77 606	Mar 50 Dejuren+ BI FISSION CH.	+
	9.5+7			Data	EXFOR11174.005	Jun 76 . 1 PT. SIG=0.868+ – 0.005 B.	
Total	1.4+7		LAS Expt	Rept	LA – 1279	Jul 51 Meyer+,TRANS,T–D NEUTS,3.23+ – 0.03B	
Total	3.5–5	4.5–4	BNL Expt	Priv	MEYER	53 Meyer. DATA IN BNL–325,DATACENTERS.	+
	3.5–5	4.5–4		Data	EXFOR11019.002	Jun 76 . 36 PTS. SIGMA.	
Total	1.7–2	2.5–2	FAR Expt	Rept	CEA – 162	Jan 53 Ertaud+.GRPHT FILTRE.TRNSM.4ES	
Total	Maxwl		CCP Expt	Conf	55Geneva 5 13	Aug 55 Geraseva+.VAL GVN,STANDARD–VAL,P662	
Total	4.5–1	1.9+2	MTR Expt	Priv	FLUHARTY	59 Fluharty. DATA IN BNL–325.	+
	5.6+0	2.0+3		Data	EXFOR11015.002	Jun 76 . 96 PTS. SIGMA.	
Total	5.0–4	9.0+0	UK Eval	Rept	AEEW – R – 351	Feb 64 Barrington+(WIN).UKNDL FILE.	
Total	1.4+0		ORL Expt	Jour	NP 61 381	Jan 65 Rayburn+ IN RES. TRNS CS=10.6+ – 0.1 B	+
	1.4+0			Data	EXFOR11026.003	Jun 76 . 1 PT. SIGMA.	
Total	2.0–3	1.0+0	GA Theo	Conf	65Karlsrhe 1 385	May 65 Young.SCATT KERNEL,GRPH TH CFD XPT.	
Total	1.0–3	1.0+0	GA Expt	Conf	66S.Diego 1 151	Feb 66 Beyster+ COMPARED WITH SCATT LAW	
Total	1.0–3	1.0+0	GA Theo	Rept	GA – 7283 22	Jul 66 Haywood.MODEL CURVE CFD OTHERS	
Total	–3	+0	GA Revw	Rept	GA – 7952	Apr 67 Beyster+ COMPARISON OF TH+EXPT CURV	
Total	1.0–2	1.0+1	GRC Expt	Prog	EANDC(OR)87L	Sep 69 Dritsa+	
Total	1.3+2		MUN Expt	Jour	PL/B 36 208	Sep 71 Dilg+ TRANS EXPT COBALT RESON NS	+
	1.3+2			Data	EXFOR20596.004	Jun 76 1PNT.	
Total	5.0–3	1.5–1	GEL Expt	Prog	EANDC(E)150U	May 72 Deruytter+,COMPAR SCATT MODELS	
Total	–3	1.0+1	IKE Theo	Rept	IKE–6–61/1	Jan 73 Keinert.DATA LIBRARY	
Total	5.0–4	1.0+1	CAB Expt	Rept	INIS – MF – 1335	Aug 74 Kropff+ 2ODEGC,TRANS,TOF.TBL+GRAPHS	+
	5.0–4	1.3+1		Data	EXFOR30283.002	Dec 74 80 DATA LINES	
Elastic	5.0–4	9.0+0	UK Eval	Rept	AEEW – R – 351	Feb 64 Barrington+(WIN).UKNDL FILE.	
Elastic	1.1+0	1.5+7	LRL Theo	Jour	NUK 10 259	Nov 67 Perkins.AGE+FAST EFFECT FOR FISS N	
Diff Elastic	5.0–4	9.0+0	UK Eval	Rept	AEEW – R – 351	Feb 64 Barrington+(WIN).UKNDL FILE.	
Diff Elastic	–3	1.0+1	IKE Theo	Rept	IKE–6–61/1	Jan 73 Keinert.DATA LIBRARY	
Thermal Scat	Cold		CHI Expt	Jour	PR 70 815	Dec 46 Anderson+ 18 DEG K. CS GIVEN.	
Thermal Scat	5.0+5	1.5+6	UPP Theo	Jour	AF 6 243	Apr 53 Holte.CALC STAT SPCE–E DISTR SLWDWN	
Thermal Scat	–1		SAC Expt	Conf	55Geneva 5 77	Aug 55 Jacrot+SPECTRUM OF SCATTRD NS,P357	
Thermal Scat	Maxwl		AE Expt	Jour	AF 15 145	Apr 59 Sjoestrand.DIFFUSION COOLING COEFF.	
				Eval	AF 15 147	Apr 59 – .CORR TO DIFFSN COOL COEF	
Thermal Scat	5.0–4	1.0–1	GA Expt	Conf	60Wien 511	Oct 60 Whittemore. CURVE, REL LOW TEMPS.	
Thermal Scat	3.5–2	1.5–1	HAR Comp	Rept	AERE – R – 3931	Jan 62 EGELSTAFF TABLES FOR 24 DEGC	
Thermal Scat	1.0–4	4.0–3	MUN Expt	Prog	EANDC(E)23L	Feb 62 Gissler+,AT 4 + 77 DEG K	
Thermal Scat	3.4–2	2.5–1	CRC Expt	Conf	62BNL 1 26	Apr 62 Haywood+ 20 150DEGC S(A,B)+P(BETA)	
	3.5–2	1.4–1		Conf	60Wien 309	Jul 62 Egelstaff+ 293DEGK	
Thermal Scat	4.0–2	1.0–1	CRC Expt	Rept	AERE – R – 4041	Apr 62 Egelstaff. 293+423 DEG K.RVW SCT LAW	
	–2	–1		Rept	AERE – R – 4019	Apr 62 – . 293 DEG K.SCT LAW. GRPH.	
Thermal Scat	5.0–3		AE Expt	Jour	JNE 16 81	Feb 62 Larsson+ N–SPECTRUM AT 2 ANGLES.	
				Conf	62Chalk R. 1 317	Sep 62 – +,N SPECT,–9TO300DEGC,2 ANGS	
	Cold			Rept	AE – 47	Dec 60 – +.E+INEL N.SVRL AS.20–90DEGC	
Thermal Scat	–		HAR ExTh	Conf	62Chalk R. 1 65	Sep 62 Egelstaff.S VS ALFA CURVE CFD TH	
Thermal Scat	Maxwl		EE Theo	Jour	PPS 81 276	Feb 63 Butler.NELKIN MODEL WITH COHERENCE	
Thermal Scat	Maxwl		EE Theo	Jour	PPS 81 294	Feb 63 Butler.NELKIN MODEL WITH COHERENCE	
Thermal Scat	3.4–2	1.1–1	ANL Eval	Rept	RPC – 9	Mar 63 Greenspan+ ADDENDA RPCC NEWSLTR 4.	
				Rept	RPC – 4	Apr 62 – +. AT 293,423 DEG K	
Thermal Scat	Cold		BUC Expt	Conf	64Geneva § 673	May 64 Mateescu+ S(A,B),P(B),SPECTRA	
Thermal Scat	Maxwl		HAR Expt	Rept	AERE – R – 4582	May 64 Haywood.295–423DEG K.SPOT INCIDT ES	
Thermal Scat	Maxwl		GA Theo	Prog	GA – 5486	Jul 64 Beyster+CALC SCAT LAW AND TOT SIG	

1 Hydrogen D2O

Quantity	Energy (ev) Min	Max	Lab	Type	Documentation Ref Vol Page	Author, Comments Date	Data
Thermal Scat	2.0 – 3	1.0 – 1	BUC	Expt Jour	RRP 9 737	Aug 64 Teutsch+ N – SPEC AT 2 ANGLES,2 TEMPS	
	4.9 – 3			Rept	IFA – FN – 24	64 – +,TOF,SCT N SPECS,GRAPHS,THS	
Thermal Scat	Cold		JUL	ExTh Jour	ZN/A 19 1422	Dec 64 Gissler.SCAT SIG AT SMALL ANG.	
Thermal Scat		+0	KTH	Revw Conf	64Bombay 2 3	Dec 64 Larsson. LIQUID DYNAMICS AND N SCAT	
Thermal Scat	4.0 – 2		GA	Theo Conf	65Karlsrhe 1 385	May 65 Young. SCATT KERNEL, TH CFD XPT.	
Thermal Scat	6.0 – 3	8.0 – 1	GA	Expt Conf	65Karlsrhe 1 407	May 65 Beyster+ GRAPHS.	
	8.0 – 3	1.0 + 0		Rept	GA – 6295	Mar 65 – +SCAT X – SECT AND ANG.DISTRBT	
Thermal Scat	2.2 – 2	1.0 – 1	MUN	ExTh Jour	NUK 7 281	Jul 65 Kornbichler.ANGDIST.MU,DIFF C VS T	
Thermal Scat	1.0 – 3	9.0 – 1	JAE	Theo Rept	JAERI – 1095	Dec 65 BY NELKIN MDL,KERNEL IS CFD C EXP	
Thermal Scat	6.3 – 3		GA	Expt Conf	66S.Diego 1 151	Feb 66 Beyster+ COMPARED WITH SCATT LAW	
	1.0 – 1	1.0 + 0		ExTh Abst	ANS 8 459	Nov 65 – + AVG COS MEASURED,CFD TH	
	Maxwl			Expt Prog	GA – 5798 19	Oct 65 – +SCAT KERNEL CFD XPT SIG	
Thermal Scat		2.0 + 6	AE	Expt Jour	AF 31 335	Apr 66 Moeller.TIME,SPACE DISTR. THRMALIZN	
				Rept	AE – 216	Mar 66 – . SLOWING – DOWN T DIST. D2O	
	+6			Conf	65Karlsrhe 1 155	May 65 – .TIME+SPACE DEP.PULSD SOURCE	
Thermal Scat	0.0 + 0	1.0 + 0	AE	Theo Rept	AE – 228	Jun 66 Purohit.INT PRMS OF GEN FREQCY SPEC	
				Rept	AE – 226	Apr 66 – .TIME – DEP SPEC.SVRL DET,MDLS	
				Conf	65Karlsrhe 1 273	May 65 – .CD,SM,GD RATES.3 MODELS	
	–			Eval Conf	65Karlsrhe 1 289	May 65 – +.M2 PARM DED FR EXPS CFD TH	
	0.0 + 0	1.0 + 0		Theo Rept	AE – 154	Sep 64 – .HINDRD ROTS.INTGRL PRMS DER	
Thermal Scat	1.0 – 3	1.0 + 0	GA	Theo Prog	GA – 7283 22	Jul 66 Gasket.CALCS HAYWOOD MDL CURVES,CFD	
Thermal Scat	Maxwl		MTR	Theo Rept	IN – 1020	Aug 66 Mcmurry.NELKIN+MCMURRY – RUSSELL PARS	
Thermal Scat	Maxwl		JAE	Theo Prog	EANDC(J)7L21	Jan 67 Gotoh.GENERALIZED SPECT IS GIVN	
Thermal Scat	7.0 – 2		GA	Revw Rept	GA – 7952	Apr 67 Beyster+ COMPARISON OF TH+EXPT CURV	
Thermal Scat	None		BNW	Comp Rept	BNWL – 436	Jun 67 Harling. 299 DEG K,S(A,B)+DIFF SIGS.	
Thermal Scat	None		CRC	Theo Conf	67Ann Arbr 1 261	Jul 67 Jarvis.PPR23.APLICATN OF SCAT – MODEL	
Thermal Scat	– 3	+0	GA	Expt Conf	67Ann Arbr 1 509	Jul 67 Neill+PPR55.INTGRL – XPT OKS MOLEC – TH	
Thermal Scat	– 3	+1	HAR	Theo Conf	67Ann Arbr 1 361	Jul 67 Haywood+PPR19.540DEG K,CFD EXPT	
Thermal Scat	+0	+7	WUR	Expt Conf	67Ann Arbr 2 149	Jul 67 Wydler.PPR9.TEST = DIFUSS/SCAT MODELS	
Thermal Scat	2.0 – 4	1.0 – 1	THS	Theo Jour	NUK 10 129	Sep 67 Pucher+ NELKIN MOD WITH CORRECTIONS	
				Diss	PUCHER	Jul 67 – + (THESIS)	
Thermal Scat	Cold		TIT	Theo Jour	NST 4 625	Dec 67 Kadotani+.COH SCATT C BUTLER – MDL	
Thermal Scat	2.0 – 1		BNW	Expt Conf	68Copenhgn 1 507	May 68 Harling.PPR80.SIG(E'),LIQUID+SOLID	
Thermal Scat	1.0 – 1	2.1 – 1	BNW	Expt Jour	NSE 33 41	Jul 68 Harling. S(A,B)+ANGDIST. 299 DEG K.	
Thermal Scat	5.6 – 2	1.0 – 1	HAR	Expt Rept	AERE – R – 5832	Jul 68 Page.H2O – D2O MIXT,2ES,300DEGK,S(AB)	
	5.5 – 2	1.1 – 1		Rept	AERE – R – 5408	Feb 67 – .S(A,B) AT 540 DEG K.	
Thermal Scat	1.6 – 1	6.5 – 1	GA	Expt Jour	NSE 33 195	Aug 68 Whittemore. 300DEG K,THETA = 30 – 120DEG	
Thermal Scat	Maxwl		KFK	Revw Jour	NUK 11 282	Oct 68 Glaeser. SCAT CALC CFD EXPT	
				Expt Rept	KFK – 602	Jul 67 – .EXPT CFD TH OF THR SCAT	
Thermal Scat	Cold		MUN	Expt Jour	ZP 219 300	Jan 69 Koester+ COH SCAT AMP.CHRISTNSN FTR.	+
	1.0 – 3			Jour	ZAP 14 738	Dec 62 Maier – Leibniz. COH SCAT AMP. REFRAKT	
	Cold			Data	EXFOR20812.003	Dec 78 1PNT.COHERENT SCT AMPLITUDE.	
Thermal Scat	– 3	– 1	CRC	Expt Rept	CRNL – 272	Feb 69 Thorson.DESCRIPT OF DATA TAPE FORMT	
Thermal Scat	Maxwl		GIT	Theo Jour	TNS 6 126	Jul 69 Mcghee+ PULSED – NEUT – XPT,DIFFUS – PARS	
Thermal Scat	Maxwl		JAE	Theo Rept	JAERI – 1181 27	Sep 69 Kadotani+.CALC C COHERENT SCAT	
Thermal Scat	Maxwl		THS	Revw Jour	AKE 14 97	Oct 69 Emendoerfer. VARIOUS SCAT MODELS	
Thermal Scat	– 3	– 2	HLT	Expt Prog	INDC(FIN) – 2G	70 Palmgren+ TOTAL SIGMA EXPT,NO DATA	
Thermal Scat	– 3	– 1	BUC	Revw Jour	SCF 22 365	Apr 70 Purica.THESIS,TBLS,NEUT THERMALIZTN	
Thermal Scat	Maxwl	Fiss	WIN	Eval Conf	70Helsinki 1 721	Jun 70 Story.110.EVALUATN PROBLEMS,TBL CRV	
Thermal Scat	5.0 – 3	1.7 – 1	CCP	Expt Jour	AE 29 91	Aug 70 Goshchitskij+ SCAT LENGTH(E) GRAPH	
				Jour	SJA 29 786	Aug 70 TRANSLATN.*	
Thermal Scat	1.0 – 3	1.0 + 0	BUC	Theo Jour	RRP 16 587	May 71 Rapeanu+ CODE TO CALCULATE 2DIFFSIG	
				Rept	IFA – DNBR – 3	71 . DETAILS DESCRIBED.	
	1.0 – 3	9.6 – 1		Rept	IFA – DNBR – 2	70 Stefan+ SCAT CODE,KOPPEL – YOUNG TH	
Thermal Scat	Pile		KFK	Expt Rept	KFK – 1497	Oct 71 Renker. PHONON DISPERSION,T = 90K	
Thermal Scat	Maxwl		THS	Theo Jour	AKE 18 219	Nov 71 Royl. CADILHAC SCAT KERNEL	
Thermal Scat	Cold		MUN	Expt Jour	ZN/A 29 1284	Jun 74 Nistler. COH SCAT AMP. TOT REFLECT.	+
				Jour	PL/B 36 208	Sep 71 Dilg+COH SCAT AMP. SUPERSEDED.	
	1.5 – 4	4.2 – 3		Data	EXFOR20601.003	Jun 76 1PNT.COH.SC.AMP.	
Thermal Scat	+0		WIN	Eval Prog	NEANDC(UK)160	Jul 74 Butland. NEW DATA AT 7 TEMPS	
Thermal Scat	– 3	1.9 + 0	THS	Theo Rept	IKE – 6 89 15	Jun 75 Keinert. DATA LIBRARY	
Scattering	1.0 – 3	9.6 – 1	BUC	Theo Rept	IFA – DNBR – 2	70 Stefan+ SCAT CODE,KOPPEL – YOUNG TH	
Scattering	– 3	1.0 + 1	IKE	Theo Rept	IKE – 6 – 61/1	Jan 73 Keinert.DATA LIBRARY	
Absorption	5.0 – 4	9.0 + 0	UK	Eval Rept	AEEW – R – 351	Feb 64 Barrington+(WIN).UKNDL FILE.	

1 Hydrogen D2O

Quantity	Energy (ev) Min	Max	Lab	Type	Documentation Ref Vol Page	Author, Comments Date	Data
Absorption	2.5−2		HAR	Expt	Jour JNE 23 625	Dec 69 Silk+ SIG=1.311+−.052MB.PULSD EXPT.	+
					Jour JNE 23 369	Jul 69 − + SIG=1.236+−0.103MB	
					Jour JNE 23 1	Mar 69 − .SIG=1.236+−.103MB PULSED EXPT.	
					Rept AERE−M−2034	May 68 − + PULSED EXPT.	
	2.5−2				Data EXFOR20460.003	Jan 76 1PNT.SIGMA.	
(n,γ)	Maxwl		CRC	Expt	Jour NSE 28 286	May 67 Merritt+ 2200 M/SEC CS. CFD.	
Nonelastic γ	2.5−2	2.4+6	OSA	Expt	Jour SCP 31 195	Mar 37 Kikuchi+.INTERACTION WITH DEUTERON	

1 Hydrogen TXX

Quantity	Energy (ev) Min	Max	Lab	Type	Documentation Ref Vol Page	Author, Comments Date	Data
Thermal Scat	−3	−1	FTI	Theo	Jour ZET 33 625	Sep 57 Ansel'M.DT,SCHWINGER THEORY	
Thermal Scat	−3	−1	FTI	Theo	Jour ZET 33 625	Sep 57 Ansel'M.HT,SCHWINGER THEORY	

3 Lithium CMP

Quantity	Energy (ev) Min	Max	Lab	Type	Documentation Ref Vol Page	Author, Comments Date	Data
Thermal Scat	None		BNL	Expt	Prog WASH−1013 9	Nov 58 Mcreynolds+LIH,1ST LVL BY E G=.085EV	
Thermal Scat	4.0−3	1.6−1	KUR	Expt	Rept IAE−756	64 ZEMLIANOV LI7H+LI7D,DIFF−SIG−CURVS	
					Rept LA−TR−65−3	65 . ENGL OF IAE−756	
Thermal Scat	Cold		KRK	Revw	Rept INP−600/PS	Apr 68 Janik.NS SCATT LI2SO4.H2O	
Thermal Scat	5.0−3		KRK	Expt	Rept INP−601/PS	Apr 68 Bajorek+ LI2SO4.H2O,IBR DUBNA,HBOND	
Thermal Scat	5.0−3		KRK	Expt	Rept INP−601/PS	Apr 68 Bajorek+ LICL.H2O,IBR DUBNA,H BONDS	
Thermal Scat	5.0−3		KRK	Expt	Rept INP−601/PS	Apr 68 Bajorek+ LICLO4.3H2OIBR DUBNA,HBOND	
Thermal Scat	−3		TRM	Expt	Conf 68Bombay 3 217	Dec 68 Thaper+ LICL.H2O,CRYST−WATER DYNAMC	
Thermal Scat	5.0−2		KIL	Expt	Jour AKE 21 275	Jul 73 Jacobs+ NEUT DIFFR EXPT ON LIND2	
Thermal Scat	Cold		GRE	Expt	Jour PL/A 48 493	Jul 74 Chieux+ SMALL ANGLE SCAT,GRAPH	
Scattering	2.6+4	2.8+4	RIC	Expt	Conf 55Geneva 4 92	Aug 55 Bonner.LIF,(P578),CURVE VDG CFD C−W	
Scattering	5.0+5	9.1+6	ORL	Expt	Jour NIM 52 181	Jun 67 Verbinski+ LIH,DIFFSIG.	

4 Beryllium CMP

Quantity	Energy (ev) Min	Max	Lab	Type	Documentation Ref Vol Page	Author, Comments Date	Data
Total	−3	1.0+1	IKE	Theo	Rept IKE−6−61/1	Jan 73 Keinert.DATA LIBRARY, BE−OXID	
Diff Elastic	−3	1.0+1	IKE	Theo	Rept IKE−6−61/1	Jan 73 Keinert.DATA LIBRARY, BE−OXID	
Thermal Scat	−3	1.9+0	THS	Theo	Rept IKE−6 89 39	Jun 75 Keinert. DATA LIBRARY BE−OXIDE	
Scattering	−3	1.0+1	IKE	Theo	Rept IKE−6−61/1	Jan 73 Keinert.DATA LIBRARY, BE−OXID	

4 Beryllium OXI

Quantity	Energy (ev) Min	Max	Lab	Type	Documentation Ref Vol Page	Author, Comments Date	Data
Evaluation	1.0−3	1.0+3	UK	Eval	Rept AEEW−R−351	Feb 64 Barrington+(WIN).UKNDL FILE.	
Evaluation	1.4−1		HAR	Eval	Rept AERE−R−4732	Sep 64 Haywood+.THERMAL SCATT LAW 22 DEG C	
Total	3.0−3	1.0+1	GA	Expt	Abst BAP 5 288	Apr 60 Walton+ TOF. DIFFERS FROM BNL325.	
Total	−3	2.0−2	GA	Expt	Conf 60Wien 511	Oct 60 Whittemore+ CURVE. REL LOW TEMPS.	
Total	3.0+4	6.8+5	DKE	Expt	Prog WASH−1034 10	Dec 61 Borgonovi+ UC. COHERENT SIG CALCTD.	
Total	Cold		TRM	ExTh	Conf 62Madras 384	Feb 62 Begum+.SIGMA AS FUNCT OF TEMP,CURVE	
Total	2.5−3	1.0+1	CCP	Expt	Jour AE 13 250	Sep 62 4TO10PC E RSLN 4TEMPS290−1500K ZHEZ	
Total	1.0−3	1.0+3	UK	Eval	Rept AEEW−R−351	Feb 64 Barrington+(WIN).UKNDL FILE.	
Total	2.0−3	4.0−1	GA	Expt	Conf 66S.Diego 1 151	Feb 66 Beyster+ COMPARED WITH SCATT LAW	
Total	None		GA	Theo	Prog WASH−1127 50	Apr 69 Borgonovi. CALC FROM SCT. CFD. NDG.	
Total	5.0+5	1.7+7	CCP	Expt	Jour AE 27 141	Aug 69 Kukhtevich+ TRANSMISSN+RES SHIELDNG	
					Jour SJA 27 76	Aug 69 .TRANSLATN.SEE ALSO P 852	
Total	Maxwl		KTO	Expt	Prog EANDC(J)26L34	Aug 72 Kanda+.NDG	
Elastic	3.6−3	1.3−1	TRM	Expt	Jour JNE 7 45	Aug 58 Bhandari+ THEORY COMPARED WITH EXPT	
Elastic	1.0−3	1.0+3	UK	Eval	Rept AEEW−R−351	Feb 64 Barrington+(WIN).UKNDL FILE.	
Diff Elastic	1.0−3	1.0+3	UK	Eval	Rept AEEW−R−351	Feb 64 Barrington+(WIN).UKNDL FILE.	
Thermal Scat	3.0−3	5.0−1	ANL	ExTh	Jour PR 71 589	May 47 Fermi+ TOF. TRNS. GRPH. CFD TH.	+
	2.8−2	5.0−1		Expt	Data EXFOR11248.	Jun 76 . 57 PTS. SIGMA OVER 2 E RANGES.	
Thermal Scat	−1		SAC	Expt	Conf 55Geneva 5 77	Aug 55 Jacrot+NDG,SLOW CHOPPER PPR 357	
Thermal Scat	3.6−4	1.3−1	TRM	Expt	Jour JNE 7 45	Aug 58 Bhandari+ 1+2PHONON INEL, SIGTRANSP	
Thermal Scat	Maxwl		AE	Eval	Jour AF 15 147	Apr 59 Sjoestrand.CORR TO DIFFSN COOL COEF	
Thermal Scat	None		ANL	Theo	Jour AF 16 385	Feb 60 Singwi.CALC DIFFSN COOL COEF CF EXP	
Thermal Scat	1.6−2	9.8−2	ANL	Eval	Rept RPC−5	May 62 Greenspan+. AT 293,DEG K	

4 Beryllium OXI

Quantity	Energy (ev) Min	Max	Lab	Type	Documentation Ref Vol Page	Date	Author, Comments	Data
Thermal Scat	1.7−2	1.3−1	CRC	Expt Rept	AERE−NP/GEN−28	Jul 62	Sinclair.CHOPPER TOF	
Thermal Scat	−		HAR	ExTh Conf	62Chalk R. 1 65	Sep 62	Egelstaff.SCAT LAW DATA,FREQENCY FN	
Thermal Scat	1.4−1		HAR	Eval Rept	AERE−R−4732	Sep 64	Haywood+.AT 22 DEG C	
Thermal Scat	1.0−3	9.0−1	JAE	Theo Rept	JAERI−1095	Dec 65	BY PARKS THEO,KERNEL IS CFD C EXP	
Thermal Scat	0.0+0	1.0+0	AE	Theo Rept	AE−228	Jun 66	Purohit.INT PRMS OF GEN FREQCY SPEC	
	−			Eval Conf	65Karlsrhe 1 289	May 65	− +.M2 PARM DED FR EXPS CFD TH	
	0.0+0	1.0+0		Theo Conf	65Karlsrhe 1 273	May 65	− .THRMLZN T/T(GAS) VS TEFF/T	
Thermal Scat	None		GA	Theo Prog	GA−7283 30	Jul 66	Young+ SCT KERNEL. TBP NSE.	
Thermal Scat	Maxwl		KFK	Expt Rept	KFK−602	Jul 67	Glaeser.EXPT CFD TH OF THR SCAT	
Thermal Scat	−		KUR	Expt Conf	67Ann Arbr 2 379	Jul 67	Zhezherun.PPR86.N−PULS DECAY IN BEO	
Thermal Scat	Maxwl		AUA	ExTh Jour	JNE 22 717	Dec 68	Ritchie+EXTRAP−DIST,PULSD ASSEMBLY	
Thermal Scat	−3		AUA	Expt Jour	JNE 22 735	Dec 68	Rainbow+LIMIT OF LAMDA(BUCKLING 2)	
Thermal Scat	2.0−2	3.5+2	AUA	Expt Rept	AAEC/TM−497	Apr 69	Dalton.LATTICE,N−SPEC OKS DATA−SETS	
Thermal Scat	None		GA	Theo Prog	WASH−1127 50	Apr 69	Borgonovi. NDG. SCT LAW CALC.	
Thermal Scat	−		LON	Theo Jour	JNE 23 211	Apr 69	WOOD CAL WAVE PARAMS.FROM FREQ SPEC	
Thermal Scat	Maxwl		JAE	Theo Rept	JAERI−1181 62	Sep 69	Iijima+.CALC OF SCAT SIG	
Thermal Scat	−3	−1	BUC	Revw Jour	SCF 22 365	Apr 70	Purica. X=1,THESIS,TBLS,THERMALIZTN	
Thermal Scat	Maxwl		JUL	Theo Jour	AKE 17 103	Mar 71	Schroeder. DIFFERENT SCAT LAW TH	
				Rept	JUEL−668−RG	Jul 70	− . SCAT LAW CALCULATION	
				Rept	JUEL−610−RG	Aug 69	− .PHONON SPEC, SCAT TH	
Thermal Scat	Pile		JUL	Comp Rept	JUEL−875−RX	Aug 72	Scharenberg.DATA ON USE AS N−FILTER	
Scattering	3.1+6		LAS	Expt Jour	PR 70 602	Nov 46	Manley+ BACKSCATT. 1.4,1.7MEV BIAS.	
Scattering	2.0+5	3.0+6	LAS	Expt Rept	PR 72 881	Nov 47	Barschall+ POOR GEOM+BCKSCT.PER MOL	
Scattering	3.6−4	1.3−1	TRM	Theo Jour	JNE 7 45	Aug 58	Bhandari+ ELASTIC+1+2PHONON INEL	
Scattering	9.0−4	3.7−3	AUL	Expt Jour	PM 8 43	Jan 63	Sabine+.DEFECT SCAT IN IRRADIAT BEO	
Absorption	3.0+6	1.5+7	FEI	Expt Book	SPN 205	61	.ENGL TRANSL OF NEJTRONFIZ 278	
				Book	NEJTRONFIZ 278	61	Kukhtevich+ SIGMA AT 2ES	
Absorption	Maxwl		CCP	Expt Jour	AE 14 193	Feb 63	Zhezherun.PULSED SOURCE, 11.8+−.4MB	
				Jour	JNE 18 279	May 64	TRANSLATN.*	
				Jour	SJA 14 183	Dec 63	TRANSLATN.*	
Absorption	1.0−3	1.0+3	UK	Eval Rept	AEEW−R−351	Feb 64	Barrington+(WIN).UKNDL FILE.	
Absorption	Maxwl		TRM	Expt Conf	67Kanpur § N123	Feb 67	Joshi.PLSD NEUT.XACT MEAS OF SIGMA	
(n,2n)	Fiss		JUL	Expt Jour	AKE 17 223	Jul 71	Demmeler+ FAST FISS FACT,CFD TH	
				Rept	JUEL−652−RG	Apr 70	− . FAST FISS FACTOR EXPT	
				Jour	NUK 12 175	May 69	Kirch+ FAST FISS FACTOR EXPT	
				Rept	JUEL−547−RG	68	− . FAST FISS FACTOR DETERMINAT	

5 Boron CMP

Quantity	Energy (ev) Min	Max	Lab	Type	Documentation Ref Vol Page	Date	Author, Comments	Data
Total	−2		COL	Expt Jour	PR 83 746	Aug 51	Tittman+B2O3,RATIO SCATT/TOT.TRANSM	
Thermal Scat	Maxwl		TRM	Expt Conf	72Chandigr 3 613	Dec 72	Begum+WEAK FERRO MAGNETISM IN FEBO3	
Absorption	3.0+6	1.5+7	FEI	Expt Book	NEJTRONFIZ 278	61	Kukhtevich+ SIGMA AT 2ES	
	4.0+6	1.5+7		Book	NEJTRONFIZ 263	61	Broder+ REMOVAL CS, GRAPH CFD	
	3.0+6	1.5+7		Book	SPN 205	61	.ENGL TRANSL OF NEJTRONFIZ 278	
	4.0+6	1.5+7		Book	SPN 194	61	.ENGL TRANSL OF NEJTRONFIZ 263	
Inelastic γ	4.0+5	1.2+6	RPI	Expt Prog	RPI−328−56 37	Mar 66	Hockenbury+ PULSE−HEIGHT SPEC GIVEN	

6 Carbon CMP

Quantity	Energy (ev) Min	Max	Lab	Type	Documentation Ref Vol Page	Date	Author, Comments	Data
Diff Elastic	7.0−2		CRC	Expt Jour	PR 75 1609	May 49	Alcock+CO2,CRYSTSP,5−90DEG,GAS/LIQ	
Thermal Scat	3.0−3		ANL	Expt Jour	PR 71 666	May 47	Fermi+CO2,GAS,ROOM T,CFD NON INTERF	
Thermal Scat	+0		COL	Expt Prog	WASH−1046 35	Jan 64	Schiellerup.CRICL POINT,CF HOVE TH.	
Thermal Scat	3.1−3		JUL	Expt Conf	68Copenhgn 1 599	May 68	Mika+ SOLID+LIQUID CARBON−MONOXIDE	
				Conf	69Wien 19	Dec 69	− + CARBON NONOXIDE.	
Thermal Scat	2.0−2	5.0−2	MTR	Expt Conf	68Copenhgn 2 205	May 68	Carpenter+C2F6,PPR88,5TO105DEG ANG,	
	Maxwl			Conf	67Ann Arbr 1 293	Jul 67	− +C2F6,PPR68,GAS,2QUANTUM−T	
Thermal Scat	Cold		MIT	Theo Jour	JCP 62 936	Feb 75	Berney.CO2 VIB SPECT.400−1800 1/CM	
Thermal Scat	Cold		MUN	Expt Jour	ZP/A 272 189	Feb 75	Koester+COH.SCT.AMP. CCL4,C2CL4 ETC	
(n,γ)	+3	+5	AUA	Expt Prog	AAEC/PR−36P 11	Mar 72	Allen+ CF2.ORELA,DATA TB ANALYZD,NDG	
Spect (n,γ)	Pile		BRK	Expt Jour	PR 80 90	Oct 50	Wilson.CCL4,ION CHAMBER	
Reson Params	+3	+5	AUA	Expt Prog	AAEC/PR−36P 11	Mar 72	Allen+ CF2.ORELA,DATA TB ANALYZD,NDG	

7 Nitrogen CMP

Quantity	Energy (ev) Min	Max	Lab	Type	Documentation Ref Vol Page	Author, Comments Date	Data
Total	1.0+5	8.9+5	DKE Expt	Prog	WASH – 1034 10	Oct 61 Bilputh+BE3N2,SIG FOR N,STEPS 1KEV	
Thermal Scat	3.0–3		ANL Expt	Jour	PR 71 666	May 47 Fermi+N2O,GAS,ROOM T CFD NON INTERFR	
(n,α)	1.4+7		SAH Expt	Conf	62Madras 46	Feb 62 Sen.CNO,NDG,EXPT DESCRIBED	

7 Nitrogen AIR

Quantity	Energy (ev) Min	Max	Lab	Type	Documentation Ref Vol Page	Author, Comments Date	Data
Total	2.5+5	1.5+7	USA Theo	Rept	D2 – 1851	May 57 Pearson.OPTMOD CALCULATION. TABLE	
Total	3.0+5	5.0+6	CCP Expt	Jour	AE 26 454	May 69 Terekhin+SIG–TBL,15NEUT–ES,CFD CALC	
				Jour	SJA 26 74	May 69 .TRANSLATION. SEE ALSO P 852	
Total	1.4+7		CCP Expt	Jour	YK – 9 50	72 Maslov+ FROM TRANS,SIG GIVEN	+
				Rept	INDC(CCP)–42	Aug 74 .P10. ENGLISH OF YK–9	
	1.4+7			Data	EXFOR40136.028	Feb 73 .1 DATA LINE	
Total	5.0–7	5.0–5	MUN Expt	Jour	ZP 250 166	Feb 72 Steyerl+,TOF TRANS AT 298 DEG K	
Diff Elastic	3.0+5	3.0+6	USA Theo	Rept	CVAC – 251T	Aug 54 Weller+ ALSO 1.0 MEV,TBLS+CURVES.	
Scattering	2.5+5	1.5+7	USA Theo	Rept	D2 – 1851	May 57 Pearson.OPTMOD CALCULATION. TBL+CRVS	
Scattering	3.3+5	1.4+7	CCP Theo	Jour	AE 28 168	Feb 70 Mordashev.SCAT NEUT FLUX+DOSIS DIST	
				Jour	EAF 28 2 96	70 . FRENCH OF AE 28 168	
Spect (n,γ)		1.4+7	CCP Theo	Jour	AE 28 168	Feb 70 Mordashev. GAM INTENS+DOSIS DISTR	
				Jour	EAF 28 2 96	70 . FRENCH OF AE 28 168	
Inelastic γ	6.0+6	1.4+7	GDT Theo	Rept	NARF – 60 – 22T	Aug 60 Wells.MONTE CARLO CALC.GAM E+ANG DST	

7 Nitrogen AMM

Quantity	Energy (ev) Min	Max	Lab	Type	Documentation Ref Vol Page	Author, Comments Date	Data
Total	5.0–3	2.0–1	KRK Expt	Conf	62Chalk R. 1 405	Sep 62 Janik+,TOT SIG PER P CFD K–N TH	
Total	2.5–2	2.3–1	KIL Expt	Prog	EANDC(E)66U	Feb 66 Broeker+ TBC.XTLSPECTROM	
Total	3.7–2	2.4–1	KIL Expt	Conf	67Juelich 232	Apr 67 MATUSSEK SIG(P)IN NH4C8O4H5 CRYSTAL	
Total	Cold		COL Expt	Prog	WASH – 1136 31	Sep 69 Markisz+ METHYLAMMONIUM CHLORDE.NDG.	
Thermal Scat	1.5–2	5.0–1	GWU Theo	Jour	PR 60 18	Jul 41 Sachs+ MASS TENSOR METHOD.	
Thermal Scat	3.0–2	1.1–1	IFJ Expt	Jour	APP 18 255	59 Wanic.NH3,TRANS,REL AG,CFD K–N,GRPH	
Thermal Scat	2.0–2	1.1–1	KRK ExTh	Jour	APP 18 255	May 59 Wanic.SIG CFD KRIEGER–NELKEN TH	
Thermal Scat	1.0–2	1.5–1	WWA Expt	Rept	INR – 117/OFJ	Nov 59 Janik+.GASEOUS NH3,CFD SIG THEOR	
Thermal Scat	Cold		COL Expt	Prog	WASH – 1034 8	Dec 61 Rush+NH4PF6,23DEG AND –190DEG C	
Thermal Scat	5.8–3	1.9–1	IFJ Expt	Rept	INP – 214	Oct 62 Janik+ NH3 LIQU+GAS,GRPH OKS K–N	
	4.0–4	–1		Revw	INP – 255	Apr 63 – +NH3+SALTS,SIG/H CFD K–N,GRPHS	
	5.8–3	1.9–1		Expt	Jour PHY 26 449	Apr 60 *EARLIER EXPT	
Thermal Scat	Cold		MTR Expt	Prog	IDO – 16977 32	Dec 63 Strong+,INEL SIGS FOR 3 STATES,CRVS	
Thermal Scat	4.9–3		UJK Expt	Jour	APP 25 141	Jan 64 Czerlunczakiewicz+ THEO CFD EXPT	
Thermal Scat	Cold		BNL Expt	Prog	WASH – 1048 15	Jun 64 Otnes+ NH4CLO4. NDG. SACHS–TELL.	
Thermal Scat	Cold		BNL Expt	Prog	WASH – 1048 15	Jun 64 Otnes+ NH4PF6. NDG. SACHS–TELL.	
Thermal Scat	–2		WWA Expt	Jour	NKA 9 511	Jul 64 Aleksandrowicz+ BRIEF.THERM VIBR,NDG	
Thermal Scat	Pile		KRK Revw	Rept	INP – 368	Nov 64 Janik.REV MOLECL DYNAMICS ,BOMBAY64	
Thermal Scat	7.8–1		TRM Expt	Conf	65Calcutta 292	Feb 65 Padmanabhan+(NH4)2C2O4.H2O,STRUCTR	
Thermal Scat	2.5–2	1.0–1	MTR Expt	Jour	JCP 42 1568	Mar 65 Brugger+ PHASED CHOP. 3 ES.	
Thermal Scat	Maxwl		COL Expt	Prog	WASH – 1068 42	Mar 66 Leung+ NH4CL04. NDG.	
Thermal Scat	Maxwl		COL Expt	Prog	WASH – 1068 42	Mar 66 Leung+,(NH4)2CR2O7,NDG	
Thermal Scat	Maxwl		COL Expt	Prog	WASH – 1068 42	Mar 66 Leung+,NH4HSO4,NDG	
Thermal Scat	Maxwl		COL Expt	Prog	WASH – 1068 42	Mar 66 Leung+,(NH4)2SO4,NDG	
Thermal Scat	–		DUB Expt	Conf	66Dubna 179	Jul 66 Parlinski+,NH4CL AT –160DEG,N SPECT	
Thermal Scat	–		KFI Theo	Jour	PHY 32 1571	Sep 66 Kosaly+ TH FOR ROTL FREEDOM OKS XPT	
Thermal Scat	5.0–3		TRM Theo	Jour	PPS 89 379	Oct 66 Venkataraman+. NH3 GAS. CFD EXPT	
Thermal Scat	1.0–2	1.3–1	DUB Expt	Rept	JINR – E3 – 3035	Dec 66 Bajorek+NH4VO,SCAT NEUT VS E(N),GRPH	
	5.0–3	1.5–1		Rept	JINR – E3 – 3037	Dec 66 – +SCNH2,SCAT NEUT VS E(N) GRPH	
Thermal Scat	–3	–2	KRK Expt	Rept	JINR – E3 – 3056	Dec 66 Bajorek+ (CO(NH3)6)I3,FREQU – DISTR	
Thermal Scat	–2	+0	COL Expt	Prog	NYO – GEN72 – 132	Jan 67 Leung+(NH4)2S2O8, TEMP DEPEND, NDG	
Thermal Scat	–2	+0	COL Expt	Prog	NYO – GEN72 – 132	Jan 67 Leung+(NH4)2SIF6, TEMP DEPEND, NDG	
Thermal Scat	4.6–3		HAR Expt	Jour	PPS 92 912	Dec 67 Webb.EXPT AT 20 100DEGC CFD THEORY	
	5.0–3			Conf	62Chalk R. 1 457	Sep 62 – .DIFF SIG 20 – 90DEG AT 21DEGC	
Thermal Scat	–3		KRK Revw	Rept	INP – 600/PS	Apr 68 Janik.AMMONIA GAS AND NH4+ ION	
Thermal Scat	Maxwl		TOH Expt	Priv	KIMURA+	Dec 69 .TOF.BE–DETECTOR.INELASTIC SCAT SIG	
Thermal Scat	–3	–1	TRM Expt	Prog	BARC – 474 14	70 Kim+ AMMONIUM SALTS,NH4 REORIENTATN	
Thermal Scat	5.0–3		IFJ Expt	Rept	INP – 726/PS	Oct 70 Janik+,NH4 ROTAT IN NH4CLO4,IBRDUBN	
	9.9–4	4.9–3		ExTh Rept	INP – 360	Oct 64 – + FREE ROTATION NH4 IN NH4CLO4	

7 Nitrogen AMM

Quantity	Energy (ev) Min	Max	Lab	Type	Documentation Ref Vol Page	Author, Comments Date	Data
Thermal Scat	−3		TRM Expt	Conf	70Madurai 3 457	Dec 70 Goyal+ SOLID AMMONIA,FREQUENCY,TBL	
				Rept	BARC − 557 85	71 . GRAPH GIVEN	
Thermal Scat	None		BUC Theo	Jour	SCF 23 699	71 Trepadus.GAUSS APPROX.CRVS CFD EXPT	
Thermal Scat	5.7 − 4	3.0 − 2	DLH Theo	Conf	72Bombay 3 423	Feb 72 Bansal+ SOLID NH4,CALC TOT SIG,GRPH	
Thermal Scat	5.0 − 3		TRM ExTh	Conf	72Grenoble 477	Mar 72 Dasannacharya+ 3ANGS,CFD THEO,GRPH	
	−3			Conf	72Bombay 3 205	Feb 72 − + NH4,ROTATING CRYSPEC	
Thermal Scat	−3		TRM Expt	Prog	BARC − 878 70	76 Venkatash+ NH4 − SALTS.E − SPECS,GRAPHS	
Scattering	6.8+6	+7	COL Expt	Jour	PRL 5 507	Dec 60 Rush+ NH4BR, − CL, − F, − I,SIG/P,10ANG	

8 Oxygen CMP

Quantity	Energy (ev) Min	Max	Lab	Type	Documentation Ref Vol Page	Author, Comments Date	Data
Diff Elastic	1.5+7		ALB Expt	Prog	A − ALB − 75 27	Jun 75 Benenson+TOF.3 ANGS.NDG.TBC.	
Diff Inelast	1.5+7		ALB Expt	Prog	A − ALB − 75 27	Jun 75 Benenson+3 ANG. 6.05,6.13 MEV LVLS.	
Nonelastic γ	1.0+6	2.0+7	ORL Expt	Rept	ORNL − TM − 5024	Sep 75 Morgan.SECONDRY G SPEC.SIO2.GRPH.TBL	
n Emission	1.0+6	2.0+7	ORL Expt	Rept	ORNL − TM − 5024	Sep 75 Morgan.SECONDRY N SPEC.SIO2.GRPH.TBL	

9 Fluorine CMP

Quantity	Energy (ev) Min	Max	Lab	Type	Documentation Ref Vol Page	Author, Comments Date	Data
Thermal Scat	3.0 − 3	1.0 − 1	ANL Expt	Jour	PR 71 666	May 47 Fermi+CF4,GAS ROOM T.CF NON INTERFR	
Thermal Scat	7.0 − 2		CRC Expt	Jour	PR 83 1100	Sep 51 Alcock+CF4,SCATT INTENSITY VS ANGLE	
(n,γ)	+3	+5	AUA Expt	Prog	AAEC/PR − 36P 11	Mar 72 Allen+ CF2.ORELA,DATA TB ANALYZD,NDG	
Reson Params	+3	+5	AUA Expt	Prog	AAEC/PR − 36P 11	Mar 72 Allen+ CF2.ORELA,DATA TB ANALYZD,NDG	

11 Sodium CMP

Quantity	Energy (ev) Min	Max	Lab	Type	Documentation Ref Vol Page	Author, Comments Date	Data
Diff Elastic	Cold		MHG ExTh	Abst	DA/B 27 508	Aug 66 Werner.MOSAIC XTAL,SECONDY EXTINCTN	
Thermal Scat	3.3 − 3	5.0 − 3	WAT Expt	Jour	PR 86 271	May 52 Weiss.NAF,APPARENT SIGMA(TRANSMISSN)	
Thermal Scat	Pile		KRK Revw	Rept	INP − 368	Nov 64 Janik.NAH2F3 MOLEC DYNMICS,BOMBAY64	
Thermal Scat	Cold		LRL Expt	Jour	JAP 37 1040	Mar 66 Sparks+ NAO2. N DIFFR. MAG PROPS.	
Thermal Scat	5.1 − 3	5.8 − 2	HAR Expt	Jour	PR 153 923	Jan 67 Buyers.NAF,PHONON SPECTRUM ONLY(TOF)	
Thermal Scat	Cold		AE Expt	Conf	68Copenhgn 1 295	May 68 Almqvist+.NACL.PHON DISP. 80K. TBC	
Thermal Scat	Maxwl		UJV Theo	Rept	UJV − 2275	69 Krivy. DIAMOND,DEBYE TEMP,EXPTS CFD	
Thermal Scat	Cold		MTR Expt	Prog	WASH − 1127 77	Apr 69 Schmunk. NACL. DISPERSN 300DEGK. TBC	
Thermal Scat	−3	+0	BHU Theo	Conf	69Roorke 3 138	Dec 69 Singh+NAF,DISPERSION GRAPH OKS EXPTS	
Thermal Scat	5.6 − 2		MTR Expt	Conf	69Wien 204	Dec 69 Randolph+ STATISTICAL CHOPPER,GRPHS	
Thermal Scat	2.0 − 2	1.0 − 1	ANK Expt	Prog	INDC(TUR) − 2G	Apr 71 Bayvas. REFLECTIVITY VERSUS NEUT − E	
Spect (n,γ)	2.0+5	8.7+6	CCP Revw	Conf	60Vienna 261	Oct 60 Groshev+.GRAPH,MAGNETIC COMPTONSPEC	

12 Magnesium CMP

Quantity	Energy (ev) Min	Max	Lab	Type	Documentation Ref Vol Page	Author, Comments Date	Data
Total	5.0 − 2	3.0 − 1	BNL Expt	Conf	58Geneva 16 297	Sep 58 Mcreynolds+MGH2,(PPR1540)CURV CFD TH	
Total	7.6 − 2	4.5 − 1	GA Expt	Jour	PR 113 806	Feb 59 Whittemore+MGH2,H CS ONLY ABITRARY S	
Total	1.4+0		ORL Expt	Jour	NP 61 381	Jan 65 Rayburn+ RES E=1.44 EV, SIG=7.8B	
Thermal Scat	5.0 − 3		BNL Expt	Abst	BAP 7 499	Aug 62 Safford+MGO2H,(TA1),E LVL INVESTIGTN	
Thermal Scat	6.0 − 2	4.3 − 1	IFJ Revw	Rept	INP − 255	Apr 63 Janik+ HYDRIDE,CFD FERMI − THEO,GRAPH	
Thermal Scat	Cold	2.5 − 2	CAV ExTh	Jour	PPS 90 657	Mar 67 Peckham.MGO,PHONON FREQ DN.SHELL MOD	
Thermal Scat	Cold		MTR Expt	Prog	WASH − 1127 77	Apr 69 Schmunk.MG2SN,DISPERSN RELATN 300D K	
Thermal Scat	−3		TRM Expt	Conf	70Madurai 3 697	Dec 70 Begum+MAGNTC EXCH INTGRL,MGXMNFE2O4	
Thermal Scat	4.1 − 3		DUB ExTh	Conf	72Grenoble 157	Mar 72 Eschrig+ INEL SCAT GAS,5TS,TOF,GRPH	
Thermal Scat	Pile		JUL Comp	Rept	JUEL − 875 − RX	Aug 72 Scharenberg.MGO,DATA ON USE(N − FILTR)	

13 Aluminium CMP

Quantity	Energy (ev) Min	Max	Lab	Type	Documentation Ref Vol Page	Author, Comments Date	Data
Total	1.4+7		ROM Expt	Jour	NC 10 281	Mar 53 Ageno+AL2O3,LI TARGET TRANSM.8.77B	
Total	1.4+0		ORL Expt	Jour	NP 61 381	Jan 65 Rayburn+ AL2O3,RES E 1.44EV. 15.1 B.	
Total	2.0+0	3.0+0	HAR Expt	Prog	AERE − PR/NP20	Mar 73 Moxon+AL2O3.TBL.SIG = 14.340+ − 0.178B	
Total	1.0 − 5	5.0 − 4	MUN Expt	Conf	JINR − D3 − 7991	Apr 74 Steyerl+ P42.AL − ZN HOM+AGED,SIG − CURV	
	4.0 − 6	7.0 − 6		Conf	JINR − D3 − 7991	Apr 74 − + P42.OXI,PERP − TRANS,CRV+GRPH	

13 Aluminium CMP

Quantity	Energy (ev) Min	Max	Lab	Type	Documentation Ref Vol Page	Author, Comments Date	Data
Diff Elastic	4.2 – 3		JUL Expt	Rept	JUEL – 1158	Feb 75 Bauer. CU – ALLOY, MN – ALLOY	
Thermal Scat	Maxwl		DUB Expt	Rept	JINR – P14 – 5624	Feb 71 Kroo+ DIFF SCAT, AL(MN), GRPH	
Thermal Scat	Pile		BUC Expt	Prog	INDC(SEC) – 35	Sep 73 Cosneanu+ P176.AL – SI,AL – ZN ALLOY,NDG	
Thermal Scat	4.9 – 3		CCP Expt	Jour	FTT 18 2509	Sep 76 Alekseev+ CE – ,ND – AL3 POLYC.DOUBLDIFF	
				Jour	SPS 18 1466	Sep 76 . ENGL OF FTT 18,2509.	
Scattering	3.1 + 6		LAS Expt	Jour	PR 70 602	Nov 46 Manley+ AL2O3,1.4,1.7MEV BIAS.SIGMA.	

14 Silicon CMP

Quantity	Energy (ev) Min	Max	Lab	Type	Documentation Ref Vol Page	Author, Comments Date	Data
Total	2.0 – 7	5.0 – 5	MUN Expt	Jour	ZP 250 166	Feb 72 Steyerl+,TOF TRANS AT 90+297 DEG K	
Thermal Scat	5.0 – 3		MOL ExTh	Conf	72Grenoble 489	Mar 72 Hautecler+ SCAT SIG, TOF, GRPH	
Thermal Scat	8.2 – 4	5.1 – 3	IEA Expt	Rept	IEA – 320	Dec 73 Amaral+(PDMS),ROOM – TEMP.TOF.TBL+GRPH	
Thermal Scat	Cold		TRM Theo	Rept	BARC – 768 115	74 Thaper+(SI – H4).SING+MULT – SCT,2 ANGLS	
Scattering	3.1 + 6		LAS Expt	Jour	PR 70 602	Nov 46 Manley+ SIC,1.41.7MEV BIAS. SIGMA.	
Nonelastic γ	1.0 + 6	2.0 + 7	ORL Expt	Rept	ORNL – TM – 5024	Sep 75 Morgan.SECONDRY G SPEC.SIO2.GRPH.TBL	
n Emission	1.0 + 6	2.0 + 7	ORL Expt	Rept	ORNL – TM – 5024	Sep 75 Morgan.SECONDRY N SPEC.SIO2.GRPH.TBL	

14 Silicon OXI

Quantity	Energy (ev) Min	Max	Lab	Type	Documentation Ref Vol Page	Author, Comments Date	Data
Total	Cold		NYU Expt	Jour	PR 55 1101	Jun 39 Whitaker+SIGS FOR SINGLE+POLY – CRYST	
Total	Maxwl		NYU Expt	Jour	PR 57 551	Mar 40 Whitaker+ ALSO EPI – CD. B,RH DETECT.	
Total	Maxwl		COL Expt	Jour	PR 57 976	Jun 40 Beyer+INTERFERENCE. POLY – ,MONOCRYST	
Total	Maxwl		COL Expt	Jour	PR 59 489	Mar 41 Hanstein. TRNS. QUARTZ CRYSTAL.	
Total	9.0 – 1		COL Expt	Jour	PR 59 489	Mar 41 Hanstein. TRNS. QUARTZ CRYSTAL,SAND.	
Total	Maxwl		JAP Expt	Jour	JMJ 25 530	Aug 43 Kimura+QUARZ,TRANS.IN FIG.VARIOUS T	
Total	Maxwl		CHI Expt	Jour	PR 70 815	Dec 46 Anderson+PYREX,C – FILTERED NS TO 18DK	
Total	6.3 – 4	3.5 – 3	UK Expt	Jour	PM 3 1280	Nov 58 Mitchell+ NORMAL+IRRADIATED SAMPLES	
Total	7.0 – 4	1.0 + 0	COL Expt	Jour	RSI 36 48	Jan 65 Rustad+ CS QUARTZ CRYSTAL. CURVES.	
Total	1.4 + 0		ORL Expt	Jour	NP 61 381	Jan 65 Rayburn+ TRNS. RES E, 1.44EV. 9.4 B.	
Total	7.0 – 4	3.0 + 0	COL Expt	Jour	RSI 36 887	Jul 65 Rustad+ FUSED,CRYSTAL QUARTZ.CURVES.	
Total	– 2	+ 1	KUR Expt	Jour	IZV 32 1719	Oct 68 Govor+ XPTL MACROSC – SIG(NEUT – E)GRPH	
				Jour	BAS 32 1584	Oct 69 . ENGL OF IZV 32 1719	
Total	1.3 + 2		MUN Expt	Jour	PL/B 36 208	Sep 71 Dilg+ SIO2. TRANS EXPT. CO RES NS.	+
	1.3 + 2			Data	EXFOR20596.006	Jun 76 1PNT.	
Total	2.0 – 7	5.0 – 5	MUN Expt	Jour	ZP 250 166	Feb 72 Steyerl+,TOF TRANS AT 90+296 DEG K	
	1.0 – 7	6.0 – 5		Jour	PL/B 29 33	Mar 69 – + GLASS. SUPERSEDED.	
Total	2.0 + 5	2.0 + 7	ORL Expt	Rept	ORNL – 4823	Dec 72 Perey+ TRNS ORELA. GRPHS. CFD.	
Total	2.0 + 0	3.0 + 0	HAR Expt	Prog	AERE – PR/NP20	Mar 73 Moxon+TRANS.TBL.SIG = 9.680+ – 0.074B	
Total	1.2 + 0	5.2 + 0	MUN Expt	Jour	ZN/A 31 115	Feb 76 Waschkowski. TRANS. RH,AG RES DET.	+
	1.3 + 0	5.2 + 0		Data	EXFOR20603.002	Jun 76 2PTS.	
Thermal Scat	– 3	– 1	UJV Expt	Jour	AE 28 413	May 70 Chalupa+ OSCILLATING – QARTZ EXPTS	
				Jour	SJA 28 523	70 . ENGL OF AE 28 413	
				Jour	EAF 28 5 44	70 . FRENCH OF AE 28 413	
Thermal Scat	4.6 – 2		UJV Expt	Jour	PL/A 37 403	Dec 71 Michalec+ VIBRATE CRYST T – MODULATON	
Thermal Scat	Pile		JUL Comp	Rept	JUEL – 875 – RX	Aug 72 Scharenberg.DATA ON USE AS N – FILTER	
Thermal Scat	1.1 – 5	1.9 – 5	ILL Expt	Jour	JNC 16 93	Oct 74 Roth+ SMALL – ANG SIG(WAVEL,TEMP),GRPH	
Scattering	3.1 + 6		LAS Expt	Jour	PR 70 602	Nov 46 Manley+ BACKSCATT. 1.4,1.7MEV BIAS.	
Scattering	2.0 – 4	1.0 + 0	LON Theo	Jour	NAT 215 615	Aug 67 King.RANDOM NET MODEL AGREES EXPT	
(n,γ)	Maxwl		COL Expt	Jour	PR 50 738	Oct 36 Fink. RATE OF ABSORPTION ONLY	

16 Sulphur CMP

Quantity	Energy (ev) Min	Max	Lab	Type	Documentation Ref Vol Page	Author, Comments Date	Data
Total	Cold		NYU Expt	Jour	PR 60 155	Aug 41 Whitaker+ CS2,RA – BE,PARAFFIN. 9.0 B.	
Total	5.0 – 3	2.0 – 1	KRK Expt	Conf	62Chalk R. 1 405	Sep 62 Janik+,CH3SH,TOT PER P CFD K – N TH	
Total	5.4 – 3	1.9 – 1	IBJ Expt	Rept	NKA 10 201	Jul 65 Borowski+ CH3SH.TOTSIG/PROT VS EN	
Elastic	Maxwl		POL Expt	Jour	BPC 5 295	57 CH2SH,194.1+ – 5B,ABST=PA60 9297 N/57	
Thermal Scat	Cold		NYU Expt	Jour	PR 60 155	Aug 41 Whitaker+CS2,RA – BE,PARAFIN.8.5B	
Thermal Scat	Maxwl		KRK ExTh	Jour	APP 11 146	Nov 52 Janik+ H2SO4,RA – BE SOURCE,B – ION CHAMB	
				Jour	APP 11 330	May 53 .CFD SACHS – TELLER.ALSO APP 12 45 53	
Thermal Scat	Maxwl		IBJ Theo	Jour	BPP 4 269	May 56 Kolos. CH3SH, HINDERED ROTATION	
Thermal Scat	Maxwl		POL Expt	Jour	APP 16 5 335	57 Budzinowski.CH3SH,195+ – 5B CFD THEOR	

16 Sulphur CMP

Quantity	Energy (ev) Min	Max	Lab	Type	Documentation Ref Vol Page	Author, Comments Date	Data
Thermal Scat	−2		KRK ExTh	Jour	BPP 5 295	Mar 57 Janik+CH3SH,RA+BE SOURC,POT BARRIER	
				Jour	APP 16 335	Sep 57 − + CONTINUATION OF BPP 5 295	
(n,γ)	Cold		NYU Expt	Jour	PR 60 155	Aug 41 Whitaker+ CS2. NG=TOT−SCT.	

17 Chlorine CMP

Quantity	Energy (ev) Min	Max	Lab	Type	Documentation Ref Vol Page	Author, Comments Date	Data
Total	9.5+7		BRK Expt	Jour	PR 77 606	Mar 50 Dejuren+CCL4,BY FISSION CH	
Total	1.5+4	6.0+5	DKE Expt	Jour	AP 84 165	May 74 Pineo+CSCL.TRNS.AVG CS.TBL.OPTMDL.	+
	1.0+5	6.5+5		Jour	AP 84 165	May 74 − + KCL.AVG TOT CS.GRPH.TBL.	
	1.5+4	6.0+5		Abst	DA/B 31 6821	May 71 .2 EN RANGES.AVG CS CFD OPTMDL.	
	1.5+4	6.0+5		Diss	PINEO	70 .KCL.AVG CS.GRPHS.STF CALC.TBL.CFD	
	1.5+4	6.0+5		Data	EXFOR10542.001	Jan 79 . DATA UNOBTAINABLE FROM AUTHORS.	
Total	+4	+5	ORL Expt	Prog	ORNL−4937 198	May 74 Good+KCL CMP.GRPH.TBC.	
Potntal Scat	3.0+3	6.5+5	DKE Expt	Jour	AP 84 165	May 74 Pineo+KCL.S WAVE SCT LENGTH.TBL.CFD.	
				Abst	DA/B 31 6821	May 71 .THESIS ABST.	
				Diss	PINEO	70 .KCL.SCT LENGTH CURV,TBL.CFD.	
				Diss	PINEO	70 .TBL.GRPHS.CFD TO 3 COLLECTIVE MDLS.	
Thermal Scat		3.3−2	UPP Theo	Jour	AF 13 199	Mar 58 Sjoelander. KCL.1 AND 2 PHONON CALCS	
				Jour	AF 14 361	May 58 − . ALSO P205.CORRECTIONS.	
Thermal Scat	5.0−3		BNL Expt	Abst	BAP 7 500	Aug 62 Boutin+ HCL. LIQ,SOLID SPEC. NDG.	
Thermal Scat	1.0−2		MSU Theo	Conf	67Ann Arbr 1 283	Jul 67 Summerfield+HCL,PPR65.TH−SIG(E,E')	
Thermal Scat	−		ISL Expt	Prog	IA− 1218 57	Aug 70 Epstein+RB2 MN CL4 ,MAGNETC STRUCT.	
Thermal Scat	−		ISL Expt	Prog	IA− 1218 56	Aug 70 Schachar+TL MN CL3 MAGNETC STRUCT	
Thermal Scat	None		FRK Theo	Jour	PL/A 34 118	Feb 71 Jex.ND4CL,BREATHING SHELL MODEL 85D	
Thermal Scat	Maxwl		OSA Theo	Jour	NST 8 3	Jun 71 Nishigori+HCL,PHTON TYPE EXPANSION	
Thermal Scat	Cold		MUN Expt	Jour	PRL 27 956	Oct 71 Koester+COH.SCAT.AMP.CCL4,4−CLETHYLN	
				Jour	ZP/A 272 189	Feb 75 − +COH.SCT.AMP. CCL4,C2CL4 ETC	
				Jour	PRL 27 956	Oct 71 − +CLOROBENZ,6−CLBUTADN. REFLCT	
				Jour	ZP 198 187	Dec 66 − + OLD EXPT.SUPERSEDED	
Thermal Scat	Maxwl		TOK Expt	Jour	JPJ 32 1019	Apr 72 Niimura+HCL,CRYST STRUCT BY N DIFFRC	
Thermal Scat	4.0−2	3.5−1	KIG Expt	Jour	AKE 28 2 138	76 Suszin. H + CL SIG IN CHLOROFORM	
				Rept	GKSS−76/E/60	76 − . H+CL IN CLOROFORM.	
Scattering	Maxwl		JAP Expt	Jour	PR 79 544	Aug 50 Kimura.NH4CL.−60 TO 0 DEGC CURVE	
Strnth Fnctn	3.0+3	6.5+5	DKE Expt	Abst	DA/B 31 6821	May 71 Pineo.S,P,D WAVE.THESIS ABST.KCL	
				Diss	PINEO	70 . KCL TBLS,GRPHS.CFD CALC,EXPTS.	

19 Potassium CMP

Quantity	Energy (ev) Min	Max	Lab	Type	Documentation Ref Vol Page	Author, Comments Date	Data
Total	1.0+5	6.5+5	DKE Expt	Jour	AP 84 165	May 74 Pineo+ KCL. AVG TOT CS. GRPH. TBL.	+
				Abst	DA/B 31 6821	May 71 − .2 E RANGE AVGS.CFD OPTMDL.	
	1.5+4	6.0+5		Diss	PINEO	70 .KCL.AVG CS.GRPHS.STF CALC.TBL.CFD	
	1.5+4	6.0+5		Data	EXFOR10542.006	Jan 79 . DATA UNOBTAINABLE FROM AUTHORS.	
Total	+3	+4	ORL Expt	Prog	ORNL−4937 198	May 74 Good+KCL CMP.GRPH.TBC.	
Potntal Scat	3.0+3	6.5+5	DKE Expt	Jour	AP 84 165	May 74 Pineo+KCL.S WAVE SCT LENGTH.TBL.CFD.	
				Abst	DA/B 31 6821	May 71 .THESIS ABST.	
				Diss	PINEO	70 .TBL.GRPHS.CFD TO 3 COLLECTIVE MDLS.	
				Diss	PINEO	70 .KCL.SCT LENGTH CURV,TBL.CFD.	
Thermal Scat	Maxwl		KRK Revw	Rept	INP−368	Nov 64 Janik.K2HPO4+K2HPO4+K3PO4,REVIEW	
Thermal Scat	Pile		KRK Revw	Rept	INP−368	Nov 64 Janik.KH2F3,REV MOL DYNAMIC 64BOMBAY	
Thermal Scat	Pile		KRK Revw	Rept	INP−368	Nov 64 Janik. KHF2,REVW MOL DYNAMICS	
Thermal Scat	Cold		BNL ExTh	Jour	JAP 37 1041	Mar 66 Cooper+ KMNF3 N DIFFR. MAGN PROPS.	
Thermal Scat	Cold		HAR Expt	Jour	JAP 37 1054	Mar 66 .KMNF3,MAGNETIC PROPS FROM N DIFF.XP	
				Jour	JAP 36 1092	Mar 65 .KMNF3,N PARAMAGNETIC SCAT XPT	
Thermal Scat	Cold		LRL Expt	Jour	JAP 37 1040	Mar 66 Sparks+ KO2. N DIFFR. MAGN PROPS.	
Thermal Scat	Cold		ORL Expt	Jour	JAP 37 1047	Mar 66 Smith+ KO2. N DIFFR. MAGN PROPS.	
Thermal Scat	None		MTR Expt	Conf	66Dubna 35	Jul 66 Brugger+KNO3 PHASE IV,DIFF PATTERN	
Thermal Scat	Cold		NJS Expt	Jour	PL/A 26 8	Dec 67 Blinc+ KH2PO4,QUASIELAST SCAT EXPT	
Thermal Scat	−		ISP Expt	Jour	PL/A 27 582	Sep 68 Schenk+ N−INTERFERENCE(KH2PO4 SCAT)	
Thermal Scat	−3	+0	IND Theo	Conf	68Bombay 3 39	Dec 68 DHIRANJAN ROY+ K−IODIDE,CALC PHONON	
Thermal Scat	−3	+1	IND Theo	Conf	68Bombay 3 39	Dec 68 Dhiranjan Roy+KBR,CALCTD DISPERSN	
Thermal Scat	−3	+0	TRM Expt	Jour	68Bombay 1 177	Dec 68 SATYA MURTY+ KMNF3,MAGNETIC SCATTNG	
Thermal Scat	Maxwl		UJV Theo	Rept	UJV−2275	69 Krivy. DEBYE TEMP,BRAGG+OTHER EXPTS	
Thermal Scat	Maxwl		BNL Expt	Jour	JPJ 26 674	Mar 69 Minkiewicz+KMNF3,SOFT PHONON MODE ZB	
Thermal Scat	−3	−1	CRC Revw	Conf	69Wien 1	Dec 69 Woods+ POTASSIUM IODIDE,XPT DESCRBD	

19 Potassium CMP

Quantity	Energy (ev) Min	Max	Lab	Type	Documentation Ref Vol Page	Date	Author, Comments	Data
Thermal Scat	−3	−1	TRM	Expt Conf	69Roorke 3 29	Dec 69	Thaper+K2C2O4,OXALATE,WATER−BINDING	
Thermal Scat	−3	−2	ISL	Expt Prog	IA− 1218 51	Aug 70	Pelah+(KH2 PO4),FERROELECTRIC, NDG	
Thermal Scat	4.7−3		TRM	Expt Rept	BARC−557 74	71	USHA DENIZ+ KMNF3,N−SPEC,3 TS,GRPHS	
Thermal Scat	Maxwl		ISS	Expt Jour	JPJ 35 1608	Dec 73	Hirakawa+.PARAMAGNETIC SCATT.K2CUF4	
Thermal Scat	None		ORL	ExTh Jour	PRL 33 412	Aug 74	Walton+ DEFECT−PHON SCT IN KCL−CN.	
Thermal Scat	None		TOK	Expt Jour	JPJ 37 660	Sep 74	Ikeda.CRITICAL SCATT. K2(CO,CU,MN)F4	
	Maxwl			Jour	JPJ 35 722	Sep 73	− +KCUF3 MAGNETIC NEUTRON DIFFR.	
	Maxwl	2.5−2		Jour	JPJ 35 617	Aug 73	− +.CRITICAL MAG.SCATT. K2.MN.F3	
Thermal Scat	None		JAE	Theo Jour	JPJ 38 21	Jan 75	Betsuyaku. THEORY,PARAMAGNET KMNF3	
	8.0−3			Expt Jour	JPJ 37 975	Oct 74	− +.PARAMAGNETIC SCATT. KMNF3	
Nonelastic	1.4+7		CCP	Expt Jour	AE 1 4 155	Sep 56	FLEROV+.SPHERE TRANSM, 1200+ −30MB	
				Jour	JNE 4 529	Apr 57	TRANSLATN.*	
				Jour	SJA 1 617	56	TRANSLATN.*	
Strnth Fnctn	3.0+3	6.5+5	DKE	Expt Abst	DA/B 31 6821	May 71	Pineo.S,P,D WAVE.THESIS ABST.KCL	
				Diss	PINEO	70	. KCL TBLS,GRPHS.CFD CALC,EXPTS.	

20 Calcium CMP

Quantity	Energy (ev) Min	Max	Lab	Type	Documentation Ref Vol Page	Date	Author, Comments	Data
Total	6.0−3	1.0+4	COL	Expt Jour	PR 73 963	May 48	Havens+ SLOW TRANSMISSION. TOF.	
Total	1.6−3		ANL	Expt Jour	PR 75 1098	Apr 49	Krueger+MULTISCAT,POWDER VS CRYSTAL	
Total	1.0−3	4.0−2	ANL	Expt Conf	58Geneva 14 212	Sep 58	Sidhu+.PPR680,CURV CFD THEORY	
Total	1.1−3	3.5−2	ANL	Revw Jour	JAP 30 1323	Sep 59	Sidhu+ CRYSTAL EFFECTS. CURV VS E.	
Total	+0		KIL	Expt Prog	EANDC(E)89 U	Jan 68	Brand+CAH2,CRYSTSPEC AT FRG−1	
Thermal Scat	Cold		LUQ	Expt Jour	PR 58 321	Aug 40	Rasetti. CALCITE,SCAT VS CRYSTRUCT.	
Thermal Scat	Cold		BNL	Expt Abst	BAP 7 356	Apr 62	Brajovic+ CASO4. 3 CMP SCT. NDG.	
Thermal Scat	5.0−3		BNL	Expt Jour	JPJ 7 499	Aug 62	Safford+.CAO2H,(TA1),E LVL INVESTIGT	
Thermal Scat	1.0−3	5.0−3	NJS	Expt Jour	PL/A 25 123	Jul 67	Dimic+ CA25R(CH3CH2COO)6,FREQU,GRPH	
				Rept	NIJS−R−507	Sep 67	.SEE ALSO. SAME EXPT+RESULTS	
Thermal Scat	None		OXF	Theo Jour	PPS 91 903	Aug 67	Elliott+CAF2,GROUP THEOR SELECTN	
Thermal Scat	Cold		TOH	Expt Jour	JPJ 24 446	Mar 68	.CA2FE2O5,MAGNETIC STRUCT BY N−DIFF	
				Jour	JPJ 22 939	Mar 67	Watanabe+CAFE2O4,MAGNETIC N DIFFR	
Thermal Scat	−3		TRM	Expt Conf	68Bombay 3 217	Dec 68	Thaper+ CASO4.2H2O, WATER MODES	
Thermal Scat	Maxwl		MUN	Expt Jour	ZP 228 454	Oct 69	Alefeld.CAF2,E−RESOL OF CAF2−SINGLE	
Thermal Scat	−3	+0	TRM	Expt Conf	69Roorke 3 25	Dec 69	Vijayaraghavan+CAF2,DISPERSION GRPHS	
Thermal Scat	−3	+0	TRM	Expt Prog	BARC−474 14	70	Iyengar+CAFX,ACCOUSTIC+OPTIC DIPERS	
Thermal Scat	Cold		WPI	Expt Jour	JCP 52 3952	Apr 70	Maeland.CAH2,TOF,DISTRIB.INEL.SCAT	
Thermal Scat	−3		TRM	Expt Rept	BARC−557 77	71	Vijayaraghavan+ CAO,PHONON,TBL,GRPH	
				Conf	72Bombay 3 255	Feb 72	− + CAO,DISPERSN CURVE	
				Conf	70Madurai 2 439	Dec 71	.SEE ALSO	
Thermal Scat	−3		TRM	Expt Rept	BARC−557 80	71	Vijayaraghavan+ CAF2,PHONONS,GRAPH	
Thermal Scat	5.0−3		IFJ	Expt Rept	INP−742/PS	Jan 71	Bajorek+CA(OH)2,TOF,IBR DUBNA	
Thermal Scat	Maxwl	2.5−2	JAE	Expt Jour	JPJ 35 204	Jul 73	Iizumi.ANHARMONIC LATT.VIB. CA.F2	

22 Titanium CMP

Quantity	Energy (ev) Min	Max	Lab	Type	Documentation Ref Vol Page	Date	Author, Comments	Data
Total	6.2−4	5.2−3	COL	Expt Rept	CU− 179	Oct 58	Gould.CS CURV BINDING OF H DEDUCED	
	5.7−4	3.3−3		Prog	CU− 174 21	Mar 58	− + TIH2. CHEM BINDING. GRPH.	
Total	1.5−3	6.0−2	ANL	Expt Jour	JAP 30 323	Sep 59	Sidhu+TIC,CURVE VS E SHOWS XTAL EFFC	
	1.0−3	4.0−2		Conf	58Geneva 14 212	Sep 58	− + TIC. CURV CFD TH. TBL.	
Total	5.0−2	5.0−1	SAC	Expt Jour	JPR 22 648	Oct 61	Genin+DATA COMPARED WITH THEORY	
Total	2.5−2	5.5−1	KIL	Expt Prog	EANDC(E)66U	Feb 66	BROECKER TBC.XTLSPECTRUM	
Total	5.0−2	2.2−1	SEO	Expt Prog	INDC(SEC)−18	Aug 71	Lee+ P91.TIH2,TID2,TRANS,NDG	
Thermal Scat	Cold		BNL	Expt Prog	WASH−1013 9	58	Mcreynolds+ 1ST VIB LVL E GVN.	
Thermal Scat	5.0−2	2.0−1	JAE	Expt Jour	JPJ 19 1862	Oct 64	Sakamoto.TOT−SIG FOR	
Thermal Scat	Cold		BNL	Expt Abst	BAP 10 436	Apr 65	Mozer+TIN,(AG12)POLYXTAL.OK SINGLXTL	
Thermal Scat	1.0−1	6.0−1	RPI	Expt Jour	NSE 23 194	Oct 65	PAN+ TIH2. TOF.CURV.TBL.3 VIB LVLS.	
	1.0−1	7.0−1		Abst	DA/B 29 212	Jul 68	PAN+ TIH2. ANGDIST+TOF ANALYSIS.	
	1.0−1	6.0−1		Conf	67Ann Arbr 1 407	Jul 67	Purohit+ TIH2. SIG−GRPH,CFD OTHR XPT	
	1.5−1			Rept	RPI−328−101	67	Pan+ ROOM TEMP VIBRATNL E+LVL WIDTH	
	1.0−1	1.0+0		Jour	NIM 42 197	Jul 66	PAN+ TIH2. FILTER DIFFERENCE METHOD.	
Thermal Scat	Maxwl		UJV	Theo Jour	UJV−2275	69	Krivy.TIC,DEBYE TEMP,BRAGG+OTHER XPT	
Thermal Scat	Maxwl		TOH	Expt Jour	JPJ 28 1014	Apr 70	Yamaguchi+TIO,SINGLE CRYSTAL N DIFF.	
Thermal Scat	Maxwl		TOH	Expt Prog	EANDC(J)19L 62	Aug 70	Kimura+TIO,TOF POWDER DIFFR. NDG	
				Priv	WATANABE	Dec 69	Watanabe+TIO,TOF,POWDER DIFF.PATTERN	

22 Titanium CMP

Quantity	Energy (ev) Min	Max	Lab	Type	Documentation Ref Vol Page	Date	Author, Comments	Data
Thermal Scat	Maxwl		TOH Expt	Jour	JPJ 31 452	Aug 71	Ishikawa+ FE2TIO4,MAGNET.STRUCT.	
Thermal Scat	Maxwl		THS Theo	Jour	AKE 18 261	Dec 71	Keinert. H-FREQ DIST,N-SP,TI HYBRID	

23 Vanadium CMP

Quantity	Energy (ev) Min	Max	Lab	Type	Documentation Ref Vol Page	Date	Author, Comments	Data
Total	5.7-4	3.3-3	COL Expt	Prog	CU- 174 21	Mar 58	Gould+ HYDRIDE. CHEM BINDING. GRPH.	
Total	7.0-2	7.0-1	KIL Expt	Jour	AKE 17 113	Mar 71	Brand+ VHX,(X=0.6/0.39) H SIG	
				Prog	EANDC(E)127U	Apr 70	- + CRYSTSPEC AT FRGI. VH	
Diff Inelast	2.1-3		MUN Expt	Jour	NWS 56 410	Aug 69	Alefeld+V2O3,HIGH RESOLVD SPIN-FLIP	
Thermal Scat	5.0-2	2.0-1	JAE Expt	Jour	JPJ 19 1862	Oct 64	Sakamoto.TOT-SIG FOR VHO.25,+E VIBR	
Thermal Scat	Cold		BNL Expt	Abst	BAP 10 436	Apr 65	Mozer+ BE4V96 ALLOY. POLY CRYSTAL.	
Thermal Scat	Cold		BNL Expt	Abst	BAP 10 436	Apr 65	Mozer+ V3SI. POLYXTAL.INCOH APPROX.	
Thermal Scat	0.0+0	1.0+0	ISP Expt	Conf	BNL-940 105	Sep 65	Kley.VDX(X=.20),TEMP=50,150DEG C	
	Cold			Jour	PL 14 100	Jan 65	Rubin+VHX,SPEC NS, ROOM T, 150C	
Thermal Scat	Maxwl		AUL Expt	Jour	JAP 39 3501	Jun 68	Vance + V3SI,ROOM T,NO PARAMAGNET SCAT	
Thermal Scat	Maxwl		CCP Expt	Jour	DOK 193 1022	Aug 70	Vintaikin+ VANAD-NITRIDE,STRUCTURE	
				Jour	SPD 15 776	Feb 71	TRANSLATN.*	
Thermal Scat	1.0-7	5.0-6	MUN Expt	Jour	ZP 238 208	Oct 70	Heidemann.V2O3,MAGNSPIN SCAT,N-SPEC	
Thermal Scat	Cold		SBU Theo	Jour	PL/A 35 48	May 71	Dieterich+ V3SI.LINR CHAIN MDL CALC	
Thermal Scat	8.0-2		TOH Expt	Jour	JPJ 41 974	Sep 76	Asano+ .N-DIFF, V2-H, RT-200DC	
Thermal Scat	2.0-3		SAC Expt	Conf	76Ahmedabd 3 331	Dec 76	Madhav Rao+ (V2O3).DIFFSIG(2TEMP)FIG	

24 Chromium CMP

Quantity	Energy (ev) Min	Max	Lab	Type	Documentation Ref Vol Page	Date	Author, Comments	Data
Total	1.6-3		ANL Expt	Jour	PR 75 1098	Apr 49	Krueger+ CR2O3.	
Thermal Scat	Cold		BNL Expt	Jour	JAP 36 1099	Mar 65	Corliss+ CR2O2. MAGN PROPS. N DIFFR.	
Thermal Scat	Cold		KJL Expt	Jour	PL/A 26 160	Jan 68	SAMUELSEN SPIN WAVES BY INEL SCAT	
Thermal Scat	Cold		TRM Expt	Jour	PL/A 26 3 108	Jan 68	RAO+CRBR3,INEL NEUT SCAT PARAMAGN.	
Thermal Scat	Cold		TRM Expt	Jour	PL/A 26 3 108	Jan 68	RAO+CRF3,INEL NEUT SCAT PARAMAGN	
Thermal Scat	Cold		ISS Expt	Jour	JPJ 24 263	Feb 68	Endoh+ MAGNETIC N-DIFF,CR(I-X)NI,CO	
Thermal Scat	-3	+1	TRM Revw	Conf	68Bombay 1 177	Dec 68	Satya Murty+CRBR3,SURVEY,MAGNT SCAT	
Thermal Scat	-3	+1	TRM Revw	Conf	68Bombay 1 177	Dec 68	Satya Murty+CRF3,MAGNETIC SCATTERING	
Thermal Scat	-3		TRM ExTh	Prog	BARC-401 9	69	Sataya+CRF2,EXPT,NEW PARAM-SCAT-MODL	
	-3	+1	Revw	Conf	68Bombay 1 177	Dec 68	Satya Murty+CRF2,MAGNETIC SCAT	
Thermal Scat	Maxwl		TOH Expt	Priv	TOMIYOSHI+	Dec 69	Tomiyoshi+ CR-GE.POWDER DIFFR.TOF.	
Thermal Scat	Maxwl		TOH Expt	Jour	JPJ 33 1303	Nov 72	Ohsawa+CRO.923TE MAG.N.DIF.T EFFECT	
Thermal Scat	Cold		BUC Expt	Prog	INDC(SEC)-35	Sep 73	Todireanu+ P177.CHROMIA,BRIEF,NDG	

25 Manganese CMP

Quantity	Energy (ev) Min	Max	Lab	Type	Documentation Ref Vol Page	Date	Author, Comments	Data
Total	Maxwl		COL Expt	Jour	PR 57 976	Jun 40	Beyer+ TRNS. MNO. CHEM,PHYS EFFECTS.	
Total	Maxwl		COL Expt	Jour	PR 57 976	Jun 40	Beyer+ TRNS. MNSO4. CHEM,PHYS EFFCTS	
Total	Maxwl		COL Expt	Jour	PR 57 976	Jun 40	Beyer+MNO2,INTERFERENCE EFFECT,TRANS	
Total	Maxwl		COL Expt	Jour	PR 57 976	Jun 40	Beyer+ MNS. INTERFERNCE EFFECT TRANS	
Total	Cold		BNL Expt	Rept	BNL-7645	63	Kistner+. MNO. 298DEGC CURVE	
Total	1.4+0		ORL Expt	Jour	NP 61 381	Jan 65	RAYBURN WOLLAN IN RES E 1.44EV 7.8B	
Total	-2	+0	COL Expt	Prog	NYO-GEN72-132	Jan 67	Leung+ VS TEMP TO LIQD HE,CF TH,NDG	
Diff Elastic	Cold		COL Expt	Jour	PR 77 577	Mar 50	Bendt+MN-NI,REL PHASE CHANG.COH SCAT	
Polarization	Maxwl		TRM Expt	Conf	65Calcutta 287	Feb 65	Begum+ MNALGE,SPIN DENSITY MAP TBD	
Thermal Scat		4.0-1	NYU Expt	Jour	PR 54 771	Nov 38	Whitaker+ MNSO4. MAGNETIC SCAT. TBL.	
Thermal Scat		4.0-1	NYU Expt	Jour	PR 54 771	Nov 38	Whitaker+ MNO. MAGNETIC SCAT. TABLE.	
Thermal Scat		4.0-1	NYU Expt	Jour	PR 54 771	Nov 38	Whitaker+MNS,MAGNETIC COMPON.OF SCAT	
Thermal Scat	8.0-2		ORL Expt	Jour	PR 83 333	Jul 51	Shull+ MNO. MAGN DIFF SCT CS. GRPH.	
Thermal Scat	Cold		COL Expt	Jour	PR 89 561	Feb 53	Bendt. MNF2.PARAMAG SCT.3 T. GRPH.	
Thermal Scat	Cold		COL Expt	Jour	PR 89 561	Feb 53	Bendt. MNO2,PARAMAG SCAT. 3T. GRAPH.	
Thermal Scat	Maxwl		CRC Revw	Conf	60Vienna 25	Oct 60	Brockhouse+.MN41CO59 REL TEMPERATUR	
Thermal Scat	None		OSA Theo	Jour	PTP 25 595	Apr 61	Nagai+CALC INELAST SIG BY SPIN WAVE	
Thermal Scat	Cold		BNL Expt	Rept	BNL-7645	63	Kistner+. MNO. MAGNETIC INEL SCAT	
Thermal Scat	5.1-1		TRM Expt	Conf	65Calcutta 287	Feb 65	Begum+ MNALGE-ALLOY,MAGNTC REFLECTN	
Thermal Scat	Cold		BNL Expt	Abst	JAP 36 1095	Mar 65	Will+ MNSO4. MAG PROPS. N DIFFR.	
Thermal Scat	0.0+0	1.0+0	HAR Expt	Jour	JAP 36 1092	Mar 65	Unknown. NAMNF3, PARAMAG SCATT EXPT.	
Thermal Scat	Cold		HAR Expt	Abst	JAP 36 1098	Mar 65	.MNCO3,DIFFR.OF POLARIZED NS	

25 Manganese CMP

Quantity	Energy (ev) Min	Max	Lab	Type	Documentation Ref Vol Page	Date	Author, Comments	Data
Thermal Scat	Cold		MIT Theo	Jour	JAP 36 1090	Mar 65	Dwight+ MNCR2S4. CALC CFD EXPT.	
Thermal Scat	Cold		MIT Theo	Jour	JAP 36 1090	Mar 65	Dwight+ MNCR2O4. CALC CFD EXPT.	
Thermal Scat	None		MIT ExTh	Jour	JAP 36 1088	Mar 65	Menyuk+ MNCR2S4. N DIFFR.	
Thermal Scat	Cold		BNL Expt	Jour	JAP 37 1056	Mar 66	Felcher. MNP. MAG PROPS. N DIFFR.	
Thermal Scat	Cold		HAR Expt	Jour	JAP 37 1053	Mar 66	.MNP,MAGNETIC PROP.FROM N DIFFR XPTS	
Thermal Scat	2.8−3	5.2−3	BNL Expt	Jour	PR 147 457	Jul 66	Friedman+ MNAL2O4. MAGN INL,OKS TH.	
Thermal Scat	2.8−3	5.2−3	BNL Expt	Jour	PR 147 457	Jul 66	Friedman+ MNF2. MAGN INL. OKS TH.	
Thermal Scat	−		CAV ExTh	Jour	PPS 90 657	Mar 67	Peckham.PHONON FREQ DN.SHELL MOD TH	
Thermal Scat	Cold		CRC Expt	Jour	JPJ 23 1426	Dec 67	Sakurai+ 81 PCT MNFE2O4. N DIFFR.	
Thermal Scat	None		ORL Expt	Abst	BAP 13 469	Mar 68	Moon+ MNF2. POL.INCOH SCT CFD TH.	
Thermal Scat	Cold		KTO Expt	Jour	JPJ 25 234	Jul 68	Mekata+MN2N,MAGNETIC N−DIFFRACT.EXPT	
Thermal Scat	Cold		GA Expt	Jour	PR 174 953	Oct 68	Borgonovi+ EXPTL+CALCTD ANG DIST	
Thermal Scat	−3	+0	TRM Revw	Conf	68Bombay 1 177	Dec 68	SATYA MURTY+ MN2O3 MAGNETC SCAT	
Thermal Scat	−3	+0	TRM Revw	Conf	68Bombay 1 177	Dec 68	SATYA MURTY+RB MN F3,MAGNETISM	
Thermal Scat	−3	+0	TRM Revw	Conf	68Bombay 1 177	Dec 68	SATYA MURTY+MNF2, MAGNETISM	
Thermal Scat	−3	+0	TRM Revw	Conf	68Bombay 1 177	Dec 68	SATYA MURTY+ MNO MAGNETIC SCAT	
Thermal Scat	−3	+0	TRM Revw	Conf	68Bombay 1 177	Dec 68	SATYA MURTY+MNSO4,MAGNETIC SCATTNG	
Thermal Scat	−		KJL Expt	Jour	PNV 3 203	69	Andresen+.MN−SE. 150K ANOMALY.ABSTR	
Thermal Scat	−3		TRM ExTh	Prog	BARC−401 9	69	Sataya+ PARAMAG SCAT−MODEL OKS EXPT	
Thermal Scat	3.0−2		IBJ Expt	Rept	INR−1137/II/PS	Nov 69	Fayek+MN3O4,CRYST PARAM+MAGN STRUCT.	
Thermal Scat	−3	−1	CRC Revw	Conf	69Wien 1	Dec 69	Woods+(MN F2) TWO EXPTS REVIEWED	
Thermal Scat	4.5−3	6.3−2	TRM Expt	Conf	69Roorke 3 498	Dec 69	Deniz+ CRITICAL MAGNETIC SCAT,GRPHS	
Thermal Scat	None		TRM Theo	Rept	BARC−557 71	71	Madhav Rao.MNO,NSPEC CFD EXPT,GRPHS	
	−3			Conf	68Bombay 3 148	Dec 68	MADHAV RAO+2DIFF SIG GRPHS CFD XPT	
Thermal Scat	6.0−2		IBJ ExTh	Rept	INR−1269/II/PS	Jan 71	Fayek+ZN.87MN.13FE2O4 MAGN STRUCT	
	3.0−2		Expt	Rept	INR−1137/II/PS	Nov 69	− +ZN−MN ALLOYS.PARAM MAGN+CRYS	
	4.0−4			Rept	INR−1140/II/PS	Nov 69	− +ZN.87 MN.13 FE2O4 MAGN STRUC	
Thermal Scat	−3		TRM Expt	Conf	72Bombay 3 517	Feb 72	Rakhecha+ MNFE3O4,MAGNET SCAT,GRAPH	
Thermal Scat	None		BUC Expt	Prog	INDC(SEC)−28	Sep 72	.SAME AS INDC(RUM)−3 15	
Thermal Scat	2.0−3	3.0−1	KFI Expt	Rept	KFKI−73−4	Apr 73	Kroo+ INCOH MAGNET SCAT AT T=80,300K	
Thermal Scat	Maxwl	2.5−2	TOH ExTh	Jour	JPJ 36 112	Jan 74	Kohgi+.SPIN WAVE,MNO, BY NEUT SCATT	
Thermal Scat	Maxwl	2.5−2	KTO Expt	Jour	JPJ 36 438	Feb 74	Yamaoka+.MAG STRUCTR,GAM PHASE,MN−IR	
Thermal Scat	Maxwl		TOH Expt	Jour	JPJ 37 1242	Nov 74	Tsuzuki+.N−DIFF,PARAMAG,TOF,MNGEO3	
Thermal Scat	1.3−2	6.0−2	JAE Expt	Jour	JPJ 41 811	Sep 76	Funahashi+.MAG INEL, MAGNON,MN−CR−SB	
Scattering	−		CCP Theo	Jour	UFN 76 239	Feb 62	Zhdanov+.CURVE,MAGNETIC SCATTERING	
				Jour	SPU 5 104	Jul 62	. ENGL OF UFN 76 239	
Scattering	−1		CCP Expt	Jour	DOK 170 1300	Sep 66	Sirota+.MANGANTELLURID AT LOW TEMPS	
				Jour	SPD 11 888	67	. ENGL OF DOK 170 1300	
Scattering	2.8−3		HAR Expt	Jour	PPS 1C 333	Apr 67	Martin.EFFECT IRRADN DEFECTS,CFD TH	
Absorption	Maxwl		AUS Expt	Jour	OAWS 158 123	Nov 49	Lintner.MNO2,RN−BE SOURCE SPHER.DEV.	

26 Iron CMP

Quantity	Energy (ev) Min	Max	Lab	Type	Documentation Ref Vol Page	Date	Author, Comments	Data
Total	Cold		NYU Expt	Jour	PR 55 1101	Jun 39	Whitaker+SIGS FOR SINGLE+POLY−CRYST	
Total	Maxwl		COL Expt	Jour	PR 57 976	Jun 40	Beyer+INTERFERENCE. POLY−,MONOCRYST	
Total	Maxwl		COL Expt	Jour	PR 57 976	Jun 40	Beyer+FE2O3,INTERFER EFFECT TRANSM.	
Total	2.4−3		KFI Expt	Conf	61Wien 3 205	Oct 61	Szabo+FE−AL,6.3+16.6PC AL,CRV SIG(T)	
Total	1.4+0		ORL Expt	Jour	NP 61 381	Jan 65	Rayburn.FE2O3,IN RES 1.44EV 36.5B	
Total	2.4+4		RPI Expt	Prog	USNDC−1 178	May 72	Block.STEEL,TYPE C1018.TRANS.CURVE	
Diff Elastic	6.0−1		OSA Theo	Jour	JPJ 18 74	Jan 63	Nagai.FECL2,CFD EXP (PR 113 497)	
Polarization	None		KIL Expt	Conf	67Juelich 223	Apr 67	Birkner+FENI3,POL BEAM,DEPOL VS 1/H	
				Conf	67Juelich 223	Apr 67	− +FERIT,POL BEAM,DEPOL VS 1/H	
Polarization	−3	−1	TRM Expt	Prog	BARC−401 9	69	Sataya+ (ZN−NI,MG−MN,ZN−CO) FE2 O4	
Polarization	−3	−2	TRM Expt	Conf	69Roorke 3 518	Dec 69	Begum+ SPINEL−FERRITES,MAGNTC STRUC	
Polarization	−3	−1	FTI Theo	Jour	ZET 58 199	Jan 70	Maleev+ FERROMAGNETS, DEPOLARIZATN	
				Jour	JET 31 111	Jul 70	TRANSLATN.*	
Thermal Scat		4.0−1	NYU Expt	Jour	PR 54 771	Nov 38	Whitaker+FE2O3 MAGNT COMPON.OF SCAT	
Thermal Scat	8.0−2		ORL Expt	Jour	PR 83 333	Jul 51	Shull+ FEO. MAGN DIFF SCT CS. GRAPH.	
Thermal Scat	Cold		CCP Theo	Jour	ZET 33 1010	Oct 57	Maleev.FERROMAGNETICS,SPIN WAVE TH	
				Jour	JEL 12 243	Oct 70	*ENGL OF ZET 33 1010	
Thermal Scat	Maxwl		KRK Revw	Jour	PF 11 257	May 60	Wanic+ CRITIC TEMP IN MAGNETICS,SCAT	
				Jour	PF 9 429	Jul 58	Janik+ INVEST OF MAGNETIC SUBSTANCE	
Thermal Scat	Cold		LRL Expt	Jour	JAP 31 356	May 60	Sparks+ JAP SUPPL.FE−S POLYXTL DIFFR	
Thermal Scat	Maxwl		WWATheo	Jour	APP 19 691	Nov 60	Kocinski. FERRIMAGN, EL+INEL SCATT	
Thermal Scat	2.4−3		KFI Expt	Conf	61Wien 3 205	Oct 61	Szabo+FE−AL,6.3+16.6PC AL,CRV SIG(T)	
Thermal Scat	−2		TRM Expt	Conf	62Madras 363	Feb 62	Iyengar. FEGE2,FESN2.NDG,TBP IN JPJ	

26 Iron CMP

Quantity	Energy (ev) Min	Max	Lab	Type	Documentation Ref Vol Page	Date	Author, Comments	Data
Thermal Scat	Cold		BNL Expt	Rept	BNL – 7645	63	Kistner+. MNZNFE2O4. MAGN INEC SCAT	
Thermal Scat	4.3 – 2		IFJ Expt	Rept	INP – 280	Oct 63	Krasnicki+ PYRRHOTITE,MAGNON SCAT	
				Rept	INP – 279	Sep 63	Wanic.PYRRHOTITE(FE7S8),MAGNON SCAT	
Thermal Scat	– 3		ITE Expt	Rept	ITE – 355	65	Alichanov.ALFA – FE2O3,3 – AXIS – SPECTR	
Thermal Scat	Cold		BNL Expt	Abst	JAP 36 1093	Mar 65	Arrot. FEMN. N DIFFR. XTL MAG PROPS.	
Thermal Scat	Cold		JAP Expt	Jour	JAP 36 1094	Mar 65	Katsuragi+.FE2AS PROPS XTL.N DIFF	
Thermal Scat	– 1		WWAExTh	Rept	INR – 665/II/PS	Nov 65	. FE3W3C,FE6W6C.CFD X – RAY RESULTS	
Thermal Scat	– 3		POL ExTh	Jour	APP 30 125	Jul 66	Oles.GA2O3FEO – FE2O3FEO,MAGN.STRUCT.	
Thermal Scat	8.0 – 2		JAE Expt	Jour	JPJ 21 1932	Oct 66	Watanabe+ FE – GE ALLOY,POLYCRYS DIFF	
Thermal Scat	Maxwl		CCP Theo	Jour	ZET 51 1423	Nov 66	Izyumov+ FERROMAGNETS,MAGNON – SPEC	
				Jour	JET 24 960	May 67	TRANSLATN.*	
Thermal Scat	8.2 – 2		BNL Expt	Jour	PR 154 508	Feb 67	Alperin+ FE3O4. POL N MAGNON SCT.	
Thermal Scat	Cold		JAP Expt	Jour	JPJ 22 674	Feb 67	Yoshii+FEMNAS,MAGNETIC DIFFRACTION	
Thermal Scat	Maxwl		IFU Theo	Jour	ZET 52 787	Mar 67	Akhiezer+ FLUCTUATN IN FERROMAGNETS	
				Jour	JET 25 517	Sep 67	TRANSLATN.*	
Thermal Scat	Cold		KYU Expt	Jour	JPJ 22 924	Mar 67	Kawaminami+.MAGNETIC N DIFFR,FE7SE8	
Thermal Scat	7.0 – 2		NRL Expt	Jour	PR 156 632	Apr 67	Saenz+ MAGNETITE MAGNON SPEC PARAMS	
Thermal Scat	Cold		TOH Expt	Jour	JPJ 22 1210	May 67	Yamaguchi+FESN,MAGNETIC N DIFFR	
Thermal Scat	None		ORL Theo	Rept	ORNL – P – 3349	Jun 67	Thompson. FERROMAGNETICS TBP PR	
Thermal Scat	Cold		ISS Expt	Jour	JPJ 23 205	Aug 67	Ishikawa+.MAGNETIC STRUCT BY N – DIFF	
Thermal Scat	6.5 – 2		KRK Expt	Rept	INP – 578	Sep 67	Szytula+.GOETHITE,STRUCTURE,SPINS	
Thermal Scat	Cold		BNL Expt	Jour	JAP 39 455	Feb 68	Menzinger+ FE – NI ALLOYS.SPIN DISPERS	
Thermal Scat	Cold		KFI Expt	Jour	JAP 39 453	Feb 68	Kroo+ TOF,DILUTE ALLOY,INELAS SCATT	
Thermal Scat	Maxwl		MOS Theo	Jour	ZET 54 571	Feb 68	Pushkarov+ DISLOCATN IN FERROMAGNET	
				Jour	JET 27 307	Aug 68	TRANSLATN.*	
Thermal Scat	7.0 – 2		KJL Expt	Conf	68Copenhgn 2 395	May 68	Steinsvoll+.FE – SI.POLR CHOP.TOF SP.	
Thermal Scat	Maxwl		AUL Expt	Jour	JPJ 25 367	Aug 68	Vance+FEMN,PARAMAGNETIC NEUT.SCATT.	
Thermal Scat	– 2		IFU Theo	Jour	UFZ 13 1682	Oct 68	Dzyub. MAGN SCAT EXPT OKS TH,TBL	
				Jour	UPJ 13 1196	Apr 69	TRANSLATN.*	
Thermal Scat	– 3	+0	TRM Expt	Conf	68Bombay 3 173	Dec 68	Youssef+ NIFE2O4,MAGNET – SCAT,SPINEL	
Thermal Scat	– 3	+0	TRM Expt	Conf	68Bombay 3 178	Dec 68	Youssef+ COFE2O4,MAGNET – SCAT,SPINEL	
Thermal Scat	– 3	+1	TRM Revw	Conf	68Bombay 1 177	Dec 68	Satya Murty+FE3O4,MAGNETIC SCAT	
Thermal Scat	– 3	– 1	TRM Expt	Prog	BARC – 401 9	69	Sataya+ (ZN – NI,MG – MN,ZN – CO) FE2 O4	
Thermal Scat	– 3		TRM ExTh	Prog	BARC – 401 9	69	Sataya+FEF2,EXPT,NEW PARAM – SCAT – MODL	
	– 3	+0		Revw Conf	68Bombay 1 177	Dec 68	Satya Murty+ FEF2,MAGNETIC SCATTRNG	
Thermal Scat	Cold		BNL Theo	Jour	PR 180 613	Apr 69	Sokoloff.LOW TEMP FERROMAGNETICS	
Thermal Scat	– 2		CCP Expt	Jour	ZET 56 1217	Apr 69	Aleshko+ BA – SC(X) – FE(12 – X) – O(19)	
				Jour	JET 29 655	Oct 69	TRANSLATN.*	
Thermal Scat	Maxwl		KTO Expt	Jour	JPJ 27 1470	Dec 69	Nakamura+ N – DIFF.FE65(NI – MN)35,135DK	
Thermal Scat	5.4 – 2		TRM Expt	Conf	69Roorke 3 513	Dec 69	Murthy+ FE – MN – GE, MAGNETIC STRUCTUR	
Thermal Scat	– 3	– 2	TRM Expt	Conf	69Roorke 3 522	Dec 69	RAO+ TL – MN – F3,ZN – FE2 – O4,MAGNETC STR	
				Conf	69Roorke 3 530	Dec 69	.SEE ALSO *PARAM – SCAT	
Thermal Scat	– 3	– 2	TRM Expt	Conf	69Roorke 3 526	Dec 69	Murthy+ ZN – FE2 – O4,MN – AL2 – O4,EXCH – IN	
Thermal Scat	– 3	– 1	FTI Theo	Jour	ZET 58 199	Jan 70	Maleev+ FERROMAGNETS, SPIN WAVES	
				Jour	JET 31 111	Jul 70	TRANSLATN.*	
Thermal Scat	7.0 – 3		IFJ Expt	Rept	INP – 695/PS	Feb 70	Szytula+ MAGN STRUCT BETA – FEOOH	
Thermal Scat	4.0 – 4	7.0 – 3	IFJ Expt	Rept	INP – 696/PS	Feb 70	Oees+,POLYCRYST GAMMA – F5OOH,NEELTEM	
Thermal Scat	– 3		SAC Expt	Rept	IAEA 124 231	Feb 70	Hennion+ FE3O4,EXCHANGE INTEGR,GRPH	
Thermal Scat	5.4 – 2		TOK Expt	Rept	JAERI – 1197 36	Aug 70	Ishikawa+,FEMN,MAGNETIC CRITIC SCATT	
Thermal Scat		6.5 – 2	CCP Expt	Jour	ZEP 12 356	Oct 70	Arkhipov+ 8ALLOYS,MAGN.DIFFUSE SCAT	
				Jour	JEL 12 243	Oct 70	TRANSLATN.*	
Thermal Scat	5.4 – 3	8.0 – 3	BUC Expt	Prog	INDC(RUM) – 2G	71	Rapeanu+FE – MO,MO – IMPURITY,CRIT.SCAT	
Thermal Scat	5.4 – 3	8.0 – 3	BUC Expt	Prog	INDC(RUM) – 2G	71	Rapeanu+FE – CR,CR – IMPURITY,CRIT.SCAT	
Thermal Scat	6.0 – 2		IBJ Expt	Rept	INR – 1282/II/PS	Apr 71	Ligenza.FESN,MAGN STRUCT,SPIN FLIP	
				ExTh Rept	INR – 1290/II/PS	Mar 71	– .FESN,MAGN STRUCT,SPIN FLIP	
Thermal Scat	Maxwl		TOH Expt	Jour	JPJ 31 452	Aug 71	Ishikawa+.FE2TIO4	
Thermal Scat	6.4 – 2		CCP Expt	Jour	ZET 61 1501	Oct 71	Arkhipov+ FE – NI ALLOY,MAGNETIC SCAT	
				Jour	JET 34 799	Apr 72	*ENG OF ZET 61 1501	
Thermal Scat	–		UFT Theo	Jour	PL/A 37 63	Oct 71	Akhiezer+ SCAT AT TRANSITION POINTS	
Thermal Scat	8.1 – 2		OSA Expt	Jour	PL/A 37 333	Dec 71	Kunitomi+FE – RH,SCATT AT TRANSITN.PT	
Thermal Scat	– 3		TRM Expt	Conf	72Bombay 3 517	Feb 72	Rakhecha+ FE3O4,MNFE3O4,MAGNET SCAT	
Thermal Scat	Maxwl		TIT Expt	Jour	JPJ 33 1296	Nov 72	Abe+.FE2MOO4 MAG.N.DIF 420,90DEGK	
Thermal Scat	Maxwl		TOH Expt	Jour	JPJ 33 1292	Nov 72	Yamaguchi+FE1.22SB MAG.N.DIF 99DEGK	
Thermal Scat	Maxwl		TRM Expt	Conf	72Chandigr 3 577	Dec 72	Srinivasan+FE3O4 MAGNETC FORM FACTOR	
Thermal Scat	Maxwl	2.5 – 2	TOH Expt	Jour	JPJ 34 58	Jan 73	Yashiro+ FE – SB. MAGNETIC NEUT DIFFR	
Thermal Scat	Maxwl	2.5 – 2	JAP Expt	Jour	JPJ 35 426	Aug 73	Adachi+.N DIFFRACTION (CO.MN).FE	
Thermal Scat	Maxwl		HIR Expt	Jour	JPJ 35 706	Sep 73	Komura+FE.65NI.35 MAG.N – DIFFUSE SCAT	
Thermal Scat	Maxwl		HIR Expt	Jour	JPJ 35 1554	Nov 73	Kadomatsu+FE(PD.53PT.47)3 MAG.N – DIFF	

26 Iron CMP

Quantity	Energy (ev) Min	Max	Lab	Type	Documentation Ref Vol Page	Author, Comments Date	Data
Thermal Scat	Maxwl		TOH Expt	Jour	JPJ 35 1616	Dec 73 Ishikawa+.CRITICAL MAG.SCATT.FE5MN5	
Thermal Scat	1.3−2	5.3−2	TOH Expt	Jour	JPJ 39 675	Sep 75 Ishikawa+.FE−NI−CR ALLOY MAGN.SCATT.	
Thermal Scat	1.3−2	5.2−2	TOK Expt	Jour	JPJ 39 949	Oct 75 Shirane+.MAG SCAT,105K,MAGNETITE	
Thermal Scat	Maxwl	2.5−2	TOH Expt	Jour	JPJ 41 1195	Oct 76 Tajima+.MAG INEL, MAGNON,GAMMA−FE−MN	
(n,γ)	2.5−2		ORL Revw	Rept	ORNL−TM−3957	Oct 72 Maerker.STAINLESS STEEL 1.0−10MEV G	
Nonelastic γ	Fast		ORL Expt	Rept	ORNL−TM−3974	Oct 72 Maerker.STAINLESS STEEL 90DEG SIG	

27 Cobalt CMP

Quantity	Energy (ev) Min	Max	Lab	Type	Documentation Ref Vol Page	Author, Comments Date	Data
Total	Maxwl		COL Expt	Prog	WASH−1068 42	Mar 66 Leung+,COSO4−7H2O,NDG	
Polarization	Maxwl		UJV Expt	Jour	CZJA 19 267	May 69 Michalec+ CO−FE(8PC)ALLOY,MAGN SCAT	
Thermal Scat	8.0−2		ORL Expt	Jour	PR 83 333	Jul 51 Shull+ CO−O. MAGN DIFF SCT CS.	
Thermal Scat	Cold		CRC Expt	Jour	JAP 39 1116	Feb 68 Martel+COF2,CRYST SP,NEUT DIST VS T	
Thermal Scat	Maxwl		UJV Expt	Jour	CZJA 19 267	May 69 Michalec+ CO−FE(8PC)ALLOY,MAGN SCAT	
Thermal Scat	7.5−2		UJV Expt	Jour	CZJB 19 1608	Dec 69 Chalupa+ DIFFRACTN−INFL ON GAM−INT	
Thermal Scat	5.0−3	1.0−1	IFJ Expt	Jour	APPA 38 467	70 Ijanik+IBR INEL N SCT ON CO(NH3)6.I2	
Thermal Scat	−3		TRM Expt	Conf	70Madurai 3 689	Oct 70 Murthy+CO−FE,MAGNTC SCATTRNG AT300K	
	−3	+0		Revw Conf	68Bombay 1 177	Dec 68 Satya Murty+ CO.92FE.08,MAGNET9SM	
Thermal Scat	−3		TRM Expt	Conf	70Madurai 3 689	Oct 70 Murthy+CO−MN,MAGNTC SCATTRNG AT300K	
Thermal Scat	−3		TRM Expt	Conf	70Madurai 3 693	Dec 70 Begum+MAGNTC SCAT,300K90K4K,CO2TIO4	
Thermal Scat	Maxwl		TRM Expt	Conf	72Chandigr 3 583	Dec 72 Paranjpe+CO.9FE MAGNETC FORM FACTOR	
Spect (n,γ)	7.5−2		UJV Expt	Jour	CZJB 19 1608	Dec 69 Chalupa+ DIFFRACTN−INFL ON GAM−INT	

28 Nickel CMP

Quantity	Energy (ev) Min	Max	Lab	Type	Documentation Ref Vol Page	Author, Comments Date	Data
Total	Maxwl		COL Expt	Jour	PR 57 976	Jun 40 Beyer+ NIO. TRNS. CHEM,PHYS EFFECTS.	
Total	−2	+0	COL Expt	Jour	PR 83 746	Aug 51 Tittman+NI2B,RATIO SCATT/TOT TRANSM.	
Total	6.9−3	1.1−1	ORL Expt	Jour	PR 96 1297	Dec 54 Allen+ NIO. TRNS. GRPH CFD CALC.	
	2.5−2			Rept	TID−14868	Jun 53 −. THESIS. SEE ALSO	
Diff Elastic	Cold		JUL Expt	Rept	JUEL−1162	Feb 75 Stockmeyer. H+D CHEMISORBED ON NI	
Thermal Scat	8.0−2		ORL Expt	Jour	PR 83 333	Jul 51 Shull+ NIO. MAGN DIFF SCT CS. GRAPH.	
Thermal Scat	0.0+0	1.0+0	GES Expt	Jour	JAP 31 2000	Jun 60 Roth. NIO. N DIFFR.DOMAIN STUDY.	
Thermal Scat	−3	−2	CCP Expt	Jour	ZET 52 665	Mar 67 Zemlyanov+NI−BE,NI CFD.6PC BE−ALLOY	
				Jour	JET 25 436	Sep 67 TRANSLATN.*	
Thermal Scat	5.0−3	1.0−1	IFJ Expt	Jour	APPA 38 467	70 Ijanik+IBR INEL N SCT ON NI(NH3)6.I2	
Thermal Scat	4.0−4	3.0−2	IFJ Expt	Rept	NP−723L	Aug 70 Szytula+,NI(OH)2 POLYCRYST.MAGN STR	
Thermal Scat	6.4−2		CCP Expt	Jour	ZET 61 1501	Oct 71 Arkhipov+ FE−NI ALLOY,MAGNETIC SCAT	
				Jour	JET 34 799	Apr 72 *ENG OF ZET 61 1501	
Thermal Scat	Maxwl	2.5−2	TOK Expt	Jour	JPJ 36 431	Feb 74 ITO+.MAG FORM FACTOR IN NI.95−CR.05	
Thermal Scat	2.0−2		JAE Expt	Jour	JPJ 37 983	Oct 74 Betsuyaku+.N−DIFFRACTION, NI.9CU.1S2	
Thermal Scat	8.0−2		TOK Expt	Jour	JPJ 38 115	Jan 75 Miyadai+.MAG.N−DIFF, NIS2 PYRITE STR	
Thermal Scat	−3		TRM Expt	Conf	76Ahmedabd 3 343	Dec 76 Chakravarthy+ NI−RU COMP.POLARIZD NS	

29 Copper CMP

Quantity	Energy (ev) Min	Max	Lab	Type	Documentation Ref Vol Page	Author, Comments Date	Data
Total	Maxwl		COL Expt	Jour	PR 57 976	Jun 40 Beyer+CU2O,INTERFER.EFFECT.TRANSM.	
Total	Maxwl		COL Expt	Jour	PR 57 976	Jun 40 Beyer+CU2S,INTERFER.EFFECT.TRANSM.	
Total	Maxwl		COL Expt	Jour	PR 57 976	Jun 40 Beyer+CUO,INTERFER.EFFECT.TRANSM.	
Total	Maxwl		COL Expt	Jour	PR 57 976	Jun 40 Beyer+CUS,INTERFER.EFFECT.TRANSM.	
Total	2.4−3		KFI Expt	Conf	61Wien 3 205	Oct 61 Szabo+. BETA−BRASS,SIG(TEMP)−GRPH	
Total	Maxwl		COL Expt	Prog	WASH−1068 42	Mar 66 Leung+,CUSO4−5H2O,NDG	
Total	5.0−6	1.1−5	MUN Expt	Conf	JINR−D3−7991	Apr 74 Steyerl+ P42.OXI,PERP−TRANS,CRV+GRPH	
Diff Elastic	Cold		COL Expt	Jour	PR 77 577	Mar 50 Bendt+CU−NI,PHASE CHANGE COH SCAT	
Thermal Scat	2.4−3		KFI Expt	Conf	61Wien 3 205	Oct 61 Szabo+. BETA−BRASS,SIG(TEMP)−GRPH	
Thermal Scat	Cold		BNL Expt	Abst	JAP 36 1093	Mar 65 Arrot. CU−MN. N DIFFR. XTL MAG PRODS	
Thermal Scat	None		OXF Theo	Jour	PPS 91 903	Aug 67 Elliott+CU2O,GROUP THEOR SELECT.RULE	
Thermal Scat	Maxwl		TOK Expt	Jour	JPJ 33 1483	Nov 72 Hirakawa+K2CUF4 MAG.N.SCAT T EFFECT	
Thermal Scat	Cold		JUL Expt	Jour	PL/A 53 305	Jun 75 Loewenhaupt+SPIN RELAXATION IN CUFE	
Thermal Scat	1.3−2	4.1−2	TOK Expt	Jour	JPJ 41 965	Sep 76 Hoshino+.PHONON DISPERSION, CU.BR	
Thermal Scat	8.0−2		TOK Expt	Jour	JPJ 41 1707	Nov 76 Harada+.ANHARMONIC EFFECT,CU−BR	

30 Zinc CMP

Quantity	Energy (ev) Min	Max	Lab	Type	Documentation Ref Vol Page	Author, Comments Date	Data
Total	Maxwl		COL Expt	Jour	PR 57 976	Jun 40 Beyer+ ZNO. TRNS. INTERFERENCE EFFCT	
Total	Maxwl		COL Expt	Jour	PR 57 976	Jun 40 Beyer+ZNS,INTERFERENCE EFFECT TRANSM	
Total	1.6−3		ANL Expt	Jour	PR 75 1098	Apr 49 Krueger+ MULTISCAT EFFECTS ZNO POWDR	
Total	Maxwl		COL Expt	Prog	WASH−1068 42	Mar 66 Leung+,ZNSO4−7H2O,NDG	
Diff Inelast	4.2−3		MOL Expt	Prog	EANDC(E)127	Apr 70 Hautecler+, BR2 TOF SPECTROMETER	
Thermal Scat	−2		WWA Expt	Jour	NKA 9 523	Jul 64 Buras.DIFFRACTN−PATTERN BY TOF,GRPH	
Thermal Scat	Cold		TRM Expt	Conf	68Madras 2 355	Feb 68 Natera+ ZN−NI−FERRITES,ANGDIST,GRPH	
Thermal Scat	Cold		JUL Expt	Rept	JUEL−673−FF	Jul 70 Wegener.TOF INEL SCAT, PHONONS EXPT	
Thermal Scat	−3		TRM Expt	Conf	70Madurai 3 697	Dec 70 Begum+ MAGNTC EXCH INTGRL,ZNCR2O4	

34 Selenium CMP

Quantity	Energy (ev) Min	Max	Lab	Type	Documentation Ref Vol Page	Author, Comments Date	Data
Thermal Scat	Maxwl		KYU Expt	Jour	JPJ 29 649	Sep 70 Kawaminami+FE7SE8,MAGN NEUT DIFFR	
Thermal Scat	−		SAC Expt	Jour	PL/A 36 376	Sep 71 Hennion+ZN−SE,PHONON DISPERSN CURVS	
Thermal Scat	Maxwl		TOK Expt	Jour	JPJ 32 1670	Jun 72 Sato.NEUTRON DIFFR CS.H3.(SE.O3)2	

35 Bromine CMP

Quantity	Energy (ev) Min	Max	Lab	Type	Documentation Ref Vol Page	Author, Comments Date	Data
Total	1.5+4	6.0+5	DKE Expt	Jour	AP 84 165	May 74 Pineo+RBBR.TRNS.AVG CS.TBL.OPTMDL.	+
	1.0+5	6.5+5		Abst	DA/B 31 6821	May 71 −.2 EN RANGES.AVG CS CFD OPTMDL.	
	1.5+4	6.0+5		Diss	PINEO	70 .RBBR.AVG CS.GRPHS.STF CALC.TBL.CFD	
	1.5+4	6.0+5		Data	EXFOR10542.011	Jan 79 . DATA UNOBTAINABLE FROM AUTHORS.	
Potntal Scat	3.0+3	6.5+5	DKE Expt	Jour	AP 84 165	May 74 Pineo+RBBR.S WAVE SCT LENGTH.TBL.CFD	
				Abst	DA/B 31 6821	May 71 .THESIS ABST.	
				Diss	PINEO	70 .TBL.GRPHS.CFD TO 3 COLLECTIVE MDLS.	
				Diss	PINEO	70 .RBBR.SCT LENGTH CURV,TBL.CFD	
Thermal Scat	5.0−3		BNL Expt	Abst	BAP 7 500	Aug 62 Boutin+ HBR. 90 DEG.SOLID,LIQ SPEC.	
Thermal Scat	3.0−1	6.0−3	HLT Expt	Conf	68Copenhgn 2 237	May 68 Tunkelo+RUBBER,NOMAL+STRETCHD.CRYST	
Strnth Fnctn	3.0+3	6.5+5	DKE Expt	Abst	DA/B 31 6821	May 71 Pineo.S,P,D WAVE.THESIS ABST.RBBR	
				Diss	PINEO	70 .RBBR TBLS,GRPHS.CFD CALC.EXPTS.	

37 Rubidium CMP

Quantity	Energy (ev) Min	Max	Lab	Type	Documentation Ref Vol Page	Author, Comments Date	Data
Total	1.5+4	6.0+5	DKE Expt	Jour	AP 84 165	May 74 Pineo+RBBR.TRANS AVG CS.TBL.OPTMDL	+
	1.0+5	6.5+5		Abst	DA/B 31 6821	May 71 −.2 EN RANGES.AVG CS CFD OPTMDL.	
	1.5+4	6.0+5		Diss	PINEO	70 .RBBR.AVG CS.GRPHS.STF CALC.TBL.CFD	
	1.5+4	6.0+5		Data	EXFOR10542.011	Jan 79 . DATA UNOBTAINABLE FROM AUTHORS.	
Potntal Scat	3.0+3	6.5+5	DKE Expt	Jour	AP 84 165	May 74 Pineo+RBBR.S WAVE SCT LENGTH.TBL.CFD	
				Abst	DA/B 31 6821	May 71 .THESIS ABST.	
				Diss	PINEO	70 .RBBR.SCT LENGTH CURV,TBL.CFD	
				Diss	PINEO	70 .TBL.GRPHS.CFD TO 3 COLLECTIVE MDLS.	
Thermal Scat	−3	−2	ISL Expt	Prog	IA−1218 51	Aug 70 Pelah+RB H2 PO4,TOF SPECTRUM,NDG	
Strnth Fnctn	3.0+3	6.5+5	DKE Expt	Abst	DA/B 31 6821	May 71 Pineo.S,P,D WAVE.THESIS ABST.RBBR	
				Diss	PINEO	70 .RBBR TBLS,GRPHS.CFD CALC.EXPTS.	

38 Strontium CMP

Quantity	Energy (ev) Min	Max	Lab	Type	Documentation Ref Vol Page	Author, Comments Date	Data
Diff Elastic	1.5+7		ALB Expt	Prog	A−ALB−75 27	Jun 75 Benenson+TOF.3 ANGS.NDG.TBC	
Diff Inelast	1.5+7		ALB Expt	Prog	A−ALB−75 27	Jun 75 Benenson+3 ANGS.2.73 MEV LVL.	
Thermal Scat	Cold		TIT Expt	Jour	JPJ 24 219	Jan 68 Nakayama+. SR(FEMO)O6 MAG N−DIFFRAC	
Thermal Scat	Maxwl		BNL Expt	Jour	JPJ 26 396	Feb 69 Yamada+SRTIO,OPTICAL PHONON,4.5−300K	
Thermal Scat	−3	+0	TRM Expt	Prog	BARC−474 14	70 Iyengar+SRFX,ACOUSTIC+OPTIC DISPERSN	
Thermal Scat	Cold		WPI Expt	Jour	JCP 52 3952	Apr 70 Maeland+SRH2 TOF DISTRIBT INEL SCAT	
Thermal Scat	−		AML Expt	Jour	PL/A 35 286	Jun 71 Mair+SRF2,STRUCT FACTORS 22TO770DEG	
Thermal Scat	Cold		JUL Expt	Jour	PL/A 51 297	Mar 75 Topler+STUDY OF SRTIO3 BY SCAT	

39 Yttrium CMP

Quantity	Energy (ev) Min	Max	Lab	Type	Documentation Ref Vol Page	Author, Comments Date	Data
Total	7.5-2	5.0-1	GA	Expt Jour	PR 113 806	Feb 59 Whittemore+ YH CS. ARBITRARY SCALE.	
Total	1.0-1	7.0-1	KIL	Expt Jour	AKE 17 113	Mar 71 Brand.YHX (X=1.88)HYDROGEN SIGMA	
Total	-3	1.0+1	IKE	Theo Rept	IKE-6-61/1	Jan 73 Keinert.DATA LIBRARY, Y-HYDRID	
Diff Elastic	-3	1.0+1	IKE	Theo Rept	IKE-6-61/1	Jan 73 Keinert.DATA LIBRARY, Y-HYDRID	
Diff Inelast	1.8-1		THS	Theo Jour	AKE 18 261	Dec 71 Keinert. SIG VS E,3 ANGS.Y HYDRIDE	
Thermal Scat	None		BNL	Expt Prog	WASH-1013 10	Nov 65 Mcreynolds+ YH. 1ST VIB LVL GIVEN.	
Thermal Scat	2.5-2		ANL	ExTh Jour	JCP 35 1950	Oct 61 Atoji. YCL2. TBL.	
Thermal Scat	7.0-2	5.0-1	IFJ	Revw Jour	INP-255	Apr 63 Janik+ HYDRIDE,CFD FERMI-THEO,GRAPH	
Thermal Scat	Cold		ORL	Revw Jour	JAP 36 1078	Mar 65 Koehler+ ALLOY MAG PROPS. N DIFFR.	
Thermal Scat	1.8-1	1.9-1	GA	ExTh Prog	GA-6583	Dec 65 Whittemore.YH2,NEUT VEL SELTR AT 2ES	
Thermal Scat	1.8-1	1.9-1	GA	Expt Prog	GA-6583	Dec 65 Whittemore.YHX,(X=1.87,2.50)CRV	
Thermal Scat	Cold		NRL	Expt Jour	JAP 37 1050	Mar 66 Ferguson+ MAGN PROPS. N DIFFR.	
Thermal Scat		5.0-3	ANL	Expt Jour	JCP 45 3817	Nov 66 Rush+ YH2,YD2,YH3,YD3 VIB SPECT CFD.	
Thermal Scat	7.0-2		NRL	Expt Jour	PR 156 632	Apr 67 Saenz+ Y-FE GARNET MAGNON SPECTRA	
Thermal Scat	-		ISL	Expt Prog	IA-1218 55	Aug 70 Pinto+(Y FE O3)SUBLATTICE-MAGNETZTN	
Thermal Scat	Maxwl		THS	Theo Jour	AKE 18 261	Dec 71 Keinert.YHX,X=1.75,H-FREQ DIST,N-SPC	
Thermal Scat	-3	1.9+0	IKE	Theo Rept	IKE-6 89 31	Jun 75 Keinert. DATA LIBRARY Y-HYDRIDE	
Scattering	5.0-2	4.5-1	BER	Expt Jour	AKE 14 370	Oct 69 Vorderwisch+ YH2.8,1.9.TOT,NP,SCT	
Scattering	-3	1.0+1	IKE	Theo Rept	IKE-6-61/1	Jan 73 Keinert.DATA LIBRARY, Y-HYDRID	
(n,p)	Maxwl		THS	Theo Jour	AKE 18 261	Dec 71 Keinert.YHX,TOT SIG,CFD EXPT	

40 Zirconium CMP

Quantity	Energy (ev) Min	Max	Lab	Type	Documentation Ref Vol Page	Author, Comments Date	Data
Thermal Scat	Maxwl		UJV	Theo Rept	UJV-2275	69 Krivy.ZRC,DEBYE T,BRAGG+OTHER EXPTS	

40 Zirconium HYD

Quantity	Energy (ev) Min	Max	Lab	Type	Documentation Ref Vol Page	Author, Comments Date	Data
Total	6.2-4	5.2-3	COL	Expt Rept	CU-179	Oct 58 Gould.CS CURV BINDING OF H DEDUCED	
	5.7-4	3.3-3		Prog	CU-174 21	Mar 58 - + CHEM BINDING. GRAPH.	
Total	5.0-2	5.5-1	GA	Expt Jour	PR 113 806	Feb 59 Whittemore+ H CS IN ZRH. CURVE.	
Total	Pile		SAC	Expt Prog	EANDC(E)23L	Feb 62 Genin.CRYST SPECT TBP IN JPR	
	5.0-2	5.0-1		Jour	JPR 22 648	Oct 61 - +DATA COMPARED WITH THEORY	
Total	1.0-3	5.5-1	GA	ExTh Rept	GA-4490	Jan 64 Whittemore+ TOF. OLD+NEW. CFD TH.	
Total	2.5-2	2.3-1	KIL	Expt Prog	EANDC(E)66U	Feb 66 Broecker+ TBC XTL SPECTROM	
Total		7.5-1	GA	Theo Conf	66Wash. 91	Mar 66 Beyster.X=1.87,CALCTD CRV CFD EXPT	
Total	7.0-4	1.0+1	GA	ExTh Prog	GA-7091 41	Apr 66 Beyster.COMPD WITH TH FROM SCAT LAW	
	1.0-3	5.0-1		Expt Conf	66S.Diego 1 151	Feb 66 - + COMPARED WITH SCATT LAW	
Total	-3	+1	GA	Revw Rept	GA-7952	Apr 67 Beyster+ COMPARISON OF TH+EXPT CURV	
Total	1.0-4	1.0+0	KFK	Theo Conf	67Ann Arbr 2 411	Jul 67 Reichardt.PPR15.SCAT-KERN-CALC=EXPT	
Total	1.0-1		KIL	Expt Prog	AKE 12 385	Dec 67 Schmidt.ZRHDX,GRPH,FN OF H+D-CONC	
	5.0-2	5.0-1		Jour	AKE 12 385	Dec 67 - .GRPH, CFD TH	
	5.0-2	4.3-1		Conf	67Juelich 229	Apr 67 - .SIG(D) IN ZR-D1.76,CRYST SP	
	1.0-1	7.3-1		Conf	67Juelich 229	Apr 67 - .SIG(HD1.95)IN ZRH(.6)D(1.2)	
Total	9.4-3	2.0+0	GA	Expt Prog	GA-9194 11	Jan 69 Slaggie+ X=1.81 TABLE+CURVE CFD TH	
Total	2.7-4	1.7-3	HLT	Expt Jour	JNE 25 189	May 71 Saastamoinen+ 4TEMPS,20-270DEG C	
Total	-3	1.0+1	IKE	Theo Rept	IKE-6-61/1	Jan 73 Keinert.DATA LIBRARY	
Diff Elastic	1.0-2	1.0+0	GA	Expt Jour	NUK 12 143	Mar 69 Carriveau+ LINAC EXPT CFD TH	
Diff Elastic	-3	1.0+1	IKE	Theo Rept	IKE-6-61/1	Jan 73 Keinert.DATA LIBRARY	
Diff Inelast	1.0-1	7.0-1	RPI	Expt Jour	NSE 23 195	Oct 65 PAN+ TOF. CURV, TBL, 3 VIB LEVELS.	
Thermal Scat	-2	4.0-1	BNL	Expt Conf	58Geneva 16 297	Sep 58 Mcreynolds+.PPR1540,CURV CFD THEORY	
Thermal Scat	Cold		MTR	Expt Jour	NSE 5 99	Feb 59 Brugger+,THETA=90DEG CURVE	
Thermal Scat	1.0-1	5.0-1	KRK	ExTh Jour	NKA 4 241	May 59 Teller-Sig+THERMLIZ CFD KOLOS+K-NTH	
Thermal Scat	-2	2.0-1	GA	Expt Abst	BAP 5 17	Jan 60 Whittemore+ 30-140DEG FOR SIG TRANS	
Thermal Scat	1.0-3	4.0-1	GA	Expt Abst	BAP 5 463	Nov 60 Mcreynolds+ CS MEAS. CFD MDLS.	
Thermal Scat	5.0-2	5.5-1	CSD	Expt Conf	61Wien 2 91	Oct 61 Haas+ X=1.5,SIG(E) FOR H.	
Thermal Scat	5.0-2	5.5-1	IFJ	Revw Jour	INP-255	Apr 63 Janik+ SIG/H CFD FERMI-THEO,GRAPH	
Thermal Scat	1.0-1	4.0-1	GA	Expt Rept	GA-4490	Jan 64 Whittemore+. CURVES.TOT,EL,AND INEL	
Thermal Scat	1.0-2	1.0+0	GA	ExTh Jour	NSE 19 230	Jun 64 Young+ 4 TEMPS. SPEC. CFD TH.	
Thermal Scat	9.7-2	3.9-1	GA	Expt Prog	GA-5554 67	Sep 64 Whittemore.LINAC CHOPPER.MEAS 4A(S)	
	1.0-3	5.5-1		Prog	GA-4434 31	Sep 64 - .LINAC CHOPPER TOT SIG(H)	
Thermal Scat	2.0-2		FEI	Expt Rept	FEI-10	65 .TOF.GRAPH SIG UNDER ANGLE 80,2TEMPS	
Thermal Scat	9.1-3	4.1-1	GA	Expt Conf	65Karlsrhe 1 407	May 65 Beyster+ GRAPHS.	
				Rept	GA-6295	Mar 65 .IDENTICAL TO 65KRLSRH,P407.	

40 Zirconium HYD

Quantity	Energy (ev) Min	Max	Lab	Type	Documentation Ref Vol Page	Date	Author, Comments	Data
Thermal Scat	2.2-2	1.0-1	MUN	ExTh Jour	NUK 7 281	Jul 65	Kornbichler.ANGDIST.MU,DIFF C VS T	
Thermal Scat	1.8-1	5.0-1	BNW	Expt Conf	BNL-940 96	Sep 65	Harling. LEVELS AT 141, 281, 411MV	
Thermal Scat	1.0-1	6.0-1	RPI	Expt Jour	NSE 23 194	Oct 65	PAN+ TOF. CURV,TBL. 3 VIB LVLS.	
	1.0-1	7.0-1		Abst	DA/B 29 212	Jul 68	PAN. ANGDIST+TOF ANALYSIS.	
	1.6-1	6.7-1		Conf	67Ann Arbr 1 407	Jul 67	Purohit+PPR46.SIG-GRPHS,CFD TH+XPTS	
	1.0-1	1.0+0		Jour	NIM 42 197	Jul 66	PAN+ELECTR.LINAC FILTR.DIFFER.METHD	
Thermal Scat	-2		IFU	Expt Prog	INDSWG-126 21	66	Vertebnyj.ZR-D1.6,FEW REMARKS NDG	
Thermal Scat	1.0-3	1.0+0	GA	ExTh Conf	66S.Diego 1 27	Feb 66	Koppel. COMPARED WITH THEO OF SCTLAW	
Thermal Scat	6.0-3	1.0+0	GA	Expt Conf	66S.Diego 1 151	Feb 66	Beyster+ COMPARED WITH SCATT LAW	
	9.1-3	4.2-1		Prog	GA-6824 103	Nov 65	- .COMPD WITH TH FROM SCAT LAW	
Thermal Scat	2.3-1		BNW	Expt Prog	WASH-1068 153	Mar 66	Smith+ CS,THETA=15 DEG. NDG.	
Thermal Scat	1.8-1	5.0-1	BAT	Expt Jour	RSI 37 697	Jun 66	Harling. TOF. CURVES.	
Thermal Scat	2.4-2		FEI	Expt Conf	66Dubna 196	Jul 66	Liforov+,GRAPH N SPECTRUM,ZRH1.46	
	-3	1.0+1	GA	Expt Conf	67Ann Arbr 1 493	Jul 66	Beyster+PPR75.X=1.85,293+700 DEG K	
	1.0-2	5.0-1		Prog	GA-6930 20	Jan 66	- + MULTISCAT CORR/T. CURVES.	
Thermal Scat	2.4-1		GA	Theo Prog	GA-7898 17	Mar 67	Beyster+. DOUBLE DIFF SIG. CURVES	
	-2		GA	Revw Rept	GA-7952	Apr 67	Beyster+ STATUS OF TH+EXPT,CURVES	
	7.8-3	8.2-1	GA	Expt Rept	GA-8345	Jun 67	Carriveau.TOF 296+700DEGK CFD TH	
	1.0-2	2.0+0		ExTh Prog	GA-7091 37	Apr 66	Beyster. TOF. 2 TEMPS. CFD TH.	
Thermal Scat	-3	-1	CRC	Expt Conf	67Ann Arbr 1 373	Jul 67	Thorson. TOF, CURVES, FULL INFORMTN	+
	-3	+0		Rept	CRNL-272	Feb 69	.TAPE FORMAT	
	-3	-1		Rept	AECL-2915	Jun 67	.SUPERSEDED.	
Thermal Scat	None		CRC	Theo Conf	67Ann Arbr 1 261	Jul 67	Jarvis.PPR23.APLICATN OF SCAT-MODEL	
	1.9-2	8.2-1	GA	Expt Prog	GA-8085	Jul 67	Beyster+ CURVS 7ES 296+700DEGK	
	5.7-1		GA	Theo Conf	67Ann Arbr 1 311	Jul 67	Slaggie.PPR53. GRPH,MULT-SCAT-CORRC	
	Maxwl		GIT	Theo Conf	67Ann Arbr 1 555	Jul 67	Kallfelz+PPR69.X=1.7,SCAT-KERNELS	
	+7		HLT	Theo Conf	67Ann Arbr 2 257	Jul 67	Manninen.PPR13.SCAT-MODL/THERMALIZN	
	-1	+1	KFK	Theo Conf	67Ann Arbr 2 411	Jul 67	Reichardt.PPR15.SCAT-KERN/THERMALZN	
	Maxwl			ExTh Rept	KFK-305	May 65	Kallfelz+TIME DEPENDENT N SPEC	
Thermal Scat	-		THS	Theo Jour	NUK 10 89	Jul 67	Roehrborn+NELKIN MDL N.DISTRIBUTION	
				Rept	BMWF-FBK66-40	Dec 66	- + EQUIVALENT REPT.	
Thermal Scat	2.0-3	1.0+0	GA	Theo Prog	GA-8449	Jan 68	Beyster+ X=1.85 EXPT+TH CFD CURVS	
Thermal Scat	5.2-3	5.0-1	BIR	Expt Conf	68Copenhgn 2 299	May 68	Beg+PPR117.DOWN-SCAT-EXPT,CRV GVN	
Thermal Scat	Maxwl		KIG	Theo Jour	AKE 13 177	Jun 68	Lahann+ THR NEUT SPECT CALC	
Thermal Scat	Maxwl		KFK	ExTh Jour	NUK 11 282	Oct 68	Glaeser. SCAT CALC CFD EXPT	
				Expt Rept	KFK-602	Jul 67	- .EXPT CFD TH OF THR SCAT	
	-3	+1		Revw Conf	67Ann Arbr 1 235	Jul 67	- .PPR104.SCAT-LAW IN MODERATR	
	1.8-2	9.0-2		Expt Rept	KFK-264	Dec 64	- + SUPERSEDED	
Thermal Scat	Maxwl		KFK	Expt Jour	NUK 12 84	Jan 69	Knoche.DIFFUS PARAMS+RETHERMALI SIG	
Thermal Scat	Maxwl		KRU	Theo Jour	AKE 14 295	Aug 69	Mehner.ZRHYD,SIG CALC CFD EXPT	
Thermal Scat	Maxwl		THS	Revw Jour	AKE 14 97	Oct 69	Emendoerfer. VARIOUS SCAT MODELS	
Thermal Scat	3.0-3	3.0-1	KRU	Theo Jour	AKE 16 201	70	Baltz.ZRHYD,EINSTEIN CRYS AS SCAT MD	
	-3	+0	HLT	Expt Prog	INDC(FIN)-1G	Apr 70	Palmgren+ SUBTHERMAL CROSS-SECTION	
Thermal Scat	Maxwl		PSU	Theo Abst	DA/B 30 5078	May 70	Mariani.SIGCOH CFD EXPT.1-PHON INEL	
Thermal Scat	Maxwl		CCP	ExTh Jour	AE 29 201	Sep 70	Antonov+ DIFFUSN PARS VS TEMPERATUR	
Thermal Scat	Cold		HLT	Expt Jour	JNE 25 189	May 71	Saastamoinen+ FREQ SPEC TO FIT TOT.	
Thermal Scat	1.7-1	2.4-1	BNW	Expt Abst	BAP 16 851	Aug 71	Clune+.2ES. X=0.54,1.03,1.56,2.00	
Thermal Scat	Maxwl		THS	Theo Jour	AKE 18 219	Nov 71	Royl. CADILHAC SCAT KERNEL, X=1.85	
	2.4-1			Jour	AKE 17 209	May 71	Keinert.DIFF INELAST SCAT CFD EXPT	
	5.7-1			Jour	AKE 17 209	May 71	- .SCAT DIFFSIG,3 ANGS,CFD EXP	
	5.0-3	5.0-1		Jour	AKE 17 209	May 71	- .X=1.92,AVG COS SCAT ANG	
				Jour	AKE 17 209	May 71	- .TOT SCAT SIG,CFD EXPT	
	1.0-2	5.0-1		Jour	AKE 17 209	May 71	- .X=1.85,ANG SCAT SIG,CFD EXP	
	2.4-1			Jour	AKE 17 209	May 71	- .SCAT DIFFSIG,4 ANGS,CFD EXP	
	2.0-3	1.0+0		Jour	AKE 17 209	May 71	- .X=1.75,NEUT SPEC,CFD EXPT	
	6.4-2	8.8-1		Jour	AKE 17 209	May 71	- .X=1.85,ANGDIST,CFD EXPT	
Thermal Scat	Maxwl		JAE	Theo Rept	JAERI-1220	Apr 72	Nakahara+.SCAT KARNEL AT HIGH TEMP	
Thermal Scat	2.2-2	2.1-1	FEI	Expt Conf	75Kiev 2 123	May 75	Parfenov+ DOUBLDIFFSIG,2ES.TBL+GRAPH	
Thermal Scat	-3	1.9+0	THS	Theo Rept	IKE-6 89 25	Jun 75	Keinert. DATA LIBRARY	
Scattering	-3	1.0+1	IKE	Theo Rept	IKE-6-61/1	Jan 73	Keinert.DATA LIBRARY	
Absorption	Maxwl		IFB	Theo Prog	YFI-7 45	Apr 69	Naumov+ CODES FOR EFFECTIV-SIG,TBL	
				Rept	INDC(CCP)-7U48	Feb 70	TRANSLATN.*	

41 Niobium CMP

Quantity	Energy (ev) Min	Max	Lab	Type	Documentation Ref Vol Page	Author, Comments Date	Data
Total	5.0−2	4.0−1	KIL Expt	Jour	AKE 17 113	Mar 71 Brand.NBDX(X=0.86)DEUTERON SIGMA	
	1.0−1	8.0−1		Jour	AKE 17 113	Mar 71 − .NBHX(X=0.6/0.9),HYDROGEN SIGM	
Thermal Scat	5.0−2	2.0−1	JAE Expt	Jour	JPJ 19 1862	Oct 64 Sakamoto.NBHX(X=0.85)TOT−SIG,VIBR.E	
Thermal Scat	−		ISP Expt	Conf	BNL−940 105	Sep 65 Kley.NBHX(X=.03)TEMP=33DEG C	
Thermal Scat	1.0−1	7.0−1	RPI Expt	Abst	DA/B 29 212	Jul 68 PAN. NBH,ANGDIST+TOF ANALYSIS.	
	2.4−1			Conf	67Ann Arbr 1 407	Jul 67 Purohit+NBH,PPR46.XPTL 2DIFF−SIG	
				Rept	RPI−328−101	67 Pan+NBH,DOUBLE DIFF SIG,VIBR E+LVL	
Thermal Scat	Maxwl		TOH Expt	Prog	EANDC(J)19L62	Aug 70 Kimura+.NBD,TOF POWDER DIFFR.NDG	
Thermal Scat	Cold		JUL Expt	Rept	JUEL−935FF	Mar 73 Conrad.NBDX,DIFFUSE SCAT EXPT	

46 Palladium CMP

Quantity	Energy (ev) Min	Max	Lab	Type	Documentation Ref Vol Page	Author, Comments Date	Data
Total	6.2−4	5.2−3	COL Revw	Prog	CU− 179 154	Oct 58 Gould.PDH,CURVE DIFF CONCENTR OF H	
	5.7−4	3.3−3	Expt	Prog	CU− 174 21	Mar 58 − + PDH. CHEM BINDING. CURVE.	
Thermal Scat	1.0−2	2.5−1	IFJ Revw	Rept	INP−255	Apr 63 Janik+ HYDRIDE,CFD FERMI−THEO,GRAPH	
Thermal Scat	None		ISP Expt	Rept	BNL−940 105	Sep 65 Kley.PDHX,X=.015,.03. TEMP=33DEG C	
Thermal Scat	3.0−2		IBJ Expt	Rept	INR−1226/II/PS	Oct 70 Maliszewski+.PD−FE(1PERCENT FE)	

47 Silver CMP

Quantity	Energy (ev) Min	Max	Lab	Type	Documentation Ref Vol Page	Author, Comments Date	Data
Thermal Scat		−3	TRM Expt	Conf	68Bombay 3 23	Dec 68 Vijayaraghavan+AGCL,DISPERSN 78DEGK	
(n,p)	1.7+6	1.6+7	FRK Expt	Prog	IKF−32 80	74 Henig+ AGCL,SIG CFD CALC,GRAPH	
(n,α)	1.8+7		RI Expt	Jour	YF 3 449	Mar 66 Kuzmin+.AG−BR,TOT,(ANG+E−DSTR)ALF	+
				Jour	SNP 3 325	Sep 66 TRANSLATN.*	
(n,α)	1.7+6	1.6+7	FRK Expt	Prog	IKF−32 80	74 Henig+ AGCL,SIG CFD CALC,GRAPH	

48 Cadmium CMP

Quantity	Energy (ev) Min	Max	Lab	Type	Documentation Ref Vol Page	Author, Comments Date	Data
Thermal Scat	None		MIT Expt	Prog	MIT−3031 4	Mar 67 Shull.CDS,MAGNET.SPIN−ORBIT SCAT	
Thermal Scat	1.3−2	1.1−1	KUR Expt	Jour	ZEP 12 80	Jul 70 Shil'Stein+CDS,COHER.+RES INTERACTN	
				Jour	JEL 12 80	Jul 69 .TRANSLATN.*0,NO 2	
Thermal Scat	8.0−2	1.2−1	CCP Expt	Jour	ZEP 13 214	Mar 71 Shil'Shtein+CDS,BRAGG−PEAK (N,GAM)	
				Jour	JEL 13 214	Mar 71 TRANSLATN.*	
(n,γ)	8.0−2	1.2−1	CCP Expt	Jour	ZEP 13 214	Mar 71 Shil'Shtein+CDS,(N,GAM)CFD BRAGG.PK	
				Jour	JEL 13 214	Mar 71 TRANSLATN.*	

49 Indium CMP

Quantity	Energy (ev) Min	Max	Lab	Type	Documentation Ref Vol Page	Author, Comments Date	Data
Thermal Scat	Maxwl		UJV Theo	Rept	UJV−2275	69 Krivy.INSB,DEBYE TEMP,BRAGG+OTHER EX	

50 Tin CMP

Quantity	Energy (ev) Min	Max	Lab	Type	Documentation Ref Vol Page	Author, Comments Date	Data
Thermal Scat	Cold		BUC Expt	Jour	RRP 19 717	Jul 74 Rapeanu+ LIQUID.SN−BI.SIG(E') CFD TH	
Thermal Scat	Maxwl		JAE Expt	Jour	JPJ 38 443	Feb 75 Iizumi+.NEUT.DIFF.,PHASE TRANS.,SNTL	

51 Antimony CMP

Quantity	Energy (ev) Min	Max	Lab	Type	Documentation Ref Vol Page	Author, Comments Date	Data
Thermal Scat	8.0−3		JAP Expt	Jour	JPJ 40 1347	May 76 Iida+.LIQ STRUCT−FACT BY N−DIF SB−ZN	

52 Tellurium CMP

Quantity	Energy (ev) Min	Max	Lab	Type	Documentation Ref Vol Page	Author, Comments Date	Data
Thermal Scat	Cold		WWA Expt	Priv	LECIEJEWIC	65 Leciejewic.TEO2,STRUCT.INVEST.N.DIFF	

53 Iodine CMP

Quantity	Energy (ev) Min	Max	Lab	Type	Documentation Ref Vol Page	Author, Comments Date	Data
Total	1.5+4	6.0+5	DKE Expt	Jour	AP 84 165	May 74 Pineo+ CSI.TRNS.AVG CS.TBL.OPTMDL.	+
	1.0+5	6.5+5		Abst	DA/B 31 6821	May 71 - .2 EN RANGES.AVG CS CFD OPTMDL.	
	1.5+4	6.0+5		Diss	PINEO	70 .CSI. AVG CS.GRPHS.STF CALC.TBL.CFD.	
	1.5+4	6.0+5		Data	EXFOR10542.012	Jan 79 . DATA UNOBTAINABLE FROM AUTHORS.	
Potntal Scat	3.0+3	6.5+5	DKE Expt	Jour	AP 84 165	May 74 Pineo+CSI.S WAVE SCT LENGTH.TBL.CFD	
				Abst	DA/B 31 6821	May 71 .THESIS ABST.	
				Diss	PINEO	70 .TBL.GRPHS.CFD TO 3 COLLECTIVE MDLS.	
				Diss	PINEO	70 .CSI.SCT LENGTH CURV,TBL.CFD.	
Strnth Fnctn	3.0+3	6.5+5	DKE Expt	Abst	DA/B 31 6821	May 71 Pineo.S,P,D WAVE.THESIS ABST.CSI	
				Diss	PINEO	70 . CSI TBLS,GRPHS.CFD CALC,EXPTS.	

55 Cesium CMP

Quantity	Energy (ev) Min	Max	Lab	Type	Documentation Ref Vol Page	Author, Comments Date	Data
Total	1.0+5	6.5+5	DKE Expt	Jour	AP 84 165	May 74 Pineo+ CSI. AVG TOT CS. TBL,GRPH.	+
				Abst	DA/B 31 6821	May 71 - .2 EN RANGES.AVG CS CFD OPTMDL.	
	1.5+4	6.0+5		Diss	PINEO	70 .CSI. AVG CS.GRPHS.STF CALC.TBL.CFD.	
	1.5+4	6.0+5		Data	EXFOR10542.012	Jan 79 . DATA UNOBTAINABLE FROM AUTHORS.	
Potntal Scat	3.0+3	6.5+5	DKE Expt	Jour	AP 84 165	May 74 Pineo+CSI. S WAVE SCT LENGTH.TBL.CFD	
				Abst	DA/B 31 6821	May 71 .THESIS ABST.	
				Diss	PINEO	70 .TBL.GRPHS.CFD TO 3 COLLECTIVE MDLS.	
				Diss	PINEO	70 CSI.SCT LENGTH.CURV.TBL.CFD	
Thermal Scat	–		ISL Expt	Prog	IA- 1218 57	Aug 70 Epstein+(CS2 MN CL4)MAGNETC STRUCT	
Thermal Scat	1.3 – 3		JAE Expt	Jour	JPJ 37 1393	Nov 74 Hirotsu+.N - DIFF,PHASE CHANGE,CSPBBR3	
(n,p)	1.4+7		CIS Expt	Jour	NC 20 903	Jun 61 Marccazzan+ALPHA+PROTON E DISTRIBUT.	
(n,p)	1.2+7	2.2+7	CIS Theo	Jour	PL/B 36 447	Oct 71 Milazzo – Colli+ CALC P SPEC CFD EXPT	
(n,p)	2.1+7		TUD Theo	Rept	ZFK – 261 77	Aug 73 Seeliger. CS – I,EXCITON – MODEL P – SPEC.	
(n,α)	1.4+7		CIS Expt	Jour	NC 20 903	Jun 61 Marccazzan+0.8+ – 0.2MB INTEGR E DIST.	
(n,α)	1.2+7	2.2+7	CIS Theo	Jour	PL/B 36 447	Oct 71 Milazzo – Colli+ CALC A SPEC CFD EXPT	
(n,α)	1.4+7		HAM Expt	Jour	NP/A 186 65	May 72 Bormann+ A ANGULAR DIST. DIR INTR.	+
	1.4+7			Data	EXFOR20471.	Jan 76 8PTS.D/DA,SIGMA,DIR.INT..	
Strnth Fnctn	3.0+3	6.5+5	DKE Expt	Abst	DA/B 31 6821	May 71 Pineo.S,P,D WAVE.THESIS ABST.CSI	
				Diss	PINEO	70 . CSI TBLS,GRPHS.CFD CALC,EXPTS.	

56 Barium CMP

Quantity	Energy (ev) Min	Max	Lab	Type	Documentation Ref Vol Page	Author, Comments Date	Data
Total	Maxwl		COL Expt	Prog	WASH – 1068 42	Mar 66 Leung+,BACL2 – 2H2O,NDG	
Total	Cold		KIL Expt	Prog	EANDC(E)89 U	Jan 68 Brand+BAH2,CRYSTSPEC AT FRG – 1	
Thermal Scat	Cold		WPI Expt	Jour	JCP 52 3952	Apr 50 Maeland.BAH2,TOF DISTRIBUTN INEL	
Thermal Scat	– 3		TRM Expt	Conf	68Bombay 3 217	Dec 68 Thaper+ BA(CLO3)2.H2O., WATER MODES	
	– 3	– 1		Conf	69Roorke 3 29	Dec 69 - +BA(CLO3)2,CHLORATE,WATER – MOL	
	– 3			Conf	68Madras 265	Feb 68 SEE ALSO *ALSO P529	

57 Lanthanum CMP

Quantity	Energy (ev) Min	Max	Lab	Type	Documentation Ref Vol Page	Author, Comments Date	Data
Total	Pile		SAC Expt	Prog	EANDC(E)23L	Feb 62 Genin. CRYSTAL SPECTROMETER. LAH2.	
	5.0 – 2	5.0 – 1		Jour	JPR 22 648	Oct 61 - + DATA CFD THEORY. LAH2	
Polarization	1.0 – 3	1.0+6	DUB Expt	Jour	YF 10 1178	Dec 69 Lushchikov+ LA2 MG3(NO3)12 . 24H2O	
				Jour	SNP 10 669	Jun 70 . ENGL OF YF 10 1187	
Thermal Scat	Cold		HAR Expt	Jour	JAP 36 1092	Mar 65 .N PARAMAGNETIC SCAT XPT LAFEO3	
				Jour	JAP 36 1092	Mar 65 .N PARAMAGNETIC SCAT XPT LACRO3	
				Jour	JAP 36 1092	Mar 65 N PARAMAGNETIC SCAT XPT LAMNO3	
Thermal Scat	Cold		ORL Revw	Jour	JAP 36 1078	Mar 65 Koehler. R – LA. MAG PROP. N DIFF.	
Thermal Scat	5.0 – 3		KRK Expt	Rept	INP – 601/PS	Apr 68 Bajorek+ LA2MG3(NO3)12.24H2O H BOND	
Thermal Scat	– 3	+0	TRM Revw	Conf	68Bombay 1 177	Dec 68 SATYA MURTY+ LACRO3,MAGNETIC SCAT	
Thermal Scat	– 3	+0	TRM Revw	Conf	68Bombay 1 177	Dec 68 SATYA MURTY+ LAFEO3,MAGNETIC SCAT	

58 Cerium CMP

Quantity	Energy (ev) Min	Max	Lab	Type	Documentation Ref Vol Page	Author, Comments Date	Data
Total	1.5 – 3	5.0 – 1	GVE Expt	Jour	HPA 25 79	Feb 52 Verdaguer+CEO2,TOF COH.EFFECTS	

58 Cerium CMP

Quantity	Energy (ev) Min	Max	Lab	Type	Documentation Ref Vol Page	Author, Comments Date	Data
Total	1.5 – 3	5.0 – 1	JNE	Expt Jour	HPA 25 79	Feb 52 Verdaguer+ CEO2,TOF,COH EFFECTS	
				Rept	JEN – 15	56 – + SEE HPA 25 79.	
Thermal Scat	Maxwl		THS	Theo Jour	AKE 18 261	Dec 71 Keinert. H – FREQ DIST,N – SP,CE HYDRID	

59 Praseodymium CMP

Quantity	Energy (ev) Min	Max	Lab	Type	Documentation Ref Vol Page	Author, Comments Date	Data
Thermal Scat	Cold		IOW	Revw Jour	JAP 33 428	Jan 62 Eyring+ PR2O3. CRYSTAL PARS.	
Thermal Scat	– 3		DUB	Revw Rept	JINR – P3 – 6732	72 Khennig. PR+++ PARAMAGNET SCAT GRPHS	
Scattering	5.0 – 1	1.0 +2	IJI	Expt Jour	ZET 67 869	74 Akopian+(PR02) POLYCRYSTAL,CURVE	
				Jour	JET 40 430	Mar 75 . ENGLISH OF ZET 67 869	

60 Neodymium CMP

Quantity	Energy (ev) Min	Max	Lab	Type	Documentation Ref Vol Page	Author, Comments Date	Data
Total	1.4 +0		ORL	Expt Jour	NP 61 381	Jan 65 Rayburn.ND2O3,IN RES 1.44EV 54.6B	
Thermal Scat	Cold		SAC	Expt Jour	PL/A 26 263	Feb 68 HAMMANN (ND GA GARNET)ANTIFER.MAGN.	

62 Samarium CMP

Quantity	Energy (ev) Min	Max	Lab	Type	Documentation Ref Vol Page	Author, Comments Date	Data
(n,α)	Maxwl		TAM	Expt Jour	PL/B 36 74	Aug 71 Mueller+SM2O3 CRYSTL LATTICE EFFECT	
(n,α)	Maxwl		TAM	Expt Jour	PL/B 36 74	Aug 71 Mueller+SMI3 CRYSTAL LATTICE EFFECT	

65 Terbium CMP

Quantity	Energy (ev) Min	Max	Lab	Type	Documentation Ref Vol Page	Author, Comments Date	Data
Thermal Scat	Cold		ORL	Expt Jour	JAP 36 1096	Mar 65 Cable+ TB – AG(PD,IN)CMP. N DIFFR.	
Thermal Scat	Cold		ORL	Revw Jour	JAP 36 1078	Mar 65 Koehler. TB – LA. MAG PROP. N DIFFR.	
Thermal Scat	Cold		ORL	Revw Jour	JAP 36 1078	Mar 65 Koehler. TB – LU. MAG PROP. N DIFFR.	
Thermal Scat	Cold		ORL	Revw Jour	JAP 36 1078	Mar 65 Koehler+ TB – Y. MAG PROPS. N DIFFR.	

66 Dysprosium CMP

Quantity	Energy (ev) Min	Max	Lab	Type	Documentation Ref Vol Page	Author, Comments Date	Data
Thermal Scat	Cold		ORL	Revw Jour	JAP 36 1078	Mar 65 Koehler+ DY – LA. MAG PROPS. N DIFFR.	
Thermal Scat	Cold		GRE	Expt Jour	PL/A 34 361	Apr 71 Sayetat+DYVO4,NEEL PT+MAGNT MOMENT	

68 Erbium CMP

Quantity	Energy (ev) Min	Max	Lab	Type	Documentation Ref Vol Page	Author, Comments Date	Data
Thermal Scat		– 2	BON	Expt Jour	PL/A 36 50	Aug 71 Bargouth+ER – AL,MAGNETIC STRUCTURE	

70 Ytterbium CMP

Quantity	Energy (ev) Min	Max	Lab	Type	Documentation Ref Vol Page	Author, Comments Date	Data
Thermal Scat	Cold		WPI	Expt Jour	JCP 52 3952	Apr 70 Maeland.(YB H2),TOF DISTN INEL SCAT	
Thermal Scat	Cold		ANL	Expt Jour	JCP 52 6430	Jun 70 Atoji+YBC2,DIFF SIG 5AND300DEGK	
Thermal Scat	–		ISL	Expt Prog	IA – 1218 55	Aug 70 Friedman+(YB FE O3),MAGNETC STRUCT	
	None			Prog	IA – 1218 55	Aug 70 Pinto+(YB FE O3)SUBLATTIC – MAGNETZTN	

72 Hafnium CMP

Quantity	Energy (ev) Min	Max	Lab	Type	Documentation Ref Vol Page	Author, Comments Date	Data
Total	7.3 – 2	7.3 – 1	KIL	Expt Jour	AKE 19 262	Apr 72 Brand+ CRYSTSPEC .CURVE.	
				Prog	EANDC(E)127U	Apr 70 – + CRYSTSPEC AT FRGI.HFHX,X = 1.99	
Total	None		BER	Expt Rept	HMI – B – 133 58	Jun 73 .HFH1.85,1.59.CRYST SPEC..277EV RES	

73 Tantalum CMP

Quantity	Energy (ev) Min	Max	Lab	Type	Documentation Ref Vol Page	Date	Author, Comments	Data
Total	Pile		SAC	Expt Prog	EANDC(E)23L	Feb 62	Genin.CRYST SPECT TBP IN JPR	
Total	5.0−2	4.0−1	KIL	Expt Jour	AKE 17 113	Mar 71	Brand.TADX(X=0.63),DEUTERON SIGMA	
	1.0−1	7.0−1		Jour	AKE 17 113	Mar 71	− .TAHX(X=0.52/0.62),H SIGMA	
	7.0−2	7.0−1		Prog	EANDC(E)127U	Apr 70	− + CRYSTSPEC AT FRGI. TAH	
	7.3−2	7.3−1		Jour	AKE 14 449	Nov 69	− . TAHX(X=0.52) TOT SIG. GRPH	
Thermal Scat	5.0−2	2.0−1	JAE	Expt Jour	JPJ 19 1862	Oct 64	Sakamoto.TAHX(X=0.7)TOT SIG, VIBR.E	
Thermal Scat	3.8−3		RIS	Expt Conf	68Copenhgn 1 35	May 68	Als − Nielsen.TA − NB.LCLZD,BAND PHON,	

74 Tungsten CMP

Quantity	Energy (ev) Min	Max	Lab	Type	Documentation Ref Vol Page	Date	Author, Comments	Data
Thermal Scat	Maxwl		TOH	Expt Priv	TANAKA	Dec 69	Tanaka+WOB,POWDER DIFFRACTION PATTRN	

75 Rhenium CMP

Quantity	Energy (ev) Min	Max	Lab	Type	Documentation Ref Vol Page	Date	Author, Comments	Data
Thermal Scat	−		WWA	Expt Conf	66Dubna 17	Jul 66	Buras.CR − RE,SINCLE XTAL	

79 Gold CMP

Quantity	Energy (ev) Min	Max	Lab	Type	Documentation Ref Vol Page	Date	Author, Comments	Data
Thermal Scat	Maxwl	2.5−2	OSA	Expt Jour	JPJ 34 1197	May 73	Nakai+.DIFFUSE MAG.SCATT. AU.CR	
	Maxwl			Jour	JPJ 29 978	Oct 70	− +.AU − CR,MAG.FORM FACTR BY DIFF	

80 Mercury CMP

Quantity	Energy (ev) Min	Max	Lab	Type	Documentation Ref Vol Page	Date	Author, Comments	Data
Total	Maxwl		COL	Expt Jour	PR 49 453	Mar 36	Mitchell.HGO,TRANSM,CD STOPPED+EPICD	

82 Lead CMP

Quantity	Energy (ev) Min	Max	Lab	Type	Documentation Ref Vol Page	Date	Author, Comments	Data
Diff Elastic	7.1−5		JUL	Expt Rept	JUEL−1158	Mar 75	Seitz. BI − ALLOY	
Thermal Scat	Cold		WWA	Expt Priv	LECIEJEWIC	65	Leciejewic.PBO,STUCT.INVEST BY N DIF	
Thermal Scat	−3	−2	CCP	Expt Jour	ZET 49 449	Aug 65	Chernoplekov+MG − PB,2.8PC PB+PURE MG	
				Jour	JET 22 315	Feb 66	TRANSLATN.*	
Thermal Scat	−		WWA	Expt Conf	66Dubna 17	Jul 66	Buras.POWDERED PBTIO3,DIFFRACTION	
Thermal Scat	−		BUC	Expt Jour	SCF 24 783	Jul 72	Mateescu+ PB − BI ALLOY,S DETERMINED	
Absorption	3.0+6		FEI	Expt Book	NEJTRONFIZ 278	61	Kukhtevich+ PB3O4, SIGMA GIVEN	
				Book	SPN 205	61	.ENGL TRANSL OF NEJTRONFIZ 278	

83 Bismuth CMP

Quantity	Energy (ev) Min	Max	Lab	Type	Documentation Ref Vol Page	Date	Author, Comments	Data
Thermal Scat	Maxwl		DUB	Expt Conf	64Bombay 2 513	Dec 64	Sosnonska+,TOF,N DIFFRACTION CURVS	
				Rept	JINR−P−1909	Jan 65	.	
				Rept	BNL−TR−81	65	. ENGL OF JINR−P−1909	
Thermal Scat	−		WWA	Expt Conf	66Dubna 17	Jul 66	Buras.POWDERED BIFEO3,DIFFRACTION	
Thermal Scat	−		BUC	Expt Jour	SCF 24 783	Jul 72	Mateescu+ PB − BI ALLOY,S DETERMINED	
Thermal Scat	Cold		BUC	Expt Jour	RRP 19 717	Jul 74	Rapeanu+ LIQUID.SN − BI.SIG(E') CFD TH	

90 Thorium CMP

Quantity	Energy (ev) Min	Max	Lab	Type	Documentation Ref Vol Page	Date	Author, Comments	Data
Total	4.5−3	2.8−2	AE	Expt Rept	AE−222	Mar 66	Beshai.THO2,TOF CALC BRAGG EDGES	+
	4.0−3	2.8−2		Data	EXFOR20161.002	May 74	1PNT.	
Thermal Scat	1.0−1	7.0−1	RPI	Expt Abst	DA/B 29 212	Jul 68	PAN. THH2,ANGDIST+TOF ANALYSIS.	
	None			Conf	67Ann Arbr 1 407	Jul 67	Purohit+ THH2,(PPR46)SIG − GRPH CFD XP	
Res Int Abs	None		WIN	Expt Jour	JNAB 16 335	Jul 62	Moore+THO2,CD TUBED OSC.RANGE OF S/M	

92 Uranium CMP

Quantity	Energy (ev) Min	Max	Lab	Type	Documentation Ref Vol Page	Author, Comments Date	Data
Total	3.8−3	9.4+0	GA Expt	Rept	GA− 8782	Jul 68 Borgonovi+TRANS 77ES TABLE+CURVE	
Total	5.0−2	5.0−1	CAI Expt	Jour	AKE 13 458	Dec 68 Saad. EFFECT CHEM BOND ON SCAT SIG	
Total	3.4−2	1.8−1	KIL Expt	Jour	AKE 14 72	Jan 69 Saad. EFFECT CHEM BOND ON SCAT SIG	
Total	6.0−3	3.5+0	RPI Expt	Jour	NSE 47 349	Mar 72 Yeater+. CURV SIG VS.E. CFD THEORY	
				Rept	RPI−328−148	Dec 68 .SUPERSEDED	
Thermal Scat	None		BNL Expt	Prog	WASH−1013 10	58 Mcreynolds+ 1ST VIB LVL. HYDRIDE.	
Thermal Scat	7.0−3	2.5−2	WWAExpt	Jour	BPC 13 291	Apr 65 Murasik+.ANTIFERROMAGNETIC UOTE	
Thermal Scat		5.0−3	ANL Expt	Jour	JCP 45 3817	Nov 66 Rush+ UH3,UD3 VIB SPECT 970+710 1/CM	
Thermal Scat	None		GA Theo	Prog	GA− 9753 22	67 Borgonovi+,COHERENT SIG CALCTD	
Thermal Scat	None		GA Theo	Prog	GA− 8085	Jul 67 Beyster+ S(A,B) CALC AT RM TEMP NDG	
Thermal Scat	1.3−1		RPI Expt	Conf	67Ann Arbr 1 407	Jul 67 Purohit+ UC,HYDRIDES. 2DIFF GRPH,CFD	
				Rept	RPI−328−101	67 Pan+ DIFF SIG QUALITAT RESULTS ONLY	
Thermal Scat	Cold		GA Theo	Rept	GA− 8675	Dec 68 Slaggie. UC. LATTICE MDL.	
Thermal Scat	Cold		MTR Expt	Prog	WASH−1127 77	Apr 69 Schmunk. TBD. UC. NDG.	
Thermal Scat	9.2−2	1.6−1	RPI Expt	Jour	NSE 47 349	Mar 72 Yeater+. DOUBLE DIFF SIG. 3 ES.	
				Rept	RPI−328−148	Dec 68 .SUPERSEDED	

92 Uranium OXI

Quantity	Energy (ev) Min	Max	Lab	Type	Documentation Ref Vol Page	Author, Comments Date	Data
Evaluation	4.0−2	1.8−1	ANL Eval	Rept	RPC− 7	62 Greenspan+.THERMAL SCATTERING LAW	
Total	1.5−3	5.0−1	GVE Expt	Jour	HPA 25 79	Feb 52 Verdaguer+TOF COH EFFECTS	
Total	1.5−3	5.0−1	JNE Expt	Jour	HPA 25 79	Feb 52 Verdaguer+ TOF, COH EFFECTS	
				Rept	JEN− 15	56 − + SEE HPA 25 79.	
Total	6.6+0	6.8+0	ANL Expt	Jour	PR 127 461	Jul 62 Jackson+U3O8.CRYSTAL AT 4−297DEG K	
Total	4.5−3	2.8−2	AE Expt	Rept	AE− 222	Mar 66 Beshai.TOF CALC BRAGG EDGES.20DEG C	+
	4.0−3	2.8−2		Data	EXFOR20161.004	May 74 1PNT.	
Total	1.3−3	8.2−2	IEA Expt	Rept	IEA− 254	Nov 71 Rodriguez+ SIG(LAMBDA) CRV	+
				Rept	EANDC(BZL)2 1	May 69 * DATA TABLE	
				Rept	IEA− 152 91	Oct 67 * IN PORTUGESE	
				Jour	CEC 19 409	67 .EXPERIMENT DESCRIBED	
	1.3−3	8.2−2		Data	EXFOR30168.002	Nov 68 125 POINTS, SIG VS LAMBDA, PRIV COM	
Thermal Scat	4.0−2	1.8−1	ANL Eval	Rept	RPC− 7	62 Greenspan+. AT 293,698 DEG K	
Thermal Scat	3.8−2	1.8−1	CRC Expt	Conf	62Chalk R. 2 213	Sep 62 Thorson+ S(AB) 20DEGC	
				Rept	AECL−1577	62 .SAME	
Thermal Scat	−3	−1	CRC Expt	Conf	67Ann Arbr 1 373	Jul 67 Thorson+HAYWOOD. TOF, CURVES	+
				Rept	CRNL− 272	Feb 69 .TAPE FORMAT	
				Rept	AECL−2915	Jun 67 .SEE ALSO	
				Conf	62Chalk R. 2 213	Sep 62 .PRELIMINARY.	
Thermal Scat	None		CRC Theo	Conf	67Ann Arbr 1 261	Jul 67 Jarvis.PPR23.APLICATN OF SCAT−MODEL	
Thermal Scat	3.4−1		RPI Expt	Conf	67Ann Arbr 1 407	Jul 67 Purohit+ PPR46.2DIFF−SIG−GRPH,CFD TH	
Thermal Scat	None		GA Theo	Prog	GA− 9753 22	Oct 67 Borgonovi+,COHERENT ELAST SIG CALCT	
Thermal Scat	Cold		MTR Expt	Prog	WASH−1127 77	Apr 69 Schmunk. NDG. TBD.	
Thermal Scat	Maxwl		GA Theo	Jour	NUK 12 205	Aug 69 Young+ ELAS+INELAS SCAT CALC	
	None			Rept	GA− 8760	Jul 68 − + SCT LAW.	
Thermal Scat	1.3−3	8.0−2	IEA Theo	Rept	IEA− 254	Nov 71 Rodrigues+ CALC COHER+INCO SIG,GRPH	
Thermal Scat	6.7+0	6.0+2	CAI Theo	Jour	AKE 22 51	Sep 72 Saad+ INTERMEDIATE RESON−INTEG CALC	
Absorption	2.5−2		IEA Expt	Rept	IEA− 152 91	Oct 67 Rodriguez+ THERMAL ABSORPTION SIGMA	+
				Jour	CEC 19 490	67 . EXPT DESCRIBED	
	2.5−2			Data	EXFOR30168.003	Nov 68 .0253EV ABSORPTION SIGMA	
Absorption	1.3−3	8.0−2	IEA ExTh	Rept	IEA− 254	Nov 71 Rodrigues+ EXPTL TOT−CALC SCAT,GRPH	
Res Int Abs	Pile		AE Expt	Conf	59Vienna 109	Sep 59 Plomberg+GRPHS,TEMPERATURE−INFLUENC	
Res Int Abs	Pile		HAR Eval	Conf	59Vienna 74	Sep 59 Bolton. BEST FIT FORMULA,OTHER XPTS	
Res Int Abs	−		WIN Expt	Jour	JNAB 16 335	Jul 62 Moore+ CD TUBED OSC. RANGE OF S/M	
				Rept	AEEW−R−57	Aug 61 − + EQU TO JNE(A+B)16 335	
Res Int Abs	+2	+3	NIL Theo	Rept	PINST−RT−1	68 Bhatti+VAL GVN,D20 CLUSTER LATTICE	
Res Int Abs	5.0+0	6.0+1	ANL Theo	Jour	NSE 39 32	70 Hwang. MULTLVL,CFD SINGL,SHIELDD.TBL	
Res Int Abs	None		DEL Expt	Abst	DA/B 30 3817	Feb 70 Dekker.LOCAL REACTOR OSCL.300−900K	
(n,γ)	1.0+3	1.2+3	ANL Theo	Jour	NSE 39 32	70 Hwang. MULTLVL,DOPPLER EFF.GRPH+TBL	
(n,γ)	4.4+1	6.0+1	ANL Theo	Jour	NSE 39 32	70 Hwang. MULTLVL,CFD SINGL,SHIELDD.GRF	
(n,γ)	+3		ANL Theo	Conf	BNL−50387 39	Apr 73 Hwang. CALC SINGL+MULTI−LVL AVG SIG	
Res Int Capt	Pile		BET ExTh	Conf	62Wien 211	May 62 Klein+ FUEL ROD EFF RES INT,ACT+CALC	
Fission	None		TRM Expt	Prog	BARC−614 21	72 Jain+ FAST FIS RATIO, CFD CALC,NDG.	
Fission	+3		ANL Theo	Conf	BNL−50387 39	Apr 73 Hwang. CALC SINGL+MULTI−LVL AVG SIG	
	4.4+1	6.0+1		Jour	NSE 39 32	70 −. MULTLVL,CFD SINGL,SHIELDD.GRF	
	1.0+3	1.2+3		Jour	NSE 39 32	70 −. MULTLVL,DOPPLER EFF.GRPH+TBL	

92 Uranium OXI

Quantity	Energy (ev) Min	Max	Lab	Type	Documentation Ref Vol Page	Date	Author, Comments	Data
Res Int Fiss	5.0+0	6.0+1	ANL	Theo Jour	NSE 39 32	70	Hwang. MULTLVL,CFD SINGL,SHIELDD.TBL	
Delayd Neuts	2.5−2		IRT	Expt Jour	NSE 61 426	Nov 76	Lukens+ UO2,U3O8 DIFFERENCE IN NUD.	
Fiss Yield	1.4+7		BAS	Expt Abst	HPA 44 601	Aug 71	Schacher+ FISS TRACK METHOD	
Reson Params	1.3+0	6.0+1	ANL	Theo Jour	NSE 39 32	70	Hwang. TOT−WID AT 6 INTERVLS,MULTLVL	

94 Plutonium CMP

Quantity	Energy (ev) Min	Max	Lab	Type	Documentation Ref Vol Page	Date	Author, Comments	Data
(n,γ)	+3		ANL	Theo Conf	BNL−50387 39	Apr 73	Hwang.(OXI).SINGL+MULTI−LVL AVG SIG	
	1.3+3	1.4+3		Jour	NSE 39 32	70	−.(OXI).MULTLVL,DOPPLER.GRPH+TBL	
Fission	+3		ANL	Theo Conf	BNL−50387 39	Apr 73	Hwang.(OXI).SINGL+MULTI−LVL AVG SIG	
	1.3+3	1.4+3		Jour	NSE 39 32	70	−.(OXI).MULTLVL,DOPPLER.GRPH+TBL	
Res Int Fiss	2.0+1	1.2+2	NIL	Theo Rept	PINST−73 1	Feb 73	Bhatti+ CRYSTL BINDING EFF ON PU−239	
Reson Params	1.3+3	1.4+3	ANL	Theo Jour	NSE 39 32	70	Hwang.(OXI).AVG F+RED+N−WID,MULTLVL	
Reson Params	7.6+0	8.1+0	NIL	Theo Rept	PINST−73 1	Feb 73	Bhatti+ CRYSTL BINDING EFF ON PU−239	

A.1

Annex
A DETAILED EXPLANATION OF THE CINDA LISTING

Each of the main information fields mentioned in the introductory section is here described in greater detail.

1. Element and Isotope, or Chemical Compound

The target in a neutron-induced reaction is given in bold script at the top of the page or whenever the isotope mass number is changing. There are three groups of entries:

  a. Natural elements or separated isotopes
  b. Collective denominations MANY and FPROD
  c. Molecules, or mixtures of elements, called COMPOUNDS

a.   **Elements or their isotopes.** This group forms the overwhelming majority of the entries, with the target described by the element number and name followed by the mass number when the entry refers to a particular isotope of that element. When the target isotope is in a metastable state, this is indicated in the comment. Where the natural element is monoisotopic, the mass number is always listed. Additionally, all data on hydrogen not referring specifically to the heavier isotopes are listed under '1 Hydrogen 001'; the heavier isotopes appear in separate listings as '1 Deuterium 002' and '1 Tritium 003'. Elements in this category are:

H	1	*N	14	Sc	45	Nb	93	Tb	159	Th	232
D	2	*O	16	*V	51	Rh	103	Ho	165		
T	3	F	19	Mn	55	I	127	Tm	169		
*He	4	Na	23	Co	59	Cs	133	*Ta	181		
Be	9	Al	27	As	75	*La	139	Au	197		
*C	12	P	31	Y	89	Pr	141	Bi	209		

*   nearly monoisotopic

Each successive element through the periodic table begins on a new page.

CINDA is exclusively concerned with neutron work plus a small number of photon-induced reactions, and with two exceptions the target nucleus in neutron (or photon) bombardment is entered. Sometimes a reaction such as $^{13}C(\alpha,n)^{16}O$ is useful insofar as it helps determine the (n,α) cross-section or resonance parameters of ^{16}O, and may be listed under ^{16}O 'Reson Params', or ^{16}O '(n,α)', with the comment INV. or INVERSE. The other exception is for information on spontaneous fission, where obviously only the fissioning nucleus is involved. But the fission product yield resulting from fission induced by thermal neutrons incident on ^{235}U is entered under ^{235}U and not ^{236}U.

b.   **Collective denominations.** FPROD stands for mixed fission products, MANY for references containing results of a single type which may be applicable for many species. Examples might be references which give a general prediction for a neutron strength function versus A, or state general conclusions about parameters of level densities, or a useful theoretical paper with recipes for calculating elastic scattering angular distributions. - These collective entries follow the separate elements in this CINDA listing.

c.   **Molecules or mixtures.** In the scattering of thermal neutrons the phenomena may depend not only on the separate nuclei of the scatterer but also on the chemical composition and physical state of the sample. In such circumstances, where the nuclei of more than one element are involved, the page is headed by a compound abbreviation. The abbreviations used are explained in Table 1.

Where only one element is involved, the entry is normally made under the main listing no matter what physical form. Thus data for graphite or diamond are to be found under Carbon.

A.2

2. Quantity (for definitions see Table 2)

The "Quantities" are 12-character abbreviations of the type descriptions for microscopic nuclear data — cross-sections, spectra, resonance parameters, resonance integrals, etc. — which are reported in the references here indexed. Table 2 lists all the quantities now used: the abbreviations are in general easily understood, though some are rather comprehensive (for example, 'Diff Inelast' includes both angular distributions and energy spectra of scattered neutrons), and study of the precise definitions is recommended when making requests to the centres for special retrievals from CINDA. Users may be unfamiliar with a few of the "collective" cross-sections, and the "sum rules" may be helpful as given on page XXV of the introduction.

3. Energy

The two columns show the minimum and maximum values of the incident neutron energies covered by the experiment or, for (γ,n) and (γ,f) reactions, the range of photon energies. The first two significant figures of these energies are given, followed by the power of 10 needed to express them in units of eV, with a minus sign on the exponent if below 1 eV. Thus:

1.9+2	is to be read	1.9×10^2 eV = 190 eV
2.4+6	is to be read	2.4×10^6 eV = 2.4 MeV
1.4+7	is to be read	1.4×10^7 eV = 14 MeV
2.5−2	is to be read	2.5×10^{-2} eV = 0.025 eV
+0	is to be read	in the range of some eV
+5	is to be read	in the range of some hundred keV
−.2+0	is to be read	−0.2 eV

Similarly the exponent 0 at the right of E_{min} and 3 at the right of E_{max} means "in the eV range". For resonance parameters the energies given refer to the highest and lowest resonance energies and not to the energy limits of the experiment.

Where only one energy is involved, such as the energy of a resonance, it is put in the E_{min} columns. Where one is dealing with a negative resonance, i.e. corresponding to a level below the neutron binding energy, the value would be preceded by a minus sign (−).

Where, as in resonance integrals, there is no upper bound, E_{min} gives the low energy limit of the integral. It occasionally occurs that a measurement is valid for all neutrons below a certain energy, as for example when the strength function is measured by counting all the resonances up to a given energy and dividing by this maximum energy. Another example is a measurement in a bremsstrahlung spectrum, where the upper energy limit of the spectrum will be found entered in the E_{max} columns.

A continuous neutron spectrum is indicated by one of several standard alphabetic abbreviations:

Cold	Subthermal spectrum
Maxwl	Thermal, normally used for experiments measured in or corrected to a Maxwellian distribution characteristic of 293°K. Variations may be indicated in the "comments" section. It is known that some erroneous entries exist where Maxwl means 'in the thermal energy range' or even 'at 0.0253 eV', which is usually entered in numerical form.
Pile	Real pile spectrum (depends on the source)
Fast	Fast reactor spectrum
Fiss	Fission spectrum, normally ^{235}U fissioned by thermal neutrons

Other alphabetic energy-entries are:

Thrsh Up   From the threshold energy upwards (for excitation functions)
None   No data given for energy
Spont   Spontaneous (for spontaneous fission)

4. Lab (see Table 4)

A three-character abbreviation shows the laboratory or institution where the work was done or the home laboratory of the first author.

5. Type

The general character of the information is shown in two abbreviations. The first describes the nature of the work referenced: experimental, theoretical, review, etc. The second describes the type of reference containing the information: journal, report, conference proceedings, abstract ...

Data Type

Expt   experiment
Theo   theoretical calculation
ExTh   mixture of experiment and calculation
Comp   compilation of experimental information
Eval   a listing of 'digested' or evaluated data
Revw   a review or survey of information in a given field

Type of Reference

Abst   scientific meeting abstract
Book   book
Conf   conference proceedings or preprints
Diss   dissertation
Jour   journal article
Prep   preprint
Priv   private communication (in all forms)
Prog   progress report (as in quarterlies)
Rept   report (not otherwise covered)
Data   numerical data in computer files

6. Documentation (see Table 3 for reference codes)

This section shows where to find the article or report containing the information. Generally speaking the sources of information fall into four categories which are treated differently:

a. Published periodicals
b. Conference contributions and proceedings
c. Numbered reports
d. Unpublished material and private communications

a. **Published periodicals.** Here the reference usually consists of the periodical abbreviation in two to four letters, followed by the volume number (the issue number where needed), the page number, and the date by month and year.

b. **Conferences.** Conferences are identified by the last two digits of the year of the conference followed by an abbreviation of its location, except when the proceedings are published in a regular journal or report series. For example, 65 Antwerp refers to the conference held in Antwerp in 1965, the International Conference on the Study of Nuclear Structure with Neutrons. The abbreviation is followed by the volume number (if there is more than one) and then by the page number from the published proceedings, whilst the paper number will be prefixed by a § sign. The date is always that of the conference. The conference codes are listed at the beginning of Table 3.

c. **Numbered reports.** The customary report abbreviation is entered, with its number and date of issue. These report codes are included in Table 3.

d. **Unpublished material and private communications.** An effort is made to keep track in CINDA of private communications and preprints, the publication of which is not imminent, when the author is willing to let their existence be known.
Such material is entered under the author's name in the form

       Priv Newson Aug 63

Further information can be obtained from Newson or from the CINDA centres.

e. **Numerical data in computer files.** Numerical data stored in generally available computer libraries are indexed by a code defining the library and an accession-number, by which data sets can be identified when requesting them from a data centre or when quoting them in a publication, for example:
       EXFOR 10234.005 Feb 71
       UKNDL-DFN 123D Nov 73

The date given is usually the date of entry in the library or the date of the last revision. The libraries indexed in this issue are briefly described in Sect. 8 below. The codes by which they are defined are included in Table 3 of the Annex.

7. Comments

The preceding sections of the entry are reasonably standardized and contain most of the information needed by the user to direct his attention to a certain reference. The Comments section allows CINDA indexers to include further information in free format about the work referenced, often sufficient to tell the user whether the reference is worth his further attention. The style and amount of information in the Comments section depends upon the particular indexer. In general the section may indicate

  One author's name (+ stands for et al.)
  Further specification about the quantity measured
  The method of measurement
  The number of points measured
  How the data are presented (or if numbers are given at all)
  The state of completeness of the experiment
  Whether there is a comparison with theory
  (Actual results; this information should be treated with caution!)

It might be appropriate at this point to issue a WARNING AGAINST USING INFORMATION GIVEN IN THE COMMENTS SECTION WITHOUT CONSULTING THE ORIGINAL ARTICLE.

A.5

The sole purpose of the Comments section is to help the user decide whether the reference is of interest. Because of space limitations the information in the comments is severely compressed and incomplete; it must not in any way be used as a substitute for the original reference. The high degree of compression attempted in presenting any useful information in limited space has led to abbreviations which depend to some extent on the temperament of indexers. An attempt has been made to standardize the abbreviations. A list of the abbreviations used in CINDA, both current and superseded, is given in Table 5. For the most part they can be reconstituted into plain language simply by supplying missing vowels and occasionally final syllables. It must be admitted that in the past the compression of the comments has been carried out to the point of unintelligibility, in a number of entries. The present practice is to make the comments clear and understandable even at the expense of added information.

8. Numerical data libraries indexed in CINDA

Entries are often marked with a cross (+) in the right-hand margin of the page, under the heading 'Data'. The cross shows that at least some of the numerical data from the reference are on file and can be obtained on request from one of the four co-operating centres. In many of these cases a "data-index line" appears either below the bibliographic reference(s) of a given work or by itself; it contains in the 'Documentation' field the file name and, for some files, a data accession-number of the form:

    EXFOR 10234.005,
    UKNDL-DFN 234D,
    BENZI-DFN 789,
    AUSTR-DFN 249,
    KEDAK-3,
    VIEN-V0002.003,
    JNDC-FFP-WG,
    JENDL-1,
    CNEN-CEA,
    SOKRATOR-1001.

Such entries show the energy range covered by the numerical data actually on file, and in the 'Comment' field carry further information defining the quantity measured, the number of data points, etc. The date given behind the accession-number is usually the date of entry into the library or the date of the last revision to the data.

Those experimental data which have been compiled at the four neutron data centres before the EXFOR agreement came into force, remain tagged with a cross (+) only, attached to a normal literature reference at the right-hand margin.

The data libraries indexed in the present issue are the following:

a. **EXFOR** is a computerized system of codes and formats used for the exchange of experimental neutron nuclear data and associated physics information between the Four Neutron Data Centres issuing CINDA (see p. VII of the introduction). Each regional centre, having different computer facilities and user needs, operates its own internal storage and retrieval system (e.g. CSISRS, NEUDADA) optimized for its needs and facilities. EXFOR is compatible with these centre-internal systems so that all data compiled at one centre are easily transmitted, through EXFOR, into the internal system of the other centres thus becoming available to users all over the world. The EXFOR accession-numbers given in CINDA apply also to the internal system of each of the Four Centres. More detailed information on the EXFOR system can be obtained from each of the Four Centres.

b. **UKNDL** — the **UKAEA N**uclear **D**ata **L**ibrary — is indexed in CINDA for those parts which are generally available, that is: complete sets of evaluated neutron nuclear data for 23 lighter nuclides or elements ($Z \leq 29$) and for 8 transactinium nuclides ($Z \geq 90$), and evaluations of 20 specific reactions used in neutron dosimetry. The format is described in AWRE/0-70/63 (Sep 1973) by K. Parker.

c. **BENZI** — the Bologna Neutron Data Library for Fission Products — was issued in the years 1966—1971 and contains evaluated neutron cross-sections (mainly (n,γ)) for 247 fission product nuclei. It has the format of the UKNDL.

d. **AUSTR** — the Australian Neutron Data Library for Fission Products — was issued in Nov 1971 and contains evaluated total, elastic, non-elastic, inelastic, capture and transport neutron cross-sections for 192 fission product nuclei. It has the format of the UKNDL.

e. **KEDAK-3**, the Karlsruhe Evaluated Nuclear Data Library, was issued in October 1975 and contains evaluated neutron cross-sections between 1 MeV and 15 MeV for 46 target-isotopes or elements.

f. **VIEN** — a collection of **V**arious **I**nternational **E**valuated **N**eutron data has been started by the IAEA Nuclear Data Section in EXFOR format to include such evaluated data which are not part of one of the established evaluated data libraries.

g. **JENDL-1**, the Japanese Evaluated Neutron Data Library was issued in October 1977 and contains evaluated neutron cross-sections for 72 target isotopes or elements; in ENDF/B format.

h. **JNDC-FFP-WG**, Evaluations of the **J**apanese **N**eutron **D**ata **C**ommittee — **F**ission **P**roduct **W**orking **G**roup, issued in November 1977; containing evaluated neutron cross-sections of 62 fission product isotopes in ENDF/B format, 34 of which have been indexed in CINDA.

i. **CNEN-CEA** the evaluated data library from the CNEN (Bologna, Italy)—CEA (Saclay, France) collaboration. Preliminary evaluations issued in January 1978 contain neutron cross-section data for 63 fission products in the ENDF/B format.

j. **SOKRATOR**, the USSR evaluated neutron data library, contains at present evaluated neutron cross-section data for 47 isotopes (for 37 of them only differential and integral elastic cross-sections). The evaluation is continuing, the format is similar to the UKNDL-format.

Numerical data are available to requestors either as listings or on computer-readable media, usually magnetic tape, and in a standard format. For requestors wishing to use the data as input to computer programs, the saving in data preparation work is clear. A less obvious advantage of requesting data from regional centres is that especially for larger data sets it frequently happens that only a curve or other qualitative description of the experimental results appears in the published literature. The original numbers can often be supplied only by the data centres; see their addresses on page VII of the introduction.

More detailed documentation on formats and contents of available nuclear data libraries as well as retrievals from these libraries can be requested from the data centres. Their services are advertised in the Newsletters of the US National Neutron Cross-Section Center, and the IAEA report CINDU-11 (March 1976) and its supplement 1 (April 1977) of the IAEA Nuclear Data Section, and the report series Jadernye Konstanty of the USSR Nuclear Data Centre.

ACKNOWLEDGEMENTS

CINDA began in 1956 as a private index maintained by Prof. H. Goldstein and his then colleagues at Nuclear Development Associates. Computer operation of the file dates from 1963, when the original punched cards were translated into computer format at Columbia University, and outside indexers were enlisted, to be joined in 1964 by the NEA Neutron Data Compilation Centre (CCDN), who maintained an identical master file at Saclay, the IAEA Nuclear Data Section (1965) and the USSR Nuclear Data Centre (1966). Readers send in their contributions to regional centres, who carry out checking operations and cover the remaining literature from their area; U.S. and Canadian operations were transferred in 1966 to TIC, Oak Ridge, and in 1974 to NNDC Brookhaven. The original Fortran programs, later adapted to run at CCDN and in Oak Ridge, have been replaced by PL/1 programs better suited to the file's increased size and to changes in the computer environment in which CINDA is maintained. Special tapes prepared by the NEA Data Bank at Saclay (previously CCDN) are then converted by the IAEA Nuclear Data Section for input to the photo-typesetting process by which this book is produced. CINDA's founder, Prof. H. Goldstein of Columbia University, has taken a leading part in its continued development, both as Chairman of the US CINDA Steering Group and as a CINDA indexer.

The Physicists at each Centre responsible for CINDA are:
- Brookhaven: C. Dunford
- Obninsk: V.N. Manokhin
- Saclay: P.D. Johnston
- Vienna: H.D. Lemmel and G. Lammer

The indexers in the Centres and the outside indexers are listed below. The editors wish to express their extreme gratitude to all these people, and to past collaborators, whose work together makes up CINDA as it now stands.

- Abrahams, K., (to 1972), Reactor Centrum Nederland, Netherlands
- Almen-Ramstroem, E., Studsvik, Sweden
- Balakrishnan, M., Bhabha Atomic Research Centre, Trombay, Bombay, India
- Behrens, H., ZAED Karlsruhe, Fed. Rep. of Germany
- Benzi, V., (to 1972), Centro di Calcolo del CNEN, Italy
- Bluet, J.C., CEN Cadarache, France
- Brunner, J., (to 1970), Eidg. Institut für Reaktorforschung, Switzerland
- Butland, A.T.D., AEE Winfrith, United Kingdom
- Calamand, A., (to 1975), Nuclear Data Section, IAEA
- Dayday, N., Nuclear Data Section, IAEA
- Depisch, R., (to 1968), Nuclear Data Section, IAEA
- Derrien, H., (to 1978), NEA Data Bank, France
- Gerwin, H., Kernforschungsanlage Jülich, Fed. Rep. of Germany
- Gruppelaar, H., ECN Petten, Netherlands
- Hanna, G.C., (to 1967), Chalk River Laboratories, Canada
- Højerup, F., Risø Research Establishment, Denmark
- Holden, N., (to 1977), NNDC Brookhaven, USA
- Hopkins, J., (to 1967), Los Alamos Scientific Laboratory, USA
- Howerton, R.J., (to 1967), Lawrence Radiation Laboratory, USA
- Junker, K., Eidg. Institut für Reaktorforschung, Switzerland
- Kaas P., (to 1971), Nuclear Data Section, IAEA
- Kalos, M.H., (to 1967), New York University, USA
- Kuchowicz, B., University of Warsaw, Poland
- Lammer, M., (to 1974), Nuclear Data Section, IAEA
- Legrand, A.M., NEA Data Bank, France
- Lemley, J., (to 1975), Nuclear Data Section, IAEA

Lesca, L., (to 1976) CCDN Saclay, France
L'Hériteau, J.P., CEN, Saclay, France
Liskien, H., Bureau Central de Mesures Nucléaires, EURATOM
Lubitz, C.R., (to 1967), Knolls Atomic Power Laboratory, USA
Manero, F., JEN Madrid, Spain
Mather, D.S., AWRE Aldermaston, United Kingdom
McLane, V., NNDC Brookhaven, USA
Møller, H.B., (to 1971), Risø Research Establishment, Denmark
Momota, T., JAERI, Tokai Research Establishment, Japan
Nakasima, R., Hosei University, Japan
Ohlig, U., Kernforschungsanlage Jülich, Fed. Rep. of Germany
Okamoto, K., Nuclear Data Section, IAEA (to 1974 at CCDN Saclay)
Parker, K., (to 1967), AWRE Aldermaston, United Kingdom
Paulsen, A., Bureau Central de Mesures Nucléaires, EURATOM
Poortmans, F., Centre d'Etude de l'Energie Nucléaire, Belgium
Popov, V.I., Nuclear Data Centre, Obninsk
Porter, D., (to 1970), AWRE Aldermaston, United Kingdom
Reffo, G., Centro di Calcolo del CNEN, Italy
Ribon, P., CEN, Saclay, France
Robertson, J.C., Dundee College of Technology, United Kingdom
Schust, J., Kernforschungszentrum Karlsruhe, Fed. Rep. of Germany
Schwerer, O., Nuclear Data Section, IAEA
Sowerby, M.B., AERE Harwell, United Kingdom
Story, J.S., AEE Winfrith, United Kingdom
Tanaka, S., JAERI, Tokai, Japan
Tarasko, L.S., Nuclear Data Centre, Obninsk
Thompson, G., (to 1977), NNDC Brookhaven, USA
Tisljar, M., Reaktorzentrum Seibersdorf, Austria
Tubbs, N.A., NEA Data Bank Saclay, France
Waite, G., NNDC Brookhaven, USA
Wallin, L., FOA, Stockholm, Sweden
Whitehead, L., (to 1974), TIC Oak Ridge, USA
Winiwarter, P., (1973), Nuclear Data Section, IAEA
Wood, I., Kjeller, Norway
Yaghubian, R., (to 1977), Nuclear Data Section, IAEA

Each of the four Data Centres responsible for CINDA has devoted a special effort to the cleanup of the CINDA file in order to render the information in this book more accurate. NNDC wishes to thank the physicists and data aides who participated in its cleanup project: C. Dunford, G. Waite, M. Bhat, M. Divadeenam, T. Burrows, J. Tuli, S. Pearlstein, A. Prince, P. Rose, B. Magurno, L. Levitt, L. Peker, G. Thompson, V. McLane, J. Stehn (physicists), and A. Daly, M. Blennau, P. Dixon, S. Santos, J. Jensen, J. Roys (data aides). At the NEA Data Bank the cleanup was performed by H. Derrien and P.D. Johnston; at the two other Centres the revisions were done by the designated CINDA indexers.

All file maintenance operations are carried out at the NEA Data Bank (previously CCDN), Saclay. The physicists responsible for the development of the computer programs are: W. Schuler and G. Danet (both NEA-DB). The conversion of the file for input to the photo-typesetting process is made by the IAEA Nuclear Data Section. A duplicate copy of the CINDA masterfile is kept by NNDC, Brookhaven.

The editors wish to acknowledge also the work of all the programmers who have helped in the earlier development of CINDA:

Attree, Mrs. P.M., Nuclear Data Section, IAEA
Battershill, I., Nuclear Data Section, IAEA
Burt, J., NNDC Brookhaven
Dudey, Mrs. R., Columbia University, New York, USA
Hirschbichler, Mrs. F., Nuclear Data Section, IAEA
Jones, J., TIC Oak Ridge, USA
Kidd, E., Union Carbide Corp., Oak Ridge, USA
Kortmann, H., CCDN Saclay, France
McLaughlin, K., Nuclear Data Section, IAEA
Miller, Mrs. A., Union Carbide Corp., Oak Ridge, USA
Paris, Mrs. F., CCDN Saclay, France
Pellegrino, L., CCDN Saclay, France
Radet, Mrs. M., CCDN Saclay, France
Rickeby, C., CCDN Saclay, France
Schofield, A., CCDN Saclay, France
Tubbs, N., CCDN Saclay, France
Willars, H., CCDN Saclay, France

TABLE 1: ABBREVIATIONS FOR MOLECULES AND MIXTURES

For those molecules and mixtures which are of primary interest with respect to neutron cross-sections, the following abbreviations are used:

1 Hydrogen	BNZ	Benzene
1 Hydrogen	CXX	Organic compounds not covered by special code
1 Hydrogen	MTH	Methane CH_4
1 Hydrogen	PFN	Paraffin
1 Hydrogen	PHL	Phenyl (di-, ter-, poly-)
1 Hydrogen	PLE	Polyethylene
1 Hydrogen	WTR	Water (H_2O), ice, steam
2 Deuterium	DXX	Deuterium compounds except D_2O and Zr-deuteride. Includes mixed H-D compounds.
2 Deuterium	D2O	Heavy water, D_2O and HDO
3 Tritium	TXX	Tritium compounds except Zr-tritide. Includes mixed H-T and D-T compounds.
4 Beryllium	OXI	Beryllium oxide
7 Nitrogen	AIR	Air
7 Nitrogen	AMM	Ammonia compounds
14 Silicon	OXI	Silicon oxide (glass, mica)
40 Zirconium	HYD	Zirconium hydride (+ deuteride and tritide)
92 Uranium	OXI	Uranium oxide

Other chemical compounds which occur in CINDA less frequently, are coded by 'CMP' following an element name. The element listed is usually the element of greatest interest for reactor physics or the element responsible for the major component of the cross-section of this compound in the energy range considered. The formula of the compound is mostly given in the comment field.

TABLE 2: QUANTITY DEFINITIONS

(Notation used is that of H. Goldstein: "Nomenclature Scheme for Experimental Monoenergetic Nuclear Cross Sections", Fast Neutron Physics, Vol.II, p.2227, Interscience, New York (1963).)

Evaluation   **Definition:** A complete and consistent set of cross-sections in some energy range. In most cases, separate entries are prepared in addition for each quantity given in the evaluation. (A "best value" derived from comparing different $\overline{\nu}$ measurements would be entered under 'Nu' only.)

Total $\sigma_{nT}(E)$ **Definition:** The total neutron cross-section. This includes papers reporting transmission data without explicit derivation of the total cross-section.

Elastic $\sigma_{n,n}(E)$ **Definition:** The total elastic scattering cross-section, integrated over all angles. Scattering amplitude measurements are entered under 'Elastic', with a note in the comment, though a few may be found under 'Thermal Scat'.

Diff Elastic $\sigma_{n,n}(E,\theta)$ **Definition:** Angular distribution (not normalized) or differential scattering cross-section (normalized) for elastically scattered neutrons. Where the author has integrated a distribution already normalized at one angle to give the total elastic scattering cross-section, this will be found under 'Elastic'. **Note:** Prior to introducing the quantity 'Polarization', many polarization measurements involving elastic scattering have been entered under 'Diff Elastic', with a note in the comment; not all of these entries have yet been corrected.

Polarization   **Definition:** All polarization measurements for neutrons in the exit channel, following scattering or any other reaction. **Note:** This quantity was introduced in 1969; previously, polarization following elastic scattering has been indexed under 'Diff Elastic'.

Potntal Scat   **Definition:** A theoretical construct: that part of the scattering cross-section which does not depend on spin-orbit coupling, and which corresponds physically to scattering by a hard sphere. **Use:** For the non-resonant part of the scattering cross-section in the resonant region. This quantity is currently not much found in the literature.

Tot Inelastc $\sigma_{n,n'}(E)$ **Definition:** Total cross-section for neutron inelastic scattering, i.e. for neutron excitation of levels in the target nucleus which decay to the ground state by gamma ray emission. **Use:** Only for the cross-section integral over all levels excited and all angles. Angular distribution of inelastic neutrons and cross-sections for excitation of specific levels are entered under 'Diff Inelast'. Inelastic slow neutron scattering, where energy is lost to or gained from molecular or crystal excitations, is entered under 'Thermal Scat'. **Note:** Some literature uses the term "inelastic" where "non-elastic" is meant in the sense of these definitions.

Table 2

Diff Inelast $\sigma_{n,n'}(E,\theta)$ Definition: Angular distributions
$\sigma_{n,n'}(E; E')$ or energy spectra of inelastically
$\sigma_{n,n'}(E; E',\theta)$ scattered neutrons, or partial
cross-sections for inelastic

scattering: **Examples of use:**
1) the angular distribution of inelastically scattered 14 MeV neutrons from ^{40}Ca;
2) the energy spectrum recorded at 90° scattering angle for inelastically scattered neutrons;
3) cross-sections for scattering to the 6.14 MeV level in O^{16}, the reaction ^{16}O(n,n')^{16}O;
4) cross-section for excitation of metastable state by inelastic scattering, like ^{107}Ag (n,n') ^{107m}Ag.

Note: As for 'Tot Inelast', the category covers only **nuclear** scattering.

Thermal Scat Definition: Information on the elastic and inelastic scattering of slow neutrons in gases, liquids, crystals, etc., where chemical binding forces, molecular or crystal vibrations etc. are involved. Papers with main emphasis on solid state physics which do not give microscopic data are generally not included. **Note:** The classification of slow neutron data has not been fully consistent, and some molecular scattering data will be found under 'Elastic', 'Diff Inelast', etc.

Scattering $\sigma_{nS}(E)$ Definition: Information on the
$\sigma_{nS}(E,\theta)$
total scattering cross-section, ($\sigma_{nS} = \sigma_{n,n}(E) + \sigma_{n,n'}(E)$). Use: For experiments at neutron energies above threshold for inelastic scattering, below the (n, 2n) threshold, and in which neutron energy groups are not resolved. For data above the (n, 2n) threshold see under 'Nonelastic'. For data at energies below about 1 eV, where molecular and crystalline binding energies are involved, see under 'Thermal Scat'.

Nonelastic $\sigma_{nX}(E)$ Definition: The sum cross-section
$\sigma_{nX}(E,\theta)$ for all nonelastic processes,
$\sigma_{nX}(E; E',\theta)$ $\sigma_{nX} = \sigma_{nT} - \sigma_{n,n} = \sigma_{n,n'} + \sigma_{n,2n} + \sigma_{n,3n}$
$+ \sigma_{n,f} + \sigma_{n,p} + \sigma_{n,d} + \sigma_{n,\gamma} + \ldots$

Absorption $\sigma_{nA}(E)$ Definition: The absorption cross-section, $\sigma_{nA} = \sigma_{nT} - \sigma_{nS}$, i.e. the sum of all partial cross-sections except for elastic and inelastic scattering. If σ_{nA} is equal to $\sigma_{n\gamma}$, see under '(n,γ)'. For fissile nuclides below the (n, 2n) or (n, p) threshold, absorption equals capture plus fission: $\sigma_{nA} = \sigma_{n,\gamma} + \sigma_{n,f}$.

Res Int Abs $\displaystyle\int_{E_{min}}^{E_{max}} \frac{\sigma_{nA}(E)}{E} dE$ Definition: The resonance integral for absorption, capture or activation. **Note:** Relevant information may be found also under 'Res Int Capt'.

(n,γ) $\sigma_{n,\gamma}(E)$ Definition: Radiative capture cross-section, $\sigma_{n,\gamma}$.

Table 2

Res Int Capt
$$\int_{E_{min}}^{E_{max}} \frac{\sigma_{n,\gamma}(E)}{E} dE$$

Definition: Resonance integral for radiative capture. **Note:** Relevant information may be found also under 'Res Int Abs'.

Spect (n, γ)

Definition: Spectrum of gamma rays or conversion electrons following neutron capture. **Note:** The term 'gamma decay' includes the competing processes of internal conversion and pair production, so that conversion electron spectra from neutron capture would be entered under 'Spect (n, γ)' with an appropriate comment. Entries are made under the target nucleus; however a few entries may exist, where inadvertently the compound nucleus was coded. Information on delayed gammas following beta decay is not entered in CINDA; only incidentally entries may refer also to such information.

Inelastic γ
$\sigma_{n,n'}(E; E_\gamma)$
$\sigma_{n,n'}(E; E_\gamma, \theta)$

Definition: Information on production cross-section, angular distributions or energy spectra for gamma rays following the inelastic scattering of neutrons. **Note:** Many inelastic scattering experiments measure the production cross-section for a specific gamma ray. This cross-section will in general differ from the cross-section for excitation of its state of origin, but will be equal if gamma-ray cascades to and from the level can be excluded. In this case, the entry may also be found under 'Diff Inelast'.

Nonelastic γ
$\sigma_{nG}(E)$
$\sigma_{nG}(E, E_\gamma)$
$\sigma_{nG}(E; E_\gamma, \theta)$

Definition: Information on gamma rays from unseparated nonelastic processes.
Use: Covers production cross-sections, angular distributions and energy spectra. Not used for gamma rays which can be assigned to one of the definite processes:
a) Inelastic scattering (see 'Inelastic γ')
b) Fission or fission fragments (see 'Spect Fiss γ' or 'Fiss Prod γ')
c) Radiative capture (see 'Spect (n, γ)')
d) Gamma rays following (n,p) or other charged particle reactions (see '(n, p)', etc.)

(n,2n)
$\sigma_{n,2n}(E)$
$\sigma_{n,2n}(E, E')$
$\sigma_{n,2n}(E; E', \theta)$

Definition: Information on (n, 2n) and (n, 2nC) reactions (C = charged particles), including integral and differential data. **Note:** The proton spectrum from the reaction d(n, 2n p) is also entered under this quantity; compare the 'Lightest particle rule' at the end of Table 2.
When the neutrons from the (n, 2n) were not separated from the inelastically scattered neutrons, see under 'n Emission'.
The reactions (n, 2 n f) and (n, 3n) are not included under this quantity.

Table 2

(n, xn) x > 2	$\sigma_{n,3n}(E)$ etc........	**Definition**: Information on (n, 3n), (n,4n), (n, 3n C) and other reactions producing at least 3 neutrons

(C = charged particles). Details are similar as for (n,2n). See also under 'n Emission'.

n Emission $\sigma_{nM}(E)$
$\sigma_{nM}(E,\theta)$
$\sigma_{nM}(E; E',\theta)$

Definition: The sum cross-section for all nonelastic processes resulting in neutron emission, weighted for the number of neutrons produced:
$$\sigma_{nM} = \sigma_{n,n'} + 2\sigma_{n,2n} + 3\sigma_{n,3n} + \bar{\nu}\sigma_{n,f} + \sigma_{n,np} + \ldots$$

Information on reactions emitting one or more charged particles only is listed under:

(n, p)	$\sigma_{n,p}(E)$	proton(s) emitted
(n, d)	$\sigma_{n,p}(E,\theta)$	deuteron(s) emitted
(n, t)	etc...	triton(s) emitted
(n, He3)		helium-3 particle(s) emitted
(n, α)		alpha particle(s) emitted

Use: Total or partial cross-sections, angular or energy distribution, ratios between groups to different levels of the product nucleus, etc.

Information on reactions emitting one neutron and one or more charged particles is listed under:

(n, np)	$\sigma_{n,np}(E)$	proton(s) emitted
(n, nd)	$\sigma_{n,np}(E,\theta)$	deuteron(s) emitted
(n, nt)	etc...	triton(s) emitted
(n, nα)		alpha particle(s) emitted

If two (or more) **neutrons** are emitted '(n,2n)' or '(n,xn) x > 2' will be used.

Fission $\sigma_{n,f}(E)$

Definition: The cross-section for neutron induced fission, or for inelastic scattering to the spontaneously fissioning isomer. The following quantities cover details of the fission reaction. **Note**: Information on fission neutrons, fragments and gammas from **spontaneous fission** can be found under the corresponding quantities for neutron induced fission.

Res Int Fiss $\int_{E_{min}}^{E_{max}} \frac{\sigma_{n,f}(E)}{E} dE$

Definition: Resonance integral, fission.

Alpha $\alpha = \dfrac{\sigma_{n,\gamma}}{\sigma_{n,f}}$

Definition: The capture to fission cross-section ratio.

Table 2

Eta $$\eta = \frac{\bar{\nu}\sigma_{n,f}}{\sigma_{n,\gamma} + \sigma_{n,f}}$$ **Definition:** The number of neutrons emitted per absorption. **Use:** For fissionable elements only. For non-fissionable elements 'n Emission' is used.

Nu ν **Definition:** ν, the number of prompt neutrons emitted per fission. **Use:** Information covered includes $\bar{\nu}$ (the average number of fission neutrons, prompt or total), the probability distribution of ν per individual fission and angular distributions for fission neutrons. **Note:** Information on neutrons from a given fragment is entered under 'Frag Neuts', that for delayed neutrons in general under 'Delayd Neuts'.

Delayed Neuts **Definition:** Information on yields, energies, etc., of **delayed** neutrons from fission.

Frag Neuts **Definition:** Information on neutrons emitted by a given fission fragment. **Note:** Distributions of ν vs. fragment mass are entered under this quantity.

Spect Fiss n **Definition:** Spectrum of neutrons emitted in fission. **Use:** For spectra, mean energies, etc.

Spect Fiss γ **Definition:** Spectrum of prompt gamma rays emitted in fission. See also under 'Fiss Prod γ'.

Fiss Prod γ **Definition:** Prompt γ-rays emitted in fission when they are assigned to fission products (otherwise see 'Spect Fiss γ'), and all delayed γ-rays from the unseparated fission products. **Use:** Spectra, mean energies, yields, etc. **Note:** A very few entries for fission product betas appear under this heading. Also K, L, M X-rays from fission products are entered here. The quantities 'Fiss Prod γ' and 'Spect Fiss γ' are not always separable.

Fiss Prod β **Definition:** Spectra, mean energies etc. of β-rays from the unseparated fission products. **Note:** Information on fission product beta-rays may also be found under 'Fiss Prod γ'.

Fiss Yield **Definition:** Yields of fission products or fission fragments (prompt, direct, chain or cumulative). Entries for ternary fission probabilities are found in this category.

Frag Spectra **Definition:** The energy or angular distribution of fission products. **Note:** Before January 1966, this information was entered under 'Fiss Yield'.

Frag Charge **Definition:** Information on the charge distribution of fission fragments, charge dispersion, most probable charge $Z_p(A)$, fractional yields etc.

Table 2

Reson Params Γ, Γ_f, J, D, etc.   **Definition:** All resonance parameter information, such as total width, partial widths for fission, gamma emission or particle emission, spins of resonances, average level spacing, Adler-Adler parameters, etc. Note that resonance parameters like other quantities are entered under the target nucleus, not under the compound nucleus. The energy limits do not refer to the neutron-energy range of the experiment but to the lowest and highest resonance energy observed.

Strnth Fnctn S_0, S_1 **Definition:** The strength function

$$\frac{\langle\Gamma\rangle}{D} = \frac{\Sigma_i \Gamma_i}{\Delta E},$$ where Γ_i is the reduced neutron width, D the mean level spacing, and $\Delta E = E_{max} - E_{min}$. The energy limits refer to resonance energies. Entries are found under the target nucleus.

Lvl Density   **Definition:** Information on level density parameters, like spin cut-off factor, parameter "a", nuclear temperature; the level density obtained from cross-sections in unresolved resonance regions is also entered under this quantity.

(γ, n) $\sigma_{\gamma,n}(E_\gamma)$ **Definition:** Information on (γ, n) reactions. **Use:** Restricted to $E_\gamma \leqslant 15$ MeV and to the following target nuclei: D, ^{6}Li, ^{7}Li, ^{9}Be, ^{13}C, ^{17}O. However, a few such entries for other elements may have been entered incidentally. In the energy field the energy range of the incident gammas is given.

Photo-Fissn   **Definition:** Information on gamma ($E\gamma \leqslant 15$ MeV) induced fission. **Use:** Cross-section, yields and spectra of neutrons, fragments, gammas, etc.

Cross-Section Hierarchy

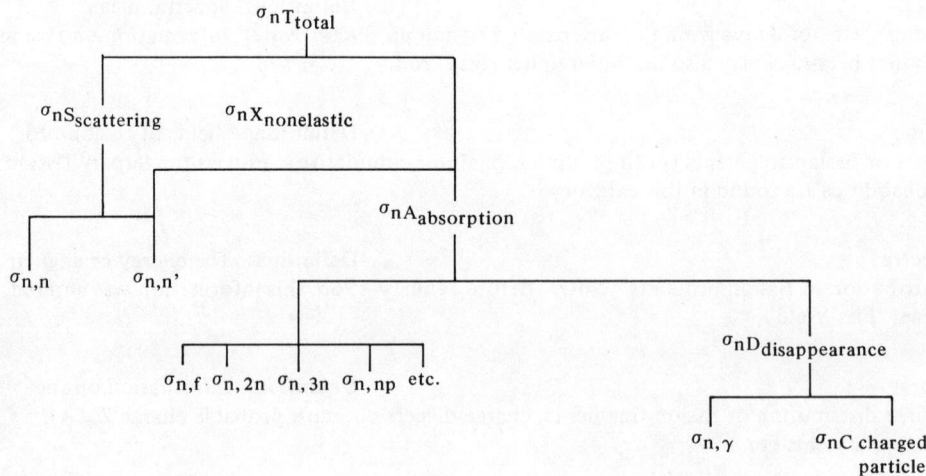

Table 2

Lightest-Particle Rule

Note that reactions with light nuclei are listed always under the raction type with the lighter outgoing particle, e.g.

Li^6 (n,α)   is listed under Li^6 (n,t)
Li^6 (n,d)   is listed under Li^6 (n, nd)
C^{12} (n,3α)   is listed under C^{12} (n,nα)

TABLE 3: REF CODES

Abbreviations for Conference Proceedings, Journals and Reports which are entered in the 'Documentation' field of CINDA in the 'Ref' column.
(Note to CINDA indexers: this list should not be used for coding new entries because it includes codes which are out of date but still existing in the file.)

Code	Description	Country
55ANS	NUCLEAR SCIENCE AND ENGINEERING CONGRESS, CLEVELAND, 12-16 DECEMBER 1955.	USA
55Geneva	FIRST INTERNATIONAL CONFERENCE ON THE PEACEFUL USES OF ATOMIC ENERGY, GENEVA, 8-20 AUG. 1955	U.N.
55Moscow	CONF. OF THE USSR ACAD. SCI. ON PEACEFUL USES OF ATOMIC ENERGY. MOSCOW, 1-5 JULY 1955	USSR
56BNL	CONFERENCE ON RESONANCE ABSORPTION OF NEUTRONS. BROOKHAVEN NAT'L LAB, 24-25 SEPT 1956 PUBL AS BNL-433	USA
56Kiev	KIEV CONFERENCE, KIEV, 1956	USSR
57ANS	AMERICAN NUCL. SOCIETY MEETING, NEW YORK, N.Y., 28-31 OCOTBER 1957	USA
57Col.Univ	INT. CONF. ON NEUTRON INTERACTIONS WITH NUCLEI, COLUMBIA UNIV., NEW YORK, SEP 1957. PUBL. AS TID-7547	USA
57Paris	UNESCO CONF. ON RADIOISOTOPES IN SCIENT. RESEARCH, PARIS 9-20 SEP 1957, EDITED BY EXTERMANN AND PUBL. 1958 BY PERGAMON PRESS, VOLUME 1 = RISR1	FRANCE
58Geneva	SECOND UN CONF. ON THE PEACEFUL USES OF ATOMIC ENERGY, GENEVA, 1-13 SEP 1968	U.N.
58Paris	INT. CONGRESS ON NUCL. PHYSICS, NUCL. INTERACTIONS AT LOW ENERGIES AND NUCL. STRUCTURE. PARIS, 7-12 JUL 1958	FRANCE
59ANL	CONFERENCE ON PHYSICS OF BREEDING, ARGONNE NATIONAL LAB, 19-21 OCT 1959. PROC PUBL AS ANL-6122	USA
59Calcutta	SYMPOSIUM ON LOW-ENERGY NUCLEAR PHYSICS CALCUTTA 19-21 FEB. 1959	INDIA
59London	INT. CONF. ON NUCL. FORCES AND THE FEW-NUCLEON PROBLEM, LONDON 1959 (PUBL. 1960).	UK
59Tashkent	CONFERENCE ON THE PEACEFUL USES OF ATOMIC ENERGY. TASHKENT, USSR, 28 SEPT - 3 OCT 1959.	USSR
59Vienna	IAEA PANEL ON HEAVY WATER LATTICES, VIENNA SEP 1959 PUBLISHED 1960 AS STI/PUB/17	IAEA
60Basel	CONF. OF THE SWISS PHYSICAL SOCIETY ON POLARISATION PHENOMENA IN NUCL. REACTIONS, 4-8 JULY 1960. PUBL. AS SUPPL. TO HELV. PHYS. ACTA VOL.33 (1960).	SWITZERLAND
60Kingston	UNITED NATIONS CONFERENCE ON NUCLEAR STRUCTURE. KINGSTON, CANADA, 29 AUG - 3 SEP 1960	U.N.
60London	INT. CONF. ON NUCL. FORCES AND THE FEW NUCLEON PROBLEM, LONDON 1959 (PUBL. 1960)	UK
60S-Vienna	IAEA SYMPOSIUM ON SELECTED TOPICS IN RADIATION DOSIMETRY, VIENNA JUNE 1960, PUBLISHED 1961 AS STI/PUB/25	IAEA
60Vienna	IAEA SYMPOS. ON PILE NEUTRON RESEARCH, VIENNA 17-21 OCT. 1960, PUBLISHED BY IAEA JAN. 1962	IAEA
60Waltair	SYMPOSIUM ON LOW ENERGY NUCLEAR PHYSICS, WALTAIR 24-26 FEB 1960	INDIA
60Wien	IAEA SYMPOSIUM ON INELASTIC SCATTERING OF NEUTRONS IN SOLIDS AND LIQUIDS. VIENNA, 11-14 OCT 1960.	IAEA
61Bombay	NUCLEAR PHYSICS SYMPOSIUM, BOMBAY, FEBUARY 1961	INDIA
61Brussels	COLLOQUIUM ON NEUTRON TIME-OF-FLIGHT METHODS, BRUSSELS 1961	BELGIUM
61Bucharst	INT. CONF. ON PHYSICS AND TECHNIQUE OF RESEARCH REACTORS, BUCURESTI, 10-17 NOV 1961. PROCEED. PUBL. AS SUPPL. TO REVUE ROUM. DE PHYS. VOL. 6 (1961)	ROMANIA
61Manchstr	RUTHERFORD JUBILEE INTERNATIONAL CONFERENCE MANCHESTER 4-8 SEP. 1961 PROCEEDINGS BY J.B. BIRKS EDITOR, LONDON 1961	UK

Table 3   REF CODES

Code	Description	Country
61RPI	SYMPOSIUM ON NEUTRON PHYSICS. RENSSELAER POLYTECH.INST.,TROY,N.Y., MAY 1961 EDITED BY M.L.YEATER AS 'NEUTRON PHYSICS'	USA
61Saclay	EANDC CONFERENCE ON TIME OF FLIGHT METHODS, SACLAY 24-27 JULY 1961 = NEUTTOF(EANDC)	FRANCE
61Vienna	IAEA SEMINAR ON THE PHYSICS OF FAST AND INTERMEDIATE REACTORS. VIENNA, 3-11 AUG 1961, IAEA STI/PUB/49.	IAEA
61Wien	IAEA SYMP. ON THE PROGRAMMING AND UTILIZATION OF RESEARCH REACTORS,VIENNA OCT 1961, PUBLISHED 1962	IAEA
62BNL	PROCEEDINGS OF THE BROOKHAVEN CONFERENCE ON NEUTRON THERMALIZATION,BROOKHAVEN NATIONAL LAB., UPTON,N.Y,APRIL 30-MAY 2,1962.PUBLISHED AS BNL-719	USA
62Chalk R.	INELASTIC SCAT OF NEUTRONS IN LIQUIDS+SOLIDS, SYMPOSIUM CHALK RIVER, 10-14 SEP 1962	CANADA
62Harwell	SYMPOS.ON NEUTRON DOSIMETRY,HARWELL,DEC.1962 PUBLISHED BY IAEA,VIENNA,MAY 1963	UK
62Madras	NUCL. PHYSICS SYMPOS., MADRAS, 28FEB-2MARCH 1962	INDIA
62Mexico	4TH INTER-AMERICAN SYMPOSIUM ON THE PEACEFUL APPLICATIONS OF NUCLEAR ENERGY, MEXICO CITY, 9-13 APRIL 1962	MEXICO
62Padua	DIRECT INTERACTIONS AND NUCLEAR REACTION MECHANISMS, PADUA, SEPTEMBER 3-8, 1962. GORDON AND BREACH NEW YORK 1963	ITALY
62Wien	IAEA PANEL ON LIGHT WATER LATTICES, VIENNA MAY-JUNE 1962, PUBLISHED 1962 AS STI/DOC/10/12	IAEA
63Amsterdm	IAEA SYMP. ON EXPONENTIAL AND CRITICAL EXPERIMENTS, AMSTERDAM 2-6 SEP 1963, PUBL. 1962 AS STI/PUB/79	IAEA
63ANL	INTERNATIONAL CONFERENCE ON NUCLEAR PHYSICS WITH REACTOR NEUTRONS,ARGONNE NATIONAL LAB.,ARGONNE, ILLINOIS, OCTOBER 15-17,1963.PUBLISHED AS ANL-6797	USA
63Bombay	SYMPOSIUM ON NUCLEAR PHYSICS AND SOLID STATE PHYS., BOMBAY, 27FEB-2MARCH 1963	INDIA
63Gatlinbg	AM. PHYS. SOC. FALL MEETING, GATLINBURG, OCT 1963	USA
63Houston	INTERNATIONAL CONFERENCE ON FAST NEUTRON PHYSICS, RICE UNIVERSITY, HOUSTON, TEXAS, 26-28 FEB 1963, PROCEEDINGS PUBLISHED AS 'PROGRESS IN FAST NEUTRON PHYSICS' BY UNIV.OF CHICAGO PRESS, 1963.	USA
63Karlsrhe	NEUTRON PHYSICS CONFERENCE, KARLSRUHE 8-10 OCT 1963	GERMANY
63Manchstr	CONF. ON LOW AND MEDIUM ENERGY NUCL. PHYS.,MANCHESTER, SEPTEMBER 1963	UK
63S.Paulo	SYMPOSIUM ON UTILISATION OF RESEARCH REACTORS, SAO PAULO, 4-8 NOVEMBER 1963	BRAZIL
64Bombay	IAEA SYMPOSIUM ON INELASTIC SCATTERING OF NEUTRONS IN SOLIDS AND LIQUIDS, BOMBAY 15-19 DEC 1964, PUBLISHED 1965 AS STI/PUB/92	IAEA
64Chandgrh	NUCLEAR PHYSICS AND SOLID STATE PHYSICS SYMP., CHANDIGARH 24-28 FEB 1964	INDIA
64Geneva	THIRD INTERNATIONAL CONFERENCE ON THE PEACEFUL USES OF ATOMIC ENERGY, GENEVA, 31 AUG - 9 SEP 1964	U.N.
64Paris	COMPTES RENDUS DU CONGRES INTERNATIONAL DE PHYSIQUE NUCLEAIRE, PARIS, 2-8 JUILLET 1964	FRANCE
64Vienna	IAEA PANEL ON USE OF PLUTONIUM FOR POWER PRODUCTION VIENNA 7-11 DEC 1964, PUBL. 1965 AS STI/DOC/10/49	IAEA
64Wien	IAEA PANEL ON IN-PILE DOSIMETRY, VIENNA JULY 1964, PUBLISHED 1965 AS STI/DOC/10/46	IAEA
65Antwerp	INT.CONF.ON THE STUDY OF NUCLEAR STRUCTURE WITH NEUTRONS, ANTWERP 19-23 JULY 1965. PROCEEDINGS GIVE FOR SOME PAPERS ABSTRACT ONLY. FOR FULL PAPERS SEE EANDC-50. FOR TECHNICAL MINUTES SEE EANDC-44.	BELGIUM
65Calcutta	SYMPOSIUM ON NUCL. PHYSICS AND SOLID STATE PHYS., CALCUTTA 8-13 FEB 1965 'VOL.1'= SOLID STATE PHYSICS,'VOL.2'=NUCL. PHYSICS	INDIA

REF CODES   Table 3

Code	Description	Location
65IAEA	IAEA SYMPOSIUM ON PERSONNEL DOSIMETRY FOR RADIATION ACCIDENTS. VIENNA, 8-12 MARCH 1965.	IAEA
65KFK	INTERNATIONAL SYMPOSIUM ON POLARIZATION PHENOMENA IN NUCLEI, KARLSRUHE, 6-10 SEPT 1965	GERMANY,F.R.
65Karlsrhe	IAEA SYMPOSIUM ON PULSED NEUTRON RESEARCH, KARLSRUHE 10-14 MAY 1965, (PREPRINTS SM-62/...), PROCEEDINGS PUBL. AS STI/PUB/104, VIENNA, AUG.1965	IAEA
65Salzburg	IAEA SYMPOSIUM ON PHYSICS AND CHEMISTRY OF FISSION, SALZBURG, AUSTRIA, 22-26 MARCH 1965. PREPRINT-CODE = SM-60/... PUBLISHED BY IAEA, VIENNA, JULY 1965 (STI/PUB/101)	IAEA
66ANL	INTERNATIONAL CONF. ON FAST CRITICAL EXPERIMENTS AND THEIR ANALYSIS, ARGONNE 10-13 OCTOBER 1966, PUBLISHED AS ANL-7320	USA
66Argonne	CONF. ON SLOW NEUTRON CAPTURE GAMMA-RAY SPECTROSCOPY, ARGONNE, 2-4 NOV 1966.PUBL. AS ANL-7282, NOV 1968	USA
66Berkeley	RADIATION MEASUREMENTS IN NUCLEAR POWER CEGB CONFERENCE, BERKELEY, 12-16 SEPT 1966	UK
66Bombay	SYMPOSIUM ON NUCLEAR PHYSICS AND SOLID STATE PHYS., BOMBAY 21-25 FEB 1966	INDIA
66Dubna	IAEA PANEL ON RESEARCH AND APPLICATIONS OF NUCLEAR PULSED SYSTEMS, DUBNA 18-22 JULY 1966, PUBLISHED JULY 1967 AS STI/PUB/144	IAEA
66Gatlinbg	INT. CONF. ON NUC. PHYS.,GATLINBURG,TENN,12-17SEP 1966	USA
66Lyon	COLLOQUE SUR LES NOYAUX LEGERS 26-28 JAN. 1966,LYON	FRANCE
66Moscow	CONF. ON NUCL. SPECTROSCOPY, MOSCOW 1966. PUBL. IN IZV VOLS 30-31	USSR
66OXFORD	CONF. ON NUCL. STRUCT. AND ELEMENTARY PARTICLES, OXFORD, 30 MARCH - 1 APRIL 1966.	UK
66Paris	FIRST IAEA CONFERENCE ON NUCLEAR DATA FOR REACTORS PARIS, 17-21 OCT 1966. PREPRINT-CODE = CN-23/... PROCEEDINGS PUBL.BY IAEA,VIENNA,1967 (STI/PUB/140) SUPPLEMENT WITH ADDITIONAL PAPERS SEE INDC-156	IAEA
66S.Diego	ANS CONF. ON REACTOR PHYSICS IN THE RESONANCE AND THERMAL REGIONS. SAN DIEGO,CALIF, 7-9 FEB 1966	USA
66Trieste	LECTURES ON FUNDAMENTALS IN NUCLEAR THEORY. TRIESTE, OCT-DEC 1966. PUBL. BY IAEA,VIENNA, AUG 1967	ITALY
66Vienna	IAEA SYMPOSIUM ON STANDARDIZATION OF RADIONUCLIDES VIENNA 10-14 OCT 1966, PUBL. 1967 AS STI/PUB/139	IAEA
66Wash.	CONFERENCE ON NEUTRON CROSS-SECTION TECHNOLOGY, WASHINGTON D.C. 22-24 MAR 1966,PUBL. AS AEC REPORT CONF-660303	USA
67Ann Arbr	IAEA SYMPOSIUM ON NEUTRON THERMALIZATION AND REACTOR SPECTRA, ANN ARBOR,MICHIGAN,17-21 JULY 1967, PUBLISHED 1968 AS STI/PUB/160	IAEA
67Bordeaux	COLLOQUE DE PHYS. NUCL.,NOYAUX MOYENS ET NOYAUX LOURDS. FRENCH PHYSICAL SOCIETY, BORDEAUX, 22-24 MAR 1967	FRANCE
67Brela	SYMPOSIUM ON LIGHT NUCLEI, FEW BODY PROBLEMS AND NUCLEAR FORCES, BRELA, 26 JUNE - 5 JULY 1967	YUGOSLAV.
67Brussels	IAEA SYMPOSIUM ON PLUTONIUM AS A REACTOR FUEL, BRUSSELS 13-17 MARCH 1967, PUBLISHED SEPT 1967 AS STI/PUB/153	IAEA
67Gainsvll	CONF. ON NUCLEON-NUCLEON INTERACTION. GAINSVILLE, 23-25 MAR 1967. PUBL. IN REV. MOD. PHYS. 39 (3) 1967	USA
67Juelich	CONF.ON NEUTRON PHYSICS AT RESEARCH REACTORS JUELICH, GERMANY, 25-28 APRIL 1967.	GERMANY,F.R.
67Kanpur	SYMPOSIUM ON NUCLEAR PHYSICS AND SOLID STATE PHYS., KANPUR 28 FEB - 3 MARCH 1967	INDIA
67Karlsrhe	IAEA SYMPOS ON FAST REACTOR PHYS. AND RELATED SAFETY PROBLEMS,KARLSRUHE 30 OCT - 3 NOV 1967 PUBLISHED BY IAEA,VIENNA 1968	GERMANY,F.R.
67Kharkov	CONF. ON NUCLEAR SPECTROSCOPY AND NUCL. STRUCTURE, KHARKOV JAN-FEB 1967	USSR

Table 3   REF CODES

Code	Description	Country
67Krakow	SEMINAR ON NUCL. SPECTROSCOPY., KRAKOW, MAY 1967, PROGRAM AND ABSTRACTS PUBLISHED AS INP-543	POLAND
67Lublin	20TH POLISH PHYSICS CONGRESS,1967,LUBLIN	POLAND
67Schafhsn	SWISS PHYSICAL SOCIETY, AUTUMN MEETING, SCHAFFHAUSEN, 29 SEPT - 1 OCT 1967	SWITZERLAND
67Tokai	IAEA MEETING ON UTILIZATION OF RESEARCH REACTORS, TOKAI,JAPAN, OCT.1967	IAEA
67Tokyo	INT. CONF. ON NUCLEAR STRUCTURE, 7-13 SEP 1967 PUBLISHED AS SUPPLEMENT TO JPJ VOL.24 (1968)	JAPAN
67Vienna	IAEA PANEL ON DELAYED FISSION NEUTRONS, VIENNA 24-27 APRIL 1967, PUBL. JUNE 1968 AS STI/PUB/176	IAEA
67Wien	IAEA PANEL ON FUEL BURN-UP PREDICTIONS IN THERMAL REACTORS, VIENNA 10-14 APRIL 1967, PUBL. JAN 1968 AS STI/PUB/172	IAEA
68Bombay	SYMPOSIUM ON NUCLEAR PHYSICS AND SOLID STATE PHYS., BOMBAY 28-31 DEC 1968 = 68PNS	INDIA
68Copenhgn	IAEA SYMPOSIUM ON NEUTRON INELASTIC SCATTERING, COPENHAGEN 20-25 MAY 1968,PUBL. 1968 AS STI/PUB/187	IAEA
68Debrecen	CONFERENCE ON ELECTRON CAPTURE AND HIGHER ORDER PROCESSES IN NUCLEAR DECAYS, DEBRECEN, JULY 1968	HUNGARY
68Dubna	UK-USSR SEMINAR ON NUCLEAR DATA FOR REACTOR COMPUTATIONS, DUBNA JUNE 1968	USSR
68DUBSY	SYMPOSIUM ON NUCLEAR STRUCTURE,DUBNA 4-11 JULY 1968 PUBLISHED AS JINR-D-3893 AND BY IAEA AS STI/PUB/189	IAEA
68JINR	IAEA PANEL ON THE FUTURE OF NUCLEAR STRUCTURE STUDIES, DUBNA 1-3 JULY 1968, PUBL. JULY 1969 AS STI/PUB/200	IAEA
68Madras	SYMPOSIUM ON NUCLEAR PHYSICS AND SOLID STATE PHYS., MADRAS,INDIA, 27 FEB TO 1 MARCH 1968 VOL.1 = NUCLEAR PHYSICS VOL.2 = SOLID STATE PHYSICS NOTE= THE VOL-NR IS NOT PRINTED ON THE COVER.	INDIA
68Riga	18TH ANNUAL CONF. ON NUCLEAR SPECTROSCOPY AND NUCL. STRUCTURE, RIGA JAN-FEB 1968	USSR
68Wash.	2ND CONFERENCE ON NUCLEAR CROSS-SECTIONS AND TECHN., WASHINGTON D.C. 4-7 MARCH 1968, PUBLISHED AS NBS SPECIAL PUBLICATION 299	USA
69Bochum	INTERNAT. CONF. ON CLUSTERING PHENOMENA IN NUCLEI, BOCHUM, 21-24 JULY 1969.PUBLISHED BY IAEA AS STI/PUB/232, NOVEMBER 1969	GERMANY,F.R.
69Chandigr	CHEMISTRY SYMPOSIUM, CHANDIGARH 23-26 SEP 1969	INDIA
69Erevan	19.ANNUAL CONF.NUCL.SPECTROSCOPY + NUCL.STRUCTURE EREVAN, 27.JAN-4.FEB.1969. SOME PAPERS PUBLISHED IN IZV VOL.33,NOS.4,8,10 AND VOL.34,NO.1	USSR
69Kinshasa	PEACEFUL USES OF ATOMIC ENERGY IN AFRICA, KINSHASA JULY-AUG 1969, PUBLISHED 1970 BY IAEA AS STI/PUB/233	IAEA
69London	INT.CONF. PHYSICS OF FAST REACTOR OPERATION AND DESIGN.LONDON,24.-26.JUNE 1969.	UK
69Montreal	INT. CONF. ON PROPERTIES OF NUCLEAR STATES, MONTREAL, CANADA, 25-30 AUG 1969	CANADA
69Roorke	NUCL. PHYS. AND SOLID STATE PHYS. SYMPOS.,ROORKEE 28-31 DECEMBER 1969. VOL.1 = INVITED TALKS, VOL.2 = NUCL. PHYS., VOL.3 = SOLID STATE PHYS.	INDIA
69Studsvik	SYMPOSIUM ON NEUTRON CAPTURE GAMMA-RAY SPECTROSCOPY, STUDSVIK, 11-15 AUGUST 1969, PUBLISHED BY IAEA 1969 AS STI/PUB/235	SWEDEN
69Trieste	LECTURES ON THEORY OF NUCLEAR STRUCTURE, TRIESTE, 7JAN-31MARCH 1969, PUBLISHED BY IAEA,VIENNA, JULY 1970 AS STI/PUB/249	IAEA IAEA
69Vienna	IAEA SYMPOSIUM ON PHYSICS AND CHEMISTRY OF FISSION, VIENNA, 28JULY-1AUG 1969, PUBLISHED 1969 AS STI/PUB/234	IAEA

REF CODES Table 3

Code	Description	Country
69Wien	IAEA PANEL ON INSTRUMENTATION FOR NEUTRON INELASTIC SCATTERING RESEARCH, VIENNA 1-5 DEC 1969 PUBL. OCT.1970 AS STI/PUB/275	IAEA
70ANL	EANDC SYMPOS.ON NEUTRON STANDARDS AND FLUX NORMALIZATION,ARGONNE NAT'L LAB,21-23 OCT.1970. PUBLISHED BY USAEC-DTIE AS CONF-701002,AUG.1971	USA
70Barcelna	7.COLLOQUE INTERNATIONAL DE PHOTOGRAPHIE CORPUSCULAIRE ET DES DETECTEURS VISUELS SOLIDES BARCELONA, SPAIN, 7-11 JULY 1970. PROCEEDINGS IN 2 VOLS BY P.CUER AND R.SCHMITT, STRASBOURG, FRANCE. ALSO KNOWN AS CONF-700705.	SPAIN
70Chicago	ANNUAL MEETING OF THE AMERICAN PHYSICAL SOCIETY, CHICAGO,26-29 JAN 1970. SYMPOS. OF THE DIVISION OF NUCLEAR PHYSICS	USA
70Helsinki	SECOND IAEA CONFERENCE ON NUCLEAR DATA FOR REACTORS HELSINKI, 15-19 JUNE 1970. PREPRINT-CODE = SM-122/.. PROCEEDINGS PUBL.BY IAEA,VIENNA,1970 (STI/PUB/259)	IAEA
70Madison	INTERNATIONAL SYMPOSIUM ON POLARIZATION PHENOMENA IN NUCLEAR REACTIONS, MADISON, 31 AUGUST TO 4 SEPTEMBER 1970	USA
70Madurai	NUCL. PHYS. SOLID STATE PHYS. SYMPOS., MADURAI, 27 - 30 DECEMBER 1970. VOL.1 = INVITED TALKS, VOL.2 = NUCL. PHYS., VOL.3 = SOLID STATE PHYS.	INDIA
71Albany	INT. CONF. ON STATISTICAL PROPERTIES OF NUCLEI, ALBANY, 23-27 AUG 1971, PROCEEDINGS PUBL. BY PLENUM PRESS, NEW YORK, 1972	USA
71Canterby	CONF.ON CHEM.NUCL.DATA,MEASUREMENTS AND APPLICAT., UNIV.OF KENT,CANTERBURY,20-22 SEPT 1971	UK
71Kiev	CONF. ON NEUTRON PHYS., KIEV 24-28 MAY 1971. PROCEED. PUBL. AS 'NEJTRONNAJA FIZIKA', KIEV 1972.	USSR
71Knoxvill	3RD CONFERENCE ON NEUTRON CROSS-SECTIONS AND TECHNOLOGY, UNIVERSITY OF TENNESSEE, KNOXVILLE, 15-17 MAR 1971. PUBL. AS CONF-710301	USA
71Moscow	CONFERENCE ON NUCLEAR SPECTROSCOPY, MOSCOW, FEB 1971.	USSR
71Vienna	IAEA CONSULTANTS MEETING ON PROMPT FISSION NEUTRON SPECTRA, VIENNA, 25-27 AUG 1971, PROCEEDINGS PUBLISHED AS STI/PUB/329 BY IAEA, 1972	IAEA
72Bombay	14.NUCL.AND SOLID STATE PHYSICS SYMP, BOMBAY, 1-4 FEB 1972. VOL.1(=VOL.14A)=INVITED TALKS, VOL.2(=VOL.14B)=NUCLEAR PHYSICS, VOL.3(=VOL.14C)=SOLID STATE PHYSICS.	INDIA
72Budapest	CONFERENCE ON NUCL.STRUCTURE AND STUDY WITH NEUTRONS.BUDAPEST,31 JULY - 5 AUGUST 1972.	HUNGARY
72Chandigr	15.NUCL. PHYS. + SOLID STATE PHYS. SYMPOS. CHANDIGARH 28 DEC 72 - 1 JAN 73. VOL.1(=VOL.15A)=INVITED TALKS, VOL.2(=VOL.15B)=NUCLEAR PHYSICS, VOL.3(=VOL.15C)=SOLID STATE PHYSICS.	INDIA
72Grenoble	IAEA SYMPOSIUM ON NEUTRON INELASTIC SCATTERING, GRENOBLE, 6-10 MARCH 1972, PROCEEDINGS PUBLISHED BY IAEA, VIENNA 1972 AS STI/PUB/308	IAEA
72Kiamesha	CONF. ON NEW DEVELOPMENTS IN REACTOR PHYSICS AND SHIELDING, KIAMESHA LAKE, NEW YORK, 12-15 SEPT 1972. PUBL IN 2 VOLS AS CONF-720901.	USA
72Kiev	22. CONF. ON NUCL. SPECTROSCOPY AND NUCL. STRUCTURE, KIEV, 25-28 JAN 1972. SOME PAPERS PUBL. IN IZV 36,NO 4.	USSR
72LosAngls	INT. CONF. ON FEW-PARTICLE PROBLEMS IN THE NUCLEAR INTERACTION, LOS ANGELES, 28 AUG - 1 SEPT 1972 PROC.PUBL. BY NORTH-HOLLAND, AMSTERDAM, AND ELSEVIER, NEW YORK, 1972.	USA
72Predeal	SUMMER SCHOOL ON NUCL. DATA AND REACTOR PHYSICS, PREDEAL, SEPT. 1972. PROC. BY I.PURICA, BUCURESTI.	ROMANIA
72Vienna	IAEA PANEL ON NEUTRON STANDARD REFERENCE DATA, VIENNA,20-24 NOV 1972,PROCEEDINGS PUBLISHED 1974 BY IAEA AS STI/PUB/371.	IAEA

Table 3 — REF CODES

Code	Description	Country
73Bangalor	16TH NUCL. AND SOLID STATE PHYSICS SYMP., BANGALORE 27-31 DEC 1973. VOL.1(=VOL.16A)=INVITED TALKS, VOL.2(=VOL.16B)=NUCLEAR PHYSICS, VOL.3(=VOL.16C)=SOLID STATE PHYSICS	INDIA
73Bologna	IAEA PANEL ON FISSION-PRODUCT NUCLEAR DATA BOLOGNA, ITALY, 26-30 NOV 1973. PROCEEDINGS PUBL. AS IAEA-169 (3 VOLUMES),1974	IAEA
73Kiev	2ND NAT'L SOVIET CONF. ON NEUTRON PHYSICS, KIEV, 28MAY - 1JUNE 1973. PROC. PUBL. BY F.E.I. OBNINSK,1974	USSR
73Munich	INT.CONF ON NUCLEAR PHYSICS,MUNICH 27AUG-1SEP1973, PROC. IN 2 VOLS PUBLISHED 1973 BY NORTH-HOLLAND/ELSEVIER	GERMANY,FR
73Pacif.Gr	INT. CONF. ON PHOTONUCLEAR REACTIONS AND APPLICATIONS, PACIFIC GROVE, CALIF.,26-30 MARCH 1973. PUBLISHED IN 2 VOLS. AS CONF-730301	USA
73Paris	SYMPOSIUM ON APPLICATIONS OF NUCLEAR DATA IN SCIENCE AND TECHNOLOGY, PARIS, 13-16 MARCH 1973, PROCEEDINGS PUBLISHED BY IAEA VIENNA 1973	IAEA
73Petten	TRIPARTITE SYMP. ON NUCLEAR PHYS. WITH THERMAL AND RESONANCE-ENERGY NEUTRONS. PETTEN,22-25 MAY 1973	NETHERLANDS
73Rochestr	3.IAEA SYMPOSIUM ON THE PHYSICS AND CHEMISTRY OF FISSION. ROCHESTER, NY, USA, 13-17 AUGUST 1973	USA
73Tbilisi	23.CONF ON NUCL.SPECTROSCOPY AND NUCL.STRUCTURE, TBILISI, USSR, FEB.1973	USSR
73Tokai	AESJ 1973 TOPICAL MEETING ON FAST REACTOR PHYSICS, 11-12 JUNE 1973, TOKAI	JAPAN
74Amsterdm	INT. CONF. ON NUCLEAR STRUCTURE AND SPECTROSCOPY AMSTERDAM, 9-13 SEP 1974	NETHERLANDS
74Bombay	17TH NUCL. AND SOLID STATE PHYSICS SYMP., BOMBAY 27-31 DEC 1974. VOL.2 SHOULD READ...17B, VOL.3 ...17C	INDIA
74Calcutta	INT. SYMP. ON RADIATION PHYSICS, CALCUTTA, 30 NOV - 4 DEC 1974. PROCEED. PUBL BY NAT. BUR. OF STANDARDS, USA, AS NBS-SP-461 (JAN 1977)	INDIA
74Columbia	2ND INTERN. CONF. ON NUCL. METHODS IN ENVIRONMENTAL RESEARCH, COLUMBIA, MISSOURI, 29-31 JULY 1974, PUBLISHED AS CONF-740701	USA
74Dacca	PHYSICS SYMP., DACCA, 18-21 NOV 1974. PROCEED. PUBL. IN NUCL. SCI. APPL./B, SUPPL.1 (APRIL 1977)	BANGLA DESH
74Kharkov	24TH ANNUAL CONF. ON NUCL. SPECTROSCOPY AND NUCL. STRUCTURE, KHARKOV, 29JAN-1FEB 1974. SOME PAPERS PUBL. IN IZV 38 NO.4 (1974).	USSR
74Petten	2ND INT. SYMPOSIUM ON NEUTRON CAPTURE GAMMA RAY SPECTROSCOPY AND RELATED TOPICS, PETTEN, 2-6 SEP 1974	NETHERLANDS
75Calcutta	18TH NUCL. AND SOLID STATE PHYSICS SYMPOS., CALCUTTA, DEC 1975. VOL.1...READ VOL.18A, VOL.2...READ VOL.18B, VOL.3...READ VOL.18C	INDIA
75Debrecen	SYMP. ON FAST NEUTRON INTERACTIONS AND THE PROBLEMS OF HIGH CURRENT NEUTR. GENERATORS, DEBRECEN, 27-30 AUG 1975. PROC. PUBL. IN AK 18(2) 1976	HUNGARY
75Delhi	7TH INTERN. CONF. ON FEW-BODY PROBLEMS IN NUCLEAR AND PARTICLE PHYSICS, DELHI, 29DEC 1975 - 3JAN 1976	INDIA
75Gothenbg	CONFERENCE IN PHYSICS,10-12 JUNE 1975, GOTHENBURG	SWEDEN
75Harwell	EUROPHYSICS CONF. ON NUCL. INTERACTIONS AT MEDIUM AND LOW ENERGIES, 24-26MARCH 1975	UK
75Karlsrhe	SEMINAR ON PHYSICAL, DOSIMETRY AND BIOMEDICAL ASPECTS OF CF-252, KARLSRUHE, 14-18 APRIL 1975, PUBL. IN IAEA-STI/PUB-418, NOV. 1976	GERMANY, F.R.
75Kiev	3RD ALL-UNION CONF. ON NEUTRON PHYSICS, KIEV, 9-13 JUNE 1975. PROCEEDINGS PUBLISHED IN 6 VOLUMES, MOSKVA, 1976.	USSR
75Leningrd	25TH ANNUAL CONF. ON NUCL. SPECTROSCOPY AND NUCL. STRUCTURE, LENINGRAD, JANUARY 1975	USSR
75Wash.	4TH CONF. ON NUCLEAR CROSS-SECTIONS AND TECHNOLOGY, WASHINGTON D.C., 3-7 MARCH 1975	USA

REF CODES

Table 3

Code	Description	Country
75Zurich	4TH INTERN. SYMPOSIUM ON POLARIZATION PHENOMENA IN NUCLEAR REACTIONS. ZURICH, 25-29 AUGUST 1975.	SWITZERLAND
76Ahmedabd	19. NUCL. PHYS. AND SOLID STATE PHYS. SYMP., AHMEDABAD 27-31 DEC 1976. VOL.1...READ VOL.19A, VOL.2...READ VOL.19B, VOL.3...READ VOL.19C.	INDIA
76ANL	MEETING ON FAST NEUTRON CROSS SECTIONS OF U-233,235, 238 AND PU-239, ARGONNE, 28-30 JUNE 1976. SOME PAPERS PUBL. IN CONF-7606-47.	USA
76Baku	26TH ANNUAL CONF. ON NUCL. STRUCTURE AND SPECTROSCOPY, BAKU, 3-6 FEB 1976. SOME PAPERS PUBL. IN IZV 40(4)1976	USSR
76Bombay	SYMPOSIUM ON REACTOR PHYSICS, BOMBAY, 1-3 MAR 1976. PROC. BY ENGG. SCIENCES COMMITTEE OF ATOMIC ENERGY, GOVT. OF INDIA, BOMBAY, 1978.	INDIA
76Corsica	3RD INT. CONF. ON NUCLEI FAR FROM STABILITY, CARGESE, CORSICA, 19-26 MAY 1976. PROCEEDINGS PUBLISHED AS CERN-76-13 (1976)	FRANCE
76Garmisch	9TH SYMPOSIUM ON FUSION TECHNOLOGY, GARMISCH, 14-18 JUNE 1976. PROCEEDINGS PUBL. IN PERGAMON PRESS	GERMANY,F.R.
76Lowell	INT. CONF. ON INTERACTIONS OF NEUTRONS WITH NUCLEI, LOWELL, MASSACHUSETTS, 6-9 JULY 1976	USA
77BNL	SYMPOS. ON NEUTRON CROSS SECTIONS FROM 10 TO 40 MEV, BROOKHAVEN NATIONAL LAB., N.Y., 3-5 MAY 1977 PROC. PUBL. IN BNL-NCS-50681.	USA
77Geel	SPECIALIST'S MEETING ON NEUTRON DATA OF STRUCTURAL MATERIALS FOR FAST REACTORS, CBNM GEEL, 5-8 DEC 1977	BELGIUM
77Kiev	4TH ALL UNION CONF. ON NEUTRON PHYSICS, KIEV, 18-22 APR 1977	USSR
77Mannheim	REAKTORTAGUNG 1977, MANNHEIM, MAR 1977, ZAED,KARLSRUHE	GERMANY, F.R.
77NBS	SYMP. ON NEUTRON STANDARDS AND APPLICATIONS, NAT.BUREAU OF STANDARDS, GAITHERSBURG, 28-31 MAR 1977	USA
77Paris	MEETING OF THE TECHN. COMMITTEE ON NATURAL FISSION REACTORS, PARIS, 19-21 DEC 1977. PROC. PUBL. 1978 BY IAEA, VIENNA.	FRANCE
77Tashkent	27TH ANNUAL CONF. ON NUCL. SPECTROSCOPY AND NUCL. STRUCTURE, TASHKENT, 23-25 MARCH 1977. SOME PAPERS PUBL. IN IZV 41(6,8,10), 42(1).	USSR
77Vienna	SYMP. ON NEUTRON INELASTIC SCATTERING, VIENNA, 17-21 OCT 1977. PROC. PUBL. IN 2 VOLS BY IAEA, VIENNA.	IAEA
78Alma-Ata	28TH ANNUAL CONF. ON NUCL. SPECTROSCOPY AND NUCL. STRUCTURE, ALMA-ATA, MARCH 1978. SOME PAPERS PUBL. IN IZV 42(4,9,11).	USSR
78Harwell	INT. CONF. ON NEUTRON PHYSICS AND NUCLEAR DATA FOR REACTORS AND OTHER APPLIED PURPOSES, AERE HARWELL, 25-29 SEPT 1978.	UK
A	ATOMICS,CONT.AS ATOMICS AND NUCL.ENERGY,LONDON	UK
A-ALB-	STATE OF NEW YORK AT ALBANY ,REPORT SERIES	USA
A-ARK-	U. OF ARKANSAS REPORT SERIES	USA
A-WAU-	UNIV. OF WASHINGTON,SEATTLE. ANNUAL PROGRESS REPORT	USA
AAB	ANAIS ACAD. BRASIL.CIENC.	BRAZIL
AAEC/	AUSTRALIAN AEC REPORTS	AUSTRALIA
AAF	ANNALES ACAD. SCI. FENNICAE, SERIES A6: PHYSICA	FINLAND
ABAGJAN	GRUPPOVYE KONSTANTY DLJA RASCHETA JADERNYKH REAKTOROV, ATOMIZDAT MOSKVA 1964 ENGLISH TRANSLATION = GROUP CONSTANTS FOR NUCLEAR REACTOR CALCULATIONS, CONSULT. BUREAU NEW YORK 1964	USSR
AC	ANALYTICAL CHEMISTRY	USA
ACA	ANALITICA CHIMICA ACTA	NETHERLANDS
ACH	ANGEWANDTE CHEMIE	GERMANY,F.R.
ACJ	ACTA CHEM. SCANDINAVICA	DENMARK
ACR	ACTA CRYSTALLOGRAPHICA	DENMARK
ACRA	ACTA CRYSTALLOGRAPHICA,PART A. STARTED VOL.26,1970	DENMARK
ACRB	ACTA CRYSTALLOGRAPHICA,PART B. STARTED VOL.26,1970	DENMARK

Table 3   REF CODES

Code	Description	Country
ACRH-	ARGONNE CANCER RESEARCH HOSPITAL REPORTS	USA
ACS	JOURNAL OF AMERICAN CHEMICAL SOC.	USA
ACSA	ACTA CHEMICA SCANDINAVICA, SERIES A.	DENMARK
ACT.EL	THE ACTINIDE ELEMENTS. NATIONAL NUCLEAR ENERGY SERIES, DIV IV, VOL 14A, 1954. MC GRAW HILL 1954, EDITORS G.T. SEABORG AND J.J. KATZ	USA
AD-	DEPT OF DEFENSE, REPORT SERIES	USA
ADP	ANNALEN DER PHYSIK	GERMAN D.R.
AE	ATOMNAYA ENERGIYA /SJA//EAF/(/JNE/)	USSR
AE-	AKTIEBOLAGET ATOMENERGI REPORTS, STOCKHOLM/STUDSVIK	SWEDEN
AE/S	ATOMNAJA ENERGIJA, SUPPLEMENT	USSR
AEA	ATOMIC ENERGY IN AUSTRALIA	AUSTRALIA
AEC(NZ)-	NEW ZEALAND A.E.C. REPORTS (THE ORIGINAL CODE IS 'AEC-' AND (NZ) IS ADDED FOR CLARIFICATION)	NEW ZEALAND
AEC-TR-	DIV.OF TECH.INFORM.EXT.AEC TRANSLATIONS	USA
AECD-	(CONT.OF MDDC-)D.T.I.E.REPORT SER.DISCONT.1960	USA
AECD/	REPORTS OF ATOMIC ENERGY CENTRE, DACCA	BANGLA DESH
AECL-	ATOMIC EN. OF CAN. LIM., CHALK RIVER, REPORT SERIES	CANADA
AECLPRCM	SHOULD READ:'PR-CN'. CHALK RIVER REPORTS	CANADA
AECU-	DIV.OF TECH.INFORM.EXT.AEC REPORT SERIES.EXTINCT	USA
AEET-	ATOMIC ENERGY EST. TROMBAY REPORT SERIES, EXTINCT	INDIA
AEEW-	AEEW-WINFRITH REPORT SERIES	UK
AEJ	J.AT.ENERGY SOC.JAPAN (NIPPON GENSHIRYOKU GAKKAISHI)	JAPAN
AERE-	AERE-HARWELL REPORT SERIES	UK
AES-	AKTIEBOLAGET ATOMENERGI, STUDSVIK, REPORTS(IN SWEDISH)	SWEDEN
AF	ARKIV FOR FYSIK	SWEDEN
AFOSR-	DEPT. OF DEFENSE REPORTS	USA
AFSWC-	AIR FORCE SPEC.WEAPONS CENTER, KIRTLAND	USA
AFSWP-	ARMED FORCES SPECIAL WEAPONS PROJECT	USA
AFWL-	AIR FORCE WEAPONS LAB, KIRTLAND, NEW MEXICO	USA
AHP	ACTA PHYS. ACAD. SCI. HUNG.	HUNGARY
AHSB(S)R-	UKAEA, HEALTH+SAFETY BRANCH, RISLEY, REPORTS.	UK
AI-	ATOMICS INTERNATIONAL, CANOGA PARK, CALIF. REPORTS	USA
AI-AEC	ATOMICS INTERNAT., AEC RESEARCH AND DEVEL.REPORTS	USA
AIAECMEMO	ATOMICS INTERNATIONAL, CANOGA PARK CALIFORNIA MEMO TO THE AEC	USA
AIF	ANALES DEL INSTITUTO DE FISICA, PUBL.1955 ONLY	MEXICO
AIP	ADVANCES IN PHYSICS (SUPPL. TO PHIL. MAG.)	UK
AJ	ASTROPHYSICAL JOURNAL	USA
AJN	ARAB JOURNAL OF NUCL. SCIENCE AND APPLICATION	EGYPT
AJP	AMERICAN J. OF PHYSICS	USA
AJS	AUSTRALIAN J. SCI.	AUSTRALIA
AK	ATOMKI KOZLEMENYEK	HUNGARY
AKE	ATOMKERNENERGIE	GERMANY, F.R.
AKO-UK-	INTERNAL ALDERMASTON REPORTS	UK
AKS	ATOMKI KOZLEMENYEK, SUPPLEMENT	HUNGARY
ALBERTA-	REPTS OF NUCL.RES.CENTRE, UNIV.OF ALBERTA, EDMONTON	CANADA
ANA	ANALYST (LONDON)	UK
ANCR-	AEROJET NUCL.COMP., NAT.REACTOR TEST.STATION REPORTS	USA
ANE	ANNALS OF NUCL. ENERGY. VOL.1 IS CALLED: 'ANNALS OF NUCL. SCIENCE AND ENGINEERING'	UK
ANL-	ARGONNE NATN'L LABORATORY, REPORT SERIES	USA
ANS	TRANS. AMER. NUCL. SOC.	USA
ANU-	REPTS OF AUSTRALIAN NATIONAL UNIV., CANBERRA	AUSTRALIA
AP	ANN. PHYS. (NY)(ANNALS OF PHYSICS)	USA
APA	ACTA PHYSICA AUSTRIACA	AUSTRIA
AP/CTR/TM-	TECHNICAL MEMO OF APPLIED PHYS. DIV., ANL	USA
APDA-	ATOMIC POWER DEVEL. ASS. REPORT SERIES, DETROIT	USA
APED-	GEN.EL.CO., AT.POWER EQUIPMENT DEP., SAN JOSE CALIF.	USA
APEX-	GEN.EL.CO., AIRCRAFT NUCL.PROP.DEPT., CINC., EXTINCT.	USA
APH	ANNALES DE PHYSIQUE (PARIS)	FRANCE
APL	APPLIED PHYSICS LETTERS	USA

REF CODES   Table 3

Code	Description	Country
APP	ACTA PHYSICA POLONICA	POLAND
APPA	ACTA PHYSICA POLONICA SECTION A	POLAND
APPB	ACTA PHYSICA POLONICA SECTION B	POLAND
ARB.BER-	KERNFORSCHUNGSZENTRUM KARLSRUHR, PROGR. REPORTS	GERMANY, FR
AREAEE-	REPTS BY ARAB REPUBLIC OF EGYPT, AT.E. ESTABLISHMENT	EGYPT
ARF-	ARMOUR RESEARCH FOUNDATION REPORTS	USA
ARI	INTERN. J. OF APPLIED RADIATION AND ISOTOPES	UK
ARN	ANNUAL REVIEW OF NUCLEAR SCIENCE	USA
ARS	ANALES DE FISICA Y QUIMICA, FORMERLY CALLED: ANALES REAL SOC. ESPAN. FIS. QUIM. (MADRID)	SPAIN
ASL	ACTA PHYSICA SLOVACA	CZECHOSLOV.
ASS	ANNALES DE LA SOCIETE SCIENT. DE BRUXELLES, SER. I	BELGIUM
ATP	ATOMPRAXIS	GERMANY, F.R.
ATW	ATOMWIRTSCHAFT, ATOMTECHNIK (FORMERLY ATOMWIRTSCHAFT)	GERMANY, F.R.
AUJ	AUSTRALIAN J. PHYS.	AUSTRALIA
AUSTR-DFN-	AUSTRALIAN LIBRARY OF EVALUATED NEUTRON CROSS-SECTIONS FOR FISSION-PRODUCT NUCLEI, AVAILABLE FROM NEUTRON DATA CENTRES. FOR DETAILS, SEE ANNEX P. A.5	AUSTRALIA
AWRE-	AWRE-ALDERMASTON REPORT SERIES	UK
BAP	BULL. AM. PHYS. SOC.	USA
BARC-	TROMBAY REPORT SERIES, FORMERLY AEET-	INDIA
BAS	BULL. ACAD. SCI. USSR, PHYS. SER.(COLUMBIA TRANSL.)	//IZV//
BAW-	BABCOCK AND WILCOX CO, LYNCHBURG, REPORT SERIES	USA
BCF	BULL. DE LA SOCIETE CHIMIQUE DE FRANCE	FRANCE
BCS	BULL. DE LA CLASSE DES SCIENCES, ACAD. ROY. BELG.	BELGIUM
BENZI-DFN-	BOLOGNA LIBRARY OF EVALUATED NEUTRON CROSS-SECTIONS FOR FISSION-PRODUCT NUCLEI, AVAILABLE FROM NEUTRON DATA CENTRES. FOR DETAILS, SEE ANNEX PAGE A.5	ITALY
BJA	BRITISH J. OF APPLIED PHYSICS	UK
BJAS	BRITISH J. OF APPLIED PHYSICS SUPPLEMENT	UK
BKN	BULL. INST. BORIS KIDRIC, VOL.18 NUCL.ENG.	YUGOSLAVIA
BKP	BULL. INST. BORIS KIDRIC, VOL.18 PHYSICS	YUGOSLAVIA
BLG-	CENTRE D'ETUDE DE L'ENERGIE NUCL., BRUXELLES	BELGIUM
BMI-	BATTELLE MEMORIAL INST., COLUMBUS OHIO, REPORTS	USA
BMWF-	BUNDESMINISTERIUM F.WISSENSCH.FORSCHG., BAD GODESBG.	GERMANY, F.R.
BNL-	BROOKHAVEN NATIONAL LAB. REPORT SERIES	USA
BNWL-	BATTELLE-NORTHWEST, RICHLAND, REPORT SERIES	USA
BOS	TRANSACTIONS OF THE BOSE RESEARCH INST., CALCUTTA	INDIA
BPC	BULL. ACAD. POLON. SCI., SER. SCI. CHIM.	POLAND
BPP	BULL. ACAD. POLON. SCI., SER. SCI. MATH. ASTRO. PHYS.	POLAND
BR-	EARLY REPORTS FROM CAVENDISH LAB, EXTINCT	UK
BRL-	BALLISTIC RESEARCH LABS REPORTS	USA
BSI	BOLLETINO DELLA SOCIETA ITALIANA DI FISICA	ITALY
BTI	BULL. OF THE TOKYO INST. OF TECHNOLOGY, ENGL. EDITION	JAPAN
BUP-	BERGEN UNIV., DEPARTM. OF PHYSICS. REPORT SERIES	NORWAY
CC-	CHICAGO UNIV., METALLURGICAL LAB REPORTS	USA
CCDN-	NEUTRON DATA COMP. CENTRE, SACLAY. REPORTS	FRANCE
CCEN-	COMUN. CENTRO EN. NUCL., UNI.FED.PERNAMBUCO, RECIFE	BRAZIL
CDP	CAHIERS DE PHYSIQUE	FRANCE
CEA-	CENTRE D'ETUDES NUCLEAIRES, SACLAY, REPORT SERIES	FRANCE
CEC	CIENCIA E CULTURA	BRAZIL
CEC-	C.N.E.N. CENTRO DI CALCOLO REPORTS	ITALY
CEN(BG)-	CENTRE D'ETUDES NUCLEAIRES, BORDEAUX-GRADIGNAN. REPORTS	FRANCE
CF-	CHICAGO UNIV., METALLURGICAL LAB REPORTS	USA
CHP	CHINESE J.PHYS. (TAIWAN)	FORMOSA
CISE-	CENTRE INFORMAZIONI STUDI ESPERIENCE, MILAN	ITALY
CJC	CAN. J. CHEM.	CANADA
CJP	CAN. J. PHYS.(FORMERLY CAN J. OF RESEARCH VOL 1-28)	CANADA
CJR	CAN. J. OF RESEARCH (EXTINCT)	CANADA
CNAEM-	CEKMECE NUCL. RES.+TRAINING CENTER, REPORTS.	TURKEY
CNEA-	COMISION NACIONAL DE ENERGIA ATOMICA REPORT SER.	ARGENTINA
CNEN-CEA	EVAL. DATA LIBRARY FROM CNEN(ITALY)-CEA(FRANCE) COLLABORATION. SEE ANNEX SECT. 8 (PAGE A.5)	FRANCE-ITALY

Table 3   REF CODES

Code	Description	Country
CNEN-RT/FI-SAME AS 'RT/FI-'. COMITATO NAZIONALE PER L'EN. NUCL.		ITALY
CONF-	CONFERENCE PROCEEDINGS	USA
COO-	CHICAGO OPERATIONS OFFICE, AEC, CONTRACT REPORTS	USA
CP-	CHICAGO UNIV., METALLURGICAL LAB REPORTS	USA
CR	COMPTES RENDUS	FRANCE
CR-	COLUMBIA UNIVERSITY REPORT SERIES	USA
CRB	COMPTES RENDUS DE L'AC. BULGARE DES SCIENCES	BULGARIA
CRC-	NATN'L RES. COUN. OF CAN. CHALK RIVER, REPORT SERIES	CANADA
CRGP-	CHALK RIVER, ONTARIO. EARLY REPORTS	CANADA
CRNL-	A.E.C.L. CHALK RIVER REPORTS	CANADA
CRP-	CHALK RIVER REPORTS	CANADA
CRR-	CHALK RIVER REPORTS	CANADA
CRRP-	CHALK RIVER REPORT SERIES	CANADA
CRT-	NATN'L RES. COUNC. OF CAN., CHALK RIVER REPORT SERIES	CANADA
CS	CURRENT SCIENCE	INDIA
CS-	CHICAGO UNIV., METALLURGICAL LAB REPORTS	USA
CU-	COLUMBIA U., NEW YORK REPORT SERIES	USA
CUD-	REPORTS OF COLUMBIA UNIV., NEW YORK	USA
CVAC-	CONS. VULTEE AIRCRAFT CORP., REPORT SERIES. EXTINCT	USA
CWR-	CURTISS-WRIGHT CORP. REPORT SERIES EXTINCT	USA
CZJ	CZECHOSLOVAK JOURNAL OF PHYSICS	CZECHOSLOV.
CZJA	CESK.CAS.FYS. = CZECH.J.PHYS., PART A	CZECHOSLOV.
CZJB	CZECHOSLOVAK JOURNAL OF PHYSICS, PART B	CZECHOSLOV.
D2-	BOEING AIRPLANE CO., SEATTLE EXTINCT	USA
DA	DISSERTATION ABSTRACTS	USA
DA/B	DISSERTATION ABSTRACTS SECTION B	USA
DASA-	DEFENSE ATOMIC SUPPORT AGENCY REPORTS	USA
DC-	GEN.EL.CO., AIRCRAFT NUCL.PROP.PROJ. EXTINCT	USA
DNA-	DEFENSE NUCLEAR AGENCY, WASHINGTON D.C., REPORTS	USA
DOE-NDC-	U.S. DEPT. OF ENERGY, NUCL. DATA COMM, REPORTS	USA
DOK	DOKLADY AKADEMII NAUK SSSR /SPD/	USSR
DP-	DU PONT, SAVANNAH RIVER REPORTS	USA
DUB-	DUBNA REPORT SERIES, ALSO KNOWN AS JINR-REPORTS	USSR
EAF	ENERGIE ATOMIQUE	//AE//
EANDC-	EUROPEAN-AMERICAN NUCL.DATA COMMITTEE DOCUMENTS	NEA
ECN-	NETHERLANDS ENERGY RESEARCH FOUNDATION, REPORTS	NETHERLANDS
EDF-	REPORTS, ELECTRICITE DE FRANCE	FRANCE
EEN	ERGEBNISSE DER EXAKTEN NATURWISSENSCHAFTEN	GERMANY,F.R.
EIR-	EIDG.INST.REAKTORFORSCH.WUERENLINGEN REPORT SERIES	SWITZERLAND
EN	ENERGIA NUCLEARE (MILAN)	ITALY
EON	EURONUCLEAR (EXTINCT MAY 1966)	UK
EPRI-	ELECTRIC POWER RES. INST., PALO ALTO, CA., REPORTS	USA
ERDA-	US ENERGY RES. AND DEVELOPMENT ADMINISTR., REPORT-SERIES	USA
EUR-	EURATOM REPORTS (FROM BCMN)	EURATOM
EXFOR	EXFOR EXPERIMENTAL NEUTRON DATA LIBRARY, AVAILABLE FROM NEUTRON DATA CENTERS. SEE ALSO ANNEX PAGE A.5	4 CENTERS
FDP	FORTSCHRITTE DER PHYSIK	GERMAN D.R.
FEI-	FIZ.-ENERG.INSTITUT, OBNINSK, REPORT SERIES	USSR
FIZ	FIZIKA	YUGOSLAVIA
FIZS	FIZIKA, SUPPLEMENT	YUGOSLAVIA
FNP	FAST NEUTRON PHYSICS, MARION AND FOWLER, N.Y., 1960	USA
FOA4-	RES. INST. OF NAT'L DEFENCE DEP'T 4, REPORTS	SWEDEN
FRA-TM-	FRA TECHNICAL MEMORANDUM SERIES, ANL	USA
FRC	'FAST REACTOR CROSS SECTIONS', S.YIFTAH ET AL. INTERNATIONAL SERIES OF MONOGRAPHS ON NUCLEAR ENERGY, PERGAMON PRESS 1960	USA
FRM-	FORSCHUNGSREAKTOR MUENCHEN, REPORT SERIES	GERMANY,F.R.
FRNC-TH-	FRENCH NON CEA REPORTS	FRANCE
FTT	FIZIKA TVERDOGO TELA /SPS/	USSR
FZK-	REPORTS GENERAL DYNAMICS, FORT WORTH, TEXAS	USA
GA-	GENERAL ATOMIC DIV., GEN.DYN.CORP, REPORT SERIES	USA
GACD-	GENERAL ATOMIC DIV., GEN.DYN.CORP, REPORT SERIES	USA

REF CODES   Table 3

Code	Description	Country
GAMD-	GENERAL ATOMICS REPORTS	USA
GAMMAATLAS	ATLAS OF GAMMA-RAY SPECTRA FROM THE INELASTIC SCATTERING OF FAST NEUTRONS, MOSCOW, ATOMIZDAT 1978 (=INDC(CCP)-120)	USSR
GEAP-	REPORTS GENERAL ELECTRIC CO, CALIFORNIA	USA
GEMP-	GEN.EL.CO.FLIGHT PROP.LAB.CINCINNATI REPORT SERIES	USA
GKSS-	GES.F.KERNENERGIE-VERWERTUNG IN SCHIFFBAU U.SCHIFFAHRT	GERMANY, FR
GSI-J-	GESELLSCHAFT F. SCHWERIONENFORSCHUNG, DARMSTADT.REPORTS	GERMANY, F.R.
GULF-	GULF RADIATION TECHNOL., SAN DIEGO REPORTS	USA
HASL-	USAEC HEALTH AND SAFETY LAB, NEW YORK, REPORT-SERIES	USA
HCA	HELVETICA CHIMICA ACTA	SWITZERLAND
HEDL-TME-	HANFORD ENGINEERING DEVELOPMENT LABS, REPORTS	USA
HMI-	HAHN-MEITNER INSTITUT, BERLIN, REPORT SERIES	GERMANY, F.R.
HNS-	HAZLETON-NUCLEAR SCIENCE CO. REPORTS	USA
HP	HEALTH PHYSICS	UK-USA
HPA	HELV. PHYS. ACTA	SWITZERLAND
HW-	HANFORD REPORT SERIES(FROM 1965 BNWL)	USA
HW-SA-	GEN.EL.CO., HANFORD AT.PROD.OP.REP.SER.(NOW BNWL)	USA
IA-	ISRAEL AEC, REHOVOT, REPORT SERIES	ISRAEL
IAE-	REPORTS FROM INST. ATOMNOJ ENERGII, KURCHATOV, MOSKVA	USSR
IAEA-	TECHNICAL REPORTS PUBLISHED BY IAEA, VIENNA	IAEA
IAN-	INST. DE ASUNTOS NUCLEARES, BOGOTA, REPORT SERIES	COLOMBIA
IBK	BULL. INST. BORIS KIDRIC, VOL.1-17	YUGOSLAVIA
ICD-	BULL.INF.CENT.PO JADERNYM DANNYM, OBNINSK	USSR
ICP-	ALLIED CHEM.CORP., IDAHO CHEM.PROGRAMS REPORTS	USA
IDO-	REPORTS OF PHILIPS PETROLEUM COMP., IDAHO FALLS	USA
IEA-	INSTITUTO DE ENERGIA ATOMICA, UNIVERSIDADE SAO PAULO	BRAZIL
IET	INSTR. AND EXPTL TECHNIQUES, ENGL TRANSL OF PTE STARTED 1958, UP TO 1970 NO VOLUME NUMBER. STARTING WITH VOL 14 1971 THE VOL-NR IS PRINTED ON THE COVER NOTE= AN ARTIFICIAL VOL-NR IS GIVEN UP TO 1970, STARTING WITH VOL 1(1958)	//PTE//
IF-	AKADEMIJA NAUK UKRAINSKAJA, KIEV, REPORTS	USSR
IFA-	ROMANIAN ACAD. SCI. INST. ATOMIC PHYS., REPORTS	ROMANIA
IFI	IZVESTIJA NA FIZICHESKIJA INSTITUT S ANEB / BULL. DE L'INST. DE PHYSIQUE ET DE RECHERCHE ATOMIQUE	BULGARIA
IFIN-NR-	INST. DE FIZ. SI ING. NUCLEARA, BUCHAREST. REPORTS	ROMANIA
IFUSP/P-	U. OF SAO PAOLO, INST. OF PHYS., REPORT SERIES	BRAZIL
IITRI-	REPORTS OF ILLINOIS INST. OF TECHNOLOGY	USA
IJP	INDIAN J. PHYS.	INDIA
IKDA-	INST. F. KERNPHYSIK DARMSTADT, REPORTS	GERMANY, F.R.
IKE-	INST. F. KERNENERGETIK, STUTTGART, REPORTS	GERMANY, FR
IKF-	INSTITUT FUR KERNPHYSIK, FRANKFURT REPORT SERIES	GERMANY, F.R.
IN-	REPORTS OF IDAHO NUCLEAR CORP., IDAHO FALLS, IDAHO	USA
INDC-	INTERN. NUCL. DATA COMMITTEE, REPORT SERIES	IAEA
INDSWG-	INTERN. NUCL. DATA SCI. WORK. GROUP, CONT'D AS INDC-	IAEA
INER-	INST. OF NUCL. ENERGY RESEARCH, REPORTS	FORMOSA
INFN/BE-	INST. NAZIONALE FISICA NUCLEARE, FLORENCE. REPORTS	ITALY
INIS-MF-	INIS MICROFICHES, IAEA, VIENNA	IAEA
INP-	INST.FIZ.JADROWEJ (NUCL.PHYS.)PAN KRAKOW, REPORTS	POLAND
INR-	INST. BADAN JADROWYCH (NUCL.RES.), WARSAW, REPORTS	POLAND
INS-	INST. OF NUCLEAR SCIENCES, PROGRESS REPORTS	NEW ZEALAND
INTELRT-	INTELCOM RADIATION TECHNOLOGY, REPORTS	USA
IP	ISOTOPENPRAXIS	GERMAN D.R.
IPA	INDIAN J. OF PURE AND APPLIED PHYSICS	INDIA
IPF-SP-	INST. DE PHYSIQUE, UNIV. DE FRIBOURG, REPORTS	SWITZERLAND
IPNO-TH-	INST. DE PHYS. NUCLEAIRE, ORSAY. REPORT SERIES-THESIS	FRANCE
IRE	IEEE TRANS.ON NUCL.SCI.(VOLS 1-9=IRE TRANS.NUCL.SC.)	USA
IRT-	INTELCOM RADIATION TECHNOLOGY, REPORT SERIES	USA
IS-	IOWA STATE UNIV. REPORTS	USA
IS-T-	IOWA STATE UNIV., THESIS-REPORTS	USA
IS/P	BNL REPORT SERIES	USA

Table 3   REF CODES

Code	Description	Country
ISN-	INST. DES SCIENCES NUCL., UNIV. DE GRENOBLE. REPORTS	FRANCE
ITE-	REPTS OF ITEF (INST.TEOR.EXP.FIZ.) MOSCOW	USSR
IVU	IZV. VYSSHIKH UCHEB. ZAVEDENIJ, FIZIKA	USSR
IZL	IZV.AKAD.NAUK LATV.SSR,SER.FIZ.	USSR
IZV	IZV. AKAD. NAUK SSSR, SER. FIZ /BAS/	USSR
JAERI-	ATOMIC ENERGY RESEARCH INST.,TOKYO	JAPAN
JAP	J. APPL. PHYS.	USA
JCP	J. CHEM. PHYS.	USA
JE	JADERNA ENERGIE	CZECHOSLOV.
JEL	JETP LETTERS	//ZEP//
JEN-	JUNTA DE ENERGIA NUCLEAR,REPORTS	SPAIN
JENDL-1	JAPANESE EVAL. NUCL. DATA LIBRARY. SEE ANNEX SECT.8	JAPAN
JENER-	JOINT ESTABL. NUCL. RES., KJELLER REP. SERIES	NORWAY
JET	SOVIET PHYS.-JETP	//ZET//
JFI	J. FRANKLIN INST.	USA
JIN	J. INORG. NUCL. CHEM.	UK
JINL	INORGAN. AND NUCL. CHEM. LETTERS	UK
JINR-	JOINT INST. FOR NUCL. RES., DUBNA. REPORTS	USSR
JMJ	PROC.PHYS-MATH.SOC.OF JAPAN	JAPAN
JMS	JOURNAL OF MASS SPECTROMETRY AND ION PHYSICS	NETHERLANDS
JNAB	J. NUCL. ENERG. SECTION A/B	UK
JNC	JOURNAL OF NONCRYSTALLINE SOLIDS	NETHERLANDS
JNDC-FFP-WG	JAPANESE NUCL. DATA COMM.,EVAL. FISSION PRODUCT DATA LIBRARY. SEE ANNEX SECT. 8 (PAGE A.5)	JAPAN
JNE	J. NUCL. ENERG.	UK
JNEA	J. NUCL. ENERG. SECTION A	UK
JNEB	J. NUCL. ENERG. SECTION B	UK
JNM	JOURNAL OF NUCLEAR MATERIALS	NETHERLANDS
JP/A	J.OF PHYSICS,PT.A= MATHEMATICAL+GENERAL PHYSICS	UK
JP/C	J.OF PHYSICS,PT.C= SOLID STATE PHYSICS	UK
JP/D	J.OF PHYSICS,PT.D= APPLIED PHYSICS	UK
JP/F	J.OF PHYSICS,PT.F= METAL PHYSICS	UK
JP/G	J.OF PHYSICS,PT.G= NUCLEAR PHYSICS	UK
JPAL	JOURN. OF PHYSICS,PT.A,LETTERS TO THE EDITOR	UK
JPC	JOURNAL DE CHIMIE PHYSIQUE ET DE PHYSICOCHIMIE BIOLOG.	FRANCE
JPJ	J. PHYS. SOC. JAPAN	JAPAN
JPJO	PROC.PHYS.-MATH.SOC.JAP., CONTIN'D 1946 AS JPJ	JAPAN
JPR	JOURNAL DE PHYSIQUE(VOLS 1-23=J.PHYS.RADIUM)	FRANCE
JPRA	JOURNAL DE PHYSIQUE, SUPPL.A, PHYSIQUE APPLIQUEE	FRANCE
JPRC	JOURNAL DE PHYSIQUE, COLLOQUE	FRANCE
JPRL	JOURNAL DE PHYSIQUE-LETTRES.START VOL.35,NO 1,JAN.1974	FRANCE
JPRS	JOURNAL DE PHYSIQUE, SUPPL.S, SOCIETE FRANCAISE	FRANCE
JRC	JOURNAL OF RADIOANALYTICAL CHEMISTRY, STARTED 1968	NETHERLANDS
JU-RR-	JYVAESKYLAE UNIV.,DEPARTMENT OF PHYSICS REPORTS	FINLAND
JUEL-	KERNFORSCHUNGSANLAGE JUELICH, REPORT SERIES	GERMANY,F.R.
KAPL-	KNOLLS ATOMIC POWER LAB., REPORT SERIES,	USA
KAPL/CSNL	KNOLLS AT.POW.LAB. CROSS-SECTION NEWSLETTERS	USA
KDK-	SWEDISH NUCLEAR DATA COMMITTEE REPORTS	SWEDEN
KDV	KGL.DANSKE VIDENSKAB. SELSKAB, MAT.-FYS. MEDD.	DENMARK
KE	KERNENERGIE	GERMAN D.R.
KEDAK-	KARLSRUHE EVALUATED NUCLEAR DATA LIBRARY, AVAILABLE FROM NEUTRON DATA CENTERS. SEE ALSO ANNEX PAGE A.5	GERMANY, F.R.
KFI	KFKI(KOZP. FIZ. KUTATO INTEZET) KOZLEMENYEK	HUNGARY
KFK-	KERNFORSCHUNGSZENTRUM KARLSRUHE REPORT SERIES	GERMANY,F.R.
KFKI-	CENTRAL RESEARCH INST. OF PHYSICS,ACAD.OF SCIENCES	HUNGARY
KFKI-YB-	KFKI-YEARBOOK	HUNGARY
KFKN	KFK-NACHRICHTEN	GERMANY,F.R.
KHFTI-	UKRAINSK. FIZ. TEKHN. INST.,KHARKOV. REPORTS	USSR
KIYAI-	REPORTS BY INST. JADERNYKH ISSLEDOVANIJ,KIEV	USSR
KNS	JOURNAL OF THE KOREAN NUCLEAR SOCIETY	KOREA
KPS	JOURNAL OF THE KOREAN PHYSICAL SOCIETY	KOREA
KR-	KJELLER REPORTS	NORWAY

REF CODES Table 3

Code	Description	Country
KRI	KRISTALLOGRAFIYA /SPC/	USSR
KSF	KRATKIE SOOBSHCHENIYA PO FIZIKE /SPL/	USSR
KT	KERNTECHNIK (DURING SOME TIME CALLED: 'KERNTECHNIK, ISOTOPENTECHNIK UND -CHEMIE')	GERMANY,F.R.
KUR-	INST. ATOMNOJ ENERGIJ,KURCHATOV, REPORTS. NOW THESE REPORTS HAVE THE CODE 'IAE-'	USSR
KURRI-TR	KYOTO-UNIV.,RESEARCH REACTOR INST.,TECHN. REPORTS	JAPAN
LA-	LOS ALAMOS SCIENTIFIC LAB. REPORT SERIES	USA
LA-TR-	LOS ALAMOS SCI.LAB,TRANSLATION REPORT SERIES	USA
LADC-	LOS ALAMOS REP. SER. CLOSED SEPT.1964	USA
LAMS-	LOS ALAMOS SC.LAB.REPORT SERIES CLOSED SEPT.1964	USA
LAPENAS	NEUTRON SPECTRA MEASUREMENTS BY ACTIVATION TECHNIQUES (ZINATNE, RIGA, USSR, 1975). IN RUSSIAN	USSR
LBL-	LAWRENCE BERKELEY LAB REPORTS	USA
LEB	AK.NAUK SSSR, ISSLEDOVANIJA PO NEJTRONNOJ FIZIKE, TRUDY FIZICHESKOGO INSTITUTA IM.P.N.LEBEDEVA. = STUDIES IN NEUT.PHYS,PUBL.OF THE FIZ.INST.LEBEDEV	USSR
LFF-	FORSKININGSRADENS LABORATORIUM, STUDSVIK	SWEDEN
LIB/TRANS-	TRANSLATION SERIES,ORIGINAL CODE IS AAEC-LIB/TRANS-	AUSTRALIA
LIJAF-	LENINGRAD INST. NUCL. PHYSICS, REPORTS	USSR
LMSC-	LOCKHEED AIRCRAFT CO. REPORTS	USA
LMSD-	LOCKHEED AIRCRAFT CORP. REPORT SERIES	USA
LNS	INST.RUDJER BOSKOVIC REPORTS	YUGOSLAVIA
LPC-T-	LABORATOIRE DE PHYS. CORPUSCULAIRE, THESES	FRANCE
LR-	REPORTS OF INST.INVESTIGACION AERONAUTICA Y ESP.	ARGENTINA
LRL-	CALIF.RES.AND DEVELOP.CO. REPORT SERIES	USA
LS-	SOREQ NUCL. RESEARCH CENTRE, REPORTS	ISRAEL
LU-NP-	LUND UNIVERSITY, REPORTS	SWEDEN
LYCEN-	UNIV.OF LYON REPORTS	FRANCE
MAB	MONATSBER.DEUT.AKAD.WISS.BERLIN	GERMANY,F.R.
MAINZ-	MAINZ UNIVERSITY, REPORTS	GERMANY, F.R.
MC-	NAT.RES.COUNCIL OF CANADA,MONTREAL LABS REPORTS	CANADA
MDDC-	MANHATTAN DISTR.,OAK RIDGE, CONTINUED AS AECD-	USA
MED	MEDICAL PHYSICS	USA
MET	METROLOGIA	GERMANY,F.R.
MF-	JUNTA ENERGIA NUCLEAR, MADRID, REPORTS	SPAIN
MFF	MAGYAR FIZIKAI FOLYOIRAT	HUNGARY
MIT-	MASS. INST. OF TECHNOLOGY, CAMBRIDGE, REPORTS	USA
MITNE-	MIT,DEP'T OF NUCL.ENGINEERING, REPORT SERIES	USA
MLM-	MOUND LAB MIAMISBURG REPORTS	USA
MNC-	REPORTS BY MARYLAND UNIV,DEPT.OF CHEMISTRY	USA
MSL	MEMOIRES DE LA SOC. ROY. DES SCIENCES DE LIEGE	BELGIUM
MTR-L-	IDAHO NUCLEAR CORPORATION, REPORTS	USA
N-	NASA REPORTS, USUALLY N68-, N70- ETC	USA
NAA-	NORTH AMERICAN AVIATION, DOWNEY,CALIF, REPORT SER.	USA
NAP	NUCL. APPLICATIONS, VOL.7(1969)-VOL.9(1970) IS CALLED: 'NUCL. APPL. AND TECHNOLOGY'	USA
NARF-	NUCLEAR AEROSPACE RESEARCH FACILITY	USA
NASA-	NASA REPORTS	USA
NAT	NATURE	UK
NB.GS.COMP.	NOBLE GAS COMPOUNDS (ED. H.H.HYMAN, CHICAGO PRESS 1963)	USA
NBS-MONO-	NAT'L BUREAU OF STANDARDS, MONOGRAPHS	USA
NC	NUOVO CIMENTO	ITALY
NC/A	NUOVO CIMENTO SECTION A	ITALY
NC/B	NUOVO CIMENTO, SECTION B, STARTING WITH VOL.40 NO.1, NOVEMBER 1965	ITALY
NCL	LETTERE AL NUOVO CIMENTO	ITALY
NCS	NUOVO CIMENTO (SUPPL.)	ITALY
NCSAC-	REPORTS TO THE AEC NUCL.CROSS-SECT.ADVISORY COMMIT.	USA
ND/A	NUCLEAR DATA TABLES	USA
NDA-	UNITED NUCLEAR CORP. REPORT SERIES EXTINCT	USA

Table 3   REF CODES

Code	Description	Country
NDF	NOTAS DE FISICA, CENTRO BRASIL. DE PESQUISAS FIS.	BRAZIL
NDL-TR-	ARMY CHEM. CORPS NUCL. DEF. LAB., MD. REPORT SERIES	USA
NE	NUCL. ENGINEERING INTERNATIONAL, FORMERLY:'NUCL.ENGG.'	UK
NEANDC-	NEA NUCL. DATA COMMITTEE REPORTS	NEA
NEDO-	REPORTS OF GENERAL ELECTRIC COMP., SAN JOSE, CALIF.	USA
NEJTRONFIZ	NEJTRONNAJA FIZIKA, MOSCOW 1961. TRANSLATED AS 'SOVIET PROGRESS IN NEUTRON PHYSICS', CONS. BUREAU, NEW YORK.	USSR
NIIAR-	REPORTS OF INST. ATOMNYKH REAKTOROV, MELEKESS,	USSR
NIJS-	REPORTS OF NUK. INST JOSEF STEFAN, LJUBLJANA	YUGOSLAVIA
NIKOLAEV	ANIZOTROPIJA UPRUGOGO RASSEJANIJA NEJTRONOV, MOSKVA, ATOMIZDAT 1972 (IN RUSSIAN, = ANISOTROPY OF ELASTICALLY SCATTERED NEUTRONS. ENGL. TRANSLATION PUBLISHED AS INDC(CCP)-71, JAN. 1976)	USSR
NIM	NUCLEAR INSTRUMENTS AND METHODS	NETHERLANDS
NKA	NUKLEONIKA	POLAND
NP	NUCLEAR PHYSICS	NETHERLANDS
NP-	D.T.I.E NUMBERING OF NON PROJECT REPORTS	USA
NP/A	NUCLEAR PHYSICS, SECTION A	NETHERLANDS
NP/B	NUCLEAR PHYSICS SECTION B	NETHERLANDS
NPW	NUCLEAR POWER VOLUME 1, ABSORBED 1963 BY NUCL. ENG.	UK
NRCN-	ISRAEL A.E.C., BEER-SHEBA, NUCL. RESEARCH CENTER NEGEV REPORTS	ISRAEL
NRDC-	AERE-HARWELL REPORT SERIES	UK
NRITB-	NUCLEAR RES. INST., TUWAITHA, BAGHDAD. REPORTS	IRAQ
NRL-	NAVAL RES. LAB. WASHINGTON DC, REPORT SERIES	USA
NSA	NUCLEAR SCIENCE ABSTRACTS	USA
NSE	NUCLEAR SCIENCE AND ENGINEERING	USA
NSF	NUCLEAR SCIENCE, TAIWAN = HO TZU K'O HSUEH	FORMOSA
NSP	NUCLEAR SCIENCE AND APPLICATIONS	BANGLA DESH
NSPA	NUCLEAR SCIENCE AND APPLICATIONS SECTION A	BANGLA DESH
NSPB	NUCLEAR SCIENCE AND APPLICATIONS SECTION B	BANGLA DESH
NST	NUCLEAR SCIENCE AND TECHNOLOGY	JAPAN
NT	NUCLEAR TECHNOLOGY, FROM VOL 10(1971)	USA
NUC	NUCLEONICS	USA
NUK	NUKLEONIK	GERMANY, F.R.
NWS	NATURWISSENSCHAFTEN	GERMANY, F.R.
NYA	TRANS N.Y. ACAD. SCI.	USA
NYO-	NEW YORK OPERATIONS OFFICE CONTRACT REPORTS	USA
NYO-GEN-	COLUMBIA UNIV. NEW YORK, REPORTS	
OAP-	CALIF. INST. OF TECHNOLOGY, ORANGE AID PREPRINTS	USA
OAW	OESTERR. AKAD. WISS., MATH-NATURW. KL., SITZUNGSBER.	AUSTRIA
OAWA	OESTERR. AKAD. WISS., MATH+NATURW. ANZEIGER	AUSTRIA
OAWS	(PREV. OAW) OESTERR. AKAD. WISS., MATA+NATURW, SITZBER	AUSTRIA
OE	ONDE ELECTRIQUE	FRANCE
ORNL-	OAK RIDGE NATN'L LAB. REPORT SERIES	USA
ORNL-P-	OAK RIDGE NATN'L LAB. PREPRINTS	USA
ORNL-TM-	OAK RIDGE NATN'L LAB. TECHNICAL MEMOS	USA
ORNL-TR-	OAK-RIDGE NATN'L LAB. TRANSLATIONS	USA
ORO-	OAK RIDGE OPERATIONS OFFICE CONTRACT REPORTS	USA
PA	PHYSICS ABSTRACTS	UK
PAN-	POLISH ACADEMY OF SCIENCES, COMPARE INR- OR INP-	POLAND
PC	PHYSICS IN CANADA (BULL. OF THE ASSOC. OF PHYSICISTS)	CANADA
PCJ	J. OF PHYSICAL CHEMISTRY (BY AM. CHEM. SOCIETY)	USA
PCP	PROC. CAMBRIDGE PHIL. SOC.	UK
PCS	J. OF PHYSICS AND CHEMISTRY OF SOLIDS	UK
PEL-	ATOMIC ENERGY BOARD, PELINDABA, REPORTS	SOUTH AFRICA
PF	POSTEPY FIZYKI	POLAND
PHY	PHYSICA	NETHERLANDS
PIA	PROC. INDIAN ACAD. SCI., SECT A	INDIA
PIC2	READ 58GENEVA	
PINST-	PAKISTAN INST. NUCL. SCI. TECH., REPORTS (NOTE: ORIGINAL CODE 'PINST-NPD-' IS 'NPD-' ONLY)	PAKISTAN

REF CODES

Table 3

PL	PHYSICS LETTERS	NETHERLANDS
PL/A	PHYSICS LETTERS, SECTION A	NETHERLANDS
PL/B	PHYSICS LETTERS, SECTION B	NETHERLANDS
PM	PHILOSOPHICAL MAGAZINE	UK
PMB	PHYSICS IN MEDICINE AND BIOLOGY	UK
PMPA	PROCEEDINGS OF THE METAL POWDER ASSOCIATION	USA
PNE	PROGRESS IN NUCL.EN. SERIES 1,PHYS.AND MATHEMATICS HUGHES,LANDERS AND HOROWITZ,LONDON 1958	UK
PNE-	USAEC REPORTS ON PEACEFUL NUCLEAR EXPLOSIONS	USA
PNR/SETR-	CADARACHE REPORTS	FRANCE
PNS	PROC. NUCL. AND SOLID STATE PHYS. SYMP.	INDIA
PNV	PHYSICA NORVEGICA	NORWAY
PPA	PROCEEDINGS OF PAKISTAN ACAD. SCI.	PAKISTAN
PPAR-	PRINCETON PENNSYLVANIA ACCELERATOR REPORTS (EXTINCT)	USA
PPS	PROC. PHYS. SOC. (LONDON)	UK
PPSA	PROC. PHYS. SOC. (LONDON) SECTION A	UK
PR	PHYSICAL REVIEW	USA
PR-	AT.EN.OF CAN.LTD, CHALK RIVER, REPORT SERIES	CANADA
PR/A	PHYS. REV. PART A	USA
PR/B	PHYS.REV.,PART B	USA
PR/C	PHYS.REV.,PT.C= NUCLEAR PHYSICS. START VOL.1,1970	USA
PR/D	PHYS.REV.,PT.D= PARTICLES AND FIELDS. START VOL.1,1970	USA
PREA	PROC.ROY.SOC.EDINBURGH, SER.A	UK
PRL	PHYS. REV. LETTERS	USA
PRM	PRAMANA	INDIA
PROKOFJEV	SPECTRA OF ELECTROMAGNETIC TRANSITIONS AND LEVEL SCHEMES FOLLOWING THERMAL NEUTRON CAPTURE BY NUCLIDES WITH A=143-193. RIGA,PUBL.HOUSE ZINATNE,1973,LATVIJA, USSR.(IN RUSSIAN AND ENGLISH)	USSR
PRS	PROC. ROY. SOC. (LONDON)	UK
PRSA	PROC. ROY. SOC. (LONDON) SECTION A	UK
PS	PHYSICA SCRIPTA, JOURNAL STARTED 1970	SWEDEN
PSS	PHYSICA STATUS SOLIDI	GERMANY,F.R.
PT	PHYSICS TODAY	USA
PTB-	PHYS. TECHN. BUNDESANSTALT, BRAUNSCHWEIG, REPORTS	GERMANY, FR
PTE	PRIBORY I TEKHNIKA EKSPERIMENTA FOR ENGL. TRANSLATION SEE IET NOTE= NO VOL-NR PRINTED ON THE COVER.AN ARTIFICIAL VOL-NR IS GIVEN,STARTING WITH VOL 1(1956)	USSR
PTP	PROGR. THEORET. PHYS. (KYOTO)	JAPAN
PTUM-E-	TECHN. UNIV. MUENCHEN, REPORTS	GERMANY, FR
PUC-	REPORTS PRINCETON UNIVERSITY,N.J.,PALMER PHYS. LAB.	USA
PWAC-	PRATT AND WHITNEY AIRCRAFT DIV.,HARTFORD,REP.SERIES	USA
RAK	RADIOKHIMIYA /SRA/	USSR
RBF	REVISTA BRASILEIRA DE FISICA	BRAZIL
RCA	RADIOCHIMICA ACTA	GERMANY,F.R.
RCN-	REACTOR CENT.NEDERLAND,PETTEN,REPORT SERIES	NETHERLANDS
RCS	RADIOCHEM. STUDIES, VOL.2, FISSION PRODUCTS (1951)	USA
RD/B/	CENTR. ELECTR. GENER. BOARD,BERKELEY LABS, REPORTS	UK
REA	ATOMIC ENERGY REVIEW	IAEA
RFA-	AKTIEBOLEGAT ATOMENERGI STOCKHOLM, REPORT SERIES	SWEDEN
RFP-	DOW CHEMICAL COMPANY, ROCKY FLAT DIV., REPORT-SERIES	USA
RFR-	AKTIEBOLAGET ATOMENERGI, STOCKHOLM REPORT SERIES	SWEDEN
RFT	REACTOR AND FUEL-PROCESSING TECHNOLOGY	USA
RI-	KHLOPIN RADIEV. INST.,LENINGRAD, REPORT SERIES	USSR
RISO-	RISO RESEACH INST. REPORT SERIES	DENMARK
RL-	LAWRENCE RADIATION LAB,BERKELEY,CALIFORNIA. REPORTS	USA
RLO-	USAEC MISCELLANEOUS REPORT SERIES	USA
RMF	REVISTA MEXICANA DE FISICA	MEXICO
RMP	REVIEW OF MODERN PHYSICS	USA
RPA	REVUE DE PHYSIQUE APPLIQUEE	FRANCE
RPC-	RADIOPLANE CO.,VAN NUYS,CALIF.,REPORT SERIES	USA

Table 3 — REF CODES

Code	Description	Country
RPI-	RENSSELAER POLYTECNIC INST., REPORTS	USA
RPP	REPORTS ON PROGRESS IN PHYSICS	UK
RRC-	REACTOR RESEARCH CENTRE KALPAKKAM, REPORTS	INDIA
RRL	RADIOCHEMICAL AND RADIOANALYTICAL LETTERS	HUNGARY+SWITZ
RRP	REVUE ROUMAINE DE PHYSIQUE	ROMANIA
RSI	REVIEW OF SCIENTIFIC INSTRUMENTS	USA
RST	REACTOR SCIENCE AND TECHNOLOGY. NOW: JNE/AB	UK
RT/FI-	COMITATE NAZIONALE PER L'EN. NUC. FIZ.	ITALY
RT/FIMA-	COMITATE NAZIONALE PER L'EN. NUC. FIZ. MAT.	ITALY
S-	AKTIEBOLAGET ATOMENERGI, STOCKHOLM, PROGR. REPORTS	SWEDEN
SC-	SANDIA CORP., ALBUQUERQUE, NEW MEXICO, REPORTS	USA
SCF	STUDII SI CERCETARI DE FIZICA	ROMANIA
SCI	SCIENCE, (AMER. ASSN. FOR ADV. OF SCI.)	USA
SCP	SCI. PAPERS OF THE INST. PHYS. CHEM. RESEARCH (TOKYO)	JAPAN
SCR-	SANDIA CORP., ALBUQUERQUE, N. MEX.,CONT'D AS SC-R-	USA
SGAE-PH-	OESTER. STUDIENGES. F. ATOMENERGIE,SEIBERSDORF	AUSTRIA
SJA	SOVIET ATOMIC ENERGY	//AE//
SJAS	SOVIET ATOMIC ENERGY, SUPPLEMENT	//AE/S//
SNP	SOVIET J. OF NUCL. PHYS.	//YF//
SOKRATOR	USSR EVAL. NUCL. DATA LIBRARY, AVAILABLE FROM NEUTRON DATA CENTERS. SEE ALSO ANNEX PAGE A.5	USSR
SPC	SOVIET PHYSICS-CRYSTALLOGRAPHY	//KRI//
SPD	SOVIET PHYSICS - DOKLADY	//DOK//
SPL	SOVIET PHYSICS - LEBEDEV INST. REPORT	//KSF//
SPN	SOVIET PROGRESS IN NEUTRON PHYSICS, NEW YORK 1961 (ENGL. TRANSL. OF NEJTRONFIZ,SEE THERE.)	USA
SPS	SOVIET PHYSICS-SOLID STATE	//FTT//
SPU	SOVIET PHYS.-USPEKHI	//UFN//
SRA	SOVIET RADIOCHEMISTRY	//RAK//
SSC	SOLID STATE COMMUNICATIONS	UK,USA
STI/DOC/10-	IAEA TECHNICAL REPORT SERIES	IAEA
STI/PUB	IAEA PUBLICATIONS	IAEA
SUNI-	REPTS BY SOUTHERN UNIVERSITIES NUCLEAR INST.	SOUTH AFRICA
TDS-	AECL, NUCL.POW.PLANT DIV., REPORT SERIES	CANADA
THAI-	REPTS ATOMIC ENERGY FOR PEACE,BANGKOK	THAILAND
TI-	ATOMICS INTERNATIONAL, NORTH AMERICAN ROCKWELL, TECHNICAL INFORMATION REPORTS	USA
TID-	DIV.OF TECH.INFORM.EXT., AEC REPORT SERIES	USA
TNCC-	TRIPARTITE NUCL. CROSS-SECT. COMMITTEE. EXTINCT	USA/UK/CAN
TNS	THE NUCLEUS	PAKISTAN
TNSD-R-	TECHNION NUCLEAR SCIENCE DEPT. REPORTS	ISRAEL
TRANSU.EL.	'THE TRANSURANIUM ELEMENTS', NATIONL NUCLEAR ENERGY SERIES, DIV. IV, VOL. 14B, 1949	USA
TU-05-	TECHNISCHE UNIV. DRESDEN, SEKTION PHYSIK, REPORTS	DDR
U/KTY-	UNIVERSITY OF KENTUCKY REPORTS	USA
UARAEE-	UNITED ARAB REPUBLIC,ATOMIC ENERGY ESTABLISHMENT	EGYPT
UCID-	UNIV.OF CALIF.,LAWRENCE RADIATION LAB,REPORTS	USA
UCRL-	CALIFORNIA U. REPORT SERIES	USA
UFN	USPEKHI FIZ. NAUK /SPD/	USSR
UFZ	UKRAINSKIJ FIZICHNIJ ZHURNAL /UPJ/	USSR
UJF-	USTAV JAD.FYZIKY (INST.NUCL.PHYS.) REPORTS	CZECHOSLOV.
UJV-	USTAV JAD.VYZKUMU(INST.NUCL.RES.),PRAGUE REP'T SER.	CZECHOSLOV.
UK-	U.K.A.E.A. RESEARCH GROUP REPORT SERIES	UK
UK/C-	REPTS ATOM.EN.OF CANADA,CHALK RIVER PROJECT	CANADA
UKNDC-	UK NUCLEAR DATA COMMITTEE, REPORT SERIES	UK
UKNDL-DFN-	UK LIBRARY FOR EVALUATED NEUTRON DATA. AVAILABLE FROM NEUTRON DATA CENTRES. SEE ANNEX PAGE A.5	UK
UMO-	UNIVERSITY MICROFILMS ORDER NUMBER THESES CAN BE ORDERED WITH THIS NUMBER FROM UNIVERSITY MICROFILMS LTD.	UK+USA
UNC-	UNITED NUCLEAR CORP., REPORT SERIES	USA
UNIV-MI-	UNIV. OF MICHIGAN, REPORT SERIES	USA

REF CODES Table 3

Code	Description	Country
UPJ	UKRAINIAN PHYSICS JOURNAL	//UFZ//
UPP-	UPPSALA UNIV., ANNUAL REPORT	SWEDEN
UR-	REPORTS OF UNIV. ROCHESTER, NEW YORK	USA
USNDC-	REPORTS TO THE US NUCL.DATA COMMETTEE	USA
USNRDL-	NAVAL RADIOLOG. DEF.LAB., SAN FRANCISCO REP.SERIES	USA
VBF	VESTSI AKADEMII NAVUK BELARUSKAI SSR, SERIJA FIZIKA-ENERGETYCHNYKH NAVUK	USSR
VIEN-V	COMPUTER FILE CONTAINING SELECTED EVALUATED NEUTRON DATA NOT CONTAINED IN ANOTHER EVALUATED DATA LIBRARY. AVAILABLE FROM NEUTRON DATA CENTERS, SEE ANNEX PAGE A.5	IAEA
WADC-	WRIGHT AIR DEV. CENTER, OHIO, REPORT SERIES	USA
WADD-TR-	WRIGHT AIR DEV., OHIO, REPORT SERIES	USA
WANL-TME	WESTINGHOUSE ASTRO-NUCLEAR LAB, PITTSBURG	USA
WAPD-	WESTINGHOUSE, ATOMIC POWER DIV., REPORT SERIES	USA
WARD-	WESTINGHOUSE ELECTRIC CORP., MADISON, PA. ADVANCED REACTORS DIVISION REPORTS	USA
WASH-	AEC, WASHINGTON REPORTS TO THE NCSAG	USA
WCAP-	WESTINGHOUSE ELECTRIC CORP. COMMERCIAL ATOMIC POWER REPORT SERIES	USA
XDC-	GEN.EL.CO., CINCINNATI, REPORT SERIES.FINISHED	USA
YF	YADERNAYA FIZIKA /SNP/	USSR
YFI-	JADERNO-FIZICHESKIE ISSLEDOVANIJA (PROGRESS REPORTS)	USSR
YK-	JADERNYE KONSTANTY, OBNINSK REPORTS	USSR
YTN	YUAN TZU NENG (ATOMIC ENERGY)	CHINA
ZAED-M-	ZENTRALSTELLE F. ATOMENERGIE-DOKUMENTATION, REPORTS	GERMANY,F.R.
ZAP	Z. ANGEW. PHYS.	GERMANY,F.R.
ZEC	ZEITSCHRIFT FUER ELECTROCHIMIE	GERMANY,F.R.
ZEP	ZET LETTERS TO THE EDITOR /JEL/	USSR
ZET	ZH. EKSPERIM. I TEOR. FIZ. /JET/	USSR
ZFK-	REPORTS BY ZENTRALINST. F. KERNFORSCHUNG, ROSSENDORF	GERMAN D.R.
ZK	Z. KRISTALLOGRAPHIE	GERMANY,F.R.
ZMP	Z. ANGEW. MATH. PHYS.	SWITZERLAND
ZN/A	ZEITSCHRIFT F.NATURFORSCHUNG, SECTION A	GERMANY,F.R.
ZP	Z. PHYSIK	GERMANY,F.R.
ZP/A	Z. PHYSIK,SECT.A=ATOMS AND NUCLEI. START VOL.272,1975	GERMANY,F.R.
ZPF	Z.PHYSIK.CHEM.(FRANKFURT)	GERMANY,F.R.

TABLE 4: LAB CODES

Abbreviations for laboratories and institutions which are entered in the 'Lab' field of the CINDA entries. (Note to CINDA indexers: this list should not be used for coding new entries because it includes codes which are out of date but still existing in the file.)

Code	Institution	Country
AAA	GROUPEMENT ATOMIQUE ALSACIEN ATLANTIQUE, H/SEINE	FRANCE
AAU	INSTITUTE OF PHYSICS, UNIV. OF AARHUS	DENMARK
ABC	ACADEMIA BRASILEIRA DE CIENCIAS, RIO DE JANEIRO	BRAZIL
ABD	US ARMY RES.+DEVEL.CENTER, ABERDEEN, MARYLAND	USA
ACC	ALLIED CHEMICAL CORPORATION, IDAHO FALLS	USA
AE	STUDSVIK ENERGITEKNIK AB	SWEDEN
AFW	AIRFORCE WEAPONS LAB., KIRTLAND, NEW MEXICO	USA
AGN	AEROJET-GENERAL NUCLEONICS, SAN RAMON, CALIFORNIA	USA
AI	ATOMICS INTERNATIONAL, CANOGA PARK, CALIF.	USA
ALA	U. OF ALBERTA, EDMONTON, ALA.	CANADA
ALB	STATE UNIVERSITY OF NEW-YORK, ALBANY, N.Y.	USA
ALD	AWRE, ALDERMASTON	UK
ALG	ALGERIA	ALGERIA
ALS	ALABAMA STATE UNIVERSITY, MONTGOMERY, ALABAMA	USA
ALU	ALLAHABAD UNIVERSITY, ALLAHABAD	INDIA
AMH	AMHERST COLLEGE, AMHERST, MASS.	USA
AML	U. OF MELBOURNE	AUSTRALIA
AMS	U. OF AMSTERDAM	NETHERLANDS
AMU	ARYA-MEHR UNIV. OF TECHNOLOGY, TEHERAN	IRAN
ANA	UNITED STATES NAVAL ACADEMY, ANNAPOLIS, MARYLAND	USA
ANC	AEROJET NUCL. CORP., IDAHO FALLS, IDAHO	USA
AND	ANDREWS UNIV., BERRIEN SPRINGS, MICHIGAN	USA
ANK	ANKARA, UNIVERSITY OR MIDDLE EAST T.U.	TURKEY
ANL	ARGONNE NATIONAL LAB., ARGONNE, ILLINOIS	USA
APD	ATOMIC POWER DEVELOPMENT ASSOCIATES, DETROIT, MICHIGAN	USA
ARF	ARMOUR RESEARCH FOUNDATION, CHICAGO, ILL.	USA
ARG	ARGENTINA	ARGENTINA
ARK	U. OF ARKANSAS, FAYETTEVILLE	USA
ARL	AEROSPACE RESEARCH LABS, WRIGHT-PATTERSON, OHIO	USA
ASU	ARIZONA STATE UNIV., TEMPE, ARIZONA	USA
ASY	U. OF SYDNEY	AUSTRALIA
ATH	NRC DEMOKRITOS, ATHENS	GREECE
ATI	ATOMINST. DER OESTERR. HOCHSCHULEN, VIENNA	AUSTRIA
AUA	A.A.E.C. RESEARCH ESTABLISHMENT, LUCAS HEIGHTS, N.S.W.	AUSTRALIA
AUB	AUBURN UNIVERSITY, ALABAMA	USA
AUF	FLINDERS UNIV, BEDFORD PARK, ADELAIDE	AUSTRALIA
AUL	AUSTRALIA	AUSTRALIA
AUS	AUSTRIA	AUSTRIA
AUW	LAB. FOR NUCL. RESEARCH, ANDRAH UNI., WALTAIR	INDIA
B+W	BABCOCK AND WILCOX CO., LYNCHBURGH, VA.	USA
BAN	BANGLA DESH	BANGLA DESH
BAR	BARTOL RESEARCH FOUNDATION, SWARTHMORE, PENNSYLVANIA	USA
BAS	U. OF BASEL	SWITZERLAND
BAT	BATTELLE MEMORIAL INST., COLUMBUS, OHIO	USA
BAU	BARI, UNIVERSITY	ITALY
BCM	BOSTON COLLEGE, CHESTNUT HILL, MASS.	USA
BCT	BATTERSEA COLLEGE OF TECHNOLOGY, LONDON, ENGLAND	UK
BEH	BERLIN, HUMBOLDT UNIVERSITAET, AND DAW ZEUTHEN	GERMAN D.R.
BEL	BELL TELEPHONE LABS., MURRAY HILL, N.J.	USA
BEP	BERLIN, VEB ATOMKRAFTWERK PANKOW	GERMAN D.R.
BER	BERLIN, HAHN-MEITNER-INSTITUT	GERMANY, FR
BET	WESTINGHOUSE, BETTIS ATOMIC POWER LAB. PITTSBURGH	USA
BFR	FREIBERG, BERGAKADEMIE	GERMAN D.R.
BGK	OFFICE OF THE ATOMIC ENERGY FOR PEACE, BANGKOK	USA
BGN	U. OF BERGEN	NORWAY
BHU	BANARAS HINDU UNIV, VARANASI	INDIA
BIA	U. OF ASTON, BIRMINGHAM	UK
BIR	U. OF BIRMINGHAM	UK

Table 4　　　　　　　　　　　　　　　　　LAB CODES

Code	Institution	Country
BKB	INST. BORIS KIDRIC, VINCA NEAR BEOGRAD	YUGOSLAVIA
BLA	INST. OF NUCL. RES. AND NUCL. EN., BULG. AC. SCI., SOFIA	BULGARIA
BLG	BELGIUM	BELGIUM
BLN	BROOKLYN COLLEGE, NEW YORK CITY	USA
BNL	BROOKHAVEN NATIONAL LAB., UPTON, N.Y.	USA
BNW	BATTELLE-NORTHWEST, RICHLAND, WASH. (FORM. HANF. AT. PROD.)	USA
BOC	BOCHUM, UNIVERSITAET	GERMANY
BOE	BOEING SCI. RES. LABS, SEATTLE, WASH	USA
BOL	CNEN BOLOGNA	ITALY
BON	BONN, UNIVERSITY	GERMANY, FR
BOR	U. OF BORDEAUX, TALENCE (GIRONDE) AND C.E.A. BORDEAUX	FRANCE
BOS	BOSE INST., CALCUTTA	INDIA
BRC	CEN BRUYERE LE CHATEL	FRANCE
BRD	UNIV. OF BRADFORD, ENGLAND	UK
BRI	U. OF BRISTOL	UK
BRK	U. OF CALIFORNIA, LAWRENCE BERKELEY LAB., BERKELEY	USA
BRL	BALLISTIC RES. LABS, ABERDEEN, PROVING GROUNDS, MD.	USA
BRN	BROWN U., PROVIDENCE, RHODE ISLAND	USA
BRU	U. OF BRUXELLES	BELGIUM
BSP	SAO PAULO, SEE IEA OR USP	BRAZIL
BUC	INST. DE FIZICA SI INGENERIE NUCLEARA, BUCHAREST	ROMANIA
BUF	STATE UNIV. OF NEW YORK, BUFFALO, N.Y.	USA
BUL	BULGARIA	BULGARIA
CAB	UNIV. SAN CARLOS Y CENTRO ATOMICO, BARILOCHE	ARGENTINA
CAD	CADARACHE, BOUCHES DU RHONE, ST. PAUL-LEZ-DURANCE	FRANCE
CAI	AEE, CAIRO	EGYPT
CAL	CALIFORNIA INSTITUTE OF TECH., PASADENA, CALIFORNIA	USA
CAN	CANADA	CANADA
CAR	CARNEGIE INSTITUTE OF TECH., PITTSBURGH, PA.	USA
CAS	CENTRO DI STUDI NUCLEARI DELLA 'CASACCIA', ROME	ITALY
CAT	U. OF CATANIA	ITALY
CAV	CAVENDISH LAB., CAMBRIDGE	UK
CAW	CARNEGIE INSTITUTE, WASHINGTON D.C.	USA
CBE	COMBUSTION ENGINEERING, WINDSOR, CONNECTICUT	USA
CBR	AUSTRALIAN NATIONAL U., CANBERRA	AUSTRALIA
CCH	UKAEA REACTOR MATERIALS LAB, CULCHETH, WARRINGTON	UK
CCP	USSR	USSR
CEA	COMMISSARIAT A L'ENERGIE ATOMIQUE, PARIS	FRANCE
CEG	CENTRAL ELECTRICITY GENERATING BOARD, BERKELEY LABS	UK
CER	CERN, GENEVA	SWITZERLAND
CHF	TAIWAN	TAIWAN
CHI	U. OF CHICAGO, ILLINOIS	USA
CHL	CHILE	CHILE
CHP	PEOPLES REPUBLIC OF CHINA	CHINA
CHU	CHARLES UNIV., FACULT. OF MATHEM. AND PHYSICS, PRAGUE	CZECHOSLOV.
CIS	C.I.S.E., MILAN	ITALY
CJD	CENTR PO JADERNYM DANNYM, OBNINSK	USSR
CLA	U. OF CALIFORNIA, LOS ANGELES	USA
CLC	CALCUTTA, SEE SAH, BOS, IAC OR ISI	INDIA
CLE	UNIVERSITE DE CLERMONT, CLERMONT-FERRAND	FRANCE
CLI	CLINTON LABS, KNOXVILLE, TENN.	USA
CLS	CLEVELAND STATE UNIV., CLEVELAND, OHIO	USA
CLU	COLORADO U., BOULDER, COLORADO	USA
CNA	CEKMECE NUCLEAR RESEARCH CENTER, ISTAMBUL.	TURKEY
CNE	COM. NACIONAL DE ENERG. ATOM., BUENOS AIRES	ARGENTINA
CNM	CENTRO NUCLEAR DE MEXICO, MEXICO CITY	MEXICO
COL	COLUMBIA U., NEW YORK CITY, N.Y.	USA
CON	CONVAIR, SAN DIEGO, CALIFORNIA	USA
COP	U. OF COPENHAGEN	DENMARK
COR	CORNELL UNIV, ITHACA, N.Y.	USA
CPO	AECL COMMERCIAL PRODUCTS, OTTAWA	CANADA
CRC	A.E.C.L. CHALK RIVER, ONTARIO	CANADA
CRL	CARLETON UNIVERSITY, OTTAWA, ONTARIO	CANADA
CSD	U. OF CALIFORNIA, SAN DIEGO	USA

LAB CODES

Table 4

Code	Institution	Country
CSE	CASE WESTERN RESERVE UNIVERS., CLEVELAND, OHIO	USA
CSI	COLUMBIA SCIENTIFIC INDUSTRIES CORP., LAFAYETTE, LA.	USA
CSR	CZECHOSLOVAKIA	CZECHOSLOV.
CTH	CHALMERS U. OF TECHNOLOGY, GOTHENBURG	SWEDEN
CUA	THE CATHOLIC UNIVERSITY OF AMERICA, WASHINGTON D.C.	USA
CUW	CURTISS-WRIGHT CORPORATION, QUEHANNA, PENNSYLVANIA	USA
CZA	CZECH. ACAD. OF SCIENCES, PRAGUE	CZECHOSLOV.
DAC	DACCA UNIVERSITY, AND ATOMIC EN. CENTRE, DACCA	BANGLA DESH
DAV	U. OF CALIFORNIA, AT DAVIS	USA
DEB	ATOMMAG KUTATO INTEZETE, DEBRECEN	HUNGARY
DEL	TECHNICAL U., DELFT	NETHERLANDS
DEN	DENMARK	DENMARK
DGE	CEC DOSIMETRY GROUP, GEEL (FORMERLY EURATOM)	BELGIUM
DKE	DUKE U., DURHAM, NORTH CAROLINA	USA
DLH	DELHI UNIVERSITY	INDIA
DOD	DEPT. OF DEFENSE, DASA. WASHINGTON, D.C.	USA
DOF	DIAMOND ORDNANCE FUSE LABORATORY	USA
DOU	DOUNREAY EXPERIMENTAL REACTOR ESTABLISHM., THURSO	UK
DUB	JOINT INSTITUTE FOR NUCLEAR RESEARCH, DUBNA	USSR
DUR	U. OF DURHAM	UK
EDF	ELECTRICITE DE FRANCE, PARIS	FRANCE
EDG	U. OF EDINBURGH, SCOTLAND	UK
EE	ENGLISH ELECTRIC CO, WHEATSTONE, LEICS	UK
EGG	EG+G, INC., SANTA BARBARA DIVISION, GOLETA, CALIF.	USA
ELU	EOTVOS LORAND UNIV., THEOR. PHYSICS INST., BUDAPEST	HUNGARY
EMY	EMORY UNIVERSITY, ATLANTA, GEORGIA	USA
ENI	ENI, SAN DONATO, MILAN	ITALY
ENS	ECOLE NORMALE SUPERIEURE, PARIS	FRANCE
ETH	EIDGENOESSISCHE TECHNISCHE HOCHSCHULE, ZURICH	SWITZERLAND
ETS	EAST TEXAS STATE UNIVERSITY	USA
FAR	CEA FONTENAY-AUX-ROSES, SEINE	FRANCE
FEI	FIZIKO-ENERGETICHESKIJ INSTITUT, OBNINSK	USSR
FIR	U. OF FIRENZE	ITALY
FLA	U. OF FLORIDA, GAINESVILLE, FLORIDA	USA
FOA	RESEARCH INSTITUTE OF NAT'L DEFENSE, STOCKHOLM	SWEDEN
FR	FRANCE	FRANCE
FRB	FREIBURG/BREISGAU, UNIVERSITAET	GERMANY, FR
FRK	FRANKFURT, J.W. GEOTHE-UNIVERSITAET	GERMANY, FR
FRS	U. OF FRIBOURG	SWITZERLAND
FSU	FLORIDA STATE U., TALLAHASSEE, FLORIDA	USA
FTI	FIZIKO-TEKHNICHESKIJ INST. IOFFE, LENINGRAD+GATCHINA	USSR
FUL	VRIJE UNIVERSITEIT TE AMSTERDAM, DE BOELELAAN	NETHERLANDS
GA	GULF ENERGY AND ENVIRONM. SYSTEMS, SAN DIEGO, CAL.	USA
GDT	GENERAL DYNAMICS, FORT WORTH, TEXAS	USA
GEA	GE, AIRCRAFT NUCL. PROPULSION DEPT., CINCINNATTI, OHIO	USA
GEB	GEN. EL. BREEDER REACT. DEVELOP. OPER., SUNNYVALE, CALIF.	USA
GEF	GE, SPACE SCIENCES LAB., VALLEY FORGE, PENN.	USA
GEL	B.C.M.N. GEEL, CEC (FORMERLY EURATOM)	BELGIUM
GEN	GENERAL ELECTRIC - NUCLEAR MATERIALS, PA.	USA
GEO	U. OF GEORGIA, ATHENS, GEORGIA	USA
GEP	GE, NUCLEONICS LAB., PLEASANTON, CA.	USA
GER	GERMANY, FED. REP. OF	GERMANY, FR
GES	GE, SCHENECTADY, N.Y. (OTHER THAN KAPL)	USA
GEV	GE, VALLECITOS ATOMIC LAB., SAN JOSE, CA.	USA
GFK	GESELLSCHAFT ZUR FOERDERUNG DER KERNENERGIE, GRAZ	AUSTRIA
GGA	GULF GENERAL ATOMIC, SAN DIEGO, CALIFORNIA	USA
GHT	U. OF GHENT	BELGIUM
GIT	GEORGIA INST OF TECHNOLOGY ATLANTA	USA
GKS	STATE COMMITTEE ON STANDARDS, MOSCOW	USSR
GLS	U. OF GLASGOW, SCOTLAND	UK
GOE	GOETTINGEN, UNIVERSITY	GERMANY, FR
GOR	UNIVERSITY OF GORKIJ, GORKIJ	USSR
GRC	GREECE	GREECE
GRE	GRENOBLE (CEA AND UNIVERSITY)	FRANCE

Table 4 LAB CODES

GRN	GRONINGEN	NETHERLANDS
GSF	GODDARD SPACE FLIGHT CENTER	USA
GSU	GEORGIA STATE UNIVERSITY, ATLANTA	USA
GVA	GENOVA, UNIVERSITY+INFN	ITALY
GVE	U. OF GENEVA	SWITZERLAND
GWU	GEORGE WASHINGTON U., WASHINGTON D.C.	USA
HAM	HAMBURG, UNIVERSITAET	GERMANY,FR
HAN	HANFORD ATOMIC PRODUCTS, RICHLAND, WASH. (LATER BNW)	USA
HAR	AERE HARWELL, BERKSHIRE	UK
HEB	HEBREW UNIVERSITY, JERUSALEM	ISRAEL
HED	HANFORD ENGINEERING DEVELOPMENT LAB, RICHLAND, WASH.	USA
HEI	HEIDELBERG, UNIV. + MAK-PLANCK-INST.	GERMANY,FR
HFA	TECHNION - ISRAEL INST. OF TECHNOLOGY, HAIFA	ISRAEL
HIR	UNIV.OF HIROSHIMA	JAPAN
HKU	CHINESE U. OF HONG KONG	HONG KONG
HLS	U. OF HELSINSKI, HELSINSKI	FINLAND
HLT	TECH. UNIV. OF HELSINKI, OTANIEMI	FINLAND
HNS	HAZLETON-NUCLEAR SCIENCE CORP., PALO ALTO, CALIFORNIA	USA
HRV	HARVARD U, MASSACHUSETTS	USA
HSL	USAEC HEALTH AND SAFETY LAB., NEW YORK	USA
HUN	HUNGARY	HUNGARY
HYO	HYOGO AGRICULTURAL U., SASAYAMA	JAPAN
IAC	IND. ASS. CULT. OF SCI., JADHAVPUR, CALCUTTA	INDIA
IAE	INTERN. ATOMIC ENERGY AGENCY, VIENNA	AUSTRIA
IAK	INST.FUER ANGEWANDTE KERNPHYSIK, KARLSRUHE	GERMANY,FR
IAN	INSTITUTO DE ASUNTOS NUCLEARES, BOGOTA	COLOMBIA
IAP	INST.FOR ADVANCED STUDIES, PRINCETON	USA
IBJ	INST. BADAN JADR. = NUCL. RES. INST., SWIERK+WARSZAWA	POLAND
IBM	IBM RESEARCH LAB, SAN JOSE, CALIF.	USA
ICD	CENTR PO JADERNYM DANNYM, OBNINSK	USSR
ICP	INST. OF CHEMICAL PHYSICS, MOSCOW	USSR
IEA	INSTITUTO DE ENERGIA ATOMICA, SAO PAULO	BRAZIL
IEN	INSTIT. DE ENGENHARIA NUCLEAR, RIO DE JANEIRO	BRAZIL
IFB	INSTITUT FIZIKI A.N. BELORUSSKOJ SSR, MINSK	USSR
IFJ	INST.FIZ.JADR. = INST.NUCL.PHYSICS, KRAKOW	POLAND
IFL	INST. FIZ. A.N. LATVIJSKOJ SSR, RIGA	USSR
IFM	UNIVERSITY OF MEXICO, INST. DE FISICA, MEXICO CITY	MEXICO
IFP	INST. FIZICHESKIKH PROBLEM, MOSKVA	USSR
IFS	INST. FUER STRAHLENPHYSIK, STUTTGART	GERMANY,FR
IFU	INST. FIZIKI A.N. UKRAINSKOJ SSR, KIEV. AROUND 1970 THE NUCLEAR PHYSICS PART OF THIS INSTITUTE BECAME A SEPARATE INSTITUTE, SEE 'IJI'	USSR
II	INST. OF ISOTOPES, HUNG. ACAD. OF SCI., BUDAPEST	HUNGARY
IID	INDIAN INST. OF TECHNOLOGY, DELHI	INDIA
IIK	INDIAN INST. OF TECHNOLOGY, KHARAGPUR	INDIA
IIT	ILLINOIS INST. OF TECHNOLOGY, CHICAGO	USA
IJE	INST. JADERN. ENERG., A.N. BELORUSKOJ SSR, MINSK	USSR
IJI	INST. JADERNYKH ISSLEDOVANIJ A.N. UKRAINSKOJ SSR, KIEV. BEFORE ABOUT 1970 IT WAS PART OF 'IFU', SEE THERE	USSR
IKE	INSTITUT FUER KERNENERGETIK, STUTTGART	GERMANY, FR
ILL	INSTITUT LAUE-LANGEVIN, GRENOBLE	FRANCE
INA	BENSBERG, INTERATOM	GERMANY,FR
IND	INDIA	INDIA
INL	IDAHO NUCLEAR ENGINEERING LAB., IDAHO FALLS	USA
INR	INST. F. NEUTRONENPHYSIK + REAKTOREN TECHN., KARLSRUHE	GERMANY,FR
IOW	IOWA STATE U., AMES, IOWA	USA
IPS	RESEARCH INST. OF PHYSICS(FORM. NOBEL INST.) STOCKHOLM	SWEDEN
IRE	INST. FOR RADIOPHYSICS + ELECTRONICS, KHARKOV	USSR
IRK	INSTITUT FUR RADIUMFORSCHUNG UND KERNPHYSIK, VIENNA	AUSTRIA
IRN	IRAN	IRAN
IRT	INTELCOM RADIATION TECHNOLOGY, SAN DIEGO, CALIFORNIA	USA
IRV	UNIVERSITY OF CALIFORNIA, IRVINE, CALIF.	USA
ISL	ISRAEL	ISRAEL
ISP	CEC ISPRA, FORMERLY EURATOM	ITALY

LAB CODES

Table 4

ISS	U. OF TOKYO, INST. OF SOLID STATE PHYSICS	JAPAN
IST	IMP. COLL. OF SCI.+TECHN., LONDON	UK
ISU	IDAHO STATE UNIV., POCATELLO, IDAHO	USA
ITE	INST. TEORETICHESKOI I EXPERIMENTALNOI FIZIKI MOSCOW	USSR
ITJ	INST. OF NUCLEAR TECHNIQUES, KRAKOW	POLAND
ITK	INDIAN INST. OF TECHNOLOGY, KANPUR	INDIA
ITM	INST. TECHNOL. DE MONTERREY	MEXICO
ITU	CEC INST. FOR TRANSURANIUM ELEMENTS, KARLSRUHE	GERMANY, FR
ITY	ITALY	ITALY
IVI	INST. VENEZUAL. DE INVESTIGACION CIENTIFICA, CARACAS	VENEZUELA
JAE	JAPAN ATOMIC ENERGY RESEARCH INST. TOKAI	JAPAN
JAP	JAPAN	JAPAN
JHU	JOHNS HOPKINS U., BALTIMORE, MARYLAND	USA
JIA	INST. JADERNYKH ISSLEDOVANIJ A.N. SSSR, MOSCOW	USSR
JLU	GIESSEN, J. LIEBIG-UNIVERSITAET	GERMANY, FR
JNA	JENA, UNIVERSITAET	GERMAN D.R.
JNE	JUNTA ENERGIA NUCLEAR, MADRID	SPAIN
JUL	JUELICH, KERNFORSCHUNGSANLAGE	GERMANY, FR
JYV	JYVAESKYLAE UNIV.	FINLAND
KAL	KALPAKKAM REACTOR RESEARCH CENTRE, KALPAKKAM, TAMILNADU	INDIA
KAN	U. OF KANSAS, LAWRENCE, KANSAS	USA
KAP	KNOLLS ATOMIC POWER LAB., SCHENECTADY, NEW YORK	USA
KAZ	INST. JADERN. FIZIKI, KAZAKHSTAN	USSR
KEN	U. OF KENT, CANTERBURY	UK
KFI	CENTRAL RES. INST. F. PHYSICS, KFKI, BUDAPEST	HUNGARY
KFK	KARLSRUHE, KERNFORSCHUNGSZENTRUM	GERMANY, FR
KFT	KHARKOVSKIJ FIZIKO-TECHNICHESKIJ INST., KHARKOV	USSR
KGU	GOSUDARSTVENNYJ UNIV. (STATE U.), KIEV	USSR
KIG	GEESTHACHT, GKSS	GERMANY, FR
KIL	KIEL, UNIVERSITAET	GERMANY, FR
KJL	INSTITUTT FOR ATOMENERGI, KJELLER	NORWAY
KLN	KOELN, UNIVERSITAET	GERMANY, FR
KON	KONAN U., KOBE	JAPAN
KOR	REPUBLIC OF KOREA	KOREA
KOS	KOSSUTH UNIV., INST. FOR EXP. PHYSICS, DEBRECEN	HUNGARY
KQU	KINGSTON, QUEEN'S UNIVERSITY, ONTARIO	CANADA
KRK	INSTITUT FIZYKI JADROWEJ PAN+UNIVERSITY, KRAKOW	POLAND
KRU	KARLSRUHE, UNIVERSITAET	GERMANY, FR
KSU	KANSAS STATE UNIVERSITY, MANHATTAN, KANSAS	USA
KTH	ROYAL INSTITUTE OF TECHNOLOGY, STOCKHOLM	SWEDEN
KTO	KYOTO U.	JAPAN
KTY	U. OF KENTUCKY, LEXINGTON, KENTUCKY	USA
KUK	UNIVERSITY OF KURUKSHETRA	INDIA
KUR	I.V. KURCHATOV ATOMIC ENERGY INST., MOSCOW	USSR
KUS	KOREA UNIV., SEOUL	KOREA
KYU	KYUSHU UNIVERSITY, DEPARTMENT OF NUCL. ENG. FUKUOKA	JAPAN
LAH	ATOMIC ENERGY CENTER, LAHORE	PAKISTAN
LAN	LANGLEY RESEARCH CENTRE, NASA LANGLEY STATION, VA.	USA
LAS	LOS ALAMOS SCIENTIFIC LAB., NEW MEXICO	USA
LAU	U. OF LAUSANNE	SWITZERLAND
LBL	LAWRENCE BERKELEY LAB, BERKELEY, CALIF.	USA
LEB	LEBEDEV-FIZ-TEKH INST. (FIAN), MOSCOW	USSR
LEI	U. OF LEIDEN	NETHERLANDS
LIE	U. OF LIEGE	BELGIUM
LIN	LENINGRAD INST. NUCL. PHYS., USSR ACAD. SCI., GATCHINA	USSR
LMS	LOCKHEED MISSILES AND SPACE DIV., PALO ALTO, CALIF.	USA
LND	LUND UNIV. + TECHNICAL UNIV.	SWEDEN
LOK	LOCKHEED AIRCRAFT, SUNNYVALE, CALIF.	USA
LON	U. OF LONDON	UK
LOU	LODZ, UNIVERSITY	POLAND
LRC	NASA LEWIS RES. CENTRE, CLEVELAND, OHIO	USA
LRL	LAWRENCE LIVERMORE LABORATORY, LIVERMORE, CALIF. FORMERLY LAWRENCE RADIATION LABORATORY.	USA
LSU	LOUISIANA STATE U.	USA

Table 4   LAB CODES

Code	Institution	Country
LTI	UNIVERSITY OF LOWELL, MASS.	USA
LUQ	LAVAL UNIVERSITY, QUEBEC	CANADA
LVN	U. OF LOUVAIN	BELGIUM
LVP	U. OF LIVERPOOL	UK
LYO	U. OF LYON, VILLEURBANNE (RHONE)	FRANCE
MAG	MAGI, ELMSFORD, NEW YORK	USA
MAN	U. OF MANCHESTER	UK
MBG	MARBURG, UNIVERSITAET	GERMANY, FR
MCG	MCGILL U., MONTREAL	CANADA
MCM	MCMASTER U., ONTARIO	CANADA
MES	INSTITUTO DI FISICA DELL'UNIVERSITA, MESSINA	ITALY
MEX	MEXICO	MEXICO
MGA	MAHATMA GHANDI SCI.INST., NAVARANGAPURA, AHMEDABAD	INDIA
MGW	MONTREAL, SIR GEORGE WILLIAMS UNIVERSITY	CANADA
MHG	U. OF MICHIGAN	USA
MIF	MOSCOW INST. OF ENGINEERING PHYSICS, MOSCOW	USSR
MIL	U. OF MILAN	ITALY
MIN	U. OF MINNESOTA, MINNEAPOLIS	USA
MIP	POLITECNICO DI MILANO	ITALY
MIS	U. OF MISSOURI, COLUMBIA	USA
MIT	MASSACHUSETTS INST. OF TECH., MASSACHUSETTS	USA
MNA	UNIV. OF MANITOBA, CYCLOTRON LAB., WINNIPEG	CANADA
MND	MOUND LAB., MIAMISBURG, OHIO	USA
MNZ	MAINZ, UNIVERSITAET	GERMANY, FR
MOL	CEN MOL	BELGIUM
MON	U. OF MONTREAL	CANADA
MOS	U. OF MOSCOW + MOSCOW STATE U.	USSR
MRC	NATIONAL RESEARCH COUNCIL, MONTREAL LAB	CANADA
MRY	MARYLAND U., COLLEGE PARK, MARYLAND	USA
MSU	MICHIGAN STATE U., E. LANSING, MICHIGAN	USA
MTR	IDAHO NUCL.CORP., IDAHO FALLS, IDAHO	USA
MTS	MIDDLE TENNESSEE STATE UNIV., MURFREESBORO, TENN.	USA
MTU	MONTANA STATE UNIVERSITY, MISSOULA, MONTANA	USA
MUA	MUSLIM UNIVERSITY, ALIGARH	INDIA
MUN	MUENCHEN, TECHNISCHE UNIVERSITAET	GERMANY, FR
MUR	MURRAY STATE UNIVERSITY	USA
MUU	MUENCHEN, UNIVERSITAET	GERMANY, FR
MVE	METROPOLITAN-VICKERS ELECTRICAL, HV LAB	UK
NAG	UNIV. OF NAGOYA	JAPAN
NAL	FERMI NATIONAL LABORATORY, BATAVIA, ILLINOIS	USA
NAP	U. OF NAPLES	ITALY
NBI	NIELS BOHR INST., COPENHAGEN	DENMARK
NBS	NATIONAL BUREAU OF STANDARDS, WASHINGTON, D.C.	USA
NCA	U. OF NORTH CAROLINA, RALEIGH, NORTH CAROLINA	USA
NCS	NORTH CAROLINA STATE COLLEGE, RALEIGH	USA
NDA	NUCLEAR DEVELOPMENT ASSOCIATES, INC.	USA
NDC	NEA DATA BANK, SACLAY	FRANCE
NDL	US ARMY NUCLEAR DEFENCE LAB., EDGEWOOD ARSENAL, MD.	USA
NEB	NORTH EASTERN UNIVERSITY, BOSTON	USA
NED	NETHERLANDS	NETHERLANDS
NEG	ISRAEL A.E.C, BEER-SHEBA, NUCL. RESEARCH CENTER NEGEV	ISRAEL
NEL	NUCLEAR EFFECTS LAB., US ARMY, EDGEWOOD ARSENAL, MD.	USA
NEU	U. OF NEUCHATEL	SWITZERLAND
NEW	U. OF NEWCASTLE-ON-TYNE	UK
NIG	NIPPON ATOMIC INDUSTRY GROUP	JAPAN
NIH	NATIONAL INST. OF HEALTH, BETHESDA, MA.	USA
NII	NIIGATA UNIVERSITY, NIIGATA	JAPAN
NIL	PAKISTAN INST. OF NUCLEAR SC. AND TECHN., NILORE	PAKISTAN
NIN	RUTHERFORD LAB, CHILTON, BERKS	UK
NIR	NAUCHNO-ISSLEDOV. INST. ATOMN. REAKTOROV, DIMITROVGRAD	USSR
NIU	NORTH ILLINOIS UNIVERSITY, DEKALB	USA
NJS	INST. JOZEF STEFAN, LJUBLJANA	YUGOSLAVIA
NMX	U. OF NEW MEXICO, ALBUQUERQUE	USA
NOL	U.S. NAVY ORDNANCE LAB., SILVER SPRINGS, MARYLAND	USA

LAB CODES

Table 4

NOR	NORWAY	NORWAY
NOT	U. OF NOTRE DAME, SOUTH BEND, IND.	USA
NPL	NATIONAL PHYSICAL LABORATORY, TEDDINGTON,	UK
NRD	U.S. NAVAL RADIOLOGICAL DEFENSE LAB., SAN FRANCISCO	USA
NRI	NUCL.RES.INST., TUWAITHA, BAGHDAD	IRAQ
NRL	U.S. NAVAL RESEARCH LAB., WASHINGTON, D.C.	USA
NRP	NAT'L RADIOLOGICAL PROTECTION BOARD, HARWELL	UK
NSU	NATIONAL SEOUL UNIVERSITY, SEOUL	KOREA
NSW	UNIV. OF NEW SOUTH WALES	AUSTRALIA
NTS	NORTH TEXAS STATE UNIVERSITY	USA
NTU	NATIONAL TAIWAN UNIVERSITY, TAIPEI	TAIWAN
NWU	NORTHWESTERN U., EVANSTON, ILLINOIS	USA
NYB	N.Y. STATE U. AT BUFFALO, N.Y.	USA
NYU	NEW YORK U. NEW YORK CITY	USA
NZA	U. OF AUCKLAND	NEW ZEALAND
NZH	INST. OF NUCLEAR SCIENCES, LOWER HUTT	NEW ZEALAND
NZL	NEW ZEALAND	NEW ZEALAND
NZW	VICTORIA UNIV. OF WELLINGTON	NEW ZEALAND
OAU	OAK RIDGE ASSOCIATED UNIVERSITIES, OAK RIDGE,TENN.	USA
OBR	OBERLIN COLLEGE, OBERLIN, OHIO	USA
OHO	OHIO U., ATHENS, OHIO	USA
OKL	U. OF OKLAHOMA	USA
ORE	UNIV. OF OREGON, EUGENE, OREGON	USA
ORL	OAK RIDGE NATIONAL LAB., TENNESSEE	USA
ORU	OREGON STATE UNIV., CORVALLIS, OREGON	USA
OSA	OSAKA U., OSAKA	JAPAN
OSL	U. OF OSLO, OSLO	NORWAY
OSP	RADIATION CENTRE OF OSAKA PREFECTURE, SAKAI, OSAKA	JAPAN
OSU	OHIO STATE U., COLUMBUS	USA
OTC	NAT. RES. COUNCIL, OTTAWA	CANADA
OTU	U. OF OTTAWA, ONTARIO	CANADA
OUL	UNIVERSITY OF OULU, OULU	FINLAND
OXF	U. OF OXFORD	UK
PAD	U. OF PADUA	ITALY
PAH	UNIVERSITY OF PAHLAVI,DANESHGAH, SHIRAZ	IRAN
PAK	PAKISTAN	PAKISTAN
PAR	U. OF PARIS, INCLUDING ORSAY.	FRANCE
PAT	PUNJABI U, PATIALA	INDIA
PAV	U. OF PAVIA	ITALY
PCF	COLLEGE DE FRANCE,PARIS	FRANCE
PCT	PICATINNY ARSENAL, DOVER, NEW JERSEY	USA
PEL	A.E. BOARD, PELINDABA, PRETORIA	SOUTH AFRICA
PEN	U. OF PENNSYLVANIA, PHILADELPHIA, PENNSYLVANIA	USA
PIC	PEDAGOGICAL INST., CONSTANTZA	RUMANIA
PNC	POWER REACTOR + NUCL. FUEL DEVELOPM. CORP., MURAMATSU	JAPAN
POL	POLAND	POLAND
PPO	PHILLIPS PETROLEUM, BARTLESVILLE,OKLAHOMA	USA
PR	PUERTO RICO	PUERTO RICO
PRA	PHYS. RESEARCH LABORATORY, AHMEDABAD	INDIA
PRT	PORTUGAL	PORTUGAL
PRW	PRATT + WHITNEY, MIDDLETOWN, CONN.	USA
PSU	PENN. STATE U., UNIVERSITY PARK, PA.	USA
PTB	PHYS.-TECHN. BUNDESANSTALT, BRAUNSCHWEIG	GERMANY,FR
PTN	U. OF PRINCETON, PRINCETON,NEW JERSEY	USA
PUC	PANJAB UNIVERSITY, CHANDIGARH	INDIA
PUP	UNIV. OF PITTSBURGH, PENNSYLVANIA	USA
PUR	PURDUE U., LAFAYETTE, INDIANA	USA
QML	QUEEN MARY COLLEGE, LONDON	UK
QUC	UNIV. COLL., TOWNSVILLE, QUEENSL.	AUSTRALIA
RAM	ATOMIC ENERGY CENTRE,RAMNA,DACCA	BANGLA DESH
RAN	THE RAND CORPORATION, SANTA MONICA, CALIFORNIA	USA
RBZ	INSTITUTE 'RUDER BOSKOVIC', ZAGREB	YUGOSLAVIA
RCN	ENERGY RESEARCH FOUNDATION, PETTEN	NETHERLANDS
REA	U. OF READING	UK

Table 4   LAB CODES

Code	Laboratory	Country
RED	REDSTONE ARSENAL, ALABAMA	USA
REH	REHOVOTH LAB, ISRAEL AEC	ISRAEL
REN	RENO METALLURGY RES. CENTER, RENO, NEVADA	USA
RES	DIVISION OF RESEARCH, USAEC, WASHINGTON, D.C.	USA
RHI	RHODE ISLAND UNIVERSITY, KINGSTON	USA
RI	RADIEVYJ INST. KHLOPIN, LENINGRAD	USSR
RIC	RICE INSTITUTE, HOUSTON, TEXAS	USA
RIO	CENTRO BRAZILIERO DE PESQUISAS FISICAS, RIO DE JANEIRO	BRAZIL
RIS	RISO, ROSKILDE	DENMARK
RLY	UKAEA, RISLEY	UK
ROC	U. OF ROCHESTER, ROCHESTER, NEW YORK	USA
ROM	U. OF ROME	ITALY
ROS	ZENTRALINST. F. KERNFORSCHUNG, ROSSENDORF	GERMAN D.R.
RPI	RENSSELAER POLYTECHNIC INST., TROY, NEW YORK	USA
RR	ROLLS-ROYCE	UK
RUM	ROMANIA	ROMANIA
RUT	RUTGERS - THE STATE UNIV., NEW BRUNSWICK, NEW JERSEY	USA
SAC	CEN SACLAY, ESSONNE	FRANCE
SAF	SOUTH AFRICA	SOUTH AFRICA
SAH	SAHA INSTITUTE, CALCUTTA	INDIA
SAI	SCIENCE APPLICATIONS INC., LAJOLLA, CALIFORNIA	USA
SAL	SORIN, NUC. RES CENTRE SALUGGIA	ITALY
SAN	UNIVERSIDAD DE CHILE, SANTIAGO	CHILE
SAS	U. OF SASKATCHEWAN, SASKATOON, SASKATCHEWAN	CANADA
SBL	DEPT. OF PHYSICS, POLYTECHNIC OF SOUTH BANK, LONDON	UK
SBU	SAARBRUECKEN, UNIVERSITAET DES SAARLANDES	GERMANY, FR
SC	SANDIA CORP., ALBUQUERQUE, NEW MEXICO	USA
SCT	U. OF CAPE TOWN	SOUTH AFRICA
SCU	USSR STATE COMM. FOR ATOMIC ENERGY, MOSCOW	USSR
SDC	SAN DIEGO STATE COLLEGE, SAN DIEGO, CALIFORNIA	USA
SEO	ATOM. ENERGY RES. INST., SEOUL	KOREA
SF	FINLAND	FINLAND
SFU	SIMON FRAZER UNIVERSITY, BURNABY, B.C.	CANADA
SGA	OESTERR. STUDIENGES. F. ATOMENERGIE, VIENNA+SEIBERSDORF	AUSTRIA
SHE	U. OF SHEFFIELD	UK
SHI	INSTIT. OF NUCL. ENERGY RES., LUNG TAN	TAIWAN
SHR	SHIP RESEARCH INST., MINISTRY OF TRANSPORT	JAPAN
SKU	CURIE-SKLODOWSKA UNIVERSITY, LUBLIN	POLAND
SLO	SLOVAK ACADEMY OF SCIENCES, PHYSICS INST., BRATISLAVA	CZECHOSLOV.
SLU	ST. LOUIS UNIVERSITY, MISSOURI	USA
SMU	SOUTHERN METHODIST UNIVERSITY, DALLAS, TEXAS	USA
SNI	SOUTHERN UNIV. NUCLEAR INST., BATON ROUGE, LA.	USA
SOC	SOCONY MOBIL OIL CO., DALLAS, TEXAS	USA
SOR	SOREQ RES. CENTRE, ISRAEL AEC, YAVNE	ISRAEL
SPN	SPAIN	SPAIN
SRC	SCOTTISH REACTOR CENTRE, E. KILBRIDE, SCOTLAND	UK
SRI	STANFORD RESEARCH INSTITUTE, MENLO PARK, CALIFORNIA	USA
SRL	SAVANNAH RIVER LAB., AIKEN, S.C.	USA
SSX	U. OF SUSSEX, BRIGHTON	UK
STB	STATE UNIV. OF NEW YORK, STONY BROOK, N.Y.	USA
STF	STANFORD U., MENLO PARK, CALIFORNIA	USA
STL	U. OF STELLENBOSCH	SOUTH AFRICA
STM	ST. MARY'S COLLEGE, ST. MARY'S CITY, MARYLAND	USA
STR	NUCLEAR RES. CENTRE, STRASBOURG-CRONENBOURG	FRANCE
SUI	STATE UNIV. IOWA, IOWA CITY	USA
SUK	SHIVAJI UNIVERSITY, KOLHAPUR	INDIA
SUL	LENINGRAD STATE UNIV., LENINGRAD	USSR
SUN	SOUTHERN UNIVERSITIES NUC. INST., FAURE, C.P.	SOUTH AFRICA
SWD	SWEDEN	SWEDEN
SWL	UNIV. OF SOUTHWESTERN LOUISIANA, LAFAYETTE, LA.	USA
SWR	STUDSVIK SCI. RES. LAB. (INCLUDING VAN DE GRAAFF LAB.)	SWEDEN
SWT	SWITZERLAND	SWITZERLAND
SYR	SYRACUSE UNIV. NEW YORK	USA
TAM	TEXAS AGRICULT. AND MECHANICAL COLLEGE	USA

LAB CODES

Table 4

Code	Institution	Country
TAT	TATA INSTITUTE, BOMBAY	INDIA
TEH	TEHERAN UNIVERSITY NUCLEAR CENTRE, TEHERAN	IRAN
TEL	TEL AVIV UNIVERSITY	ISRAEL
TEN	UNIVERSITY OF TENNESSEE	USA
TEX	U. OF TEXAS, AUSTIN, TEXAS	USA
THA	AACHEN, TECHNISCHE HOCHSCHULE	GERMANY,FR
THB	TECHNISCHE HOCHSCHULE BRAUNSCHWEIG	GERMANY, FR
THD	DARMSTADT, TECHN. HOCHSCHULE	GERMANY,FR
THS	STUTTGART, UNIVERSITAET	GERMANY,FR
THU	NATIONAL TSING HUA UNIV., HSIN-CHU	TAIWAN
TIL	LENINGRADSKIJ TECHNOLOG.INST.LENSOVETA,LENINGRAD	USSR
TIT	TOKYO INSTITUTE OF TECHNOLOGY, TOKYO	JAPAN
TKU	TURKU UNIVERSITY	FINLAND
TNC	TEXAS NUCLEAR CORP., AUSTIN, TEXAS	USA
TNL	TRIANGLE UNIVERSITIES NUCL.LAB., DURHAM,NORTH CAROLINA	USA
TOH	TOHOKU UNIVERSITY, SENDAI	JAPAN
TOK	TOKYO U.	JAPAN
TOR	U. OF TORONTO	CANADA
TOU	U. OF TOULOUSE,TOULOUSE (HAUTE GARONNE)	FRANCE
TPG	UNIVERSITY OF GRAZ, INST. FUER THEOR. PHYSIK	AUSTRIA
TPI	TOMSKIJ POLITEKHNICHESKOI INST., TOMSK	USSR
TPT	INTERN. CENTRE FOR THEORETICAL PHYSICS, TRIESTE	ITALY
TRI	U. OF TRIESTE	ITALY
TRM	BHABHA ATOMIC RES. CENTRE, TROMBAY, BOMBAY	INDIA
TUD	TECHNISCHE UNIV. DRESDEN, DRESDEN + PIRNA	GERMAN D.R.
TUE	TUEBINGEN, UNIVERSITAET	GERMANY,FR
TUK	TURKEY	TURKEY
TUL	TULANE U., NEW ORLEANS, LOUISIANA	USA
TUP	POLITECNICO DI TORINO,TURIN	ITALY
TUR	U. OF TORINO	ITALY
UAG	U. OF ALGER (INCLUDING INST. D'ETUDES NUCLEAIRES)	ALGERIA
UAL	UNIVERSITY OF ALABAMA	USA
UAR	EGYPT	EGYPT
UBA	UNIVERSIDAD DE BUENOS AIRES	ARGENTINA
UBC	U. OF BRITISH COLUMBIA, VANCOUVER, BRITISH COLUMBIA	CANADA
UBE	BERN, UNIVERSITAET	SWITZERLAND
UBO	BOLOGNA, UNIVERSITA + IST.NAZ.DI FIS.NUCL.	ITALY
UCB	UNITED NUCLEAR CORP., TUXEDO, NY	USA
UCD	UNIVERSITY COLLEGE,DUBLIN	EIRE
UCN	U. OF CINCINNATI, CINCINNATI, OHIO	USA
UCS	UNION CARBIDE STERLING FOREST RES.CENTRE,TUXEDO.NY	USA
UEC	UNIV. ESTADUAL DE CAMPINAS	BRAZIL
UEN	ERLANGEN+NUERNBERG, UNIVERSITAET	GERMANY,FR
UFP	UNIV.FEDERAL DE PERNAMBUCO+C.E.N.,RECIFE	BRAZIL
UFT	UKRAINSKIJ FIZIKO-TEKHNICHESKIJ INSTITUT, KHARKOV	USSR
UI	U. OF ILLINOIS	USA
UIA	UNIV. INSTELLING, ANTWERP	BELGIUM
UJK	JAGELLONIAN UNIVERSITY, KRAKOW	POLAND
UJV	USTAV JAD. VYZKUMU (INST. NUCL. RES.), REZ U PRAHY	CZECHOSLOV.
UK	UNITED KINGDOM	UK
UKW	WINDSCALE REACTOR DEVELOPMENT LABS. UKAEA	UK
UMT	UNIVERSITY OF MONTANA, HELENA, MONTANA	USA
UMX	UNI. NACIONAL AUTONOMA DE MEXICO	MEXICO
UNC	UNITED NUCLEAR CORP., ELMSFORD, N.Y.	USA
UPA	UNIVERSIDAD DE LA PLATA, BUENOS AIRES	ARGENTINA
UPP	U. OF UPPSALA	SWEDEN
URJ	UNIVERSITY OF RAJESTAN, JAIPUR	INDIA
URR	UNIV. OF ROORKEE,ROORKEE	INDIA
URU	URUGUAY	URUGUAY
USA	UNITED STATES	USA
USC	U. OF SOUTHERN CALIFORNIA, LOS ANGELES	USA
USP	UNIV. DE SAO PAULO, SAO PAULO	BRAZIL
UST	UNIVERSITY OF STOCKHOLM	SWEDEN
UTR	U. OF UTRECHT	NETHERLANDS

Table 4 LAB CODES

Code	Institution	Country
UZB	INST. JADERNOJ FIZIKI A.N. UZBEKSKOJ SSR, TASHKENT	USSR
VAL	VALENCIA UNIVERSITY	SPAIN
VBT	VANDERBUILT UNIV.	USA
VIP	VIRGINIA POLYTECHNIC	USA
VIR	U. OF VIRGINIA, CHARLOTTESVILLE, VA.	USA
VLD	UNIV. DE VALLADOLID	SPAIN
VNS	VIETNAM, NORTH AND SOUTH	VIETNAM
VNV	CENTRE D'ETUDES DE LIMEIL, VILLENEUVE-ST.GEORGES	FRANCE
WAD	WRIGHT AIR DEVELOPMENT CENTER, OHIO	USA
WAI	WESTERN AUSTRAL. INST. OF TECHNOLOGY, WEST BENTLEY	AUSTRALIA
WAL	WESTINGHOUSE ASTRONUCLEAR LAB., PITTSBURGH	USA
WAP	WESTINGHOUSE ATOMIC POWER DIV., PITTSBURGH, PENNS.	USA
WAS	WASHINGTON U., ST LOUIS, MISSOURI	USA
WAT	WATERTOWN ARSENAL, WATERTOWN, MASS.	USA
WAU	U. OF WASHINGTON, SEATTLE	USA
WAY	WAYNE STATE UNIVERSITY, DETROIT, MICHIGAN	USA
WES	WESTINGHOUSE RESEARCH LAB., PITTSBURGH, PENN.	USA
WEW	WESTINGHOUSE ADVANCED REACTOR DIV., PITTSBURGH, PENN.	USA
WIN	AEE WINFRITH, DORSET	UK
WIS	U. OF WISCONSIN, MADISON	USA
WIT	UNIV. OF WITWATERSRAND, JOHANNESBURG	SOUTH AFRICA
WKU	WESTERN KENTUCKY UNIV., BOWLING GREEN, KENTUCKY	USA
WLY	WESLEYAN UNIV., MIDDLETOWN, CONN.	USA
WMU	WESTERN MICHIGAN UNIVERSITY	USA
WPI	WORCESTER POLYTECH. INST	USA
WSU	WASHINGTON STATE UNIV., PULLMAN	USA
WUC	WOLLONGONG UNIVERSITY COLLEGE, WOLLONGONG	AUSTRALIA
WUR	EIDG.INSTITUT FUER REAKTORFORSCHUNG, WUERENLINGEN	SWITZERLAND
WUU	WUERZBURG, UNIVERSITAET	GERMANY, FR
WVU	U. OF WEST VIRGINIA, MORGANTOWN	USA
WWA	U. OF WARSAW+PAN.	POLAND
WWS	WESTERN WASHINGTON STATE COLLEGE, BELLINGHAM	USA
WZI	WEIZMANN INST., REHOVOTH	ISRAEL
YAL	YALE U., NEW HAVEN, CONNECTICUT	USA
YAM	YAMANASHI U., KOFU	JAPAN
YOK	RIKKYO (ST.PAULS)U., YOKOSUKA, INST. FOR AT. ENERGY	JAPAN
YUG	YUGOSLAVIA	YUGOSLAVIA
ZAG	U. OF ZAGREB	YUGOSLAVIA

TABLE 5: SOME ABBREVIATIONS USED IN "Comments"

(Note to CINDA indexers: this list should not be used for coding new entries because it includes codes which are out of date but still existing in the file.)

A, ALF	Alpha particle, Mass number	EV	Electron volt
A-WID	Alpha width	EXCIT	Exitation
ABS	Absolute, Absorption	EXCTD	Excited
ABSL	Absolute	EXP	Exponential
ABST, ABSTR	Abstract	EXPT	Experiment
ACC	Accuracy	EXPTAL	Experimental
ACT	Activation, Activity	F	Fermis
ACTIV	Activation, Activity	F-WID	Fission width
ANAL	Analysis	FC	Fast chopper
ANG	Angle	FIG	Figure (graph) given
AS	Angles	FISS	Fission
AV, AVG	Average	FN	Function
B	Barns	FP	Submitted for publication in this form
BIN	Binary		
C	With	FR	French
C-W	Cockcroft-Walton	FRAG	Fragment
CALC	Calculated	FREQ	Frequency
CAPT	Capture	FWD	Forward
CF	See also, Compare	G	Gamma ray
CFD	Compared	G	Statistical weight (as in 2G WN)
CH	Chamber	G-WID	Gamma width
COEF	Coefficient	GAM	Gamma ray
COH	Coherent	GE-LI	Germanium-Lithium detector
COINC	Coincidence	GEOM	Geometry
COMPNUC	Compound Nucleus	GND	Ground state
CONT	Continuous	GRPH	Graph
CORR, CORREL	Correlation	GS	Gamma rays
CORRC	Correction	GVN	Given (as in VAL GVN)
CRV	Curve	H	Hours
CRYST	Crystal	H-F	Hauser-Feshbach
CS	Cross-section	HL	Half-life
CURV	Curve	I	Nuclear spin
D	Days, Level spacing	IA	Isotopic Assignment
D	Decimal in older entries	INEL	Inelastic
DEG	Degree	INT, INTENS	Intensity, Intensities
DEGC	Degrees centigrade	INTEG	Integral
DEGK	Degrees Kelvin	INV	Inverse reaction
DEL	Differential elastic scattering	ISOM	Isomer, Isomeric state
DET	Detector, detected	ISOTR	Isotropic
DFN	Level spacing function	J	Total angular momentum
DIFF	Differential	K-N	Krieger-Nelkin
DIST	Distribution	KB	Kilobarn
DISTR	Distribution	KE	Kinetic energy
DRVD	Derived	KEV	Kiloelectron volts
DSIG	Differential cross section	KIN-E	Kinetic energy
DTCTR	Detector	L	Orbital angular momentum
E	Energy	LEG COEF	Legendre coefficients
ELAS	Elastic	LINAC	Linear accelerator

Table 5

EN	Energy, neutron energy	LRA	Long-range alphas
ENG, ENGL	English	LVL	Level, State
ES	Energies	M	Minutes
M	Minus, less than, below	/SR	Per Steradian (as in 50 MB/SR)
M-R	Moxon-Rae detector	S	Seconds
MAX	Maximum	S	Cross-section
MB	Millibarn	SC	Scintillator, slow chopper
MD	Monotonically decreasing	SC-T	Scintillator tank
MEAN	Average	SCAT, SCT	Scattering
MEDT	Intermediate structure	SCH	Scheme
META	Metastable (state)	SCINT	Scintillator
MEV	Million electron volts	SEL	Elastic scattering
MI	Monotonically increasing	SIG	Cross-section
MIN	Minutes	SNE	Sigma nonelastic
MS	Millisecond	SPEC	Spectrum, Spectrometer
MUB	Microbarn	SPECT	Spectrum, Spectrometer
MULTISCAT	Multiple scattering	SPH	Sphere, spherical
MUS	Microsecond	SPRSDD	Superseded
N	Neutron	SQ	Square
N-WID	Neutron width	STAT MDL	Statistical model
NDG	No data given	S0, S1	Strength function, $L = 0$, $L = 1$, etc.
NEUT	Neutrons		
NG	(n, gamma)	T	Temperature, Time, Triton
NORM	Normalized	T-WID	Total width
NP	(n, proton) etc.	TBC	To be completed
NS	Neutrons	TBD	To be done, proposed
NS	Nanoseconds	TBG	To be given
OBS	Observed	TBL	Table
OKS	Confirms, Agrees with	TBP	To be published
OPTMDL	Optical model	TD5	Half-life
OSC	Oscillator	TER, TERN	Ternary
OTH, OTHR	Other(s) (as in CFD OTH, = compared to other results)	TH	Theory, calculation
		THR	Thermal
P	Proton	THRS	Threshold
P	Plus, greater than	TOF	Time of flight
P-B	Perey-Buck	TOT	Total
P-T	Porter-Thomas	TR	Threshold
PAR	Parameter	TRANS	Transmission
PARAM	Parameter	TRANSL	Translation
PARS	Parameters	TRNS	Transmission
PC	Per cent	VAL	Value
PI	Parity	VAR	Variation
PK, PKS	Peak, Peaks	VDG	Van de Graaff
PM	Plus or minus	VEL	Velocity
POL	Polarization, polarized	VS	Versus
POLRZ	Polarization, polarized	W DIST	Wigner distribution
PS	Protons	W-D	Wigner distribution
PSR	Per Steradian	WF	Fission width
Q	Doubtful, Query	WG	Gamma width
R	Nuclear radius (as in $R = 7F$)	WID	Width
REF	Reference	WN	Neutron width
REL	Relative to	WT	Total width

RES	Resonance	XPT	Experiment
RESOL	Resolution	XTAL	Crystal
RESON	Resonance	XTL	Crystal
REVW	Review	Y	Years
RSLN	Resolution	YLD	Yield
RVW	Review	Z	Atomic number
X	Wrong, negative (prefix)	ZP	Most probable charge of fission-fragments
XCIT	Excitation		

HOW TO ORDER IAEA PUBLICATIONS

 An exclusive sales agent for IAEA publications, to whom all orders and inquiries should be addressed, has been appointed in the following country:

UNITED STATES OF AMERICA   UNIPUB, 345 Park Avenue South, New York, NY 10010

 In the following countries IAEA publications may be purchased from the sales agents or booksellers listed or through your major local booksellers. Payment can be made in local currency or with UNESCO coupons.

ARGENTINA	Comisión Nacional de Energía Atomica, Avenida del Libertador 8250, RA-1429 Buenos Aires
AUSTRALIA	Hunter Publications, 58 A Gipps Street, Collingwood, Victoria 3066
BELGIUM	Service du Courrier de l'UNESCO, 202, Avenue du Roi, B-1060 Brussels
CZECHOSLOVAKIA	S.N.T.L., Spálená 51, CS-113 02 Prague 1 Alfa, Publishers, Hurbanovo námestie 6, CS-893 31 Bratislava
FRANCE	Office International de Documentation et Librairie, 48, rue Gay-Lussac, F-75240 Paris Cedex 05
HUNGARY	Kultura, Hungarian Trading Company for Books and Newspapers, P.O. Box 149, H-1389 Budapest 62
INDIA	Oxford Book and Stationery Co., 17, Park Street, Calcutta-700 016 Oxford Book and Stationery Co., Scindia House, New Delhi-110 001
ISRAEL	Heiliger and Co., Ltd., Scientific and Medical Books, 3, Nathan Strauss Street, Jerusalem
ITALY	Libreria Scientifica, Dott. Lucio de Biasio "aeiou", Via Meravigli 16, I-20123 Milan
JAPAN	Maruzen Company, Ltd., P.O. Box 5050, 100-31 Tokyo International
NETHERLANDS	Martinus Nijhoff B.V., Booksellers, Lange Voorhout 9-11, P.O. Box 269, NL-2501 The Hague
PAKISTAN	Mirza Book Agency, 65, Shahrah Quaid-e-Azam, P.O. Box 729, Lahore 3
POLAND	Ars Polona-Ruch, Centrala Handlu Zagranicznego, Krakowskie Przedmiescie 7, PL-00-068 Warsaw
ROMANIA	Ilexim, P.O. Box 136-137, Bucarest
SOUTH AFRICA	Van Schaik's Bookstore (Pty) Ltd., Libri Building, Church Street, P.O. Box 724, Pretoria 0001
SPAIN	Diaz de Santos, Lagasca 95, Madrid-6 Diaz de Santos, Balmes 417, Barcelona-6
SWEDEN	AB C.E. Fritzes Kungl. Hovbokhandel, Fredsgatan 2, P.O. Box 16356, S-103 27 Stockholm
UNITED KINGDOM	Her Majesty's Stationery Office, P.O. Box 569, London SE 1 9NH
U.S.S.R.	Mezhdunarodnaya Kniga, Smolenskaya-Sennaya 32-34, Moscow G-200
YUGOSLAVIA	Jugoslovenska Knjiga, Terazije 27, P.O. Box 36, YU-11001 Belgrade

---

 Orders from countries where sales agents have not yet been appointed and requests for information should be addressed directly to:

 Division of Publications
International Atomic Energy Agency
Kärntner Ring 11, P.O. Box 590, A-1011 Vienna, Austria